Who's Who in Frontiers of Science and Technology

Who'sWho In Frontiers of Science and Technology

Biographical Titles Currently Published by Marquis Who's Who

Who's Who in America

  Who's Who in America supplements:

    Who's Who in America Birthdate Index

    Who's Who in America Classroom Project Book

    Who's Who in America College Alumni Directory

    Who's Who in America Index:

      Geographic Index, Professional Area Index

Who Was Who in America

  Historical Volume (1607-1896)

  Volume I (1897-1942)

  Volume II (1943-1950)

  Volume III (1951-1960)

  Volume IV (1961-1968)

  Volume V (1969-1973)

  Volume VI (1974-1976)

  Volume VII (1977-1981)

  Volume VIII (1982-1985)

  Index Volume (1607-1985)

Who Was Who in American History—Arts and Letters

Who Was Who in American History—The Military

Who Was Who in American History—Science and Technology

Who's Who in the World

Who's Who in the East

Who's Who in the Midwest

Who's Who in the South and Southwest

Who's Who in the West

Who's Who in American Law

Who's Who of American Women

Who's Who in Finance and Industry

Who's Who in Frontiers of Science and Technology

Who's Who in Religion

World Who's Who in Science

Directory of Women in Marquis Who's Who Publications

Index to Who's Who Books

Directory of Medical Specialists

Marquis Who's Who Directory of Online Professionals

Marquis Who's Who Directory of Computer Graphics

Marquis Who's Who in Cancer: Professionals and Facilities

Marquis Who's Who in Rehabilitation: Professionals and Facilities

Marquis International Who's Who in Optical Science and Engineering

Who's Who
in Frontiers of Science and Technology®

2nd edition

MARQUIS
Who's Who

Marquis Who's Who, Inc.
200 East Ohio Street
Chicago, Illinois 60611 U.S.A.

Library of Congress Catalog Card Number 82-82015
International Standard Book Number 0-8379-5702-8
Product Code Number 030342

Distributed in Europe by
Thompson, Henry Limited
London Road
Sunningdale, Berks
SL5 OEP, England

Distributed in Asia by
United Publishers Services Ltd.
Kenkyu-Sha Bldg.
9, Kanda Surugadai 2-Chome
Chiyoda-Ku, Tokyo, Japan

Manufactured in the United States of America

Table of Contents

Preface

The second edition of *Who's Who in Frontiers of Science and Technology* meets the need for biographical information on individuals engaged in the forefront fields of science. The volume includes approximately 14,000 scientists and technologists who are currently working in North America in the frontier areas of their respective specialties.

The biographical sketches include the content elements found in *Who's Who in America,* including vital statistics, education, career history, awards, publications, and memberships. In addition, using a computer-coded list of frontier fields and subspecialties, each biographee has provided his or her subspecialties of science and a description of current research or work interest. This narrative statement of current work enables the biographee to describe narrower subspecialties than those covered in the list. The information on specialties is also found in the Index of Fields and Subspecialties, in which biographees are listed under approximately 420 subspecialties arranged within 23 major fields.

The challenge of defining frontier areas of science was met by going to the scientific community for current descriptions of fields at the cutting edge of science and technology. Research by Marquis staff resulted in a two-fold general description of frontier science that included both new directions in traditional fields of research, such as genetic engineering and gravitational biology, and work using the most advanced technology, like lasers and computers. Based on these descriptions, Marquis researchers developed a working list of frontier topics covering fields from agriculture to zoology. This working list was sent to 1,500 scientists, including editors of scholarly scientific journals, for additions, deletions, and other changes and comments. The scientists' comments were embodied in the expanded final list of frontier subspecialties, which became the basis for definition of frontiers of science in each field. For the second edition, the subspecialty list has been revised and updated, based on recommendations from members of the Board of Advisors and from other scientists.

The list was sent to each biographee, who was asked to select one or two subspecialties that reflected personal research or work interest. Thus, the comprehensive Index and the sketches contain two subspecialty entries for many listees in *Who's Who in Frontiers of Science and Technology.* If a subspecialty was found in more than one field of science, the name of the field was appended to the subspecialty description in the sketch, as in Biomass (agriculture) and Biomass (energy science and technology). Biographees with subspecialties not encompassed in the list are found in the Index at the end of each major field under the category "Other."

The Index serves two important reference functions. It provides a current listing of the frontier fields of science and technology, as defined by those within the fields. It also allows additional access to sketch information beyond biographee names: the user can find practitioners within specific new fields of science and technology.

Most biographees furnished their own data and reviewed the sketches to assure accurate, current information. In some cases where individuals failed to supply needed information, Marquis staff members compiled the data through independent research. Such sketches are denoted by an asterisk. Brief key information is provided in the sketches of selected individuals, new to this edition, who did not submit data. Cross-references to current information in *Who's Who in America* appear for others.

As in all Marquis Who's Who biographical volumes, the principle of current reference value determined selection of biographees. Reference interest is based on either position of responsibility or noteworthy achievement. Those in high positions related to frontiers of science include many eminent scientists. The noteworthy achievers are not all familiar names, since much advanced scientific research is being conducted by younger practitioners who are not yet known outside their own fields.

Adele Hast, Ph.D.
Editor-in-Chief

Board of Advisors

Marquis Who's Who gratefully acknowledges the contribution of the following distinguished individuals to the second edition of *Who's Who in Frontiers of Science and Technology*. Members of the Board of Advisors have nominated outstanding scientists and technologists for inclusion in the book and have made themselves available for review and evaluation of contents. However, the Board of Advisors, either collectively or individually, is in no way responsible for the selection of names or for the accuracy of the information in this volume.

Bruno A. Boley, Sc.D.
Dean, Technological Institute
Northwestern University

Robert E. Boyer, Ph.D.
Dean, College of Natural Sciences
University of Texas at Austin

Theodore Cooper, M.D., Ph.D.
Executive Vice President
The Upjohn Company

Charles H. Davis, Ph.D.
Dean, Graduate School of
  Library and Information Science
University of Illinois at
  Urbana-Champaign

Dorothy E. Denning, Ph.D.
SRI International
Menlo Park, California

Herman Feshbach, Ph.D.
Head, Department of Physics
Massachusetts Institute of Technology

Walter Freiberger, Ph.D.
Professor, Division of
  Applied Mathematics
Brown University

Yuan-Cheng B. Fung, Ph.D.
Professor, Department of
  Bioengineering & Applied Mechanics
University of California,
  San Diego

Pierre M. Galletti, M.D., Ph.D.
Vice President, Division of
  Biology and Medicine
Brown University

Lawrence D. Grouse, M.D., Ph.D.
Senior Medical Editor
Lifetime Television Network

Donald L. Hammond, D.Sc.
Director, Hewlett-Packard
  Laboratories
Bristol, England

Lee N. Miller, Ph.D.
Managing Editor
Ecological Society of America
Cornell University

Jeremiah P. Ostriker, Ph.D.
Director, Princeton University
  Observatory

Charles A. Wert, Ph.D.
Head, Department of Metallurgy
  and Mining Engineering
University of Illinois at
  Urbana-Champaign

Sylvan H. Wittwer, Ph.D.
Director Emeritus, Agricultural
  Experiment Station
Michigan State University

Standards of Admission

Selection of biographees for *Who's Who in Frontiers of Science and Technology* is determined by reference interest, based on involvement in research or other work at the frontiers of science. Reference interest derives from either or both of two factors: (1) incumbency in a defined position or (2) attainment of a significant level of achievement.

Admission based on position includes the following examples:

Heads of selected university research institutes and programs

Directors of selected independent research institutes

Directors of selected governmental research centers

Heads of selected industrial research laboratories

Principals of selected consulting organizations

Deans of selected academic divisions

Selected members of honorary organizations in science, such as the National Academy of Sciences, the National Academy of Engineering, and the Institute of Medicine

Recipients of selected national and international awards in science

Admission by the factor of significant achievement is based on objective criteria for measuring accomplishments within the scientific profession.

Key to Information

❶ **DAVIES, STEPHEN FRANCIS,** ❷ physics educator; ❸ b. Evanston, Ill., Oct. 8, 1930; ❹ s. Paul Harwell and Mary Louise (Ryan) D.; ❺ m. Elizabeth C. Swan, June 10, 1956; ❻ children: Robert Dwight, Mary Adele, William Fremont. ❼ B.S., Princeton U., 1953; Ph.D., MIT, 1959. ❽ Cert. safety profl., Mass. ❾ Research asst. radiation lab. physics dept. MIT, Cambridge, 1959-61; assoc. physicist Battelle Meml. Inst., Columbus, Ohio, 1961-64; asst. prof. physics Columbia U., N.Y.C., 1965-69, assoc. prof., 1969-75, prof. radiation physics, 1975 –; vis. scientist Am. Inst. Physics, 1978; vis. prof. Rensselaer Poly. Inst., Troy, N.Y., 1981-82; chmn. commn. radiation physics Internat. Union Pure and Applied Physics, 1979-81; mem. Nat. Sci. Bd., 1982 –. ❿ Editor: Radiation Testing Standards, 1976; contbr. articles to profl. jours. ⓫ Trustee Cornell U.; bd. dirs. Fairfield County chpt. Am. Cancer Soc., Greenwich Civic Orch. ⓬ Served with USN, 1948-49. ⓭ Recipient Research prize N.Y. Acad. Scis., 1980; fellow Sloan Found., 1974-76, Guggenheim Found., 1981. ⓮ Mem. AAAS, Am. Phys. Soc., Nat. Acad. Scis., Am. Nuclear Soc., Sigma Xi. ⓯ Republican. ⓰Episcopalian. ⓱ Clubs: Down Town (N.Y.C.); Rolling Meadows Country. ⓲ Lodge: Masons. ⓳ Current work: Research in nondestructive testing. ⓴ Subspecialties: Radiation physics; Nuclear physics. ㉑ Home: 411 Wolf Pit Rd Greenwich CT 06830 ㉒ Office: Dept Physics Columbia U New York NY 10002

KEY

❶ Name
❷ Occupation
❸ Vital statistics
❹ Parents
❺ Marriage
❻ Children
❼ Education
❽ Professional certifications
❾ Career
❿ Writings and special achievements
⓫ Civic and political activities
⓬ Military record
⓭ Awards and fellowships
⓮ Professional and association memberships
⓯ Political affiliation
⓰ Religion
⓱ Clubs
⓲ Lodges
⓳ Current work
⓴ Subspecialties
㉑ Home address
㉒ Office address

Table of Abbreviations

The following abbreviations and symbols are frequently used in this book.

*An asterisk following a sketch indicates that it was researched by the Marquis Who's Who editorial staff and has not been verified by the biographee.

A.A. Associate in Arts
AAAL American Academy of Arts and Letters
AAAS American Association for the Advancement of Science
AAHPER Alliance for Health, Physical Education and Recreation
AAU Amateur Athletic Union
AAUP American Association of University Professors
AAUW American Association of University Women
A.B. Arts, Bachelor of
AB Alberta
ABA American Bar Association
ABC American Broadcasting Company
AC Air Corps
acad. academy, academic
acct. accountant
accg. accounting
ACDA Arms Control and Disarmament Agency
ACLU American Civil Liberties Union
ACP American College of Physicians
ACS American College of Surgeons
ADA American Dental Association
a.d.c. aide-de-camp
adj. adjunct, adjutant
adj. gen. adjutant general
adm. admiral
adminstr. administrator
adminstrn. administration
adminstrv. administrative
ADP Automatic Data Processing
adv. advocate, advisory
advt. advertising
A.E. Agricultural Engineer (for degrees only)
A.E. and P. Ambassador Extraordinary and Plenipotentiary
AEC Atomic Energy Commission
aero. aeronautical, aeronautic
aerodyn. aerodynamic
AFB Air Force Base
AFL-CIO American Federation of Labor and Congress of Industrial Organizations
AFTRA American Federation TV and Radio Artists
agr. agriculture
agrl. agricultural
agt. agent
AGVA American Guild of Variety Artists
agy. agency
A&I Agricultural and Industrial
AIA American Institute of Architects

AIAA American Institute of Aeronautics and Astronautics
AID Agency for International Development
AIEE American Institute of Electrical Engineers
AIM American Institute of Management
AIME American Institute of Mining, Metallurgy, and Petroleum Engineers
AK Alaska
AL Alabama
ALA American Library Association
Ala. Alabama
alt. alternate
Alta. Alberta
A&M Agricultural and Mechanical
A.M. Arts, Master of
Am. American, America
AMA American Medical Association
A.M.E. African Methodist Episcopal
Amtrak National Railroad Passenger Corporation
AMVETS American Veterans of World War II, Korea, Vietnam
anat. anatomical
ann. annual
ANTA American National Theatre and Academy
anthrop. anthropological
AP Associated Press
APO Army Post Office
Apr. April
apptd. appointed
apt. apartment
AR Arkansas
ARC American Red Cross
archeol. archeological
archtl. architectural
Ariz. Arizona
Ark. Arkansas
ArtsD. Arts, Doctor of
arty. artillery
ASCAP American Society of Composers, Authors and Publishers
ASCE American Society of Civil Engineers
ASHRAE American Society of Heating, Refrigeration, and Air Conditioning Engineers
ASME American Society of Mechanical Engineers
assn. association
assoc. associate
asst. assistant
ASTM American Society for Testing and Materials
astron. astronomical
astrophys. astrophysical
ATSC Air Technical Service Command
AT&T American Telephone & Telegraph Company

atty. attorney
AUS Army of the United States
Aug. August
aux. auxiliary
Ave. Avenue
AVMA American Veterinary Medical Association
AZ Arizona

B. Bachelor
b. born
B.A. Bachelor of Arts
B.Agr. Bachelor of Agriculture
Balt. Baltimore
Bapt. Baptist
B. Arch. Bachelor of Architecture
B.A.S. Bachelor of Agricultural Science
B.B.A. Bachelor of Business Administration
BBC British Broadcasting Corporation
B.C., BC British Columbia
B.C.E. Bachelor of Civil Engineering
B. Chir. Bachelor of Surgery
B.C.L. Bachelor of Civil Law
B.C.S. Bachelor of Commercial Science
B.D. Bachelor of Divinity
bd. board
B.E. Bachelor of Education
B.E.E. Bachelor of Electrical Engineering
B.F.A. Bachelor of Fine Arts
bibl. biblical
bibliog. bibliographical
biog. biographical
biol. biological
B.J. Bachelor of Journalism
Bklyn. Brooklyn
B.L. Bachelor of Letters
bldg. building
B.L.S. Bachelor of Library Science
Blvd. Boulevard
bn. battalion
B.&O.R.R. Baltimore & Ohio Railroad
bot. botanical
B.P.E. Bachelor of Physical Education
br. branch
B.R.E. Bachelor of Religious Education
brig. gen. brigadier general
Brit. British, Britannica
Bros. Brothers
B.S. Bachelor of Science
B.S.A. Bachelor of Agricultural Science
B.S.D. Bachelor of Didactic Science
B.S.T. Bachelor of Sacred Theology
B.Th. Bachelor of Theology
bull. bulletin
bur. bureau
bus. business
B.W.I. British West Indies

CA California

CAA Civil Aeronautics Administration
CAB Civil Aeronautics Board
Calif. California
C.Am. Central America
Can. Canada, Canadian
CAP Civil Air Patrol
capt. captain
CARE Cooperative American Relief Everywhere
Cath. Catholic
cav. cavalry
CBC Canadian Broadcasting Company
CBI China, Burma, India Theatre of Operations
CBS Columbia Broadcasting System
CCC Commodity Credit Corporation
CCNY City College of New York
CCU Cardiac Care Unit
CD Civil Defense
C.E. Corps of Engineers, Civil Engineers (in firm's name only or for degree)
cen. central (To be used for court system only)
CENTO Central Treaty Organization
CERN European Organization of Nuclear Research
cert. certificate, certification, certified
CETA Comprehensive Employment Training Act
CFL Canadian Football League
ch. church
Ch.D. Doctor of Chemistry
chem. chemical
Chem.E. Chemical Engineer
Chgo. Chicago
chirurg. chirurgical
chmn. chairman
chpt. chapter
CIA Central Intelligence Agency
CIC Counter Intelligence Corps
Cin. Cincinnati
cir. circuit
Cleve. Cleveland
climatol. climatological
clin. clinical
clk. clerk
C.L.U. Chartered Life Underwriter
C.M. Master in Surgery
C.&N.W.Ry. Chicago & Northwestern Railway
CO Colorado
Co. Company
COF Catholic Order of Foresters
C. of C. Chamber of Commerce
col. colonel
coll. college
Colo. Colorado
com. committee
comd. commanded
comdg. commanding
comdr. commander
comdt. commandant

commd. commissioned
comml. commercial
commn. commission
commr. commissioner
condr. conductor
Conf. Conference
Congl. Congregational, Congressional
Conglist. Congregationalist
Conn. Connecticut
cons. consultant, consulting
consol. consolidated
constl. constitutional
constn. constitution
constrn. construction
contbd. contributed
contbg. contributing
contbn. contribution
contbr. contributor
Conv. Convention
coop. cooperative
CORDS Civil Operations and Revolutionary Development Support
CORE Congress of Racial Equality
corp. corporation, corporate
corr. correspondent, corresponding, correspondence
C.&O.Ry. Chesapeake & Ohio Railway
C.P.A. Certified Public Accountant
C.P.C.U. Chartered Property and Casualty Underwriter
C.P.H. Certificate of Public Health
cpl. corporal
CPR Cardio-Pulmonary Resuscitation
C.P.Ry. Canadian Pacific Railway
C.S. Christian Science
C.S.B. Bachelor of Christian Science
CSC Civil Service Commission
C.S.D. Doctor of Christian Science
CT Connecticut
ct. court
crt. center
CWS Chemical Warfare Service
C.Z. Canal Zone

d. daughter
D. Doctor
D.Agr. Doctor of Agriculture
DAR Daughters of the American Revolution
dau. daughter
DAV Disabled American Veterans
D.C.,DC District of Columbia
D.C.L. Doctor of Civil Law
D.C.S. Doctor of Commercial Science
D.D. Doctor of Divinity
D.D.S. Doctor of Dental Surgery
DE Delaware
dec. deceased
Dec. December
def. defense
Del. Delaware
del. delegate, delegation

Dem. Democrat, Democratic
D.Eng. Doctor of Engineering
denom. denomination, denominational
dep. deputy
dept. department
dermatol. dermatological
desc. descendant
devel. development, developmental
D.F.A. Doctor of Fine Arts
D.F.C. Distinguished Flying Cross
D.H.L. Doctor of Hebrew Literature
dir. director
dist. district
distbg. distributing
distbn. distribution
distbr. distributor
disting. distinguished
div. division, divinity, divorce
D.Litt. Doctor of Literature
D.M.D. Doctor of Medical Dentistry
D.M.S. Doctor of Medical Science
D.O. Doctor of Osteopathy
D.P.H. Diploma in Public Health
D.R. Daughters of the Revolution
Dr. Drive, Doctor
D.R.E. Doctor of Religious Education
Dr.P.H. Doctor of Public Health, Doctor of Public Hygiene
D.S.C. Distinguished Service Cross
D.Sc. Doctor of Science
D.S.M. Distinguished Service Medal
D.S.T. Doctor of Sacred Theology
D.T.M. Doctor of Tropical Medicine
D.V.M. Doctor of Veterinary Medicine
D.V.S. Doctor of Veterinary Surgery

E. East
ea. eastern (use for court system only)
E. and P. Extraordinary and Plenipotentiary
Eccles. Ecclesiastical
ecol. ecological
econ. economic
ECOSOC Economic and Social Council (of the UN)
E.D. Doctor of Engineering
ed. educated
Ed.B. Bachelor of Education
Ed.D. Doctor of Education
edit. edition
Ed.M. Master of Education
edn. education
ednl. educational
EDP electronic data processing
Ed.S. Specialist in Education
E.E. Electrical Engineer (degree only)
E.E. and M.P. Envoy Extraordinary and Minister Plenipotentiary
EEC European Economic Community
EEG Electroencephalogram
EEO Equal Employment Opportunity
EEOC Equal Employment Opportunity Commission

EKG Electrocardiogram
E.Ger. German Democratic Republic
elec. electrical
electrochem. electrochemical
electrophys. electrophysical
elem. elementary
E.M. Engineer of Mines
ency. encyclopedia
Eng. England
engr. engineer
engring. engineering
entomol. entomological
environ. environmental
EPA Environmental Protection Agency
epidemiol. epidemiological
Episc. Episcopalian
ERA Equal Rights Amendment
ERDA Energy Research and Development
    Administration
ESEA Elementary and Secondary
    Education Act
ESL English as Second Language
ESSA Environmental Science Services
    Administration
ethnol. ethnological
ETO European Theatre of Operations
Evang. Evangelical
exam. examination, examining
exec. executive
exhbn. exhibition
expdn. expedition
expn. exposition
expt. experiment
exptl. experimental

F.A. Field Artillery
FAA Federal Aviation Administration
FAO Food and Agriculture Organization
    (of the UN)
FBI Federal Bureau of Investigation
FCA Farm Credit Administration
FCC Federal Communication Commission
FCDA Federal Civil Defense
    Administration
FDA Food and Drug Administration
FDIA Federal Deposit Insurance
    Administration
FDIC Federal Deposit Insurance
    Corporation
F.E. Forest Engineer
FEA Federal Energy Administration
Feb. February
fed. federal
fedn. federation
FERC Federal Energy Regulatory
    Commission
fgn. foreign
FHA Federal Housing Administration
fin. financial, finance
FL Florida
Fla. Florida
FMC Federal Maritime Commission

FOA Foreign Operations Administration
found. foundation
FPC Federal Power Commission
FPO Fleet Post Office
frat. fraternity
FRS Federal Reserve System
FSA Federal Security Agency
Ft. Fort
FTC Federal Trade Commission

G-1 (or other number) Division of General
    Staff
Ga., GA Georgia
GAO General Accounting Office
gastroent. gastroenterological
GATT General Agreement of Tariff and
    Trades
gen. general
geneal. genealogical
geod. geodetic
geog. geographic, geographical
geol. geological
geophys. geophysical
gerontol. gerontological
G.H.Q. General Headquarters
G.N. Ry. Great Northern Railway
gov. governor
govt. government
govtl. governmental
GPO Governmental Printing Office
grad. graduate, graduated
GSA General Services Administration
Gt. Great
GU Guam
gynecol. gynecological

hdqrs. headquarters
HEW Department of Health, Education
    and Welfare
H.H.D. Doctor of Humanities
HHFA Housing and Home Finance Agency
HHS Department of Health and Human
    Services
HI Hawaii
hist. historical, historic
H.M. Master of Humanics
homeo. homeopathic
hon. honorary, honorable
Ho. of Dels. House of Delegates
Ho. of Reps. House of Representatives
hort. horticultural
hosp. hospital
HUD Department of Housing and Urban
    Development
Hwy. Highway
hydrog. hydrographic

IA Iowa
IAEA International Atomic Energy Agency
IBM International Business Machines
    Corporation
IBRD International Bank for
    Reconstruction and Development

ICA International Cooperation
    Administration
ICC Interstate Commerce Commission
ICU Intensive Care Unit
ID Idaho
IEEE Institute of Electrical and Electronics
    Engineers
IFC International Finance Corporation
IGY International Geophysical Year
IL Illinois
Ill. Illinois
illus. illustrated
ILO International Labor Organization
IMF International Monetary Fund
IN Indiana
Inc. Incorporated
ind. independent
Ind. Indiana
Indpls. Indianapolis
indsl. industrial
inf. infantry
info. information
ins. insurance
insp. inspector
insp. gen. inspector general
inst. institute
instl. institutional
instn. institution
instr. instructor
instrn. instruction
intern. international
intro. introduction
IRE Institute of Radio Engineers
IRS Internal Revenue Service
ITT International Telephone & Telegraph
    Corporation

JAG Judge Advocate General
JAGC Judge Advocate General Corps
Jan. January
Jaycees Junior Chamber of Commerce
J.B. Jurum Baccolaureus
J.C.B. Juris Canoni Baccalaureus
J.C.D. Juris Canonici Doctor,
    Juris Civilis Doctor
J.C.L. Juris Canonici Licentiatus
J.D. Juris Doctor
j.g. junior grade
jour. journal
jr. junior
J.S.D. Juris Scientiae Doctor
J.U.D. Juris Utriusque Doctor
jud. judicial

Kans. Kansas
K.C. Knights of Columbus
K.P. Knights of Pythias
KS Kansas
K.T. Knight Templar
Ky., KY Kentucky

La., LA Louisiana
lab. laboratory

lang. language
laryngol. laryngological
LB Labrador
lectr. lecturer
legis. legislation, legislative
L.H.D. Doctor of Humane Letters
L.I. Long Island
lic. licensed, license
L.I.R.R. Long Island Railroad
lit. literary, literature
Litt.B. Bachelor of Letters
Litt.D. Doctor of Letters
LL.B. Bachelor of Laws
LL.D. Doctor of Laws
LL.M. Master of Laws
Ln. Lane
L.&N.R.R. Louisville & Nashville Railroad
L.S. Library Science (in degree)
lt. lieutenant
Ltd. Limited
Luth. Lutheran
LWV League of Women Voters

m. married
M. Master
M.A. Master of Arts
MA Massachusetts
mag. magazine
M.Agr. Master of Agriculture
maj. major
Man. Manitoba
Mar. March
M.Arch. Master in Architecture
Mass. Massachusetts
math. mathematics, mathematical
MATS Military Air Transport Service
M.B. Bachelor of Medicine
MB Manitoba
M.B.A. Master of Business Administration
MBS Mutual Broadcasting System
M.C. Medical Corps
M.C.E. Master of Civil Engineering
mcht. merchant
mcpl. municipal
M.C.S. Master of Commercial Science
M.D. Doctor of Medicine
Md, MD Maryland
M.Dip. Master in Diplomacy
mdse. merchandise
M.D.V. Doctor of Veterinary Medicine
M.E. Mechanical Engineer (degree only)
ME Maine
M.E.Ch. Methodist Episcopal Church
mech. mechanical
M.Ed. Master of Education
med. medical
M.E.E. Master of Electrical Engineering
mem. member
meml. memorial
merc. mercantile
met. metropolitan

metall. metallurgical
Met.E. Metallurgical Engineer
meteorol. meteorological
Meth. Methodist
Mex. Mexico
M.F. Master of Forestry
M.F.A. Master of Fine Arts
mfg. manufacturing
mfr. manufacturer
mgmt. management
mgr. manager
M.H.A. Master of Hospital Administration
M.I. Military Intelligence
MI Michigan
Mich. Michigan
micros. microscopic, microscopical
mid. middle (use for Court System only)
mil. military
Milw. Milwaukee
mineral. mineralogical
Minn. Minnesota
Miss. Mississippi
MIT Massachusetts Institute of Technology
mktg. marketing
M.L. Master of Laws
MLA Modern Language Association
M.L.D. Magister Legnum Diplomatic
M.Litt. Master of Literature
M.L.S. Master of Library Science
M.M.E. Master of Mechanical Engineering
MN Minnesota
mng. managing
Mo., MO Missouri
moblzn. mobilization
Mont. Montana
M.P. Member of Parliament
M.P.E. Master of Physical Education
M.P.H. Master of Public Health
M.P.L. Master of Patent Law
Mpls. Minneapolis
M.R.E. Master of Religious Education
M.S. Master of Science
MS, Ms. Mississippi
M.Sc. Master of Science
M.S.F. Master of Science of Forestry
M.S.T. Master of Sacred Theology
M.S.W. Master of Social Work
MT Montana
Mt. Mount
MTO Mediterranean Theatre of Operations
mus. museum, musical
Mus.B. Bachelor of Music
Mus.D. Doctor of Music
Mus.M. Master of Music
mut. mutual
mycol. mycological

N. North
NAACP National Association for the
    Advancement of Colored People
NACA National Advisory Committee for
    Aeronautics

NAD National Academy of Design
N.Am. North America
NAM National Association of Manufacturers
NAPA National Association of Performing
    Artists
NAREB National Association of Real
    Estate Boards
NARS National Archives and Record
    Service
NASA National Aeronautics and Space
    Administration
nat. national
NATO North Atlantic Treaty Organization
NATOUSA North African Theatre of
    Operations
nav. navigation
N.B., NB New Brunswick
NBC National Broadcasting Company
N.C., NC North Carolina
NCCJ National Conference of Christians
    and Jews
N.D., ND North Dakota
NDEA National Defense Education Act
NE Nebraska
NE Northeast
NEA National Education Association
Nebr. Nebraska
NEH National Endowment for Humanities
neurol. neurological
Nev. Nevada
NF Newfoundland
NFL National Football League
Nfld. Newfoundland
N.G. National Guard
N.H. NH New Hampshire
NHL National Hockey League
NIH National Institutes of Health
NIMH National Institute of Mental Health
N.J., NJ New Jersey
NLRB National Labor Relations Board
NM New Mexico
N.Mex. New Mexico
No. Northern
NOAA National Oceanographic and
    Atmospheric Administration
NORAD North America Air Defense
NOW National Organization for Women
Nov. November
N.P.Ry. Northern Pacific Railway
nr. near
NRC National Research Council
N.S., NS Nova Scotia
NSC National Security Council
NSF National Science Foundation
N.T. New Testament
NT Northwest Territories
numis. numismatic
NV Nevada
NW Northwest
N.W.T. Northwest Territories
N.Y., NY New York
N.Y.C. New York City

NYU New York University
N.Z. New Zealand

OAS Organization of American States
ob-gyn obstetrics-gynecology
obs. observatory
obstet. obstetrical
O.D. Doctor of Optometry
OECD Organization of European
 Cooperation and Development
OEEC Organization of European
 Economic Cooperation
OEO Office of Economic Opportunity
ofcl. official
OH Ohio
OK Oklahoma
Okla. Oklahoma
ON Ontario
Ont. Ontario
ophthal. ophthalmological
ops. operations
OR Oregon
orch. orchestra
Oreg. Oregon
orgn. organization
ornithol. ornithological
OSHA Occupational Safety and Health
 Administration
OSRD Office of Scientific Research and
 Development
OSS Office of Strategic Services
osteo. osteopathic
otol. otological
otolaryn. otolaryngological

Pa., PA Pennsylvania
P.A. Professional Association
paleontol. paleontological
path. pathological
P.C. Professional Corporation
PE Prince Edward Island
P.E.I. Prince Edward Island (text only)
PEN Poets, Playwrights, Editors, Essayists
 and Novelists (international association)
penol. penological
P.E.O. women's organization (full name
 not disclosed)
pfc. private first class
PHA Public Housing Administration
pharm. pharmaceutical
Pharm.D. Doctor of Pharmacy
Pharm. M. Master of Pharmacy
Ph.B. Bachelor of Philosophy
Ph.D. Doctor of Philosophy
Phila. Philadelphia
philharm. philharmonic
philol. philological
philos. philosophical
photog. photographic
phys. physical
physiol. physiological
Pitts. Pittsburgh
Pkwy. Parkway

Pl. Place
P.&L.E.R.R. Pittsburgh & Lake Erie
 Railroad
P.O. Post Office
PO Box Post Office Box
polit. political
poly. polytechnic, polytechnical
PQ Province of Quebec
P.R., PR Puerto Rico
prep. preparatory
pres. president
Presbyn. Presbyterian
presdl. presidential
prin. principal
proc. proceedings
prod. produced (play production)
prodn. production
prof. professor
profl. professional
prog. progressive
propr. proprietor
pros. atty. prosecuting attorney
pro tem pro tempore
PSRO Professional Services Review
 Organization
psychiat. psychiatric
psychol. psychological
PTA Parent-Teachers Association
ptnr. partner
PTO Pacific Theatre of Operations,
 Parent Teacher Organization
pub. publisher, publishing, published
pub. public
publ. publication
pvt. private

quar. quarterly
q.m. quartermaster
Q.M.C. Quartermaster Corps.
Que. Quebec

radiol. radiological
RAF Royal Air Force
RCA Radio Corporation of America
RCAF Royal Canadian Air Force
RD Rural Delivery
Rd. Road
REA Rural Electrification Administration
rec. recording
ref. reformed
regt. regiment
regtl. regimental
rehab. rehabilitation
rep. representative
Rep. Republican
Res. Reserve
ret. retired
rev. review, revised
RFC Reconstruction Finance Corporation
RFD Rural Free Delivery
rhinol. rhinological
R.I., RI Rhode Island

R.N. Registered Nurse
roentgenol. roentgenological
ROTC Reserve Officers Training Corps
R.R. Railroad
Ry. Railway

s. son
S. South
SAC Strategic Air Command
SALT Strategic Arms Limitation Talks
S.Am. South America
san. sanitary
SAR Sons of the American Revolution
Sask. Saskatchewan
savs. savings
S.B. Bachelor of Science
SBA Small Business Administration
S.C., SC South Carolina
SCAP Supreme Command Allies Pacific
Sc.B. Bachelor of Science
S.C.D. Doctor of Commercial Science
Sc.D. Doctor of Science
sch. school
sci. science, scientific
SCLC Southern Christian Leadership
 Conference
SCV Sons of Confederate Veterans
S.D., SD South Dakota
SE Southeast
SEATO Southeast Asia Treaty
 Organization
sec. secretary
SEC Securities and Exchange Commission
sect. section
seismol. seismological
sem. seminary
s.g. senior grade
sgt. sergeant
SHAEF Supreme Headquarters Allied
 Expeditionary Forces
SHAPE Supreme Headquarters Allied
 Powers in Europe
S.I. Staten Island
S.J. Society of Jesus (Jesuit)
S.J.D. Scientiae Juridicae Doctor
SK Saskatchewan
S.M. Master of Science
So. Southern
soc. society
sociol. sociological
S.P. Co. Southern Pacific Company
spl. special
splty. specialty
Sq. Square
sr. senior
S.R. Sons of the Revolution
SS Steamship
SSS Selective Service System
St. Saint, Street
sta. station
stats. statistics
statis. statistical

S.T.B. Bachelor of Sacred Theology
stblzn. stabilization
S.T.D. Doctor of Sacred Theology
subs. subsidiary
SUNY State University of New York
supr. supervisor
supt. superintendent
surg. surgical
SW Southwest

TAPPI Technical Association of Pulp
  and Paper Industry
Tb Tuberculosis
tchr. teacher
tech. technical, technology
technol. technological
Tel.&Tel. Telephone & Telegraph
temp. temporary
Tenn. Tennessee
Ter. Territory
Terr. Terrace
Tex. Texas
Th.D. Doctor of Theology
theol. theological
Th.M. Master of Theology
TN Tennessee
tng. training
topog. topographical
trans. transaction, transferred
transl. translation, translated
transp. transportation
treas. treasurer
TV television
TVA Tennessee Valley Authority
twp. township
TX Texas
typog. typographical

U. University
UAW United Auto Workers
UCLA University of California
  at Los Angeles
UDC United Daughters of the Confederacy
U.K. United Kingdom
UN United Nations
UNESCO United Nations Educational,
  Scientific and Cultural Organization
UNICEF United Nations International
  Children's Emergency Fund
univ. university
UNRRA United Nations Relief and
  Rehabilitation Administration
UPI United Press International
U.P.R.R. United Pacific Railroad
urol. urological
U.S. United States
U.S.A. United States of America
USAAF United States Army Air Force
USAF United States Air Force
USAFR United States Air Force Reserve
USAR United States Army Reserve
USCG United States Coast Guard

USCGR United States Coast Guard
  Reserve
USES United States Employment Service
USIA United States Information Agency
USMC United States Marine Corps
USMCR United States Marine Corps
  Reserve
USN United States Navy
USNG United States National Guard
USNR United States Naval Reserve
USO United Service Organizations
USPHS United States Public Health
  Service
USS United States Ship
USSR Union of the Soviet Socialist
  Republics
USV United States Volunteers
UT Utah

VA Veterans' Administration
Va., VA Virginia
vet. veteran, veterinary
VFW Veterans of Foreign Wars
V.I., VI Virgin Islands
vice pres. vice president
vis. visiting
VISTA Volunteers in Service to America
VITA Volunteers in Technical Service
vocat. vocational
vol. volunteer, volume
v.p. vice president
vs. versus
Vt., VT Vermont

W. West
WA Washington (state)
WAC Women's Army Corps
Wash. Washington (state)
WAVES Women's Reserve, U.S. Naval
  Reserve
WCTU Women's Christian Temperance
  Union
we. western (use for court system only)
W. Ger. Germany, Federal Republic of
WHO World Health Organization
WI, Wis. Wisconsin
W.I. West Indies
WSB Wage Stabilization Board
WV West Virginia
W.Va. West Virginia
WY Wyoming
Wyo. Wyoming

YK Yukon Territory (for address)
YMCA Young Men's Christian Association
YMHA Young Men's Hebrew Association
YM & YWHA Young Men's and Young
  Women's Hebrew Association
Y.T. Yukon Territory
YWCA Young Women's Christian
  Association
yr. year

zool. zoological

Alphabetical Practices

Names are arranged alphabetically according to the surnames, and under identical surnames according to the first given name. If both surname and first given name are identical, names are arranged alphabetically according to the second given name. Where full names are identical, they are arranged in order of age—with the elder listed first.

Surnames beginning with De, Des, Du, however capitalized or spaced, are recorded with the prefix preceding the surname and arranged alphabetically, under the letter D.

Surnames beginning with Mac and Mc are arranged alphabetically under M.

Surnames beginning with Saint or St. appear after names that would begin Sains, and are arranged according to the second part of the name, e.g., St. Clair before Saint Dennis.

Surnames beginning with Van, Von, or von are arranged alphabetically under the letter V.

Compound hyphenated surnames are arranged according to the first member of the compound. Compound unhyphenated surnames are treated as hyphenated names.

Parentheses used in connection with a name indicate which part of the full name is usually deleted in common usage. Hence Abbott, W(illiam) Lewis indicates that the usual form of the given name is W. Lewis. In such a case, the parentheses are ignored in alphabetizing. However if the name is recorded Abbott, (William) Lewis, signifying that the entire name William is not commonly used, the alphabetizing would be arranged as though the name were Abbott, Lewis.

Who'sWho in Frontiers of Science and Technology

AAGAARD, GEORGE NELSON, medical educator; b. Mpls., Aug. 16, 1913; s. George N. and Lucy T. (Nelson) A.; m. Lorna D. Docken, Aug. 26, 1939; children: Diane Louise, George Nelson, Richard Nelson, David Nelson, Steven Nelson. B.S., U. Minn., 1934, M.B., 1936, M.D., 1937. Intern Mpls. Gen. Hosp., 1936-37; successively fellow, instr., asst. prof. internal medicine U. Minn. Med. Sch., 1941-47, assoc. prof., dir. continuing med. edn., 1948-51; prof. medicine, dean Southwestern Med. Sch., U. Tex., 1952-54; dean U. Washington Sch. Medicine, 1954-64, prof. medicine, 1954-78, disting. prof. medicine and pharmacology, 1978—, head div. clin. pharmacology, 1964-79; mem. Nat. Adv. Council for Health Research Facilities USPHS, 1954-58; mem. nat. adv. heart council NIH, 1961-65; mem. spl. med. adv. group VA, 1970-74; chmn. bd. trustees Network for Continuing Med. Edn., 1966-78. Bd. dirs., editorial bd.: Western Jour. Medicine. Mem. Am. Heart Assn. (trustee), Assn. Am. Med. Colls. (pres. 1960-61), AMA (dir., chmn. com. continuing profl. edn. programs 1972), Pharm. Mfrs. Assn. Found. (mem. sci. adv. com. 1967-74), Am. Soc. Clin. Pharmacology and Therapeutics (pres. 1977, Elliot award 1983), N.Y. Acad. Scis., A.A.A.S., Washington, King County med. socs., Alpha Omega Alpha. Subspecialties: Internal medicine; Pharmacology. Home: 8001 Sand Point Way NE C66 Seattle WA 98115

AAROE, WILLIAM HENRY, state official, industrial hygienist; b. Perth Amboy, N.J., June 18, 1920; s. Christian P. and Hilda (Petersen) A.; m. Mildred Isabella Ramsay, Sept. 21, 1946; children: Wendy Lou, William Christian; m. Donna Jean Armstead, July 2, 1984. B.S. in San. Engring, Rutgers U., 1942; M.P.H., U. Mich., 1960. Engr./draftsman Raritan Copper Works, Perth Amboy, 1946-48; field engr. Pitometer Co., Inc., N.Y.C., 1948-49; pub. health engr. N.J. Dept. Health, Trenton, 1950-58, prin. pub. health engr. and radiation physicist, 1958-59, radiation physicist, 1960-62, chief radiol. health program, 1962-70; dep. dir. office radiation control N.Y.C. Dept. Pub. Health, 1970-74; acting chief environ. engring. sect. Phila. Dept. Pub. Health, 1975-76, chief occupational and radiol. health sect., 1974-76; dir. indls. hygiene div. W.Va. Dept. Health, South Charleston, 1977—; guest lectr. Rutgers U. Extension, 1963-70, Manhattan Coll., 1972; adj. asst. prof. environ. medicine NYU Med. Ctr., 1973-76; chmn. Conf. Radiol. Health, 1969. Contbr. articles to profl. jours. Served to lt. comdr. USNR, 1943-62; to capt. USPHSR, 1962—. Mem. AAAS, Am. Water Works Assn., Health Physics Soc., Conf. Radiation Control Program Dirs., Am. Conf. Govtl. Indsl. Hygienists (chmn. waste disposal com.), Commd. Officers Assn. USPHS, Am. Indsl. Hygiene Assn., Health Physics Soc., Am. Nuclear Soc., Planetary Soc., Air Pollution Control Assn., Internat. Platform Assn. Subspecialties: Nuclear physics; Toxicology (medicine). Home: 5308 Pamela Circle Cross Lanes WV 25313 Office: 151 11th Ave South Charleston WV 25303

AARSSEN, LONNIE WILLIAM, biology educator; b. Chatham, Ont., Can., May 19, 1955; s. William Alexander and Shirley Mae (Lawrence) A.; m. Brenda Jean Kilgren, Feb. 19, 1983. B.Sc. with honors, U. Western Ont., London, Can., 1978; Ph.D., U. B.C., Vancouver, Can., 1983. Lectr., Queen's U., Kingston, Ont., Can., 1982-83, asst. prof. biology, 1983—. Contbr. articles to profl. jours. and chpts. to books. Nat. Scis. and Engring. Research Council Can. grantee, 1983. Mem. Brit. Ecol. Soc., Ecol. Soc. Am., Can. Bot. Assn., Internat. Soc. Plant Population Biologists. Current work: Plant population dynamics in relation to community organization and development; neighbour interactions, ecotypic variation, co-evolution of competitors, mechanisms of coexistence. Subspecialties: Population biology; Species interaction. Home: Box 84 Yarker ON K0K 3N0 Canada Office: Dept Biology Queen's Univ Kingston ON K7L 3N6 Canada

ABBEY, GEORGE WILLIAM SAMUEL, engineer; b. Seattle, Aug. 21, 1932; s. Sam and Brenta (Gibby) A.; m. Joyce Rohel Wilderman, Sept. 13, 1955 (div. 1980); children—George William Samuel, Joyce, Suzanne, James, Andrew. B.S., U.S. Naval Acad., 1954; M.S. in Elec. Engring., U.S. Air Force Inst. Tech., 1959. System engr. Dyna-Soar program U.S. Air Force, Dayton, Ohio, also Boeing Co., Seattle, 1959-64; chief system int. (Apollo), NASA, Johnson Space Ctr., Houston, 1964-67, tech. asst. to program mgr., Apollo, 1967-69, tech. asst. to dir., 1969-76, dir. flight ops., 1976-83, dir. flight crew ops., 1983—. Contbr. articles to profl. jours. Served to maj. USAF, 1954-67. Recipient Dist. Servicel medal, NASA, 1972, 81, Exceptional Service medal, 1969; Cert. of Commendation, 1968; Medal of Freedom, Pres. U.S., 1970, others. Fellow Am. Astron. Soc., U.S. Naval Inst., AIAA; mem. Naval Acad. Alumni Assn. Current work: Director of space shuttle flight crew operations. Select, train and prepare and direct space shuttle astronaut activities. Subspecialties: Aerospace engineering and technology; Electrical engineering. Office: Johnson Space Center NASA Houston TX 77058

ABBOTT, DALLAS HELEN, marine geophysicist, researcher; b. Auburn, Maine, July 3, 1952; d. Edward Farrington and Maude (McCurry) Abbott; m. William Henry Menke, Aug. 24, 1977. B.S., MIT, 1974; Ph.D., Columbia U., 1982. Asst. prof. marine geophysics Oreg. State U., 1982—. Contbr. articles to sci., profl. jours. Mem. Am. Geophys. Union, Geol. Soc. Am. Current work: Submarine hydrothermal activity; heat flow; Archaen tectonics; sediment slides; turbidity currents; sea level history. Office: Geophysics Dept Oreg State U OCII Corvallis OR 97331

ABBOTT, WILLIAM HAROLD, JR., micropaleontologist; b. Atlanta, Mar. 23, 1944; s. William Harold and Mary Elizabeth (Casteel) A.; m. Eloise May Jones, Aug. 23, 1969; 1 child, John Casteel. B.S., Ga. State U., 1969; M.S., Northeast La. State U., 1970; Ph.D., U. S.C., 1972. Asst. prof. U. S.C., Beaufort, 1972-74; coastal plains geologist S.C. Geol. Survey, Columbia, 1974-80; sr. staff paleontologist Mobil Oil Co., Dallas, 1980—. Contbr. articles to profl. jours. Editor: Studies in North American Cenozoic Correlations, 1984. Mem. Geol. Soc. Am., Am. Assn. Petroleum Geologists, Soc. Econ. Paleontologists and Mineralogists, (diatom working group chmn. 1983—). Methodist. Current work Utilize fossil diatoms and calcareous nannoplankton for worldwide correlations of geologic units and interpretation of environment deposition. Subspecialties: Paleontology; Paleontology, paleoecology. Home: PO Box 1007 Midlothian TX 76065 Office: Mobile Exploration Producing Services PO Box 900 Dallas TX 75221

ABBRECHT, PETER HERMAN, physiologist, educator; b. Toledo, Nov. 27, 1930; s. Hermann Richard and Paula Katherine (Schwenk) A.; m. Anne Patterson Lampman, Feb. 16, 1957; children—Elaine, Brian. B.S., Purdue U., 1952; M.S., U. Mich., 1953, Ph.D. in Chem. Engring, 1957, M.D., 1962. Diplomate: Am. Bd. Internal Medicine. Sr. chem. engr. Minn. Mining & Mfg. Co., Detroit, 1956-58; intern U. Calif. Hosp., Los Angeles, 1962-63; mem. faculty U. Mich. Med. Sch., Ann Arbor, 1963-80, prof. physiology, 1972-80, chmn. bioengring. program, 1972-77, prof. internal medicine, 1976-80; prof. internal medicine and physiology Uniformed Services U. of Health Scis., Bethesda, Md.; and cons. physician Walter Reed Army Med. Center, 1980—; guest scientist Naval Med. Research Inst., 1980-82; resident in internal medicine U. Mich. Hosp., 1971-72, fellow in pulmonary disease, 1974-75; vis. prof. bioengring. U. Calif., San Diego, 1973; dir. physiology and biomed. engring. program NIGMS-NIH, 1977-78; cons. VA, NASA, Air Force Office Sci. Research, NIH, NSF; mem. nat. research resources advisory council, 1975-78. Editor in chief: Internat. Jour. Biomed. Engring, 1972-74; Editorial bd.: Jour. Biomechanics; editor-in-chief: Annals Biomed. Engring., 1979-84. Contbr. articles to profl. jours. Recipient outstanding research award Mich. Heart Assn., 1960; research career devel. award NIH, 1969-73. Fellow Am. Coll. Chest Physicians, ACP; mem. Biomed. Engring. Soc. (dir. 1970-72); Mem. Am. Physiol. Soc., Am. Thoracic Soc., Soc. Exptl. Biology and Medicine. Current Work: Control of respiration; high frequency ventilators. Subspecialties: Physiology (medicine); Biomedical engineering. Home: 2806 Spencer Rd Chevy Chase MD 20815

ABDEL-LATIF, ATA ABDEL-HAFEZ, biochemist, educator; b. Palestine, Jan. 22, 1933; s. Abdel-hafez M. and Ayshah A. (Abour) Abdel-L.; m. Iris K. Graham, Sept. 10, 1957; children: Rhonda, David, Joseph, Rhadi. B.S. in Chemistry, DePaul U., 1955, M.S. in Chemistry, 1958; Ph.D. in Biochemistry, Ill. Inst. Tech., 1963. Postdoctoral fellow U. Ill., Chgo., 1963-65; med. research assoc. U. Ill.-State of Ill. Pediatric Inst., Chgo., 1965-67; assoc. prof. biochemistry Med. Coll. Ga., 1967-74, prof. cell and molecular biology, 1974—. Contbr. articles on biochemistry of nerve and muscle to profl. publs. NIH grantee, 1963—. Mem. Am. Soc. Biol. Chemistsy, Am. Physiol. Soc., Internat. Soc. Neurochemistry, others. Current Work: Effects of neurotransmitters on phospholipid metabolism in nerve and muscle. Release of arachidonate from membrane phospholipids for prostaglandin synthesis in nerve and muscle. Subspecialty: Biochemistry (medicine). Home: 123 Avondale Dr Augusta GA 30907 Office: Dept Cell and Molecular Biology Med Coll GA Augusta GA 30912

ABDOU, MOHAMED AZIZ, nuclear engineer; b. Egypt, July 10, 1945; came to U.S., 1969, naturalized, 1980; s. Abdelaziz A. Abdou and Ensaf M. Basha; m. Zahira M. El-Derini, Sept. 17, 1969; 1 child, Shareef. B.S., U. Alexandria, Egypt, 1967; M.S., U. Wis., 1971, Ph.D., 1973. Nuclear engr. Argonne (Ill.) Nat. Lab., 1974-78, assoc. dir. fusion power program, 1979-83; head fusion sect., applied physics div.; assoc. prof. Ga. Inst. Tech., Atlanta, 1978-79; mgr. nuclear engring. and materials br. Fusion Engring. Design Center, Oak Ridge Nat. Lab., 1982-83; prof. mech., aerospace and nuclear engring. dept. UCLA, 1983—. Mem. Am. Nuclear Soc. Current Work: Development of fusion engineering and technology; special interest in nuclear components (first wall, blanket, shield, impurity control) of fusion reactors and overall fusion reactor system analysis and design. Subspecialties: Nuclear fusion; Nuclear fission. Office: 6288 Boelter Hall UCLA Los Angeles CA 90024

ABDOU, NABIH I., physician, educator; b. Cairo, Egypt, Oct. 11, 1934; came to U.S., 1962, naturalized, 1972; s. Ibrahim and Galila (Azer) A.; m. Nancy L. Layle, Aug. 26, 1939; children: Mark L., Marie L. M.D., Cairo U., 1959; Ph.D., McGill U., 1969. Prof. medicine U. Kans. Med. Center, Kansas City, 1978—. Fulbright scholar, 1962-65. Fellow A.C.P., Am. Acad. Allergy; mem. Am. Assn. Immunologists, Am. Rheumatism Assn., Central Soc. Clin. Research. Current Work: Cellular immunology, autoimmunity. Subspecialties: Immunology (medicine); Allergy. Office: U Kans Med Center 4035B Kansas City KS 66103

ABDULHAY, GAZI, obstetrician, genecologist, educator; b. Antakya-Hatay, Turkey, Sept. 14, 1948; s. Ali and Mediha (Bekfilavi) A.; m. Suzanne Moorman, Aug. 18, 1979; 1 child, Leyla. M.D. (Turkish Sci. and Tech. Research Assn. scholar), U. Istanbul, 1972. Diplomate: Am. Bd. Ob-Gyn. Extern Soldier's Home, Chelsea, Mass., 1972-73; intern Rush-Presbyn.-St. Luke's Med. Ctr., Chgo., 1973-74, resident in ob-gyn, 1974-77; clin. fellow in gynecologic oncology Georgetown U., Washington, 1977-78, U. Calif.-Irvine, 1978-80; asst. prof. ob-gyn Oreg. Health Scis. U., Portland, 1980—, chief gynecologic oncology, 1980—. Contbr. numerous sci. articles to profl. jours. Mem. Med Assn. Arab Ams., Am. Coll. Ob-Gyn, AMA, Soc. Gynecologic Oncologists, ACS, Western Assn. Gynecologic Oncologists. Current Work: Cervical cancer interferon in gynecological malignancies; clinical and basic science research related to gynecologic oncology. Subspecialties: Oncology; Gynecological oncology. Home: 4268 Albert Circle Lake Oswego OR 97034 Office: 3181 SE Sam Jackson Park Rd Portland OR 97201

ABDULLA, ABDULLA MOHAMMED, cardiologist, medical educator; b. Bombay, India, June 20, 1942; came to U.S., 1971; s. Mohammed Abedeen and Zubaida (Siddick) A.; m. Shahien Shahzada, Dec. 20, 1970 (div. 1978); children: Aaliya, Mikaal; m. Sue Ann Swan, Apr. 6, 1979; 1 child, Siara. B.Sc. (honors), U. Karachi, Pakistan, 1965, M.B., B.S., 1970. Diplomate: Am. Bd. Internal Medicine, Am. Bd. Cardiology. Intern Dow. Med. Coll., U. Karachi, Pakistan, 1970-71; intern Mt. Carmel Mercy Med. Center, Detroit, 1971-72, resident in internal medicine, 1972-74; fellow in cardiology Med. Coll. Ga., Augusta, 1974-76, attending physician in cardiology, 1976—, asst. chief cardiology, 1983—, assoc. prof. medicine, 1980-85, prof. medicine, 1985—, dir. hemodynamics lab., 1984—; cons. computer aided instructions to med. schs., 1980—, lectr. in field. Author: Cardiovascular Physical Diagnosis, 1983; contbr. chpts. to books; reviewer: Jour. AMA, 1982—, Jour. Am. Acad. Dermatology, 1982—; Contbr. to profl. jours. Fellow Am. Coll. Cardiology, ACP; mem. So. Soc. Clin. Investigations, AMA, So. Med. Assn. (vice chmn. chest diseases sect. So. chpt. 1982), Am. Heart Assn. (teaching scholar 1980-83), Ga. Heart Assn. (dir. 1982—). Republican. Developer multi-media computer-aided learning in med. edn., (Gov.s award of Excellence Am. Coll. Cardiology 1982), 1980. Current Work: Cardiac diseases; computer-assisted learning; medical education. Subspecialty: Cardiology. Home: 2333 Kings Way Augusta GA 30904 Office: Med Coll GA 15th St Suite 6125 Augusta GA 30912

ABEL, CARLOS ALBERTO, immunologist; b. Buenos Aires, Argentina, May 7, 1930; came to U.S., 1959, naturalized, 1969; s. Carlos Alberto and Rosa Blanca (Molinero) A.; m. Amalia Carmen Minieri, June 15, 1959; B.S., M. Belgrano Coll., 1948; M.D., U. Buenos Aires, 1957. Intern, St Joseph's Hosp., Providence, 1959-60; resident in pediatrics U. Md. Hosp., 1964-66; fellow in pediatrics U. Md., Balt., 1960-64, resident in pediatrics, 1964-66; advanced research fellow Scripps Clinic, La Jolla, Calif., 1966-69; vis. scientist U. Oxford, Eng., 1969-70; mem. div. basic immunology Nat. Jewish Hosp., Denver, 1970-84; sr. scientist Med. Research Inst., San Francisco, 1984—; vis. scholar U. Calif.-Berkeley, 1982. Contbr. articles to profl. jours. Mem. Am. Assn. Immunologists, Am. Assn. Pathologists, Biochem. Soc. (Eng.), British Soc. for Immunology, Sociedad Argentina de Immunologia, Asociacion Latino Americana Immunologia. Democrat. Roman Catholic. Current work: Structure and function of glycoproteins from the surface of lymphocytes: study of their role in cell-cell interactions. Home: 523 Cragmont Ave Berkeley CA 94708 Office: Med Research Inst 2200 Webster St San Francisco CA 94115

ABEL, ERNEST LAWRENCE, research scientist; b. Toronto, Ont., Can., Feb. 10, 1943; s. Jack and Rose (Tarshes) A.; m. Barbara Ellen Buckley; two children. B.A. in Psychology, U. Toronto, 1965, M.A. in Psychology, 1967, Ph.D. in Psychology, 1971. Postdoctoral fellow U. N.C., Chapel Hill, 1971-73; research asst. prof. in pediatrics SUNY-Buffalo, 1981—, research assoc. prof. in psychology, 1981—; acting dep. dir. Research Inst. Alcoholism, Buffalo, 1983-84, prin. supr. research, 1984-85, research scientist VI, 1984-85; prof. obstetrics Wayne State U., Detroit, 1985—, prof. psychology, 1985—; dir. ops. Mott Ctr. for Human Growth and Devel., Detroit. Author: Marihuana, Tobacco, Alcohol and Reproduction, 1983; Drugs and Sex, 1984; Smoking and Reproduction: An Annotated Bibliography, 1984; Fetal Alcohol Syndrome/-Fetal Alcohol Effects, 1984. Contbr. revs. to profl. publs. Grantee Nat. Inst. on Drug Abuse, 1984—, Nat. Inst. Alcoholism and Alcohol Abuse, 1983—, Health Research Council, 1981-82. Mem. Western N.Y. Task Force on Prevention of Mental Retardation and Developmental Disabilities (chmn. fetal alcohol subcom. 1981-83), Research Soc. on Alcoholism (pres. fetal alcohol study group 1985—), Teratology Soc., N.Y. Acad. Scis., Behavioral Teratology Soc. (pres. 1983-84). Current work: Epidemiological investigations of alcohol and violence, behavioral and pharmacological studies of effects of pre-and postnatal exposure to drugs. Subspecialties: Reproductive biology (medicine); Pediatrics. Office: Mott Ctr for Human Growth and Devel 275 E Hancock St Detroit MI 48201

ABEL, LARRY ALLEN, neuroscience researcher, educator; b. Pitts., Dec. 21, 1949; s. Edgar Mannist and Cecilia (Carpe) A. B.S. in Elec. Engring., Carnegie-Mellon U., 1971, M.S., 1972, Ph.D., 1976. Postdoctoral fellow Bascom Palmer Eye Inst., U. Miami, Fla., 1976-78; research assoc. dept. neurology U. Pitts., 1978-79, research asst. prof., 1979-80; biomed. engr., co-dir. ocular motor neurophysiology lab. Research Service, VA Med. Ctr., Cleve., 1980—; asst. prof. dept. neurology, also dept. biomed. engring. Case Western Res. U., Cleve., 1980—. Co-author jour. articles and book chpts. Grantee Health Research and Services Found., Pitts., 1979, VA, Cleve., 1982—. Mem. IEEE, Assn. Research in Vision and Ophthalmology, Soc. Neurosci. Jewish. Current work: Application of systems engineering techniques to study of control of eye movements and to visual perception. Subspecialties: Biomedical engineering; Neurophysiology. Home: 3745 Woodridge Rd Cleveland Heights OH 44121 Office: Dept Neurology Case Western Res U 2074 Abington Rd Cleveland OH 44106

ABELA, GEORGE SAMIH, medical educator, internist; b. Tripoli, Lebanon, Jan. 1, 1950; came to U.S., 1976, naturalized, 1983; s. Anthony George and Maro (Kozma) A.; m. Sonia Zablit, May 14, 1977; children—Oliver George, Andrew John. B.Sc. in Chemistry and Biology, Am. U. of Beirut, 1971, M.Sc. in Pharmacology, 1974, M.D., 1976. Diplomate Am. Bd. Internal Medicine. Intern in pathology Emory U., Atlanta, 1976-77, resident in medicine, 1977-80; fellow in cardiology U. Fla., Gainesville, 1980-83, asst. prof. medicine and cardiology, 1983—. Research fellow Am. Heart Assn., 1982-83; Merck fellow Am. Coll. Cardiology, 1982-83; recipient New Investigator Research award NIH, 1983-86. Fellow Am. Soc. for Lasers in Medicine, Am. Coll. Cardiology (assoc.); mem. Am. Heart Assn., ACP. Current work: Development and application of lasers and optics to treatment of cardiovascular diseases. Subspecialties: Laser medicine; Cardiology. Office: Dept Medicine-Cardiology Box J-277 JHMHC Gainesville FL 32610

ABELES, TOM PETER, renewable energy consultant, researcher; b. Louisville, Feb. 25, 1941; s. Gerd Hans and Ilse Rachael (Lowenstein) A.; m. Ruth Elaine Brink, 1980; children: Katrina Victoria Brink, Christopher Mathew. B.S. cum laude (Nat. Merit Scholar), Wilmington (Ohio) Coll., 1963; Ph.D. (NDEA scholar), U. Louisville, 1969. Asso. prof. U. Wis., Green Bay, 1970-76; pres., chmn. bd. i.e. assocs., inc., Mpls., 1976—. Contbr. articles to profl. jours. Fellow, v.p. Minn. chpt. Partners of the Ams. Mem. Soc. Gen. Systems Research, World Future Soc., others. Current Work: Research and development of renewable energy, financial and economic development, energy systems, agricultural energy management, overseas energy development, policy analysis. Subspecialties: Biomass (energy science and technology); Solar energy. Office: i e associates 3704 11th Ave S Minneapolis MN 55407

ABELSON, JOHN N., molecular biologist. Prof. div. of biology Calif. Inst. Tech. Elected Nat. Acad. Scis., 1985. Subspecialty: Molecular biology. Office: Calif Inst Tech Div of Biology Pasadena CA 91125

ABEND, KENNETH, electrical engineer; educator; b. N.Y.C., Jan. 14, 1936; s. Isadore and Sadie A.; m. Judith Segal, June 26, 1966; children—Cary, Illysa, Debra, Lori. B.E.E. cum laude, CCNY, 1958; M.S. in Elec. Engring., U. Pa., 1963, Ph.D., 1966. Sr. research engr. Philco Research Lab., Phila., 1958-63; engring. research specialist Philco-Ford Corp., Blue Bell, Pa., 1964-68; sr. engring. specialist Ford-Aerospace & Communication, Willow Grove, Pa., 1968-76; prin. mem. engring. staff RCA Govt. Systems Div., Moorestown, N.J., 1976-84; mgr. adv. signal processing Interspec, Conshohocken, Pa., 1984—; assoc. mem. grad. faculty elec. engring. dept., Pa. State U., King Prussia, 1967—; adj. assoc. prof. systems engring. dept. U. Pa., Phila., 1972—. Contbr. articles to profl. jours. Fellow U. Pa., 1963. Mem. IEEE (sr.), Sigma Xi, Eta Kappa Nu. Lodge: B'nai B'rith. Current work: Research and development and analysis of advanced digital and statistical signal processing systems and techniques for radar, communications and pattern recognition. Subspecialties: Electrical engineering; Systems engineering. Home: 623 Killdeer Ln Huntingdon Valley PA 19006 Office: Interspec 1100 E Hector St Conshohocken PA 19428

ABERCROMBIE, RONALD FORD, researcher, educator; b. Greenville, S.C., June 10, 1946; s. Paul Robert and Pauline Hazel (Morillo) A.; m. Janice Lee Nale, May 31, 1969. B.S. in Physics, U. N.C., 1968; M.S. in Physics, U. Md., 1972, Ph.D. in Biophysics, 1976. Asst. prof. U. Md., Balt., 1976-82; research assoc. Washington U., St. Louis, 1980-82; asst. prof. Emory U. Med. Sch., Atlanta, 1982—. Contbr. articles to profl. jours. Served with U.S. Army, 1969-70. Recipient Grass Found. fellow, 1976; Am. Heart Assn. award, 1979; NIH award, 1982—. Mem. Soc. Gen. Physiologists, Biophys. Soc., N.Y. Acad. Scis., AAAS, Am. Assn. Physics Tchrs. Current work: Description of diffusion and binding of intracellular ions, especially $Ca2+$ and $H+$; ionic hemeostasis in neurons and transport of ions across membranes. Subspecialties: Biophysics (biology); Neurobiology. Home: 4118 Yuma Dr Clarkston GA 30021 Office: Emory U Sch Medicine Room 244 Physiology Bldg Atlanta GA 30322

ABERG, GUNNAR A.K., pharmacologist; b. Falkenberg, Sweden, Mar. 16, 1936; came to U.S., 1978, naturalized, 1980; s. Thorsten Gustaf and Birgit (Lindahl) A.; m. Britt-Marie Wiman, Jan. 15, 1964 (div. Apr. 1974); 1 dau., Maria; m. Laurie Jane Seagondollar, May 27, 1978; 1 son, Peter. Ph.D. in Physiology, U. Gothenberg, Sweden, 1965; Ph.D. in Pharmacology, U. Linkoping, Sweden, 1972. Sect. head Bofors Nobel-Pharma, Molndal, Sweden, 1964-68, dir. pharmacology, 1968-73; group leader Haessle, Gothenburg, 1973-78; dir. cardiovascular pharmacology Astra, Worcester, Mass., 1978-80, Ciba-Geigy, Summit, N.J., 1980-82; dir. pharmacology Squibb Corp., Princeton, N.J., 1982—; assoc. prof. U. Linkoping, 1974—. Contbr. articles to profl. jours. Served with Swedish Army, 1956-57. Lutheran. Patentee in field. Current Work: Cardiovascular drug research. Subspecialties: Pharmacology; Membrane biology. Home: 519 Bergen St Lawrenceville NJ 08648 Office: Squibb Inst for Med Research PO Box 4000 Princeton NJ 08540

ABERMAN, HAROLD MARK, veterinarian, biomedical engineer; b. Chgo., Aug. 5, 1956; s. Howard Oscar and Goldie Esther (Imyak) A. B.S. in Biology, Purdue U., 1979, D.V.M., 1983; B.S.E., 1985; postgrad., 1985—. Research technician Purdue U., West Lafayette, 1978-80; summer fellow Lovelace Biomed., Albuquerque, 1981; NIH fellow, 1983—. Recipient Vet. Student award Lake Shore Kennel Club, 1982; Gordon Research Found. grant-in-aid, 1984. Mem. Am. Vet. Med. Assn., Am. Animal Hosp. Assn. Jewish. Current work: Long term bone remodeling under non-invasive steady state conditions; bone blood flow measurements per non-invasive quantitative methods. Subspecialties: Biomaterials; Artificial organs and prostheses. Home: 122 Waldron Apt 1 West Layfayette IN 47906 Office: Biomed Engring Ctr Purdue U West Lafayette IN 47907

ABERNATHY, BILL J., energy engineer, educator, consultant; b. Cape Girardeau, Mo., Oct. 19, 1922; s. Leonard W. and Anna E. (Austin) A.; m. June E. Abernathy, June 19, 1923; children: Janice Abernathy Ririe, Barbara Abernathy Rummel, Steven. Vocat. class A credential, UCLA. Mem. faculty Orange Coast Coll., 1961-83, successively asst. prof. energy engring., assoc. prof., later prof. energy engring., dean tech. div., cons. energy, now ret.; dir. energy audit and solar seminars energy mgmt. trainer. Served with USN. Decorated Presdl. citation. Patentee portable recompression chamber. Current Work: Energy conservation in residential and commercial structures; passive solar energy. Subspecialty: Solar energy. Office: 3303 Harbor Blvd Costa Mesa CA 92626

ABID, SYED HASAN, virologist; b. Delhi, India, Apr. 27, 1945; came to U.S., 1968, naturalized, 1976; s. Syed Mohammad and Sahar Zainab (Bilgrami) Askari; m. Barbara Bozena, Dec. 1, 1973; children: Sahra Sheerin, Anisa Farah. M.Sc., U. Karachi, Pakistan, 1966; M.S., No. Ill. U., DeKalb, 1970; Ph.D., U. Ill., 1975. Lectr. dept. biol. scis. U. Ill., Chgo., 1970-71; teaching asst. dept. microbiology U. Ill. Med. Ctr., 1971-74, research assoc. dept. biochemistry,

1975; virologist research dept. Met. San. Dist. Greater Chgo., 1975-83; dir. virology program Pub. Health Labs., Westchester County, Valhalla, N.Y., 1983—; cons. dept. microbiology and botany U. Kuwait, 1981—; cons. United Nations Devel. Programme, 1983—. Recipient Summer Study award Internat. Inst. Edn., 1969; Am. Cancer Soc. instl. grantee, 1973-74. Mem. Am. Soc. Microbiology. Islam. Current Work: Development of new methods for virus detection in environmental and clinical specimen, development of methods and detection of mutagens and carcinogens using short term mutagenic/carcinogenic tests in environmental samples; assessment of health risks resulting due to microbial and chemical burden in the environment. Subspecialties: Animal virology; Cell and tissue culture.

ABIDI, SHARON LOW, research chemist, consultant; b. Hsin Chu, Taiwan, China, Nov. 6, 1934; came to U.S., 1962, naturalized, 1972; d. Anan and Lu Mei (Liu) Low; m. Mir Syed Faiyaz Ali Abidi, Nov. 24, 1964. B.S., Cheng Kung U., 1960; M.A., U. Calif.-Santa Barbara, 1964; Ph.D., U. Maine, 1969. Various positions with various universities, 1960-74; research assoc. Am. Health Found., N.Y.C., 1974-76; sr. scientist Meloy Labs., Springfield, Va., 1976-78; research chemist Brown & Williams Tobacco Co., Louisville, 1978; Nat. Fishery Research Lab., La Crosse, Wis., 1978—. Contbr. articles to profl. jours. Mem. Am. Chem. Soc., Sigma Xi. Current work: Research work in chemistry pertaining to Synthetic Organic Chemistry and developing methodology utilizing modern analytical tools. Subspecialties: Organic chemistry; Analytical chemistry. Home: 1705 LaCrescent St #127 LaCrosse WI 54603 Office: Nat Fishery Research Lab 2630 Fanta Reed Rd LaCrosse WI 54603

ABLASHI, DHARAM VIR, virologist, immunologist, lecturer, researcher; b. Lahore, India, Oct. 8, 1931; came to U.S., 1959, naturalized, 1970; s. Maharaj Krishan and Lajwanti Devi D.; m. Kristine Louise Upper, Aug. 13, 1966; children: Kerin Louise, Davinder Kumar, Sameer Kumar. Diploma radio engring., Poly. Tech. Inst., Delhi, India, 1950; D.V.M., Panjab Veterinary Coll., India, 1955; M.S., U. R.I., 1962. Sr. research assoc. Indian Veterinary Research Inst., Izatnagar, India, 1955-59; research assoc. Animal Pathology dept. U. R.I., Kingston, 1960-66; research veterinarian Cobb Breeding Corp., Concord, Mass., 1967-69; research viorologist Flow Labs., Inc., Rockville, Md., 1967-69; research microbiologist Nat. Cancer Inst. NIH, Bethesda, Md., 1969-73, head primate virus sect., 1973-79; microbiologist Nat. Cancer Inst. NIH (Lab. Cellular and Molecular Biology), 1979—; mem. Nat. Cancer Inst. NIH (Primate Exec. Com.), 1972-77; mem. internat. faculty WHO/Internat. Agy. Research on Cancer, Lyon, France, 1974-76, 78; cons. in field. Editor: (with others) Epstein Barr Virus Production, Concentration and Purification, 1975, Nasopharyngeal Carcinoma, 1980, Nasopharyngeal Carcinoma-Current Concepts and Prospects, 1983; contbr. (with others) numerous articles to profl. jours. Chmn. Environ. com. Chincoteague Bay Trails END Assn. Inc., 1977—, dir., 1979—. NIH grantee, 1963-65. Mem. Am. Soc. Microbiology, Am. Assn. Cancer Research, Internat. Assn. Comparative Research on Leukemia and Related Diseases, Soc. Exptl. Biology and Medicine, Veterinary Cancer Soc. Republican. Hindu. Current Work: Etiologic role, mechanism of action and control of DNA viruses of primates with oncogenesis with particular emphasis on herpesviruses; study in nasopharyngeal carcinoma in relation to virus, chemicals, etc. Subspecialties: Cancer research (medicine); Virology (medicine).

ABLIN, RICHARD JOEL, immunologist; b. Chgo., May 15, 1940; s. Robert B. and Minnie E. (Gordon) A.; m. Linda L. Lutwack; 1 son, Michael D. A.B., Lake Forest Coll., 1962; Ph.D., SUNY, Buffalo, 1967. Diplomate: Am. Bd. Clin. Immunology and Allergy; cert. Nat. Registry Microbiologists. Instr., research asst. Rosary Hill Coll., Buffalo, 1965-66; USPHS postdoctoral fellow in microbiology SUNY Sch. Medicine-Buffalo, 1966-68; AID research cons. Paraguay Program in Med. Edn., 1968; dir. div. immunology Millard Fillmore Hosp., Buffalo, 1968-70; head immunology sect. renal unit and cons. med. staff Meml. Hosp. of Springfield, Ill., 1970-73; asst. prof. medicine So. Ill. U. Sch. Medicine, Springfield, 1971-73; cons. med. staff dept. pediatrics St. Johns Hosp., Springfield, 1971-73; dir. immunobiology sect. div. urology dept. surgery Cook County Hosp. and Hektoen Inst. Med. Research, Chgo., 1973-75, sr. sci. officer div. immunology, 1976-83; sr. sci. staff, clin. immunologist Cook County Hosp., 1973-75; assoc. prof. microbiology Univ. Health Scis./Chgo. Med. Sch., 1973-74; research assoc. prof. urology, dir. immunology unit, dept. urology Health Scis. Ctr., SUNY-Stony Brook, 1983—. Editor or contbg. editor numerous sci. jours. and books; contbr. articles to sci. publs. Fellow Am. Assn. Clin. Immunology and Allergy, Am. Coll. Cryosurgery (v.p. 1977-79), Nat. Acad. Clin. Biochemistry; mem. AAAS, Am. Assn. Cancer Research, Am. Assn. Immunologists, Am. Fedn. Clin. Research, Am. Soc. Immunology of Reprodn., Assn. Clin. Scientists, Brit. Assn. Surg. Oncology (overseas mem.), Buffalo Collegium of Immunology, Internat. Soc. Andrology, Internat. Soc. Chronobiology, Internat. Soc. Cryosurgery (U.S. del. 1980-83, pres. 1977-80, hon. life pres.), Internat. Soc. Immunology of Reprodn., Japan Soc. Low Temperature Medicine, N.Y. Acad. Scis., Reticuloendothelial Soc., Soc. Cryobiology, Soc. Exptl. Biology and Medicine, Soc. Protozoologists, Soc. Study Reprodn., Transplanation Soc., Sigma Xi. Current Work: Aberrations of immunologic responsiveness; immunologic consequences of experimentally and clinically induced hypo- and hyperthermia; immunoparasitic relationships; transplantation and tumor antigens. Subspecialties: Immunology (medicine); Cancer research (medicine). Office: Dept Urology Health Scis Ctr SUNY Stony Brook NY 11794

ABLOWITZ, MARK JAY, mathematics and computer science educator; b. Bronx, N.Y., June 5, 1945; s. Ben and Mae (Markoff) A.; m. Enid Bate, June 9, 1968. B.A., U. Rochester, 1967; Ph.D., MIT, 1971. Teaching asst. MIT, Cambridge, Mass., 1967-71, instr., 1970; asst. prof. math. Clarkson Coll. Tech., Potsdam, N.Y., 1971-75, assoc. prof. math., 1975-76, prof. math. and computer sci., 1977—, chmn. dept. math. and computer sci., 1979—. Author: (with H. Segur) Solitons and the Inverse Scattering Transform, 1981. Recipient Clarkson Graham Research award Clarkson Coll. Tech., 1976; Sloan fellow, 1975-77; Guggenheim fellow, 1984. Mem. Soc. Indsl. and Applied Math., Math. Assn. Am., Am. Math. Soc., Sigma Xi, Tau Beta Pi. Current work: Solutions of nonlinear evolution equations of physical interest. Subspecialty: Applied mathematics. Office: Dept Math and Computer Sci Clarkson Coll Tech Potsdam NY 13676

ABOOD, LEO GEORGE, educator; b. Erie, Pa., Jan. 15, 1922; s. George E. and Sara (Muffet) A.; m Lois Wuchner, Sept. 25, 1947; children—George T., Mary E. B.S., Ohio State U., 1943; Ph.D., U. Chgo., 1950. Instr. physiology U. Chgo., 1950-52; assoc. prof. biochemistry U. Ill., Chgo.-1954-63, prof., 1963-65; prof. brain research and biochemistry U. Rochester, N.Y., 1965—; mem. biomed. research com. Nat. Inst. Drug Abuse; mem. com. on anticholinergics, com. risk assessment of chemi. agt. stockpile Nat. Acad. Sci., 1981—; trustee Brain Research Found.; dir. sci. Huxley Research Inst. Editorial bd. Experimental Neurology, 1974, Jour. Neurosci. Research, 1974. Contbr. numerous articles to profl. jours. Patentee in field. Served with USNR, 1943-46. Mem. Am. Chem. Soc., Am. Physiol. Soc., Soc. Neurosci., Am. Soc. Neurochemistry. Subspecialties: Neurochemistry; Molecular pharmacology. Home: 45 Crandon Way Rochester NY 14618 Office: Ctr Brain Research U Rochester Med Ctr Rochester NY 14642

ABOU-DONIA, MARTHA MAY, neurochemist; b. Cedar Creek, Ark., June 6, 1944; d. James S. and Helen E. (Hughes) Davis; m. Mohamed Bahie-el-dien Abou-Donia, Feb. 1, 1967; children: Tarek, Sheref, Suzanne. B.S., U. Calif.-Davis, 1965; M.S., U. Calif.-Berkeley, 1967; Ph.D., Duke U., 1981. Sr. research technician dept. biochemistry and animal sci. Tex. A&M U., 1967-70; sr. research technician dept. pharmacology Duke U., Durham, N.C., 1973-74; research scientist I dept. microbiology Burroughs Wellcome Co., 1974-77, research scientist II dept. medicinal biochemistry, 1977-82, research scientist III, 1982-85, clin. research scientist dept. clin. neurosci., anesthesia/analgesia sect., 1985—. Contbr. articles to profl. jours. Mem. Soc. Neurosci. Current Work: Regulatory role of pteridine cofactor in peripheral and central nervous system. Subspecialties: Neurochemistry; Neuropharmacology. Home: 106 Catawba Ct Chapel Hill NC 27514 Office: 3030 Cornwallis Rd Research Triangle Park NC 27709

ABOU-GHARBIA, MAGID ABDEL-MEGEID, medicinal chemist; b. Cairo, Egypt, Dec. 1, 1949; came to U.S., 1974; s. Abdel-Megid and Neamat (Afify) A.; m. Lamaat Shalaby, Jan. 13, 1973; children—Neveen, Shereen, Kareem. B.Sc. in Pharmacy, Cairo U., 1971, M.Sc. in Chemistry, 1974; Ph.D., U. Pa., 1979. Lectr., Cairo U., Egypt, 1971-74; grad. faculty U. Pa., Phila., 1974-78; vis. research assoc. Sch. Pharmacy, Temple U., Phila., 1978-79, NIH postdoctoral fellow, Sch. Medicine, 1979-82; sr. research chemist Wyeth Labs., Radnor, Pa., 1982-84, supr., 1985—. Contbr. articles to profl. jours. Patentee in field. NIH fellow, 1979-82; U. Pa. fellow, 1977-78. Fellow Sigma Xi; mem. Am. Chem. Soc., Phila. Organic Chemist Club, Royal Inst. Chemistry. Republican. Moslem. Current work: Synthesis of biologically active compounds for cardiovascular and central nervous systems. Subspecialties: Organic chemistry; Synthetic chemistry. Office: Wyeth Labs PO Box 8299 Philadelphia PA 19101

ABRAHAM, GEORGE, research physicist, engineer; b. N.Y.C., July 15, 1918; s. Herbert and Dorothy (Jacoby) A.; m. Hilda Mary Wenz, Aug. 26, 1944; children: Edward H., Dorothy J., Anne H., Alice J. Sc.B., Brown U., 1940; S.M., Harvard U., 1942; Ph.D., U. Md., 1972; postgrad., MIT, George Washington U. Registered profl. engr., D.C. Chmn. bd., pres. bd. Intercollegiate Broadcasting System, N.Y., 1941—; radio engr. RCA, Camden, N.J., 1941; with Naval Research Lab., Washington, 1942—, head sci. edn., head exptl. devices and microelectronics sects., 1945-69, head systems applications Office of Dir. Research, 1969-75, research physicist Office Research and Tech. Applications, cons., 1975—; lectr. U. Md., 1945-52, George Washington U., 1952-67, Am. U., 1979; indsl. cons.; mem. Bd. Registration Profl. Engrs. Contbr. chpts. to books, articles to profl. jours. Chmn. bd. Canterbury Sch., Accokeek, Md.; mem. schs. and scholarships com. Harvard U.; active PTA, Boy Scouts Am. Served to capt. USNR, World War II. Recipient Group Achievement award Fleet Ballistic Missile Program U.S. Navy, 1963; Edison award Naval Research Lab., 1971; Navy Research Publ. awards, 1974, 85; Patent awards, 1959-75; D.C. Sci. citation, 1982; others. Fellow IEEE (Harry Diamond award 1981, Centennial award 1984), Washington Acad. Scis. (pres. 1974-75), N.Y. Acad. Scis., AAAS; Mem. Am. Phys. Soc., Am. Assn. Physics Tchrs., Am. Soc. Naval Engrs., Washington Soc. Engrs. (pres. 1974, award 1981), Philos. Soc. Washington, AAUP, Sierra Club, Sigma Xi, Sigma Pi Sigma, Tau Beta Pi, Sigma Tau, Eta Kappa Nu, Iota Beta Sigma. Clubs: Cosmos (Washington), Harvard (Washington); Appalachian Mountain (Boston); Sierra (San Francisco). Patentee in field. Current Work: Solid state electronics, microelectronics, multivalued logic implementation, solid state physics, electrical engineering. Subspecialties: Computer engineering; Integrated circuits. Home: 3107 Westover Dr SE Washington DC 20020 Office: Naval Research Lab Washington DC 20375

ABRAHAM, KUZHIKALAIL MATHEW, research chemist; b. Ranny-Perinad, India, Jan. 17, 1945; came to U.S., 1968, naturalized, 1978; s. Kuzhikalail Abraham and Aleyamma (Chacko) Mathew; m. Deborah Ruth Van Hoek, Mar. 3, 1973. B.Sc., Kerala U., 1965, M.Sc., 1967; Ph.D., Tufts U., 1973. Postdoctoral research assoc. Vanderbilt U., Nashville, 1973-75, MIT, Cambridge, Mass., 1975; sr. scientist EIC Labs. Inc., Newton, Mass., 1976-79, group leader, 1979-84, head lithium battery research, 1984—; plenary lectr. 2d Internat. Lithium Battery Meeting, Paris, 1984, Soc. for Advancement Electrochem. Sci. and Tech., Madras, India, 1984; lectr. NATO Advanced Study Inst., Lisbon, Portugal, 1984. Contbr. chpts. to books, articles to profl. jours. Patentee in field. Recipient Invention award NASA, 1983; Nat. Merit scholar, 1966-67. Mem. Am. Chem. Soc., Electrochem. Soc. (treas. Boston sect. 1984-85, vice chmn. 1985-86), N.Y. Acad. Sci., Sigma Xi. Current work: Research and development work on high energy density batteries including primary and secondary lithium batteries. Subspecialty: Electrochemical energy storage and conversion. Home: 57 Colonial Rd Needham MA 02192 Office: E I C Laboratories Inc 111 Downey St Norwood MA 02062

ABRAHAM, MARVIN MEYER, physicist; b. N.Y.C., Dec. 8, 1930; s. Raymond and Esther (Matza) A.; m. Reeva Swidler, Sept. 2, 1958; children—Seth, Naomi, David. B.S., CCNY, 1953; M.S., U. Calif.-Berkeley, 1954, Ph.D., 1958. Researcher Argonne Nat. Lab., Ill., summer 1958; Lawrence Berkeley Lab., 1960-63; research fellow Clarendon Lab., Oxford U., Engl. 1958-60; vis. prof. Internat. Atomic Energy Authority, San Carlos de Bariloche, Argentina, 1962-63; research staff Solid State div. Oak Ridge Nat. Lab., Tenn., 1963—. Contbr. articles to profl. jours. Patentee in field. Fulbright-Hays fellow, 1958, 59; N.Y. State Regents scholar, 1949-53. Fellow Am. Phys. Soc., Am. Ceramic Soc. Current work: Electron paramagnetic resonance in solids. Subspecialties: Condensed matter physics; High-temperature materials. Office: Oak Ridge Nat Lab Solid State Div PO Box X Oak Ridge TN 37831

ABRAHAMS, ATHOL DENIS, geography researcher, geography educator; b. Sydney, New South Wales, Australia, Mar. 10, 1946; came to U.S., 1977; s. Alfred George and Muriel Clare (McTaggart) A.; m. Lesley Jane Hungerford, June 9, 1968 (div. 1975); 1 child, Katharine Jane; m. Helen Lorraine Oak, Jan. 3, 1976. B.A. with honors, U. Sydney, 1966, Ph.D., 1971. Killam postdoctoral fellow U. Alta., Edmonton, Can., 1971-73; lectr. U. New South Wales, Sydney, 1973-77; assoc. prof. SUNY-Buffalo, 1977-84, prof., 1984—. Editor: Hillslope Processes, 1985; assoc. editor Annals of Assn. Am. Geographers Jour., 1982—. Contbr. articles to profl. jours. New South Wales Tchrs. Coll. scholar 1963-66; Australian Govt. Commonwealth postgrad. scholar 1967-71. Fellow Geol. Soc. Am.; mem. Assn. Am. Geographers (sec., treas. geomorphology splty. group 1983-84, chmn. 1984—), Brit. Geomorphological Research Group, Am. Geophys. Union. Current work: Analysis of channel networks and their drainage basins; analysis of river channel morphology; analysis of desert hillslopes and the processes that form them. Subspecialties: Hydrology; Geomorphology. Office: Dept Geography SUNY Buffalo NY 14260

ABRAHAMS, CLARK RICHARD, operations research manager, consultant; b. San Francisco, Mar. 7, 1951; s. Harold Jay and Ida (Krasne) A.; m. Judy Carolyn Whitesides, Oct. 24, 1980; 1 son, Robert Bradford. A.B., U. Calif.-Berkeley, 1973; M.S., Stanford U., 1974. Project mgr. Standard Oil Co. of Ind., Chgo., 1974-76; project mgr. Fair, Isaac & Co., Inc., San Rafael, Calif., 1976-78; pres. StatComp, San Francisco, 1978-80; asst. v.p. Bank of Calif., San Francisco, 1980-81; corp. mgr. ops. research Barclays Am. Corp., Charlotte, N.C., 1981—; pres. StatComp, Charlotte, N.C., 1983—. Inventor: computerized process Genosys, 1978, Credit Management Tool RE&PF Systems, 1979. Mem. Am. Statis. Assn., Ops. Research Soc. Am. Democrat. Presbyterian. Club: Mt. Diablo Jaycees. Current Work: Discrete multivariate statistics; design implementation of statistical computing software; automated generation-selection of optimal statistical decision models; stochastic modeling of consumer behavior; financial modeling. Subspecialties: Operations research (mathematics); Statistics. Home: 216 Altondale Ave Charlotte NC 28207 Office: Barclays Am. Corp 201 S Tryon St Charlotte NC 28231

ABRAHAMS, SIDNEY CYRIL, physicist, crystallographer; b. London, May 28, 1924; came to U.S., 1948, naturalized, 1963; s. Aaron Harry and Freda (Cohen) A.; m. Rhoda Banks, May 1, 1950; children—David Mark, Peter Brian, Jennifer Anne. B.Sc., U. Glasgow (Scotland), 1946, Ph.D., 1949, D.Sc., 1957; Fil.Dr. (hon.), U. Uppsala (Sweden), 1981. Postdoctoral fellow U. Minn., Mpls., 1949-50; staff mem. div. indsl. cooperation MIT, Cambridge, 1950-54; Imperial Chem. Industries fellow U. Glasgow, 1954-57; mem. tech. staff AT&T Bell Labs., Murray Hill, N.J., 1957—; vis. prof. U. Bordeaux (France), 1979. Editor jour. Acta Crystallographica, 1978—; book rev. editor jour. Ferroelectrics, 1975—. Contbr. articles to profl. publs. Chmn. com. chem. crystallography Nat. Acad. Sci., 1968-76, USA Nat. Com. Crystallography, 1970-72, Am. Inst. Physics Pub. Policy Com., 1982—, IUCr Commn. on Jours., 1978—, IUCr Commn. on Crystallographic Nomenclature, 1978—. Recipient Disting. Tech. Staff award AT&T Bell Labs., 1982. Fellow Am. Phys. Soc., AAAS; mem. Am. Crystallographic Assn. (pres. 1968, mng. editor jour.). Republican. Presbyterian. Current work: Physics of condensed matter, particularly elucidation by diffraction methods of relationships between macroscopic properties and atomic arrangement in crystals. Subspecialties: Condensed matter physics; Crystallography. Office: AT&T Bell Labs Murray Hill NJ 07974

ABRAHAM-SHRAUNER, BARBARA WAYNE, physicist, educator; b. Morristown, N.J., June 21, 1934; d. Leonard Gladstone and Ruth Elizabeth (Thrasher) Abraham; m Ely Shrauner, 1965; children—Elizabeth Ann, Jay Arthur. B.A., U. Colo., 1956; A.M., Radcliffe Coll., 1957; Ph.D., Harvard U., 1962. Postdoctoral research assoc. Free U. Brussels, 1962-64; resident research assoc. NASA-Ames Research Ctr., Moffett Field, Calif., 1964-65, cons., 1967; asst. prof. dept. elec. engring. Washington U., St. Louis, 1966-69, assoc. prof., 1969-77, prof., 1977—; with Los Alamos Sci. Lab., 1975-76, cons., collaborator, 1979, 84. Contbr. articles to profl. jours. Mem. Am. Phys. Soc. (com. on status of woman in physics div. 1978-80, exec. com. plasma physics 1981-83), Am. Geophys. Union, AAUP (local exec. com. 1979-82), Phi Beta Kappa, Sigma Xi, Sigma Pi Sigma, Eta Kappa Nu. Current work: Lie point transformation solutions of the Vlasov-Maxwell equations for plasmas, transport properties of III-V semiconductors in high electric fields. Subspecialties: Plasma physics; Microelectronics. Home: 7452 Stratford Saint Louis MO 63130 Office: Dept Elec Engring Washington U Lindell Blvd Saint Louis MO 63130

ABRAHAMSON, EARL ARTHUR, analytical chemist, consultant in research computing; b. Aberdeen, S.D., June 5, 1924; s. Earl A.C. and Selma (Locken) A.; m. Dorothy Bergesen, Aug. 1948; children—Kris Leigh, Jill Anne, Kirsten Lynne. B.S. in Chemistry, U. N.D., 1948; Ph.D. in Analytical Chemistry, U. Kans., 1951. Research chemist DuPont, Wilmington, Del., 1951-53, sect. supr., 1953-58, asst. div. head, 1958-70, supr. computer group, 1970-84, supr. computer planning, 1984—. Contbr. articles to profl. jours. Mem. Sch. Bd. Mt. Pleasant Pub. Schs., Wilmington, 1965-76, pres. 1972-76; pres. Del. Sch. Bd. Assn., Dover, 1971-72. Eastman Kodak fellow, 1951. Fellow AAAS; mem. Am. chem. Soc., Research Soc. Am., Wilmington Skating Club (pres. 1968-69). Republican. Lutheran. Current work: On-line data acquisition and analysis from analytical instruments automation of technical library. Subspecialties: Analytical chemistry; Information systems, storage, and retrieval (computer science). Office: E I DuPont de Nemours Experimental Station Wilmington DE 19898

ABRAHAMSON, WARREN GENE, II, biologist, educator; b. Ludington, Mich., Mar. 26, 1947; s. Warren Gene and Alice Enid (Johnson) A.; m. Christy Raye Abrahamson, Aug. 16, 1969; 1 dau., Jill Raye. B.S. in Botany, U. Mich., 1969; M.S. in Biology, Harvard U., 1971, Ph.D., 1973. Asst. prof. biology Bucknell U., Lewisburg, Pa., 1973-79, assoc. prof., 1979-83, David Burpee prof. plant genetics, 1983—; vis. asst. prof. Mich. State U., East Lansing, 1976; research fellow Archbold Biol. Sta., Lake Placid, Fla., 1980-81, research assoc., 1976—. Contbr. articles to sci. jours. Recipient Bradley-Moore-Davis award U. Mich., 1969; Lindback award Bucknell U., 1975-76; Class of 1956 Lectureship, 1982-83; NSF grantee, 1974—. Mem. Audubon Soc. (chpt. program chmn. 1978-80, chpt. pres. 1982—, William Dutcher award 1984), Bot. Soc. Am., Ecol. Soc. Am., Fla. Acad. Sci., Internat. Soc. Plant Population Biologists, Soc. Study of Evolution, Torrey Bot. Club, Sigma Xi, Phi Sigma. Democrat. Methodist. Current Work: Plant-insect interactions, goldenrod-stem gall insect-parasitoid guild interaction, plant life histories, fire ecology of Florida. Subspecialties: Evolutionary biology; Population biology. Home: 153 Mountain View Rd Lewisburg PA 17837 Office: Dept Biology Bucknell U Lewisburg PA 17837

ABRAMS, GARY MITCHELL, neurologist, researcher; b. N.Y.C., June 9, 1949; s. Abraham and Harriet (Vogel) A.; m. Joan Roth, July 4, 1971; children—Bryan Curtis, Lindsey Jane. B.A. cum laude, SUNY-Buffalo, 1970; M.D., U. Pitts., 1974. Med. intern U. Pitts., 1974-75; resident in neurology Columbia-Presbyn. Hosp., N.Y.C., 1975-77, chief resident neurology, 1977-78; fellow neuroendocrinology Columbia U., N.Y.C., 1978-79; asst. prof. neurology Coll. Physicians and Surgeons, Columbia U., 1980—; vis. scientist Nat. Inst. Med. Research, London, 1979-80. Contbr. articles to profl. jours. Ad hoc reviewer Neurology jour., 1981. Mem. Am. Acad. Neurology (assoc.), Internat. Assn. Study Pain, Soc. Neurosci., AAAS, Phi Beta Kappa. Neuropeptides, pain, neuroendocrinology. Subspecialties: Neurology; Neuroendocrinology. Office: Dept Neurology Columbia U 650 W 168th St New York NY 10032

ABRAMS, GERALD DAVID, pathologist, educator; b. Detroit, Apr. 27, 1932; s. Arthur and Esther (Kushner) A.; m. Gloria Sandra Turner, June 6, 1954; children—Kathryn Ruth, Nancy Susan. B.A., Wayne State U., 1951; M.D., U. Mich., 1955. Diplomate Am. Bd. Pathology. Resident in pathology U. Mich., Ann Arbor, 1955-60, instr. pathology, 1959-60, asst. prof. pathology, 1963-66, assoc. prof. pathology, 1966-69, prof. pathology, 1969—; cons. physician VA Med. Ctr., Ann Arbor, 1963—; dep. med. examiner Washtenaw County, Ann Arbor, 1963—. Contbr. chpts. to books, articles to profl. jours. Served to capt. U.S. Army, 1961-62. Recipient Borden Research award U. Mich., 1955, Kaiser Permanente award, 1978; Markle Found. scholar Acad. Medicine, 1963-68. Mem. Am. Assn. Pathologists, Internat. Acad. Pathology, AAAS, Mich. Soc. Pathologists. Current work: Diagnostic anatomic pathology; experimental pathology-cardiovascular and gastrointestinal disease. Subspecialty: Pathology (medicine). Office: U Mich Dept Pathology M5218 Ann Arbor MI 48109

ABRAMS, RICHARD FRANCIS, engineering, systems development manager; b. Cambridge, Mass., Nov. 14, 1948; s. Abraham and Dorothea (Bannen) A.; m. Jean Parker, June 10, 1972; children: Keith, Julie. B.S. in Chem. Engring, Worcester Polytech. Inst., 1970. Pilot plant supr. Artisan Industries Inc., Waltham, Mass., 1971-74; process engr. CTI Cyrogenics, Waltham, 1974-76; supr. process engring. Helix Tech, Westboro, Mass., 1976-78, task force leader, 1978-80; mgr. engring./devel. Koch Process Systems (formerly Helix/CTI), 1980—. Men. Am. Inst. Chem. Engrs., Am. Nuclear Soc. Patentee improved control system, 1980, radioactive waste process, 1982. Current Work: Develop and design radioactive waste treatment systems for nuclear facilities, gaseous and solid wastes. Subspecialties: Nuclear engineering; Gas cleaning systems. Home: 9 Jasper St Westboro MA 01581

ABRAMS, THOMAS WILLIAM, neurobiologist; b. N.Y.C., Dec. 24, 1950; s. Oscar and Evelyn (Korn) A. B.A., Carleton Coll., 1972; Ph.D., U. Wash., 1982. Postdoctoral fellow Columbia U., N.Y.C., 1981-84; research assoc. Howard Hughes Med. Inst., N.Y.C., 1984—. Mem. AAAS, Soc. Neurosci. Current work: Cellular mechanisms for regulation of synaptic strength during learning and development; these mechanisms include neuronal activity, calcium influx and cyclic nucleotides. Subspecialties: Neurophysiology; Cell biology. Office: Ctr for Neurobiology and Behavior and Howard Hughes Med Inst 722 W 168th St New York NY 10032

ABRAMSON, HYMAN NORMAN, engineering and scientific research executive; b. San Antonio, Mar. 4, 1926; s. Nathan and Pearl (Westerman) A.; m. Idelle Rebecca Ringel, Apr. 20, 1947; children—Phillip David, Mark Donald. B.S.M.E., Stanford U., 1950, M.S. in Engring. Mechanics, 1951; Ph.D. in Engring. Mechanics (So. Fellowship Fund fellow), U. Tex., Austin, 1956. Engr. U.S. Naval Air Missile Test Center, Point Mugu, Calif., 1947-48; project engr. Chance Vought Aircraft Co., Dallas, 1951-52; assoc. prof. aero. engring. Tex. A&M U., 1952-55; sect. mgr., dept. dir. S.W. Research Inst., San Antonio, 1956-72, v.p. div. engring. scis., 1972-85, exec. v.p., 1985—; mem. research adv. com. USCG; adv. panel engring. mechanics NSF; com. U.S. Dept. Commerce. Author: An Introduction to the Dynamics of Airplanes, 1958, reprinted, 1971; contbr. numerous articles to profl. publs.; editor: (with others) Applied Mechanics Surveys, 1966, The Dynamic Behavior of Liquids in Moving Containers, 1966; assoc. editor: (with others) Applied Mechanics Revs, 1954—; editorial adv. bd.: (with others) Jour. Computers and Structures, 1970—, Aeros. and Astronautics, 1975—. Mem. Greater San Antonio C. of C., and City of San Antonio Market Sq. Adv. Com., 1973-77; mem. U.S. Bicentennial Com. of San Antonio, 1975-76. Served with USN, 1943-45. Mem. AIAA (Disting. Service award 1973, dir.), ASME (v.p.; hon.), Nat. Acad. Engring., Soc. Naval Architects and Marine Engrs., AAAS, Sigma Xi. Republican. Jewish. Current Work: Fluid-structure interaction. Subspecialties: Theoretical and applied mechanics; Fluid mechanics. Home: 1511 Spanish Oaks Dr San Antonio TX 78213 Office: 6220 Culebra Rd San Antonio TX 78284

ABSALOM, CONSTANCE MARY, geologist; b. Woodbury, N.J., Sept. 30, 1948; d. Joseph Vincent and Mary Patricia (Logue) O'Connor; m. Frank G. Absalom, June 20, 1970; 1 child, William Henry. B.S., Rutgers U., 1976; postgrad. Temple U., 1981, U. Pa., 1981-83. Cert. geologist, Ind. Lab instr. Rutgers U., Camden, N.J., 1969-70; sci. tchr. Sacred Heart Sch., Mt. Holly, N.J., 1970-71; geologist Site Engrs., Voorhees, N.J., 1971-72, 78-79, Sippel & Masteller, Marlton, N.J., 1977, Stone & Webster, Cherry Hill, N.J., 1979—. Named Toastmaster of Yr., 1982; Outstanding Woman of Yr., YWCA, 1981. Mem. Geol. Soc. Am. Roman Catholic. Lodge: Toastmasters. Current work: Detailed geologic mapping and fault dating at nuclear power plant sites. Subspecialties: Cryptography and data security; Geology. Home: 1706 Cottage St Hainesport NJ 08036 Office: Stone & Webster Engring Corp 3 Executive Campus Route 70 Cherry Hill NJ 08034

ABSOLOM, DARRYL ROBIN, immunologist; b. Germiston, Transvaal, S. Africa, Dec. 15, 1954; s. George Dalziel and Margaret (Marlowe) A. B.Sc., U. Cape Town, S. Africa, 1973, B.Sc. with honors, 1974, Ph.D., 1977. Research asst. prof. SUNY-Buffalo, 1978-82, research assoc. prof., 1983—; cancer scientist Roswell Park Meml. Inst., Buffalo, 1978-79; sr. scientist Hosp. for Sick Children, Toronto, Ont., Can., 1982—; asst. prof. U. Toronto, 1982-83, assoc. prof., 1983—. Editor: Molecular Immunology, 1983; Editorial advisor: Immunological Communication Jour, 1980—, Preparative Biochemistry Jour, 1980—, Biol. Dispersions and Surfaces Jour, 1983—. Rotary Internat. Scholarship awardee, 1977; Ont. Heart Found. Fellowship awardee, 1978-82; Can. Heart Found. Sr. Fellowship awardee, 1983—. Mem. Internat. Surface Sci. Group, Am. Soc. Artificial Internal Organs, N.Y. Acad. Sci., Am. Chem.

Soc. Current Work: Biomaterials, cell adhesion, protein adsorption, phagocytosis, cell-cell interactions, applied surface thermodynamics, antigen-antibody interactions. Subspecialties: Biomaterials; Biophysics (biology). Office: Hosp for Sick Children Research Inst 555 University Ave Toronto ON M5G 1X8 Canada

ABUZZAHAB, FARUK SAID, SR., psychiatrist, educator; b. Beirut, Lebanon, Oct. 12, 1932; came to U.S., 1959, naturalized, 1978; s. Said Salim and Nehmat (Muezzin) A.; m. Kathryn Buoen, Oct. 1982; children: Nada, Jennifer, Faruk, Jeffrey, Mark, Brita, Omar. M.D., Am. U. Beirut, 1959; Ph.D., U. Minn., 1968. Diplomate: Am. Bd. Psychiatry and Neurology. Rotating intern Am. U. Hosp., Beirut, 1958-59; jr., then sr. asst. resident Johns Hopkins Hosp., Balt., 1959-62; vis. resident psychiatry Balt. City Hosp., 1960-62; fellow dept. psychiatry Johns Hopkins U. Sch. Medicine, 1959-62; research psychiatrist Henry Phipps Psychiat. Clinic, 1959-62; research fellow depts. psychiatry and pharmacology U. Minn., Mpls., 1962-66, instr., 1966-67, asst. prof., 1967-71, clin. asst. prof., 1971-73, clin. asso. prof., 1973-79, clin. prof., 1979—; clin. dir. Hastings (Minn.) State Hosp., 1963-78; practice medicine specializing in adult psychiatry and clin. psycho-pharmacology, Mpls., 1965-73; staff psychiatrist Dunn County Health Care Center, Menomonie, Wis., 1971—; active med. staff St. Mary's Hosp., Mpls., 1971—; asso. in psychiatry Fairview Hosp., Mpls., 1971—, also cons.; pres. Clin. Psychopharmacology Cons., P.A., Mpls., 1973—. Editorial adv. bd.: Jour. Practical Therapeutics, 1979—, Am. Jour. Psychiatry, 1980—; Contbr. articles to sci. publs. Adminstr. Pharmacopsychiatry Fund, Minn. Med. Found., Mpls., 1972—. Fellow Am. Psychiat. Assn., Am. Coll. Clin. Pharmacology; mem. Johns Hopkins Med. and Surg. Soc., Med. Alumni Assn. of Am. U. Beirut (life), AMA, Minn. Psychiat. Soc. (program and CME chmn. 1983-85), Minn. State Med. Soc., Hennepin County Med. Soc., Hennepin County Psychiat. Soc. (pres. 1976-78), Am. Soc. Clin. Pharmacology and Therapeutics, Soc. Biol. Psychiatry, Minn. Soc. Neurol. Sci., Collegium Internationale Neuropsychopharmacologicum, Am. Soc. Pharmacology and Exptl. Therapeutics, Am. Assn. Geriatric Psychiatry, Sigma Xi, Alpha Omega Alpha. Current Work: Psychopharmacology, neuropsychopharmacology research, teaching and clinical practice. Subspecialties: Psychiatry; Psychopharmacology. Home: 2601 E Lake of Isles Blvd Minneapolis MN 55408 Office: 606 24th Ave S Suite 818 Minneapolis MN 55454

ACHENBACH, JAN DREWES, engineering scientist, educator; b. Leeuwarden, Netherlands, Aug. 20, 1935; came to U.S., 1959, naturalized, 1978; s. Johannes and Elizabeth (Schipper) A.; m. Marcia Graham Fee, July 15, 1961. Kand. Ir., Delft U. Tech., 1959; Ph.D., Stanford U., 1962. Preceptor Columbia U., 1962-63; asst. prof. Northwestern U., Evanston, Ill., 1963, assoc. prof., 1966-69, prof. dept. civil engring., 1969—, Walter P. Murphy prof. civil engring. and applied math., 1981—; vis. assoc. prof. U. Calif., San Diego, 1969; vis. prof. Tech. U. Delft, 1970-71; cons. EPRI, 1983—; prof. Huazhong Inst. Sci. and Tech., 1981; mem. at large U.S. Nat. Com. Theoretical and Applied Mechanics, 1972-78. Author: Wave Propagation in Elastic Solids, 1973, A Theory of Elasticity with Microstructure for Directionally Reinforced Composites, 1975, (with A.K. Gautesen and H. McMaken) Ray Methods for Waves in Elastic Solids, 1982; editor: (with J. Miklowitz) Modern Problems in Elastic Wave Propagation, 1978; editor-in-chief: Wave Motion, 1979—. Recipient award C. Gelderman Found., 1970, C.W. McGraw Research award Am. Soc. Engring. Edn., 1975. Fellow Am. Acad. Mechanics (pres. 1978-79), ASME; mem. Am. Geophys. Union, AIAA., U.S. Nat. Acad. Engring. Current Work: The propagation of mechanical disturbances in solids; with applications to scattering of ultrasonic waves by cracks for nondestructive evalutation of materials and acoustic radiation by material damage regions; fracture mechanics. Subspecialties: Theoretical and applied mechanics; Applied mathematics. Home: 574 Ingleside Park Evanston IL 60201 Office: Dept Civil Engring Northwestern U Evanston IL 60201

ACHORD, JAMES LEE, medical educator; b. Dayton, Ohio, Sept. 24, 1931; s. Lonnie M. and Ethel (Collins) A.; m. Pat Moore, Dec. 18, 1954; children: Michael, Ann, Andrew. M.D., Emory U., 1956. From instr. to asst. prof. Emory Med. Sch., Atlanta, 1962-71; med. dir. Med. Center Central Ga., Macon, 1971-75; prof., assoc. dean East Tenn. State U. Sch. Medicine, Johnson City, 1975-76; prof. medicine, dir. digestive diseases U. Miss. Sch. Medicine, Jackson, 1976—; chief of staff Univ. Med. Center, Jackson, 1981-82. Editor: Chronic Inflammatory Bowel Disease, 1974; author articles. Mem. adminstrv. bd. Meth. Ch., Jackson, 1983. Served to capt. M.C. U.S. Army, 1957-59. Fellow Am. Coll. Gastroenterology (pres. 1984), A.C.P., Am. Gastroenterological Assn., Am. Assn. for Study of Liver Disease, Fedn. Digestive Disease Socs. (vice chmn. 1982-83), Ga. Gastroenterological Soc. (founding pres. 1971-73). Current Work: Liver disease, peptic ulcer disease, others. Subspecialties: Gastroenterology; Internal medicine. Home: 202 Wexford Ct Jackson MS 39208 Office: U Miss Sch Medicine 2500 N State St Jackson MS 39216

ACHTER, EUGENE KENNETH, biomedical instrumentation developer; b. Bklyn., Oct. 24, 1944; s. Sam and Jennie (Rabinewitz) A. Sc.B. in Chemistry, Brown U., 1966; M.S., U. Chgo., 1969, Ph.D., 1969. Sr. asst. scientist USPHS/NIH, Bethesda, Md., 1969-71; sr. staff fellow NIH, 1971-73; project mgr. Am. Instrument Co., div. Travenol Labs., Silver Springs, Md., 1973-78; mem. tech. staff Aerospace Corp., Washington, 1978-82; project dir. blood gas systems Nova Biomedical, Waltham, Mass., 1982—. Patentee in field. Served with USPHS, 1969-71. Current work: Biomed instrumentation devel., blood gas. Subspecialties: Biomedical engineering; Clinical chemistry. Office: Nova Biomedical 200 Prospect St Waltham MA 02254-9141

ACKERMAN, MICHAEL JAN, biomedical engineer, consultant; b. Bklyn., Apr. 11, 1946; s. Harry and Gertrude (Scherer) A.; m. Judy Ellen Lipton, July 3, 1967; children—Lorrie Faith, Jeremy David. B.A., Hofstra U., 1966; M.A., Clark U./Worcester Poly. Tech., 1969; Ph.D., U. N.C., 1971. Head instrumentation div. Naval Med. Research Inst. Bethesda, Md., 1975-79, head bioengring. br., 1979-84, head biomed. engring. br., 1984—; adj. asst. prof. George Washington U., 1973-75; cons., 1975—; lectr. Georgetown U., 1983—. Contbr. articles to profl. jours. Pres., Parkwood Residents Assn., 1983. Served to lt. USN, 1972-75. Recipient Cash award USN, 1982, 83, 84. Mem. Symposium for Computer Applications in Med. Care (pres. 1981-82, bd. dirs. program chmn. 1985), Am. Assn. Med. Systems and Informatics (charter mem., bd. dirs. 1983—), U.S. Council for Med. Info. '86 (treas. 1983—), Undersea Med. Soc., IEEE, Assn. Computing Machinery. Current work: Use of computer for on-line analysis of medical data, effects of hyperbaric environment on central nervous system. Subspecialties: Biomedical engineering; Biomedical engineering. Office: Naval Med Research Inst Mail Stop 38 Bethesda MD 20814

ACKERMAN, NEIL RICHARD, pharmacologist, immunologist; b. Balt., May 1, 1943; s. Bernard Marvin and Florence (Berger) A.; m. Lorraine Kessler, May 30, 1964; 1 child, Anne Dee. B.A., U. Md., 1965, B.S., 1966, Ph.D., 1969. Pharmacologist, Pfizer Inc., Groton, Conn., 1971-76; postdoctoral fellow Stanford U., Calif., 1969-71; treas. Pulmonary Research Group, N.Y.C., 1971-76; dept. head Syntex Research Co., Palo Alto, Calif., 1976-82; mgr. E.I. DuPont Co., Wilmington, Del., 1982—. Contbr. articles to med. and sci. jours. Mem. AAAS, Am. Soc. Pharmacology and Exptl. Therapeutics, Phi Kappa Phi. Current work: Arthritis, inflammatory diseases, autoimmune diseases, dermatology, pulomonary diseases. Subspecialties: Pharmacology; Rheumatology. Office: EI DuPont Co Exptl Sta E-400 Wilmington DE 19898

ACKERMAN, ROBERT HAROLD, neuroscientist, neurologist/neuroradiologist; b. N.Y.C., June 1, 1935; s. Myron and Leona (Auerbach) A. B.A. in History, Brown U., 1957; postgrad., Columbia U., 1959-60; M.D., U. Rochester, 1964; M.P.H., Harvard U., Boston, 1972. Diplomate: Am. Bd. Psychiatry and Neurology, Am. Bd. Radiology. Rotating intern Bassett Hosp., Cooperstown, N.Y., 1964-65; resident in medicine U. N.C.-Chapel Hill, 1965-66, resident in neurology, 1966-68; fellow in neuropathology Mass. Gen. Hosp., Boston, 1968-69, resident in neurology, 1969-70, fellow in neuroradiology, 1972-75, dir. Carotid Evaluation lab. and Lab. Cerebral Blood Flow and Metabolism, 1975—, assoc. neurologist, assoc. radiologist, 1980—; cerebrovascular research fellow Nat. Hosp. Nervous Diseases, London, 1970-71; instr. in neurology Harvard U., 1972-75, asst. prof. radiology, 1975-80, assoc. prof., 1980—; cons. to dept. pharm. research New Eng. Nuclear Corp., 1982. Contbr. numerous articles to profl. jours.; editorial bd.: Archives Neurology, 1980—, Stroke, 1980—. Served to pfc. USAR, 1958-64. Dalton scholar, 1970; Nat. Insts. Neurol. and Communicative Disorders and Stroke spl. fellow, 1972-75; grantee, 1979, 81. Fellow Am. Acad. Neurology, Am. Heart Assn. Stroke Council (exec. com. 1979-81); mem. Am. Assn. Neuropathologists, Am. Coll. Radiology, AMA, Am. Neurol. Assn., Am. Soc. Neuroradiology, Assn. Univ. Radiologists, Soc. Neurosci., Soc. Nuclear Medicine. Clubs: Harvard of N.Y, Eastern Point Yacht. Current Work: Development and application of new technology for diagnosis and treatment cerebrovascular and other neurological diseases; measurement of cerebro vascular and brain physiology. Subspecialties: Neurology; Diagnostic radiology. Home: Edgemoor Rd Gloucester MA 01930 Office: Mass Gen Hosp Boston MA 02114

ACKERMAN, ROY ALAN, biochemical engineer, research corporation executive; b. Bklyn., Sept. 9, 1951; s. Jack and Estelle (Kuchlik) A.; married; children—Shanna Avrah, Shira Beh. B.S. in Chem. Engring., Poly. Inst., Bklyn., 1972; M.S. in Chem. Engring. and Biochem. Engring., MIT, 1974; Ph.D. in Chem. Engring., U. Va. and U.B.H., 1985. Registered profl. engr. Chem. engr. Tri-Flo Research Labs., Ltd., Queens, N.Y., 1972-74; sr. project engr. Thetford Corp., Ann Arbor, Mich., 1975; dir. research and devel. Astre Corporate Group, Charlottesville, Va., 1976-79, tech. dir., 1979—, also dir.; adj. prof. biomed. tech. George Washington U., Washington, 1977, 80, NYU, N.Y.C., 1979-80, Poly. Inst. N.Y., Bklyn., 1980-81; dir. Biofiltration Technols., Ltd., Manhasset, N.Y., 1980-82, Indsl. Microgenics, Ltd., Charlottesville and Roanoke, Va., 1980—, Edlaw Preparations, Inc., Farmingdale, N.Y., 1982—, Bicarbodyte Corp., Charlottesville, 1984—. Holder 10 U.S. patents; contbr. over 30 tech. articles to profl. publs. Bd. dirs. Jaycees, Charlottesville, 1979, adminstrv. v.p., 1980; mem. Albemarle County (Va.) Citizens Zoning Rev. Com., 1980-81, Charlottesville-Albemarle Airport Bd., 1983—. Samuel Ruben scholar, 1968-72. Mem. Am. Inst. Chemists, Am. Inst. Chem. Engrs., Am. Chem. Soc., Am. Soc. Microbiology, Am. Soc. Artificial Internal Organs, Soc. Indsl. Microbiology, Internat. Soc. Artificial Organs, Water Pollution Control Fedn. Current Work: Medical device design and development; genetic engineering; hemodialysis; genetic recombination; respiratory therapy; hazardous waste treatment; water reuse and recycling. Subspecialties: Enzyme technology; Artificial organs and prostheses. Office: AstreCorporate Group 1130 E Market St PO Box 5072 Charlottesville VA 22905

ACKERMANN, NORBERT JOSEPH, JR., energy technology company executive; b. Chattanooga, July 3, 1942; s. Norbert Joseph and Lusella (Smith) A.; divorced (div.); children: Dori, Nancy, Andy, Jill. B.S., U. Tenn., 1965, M.S., 1967, Ph.D., 1971. Research instr. U. Tenn., Knoxville, 1967-68; nuclear engr. Union Carbide, Oak Ridge, 1968-71, head fast reactor measurement methods, 1971, head reactor controls devel. sect., 1971-76; pres. Tech. for Energy Corp., Knoxville, 1975—; dir. spl. instrumentation group Three Mile Island Recovery Operation, 1979; mem. adv. bd. dirs. United Am. Bank; bd. dirs. Energy Opportunities Consortium's Innovation Ctr. Contbr. articles in field of power plant surveillance and diagnostics and specialized measurement systems to profl. jours. Bd. dirs. Jr. Achievement. Herman Hickman fellow, 1966-67; AEC fellow, 1966-68; recipient Outstanding Engring. Alumunus award U. Tenn. Coll. Engring., 1974. Mem. Am. Nuclear Soc., IEEE, Am. Mgmt. Assn., AAAS, Energy Conservation Soc., Southeastern Conf. Football Ofcls. Assn. Current Work: Technical services and instrumentation and computer systems business serving the electric power industry. Subspecialty: Nuclear engineering. Home: 12220 Bluff Shore Dr Knoxville TN 37922 Office: 1 Energy Ctr Pellissippi Pkwy Knoxville TN 37922

ACOSTA, GUSTAVO, physician, clin. researcher; b. Cardenas, Cuba, Sept. 13, 1933; came to U.S., 1962, naturalized, 1969; s. Gustavo and Daria R. (Rua) A.; m. Josefina A. Acosta, Dec. 27, 1958; children: Gustavo, Marie. B.S., Trinitarian Coll., Cardenas, 1951; student medicine, U. Havana, 1961; M.D., U. Salamanca, Spain, 1963. Intern U. Salamanca, 1963; staff physician Huntington (W.VA.) State Hosp., 1964-66; asst. sect. chief Osawatomie (Kans.) State Hosp., 1966-69; regional med. dir. Latin Am. region Am. Cyanamid Internat. (Lederle Labs), 1970-71; asso. med. dir. Internat. div. Abbott Labs., 1971-76; asso. dir. corp. med. affairs Marion Labs., 1976-79; asso. dir. clin. research dept. Stuart Pharms. div. ICI Ams., Inc., Wilmington, Del., 1979—. Author: The Role of the Physician in the Pharmaceutical Industry, 1980; editorial council: Medico Intermaericano. Recipient Presdl. awards Abbott Labs., 1974, 75. Mem. Am. Soc. Clin. Pharmacology and Therapeutics, Neurosci. Soc., Am. Burn Soc., Internat. Soc. Burn Injuries, Internat. Anesthesia Research Soc. Republican. Roman Catholic. Current Work: Extensive clin. research in C.N.S. and anesthesiology, as well as infectious diseases. Subspecialties: Anesthesiology; Psychiatry.

ADAIR, ROBERT KEMP, physicist, educator; b. Ft. Wayne, Ind., Aug. 14, 1924; s. Robert Cleland and Margaret (Wiegman) A.; m. Eleanor Reed, June 21, 1952; children—Douglas McVeigh, Margaret Guthrie, James Cleland. Ph.B., U. Wis., 1947, Ph.D., 1951. Instr. U. Wis., 1950-53; physicist Brookhaven Nat. Lab., 1953-58; mem. faculty Yale, 1958—, prof. physics, 1961-72, Eugene Higgins prof. physics, 1972—, chmn. dept., 1967-70, dir. div. phys. scis., 1977—. Author: (with Earle C. Fowler) Strange Particles, 1963, Concepts in Physics, 1969; Assoc. editor: Phys. Rev, 1963-66; assoc. editor Phys. Rev. Letters, 1974-76, editor 1978-83. Served with inf. AUS, 1943-46. Guggenheim fellow, 1954; Ford Found. fellow, 1962-63; Sloane Found. fellow, 1962-63. Fellow Am. Phys. Soc. (chmn. div. particles and fields 1972-73); mem. Nat. Acad. Scis. Subspecialties: Nuclear physics; Particle physics. Home: 50 Deepwood Dr Hamden CT 06517 Office: JW Gibbs Lab Yale Univ New Haven CT 06520

ADAMCZAK, ROBERT LEONARD, chemist; b. Buffalo, Aug. 16, 1927; s. Leo Stanley and Lottie Dorothy (Pawlak) A.; m. Patricia Chupinski, Aug. 23, 1958; children: Michael R., Bruce W., Karen M. B.A., U. Buffalo, 1951, M.A., 1954, Ph.D. in Phys. Chemistry, 1956. Chemist Olin-Mathieson Corp., Niagara Falls, N.Y., 1951-53; research chemist Esso Research & Engring. Co., Linden, N.J., 1957-59; inorganic polymer chemist USAF Material Lab., Dayton, Ohio, 1959-60, chief tribology/lubrication br., 1960-68, sci. adminstr., 1968-75; chief of plans Wright Aero Labs., Wright-Patterson AFB, Ohio, 1975—. Contbr. articles to profl. jours. Served with U.S. Army, 1947-48. Union Carbide fellow, 1954-55. Fellow Am. Inst. Chemists, ASME; mem. Am. Chem. Soc., Ohio Acad. Sci., N.Y. Acad. Sci., Am. Soc. Lubrication Engrs., Sigma Xi. Republican. Roman Catholic. Current Work: Planning for future aerospace technology capabilities. Subspecialties: Aerospace engineering and technology; Aeronautical engineering. Home: 7556 Beldale Ave Huber Heights OH 45424 Office: Wright Aero Labs AFWAL/XR Wright-Patterson AFB OH 45433

ADAMS, CHARLES HENRY, retired animal science educator; b. Burdick, Kans., Nov. 7, 1918; s. Henry Lory and Bertha Frances (Westbrook) A.; m. Eula Mae Peters, Apr. 23, 1943. B.S., Kans. State U., 1941, M.S., 1942; Ph.D., Mich. State U., 1964. Instr. Kans. State U., Manhattan, 1946-47; asst. prof. animal sci. U. Nebr.-Lincoln, 1947-64, assoc. prof., 1964-70, prof., 1970-83, prof. emeritus, 1983—, asst. dean Coll. Agr., Inst. Agrl. and Natural Resources, 1973-83. Served to lt. U.S. Army, 1943-46. Fellow Am. Soc. Animal Sci. (Disting. Teaching award 1972); mem. Am. Meat Sci. Assn. (Disting. Teaching award 1969), Inst. Food Tech., AAAS, Lincoln C. of C., Sigma Xi, Alpha Zeta. Republican. Mem. Disciples of Christ Ch. Lodge: Rotary. Home: 7101 Colby St Lincoln NE 68505

ADAMS, DAVID ARTHUR, environmental science educator; b. Lakewood, Ohio, Nov. 26, 1931; s. Arthur Joseph and Ruth Elizabeth (Joy) A.; m. Patricia Holmes Smith, Dec. 22, 1955; 1 child, David Arthur. B.S., N.C. State U., 1953, M.S., 1957, Ph.D., 1962. Chief naturalist N.C. Div. State Parks, Raleigh, 1957-59; commr. N.C. Div. Comml. and Sports Fisheries, 1963-68; staff mem. Nat. Council Marine Research and Engring. Devel., Washington, 1968-69; pres. Coastal Zone Resources Corp., Wilmington, N.C., 1969-76; asst. sec. natural resources N.C. Dept. Natural Resources and Comml. Devel., Raleigh, 1976-78; assoc. prof. environ. sci. N.C. State U., Raleigh, 1978—, coordinator Ctr. Environ. Studies, 1982—; mem. Pres.'s Commn. on Marine Sci., Engring. and Resources, Washington, 1967-69. Contbr. articles to profl. jours. Served to 1st lt. U.S. Army, 1953-55. Recipient Disting. Citizen's award Gov. N.C., 1968. Mem. Nat. Assn. Environ. Profls. (cons., bd. dirs.), Ecol. Soc. Am., Sigma Xi, Phi Kappa Phi. Democrat. Methodist. Current work: Institutional issues natural resource management; wildlife habitat modeling; land use simulation. Subspecialties: Resource management; Ecology (environmental science). Home: 7521 Haymarket Ln Raleigh NC 27609 Office: Dept Forestry NC State Univ Box 8002 Raleigh NC 27695

ADAMS, DAVID BACHRACH, psychology educator; b. Mo., 1939; s. Robert M. and Elizabeth (Bachrach) A. B.A., Columbia Coll., 1962; Ph.D., Yale U., 1967. Fellow Yale U., 1968-70; prof. dept. psychology Wesleyan U., 1970—; mem. Nat. Acad. Sci. Exchange to Soviet Union, 1976; Fulbright exchange lectr. in, Soviet Union, 1981. Contbr. articles in field to profl. jours. Pres. Conn. Assn. Am.-Soviet Friendship. Mem. Internat. Soc. Research on Aggression, Behavior Genetics Assn., Neurosci. Soc., Animal Behavior Soc., Am. psychol. Assn., AAAS. Current Work: Human and animal social behavior; neural and cultural factors; this includes brain mechanisms of aggression, ethological studies and cultural studies of human sex and warfare. Subspecialties: Physiological psychology; Comparative neurobiology. Office: Dept Psychology Wesleyan U Middletown CT 06457

ADAMS, DONALD FREDERICK, mech. engr., educator, cons.; b. Streator, Ill., Sept. 25, 1935; s. Fred Mathew and Margaret Ann (Doerr) A.; m. Roberta Ann, June 22, 1957; children: David Allan, Daniel Scott, Douglas John, Jayne Lynn. B.S., U. Ill., 1957, Ph.D. in Applied Mechanics, 1963; M.S., U. So. Calif., 1960. Registered profl. engr., Wyo. Engr. Northrop Aircraft, Hawthorne, Calif., 1957-60; instr. U. Ill., 1960-63; supr. Aeronutronic div. Ford Motor Co., Newport Beach, Calif., 1963-67; mem. staff Rand Corp., Santa Monica, Calif., 1967-72; assoc. prof. mech. engring. U. Wyo., 1972-75, prof., 1975—, legal and indsl. cons.; internat. travel for UN Indsl. Devel. Orgn. Contbr. numerous articles to profl. publs. Named Outstanding Faculty Mem. U. Wyo., 1973. Mem. AIAA, ASME, ASTM, Soc. Automotive Engrs. (Ralph-Teetor award 1978), Am. Acad. Mechanics, Wyo. Engring. Soc., Nat. Soc. Profl. Engrs., Wyo. Soc. Profl. Engrs., Am. Soc. Metals, Soc. Exptl. Stress Analysis, Am. Soc. Engring. Edn. Roman Catholic. Current Work: Fiber reinforced composite materials. Subspecialties: Composite materials; Solid mechanics. Home: 421 S 19th St Laramie WY 82070 Office: Mech Engring Dept U Wyo Laramie WY 82071

ADAMS, DONALD ROBERT, anatomist, educator; b. Red Bluff, Calif., Aug. 3, 1937; s. Robert William and Nellie May (Longcor) A.; m. Carol Gene Gribler, July 19, 1974; children: Shawn Ryan, Robert James. A.B. in Zoology, U. Calif., Davis, 1960, Ph.D. in Anatomy, 1970; M.A. in Biology, Chico (Calif.) State Coll., 1967. Tchr. Malangali Govt. Secondary Sch., Tanganyika, East Africa, 1961-63, C.K. McClatchy Sr. High Sch., Sacramento, 1964-65; asst. prof. anatomy Mich. State U., 1970-74; asst. prof. vet. anatomy Iowa State U., Ames, 1974-76, assoc. prof., 1976—. Named Norden Outstanding Tchr. Coll. Vet. Medicine, 1982. Mem. AAAS, Am. Assn. Anatomists, Am. Assn. Vet. Anatomists, World Assn. Vet. Anatomists, Iowa Microbeam Soc. Republican. Current Work: Morphological adaption of vertebrates to environ. factors with emphasis on upper respiratory system. Subspecialties: Anatomy and embryology; Pulmonary medicine. Home: 812 Onyx Circle Ames IA 50010 Office: 1034 Coll of Veterinary Medicine Ames IA 50011

ADAMS, JAMES HALL, JR., research physicist; b. Statesville, N.C., Aug. 7, 1943; s. James Hall and Mary Elizabeth (Powell) A.; m. Rebekah Ellis, June 4, 1968; children: Mary Amanda, David Alexander. B.S., N.C. State U., 1966, M.S., 1968, Ph.D., 1972. Research asst. Johnson Space Center, Houston, 1968-72; research assoc. NRC, Washington, 1972-74; research physicist U.S. Naval Research Lab., Washington, 1974—. Mem. AAAS, IEEE, Am. Phys. Soc., Am. Geophys. Union, Am. Astron. Soc. Current Work: Cosmic ray composition, low energy cosmic rays origin, cosmic ray physics, magnetospheric physics, cosmic ray effects on microelectronics. Subspecialty: Cosmic ray high energy astrophysics. Office: US Naval Research Lab Code 4022 Washington DC 20375

ADAMS, JAMES PAUL, nuclear engineer, physicist; b. Delta, Utah, May 1, 1943; s. Paul Monroe and Louise (Cruikshank) A.; m. Mary Ann Pace, Aug. 18, 1967; children—Kristen Ann, Paul David, Amy Louise, Rebecca Jane, James Max. B.S., Brigham Young U., 1968; Ph.D. Iowa State U., 1972. Postdoctoral researcher U. Notre Dame, South Bend, Ind., 1972-74; nuclear power engr. U.S. Dept. Energy, Arlington, Va., 1974-79; sr. scientist EG&G Idaho, Inc., Idaho Falls, 1979—. Contbr. articles to profl. publs. Com. chmn. Teton Peaks council Boy Scouts Am., 1968-70, 81-83. Mem. Am. Phys. Soc., Am. Nuclear Soc., Sigma Xi, Sigma Pi Sigma (pres. 1964-65), Phi Beta Pi. Republican. Mormon. Current work: Nuclear specialist, thermal and hydraulics of reactors. Subspecialties: Nuclear physics; Nuclear fission. Home: 2285 Richards Ave Idaho Falls ID 83401 Office: EG&G Idaho Inc PO Box 1625 Idaho Falls ID 83415

ADAMS, JAMES ROLF, ecological services administrator, biologist; b. Santa Barbara, Calif., Aug. 5, 1932; s. Elmo W. and Ann M. (Miller) A.; m. Maryline Poole, Aug. 2, 1978; children—Katherine Adams, Ruth Adams. B.S. in Fisheries, Humboldt State U., 1958, M.S. in Fisheries, 1960, Ph.D. in Fisheries, U. Wash., 1975. Biologist, U.S. Fish and Wildlife Services, Auke Bay, Alaska, 1953-62; biologist Pacific Gas & Electric Co., San Ramon, Calif., 1962-71, sr. biologist, 1971-76, supervising biologist, 1976-83, dir., 1983—; mem. water quality com. Nat. Acad. Scis., Washington, 1970-72; mem. comn. on power plant siting Nat. Acad. Engring., Washington, 1971-72; mem. research steering com. Edison Electric Inst., N.Y.C., 1969-76. Mem. Am. Fisheries Soc., Am. Inst. Fishery Research Biologists, AAAS, Assn. Power Biologists, Western Soc. Naturalists. Subspecialties: Ecosystems analysis; Resource management. Home: 1170 Keeler Ave Berkeley CA 94708 Office: Dept Engring Research Pacific Gas Electric Co 3400 Crow Canyon Rd San Ramon CA 94583

ADAMS, JAMES RUSSELL, food scientist; b. Malvern, Ark., Apr. 14, 1953; s. James Gerald and Mary Pauline (Russell) A.; m. Deborah Sue Hausermann, May 28, 1982; 1 child: Ryan David. B.S. in Biology, Ark. Tech. U., 1975. Dir. quality assurance and research and devel. Atkins Pickle Co. sub. Dean Foods, Atkins, Ark., 1975-85; dir. research and devel. Bloch & Guggenheimer, Hurlock, Md., 1985—. Contbr. to research paper in field. Mem. Inst. Food Technologists, Internat. Assn. Quality Circles, N.Y. Acad. Scis. Republican. Am. Baptist. Current Work: Refining fermentation techniques currently used in industry to improve quality and texture of raw material; low salt brining and processing for new products. Subspecialty: Food science and technology. Office: Bloch & Guggenheimer Inc PO Box 850 Hurlock MD 21643

ADAMS, JOHN DAVID, consultant, lecturer; b. Wooster, Ohio, Sept. 13, 1942; s. Lyman Harry and Catherine Ruth (Whittlesey) A.; m. Sarah Jane Dalbey, Aug. 15, 1964; children: Samantha Lee, Gillian Lindsey. A.B. in Math, Wittenberg U., 1963; B.S. in Mgmt. Sci, Case Inst. Tech., 1965; Ph.D. in Orgnl. Behavior, CAse-Western Res. U., 1965. Cert. Consultants Internat. Vis. lectr. U. Leeds, Yorkshire, U.K., 1969-71; mgr. Nat. Tng. Labs. Inst., Washington, 1971-74, div. dir., 1974-75, consultant, Arlington, Va., 1975—. Author: Transition, 1976, Understanding and Managing Stress (3 vols.), 1980; editor: New Technology in Organizational Development, Vol. 2, 1975, Organizational Development in Health Care Organizations, 1982. Bd. trustees Potomac Rugby Union, 1975—. NDEA fellow, 1965-69. Mem. Am. Psychol. Assn., Assn. Humanistic Psychology, Orgn. Devel. Network (dir. 1971-74), Blue Key, Tau Beta Pi. Current Work: Health protection, risk reduction, stress management, belief systems, personal peak performance, personal transformation, expanded consciousness, cultural hypnosis, paradigm shift, holistic. Subspecialties: Social psychology; Preventive medicine. Home and Office: 2914 27th St N Arlington VA 22207

ADAMS, KARYL ANN, defense aeronautical laboratory electronics enginner, computer systems analysist; b. Urbana, Ohio, Jan. 8, 1952; d. Robert Vincent Adams and Mildred Marie (Neff) Richardson. B.S., Ohio No. U., 1975; M.S., Air Force Inst. Tech., 1985. Elec. engr. Air Force Aerospace Med. Research Lab., Wright Patterson AFB, Ohio, 1975, Air Force Flight Dynamics Lab., 1976-79; electronics engr. Air Force Wright Aero. Lab., 1980—, guest lectr., 1976—; computer graphics researcher Air Force Wright Aero. Lab. (Control Synthesis Br.), 1980—. Activity organizer Campus Chest-United Way, Ada, Ohio, 1971-75. Olin fellow Washington U., St. Louis, 1975; recipient Sustained Superior Performance award U.S. Air Force, 1977, 85, Spl. Act of Service award, 1981; named Jr. Scientist and Engr. of Yr. Air Force Flight Dynamics Lab., 1978. Mem. Assn. Computing Machinery, IEEE, Mortarboard, Alpha Omicron Pi. Methodist. Current Work: Managing a technical team evaluating the performance of the forward swept wing technology demonstrator; developing an interactive graphics environment for the design of cockpit displays for advanced aircraft systems. Subspecialties: Aerospace engineering and technology; Computer engineering. Home: 7578 Mount Hood Huber Heights OH 45424 Office: Air Force Wright Aero Labs Wright Patterson AFB OH 45341

ADAMS, MAX D., pharmacologist, researcher; b. St. Marys, W.Va., July 25, 1941; s. Guy and Alfarata (Johnson) A.; m. Mergie Ann Wilson, July 5, 1963; children: Julie, Christy. B.S., W. Va. U., 1965; M.S., Purdue U., 1968, Ph.D. in Pharmacology, 1970. Diplomate: Am. Bd. Toxicology. Instr. Med. Coll. Va., 1972-76, asst. prof., 1972-76; sr. research pharmacologist Mallinckrodt, Inc., St. Louis, 1977-81, research mgr. pharmacology and toxicology, 1981-84, assoc. dir. pharmaceutics and device research and devel., 1984—. Mem. Am. Soc.

Pharmacology and Exptl. Therapeutics. Methodist. Current Work: Pharmacology and toxicology of diagnostic pharmaceuticals. Subspecialties: Pharmacology; Toxicology (medicine). Home: 3069 Winding River Dr Saint Charles MO 63303

ADAMS, ROBERT MCCORMICK, anthropologist, institution executive; b. Chgo., July 23, 1926; s. Robert McCormick and Janet (Lawrence) A.; m. Ruth Salzman Skinner, July 24, 1953; 1 dau., Megan. Ph.B., U. Chgo., 1947, M.A., 1952, Ph.D., 1956, Archaeol. field tng. in, Jarmo, Iraq, 1950-51. Yucatan, Mexico, 1953, field studies history irrigation and urban settlement, Iraq, Saudi Arabia, and, Iran, 1956—, reconnaissance and excavation ancient Mayan settlement patterns, Chiapas, Mexico, 1958-61; mem. faculty and staff Oriental Inst. U. Chgo., 1955-84; asso prof. Oriental Inst., 1961-62, prof. Oriental Inst., 1962-84, dir. Oriental Inst., 1962-68, 81-83, dean div. social scis., 1970-74, 79-80, provost, 1982-84; sec. Smithsonian Inst., Washington, 1984—; resident dir. Baghdad Sch., Am. Schs. Oriental Research, 1968-69; chmn. assembly behavioral and social scis. NRC 1972-76. Author: Land Behind Baghdad, 1965, The Evolution of Urban Society, 1966, (with H.J. Nissen) The Uruk Countryside, 1972, Heartland of Cities, 1981; Editor: (with C. H. Kraeling) City Invincible: A Symposium on Urbanization and Cultural Development in the Ancient Near East, 1960, (with C.S. Schelling) Corners of Foreign Field, 1979, (with N.J. Smelser and D.J. Treiman) Behavioral and Social Science Research: A National Resource, 1982. Trustee Nat. Humanities Center, 1976-83, Russell Sage Found., 1978—. Served with USNR, 1944-46. Fellow Am. Acad. Arts and Scis., Middle East Studies Assn., Iraqi Acad. (asso.), AAAS, Am. Anthrop. Assn., mem. Soc. Am. Archaeology, German Archaeol. Inst., Nat. Acad. Scis., Am. Philos. Soc., Sigma Xi. Office: Smithsonian Inst Office of the Sec 100 Jefferson Dr SW Washington DC 20560*

ADAMS, WILLIAM HENRY, chemist, educator; b. Balt., Dec. 21, 1933; s. William Henry and Mary Ellen (Verlander) A.; m. Violeta Lourdes Flores, Dec. 20, 1958 (dec.); 1 dau., Maryna Noelle. A.B., Johns Hopkins U., 1955; S.M., U. Chgo., 1956, Ph.D., 1960. Asst. prof. Pa. State U., 1962-66; asst., then assoc. prof. Rutgers U., New Brunswick, N.J., 1966-75, prof., 1975—. NSF postdoctoral fellow, 1960-62. Mem. Am. Phys. Soc., Am. Chem. Soc., AAAS. Current Work: Quantum theory of intermolecular interactions. Subspecialty: Theoretical chemistry. Home: 3 Meadowbrook Ln Piscataway NJ 08854 Office: Dept Chemistry Rutgers U New Brunswick NJ 08903

ADBEL-GHAFFAR, AHMED MANSOUR, structural engineering educator; b. Mansourah, Egypt, Apr. 30, 1947; came to U.S., 1972; naturalized, 1981; s. Mansour A. and Nafissa E. (Kasem) A-G.; m. Cathleen Crane, Oct. 12, 1975; children—Samy A. M., Tarek A.M. B.Sc. in Civil Engring., Cairo U., 1970; M.Sc., Calif. Inst. Tech., 1973, Ph.D., 1976. Cons. engr. Bakhoum & Moharram, Cairo, 1970-72; instr. Cairo U., 1970-72; research fellow Calif. Inst. Tech., Pasadena, 1976-78; asst. prof. U. Ill.-Chgo., 1978-79, Princeton U., N.J., 1979-83, assoc. prof., 1983—, dir. grad. studies dept. civil engring., 1984—. Assoc. editor Soil Dynamics and Earthquake Engring., 1980. contbr. articles to profl. jours. Recipient Rheinstein Research award Princeton U., 1981; Norman Sollenberger Faculty award Princeton U., 1984. Mem. ASCE (Raymond C. Reese Research prize 1982, Thomas A. Middlebrooks award 1982), Earthquake Engring. Research Inst., Am. Acad. Mechanics, Internat. Assn. Bridge and Structural Engring., Internat. Soc. Soil Mechanics and Found. Engring. Moslem. Current work: Earthquake engineering, particularly stuctural dynamics and seismic response analysis of large scale civil engineering structures such as cable-supported bridges and dams; full scale dynamic testing of structures. Subspecialties: Civil engineering; Theoretical and applied mechanics. Home: 52 Dodds Lane Princeton NJ 08540 Office: Civil Engring Dept Princeton U Princeton NJ 08544

ADDIS, JAMES THEODORE, aquatic ecologist; b. Sandusky, Ohio, Aug. 29, 1937; s. Clifford Howard A. and Naomi (Delinger) Nichols; m. Ann Washburn, Nov. 19, 1971; children—Steven D., Bonnie L. B.Sc. in Agr., Ohio State U., 1961, M.Sc. in Zoology, 1963, postgrad., 1965. Research assoc. Ohio State U., Columbus, 1963-65, instr. dept. zoology, 1968-74; supr. inland fisheries research Ohio Dept. Natural Resources, Ashley, 1965-68; dist. fish mgr. Wis. Dept. Natural Resources, Madison, 1974-76, dir. bur. fish mgmt., 1976—; chmn. Lake Superior and Lake Michigan coms. Great Lakes Fisheries Commn. Contbr. articles to profl. jours. Chmn. Middleton Transp. Commn., 1983; pres. Century Harbor Property Owners Assn., 1984—. Mem. Am. Fisheries Soc., Wis. Acad. Sci., Arts and Letters, Internat. Assn. Fish and Wildlife Agys., Trout Unltd., Wis. Wildlife Fedn., Isaac Walton League Am., Sigma Xi. Current work: Management of fisheries and aquatic resources primarily from view of an adminstrator; fish populations, resource allocation, environmental protection. Subspecialties: Resource management; Limnology. Home: 2829 Century Harbor Rd Middleton WI 53562 Office: Wis Dept Natural Resources Box 7921 Madison WI 53562

ADDY, JOHN KEITH, chemist, educator; b. Sheffield, Eng., June 30, 1937; came to U.S., 1966, naturalized, 1976; s. John Arthur and Gladys (Powell) A.; m. Jean Elizabeth Powell, July 23, 1963; children: John David, June Elizabeth. B.Sc. with spl. honors, Kings Coll., U. London, 1958; Ph.D., U. Southampton, Eng., 1962. Postdoctoral research assoc. U. Oreg., 1961-62; Lectr. chemistry N.E. Essex Coll., Colchester, Eng., 1962-63, John Dalton Coll. Tech., Manchester, Eng., 1963-66; asst. prof. chemistry Wagner Coll., Staten Island, N.Y., 1966-69, assoc. prof., 1969-74, prof., 1974—. Contbr. articles to chem. jours. Fellow Royal Soc. Chemistry (treas. U.S. sec. 1981—); mem. Am. Chem. Soc. (nat. councillor 1975-81). Mem. Evangelical Free Ch. Am. Lodge: Rotary (dir. 1976-84). Current Work: Crystal structure of polymers. Subspecialties: Physical chemistry; Polymer chemistry. Home: 166 Chelsea St Staten Island NY 10307 Office: Dept Chemistry Wagner Coll Staten Island NY 10301

ADELI, HOJJAT, civil engineer, educator; b. Langrood, Iran, June 3, 1950; came to U.S., 1974, naturalized, 1983; s. Jafar and Mokarram (Soofi) A.; m. Nahid Dadmehr, Feb., 1979; children—Amir, Anahita. M.S. in Civil Engring. U. Teheran, Iran, 1973; Ph.D. in Civil Engring., Stanford U., 1976. Asst. prof. Northwestern U., Evanston, Ill., 1977; asst. prof. U. Teheran, 1978-81, assoc. prof., 1981-82; assoc. prof. U. Utah, Salt Lake City, 1982-83, Ohio State U., Columbus, 1983—; cons. Atomic Orgn. of Iran, Teheran, 1978-79, Iran Ministry of Housing, Teheran, 1979-82. Author: How Can the Casualties and Damages Due to Earthquakes in the Cities Be Reduced, 1979; Strength of Materials-Including 1000 Problems, 1980, 2nd edit. 1984; Small Buildings in Earthquake Regions, 1980, 2nd edit., 1984; Earthquake Engineering, 1980; Analysis of Structures, 1981. Contbr. articles to profl. jours. Recipient First Degree Medal of Knowledge, Iran Ministry of Higher Edn., 1973. Mem. ASCE, Earthquake Engring. Research Inst. Current work: Computer-aided analysis and design of structures, artificial intelligence, software engineering. Subspecialties: Civil engineering; Computer-aided design. Home: 1131 Firth Ave Worthington OH 43210 Office: Dept Civil Engring 470 Hitchcock Hall 2070 Neil Ave Ohio State U Columbus OH 43210

ADELMAN, GEORGE, editor, librarian, consultant; b. Boston, Sept. 17, 1926; s. Morris and Anna (Cohen) A.; m. Sondra Cohen, July 15, 1957; children: Merle, Marjorie. B.A., Dartmouth Coll., 1947; M.A. in Psychology, Boston U., 1950; M.S. in Library Sci., Simmons Coll., 1950. Gen. mgr. Mass. Chem. Co., Boston, 1947-55; reference librarian Boston Public Library, 1950-55; tech. info. officer U.S. Office of Naval Research, Boston, 1955-64; dir. publs., editor, librarian Neuroscis. Research Program M.I.T., Boston, 1964-82, editorial cons., 1983—, cons. in field. Editor: Neuroscis. Research Program Bull., 1965-82; co-editor: The Organization of the Cerebral Cortex, 1981, The Neurosciences: Paths of Discovery, 1977, The Neurosciences: Study Program I-IV, 1967-77, Neurosciences Symposium Summaries, 1968-80; editor-in-chief: Ency. Neurosci., 1983—; contbr. articles and revs. on neuroscis. to profl. jours. Active Boston Mus. Fine Arts. Served with USN, 1943-46. Recipient Meritorious Service award Office Naval Research, 1963. Mem. Soc. Neurosci., Council Biology Editors. Democrat. Jewish. Club: Print and Drawing. Current Work: editorial and program consultant. Subspecialty: Interdisciplinary neuroscience. Home: 1904 Beacon St Brookline MA 02146

ADELMAN, SAUL JOSEPH, physics educator; b. Atlantic City, N.J., Nov. 18, 1944; s. Benjamin and Kitty (Sandler) A.; m. Carol Jeanne Sugerman, Mar. 28, 1970; children: Aaron, Barry, David. B.S. in Physics, U. Md., 1966; Ph.D., Calif. Inst. Tech., 1972. NAS/NRC postdoctoral resident research assoc. NASA Goddard Space Flight Center, Greenbelt, Md., 1972-74; asst. prof. astronomy Boston U., 1974-78; asst. prof. physics The Citadel, Charleston, S.C., 1978-83, assoc. prof., 1983—; NRC-NASA research assoc., 1984-86. Author: Bound for the Stars, 1981, (with Benjamin Adelman); contbr. articles to profl. jours. NASA grantee, 1975-76, 79-81, 82—; NSF grantee, 1976-79, 81-82. Fellow Royal Astron. Soc., British Interplanetary Soc.; mem. Internat. Astron. Union, Am. Astron. Soc., Optical Soc. Am., Astron. Soc. Pacific, Phi Beta Kappa, Phi Kappa Phi, Sigma Xi, Sigma Pi Sigma. Current Work: Research peculiar B and A type stars; main sequence B, A and F type stars, planetary engineering; photoelectric spectrophotometry. Subspecialty: Optical astronomy. Home: 1434 Fairfield Ave Charleston SC 29407 Office: Dept Physics The Citadel Charleston SC 29409

ADELMAN, STEVEN A., chemistry educator, research scientist; b. Chgo., July 4, 1945; s. Hyman and Sarah A.; m. Barbara Stolberg, May 12, 1974. Ph.D. (NSF fellow), Harvard U., 1972. Postdoctoral fellow MIT, Cambridge, 1972-73; U. Chgo., 1973-74; asst. prof. chemistry Purdue U., West Lafayette, Ind., 1975-77, assoc. prof., 1977-82, prof., 1982—; vis. faculty Columbia U., 1982-83, U. Paris, 1985; cons. Exxon Research Co., Exxon Labs., Los Alamos Nat. Lab., Contbr. articles on chemistry to profl. jours. Alfred P. Sloan fellow, 1976-80; Guggenheim fellow, 1982-83; NSF grantee, 1976—. Mem. Am. Chem. Soc., Am. Phys. Soc., AAAS. Current Work: Applications of statistical mechanics to problems in chemistry, theories for chemical reaction dynamics in liquid solution. Subspecialties: Theoretical chemistry; Statistical mechanics. Home: 2827 Wilshire St West Lafayette IN 47906 Office: Dept Chemistry Purdue U West Lafayette IN 47906

ADHAV, RATNAKAR SHANKAR, physicist, consultant; b. Sakri, Bombay, India, Oct. 30, 1927; came to U.S., 1976; s. Shankar Dhondu Adhav and Shevanti (Ramachndra) Thombre; m. Nalini Sadashiv Satpute, June 17, 1953; children—Sanjay, Geeta, Shailesh. B.S., Fergusson Coll., Poona, India, 1949; M.S., U. Poona, 1952; Ph.D. in Physics, U. Gujarat, India, 1958. Lectr. in physics Gujarat Coll., Ahmedabad, India, 1952-58; postdoctoral fellow Nat. Research Council, Ottawa, Ont., Can., 1958-60; research physicist Govt. of Can., Ottawa, 1960-63, EDO (Can.) Ltd., Cornwall, 1963-69; dir. research Quantum Tech. Inc., Toronto, 1969-76, pres., Sanford, Fla., 1976. Patentee in field. Pres., PTA, Cornwall, Can., 1955, India Assn., Sanford, 1984. Mem. IEEE (chmn. subsect. 1966), Optical Soc. Current work: Frequency doubling of lasers; electro-optic devices for laser; nonlinear materials-growth and characterization. Subspecialty: Optical engineering. Office: Quantum Tech Inc 2620 Iroquois Ave Sanford FL 32771

ADKINSON, N. FRANKLIN, JR., physician, educator; b. Forest City, N.C., May 18, 1943; s. N. Frank and Estelle (Stembridge) A.; m. Judy Faye Hyder, Aug. 20, 1966; children: Anna Estelle, Carter Franklin. B.A. with highest honors, U. N.C., Chapel Hill, 1965; M.D., Johns Hopkins U., 1969. Intern, resident Osler Med. Service, Johns Hopkins Hosp., Balt., 1969-71; clin. assoc. Lab. Immunology Nat. Cancer Inst., Bethesda, Md., 1971-73; mem. faculty Johns Hopkins U. Sch. Medicine, Balt., 1973—, assoc. prof. medicine, 1980—. Served to surgeon USPHS, 1971-73. NIH grantee. Mem. Am. Acad. Allergy, AAAS; mem. Am. Soc. Clin. Investigation; Mem. Am. Fedn. Clin. Research. Current Work: Drug hypersensitivity states; IgE methodology; arachidonate metabolism in inflammation. Subspecialties: Allergy; Immunology (medicine). Office: Johns Hopkins U at Good Samaritan Hosp 5601 Loch Raven Blvd Baltimore MD 21239

ADKISSON, PERRY LEE, university official; b. Hickman, Ark., Mar. 11, 1929; s. Robert Louise and Imogene (Perry) A.; m. Frances Rozelle, Dec. 29, 1956; 1 dau., Jean Amanda. B.S., U. Ark., 1950, M.S., 1954; Ph.D. in Entomology, Kans. State U., 1956. Asst. prof. entomology U. Mo., 1956-58; asso. prof. Tex. A&M U., 1958-63, prof., 1963-67, Disting. prof., head dept. entomology, 1967-78, v.p. for agr. and renewable resources, 1978-80, dep. chancellor for agr., 1980-83, dep. chancellor, 1983—; cons. Internat. AEC, Vienna, 1969-74; Chmn. sci. adv. panel Gov. Tex. on Agrl. Chems., 1970-72; chmn. Tex. Pesticide Adv. Com., 1971—; mem. panel experts on integrated pest control UN/FAO, Rome, 1971—; mem. Structural Pest Control Bd., Tex., 1971-78, NRC World Food and Nutrition Study Team, 1977; chmn. com. biology pest species NRC, 1974; mem. environ. studies bd., study group problems pest control Nat. Acad. Sci.-NRC, 1972—; mem. vis. group Internat. Center Insect Physiology and Ecology, Nairobi, Kenya, 1974-75; mem. U.S. directorate UNESCO Man and the Biosphere Program, 1975; mem. governing bd. Internat. Crops Research Inst. for Semi-Arid Tropics, 1983—; mem. bd. agr. NRC, 1985—; mem. Nat. Sci. Bd., 1985—. Mem.: editorial com. Ann. Rev. Entomology, 1973—; contr. articles to profl. jours. Served with M.C. AUS, 1951-53. Recipient Alexander Von Humboldt award, 1980; Disting. Alumnus award Kans. State U., 1980; USPHS postdoctoral fellow Harvard U., 1963-64. Fellow AAAS, Entomol. Soc. Am. (governing bd. 1971-79, pres. 1974, Bussart Meml. award 1967); mem. Kans. Entomol. Soc., Internat. Orgn. Biol. Control, Am. Registry Profl. Entomologists (governing council 1976-78, pres. 1977), Nat. Acad. Scis., Phi Kappa Phi, Sigma Xi. Current Work: Research in insect physiology, photoperiodism, ecology and integrated control of crop pests. Subspecialty: Integrated pest management.

ADLAKHA, RAMESH CHANDER, cell biologist, educator; b. New Delhi, India, July 31, 1949; came to U.S., 1980; s. Lok Nath and Sita Rani (Dudeja) A. B.Sc., Delhi U., 1969; M.Sc., Indian Inst. Tech. Delhi, 1971; D.Sc., U. Paris, 1980. Chemist, Indian Agr. Research Inst., New Delhi, 1971-72; sr. research fellow Council Sci. and Indsl. Research, New Delhi, 1972-75; vis. research fellow Institut de Chimie des Substances Naturelles, Centre Nationale de la Recherche Scientifique, France, 1975-80; research assoc. U. Tex. M.D. Anderson Hosp., Houston, 1980-83, asst. prof. cell biology, 1983—; asst. prof. Grad. Sch. Biomed. Scis., Houston, 1984—. Contbr. articles to cell profl. publs. Mem. exec. com. L'Alliance Française de Houston, 1983—, v.p., 1985—. Nat. Merit scholar Govt. India, 1969; merit scholar Indian Inst. Tech., 1969-71; French Govt. scholar, 1975-80. Mem. Am. Soc. Cell Biology, Am. Assn. Cancer Research, Internat. Cell Cycle Soc., AAAS. Hindu. Current work: Biochemical regulation of cell cycle; characterization of chromosome condensation and decondensation factors; role of non-histone protein phosphorylation in mitosis; role of polyamines in mammalian cell proliferation. Subspecialties: Cell biology; Cell biology (medicine). Home: 1401 Braeswood #13 Houston TX 77030 Office: Dept of Chemotherapy Research Univ Tex M D Anderson Hosp and Tumor Inst 6723 Bertner Houston TX 77030

ADLER, FRED PETER, electronics executive; b. Vienna, Austria, Mar. 29, 1925; came to U.S., 1942; s. Michael and Ellida (Bronner) A.; m Christine Austin, 1971; children—Michael Steven, Andrew David. B.E.E. with honors, UCLA, 1945; M.E.E., Calif. Inst. Tech., 1948, Ph.D. magna cum laude, 1950. Elec. engr. Gen. Electric Co. Research and Cons. Labs., 1945-47; project engr. Jet Propulsion Lab. Hughes Aircraft Co., Culver City, Calif., 1950, sr. staff physicist, 1954-57, mgr. advanced planning, 1957-59, dir. advanced project lab., 1959-61, v.p., mgr. space systems div., 1961-66, v.p., asst. group exec. Aerospace Group, 1966-70, v.p., group exec., 1973-81, sr. v.p. corp., pres. EDSG Group, El Segundo, Calif., 1981—; pres., chmn. bd. HBH, 1979—. Author: (with others) Guided Missile Engineering, 1959. Contbr. articles to profl. jours. Fellow AIAA; mem. N.Y. Acad. Sci., Def. Sci. Bd. (assoc.), Sigma Xi, Tau Beta Pi. Office: Hughes Aircraft Co PO Box 902 (E1/A102) El Segundo CA 90245

ADLER, IRVING, mathematics educator, author, researcher in mathematical biology; b. N.Y.C., Apr. 27, 1913; s. Marcus and Celia (Kress) A.; m. Ruth Relis, June 2, 1935 (dec. 1968); children: Stephen Louis, Peggy Adler Robohm; m. Joyce Theresa Lifshutz, Sept. 16, 1968. B.S., CCNY, 1931; M.A., Columbia U., 1938, Ph.D., 1961. Math. tchr. pub. high schs., N.Y.C., 1932-46; chmn. math. dept. Textile High Sch., N.Y.C., 1946-52; nat. dir. Nat. Council Arts, Scis. and Professions, N.Y.C., 1953-54; instr. Columbia U., N.Y.C., 1957-60, Bennington (Vt.) Coll., 1961, free lance author, 1954—; cons. ednl. policies commn. NEA, Washington, 1940-41; keynote speaker Conf. State Suprs. of Math., U.S. Office Edn., 1961. Author: The New Mathematics; 54 other books; co-author: The Reason Why Series, 1960-77; contbr. articles to profl. publs. Pres. Vt. in Miss. Corp., Vt. and Miss., 1965-67; mem. Sch. Bd. Shaftsbury, Vt., 1976-82, chmn., 1979-80; mem. sch. bd. Mt. Anthony High Sch. Dist., Bennington, Vt., 1981-84; sec. county com. Democratic party, Bennington, 1972-75. Recipient awards for sci. books for children Nat. Sci. Tchrs. Assn. and Children's Book Council, 1972, 75, 80; award N.Y. State Assn. Supervision and Curriculum Devel., 1961. Fellow AAAS, Vt. Acad. Arts and Scis. (pres. 1978-81); mem. Am. Math. Soc., Math. Assn. Am., Soc. Indsl. and Applied Math., Nat. Council Tchrs. of Math., Phi Beta Kappa, Kappa Delta Pi. Jewish. Current Work: Models of phyllotaxis; models of pre-biotic chemical evolution. Subspecialties: Morphology; Applied mathematics. Home: RD 2 North Bennington VT 05257

ADLER, JULIUS, biologist, biochemist, educator; b. Edelfingen, Germany, Apr. 30, 1930; came to U.S., 1938, naturalized, 1943; s. Adolf and Irma (Stern) A.; m. Hildegard Wohl, Oct. 15, 1963; children: David Paul, Jean Susan. A.B., Harvard U., 1952; M.S., U. Wis., 1954, Ph.D., 1957; Postdoctoral fellow, Washington U., St. Louis, 1957-59, Stanford U., 1959-60. Asst. prof. biochemistry and genetics U. Wis., Madison, 1960-63, asso. prof., 1963-66, prof., 1966—, Edwin Bret Hart prof. biochemistry and genetics, 1972—, Steenbock prof. microbiol. scis., 1982—. Research, publs. in field. Mem. Am. Acad. Arts and Scis., Nat. Acad. Scis. Current Work: Behavior of simple organisms, especially bacteria. Subspecialties: Biochemistry (biology); Molecular biology. Home: 1234 Wellesley Rd Madison WI 53705 Office: Dept Biochemistry U Wis Madison WI 53706

ADLER, LEONORE LOEB, psychologist; b. Karlsruhe, Ger., May 2, 1921; came to U.S., 1938, naturalized, 1944; d. Leo and Elsie (Laemle) Loeb; m. Helmut Ernest Adler, May 22, 1943; children: Barry Peter, Beverly Sharmaine, Evelyn Renee. B.A., Queen's Coll., CUNY, 1968; Ph.D., Adelphi U., 1972. Research asst. dept. mammalogy Am. Mus. Natural History, N.Y.C., 1956-84; adj. asst. prof. dept. psychology Coll. S.I., CUNY, 1974-80; research assoc. Mystic (Conn.) Marine-life Aquarium, 1976—; adj. asst. prof. dept. psychology York Coll., CUNY, 1978-80; dir. Inst. Cross-Cultural and Cross-Ethnic Studies, assoc. prof. psychology Molloy Coll., Rockville Centre, N.Y., 1980—. Author, editor: Cross Cultural Research at Issue, 1982; author, translator: This is the Dachshund, 1966, 75; editor, co-author: Issues in Cross-Cultural Research, 1976; mng. editor: Internat. Jour. Group Tensions, 1978-84. Fellow N.Y. Acad. Scis. (sect. psychology and women in sci.); mem. Am. Psychol. Assn., (mem. women's network 1982—), N.Y. State Psychol. Assn. (pres. div. social psychology 1978-79, 80-82, pres. div. acad. psychology 1982-83, chair com. women's issues 1982-84; Kurt Lewin award 1985), Eastern Psychol. Assn. (bd. dirs.), Internat. Council Psychologists (chair publs. policy com. 1981-83, treas. 1983-85), Internat. Assn. Cross-Cultural Psychology, Soc. Cross-Cultural Research, Assn. Women in Sci., Animal Behavior Soc., Internat. Orgn. Study Group Tensions, Internat. Soc. History Behavioral and Social Scis., Internat. Soc. Comparative Psychology, Queens County Psychology Assn. (pres.-elect 1985-86). Current Work: Cross-cultural research with children's drawings, social distances, attitudes, sea mammals. Subspecialties: Social psychology; Comparative psychology. Home: 162-14 86th Ave Jamaica NY 11432 Office: Inst Cross-Cultural & Cross-Ethnic Studies Molloy Coll 1000 Hempstead Ave Rockville Centre NY 11570

ADLER, ROBERT, electronics engineer; b. Vienna, Austria, Dec. 4, 1913; came to U.S., 1940, naturalized, 1945; s. Max and Jenny (Herzmark) A.; m. Mary F. Buehl, 1946. Ph.D. in Physics, U. Vienna, 1937. Asst. to patent atty., Vienna, 1937-38; lab. Sci. Acoustics, Ltd., London, Eng., 1939-40, Asso. Research, Inc., Chgo., 1940-41; research group Zenith Radio Corp., Chgo., 1941-52, asso. dir. research, 1952-63, v.p., 1959-77, dir. research, 1963-77, EXTEL Corp., Northbrook, Ill., 1978-79, v.p. research, 1979-82; tech. cons. Zenith Corp., 1982—. Contbr. numerous articles profl. publs. Fellow IEEE (Edison medal 1980); mem. Nat. Acad. Engring. Developed various electron beam tubes for frequency modulation transmitters, for TV receivers, electron beam parametric amplifier; pioneer ultrasonic remote control for TV, ultrasonic light deflection for laser projection TV. Current Work: Improvement of cathode ray tubes; applications of optics and acoustics (particularly surface acoustic waves) in information display and information access devices. Subspecialties: Electronics; Acoustics. Home: 327 Latrobe Ave Northfield IL 60093 Office: Zenith Ctr 1000 Milwaukee Ave Glenview IL 60025

ADLER, STEPHEN LOUIS, physicist; b. N.Y.C., Nov. 30, 1939; s. Irving and Ruth (Relis) A.; children: Jessica Wendy, Victoria Stephanie, Anthony Curtis. A.B. summa cum laude, Harvard U., 1961; Ph.D., Princeton U., 1964. Jr. fellow Soc. of Fellows Harvard U., 1964-66; research assoc. Calif. Inst. Tech., 1966; mem. Inst. for Advanced Study, Princeton U., N.J., 1966-69; prof. Sch. Natural Scis., Inst. for Advanced Study, 1969-79, N.J. Albert Einstein prof., 1979—; vis. lectr. dept. physics Princeton U., 1969—; cons. in field. Author: (with R.F. Dashen) Current Algebras, 1968; contbr. articles to profl. jours. Fellow Am. Acad. Arts and Scis., Am. Phys. Soc.; mem. Nat. Acad. Scis., Phi Beta Kappa, Sigma Xi. Current Work: Quantum gravitation; effective action models for quark confinement; Quaternionic field theory. Subspecialties: Particle physics; Theoretical physics. Home: 287A Nassau St Princeton NJ 08540 Office: Inst for Advanced Study Princeton NJ 08540

ADRIAN, DONALD JAMES, communication systems consultant, researcher; b. Huntington Park, Calif., July 10, 1929; s. James Albert and Linnie Josephine (Butcher) A.; m. Doris Faye Edmiston, Apr. 11, 1954; children—Nancy Ann, Thomas James, Steven Ray. B.S., Calif. State Poly. U., 1952; M.A., UCLA, 1964. Physicist, Nat. Bur. Standards, Corona, Calif., 1952-53; electronic scientist Naval Ordnance Lab., Corona, 1953-60; lab. dir. Aero Geo Astro Corp., Corona, 1960-65, Astrophysics Research Corp., Norco, Calif., 1965-72; v.p., dir. Megatek Corp., San Diego, 1972-82; cons., Leucadia, Calif., 1982—. Patentee in radar, navigation, electronics; contbr. articles to profl. jours. Recipient U.S. Navy Superior Achievement award, 1958. Mem. IEEE, Am. Geophys. Union, Inst. Navigation, Bioelectromagnetics Soc., Optical Soc. Am., AAAS. Democrat. Methodist. Current work: VLF navigation, electromagnetic bioeffects, signal processing, computer based systems, atmospheric optics, radio propagation. Subspecialties: Electronics; Systems engineering. Home: 287 La Costa Ave Leucadia CA 92024

ADVANI, SUNDER HASHMATRAI, engineering educator, researcher; b. Hyderabad, Pakistan, Aug. 10, 1941; s. Hashmatrai C. and Rukmani H. (Idnani) A.; m. Monica Jhangiani, Aug. 9, 1968; children—Anjali, Sunil. B.S.M.E., Bombay U., India, 1961; M.S., Stanford U., 1962, Ph.D., 1965. Mem. tech staff Northrop Corp., Hawthorne, Calif., 1965-67; assoc. prof. W.Va. U., Morgantown, 1967-74, prof., 1974-78; prof., chmn. Ohio State U., Columbus, 1978—, assoc. dean, 1984—; cons. NIH, Bethesda, Md., 1974, DOE, Washington, 1983, SOHIO, Cleve., 1983—, Gulf, Pitts., 1985. Assoc. editor Energy Resources Tech., 1982—. Contbr. articles to profl. jours. Grantee numerous orgns. Fellow ASME; mem. Am. Acad. Mechanics, Am. Soc. Engring. Edn. Current work: Research in solid mechanics; engineering education. Subspecialties: Fracture mechanics; Theoretical and applied mechanics. Home: 3841 Criswell Dr Columbus OH 43220 Office: Ohio State Univ 155 W Woodruff Columbus OH 43210

AFFATATO, JOSEPH FRANK, marketing executive; b. Bklyn., June 26, 1952; s. Joseph and Anna (Russo) A.; m. Linda Marie Borodich, Nov. 4, 1972. Student NYU Sch. Engring., 1969, Poly. Inst. Bklyn., 1970-72, Columbia U., 1973-74. Engr., IBM Corp., N.Y.C., 1973-76; regulatory tech. mgr. Memorex Corp., Santa Clara, Calif., 1976-79; OEM system mgr. Hazeltine Corp., Commack, N.Y., 1980-82; mktg. support mgr. Corvus Systems, San Jose, Calif., 1982-83; mktg. mgr. Gen. Optronics, Edison, N.J., 1983-84, NSG America, Somerset, N.J., 1985—; v.p. Data Retention Labs., N.Y.C., 1979-80; cons. Synergetic Systems, S.I., 1982—; sr. cons. Integrated Optical Systems, Alexandria, Va., 1984—. Mem. Republican Presdl. Task Force, Washington, 1984, Republican Senatorial Club, Nat. Senatorial Congl. Com., 1985. ROTC scholar, 1970; U.S. Naval Res. Officers Assn. scholar, 1970; NYU Sch. Engring. grantee, 1969. Mem. N.Y. Acad. Sci., Am. Phys. Soc., Optical Soc. Am., AAAS. Roman Catholic. Lodge: Lions. Current work: Long haul fiber optics systems using single mode fiber and InGaAsP lasers emitting at 1330 and 1550 NM. Also research in bio-cybernetics. Subspecialties: Fiber optics; Artificial intelligence. Home: 1100 Clove Rd Suite L-O Staten Island NY 10301 Office: NSG America World's Fair Dr Somerset NJ 08873

AFSHAR, SIROOS K., software engineer; b. Qom, Iran, July 3, 1949; came to U.S., 1975, naturalized, 1980; s. Bagher and Mastooreh Afshar-Khajev; m. Simin Manii, Aug. 11, 1974; children: Pedram, Afsheen. B.S.E.E., Sharif U., Tehran, Iran, 1972; M.S.E.E., U. Mich., 1976, Ph.D., 1979. Design engr. Nat. Iranian Oil Co., Tehran, 1972-75; research asst. U. Mich., Ann Arbor, 1976-79; asst. prof. La. State U., Baton Rouge, 1979-82; mem. tech. staff AT&T Info. Systems, Lincroft, N.J., 1982—; adj. prof. Monmouth Coll., N.J., 1985; Predoctoral fellow U. Mich., 1978. Recipient Outstanding Achievement award U. Mich., 1979. Mem. IEEE, Assn. Computing Machinery, Soc. Indsl. and Applied Math., Math. Assn. Am., Phi Kappa Phi, Tau Beta Pi, Eta Kappa Nu. Current Work: Research and development in computer interconnection networks. Subspecialties: Software engineering; Algorithms. Home: 10 Constitution Ct Manalapan NJ 07726 Office: AT&T Info Systems 307 Middletown-Lincroft Rd Lincroft NJ 07738

AGARD, EUGENE THEODORE, medical physicist; b. Barbados, W.I., Aug. 15, 1932; came to U.S., 1959; s. Samuel and Pearl Doris (Best) A.; m. Joyce Elaine Phillips, June 8, 1960; children: Noel A., Ian C., Wendy T., Linda G. B.Sc. with 1st class honors, U. W.I., Jamaica, 1954-56; M.Sc., U. London, 1958; Ph.D., U. Toronto, Ont., Can., 1970. Cert. Am. Bd. Radiology. Asst. physisist Mass. Gen. Hosp., Boston, 1959-63; lectr., U. W.I., Trinidad, 1963-72; dir med. physics program P.R. Nuclear Center, 1972-76; asso. clin. prof. Wright State U., Dayton, 1977-80; med. physicist, radiation safety officer Kettering Med. Center, Dayton, Ohio, 1976-84; cons. in radiol. physcis, 1984—; cons., researcher. Contbr. articles to profl. jours. Mem. Am. Assn. Physicists in Medicine (mem. internat. relations com. 1974-77), Health Physics Soc. (chmn. affirmative action com. 1980-81), Miami Valley Alt. Energy Assn. (dir. 1980-81), Radiol. Soc. N. Am., Am. Coll. Radiology. Christian. Current Work: Radiation dosimetry and biological effects of radiation. Subspecialties: Biophysics (physics); Imaging technology. Office: PO Box 2086 Dayton OH 45429

AGARWAL, ASHOK KUMAR, chemical engineer, researcher; b. Firozabad, India, Aug. 14, 1950; came to U.S., 1975, naturalized, 1983; s. Satyanarain and Shakuntla Devi (Garg) A.; m. Neena Garg, Dec. 28, 1981. B.Tech. in Chem. Engring., Indian Inst. of Tech., Kanpur, 1971, M. Tech. in Chem. Engring., 1974; Ph.D. in Chem. Engring., W.Va. U., 1978. Project engr. Indian Cons. Bur., New Delhi, 1974; research assoc. W.Va. U., Morgantown, 1978; sr. research chem. engr. Monsanto Research Corp., Miamisburg, Ohio, 1978-84; contract mgr. Monsanto Co., Dayton, Ohio, 1984—. Contbr. articles to sci. jours. Recipient Gold Medal Agarwal Inter Coll., 1966, Shalimar Gold medal Indian Pulp and Paper Tech. Assn., 1974. Mem. Am. Inst. Chem. Engrs. (profl. devel. recognition cert.). Mem. editorial bd. Energy Progress jour., 1981—. Current work: Process development; synthetic fuels devel., underground coal gasification; reaction kinetics; catalysis; reactor engineering; state-of-the-art instrumentation development; hazardous wastes and environmental engineering, reservoir engineering, computer simulation and process analysis as related to design and process improvement. Subspecialties: Chemical engineering; Coal. Home: 2125 Imperial Rd West Carrollton OH 45449 Office: Monsanto Co 1515 Nicholas Rd Dayton OH 45418

AGGARWAL, MAHESH CHAND, mechanical engineering educator; b. M.Nagar, India, Nov. 1, 1947; came to U.S., 1971, naturalized, 1979; s. Roop Chand and Daya (Vati) A.; m. Anita Agrawal, Dec. 29, 1972; children—Payal, Parag. B.Tech., India Inst. Tech., Kanpur, 1971; M.S., Marquette U., 1973; Ph.D., U. Mich., 1978. Research asst. Marquette U., Milw., 1971-72, teaching asst., 1972; teaching fellow U. Mich., Ann Arbor, 1973-74, 77-78; asst. prof. Gannon U., Erie, Pa., 1978-82, chmn. mech. engring. dept., 1981-82, 83-84, assoc. prof. mech. engring., 1982—; cons. Autoclave Engring., Erie, 1980—, Amsco, Erie, 1981-84. Author: Heat Transfer Lab Manual, 1981, 83; Fluid Mechanics Lab Manual, 1981, 83. Editor ann. energy seminar proceeding, 1979—. India Inst. Tech. scholar 1966-71, Uttar Pradesh Edn. Bd. scholar 1960-62, 64-65. Mem. ASME, Northwestern Inventor Council. Hindu. Current work: Heat recovery and storage from low temperature waste heat; heat transfer as applied to very high temperature and very high pressure. . Home: 4241 W 32nd St Erie PA 16506Office: Gannon U University Sq Erie PA 16541

AGHEVLI, REZA, electrical and computer engineer, researcher; b. Tehran, Iran, Jan. 7, 1943; came to U.S., 1966, naturalized, 1985; s. Abolhassan and Tahereh (Mokhtar-Massoumi) A.; m. Azita Naghavi, June 29, 1973; children—Arash, Kaveh. B.S.E. in Elec. Engring., with honors, U. Tehran, 1965, M.S.E. in Elec. Engring., 1967, M.S. in Physics, 1971; Ph.D. in Elec. Engring. U. Mich., 1972. From asst. prof. to assoc. prof. elec. engring. Tehran Poly. U., 1972-76; mng. dir. Ednl. Equipment Industries, Inc., Tehran, 1977-80; vis. assoc. prof. U. Santa Clara, Calif., 1981-82; mem. tech. staff AT&T Bell Labs., Allentown, Pa., 1982—. Contbr. articles to profl. jours. NSF grantee, 1968-72. Fullbright-Hayes Found. scholar, 1975-76; Mem. IEEE, Am. Phys. Soc., Sigma Xi. Current work: Microelectronics, CAD tools and methodologies for VLSI design, semiconductor device modeling. Subspecialties: Microelectronics; Semiconductors. Office: AT&T Bell Labs 1247 S Cedar Crest Blvd Allentown PA 18103

AGNEW, DOUGLAS CRAIG, environmental consultant; b. East Meadow, N.Y., June 6, 1957; s. Edwin Lee and Mary Margaret (Reardon) A. B.S. in Environ. Biology, Stockton State Coll., 1979. Aquatic biologist Lakes and Waterways Mgmt. Inc., Pompano Beach, Fla., 1979-80, div. mgr., Tampa, Fla., 1980-82, v.p., 1982; environ. cons., pres. Aqua Sci., Inc., Dunedin, Fla., 1982—. Active Greater Tampa C. of C., Environ. Quality Council. Served with USCGR, 1976-82. Mem. Fla. Aquatic Plant Mgmt. Soc., Marine Tech. Soc., N. Am. Lake Mgmt. Soc. Subspecialties: Ecosystems analysis; Resource management. Home: 129 Edgewater Terr Dunedin FL 33528 Office: Aqua Sci Inc 129 Edgewater Terr Dunedin FL 33528

AGNEW, HAROLD MELVIN, physicist; b. Denver, Mar. 28, 1921; s. Sam E. and Augusta (Jacobs) A.; m. Beverly Jackson, May 2, 1942; children: Nancy E. Agnew Owens, John S. A.B., U. Denver, 1942; M.S., U. Chgo., 1948, Ph.D., 1949. With Los Alamos Sci. Lab., 1943-46, alt. div. leader, 1949-61, leader weapons div., 1964-70, dir., 1970-79; pres. GA Techs. Inc., San Diego, 1979-84, dir., 1984—; sci. adviser Supreme Allied Comdr. in Europe, Paris, France, 1961-64; Chmn. Army Sci. Adv. Panel, 1965-70, mem., 1970-74; mem. aircraft panel Pres.'s Sci. Adv. Com., 1965-73; mem. USAF Sci. Adv. Bd., 1957-69, Def. Sci. Bd., 1965-70, Gov. N.Mex. Radiation Adv. Council, 1959-61; sec. N.Mex. Health and Social Services, 1971-73; chmn. gen. adv. com. ACDA, 1974-77, mem., 1977-81; mem. aerospace safety adv. panel NASA, 1968-74; mem. U.S. Army Sci. Bd., 1978-80, White House Sci. Council, 1982—; mem. council engring. NRC, 1978-82, trustee council engring., 1982—; mem. Los Alamos Bd. Ednl. Trustees, 1950-55, pres., 1955; mem. Woodrow Wilson Nat. Fellowship Found., 1973—; trustee San Diego Mus. Art, 1983—; mem. N.Mex. Senate, 1955-61; sec. N.Mex. Legis. Council, 1957-61; chmn. N.Mex. Senate Corp. Commn., 1957-61; bd. dirs. Fedn. Rocky Mountain States, Inc., 1975-77. Recipient Ernest Orlando Lawrence award AEC, 1966; Enrico Fermi award Dept. Energy, 1978. Fellow Am. Phys. Soc., AAAS; mem. Nat. Acad. Scis., Nat. Acad. Engring. (Assembly of Engring.), Council on Fgn. Relations, Phi Beta Kappa, Sigma Xi, Omicron Delta Kappa. Subspecialty: Nuclear physics. Home: 322 Punta Baja Solana Beach CA 92075 Office: PO Box 81608 San Diego CA 92138

AGNEW, WILLIAM GEORGE, mech. engr., engring. lab. adminstr.; b. Oak Park, Ill., Jan. 12, 1926; s. Dupre L. and Marion S. (Roberts) A.; m. Norma Jean Light, Mar. 9, 1957; children—Brian R., Daniel D., Dalen W. B.S. in Mech. Engring, Purdue U., 1948, M.S. in Mech. Engring, 1950, Ph.D., 1952. Research engr. Project Squid, U.S. Navy, Purdue U., 1948-50; with General Motors Research Labs., Warren, Mich., 1952—, dept. head fuels and lubricants, 1967-70, dept. head emissions research, 1970-71, tech. dir., 1971—. Contbr. articles to profl. jours. Served with Manhattan Dist. U.S. Army, 1944-46. Mem. Soc. Automotive Engrs. (Horning Meml. award 1960), ASME, Combustion Inst. (bd. dirs. 1960-76), Nat. Acad. Engring., AAAS, Engring. Soc. Detroit, Sigma Xi. Current Work: Combustion, engines, vehicle structures, aerodynamics, fules, lubricants, energy resources, power transmissions, air pollution, atmospheric chemistry, auto safety. Subspecialties: Mechanical engineering; Combustion processes. Home: 3450 31 Mile Rd Romeo MI 48065 Office: Research Laboratories General Motors Technical Center Warren MI 48090

AGNEW, WILLIAM SCOTT, neuroscientist, educator; b. Salina, Kans., Dec. 16, 1946; s. Boyd Fergusson and Betty June (Johnson) A.; m. Jean Susanne Swedes, Aug. 14, 1972 (div. 1984). A.B., UCLA, 1969, Ph.D., 1976. Research fellow Calif. Inst. Tech., Pasadena, 1976-80; asst. prof. physiology Yale U. Sch. Medicine, New Haven, 1980-85, assoc. prof., 1985—. Postdoctoral fellow Muscular Dystrophy Assn., 1976, NIH, 1977-80. Mem. Am. Chem. Soc., N.Y. Acad. Scis., Soc. Neurosci., Soc. Gen. Physiology. Current work: Molecular basis of electrical events in neuronal cells. Subspecialty: Neurochemistry. Office: Dept Physiology Yale U Sch Medicine 333 Cedar St New Haven CT 06510

AGOSIN, MOISES K., zoology educator and researcher; b. Marseilles, France, Dec. 1, 1922; came to U.S., 1968, naturalized, 1974; s. Abraham W. and Raquel A.; m. Frida, June 18, 1948; children—Cynthia Regina, Marjorie Stella, Mario Daniel. M.D., U. Chile, Santiago, 1948. Postdoctoral fellow Rockefeller Found., Bethesda, Md., 1952-54; research assoc. NIH, Bethesda, 1955; prof. extraordinary U. Chile, 1956-60, dept. head, 1961-67; research prof. zoology U. Ga., Athens, 1968—; vis. prof. U. Calif.-Berkeley, 1961, U. London, 1965; cons. WHO, Panama, Geneva, Lima, Peru, 1958, 62, 67, 84. Collaborating author: The Physiology of Insects, 1974; Insect Biochemistry, 1978; Insect Biochemistry, Physiology and Pharmacology, 1984. Fellow Am. Acad. Microbiology,. Chilean Acad. Scis.; mem. Am. Chem. Soc., Am. Soc. Biol. Chemists, Biochem. Soc. (London). Current work: Drug detoxication systems in invertebrates. Subspecialties: Biochemistry (biology); Parasitology. Home: 177 Deertree Dr Athens GA 30605 Office: Univ of Ga 110 Riverbend Rd Athens GA 30602

AGOSTA, WILLIAM CARLETON, chemist, educator; b. Dallas, Jan. 1, 1933; s. Angelo N. and Helen Carleton (Jones) A.; m. Karin Solveig Engstrom, July 2, 1958; children—Jennifer Ellen, Christopher William. B.A., Rice Inst., 1954; A.M., Harvard U., 1955, Ph.D., 1957. NRC postdoctoral fellow Oxford (Eng.) U., 1957-58; Pfizer postdoctoral fellow U. Ill., Urbana, 1958-59; asst. prof. U. Calif., Berkeley, 1959-61; liaison scientist U.S. Navy, Frankfurt, Germany, 1961-63; asst. prof. Rockefeller U., 1963-67, asso. prof., 1967-74, prof., 1974—; cons. in field; officer, dir. Chiron Press, Inc. Contbr. articles to profl. jours. John Angus Erskine fellow U. Canterbury (N.Z.), 1981. Mem. Am. Chem. Soc., Chem. Soc. London, Interam. Photochem. Soc., European Photochemistry Assn., Am. Soc. Photobiology, Phi Beta Kappa, Sigma Xi. Current Work: Organic photochemistry, conformational analysis, mammalian pheromones. Subspecialties: Organic chemistry; Photochemistry. Home: 32 Washington Sq New York NY 10011 Office: Rockefeller U 1230 York Ave New York NY 10021

AGRAWAL, GOVIND PRASAD, physicist, researcher; b. Kashipur, India, July 24, 1951; came to U.S., 1977; s. Amarnath and Sushila (Devi) A.; m. Anne L. Frette-Damicourt, July 22, 1977; children—Sipra, Caroline. B.S., U. Lucknow, 1969; M.S., Indian Inst. Tech., New Delhi, 1971, Ph.D., 1974. Attache de recherche Ecole Polytechnique France, Palaiseau, 1974-76; research assoc. CUNY, 1977-80; research scientist Quantel, Orsay, France, 1980-81; mem. tech. staff AT&T Bell Labs., Murray Hill, N.J., 1982—. Contbr. articles to profl. jours. Recipient Gold medal U. Lucknow, 1969; Govt. of India scholar, 1965; Council Sci. and Indsl. Research fellow, 1971. Mem. IEEE, Am. Phys. Soc., Optical Soc. Am. Current work: Semiconductor lasers, optical fiber communication. Optical bistability, phase conjugation, nonlinear spectroscopy. Subspecialties: Semiconductor lasers; Theoretical physics. Office: AT&T Bell Labs 600 Mountain Ave Murray Hill NJ 07974

AGRAWAL, HARISH CHANDRA, neurobiologist, researcher; b. Allahabad, Uttar Pradesh, India; came to U.S., 1970, naturalized, 1982; s. Shambhu and Rajmani Devi A.; m. Daya Kumari Bhushan, Feb. 6, 1960; children: Sanjay, Sanjeev. B.Sc., Allahabad U., 1957, M.Sc., 1959, Ph.D., 1964. Med. research assoc. Thudichum Psychiat. Lab., Galesburg, Ill., 1964-68; lectr. dept. biochemistry Charing Cross Hosp., London, 1968-70; prof. pediatrics Wash. U. Sch. Medicine, St. Louis, 1970—, also prof. neurology, assoc. prof. neuropatholgy; mem. neurology study sect. NIH, 1979-82. Author: Handbook of Neurochemistry, 1969, Developmental Neurobiology, 1970, Biochemistry of Developing Brain, 1971, Membranes and Receptors, 1974, Proteins of the Nervous System, 1980, Biochemistry of Brain, 1980, Handbook of Neurochemistry, 1983. Jr. research fellow Council Sci. and Indsl. Research, New Delhi, 1960-62; sr. research fellow, 1963-64; recipient Research Career Devel. award Nat. Inst. Neurol. and Communicative Disorders, 1974-79. Mem. Internat. Soc. Neurochemistry, Internat. Brain Research Orng., Am. Soc. Neurochemistry, Am. Soc. Biol. Chemists, Am. Soc. Physiologists Soc., Soc. Neurosci. Current Work: Acylation, glycosylation and phosphorylation of proteins of myelin, myelin or glial surface antigens responsible for demyelination of neural tissues; proteins of neurofilaments and their involvement in Alzheimer's disease. Subspecialties: Neurochemistry; Neurobiology. Home: 18 Chafford Woods Saint Louis MO 63144 Office: Dept Pediatrics Washington U 400 S Kingshighway Blvd PO Box 14871 Saint Louis MO 63178

AGRAWAL, KRISHNA CHANDRA, pharmacology, educator, consultant, researcher; b. Calcutta, India, Mar. 15, 1937; came to U.S., 1962; s. Prasadi Lal and Asarfi Devi (Agrawal) A.; m. Mani Agrawal, Dec. 2, 1960; children: Sunil, Lina, Nira. B.S. in Pharmacy, Andhra U., Waltair, India, 1959, M.S. in Pharmacy, 1960; Ph.D., U. Fla., 1965; cert. in pharm. chemistry. Research asso. dept. pharmacology Yale U. Sch. Medicine, New Haven, 1966-69, instr., 1969-70, asst. prof., 1970-76, asso. prof., 1976; assoc. prof. dept. pharmacology Tulane U. Sch. Medicine, New Orleans, 1976-81, prof., 1981—; cons. mem. Southeastern Cancer Study Group, 1980—; mem. adv. com. on instnl. grants Am. Cancer Soc., 1980—. Contbr. numerous articles on cancer chemotherapy and devel. of radiosensitizing agts. for use in radiotherapy to sci. jours. Nat. Cancer Inst. grantee, 1976—; WHO grantee, 1979-82; La. Bd. Regents grantee, 1981-82, 83-84. Fellow Am. Inst. Chemists; mem. Am. Chem. Soc., Am. Assn. for Cancer Research, Radiation Research Soc., Am. Soc. Pharmacology and Exptl. Therapeutics, Sigma Xi. Patentee radiosensitizers for hypoxic tumor cells and compositions thereof. Current Work: Development of anticancer agents; development of radiation sensitizing agents for selective sensitization of hypoxic tumor cells to radiotherapy; studies related to molecular mechanism of action of hyperthermia and cancer chemotherapeutic agents. Subspecialties: Molecular pharmacology; Cancer research (medicine). Home: 6760 Bamberry Dr New Orleans LA 70126 Office: Dept Pharmacology Tulane U Sch Medicine New Orleans LA 70112

AGRAWAL, RAM KUMAR, mechanical engineer, consultant; b. Chhattar, Haryana, India, Aug. 15, 1938; came to U.S., 1968, naturalized, 1977; s. Lakhi Ram and Chandroli Devi A.; m. Bimla Kumari, Apr. 4, 1945; children: Vipin K., Vini K., Vina K., Binu K. B.S. in M.E, G.N. Engring. Coll., Ludhiana, India, 1964; M.S. in M.E, U. Houston, 1970; Ph.D., Tex. A&MU., 1973. Registered profl. engr., Tex. Lectr. mech. engring. Bits, Pilani, India, 1965-68; research asst., instr. U. Houston, 1968-70; instr., cons. Tex. A&MU., 1970-73; sr. and prin. mech. engr. Heat Research Corp., Houston, 1973-78; pvt. practice cons. engring., Houston, 1978-80; sr. mech. engr. Fluor Engrs. Inc., Houston, 1980—. Mem. ASME. Current Work: Specific interests in designing and engineering of direct fired equipments such as pyralysis furnaces, reformer furnaces, fired heaters and boilers. Subspecialty: Mechanical engineering.

AGRIOS, GEORGE N., plant pathologist, educator; b. Galarinos, Halkidiki, Greece, Jan. 16, 1936; came to U.S., 1963, naturalized, 1966; s. Nicholas G. and Olga (Kotsioudis) A.; m. Annette E. Braynard, Nov. 11, 1962; children: Nicholas, Anthony, Alexander. B.S., U. Thessaloniki, Greece, 1957; Ph.D., Iowa State U., Ames, 1960. Asst. prof. dept. plant pathology U. Mass., Amherst, 1963-69, assoc. prof., 1969-75, prof., 1975—. Author: Plant Pathology, 1969, 2d edit, 1978. Served with C.E. Greek Army, 1960-61. Mem. Am. Phytopath. Soc., Can. Soc. Plant Pathology, AAAS, N.Y. Acad. Scis., Am. Tissue Culture Assn. Greek Orthodox. Current Work: Transmission of viruses through tissue culture techniques. Detection, identification and manipulation of genes for resistance to viruses through tissue culture techniques; effect of antiviral compounds. Subspecialties: Plant virology; Plant cell and tissue culture. Home: 20 Valley View Circle Amherst MA 01002 Office: Dept Plant Pathology U Mass Amherst MA 01003

AGUIAR, ADAM MARTIN, chemistry educator, cons., researcher; b. Newark, Aug. 11, 1929; s. Joaquim and Emilea (Nunes) A.; m. Harriet Joan Greenberg, Dec. 23, 1940; m. Laura Estelle Brand, July 10, 1957; children: Justine Diane, David Laurence. B S., Fairleigh Dickinson U., 1955; M.A., Columbia U., 1957, Ph.D. (Union Carbide fellow), 1960. Chemist Otto B. May, Newark, 1948-55; NIH Postdoctoral fellow Columbia, U., N.Y.C., 1959-60; prof. chemistry Tulane U., New Orleans, 1963-72; research fellow Roche Inst. Molecular Biology, 1982, Tulane U., 1969-70; dean grad. and research programs William Paterson Coll., Wayne, N.J., 1972-73; prof. chemistry Fairleigh Dickinson U., Madison, N.J., 1973—; pres. Seltox Corp., N.J.; vice chmn. Seltox Internat. Corp., Nev.; pres. A & B Assos.; cons. chemists; hon. research prof. Birkbeck Coll., U. London, 1970, Rutgers U., 1973-74. Contbr. articles on chemistry to profl. jours. numerous research grants, 1972-77. Mem. Am. Chem. Soc., AAAS, N.Y. Acad. Scis., Oral Health Research Center (Fairleigh Dickinson U. Dental Sch. Hackensack, N.J.), Sigma Xi. Current Work: The synthesis and development of novel organophosphorus medicinals for third world and other protozoal and parasitic diseases. Subspecialties: Organic chemistry; Medicinal chemistry. Home: 530 Valley Rd 5F Upper Montclair NJ 07043 Office: Madison Ave 11-C Madison NJ 07940

AHEARNE, DANIEL PAUL, physicist; b. New Britain, Conn., Apr. 23, 1931; s. Daniel Paul and Balbena Marion (Baloski) A.; m. Germaine Marie Sirois, Feb. 4, 1954; children: Michael Jude, Douglas James. B.S. in Applied Physics, Calif. State U., 1962; postgrad, UCLA, 1963-65, U. N.Mex., 1966-67, N.Mex. Inst. Tech., 1967-69. Jr. engr. Gen. Dynamics/Electronics, San Diego, 1961-62; physicist N. Am. Rockwell, Los Angeles, 1963-65; weapons system research staff TRW Systems, Redondo Beach, Calif., 1965-66; br. chief U.S. Air Force Weapon Lab., Kirtland AFB, N. Mex., 1967-69; chief scientist Safeguard Systems Comm. Agy., Washington, 1969-70; pres. Mesa Cons., 1971-73; tech. dir. ITT Grinnell, Washington, 1981—; cons. in field; asso. adminstr. FEA, 1974-75; pres. Team Inc., 1976-81; tech. dir. ITT Grinnell Energy Products Group, 1981-82; participant USAF Communications Master Plan Formulation, others. Contbr. articles to profl. jours. Exec. dir. Dem. Party., N.M., 1970-72. Served with U.S. Army, 1948-57. Decorated D.S.C., Silver Star, Bronze Star medals (2), Purple Heart (3).; Nuclear Sci. fellow, 1962; N. Am Rockwell Corp. fellow, 1964; Colo. U. research assistantship, 1965. Mem. Am Phys. Soc., N.Y. Acad. Sci., Va. Acad. Sci., Ala. Acad. Sci. Roman Catholic. Patentee in field. Current Work: Work relating to energy systems including laser, nuclear, and solar energy systems; weapons system and thermonuclear design and effects analysis/design. Subspecialties: Plasma physics; Laser fusion.

AHLEN, JOHN WILLIAM, III, science administrator; b. Oak Park, Ill., Jan. 4, 1947; s. John William and Helen Beatrice (Damaske) A.; m. Andrea Louise Grabow, Aug. 31, 1970; children—John William, Jenny Kristin. B.S., U. Ill.-Chgo., 1969, Ph.D., 1974. Staff scientist Ill. Legis. Council, Springfield, 1974-78, sr. staff scientist, 1978-82, asst. dir. sci. and tech., 1982-84; exec. dir. Ark. Sci. and Tech. Authority, Little Rock, 1984—; vis. asst. prof. U. Ill., Urbana-Champaign, 1977-78; adj. asst. prof. Sangamon U., Springfield, 1974-79, 81-82, So. Ill. U. Sch. Medicine, Springfield, 1974-84. Contbr. chpt. in textbook. Mem. Gov.'s Sci. and Tech. Task Force, 1977-78. USPHS trainee in bioengring., 1969-73. Mem. Am. Soc. Mech. Engrs., IEEE, N.Y. Acad. Scis., Sigma Xi. Club: Sertoma (Springfield) (bd. dirs. 1983-84). Current work: Science adviser in state government agency concerned with developing science, engineering, and technology resources in education, research, and economic development. Subspecialties: Biomedical engineering; Human information processing. Home: 12717 Pleasant Forest Little Rock AR 72212 Office: Ark Sci and Tech Authority 200 Main St Suite 210 Little Rock AR 72201

AHLUWALIA, BHAGWAT DATTA, radiol. physicist, educator; b. Pindibhatian, India, Apr. 28, 1939; came to U.S., 1965, naturalized, 1978; s. Shri Kundan Lal and Gauran A.; m. Ekta Walia, Mar. 11, 1972; children: Ana, Atul, Sumit. B.Sc., Hons Sch., 1963; M.Sc., Hons Sch., Panjab U., 1964; Ph.D., Boston U., 1972. Diplomate, Am. Bd. Am. Bd. Sci. in Nuclear Medicine Radiology. Asst. physicist dept. radiology Mass. Gen. Hosp., Boston, 1973-77; assoc. Harvard U. Med. Sch., dept. radiology, 1973-77; vis. scientist dept. radiation therapy Postgrad. Inst. Medicine and Research, Chandigarh, India, 1979; asst. prof., radiol. physicist U. Okla. Health Sci. Center, Oklahoma City, 1977-84, assoc. prof., dir. Office Radiol. Safety, 1983—. Recipient Medal Panjab U., 1963, Young Investigator award NIH, 1975; Ford Found. grantee, 1965. Mem. Am. Assn. Physicists in Medicine, Soc. Nuclear Medicine, Health Physics Assn., IEEE. Current Work: Med. physics, imaging and therapy. Subspecialty: Medical physics.

AHLUWALIA, HARJIT SINGH, educator; b. Bombay, India, May 13, 1934; s. Sewa Singh and Jaswant (Kaur) A.; m. Manjit Kaur, Nov. 29, 1964; children: Suvinder Singh, Davinder Singh. B.Sc. with honors, Panjab U., 1953; Ph.D., Gujarat U., 1960. Sr. research fellow Phys. Research Lab., Ahmedabad, India, 1954-62; tech. assistance expert UNESCO, Paris, 1962-63; research assoc. Southwest Ctr. for Advanced Studies, Dallas, 1963-64; vis. prof. IAEA, Vienna, 1965-67; sci. dir. Lab. de Fisica Cosmica, U. Mayor de San Andres, LaPaz, Bolivia, 1965-67; vis. prof. Pam Am U., Washington, 1967-68; prof. U. N.Mex., 1968—; nat. rep. of Bolivia Internat. Union Pure and Applied Physics, 1966-69, Com. on Space Research, 1966-69, Space and Radiation Monitoring Orgn., 1966-69; high energy group sec. to Internat. Council Sci. Unions, 1974—; mem. Cosmic Ray Commn. Internat. Union Pure and Applied Physics, 1966-69. Contbr. articles to profl. jours. Research grantee USAF, 1962-68; Research grantee NSF, 1964-67, 69-71, 76-77, 78-81; Research grantee NASA, 1972-73, 73-77; Research grantee Sandia Nat. Lab., 1969-71. Mem. Am. Geophys. Union, Am. Phys. Soc., IEEE, Am. Astron. Soc., Internat. Astron. Union, Sigma Xi. Democrat. Sikh. Current Work: Study of cosmic ray intensity variations and anistropies. Subspecialty: Plasma physics. Home: 13000 Cedar Brook NE Albuquerque NM 87111 Office: 800 Yale Blvd NE Albuquerque NM 87131

AHMAD, IMAD AL DEAN, astronomer, computer programmer, consultant; b. Aug. 11, 1948; s. Hassan and Qudsia (Holazada) A.; m. Alexis Walser (div.); m. Frances Eddy, June 11, 1980. B.A. cum laude, Harvard Coll., 1970; Ph.D., U. Ariz., 1975. Research assoc. Harvard Coll. Obs., Cambridge, Mass., 1975-76; sr. scientist Am. Sci. and Engring., Cambridge, 1976-77; research assoc. U. Md., College Park, 1977-79, lectr., 1983—; sr. staff scientist Andrulis Research Corp., Bethesda, Md., 1979-81; chief scientist Imad-Ad-Dean, Inc., Bethesda, 1981—. Contbr. articles to sci. jours. Sec., East Bethesda Civic Assn., 1984; chmn. Md. Libertarian Party, Bethesda, 1981, mem. platform com., 1983, parliamentarian, 1983. Harvard scholar, 1966. Mem. Am. Astron. Soc. (hist. astronomy div.), Washington Area Astronomers (organizing com. 1981—). Muslim. Current work: Stellar winds, binary interactions, ultraviolet spectroscopy, solar physics, X-ray astronomy, radio astronomy, history of science, Islamic ethno-astronomy. Subspecialties: Ultraviolet high energy astrophysics; X-ray high energy astrophysics. Home: 4323 Rosedale Ave Bethesda MD 20814 Office: Imad-Ad-Dean Inc 4323 Rosedale Ave Bethesda MD 20814

AHNELL, JOSEPH EUGENE, chemist, instrumentation scientist; b. Pitts., Mar. 24, 1942; s. Joseph Eugene Fromelius and Sarah Dorothy (Smith) Ahnell; m. Ellen Rose Kerman, June 7, 1973 (div. 1981). B.A. in Chemistry, U. So. Fla., 1965, B.A. in Physics, 1965; M.A. in Phys. Chemistry, Johns Hopkins U., 1968, Ph.D. in Phys. Chemistry, 1972. Instr. chemistry CCNY, N.Y.C., 1971; instrumentation mgr. in chemistry, Johns Hopkins U., Balt., 1972-75; sr. scientist Johnston Labs., Balt., 1976-80, project mgr. research and devel., 1981-83, program mgr. research and devel., 1984—; cons. scientist B&R Instruments, Pasadena, Md., 1973-77. Patentee, co-patentee in field. Mem. Am. Chem. Soc., Am. Phys. Soc., Am. Soc. Microbiology. Democrat. Roman Catholic. Current work: Flow cytometry, bacterial detection, identification, susceptibility testing, instrumentation, electrochemistry, chromatography. Subspecialties: Bioinstrumentation; Microbiology (medicine). Home: 4519 Hydes Rd Hydes MD 21082 Office: Johnston Labs 383 Hillen Rd Towson MD 21204

AIKMAN, GEORGE CHRISTOPHER LAWRENCE, astronomer; b. Ottawa, Ont., Can., Nov. 11, 1943; s. Cecil Howard and Gwendolen Ellery (Read) A.; m. Beverly Mildred Boylan, May 27, 1972 (div.); children: Michael Donovan, Tabatha Karen.; m. Judith Anne Rackharm, Nov. 19, 1983. B.Sc. with honors, Bishop's U., Lennoxville, Que., 1965; M.Sc., U. Toronto, 1968. Research officer Dominion Astrophys. Obs., Victoria, B.C., Can., 1968—, assoc. research officer, 1979—. Contbr. articles in field to profl. jours. Mem. Am. Astronom. Soc., Canadian Astron. Soc., Royal Astron. Soc. Can., Astron. Soc. Pacific. Current Work: Origin of chem. peculiarities in stars. Subspecialty: Optical astronomy. Office: Dominion Astrophys Obs 5071 W Saanich Rd Rural Route 5 Victoria BC V8X 4M6 Canada

AISENBERG, ALAN C., research physician; b. N.Y.C., Dec. 7, 1926; s. Jacob and Celia (Able) A.; m. Nadya L. Margulies, Oct. 2, 1952; children: James, Margaret. S.B., Harvard U., 1945, M.D., 1950; Ph.D., U. Wis., 1956. Diplomate Am. Bd. Internal Medicine. Intern and resident in medicine Presbyn. Hosp., N.Y.C., 1950-53; Am. Cancer Soc. fellow U. Wis., 1954-56; asst. in medicine Mass. Gen. Hosp., 1957-61; instr. medicine Harvard Med. Sch., 1957-61; asst. physician Mass. Gen. Hosp., 1961-69, physician and head lymphoma clinic, 1969-84, prof., 1984—; asst. prof. medicine Harvard Med. Sch., 1961-69, assoc. prof., 1969—. Author: Glycolysis and Respiration of Tumors, 1961, also over 100 articles. Guggenheim fellow, 1964. Mem. Am. Assn. Immunologists, Am. Assn. Cancer Research, Am. Assn. Clin. Oncology, Am. Fedn. Clin. Research, ACP. Current Work: Cellular immunology, malignant lymphoma. Subspecialties: Cancer research (medicine); Oncology. Home: 124 Chestnut St Boston MA 02108 Office: Mass Gen Hosp Boston MA 02114

AISNER, JOSEPH, physician, oncologist, cancer researcher; b. Munich, Germany, Jan. 5, 1944; came to U.S., 1948, naturalized, 1954; s. Philip and Faye A.; m. Seena C. Feldman, June 26, 1948; children: Dara L., Leon A. B.S. in Chemistry, Wayne State U., 1965, M.D., 1970. Diplomate: Am. Bd. Internal Medicine, Sub-Bd. Oncology. Intern Sinai Hosp., Detroit, 1970-71; resident in internal medicine Georgetown U. Hosp., Washington, 1971-72; clin. assoc. Balt. Cancer Research Ctr., Nat. Cancer Inst., 1972-74, sr. investigator,

1974-76, chief med. oncology, 1976-81; head div. med. oncology U. Md. Cancer Ctr., Balt., 1981—, prof. medicine and oncology, 1982—, dep. dir. clin. affairs, 1982—; cons. in field. Contbr. numerous articles and abstracts to sci. jours., also chpts. to books. Served with USPHS, 1972-81. Mem. ACP, Am. Soc. Clin. Oncology, Am. Soc. Hematology, Am. Fedn. Clin. Research, AAAS, Cancer Leukemia Group B, Am. Assn. Cancer Research. Current Work: Cancer research. Subspecialties: Cancer research (medicine); Oncology. Home: 1404 Berwick Rd Ruxton MD 21204 Office: 22 S Greene St Baltimore MD 21201

AIST, JAMES ROBERT, plant pathologist; b. Cheverly, Md., Feb. 20, 1945; s. Arthur Stewart and Carolyn Roberta (Thornberg) A. B.S., U. Ark., 1966, M.S., 1968; Ph.D., U. Wis., 1971. NATO postdoctoral fellow Swiss Fed. Inst. Tech., Zurich, 1971-72; asst. prof. Cornell U., Ithaca, N.Y., 1972-78, assoc. prof., 1978—; vis. assoc. research biologist U. Calif., Irvine, 1979-80. Asso. editor: Phythopathology, 1979-82, Exptl. Mycology, 1978—; contbr. articles to profl. jours. NSF grantee, 1976—; Dep. Def. grantee, 1978-80; USDA grantee, 1979—. Mem. AAAS, Am. Phytopathological Soc., Am. Soc. Cell Biology. Roman Catholic. Current Work: Plant disease resistance, mitosis, analytical microscopy research. Subspecialties: Plant pathology; Cell biology. Home: 414 Snyder Hill Rd Ithaca NY 14850 Office: Dept Plant Pathology Cornell U Ithaca NY 14853

AITKEN, PETER GIL, neurobiologist, educator; b. N.Y.C., Mar. 7, 1947; s. Hugh Walter and Laura Isabell (Tapia) A.; m. Kathryn Ann Conte, June 22, 1973; 1 child, Benjamin Joseph. B.S., U. Rochester, 1972; M.A., SUNY-Brockport, 1974; Ph.D., U. Conn., 1978. Lectr. Cornell U., Ithaca, N.Y., 1978-79, postdoctoral fellow, 1979-82; asst. med. research prof. Duke U., Durham, N.C., 1982—. Contbr. articles to profl. jours. Recipient Nat. Research Service award NIH, 1979. Mem. AAAS, Soc. for Neurosci., Sigma Xi. Current work: Function of nervous system with particular relevance to disease processes; epilepsy. Subspecialties: Neurobiology; Neurophysiology. Office: Dept of Physiology Duke Univ Med Ctr Durham NC 27710

AKASOFU, SYUN-ICHI, geophysicist; b. Nagano-Ken, Japan, Dec. 4, 1930; came to U.S., 1958; s. Shigenori and Kumiko (Koike) A.; m. Emiko Endo, Sept. 25, 1961; children: Ken-Ichi, Keiko. B.S., Tohoku U., 1953, M.S., 1957; Ph.D., U. Alaska, 1961. Sr. research asst. Nagasaki U., 1953-55; research asst. Geophys. Inst., U. Alaska, 1958-61, mem. faculty, 1961—, prof. geophysics, 1964—. Author: Polar and Magnetospheric Substorms (Russian edit. 1971), 1968, The Aurora: A Discharge Phenomenon Surrounding the Earth (in Japanese), 1975, Physics of Magnetospheric Substorms, 1977, Aurora Borealis: The Amazing Northern Lights (Japanese edit. 1981), 1979; co-author: Sydney Chapman, Eighty, 1968, Solar-Terrestrial Physics (Russian edit. 1974); editor: Dynamics of the Magnetosphere, 1979; co-editor: Physics of Auroral Arc Formation, 1980—; editorial bd. Planet and Space Sci.; co-editor: Space Sci. Revs.; assoc. editor Jour. Geophysical Research, Jour. Geomagnetism and Geoelectricity. Recipient Chapman medal Royal Astron. Soc., 1976, award Japan Acad., 1977; named Disting. Alumnus U. Alaska, 1980. Fellow Am. Geophys. Union (John Adam Fleming medal 1979); mem. AAAS, Sigma Xi. Current Work: Auroral physics, magnetospheric physics. Subspecialties: Aeronomy; Plasma physics.

AKBAR, HUZOOR, pharmacologist, educator, researcher; b. Karachi, Pakistan, Dec. 2, 1948; came to U.S., 1977; s. Hasan and Taeed Fatima (Rehbar) A.; m. Ildiko St. George, Apr. 9, 1977; children: Vazeer Daniel, Imran Shaan. B.S. with honors, Karachi U., Pakistan, 1971; M.S., 1972; Ph.D., Australian Nat. U., Canberra, 1978. Research asoc. in pathology Vanderbilt U., Nashville, 1977-78; in medicine Boston U., 1978-79; in pharmacology Ohio State, Columbus, 1979-81; asst. prof. pharmacology and biomed. sci. Ohio U., Athens, 1981—. Contbr. articles on pharmacology to profl. jours. Am. Heart Assn. grantee, 1982-85; Am. Osteo. Assn. grantee, 1984—. Mem. Am. Physiol. Soc., Internat. Soc. on Thrombosis and Haemostatis, Am. Soc. for Pharmacology and Exptl. Therapeutics. Current Work: Mechanisms of blood platelet aggregation and secretion as well as the mechanisms of the actions of drugs which inhibit aggregation and secretion from platelets. Subspecialties: Pharmacology; Hematology. Home: 24 Ball Dr Wonderhills Athens OH 45701 Office: Irvine Hall 416 Athens OH 45701

AKCASU, OSMAN ERSED, electronic engineer, solid-state physicist; b. Istanbul, Turkey, Nov. 3, 1955; came to U.S., 1981; s. Huseyin Alaeddin and Seminur Mahan (Germaner) A.; m. Fatma Ayse Kublay, Oct. 13, 1980; children—Umit Mahan, Ayse Ebru. B.E.E., Tech. U. Istanbul, 1977; Ph.D., U. Bradford, Eng., 1980. Assoc. prin. engr. Harris Semiconductor Co., Melbourne, Fla., 1981-84; sr. staff device engr. Fairchild Camera and Instrument Corp., Puyallup, Wash., 1984—. Contbr. articles to profl. jours. Patentee in field. Mem. IEEE. Current work: Semiconductor device modeling; physics; mathematical analysis of multidimensional non-linear systems; semiconductor process development; characterization. Subspecialties: Microchip technology (engineering); Applied mathematics. Home: 13011 Meridian S Apt #I-202 Puyallup WA 98373 Office: Fairchild Camera and Instrument Corp 1111 39th Ave SE PO Box 5000 Puyallup WA 98373

AKERA, TAI, pharmacologist, educator; b. Wakayama, Japan, July 13, 1932; came to U.S., 1971; s. Jibusuke and Ayako (Omata) A.; m. Chiseko Masuda; children: Atsushi, Yuka, Chika. M.D., Keio U., Tokyo, 1958, Ph.D., 1965. Diplomate: med. diplomate Japanese Ministry Welfare. Intern Keio U. Hosp., 1958-59; postdoctoral fellow U. Mich., Ann Arbor, 1962-64; instr. Keio U., 1964-66, asst. prof., 1966-71; vis. asst. prof. dept. pharmacology and toxicology Mich. State U., East Lansing, 1967-70, asso. prof., 1971-74, prof., 1974—; mem. pharmacology study sect. NIH, 1985-89. Contbr. over 120 articles to profl. jours., also rev. papers. NIH grantee, 1972—; Mich. Heart Assn. grantee, 1972-82. Mem. Japanese Med. Assn., Japanese Pharmacology Soc., Am. Soc. for Pharmacology and Exptl. Therapeutics. Current Work: Cardiotonic drugs; ion transport across the cell membranes; basic research on mechanisms of drug actions and reactions. Subspecialties: Pharmacology; Toxicology (medicine). Home: 1873 Ridgewood Dr East Lansing MI 48823 Office: Dept Pharmacology and Toxicology Mich State U East Lansing MI 48824

AKERS, STUART WILLIAM, plant-stress physiologist; b. Sentinel, Okla., July 6, 1945; s. William Frederick and Nettie Rachel (Holt) A.; m. Carolyn Sue Pruett, Dec. 20, 1970; children: Jonathan S., Susan C. B.S., U. Okla., 1967; M.S., N.C. State U., 1969, Ph.D., 1975. Asst. prof. S.W. Okla. State U., Weatherford, 1975-76; research assoc U. Ky., Lexington, 1976-77, Purdue U., West Lafayette, Ind., 1977-81; asst. prof. Okla. State U., Stillwater, 1981—. Served as 1st lt. U.S. Army, 1969-71. Decorated Bronze Star. Mem. Am. Soc. Plant Physiologist, Am. Soc. Horticulture Sci., Plant Growth Regulator Soc. Am. Democrat. Methodist. Current Work: Investigations on plant response to environmental stresses that limit horticultural crop productivity and propagation effectiveness. Subspecialty: Plant physiology (agriculture). Home: 1017 E Ridgecrest Ave Stillwater OK 74074

ALAPOUR, ADEL, nuclear engineer; b. Tehran, Iran, June 17, 1948; came to U.S., 1974; s. Mostafa and Mehry (Latifi) A.; m. Cynthia Ann Jackson, Feb. 20, 1980; children: Kavon A., Vida N. B.S.M.E., Arya-Mehr U. Tech.-Iran, 1970; M.S.N.E., Ga. Inst. Tech., 1975, Ph.D., 1980. Operation coordinator Iran Electric Power Generation & Transmission Co., Tehran, 1970-72, plant analyst, 1972-74; grad. research asst. dept. nuclear engring. Ga. Inst. Tech., Atlanta., 1974-78; nuclear engr. Brookhaven Nat. Lab., Upton, N.Y., 1978-80; nuclear engr. So. Co. Services Inc., Birmingham, Ala., 1980-81, sr. engr., 1981—. Mem. Am. Nuclear Soc. (Birmingham sect. chmn. 1982-83, dir. 1983—), N.Y. Acad. Scis., So. Co. Services Leadership Devel. Assn., Sigma Xi. Current Work: Steady state and time dependent analysis of Nuclear reactor systems. Subspecialties: Nuclear engineering; Nuclear fission. Home: 5193 Selkirk Cir Birmingham AL 35243 Office: So Co Services Inc PO Box 2625 Birmingham AL 35202

ALBACH, RICHARD ALLEN, microbiology educator; b. Chgo., Mar. 31, 1930; s. Maurice and Martha (Silverman) A.; m. Janice Elaine Boewe, Jan. 23, 1962; children: Michael, Karren, Kimala, David, Brian, Julie, Barry. B.S., U. Ill., 1956, M.S., 1958; Ph.D., Northwestern U., 1963. Asst. prof. U. Health Scis., Chgo. Med. Sch., 1968-69, North Chicago, Ill., assoc. prof., 1969-73, prof., 1973—, vice chmn., 1975-82, acting chmn., 1982-84; editorial cons. Yearbook Med. Pubs., Chgo., 1975-81. Contbr. articles to profl. jours. Served with U.S. Army, 1953-55. NIH grantee, 1965-78; LAbbott Found. fellow, 1961; Trustees Research award Chgo. Med. Sch., 1968; Teaching Prof. of the Yr., 1976, 78, 82. Fellow Am. Acad. Microbiology; mem. Am. Soc. Microbiology, Soc. Protozoologists (exec. com. 1984—), Am. Soc. Parasitologists, Ill. Soc. Microbiology (membership chmn. 1969-70). Current Work: Molecular biology of parasitic protozoa. Subspecialties: Microbiology (medicine); Parasitology. Address: Univ Health Sci Chicago Med Sch 3333 Green Bay Rd North Chicago IL 60064

ALBANO, WILLIAM A., surg. oncologist; b. Summit, N.J., Aug. 6, 1945; s. Alexander and Marguerite (Pedecine) A.; m. Marjo Friese, Aug. 20, 1968; children: William, Alexander, Andrew, Michelle. B.S., Seton Hall U., 1967; M.D., Creighton U., 1971. Diplomate: Am. Bd. Surgery. Resident in surgery Creighton U., Omaha, 1971-75; fellow in surg. oncology City of Hope, Duarte, Calif., 1975-76; asst. prof. surgery, chief div. surg.oncology Creighton Cancer Center, Omaha, 1976—. Contbr. articles to profl. jours. Fellow Soc. Surg. Oncology, A.C.S., Southwestern Surg. Soc.; mem. North Central Cancer Group, Nebr. Cancer Soc. (pres. 1981-82). Current Work: Hereditary cancer. Subspecialties: Surgery; Cancer research (medicine). Office: Creighton Cancer Center 601 N 30th St Omaha NE 68131

ALBAUGH, FRED WILLIAM, nuclear engineer; b. Albia, Iowa, Apr. 13, 1917, s. Loren Eugene and Blanche (Kussart) A.; m. Edrey Elizabeth Smith, Nov. 25, 1944; children—Jeffrey S., James F., Jean E. B.A. in Chemistry, UCLA, 1935; Ph.D. in Chemistry, U. Mich., 1941. Lic. petroleum engr., Calif. Chemist Standard Oil of Calif., Richmond, 1935-37; research engr. Union Oil Co., Wilmington, Calif., 1941-43, 45-47; sect. chief Manhattan Project, U. Chgo., 1944-45; research and devel. mgr. Gen. Electric Co., Hanford, Wash., 1947-65; research and devel. mgr., lab. dir. Battelle Northwest Labs., Hanford, 1965-76; pvt. cons. to nuclear industry, Richland, Wash., 1976—; AEC missions to Australia, Euratom, Can., 1958-66; mem. AEC-Gen. Electric task force on Hanford diversification, 1963-64. Contbr. articles to profl. jours. Patentee in field. Mem. Wash. State Human Rights Com., 1966-68, Bonneville Regional Adv. Council, 1966-76; adminstrv bd. Tri-City Univ. Ctr., Richland, 1980—; chmn. Utility Adv. Bd., Richland, 1977—. Recipient Community Service award Tri-City Nuclear Indsl. Council, 1976; Am. Petroleum Inst. fellow, 1937-41. Fellow Am. Nuclear Soc.; mem. Nat. Acad. Engring., Am. Chem. Soc., AAAS. Republican. Methodist. Lodge: Kiwanis (pres. Richland 1980-81). Current work: Research and development management consultation; national and Pacific Northwest regional energy supply; nuclear energy technology. Subspecialty: Nuclear fission. Office: care Battelle Northwest Labs PO Box 999 Richland WA 99352

AL-BAZZAZ, FAIQ JABER, physician, educator, researcher; b. Baghdad, Iraq, July 1, 1939; came to U.S., 1966; s. Jaber Mehdi and Fadelah Hassoun (Ismail) Al-B.; m. Paulette Dodds, Nov. 15, 1969; children: Nesreen, Basheer, Senan. M.B., Ch.B., U. Baghdad, 1962. Diplomate: Am. Bd. Internal Medicine, Am. Bd. Pulmonary Diseases. Gen. practice Medicine, 1965; resident Mosul Med. Coll., 1965-66, U. Miss. Med. Center, 1966-68, U. Minn. and Mpls. VA. Hosp., 1968-69; clin. and research fellow Mass. Gen. Hosp. and Harvard U., Boston, 1969-71; asst. prof. medicine U. Ill., Chgo., 1971-78, assoc. prof. clin. medicine, 1978-81, assoc. prof. medicine, 1981—; chief respiratory and critical care sect. West Side VA Med. Ctr., Chgo., 1977—. Contbr. articles to profl. jours. Chgo. Lung Assn. grantee, 1972, 73, 77; VA grantee, 1976—; Am. Heart Assn. grantee, 1979-81. Fellow ACP, Am. Coll. Chest Physicians, Royal Coll. Physicians Can.; mem. Am. Physiol. Soc., Central Soc. Clin. research, Am. Thoracic Soc., Am. Fedn. Clin. Research. Moslem. Current Work: Elucidation of mechanisms of ion and fluid transport across respiratory epithelia; role of cyclic nucleotides, cytosolic calcium and prostaglandins in modulation of membrane and paracellular conductance; role of neuropeptides in regulation of ion transport. Subspecialties: Pulmonary medicine; Membrane biology. Home: 343 Jefferson Woodstock IL 60098

ALBEE, ARDEN LEROY, geology educator, administrator; b. Port Huron, Mich., May 28, 1928; s. Emery A. and Mildred H. (Tool) A.; m. Ann M. Hood, July 12, 1953 (div. 1977); children—Janet, Carol, James, Mary; m. Charlene H. Ettenheim, Jan. 1, 1978; stepchildren—Margaret, Kathy, Ginger, George. B.A., Harvard U., 1950, M.A., 1951, Ph.D., 1957. Registered geologist, Calif. Geologist, U.S. Geol. Survey, 1950-59; chief scientist Calif. Inst. Jet Propulsion Lab., Pasadena, 1978-84, project scientist Mars Geosci. Climatology Observer Project, 1984—; prof. geology Calif. Inst. Tech., 1959—, dean grad. studies, 1984—; cons. Los Angeles Dept. of Water and Power, 1964-70, Converse Davis & Assocs., 1964-73, Fugro Inc., 1974-78; mem., chmn. numerous NASA working groups. Contbr. numerous articles to sci. jours.; editor Ann. Rev. Earth and Space Scis., 1978—. Recipient NASA medal for Exceptional Sci. Achievement, 1976. Fellow Geol. Soc. Am. (editor 1970—); mem. Microbean Analysis Soc., Mineral. Soc. Am. (editor 1972-76, counselor 1978-80), Am. Astron. Soc., Geochem. Soc. (counselor 1980-84). Presbyterian. Subspecialties: Petrology; Planetology. Home: 2040 Midlothian Dr Altadena CA 91001 Office: Calif Inst Tech 1201 E California Blvd (170-25) Pasadena CA 91125

ALBEN, KATHERINE TURNER, research scientist; b. Bridgeport, Conn., Apr. 28, 1947; M. Jonathan and Mary Barbara (Haberzetle) T.; m. Richard Samuel Alben, May 7, 1971; children—Jonah, Elissa, Silas. A.B. magna cum laude in Chemistry, Mt. Holyoke Coll., 1969; M.Phil. in Phys. Chemistry, Yale U., 1971, Ph.D. in Phys. Chemistry, 1976. Research scientist I, N.Y. State Dept. Health, Albany, 1977-80, research scientist II, 1980—. Contbr. articles to profl. jours. Mem. Am. Chem. Soc., Am. Water Works Assn. (organics research com. 1982-85), Sigma Xi. Current work: Potable water treatment processes to remove organic contaminants; chemical analysis and mathematical models describing fate and transport of organics in drinking water treatment. Home: 1705 Dorwaldt Blvd Schenectady NY 12309 Office: NY State Dept Health Empire Plaza Albany NY 12201

ALBERS, HENRY ELLIOTT, biomedical researcher; b. Ames, Iowa, Apr. 7, 1953; s. Henry H. and Marjorie (Klein) A. B.A., U. Nebr., Lincoln, 1974; M.S., Tulane U., 1978, Ph.D., 1979. Research fellow in physiology Harvard Med. Sch., Boston, 1979-82; research assoc. in endocrinology Worcester Found. for Exptl. Biology, Shrewsbury, Mass., 1981-82; sr. research assoc. Worcester Found. Exptl. Biology, 1982-84; asst. prof. physiology U. Mass. Med. Sch., Worcester, 1984—. Contbr. sci. articles to profl. jours. USPHS grantee, 1982—. Mem. Soc. Neurosci., Internat. Soc. Chronobiology. Current Work: Studies of the neural and hormonal control of circadian behavior. Subspecialties: Physiology (biology); Neuroendocrinology. Home: 104 Lakeside Dr Shrewsbury MA 01545 Office: U Mass Med Sch Worcester MA

ALBERS, PETER HEINZ, wildlife research biologist; b. S.I., N.Y., May 4, 1943; s. Heinz Amandus and Gertrude (Bauer) A.; m. Bernadette Ann Martin, May 20, 1972; children—Bridget, Eric. B.S., U. Mont., 1965; M.S., U. Guelph, 1966; Ph.D., U. Mich., 1975. Instr. U. Maine, Orono, 1975; wildlife research biologist U.S. Fish and Wildlife Service Patuxent Wildlife Research Ctr., Laurel, Md., 1976—. Contbr. articles to profl. jours. Baseball coach Boys and Girls Club, Bowie, Md., 1984. Served to capt. U.S. Army, 1966-70, Vietnam. Recipient spl. achievement award U.S. Fish and Wildlife Service, 1982. Mem. Wildlife Soc., Ecol. Soc. Am., Sigma Xi. Democrat. Current work: Effects of environmental contaminants on wildlife, petroleum, acid deposition, metals, pesticides. Subspecialties: Environmental toxicology; Wildlife management. Office: US Fish and Wildlife Service Patuxent Wildlife Research Ctr Laurel MD 20708

ALBERS, ROBERT CHARLES, theoretical solid state physicist; b. San Jose, Calif., Feb. 11, 1949; s. Charles John and Beulah Elizabeth (Reibenspies) A.; m. Shirley Giurlani, May 6, 1978; children—Carolyn Anne, Kathryn Elizabeth. B.S., U. Santa Clara, 1971; M.A., Cornell U., 1974, Ph.D., 1977. Mem. staff Los Alamos Nat. Lab., N.Mex., 1977—. Mem. Am. Phys. Soc., AAAS. Current work: Solid state theory, electronic band structure calculations, high-pressure physics, x-ray absorption in solids, anharmonic phonon theory. Subspecialties: Condensed matter physics; Theoretical physics. Office: Los Alamos Nat Lab Los Alamos NM 87545

ALBERS, WALTER ANTHONY, JR, science manager, researcher; b. McKeesport, Pa., July 19, 1930; s. Walter Anthony and Mary Dorothy (Roberts) A.; m. Nancy Ann Rock, Aug. 2, 1952 (dec. June 1966); m. Betty Grace McKinley, June 24, 1967; children—Patricia, Kevin, Jodie, Gaylen, Kurt. B.S., Wayne State U., 1952, M.S., 1954, Ph.D., 1960. Mem. tech. staff Bell Telephone Labs., Allentown, Pa., 1954-57; research assoc. Wayne State U., Detroit, 1957-59; sr. research scientist Bendix Corp. Research Labs., Southfield, Mich., 1959-62; supr. solid state physics Gen. Motors Research Labs., Warren, Mich., 1962-72, head societal analysis dept., 1972—. Editor: Physics of Optoelectronic Materials, 1970; Societal Risk Assessment, 1980. Contbr. articles to profl. jours. Bd. dirs. Men's Dist. Golf Assn., 1983; mem. adv. com. United Way Am., Alexandria Va., 1982—. Mem. Am. Phys. Soc., AAAS, Am. Mgmt. Assn., Soc. for Risk Analysis, Sigma Xi. Club: Farmington Hills Country (Mich.) (pres. 1979-80). Current work: Head of interdisciplinary group of scientists who research social and behavioral aspects of the interface between corporations and society. Subspecialties: Condensed matter physics; Operations research (mathematics). Home: 2068 S Hammond Lake Dr West Bloomfield MI 48033 Office: Gen Motors Research Labs 12 Mile and Mound Rd Warren MI 48090

ALBERT, PAUL ANDRE, metallurgist, physicist, consultant; b. Van Buren, Maine, Apr. 14, 1926; s. Armand Louis and Marie (Lussier) A.; m. Jeanne Terese Kachman, June 28, 1955; children—John Paul, Madeleine Jeanne, Peter Andrew, Charles Joseph, Anthony James, Angeline Marie, David Armand, Lawrence Louis. B.S. in Engring. Physics, U. Maine, 1949; M.S. in Metallurgy, NYU, 1954, Sc.D. in Metallurgy, 1955. Supervising metallurgist Westinghouse Research, Pitts., 1955-64; sr. engr. IBM, Yorktown Heights, N.Y., 1964-67, research staff mem., Burlington, Vt., 1967-71, San Jose, Calif., 1971-81; pres. Albert Cons., Inc., San Jose, 1981—, Persyst, Inc., San Jose, 1982—. Author tech. papers on magnetic materials and devices; patentee (10). Mem. adv. bd. Youth Sci. Inst., San Jose, 1981—. Served with USAAC, 1944-45. Mem. IEEE. Club: San Jose Country. Current work: Magnetic storage of information, from the standpoint of materials and devices and their interrelations. Subspecialties: Electronic materials; Magnetic physics. Home: 10473 Anderson Rd San Jose CA 95127 Office: Albert Consulting Inc 636 Giguere Ct San Jose CA 95133

ALBERTS, WALTER WATSON, health science administrator; b. Los Angeles, Dec. 31, 1929; s. Hugo William and Ruth Lucia (Watson) A.; m. Marilyn West, Mar. 22, 1959; children: Allison C., Allan W. A.B., U. Calif. Berkeley, 1951, Ph.D., 1956. Research physiologist U. Calif. Med. Ctr., San Francisco, 1955-56; biophysicist Mt. Zion Hosp. and Med. Ctr., San Francisco, 1956-72; grants assoc. NIH, Bethesda, Md., 1972-73, spl. asst. to assoc. dir. collaborative and field research, 1973-74, head research contracts sect., 1974-75; asst. dir. contract research programs, extramural activities program Nat. Inst. Neurol. and Communicative Disorders and Stroke, NIH, 1975-77; adminstrv. dir. Smith Kettlewell Inst., San Francisco, 1977-78; dep. dir. fundamental neurosci. program Nat. Inst. Neurol. and Communicative Disorders and Stroke, NIH, Bethesda, Md., 1979—. Contbr. articles to profl. jours. Nat. Inst. Neurol. Diseases and Blindness research career program awardee, 1963-68. Fellow AAAS; mem. Am. Physiol. Soc., Biophys. Soc., IEEE, Soc. Neurosci., Sierra Club, Phi Beta Kappa, Sigma Xi. Congregationalist. Current Work: Neurophysiology, biological and medical physics, particularly the central nervous system of man. Subspecialties: Neurophysiology; Biophysics (physics). Home: 9205 Friars Rd Bethesda MD 20817 Office: NIH Bethesda MD 20892

ALBERTSON, CLARENCE ELMO, JR, chemist; b. Rockwood, Tenn., Oct. 7, 1922; s. Clarence E. and Eleanor A. (Reemelin) A.; m. Helen L. Wolfe, Dec. 27, 1947; children—Barbara Jill, Pamela Sue, Charles Alan. A.B., Miami U., Oxford, Ohio, 1943; M.S., U. Cin., 1948, Ph.D., 1949; postdoctoral fellow Purdue U., 1949-50. Phys. chemist Robertshaw Fulton Co., Pitts., 1950-51; phys. chemist Borg-Warner Corp., Bellwood, Ill., 1951-68, mgr. phys. chemistry, Des Plaines, Ill., 1968-78, sr. scientist, 1978—. Contbr. tech. papers Am. Chem. Soc., ASHRAE, Am. Electroplaters Soc., others. Patentee in fields of friction materials, electroplating, refrigeration, sensors. Mem. Villa Park Environ. Control Bd., Ill., 1973-75. Recipient Henry Hochstetter award U. Cin., 1948. Fellow Am. Inst. Chemists; mem. Am. CHem. Soc., Am. Soc. Lubrication Engrs. (trustee 1975-78), Electrochem. Soc. (sec. chmn. 1978-80), Am. Electroplaters Soc. Republican. United Methodist. Current work: Friction materials, composites, sensors, lubricants. Subspecialties: Physical chemistry; Materials (engineering). Home: 240 S Monterey Ave Villa Park IL 60181 Office: Borg-Warner Research Ctr Wolf & Algonquin Rds Des Plaines IL 60018

ALBINI, BORIS, immunopathologist, researcher; b. Zagreb, Croatia, Yugoslavia, Mar. 7, 1943; came to U.S., 1974, naturalized, 1977; s. Julius and Maja (Skojic) A.; m. Christine Helen Seymanski, Dec. 16, 1978; children: Thomas, Paul. M.A., Acad. Music, Vienna, Austria, 1963; M.D., U. Vienna, 1969. Intern surgery Floridsdorf Hosp., Vienna, Austria, 1969-70; clin. asst. prof. exptl. pathology U. Vienna, 1970-73; research asst. prof. microbiology SUNY-Buffalo, 1974-76, asst. prof., 1976-78, assoc. prof., 1978-83, prof., 1983—, res. prof. medicine, 1985—. Author: (with others) The Immunopathology of the Kidney, 1979. Co-editor: (with others) Immunopathology, 1979; Immunofluorescence and Related Cytochemical Methods, 1983; Antibodies: Their Protective, Destructive and Regulatory Role, 1985. Assoc. editor: (with others) Clin. Exptl. Immunology, 1980; Immunological Communications, 1981; Internat. Archives Allergy and Applied Immunology, 1981. Vice-pres. Friends of Vienna, Buffalo, 1976—. Mem. Assn. Immunology, Am. Assn. Immunology, Assn. Immunology of Austria. Current Work: Immunopathology of kidney diseases, immune response in immune complex-mediated diseases, immunopathology and autoimmunity in spontaneous autoimmune thyroiditis of obese strain chickens, immunopathology of the gastrointestinal tract. Subspecialties: Immunology (medicine); Nephrology. Home: 31 Kim Circle Williamsville NY 14221 Office: SUNY-Buffalo 240B Cary Hall Buffalo NY 14214

ALBRECHT, THOMAS BLAIR, microbiology educator; b. Phila., July 31, 1943; s. Blair Robson and Deborah Hawley (Smedley) A.; m. Isis de Alencar, July 28, 1967; children: Christine, Thomas Edward, Alan Wayne. B.S., Brigham Young U., 1967, M.S., 1969, Ph.D., Pa. State U., 1973. Research fellow Harvard U., 1974-75; asst. prof. microbiology U. Tex., 1976-80, assoc. prof., 1980—. Contbr. articles in field to profl. jours. Grantee NIH, 1976-79, 84—, Moody Found., 1979-82, Cooper Labs., Inc., 1979-85, EPA, 1985—. Mem. Am. Soc. Microbiology., Am. Soc. Cell Biology, Soc. Exptl. Biology and Medicine, Sigma Xi. Current Work: Cell responses to herpes virus, particularly human cytomegalo-viruses. Subspecialties: Microbiology (medicine); Cell biology (medicine). Home: 1905 Back Bay Dr Galveston TX 77551 Office: Microbiology U Texas Med Br Galveston TX 77550

ALBRIGHT, JOHN RUPP, physics educator; b. Wilkes-Barre, Pa., June 10, 1937; s. John Rupp and Salome (Shettel) A.; m. Christina Lamson Bischoff, June 11, 1960 (div. 1984); children—Helen Jane Albright Black, Catherine Louise Albright Pottorff, John Rupp, III; m. Elizabeth Helen Peters, March 1984. A.B., Susquehanna U., 1959; M.S., U. Wis., 1961, Ph.D., 1964. Asst. prof. physics Fla. State U., Tallahassee, 1963-70, assoc. prof., 1970-78, prof., 1978—, assoc. chmn., 1980-85; reviewer Textbook Publishers, 1965—. Co-author: Introduction to Atomic and Nuclear Physics, 1972; contbr. articles profl. jours. Fellow Sci. Research Council of Great Britian, 1976, Cavendish Lab. Cambridge, U.K.; mem. Am. Phys. Soc., Am. Assoc. Physics Tchrs. Lutheran. Current work: Mathematical techniques in physics, including computational methods, special function theory. Subspecialties: Particle physics; Theoretical physics. Home: Route 3 Box 4060 Havana FL 32333 Office: Dept Physics Fla State U Tallahassee FL 32306

ALBRIGHT, ROBERT LEE, research scientist; b. Leola, Pa., Jan. 28, 1932; s. Martin Albright and Ida (Wolgemuth) Buchen; m. Wanda Cardella Sprow, Sept. 20, 1959; children—Rhonda Fae, Colleen Dawn. B.S. in Chemistry, Elizabethtown Coll. (Pa.), 1954; Ph.D. in Organic Chemistry, U. Ill., 1958. Research chemist process design Rohm and Haas Co., Phila., 1958-64, research chemist fluid process chemistry, 1964-70, sr. chemist, plant chemist, 1970-78, sr. chemist, dir. devel., 1978-82, research fellow, 1982—; lectr. dept. chemistry Elizabethtown Coll., 1959, Holy Family Coll., Phila., 1963. Contbr. articles to profl. jours. Mem. Am. Chem. Soc., Thermal Analysis Forum of Delaware Valley (councillor 1978, 81, pres. 1980). Republican. Baptist. Current work: Design and synthesis of kinetically effective polymers for anchoring catalytic agents and enzymes; synthesis of porous polymers for performing separations; catalysis; absorption; ion exchange; reactions mechanisms. Subspecialties: Polymer chemistry; Synthetic chemistry. Home: 36 Autumn Rd Churchville PA 18966 Office: Rohm and Haas Co 727 Norristown Rd Spring House PA 19477

ALBURGER, DAVID ELMER, nuclear physicist; b. Phila., Oct. 6, 1920; s. Elmer R. and Josephine (Reid) A.; m. Mary Mickle, Oct. 6, 1945; children—David R., Mary Jo, Evelyn A., Andrew R. B.A., Swarthmore Coll., 1942; M.S., Yale U., 1946, Ph.D., 1948. Radar engr. Naval Research Lab., Washington, 1942-45; sr. physicist Brookhaven Nat. Lab., Upton, N.Y., 1948—. Mem. fellowship awards com. NSF, 1959-62. Contbr. articles to profl. jours. Pres., Bellport Sch. Bd., N.Y., 1966-69. Served as ensign USNR, 1944-45. Sterling fellow, 1947-48; NSF fellow, Stockholm, 1952-53. Fellow Am. Phys. Soc. Current work: Properties of nuclear energy levels as observed in radioactivity and nuclear reactions. Subspecialty: Nuclear physics. Home: 290 Beaver Dam Rd Brookhaven NY 11719 Office: Brookhaven Nat Lab Upton NY 11973

ALCENA, VALIERE, internist, educator; b. Haiti, West Indies, Aug. 24, 1934; came to U.S., 1960, naturalized, 1965; s. Lamartine and Florisane (Lacoste) A. B.A., Queens Coll., Flushing, N.Y., 1970; M.D., Albert Einstein Coll., Bronx, N.Y., 1973. Diplomate: Am. Bd. Internal Medicine. Intern Montefiore Hosp. and Med. Center, Bronx, N.Y., 1973-74, resident in medicine, 1974-74, chief resident, 1975-76, fellow in hematology, 1976-77, fellow in oncology, 1977-78; clin. instr. medicine Albert Einstein Coll., Bronx, N.Y., 1978—; clin. instr. medicine in psychiatry Cornell U. Med. Sch., N.Y.C., 1978—; adj. attending physician in medicine Montefiore Hosp., Bronx, 1978—, asst. attending physician in oncology, 1980—; assoc. attending physician in medicine and hematology White Plains (N.Y.) Hosp., 1978—; assoc. attending physician in medicine St. Agnes Hosp., White Plains, 1978—; clin. affiliate, cons. medicine N.Y. Hosp., White Plains, 1978—. Contbr. sci. articles to profl. publs. Chmn. public end. com. Am. Cancer Soc., Central Westchester, N.Y., 1979-81, v.p., 1982; mem. exec. com. Westchester chpt., 1983—, mem. bd. dirs., 1982—; pres. Central Westchester unit, Am. Cancer Soc., 1983. King-Kennedy scholar, 1968-69. Mem. AMA, Am. Soc. Clin. Oncology, Am. Soc. Hematology, ACP, Nat. Soc. Internal Medicine, N.Y. Soc. Internal Medicine, Westchester Soc. Internal Medicine. Democrat. Roman Catholic. Current Work: Academic solo practitioner; clinical teaching. Subspecialties: Chemotherapy; Hematology. Home: 137 Trails End New City NY 10956 Office: 170 Maple Ave White Plains NY 10601

ALCORN, STANLEY MARCUS, plant pathologist; b. Modesto, Calif., June 18, 1926; s. Timothy Marshall and Marian (Boehne) A.; m. Esther Eastvold, June 19, 1949; children: Steven, Joseph, Eric, Mark. A.A., Modesto Jr. Coll., 1946; B.S., U. Calif., 1948, Ph.D., 1953. Postdoctoral fellow U. Calif., Berkeley, 1953-55; plant pathologist U.S. Dept. Agr., Tucson, Ariz., 1955-63; assoc. prof. U. Ariz., Tucson, 1963-65, prof. plant pathology, 1965—. Served with USAAF, 1944-45. Fellow AAAS; mem. Am. Phytopath. Soc., Am. Soc. Microbiology, Am. Soc. Hort. Sci., Am. Farm Bur., Guayule Rubber Soc., Sigma Xi. Republican. Methodist. Current Work: Diseases of new crops, of cacti, phytobacteriaology, soil-borne fungi, etiology, epidemiology, control, guayule, jojoba, guar, cacti, bio-mass plants. Subspecialty: Plant pathology. Office: Dept. Plant Pathology U Ariz Tucson AZ 85721

ALDEN, CARL LESLIE, veterinary pathologist; b. Centerville, Iowa, Oct. 14, 1944; s. Carl Miller and Lelah Belle Francis (Benz) A.; m. Patricia Ann Blum, May 10, 1964; children—Cynthia Lynne, Christopher Nathan, Jeremy Russell. M.Sc., Ohio State U., 1976, D.V.M., 1968. Vet. pathologist Ohio Dept. Agr., Reynoldsburg, 1972-76; asst. prof., coordinator div. comparative pathology W.Va. U., Morgantown, 1976-77; vet. pathologist, sect. head Proctor & Gamble Co., Cin., 1977—; cons. pathologist Ohio Dept. Agr., 1976—; lectr. nat. and internat. meetings on nephrotoxicity, hydrocarbon nephropathy, detergent builder nephropathy. Author: Color Atlas for Small Animal Necropsy, 1981. Contbr. numerous articles to profl. publs. Coach Harrison Select Boys Soccer, Ohio, 1980-84; asst. coach boys soccer team Harrison High Sch., 1985; mem. S.W. Local Sch. Bd., Harrison, 1985; mem. pastor parish com. Harrison United Meth. Ch., 1985. Served with U.S. Army, 1968-71; lt. col. Ohio Air N.G. Mem. Am. Coll. Vet. Pathology (diplomate; chmn. renal pathology spl. interest group 1984, toxicology spl. interest group 1985), Am. Vet. Med. Assn., Ohio Vet. Med. Assn. (chmn. comparative medicine sect. 1981-84), Am. Assn. Vet. Lab. Diagnosticians, Am. Assn. Lab. Animal Medicine, AAAS, Midwest Assn. Vet. Lab. Diagnosticians, Cin. Vet. Med. Assn., Soc. Toxicologic Pathology (chmn. Gt. Lakes discussion group). Republican. Methodist. Club: Harrison Soccer. Current work: Renal pathology; toxicologic pathology; investigative nephrotoxicology. Subspecialty: Pathology (veterinary medicine). Office: Procter & Gamble Co PO Box 39175 Cincinnati OH 45247

ALDER, BERNI JULIAN, physicist; b. Duisburg, Ger., Sept. 9, 1925; came to U.S., 1941, naturalized, 1944; s. Ludwig and Ottilie (Gottschalk) A.; m. Esther Berger, Dec. 28, 1956; children—Kenneth, Daniel, Janet. B.S., U. Calif., Berkeley, 1947, M.S., 1948; Ph.D., Calif. Inst. Tech., 1951. Instr. chemistry U. Calif., Berkeley, 1951-54; theoretical physicist Lawrence Livermore Lab., Livermore, Calif., 1955—; van der Waals prof. U. Amsterdam, Netherlands, 1971; prof. associé U. Paris, 1972. Author: Methods of Computational Physics, 1963; editor: Jour. Computational Physics, from 1966. Served with USN, 1944-46. Guggenheim fellow, 1954-55; NSF sr. postdoctoral fellow, 1963-64. Fellow Am. Phys. Soc.; mem. Nat. Acad. Scis., Am. Chem. Soc. (Joel Henry Hildebrand award in theoretical and exptl. chemistry of liquids 1985). Republican. Jewish. Current Work: Computer simulation of classical and quantum mechanical many-bodied systems. Subspecialties: Statistical physics; Theoretical chemistry. Office: PO Box 808 Lawrence Livermore Lab Livermore CA 94550

ALDER, EDWIN FRANCIS, agricultural researcher; b. Hugo, Okla., Sept. 1, 1927; s. Joseph B. and Mary Frances (Alder) A.; m. Ann Ruth Wilson, Feb. 10, 1951; children—Gwendolyn Ann, Jan Allison, Martha Ellen, Steven Edwin. B.S., U. Okla., 1951, Ph.D., 1956; M.S., U. Chgo., 1952; postgrad. U. Bergen, Norway, 1953-54. Instr. Ark. State Coll., Jonesboro, 1953, U. Ark., Fayetteville, 1955-57; sr. plant physiologist Eli Lilly & Co., Greenfield, Ind., 1957-66, dir. agrl. research, Indpls., 1966-74, v.p. Lilly Research Labs, 1974—, also dir. Served with USN, 1945-48, MTO. Fulbright scholar U.S. Govt., Bergen, Norway, 1953-54; Wychwood fellow U. Chgo., 1951. Mem. Phi Beta Kappa, Phi Eta Sigma. Current Work: Agricultural research. Subspecialties: Plant physiology (agriculture); Animal physiology. Home: 10140 E Troy Ave Indianapolis IN 46239

ALDERFER, RONALD GODSHALL, ecologist; b. Harleysville, Pa., July 14, 1943; s. Allen A. and Eva (Godshall) A.; m. Constance Joan Beachy, Aug. 21, 1965; children—Philip Wendell, Kristin Nicole. A.B., Washington U., St. Louis, 1965, Ph.D., 1969. Cert. sr. ecologist; cert. environ. profl. Asst. prof. biology U. Chgo., 1969-75; chief ecologist Harland Bartholomew & Assocs., St. Louis, 1975-81; assoc. v.p., Midwest regional mgr. Environ. Sci. & Engring., Inc., St. Louis, 1981—; chmn. environ. com. Regional Commerce and Growth Assn., St. Louis, 1984. Contbr. articles to profl. jours. Mem. AAAS, Nat. Assn. Environ. Profls. (bd. dirs.), Ecol. Soc. Am., Soc. Environ. Toxicology and Chemistry. Current work: Site investigation, remedial planning and implementation of corrective action at abandoned and active waste disposal sites; environmental planning for the siting of industrial facilities; air emission control planning. Subspecialties: Ecology (environmental science); Environmental toxicology. Home: 15574 Highcroft Dr Chesterfield MO 63017 Office: Environ Sci and Engring Inc 11665 Lilburn Park Rd Saint Louis MO 63146

ALDERMAN, MICHAEL HARRIS, public health educator; b. New Haven, Mar. 26, 1936; s. Julius and Ann (Vener) A.; m. Betsy Feinstein, July 21, 1968; children: John F., Peter B. B.A. magna cum laude, Harvard Coll., 1958; M.D., Yale U., 1962; postgrad., Johns Hopkins Sch. Pub. Health, 1965-66. Vis. physician, assoc. dir. Albert Einstein Coll. Medicine, Bronx, N.Y., 1962-64, 68-70; prof. pub. health and medicine Cornell U. Med. Ctr., N.Y.C., 1964-68, 70—; chmn. dept. epidemiology and social medicine Albert Einstein Coll. Medicine, N.Y.C., 1984—; vis. lectr. U. West Indies, Jamaica, 1970-71; chmn. bd. African Med. Research Found., N.Y.C., 1981—; cons. UN Med. Service, N.Y.C., 1981; mem. exec. com. Nat. Council on Internat. Health, Washington; mem. Nat. Bd. Med. Examiners. Editor: Clinical Medicine for the Occupational Physician, 1982, Hypertension: The Nurse's Role in Ambulatory Care, 1977. Served with USPHS, 1964-66. Glorney Raisbeck fellow N.Y. Acad. Medicine, 1967-68; traveling fellow WHO, Switzerland, 1973, 77. Fellow Am. Acad. Physicians; mem. Am. Heart Assn. (fellow Council on Epidemiology), Am. Fedn. Clin. Research, Internat. Assn. Occupational Health, Soc. Epidemiological Research, N.Y. Heart Assn. (chmn. council on community programs 1975), Am. Soc. Tropical Medicine and Hygiene, N.Y. Acad. Medicine, Am. Pub. Health Assn., Council on Fgn. Relations; Explorers Club, N.Y. State Civil Rights Commn. Clubs: Century, Harvard (N.Y.C.). Current Work: The epidemiology of high blood pressure and its treatment in the community as well as health in the developing world. Subspecialties: Internal medicine; Epidemiology. Office: Albert Einstein Coll Medicine 1300 Morris Park Ave Bronx NY 10461

ALDERSON, LOUIS EVERETT, wildlife biologist; b. Adrian, W.Va., Feb. 12, 1921; s. Frank Auburn and Charlotte Bierne (Walker) A.; m. Leta May Gourley, Jan. 19, 1945; children—John Edward, David Walker. A.B., U. W.Va., 1947; M.S., U. Wyo., 1949; Ph.D., Pacific West U., 1982. Grad. asst. Wyo. Game and Fish Commn., Laramie, 1948-49; dist. game mgr. W.Va. Conservation Commn., Hamlin, 1949-55; resident mgr. Union Carbide Club, Inc., Glen, W.Va., 1956-57; wildlife research biologist U.S. Fish and Wildlife Service, Fort Worth, 1957-70; v.p. Coastal Ecosystems Mgmt., Inc., Fort Worth, 1971—, also dir.; mem. tech. staff Tex. br. U.S. Study Commn. Fort Worth, 1964-65; bd. dirs. Tex. Orgn. Endangered Species, Author: (study) Revise U.S. Wetlands, 1963; Texas Coast Hurricane Portection, 1964; Terlingua Ranch Game, 1972; Measure Wildlife Habitat Diversity, 1985. Mem. exec. com. Internat. Student Orgn., Tex. Christian U., Fort Worth, 1973; precinct chmn. Tarrant County Republicans, 1976—, election judge, 1976-82, exec. com., 1976—. Served to capt. U.S. Army, World War II. Mem. Wildlife Soc. (cert.), Am. Soc. Mammalogists, Soc. Range Mgmt., Audubon Soc., DAV, Benzene Ring, Scabbard and Blade, Sigma Xi. Roman Catholic. Current work: Wildlife habitat and population studies via various methods; multi-disciplinary research in biology, geology, chemistry, physics. Office: Ecosystems Mgmt Inc 1031 N Henderson St Fort Worth TX 76107

ALDINGER, RANDOLPH RHETT, physics educator, researcher; b. Bowdle, S.D., Feb. 3, 1955; s. Eugene and Olivia Helena (Barth) A.; m. Melinda Sue Mathews, Aug. 8, 1975. A.S., Aberdeen Sch. Commerce, 1976; student U. Minn., 1976-79; B.S., Ariz. State U., 1980; Ph.D., U. Tex., 1984. Math. instr. Austin Community Coll. (Tex.), 1983-84; asst. prof. physics Eastern Ill. U., Charleston, 1984—. Contbr. articles to profl. publs. Profl. devel. scholar U. Tex., 1984; Eastern Ill. U. faculty research grantee, 1985. Mem. Am. Assn. Physics Tchrs., Am. Phys. Soc., Nat. Sci. Tchrs. Assn. Research or work interests: Group theoretical descriptions of hadrons, constrained Hamiltonian systems and hadronic string models Subspecialties: Particle physics; Theoretical physics. Home: 630 W Grant Ave Charleston IL 61920Office: Dept Physics Eastern Ill Univ Charleston IL 61920

ALDISSI, MAHMOUD, research chemist, government official; b. Jalameh, Jordan, Sept. 15, 1952; s. Ali Yousef and Amneh (Hussein) A.; m. Barbara Elva Townsend, Sept. 16, 1983; 1 child, Andrew A.T. B.S., U. Montpellier, France, 1976, M.S., 1978, Ph.D., 1981. Came to U.S., 1981. Postdoctoral fellow U. Pa., Phila., 1981-82; postdoctoral fellow Los Alamos Nat. Lab., 1982-84, staff mem., research chemist, 1984—. Patentee in field. Mem. Am. Chem. Soc. (div. polymeric materials sci. and engring.). Current work: Research on polymeric materials which exhibit unique electronic and optical properties, ie., high electrical conductivities which are candidates for potential technological applications. Subspecialties: Polymer chemistry; Polymers (materials science). Office: Materials Sci and Tech Los Alamos National Lab PO Box 1663 Los Alamos NM 87545

ALDRICH, RALPH EDWARD, physicist; b. Worcester, Mass., Jan. 29, 1940; s. Richard Hodgdon and Florence (Higginbottom) A.; m. Nancy Cook, Aug. 10, 1968. A.B., Amherst Coll., 1961; M.S., U. Nebr., 1963; Ph.D., Tufts U., 1967. Sr. mem. tech. staff Itek Central Research Lab., Lexington, Mass., 1967-76, mgr. material group, 1976; mgr. device tech. Itek Optical Systems, Lexington, 1976—. Contbr. articles to profl. jours. Patentee in field. Mem. Am. Phys. Soc. Current work: Adaptive optics, piezoelectric materials. Subspecialty: Holography. Office: Itek Optical Systems 10 Maguire Rd Lexington MA 02173

ALDRIDGE, MELVIN DAYNE, electrical engineer, educator, cons.; b. Crab Orchard, W.Va., July 20, 1941; s. William Bert and Gladys Revel (Deck) A.; m. Nancy Dickinson, June 6, 1963; children: Kenrick Lee, Randal Jay. B.S.E.E., W.Va. U., 1963; M.E.E., U. Va., 1965, D.Sc., 1968. Registered profl. engr., W.Va. Electronic engr. NASA, 1963-68; asst. prof. dept. elec. engring. W.Va. U., Morgantown, 1968-72, assoc. prof., 1972-76, prof., 1976-84, dir. Energy Research Ctr., 1978-84; prof. elec. engring., dir. engring. expt. stat., asst. dean for research Auburn U., 1984—. cons. in field. Contbr. articles on electronic monitoring and control in coal mines to profl. jours. Mem. IEEE, Am. Soc. for Engring. Edn., Soc. Mining Engrs., Ala. Soc. Profl. Engrs. (Outstanding Young Engr. award 1978), Sigma Xi. Baptist. Current Work: Application of electronics to coal mining and related activities; research administrator. Subspecialties: Electrical engineering; Coal. Home: 254 Carter St Auburn AL 36830 Office: 108 Ramsay Hall Auburn University AL 36849

ALESSANDRO, DANIEL, med. physicist; b. Senglea, Malta, Feb. 16, 1933; s. Joseph and Elsie A.; married; children: Paul J., Deborah A. B.S., Bklyn. Coll., 1960; M.S., N.Y. U., 1964, postgrad., 1967-70. Physicist Columbia-Presbyn. Med. Center, N.Y.C., 1960-62, N.Y. U. Med. Center, N.Y.C., 1962-70, Overlook Hosp., Summit, N.J., 1971-74; physicist St. Elizabeth Hosp., Elizabeth, N.J., 1977-82, cons. physicist, 1969—; physicist Good Samaritan Hosp., Suffern, N.Y., 1969—, cons. physicist, 1969—. Served with USN, 1951-55. Mem. Am. Assn. Pysicists in Medicine, N.J. Med. Physics Soc. (co-founder 1974, pres. 1977—78). Roman Catholic. Current Work: Physics research. Subspecialty: Medical physics.

ALESSI, NORMAN EMIL, psychiatrist, educator; b. Birmingham, Ala., Mar. 25, 1950; s. Joseph Samuel and Lucy (D'Zuana) A.; m. Barbara Alene McCaslin, May 28, 1983. B.S., Emory U., 1972, M.D., 1976. Diplomate Am. Bd. Psychiatry and Neurology. Psychiat. intern U. Mich., Ann Arbor, 1976-77, resident, 1977-80, fellow child psychiatry, 1978-81, research fellow, 1981-83, asst. prof. psychiatry, 1983—, research dir., 1983—; research cons. Dept. Mental Health, Lansing, Mich., 1981-82. Contbr. articles to profl. jours. Mem. Am. Psychiat. Assn., Am. Acad. Child Psychiatry, Soc. for Neurosci. Current work: Neurobiology of affective disorders among children and adolescents; phenotypic plasticity of opioid peptides during ontogency. Subspecialties: Psychopharmacology; Developmental biology. Office: U Mich Mental Health Research Inst 205 Washtenaw Pl Ann Arbor MI 48109

ALEVY, YAEL GRIS, immunologist; b. Krakow, Poland, May 13, 1948; d. Leon Arie and Deborah (Friedman) G.; m. Mitchell Alan Alevy, July 15, 1973. B.Sc., Bar-Ilan U., Ramat Gan, Israel, 1971; Ph.D., Albert Einstein Coll. Medicine, Bronx, N.Y., 1975. Postdoctoral fellow dept. microbiology and immunology Washington U. Sch. Medicine, St. Louis, 1975-77; research assoc. St. Louis U. Sch. Medicine, 1977-79, asst. research prof., 1979-83, assoc. prof. dept. medicine, 1983—. Contbr. articles to profl. jours. NIH grantee, 1980-86. Mem. Am. Assn. Immunologists, N.Y. Acad. Scis., AAAS. Current Work: Immune response and immunoregulation in uremia, experimental animal model; immune response and immunoregulation in patients with chronic uremia maintained on hemodialysis; immunoregulation of IgE synthesis in vitro. Subspecialty: Immunobiology and immunology. Home: 11916 Kendon Dr St Louis MO 63131 Office: 1402 S Grand Blvd 208 Doisy Hall St Louis MO 63104

ALEXANDER, DENNIS JAY, engineering company administrator; b. Washington, July 20, 1944; s. James Wesley and Judie O'Del (Hamilton) A.; m. Brenda Joyce Allison, July 4, 1970; children: Brian Keith, James Michael. B.S. in Indsl. Engring, U. Okla., Norman, 1967; postgrad., U.S. Naval Nuclear Power Sch., Mare Island, Calif., 1967. Lead power engr. Stone & Webster Engring. Corp., Boston, 1972-75, mgr. power div., Cherry Hill, N.J., 1975-79, asst. mgr. engring., 1979-80, project mgr., 1980—. Served to lt. USN, 1967-72. Mem. Am. Nuclear Soc., Frankford Radio Club (pres. awards chmn.). Lodge: K.C. Current Work: Managing and directing the technical and administrative aspects of large and small projects. Most of these projects are in the electrical power industry. Subspecialties: Nuclear engineering; Mechanical engineering. Home: RD 3 Butterworth Bogs Rd Vincentown NJ 08088 Office: Stone & Webster Engring Corp PO Box 5200 Cherry Hill NJ 08034

ALEXANDER, EDWARD RUSSELL, disease research administrator; b. Chgo., June 15, 1928; s. Russell Green and Ethelyn Satterlee (Abel) A. Ph.B., U. Chgo., 1948, B.S., 1950, M.D., 1953. Intern Cin. Gen. Hosp.; chief surveillance sect. Communicable Disease Center, Atlanta, 1955-57, 59-60; resident, instr. dept. pediatrics U. Chgo., 1954-55, 57-59; asst. prof. dept. preventive medicine and dept. pediatrics U. Wash., Seattle, 1961-65, assoc. prof., 1965-69, prof., 1969-79; chmn. dept. epidemiology U. Wash. (Sch. Pub. Health), 1970-75; prof. dept. pediatrics U. Ariz., Tucson, 1979-83; chief research br., Div STD, Centers for Disease Control, Atlanta, 1983—. Contbr. articles to profl. jours. Markle scholar, 1962-67. Mem. Am. Acad. Pediatrics, Am. Pediatric Soc., Am. Pub. Health Assn., Assn. Tchrs. Preventive Medicine, Am. Epidemiol. Soc., Soc. Epidemiol. Research, Internat. Epidemiol. Soc., King County Med. Soc. Current Work: Infectious disease epidemiology with particular concern for sexually transmitted disease and its maternal neonatal consequences. Subspecialties: Epidemiology; Microbiology (medicine). Office: Research Br Div STD Centers for Disease Control Atlanta GA 30333

ALEXANDER, HAROLD, biomedical engineering, educator, consultant, researcher; b. N.Y.C.; s. Jack and Freda (Koltun) A.; m. Sheila E., Dec. 20, 1964; children: Robin, Andrea. B.S., N.Y.U., 1962, M.S., 1963, Ph.D., 1967. Head Lab. for Balloon Tech., 1968-73, asst. prof., 1968-71, assoc. prof., 1971-77; co-dir. Lab. for Balloon Tech. (Med. Engrging. Lab.), 1973-77; assoc. prof. surgery U. Medicine and Dentistry N.J.-N.J. Med. Sch., Newark, 1977-81, prof., 1981—; dir. U. Medicine and Dentistry N.J.-N.J. Med. Sch. (Orthopaedic Research Labs.), 1977—; cons. med. device industry; officer CAS, Inc. Contbr. articles to profl. jours. Recipient Founder's Day award N.Y.U., 1967, Outstanding Research Paper award Internat. Research Soc. for Orthopaedics and Traumatology, 1981. Mem. Orthopaedic Research Soc., ASME, ASTM, Sigma Xi, Sigma Gamma Tau. Co-patentee bio-adsorbable composite tissue scaffold. Current Work: Research and development of orthopaedic implants; orthopaedic biomechanics educator; manufacturing and sales of medical devices. Subspecialties: Biomedical engineering; Physiology (medicine). Home: 47 Elmwood Pl Short Hills NJ 07078 Office: Sect Orthopaedic Surgery U Medicine and Dentistry NJ-NJ Med Sch 100 Bergen St Newark NJ 07103

ALEXANDER, JAMES L., behavioral ecologist, educator, research; b. San Francisco, June 5, 1945; s. William Preston and Lenore E. (Funk) A.; m. Elizabeth Pascoe, Sept. 3, 1977; children: Alan James, Lauren Elizabeth. B.B.A., U. Tex.-Austin, 1967; M.A., U. Houston, 1977, Ph.D., 1978. Research asst. in psychiatry Baylor Coll. Medicine, Houston, 1972-73, asst. prof. rehab., 1979—; research asst. in behavioral ecology Inst. for Rehab. and Research, Houston, 1973-78, assoc. dir. behavioral ecology, 1978-79, dir. behavioral ecology, 1979—; clin. asst. profl. psychology U. Houston, 1978—; project dir. U. Houston (Systems Ctr.), 1982—; v.p. Planning Assocs., Houston, 1982—; vis. architecture critic Rice U., Houston, 1976. Developer: measurement tool self-observation and report technique, 1982. Served to lt. U.S. Army, 1968-71, Vietnam. Decorated Bronze Star; recipient Outstanding Community Service award Pres. Carter, 1979. Mem. Am. Congress Rehab. Medicine, Am. Psychol. Assn., AAAS, Sigma Xi. Current Work: Current research interests involve applying the principles of behavioral ecology: (1) to establish better systems of outpatient and follow-up care for physically disabled persons, and (2) to study the processes of adjustment to a physical disability. Further interests include applying the perspective of behavorial ecology to solve problems in business, health care, government, and educational organizations. Subspecialties: Behavioral ecology; Physical medicine and rehabilitation. Office: Inst for Rehab and Research 1333 Moursund Houston TX 77030

ALEXANDER, JAMES WESLEY, surgeon, educator, researcher; b. El Dorado, Kans., May 23, 1934; s. Rossiter and Merle Alexander; m. Maureen Louise Strohofer, Oct. 19, 1984; children—Joseph, Judith, Randolph, Elizabeth, John Charles. Student Tex. Tech. Coll., 1951-53; M.D., U. Tex., 1957; postgrad., U. Cin., 1958-64, U. Minn., 1966-67. Diplomate Am. Bd. Surgery, Am. Bd. Thoracic Surgery. Intern, Cin. Gen. Hosp., 1957-58; resident in surgery U. Cin.-Cin. Gen. Hosp., 1958-64; mem. staff Univ. Hosp., 1963—, Cin. VA Hosp., 1966—, Christian R. Holmes Hosp., 1966—, The Christ Hosp., 1968—, Cin. Shriners Burns Inst., 1968—, Jewish Hosp., Cin., 1972—; instr. in surgery U. Cin. Coll. of Medicine, 1962-64, asst. prof., 1966-69, assoc. prof. surgery, 1969-75, prof. surgery, 1975—; instr. pediatrics, research asst. in microbiology Univ. Minn., 1966-67; dir. transplantation div. and surg. immunology lab. Univ. Cin. Coll. of Medicine, 1967—; dir. research Shriners Burns Inst. Cin. Unit, 1979—; cons. NIH, 1967—, renal diseases and transplantation Regional Med. Program, 1972-73. Editor: Problems in General Surgery, 1984. Contbr. articles to profl. jours. Served to capt. U.S. Army, 1964-66, to maj. M.C. USAR, 1967-68. Mem. editorial bd. Journ. Clin. Surgery, 1981-82, Annals of Surgery, 1975—, Circulatory Shock, 1979—, J. Burn Care and Rehab., 1979—. Grantee USPHS, 1968-85, Upjohn, 1971, Syntex Corp., 1972, Eli Lilly Co., 1972, Ross Labs., 1980, 3M Co., 1982, 84, Ortho Pharm., 1985, Johnson & Johnson, 1984-85; fellow Am. Cancer Soc., 1960-61, 1961-63, 1966-68. Fellow ACS; mem. Am. Burn Assn. (v.p. 1982-83, pres. 1984-85), Am. Soc. Transplant Surgeons, Am. Surg. Assn., Surg. Infection Soc. (sec. 1981-84), Am. Assn. Immunologists, Am. Soc. Transplant Surgeons, Am. Soc. Parenteral Enteral Nutrition, Assn. Acad. Surgery, Cin. Acad. Medicine, Cin. Surg. Soc., Internat. Soc. Burn Injuries, Ohio State Med. Assn., Soc. Univ. Surgeons, Univ. Cin. Grad. Surg. Soc., Phi Eta Sigma, Alpha Omega Alpha, Alpha Epsilon Delta Current Work: Surgery, immunology, transplantation. Subspecialties: Transplant surgery; Transplantation. Home: 2869 Grandin Rd Cincinnati OH 45208 Office: Dept of Surgery Univ Cin Med Ctr 231 Bethesda Ave Cincinnati OH 45267

ALEXANDER, JOHN MACMILLAN, chemistry educator; b. Columbia, Mo., Aug. 17, 1931; s. John Macmillan and Victoria (Holladay) A.; m. Betty Jo Linton, Aug. 1, 1953; children—Mary Jo, John Macmillan III, Frank Linton, James Holladay. B.S., Davidson Coll., 1953; Ph.D., MIT, 1956. Research assoc. MIT, Cambridge, 1956-57; research chemist Lawrence Berkeley Lab., Calif., 1957-63; assoc. prof. chemistry SUNY, Stony Brook, 1963-67, prof., 1968—. Contbr. articles to profl. jours. Mem. program adv. com. Tandem Accelerator, Brookhaven Nat. Lab., 1977—. Sloan Found. fellow, 1964-67; Guggenheim fellow, 1969-70. Mem. Am. Chem. Soc., Am. Phys. Soc., Phi Beta Kappa. Democrat. Presbyterian. Club: Midget Ocean Racing. Current work: Radioactivity, high energy nuclear reactions, fission, spallation, heavy ion reactions, elastic and inelastic scattering fusion, energy and spin dissipation, evaporative decay. Subspecialties: Nuclear chemistry; Nuclear physics. Home: 14 Highwood Rd Setauket NY 11733 Office: Chemistry Dept SUNY Stony Brook NY 11794

ALEXANDER, JONATHAN, cardiologist, consultant; b. N.Y.C., Nov. 29, 1947; s. Josef and Hannah (Margolis) A.; m. Karen Deborah Einhorn, Aug. 8, 1971; children: Jessica, Beth, Daniel Lewis. B.A., Harvard U., 1968; M.D., Albert Einstein Coll. Medicine, 1973. Intern, resident Yale-New Haven Hosp., 1973-76; fellow dept. cardiology Yale U. Sch. Medicine, New Haven, 1976-78, asst. clin. prof. medicine, 1978-83, assoc. clin. prof. medicine, 1983—; attending physician Danbury (Conn.) Hosp., 1978—, West Haven (Conn.) Vets. Hosp., 1978—, New Milford (Conn.) Hosp., 1980—; dir. cardiac rehab. unit and nuclear cardiology Danbury (Conn.) Hosp., 1978—. Bd. dirs. Ives Festival Artists, Danbury, Conn., 1979-82; sec. bd. dirs. Western Conn. Symphony Orch., Danbury, 1981-83. Recipient Samuel Kushlan award Yale-New Haven Hosp., 1974, Revlon award 11th Internat. Congress Chemotherapy, 1983. Fellow ACP, Am. Coll. Cardiology, Am. Coll. Chest Physicians, Am. Heart Assn.; mem. Soc. Nuclear Medicine, N.Y. Acad. Scis., Alpha Omega Alpha. Jewish. Current Work: Hospital-based cardiologist directing cardiac rehabilitation and nuclear cardiology programs. Subspecialties: Cardiology; Internal medicine. Office: Cardiology Dept Danbury Hosp Danbury CT 06877

ALEXANDER, LECKIE FREDERICK, mechanical engineering, educator, consultant; b. Dundee, Scotland, Mar. 26, 1929; came to U.S., 1978; s. Frederick and Mary Baxter (Barclay) L.; m. Alison Elizabeth Wheelwright, Mar. 30, 1957; children: Gavin F., Gregor W., Sean C. B.S.C., St. Andrews U., 1949; M.S., Stanford U., 1955, Ph.D., 1958. Cons. civil engr. Mott, Hay & Anderson, London, 1949-51; Forschungsassistent Technische Hochschule, Hanover, W.Ger., 1957-58; univ. lectr. Cambridge (Eng.) U., 1958-68; fellow and dir. studies Cambridge (Eng.) U. (Pembroke Coll.), 1959-68; prof. engring. U. Leicester, Eng., 1968-78; prof. mech. engring. and theoretical and applied mechanics U. Ill., Urbana, 1978—, head dept. theoretical and applied mechanics, 1984—; cons. solid mechanics. Author: (with E. C. Pestel) Matrix Methods in Elaso-mechanics, 1963; contbr. numerous articles to profl. jours.; editorial bd. various jours. Bd. govs. Bedales Sch., Petersfield, Eng., 1975-78. Served to flight lt. RAF, 1951-54. Recipient Halliburton award U. Ill., 1982. Fellow Am. Acad. Mechanics; mem. ASME. Current Work: Strength of materials, computer-aided design. Subspecialties: Theoretical and applied mechanics; High-temperature materials. Home: 50 Lake Park Champaign IL 61820 Office: 104 S Wright St Urbana IL 61801

ALEXANDER, MARY LOUISE, biology educator; b. Ennis, Tex., Jan. 15, 1926; d. Emmett F. and Florence (Hill) A. B.A., U.Tex., 1947, M.A., 1949, Ph.D., 1951. Instr., research asst. Genetics Found., U. Tex., Austin, 1944-51, research asst., 1962-67; postdoctoral fellow biology div. AEC, Oak Ridge, 1951-52; postdoctoral research fellow dept. zoology U.Tex., Austin, 1952-55; research assoc. M.D. Anderson Hosp. and Tumor Inst., Houston, 1956-58, asst. biologist, 1959-62; research cons. Brookhaven Nat. Lab., Upton, N.Y., 1955; researcher Oak Ridge Inst. Nuclear Studies, 1951-77; assoc. prof. biology

S.W. Tex State U., San. Marcos, 1966-69, prof., 1970—. Nat. Cancer Inst. fellow Inst. Animal Genetics, Edinburgh, Scotland, 1960-61. Mem. Genetics Soc. Am., Radiation Research Soc., Am. Soc. Human Genetics, Sigma Xi, Gamma Phi Beta, Phi Sigma, Alpha Epsilon Delta. Current Work: Mutagensis. Subspecialties: Gene actions; Animal genetics. Home: Hunter's Glen Route 2 Box 119 San Marcos TX 78666 Office: Dept Biology SW Tex State U San Marcos TX 78666

ALEXANDER, MICHAEL NORMAN, condensed matter physicist; b. Washington, Mar. 27, 1941; s. Samuel Nathan Alexander and Eleanor Frances (Magazine) Huntoon; m. Judith Rosemary Deutsch, June 14, 1964; children—Daniel Lev, Shana Nicole. A.B., Harvard U., 1962; Ph.D., Cornell U., 1967. Research physicist Army Materials and Mechanics Research Ctr., Watertown, Mass., 1967-79; sr. mem. tech. staff GTE Labs. Inc., Waltham, Mass., 1979—. Contbr. articles to profl. jours, Subcommittee chmn. Wetlands Adv. Com. Lexington Mass., Planning Bd., 1974-75; guidance adv. com. High Sch., Lexington, 1984—. Mem. Am. Phys. Soc., (exec. com. New Eng. sect. 1984—), Optical Soc. Am., Electrochemical Soc., AAAS, Sigma Xi, Phi Kappa Phi. Jewish. Current work: Deep-level defects in semiconductors; luminescence of ions in insulators; metal-nonmetal transition in semi-conductors; nuclear magnetic resonance studies of metals and alloys, and of molecular motion. Subspecialties: Condensed matter physics; Semiconductors. Office: GTE Labs Inc 40 Sylvan Rd Waltham MA 02254

ALEXANDER, MILLARD HENRY, chemist, educator; b. Boston, Feb. 17, 1943; s. Benjamin and Marie M. (Mayer) A.; m. Francoise Bore, Dec. 23, 1966 (div.); 1 dau., Stephanie Andrea. B.A. magna cum laude, Harvard Coll., 1964; Ph.D., U. Paris-South, 1967. Research fellow Harvard U., 1968-71, lectr. summer sch., 1971; asst. prof. Inst. Molecular Physics, U. Md., College Park, 1971-72, asst. prof. dept. chemistry, 1972-75, assoc. prof., 1975-79, prof., 1979—. Contbr. numerous articles to profl. jours. Recipient Outstanding Young Tchr. award D.C. Inst. Chemists, 1977. Fellow Am. Phys. Soc.; mem. Am. Chem. Soc. Current Work: Theory of inelastic and reactive collisions involving atoms and molecules. Subspecialties: Theoretical chemistry; Atomic and molecular physics. Office: Dept Chemistry U Md College Park MD 20742

ALEXANDER, NANCY JEAN, molecular geneticist; b. Ithaca, N.Y., Jan. 14, 1947; d. Ralph William and Gladys (Robin) A. B.S., SUNY, Oswego, 1968; M.A., Duke U., 1971, Ph.D., 1977. Research assoc. Ohio State U., Columbus, 1977-80; molecular geneticist No. Regional Research Lab., U.S. Dept. Agr., Peoria, Ill., 1980—. Mem. Genetics Soc. Am., Am. Soc. Cell Biology, Am. Soc. Microbiology, Sigma Xi. Current Work: Conversion of biomass to useful chemicals using genetic engineering techniques. Subspecialties: Genetics and genetic engineering (agriculture); Biomass (agriculture). Address: 1815 N University St Peoria IL 61604

ALEXANDER, NELSON EUGENE, electronics scientist, consultant; b. Burnham, Pa., Jan. 5, 1908; s. Albert Wilson and Elizabeth Olive (Alexander) A.; m. Lenore Lillian Hummel, Apr. 8, 1933 (dec. 1979); children—James Garth, Susanne Gardner; m. Linda Ruth Erhardt, June 15, 1980. B.S. in Electrochem. Engring., Pa. State U., State College, 1931. Test engr. Atlantic Refining Co., Phila., 1934-42; instr. rockets Nat. Def. Research Commn., Cumberland, Md., 1942-47; electronics scientist Fort Detrick, Frederick, Md., 1947-65, NIH, Bethesda, Md., 1965-68, exec. sec. Florence Agreem Commn., NIH, 1968-79, sci. cons., 1979—. Contbr. articles to profl. jours. Patentee in field. Recipient Naval Ordanance Devel. award U.S. Navy, 1946; Best Tech. Paper award Inst. Radio Engrs., 1957; fellow Sec. Army, 1960. Mem. IEEE (sr.), Biophysical Soc. (charter), Electron Microscopy Soc., Optical Soc. Am., Soc. Automotive Engrs., Sigma Xi. Current work: Evaluate and recommend duty free entry applications nationally for biomedical instruments. Subspecialties: Bioinstrumentation; Biophysics (biology). Home: 1201 Motter Ave Frederick MD 21701Office: Nat Inst Health Bldg 13 Room 3W13 Bethesda MD 20205

ALEXANDER, PETER, energy technology company executive, physicist, geophysicist; b. N.Y.C., Feb. 14, 1935; s. John and Beatrice (Strauss) A.; m. Iris Rubin, June 7, 1956; children: Susan, Robin, Scott. B.S. in Physics, MIT, 1956; Ph.D. in Physics (X-R fellow), Purdue U., 1961; research fellow, Calif. Inst. Tech., 1961-63. Mgr. physics dept. Teledyne Inc., Westwood, N.J., 1965-72; head adv. tech. br. Office Naval Intelligence, Washington, 1972-74; dir. adv. tech. div. Bendix Corp., Grand Junction, Colo., 1974-77; mgr. energy tech. TRW Inc., Denver, 1977-83; dir. engring. Schlumberger, Houston, 1983—; presenter numerous symposia in, U.S. and Europe. Author of numerous technical papers, patents and tech. reports. Recipient NASA patent award. Mem. Am. Nuclear Soc. (chmn. Nuclear Standards commn. 1973-74), IEEE, Soc. for Control & Instrumentation Energy Processes (dir. 1980), Soc. Exploration Geophysicists, Am. Physical Soc. Current Work: Development of sensors, down hole mechanical and electronic tools, reservoir analysis techniques and operational approaches for reservoir diagnostics; Insitu extraction technology. Development of technology for disposal of high and low level nuclear wastes. Subspecialty: Oil shale. Office: Flopetrol Johnston Schlumberger Box 36369 Houston TX 77036

ALEXANDER, PETER JOHN, aquatic biologist; b. Milw., July 9, 1953; s. Leonard C. and Helen (Ellis) A. B.S., U. Wis.-Green Bay, 1975; postgrad. Calif. State U.-Hayward, 1977—. Aquatic researcher U. Wis.-Green Bay, 1973-74; biologist U.S. Geol. Survey, Menlo Park, Calif., 1979-81; aquatic biologist East Bay Regional Park Dist., Oakland, Calif., 1977—. Mem. Am. Soc. Limnology and Oceanography, Am. Soc. Freshwater Ecology, Grissley Peak Flyfishing Conservation Club (conservation com. 1983—). Current work: Limnology; aquatic biology; lake restoration; advances in erosion control; rainbow trout habitat research; research native and historical trout populations in California. Subspecialties: Ecosystems analysis; Resource management. Home: 650 Broadmoor Blvd San Leandro CA 94577 Office: East Bay Regional Park Dist 11500 Skyline Blvd Oakland CA 94619

ALEXANDER, RONALD CLIFFORD, computer scientist; b. Portland, Oreg., Sept. 20, 1949; s. Raymond Eugene and Arlene Katherine Bertha (Schmeckpepper) A.; m. Kay Ann Joncas, Apr. 22, 1972. A.A., Portland Community Coll., 1971; B.S. in Math., SUNY-Albany, 1978; B.S.E.E., U. Portland, 1979. Optical computer researcher Oreg. Grad. Ctr., Beaverton, 1979-80; automatic test system designer Naval Undersea Weapons Engring. Sta., Keyport, Wash., 1980-82; evaluation engr. Harry Diamond Labs., Adelphi, Md., 1982-83; quality engr. Intel Systems, Hillsboro, Oreg., 1984—; tng. cons. Emanual Hosp., Portland, 1971-73, Bonneville Power Adminstrn., Portland, 1979-80, theater ads on film, Portland, 1969—. Patentee interface for HPATS-80, event driven susceptability measurements. Trustee Portland Highland Games Assn., 1978—; founder Met. Hospitals Credit Union, Portland, 1972. Served with USN, 1973-77. Mem. IEEE, Internat. Test and Evaluation Assn. (charter), Eta Kappa Nu, Theta Beta. Democrat. Lutheran. Clubs: Clan Donald (Oreg. state commr. 1978), Mensa. Lodge: Grange. Current work: Application of process logic to manufacturing. Subspecialties: Systems engineering; Operations research (engineering). Home: 57740 Timber Rd E Vernonia OR 97064 Office: Intel Systems 5200 NE Elam Young Pkwy Hillsboro OR 97123

ALEXANDER, SAMUEL ADAM, plant pathologist; b. Tallulah, La., May 15, 1941; s. Lloyd Cleveland and Ruby Bell (Osborne) A.; m. Connie Hall, May 30, 1949; children: Adam Hall, Scott Lloyd, Amy Elizabeth. B.S., La. Tech. U., 1964, M.S., 1970; Ph.D., Va. Poly. Inst. and State U., 1973. Grad. research asst. dept. botany and bacteriology La. Tech. U., 1968-70; grad. research asst. dept. plant pathology and physiology Va. Poly. Inst. and State U., 1970-73; research assoc. dept. plant pathology Pa. State U., 1974-76; asst. prof. plant pathology Va. Poly. Inst. and State U., Blacksburg, 1976-82, assoc. prof., 1982—. Contbr. articles to profl. jours. Served with U.S. Army, 1965-68. Mem. Am. Phytopathological Soc., Soc. Am. Foresters, Sigma Xi, Phi Sigma, Gamma Sigma Delta. Current Work: Root diseases of forest trees, development of predictive models, and application of integrated forest pest management strategies. Subspecialties: Plant pathology; Integrated pest management. Office: Dept Plant Pathology and Physiology Va Poly Inst and State U Blacksburg VA 24061

ALEXANDER, WILLIAM DAVIDSON, III, consulting engineer; b. Charlotte, N.C., June 20, 1911; s. William Davidson and Elizabeth (Galt) A.; m. Louise York, Nov. 14, 1936 (dec. Nov. 1983); 1 child, William Davidson IV. B.S., Va. Mil. Inst., 1934; C.E., N.C. State U., 1953. Commd. 2d lt. U.S. Army, 1940, advanced through grades to col. U.S. Air Force, 1951, ret., 1962; v.p. SSV&K Engrs., N.Y.C., 1962-75, pres., 1974-75; asst. gen. mgr. transit system devel. Met. Atlanta Regional Transit Authority, 1975-79; cons. engr., Pawleys Island, S.C., 1979—. Decorated Legion of Merit. Fellow ASCE, Soc. Am. Mil. Engrs.; mem. Nat. Acad. Engring. Current work: Engineering Management, contract negotiations, arbitration. Subspecialty: Transportation engineering.

ALEXANDER, WILLIAM NEBEL, dentist, former army officer, educator; b. Pitts., May 22, 1929; s. William Harrison and Ida Margaret (Nebel) A.; m. Lorrain Michaela Berg, Nov. 29, 1958; children: Kathleen, Gregory, Christopher, Jeffrey, Steven. Student, St. Vincent Coll., 1947-49; D.D.S., U. Pitts., 1953; cert., U. Pa., 1961; M.S. in Edn, Jackson State U., 1982. Diplomate Am. Bd. Oral Medicine (bd. dirs. 1985—). Commd. 2d lt. U.S. Army, 1952, advanced through grades to col., 1972; chief oral medicine service (Letterman Army Med. Ctr.), San Francisco, 1961-66; chief clinician (464th Med. Detachment), Kaiserslautern, W.Ger., 1966-69; comdg. officer (257th and 499th Med. Detachment), Vietnam, 1969-70; dir. gen. dental residency (Darnall Army Hosp.), Ft. Hood, Tex., 1970-74; dir. and chmn. dental edn. (Madigan Army Med. Ctr.), Tacoma, 1974-78; ret., 1978; prof., dir. patient admissions U. Miss. Sch. Dentistry, Jackson, 1978—, mem. faculty senate, 1985—; cons. oral medicine; dental cons. Miss. State Dept. Edn., Jackson, 1980—. Co-editor: Problem Oriented Dental Record, 1980-81; contbg. author: Oral Health of the Elderly, 1983; author manual/clin. lab. medicine for dentists, 1980-81; video tape TMJ/MFPD Syndrome Diagnosis, 1977. Tchr. piloting U.S. Power Squadrons, San Francisco, Tacoma, 1965-78; co-chmn. parish council Christ the King Parish, Belton, Tex., 1971-83; usher-greeter St. Paul's Parish, Brandon, Miss., 1978—. Decorated Bronze Star, Legion of Merit. Fellow Am. Coll. Dentists, Am. Acad. Oral Medicine; mem. Internat. Assn. Dental Research, AAAS, Omicron Kappa Upsilon (pres. chpt. 1983), Sigma Xi, Phi Kappa Phi. Republican. Roman Catholic. Clubs: Presidio Yacht (San Francisco); Loyal Order of Boar. Current Work: Diagnosis and treatment of temporomandibular joint disturbances, research and treatment oral manifestation of systemic disease, geriatric oral diseases. Subspecialties: Oral pathology; Oral Medicine. Home: 300 Forest Point Dr Brandon MS 39042 Office: U Miss Med Center 2500 MS State St Jackson MS 39216

ALEXEFF, IGOR, electrical engineering educator, researcher; b. Pitts., Jan. 5, 1931; s. Alexander and Tamara (Tchirkow) A.; m. Anne Irene Fabina, Feb. 4, 1954; children—Alexander, Helen. B.A., Harvard U., 1952; M.S., U. Wis., 1957, Ph.D., 1959. Registered profl. engr., Tenn. Research engr. Westinghouse Co., Pitts., 1952-53; postdoctoral fellow U. Zurich, Switzerland, 1959-60; group leader Oak Ridge Nat. Lab., 1960-70; prof. U. Tenn., Knoxville, 1970—; vis. prof., Japan, India, South Africa, Brazil, Author publs. in field. Patentee in field. Pres. So. Appalachian Sci. and Engring. Fair, Knoxville, 1984-85. Recipient Weinberg award Oak Ridge Nat. Lab.; Chancellor's research scholar U. Tenn., 1984. Fellow Am. Phys. Soc. (sec. treas. physics div. 1983—), IEEE (chmn. plasma soc. 1983-84, Centennial medal 1984); mem. Mensa, Tenn. Inventors Assn. (pres. Knoxville 1983- 84), Sigma Xi. Democrat. Eastern Orthodox. Current work: Sub-millimeter microwave generation. Subspecialties: Plasma (energy science and technology); Nuclear fission. Home: 2790 Turnpike Oak Ridge TN 37830 Office: Univ Tenn Ferris Hall Knoxville TN 37996-2100

ALFANO, ROBERT RICHARD, physicist, consultant, educator; b. N.Y.C., May 7, 1941. B.S., Fairleigh Dickinson U., 1963, M.S. in Physics, 1964; Ph.D. in Physics, N.Y. U., 1972. Mem. research staff GTE, 1964-72; prof. physics CCNY, 1972—, Herbert Kayser prof. elec. engring., 1984—, dir. Inst. for Ultrafast Spectroscopy and Lasers, 1982—, dir. Photonic Engring. Labs., 1985—. Contbr. numerous articles to profl. jours. A.P. Sloan fellow, 1974-78. Fellow Am. Phys. Soc.; mem. Am. Biophys. Soc. Patentee in field. Current Work: Picosecond and femtosecond lasers and techniques, ultrafast spectroscopy in materials. Subspecialties: Condensed matter physics; Biophysics (physics). Office: CCNY CUNY Convent Ave and 138th St New York NY 10031

ALFIDI, RALPH JOSEPH, radiologist, educator; b. Rome, Italy, Apr. 20, 1932; s. Lucas and Angeline (Panella) A.; m. Rose Esther Senesac, Sept. 3, 1956; children: Sue, Lisa, Christine, Catherine, Mary, John. A.B., Ripon (Wis.) Coll., 1955; M.D., Marquette U., Milw., 1959. Intern Oakwood Hosp., Dearborn, Mich., 1959-60; resident, chief resident, A.C.S. fellow U. Va., 1960-63; practice medicine, specializing in radiology, Cleve., 1965—; staff mem. Cleve. Clinic, 1965-78, head dept. hosp. radiology, 1968-78; dir. dept. radiology Univ. Hosps., Cleve.; cons. VA Hosp., Hillcrest Hosp., Cleve.; chmn. dept. radiology Case Western Res. U. Sch. Medicine, 1978—; Chmn. staff Cleve. Clinic Found., 1975-76. Author: Complications and Legal Implications of Special Procedures, 1972, Computed Tomography of the Human Body: An Atlas of Normal Anatomy, 1977; Editor: Whole Body Computed Tomography, 1977; Contbr. articles to radiology jours. Served to capt., M.C. U.S. Army Res., 1963-65. Picker Found. grantee, 1969-70; NRC grantee, 1969-70. Fellow Am. Coll. Radiology; mem. AMA, Radiol. Soc. N. Am., Am. Roentgen Ray Soc., Am. Heart Assn., Soc. Cardiovascular Radiology, Soc. Gastrointestinal Radiology, Soc. Computed Body Tomography (pres. 1977-78), Eastern Radiol. Soc., Ohio Radiol. Soc., Cleve. Radiol. Soc. (pres. 1976-77). Roman Catholic. Clubs: Hillbrook, Chagrin Valley Racquet, Kirtland Country. Current Work: Research in NMR imaging gating of vascular and other systems; positron emission tomography of CNS, vascular system, and oncology. Subspecialties: Diagnostic radiology; Imaging technology. Home: 742 Coy Ln Chagrin Falls OH 44022 Office: Case Western Res U Dept Radiology 2074 Abington Rd Cleveland OH 44106

ALFORD, GEARY SIMMONS, experimental clinical psychologist, educator; b. McComb, Miss., Apr. 11, 1945; s. Percy Knapp and Murrell (Dodds) A.; m. Catherine Elizabeth Alford; children: Alexander Geary, Zeb Burton. Diploma, Goethe-Inst., 1965; B.A., Millsaps Coll., 1968; M.A., U. Ariz., 1971, Ph.D., 1972. Intern, then resident in psychology U. Miss. Med. Center, Jackson, 1971-72, clin. asst. prof., 1972-73, asst. prof., 1973-79, assoc. prof. psychiatry-psychology, 1980—, asst. prof. pharmacology-toxicology, 1979—, clin. asst. prof. family medicine, 1975—; cons. in field; dir. Protective Service Life Ins. Co., Jackson, 1976—; mem. adv. bd. Drug Research and Edn. Assn. Miss. Contbr. articles, chpts. to profl. publs.; editorial bd.: Behavior Modification, 1982—; editorial reviewer for various nat., internat. profl. jours. Chmn. Diocesan Comm. on Alcohol and Drug Dependency, Episcopal Diocese Miss., 1980—. Sigma Xi traveling scholar, 1971; Nat. Inst. Drug Abuse postdoctoral fellow, 1975; Nat. Inst. Alcoholism and Alcohol Abuse postdoctoral fellow, 1976. Fellow Behavior Therapy and Research Soc. (clin.); mem. Am. Psychol. Assn., Miss. Psychol. Assn. (pres. 1977-78), Assn. Advancement Behavior Therapy, Sigma Xi. Current Work: Development and evaluation of behavioral therapeutic procedures derived from basic experimental psychology; clinical neuropharmacology, addictive disorders and their treatment. Subspecialties: Behavioral psychology; Neuropharmacology. Home: 20 Sheffield Crescent Jackson MS 39211 Office: Dept Psychiatry and Human Behavior U Miss Med Center 2500 N State St Jackson MS 39216

ALFVEN, HANNES OLOF GOSTA, physicist, educator; b. May 30, 1908. Ph.D., U. Uppsala, Sweden, 1934. Prof. theory of electricity Royal Inst. Tech., Stockholm, 1940-45, prof. electronics, 1945-63, prof. plasma physics, 1963-73; prof. applied physics and info. sci. U. Calif., San Diego, 1967—; past mem. Swedish Sci. Adv. Council, Swedish Atomic Energy Commn.; past bd. govs. Swedish Def. Research Inst., Swedish Atomic Energy Co.; past sci. adv. Swedish Govt.; past pres. Pugwash Confs. Sci. and World Affairs; mem. panel comets and astroids NASA. Author: Cosmical Electrodynamics, 1950, On the Origin of the Solar System, 1954, Cosmical Electrodynamics: Fundamental Principles, 1963, Worlds-Antiworlds, 1966, The Tale of the Big Computer, 1968, Atom, Man and the Universe, 1969, Living on the Third Planet, 1972, Evolution of the Solar System, 1976, Cosmic Plasma, 1981. Recipient Nobel prize for physics, 1970; Lomonsov Gold medal USSR Acad. Scis., 1971; Franklin medal, 1971. Mem. Swedish Acad. Scis., Akademia NAUK (USSR), U.S. Acad. Scis. (fgn. asso.), Royal Soc. (fgn. mem.), numerous others. Subspecialty: Plasma physics. Office: Dept Electrical Engineering and Computer Science U Calif La Jolla CA 92093*

ALGER, JEFFRY ROY, biochemical researcher; b. Seattle, Jan. 27, 1954; s. James V. Alger and Janet L. (Clark) Durance. B.S., Wash. State U., 1975; M.S., Yale U., 1977, M.Phil., 1978, Ph.D., 1979. Postdoctoral assoc. Yale U., New Haven, 1979-82, research assoc., 1982-83, asst. prof. radiology, molecular biophysics, and biochemistry, 1984—. Contbr. numerous articles to profl. jours. Mem. AAAS, Am. Chem. Soc. Current work: The application of nuclear magnetic resonance technology to the study of metabolism in living subjects, with the eventual goal of developing clinical diagnostic protocols based on NMR. Subspecialties: Nuclear magnetic resonance; Biophysical chemistry. Office: Yale U Box 6666 New Haven CT 06511

ALI, ABDUL WAHAB, physicist; b. Arbil, Iraq, Feb. 28, 1933; m. Marie G. Monte, 1958; children—Delair, Gianne. B.Sc., Higher Techrs. Coll., Baghdad, Iraq, 1953; M.Sc., U. Md., 1961, Ph.D., 1965. Research assoc. Catholic U., Washington, 1965-66, research asst. prof. physics, 1966-68, research assoc. prof., 1968-69; research physicist Naval Research Labs., Washington, 1969—, sr. physicist cons. Plasma Physics div., 1974-84. Contbr. articles to profl. jours. Pres. Kurdish-Am. Soc., Washington, 1975-77. Subspecialties: Plasma physics; Theoretical physics. Home: 11416 Spur Wheel Ln Potomac MD 20854 Office: Naval Research Lab Washington DC 20854

ALIG, ROGER CASANOVA, physicist, electrical engineer; b. Indpls., Nov. 7, 1941; s. Daniel Bell and Dora (Frank) A.; m. Marcia Pritchard, Dec. 22, 1963; children—Paul, Graham, Heidi. B.A., Wabash Coll., 1963; M.S., Purdue, U., 1965, Ph.D., 1967. Mem. tech staff RCA Labs., Princeton, N.J., 1967—. Patentee in field. Contbr. articles to profl. jours. Bd. dirs. Family Service Agy., Princeton, 1978—. Recipient Sarnoff medal RCA Corp., 1983vis. prof. OAS, Sao Carlos, Sao Paulo, 1970; NASA fellow, 1963. Mem. Am. Phys. Soc., Sigma Xi, Phi Beta Kappa, Tau Kappa Epsilon. Current work: Electron optics for cathode ray display tubes; theory of transport phenomena in semiconductors. Subspecialties: Computer-aided design; Condensed matter physics. Home: 17 Landing Ln Princeton NJ 08550 Office: RCA Labs Princeton NJ 08540

ALIKHAN, MAHMOOD, physician, consultant; b. Rampur, U.P., India, Nov. 15, 1945; came to U.S., 1970; s. Anwar and Nadir (Jehan) A.; m. Linda Dorothy Linn, Oct. 16, 1971; children—Leah, Loren. M.B., B.S., Dow Med. Coll., Karachi, Pakistan, 1968; M.P.H., John Hopkins U., 1981. Diplomate: Am. Bd. Internal Medicine. House officer cardiology and surgery Jinnah and Civil Hosp., Karachi, Pakistan, 1969-70; intern and resident in medicine Union Meml., Balt., 1970-73; NIH fellow in cardiology U. Vt., Burlington, 1973-75; asst chief clin. investigations USPHS Hosp., Balt., 1975-81; assoc. chief and dir. cardiac catheterization lab. USPHS, Balt., 1977-81; dir. cardiology floor and rehab. Greater Balt. Med. Ctr., 1982—; dir. Greater Balt. Med. Ctr. Med. Assoc., Towson, Md., 1982—; v.p. and dir. Clin. Assocs. P.A., Towson, 1982—. Fellow Am. Coll. Cardiology, Am. Coll. Chest Physicians, Am. Coll. Angiology; mem. ACP, Am. Fedn. Clin. Research. Current Work: Cardiovascular physiology; cardiac catheterization and angiography; cardiovascular epidemiology; cardiovascular diseases in the elderly. Subspecialties: Cardiology; Gerontology. Home: 1602 Pot Spring Rd Timonium MD 21093Office: Clin Assocs P A 660 Kenilworth Dr Towson MD 21204

ALIPHAS, AMNON, engineering scientist, educator; b. Mexico City, Sept. 19, 1953; came to U.S., 1976; s. Avner and Esther (Cymet) A.; m. Perla Brzezinski, Aug. 14, 1976; children—Avner, Tally. B.Sc. in Elec. Engring., Nat. U., Mexico City, 1976; M.Sc. in Elec. Engring., Stanford U., 1978, Ph.D. in Elec. Engring., 1981. Registered profl. engr. Sr. engr. Wang Labs., Lowell, Mass., 1981-83; sr. scientist signal processing Kurzweil Applied Intelligence, Waltham, Mass., 1983—; adj. prof. engring. Boston U., 1982—. Recipient Internat. Bible Contest award Israeli Govt., 1971; award Mexican govt., 1978. Mem. IEEE, Acoustics Speech and Signal Processing Assn. Current work: Speech recognition; speech compression; digital filtering structures; algorithms. Subspecialties: Algorithms; Artificial intelligence. Home: 18 Peregrine Rd Newton MA 02159 Office: Kurzweil Applied Intelligence Waltham MA 02154

ALKADHI, KARIM ABDEL, pharmacology educator, researcher; b. Baghdad, Iraq, July 29, 1938; came to U.S., 1965; s. Mohamed Saeed Alkadhi and Fatema Majeed; m. Ann L. Bragdon, Sept. 22, 1967; children—Selwa, Isam, Rheim. B.Sc., Coll. Pharmacy, Baghdad, 1960; M.Sc., U. Conn., 1967; Ph.D., SUNY-Buffalo, 1972. Asst. prof. Sch. Medicine U. Benghazi, Libya, 1973-75; asst. prof. Sch. Medicine, Mustansiryia U., Baghdad, 1975-78, assoc. prof., 1978-80; research assoc. prof. pharmacology U. Conn. Health Ctr., Farmington, 1980-81; asst. prof. pharmacology U. Houston, 1981—. Contbr. articles to profl. jours. Mem. Brit. Pharm. Soc., Soc. for Neurosci, Soc. Exptl. Biology and Medicine, Am. Soc. Pharmacology and Exptl. Therapeutics. Current work: Pharmacology and physiology of cholinergic synaptic transmission at sympathetic ganglia and neuromuscular junction of skeletal muscles. Subspecialties: Pharmacology; Neurophysiology. Office: Dept Pharmacology Univ Houston University Park Houston TX 77004

ALKALAY, DAVID, chemist; b. Sofia, Bulgaria, Sept. 15, 1928; came to U.S., 1957; s. Shelomo and Leah A.; m. Marcella D. Podolan, Mar. 30, 1961; children—John Edward. Chem. Engr., Sofia Poly., 1952; M.S. in Chemistry, U. Maine, 1959. Chemist, CIBA-Geigy Corp., Summit, N.J., 1961-68, lab. supr., 1969-71, sr. research scientist, Ardsley, N.Y., 1972-79, mgr. clin. pharmacokinetics and disposition, 1980—. Contbr. articles to profl. jours. Mem. Am. Soc. Mass Spectrometry, Am. Chem. Soc., Am. Soc. Clin. Pharmacology and Therapeutics, N.Y. Acad. Scis., Sigma Xi (pres. Westchester chpt. 1984-85). Current work: Analytical chemistry; biomedical mass spectrometry; human drug metabolism; pharmacokinetics. Subspecialties: Analytical chemistry; Pharmacokinetics. Home: 27 Revere Rd Ardsley NY 10502 Office: CIBA-Geigy Corp 444 Saw Mill River Rd Ardsley NY 10502

ALKANA, RONALD LEE, neuroscientist, pharmacologist, educator; b. Los Angeles, Oct. 17, 1945; s. Sam A. and Madelyn J. Davis; m. Linda Kelly, Sept. 12, 1970; 1 child, Alexander Philippe Kelly. Lic. pharmacist, Calif., Nev. Zoology student UCLA, 1966; Pharm.D. U. So. Calif., 1970; Ph.D. U. Calif.-Irvine, 1975; Postdoctoral fellow Nat. Inst. on Alcohol Abuse and Alcoholism U. Calif.-Irvine, 1974-76, resident assisting dir., div. neurochemistry, dept. psychiatry, 1976; asst. prof. pharmacology and toxicology Sch. Pharmacy U. So. Calif., Los Angeles, 1976-82, assoc. prof., 1982—; cons. Nat. Alcohol Research Center U. Calif. - Irvine. Contbr. articles on pharmacology and behavior to profl. jours. Nat. Inst. on Alcohol Abuse and Alcoholism grantee, 1980-85. Mem. Am. Soc. for Pharmacology and Exptl. Therapeutics, Research Soc. on Alcoholism, Am. Coll. Clin. Pharmacology, Internat. Soc. Biomed. Research on Alcoholism, Soc. for Neurosci., Sigma Xi. Current Work: Effects of drugs on brain and behavior, biological basis of behavior, hyperbaric induced antagonism of ethanol's behavioral effects, ethanol's effects on learning and memory, temperature dependence of ethanol's effect. Subspecialties: Neuropharmacology; Psychobiology. Office: 1985 Zonal Ave Los Angeles CA 90033

ALKON, DANIEL LEON, research scientist; b. Phila., Dec. 6, 1942. B.A., U. Pa., 1965; M.D., Cornell U., 1969. Intern, Mt. Sinai Hosp., N.Y.C., 1970; research assoc. Nat. Inst. Neurol. and Communicative Disorders and Stroke, NIH, Bethesda, Md., 1970-72, sr. staff fellow, 1972-74, sect. chief neural systems Lab of Biophysics, Woods Hole, Mass., 1975—. Recipient Commendation medal USPHS, 1981. Mem. Biophys. Soc., Soc. Gen. Physiology, Soc. Neurosci., Marine Biol. Lab. Corp., AAAS. Current work: Biophysical and biochemical basis of associative learning Subspecialty: Neurophysiology. Office: NIH Sect on Neural Systems Lab Biophysics Marine Biol Lab Woods Hole MA 02543

ALLAN, BARRY DAVID, physical chemist; b. Steubenville, Ohio, Jan. 20, 1935; s. John Young and Frances Lucy (Halbrunner) A.; m. Inge Elisabeth Bergeler, Aug. 5, 1961; children—Barbara Diane, Stephen Barry. B.S., Ariz. State U., 1956; M.S., U. Ala., 1964, Ph.D., 1968. Chemist White Sands Missile Range, N.Mex., 1956; aero. fuels researcher Army Missile Command, Redstone Arsenal, Ala., 1958-62, research chemist, 1962-68, group leader, 1968—; prof. J.C. Calhoun Coll., Decatur, Ala., 1969-73, Athens Coll., Ala., 1970-73, U. Ala., Huntsville, 1974-76; cons., 1965; reviewer NSF, 1973. Contbr. articles to profl. jours. Patentee in field. Active Huntsville Civic Assn., 1961. Served to capt. AUS, 1956-58. Recipient Army Research and Devel. Achievement award 1962, Navy commendation, 1968, Army commendation, 1971, 72. Mem. Am. Chem. Soc. (treas. 1969-73, pres. 1974-76), Combustion Inst., Pasteur Soc., Assn. U.S. Army, N.Y. Acad. Scis., Joint Army, Navy, NASA, Air Force Propellant Characterization Group on Fluids and Materials, Sigma Xi, Gamma Sigma Epsilon, Theta Chi. Current work: Advanced technology on propellants and propulsion systems. Subspecialties: Physical chemistry; Analytical chemistry. Office: US Army Missile Command AMSMI-RK Redstone Arsenal AL 35809

ALLAN, DOUGLAS CLIPPINGER, research physicist; b. Bryn Mawr, Pa., May 2, 1956; s. William Donald and Joyce (Clippinger) A.; m. Carol Lola Brinton, July 21, 1979. B.S., Hofstra U., 1978; Ph.D., MIT, 1982. Postdoctoral researcher MIT, Cambridge, 1982, U. Pa., Phila., 1982-84; sr. scientist Corning

Glass Works, N.Y., 1985—. Author: The Physics of Hydrogenated Amorphous Silicon II, 1984. NSF fellow, 1978. Mem. Am. Phys. Soc. Current work: Theoretical research and description of ground state and excitations of bonded materials; study of vibrational modes on semiconductor surfaces. Subspecialty: Condensed matter physics. Home: 147 W 5th St Corning NY 14830 Office: Corning Glass Works Sullivan Park Corning NY 14831

ALLAN, JAMES CLARK, engineering company executive; b. Arbroath, Scotland, Oct. 4, 1945; came to U.S., 1982; s. James Alexander and Margaret A. (Clark) A.; m. Lesley Melville Macfarlane, Mar. 9, 1968; children—Ian, Douglas. B.Sc. in Electronic Physics, U. St. Andrews, Scotland, 1966; M.Sc. in Control Systems, U. Edinburgh, Scotland, 1967. Design engr. Brit. Aircraft Corp., 1967-69; mfg. mgr. Burroughs Corp., Scotland, 1969-81; mgr. thin film heads Memorex Corp., Santa Clara, Calif., 1981-83; v.p. tech. Grenex Inc., Fremont, Calif., 1983—; lectr. Paisley Tech. Coll., Scotland, 1969-72. Patentee digital tape cassette drive, interpolative servo system, flexible disk cleaning system. Mem. IEEE. Republican. Current work: Disk drive techology, magnetic recording, technology on disk media, vertical and high density longitudinal recording, thin film head technology. Subspecialties: Magnetic physics; Applied magnetics. Office: Grenex Inc 47050 Kato Rd Fremont CA 94538

ALLARD, ROBERT WAYNE, geneticist, educator; b. Los Angeles, Sept. 3, 1919; s. Glenn A. and Alma A. (Roose) A.; m. Ann Catherine Wilson, June 16, 1944; children: Susan, Thomas, Jane, Gillian, Stacie. B.S., U. Calif.-Davis, 1941; Ph.D., U. Wis., 1946. From asst. to assoc. prof. U. Calif.-Davis, 1946—, prof. genetics, 1955—. Author books; contbr. articles to profl. jours. Served to lt. USNR. Recipient Crop Sci. award Am. Soc. Agronomy, 1964, DeKalb Disting. Career award Crop Sci. Soc. Am., 1983; Guggenheim fellow, 1954, 60; Fulbright fellow, 1955. Mem. Nat. Acad. Scis., Am. Acad. Arts and Sci., Am. Soc. Naturalists (pres. 1974-75), Genetics Soc. Am. (pres. 1983-84), Am. Acad. Arts and Scis., Phi Beta Kappa, Sigma Xi, Alpha Gamma Rho, Alpha Zeta. Democrat. Unitarian. Current Work: Population genetics, evolutionary genetics, plant breeding. Subspecialty: Genetics and genetic engineering (biology). Home: 2515 Bombadil Ln Davis CA 95616

ALLAUDEEN, HAMEEDSULTHAN SHEIK, molecular biologist; b. Punganur, India, Apr. 12, 1943; s. Hameed Sulthan and Jannath Beevi; m. Sadhika; children: Jerina, Nazima. Ph.D., Indian Inst. Sci., Bangalore, India, 1971. Research staff scientist molecular biophysics and biochemistry dept. Yale U., New Haven, 1971-73, lectr. pharmacology dept., 1975-77, asst. prof., 1977-; asst. div. natural product pharmacology Smith Kline & French Labs., Phila., 1982—. Contbr. articles to profl. jours. Leukemia Soc. Am. fellow, 1973-75. Mem. Am. Assn. Cancer Research, Am. Soc. Microbiology. Current Work: Molecular virology; regulation of DNA replication in tumor cells. Subspecialties: Cancer research (medicine); Molecular pharmacology. Home: 738 Champlain Dr King of Prussia PA 19403 Office: Smith Kline & French Labs Philadelphia PA 19101

ALLCOCK, HARRY REX, chemistry educator; b. Loughborough, Eng., Apr. 8, 1932; m. Noreen Raworth. B.Sc., U. London, 1953, Ph.D., 1956. Research scientist, then sr. research scientist Am. Cyanamid Co., Stamford, Conn., 1961-66; assoc. prof. chemistry Pa. State U., 1966-70, prof., 1970—, now Evan Pugh Prof. chemistry. Recipient award in polymer chemistry Am. Chem. Soc., 1985. Subspecialty: Polymer chemistry. Office: Pennsylvania State Univ Dept of Chemistry University Park PA 16802

ALLDREDGE, GERALD PALMER, physics educator, chemistry and materials science researcher; b. Hereford, Tex., Oct. 20, 1935; s. John Hobson and Mary Ruth (Palmer) A.; m. Mary McPhail Gray, June 18, 1983; children—Elizabeth C., Morgan M. B.A., Tex. Tech U., 1958, M.S., 1960; postgrad. U. Calif., 1958-59; Ph.D., Mich. State U., 1966. Grad. research asst. physics Tex. Tech U., Lubbock, 1959-60, Mich. State U., East Lansing, 1960-64; asst. prof. physics So. Ill. U., Carbondale, 1964-68; faculty research scientist physics U. Tex., Austin, 1968-75; assoc. prof. physics U. Mo.-Rolla, 1975-79, sr. investigator Ctr. for Materials Research, 1975-77; assoc. prof. physics U. Mo., Columbia, 1979—; resident research assoc. solid state sci. div. Argonne Nat. Lab., Lemont, Ill., part-time 1965, 66; guest prof. Tech. U. Denmark, Lyngby, 1983-84; vis. scientist theoretical physics div. U.K. Atomic Energy Research Establishment-Harwell, Didcot, Eng., 1984; vis. prof. physics U. Calif.-Irvine, 1984. Contbr. articles to profl. jours. Woodrow Wilson Nat. Fellowship Found. fellow, 1958; NSF/Mich. State U. fellow, 1962; research grantee NSF, Air Force Office Sci. Research, NATO, others. Mem. Am. Phys. Soc., Am. Chem. Soc., Materials Research Soc., Assn. for Computing Machinery, Am. Assn. for Engring. Edn., Soc. for Indsl. and Applied Math., Am. Assn. Physics Tchrs., AAAS, Am. Ceramic Soc. Am. Vacuum Soc., IEEE, Computer Soc., Sierra Club, Audubon Soc., Sigma Xi. Current work: Theoretical/computational studies of the physics and chemistry of solid surfaces and interfaces—including electronic structure, atomic structure and dynamics, interactions of molecules with surfaces, and interpretation of experimental probes of such physical systems with low-energy electron diffraction, photoelectron spectroscopies, inelastic electron-tunneling spectroscopy, and inelastic neutron scattering. Subspecialties: Condensed matter physics; Theoretical chemistry. Home: 600 Morningside Dr Columbia MO 65201 Office: Dept Physics and Astronomy Univ Missouri Columbia MO 65211

ALLEN, ARTHUR L., university dean, agricultural research administrator; b. Los Angeles, June 7, 1944; m. Gwen; children—Monica, Traci; m. Denise; 1 child, Christopher. B.S., Ark. AM&N Coll., Pine Bluff, Ark., 1966; M.S., Okla. State U., 1968; Ph.D., U. Ill., 1971. Assoc. prof. Langston U., Okla., 1971-74, Ala. A&M U., Normal, 1974-76; Title XII officer U. Ark.-Pine Bluff, 1977—, asst. dean for resident instrn., 1978-79, assoc. prof. div. agr. and tech., asst. dir. Research Ctr., asst. adminstr. 1890 Coop. Extension Programs, 1978-82, prof., adminstr. 1890 Agrl. Programs, 1982—, dean div.agr. and tech., 1982—. Mem. Am. Chem. Soc., Soil Sci. Soc. Am., Crop Sci. Soc.Am., Assn. Research Dirs., Nat. Assn. State Land-Grant Colls. and Univs., Sigma Xi, AlphaKappa Mu, Beta Kappa Chi, Gamma Sigma Delta. Subspecialties: Soil science; Agricultural research administration. Office: UAPB Research Ctr PO Box 82 U Ark-Pine Bluff Pine Bluff AR 71601

ALLEN, CHARLES EUGENE, educator; b. Burley, Idaho, Jan. 25, 1939; s. Charles William and Elsie Permelia (Fowler) A.; m. Connie Jeanette Block, June 19, 1966; children—Kerry Janelle, Tamara Sue. B.S., U. Idaho, 1961; M.S., U. Wis., 1963, Ph.D., 1966. Research asst. U. Wis., Madison, 1961-65; NSF fellow Commonwealth Sci. and Indsl. Research Orgn., Div. Food Research, Sydney, Australia, 1966-67; mem. faculty depts. animal sci. and food sci. and nutrition U. Minn., St. Paul, 1967—, prof., 1972—, dean, assoc. dir. Coll. Agr., 1984—; vis. prof. animal sci. Pa. State U., 1978. Contbr. articles profl. jours. Pres. Falcon Heights P.T.A., 1973-74. Mem. Am. Soc. Animal Sci., Nat. Inst. Food Technologists, Am. Meat Sci. Assn., Am. Inst. Nutrition, Minn. Inst. Food Technologists, Sigma Xi. Lutheran. Current work: Animal growth biology and biotechnology; food science and human nutrition. Subspecialties: Animal nutrition; Food science and technology. Office: 1420 Eckles Ave Saint Paul MN 55108

ALLEN, CHARLES MARSHALL, JR, biochemistry educator; b. Cortland, N.Y., Sept. 13, 1938; s. Charles M. and Doris M. Allen; m. Mary Janet Carr, Nov. 9, 1963; children—Christopher Paul, Benjamin David. B.S., Syracuse U., 1960; Ph.D., Brandeis U., 1964. Research fellow Harvard U., 1964-67; asst. prof. U. Fla., Gainesville, 1967-73, assoc. prof., 1973-79, prof. biochemistry, 1979—; vis. prof. U. Nottingham Eng., 1980-81. Contbr. articles to profl. jours. Grantee: NIH, NSF, 1967—. Current work: Enzymology, lipid metabolism; bio organic chemistry; enzyme mechanisms; metabolic regulation. Subspecialty: Biochemistry (medicine). Office: Dept Biochemistry J Hillis Miller Health Ctr Gainesville FL 32610

ALLEN, CLARENCE RODERIC, geologist, educator; b. Palo Alto, Cal., Feb. 15, 1925; s. Hollis Partridge and Delight (Wright) A. B.A., Reed Coll., 1949; M.S., Cal. Inst Tech., 1951, Ph.D., 1954. Asst. prof. geology U. Minn., 1954-55; mem. faculty Cal. Inst. Tech., 1955—, prof. geology and geophysics, 1964—; interim dir. Seismological Lab., 1965-67, acting chmn. division of geological scis., 1967-68; Chmn. cons. bd. earthquake analysis Cal. Dept. Water Resources, 1965-74; chmn. geol. hazards adv. com. for program Cal. Resources Agy., 1965-66; mem. earth scis. adv. panel NSF, 1965-68, chmn., 1967-68, mem. adv. com. environmental scis., 1970-72; mem. U.S. Geol. Survey adv. panel to Nat. Center Earthquake Research, 1966-75, Cal. Mining and Geology Bd., 1969-75, chmn., 1975; mem. task force on earthquake hazard reduction Office Sci. and Tech., 1970-71. Served to 1st lt. USAAF, 1943-46. Recipient G.K. Gilbert award seismic geology Carnegie Instn., 1960. Fellow Am. Geophys. Union, Geol. Soc. Am. (counselor 1968-70, pres. 1973-74), Am. Acad. Arts Scis.; mem. Am. Assn. Petroleum Geologists, Nat. Acad. Scis., Earthquake Engring. Research Inst., Seismological Soc. Am. (dir. 1970—, pres. 1975-76), Assn. Engring. Geologists, Nat. Acad. Engring., Soc. Exploration Geophysicists, Phi Beta Kappa. Current Work: Seismotectonics; Evaluation of seismic hazard. Subspecialties: Geophysics; Tectonics. Home: 1000 E California St Apt 306 Pasadena CA 91106

ALLEN, DONALD ORRIE, pharmacologist, educator; b. Belding, Mich., Jan. 11, 1939; s. Orrie Burt and Bessie E. (Elmendorf) A.; m. Arlene E. Stalberger, Dec. 30, 1961; children: Michael, Mark, Kelley, Paul. B.S., Ferris Inst., Big Rapids, Mich., 1962; Ph.D., Marquette U., Milw., 1967. Asst. prof. Ind. U. Sch. Medicine, 1967-72, asso. prof., 1972-75; prof. pharmacology U. S.C. Sch. Medicine, Columbia, 1975—, chmn. dept., 1977—. Contbr. articles to profl. jours. Grantee NIH; Grantee Am. Diabetes Assn. Mem. Am. Soc. Pharmacology and Exptl. Therapeutics, Internat. Soc. Biochem. Pharmacology, Southeastern Pharmacology Soc. Roman Catholic. Current Work: Control of metabolism, cyclic nucleotides, hormone action, adipose tissue, lipolysis. Subspecialties: Cellular pharmacology; Biochemistry (medicine). Office: Dept Pharmacology Sch Medicine Univ SC Columbia SC 29208

ALLEN, DOUGLAS MARK, electrochemical engineer; b. Dayton, Ohio, May 31, 1958; s. George Thomas and Lillie Mae (Daniels) A. B.S. in Mech. Engring., U. Dayton, 1980, M.S., 1982. Computer programmer U. Dayton Research Inst., 1976-80; electrochem. engr. Air Force Wright Aero. Labs., Wright Patterson AFB, Ohio, 1980—; cons. Corning Glass Co., Greenville, Ohio, 1982—, U. Dayton Sch. Engring., 1981—. Contbr. articles to profl. jours. Bd. dirs. Shaping the 80's, Dayton, 1982, Creativity 80's, Dayton, 1983. Recipient Sustained Superior Performance award U.S. Air Force, 1983, 84. Mem. AIAA, Mensa, Dayton Dressage and Combined Tng. Assn. Republican. Current work: Research and development of batteries and fuel cells for air force aerospace applications including satellites, aircraft and missiles, development of sodium/sulfur satellite batteries. Subspecialties: Aerospace engineering and technology; Materials. Home: 11588 Sweet Potato Ridge Rd Brookville OH 45309Office: Air Force Wright Aero Labs AFWAL/POOC Wright Patterson AFB OH 45449

ALLEN, DURWARD LEON, biologist, educator; b. Uniondale, Ind., Oct. 11, 1910; s. Harley J. and Jennie M. (LaTurner) A.; m. Dorothy Ellen Helling, Sept. 23, 1935; children—Stephen R., Harley W., Susan E. A.B., U. Mich., 1932; Ph.D., Mich. State Coll., 1937; L.H.D. (hon.), No. Mich. U., 1971; D.A. (hon.), Purdue U., 1985. Game research biologist Mich. Dept. Conservation, 1935-46; wildlife research biologist U.S. Fish and Wildlife Service, Laurel, Md., 1946-50, asst. chief br. wildlife research, Washington, 1951-54; prof. wildlife ecology Purdue U., West Lafayette, Ind., 1954—; Mem. Adv. Bd. on Nat. Parks, Monuments and Historic Sites, U.S. Dept. Interior, 1966-72, chmn., 1971-72; Chmn. Nat. Sci. Adv. Com. on Fish and Wildlife and Parks, U.S. Dept. Interior, 1975-76. Author: Michigan Fox Squirrel Management, 1943, Pheasants Afield, 1953, Our Wildlife Legacy, 1954, The Life of Prairies and Plains, 1967, Wolves of Minong, 1979; Editor: Pheasants in North America, 1956. Recipient medal of honor Angler's Club of N.Y., 1956. Fellow AAAS; mem. Wildlife Soc. (hon. life mem., pres. 1956-57, Annual Tech. Publ. award 1946, Annual Conservation Edn. award 1955, Leopold Meml. medal 1968), Am. Soc. Mammalogists, Ecol. Soc. Am., Washington Biologists' Field Club, Am. Inst. Biol. Scis., Am. Forestry Assn. (bd. dirs.), Wilderness Soc., Outdoors Writers Assn. Am. (Jade of Chiefs award 1968), Nature Conservancy, Conservation Found., Nat. Parks and Conservation Assn., Ind. Acad. Sci., Nat. Audubon Soc. (bd. dirs. 1975-84), Seminarium Botanicum, Sigma Xi, Phi Sigma, Xi Sigma Pi. Clubs: Boone and Crockett, Cosmos (Washington); Explorers (N.Y.C.). Current work: Species adaptations, predator-prey relationships, habits and biology of birds and mammals. Subspecialties: Resource conservation; Ecology (biology). Home: 1010 Windwood Lane West Lafayette IN 47906

ALLEN, GARY CURTISS, earth science educator, consultant; b. Stockton, Calif., July 18, 1939; s. Curtiss Wright and Helen Lucille (McElroy) A.; m. Ruth Lee Mayeux, June 5, 1965; children—Adrienne Lucille, Christopher Gary. B.S. in Chemistry, Stanford U., 1961; M.A. in Geology, Rice U., 1963; Ph.D., in Geochemistry, U., N.C., 1968. Sect. head div. mineral resources state of Va., Charlottesville, 1966-68; asst. prof. La. State U., New Orleans, 1968-72; assoc. prof. dept. earth scis. U. New Orleans, 1972-78, prof., 1978—; pres. Sunbelt Assoc. Inc., New Orleans, 1978—; dir. Am-Guy Mining Ltd., Georgetown, Cayman Island. Contbr. articles to profl. jours. Mem. St. Frances Cabrini Sch. Bd., New Orleans, 1979-82. NASA fellow, 1963-66; grantee various fed. agys. Mem. Geol. Soc. Am., Am. Chem. Soc., Mineral. Soc. Am., Geochem. Soc. Am., Nat. Asbestos Council, Sigma Xi (pres. U. New Orleans 1977-78). Current work: Research in metamorphic petrology; archeological geochemistry; environmental mineralogy. Subspecialties: Geochemistry; Petrology. Home: 6961 Mayo Blvd New Orleans LA 70126 Office: Dept Earth Scis U New Orleans New Orleans LA 70148

ALLEN, GARY IRVING, neurophysiologist; b. Lockport, N.Y., Apr. 7, 1942; s. Ralph Willard and Lois Marie (Chamberlin) A.; m. Elaine Irene Main, June 13, 1964; children: Michelle Irene, Elisa Joy, Scott Jeremy. B.S. in E.E, Cornell U., 1965; Ph.D. in Physiology, SUNY, Buffalo, 1969. Asst. prof. Lab. Neurobiology, dept. physiology Sch. Medicine, SUNY, Buffalo, 1971-75; asst. prof., dir. Lab. Neurobiology, dept. physiology Sch. Medicine, SUNY (Lab. Neurobiology), 1975-76; lectr., vis. scholar dept. physiology and anatomy U. Calif., Berkeley, 1976-79; dir. Christian Embassy at UN, 1979-83, pres. Christian Mission for UN, 1983—; adj. asst. prof. dept. physiology N.Y. Med. Coll., Valhalla, N.Y., 1981-85. Contbr. articles to profl. jours. Mem. Am. Physiol. Soc., Soc. for Neurosci., Internat. Brain Research Orgn., Am. Sci. Affiliation (Met. N.Y. exec. council 1983-84), Soc. Internat. Devel., Council Religion and Internat. Affairs, Asia Soc., Am.-Nepal Soc. Current Work: Cerebro-cerebellar loops in initiation and control of movement. Subspecialty: Neurophysiology. Home: 965 Knollwood Rd White Plains NY 10603

ALLEN, GIL C., chiropractor, neurophysiologist; b. Queens, N.Y., July 2, 1945; s. Harrison and Ethel (Garby) A.; m. Rise Hepner, May 30, 1968; children: Jonathan, Douglas. B.A., Queens Coll., 1969, M.A., 1972; M.S., U. Bridgeport, 1980; Ph.D., CUNY, 1978; D.C., Nat. Coll. Chiropractic, 1966. Practice chiropractics, nutrition, applied kinesiologist, neurophysiologist, acupuncturist, Flushing, N.Y., 1968—. Mem. Am. Biomagnetic Assn., Am. Soc. Clin. Hypnosis, N.Y. Acad. Scis., Council on Nutrition, Council on Roentgenology, Tridology Soc. Am., Am. Chiropractic Assn., Soc. Neurosci., Found. Chiropractic Edn. and Research, N.Y. State Chiropractic Assn. (pres. Queens dist.). Current Work: Developing new treatment procedures to better handle chronic ailments as well as the physical, emotional, biochemical, biomechanical and psychological concomitants of such ailments; all encompassing holistic health care concepts. Subspecialty: Neurophysiology. Office: 142-01 37th Ave Flushing NY 11354

ALLEN, HENRY LEIGH, researcher; b. Phila., Apr. 26, 1945; s. Sydney and Edith (Gamson) A.; 1 child, Lisa E. B.A., Pa. State U., 1967; V.M.D., U. Pa., 1971. Lic. veternarian, Pa. Resident in pathology U. Pa. Veterinary Sch., Phila., 1971-73, instr., Pathology, 1973-75; research fellow Merck Sharp and Dohme Research Labs., West Point, Pa., 1975-77, sr. research fellow, 1977-79, dir. toxicology and pathology, 1979-84, sr. investigator, 1984—. Contbr. articles to profl. jours. Subspecialties: Pathology (veterinary medicine); Toxicology (medicine). Office: 44-1 MSDRL West Point PA 19486

ALLEN, HOWARD JOSEPH, cancer research scientist; b. Gloversville, N.Y., Mar. 11, 1941; s. Howard Joseph and Beatrice (Leona) A.; m. June Ellen Lansing, Dec. 21, 1959; children—Tina, Theresa, Howard III, Scott, Craig (dec.). B.S., SUNY-Albany, 1965; Ph.D., SUNY-Buffalo, 1970. Research assoc. Fla. State U., 1970-72; cancer research scientist Roswell Park Meml. Inst., Buffalo, 1970—; asst. prof. biochemistry, SUNY-Buffalo, 1974—; research prof. cancer Niagra U., N.Y., 1976—. Contbr. articles to profl. jours. Fellow NIH, SUNY-Buffalo Faculty. Mem. Am. Cancer Research, Am. Soc. Cell Biology, Am. Soc. Biol. Chemists, Am. Zoology Soc., Am. Chem. Soc. Democrat. Roman Catholic. Current work: Chemistry genetics and function of mammalian tissue lectins. Subspecialties: Biochemistry (biology); Cell biology. Home: 372 Fletcher St Tonawanda NY 14150 Office: Roswell Park Meml Inst 666 Elm St Buffalo NY 14263

ALLEN, JONATHAN, electrical engineering educator; b. Hanover, N.H., June 4, 1934; married, 1960; 2 children. A.B., Dartmouth Coll., 1956, M.S., 1957; Ph.D. in Elec. Engring, MIT, 1968. Supr. human factors engring. Bell Telephone Labs., 1961-67; asst. prof. elec. engring. MIT, Cambridge, 1968-72, assoc. prof. elec. engring., 1972-75, prof., 1975—, assoc. dir. research lab. electronics, 1976-81, dir., 1981—; cons. Lincoln Lab., IBM, Data Gen. Corp. Fellow IEEE. Subspecialty: Electronics. Office: Dept Elec Engring MIT Cambridge MA 02139*

ALLEN, LEW, JR., laboratory executive, former air force officer; b. Miami, Fla., Sept. 30, 1925; s. Lew and Zella (Holman) A.; m. Barbara Frink, Aug. 19, 1949; children: Barbara Allen Miller, Lew, Marjorie Allen Dauster, Christie Allen Jameson, James Gilbert. B.S., U.S. Mil. Acad., 1946; M.S., U. Ill., 1952, Ph.D., 1954. Commd. 2d lt. USAAF, 1946; advanced through grades to gen. USAF, 1977; physicist AEC, Los Alamos, 1954-57, Air Force Weapons Lab., 1957-61; mem. staff Office Sec. Def., 1961-65; with Air Force Space Program, 1965-72; dir. Nat. Security Agy., Ft. Meade, Md., 1973-77; comdr. Air Force Systems Command, 1977; vice chief staff USAF, 1978, chief staff, 1978-82, ret., 1982; dir. Jet Propulsion Lab., Pasadena, Calif., 1982—. Decorated D.S.M. (5), Legion of Merit with 2 oak leaf clusters, Joint Service Commendation medal. Mem. Am. Phys. Soc., Am. Geophys. Union, Nat. Acad. Engring., Sigma Xi. Subspecialty: Space science research management. 1040 S Arroyo Blvd Pasadena CA 91105 Office: Jet Propulsion Lab California Inst Tech 4800 Oak Grove Dr Pasadena CA 91125

ALLEN, ROBERT ARTHUR, clinical psychologist; b. Stockton, Calif., July 24, 1952; s. Arthur Hagy and Peggy Irmgard (Oetjen) A.; m. Joann May Meluskey, Aug. 3. B.A., DePauw U., 1975; M.A., U. Ottawa, Ont., Can., 1977; Ph.D., Calif. Sch. Profl. Psychology, 1980. Lic. clin. psychologist, Calif. Postdoctoral intern/research asst. Stanford U. Med. Center, 1977-81; psychologist No. Calif. Psychol. Services, San Francisco, 1979-82, pvt. practice clin. psychology, Cupertino, Calif. Contbr. articles to profl. jours. Mem. Am. Psychol. Assn., Calif. Psychol. Assn., Biofeedback Soc. Am., Am. Assn. Study Headache. Current Work: Research in psychobiology and neuropsychology. Subspecialties: Neuropsychology; Psychobiology. Office: 20333 Stevens Creek Blvd Cupertino CA 95014

ALLEN, ROBERT BURNELL, research scientist; b. Pitts., Sept. 16, 1951; s. James Burnell and Mary (Thomas) A.; m. Letty Carmen Carrera, Dec. 29, 1978; 1 child, Dianne K.; stepchildren—Daniel J. Espinoza, Dean F. Espinoza, B.A., Reed Coll., 1973; Ph.D., U. Calif.-San Diego, 1978. Mem. tech. staff Bell Labs., Murray Hill, N.J., 1978-83, Bell Communication Research, Morristown, N.J., 1984—. Editor-in-chief Assn. Computer Machinery Transactions on Office Info. Systems, 1984—. Subspecialties: Information systems, storage, and retrieval (computer science); Human factors engineering. Office: Bell Communications Research 2A-367 Morristown NJ 07960

ALLEN, ROBERT CARTER, pathology educator; b. Natick, Mass., Feb. 5, 1930; s. Roy Henry and Helen Louise (Carter) A.; m. Carol Lillian Chase, Oct. 26, 1956; children: Robert Carter, Roger, Chase. B.S., U. Vt., 1952, M.S., 1955; Ph.D., Va. Poly. Inst., 1959. Postdoctoral fellow Jackson Meml. Lab., Bar Harbor, Maine, 1960-62; sr. scientist Oak Ridge (Tenn.) Nat. Lab., 1962-68, Oak Ridge Tech. Enterprises Corp., 1968-73; assoc. prof. pathology Med. U. S.C., Charleston, 1973-76, prof. pathology, 1981—, prof., chmn. lab. animal medicine, 1976-85; cons. Corning Med., Sullivan Park, N.Y., 1979, Upjohn, Kalamazoo, Mich, 1980, E.I. duPont de Nemours & Co., Wilmington, Del., 1982. Author, sr. editor: Electrophoresis, 1981, Marker Proteins of Immflamation, 1982, Electrophoresis and Isoelectric Focusing, 1974; sr. author: Gel Electrophoresis and Isoelectric Focusing of Proteins, 1984; assoc. editor: Electrophoresis, 1980—. Mem. Electrophoresis Soc. (pres. 1980-82, sec.-treas. 1980—). Clubs: Sertoma (Charleston, S.C.); Hobcaw Yacht (Mount Pleasant, S.C.) (mem. bd. 1975-76). Current Work: Development of methodology for the study of genetic polymorphisms and molecular expressions of disease. Subspecialties: Genetics and genetic engineering (medicine); Pathology (medicine). Home: 501 Palm Blvd Isle of Palms SC 29451 Office: Med U SC 171 Ashley Ave Charleston SC 29425

ALLEN, ROBERT CHARLES, physician, biochemist; b. Pueblo, Colo., Aug. 12, 1945; s. Noel Charles and Gladys Louise (Puig) A.; m. Joan Marie Lindsay, June 26, 1976; children—Robert Lindsay, Christina Marie. B.S., Southeastern La. U., 1967; Ph.D., Tulane U., 1973, M.D., 1977. Diplomate Am. Bd. Pathology. Assoc. in biochemistry, Tulane U., New Orleans, 1973-76; commd. capt. M.C. U.S. Army, 1977, advanced through grades to maj., 1980; intern Brooke Army Med. Center, Ft. Sam Houston, Tex., 1977-78, resident in clin. pathology, 1983-85; infectious disease officer U.S. Army Inst. Surg. Research, 1978—. Contbr. articles to profl. jours. Served with U.S. Army, 1968-70. Recipient Clin. Pathology award La. Pathology Soc., 1977; Leah Seidman award Tulane U., 1977. Mem. Am. Assn. Immunology, Am. Chem. Soc., AMA, Am. Soc. Biol. Chemistry, Am. Soc. Photobiology, Am. Soc. Microbiology, Biophys. Soc., Surg. Infection Soc., Reticuloendothelial Soc., Sigma Xi. Discovered the phenomenon of native granulocytic leukocyte luminescence. Current Work: Excited state and radical chemistry; chemiluminescence and single photon counting; biological redox mechanisms; information aspects of humoral immune systems; phagocyte microbicidal mechanisms. Subspecialties: Infectious diseases; Biochemistry (medicine).

ALLEN, THERESA OHOTNICKY, research psychologist; b. Torrington, Conn., Apr. 27, 1948; d. Frank Richard and Helen Theresa (Drozdenko) Ohotnicky; m. Thomas Atherton Allen, Aug. 12, 1972; children: Melanie Atherton, Abigail Baldwin. B.A., U. Conn., 1970; M.S., Villanova U., 1975; Ph.D., Duke U., 1978. Fellow in neurol. sci. U. Pa., Phila., 1978-80, fellow in psychology, 1980-81, research assoc. dept. psychology, 1981-84; research specialist dept. elec. and computer engring. Drexel U., 1983-84; biomed. research cons. to bus. and industry, 1985—. Contbr. articles in field to profl. jours. Mem. AAAS, Animal Behavior Soc., Soc. Study of Reproduction, Soc. for Neurosci., Sigma Xi. Subspecialties: Neurobiology; Ethology. Office: 728 Dodds Ln Gladwyne PA 19035

ALLEN, THOMAS CORT, JR., plant pathologist; b. Madison, Wis., Oct. 28, 1931; s. Thomas Cort and Esther Elsa (Liening) A.; m. Donna Jeanne Hillebrand, June 27, 1953; 1 dau., Kathleen Deanne Gillispie. B.S., U. Wis., Madison, 1953; Ph.D., U. Calif., Davis, 1956. Head microbiology sect. Agrl. Research Lab., Stauffer Chem. Co., Mountain View, Calif., 1958-62; asst. prof. dept. botany and plant pathology Oreg. State U., Corvallis, 1962-66, assoc. prof., 1966-76, prof., 1976—; community edn. art instr. Linn-Benton Community Coll., 1972—; artist-in-residence Coll. Agrl. Scis., Oreg. State U., 1983—. Pres. Corvallis Arts Center, 1963-64. Served as 1st lt. U.S. Army, 1956-58. Allied Chem. Co. fellow, 1957; NSF fellow, 1964; NATO sr. fellow, 1970. Fellow Royal Hort. Soc. London; mem. Am. Phytopath. Soc., Electron Microscopy Soc. Am., Oreg. Electron Microscopists (pres.), Watercolor Soc. Oreg. (pres.), Sigma Xi (chpt. pres., regional lectr.). Republican. Congregationalist. Club: Soc. Preservation Barbershop Quartet Singing in Am. Lodge: Rotary. Patentee in field. Current Work: Creation of virus-free plants in tissue culture, electronmicroscopy, ultrastructural pathology, ornamentals and potatoes. Subspecialties: Plant virology; Plant pathology. Home: 3989 SW Fairhaven Ct Corvallis OR 97333 Office: Dept Botany Oreg State U Corvallis OR 97331

ALLER, LAWRENCE HUGH, astronomer; b. Tacoma, Sept. 24, 1913; s. Leslie E. and Lenabelle (Davis) A.; m. Rosalind Duncan Hall, Apr. 24, 1941; children—Hugh Duncan, Raymond Donald, Gwendolyn Jean. A.B., U. Calif., 1936; M.A., Harvard, 1938, Ph.D., 1942. Jr. fellow Soc. Fellows, Harvard U., 1939-42, instr. physics, 1942-43; research physicist U. Calif. at Berkeley, 1943-45; asst. prof. astronomy Ind. U., 1945-48; asso. prof. U. Mich., 1948-54, prof. astronomy, 1954-62; vis. prof. Australian Nat. U., Canberra, 1960-61, U. Toronto, 1961-62; prof. astronomy U. Calif. at Los Angeles, 1962—; Guest investigator Dominion Astrophys. Obs., 1951, Mt. Wilson Obs.; vis. prof. U. Sydney, U. Tasmania, 1968-69, U. Queensland, 1977-78; guest investigator C.S.I.R.O. Australia, 1968-69, 71, 77-78, Anglo-Australian Obs., 1978. Author: Atoms, Stars and Nebulae, 2d edit, 1971, Astrophysics, 1954, Gaseous Nebulae, 1956, Abundances of the Elements, 1961, Atmospheres of the Sun and Stars, 1963, Physics of Thermal Gaseous Nebulae, 1984. Mem. Internat. Astron. Union, Royal Astron. Soc., Am. Acad. Arts and Scis., Nat. Acad. Scis. Current Work: Determination of chemical compositions of nebulae stars; physical progress in attenuated nebulae plasmas. Subspecialty: Optical astronomy. Home: 18118 W Kingsport Dr Malibu CA 90265

ALLEY, KEITH EDWARD, anatomist; b. Palm Springs, Calif., June 27, 1943; s. William and Kathryn (Carmody) A.; m. Jean Lane Doyle, June 18, 1966; 1 son, Colin. D.D.S., U. Ill., 1968, Ph.D., 1972. Postdoctoral trainee U. Ill. Coll. Medicine, Chgo., 1968-72; spl. fellow in physiology U. Iowa, Iowa City, 1972-74; asst. prof. anatomy Case Western Res. U., Cleve., 1974-80, assoc. prof. oral biology, 1980-85; prof., chmn. dept. oral biology Ohio State U., Columbus, 1985—. Contbr. articles to profl. jours., chpts. to books. NIH grantee, 1977-82. Mem. Soc. Neurosci., AAAS, Internat. Assn. Dental Research. Current Work: Development of neuronal systems responsible for motor activity. Subspecialties: Comparative neurobiology; Oral biology. Home: 6924 Lakebrook Blvd Worthington OH 43085 Office: 305 W 12th Ave Columbus OH 43210

ALLIS, DEO G., ceramic engineer, glass technologist; b. Hornell, N.Y., Sept. 10, 1920; s. Deo G. and Carrie (Drake) Allis; m. Helen J. Seivers, Dec. 3, 1927; children—Karen June, Steven Lee. B.S., Alfred U., 1949. Lab technician Hartford Empire Co., Conn., 1949-50; tech. control staff Libbey Owens Ford, Charleston, W.Va., 1950-54, shift supt. window glass, 1954-56, furnace engr. ceramics, Toledo, Ohio, 1956—, ret., 1985; pvt. practice cons., Toledo, 1985—. Deacon, Grace Lutheran Ch. Served with AUS, 1942-45; PTO. Mem. Am. Ceramic Soc., (treas. Northwest Ohio sect. 1975-78), ASTM, Nat. Inst. Ceramic Engrs. Lodges: Masons, Shriners. Current work: Glass furnace design; material specification operation. Subspecialties: Ceramic engineering; Ceramics. Home: 2947 Elsie Ave Toledo OH 43613 Office: Libbey Owens Ford Co Inc 1701 E Broadway Toledo OH 43605

ALLISON, DAVID COULTER, surgeon; b. Detroit, June 2, 1942; s. William David and Dorothy (Watson) A.; m. Elizabeth Ward, Sept. 19, 1970; children: Tiffany, Elizabeth, Mathew. M.D., U. Mich., 1967; Ph.D., U. Chgo., 1976. Diplomate: Am. Bd. Surgery. Intern U. Chgo., 1967-68, resident, 1974-78, practice medicine, specializing in surgery, Albuquerque, 1978—; faculty dept. surgery U. N.Mex., Albuquerque, 1978—; asst. chief surgery VA Med. Center, Albuquerque, 1978—. Contbr. articles to profl. jours. Served to capt. U.S. Army, 1968-70. VA grantee, 1981, 82. Fellow ACS; mem. Histochemistry Soc., Soc. Cell Kinetics. Current Work: Cytometry of cancer and TCDD exposed cells to identify factors associated with tumor progression and cell damage. Subspecialties: Surgery; Cell biology (medicine). Office: Univ NM Med Sch 2211 Lomas Blvd NE Dept Surgery Albuquerque NM 87131

ALLMAN, NORRIS C., nuclear engineer; b. Bklyn., May 30, 1952; s. Bernard and Florence (Boxill) A.; m. Migail Igus, Apr. 24, 1976; 1 son, Ryan. B.S. in Physics, Poly. Inst. Bklyn., 1975, M.S. in Nuclear Engring. Engr. Pub. Service Co., Newark, 1976-77, lead engr., 1977-79, sr. engr., 1979-81, prin. staff radiation analyst, 1981—; instr. physics Essex County Coll. Mem. Am. Nuclear Soc., ASME, Health Physics Soc. Current Work: Provide health physics calculation to estimate environmental radiation levels outside nuclear power plants. Subspecialty: Nuclear fission. Home: 536 Pierson St Westfield NJ 07090 Office: 80 Park Plaza Suite T-22-A Newark NJ 07101

ALLMANN, DAVID WILLIAM, biochemist, educator; b. Peru, Ind., May 20, 1935; s. Frederick Carl and Eunice (Vermillion) A.; m. Mary Ann Van Der Weele, Feb. 11, 1956; children: Victoria Lynn, Judith Ann. B.S., Ind. U.-Bloomington, 1958, Ph.D., 1964. Postdoctoral researcher Inst. Enzyme Research, Madison, Wis., 1964-66, asst. prof., 1966-70; assoc. prof. biochemistry Ind. U. Sch. Medicine, Indpls., 1970-80, prof., 1980—. Contbr. numerous articles, abstracts to profl. jours. Nat. Inst. Dental Research grantee, 1977-83. Mem. Am. Assn. Dental Research (sec./treas. Pharmacology Toxicology and Therapeutics Group 1981-84, pres.-elect 1984-85, pres. 1985), Am. Assn. Dental Schs. (pres. Nutrition Sect. 1980, pres. pharmacology group 1985), Am. Inst. Nutrition, Am. Assn. Biol. Chemists, European Orgn. Caries Research. Clubs: Red Devil Rooters (Indpls.) (pres. 1982), Band Booster (Indpls.) (pres. 1976). Current Work: Determination of metabollic effects of Na F in vivo and in vitro. Subspecialty: Biochemistry (medicine). Home: 4101 Melbourne Rd Indianapolis IN 46208 Office: Dept Biochemistry Ind U Sch Medicine 635 Barnhill Dr Indianapolis IN 46223

ALLOCCA, JOHN ANTHONY, medical research scientist; b. Bklyn., Aug. 27, 1948; s. Frank and Dorothy (Aulicino) A.; married; children: Jennifer, Jerry. A.A.S., SUNY-Farmingdale, 1972; B.A., SUNY-Old Westbury, 1975; M.S., Poly. Inst. N.Y., 1979; D.Sc., Pacific Western U., 1981. Adminstr. Hofstra U., 1967-71; psychotherapist Creedmore State Hosp., 1975-76; biomed. engr. Doll Research Inc., 1971-77; research scientist Albert Einstein Coll. Medicine, 1977-78; research cons. L.I. Coll. Hosp., 1979-80; research scientist, tech. dir. pulmonary labs. Mt. Sinai Med. Center, 1980-82; research scientist Langer Biomech. Group, Inc., 1983-84; pres./research scientist Andromeda Research, Inc., 1984—. Mem. IEEE, Assn. Advancement Med. Instrumentation, AAAS, Am. Assn. Physicists in Medicine, N.Y. Acad. Scis. Current Work: Biomedical research, biophysics. Subspecialties: Neurology; Biophysics (physics). Home: 90 Moffett St Oyster Bay NY 11771

ALMEYDA, GUILLERMO FELIX, atmospheric science educator; b. Chincha, Per, Nov. 20, 1946; came to U.S. 1983; s. Santos and Margarita Almeyda; m. Mercedes E. Almeyda, Aug. 6, 1975. B.S., Colo. State U., 1970, M.S., 1972; Ph.D., U. Nev.-Reno, 1986. Asst. prof. Universidad Nacional Agraria, La Molina, Lima, Peru, 1972-74, assoc. prof., 1974-79, prof., 1979—; weather forecaster Panamericana TV, Lima, 1980-83; v.p. sci. com. Ministry of Interior, 1977-83. Contbr. articles to profl. jours. Mem. Accion Popular, Lima, 1980—. Mem. Am. Phys. Soc., Am. Meteorol. Soc., Sigma Xi. Current work: Research in modeling of stratus and cumulus clouds over the Pacific Ocean during El Niño phenomenum; boundary layer development. Subspecialty: Synoptic meteorology. Home: 1775 Evans Ave Apt 404 Reno NV 89512 Office: Desert Research Inst U Nev System Atmospheric Scis Center PO Box 60220 Reno NV 89506

ALPEN, EDWARD LEWIS, biophysicist, educator; b. San Francisco, May 14, 1922; s. Edward Lawrence and Margaret Lilly (Shipley) A.; m. Wynella June Dosh, Jan. 6, 1945; children: Angela Marie, Jeannette Elise. B.S., U. Calif., Berkeley, 1946, Ph.D., 1950. Br. chief, then dir. biol. and med. scis. Naval Radiol. Def. Lab., San Francisco, 1952-68; mgr. environ. and life scis. Battelle Meml. Inst., Richland, Wash., 1968-69, asso. dir., then dir. Pacific N.W. div., 1969-75; dir. Donner Lab., U. Calif., Berkeley; also asso. dir. Lawrence Berkeley Lab., 1975—; prof. biophysics U. Calif., Berkeley, 1975—, prof. radiology, San Francisco, 1976—; mem. Nat. Council Radiol. Protection, 1969—; Mem. Gov. Wash. Council Econ. Devel., 1973-75; bd. dirs. Wash. Bd. Trade, 1973-76. Author papers, abstracts in field. Served to capt. USNR, 1942-46, 50-51. Recipient Navy Sci. medal, 1962, Disting. Service medal Dept. Def., 1963, Sustaining Members medal Assn. Mil. Surgeons, 1971; fellow Guggenheim Found., 1960-61; sr. fellow NSF, 1958-59. Fellow Calif. Acad. Scis.; mem. Bioelectromagnetics Soc. (pres. 1979-80), Am. Physiol. Soc., Radiation Research Soc., Soc. Exptl. Biology and Medicine, Biophys. Soc., Am. Philatelic Soc., Sigma Xi. Episcopalian. Current Work: Radiation biology. Subspecialty: Biophysics (physics). Home: 1182 Miller Ave Berkeley CA 94708 Office: 466 Donner U Calif Berkeley CA 94720

ALPER, ALLEN MYRON, precision materials company executive; b. N.Y.C., Oct. 23, 1932; s. Joseph and Pauline (Frohlich) A.; m. Barbara Marshall, Dec. 20, 1959; children: Allen Myron, Andrew Marshall. B.S., Bklyn. Coll., 1954; Ph.D. (Univ. fellow, Dyckman Inst. scholar, Univ. Pres's. scholar), Columbia U., 1957. Sr. mineralogist Corning Glass Works, N.Y., 1957-59, research mineralogist, 1959-62, mgr. ceramic research, sr. research asso., 1962-69; with GTE Sylvania Inc. div. Sylvania Inc., Towanda, Pa., 1969—, chief engr., 1971-72, dir. research and engring., 1972-78, mgr. ops., from 1978; now pres. GTE Walmet, Royal Oak, Mich.; mem. Pa. Gov's Adv. Panel on Materials, 1971—; chmn. adv. com. Materials Research Lab., Pa. State U.; mem. adhoc adv. com. Phase Equilibria Data Center, 1983. Editor: Phase Diagrams: Materials Science and Technology, 1970, High Temperature Oxides, 1970-71; editorial bd.: High Temperature Sci. jour, 1969—, High Temperature Chemistry, 1973—, Materials Handbook, 1974—; editor: Materials Sci. and Tech. Series, 1972—; contbr. articles to profl. jours. Mem. exec. bd. Gen. Sullivan council Boy Scouts Am. Recipient Bklyn. Coll. award Disting. Achievement, 1983; N.Mex. Bur. Mines. grantee, 1954-57; also fellow. Fellow Am. Ceramic Soc., Geol. Soc. Am., Am. Inst. Chemists; mem. Brit. Ceramic Soc., Am. Soc. Metals, Am. Chem. Soc., Sigma Xi. Presbyterian. Club: Towanda Country. Patentee in field. Current Work: Ceramic, carbides, nitrides, phase equilibria, new compounds, composites, new materials, high temperature materials (research, development and engineering). Subspecialties: Composite materials; High-temperature materials. Home: 880 Great Oaks Blvd Rochester MI 48063 Office: GTE Walmet Royal Oak MI 48068

ALPER, HOWARD, chemistry educator; b. Montreal, Que, Can., Oct. 17, 1941; s. Max and Frema (Weinstein) A.; m. Anne Elizabeth, June 4, 1966; children: Ruth, Lara. B.Sc. in Chemistry with honors, Sir George Williams U., Can., 1963; Ph.D., McGill U., 1967. NATO postdoctoral fellow, 1967-68; asst. prof. SUNY-Binghamton, 1968-71, assoc. prof., 1971-74; assoc. prof. chemistry U. Ottawa, Ont., Can., 1975-77, prof., 1978—, chmn. dept., 1982-85. Contbr. 201 articles to sci. jours. Recipient E.W.R. Steacie award Natural Scis. and Engring. Research Council Can., 1980; John Simon Guggenheim fellow, 1985—. Fellow Royal Soc. Can., Mem. Am. Chem. Soc., mem. Chem. Inst. Can. (inorganic chemistry award 1980, catalysis award 1984), Chem. Soc. (London). Patentee in field (5). Current Work: Metal complexes as catalysts, reagents, and intermediates in synthesis; phase transfer catalysis. Subspecialties: Organic chemistry; Inorganic chemistry. Office: 365 Nicholas St Ottawa ON KIN 9B4 Canada

ALPHIN, REEVIS STANCIL, pharmacologist, drug. co. adminstr.; b. Mt. Olive, N.C., Apr. 21, 1929; s. Fred and Carla (Dail) A.; m. Barbara Gilliam, Sept. 3, 1955; children: Robert Stancil, Carla Gilliam. B.A., U. N.C., 1951; M.A., Duke U., 1955; Ph.D., Med. Coll. Va., 1966. Pharmacologist Eli Lilly Co., Indpls., 1956-60; group mgr. pharmacology A.H. Robins Co., Richmond, Va., 1960-71, asso. dir. pharmacology, 1971—. Contbr. numerous articles to profl. publs. Served to capt. USAF, 1951-53. Mem. AAAS, N.Y. Acad. Scis., Am. Physiol. Soc., Am. Pharmacology Soc. Presbyterian. Lodge: Masons. Patentee in field. Current Work: Research in area of gastrointestinal pharmacology. Subspecialties: Molecular pharmacology; Gastroenterology.

AL SAADI, ABDUL AMIR, clinical geneticist, cytogeneticist; b. Baqubah, Iraq, Oct. 20, 1935; s. Zahra J. and Majeed S. A.S.; m. Karen Eileen Svendsen, Nov. 20, 1961; children: Neda, Yasmin, Sami, Laith. B.Sc. magna cum laude, U. Baghdad, 1955; M.A., U. Kans., 1959; Ph.D., U. Mich., 1963. Research asso. U. Mich., 1963-65, asst. prof., 1965-70; chief genetics William Beaumont Hosp., Royal Oak, Mich., 1970—; dir. Sch. Histotech., 1976—; clin. prof. Wayne State U., 1973—, Oakland U., 1977—. Contbr. numerous articles to profl. jours., chpts. to books. Mem. Am. Soc. Human Genetics, Am. Soc. Cell Biology, Am. Assn. Cancer Research, Tissue Culture Assn., AAAS, Am. Thyroid Assn., Am. Fedn. Clin. Research. Current Work: Clinical genetics, role of chromosomal abnormalities in cancer. Subspecialties: Genetics and genetic engineering (medicine); Cell biology (medicine). Home: 2325 Adare St Ann Arbor MI 48108 Office: William Beaumont Hosp Royal Oak MI 48072

AL-SARRAF, MUHYI, oncologist, educator, researcher; b. Baghdad, Iraq, Sept. 15, 1938; came to U.S., 1963, naturalized, 1971; s. Abdul Hussien K. and Neisemah J. (Jawad) Al-S.; m. Ellen Grace Connors, Aug. 29, 1976; children: Renee, Ramsey. M.B., Ch.B., Baghdad U., 1961. Diplomate: Am. Bd. Internal Medicine.; Lic. physician, Mich., Ill. Intern Providence Hosp., Washington, 1963-64; resident in internal medicine Grace Hosp., Detroit, 1964-67; fellow in oncology Wayne State U., Detroit, 1967-68; Detroit Inst. Cancer Research, 1967-68; instr. oncology Wayne State U., 1968-69, asst. prof., 1970-73, assoc. prof., 1973-81, prof., 1981—; mem. Met. Detroit Cancer Control Program, Comprehensive Cancer Center Met. Detroit; vis. prof. Med. City Teaching Hosp. and Med. Coll., Baghdad U., 1975, U. Okla. Health Scis. Center and Okla. Med. Research Found., 1975, Cancer Control Agy. B.C., Vancouver, 1975; chief oncology div., acting chief hematology div. King Faisal Specialist Hosp. and Research Center, Riyadh, Saudi Arabia, 1975-76; mem. diagnostic research adv. com. div. cancer biology and diagnosis Nat. Cancer Inst., NIH, HEW, 1980—; mem. staff Grace, Detroit Gen., Harper, Hutzel hosps.; cons. VA. Author: Immunosuppressive Therapy, 1971; contbr. articles and abstracts to profl. jours., chpts. to books. Fellow Royal Coll. Physicians Can., ACP.; mem. Wayne County Med. Soc., Mich. Med. Soc., Am. Soc. Clin. Oncology, Am. Assn. Cancer Research, Detroit Physiol. Soc., Am. Assn. Cancer Edn., Am. Soc. Preventive Oncology (founding mem.), S.W. Oncology Group, Radiation Therapy Oncology Group. Current Work: Teaching and tng. med. oncologists, clin. trials, tumor markers, tumor immunology. Subspecialties: Cancer research (medicine); Chemotherapy. Home: 2952 Westview Ct N Bloomfield Hills MI 48013 Office: 3990 John R St Detroit MI 48201

ALSPAUGH, MARGARET ANN, immunologist, educator, researcher; b. Detroit, Apr. 7, 1938; d. Robert Eugene and Frances (Zemanek) A. B.A. in Biology, U. Hawaii, 1965; Ph.D. in Immunology (NIH predoctoral fellow), Wash. State U., 1972; now student U. Mo.-Columbia Sch. Medicine. Asst. in biology Eastern Mich. U., 1958-59, asst. in chemistry, 1959-61; fellow Scripps Clinic and Research Found., 1972-77; asst. prof. medicine and microbiology La. State U., 1977-79, assoc. prof, 1979-80, dir. Clin. Rheumatology Lab., 1977-80; assoc. prof. medicine and pathology, assoc. scientist Cancer Research Center, U. Mo., Columbia, 1980—, co-dir. Antinuclear Antibody Lab., 1980—; cons. Abbott Labs. Contbr. chpt., articles to profl. publs. NIH postdoctoral fellow, 1972-75; Am. Assn. Immunologists travel fellow, 1974; Arthritis Found. fellow, 1975-78. Mem. Am. Rheumatism Assn., Am. Assn. Immunologists, Am.Fedn. Clin. Research. Discovered antigen-antibody systems. Current Work: Research on role of discovered antigen-antibody systems in pathogenesis of forms of arthritis and breast cancer; research projects on melanoma. Subspecialties: Immunology (medicine); Rheumatology.

ALTAN, TAYLAN, mechanical engineer; b. Trabzon, Turkey, Feb. 13, 1938; came to U.S., 1962, naturalized, 1971; s. Seref and Sadife (Baysal) A.; m. Susan Barbara Borah, July 18, 1964; children: Peri, Aylin. Diploma Engr., Tech. U. Hannover, 1962; Ph.D., U. Calif., Berkeley, 1966. Research scientist E.I. duPont de Nemours & Co., Wilmington, Del., 1966-68; sr. research leader Battelle Columbus Lab., Columbus, Ohio, 1968—; adj. prof. Ohio State U., 1977—. Co-author: Forging Equipment, Materials and Practices, 1973; sr. author: Metalforming: Fundamentals and Applications, 1983. Mem. Internat. Prodn. Engring. Research Inst., Am. Soc. Metals (chmn. forging com. 1978—), Soc. Mfg. Engrs., ASME (chmn. prodn. div. 1976). Current Work: Forging, extrusion, rolling, sheet metal forming, computer aided design and manufacturing, materials processing, behavior of materials. Subspecialties: Materials processing; Solid mechanics. Home: 1380 Sherbrook Pl Columbus OH 43209 Office: 505 King Ave Columbus OH 43201

ALTEROVITZ, SAMUEL ADAR, physicist; b. Bucharest, Roumania, Aug. 25, 1939; came to U.S., 1981; s. Nathan and Bracha (Schiller) A.; m. Dalia Grinberg, Oct. 6, 1970; children—Gil, Ron. M.Sc., Hebrew U., Jerusalem, 1964; Ph.D., Tel Aviv U., 1971. Sr. research assoc. NASA, Cleve., 1976-78, research physicist, 1983—; sr. lectr. Tel Aviv U., 1978-81, assoc. prof., 1982-83; sr. scientist U. Nebr., Lincoln, 1981-82. Contbr. chpts. to books, articles to profl. jours. Recipient Young Scientist award Bath Sheva de Rotschild Fund, Tel-Aviv, 1974. Mem. Am. Phys. Soc. Jewish. Current work: Semiconducting and superconducting materials, especially at low temperature. Subspecialties: Condensed matter physics; Low temperature physics. Home: 19219 Story Rd Rocky River OH 44116 Office: NASA Lewis Research Ctr MS 54-5 21000 Brook Park Rd Cleveland OH 44135

ALTMAN, LEONARD, allergist, educator; b. Fresno, Calif., Sept. 1, 1944; s. Martin and Ida (Sharnoff) A.; m. Gaylene Bouska, Dec. 26, 1970; children: Jonathan D., Matthew C. B.A., U. Pa., 1965; M.D. cum laude, Harvard U., 1969. Diplomate: Am. Bd. Internal Medicine, 1975, Am. Bd. Allergy and Immunology, 1980. Intern U. Wash. Affiliated Hosps., Seattle, 1969-70, resident in medicine, 1970-71; chief med. resident and instr. medicine Harborview Med. Ctr., 1974-75, asst. prof. medicine div. allergy and infectious diseases dept. medicine, 1975-79, assoc. prof. medicine, 1979—, chief allergy div., 1979—; research assoc. immunology sect. lab. Microbiology and Immunology Nat. Inst. Dental Research, NIH, Bethesda, Md., 1971-73, sr. research assoc., 1973-74. Contbr. articles to profl. jours. Served to lt. comdr. USPHS, 1971-74. Fellow Am. Acad. Allergy, ACP; mem. Am. Assn. Immunologists, Western Soc. Clin. Research, AAAS, Am. Fedn. Clin. Research, Reticuloendothelial Soc., Puget Sound Allergy Soc. (pres. 1977), Infectious Disease Soc. Am., King County Med. Soc., Wash. State Med. Assn. Current Work: Phagocyte function, lung injury, leukocyte chemotaxis. Subspecialties: Immunology (medicine); Allergy. Home: 1015 Belmont Pl E Seattle WA 98102 Office: Dept Medicine U Wash Seattle WA 98195

ALTSCHULER, MARTIN DAVID, med. physicist, educator; b. Bklyn., Feb. 25, 1940; s. Frank Philip and Sarah Gertrude (Cloder) A.; m. Susan Jane, Sept. 2, 1962; children: Steven Jeffrey, Daniel Lewis, Rachel Lyra. B.S. summa cum laude, Poly. Inst. Bklyn., 1960; M.S., Yale U., 1961, Ph.D., 1964. Scientist High Altitude Obs., Nat. Center Atmospheric Research, Boulder, Colo., 1965-76; assoc. prof. adj. dept. astrogeophysics U. Colo., Boulder, 1966-76; assoc. prof. computer sci. SUNY-Buffalo, 1976-81; assoc. prof. radiation therapy Sch. Medicine, U. Pa., 1981—; fellow, mem. summer faculty Air Force Office Sci. Research, 1981. Contbr. numerous articles to profl. jours. Recipient Career Devel. award NIH, 1977-82. Mem. Am. Phys. Soc., Am. Astron. Soc., Internat. Astron. Union, Am. Assn. Physicists in Medicine, Soc. Photo-Optical Instrumentation Engrs., IEEE. Patentee topographic comparator, brachytherapy algorithms. Current Work: Three-dimensional mapping of human body: interior: CAT scanning and x-rays for cardiology, brachytherapy and treatment planning; exterior: laser mapping for anthropometry. Subspecialties: Mathematical software; Biomedical engineering. Office: Hosp U Pa Dept Radiation Therapy 3400 Spruce Philadelphia PA 19104

ALTURA, BURTON MYRON, physiologist, educator; b. N.Y.C., Apr. 9, 1936; s. Barney and Frances (Dorfman) A.; m. Bella Tabak, Dec. 27, 1961; 1 dau., Rachel Allison. B.A., Hofstra U., 1957; M.S., N.Y. U., 1961, Ph.D. (USPHS fellow), 1964. Teaching fellow in biology N.Y. U., N.Y.C., 1960-61; instr. exptl. anesthesiology Sch. Medicine, 1964-65, asst. prof., 1965-66; asst. prof. physiology and anesthesiology Albert Einstein Coll. Medicine, N.Y.C., 1967-70, assoc. prof., 1970-74, vis. prof., 1974-76; prof. physiology SUNY Downstate Med. Center, Bklyn., 1974—; research fellow Bronx Mcpl. Hosp. Center, 1967-76; mem. spl. study sect. on toxicology Nat. Inst. Environ. Health Scis., 1977-78; mem. Alcohol Biomed. Research Rev. Com., Nat. Inst. Alcohol Abuse and Alcoholism, 1978—; adj. prof. biology Queens Coll., CUNY, 1983—; cons. NSF, Nat. Heart, Lung and Blood Inst., CUNY, Miles Inst., Upjohn Co., Bayer AG, Ciba-Geigy, Zyma SA.; organizer, condr. symposia. Author: Microcirculation, 3 vols., 1977-80, Vascular Endothelium and Basement Membranes, 1980, Pathophysiology of the Reticuloendothelial System, 1981, Ionic Regulation of the Microcirculation, 1982; editor-in-chief: Physiology and Patho-physiology Series, 1976—, Microcirculation, 1980—, Magnesium: Exptl. and Clin. Research, 1981—; mem. editorial bd.: Jour. Circulatory Shock, 1973—, Advances in Microcirculation, 1976—, Jour. Cardiovascular Pharmacology, 1977—, Prostaglandins and Medicine, 1978—, Substance and Alcohol Actions/Misuse, 1979—, Alcoholism: Clin. and Exptl. Research, 1982—; assoc. editor: Jour. of Artery, 1974—; asso. editor: Microvascular Research, 1978—, Agents and Actions, 1981—; contbr. over 450 articles to profl. jours. Recipient Research Career Devel. award USPHS, 1968-72; travel awards NIH, 1968; travel awards Am. Soc. Pharm. and Exptl. Therapeutics, 1969; NIH grantee, 1968—; NIMH grantee, 1974-78; Nat. Inst. Drug Abuse grantee, 1979—. Fellow Am. Heart Assn. (mem. council on stroke 1973—, council basic sci. 1969—, council on thrombosis 1971—, council on circulation 1978—, council on high blood pressure 1978—, cardiovascular A study sect. 1978-81), Am. Coll. Nutrition; mem. Microcirculatory Soc. (past mem. exec. council, mem. nominating com. 1973-74); fellow Am. Physiol. Soc. (mem. circulation group 1971—, public info. com. 1980—); mem. Soc. Exptl. Biology and Medicine (editorial bd. 1976—), AAUP, Am. Public Health Assn., Am. Chem. Soc. (div. medicinal chemistry), Am. Soc. Pharm. and Exptl. Therapeutics, Endocrine Soc., Harvey Soc., Am. Coll. Toxicology, Research Soc. on Alcoholism, Am. Thoracic Soc., Soc. for Neurosci., Shock Soc. (founding), Am. Fedn. Clin. Research, AAAS, European Conf. Microcirculation, Internat. Anesthesia Research Soc., Internat. Soc. Thrombosis and Haemostasis, Internat. Soc. Biomed. Research on Alcoholism (founding mem.), Internat. Soc. Biorheology, Soc. Environ. Geochemistry and Health, Soc. Neurosci., Reticuloendothelial Soc., Gerontol. Soc., Internat. Platform Assn., Am. Inst. Biol. Sci., Assn. Gnotobiotics, Am. Microscopical Soc., Am. Soc. Zoologists, Am. Soc. Cell Biology, Am. Soc. Bone and Mineral Research, N.Y. Acad. Scis., Am. Public Health Assn., N.Y. Heart Assn., Sigma Xi. Current Work: Excitation contraction coupling of vascular smooth muscle, microcirculation; role of magnesium in cardiovascular patho-physiology; cardiovascular research. Subspecialties: Physiology (medicine); Pharmacology. Office: 450 Clarkson Ave Brooklyn NY 11203

ALVARES, ALVITO PETER, pharmacologist, educator, science researcher; b. Bombay, India, Dec. 25, 1935; came to U.S., 1958, naturalized, 1971; s. Amancio and Diva A.; m. Joy Ann Schmidt, Aug. 31, 1969; children: Christopher, Kevin. B.Sc., U. Bombay, 1955, B.Sc. in Tech., 1957; M.S. in Biochemistry, U. Detroit, 1961; Ph.D. in Pharmacology, U. Chgo., 1966. Sr. research biochemist Burroughs Wellcome & Co., 1967-70; research asso. Rockefeller U., N.Y.C., 1970-71, asst. prof., 1972-75, asso. prof., 1975-77; asso. prof. dept. pharmacology Uniformed Services U. Health Scis., Bethesda, Md., 1977-78, prof., 1978—. Mem. editorial bd.: Pharmacology, Clin. Pharmacology and Therapeutics; contbr. numerous articles to sci. jours., chpts. in books. Recipient career devel. award NIH, 1975-77; Irma T. Hirschl scholar, 1975-77. Mem. Am. Soc. Pharmacology and Exptl. Therapeutics, Am. Soc. Biol. Chemists, Am. Soc. for Clin. Pharmacology and Therapeutics, Soc. Toxicology, N.Y. Acad. Scis. Current Work: Professor of pharmacology; research in toxicology; teach medical and graduate students; environmental toxicological research. Subspecialties: Molecular pharmacology; Toxicology (medicine). Office: Dept Pharmacology Uniformed Services U 4301 Jones Bridge Rd Bethesda MD 20814

ALVAREZ, LUIS W., physicist; b. San Francisco, June 13, 1911; s. Walter C. and Harriet S. (Smyth) A.; m. Geraldine Smithwick, 1936; children: Walter, Jean; m. Janet L. Landis, 1958; children: Donald and Helen. B.S., U. Chgo., 1932, M.S., 1934, Ph.D., 1936, Sc.D., 1967; Sc.D., Carnegie-Mellon U., 1968, Kenyon Coll., 1969, Notre Dame U., 1976, Ain Shams U., Cairo, 1979, Pa. Coll. Optometry, 1982. Research asso., instr., asst. prof., asso. prof. U. Calif., 1936-45, prof. physics, 1945-78, prof. emeritus, 1978—; assoc. dir. Lawrence Radiation Lab., 1954-59, 75-78; radar research and devel. Mass. Inst. Tech., 1940-43, Los Alamos, 1944-45; dir. Hewlett Packard Co. Recipient Collier Trophy, 1946; Medal for Merit, 1948; John Scott medal, 1953; Einstein medal, 1961; Nat. Medal of Sci., 1964; Michelson award, 1965; Nobel prize in physics, 1968; Wright prize, 1981; named Calif. Scientist of Year, 1960; named to Nat. Inventors Hall of Fame, 1978. Fellow Am. Phys. Soc. (pres. 1969); mem. Nat. Acad. Scis., Nat. Acad. Engring., Am. Philos. Soc., Am. Acad. Arts and Scis., Phi Beta Kappa, Sigma Xi; assoc. mem. Institut D'Egypte. Current Work: Experimental and theoretical aspects of the major biological paleo-extinctions; stabilized optical devices; particle physics. Subspecialties: Particle physics; Biophysics (physics). Office: Univ Calif Dept Physics Berkeley CA 94720

ALVAREZ, WALTER, geology educator; b. Berkeley, Calif., Oct. 3, 1940; s. Luis W. and Geraldine (Smithwick) A.; m. Mildred M Millner, May 8, 1965. B.A., Carleton Coll., 1962; Ph.D., Princeton U., 1967. Sr. geologist Am. Overseas Petroleum Ltd., The Hague, Netherlands, 1967-68, Tripoli, Libya, 1968-70; NATO fellow British Sch. Archaeology, Rome, 1970-71; research assoc. Lamont-Doherty Geol. Obs., Columbia U., Palisades, N.Y., 1971-77; asst. prof. geology dept. geology and geophysic U. Calif.-Berkeley, 1977-79, assoc. prof., 1979-81, prof., 1981—. Fellow Geol. Soc. Am.; mem. Am. Geophys. Union, AAAS, Societa Geologica Italiana, Sigma Xi. Current Work: Mass extinctions; paleomagnetism; plate tectonics; apennine structure, stratigraphy, tectonics; mediterranean tectonics. Subspecialties: Tectonics; Geophysics. Address: Dept Geology and Geophysics Univ Calif Berkeley CA 94720

ALVES, LEO MANUEL, plant physiologist; b. Phila., May 21, 1945; s. Manuel Louis and Rose Catherine (Fargoniere) A. B.S., St. Norbert Coll., 1968; Ph.D., U. Chgo., 1975. Asst. prof. Lincoln U., Pa., 1975-76; research plant pathologist Eastern Regional Research Center, Agrl. Research Service, U.S. Dept. Agr., Phila., 1976-78, collaborator, 1978—; research assoc., asst. prof. Manhattan Coll., Bronx, N.Y., 1978-84; chmn., assoc. prof., research assoc. biology dept. Manhattan Coll.-Coll. Mount St. Vincent, Bronx, 1984—. Contbr. articles in field to profl. jours. Mem. Am. Phytopath. Soc., Am. Soc. Hort. Sci., Am. Soc. Plant Physiologists, Japanese Soc. Plant Physiologists, Sigma Xi. Club: Mensa. Current Work: Researcher in exploring the role of sesquiterpenoid stress metabolites in the mediation of expression of disease resistance in the plants of the Solanaceae. Subspecialties: Plant physiology (biology); Plant pathology. Office: Manhattan College Plant Morphogenesis Laboratory Bronx NY 10471

AMAR, AMAR DEV, productions/operations systems designer, educator; b. Bhakkar, Punjab, India; came to U.S., 1972, naturalized, 1981; s. Prem Datt Shakir and Kaushlaya (Khirbat) Shakir; m. Sneh Lata Chopra, Mar. 16, 1975; children: Harpriye Amar Juneja, Januj Amar Juneja. B.S. with honors, Panjab U., 1969; M.S., Mont. State U., 1973; M.B.A., Baruch Coll., 1980; Ph.D., CUNY, 1980, M.Phil., 1980. Engr.-in-charge Orisun Machine Tools, Chandigarh, India, 1966-67; asst. engr. Teledyne Pacific Indsl. Controls, Oakland, Calif., 1972; indsl. design engr. Vornado/Store Decor Co., Garfield, N.J.,

1973-76; systems analyst Arkwin Industries, Inc., Westbury, N.Y., 1977, 82; adj. asst. prof. Baruch Coll., N.Y.C., 1978-81; project assoc. Research Found. CUNY, N.Y.C., 1980-82; asst. prof. prodns./ops. systems Montclair State Coll., Upper Montclair, N.J., 1975-83; dir. Montclair State Coll. (Mgmt. Devel. Center), 1981-83; assoc. prof. prodn./ops. mgmt. and indsl. relations Seton Hall U., South Orange, N.J., 1983—; cons. in field. Mem. Inst. Indsl. Engrs. (sr.), Inst. Mgmt. Scis., Am. Prodn. and Inventory Control Soc., Ops. Research Soc. Am. Current Work: Scheduling large systems, ordering, combinatorics; planning outputs, establishing sequence, workcenter planning, scheduling activities and events in a large system. Subspecialties: Distributed systems and networks; Industrial engineering. Home: 134 Christie St Edison NJ 08820 Office: Dept Mgmt and Indsl Relations Seton Hall U South Orange NJ 07079

AMAR, PRAVEEN KUMAR, environmental scientist, engineering educator; b. Amritsar, Punjab, India, May 15, 1949; came to U.S., 1969, naturalized, 1982; s. Lal Chand and Vidya Vati (Kubba) A.; m. Mabel Hsiao-Ping Han, Oct. 9, 1976; children—Christopher Anil, Jonathan Ajay. B.S. in Mech. Engring., Punjab Engring. Coll., 1969; M.S., UCLA, 1971, Ph.D., 1977. Registered engr., Calif. Environ. scientist Pacific Environ. Services, Santa Monica, Calif., 1973-75; instr. mech. engring. Calif. State U.-Sacramento, 1978—; sr. air pollution specialist Calif. Air Resources Bd., Sacramento, 1977—. Contbr. articles to profl. jours. Mem. AAAS. Democrat. Current work: Perform and manage research on California's acid deposition (acid rain) program-$18 million research 1983-87. Subspecialties: Environmental engineering; Acid rain. Home: 1545 Pebblewood Dr Sacramento CA 95833 Office: Research Div Calif Air Resources Bd 1800 15th St Sacramento CA 95814

AMAREL, SAUL, computer scientist, educator; b. Thessaloniki, Greece, Feb. 16, 1928; s. Albert and Sol (Pelossof) Amario; m. Marianne Kroh, Dec. 20, 1953; children—Dan, David. Came to U.S., 1957, naturalized, 1962. B.Sc., Israel Inst. Tech., Haifa, 1948, Ingenieur E.E., 1949; M.S., Columbia U., 1953, D.Egn. Sci., 1955. Sci. dep. Israel Ministry Def., Israel, 1948-52, project leader control and computer systems, 1955-57; research engr. Electronic Research Lab., Columbia, 1953-55; head computer theory research RCA Labs., Princeton, N.J., 1957-69; prof. chmn. dept. computer sci. Rutgers U., New Brunswick, 1969-84; dir. Lab. Computer Sci., Research, 1977—; dir. Rutgers Research Resource in Computers in Medicine, 1971-83; vis. prof. computer sci. Carnegie Mellon U., 1966; vis. scholar Stanford U., 1979. Mem. chem./biol. info. handling rev. com. NIH, 1971-75; mem. info. scis. adv. com. N.J. Dept. Higher Edn., 1973-76; mem. nat. adv. com. BIONET; mem. exec. and adv. coms. SUMEX-AIM, 1974—; vis. research fellow SRI Internat., 1983; vis. research scientist Carnegie Mellon U., 1985. Mem. editorial bd. Artificial Intelligence, Internat. Jour., 1969—, Jour. Computer Langs., 1974—; contbr. articles to sci. jours. Trustee Ramapo Coll. N.J., 1969-73; bd dirs. N.J. Ednl. Computer Network, 1975-80. Mem. IEEE (sr.), Soc. Indsl. and Applied Math, Assn. Computing Machinery, AAAS, Am. Assn. Artificial Intelligence (exec. council 1982—). Sigma Xi. Current work: Poblems of representation in artificial intelligence; theory formation; machine learning; expert systems. Subspecialties: Artificial intelligence; Theoretical computer science. Office: Rutgers U New Brunswick NJ 08903

AMBLER, ERNEST, government official; b. Bradford, Eng., Nov. 20, 1923; came to U.S., 1953, naturalized, 1958; s. William and Sarah Alice (Binns) A.; m. Alice Virginia Seiler, Nov. 19, 1955; children: Christopher William, Jonathan Ernest. B.A., New Coll., Oxford U., 1945, M.A., 1949, Ph.D., 1953. With Armstrong Siddeley Motors, Ltd., Coventry, Eng., 1944-48; Nuffield Research fellow Oxford U., 1953; with Nat. Bur. Standards, Commerce Dept., 1953—, div. chief inorganic materials div., Washington, 1965-68; dir. Inst. for Basic Standards, Washington, 1968-73; dep. dir. Nat. Bur. Standards, Washington, 1973, acting dir., 1975-78, dir. bur., 1978—; Liaison rep. to div. phys. scis. Nat. Acad. Sci.-NRC, 1968-69; Sponsor's del. Nat. Conf. Standards Lab., 1968; U.S. rep. Internat. Com. on Weights and Measures, 1972—. D.C. mem. bd. govs. Israel/U.S. Binat. Indsl. Research and Devel. Found.; mem. Md. High Tech. Roundtable. Recipient Arthur S. Flemming award Washington Jr. C. of C., 1961; John Simon Guggenheim Meml. Found. fellow, 1963; recipient William A. Wildmack award in metrology, 1976, Pres.'s award for Distinguished Fed. Civilian Service, 1977. Fellow AAAS, Am. Phys. Soc. (editor Rev. Modern Physics 1966-69); mem. Washington Acad. Scis. Patentee low temperature refrigeration apparatus. Subspecialties: Low temperature physics; Condensed matter physics. Office: Nat Bur Standards Washington DC 20234

AMBRE, JOHN JOSEPH, physician, toxicologist, pharmacologist, educator; b. Aurora, Ill., Sept. 14, 1937; s. Frederick Mathias and Cecelia Angela (Petit) A.; m. Anita Marie Sievert, Nov. 3, 1962; children: Susan, Peter, Denise, Matthew. B.S., Notre Dame U., 1959; M.D., Loyola U.-Chgo., 1963; M.S., U. Iowa, 1970, Ph.D., 1972. Med. fellow Mayo Clinic, Rochester, Minn., 1966-68; asst. to assoc. prof. U. Iowa Coll. Medicine, Iowa City, 1972-78; med. dir. CBT Labs., Highland Park, Ill., 1978—; assoc. prof. Northwestern U. Med. Sch., Chgo., 1980—; cons. Abbott Labs., North Chicago, Ill.; toxicology cons. Metpath Labs., Teterboro, N.J.; cons. Hyland Diagnostics, Round Lake, Ill., 1981. Author: Drug Assay, 1983; editorial bd. Jour. Analytical Toxicology; contbr. articles to sci. publs. Served to capt. AUS, 1964-66. U. Iowa VA Clin. Investigator, 1973. Mem. Am. Fedn. Clin. Research, Am. Soc. Clin. Pharmacology and Therapeutics, Am. Soc. Pharmacology and Exptl. Therapeutics, Am. Assn. Clin. Chemistry, AAAS. Drug patentee, 1972. Current Work: Clinical pharmacology; clinical toxicology; drug analysis in biological fluids; therapeutic drug monitoring; drug metabolism; drug metabolite identification; metabolism of drugs and chemicals causing poisoning especially drugs of abuse. Subspecialties: Pharmacology; Toxicology (medicine). Home: 1210 Walden Ln Deerfield IL 60015 Office: Northwestern U Med School 303 E Superior Chicago IL 60611

AMDAHL, GENE MYRON, computer company executive; b. Flandreau, S.D., Nov. 16, 1922; s. Anton E. and Inga (Brendsel) A.; m. Marian Quissell, June 23, 1946; children: Carlton Gene, Beth Delaine, Andrea Leigh. B.S.E.E., S.D. State U., 1948, D.Eng. (hon.), 1974; Ph.D., U. Wis., 1952, D.Sc. (hon.), 1979; D.Sc. (hon.), Luther Coll., 1980, Augustana Coll., 1984. Project mgr. IBM Corp., Poughkeepsie, N.Y., 1952-55; group head Ramo-Wooldridge Corp., Los Angeles, 1956; mgr. systems design Aeronutronics, Los Angeles, 1956-60; mgr. systems design advanced data processing systems IBM Corp., N.Y.C., Los Gatos, Calif., Menlo Park, Calif., 1960-70; founder, chmn. Amdahl Corp., 1970-80, Trilogy Ltd., 1980—. Served with USN, 1942-44. Recipient Disting. Alumnus award S.D. State U., 1973, Data Processing Man of Yr. award Data Processing Mgmt. Assn., 1976, Disting. Service citation U. Wis., 1976, Michelson-Morley award Case-Western Res. U., 1977, Harry Goode Meml. award for outstanding contbns. to design and manufacture of large, high-performance computers Am. Fedn. Info. Processing Socs., 1983; IBM fellow, 1965; IEEE fellow, 1969. Fellow Brit. Computer Soc.; mem. Nat. Acad. Engring.; IEEE (W.W. McDowell award 1976), Quadrato della Radio, Pontecchio Marcon. Lutheran. Club: La Rinconada Country (Saratoga, Calif.). Patentee in field. Current Work: Advanced large scale integrated circuitry and high performance computer organization. Subspecialties: Computer architecture; Computer engineering. Home: 165 Patricia Dr Atherton CA 94025 Office: Trilogy Systems 10500 Ridgeview Ct Cupertino CA 95014

AMER, AHMAD (EL SAYED), engring. and fabrication co. exec., metall. engr., cons.; b. Cairo, Egypt, June 17, 1940; came to U.S., 1968, naturalized, 1973. B.S. in Metall. Engring, Cairo U., 1964. Registered profl. engr., Calif. Process metallurigst Gen. Orgn. for Industrialization, Cairo, 1964-1968; plant metallurgist Phoenix Steel Corp., Claymont, Del., 1968-71; mgr. quality control Pipeco Steel Co., Wilmington, Del., 1971-72; chief metallurgist Cann & Saul Co., Royersford, Pa., 1972-74; sr. metall. engr. Bechtel Power Corp., Gaithersburg, Md., 1974-77; pres. Amer Indsl. Techs., Inc., Wilmington, 1977—. Mem. ASME, Am. Welding Soc., Am. Soc. Metals. Club: Rodney Sq. Lodges: Masons; Shriners. Developed process for continuous casting of high strength low alloy steel, process for rolling, heat treating and testing explosive-bonded titanium cladding. Current Work: Fabrication of pressure vessels and piping, weldments for nuclear and chem. processing industries. Subspecialties: Materials processing; Nuclear engineering. Home: 1515 Forsythia Ave Wilmington DE 19810 Office: 1000 S Madison St Wilmington DE 19801

AMER, M. SAMIR, pharm. co. exec., researcher; b. Egypt, Sept. 2, 1935; s. M. Mohamed and Zeinab H. (Saad) A.; m. Laila E. El-Fatatry, June 12, 1958; children: Amre S., Nancy S., Mona S., Suzanne S. Ph.D., U. Ill., 1962; M.B.A., Columbia U., 1980. Dir. cardiovascular research Mead Johnson & Co., Evansville, Ind., 1969-77; dir. biol. research Bristol Myers Internat., N.Y.C., 1977-82, dir. strategic mktg., 1982—. Contbr. articles to profl. jours. Mem. Am. Soc. Pharmacology and Exptl. Therapeutics, Am. Soc. Biol. Chemists. Current Work: Mechanisms of hormone action, blood pressure control, strategic marketing, new trends in pharmacology and medicine. Subspecialties: Molecular biology; Pharmacology. Home: 155 North St Greenwich CT 06830 Office: Bristol Myers Internat 345 Park Ave New York NY 10154

AMERO, BERNARD ALAN, process engineer, chemist; b. Malden, Mass., Feb. 29, 1948; s. Bernard Franklin and Mary Geraldine (Amirault) A. B.S., Providence Coll., 1970; Ph.D., Ohio State U., 1976. Sr. staff process engr. Champion Internat., West Nyack, N.Y., 1976—. Mem. Am. Chem. Soc., TAPPI, Can. Pulp and Paper Assn. Club: Crab Apple Computer (Spring Valley, N.Y.). Subspecialties: Physical chemistry; Graphics, image processing, and pattern recognition. Home: Normandy Village Bldg 15 Unit 2 Nanuet NY 10954 Office: Champion Internat Tech Ctr Bldg One West Nyack NY 10994

AMES, BRUCE N(ATHAN), biochemist, geneticist; b. N.Y.C., Dec. 16, 1928; s. Maurice U. and Dorothy (Andres) A.; m. Giovanna Ferro-Luzzi, Aug. 26, 1960; children: Sofia, Matteo. B.A., Cornell U., 1950; Ph.D., Calif. Inst. Tech., 1953. Chief sect. microbial genetics NIH, Bethesda, Md., 1953-68; prof. biochemistry U. Calif., Berkeley, 1968—. Mem. Nat. Cancer Adv. Bd. Recipient Eli Lilly award Am. Chem. Soc., 1964, Flemming award, 1966; Rosenstiel award, 1976; FASEB award, 1976; Environ. Mutagen Soc. award, 1977; Felix Wankel award, 1978; John Scott medal, 1979; New Brunswick award, 1980; Corson medal, 1980; Mott prize, 1983; Gairdner award, 1983; Tyler prize for environ. achievement, 1985. Mem. Am. Soc. Biol. Chemists, Am. Soc. Microbiology, Environ. Mutagen Soc., Genetics Soc., Am. Assn. Cancer Research, Soc. of Toxicology, Am. Chem. Soc., Am. Acad. Arts and Scis., Nat. Acad. Scis. Research, publs. on bacterial molecular biology, histidine biosynthesis and its control; RNA and regulation; mutagenesis; detection of environmental mutagens and carcinogens, genetic toxicology, oxygen radicals and disease. Current Work: Mutagens; biochemical genetics. Subspecialties: Biochemistry (biology); Genetics and genetic engineering (biology). Home: 1324 Spruce St Berkeley CA 94709 Office: Univ Calif Dept Biochemistry Berkeley CA 94720

AMES, LYNFORD LENHART, chemist, educator, researcher; b. Fresno, Ohio, May 20, 1938; s. Robert Jonathan and Magalene Elaine (Miller) A.; m. Judith Elaine Kilbourne, Mar. 23, 1963; children: Graham, Constance. B.S., Muskingum Coll., 1960; Ph.D., Ohio State U., 1965. NSF postdoctoral fellow Oxford (Eng.) U., 1965-66; asst. prof. N. Mex. State U., 1966-70, assoc. prof., 1970-78, prof., 1978—, head dept. chemistry, 1976—. Mem. Am. Chem. Soc., AAAS, Sigma Xi. Republican. Presbyterian. Lodge: Rotary. Current Work: High temperature chemistry; spectroscopy. Subspecialties: High temperature chemistry; Physical chemistry. Home: 685 Farney Rd Las Cruces NM 88005 Office: Box 3C N Mex State U Las Cruces NM 88005

AMES, WILLIAM FRANCES, applied mathematician; b. Brandon, Man., Can., Dec. 8, 1926; came to U.S., 1932, naturalized, 1941; s. Paul Main and Della Johanna (Hebel) A.; m. Theresa Danielson, Nov. 5, 1924; children—Karen Anne, Susan Lynn, Pamela Margaret. B.S., U. Wis., 1949, M.S., 1950. Research engr. DuPont Co., Newark, Del., 1954-59; prof. math. U. Del.-Newark, 1959-67, U. Iowa, Iowa City, 1967-74; dir., Regent's prof. Ga. Tech. Inst., Atlanta, 1974—; cons. DuPont Co., Newark, 1959-62, Naval Underwater Systems Center, Newport, R.I., 1982—. Author: Nonlinear Partial Differential Equations, Vol. I, 1965, Vol. II, 1972; Nonlinear Ordinary Differential Equations, 1968; Numerical Methods Partial Differential Equations, 1967, 77. Contbr. articles to profl. jours. Served to lt. (j.g.) USN, 1944-46, 51-52. Recipient Humboldt prize Fed. Republic Germany, 1973; fellow NSF, 1963, NATO, 1972, 80. Mem. Soc. Indsl. and Applied Math. (council 1978-84), Internat. Soc. Math. Computers in Simulation (bd. dirs. 1984—). Democrat. Presbyterian. Current work: Senior researcher in nonlinear partial differential equations of physics and engineering science. Subspecialties: Applied mathematics; Numerical analysis (mathematics). Office: School of Mathematics Georgia Inst Tech Atlanta GA 30332

AMICK, JAMES ALBERT, research chemist; b. Lawrence, Mass., Feb. 18, 1928; s. Chester A. and Marcella E. (Hoover) A.; m. Nancy J. Scott, Sept. 9, 1961; 1 dau., D'Maris Ann. A.B., Princeton U., 1949, M.A., 1951, Ph.D., 1952, postgrad., 1952-53. Research scientist RCA Labs., Princeton, N.J., 1953-57, group leader, 1957-71; mgr. Materials and Process Lab., RCA Solid State, Raritan, N.J., 1971-76; research assoc. Exxon Research, Linden, N.J., 1976-80, sr. research assoc., 1980—; area mgr., 1983. Author: (with others) Semiconductor Thin Films, 1964; Photoelectronic Materials and Devices, 1965. Contbr. articles to profl. jours. Patentee in field. Recipient David Sarnoff Team award RCA Corp., 1967; 3 RCA Lab. Achievement awards. Fellow Am. Inst. Chemists; mem. Electrochem. Soc. (div. sec. 1978-79, div. chmn. 1980-82, soc. sec. 1982—). Lodge: Masons. Current work: Silicon device technology, materials characterization; chemical vapor deposition techniques; thin film strain gauges. Subspecialties: Solar energy; Materials (engineering). Home: 76 Leabrook Ln Princeton NJ 08540 Office: Exxon Research Route 22E Annandale NJ 08801

AMIDON, GORDON LEWIS, pharmaceutics educator; b. Apr. 27, 1944; s. George Walter and Ester Ann (McIntire) Am; m. Pamela Jayne Aruri, Aug. 27, 1966; children—Keith E., Kevin S., Eric D., Christopher M. B.S. in Pharmacy, SUNY-Buffalo, 1967; M.A. in Math., U. Mich., 1970, Ph.D. in Pharmaceutics, 1971. Asst. prof. U. Wis.-Madison, 1971-76; assoc. prof. 1976-81; adj. prof., U. Kans., 1981-83; dir. pharm. chem. research INTERx Research Corp., Lawrence, Kans., 1981-83; dir. research Smith Kline Consumer Products, Phila., 1983—; prof. pharm. U. Mich., Ann Arbor, 1983—. Mem. editorial bd.: Internat. Jour. Pharmaceutics, 1980—. Contbr. articles to profl. jours. Fellow Acad. Pharm. Scis. (chmn. basic pharmaceutics sect. 1984—); mem. Am. Pharm. Assn., AAAS. Current work: Transport phenomena, diffusion plus chemical and enzymatic reaction, obsorption of drugs and prodrugs, cellular transport of peptides and peptide analogues, solubility estimation and solution thermodynamics Subspecialty: Pharmaceutical research and development. Office: Coll Pharmacy Univ Mich Church/Geddes Ann Arbor MI 48109

AMIDON, GREGORY EVERETT, pharmaceutical chemist, researcher; b. Seneca Falls, N.Y., Jan. 13, 1952; s. George Amidon and Esther Ann (McIntire) McElligott; m. Elizabeth Platten, May 26, 1974. B.S. in Medicinal Chemistry, U. Mich., 1974, M.S., 1978; Ph.D., 1979. Summer scholar The Upjohn Co., Kalamazoo, Mich., 1974, scientist, 1979-83, research scientist, 1983—; teaching asst. U. Mich., Ann Arbor, 1974-75, research asst., 1975-79. Mem. Am. Pharm. Assn. (Ebert prize 1983), Acad. Pharm. Scis., Rho Chi. Current work: Oral controlled release, physical properties of solids, preformulation and formulation development of pharmeceuticals Subspecialty: Drug delivery systems. Office: The Upjohn Co 7000 Portage St Kalamazoo MI 49001

AMIRKHANIAN, JOHN DAVID, geneticist; b. Esfahan, Iran, Nov. 10, 1927; came to U.S., 1979, naturalized, 1979; s. Gregor D. and Astghik H. (Alexanderian) A.; m. Romelia Grigorian, Jan 30, 1957; children: Varoujan, Areg, Aspet. B.Sc., Tehran U., 1973; Ph.D., U. London, 1977. Calif. community coll. instr. biol. sci. (cert.). Vis. prof. U. So. Calif, Los Angeles, 1979-81; research assoc. Natural History Mus., Los Angeles County, 1980—; asst. prof. Sch. Pub. Health, Tehran U., 1977-79; sr. asst. prof. Charles Drew Postgrad. Med. Sch., Los Angeles, 1982—. Contbr. articles to profl. jours. WHO grantee, 1969; recipient Sci. Research prize Sci. Research Council of Tehran U., 1973. Fellow Linnean Soc. London, N.Y. Acad. Sci.; mem. Genetics Soc. Am., Genetical Soc. Eng., Inst. Biology London. Mem. Apostolic Ch. of Armenia. Current Work: Genetic repair and recombination in eukaryotes. Subspecialties: Mutagenesis; Environmental toxicology. Office: Lab C Charles R Drew Postgrad Med Sch 1621 E 120th St Los Angeles CA 90059

AMJAD, HASSAN, physician; b. Jhang, Punjab, Pakistan, Nov. 27, 1947; came to U.S., 1971, naturalized, 1980; s. Jafar and Anwer (Fatima) H.; m. Lolita Quezon, Oct. 27, 1973; children: Urooj, Quartel Ayne, Shabnaum. M.D., King Edward Med. Coll., Pakistan, 1970. Diplomate: Am. Bd. Internal Medicine, Am. Bd. Hematology. Intern Riverside Hosp., Toledo, Ohio, 1971-72, SUNY-Buffalo, 1972-73, William Beaumont Hosp., Royal Oak, Mich., 1972-73; resident Wayne State U. Sch. Medicine-Harper Grace Hosp., Detroit, 1974-76; asst. clin. prof. medicine Marshall U. Med. Ctr., Huntington, W.Va., 1977-82; chief med. services VA, Beckley, W.Va., 1980-82; chief medicine Plateau Med. Ctr., Oak Hill, W.Va., 1982—, dir. Jafary Med. Clinics, 1982—; cons. in medicine and cancer diseases Appalachian Regional Hosp., 1977—; also Raleigh Gen. Hosp. Contbr. articles to profl. jours. Bd. dirs. Am. Cancer Soc., Raleigh County, W.Va., 1981—, Raleigh County Heart Assn., 1981—. Recipient Hands and Heart award VA, 1981. Fellow ACP, Internat. Soc. Internal Medicine, Internat. Soc. Hematology, Am. Coll. Chest Physicians; mem. Am. Soc. Hematology, Am. Soc. Clin. Oncology, AAAS, Am. Fedn. Clin. Research. Muslim. Current Work: Biomedical use of lasers, recombinant DNA, health care in underdeveloped. Subspecialties: Chemotherapy; Hematology. Address: 32 Hummingbird Ln Beckley WV 25801

AMMAR, RAYMOND G., physics educator; b. Kingston, Jamaica, July 15, 1932; came to U.S., 1961, naturalized, 1965; s. Elias George and Nellie (Khaleel) A.; m. Carroll Ikerd, June 17, 1961; children—Elizabeth, Robert, David. A.B., Harvard U., 1953; Ph.D., U. Chgo., 1959. Research assoc. Enrico Fermi Inst., U. Chgo., 1959-60; asst. prof. physics Northwestern U., Evanston, Ill., 1960-64, assoc. prof., 1964-69; cons. Argonne Nat. Lab. Ill., 1965-69, vis. scientist, 1971-72; vis. scientist Fermilab, Batavia, Ill., (summers) 1976-81; prof. physics U. Kans., Lawrence, 1969—; vis. scientist Deutsches Elektronen Synchrotron (DESY), Hamburg, Fed. Republic Germany, 1982-85; on sabbatical leave at Fermilab and DESY, 1984-85. Contbr. articles to sci. jours. NSF grantee, 1962—. Fellow Am. Phys. Soc.; mem. AAUP. Current work: Experimental elementary particle physics. Subspecialties: Particle physics; Nuclear physics. Home: 1651 Hillcrest Rd Lawrence KS 66044 Office: Physics Dept U Kans Lawrence KS 66045

AMOLS, HOWARD IRA, med. physicist, educator, researcher; b. N.Y.C., Feb. 11, 1949; s. Nathan and Esther Ruth (Rauchwarger) A.; m. Koren Lynn, Sept. 1, 1970; children: Amy, Rachel. B.S. summa cum laude in Physics N.Y. State Regents scholar), Cooper Union, 1970; M.S., Brown U., 1973; Ph.D. in Physics (NDEA Title IV grad. fellow, 1970-73), 1974. Nat. Cancer Inst. postdoctoral fellow Los Alamos (N.Mex.) Nat. Lab., 1974-76, staff mem., 1974-79; asst. prof. radiology U. N.Mex., Albuquerque, 1979-81; assoc. physicist R.I. Hosp., Providence, 1981-84, chief physicist radiation therapy, 1984—; asst. prof. radiation medicine Brown U., Providence, 1981-84, assoc. prof., 1984—; vis. scientist Karlsruhe Nuclear Research Center, W. Ger., 1977-78. Contbr. articles to profl. jours. Prin. investigator, research grantee Nat. Cancer Inst., 1981—. Mem. Radiation Research Soc., Am. Assn. Physicists in Medicine, Am. Coll. Med. Physics, Soc. Physics Students, Sigma Xi. Current Work: Dosimetry, microdosimetry, radiobiology. Subspecialties: Oncology; Radiology. Home: 22 Sutton Pl Cranston RI 02910 Office: RI Hosp Dept Radiation Oncology Providence RI 02902

AMOS, DENNIS BERNARD, physician; b. Bromley, Eng., Apr. 16, 1923; married; 5 children. M.B., B.S., U. London, 1951; M.D., 1963. Intern Guy's Hosp., London, 1951; from assoc. cancer research scientist to prin. cancer research scientist Roswell Park Meml. Inst., 1956-62; James B. Duke prof. immunology and exptl. surgery Med. Center, Duke U., Durham, N.C., 1962—; research fellow Guy's Hosp., London, 1952-55; sr. research fellow Roswell Park Meml. Inst., 1955-56; chmn. human lymphocyte-antigen standards com. AACHT and NIH/Nat. Inst. Allergy and Infectious Diseases; mem. nomenclature com. luekocyte antigens WHO, Internat. Union Immunol. Socs. Mem. Am. Assn. Immunologists, Am. Assn. Cancer Research, Transplantation Soc., Am. Assn. Clin. Histocomptabilitiy Testing, Inst. Medicine, Nat. Acad. Scis. Subspecialties: Immunology (medicine); Transplantation. Office: Duke U Med Center Box 3010 Durham NC 27710

AMUNDSEN, KEITH BYRON, electrical engineer; b. Freeport, N.Y., July 1, 1954; s. Lloyd Alfred and Joyce Lynn (Cassidy) Amundsen Garing. B.S. in Elec. Engring, MIT, 1976; M.S. in Computer Architecture, U. Calif.-Berkeley, 1976-77. Lab. asst. MIT Digital Systems Lab., Cambridge, 1973; engr. Long Island (N.Y.) Lighting Co., 1974-76; teaching asst. digital lab., instr. analog lab. U. Calif.-Berkeley, 1976-77; prin. engr. Digital Equipment Corp., Maynard, Mass., 1977—; pres. Solar Wind Assocs., Cambridge, 1978—; cons. in field. Editor: Digital Equipment Co. Unibus Handbook, 1979; puslisher: Massbus Interface Standard, 1979. Recipient Bausch & Lombe award in physics, 1972. Mem. IEEE, Assn. Computing Machinery, Am. Nat. Standards Inst. (U.S. del. to Internat. Standards Orgn.), Sigma Xi, Pi Lambda Phi. Republican. Lutheran. Club: Unqua Corinthian Yacht. Current Work: Communication architecture; VLSI architecture; multiprocessors. Subspecialties: Distributed systems and networks; Computer architecture. Home: 44 Dorothy Rd Arlington MA 02174 Office: 146 Main St ML 3-5/U26 Maynard MA 01754

ANCKER-JOHNSON, BETSY, physicist, automotive company executive; b. St. Louis, Apr. 29, 1927; d. Clinton James and Fern (Lalan) A.; m. Harold Hunt Johnson, Mar. 15, 1958; children: Ruth P. Johnson, David H. Johnson, Paul A. Johnson, Martha H. Johnson. B.A. in Physics with high honors (Pendleton scholar), Wellesley Coll., 1949; Ph.D. magna cum laude, U. Tuebingen, Germany, 1953; D.Sc. (hon.), Poly. Inst. N.Y., 1979, Trinity Coll., 1981, U. So. Calif., 1984, Alverno Coll., 1984; LL.D. (hon.), Bates Coll., 1980. Instr., jr. research physist U. Calif., 1953-54; physicist Sylvania Microwave Physics Lab., 1956-58; mem. tech. staff RCA Labs., 1958-61; research specialist Boeing Co., 1961-70, exec., 1970-73, asst. sec. commerce for sci. and tech., 1973-77; dir. phys. research Argonne Nat. Lab., Ill., 1977-79; v.p. environ. activities staff Gen. Motors Tech. Center, Warren, Mich., 1979—; affiliate prof. elec. engring. U. Wash., 1964-73; dir. Gen. Mills; mem. Energy Research Adv. Bd. Dept. Energy. Author. Mem. staff Inter-Varsity Christian Fellowship, 1954-56; Trustee Wellesley Coll., 1972-77. AAUW fellow, 1950-51; Horton Hollowell fellow, 1951-52; NSF grantee, 1967-72. Fellow Am. Phys. Soc. (councillor-at-large 1973-76), IEEE; mem. Nat. Acad. Engring., Phi Beta Kappa, Sigma Xi. Patentee in field. Office: Environmental Activities Staff GM Technical Center Warren MI 48090

ANCONA, ANTONIO, nuclear physicist, consultant; b. Bari, Puglia, Italy, Mar. 9, 1945; came to U.S., 1961; s. Francesco and Maria (Scotella) A.; m. Carole Louise Prindle, June 30, 1978. B.S.E.E., U. Hartford, 1968; M.S.N.S., Rensselaer Poly. Inst., 1970, Ph.D. in Nuclear Engring, 1977. Electronic engr. Chandler Evans Co., West Hartford, Conn., 1968-70; physicist Combustion Engring. Co., Windsor, Conn., 1970-75; research asst. Rensselaer Poly. Inst., 1975-77; nuclear physicist Nuclear Assocs. Internat., Rockville, Md., 1977—; prin. Ancona & Assocs., Annapolis, Md., 1979—. Contbr.: articles to Nuclear Sci. and Engring, Transactions Am. Nuclear Soc. Recipient Outstanding Achievement award Control Data Corp., Mpls., 1979. Mem. Am. Nuclear Soc., Nat. Soc. Profl. Engrs. Patentee digital function generator, digital controlled oscillator. Current Work: Research in advanced iteration schemes for diffusion and transport theory solutions of nuclear reactor neutron flux. Subspecialties: Nuclear physics; Numerical analysis (computer science). Home: 2616 Quiet Water Cove Annapolis MD 21401 Office: Nucleare Assocs Internat 6003 Executive Blvd Rockville MD 20852

ANDERLE, RICHARD JOHN, mathmetician; b. N.Y.C., Oct. 8, 1926; s. Joseph and Jennie Helen (Styskal) A.; widower. B.A., Bkyln. Coll., 1948; D.Sc. (hon.), Ohio State U., 1981. Mathematician Naval Surface Weapons Ctr., Dahlgren, Va., 1948-59, chmn. br. Exterior Ballistics, 1959-60, Astronautics, 1960-80, research assoc., 1981-85; sr. systems engr. Gen. Electric Co., King of Prussia, Pa., 1985—; lctr. Am. U., D.C., 1964-65; cons. Commn. Internat. Astron. Union, 1970—. Contbr. articles to profl. jours. Councilman Christ Lutheran Ch., Fredericksburg, 1963-65, treas., 1963-64, fin. sec., 1976-84. Recipient Superior Service award USN, John Adolphus Dahlgren award Naval Surface Weapons Ctr., Corresponding Astronomer award Royal Belgian Obs. Brussels, 1984. Fellow Am. Geophys. Union (pres. 1980-82); mem. IEEE, AIAA, Am. Congress Surveying and Mapping, Inst. Navigation, Internat. Assn. Geodesy (pres. advanced tech. sect. 1983—). Current work: Determination of precise orbits of satellites. Subspecialties: Astronautics; Geophysics. Home: PO Box 469 Southeastern PA 19399Office: Gen Electric Co Space Systems Div PO Box 8555-43A30 Philadelphia PA 19101

ANDERS, JAMES EDWARD, hydraulics consultant; b. Tulsa, Jan. 14, 1925; s. Walter Lesene and Elizabeth Jane (James) A.; m. Dolores Ellen Fish, Oct. 22, 1946 (div. June 1969); children—Christine Anders Paris, James E., Jr., Betty Anders Daniels; m. Jessie Lyvers McHaffie, Aug. 11, 1979; stepchildren—John R., Jr., Susan McHaffie Proia, Amy McHaffie Zeien. B.S.M.E., Lehigh U., 1951. Test. engr. Nat. Lead Co., South Amboy, N.J., 1951-53; hydraulics engr. Bethlehem Steel Corp., Pa., 1953-83; pres. Hydraulics Assocs., Bethlehem, Pa., 1983—. Author: Industrial Hydraulics Troubleshooting, 1983. Contbr. Ency. of Sci. and Tech., 1984. Served with USAAF, 1943-45. Mem. Fluid Power Soc. (chpt. pres. 1974-76, 84-85), Am. Soc. Lubrication Engrs.

Republican. Presbyterian. Current work: Consulting and teaching industrial and mobile hydraulics. Subspecialty: Power hydraulics. Home: 256 8th Ave Bethlehem PA 18018

ANDERSEN, CYRIL F., mechanical engineer, consultant; b. Grace, Idaho, May 3, 1927; s. Leo Nels and Emma (Fraser) A.; m. Dorothy Louise Spencer, July 21, 1947; children—David, Paul (dec.), Jon. Student Utah State U., 1945-47; B.S.M.E., U. Utah, 1958, M.S.M.E. in Applied Mechanics, 1962; postgrad. Brigham Young U., 1962-69. Mech. engr. Sperry Rand Corp., Salt Lake City, 1958-69; Viking cognizance engr. Jet Propulsion Lab., Pasadena, Calif., 1969-70; chief engr. Devel. Corp. Am., Salt Lake City, 1970-72, Powermatic Corp., Salt Lake City, 1972-73; engr. Eimco P.E.C., Salt Lake City, 1973—; test cons. U. Utah, Salt Lake City, 1969; structural cons. Delta Reinforced Plastics, Salt Lake City, 1981—. Inventor artificial trachea. Co-author lab. procedures for artificial heart test. Active Red Butte Dist. council Boy Scouts Am., 1955-62; campaign vol. Salt Lake City Democratic party 1976; adviser, fundraiser Salt Lake City Jr. Achievement, 1978-83. Mem ASME (treas. 1982-83), Inernat. Soc. Inventors and Designers, Salt Lake City Toastmasters (treas. 1979-80), Pi Tau Sigma, Tau Beta Pi. Current work: Stress, deflection and vibration analysis; development of mechanical automatic bicycle transmission. Subspecialties: Theoretical and applied mechanics; Fluid mechanics. Home: 1491 Ute Dr Salt Lake City UT 84108 Office: Eimco PEC 669 W 2d S Salt Lake City UT 84110

ANDERSEN, DOUGLAS CRAIG, ecologist, ecology educator; b. Tacoma, Sept. 30, 1946; s. Glenn Woodrow Andersen and Julienne Marie (Omejc) Bramsche; m. Sherry Lee Bokker, Sept. 11, 1971 (div. Feb. 1984); 1 child, Craig Douglas. B.S., U. Wash., 1973; M.A., U. Kans., 1975; Ph.D., Utah State U., 1980. Research asst. prof. Utah State U., Logan, 1980-81; asst. prof. ecology Purdue U., West Lafayette, Ind., 1981—. Contbr. articles to profl. jours. Served with U.S. Army, 1968-70, Vietnam. NSF grantee. Mem. Ecol. Soc. Am., Am. Soc. Mammalogists, Wildlife Soc., Am. Soc. Naturalists. Current work: Physiological and nutritional ecology of birds and mammals; the roles of animals and disturbance in ecosystems. Subspecialties: Ecology (biology); Species interaction. Office: Dept Forestry and Natural Resources Purdue U West Lafayette IN 47907

ANDERSEN, PER HOLME, astrophysicist; b. Herning, Denmark, Aug. 31, 1945; emigrated to Can., 1954, naturalized, 1968; s. Carl and Vera Johanne (Petersen) A. B.Sc. with honors in Astronomy, U. Victoria, B.C., 1968; M.Sc. in Astronomy, U. Western Ont., 1970; Ph.C. in Astronomy, U. Wash.-Seattle, 1973. Lectr. dept. physics and astronomy Brandon (Man.) U., 1979-80; asst. prof. dept. physics Brock U., St. Catharines, Ont., 1980-81; asst. prof. dept. math. and astronomy U. Man.-Winnipeg, 1981—, NRC of Can. scholar, 1968-70. Contbr. articles in field to profl. jours. Mem. Am. Astron. Soc., Canadian Astron. Soc. Current Work: Theory and observation of stellar atmospheres, mass loss, spectral line formation, novae. Subspecialties: Optical astronomy; Theoretical astrophysics. Office: U Manitoba 347 University Coll Winnipeg MB R3T 2N2 Canada

ANDERSON, ALBERT GORDON, research chemist; b. Evanston, Ill., Nov. 21, 1945; s. Axel Waldemar and Virginia Ruth (Carlson) A.; m. Christine Ruth Minton, Aug. 25, 1973; children—Robert Axel, Barbara Ruth. A.A., Santa Rosa Jr. Coll., 1965; B.A., Sacramento State U., 1967; Ph.D., U. Utah, 1977. Research chemist E.I. DuPont de Nemours & Co., Wilmington, Del., 1977—. Patentee in field. Served with AUS, 1969-72. Mem. Am. Chem. Soc., Optical Soc. Am. Subspecialties: Organic chemistry; Electro-optics. Home: 2410 St Francis St Wilmington DE 19808 Office: EI DuPont de Nemours & Co E328/204 Experimental Sta Wilmington DE 19898

ANDERSON, ALFRED BENNETT, chemistry educator, researcher; b. Ithaca, N.Y., Feb. 16, 1942; s. Alfred Leonard and Evelyn (Bennett) A.; m. Lynn Marie Santeler, Mar. 15, 1975. A.B., Cornell U., 1964; Ph.D., Johns Hopkins U., 1970. Postdoctoral fellow Ind. U., Bloomington, 1971-72, Cornell U., Ithaca, N.Y., 1972-74, U. Calif.-Santa Barbara, 1977-78; J.W. Gibbs instr. Yale U., New Haven, 1974-76, instr., 1976-77; asst. prof. chemistry Case Western Res. U., Cleve., 1979-81, assoc. prof., 1981—. Contbr. numerous articles to sci. jours. Recipient numerous research grants from fed. and pvt. orgns. Mem. Am. Chem. Soc., Am. Phys. Soc., Sigma Xi. Current work: Predicting and understanding molecular structures and reaction mechanisms in areas of inorganic, surface, and solid state chemistry by using quantum theory. Subspecialties: Surface chemistry; Theoretical chemistry. Office: Chemistry Dept Case Western Res U Cleveland OH 44106

ANDERSON, ANSEL COCHRAN, physics educator; b. Warren, Pa., Sept. 17, 1933; s. Andrew Conrad and Elpha (Cochran) A.; m. Janet Arlene Belles, June 11, 1955; children—Gail Marie, Alan Belles. B.S., Allegheny Coll., 1959; M.A., Wesleyan U., 1957; Ph.D., U. Ill., 1961. Asst. prof. physics U. Ill., Urbana, 1964-66, assoc. prof., 1966-69, prof., 1969—. Contbr. articles to profl. jours. Guggenheim fellow, 1966-67; Hays-Fulbright grantee, 1966-67; NSF fellow, 1958-60. Fellow Am. Phys. Soc. Current work: Defects; disordered materials. Subspecialties: Condensed matter physics; Low temperature physics. Home: 1911 McDonald Dr Champaign IL 61821 Office: Dept Physics U Ill Urbana IL 61801

ANDERSON, CARL WILLIAM, molecular biologist, geneticist; b. Washington, May 19, 1944; s. Carl Elmore and Laverne Ann-Marie (Larsen) A.; m. Mary Elizabeth Daniell, Apr. 20, 1968; children: Carl E., Christine E. B.A., Harvard Coll., 1966; Ph.D. in Microbiology, Washington U., St. Louis, 1970. With Cold Spring Harbor Lab., N.Y., 1970-75; genetecist biology dept. Brookhaven Nat. Lab., Upton, N.Y., 1975—; assoc. prof. microbiology SUNY, Stony Brook. Mem. AAAS, Am. Soc. Microbiology, Am. Soc. Virology. Current Work: Regulation of gene expression, molecular biology of DNA tumor viruses, protein phosphorylation. Subspecialties: Molecular biology; Virology (biology). Home: 23 Shelbourne Ln Stony Brook NY 11790 Office: Biology Dept Brookhaven Nat Lab Upton NY 11973

ANDERSON, CRAIG JAY, environmental chemist; b. Duluth, Minn., Aug. 9, 1951; m. Debbi Lee Rossiter, June 28, 1975; children—Bridget, Aaron, Benjamin. B.S., Coll. of St. Scholastica, Duluth, 1973; M.S., U. Minn., 1979. Chemist, EPA, Duluth, 1974-75; analytical chemist Buckbee-Mears Co., St. Paul, 1976-77, U. Wis.-Superior, 1977-78; sr. environ. chemist Minn. Power & Light Co., Duluth, 1979—. Chmn. bd. trustees Twin Ports Bible Fellowship Ch., Duluth, 1982-83, chmn. bd. elders, 1983-84; bd. dirs. Lakeview Christian Acad. Sch., Duluth, 1984—. Mem. Am. Chem. Soc. Current work: Acid rain, environmental chemistry of coal fired power plants, toxicity of heavy metals in aquatic systems, coal and coal ash chemistry. Subspecialties: Analytical chemistry; Environmental chemistry. Office: Minn Power & Light Co 30 W Superior St Duluth MN 55802

ANDERSON, DAVID WALTER, physicist, educator; b. Heron Lake, Minn., June 18, 1937; s. Walter O. and Martha G. (Anderson); m. Jane L. Friedlund, Dec. 17, 1960; children: Bonnie Jean, Brian David. B.S. summa cum laude, Hamline U., 1959; Ph.D., Iowa State U., 1965. Diplomate: in radiol. physics Am. Bd. Radiology. Prof. radiation physics U. Okla. Health Scis. Ctr., Oklahoma City, 1975-82; dir. radiol. physics, prof. radiology City of Faith Med. and Research Ctr., Tulsa, 1982—; cons. in radiol. physics, 1972—. Author: Absorption of Ionizing Radiation, 1984. Contbr. numerous articles to profl. jours. AEC postdoctoral research fellow, 1965-66. Mem. Am. Assn. Physicists in Medicine, Am. Phys. Soc., Am. Coll. Radiology, Soc. Magnetic Resonance Imaging, Christian Med. soc., Soc. Nuclear Medicine. Democrat. Methodist. Current Work: Radiological physics, radiation dosimetry, magnetic resonance imaging, photonuclear physics. Subspecialties: Biophysics (physics); Biomedical engineering. Office: Radiology Dept 8181 S Lewis Ave Tulsa OK 74136

ANDERSON, DON LYNN, educator, geophysicist; b. Frederick, Md., Mar. 5, 1933; s. Richard Andrew and Minola (Phares) A.; m. Nancy Lois Ruth, Sept. 15, 1956; children: Lynn Ellen, Lee Weston. B.S., Rensselaer Poly. Inst., 1955; M.S., Calif. Inst. Tech., 1959, Ph.D., 1962. With Chevron Oil Co., Mont., Wyo., Calif., 1955-56; with Air Force Cambridge Research Center, Boston, 1956-58, Arctic Inst. N.Am., Boston, 1958; mem. faculty Calif. Inst. Tech., Pasadena, 1962—, asso. prof. geophysics, 1964-68, prof., 1968—, dir. seismol. lab., 1967—; Prin. investigator King Mars Seismic Expt.; mem. various coms. NASA, Nat. Acad. Scis.; chmn. seismology com. Nat. Acad. Sci., 1975, mem. Acad., 1982—. Asso. editor: Jour. Geophys. Research, 1965-67, Tectonophysics, 1974-77; editor: Physics of the Earth and Planetary Interiors. Recipient Exceptional Sci. Achievement award NASA, 1977; Sloan Found. fellow, 1965-67. Fellow Am. Geophys. Union (James B. Macelwane award, 1966, pres. tectonophysics sect. 1971-72, chmn. Macelwane award com. 1975), Geol. Soc. Am. (asso. editor bull. from 1971); mem. Am. Acad. Arts and Scis., AAAS, Royal Astron. Soc., Seismol. Soc. Am., Sigma Xi. Current Work: Composition of earth, seismology. Subspecialty: Geophysics. Office: Calif Inst Tech Seismology Lab Pasadena CA 91125

ANDERSON, DONALD KEITH, chem. engr.; b. Iron Mountain, Mich., July 15, 1931; s. Milton Eugene and Edna Olive (Van Court) A.; m. Gina Dale Garrett, July 12, 1957; children—Shannon Elizabeth, Amanda Juliet. B.S., U. Ill., 1956; M.S., U. Wash., 1958, Ph.D., 1960. Asst. prof. chem. engring. Mich. State U., 1960-64, asso. prof., 1964-69, prof. chem. engring. and physiology, 1970—, chmn. dept. chem engring., 1977—; cons. to industry. Contbr. numerous articles to profl. jours. Recipient Disting. Faculty award Mich State U., 1973. Mem. Am. Inst. Chem. Engrs., Am. Chem. Soc., Am. Soc. Engring. Edn., Sigma Xi, Tau Beta Pi, Sigma Tau, Phi Lambda Upsilon, Omega Chi Epsilon. Club: Lions. Current Work: Mass transfer, diffusion. Subspecialties: Chemical engineering; Physiology (biology). Office: Dept Chem Engring Mich State U East Lansing MI 48824

ANDERSON, DUWAYNE MARLO, earth and polar scientist, university administrator; b. Lehi, Utah, Sept. 9, 1927; s. Duwayne LeRoy and Fern Francell (Fagan) A.; m. June B. Hodgin, Apr. 2, 1980; children by previous marriage: Lynna Nadine, Christopher Kent, Lesleigh Leigh. B.S., Brigham Young U., 1954; Ph.D. (Purdue Research Found. fellow), Purdue U., 1958. Prof. soil physics U. Ariz., Tucson, 1958-63; research scientist, chief earth scis. br. (Cold Regions Research and Engring. Lab.), Hanover, N.H., 1963-76; chief scientist, div. polar programs NSF, Washington, 1976-78, mem. Viking sci. team, 1969-76; dean faculty natural scis. and math. SUNY, Buffalo, 1978-84; univ. assoc. provost for research Tex. A&M U., College Station, 1984—; Pegrum lectr. SUNY, 1980; cons. NASA, 1964—, NSF, 1979-81, U.S. Army Cold Regions Research and Engring. Lab., Hanover, N.H., 1979—; sr. U.S. rep., Antarctica, 1976, 77, vis. prof., lectr. numerous univs. Editor: (with O.B. Andersland) Geotechnical Engineering for Cold Regions, 1978; Cons. editor: Soil Sci, 1965—, (with O.B. Andersland) Cold Regions Sci. and Tech, 1978-82; Contbr. numerous sci. and tech. articles to profl. jours. Bd. dirs. Ford K. Sayre Meml. Ski Council, Hanover, 1969-71; bd. dirs. Grafton County Fish and Game Assn., 1965—, pres., 1968-70; bd. dirs. Hanover Conservation Council, 1970-76, v.p., 1970-73; bd. dirs. Buffalo Mus. Sci., 1980-84, v.p., 1982-84; bd. dirs. Houston Area Research Ctr., 1984—; councilor Tex. A.&M. Research Found., 1984—. Served with USAF, 1946-49. Recipient Sci. Achievement award Cold Regions Research and Engring. Lab., 1968; Sec. of Army Research fellow, 1966. Fellow Am. Soc. Agronomy; mem. Am. Polar Soc., Am. Geophys. Union (spl. task force on cold regions hydrology 1974—), AAAS, Soil Sci. Soc. Am., Niagara Frontier Assn. Research and Devel. Dirs. (pres. 1983-84), Sigma Xi, Sigma Gamma Epsilon. Republican. Current Work: Behavior of earth materials at low temperatures; surface chemistry of clay minerals; planetary geology. Subspecialties: Geochemistry; Arctic studies. Home: 8720 Bent Tree Dr College Station TX 77840 Office: 305 E Bizzell Hall Tex A&M U College Station TX 77843

ANDERSON, ERIC EDWARD, health care consulting firm executive; b. Mpls., Jan. 24, 1951; s. Charles Eric and Elizabeth B. (Engstr) A.; m. Florence Kaye, June 18, 1978; children—Cara Elizabeth, Evan Travis. B.A. in Psychology summa cum laude, U. Minn.-Mpls., 1973; M.A. in Theology Fuller Theol. Sem, 1977, Ph.D. in Clin. Psychology, 1978. Lic. cons. psychologist, Minn. Research asst. Fuller Theol. Sem., 1973-76; instr. in psychology Pasadena City Coll., 1976-78; intern in psychology Long Beach (Calif.) VA Hosp., 1977-78; postdoctoral intern U. Minn.,-Mpls., 1978-79, asst. prof. health psychology, coordinator tng. in aging, 1979-83, dir. profl. services Kiel Clinic. Mpls., St. Paul, 1979-83, group v.p., 1983-84, pres., 1984—; cons. in field; expert witness First Examiner Hennepin County (Minn.) 4th Jud. Dist., 1982—. Contbr. chpt., articles to profl. publs.; editorial cons.: Jour. Gerontology, 1981—. Recipient Outstanding Achievement award Am. Acad. Achievement, 1969. Mem. Am. Psychol. Assn., Minn. Psychol. Assn., Gerontol. Soc. Am., Phi Beta Kappa. Current Work: Psychology of aging, promotion of mental health, life span development, health psychology. Subspecialties: Developmental psychology; Behavioral psychology. Office: Kiel Profl Services Inc 1100 Commerce Bldg 4th and Wabash Sts Saint Paul MN 55101

ANDERSON, FRANZ ELMER, sedimentologist, educator; b. Cleve., July 23, 1938; s. Elmer C. and Flo (Jordan) A.; m. Harmony Wilson, Apr. 22, 1965 (div. Juen 1973); children: Toren, Tristan; m. Ann Laundon, July 31, 1976; 1 dau., Brynanne. B.A., Ohio Wesleyan U., 1960; M.S., Northwestern U., Evanston, Ill., 1962; Ph.D., U. Wash.-Seattle, 1967. Research asst. U. Wash.-Seattle, 1965-67; asst. prof. U. N.H.-Durham, 1967-71, assoc. prof., 1971-82, prof. dept. earth scis., 1982—. Author: Introduction to Oceanography Lab Manual, 1978. Fulbright grantee Izmir, Turkey, 1973; Nat. Environ. Research Council sr. fellow Scotland, 1980-81. Fellow Geol. Soc. Am; mem. Soc. Econ. Paleontologists/Mineralogists, Internat. Assn. Sedimentologists, Marine Edn. Assn., New Eng. Estuarine Research Soc. Current Work: Estuarine sedimentation, especially processes which control intertidal fine-grained sediment erosion and deposition. Subspecialties: Sedimentology; Oceanography. Home: 74 Shore Rd Cape Neddick ME 03902 Office: Jackson Estuarine Lab U NH Durham NH 03824

ANDERSON, GARY ALLAN, veterinary pathologist; b. Faulkton, S.D., Dec. 3, 1951; s. Harold LeRoy and Bonnie Mae (Bukaske) A.; m. Amelia Marie Christiansen, Aug. 26, 1972; children—Andy, Kyle. A.A., Central Coll., Kans., 1972; B.S., S.D. State U., 1975; D.V.M., M.S., Kans. State U., 1979; Ph.D., U. Calif.-Davis, 1984. Instr. pathology Kans. State U., Manhattan, 1979; pathology resident U. Calif.-Davis, 1979-80, research assoc., 1980-83; research pathologist U. Nebr., Lincoln, 1983—; cons. to industry. Contbr. articles to profl. jours. Active City Recreation Program, Lincoln, 1984-85. NIH fellow, 1979; U.S. Dept. Agr. grantee, 1983, 84. Mem. Am. Animal Health Assn., AVMA, Am. Assn. Vet. Immunologists, AAAS, Phi Zeta, Phi Kappa Phi. Mem. Wesleyan Ch. Current work: Immunopathogenic mechanisms of infectious diseases in food animals; immunobiology of fetuses and neonates and respiratory diseases; hybridoma technology for diagnostic and research applications; vaccine development and immunomodulation. Subspecialties: Pathology (veterinary medicine); Immunobiology and immunology. Home: 2521 Winchester N Lincoln NE 68512 Office: U Nebr East Campus Lincoln NE 68583

ANDERSON, GREGORY JOSEPH, biologist, educator; b. Chgo., Nov. 26, 1944. B.S. (Kiwanis Club of Pipestone, Minn., fellow), St. Cloud State Coll., 1966; Ph.D. (Floyd Meml. fellow), Ind. U., 1971. Asst. prof. U. Nebr., Lincoln, 1971-73; assoc. prof. biology U. Conn., 1973-78, prof., 1978—; vis. scientist Research Inst., U. Adelaide, South Australia, Australia, 1979-80; Sigma Xi grantee, U. Nebr. Research Council grantee, S. Am., 1972; mem. organizing com. 2d Internat. Symposium on Solanaceae, 1981; speaker profl. seminars; adv. panel NSF, 1983-86. Contbr. articles, chpts., revs. to profl. publs. U. Conn. Research Found. grantee, 1973, 74, 75, 79, 80, 81; NSF grantee, 1978, 79, 81. Mem. AAUP, Am. Soc. Naturalists, Am. Soc. Plant Taxonomists (George R. Cooley award 1981), Bot. Soc. Am., Internat. Assn. Plant Taxonomy, Soc. Econ. Botany (governing council 1978-81, sec. 1981-84, v.p. 1985-86, pres. elect 1985-86), Soc. Study Evolution, Sigma Xi. Club: Joshuas Tract Land Trust. (vice chmn.). Current Work: Plant systematics and evolution; economic botany; reproductive and pollination biology. Subspecialties: Evolutionary biology; Systematics. Office: U Conn Ecology and Evolutionary Biology Box U-43 Storrs CT 06268

ANDERSON, JAMES ALFRED, psychologist, neuroscientist, researcher, educator; b. Detroit, July 31, 1940; s. Courtney Alfred and Catherine Plummer (Bullock) A.; m. Diana M. De Vincenzi, Nov. 1, 1969; 1 son, Eric David. S.B., M.I.T., 1962, Ph.D., 1967. Postdoctoral fellow depts. anatomy, physiology Brain Research Inst., Space Biology Lab., UCLA, 1967-71; research asso., postdoctoral fellow Rockefeller U., N.Y.C., 1971-73; asst. prof. divs. applied math. and biol. and med. scis. Brown U., Providence, 1973-77, asst. prof. psychology and neurosci., 1977-78, assoc. prof. dept. psychology and Center for Neural Sci., 1978—. Editor: (with Geoffrey Hinton) Parallel Models of Associative Memory, 1981; contbr. (with Geoffrey Hinton) articles to profl. jours. NSF grantee, 1977-78, 80—. Mem. Soc. for Neurosci., Soc. for Math. Psychology, Psychonomic Soc., Cognitive Sci. Soc., Sigma Xi. Current Work: Mathematical models of cognition; models of cognitive function inspired by the structure and properties of the nervous system. Subspecialties: Cognition; Neurophysiology. Home: 22 Blaisdell Ave Pawtucket RI 02860 Office: Dept Psychology Brown U Providence RI 02912

ANDERSON, JAMES BRYAN, mathematician, engineer; b. Sandusky, Ohio, Aug. 23, 1950; s. Rodney Jack and Ann Marie (Glenn) A. B.S., U. Toledo, 1977, M.S., 1980, M.S. in Engring. Sci, 1982. Systems analyst (project leader) Teledyne Continental Aircraft Co., Toledo, 1980-82; sr. engr. FMC Corp., Mpls., 1982—. Contbr. articles to profl. jours. Mem. Am. Soc. Computing Machinery, Soc. Indsl. and Applied Math., AIAA, Pi Mu Epsilon, Eta Kappa Nu. Current Work: Laser welding simulation, finite difference schemes for partial differential equations, two point boundary value problems associated with optimal process control; system reliability simulation. Subspecialties: Numerical analysis (computer science); Mathematical software. Home: 7862 Yates Ave N Brooklyn Park MN 55443 Office: FMC Corp No Ordnance 4800 East River Rd Minneapolis MN 55421

ANDERSON, JAMES EMMONS, chemist; b. Hartford, Conn., July 31, 1938; s. William Joseph and Edith Dean (Bottorff) A.; m. Elizabeth Murphy, June 16, 1962. B.S., Union Coll., 1960; Ph.D., Princeton U., 1963. Postdoctoral research fellow Bell Telephone Labs., Murray Hill, N.J., 1963-65; research scientist Ford Motor Co., Dearborn, Mich., 1965—, now prin. research scientist; vis. adj. prof. U. Mich., Ann Arbor, 1979—; chmn. Gordon Research Conf., 1968, vice chmn., 1984. Mem. editorial bd. Jour. Membrane Sci., 1979—. Contbr. articles to profl. jours. Humboldt Stiftung fellow, 1975-76. Fellow Am. Phys. Soc.; mem. Am. Chem. Soc., AAAS. Subspecialties: Physical chemistry; Polymer chemistry. Home: 2872 Glacier Way Ann Arbor MI 48105 Office: Sci Research Lab Ford Motor Co Room 3199 Dearborn MI 48121

ANDERSON, JAMES GILBERT, chemistry educator; b. Spokane, Wash., Feb. 4, 1944; s. Paul Alexander and Mary (Gilbert) Hamblen; m. Cynthia Burgess, Dec. 22, 1984; B.S. in Physics, U. Wash., 1966; Ph.D. in Astrogeophysics, Oxford U., 1970. Postdoctoral fellow, then asst. prof. U. Pitts., asst. prof., until 1975; research scientist, assoc. prof. U. Mich., Ann Arbor, 1975-78; prof. chemistry Harvard U., Cambridge, Mass., 1978—. Mem. Am. Geophys. Union, Am. Phys. Soc., Am. Chem. Soc. Subspecialties: Kinetics; Space chemistry.

ANDERSON, JAMES OTTO, research plant scientist, consultant, educator; b. Eighty Four, Pa., Aug. 3, 1945; s. Otto Frank and Ethel Marie (Irey) A.; m. Martha Alene Cain, Sept. 9, 1966; 1 dau., Heather Lynn. B.S. in Edn, Calif. (Pa.) State Coll., 1967; Ph.D., W.Va. U., 1972. NDEA fellow in plant sci. W.Va. U., Morgantown, 1967-71, Inst. Biol. Sci. fellow, 1971-72; vis. scientist Inst. Low Temperature Sci., Hokkaido U., Sapporo, Japan, 1972-73; research assoc. U.S. Dept. Agr. Pasture Lab., Pa. State U., University Park, 1973-75; postdoctoral research scientist W. Alton Jones Cell Sci. Ctr., Lake Placid, N.Y., 1975-76; adj. asst. prof. plant sci. U. Ariz., Tucson, 1976—; pres. Vari-Ident Labs., Tucson, 1982—. Author computer based inventory program. Japan Soc. Sci. fellow, 1972. Mem. Soc. Cryobiology, Am. Soc. Plant Physiologists, Internat. Soc. Plant Tissue Culture, N.Y. Acad. Scis., Sigma Xi. Clubs: Tucson Rod and Gun, W.Va. Wildwater. Current Work: Plant biotechnology (plant tissue culture, protoplast fusion), plant germplasm conservation and biochemical identification of varieties, plant physiology (crop productivity and stress). Subspecialties: Genetics and genetic engineering (agriculture); Plant cell and tissue culture. Home: 5075 E Cooper St Tucson AZ 85711 Office: Dept Plant Scis Univ Ariz Tucson AZ 85721

ANDERSON, JAY OSCAR, poultry nutritionist; b. Brigham, Utah, Dec. 5, 1921; s. Oscar Carl and Ada Ruth (Petersen) A.; m. Nelda Elaine Huber, Jan. 12, 1944; children: Wayne J., Raymond C., Russell K., Elaine Anderson Young, Dale H., Keith J. M.S., U. Md., 1948, Ph.D., 1950. Chemist, Merck & Co., Rahway, N.J., 1950-51; asst. prof. animal sci. Utah State U., Logan, 1951-54, assoc. prof., 1954-59, prof., 1959-84; with Anderson Animal Clinic, Mesa, Ariz., 1984—. Contbr. articles to profl. jours. Served to 1st lt. U.S. Army, 1943-46. Mem. Poultry Sci. Assn., Am. Inst. Nutrition, AAAS, World Poultry Sci. Assn., Sigma Xi, Phi Kappa Phi. Mormon. Current Work: Protein and amino acid requirements of poultry. Subspecialties: Animal nutrition; Nutrition (biology).

ANDERSON, JOHN MELVIN, physicist; b. Kansas City, Mo., Oct. 9, 1924; s. Melvin Carrol and Myrtle (Wooley) A.; m. Lois Emma Koester, Oct. 14, 1926; children—Charles Melvin, James Melvin, Ruth Carol, Julie Carol. B.S. in Elec. Engring., U. Ill., 1947, M.S., 1948, Ph.D., 1955. Research assoc. U. Ill., Urbana, 1948-55; physicist Gen. Electric Co., Schenectady, N.Y., 1955—. Contbr. articles to profl. jours. Patentee in field. Served with Signal Corps, U.S. Army, 1943-46. Fellow IEEE, Am. Phys. Soc.; mem. Sigma Xi, Tau Beta Pi, Eta Kappa Nu. Current work: Research in gaseous electronics and development of plasma related devices; electrical discharge lamp research and development. Subspecialties: Plasma physics; Plasma engineering. Home: 17 Cedar Ln Scotia NY 12302 Office: Gen Electric Co PO Box 8 Schenectady NY 12301

ANDERSON, JOHN ROBERT, psychologist; b. Vancouver, B.C., Can., Aug. 27, 1947; came to U.S., 1968, permanent resident, 1974; s. John Leonard and Adeline (Langraff) A.; m. Lynne Marie Reder, Mar. 29, 1973; children—John Frank, Abraham Robert. B.A., U. B.C., 1968; Ph.D., Stanford U., 1972. Asst. prof. psychology Yale U., New Haven, 1972-73, prof., 1976-78; jr. fellow U. Mich., Ann Arbor, 1973-76; prof. psychology and computer sci. Carnegie Mellon U., Pitts., 1978—. Author: Language, Memory and Thought, 1976; Cognitive Psychology and Its Implications, 1980, 2d edit., 1985; Cognitive Skills and Their Acquisitions, 1981; The Architecture of Cognition, 1983; Human Associative Memory, 1973. Mem. Am. Psychol. Assn., Am. Assn. Artificial Intelligence, Psychonomics Soc., Cognitive Sci. Soc. Subspecialties: Cognition; Artificial intelligence. Office: Carnegie Mellon U Dept Psychology Pittsburgh PA 15213

ANDERSON, KINSEY A., physicist, educator; b. Preston, Minn., Sept. 18, 1926; s. Malvin R. and Allene (Michener) A.; m. Lilica Athena Vassiliades, May 29, 1954; children—Danae, Sindri. B.A., Carleton Coll., 1949; Ph.D., U. Minn., 1955. Research assoc., faculty U. Iowa, Iowa City, 1955-59; Guggenheim fellow Royal Inst. Tech., Stockholm, Sweden, 1959-60; faculty U. Calif. at Berkeley, 1960—, prof. physics, 1966—; dir. Space Sci. Lab., 1970-79; Cons. NSF, NASA. Contbr. numerous articles to profl. jours. Mem. Nat. Acad. Scis., Am. Geophys. Union, Am. Phys. Soc., Am. Astron. Soc., Internat. Astron. Union, Phi Beta Kappa, Sigma Xi. Research in space plasma physics, magnetospheric particles, magnetic and electric fields using balloon, rocket and satellite instruments. Subspecialty: Solar physics. Home: 8321 Buckingham Dr El Cerrito CA 94530 Office: Space Sci Lab U Calif Berkeley CA 94720

ANDERSON, LUCY MACDONALD, cancer researcher; b. Huntington, W.Va., Oct. 10, 1942; d. Frederic Arthur and Mary Emily (Holton) M.; m. Robert S. Anderson, Aug. 29, 1964; children—Robert S., Donald P. A.B., Bryn Mawr Coll., 1964; Ph.D., U. Pa., 1968. Research assoc. U. Pa., Phila., 1968-70; postdoctoral fellow U. Minn., Mpls., 1970-73; asst. mem. Sloan-Kettering Inst., Rye, N.Y., 1973-82; spl. expert Nat. Cancer Inst., Frederick, Md., 1982—. Contbr. articles to profl. jours. NSF fellow, 1964, also others. Mem. Am. Assn. Cancer Research. Episcopalian. Current work: Transplacental/-perinatal carcinogenesis; metabolic activation and detoxification of carcinogens; modulation of tumorigenesis; analysis of dose-response; polycyclic aromatic hydrocarbons, nitrosamines, polychlorinated biphenyls. Subspecialties: Cancer research (medicine); Biochemistry (biology). Home: 12795 Buttercup Ct West Friendship MD 21794 Office: Lab Comparative Carcinogenesis Nat Cancer Inst Bldg 538 Fort Detrick Frederick MD 21701

ANDERSON, LYNN M., government research center scientist. Physicist Space Experiments Office, NASA Lewis Research Ctr., Cleve. Subspecialty: Solar energy. Office: NASA Lewis Research Ctr 21000 Brookpark Rd Cleveland OH 44135

ANDERSON, MAURITZ GUNNAR, biology educator, consultant, researcher; b. Chgo., Aug. 11, 1918; s. Carl Gunnar and Signe (Holme) A.; m. Jeannette Stacey, Dec. 12, 1942; children: William Stacey, John Gunnar. A.B., U. Mich., 1942; postgrad., Harvard U., 1946-47; M.S. in Botany, Ind. U., 1962; postgrad., Northwestern U. Med. Ch., 1953-54; Ph.D. in Mycology, Va. Poly. Inst. and State U., 1976. Supr. histology and microscopy div. Swift and Co., Chgo., 1949-56, research histologist and microsocopist, 1958-63; chief histologist Norwich Pharm. Co., N.Y., 1957; instr. Towson (Md.) State U., 1963-64, asst. prof., 1964-69, assoc. prof., 1969-82, prof., 1982—; cons. McCrone Assocs., Chgo., McCormick Spices, Balt., Best Foods Products, Union, N.J., T.J. Lipton Co., Englewood Cliffs, N.J.; mem. del. applied microbiologists, also citizens' ambassador to Republic of China, 1984. Bd. dirs. YMCA, Wheaton, Ill., 1959,60, Y Men's chmn., 1953-54; organizer, chmn. Y Men's Club; organizer and coach swim team YMCA, 1953; swim team coach City of Wheaton, 1964; pres. PTA, Wheaton, 1960. Recipient Spl. Service award YMCA, Wheaton, 1962; Towson State U. yearbook dedicated in honor, 1968. Mem. Am. Bot. Soc., Mycological Soc. Am., Inst. Food Technologists (nat. and local chpts.), Am. Assn. Feed Microscopists, Am. Inst. Biol. Scis., Internat. Soc. Aerobiology, AAUP, Sigma Xi, Beta Beta Beta, Phi Gamma Delta. Clubs: Ind. U. Alumni, U. Mich., Va. Poly. Inst. and State U. Alumni, M of U. Mich. Discoverer method of puffing bacon rinds, 1958, method of destroying Trichinella spiralis in meat infested therewith, 1967. Current Work: Nutrition of aquatic molds and microscopy of industrial products. Subspecialties: Microbiology; Microscopy. Home: 18 Maryland Ave Towson MD 21204 Office: Dept Biol Scis Towson MD 21204

ANDERSON, NEIL ALBERT, educator; b. Mpls., Oct. 21, 1928; s. Seth Albert and Hedvig Mary (Johnson) A.; m. Barbara Ann Anderson, Aug. 6, 1960; children: Mary, Elizabeth. B.S., U. Minn., 1951, M.S., 1957, Ph.D., 1960. Asst. prof. plant pathology U. Minn., St. Paul, 1960-64, asso. prof., 1964-70, prof., 1970—. Served with U.S. Army, 1952-54. Mem. Am. Phytopath. Soc., Mycological Soc. Am., AAAS, Sigma Xi. Current Work: Researcher in genetics of parasitism. Subspecialties: Plant pathology; Gene actions. Office: University of Minnesota Dept Plant Pathology 312 Stakman Hall St Paul MN 55108

ANDERSON, PHILIP WARREN, physicist; b. Indpls., Dec. 13, 1923; s. Harry W. and Elsie (Osborne) A.; m. Joyce Gothwaite, July 31, 1947; 1 dau., Susan Osborne. B.S., Harvard U., 1943, M.A., 1947, Ph.D., 1949; D.Sc. (hon.), U. Ill., 1979. Mem. staff Naval Research Lab., 1943-45; mem. tech. staff Bell Telephone Labs., Murray Hill, N.J., 1949-84, chmn. theoretical physics dept., 1959-60, asst. dir. phys. research lab., 1974-76, cons. dir., 1976-84; Fulbright lectr. U. Tokyo, 1953-54; Loeb lectr. Harvard U., 1964; prof. theoretical physics Cambridge (Eng.) U., 1967-75; prof. physics Princeton U., 1975—; Overseas fellow Churchill Coll., Cambridge U., 1961-62; fellow Jesus Coll., 1969-75, hon. fellow, 1978—. Author: Concepts in Solids, 1963, Basic Notions of Condensed Matter Physics, 1984. Recipient Oliver E. Buckley prize Am. Physical Soc., 1964; Dannie Heinemann prize Göttingen (Ger.) Acad. Scis., 1975; Nobel prize in physics, 1977; Guthrie medal Inst. of Physics, 1978; Nat. Medal Sci., 1982. Fellow Am. Phys. Soc., Am. Acad. Arts and Scis., AAAS; mem. Nat. Acad. Scis., Royal Soc. (fgn.), Phys. Soc. Japan, European Phys. Soc. Research in quantum theory, especially theoretical physics of solids, spectral line broadening, magnetism, superconductivity. Subspecialty: Theoretical physics. Address: Princeton U Dept Physics Princeton NJ 08544

ANDERSON, RALPH ROBERT, animal science educator; b. Fords, N.J., Nov. 1, 1932; s. Harry W. and Johanna K. (Damgaard) A.; m. LaVeta Ann Phillips, Jan. 28, 1961; children: Richard, Laura. B.S., Rutgers U., 1953, M.S., 1958; Ph.D., U. Mo.-Columbia, 1961. Cert. animal scientist. Instr. U. Mo., Columbia, 1961-62, asst. prof., 1965-68, assoc. prof., 1968-76, prof. animal sci., 1976—; asst. prof. Iowa State U., Ames, 1962-64; trainee in endocrinology U. Wis., Madison, 1964-65. Editor: Relaxin, 1982; co-editor: The Endocrine Pancreas, 1979, Hormones and Energy Metabolism, 1979, The Renin-Angiotension System, 1980. Served with U.S. Army, 1954-56. NIH predoctoral fellow U. Mo., 1960-61; NIH postdoctoral fellow U. Wis., 1964-65; Fulbright fellow N.Z., 1973-74; recipient Grad. Superior Teaching award Gamma Sigma Delta, U. Mo., 1982. Mem. Endocrine Soc., Am. Physiol. Soc., Am. Dairy Sci. Assn. (bd. editors), Sigma Xi. Club: Track. Lodge: Kiwanis. Current Work: Hormones effecting mammary growth and lactation; present emphasis is on effects of relaxin, placental lactogen, estrogens and progesterone in vivo and in vitro. Subspecialties: Animal physiology; Endocrinology. Home: 2517 Shepard Blvd Columbia MO 65201 Office: Dept Dairy Sci Univ Mo 162 Animal Sci Research Center Columbia MO 65211

ANDERSON, REBECCA J., pharmacologist, educator; b. Ft. Madison, Iowa, Aug. 21, 1949; s. Charley R. and Anna L. (Herrmuth) A. B.A. cum laude, Coe Coll., Cedar Rapids, Iowa, 1971; Ph.D. with distinction, Georgetown U., 1975. Adj. assoc. prof. toxicology U. Mich., 1983—; Med. Research Council Can. fellow U. Toronto, 1975-77; asst. prof. pharmacology George Washington U., 1977-80, assoc. prof., 1980-83; group leader neuro. diseases Warner-Lambert Co., Ann Arbor, Mich., 1983—; cons. Bur. Med. Devices, Life Systems, Inc. Contbr. articles to profl. jours. Mem. Soc. Neurosci., Am. Soc. Pharmacology and Exptl. Therapeutics, Am. Eplepsy Soc., Am. Chem. Soc., AAAS, Biometric Soc., Sigma Xi, Phi Kappa Phi. Current Work: Neuropharmacology of motor systems, environmental and industrial neurotoxicology. Subspecialties: Neuropharmacology; Toxicology (medicine). Office: Dept Pharmacology Warner-Lambert Co 2800 Plymouth Rd Ann Arbor MI 48105

ANDERSON, RICHARD COOPER, consultant, electronics engineer; b. Berkeley, Calif., Jan. 30, 1935; s. Harold Rudolph and Elsie Carolyn (Karsten) A.; m. Linda Euler, July 21, 1962; children: Kristin Ruth, Karen Lynn. M.S.E.E., Stanford U., 1957; postgrad., U. Md., 1958-60. Engr. Fairchild Semicondr., Palo Alto, Calif., 1960-66; mgr. computer systems engring. Varian Assocs., Palo Alto, 1966-72; program dir. Am. Videonetics, Sunnyvale, Calif., 1973-75; pres. R.C. Anderson, Inc., Los Altos, Calif., 1975—. Served to lt. comdr. U.S. Navy, 1957-60. Mem. IEEE, Profl. and Tech. Cons. Assn. Patentee in field. Current Work: Development of custom integrated circuits; custom integrated circuits, VLSI; silicon foundry; IC design and tooling standards. Subspecialties: Integrated circuits; Computer engineering. Office: 900 N San Antonio Rd Suite 204 Los Altos CA 94022

ANDERSON, RICHARD LOUIS, electrical engineering educator; b. Mpls., Feb. 4, 1927; s. Ben Walter and Anna Elizabeth (Zitcowicz) A.; m. Claire Louise Petersen, Sept. 15, 1951; children—Gretchen, Betty Lise, Karl. B.E.E., U. Minn.-Mpls., 1950, M.E.E., 1952; Ph.D., Syracuse U., 1960; Sc.D. (hon.), U. Sao Paulo, Brazil, 1969. Research asst. U. Minn.-Mpls., 1950-52; research engr. IBM Corp., Poughkeepsie, N.Y., 1952-61; assoc. prof. elec. engring. Syracuse U., N.Y., 1961-66, prof. elec. engring., 1966-79; prof. elec. engring. and materials sci. U. Vt., Burlington, 1979—, dir. dept. materials sci., 1981—; Fulbright-Hayes prof. U. Madrid, Spain, 1960-61, U. Sao Paulo, Brazil, 1967-69. Contbr. numerous articles to sci. jours.; patentee electronics. Served with USNR, 1944-47. Fellow IEEE; mem. Am. Phys. Soc., Brazilian Phys. Soc., AAUP, Electrochem. Soc., Sigma Xi. Current work: Semiconductor device electronics; low temperature electronics; physics of failure. Subspecialties: Semiconductors; Microelectronics. Home: RD #2 Box 37A Charlotte VT 05445 Office: U Vermont 309 Votey Bldg Burlington VT 05405

ANDERSON, RICHARD ORR, fishery scientist; b. Evanston, Ill., Oct. 23, 1929; s. Anders A. and Grace (Orr) A.; m. Joan Veh, June 13, 1951; children—Barbara, Donna. B.S., U. Wis., 1951; M.S., U. Mich., 1953, Ph.D., 1959. Research assoc. Inst. Fish Research, Ann Arbor, Mich., 1955-58; instr. U. Mich., Ann Arbor, 1958-59; biologist-in-charge Wolf Lake Hatchery, Dept. Nat. Resources, Mattawan, Mich., 1959-63; leader Coop. Fishery Research Unit., Sch. Forestry, Fishes and Wildlife, U. Mo., Columbia, 1963—, prof., 1977—; co-chmn. Mo. Agr. Adv. Council, 1983-84; tech. mem., bd. dirs. Mo. Fish Farmers Assn., 1980—. Contbr. articles to profl. jours. Recipient Sport Fishing Inst. Commendation award, 1975; Gulf Oil Corp. fellow, 1984. Mem. Am. Fisheries Soc. (award of excellence 1983), N.Am. Benthological Soc., Internat. Assn. Theoretical and Applied Limnology. Current work: Fishery management, agriculture population dynamics. Subspecialties: Resource conservation; Ecology (biology). Home: Route 7 Box 101AA Columbia MO 65202 Office: Sch Forestry Fisheries and Wildlife U Mo Stephens Hall Columbia MO 65211

ANDERSON, ROBERT SIMPERS, immunologist; b. Bryn Mawr, Pa., Jan. 4, 1939; s. Paul Alexander Anderson and Ella (Trew) Simpers; m. Lucy Anne Macdonald, Aug. 29, 1964; children: Robert Simpers, Donald Paul. B.S., Drexel U., 1961; M.S., Hahnemann Med. U., 1968; Ph.D., U. Del., 1971. Postdoctoral fellow U. Minn., 1970-73; asst. mem. Sloan-Kettering Inst. Cancer Research, 1973-82, lab. head, 1974-82; asst. prof. Cornell U., 1975-82; immunologist Aberdeen Proving Ground, Md., 1982—. Contbr. articles to profl. jours; mem. editorial bd.: Jour. Invertebrate Pathology, 1977-83, Jour. Comparative and Developmental Immunology, 1977-83. Mem. Marshland Conservancy, Rye, N.Y., 1978-82. Whitehall Found. grantee, 1974-81; NSF grantee, 1977-83; EPA grantee, 1980-83; Griffis Found. grantee, 1981-83. Mem. Am. Assn. Immunologists, Am. Entomol. Soc., Am. Soc. Zoologists, Internat. Soc. Developmental and Comparative Immunology, N.Y. Acad. Scis., Phila. Physiol. Soc., Soc. Invertebrate Pathology, Sigma Xi. Republican. Episcopalian. Current Work: The effects of environmental chemicals on immune response. Subspecialties: Immunotoxicology; Environmental toxicology. Office: Chem Research and Devel Ctr Biotech Div Aberdeen Proving Ground MD 21010

ANDERSON, ROGER CLARK, biologist, educator; b. Wausau, Wis., Oct. 30, 1941; s. Jerome Alfred and Virginia S. (Anderson); m. Mary Rebecca Blocher, Aug. 5, 1967; children: John Allen, Nancy Lynn. B.S., Wis. State Coll., 1963; M.S., U. Wis., Madison, 1965, Ph.D., 1968. Asst. prof. botany So. Ill. U., Carbondale, 1968-70; asst. prof. U. Wis., Madison, 1970-73; assoc. prof. biology Central State U., Edmond, Okla., 1973-76; assoc. prof. Ill. State U., Normal, 1976-79, prof., 1980—; dir. U. Wis.-Madison Arboretum, 1973-76. Contbr. articles on biology to profl. jours. Treas. Miller Park Zoo Bd., 1982; pres. So. Ill. Audubon Soc., 1970; chmn. McLean County Parks and Recreation Adv. Council, 1983-85; mem. Ill. Nature Preserves Commn., 1985. NSF grantee, 83, 85-86; Dept. Agr. grantee, 1982; Ill. Dept. Conservation grantee, 1981-83; Met. San. Dist. Greater Chgo. grantee, 1978-79. Mem. Am. Bot. Soc., Ecol. Soc., Am., Ill. Acad. Sci., Sigma Xi. Current Work: Community ecology of Grasslands. Subspecialty: Ecology (environmental science). Home: 14 McCormick Blvd Normal IL 61761 Office: Dept Biology Ill State U Normal IL 61761

ANDERSON, STANLEY HELMER, wildlife biologist, researcher; b. San Francisco, Aug. 6, 1939; s. Helmer and Tyra (Sahlin) A.; m. Donna Lawrence, Feb. 27, 1965; children—Rebecca, Gregory. B.A., U. Redlands, 1961; M.A., Oreg. State U., 1968, Ph.D., 1970. Asst. prof. Kenyon Coll., Gambier, Ohio, 1970-75; scientist Oak Ridge Assoc. U., Tenn., 1975-76; sect. chief Patuxent Research Ctr., Laurel, Md., 1976-80; prof. zoology, leader Wyo. Coop. Research Unit, U. Wyo., Laramie, 1980—. Co-author: Environmental Science, 1980, 83; author: Managing our Wildlife Resource, 1985; also articles. Served to lt. USN, 1963-66. Mem. Am. Ornithologists Union (rep. 1978—), Wildlife Soc. (state bd. dirs. 1984—), Am. Inst. Biol. Scis., Ecology Soc., Cooper Ornithol. Soc., Sigma Xi. Current work: Evaluation of impacts of habitat alteration due to human impact (energy development, agriculture, fire, etc.) on wildlife habitat and wildlife populations. Subspecialties: Ecosystems analysis; Population biology. Home: 1062 Arapaho Dr Laramie WY 82070 Office: U Wyo Zoology Dept Box 3166 University Station Laramie WY 82071

ANDERSON, THOMAS EDWARD, neuroscience researcher, educator; b. Evergreen Park, Ill., Dec. 9, 1947; s. Nils Edward and Marion Elizabeth (Senn) A.; m. Nita Fay Golightly, May 21, 1971; children—Kristin Lee, Linse Nils, Lorien Bernice. B.A. in Math and Physics, Hamline U., 1968; M.A. in Math., U. Tex., 1972; Ph.D. in Neurosci., U. Mich., 1977. Postdoctoral fellow dept zoology U. Tex., Austin, 1977-79; assoc. sr. research scientist Gen. Motors Research Labs., Warren, Mich., 1979-81, sr. research scientist, 1981-82, staff research scientist, 1982—; speaker Am. Cancer Soc., Detroit, 1983; adj. prof. dept. elec. and computer engring. Wayne State U., Detroit, 1984—; reviewer Tech. Research Found., Washington, 1984—. Contbr. articles to profl. jours. NIH fellow U. Mich., 1975, U. Tex., 1977. Mem. Soc. Neurosci., Mich. Neurosci. Soc. (membership chmn. 1984—), Am. Assn. Automotive Medicine, Soc. Automotive Engrs., Sigma Xi. Current work: Pathophysiologic mechanisms of spinal cord and brain injury; interventions to reduce severity and improve outcome. Subspecialties: Neurophysiology; Biomedical engineering. Office: Gen Motors Research Labs Biomed Dept Warren MI 48090

ANDERSON, W. FRENCH, government research scientist; b. Tulsa, Dec. 31, 1936; s. Daniel French and LaVere Frances (Schoenfelt) A.; m. Kathryn Dorothy Duncan, June 24, 1961. A.B. magna cum laude, Harvard U., 1958, M.D. magna cum laude, 1963; M.A. with honors, Cambridge (Eng.) U., 1963. Diplomate: Nat. Bd. Med. Examiners. Intern Children's Hosp., Boston, 1963-64; Head sect. human biochemistry Lab. Clin. Biochemistry, Nat. Heart Inst., NIH, 1968-71; head sect. molecular hematology Lab. Clin. Biochemistry, Nat. Heart Inst., NIH 1971-73; chief molecular hematology br. Lab. Clin. Biochemistry, 1973-77, chief Lab. Clin. Biochemistry, later Lab. Molecular Hematology, 1977—; adj. prof. grad. genetics program George Washington U.; mem. faculty dept. medicine and physiology NIH Grad. Program. Author 3 books.; contbr. numerous articles to profl. jours. Served as commd. officer USPHS, 1965-67. Recipient ann. award for sci. achievement biol. scis. Washington Acad. Scis., 1971, Superior Service award HEW, 1975, Thomas B. Cooley award for sci. achievement Cooley's Anemia Blood and Research Found. for Children, 1977, Outstanding Performance award HHS, 1982. Mem. Am. Chem. Soc., Am. Fedn. Clin. Research, Am. Soc. Cell Biology, Am. Soc. Biol. Chemists, Am. Soc. Clin. Investigation, Am. Soc. Hematology, Am. Soc. Human Genetics, Assn. Am. Physicians, Peripatetic Club, Hastings Center. Current Work: Gene therapy; genetic engineering; molecular genetics. Subspecialties: Genetics and genetic engineering (medicine); Molecular biology. Office: National Institutes of Health Bldg 10 Room 7D 20 Bethesda MD 20205

ANDERSON, WAYNE IAN, veterinarian, pathologist; b. N.Y.C., May 21, 1952; s. Bertram and Sylvia (Becker) A. B.S. cum laude, U. Del., 1973; M.S., U. Ga., 1975, Ph.D., 1978, D.V.M., 1981. Lic. veterinarian, Ala., Ga. Grad. research asst. dept. poultry sci. U. Ga., Athens, 1973-77; vet. diagnostician Vet. Diagnostic Lab., Albertville, Ala., 1981-82; field veterinarian U.S. Dept. Agr., Athens, 1982-85; resident in pathology N.Y. State Coll. Vet. Medicine, Cornell U., Ithaca, 1985—. Contbr. numerous articles to profl. jours. Active numerous charitable and religious orgns. Recipient letters of commendation U.S. Dept. Agr., 1983; Southeastern profl. cons. scholar U. Ga. Coll. Vet. Medicine, 1978; Mem. AVMA, Am. Assn. Avian Pathologists, Assn. Avian Veterinarians, Am. Assn. Swine Practitioners, Poultry Sci. Assn., Sigma Xi, Alpha Zeta, Phi Kappa Phi, Gamma Sigma Delta. Current work: Engaged in the gross and histopathological examination of tissue to determine the etiology of domestic animal diseases. Subspecialties: Pathology (veterinary medicine); Animal pathology. Home: 245 University Circle Athens GA 30605 Office: Dept Pathology NY State Coll Vet Medicine Cornell U Ithaca NY 14853

ANDRE, MICHAEL, medical physicist; b. Des Moines, Apr. 25, 1951; s. Paul Leo and Pauline (Vermie) A. B.A., Central U. Iowa, 1972; postgrad., U. Ariz., 1972-73; M.S., UCLA, 1975, Ph.D. in Med. Physics, 1979. Research assoc. Inst. Atmospheric Physics, Tucson, 1972-73; mem. tech. staff Hughes Aircraft Co., Los Angeles, 1973-74; researcher UCLA, 1974-77; med. radiation physicist Los Angeles County Olive View Med. Center, Los Angeles, 1977-81; asst. prof. radiol. scis. UCLA Sch. Medicine, 1980-81; asst. prof. radiology U. Calif. and VA Med. Ctr., San Diego, 1981—; sr. radiation physicist Cedars-Sinai Med. Ctr., Los Angeles, 1980—. Contbr. articles to profl. jours. Coordinator Ariz. Public Interest Research Group, 1972-73. Recipient Cum Laude award Radiol. Soc. N.Am., 1979; Louis B. Silverman award Health Physics Soc., 1979. Mem. Am. Assn. Physicists in Medicine, Soc. Photo-optical Instrumentation Engrs., Soc. Nuclear Medicine, American Alpine Sierra Club. Current Work: Digital image processing of CT, ultrasound, x-ray data. Subspecialties: Medical physics; Diagnostic radiology. Home: 536 Glenmont Dr Solana Beach CA 92075 Office: Dept Radiology U Calif V114 3350 La Jolla Village Dr La Jolla CA 92161

ANDREASSI, JOHN L(AWRENCE), psychology educator, researcher; b. N.Y.C., Oct. 23, 1934; s. Croce and Agnes M. (Aiello) A.; m. Gina Bearzatto, Mar. 29, 1969; children: John L., Jeanine, Cristina. B.A., CCNY, 1956; M.A., Fordham U., 1959; Ph.D., Case Western Res. U., 1964. Lic. psychologist, N.Y. Psychologist Dunlop & Assos., Stanford, Conn., 1958-61; USPHS fellow Western Res. U., Cleve., 1961-64; psychologist researcher U.S. Naval Tng. Device Center, Sands Point, N.Y., 1964-67; assoc. prof. N.Y. U., N.Y.C., 1967-73; prof. psychology Baruch Coll., CUNY, N.Y.C., 1973—; cons. ITT, Paramus, N.J., 1960-61, Naval Applied Scis. Lab., Bklyn., 1969-72. Author: Psychophysiology, 1980; contbr. articles to profl. jours., sect. to ency. Research awardee Office Naval Research, 1969-73, 73-79; Research awardee Air Force Office Sci. Research, 1979—. Fellow Internat. Orgn. Psychophysiology (bd. dirs. 1981—, editorial bd.); mem. Am. Psychol. Assn. Current Work: Research on event-related brain potentials and related sensory-perceptual processes, especially with respect to brain hemispheric differences in performance and physiological response. Subspecialties: Physiological psychology; Sensory processes. Home: 38 Gainsborough Rd Scarsdale NY 10583 Office: Baruch Coll Box 512 17 Lexington Ave New York NY 10010

ANDREEFF, MICHAEL, physician, researcher, educator; b. Berlin, Mar 11, 1943; came to U.S., 1977; s. Ljuben A. and Ursula H. (Nitzsche) A. Student, U. Muenster, 1962-64; M.D. magna cum laude, U. Heidelberg, 1968, Ph.D., 1976. Intern Mcpl. Hosp., Ludwigshafen, Germany, 1968-70; resident in medicine, sci. asst. U. Heidelberg, Germany, 1970-75; vis. scientist Karolinska Inst., Stockholm, 1973; staff clinician U. Mainz, Germany, 1976-77; mem. med. faculty U. Heidelberg, 1976—; vis. investigator Sloan-Kettering Inst. for Cancer Research, N.Y.C., 1977-79, assoc., 1979—; assoc. prof. medicine Cornell U., 1982—; asst. attending hematopathologist, asst. attending physician Leukemia/Lymphoma Service, Meml. Hosp., N.Y.C., 1981—. Contbr. numerous articles to profl. jours. Grantee German Research Council, 1977; Grantee Nat. Cancer Inst., 1980; Grantee Am. Cancer Soc., 1980. Mem. German Cancer Soc., German Soc. Hematology and Oncology, European Study Group for Cell Proliferation, European Assn. Cancer Research, Am. Assn. Cancer Research, Am. Soc. Clin. Oncology, Cell Kinetics Soc., N.Y. Acad. Sci. Current Work: Hematology, laser in medicine, flow cytometry, leukemia cell biology, chemotherapy of cancer. Subspecialties: Hematology; Cell study oncology. Office: Meml Sloan-Kettering Cancer Center 1275 York Ave New York NY 10021

ANDREIS, HENRY JEROME, sugar company executive, soil technologist; b. Milw., Sept. 1, 1931; s. Henry Rico and Elizabeth (Burback) A.; m. Audrey N. Kowalski, Apr. 24, 1954; children—Terry, Barbara, Henry, Mary, Linda. B.S., U. Wis.-Madison, 1954, M.S., 1955. Soil technologist U.S. Sugar Corp., Clewiston, Fla., 1955-69, first asst., 1969-81, v.p., dir., 1981—; cons. sugarcane prodn. Inventor silage from sugarcane bagasse, sulfur managanese fertilizer. Bd. dirs. Hendry County Soil and Water Conservation Dist., 1983-85; mem. sugarcane adv. bd. Dept. Agr., 1984-85. Calumet-Hecla Consol. Copper Co. fellow. Mem. Am. Soc. Agronomy, Crop Sci. Soc. Am., Soil Sci. Soc. Am., Am. Soc. Sugar Cane Technologists (exec. com.), Internat. Soc. Sugar Cane Technologists, Internat. Soc. Soil Sci., Soil and Crop Sci. Soc. Fla. (cons. editor jour. 1971-72), Hendry County Farm Bur. (exec. com. 1968-72, pres. 1970-71), Palm Beach County Bowling Assn. Clubs: Clewiston Golf (pres.), S.W. Fla. Lake Okeechobee Bass (Clewiston) (v.p.). Lodge: Elks. Current work: Sugarcane agronomy, soil fertility, fertilizers, pastures. Subspecialties: Agronomy; Soil science. Office: US Sugar Corp PO Drawer 1207 111 Ponce De Leon St Clewiston FL 33440

ANDRES, RONALD PAUL, chemical engineer, educator; b. Chgo., Jan. 9, 1938; s. Harold William and Amanda Ann (Breuhaus) A.; m. Jean Mills Elwood, July 15, 1961; children—Douglas, Jennifer, Mark. B.S., Northwestern U., 1959; Ph.D., Princeton U., 1962. Asst. prof. Princeton U., 1962-68, asso. prof., 1968-76, prof. chem. engring., 1976-81, Purdue U., West Lafayette, Ind., 1981—; head Purdue U. (Sch. Chem. Engring.), 1981—. Mem. Am. Chem. Soc., Am. Inst. Chem. Engrs., AAAS, Sigma Xi, Tau Beta Pi, Pi Mu Epsilon, Phi Lambda Upsilon, Phi Eta Sigma. Current Work: Physics and chemistry of small molecular clusters; metal clusters, catalysis; nucleation; atmospheric chemistry. Subspecialties: Chemical engineering; Surface chemistry. Office: Sch Chem Engring Purdue U West Lafayette IN 47907

ANDREW, CLIFFORD GEORGE, neuroscientist, neurologist; b. St. Louis, Sept. 10, 1946; s. Eugene Ashton and Anna Louise (Hanish) A.; m. Louise Collier Briggs, June 13, 1970; children: Galen Michael, Amalie Linnea. A.B. (Coll. scholar), Columbia U., 1968; Ph.D. in Biochemistry, Duke U., 1974, M.D. (Duke Avelor scholar), 1975. Diplomate: Am. Bd. Psychiatry and Neurology. Intern Duke U. Hosp., 1975-1976; resident in neurology Johns Hopkins U., 1976-79, neuromuscular fellow, 1979-80, asst. prof. neurology, 1980—. Contbr. articles to profl. jours. Recipient Tchr. Investigator Devel. award Nat. Inst. Neurologic Communicative Disease and Stroke, 1980—; Muscular Dystrophy Assn. basic research grantee, 1981—. Mem. Columbia Chemists, AAAS, Am. Soc. Neurochemistry, Neuroscis. Soc., Am. Acad. Neurology, Physicians for Social Responsibility, Chesapeake Bay Found., Severn River Assn., Pointfield Landing Community Assn. Independent Democrat. Presbyterian. Patentee Intern bd. game, microcomputer game. Current Work: Interested in role of biol membranes and their constituent proteins and glycoproteins in neuromuscular devel., function, and disease; investigating membrane factors responsible for developmentally regulated muscle susceptibility to Coxsackie A2 Virus. Subspecialties: Neurobiology; Membrane biology. Home: 474 Old Orchard Cirle Point Field Landing on the Severn Millersville MD 21108 Office: Dept Neurology 5134 Meyer Neuroscis Center Johns Hopkins U Sch Medicine Baltimore MD 21205

ANDREWS, HUGH ROBERT, nuclear physicist, researcher; b. Frederickon, N.B., Can., Apr. 29, 1940; s. John V. and Bertha T. (Smith) A.; m. Josephine D. Kennedy, May 22, 1971; children: J. Matthew, E. Louise. B.Sc. (Lord Beaverbrook scholar), U. N.B., 1962; A.M., Harvard U., 1963, Ph.D., 1970. Research officer Chalk River Nuclear Labs., Atomic Energy of Can., 1971—. Contbr. articles to sci. publs. Recipient prize Can. Math. Congress, 1958, Rutherford prize Royal Soc. Can., 1968; Frank Knox fellow, 1962-64. Mem. Can. Assn. Physicists, Am. Phys. Soc., Can. Nuclear Soc., N.Y. Acad. Scis., Sigma Xi. Anglican. Current Work: Experimental nuclear structure, particularly high spin states; gamma spectroscopy; hyperfine interactions; energy loss phenomena; ultra-sensentive mass spectrometry. Subspecialties: Nuclear physics; Condensed matter physics. Home: 66 Rutherford Ave PO Box 1356 Deep River ON KOJ 1PO Canada Office: Chalk River Nuclear Labs Station 49 Chalk River ON K0J 1J0 Canada

ANDREWS, PETER WALTER, developmental biologist, educator, researcher; b. London, June 5, 1950; s. Walter and Sheila A.; m. Dale Joan Andrews, Sept. 26, 1981; 1 dau., Whitney Elizabeth. B.Sc. with 1st class honors in Biochemistry, U. Leeds, Eng., 1971; D.Phil., Oxford (Eng.) U., 1975. Research fellow Inst. Pasteur, Paris, 1974-75, Sloan-Kettering Inst., N.Y.C., 1976-78; research investigator Wistar Inst., Phila., 1978-80, research assoc., 1980-82, asst. prof., 1983—. Contbr. articles to sci. jours. Mem. Soc. Developmental Biology. Current Work: Analysis of cellular differentiation, especially using human and mouse teratocarcima cell lines and employing immunogenetic approaches that include the use of monoclonal antibody-defined differentiation antigens; preparation of new hybridomas. Subspecialties: Developmental biology; Cell and tissue culture. Office: Wistar Inst 36th and Spruce Sts Philadelphia PA 19104

ANDREWS, ROGER CHARLES, radiation and nuclear effects scientist, physics educator; b. N.Y.C., Mar. 13, 1941; s. George Wallace and Mary (Spehr) A.; m. Barbara Ann Weaver, Dec. 24, 1976 (div. May 1980); children—David, Deborah, Craig. B.S. in Engring., U.S. Mil. Acad., 1962; M.S. in Physics, Naval Postgrad. Sch., 1969; M.B.A. in Mgmt., Fairleigh Dickinson U., 1973; Ph.D. in Engring. Adminstrn., George Washington U., 1981. Assoc. prof. physics U.S. Mil. Acad., West Point, N.Y., 1970-74; mgr. tech. devel. Research and Devel. Office, C.E., Washington, 1974-76; mgr. infra-red devel. Night Vision Lab., Washington, 1976-78; mem. sci. adv. group Def. Nuclear Agy., Alexandria, Va., 1978-82; chief radiation effects McDonnell Douglas Astronautics Co., St. Louis, 1982—; U.S. rep. on infrared tech. NATO, Brussels, 1976-78, on Identification Friend or Foe, 1976-78. Contbr. numerous articles to tech. jours. Chmn. Christian Social Concerns Commn., United Methodist Ch., Washington, 1980; mem. adminstrv. bd. Met. United Meth. Ch., Washington, 1981. Served to lt. col. U.S. Army, 1962-82. Decorated Legion of Merit. Mem. IEEE, Am. Soc. Mil. Engrs. (program chmn. 1978). Republican. Presbyterian. Club: Creve Coeur Country. Current work: Hardening of electrical and electro-optic devices to the effects of nuclear weapons. Subspecialties: Nuclear physics; Atomic and molecular physics. Home: 12621 Conway Rd Saint Louis MO 63141 Office: McDonnell Douglas Corp Dept E451 PO Box 516 Saint Louis MO 63166

ANDRIA, GEORGE DANIEL, manufacturing company executive; b. Hibbing, Minn., Aug. 4, 1941; s. Chris and Mary (Coppeletti) A.; m. Kathleen Patricia Brady, June 21, 1964; children—Frances M., Patricia M., Kathleen M., Bridgett M., George D. B.A., St. Johns U., 1963; M.S., St. Louis U., 1965, Ph.D., 1968. Asst. prof. Fontbonne Coll., Clayton, Mo., 1967-68, U. Pitts., 1968-73; mgr. sci. computing Bituminous Coal Research, Monroeville, Pa., 1973-81; dir. sci. systems Am. Greetings Corp., Cleve., 1981—; cons. Alcoa Aluminum, Pitts., 1970-71, Fuller Roth & Smith, Pitts., 1971-72, Bituminous Coal Research, Pitts., 1972-73. Contbr. articles to profl. jours. St. Louis U. fellow 1965-68. Mem. Soc. Indsl. and Applied Math., Assn. Computing Machinery, Operations Research Soc. Am. Roman Catholic. Current work: Management science, operations research, statistics, scientific computing. Subspecialties: Mathematical software; Artificial intelligence. Home: 4841 Pin Oak Dr Akron OH 44313 Office: Am Greetings 10500 American Rd Cleveland OH 44144

ANDROULAKIS, JOHN GEORGE, mechanical engineer; b. Archanes, Crete, Greece, May 15, 1924; came to U.S., 1953, naturalized, 1962; s. George John and Maria Stylianos (Terjakis) A.; m. Vassiliki John Androulakis, Jan. 3, 1959; children: George John. B.Engring., Ecole Nationale Superieure du Genie Maritime, France, 1953; M.S.M.E., Poly. Inst. Bklyn., 1955. Design engr. H.N. Whittelsey, Inc., N.Y.C., 1954-58; devel. engr. Brookhaven Nat. Lab., Upton, N.Y., 1958-64; project engr. Grumman Aerospace Corp., Bethpage, N.Y., 1964-75; tech. dir. Intersystem Design & Tech. Corp., Lauderdale, Fla., 1975-80; prin. mem. tech. staff RCA/AStro Electronics, Princeton, N.J., 1980—. Contbr. articles to profl. jours. Served with Greek Air Force, 1942-46. Decorated Brit. Mil. Medal. Greek Orthodox. Patentee in field. Current Work: Meteorol. and communication satellite design. Subspecialties: Aerospace engineering and technology; Satellite studies.

ANDRUSHKIW, ROMAN IHOR, mathemetician, educator, consultant; b. Lviw, Ukraine, May 3, 1937; came to U.S., 1949; s. Joseph Wasyl and Sofia A.; m. Svitlana Maria Lutzky, Nov. 22, 1975; 1 son, Pavlo Marian. B.E., Stevens Inst. Tech., 1959, Ph.D. in Math., 1973; M.S. E.E., Newark Coll. Engring., 1964; M.S.in Math, U. Chgo., 1967. Elec. engr. Weston Instruments and Electronics, Newark, 1959-64; instr. Newark Coll. Engring., 1964-66, 68-70; research asst. U. Chgo., 1966-68; asst. prof. N.J. Inst. Tech., Newark, 1970-78, assoc. prof. math., 1978-84, prof. math., 1984—; cons., instr. Bendix Corp., Teterboro, N.J., 1981-82; cons. E.T. Killam Assos., Millburn, N.J., 1982; reviewer Am. Math. Soc., Ann Arbor, Mich., 1977—; speaker meetings and confs. Contbr. numerous sci. papers and abstracts to profl. pubs. Assoc. dir. Newark chpt. Plast, Inc., 1980-82. NSF grantee, 1966. Mem. Soc. Computer Simulation, Soc. Indsl. and Applied Math., Internat. Assn. Math. and Computers in Simulation, Am. Math. Soc., Shevchenko Sci. Soc. (exec. council 1974—), Ukranian Engrs. Soc. Am. Inventor, patentee. Current Work: Finite difference and finite element analysis of initial-boundary value problems in fluid dynamics, heat and mass transfer, wave propagation, Stefan-type problems; spectral theory and eigenvalue approximation of operator-valued functions. Subspecialties: Applied mathematics; Numerical analysis (computer science). Office: NJ Inst Tech 323 Dr Martin Luther King Jr Blvd Newark NJ 07102

ANDRYSCO, ROBERT MICHAEL, specialist in human, animal relations, researcher; b. Cleve., Nov. 11, 1954; s. Robert and Bernice Beatrice A.; m. Paula Ann Hohenbrink, Oct. 17, 1982. B.S. in Biology and Chemistry, Ashland Coll., 1976; M.S. in Vet. Physiology and Pharmacology, Ohio State U., 1978, Ph.D. in Vet. Medicine and Psychology, 1982. Surg. asst. Brookville Animal Hosp., Parma, Ohio, 1975; research asso. Ohio Agrl. Research and Devel. Center, Wooster, 1976; grad. research assoc., teaching asso. vet. physiology Ohio State U., Columbus, 1976-78, grad. research asso., 1978-81, specialist in human and animal relations, Columbus, Ohio, 1980—; cons. Capital Area Humane Soc., Columbus; 14 Columbus area vet. clinics Ohio State U. Vet. Clinic, others. Contbr. articles on human-animal relations to profl. jours. Named Outstanding Young Man of Am. U.S. Jaycees, 1979. Mem. Soc. for Neurosci., European Brain and Behavior Soc., Brit. Brain Research Assn., Delta Soc. Roman Catholic. Current Work: Pet-facilitated therapy: companion animal behavior modification; establishment of Campanion Animal Services, Inc. Subspecialty: Human/animal bond.

ANFINSEN, CHRISTIAN BOEHMER, biochemist; b. Monessen, Pa., Mar. 26, 1916; s. Christian Boehmer and Sophie (Rasmussen) A.; m. Florence Bernice Kenenger, Nov. 29, 1941; children: Carol Bernice, Margot Sophie, Christian Boehmer; m. Libby Shulman Ely, 1979. B.A., Swarthmore Coll., 1937, D.Sc., 1965; M.S., U. Pa., 1939, D.Sc., 1967; Ph.D., Harvard U., 1943; D.Sc. (hon.), Georgetown U., 1967, Swarthmore Coll., 1965, N.Y. Med. Coll., 1969, Gustav Adolphus U., 1975, Brandeis U., 1977, Providence Coll., 1978; M.D. (hon.), U. Naples, 1981. Am.-Scandinavian Found. fellow Carlsberg Lab., Copenhagen, 1939; sr. cancer research fellow Nobel Inst., Stockholm, 1947; Markle scholar, 1948—; asst. prof. biol. chemistry Harvard U. Med. Sch.; prof. biochemistry Harvard Med. Sch., 1962-63; Guggenheim fellow Weizmann Inst., Rehovot, Israel, 1958; chief lab. cellular physiology and metabolism Nat. Heart Inst., Bethesda, Md., 1950-62; chief lab. chem. biology Nat. Inst. Arthritis and Metabolic Diseases, Bethesda, 1963-82; mem. faculty dept. biology Johns Hopkins U., Balt., 1982—Bd. govs. Weizmann Inst. Sci., Rehovot, Israel. Author: The Molecular Basis of Evolution, 1959; Contbr. to sci. publs. Recipient Rockefeller Public Service award, 1954-55; Nobel prize in chemistry, 1972; Myrtle Wreath Hadassah, 1977. Mem. Am. Soc. Biol. Chemists (pres. 1971-72), Am. Acad. Arts and Scis., Am. Philos. Soc., Nat. Acad. Scis., Washington Acad. Scis., Fedn. Am. Scientists (treas. 1958-59, vice chmn. 1959-60, 73-76), Pontifical Acad. Sci. Current Work: Proteins. Subspecialty: Biochemistry (biology). Home: 1740 Vineyard Trail Epping Forest Annapolis MD Office: Dept Biology Johns Hopkins U. 34th and Charles St Baltimore MD 21218

ANGELES, MARSHALL ROBERT, chemist; b. N.Y.C., Apr. 7, 1945; s. Modesto and Alexandra (Haluko) A.; m. Patricia Lynch, June 21, 1975; children—Matthew, Elena-Rose, Dennis. B.S. in Chemistry, Manhattan Coll., 1966; M.S. in Organic Chemistry, St. Joseph's U., Phila., 1969; postgrad. Villanova U., 1969-71. Research asso. Rhône-Poulenc, New Brunswick, N.J., 1973-79; sr. chemist Merck & Co., Inc., Rahway, N.J., 1979—. Patentee in field. Mem. Adv. bd. Indsl. and Chem. News, 1983—. Mem. Am. Chem. Soc. Democrat. Roman Catholic. Current work: Process research and optimization, new leads exploration and evaluation, synthetic chemistry via organometallic intermediates. Subspecialties: Organometallics; Organic chemistry. Office: Merck & Co Inc PO Box 2000 Rahway NJ 07065

ANGELL, CHARLES LESLIE, research chemist; b. Budapest, Hungary, July 4, 1926; came to U.S., 1957; m. Marianne Haley, Sept. 20, 1958; children—Steve J., Catharine M. B.S., U. Sydney, 1949, M.S., 1950; Ph.D., Cambridge U., Eng., 1955. Sr. Chemist Central Sci. Lab. Research Inst., Union Carbide Corp., Tarrytown, N.Y., 1958-70, research chemist, 1970—. Contbr. articles to profl. jours. Bd. dirs. United Way of No. Westchester, N.Y., 1972-83, pres.-elect., 1984—. Recipient Marshall Meml. award United Way, 1984; Community Service award Union Carbide Corp., 1983. Mem. Royal Soc. Chemistry, Coblenz Soc. (pres. 1969-71), Soc. Applied Spectroscopy (chmn. N.Y. sect. 1982), Am. Chem. Soc., ASTM (vice chmn. com. raman spectroscopy). Current work: Infrared and raman spectroscopy of surfaces and catalytic systems; experimental development of techniques; applications to molecular sieves. Subspecialties: Surface chemistry; Catalysis chemistry. Office: Union Carbide Corp Tarrytown NY 10591

ANGELO, MICHAEL JAMES, bio-engineer, research chemical engineer; b. Rahway, N.J., Nov. 5, 1954; s. James Eugene and Lucy (Panaccione) A.; m. Carla Ann Demicco, May 19, 1984. B.S., Rensselear Poly. Inst. 1976; Ph.D., U. Del., 1981. Sr. scientist mah. scis. central research Gen. Foods Tech. Ctr., Tarrytown, N.Y., 1980—. Contbr. articles to profl. jours. Mem. Am. Inst. Chem. Engrs., Am. Chem. Soc., AAAS, Tau Beta Pi. Roman Catholic. Current work: Pharmacokinetic modeling applications in toxicology and nutrition research; enzyme kinetic modeling; applied math consultant in food research. Subspecialties: Pharmacokinetics; Chemical engineering. Office: Gen Foods Tech Ctr 555 S Broadway Tarrytown NY 10591

ANGLIN, JAMES RICHARD, research chemist; b. Toronto, Ont., Can., Nov. 10, 1946; s. Arthur Baker and Elizabeth Mary (Wales) A.; m. Esther Joy Boykin, Apr. 4, 1977; children—Emily Claire, Elaina Marie. B.Sc., Queen's U., Kingston, Ont., Can., 1969; Ph.D., MIT., 1974. Postdoctoral fellow, research assoc. U. Alberta, Edmonton, Can., 1974-77; vis. asst. prof. Bucknell U., Lewisburg, Pa., 1977-78; research chemist Gulf Research & Devel. Co., Harmarville, Pa., 1978—. Patentee in field. NRC of Can. postdoctorate fellow U. Alta., 1974-76, research assoc., 1977, postgrad. scholar, 1969, Uniroyal fellow MIT, 1974. Mem. Am. Chem. Soc., Soc. Automotive Engrs. (Pitts. sect. vice chmn. for student activities 1984-85). Current work: Chemistry and technology of fuels and lubricants, diesel fuel low temperature filterability, octane improvers, petrochemicals, organometallics. Subspecialties: Fuels; Organometallics. Home: 4705 Pembroke Ct Allison Park PA 15101 Office: Gulf Research & Devel Co PO Drawer 2038 Pittsburgh PA 15230

ANGUS, JOHN COTTON, chemical engineering educator; b. Grand Haven, Mich., Feb. 22, 1934; s. Francis Clark and Margaret (Cotton) A.; m. Caroline Helen Gezon, June 25, 1960; children—Lorraine Margaret, Charles Thomas. B.S. in Chem. Engring, U. Mich., 1956, M.S., 1958, Ph.D. in Engring, 1960. Registered profl. engr., Ohio, Mich. Research engr. Minn. Mining & Mfg. Co., St. Paul, 1960-63; prof. Case Inst. Tech., Cleve., 1963-67, prof. chem. engring., 1967—, chmn. dept., 1974-80; vis. lectr. U. Edinburgh, Scotland, 1972-73; vis. prof. Northwestern U., 1980-81. Vice pres. ARC, Inc.; trustee Ohio Coal Research Lab.; chmn. bd. trustees Ohio Scottish Games. NSF fellow, 1956-57; NATO sr. fellow, 1972-73. Mem. Am. Inst. Chem. Engrs., Am. Chem. Soc., Electrochem. Soc., Sigma Xi, Tau Beta Pi, Phi Lambda Upsilon. Research in fields of crystal growth, laser applications, coal gasification, sulfur removal processes, electrochemical devices, thermodynamics. Subspecialties: Chemical engineering; Electrochemistry. Home: 2716 Colchester Rd Cleveland OH 44106 Office: Dept Chem Engring Case Western Res U Cleveland OH 44106

ANGUS, ROBERT DALE, veterinarian; b. American Falls, Idaho, Oct. 2, 1930; s. Stephen Robert and Afton (Parker) A.; m. Vivien June Wheeler, May 10, 1961; children—Stephen Wade, Jyll, Scot Alan, Ryan Dee, Jeff Davis. B.S., U. Calif.-Davis, 1954, D.V.M., 1956; M.P.H., U. Minn., 1967. Lic. veterinarian, Colo., Idaho. Instr. clinics, surgery Colo. State U., Fort Collins, 1956-57; veterinarian Dept. Agr., Idaho, 1957-65, St. Paul, 1965-70, Nat. Vet. Services Labs., Ames, Iowa, 1970—. Contbr. articles to profl. jours. Active local chs. Ch. of Jesus Christ of Latter-Day Saints, 1952—. Mem. AVMA, Nat. Assn. Fed. Veterinarians, Phi Zeta. Current work: Diagnostic veterinary medicine—improvement, development, and evaluation of diagnostic tests, reagents, and procedures for disease processes. Subspecialties: Microbiology (veterinary medicine); Immunobiology and immunology. Home: 3108 Northwood Ames IA 50010 Office: Dept Agr Nat Vet Services Labs PO Box 844 Ames IA 50010

ANISMAN, HYMIE, psychologist, educator, researcher; b. Munich, Germany, Apr. 3, 1948; emigrated to Can., 1950; s. Simon M. and Helen (Pulver) A.; m. Maida S. Silverstone, Aug. 30, 1969; children: Simon, Rebecca, Jessica. B.A., Sir George Williams U., Montreal, Que., 1969; M.A., Meml. U. Nfld., St. John's, 1970; Ph.D., U. Waterloo, Ont., 1972. Asst. prof. U. Waterloo, 1972-73, Wilfred Laurier U., Waterloo, 1973-74; asst. prof. Carleton U., Ottawa, Ont., 1974-76, assoc. prof., 1976-82, prof., 1982—. Editor: Psychopharmacology of Aversive Motivated Behavior, 1978; contbr. articles to profl. jours. Fellow Can. Psychol. Assn.; mem. Am. Psychol. Assn., AAAS, Soc. for Neurosci. Current Work: Stress and its relation to neurochemical change. Implications for physical and pscyhological pathology. Subspecialties: Neuropharmacology; Neuropsychology. Office: Carleton Univ Ottawa ON K1S 5B6 Canada

ANNINO, RAYMOND, chemistry researcher; b. N.Y.C., Sept. 5, 1927; s. Joseph and Jane (O'Connell) A.; m. Marie Ellin Ott, Oct. 21, 1950; children—Douglas, Stephen, Brian, Lauren, Jill. B.A., Columbia U., 1950; Ph.D., Okla. State U., 1955. Researcher Nat. Dairy Research Lab., Oakdale, L.I., N.Y., 1950-53; supr. analytical research Westvaco Chlor Alkali, FMC, South Charleston, W.Va., 1955-57; asst. prof. chemistry Northeast La. State U., Monroe, 1957-60; asst. prof. chemistry, assoc. prof. Canisius Coll., Buffalo, 1960-67; sr. research scientist Foxboro Co., Mass., 1967-72; prof., chmn. dept. chemistry Canisius Coll., Buffalo, 1972-81, prin. research scientist, Foxboro, 1981—; sci. advisor FDA, Buffalo and Washington, 1972-81; maitre de reserche Ecole Polytechnique, Paris, 1977-78. Author: The Use of Personal Computers in the Laboratory. Contbr. articles to profl. jours., chpts. to books. Served with USN, 1945-47; PTO. Recipient Disting. Chromatographers award Northeast Regional Chromatography Discussion Group, 1982; IR-100 award Research and Devel. Mag. Competition, 1975, others. Mem. Am. Chem. Soc. (Jacob Schoelkopf medal 1983, chmn. analytical group local chpt. 1962); Soc. Applied Spectroscopy (chmn. local sects. 1966-67, 73-74), Sigma Xi, Phi Lambda Upsilon, Sigma Pi Sigma. Current work: Chromatography instrumentation and theory, column technology, use of fluidic, no moving part, devices, optical to pneumatic and pneumatic to optical conversion processes. Subspecialty: Analytical chemistry. Home: 9 Winchester North Smithfield RI 02895 Office: Foxboro Co D 330 01-2 38 Neponset Ave Foxboro MA 02035

ANNIS, LAWRENCE VINCENT, JR., clinical psychologist, mental health administrator; b. Augusta, Ga., Dec. 28, 1946; s. Lawrence Vincent and Betty (Allen) A.; m. Kathy Ann Kirkwood, June 12, 1971 (div. Aug. 1973); m. Christy Adele Baker, Aug. 22, 1982. B.A., Augusta Coll., 1968; M.A., Western Carolina U., Cullowhee, N.C., 1974; Ph.D., U. Miss., 1981. Staff psychologist Alpine Psychoedn. Center, Gainesville, Ga., 1974-75; psychologist N. Miss. Retardation Center, Oxford, 1978-79; psychology intern Devereux Found., Devon, Pa., 1979-80; sr. behavior specialist Gracewood State Sch., Ga., 1980-81; clin. psychologist Fla. State Hosp., Chattahoochee, 1981-84; supervising clin. psychologist Fla. Corrections Mental Health Instn., 1984—. Served with USN, 1969-72. Mem. Internat. Council Psychologists, Am. Psychol. Assn., Southeastern Psychol. Assn. Unitarian. Current Work: Forensic psychology, sex offender rehabilitation. Subspecialty: Behavioral psychology. Office: Forensic Service Fla State Hosp Chattahoochee FL 32324

ANSARI, GHULAM A. S., biochemist, educator; b. Barabanki, India, Oct. 4, 1947; came to U.S., 1974; s. Ghulam Matin and Basirunisa Ansari; m. Naseem Hasan, Apr. 11, 1974; 1 child, Faheem Ahmad. B.Sc., Aligarh Muslim U., India, 1966, M.Sc., 1969, M.Ph., 1970, Ph.D., 1973. Asst. prof. Aligarh Muslim U., India, 1973-74; postdoctoral fellow U. Idaho, Moscow, 1974-76; research assoc. U. Tex. Med. Br., Galveston, 1976-79, asst. prof. biochemistry, 1980—. Contbr. articles to various jours. Mem. Am. Chem. Soc., Royal Soc. Chemistry, Sigma Xi. Current work: Toxicity of halogenated hydrocarbons, prevention of chemical carcinogenesis by food antioxidants, carcinogen present in food. Subspecialties: Biochemistry (biology); Toxicology (agriculture). Home: 7662 Chantilly Circle Galveston TX 77551 Office: U Tex Med Br 626 Basic Sci Bldg Galveston TX 77550

ANSELL, GEORGE STEPHEN, metallurgist, educator; b. Akron, Ohio, Apr. 1, 1934; s. Frederick Jesse and Fanny (Soletsky) A.; m. Marjorie Boris, Dec. 18, 1960; children: Frederick Stuart, Laura Ruth, Benjamin Jesse. B.Met.E., Rensselaer Poly. Inst., 1954; M.Met.E., 1955, Ph.D., 1960. Registered profl. engr., N.Y. State. Phys. metallurgist U.S. Naval Research Lab., Washington, 1957-58; faculty Rensselaer Poly. Inst., Troy, N.Y., 1960—, Robert W. Hunt prof. metall. engring., 1965—, chmn. materials div., 1969-74, dean engring., 1974—; Cons. to pvt. cos. Recipient Curtis W. McGraw award Am. Soc. for Engring. Edn., 1971. Fellow Am. Soc. for Metals (Alfred H. Geisler award Eastern N.Y. chpt. 1964, Bradley Stoughton award 1968), Metall. Soc.; mem. Am. Inst. Mining, Metall. and Petroleum Engrs. (Hardy Gold medal 1961, chmn. Inst. Metals div. 1974), Nat. Soc. Profl. Engrs., Sci. Research Soc. Am., Sigma Xi, Tau Beta Pi, Phi Lambda Upsilon. Research, publs. on theoretical and exptl. analysis of relationships between defect structure and properties of crystaline solids. Subspecialties: Metallurgy; High-temperature materials. Home: 6 Colonial Green Loudonville NY 12211 Office: Sch of Engring Rensselaer Poly Inst Troy NY 12181

ANSELMO, VICTOR JOHN, engineer; b. Bklyn., Aug. 21, 1940; s. Peter Joseph and Helen Tillie (Koslowsky) A.; m. Mary Catherine Root, Sept. 8, 1962; children—Victor John, Joseph Frederick, Michele Marie, John Vito. B.S., U. Md., 1963; M.S., So. Meth. U., 1966; Ph.D., Okla. State U., 1971; M.B.A., Pepperdine U., 1980. Sr. engr. Jet Propulsion Lab., Calif. Inst. Tech., Pasadena, Calif., 1970-78, sr. scientist, 1978-82, mem. tech. staff, 1980-82, mgr. soldier machine interface, 1982-84; dep. dir. space sta. engring. NASA, Washington, 1984-85; mgr. artificial intelligence ctr. Boeing Computer Services, Bellevue, Wash., 1985—. Patentee multispectral image diagnosis system. Contbr. articles to profl. jours. Choral dir. Los Angeles area churches, 1970-83, youth orgn. coordinator, 1970-80; youth sports coach La Canada City Sports Leagues, 1975-80. NIH fellow, 1972. Mem. IEEE, Am. Mgmt. Assn., Am. Assn. Artificial Intelligence, AIAA, Roman Catholic. Current work: Manager artificial intelligence center; development of advanced automation plan for space station; application of artificial intelligence and robotics. Subspecialties: Robotics; Artificial intelligence. Home: 3320 217th Pine Redmond WA 98052 Office: Boeing Computer Services Artificial Intelligence Ctr Bellevue WA

ANSON, JAMES GREG, kinesiologist, researcher, educator; b. Te Aroha, N.Z., Feb. 28, 1945; came to U.S., 1981; s. James Midgley and Sarah Eugenie (McNiel) A.; m. Erin Diana Wylie, Jan. 5, 1974; children—Jason James, Mark Wylie. Diploma in Phys. Edn., U. Otago, Dunedin, N.Z., 1974; M.S., U. Wyo., 1977; Ph.D., Pa. State U., 1980. Cert. tchr., N.Z. Secondary sch. tchr. Te Aroha Coll., N.Z., 1966-67, Papatoetoe High Sch., Auckland, N.Z., 1970; tchr. N.Z. Vol. Service Abroad, Guadalcanal, Solomon Islands, 1968-69; lectr. Cumberland Coll. Health Scis., Sydney, Australia, 1980-81; acting asst. prof. U. Wash., Seattle, 1981-83; asst. prof. Oreg. State U., Corvallis, 1983-85, dir. Motor Behavior Lab., 1983-85, lectr. U. Otago, Dunedin, N.Z., 1985—. Contbr. articles to sci. jours. Mem. Soc. Neurosci., AAAS, N.Am. Soc. Psychology of Sport and Phys. Activity, Phi Kappa Phi, Phi Delta Kappa, Kappa Delta Pi. Current work: Human motor control and motor development, specifically the study of factors underlying planning, initiating and control of simple and complex rapid arm movements. Subspecialties: Neuropsychology; Cognition. Office: Faculty Phys Edn U Otago Box 56 Dunedin NZ

ANTAL, MICHAEL JERRY, JR., energy specialist and consultant; b. Monroe, Mich., May 18, 1947; s. Michael Jerry and Carolyn Sarah (McAdam) A.; m. Ann Gorsuch Slaughter, July 14, 1949; children: Dickinson James, Rachel Caroline. A.B., Dartmouth Coll., 1969; M.S., Harvard U., 1970, Ph.D., 1973. Mem. staff Los Alamos Sci. Lab., N.Mex., 1973-75; asst. prof. mech. and aerospace engring. Princeton U., 1975-81; Coral Industries prof. renewable energy resources U. Hawaii, Honolulu, 1981—; cons. Council on Environ. Quality, Office Tech. Assessment, Exxon Corp. Contbr. articles to sci. jours. Recipient numerous grants fed. and state agys. Mem. Am. Chem. Soc., Am. Phys. Soc., Soc. Indsl. and Applied Math., Combustion Inst., AAAS. Christian Scientist. Current Work: Pyrolysis chemistry, supercritical fluids, thermochemical biomass conversion, high temperature solar thermal energy. Subspecialties: Biomass (energy science and technology); Solar energy. Home: 357 Opihikao St Honolulu HI 96825 Office: U Hawaii 2540 Dole St Honolulu HI 96822

ANTCLIFF, RICHARD RAYMOND, research physicist; b. Jersey City, N.J., June 31, 1955; s. Frederick Antcliff and Grace (Martin) Antcliff Lemke; m. Joanne Nix, May 28, 1977; 1 child, Barbara Jo. B.A., Berry Coll., 1977; Ph.D., U. Ga., 1981. Research physicist Systems Research Labs, Inc., Dayton, Ohio, 1981—. Contbr. articles to profl. jours. Deacon, Sunday sch. tchr. Liberty Bapt. Ch., Hampton, Va., 1983-84. Named one of Outstanding Young Men Am., 1984. Mem. Am. Chem. Soc., Optical Soc. Am., Soc. Applied Spectroscopy, Am. Sci. Affiliation. Current work: Application of CARS to combustion diagnostics of hypersonic scramjets. Subspecialties: Laser spectroscopy; Physical chemistry. Office: Systems Research Labs Inc NASA Langley Research Ctr MS 168 Hampton VA 23665

ANTLER, MORTON, scientist, researcher; b. N.Y.C., Apr. 27, 1928; s. Max and Anna Antler; m. Esther Baron, June 10, 1950; children—Francine, Douglas, Laurel. B.A., NYU, 1948; Ph.D. in Chemistry, Cornell U., 1953. Research chemist Ethyl Corp., Detroit, 1953-58; supervising phys. chemist Borg Warner Research Ctr., Des Plaines, Ill., 1958-59; adv. chemist IBM, Endicott, N.Y., 1959-63; dep. dir. research Burndy Corp., Norwalk, Conn., 1963-70; mem. tech. staff AT&T Bell Labs., Columbus, Ohio, 1970—; chmn. adv. com. Internat. Confs. on Elec. Contact Phenomena, 1984—. Contbr. articles to profl. jours. Recipient Honor award Electronic Connector Study Group, Inc., Camden, 1975; Ragnar Holm Sci. Achievement award Ill. Inst. Tech., Chgo., 1980. Mem. IEEE (sr., chmn. CHMT elec. contacts com. 1981—), Am. Chem. Soc., ASTM, Am. Electroplaters' Soc. (Precious Metal Plating award 1968, 71), Am. Soc. Lubrication Engrs. (Capt. Alfred E. Hunt Meml. award 1971), Sigma Xi. Current work: Electrical Contacts; friction; lubrication and wear, corrosion science; environmental effects on materials. Subspecialties: Materials (engineering); Electrical contacts and tribology. Home: 821 Strawberry Hill Rd E Columbus OH 43213 Office: AT&T Bell Labs 6200 E Broad St Columbus OH 43213

ANTMAN, KAREN SUE HAMM, physician, b. Camden, N.J., July 26, 1948. B.S., magna cum laude in Chemistry, Muhlenberg Co., 1970; M.D., Columbia U., 1974. Diplomate Am. Bd. Internal Medicine, Am. Bd. Medical oncology. Intern, Columbia-Presbyn. Hosp., 1974-75; resident Columbia Presbyn. Med. Ctr., N.Y.C., 1975-77; clin. fellow in oncology Dana-Farber Cancer Inst., Harvard Med. Sch., 1977-78, instr. medicine, Boston, 1979-83, asst. prof. medicine, 1983—; asst. medicine Brigham and Women's Hosp., Boston, 1977-79, jr. assoc. medicine, 1979-82, assoc. physician, 1982—, clin. assoc. Dana-Farber Cancer Inst., 1979-83, asst. physician, 1983—. Contbr. articles to profl. jours. Chistian N. Lindbach Found. scholar, 1969-70; fellow Johanna C. Wood, 1979-80, Nat. Cancer Inst., 1980-81, Am. Cancer Soc., 1981-84. Mem. ACP, Am. Soc. Clin. Oncology, Am. Assn. Cancer Research. Home: 14 Briar Ln Weston MA 02193 Office: Dana Farber Cancer Inst 44 Binney St Boston MA 02115

ANTMAN, STUART SHELDON, mathematician; b. Bklyn., June 2, 1939; s. Mitchell and Gertrude (Siegel) A.; B.S., Rensselaer Poly. Inst., 1961; M.S., U Minn., 1963, Ph.D., 1965; m. Wilma G. Richlin, Mar. 24, 1968; children—Rachel A., Melissa D. Vis. mem. Courant Inst., N.Y. U., 1965-67, asst. prof., 1967-69, assoc. prof., 1969-72; vis. fellow U. Oxford, Eng., 1969-70, Heriot Watt U., Edinburgh, Scotland, summer 1972, 77; prof. math. U. Md., 1972—; mem. Applied Math. Summer Inst., Dartmouth Coll., 1973; prof. Ecole'd Ete d'Analyse Numerique, France, summer 1974; vis. prof. U. Paris, summer 1975, Brown U., 1978-79, Ecole Polytechnique, summer 1979, Math. Scis. Research Inst., Berkeley, Calif., 1983, U. P. and M. Curie, Paris, spring 1983, Math. Research Ctr., U. Wis., spring 1984, Inst. Math. and Applications, U. Minn., winter 1985. Editor: (with J.B. Keller) Bifurcation Theory and Nonlinear Eigenvalue Problems, 1969; co-editor Springer Tracts in Natural Philosophy, 1972-80; editorial bd. Archive for Rational Mechanics and Analysis, 1972—, Acta Applicandae Mathematicae, 1982—. Mem. U.S. Nat. Com. Theoretical and Applied Mechanics, 1980—. NSF grantee, 1972—; Guggenheim fellow, 1978-79. Mem. Am. Math. Soc. (editorial com. proc. symposia 1986—), Math. Assn. Am., Soc. Indsl. and Applied Math., Soc. Natural Philosophy (sec. 1974-76). Current work: Nonlinear problems of solid mechanics; stability theory; nonlinear analysis; bifurcation theory. Subspecialties: Applied mathematics; Solid mechanics. Office: Dept Math U Md College Park MD 20742

ANTZELEVITCH, CHARLES, physiologist, pharmacologist, educator; b. Ramat-Gan, Israel, Mar. 25, 1951; came to U.S., 1959; s. Chaim Asher and Frida (Hassman) A.; m. Brenda Reisner, June 24, 1973; children—Daniel Avi, Lisa Rachel. B.A., Queens Coll., 1973; Ph.D., Upstate Med. Ctr., SUNY-Syracuse, 1978. NIH postdoctoral fellow Masonic Med. Research Lab., Utica, N.Y., 1977-80, research scientist, cardiology dept., 1980-83; assoc. prof. pharmacology dept. Upstate Med. Ctr., 1983—; sr. research scientist cardiology dept. Masonic Med. Research Lab., 1984, dir. research and adminstrn., 1984—; program dir. minority high sch. student research apprentice program NIH, 1984; program dir. NIH tng. grant, 1985—; ad hoc reviewer NIH study sect., 1985. NIH fellow, 1973-77, 77-80. Mem. Am. Heart Assn., (basic sci. council, 1982—, vice chmn. research peer rev. com. N.Y. 1982), Central N.Y. Heart Assn. (Van Horne award 1981-84), AAAS, Am. Physiol. Soc., Cardiac Electrophysiol. Soc., N.Y. Acad. Scis., Internat. Soc. Heart Research. Lodge: Masons. Current work: Cardiac physiology and pharmacology related to arrhythmias. Subspecialties: Physiology (medicine); Cardiology. Office: Masonic Med Research Lab 2150 Bleecker St Utica NY 13504

ANURAS, SINN, medical educator, gastroenterologist; b. Bangkok, Thailand, Apr. 6, 1941; came to U.S., 1967, naturalized, 1979; s. Tiang and Rattana (Suppipat) A.; m. Jitra Suppamongkol, Aug. 9, 1969; children—Julia, Sandra. M.D., Chulalongkorn U., 1966. Diplomate Am. Bd. Internal Medicine. Intern, Resurrection Hosp., Chgo., 1967-68; resident in gastroenterology U. Iowa, 1972-74, asst. prof., 1975-80, assoc. prof. gastroenterology, 1980—. Contbr. papers to profl. lit. Fellow ACP; mem. Am. Gastroent. Assn., Am. Assn. for Study Liver Disease, Central Soc. for Clin. Research, Am. Physiol. Soc. Republican. Buddhist. Current work: Gastrointestinal motility, smooth muscle diseases. Subspecialties: Gastroenterology; Genetics and genetic engineering (medicine). Home: 55 Arbury Dr Iowa City IA 52240 Office: Dept Gastroenterology-Internal Medicine Univ Iowa Med Sch Newton Rd Iowa City IA 52242

APEL, JOHN RALPH, physicist; b. Absecon, N.J., June 14, 1930; s. Ezio A. and Grace A. (Rose) Baltera; m. Martha Eleise Davis, Sept. 8, 1956; children: Denise Alison, Jacqueline Jeanne. B.S., U. Md., 1957, M.S., 1961; Ph.D. (William S. Parsons fellow), Johns Hopkins, 1970. With Applied Physics Lab., Johns Hopkins U., Laurel, Md., 1957-70, 82—; sr. physicist Applied Physics Lab., Johns Hopkins, 1961-70, asst. group supr., 1966-70; asst. dir. Applied Physics Lab., John Hopkins U., 1982—; dir. Ocean Remote Sensing Lab., Atlantic Oceanographic and Meteorol. Labs., Miami, Fla., 1970-75, Pacific Marine Environ. Lab., NOAA, Seattle, 1976-81; Adj. prof. physics U. Miami, 1970-76; affiliate prof. atmospheric scis. and oceanography U. Wash., 1976-81; cons. NASA, Dept. Def., 1971—, UNESCO, Intergovtl. Oceanographic Commn., 1975—; chmn. ocean dynamics adv. sub com. NASA, 1973-76; mem. Internat. Union of Radio Scis., Commn. F, 1974—, Inter-Union Commn. Radio Meteorology, 1975-82; Sr. fellow Joint Inst. for Study of Atmosphere and Ocean, 1977-81; chmn. Sea Use Council Sci. and Tech. Bd., 1977-81; sr. fellow Joint Inst. for Marine and Atmospheric Research, 1978-81; chmn. aerospace and remote sensing Internat. Council for Exploration of Sea, 1979—; trustee Pacific Sci. Center, 1977-81; mem. Sci. Commn. Ocean Research, 1980—. Contbg. author: Ballistic Missile and Space Technology, Vol. 4, 1961,

Advances in Geophysics, Vol. 9, 1962, Advances in Astronautical Sciences, Vol. 30, 1974, Remote Sensing: Energy-Related Studies, 1975, Annual Review of Earth and Planetary Sciences, vol. 8, 1980; guest co-editor: Boundary Layer Meteorology, 1977; Contbr. articles to profl. jours. Served with USNR, 1951-52. Recipient Disting. Authorship award Nat. Oceanic and Atmospheric Adminstrn., 1976; Gold medal for meritorious service Dept. Commerce, 1974. Mem. Am. Phys. Soc., Am. Meteorol. Soc., N.Y. Acad. Scis., AAAS, Am. Geophys. Union, Sigma Xi, Sigma Pi Sigma, Phi Eta Sigma, Phi Delta Theta. Clubs: Cosmos (Washington); Explorers (N.Y.C.). Current Work: Physical oceanography; remote sensing. Subspecialty: Physics laboratory administration. Home: 14605 Carrolton Rd Rockville MD 20853 Office: Applied Physics Lab Johns Hopkins Rd Laurel MD 20707

APICELLA, MICHAEL ALLEN, med. researcher; b. Bklyn., Apr. 4, 1938; s. Anthony and Fay (Kahn) A.; m. Agnes Maria, Dec. 16, 1961; children: Michael P., Christopher A., Peter N. B.A., Coll. Holy Cross, 1959; M.D., SUNY Downstate Med. Ctr., 1963. Diplomate: Am. Bd. Internal Medicine. Intern, then resident Ohio State U., Columbus, 1963-66; fellow in medicine Johns Hopkins Hosp., Balt., 1966-68, practice medicine, San Antonio, 1968-70, Buffalo, 1970-78, 81—, Reno, 1979-81; prof. medicine and microbiology Med. Sch. SUNY-Buffalo, 1970—. Contbr. articles to profl. jours. Served to maj. USAF, 1968-70. Recipient USPHS career devel. award, 1974-79. Mem. Infectious Disease Soc., Central Soc. Clin. Research, Western Soc. Clin. Research, Am. Soc. Microbiology. Roman Catholic. Current Work: bacterial antigens and their relationship to human disease. Subspecialties: Internal medicine; Infectious diseases. Office: Med Sch SUNY Buffalo NY 14215

APIRION, DAVID, geneticist; b. Petah-Tikva, Israel, July 17, 1935; came to U.S., 1963, naturalized, 1970; s. Shlomo Zalman and Zehava Golda (Shevkes) A.; m. Mary Riddle McKinley, Sept. 10, 1963 (div.); children: Jonathan, Michael, Alison. M.Sc., Hebrew U., Jerusalem, 1960; Ph.D., Glasgow U., 1963. Lectr. Glasgow U., 1963; research fellow Harvard U., Cambridge, Mass., 1963-65; asst. prof. Washington U., St. Louis, 1965-70, assoc. prof., 1970-78, prof. microbiology/immunology, 1978—. Contbr. over 160 articles to profl. jours. Active Big Bros. of St. Louis. Served with Israeli Army, 1953-55. Jewish. Current Work: RNA processing, differentiation. Subspecialties: Biochemistry (biology); Genetics and genetic engineering (biology). Home: 408 S Hanley Clayton MO 63105 Office: 660 S Euclid St PO Box 8093 Saint Louis MO 63110

APKARIAN, VARTKESS ARA, chemistry educator; b. Damascus, Syria, Sept. 2, 1955; came to U.S., 1973; s. Artine Apkar and Sona (Babikian) A.; m. Alice Louise Batts, Sept. 6, 1980. B.Sc. in Chemistry, U. So. Calif., 1976; Ph.D. in Chemistry, Northwestern U., 1980. Postdoctoral fellow Northwestern U., Evanston, Ill., 1980-81, Cornell U., Ithaca, N.Y., 1981-83; asst. prof. chemistry U. Calif.-Irvine, 1983—. Contbr. articles to profl. jours. Chmn. Tekeyan Cultural Assn., Chgo., 1978-80. Young faculty in chemistry fellow Dreyfus Found., Cottrell Found., Petroleum Research Found., 1983. Mem. Chem. Soc., Am. Phys. Soc. Club: Armenian Gen. Benevolent Union. Current work: Photo-physics and photochemistry in the solid state, energy transfer, optical and chemical lasers in solids and laser induced reactions. Subspecialties: Physical chemistry; Laser-induced chemistry. Office: Dept Chemistry U Calif Irvine CA 92717

APOSTAL, MICHAEL CHRISTOPHER, engring. mechanics research and devel. co. exec., energy-related tech. cons. co. exec., educator; b. Monterey, Calif., July 21, 1944; s. Emanuel and Iris (Kalman) A.; m. Rose Maryann Parente, June 7, 1980; 1 dau., Nikki. B.S. in Civil Engring., U. R.I., 1967; M.S. in Civil Engring, U. Conn., 1974; Ph.D. in Civil Engring, SUNY, Buffalo, 1974. Sr. structures engr. Bell Aerospace Corp., Buffalo, 1969-74; sr. structures engr. Marc Analysis Research Corp., Providence, 1974-76; pres. Jordan, Apostal, Ritter Assos., Inc., Davisville, R.I., 1977—; v.p. Drilling Resources Devel. Corp. subs. Jordan, Apostal, Ritter Assos., Inc., Tulsa, 1980—; adj. asso. prof. civil and environ. engring. U. R.I.; Mem. North Kingstown (R.I.) C. of C. Contbr. articles to profl. jours. Mem. ASME, Soc. Petroleum Engrs., Soc. Computer Simulation, Petroleum Club R.I. Greek Orthordox. Clubs: Warwick (R.I.); Sportsman's Assn. Current Work: Numerically modeling (using the finite element method) three-dimensional dynamic behavior characteristics of a rotating, drilling, bottom hole assembly. Subspecialties: Fracture mechanics; Theoretical and applied mechanics. Office: Jordan Apostal Ritter Assos Inc Adminstrn Bldg 7 Davisville RI 02854

APOSTOLOU, SPYRIDON F., med. devices mfg. co. exec.; b. Athens, June 9, 1944; came to U.S., 1965, naturalized, 1970; s. Photios K. and Maria A. (Gikontes) A.; m. Christina O. Nerrie, Dec. 12, 1981. B.S. in Physics, Bradley U., 1968; M.S., Rensselaer Poly. Inst., 1970; Ph.D. in Solid State Physics, Washington U., St. Louis, 1972; Sc.D. in Mech. Engring. and Material Engring, 1976. Postdoctoral researcher Sch. Engring., Washington U., 1976-77; project engr. Becton-Dickinson, Rutherford, N.J., 1977-78, mgr. materials, 1979-80, asst. dir. research and devel., 1980-81, dir. sci. and tech., 1981—. Contbr. articles to profl. jours. Mem. Soc. Plastics Engrs. (chmn. mktg. div.), Am. Mgmt. Assn., N.Y. Acad. Sci. Greek Orthodox. Current Work: Metallurgy technology, polymeric and radiation technology, needle technology, coating and lubrication technology, new processes, new materials technology. Subspecialties: Biomaterials; Polymer physics. Office: Stanley St East Rutherford NJ 07070

APP, ALVA AGEE, agriculturalist; b. Bridgeton, N.J., Feb. 19, 1932; s. Frank and Helen (Minch) A.; m. Barbara Green, Apr. 2, 1955 (div. May 1981); children—Jeffrey, Linda, Marylou. B.S., Cornell U., 1953; M.S., Rutgers U. 1955, Ph.D., 1956. Research assoc. Johns Hopkins U., Balt., 1961-64; dir. cell physiology Boyce Thompson Inst., Yonkers, N.Y., 1965-76, dir. nitrogen & crop yields, Ithaca, N.Y., 1976-81; dep. dir. Internat. Centre of Insect Physiology & Ecology, Nairobi, Kenya, 1981-83; di. agrl. scis. Rockefeller Found., N.Y.C., 1983—; mem. Sci. Adv. Bd. Ohio State U., Columbus, 1984—. Contbr. articles to profl. jours. Bd. dirs. Agrl. Missions Nat. Council Chs., N.Y.C., 1974-77. Served to 1st lt. U.S.A.F., 1956-58. Grantee Nat. Sci. Found., UN Devel. Programme. Fellow AAAS; mem. Am. Chem. Soc., Am. Soc. Agronomy; Tissue Culture Assn., Am. Soc. Plant Physiology, Sigma Xi. Current work: Director program in international agriculture. Subspecialties: Agronomy; Plant physiology (agriculture). Office: Rockefeller Found 1133 Ave of Americas New York NY 10036

APPEL, ANTOINETTE RUTH, neuropsychologist; b. N.Y.C., Mar. 31, 1943; d. Leon S. and Augusta (Marienberg) A. B.A., U. Vt., Burlington, 1964; M.A., Mt. Holyoke Coll., 1965; Ph.D., CUNY, 1972. Lic. psychologist, Conn, Mass., R.I. Diplomate Am. Bd. Profl. Neuropsychology. Fellow, instr. Mt. Sinai Sch. Medicine, N.Y.C., 1971-74; asst. prof. So. Ill. U. Sch. Medicine, Carbondale, 1974-76; USPHS intern Conn. Valley Hosp., Middletown, 1976-77; asst. prof. U. Conn. Health Ctr., Farmington, 1977-79, Brown U., Providence, 1979-83; cons., Providence, 1981-83; neuropsychologist Butler Hosp., Providence, 1979-81; dir. neuropsychol. assessment and treatment Center Neurol. Scis., Fort Lauderdale, Fl, 1983—; cons. Fuller Meml. Hosp., Attleboro, Mass., 1979-81, VA Hosp., Providence, 1979-81, Dept. Social Rehab. Services, Providence, 1981-83. Contbr. articles to profl. jours. Bd. dirs. Sojourner House, Providence, 1979-81, Hartford (Conn.) Interval House, 1978-79, Combined Hosp. Alcoholism Program, Hartford, 1978. Served with WAC, 1963-64. Recipient cert. of recognition Psi Chi, 1974; Hartford Salute award Greater Hartford Conv. Bur., 1979. Mem. Am. Psychol. Assn., Eastern Psychol. Assn., N.Y. Acad. Scis., Sigma Xi, Psi Chi. Democrat. Inventor eye movement monitor. Current Work: Methods of identifying physical diseases which masquerade as psychiatric syndromes; mechanisms of dysfunction in closed head injuries Subspecialties: Neuropsychology; Health services research. Home: 6622 Racquet Club Dr Lauderhill FL 33319 Office: Center Neurol Services 5601 N Dixie Hwy Suite 407 Fort Lauderdale FL 33334

APPEL, BRUCE RICHARD, chemist; b. Los Angeles, Sept. 4, 1936; s. Marvin and Jeanette (Horowitz) A.; m. Teresa Nakahara, July 10, 1959; children—Leah, Kenneth. B.S., U. Calif.-Berkeley, 1958, Ph.D., UCLA, 1964. Research chemist Shell Devel. Co., Emeryville, Calif., 1964-72; group leader Calif. Dept. Health Services, Berkeley, 1972—; instr. extension dept. U. Calif.-Berkeley, 1975-79; cons. various govt. and pvt. orgns. Editor: Chemistry of Atmospheric Aerosols, 1978. Contbr. chpts. to books, articles to profl. jours. Served to capt. U.S. Army, 1958-60. U.S. Rubber Co. fellow, 1963; Shell Oil Co. exchange scientist, 1968. Mem. Am. Chem. Soc. Democrat. Current work: Chemistry of atmospheric particles and gases, sampling and analytical methodology. Subspecialty: Atmospheric chemistry. Office: Calif Dept Health Services 2151 Berkeley Way Berkeley CA 94707

APPEL, JAMES BARRY, psychology educator, behavioral pharmacologist; b. N.Y.C., Feb. 18, 1934; s. Harold and Ruth (Shifte) A.; m. Hope Mag, Nov. 24, 1965. A.B., Columbia U., N.Y.C., 1955; Ph.D., Ind. U., 1960; postgrad. Ind. U. Med. Center, Indpls., 1959-60. Research asst. Yale U., New Haven, 1960-61, asst. prof., 1961-66; assoc. prof. U. Chgo., 1966-72; mem. faculty U. S.C., Columbia, 1972—, prof. psychology, 1972—; dir. gen. exptl. psychology program, 1984—; vis. prof. Med. Research Council unit Univ. Coll., London, Eng., 1978. Contbr. articles to various publs. Research grantee USPHS, Nat. Inst. Drug Abuse, 1973—. Fellow AAAS, Am. Coll. Neuropsychopharmacology, Am. Psychol. Assn.; mem. Soc. Neurosci. (chpt. pres. 1982-83), Behavioral Pharmacology Soc., Soc. Stimulus Properties of Drugs (pres. 1981-82). Current Work: Mechanisms of action of hallucinogenic and related psychoactive drugs in vivo; history and logic of psychology; learning. Subspecialties: Behavioral psychology; Psychopharmacology. Home: 3034 Stepp Dr Columbia SC 29204 Office: Dept of Psychology U SC Columbia SC 29208

APPELBAUM, JOEL A(LAN), physicist; b. Bklyn., Dec. 30, 1941; s. Emmanuel and Sylvia A. A.; m. Muriel Rothenburg, Sept. 1, 1963; 1 child, Robert. B.S. in Physics, CCNY, 1963; M.S., U. Chgo., 1964, Ph.D. in Physics, 1966. Mem. tech staff Bell Labs., Murray Hill, N.J., 1967-68, mem. staff dept. theoretical physics, 1969-78, supr. econ. analysis, 1978-80, head demand econs., Holmdel, N.J., 1980-82, head bus. planning dept., 1982-83, dir. strategic planning, 1983-84; dir. venture tech. AT&T-Techs., Berkeley Heights, N.J., 1984—; asst. prof. physics U. Calif.-Berkeley, 1968-69; vis. lectr. Ecole Polytechnique Federale de Lausanne, Berlin, 1973; instr. theoretical physics U. Colo., Boulder, 1970. Contbr. numerous articles to profl. jours. Fellow Am. Phys. Soc. (Davison Germer prize 1979), AAAS; mem. Inst. Mgmt. Sci., Ops. Research Soc. Am. Phi Beta Kappa. Current work: Formation of high technology businesses within AT&T. Subspecialties: Condensed matter physics; Systems engineering. Home: 100 W Dudley Ave Westfield NJ 07770 Office: AT&T Tech One Oak Way Room 4EC102 Berkeley Heights NJ 07927

APPLE, MARTIN ALLEN, computer-biotech. co. exec.; b. Duluth, Minn., Sept. 17, 1939; s. Samuel Ben and Sylvia (Mintz) A.; m. Grace Ann Canfield, 1960; children: Deborah Dawn, Pamela Ruth, Nathan Herschel, Rebeccah Lynn. A.B., U. Minn., 1959, M.Sc., 1963; Ph.D., U. Calif., 1968. Asst. prof. U. Calif., 1971-78; asst. prof. Sch. Pharmacy and Cancer Research Inst., U. Calif., 1971-78; pres., chief exec. officer Internat. Plant Research Inst., Inc., San Carlos, Calif., 1978-82; adj. prof. U. Calif., San Francisco, 1982; chmn., chief exec. officer Ean-Tech, Daly City, Calif., 1982—; dir. Internat. Plant Research Inst., San Carlos, 1978-82, Conation Techs., San Francisco, 1982—. Contbr. articles in field to profl. jours. Chmn. Zone 7 Sch. Council, San Francisco, 1970-72. Recipient awards Am. Cancer Soc., 1970, 71, 73, 75, Grantee NIH, 1973-78, Grantee U. Calif., 1975-78. Fellow Am Inst. Chemists, Am. Coll. Clin. Pharmacologists; mem. AAAS, Am. Inst. Chemists, Am. Coll. Clin. Pharmacology, Am Soc. Pharmacology and Exptl. Therapeutics, Phi Beta Kappa. Patentee in field. Current Work: Biomolecular computer components, artificial intelligence, bioactive molecule design exec., computer software-genetic engring. product design and mktg. Subspecialties: Genetics and genetic engineering (agriculture); Artificial intelligence. Office: 699-A Serramonte Blvd Daly City CA 94015

APPLEBY, JOHN FREDERICK, physicist; b. Houston, Aug. 22, 1948; s. Walter Goode and Helen Marie (Norris) A.; m. Jeannine Poma, Dec. 28, 1977; 1 dau, Danielle Jeanne-Helen. B.A., Oberlin Coll., 1970; M.S., U. Mass.-Amherst, 1972; Ph.D., SUNY-Stony Brook, 1980. Research scientist Planetary Sci. Inst., Pasadena, 1979-81; sr. scientist Jet Propulsion Lab., Pasadena, 1981—. Contbr. articles to profl. jours. Mem. Am. Astron. Soc. (div. planetary sci.), Sigma Xi. Current Work: Atmospheric structures of the Jovian Planets and Titan; remote retrieval of atmospheric parameters; non-local thermodynamic equilibrium processes; Jupiter's clouds and NH3 ice scattering. Subspecialties: Planetary atmospheres; Planetary science. Office: 4800 Oak Grove Dr MS 183 301 Pasadena CA 91109

APPLETON, B. R., solid state physicist, materials consultant; b. Pampa, Tex., Nov. 24, 1937; s. Claude and Dulsey (Smoot) A.; m. Priscilla Pepper, Sept. 11, 1959; children—William, Todd, Thomas. B.S., U. Mo., 1960; Ph.D., Rutgers U., 1966. Research scientist Bell Labs., Murray Hill, N.J., 1966-67; group leader Oak Ridge Nat. Lab., 1967-78, sect. head solid state div., 1978-82, dir. Surface Modification Ctr., 1981—; owner Custom Goniometer Systems, Oak Ridge, 1968—. Author 5 books. Contbr. articles to sci. jours. Recipient award for Outstanding Research Dept. Energy, 1980. Fellow Am. Phys. Soc.; mem. Materials Research Soc. (v.p. 1984), Nat. Research Council (socio state scis. com.). Current work: Ion beam and laser processing, ion implantation pulsed laser processing. Subspecialties: Condensed matter physics; Materials processing. Home: 1025 W Outer Dr Oak Ridge TN 37830 Office: Oak Ridge Nat Lab Oak Ridge TN 37831

APPLEWHITE, THOMAS HOOD, chemist; b. Imperial, Calif., Dec. 30, 1924; s. Thomas and Lottie Lea (McCamy) A.; m. Harriet Mary Kaplan, June 3, 1945; children—Pamela Emily, Thomas Ted. A.A., Pasadena City Coll., 1951; B.S., Calif. Inst. Tech., 1953, Ph.D., 1957. Research chemist Dow Chem. Corp., Pitts., 1956-59, U.S. Dept. Agr., Western Regional Lab., Albany, Calif., 1959-63, investigation leader, 1963-67; research dir. PVO Internat., Richmond, Calif., 1967-69; mgr. edible oil products Kraft, Inc., Glenview, Ill., 1969-78, dir. research services, 1978—. Contbr. articles to profl. jours. Patentee in field. Assoc. editor: Jour. Am. Oil Chemists Soc., 1967—. Editor: Bailey's Ind. Fat and Oil Products, 1985. Served with USN, 1942-45; ETO; ATO; PTO. NSF fellow, 1955; Service award, Nat. Assn. Margarine Mfg., 1980; Kraft Merit award, 1982; A.E. Bailey medal, N.C. Am. Oil Chem. Soc., 1982. Mem. Am. Chem. Soc., Inst. Food Technologists, Am. Oil Chemists' Soc. (pres. 1977-78), Sigma Xi. Presbyterian. Current work: Chemistry and biochemistry of lipids, proteins and carbohydrates; fats in health, nutrition and disease; automated information handling; automation and instrumentation in analytical chemistry. Subspecialties: Food science and technology; Biochemistry (biology). Home: 205 W Olive Prospect Heights IL 60070 Office: Kraft Inc 801 Waukegan Rd Glenview IL 60025

APRISON, MORRIS HERMAN, biochemist, neurobiologist, educator; b. Milw., Oct. 6, 1923; s. Henry and Ethel (Mollin) A.; m. Shirley Reder, Aug. 21, 1949; children—Barry, Robert. B.S. in Chemistry, U. Wis., 1945, tchrs. cert., 1947, M.S. in Physics, 1949, Ph.D. in Biochemistry, 1952. Grad. teaching asst. in physics U. Wis.-Madison, 1947-49, grad. research asst. in pathology Sch. Medicine, 1950-51, grad. research asst. in biochemistry, 1951-52; tech. asst. in physics Inst. Paper Chemistry, Appleton, Wis., 1959-50; biochemist, prin. investigator, head biophysics sect. Galesburg State Research Hosp., Ill., 1952-56; prin. research investigator in biochemistry Inst. Psychiat. Research; asst. prof. depts. biochemistry and psychiatry Ind. U. Med. Sch., Indpls., 1956-60, assoc. prof., 1960-64, prof. biochemistry, 1964-78, disting. prof. psychiatry and biochemistry 1978, disting. prof. neurobiology and biochemistry, 1978—, chief neurobiology sect., 1969-74; mem. exec. com. dept. psychiatry, exec. adminstr. Inst. Psychiat. Research, 1973-74, dir. inst., 1974-78, chief sect. applied and theoretical neurobiology, 1978—; co-chmn. session on neurotransmitters 23d internat. Physiol. Congress, 1965; chmn. session neurochemistry and neuropharmacology 25th Congress, 1971; ad hoc mem. study sect. psychopharmacology NIMH, 1967-71, mem. neuropsychology study sect., 1970-74; mem. molecular and cellular neurobiology program adv. panel NSF, 1984-86; vis. prof. 4th ASPET Workshop, Vanderbilt U., 1972; guest scholar Grad. Sch., Kans. State U., 1973. Adv. editor: Neurosci. Research, 1968-73, Jour. Biol. Psychiatry, 1968-83, Neuropharmacology, 1969—, Jour. Neurochemistry, 1972-75, Pharmacology, Biochemistry and Behavior, 1973—, Jour. Comparative and General Pharmacology, 1974-75, Gen. Pharmacology, 1975—, Jour. Devel. Psychobiology, 1974-77; regional editor: Life Sci., 1970-73; co-editor: Advances in Neurochemistry, 1973—; mem. editorial bd.: Jour. Neurochemistry, 1975-79; dep. chief editor, 1980-83; mem. editoial bd.: Neurochem. Research, 1975-82; co-editor 7 books, also series; contbr. articles to profl. jours., chpts. to books. Mem. Ind. regional adv. bd. Anti-Defamation League, 1973-76; bd. overseers St. Meinrad Sem., 1974-77. Served with USNR, 1944-46. Mem. Am. Physiol. Soc., Biophys. Soc., Soc. Biol. Psychiatry (program com. 1974-75, co-chmn. 1975-76, gold medal 1975), Internat. Brain Research Orgn., Internat. Soc. Neurochemistry (co-chmn. session 1st internat. meeting Strasbourg, France 1967, 4th meeting Tokyo 1973, 7th meeting, Jerusalem, 1979, council 1973-75, sec. 1975-79, chmn. 1979-81, publication com. 1975-83, nominating com. 1983—), Am. Soc. Neurochemistry (co-chmn. session 1970, 71, 73, 80, 81, council 1971-73, 75-79, chmn. sci. program com. 1972, mem. 1973), Soc. for Neurosci. (pres. Indpls. chpt. 1970-71), Sigma Xi. Current work: Neurotransmitters, receptors, applied theoretical neurobiology, development of Animal Models for studying depression and psychosomatic disease. Subspecialties: Neurobiology; Neurochemistry. Office: Inst Psychiatric Research Ind Univ Sch Medicine 791 Union Dr Indianapolis IN 46223

APT, KENNETH ELLIS, nuclear chemist, research manager; b. Bellingham, Wash., Apr. 27, 1945; s. William H. and Clara R. (Dahlke) A.; m. Linda K. Trocki, Mar. 10, 1982; children—Aimee C., Julie R. B.A. cum laude, Western Wash. Univ., 1967; Ph.D., MIT, 1971. Staff mem. Los Alamos Nat. Lab, N.Mex., 1971-78, asst. assoc. dir., 1980-84, assoc. chemistry div. leader, 1984—; internat. nuclear safeguards officer Internat. Atomic Energy Agy., Vienna, Austria, 1978-80. Contbr. referred jour. articles, reports, articles to sci. symposia proces. NSF grad. trainee, 1970; NATO postdoctoral fellow (declined 1971). Mem. Am. Chem. Soc. (div. Nuclear chemistry and tech.), AAAS. Current work: Sci. research management and program management. Subspecialty: Nuclear chemistry. Office: Los Alamos Nat Lab PO Box 1663 Los Alamos NM 87545

ARAI, TADASHI, physicist; b. Tokyo, June 18, 1926; came to U.S., 1956; s. Minoru and Kazu (Momose) A.; m. Gerda J. Wessel; 3 children. B.S. in Physics, U. Tokyo, 1951; Ph.D. in Physics, U. Kyoto, Japan, 1955. Research scientist Carnegie Inst. Tech., Pitts., 1956-59, U. Uppsala, Sweden, 1959-60; vis. prof. U. Messina, Italy, 1970-71; physicist Argonne Nat. Lab., Ill., 1960-79, 1983—; vis. prof. U. Iowa, Iowa City, 1979-80, Howard U., Washington, 1980-83. Contbr. articles to profl. jours. Mem. Am. Phys. Soc., Phys. Soc. Japan, Sigma Chi. Subspecialties: Theoretical physics; Condensed matter physics.

ARAKAWA, EDWARD TAKASHI, physicist; b. Honolulu, Apr. 8, 1929; B.S., Samford U., 1951; M.S., La. State U., 1953; Ph.D., U. Tenn., 1957. Research assoc. Oak Ridge Assoc. Univs., 1953-57; sr. research staff Oak Ridge Nat. Lab., 1957—. Fellow Optical Soc. Am., Am. Phys. Soc. Current work: Optical properties of solids, soft x-ray spectroscopy, resonance ionization mass spectroscopy, photoacoustics. Subspecialty: Condensed matter physics. Home: 111 Amherst Ln Oak Ridge TN 37830 Office: Oak Ridge Nat Lab 4500S H 160 Oak Ridge TN 37830

ARAUJO, ROGER JEROME, research chemist; b. Fall River, Mass., Mar. 13, 1934; s. Christopher Jerome and Dora Eva (Limoge) a.; m. Helene Lorraine Methot, Apr. 2, 1954 (div. 1975); children—Rochelle, Wendyl, Lynn, Renee; m. Carol Freese, Mar. 18, 1978. B.S., Durfee Coll., 1956; Ph.D., Brown U., 1962. Research chemist Corning Glass Works, N.Y., 1961-70, research mgr., 1970-82, sr. research assoc., 1982—. Contbr. articles to profl. jours. and encys. Patentee in field. Alderman, City Council, Corning, 1972-75. Mem. Am. Chem. Soc., Am. Ceramic Soc., Sigma Xi (treas. local chpt.). Democrat. Roman Catholic. Current work: Physics of photochromic glasses, statistical mechanics of glass structure, reaction of hydrogen with fiber optics. Subspecialties: Photochemistry; Statistical mechanics. Home: 721 Seneca Dr Horseheads NY 14845 Office: Corning Glass Works Sullivan Park Corning NY 14831

ARAVE, CLIVE WENDELL, animal scientist, educator; b. Idaho Falls, Idaho, May 12, 1931; s. Joseph Clarence and Rhoda Elvera (Peterson) A.; m. Carley McMurtrey, Oct. 10, 1950; children: Wendy, Stephanie, Joe, Christine, Lorraine, James. B.S., Utah State U., 1956, M.S., 1957; Ph.D., U. Calif.-Davis, 1963. Asst. mgr. Lavacre Farms, Modesto, Calif., 1957-59; asst. prof. agr. Calif. State U.-Chico, 1963-65; asst. prof. to assoc. prof. animal, dairy and vet. scis. Utah State U.-Logan, 1965—. Contbr. articles to profl. jours. Served to sgt. AUS, 1951-53. U.S.-N.Z. Coop. Sci. Program grantee NSF, 1980-81. Mem. Am. Dairy Sci. Assn., Animal Behavior Soc., Sigma Xi, Phi Kappa Phi. Republican. Mormon. Lodge: North Logan Lions. Current Work: Genetic polymorphisms, animal sensory perception, early experience, animal behavior, sensory perception, operant conditioning, social behavior, early experience. Subspecialties: Animal genetics; Behaviorism. Home: 1460 E 2100 N Logan UT 84321 Office: Utah State U UMC 48 Logan UT 84322

ARCH, STEPHEN WILLIAM, biology educator, neurochemical researcher; b. Los Angeles, May 15, 1942. A.B., Stanford U., 1964; Ph.D., U. Chgo., 1970. Postdoctoral fellow Calif. Inst. Tech., Pasadena, 1970-72; asst. prof. Reed Coll., Portland Oreg., 1972-77, assoc. prof., 1977-83, prof., 1983—; cons. NIH, Bethesda, Md., 1982—. Contbr. articles to profl. jours. Grantee Alfred P. Sloan Found., Med. Res. Found. Oreg., NSF, NIH. Mem. Soc. General Physiologists, Soc. Neurosci. Current work: biosynthesis, posttranslational routing, and secretion of neuropeptides. Subspecialties: Neurochemistry; Cell biology. Office: Biological Laboratories Reed Coll 3203 SE Woodstock Blvd Portland OR 97202

ARCHER, JUANITA ALMETTA HINNANT, physician, educator; b. Washington, Nov. 3, 1934; d. Roy E. and Anna O. (Blakeney) Hinnant; m. Frederick I. Archer, June 8, 1958. B.S., Howard U., 1956, M.S., 1958, M.D., 1965. Intern Freedmen's Hosp., Washington, 1965-66; resident Howard U., Washington, 1966-68, fellow, 1970-71, instr., 1971-75, asst. prof., 1975-78, assoc. prof. medicine, 1978—; attending staff D.C. Gen. Hosp.; attending staff, dir. endocrine metabolic lab. Howard U. Hosp., Washington, 1975; cons. NIH, 1979-82, Gen. Clin. Research Ctr., 1979—, Nat. Inst. Allergy and Metabolic Disease, 1979. Am. Diabetes Assn. grantee, 1976; NIH grantee, 1979; Howard U. Women's Aux. grantee, 1981; Josiah Macy Found. faculty fellow, 1974-77. Baptist. Current Work: Insulin action and insulin receptor activity in human erthrocytes. Subspecialties: Receptors; Internal medicine. Home: 4305 Ranger Ave Temple Hills MD 20748 Office: Howard U Hosp 2041 Georgia Ave NW Washington DC 20060

ARCHER, MICHAEL CHRISTOPHER, cancer researcher, educator; b. Stoke-on-Trent, Eng., May 9, 1943; s. William Thomas and Mabel (Bailey) A.; m. Carolyn D. Hoskins, Oct. 10, 1970; children: Emily Winpenny, Jason Warwick, Elliot William George. M.A., Cambridge (Eng.) U., 1965; M.Sc., U. Warwick, Eng., 1967; Ph.D., U. Toronto, Ont., Can., 1970. Research assoc. dept. applied biol. scis. M.I.T., 1970-72, asst. prof., 1972-76, assoc. prof., 1976-79; assoc. prof. dept. med. biophysics U. Toronto, 1979-82; sr. scientist Ont. Cancer Inst., Toronto, 1979-82, prof., sr. scientist, 1982—; cons. in field. Contbr. articles to profl. jours. Recipient Future Leader award Nutrition Found., 1974-76; NIH grantee, 1977—. Mem. Royal Soc. Chemistry (fellow), Am. Chem. Soc., AAAS, Am. Soc. Biol. Chemists, Soc. Toxicology, Am. Assn. Cancer Research. Current work: Chemical carcinogenesis. Subspecialties: Cancer research (medicine); Toxicology (medicine). Office: Ont Cancer Inst 500 Sherbourne St Toronto M4X 1K9

ARCHER, RICHARD EARL, product designer and alternative energy design cons.; b. Springfield, Ill., Aug. 24, 1945; s. Earl Wiley and Era Marie (Fentress) A.; m. Elizabeth Lou Lutz, Aug. 9, 1969; children: Jeremy Richard, William Earl. B.A. in Design, So. Ill. U., Carbondale, 1970; M.S., Gov.'s State U., 1979. Instr. design So. Ill. U., 1971-79, coordinator design program, 1979-80, asst. prof. comprehensive planning and design, 1980—; dir. Applied Alternatives.; Mem. Nat. Alcohol Fuels Commn., 1980; chmn. Carbondle Energy Futures Task Force, 1980-81; mem. Ill. Legislature Alternative Energy Commn., 1981—; mem. adv. panel U.S. Congl. Office Tech. Assessment, 1982. Editor: Ill. Solar Resource Adv. Council Grants Newsletter, 1979-81; contbr. articles to profl. jours. Recipient Outstanding Tchr. Year award Coll. Human Resources, So. Ill. U., 1979; U.S. Dept. Energy grantee, 1979-81; U.S. Dept. Labor grantee, 1978-79; Ill. Dept. Energy grantee, 1980-81. Mem. Internat. Solar Energy Soc., Am. Wind Energy Assn., Internat. Biomass Inst., Nat. Alcohol Fuels Producers Assn., Solar Lobby (dir.). Current Work: Solar energy, ethanol prodn., energy and chem. feedstocks from biomass, community econs. of conservation and alternative energy. Subspecialties: Solar energy; Biomass (energy science and technology). Home: Box 168 Rural Route 1 DeSoto IL 62924 Office: Design Program Bldg 0720 So Ill U Carbondale IL 62901

ARCHER, ROBERT ALLEN, medicinal researcher; b. Reading, Pa., Apr. 3, 1936; s. Francis Emerson and Susanne Agnes (Matlock) A.; m. Joyce Ann Packard, June 21, 1963; children—Lisa Ann, Gregory Allen, Timothy Andrew. A.B., Harvard U., 1958; M.S., U. Del., 1960; Ph.D., Stanford U., 1963. Postdoctoral fellow Columbia U., 1963-64; sr. organic chemist Lilly Research Labs., Eli Lilly & Co., Indpls., 1964-72, research scientist, 1972-77, research assoc., 1977—. Contbg. author: Cannabinoids in Drug Research, 1985. Contbr. articles to sci. jours. Patentee in drugs and drug mfg. processes. Trumpet player Philharm. Orch. Indpls., 1964—. Mem. Am. Chem. Soc., AAAS, Sigma Xi.

Club: Harvard of Ind. (chmn. schs. com. 1964-81). Current work: Research on connective tissue, degenerative diseases, especially arthritis and osteoarthritis; collagen and proteoylcan metabolism and degradation; central nervous system drugs, expecially cannabinoids. Subspecialties: Immunology (medicine); Rheumatology. Home: 5563 N Pennsylvania St Indianapolis IN 46220 Office: Lilly Research Labs MC 705 Eli Lilly & Co Bldg 98C-4 Indianapolis IN 46285

ARCHER, STEVEN RONALD, plant ecologist, educator; b. Sioux Falls, S.D., Sept. 23, 1953; s. Ronald Franklin and Carol Marguarite (Wright) A.; m. Gwendolyn Maureen Allen, Aug. 16, 1975; children—Jordan, Cadie. B.A., Augustana Coll., 1975; M.S., Colo. State U., 1980, Ph.D., 1983. Research assoc. Augustana Coll., 1976-78; grad. teaching asst. Colo. State U., 1978-80, instr., 1980-82, grad. research asst., 1982-83; asst. prof. ecology Tex. A&M U., College Station, 1983—; ecol. cons. Augustana Research inst., 1977-78, U.S. Forest Service, Chadron, Nebr., 1979, Seward, Alaska, 1980. Contbr. articles to profl. jours. Counselor, Sioux Vocat. Sch. for Handicapped, S.D., 1972, Problems in Living Ctr., 1975; bd. dirs. prairies restoratiun project S.D. Bicentennial Commn., 1974. Terwillage Meml. scholar, 1982. Mem. Ecol. Soc. Am., Soc. Range Mgmt., Sigma Xi, Phi Kappa Phi. Democrat. Lutheran. Current work: Role of herbivores in mediating plant processes at individual; population and community levels; local distribution of photsynthetic pathways; ecology of shrubs and shrublands. Subspecialties: Ecology (biology); Population biology. Home: 1100 Hawktree St College Station TX 77840 Office: Range Sci Dept Tex A&M Univ College Station TX 77843-2126

ARCHIBALD, JAMES DAVID, paleontologist, biology educator; b. Lawrence, Kans., Mar. 23, 1950; s. James Russell and Donna Lee (Acord) A. B.Sc. in Geology, Kent State U., 1972; Ph.D. in Paleontology, U. Calif.-Berkeley, 1977. Gibbs instr. dept. geology Yale U., New Haven, 1977-79; asst. prof., 1979-83; assoc. prof. biology San Diego State U., Calif., 1983—; curator mammals Peabody Mus. Nat. Hist., Yale U., 1979-83; research assoc. Mus. Paleontology, U. Calif., Berkeley, 1983—. Author: Study of Mammals Across Cretaceous Tertuary Boundary, 1982. Assoc. editor Jour. Vertebrate Paleontology, 1984—. Contbr. articles to profl. jours. Fellow San Diego State U.; grantee Sigma Xi, Nat. Geol. Soc., NSF, Am. Chem. Soc. Mem. Am. Soc. Mammalogists, Soc. Vertebrate Paleontology, Soc. Systemic Zoology, Paleontol. Soc., Geol. Soc. Am. Current work: Systematics and evolution of Cretaceous and Tertiary mammals; biostratigraphy, paleontology, stratigraphy. Subspecialties: Paleobiology; Systematics. Office: Dept Biology San Diego State U San Diego CA 92182

ARCHIBALD, PATRICIA A., biologist, educator; b. Olney, Ill., July 18, 1934; d. Stanley Ray and Mabel Ellen (Seed) A. B.S., Ball State U., 1953, M.A. in Biol. Sci, 1961; Ph.D. in Botany, U. Tex.-Austin, 1969. Mem. faculty Slippery Rock U. (Pa.), 1969—, prof. biology, 1979—; sci. rev. adminstr. competitive grants program EPA, 1980-82; exchange scientist Czechoslovak Acad. Sci., 1977, USSR Acad. Sci., 1978. Contbr. articles to sci. jours. Mem. Am. Phycol. Soc., Brit. Phycol. Soc., Internat. Phycol. Soc., Am. Assn. Systematics. Subspecialties: Phycology (Algology); Morphology. Home: PO Box 429 Grove City PA 16127 Office: Slippery Rock U Slippery Rock PA 16057

ARENBERG, IRVING KAUFMAN, physician, educator; b. East Chicago, Ind., Jan. 10, 1941; m. Carol Rakita; children—Daniel Kaufman, Michael Harrison, Julie Gayle. B.A., U. Mich., 1963, M.D., 1967. Cert. Am. Bd. Otolarnygology; lic. physician Mich., Mo., Calif., Ill., Fla., Wis., Colo. Intern, Chgo. Wesley Meml. Hosp., Northwestern U.-McGaw Med. Ctr., Chgo., 1967-68; asst. resident in surgery St. Luke's Hosp., St. Louis, 1968-69; sr. asst. resident otolaryngology Barnes and Allied Hosps., Washington U. Sch. Medicine, St. Louis, 1970-71, assoc. resident, 1971-73, chief resident, 1973-74, fellow in neurotology, 1974-75; vis. scientist Swedish Med. Research Council, Royal Acad. Hosp., U. Uppsala, Sweden, 1975-76; asst. prof. surgery div. otolaryngology U. Wis. Hosps. and Clinics, 1976-80; chief otolaryngology dept. surgery VA Hosp., Madison, 1976-80; clin. assoc. prof. dept. otolaryngology U. Colo. Med. Ctr., Denver, 1980—; cons., lectr., vis. prof. in medicine. Contbr. articles to profl. jours. Editor numerous profl. jours. Served as lt. comdr. USNR. 1964-74. Recipient numerous awards for excellence in medicine and edn., most recent: Calicetti prize and Gold medal for Ear Research, U. Bologna, 1983. Fellow Am. Acad. Ophthalmology and Otolaryngology, Royal Coll. Health, Am. Coll. Surgeons, Internat. Coll. Surgeons; mem. AMA, Assn. Research Otolaryngology, Am. Neurotology Soc., Am. Auditory Soc., Triologic Soc., Underwater Med. Soc., Soc. Mil. Otolaryngologists, Am. Council Otolaryngology, AAUP, Internat. Platform Assn., AAAS, Electron Microscopy Soc. Am., Am. Assn. Anatomists, Am. Soc. Cell Biology, Central States Electron Microscopy Soc., N.Y. Acad. Scis., Sigma Xi, numerous others. Current Work: Inner ear disease. Subspecialty: Pathology (medicine). Office: Colo Ear Clinic 2480 S Downing Suite 200 Denver CO 80210

ARIANO, MARJORIE A., research scientist, educator; b. Tokyo, Japan, Feb. 13, 1951; d. Richard A. and Marjorie W. (Farr) A. B.S., UCLA, 1972, Ph.D., 1977. Postdoctoral fellow in molecular biology U. So. Calif., 1977-80; asst. prof. anatomy and neurobiology U. Vt., Burlington, 1980-86, assoc. prof., 1986—. Mem. sci. research bd. Vt. Heart Assn.; sci. reviewer Hereditary Disease Found., NSF. Contbr. articles to profl. publs. Grantee NIH, Vt. Heart Assn., NSF, 1972—. Mem Soc. Neurosci. Current Work: Role of cyclic Nucleotides in mediation of neural transmission within the basal ganglia and sympathetic ganglia. Subspecialties: Neurochemistry; Immunology (medicine). Office: Dept Anatomy and Neurobiology Given Med Bldg Burlington VT 05405

ARIS, RUTHERFORD, applied mathematician, educator; b. Bournemouth, Eng., Sept. 15, 1929; came to U.S., 1955, naturalized, 1962; s. Algernon Pollock and Janet (Elford) A.; m. Claire Mercedes Holman, Jan. 1, 1958. B.Sc. (spl.) with 1st class honours in Math, London (Eng.) U., 1948, Ph.D., 1960, D.Sc., 1964; D.Sc. (hon.), U. Exeter, 1984, Clarkson U., 1985; student, Edinburgh (Scotland) U., 1948-50. Tech. officer Billingham div. I.C.I. Ltd., 1950-55; research fellow U. Minn., 1955-56; lectr. tech. math. Edinburgh U., 1956-58; mem. faculty U. Minn., 1958—, prof. chem. engring., 1963—, Regents' prof., 1978—; O.A. Hougen vis. prof. U. Wis., 1979; Sherman Fairchild Disting. Scholar Calif. Inst. Tech., 1980-81; cons. to industry, lectr., 1961—. Author: Optimal Design of Chemical Reactors, 1961, Vectors, Tensors and the Basic Equations of Fluid Mechanics, 1962, Discrete Dynamic Programming, 1964, Introduction to the Analysis of Chemical Reactors, 1965, Elementary Chemical Reactor Analysis, 1969, (with N.R. Amundson) First-Order Partial Differential Equations with Applications, 1973, (with W. Strieder) Variational Methods Applied to Problems of Diffusion and Reaction, 1973, The Mathematical Theory of Diffusion and Reaction in Permeable Catalysts, 1975, Mathematical Modelling Techniques, 1978, Chemical Engineering in the University Context, 1982; co-editor An Index of Scripts for E.A. Lowe's Codices Latini Antiquiores, 1982; Springs of Scientific Creativity, 1982. Sr. research fellow NSF, 1964-65; Guggenheim fellow, 1971-72; Recipient E. Harris Harbison award for distinguished teaching, 1969; Alpha Chi Sigma award Am. Inst. Chem. Engrs., 1969; Chem. Engring. lectr. award Am. Soc. Engring. Edn., 1973. Fellow Inst. Math. and Applications; mem. Nat. Acad. Engring., Soc. Nat. Philosophy, Soc. for Math. Biology, Soc. Indsl. and Applied Math., Am. Chem. Soc., Am. Inst. Chem. Engrs. (R.H. Wilhelm award 1975, Lewis award 1981), Mediaeval Acad. Am., Soc. Scribes and Illuminators, Soc. Textual Scholarship, Internat. Soc. Math. Modeling. Lutheran. Current Work: Mathematical modelling of chemical reactors; Latin palaeography. Subspecialties: Applied mathematics; Chemical engineering. Office: Dept of Chemical Engineering Univ of Minnesota Minneapolis MN 55455

ARISON, BYRON H., chemist. B.S., U. Mich., 1944; M.S., Poly. Inst. Bklyn., 1953, Ph.D., 1967. Chemist, Manhattan project E.I. DuPont, 1943-45; Merck MSDRL, 1947-67, assoc. chemist, 1964-67, sr. research chemist, 1967-69, research fellow, 1969-73, sr. research fellow, 1973-75, sr. investigator, 1975—. Contbr. numerous articles to profl. jours. Patentee in field. Served with U.S. Army, 1945-46. Mem. Am. Chem. Soc. Home: 88 Century Lane Watchung NJ 07060

ARKILIC, GALIP MEHMET, applied scientist, educator; b. Sivas, Turkey, Mar. 10, 1920; came to U.S., 1943, naturalized, 1960; s. Sabir Mehmet and Zehra Fatima (Hocazade) A.; m. Ann A. Bryan, Mar. 31, 1956; children: Victor, Dennis, Layla, Errol. B.M.E., Cornell U., 1946; M.S., Ill. Inst. Tech., 1948; Ph.D., Northwestern U., 1954. Mech. engr. Miehle Printing Press and Mfg. Co., Chgo., 1948-49, analyst, 1954-56; research and devel. engr. Mech. and Chem. Industries, Turkey, 1949-52; asst. prof. Pa. State U., University Park, 1956-58; asso. prof. dept. civil engring. George Washington U., Washington, 1958-63, prof. applied sci., 1963—, chmn. dept. engring. mechanics, 1966-69; asst. dean George Washington U. (Sch. Engring. and Applied Sci.), 1969-74. Contbr. articles to sci. jours. Vice pres. Courtland Civic Assn., Arlington, Va., 1965-66; pres. Am. Turkish Assn., Washington, 1967-71. Served to 2d lt. Turkish Army, 1939-41. Recipient Disting. Leadership award Am. Turkish Assn., 1972; Recognition of Service award Sch. Engring. and Applied Sci., George Washington U., 1976; Air Force Office of Sci. Research grantee, 1963-69. Mem. ASME, AAUP, Am. Acad. Mechanics, Sigma Xi. Club: George Washington U. (Washington). Current Work: Analysis of plates and shell structures, applied ordinary differential equationss. Subspecialties: Theoretical and applied mechanics; Applied mathematics. Home: 8403 Camden St Alexandria VA 22308 Office: George Washington U Washington DC 20052

ARMISTEAD, WILLIS WILLIAM, university administrator; b. Detroit, Oct. 28, 1916; s. Eber Merrill and Josephine Brunell (Kindred) A.; m. Martha Sidney Clark, Sept. 17, 1938 (dec. 1964); children: Willis William, Jack Murray, Sidney Merrill; m. Mary Wallace Nelson, 1967. D.V.M., Tex. A. and M. Coll., 1938; M.Sc., Ohio State U., 1950; Ph.D., U. Minn., 1955. Diplomate: hon. diplomate; Am. Coll. Veterinary Surgeons, Am. Coll. Veterinary Preventive Medicine. Pvt. practice veterinary medicine, 1938-40; instr. Sch. Veterinary Medicine, Tex. A. and M. Coll, 1940-42, asst. prof. to prof., 1946-53; dean Sch. Veterinary Medicine, 1953-57, Coll. Veterinary Medicine, Mich. State U., East Lansing, 1957-74, Coll. Veterinary Medicine, U. Tenn., Knoxville, 1974-79; v.p. agr. U. Tenn. System, 1979—; collaborator animal diseases and parasite research div. Dept. Agr., 1954-65; cons., adviser commn. veterinary edn. of South So. Regional Edn. Bd., 1953-56; mem. gov.'s sci. adv. bd., 1958-60; nat. cons. to Air Force Surgeon Gen., 1960-62; mem. adv. council Inst. Lab. Animal Resources, NRC, 1962-66; pres. Assn. Am. Veterinary Med. Colls., 1964-65, 73-74; veterinary med. resident investigators selection com. U.S. VA, 1967-70; veterinary medicine rev. com. Bur. Health Professions Edn. and Manpower Tng., HEW, 1967-71; mem. Nat. Bd. Veterinary Med. Examiners, 1970-74; mem. adv. panel for veterinary medicine Inst. Medicine, Nat. Acad. Scis., 1972-74; mem. bd. agr. and renewable resources NRC, 1976-77; 1st Allam lectr. Am. Coll. Veterinary Surgeons, 1972. Contbg. author: Canine Surgery, rev. edit, 1957, Canine Medicine, rev. edit, 1959; editor: The N.Am. Veterinarian, 1950-56, Jour. Veterinary Med. Edn, 1974-80; assoc. editor: Jour. Am. Animal Hosp. Assn, 1964-70; contbr. tech. articles to profl. jours. Bd. dirs. Tenn. Farm Bur. Fedn., 1979—. Served from 1st lt. to maj. Veterinary Corps AUS, 1942-46. Recipient Meritorious Service award Selective Service System, 1972; hon. alumnus Mich. State U., 1972; Recipient Disting. Alumnus award Coll. Vet. Medicine, Tex. A. and M. U., 1980. Mem. AAAS, U.S. Animal Health Assn., Am. Veterinary Med. Assn. (pres. 1957-58, award 1977), Tex Veterinary Med. Assn. (pres. 1947-48), Mich. Veterinary Med. Assn. (trustee Edn. and Sci. Trust 1970-74), Tenn. Veterinary Med. Assn., Inst. Medicine of Nat. Acad. Scis., N.Y. Acad. Scis., Sigma Xi, Phi Kappa Phi, Alpha Zeta, Phi Zeta, Omega Tau Sigma (nat. Gamma Award Ohio State U. 1962). Episcopalian. Club: Rotary. Subspecialties: Agricultural research, administration; Veterinary medical research, administration. Home: 1101 Cherokee Blvd Knoxville TN 37919 Office: Box 1071 Knoxville TN 37901

ARMITAGE, JAMES OLEN, physician; b. Los Angeles, Dec. 19, 1946; s. Bernard O. and Thelma A. (Young) A.; m. Nancy Elaine Roker, Aug. 12, 1967; children: Amy Jolane, Gregory Olen, Anne Marie, Joel Donald. B.S., U. Nebr.-Lincoln, 1969; M.D., U. Nebr.-Omaha, 1973. Diplomate: Am. Bd. Internal Medicine with subsplty. in med. oncology. Intern, resident U. Nebr. Med. Center, Omaha, 1973-75; fellow U. Iowa Hosp. and Clinics, Iowa City, 1975-77; practice medicine specializing in oncology, hematology, Omaha, 1977-79; asst. prof. medicine, dir. bone marrow transplanation unit U. Iowa, 1979-82; asso. prof. medicine, vice chmn. dept. internal medicine U. Nebr.-Omaha, 1982—. Contbr. articles to profl. jours. Mem. Central Soc. Clin. Research, Am. Soc. Hematology, Am. Assn. Cancer Research, Am Soc. Clin. Oncology, Internat. Soc. Exptl. Hematology, ACP, Phi Beta Kappa, Alpha Omega Alpha. Current Work: Bone marrow transplantation; mgmt. leukemia and lymphona. Subspecialties: Oncology; Marrow transplant. Home: 3716 S 94th Circle Omaha NE 68124 Office: 42d and Dewey Ave Omaha NE 68105

ARMSTRONG, ANDREW THURMAN, chemical consultant, educator; b. Haslet, Tex., May 26, 1935; s. Andrew Thurman and Ila (Kitchen) A.; m. Kay Frances Masters, Sept. 7, 1938; children: Michael Andrew, Marion Kay, Benjamin Neil. B.S., North Tex. State U., 1958, M.S., 1959; Ph.D., La. State U., 1967. Asst. prof. chemistry U. Tex., Arlington, 1969-74, assoc. prof. chemistry, 1974-84; pres., owner Armstrong Forensic Lab., Arlington, 1981. Contbr. articles to profl. jours. Mem. Tarrant County Adv. Council on Arson. Recipient White Helmet award Arlington Fire Dept., 1976; named Outstanding Tchr. Sch. Sci., U. Tex., Arlington, 1975-76. Fellow Am. Inst. Chemists; mem. Am. Chem. Soc. (W.T. Doherty award Dallas-Fort Worth Chpt. 1982), Am. Assn. Forensic Scientists, Am. Assn. Indsl. Hygiene. Baptist. Current Work: Forensic chemistry of fire utilizing. Subspecialty: Analytical chemistry. Office: 3008 W Division Suite C Arlington TX 76012

ARMSTRONG, DALE DEAN, accelerator physicist; b. Salina, Kans., Aug. 18, 1927; s. Ronald Eugene and Viva Beatrice (Woodin) A.; m. Jurhee Louise Galloway, Mar. 1, 1952; children—Dale Dean, Harold Galloway, Amy Denton. B.S. in Engring. Physics, U. Colo., 1957; M.S. in Physics, U. N.Mex., 1961, Ph.D. in Physics, 1965. Staff mem. Los Alamos Nat. Lab., N.Mex., 1957-76, 78-80, assoc. group leader, 1976-78, dep. group leader, 1980—. Contbr. articles to profl. jours. Served with USN, 1945-46. Mem. Am. Phys. Soc. Republican. Current work: Accelerator research and development in support of the fusion reactor materials program and in support of strategic defense programs. Subspecialty: Nuclear physics. Home: 1391 44th St Los Alamos NM 87544 Office: Los Alamos Nat Lab PO Box 1663 Los Alamos NM 87545

ARMSTRONG, DONALD, educator; b. Hamilton, Ont., Can., July 20, 1933; s. Alfred George and Dorothy Emma (Burden) A.; m. Christine Marie Medeiros, June 13, 1954; children: Donald, David, Dennis, Sandra, Kenneth, Elizabeth. B.S., San Diego State U., 1957; M.S., U. Colo., 1969; Ed.D., U. Tulsa, 1974; Ph.D., U. Oslo, 1980. Instr. San Diego State U., 1960-62, U. Oreg. Med. Sch., Portland, 1963-67, U. Colo. Med. Ctr., Denver, 1967-70; clin. chemist, dir. research ctr. Hillcrest Med. Ctr., Tulsa, 1970-74; asst. prof. U. Colo. Med. Ctr., 1974-81; assoc. prof. U. Fla. Med. Sch., Gainesville, 1981—; dir., clin. chemist Allied Vet. Med. Lab., Tulsa, 1970-74; research cons. Hillcrest Med. Ctr., Tulsa, 1974-76; cons., clin. chem. toxicologist Ft. Lyons VA Hosp., Colo., 1975-81; cons. Sigma Chem. Co., St. Louis, 1979—. Editor: Ceroid-Lipofuscinosis (Batten's Disease), 1982, Free Radicals in Molecular Biology and Aging, 1984. Bd. dirs. N. Fla. Sight Found.; fields events Official U. Fla. Track Office. Served with U.S. Army, 1953-55. Children's Brain Disease grantee, 1973-85; March of Dimes grantee, 1974; Hillcrest Med. Ctr. grantee, 1974-78; Nat. Retinitis Pigmentosa Found. grantee, 1975-76. Mem. Am. Aging Assn. (bd. dirs. 1975-85, symposium chmn. 1983-85, pres. 1985-86), Assn. Research in Vision and Ophthalmology, Research to Prevent Blindness, Ophthalmic Assn. Democrat. Roman Catholic. Club: Lions (Gainesville, Fla.). Current Work: Autoxidation of membrane lipids induced by free radicals and the subsequent formation of fluorescent materials. Subspecialties: Biochemistry (biology); Ophthalmology. Home: 2036 NW 20th Ln Gainesville FL 32605 Office: U Fla Box J-284 Gainesville FL 32610

ARMSTRONG, JOHN ALLAN, physicist, research and development executive; b. Schenectady, July 1, 1934; s. Orlo Lucius and Mary Kathryn (Moffitt) A.; m. Elizabeth Saunders, Sept. 20, 1958; children: Sarah Richardson, Jennifer Mary. A.B., Harvard U., 1956, Ph.D., 1961. Postdoctoral fellow Harvard U., 1961-63; mem. research staff IBM, Yorktown Heights, N.Y., 1963-74, dir. phys. scis., 1975-80, mem. corp. tech. com., 1980-81; mgr. materials and tech. devel. IBM (Gen. Tech. Div. Lab.), East Fishkill, N.Y., 1981-83, v.p. logic and memory research div., Yorktown Heights, 1983—. Contbr. articles to profl. jours. Fellow Am. Phys. Soc., Optical Soc. Am.; mem. AAAS. Current Work: Director of semiconductor materials, device and circuit research; semiconductor packaging. Subspecialties: Microchip technology (engineering); Laser spectroscopy. Office: IBM Research Box 218 Yorktown Heights NY 10598

ARMSTRONG, NEAL EARL, civil engineering educator; b. Dallas, Jan. 29, 1941; married; 3 children. B.A., U. Tex., 1962, M.A., 1965, Ph.D., 1968. Research engr. Engring. Sci., Inc., 1967-68; asst. office mgr., cons. san. engring., 1968-70; mgr. Washington Research and Devel. Lab., 1970-71; assoc. prof. U. Tex.-Austin, 1971-79, prof. civil engring., 1979—. Mem. ASCE, Ecol. Soc. Am., Am. Soc. Limnology and Oceanography, Water Pollution Control Fedn., Internat. Assn. Water Pollution Research, Estuarine Research Fedn. (v.p. 1975-77). Current Work: Water quality management, water pollution ecology, water quality modelling. Subspecialties: Environmental engineering; Ecology (environmental science). Office: Dept Civil Engring U Tex Austin TX 78712

ARMSTRONG, NEIL A., computer systems company executive, former astronaut; b. Wapakoneta, Ohio, Aug. 5, 1930; s. Stephen A.; m. Janet Shearon; children: Eric, Mark. B.S. In Aero. Engring, Purdue U., 1955; M.S. in Aero. Engring, U. So. Calif. With Lewis Flight Propulsion Lab., NACA, 1955; then aero. research pilot for NACA (later NASA, High Speed Flight Sta.), Edwards, Calif.; astronaut Manned Spacecraft Center, NASA, Houston, 1962-70; command pilot Gemini 8, Mar. 1966; comdr. Apollo II; dep. asso. adminstr. for aeros. Office Advanced Research and Tech., Hdqrs. NASA, Washington, 1970-71; prof. aerospace engring. U. Cin., 1971-79; chmn. bd. Cardwell Internat., Ltd., Lebanon, Ohio, 1980-82; chmn. CTA, Inc., 1982—; dir. Gates Learjet Corp., Cin. Gas & Electric Co., Eaton Corp., Taft Broadcasting Co., Cin. Milacron, UAL, Inc. Trustee, Cin. Mus. Natural History. Served as naval aviator USN, 1949-52, Korea. Recipient numerous awards, including Octave Chanute award Inst. Aero. Scis., 1962, Presdl. Medal for Freedom, 1969, Exceptional Service medal NASA, Hubbard Gold medal Nat. Geog. Soc., 1970, Kitty Hawk Meml. award, 1969, Pere Marquette medal, 1969, Arthur S. Fleming award, 1970, Congl. Space Medal of Honor, Explorers Club medal. Fellow AIAA (hon., Astronautics award 1966), Internat. Astronautical Fedn. (hon.), Soc. Exptl. Test Pilots; mem. Nat. Acad. Engring. 1st man to walk on moon, 1969. Subspecialty: Astronautics. Office: 31 N Broadway Lebanon OH 45036

ARMSTRONG, THOMAS PEYTON, physics educator, researcher; b. Atchison, Kans., Nov. 24, 1941; s. Floyd Draper and Mary Elizabeth (Wohlgemuth) A.; m. Jeanette Carol Fry, June 9, 1962; children—Elizabeth, Stuart. B.S., U. Kans., 1962; M.S., U. Iowa, 1964, Ph.D. 1966. Postdoctoral asst. U. Iowa, Iowa City, 1966-67; research assoc. U.K. Atomic Energy, Culham, Eng., 1967-68; asst. prof. physics U. Kans., Lawrence, 1968-72, assoc. prof., 1972-75, prof., 1975—; co-investigator NASA Goddard Explorer 47 and 50, Greenbelt, Md., 1972—, Jet Propulsion Lab., Voyager 1 and 2, Pasadena, Calif., 1973—, Jet Propulsion Lab., Galileo, Pasadena, 1979—. Contbr. articles to profl. jours. Recipient Higuchi Research Achievement award U. Kans., 1983. Mem. Am. Geophys. Union, Am. Phys. Soc., AAAS. Current work: Planetary exploration, space plasma physics, numerical simulation, nonlinear waves and plasma instabilities. Subspecialty: Plasma physics. Home: 3217 W 9th St Lawrence KS 66044 Office: Dept Physics and Astronomy U Kans Lawrence KS 66044

ARNAOUT, M. AMIN, nephrologist, educator; b. Sidon, Lebanon, Aug. 8, 1949; came to U.S., 1976, naturalized, 1981; s. Ala Eddine and Insaf (Kublan) A.; m. Amal Kawwa, Oct. 23, 1975; children—Ramy, Rima. B.S., Am. U., Beirut, 1969, M.D. with distinction, 1974. Diplomate Am. Bd. Internal Medicine, Am. Bd. Nephrology. Intern, Am. U. Hosp., Beirut, 1974-75, resident, 1975-76; fellow Johns Hopkins Hosp., Balt., 1976; fellow Children's Hosp., Boston, 1976-78; instr. Harvard Med. Sch., 1978-82, asst. prof. 1982—; established investigator Am. Heart Assn., 1982—. Mem. Am. Soc. Nephrology, Internat. Soc. Nephrology, Am. Assn. Immunologists, Fedn. Am. Socs. Exptl. Biology, Am. Soc. Pediatric Research. Current work: Nephrology, membrane biology; receptors; complement system, phagocytosis. Subspecialties: Membrane biology; Immunobiology and immunology. Office: Childrens Hosp 300 Longwood Ave Boston MA 02115

ARNETT, WILLIAM DAVID, astrophysicist. Prof. dept. astronomy Dept. Astrophysics and Physics U. Chgo. Subspecialty: Theoretical astrophysics. Office: U Chgo Chicago IL 60637

ARNOLD, DEAN EDWARD, fishery biologist, limnologist, educator; b. Elmira, N.Y., Apr. 8, 1939; s. Edward Frank and Dorothy Josephine (Evertts) A.; m. Altheda Jane Watkins, June 27, 1965 (div. Jan. 1980); m. Juliet Keith Johnson, Aug. 23, 1980; children—Margaret Jean, David Edward. A.B., U. Rochester, 1961; M.S., Cornell U., 1965, Ph.D., 1969. Research assoc. Cornell U., Ithaca, N.Y., 1964-66; research limnologist U. Mich., Ann Arbor, 1969-72; research fishery biologist U.S. Fish and Wildlife Service, University Park, Pa., 1973—; adj. asst. prof. Pa. State U., University Park, 1973—; cons., ptnr. Environ. Research Group, Inc., Ann Arbor, 1972-75. Editor: Research of the Cooperative Fish and Wildlife Units, 1976. Contbr. articles to sci. jours. Asst. scoutmaster Boy Scouts Am., State College, Pa., 1981—; mem. choir Grace Luth. Ch., State College, 1979—; mem. State Coll. Mcpl. Band, 1974—. Served to lt. (j.g.), USN, 1961-63, ETO. Grantee AEC, 1970, NIH, 1968, EPA, 1979, U.S. Fish and Wildlife Service, 1980—, Pa. Power & Light Co., 1983—. Mem. Am. Fisheries Soc. (regional pres. 1982-83, assoc. editor), Am. Inst. Fishery Research Biologists (Thompson award 1972), N.Am. Benthological Soc., Assn. for Great Lakes Research, Am. Philatelic Soc., Nat. Ry. Hist. Soc. (editor 1978-81), Sigma Xi. Democrat. Lutheran. Current work: Aquatic effects of acid precipitation, water quality requirements of fishes, management/manipulation of lakes and streams. Subspecialty: Ecology (environmental science). Office: Pa Coop Fish and Wildlife Research Unit 7 Ferguson Bldg University Park PA 16802

ARNOLD, JAMES RICHARD, chemist, educator; b. New Brunswick, N.J., May 5, 1923; s. Abraham Samuel and Julia (Jacobs) A.; m. Louise Clark, Oct. 11, 1952; children: Robert C., Theodore J., Kenneth C. A.B., Princeton U., 1943, M.A., 1945, Ph.D., 1946. Postdoctoral fellow Inst. Nuclear Studies, U. Chgo., 1946-47, mem. faculty, 1948-55; NRC fellow Harvard U., 1947-48; mem. faculty chemistry Princeton U., 1955-58; asso. prof. chemistry U. Calif., San Diego, 1958-60, prof., 1960—, Harold C. Urey prof., 1983—, chmn. dept. chemistry, 1960-63; asso. Manhattan Project, 1943-46; dir. Calif. Space Inst., 1980—; mem. various bds. NASA, 1959—; mem. space sci. bd. Nat. Acad. Sci., 1970-74, mem. com. on sci. and public policy, 1973-77. Mem. editorial bd.: Ann. Rev. Nuclear Chemistry, 1972; asso. editor: Revs. Geophysics and Space Physics, 1972-75, Moon, 1972—; contbr. articles to profl. jours. Pres. Torrey Pines Elem. Sch. PTA, 1964-65; pres. La Jolla Democratic Club, 1965-66; mem. nat. council World Federalists-U.S.A., 1970-72. Recipient E.O. Lawrence medal AEC, 1968; Leonard medal Meteoritical Soc., 1976; asteroid 2143 named Jimarnold in his honor, 1980; Guggenheim fellow India, 1972-73. Mem. Nat. Acad. Sci., Am. Acad. Arts and Scis., Am. Chem. Soc., AAAS, Fedn. Am. Scientists, World Federalist Assn., Internat. Acad. Astronautics (corr.). Subspecialty: Satellite studies.

ARNOLD, ORVILLE EDWARD, cons. engr.; b. Sparta, Wis., Sept. 30, 1933; s. Donald E. and Lenice K. (Reilly) A.; married; children: Donald, David, Beth, Sandra. B.S.C.E., U. Wis.-Madison, 1955. Registered profl. engr., Wis. Design engr. Inland Steel Co., East Chicago, Ind., 1955-56; chief structural engr. Flad & Assocs. (Architects), Madison, Wis., 1956-63; pres. Arnold & O'Sheridan Cons (Engrs.), Madison, 1964—. Bd. dirs. Madison Opportunity Ctr., Hospice Care.; pres. Mendota/Monoma Lake Problems Assn., 1974. Recipient Engr. of Yr. in Pvt. Practice award Wis. Soc. Profl. Engrs., 1978; Disting. Service citation U. Wis. Coll. Engring., 1982. Mem. Nat. Soc. Profl. Engrs., Wis. Soc. Profl. Engrs., ASCE (pres. Wis. sect. 1972), Am. Concrete Inst. Roman Catholic. Current Work: Design of structural, mechanical and electrical engineering systems for buildings. Subspecialty: Civil engineering. Home: 1521 Edgehill Dr Madison WI 53705 Office: 815 Forward Dr Madison WI 53711

ARNOLD, WILLIAM HOWARD, energy company executive; b. Jefferson Barracks, Mo., May 13, 1931; s. William Howard and Elizabeth Welsh (Mullen) A.; m. Josephine Inman Routheau, June 13, 1952; children: William, Frances, Edward, David, Thomas. A.B., Cornell U., 1951; A.M., Princeton U., 1953, Ph.D., 1955. Instr., research assoc. Princeton U., 1955; sr. engr., mgr. reactor physics Westinghouse Atomic Power Div., Pitts., 1955-61; dir. nuclear fuel mgmt. NUS Corp., Washington, 1961-62; various mgmt. positions to gen. mgr. PWR Systems, Pitts., 1962-79; pres. Westinghouse Nuclear Internat., Pitts., 1979-80, gen. mgr. Advanced Reactor div., 1981—, gen. mgr. Advanced Energy Systems div., 1983—; tchr. nuclear tech. U. Pitts., 1957, U. Ala., 1963. Contbr. articles to profl. jours. Fellow Am. Nuclear Soc., AAAS; mem. Nat. Acad. Engring., Am. Phys. Soc., Sigma Xi. Clubs: Longue Vue Country, Chevy Chase. Subspecialty: Nuclear engineering. Office: Box 158 Madison PA 15663

ARNS, ROBERT GEORGE, physics educator, educational administrator, consultant; b. Buffalo, July 24, 1933. B.S., Canisius Coll., 1955; M.S., U. Mich., 1956, Ph.D., 1960. Asst. prof., assoc. prof. SUNY-Buffalo, 1960-64; assoc. prof., prof. Ohio State U., Columbus, 1964-77, vice provost, 1971-73, assoc. provost, 1975-77; prof. physics U. Vt., Burlington, 1977—, v.p. acad. affairs,

1977—. Contbr. articles to sci. jours. NSF grantee, 1960-77. Mem. Am. Phys. Soc., Strategic Mgmt. Soc. (founding mem.). Current work: Nuclear structure physics, solar energy systems, management information and decision support systems, data communications, strategic planning and management. Subspecialties: Nuclear physics; Distributed systems and networks. Office: U Vt Waterman Bldg Burlington VT 05405

ARNSDORF, MORTON FRANK, cardiologist; b. Chgo., Aug. 7, 1940; s. Selmar N. and Irmgard C. (Steinmann) A.; m. Mary Hunter Tower, Dec. 26, 1963 (div. 1982). B.A. magna cum laude, Harvard U., 1962; M.D., Columbia U., 1966. Diplomate: Am. Bd. Internal Medicine. Housestaff officer U. Chgo., 1966-69; fellow cardiology Columbia-Presbyn. Med. Ctr., N.Y.C., 1969-71; asst. prof. medicine U. Chgo., 1973-79, assoc. prof., 1979-83, prof., 1983—, chief sect. cardiology, 1981—; mem. pharmacology study sect. NIH, 1981-84. Contbr. articles to profl. jours. Served to maj. USAF, 1971-73. Recipient Research Career Devel. award. NIH, 1976-81; research grantee Chgo. Heart Assn., 1976-78; research grantee NIH, 1977—. Fellow Am. Coll. Cardiology; mem. Am. Heart Assn. (dir. 1981-83, chmn. exec. com. basic sci. council 1981-83, steering com. 1983—), Chgo. Heart Assn. (bd. govs., past chmn. research council, chmn. patient care com.), AMA, Am. Fedn. Clin. Research, Assn. Univ. Cardiologists, Cardiac Electrophysiol Soc. (sec.-treas. 1985—), Central Soc. Clin. Research (council), Chgo. Med. Soc., Ill. Med. Soc. Club: Quadrangle. Current Work: Cellular electrical activity assessed by microelectrode techniques in mammalian heart tissue; mechanism of arrhythmogeneis and the manner in which antiarrhythmic drugs work. Subspecialty: Cardiology. Office: Chief Sect Cardiology Univ Chicago Hosps and Clinics Box 423 950 E 59th St Chicago IL 60637

ARONIN, NEIL, endocrinologist, educator; b. Washington, Mar. 16, 1948; s. David and Thelma (Borenstein) A.; m. Marion DiFiglia, Jan. 1, 1980; children: Elizabeth H., Leah M. B.A. magna cum laude, Duke U., 1970; M.D., U. Pa., 1974. Diplomate: Am. Bd. Internal Medicine, subsplty. bd. endocrinology and metabolism. Intern in medicine Duke U. Med. Center, Durham, N.C., 1974-75, resident, 1975-77; clin. fellow in endocrinology and metabolism Mt. Sinai Med. Center, N.Y.C., 1977-79, instr. dept. medicine, 1979-80; NIH research fellow in neuroendocrinology, dept. neourology Mass. Gen. Hosp.-Harvard Med. Sch., Boston, 1979-81; asst. prof. medicine and physiology U. Mass. Med. Center, Worcester, 1981—; clin. assoc. in neurendocrinology Mass. Gen Hosp., 1981—. NIH grantee, 1982—. Mem. Soc. Neurosci., Endocrine Soc., N.Y. Acad. Scis., Am. Fedn. Clin. Research. Democrat. Jewish. Current Work: Anatomy and physiology of peptide systems in brain; regulation of hypothalamic-pituitary axis. Subspecialty: Neuroendocrinology.

ARONOW, SAUL, geology educator, consultant; b. Bklyn., Dec. 10, 1923; s. Samuel Judah and Rebecca (Mirel) A.; m. Judith Zuckerman, Feb. 17, 1948; children—Jessie Judith, Kurt Albert, Rebecca Ellen. B.A., Bklyn. Coll., 1945; M.S., State U. Iowa, 1946; Ph.D., U. Wis., 1955. Geologist, U.S. Geol. Survey, Grand Forks, N.D., 1948-52; prof. geology Lamar U., Beaumont, Tx. 1955—; cons. Minn. Geol. Survey, St. Paul, 1971-78, Tex. Bur. Econ. Geology, Austin, 1963-69, Soil Conservation Service, Temple, Tex., 1965—. Contbr. articles to profl. jours. Fellow Geol. Soc. Am.; mem. AAAS, Soil Sci. Soc. Am., Sigma Xi. Current work: Soils, glacial geology, geomorphology, Pleistocene of Gulf Coast. Subspecialties: Geology; Geomorphology. Home: 5590 Frost Beaumont TX 77706 Office: Dept Geology Box 10031 Lamar Univ Sta Beaumont TX 77710

ARONSON, CARL EDWARD, pharmacologist, toxicologist, educator; b. Providence, Mar. 14, 1936; s. Carl Ivar and Ruth (Workman) A.; m. Marjorie B. Aronson, Dec. 17, 1960; children: Linda, Kristen. A.B., Brown U., 1958; Ph.D., U. Vt., 1966; M.A. (hon.), U. Pa., 1973. Research technician Worcester Found. Exptl. Biology, Shrewsbury, Mass., 1959-60; postdoctoral fellow U. Pa., 1965-67, lectr., 1965-74, instr., 1967-70, assoc. dept. pharmacology, 1970-71, asst. prof., 1971-73, head labs. pharmacology and toxicology dept. animal biology, 1972—, assoc. prof., 1973—, acting assoc. dean student affairs, 1974-75; cons. in field. Contbr. numerous articles to profl. jours. Active numerous civic orgns. Served with USAFR, 1958-65. Recipient Norden Disting. Tchr. award U. Pa., 1982. Mem. AAUP, Am. Acad. Vet. Pharmacology and Therapeutics (pres. 1983), Am. Acad. Vet. Pharmacology and Therapeutics (pres. 1983-85), Am. Acad. Veterinary and Comparative Toxicology, Am. Soc. Pharmacology and Exptl. Therapeutics, John Morgan Soc., Physiol. Soc. Phila., Sigma Xi. Current Work: Biomedical pharmacology and toxicology with emphasis on in vitro methods of assessment of cardiotoxicity of drugs and chemicals. Subspecialties: Pharmacology; Toxicology (medicine). Office: Labs Pharmacology and Toxicology U Pa Sch Vet Medicine 3800 Spruce St Philadelphia PA 19104

ARONSON, MIRIAM KLAUSNER, gerontologist, consultant, research, educator; b. N.Y.C., July 12, 1940; d. Joseph and Martha (Sklower) Klausner; children: Eric, Andrew, Elliott. A.B., Barnard Coll., N.Y.C., 1961; M.Ed., Tchrs. Coll. Columbia U., 1970, ED.D., 1980. Cons., researcher geriatric facilities, N.Y. and N.J., 1969-75; dir. geriatric program Soundview-Throgs Neck Community Mental Health Ctr., Bronx, N.Y., 1975-78; chief services to elderly Bronx-Lebanon Hosp. Community Mental Health Ctr., Bronx, 1978-79; dir. longterm Care Gerontol. Ctr. Albert Einstein Coll. Medicine, Bronx, 1979—, asst. prof. neurology and psychiatry, 1980-85, assoc. prof., 1985—, prin. investigator senile dementias, risks and course, 1984—. Author, dir.: film series Teaching series on Alzheimers Disease, 1980; author (with R. Bennett and B. Gurland) film The Acting Out Elderly, 1983. Mem. Hillsdale (N.J.) Bd. Health, 1975-82, pres., 1977-81; mem. planning and policy com. Outreach Health Service Program, Bergen County, N.J., 1976. N.Y. State Regents scholar, 1957-61; Adminstrn. Aging grantee, 1968-70, 74-75; Nat. Council Community Mental Health Ctrs. Best Outreach Program award, 1976; Alzheimers Disease Soc. Greater N.Y. award, 1982. Fellow Gerontol. Soc. Am. (dir. task force on long team care 1981-85), Am. Orthopsychiat. Soc. (program com. 1985-86); mem. Am. Geriatrics Soc., Nat. Alzheimers Disease and Related Disorders Assn. (dir. edn. and pub. awareness com. 1979-84, cons. 1985—), Western Gerontol. Soc. (bd. dirs. 1983-85). Current Work: Current research, practice and education interests relate to risk factors for and clinical course of Alzheimer's Disease and other dementing illnesses and their impact on the family. Subspecialty: Gerontology. Home: 305 Ell Rd Hillsdale NJ 07642 Office: Albert Einstein College of Medicine Resnick Gerontology Center 1300 Morris Park Ave Belfer Bldg 802 Bronx NY 10461

ARONSON, STANLEY MAYNARD, educator, physician; b. N.Y.C., May 28, 1922; s. Eliuh and Lena (Hassner) A.; m. Betty Ellis, June 3, 1947; children: Susan, Lisa, Sarah. B.S., CCNY, 1943; M.D., N.Y. U., 1947; M.A., Brown U., 1971; M.P.H., Harvard U. Sch. Public Health, 1981. Diplomate: Am. Bd. Pathology., Am. Bd. Neuropathology. Residency tng. Bellevue Hosp.; Residence tng. Meml. Center for Cancer, Mt. Sinai Hosp., all N.Y.C., 1947-53; faculty Columbia Coll. Physicians and Surgeons, 1951-54; prof. pathology, asst. dean SUNY, Bklyn., 1954-70; prof. med. sci., dean medicine Brown U., 1970-81, Univ. prof. med. sci., 1981—; dir. labs. Kings County Hosp. Center, Bklyn., 1965-70; pathologist-in-chief Miriam Hosp., Providence, 1970-75; vis. prof. community medicine Dartmouth Coll. Med. Sch., 1982—; lectr. Yale Sch. Medicine, 1964-65; lectr. pathology Tufts U. Sch. Medicine, 1978—; cons. physician neuropathology Jewish Chronic Disease Hosp., Bklyn., 1951—, NIH, 1962—; cons. physician R.I. Hosp., Roger Williams Hosp., Meml. Hosp., Providence VA Hosp., Butler Hosp., Providence, Luth. Med. Center, N.Y.C. Author: (with B.W. Volk) Cerebral Sphingolipidoses, 1962, Inborn Disorders of Sphingolipid Metabolism, 1966, Sphingolipids, Sphingolipidoses and Allied Disorders, 1972, (with A. Sahs and E Hartman) Guidelines for Stroke Care, 1976; (with Adachi and Hirano) Pathology of the Myelinated Axon, 1985; also numerous articles; mem. editorial bd.: Jour. Submicroscopic Cytology, R.I. Med. Jour., Jour. Neuropathology and Exptl. Neurology. Mem. Nat. Adv. Commn. on Multiple Sclerosis, 1973-74; commr. U.S. Commn. Control of Huntington's Disease, 1976—; mem. NIH Perinatal Research Commn., Joint Commn. on Stroke Facilities; chmn. Legis. Commn. Dementia Related to Aging; mem. med. adv. bd. Nat. Multiple Sclerosis Soc., Dysautonomia Found., Nat. Tay-Sachs Assn., Nat. Fund for Med. Edn., Hospice R.I., Interfaith Health Care Ministries. Served with U.S. Army, 1942-46. Mem. AMA, Am. Neurol. Assn., Am. Assn. Neuropathology (pres. 1971-72), Am. Public Health Assn., Am Coll. Epidemiology, N.Y. Acad. Medicine, Am. Acad. Neurology, Am. Assn. Pathologists and Bacteriologists, Internat. Soc. Neuropathology, Assn. Am. Med. Colls., N.Y. Neurol. Soc. Research on genetics epidemiology, pathology and diagnostic features of cerebral degenerative diseases, population dynamics, pathology and epidemiology of cerebral vascular disease and stroke. Subspecialties: Pathology (medicine); Preventive medicine. Home: 26 Elm St Rehoboth MA 02769 Office: Office Med Affairs Brown U Providence RI 02912

ARROW, KENNETH JOSEPH, economist, educator; b. N.Y.C., Aug. 23, 1921; s. Harry I. and Lillian (Greenberg) A.; m. Selma Schweitzer, Aug. 31, 1947; children—David Michael, Andrew. B.S. in Social Sci., CCNY, 1940; M.A., Columbia U., 1941, Ph.D., 1951, D.Sc., 1973; LL.D. (hon.), U. Chgo., 1967, City U. N.Y., 1972, Hebrew U. Jerusalem, 1975, U. Pa., 1976, D.Social and Econ. Scis., U. Vienna, Austria, 1971, D.Social Scis., Yale, 1974, Doctor, Université René Descartes, Paris, 1974; Dr.Pol., U. Helsinki, 1976; M.A. (hon.), Harvard U., 1968; D., Universite Aix-Marseille, 1985; D.Litt., U. Cambridge, 1985. Research asso. Cowles Commn. for Research in Econs., 1947-49; asst. prof. econs. U. Chgo., 1948-49; acting asst. prof. econs. and statistics Stanford, 1949-50, asso. prof., 1950-53, prof. econs., statistics and ops. research, 1953-68; prof. econs. Harvard, 1968-74, James Bryant Conant univ. prof., 1974-79; exec. head dept. econs. Stanford U., 1954-56, acting exec. head dept., 1962-63, Joan Kenney prof. econs. and prof. ops. research, 1979—; economist Council Econ. Advisers, U.S. Govt., 1962; cons. RAND Corp. Author: Social Choice and Individual Values, 1951, Essays in the Theory of Risk Bearing, 1971, The Limits of Organization, 1974, Collected Papers, Vols. I and II, 1983; Co-author: Mathematical Studies in Inventory and Production, 1958, Studies in Linear and Nonlinear Programming, 1958, Time Series Analysis of Inter-industry Demands, 1959, Public Investment, The Rate of Return and Optimal Fiscal Policy, 1971, General Competitive Analysis, 1971, Studies in Resource Allocation Processes, 1977. Served as capt. AUS, 1942-46. Social Sci. Research fellow, 1952; fellow Center for Advanced Study in the Behavioral Scis., 1956-57, Churchill Coll., Cambridge, Eng., 1963-64, 70, 73; Guggenheim fellow, 1972-73; Recipient John Bates Clark medal Am. Econ. Assn., 1957; Alfred Nobel Meml. prize in econ. scis., 1972. Fellow Am. Acad. Arts and Scis. (v.p. 1979-81), Econometric Soc. (v.p. 1955, pres. 1956), Am. Statis. Assn., Inst. Math. Statistics, Am. Econ. Assn. (mem. exec. com. 1967-69, pres. 1973), AAAS (chmn. sect K 1983), Internat. Econ. Assn. (pres. 1983-86), Internat. Soc. for Inventory Research (pres. 1983-84); mem. Nat. Acad. Scis., Am. Philos. Soc., Inst. Mgmt. Scis. (pres. 1963, chmn. council 1964), Finnish Acad. Scis. (fgn. hon.), Brit. Acad. (corr.), Western Econ. Assn. (pres. 1980-81). Current work: Optimal use of information for decisions by individuals and organizations. Subspecialty: Operations research (mathematics). Office: Dept Econ Stanford U Stanford CA 94305

ARSENEAU, JAMES CHARLES, medical oncologist, researcher; b. Syracuse, N.Y., Aug. 29, 1942; s. James Howard and Glenna (Wurth) A.; m. Jane Ellen Macy, July 2, 1966; children: Marc, David. A.B., Syracuse U., 1964; M.D., Albany (N.Y.) Med. Coll., 1968. Cert. Am. Bd. Internal Medicine. Intern Strong Meml. Hosp., Rochester, N.Y., 1968-69, resident, 1969-70; instr. trainee U. Rochester, 1968-70; clin. assoc. Nat. Cancer Inst., Bethesda, 1970-73; fellow med. oncology U. Rochester, 1973-74, asst. prof. oncology, 1974-80, assoc. prof., 1980—; chmn. new drug com. Gynecologic Oncology Group, Phila., 1980—, mem. exec. com., 1982—; co-chmn. Melanoma group Eastern Coop. Oncology Group, Madison, Wis., 1980—. Cons. editor: Investigational New Drugs, 1982—; contbr. articles to profl. jours. Bd. dirs. United Cancer Council, Rochester, 1977-80, Make Today Count, 1977—. Served with USPHS, 1970-73. Wilson fellow, 1973-74; Am. Cancer Soc. fellow, 1974-77. Mem. AMA, N.Y. State Med. Soc., Rochester Acad. Medicine, Am. Soc. Clin. Oncology, N.Y. Acad. Scis. Republican. Current Work: Clincial research of new anti-neoplastic drugs, biologicals, anti-cancer agents clinical studies of new anti-cancer therapies. Subspecialties: Chemotherapy; Cancer research (medicine). Home: 24 Vincent Dr Pittsford NY 14534

ARTHUR, MICHAEL EDWARD, ceramic engineer; b. Ashland, Ky., Dec. 12, 1943; s. Edward F. and Charlene (Hickman) A.; m. Elizabeth Pizar, July 25, 1981; children—Michael Edward. B.S. in Ceramic Engring., Ga. Inst. Tech., 1966, M.S., 1969; M.B.A., U. Chgo., 1983. Registered profl. engr., Wis. Metallurgist, Armco Steel, Ashland, 1966-67; product engr. Tex. Instruments, Dallas, 1969-70; staff engr. McGraw-Edison, Milw., 1971-84; mgr. engring. Murata Erie N.A., State College, Pa., 1984—. Editor Ceramic-Metal Systems Bibliography, 1970-74. Patentee in field. Author articles. Mem. Greendale (Wis.) Telecommunications Bd., 1982-83. Mem. Am. Ceramic Soc., Keramos, Nat. Inst. Ceramic Engrs., Sigma Xi (recipient undergrad. research award 1967). Current work: Dielectric ceramic materials and processing for monolithic ceramic capacitors. Subspecialties: Ceramic engineering; Electronic materials. Home: 1329 Sandpiper Dr State College PA 16801 Office: Murata Erie NA 1900 W College Ave State College PA 16801

ARUNKUMAR, KOOVAPPADI ANANTHASUBRAMONY, physicist, educator; b. Tiruchirapally, India, June 19, 1949; came to U.S., 1979, naturalized, 1982; s. Koovappadi Subramani and Jayalakshmi (Arunachalam) Ananthasubramony; m. Radha Arunkumar, Aug. 20, 1976; 1 child, Amiethab. B.Sc., U. Kerala, India, 1969, M.Sc., 1971; Ph.D., Indian Inst. Tech., Madras, 1975, U. Hull, Eng., 1979. Vis. asst. prof. U. Ky., Lexington, 1979-80, sr. research assoc., 1980-83, asst. research prof., 1983-84; sr. design engr. Apollo Lasers, Calif., 1984-85; sr. scientist Spectron Devel. Labs., Costa Mesa, Calif., 1985—. Contbr. articles to profl. jours. Indian Inst. Tech. research fellow, 1971-72; Council Sci. and Indsl. Research jr. research fellow, 1972-75; U.K. Commonwealth scholar, 1975-79. Mem. Am. Phys. Soc., Smithsonian Instn., Sigma Xi. Hindu. Current Work: Laser systems, holography, free electron lasers, laser plasma interaction, surface enhanced Raman scattering. Laser Raman spectroscopy, fiber optics. Home: 1250 Adams Ave V102 Costa Mesa CA 92626 Office: Spectron Devel Lab 3303 Harbor Blvd Suite G-3 Costa Mesa CA 92626

ARVIDSON, RAYMOND ERNST, planetary geology educator; b. Bklyn., Jan. 22, 1948; m. Eloise Kettleson, 1969; 2 children. B.A., Temple U., 1969; M.S., Brown U., 1971, Ph.D., 1974. Research assoc. in planetary geology Brown U., Providence, 1973; asst. prof. earth and planetary scis. Washington U., St. Louis, 1974-78, assoc. prof., 1978-84, prof., 1984—, fellow McDonnell Ctr. for Space Scis., 1976—, dir. Washington U./NASA Planetary Image Facility, 1978—; vis. scientist Lowell Obs., 1972, Lunar Sci. Inst., 1974; vis. prof. U. Rome, 1974; in residence for Viking mission Jet Propulsion Lab., Calif. Inst. Tech., 1976; mem. Viking Lander Imaging Flight Ops. Team, 1975-82, team leader, 1978-82; mem. space sci. bd., chmn. com. on data mgmt. and computation Nat. Acad. Sci., 1981-84; mem. Venus Radar Mapper Team, 1979—; mem. end-end info. system rev. panel NASA, 1981-83, mem. earth observing system sci. steering com., 1982—, mem. imaging spectrometer sci. adv. group, 1984—, mem. planetary imaging spectrometer instrument sci. design team, 1984—, chmn. earth observation system data panel, 1984. Assoc. editor Jour. Geophys. Research, 1981-84, Cambridge U. Press, 1983—. Mem. Am. Soc. Photogrammetry, Am. Geophys. Union (sec. planetology div. 1984-85), AIAA, AAAS, Geol. Soc. Am. (sec. planetary geology div. 1984), Planetary Soc. Subspecialties: Planetology; Remote sensing (geoscience). Home: 1612 Forestview Ridge Ln Ballwin MO 63021 Office: Dept Earth and Planetary Sci Washington U Saint Louis MO 63130

ARVIND, computer science educator and researcher, consultant; b. Lucknow, India, May 15, 1947; s. Devki Nandan and Rukmani (Mithal); m. Gita Singh Mithal, Dec. 4, 1973; children: Divakar Singh, Prabhakar Singh. B.Tech. in Elec. Engring, Indian Inst. Tech., Kanpur, 1969; M.S. in Computer Sci, U. Minn., 1972; Ph.D. in Computer Sci, 1973. Asst. prof. info. and computer sci. U. Calif.-Irvine, 1974-78; assoc. prof. elec. engring. and computer sci. MIT, 1979—; cons. IBM, TRW Array Processors, numerous other cos. Contbr. articles to profl. jours. Mem. Assn. Computing Machinery, IEEE (sr.). Current Work: Dataflow architectures and functional programming languages; data flow; functional languages; parallel computing. Subspecialties: Computer architecture; Programming languages. Home: 34 Lombard Rd Arlington MA 02174 Office: MIT Lab for Computer Sci 545 Technology Square Cambridge MA 02139

ASANUMA, HIROSHI, physiologist; b. Kobe, Japan, Aug. 17, 1926; came to U.S., 1965, naturalized, 1966; s. Kisaburo and Yukiko (Takahashi) A.; m. Reiko Shimasu, Dec. 18, 1953; children—Chisato, Mari. M.D., Keio U., Tokyo, 1952; D.Med.Sci., Kobe (Japan) Med. Coll., 1959. Intern Saseikai Hosp., Kobe, 1952-53; instr. dept. physiology Kobe Med. Coll., 1953-59; asst. prof. dept. physiology Osaka City U. Med. Sch., 1959-65; asso. prof. dept. physiology N.Y. Med. Coll., N.Y.C., 1965-71, prof., 1971-72, Rockefeller U., N.Y.C., 1972—; guest investigator Rockefeller Inst., 1961-63. Contbr. articles to profl. jours. Rockefeller Found. Internat. fellow, 1961-62; City of N.Y. Career Scientist awardee, 1965-72. Mem. Am. Physiol. Soc., Japanese Physiol. Soc., Harvey Soc., Soc. for Neurosci. Current Work: To study the functional role of sensory input to the motor cortex during willed movements. Subspecialties: Neurophysiology; Neurobiology. Home: 505 E 79th St New York NY 10021 Office: Rockefeller U 1230 York Ave New York NY 10021

ASATO, YUKIO, biologist; b. Waipahu, Hawaii, Jan. 19, 1934; s. Kame and Kama (Tamashiro) A.; m. Sue Akemi, Nov. 12, 1937; children: April A., Lynn K. B.A., U. Hawaii, 1957, M.S., 1966, Ph.D., 1969. Postdoctoral research scientist NASA, Moffett Field, Calif., 1969-71; asst. prof. Southereastern Mass. U., North Dartmouth, 1971-75, assoc. prof., 1975-80, prof. biology, 1980—. Contbr. articles to profl. jours. Served with AUS, 1957-60. Mem. Am. Soc. Microbiology, AAAS, Genetic Soc. Am. Current Work: Research in molecular biology of the blue-green bacteria; regulation of cell cycle events in cyanobacteria. Subspecialties: Genome organization; Molecular biology. Office: Dept Biology Southeastern Mass Univ North Dartmouth MA 02747

ASAWA, GEORGE NOBUO, dentist; b. Norwalk, Calif., Apr. 29, 1925; s. Zensuke and Moto (Murata) A.; m. Masako Sadao, July 7, 1957; 1 dau., Elizabeth. B.A., U. Calif.-Berkeley, 1950, B.S., 1953; D.D.S., Washington U., St. Louis, 1963. Clin. asst. prof. U. So. Calif. Sch. Dentistry, Los Angeles, 1979—. Fellow Acad. Gen. Dentistry; mem. Internat. Assn. Dental Research, Am. Assn. Dental Research, Fedn. Internat. Dentaires, Am. Dental Assn. Democrat. Quaker. Current Work: Teaching prosthodontics at University Southern California School of Dentistry. Subspecialty: Prosthodontics. Home: 930 S Knott Ave Anaheim CA 92804

ASBURY, ARTHUR KNIGHT, neurologist, educator; b. Cin., Nov. 22, 1928; s. Eslie and Mary (Knight) A.; m. Carolyn Holstein, May 17, 1980; children by previous marriage: Dana, Patricia Knight, William Francis. Grad., Phillips Acad., Andover, Mass., 1946; student, Stanford, 1947-48; B.S., U. Ky., 1951; M.D., U. Cin., 1958; M.A. (hon.), U. Pa., 1974. Intern in medicine Mass. Gen. Hosp., Boston, 1958-59, resident, 1959-63, fellow, 1963-65, staff neurologist, 1965-69; chief neurology San Francisco VA Hosp., 1969-74; prof. dept. neurology U. Pa., Phila., 1974—, chmn. dept. neurology, 1974-82; teaching fellow Harvard Med. Sch., 1958-65, instr., 1965-68, assoc., 1968-69; assoc. prof. neurology U. Calif. at San Francisco, 1969-73, prof., vice-chmn., 1969-74. Sr. editor: Internat. Med. Rev. Series-Neurology, Butterworth & Co., London, 1980—; Asso. editor: Archives of Neurology, 1975-76; Assoc. editor: Annals of Neurology, 1976-81; mem. editorial bd.: Muscle and Nerve, 1977—, Neurology, 1981—, Jour. Neuropathology and Exptl. Neurology, 1981-83; chief editor: Annals of Neurology, 1985—; contbr. chpts. to med. textbooks, articles to med. jours. Vice-pres., bd. dirs. Forest Retreat Farms Inc., Carlisle, Ky., 1970—. Served with AUS, 1951-53. USPHS grantee, 1967—; Muscular Dystrophy Assn. grantee, 1974—. Fellow Am. Acad. Neurology (v.p. 1977-79); mem. Am. Neurol. Assn. (councillor 1976-81, pres. 1982-83), Am. Assn. Neuropathologists (v.p. 1983-84), Soc. Neurosci., Assn. Univ. Profs. Neurology (pres. 1980-82). Episcopalian (vestryman). Subspecialty: Neurology. Home: 2409 Naudain St Philadelphia PA 19146 Office: Dept Neurology Hospital Univ Pa Philadelphia PA 19104

ASCHER, MICHAEL CHARLES, public transit executive; b. N.Y.C., Jan. 8, 1944; s. Benjamin Paul and Miriam (Schechter) A.; m. Alexa Fern Rubin, June 12, 1966; children: Stacey Nicole, Jennifer Sharyn. B.M.E., CCNY, 1966; M.S. in Engring, L.I. U., 1971. Registered profl. engr., N.Y., N.J., Tenn. Mech. engr. L.I. Lighting Co., Hicksville, N.Y., 1966-72; sr. engr. and supr. engr. Burns and Roe, Inc., Hempstead, N.Y., 1972-76, project mgr., Woodbury, N.Y., 1976-78, project engring. mgr., Oradell, N.J., 1978-79, project mgr., 1979-83, dep. dir., 1983-84; v.p., chief engr. N.Y.C. Transit Authority, 1985—. Contbr. tech. articles to profl. publs. Tech. del. L.I. (N.Y.) Space Shuttle Task Force, 1972. Mem. ASME (chmn. L.I. exec. com. 1971-72, Valued Service cert. 1972, 75), Nat. Soc. Profl. Engrs., Assn. L.I. Engrs. and Scientists (vice chmn. 1972-73). Lodge: B'nai B'rith (treas. Oradell chpt. 1979-80). Current Work: Responsible for restoration of N.Y.C. mass transit system. Subspecialty: Mechanical engineering. Office: New York City Transit Authority 370 Jay St Brooklyn NY 11201

ASHCROFT, NEIL WILLIAM, physics educator; b. London, Nov. 27, 1938; married, 1961; 2 children. B.Sc., U. N.Z., 1958, M.Sc. with honors, 1960; Ph.D., U. Cambridge, 1964. Sci. research council sr. fellow Cavendish Lab. U. Cambridge, 1973-74, vis. fellow Clare Hall, 1973-74; research assoc. theoretical physics Cornell U., Ithaca, N.Y., 1965-66, from asst. prof. to assoc. prof., 1966-75, prof. physics, 1975—; dir. Cornell U. (Lab. Atomic and Solid State Physics), 1979-84; assoc. dir. Cornell High Energy Synchrotron Source, 1979—; cons. Los Alamos Nat. Lab. John Simon Guggenheim Mem. fellow, 1984-85, Royal Soc. guest fellow, 1984-85, Overseas fellow Churchill Coll., Cambridge Eng., 1984-85. Fellow AAAS, Am. Phys. Soc. (vice chmn. div. condensed matter physics 1985-86); mem. Am. Inst. Physics. Subspecialties: Condensed matter physics; Theoretical physics. Office: Clark Hall Cornell U Ithaca NY 14853

ASHER, ROBERT BERNARD, engineering program administrator, researcher; b. Chgo., June 15, 1941; s. Ben and Edwina Ruth (Deutschle) A.; m. Linda Louise Parker, May 15, 1965; children—Christina Dawn, Kimberly Diane, Heidi Darlene. B.S. in Engring., Okla. State U., 1969, M.S., 1971, Ph.D., 1974. Commd. 2d lt. U.S. Air Force, 1969, advanced through grades to capt., 1977; computer analyst Air Force Satellite Control Facility, Sunnyvale, Calif., 1964-66; tech. mgr. Air Force Avionics Lab. Wright-Patterson AFB, Ohio, 1971-74; vis. scientist Stanford U. Info. Scis. Lab., Calif., 1975; research assoc. F.J. Seiler Research Lab., U.S. Air Force Acad., Colo., 1974-77; cons. Optical Scis. Co., Placentia, Calif., 1977-78; asst. prof. dept. elec. engring. Tex. Tech U., Lubbock, 1978-79; program mgr. Orincon Corp., San Diego, 1978-79; sr. staff scientist, tech. supr. Lockheed Palo Alto Research Labs., Calif., 1979-81; program dir. Sandia Nat. Labs., Albuquerque, 1981-85; assoc. dir. Space and Flight Systems Lab., U. Colo., Colorado Springs, 1981—. Contbr. articles to profl. jours. Elder, Pulpit Rock Ch., Colorado Springs, Colo., 1975-77; dir. adult edn. Grace Ch., Albuquerque, 1981-83; Bible tchr. Hope Evangelical Free Ch., Albuquerque, 1983—. Mem. IEEE, Optical Soc. Am. SPIE. Republican. Current work: Development and research of key technologies for space weapons for the strategic defense initiative. Subspecialties: Systems engineering; Graphics, image processing, and pattern recognition. Home: 5410 Candlewood Ct NE Albuquerque NM 87111 Office: U Colo Colorado Springs CO Also: 1900 Randolph Dr SE Albuquerque NM 87106

ASHLEY, HOLT, aeronautical scientist, educator; b. San Francisco, Jan. 10, 1923; s. Harold Harrison and Anne (Oates) A.; m. Frances M. Day, Feb. 1, 1947. Student, Calif. Inst. Tech., 1940-43; B.S., U. Chgo., 1944; S.M., Mass. Inst. Tech., 1948, Sc.D., 1951. Faculty Mass. Inst. Tech., 1946-67, prof. aero., 1960-67; prof. aeros. and astronautics and mech. engring. Stanford U., 1967—; spl. research aeroelasticity, aerodynamics; cons. govt. agys., research orgns., indsl. corps.; dir. office of exploratory research and problem assessment and div. advanced tech. applications NSF, 1972-74; mem. sci. adv. bd. USAF, 1958-80; research adv. com. structural dynamics NASA, 1952-60, research adv. com. on aircraft structures, 1962-70, chmn. research adv. com. on materials and structures, 1974-77; mem. Kanpur Indo-American program Indian Inst. Tech., 1964-65; AIAA Wright Bros. lectr., 1981. Co-author: Aeroelasticity, 1955, Principles of Aeroelasticity, 1962, Aerodynamics of Wings and Bodies, 1969, Engineering Analysis of Flight Vehicles, 1974. Mem. Greater Boston coordinating council Boy Scouts Am., also mem.-at-large and adviser air explorer squadron. Recipient Goodwin medal M.I.T., 1952; Exceptional Civilian Service award U.S. Air Force, 1972, 80; Public Service award NASA, 1981; named one of 10 outstanding young men of year Boston Jr. C. of C., 1956. Fellow Am. Acad. Arts and Scis.; hon. fellow AIAA (assoc. editor jour., v.p. tech. 1971, pres. 1973, Structures, Structural Dynamics and Materials award 1969); mem. Am. Meterol. Soc. (profl., recipient 50th Anniversary medal 1971), ASME (chmn. exec. com. aerospace div. 1982), AAAS, Nat. Acad. Engring. (aeros. and space engring. bd. 1977, council 1985—), Phi Beta Kappa, Sigma Xi, Tau Beta Pi. Current Work: Aeroelasticity; unsteady aerodynamics; wind energy. Subspecialties: Aeronautical engineering; Aerospace engineering and technology. Address: 475 Woodside Dr Woodside CA 94062

ASHOK, S., engineering educator; b. Coimbatore, Tamilnadu, India, July 17, 1947, came to U.S., 19; s. C.R. Somasundaram and Vasantha (Devi) Ashok; m. Lavanya Dilli, Oct. 19, 1980. B.E. with honors, U. Madras, India, 1968; M.Tech., Indian Inst. Tech., Kanpur, 1970; Ph.D., Rensselaer Poly. Inst., 1978. Research asst. Indian Inst. Tech., Kanpur, 1969-70; grad. asst. Rensselaer Poly. Inst., Troy, N.Y., 1970-76, instr., 1977-78; asst. prof. Pa. State U., University Park, 1978-83, assoc. prof. engring. sci., 1983—; staff Gen. Elec. Corp. Research and Dev., Schenectady, N.Y., 1973. Contbr. articles to profl. jours.; patentee in field. Vol., Samaritan Hosp., Troy, 1970-73. Recipient Allen

Dumont award Rensselaer Poly. Inst., 1979, faculty research award Pa. State Engring. Soc., 1983; Humboldt fellow, 1983. Fellow IETE (India); mem. IEEE (sr.), Electrochem. Soc., N.Y. Acad. Sci., ACLU, Sigma Xi. Current work: Semiconductor interface phenomena; ion-assisted processing and its influence on semiconductor surfaces; thin films for semiconductor devices, sensors and solar cells. Subspecialties: Semiconductors; Microelectronics. Home: 445 Waupelani Dr I-21 State College PA 16801 Office: Pa State Univ 130 Hammond Bldg University Park PA 16802

ASHTEKAR, ABHAY VASANT, physicist, educator; b. Shirpur, India, July 5, 1949; came to U.S., 1969; s. Vasant Dhuleshwar and Vimala (Nandrekar) A.; m. Anne Magnon, Mar. 26, 1975. B.Sc. with honors, U. Bombay India, 1969; Ph.D., U. Chgo., 1974. Postdoctoral fellow Math. Inst., Oxford, Eng., 1974-76; research assoc. Enrico Fermi Inst., Chgo., 1976-78; maitre de conf. U. de Clermont-FD, France, 1978-80; asst. prof., then assoc. prof. physics Syracuse, U., N.Y., 1980-83, prof., 1984—; chaire de gravitation U. de Paris, 1983—; Gastwissenenschaftler Max Planck Inst., Munich, Fed. Republic Germany, 1976, 78, 79, 85; vis. scientist Raman Research Inst., Bangalore, India, 1973, 79. Co-translator: On Manifolds with Affine Connections and Relativity, 1984. Author: Quantum Gravity, 1985. Contbr. articles to research jours., chpts. to books. Recipient 1st Gravity prize Gravity Research Found., 1977; Sloan research fellow, 1981—; grantee NSF, 1980—, French Edn. Ministry, 1978-80. Mem. Bibliopolis (sci. com., internat. editorial bd. 1982—), Am. Phys. Soc., Internat. Soc. Math. and Physics, Internat. Soc. Gen. Relativity and Gravity. Current work: General relativity, quantum field theory, quantum gravity, conceptual foundations of physics, differential geometry. Subspecialties: Relativity and gravitation; Theoretical physics. Office: Physics Dept Syracuse U Syracuse NY 13210

ASMUS, JOHN FREDRICH, physicist; b. Pasadena, Calif., Jan. 30, 1937; s. William F. and Eleanor E. (Kocher) A.; m. Barbara Ann Flaherty, Feb. 23, 1963; children—Joanne M., Rosemary H. B.S. in E.E, Calif. Inst. Tech., 1958, M.S., 1959, Ph.D. in E.E. and Physics, 1965. Head optical systems dept. Aero Geo Astro Corp., Alexandria, Va., 1960-64; head laser dept. Gulf Gen. Atomic, San Diego, Calif., 1964-69; research staff Inst. Def. Analyses, Arlington Va., 1969-71; v.p. Sci. Applications, Inc., Albuquerque, 1971-73; lectr. U. Calif., Davis, 1974, research physicist, co-founder art and sci. center, San Diego, 1973—; cons.; mem. adv. group on electron devices Smithsonian Assos. Contbr. sci. articles to profl. jours. Schlumberger fellow, 1959-60; Tektronix fellow, 1960-61. Mem. Internat. Inst. Conservation of Historic and Artistic Works, IEEE, Am. Inst. Conservation, Nat. Trust Historic Preservation, Venice Soc., Bay Area Art Conservation Guild, Sigma Xi, Tau Beta Pi. Patentee metallic vapor laser, embedded pinch laser; introduced laser, ultrasonic and computer image enhancement techniques to art conservation. Current work: Surface preparation, laser applications, art restoration, digital image processing, laser effects. Subspecialty: Excimers. Home: 8239 Sugarman Dr LaJolla CA 92037 Office: IGPP A 025 University California San Diego La Jolla CA 92093

ASMUSSEN, JES, JR., electrical engineering educator, researcher, consultant; b. Milw., June 12, 1938; s. Jes and Anita (Weltzien) A,; m. Judith Adele Knopp, June 18, 1960 (div. 1980); children—Kirsten, Jes III, Stig. B.S.E.E., U. Wis., 1960, M.S.E.E., 1964, Ph.D. in Elec. Engring., 1967. Design and devel engr. Louis Allis Co., Milw., 1960-62; asst. prof. elec. engring. Mich. State U., East Lansing, 1967-71, assoc. prof., 1971-75, prof., 1975—, acting assoc dir. div. engring. research, 1983-84; cons. Kimberly Clark Corp., Lear Siegler Corp., NASA, Lewis Research Ctr., S.D. Warren/Scott Paper Co., 1971—. Contbr. articles to profl. jours. Grantee NSF, Dept. Energy, NASA, Def. Advanced Research Projects Agy., 1971—. Mem. IEEE, AIAA, Sigma Xi. Current work: Microwave discharges (plasma) as applied to microchip technology and electric propulsion engines for spacecraft propulsion, microwave technology for materials processing, wind power engineering. Subspecialties: Electrical engineering; Aerospace engineering and technology. Home: 4138 Luff Ct Okemos MI 48864 Office: Elec Engring Dept Mich State Univ East Lansing MI 48824

ASQUITH, RICHARD LAVERNE, veterinary researcher; b. Galesburg, Ill., May 31, 1928; s. Leon and Leatha Lavina (Fleming) A.; m. Jeannine Lou Whitcomb, Oct. 22, 1950; children—Anthony, Adam, Andrew. B.S., Mich. State Coll., 1954; B.S., Mich. State U., 1956, D.V.M., 1958. Gen. practice vet. medicine, Pekin, Ill., 1958-65, Springfield, Ill., 1965-75; mem. faculty Springfield Coll., 1965-75; staff veterinarian Ill. Dept. Agr., 1972-74; faculty U. Fla., Gainesville, 1975—. Author: (with others) Aflatoxin and Aspergillus flavus in corn, 1983. Contbr. articles to profl. jours. Served to 1st lt. U.S. Army, 1950-52. Mem. AVMA, Am. Assn. Equine Practitioners, Am. Coll. Cryosurgery, Sigma Gamma Epsilon, Gamma Sigma Delta. Club: Key (Ill.) Lodge: Elks. Current work: Distribution and biology of equine parasitism/equine mycotoxicology. Subspecialties: Preventive medicine (veterinary medicine); Toxicology (agriculture). Home: 2336 SE 12th St Ocala FL 32670 Office: Horse Research Ctr 2825 NW 100th St Ocala FL 32675

ASTENAH-ASL, ABOLHASSAN, civil engineering educator; b. Tabriz, Iran, Jan. 7, 1948, came to U.S., 1978; s. Ebrahim and Sahineh Astaneh-Asl; m. Mehry Adrangi, Oct. 11, 1973; children—Kaveh, Cyrus. M.S. in Civil Engring., Tehran Poly., Iran, 1969; M.S. in Structures, U. Mich., 1979, Ph.D., 1982. Structural engr. Nava Co., Iran, 1973-76; ptnr. Dillon Constrn. Co., Iran, 1976-80; research asst. U. Mich., Ann Arbor, 1979-82; asst. prof. U. Okla., Norman, 1982—; structural cons., Oklahoma City, 1982—. Contbr. articles to profl. jours. U. Mich. fellow, 1980. Mem. ASCE, Earthquake Engring. Research Inst., Am. Inst. Steel Constrn., Am. Soc. Engring. Edn., Nat. Civil Engring. Honor Soc. Current work: Behavior of steel structures and connections subjected to earthquake loads; behavior of steel connections; evaluation of existing structures. Subspecialties: Civil engineering; Structural engineering. Home: 809 Branchwood Ct Norman OK 73069 Office: U Okla 202 W Boyd Room 334 Norman OK 73019

ATAL, BISHNU SAROOP, speech scientist; b. Kanpur, India, May 10, 1933; s. Jagannath Prasad and Lakshmi Devi (Kakshmi) A.; m. Kamla, July 3, 1959; children—Alka, Namiha. B.Sc. with honours, U. Lucknow, India, 1952; D.I.I.Sc., Indian Inst. Sci., 1955; Ph.D., Poly. Inst. Bklyn., 1968. Sr. research asst. Indian Inst. Sci., Bangalore, 1955-56, lectr., 1957-60; sr. research fellow Central Elec. Engring. Research Inst., Pilani, Raj, India, 1960-61; mem. tech. staff Bell Labs., Murray Hill, N.J., 1961-85, head acoustic research, 1985—. Fellow Acoustical Soc. Am., (editor speech com. 1981-83), IEEE (Centennial medal 1984, Tech. Achievement award). Current work: Man machine communication by voice - synthesis, recognition, and coding (encryption) of speech by computers. Subspecialties: Man machine communication by voice; Telecommunications. Office: AT&T Bell Labs 600 Mountain Ave Murray Hill NJ 07974

ATALLAH, YOUSEF HANNA, toxicologist, researcher; b. Shebin El-Kom, Menofia, Egypt, May 27, 1936; came to U.S., 1961; s. Hanna and Helen (Mansour) A.; m. Mary Habib Ibrahim, May 28, 1968; children—Jackie, Hany, Joann. B.Sc., Ain Shams U., Cairo, 1956, M.Sc., 1959; Ph.D., La. State U., 1964. Diplomate Am. Bd. Toxicology. Assoc. prof. Nat. Research Ctr., Cairo, 1966-71; prof. U. Algeria, Algiers, 1971-73; sr. research fellow U. Ky., Lexington, 1973-74; mgr. environ. studies Velsicol Chem. Corp., Chgo., 1974-82, dir. environ. sci., 1982—; speaker univs., sci. forums. Contbr. numerous articles to sci. jours., chpts. to books. Patentee biotech. field. Mem. Soc. Toxicology (chmn. com. 1984), Soc. Environ. Toxicology and Chemistry, Am. Chem. Soc., Entomol. Soc. Am., AAAS, Internat. Soc. Ecotoxicology and Environ. Safety. Coptic Orthodox (bd. dirs. 1976—). Current work: Metabolism and pharmacokinetics, environmental toxicology, risk assessment of chemicals. Subspecialties: Environmental toxicology; Toxicology (medicine). Home: 411 Helena Ave Mount Prospect IL 60056 Office: Velsicol Chem Corp 341 E Ohio St Chicago IL 60611

ATANASOFF, JOHN VINCENT, theoretical physicist; b. Hamilton, N.Y., Oct. 4, 1903; s. John and Iva Lucina (Purdy) A.; m. Lura Meeks, June 1926 (div.); children—Elsie L. Atanasoff Whistler, Joanne C. Atanasoff Gathers, John V. II.; m. Alice Crosby, June 17, 1949. B.S.E.E., U. Fla., 1925, Sc.D. (hon.), 1974; M.S., Iowa State U., 1926; Ph.D. in Theoretical Physics, U. Wis.-Madison, 1930; Sc.D. (hon.), Moravian Coll., 1981; Litt.D., Western Md. Coll., 1984. Instr. math. Iowa State U., 1926-29, assoc. prof., 1930-42; instr. math. U. Wis., 1929-30; chief acoustics div U.S. Naval Ordnance Lab., 1942-49; chief scientist U.S. Army Field Forces, 1949-50; dir. U.S. Navy Fuze Program, NOL; pres. Ordnance Engring. Corp., 1952-56; v.p. Aerojet Gen. Corp., 1956-61; pres. Cybernetics, Inc., 1961—. Patentee in field; inventor first electronic digital computer. Recipient Disting. Service award U.S. Navy, 1945; citation Eastern Seis. Soc. Am., 1947, citation Admiral Bur. of Ordnance, 1947, Disting. Achievement Citation, Iowa State U. Alumni assn., 1983, Computer Pioneer medal, IEEE, 1984, Computing Appreciation award EDUCOM, 1985, Gov.'s Sci. medal State of Iowa, 1985, Order of Bulgaria 1st class, 1985, Holley medal ASME, named to Order of Cyril and Methodius 1st class, Bulgaria, 1970, Iowa Inventors Hall of Fame, 1978. Mem. Bulgarian Acad. Scis. (fgn.), Phi Beta Kappa, Sigma Xi, Tau Beta Pi, Phi Kappa Phi, Pi Mu Epsilon, Sigma Tau. Club: Cosmos. Home: 11928 E Baldwin Rd Monrovia MD 21770

ATCHLEY, BILL LEE, science center executive, engineering educator, engineer; b. Cape Girardeau, Mo., Feb. 16, 1932; m. Pat Limbaugh, Aug. 24, 1954; children—Julie, Pam, David. B.S., U. Mo., 1957, M.S., 1959; Ph.D. in Civil Engring., Tex. A&M U., 1965. Registered profl. engr., S.C. Assoc. prof. U. Mo., Rolla, 1961-66, prof. engring. mechanics, 1966-75; dean engring. W.Va. U., Morgantown, 1975-79; pres. Clemson U., S.C., 1979-85; pres., chief exec. officer Nat. Sci. Ctr. for Communications and Electronics Found., Inc., 1985—; chmn. S.C. Council Pres., 1980-81; chmn. research-edn. Gov.'s Council of Alcohol Fuels, 1980; mem. com. energy and environment Nat. Assn. State Univs. and Land-Grant Colls., 1981—; mem. Nat. Com. on Synthetic Fuels, Nat. Coal Council. Active Willow Island Commn., W.Va., bd. dirs. Bicentennial Com., Rolla, Mo., Blue Ridge council #551 Boy Scouts Am., First Methodist Ch. Served in U.S. Army, 1952-54. Ford Found. fellow; recipient Disting. Service award City of Rolla, 1975; invited contbr. Phillips Agenda of Social Values, Phillips Petroleum Co. Mem. Am. Soc. Engring. Edn. (Midwest chmn. 1971), ASCE, Nat. Soc. Profl. Engrs., Newcomen Soc. North Am., State Bd. Registration for Profl. Engrs., Morgantown C. of C., W.Va. C. of C. Lodges: Rotary; Rolla Lions. Subspecialty: Civil engineering. Office: PO Box 992 Clemson SC 29633

ATKINSON, MARK ARTHUR LEONARD, biochemist; b. London, Eng., Feb. 21, 1952; s. John Leonard and Gwenda Mary (Loveday) A.; m. Lynn Dickerson Morrow, June 13, 1984. B.A., Oxford U., 1974, M.A., 1975, D.Phil., 1979. Postdoctoral fellow Yale U., New Haven, 1979-82; vis. assoc. Nat. Heart, Lung, and Blood Inst., NIH, Bethesda, Md., 1982—. Erin research scholar Linacre Coll., Oxford U., Eng., 1976; James Hudson Brown and Alexander B. Coxe fellow Yale U., 1981. Mem. AAAS, Biophys. Soc., Am. Soc. Cell Biology, Am. Soc. Biol. Chemists, Club: Leander (Henley, Eng.). Current work: Structure and regulation of non-muscle cell myosins and their interactions with other cytoskeletal components. Subspecialties: Biochemistry (biology); Cell biology. Home: 1 Bannister Ct Gaithersburg MD 20879 Office: Nat Heart Lung and Blood Inst Lab of Cell Biology NIH Bldg 3 Room B1-22 Bethesda MD 20205

ATKINSON, STEVEN ALBERT, engineering administrator, heat transfer analyst; b. Powell, Wyo., Sept. 15, 1940; s. Albert Nye and Minnie Bell (Watson) A.; m. Patsy Marie Grimes, June 26, 1962; children: Aaron, John, Mark. B.S. in M.E, Colo. State U., 1962; M.S. in M.E, U. Idaho, Moscow, 1969. Registered profl. engr., Idaho. Reactor operator Atomic Energy Div., Phillips Petroleum Co., Idaho Falls, 1962-64, engr., 1964-66; sr. engr. Idaho Nuclear Corp., Idaho Falls, 1966-71; assoc. project engr. Aerojet Nuclear Corp., Idaho Falls, 1971-76; project engr., engring. supr. EG & G Idaho, Inc., Idaho Falls, 1976-80, sr. engring. specialist, 1980—. Contbr. articles to profl. jours. Chmn. Bonneville County Young Republicans, Idaho Falls, 1967; elder, chmn. commn. First Presbyn. Ch., 1975-77; chmn. membership Boy Scouts Am., Idaho Falls, 1980-83, leader webelos den, 1982-83, troop treas. Boy Scouts Am., 1984—. Mem. ASME (treas. Idaho sect. 1976-77, sec. 1977-80), Am. Nuclear Soc. Club: Toastmasters. Current Work: Analysis methods and technological assessments for advanced nuclear power reactors for earth and space emphasizing nuclear reactor accident analysis and safety design including statistical and probabilistic methods. Subspecialties: Nuclear engineering; Mechanical engineering. Home: 1034 Mojave St Idaho Falls ID 83401 Office: EG & G Idaho Inc PO Box 1625 Idaho Falls ID 83415

ATLAS, DAVID, research scientist; b. Bklyn., May 25, 1924; s. Isadore and Rose (Jaffee) A.; m. Lucille Rosen, Sept. 26, 1948; children: Joan Linda, Robert Fred. B.Sc., NYU, 1946; M.Sc., MIT, 1951, D.Sc. in Meteorology, 1955. Chief weather radar br. Air Force Cambridge Research Labs., Bedford, Mass., 1948-66; prof. meterology U. Chgo., 1966-72; dir. atmospheric tech. div. Nat. Center for Atmospheric Research, Boulder, Colo., 1972-73, dir. nat. hail research expt., 1974-75; dir. lab. for atmospheric sci. NASA, Goddard Space Flight Center, Greenbelt, Md., 1977-84; sr. research assoc. dept. meteorology U. Md., 1985—; disting. vis. scientist Jet Propulsion Lab., Calif. Inst. Tech., 1984—; chmn. Nat. Acad. Scis. Panel Remote Atmospheric Probing, also mem. com. on atmospheric scis., 1975-82. Served as 1st lt. USAAF, 1943-46. Recipient Loeser award Air Force Cambridge Research Labs., 1957, O'Day award, 1964; Robert M. Losey award AIAA, 1966; NASA Outstanding Leadership medal, 1982; Presdl. Meritorious Sr. Exec. award, 1983; NSF sr. postdoctoral fellow Imperial Coll., London, Eng., 1959-60. Fellow Am. Meteorol. Soc. (councilor 1961-64, 72-74, Meisinger award 1957, asso. editor publs. 1957-74, pres. 1975—Cleveland Abbé award 1983), Am. Geophys. Union, Am. Astronautical Soc., Royal Meteorol. Soc., AAAS (chmn.-elect atmospheric and hydrospheric scis. sect. 1985); mem. Internat. Radio Sci. Union (pres. inter-union commn. on radio meteorology 1969-72). Inventor weather radar devices. Current Work: Meterology and climatology; satellite meterology, radar meterology, remote sensing, research management. Subspecialties: Meteorology; Remote sensing (atmospheric science). Home: 7420 Westlake Terr Bethesda MD 20817

ATLAS, STEVEN ALAN, internist, educator; b. N.Y.C., Sept. 3, 1946; s. Louis and Lillian (Weinberger) A. B.A., Johns Hopkins U., 1968, M.D., 1971. Diplomate Nat. Bd. Med. Examiners, Am. Bd. Internal Medicine. Intern, then resident N.Y. Hosp., N.Y.C., 1971-73; research assoc. NIH, Bethesda, Md., 1973-76; instr., then asst. prof. Cornell U. Med. Ctr., N.Y.C., 1976-82, assoc. prof., 1982—; asst. attending physician N.Y. Hosp., N.Y.C., 1977-82, assoc. attending physician, 1982—. Contbr. articles to profl. jours. Served as surgeon USPHS, 1973-76. Recipient Research Career Devel. award NIH, 1979-84. Fellow Council for High Blood Pressure Research of Am. Heart Assn.; mem. Am. Soc. Clin. Investigation, Am. Fedn. Clin. Research, Endocrine Soc., N.Y. Acad. Scis. Democrat. Jewish. Current work: Hypertension research; biochemistry and physiology of renin-angiotensin system and vasoactive natriuretic hormones (atrial natriuretic factor); biochemistry proteolytic enzymes. Subspecialties: Biochemistry (medicine); Endocrinology. Home: 1161 York Ave New York NY 10021 Office: NY Hosp Cornell Med Ctr 525 E 68th St New York NY 10021

ATLURI, SATYA NADHAM, educator in theoretical and applied mechanics, consultant; b. Gudivada, India, Oct. 7, 1945; came to U.S., 1966, naturalized, 1976; s. Tirupati Rao and Tulasi (Devi) A.; m. Revati Adusumilli, May 17, 1972; children—Neelima, Niroupa. B.E., Andhra U. (India), 1964; M.E., Indian Inst. Sci., 1966; Sc.D., MIT, 1969. Researcher MIT, Cambridge, 1966-71; asst. prof. U. Wash., Seattle, 1971-74; assoc. prof. Ga. Tech. Inst., Atlanta, 1974-77, prof., 1977-79, Regents' prof. mechanics, 1979—, dir. Ctr. Computational Mechanics, 1980—. Editor, author: Hybrid and Mixed Finite Element Methods, 1983; Computational Methods in Mechanics of Fracture, 1985; Finite Element Handbook, 1985; editor-in-chief Internat. Jour. Computational Mechanics; mem. editorial bd. Internat. Jour. Numerical Methods in Engring., Computers and Structures, Engring. Fracture Mechanics, and Applied Mechancis Revs.; contbr. articles to profl. jours. Recipient Gold medal Andhra U., 1964; Roll of Honors award Indian Inst. Sci., 1966; grantee NSF, U.S. Air Force Office Sci. Research, Office Naval Research, NASA, WPAFB, others. Fellow Am. Acad. Mechanics; mem. ASME (com. chmn. 1983—), ASCE (assoc. editor jour. 1982-85), AIAA (assoc. editor jour. 1983—). Current work: Computational mechanics, constitutive modeling, mechanics of fracture and materials, control of large space structures, continuum mechanics, and structural integrity analyses. Subspecialties: Theoretical and applied mechanics; Fracture mechanics. Home: 2794 Woodland Park Dr NE Atlanta GA 30345 Office: Ga Inst Tech Sch Civil Engring Atlanta GA 30332

ATTALLAH, ABDELFATTAH, immunobiologist; b. Dakahlia, Egypt, Feb. 2, 1944; s. Mohamed M. A. B.S., Alexandria (Egypt) U., 1967; D.E.A., Paris U., 1971; Ph.D., George Washington U., 1974. Research scientist Research Found. Children's Nat. Med. Ctr., Washington, 1972-76; research scientist Naval Med. Research Inst., Bethesda, Md., 1976-78; chief immunology sect. Nat. Ctr. Drugs and Biologics, NIH, Bethesda, 1978—; vis. scientist Naval Med. Research Inst., 1978-82; adj. prof. Georgetown U., 1982—, George Washington U. Contbr. chpts. to books, articles to profl. jours. Mem. Am. Assn. Immunologists, AAAS, Am. Soc. Microbiology, N.Y. Acad. Scis., Assn. Egyptian-Am. Scholars, Sigma Xi. Current Work: Cell biology, cell and tissue culture, immunobiology, infectious diseases, genetics and genetic engring. and cancer research. Subspecialties: Cellular engineering; Immunopharmacology. Home: 5919 Beech Ave Bethesda MD 20817 Office: FDA 8000 Rockville Pike Bethesda MD 20205

ATTARD, JOHN, medicinal chemist, educator; b. Victoria, Gozo, Malta, May 26, 1943; came to U.S., 1971; s. Felix and Carmen (Gatt) A. B. in Chemistry with honors, U. London, 1969; M. in Chemistry, Catholic U. Am., 1973. Instr. chemistry Dept. Edn., Victoria, Malta, 1960-65; chemist May & Baker Ltd, Dagenham, Eng., 1969-71; organic chemist Thiokol Corp., Santa Fe Springs, Calif., 1973-75; radiochemist ICN Pharm., Irvine, Calif., 1975-76; medicinal chemist Allergan Pharm. subs. SKB, Irvine, 1977—; teaching asst. Catholic U. Am., 1971-73; instr. chemistry Saddleback Community Coll., Irvine, 1981-83. Mem. Am. Chem. Soc. Current work: Multistep syntheses of new organic compounds of potential therapeutic value. Subspecialties: Medicinal chemistry; Synthetic chemistry. Home: 9786 Continental Dr Huntington Beach CA 92646 Office: Allergan Pharm Co 25252 Dupont Dr Irvine CA 92713

ATTAYA, HOSNY M(OUSTAFA), nuclear engineer, consultant; b. Alexandria, Egypt, Nov. 29, 1945; came to U.S., 1976, naturalized, 1983; s. Moustafa K. Attaya and Zakia (Ali) Ali; m. Hala T. Abou-El-Nasr, Ot. 6, 1977; children: Shariff, Nabil. B.S. in Nuclear Engring, U. Alexandria, 1967, M.S. in Nuclear Engring, 1974; M.S. in Nuclear Engring, U. Wis.-Madison, 1977, Ph.D., 1981. Research assoc. Atomic Energy Authority of Egypt, Cairo, 1967-76; research asst. U. Wis.-Madison, 1976-81, project assoc., 1981-84, asst. scientist, 1984—; cons. Fusion Power Assocs., GAithersburg, Md., 1982-83. Mem. Am. Nuclear Soc., Am. Soc. Metals, Metall. Soc. Current Work: Materials particle transport in material, magneto-statico; magnet design in fusion reactors; interactions of ferro-magnetic materials in magnetic fusion reactors. Subspecialties: Nuclear engineering; Nuclear fusion. Home: 4801 Sheboygan Ave Apt 702 Madison WI 53705 Office: Dept Nuclear Engring U Wis-Madison 1500 Johnson Dr Madison WI 53706

ATTILIO, DONALD ERNEST, oil company executive; b. Newport, R.I., Sept. 24, 1949; s. Carmen and Alice Joyce (Perez) A.; m. Robyn Marie Underwood, May 14, 1977 (div. Mar. 1983); 1 child, Donald Ernest. B.A. in Pol. Sci., U. Southwest La., 1978. Pres. Pegasus Oil Co., Lafayette, La., 1978-81, Ashdon Industries, Houston, 1981-82, Att Litt Enterprises, Houston, 1982—; pres. Ameriquest, Inc., Lafayette, 1978-82, chmn. bd., chief exec. officer, Lafayette, 1982—. Served with USN, 1969-73. Mem. Soc. Exploration Geophysicists, Marine Tech. Soc., Miami Geol. Soc., U.S. Naval Inst., Ocean Research and Edn. Soc., Navy League, Geothermal Resources Council. Episcopalian. Club: Safari Internat. (Lafayette). Current work: Oil exploration; underwater archaelogical research. Subspecialties: Fuels; Ocean energy conversion. Home: PO Box 57 Sugarloaf Key FL 33044 Office: Ameriquest Inc PO Box 51773 Lafayette LA 70505

ATTINGER, ERNST OTTO, biomedical engineering education administrator; b. Zurich, Switzerland, Dec. 27, 1922; came to U.S., 1952, naturalized, 1965; s. Ernst and Martha (Padrutt) A.; m. Francoise Marie L. Daubige, Feb. 4, 1947; children: Christopher, Nathalene, Joelle. B.A., Winterthur, Switzerland, 1941; M.D., Zurich U., 1948; M.S., Drexel Inst. Tech., 1961; Ph.D. in Biomed Engring., U. Pa., 1965. Research fellow Am. Heart Assn. Tufts U., Boston, 1956-59; sr. investigator Presbyn. Hosp., Phila, 1961-62; research dir. Presbyn. Hosp. U. Pa. Med. Center, Phila., 1962-67; chmn. div. biomed. engring. U. Va., Charlottesville, 1967—, Harry Douglas Forsyth prof. applied sci., 1984—. Author: Pulsatile Blood Flow, 1964, Global Systems Dynamics, 1970, Biomedical Engineering in Dentistry, 1977. Recipient Pres.'s and Visitor's Research prize U. Va., 1976. Fellow IEEE; mem. Biomed. Engring. Soc., Am. Physiol. Soc., N.Y. Acad. Scis., Sigma Xi. Current Work: Analysis of biological systems, systems analysis of control hierarchies, assessment of health care technology. Subspecialties: Biomedical engineering; Systems engineering. Office: Med Center Dept Biomed Engring U Va Box 377 Charlottesville VA 22908

ATTIX, FRANK HERBERT, medical physics educator, researcher; b. Portland, Oreg., Apr. 2, 1925; s. Ulysses Sheldon and Alma Katherine (Michelsen) A.; m. Evelyn Louise Van Scoy, Apr. 19, 1946; m. Shirley Adeline Lohr, Jan. 24, 1959; children: Shelley Anne, Richard Haven. A.B. in Physics with honors, U. Calif., Berkeley, 1949; M.S. in Physics, U. Md., College Park, 1953. With NIH, Bethesda, Md., 1949-50, Nat. Bur. Standards, Washington, 1950-57, Am. Car & Foundry Co., Washington, 1957-58, Naval Research Lab., Washington, 1958-76; prof. med. physics U. Wis., Madison, 1976—. Editor in chief, contbg. author: Radiation Dosimetry, 2d edit. vols. I-III, 1966-69; contbr. other books, sci. papers to publs. Served to lt. USN, 1943-46. Recipient ann. award for applied sci. Research Soc. Am.-Naval Research Lab., 1969. Mem. Am. Phys. Soc., Am. Assn. Physicists in Medicine (bd. dirs. 1978-80), Health Physics Soc. (bd. 1968-71), Phi Beta Kappa, Sigma Xi, Sigma Pi Sigma. Club: August Derleth Soc. (Sauk City, Wis.) (bd.). Patentee. Current Work: Radiol. physics and dosimetry. Subspecialties: Medical physics; Radiation dosimetry. Home: 3333 Westview Ln Madison WI 53713 Office: U Wis 1300 University Ave Room 1530 Madison WI 53706

ATTWOOD, DAVID THOMAS, physics researcher, educator, administrator; b. N.Y.C., Aug. 15, 1941; s. David Thomas and Josephine (Banks) A.; children—Timothy David, Courtney Catherine, Kevin Richard. B.S., Hofstra U., 1963; M.S., Northwestern U., 1965; postgrad. Poly. Inst. Bklyn., 1965-66; D.Sci. in Plasma Physics, NYU, 1972. Research physicist Gen. Applied Sci. Lab., Westbury, N.Y., 1965-68; group leader laser-fusion diagnostics Lawrence Livermore Nat. Lab., Calif., 1972-83; lectr. applied sci. U. Calif.-Davis, 1978-83, mem. student policy com. for Lawrence Livermore Nat. Lab./U. Calif.-Davis; sr. staff scientist Lawrence Berkeley Lab., U. Calif., 1983—, dir. Ctr. for X-Ray Optics, 1983—; mem. U. Rochester/Dept. Energy steering com. for Nat. Laser User Facility, 1979-82; mem. site rev. coms. NIH and NSF, 1983, 84; organizer Am. Inst. Physic's Topical Conf. on Low Energy X-Ray Diagnostics, Monterey, Calif., 1981; chmn. program subcom. on laser fusion and laser-plasma interactions, Conf. on Laser Engring. and Optics, 1983; workshop leader working group on short wavelength optics, Conf. on Free Electron Lasers for Extreme Ultraviolet, 1983. Bd. dirs. Mustang Soccer Club, 1976-84. Editor: (with B.L. Henke) Low Energy X-Ray Diagnosis, 1981. Contbr. articles to profl. jours. Tech. reviewer sci. jours. Recipient joint invitations from Acads. of Sci. of U.S. and USSR to visit and lectr. in Soviet Union, 1983. Mem. AAAS, Am. Phys. Soc., Optical Soc. Am. (chmn. tech. group for x-ray and ultraviolet techniques 1983—, program com. Conf. on Extreme Ultraviolet Lasers 1982, 84), Sigma Xi. Current work: Techniques for phase sensitive x-ray experiments, including optics and partially coherent x-ray sources; x-ray microholography; physics of laser-plasma interactions. Subspecialties: Holography; Plasma physics. Office: Lawrence Berkeley Lab 1 Cyclotron Rd Berkeley CA 94720

ATWATER, ILLANI JEANNE, cell physiologist; b. Los Angeles, May 28, 1941; d. Eugene and Elizabeth Ruth (Ransom) A.; m. Eduardo Rojas, June 15, 1967; children—Felipe, Alejandro, Manuel, Andrea Rojas; adopted children—Mario, Jorge, Leo, Rodolfo, Hugo, Juan, German, Sofia. B.S., U. Calif.-Berkeley, 1963; Doctorate de l'Université, Pierre et Marie Curie U., Paris, 1977. Asst. prof. U. Chile, Santiago, 1965-74; research assoc. Physiol. Inst., U. Saarlandes, Homburg, Germany, 1974-75, École Normale Supérieure, Paris, 1975-76; sr. research assoc. U. East Anglia, Norwich, Eng., 1976-83; prof. Instituto Politechico National, Mexico City, 1981-82; spl. expert NIH, Bethesda, Md., 1984—. Contbr. articles to profl. jours. Mem. Physiol. Soc., Biophys. Soc., Am. Diabetes Assn., European Assn. for Study Diabetes, Brit. Diabetic Assn., N.Y. Acad. Scis. Current work: The evolvement of membrane potential in the process of hormone secretion at the cellular level; the development of bioelectrodes using cell receptors for very sensitive hormone assays. Subspecialties: Biophysics (biology); Neuroendocrinology. Office: Lab Cell Biology and Genetics NIH NIADDK Bldg 4 Room 312 Bethesda MD 20205

ATWOOD, DONALD KEITH, oceanographer, chemist; b. Burlington, Vt., June 5, 1933; s. Fred Charles and Agatha Marie (Morrissette) A.; Jo Ann Marie Sebesta, Oct. 17, 1954 (div. 1980); children—Joseph Michael, Janet Marie, Daniel John, Sarah Katharine. B.S. in Chemistry magna cum laude, St. Michael's Coll., 1955; Ph.D., Purdue U., 1960. Sr. research specialist Exxon Prodn. Research, Houston, 1960-69; assoc. prof. U. P.R., Mayaguez, 1969-76; dir. ocean chem. div. Atlantic Oceanographic and Meteorol. Labs., NOAA, Miami, Fla., 1976—; subject leader Chem. Oceanography Coop. Investigation

Caribbean and Adjacent Regions, Intergovtl. Oceanographic Commn. (IOC), Paris, 1972-76; dir. Caribbean Pollution Monitoring program Integovtl. Oceanographic Commn. Regional Subcom. for Caribbean and Adjacent Regions. IOC, Paris, 1979—; developer, tchr. various chem. oceanography courses P.R., served on various NSF panels, 1974-80. Contbr. articles to profl. jours. Recipient Cert. of Recognition, NOAA, 1982; grantee NSF. Mem. Am. Chem. Soc., Am. Soc. Limnology and Oceanography, Am. Geophys. Union, AAAS, Sigma Xi, Phi Lamda Upsilon, Delta Epsilon Sigma. Club: Team Miami. Current work: Basic research in environmental controls exerted by the ocean on marine resources. Subspecialties: Oceanography; Sea floor spreading. Office: NOAA-AOML 4301 Rickenbacker Causeway Miami FL 33149

ATWOOD, JOAN DOLORES, psychology educator, psychotherapist, researcher, counselor; b. Queens, N.Y., Sept. 15, 1943; d. Louis and Helen (Juarez) Armagno; m. William R. Atwood, Mar. 21, 1981; children: Debby, Barbara, Lisa, Janine, Brian. B.A. in Psychology magna cum laude, SUNY-Stony Brook, 1973, M.A. in Psychology, 1975, M.A. in Sociology, 1977, Ph.D. in Sociology, 1981. Research assoc. dept. psychology SUNY-Stony Brook, 1973-75, dept. psychiatry, 1975-80; asst. prof. psychology SUNY-Farmingdale, 1980—; cons. Biofeedback Services, 1975—, pvt. practice counseling, 1975—, workshop/group coordinator, 1975—. Author: Making Contact with Human Sexuality, 1981. Mem. Citizens Alliance, Nassau, N.Y., 1980—; mem. task force NOW, Nassau, 1981—. Fellow Internat. Council Sex Edn. and Parenthood; mem. Am. Psychol. Assn., Am. Assn. Sex Educators, Counselors, and Therapists, Sex Info. and Edn. Council U.S. (assoc.), Am. Assn. Marriage and Family Therapists (clin.), Environ. Control Assn., Phi Alpha Sigma. Current Work: Marriage, family and sex therapy; sexual behavior; social relationships. Subspecialties: Social psychology; Developmental psychology. Home: 542 Lakeview Ave Rockville Centre NY 11570 Office: SUNY Route 110 Farmingdale NY 11375

AUBE, CLAUDE B., pathologist, research station administrator; b. St. Vallier, Que., Can., May 20, 1936; s. Albert and Clotilde A.; m. Claire Baribeau, Sept. 5, 1960; children—Mireille, Martin. M., McGill U., 1963, Ph.D., 1965. Research scientist Can. Dept. Agr., 1965-71; asst. prof. Laval U., after 1968, also dir. grad. students; with Can. Dept. Agr., 1972—, dir. research program service, 1976-78, program specialist, Ste. Jean-sur-Richieleu, Que., 1978-80, dir. Research Sta., 1980—. Bd. dirs. Sport Ctr. of La Pocatiere, 1965-66, pres., 1966-67. Mem. Can. Phytopathological Soc., Am. Phytopathological Soc., Que. Soc. Protection Plants (bd. dirs. 1969-72), Internat. Soc. Phytopathology (Can. del. 1971—). Subspecialty: Plant pathology. Office: Agr Can Research Sta 430 Govin Blvd Saint Jean-Sur-Richelieu PQ J3B 6Z8 Canada

AUBEL, JOSEPH LEE, physicist, educator; b. Lansing, Mich., Sept. 7, 1936; s. Lee M. and Bertha C. (Sears) A.; m. Elvira Marie Ruhlig, July 1, 1967; 1 child, Edward Lee. B.S., Mich. State U., 1958, Ph.D., 1964. Asst. prof. U. South Fla., Tampa, 1964-74, assoc. prof., 1974—. Contbr. articles to profl. jours. Mem. Optical Soc. Am., Am. Assn. Physics Tchrs. (pres. Fla. sect. 1981), Am. Sci. Affiliation. Democrat. Lutheran. Current work: Electrolyte electroreflectance of semiconductors; Raman spectroscopy. Subspecialties: Atomic and molecular physics; Condensed matter physics. Home: 315 Bahamas Temple Terrace FL 33617 Office: U South Fla Physics Dept Tampa FL 33620

AUBURG, C(HARLES) DOUGLAS, mechanical engineering supervisor; b. Vancouver, Wash., Apr. 13, 1942; s. Charles E. and Josephine (Imsdahl) A.; m. Tamara A. Ketola, Sept. 15, 1962; children—Josephine A., David C. B.S.M.E., Wash. State U., 1965; M.Pub. Adminstrn., Lewis and Clark Coll., 1984. Design engr. Longview Fibre Co., Wash., 1965-67, mech. test engr. Bonneville Power Adminstrn., Vancouver, 1967-74, heavy equipment engr., 1974-75; mgmt. trainee, Washington, 1975-76, asst. to chief engr., Portland, Oreg., 1976-77, energy engr., 1977-82, energy supr., 1982—; industry research advisor Elec. Power Research Inst., Palo Alto, Calif., 1983-85. Mem. Assn. Energy Engrs. (sr., cert. energy mgr. 1983), ASHRAE (task group sec. 1982-84, task group vice chmn. 1985-86, Oreg. govtl. affairs com. 1983-84), ASME, Am. Soc. Engring. Mgrs. (nat. conv. 1984-85), Nat. Model R.R. Assn. Club: Columbia Gorge Model R.R. (chmn. bd. 1980-82, sec. 1982) (Portland). Current work: Manager research program in support of utility energy conservation program. Subspecialty: Energy conservation engineering. Home: 7215 NE 61st Ave Vancouver WA 98661 Office: Bonneville Power Adminstrn PO Box 3621-EPC Portland OR 97208

AUDETTE, LOUIS GIRARD, II, energy co. exec.; b. Orange, N.J., Sept. 24, 1939; s. Charles LaPointe and Mary Ford (Haggart) A.; m. Anna Brita Held, Aug. 15, 1964; children: Jessie, Alexis. B.A., Yale U., 1962, B.F.A., 1963, M.S., 1965. Instr. anatomy and dir. med. TV Yale U., New Haven, 1964-69; dir. dept. biomed. communications U. Conn. Health Ctr., Farmington, 1969-78; regional library cons. for New Eng. Nat. Library of Medicine, Bethesda, Md., 1977-79; dir. learning resources ctr. Project HOPE, Alexandria, Egypt, 1977-78; founder, pres. New Eng. Alt. Fuels, Inc., Brattleboro, Vt., 1979—; adv. Vt. Energy Office, N.H. Gov.'s Council on Energy. Chmn. Brattleboro Alternative Energy Com., 1980; mem. Monadnock Energy Project. Dept. of Energy appropriate tech. grantee, 1980-81. Current Work: Development of small scale modular power plants using non-traditional fuels such as cellulosic waste, landfill gas, wood chips. Subspecialties: Fuels and sources; Combustion processes. Office: 67 Main St Brattleboro VT 05301

AUER, PETER LOUIS, plasma physicist, educator; b. Budapest, Hungary, Jan. 12, 1928; came to U.S., 1937, naturalized, 1942; s. Laszlo and Irma (Morgenstern) A.; m. Rheta E. Siegel, Aug. 27, 1952; children—Deborah, Douglas, Andrea, Matthew. A.B., Cornell U., 1947; Ph.D., Calif. Inst. Tech., 1951. Physicist Gen. Electric Research Lab., Schenectady, 1954-61; head plasma physics Sperry Rand Research Center, Sudbury, Mass., 1961-64; dir. Ballistic Missile Def., Office Sec. Def., Washington, 1964-66; prof. aerospace engring. Cornell U., Ithaca, N.Y., 1966—, dir. lab. plasma studies, 1967-74; cons. Office Sec. Def., Gen. Electric Co., Electric Power Research Inst., AEC, NRC, Nat. Acad. Scis., Dept. of Energy, Inst. for Energy Analysis; vis. scientist Frascati, Italy, 1960-61; vis. prof. Oxford U., 1972-73. Editor: Plasma Physics, 1970; asso. editor: Energy, 1976; Contbr. articles to profl. jours. Guggenheim fellow, 1960-61. Fellow Am. Phys. Soc. Pantentee in field. Current Work: Plasma physics and fusion reactor studies. Subspecialties: Plasma physics; Fusion. Home: 220 Devon Rd Ithaca NY 14850

AUERBACH, OSCAR, pathologist, educator; b. N.Y.C., Jan. 1, 1905; s. Max and Jennie (Geller) A.; m. Dora Herman, Mar. 20, 1932 (dec. Apr. 1984); children: Richard C., Bruce E.; m. Lana Halmy, Nov. 13, 1984. B.S., N.Y.U., 1925; M.D., N.Y. Med. Coll., 1929. Diplomate: Am. Bd. Pathology. Intern Morrisania Hosp., N.Y.C., 1929-31; research fellow U. Vienna, 1931-32; pathologist Sea View Hosp., S.I., N.Y., 1932-47; chief lab. VA Hosp., Staten Island, 1947-51, East Orange, N.J., 1952-59, sr. med. investigator, 1960-78; disting. physician VA Med. Center, East Orange, 1978-83, sr. med. investigator, disting. physician emeritus, 1983—; prof. pathology U. Medicine and Dentistry, Newark, N.J., 1966-69, 71—, asst. dean student affairs, 1980-83; vis. instr. Washington U. Med. Sch., St. Louis, 1944; assoc. prof. pathology N.Y. Med. Coll., 1949-61, prof., 1962-71; cons. pathologist Richmond Gen. Hosp., S.I., 1938-47, VA Hosp., Castle Point, N.Y., 1946-47, East Orange Gen. Hosp., 1962-68, St. Vincent's Med. Center, S.I., 1965-78, St. Barnabas Med. Center, Livingston, N.J., 1973—. Contbr. articles in field to profl. jours. Served to lt. M.C. USN, 1944-46. Named Sr. Med. Investigator VA, 1960; recipient Career Service award Nat. Civil Service League, 1963, cert. of Commendation Adminstrn. Vets. Affairs, 1963, Selman Waksman award Am. Coll. Chest Physicians, 1968, Miriam Goldberg Levin Meml. award, 1970, Edward J. Ill award Acad. Medicine N.J., 1971, Golden Apple award N.J. Med. Sch. Student AMA, 1973, Alumni Sci. medal N.Y. Med. Coll., 1973, Spl. award Coll. Medicine and Dentistry N.J., N.J. Med. Sch., 1978, Trudeau medal Am. Lung Assn., 1979, Dennis J. Sullivan award of merit N.J. Pub. Health Assn., 1979, Exceptional Merit award Pres. Coll. Medicine and Dentistry N.J., 1981, Disting. Scientist award Grad. Student Assn. Coll. Medicine and Dentistry N.J., 1981, Golden Apple award N.J. Med. Sch. Student Council, 1982. 1982, 84, 85, Excellence in Teaching award Univ. Found. Fellow ACP; mem. Internat. Assn. Study Lung Cancer, AMA, Am. Assn. Pathologists and Bacteriologists, Am. Trudeau Soc., Assn. Am. Med. Colls., Am. Assn. Thoracic Surgeons, Mexican Soc. Study Tb and Chest Diseases (hon.), Soc. Pathologists and Chilean Soc. Study Chest Diseases (hon.), N.Y. Acad. Medicine, Am. Lung Assn. (hon., life), Cuban Soc. Anatomical Pathologists (hon.), Sigma Xi. Subspecialties: Pathology (medicine); Cancer research (medicine).

AUGENSEN, HARRY JOHN, astronomer, physicist, educator; b. Chgo., July 18, 1951; s. Harry Clarence and Margaret Barbara (Schramm) A.; m. Anna DiEgidio, Oct. 17 1981. B.A., Elmhurst Coll., 1973; M.S. in Astronomy, Northwestern U., 1974, Ph.D. in Astronomy, 1978. Lectr. in physics and astronomy Northwestern U., 1978-80; lectr. in astronomy Swarthmore Coll., 1980-82; lectr. in astronomy Widener U., 1981, asst. prof. physics and astronomy, 1982—; coordinator Astro-Sci. Workshop, Chgo., 1979-80; lectr. Harlow Shapley Vis. Lectureship Series at Colls. and Univs.; summer faculty fellow NASA-Goddard Space Flight Center, 1982; vis. observer Cerro Tololo Obs., 1976, 77, 81. Contbr. articles to profl. jours. Recipient Small Grant award Am. Astron. Soc., 1981. Mem. Am. Astron. Soc., Royal Astron. Soc., Astron. Soc. Pacific, Sigma Xi. Presbyterian. Current Work: Astronomy edn.; planetary nebulae; high-velocity stars; Internat. Ultraviolet Explorer satellite observations of central stars of planetary nebulae; optical spectroscopy of central stars. Subspecialties: Optical astronomy; Ultraviolet high energy astrophysics. Home: 217 Plush Mill Rd Wallingford PA 19086 Office: Kirkbride Hall Widener U Chester PA 19013

AUGUST, GILBERT PAUL, pediatric endocrinologist; b. Jersey City, Sept. 18, 1936; m. Bernice Ide, July 3, 1960; children: Sharon, Lauren. B.S., CCNY, 1958; M.D., NYU, 1962. Diplomate: Am. Bd. Pediatrics. Intern Bellevue Hosp., N.Y.C., 1962-63, resident in pediatrics, 1963-65; endocrinologist Children's Hosp. of D.C., Washington, 1969—; mem. cert. subcom. for pediatric endocrinology Am. Bd. Pediatrics, 1977-81. Author: Pediatric Endocrinology, 1983. Served as surgeon USPHS, 1965-67. Mem. Endocrine Soc., Lawson Wilkins Pediatric Endocrine Soc. Current Work: Somatomedin and MSA receptors. Subspecialties: Pediatrics; Endocrinology. Office: Children's Hospital National Medical Center 111 Michigan Ave NW Washington DC 20010

AUKRUST, EGIL, metallurgist; b. Lom, Norway, June 16, 1933; s. Paal and Torlang (Borresen) A.; m. Rose, Mar. 23, 1962. Diploma Engr., Tech. U. Norway, 1957, Dr. Ing., 1960. Research assoc. Pa. State U., University Park, 1960-62; research engr. Jones & Laughlin Steel Corp., Pitts., 1962-65, research supr., 1965-69, asst. dir. process metallurgy, 1969-71, dir. process metallurgy, 1971-74, gen. mgr. research, 1974-81, sr. dir. tech., 1981-84; sr. tech. dir. LTV Steel Co., Independence, Ohio, 1984—. Contbr. articles to profl. jours. Served with Norwegian Army, 1952-53. Mem. Am. Iron and Steel Inst., Indsl. Research Inst., Metals Soc. (U.K.), AIME, Assn. Iron and Steel Engrs., Am. Soc. Metals, Engrs. Soc. Western Pa. Subspecialty: Metallurgical engineering. Home: 23200 Lake Rd Bay Village OH 44140 Office: LTV Steel Co Research Ctr 6801 Brecksville Rd Independence OH 44131

AULL, JOHN LOUIS, biochemist, educator, researcher; b. Newberry, S.C., May 7, 1939; s. Louis Eugene and Helen (Lomineck) A.; m. Judy Capps, June 1, 1963; children: Amber Kristina, Ashley Caroline. A.B. in Chemistry, U. N.C., Chapel Hill, 1964; Ph.D. in Biochemistry, N.C. State U., 1972. Postdoctoral research asso. U. S.C., 1973; asst. prof. chemistry Auburn U., 1974-80, assoc. prof., 1980—. Contbr. articles to profl. jours. Served to lt. USN, 1964-67. Decorated Nat. Service medal.; NIH grantee, 1979—. Mem. Am. Soc. Biol. Chemists, Am. Chem. Soc. (chmn. local sect.). Episcopalian. Current Work: Biochemistry-enzymology; enzyme inhibition; nuclear magnetic resonance studies of enzymes. Subspecialties: Biochemistry (biology); Magnetic resonance imaging. Home: 1029 Cumberland Dr Auburn AL 36830 Office: 305 Saunders Hall Dept Chemistry Auburn U Auburn AL 36849

AULT, ADDISON, chemist, educator; b. Boston, July 3, 1933; s. Warren Ortman and Myrtle Lavina (Wilcock) A.; m. Janet Ruth Meade, Aug. 23, 1958; children: Margaret Ruth, Warren James, Addison David, Peter Harwell, Emily Elizabeth. B.A., Amherst Coll., 1955; Ph.D., Harvard U., 1960. Asst. prof. Grinnell Coll., Iowa, 1959-61; research asso. Argonne (Ill.) Nat. Lab., 1961-62; prof. chemistry Cornell Coll., Mt. Vernon, Iowa, 1962—. Author: Problems in Organic Structure Determination, 1967, Techniques and Experiments for Organic Chemistry, 1973, 2d edit., 1976, 3d edit., 1980, 4th edit., 1983, (with G.O. Dudek) NMR: An Introduction to Proton Nuclear Magnetic Resonance Spectroscopy, 1976, (with Margaret Ault) A Handy and Systematic Catalog of NMR Spectra, 1980; (with Marc Loudon) Solutions Manual to accompany Organic Chemistry, 1984. NSF Sci. Faculty fellow, 1967. Mem. Am. Chem. Soc., Chem. Soc. (London), AAAS, AAUP, Phi Beta Kappa, Sigma Xi. Current Work: Stereochemistry; nuclear magnetic resonance; enzyme kinetics. Subspecialty: Organic chemistry. Home: 519 N 2d St W Mount Vernon IA 52314 Office: Cornell Coll Mount Vernon IA 52314

AUPPERLE, KENNETH ROBERT, computer architecture specialist; b. Bklyn., Aug. 27, 1957; s. Robert Wolfgang and Margarete Elisabeth (Fischer) A.; m. Laura Jean Marie Welch, Aug. 8, 1981. B.S. in Elec. Engring, Poly. Inst. N.Y., 1979, M.S. in Computer Sci, 1979. Regional computer architecture specialist Intel Corp., Hauppauge, N.Y., 1979—; adj. lectr. Poly. Inst. N.Y., Farmingdale, 1979—. Mem. IEEE, Assn. Computing Machinery, Tau Beta Pi. Lutheran. Current Work: Software and system architecture considerations in microprocessor systems. Subspecialties: Computer engineering; Computer architecture. Office: 300 Vanderbilt Motor Pkwy Hauppauge NY 11787

AURAND, LEONARD WILLIAM, food chemist, researcher, educator; b. Shamokin Dam, Pa., Feb. 5, 1920; s. James Wilson and Esther Matilda (Weissinger) A.; m. Eleanor May Nichols, Feb. 22, 1943; children: Rebecca Louise Aurand Newton, Thomas James, Sarah Jane Aurand Anderson. B.S., Pa. State U., 1941, Ph.D., 1949; M.S., U. N.H., 1947. Asst. prof. N.C. State U., 1949-55, assoc. prof., 1955-60, prof. food sci. and biochemistry, 1960—. Author: Food Composition and Analysis, 1963, Food Chemistry, 1973, Laboratory Manual in Food Chemistry, 1977; contbr. numerous articles to profl. jours. Cert. hunger interpreter Bd. Global Ministeries, United Methodist Ch., N.Y.C., and, N.C. Conf. United methodist Ch. Served with USNR, 1942-46. Mem. Am. Inst. Nutrition, Inst. Food Technologists. Democrat. Lodge: Masons. Current Work: Lipid oxidation in foods and problems of hunger in U.S. and Third World nations. Subspecialties: Food science and technology; Nutrition (biology). Home: 921 Trailwood Dr Raleigh NC 27606 Office: 236 Schaub Hall NC State U Raleigh NC 27650

AUSTEN, K(ARL) FRANK, physician; b. Akron, Ohio, Mar. 14, 1928; s. Karl and Bertle (Jehle) A.; m. Joycelyn Chapman, Apr. 11, 1959; children: Leslie Marie, Karla Ann, Timothy Frank, Jonathan Arthur. A.B., Amherst Coll., 1950; M.D., Harvard U., 1954. Intern in medicine Mass. Gen. Hosp., 1954-55, asst. resident, 1955-56, sr. resident, 1958-59, chief resident, 1961, asst. in medicine, 1962-63, asst. physician, 1963-66, chief pulmonary unit, 1964-66, also cons. in medicine; practice medicine, specializing in internal medicine, allergy and immunology, Boston, 1962—; USPHS postdoctoral research fellow Nat. Inst. Med. Research, Mill Hill, London, 1959-61; asst. in medicine Harvard Med. Sch., 1960-1961, instr., 1961-62, asso. in medicine, 1962-64, asst. prof., 1965-66, asso. prof., 1966-68, prof., 1969-72, Theodore B. Bayles prof., 1972—; physician-in-chief Robert B. Brigham Hosp., 1966-80; physician Peter Bent Brigham Hosp., 1966-80; chmn. dept. rheumatology and immunology Brigham and Women's Hosp., 1980—; mem. fellowship subcom. Arthritis Found., 1968-71, chmn., 1971; mem. council Infectious Disease Soc. Am., 1969-71; mem. arthritis tng. grants com. Nat. Inst. Arthritis and Metabolic Diseases, NIH, 1970-73; mem. directing group, task force on immunology and disease Nat. Inst. Allergy and Infectious Diseases, 1972-73; bd. dirs. Arthritis Found., 1972-75, mem. manpower study com., 1972-73, chmn. research com., 1972—; chmn. research com. Med. Found., Inc., 1972-76; mem. Am. Bd. Allergy and Immunology, 1973-78, Nat. Commn. on Arthritis and Related Musculoskeletal Diseases, 1975-76, Allergy and Immunology Research Commn., 1975—, chmn., 1976-79. Mem. editorial bd.: Arthritis and Rheumatism, 1968-81, Proc. of Transplantation Soc, 1968—, Jour. Infectious Diseases, 1969-79, Jour. Exptl. Medicine, 1971—, Immunol. Communications, 1972—, Clin. Immunology and Immunopathology, 1972—, Proc. of Nat. Acad. Scis, 1978—, Clin. and Exptl. Immunology, 1978—, Immunopharmacology, 1979—, Receptors and Recognition, 1980—, Rheumatology Internat, 1980—, Clin. Immunology Revs, 1981—; contbr. articles to profl. jours. Trustee Amherst Coll., 1981—. Served to capt., M.C. U.S. Army, 1956-58. Mem. Nat. Acad. Scis. (chmn. sect. on med. microbiology and immunology 1983—), Am. Soc. Pharm. and Exptl. Therapeutics, Am. Soc. Exptl. Pathology, Am. Assn. Immunologists (pres. 1977-78), Brit. Soc. Immunology, Am. Soc. Clin. Investigation, Am. Rheumatism Assn., A.C.P., Transplantation Soc., Am. Acad. Arts and Scis., Assn. Am. Physicians (recorder 1978-84), Am. Acad. Allergy (exec. com. 1970-72, sec. 1977-80, pres. 1981), Fedn. Am. Soc. Exptl. Biology (dir. 1977—). Current Work: Molecular and cell biology, immunopharmacology of mediators of inflammation. Subspecialties: Immunobiology and immunology; Internal medicine. Home: 34 Bradford Rd Wellesley Hills MA 02181 Office: Brigham and Women's Hosp 75 Francis St Boston MA 02115 also 250 Longwood Ave Boston MA 02115

AUSTEN, W(ILLIAM) GERALD, surgeon. Chief of surgery Mass. Gen. Hosp., Boston; Churchill prof. surgery Harvard Med. Sch. Subspecialty: Surgery. Office: Mass Gen Hosp 55 Fruit St Boston MA 02114*

AUSTER, PETER JAY, marine fisheries ecologist; b. Middletown, Conn., Aug. 11, 1956; s. David and Norma Louise (Brenner) A. B.S., U. Conn., 1978, M.S., 1985. Marine mammalogist U. R.I., Narragansett, 1979; fisheries biologist observer program Northwest and Alaska Fisheries Ctr., Nat. Marine Fisheries Service, Seattle, 1978, 80, 81; staff scientist NOAA's Nat. Undersea Research Program, U. Conn. at Avery Point, Groton, 1983—, mus. assoc. Mus. Nat. History, Storrs, 1983—; fisheries cons. Analysis & Tech. Inc., Stonington, Conn., 1983—; edn. com. Schooner, Inc., New Haven, Conn., 1979-80. Contbr. articles to profl. jours. Mem. Nat. Shellfisheries Assn., Am. Soc. Zoologists, New Eng. Estuarine Research Soc., Am. Inst. Fishery Research Biologists (assoc.). Current work: Descriptions of fish and crustacean predator-prey interactions and foraging techniques; abiotic effects on small scale spatial distribution as it relates to foraging and resource partitioning. Subspecialties: Marine biology; Behavioral ecology. Home: 12 Denison Ave Mystic CT 06355 Office: NOAA's Nat Undersea Research Program Univ Connecticut Groton CT 06340

AUSTIN, EDWARD MARVIN, mech. engr.; b. Rome, Ga., Nov. 15, 1933; s. Marvin Hart and Sarah Katherine (Youngblood) A.; m. Elizabeth Maria Geisz, Dec. 17, 1955; children: Jean, Diane, Judy. B.M.E., Ga. Inst. Tech., 1955, M.S. M.E., 1957. Registered profl. engr., N.C. Assoc. aircraft engr. Lockheed Aircraft Corp., Marietta, Ga., 1955; sr. engr. Safeguard System, Western Electric Co., Greensboro, N.C., 1968-71; project engr. Sandia Nat. Labs., Albuquerque, 1957—. Pres. Heights br. YMCA, Albuquerque, 1974-75. Mem. ASME, Nat. Soc. Profl. Engrs., Sigma Xi, Phi Eta Sigma, Pi Tau Sigma, Kappa Kappa Sigma, Tau Beta Pi, Phi Kappa Phi. Current Work: Project engineer for nuclear warhead development. Subspecialties: Systems engineering; Nuclear fission. Home: 3017 Matador Dr NE Albuquerque NM 87111 Office: Sandia Nat Labs Box 5800 Albuquerque NM 87185

AUSTIN, STEVEN ARTHUR, geologist; b. Stanford, Calif., Jan. 25, 1948; s. Arthur Wyatt and Dorothy (Janes) A. B.S. in Geology, U. Wash., 1970; M.S. in Geology, San Jose State U., 1971; Ph.D., Pa. State U., 1979. Research assoc. in geology Inst. Creation Research, El Cajon, Calif., 1979—; resident geologist Keymar Resources, Inc., El Cajon, 1983—. Author: Catastrophes in Earth History, 1984. Deacon, College Ave. Bapt. Ch., San Diego, 1984—. Mem. Am. Assn. Petroleum Geologists, Soc. Econ. Paleontologists and Mineralogists, Geol. Soc. Am. Current work: Catastrophic geologic processes and catastrophism in geology; origin of coal and oil; stratigraphy; sedimentology; origin of life; volcanoes that changed history. Subspecialties: Geology; Coal. Home: PO Box 2892 El Cajon CA 92021 Office: Inst Creation Research 2100 Greenfield Dr El Cajon CA 92021

AUSTRIAN, ROBERT, physician; b. Balt., Apr. 12, 1916; s. Charles Robert and Florence (Hochschild) A.; m. Babette Friedmann, Dec. 29, 1963; stepchildren: Jill Bernstein, Toni Bernstein. A.B., Johns Hopkins U., 1937, M.D., 1941; D.Sc. honoris causa, Hahnemann Med. Coll., 1980, Phila. Coll. Pharmacy and Sci., 1981. Diplomate: Am. Bd. Internal Medicine. House officer Johns Hopkins Hosp., 1941-50, asst. dir. med. out-patient dept., 1951-52; assoc. prof. medicine, then prof. medicine SUNY Coll. Medicine, 1952-62; John Herr Musser prof., chmn. dept. research medicine U. Pa. Sch. Medicine, 1962—; attending physician Hosp. U. Pa.; Tyndale vis. lectr. and prof. Coll. Medicine U. Utah, 1964; spl. research on infectious diseases, bacterial genetics; mem. Meningococcal Infections Commn., 1964-72, Commn. on Acute Respiratory Disease, 1965-72, Commn. Streptococcal and Staphylococcal Diseases, 1970-72, Armed Forces Epidemiol. Bd.; cons. surg. gen. U.S. Army Research and Devel. Command, 1966-69; mem. subcom. streptococcus and pneumococcus Internat. Com. Bacteriol. Nomenclature; mem. allergy and immunology study sect. Nat. Inst. Allergy and Infectious Diseases, 1965-69, mem. bd. sci. counselors, 1967-70, chmn., 1969-70. Mem. editorial bd.: Jour. Bacteriology, 1964-69, Am. Rev. Respiratory Diseases, 1963-66, Bacteriol. Rev, 1967-71, Jour. Infectious Diseases, 1969-74, Antimicrobial Agents and Chemotherapy, 1972—, Infection and Immunity, 1973-81, Revs. of Infectious Diseases, 1979—, Vaccine, 1983—. . Trustee Johns Hopkins U., 1963-69. Served to capt. M.C. AUS, 1943-45. Recipient U.S. Typhus Commn. medal, 1947; Albert Lasker Clin. Med. Research award, 1978; Phila. award, 1979; Willard O. Thompson award Am. Geriatric Soc., 1981, others. Fellow ACP (master, James D. Bruce Meml. award 1979), N.Y. Acad. Scis., Am. Acad. Microbiology, AAAS (chmn. sect. on med. scis. 1975); mem. Assn. Am. Physicians, Am. Soc. Clin. Investigation, Am. Clin. and Climatol. Assn. (pres. 1984), Am. Soc. Microbiology (v.p. N.Y. br. 1961-62), Nat. Acad. Scis., Soc. Exptl. Biology and Medicine, Harvey Soc., Am. Fedn. Clin. Research, Balt. Med. Soc., Am. Assn. Immunologists, N.Y. Acad. Medicine (sec. sect. microbiology 1961-62), Phila. County Med. Soc. (Strittmatter award 1979), Coll. Physicians Phila. (award of Meritorious Service 1980), Interurban Clin. Club (pres. 1970), Infectious Disease Soc. Am. (pres. 1971, Maxwell Finland lecture award 1974), Johns Hopkins Soc. Scholars, Phi Beta Kappa, Sigma Xi, Alpha Omega Alpha, Omicron Delta Kappa. Club: 14 W. Hamilton Street (Balt.). Current Work: Studies of the epidemiology, bacteriology and prevention by vaccination of pneumococcal infection. Subspecialties: Infectious diseases; Microbiology (medicine). Address: Dept Research Medicine U Pa Sch Medicine Philadelphia PA 19104

AUSUBEL, FREDERICK MICHAEL, biologist. Prof. genetics Harvard Med. Sch., Boston. Subspecialty: Genetics and genetic engineering (biology). Office: Harvard Med Sch 25 Shattuck St Boston MA 02115

AVADIAN, JOHN MARK, computer scientist, distributed system architectures consultant; b. La Reole, Gironde, France, Nov. 29, 1943; came to U.S., 1970; s. Simon and Linda (Ruffini) A.; m. Jacqueline Verdier, Aug. 10, 1968; 1 dau., Cecile. Math. cert., U. Bordeaux, France, 1963; M.B.A., Pepperdine U., 1979; M.S. in Computer Sci, UCLA, 1982. Systems programmer IBM, Poughkeepsie, N.Y., 1968-71; data systems specialist Computer Sci. Corp., N.Y.C., 1971-73, sr. tech. cons., El Segundo, Calif., 1974-79; research mgr. Systems Devel. Corp., Santa Monica., Calif., 1973-74; chief architect Transaction Tech.Inc., Los Angeles, 1979-81; prin. scientist InnovaTech Corp., Los Angeles, 1981—, also dir.; dir. Calsoft Mgmt. Cons., Los Angeles, 1981—, Credifax, Inc., Los Angeles, 1982—; tech. cons. Internat. Cons., El Toro, Calif., 1982—. Served to 1st lt. French Air Force, 1966-68. Mem. Assn. Computing Machinery. Current Work: Research in architectural design of distributed cognitive systems involving multiple interacting, non-cooperating systems; specializing in models of distributed heterogenous systems with emphasis on conflicts, security problems, logistics issues, etc., regarding the distribution of algorithms; postulating that algorithm ownership and distribution control, which is often ignored, is as important as data management. Subspecialties: Distributed systems and networks; Software engineering. Office: InnovaTech Corp 12304 Santa Monica Blvd Los Angeles CA 90025

AVERY, JAMES KNUCKEY, dental educator; b. Holly, Colo., Aug. 6, 1921; s. Willard Smith and Bertha (Knuckey) A.; m. Dorothy Jane Thuerk, Aug. 26, 1950; children—Nancy Jane, David Lloyd, Robert Hugh. B.A., U. Rochester, 1948, Ph.D., 1952; D.D.S., U. Kansas City, 1945. Instr. anatomy U. Rochester Dental Sch., 1952-54; mem. faculty U. Mich. Med. and Dental Sch., 1954—; prof. oral biology Sch. Dentistry, 1963—, prof. anatomy, 1970—, chmn. dept. oral biology, 1977—; dir. Dental Research Inst., 1975—; mem. dental tng. com. NIH, 1964-68; research cons. VA, Ann Arbor, 1964—. Editorial bd.: Jour. Dental Research, 1968-72. Served to lt. (j.g.) USNR, 1945-47. Recipient award Acad. Dental Medicine. Fellow Am. Coll. Dentists, AAAS (chmn. dentistry sect. 1976); mem. ADA (cons. sci. session 1960-70), Internat. Assn. Dental Research (pres. 1974-75), Am. Assn. Anatomists, Electron Microscopic Soc. Am., Teratology Soc., Sigma Xi (hon.), Omicron Kappa Upsilon o3(hon.). Specialty: Oral biology. Home: 2475 Placid Way Ann Arbor MI 48105

AVERY, ROBERT TOLMAN, electro-mech. engr.; b. San Luis Obispo, Calif., Feb. 7, 1926; s. Harold Tolman and Elizabeth Ella (Murphey) A.; m. Beverly Gail Beckman, July 11, 1948; children: Scott Murphey, Leslie Ann. B.S., U. Minn., 1946; M.S., Stanford U., 1948; D.Eng., U. Calif.-Berkeley, 1974. Registered profl. engr., Calif. Bridge engr. State of Calif., San Francisco, 1948-50; design engr. U. Calif. Radiation Lab., Berkeley, 1950-54; research engr. Chromatic TV Labs., Oakland, Calif., 1954-55; sr. engr. Varian Assos.,

Palo Alto, Calif., 1955-61; project mgr. Brobeck Assocs. (Cons. Engrs.), Berkeley, 1961-66; sr. staff scientist Lawrence Berkeley Lab., U. Calif., 1966—; cons. in field. Contbr. articles to profl. jours. Mem. Nat. Soc. Profl. Engrs., IEEE, ASME, Internat. Soc. Rock Mechanics. Patentee in field. Current Work: Engineering design of novel particle accelerators, electromagnets, vacuum systems and related equipment. Subspecialties: Mechanical engineering; Applied magnetics. Home: 1408 Camino Peral Moraga CA 94556 Office: 1 Cyclotron Rd Berkeley CA 94720

AVERY, WILLIAM HINCKLEY, physicist; b. Ft. Collins, Colo., July 25, 1912; s. Edgar Delano and Mabel Abbey (Gordon) A.; m. Helen Wallace Palmer, July 18, 1937; children—Christopher, Patricia (Mrs. W. Randolph Bartlett, Jr.). A.B., Pomona Coll., 1933; A.M., Harvard, 1935, Ph.D., 1937. Postdoctoral research asst. infrared spectroscopy Harvard, 1937-39; research chemist Shell Oil Co., St. Louis, Houston, 1939-43; head propulsion div. Allegany Ballistics Lab., Cumberland, Md., 1943-46; cons. in physics and chemistry Arthur D. Little Co., Cambridge, Mass., 1946-47; profl. staff mem. Applied Physics Lab., Johns Hopkins, Laurel, Md., 1947-73, asst. dir. exploratory devel., 1973-78, dir. ocean energy programs, 1978—; mem. various coms. DOD, NASA, NRC, Nat. Acad. Scis.; Nat. Acad. Engring., 1955—; mem. tech. adv. bd. panel on SST environ. research Dept. Commerce, 1971; mem. subcom. AEC, Pres.'s Energy Report, 1973. Contbr. articles to profl. jours. Recipient C.N. Hickman award, 1951, Presdl. certificate of merit, 1948, Naval Ordnance Devel. award, 1945. Fellow Am. Inst. Aeros. and Astronautics (tech. dir. 1968-71); mem. Am. Chem. Soc., Combustion Inst. (dir. 1960-80, Sir Alfred C. Egerton Gold medal 1971), Phi Beta Kappa. Club: Cosmos (Washington). Current work: Fuels and electric power from ocean thermal energy conversion. Subspecialties: Combustion processes; Ocean energy conversion. Home: 724 Guilford Ct Silver Spring MD 20901 Office: Johns Hopkins Rd Laurel MD 20707

AVITZUR, BETZALEL, engineering educator; b. Haifa, Israel, May 7, 1925; came to U.S., 1955, naturalized, 1972; s. Shrage and Nehama (Voronowsky) A.; m. Pnina Stuerman, Aug. 9, 1955; children—Amir, Orly, Tal, Ron. B.S., Dip.Ing., Technion-Israel Inst. Tech., Haifa, 1949; M.S., U. Mich., 1956, Ph.D. in Mech. Engring., 1960. Research and devel. engr. Ministry Def., Israel, 1949-54; engr., dept. mgr. Vulcan Foundaries, Haifa, 1954-55; research and devel. engr. Micrometrical Dev., Ann Arbor, Mich., 1956-58; asst. research student U. Mich., Ann Arbor, 1958-59; research engr. Ford Motor Co., Dearborn, Mich., 1959-61; sr. lectr. Technion-Israel Inst. Tech., Haifa, 1961-64; prof. engring. Lehigh U., Bethlehem, Pa., 1964—; asst. research engr. U. Calif., Berkeley, 1963; cons. in field; pres. Metal Forming Inc., Allentown, Pa., 1972—. Author: Metal Forming: Processes and Analysis, 1968, 2d edit., 1979; Metal Forming: The Application of Limit Analysis, 1980; Handbook of Metal Forming Processes, 1983. Editor: (with C. Van Tyne) Production to Near Net Shape, Source Book, 1983. Contbr. articles to profl. jours. Recipient Meritorious Service award Wire Assn., 1969. Fellow ASME; mem. N.Am. Mfg. Research Inst. (founding) Am. Soc. Metals. Current work: Studies in the characterization of friction. Strip rolling, flow through conical converging dies, development of numerical procedures including FEM, and the introduction of ultrasonics in metal forming. Subspecialties: Mechanical engineering; Metallurgical engineering. Office: Lehigh U Whitaker Lab 5 Bethlehem PA 18015

AVNER, BARRY PAUL, biomedical consultant, educator, inventor; b. Chgo., June 19, 1944; s. Alex and Beatrice (Gerber) A.; m. Belina Rothman, Dec. 27, 1973; children—Jeremy Isaiah, Michael David. B.A., SUNY-Buffalo, 1966, Ph.D., 1970, postgrad., 1971; postgrad. U. Calif.-San Francisco, 1973. Asst. prof. pharmacology U. N.Mex. Med. Sch., Albuquerque, 1973-81; assoc. scientist Lovelace Med. Found., Albuquerque, 1981-83; asst. v.p., dir. research Summa Med. Corp., Albuquerque, 1983-84; div. chief monoclonal antibody prodn. Biotherapeutics Inc., Franklin, Tenn., 1985—. Contbr. articles to profl. jours. Patentee in field. Grantee Research Allocations Com., 1973, 76, NSF, 1974-77; N.Mex. Lung Assn., 1976, NIH, 1977-80, 80, 80-83, Boerhinger Ingelheim, 1981-83, Lovelace Med. Found., 1981-83. Mem. Am. Soc. Pharmacology and Exptl. Therapeutics, Am. Chem. Soc. (div. biol. chemistry), N.Y. Acad. Scis., Western Pharmacology Soc., AAAS, Soc. Analytical Cytology, Rho Chi. Democrat. Jewish. Current work: Developed hybridoma technology (human), flow cytometry applications in immunodiagnosis; consultant/advisor to start up biotechnology companies. Subspecialties: Immunopharmacology; Cell and tissue culture. Office: Biotherapeutics Inc 400 Eddy Ln Franklin TN 37062

AXE, JOHN DONALD, physical chemist. Sr. physicist Brookhaven Nat. Lab., Upton, N.Y. Subspecialty: Physical chemistry. Office: Brookhaven Nat Lab Upton NY 11973

AXEL, LEON, radiologist; b. Lakewood, N.J., Nov. 1, 1947; s. Milton and Alice (Terry) A. B.S., Syracuse U., 1967; Ph.D., Princeton U., 1971; M.D., U. Calif., San Francisco., 1976. Diplomate: Am. Bd. Radiology. Clin. instr. U. Calif., San Francisco, 1980-81; asst. prof. radiology U. Pa., Phila., 1981—. Mem. AAAS, Radiol. Soc. N.Am., Am. Roentgen Ray Soc., Am. Assn. Physicists in Medicine, Soc. Magnetic Resonance in Medicine, Am. Inst. Ultrasound in Medicine. Current Work: Computed tomography, ultrasound, nuclear magnetic resonance, noninvasive measurement of blood flow. Subspecialties: Diagnostic radiology; Imaging technology. Office: Dept Radiology 3400 Spruce St Philadelphia PA 19104

AXEL, RICHARD, pathologist; b. Bklyn., July 2, 1946; married, 1975. A.B., Columbia U., 1967; M.D., Johns Hopkins U., 1970. Intern pathology Columbia U. Coll. Physicians and Surgeons, 1970-71; fellow pathology and oncology Inst. Cancer Research, 1971-72; joint appointment vis. fellow dept. pathology Columbia U., 1971-72; research assoc. NIH, 1972-74; asst. prof. dept. pathology and inst., 1974-78; prof. dept. pathology and biochemistry and Inst. Cancer Research, Columbia U., N.Y.C., 1978—; asst. attending physician Presbyn. Hosp., N.Y.C., 1974—. Recipient Young Scientist award Passano Found., 1979; Waterman award, 1982. Mem. Am. Acad. Arts and Scis., Nat. Acad. Scis. Subspecialty: Genetics and genetic engineering (medicine). Office: Inst Cancer Research 701 W 168th St New York NY 10032

AXELROD, JULIUS, biochemist, pharmacologist; b. N.Y.C., May 30, 1912; s. Isadore and Molly (Leichtling) A.; m. Sally Taub, Aug. 30, 1938; children—Paul Mark, Alfred Nathan. B.S., Coll. City N.Y., 1933; M.A., N.Y. U., 1941, D.Sc. (hon.), 1971; Ph.D., George Washington U., 1955, LL.D. (hon.), 1971, D.Sc., U. Chgo., 1965, Med. Coll. Wis., 1971; LL.D., Coll. City N.Y., 1972; Dr.h.c., U. Panama, 1972; Sc.D., Med. Coll. Pa., 1974; Dr. honoris causa, U. Paris (Sud), 1982. Chemist Lab. Indsl. Hygiene, 1935-46; research asso. 3d N.Y. U. research div. Goldwater Meml. Hosp., 1946-49; asso. chemist sect. chem. pharmacology Nat. Heart Inst., NIH, 1949-50, chemist, 1950-53, sr. chemist, 1953-55; acting chief sect. pharmacology Lab. Clin. Sci. NIMH, 1955, chief sect. pharmacology, 1955-84, now guest worker Lab. Cell Biology; Otto Loewi meml. lectr. N.Y. U., 1963; Karl E. Paschkis meml. lectr. Phila. Endocine Soc., 1966; NIH lectr., 1967; Nathanson meml. lectr. U. So. Calif., 1968; James Parkinson lectr. Columbia U., 1971; Wartenberg lectr. Am. Acad. Neurology, 1971; Arnold D. Welch lectr. Yale U., 1971; Harold Carpenter Hodge distinguished lectr. toxicology U. Rochester, 1971; Bennett lectr. Am. Neurol. Assn., 1971; Harvey lectr., 1971; Mayer lectr. Mass. Inst. Tech., 1971; distinguished prof. sci. George Washington U., 1972; Salmon lectr. N.Y. Acad. Medicine, 1972; Eli Lilly lectr., 1972; Mike Hogg lectr. U. Tex., 1972; Fred Schueler lectr. Tulane U., 1972; vis. scholar Herbert Lehman Coll. City U. N.Y., 1973; cons. George Washington U., 1959—; panelist U.S. Bd. Civil Service Examiners, 1958-67; mem. research adv. com. United Cerebral Palsy Assn., 1966-69; mem. psychopharmacology study sect. NIMH, 1970-74; mem. Internat. Brain Research Orgn.; mem. research adv. com. Nat. Found.; vis. com. Brookhaven Nat. Lab., 1972-76; bd. overseers Jackson Lab., 1974. Editorial bd. Jour. Pharmacology and Exptl. Therapeutics, 1956-72, Jour. Medicinal Chemistry, 1962-67, Circulation Research, 1963-71, Currents in Modern Biology, 1966-72; editorial adv. bd.: Communication in Behavioral Biology, 1967-73, Jour. Neurobiology, 1968-77, Jour. Neurochemistry, 1969-77, Jour. Neurovisceral Relation, 1969, Rassegna di Neurologia Vegetativa, 1969—, Internat. Jour. Psychobiology, 1970-75; hon. cons. editor: Life Scis., 1961-69; co-author: The Pineal, 1968; contbr. papers in biochem. actions and metabolism of drugs, hormones, action of pineal gland, enzymes, neurochem. transmission to profl. jours. Recipient Meritorious Research award Assn. Research Nervous and Mental Diseases, 1965; Gairdner award distinguished research, 1967; Nobel prize med. physiology, 1970; Alumni Distinguished Achievement award George Washington U., 1968; Superior Service award HEW, 1968; Distinguished Service award, 1970; Claude Bernard professorship and medal U. Montreal, 1969; Distinguished Service award Modern Medicine mag., 1970; Albert Einstein award Yeshiva U., 1971; medal Rudolf Virchow Med. Soc., 1971; Myrtle Wreath award Hadassah, 1972. Fellow Am. Acad. Arts and Scis., Am. Soc. Neuropsychopharmacology; mem. German Pharmacol. Soc. (corr.), Am. Chem. Soc., Am. Soc. Pharmacology and Exptl. Therapeutics (Torald Sollmann award 1973), Am. Soc. Biol. Chemists, AAAS, Nat. Acad. Scis., Am. Neurol. Assn. (hon.), Royal Soc. London (fgn.), Inst. Medicine (sr.), Sigma Xi, Am. Psychopathol. Assn. (hon.). Subspecialty: Pharmacology. Office: NIMH Lab Cell Biology 900 Rockville Pike Bethesda MD 20014

AXELROD, NORMAN NATHAN, optical engineering company executive; b. N.Y.C., Aug. 26, 1934; s. Louis E. and Sadie (Katz) A.; m. Victoria Ann Grant, Mar. 21, 1975; children: Lauren, Brian. A.B., Cornell U., 1954; Ph.D., U. Rochester, 1960. Postdoctoral fellow U. London, 1960-61, NASA Goddard Space Flight tr., 1959-60; asst. prof. U. Del., 1961-65; mem. tech. staff Bell Telephone Labs., Murray Hill, N.J., 1965-72; prin., pres. Norman N. Axelrod Assocs., N.Y.C., 1972—. Mem. Optical Soc. Am., IEEE. Current Work: Plan, design and develop optical and laser systems; materials characterization, sensing, industrial automation; data storage/retrieval/reproduction/display. Subspecialties: Optical engineering; Laser data storage and reproduction. Home: 445 E 86th St New York NY 10028 Office: 56 W 45th St New York NY 10036

AXELROOD, HELEN BLAU, psychologist; b. Chgo., Feb. 13; d. Morris and Goldie (Bookstien) Blau; m. Jack Axelrood, June 27, 1948; children: Lisa, Barney, Larry Michael. B.A., Roosevelt U., 1951, M.A., 1977; Ph.D., Marquette U., 1982. Tchr., art dir., teaching supr. Chgo. schs., 1951-75; pvt. practice psychotherapy, Evanston, Ill., 1977—; intern in drug and alcohol rehab. Luth. Gen. Hosp., Park Ridge, Ill., 1979; dir. Weight Care Inst. and Counseling Clinic, Evanston, 1981—; lectr. on eating disorders to various Chgo. area groups and orgns. TV and state actress and writer, Chgo., 1951-74. Recipient Dedicated Service award Beth Emet Temple, Evanston, 1960; Outstanding Service award Temple Beth El, Chgo., 1970. Mem. Am. Psychol. Assn., Am. Personnel and Guidance Assn., Assn. Specialists in Group Work, Ill. Psychol. Assn., Ill. Personnel and Guidance Assn. Current Work: Research on personality differences with weight changes. Subspecialty: Behavioral psychology. Home: 2022 Hawthorne Ln Evanston IL 60201 Office: Weight Care Institute & Counseling Clinic 1601 Sherman St Suite 402 Evanston IL 60201

AYASLI, SERPIL, physicist, electrical engineer; b. Ankara, Turkey, May 22, 1951; came to U.S., 1979; B.S.E.E., Middle East Tech. U., Ankara, Turkey, 1973, M.S., 1975, Ph.D., 1978. Teaching asst. physics dept. Middle East Tech. U., 1974-78, instr., 1978-79; postdoctoral researcher M.I.T., Cambridge, 1979-82; mem. staff Lincoln Lab., Lexington, 1982—. Contbr. articles in field to profl. jours. Mem. Am. Astron. Soc. Current Work: Research and data analysis on radars, electromagnetic wave propagation. Subspecialties: Theoretical astrophysics; X-ray high energy astrophysics. Office: MIT Lincoln Lab PO Box 73 Lexington MA 02173

AYERS, ARNOLD LESLIE, SR., chemical engineer, retired; b. Dayton, Ohio, July 30, 1917; s. Leslie Arnold and Marie Antoinette (Ritter) A.; m. Doris Evelyn Lotspeich, Mar. 19, 1938; children: Arnold Leslie, Kenneth Duanne, Vicki Lynn Ayers Kershaw. B.S. in Chem. Engring, Iowa State U., 1938. Research chemist Magic City Printing Co., Omaha, 1938-40; sr. chem. engr. Phillips Petroleum Co., Bartlesville, Okla., 1940-51, supt. ops., Idaho Falls, Idaho, 1951-67; tech. dir. Allied Chem. Corp., Morristown, N.J., 1967-71, Allied-Gen. Nuclear Service, Barnwell, S.C., 1971-79; mgr. TWTF project EG&G-Idaho, Inc., Idaho Falls, 1979-82, cons., 1982-85, retired; cons. Gorleban Hearings, Lower Saxony-State, Hanover, Fed. Republic Germany, 1979. Served to maj. U.S. Army, 1942-45. Recipient Merit award Chem. Engring., 1972; prof. Achievement citation Iowa State U.-Ames, 1975. Fellow Am. Inst. Chem. Engrs.; mem. Am. Nuclear Soc., Am. Chem. Soc. Patentee electro pulse separater, method of dissolving spent nuclear fuel. Subspecialties: Chemical engineering; Nuclear engineering. Home: 887 Linden Pl Idaho Falls ID 83401

AYLES, G. BURTON, genetcist; b. Prince Albert, Sask., Can., Nov. 28, 1945; s. W. George and Leonis W. (Farnsworth) A. B.Sc., U. B.C., 1967, M.Sc., 1969; Ph.D., U. Toronto, 1972. Research scientist Freshwater Inst., Winnipeg, Man., Can., 1972-80, regional planning officer, 1980-82, dir. research, 1982—. Contbr. articles to profl. jours. Current Work: Aquaculture, genetics of fish. Subspecialties: Genetics and genetic engineering (biology); Animal genetics. Office: 501 University Crescent Winnipeg MB R3T 2N6 Canada

AYOUB, GEORGE TANIOS, engineering company executive; b. Lebanon, Jan. 24, 1951; s. Tanios Tannoos and Hellen (Ishaya) A. E.E., U. St. Joseph, Lebanon, 1974; Ph.D., U. Nebr.-Lincoln, 1976, M.B.A., 1978. Project mgr., sr. engr. Marathon Oil Co., 1978-80, research scientist, Denver, 1980-82; sr. staff exec. AREC, Abu Dhabi, United Arab Emirates, 1982—. Author: Optical Characterization of Thin Films on Water by Ellipsometry, 1978, New Applications of Coherency in Seismic Exploration, 1983. U. Nebr. grantee, 1974; U. Nebr. postdoctoral fellow, 1976. Mem. Soc. Exploration Geophysicists, Optical Soc. Am., Sigma Xi. Current Work: Exploration techniques - computer science applied to exploration and production of petroleum, signal processing and fiber optics. Subspecialties: Petroleum engineering; Geophysics. Office: PO Box 7658 Abu Dhabi UAE

AYRES, DAVID SMITH, physics researcher; b. Boston, June 14, 1939. B.S., Williams Coll., 1961; M.A., U. Calif.-Berkeley, 1963, Ph.D., 1968. Jr. engr. Sprague Electric, Visalia, Calif., 1961; teaching, research asst. U. Calif.-Berkeley, 1961-63, 65-68; vol. tchr. U.S. Peace Corps, U. Nigeria, 1963-65; postdoctoral fellow Lawrence Radiation Lab., Berkeley, 1968-69; successively postdoctoral fellow, asst. physicist, physicist, Argonne Nat. Lab., Ill., 1969-84, sr. physicist, 1984—. Fellow Am. Phys. Soc.; mem. AAAS. Current work: Search for nucleon decay and other underground physics; detectors and instrumentation for colliding beam experiments; electronics and data acquisition; meson spectroscopy; tests of fundamental conservation laws. Subspecialty: Particle physics. Office: Argonne Nat Lab Bldg 362 HEP Argonne IL 60439

AZARNOFF, DANIEL LESTER, pharm. co. exec.; b. Bklyn., Aug. 4, 1926; s. Samuel J. and Kate (Asarnow) A.; m. Joanne Stokes, Dec. 26, 1951; children: Rachel, Richard, Martin. B.S., Rutgers U., 1947, M.S., 1948; M.D., U. Kans., 1955. Instr. anatomy U. Kans., 1949-50, research fellow, 1950-52, intern, 1955-56, Nat. Heart Inst. resident research fellow, 1956-58, asst. prof. medicine, 1962-64, assoc. prof., 1964-68, dir. clin. pharmacology study unit, 1964-68, assoc. prof. pharmacology, 1965-68, prof. medicine and pharmacology, 1968; dir. (Clin. Pharmacology-Toxicology Center), 1967-68, Disting. prof., 1973-78; also prof. medicine; Nat. Inst. Neurol. Diseases and Blindness pl. trainee Washington U., St. Louis, 1958-60; asst. prof. medicine St. Louis U., 1960-62; vis. scientist, Fulbright scholar Karolinska Inst., Stockholmm, 1968; sr. v.p. worldwide research and devel. G.D. Searle & Co., Chgo., 1978; pres. Searle Research and Devel., Skokie, Ill., 1979—; prof. pathology, clin. prof. pharmacology Northwestern U., 1978—; William N. Creasy vis. prof. clin. pharmacology Med. Coll. Va., 1975; Bruce Hall Meml. lectr. St. Vincents Hosp., Sydney, 1976; 7th Sir Henry Hallett Dale lectr. Johns Hopkins U., 1978; professorial lectr. U. Chgo., 1979; dir. 2d Workshop on Prins. Drug Evaluation in Man, 1970; chmn. com. on problems of drug safety NRC-Nat. Acad. Sci., 1972-76; cons. numerous govtl. agencies. Editorial bd. Jours., AMA, many others; editor: Rev. of Drug Interactions, 1974-77, Yearbook of Drug Therapy, 1977-79; series editor: Monographs in Clin. Pharmacology, 1977-. Served with AUS, 1945-46. Recipient Ginsburg award in phys. diagnosis U. Kans. Med. Center, 1953, Outstanding Intern award, 1956, Ciba award for gernotol. research, 1958, Rectors medal U. Helsinki, 1968; John and Mary R. Markle scholar, 1962; Burroughs Wellcome scholar, 1964. Fellow ACP, N.Y. Acad. Scis.; mem. Am. Soc. Clin. Nutrition, Am. Nutrition Inst., Am. Soc. Pharmacology and Exptl. Theapeutics (chmn. clin. pharmacology div. 1969-71, exec. com. 1966-73, 78—, del. 1975-78, bd. publ. trustees), Am. Soc. Clin. Pharmacology and Therapeutics, Am. Fedn. Clin. Research, Brit. Pharmacol. Soc., AMA (vice chmn. council on drugs 1971-72), Central Soc. Clin. Research, Royal Soc. Promotion of Health, Inst. Medicine Nat. Acad. Scis., Soc. Exptl. Biology and Medicine (Councillor), Internat. Union Pharmacologists (sec. clin. pharmacology sect.), Sigma Xi. Current Work: Integrate development of new drugs, including those produced by bioengineering. Subspecialties: Pharmacology; Internal medicine. Home: 1030 Lake Shore Blvd Evanston IL 60202 Office: 4901 Searle Pkwy Skokie IL 60077

AZAROFF, LEONID VLADIMIROVITCH, physics educator; b. Moscow, June 19, 1926; came to U.S., 1939, naturalized, 1945; s. Vladimir Ivanovitch and Maria Yulievna (Odlen) A.; m. Carmen Wade, Mar. 9, 1946 (div. July 1968); m. Beth Sulzer, Mar. 4, 1972; children: David, Richard, Lenore. B.S. cum laude, Tufts Coll., 1948; Ph.D., M.I.T., 1954. Research physicist Armour Research Found., Chgo., 1953-54, sr. scientist, 1954-57; asso. prof. metall. engring. Ill. Inst. Tech., 1957-61, prof., 1961-66; prof. physics, dir. Inst. Material Sci., U. Conn., 1966—; guest physicist Brookhaven Nat. Lab., 1961, 62, 64; vis. prof. U. Mass., 1978-79, 85-86; cons. Owens-Ill., Philips Electronics, Hilger-Watts, Inc.; U.S. del. Internat. Union Crystallography, teaching commn., 1963-69; dir. Conn. Product Devel. Corp., Rogers Corp. Asso., Conn. Devel. Corp., 1977—. Author: 7 books, including X-Ray Diffraction and X-Ray Spectroscopy, 1973; also articles. Served with AUS, 1944-46. Fellow Am. Phys. Soc. (cons. editor), Mineral. Soc. Am.; mem. AAAS (dir.), IEEE (sr.), Am. Soc. Engring. Edn., Conn. Acad. Sci. and Engring. (pres. 1976-82), Am. Crystallographic Assn., Am. Inst. Mining Engrs., Internat. Union Physics, Internat. Union Crystal Growth, Sigma Xi, Phi Kappa Phi, Sigma Pi Sigma. Current Work: Electronic structure of alloys; liquid crystal structures. Subspecialties: Metallurgy; Crystallography. Home: PO Box 103 Storrs CT 06268

AZHIR, ARASTEH, biotechnologist, biophysicist; b. Tehran, Iran, Jan. 31, 1947; came to U.S., 1981; s. Ahmad and Effat (Sadri) A.; m. Khosro Amirsolymanie, Jan. 14, 1970; children—Naz, Saghi. B.S. in Biochemistry and Math., Queen Elizabeth London U., 1968; M.Ph. in Biophysics, Kings' Coll., London U., 1971; Ph.D. in Biophysics, Tehran U., 1972. Asst. prof. Tehran U., 1971-80; research coordinator Middlesex Hosp., London U., 1980-81; cons. U. Calif.-San Francisco, 1982-83; mgr. product rev. and testing Intelligenetics, Palo Alto, Calif., 1983—. Author: Elementary Topics in Biophysics, 1979; The Physical Principle of Radiology, 1983. Contbr. articles to profl. jours. Mem. Biophys. Soc., Am. Med. Writers Assn., Soc. Math. Biology. Current work: Computer science applied to molecular biology. Subspecialties: Biophysics (biology); Biochemistry (biology). Home: 46 Surrey Ln San Rafael CA 94903 Office: Intelligenetics 124 University Ave Palo Alto CA 94301

AZZIZ, NESTOR JALIL, physics educator; b. Durazno, Uruguay, Dec. 11, 1932; s. Mateo and Saturnina (Jozami) A.; m. Juana Maria Baumgartner, Mar. 30, 1957; children: Ricardo, Rodolfo, Cecilia, Eduardo. B.Engring., U. Uruguay, 1958; M.S. in Nuclear Tech, U. P.R., 1960; Ph.D., Pa. State U., 1963. Pres. Azziz Heating, Montevideo, Uruguay, 1951-59; fellow physicist Westinghouse Atomic Power Div., Pitts., 1963-70; prof. dept. physics U. P.R., Mayaguez, 1971—; cons. and lectr. in field. Contbr. articles to profl. jours. Dept. Energy grantee, 1976-78. Mem. N.Y. Acad. Sci., Am. Phys. Soc. Patentee in field. Current Work: Pure physics, theoretical physics and applied physics. Subspecialties: Nuclear physics; Atomic and molecular physics. Office: Dept Physics University of Puerto Rico Mayaguez PR 00708

BAAS, ERVIN JUNIOR, veterinarian; b. Sibley, Iowa, Jan. 24, 1932; s. Jacob and Gertrude Irene (Den Beste) B.; m. Maryilyn Jean Canby, July 19, 1981; children—Valerie, Brett. B.S., U. Minn., 1958, D.V.M., 1960; Ph.D., U. Calif.-Davis, 1971. Diplomate Coll. Lab. Animal Medicine. Gen. practice vet. medicine, Marshall, Minn., 1960-67; chief carnivore unit NIH, Bethesda, Md., 1971-84; staff veterinarian Nat. Inst. Arthritis, Diabetes, Digestive and Kidney Diseases, Bethesda, Md., 1984—. Served with USAF, 1951-54. Mem. AVMA, Am. Coll. Lab. Animal Medicine, Am. Soc. Clin. Pathology, D.C. Acad. Vet. Medicine, Phi Zeta. Presbyterian. Subspecialties: Laboratory animal medicine; Pathology (veterinary medicine). Office: Nat Inst Arthritis Diabetes Digestive and Kidney Diseases Bldg 4 B1-11 Wisconsin Ave Bethesda MD 20205

BABAYAN, VIGEN KHACHIG, university/hospital nutritionist, chemist; b. Erivan, Armenia, Jan. 1, 1913; came to U.S., 1922, naturalized, 1929; s. Khosrov and Nectar (Kouyoumdjian) B.; m. Kanare Edgarian, Nov. 15, 1942; children—Tamar, Richard, Sona. B.A., NYU, 1938, Ph.D., 1943. Chemist, E.F. Drew & Co., Boonton, N.J., 1938-41; dir. research and devel. Ridbo Labs., Patterson, N.J., 1941-48; chief chemist Theobold Industries, Kearny, N.J., 1948-49; v.p., dir. research and devel. Drew Chem. Corp., N.Y.C., Boonton, 1949-64; v.p., dir. research and devel. and quality control Stokely-Van Camp, Inc., Indpls., 1964-78, v.p. sci. and tech., 1978-82; asst. prof. medicine Ind. U. Med. Sch., Indpls., 1968-77; vis. scientist St. Luke's Hosp., Columbia U. Sch. Medicine, N.Y.C., 1979—; sr. research assoc. New Eng. Deaconess Hosp., Harvard U. Med. Sch., Boston, 1979-82, dir. research, nutrition/metabolism lab. Cancer Research Inst., 1983—; mem. adv. com. NRC. Contbr. sect. to ency., numerous articles to profl. lit. Patentee in field. Mem. central exec. com. Armenian Apostolic Ch., 1972-80; active Armenian Cultural Assn. Am., 1976—, Armenian Folk Festival Com., 1962-65, Armenian Nat. Com., 1976—, Armenian Relief Soc., 1932—. Recipient Glycerine Assn. award, 1964, U.S. Army Appreciation for Patriotic Civilian Service award, 1976. Mem. AAAS, Am. Assn. Candy Technologists, Am. Assn. Cereal Chemists, Am. Chem. Soc., Am. Frozen Food Inst., Am. Inst. Nutrition, Am. Oil Chemists Soc., Am. Oil Chemists Soc. Found., Am. Soc. for Clin. Nutrition, Am. Soc. for Parenteral and Enteral Nutrition, Assn. Research Dirs., Fedn. Am. Socs. for Exptl. Biology, Grocery Mfrs. Assn., Inst. Food Technologists (Sci. Achievement award 1977, fellow 1977, 83), Inst. Shortening and Edible Oils, Nat. Confectioners Assn., Nat. Food Processors Assn., N.Y. Acad. Scis., N.Am. Assn. for Study Obesity, Nutrition Today Soc., Research and Devel. Assocs., Soap and Detergent Assn. Current work: Medium chain triglycerides and structured lipids in nutrition and aid in the critically ill patients. Subspecialties: Nutrition (medicine); Health services research. Home: 178 Beethoven Ave Waban MA 02168 Office: Harvard U Med Sch New Eng Deaconess Hosp Cancer Research Inst 194 Pilgrim Rd Boston MA 02215

BABB, ALBERT LESLIE, nuclear engineering educator; b. Vancouver, C., Can., Nov. 7, 1925; came to U.S., 1948, naturalized, 1954; s. Clarence Stanley and Mildred (Gutteridge) B.; m. Marion A. McDougall; children: Eugene Matthew, Philip Leslie, Christine Louise. B.A. Sc., U. B.C., 1948; M.S., U. Ill., 1949, Ph.D., 1951; student, Internat. Sch. Nuclear Sci. and Engring., Argonne Nat. Lab., 1956-57. Chem. engr. Nat. Research Council Can., 1948; research engr. Rayonier Inc., 1951-52; mem. faculty U. Wash., Seattle, 1952—, chmn. nuclear engring. group, 1957-65, prof. chem. engring., 1960—, dir. nuclear reactor labs., 1962-72, prof. nuclear engring., 1965—, chmn. dept. nuclear engring., 1965-81, acting chmn., 1984—, acting chmn. dept. chem. engring., 1985; del. Japan-U.S. Seminar on Nuclear Engring. Edn., 1974; lectr. hemodialysis engring. USSR Ministry of Health, Moscow, 1976; lectr. biomed. engring. Norwegian Nephrological Soc., Oslo, 1980; lectr. hemodialysis engring. Kuratorium für Hemodialyse, Munster, Germany, 1980, Clinique Iser, Munich, W. Germany, 1980, Meml. Hosp., Hvidovre, Denmark, 1980, State Hosp., Copenhagen, 1980; cons. in field. Contbr. chpts. to books., articles to profl. jours. Active local services to Children's Orthopaedic Hosp., Northwest Artificial Kidney Ctr.; trustee Pacific Sci. Ctr. Found., mem. exec. com., 1973-80. Recipient citation Wash. Joint Legis. Com. Nuclear Energy, 1968; named Engr. of Yr. Wash. State Profl. Engrs. Assn., 1969; award for excellence Sigma Xi. Fellow Am. Inst. Chem. Engrs., Am. Inst. Chemists; mem. Am. Nuclear Soc. (dir. 1976—), Am. Inst. Chem. Engrs. (Engr. of Distinction), Engrs. Joint Council, Nat. Acad. Engring. (membership com.), Am. Soc. Engring. Edn. (chmn. nuclear engring. div. 1965-66), Am. Nephrology Soc., Am. Soc. Artificial Internal Organs, European Dialysis and Transplantation Assn., Sigma Xi, Tau Beta Pi, Pi Mu Epsilon, Alpha Chi Sigma. Presbyterian. Co-inventor of artificial kidney systems, techniques for early diagnosis of cystic fibrosis in children using nuclear reactors, formulated dialysis index for hemodialysis patients; co-inventor system for treatment of sickle cell anemia, computerized insulin pump for diabetics; patentee of stabilizing structures in permafrost, artificial kidneys and artificial pancreas. Current Work: Mathematical modelling of human respiratory systems; synthetic fuel producing nuclear energy systems, dialysis engineering. Subspecialties: Biomedical engineering; Nuclear fission. Home: 3237 Lakewood Ave S Seattle WA 98144 Office: Dept Nuclear Engring U Wash Seattle WA 98195

BABCHIN, ALEXANDER JOSEPH, chemistry and engineering researcher, consultant, educator; b. Moscow, May 20, 1938; came to U.S., 1977, naturalized, 1985; s. Joseph S. and Tilia (Kapshitsky) B. M.S. in Chem. Engring., Moscow Inst. Chem. Engring., 1961; Ph.D. in Phys. Chem., Nat. Research Inst., Moscow, 1966. Registered profl. engr. Sr. engr. Nat. Research Inst., 1962-66, lab dir., 1966-72; sr. research fellow Technion, Haifa, Israel, 1973-77; assoc. prof. Inst. Paper Chem., Appleton, Wis., 1977-81; sr. research assoc. Inst. Applied Chem. Physics, CUNY, 1981-84, Electrochem. Tech. Corp., Seattle, 1984—. Mem. editorial bd. Jour. Colloid and Interface Sci., 1983-85. Contbr. numerous articles to profl. jours. Patentee in field. Mem. N.Y. Acad. Scis., Am. Chem. Soc., Internat. Assn. Colloid and Interface Sci., Physico-Chem. Hydrodynamics Internat. Assn. (sci. sec. provisional council 1982-84). Current work: Ionic transport and osmotic flow through membranes; electrochemistry of corrosion. Subspecialties: Surface chemistry; Fluid mechanics. Office: Electrochemical Tech Corp 3935 Leary Way NW Seattle WA 98107

BABCOCK, GEORGE FRANCIS, immunologist, educator; b. Buffalo, Jan. 20, 1948; s. George F. and Iris E. (Dickerson) B. B.S., Muskingum Coll., 1970; M.S., N.D. State U., 1972; Ph.D., U. Nebr., 1975. Research assoc. U. N.C., Chapel Hill, 1978-79; asst. prof. surgery, asst. immunologist U. Tex. Cancer Ctr., M.D. Anderson Hosp., Houston, 1979-83; assoc. prof. surgery, adj. assoc. prof. pathology U. Cin., 1983—; asst. dir. research Shriners Burns Inst., Cin Unit, 1983—. Producer, licensed monoclonal antibody (Leu 11), 1982. Recipient Nat. Research Service award NIH, 1975. Mem. Am. Assn. Cancer Research, AAAS, Am. Assn. Immunologists, Am. Soc. Microbiology, N.Y. Acad. Scis., Reticuloendothelial Soc., Sigma Xi, Alpha Epsilon Delta. Current work: Research in area of immunology especially as it related to tumors and infectious disease; humoral and cell-mediated immune responses to primary and transplanted tumors both in vivo and in vitro; detection, isolation and purification of tumor specific antigens; immunotherapy of tumors and infections; study of immune surveillance; genetic control of immune responses; and mechanisms of action of biological response modifier. Subspecialties: Infectious diseases; Immunogenetics. Home: 3535 Erie Ave Cincinnati OH 45208 Office: Dept Surgery U Cin Med Ctr 231 Bethesda Ave Cincinnati OH 45267

BABCOCK, HORACE WELCOME, astronomer; b. Pasadena, Calif., Sept. 13, 1912; s. Harold Delos and Mary Geddie (Henderson) B.; 1940 (div. 1958); children—Ann Lucille, Bruce Harold; m. Elizabeth Mae Aubrey, 1958; 1 son, Kenneth L. B.S., Calif. Inst. Tech., 1934; Ph.D., U. Calif., 1938; D.Sc. (hon.), U. Newcastle-upon-Tyne (Eng.), 1965. Asst. Lick Obs., Mt. Hamilton, Calif., 1938-39; instr. Yerkes and McDonald Obs., Williams Bay, Wis., Ft. Davis, Tex., 1939-41; with Radiation Lab., MIT, 1941-42, Rocket-Project, Calif. Inst. Tech., 1942-45; staff mem. Mt. Wilson and Palomar Obs., Carnegie Instn. of Washington, Calif. Inst. Tech., Pasadena, 1946—; dir. Mt. Wilson and Palomar Obs., 1964-78. Author sci. and tech. papers in profl. jours. Recipient USN Bur. Ordnance Devel. award, 1946; Draper medal Nat. Acad. Scis., 1957; Eddington medal Royal Astron. Soc., 1958; Gold medal, 1970; Bruce medal Astron. Soc. Pacific, 1969. Mem. Royal Astron. Soc. (asso.), Societé Royale des Sciences de Liege (corr. mem.), Am. Philos. Soc., Am. Acad. Arts and Scis., Nat. Acad. Scis. (councilor 1973-76), Am. Astron. Soc. (councilor 1956-58), Astron. Soc. Pacific, Internat. Astron. Union, Tau Beta Pi. Subspecialty: Optical astronomy. Home: 2189 N Altadena Dr Altadena CA 91001 Office: Mt Wilson and Las Campanas Observatories Carnegie Instn Of Washington 813 Santa Barbara St Pasadena CA 91101

BABISH, RICHARD CONSTANTINE, optical engineer; b. Beverly, Mass., Sept. 17, 1918; s. Constantine M. and Anna (Bennett) B.; m. Josita M. Dolan, May 20, 1945; children—James F., Joan M. B.S. in Physics, MIT, 1946. Lab asst. Paramount News, N.Y.C., 1940-42; engr. to v.p. Vitarama Corp., Huntington, N.Y., 1942-54; mem. staff Radiation Lab MIT, Cambridge, 1944-45; tech. dir. Cinerama, Oyster Bay, N.Y., 1952-54, Cinemiracle, N.Y.C., Los Angeles, 1954-56; engr., branch-chief, tech. dir. Perkin-Elmer, Norwalk, Conn., 1949-84; mem. tech. adv. bd. in optics Western Conn. State Coll., Danbury, 1983-84, Waterbury State Tech. Coll., 1983-84. Patentee in field. Fellow Optical Soc. Am.; mem. Soc. Photog. Instrumentation Engrs., Soc. Motion Picture and TV Engrs., AAAS, Southwest Conn. Chapter Optical Soc. Am. (treas., pres.). Current work: Optical and photographic instrumentation and systems engineerings, research and development optical design, metrology and fabrication, aerospace and astronomical optical system design manufacture. Subspecialties: Optical engineering; Aerospace engineering and technology. Home: 74 Rivergate Dr Wilton CT 06897 Office: Perkin-Elmer Corp Main Ave Norwalk CT 06856

BABITCH, JOSEPH AARON, biochemistry educator; b. Detroit, July 14, 1942; s. David Ira and Adele June (Wexler) B.; m. Marianne Ingrid Wanninger, Dec. 22, 1964; children—Tanya, Maxwell. B.S., U. Mich., 1965; Ph.D., UCLA, 1971; postdoctoral, U. Cambridge, 1971-72, U. Goteborg, Sweden, 1972-73. Asst. prof. Tex. Christian U., Ft. Worth, 1973-78, assoc. prof. biochemistry, 1978—; adj. asst. prof. neurology U. Tex. Health Scis. Ctr., Dallas, 1977—. Contbr. articles to profl. jours. Recipient Research Career Devel. award NIH, 1978-83; NIH grantee, 1975—. Mem. Soc. Neurosci., Am. Soc. Neurochemistry, Internat. Soc. Neurochemistry, Am. Soc. Cell Biology. Current work: Calcium-binding proteins; neurotransmitter release. Subspecialties: Biochemistry (medicine); Neurochemistry. Home: 2230 Warner Rd Ft Worth TX 76110 Office: Tex Christian U Chemistry Dept Ft Worth TX 76129

BABOIAN, ROBERT, corrosion engineer, researcher; b. Watertown, Mass., Nov. 17, 1934; s. Charles H. and Rose M. (Nazarian) B.; m. Roberta Joan Sanderson, June 20, 1959; children—Robert C., Laura J., Susan M., Rosann M. B.S., Suffolk U., 1959; Ph.D. Rennselaer Polytech. Inst., 1964. Sr. research assoc. U. Toronto, Ont., Can., 1965-66; mem. tech. staff Tex. Instruments, Attleboro, Mass., 1966-69, head corrosion lab, 1969—; chmn. bd. evaluation Ctr. Materials Sci. Nat. Bur. Standards, Gaitlesberg, Md., 1983-84; cons. Statue of Liberty Restoration Program. Editor: Galvanic and Pitting Corrosion, 1976; Electrochemical Techniques for Corrosion, 1977; Automotive Corrosion by Deicing Salts, 1981; Laboratory Corrosion Tests and Standards, 1985. Contbr. numerous articles to tech. jours. Patentee in field. Postdoctoral fellow Ford Found., U. Toronto, 1964, Tex. Instrument fellow, 1980. Mem. Fed. Materials Socs. (trustee 1984—), ASTM (treas. 1984—, v.p. bd. dirs. 1983—, award of appreciation 1979), Nat. Assn. Corrosion Engrs. (bd. dirs. 1981-84, citation of recognition 1977), Soc. Automotive Engrs. (chmn. auto corrosion com. 1984—), Am. Chem. Soc., Electrochem. Soc. United Church of Christ. Current work: Research and development of corrosion resistant materials and devices for corrosion control, use of electrochemical techniques for corrosion investigations. Subspecialties: Corrosion; Materials. Office: Tex Instruments Inc 34 Forest St Attleboro MA 02703

BABRAKZAI, NOORULLAH, biologist, educator, researcher; b. Nadershah Koat, Afghanistan, May 10, 1945; came to U.S., 1970; s. Said Akbar and Amila Bibi B.; m. Sami Ann, June 30, 1984. B.Sc., U. Peshawar, Abbottabad, Pakistan, 1965, M.Sc., 1967; Ph.D., U. Ariz., 1975. Lectr. Kabul (Afghanistan) U., 1968-70; grad. asst. U. Ariz., 1971-75, research asst. prof., 1977-81; teaching assoc. Pima Community Coll., Tucson, 1980-81; asst. prof. dept. biology Central Mo. State U., 1981—. Recipient Gold medal in zoology U. Peshawar, 1967; Meritorious Teaching Asst. award U. Ariz. Found., 1975. Mem. AAAS, Am. Malacological Union, Am. Soc. Zoologists, Mo. Acad. Sci., Sigma Xi. Current Work: Cytology, cytotaxonomy, cytogenetics of pulmonate land snails. Subspecialty: Cytology and histology. Home: 610 Christopher Warrensburg MO 64093 Office: Dept Biology Central Mo State Univ Warrensburg MO 64093

BABU, UMA MAHESH, diagnostic scientist, immunologist; b. Mysore City, India, Mar. 29, 1947, came to U.S., 1968; d. Chinnaswamy and Rajalaksmi (Kusuma) Setty; m. Vimala Babu, Nov. 16, 1975; 1 child, Ravi Kiran. B.S., U. Mysore, India, 1968; Ph.D., U. Nebr., 1974. Postdoctoral U. Manitoba, Can., 1974-77; research assoc. Thomas Jefferson U., Phila., 1977-83, research asst. prof., 1983-84; sr. scientist Pitman-Moore, Washington Crossing, N.J., 1984—. Contbr. articles to profl. jours. Fellow Am. Field Service; Am. Assn. Immunologists, N.Y. Acad. Scis., Sigma Xi, Phi Lamda Upsilon. Current work: Immunology; immunochemistry; immunogenetics; diagnostics; vaccines. Subspecialties: Immunology (agriculture); Biophysical chemistry. Home: 1 Barbet Dr Voorhees NJ 08043 Office: Pitman-Moore PO Box 344 Bear Tavern Rd Washington Crossing NJ 08560

BABUIN, MICHAEL LOUIS, geologist; b. Raleigh, N.C., Apr. 18, 1958; s. Renato John and Patricia (Goodwin) B.; m. Teresa Joy Wehunt, July 11, 1981; 1 child, Lisa Marie. B.S., Campbell U., 1980; postgrad. S.D. Sch. Mines, 1980-82; M.S., Old Dominion U., 1984. Lab. asst. Campbell U., Buies Creek, N.C., 1978-79; geol. technician N.C. Geol. Survey, Raleigh, 1980; cartographer Landmark Engring., Cary, N.C., 1981; field geologist Compañia Minera de Cobalto y Tex., 1983; research asst. Old Dominion U., Norfolk, Va., 1982—. Contbr. article to profl. jour. Mem. Geol. Soc. Am., Soc. Econ. Paleontologists and Mineralogists, Am. Assn. Stratigraphic Palynologists, Am. Assn. Petroleum Geologists (jr.), Am. Inst. Mining Engrs. Current work: Determination of depositional processes in fluvial systems throughout the humid tropics; tropical hydrology and geomorphology from these areas of the world. Subspecialties: Tropical geomorphology; Sedimentology. Office: Dept Geophysical Sci Old Dominion U Norfolk VA 23508

BACH, DEBORAH, psychologist; b. Springfield, Mass., Dec. 7, 1937; d. Kenneth William and Ethel (Martin) Donaldson; m. Edward August Bach, Mar. 26, 1958 (div. 1980); children: Cynthia, Hillary, Melanie, Edward, Andrea. B.S. in Edn. and B.A. in Psychology, Am. Internat. Coll., 1975, M.S., 1977, M.A., 1980. Cert. social worker, Mass. Tchr. Hampden (Mass.) Schs., 1963-74; instr. Springfield (Mass.) Tech. Community Coll., 1977; psychologist Providence Hosp., Holyoke, Mass., 1976—; cons. drug edn. Springfield schs., 1976—, Concerned Parents, Region I, Mass., 1976—; psychol. evaluator Springfield Police Cadets, 1982. Mem. Republican Town Com., Wilbraham, Mass., 1970-71; v.p. PTO, Wilbraham, 1972-73; del. White House Conf. on Families, 1980. Mem. Am. Psychol. Assn., LWV. Republican. Roman Catholic. Current work: Personality assessment/research of drug-dependent individuals. Subspecialty: Clinical psychology. Office: 210 Elm St Holyoke MA 01040

BACH, MARILYN LEE, immunology educator, education council science researcher; b. Lynn, Mass., Apr. 24, 1937; d. Samuel and Ida (Callum) Brenner; m. Fritz Heinz Bach, June 18, 1958 (div. Sept. 1980); children: David, Peter, Wendy. B.S., Simmons Coll., 1958; postgrad., MIT, 1958-60; Ph.D., N.Y. U., 1960. Fellow in oncology U. Wis.-Madison, 1966-67, project assoc. dept. genetics, 1967-68, research assoc. dept. med. genetics, 1968-70, asst. prof., 1970-75, assoc. prof. dept. genetics, 1975-78; assoc. prof. depts. of lab. of medicine/pathology Med. Sch., Sch. Pub. Health-Health Services Research Ctr., U. Minn., Mpls., 1978—; vis. prof. U. Leiden, Netherlands, 1973; invited lectr. U. Hosp. Bloodbank, 1974; sci. liaison Office for Med. Applications of Research, NIH, Bethesda, Md., 1979-80; spl. asst. to dir. for program devel. Nat. Inst. Allergy and Infectious Disease, 1980-81; fellow in sci. and pub. policy Brookings Instn., Washington, 1981-82; vis. fellow Am. Council on Edn., Washington, 1982—. Contbr. sects. to books, numerous articles in field to profl. jours.; patentee primed lymphocyte typing, use of lymphocyte blastoid cell lines for primed lymphocyte typing. Mem. nat. adv. council Nat. Inst. Allergy and Infectious Disease, 1974-77; mem. Basil O'Connor starter research grant panel Nat. Found., N.Y.C., 1975-78. Recipient Founders Day award N.Y. U., 1967, Faculty Research award Am. Cancer Soc., 1971. Mem. Am. Assn. Immunologists (chmn. nominating com. 1978-79, com. mem. on status of women 1982—), AAAS, Transplantation Soc. (editorial bd. Transplantation 1974-77, symposium lectr. internat. congress 1976). Democrat. Jewish. Club: MIT (Washington). Current Work: Research directed at genetic and cellular immunology mechanisms of transplantation; concurrent interest in science policy, particularly university/industry relationships. Subspecialties: Immunogenetics; Transplantation. Home: 5412 Lambeth Rd Bethesda MD 20814 Office: Am Council on Edn Suite 824 1 Dupont Circle Washington DC 20036

BACHMAN, WALTER CRAWFORD, ship designer, marine cons.; b. Pitts., Dec. 24, 1911; s. Clarence E. and Mary Elizabeth (Crawford) B.; m. Helen Elizabeth Van Cleaf, Mar. 25, 1938; children—Van Cleaf, Elizabeth Crawford Bachman Ramjoué. B.S. in Indsl. Engring, Lehigh U., 1933, M.S., 1935. Tchr. mech. engring. Lehigh U., 1935-36; marine engr. Fed. Shipbldg. and Dry Dock Co., 1936; marine engr. Gibbs & Cox, Inc., N.Y.C., 1936-70, chief engr., 1958-63, v.p., chief engr., 1963-70, marine cons., Short Hills, N.J., 1970—. Fellow ASME; mem. Nat. Acad. Engring. (mem. marine bd. 1967-75), Soc. Naval Architects and Marine Engrs., Am. Soc. Naval Engrs., N.Y. Acad. Scis. Club: Yacht (Beaulieu-St. Jean). Subspecialties: Mechanical engineering; Ocean engineering. Address: 21 Wayside Short Hills NJ 07078

BACHRACH, HOWARD L., biochemist; b. Faribault, Minn., May 21, 1920; s. Harry and Elizabeth (Panovitz) B.; m. Shirley F. Lichterman, June 13, 1943; children: Eve E., Harrison J. B.A. in Chemistry, U. Minn., 1942, Ph.D. in Biochemistry, 1949. Research asst. explosives research lab. Nat. Def. Research Com. project Carnegie Inst. Tech., Pitts., 1942-45; research asst. U. Minn., Mpls., 1945-49; biochemist foot-and-mouth disease mission U.S. Dept. Agr., Denmark, 1949-50; research biochemist and virus lab. U. Calif.-Berkeley, 1950-53; chief scientist and head biochem. and phys. investigation Plum Island Animal Disease Center, USDA, Greenport, N.Y., 1953-80, research chemist, advisor to dir., 1981—; sr. exec. U.S. Dept. Agr., 1979; mem. viral and rickettsial grants subcom. Walter Reed Army Inst. Research, 1982-85, Recipient Naval Ordnance Devel. award, 1945; Certificate of Merit U.S. Dept. Agr., 1960; Disting. Service award U.S. Dept. Agr., 1982; Presdl. citation, 1965; Recipient U.S. Sr. Exec. Service award, 1980; AAAS Newcomb Cleveland prize, 1982; Nat. Award for Agrl. Excellence, 1983; Alexander von Humboldt award, 1983; Nat Medal of Sci., 1985. Fellow N.Y. Acad. Scis.; mem. Am. Coll. Veterinary Microbiologists (hon.), Am. Chem. Soc. (Kenneth A. Spencer award 1983), Nat. Acad. Scis., Am. Soc. Virology, Sigma Xi., Gamma Alpha, Phi Lambda Upsilon. Current Work: Structure and function of viruses; virionome strategies; cloned subunit protein vaccines; mapping and synthesis of antigenic sites. Subspecialties: Animal virology; Genetics and genetic engineering (veterinary medicine). Home: Dayton Rd Southold NY 11971

BACIOCCO, ALBERT JOSEPH, JR., naval officer; b. San Francisco, Mar. 4, 1931; s. Albert Joseph and Florence Beatrice (Wiegner) B.; m. Mary Jane Rivera, June 25, 1955; children: David Anthony, Debra Ann, Andrew Joseph, Mary Susan. B.S., U.S. Naval Acad., 1953. Commd. ensign U.S. Navy, 1953; advanced through grades to vice adm.; comdr. U.S.S. Gato, 1965-69; with Submarine Div. 42, 1969-71, Submarine Squadron 4, Charleston, S.C., 1974-76, Submarine Group 6, 1981-83, Naval Base, Charleston, S.C., 1982; mem. chief naval ops. staff, Washington, 1971, 77-78; chief naval research, chief naval devel., dep. chief naval material, Arlington, Va., 1978-81; dir. research, devel, test and evaluation Dept. Navy, Washington, 1983—. Decorated D.S.M., Legion of Merit (4), Meritorious Service medal, Navy Commendation medal. Mem. U.S. Naval Inst., Am. Def. Preparedness Assn., Am. Soc. Naval Engrs., U.S. Naval Acad. Alumni Assn. Roman Catholic. Subspecialty: Research administration.

BACKER, DONALD CHARLES, astronomer; b. Plainfield, N.J., Nov. 9, 1943. B.Engring., Cornell U., 1966, Ph.D., 1971; M.Sc., U. Manchester, Eng., 1968. Research assoc. Nat. Radio Astronomy Obs., Charlottesville, Va., 1971-73; NRC fellow Goddard Space Flight Ctr., 1973-75; assoc. research astronomer, assoc. adj. prof. U. Calif., Berkeley, 1975—. Mem. Am. Astron. Soc., Internat. Radio Sci. Union, Internat. Astron. Union, AAAS. Current Work: Compact radio sources in our galaxy; pulsars; radio interferometry. Subspecialty: Radio and microwave astronomy. Office: 601 Campbell Hall U Calif Berkeley CA 94720

BACKMAN, THOMAS WILLIAM HIGHTOWER, ecologist, educator, researcher; b. San Diego, May 25, 1948; s. William Eerro and Theola Gladys (Cowen) B.; m. Brenda Lee Hightower, June 28, 1980. B.S. in Biology, San Diego State U., 1973, M.S. in Biology, 1976; Ph.D. in Fisheries, U. Wash., 1984. Research asst. Seattle Pacific U., 1976-80; teaching asst. U. Wash., Seattle, 1981; prof. ecology U. Autonomous de Baja Calif., Ensenada, Mex., 1981-82; statistician U.S. Navy, San Diego, 1982-84; adj. prof. Calif. Sch. Profl. Psychology, San Diego, 1984-85; research biologist Ocean Garden Products, Inc., San Diego, 1985—; prin. investigator Northwest Cons. Co., Winslow, Wash., 1975-76. Mem. Aquatic Plant Mgmt. Soc., Am. Soc. Limnology and Oceanography, Citizens for Century III, Nat. Assn. Underwater Instrs., Ecol. Soc. Am., Marine Sci. Soc. (chmn. scholarship com. 1979, sec. 1980), U.S. Coast Guard Aux. (aid to navigation officer 1984). Club: Bus Divers (sci. officer 1983-84). Current work: Long term marine ecological research. Subspecialties: Ecology (biology); Marine biology.

BACKUS, CHARLES EDWARD, electrical engineer, consultant researcher, educator; b. Wadestown, W.Va., Sept. 17, 1937; s. Clyde Harvey and Opal Daisy (Strader) B.; m. Judith Ann, Sept. 1, 1957; children: David, Elizabeth, Amy. B.S.M.E., Ohio U., 1959; M.S., U. Ariz., 1961, Ph.D., 1965. Supr. system dynamic analysis Westinghouse Astronuclear Lab., Pitts., 1965-68; asst. prof. engring. Ariz. State U., 1968-71, assoc. prof., 1971-76, prof., 1976—; asst. dean Ariz. State U. Sch. Engring., 1979—; dir. Ariz. State U. Center for Research, 1980—; with Los Alamos Sci. Lab., summers 1969-72, Lawrence Livermore (Calif.) Lab., summer 1973; cons. in field. Author 70 papers on photovoltaics and advanced energy conversion. Recipient Faculty Achievement award Ariz. State U. Alumni Assn., 1976. Fellow IEEE; mem. Am. Nuclear Soc., AAAS, Am. Soc. Engring. Edn., ASME, IEEE, Internat. Solar Energy Soc., Mesa C. of C., Sigma Xi, Pi Mu Epsilon, Tau Beta Pi. Methodist. Current Work: Research on photovoltaic concentration. Subspecialty: Solar energy.

BACKUS, GEORGE EDWARD, geophysicist, educator; b. Chgo., May 24, 1930; s. Milo Morlan and Dora Etta (DAre) B.; m. Elizabeth Evelyn Allen, Nov. 25, 1961; m. Varda Esther Peller, Jan. 8. 1977; children: Benjamin, Brian, Emily. Ph.B., U. Chgo., 1947, S.B., 1948, S.M., 1950, Ph.D., 1956. Asst. examiner U. Chgo., 1949-50; jr. mathematician Inst. Air Weapons Research, Chgo., 1951-53; physicist Project Matterhorn, Princeton, N.J., 1957-58; asst. prof. math. M.I.T., 1958-60; assoc. prof. geophysics U. Calif.-San Diego, 1960-62, prof., 1962—. Research publs. in theoretical seismology, geomagnetism, plate tectonics, sci. inference, differential geometry and numerical analysis. Guggenheim fellow, 1963, 70; AEC grantee, 1954-57; NSF grantee, 1963-74, 83—. Fellow Am. Geophys. Union; mem. U.S. Nat. Acad. Scis., Am. Acad. Arts and Scis., Royal Astron. Soc., N.Y. Acad. Scis., Am. Math. Soc., Am. Phys. Soc. Current Work: Anisotrpic elasticity; electrical conductivity of earth's mantle; motion of earth's core; geomagnetic dynamo theory. Subspecialties: Geophysics; Planetary science. Office: IGPP U Calif-San Diego A-025 La Jolla CA 92093

BACKUS, JOHN, computer scientist; b. Phila., Dec. 3, 1924; s. Cecil Franklin and Elizabeth (Edsall) B.; m. Una Stannard, 1968; children: Karen, Paula. B.S., Columbia U., 1949, A.M., 1950 D.Univ. (hon.), U. York, Eng., 1985. Programmer IBM, N.Y.C., 1950-53, mgr. programming research, 1954-59; staff mem. IBM T.J. Watson Research Center, Yorktown Heights, N.Y., 1959-63; IBM fellow IBM Research, Yorktown Heights and San Jose, Calif., 1963—. Editorial bd.: Internat. Jour. Computer and Info. Scis. Served with AUS, 1943-46. Recipient W. Wallace McDowell award IEEE, 1967; Nat. medal of Sci., 1975; Harold Pender award Moore Sch. Elec. Engring., U. Pa., 1983; Achievement award Indsl. Research Inst., Inc., 1983. Mem. Nat. Acad. Engring., Nat. Acad. Scis., Am. Acad. Arts and Scis., Assn. Computing Machinery (Turing award 1977), Am. Math. Soc., European Assn. Theoretical Computer Sci. System designer IBM 704, Fortran programming lang., Backus-Naur Form Lang., function level programming; mem. design group ALGOL 60 lang. Current Work: Function level programming; algebra of programs; algebraic transformation and optimization; functional equations, combinatory foundations for programming. Subspecialties: Programming languages; Foundations of computer science. Home: 91 St Germain Ave San Francisco CA 94114 Office: Dept K51 Bldg 80 IBM Almaden Research Ctr 650 Harry Rd San Jose CA 95120

BACON, VINTON WALKER, civil engineer, educator; b. Estelline, S.D., Dec. 21, 1916; s. Ernest Vinton and Emma Omar (Edwards) B.; m. Margaret Ann Pratt, May 29, 1940; children—Robert Vinton, Kathryn Ann, Don Edwards, Vinton Walker. A.A., Los Angeles Jr. Coll., 1937; B.S. in Civil Engring, U. Calif., Berkeley, 1940. Diplomate: Am. Acad. Environ. Engrs. Engrs. East Bay City Sewage Disposal Survey, Berkeley, 1940-41; designer Los Angeles County Sanitation Dists., 1941-43, 46; office engr. Orange County Sewerage Survey, Santa Ana, Calif., 1946-49; exec. officer Calif. State Water Pollution Control Bd., Sacramento, 1950-56; exec. sec. N.W. Paper and Pulp Assn., Tacoma, 1956-62; gen. supt. Met. San. Dist. Greater Chgo., 1962-70; prof. civil engring. U. Wis., Milw., 1970-83, prof. emeritus, 1983—; cons. in field. Contbr. numerous papers to profl. jours. Chmn. Wis. Gov.'s Solid Waste Recycling Task Force, 1971-76; mem. Wis. Solid Waste Recycling Authority, 1974-76; mem. Milw. Met. Sewerage Commn., 1982—; chmn. U.S. sect. sci. adv. bd. Internat. Joint Commn., 1983—. Served with USPHS, 1943-46. Named Constrn. Man of Year Engring. News-Record, 1967; Recipient Silver Beaver award Boy Scouts Am., 1962; Gordon Maskew Fair award Am. Acad. Environ. Engrs., 1985. Fellow ASCE (awards 1956, 67), Inst. Water Resources (hon.), Am. Pub. Health Assn.; mem. Water Pollution Control Fedn., Am. Water Works Assn., Nat. Acad. Engrs. Originator deep tunnel project and land utilization of sewage sludge project Met. San. Dist. Greater Chgo., 1965. Current Work: Wastewater reclamation and reuse, sewage sludge application to enhance crop production, toxicology aspects of reuse of waters and sludge, socio economic aspects of points non point sources of wastes. Subspecialties: Civil engineering; Water supply and wastewater treatment. Home: 4634 N Wilshire Rd Milwaukee WI 53211

BADER, FREDRIC GEORGE, biochemical engineer; b. Muskegon, Mich., Sept. 29, 1947; s. John Julius and Elizabeth Jean (Scheide Mantel) B.; m. Ann Margaret Kane, Aug. 30, 1969; children—Fredric Robert, Ann Kathryn, Kathleen Marie. B.S. in Chem. Engring., U. Mich., 1969; Ph.D. in Chem. Engring., U. Minn., 1974. Asst. prof. U. Mich., Ann Arbor, 1974-77; scientist Upjohn Co., Kalamazoo, 1977-83; mgr. fermentation pilot plants Bristol-Meyers Co., Syracuse, N.Y., 1983—; DuPont prof., 1974; cons. Dow Chem. Co., Midland, Mich., 1975-77. Author: Microbial Population Dynamics I, 1981. Contbr. articles to profl. jours. Patentee in field. Pres. and founder O & A Marriage Encounter of Kalamazoo, 1982. Corp. fellow U. Minn., 1970. Mem. Am. Inst. Chem. Engrs., Am. Chem. Soc., Phi Lambda Upsilon, Tau Beta Pi. Republican. Roman Catholic. Current work: Fermentation, environmental effects on microbial physiology; sterilization; oxygen mass transport; mechanical mixing; modelling of microbial growth. Subspecialty: Microbiology. Home: 7502 Northfield Ln Manlius NY 13104 Office: Indsl Div Bristol-Meyers Co PO Box 4755 Syracuse NY 13221-4755

BADGER, THOMAS MARK, neuroendocrinologist, nutritionist, educator; b. Modesto, Calif., Mar. 21, 1945; s. Robert Albert and Valeria (Eaves) B.; m. Cheryl Ann Jordan, Aug. 26, 1967; 1 child, Mark. B.S., Calif. State U., 1968; M.S., U. Mo., 1970, Ph.D., 1973. Research assoc. U. Mo., Columbia, 1973-74; instr. Washington U., St. Louis, 1974-77; asst. prof. Harvard Med. Sch., Boston, 1977-82, assoc. prof., 1982—, dir. basic research Vincent Labs., Mass. Gen. Hosp., 1979—; mem. study section NIH, 1982-83; reviewer sci. pubs. Contbr. articles to profl. jours. Coach, youth baseball, soccer and basketball YMCA and City of Newton, 1979—; active PTA, Newton Lower Falls Improvement Assn. NIH fellow, 1968-70, 74-77. Mem. Am. Inst. Nutrition, Endocrine Soc., Soc. for Reprodn., Soc. Exptl. Biology and Medicine, Sigma Xi, Gamma Sigma Delta, Phi Lambda Upsilon. Current work: Research on neuroendocrinology of reproduction and growth, mechanisms of hormone and drug actions, mechanisms of nutrient interactions on hypothalmic and pituitary physiology. Subspecialties: Neuroendocrinology; Nutrition (medicine). Home: 31 Clearwater Rd Newton MA 02162 Office: Gynecology Dept Mass Gen Hosp 32 Fruit St Boston MA 02114

BAEDECKER, PHILIP ACKERMAN, analytical chemist, researcher; b. East Orange, N.J., Dec. 19, 1939; s. Harold John and Audrey Sarah (Ackerman) B.; m. Mary Josephine LaFuze, Jan. 2, 1966; 1 child, Cheryl Elise. B.S., Ohio U., 1961; M.S., U. Ky., 1964, Ph.D., 1967. Research assoc. Mass. Inst. Tech., Cambridge, 1967-68; asst. research chemist U. Calif., Los Angeles, 1968-73; research chemist U.S. Geol. Survey, Reston, Va., 1974-81, chief br. analytical chemistry, 1981—. Contbr. articles to profl. jours. Pres. Reston Community Players, Reston, 1978, Friends of the Reston Community Ctr., 1979. Fellow Haggin, 1963, Murrill, 1964, Tenn. Eastman, 1965, NSF, 1966. Mem. Am. Chem. Soc., AAAS, Meteoritical Soc., Sigma Xi. Current work: Studies concerning the chemical history of meteorites and lunar samples; neutron activation analysis applied to geochemical problems, computeranalysis of gamma-ray spectra, decay scheme studies. Subspecialties: Analytical chemistry; Geochemistry. Office: U S Geol Survey 12201 Sunrise Valley Dr Reston VA 22092

BAEN, SPENCER R., university research center administrator; b. San Antonio, Mar. 20, 1921; s. John Spencer and Grace (Roe) B.; m. Joyce Kirkland, July 25, 1944 (dec. 1982); children—Kay Baen Brooks, John Spencer II, Peter Roe, Steven Paul; m. Pauline Scott, B.S., Tex. A&M U., 1943; M.S.M.E., Calif. Inst. Tech., 1947, Ph.D., 1950. Registered profl. engr., Commd. 2d lt. U.S. Army, 1950, advanced through grades to col., with missile research and devel. program, 1950-59, missile, Pentagon, Washington, 1959-63, Shillelagh missile project mgr., Redstone Arsenal, Ala., 1965-68; asst. dir. Tex. Engring. Sptl. Sta., Tex. A&M U., 1970—, dir. Ctr. for Energy and Mineral Resources, 1978—; mem. Coal and Ligmite Adv. Council, Tex., 1979-83, Energy from Agr. Adv. Council, 1979-83. Mem. Arts Council of Brazos Valley, Bryan (Tex.), 1972-76; pres. Bryan-College Station Chamber Orch., 1973-78. Decorated Legion of Merit U.S. Army, Mem. Tex. Soc. Profl. Engrs. (bd. dirs. 1973-77), Nat. Assn. State Univs. and Land Grant Colls (energy and environ. com. 1980—), Sigma Xi, Tau Beta Pi, Pi Tau Sigma. Episcopalian. Lodge: Optimists. Current work: Coordinate and develop energy and mineral related programs in research teaching and public service - technology transfer.

Subspecialty: Research and development management. Office: Ctr for Energy and Mineral Resources Tex A&M U College Station TX 77843

BAER, ERIC, science educator; b. Nieder-Weisel, Germany, July 18, 1932; came to U.S., 1947, naturalized, 1952; s. Arthur and Erna (Kraemer) B.; m. Ana Golender, Aug. 5, 1956; children: Lisa, Michelle. M.A., Johns Hopkins, 1953, D.Engring., 1957. Research engr., polychems. dept. E.I. du Pont de Nemours & Co., Inc., 1957-60; asst. prof. chemistry and chem. engring. U. Ill., 1960-62; assoc. prof. engring. Case Inst. Tech., 1962- 66; prof., head dept. polymer sci. Case Western Res. U., 1966-78; dean Case Inst. Tech., 1978-83, Leonard Case prof. macromolecular sci., 1984—; cons. to industry, 1961—. Author articles in field.; Editor: Engineering Design for Plastics, 1963, Polymer Engineering and Science, 1967—. Recipient Curtis W. McGraw award ASEE, 1968. Mem. Am. Chem. Soc. (Borden award 1981), Am. Phys. Soc., Am. Inst. Chem. Engring., Soc. Plastics Engring. (internat. award 1980), Plastics Inst. Am. (trustee). Subspecialties: Polymer chemistry; Physical chemistry. Home: 2 Mornington Ln Cleveland Heights OH 44106 Office: Case Western Res Univ Cleveland OH 44106

BAER, THOMAS STRICKLAND, health and environmental safety executive; b. Huntington, W.Va., May 24, 1942; s. Peter Harrison and Virginia (Strickl) B.; m. Margaret Thresa Durkin, Nov. 21, 1964; children: Kathleen Nancy, Thomas Holman. B.S., U.S. Naval Acad., 1964; M.S., U. Cin., 1971, Ph.D., 1973. Sta. engr. Met. Edison Co., Middletown, Pa., 1973-74; v.p., gen. mgr. Protective Packaging Inc., Louisville, 1974-76; v.p. Nuclear Engring. Co., Louisville, 1976-81; project mgr. hazardous chem. waste dept. Bechtel Nat. Inc., Oak Ridge, 1981—. Cub scout leader Old Ky. Home council, Louisville, 1975-78, commr., 1978-81; scoutmaster Great Smokey Mountain council Boy Scouts Am., Knoxville, Tenn., 1981—. Served to lt. USN, 1964-69, Vietnam. Mem. Am. Nuclear Soc., Health Physics Soc., Scientists and Engrs. for Secure Energy, Am. Soc. Engring. Mgmt., Soc. Am. Mil. Engrs. Republican. Roman Catholic. Current Work: Development of methods and technique to safely dispose of hazardous materials. Subspecialties: Nuclear engineering; Environmental engineering. Home: 1004 High Springs Rd Knoxville TN 37922 Office: Bechtel Nat Inc Oak Ridge TN 37830

BAER, WALTER S., communications company executive; b. Chgo., July 27, 1937; s. Walter S. Jr. and Margaret S. (Mayer) B.; m. Miriam R. Schenker, June 18, 1959; children—David W., Alan B. B.S., Calif. Inst. Tech., 1959; Ph.D., U. Wis., 1964. Research physicist Bell Telephone Labs., Murray Hill, N.J., 1964-66; fellow White House, Washington, 1966-67, mem. sci. adv. staff, 1967-69; cons., sr. scientist RAND Corp., Santa Monica, Calif., 1970-81; dir. energy policy program, 1978-81; dir. advanced tech. Times Mirror Co., Los Angeles, 1981—; cons. in field; dir. Aspen Cable TV Workshop, Colo., 1972-73; mem. computer sci. and engring. bd. Nat. Acad. Scis., 1969-72; mem. cable TV adv. com. FCC, 1972-73; adv. council Aspen Program on Communications, 1974—. Author: Interactive Television, 1971; Cable Televison: A Handbook for Decisionmaking, 1973, also articles. Editor: The Electronic Box Office, 1974; wc/RAND Cable Television Series, 1974; editorial bd. Telecommunications Policy, 1976—. Visitor European Community, 1978; mem. corp. adv. bd. World Wildlife Fund; mem. adv. com. communications law program UCLA. Recipient award for excellence in teaching U. Wis., 1960; Preceptor award Broadcast Industry Conf., 1974; NSF fellow U. Wis. Fellow AAAS; mem. Am. Phys. Soc. (Congressional fellows selection com. 1976—), Internat. Inst. Communications, IEEE, Sigma Xi. Subspecialty: Telecommunications. Home: 560 Latimer Rd Santa Moinca CA 90402

BAES, CHARLES FREDERICK, JR., research chemist; b. Cleve., Dec. 2, 1924; s. Charles Frederick and Edna Irene Ridenaur; m. Julia R. Rodriguez, Jan. 9, 1948; children—Charles Frederick III, Linda Marie, Sandra Jean. B.S., Rutgers U., 1946; M.S., U. So. Calif., 1948, Ph.D., 1950; postgrad. Columbia U., N.Y.C., 1950-51. Research chemist Oak Ridge Nat. Lab., 1951—; vis. prof. chemistry William and Mary Coll., Williamsburg, Va., 1972-73. Author: Hydrolysis of Cations, 1976. Contbr. numerous articles to profl. jours. Current work: Separations chemistry, solution chemistry, environmental chemistry, research on solvent extraction, the CO2 problem, aquous solution chemistry. Subspecialties: Thermodynamics; Physical chemistry. Home: 102 Berwick Dr Oak Ridge TN 37830 Office: S216-4500S Oak Ridge Nat Lab PO Box X Oak Ridge TN 37831

BAETZOLD, ROGER CHARLES, research chemist; b. Warsaw, N.Y., Feb. 26, 1942; s. Maynard Charles and Mary Katharine (Tuttle) B.; m. Gail Frances Petz, Jan. 25, 1964; children—John, Edward, Anne, David. B.A., U. Buffalo, 1963; Ph.D., U. Rochester, 1966. Chemist Eastman Kodak Co., Rochester, N.Y., 1966—. Mem. Am. Chem. Soc., Am. Vacuum Soc. Current work: Theory of surface reactions, electronic structure calculations, metal clusters. Subspecialties: Catalysis chemistry; Theoretical chemistry. Office: Eastman Kodak Co Chemistry Div Lake Ave Rochester NY 14650

BAGBY, MARVIN ORVILLE, chemist; b. Macomb, Ill., Sept. 27, 1932; s. Byron Orville and Geneva Floriene (Filbert) B.; m. Mary Jean Jennings, Aug. 31, 1957; children—Gary Lee, Gordon Eugene. B.S., Western Ill. U., 1957, M.S., 1957. With USDA Agr. Research Service, No. Regional Research Ctr., Peoria, 1957—, research leader, 1974-80, mgr. Northern Agrl. Energy Ctr., 1980—; tchr. adviser USDA Sci. and Edn. Adminstrn., Washington, 1975-81, Council Great Lakes Govs., Madison, Wis., 1984; mem. Sec. Agr. Task Force on Critical Materials, 1984. Contbr. articles to profl. jours.; patentee in processing and use of agrl. materials. Served with AUS, 1953-55. Recipient Performance awards USDA, 1961, 81, Alumni Achievement award Western Ill. U., 1980. Fellow Am. Inst. Chemists; mem. Am. Chem. Soc., Am. Oil Chemists' Soc., AAAS, TAPPI, (sec. nonwood plant fibers com. 1976-82), N.Y. Acad. Sci., Am. Soc. Agrl. Engrs. Current work: Plant biomass for liquid fuels, chemicals, materials (vegetable oils cellulose, hemicellulose, lignin, whole plant oils, hydrocarbons, phenolics, fermentation substrate conversion, alternative crops for chemicals and materials). Subspecialty: Biomass (energy science and technology). Office: Northern Regional Research Ctr USDA 1815 N University St Northern Agrl Energy Ctr Peoria IL 61604

BAGLEY, BRIAN G., materials science researcher; b. Racine, Wis., Nov. 20, 1934; s. Wesley John and Ethel Sophie (Rasmussen) B.; m. Dorothy Elizabeth Olson, Nov. 20, 1959; children: Brian John, James David, Kristin Marie. B.S., U. Wis., 1958, M.S., 1959; A.M., Harvard U., 1964, Ph.D., 1968. Mem. tech. staff Bell Labs., Murray Hill, N.J., 1967—. Contbr. articles in field to profl. jours.; patentee in field. Served to lt. U.S. Army, 1960-61. Xerox predoctoral fellow Harvard U., 1964-66; R.J. Painter fellow, 1966-67. Mem. Am. Phys. Soc., Materials Research Soc. Lutheran. Current Work: Basic research in the physics and chemistry of amorphous materials, including preparation, characterization and applications in electronic and optical devices. Subspecialties: Electronic materials; Fiber optics. Home: 467 Ridge Rd Watchung NJ 07060 Office: Bell Labs Rm 1D-445 600 Mountain Ave Murray Hill NJ 07974

BAGLIO, JOSEPH ANTHONY, materials scientist; b. N.Y.C., May 16, 1937; s. Albert Salvatore and Theresa N. (Vilardi) B.; m. Helen Sylvia Peters; children—Frances, Christine. B.S., St. John's U., 1958; Ph.D., Rutgers U., 1965. Chemist, U.S. AEC, New Brunswick, N.J., 1958-60; asst. mem. tech. staff RCA Labs., Princeton, N.J., 1960-61; teaching asst., fellow Rutgers U., New Brunswick, 1961-65; prin. investigator GTE Labs., Waltham, Mass., 1965—. Contbr. articles to profl. jours. Patentee in field. Mem. Am. Chem. Soc., Electrochem. Soc., Sigma Xi (pres. chpt. 1984-85). Current work: Chemistry and physics of semiconductor surfaces, solid state materials synthesis and evaluation with emphasis on dielectrics for control and reduction of surface states on compound semiconductors. Subspecialties: Solid state chemistry; Electronic materials. Home: 8 Forest Hill Dr Andover MA 01810 Office: GTE Labs 40 Sylvan Rd Waltham MA 02254

BAGWELL, JOYCE MARIE BURRIS, geology-chemistry educator, researcher; b. Charleston, S.C., July 6, 1932; d. Chalmers Eugene and Jennie Louise (Hall) Burris; m. W. Howard Bagwell, June 12, 1954; children: W. Howard Jr., John Frederick. B.A., Furman U., Greenville, S.C., 1954; M.S., Clemson U., S.C., 1962. Tchr. Pendleton (S.C.) High Sch., 1954-55; tchr. sci. S.W. Daniel High Sch., Clemson, 1955-57, 58-60, McCants Jr. High Sch., Anderson, S.C., 1960-65; tchr. biology Anderson Jr. Coll., 1962-63; tchr. sci. 1st Baptist High Sch., Charleston, 1966-67; asst. prof. geology and chemistry Baptist Coll., Charleston, 1967—; prin. investigator lower S.C. mini-network U.S. Geol. Survey, 1976—. Contbr. articles to profl. jours. Mem. Eastern Seismological Soc. Am., Nat. Tchrs. Assn., S.C. Tchrs. Assn., Alpha Delta Kappa. Republican. Baptist. Current Work: Isoseismal studies of felt earthquakes in lower South Carolina; monitoring eleven station, thirty one channel seismic network in lower South Carolina; teaching chemistry and geology. Subspecialties: Geology; Seismology. Home: 127 Sycamore Dr Summerville SC 29483 Office: Dept Chemistry/Geology Baptist Coll PO Box 10087 Charleston SC 29411

BAHARY, WILLIAM SHAUL, chemist, researcher; b. Kermanshah, Iran, Jan. 20, 1936; came to U.S., 1951, naturalized, 1956; s. Shaul S. and Victoria (Menashi) B.; m. Susan C. Kurshan, Nov. 23, 1979. B.A., Harvard U., 1957; M.A., Columbia U., 1958, Ph.D., 1961. Sr. research chemist Tex.-U.S. Chem. Co., Parsippany, N.J., 1961-68; vis. asst. prof. Fairleigh Dickinson U., Teaneck, N.J., 1968-73; adj. asst. prof. Stevens Inst. Tech., Hoboken, N.J., 1973-79; supervising engr. Duracell, Inc., Tarrytown, N.Y., 1979—; treas. Bahary & Co., Pearl River, N.Y., 1960—. Contbr. articles to profl. jours. Patentee in field. Mem. Am. Chem. Soc., AAAS, Hudson-Bergen Chem. Soc. (div. program dir. 1975-79). Democrat. Jewish. Club: Harvard (N.Y.). Current work: Research and development work on batteries, especially polymer and biopolymer applications in electrochemical cells. Subspecialties: Electrochemistry; Polymer chemistry. Home: 325 E 79th St New York NY 10021 Office: Duracell Inc S Broadway Tarrytown NY 10591

BAHE, LOWELL WARREN, chemistry educator, researcher; b. Sycamore, Ill., Jan. 30, 1927; s. Herman William and Myra May (Snow) B.; m. Virginia Ruth Peterson, June 12, 1954 (div.); children: Margaret, Laurel, Ellen. B.S., Purdue U., 1949; M.A., Princeton U., 1951, Ph.D., 1953. Research chemist Allis Chalmers Mfg. Co., West Allis, Wis., 1953-57; asst. prof., then assoc. prof., prof. chemistry U. Wis., Milw., 1957—. Contbr. articles on chemistry to profl. jours. Served with USN, 1945-46. Mem. Am. Chem. Soc., Wis., Acad. Arts, Letters and Sci., Sigma Xi. Unitarian. Current Work: Electrolyte solutions, dielectric constants, research on behavior of ions in media with high dielectric constants. Subspecialties: Physical chemistry; Thermodynamics. Home: 2106 E Newton Blvd Shorewood WI 53211 Office: Chemistry Dept U Wis Milwaukee WI 53201

BAHNER, CARL TABB, chemist, educator; b. Conway, Ark., July 14, 1908; s. Gustavus Lonsford and Augusta Thomas (Moore) B.; m. Mary Catharine Garrott, Sept. 17, 1931; children: Thomas Maxfield, Mary Catharine, Frances Jane. A.B., Hendrix Coll., 1927; M.S., U. Chgo., 1928; Th.M., So. Bapt. Theol. Sem., 1931; postgrad., Yale U., 1931-32; Ph.D., Columbia U., 1937. Head physics dept. Union U., 1936-37; head chemistry dept., prof. Carson-Newman Coll., Jefferson City, Tenn., 1937-67, research coordinator, 1967-73; assoc. prof. Walters State Community Coll., Morristown, Tenn., 1973-78; prof. chemistry Bluefield (Va.) Coll., 1979—; cons. TVA, 1941-45; med. div. Oak Ridge Inst. Nuclear Studies, 1950-56, Oak Ridge Nat. Labs., 1948-80; head natural sci unit, test devel. sect. U.S. Civil Service, 1945; sr. research chemist Roswell Park Meml. Hosp., 1956; research chemist Chester Beatty Research Inst., 1957. Contbr. articles to profl. jours. Chmn. Charter Revision Com., City of Jefferson City, 1978-79. Recipient Fla. award Fla. sect. Am. Chem. Soc., 1964; award for excellence in chemistry teaching Mfg. Chemists Assn., 1967; Hendrix Coll. Disting. Alumnus award, 1969; Algernon Sydney award, 1969; Disting. Service award Walters State Community Coll., 1978. Fellow AAAS, Am. Inst. Chemists, Tenn. Acad. Sci. (pres. 1951); mem. Am. Assn. Cancer Research, AAUP, Am. Chem. Soc. (chmn. E. Tenn. sect. 1951), Tenn. Inst. Chemists (pres. 1972-73), W.Va. Acad. Sci., Sigma Xi, Alpha Chi, Phi Lambda Upsilon, Sigma Pi Sigma. Patentee in field. Current Work: Cancer chemotherapy, carcinogenesis, structure activity relations; radiation effects on organic compounds. Subspecialties: Organic chemistry; Chemotherapy. Home: PO Box 549 Jefferson City TN 37760 Office: Bluefield Coll Bluefield VA 24605

BAI, TAEIL, astrophysicist; b. Jeonnam, Korea, July 16, 1945; came to U.S., 1972; s. Jong-hun and Soo-bong (Suh) B.; m. Suin Kim; children: Samuel, Jean, Helen. B.S., Kyung Hee U., Seoul, Korea, 1967; Ph.D., U. Md., 1977. Research assoc. U. Md., 1977-78; postgrad. research physicist U. Calif.-San Diego, 1978-80; asst. research physicist U. San Diego, 1980-82; sr. research assoc. Stanford U., Calif., 1982—. Contbr. articles to profl. jours. Served with Korean Army, 1967-69. Recipient Donald E. Billings award in astrogeophysics U. Colo., Boulder, 1978. Mem. Am. Phys. Soc., Am. Astron. Soc. Current Work: High energy phenomena in solar flares; x-ray astronomy. Subspecialty: Solar physics. Office: Inst Plasma Research Stanford U Stanford CA 94305

BAILEY, ALFRED WILLIAM, veterinarian; b. Lamont, Wash., Sept. 1, 1935; s. Fred and Ila May (Schuster-Curtis) B.; m. Patricia Catherine Seals, Dec. 27, 1960; children—Barbara Ellen, Bryan David. D.V.M., Wash. State U., 1960; M.P.H., U. Okla.-Norman, 1982. Registered profl. sanitarian, Okla. Veterinarian, Anacortes, Wash., 1963, Lynnwood, Wash., 1964; veterinary med. officer U.S. Dept. Agr., Ellensburg, Wash., 1964-70, Phoenix, 1970-72, Salem, Oreg., 1972-75, state program dir., Oklahoma City, 1975—. Mem. Assn. Children with Learning Disabilities, 1976—. Mem. AVMA, Okla. Veterinary Med. Assn., So. States Animal Health Assn., Can. Veterinary Med. Assn., B.C. Veterinary Med. Assn., U.S. Animal Health Assn. (mem. com. on pub. health and environ. quality 1980—). Lodge: Order Eastern Star. Current work: Veterinary public health and preventive medicine; meat and poultry inspection; regulatory involvement with antibiotic and pesticide residues. Subspecialties: Preventive medicine (veterinary medicine); Food science and technology. Home: 10200 Ski Dr Oklahoma City OK 73132 Office: Okla Dept Agr 2800 N Lincoln Blvd Oklahoma City OK 73132

BAILEY, FREDERICK EUGENE, JR., polymer scientist; b. Bklyn., Oct. 8, 1927; s. Frederick Eugene and Florence (Berkeley) B.; m. Mary Catherine Lowder, May 7, 1979. B.A., Amherst Coll., 1948; M.S., Yale U., 1950; Ph.D., 1952. Sr. chemist Union Carbide Research Devel., 1952-59, group leader, 1959-62, asst. dir., 1962-69, mgr. mktg. research, N.Y.C., 1969-71, sr. research scientist, South Charleston, W.VA., 1971—; adj. prof. chemistry Marshall U., Huntington, W.Va., 1975—; adj. prof. chem. engring. W.Va. Coll. Grad. Studies, 1981—; lectr. polymer chemistry U. Charleston, Morris Harvey Coll., 1962-63, 65; mem. grad. faculty W.Va. U., 1959-61; chmn. Gordon Research Conf. on Polymers, W. Coast, 1972, N.H., 1984; mem. Gordon Research Conf. Council. Author: Polyethylene Oxide, 1976; editor: Initiation of Polymerization, 1983; (with K.N. Edwards) Urethane Chemistry and Applications, 1981. Addison Brown scholar Amherst Coll., 1948; Forrest Jewett Moore fellow, 1949. Fellow AAAS, Am. Inst. Chemists (cert. chemist), N.Y. Acad. Scis.; mem. Am. Chem. Soc. (chmn. divisional officer caucus 1980-85, chmn. div. polymer chemistry 1976, councilor div. 1978—, com. sci. 1978, 82-83, gen. sec. Macromolecular secretariat 1978, Top Dog award 1983). Republican. Episcopalian. Clubs: Williams (N.Y.C.); Tennis (Charleston, W.Va.). Patentee in field. Current Work: Synthesis and characterization of high polymer systems and market applications of such systems, current emphasis on polyurethane materials. Subspecialties: Polymer chemistry; Polymer physics. Home: 848 Beaumont Rd Charleston WV 25314 Office: Union Carbide Corp Tech Center South Charleston WV 25303

BAILEY, JAKE S., elec. engr.; b. Middlesboro, Ky., Dec. 29, 1927; s. Charles Wise and Mary Elizabeth (Nice) B.; m. Barbara Jean McClelland, Sept. 11, 1947; children: Linda Heguy, Mimi McDonough, Alan. B.S., U. Ala., 1949; postgrad., U. Minn., 1954. Registered profl. engr., N.Y., N.J., Pa., Del., Md., Fla., Kans. Substa. design engr. Memphis Light Gas and Water, 1949-52; project electronics engr. Boeing Corp., Wichita, Kans., 1952-54; autopilot design engr. Honeywell Aero., Mpls., 1954-58; electronics design supr. Link/Singer, Binghamton, N.Y., 1958-60; Mgr. exptl. methods Gen. Electric Aerospace, Phila., 1960-69; pres. B&G Corp., Valley Forge, Pa., 1969-74; elec. engring. cons., Phoenixville, Pa., 1974-81; mgr. elec. engring. ADCI, Milan, Italy, 1981; chief elec. engr. Haines, Lundbere Waehler, N.Y.C., 1981—. Served with USNR. Sr. mem. IEEE; Mem. Illumination Engrs. Soc., Aircraft Owners and Pilots Assn. Current Work: Electrical design, control design, energy studies. Subspecialties: Electrical engineering; Electronics. Office: 2 Park Ave New York NY 10016

BAILEY, LEONARD LEE, thoracic surgeon, educator; b. Takoma Park, Md., 1942. M.D., Loma Linda U., Sch. Medicine, 1969. Intern Loma Linda U. Med. Ctr., Calif., 1969-70, researcher in gen. surgery, 1970-73, researcher in thoracic and cardiovascular surgery, 1973-74, dir. pediatric cardiac surgery, asst. prof. surgery, 1975—; researcher in cardiovascular surgery Hosp. for Sick Children, Toronto, Ont., Can., 1974-75. Subspecialties: Cardiac surgery; Transplant surgery. Office: Loma Linda Med Ctr Dept Surgery Loma Linda CA 92350

BAILEY, STUART LOHR, project engineer; b. Harper, Kans., Apr. 1, 1927; s. Vernon A. and Esther Rhea (Goodnight) B.; m. Anita Jo Bean, Feb. 22, 1927; children: Michael, Patti. Student, Okla. State U., 1946-48. Draftsman O.E.M. Mfg. Co., Houston, 1948-56, supr., 1956-65, design engr., 1965-67, sr. engr., 1967-79, sr. test. engr., 1979-81, project engr., 1981—. Mem ASME. Republican. Patentee valves; single acting piston. Current Work: Development of oil field drilling equipment; create, develop, test, prodn. specifications, quality assurance, manufacturing trouble shooting, performance analysis. Subspecialties: Mechanical engineering; Materials (engineering). Home: 15215 Moss Way San Antonio TX 78232 Office: 6110 Rittiman Rd San Antonio TX 78218

BAILEY, WILLIAM F., chemist, educator, researcher; b. N.J., Dec. 8, 1946. B.S., St. Peters Coll., 1968; Ph.D., U. Notre Dame, 1973. Postdoctoral assoc. U. N.C., 1973, Yale U., 1974-75; asst. prof. chemistry U. Conn., 1975-80, assoc. prof., 1980—; cons. in field. Contbr. numerous articles, abstracts to profl. publs. Mem. Am. Chem. Soc. Current Work: Molecular structure and energetics; Carbon-13 nuclear magnetic resonance; conformational analysis; chemistry of group I organometalics; wear behavior of dental restoratives. Subspecialties: Organic chemistry; Nuclear magnetic resonance.

BAILEY, WILLIAM JAMES, public health educator, drug abuse prevention consultant; b. Gary, Ind., Nov. 5, 1947; s. William Arthur and Alice Jeanne (Tittle) B. B.S., Ind. U., 1976, M.S., 1977, M.P.H., 1979, postgrad., 1979-83. Drug abuse cons., Bloomington, Ind., 1974-80, coordinator risk reduction project, lectr. pub. health, 1980—. Author: Drug Use In American Society, 1981; editor: periodical Bibliog. Index of Health Edn. Periodicals, 1981—. Pub. edn. chmn. Am. Cancer Soc.-Monore County, Bloomington, 1981—. Mem. Am. Pub. Health Assn., Assn. for Ednl. Communication and Tech., Eta Sigma Gamma. Republican. Roman Catholic. Current Work: Research in prevention of drug abuse particularly in university students and adolescents, including multivariate causation models of drug problems (tobacco, alcohol, illicit drugs); development of automated information retrieval systems in health education. Subspecialties: Preventive medicine; Information systems (Information science). Home: Apt 2-T 800 N Smith Rd Bloomington IN 47401 Office: Ind U Dept Health Edn HPER Bldg Room 116 Bloomington IN 47405

BAINBRIDGE, KENNETH TOMPKINS, physicist, educator; b. Cooperstown, N.Y., July 27, 1904; s. William Warin and Mae (Tompkins) B.; m. Margaret Pitkin, Sept. 8, 1931 (dec. 1967); children: Martin Keeler, Joan, Margaret Tompkins; m. Helen Brinkley King, Oct. 11, 1969. S.B., Mass. Inst. Tech., 1926, S.M., 1926; M.A., Princeton, 1927, Ph.D., 1929; M.A. (hon.), Harvard, 1942. Physicist, 1928-29; Nat. Research Council fellow Bartol Research Found., 1929-31, Bartol Research Found. fellow, 1931-33; Guggenheim Meml. Found. fellow at Cavendish Lab., Cambridge, Eng., 1933-34; asst. prof. physics Harvard, 1934-38, asso. prof., 1938-46, prof., 1946—, chmn. dept. physics, 1953-55, George Vasmer Leverett prof. physics, 1961-75, emeritus, 1975—, now design cons. linear direct current motors; tech. cons. Nat. Def. Research Council, 1940-44, M.I.T. Radiation Lab., 1940-43, Los Alamos Lab., 1943-45; dir. Alamogordo Atomic Bomb Test, Feb.-Sept. 1945. Contbr.: tech. articles to Jour. of Franklin Inst. Trustee Asso. Univs., Inc., 1957-59; Mem. 7th Solvay Chemistry Congress, 1947. Awarded Louis Edward Levy medal Franklin Inst., 1933; Presdl. certificate of merit for work on radar, 1948. Mem. Am. Phys. Soc., Nat. Acad. Scis., Am. Acad. Arts and Scis., Alpha Tau Omega, Tau Beta Pi. Holder of patents on photo electric cells, electronic multiplier and electro magnetic pumps. Current Work: Linear D.C. motors. Subspecialties: Nuclear physics; Applied magnetics. Address: 5 Nobscot Rd Weston MA 02193

BAIR, SCOTT SLAYBAUGH, III, research mechanical engineer; b. Balt., Apr. 17, 1950; s. Scott Slaybaugh and Joan Patricia (Matthews) B.; m. Lynn Broom, Jan. 23, 1971; children: Christianne, Carribeth, Brennan. B.S. in Mech. Engring, Ga. Tech. Inst., 1972, M.S., 1974. Research engr. Ga. Inst. Tech., Atlanta, 1974—. Contbr. articles to profl. jours. Mem. ASME. Patentee in field. Current Work: Tribology, high pressure rheology. Subspecialties: Mechanical engineering; Fluid mechanics. Home: 1603 Trentwood Pl Atlanta GA 30319 Office: Dept Mech Engring Ga Inst Tech Atlanta GA 30332

BAIRD, HENRY WELLES, III, pediatric neurologist; b. Fort Leavenworth, Kans., Oct. 10, 1922; s. Henry Welles and Elizabeth (Tower) B.; m. Eleanora C. Gordon, Apr. 21, 1950; children: Henry Welles IV, Douglas G., Bruce C., Matthew C. B.S., Yale U., 1945, M.D., 1949. Fellow, resident neurology and pediatrics Temple U. Sch. Medicine, Phila., 1950-53, faculty pediatrics, 1953-84, assoc. prof., 1963-68, prof. pediatrics, 1968—, practice medicine specializing in pediatric neurology, Phila., 1953—; attending pediatrician St. Christopher's Hosp. for Children, Phila., 1966-84. Author: The Child with Convulsions, 1972, Neurologic Evaluation of Infants and Children, 1983; Mem. editorial bd.: Devel. Medicine and Child Neurology, 1971—, editor, 1977—; contbr. articles to profl. jours. Served to capt. M.C. AUS, 1950-56. Mem. Soc. Pediatric Research, Am. Acad. Pediatrics, Am. Acad. Cerebral Palsy. Current Work: Research in pediatric neurology, convulsive disorders, electro-encephalography and evoked cortical responses. Subspecialties: Pediatrics; Neurophysiology. Office: 5A Netherhall Gardens London NW3 5RN England*

BAIRD, RICHARD WILLIAM, photolithography engineer; b. Lockport, N.Y., Oct. 29, 1953; s. William George and Jane Elizabeth (Kelly) B. B.S. in Chemistry, Calif. Inst. Tech., 1976; S.M. in Chem. Engring., MIT, 1979. Research asst. MIT, Cambridge, Mass., 1979-82; process engr. Monolithic Memories, Inc., Sunnyvale, Calif., 1982-84; photolithography engr. solid state div. Varian Assocs., Santa Clara, Calif., 1984-85, Avantek, Inc., Santa Clara, 1985—. Patentee in field. Mem. Soc. Photo-Optical Instrumentation Engrs., Am. Astron. Soc., L-5 Soc. (sec. Silicon Valley chpt. 1984—). Current work: Novel photolithographic techniques for submicron image geometries, dry process techniques (plasma, etc.) for semiconductors. Subspecialty: Microchip technology (materials science). Home: 1271 Vicente Dr #177 Sunnyvale CA 94086 Office: Avantek Inc 3175 Bowers Ave Santa Clara CA 95054

BAIREY, MILES HUXTABLE, veterinarian, laboratory administrator; b. Sioux Falls, S.D., Apr. 30, 1934; s. Guy H. and Mary Annabelle (Huxtable) B.; m. Janice Lee Smith, Jan. 8, 1956; children—Michael, Mark, Melody, Monica, Jason. A.Agr., S.D. State Coll., 1954; B.S., U. Minn., 1959, D.V.M., 1961; M.S., Mont. State U., 1968. Owner Highmore Vet. Service, S.D., 1961-65; inspecting veterinarian U.S. Dept. Agr., Ames, Iowa, 1965-68, lab. sect. head Nat. Vet. Services Lab., 1969-79, lab. chief, 1979—. Pres. Highmore Booster Club, 1961-65; active Luth. Ch. Council, Highmore, 1962-65, Meml. Luth. Ch. Council, Nevada, Iowa, 1972-74; pres. Nevada Community Sch. Dist., 1979-84. Recipient Merit award Vet. Services, 1971, 74, Outstanding Rating award, 1972; cert. of Appreciation Animal and Plant Health Inspection Service, 1978; Merit award Avian Influenza Task Force, 1984. Mem. AVMA, Nat. Assn. Fed. Veterinarians (bd. dirs. 1971-75, regional rep. 1975-79), Am. Assn. Microbiologists, Phi Zeta. Lutheran. Club: Kiwanis (v.p. 1964-65). Current work: Veterinary biologic bacterial test development-pasteurella salmonella, brucella, mycobacterium. Subspecialty: Microbiology (veterinary medicine). Home: RR 1 Nevada IA 50201 Office: Nat Vet Services Lab PO Box 844 Ames IA 50010

BAISE, WALKER NATHAN, loss prevention executive; b. Tampa, Fla., Apr. 11, 1931; s. Walker Nathan Baise and Lucille (Fountain) Baise Smith; m. Sandra Louise Rogers, Mar. 26, 1983. B.S. in Geology, U. Fla., 1957; postgrad. Calif. State U.-Fullerton, 1963-64. Geophysicist Continental Oil Co., Ponca City, Okla., 1957-63; engr. Rockwell Internat., Fullerton, Calif., 1963-69; cons. Marsh & McLennan, N.Y.C., 1970-83; pres. Loss Prevention Services, El Paso, 1983—; fin. officer energy and environ. com. N.Y. Bd. Trade, N.Y.C., 1976-77. Served with U.S. Army, 1951-54, Korea. Mem. Soc. Exploration Geophysicists, Am. Geol. Soc., El Paso Indsl. Safety Council, El Paso County Hist. Soc. Republican. Lodge: Elks. Subspecialties: Human factors engineering; Information systems (Information science). Office: Loss Prevention Services 6221 Palo Alto Ave El Paso TX 79912

BAJPAI, SHYAM N, electrical engineering educator; b. Kakor Buzurg, Uttar Pradesh, India, Oct. 15, 1947; came to U.S., 1981; s. Chandrika Prasad and Ram (Beti) Bajpai; m. Mira Devi, May 11, 1971; children—Vivek, Vipul. B.S., Kanpur U., India, 1967; M.S., Agra U., India, 1970; Ph.D., Indian Inst. Tech., New Delhi, 1980. Asst. prof. Kanpur U. Christ Ch. Coll., 1971-81, SUNY-Stony Brook, 1983—; teacher fellow Indian Inst. Tech., 1977-80; sr. engr. Westinghouse Research and Devel. Ctr., Pitts., 1981-82; vis. assoc. prof. U. Tex., 1983. Contbr. articles to profl. publs. Recipient Invention award Westinghouse Electric Corp., 1984; Univ. Grants Commn. (India) fellow,

1977-80; Bursary scholar, 1966-67; Govt. Uttar Pradesh scholar, 1965-66, 61-65. Mem. IEEE (sr.), Indian Assn. Physics Tchrs. (nat. steering com.), IEEE Magnetic Soc., IEEE MTT Soc. Current work: Working on novel emerging magnetostatic wave technology applicable directly at microwave frequencies; magnetostatic wave devices that are potentially useful in microwave communication and radar systems and broad band phased array antennas. Subspecialties: Applied magnetics; Microelectronics. Home: 44-92-A Piedmont Dr Port Jefferson Station New York NY 11776 Office: Dept Elec Engring SUNY Stony Brook NY 11794

BAK, DAVID ARTHUR, chemist; b. Yankton, S.D., Feb. 6, 1939; s. Arthur E. and Helen E. (Munkvold) B.; m. Rita Mae Bak, Nov. 29, 1964 (div.); children: John David, Mikkle DeWayne. B..A., Augustana Coll., 1961; Ph.D., Kans. State U., 1965. Teaching Asst. Kans. State U., Manhattan, 1961-62, research asst., 1962-65; research assoc. Mich. State U., 1965-66; vis. prof. chemistry N. Tex. State U., Denton, 1977-78; asst. prof. chemistry Hartwick Coll., Oneonta, N.Y., 1966-71, assoc. prof., 1971-77, prof., 1977—, chmn. dept., 1974-85, chmn. div. phys. and life scis., 1976-77. Commr., merit badge counselor Boy Scouts Am., 1976—; trustee, com. faculty rep., Hartwick Coll., 1972, 74, 82. Served with U.S. Army, 1957-60. Mem. Am. Chem. Soc., Sigma Xi, Phi Lambda Upsilon. Current Work: Organic synthetic electrochemistry, intramolecular nonconjugated pi electron interactions. Subspecialty: Organic chemistry. Home: 109 Clinton St A Oneonta NY 13820 Office: Hartwick Coll Oneonta NY 13820

BAK, MARTIN JOSEPH, electronics engineer; b. Washington, Apr. 15, 1947; s. Anthony F. and Irene L. (Hutton) B.; m. Tina Mauree Bak, Apr. 11, 1949; children: Mauree, E., H., Cheryl I. H., Brian H. B.S.E.E., U. Md. Electronics test technician Electronics for Life Scis. Inc., Rockville, Md., 1964-69; electronics engr. Nat. Inst. Neurol. and Communicative Disorders and Stroke, Lab. Neural Control, NIH, Bethesda, MD., 1970—; also cons. Contbr. articles to profl. jours. Patentee in field. Served with USAR, 1969-75. Mem. Soc. Neurosci., IEEE, AAAS. Current Work: Design of instrumentation for acquisition and processing of neurological signals. Design of chronically implantable electrodes for long-term recording and stimulation of neural tissue. Subspecialties: Electronics; Biomedical engineering. Office: Bldg 36 Room 5A-29 Bethesda MD 20205

BAKER, DALE B, information service administrator; b. Bucyrus, Ohio, Sept. 19, 1920; m. 1947; 3 children. B.S. in Chem. Engring., Ohio State U., 1942, M.S., 1948. Chemist supr. E.I. DuPont de Nemours and Co., 1942-45, asst. editor, 1946-50, assoc. editor, 1951-57; dir. Chem. Abstracts Service, Columbus, Ohio, 1958-83, dep. exec. dir., 1983—. Recipient Merit award Am. Soc. Info. Sci., 1983, Patterson Crane award Am. Chem. Soc. Subspecialty: Information systems (Information science). Office: Chem Abstracts Service PO Box 3012 Columbus OH 43210

BAKER, DANIEL CLIFTON, surgery educator; b. N.Y.C., Dec. 11, 1942; s. Daniel Clifton and Geraldine Elizabeth (Dieck) B.; m. Mary Bradwell Conley, Feb. 9, 1974; children: Daniel Clifton IV, John Conley. A.B., Columbia U., 1964, M.D., 1968. Asst. prof. plastic surgery NYU Med. Sch., 1979-84, assoc. prof., 1984—; cons. in field. Editor: Facial Paralysis, 1979, Symposium on Rhinoplasty, 1983. Served to maj. U.S. Army, 1970-72, Vietnam. Recipient alumni achievement award Farleigh Dickinson U., 1980. Mem. N.Y. County Med. Soc., Am. Soc. Plastic and Reconstructive Surgeons, Internat. Soc. Reconstructive Microsurgery, Am. Soc. Aesthetic Plastic Surgery (best. sci. presentation 1979). Clubs: N.Y. Athletic; Meadow (Southampton, N.Y.). Current Work: Primary interest and specialization in plastic and reconstructive surgery of the face and neck, reconstructive surgery and microsurgery following trauma and cancer. Subspecialties: Surgery; Microsurgery. Home: 630 Park Ave New York NY 10021 Office: Inst Reconstructive Plastic Surgery 550 1st Ave New York NY 10016

BAKER, DONALD JAMES, oceanographer, businessman; b. Long Beach, Calif., Mar. 23, 1937; s. Donald James and Lillian Mae (Pund) B.; m. Emily Lind Delman, Sept. 7, 1968. B.S., Stanford U., 1958; Ph.D., Cornell U., 1962. Postdoctoral fellow Grad. Sch. Oceanography, U. R.I., Kingston, 1962-63; NIH fellow in chem. biodynamics Lawrence Radiation Lab., U. Calif., Berkeley, 1963-64; research fellow, asst. prof., assoc. prof. phys. oceanography Harvard U., 1964-73; research prof. dept. oceanography, sr. oceanographer, applied physics lab. U. Wash., Seattle, 1973-77; sr. fellow Joint Inst. for Study Atmosphere and Ocean, 1977—, prof., dept. oceanography, 1979—, chmn. dept. oceanography, 1979-81; dean Coll. Ocean and Fishery Scis., 1981-83; disting. vis. scientist Jet Propulsion Lab., Calif. Inst. Tech., Pasadena, 1982—; group leader deep-sea physics group Pacific Marine Environ. Lab., NOAA, Seattle, 1977-79; co-chmn. exec. com. Internat. So. Ocean Studies (NSF project), 1974-84; bd. govs. Joint Oceanographic Instns., Inc., 1979—, pres., 1983—; vice-chmn. joint panel, global weather experiment Nat. Acad. Scis., 1976-81, mem. ocean scis. bd., ocean scis. policy bd., ocean studies bd., 1979—, mem. com. on atmospheric scis., 1978-81, mem. climate research com., 1979—; mem. space and earth sci. adv. com. NASA, 1982—; mem. environ. panel Navy Research Adv. Com., 1983—. Co-editor in chief: Dynamics of Atmospheres and Oceans Jour, 1975-79; Contbr. sci. articles to profl. jours. Fellow Explorers Club; mem. Am. Geophys. Union, Am. Meteorol. Soc. (council 1982—), Sigma Xi. Patentee deep-sea pressure gauge. Current Work: General ocean circulation, air-sea interaction in polar regions, ocean instrumentation, ocean measurements from satellites, research management. Subspecialties: Oceanography; Remote sensing (geoscience). Office: Joint Oceanographic Instns Inc 1755 Massachusetts Ave NW Washington DC 20036

BAKER, HERBERT GEORGE, botany educator; b. Brighton, Eng., Feb. 23, 1920; came to U.S., 1957; s. Herbert Reginald and Alice (Bambridge) B.; m. Irene Williams, Apr. 4, 1945; 1 child, Ruth Elaine. B.S., U. London, 1941, Ph.D., 1945. Research chemist, asst. plant physiologist Hosa Research Labs., Sunbury-on-Thames, Eng., 1940-45; lectr. botany U. Leeds, Eng., 1945-54; research fellow Carnegie Instn., Washington, 1948-49; prof. botany U. Coll. Ghana, 1954-57; faculty U. Calif., Berkeley, 1957—, assoc. prof. botany, 1957-60, prof., 1960—, dir. bot. garden, 1957-69. Author: Plants and Civilization, 1965, 70, 78; Editor: (with G.L. Stebbins) Genetics of Colonizing Species, 1965; series editor: Bot. Monographs, 1971—; Contbr. articles to sci. jours. Fellow AAAS (pres. Pacific div.), Assn. Tropical Biology; mem. Am. Inst. Biol. Sci., Am. Acad. Arts and Sci., Ecol. Soc. Am., Soc. for Study Evolution (past pres.), Bot. Soc. Am. (past pres.), Sigma Xi. Current Work: Reproductive biology of plants (pollination biology, breeding systems, population structure) especially of tropical species. Evolution and ecology of plants under human influence, particularly weeds. Chemistry of nectar and pollen. Subspecialties: Evolutionary biology; Ecology (environmental science). Home: 635 Creston Rd Berkeley CA 94708

BAKER, HERMAN, vitaminologist, nutritionist, educator; b. N.Y.C., Jan. 22, 1926; s. Harry and Fannie (Becker) B.; m. Shirley Levitz, Nov. 15, 1952; children—Elliott, Joel. B.S., CCNY, 1946; M.S., Emory U., 1948; Ph.D., NYU, 1956. Cert. specialist in human nutrition Am. Bd. Nutrition. Research fellow Columbia U., N.Y.C, 1948-50; research assoc. Mt. Sinai Hosp., N.Y.C., 1950-60; assoc. prof. medicine N.J. Med. Sch., Newark, 1960-70, prof., 1970—, dir. vitamin labs., 1960—, dir. nutrition, 1970—. Author: Clinical Vitaminology, 1968; also numerous articles on clin. nutrition, 1950—. Fellow Am. Coll. Nutrition, Interat. Acad. Preventive Medicine (hon.); mem. Am. Soc. Clin. Nutrition, Soc. Exptl. Biology and Medicine. Current work: Relationships of vitamin metabolism in human health and disease. Subspecialties: Nutrition (medicine); Health services research. Home: 27 Wilk Rd Edison NJ 08837 Office: NJ Med Sch 100 Bergen St Newark NJ 07103

BAKER, IRENE, research botanist; b. Tredegar, Gwent, Wales, Feb. 22, 1918; d. William John and Mary Jane (Jones) Williams; m. Herbert George Baker, Apr. 4, 1945; 1 dau., Ruth Elaine. B.Sc. with honors, U. Wales, 1940, diploma in edn, 1941. Lectr. in biology Leeds Tech. Coll., Eng., 1945; research asst. zoology U. Leeds, 1945-48; research assoc. Govt. of Tsetse Control, Ghana, 1954-57; asst., then lectr. biology Mills Coll., 1958-69; research assoc. botany U. Calif.-Berkeley, 1974—. Contbr. articles sci. jours., chpts. in books. Mem. Bot. Soc. Am., Soc. Woman Geographers, Biosystematists, Sigma Xi. Current Work: Pollination biology and chemistry of flower products. Subspecialty: Reproductive biology. Home: 635 Creston Rd Berkeley CA 94708 Office: Botany Dept U Calif Berkeley CA 94720

BAKER, LAURENCE HOWARD, osteopathic internist, educator; b. Bklyn., Jan. 14, 1943; s. Jacob and Sylvia (Tannenbaum) B.; m. Maxine V. Friedman, July 25, 1964; children: Mindy, Jennifer. B.A., Bklyn. Coll., 1962; D.O., U. Osteopathic Medicine and Surgery-Des Moines, 1966. Intern Flint (Mich.) Osteo. Hosp., 1966-67; resident in internal Medicine Detroit Osteo. Hosp., 1967-68; mem. faculty Wayne State U., Detroit, 1972—, prof. internal medicine, 1979—, chief oncology div. Med. Center, 1982—; coordinator cancer program, 1981—; dep. dir. Comprehensive Cancer Center, Detroit, 1981—. Editor: New Agents and Pharmacology Soft Tissue Sarcomas, 1983. Assoc. chmn. S.W. Oncology Group, San Antonio, 1981—; chmn. Intergroup Sarcoma Study Group, Detroit, 1982—. Served to maj. U.S. Army, 1968-70, Viet Nam War. Mem. Am. Soc. Cancer Research, Am. Soc. Clin. Oncology, Am. Soc. Clin. Pharmacology and Therapeutics, Am. Soc. Clin. Research; Am. Soc. Cancer Edn. . Current Work: Anticancer drug development. Subspecialties: Cancer research (medicine); Chemotherapy. Office: Wayne State Univ Univ Health Center 4201 Saint Antoine St 7C Detroit MI 48201

BAKER, PAUL MANUEL AVILES, land use and development planner, consultant; b. Washington, Sept. 2, 1955; s. Bruce Arnold and Dolores Joyce (Aviles) B. Student William and Mary Coll., 1973-75; B.S. in Zoology, U. Wis.-Madison, 1980; M.Planning, Sch. Architecture, U. Va., 1984. Environ. specialist Wis. Dept. Natural Resources, Madison, 1979-80; environ. scientist HDR, Inc., Alexandria, Va., 1981-83; environ. analyst LABAT-Anderson, Inc., Arlington, Va., 1983-84; land planner Patton, Harris, Rust & Assocs., Fairfax, Va., 1984; asst. dir. mktg. Consumer Health Services, Alexandria, Va., 1985—; pres. Baker Farwell Assocs. Cons. Group, Arlington, 1983—. Author various environ. impact statements. Commr. Environ. Policy Commn., Alexandria, 1982-85. Mem. Ecol. Soc. Am., Am. Planning Assn. (student rep. Va. chpt. 1983-84 teller com., polit. corr.), Am. Inst. Cert. Planners (cert.), AAAS, Am. Inst. Biol. Scis. (polit. corr.), No. Va. Student Planning Assn. (pres. 1983-84). Episcopalian. Current work: Demographic and market analysis; development feasibility studies; analysis of land use/resource conservation; development of ecologically sensitive systems of development and land use. Subspecialties: Ecosystems analysis; Resource conservation. Home: 1002 N Columbus St Alexandria VA 22314 Office: Consumer Health Services Inc 600 Cameron St Suite 300 Alexandria VA 22314

BAKER, THOMAS, pharmacology educator, research consultant; b. Mineola, N.Y, Sept. 19, 1933; s. Raymond Ira and Agatha (Carroll) B.; m. Marion Whitaker, Feb. 7, 1933; children: Patricia Anne, Susan, Thomas, Peter, David, Marian. B.A., Hunter Coll., CUNY, 1968; M.S., Cornell U., 1971. Assoc. research prof. Cornell U. Med. Coll., N.Y.C., 1962-82; dir. research dept. anesthesiology St. Joseph's Hosp. and Med. Ctr., Paterson, N.J., 1983—, research cons. to anesthesiology dept., Paterson, N.J., 1981-83. Contbr. articles on pharmacology to profl. jours. Mem. Ramapo Voluntary Ambulance Corps. NIH grantee, 1971-82. Mem. AAAS, Am. Soc. Pharmacology and Exptl. Therapeutics, N.Y. Acad. Scis., Soc. Exptl. Biology and Medicine, Soc. Neurosci., Soc. Toxicology. Current Work: Effects of drugs and toxic agents on the nervous system, neuropharmacology, neurotoxicology. Subspecialties: Neuropharmacology; Toxicology (medicine). Office: 703 Main St Paterson NJ 07503

BAKER, WILLIAM OLIVER, research chemist; b. Chestertown, Md., July 15 1915; s. Harold May and Helen (Stokes) B.; m. Frances Burrill, Nov. 15, 1941; 1 son, Joseph Burrill. B.S., Washington Coll., 1935, Sc.D., 1957; Ph.D., Princeton, 1938; Sc.D., Georgetown U., 1962, U. Pitts., 1963, Seton Hall U., 1965, U. Akron, 1968, U. Mich., 1970, St. Peter's Coll., 1972, Poly. Inst. N.Y., 1973, Trinity Coll., Dublin, Ireland, 1975, Northwestern U., 1976, U. Notre Dame, 1978, Tufts U., 1981, N.J. Coll. Medicine and Dentistry, 1981; D.Eng., Stevens Inst. Tech., 1962, N.J. Inst. Tech., 1978; LL.D., U. Glasgow, 1965, U. Pa., 1974, Kean Coll., N.J., 1976, Lehigh U., 1980, Drew U., 1981; L.H.D., Monmouth Coll., 1973, Clarkson Coll. Tech., 1974. With Bell Telephone Labs., 1939-80, in charge polymer research and devel., 1948-51, asst. dir. chem. and metall. research, 1951-54, dir. research, phys. scis., 1954-55, v.p. research, 1955-73, pres., 1973-79, chmn. bd., 1979-80; dir. Ann. Revs., Inc., Summit and Elizabeth Trust Co.; vis. lectr. Northwestern U., Princeton U., Duke; Schmitt lectr. U. Notre Dame, 1968; Harrelson lectr. N.C. State U., 1971; Herbert Spencer lectr. U. Pa., 1974; Charles M. Schwab Meml. lectr. Am. Iron and Steel Inst., 1976; NIH lectr., 1958, Metall. Soc. Am. Inst. Mining Engrs./Am. Soc. Metals disting. lectr., 1976; Miles Conrad Meml. lectr. Nat. Fedn. Abstracting and Indexing Services, 1977; Wulff lectr. M.I.T., 1979; other lectureships; cons. Office Sci. and Tech., from 1977; Mem. Princeton Grad. Council, 1956-64; bd. visitors Tulane U., from 1963; mem. commn. sociotech. systems NRC, 1974-78, also chmn. adv. bd. on mil. personnel supplies, 1964-78; mem. com. on phys. chemistry of div. chemistry and chem. tech., 1963-70; also steering com. Pres.'s Food and Nutrition Study Commn. Internat. Relations Nat. Acad. Scis.-NRC, 1975; mem. panel on phys. chemistry Office Naval Research, 1948-51; past mem. Pres.'s Sci. Adv. Com., 1957-60; nat. sci. bd. NSF, 1960-66; past chmn. Nat. Sci. Info. Council, 1959-61; mem. sci. adv. bd. Nat. Security Agy., 1959-76, cons., from 1976; cons. Dept. Def., 1958-71, Dept. Def. (to spl. asst. for sci. and tech.), 1963-73, Dept. Def. (to); Panel of Ops. Evaluation Group, USN, 1960-62; mem. N.J. Bd. Higher Edn., from 1967, exec. com., from 1970; vice chmn., 1970-72; mem. liaison com. for sci. and tech. Library of Congress, 1963-73; mem. Pres.'s Fgn. Intelligence Adv. Bd., 1959-77; chmn. Pres.'s Adv. Group Anticipated Advances in Sci. and Tech., 1975-76; vice chmn. Pres.'s Com. Sci. and Tech., 1976-77; bd. regents Nat. Library Medicine, 1969-73; bd. visitors Air Force Systems Command, 1962-73; mem. mgmt. adv. council Oak Ridge Nat. Lab., from 1970; mem. Nat. Commn. on Libraries and Info. Scis., 1971-75, Commn. on Critical Choices for Ams., 1973-75, Nat. Cancer Adv. Bd., 1974-80; mem. panel adv. Inst. Materials Research, Nat. Bur. Standards, 1966-69; mem. Council Trends and Perspectives, U.S. C. of C., 1966-74; chmn. tech. panels adv. to Nat. Bur. Standards, Nat. Acad. Scis.-NRC, 1969-78; mem. Nat. Council Ednl. Research, 1973-75; mem. energy research and devel. adv. council Energy Policy Office, 1973-75; mem. Project Independence adv. com. Fed. Energy Adminstrn., 1974-75, Gov.'s Com. to Evaluate Capital Needs N.J., 1974-75; mem. governing bd. Nat. Enquiry into Scholarly Communication, 1975-79; adv. council N.J. Regional Med. Library, from 1975, Fed. Emergency Mgmt. Adv. Bd., from 1980; Gas Research Inst. Adv. Bd., from 1978; mem. adv. bd. N.J. Sci./Tech. Center, from 1980; Mem. sci. adv. bd. Robert A. Welch Found., from 1968; vis. com. for chemistry Harvard, 1959-72; mem. council Marconi Fellowships, from 1978; vis. com., div. chemistry and chem. engring. Calif. Inst. Tech., 1969-72; vis. com. on scis. and math. Drew U.; asso. in univ. seminar on tech. and social change Columbia, from 1969; vis. com., dept. materials sci. and engring. M.I.T., 1973-76; bd. overseers Coll. Engring. and Applied Sci. U. Pa., from 1975; bd. dirs. Council on Library Resources, from 1970, Health Effects Inst., from 1980; Clin. Scholar Program Robert Wood Johnson Found., 1973-76, Third Century Corp., 1973-76. Contbr.: High Polymers, 1945, Symposium on Basic Research, AAAS, 1959, Rheology, Vol. III, 1960, Technology and Social Change, 1964, Science: The Achievement and the Promise, 1968, Ann. Rev. Materials Sci, 1976, various other books.; Mem. editorial adv. bd.: Jour. Info. Sci; past mem. adv. editorial bd.: Chem. and Engring. News; hon. editorial adv. bd.: Carbon; Contbr. numerous articles to tech. jours. Trustee Urban Studies, Inc., 1960-78; trustee Aerospace Corp., 1961-76, Carnegie-Mellon U., Princeton, Fund N.J., Harry Frank Guggenheim Found., Gen. Motors Cancer Research Found., Charles Babbage Inst., Newark Mus.; trustee Rockefeller U., from 1960, chmn., from 1980; trustee Andrew W. Mellon Found., chmn., from 1975. Named 1 of 10 top scientists in U.S. industry, 1954; recipient Perkin medal, 1963; Honor scroll Am. Inst. Chemist, 1962; award to execs. ASTM, 1967; Edgar Marburg award, 1967; Indsl. Research Inst. medal, 1970; Frederik Philips award IEEE, 1972; Indsl. Research Man of Year award, 1973; Procter prize Sigma Xi, 1973; James Madison medal Princeton, 1975; Mellon Inst. award, 1975; Soc. Research Adminstrs. award for distinguished contbns., 1976; von Hippel award Materials Research Soc., 1978; Fahrney medal Franklin Inst., 1977; N.J. Sci/Tech. medal, 1980; Harvard fellow, 1937-38; Procter fellow, 1938-39; Jefferson medal N.J. Patent Law Assn., 1981; David Sarnoff prize AFCEA, 1981. Fellow Am. Phys. Soc., Am. Inst. Chemists (Gold medal 1975), Franklin Inst., Am. Acad. Arts and Scis.; mem. Dirs. of Indsl. Research, Am. Chem. Soc. (past mem. com. nat. def., cons., past mem. com. chemistry and pub. affairs, Priestley medal 1966, Parsons award 1976, Willard Gibbs award 1978, Madison Marshall award 1980), Am. Philos. Soc., Nat. Acad. Scis. (council 1969-72, com. sci. and pub. policy 1966-69), Nat. Acad. Engring., Inst. Medicine (council 1973-75), Indsl. Research Inst. (dir. 1960-63), Sigma Xi, Phi Lambda Upsilon, Omicron Delta Kappa. Clubs: Chemists of N.Y. (hon.), Cosmos, Princeton of Northwestern N.J. Holder 13 patents. Current Work: Formation and structure of polymers; viscoelasticity of biopolymers; ultrathin films for information storage and integrated circuit patterns; photonics for communication systems; organization of research and development. Subspecialties: Solid state chemistry; Materials (engineering). Office: care AT&T Labs 600 Mountain Ave Murray Hill NJ 07974*

BAKER, WILLIAM RAY, chemist; b. Yakima, Wash., Dec. 15, 1951; s. Ray Charles and Helen Teresa (Rink) B.; m. Mindy Gail Ross, Dec. 28, 1974. B.S., U. Wash., 1974; Ph.D., U. Ill., 1979. Postdoctoral research assoc. U. Calif.-Berkeley, 1979-81; research assoc. Abbott Labs., North Chicago, Ill., 1981—. Contbr. articles to profl. jours. Mem. Am. Chem. Soc., AAAS. Current work: Developing new synthetic methods; organotitanium chemistry; chemical modification of macrolide natural products for use as new antibiotics. Subspecialty: Organic chemistry. Home: 6 Constitution Ct Vernon Hills IL 60061 Office: Abbott Labs Abbott Park North Chicago IL 60064

BAKSAY, LASZLO ANDREW, physicist, educator; b. Budapest, Hungary, July 22, 1945; came to U.S., 1978, naturalized, 1981; s. Laszlo and Jolan (Bethlen) B.; m. Marika Gallo, July 16, 1983. Dipl. Phys., RWTH Aachen, 1972, Dr. rer. nat., 1978, Staatsexamen, 1979. Chercheur visiteur CERN, Geneva, 1972-75; research assoc. RWTH, Aachen, Fed. Republic Germany, 1975-78; vis. scientist Stanford U. Calif., 1978-82; asst. prof. physics Northeastern U., Boston, 1978-83; staff scientist Lawrence Berkeley Lab., Calif., 1982-83; assoc. prof. physics U. Dallas, Irving, Tex., 1983-85; mem. faculty dept. physics Union Coll., Schenectady, 1985—; textbook cons. to several pubs., 1980-82. Contbr. articles to profl. publs. Henkel scholar, 1967-72; Thyssen scholar, 1968-72, research scholar Fed. Republic Germany, 1972-74. Mem. Am. Phys. Soc., Deutsche Physikalische Gesellschaft, European Phys. Soc. Current work: Experimental elementary particle physics, development of new particle detectors at high pressures, instrumentation, experiments on proton decay and muon neutrino mass. Subspecialties: Particle physics; Electronics. Office: Dept Physics Union College Schenectady NY 12308

BAKSI, SAMARENDRA NATH, endocrinologist; b. Rajshahi, India, Dec. 28, 1940; s. Rishi and Haribhabini (Majumdar) B.; m. Shila Baksi, Aug. 16, 1971; children: Samudra Neal, Subir Kumar. B.V.Sc., Bihar U., India, 1960; M.S., U. Mo., Columbia, 1967, Ph.D., 1971. Fellow in reproductive physiology Worcster Found. Exptl. Biology, Shrewsbury, Mass., 1971-72; vis. fellow Nat. Inst. Environ. Health Sci., NIH, Research Triangle Park, N.C., 1972-74; research assoc. in pharmacology U. Tex. Med. Br., Galveston, 1975; research assoc. in pharmacology Tex. Tech. U. Health Scis. Center, Lubbock, 1976-79, research assoc. in physiology, 1980-83; asst. prof. physiology and pharmacology Coll. Vet. Medicine Wash. State U., 1984—. Contbr. articles to sci. jours. Mem. Endocrine Soc., Am. Physiol. Soc., Am. Soc. Pharmacology and Exptl. Therapeutics, Am. Soc. Bone and Mineral Research. Current Work: Neurotransmitter physiology; central catecholamine metabolism alteration by estrogen, lead and calcium. Regulation of vitamin D endocrine system. Dopamine receptor physiology; toxicology. Subspecialties: Neuroendocrinology; Molecular pharmacology. Home: Route 2 Box 754 Pullman WA 99163 Office: Washington State U Coll Vet Medicine Pullman WA 99164

BAKUZONIS, CRAIG WILLIAM, clinical engineer; b. Schenectady, N.Y., Mar. 10, 1955; s. Joseph Konstanty and Margaret Elfrida (Borcherding) B. B.S., Rensselaer Poly. Inst., 1977, M.Engring., 1978. Clin. engr. Albany Med. Ctr., N.Y., 1978-80; chief clin. engr. Ellis Hosp., Schenectady, 1980-85; clin. engr. Geisinger Med. Ctr., Danville, Pa., 1985—; instr. Rensselaer Poly. Inst., Troy, N.Y., 1980-85. Mem. IEEE, Assn. Advancement Med. Instrumentation, Am. Soc. Hosp. Engring., Tau Beta Pi. Current work: Patient care monitoring, arrhythmic monitoring, anesthesic, critical care, respiratory therapy. Subspecialties: Bioinstrumentation; Biomedical engineering. Home: 108 Ridgeview Danville PA 17821 Office: Geisinger Med Ctr Danville PA 17822

BALANIS, GEORGE NICK, electrical engineer; b. Athens, Greece, Oct. 7, 1944; came to U.S., 1963, naturalized, 1977; s. Nicholas G. and Mary (Traganoudaki) B.; m. Toula Koutis, Nov. 15, 1971; 1 son, Nikolas. B.S. with honors, Calif. Inst. Tech., 1967, M.S., 1968, Ph.D., 1972. Research asst. Calif. Inst. Tech., Pasadena, 1968-71; staff scientist Applied Theory, Inc., Los Angeles, 1971-77, Arete Assocs., Los Angeles, 1977-80; sr. engr. Garrett Airesearch, Torrance, Calif., 1980—. Contbr. articles to profl. jours. Mem. IEEE, ASME, Soc. Indsl. and Applied Math., Am. Math. Soc., Am. Acad. Mechanics, Tau Beta Pi, Sigma Chi. Greek Orthodox. Current Work: Inverse scattering, computer aided engineering. Subspecialties: Applied mathematics; Electrical engineering. Home: 2349 Hill St Santa Monica CA 90405

BALASCIO, JOSEPH FRANCIS, mfg. co. exec.; b. Wilkes-Barre, Pa., Aug. 14, 1941; s. Joseph Francis and Anna Marie (Fristic) B.; m. Irma Marie Wagner, Sept. 10, 1966; children: John, Johanna, Catherine. B.S., King's Coll., Wilkes-Barre, 1963; M.S., Pa. State U., 1966, Ph.D. in Solid State Sci., 1972. Sr. scientist ISOMET Corp., Oakland, N.J., 1972-74, mgr. crystal dept., Springfield, Va., 1975-76; sr. staff engr. Motorola, Inc., Carlisle, Pa., 1976-82, prin. staff engr., 1982—; assoc. mem. sci. adv. bd. assn., 1981—. Contbr. articles to profl. jours. Mem. Am. Chem. Soc., Am. Ceramic Soc., Optical Soc. Am., Am. Assn. Crystal Growth. Current Work: Research and development on the growth of alpha quartz single crystals so that this material may be routinely fabricated employing semiconductor processing technology and used in satellite applications. Subspecialties: Solid state chemistry; Crystallography. Home: 734 Sherwood Dr Carlisle PA 17013 Office: 2510 Ritner Hwy Carlisle PA 17013

BALAZS, TIBOR, research toxicologist; b. Sarbogard, Hungary, Mar. 1, 1922; came to U.S., 1963, naturalized, 1968; s. Armin and Bella (Stern) B.; m. Eva Bokor, Dec. 18, 1949; 1 dau., Anna. Mag. Pharm. Peter Pazmany U., Budapest, Hungary, 1948; D.V.M. Vet. U. Budapest, 1949; Toxicologist Food and Drug Directorate Ottawa, Ont., Can., 1959-63; research group leader Lederle Lab., Pearl River, N.Y., 1963-69; asst. dir. Smith Kline Co., Phila., 1969-71; chief drug toxicology br., div. drug biology Nat. Ctr. Drugs and Biologics, FDA, Washington, 1971—; vis. prof. pharmacology Howard U. Coll. Medicine. Research numerous publs. in drug toxicology; editor: Cardiac Toxicology, 1981. Recipient Commendable Service award FDA, 1978, Merit award, 1982. Fellow Am. Coll. Vet. Toxicology; mem. Am. Soc. Pharmacology and Exptl. Therapeutics, Soc. Toxicology, (Arnold J. Lehmann award 1984), AVMA, Acad. Toxicol. Scis. (diplomate). Current Work: Direct and conduct drug toxicology research. Subspecialties: Pharmacology; Toxicology (medicine). Office: 200 C St SW Washington DC 20204

BALBINDER, ELIAS, biologist; b. Warsaw, Poland, Jan. 22, 1926; s. Aaron Lejba and Chaja Pessa (Kratka) B.; m. Evelyn Weissman, May 10, 1955 (dec.); children: Rachel Naomi, Sara Elizabeth; m. Glory Hirshfeld, May 17, 1980. B.S., U. Mich., 1949; Ph. D., Ind. U., 1957. Research assoc. Carnegie Inst. Wash., Cold Spring Harbor, N.Y., 1957-60; Am. Cancer Soc. postdoctoral research fellow U. Calif., San Diego, 1960-62; asst. prof. genetics Syracuse U., 1962-67, assoc. prof., 1967-71, prof., 1971-76; dir. genetics and carcinogenesis Am. Med. Center-Cancer Research Center, Lakewood, Colo., 1976-82; adj. prof. biochemistry, biophysics and genetics U. Colo. Health Scis. Ctr., Denver, 1982—; mem. genetic biology panel NSF, 1977-79. Contbr. articles to profl. jours. NSF, NIH grantee, 1963-78; Fulbright Hays awardee Argentina, 1963; Fulbright Hays awardee Colombia, 1982; NIH spl. fellow Osaka (Japan) U., 1970. Fellow AAAS; mem. Am. Soc. Microbiology, Genetics Soc. Am., Environ. Mutagen Soc., Sigma Xi. Current Work: Research in role of DNA repair, mutagens/carcinogens in causing rearrangements. Subspecialties: Gene actions; Cancer research (medicine). Home: 2160 E Columbia Pl Denver CO 80210 Office: 4200 E 9th Ave Denver CO 80262

BALCERZAK, STANLEY PAUL, physician; b. Pitts., Apr. 27, 1930; s. Stanley P. and Margaretta R. (Giel) B.; m. Mary E. Kicher, Aug. 29, 1953; children: Paul, William, Margaret, John, James, Thomas, Eric. B.S., U. Pitts., 1953; M.D., U. Md., 1955. Diplomate: Am. Bd. Internal Medicine. Intern U. Pitts., 1955-56; asst. resident medicine U. Chgo., 1956-59, chief resident, 1959-60, instr. medicine, 1959-60; instr. medicine, asst. prof. U. Pitts., 1962-67; asso. prof. medicine Ohio State U., Columbus, 1967-71, prof., 1971—, dir. div. hematology and oncology, 1969—; mem. med. adv. com. ARC, 1975—; mem. clin. fellowship review com. Am. Cancer Soc., 1976-82. Contbr. articles in field to profl. jours. Served with U.S. Army, 1960-62. Fellow ACP; mem. Am. Soc. Clin. Oncology, Am. Assn. Cancer Research, Am. Fedn. Clin. Research, Am. Soc. Hematology, Central Soc. Clin. Research (councillor 1980—), S.W. Oncology Group (chmn. sarcoma com. 1981—), Polycythemia Vera Study Group (standardization com., publication com., quality control com. 1969—, myeloproliferative com. 1973—), Phi Beta Kappa, Alpha Omega Alpha. Subspecialty: Hematology. Office: 410 W 10th Ave N-1035 Columbus OH 43210

BALDESCHWIELER, JOHN DICKSON, chemist, educator; b. Elizabeth, N.J., Nov. 14, 1933; s. Emile L. and Isobel (Dickson) B.; m. Marcia Ewing,

June 20, 1959; children—John Eric, Karen Anne, David Russell. B. Chem. Engring., Cornell U., 1956; Ph.D., U. Calif. at Berkeley, 1959. From instr. to asso. prof. chemistry Harvard U., 1960-65; faculty Stanford (Calif.) U., 1965-71, prof. chemistry, 1967-71; chmn. adv. bd. Synchrotron Radiation Project, 1972-75; vis. scientist Synchrotron Radiation Lab., 1977; dep. dir. Office Sci. and Tech., Exec. Office Pres., Washington, 1971-73; prof. chemistry Calif. Inst. Tech., Pasadena, 1973—, chmn. div. chemistry and chem. engring., 1973-78; OAS vis. lectr. U. Chile, 1969; spl. lectr. in chemistry U. London, Queen Mary Coll., 1970; vis. scientist Bell Labs., 1978; Mem. Pres.'s Sci. Adv. Com., 1969—, vice chmn., 1970-71; mem. Def. Sci. Bd., 1973-80, vice chmn., 1974-76; mem. carcinogenesis adv. panel Nat. Cancer Inst., 1973—; mem. com. planning and instl. affairs NSF, 1973-77; adv. com. Arms Control and Disarmament Agy., 1974-76; mem. Nat. Acad. Sci. Bd. Sci. and Tech. for Internat. Devel., 1974-76, ad hoc com. on fed. sci. policy, 1979, task force on synfuels, 1979; mem. Pres.'s Com. on Nat. Medal, 1974-76, Pres.'s Adv. Group on Sci. and Tech., 1975-76; mem. governing bd. Reza Shah Kabir U., 1975—; mem. Sloan Commn. on Govt. and Higher Edn., 1977-79, U.S.-USSR Joint Commn. on Sci. and Tech. Cooperation, 1977-79; vice chmn. del. on pure and applied chemistry to People's Republic of China, 1978, mem. com. on scholarly communication with, 1978—; mem. research adv. council Ford Motor Co., 1979—; mem. Chem. and Engring. Adv. Bd., 1981—. Mem. editorial adv. bd.: Chem. Physics Letters, 1979—. Served to 1st lt. AUS, 1959-60. Sloan Found. fellow, 1962-64, 64-65; recipient Fresenius award Phi Lambda Upsilon, 1968. Mem. Nat. Acad. Scis., Am. Chem. Soc. (award in pure chemistry 1967), Council on Sci. and Tech. for Devel., Am. Acad. Arts and Scis., Am. Philos. Soc. Current Work: Drug delivery via encapsulation using phospholipid vesicles. Molecular spectroscopy and structure determination using EXAFS. Subspecialties: Physical chemistry; Nuclear magnetic resonance. Home: 619 S Hill Ave Pasadena CA 91106 Office: PO Box 5886 Pasadena CA 91107

BALDO, GEORGE JESSE, neurophysiologist, physiology educator; b. Herkimer, N.Y., Aug. 14, 1952; s. Sullivan George and Dellalouise (Crane) B.; m. Linda Kathryn Brown, Aug. 22, 1981. B.S. with honors, Union Coll., 1974; Ph.D., SUNY-Stony Brook, 1982. Tchr. asst. Bd. Coop. Ednl. Services II, Patchogue, N.Y., 1974-76; tchr. asst. SUNY-Stony Brook, 1977-81, research assoc., 1981-83, research asst. prof., 1985—. Contbr. articles to profl. jours. Mem. Consumer Services Com., Stony Brook, Civic Assn., South Setauket Park, 1981-83. Mem. AAAS, Am. Physiol. Soc., Sigma Xi. Republican. Roman Catholic. Club: Nat. Corvette Owners Assn. (N.Y.C.). Current Work: Synaptic transmission at the neuromuscular junction; factors controlling the release of neurotransmitter from motor nerve terminals. Subspecialty: Neurophysiology. Office: Dept Physiology and Biophysics Health Scis Center SUNY-Stony Brook Stony Brook NY 11794

BALDONADO, ARDELINA-ERIKA ALBANO, nursing educator; b. Ilocos, Norte, Philippines, May 18, 1936; came to U.S., 1960; d. Rosalino and Jovita Crisencia (Acosta) Albano; m. Alfredo Pulido Baldonado, Feb 2, 1963; children: Rozelda Fredelyn, Bradshaw Mark, Erika Gina. B.S.N., Santo Thomas U., Manila, Philippines, 1959; M.S., DePaul U., 1965; Ph.D., Loyola U., 1982. Instr. nursing edn. dept. Northwestern U., Chgo., 1966-70; instr. U. Ill. Coll. Nursing, Chgo., 1973-76; asst. prof. nursing Loyola U., Chgo., from 1976, now assoc. prof. nursing, asst. dean and dir. undergrad. nursing program; acting chmn. St. Francis Hosp. Sch. Nursing, 1972-73; research coordinator Hospice of the Northshore, Wilmette, Ill., 1982—. Author: Cancer Nursing: A Holistic Multidisciplinary Approach, 1978, 82; contbr. articles to profl. jours. Mem. Am. Edn. Research Assn., Am. Nurses Assn., Council Nurse Researchers, Ill. Nurses Assn., Philippine Nurses Assn. Chgo. (v.p. 1966-67, bd. dirs. 1967-70), Ill. League Nursing, Am. Assn. Critical Care Nurses, Nat. League Nursing. Roman Catholic. Current Work: Meta-analysis of research; cancer research; pain and symptom control; correlation of personality traits and job characteristics and professional success; application of nursing theoretical formulations by graduate students during clinical practicum. Subspecialties: Research methodology; Behavioral psychology. Home: 1808 Dobson St Evanston IL 60202 Office: Loyola U Chgo Niehoff Sch Nursing 6525 N Sheridan Rd Chicago IL 60626

BALDWIN, THOMAS OAKLEY, biochemist, educator; b. Jackson, Miss., June 3, 1947; s. Louis Oakley and Elizabeth (Thornton) B.; m. Miriam Ziegler, Apr. 15, 1978; children—Rebecca Jo, Ruth Elizabeth. B.S. in Chemistry, U. Tex., 1969, Ph.D., 1971. Research fellow tutor Harvard U., Cambridge, Mass., 1972-75; asst. prof. U. Ill., Urbana, 1975-81; instr. Marine Biol. Lab., Woods Hole, Mass., 1977-78; assoc. prof. Tex. A&M U., College Station, 1981—; cons. Upjohn Co., Kalamazoo Mich. Contbr. articles to profl. jours. Robert A. Welch Found. scholar, 1967-69; USPHS trainee, 1969-71, fellow, 1972-74; grantee USPHS, 1978—, NSF, 1976—, Upjohn Co., 1980-84, Welch Found., 1982-85. Mem. AAAS, Biophys. Soc., Am. Chem. Soc. (treas. local sect. 1979-81), Am. Soc. Photobiology, Am. Soc. Microbiology, Am. Soc. Biol. Chemists. Current work: Applications of recombinant DNA technology to study fundamental properties and structures of enzymes. Subspecialties: Biochemistry (medicine); Enzyme technology. Home: 801 Delma Dr Bryan TX 77802 Office: Dept Biochemistry Tex A&M U College Station TX 77843

BALICK, MICHAEL JEFFREY, biologist, adminstr., cons.; b. Phila., July 21, 1952; s. Jacob and Lillian (Rosen) B.; m. Daphne Allon, Aug. 19, 1980. Student, Tel Aviv U., 1972-73; B.S., U. Del., 1975; A.M., Harvard U., 1976, Ph.D. in Biology, 1980. Research asst. Bot. Mus. of Harvard U., Cambridge, Mass., 1979-80, research assoc. in plant domestication, 1980—; exec. asst. to pres., asst. curator N.Y. Bot Garden, Bronx, 1980—; adj. asst. prof. CUNY, 1982—, agribus. cons. Contbr. articles on biology to profl. jours. Recipient G. H. M. Lawrence Meml. award, 1979; Charles A. Lindbergh grantee, 1980. Fellow Linnean Soc.; mem. Internat. Assn. Plant Taxonomy, Soc. for Econ. Botany, Palm Soc., Am. Assn. Bot. Gardens and Arboreta, Sigma Xi. Current Work: Exploration for and identification of little known useful plants, especially palms, of New World Tropics, follow-up agronomic domestication studies. Subspecialties: Taxonomy; Economic botany. Office: New York Botanical Garden Bronx NY 10458

BALINSKY, DORIS, research biochemist, educator, administrator; b. Frankfurt, Ger., Dec. 3, 1934; came to U.S., 1975; d. Robert Emil and Else Leonore (Machol) Goldschmidt; m. John Boris Balinsky, Mar. 29, 1958; children: Andrew Paul, Martin George. Research biochemist South African Inst. Med. Research, Johannesburg, 1960-76, head enzyme research unit, 1969-76; research assoc. Columbia U., 1975-76; adj. assoc. prof. dept. biochemistry and biophysics Iowa State U., 1978-80, adj. prof. biochemistry, 1980-85; sr. physiologist U.S. Dept. Agr., Washington, D.C., 1985—. Contbr. articles in field to profl. jours. Witwatersrand Council Edn. fellow, 1957-59; AAUW fellow, 1968-69; recipient Rebecca Lurie Brown prize, 1955. Mem. Am. Soc. Biol. Chemists, Am. Assn. Cancer Research, Sigma Xi, Iota Sigma Pi. Current Work: Biochemical, especially isozymic changes in cancer and in aging. Subspecialties: Biochemistry (medicine); Cancer research (medicine). Office: USDA JS Morrill Bldg Rm 112 Washington DC 20251

BALL, LARRY LENNOX, medical company executive; b. Fort Worth, June 17, 1940; s. Fred Mathew and Virginia Elizabeth (Apperson) B.; children—Jodi Camille, Stephanie Kay, Patrick Lennox. B.S., U.S. Air Force Acad., 1964; M.S., U. So. Calif., 1972; M.S., San Jose State U., 1978; Ph.D., Stanford U., 1980. Hardware and software engr. Ford Aerospace, Palo Alto, Calif., 1970-72; mgr. engring. dept., Pasadena, Calif., 1972-74; NIH grantee, Stanford U., Calif., 1975-79; NIH fellow UCLA, 1980-81; pres. Audio Cybernetics, Ltd., Palo Alto, Calif., 1982—; adj. prof. San Jose State U., Calif., 1975—. Served with USAF, 1964-70. Mem. Soc. for Neurosci. Democrat. Episcopalian. Current work: Artificial intelligence approaches to problem solving and diagnostic testing results in multi modal clinical environments. Subspecialties: Artificial intelligence; Neurophysiology. Home: 89 Watkins Ave Atherton CA 94025 Office: Audio Cybernetics Ltd 460 California Ave Palo Alto CA 94306

BALL, LAURENCE ANDREW, biochemist, educator, researcher; b. York, Yorkshire, Eng., July 9, 1944; s. Laurence Elinger and Christine Mary (Howe) B.; m. Ann Marguerite, July 20, 1968; children: Jennifer Susan, Katherine Sarah. B.A., Oxford (Eng.) U., 1966, Ph.D., 1969. Postdoctoral fellow U. Wis., 1969-71, assoc. prof., Madison, 1979-82, prof. biochemistry and biophysics, 1982—; sci. staff mem. Nat. Inst. Med. Research, Mill Hill, London, Eng., 1972-74; asst. prof. in residence U. Conn., Storrs, 1974-78, assoc. prof., 1978-79; active NIH Study Sect. Virology, 1980—. Editorial bds.: Virology, Jour. Interferon Research; contbr. writings to profl. publs. in field. Recipient NIH Research Career Devel. Award, 1978—; NIH research grantee, 1979—, 81—. Mem. Am. Soc. Microbiology, Am. Soc. Virology, Am. Soc. Biol. Chemists. Current Work: Control of gene expression of animal viruses; mechanism of action of interferon. Subspecialties: Biochemistry (biology); Virology (biology). Office: 1525 Linden Dr Biophysics Lab Madison WI 53706

BALLMANN, DONALD LAWRENCE, geologist; b. Dayton, Ohio, Apr. 25, 1927; s. Adam Ignatius and Martha Marie (Barhorst) B.; m. Miriam Alice Nelson, June 4, 1972. B.A. in Philosophy, St. Josephs Coll., 1954; B.S. in Geology, U. Ill., 1955, M.S., 1956, Ph.D., 1959. Cert. profl. geologist. Faculty mem. St. Joesphs Coll., Rensselaer, Ind., 1956-72, acad. dean, 1963-68, dir. devel. founds. and govt. relations, 1968-72; project mgr. Damesand Moore, Park Ridge, Ill., 1973-75, assoc., 1975-83; engring. geology group leader Office Nuclear Waste Isolation, Battelle Labs., Columbus, Ohio, 1983-84, sr. engring. geologist, project mgr., 1984—. Author bull., also numerous reports. Mem. Geol. Soc. Am., Am. Assn. Petroleum Geologists, Soc. Econ. Paleontologists and Mineralogists, AAAS, Am. Nuclear Soc., Am. Inst. Profl. Geologists, Sigma Xi. Roman Catholic. Current work: Site investigations for a geologic repository for civilian nuclear waste. Subspecialty: Geology. Home: 946 Cross Country Dr Worthington OH 43085 Office: Battelle Project Management Div 505 King Ave Columbus OH 43201

BALLY, JOHN, astrophysicist; b. Szombathely, Hungary, Jan. 11, 1950; s. Istvan and Livia (Bally) Pogacsas; m. Kim Ruhland, June 12, 1982. M.A., U. Calif.-Berkeley, 1972; M.S., U. Mass., Amherst, 1977, Ph.D., 1980. Research asst. Five Coll. Radio Astronomy Obs., U. Mass., Amherst, 1977-80; staff AT&T Bell Labs., Holmdel, N.J., 1980—. Mem. Am. Astron. Soc. Current Work: Investigation of physics of star formation; radio astron. observations of energetic outflows in star forming clouds, molecular cloud structure; instrumentation, superconducting (SIS) receivers, microwave and mm-wave electronics. Subspecialty: Radio and microwave astronomy. Office: HOH L-245 AT&T Bell Labs Holmdel NJ 07733

BALSTER, ROBERT LOUIS, psychopharmacology educator; b. St. Cloud, Minn., Oct. 12, 1944; s. Louis and Marion M. (Vandergon) B.; m. Sandra K. Herwig, June 25, 1966; 1 dau., Sarah E. B.A., U. Minn., 1966; Ph.D., U. Houston, 1970. Postdoctoral fellow in psychiatry and pharmacology U. Chgo., 1970-72; assoc. in med. psychology Duke U. Med. Sch., 1972-73, asst. prof. med. psychology, 1973; asst. prof. pharmacology and toxicology Med. Coll. Va., Va. Commonwealth U., Richmond, 1973-78, assoc. prof., 1978-84, prof., 1984—, dir. grad. studies in pharmacology, 1980—; govt. cons. Editor: Current Status of Behavioral Pharmacology, 1985. Contbr. articles, book chpts, papers and abstracts to profl. lit. Fellow Am. Psychol. Assn.; mem. Am. Soc. Pharmacology and Exptl. Therapeutics, Behavioral Pharmacology Soc. Current Work: Laboratory research in area of drug abuse. Subspecialties: Psychopharmacology; Physiological psychology. Office: Pharmacology Dept Virginia Commonwealth U Richmond VA 23298

BALTIMORE, DAVID, microbiologist, educator; b. N.Y.C., Mar. 7, 1938; s. Richard I. and Gertrude (Lipschitz) B.; m. Alice S. Huang, Oct. 5, 1968; 1 dau., Teak. B.A. with high honors in Chemistry, Swarthmore Coll., 1960; postgrad., Mass. Inst. Tech., 1960-61; Ph.D., Rockefeller U., 1964. Research assoc. Salk Inst. Biol. Studies, LaJolla, Calif., 1965-68; assoc. prof. microbiology Mass. Inst. Tech., Cambridge, 1968-71, prof. biology, 1972—, Am. Cancer Soc. prof. microbiology, 1973-83, dir. Whitehead Inst. Biomed. Research, 1982—. Editorial bd.: Jour. Virology. Recipient Gustav Stern award in virology, 1971; Warren Triennial prize Mass. Gen. Hosp., 1971; Eli Lilly and Co. award in microbiology and immunology, 1971; U.S. Steel Found. award in molecular biology, 1974; Gairdner Found. ann. award, 1974; Nobel prize in physiology or medicine, 1975. Fellow AAAS; mem. Nat. Acad. Scis., Am. Acad. Arts and Scis., Pontifical Acad. Scis. Current Work: Abelson murine leukemia virus, poliovirus replication, gene expression, immunoglobulin transcription. Subspecialties: Molecular biology; Immunobiology and immunology. Home: 26 Reservoir St Cambridge MA 02138 Office: Whitehead Inst Biomed Research Cambridge MA 02142

BALZHISER, RICHARD EARL, energy researcher; b. Elmhurst, Ill., May 27, 1932; married, 1951; 4 children. B.S.E., U. Mich., 1955, M.S.E., 1956, Ph.D., 1961. Prof. chem. engring. U. Mich., 1961-71, chmn., 1970-71; asst. dir. Office Sci. and Tech., 1971-73; dir. Fossil Fuel and Advanced Systems, 1973-79; v.p. research and devel. Elec. Power Research Inst., Palo Alto, Calif., 1979—; cons. Allegany Ballistics Lab., 1961-62, E. I. duPont de Nemours & Co., Inc., 1967-70; White House fellow, 1967-68; cons. prof. Stanford U., 1974-79; mem. adv. bd. U. Calif.-Berkeley, 1974-77, Argonne Nat. Lab., 1974-80, Oak Ridge Nat. Lab., 1976-79, Calif. Tech. Energy Com., from 1976, Gas Research Inst., from 1979, Inst. Energy Analysis, from 1980. Mem. AAAS, Am. Inst. Chem. Engrs., AIME. Subspecialty: Energy research management. Office: Elec Power Research Inst PO Box 10412 Palo Alto CA 94303

BAMBERGER, CARLOS ENRIQUE LEOPOLDO, chemist; b. Offenbach, Hessen, Germany, Mar. 26, 1933; came to U.S., 1966; s. Hermann and Theresa (Wolf) B.; m. Elena Regina Gidekel, July 11, 1959; children—Gustavo E., Sylvia K., Roberto H. Chem. technician, Indsl. High Sch.-Buenos Aires, 1952; Dr.Chemistry, U. Buenos Aires, 1958. Research asst. to sect. head Com. Nac. Energia Atomica, Buenos Aires, 1957-61; postdoctoral fellow IAEA, Oak Ridge, Tenn., 1961-63; head beryllium div. Com. Nac. Energia Atomica, Buenos Aires, 1963-66; research staff mem. Oak Ridge Nat. Lab., Tenn., 1966-80; group leader, 1980—. Contbr. articles to jours., chpts. to books. Patentee in field. Fellow AAAS; mem. Am. Chem. Soc., Am. Ceramic Soc. Jewish. Current work: Research on synthesis and characterization of actinide compounds relevant to nuclear waste disposal; research on synthesis of advanced non-oxide refractory compounds. Subspecialties: High temperature chemistry; Inorganic chemistry. Home: 165 Nebraska Ave Oak Ridge TN 37830 Office: Oak Ridge Nat Lab PO Box X Oak Ridge TN 37831

BAMBURG, JAMES ROBERT, biochemistry educator, researcher; b. Chgo., Aug. 20, 1943; s. Leslie H. and Rose M. (Abrahams) B.; m. Laurie S. Minamide, June 22, 1985; children: Eric G., Leslie A. B.S. in Chemistry, U. Ill., 1965; Ph.D. in Biochemistry, U. Wis., 1969; postgrad., Stanford U., 1969-71. Asst. prof. biochemistry Colo. State U., 1971-76, assoc. prof., 1976-81, prof., 1981—, interim chmn., 1982-85; vis. prof. Cambridge (Eng.) U. Med. Sch., 1978-79, London, Eng., 1985-86; mem. Biomedl Sci. Study sect. NIH, 1980-85. Contbr. articles in field to profl. jours. W.H. Peterson fellow, 1968; Nat. Multiple Sclerosis Soc. fellow, 1969-71; Guggenheim fellow, 1978-79. Mem. Am. Soc. Biol. Chemists, Am. Soc. Cell Biology, Am. Chem. Soc., Internat. Soc. Neurochemistry. Current Work: Role of cytoskeletal proteins in cell motility and nerve growth. Subspecialties: Biochemistry (biology); Cell biology. Office: Department of Biochemistry Colorado State University Fort Collins CO 80523

BAME, SAMUEL JARVIS, JR., research scientist; b. Lexington, N.C., Jan. 12, 1924; s. Samuel Jarvis and Stella Blanche (Davis) B.; m. Joyce Carleton Fancher, June 21, 1956; children: Karen, Dorthe, Barbara. B.S., U. N.C., 1947; Ph.D., Rice U., 1951. Staff mem. Los Alamos (N.Mex.) Nat. Lab., 1951-81, fellow, 1981—; mem. numerous NASA adv. coms. Contbr. articles to profl. jours. Served with AUS, 1943-46. Recipient Disting. Performance award Los Alamos Nat. Lab., 1980. Fellow Am. Phys. Soc., AAAS, Am. Geophys. Union. Current Work: Study of interplanetary solar wind and magnetospheric plasmas; design and implementation of space instrumentation for scientific studies; analysis and interpretation of data received from space. Subspecialties: Space plasma physics; Solar physics. Home: 164 Dos Brazos Los Alamos NM 87544 Office: MS D438 Los Alamos Nat Lab Los Alamos NM 87545

BAMFORD, THOMAS TRUMAN, business executive; b. Ipswich, Mass., June 10, 1926; s. Robert and Isabel (Nutt) B.; m. Calypso Giantis, Apr. 21, 1974; children—Sandra, Shiela, Robert, William, Deidre, Tracy. B.S. in Chem. Engring, Worcester Poly. Inst., 1949, M.S., 1950. Research engr. Lever Brothers Co., Cambridge, Mass., 1950-52; mem. sr. staff Arthur D. Little, Inc., Cambridge, 1952-74; pres. Bamford Assos., Inc., Ipswich, 1974-79; v.p. research and devel. FMC Corp., Chgo., 1979—; dir. Centocor, Inc., Malvern, Pa., IMRX, Inc., Phila.; asso. prof. mgmt. of tech. U. N.H., 1971-72. Author: Executive Zoo, 1974. Served with USN, 1944-46. Mem. Indsl. Research Inst. Clubs: Mid-Am., Courtside, Forest Country. Address: FMC Corp 200 E Randolph St Chicago IL 60601

BAMJI, SOLI SHAVAX, physicist; b. Bombay, India, Nov. 28, 1947; came to U.S., 1971; naturalized, 1973; s. Shavax and Kolan (Daji) B.; m. Farida S. Jamooji, Dec. 27, 1974; children—Carl, Michelle. B.S., U. Bombay, 1968; M.S., U. Scranton, 1972; Ph.D., Va. State U., 1977. Postdoctoral fellow Dept. Nat. Def., St. Jean, Que., Can., 1977-80; research assoc. Nat. Research Council, Ottawa, Ont., Can., 1980-81, asst. officer research, 1981-82, assoc. officer, 1982—; cons. Coll. Militaire Royal, St. Jean, 1980-81. Contbr. articles to profl. jours. R.D. Sethna Fund scholar, 1971. Mem. IEEE (sr.; best tech. paper award 1982), Am. Inst. Physics, Sci. Assn. (chmn. Ottawa sect. 1983-85). Current work: Charge storage and transport in polymers; electrets; electroluminescence in polymeric materials; mechanisms of degradation in high voltage insulation. Subspecialties: Polymer physics; Polymer engineering. Home: 1599 Boyer Rd Ottawa ON K1C 3H4 Canada Office: Nat Research Council Canada M-50 Montreal Rd Ottawa ON K1A OR8 Canada

BAN, STEPHEN DENNIS, mechanical engineer; b. Gary, Ind., Dec. 16, 1940; married, 1966; 3 children. B.S.M.E., Rose Poly. Inst., 1962; M.S.M.E., Case Inst. Tech., 1964, Ph.D., 1967. Research engr. Battelle Meml. Inst., 1967-68, sr. research engr., 1968-69, sr. project leader, 1969-70, assoc. chief fluid and gas dynamics div., 1970-71, chief, 1971-77; dir. R&D devel. & testing lab. Bituminous Material Co., 1977-80; adj. prof. mech. engring. Rose Hulman Inst. Tech., 1980—; mem. staff Gas Research Inst., Chgo., 1980—; v.p., 1980-83, sr. v.p., 1983—. Mem. AIAA, Sigma Xi. Subspecialty: Mechanical engineering. Office: Gas Research Inst 8600 W Bryn Mawr Chicago IL 60631

BANASZAK, KONRAD JOSEPH, hydrogeologist, geochemist; b. East Chgo., Indpls. Oct. 6, 1944; s. Joseph Albert and Stella Louise (Karczewska); m. S. Jennifer Sugarman, Aug. 29, 1971; 1 child, Caille Peri Sugarman-Banaszak. B.S., Beloit Coll., 1966; M.S., Northwestern U., 1969, Ph.D., 1975. Cert. profl. geologist, Ind. Asst. prof. U. Miss., 1971-77; assoc. prof. Ind. U.-Purdue U., Indpls., 1977-79; hydrogeologist Office Surface Mining, Indpls., 1979-81, supervisory hydrologist U.S. Geol. survey, 1981—. Recipient Outstanding Tch. of Yr. award Sch. of Engring., U. Miss., 1975. Mem. Am. Inst. Profl. Geologists (section pres. 1984), Am. Inst. Hydrology, Geochem. Soc., Geol. Soc. Am. Jewish. Current work: Geochemical reacions in ground-water and between ground water and earth materials; Impacts of coal mining on ground water and water quality and treatment technologies. Subspecialties: Hydrogeology; Geochemistry. Home: 1115 West 79th St Indianapolis IN 46260 Office: US Geol Survey 6023 Guion Rd Indianapolis IN 46254

BANCHOFF, THOMAS FRANCIS, See *Who's Who in America*, 43rd edition.

BANDER, MYRON, physics educator, university dean; b. Belzyce, Poland, Dec. 11, 1937; came to U.S., 1949, naturalized, 1956; s. Elias and Regina (Zielonka) B.; m. Carol Jean Heimberg, Aug. 20, 1967. B.A., Columbia U., 1958, M.A., 1959, Ph.D., 1962. NSF postdoctoral fellow, various locations, 1962-63; research assoc. Stanford Linear Acceleration Ctr., Calif., 1963-66; asst. prof. physics U. Calif.-Irvine, 1966-68, assoc. prof., 1968-74, prof., 1974—, dean Sch. Phys. Scis., 1980—. Sloan fellow, 1968—. Fellow Am. Phys. Soc. Current work: Elementary particle theory; field theory; statistical mechanics. Subspecialties: Particle physics; Statistical physics. Office: U Calif Sch Phys Scis Irvine CA 92717

BANDURSKI, BRUCE LORD, ecologist and environmental scientist; b. Waterbury, Conn., June 28, 1940; s. Stanley Alexander Bandurski and Virginia Ann (VanRensselaer) Bandurski Hinckley. B.S. with honors Mich. State U., 1962; postgrad. George Washington U., 1964-65, U.S. Dept. Agr. Grad. Sch., 1965-66. Park ranger Nat. Park Service, 1962-63; sci. reference analyst USPHS, Washington, 1963-65; intelligence ops. specialist U.S. Army, Washington, 1965-66; analyst planner U.S. Dept. Interior, Washington, 1966-74, coordinator, br. chief, 1974-84, on detail as ecologist, ecomgmt. advisor Internat. Joint Commn. U.S. and Can., 1983-85, ecomgmt. advisor, ecologist, 1985—; mem. faculty U.S. Dept. Agr. Grad. Sch., 1968—; mem. subcom. Fed. Interagy. Com. on Edn., 1967—; watch dir., dep. and acting mission dir. U.S. Man-in-Sea program, St. John, V.I., 1970; chmn. Conservation Roundtable of Washington, 1970-71; chmn. com. on definitions, spl. com. on environ. protection U.S. nat. com. World Energy Conf., Washington, 1981—; initiator, dir. Binat. Workshop on Transboundary Monitoring, 1984. Writer planning and recreation impact mgmt. series, 1967-73; author U.S. Bur. Land Mgmt. Environ. Mgmt. Procedures 1976-84 (Achievement award 1978, 79, 84). Active various natural resource stewardship orgns. and fed. civil service interagy. orgns. Mem. Ecol. Soc. Am. (charter Met. Washington chpt.), Internat. Assn. for Ecology, Am. Soc. Naturalists. Current work: Complementarities between holism and reductionism as they pertain to governance of man/environs relations. Subspecialty: Transdisciplinary ecomanagement. Home: Bandura/Point of Maine/Starboard Bucks Harbor ME 04618 Office: Internat Joint Commn US and Can 2001 S St NW 2d Floor Washington DC 20440

BANE, GILBERT WINFIELD, JR., marine sciences educator, fisheries researcher; b. San Diego, Dec. 11, 1931; s. Gilbert Winfield and Eva (Chaffin) B.; m. Anneka Wright, Oct. 5, 1970; children—Cynthia, Victoria, Robert. B.S., San Jose State U., 1954; M.S., Cornell U., 1961, Ph.D., 1963. Prof., dir. marine sci. Southampton Coll., N.Y., 1969-73; chmn. natural scis. St. Francis Coll., Biddleford, Maine, 1973-75; dir. Environ. Studies U. N.C., Wilmington, 1975-82, dir. marine scis., 1975-82; dir. fisheries Inst. La. State U., Baton Rouge, 1982—. Author books. Contbr. articles to profl. jours. Fellow Am. Inst. Fisheries Research Biologists; mem. Am. Fisheries Soc., Am. Soc. Ichthyologists and Herpetologists. Current work: Racial determination of stocks of fishes in the Gulf of Mexico; ecology of important marine fishes and sharks in the Gulf of Mexico Subspecialty: Fishery biology. Office: Fisheres Inst La State Univ Baton Rouge LA 70803

BANERJEE, AMIYA KUMAR, molecular virologist, educator; b. Rangoon, Burma, May 3, 1936; came to U.S., 1965, naturalized, 1978; s. Phanindra Nath and Bibhati (Ghosal) B.; m. Sipra Datta, Jan. 23, 1965; children: Antara, Arjun. M.A., Calcutta U., 1958, Ph.D., 1964, D.Sc., 1970. Research assoc. Albert Einstein Coll. Medicine, Yeshiva U., Bronx, N.Y., 1966-69; asst. mem. Roche Inst. Molecular Biology, Nutley, N.J., 1970-73, assoc. mem., 1974-79, full mem., 1980—; adj. prof. dept. cell biology N.Y.U. Med. Sch., N.Y.C., 1980—; adj. prof. dept. microbiology U. Medicine and Dentistry N.J., 1985—. Mem. virology study sect. NIH. Editorial bd.: Jour. Virology, Virology; Contbr. articles and abstracts to sci. jours. Recipient Phoebe Weinstein award NIH, 1977. Mem. AAAS, Am. Soc. Biol. Chemists, Am. Soc. Microbiology, Harvey Soc., N.Y. Acad. Scis. Club: Tagore Soc. (N.Y.C.). Current Work: I am primarily interested in the molecular biology of vesicular stomatitis virus gene expression. Areas studied include: mode of genome transcription and replication in vitro, structure and function of the genetic material, biochemical functions of purified viral proteins, mechanisms of defective virus production and the interference phenomenon. Subspecialties: Virology (veterinary medicine); Molecular biology. Home: 113 Fairway Ave Verona NJ 07044 Office: Roche Institute of Molecular Biology Nutley NJ 07110

BANERJEE, KRISHNADAS, radiol. physicist; b. Calcutta, India, Jan. 3, 1934; came to U.S., 1961, naturalized, 1977; s. Ramkanai and Hemlata (Mukherjee) B.; m. Rama Dhar, June 19, 1968; 1 dau., Rini. M.S., Calcutta U., India, 1956; Ph.D., U. Pitts., 1965. Cert. radio. physicist Am. Bd. Radiology. Research fellow Saha Inst. Nuclear Physics, Calcutta, 1967-69; postdoctoral fellow U. Pitts., 1969-70; dir. radiol. physics and radiation biology St. Francis Gen. Hosp., Pitts., 1970—; adj. prof. radiol. physics U. Pitts. Grad. Sch. Public Health, Pitts., 1978—. Fulbright scholar, 1961. Mem. Am. Assn. Physicists in Medicine, Health Physics Soc., Radiol. Soc. N.Am. Hindu. Current Work: Radiological physics, nuclear medicine, radiation therapy, medical physics, nuclear magnetic resonance. Subspecialties: Radiological physics; Biophysics (physics). Home: 641 Ravencrest Rd Pittsburgh PA 15215 Office: St Francis Gen Hosp Pittsburgh PA 15201

BANERJEE, SANJAY KUMAR, electrical engineer, researcher; b. Khartoum, Sudan, Feb. 24, 1958; came to U.S., 1979; s. Sunil Chandra and Anima (Mukherjee) B.; m. Jaba Chatterjee, June 18, 1983. B.Tech., Indian Inst. Tech., 1979; M.S., U. Ill., 1981, Ph.D., 1983. Research assoc. Coordinated Sci. Lab., Urbana, Ill., 1979-83; asst. prof. U. Ill., Urbana, 1983; mem. tech. staff Tex. Instruments, Dallas, 1983—. Patentee; contbr. articles to profl. jours. Recipient Nat. Sci. Talent scholarship Govt. India, 1974; Jagadis Bose Sci. scholarship, 1975; Silver medal Indian Inst. Tech., 1979; Swapan Saha Gold medal, 1979. Mem. IEEE, Phi Kappa Phi. Current work: Ion implantation and transient annealing of semiconductors; three-dimensional integrated circuits; polysilicon device physics. Subspecialties: Microchip technology (engineering); Semiconductors. Home: 1107 Haynes Richardson TX 75081 Office: Texas Instruments PO Box 225621 MS 369 Dallas TX 75265

BANERJEE, SIPRA, biochemist, educator; b. Calcutta, India, Feb. 20, 1939; came to U.S., 1965, naturalized, 1978; d. Sanmatha Nath and Sudharani Datta; m. Amiya Banerjee, Jan. 23, 1965; children: Antara, Arjun. Ph.D. in Biochemistry, Calcutta U., 1965. Postdoctoral fellow dept. biochemistry Albert Einstein Coll. Medicine, Bronx, N.Y., 1966-69; research biochemist, dept. pharmacology N.Y. Med. Coll., N.Y.C., 1969-70; fellow dept. biochemistry and drug metabolism Hoffman-LaRoche Inc., Nutley, N.J., 1972-73; assoc. research scientist, dept. environ. medicine N.Y.U. Med. Ctr., N.Y.C., 1972-78; asst. prof. Inst. Environ. Medicine, 1978-85, research prof., 1985—. Contbr. articles to profl. jours. Mem. Am. Soc. Biol. Chemists, Am. Assn. for Cancer Research, N.Y. Acad. Scis. Clubs: Milani (Bay Shore, N.Y.); Kallol (N.J.). Current Work: Biochemical studies of molecular mechanisms of chemical carcinogenesis. Subspecialties: Biochemistry (biology); Cancer research (medicine). Home: 113 Fairway Ave Verona NJ 07044 Office: 550 1st Ave MSB Room 207 New York NY 10016

BANERJEE, SUJIT, environmental scientist, research chemist; b. Calcutta, India, Jan. 5, 1950; came to U.S. 1977; s. Debidas and Sujata (Mukerji) B.; m. Anuradha Sengupta, Jan. 2, 1978; 1 child, Joya. B.Sc., Indian Inst. Tech., Kharagpur, 1969; M.Sc., Concordia U., Montreal, 1972, Ph.D., 1974. Postdoctoral fellow McMaster U., Hamilton, Ont., Can., 1974-76; sr. scientist Syracuse Research Corp., N.Y., 1977-83, cons., 1984—; group leader Brookhaven Nat. Lab., Upton, N.Y., 1983—; cons. Gulf Oil, Pitts., 1982, Tech. Database Services, N.Y.C., 1983. Contbr. articles to profl. jours., chpts. to books. Patentee in field. Grantee NIH, 1978-81, EPA, 1978—, Nat. Bur. Standards, 1980-83, Nuclear Regulatory Commn., 1984—. Mem. Am. Chem. Soc., Soc. Environ. Toxicology and Chemistry. Current work: Research on mechanisms of chemical; biological and environmental processes, development of new techniques in analytical chemistry. Subspecialties: Environmental chemistry; Analytical chemistry. Office: Brookhaven Nat Lab Bldg 535A Upton NY 11973

BANERJEE, UTPAL, computer scientist; b. Calcutta, India, Aug. 4, 1942; came to U.S., 1965, naturalized, 1970; s. Santosh Kumar and Santi Rani (Mukherjee) B.; m. Aloka Mukherjee, June 11, 1969; 1 dau., Sanchita. B.Sc., Calcutta U., 1961, M.Sc., 1963; M.S., Carnegie-Mellon U., Pitts., 1967, Ph.D., 1970; M.S., U. Ill., Urbana-Champaign, 1976, Ph.D., 1979. Asst. prof. math. U. Cin., 1969-75; prin. analyst Honeywell, Phoenix, 1979-81; mem. research staff Fairchild Labs., Palo Alto, Calif., 1981-82; cons. Control Data Corp., Sunnyvale, Calif., 1982—. Contbr. articles to profl. jours. Mem. Am. Math. Soc., Math. Assn. Am., Assn. Computing Machinery, IEEE, Sigma Xi. Current Work: Parallel processing for supercomputers. Subspecialties: Computer architecture; Algorithms. Office: MS SVL 144F Control Data Corp Box 3492 Sunnyvale CA 94088

BANIK, NARENDRA LAL, neuroscientist; b. Ganganagar, Bengal, India, Jan. 2, 1938; s. Surendra Lal and Radharani B.; m. Meena Banik, Mar. 7, 1968; children: Manendu, Nandini. B.Sc., U. Calcutta, 1959; M.Sc., U. London, 1966, Ph.D. in biochemistry, 1970. Research asst. Inst. Psychiatry, London, 1962-65; research asst. Charing Cross Hosp. Med. Sch., London, 1966-70; lectr. Inst. Neurology, London, 1970-74; research asso. Stanford U., 1974-76; asst. prof. Med. U. S.C., Charleston, 1977-80; assoc. prof. U. S.C., 1980—. Contbr. articles to profl. jours. NATO grantee, 1971; Welcome Research Found., grantee, 1974. Mem. Biochem. Soc. London, Internat. Soc. Neurochemistry, Am. Soc. Neurochemistry, AAAS, Soc. Neurosci., Am. Soc. Biol. Chemists. Current Work: Membrane biochemistry, myelination and mechanism of demyelination, spinal cord injury research. Subspecialties: Neurochemistry; Biochemistry (biology). Home: 750 Olney Rd Charleston SC 29407 Office: 171 Ashley Ave Neurology Charleston SC 29425

BANISTER, JOHN ROBERT, physicist; b. Wayne, Nebr., Feb. 4, 1923; s. John Clark and Laura Ethel (Taylor) B.; m. Jeanne Frances Weppler, Dec. 23, 1950; children—John Conrad, Stephen James, Gayle Frances. B.S. in Physics, Iowa State U., 1948, Ph.D. in Physics, 1953. Graduate research asst. Iowa State U., Ames, 1948-53; staff mem. Sandia Labs, Albuquerque, 1953-60, div. supr., 1960-64; dept. mgr., 1964-77, div. supr., 1977—. Contbr. articles to profl. jours. Inventor Snob and Greg Gages. Served to staff sgt. U.S. Army, 1943-46. Grantee NSF, 1973. Fellow Am. Phys. Soc.; mem. Am. Geophys. Union, AAAS, Sigma Xi, Phi Kappa Phi. Republican. Methodist. Current work: Supervisor of ground motion and seismic division; weapon effect studies, detection and discrimation of nuclear tests. Subspecialties: Fluid dynamics; Seismology. Home: 1205 Jefferson NE Albuquerque NM 87110 Office: Sandia Nat Labs PO Box 5800 Albuquerque NM 87185

BANITT, ELDEN HARRIS, medicinal chemist; b. Red Wing, Minn., Apr. 7, 1937; s. Henry George and Emilie (Diercks) B.; m. Kay Starz, Aug. 1, 1959; children—Lynn R., Lee S. B.A., St. Olaf Coll., 1959; Ph.D., U. Wis.-Madison, 1964; postdoctoral fellow U. Calif.-Berkeley, 1964-65. Sr. chemist 3M, St. Paul, Minn., 1965-69; research specialist Riker/3M, St. Paul, 1969-75, sr. research specialist, 1975—. Mem. Am. Chem. Soc. Lutheran. Current work: New molecule research on organic compounds of medicinal interest, drug discovery. Subspecialties: Organic chemistry; Synthetic chemistry.

BANJAVIC, RICHARD ALAN, educator, consultant; b. Chgo., June 13, 1947; s. John and Dorothy (Kostadin) B.; m. Judith Caplan Banjavic, Jan. 29, 1982. B.A. in Physics with honors, Johns Hopkins U., 1969; M.S. in Physics, U. Ill., 1971; M.S. in Radiol. Physics, U. Wis., Madison, 1973, Ph.D., 1978. Research assoc. Materials Sci. Lab., U. Ill., 1970-72; research asst. nuclear medicine U. Wis., 1972-74, research asst. radiotherapy physics and ultrasound, 1974-78, postdoctoral research assoc. ultrasound, 1978-79; research assoc. ultrasound U. Colo. Health Sci. Center, Denver, 1979-80, instr., 1980-81, asst. prof., 1981-83; ultrasound physicist Rocky Mountain Med. Physics, Inc., Denver, 1983-84; pres. Acoustic Enterprises, Inc.; asst. prof., chief med. physics U. Mo., Columbia, 1985—; cons. in field. Contbr. articles in field to profl. jours. Served with USNR, 1971-80. Woodrow Wilson fellow, 1969; NSF fellow, 1970. Fellow Am. Inst. Ultrasound in Medicine, Am. Assn. Physicists in Medicine, Assn. Advancement Physics, Acoustical Soc. Am., Soc. Magnetic Resource Imaging, IEEE. Democrat. Roman Catholic. Current Work: Study of diagnostic ultrasonic imaging itself as a separate modality and in conjunction with the other types of diagnostic modalities presently available. Subspecialties: Imaging technology; Acoustics.

BANK, HARVEY LEONARD, pathology educator; b. Bklyn., Feb. 13, 1943; s. Myron and Ruth B.; m. Ellen Shield, Aug. 22, 1965; children—Daniel, Laura, Michael. B.A., CUNY, 1965; postgrad. NYU, 1966-68; Ph.D., U. Tenn., 1968-72; postdoctoral fellow Duke U., 1972-73. Technician, Lamont Geol. Obs., 1965-67; sr. technician Reckefeller U., 1967-68; guest investigator Nat. Inst. Environ. Issues, 1972-73; assoc. Med. U. S.C., Charleston, 1973-74, asst. prof., 1974-79, assoc. prof., 1979—; research coordinator Cryolife Inc., 1985—; cons. EPA, 1979—. Contbr. articles to profl. jours. NIH grantee 1986-78; Smith, Kline, French fellow, 1973-75. Mem. Soc. Cryobiology (treas. 1977-80, chmn. various coms.), Am. Soc. Cell Biology, Biophys. Soc., Electron Miscroscopic Soc. Am., Southeast Soc. Electron Microscopy (chmn. Ruska award com.), AAAS, Microbeam Analysis Soc., Sigma Xi (Charleston chpt. v.p. 1978-79, pres. 1979-80, chmn. various coms.). Home: 131 Winchester Dr Charleston SC 29407 Office: Dept Pathology Med U SC 171 Ashley Ave Charleston SC 29425

BANKA, VIDYA SAGAR, cardiologist; b. Lyallpur, India, Mar. 5, 1941; came to U.S., 1970; s. Ram Ch and Hukam (Devi) B.; m. Reena Sagar Banka, Jan. 26, 1972; children: Sahil, Sarovar. M.B.B.S., Med. Coll. Amritsar, India, 1964; M.D., Panjab U., India, 1967. Diplomate: Am. Bd. Internal Medicine. Registrat incardiology Postgrad. Inst. Med. Edn. and Research, Chandigarh, India, 1967-69; dir. cardiac catheterization labs. Presbyn. U. Pa. Med. Center, Phila., 1974-83; dir. interventional cardiovascular medicine Episcopal Hosp., Phila., 1983—, dir. div. Cardiology, 1985—; assoc. prof. medicine U. Pa. Sch. Medicine, Phila., 1979-82, assoc. prof. clin. medicine, 1982—; prof. medicine Temple U., 1985—. Author: A Clinical and Angiographic Approach to Coronary Heart Disease, 1978. Fellow ACP, Am. Coll. Cardiology, Am. Coll. Chest Physicians, Am. Heart Assn. (council clin. cardiology). Patentee in field. Current Work: Coronary heart disease; coronary angioplasty and use of laser during angioplasty. Subspecialty: Cardiology. Home: 237 Stacey Rd Narberth PA 19072 Office: Div Cardiology Episcopal Hosp Front St and Lehigh Ave Philadelphia PA 19125

BANKERT, RICHARD BURTON, immunologist; b. Phila., Apr. 22, 1940; children: Lauren, Darin. B.A., Gettysburg Coll., 1962; V.M.D., U. Pa., 1968, Ph.D., 1973. Postdoctoral fellow U. Pa., 1968-70, postdoctoral research fellow in immunology, 1970-72; assoc. veterinarian Atlantic Vet. Clinic, Pomona, N.J., 1968-69; owner, mgr. Spruce Hill Vet. Clinic, Pa., 1968-73; assoc. chief molecular immunology Roswell Park Meml. Inst., Buffalo, 1973—; prof. cell and molecular biology SUNY-Buffalo. Served with AUS. Nat. Cancer Inst. grantee, 1978—; Am. Cancer Soc. grantee, 1979—; Allergy and Immunology grantee, 1983—. Mem. AVMA, AAAS, Am. Assn. Immunologists, N.Y. Acad. Scis., Sigma Xi. Current Work: Immunology, microbiology. Subspecialties: Immunology (agriculture); Cancer research (veterinary medicine).

BANKHURST, ARTHUR DALE, physician, educator; b. Cleve., July 21, 1937; s. John William and Daisy (Howard) B.; m. Lois Hull, Feb. 20, 1969; children: Anne, Claire, Benjamin, Noah. B.S., M.I.T., 1958; M.D., Case Western Res. U., 1962. Diplomate: Am. Bd. Internal Medicine., subsplty. bd. rheumatology. Intern in medicine Univ. Hosps. of Clev., 1962-63, resident, 1965-69; research fellow Walter and Eliz Hall Inst., Melbourne, Australia, 1969-71, WHO, Geneva, Switzerland, 1971-73; asst. prof. medicine U. N.Mex., Albuquerque, 1973-77, assoc. prof., 1977-81, prof., 1981—, chief clin. immunology and rheumatic diseases, 1979—; cons. N.Mex. Profl. Standard Rev. Orgn.; chief of rheumatology Albuquerque VA Med. Center. Contbr. articles to numerous profl. jours. Served to lt. comdr. U.S. Navy, 1963-65. Cleveland fellow Walter and Eliza Hall Inst., 1969-71; Nat. Arthritis Found. sr. investigator, 1974-79. Mem. AAAS, Am. Assn. Immunologists, Am. Fedn. Clin. Research, Am. Rheumatic Assn., Brit. Soc. Immunology, Western Soc. Clin. Investigation. Subspecialties: Immunology (medicine); Immunopharmacology. Office: Dept Medicine 2211 Lomas Blvd NE Albuquerque NM 87131

BANKOFF, SEYMOUR GEORGE, engineering educator; b. N.Y.C., Oct. 7, 1921; s. Jacob and Sarah (Rashkin) B.; married; 4 children; B.S. in Mineral Dressing, Columbia U., 1940, M.S. 1941; Ph.D. in Chem. Engring., Purdue U., 1952. Chem. engr. Sinclair Refining Co., East Chicago, Ind., 1941-42; tetryl process engr. E.I. duPont de Nemours & Co., Childersburg, Ala., 1942-43; subgroup leader U. Chgo. Metall. Lab., 1943-44; engr. Hardford Engring. Works, Richland, Wash., 1944-45, Plastics div., Arlington, N.J., 1945-48; asst. prof. Rose Poly. Inst., Terre Haute, Ind., 1948-51, assoc. prof., 1951-53, prof. chem. engring., 1953, head dept., 1954-59; prof. Northwestern U., Chgo., 1959—, Walter P. Murphy prof. chem. engring., 1971, prof. chem. and nuclear engring., 1975, prof. chem., mech. and nuclear engring., 1979; chmn. vis. com. Brookhaven Nat. Lab., 1981-82; mem. vis. com. Oak Ridge Nat. Lab., 1983—; cons. Elec. Power Research Inst., Brookhaven Nat. Lab., U.S. Nuclear Regulatory Commn., Los Alamos Nat. Lab., Fauske & Assoc., Inc., Westinghouse Elecric Corp. Patentee Polymeric tetrafluoroethylene dispersions, receptacle. Mem. editorial bd. Internat. Jour. Multiphase Flow, 1973—, Chem. Engring. Communications, 1972-79, Indsl. and Engring. Chemistry and I and EC Fundamentals Quar., Nuclear Engring. and Design, 1984. U.S.-Israel Fulbright exchange lectr., 1967; U.S.-Scandinavia Fulbright exchange lectr.; Wolfson lectr., Israel, 1970; Shell prof., Imperial Coll. London, 1966-67; Fulbright scholar, 1966-67; NSF fellow; Guggenheim fellow. Fellow Am. Inst. Chem. Engrs., Internat. Ctr. Heat and Mass Transfer (Yugoslavia), ASME (research com. heat transfer div.); mem. Am. Nuclear Soc., Am. Energy Independence (adv. bd.). Current work: Two-phase flow and heat transfer; nuclear reactor safety thermalhydraulics. Subspecialties: Chemical engineering; Nuclear fission. Office: Northwestern U Dept Chem Engring Evanston IL 60201

BANKS, WILLIAM LOUIS, JR., biochemistry and surgery educator, cancer center administrator; b. Paterson, N.J., Mar. 25, 1936; s. William Louis and Martha (Roughgarden) B.; m. Sharon R. Hazelton, Aug. 1, 1965; 1 child, Heather Michelle. B.S., Rutgers U., 1958; M.S., Bucknell U., 1961; Ph.D., Rutgers U., 1963. Teaching asst. Bucknell U., 1958-60; research asst. Rutgers U., 1960-62; lectr. chemistry St. Mary's U., 1963-65; asst. prof. biochemistry Med. Coll. Va., 1965-69, assoc. prof., 1969-74, prof., 1974—; co-dir. Massey Cancer Ctr., 1974—. Contbr. in field. Bd. dirs. Epilepsy Found. Va., 1974-76. Served to capt. USAF, 1963-65. Johnson & Johnson Research fellow, 1962-63; Alfred P. Sloan Found. Faculty scholar, 1975-76; grantee in field. Mem. AAAS, Am. Assn. Cancer Edn., Am. Assn. Cancer Research, AAUP, Am. Chem. Soc., Am. Council on Sci. and Health, Am. Inst. Nutrition, N.Y. Acad. Sci., Nutrition Today Soc., Soc. Exptl. Biology and Medicine, Sigma Xi, Rho Chi, Sigma Zeta. Current Work: Nutrition and cancer. Subspecialties: Biochemistry (medicine); Oncology. Office: Medical College Virginia PO Box 37 Richmond VA 23298

BAPNA, MAHENDRA SINGH, biomaterials educator, researcher; b. Udaipur, Rajasthan, India, Sept. 8, 1939; came to U.S., 1962; s. Both Lal and Chagan Bai (Nahar) B.; m. Prabha Bhandari, May 31, 1966; children: Manish, Mitali. B.Sc., Rajasthan U., Udaipur, 1957; B.S. in Metallurgy, Banaras (Utar Pradesh, India) U., 1961; M.S. in Materials Sci, Marquette U., 1964; Ph.D., Northwestern U., 1969. Asst. prof. Loyola U. Chgo., Maywood, Ill., 1970-73; postdoctoral fellow Northwestern U., 1973-74; asst. prof. biomaterials Coll. Dentistry, U. Ill.-Chgo., 1974-77, assoc. prof., dir. biomaterials, 1977-83, prof., dir. biomaterials, 1983—. Contbr. articles to profl. jours. Univ. scholar, 1955-57; Murphy fellow, 1966-68; NIH grantee, 1972; univ. grantee, 1977. Fellow Acad. Dental Materials; mem. Am. Soc. Metals (hon., ednl. com.), Internat. Assn. Dental Research, Am. Assn. Dental Research, Sigma Xi. Current Work: Understanding the existing and developing new restorative dental materials; effects of oral environment on mechanical and physical properties of restorative dental materials; examining the elastic interaction among defects in anisotropic metals. Subspecialties: Biomaterials; Materials. Home: 711 N Jefferson St Hinsdale IL 60521Office: U Ill Coll Dentistry 801 S Paulina St Chicago IL 60612

BARALD, KATHARINE FRANCESCA, developmental neurobiologist, biochemist, educator; b. Greenville, S.C., May 11, 1945; d. Fred Charles and Francesca (Marion) B.; m. Douglas M. Jewett, Dec. 29, 1971; 1 child, Ethan MacNeil Barald Jewett. A.B. in Biology, Bryn Mawr Coll., 1967; M.S. in Molecular Biology, U. Wis.-Madison, 1969, Ph.D., 1974. NIH postdoctoral fellow U. Calif.-San Diego, La Jolla, 1975-76, Muscular Dystrophy Assn. Am. postdoctoral fellow, 1976-78; NIH postdoctoral fellow Stanford U., Calif., 1978-80; asst. prof. anatomy and cell biology U. Mich., Ann Arbor, 1980—; cons. various indsl. and univ. hybridloma facilities, 1979—; mem. study panel NSF, Washington, 1984—. Author jour. articles and book chpts. Mem. Soc. Neurosci., Soc. Cell Biology, Soc. Developmental Biology, AAAS, Sigma Xi. Current work: Molecular aspects of development and regeneration of the nervous system. Subspecialties: Neurobiology; Cell and tissue culture. Office: Dept Anatomy and Cell Biology U Mich 5740 Med Sci II Ann Arbor MI 48109

BARAN, JOHN STANISLAUS, medicinal chemist, researcher; b. Chgo., Feb. 7, 1929; s. John Peter and Stella (Stanczykiewicz) B.; m. Nancy Harris, June 26, 1954; children—Mariana, Cecily. B.A., U. Chgo., 1951, M.Sc., 1953; Ph.D., U. Wis.-Madison, 1955. Research investigator G.D. Searle & Co., Skokie, Ill., 1956-58, sr. research investigator, 1958-65, research fellow, 1965—; vis. lectr. U. So. Calif., 1968. Contbr. articles to profl. jours. Patentee in field. Served as sgt. Ill. N.G., 1948-51. Mem. Am. Chem. Soc., AAAS, Am. Pharm. Assn. Republican. Current work: Medicinal chemistry research in hypertension, hypercholesterolemia, fertility control; chemistry of natural products, peptides, steroids. Subspecialties: Medicinal chemistry; Organic chemistry. Home: 659 Locust St Winnetka IL 60093 Office: GD Searle and Co Inc 4901 Searle Pkwy Skokie IL 60077

BARANOV, ANDREY I(PPOLITOVICH), botanist; b. Harbin, China, Oct. 17, 1917; s. Ippolit G. and Varvara M. B.; m. Nina M., June 14, 1946; 1 dau., Elena. First class diploma (equivalent of LL.B), Harbin Law Sch., 1938; post grad., U. Wash., 1960-61; M.S. in Biology, Northeastern U., 1973. Research fellow Harbin Regional Museum, 1946-50, Academia Sinica inst. Forestry and Soil Sci., Shenyang, China, 1950-58; herbarium asst. Arnold Arboretum, Harvard U., 1963-67; bibliography researcher World Life Research Inst., Colton, Calif., 1967-68; mem. bd. advs. Inst. for Traditional Medicine and Preventive Health Care, 1979—. Author: Basic Latin for Plant Taxonomists, 1971, Studies in Begoniaceae, 1981; contbr. numerous articles to profl. jours.; author monographs. Mem. New Eng. Bot. Club, Am. Fern Soc., Bot. Soc. Am., Internat. Assn. Plant Taxonomy, Mus. Russian Culture, Sigma Xi (assoc.). Russian Orthodox. Current Work: Plant taxonomy; ethnopharmacology of Far Eastern nations, primarily study of ginseng. Subspecialties: Taxonomy; Ethnobotany. Office: PO Box 131 Cambridge MA 02140

BARBEE, STEVEN GEORGE, engineer; b. Hastings, Nebr., Feb. 2, 1953; s. James Max and Betty Lavonne (Gustafson) B.; m. Deborah Kay Hultman, June 7, 1975; children—Paul Steven, David Lyle. A.B. summa cum laude in Physics and Math., Doane Coll., 1974; M.S. in Plasma Physics, Columbia U., 1976. Project engr. IBM Corp., East Fishkill, N.Y., 1978—. Contbr. articles to profl. jours. Patentee in field. Author jour. IBM Tech. Disclosure Bull. 1979. Mem. Am. Phys. Soc., Am. Vacuum Soc., Electrochem. Soc., N.Y. Acad. Scis. Republican. Episcopalian. Current work: Development and application of new chemical vapor deposition processes to advanced bipolar digital devices; chemistry and structure of polycrystalline silicon. Subspecialties: Microchip technology (materials science); High temperature chemistry. Office: IBM E Fishkill Z48A Rt 52 Hopewell Junction NY 12533

BARBER, ANN MCDONALD, internist; b. Washington, Jan. 14, 1951; d. Charles Finch and Lois (LaCroix) B. B.S. in Math., Stanford U., 1974, M.S. in Math., 1974; M.D., Northwestern U., Chgo., 1981. Resident in internal medicine Northwestern U. Med. Ctr., Chgo., 1981-84; mathematician Div. Computer Research and Tech., NIH, Bethesda, Md., 1974-76; program anaylst engineer Mass. Gen. Hosp., Boston, 1976-77; med. staff fellow Nat. Cancer Inst., NIH, Bethesda, 1984-87. Contbr. articles to profl. jours. including Am. Jour. Medicine. Mem. Sci. Research Soc. North Am., ACP (assoc.), Am. Fedn. Clin. Research, Sigma Xi. Current work: Oncology research. Subspecialty: Chemotherapy. Office: NCI NIH 9000 Rockville Pike Bethesda MD 20205

BARBER, EUGENE JOHN, chemist; b. Kit Carson, Colo., Jan. 8, 1918; s. Emery Eugene and Addie Margaret (Craft) B.; m. Doris Margaret Pfeifer, Oct. 7, 1945; children—Gail Margaret, Thomas Allan, Daniel John, James Wallace. B.S., U. Nev., 1940; Ph.D., U. Wash., 1949. Research chemist SAM Labs. Columbia U., N.Y.C., 1942-45; research fellow U. Wash., Seattle, 1945-48; chemist Nuclear Div. Union Carbide Corp., Oak Ridge, 1948-77, sr. research sci., 1977-84; sr. research sci. Martin Marietta Energy Systems, Oak Ridge, 1984—; cons. MMES, Oak Ridge, 1984—. Contbr. articles to profl. jours.; patentee in field. Patron Community Children's Theater, Kingston, Tenn., 1984. Mem. Am. Chem. Soc. (local sect. chmn., 1963-64), AAAS, Phi Beta Kappa, Sigma Xi, Phi Kappa Phi, Phi Lambda Upsilon. Republican. Presbyterian. Lodge: Lions (Kingston). Current work: Characterization and properties of heavy metal fluorides with emphasis on processing and handling of uranium fluorides; soluability of volatile inorganic fluorides in non electrolytes. Subspecialties: Physical chemistry; Inorganic chemistry. Home: 122 Westcliff Dr PO Box 476 Kingston TN 37763 Office: Martin Marietta Energy Systems PO Box P MS271 Oak Ridge TN 37831

BARBER, JERRY RANDEL, See *Who's Who in America,* 43rd edition.

BARBER, MICHAEL JAMES, biochemistry educator, researcher; b. Kent, Eng., Aug. 8, 1950; came to U.S. 1977; s. James William and Anne Louise (Shergold) B.; m. Janet Susan Forrester, Sept. 25, 1982. B.Sc. with honors, U. Kent, 1972, M.Sc., 1973; Ph.D., U. Sussex, Eng., 1976. Postdoctoral fellow U. Sussex, Brighton, 1975-77; lectr. Open U., Brighton, 1976-77; research assoc. Duke U., Durham, N.C., 1977-81, sr. research assoc., 1981-83; asst. prof. U. South Fla., Tampa, 1983—; cons. Update Inst. Inc., Madison, Wis., 1978—, Exxon Research and Engring., Linden, N.J., 1978-79. Contbr. articles to profl. jours., chpts. to books. Postgrad. fellow U.K. Sci. Research Council, 1972-73, predoctoral fellow, 1973-75. Mem. Am. Soc. Biol. Chemists. Mem. Ch. of Eng. Current work: Mechanism of action of molybdenum enzymes, applications of spin-labels, EPR of metalloenzymes, methanogenesis, nitrogen assimilation. Subspecialties: Biochemistry (medicine); Electron spin resonance. Office: Univ South Fla Coll Med Box 7 MDC Tampa FL 33612

BARBIERI, RICHARD CHARLES, quality assurance engr., cons., educator; b. Bell, Calif., Nov. 9, 1941; s. Richard Stanley and Charlotte Francis (Nearman) Sieler; m. Joyce Ann Barbieri, June 14, 1965; children—Richard Charles, Kimberly, Susan, Darran; m. Marie Barbieri, Nov. 4, 1977. A.A.S., Wentworth Inst., Boston, 1967; B.S.I.T., Northeastern U., 1972. Test Engr. Digital Equipment Corp., Maynard, Mass., 1967-69; asst. quality assurance mgr. Environ. Equipment div. EG&T, Waltham, Mass., 1969-71; quality assurance mgr. Iotron Corp., Bedford, Mass., 1971-75; quality assurance mgr., chief test engr. Spacetac, Bedford, 1975-78; quality assurance mgr Nypro, Clinton, Mass., 1978-81; group quality assurance mgr. Dennison Mfg. Co., Framingham, Mass., 1981—82; dir. quality Electronic Designs, Inc., Hopkinton, Mass., 1982—; quality systems cons.; tchr. quality-tech.-mgmt. North Shore Community Coll., Beverly, 1982—. Scoutmaster, mem. council exec. bd. Boy Scouts Am. Served with USNR, 1961-64. Mem. Am. Soc. Quality Control (cert. quality engr., chmn. sect. seminars), Internat. Assn. Quality Circles. Current Work: Modernising quality-productivity systems using imaging technology, computer systems and organizational culture dynamics for cost effective non-stress results. Subspecialties: Information systems (Information science); Statistics. Home: Route 119 W State Rd Ashby MA 01431 Office: Framingham MA 01701

BARBORAK, JAMES CARL, chemist, educator, researcher; b. Moulton, Tex., Sept. 8, 1941; s. Victor John and Clothilda Rose (Motal) B.; m. Shirley Ann Heczko, June 7, 1969. B.S., U. Tex., Austin, 1963, Ph.D., 1968. Research scientist Uniroyal, Inc., 1968-69; postdoctoral fellow Princeton U., 1969-70, instr., 1970-72; asst. prof. chemistry U. N.C., Greensboro, 1972-76, assoc. prof., 1976-79, prof., 1979—, dir. research in organic and organometallic chemistry, 1972—. Contbr. articles to profl. jours. Am. Chem. Soc.-Petroleum Research Fund grantee, 1978. Mem. Am. Chem. Soc. Roman Catholic. Current Work: Organic chem. synthesis, especially of strained ring systems; mechanistic organometallic chemistry; organic synthesis employing organometallic intermediates. Subspecialties: Organic chemistry; Organometallics. Home: 205 Kingsdale Ct Jamestown NC 27282 Office: Dept Chemistry U NC Greensboro NC 27412

BARBOSA-SALDIVAR, JOSE LUIS, internist, endocrinologist, clinical nutritionist, educator; b. Asuncion, Paraguay, Dec. 24, 1946; came to U.S., 1972. B.Sc., Goethe Coll., Asuncion, 1964; M.D. summa cum laude, Asuncion U., 1970; postgrad, Balliol Coll., Oxford U., 1971-72; M.P.H., Harvard U., 1973. Diplomate: Am. Coll. Nutrition. Intern Bklyn. Hosp., SUNY-Downstate Med. Ctr., N.Y.C., 1974-75; resident Mt. Sinai Hosp., CUNY, N.Y.C., 1975-77; fellow in endocrinology, metabolism and nutrition Columbia U. Coll. Physicians and Surgeons, St. Luke's Hosp. and Inst. Human Nutrition; asst. attending physician St. Luke's-Roosevelt Med. Ctr., N.Y.C., 1979—; assoc. in clin. medicine Columbia U., 1979—; mem. adv. bd. Council on Mcpl. Performance, N.Y.C., 1974—. Contbr. articles to profl. jours. Soc. Oxford and Cambridge Soc., N.Y.C., 1981—. Recipient Univ. Gold medal Asuncion U., 1970, Gold Medal Goethe Coll., 1964; Hoescht prize, 1970. Fellow ACP, N.Y. Acad. Medicine, Royal Soc. Health; mem. Am. Inst. Nutrition, Am. Heart Assn., N.Y. Heart Assn., Am. Diabetes Assn., N.Y. Diabetes Assn. Roman Catholic. Clubs: Harvard (N.Y.C.); Union. Current Work: Composition of diets and metabolic balance in the treatment of obesity; composition of intravenous nutrition and its metabolic effects. Subspecialties: Internal medicine; Endocrinology. Office: 30 Central Park S New York NY 10028

BARD, ALLEN JOSEPH, educator, chemist; b. N.Y.C., Dec. 18, 1933; s. John J. and Dora (Rosenberg) B.; m. Frances Joan Segal, June 15, 1957; children: Edward David, Sara Lynn. B.S. summa cum laude, CCNY, 1955; A.M., Harvard U., 1956, Ph.D. (NSF fellow), 1958. Research chemist Gen. Chem. Co., Morristown, N.J., 1955; faculty U. Tex., Austin, 1958—, prof. chemistry, 1967—, Jack S. Josey prof., 1980-82, Norman Hackerman prof., 1982-85, Hackerman-Welch endowed chair, 1985—; cons. E.I. duPont de Nemours & Co., Wilmington, Del., Tex. Instruments, Dallas; vis. prof. Mich. State U., UCLA, U. N.C.; vis. scholar U. Ga., 1969; Fulbright prof. U. Paris, 1973; Sherman Mills Fairchild scholar Calif. Inst. Tech., 1977. Author: Chemical Equilibrium, 1966; co-author: Electrochemical Methods, 1980; Editor: Electroanalytical Chemistry-A Series of Monographs on Recent Advances, 1966—, Ency. of Electrochemistry of the Elements, 1973—, Jour. Am. Chem. Soc, 1982—; Contbr. articles to profl. jours. Recipient Ward medal, 1955; named Analyst of Year Dallas Soc. Analytical Chemists, 1976. Mem. Am. Chem. Soc. (Harrison Howe award Rochester sect. 1980, Fisher award in analytical chemistry 1984), Electrochem. Soc. (Carl Wagner Meml. award 1981), AAAS, Nat. Acad. Sci., Internat. Soc. Electrochemistry, Sigma Xi. Research on electrogenerated chemiluminescence; semicondr. electrodes for solar energy conversion; co-discoverer magnetic field effects on solution spectroscopic and chemiluminescent processes; discoverer solar photosynthesis of amino acids on semicondr. powders. Subspecialties: Analytical chemistry; Physical chemistry. Home: 6202 Mountainclimb Dr Austin TX 78731

BARDANA, EMIL JOHN, JR., physician, educator, researcher; b. N.Y.C., May 21, 1935; s. Emilio Dominico and Florencia Fellicita (Perotti) B.; m. Norma Jean Olson, July 9, 1960; children: Anthony John, Anne Michelle. B.S., Georgetown U., 1957; M.D., McGill U., 1961. Diplomate: Am. Bd. Internal Medicine, Am. Bd. Allergy and Immunology. Med. intern U. Calif. Med. Ctr., San Francisco, 1961-62; resident U. Oreg. Med. Sch., Portland, 1965-68, fellow in immunology and allergy, 1969, prof. medicine, vice chmn. dept. medicine, head allergy and clin. immunology sect., 1972—; fellow in immunology Nat. Jewish Hosp., Denver, 1969-71. Contbr. articles to profl. jours., chpts. to books. Served with USN, 1962-65. Fellow ACP (gov. Oreg. 1981-85), Am. Acad. Allergy and Immunology, Am. Coll. Chest Physicians; mem. N.Y. Acad. Scis., Alpha Omega Alpha. Roman Catholic. Club: Oswego Lake Country (Lake Oswego, Oreg.). Lodge: Sons of Italy (Portland). Subspecialties: Allergy; Immunology (medicine). Home: 12389 SW Clara Ln Lake Oswego OR 97034 Office: 3181 SW Sam Jakson Park Rd Portland OR 97201

BARDEEN, JOHN, physicist, emeritus physics educator; b. Madison, Wis., May 23, 1908; s. Charles Russell and Althea (Harmer) B.; m. Jane Maxwell, July 18, 1938; children—James Maxwell, William Allen, Elizabeth Ann Bardeen Greytak. B.S., U. Wis., 1928, M.S., 1929; Ph.D., PrincetonU., 1936. Geophysicist Gulf Research & Devel. Corp., Pitts., 1930-33; mem. Soc. Fellows Harvard, 1935-38; asst. prof. physics U. Minn., 1938-41; with Naval Ordnance Lab., Washington, 1941-45; research physicist Bell Telephone Labs., Murray Hill, N.J., 1945-51; prof. physics, elec. engring. U. Ill., 1951-75, emeritus, 1975—; mem. Pres.'s Sci. Adv. Com., 1959-62. Recipient Ballantine medal Franklin Inst., 1952; John Scott medal Phila., 1955; Fritz London award, 1962; Vincent Bendix award, 1964; Nat. Medal Sci., 1966; Morley award, 1968; medal of honor IEEE, 1971; Franklin medal, 1975; Founder's award Nat. Acad. Engring., 1984; co-recipient Nobel prizes in physics, 1956, 72; Presdl. medal of Freedom, 1977. Fellow Am. Phys. Soc. (Buckley prize 1954, pres. 1968-69); mem. Am. Acad. Arts and Sci., IEEE (hon.), Am. Philos. Soc., Royal Soc. Gt. Britain (fgn. mem.), Acad. Sci. USSR (fgn. mem.), Indian Nat. Sci. Acad. (fgn.), Japan Acad. (fgn.). Current Work: Transport in quasi-one-dimensional metals. Subspecialties: Condensed matter physics; Low temperature physics. Office: Dept Physics Univ Ill Urbana IL 61801*

BARDEEN, WILLIAM A., research physicist; b. Washington, Pa., Sept. 15, 1941; s. John and Jane (Maxwell) B.; m. Marjorie A. Gaylord; children—Charles G., Karen G. A.B., Cornell U., 1962; Ph.D., U. Minn., 1968. Research assoc. SUNY-Stony Brook, 1966-68; mem. Inst. for Advanced Study, Princeton, N.J., 1968-69; asst. prof. physics Stanford U., 1969-73, assoc. prof., 1973-75; scientist Fermilab, Batavia, Ill., 1975—; vis. scientist CERN, Geneva, Switzerland, 1971-72, Max Planck Inst., Munich, Fed. Republic Germany, 1977. Contbr. articles to profl. jours. Alfred P. Sloan Found. fellow, 1971-74; John Simon Guggenheim Meml. Found. fellow, 1985-86; recipient Alexander von Humboldt Found. award, 1977. Fellow Am. Phys. Soc. Current work: Study of fundamental structure of matter; application of quantum field theory to various aspects of theoretical particle physics. Subspecialties: Particle physics; Theoretical physics. Office: Fermilab PO Box 500 Batavia IL 60510

BARDEN, ROLAND EUGENE, biochemist, educator; b. Powers Lake, N.D., Sept.11, 1942; s. Harry S. and Sena Barden; m. Carolyn J. Eliason, Nov. 25, 1967; children: Carl, Janine, Ann. B.S., U. N.D., 1964; M.S., U. Wis., 1966, Ph.D., 1969. Postdoctoral fellow Case Western Res. U., Cleve., 1968-71; asst. prof., then assoc. prof. U. Wyo., Laramie, 1971-82, prof. chemistry, 1982—, chmn. dept., 1980-83, assoc. dean arts & scis., 1983-84, assoc. v.p. acad. affairs, 1984—; Mem. biomed. sci. study sect. NIH 1982-85; chmn. research com. Wyo. affiliate Am. Heart Assn.; mem. com. on research and edn. Assoc. Western Univs., 1981-84. Contbr. articles to sci. jours. NIH postdoctoral fellow, 1968-70; career devel. award, 1976-80. Mem. Am. Soc. Biol. Chemists, Am. Chem. Soc. Lutheran. Current Work: Enzymes, affinity labels, fossil biopolymers, academic administration, teaching and research. Subspecialties: Biochemistry (biology); Geochemistry. Office: Dept Chemistry U Wyo Laramie WY 82071

BARDIN, CLYDE WAYNE, research association executive, biomedical research; b. McCamey, Tex., Sept. 18, 1934; s. James A. and Nora Irene B.; m. Dorothy T. Krieger, Aug. 11, 1978; children: Charlotte Elaine, Stephanie Faye. B.A., Rice U., 1957; M.S., Baylor U. Coll. Medicine, 1962, M.D., 1962. Intern N.Y. Hosp., N.Y.C., 1962-63; resident, investigator Nat. Cancer Inst., Bethesda, Md., 1964-70; prof. endocrinology Milton S. Hershey Med. Ctr., Hershey, Pa., 1970-78; v.p., dir. biomed. research Population Council, N.Y.C., 1978—. Editor: books, including Cell Biology of the Testes, 1982, Current Therapy in Endocrinology, 1983; contbr. numerous articles, revs. to profl. publs. Served to comdr. USPHS, 1964-67. Mem. Am. Fedn. Clin. Research, Am. Soc. Andrology, Endocrine Soc., Soc. Study Reprodn., Am. Assn. Physicians, Am. Soc. Clin. Investigation. Current Work: Broad interest in endocrinology with particular focus on mechanism of action of androgens; direct development program for contraceptives with particular emphasis on finding methods that are suitable for use in males. Subspecialties: Endocrinology; Receptors. Home: 1148 Fifth Ave New York NY 10028 Office: Population Council 1230 York Ave New York NY 10021

BARDWELL, STEVEN JACK, physicist; b. Denver, Dec. 2, 1949; s. George Eldred and Vivian (Marinoff) B.; m. Margaret Anne Sexton, Sept. 26, 1968 (div. Oct. 1984); children—James, William; m. 2d, Patricia Gail Lunsford, Nov. 17, 1984. B.A., Swarthmore Coll., 1971; Ph.D., U. Colo., 1975. Physicist LBM Systems, N.Y.C., 1980—. Author: Beam Defense, 1983. Contbr. articles to mags. Inventor Laser Printer Interface, 1982. Mem. Am. Phys. Soc., Sigma Xi. Current work: Theoretical study of highly nonlinear continuum systems, related to interaction of radiation and matter in fluids and plasmas; technological applications to weather, energy production and computer design. Subspecialties: Plasma physics; Graphics, image processing, and pattern recognition. Home: 166 Edgars Ln Hastings-on-Hudson NY 10706 Office: LBM Systems 251 Park Ave S New York NY 10010

BARE, CHARLES EDGAR, plant physiologist; b. Allison Twp., Ill., Nov. 6, 1939; s. Kenneth Wilford and Florence Juanita (Waters) B.; m. Patricia Houle, Aug. 12, 1961; children: Charles, Theresa, Andrew, David, Ursula, Michael, Rebecca. B.S., So. Ill. U., 1966, M.S., 1969. Cert. comml. pesticide applicator. Instr. natural sci. Franconia (N.H.) Coll., 1969-72; plant physiologist, chemonarcocide unit Weed Sci. Lab., Agr. Environ. Quality Inst., Agrl. Research Service, USDA, Beltsville, Md., 1972-76, plant physiologist, 1976—. Contbr. articles to profl jours. Active Boy Scouts Am., Annapolis High Band Parents. Served with U.S. Navy, 1957-60. NSF grantee, 1971-72. Mem. Council Agrl. Sci. and Tech., Am. Soc. Agronomy, Crop Sci. Soc. Am., Soil Sci. Soc. Am., Assn. for Tropical Biology, Phi Sigma Soc. Current Work: Crop production, pest control, mode of action of herbicides. Membrane and cell biology. Subspecialties: Plant physiology (agriculture); Plant cell and tissue culture. Office: USDA-ARS-BARC-W B001 R40 Beltsville MD 20705

BAREISS, LYLE EUGENE, aerospace company executive; b. Rawlins, Wyo., Nov. 4, 1945; s. Godfrey Matthew and Vera Edith (Squires) B. B.S. in Mech. Engring, Wyo. U., 1969; postgrad., Colo. State U., 1970. Skylab systems engr. Martin Marietta Aerospace Co., Denver, 1969-73, sr. staff engr., shuttle/-spacelab contamination, 1974-79, mgr. tech. unit, contamination and laser effects, 1980—, dep. mgr. materials engring. sect., 1984-85, systems engring. spltys. sect., 1985—. Recipient Skylab Achievement award NASA, 1973; NASA New Tech. awards, 1977, 82, 85. Mem. AIAA, Sigma Alpha Epsilon. Presbyterian. Lodge: Odd Fellows. Current Work: Architect of computer model to predict contamination of U.S. satellite systems; basic research of effects of laser irradiation on satellite/booster systems and materials oxidation and glow of satellites in low-earth orbit. Subspecialties: Aerospace engineering and technology; Satellite studies. Home: 8031 E Phillips Circle Englewood CO 80112 Office: Martin Marietta Aerospace Co Box 179 Denver CO 80201

BARFIELD, WALTER DAVID, physicist; b. Gainesville, Fla., Nov. 25, 1928; s. Walter H. and Myrtle Marie (May) B. B.S. in Physics and Math. cum laude, U. Fla., 1950, M.S., 1951; postgrad., U. N.Mex., Los Alamos, 1952-56, 61, 72-73; Ph.D. in Physics, Rice U., 1961. Research asst. theoretical div. Los Alamos Nat. Lab., 1951-52, mem. staff, 1952-57, 60-63, Los Alamos Nat. Lab. (Group T-2), 1968-70, Los Alamos Nat. Lab. (Group T-4), 1971-79; staff theoretical physics div. Los Alamos Nat. Lab. (Group T-14), 1980—; tech. staff Research and Engring. Support div. Inst. Def. Analyses, Arlington, Va., 1963-67. Contbr. numerous articles to profl. jours. Mem. Am. Phys. Soc., Phi Beta Kappa, Sigma Xi. Current Work: Numerical modeling of high explosives. Subspecialties: Theoretical and applied mechanics; Radiative transfer. Home: 4647 Ridgeway Dr Los Alamos NM 87544 Office: PO Box 1663 Los Alamos NM 87545

BARGER, JAMES DANIEL, pathologist; b. Bismarck, N.D., May 17, 1917; s. Michael Thomas and Mary Margaret (Donohue) B.; m. Susie B. Helm, Nov. 20, 1945 (dec. 1951); children: James Daniel, Mary Susan; m. Josephine Steiner, May 30, 1952 (dec. 1971); children: Michael Thomas, Mary Elizabeth; m. Jane H. Ray Regan, Apr. 20, 1980. Student, St. Mary's Coll., Winona, Minn., 1934-35; A.B., B.S., U. N.D., 1939; M.D., U. Pa., 1941; M.S. in Pathology, U. Minn., 1949. Diplomate Am. Bd. Pathology; registered profl. engr., Calif. Pathologist Pima County Hosp., Tucson, 1949-50, Maricopa County Hosp., Phoenix, 1950-51; chmn. dept. pathology Good Samaritan Hosp., Phoenix, 1951-63; chief clin. pathology Sunrise Hosp., Las Vegas., 1964-68, chmn. dept. lab. medicine, 1968-81, sr. staff pathologist, 1981—. Contbr. articles to profl. jours. Served to maj. U.S. Army, 1942-45. Fellow Coll. Am. Pathologists (exec. com. 1967-84, sec.-treas. 1971-79, v.p. 1979-81, pres. 1981-83), Am. Soc. Clin. Pathologists, AAAS; mem. AMA (alt. del. 1983—), Am. Assn. History of Medicine, Internat. Acad. Pathology, Am. Assn. Pathology, N.Y. Acad. Scis., Ariz. Soc. Pathologists (pres. 1955-58), Calif. Soc. Pathologists, Am. Assn. Blood Banks, Phoenix Soc. Pathologists, Phoenix Med. History Soc., Nev. State Med. Assn., Nev. Soc. Pathologists, Am. Pub. Health Assn., Am. Acad. Forensic Scis., Am. Assn. Pathologists, Assn. Advancement of Med. Instrumentation, Am. Mgmt. Assns., Am. Soc. for Quality Control, Am. Assn. Clin. Chemists, Soc. Advancement of Mgmt., Internat. Assn. Quality Circles, Sigma Xi. Democrat. Roman Catholic. Club: Rotary. Current Work: Quality applications in medicine. Subspecialties: Pathology (medicine); Hematology. Home: 1307 Canosa Las Vegas NV 89104 Office: Sunrise Hosp PO Box 14157 Las Vegas NV 89104

BARGER, JAMES EDWIN, physicist; b. Manhattan, Kans., Dec. 28, 1934; s. Edgar Lee and Carolyn Marie (Grantham) B.; m. Mary Elizabeth Rupp, Aug. 24, 1957; children—Elaine Marie, Carolyn Ruth, James Rupp, Corinne Elizabeth. B.S., U. Mich., 1957; M.S., U. Conn., 1960; Ph.D., Harvard U., 1964. Teaching asst. Harvard U., Cambridge, 1961-64; v.p. Bolt Beranek & Newman, Inc., Cambridge, Mass., 1965-75, chief scientist phys. scis., 1975—. Mem. Methods and Procedures Com., Town of Winchester, 1967-71; trustee Winchester Hosp., 1972—; corp. mem. Mt. Vernon House, 1979—. Served with USNR, 1957-63. NSF fellowship, 1960-64. Fellow Acoustical Soc. Am.; mem. Marine Tech. Soc., AAAS, Tau Beta Pi, Pi Tau Sigma. Conglist (deacon). Club: Winchester Country. Subspecialty: Acoustics. Office: 10 Moulton St Cambridge MA 02138

BARISAS, BERNARD GEORGE, JR., chemistry educator, immunology researcher; b. Shreveport, La., July 16, 1945; s. Bernard George and Edith (Bailey) B.; m. Judith Kathleen O'Rear, May 19, 1973 (div. Sept. 1978); m. Deborah Anne Roess, Aug. 6, 1981. B.A., U. Kans., 1965, Oxford U., 1967; M. Phil., Yale U., 1969, Ph.D., 1971. NIH postdoctoral trainee Yale U., 1971-72, research assoc., 1972; NIH postdoctoral fellow U. Colo., Boulder, 1973-75; asst. prof. biochemistry St. Louis U., 1975-80, assoc. prof., 1980-81; assoc. prof. chemistry and microbiology Colo. State U., 1981—. Contbr. articles to tech. jours. Sec. Mo. Rhodes Scholarship Selection Com, 1976-81; mem. Colo. Com., 1982. Rhodes scholar, 1965; Woodrow Wilson fellow, 1965; Fulbright sr. fellow, Göttingen, 1985; recipient Research Career Devel. award NIH, 1978. Mem. Am. Soc. Biol. Chemists, Am. Assn. Immunologists, Biophys. Soc., Am. Chem. Soc., AAAS, N.Y. Acad. Scis., Soc. Applied Spectroscopy, Phi Beta Kappa, Sigma Xi, Omicron Delta Kappa, Pi Mu Epsilon, Phi Lambda Upsilon, Delta Phi Alpha. Clubs: Am. Alpine (N.Y.C.); Colo. Mountain (Denver); St. Louis Mountain (pres. 1976-77). Current Work: Application of laser optical and image processing techniques in bioinstrumentation, particularly applied to immunology and membrane biology. Subspecialties: Laser spectroscopy; Immunobiology and immunology. Home: 1701 Glenwood Dr Fort Collins CO 80526 Office: Dept of Chemistry Colorado State University Fort Collins CO 80523

BARISH, SAMUEL JOSEPH, physicist; b. N.Y.C., Jan. 23, 1944; s. Louis Mayer and Shirley Florence (Halprin) B.; m. Ruth Edelstein, Aug. 23, 1964; 1 child, Daniel Mark. B.A., Johns Hopkins U., 1965; M.S., U. Pa., 1966, Ph.D., 1972. Research fellow U. Pa., Phila., 1966-72; postdoctoral appointee Argonne Nat. Lab., Ill., 1972-75; sr. research physicist Carnegie-Mellon U., Pitts., 1975-80; interactions expts. program mgr. U.S. Dept. Energy, Washington, 1980-83, small bus. innovation research program officer, 1983—. Contbr. articles to profl. jours. Mem. Am. Phys. Soc., Western Pa. Dressage Assn. (pres. 1977), Potomac Valley Dressage Assn. (pres. 1984-85). Clubs: Aspen Hill Racquet (Wheaton, Md.); Rockville Tennis. Current work: Selection of energy research topics, evaluation of energy research proposals, selection of proposals for funding, and management of the Department of Energy Small Business Innovation Research program. Subspecialties: Particle physics; Laser fusion. Office: US Dept Energy ER-16 GTN Washington DC 20545

BARKAN, PHILIP, mech. engr.; b. Boston, Mar. 29, 1925; s. Philip and Blanche (Seifert) B.; m. Hinda Brody, Sept. 5, 1948 (dec. Aug. 1979); children—Ruth, David. B.S.M.E., Tufts U., 1946; M.S.M.E., U. Mich., 1948; Ph.D. in Mech. Engring, Pa. State U., 1953. Asst. prof. engring. research Pa. State U., 1948-51; sect. mgr. applied physics and mech. engring. Gen. Electric Co., Phila., 1953-77; prof. mech. engring. Stanford U., 1977—; vis. prof. Israel Inst. Tech., Haifa, 1971-72; cons. to electric power industry, 1977—. Contbr. numerous articles to profl. publs. Pres. bd. trustees Middletown (Pa.) Free Library, 1959-61; chmn. bd. trustees Sch. in Rose Valley, 1967-68; Democratic candidate for Middletown Twp. Supr., 1959, 61, 63; pres. Middletown Dem. Club, 1960. Served with USN, 1943-46. Recipient 1st Charles P. Steinmetz medal and award Gen. Electric Co., 1973; Electric Power Research Inst. grantee, 1979. Fellow IEEE; mem. ASME, Nat. Acad. Engring., Sigma Xi. Patentee in field. Subspecialty: Mechanical engineering. Office: Design Div Dept Mech Engring Stanford U Stanford CA 94305

BARKER, HAROLD GRANT, surgeon; b. Salt Lake City, June 10, 1917; s. Frederick George and Jennetta (Stephens) B.; m. Kathleen Butler, July 29, 1949; children—Janet Stephens, Douglas Reid. A.B., U. Utah, 1939, postgrad., 1939-41; M.D., U. Pa., 1943. Diplomate: Am. Bd. Surgery. Intern. Hosp. U. Pa., 1943-44, asst. resident in surgery, 1947-51, sr. resident in surgery, 1951-52, asst. attending surgeon, 1952-53; also asst. instr., research fellow U. Pa., 1946-51, instr., research fellow, 1951-52, assoc. in surgery, 1952-53, asst. prof. surgery, Columbia, 1953-57, assoc. prof., 1957-68, prof., 1968-82, prof. emeritus, 1982—; asst. attending surgeon Presbyn. Hosp., 1953-57, assoc. attending surgeon, 1957-69, attending surgeon, 1969—, dir. med. affairs, 1974-82; practice medicine specializing in surgery, Phila., 1952-53, N.Y.C., 1953—. Contbr. articles med. jours. Served from 1st lt. to capt., M.C. AUS, 1944-46, ETO. Fellow A.C.S.; mem. Soc. U. Surgeons, N.Y. Surg. Soc., Am. Physiol. Soc., Soc. Exptl. Biology and Medicine, AMA, Halsted Soc., N.Y. State (chmn. surg. sect. 1961-62), N.Y. County med. socs., Am. Surg. Assn., N.Y. Gastroent. Assn., Société Internationale de Chirurgie, Soc. Surgery Alimentary Tract, Allen O. Whipple Surg. Soc., Am. Assn. History Medicine, Collegium Internationale Chirurgiae Digestivae. Republican. Presbyn. Clubs: Century Assn; Manursing Island (Rye, N.Y.); Am. Yacht. Current Work: Renal physiology, gastrointestinal physiology.liver physiology, cirrhosis of liver, fluid physiology. Subspecialties: Surgery; Physiology (medicine). Home: 1 Forest Ave Rye NY 10580 Office: 161 Ft Washington Ave New York NY 10032

BARKER, LEWELLYS FRANKLIN, health care exec.; b. Balt., Sept. 9, 1933; s. William Halsey and Mary Lee (Randol) B.; m. Eileen Frances Sweeney, June 6, 1964; children: Robin Lee, Lillian Halsey, Colin MacLeod. A.B., Princeton U., 1955; M.D., Johns Hopkins U., 1959. Intern Johns Hopkins U. Hosp., Balt., 1959-60; resident in medicine Bellevue Hosp., N.Y.C., 1960-62; commd. med. officer USPHS, 1962-78; med. officer div. biologics standards NIH, Bethesda, MD., 1962-72; dep. dir. div. virology Bur. Biologics FDA, Rockville, Md., 1972-73, dir. div. blood and blood products, 1973-78; v.p. blood services ARC, Washington, 1978-81, v.p. health services, 1981—; bd. dirs. Am. Blood Commn., 1978—, Nat. Health Council, 1981—; mem. expert com. on viral diseases WHO. Recipient Meritorious service medal USPHS., 1973. Mem. AMA, AAAS, Am. Soc. Microbiology, Am. Assn. Immunologists, N.Y.Acad. Scis., Am. Epidemiological Soc., Am. Assn. Blood Banks, Internat. Soc. Blood Transmission (councilor 1976-82), Am. Clin. Climatol. Assn., Am. Public Health Assn., Phi Beta kappa. Subspecialty: Preventive medicine. Office: ARC 17th and D Sts NW Washington DC 20006

BARKLEY, LINDA DOROTHY, reliability engineer; b. San Diego, Dec. 12, 1951; d. James Falls and Helen Patricia (Yoo) B. B.A., U. San Diego, 1974; M.S., Loyola Marymount U., 1980. Sr. project engr. Hughes Aircraft Co., Los Angeles, 1978—. Mem. Women and Math. (So. Calif. coordinator 1979—), Am. Math. Soc., Assn. for Women in Math., Soc Indsl. and Appied Math, Soc. Women Engrs., Math./Sci. Interchange Los Angeles (v.p. 1980—), Pi Mu Epsilon. Current Work: Reliability studies for communication satellites. Subspecialty: Satellite studies. Office: Hughes Aircraft Co PO Box 92919 S32/C314 Los Angeles CA 90009

BARNABEO, AUSTIN EMIDIO, chemist; b. N.Y.C., Feb. 7, 1933; s. Austin and Sally Ann (Curcio) B.; m. Patricia Frances Nagle, Sept. 2, 1956; children—Susan Patricia, Evelyn Maria. B.S., Queens Coll., 1954; M.S., Bklyn. Coll., 1960. Chemist, Blackman Brands, Hackensack, N.J., 1955-56; research chemist Union Carbide Corp., Bound Brook, N.J., 1956-62, project scientist, 1962-71, research scientist, 1971-81, sr. research scientist, 1981—. Contbr. articles to profl. jours. Patentee in field. Mem. Am. Chem. Soc., Sigma Xi. Current work: Basic studies of moisture cure technologies; new applications for very low density polyethylene; development of wire and cable polyolefin products. Subspecialties: Polymer chemistry; Organic chemistry. Home: 533 Spring Valley Dr Bridgewater NJ 08807 Office: Union Carbide Corp Polyolefin Specialties Div PO Box 670 River Rd Bound Brook NJ 08805

BARNARD, DONALD ROY, entomologist; b. Santa Ana, Calif., June 7, 1946; s. Alan Whittaker and Ethel Mae (Kennedy) B.; m. Priscilla Margaret Grier, Aug. 12, 1967; children—Jennifer Erin, David Michael. B.S. in Zoology, Calif. State U., 1969, M.A. in Biology, 1972; Ph.D. in Entomology, U. Calif.-Riverside, 1977. Teaching asst. Calif. State U., Long Beach, 1969-72, U. Calif.-Riverside, 1972-77; postdoctoral fellow Colo. State U., Ft. Collins, 1977-79; research entomologist agrl. research service USDA, Poteau, Okla., 1979—; cons. WHO/FAO, 1980—, Bay Region Agrl. Devel. Project, AID, Somali Democratic Republic/U.S.A., 1981—. Contbr. articles to profl. jours. Mem. Entomol. Soc. Am., Entomol. Soc. Can., Ecol. Soc. Am. Current work: Population ecology and integrated management systems for arthropod ectoparasites of domestic livestock. Subspecialties: Integrated pest management; Ecosystems analysis. Office: Agrl Research Service USDA Box 588 Hwy 271 S Poteau OK 74953

BARNARD, THOMAS ELLIOT, electrical engineer; b. Oklahoma City, Dec. 5, 1941; s. Thomas Elvis and Verdun V. (Johnson) B. Sc.B. in Applied Math., Brown U., 1963; postgrad. So. Meth. U., 1965-66, Catholic U., 1981—. Mem. tech. staff Tex. Instruments, Dallas, 1964-69, Washington, 1969-79; staff engr. Gould Def. Electronic Div., Glen Burnie, Md., 1979—. Contbr. articles to profl. jours. Mem. IEEE, Am. Geophys. Union, AAAS. Republican. Club: Whitehurst Garden (Severna Park, Md.) (v.p. 1982-83, treas. 1983-84, pres. 1984-85). Current work: Digital signal processing-time series analysis, array processing, computer roundoff error propagation, target motion analysis, and related topics. Subspecialties: Applied mathematics; Electrical engineering. Office: Gould Def Electronics 6711 Baymeadow Dr Glen Burnie MD 21061

BARNER, HENDRICK BOYER, medical educator, cardiovascular and thoracic surgeon; b. Seattle, Feb. 23, 1933; s. Henry Adolph and Billie (Halvorson) B.; m. Mechthild Brigitta Boehnke, Mar. 6, 1961; children—Boyer Hendrick, Bjorn Oluf, Bela Mattis. B.S., U. Wash., 1954, M.D., 1957. Diplomate Am. Bd. Surgery, Am. Bd. Thoracic Surgery. Intern, resident U. Rochester, N.Y., 1957-59, 61-64, instr., 1964-65; asst. prof. St. Louis U., 1966-70, assoc. prof., 1970-73, prof. surgery, 1973—. Contbr. chpts. to books, articles to profl. jours. Bd. dirs. St. Louis Heart Assn., 1979—. Mo. affiliate Am. Heart Assn., 1980—. Served with USN, 1959-61, capt. Res. Fellow ACS; mem. Am. Surg. Assn., Am. Assn. for Thoracic Surgery, Soc. Thoracic Surgeons, Internat. Cardiovascular Soc. Current work: Cardiovascular physiology, myocardial preservation, vascular conduits. Subspecialty: Cardiac surgery. Home: 443 Sherwood Dr Webster Groves MO 63119 Office: St Louis U Inst Exptl Surgery Saint Louis MO 63119

BARNES, AARON, physicist; b. Shenandoah, Iowa, May 9, 1939; s. Charles Raymond and Avis Irene (Ross) B.; m. Barbara JoAnne Dean, Sept. 17, 1962; children: Christopher, Stephen. S.B. with honors, U. Chgo., 1961, S.M., 1962, Ph.D., 1966. NRC resident research assoc. NASA-Ames Research Center, Moffett Field, Calif., 1966-67, research scientist, theoretical and planetary studies br., 1967—; guest scientist Max Planck Institut fur Physik und Astrophysik, Garching, W.Ger., 1973. Contbr. articles to profl. jours. Hon. Woodrow Wilson fellow, 1961; interdisciplinary scientist Internat. Solar Polar Mission, 1978—; NASA grantee; recipient Outstanding Sci. Achievement award NASA, 1982. Mem. Am. Phys. Soc., Am. Astron. Soc., Am. Geophys. Union, Internat. Astron. Union, AAAS, Phi Beta Kappa, Sigma Xi. Current Work: Theory of space and astrophysical plasmas, solar wind, hydromagnetic waves and turbulence. Subspecialties: Theoretical astrophysics; Solar physics. Office: NASA-Ames Research Center 245-3 Moffett Field CA 94035

BARNES, CHARLES DEE, physiologist, researcher; b. Carroll, Iowa, Aug. 17, 1935; s. Jack Y. and Gladys R. (Beckwith) B.; m. Leona G. Wohler, Sept. 8, 1957; children: Tara L., Teagen Y., Kalee M., Kyler A. B.S., Mont. State U., 1958; M.S., U Wash., 1961; Ph.D., U. Iowa, 1962. Postdoctoral fellow U. Calif., San Francisco, 1962-64; asst. prof. Ind. U, Bloomington, 1964-68, assoc. prof., 1968-71; vis. scientist Inst. of Human Physiology, Pisa, Italy, 1968-69; prof. Ind. State U. and Ind. U. Sch. Medicine, Terre Haute, 1971-75; prof., chmn. dept. physiology Tex. Tech U. Health Scis. Center, Sch. Medicine, Lubbock, 1975-83; prof. physiology, chmn. dept. Wash. State U., Pullman, 1983—. Contbr. numerous articles on physiology to profl. jours. Mem. Am. Physiol. Soc., Internat. Brain Research Orgn., Soc. for Neuroscis., Am. Soc. for Pharmacology and Exptl. Therapeutics, Radiation Research Soc., Western Pharmacology Soc. Current Work: Brainstem-spinal cord interaction, sensory evoked potentials. Subspecialties: Neurophysiology; Neuropharmacology. Home: NW 1235 State St Pullman WA 99163 Office: Dept VCAPP Wash State U Pullman WA 99164

BARNES, FRANK STEPHENSON, electrical engineer, educator; b. Pasadena, Cal., July 31, 1932; s. Donald Porter and Thedia (Schellenberg) B.; m. Gay Dirstine, Dec. 17, 1955; children—Stephen, Amy. B.S., Princeton, 1954; M.S., Stanford, 1955, Ph.D., 1958. Fulbright prof. Coll. Engring., Baghdad, Iraq, 1957-58; research asso. Colo. Research Corp., Broomfield, 1958-59; prof. dept. elec. engring. U. Colo., Boulder, 1959—, chmn. dept., 1964-81; acting dean U. Colo. (Coll. Engring. and Applied Sci.), 1980-81; mem. G-Ed Adcom, IEEE, 1970-77; pres. IEEE Device Soc., 1974-75; Faculty Research lectr. U. Colo., 1965. Regional editor: Electronics Letters of Brit. Inst. Elec. Engrs, 1970-75. Bd. dirs. ABET, 1980-82. Recipient Curtis W. McGraw Research award, 1965; Robert L. Stearns award, 1980; Max Peter's Service award, 1985. Fellow AAAS, IEEE (editor Student Jour. 1967-70, v.p. for publ. activities 1974-75, ednl. activities bd. 1976-85), Engrs. Council Profl. Devel. (dir. 1976-82, chmn. com. advanced level accreditation 1976-78), Bioelectromagnetics Soc. (bd. dirs. 1982-83). Current Work: The effects of electromagnetic waves on biological materials; millimeter waves devices; lasers. Subspecialties: Semiconductors; Laser data storage and reproduction. Home: 225 Continental View Dr Boulder CO 80303

BARNES, GEORGE LEWIS, plant pathologist; b. Detroit, Aug. 21, 1920; s. Harold Bernard and Christina Sinclair (White) B.; m. Phyllis June Dollarhite, June 14, 1947; children: William, Jeffrey, Gregory, Susan. B.S., Mich. State U., 1948, M.S., 1950, Ph.D., Oreg. State U., 1953. With Olin Mathieson Chem. Corp., Columbus, Ohio, 1953-55, Port Jefferson Sta., N.Y., 1955-58; with U.S. Dept. Agr., Stillwater, Okla., 1958-61; plant pathologist Okla. State U., 1958-80, extension plant pathologist, 1980—. Contbr. articles to profl. jours. Served with USAAF, 1942-45. Mem. Am. Phytopath. Soc., Okla. Acad. Sci., Sigma Xi, Phi Kappa Phi. Current Work: Extension, research. Subspecialties: Integrated pest management; Plant pathology. Home: 424 N Donaldson Dr Stillwater OK 74075 Office: Dept Plant Pathology Okla State U Stillwater OK 74078

BARNES, HAROLD JOHN, veterinary medicine educator, poultry medicine clinician; b. Sydney, Australia, May 17, 1943; came to U.S., 1946, naturalized, 1960; s. Harold Irvin and Ruby Elizabeth Alice (Manley) B.; m. Nona Marie Bixler, Aug. 25, 1962; children—Valerie Marie, Melissa Elizabeth. B.S. summa cum laude, Kans. State U., 1969, D.V.M., 1970; Ph.D., Ahmadu Bello U., Zaria, Nigeria, 1976. Diplomate Am. Coll. Vet. Pathologists. Instr. Kans. State U., Manhattan, 1970-71; lectr. Ahmadu Bello U., 1971-75; asst. prof. Iowa State U., Ames, 1975-78, assoc. prof., 1978-82; prof. veterinary medicine N.C.

State U., Raleigh, 1982—. Editor: (with others) Diseases of Poultry, 8th edit., 1984. Mem. editorial bd. Avian Disease Manual, 1st and 2nd edit., 1980, 83; contbr. articles to profl. jours. Recipient Outstanding Tchr. award N.C. State U., 1984, Industry Service award Iowa Turkey Fedn., 1982. Mem. Am. Assn. Avian Pathologists (dir.-at-large 1983—), AVMA, Sigma Xi, Phi Kappa Phi, Gamma Sigma Delta, Alpha Zeta, Phi Zeta. Republican. Current work: Response of avian respiratory tract to injury, causes and pathogenesis of respiratory diseases in poultry, interaction of environment and infectious agents in avian respiratory diseases, use of management to prevent and control flock diseases, pathology of avian diseases. Subspecialties: Pathology (veterinary medicine); Poultry medicine. Home: 1601 Medfield Rd Raleigh NC 27607 Office: Sch Vet Medicine 4700 Hillsborough Raleigh NC 27606

BARNES, HUBERT LLOYD, geochemistry educator, consultant; b. Chelsea, Mass., July 20, 1928; s. George Lloyd and Mary Ellen (MacPherson) B.; m. Mary Talbot Westergaard; children: Roy Malcolm, Catherine Patricia. B.S., M.I.T., 1950; Ph.D., Columbia U., 1958. Resident geologist Peru Mining Co., Hanover, N.Mex., 1950-52; lectr. geology Columbia U., N.Y.C., 1952-54; postdoctoral fellow Geophys. Lab., Carnegie Inst., Washington, 1956-60; prof. Pa. State U., University Park, 1960—; dir. Ore Deposits Research, University Park, Sci. Systems, Inc., State College, Pa.; vis. prof. Mineralogy-Petrology Inst., Heidelberg, 1974; exchange scientist Nat. Acad. Sci., Moscow, 1974; Crosby lectr. M.I.T., Cambridge, 1983; cons. numerous corps. Author: Uranium Prospecting, 1956; editor: Geochemistry of Hydro. Ores, 1967, 79. Guggenheim fellow, 1966-67; N.L. Britton scholar, 1955-56; C.F. Davidson lectr. U. St. Andrews, Scotland, 1971; Thayer Lindsley lectr. Soc. Econ. Geologists, 1980-81; W.O. Crosby lectr. MIT, 1983; vis. prof. Academia Sinica, 1983. Fellow Mineral Soc. Am.; mem. Geochem. Soc. (councilor, pres. 1983-85), Soc. Econ. Geologists (councilor 1981-83), Am. Geologic Inst. (governing bd. 1981-83), U.S. Nat. Com. Geochemistry (chmn. 1976-78), U.S. Nat. Com. Geology. Current Work: Chemistry and geology of natural hydrothermal processes especially in geothermal and ore-forming systems. Subspecialties: Geochemistry; High temperature chemistry. Home: 213 E Mitchell Ave State College PA 16801 Office: Pa State U 235 Deike Bldg University Park PA 16802

BARNES, RONNIE CLAY, astronomy educator, planetarium administrator; b. Union City, Tenn., Sept. 10, 1941; s. William Clay and Alice Evelyn (Hays) B.; m. Sue Ann Hagerman, Sept. 3, 1966; children—Lara Ann, Matthew Clay. B.S. in Physics, Vanderbilt U., 1963; M.A. in Astronomy, Ind. U., 1966, Ph.D. in Astrophysics, 1968. Asst. prof. astronomy U. Mo., Columbia, 1968-75; assoc. prof. Lambuth Coll., Jackson, Tenn., 1975-85, prof., 1985—, chmn. div. natural sci., 1981-84, dir. M.D. Anderson Planetarium, 1984—. Research and publs. in field. NASA fellow Ind. U., Bloomington, 1964-66; NASA summer faculty fellow NASA G.C. Marshall Spaceflight Ctr., Huntsville, Ala., 1979, 80. Fellow Royal Astron. Soc.; mem. Am. Astron. Soc., Astron. Soc. of Pacific. Current work: Applications of the general theory of relativity to problems of astrophysics and determining the properties of close binary stars from mathematical models. Subspecialties: Cosmology; Binary stars. Home: 205 Westwood Jackson TN 38301Office: Lambuth Coll Dept Phys Sci Lambuth Blvd Jackson TN 38301

BARNETT, ALLEN, research pharmacologist; b. Newark, May 5, 1937; s. Samuel and Lillian (Bloomberg) B.; m. Mary Lou Victoria Selva, June 6, 1965; children: Carole, David. B.S. in Pharmacy, Rutgers U., 1959; Ph.D. in Pharmacology, SUNY-Buffalo, 1965. Registered pharmacist, N.J., N.Y. Group leader pharmacology Roche Labs., 1965-66; group leader pharmacology Schering Corp., Bloomfield, N.J., 1966-69, sect. leader, 1969-73, mgr. pharmacology, 1974-75, assoc. dir. biol. research, 1976-79, sr. assoc. dir. biol. research, 1980-84, sr. dir. biol. research, 1984—; adj. assoc. prof. Fairleigh Dickinson U. Contbr. articles to profl. jours. Served with U.S. Army, 1960-61. Mem. Am. Soc.Pharmacology and Exptl. Therapeutics, Am. Chem. Soc., Acad. Pharm. Sci., N.Y. Acad. Scis., AAAS, Am. Pain Soc., Soc. Neurosci. Current Work: Analgesia and endogenous pain suppression systems, dopamine receptors and behavior. Subspecialties: Pharmacology; Neuropharmacology. Office: Schering Corp 60 Orange St Bloomfield NJ 07003

BARNETT, HENRY JOSEPH MACAULEY, physician; b. Newcastle-on-Tyne, Eng., Feb. 10, 1922; came to Can. 1925; s. Thomas William and Sadie (Banks) B.; m. Kathleen Gourlay, Feb. 23, 1946; children—Ann, Will, Jane, Ian. M.D., U. Toronto, 1944; LL.D. Dalhousie U., 1984; D.Sc., N.Y. Inst. Tech., 1985. Jr. rotating intern Toronto Gen. Hosp., 1944, sr. med resident, 1947-48, resident in neurology, 1949-50, fellow in pathology Banting Inst., U. Toronto, 1946-47; sr. med. neurology resident Sunnybrook Hosp., Toronto, 1948-49, cons. neurology 1953-66; house staff Nat. Hosp., London, Eng., 1950-51; research asst. dept. neurology Oxford U., Eng., 1951; physician, 1952-67; cons. in neurology Clarke Inst. Psychiatry, 1953-68, Toronto Hosp., Weston, 1954-66; chief div. neurology, 1966-69; chief neurology Victoria Hosp., London, Ont., 1969-72, U. Hosp., London, 1972-84; chief dept. clin. neurol. scis. U. Hosp. London, 1974-84; clin. tchr. U. Toronto, 1952-54, assoc. in medicine, 1954-63, asst. prof., 1963-66, assoc. prof., 1966-69; prof. neurology U. Western Ont., London, 1969, chmn. dept. clin. neurol. scis., 1974-84, prof. neurology, 1984—; sci. dir. John P. Robarts Research Inst., London, 1984—; researcher in field; lectr. in field; cons. in field. Contbr. articles to profl. jours., chpts. to books. Editorial bd. Neurology, 1973-76, Jour. Neurol. Scis., 1970—, Can. Jour. Neurol. Scis., 1980—, Cerebral Circulation, 1981—, Neuroepidemiology, 1981-84; editor-in-chief Stroke, 1981—. Fellow ACP, Royal Coll. Physicians London, Med. Soc. London; mem. Hungarian Neurosurg. Soc. (hon. Mem.), Neurol. Assn. Costa Rica (hon. mem.), Can. Neurol. Soc. (pres. 1975-76), Toronto Neurol. Soc. (founding pres. 1968), Am. Assn. Neurol. Surgeons, Am. Neurol. Assn. (v.p. 1980-81), Am. Heart Assn., N.Y. Acad. Scis., Alpha Omega Alpha, others. Subspecialty: Neurology. Office: Univ Hosp PO Box 5339 Sta A 339 Windermere Rd London ON Canada

BARNETT, STOCKTON GORDON, research/development director; b. East Orange, N.J., July 18, 1939; s. Stockton and Ethel (Osborn) B.; m. Lucy Estelle Gockel, Aug. 20, 1966; 1 dau., Elizabeth Anne. B.A., Dartmouth Coll., 1961; M.S., U. Iowa, 1963; Ph.D., Ohio State U., 1966. Faculty geology and earth sci. SUNY Plattsburgh, 1966-81, prof., 1976-81; dir. research/devel. Condar Co., Hiram, Ohio, 1981—. Contbr. articles to profl. jours. Exec. com. mem Lake Champlain Commn., 1975-82. Recipient EPA award, 1979. Mem. AAAS, Soc. Econ. Paleontologists and Mineralogists, Sigma Xi. Patentee in field. Current Work: developed first smokeless woodstove and combustion controls; developed method of measuring particulate emissions from woodstoves. Subspecialties: Paleontology; Biomass (energy science and technology). Home: 11782 Mills Rd Garrettsville OH 44231 Office: PO Box 6 Hiram OH 44234

BARNETT, TIM P., research marine physicist, academic adminstrator; b. Los Angeles, Sept. 23, 1938; m. Judie Freymiller. B.A. in Physics, Pomona Coll., 1960; M.S. in Phys. Oceanography, Scripps Instn. Oceanography, U. Calif., 1962, Ph.D., 1966. Research asst. Scripps Instn. Oceanogrphy, La Jolla, Calif., 1960-64, research marine physicist, acad. adminstr., 1971—; oceanographer U.S. Navel Oceanographic Office, Washington, 1964-66; sr. scientist, mgr. Ocean Physics Westinghouse Ocean Research Lab., San Diego, 1966-71. G.F. Baker scholar. Mem. Am. Metall. Soc., Am. Geophys. Union. Current work: Climate prediction, climate dynamics, remote sensing. Subspecialties: Climatology; Remote sensing (atmospheric science).

BARNEY, DIANE JEAN, electrical engineer; b. Ann Arbor, Mich., May 18, 1951; d. Jack Allan and Dorothy Louise (Metcalf) Hathaway; m. Frederick William Barney, Dec. 16, 1978. Assocs. degree, Schoolcraft Community Coll., 1972; B.S.E.E., Va. Tech., 1983. Assoc. engr. Consumers Power Co., Jackson, Mich., 1983—. Mem. Mich. Women Hwy. Traffic Safety, 1977-83. Scholar Plymouth Rotary Club, 1969-71, State Va., 1980-83. Mem. IEEE (chmn. employment assistance com.), Power Engring. Soc, Lansing Jaycee Aux. (pres., parlimentarian, treas., community service dir.) Current work: Modeling of turbine generator torsional effects; generator and system stability. Subspecialties: Electrical engineering; Applied magnetics. Home: 612 Winifred St Jackson MI 49202 Office: Consumers Power Co 212 N Michigan Ave Jackson MI 49201

BARNHART, CHARLES ELMER, See *Who's Who in America,* 43rd edition.

BARON, JEFFREY, educator, researcher; b. Bklyn., July 10, 1942; s. Harry Leo and Terry (Goldstein) B.; m. Judith Carol, June 27, 1965; children: Stephanie Ann, Leslie Beth, Melissa Leigh. B.S. in Pharmacy, U. Conn., 1965; Ph.D. in Pharmacology, U. Mich., 1969. Research fellow in biochemistry U. Tex. Southwestern Med. Sch., Dallas, 1969-71, research asst. prof. biochemistry and pharmacology, 1971-72; asst. prof. U. Iowa, 1972-75, assoc. prof., 1975-80, prof. pharmacology, 1980—. Contbr. articles to profl. jours. USPHS fellow U. Mich., 1965-69; recipient Research Career Devel. award NIAMDD, 1975-80. Mem. Am. Soc. Pharmacology and Exptl. Therapeutics, Am. Soc. Biol. Chemists, AAAS, Am. Assn. Cancer Research, N.Y. Acad. Scis., Soc. Exptl. Biology and Medicine, Soc. Toxicology, Internat. Soc. Study Xenobiotics. Current Work: Immunohistochemistry, immunocytochemistry, chemical carcinogenesis, drug metabolism; toxicology, cellular pharmacology. Subspecialties: Cancer research (medicine); Toxicology (medicine). Home: 302 Shrader Rd Iowa City IA 52240 Office: 2-230 Bowen Sci Bld Iowa City IA 52242

BARON, MIRON, psychiatrist, educator; b. Israel, June 14, 1947; s. Ichiel and Carmela (Muzikansky) B.; m. Carmela Tal, June 5, 1974. M.D., Sackler Med. Sch., Tel Aviv,U., 1973. Diplomate: Am. Bd. Psychiatry and Neurology, Nat. Bd. Med. Examiners. Resident in psychiatry Albert Einstein Coll. Medicine, N.Y.C., 1974-77; research psychiatrist N.Y. State Psychiat. Inst., N.Y.C., 1977-80, dir. div. psychogenetics, 1980—; asst. prof. psychiatry Columbia U. Coll. Physicians and Surgeons, N.Y.C., 1977-82, assoc. prof. psychiatry, 1983—. Contbr. articles to profl. jours. Recipient A.E. Bennett research award Soc. Biol. Psychiatry, 1976, Roche Labs. award, 1976, Mead Johnson Labs. award, 1976; NIMH research scientist devel. awardee, 1978-83. Mem. Am. Psychiat. Assn., Soc. Neurosci., Am. Soc. Human Genetics, AAAS, N.Y. Acad. Sci. Current Work: Biological psychiatry, psychiatric genetics, psychoparmacology, neuroscience. Subspecialties: Psychiatry; Genetics and genetic engineering (medicine). Office: 722 W 168th St New York NY 10032

BARON, SEYMOUR, engineering and research executive; b. N.Y.C., Apr. 5, 1923; s. Benjamin and Tillie (Schuster) B.; m. Florence Chill, Aug. 27, 1950; children: Richard Mark, Paul Lawrence. B.S. Engring., Johns Hopkins U., 1944, M.S., 1947; Ph.D., Columbia U., 1950. Lab. researcher U.S. Indsl. Chem. Co., 1944-47; research asst. Columbia U., N.Y.C., 1947-50; chief engr. Burns and Roe, Inc., Oradell, N.J., 1950-64, v.p., 1964-75, sr. v.p., 1975-76, sr. corporate v.p., 1976-84, dir., 1967—; assoc. dir. Brookhaven Nat. Lab., Upton, N.Y., 1984—; adj. prof. Columbia U., Poly. Inst. Bklyn.; bd. dirs. Argonne Univs. Assn., mem. exec. com., spl. com. for reactor devel., Argonne Univs. Assn., 1976-82; mem. adv. com., engring. tech. div. Oak Ridge Nat. Lab.; mem. N.J. Commn. on Radiation Protection; mem. rev. com. on fusion and rev. com. on chem. tech. div. U. Chgo., 1983—. Fellow ASME, Am. Nuclear Soc., AAAS; mem. Am. Inst. Chem. Engrs., Nat. Acad. Engring., Sigma Xi, Phi Lambda Upsilon. Lions (Oradell). Current Work: Executive management of applied programs. Subspecialties: Mechanical engineering; Nuclear engineering. Office: Brookhaven Nat Lab Upton NY 11973

BARONE, ROBERT MICHAEL, physician/surgeon; b. Buffalo, Apr. 2, 1941; s. Michael Horace and Antoinette (Buscaglia) B.; m. Mary Margaret Wallis, Mar. 11, 1967; children: Susanne, Julie, Robert. B.S., Georgetown U., 1962; M.D., SUNY-Buffalo, 1966; M.S., U. Ill., 1970. Resident U. Ill., Chgo., 1966-72, fellow in surg. oncology, asst. prof. surg., 1972-74 staff surgeon San Diego Tumor Inst., 1980-82; assoc. clin. prof. surgery U. Calif.-San Diego, 1976—; staff surg. oncologist Oncology Assocs. of San Diego, 1982—; mem. U. Calif. San Diego Cancer Center, 1978—. Contbr. articles to profl. jours. Served to comdr. USNR, 1966-74. Recipient Chi. Surg. Research award Chi. Surg. Soc., 1971; NCI grantee, 1979—; Mead Johnson Research award, 1971. Fellow ACS, Soc. Surg. Oncology, Soc. Head Neck Surgeons, Sigma Xi; mem. Soc. Acad. Surgery, Am. Soc. Clin. Oncology, Soc. Gen. Surgeons San Diego, Calif. Med. Soc., San Diego County Med. Soc., Warren Cole Soc. Republican. Roman Catholic. Current Work: Devel. of implantable infusion system for regional delivery chemotherapy to liver; devel. implantable devices for vascular access. Subspecialties: Surgery; Head and neck surgery. Office: 3930 4th Ave San Diego CA 92103

BAROODY, WILLIAM JOSEPH, JR., research institute executive; b. Manchester, N.H., Nov. 5, 1937; s. William Joseph and Nabeeha Marion (Ashooh) B.; m. Mary Margaret Cullen, Apr. 23, 1960; children: William Joseph, Mary Nabeeha, David, Jo Ellen, Christopher, Andrew, Thomas, Philip, Paul. A.B. in English, Holy Cross Coll., 1959; postgrad. in polit. sci., Georgetown U., 1961-64; LL.D. (hon.), Seattle U., 1976, Marist Coll., 1976, Assumption Coll., 1981; Litt.D. (hon.), St. Mary of the Woods Coll., 1976. Legis. asst. and press sec. to Congressman Melvin R. Laird, 1961-68; research dir. House Republican Conf., Washington, 1968-69; asst. to sec and dep. sec. Dept. Def., Washington, 1969-73; spl. asst. to Pres. U.S., White House, 1973-74; asst. to Pres. U.S., White House, 1974-76; exec. v.p. Am. Enterprise Inst. for Pub. Policy Research, Washington, 1977-78, pres., 1978—. Publisher: Pub. Opinion mag., 1977—, Regulation mag., 1977—, Fgn. Policy and Def. Rev., 1977—, The AEI Economist, 1978—. Chmn. bd. Woodrow Wilson Internat. Ctr. for Scholars, 1982—; bd. dirs. St. Anselm Coll., Ctr. for Study of the Presidency, Wolftrap Found., Dole Found.; mem. Pres.'s Task Force on Pvt. Sector Initiatives, 1982. Served in USN, 1959-61. Recipient Disting. Civilian Pub. Service award Dept. Def., 1973. Mem. Am. Polit. Sci. Assn. Republican. Melkite Catholic. Office: 1150 17th St NW Washington DC 20036

BARR, DAVID JOHN, geological engineering educator, researcher; b. Evansville, Ind., Mar. 5, 1939; s. Ralph Emerson and Selma Louise (Sander) B., m. Kay Arlene Porter, Jan. 23, 1965; 1 child, John Matthew. Civil engr., U. Cin., 1962; M.S. in Civil Engring., Purdue U., 1964, Ph.D., 1968. Registered profl. engr., Ohio. Instr. civil engring. Purdue U., West Lafayette, Ind., 1964-68; asst. prof. U. Cin., 1968-72; assoc. prof. U. Mo., Rolla, 1972-78, prof., 1978—, dir. Mining Research Inst., 1980—. Bd. dirs., fireman Rolla Rural Fire Protection Assn., 1975—. Receipent New Technology award NASA, 1980. Mem. ASCE (chmn. aerospace div. 1976-77), Am. Soc. Photogrammetry (pres. Rolla region 1975-76), ASTM, Assn. Engring. Geologists, AIME. Presbyterian. Current work: Use of remote sensing technology for mineral exploration and geological engineering; application of artificial intelligence in manipulating resource databases. Office: Dept Geol Engring U MO 110 Mining Blvd Rolla MO 65401

BARRETT, CHARLES SANBORN, emeritus metallurgy educator; b. Vermillion, S.D., Sept. 28, 1902; s. Charles H. and Laura (Dunham) B.; m. Dorothy A. Adams, Aug. 2, 1928; 1 dau., Marjorie A. B.S., U. S.D., 1925; fellow, U. Chgo., 1927-28, Ph.D., 1928. With metallurgy dept. Naval Research Lab., 1928-32; metals research lab., dept. metall. engring. Carnegie Inst. Tech., 1932-46; prof. James Franck Inst., U. Chgo., 1946-71, emeritus, 1971—; prof., sr. research engr., adj. prof. physics U. Denver, 1970—; exchange prof. U. Birmingham, Eng., 1951-52; vis. prof. U. Denver, 1961, Stanford, 1963, U. Va., 1968, 70, Ga. Inst. Tech., 1973; Eastman prof. Oxford U., Eng., 1965-66; Mem. nat. com. on crystallography, 1950-54. Author: Structure of Metals, 1943, rev. edits., 1952, (with T.B. Massalski), 1966; Co-editor vols.: Advances in X-ray Analysis; Author tech. papers, phys. metallurgy, crystallography. Recipient Mathewson medal Am. Inst. Mining and Metall. Engrs., 1934, 44, 51, Hume-Rothery award, 1975; Howe medal Am. Soc. Metals, 1939; Clamer medal Franklin Inst., 1950; Heyn medal Deutsches Gesellschaft fûr Metallkunde, 1966; Sauveur medal Am. Soc. Metals, 1966; Gold medal Japan Inst. Metals, 1976; Acta Metallurgica Gold medal, 1982. Fellow Am. Phys. Soc., Am. Soc. Metals (hon. mem., Gold medal 1976), Am. Inst. Mining and Metall. Engrs. (chmn. Inst. Metals div. 1956, hon. mem. 1980); mem. Am. Crystallographic Assn., Nat. Acad. Scis., Inst. Metals (London), Internat. Union Crystallography (editor metals sect. Structure Reports 1949-51), Phi Beta Kappa, Sigma Xi, Delta Tau Delta, Sigma Pi Sigma, Alpha Sigma Mu. Current Work: Applied x-ray diffraction. Subspecialty: Materials. Office: Chem and Materials Sci Div Denver Research Inst U Denver Denver CO 80208

BARRETT, IZADORE, fishery biologist; b. Vancouver, B.C., Can., Oct. 4, 1926; came to U.S., 1956, naturalized, 1965; s. Samuel Barrett and Rose (Hyatt) Barrett Gordon; m. Fulvia Mercedes Quesada, July 5, 1958; children—Marcus, Byron, Norman, Dora. B.A., U. B.C., 1947, M.A., 1949; postgrad. U. Toronto, 1949-52; Ph.D., U. Wash., 1980. Chief hatchery biologist B.C. Game Commn., Vancouver, 1952-56; scientist Inter-Am. Tropical Tuna Commn., La Jolla, Calif., 1956-67; chief biologist UN Devel. Program Fishery Devel. Project, Santiago, Chile, 1967-69; fisheries adviser (Chile) FAO, UN, Santiago, 1969-70; dep. dir. Southwest Fisheries Ctr., La Jolla, 1970-77, dir., 1977—; research assoc. Scripps Inst. Oceanography, La Jolla, 1977—; mem. sci. and statis. com. Pacific Fishery Mgmt. Council, Portland, Oreg., 1977—. Contbr. articles to profl. jours. Chmn. Mayor's San Diego/LaJolla Underwater Park Com., 1978—; mem. adv. council Inst. Marine Resources, U. Calif.-San Diego, La Jolla, 1979-84; bd. govs. San Diego Sci. Fair, 1984—, San Diego Oceans Found. Ont. Research Council scholar, 1949. Fellow Am. Inst. Fishery Research Biologists (v.p. 1973-76); mem. Am. Soc. Ichtyologists and Herpetologists, Western Soc. Naturalists, Soc. for Marine Mammals, AAAS. Current work: research and analysis to provide scientific advice for management of U.S. and international marine fisheries. Subspecialty: Resource management. Office: Southwest Fisheries Ctr PO Box 271 La Jolla CA 92038

BARRETT, JAMES THOMAS, immunologist; b. Centerville, Iowa, May 20, 1927; s. Alfred Wesley and Mary Marjorie (Taylor) B.; m. Barbro Anna-Lill Nilsson, July 31, 1967; children: Sara, Robert, Annika, Nina. B.A., State U. Iowa, 1950, M.S., 1951, Ph.D., 1953. Asst. prof. bacteriology and parasitology U. Ark. Sch. Medicine, Little Rock, 1953-57; asst. prof. microbiology U. Mo.-Columbia Sch. Medicine, 1957-59, assoc. prof., 1959-67, prof., 1967—. Author: Textbook of Immunology, 4th edit, 1983, Basic Immunology and Its Medical Application, 2d edit, 1980. Editor: Contemporary Classics in the Life Sciences, 1985. Served with USN, 1944-45. NIH fellow, 1963-64; NIH Fogarty sr. fellow, 1977-78; Fulbright scholar, 1984. Mem. Am. Assn. Immunology, Am. Soc. Microbiology, Sigma Xi. Current Work: Immunology of enzyme-proenzyme pairs, toxicity of Loxosceles reclusa spider venom, anaerobic bacteria-chemotaxis, phagocytosis, platelet activation by toxins and bacteria. Subspecialties: Immunobiology and immunology; Microbiology. Home: 901 Westport Dr Columbia MO 65203 Office: Sch Medicin U Mo Columbia MO 65212

BARRIGA, OMAR OSCAR, Immunologist, parasitologist, educator; b. Santiago, Chile, Mar. 1, 1938; s. Simon S. and Elvira E. (Val) B.; m. Ines Quirland Rojas, Dec. 31, 1960; children: Omar Alexander, Alvaro Gonzalo. B.A., U. Chile, 1958, D.V.M., 1963; M.S., U. Ill., 1971, Ph.D., 1973. Asst. prof. to assoc. prof. parasitology and immunology U. Chile, 1964-68; instr. parasitology U. Ill., 1969-72; asst. prof. parasitology U. Pa., 1973-78; assoc. prof. parasitology Ohio State U., Columbus, 1979—; vis. prof. parasitology and immunology U. Fed. Rio Grande do Sul, Brazil, 1977-78; ad hoc cons. NIH and NSF. Author: The Immunology of Parasitic Infections, 1981; contbr. articles to sci. jours., chpts. in books. Recipient Disting. Tchr. award Norden Labs., 1975. Mem. Am. Soc. Parasitologists, Am. Soc. Immunologists, Am. Soc. Tropical Medicine and Hygiene, Phi Zeta, Phi Sigma. Current Work: Immunomodulation by parasitic infections, immunization for control of parasitic infections. Subspecialties: Immunology (medicine); Parasitology. Office: 1900 Coffey Rd Columbus OH 43210

BARRON, RANDALL FRANKLIN, mech. engr., educator, cons; b. Many, La., May 16, 1936; s. Benjamin Franklin and Inez (Norseworthy) B.; m. Shirley McDuffie, Mar. 14, 1958; children: Randy, Donna Carol Barron Ellard, Steven Dale, Brian Richard. B.S., La. Poly. Inst., 1958; M.S., Ohio State U., 1961; Ph.D., 1965. Registered profl. engr., La. Instr. dept. mech.engring. Ohio State U., 1958-64, asst. prof., 1965; assoc. prof. mech. engring. La. Technol. U., 1965-70, prof., 1970—, Alumni prof., 1979, dir. div. engring. research, 1975—; cons. engring., including to Riley-Beaird, 1966—. Author: Cryogenic Systems, 1966, 2d edit., 1985; contbr. articles to nat., internat. profl. jours. Player agt. Dixie Baseball, Ruston, La., 1976-83. Recipient Gold Medal award Pi Tau Sigma, 1968, award of merit La. Engring. Soc., 1969, Outstanding Research award Sigma Xi, 1971, Achievement award Engring./Sci. Council, 1981, Outstanding Teaching award Tau Beta Pi, 1981, La. Tech. Alumni Found. Prof. award, 1979. Mem. ASME, Am. Soc. Engring. Edn., Cryogenic Soc. Am., AAAS. Methodist. Lodge: Masons. Current Work: Heat transfer at cryogenic temperatures. Subspecialties: Mechanical engineering; Cryogenics. Home: 2202 Greenbriar Dr Ruston LA 71270 Office: Dept Mech Engring La Technol U Ruston LA 71272

BARRON, SARAH KATHRYN BRASWELL, zoologist, educator, researcher; b. McKinney, Tex., Nov. 6, 1941; d. Albert Dalton and Gloria Belle (Staton) Braswell; m. John Calvin Barron, June 3, 1961; 1 dau., Lucille Ann. B.S. in Math, Trinity U., 1962; Ph.D. in Zoology, U. Tex. Austin, 1982. Cert. tchr. math./English, biol./composite sci. Tchr. math. Northside Ind. Sch. Dist., San Antonio, 1963-65, Corpus Christi Ind. Sch. Dist., Tex., 1965-66; instr. math. Christopher Jr. Coll., Corpus Christi, 1966; tchr. math./English Del Valle (Tex.) Ind. Sch. Dist., 1968, Incarnate Word Acad., Corpus Christi, 1966-68; tchr. math., sci., English Holy Cross High Sch., Austin, Tex., 1969-70; teaching asst. U. Tex. Austin, 1970, 72, 1973-75, NSF genetics tng. grantee, 1975-76, research asst., 1977, 78-79, RASSL tutor, 1980-81, specialist dept. computer scis., 1981, research asst. petroleum engring. dept., 1981-82, grad. research asst. III dept. zoology, summer, 1982, postdoctoral assoc. dept. zoology, 1982—; tchr. sci. Town-Country Sch., Austin, 1976. Contbr. reports in field. Active Walnut Creek Neighborhood Assn., Austin. Nat. Inst. Aging grantee, 1982; Ken-ichi Kojima Genetics Meml. travel fellow 1981. Mem. AAAS, Assn. for Computing Machinery, Entomol. Soc. Am., Genetics Soc. Am., Soc. for Study of Evolution, Sigma Xi (grantee 1980). Presbyterian. (officer bd. edn., diaconate council for cultural missions). Current Work: Genetics of life histories of drosophila, longevity and aging in drosophila, morphometrics, life histories, temperature and humidity effects, micro-evolution. Subspecialties: Evolutionary biology; Gene actions. Home: 510 E Braker Ln Austin TX 78753 Office: Dept Zoolog U Tex Austin TX 78712

BARRON, SAUL, chemist, educator, cons.; b. N.Y.C., Feb. 24, 1917; s. Max and Sadie (Levitt) B.; m. Phyllis Levin, Sept. 6, 1941. B.S. in Chem. Engring, Lafayette Coll., Easton, Pa., 1941; M.S. in Chem. Engring, Ohio State U., 1948, Ph.D. (fellow), 1954. Registered profl. engr., Ohio, Md. Jr. naval architect Phila. Navy Yard, 1941-42; mech. engr. Wright-Patterson AFB, Ohio, 1946-51; staff scientist Martin Co., 1954-56; sr. scientist Avco, Lawrence, Mass., 1956-57; dir. research Thiokol Co., 1958-60, Bell Aerosystems Co., Wheatfield, N.Y., 1960-64; prof. chemistry SUNY, Buffalo, 1964—; pres. Space Scis. Co., Buffalo, 1964—; vis. prof. Hebrew U. Jerusalem, 1982; lectr. in field; cons. in field. Contbr. articles to tech. jours. Served to capt. USAAF, 1943-46; with USAF, 1951-52, Korea. Mem. Am. Chem. Soc. (chmn. Western N.Y. chpt.), Am. Ceramic Soc., Instruments and Control Soc., N.Y. Acad. Scis., AAUP, Sigma Xi, Tau Beta Pi, Phi Lambda Upsilon. Lodge: Masons. Current Work: Thermal behavior of polymers; temperature studies of mixtures; developing cooperative program in chemistry; research on heat transfer-cooling systems in supersonic aircraft, re-entry cooling of ballistc nose cones, low temperature testing of aircraft power plants, oscillographic data processing, material and environ. effects upon transport properties of propellants and their behavior in space, thermodynamics and combustion studies of high energy propellants, analytical procedures in chem. instrumentation, solid state physics. Subspecialties: Thermodynamics; Chemical engineering. Home: 249 Troy Del Way Buffalo NY 14221 Office: Buffalo State College 1300 Elmwood Ave Buffalo NY 14222

BARROWS, HAROLD LINDSEY, soil scientist, research administrator; b. Lookout Mountain, Tenn., Dec. 14, 1926; s. Irvin H. and Edna Louise (Seagle) B.; m. Betty Ann Callaway, Dec. 14, 1946; children—Thomas Irvin, Susan Margaret Barrows Hamill. B.S., U. Chattanooga, 1949; M.S., U. Fla., 1955, Ph.D., 1959. Cert. profl. soil scientist. Chemist, U.S. Dept. Agr.-Agrl. Research Service, Gainesville, Fla., 1949-59, plant physiologist, Bogalusa, La., 1959-60, soil scientist, Beltsville, Md., 1960-68, agrl. adminstr. Beltsville and Washington, 1968-83, dir. Nat. Soil Erosion Research Lab., Purdue U., West Lafayette, Ind., 1983—. Contbr. numerous articles to profl. jours. Served with AUS, 1945-46. Fellow Am. Soc. Agronomy, Soil Sci. Soc. Am.; mem. Am. Chem. Soc., Soil Conservation Soc. Am., AAAS, Sigma Xi, Gamma Sigma Epsilon, Gamma Sigma Delta. Current work: Use and protection of soil and water resources for sustained agricultural production. Subspecialties: Soil science; Environmental chemistry. Home: 207 E Navajo St West Lafayette IN 47906 Office: USDA-ARS Nat Soil Erosion Research Lab Purdue U Soil Bldg West Lafayette IN 47907

BARRY, ROGER GRAHAM, climatologist, educator; b. Sheffield, Eng., Nov. 13, 1935; came to U.S., 1968; s. Graham Charles and Winifred (Watson) B.; m. Valerie Tompkin, Oct. 3, 1959; children—Rachel Elena, Jane Christina. B.A. with honors, U. Liverpool, Eng., 1957; M.Sc., McGill U., Montreal, Que., Can., 1959; Ph.D., Southampton (Eng.) U., 1965. Leverhulme Research fellow U. Liverpool, 1959; lectr. U. Southampton, 1960-66, 67-68; research scientist dept. energy, mines, resources, Ottawa, Ont., Can., 1966-67; asso. prof. geography U. Colo., 1968-71, prof., 1971—; dir. World Data Center-A for Glaciology, 1976—; vis. fellow Australian Nat. U., Canberra, 1975. Co-author: Atmosphere, Weather and Climate, 1968, rev. edit., 1982; Synoptic Climatology, 1973; Mountain Weather and climate, 1981; Co-editor: Arctic and Alpine Environments, 1975; Contbr. articles to profl. jours. NSF grantee; NOAA grantee; Guggenheim fellow, 1982-83; NASA grantee; Dept. of Energy grantee.

Mem. Am. Meteorol. Soc., AAUP, Royal Meteorol. Soc., Assn. Am. Geography, Inst. Brit. Geographers, Am. Quaternary Assn., Internat. Mountain Soc. (sec.). Current Work: Climatic change, snow/ice-climate interactions, mountain climates, polar environments, synoptic climatology. Subspecialty: Climatology. Office: World Data Center-A Glaciology Box 449 U of Colo Boulder CO 80309

BARSHINGER, RICHARD N, mathematics educator, researcher; b. York, Pa., Oct. 16, 1944; s. Alfred M. and Charlotte A. (Pifer) B.; m. Patricia Stecker, June 15, 1967; children—Adrien M., James N. B.S. summa cum laude, Lebanon Valley Coll., 1966; M.A., Pa. State U., 1970; Ph.D., SUNY-Binghamton, 1981. Instr. math. Pa. State U., Scranton and Dunmore, 1970-74, asst. prof., 1974-84, assoc. prof., 1984—, liaison to arts orgns. Dunmore, 1973—. Author math. courses for corr. students, 1973-84. Contbr. articles to profl. jours. Profl. musician; performer on harpsichord and organ; music dir. Ch. of Epiphany, Glenburn, Pa., 1970—. Grantee for study of restored antique Flemish harpsichords Belgium Ministry of Edn., 1981. Mem. Math. Assn. Am., Soc. for Indsl. and Applied Math. (referree Jour. on Applied Math.). Current work: Asymptotic solutions to applied mathematics problems of a phenomenological type. Subspecialty: Applied mathematics. Office: Pa State Univ Scranton Campus 120 Ridge View Dr Dunmore PA 18414

BARSKY, ARNOLD M(ILTON), nuclear engineer; b. Chgo., June 21, 1953; s. Murray H. and Doris (Stein) B.; m. Dawn Ann Terry, Jan. 15, 1978; children: Rebecca Marie, Adam Matthew. B.S. in Physics, U. Ill., 1975, B.S. in Astronomy, 1975; M.S. in Nuclear Engring, U. Wis., 1977. Exchange student Energieonderzoek Centrum Nederland, Holland, 1975; nuclear ops. engr. Gen. Electric Knolls Atomic Power Lab., Schenectady, 1978-81, nuclear refueling engr., Windsor, Conn., 1981-83, asst. chief refueling engr., West Milton, N.Y., 1984—. Mem. Am. Nuclear Soc. Jewish. Current Work: Naval nuclear propulsion systems, refueling and pressure vessel reuse. Subspecialties: Nuclear engineering; Nuclear fission. Home: 14 Oxford Dr Wilton NY 12866 Office: General Electric Knolls Atomic Power Lab PO Box 1072 Schenectady NY 12301

BARSKY, BRIAN ANDREW, computer scientist; b. Montreal, Sept. 17, 1954; s. Arthur Harold and Audrey Barbara (Epstein) B. D.C.S., McGill U., 1973, B.Sc., 1976; M.S., Cornell U., 1978; Ph.D., U. Utah, 1981. Vis. researcher Sentralinstitutt, Oslo, 1979; instr. U. Calif., Santa Cruz, 1982—, asst. prof. computer sci., Berkeley, 1981—; adj. asst. prof. U. Waterloo, Ont., Can., 1982—. Contbr. articles to profl. jours. U. Utah fellow; Natural Scis. and Engring. Research Council scholar; U. Calif. Berkeley Regents Jr. Faculty fellow; NSF grantee, 1982—; IBM Young Faculty Devel. award, 1983, Presdl. Young Investigator award, 1985. Mem. Spl. Interest Group on Graphics (tech. program chmn. 1985), Assn. Computing Machinery, Nat. Computer Graphics Assn., IEEE Computer Soc., Can. Man-Computer Communications Soc., Soc. Indsl. and Applied Math. Current Work: Interactive three-dimensional computer graphics and computer aided geometric design and modeling. Subspecialty: Graphics, image processing, and pattern recognition. Office: Computer Sci Div Univ Calif Berkeley CA 94720

BARSTOW, DAVID ROBBINS, computer scientist; b. Middletown, Conn., Aug. 5, 1947; s. Robbins Wolcott and Margaret (Vanderbeek) B.; m. Linda Gail Francis, Dec. 27, 1970; children: Geoffrey Francis, Susanna Lin. B.A. in Math, Carleton Coll., Northfield, Minn., 1969; M.S. Stanford U, 1970, Ph.D. in Computer Sci. with distinction, 1978. J.W. Gibbs instr. dept. computer sci. Yale U., New Haven, 1977-79, asst. prof., 1979-80; program leader for software research Schlumberger-Doll Research, Ridgefield, Conn., 1980—. Author: Knowledge-based Program Construction, 1979; editor: (with others) Interactive Programming Environments, 1984; Assoc. editor: Computing Surveys; Contbr. articles to profl. jours. Mem. Assn. for Computing Machinery, IEEE, Am. Assn. for Artificial Intelligence. Current Work: Automatic programming, programming environments, industrial applications of artificial intelligence. Subspecialties: Artificial intelligence; Software engineering. Office: Schlumberger-Doll Research Old Quarry Rd Ridgefield CT 06877

BARTA, OTA, immunologist, educator; b. Ostrava, Czechoslovakia, Aug. 18, 1931; s. Otakar and Ludmila (Schirmerova) B.; m. Vera D. Dadakova, 1956; children: Marketa, Tomas. MVDr., Vet. Faculty, Agrl. U., Brno, Czechoslovakia, 1955, C.Sc., 1963; Ph.D., U. Guelph, Ont., Can., 1969; cert., Am. Coll. Vet. Microbiologists. Asst. prof. Vet. Faculty Agrl. U., Brno, 1955-61; scientist Central Research Inst. Animal Husbandry, Prague-Uhrineves, 1961-63, Inst. Vet. Med. Research, Brno, 1963-67; research asso. U. Guelph, 1967-69; asst. prof. Okla. State U., Stillwater, 1969-73, asso. prof., 1973-75, La. State U., 1975-78, prof., 1978—. Contbr. articles to profl. jours. Recipient Chaire Francqui Internationale Brussels, 1979; Silver medal U. Liege, Belgium, 1979; Fulbright sr. lectr., 1981. Mem. Am. Soc. Microbiology, Am. Assn. Immunologists, World Assn. Vet. Microbiologists, Immunologists and Specialists in Infectious Disease, AVMA, Am. Assn. Vet. Immunologists. Current Work: Clinical immunology, serum regulation of lymphocyte functions. Subspecialties: Immunology (agriculture); Clinical immunology. Office: Dept Vet Microbiology and Parasitology La State U Baton Rouge LA 70803

BARTEL, LAVON LEE, nutritional and food science educator; b. Salem, Oreg., Nov. 12, 1951; d. Harvey C. Bartel and Jeanne Marie (Siddall) Shelton; m. David G. Struck, Sept. 14, 1974. B.S., Oreg. State U., 1973, M.S., 1975; Ph.D., U. Wis., 1979. Research asst. U. Wis., Madison, 1975-79; asst. prof., chmn. dept. nutritional and food sci. Whittier Coll., Calif., 1979-82; asst. prof. U. Vt., Burlington, 1982—; food cons. Sunny Meadows and Earth's Best, Burlington, 1983—. Contbr. articles to profl. jours. Mem. Am. Dietetics Assn., Inst. Food Technologists, Am. Pub. Health Assn., Sigma Xi, Phi Sigma, Delta Kappa Gamma. Current work: Use of microcomputers in food service and clinical nutrition management, lipid metabolism in renal disease. Subspecialties: Nutrition (medicine); Food science and technology. Home: RD 2 Box 180 Richmond VT 05477 Office: U Vt Dept Human Nutrition and Foods 310 Terrill Hall Burlington VT 05405

BARTEL, NORBERT HARALD, astronomer; b. Wettendorf, W. Ger., Feb. 24, 1950; came to U.S., 1980; s. Heinrich J. and Irmgard E. (Kall) B.; m. Joan C. Bartel, Jan. 11, 1951; children: Hanna Siglinde, Robert H. Diplom in physics, Rheinische Friedrich-Wilhelms U., Bonn. W.Ger., 1976; Dr. rer. nat., Rheinische Friedric-Wilhelms U., Bonn. W.Ger., 1978. Research assoc. Max-Planck-Inst. fur Radioastronomie, Bonn, W. Ger., 1978-80; vis. scientist MIT, 1980-82; research assoc. Ctr. Astrophysics, Harvard U., 1983—Editor procs. Notes in Physics, 1985. Contbr. articles in field to profl. jours. Recipient Otto-Hahn medal Max-Planck-Gesellschaft, 1980. Mem. Am. Astron. Soc., Astronomische Gesellschaft. Current Work: Compact objects, pulsars, supernovae, galactic nuclei, quasars. Subspecialties: Infrared astronomy; Radio and microwave astronomy. Home: 6 Lombard Terr Arlington MA 02174 Office: 60 Garden St Cambridge MA 02138

BARTH, CHARLES ADOLPH, astro-geophysicist, atmospheric and space physicist; b. Phila., July 12, 1930; married, 1954; 4 children. B.S., Lehigh U., 1951; M.A., UCLA, 1955, Ph.D., 1958. Research geophysicist Inst. Geophysics, UCLA, 1957-58; research physicist Jet Propulsion Lab., Calif. Inst. Tech., 1958-65; assoc. prof. U. Colo., Boulder, 1965-67, prof. astro-geophysics, 1967—, dir. atmospheric and space physics lab., 1965—. NSF fellow Bonn, W.Ger., 1958-59; recipient NASA Disting. Service award for work on solar mesosphere Explorer Mission, 1984. Mem. AAAS, Am. Astron. Soc., Am. Geophys. Union. Subspecialties: Planetary atmospheres; Space physics. Office: Atmospheric and Space Physics Lab U Colo Boulder CO 80309*

BARTHOLOMEW, JR. GEORGE A., zoologist. Prof. zoology UCLA. Elected mem. Nat. Acad. Scis., 1985. Office: UCLA Dept Biology Los Angeles CA 90024*

BARTINE, DAVID ELLIOTT, engineering physics laboratory manager; b. Phila., Dec. 6, 1936; s. David Fenton and Elda Josephine (McClain) B.; m. Dorothy Judith Shankle, Dec. 19, 1959; children: David, Benjamin, Rebecca, Mac. B.S. in Chemistry, Eastern Bapt. Coll., 1959; M.S. in Sci. Edn, U. Pa., 1961; M.S. in Nuclear Engring, U. Mo.-Rolla, 1966, Ph.D. in Nuclear Engring, 1971. Instr. physics and chemistry Beaver Coll., Glenside, Pa., 1960-62; instr. chemistry Montgomery Jr. Coll., Takoma Park, Md., 1962-65; research staff mem. Union Carbide, Oak Ridge Nat. Lab., 1969-78, group leader, 1978-81, sect. head reactor analysis and shielding, engring. physics div., 1981—; mem. Com. to Develop Ctr. for Advancement Radiation Edn. and Research Johns Hopkins Med. Inst., Balt., 1982—; mem. nuclear engring. adv. com. U. Mo.-Rolla, 1982—; advisor Def. Nuclear Agy. on Radiation Transport Issues, Washington, 1975—; tech. coordinator Dept. Energy Fgn. Exchange, Washington, 1976—. Author: Radiation Transport Cross Section Sensitivity Analysis - A General Approach Illustrated, 1974; contbr. articles to profl. jours. Recipient citation for Three Mile Island assistance Dept. Energy. Mem. Am. Nuclear Soc. (treas. radiation protection and shielding div. 1978-80, vice chmn. 1981-82, chmn. 1982-83, outstanding service award 1978), AAAS, Sigma Xi. Methodist. Current Work: Radiation transport methods development and application, shielding integral experiments and analysis, reactor core analysis, system conceptual design studies. Subspecialties: Nuclear engineering; Nuclear fission. Office: Oak Ridge Nat Lab PO Box X Oak Ridge TN 37830

BARTLETT, ALAN CLAYMORE, geneticist; b. Price, Utah, June 17, 1934; s. Rulon Ashley and Emily Bertha (Hunter) B.; m. Vanice Rae Baker, Mar 16, 1956; children: Ravae Edith Johnson, Denice Alene Hardman, LeIsle Emily Jacobson, Trace Alan. A.S., Carbon Coll., 1954; B.A., U. Utah, 1956; Ph.D., Purdue U., 1962. Instr. Carbon Coll., Price, Utah, 1957-58, Purdue U., Lafayette, Ind., 1958-62; geneticist U.S. Dept. Agr., State College, Miss., 1962-67, Tucson, 1967-69, Phoenix, 1969—; adj. prof. Miss. State U., 1963-67; adj. faculty Ariz. State U., 1975-79. Contbr. articles to profl. jours. Pres. Tempe Assn. for Gifted, 1975-76; bd. dirs. Ariz. Assn. Gifted, 1977-78. Mem. AAAS, Ariz.-Nev. Acad. Sci., Genetics Soc. Am., Am. Genetic Assn., Entomology Soc. Am., Am. Inst. Biol. Scis. Mormon. Current Work: Development of genetic techniques for insect control. Subspecialties: Genetics and genetic engineering (agriculture); Genetics and genetic engineering (biology). Office: 4135 E Broadway Phoenix AZ 85040

BARTLETT, ALBERT ALLEN, physicist, educator; b. Shanghai, China, Mar. 21, 1923; m. Eleanor Frances Roberts, Aug. 24, 1946; 4 children. B.A. in Physics, Colgate U., 1944; M.A. in Physics, Harvard U., 1948, Ph.D. in Physics, 1951. Mem. sci. staff Los Alamos Sci. Lab., 1944-46; mem. faculty dept. physics U. Colo., Boulder, 1950—, prof., 1962—; mem. faculty Harvard U. Summer Sch., 1952, 53, 55, 56; mem. sci. staff Nobel Inst. Physics, Stockholm, 1963-64. Contbr articles to physics jours. Mem. Boulder Parks and Recreation Adv. Bd., 1967-72, vice chmn., 1969, 70, chmn., 1971; founding mem. PLAN Boulder. Recipient Thomas Jefferson award Faculty U. Colo., 1972, Robert L. Stearns award Assoc. Alumni, 1974, Medallion U. Colo. Centennial Commn., 1977, Univ. Gold medal Regents of U. Colo., 1978, Univ. award for teaching, 1981. Fellow Am. Phys. Soc., AAAS, Am. Assn. Physics Tchrs. (nat. pres. 1978, Robert A. Millikan award 1981, Disting. Service citation 1970); mem. AAUP, Phi Beta Kappa, Sigma Xi. Current work: Problems of energy consumption and of growth in demand for energy. Subspecialty: Nuclear physics. Home: 2935 19th St Boulder CO 80302 Office: Dept Physics Campus Box 390 U Colo Boulder CO 80309

BARTLETT, PAUL DOUGHTY, chemist, educator; b. Ann Arbor, Mich., Aug. 14, 1907; s. George Miller and Mary Louise (Doughty) B.; m. Mary Lula Court, June 24, 1931; children: Joanna Court (Mrs. Stephen D. Kennedy), Geoffrey McSwain, Sarah Webster. A.B., Amherst Coll., 1928, Sc.D. (hon.), 1953; M.A., Harvard U., 1929, Ph.D., 1931; Sc.D. (hon.), U. Chgo., 1954; Sc.D. Dr. honoris causa, U. Montpellier, 1967, U. Paris, 1968, U. Munich, 1977. NRC fellow Rockefeller Inst., 1931-32; instr. chemistry U. Minn., 1932-34; mem. faculty Harvard U., 1934-75, prof. chemistry, 1946-75, Erving prof. chemistry, 1948-75, Erving prof. emeritus, 1975—, chmn. dept., 1950-53; Robert A. Welch prof. chemistry Tex. Christian U., 1974-85, Robert A. Welch prof. emeritus, 1985—; George Fisher Baker lectr. Cornell U., spring 1949; vis. prof. UCLA, 1950; Walker-Ames lectr. U. Wash., 1952; guest lectr. U. Munich, Germany, 1957; speaker 15th Internat. Congress Pure and Applied Chemistry, Paris, France, 1957; Karl Folkers lectr. U. Ill., 1960; Spl. Univ. lectr. U. London, Eng., 1961; lectr. Japan Soc. for Promotion of Sci., 1978; mem. div. com. math., phys. and engring. scis. NSF, 1957-61. Author: Nonclassical Ions, 1965; also chpts. in textbooks, over 250 research papers.; Mem. editorial bd.: Jour. Am. Chem. Soc, 1945-55, Jour. Organic Chemistry, 1954-57, Tetrahedron. Recipient award in pure chemistry Am. Chem. Soc., 1938; August Wilhelm von Hofmann gold medal German Chem. Soc., 1962; Roger Adams award organic chemistry, 1963; Willard Gibbs medal, 1963; Theodore William Richards medal, 1966; Nat. Medal of Sci., 1968; James Flack Norris award in phys. organic chemistry Am. Chem. Soc., 1969, S.W. regional award, 1985; John Price Wetherill medal, 1970; Linus Pauling award, 1976; Nichols medal, 1976; James Flack Norris award in teaching chemistry, 1978; Alexander von Humboldt sr. scientist award U. Freiburg, Germany, 1976; Alexander von Humboldt sr. scientist award U. Munich, 1977; Wilfred T. Doherty award, 1980; Max Tishler award Harvard U., 1981; Robert A. Welch award, 1981; Guggenheim and Fulbright fellow, spring 1957. Hon. fellow Chem. Soc. (London; Centenary lectr. 1969, Ingold lectr. 1975); mem. Swiss Chem Soc. (hon.), Chem. Soc. Japan (hon.), Nat., N.Y. acads. scis., Am. Acad. Arts and Scis., Am. Philos. Soc., Franklin Inst. (hon.), Am. Chem. Soc. (chmn. Northeastern sect. 1953-54), Internat. Union Pure and Applied Chemistry (pres. organic div. 1967-69, program chmn. 23d internat. congress 1971), Deutsche Akademie der Naturforscher Leopoldina, Phi Beta Kappa, Sigma Xi, Phi Lambda Upsilon. Research kinetics and mechanism organic reactions. Current Work: Study of the steps by which organic chemical reactions occur, as determined by molecular structure, arrangement of atoms in space, catalysts, light, etc. Subspecialties: Organic chemistry; Reaction mechanisms. Office: Dept Chemistry Texas Christian Univ Texas Christian Univ Fort Worth TX 76129

BARTLETT, PETER GREENOUGH, engring. co. exec.; b. Manchester, N.H., Apr. 22, 1930; s. Richard Cilley and Dorothy (Pillsbury) B.; m. Jeanne Eddes, July 8, 1954; children: Peter G., Marta, Lauren, Karla, Richard E. Ph.B., Northwestern U., 1955. Engr. Westinghouse Electric Co., Balt., 1955-58; mgr. mil. communications Motorola, Inc., Chgo., 1958-60; pres. Bartlett Labs., Inc., Indpls., 1960-63; assoc. prof. elec. engring. U. S.C., Columbia, 1963-64; dir. research Eagle Signal Co., Davenport, Iowa, 1964-67; div. mgr. Struthers-Dunn, Inc., Bettendorf, Iowa, 1967-74; pres. Automation Systems, Inc., Eldridge, Iowa, 1974—. Served with U.S. Navy, 1952-54. Mem. IEEE. Republican. Presbyterian. Over 50 patents in field. Subspecialties: Electronics; Computer architecture. Office: 208 N 12th Ave Eldridge IA 52748

BARTON, KENNETH E., JR., engineer, engineering director; b. Springfield, Ill., Jan. 19, 1950; s. Kenneth E. and Almeta (Triche) B. B.S. in Elec. Engring., Howard U., 1973, M.E., 1976. Clin. mgr. Medtronic, Inc., Mpls., 1976-83; dir. engring. XOMED, Inc., Jacksonville, Fla., 1984—. Contbr. paper to profl. conf. Active, Big Bros.; bd. dirs. St. Philip Ch., St. Paul, 1979-83, YMCA, Mpls., 1980-83, River Region Drug Ctr., Jacksonville, 1984. Mem. IEEE, Nat. Tech. Assn. Episcopalian. Current work: developing implantable hearing device after 7 years developing pacemakers. Subspecialties: Electrical engineering; Biomedical engineering. Home: 11051 Reading Rd Jacksonville FL 32223 Office: XOMED Inc 6743 Southpoint Dr N Jacksonville FL 32216

BARTON, PAUL BOOTH, JR., geologist, researcher; b. N.Y.C., Sept. 30, 1930; s. Paul Booth and Dorothy Lee (Diggs) B.; m. Martha L. Ashby, June 25, 1955; children—Mark D., John E. B.S., Pa. State U., 1952; A.M., Columbia U., 1954, Ph.D., 1955. Research geologist U.S. Geol. Survey, Reston, Va., 1955—. Author tech. report and articles in field. Fellow Mineral. Soc. Am. (v.p. 1984-85; Roebling medal 1984), Geol. Soc. Am.; mem. Nat. Acad. Sci., Soc. Econ. Geologists (pres. 1979), Geochem. Soc. (councilor). Current work: Field and laboratory studies of ore deposits (especially massive sulfide and epithermal deposits); experimental study of mineral stabilities and phase relations; long-term availability of mineral resources. Subspecialty: Mineralogy. Office: MS 959 US Geol Survey Reston VA 22092

BARTON, THOMAS JACKSON, chemistry educator; b. Dallas, Nov. 5, 1940; s. Ralph and Florence (Whitfield) B.; m. Betty Burton, Oct. 1, 1966; children—Ralph, Brett. B.S., Lamar U., 1962; Ph.D., U. Fla., 1967. NIH postdoctoral fellow Ohio State U., Columbus, 1967; asst. prof. Iowa State U., Ames, 1967-75, assoc. prof., 1975-78, prof. chemistry, 1978-84, disting. prof., 1984—. Author: Organic Chemistry-An Overview, 1977. Contbr. articles to profl. jours. Recipient Gov.'s Sci. medal State Iowa, 1983. Mem. Am. Chem. Soc. (F.S. Kipping award 1982). Current work: Synthetic and mechanistic research in organosilicon chemistry. Subspecialties: Organic chemistry; Organometallics. Office: Iowa State U Chemistry Dept Ames IA 50011

BARTOS, DALE LEE, range scientist, researcher; b. Zurich, Kans., July 26, 1944; s. Herman James and Eleanor (Kern) B. B.S., Fort Hays Kans. State U., 1966, M.S., 1968; Ph.D., Colo. State U., 1972. Range scientist U.S. Forest Service, U. S. Dept. Agr., Logan, Utah, 1972-84, ops. research analyst, Ogden, Utah, 1984—. Contbr. articles to profl. jours. Recipient Albertson Book Scholarship award Ft. Hays Kansas State U., 1972; named Outstanding Young Man of Am., U.S. Jaycees, 1975. Mem. Soc. Range Mgmt., Ecol. Soc. Am., Soc. Computer Simulation, Logan Jaycees (dir. 1974), Sigma Xi. Current work: Developing simulation models of succession in western aspen-conifer ecosystems, monitoring changes as result of disturbance in aspen system. Subspecialties: Ecology (biology); Ecosystems analysis. Home: 1489 N 1525 E Logan UT 84321 Office: Intermountain Forest and Range Experiment Sta 507 25th St Ogden UT 84401

BARTOS, LEONARD FRANCIS, limnologist, educator; b. Balt., Oct. 17, 1947; s. Leonard Francis and Agnes Louise (Martin) B.; m. Mary Elizabeth Farr, Nov. 11, 1972; children—Sara Louise, Jeffrey Jay, Rebecca Lee. B.S., U. Md., 1970; M.D., Western Ill. U., 1974. Research asst. AEC, Argonne Labs., Ill., 1972-73; limnologist S.W. Fla. Water Mgmt. Dist., Brooksville, 1974-76, lab. dir., 1976-79, aquatic plant mgr., 1979-84, dept. dir. field ops., 1984—; prof. biology Pasco Hernando Community Coll., Brooksville, 1981—. Contbr. articles to profl. jours.; editor Aquatics, 1985—. Mem. Planning and Zoning Bd., Brooksville, 1984. Mem. Internat. Soc. Limnology Fla. Acad. Scis., Aquatic Plant Mgmt. Soc., Fla. Aquatic Plant Mgmt. Soc. (dir. 1981-83), Brooksville Jaycees (pres. 1980-81). Democrat. Presbyterian. Current work: Integrated aquatic plant management. Subspecialties: Integrated pest management; Limnology. Home: 461 Rogers Ave Brooksville FL 33512 Office: SW Fla Water Mgmt Dist 2379 Broad St Brooksville FL 33512

BARTUS, RAYMOND T., neuroscientist, writer, lecturer, musician; b. Chgo., May 19, 1947; s. Frank A. and Katherine (Bogus) B.; m. Cheryl Gyure, Feb. 11, 1967; children—Raymond T., Kristin Marie. B.A. in Psychology with honors, California (Pa.) State Coll., 1968; M.S. in Exptl. Psychology (NIH predoctoral asst.), N.C. State U., 1970, Ph.D. in Physiol. Psychology (NASA pre-doctoral fellow), 1972. NRC Postdoctoral assoc. Naval Med. Research Lab., Groton, Conn., 1972-73; scientist Warner-Lambert/Parke-Davis Research Labs., Ann Arbor, Mich., 1973-77, sr. scientist, 1977-78; sr. scientist CNS research Med. Research div. Am. Cyanamid Co., Pearl River, N.Y., 1978, dir. geriatric discovery program, 1979—, group leader behavioral neurosci., 1980—; adj. prof. psychiatry N.Y. U., 1980—; research affiliate Tulane U. and Delta Regional Primate Research Center, Covington, La., 1978—; adj. asst. prof. Conn. Coll., 1973; referee, program advisor, spl. sci. cons. Office Technol. Assessment, NSF, NIMH, Nat. Inst. Aging, Fedn. Am. Socs. Exptl. Biology; research cons.; speaker profl. cons. Editor in chief: Neurobiology of Aging: Experimental and Clinical Research, 1981; editorial adv. bd., referee: Jour. Gerontology, 1981—, Exptl. Aging Research, 1981-82, Pharmacology, Biochemistry and Behavior, 1981-82; referee: jours. sci. adv. bd.: jours. Anti-Aging News, 1980-84; editor sci. books. Contbr. over 100 articles to profl. jours.; editor profl. books. Nat. Research Council postdoctoral fellow, 1972-73; recipient Exceptional Sr. Research award Calif. State Coll., 1968. Mem. Soc. Neurosci., Gerontol. Soc., Am. Aging Assn. (bd. dirs.), Am. Psychol. Assn., Sigma Xi, Psi Chi. Current Work: Neurophysiology, understanding changes in brain with age and how to correct, psychopharmacology, cognition, learning, neurochemistry, psychiatry, neuropsychology, psychobiology, physiol. psychology. Subspecialties: Neuropharmacology; Gerontology. Office: American Cyanamid Co Medical Research Div Pearl River NY 10965

BASAR, TAMER, engineering educator; b. Istanbul, Turkey, Jan. 19, 1946; came to U.S., 1969, naturalized, 1981; s. Munir and Seniye (Pirilsu) B.; m. Tangul Unerdem, Dec. 27, 1975; children—Gozen, Elif. B.S.E.E., Robert Coll., Istanbul, 1969; M.S., Yale U., 1970, M.S. in Philosophy, 1971, Ph.D., 1972. Research fellow Harvard U., Cambridge, Mass., 1972-73; sr. research sci. Marmara Research Inst., Gebze, Turkey, 1973-80; assoc. prof. U. Ill., Urbana, 1980-83, prof. elec. and computer engring., 1983—; dir. Decision and Control Lab., Coordinated Sci. Lab., Urbana, Author: Dynamic Noncooperative Game Theory, 1982; editor: Modelling and Control of National Economies, 1983. Recipient TUBITAK Young Sci. award in applied math. Nat. Research Council Turkey, 1974; Sedat Simavi Found. award in math. sci. Sedat Simavi Found., Turkey, 1979. Fellow IEEE; mem. N.Y. Acad. Sci., AAAS, Sigma Xi. Current work: Control of stochastic systems; analysis and optimization of large scale systems; dynamic game theory; decision making under uncertainy; dynamic modelling of economic systems. Subspecialties: Computer engineering; Applied mathematics. Home: 1114 Scoville Urbana IL 61801 Office: U Ill 1101 W Springfield Ave Urbana IL 61801

BASCOM, WILLARD NEWELL, scientist, engineer; b. N.Y.C., Nov. 7, 1916; s. Willard Newell and Pearle (Boyd) B.; m. Rhoda Nergaard, Apr. 15, 1946; children: Willard, Anitra. Grad., Colo. Sch. Mines, 1942. Registered profl. engr., Fla., D.C. Research engr. U. Calif.-Berkeley, 1945-50, Scripps Inst. Oceanography, 1950-54; exec. sec. Nat. Acad. Scis., Washington, 1954-62; pres. Ocean Sci. & Engring., Inc., Washington, 1962-72; dir. Coastal Water Research Project, Long Beach, Calif., 1973-85. cons. to govt. and industry. Author: Waves and Beaches, 1964, A Hole in the Bottom of the Sea, 1961, Deep Water, Ancient Ships, 1976, over 100 articles. Recipient Disting. Achievement medal Colo. Sch. Mines, 1979; recipient Compass Disting. Achievement award Marine Tech. Soc., 1970. Clubs: Explorers (Explorers medal 1980), Adventurers. Patentee deep ocean search/recovery system. Current Work: Coastal ecology, archaeology. Subspecialties: Oceanography; Archaeology. Home: 5137 Vista Hermosa Long Beach CA 90815

BASEHORE, KERRY LEE, nuclear engineer, consultant; b. Hershey, Pa., Aug. 24, 1953; s. Kenneth Leroy and Jeannette Marie (Tietsworth) B.; m. Betsy Ann Chamberlain, June 14, 1975; children: Kenneth Lawrence, Carolyn Joyce, Laura Elizabeth. B.S., Pa. State U., 1975; M.S., M.I.T., 1977, Nuclear Engr., 1977. Registered profl. engr., Va. Devel. engr. Battelle N.W. Labs., Richland, Wash., 1977-80; sr. engr. Va. Electric & Power Co., Richmond, 1980-84, supr. nuclear engring., 1984—; cons. Westinghouse-Hanford Co., Richland, Wash., 1982. Tchr. Chester United Meth. Ch., Chester, Va., 1981-82. Mem. Am. Nuclear Soc. (thermal hydraulic program com. 1981—), Nat. Soc. Profl. Engrs., Sigma Xi. Republican. Methodist. Club: Engineers (Richmond). Current Work: supervision of group responsible for light water reactor safety analysis, thermal-hydraulic analysis, fuel performance and LOCA. Subspecialties: Nuclear engineering; Numerical analysis (computer science). Home: 10118 Remora Dr Richmond VA 23237 Office: Va Electric & Power Co PO Box 26666 Richmond VA 23261

BASH, FRANK NESS, astronomer, educator; b. Medford, Oreg., May 3, 1937; s. Frank Cozad and Kathleen Jane (Ness) B.; m. Susan Martin Fay, Sept. 10, 1960; children: Kathryn Fay Bash Cerveuka, Francis Lee. B.A. in Physics, Willamette U., 1959; M.A. in Astronomy, Harvard U., 1962; Ph.D. in Astronomy, U. Va., 1967. Staff scientist Lincoln Lab., M.I.T., 1962; asso. astronomer Nat. Radio Astronomy Obs., Green Bank, W.Va., 1962-64; research asst. U. Va., 1965-67; postdoctoral faculty asso. U.Tex., Austin., 1967-69, asst. prof. astronomy, 1969-73, asso. prof., 1973-81, prof., 1981—, chmn. dept. astronomy, 1982—, Frank N. Edmonds Jr. Regents prof., 1985—. Author: (with Daniel Schiller and Pilip Balamore) Astronomy, 1977; contbr. articles to profl. jours. NSF grantee, 1967—; Netherlands's NSF grantee, 1979. Mem. Am. Astron. Soc., Internat. Astron. Union, Internat. Sci. Radio Union, Tex. Assn. Coll. Tchrs. (pres. U. Tex. chpt. 1980-82). Club: Town and Gown (Austin). Current Work: Research on process of star formation in spiral galaxies. Subspecialties: Radio and microwave astronomy; Theoretical astrophysics. Office: Dept Astronomy U Tex Austin TX 78712

BASHINSKI, HOWARD STEWART, human factors engineer, visual psychophysics researcher; b. Orlando, Fla., Dec. 6, 1952; s. Isadore and Tilley (Woodward) B.; m. Laurie Ingraham, May 12, 1975 (div. July, 1980); 1 child, Brina; m. Michele Noe, May 22, 1981; children—Samantha, Caitlin. Student Ga. Inst. Tech., 1969-71; B.G.S., U. Nebr., 1975; M.S., Acadia U., 1979; Ph.D. in Exptl. Psychology, U. Colo., 1982. Postdoctoral fellow McMaster U., Hamilton, Ont., 1982-83; software engr. NCHEMS, Boulder, Colo., 1983; sr. engr. Gen. Dynamics Corp., Ft. Worth, 1984—. Served to sgt. USAF, 1972-76. Univ. fellow Acadia U., 1977-79. Nat. Scis. and Engring. Research Council scholar U. Colo., 1980-82. Current work: Psychophysics of advanced display systems, human-instrumentation visual interfacing, aircraft lighting systems, advanced displays. Subspecialties: Human factors engineering; Psychophysics. Office: Gen Dynamics PO Box 748 Fort Worth TX 76101

BASHKIN, STANLEY, physics educator; b. Bklyn., June 20, 1923; s. Max and Elizabeth B.; m. Margaret Mary Turnbull, Aug. 22, 1957; children—James K., Margaret J., John S. B.A., Bklyn. Coll., 1944; Ph.D., U. Wis.-Madison, 1950. Asst. prof. La. State U., Baton Rouge, 1950-53; research assoc. U. Iowa, Iowa

City, 1953-56, asst. prof., 1956-59, assoc. prof., 1959-62; prof. U. Ariz., Tucson, 1962—; pres. Ariz. Carbon Foil Co., Tucson, 1972—. Author numerous books. Contbr. articles to profl. jours. Recipient Outstanding Alumnus medal Bklyn. Coll.; Royal Soc. Arts and Scis. fellow, Alexander von Humboldt Found. sr. fellow, Fulbright fellow, Oxford U. sr. vis. fellow, Australian Nat. U. research fellow. Fellow Am. Phys. Soc., Optical Soc. Am.; mem. Internat. Nuclear Target Makers Soc., Royal Soc. Arts. Subspecialty: Atomic and molecular physics. Office: U Ariz Dept Physics PAS Bldg 81 Tucson AZ 85721

BASIC, JOHN NICHOLAS, SR., engring. co. exec., mech. engr.; b. Chgo., Dec. 16, 1923; s. Marin and Mary (Lucin) B.; m. Marijo C. Coleman, May 20, 1950; children: Cathe Ostrowski, John Nicholas, Sarah Ann, Margaret Mary, Kerry Eileen, Laura Rene. B.S.M.E., Ill. Inst. Tech., 1947, postgrad., 1948-51; student law, Loyola U., Chgo., 1956, 59. Registered profl. engr., Ill. Jr. engr. U. Chgo. Cyclotron Project, 1948; jr. engr to mgr. maintenance Joanna Western Mills Co., Chgo., 1949-56, dir. engring., 1959-69; chief engr. Mt. Hope Machinery Co., Taunton, Mass., 1956-59; pres., owner Basic Environ. Engring., Inc., Glen Ellyn, Ill., 1970—. Served with USNR., 1944-46, PTO. Grantee Pollution Engring. Mag., 1977, 78, 79. Mem. ASME, We. Soc. Engrs., Air Pollution Control Assn. Republican. Roman Catholic. Club: Glen Ellyn Country. Patentee in field. Current Work: Design and build systems that burn wide spectrum of wastes with same equipment; construct solid waste water wall combustion systems to burn varied wastes, extract higher energy efficiencies and with environ. acceptable standards. Subspecialties: Combustion processes; Biomass (energy science and technology). Home: 41 W 202 Whitney Rd Saint Charles IL 60174 Office: 21 W 161 HIll Ave Glen Ellyn IL 60137

BASILICO, CLAUDIO, geneticist, educator; b. Milan, Italy, Feb. 7, 1936; came to U.S., 1967; s. Vittorio and Enrica (Belloni) B.; m. Mariapia Casartelli, Oct. 7, 1961; children: Stefano, Francesca, Enrica. M.D., U. Milan, 1960. Vis. research fellow div. biology Calif. Inst. Tech., 1962; staff Internat. Lab. Genetics and Biophysics, Naples, Italy, 1963-66; research asso. dept. cell biology Albert Einstein Coll. Medicine, 1966-67; vis. research scientist dept. pathology N.Y. U. Sch. Medicine, N.Y.C., 1967-69, research asst. prof., 1969, asso. prof., 1970-75, prof. dept. pathology, 1975—; mem. Am. Cancer Soc. adv. com. on cellular and developmental biology, 1979-82. Contbr. articles to profl. jours. Trustee Cold Spring Harbor Lab., 1981—. Mem. Am. Soc. Microbiology, Am. Soc. Cell Biology, Am. Assn. for Cancer Research, Am. Soc. Virology. Current Work: Viral oncology, cell genetics, mechanisms gene expression. Subspecialties: Genome organization; Virology (biology). Office: 550 First Ave New York NY 10016

BASOLO, FRED, chemistry educator; b. Coello, Ill., Feb. 11, 1920; s. John and Catherine (Marino) B.; m. Mary P. Nutley, June 14, 1947; children: Mary Catherine, Freddie, Margaret Ann, Elizabeth Rose. B.E., So. Ill. U., 1940; M.S., U. Ill., 1942, Ph.D. in Inorganic Chemistry, 1943. Research chemist Rohm & Haas Chem. Co., Phila., 1943-46; mem. faculty Northwestern U., Evanston, Ill., 1946—, prof. chemistry, 1958—, chmn. dept. chemistry, 1969-72, Morrison prof., 1980—; cons. and lectr. in field. Co-author: (with R.G. Pearson) Mechanisms of Inorganic Reactions, 1958, (with R.C. Johnson) Coordination Chemistry, 1964; assoc. editor: (with R.C. Johnson) Inorganica Chemica Acta, 1967—, Inorganic Chemica Acta Letters, 1977—; mem. editorial bds. of numerous profl. jours. (with R.C. Johnson); contbr. (with R.C. Johnson) articles to profl. jours. Mem. adv. bd. Who's Who in America. Recipient Bailar Medal award, 1972; So. Ill. U. Alumni achievement award, 1974; Dwyer Medal award, 1976; James Flack Norris award outstanding achievement in teaching chemistry, 1981; Oesper Meml. award, 1983; Guggenheim fellow U. Copenhagen, 1954-55; Sr. NSF fellow U. Rome, 1962; NATO disting. prof. Tech. U. Munich, 1969; Japanese Soc. Promotion of Sci. fellow, 1979; NATO Sr. Scientist fellow Italy, 1981. Fellow AAAS; mem. Nat. Acad. Scis., Am. Chem. Soc. (bd. dirs. 1982—, pres. 1983, inorganic chemistry research award 1964, citation for excellence 1971, Disting. Service award 1975), Chem. Soc. (London), Italian Chem. Soc. (hon.), Sigma Xi, Alpha Chi Sigma, Kappa Delta Phi, Phi Lambda Upsilon (hon.). Subspecialties: Inorganic chemistry; Nuclear chemistry. Office: Dept Chemistry Northwestern U Evanston IL 60201

BASRI, GIBOR BROITMAN, astronomy educator; b. N.Y.C., May 3, 1951; s. Saul and Phyllis B.; m. Jessica Broitman, June 21, 1981. B.Sc., Stanford U., 1973; Ph.D., U. Colo., 1979. Postdoctoral fellow U. Calif.-Berkeley, 1979-81, asst. prof. astronomy, 1982—. Contbr. articles to profl. jours., 1979—. Chancellor's fellow U. Calif.-Berkeley, 1979-81. Mem. Am. Astron. Soc., Astron. Soc. of the Pacific, Internat. Astron. Union. Current work: Stellar atmospheres; stellar activity. Subspecialty: Ultraviolet high energy astrophysics. Home: 1090 Warfield Ave Oakland CA 94610 Office: U Calif Dept Astronomy Berkeley CA 94720

BASRI, SAUL ABRAHAM, physics educator; b. Baghdad, Iraq, Feb. 15, 1926; s. Abraham Saul and Levana (Mathalone) B.; m. Phyllis Claire Whyte, Feb. 1, 1950 (div. 1975); children—Gibor S., David A. B.S., MIT, 1948; Ph.D., Columbia U., 1953. Asst. prof. Colo. State U., Ft. Collins, 1953-56, assoc. prof., 1956-67, prof., 1967—; physicist Nat. Bur. Standards, Boulder, Colo., summers, 1956-58; Fulbright lectr. U. Rangoon (Burma), 1956-57, U. Ceylon, 1965-66; vis. prof. Technion, Haifa, Israel, 1973-74. Author: Deductive Theory of Space and Time, 1966. Contbr. articles to profl. jours. Mem. Am. Phys. Soc. Democrat. Jewish. Current work: Theoretical foundation. Subspecialty: Particle physics. Home: 1625 W Elizabeth C 3 Fort Collins CO 80521 Office: Dept Physics Colo State U Fort Collins CO 80523

BASS, HYMAN, mathematician, educator; b. Houston, Oct. 5, 1932; s. Isador and Fanny (Weiss) B.; m. Mary Ellen Popkin, June 9, 1957 (div. 1978); children: Anne Ruth, Ivan Philip; m. Dorothea Henriette Goldys, Nov. 1, 1979; 1 dau., Gabriella Sierra. B.A., Princeton U., 1955; M.S., U. Chgo., 1956, Ph.D. (NSF grad. fellow), 1959. Ritt instr. math. Columbia U., 1959-62, asst. prof., 1963-64, chmn. dept. math., 1975—; asso. prof., chmn. at Barnard Coll., 1964-65, prof., 1965—; Vis. mem. Inst. Advanced Study, Princeton, 1964, 65-66, Inst. de Hautes Etudes Scientifiques, Paris, 1968-69; vis. prof. Universidad Nacional Autónoma de Mex., 1965, Tata Inst. Fundamental Research, Bombay, 1965-66, 69, 76, 80, U. Paris, 1968, 73, 81, Cambridge U., 1973, Instituto de Matematica Pura e Applicada, Rio de Janeiro, 1977, Bar Ilan U., Israel, 1980; chmn. adv. com. pure mathematics NRC, 1970-71, mem. bd. math. scis., 1984—; adv. panel, div. math. NSF, 1973-75. Editorial bd.: Jour. Indian Math. Soc, 1968—, Cambridge Tracts in Pure and Applied Mathematics; 968: Jour. Pure and Applied Algebra, 1970—, Am. Jour. Mathematics, 1971—, North-Holland Math. Library, 1971—, Acad. Press Series in Pure and Applied Math, 1974—. NSF fellow Coll. de France, 1962-63; Sloan fellow, 1964-66; Guggenheim fellow, 1968-69; recipient Van Amridge book prize Columbia, 1969, Cole prize Am. Math. Soc., 1975. Mem. Am. Math Soc. (editorial bd. 1969—, council 1969-72), Am. Acad. Arts and Scis., Nat. Acad. Scis., London Math. Socs., Societé Mathématique de France, Soc. Collaborateurs N. Bourbaki, Math. Assn. Am., AAAS., Am. Acad. Arts and Scis., Nat. Acad. Scis. Subspecialty: Algebra and number theory. Home: 435 Riverside Dr New York NY 10025

BASS, LOUIS NELSON, agronomist, plant physiologist, govt. ofcl.; b. Iola, Kans., Mar. 7, 1919; s. Herbert and Olive (Felker) B.; m. Helen Jane Collins, Nov. 7, 1943; children—Colin David, Nelsa Louise Mullen. B.S., Upper Iowa U., 1940; M.S., U. Iowa, 1943; Ph.D., Iowa State U., 1949. Asst. prof. botany and plant pathology Iowa State U., Ames, 1949-58; plant physiologist Nat. Seed Storage Lab., USDA, Fort Collins, Colo., 1958-70, dir., 1970—, research leader seed viability and storage, 1972—; Mem. grad. faculty Colo. State U., Fort Collins, 1960—. Recipient Alumni Achievement award Upper Iowa U., 1972. Mem. Am. Soc. Agronomy (asso. editor Jour. 1971-74), Soc. Comml. Seed Technologists, Assn. Ofcl. Seed Analysts (Merit award 1975, sci. edn. editor 1962—, pres. 1971-72, mem. pub. service com. 1962—), Crop Sci. Soc. Am. (ex.-officio mem. com. for preservation of genetic stocks 1971—), Am. Soc. Hort. Sci., Internat. Seed Testing Assn. (vice chmn. seed moisture and storage com. 1974-80, chmn. seed storage com. 1980—), Am. Type Culture Collection, Sigma Xi, Gamma Sigma Delta, Epsilon Sigma Phi. Current work: Conduct research on methods of keeping seeds viable and on germination requirements of stored seed. Subspecialties: Plant physiology (agriculture); Resource conservation. Home: 1117 Fairview Fort Collins CO 80521 Office: Nat Seed Storage Lab Colo State Univ Fort Collins CO 80523

BASSETT, WILLIAM AKERS, geology educator; b. Bklyn., Aug. 3, 1931; s. Preston Rogers and Jeanne (Mordorf) B.; m. Jane Kermes, Sept. 8, 1962; children—Kari, Jeffrey, Penelope. B.A., Amherst Coll., 1954; M.A., Columbia U., 1956, Ph.D., 1959. Research assoc. Brookhaven Nat. Lab., Upton, N.Y., 1960-63; asst. prof. geology U. Rochester, N.Y., 1961-65, assoc. prof., 1965-68, prof., 1969-78; prof. Cornell U., Ithaca, N.Y., 1978—. Contbr. articles to profl. jours. NSF grantee 1962—. Fellow Geol. Soc. Am., Mineral. Soc. Am., Am. Geophys. Union; mem. AAAS, Sigma Xi (pres. Rochester chpt. 1977-78). Current work: Effects of high pressure and high temperature on the properties of minerals. Subspecialty: Mineralogy. Home: 765 Bostwick Rd Ithaca NY Office: Cornell U Dept Geol Scis Ithaca NY 14853

BASSI, SUKH DEV, microbiologist; b. Kericho, Kenya, Feb. 11, 1941; came to U.S., 1963, naturalized, 1975; s. Telu R. and Vidya B. (Gug) B.; m. Jane Gempler, Aug. 21, 1971; children: Neal, Nathah, Sean. B.A., Knox Coll., 1965; M.S., St. Louis U., 1968, Ph.D., 1970. Prof. biology Benedictine Coll., Atchison, Kans., 1971-81; tech. dir. Midwest Solvents Co., Atchison, 1981—; cons. Clark Coll., Atlanta, 1971—. Chmn. Sunflower dist. Boy Scouts Am., Atchison, 1980. Paul Harris fellow, 1982. Mem. Am. Soc. Microbiologists, Am. Chem. Soc., Assn. Am. Cereal Chemists, AAAS, C. of C. Atchison (dir. 1981, v.p. 1983), Sigma Xi. Lodges: Rotary (pres. 1979-80) (Atchison); Elks. Current Work: Biomass conversion to chemicals; genetic engineering; simultaneous production of glucose and alcohol from cellulose. Subspecialties: Biomass (energy science and technology); Enzyme technology. Home: Rural Route 3 Box 159B Atchison KS 66002 Office: Midwest Solvents Co Inc 1300 Main St Atchison KS 66002

BASSIN, N. JAY, environmental consultant; b. Tokyo, July 23, 1948; s. Jules and Beatrice (Kellner) B.; m. Carolyn Baldwin, June 20, 1970. A.B., Oberlin Coll., 1970; Ph.D., Tex. A&M U., 1975. Asst. prof. No. Ill. U., DeKalb, 1974; oceanographer U.S. Bur. Land Mgmt., Los Angeles, 1975-79; minerals and power plant projects dir. U.S. Fish & Wildlife Service, Washington, 1979-81; water resources program U.S. Nat. Park Service, Washington, 1981-83; sr. prin. Environ. Mgmt. Support, Silver Spring, Md., 1983—; cons. U.S. EPA, Washington, 1983—. Editor and author: Digital Rev., 1984—. Editor: Long Range Research Agenda, 1984. Contbr. articles to profl. jours. Fellow NSF, Tex. A&M U. Mem. Am. Water Resources Assn., AAAS, Am. Geophys. Union, Geol. Soc. Am., Washington Computer Soc. (exec. com. 1984—), Sigma Xi, Phi Kappa Phi. Current work: Strategic planning and management in natural resources; use of microcomputers in environmental management. Subspecialties: Resource management; Oceanography. Office: Environ Mgmt Support 9514 Midwood Rd Silver Spring MD 20910

BAST, ROBERT CLINTON, JR., physician; b. Washington, Dec. 8, 1943; s. Robert Clinton and Ann Christine (Borl) E.; m. Blanche Amy Simpson, Oct. 21, 1972; 1 dau.: Elizabeth Simpson. B.A. cum laude, Wesleyan U., Middletown, Conn., 1965; M.D. magna cum laude, Harvard U., 1971. Intern dept. medicine Johns Hopkins Hosp., Balt., 1971-72; research assoc., research scientist biology br. Nat. Cancer Inst., NIH, Bethesda, Md., 1972-75; jr. asst. resident Peter Bent Brigham Hosp., Boston, 1975-76; clin. fellow to assoc. physician Sidney Farber Cancer Inst., Boston, 1976-84; jr. assoc. to assoc. physician Brigham and Women's Hosp., Boston, 1977-84; asst. prof. medicine to assoc. prof. Harvard Med. Sch., Boston, 1977-84; prof. medicine Duke U. Med. Ctr., 1984—, co-dir. hematology-oncology, dir. clin. research programs Comprehensive Cancer Ctr., Durham, N.C., 1984—, also prof. microbiology/immunology; mem. exptl. immunology sect. NIH, 1983-84; mem. grant rev. com. Leukemia Soc. Am., 1985—, FDA rev. com., 1985—. cons. Boston Hosp. for Women, 1979—, Nat. Cancer Inst., 1976—. Mem. editorial bd.: Internat. Jour. Immunopharmacology, 1979—, Jour. Biol. Response Modifiers, 1982—; contbr. articles to profl. jours. Served with USPHS, 1972-75. Recipient Henry Asbury Christian award Harvard Med. Sch., 1971; Dominus award, 1984. USPHS fellow and Eli Lilly student research fellow, 1967-69; Leukemia Soc. Am. scholar, 1978-83. Mem. Am. Assn. Cancer Research, Am. Assn. Immunologists, Am. Fedn. Clin. Research, Am. Soc. Clin. Investigation, Am. Soc. Clin. Oncology, Am. Soc. Microbiology, Internat. Assn. Immunopharmacology, Reticuloendothelial Soc., Sigma Xi, Alpha Omega Alpha. Current Work: Tumor immunology, immunopharmacology, application of monoclonal antibodies to immunodiagnosis and immunotherapy of cancer. Subspecialties: Cancer research (medicine); Immunopharmacology. Home: Turkey Farm Rd Route 8 PO Box 63G Chapel Hill NC 27514 Office: Box 3843 Duke U Med Ctr Durham NC 27710

BASTAWI, ALY ELOUI, dental educator, consultant, researcher; b. Cairo, Oct. 13, 1928; came to U.S., 1961, naturalized, 1980; s. Abdel Ghafour and Amina Abdel Ghafour Mohammed; m. Khadiga Hamza, June 26, 1969; children: Akrum Eloui, Bassel Eloui. P.N.S., Cairo U., 1952, B.D.S., 1957; M.S.D., Ind. U.-Indpls., 1961; D.M.D., U. Louisville, 1975. Lectr. pedodontics Cairo U., 1965-69; asst. prof. Howard U., 1969-73, dir. postgrad. pedodontics, 1969-73; assoc. prof. U. Louisville, 1973-76, chmn. dept. pedodontics, 1976-79, prof., 1979—; dir. research, 1973-76; prof., cons. dental edn. Garyounis U., Benghazi, Libya, 1979-81, Cairo U., 1981-82. Contbr. articles to profl. jours. Internat. Coll. Dentists fellow, 1962. Mem. Am. Dental Assn., Am. Assn. Dental Schs., Am. Acad. Pedodontics, Internat. Assn. Dental Research, Egyptian Dental Assn., Omicron Kappa Upsilon. Current Work: Dental education, consultant in dental education, research in the field of psychophysiology to study anxiety in dental patients through their autonomic responses. Subspecialties: Pedodontics; Psychophysiology. Home: PO Box 22496 Louisville KY 40222 Office: University of Louisville School of Dentistry Preston St and Muhammed Ali Blvd Louisville KY

BASTEDO, WILLIAM GARDNER, government executive; b. Asbury Park, N.J., Nov. 2, 1929; s. William O. and Kathleen R. (Gardner) B.; m. Mary Lou Martinez, June 7, 1958; children: Mary Ann, William Gardner Jr., Robert G., Margaret E. B.S. in Mil. Sci., U. Md., 1952; M.S. in Pub. Adminstrn., George Washington U., 1964. Capsule communicator NASA Johnson Space Ctr., Houston, 1965-68; chief instrumentation ships div. Western Test Range, Calif., 1968-70; dep. dir. plans USAF Space and Missile Test Orgn., 1970-72; officer in charge outer space affairs U.S. Dept. State, Washington, 1972-74; tech. intelligence Def. Intelligency Agy., Washington, 1974-75; dir. internat. program support Office Internat. Affairs NASA Hdqrs., 1975-81; program mgr. Space Tracking and Data Network, 1981-84, dep. dir. ground networks div. NASA Hdqrs., 1984—; instr. Golden Gate U., part-time, 1969-72, 73. Served to col. USAF, 1952-75. Decorated Air Force Commendation medal with cluster, Air Force Meritorious Service Medal, Legion of Merit, Joint Services Commendation medal; Recipient Exceptional Service medals NASA, 1979, 81; Outstanding Service award Skylab Reentry Interagy. Task Force, 1979. Roman Catholic. Lodge: K.C. Subspecialty: Aerospace engineering and technology. Office: Code TN NASA Headquarters Washington DC 20546

BASU, AMIYA, research engineer, consultant; b. Calcutta, India, Mar. 29, 1949; came to U.S. 1972; s. Ajit and Ila (Dutta) B.; m. Malabika Mitra, Apr. 27, 1978; 1 child, Ayan. B.S.M.E., N.Mex. State U., 1974, M.S.M.E., 1975. Registered profl. engr., Ariz. Mech. engr. Ariz. Pub. Service Co., Phoenix, 1976-79, research engr., project mgr., 1979—; pres., founder Energy Engring. Cons., Phoenix, 1982—. Author: Handbook of Energy Systesm, 1984. Mem. ASME (solar energy standards com.), Blue Key, Pi Tau Sigma, Tau Beta Pi, Sigma Tau. Current work: Advanced energy systems (solar electric generation, high temperature gas-cooled nuclear reactors, cogeneration, photovoltaic systems). Subspecialties: Mechanical engineering; Solar engineering. Office: Ariz Pub Service Co PO Box 21666 MS 5629 Phoneix AZ 80036

BASU, PANKAJ KUMAR, physicist, researcher; b. Diamond Harbor, West Bengal, India, Feb. 1, 1930; came to U.S., 1969, naturalized, 1977; s. Satish Chandra and Sarasi (Ghosh) B.; m. Rina Roy, Apr. 21, 1964; children—Gautom, Lopa. B.S., Calcutta U., India, 1952; M.S., Max Planck Inst., Stuttgart, W.Va., 1963; Ph.D., U. Stuttgart, 1968. Research assoc. Rice U., Houston, Tex., 1969-70, U. Md., College Park, 1970-71; asst. prof. Howard U., Washington, 1971-72; prof. U. of D.C., Washington, 1972—; staff scientist George Washington U., Washington, 1973-76; vis. scientist Lawrence Livermore Lab., Calif., summers 1983, 85; guest worker Nat. Bur. of Standards, Gaithersburg, Md., 1982—. Author: Verfestigung n-Bestrahlter Cu-Au Einkristaue, 1968. Contbr. articles to profl. jours. Max Planck scholar Max Planck Inst., 1964; grantee NSF, 1979, Nat. Bur. Standards, 1983. Mem. Am. Phys. Soc., Am. Assn. Physics Tchrs. Democrat. Clubs: Sanskriti (sec. 1971), Indo-German Student (pres. 1961-63). Statistical physics; many body theory; theoretical solid state; chemical physics; computational physics in the area of statistical physics. Subspecialty: Statistical physics. Home: 15 Chancelet Ct Rockville MD 20852 Office: Dept of Physics 4200 Connecticut Ave NW Washington DC 20008

BATCHA, GEORGE, mechanical and nuclear engineer; b. Marblehead, Ohio, Oct. 24, 1928; s. John and Anna (Groholy) B.; m. Erika Voelker, Jan. 1, 1982; 1 child, Susan Kolodziejczyk. B.A., Bowling Green State U., 1951; M.S. in Engring. Sci., U. Toledo, 1968; certs. numerous U.S. Army tng. schs. Registered profl. engr., Ohio, Mich. With Standard Products Co., Port Clinton, Ohio, 1951, A.O. Smith Co. Landing Gear div., Toledo, Ohio, 1951, army rep. at Glenn L. Martin Co., Balt., 1952-54, Cleve. Pneumatic Tool Co., 1954-55, Hardware Stamping div. Fort Motor Co., Sandusky, Ohio, 1955-59; mech. design and test engr. Missile and Def. Engring. divs. Chrysler Corp., Detroit, 1959-62; mech. and nuclear engr. NASA, Lewis Research Ctr., Plum Brook Sta., Sandusky, 1962-74; mech. and system mgmt. engr. Armament Research and Devel. Command, U.S. Army, Dover, N.J., and Rock Island, Ill., 1974-81, mech. engr. Tank Automotive Command, Warren, Mich., 1981—. Author numerous tech. reports. Served with U.S. Army, 1952-54. Scholar, Bowling Green State U., 1948; recipient Apollo Achievement award NASA, 1969, Accomplishment awards, 1967, 68, Cost Reduction awards, 1971, 74; Dept. Army Achievement award Tank Automotive Command, 1985. Mem. Nat. Soc. Profl. Engrs., Order of Engr., Nat. Council Engring. Examiners (cert.), Am. Acad. Environ. Engrs. (diplomate), Soc. Logistics Engrs. (cert. profl. logistician), Assn. U.S. Army, Port Clinton Power Squadron of Ohio. Byzantine Catholic. Current work: Technical assessment and guidance of developmental programs of all elements of integrated logistics support in tank-automotive weapon system and equipment. Subspecialties: Mechanical engineering; Nuclear engineering. Home: 1410 Bishop Rd Gross Point Park MI 48230-1148 Office: US Army Tank Automotive Command Attn AMSTA-HC Bldg 200A Warren MI 48397-5000

BATCHELDER, MICHAEL JACK, engineering educator, consultant; b. Horton, Kans., July 4, 1945; s. David G. and LaVeta M. (Clements) B.; m. Kathleen M. Musgrave, Aug. 2, 1969; children—David Dean, Jack William, Katherine Eva. B.S. in Elec. Engring., Okla. State U., 1968, M.S., 1969; Ph.D., Va. Poly. Inst. and State U., 1974. Engr., Western Electric, Winston-Salem, N.C. and Whippany, N.J., 1969-71; asst. prof. dept. elec. engring. S.D. Sch. Mines, Rapid City, 1974-84; assoc. prof. dept. elec. engring. T.J. Watson Sch Engring. SUNY-Binghamton, 1984—; mem. faculty Hughes Aircraft, Los Angeles, summer, 1978; vis. scientist Michelsen Inst. Bergen, Norway, 1980-81; cons. Universal Instruments, Binghamton. Co-designer computer systems. Norwegian Marshall Fund grantee, 1980. Mem. IEEE (subsect. pres. 1982-83), Am. Soc. Engring. Edn. (John A. Curtis award 1983), Assn. Computing Machinery, Sigma Xi. Republican. Presbyterian. Current work: Real-time computing systems, robotics. Subspecialties: Computer engineering; Robotics. Office: SUNY TJ Watson Sch Engring Dept Elec Engring Binghamton NY 13901

BATE, ROBERT THOMAS, physicist; b. Denver, Apr. 1, 1931; s. Harold Thomas and Eunice (Redmond) B.; m. Helen Marie Giehm, Mar. 17, 1951; children—Donna Bate Kinney, Barbara Bate Wortham, Susan Bate Moore, Richard, Beverly Bate Bates. B.S. in Engring. Physics, U. Colo., 1955; M.S. in Physics, Ohio State U., 1957. Physicist U.S. Bur. Standards, Boulder, Colo., 1955; research asst. Ohio State U., Columbus, 1955-57; physicist Battelle Inst., Columbus, 1957-64, Tex. Instruments, Inc., Dallas, 1964—, br. mgr. central research labs., 1974—, sr. scientist, 1966-74; mem. Solid State scis. com. NRC, 1981-84. Contbr. numerous articles to profl. jours., chpts. to books. Patentee electronic devices. Served with USMCR, 1952-54. Tex. Instruments fellow, 1985—. Fellow Am. Phys. Soc.; mem. IEEE (sr.). Current work: Advanced semiconductor devices and architectures quantum devices. Subspecialties: Semiconductors; Condensed matter physics. Home: 3106 Kristin Ct Garland TX 75042 Office: Tex Instruments Inc PO Box 225936 MS 154 Dallas TX 75265

BATEMAN, DURWARD FRANKLIN, plant pathologist, educator; b. Tyner, N.C., May 28, 1934; s. Benny Franklin and Grace (Cale) B.; m. Shirley Eugenia Byrum, June 23, 1953; children: Cynthia Anne, Brenda Sue, Diane Mia. B.S., N.C. State Coll., 1956; M.S., Cornell U., 1958, Ph.D., 1960. Asst. prof. dept. plant pathology Cornell U., Ithaca, N.Y., 1960-65, assoc. prof., 1965-69, prof., 1969-70, prof., chmn. dept., 1970-79, tchr. grad. course in area of disease and pathogen physiology, 1963-79; field rep. dept. plant pathology Cornell U. (Grad. Sch.), 1966-69; cons. NIH, 1968; vis. prof. N.C. State U., Raleigh, 1975; assoc. dean N.C. State U. (Sch. Agr. and Life Scis.); also dir. N.C. Agrl. Research Service, 1979—; vice chmn. So. Agrl. Expt. Sta. Dirs. Assn., 1984, chmn., 1985; chmn. legis. subcom. of Expt. Sta. Com. on Policy, Nat. Assn. State Univs. and Land Grant Colls., 1983; mem. biotech. com., 1982—. Contbr. articles to profl. jours. NIH sr. fellow U. Calif., Davis, 1967. Fellow Am. Phytopath. Soc. (councilor-at-large 1973, sr. councilor-at-large 1974, v.p. 1975, pres. 1977-78); mem. AAAS, Intersoc. Consortium for Plant Protection (exec. com. 1977-80), Internat. Soc. Plant Pathology, Sigma Xi, Phi Kappa Phi, Kappa Phi Kappa, Gamma Sigma Delta. Current Work: Research administration and enzymology of plant tissue decomposition by fungi and bacteria. Subspecialties: Plant pathology; Plant physiology (agriculture). Home: 4026 Glen Laurel Ln Raleigh NC 27612

BATES, JOHN BRYANT, research scientist; b. Harlan, Ky., Mar. 11, 1942; s. Burnice Floyd and Mildred Jane (Bryant) B.; m. Sharon Elaine Craft, June 9, 1963; children—Sean, Erin. B.A., U. Ky., 1964, Ph.D., 1968; postgrad. U. Md., 1969. Research staff Oak Ridge Nat. Lab., 1969-75, group leader, sr. staff mem., 1975—. Editor: Fast Ionic Transport in Solids, 1982. Contbr. articles to profl. publs., chpts. to books. Fellow Am. Phys. Soc.; mem. Coastal Sci. Assn. (bd. dirs. 1983—). Unitarian. Club: Concord Yacht (Tenn.). Current work: Solid-solid interfaces, solid electrolytes. Subspecialties: Condensed matter physics; Ceramics. Home: 116 Baltimore Dr Oak Ridge TN 37830 Office: Oak Ridge Nat Lab PO Box X Oak Ridge TN 37831

BATES, RICHARD DOANE, JR., chemistry educator; b. Elizabeth, N.J., July 24, 1944; s. Richard Doane and Sarah Newbold (Deacon) B.; m. Ruthann Iovanni, Feb. 13, 1971; children—Spencer Deacon, Dunlea Ristine. B.A., Cornell U., 1966; M.A., Columbia U., 1967, Ph.D., 1971. Asst. prof. chemistry Georgetown U., Washington, 1973-79, assoc. prof., 1979—; vis. scholar Northwestern U., 1981. Served to 1st lt. AUS, 1971-73. NIH fellow, 1967-71 Mem. Am. Phys. Soc., Am. Chem. Soc., Laser Inst. Am., Royal Soc. Chemistry, N.Y. Acad. Scis., Canal Zone Study Group (v.p. 1981—), Delta Kappa Epsilon. Episcopalian. Current work: Laser-matter interactions; vibrational energy uptake in collisions; transient complex formation; molecular motions and interactions in gases and liquids. Subspecialties: Physical chemistry; Laser-induced chemistry. Home: 4631 Hunt Ave Chevy Chase MD 20815 Office: Georgetown U Dept Chemistry Washington DC 20057

BATES, STEPHEN ROGER DENIS, physician, educator; b. London, Aug. 17, 1944; came to U.S., 1971; s. Denis W. and Kathleen Mary (Lea) B.; m. Jeannie Almind, Dec. 28, 1968; children: Stephen, Thomas, Kristina. Student, Haileybury Coll.-Eng., 1958-62; student, U. London, 1963-68; M.B.B.S., St. George's Hosp. Med. Sch.-U. London, 1968. Diplomate: Royal Coll. Obstetricians & Gynecologists. Intern, London, 1969-70, resident in pediatrics and neurology, Cin., 1971-74; chief resident in neurology U. Cin., 1974-75, instr. pediatrics, 1975-76; asst. prof. child neurology Children's Hosp. Med. Center, Cin., 1976-81, assoc. prof., 1981—, asst. chief of staff, 1975—, dir. EEG Lab., 1976—, dir. epilepsy children's program, 1980—. Contbr. articles to profl. jours. Mem. Brit. Med. Assn., Am. Acad. Neurology, Cin. Soc. Neurology and Neurosurgery, Cin. Pediatric Soc., Child Neurology Soc., Am. Epilepsy Soc., Am. Med. Electroencephalographic Assn., AAAS. Club: Cin. Raquet. Current Work: Study of hepatic toxicity; carbamazepine and dyslipoproteinemia; migraine in childhood and relationship to dyslipoproteinemia; nitrazepam in the treatment of childhood epilepsy. Subspecialties: Neurology; Pediatrics. Home: 7054 Mt Vernon Cincinnati OH 45227 Office: Children's Hosp Med Center Elland & Bethesda Aves Cincinnati OH 45229

BATTERMAN, BORIS WILLIAM, physicist; b. N.Y.C., Aug. 25, 1930. Student Cooper Union Coll., 1949-50, Technische Hochschule, Stuttgart, Germany, 1953-54; S.B., Mass. Inst. Tech., 1952, Ph.D., 1956. Mem. tech. staff Bell Telephone Labs., Murray Hill, N.J., 1956-65; asso. prof. Cornell U., 1965-67, prof. applied and engring. physics, 1967—, Walter S. Carpenter Prof. of engring., 1985—; dir., 1974-78, Synchrotron Radiation Lab. (CHESS), 1978—; cons. x-ray diffraction; mem. U.S.A. Nat. Com. Crystallography, Nat. Acad. Sci., 1969-72. Asso. editor: Jour. Crystal Growth, 1964-74. Guggenheim fellow, 1971; Fulbright Hayes fellow, 1971; Humboldt fellow, 1983. Fellow Am. Phys. Soc. Current work: X-ray scattering in condensed matter using synchrotron radiation; instrument development for synchrotron radiation.

Subspecialty: Condensed matter physics. Office: Cornell U Clark Hall Ithaca NY 14853

BATTIN, RICHARD HORACE, aeronautical engineer; b. Atlantic City, Mar. 3, 1925; s. Horace Leslie and Martha Esther (Scheu) B.; m. Margery Katheryn Milne, Aug. 25, 1947; children: Thomas, Pamela, Jeffrey. B.S., M.I.T., 1945, Ph.D., 1951. Instr. math. M.I.T., 1946-51, research mathematician Instrumentation Lab., 1951-56, adj. prof. aeros. and astronautics, 1979—; sr. staff mem. Ops. Research Group, Arthur D. Little, Inc., Cambridge, Mass., 1956-58; tech. dir. Apollo Mission devel.; assoc. dir. Instrumentation Lab., 1958-73; assoc. head NASA Program dept. Charles Stark Draper Lab., Inc., 1973—, mem. aerospace safety adv. panel, 1980—. Author: (with J.H. Laning, Jr.) Random Processes in Automatic Control, 1956, Astronautical Guidance, 1964; Mem. editorial com.: Celestial Mechanics, 1968-74. Pres. Project Impact, 1981—; Mem. Lexington (Mass.) Town Meeting, 1956—; mem. Lexington Appropriations Com., 1958-64. Served to lt. (j.g.) Supply Corps USNR, 1945-46. Recipient Louis W. Hill Space Transp. award AIAA, 1972, Mechanics and Control of Flight award, 1978; Superior Achievement award Inst. of Navigation, 1980; Teaching award dept. aeros. and astronautics M.I.T., 1981. Fellow AIAA (asso. editor jour., chmn. astrodynamics tech. com. 1978-80, dir. tech. 1979-82), Am. Astronautical Soc.; mem. Nat. Acad. Engring., Internat. Acad. Astronautics, Celestial Mechanics Inst., Sigma Xi. Club: Hancock Men's (pres. 1974-76). Current Work: NASA space shuttle. Subspecialty: Aerospace engineering and technology. Home: 15 Paul Revere Rd Lexington MA 02173 Office: 555 Technology Sq Cambridge MA 02139

BATTOCLETTI, JOSEPH HENRY, electrical engineer, educator; b. Bridgeport, Ohio, Mar. 12, 1925; s. Joseph Matthew and Henrietta (Dzielski) B.; m. Rosemary Therese Mashl, Aug. 25, 1951; children—Mary Rose, Theresa, Anne, Elizabeth, Mary Catherine, Timothy, James. B.S. in Elec. Engring., U. Detroit, 1947; M.S. in Elec. Engring., Northwestern U., 1947; Ph.D., UCLA, 1961. Registered profl. engr., Wis. Radio engr. Motorola Inc., Chgo., 1949-51; assoc. prof. Loyola U., Los Angeles, 1951-62, Marquette U., Milw., 1963-66; prof. biomed. engring. surgery Med. Coll. Wis., Milw., 1970—; cons. Nat. Acad. Scis., Chile, S.Am., 1962-63; mgr. applied research Badger Meter, Inc., Brown Deer, Wis., 1966-70; biomed. engr. VA Med. Ctr., Wood, Wis., 1978—. Author: Electromagnetism, Man and the Environment, 1976. Co-editor: Biologic and Clinical Effects of Low-Frequency Magnetic and Electric Fields, 1974. Contbr. numerous chpts. to books, also articles. Mem. IEEE (chmn. Milw. sect. 1980-81, sect. mem. award 1975, Centennial medal, 1984), Soc. Magnetic Resonance in Medicine, Bioelectromagnetic Soc. Roman Catholic. Current work: Blood flow measurement and imaging using nuclear magnetic resonance, permanent magnet design and contruction. Subspecialties: Electrical engineering; Biomedical engineering. Home: 825 W Good Hope Rd River Hills WI 53217 Office: Med Coll Wis 8700 W Wisconsin Ave Milwaukee WI 53226

BATZEL, ROGER ELWOOD, chemist; b. Weiser, Idaho, Dec. 1, 1921; s. Walter George and Inez Ruth (Klinefelter) B.; m. Edwina Lorraine Grindstaff, Aug. 18, 1946; children: Stella Lynne, Roger Edward, Stacy Lorraine. B.S., U. Idaho, 1947; Ph.D., U. Calif. at Berkeley, 1951. Mem. staff Lawrence Livermore (Calif.) Lab., 1953—, head chemistry dept., 1959-67, assoc. dir. for chemistry, 1961-71, assoc. dir. for testing, 1961-64, assoc. dir. for space reactors, 1966-68, asso. dir. chem. and bio-med. research, 1969-71, dir. lab., 1971—. Served with USAAF, 1943-45. Named to Alumni Hall of Fame U. Idaho, 1972; recipient disting. assoc. award U.S. Dept. Energy, 1982. Fellow Am. Phys. Soc.; mem. Sigma Xi. Club: Commonwealth of Calif. (San Francisco). Subspecialty: Nuclear chemistry. Office: PO Box 808 Livermore CA 94550

BAUCH, TAMIL DANIEL, civil engineer, researcher, artist; b. Bklyn., Aug. 26, 1943; s. Marks Joseph and Mary (Heller) B. B.C.E., Rensselaer Poly. Inst., 1965. Field supt. trainee, asst. supt. Diesel Constrn. Co., N.Y.C., 1969-70; founder, dir. A.I.R. Design Group (name formerly Egge Research), 1971—; staff cons. Dome East Corp., Hicksville, N.Y., 1973-76, Child Environ. Design Inst., Poughkeepsie, N.Y., 1976-78; major cons. Bio-Energy Systems, Inc., Ellenville, N.Y., 1979—; pres. Aerius Design Group, Inc., 1982—; cons. on solar energy and energy conservation field to major corps. Contbr. to profl. publs. Patentee in field. Served to lt. (j.g.) USN, 1965-69. Mem. Mid-Hudson Renewable Energy Assn., Tau Beta Pi, Chi Epsilon. Patentee composite constrn. panel. Current Work: Development of: solar collector technology; energy conservation products; solar heated structures (homes, commercial buildings and greenhouses); experimental architecture—molded building components; sculpture and displays—use of molded glass reinforced cement components. Subspecialties: Solar energy; Energy conservation. Office: RFD 1 Box 394B Kingston NY 12401

BAUE, ARTHUR EDWARD, surgeon, educator; b. St. Louis, Oct. 7, 1929; s. Arthur Christian and Viola (Wegener) B.; m. Rosemary Dysart, Nov. 24, 1956; children—Patricia Sage, Arthur Christian II, William Dysart. A.B. summa cum laude, Westminster Coll., 1950; M.D. cum laude, Harvard, 1954. Diplomate: Am. Bd. Surgery (dir.), Am. Bd. Thoracic Surgery (dir.). Successively intern, resident, chief resident surgery Mass. Gen. Hosp., Boston, 1954-61; asst. prof. surgery U. Mo. Sch. Medicine, 1962-64; asst. prof., then asso. prof. surgery U. Pa. Sch. Medicine, Phila., 1964-67; Harry Edison prof. surgery Washington U. Sch. Medicine, St. Louis, 1967-75; surgeon-in-chief, dir. dept. surgery Jewish Hosp., St. Louis, 1967-75; chief of surgery Yale-New Haven Hosp., 1975-85; prof., chmn. dept. surgery Yale, 1975-85, Donald Guthrie prof. surgery, 1977-85; assoc. dean clin. affairs, prof. surgery St. Louis U. Sch. Medicine, 1985—; cons. surgery Nat. Bd. Med. Examiners; chmn. NIH surgery B study sect., 1978-82. Chief editor: Archives of Surgery, 1977—; mem. editorial bd.: Am. Jour. Physiology. Mem. alumni council Westminster Coll. Served to capt. USAF, 1959. John and Mary R. Markle scholar acad. medicine, 1963; recipient Research Career Devel. award USPHS, 1964. Mem. Am. Assn. Thoracic Surgery, Am. Coll. Cardiology, Am. Coll. Chest Physicians, A.C.S., Assn. Acad. Surgery, New Eng. Surg. Soc., Internat. Cardiovascular Soc., Soc. Thoracic Surgeons, Soc. Univ. Surgeons, Soc. Vascular Surgery, Internat. Soc. Surgery, Am. Assn. Surgery Trauma, Am. Assn. Artificial Internal Organs, Am. Physiol. Soc., AMA (editorial bd. jour.), Am., Central, Western surg. assns., Soc. Surgery Alimentary Tract, Alpha Omega Alpha. Current Work: Shock, circulatory failure, multiple organ failure, subcellular alterations with aschemia, abnormallities of cellular energetics and the effects of ATP-magnesium chloride. Subspecialties: Surgery; Cardiac surgery. Home: 6333 Ellenwood Ave Clayton MO 63105 Office: St Louis U Sch Medicine 1325 S Grand Blvd Saint Louis MO 63104

BAUER, DENNIS PAUL, chemist; b. Pitts., July 29, 1948; s. Frank Paul Bauer and Anne Marie (Olup) Giese; m. Beverly Ann Behn, June 5, 1971. B.S. in Chemistry, U. Cin., 1971, Ph.D. in Organic Chemistry, 1976; M.S. in Inorganic Chemistry, U. Ga., 1973; M.B.A., La. State U., 1982. Research assoc. U. Calif.-Berkeley, 1976-77; research chemist Ethyl Corp. Research and Devel., Baton Rouge, 1977-81, econs. chemist, 1981-82, research supr., 1982-83, product coordinator, 1983—. Contbr. articles to profl. jours. Patentee in field. Bd. dirs. Baton Rouge Recreation and Parks Commn., 1982—, Oak Hills Civic Assn., 1984. Grantee H. Arnold Air Force Aid Soc., 1966-71, NSF, 1976-77; Laws fellow, 1975-76. Mem. Am. Chem. Soc., Chemistry Soc. (London), AAAS, N.Y. Acad. Scis. Current work: Fine chemical synthesis and organometallic compounds. Subspecialties: Synthetic chemistry; Organometallics. Home: 11904 Towering Oaks Dr Baton Rouge LA 70810 Office: Ethyl Corp 451 Florida Blvd Baton Rouge LA 70810

BAUER, MARVIN EUGENE, remote sensing researcher, educator; b. Valparaiso, Ind., July 24, 1943; s. William Gordon and Maxine Doris (Adams) B.; m. Jean Warner, June 28, 1969. B.S.A., Purdue U., 1965, M.S., 1967; Ph.D., U. Ill., 1970. Research agronomist Purdue U., West Lafayette, Ind., 1970-82, sr. research agronomist, 1982-83; prof. remote sensing U. Minn.-St. Paul, 1983—, dir. Remote Sensing Lab., 1983—. Editor-in-chief Remote Sensing of Enrivon. Jour., 1980—. Contbr. articles to profl. jours. Mem. Am. Soc. Agronomy, Am. Soc. Photogrammetry Remote Sensing, IEEE Geosci. Remote Sensing Soc., AAAS, Council Agrl. Sci. Tech., Sigma Xi. Current work: Spectral properties of crops and application of remote sensing to crop indentification, condition assessment, and yield prediction. Subspecialties: Agronomy; Remote sensing (atmospheric science). Office: Remote Sensing Lab U Minn 110 Green Hall 1530 N Cleveland Ave Saint Paul MN 55108

BAUER, MICHAEL ANTHONY, computer scientist; b. Dayton, Ohio, Feb. 18, 1948; s. Vincent DeJohn and Stephanie (Talmant) B.; m. Angeline Blonski, May 22, 1976; children: Andrea, Michelle. B.Sc., U. Dayton, 1970; M.Sc., U. Toronto, 1971, Ph.D., 1978. Programmer Wright Patterson AFB, Dayton, Ohio, 1966-70; instr. U. Toronto, 1974; research fellow U. Edinburgh, Scotland, 1974-75; lectr. U. Western Ont., London, 1975-78, asst. prof., 1978-81, assoc. prof., 1981—; internal cons. software engring. Geac Computers Internat., 1984-85. Judge London (Ont.) Dist. Sci. Fair, 1980—. Nat. Research Council Can. scholar, 1972-74; recipient Excellence in Teaching award U. Western Ont., 1982; Teaching award Ont. Conf. Univ. Faculty Assns., 1982; sr. indsl. fellow NRC Can., 1984-85. Mem. IEEE, Assn. Computing Machinery, Soc. Indsl. and Applied Math, Can. Info. Processing Soc. Current Work: Automated tools, techniques and methods to aid in software specification, design and implementation; interfaces to computer systems and software. Subspecialties: Software engineering; Algorithms. Office: Dept Computer Sci U Western Ont London ON N6A 5B9 Canada

BAUER, RICHARD CARLTON, nuclear engineer; b. Batavia, N.Y., July 15, 1944; s. Willard Ronald and Ethel Ann. (Roth) B.; m. Madeline Joy Amreich, June 28, 1969; children: Jason Todd, Cheryl Robyn. B.S., Clarkson Coll. Tech., 1966; M.Eng., Cornell U., 1968; Ph.D., Carnegie-Mellon U., 1974. Registered profl. engr., Pa. cert. fallout shelter analyst Fed. Emergency Mgmt. Agy. Engr., sr. engr. Bettis Atomic Power Lab., West Mifflin, Pa., 1968-78, staff engr. to gen. mgr., 1978-79, mgr. reactor system performance analysis, 1979—, tng. lectr., 1975—, sec., mem. reactor safety com., 1975—. Author: Reactor Safety, Systems, Analysis, 1978. Chmn. secondary schs. com. Cornell U., Pitts. sect., 1976-78; regional v.p. Soc. Engrs., 1974-80. N.Y. State regents fellow, 1962-66; AEC spl. fellow, 1967, 68; Bettis Lab. doctoral fellow, 1968-74. Mem. Am. Nuclear Soc., Am. Inst. Chem. Engrs., Pa. Soc. Engrs. (dir. 1981-84, chmn. sustaining assocs. 1981-84, 2d v.p. 1984, 1st v.p. 1985), Nat. Soc. Prof. Engrs., N.Y. Acad. Scis., Am. Mgmt. Assn., Sigma Xi, Omega Chi Epsilon, Tau Beta Pi. Club: Triangle. Current Work: My current activities involve nuclear reactor safety, protection analysis and plant operations and lecturing; my interests also include commercial nuclear reactor operational economics, reactor testing, plant testing. Subspecialties: Nuclear engineering; Nuclear fission.

BAUER, RICHARD HENRY, educator, researcher; b. Garrison, N.D., Oct. 5, 1939; s. Richard and Martha (Sayler) B. B.A., U. Mont., Missoula, 1964, M.A., 1965; Ph.D., U. Wash., Seattle, 1970. Instr. psychology U. Houston, 1970-72; asst. prof. Kans. State U., Manhattan, 1977-81, Middle Tenn. State U., 1981—. Contbr. articles in field to profl. jours. Served with U.S. Army, 1957-59. USPHS trainee, 1964-65; NSF trainee, 1967-69; NIMH fellow, 1972-74; NIMH grantee, 1973; Upjohn Co. grantee, 1975. Mem. Am. Psychol. Assn., Midwestern Psychol. Assn., Western Psychol. Assn., N.Y. Acad. Sci., Soc. Neurosci., Psychonomic Soc., AAAS, Fedn. Am. Scientists, Internat. Acad. Research in Learning Disabilities, Internat. Soc. Devel. Psychology, Sigma Xi. Subspecialties: Neuropsychology; Physiological psychology. Office: Department of Psychology Middle Tennessee State University Murfreesboro TN 37132

BAUER, SIMON HARVEY, chemist, emeritus educator; b. Kaunas, Lithuania, Oct. 12, 1911; came to U.S., 1921, naturalized, 1927; s. Benzion and Golda (Betten) B.; m. Miriam Rosoff, June 25, 1938; children: Frederick, Deborah, Ross. B.S., U. Chgo., 1931, Ph.D., 1935. Postdoctoral fellow Calif. Inst. Tech., Pasadena, 1935-37; instr. Pa. State U., University Park, 1937-39; instr. Cornell U., Ithaca, N.Y., 1939-41, asst. prof., 1941-46, assoc. prof., 1946-50, prof. phys. chemistry, 1950-77, prof. emeritus, 1977—; fgn. adj. prof. Inst. Molecular Sci., Okazaki, Japan, 1983, cons. Los Alamos Nat. Lab., Argonne Nat. Lab., CALSPAN, Atlantic-Richfield Co., 1944—. Contbr. articles to sci. jours. Recipient Alexander von Humboldt award Humboldt Found., 1979; Guggenheim fellow, 1949; NSF sr. postdoctoral fellow, 1962. Fellow Am. Phys. Soc., AAAS; mem. Am. Chem. Soc., Combustion Inst., Sigma Xi, Phi Beta Kappa. Current Work: Molecular structure of amorphous, heterogeneous catalysts, dynamics of intramolecular transformations of very fast reactions, gas phase chemiluminescent reactions. Subspecialties: Physical chemistry; Kinetics. Home: 412 Klinewoods Rd Ithaca NY 14850 Office: Dept Chemistr Cornell U Ithaca NY 14853

BAUER, VICTOR JOHN, See *Who's Who in America,* 43rd edition.

BAUGHMAN, ROBERT A., JR., pharmaceutical chemistry researcher; b. Whitehall, Wis., Aug. 12, 1949; s. Robert A. and Charlene C. (Hronek) B.; m. Barbara Ann Neff, July 18, 1982; 1 child, Katharine Neff. B.Sc., Loyola U., Los Angeles, 1974; Pharm.D., U. Calif.-San Francisco, 1978, Ph.D., 1982. Lic. pharmacist, Calif., Nev. Research chemist Lederle Labs., Pearl River, N.Y., 1982-83, sr. research scientist, 1983-85; research scientist Genentech, Inc., South San Francisco, Calif., 1985—. Contbr. articles to profl. jours.; reviewer. Lectr., Community Health Edn., San Francisco, 1975-82; mem. San Francisco Symphony Forum, 1977-82. Served with U.S. Army, 1971-73. Mem. Am. Pharm. Assn., Acad. Pharm. Sci., Am. Chem. Soc., AAAS, Rho Chi., Phi Sigma Kappa (pres. 1973-74), Rho Pi Phi. Democrat. Roman Catholic. Current work: Effect of disease states on drug pharmacokinetics/pharmacodynamics; pharmacokinetics of compounds produced by genetic engineering technology. Subspecialties: Pharmacokinetics; Pharmacology. Office: Genentech Inc 460 Point San Bruno Blvd South San Francisco CA 94080

BAUM, CARL EDWARD, electromagnetic theorist; b. Binghamton, N.Y., Feb. 6, 1940; s. George Theodore and Evelyn Monica (Bliven) B.; B.S.E.E. with honors, Calif. Inst. Tech., 1962, M.S.E.E., 1963, Ph.D.E.E., 1969. Sr. scientist Electromagnetics, Air Force Weapons Lab., Albuquerque, 1971—; adviser U.S. Army, Navy, Air Force and tri-service agencies on EMP related matters. Composer of many musical opuses. Served to capt. U.S.A.F., 1962-71. Fellow IEEE (co-chmn. joint tech. com. nuclear electromagnetic pulse for the Antennas and Propagation Soc. and Electromagnetic Compatibility Soc. 1978—, chmn. Albuquerque joint chpt. IEEE of Antennas and Propatation Microwave Theory and Techniques and Electromagnetic Compatibility Socs. 1977); mem. N.Mex. Acad. Sci., SUMMA Found. (dir., pres. 1973—), Nat. Hon. Soc.; Internat. Biographical Assn. (life), Electromagnetics Soc. (pres. 1983-85), Am. Biographical Assn. (life), Tau Beta Pi, Sigma Xi. Subspecialty: Electrical engineering. Home: 5116 Eastern SE Unit D Albuquerque NM 87108 Office: AFWL/NTATT Kirtland AFB NM 87177

BAUM, PETER JOSEPH, research physicist, consultant, author; b. Lennox, Calif., June 4, 1943; s. Custer Charles and Persis Eugenia (Fell) B.; widowed; 1 child, Maryann Joy. B.A. in Physics, U. Calif., Santa Barbara, 1965; M.S. in Physics, U. Nev., Reno, 1967; Ph.D. in Physics (NDEA fellow 1968, NSF fellow 1969), U. Calif., Riverside, 1971; Calif. state teaching cert. astronomy, 1973. Research engr. microelectronics Autonetics Div. N.Am. Rockwell Corp., 1967-68; physicist computer analysis Corona Lab., Naval Weapons Center, 1968-70; research assoc. solar-plasma physics U.S. Air Force Office Sci. Research, 1970-74; Air Force grantee, 1972-74; research physicist solar-terrestrial plasma physics U. Calif., Riverside, 1974-85, wind energy, energy sci. program, 1980-85; mem. tech. staff Gen. Research Corp., Santa Barbara, Calif., 1985—; cons. Sandia Labs., Albuquerque, 1973-75; cons. wind energy City of Riverside Public Utilities Dept., 1980-83; instr. in astronomy Riverside City Coll., 1975-80. Author: (with A. Bratenahl) Magnetic Reconnection, 1982; contbr. (with A. Bratenahl) articles to tech. publs. Calif. Inst. Tech. Presdl. Fund grantee, 1970; NSF grantee, 1974-85; Calif. Space Inst. grantee, 1981-82. Mem. Am. Phys Soc., Am. Astron. Soc., Am. Geophys. Union (life), Phi Kappa Phi. Current Work: Dir. operation UCR 11 meter terrella experiment; lab. studies of magnetic reconnection; condr. exptl. and theoretical research in geomagnetic substorms, solar flares, magnetic energy conversion; studies wind energy potential San Gorgonio Pass region, Calif.; high energy accelerator physics and laser interactions. Subspecialties: Solar physics; High energy astrophysics. Home: 1180 Garden Ln Santa Barbara CA 93108 Office: Gen Research Corp 5383 Hollister Ave Santa Barbara CA 93111

BAUM, STANLEY, radiologist, educator; b. N.Y.C., Dec. 26, 1929; s. Herman and Fannie (Harris) B.; m. Jeanne Masch, June 29, 1958; children: Richard Arthur, Laura Dianne, Carol Lisa. B.A., N.Y. U., 1951; M.D., U. Utrecht, Holland, 1957. Intern Kings County Hosp., N.Y.C., 1957-58; resident in radiology Grad. Hosp., U. Pa., Phila., 1958-61; trainee Nat. Cancer Inst., Bethesda, Md., 1958-61; fellow cardiovascular radiology Stanford (Calif.) U., 1961-62; instr. radiology U. Pa., Phila., 1962-63, asst. prof., 1963-66, assoc. prof., 1966-70, prof., 1970—, Eugen P. Pendergrass prof. radiology, 1977—, chmn. dept. radiology, 1975—; chmn. med. bd. Hosp. of U. Pa., 1983—; chief cardiovascular radiology Mass. Gen. Hosp., Boston, 1971-75; prof. radiology Harvard Med. Sch., Boston, 1971-75; cons. Radiation Effects Research Found., Hiroshima, Japan, 1975—; cardiovascular rev. bd. Am. Heart Assn., 1970—. Editorial bd.: Investigative Radiology, 1970-80, New Eng. Jour. Medicine, 1975-76, Radiology, 1975—, Gastrointestinal Radiology, 1975-79, Jour. Continuing Edn, 1978-80, Postgrad. Radiology, 1980—. Fellow Am. Coll. Radiology, Am. Coll. Cardiology; mem. Soc. Cardiovascular Radiology (pres. 1974-76), Soc. Chmn. Acad. Radiology Depts. (sec.-treas. 1983—), Inst. of Medicine of Nat. Acad. Scis. Subspecialty: Diagnostic radiology. Home: 401 W Moreland Ave Chestnut Hill PA 19118 Office: 3400 Spruce St Philadelphia PA 19104

BAUM, THOMAS HALL, chemist, research engineer; b. White Plains, N.Y., May 10, 1955; s. Harry William and Marie Elenor (Mayone) B.; m. Caryn Leslie Giglio, Aug. 20, 1983. B.A. in Chemistry, Manhattanville Coll., 1978; M.S. in Chemistry, Poly. Inst. N.Y., 1982. Research technician II, Stauffer Chem. Co., Ardsley, N.Y., 1977; sr. technician, lab. specialist IBM, Yorktown, N.Y., 1978-82, assoc. engr., San Jose, Calif., 1982-84, sr. assoc. engr., 1984—. Contbr. articles to profl. jours. Patentee in field. Recipient award Am. Microchem. Soc., 1977; J. Hughes scholar, 1975-77; R. Beatty scholar, 1976-77. Mem. Am. Chem. Soc., Materials Research Soc. Roman Catholic. Current work: Photochemistry; laser-induced processes; laser deposition; laser etching; laser photochemistry for microelectronics. Subspecialties: Photochemistry; Laser-induced chemistry. Office: IBM K42-282 5600 Cottle Rd San Jose CA 95193

BAUMAN, ALBERT JOSEPH, applied chemistry consultant, researcher; b. San Francisco, Sept. 2, 1921; s. August Albert and Anna Cecelia (Kelly) B.; m. Lucia Eleanor Goodspeed, July 23, 1960; 1 child, Christina. B.Sc., U. So. Calif., 1953. Chemist, Aerojet/Gen., Azusa, Calif., 1953-59; biochemist City of Hope Med. Ctr., Duarte, Calif., 1959-61, Calbiochem, Los Angeles, 1961-62; mem. tech. staff Jet Propulsion Lab., Pasadena, Calif., 1962-79; pres. ESR Assocs., Inc., Sierra Madre, Calif., 1979—; cons. in field. Contbr. articles to profl. jours. Patentee in chem. detectors. Served with U.S. Army, 1943-46. Recipient Invention award NASA, 1973. Mem. Am. Chem. Soc., AAAS, Phytochem. Soc. N. Am., N.Y. Acad. Scis., Am. Def. Preparedness Soc. Democrat. Lutheran. Current work: Currently researching applied microwave/ferrite security devices and relations areas of anti-counterfeiting, tracking; also developing fine particle test systems HEPA filters. Subspecialties: Analytical chemistry; Applied magnetics. Home and office: 524 Oakdale Dr Sierra Madre CA 91024

BAUMAN, JOHN E., JR., chemistry educator; b. Kalamazoo, Mich., Jan. 18, 1933; s. John E. and Teresa A. (Wauchek) B.; m. Barbara Curry, June 6, 1964; children: John, Catherine, Amy. B.S., U. Mich., 1955, M.S., 1960, Ph.D., 1962. Chemist Midwest Research Inst., Kansas City, Mo., 1955-58; research assoc. U. Mich., Ann Arbor, 1958-61; prof. chemistry U. Mo., Columbia, 1961—. Active Mo. Symphony Soc., Columbia Audubon Soc. Recipient Faculty Alumni award U. Mo., 1969, Amoco teaching award, 1975, Purple Chalk award U. Mo., 1980. Mem. Am. Chem. Soc. (nat. lectr), Calorimetry Conf., Mo. Acad. Sci., Sigma Xi, Alpha Chi Sigma. Roman Catholic. Lodges: Kiwanis (pres. Little Dixie 1982-83); KC. Current Work: Thermodynamics of inorganic reactions in solution. Subspecialties: Inorganic chemistry; Thermodynamics. Home: 1805 Cliff Dr Columbia MO 65201 Office: 237 Chemistry Bldg Columbia MO 65211

BAUMAN, THOMAS CHARLES, metallurgist, cons.; b. Los Angeles, Nov. 26, 1945; s. Thomas and Geraldine Maxine (Ballou) B.; m. Judith Ann Smith, Dec. 23, 1970 (div.); children: Kimberley Ann, Ann Lorraine, Laura Marie.; m. Joy Lynne Mott, Jan. 23, 1984. B.Sc. in Metall. Engring. with honors, Calif. Poly. State U., 1974; M.Sc. in Mgmt. Sci. and Energy Systems Engrng, West Coast U., 1978; postgrad. in bus. adminstrn, Pepperdine U., 1982. Registered profl. engr., Calif., 1977. Research asst. Calif. Poly State U., 1972-74; grad. research asst. U. Calif., Berkeley, 1974; metallurgist Aluminum Co. Am., Corona, Calif., 1974; engr. So. Calif. Gas Co., Los Angeles, 1974-76; material application specialist R. M. Parsons Co., Pasadena, Calif., 1977-78; sr. metallurigst Borg-Warner Corp., Los Angeles, 1978, supervising metall. engr., 1979, mgr. dept. metall. engring., 1979-81, mgr. tech. services Energy Systems Devel. Center, 1981-82; gen.mgr. Thermal Electron Corp., Metall. Service Group, Los Angeles, 1982-83; engr., cons., mfg. mgmt. adminstr. Northrop Corp., 1983—; materials cons., partner METCON Inc., Los Angeles, 1977—, cons. materials application, failure analysis of metallic components. Contbr. articles to profl. jours. Served to staff sgt. USAF, 1966-70, Vietnam. Decorated Air Force Commendation medal. Mem. Am. Soc. Metals (corp. rep.), ASME, Am. Welding Soc., Nat. Assn. Corrosion Engrs. (accredited corrosion specialist 1980), Am.Mgmt. Assn. Am., Internat. Platform Assn., MENSA, Alpha Gamma Sigma. Republican. Roman Catholic. Clubs: Byron Jackson Mgmt. (Los Angeles); Am. Legion, VFW, Can. Legion Pipe Band. Current Work: Producibility of advanced weapon systems, thermal treatment of metals and their mechanical behavior. Subspecialties: Metallurgical engineering; Materials (engineering). Office: 9800 E Washington Blvd Pico Rivera CA 90660

BAUMER, (ANDREW) RONALD, mechanical engineer; b. St. Joseph, Mo., Oct. 5, 1936; s. Andrew C. Baumer and Katerine Louise (Luton) Fischer; m. Sandra Kay Zarski, Sept. 8, 1956 (div.); children—Andrew Ronald, Michael Victor, Megan Kathleen, Eric Christopher; m. Pauline Simonds, Oct. 31, 1975; 1 child, Nicola Jane Cook. B.S.M.E., U. Mich., 1959; M.S.E., U. Akron, 1963. Registered profl. engr., Tex. Research engr. B.F. Goodrich Co., Brecksville, Ohio, 1959-66, sr. project engr., Cleve., 1966-75; project mgr. Velsicol Chem. Co., Beaumont, Tex., 1975-78; project mgr. Triangle Engrs., Beaumont, 1980, mgr. hazardous waste mgmt., 1980—. Contbr. articles to profl. jours. Mem. ASME, Beaumont C. of C. (chair aviation com.). Current work: Energy conservation and hazardous waste management. Subspecialties: Hazardous waste disposal; Mechanical engineering. Office: Triangle Engrs PO Box 1309 Nederland TX 77727

BAUMGARDNER, MARION FISHER, agronomy educator; b. Wellington, Tex., Feb. 7, 1926; s. Joseph Bailey and Eva Lyle (Godfrey) B.; m. Maralee Speer, Apr. 10, 1955; children—Timothy, Jonathan, Mary. B.S., Tex. Tech U., 1950; M.S., Purdue U., 1955, Ph.D., 1964; postgrad. Yale U., 1956-57; D.Sc. (hon.), DePauw U., 1980. Cert. prof. agronomist, profl. soil scientist. Program specialist in agr. Ford Found., Buenos Aires, Argentina, 1964-66; asst. prof. agronomy Purdue U., West Lafayette, Ind., 1964-67, assoc. prof., 1967-71, prof., 1972—, dir. lab. for applications of remote sensing, 1982—; cons. for UN to various countries; Author: (with David Kingrey) Now is Tomorrow, 1975; (with others) Resource Inventory and Baseline Study Methods for Developing Countries, 1983; (with others) Land Use Planning, 1984. Mem. adv. bd. Internat. Jour. of Remote Sensing, 1979—. Contbr. articles to profl. jours. Mem. adv. bd. Internat. Ctr., West Lafayette, 1976—. Named Disting. Agrl. Alumnus, Tex. Tech U., Lubbock, 1983, Disting. Univ. Alumnus, Tex. Tech U., 1985. Fellow Soil Sci. Soc. Am., Soil Conservation Soc. Am. (Presdl. citation 1983); Am. Soc. Agronomy; mem. AAAS, Internat. Soc. Soil Sci. (vice chmn. working group on remote sensing 1980-84), Remote Sensing Soc., Tippecanoe County Hist. Soc. Lodge: Kiwanis (pres. Lafayette 1983-84). Current work: Reflectance properties of soils; aerospace inventory of natural resources and monitoring of land degradation. Subspecialties: Agronomy; Remote sensing (geoscience). Office: Lab for Applications of Remote Sensing 1291 Cumberland Ave Purdue U West Lafayette IN 47907

BAUMGARDT, BILLY R., university administrator, agricultural educator; b. Lafayette, Ind., Jan. 17, 1933; s. Raymond P. and Mildred Lucille (Cordray) B.; m. D. Elaine Blain, June 8, 1952; children—Pamela K. Farley, Teresa Jo Adolfsen, Donald Ray. B.S. in Agr., Purdue U., 1955, M.S., 1956; Ph.D., Rutgers U., 1959. From asst. prof. to assoc. prof. U. Wis., Madison, 1959-67; prof. animal nutrition Pa. State U., University Park, 1967-70, head dept. dairy animal sci., 1970-79, assoc. dir. agr. exptl. sta., 1979-80; dir. agrl. research, assoc. dean Purdue U., West Lafayette, Ind., 1980—; bd. dirs. Agr. Alumni Seed Improvement Assn., West Lafayette, 1983—; chmn. com. Ind. Corp. for Sci. and Tech., West Lafayette, 1983—; chmn.-elect Exptl. Sta. Com. on Orgn. and Policy, West Lafayette, 1984—. Contbr. chpts. to books, articles to profl. jours. Recipient Nutrition Research award Am. Dairy Sci. Assn., 1966; Wilkinson award for adminstrv. excellence Pa. State U., 1979. Fellow AAAS; mem. Am. Dairy Sci. Assn. (pres. 1984-85), Am. Soc. Animal Sci., Am. Inst. Nutrition, Sigma Xi. Club: Rotary. Subspecialties: Animal nutrition; Agricultural research administration. Home: 812 Lazy Ln Lafayette IN 47904 Office: Purdue U 116 AGAD West Lafayette IN 47907

BAUMGARTEN, REUBEN LAWRENCE, chemist, educator, cons.; b. N.Y.C., Nov. 19, 1934; s. Leon and Sonia (Jacobson) B.; m. Iris Marsha, Dec. 22, 1963; children: Lainie Nicole, Steven Craig. B.S. cum laude, CCNY, 1956; M.S., U. Mich., 1958, Ph.D., 1962. Instr. Hunter Coll. (named changed to

Lehman Coll. 1968), 1962-66, asst. prof. chemistry, 1966-71, assoc. prof., 1971-77, prof., 1977—, chmn. dept. chemistry, 1978—; cons. Marks Chem. Works. Author: Organic Chemistry—A Brief Survey, 1978. Mem. Am. Chem. Soc., Sigma Xi, Phi Lambda Upsilon. Jewish. Lodge: Free Sons of Israel. Current Work: Organic chemistry of nitrogen; Rimini-Simon test; hydroxylamines; Fredlel-Crafts reaction catalysts; mechanisms and kinetics. Subspecialty: Organic chemistry. Home: 22 Eagle Rd Edison NJ 08820 Office: Herbert H Lehman Coll Bronx NY 10468

BAUST, JOHN G., biology educator; b. Flushing, N.Y., Oct. 6, 1942; s. John G. and Frances Baust; m. Judith W. Baust, Jan. 30, 1966; children—John Morris, Christine Diana, Jessica Elizabeth. B.A. in Biology and Chemistry, SUNY-Fredonia, 1965; Ph.D. in Zoophysiology, Inst. Arctic Biology, U. Alaska, 1970. Assoc. prof. dept. biology U. Houston, 1975-78, assoc. prof., 1978-83, prof., 1983, B.J. Luyet disting. prof. cryobiology, 1984—, dir. Inst. Low Temperature Biology, 1984—; sci. advisor Am. Found. Biol. Research, Bethesda, Md., 1982-83; mem. sci. adv. panel NSF, Office of Naval Research; cons. Ralston Purina, Inc., Marifarms, Inc., Mariseed, Inc.; research scientist Bering Sea Expdn. Contbr. articles to profl. jours., revs. to jours. Pres., University Oaks Civic Assn., Houston, 1979—; precinct chmn. Houston Republican Com., 1981—; mem. and univ. rep. to Houston Ind. Sch. Dists.: Devel. of Consortium Model Schs., 1983—; mem. steering com. on campus community devel., Houston, 1980—. Recipient Antarctic Service medal NSF, 1981, Sci. Leader award, 1981, Faculty Devel. award U. Houston, 1981; Norwegian Marshall fellow, 1981-82; NSF grantee, 1970—. Mem. Am. Assn. Tissue Banks, AAAS, Am. Physiol. Soc., Soc. for Cryobiology (bd. govs. 1983—, v.p. 1981-83, chmn. local com. 1982, membership com. 1978-82, chmn. 1983—; symposium com. chmn. 1980-83), Can. Entomol. Soc., Am. Soc. Zoologists, Entomol. Soc. Am. (local com. 1978), N.Y. Acad. Scis., Soc. Exptl. Biology and Medicine, World Mariculture Soc., Phi Delta Kappa, Sigma Xi (membership com. 1982-83). Current work: Research focuses on physiological and biochemical bases of low temperature adaptation (polar and temperate environments); general cryobiology and technique development in high performance liquid chromatography. Subspecialty: Comparative physiology. Office: Dept Biology U Houston University Park Houston TX 77004

BAUTZ, GORDON THOMAS, biochemical pharmacologist; b. Bridgeport, Conn., June 6, 1942; s. Milton and Janet Bedford (Ballou) B.; m. Delmae Hannemann, June 12, 1965; children: Tracy, Jennifer. B.S., Salem (W.Va.) Coll., 1964. With U.S. Dept. Fisheries, Milford, Conn., 1964-65; assoc. scientist Mt. Sinai Hosp., N.Y.C., 1965-68; scientist Hoffmann-La Roche Inc., Nutley, N.J., 1968—. Contbr. articles and abstracts to profl. jours. Mem. Am. Soc. for Pharmacology and Exptl. Therapeutics, N.Y. Acad. Scis. Subspecialties: Neuropharmacology; Neurochemistry. Office: 314 Kingsland St Nutley NJ 07110

BAXTER, CHARLES RUFUS, medical educator, surgeon; b. Paris, Tex., Nov. 4, 1929; s. Gobel Lynwood and Thelma (Hannon) B.; m. JoAnn Lee, Apr. 1, 1956; children—David Brian, Robert Bradley, Ronald Lee. B.S., U. Tex., 1950; M.D., U. Tex.-Dallas, 1954. Intern, Parkland Meml. Hosp., Dallas, 1954-55; resident in internal medicine Sch. Medicine, U. Tex., Dallas, 1954-56, resident in surgery, 1958-62, asst. prof. surgery, 1962-64, assoc. prof., 1964-68, prof., 1968—, dir. Transplant Services and Research Ctr., 1978—; dir. Burn Research Ctr., Parkland Regional Burn Ctr., Dallas, 1964—; mem. Gov.'s Task Force on Transplants, 1984; mem. HHS Transplant Task Force, 1985. Editor Jour. Burn Care and Rehab., 1980. Contbr. articles and chpts. to publs. in field. Served as capt. U.S. Army, 1956-58. Recipient Guiseppe Whitaker Internat. Burn prize, 1984; Curtiss P. Artz Trauma award Am. Trauma Soc., 1985. Fellow ACS; mem. Am. Burn Assn. (pres. 1973-74, Harvey Allen award 1979),Am. Assn. Surgery of Trauma (pres. 1980-81), Am. Assn. Tissue Banks (bd. dirs. 1980-85), Am. Surg. Soc. Republican. Baptist. Subspecialties: Critical care; Transplant surgery. Office: U Tex Med Sch Dept Surgery 5323 Harry Hines Blvd Dallas TX 72352

BAXTER, GENE FRANCIS, chemical researcher; b. Sanish, N.D., July 25, 1922; s. Leslie Valentine and Frances Rubena (Ellertson) B.; m. Jacqueline Claire Smith, July 16, 1949 (div. Apr. 1962); children—Marsha Lynn, Michael James, Anthony Frederick; m. 2d, Elizabeth Rose Turner, Feb. 14, 1970. B.S. in Chemistry, U. Wash., 1944. Research chemist Adhesive Products Co., Seattle, 1944-46, Martin-Marietta Co., Seattle, 1946-53, group leader, 1953-62; research scientist Weyerhaeuser Co., Seattle, 1962-73; scientist Ga. Pacific Corp., Decatur, 1973-83, sr. scientist, 1983—. Patentee in field. Mem. Am. Chem. Soc., Am. Mineral Soc. Subspecialties: Organic chemistry; Polymer chemistry. Home: 195 Tiburon Dr Decatur GA 30038 Office: Ga-Pacific Tech Ctr 2883 Miller Rd Decatur GA 30035

BAXTER, JOANN CRYSTAL, dental educator, researcher; b. Pitts., Jan. 9, 1947; d. John and Helen (Halaja) March; m. Albert Donald Baxter, June 14, 1965 (div. June, 1976); m. John David Hasenmiller, June 5, 1981. D.M.D., U. Pitts., 1977, cert. Splty., 1978, M.D.S., 1979. Cert. specialist prosthodontic dentistry. Pvt. practice dentistry, Pitts., part-time, 1977-79; asst. prof. dentistry U. Pitts., 1979-80; asst. prof. prosthodontics, geriatrics U. Ill.-Chgo, 1980—; cons. VA Continuing Edn., Washington, 1981—, U. Conn., 1982—, Henrotin Hosp., Chgo., 1981, VA Hosp., Wood, Wis., 1982. Mem. Am. Coll. Prosthodontics (chairperson edn. com. 1982—), ADA, Chgo. Dental Assn. (program com. 1982—), Am. Equilibration Soc. (chmn. credentials com. 1981-82), Am. Prosthodontics Soc. Republican. Eastern Orthodox. Current Work: Prosthodontic specialist; geriatric nutrition; research geriatric dentistry; geriatric nutrition. Subspecialties: Prosthodontics; Gerontology. Office: U Ill 801 S Paulina St Chicago IL 60680

BAXTER, JOHN DARLING, physician, educator; b. Lexington, Ky., June 11, 1940; s. William Elbert and Genevive Lockhart (Wilson) B.; m. Ethelee Davidson Baxter, Aug. 10, 1963; children: Leslie Lockhart, Gillian Booth. A.B. in Chemistry, U. Ky., 1962; M.D., Yale U., 1966. Intern, then resident in internal medicine Yale-New Haven Hosp., 1966-68; USPHS research assoc. Nat. Inst. Arthritis and Metabolic Diseases, NIH, 1968-70; Dernham sr. fellow oncology U. Calif. Med. Sch., San Francisco, 1970-72, mem. faculty, 1972—, prof. medicine and biochemistry and biophysics, 1979—; dir. endocrine research Howard Hughes Med. Inst., 1973-82; chief div. endocrinology Moffitt Hosp., 1980—, dir. Metabolic Research Unit, 1981—; attending physician U. Calif. Med. Center, 1972—. Editor textbook of endocrinology and metabolism; Author research papers in field; mem. editorial bd. profl. jours. Recipient George W. Thorn award Howard Hughes Med. Inst., 1978, Disting. Alumni award U. Ky., 1980; grantee NIH; grantee Am. Cancer Soc.; grantee others. Mem. Am. Chem. Soc., Am. Soc. Clin. Investigation, Am. Thyroid Assn., Assn. Am. Physicians, Am. Fedn. Clin. Research, Endocrine Soc., Western Assn. Physicians, Western Soc. Clin. Research. Current Work: Gene structure and regulation; hormone action. Subspecialties: Genetics and genetic engineering (biology); Endocrinology. Office: 671 HSE U Calif Med Sch San Francisco CA 94143

BAY, ROGER RUDOLPH, forest service official; b. LaCrosse, Wis., Nov. 27, 1931; s. Rudolph H. and Frieda K. (Leibel) B.; m. Ruth Ann Buckley, Aug. 30, 1958; children—Roger W., Laurie A. Bay Sandman. B.S. in Forestry, U. Idaho, 1953; M.F., U. Minn., 1954; Ph.D. in Forestry, 1967. Project leader, scientist North Central Forest Exptl. Sta., Grand Rapids, Minn., 1956-70; from asst. chief to chief watershed research U.S. Forest Service USDA, Washington, 1970-73, staff asst. research, U. Washington, 1973-74, sta. dir. Intermountain Forest and Range Exptl. Sta., Ogden, Utah, 1974-83, sta. dir. Pacific Southwest Forest and Range Exptl. Sta., Berkeley, Calif., 1983—. Contbr. articles to profl. jours. Active numerous civic orgns. Mem. Soc. Am. Foresters, Am. Geophys. Union, AAAS, Am. Foresters Assn. Current work: Development of research organizations, forest watershed management, research priority setting. Subspecialty: Forestry. Office: Pacific Southwest Forest and Range Exptl Sta USDA Forest Service PO Box 245 Addison St Berkeley CA 94701

BAYBARS, ILKER, business educator; b. Gordes, Manisa, Turkey, Nov. 26, 1947; came to U.S., 1970; s. Tevfik and Emine (Basboga) B. B.S., Middle East Tech. U., Ankara, Turkey, 1969; M.S., Carnegie-Mellon U., 1972, Ph.D., 1979. Instr. Middle-East Tech. U., Ankara, Turkey, 1969-70; instr. Carnegie-Mellon U., 1978-79; acad. dir. Quantitative Skills Summer Inst., 1980; vis. asst. prof. Sch Urban Pub. Affairs, 1979-81; asst. prof. Arad. Sch. Indsl. Adminstrn., 1981—; cons. Par Ajans, Ankara, 1968-70, UN, N.Y.C., 1981—, AT&T, Bedminister, N.J., 1981—, Mellon Bank, Pitts., 1982—. Author: Graph Theory; A Self-Pace Text, 1976. Served with Turkish Army, 1976. UN Traveling grantee, 1981; NSF grantee, 1980-82; recipient Carnegie-Mellon U. Limbach Teaching award, 1981. Mem. Pitts. Turkish Am. Assn., Ops. Research Soc. Am., Inst. Mgmt. Sci., Soc. Indsl. Applications of Math., Assn. Pub. Policy Analysis and Mgmt., Sigma Xi. Current Work: Optimal design of networks; facility-capicity planning and expansion; optimal design of assembly systems; algorithms; graph theory; mathematical programming. Subspecialties: Operations research (mathematics); Algorithms. Home: 5133 Forbes Ave Pittsburgh PA 15213 Office: GSIA Carnegie Mellon U 5000 Forbes Ave Pittsburgh PA 15213

BAYER, JESSE ABRAHAM, systems engineer; b. N.Y.C., Oct. 26, 1945; s. Irving and Sarah (Dratler) B.; m. Leslie Helen Bayer, Jan. 28, 1968; children: Hannah Michelle, Ariel Ian. B.E.M.E., Cooper Union, 1967; S.M.M.E., MIT, 1969; D.Engring. Sci., Columbia U., 1974. Registered engr. in tng. Mem. tech. staff Bell Labs., Whippany, N.J., 1967-83; Disting. mem. tech. staff Bell Communications Research, Inc., 1984—. Active Friends of Orange Public Library, Friends of Turtle Back Zoo. Recipient award Cooper Union Alumni Assn., 1967. Mem. ASME. Subspecialties: Systems engineering; Software engineering. Home: 444 Prospect St South Orange NJ 07079 Office: Bell Communications Research 435 South St Room 2K 330 Morristown NJ 07960

BAYLIS, CHARLES MERRITT, electrical engineer, materials scientist; b. Cin., July 3, 1956; s. Richard Edwin and Marjory (Ackerman) B.; m. Cynthia Jean Staun, Sept. 3, 1983. A.B. in Engring. Sci., Dartmouth Coll., 1978; M.S. in Materials Sci., Stanford U., 1981; M.S. in Elec. Engring., U. Calif.-Berkeley, 1981. Assoc. engr. SRI Internat., Menlo Park, Calif., 1979-81; instr. U. Calif.-Berkeley, 1981; supr. semicondr. lab. Cin. Milacron, Cin., 1981-84; product mgr. MISA Corp., Mildford, Ohio, 1984-85; cons. epitaxial reactor tech., 1985—. Editor Proc. Custom Integrated Circuits Conf., 1983. Recipient J.G. Kemeny prize in Computing Dartmouth Coll., 1978. Mem. IEEE, Assn. Computing Machinery. Republican. Roman Catholic. Current work: Epitaxial reactor technology. Subspecialties: Computer engineering; Microchip technology (materials science). Home: 601 Almarida Dr Apt 06 Campbell CA 95008

BAYLIS, WILLIAM ERIC, physicist, educator; b. Providence, Nov. 28, 1939; s. Charles A. and Ruth W. (Weage) B.; m. Bobbye Kaye Whitenton, June 10, 1961; children: Evelyn M., Katherine R. B.Sc., Duke U., 1961; M.Sc., U. Ill., 1963; D.Sc., Tech. U. Munich, W.Ger., 1967. Postdoctoral research assoc. Joint Inst. Lab. Astrophysics, Boulder, Colo., 1967-69; asst. prof., then assoc. prof. U. Windsor, Ont., Can., 1969-78, prof. physics, 1978—; vis. scientist Max-Planck-Inst., Gottingen, W. Ger., 1976-77. Contbr. articles to profl. jours. Mem. Can. Assn. Physicists, Am. Phys Soc. Current Work: Theory of atomic interactions; pseudopotentials, pressure broadening of spectral lines, correlation effects in relativistic hartree fock calculations. Subspecialties: Atomic and molecular physics; Theoretical physics. Home: RR 2 Harrow ON N0R 1G0 Canada Office: U Windsor Physics Dept Windsor ON N9B 3P4 Canada

BAYLOR, STEPHEN MURRAY, physiologist, biophysicist; b. Galesburg, Ill., July 5, 1943; s. Hugh Murray and Elisabeth Ann (Barbou) B.; m. Philomena Ann McDonnell, July 14, 1969; children—Isolde Ann, Timothy Stephen, Elizabeth Ellen. B.A., Knox Coll., 1965; M.A., U. Ill., 1966; M.D., Stanford U., 1971. Staff assoc. Nat. Cancer Inst., Bethesda, Md., 1971-73; research assoc. Yale U., New Haven, 1973-77, asst. prof., 1977-80; asst. prof. physiology U. Pa., Phila., 1980—. Contbr. articles to profl. jours. Served with USPHS, 1971-73. NIH grantee, 1981, 84. Mem. Biophys. Soc., Soc. Gen. Physiologists. Current work: Excitation-contraction coupling in muscle; the role of calcium ion as an intracellular messenger; membrane excitability. Subspecialties: Physiology (medicine); Biophysics (biology). Home: 351 Bala Ave Bala Cynwyd PA 19004 Office: U Pa Dept Physiology G4 Philadelphia PA 19104

BAYM, GORDON ALAN, physicist, educator; b. N.Y.C., July 1, 1935; s. Louis and Lillian B.; m. Lillian Hartmann; children—Nancy, Geoffrey, Michael, Carol. A.B., Cornell U., 1956; A.M., Harvard U., 1957, Ph.D., 1960. Fellow Universitetets Institut for Teoretisk Fysik, Copenhagen, Denmark, 1960-62; lectr. U. Calif.-, Berkeley, 1962-63; prof. physics U. Ill., Urbana, 1963—; vis. prof. U. Tokyo and U. Kyoto, 1968, Nordita, Copenhagen, 1970, 76, Niels Bohr Inst., Copenhagen, 1976, U. Nagoya, 1979; vis. scientist Academia Sinica, China, 1979; mem. adv. bd. Inst. Theoretical Physics, Santa Barbara, Calif., 1978-83; mem. subcom. theoretical physics, physics adv. com. NSF, 1980-81, 84, mem. phys. adv. com., 1982-85; Mem. nuclear sci. adv. com. Dept. of Energy/NSF, 1982—. Author: Lectures on Quantum Mechanics, 1969, Neutron Stars, 1970, Neutron Stars and the Properties of Matter at High Density, 1977, (with L.P. Kadanoff) Quantum Statistical Mechanics, 1962; assoc. editor: Nuclear Physics. Recipient Alexander von Humboldt Found. sr. U.S. Scientist award, 1983; Fellow Am. Acad. Arts and Scis.; Alfred P. Sloan Found. Research fellow, 1965-68; NSF postdoctoral fellow, 1960-62. Fellow Am. Phys. Soc., AAAS; mem. Am. Astron. Soc., Internat. Astron. Union., Nat. Acad. Scis. Subspecialties: Theoretical physics; Theoretical astrophysics. Office: Loomis Lab Physics U Ill 1110 W Green St Urbana IL 61801

BAZAN, NICHOLAS GUILLERMO, ophthalmology, neurology, biochemistry educator; b. Los Sarmientos, Argentina, May 22, 1942, came to U.S., 1965-68, 81—; s. Nicolas and Tomasa (Paez) B.; m. Haydee Elvira Pasqual; children—Patricia, Andrea, Nicolas, Hernan, Maria. B.S., Colegio Nacional de Salta, Argentina, 1958; M.D., Facultad de Medicina, Argentina, 1965; D. Med. Sci., Med. Sch. U. Tucuman, Argentina, 1971. Fellow Inst. Biology, Tucuman, 1963-65; postdoctoral research fellow Coll. Physicians & Surgeons, N.Y.C., 1965-66; asst. dir., asst. prof. Clark Inst. Psychiatry, Toronto, Ont., Can., 1968-70; research assoc. Harvard Med. Sch., Boston, 1966-68; founder dir., prof., Inst. Biochemical Research, Bahia Blanca, Argentina, 1970-81; founder sch. biology U. South, Argentina, 1970; founder, 1st pres. Found. Promotion of Sci. and Culture, B. Blanca, Argentina, 1979; prof. ophthalmology, neurology, biochemistry La. State U., New Orleans, 1981—, Ernest C. and Ivette C. Villere chair research retinal degeneration, 1984—. United Nations expert to India, 1983; mem. task force devel. neurobiology USPHS, 1983-84, special rev. com. NIH, 1985. Editor: Neurochemistry of the Retina, 1980, Functions and Biosynthesis of Lipids, 1977, New Trends on Nutrition, 1981, Neural Membranes, 1983; editorial bd. Jour. Neurochemistry and Neurochemical Pathology, 1981. Contbr. articles to profl. jours. Named Ten Outstanding Young Persons in Argentina, Jr. Chamber, 1976. Grantee NIH, 1981-85 Epilepsy Found. Am., 1983, Fight for Sight, 1982, Am. Diabetes Assn., 1984. Internat. research scholar Research Prevent Blindness, 1977; scholar Council Internat. Soc. Neurochemistry, 1979-83, Gold Medal Found. G. Lorenzini, Milan, Italy, 1981; William and Mary Greve Internat. scholar, 1983-84 Mem. Internat. Soc. Neurochemistry, Am. So. Neurochemistry, Am. Soc. Biol. Chemists, Assn. Research Vision Ophthalmology, Can. Biochemical Soc., Biochemical Soc. Eng. Roman Catholic. Current work: Excitable membranes and metabolism prostaglandins. Subspecialties: Neurochemistry; Ophthalmology. Home: 6933 Lake Willow Dr New Orleans LA 70126 Office: La State U Eye Ctr 136 S Roman St New Orleans LA 70112

BAZINET, LESTER, biologist, educator; b. Escanaba, Mich., May 5, 1929; s. Archie E. and Verlie (Trombly) B. B.S., No. Mich. U., 1959; M.S., U. Mich., 1961; Ed. D., Nova U., 1977; postgrad., Stanford U., 1969, 72, 79. Biology tchr., Swartz Creek, Mich., 1960-65; instr. biology Villanova (Pa.) U., 1965-66, 67-69; prof. biology Community Coll. Phila., 1970—, head dept., 1973, 74. Author: Laboratory Manual Morphology and Evolution in the Plant Kingdom, 1973, Development and Evaluation of a Biology Laboratory Unit on Cells and Tissues, 1975, The Development and Evaluation of an A-T Program of Instruction for Introductory Biology Laboratory, 1977, Audio-Tutorial Laboratory Guide for Biology 101, 1977. Mich. Bd. Regents scholar, 1947; Backus-Jewett fellow, 1960; NSF fellow, 1969; recipient Lindback award for Disting. Teaching, 1976. Mem. N.Y. Acad. Sci., Am. Bryol. and Lichenol. Soc., Am. Bot. Soc., Phycol. Soc. Am., Mich. Bot. Club, Phila. Bot. Club, Kappa Delta Pi. Current Work: Taxonomy and systematics; marine algae; teaching biology and botany. Subspecialties: Evolutionary biology; Taxonomy. Home: 1146 S 8th St Philadelphia PA 19147 Office: 1700 Spring Garden St Philadelphia PA 19130

BAZZAZ, FAKHRI A., plant biology educator, administrator; b. Baghdad, Iraq, June 16, 1933; came to U.S., 1965; s. Abdul-Lalif and Munifa B.; m. Maarib Bazzaz, Aug. 25, 1958; children—Sahar, Ammar. B.S., U. Baghdad, 1953; M.S., U. Ill., 1960, Ph.D., 1963. Prof. U. Ill., Urbana, 1977-84, head dept. plant biology, acting dir. Sch. Life Scis., 1983-84; prof. biology Harvard U., 1984—; fellow Clare Hall, Cambridge U., Eng., 1981. Editor: Oecologia, 1983. Mem. Ecol. Soc. Am., Brit. Ecol. Soc. Office: Biol Labs Harvard U 16 Divinity Ave Cambridge MA 02138

BEACH, LEE ROY, psychologist, educator; b. Gallup, N.Mex., Feb. 29, 1936; s. Dearl and Lucile Ruth (Krumtum) B.; m. Barbara Ann Heinrich, Nov. 13, 1971. B.A., Ind. U., 1957; M.A., U. Colo., 1959, Ph.D., 1961. Aviation psychologist U.S. Sch. Aviation Medicine, Pensacola, Fla., 1961-63; human factors officer Office of Naval Research, Washington, 1963-64; postdoctoral research U. Mich., Ann Arbor, 1964-66; faculty dept. psychology U. Wash., Seattle, 1966—, prof. psychology, 1974—; cons. VA Med. Center, Seattle, 1979—. Contbr. articles to profl. jours.; author: Psychology: Core Concepts and Special Topics, 1973. Served with USN, 1961-64. Recipient Feldman Research award, 1981; NIMH fellow, 1964-66; NIH grantee, 1979—. Fellow Am. Psychol. Assn.; mem. AAAS. Current Work: Research on judgement and decision processes and on metacognition. Subspecialties: Cognition; Social psychology. Home: 2129 2d Ave W Seattle WA 98119 Office: Dept Psychology NI25 Univ Wash Seattle WA 98195

BEACH, LOUIS ANDREW, research physicist; b. Greenville, Ind., June 2, 1925; s. George Covert and Clara Christine (Kiesler) B.; m. Virginia Ann McHugh, Oct. 20, 1956; children—Andrew, Ann Marie, Ruth Christine, Covert John. B.S. in Physics, Ind. U., 1944, M.S. in Physics, 1947, Ph.D. in Exptl. Physics, 1949. Grad asst. Ind. U., Bloomington, 1946-49; research assoc. Cornell U., Ithaca, N.Y., 1949-51; nuclear physicist Naval Research Lab., Washington, 1951-55, br. head, 1955-65, sect. head, 1965-80, research physicist, 1980—; lectr. nuclear engring. Catholic U., Washington, 1960-66. Contbr. articles to profl. jours. Pres. Hillcrest Citizens Assn., Washington, 1958-60. Served with U.S. Army, 1944-46, ETO. Fellow Washington Acad. Scis.; mem. Am. Phys. Soc., AAAS, Cath. War Vets. (post comdr. 1954-56), Sigma Xi (pres. Naval Research Lab. chpt. 1963-64). Democrat. Lodge: K.C. Current work: Beta decay studies, radiation interaction with matter, shielding of nuclear radiation, nuclear reactor theory, nuclear structure, radiation damage to metals, nuclear detectors. Subspecialties: Nuclear physics; Nuclear fission. Home: 1200 Waynewood Blvd Alexandria VA 22308 Office: Code 6616 Naval Research Lab Washington DC 20375-5000

BEACH, ROBERT LEIGH, neurobiologist, consultant; b. Milford, Conn., July 4, 1948; s. Richard Booth and Georgia (Eisenman) B. B.S. in Chemistry, U. Conn., 1971, M.S. in Organic Chemistry, 1972, Ph.D. in Neurobiology, 1977. Postdoctoral fellow U. Conn., Storrs, 1977; NIH fellow U. Calif.-Irvine, 1977-79, research psychobiologist, 1979-81; research physiologist VA Med. Ctr., Kansas City, Kans., 1981-82; research assoc. prof. Kans. U. Med. Ctr., Kansas City, 1982—; cons. in field, 1983—. Contbr. articles to profl. jours. Cold Spring Harbor Summer fellow, 1975. Mem. AAAS, Am. Soc. Biol. Chemists, Am. Soc. Cell Biology, Internatl. Soc. Neurochemistry, Soc. for Neurosci., Phi Kappa Phi. Current work: Roles of cytoskeletal and extracellular matrix components in development and plasticity of neuro-neuronal and neuro-muscular synapses. Subspecialties: Neurobiology; Neurochemistry. Home: 3900 Booth #12 Kansas City KS 66103 Office: Box 282 Kans Univ Med Ctr 3900 Rainbow Blvd Kansas City KS 66103

BEACHLEY, NORMAN HENRY, mechanical engineer, educator; b. Washington, Jan. 13, 1933; s. Albert Henry and Anna Garnet (Eiring) B.; m. Marion Ruth Iglehart, July 18, 1959; children: Brenda Ruth, Rebecca Sue, Barbara Joan. B.M.E., Cornell U., 1956, Ph.D., 1966. Mem. tech. staff Hughes Aircraft Co., Culver City, Calif., 1956-57; mem. tech. staff Space Tech. Labs., Redondo Beach, Calif., 1959-63; mech. engring. professorial staff U. Wis., Madison, 1966—, prof. mech. engring., 1978—; cons. Nat. Bur. Standards, 1980—. Co-author: Introduction to Dynamic System Analysis, 1978. Served with USAF, 1957-59. Sci. and Engring. Research Council Gt. Britain fellow, 1981-82. Mem. ASME, Soc. Automotive Engrs., Sigma Xi. Research in field of energy storage powerplants for motor vehicles, 1970. Subspecialty: Mechanical engineering. Home: 2332 Fitchburg Rd Verona WI 53593 Office: U Wis 1513 University Ave Madison WI 53706

BEACOM, STANLEY ERNEST, animal nutritionist, administrator; b. Fort Macleod, Alta., Can., May 18, 1927; s. Henry Grier and Alice Louise (Young) B.; m. Cynthia Jean Lonsdale, Aug 2, 1957; children—Kathryn Jean, Connie Lynn. B.Sc. with distinction, U. Alta., 1949, M.Sc., 1951; Ph.D., McGill U., 1959. Tech. officer Agr. Can. Research Br., Melfort, Sask., 1952-53, research officer, 1953-56, research scientist, 1965-66, research dir., 1966—. Bd. dirs. Melfort Credit Union. Mem. Sask. Inst. Agrologists (past pres.), Agrl. Inst. Can., Can. Soc. Animal Sci., Melfort Agrl. Soc. Mem. United Ch. of Can. Lodge: Masons. Current work: Developing technology to improve the efficiency of utilizing harvested hay in beef finishing rations-effects of hay quality, hay to grain ratio, fines of grinding, high energy supplements, implants, additives. Subspecialty: Animal nutrition. Office: Agr Can Research Sta PO Box 1240 Melfort SK S0E 1A0 Canada

BEADLE, CHARLES WILSON, mech. engr., educator; b. Beverly, Mass., Jan. 24, 1930; s. Thomas and Jean (Wilson) B.; m. Dorothy E. Beadle, May 5, 1956; children: Steven, Sara, Gordon. B.S., Tufts U., 1951; M.S.E., U. Mich., 1954; Ph.D., Cornell U., 1961. Registered prof. engr., Calif., Mich. With Gen. Motors Research Labs., 1951-54, RCA Research Labs., 1954-57; mem. faculty U. Calif.-Davis, 1961—, prof. mech. engring., 1975—, chmn. dept., 1978—. Contbr. articles to profl. jours. Ford Found. resident in engring. practice, 1965-66. Fellow ASME, Am. Soc. Engring. Edn. Current Work: Computer-aided mechanical design. Subspecialties: Mechanical engineering; Computer-aided design.

BEAKES, JOHN HERBERT, consulting firm executive; b. Balt., Feb. 24, 1943; s. John Herbert and Martha (Ailes) B.; m. Rosemary Brown, June 11, 1966; children: Susan Dawn, Sarah Elisabeth, John Herbert. B.S., U.S. Naval Acad., 1966; M.S. in Environ. Engring, Johns Hopkins U., 1977. Registered profl. engr., Md., Pa., Tenn. Nuclear submarine officer U.S. Navy, 1966-74; sr. engr. Gen. Physics Corp., Columbia, Md., 1974-77, dir. engring. services, 1977-79, v.p., 1979-82, sr. v.p., 1982—, pres. subs. Gen. Tech. Services, 1984—. Served as lt. comdr. USN, 1966-74. Mem. Am. Nuclear Soc., ASME (exec. com. plant engring. and maintenance div. 1981-84). Republican. Presbyterian. Current Work: Operability, maintainability and reliability enhancements to power generation facilities. Subspecialties: Nuclear engineering; Information systems (Information science). Office: Gen Physics Corp 10650 Hickory Ridge Rd Columbia MD 21044

BEALL, DONALD RAY, See *Who's Who in America,* 43rd edition.

BEAN, WILLIAM JOSEPH, JR., virologist; b. Albany, N.Y., Mar. 16, 1945; s. William Joseph and Ruth Elizabeth (Lafferty) B.; m. Dianne Lee Pendleton, Sept. 28, 1968; 1 dau., Shawn Katherine. B.S., U. Maine, 1967, M.S. in Bacteriology, 1969; Ph.D. in virology, Rutgers U., 1974. Research asst. Waksman Inst. Microbiology, Piscataway, N.J., 1974-75; research assoc. St. Jude Children's Research Hosp., Memphis, 1975-77, asst. mem., 1977-82, assoc. mem., 1982—; asst. prof. microbiology U. Tenn., Memphis, 1981—. Served to lt. U.S. Army, 1968-71. Mem. Am. Soc. Microbiology, Am. Soc. Virology. Current Work: Genetics of influenza virus; molecular and biological basis of genetic changes in human and animal influenza viruses. Subspecialties: Virology (biology); Molecular biology. Home: 3981 Cheryl Dr Memphis TN 38116 Office: 332 N Lauderdale Memphis TN 38101

BEARD, ELIZABETH LETITIA, physiology and medical research educator; b. New Orleans, Apr. 2, 1932; d. Howard Horace and Irene (Handley) B. B.A., Tex. Christian U., 1952, B.S., 1953, M.S., 1955; Ph.D., Tulane U., 1961. Instr., Loyola U., New Orleans, 1955-58, asst. prof., 1958-62, assoc. prof., 1962-68, prof. physiology, researcher, 1968—; research assoc. Tulane Sch. Medicine, 1960-63, prof. med. reinforcement programs, 1968—. Soprano soloist Christ Ch. Cathedral, 1967-83, Holy Name of Jesus Ch., 1967—; pres. sch. bd. Holy Name of Jesus Ch., 1976-79; mem. Met. Mus. Art, N.Y.C., 1974—, New Orleans Mus. Art, 1975—, grad. research com. La. chpt. Am. Heart Assn., 1970-72, undergrad. research com., 1978—. Grantee NIH 1962-64, 67-69, La. Heart Assn., 1966-67, Edward Schleider Found., 1974-77, New Orleans Cancer Assn. Mem. Am. Inst. Biol. Scis., Assn. Southeastern Biologists, AAUP, AAAS, N.Y. Acad. Scis., Am. Physiol. Soc., Sigma Xi. Contbr. articles to profl. jours. Subspecialty: Physiology (biology). Home: 6127 Garfield St New Orleans LA 70118 Office: Loyola U 6363 Saint Charles Ave New Orleans LA 70118

BEARD, JAMES TAYLOR, mechanical engineering educator, consultant; b. Birmingham, Ala., Oct. 1, 1939; s. James Robison and Mary Evelyn (McArthur) B.; m. Kathryn LuClaire Lee, June 5, 1965; children: Rosemary Ann, James David. B.M.E., Auburn (Ala.) U., 1961; M.S., Okla. State U., Stillwater, 1963, Ph.D.M.E. (NDEA fellow), 1965. Registered profl. engr., Va.

Research asst. Okla. State U., 1963-65; asst. prof. mech. and aerospace engring. U. Va., Charlottesville, 1965-69, assoc. prof., 1969—, asst. provost, 1972-77, mem. faculty senate, 1983-85; ptnr. Assoc. Environ. Consultants, Charlottesville, 1971—; short course dir. EPA, 1972-82; tech. adv. com. Va. Air Pollution Control Bd. Contbr. articles to profl. jours. Elder, clk. of session Westminster Presbyn. Ch.; mem. Albemarle County Democratic Com., 1972—; treas. bd. dirs. Charlottesville Housing Found., 1969-81. Recipient Algernon Sydney Sullivan award Auburn U., 1961. Mem. ASME, ASHRAE, Am. Soc. Agrl. Engrs., Internat. Solar Energy Soc., Sigma Xi, Tau Beta Pi, Phi Kappa Phi, Pi Tau Sigma. Club: Colonnade (Charlottesville). Current Work: Heat transfer, solar energy system analysis, air pollution control, univ. engring. educator, combustion as related to air pollution control. Subspecialties: Mechanical engineering; Solar energy. Home: 412 Westmoreland Ct Charlottesville VA 22901 Office: Dept Mech and Aero Engineering U Va Charlottesville VA 22901

BEARD, LEO ROY, civil engineer; b. West Baden, Ind., Apr. 6, 1917; s. Leonard Roy and Barbara Katherine (Frederick) B.; m. Marian Janet Wagar, Oct. 21, 1939 (dec.); children: Patricia Beard Huntzicker, Thomas Edward, James Robert; m. Marjorie Elizabeth Pierce Wood, Aug. 30, 1974. A.A., Pasadena City Coll., 1937; B.S., Calif. Inst. Tech., 1939. Engr. U.S. Army C.E., Los Angeles, 1939-49; engr. Office Chief of Engrs., Washington, 1949-52; chief of Reservoir Regulation, Sacramento, 1952-64; dir. Hydrologic Engring. Center, Davis, Calif., 1964-72; prof. civil engring. U. Tex., Austin, 1972—; dir. (Center for Research in Water Resources), 1972-80; cons. Espey, Huston & Assos., Austin, 1980—; v.p. Internat. Commn. of Water Resource Systems; mem. NRC Water Sci. and Tech. Bd. Editor-in-chief: Water International; Editor: Jour. of Hydrology. Served with USNR, 1945-46. Recipient Meritorious Civilian Service award U.S. Army C.E., 1972. Fellow ASCE (water resources exec. com., Julian Hinds award 1981); mem. Internat. Water Resources Assn. (exec. bd.), Am. Water Resources Assn. (hon.), Am. Geophys. Union (pres. hydrology sect.), Nat. Soc. Profl. Engrs., Internat. Assn. Hydrol. Scis., World Meteorol. Orgn. (chmn. com. on hydrol. design data), U.S. Com. on Irrigation, Drainage and Flood Control, Univs. Council on Water Resources (exec. bd.), Nat. Acad. Engring. Current Work: All aspects of water resources management. Subspecialties: Civil engineering; Hydrology. Home: 606 Laurel Valley Austin TX 78746 Office: PO Box 519 Austin TX 78767

BEARDEN, ALAN JOYCE, biophysicist; b. Balt., Nov. 23, 1931; s. Joyce Alvin and Lillian Lavonia (Singleton) B. A.B., Johns Hopkins U., 1950, Ph.D., 1958. Asst. prof. physics Cornell U., Ithaca, N.Y., 1960-64; asst. prof. chemistry U. Calif., San Diego, 1966-68, from lectr. to asso. prof. div. med. physics, Berkeley, 1969-76, prof. biophysics, 1976—, chmn. div. med. physics, 1978-79, chmn. dept. biophysics and med. physics, 1979-84. Served with USN, 1950-54. NIH career devel. awardee, 1970-74; NIH fellow U. Calif., San Diego, 1964-66; Pollard lectr. Yale U., 1976. Fellow Am. Phys. Soc. (chmn. div. biol. physics 1978-79); mem. Biophys. Soc., Am. Soc. Photobiology, AAAS. Research in photosynthesis, bioenergetics, auditory transduction, energy transfer in biology. Subspecialty: Biophysics (physics). Office: Dept Biophysics and Med Physics U Calif Berkeley CA 94720

BEARN, ALEXANDER GORDON, physician scientist, pharmaceutical company executive; b. Surrey, Eng., Mar. 29, 1923; came to U.S., 1951; s. Edward Gordon and Rose (Kay) B.; m. Margaret Slocum, Dec. 20, 1952; children: Helen Elliot, Gordon Clarence Frederic. Ed., Epsom Coll.; M.B., B.S., Guy's Hosp., U. London, Eng., 1946; M.D., 1951; M.D. Dr. honoris causa, U. René Descartes, Paris, 1974. House physician Guy's Hosp., 1946-47; house physician, registrar Postgrad. Med. Sch., London, 1948-51; mem. staff Rockefeller Inst., N.Y.C., 1951-64, assoc. prof., 1957-64, prof., sr. physician, 1964-66; prof. medicine Cornell U., 1966—, Stanton Griffis Disting. med. prof., 1976-80, chmn. dept., 1966-77; physician-in-chief N.Y. Hosp., 1966-77; med. dir., bd. dirs., sec.-treas. Russell Sage Inst. Pathology, 1967-79; sr. v.p. med. and sci. affairs Merck, Sharp & Dohme Internat., Rahway, N.J., 1979—; Lilly lectr., 1973, Lettsomian lectr., 1976; bd. sci. cons. Sloan Kettering Inst., 1967-74; mem. Commn. Human Resources, Nat. Acad. Scis., 1974-77; chmn. div. med. scis. Assembly Life Scis., 1978—; bd. sci. counselors Nat. Inst. Arthritis, Metabolism and Digestive Diseases, 1976-80; mem. Space Sci. Bd., 1978-79; cons. genetics tng. com., div. gen. med. scis. USPHS, 1961-65, cons. genetics study sect., 1966-70; pres. Royal Soc. Medicine Found., Inc., 1976-78; now dir.; mem. bd. sci. overseers Jackson Lab., Bar Harbor; mem. Inst. Medicine, Nat. Acad. Scis. Editor: Am. Jour. Medicine; co-editor: Progress in Medical Genetics, 1962-85; assoc. editor: Cecil-Loeb Textbook of Medicine; Contbr. articles to profl. jours. Trustee Rockefeller U., Helen Hay Whitney Found. Served as med. officer RAF, 1947-49. Fellow AAAS, Royal Coll. Physicians (Edinburgh, Scotland), Royal Coll. Physicians (London, Eng.); mem. Nat. Acad. Scis., Am. Philos. Soc., Assn. Am. Physicians, Am. Soc. Clin. Investigation, Am. Soc. Human Genetics (pres. 1971), Genetics Soc. Am., Am. Soc. Biol. Chemists, Soc. Exptl. Biology and Medicine, Harvey Soc. (pres. 1972-73, Harvey lectr. 1975), Harveian Soc. London (Council 1959), Assn. Physicians Great Britain and Ireland, Med. Research Soc. Great Britain, Med. Soc. London, Am. Assn. History Medicine, Sigma Xi (pres. Rockefeller chpt. 1962-63); fgn. assoc. Norwegian Acad. Sci. and Letters; hon. mem. Sociedad Medica de Santiago, Sociedad de Biologia de Santiago. Presbyterian. Clubs: Century Assn. (N.Y.C.), Grolier (N.Y.C.); Crail Golf (Scotland). Subspecialty: Genetics and genetic engineering (medicine). Home: 1225 Park Ave New York NY 10028 Office: Merck and Co Inc PO Box 2000 Rahway NJ 07065

BEASLEY, WAYNE MACHON, materials science educator, consultant; b. Everett, Mass., May 23, 1922; s. William Francis and Elsie May (Machon) B.; m. Evelyn Harriet Eddy, Feb. 28, 1945; 1 dau., Dawn Linda. S.B. cum laude, Harvard U., 1945; S.M., M.I.T., 1965. Tchr. math. Dover (N.H.) High Sch., 1946-48; cons., Rochester, N.H., 1948-51; physicist Clarostat mfg. Co., Dover, 1951-55; sr. physicist Metals & Controls Corp., Attleboro, Mass., 1955-57; research prof. U. N.H., Durham, 1957-72, prof. materials sci., 1972-84, prof. emeritus, 1984—; materials cons., 1984—; cons. materials tech. to electronics industry in U.S. and Japan. Contbr. articles to various jours. Mem. budget com., Town of Barrington (N.H.), 1978-81; mem. roads com., 1980-81, planning bd., 1982—, Waste Disposal Study Commn., Barrington, 1975-78. Served to ensign USN, 1943-45, PTO. Mem. Am. Phys. Soc., European Phys. Soc., Internat. Soc. for Stereology, Am. Soc. for Metals (pres. N.H. chpt. 1959-60), N.H. Acad. Sci., Union Concerned Scientists, Sigma Xi. Clubs: MIT Faculty (Cambridge, Mass.); Harvard (N.H.) (v.p.). Co-patentee method of elec. noise reduction in potentiometers. Current Work: Application of quantitative stereological techniques to particle packing; research involving spinodal decomposition transformations; high-temperature phase determination (ceramics). Subspecialties: Materials; High-temperature materials. Home: 22 Weeks Ln Rochester NH 03867 Office: University of New Hampshire Kingsbury Hall Durham NH 03824

BEASON, ROBERT CURTIS, biology educator; b. Ft. Scott, Kans., May 12, 1946; s. Eugene and Lida Jane (Lawson) B.; m. Julia Ann Farthing, Aug. 10, 1967 (div. 1973); m. Delena Lorraine Sloane, Feb. 14, 1981; 1 child, Zachary Adam Sloane. B.A., Bethany Nazarene Coll., 1968; M.S., Western Ill. U., 1970; Ph.D., Clemson U., 1976. Research scientist U.S. Air Force, Kirtland AFB, N.Mex., 1970-74; grad. research asst. Clemson (S.C.) U., 1974-76; research biologist U.S. Forest Service, Columbia, S.C., 1976; vis. lectr. U. Calif.-Irvine, 1977; vis. asst. prof. Western Ill. U., Macomb, 1977-78; asst. prof. biology SUNY-Geneseo, 1978-85, assoc. prof., 1985—; cons. FAA, 1977, NASA. Reviewer: Jour. Field Ornithology, 1975—. U.S. Dept. Interior grantee, 1974; NSF grantee, 1981; Geneseo Found. grantee, 1982, 84, 85. Mem. AAAS, Am. Ornithologists Union (life), Animal Behavior Soc., Ecol. Soc. Am. Current Work: Evolution of migration; avian migration; orientation and navigation; avian behavioral ecology; role of vocalizations and behavior in avian speciation. Subspecialties: Behavioral ecology; Evolutionary biology. Home: 7673 Dutch St Rd Mount Morris NY 14510 Office: Dept Biology SUNY Geneseo NY 14454

BEATON, MICHAEL STEVE, materials engineer; b. Camden, Tenn., July 4, 1950; s. Thomas Max and Doris Marie (Jones) B.; m. Robin Terri Webster, Jan. 1, 1983; 1 child, Michael Scott. B.S., U. Tenn., 1973, M.S., 1975. Research asst. U. Tenn., 1973-75; metall. engr. Robertshaw Controls Co., Knoxville, 1975; group leader, materials engr. U. Tenn. Space Inst., Tullahoma, Tenn., 1975-79; product devel. engr. Brunswick Corp., Deland, Fla. 1979—. Patentee (pending) seamless oriented metal fiber structure. Contbr. articles to profl. jours. Recipient Merit award for contbrs. to arc welding design and engring. James F. Lincoln Arc Welding Found., 1985. Mem. Am. Soc. Metals (chpt. pres. 1982-83, coms.), Am. Ceramic Soc., ASME (coms.). Republican. Methodist. Club: Halifax. Current work: Tribiology; high temperature abradable materials; sintering; ceramic coatings, ceramic adhesives; effect of alloy microstructure on high temperature properties; near net shape fabrication. Subspecialties: Metallurgical engineering; Ceramics. Home: 2726 Palm Terr DeLand FL 32720 Office: Brunswick Corp 2000 Brunswick Ln DeLand FL 32724

BEATON, ROY HOWARD, retired nuclear industry executive; b. Boston, Sept. 1, 1916; s. John Howard and Mary Beaton (LaVoie) B.; children—Constance Beaton Reinholz, Roy Howard. B.S., Northeastern U., 1939, D.Sc. (hon.), 1967; D. Eng., Yale U., 1942. With E.I. duPont, 1942-45, plant tech. supr., 1944-45; asso. prof. chem. engring. U. Kans., Lawrence, 1946; with Gen. Electric Co., 1946-81, v.p., gen. mgr. electronic systems div., Syracuse, N.Y., 1968-74, v.p., gen. mgr. energy systems and tech. div., Fairfield, Conn., 1974-75, v.p., gen. mgr. nuclear energy systems div., San Jose, Calif., 1975-77, v.p., group exec. nuclear energy group, 1977-79, sr. v.p., group exec. nuclear energy group, 1979-81. Chmn. industry div. United Way Campaign, Santa Clara County, Calif., 1978-79. Fellow Am. Inst. Chemists, AAAS, Nat. Acad. Engring., Am. Ordnance Assn., Am. Nuclear Soc., Am. Inst. Chem. Engrs., IEEE, AIAA, Navy League U.S., Air Force Assn., Soc. Mil. Engrs., Santa Clara County Mfg. Group, Sigma Xi, Tau Beta Pi. Subspecialty: Nuclear engineering. Home: PO Box 1018 Saratoga CA 95070

BEATTIE, CRAIG WARREN, pharmacologist, educator; b. Elizabeth, N.J., Oct. 26, 1943; s. Warren Edgar and Margaret Ann (Sasz) B.; m. Jean Blankenship, Nov. 24, 1973. B.S., Fairleigh Dickinson U., 1965, M.S., 1968; Ph.D., U. Del., 1971. Postdoctoral fellow dept. pharmacology U. Ill., 1971-72; sr. research scientist Pharm. div. Penwalt Corp., 1972-73; sr. research biologist endocrine sect. dept. pharmacology Wyeth Labs., 1973-76; asst. prof. pharmacology Bowman-Gray Sch. Medicine, Wake Forest U., 1976-77; assoc. prof. pharmacology in surgery div. surg. oncology U. Ill. Sch. Medicine, 1977-83-, prof. pharmacology in surgery div. surg. oncology, 1983—, assoc. prof. pharmacology, 1977-83, prof. pharmacology, 1983—; vis. prof. Sch. Biochemistry U. New South Wales, Australia, 1983-84. Contbr. numerous articles and revs. to sci. jours., chpts. to books. Recipient award Pharm. Mfrs. Assn. Found., 1976-77; U. Del. research fellow, 1968-70; NIH postdoctoral fellow, 1970-72. Mem. Am. Soc. Pharmacology and Exptl. Therapeutics, Endocrine Soc., Am. Assn. Cancer Research, Tissue Culture Soc., Am. Soc. Zoologists, Sigma Xi. Current Work: Endocrine correlates to neoplastic transformation and gene. expression. Subspecialties: Cancer research (medicine); Receptors. Office: Div Surg Oncology U Ill 370A 840 S Wood St Chicago IL 60612

BEAUCAGE, SERGE LAURENT, nucleic acids chemist, researcher; b. St. Hyacinthe, Que., Can., Jan. 11, 1951; came to U.S., 1979; s. Rene and Therese (Bernier) B.; m. Diane Marie Desrosiers, Sept. 6, 1975; 1 child: Brian. B.S., U. Quebec, Montreal, Can., 1974; Ph.D., McGill U., Montreal, 1978. Research assoc. U. Colo., Boulder, 1979-81, U. Mich., Ann Arbor, 1981-82; sr. staff scientist Smith-Kline Beckman, Palo Alto, Calif., 1982—; cons. Genetics Inst., Boston, 1981-84. Patentee in field. Contbr. articles to profl. jours. Mem. Am. Chem. Soc. Current work: Chemistry and analysis of nucleic acids. Development of novel methodologies for the solid phase synthesis of DNA and RNA. Subspecialties: Synthetic chemistry; Biochemistry (biology). Office: 1050 Page Mill Rd Palo Alto CA 94304

BEAVEN, MICHAEL ANTHONY, research pharmacologist; b. London, Dec. 4, 1936; came to U.S., 1962, naturalized, 1968; s. Edward and Phyllis Georgina Dorcas (Barker) B.; m. Vida Helms, Feb. 1, 1964. B.Pharm., Chelsea Coll., U. London, 1959, Ph.D., 1962. USPHS vis. fellow Lab. Chem. Pharmacology, Nat. Heart, Lung and Blood Inst., NIH, Bethesda, Md., 1962-65, research pharmacologist, 1965-68, research pharmacologist exptl. therapeutics br., 1968-77, sect. chief sect. cellular pharmacolog Lab. Cellular Metabolism, 1977-82, dep. chief Lab. Chem. Pharmacology, 1982—; assoc. mem. Darwin Coll., Cambridge (Eng.) U., 1982-83. Editorial bd. Jour. Pharms. and Exptl. Therapeutics, European Jour. Pharmacy. Contbr. over 100 articles and revs. to profl. jours., also chpts. to books. Mem. Pharm. Soc. Gt. Britain, Am. Soc. Pharmacology and Exptl. Therapeutics. Current Work: Role of histamine in pathological and physiological reactions: mechanism of mast cell degranulation. Subspecialties: Pharmacology; Immunopharmacology. Office: Bldg 10 Room 8N108 NIH Bethesda MD 20892

BEAVER, BONNIE VERYLE, veterinary anatomy educator; b. Mpls., Oct. 26, 1944; d. Crawford F. and Gladys I. (Nielsen) Gustafson; m. Larry J. Beaver, Nov. 25, 1972. B.S., U. Minn., 1966, D.V.M., 1968; M.S., Tex. A&M U., 1972. Instr. vet. surgery and radiology U. Minn., St. Paul, 1968-69; instr. Tex. A&M U., College Station, 1969-72, asst. prof. vet. anatomy, 1972-76, assoc. prof., 1976-82, prof., 1982—, mem. staff Vet. Teaching Hosp., 1982—; mem. vet. medicine adv. com. HEW, 1972-74, mem. nat. adv. food and drug com., 1975; mem. nat. bd. lectureships Arabian Horse Trust, 1979—; mem. Brazos County Extension Horse Com., Tex., 1982—; v.p, mem. entry com. Brazos Valley Regional Sci. and Engring. Fair, 1974-83, chairwoman animal expt. com., 1974-84, fair dir., 1983—; exhibitor palomino quarter horses. Author: Veterinary Aspects of Feline Behavior, 1980; Horse Color, 1984; also articles. Editorial bd. Applied Animal Ethology, 1981-82, 83-84, VM/SAC, 1982-85, Applied Animal Behavior Sci., 1983—. Bd. dirs. Brazos Valley unit Am. Cancer Soc., 1976-82, v.p., 1977-82. Honored for contbns. of women veterinarians to profession Calif. Vet. Med. Assn., 1973; Outstanding Woman Veterinarian, Assn. Women Veterinarians, 1982. Mem. Palomino Horse Breeders Am. (nat. insp. 1965—, nat. bd. dirs. 1967, 68, 81—, contbg. editor 1974-81, exec. bd. 1981-82, 83-84, 84-85, v.p. and chmn. drug, medication, devices and abuse com. 1983-84, treas. 1984-85), U. Minn. Alumni Assn. (life), Tex. Palomino Exhibitors Assn. (state. bd. dirs. 1972-79, 81-82, instr. youth judging clinic 1975), Alamo Palomino Exhibitors Assn., AVMA (1st vice chmn. council on edn. 1984-85, chmn. endl. commn. for fgn. vet. grads. 1982-83, 83-84), Brazos Valley Vet. Med. Assn. (sec.-treas. 1972), Tex. Vet. Med. Assn. (chmn. editorial com. 1978-81, bd. dirs. 1980—, chmn. edn. com. 1983-84), Am. Vet. Neurology Assn., Animal Behavior Soc., Am. Soc. Vet. Ethology (founder and charter mem., pres. 1975, 76-80, exec. com. 1975—), Am. Assn. Vet. Anatomists, Am. Assn. Equine Practicioners, Assn. Am. Vet. Med. Colls., Am. Assn. Vet. Clinicians, Am. Vet. Computer Soc., AAAS, Delta Soc. (adv. com. 1983), Sigma Epsilon Sigma, Phi Zeta (nat. pres. 1979-81), Phi Delta Gamma, Gamma Sigma Delta, Phi Sigma. Current work: Domestic animal behavior. Subspecialty: Ethology. Home: Route 3 Box 354 College Station TX 77840 Office: Tex A&M U Coll Vet Medicine College Station TX 77840

BEAVER, PAUL CHESTER, parasitologist, educator; b. Glenwood, Ind., Mar. 10, 1905; s. John Chester and Blanche Emma (Murphy) B.; m. Lela E. West, Oct. 16, 1931; 1 dau., Paula Jean Beaver Chipman. A.B., Wabash Coll., 1928, D.Sc. (hon.), 1963; M.S., U. Ill., 1929, Ph.D., 1935. Diplomate: Am. Bd. Microbiology. Asst. zoology U. Ill., 1928-29, 31-34; instr. zoology U. Wyo., 1929-31; instr. biology Oak Park Jr. Coll., 1934-37; asst. prof. biology Lawrence Coll., 1937-42; biologist Wis. Dept. Health, summer 1940, Ga. Dept. Pub. Health, 1942-45; asst. prof. parasitology Tulane U. Med. Sch., 1945-47, asso. prof., 1947-52, prof., 1952—, head dept. parasitology, 1956-71, William Vincent prof. tropical diseases and hygiene, 1958-76, prof. emeritus, 1976—; dir. Internat. Center Med. Research and Tng. in Colombia, 1967-76; vis. prof. Eastern Mont. Normal Sch., summers 1935-37, Colo. State Coll., 1941, U. Mich., 1954-56, 58, U. Natal Med. Sch., Durban, South Africa, 1957; hon. vis. prof. Universidad del Valle, Cali, Colombia, 1970-76; cons. Ga. Dept. Pub. Health, 1946-53, USPHS Hosp., New Orleans, 1949-72, WHO, 1960-77; mem. com. standards and exams. Am. Bd. Microbiology, 1960-67; mem. commn. parasitic diseases Armed Forces Epidemiol. Bd., 1953-73, dir. commn. parasitic diseases, 1967-73; mem. Am. Found. Tropical Medicine, 1960-66; microbiology fellowships rev. panel NIH, 1960-63; mem. WHO expert com. on intestinal helminths, 1963, temp. adv., 1960, 61, 65, 66, 80, 81, WHO expert panel on parasitic diseases, 1963-77; bd. sci. counselors Nat. Inst. Allergy and Infectious Diseases, NIH, 1966-68; mem. NIH parasitic diseases panel U.S.-Japan Coop. Med. Sci. Program, 1965-69; mem. adv. sci. bd. Gorgas Meml. Inst. Tropical and Preventive Medicine, 1970—. Co-author: Animal Agents and Vectors of Human Disease, rev. edit, Craig & Faust's Clinical Parasitology, rev. edit.; contbg. author: Mitchell-Nelson's Pediatrics; editorial bd.: Am. Jour. Tropical Medicine and Hygiene, 1958-60, 67-70, editor-in-chief, 1960-66, 72—; asso. editor: Am. Jour. Hygiene, 1961-64, Jour. Parasitology, 1965-76, Am. Jour. Epidemiology, 1966—; editorial bd.: Transactions of Am. Micros. Soc, 1966-73, Ceskoslovenska Parasitologie, 1966-72; contbr. articles to profl. jours. Fellow Am. Acad. Microbiology (bd. govs. 1966-75), AAAS; mem. Internat. Filariasis Assn., Am. Soc. Tropical Medicine and Hygiene (councilor 1956-57, v.p. 1958, pres. 1969), Royal Soc. Tropical Medicine and Hygiene, Am. Soc. Parasitologists (councilor 1952-54, 56-59, pres. 1968), Am. Micros. Soc. (v.p. 1953, exec. com. 1955-59, 61-62), Am. Pub. Health Assn., Société Belge de Medicine Tropicale de Parasitologie et de Mycologie, Société de Pathologie Exotique (France; hon.), Sociedad Mexicana de Parasitologia (hon.), New Orleans Acad. Sci., Brazilian Soc. Tropical Medicine (hon.), Sigma Xi, Delta Omega, Alpha Omega Alpha (hon.). Club: Round Table (New Orleans). Current Work: Research and consultation on parasites causing tropical diseases, especially parasites of animals causing disease in man. Subspecialty: Parasitology. Home: 1416 Cadiz St New Orleans LA 70115 Office: 1430 Tulane Ave New Orleans LA 70112

BECCHETTI, FREDERICK DANIEL, JR., physicist; b. Mpls., Mar. 3, 1943; s. Frederick Daniel and Olga Maxine (Sestini) B. B.S., U. Minn., 1965, M.S., 1968, Ph.D., 1969. Research assoc. Niels Bohr Inst., Copenhagen, 1969-71; research assoc. Lawrence Berkeley Lab., 1971-1973; asst. prof. U. Mich., 1973-76, assoc. prof. physics, 1976-82, prof. physics, 1982—. Contbr. articles to profl. jours. NSF fellow, 1970-71. Mem. Am. Phys. Soc., IEEE, Am. Assn. Physics Tchrs. Democrat. Roman Catholic. Current Work: Nuclear models; nuclear reactions; nuclear radiation detectors; heavy ion research. Subspecialty: Nuclear physics. Office: 1049 Randall Lab Dept Physics U Mich Ann Arbor MI 48109

BECHTEL, DONALD BRUCE, research chemist; b. Paterson, N.J., Aug. 1, 1949; s. Joseph F. and Helene J. (Fiedeldey) B.; m. Kathleen Ann Bechtel, Aug. 7, 1971; children: Michael Shannon, Ryan John. B.S., Iowa State U., 1971, M.S., 1974; Ph.D. in Biology, Kans. State U., 1982. Chemist U.S. Grain Mktg. Research Lab., Manhattan, Kans., 1974-77, research chemist, 1977—. Editor: New Frontiers in Food Microstructure. Contbr. articles to sci. jours. U.S. Dept. Agr. grantee, 1982. Mem. Am. Assn. Cereal Chemistry, Bot. Soc. Am., Sigma Xi. Republican. Lutheran. Club: Optimists (Manhattan). Current Work: Formation and secretion of storage proteins in cereals. Subspecialties: Cell biology; Developmental biology. Home: 2928 Gary Ave Manhattan KS 66502 Office: 1515 College Ave Manhattan KS 66502

BECHTEL, STEPHEN DAVISON, JR., engineering company executive; b. Oakland, Calif., May 10, 1925; s. Stephen Davison and Laura (Peart) B.; m. Elizabeth Mead Hogan, June 5, 1946; 5 children. Student, U. Colo., 1943-44; B.S., Purdue U., 1946; Dr. Engring. (hon.), 1972; M.B.A., Stanford U., 1948. Registered profl. engr. N.Y., Mich., Alaska, Calif., Md., Hawaii, Ohio, D.C., Va. With Bechtel Corp., San Francisco, 1941—, pres., 1960-73; chmn. cos. in Bechtel group, 1973-80; chmn. Bechtel group (Bechtel Group Inc.), 1980—; dir. IBM Co., So. Pacific Co. Mem., vice chmn. Bus. Council; life councillor, past chmn. Conf. Bd.; mem. Presdl. Commn. Urban Housing, 1967-69, Nat. Indsl. Pollution Control Council, 1970-73, Nat. Productivity Commn., 1971-74, Cost of Living Council, 1973-74, Nat. Commn. Indsl. Peace, 1973-74, Labor-Mgmt. Group, 1974—; mem. policy com. Bus. Roundtable; trustee, chmn. bldg. and grounds com. Calif. Inst. Tech.; mem. pres.'s council Purdue U. Served with USMC, 1943-46. Decorated officer French Legion of Honor; recipient disting. alumnus award Purdue U., 1964; Ernest C. Arbuckle disting. alumnus award Stanford U., 1974; Man of Yr. award Engring. News Record, 1974; Outstanding Achievement in Constrn. award Moles, 1977; Disting. Engring. Alumnus award U. Colo., 1979; Washington award Western Soc. Engrs., 1985. Fellow ASCE; mem. Nat. Acad. Engring. (chmn.), Am. Inst. Metall. Engrs., Calif. Acad. Scis. (hon. trustee), Chi Epsilon, Tau Beta Pi. Clubs: Pacific Union (San Francisco); Claremont Country (Oakland, Calif.); Cypress Point (Monterey Peninsula, Calif.); Thunderbird Country (Palm Springs, Calif.); Vancouver (B.C.); Ramada (Houston); Bohemian, San Francisco Golf; Links (N.Y.C.), Blind Brook (N.Y.C.); Augusta (Ga.) Nat. Golf; York (Toronto); Mount Royal (Montreal). Subspecialty: Civil engineering. Office: Bechtel Group Box 3965 San Francisco CA 94119

BECK, LEE RANDOLPH, research and development corporation executive; b. Chgo., Mar. 7, 1942; s. and Beverly (Deitz) Kolner; m. Marjorie Collisson, Aug. 13, 1966; children: John, Jessica. B.A., U. Dubuque, 1965; M.S., N.Mex. Highlands U., 1966; Ph.D., Wash. State U., 1970; postgrad., Ohio State U., 1970-72. Asst. prof. dept. ob-gyn U. Ala.-Birmingham, 1972-78, assoc. prof., 1978-83, prof., 1983-85; cons. Stolle Research and Devel. Corp., Lebanon, Ohio, 1972-85, exec. v.p., 1985—. Contbr. articles on immunology and contraception to profl. jours. USPHS fellow, 1968, 70. Mem. Am. Fertility Soc., Soc. for Study of Reprodn., Soc. for Advancement of Contraception, Controlled Release Soc. Republican. Patentee in field. Current Work: Research in reproduction and immunology and controlled drug-delivery systems. Subspecialties: Immunology (medicine); Immunobiology and immunology. Office: Stolle Research and Devel Corp 2964 State Rt 42S Lebanon OH 45036

BECK, LYLE VIBERT, medical educator and researcher; b. Lebanon, Ind., Apr. 19, 1906; s. Thomas Asberry Beck and Margaret Elizateth (Patterson) Fowler; m. Dorinda Rogers Bakenhus, Mar. 9, 1940. A.B., Wabash Coll., 1928; M.S., Washington U., St. Louis, 1930; Ph.D., U. Pitts., 1933. Teaching asst. in zoology Washington U., 1928-30, NYU, N.Y.C., 1930-31, U. Pitts., 1931-33; postdoctoral fellow NYU, L.I. Coll. Medicine, U.Pa., 1933-38; staff Nat. Cancer Inst., Bethesda, Md., 1947-50; mem. faculty Hahnemann Med. Coll., 1940-47, U. Pitts., 1951-61; mem. faculty Ind. U., Bloomington, 1961-76, chmn. pharmacology, 1961-71, prof. emeritus, 1976—. Author, co-author articles, abstracts in field. Pres. Unitarian-Universalist Ch., Bloomington, 1977; pres. Bloomington Meml. Soc., 1985—; mem. Bloomington Democratic Com. Research grantee NIH, USAF, Eli Lilly Co., Upjohn Co. Mem. AAAS, Am. Chem. Soc., Am. Soc. Zoology, Am. Physiol. Soc., Am. Soc. Pharmacology and Exptl. Therapeutics, Endocrinology Soc., Am. Soc. Cancer Research, Am. Inst. Biol. Scis., Am. Soc. Cancer Research, AAUP, N.Y. Acad. Scis., Phi Beta Kappa, Sigma Xi. Current Work: Diabetes on toxicity of liver damaging organic compounds, liver damaging effects of certain halogenated organic compounds greatly enhanced in diabetic rodents, research to identify mechanisms involved. Subspecialties: Cellular pharmacology; Neuroendocrinology. Home: Apt 8 2455 Tamarack Trail Bloomington IN 47401 Office: Pharmacology Sect Med Scis Program Ind Univ Sch Medicine Bloomington IN 47405

BECK, MARY MCLEAN, physiologist, educator; b. Oak Ridge, Tenn., Sept. 14, 1946; d. Clifford Keith and Mary Elizabeth (Lassetter) Beck; m. Ron Johnson, 1983; 1 child, Lindsay McLean. B.A., Westhampton Coll. U., Richmond, 1968; M.S., U. Md., 1976, Ph.D., 1980. Bilingual sec. Max-Planck-Institut fur Plasmaphysik, Garching, W. Ger, 1972-74; grad. research asst. dept. poultry sci. U. Md., 1975-80; asst. prof. physiology U. Nebr., 1980—. Contbr. to profl. jours. Hubbard Farms scholar, 1978. Mem. Soc. Neurosci., N.Y. Acad. Sci., Nebr. Acad. Sci., Poultry Sci. Assn., Sigma Xi. Democrat. Current Work: Neural degeneration, cerebral energy metabolism avian model for seizure disorders, auditory function. Subspecialties: Neurobiology; Neurophysiology. Office: University of Nebraska 215 Baker Hall Lincoln NE 68583

BECK, NAMA, medical educator; b. Seoul, Korea, Aug. 26, 1933; came to U.S., 1964; s. Rakjoong and Yebun (Park) B.; m. Irene Whayoung, Apr. 23, 1966; children: Edmund C., Alma S. M.S., Seoul U., 1959, M.D., 1963. Diplomate: Am. Bd. Internal Medicine. Asst. prof. medicine U. Pitts., 1970-75; assoc. prof. U. Tex. Health Sci. Ctr., San Antonio, 1975-1981; prof. medicine U. Calif.-Irvine, 1981—. Contbr. articles to profl. jours. Nat. Inst. on Aging grantee, 1980. Fellow ACP; mem. Am. Soc. Nephrology, Am. Physiol. Soc., Am. Soc. Endocrinology. Current Work: Renal metabolism with emphasis on (1) calcium, phosophorus and parathyroid hormone, (2) water metabolism, (3) aging, and (4) renal vasoactive hormones. Subspecialty: Nephrology. Home: 8 Fortuna W Irvine CA 92714 Office: University of California Irvine CA 92717

BECK, PAUL ADAMS, metallurgist, educator; b. Budapest, Hungary, Feb. 5, 1908; came to U.S., 1928, naturalized, 1945; s. Philip O. and Laura (Bardos) B.; children—Paul John, Philip Odon. M.S., Mich. Coll. Mining and Tech., 1929; M.E., Royal Hungarian U. Tech. Scis., 1931; Dr.Min. (hon.), Leoben Inst. Tech., 1979. Metallurgist Am. Smelting & Refining Co., Perth Amboy, N.J., 1937-41; chief metallurgist Beryllium Corp., Reading, Pa., 1941-42; supt. metall. lab. Cleve. Graphite Bronze Co., 1942-45; faculty U. Notre Dame, 1945—, prof. metallurgy, 1949—, head dept. metallurgy, 1950-51; research prof. phys. metallurgy U. Ill., 1951-76. Co-author: The Physics of Powder Metallurgy, 1951, Metal Interfaces, 1952, Recrystallization, Grain Growth and Textures, 1966; Editor: Theory of Alloy Phases, 1956, Electronic Structure and Alloy Chemistry of Transition Elements, 1963; co-editor: Magnetic and Inelastic Scattering of Neutrons by Metals, 1968, Magnetism In Alloys, 1972. Recipient U.S. Scientist award Humboldt Found., 1978, Heyn Meml. award German Metall. Soc., 1980. Fellow Metall. Soc. of AIME (Mathewson Gold Medal award 1952, ann. lectr. 1971, Hume-Rothery award 1974), Am. Soc. Metals (Sauveur Achievement award 1976), Am. Phys. Soc., Hungarian Phys.

Soc. (hon.); mem. Nat. Acad. Engring. Current Work: Magnetism in alloys, effects of short-range atomic order on magnetic properties of alloys. Subspecialty: Metallurgy. Office: Metallurgy Bldg 1304 W Green St U Ill Urbana IL 61801

BECK, THEODORE RICHARD, chemical engineer, consultant and researcher; b. Seattle, Apr. 11, 1926; s. Theodore and Gudmunda Elin (Thorarinsdottir) B.; m. Ruth Elizabeth Schaumberger, Dec. 1, 1951; children: Randi Marie, Maren Louisa. B.S. in Chem. Engring, U. Wash., 1949, M.S., 1950, Ph.D., 1952. Registered profl. engr., Wash. Research engr. duPont Corp., Deepwater, N.J., 1952-54; group leader Kaiser Aluminum & Chem. Corp., Permanente, Calif., 1954-59; sect. head Am. Potash & Chem. Corp., Henderson, Nev., 1959-61; mem. tech. staff Boeing Co., Seattle, 1961-65, sr. basic research scientist, 1965-72; div. mgr. Flow Research, Inc., Kent, Wash., 1972-75; pres. Electrochem. Tech. Corp., Seattle, 1975—; guest lectr. U. Wash., 1963-64, research prof. and affiliate prof., 1972-80; cons. Argonne Nat. Lab., 1973-80. Editor: Corrosion div. Jour. Electrochem. Soc, 1971-75, Tutorial Lectures in Electrochem. Engring. and Tech, 1981. Bd. dirs. N. Cascades Conservation Council, Seattle, 1973-80, Seattle Youth Symphony Orch., 1975-78. Fellow Am. Inst. Chem. Engrs.; mem. AAAA, Am. Chem. Soc., Am. Electroplaters Soc., Electrochem. Soc. (pres. 1975-76, Outstanding Achievement award corrosion div. 1981, hon. mem.), Internat. Soc. Electrochemistry, Metall. Soc. of AIME, Nat. Assn. Corrosion Engrs., Sigma Xi, Tau Beta Pi, Phi Lambda Upsilon. Club: Seattle Mountaineers. Patentee, publs. in electrochem. engring. and corrosion fields. Current Work: Developer electrochem. processes and devices and solution of problems in applied electrochemistry. Research in electrochem. kinetics, elec. double layer, transport properties, current distbn. to support devel. activities. Subspecialties: Chemical engineering; Corrosion. Home: 10035 31st Ave N E Seattle WA 98125 Office: Electrochem Tech Corp 1601 Dexter Ave N Seattle WA 98109

BECK, WARREN RANDALL, materials scientist, inventor; b. Bethlehem, Pa., Feb. 14, 1918; s. Stewart Elbert and Lottie Marion (Horne) B.; m. Lois Kathryn Jones, Sept. 1, 1939 (div. 1964); children—Dianne Evelyn, Delzer, Kathryn Lynn Thostenson, Vicki Allison Martin, Constance Rae Beck; m. Carol Jean Anderson, Mar. 14, 1970. B.S. in Ceramics, Pa. State U., 1943; M.S. in Geology and Minerals, U. Minn., 1948. Research assoc. Pa. State U., Univ. Park, 1942-43; ceramist 3M Co., St. Paul, 1943-52, sect. mgr., 1952-65, lab. research mgr., 1965-74, corp. scientist, 1974—. Patentee in field (28). Contbr. articles to profl. jours. Founder Minn. sect. Am. Ceramics Soc., St. Paul, 1958 (fellow). Recipient 1-R 100 award Indsl. Research Publication, 1984. Mem. Carlton Soc., N.Y. Acad. Sci., Soc. of Glass Tech. (emeritus), Sigma Xi. Current work: Development of unique glass compositions and rapidly quenched ceramic materials and products therefrom. Subspecialties: Composite materials; Glass technology. Home: 1567 Atlantic Saint Paul MN 55106 Office: 3M Co 3M Center Saint Paul MN 55144

BECK, WILLIAM SAMSON, physician, educator, biochemist; b. Reading, Pa., Nov. 7, 1923; s. Myron Paul and Gertrude (Harris) B.; m. Helene Samuels, Oct. 24, 1947; children: Thomas Russell, Peter Dean; m. Hanne Troedsson, July 20, 1964; children: John Christopher, Paul Brooks. B.S. (Chem.), U. Mich., 1943, M.D., 1946; A.M. (hon.), Harvard U., 1971. Diplomate: Am. Bd. Internal Medicine, 1954. Instr., asst. prof. medicine UCLA, 1950-55; fellow in biochemistry NYU Coll. Medicine, 1955-57; mem. faculty dept. medicine Harvard U., 1957—, prof., 1979—, tutor in biochem. scis., 1957, prof., admission chmn. M.I.T. Div. Health Sci. and Tech., 1971—; dir. clin. labs. Mass. Gen. Hosp., 1957-75, chief hematology unit, 1957-72, dir. hematology research lab., 1957—; mem. adv. council Nat. Inst. Arthritis, Metabolism and Digestive Diseases, NIH, 1971-74; mem. hematology study sect. NIH, 1967-71. Author: Modern Science and the Nature of Life, 1957, Human Design, 1971, Hematology, 4th edit., 1985, (with G.G. Simpson), Life: An Introduction to Biology, 3d edit., 1986; contbr. articles to profl. jours. Served with AUS, 1943-46. Mem. Am. Soc. Biol. Chemists, Am. Soc. Hematology (exec. com. 1979-84), Assn. Am. Physicians, Am. Soc. Clin. Investigation, Am. Assn. Cancer Research. Current Work: Biochemistry of DNA synthesis, vitamin B12 and folic acid. Subspecialties: Hematology; Biochemistry (biology). Home: 85 Arlington St Winchester MA 01890 Office: Mass Gen Hosp Boston MA 02114

BECKER, DONALD ARTHUR, nuclear analytical chemist; b. Detroit, Feb. 14, 1938; s. Millard William Herman and Esther Laura (Pohl) B.; m. Linda Carole Knorr, Aug. 19, 1960; children—Steven Scott, Tracy Lynn. B.S. in Chemistry, Valparaiso U., 1959; M.S. in Phys. Chemistry, Fla. State U., 1961. Research chemist Nat. Bur. Standards, Washington, 1961-73, chief sect. analytical chemistry, 1973-75, asst. chief div., 1975-76, asst. to dir. Nat. Measurement Lab., 1976, mgr. program recycled oil, 1976-82, spl. asst. to dir. analytical chemistry, 1982—; chmn. various workshops on energy and environ., 1975-76; chmn. various confs., 1976-82, Contbr. articles to profl. jours. Pres., bd. dirs. Lutheran Ch., Silver Spring, Md., 1963-73; chmn. com. Seneca council Boy Scouts Am., 1980-83. Recipient Silver Medal award U.S. Dept. Commerce, 1982. Mem. Am. Chem. Soc., Am. Nuclear Soc., Soc. Environ. Geochemistry and Health, ASTM (chmn. task force nuclear methods of chem. analysis 1984—). Current work: Nuclear analytical chemistry; neutron activation analysis; nuclear reactor characterization; accuracy and precision in chemical analysis; quality assurance in analytical chemistry. Subspecialties: Analytical chemistry; Nuclear chemistry. Home: 13115 Dauphine St Silver Spring MD 20906 Office: Ctr Analytical Chemistry Nat Bur Standards Gaithersburg MD 20899

BECKER, DONALD AUGUST, ecologist, educator, planner, consultant; b. Valley City, N.D., July 27, 1938; s. August F. and Ella M. (Amundson) B.; m. Elaine R. Sandberg, Aug., 20, 1960; children: Michelle, Pamela, Donald. B.S., Valley City State Coll., 1960; M.S. in Biology, U. N.D., 1966, Ph.D. in Ecology, 1968. Assoc. prof. biology Midland Luth. Coll., Fremont, Nebr., 1968-75; environ. specialist Mo. River Basin Commn., Omaha, 1975-81; flood plan studies mgr. Mo. Basin State Assn., Omaha, 1982-83; environ. resource specialist U.S.C.E., Omaha, 1983—; cons. govtl. agys., plant ecology. Author: Mo. River Flood Studies, 1981, 82. U.S. Water Resources Council grantee, 1980-1982; Nat. Park Service grantee, 1982-1984. Mem. Nebr. Acad. Sci., Signa Xi. Current Work: Flood plain management, river ecology, land use and cover data bases, grassland ecology, plant autecology, water and related land resources planning and mangement. Subspecialties: Ecology (environmental science); Resource conservation. Office: US Army Corp Engrs Omaha NE 68102

BECKER, ERNEST I., chemistry educator, consultant, researcher; b. Cleveland, Aug. 18, 1918; s. Harry and Esther (Cohen) B.; m. Marion Ferris, Dec. 20, 1947; children: Jonathan David, Kenneth Alan, Mark Edward, Robert Neal, Paula Sarah. B.S. in Pharmacy, Western Res. U., 1941, M.S. in Chemistry, 1943, Ph.D., 1946. Instr. Poly. Inst. of Bklyn., 1946, asst. prof., 1947-51, assoc. prof., 1951-56, prof., 1956-65; prof., chemistry U. Mass., Boston, 1965—, chmn. dept., 1965-72, chmn. div. natural scis., 1965-70; cons. in field. Author 6 books on organometallic syntheses and reactions, 1 book first aid manual for chem. accidents; contbr. numerous articles on chemistry to profl. jours; book reviewer. U.S. Army grantee, 1949-53; NIH grantee, 1950-53; U.S. Army Research Office grantee, 1959-67; Fisher Sci. Co. grantee, 1981-83. Fellow N.Y. Acad. Scis., Chem. Soc. of London; mem. Am. Chem. Soc., AAAS, Am. Inst. Chemists (cert.), Nat. Sci. Tchrs. Assn., New Eng. Assn. Chemistry Tchrs. Current Work: Alkylation of heterocycles polymer synstheses, flurorescent monomers and polymers. Subspecialties: Organic chemistry; Synthetic chemistry. Home: 32 Oxford Rd Newton MA 02159 Office: Dept Chemistry U Mass Boston MA 02125

BECKER, E(RNEST) LOVELL, medical educator, consultant; b. Cin., Jan. 13, 1923; s. Ernest Louis and Sarah (Lovell) B.; children—James T., Margaret W., Frank L.; m. Eleanor Holden. A.B., Washington and Lee U., 1944; D.Sc. (hon.), 1980; M.D., U. Cin., 1948; grad. Oak Ridge Inst. Nuclear Studies, 1952. Diplomate Am. Bd. Internal Medicine. Intern, Christ Hosp., Cin., 1948-49; jr. asst. resident in medicine Med. Coll. Va. Hosp., Richmond, 1949-50, sr. asst. resident in medicine, 1950-51; mem. 3rd med. div., cardiac clinic Bellevue Hosp., N.Y.C., 1951-53, jr. attending physician 4th med. div., 1952-53, asst. attending physician 2d med. div., 1957-68; attending physician Med. Coll. Va. Hosp., 1955-57; asst. attending physician N.Y. Hosp., N.Y.C., 1957-65, assoc. attending physician, 1965-69, attending physician, 1969-78; cons. in medicine U.S. Naval Hosp., St. Albans, N.Y., 1960-73; cons. pro tem dept. medicine Meml. Hosp., N.Y.C., 1963-64, clin. asst. (wards and teaching) dept. medicine, 1964—; asst. vis. physician James Ewing Hosp., N.Y.C., 1964-73; dir. medicine Beth Israel Med. Ctr., N.Y.C., 1980—; asst. in dept. pharmacology Coll. Medicine, U. Cin., 1946-47; asst. in dept. medicine Med. Coll. Va., 1950-51, asst. prof. medicine, 1955-57; instr. dept. physiology Coll. Medicine, NYU, 1951-53; vis. investigator Oak Ridge Inst. Nuclear Studies, 1952; investigator Mount Desert Island Biol. Lab., Salisbury Cove, Maine, summers 1951, 52, 55; dir. Eugene F. DuBois Pavilion Clin. Research Ctr., N.Y. Hosp.-Cornell Med. Ctr., 1960-73; assoc. prof. medicine Med. Coll., Cornell U., 1962-69, prof., 1969-78, adj. prof., 1978—; dir. div. nephrology and hypertension, dept. medicine N.Y. Hosp.-Cornell Med. Ctr., 1967-73, dir. office continuing edn. and regional activities, 1978-78; dir. dept. grad. med. evaluation AMA, Chgo., 1978-80; prof. medicine Mount Sinai Sch. Medicine, CCNY, 1980—; spl. assignment Andean Inst. Biology, Lima and Morococha, Peru, 1954; cons. U.S. Army Icefield Ranges Research Project of Arctic Inst. North Am. and Am. Geog. Soc.; mem. exec. com. III Internat. Congress Nephrology, Washington, 1966; sec.-gen. Internat. Com. for Nomenclature and Rosology of Renal Disease; mem. research adv. com. Health Research Council of N.Y.C., mem. metabolic study sect., 1965-78; cons./lectr. U.S. Navy St. Albans Naval Hosp. and Naval Med. Research Unit No. 3, Cairo, Arab Republic of Egypt; chmn. ad-hoc com. for Establishing Criteria for Chronic Renal Disease Ctr., 1972; mem. sci. adv. com. artificial kidney - chronic uremia program Nat. Inst. Arthritis and Metabolic Disease, 1971-78; dir. continuing edn. Med. Coll., Cornell U., 1972-78; mem. steering com., chmn. kidney adv. com. Listing Program for Specialized Clin. Services, Joint Commn. on Accreditation of Hosps., 1972-77; mem. exec. com. Congress Internal Medicine, 1971; chmn. adv. com. Soc. Security Adminstrn. for Renal Provisions of HR-1, 1972-73; chmn. research adv. com. and human rights com. N.Y. Hosp.-Cornell Med. Ctr., 1960-78; chmn. med. adv. bd. Life Extension Inst., N.Y.C., 1973-78; chmn. high altitude physiology subcom. Arctic Inst. North Am., 1973—; com. on nomenclature and classification of renal disease WHO, 1975—; sec. Liaison Com. on Grad. Med. Edn., 1978-80, sec. adv. com., 1978-80; cons. to Sec. U.S. Air Force, 1983. Editorial cons. Am. Jour. Medicine, 1971—, Clin. Nephrology, 1971—; mem. editorial adv. bd. Current Contents, 1972—; chmn. editorial bd. Internat. Dictionary of Biology and Medicine, (in press); contbr. articles and abstracts to profl. jours. Creator photographic essay Cosmos Club, Washington, 1973-74, Century Assn., 1974. Mem. med. adv. bd. Nat. Kidney Found., N.Y., pres., 1970-73. Served to capt. USAF, 1953-55, col. USAFR. Recipient Lederle Med. Faculty award 1960-63; scholar med. scis. John and Mary R. Markle Found., 1955-60; fellow John E. Fogarty Internat. Ctr. for Advanced Study in Health Scis., WHO, 1974, 78. Fellow AAAS, ACP (sci. program com. 1966-72, postgrad. edn. com. 1972-78, com. for self-assessment exam. kidney sect. 1972, course dir. self-assessment exam IV 1977), N.Y. Acad. Scis., Royal Soc. Medicine, Royal Soc. Tropical Medicine and Hygiene; mem. Am. Clin. and Climatological Assn., AMA (cons. current med. info. and terminology 1980—), Am. Physiol. Soc., Am. Soc. Nephrology (fin. chmn. 1966—), Med. Strollers (pres. 1969), N.Y. Acad. Medicine (membership com.) N.Y. Clin. Soc. (sec. 1974, pres. 1975), N.Y. County Med. Soc., N.Y. Med. and Surg. Soc., Soc. Exptl. Biology and Medicine, So. Soc. Clin. Research, Harvey Soc. (N.Y. chpt.), Chgo. Inst. Medicine, Chgo. Med. Soc., Chgo. Soc. Internal Medicine, Council Fgn. Relations (N.Y. chpt.), Soc. Med. Cons. to Armed Forces, Explorers Club (pres. N.Y. chpt. 1975-76), Sons of Revolution, Am. Geographic Soc. (council), Am. Heart Assn. (exec. com. renal sect. council on circulation 1965-67, mem. adv. bd. immunology and microbiology research study com. 1970-72), N.Y. Heart Assn. (research adv. com. 1964-69, bd. dirs. 1965-70), Sigma Xi. Episcopalian. Clubs: Am. Alpine; Athenaeum (London); Bandar Log Group (Chgo.); Cosmos (Washington); Century Assn., River, Union (N.Y.C.), Meadow (Southampton, N.Y.); Himalayan Mountain, Madison Sq. Garden. Current work: Nephrology, medical administration. Subspecialties: Internal medicine; Nephrology. Home and Office: Box 422 Water Mill NY 11976

BECKER, MICHAEL MCCLELLAN, biology educator; b. Tampa, Fla., May 23, 1951; s. Jane (McClellan) B. B.S., U. South Fla., 1973; Ph.D., Calif. Inst. Tech., 1981. NSF research fellow U. South Fla., Tampa, 1971, research asst., 1973-75; NIH predoctoral trainee Calif. Inst. Tech., Pasadena, 1976-80; Anna Fuller postdoctoral fellow Harvard U., Cambridge, 1981-83; asst. prof. dept. biology U. Pitts., 1983—. Dreyfus Found. travelling scholar, 1977; recipient Herbert Newby McCoy award Calif. Inst. Tech., 1978. Mem. Am. Phys. Soc., Sigma Xi. Current work: Determination of the structure of genes. Subspecialty: Molecular biology. Office: Dept Biol Scis U Pitts 5th and Ruskin Sts Pittsburgh PA 15260

BECKER, PAUL ROBIN, ceramic engineering executive, researcher; b. Renton, Wash., June 17, 1950; s. Carl Peter and Barbara Ann (Robinson) B.; m. Judith Ann Ongna, July 28, 1973. B.S. in Ceramic Engring., U. Wash., 1972. Flight officer Braniff Airways, Dallas, 1978-80; ceramic research engr. Vought Corp., Dallas, 1980-82; v.p. engring., research engr. Carbon Carbon Advanced Tech., Carrollton, Tex., 1982—. Author article. Served to lt. USN, 1972-78. Mem. Am. Ceramic Soc. Republican. Mem. Reformed Ch. Am. Current work: Development and manufacturing of coated carbon carbon for high temperature structural application. Subspecialties: High-temperature materials; Ceramics. Home: 7208 Tumbleweed Ct Colleyville TX 76034 Office: Carbon Carbon Advanced Tech 1604 Vantage Dr Carrollton TX 75006

BECKER, ROBERT OTTO, orthopaedic surgeon, educator; b. River Edge, N.Y., May 31, 1923; s. Otto and Elizabeth (Blank) B.; m. Lillian Moller, Sept. 6, 1946; children: Lisa, Michael, Adam. B.A., Gettysburg Coll., 1946; M.D., NYU, 1948. Diplomate: Am. Bd. Orthopaedic Surgery. Intern Bellevue Hosp., N.Y.C., 1948-49; resident in orthopaedic surgery Downstate Med. Ctr., SUNY, Bklyn., 1953-56; mem. faculty SUNY Upstate Med. Ctr., Syracuse, 1956—; now prof. orthopaedic surgery; clin. prof. orthopaedic surgery La. State U. Coll. Medicine, Shreveport, 1980—. Author: Mechanisms of Growth Control, 1981, Electromagnetism and Life, 1982; The Body Electric, 1985; contbr. articles to profl. publs. Served to 1st lt. U.S. Army, 1951-53. Recipient Middleton award VA, 1960, Disting. Alumnus award NYU Coll. Medicine, 1966, Nicolas Andry award Am. Assn. Bone Joint Surgery, 1979; SUNY Faculty Exchange scholar, 1979. Mem. N.Y. Acad. Scis., AAAS. Republican. Club: Angler's (N.Y.). Current Work: Electrical control systems in living organisms; bio effects electrical currents; electrical fields; magnetic fields. Subspecialties: Biomedical engineering; Cell and tissue culture. Home and Office: Star Route Lowville NY 13367

BECKER, STEPHEN ALLAN, astronomer, astrophysicist; b. Evanston, Ill., Sept. 11, 1950; s. John Nicholas and Irene Ann (Wlodarski) B.; m. Wendee M. Brunish, May 30, 1980. B.A., Northwestern U., 1972; M.S., Case Western Res. U., 1974; Ph.D., U. Ill., 1979. Research and teaching assoc. astronomy dept. U. Ill., Urbana, 1979-80; research fellow in physics W.K. Kellogg Radiation Lab., Calif. Inst. Tech., Pasadena, 1980-82; staff mem. Los Alamos (N.Mex.) Nat. Lab., 1983—. Contbr. papers to profl. publs. and confs. Mem. Am. Astron. Soc., Planetary Soc. Roman Catholic. Current Work: Stellar evolution, star clusters, supernovae, abundance anomalies in meteorites, variable stars, nuclear reactions. Subspecialties: Theoretical astrophysics; Nuclear physics. Office: Los Alamos Nat Lab P O Box 1663 MSB220 Los Alamos NM 87545

BECKERS, JACQUES MAURICE, astronomer; b. Arnhem, Netherlands, Feb. 14, 1934; s. Wilhelmus Bartholomeus and Maria Hubertina (Hermans) B.; m. Gerda Maria van Vuurden, Apr. 7, 1959; children: Christina M., Michael P. Doctorandus Astronomy, U. Utrecht, Netherlands, 1959, Dr. Astronomy, 1964. Commonwealth Sci. and Indsl. Research Orgn. fellow, Sydney, Australia, 1959-62; astrophysicist Sacramento Peak Obs., 1962-79; dir. multiple mirror telescope obs. U. Ariz., Tucson, 1979-84; dir. Advanced Devel. Program, Nat. Optical Astronomy Observatories, Tucson, 1984—. Contbr. articles to profl. jours. Recipient Henryk Arctowski award Nat. Acad. Scis., 1975. Mem. Am. Astron. Soc., Internat. Astron. Union, Optical Soc. Am. Current Work: Solar physics, stellar atmospheres, speckle interferometry, astronomical instrumentation. Subspecialties: Optical astronomy; Solar physics. Home: 4871 E Avenida del Cazador Tucson AZ 85718 Office: ADP Nat Optical Astronomy Observatories Tucson AZ 85726

BECKJORD, ERIC STEPHEN, educator, energy researcher; b. Evanston, Ill., Feb. 17, 1929; s. Walter Clarence and Mary Amelia (Hitchcox) B.; m. Caroline Wendell Gardner, Feb. 28, 1953; children: Eric. H., Amy W., Charles A., Sarah H. A.B. cum laude, Harvard U., 1947; M.S in E.E, M.I.T., 1956. Devel. engr. Gen. Electric Co., San Jose, Calif., 1956-60, project engr., Pleasanton, Calif., 1960-63; engring. mgr. Westinghouse Electric Corp., Pitts., 1963-70; v.p. Westinghouse Nuclear Europe, Brussels, 1970-73; project dir., mgr. strategic planning-nuclear Westinghouse Electric Corp., Pitts., 1973-75; dep. dir. Office Nuclear Affairs, Fed. Energy Adminstrn., 1975; dir. div. reactor devel. and demonstration ERDA, 1976-77; dir. div. nuclear power devel. U.S. Dept. Energy, 1977-78; coordinator U.S. Dept. Energy (Internat. Nuclear Fuel Cycle Evaluation), 1978-80; dep. dir. Argonne Nat. Lab., Ill., 1980-84; vis. prof. dept. nuclear engring. MIT, 1984—; mem. reactor safety criteria Am. Standards Inst., 1965-68; mem. AEC Water Reactor Core Cooling Task Force, 1966-67. Author: Advances in Nuclear Science, 1962; contbr. articles to profl. jours. Bd. dirs. St. Edmund's Acad., Pitts., 1967-69; bd. dirs. Shady Lane Sch., 1968-70; vestryman Calvary Episcopal Ch., 1970, 75. Served to lt. (j.g.) USNR, 1951-54. Fellow Am. Nuclear Soc. (v.p., pres.-elect Belgian sect. 1972); mem. IEEE, Sigma Xi. Republican. Current Work: Teaching graduate courses in probabilistic risk assessment, thermodynamics, fluid flow, and heat transfer; research in light water reactor safety and reliability, and design improvement. Subspecialties: Nuclear fission; Electrical engineering. Home: 146 Lexington Ave Cambridge MA 02138 Office: MIT Room 24-212 Cambridge MA 02139

BECKWITH, JONATHAN ROGER, See *Who's Who in America*, 43rd edition.

BEDAIR, SALAH MOHAMED, engineering educator; b. Alexandria, Egypt, Dec. 10, 1938; came to U.S., 1963; s. Mohamed Bedair and Fawzia Katter; m. Nadia El Masry; children—Harry, Sarah. B.Sc., Alexandria U. (Egypt), 1960; M.Sc., U. Calif.-Berkeley, 1965, Ph.D., 1969. Asst. prof. Alexandria U., 1970-73, assoc. prof., 1974-77; asst. prof. Carnegie-Mellon U., Pitts., 1973-74; research engr. Research Triangle Inst., Research Triangle Park, N.C., 1977-81; head dept. nuclear engring. Alexandria U., 1981-82; prof. engring. N.C. State U., Raleigh, 1982—; cons. AT&T, Roanoke, 1984, NASA, 1983. Contbr. articles to profl. publs. Mem. IEEE, Am. Phys. Soc., Am. Soc. Metals. Current work: Semiconductor material and devices. Subspecialties: Semiconductors; Sensory processes. Office: Elec Engring Dept NC State U Raleigh NC 27695

BEDELL, GEORGE NOBLE, medical educator; b. Harrisburg, Pa., May 1, 1922; s. George Harold and Elsie Clair (Noble) B.; m. Betty Jane Goldzier, Nov. 4, 1950 (dec. 1970); children—David, Mark, Barbara, Bruce; m. Mirriel Shields Hummel, Oct. 17, 1970; stepchildren—Judith, Jeffrey, Eric, Deborah, Andrew. B.A., DePauw U., 1944; M.D., U. Cin., 1946. From asst. prof. to prof. internal medicine U. Iowa, Iowa City, 1954—. Contbr. articles to profl. jours. Del. Democratic Nat. Conv., Chgo., 1968; treas. Johnson County Dem. Central Com., Iowa City, 1958-64. Served to capt. U.S. Army, 1948-50. Recipient Career Devel. award NIH, Iowa City, 1962-72. Mem. Am. Lung Assn. (nat. bd. dirs. 1971-80, bd. dirs. Iowa 1973-81), AMA (del. 1979—), Am. Soc. Clin. Investigation, Central Soc. Clin. Research. Unitarian. Current work: Clinical pulmonary physiology; clinical pulmonary disease. Subspecialties: Pulmonary medicine; Internal medicine. Home: 327 Blackhawk St Iowa City IA 52240 Office: Univ Hosps Iowa City IA 52250

BEDELL, RALPH CLAIRON, psychologist, emeritus educator; b. Hale, Mo., June 4, 1904; s. Charles Edward and Jennie (Eaton) B.; m. Stella Virginia Bales, Aug. 19, 1929 (dec. 1968); m. Ann Sorency, Dec. 21, 1968 (dec. 1975); m. Mtra Jervey Hoyle, Feb. 14, 1976; 1 son, Brian Hoyle. B.S. in Edn, Central Mo. State U., 1926; M.A., U. Mo.-Columbia, 1929, Ph.D., 1932. Diplomate: Am. Bd. Profl. Psychology; cert. tchr. Mo. Prof. psychology, dir. guidance N.E. Mo. State U., Kirksville, 1933-37; dean faculty and student personnel Central Mo. State U., Warrensburg, 1937-38; prof. ednl. psychology, counselor edn. U. Nebr., Lincoln, 1938-50; prof., chmn. dept. psychology and edn. American U., Washington, 1950-52; sec.-gen. S. Pacific Commn., Noumea, New Caledonia, 1955-58; dir. counseling and guidance insts. U.S. Office Edn., Washington, 1958-67; prof. edn. U. Mo.-Columbia, 1967-74, prof. emeritus, 1974—; cons. and advisor in edn. Co-author: General Science for Today, 1932, rev. edit., 1936, (with Ralph K. Watkins, with Frank E. Sorenson and Harold E. Wise) Element of Pre-Flight Aeronautics, 1942; dir., editor (with Ralph K. Watkins, with Frank E. Sorenson and Harold E. Wise) textbooks for naval aviation cadets in WWII, 1942-45. Served to comdr. USNR, 1941-45. Recipient Alumnus award Central Mo. State U., 1971; award Mo. Guidance Assn., 1971; award Mo. Coll. Personnel Assn., 1982; Disting. Sr. Psychologist award Div. Counseling Psychology, Am. Psychol. Assn., 1985. Fellow Am. Psychol. Assn., Royal Soc. Health, Explorers Club (Flag award 1980); mem. Am. Personnel and Guidance Assn. (life), Mil. Order of the World Wars, U. Mo. Alumni Assn. (outstanding service to edn. award 1979), Assn. Counselor Edn. and Supervision (outstanding contribution to counselor edn. award 1967), Phi Delta Kappa, Sigma Tau Gamma (Soc. of The Seventeen, Disting. Achievement award 1985). Democrat. Unitarian. Clubs: Columbia (Mo.) Country; Army and Navy (Washington). Current Work: Cognition in counseling for career change; cross cultural problems in teacher education between the United States and Thailand. Subspecialties: Behavioral psychology; Counseling psychology. Home: 106 S Ann St Columbia MO 65201 Office: Coll Edn U Mo-Columbia 301 Hill Hall Columbia MO 65211

BEDFORD, ANTHONY, aerospace engineering educator; b. Baton Rouge, Oct. 7, 1938; s. Ernest Marcek and Thelma (Harris) B.; m. Nancy Louise Rosenblad, June 24, 1961; children—Susan Gail, Linda Elizabeth. B.S. in Aerospace Engring., U. Tex., 1961; M.S. in Aeros., Calif. Inst. Tech., 1962; Ph.D., Rice U., 1967. Registered profl. engr., Tex. Engr., Douglas Co., Santa Monica, Calif., 1962-64; staff mem. TRW Systems, Houston, 1966-68; prof. U. Tex., Austin, 1968—; cons. in field. Contbr. articles to profl. jours. Calif. Inst. Tech. scholar, 1961-62; NASA fellow, 1964-66; grantee NSF, 1969-75, Office of Naval Research, 1981-85. Mem. Soc. Engring. Sci., Am. Acad. Mechanics, Soc. Natural Philosophy, ASME. Current work: Acoustics of ocean sediments, constitutive theories for mixtures, wave propagation in mixtures. Subspecialties: Aeronautical engineering; Theoretical and applied mechanics. Home: 3510 Highland View Dr Austin TX 78731 Office: Univ Tex Austin TX 78712

BEDINGER, JOSEPH ARNOLD, nuclear plant design consultant; b. Portales, N.Mex., July 1, 1916; s. Henry Clay and Betty (Miller) B.; m. Ruth V. Jones, June 6, 1969; 1 dau., Sandra Lynn Bedinger Chase. Student, Eastern N.Mex. Jr. Coll., 1935-38, Valley Coll., 1950-51, UCLA, 1951-55. Nuclear design cons. N.Am. Aviation, Canoga Park, Calif., 1950-55, Westinghouse Corp., Richland, Wash., 1977-79, Wash. Pub. Power Supply System, Richland, 1979-80, Gulf States Utility, St. Francisville, La., 1980-82. Mem. ASME, Am. Soc. Metals, Am. Welding Soc., Am. Nuclear Soc., Soc. Automotive Engrs. Mem. Christian Ch. Current Work: Use of a computer system, with graphics, to check the nuclear plant design for interference. Subspecialties: Theoretical computer science; Computer-aided design. Home: 909 S Juniper Escondido CA 92025

BEDROSIAN, SAMUEL DER, electrical and systems engineer, educator; b. Marash, Turkey, Mar. 24, 1921; came to U.S., 1922, naturalized, 1942; s. Sahag Der and Zabel B.; m. Agnes Morjigian, Nov. 24, 1951; children—Camille, Gregory. A.B., SUNY, Albany, 1942; M.E.E., Poly. Inst. Bklyn., 1951; Ph.D., U. Pa., 1961. Project engr. Signal Corps Engring. Labs., Ft. Monmouth, N.J., 1946-49, sect. chief, 1949-54, asst. br. chief, 1954-55; systems engr. Burroughs Research Center, Paoli, Pa., 1955-60; mem. research staff U. Pa., 1960-64, asst. prof. elec. engring., 1964-68, asso. prof., 1968-73, prof. elec. and systems engring., 1973—, chmn. dept. systems engring., 1975-80; dir. dual degree MBA/MSE program for (Wharton Sch. and Sch. Engring.), 1977-82; cons. in field; organizer, gen. chmn. 22d M.W. Symposium on Circuits and Systems at Moore Sch., Phila., 1979; NAVELE Research chair prof. Naval Postgrad. Sch., Monterey, Calif., 1980-81. Contbr. numerous articles to profl. jours. Served to 1st lt., Signal Corps U.S. Army, 1943-46, PTO. Recipient Kabakjian award Armenian Students Assn. U.S.A., 1977. Fellow IEEE (guest editor Transactions on Circuits and Systems 1979); mem. Franklin Inst. (asso. editor jour. 1966—, guest editor spl. issue jour. 1973, 76), Sigma Xi, Eta Kappa Nu. Patentee in field. Current Work: Application of fuzzy, set theory to image clarification quality criteria and information content; design of computer communication network; application of graph theory to VLSI chip layout. Subspecialties: Graphics, image processing, and pattern recognition; Distributed systems and networks. Home: 35 Bryan Ave Malvern PA 19355 Office: Moore Sch U Pa 200 S 33d St Philadelphia PA 19104

BEEDLE, LYNN SIMPSON, civil engineering educator; b. Orland, Calif., Dec. 7, 1917; s. Granville L. and Carol (Simpson) B.; m. Ella Marie Grimes, Oct. 20, 1946; children: Lynn, Helen, Jonathan, David, Edward. B.S., U. Calif., 1941; M.S., Lehigh U., 1949, Ph.D., 1952. With Todd-Calif. Shipbldg. Corp., Richmond, Calif., 1941; instr. Postgrad. Sch., U.S. Naval Acad.; officer-in-charge Underwater Explosions Research div. Norfolk (Va.) Naval Shipyard, 1941-47; dir. Lehigh U. Fritz Engring. Lab., Bethlehem, Pa., 1960-84; prof. civil engring. Lehigh U., 1958-77, Univ. Disting. prof., 1978—, dir. High-Rise Inst., 1983—. Author: Plastic Design of Steel Frames, 1958, (with others) Structural Steel Design, 2d edit, 1974; editor-in-chief: (with others) Planning and Design of Tall Buildings, 6 vols., 1978-81; contbr. (with others) articles to profl. jours. Served with USNR, 1941-47. Recipient Robinson award Lehigh U., 1952, Hillman award, 1973; E.E. Howard award ASCE, 1963; Research prize, 1956; Silver medal Am. Welding Soc., 1957; Constrn. award Engring. News Record, 1965, 73; Regional Tech. Meeting award Am. Iron and Steel Inst., 1958; T.R. Higgins award Am. Inst. Steel Constrn., 1973; Engr. of Year award Lehigh Valley sect. Nat. Soc. Profl. Engrs., 1977. Fellow ASCE (hon. mem.; dir. 1974-77, dir. Lehigh Valley sect. 1977—, past chmn. structural div. exec. com., past mem. research com.); mem. Structural Stability Research Council (life mem., chmn. 1966-70, dir. 1970—), Welding Research Council, Am. Inst. Steel Constrn., Nat. Acad. Engring., Council on Tall Bldgs. and Urban Habitat (chmn. 1970-76, dir. 1976—), Internat. Assn. Bridge and Structural Engring. (hon.). Presbyn. (elder 1957—). Current Work: Urban design, plastic design, residual stresses, high-strength bolts, welded plate girders,tall buildings. Subspecialty: Civil engineering. Home: 102 Cedar Rd Hellertown PA 18055 Office: Fritz Engring Lab Lehigh Univ Bethlehem PA 18015

BEERY, KENNETH EUGENE, food scientist; b. Lancaster, Ohio, Apr. 30, 1943; s. Robert David and Lucille Ester (Scholl) B.; m. Marci Annear, Aug. 22, 1965; children: Kevin, Kendra, Kelli, Kyle. B.S., Ohio State U., 1965; Ph.D., Pa. State U., 1970. With U.S. Dept. Agr., Berkeley, Calif., 1972-75, Union Carbide Corp., Chgo., 1975-76; dir. research Archer Daniels Midland Co., Decatur, Ill., 1976-84; dir. lipid and protein research Central Soya Co., Fort Wayne, Ind. Editorial adv. bd.: Food Tech. mag, 1975-78; contbr. articles to profl. jours. Served with U.S. Army, 1970-72, lt. col. Res. Recipient Honored Grad. Student award Am. Oil Chemists Soc., 1969. Mem. Inst. Food Technologists (chmn. Iowa sect. 1978-79), AAAS, Am. Meat Sci. Assn., Am. Soc. Animal Sci., Am. Mamt. Assn., Am. Assn. Cereal Chemists, Research Soc. Am., Sigma Xi, Alpha Gamma Sigma, Gamma Sigma Delta, Alpha Zeta, Phi Tau Sigma. Current Work: Process development and anlaysis, corn, soy, wheat and grain. Subspecialties: Food science and technology; Biomass (agriculture). Office: Central Soya Co PO Box 1400 Fort Wayne IN 46801

BEETON, ALFRED MERLE, limnologist, educator; b. Denver, Aug. 15, 1927; s. Charles Frederick and Edna F. (Smith) B.; m. Mary Eileen Wilcox, July 20, 1945; children—Maureen Ann, Heather Ann, Celeste Nadine; m. Ruth Elizabeth Holland, June 4, 1966; children—Jonathan Eugene, Daniel Paul. B.S., U. Mich., 1952, M.S., 1954, Ph.D., 1958. Fishery biologist U.S. Bur. Comml. Fisheries, Ann Arbor, Mich., 1957-65, chief environ. research, 1960-65; prof. zoology U. Wis.-Milw., 1965-76; asst. dir. U. Wis.-Milw. (Center for Gt. Lakes Studies), 1965-69, assoc. dir., 1969-73; assoc. dean U. Wis.-Milw. (Grad. Sch.), 1973-76; dir. Gt. Lakes and Marine Waters Center; prof. U. Mich., Ann Arbor, 1976—; lectr. biology Wayne State U., 1957-61; lectr. civil engring. U. Mich., 1961-65; mem. research adv. council Wis. Dept. Natural Resources; mem. water quality criteria com. Nat. Acad. Scis.; cons. U.S. Army C.E., 1967-73, Met. San. Dist. Chgo., 1968-76, EPA, 1973-83; adviser to Smithsonian Instn. on projects in, Ghana, Laos, Yugoslavia, 1972-82; to WHO/Pan Am. Health Orgn. in, Venezuela, 1978; mem. environ. studies bd. NRC, 1976-82, internat. environ. program com., 1977-82. Contbr. chpts. to books; articles Ency. Brit. Mem. Internat. Assn. Theoretical and Applied Limnology, Am. Soc. Limnology and Oceanography (treas. 1962-81), Am. Soc. Zoologists, Internat. Assn. Gt. Lakes Research, Sigma Xi. Current Work: Eutrophication of the Great Lakes. Limnology of tropical man-made lakes. Subspecialties: Ecology (environmental science); Limnology. Home: 2761 Oakcleft St Ann Arbor MI 48103 Office: U Mich Ann Arbor MI 48109

BEETZ, CHARLES PERSHING, JR., physicist; b. Cin., June 11, 1947; s. Charles Pershing and Bertha Ema (Yentsch) B.; m. Virginia Lou Fogle, Dec. 21, 1968; children—Jason Andrew, Kara Emily. B.S., Morehead State U., 1970; M.S., Purdue U., 1974, Ph.D., 1978. Research assoc. Purdue U., West Lafayette, Ind., 1978-79; sr. research scient Gen. Motors Research Labs., Warren, Mich., 1979-82, asst. head physics dept., 1984—; group leader Am. Cyanamid Co., Stamford, Conn., 1982-84; topical area chmn. 17th Biennial Carbon Conf., Am. Carbon Soc., 1985. Contbr. articles to profl. jours. Mem. Am. Phys. Soc., Am. Carbon Soc., Materials Research Soc., Soc. Advancement Materials and Process Engring., Sigma Xi. Current work: Composite materials including vapor phase growth of carbon fibers, automotive composite applications, metal and ceramic matrix composite materials. Subspecialties: Condensed matter physics; Biophysics (physics). Office: General Motors Research Lab Physics Dept Warren MI 48090

BEGGS, JAMES MONTGOMERY, government official; b. Pitts., Jan. 9, 1926; s. James Andrew and Elizabeth (Mikulan) B.; m. Mary Elizabeth Harrison, Oct. 3, 1953; children—Maureen Elizabeth, Kathleen Louise, Teresa Lynn, James Harrison, Charles Montgomery. Student, So. Meth. U., 1942-44; B.S. in Engring, U.S. Naval Acad., 1948; M.B.A., Harvard U., 1955; LL.D. (hon.), Washington and Jefferson Coll., 1972; Dr. Engr. Mgmt., Embry-Riddle U., 1972; LL.D. (hon.), Salem Coll.; D.Engring., U. Ala.; LL.D., Maryville Coll. Commd. ensign U.S. Navy, 1947, advanced through grades to lt. comdr., 1954, resigned, 1954; various mgmt. positions Westinghouse Electric Corp., 1955-68, v.p. Def. and Space Center, 1968; asso. adminstr. advanced research and tech. NASA, 1968-69; undersec. Dept. Transp., 1969-73; mng. dir. Summa Corp., Los Angeles, 1973-74; exec. v.p., dir. Gen. Dynamics Corp., St. Louis, 1974-81; adminstr. NASA, Washington, 1981—; dir. ConRail, Phila., EMC, Inc., Cockeysville, Md. Vice chmn. bd. Howard County (Md.) Charter Bd., 1966-67; mem. Md. Bd. Natural Resources, 1966-67. Mem. Nat. Acad. Pub. Adminstrn., Am. Soc. Pub. Adminstrn., AIAA, Am. Soc. Naval Engrs. Clubs: Burning Tree (Bethesda Md.); Met. (Washington); Chevy Chase (Md.); St. Louis (St. Louis), Bellerive Country (St. Louis). Subspecialties: Mechanical engineering; Aerospace engineering and technology. Office: NASA 400 Maryland Ave SW Washington DC 20546

BEHBEHANI, ABBAS M., clin. virologist, educator; b. Iran, July 27, 1925; came to U.S., 1946, naturalized, 1964s; s. Ahmad M. and Roguia B (Tasougi) B.; married; children: Ray, Allen, Bita. B.A., Ind. U., 1949; M.S., U. Chgo., 1951; Ph.D., Southwestern Med. Sch., U. Tex., 1955. Asst. prof. Baylor U. Coll. Medicine, Houston, 1960-64; assoc. prof. pathology U. Kans. Sch. Medicine, Kansas City, 1967-72, prof., 1972—. Author two books, numerous articles. Fellow Am. Acad. Microbiology; mem. AAAS, Am. Soc. Microbiology, Soc. Exptl. Biology and Medicine. Moslem. Current Work: Use of tissue culture system in the study of human disease. Subspecialties: Virology (medicine); Tissue culture. Home: 5415 Hazen St Kansas City KS 66106 Office: Dept Pathology and Oncology U Kans Med Center Kansas City KS 66103

BEHNKE, WALTER ERIC, chemist, researcher; b. Fulton, N.Y., June 1, 1923; s. Otto Emil and Christine Maria (Wurster) B.; m. Mary Veronica Eagle, Jan. 29, 1954 (dec. Nov. 1983); 1 child, Kurt Richard. B.S., Stetson U., 1948; Ph.D., U. Pitts., 1954. Adhesives chemist Swift & Co., Chgo., 1953-55; devel. chemist Parke, Davis & Co., Detroit, 1955-76; group mgr., research assoc. Warner, Lambert Co., Holland, Mich., 1976—. Patentee in field. Vice pres. St. Clair Shores Symphony Orch., also bd. dirs. Served as lt. (j.g.) USN, 1943-46, PTO. Recipient commendation St. Clair Shores Symphony Orch. Bd. Dirs., 1980. Mem. Am. Chem. Soc., AAAS, Sigma Xi. Republican. Lutheran. Current work: Direct process research and scale-up operations in developing suitable chemical procedures for producing new drug substances for preclinical and clinical studies. Subspecialties: Organic chemistry; Synthetic chemistry. Home: 770 Pleasant Ridge Holland MI 49423 Office: Parke-Davis/Warner-Lambert 188 Howard Ave Holland MI 49423

BEHRENDS, RALPH EUGENE, physicist, educator; b. Chgo., May 20, 1926; s. Oluf and Marie-Therese (Ichtertz) B.; m. Ana Luisa Duran, June 29, 1954 (div. June 1961); 1 child, Jon Carlo; m. Marlene Imelda Bowman, Oct. 7, 1961 (div. Oct. 1974); 1 child, Kendra Ralene. B.S., U.S. Naval Acad., 1947; Ph.D., UCLA, 1956. Instr., UCLA, 1956-57; asst. physicist Brookhaven Nat. Lab. Upton, N.Y., 1957-59; NSF fellow Inst. for Advanced Study, Princeton, N.J., 1959-60; research assoc. U. Pa., Phila., 1960-61; asst. prof. to prof. physics Belfer Grad. Sch. Sci., Yeshiva U., N.Y.C., 61-78, prof. physics Yeshiva U., 1978—, chmn. dept., 1982—. Contbg. author: Group Theory and Applications, 1968. Contbr. articles to physics jours. Served to ensign USN, 1947-50, PTO. NSF fellow, 1959-60, grantee, 1962-70. Mem. Am. Phys. Soc., N.Y. Acad. Scis. Democrat. Current work: Elementary particle theory; phenomenology and symmetries of particle properties and reactions arising from weak, electromagnetic, and strong interactions. Subspecialties: Particle physics; Theoretical physics. Home: 330 E 70 St New York NY 10021 Office: Dept Physics Yeshiva U 2495 Amsterdam Ave New York NY 10033

BEHRMAN, RICHARD ELLIOT, pediatrician, neonatologist, university dean; b. Phila., Dec. 13, 1931; s. Robert and Vivian (Keegan) B.; m. Ann Nelson, Aug. 14, 1954; children: Amy Jane, Michael Jameson, Carolyn Ann, Hillary. A.B., Amherst Coll., 1953; J.D., Harvard U., 1956; M.D. (Univ. scholar), U. Rochester, 1960. Intern Johns Hopkins Hosp., Balt., 1960-61, resident in pediatrics, 1963-65; asst. prof. pediatrics U. Oreg. Sch. Medicine, Portland, 1965-67, assoc. prof., 1967-68; prof. U. Ill. Coll. Medicine, Chgo., 1968-71; prof., chmn. dept. Columbia U. Coll. Physicians and Surgeons, N.Y.C., 1971-76; prof., chmn. dept. Case Western Res. U. Sch. Medicine, Cleve., 1976-81, dean Sch. Medicine, 1980—; dir. dept. pediatrics Rainbow Babies and Children's Hosp., Cleve., 1976-81; chmn. bd. maternal, child and family research Nat. Acad. Sci., NRC, 1977-80; examiner Am. Bd. Pediatrics. Author: Neonatology: Diseases of the Fetus and Infant, 1973, Neonatal-Perinatal Medicine, 1977; editor: Nelson's Textbook of Pediatrics, 1978, 83; mem.: editorial bd., sect. editor fetal and neonatal medicine Jour. Pediatrics, 1970-85; asso. editor: editorial bd., sect. editor fetal and neonatal medicine Pediatric Research, 1971-80. Served with USPHS, 1961-63. Whipple scholar, 1960-61; Wyeth pediatric fellow, 1963-65. Fellow Am. Acad. Pediatrics; mem. Soc. Pediatric Research (v.p. 1976-77), Inst. Medicine of Nat. Acad. Scis., Am. Pediatric Soc., Perinatal Research Soc. (council 1970-73), Pediatric Travel Club, Soc. Gynecol. Investigation, Sigma Xi. Presbyterian. Club: Century Assn. Current Work: Neonatal intensive care; fetal physiology; health and education administration. Subspecialties: Pediatrics; Neonatology. Home: Route 2 Box 139 River Rd Gates Mills OH 44040 Office: 2101 Adelbert Rd Cleveland OH 44106

BEIER, EUGENE WILLIAM, physicist, educator; b. Harvey, Ill., Jan. 30, 1940; s. Carl Lee and Mable Lois (Sage) B.; m. Virginia Rose Hance, Sept. 8, 1974; 1 child, Jonathan. B.S., Stanford U., 1961; M.S., U. Ill., 1963, Ph.D., 1966. Research assoc. U. Ill., Urbana, 1966-67; asst. prof. U. Pa., Phila., 1967-73, assoc. prof., 1973-79, prof. physics, 1979—, prin. investigator high energy physics group, 1982—. Contbr. articles to profl. jours. Mem. Am. Phys. Soc., AAUP, Sigma Xi. Current work: Research and teaching in physics; instrumentation; data analysis. Subspecialty: Particle physics. Office: U Pa Dept Physics Philadelphia PA 19104

BEIER, ROSS CARLTON, research chemist; b. Portage, Wis., Dec. 27, 1946; s. Carl August and Jean Marie (Buzzell) B.; m. Janet Mary Bauknecht, July 27, 1974; children—Joshua Carlton, Samuel Robert. B.S. in Chemistry and Math., U. Wis.-Stevens Point, 1969; Ph.D. in Organic Chemistry, Mont. State U., 1980. Research chemist Nat. Cotton Path. Research Lab., College Station. Tex., 1979-80, Vet. Toxicology and Entomology Research Lab., College Station, 1980—; vis. mem. grad. faculty Tex. A & M U., College Station, 1982—. Contbr. articles to profl. jours. Served with U.S. Army, 1969-72. Recipient Rudy Johansson award Mont. State U., 1975. Mem. Am. Chem. Soc., N.Y. Acad. Sci., Am. Soc. Mass Spectroscopy. Republican. Current work: Chemistry and structural determination of natural products, pesticides, and their metabolites in living systems; quantitative aspects of these components as related to their toxicology. Subspecialties: Organic chemistry; Toxicology (agriculture). Office: Vet Toxicology and Entomology Lab F & B Rd PO Drawer GE College Station TX 77841

BEIGEL, MICHAEL LEE, electronic and musical product company executive; b. N.Y.C., Jan. 29, 1947; s. Jerome and Freda (Marks) B. B.E.E., MIT, 1969; B.S. in Humanities, 1970. Pres. Identic Data Inc., Cambridge, Mass., 1970-71; cons. Guild Musical Instruments, Hoboken, N.J., 1971-72; v.p. engring. Musitronics Corp., Rosemont, N.J., 1972-78, also dir.; pres. Beigel Sound Lab., Warwick, N.Y., 1981—; pres. Beigel Cons. Services, Warwick, 1978-84, EPD Tech. Corp., Elmsford, N.Y., 1984—, also dir. Contbr. articles to profl. jours. Patentee in field (7). Speaker, Midwest Acoustics Conf., Chgo., 1981. Mem. Audio Engring. Soc. (session chmn. electronic music 1982), IEEE, Acoustical Soc. of Am. Current work: Product research, development and design in industrial measurement and control, consumer products, musical products, ultrasonic products. Subspecialties: Electronics; Ultrasound. Home: 34 Echo Lane Warwick NY 10990 Office: EPD Tech Corp 12 W Main St Elmsford NY 10523

BEIRNE, OWEN ROSS, oral and maxillofacial surgeon, educator, researcher; b. Santa Maria, Calif., Jan. 18, 1947; s. Owen and Thelma (Ross) B.; m. Sheryl Martha Schochet, Aug. 23, 1970; 1 son, Samuel Lewis Schochet. B.A., U. Calif.-Berkeley, 1968; D.M.D., Harvard U., 1972; Ph.D., U. Calif.-San Francisco, 1976. Cert. oral and maxillofacial surgery; diplomate Am. Bd. Oral and Maxillofacial Surgery. Resident oral and maxillofacial surgery Harbor-UCLA Med. Ctr., Torrance, Calif., 1976-79; asst. prof. Sch. Dentistry, U. Calif.-San Francisco, 1979-85, attending staff U. Calif.-Moffitt Hosp., San Francisco, 1979-85, Mt. Zion Med. Ctr., San Francisco, 1981-85; assoc. prof. U. Wash., 1985—; cons. San Francisco Gen. Hosp., 1980-85, Calif. Children's Service, 1980-85, assoc. prof. U. Wash., 1985—, dir. oral and maxillofacial residencies program, 1985—. Contbr. articles to profl. publs. U. Calif. Cancer Coordinating Com. grantee; recipient Silver award Harvard Sch. Dental Medicine, 1972. Fellow Am. Soc. Dental Anesthesiology; Mem. AAAS, Am. and Internat. Assn. Dental Research, ADA, Am. Assn. Dental Schs., Calif. Honor Soc., Phi Beta Kappa, Omicron Kappa Upsilon. Current Work: Chemical carcinogenesis and oral cancer, preprosthetic surgery, bone grafting, teaching graduate oral and maxillofacial surgery; orthognathic surgery. Subspecialties: Oral and maxillofacial surgery; Cancer research (medicine). Home: 15618 Main St Bellevue WA 98008 Office: U Wash Dept Oral and Mixillofacial Surgery SB-24 Seattle WA 98195

BEISER, LEO, consulting physicist, researcher, author; b. N.Y.C., Sept. 18, 1924; s. Sigmund N. and Sarah (Weiner) B.; m. Edith Vegotsky, Aug. 31, 1946; children: Helene Ronnie, Steven Scott. B.S. in Physics, Hofstra U., 1964, M.A. in Physics, 1966; elec. engring. honor grad., R.C.A. Insts., 1948; postgrad. in bus. adminstrn, Alexander Hamilton Ins., 1958. Asst. chief engr. CBS, N.Y.C., 1951-56; project mgr. Polarad Electronics Corp., N.Y.C., 1956-60; staff cons. Gen. Instrument Corp., L.I., N.Y., 1960-61; research mgr. Telechrome Corp., 1961-62; staff research specialist Autometric-Raytheon Corp., 1962-63; sr. staff physicist, dir. Dennis Gabor Labs., CBS Labs., Stamford, Conn., 1963-76; pres., research dir. Leo Beiser Inc., Flushing, N.Y., 1976—; seminar leader; editorial advisor. Author: Advanced Electronic and Electro-Optical Publishing and Printing, 1977; contbr.: Laser Scanning Systems chpt. to Laser Applications, Vol. 2, 1974. Served with USAAF, 1943-46, CBI. Recipient IR-100 award for Holofacet optical scanner, 1973 (now in Smithsonian Instn.). Fellow Soc. Info. Display (recognition award 1978), Soc. Photo-Optical Instrumentation Engrs.; mem. Optical Soc. Am., Soc. Motion Picture and TV Engrs. Numerous patents and inventions in laser scanning, notably light scanning system utilizing diffraction optics. Current Work: Advanced laser scanning; holographic scanning; data storage and retrieval; optical information handling; three dimensional imaging; holography; imaging technologies. Subspecialties: Information systems, storage, and retrieval (computer science); Laser data storage and reproduction. Home and Office: 151-77 28th Ave Flushing NY 11354

BEITZ, ALVIN JAMES, neurobiologist, researcher, educator; b. Meadville, Pa., Feb. 16, 1949; s. Albert O. and Margaret (Balint) B.; m. Diane W. Beitz, Sept. 4, 1971; children: Jennifer, Scott, Stacey, Mark, Julie. B.S., Gannon Coll, 1971; Ph.D., U. Minn., 1976. Postdoctoral fellow Harvard U. Med. Sch., Boston, 1976-78; asst. prof. anatomy U. S.C., Columbia, 1978-82, asso. prof., 1982; asst. prof. Sch. Vet. Medicine, U. Minn., St. Paul, 1982-84, assoc. prof., 1984—. Contbr. articles to sci. jours. Recipient Bacaner research award Minn. Med. Found., 1978. Mem. Am. Assn. Anatomists, Soc. for Neurosci. Roman Catholic. Current Work: Research into the anatomy, biochemistry and pharmacology of pain pathways and the central nervous system pain suppression system. Subspecialties: Neurobiology; Anatomy and embryology. Home: 3517 Vivian Ave Roseville MN 55126 Office: Dept Vet Biology U Minn 1988 Fitch Ave Saint Paul MN 55108

BEKEY, IVAN, electrical engineer, government official; b. Czechoslovakia, Nov. 21, 1931; came to U.S. 1945, naturalized, 1953; s. Andrew and Elizabeth (Magyar) B.; m. Marlene Ann Woodbury, May 30, 1968; children—Lisa Ann, Suzi J. B.S. in Elec. Engring., UCLA, 1954, M.S. in Elec. Engring., 1957. With automatic controls dept. Douglas Aircraft Co., Los Angeles, 1954-57; chief electronic countermeasures-radar RCA, Los Angeles, 1957-60; mgr., dir communications-surveillance for def. systems Aerospace Corp., Los Angeles, 1960-72, dir. mission analyses, 1972-78; chief advanced concepts NASA Hdqrs., Washington, 1978-81, dir. advanced programs, 1981—. Patentee in fields of audio and dentistry. Recipient Pub. Service Achievement medal NASA, 1976, Exceptional Service medal NASA, 1983. Fellow AIAA, Washington Acad. Scis.; mem. Internat. Inst. Astronautics. Current work: Space systems, space transportation, new-innovative techniques, manual space flight, evolution, space tethers, flight demonstration programs. Subspecialty: Aerospace engineering and technology. Office: NASA Hdqrs Fed Office Bldg 10B Room B421 600 Independence Ave SW Washington DC 20546

BEKOFF, ANNE C., neurobiology educator; b. Denver, May 19, 1947; d. James Gilbert and Jean (Herres) Cox; m. Marc Bekoff, June 28, 1970. B.A., Smith Coll., 1969; Ph.D., Washington U., St. Louis, 1974. Research assoc. U. Colo. Med. Ctr., Denver, 1975-76; asst. prof. biology U. Colo., Boulder, 1976-82, assoc. prof., 1982—. Grantee NSF, 1976-83, NIH, 1983-86; research fellow Alfred P. Sloan Found., 1979-81, John Simon Guggenheim Meml. Found., 1983-84. Mem. Soc. for Neurosci., Soc. Devel. Biology, Animal Behavior Soc., AAAS. Current work: Development of motor control mechanisms, analysis of neural circuitry underlying coordinated behaviors, embryonic motility. Subspecialties: Neurophysiology; Neurobiology. Office: EPO Biology Dept Univ Colo B-334 Boulder CO 08309

BEL BRUNO, JOSEPH J(AMES), chem. physicist; b. Passaic, N.J., June 30, 1952; s. Joseph and Carmella (Nicastro) Bel B.; m. Kathleen Cassidy, Aug. 10, 1980. B.S. in Chemistry, Seton Hall U., 1974; Ph.D. in Chemistry, Rutgers U., 1980. Research chemist Am. Cyanamid, Bound Brook, N.J., 1974-76; research assoc. Princeton U., 1980-82; asst. prof. chemistry Dartmouth Coll., 1982—. Contbr. articles to profl. jours. Mem. Am. Phys. Soc., Am. Chem. Soc., Sigma Xi. Roman Catholic. Current Work: Laser-assisted chem. processes; spectroscopic and dynamical studies of van der Waals complexes; molecular energy transfer; laser spectroscopy; laser photochemistry. Subspecialties: Laser-induced chemistry; Atomic and molecular physics. Home: Scott Ave West Lebanon NH 03784 Office: Dept Chemistry Dartmouth Coll Hanover NH 03755

BELDING, HIRAM HURLBURT, IV, psychologist; b. Chgo., Nov. 26, 1942; s. Hiram Hurlburt and Nancee Curry (Reitheimer) B.; m. Margaret Irving, June 25, 1966; children: Wendy Kathleen, Lindsay Cameron. A.A., Riverside City Coll., 1966; B.A. in Psychology, San Jose State U., 1968; M.A. in Human Behavior, U.S. Internat. U., 1971, Ph.D. in Human Behavior, 1975. Lic. psychologist, S.C., Calif. Electronics technician U.S. Air Force, Denver and Las Vegas, 1960-64; dep. probation officer Riverside County Probation Dept., 1968-70; psychologist USN Med. Ctrs. (Bethesda), Md., 1974-79, USN Med. Ctrs. (Charleston), S.C., 1974-79, USN Med. Ctrs. (San Diego), 1974-79; clin. psychologist Psychol. Services of San Diego, 1978—; cons. FBI, 1979—. Served to lt. USNR, 1974-79. Mem. Am. Psychol. Assn., Calif. Psychol. Assn., Acad. Psychologists, San Diego Nat. Register Health Care Providers in Psychology, Assn. Advancement Psychology. Republican. Current Work: Individual and family psychotherapy, hypnosis for early life information and painccontrol. Subspecialty: Behavioral psychology. Home: 3664 Curtis St San Diego CA 92106 Office: Psychological Services of San Diego 3560 4th Ave San Diego CA 92103

BELIAN, RICHARD DUANE, physicist; b. Santa Fe, N.Mex., Feb. 23, 1938; s. Charles Paul and Era May (Johnson) B.; m. Mary Reyes, Mar. 3, 1962; children: Richard, Raymon, Anthony. M.S., U. N.Mex., 1967. Staff mem. Los Alamos (N.Mex.) Nat. Lab., 1967—. Contbr. articles to profl. publs. Pres. De Vargas Civitan Club, 1972-63, dist. lt. gov., 1980-81. Served with USAR, 1959-65. Mem. Am. Astron. Soc., Am. Geophys. Union. Democrat. Lodge: Elks. Current Work: Magnetospheric dynamics and substorms, magnetospheric ion composition particle energization; X-ray bursters and transients. Subspecialty: X-ray high energy astrophysics. Home: 2005 Zozobra Ln Santa Fe NM 87501 Office: Los Alamos Nat Lab Los Alamos NM 87545

BELJAN, JOHN RICHARD, medical scientist, medical educator; b. Detroit, May 26, 1930; s. Joseph and Margaret Anne (Brozovich) B.; m. Bernadette Marie Marenda, Feb. 2, 1952; children: Ann Marie, John Richard, Paul Eric. B.S., U. Mich., 1951, M.D., 1954. Diplomate: Am. Bd. Surgery. Intern U. Mich., 1954-55, resident in gen. surgery, 1955-59; dir. med. services Stuart div. Atlas Chem. Industries, Pasadena, Calif., 1965-66; from asst. prof. to assoc. prof. surgery U. Calif. Med. Sch., Davis, 1966-74, from asst. prof. to assoc. prof. engring., 1968-74, from asst. dean to assoc. dean, 1971-74; prof. surgery, prof. biol. engring. Wright State U., Dayton, Ohio, 1974-83, dean Sch. Medicine, 1974-81, vice provost Sch. Medicine, 1974-78, v.p. health affairs Sch. Medicine, 1978-81, provost, sr. v.p., 1981-83; provost, v.p. acad. affairs, dean Sch. Medicine Hahnemann U., Phila., 1983-85, spl. advisor to pres., 1985—, prof. surgery, biomed. engring., 1983—; prof. arts and scis., assoc. v.p. med. affairs Central State U., Wilberforce, Ohio, 1976—; trustee Cox Heart Inst., 1975-77, University City Sci. Ctr., Phila., 1983—, Drew Health Center, 1977-78, Wright State U. Found., 1975-83; trustee, regional v.p. Engring. and Sci. Inst. Hall of Fame, 1983—; mem. adv. bd. Space Tech. Ctr., Phila., 1985—; bd. dirs. Miami Valley Health Systems Agy., 1975-82; cons. in field. Author articles, revs., chpts. in books. Served with M.C. USAF, 1955-65. Decorated Commendation medal; Braun fellow, 1949; grantee USPHS, 1967—; NASA, 1968—. Fellow A.C.S., Royal Soc. Medicine; mem. Aerospace Med. Assn., AAUP, Inst. Aeros. and Astronautics, AMA (council on sci. affairs 1978—), Assn. Acad. Surgery, Biomed. Engring. Soc., F.A. Coller, surg. socs., Flying Physicians Assn., Pa. Med. Soc., Med. Soc. N.J., Phila. Acad. Surgery, Phila. Coll. Physicians, Burlington County Med. Soc., IEEE, Instrument Soc. Am., Royal Soc. Medicine, Soc. Internat. de Chirurgie, Phi Beta Kappa, Alpha Omega Alpha, Phi Eta Sigma, Phi Kappa Phi, Alpha Kappa Kappa. Clubs: Mich. Alumni (Dayton) (Outstanding Alumnus award 1976), Vesper (Phila.); University of Washington, Oakwood Fur, Fin and Feather. Current Work: Engineering and physical principles in biological systems and man; characterization and modelling of biological rhythms and bone repair; human performance and measurement. Subspecialties: Space medicine; Chronobiology. Home: 159 Haines Dr Moorestown NJ 08057 Office: Hahnemann Univ Broad and Vine Sts Philadelphia PA 19102

BELL, BARBARA JEAN, human factors specialist, human reliability analyst; b. Houston, Aug. 28, 1954; d. John Leon and Louise (Sturdivant) B. B.A. in Modern Langs, Tex. A&M U., 1976, M.S. in Indsl. Engring, 1979. Mem. tech staff Sandia Nat. Labs., Albuquerque, 1979-82; prin. research scientist Battelle Columbus (Ohio) Labs., 1983—; course instr. U. Wis.-Madison, 1981-82, JBF Assocs., Knoxville, Tenn., 1982-83, Det Norske Veritas, Oslo, 1982. Author: (with A.D. Swain) A Procedure for Conducting Human Reliability Analysis for Nuclear Power Plants, 1981, 2d edit., 1983. Tchr., leader Del Norte Baptist Ch., Albuquerque, 1979-82. Mem. Human Factors Soc., Am. Nuclear Soc. (exec. council TGHF 1982-85). Republican. Current Work: Human reliability analysis as part of probabilistic risk assessment, usually for nuclear power generating stations. Subspecialties: Human factors engineering; Nuclear fission. Office: Risk Assessment Group Battelle Columbus Labs 505 King Ave Columbus OH 43201

BELL, C. THOMAS, laboratory administrator, researcher; b. Batavia, N.Y., Oct. 25, 1950; s. Charles Hobart and Helen Iola (Mohart) B.; m. Susan Dunn, June 17, 1972; 1 child, Cham Brooke. B.Sc., Ohio State U., 1972, M.Sc., 1974, Ph.D., 1979. Intern Ohio State U., Columbus, 1977-78, instr., 1978-79, asst. prof., 1979; cons. CTL Engring., Columbus, 1979-81; toxicologist Ohio Dept. Agr., Columbus, 1981; lab. dir. Research and Devel. Lab., Columbus, 1981—. Advisor Coop. Extension Service Adv. Com., Columbus, 1984. Mem. Assn. Ofcl. Analytical Chemists. Current work: Investigation of physiological functions of hosts due to changing microbial and nutritional factors. Subspecialties: Animal physiology; Microbiology (veterinary medicine). Home: 874 Singing Hills Ln Worthington OH 43085 Office: Research and Devel Lab 2331 Sullivan Ave Columbus OH 43204

BELL, CHAROLETTE RENEE, school psychologist; b. St. Louis, Jan. 23, 1949; d. Jesse Leon and Victoria Larue (Hancock) B.; married; children: J. Leon III, David Anthony. B.A., Dillard U., 1970; M.A., U. No. Colo., 1973, Ed.D., 1976. Cert. sch. psychologist. G.E.D. instr. Collbran (Colo.) Civilian Job Corps Ctr., 1970-72; sch. psychologist Aurora (Colo.) Schs., 1973-76, Cherry Creek Schs., Englewood, Colo., 1976-78; researcher S.C. State Coll., Orangeburg, 1978—; cons. psychologist S.C. Dept. Social Services, Columbia, 1980—, S.C. Dept. Mental Retardation, Columbia, 1981—; ednl. psychologist Nat. Assessment of Ednl. Progress, Denver, 1978. Contbg. author: Discipline and Classroom Management, 1980. Chmn. Community Adv. Bd. for Retarded, Orangeburg, 1980—; v.p. Orangeburg Mental Health Assn., 1982—; founder, chmn. Citizens Against Sexual Assault, 1979-80. Fellow Am. Psychol. Assn.; mem. Evaluation Network, Am. Assn. Sex. Educators, Counselors and

Therapists, Assn. Black Psychologists (co-chmn. nat. testing com. 1981), Adlerian Soc. (v.p. 1982—), Alpha Kappa Alpha. Democrat. Episcopalian. Club: Altrusa. Current Work: Achievement on standardized tests by limited resource students. Subspecialty: Testing and evaluation. Home: PO Box 99 Orangeburg SC 29116 Office: SC State Coll Box 1841 Orangeburg SC 29117

BELL, CHESTER GORDON, computer engineering company executive; b. Kirksville, Mo., Aug. 19, 1934; s. Roy Chester and Lola Dolph (Gordon) B.; m. Gwendolyn Kay Druyor, Jan. 3, 1959; children: Brigham Roy, Laura Louise. B.S. in E.E, M.I.T., 1956, M.S. in E.E, 1957. Engr. Speech Communication Lab., M.I.T., 1959-60; mgr. computer design Digital Equipment Corp., Maynard, Mass., 1960-66, v.p. engring., 1972-83; chief tech. officer Encore Computer Corp., Wellesley Hills, Mass., from 1984, now vice chmn. tech.; prof. computer sci. Carnegie-Mellon U., 1966-72; dir. Inst. Research and Coordination Acoustic Music, 1976-81, Computer Mus., 1982—. Author: (with Newell) Computer Structures, 1971, (with Grason, Newell) Designing Computers and Digital Systems, 1972, (with Mudge, McNamara) Computer Engineering, 1978, (with Siewiorek, Newell) Computer Structures, 1982. Recipient 6th Mellon Inst. award, 1972. Fellow IEEE (McDowell award 1975), (Eckert-Mauchly award 1982), AAAS; mem. Nat. Acad. Engring., Assn. Computing Machinery (editor Computer Structures sect. 1972-78), Eta Kappa Nu. Current Work: computer science, computer art, electrical engineering, computer engineering. Subspecialties: Computer architecture; Computer engineering. Office: Encore Computer Corp Wellesley Hills MA 02181

BELL, GRANT RICHARD, engineering consultant; b. Janesville, Wis., Apr. 13, 1943; s. Frank Eugene and Bernadine Marie (Rankins) B.; m. Suzanne Elaine Gast, Sept. 4, 1965; children—Grant Richard II, Martha Suzanne, Geoffrey Roger. B.S.M.E., U. Wis., 1966; M.B.A. in Fin. and Real Estate, U. Tex.-Arlington, 1985. Registered profl. engr., Wis., Iowa, Tex.; registered one and two family dwelling insp. So. Bldg. Code Congress Internat. Indsl. engr. PPG Industries, Barberton, Ohio, 1966-72; chief engr. Wick Bldg. Systems, Madison, Wis., 1972-75, prodn. mgr., Marshfield, Wis., 1975-77, div. mfg. mgr., Arlington, Tex., 1979-79; cons. G.R. Bell and Assocs., Inc., Arlington, 1979—; mem. constrn. research adv. council Constrn. Research Ctr., U. Tex.-Arlington, Author homeowner's manual and profl. inspection report for systematic bldg. inspection program, 1983; engr. Tex. size mobile home, 1978; producer 1st sunken living room mobile home, 1976; modifier standard Binning frame for mobile homes; developer various additional prodn. machinery. Mem. ASME, Nat. Soc. Profl. Engrs., Tex. Soc. Profl. Engrs., ASHRAE, Internat. Conf. Bldg. Ofcls., Am. Concrete Inst., Tex. Assn. Real Estate Inspectors (cert.). Democrat. Methodist. Current work: Concrete shells, earth shelters, solar applications, theory Z, and participation management, motivation, sufficiency, manufacturing methods and machinery. Subspecialty: Construction inspection, testing-failure analysis, mgmt. orgn. (organizational behavior). Home: 5500 Summit Ridge Trail Arlington TX 76017 Office: G R Bell and Assocs Inc 5609 W Polywebb Rd Arlington TX 76017

BELL, MARVIN CARL, animal nutritionist, researcher, educator; b. Centertown, Ky., Dec. 24, 1921; s. Marvin Cyril and Ida (Coffman) B.; m. Betty Triplett, Aug. 22, 1948; children: Celia Bell Ferguson, Rachel Bell Burley. B.S. in Agr., U. Ky., 1947, M.S. in Agr., 1948; Ph.D. in Animal Nutrition, Okla. State U., 1951. Assoc. prof. research and teaching animal husbandry-vet. sci. U. Tenn., Knoxville, 1951-57; assoc. prof. U. Tenn.-AEC-Agrl. Research Lab., Oak Ridge, 1957-65, prof., 1965-74; prof. animal sci. U. Tenn., Knoxville, 1974—; cons. Oak Ridge Nat. Lab., 1965-67. Contbr. chpts., numerous articles to profl. publs. Served to maj. USAFR, 1942-46, ETO. Recipient Calcium Carbonate Co.-Nat. Feed Ingredient Assn. Travel Fellowship award, 1969; named. Disting. Alumnus U. Ky. Coll. Agr., 1984; travel grantee Internat. Congress Nutrition, Hamburg, Germany, 1966; travel grantee Internat. Congress Nutrition, Mexico City, 1973; travel grantee Internat. Congress radiation Research, Evion, France, 1970. Fellow AAAS, Am. Soc. Animal Sci.; mem. Am. Inst. Nutrition, Animal Nutrition Research Council, Council Agr. Sci. and Tech., Radiation Research Soc., Sigma Xi, Gamma Sigma Delta (Research award of Merit 1970). Methodist. Current Work: Mineral nutrition and toxicology in livestock; fallout radiation effects on livestock and protection practices. Subspecialties: Animal nutrition; Toxicology (agriculture).

BELL, NORMAN HOWARD, physician, endocrinologist, educator; b. Gainesville, Ga., Feb. 11, 1931; s. Kenneth Rush and Henrietta Maria (Howard Rankin) B.; m. Claude Handy, June 27, 1959 (dec. 1967); children—Douglas Howard, Julianne Rankin; m. Mary Virginia Baughman, Aug. 24, 1968 (div. July 1972); m. Ledlie Laird Dinsmore, Dec. 19, 1972; 1 son, Bayard Gardiner. A.B., Emory U., 1951; M.D., Duke U., 1955. Intern Duke U. Med Ctr., Durham, N.C., 1955-56, resident, 1956-57; clin. assoc. Nat. Inst. Allergy and Infectious Diseases, NIH, Bethesda, Md., 1957-59; mem. staff clin. endocrinology br. Nat. Heart, Lung and Blood Inst., NIH, Bethesda, 1959-63; asst. prof. medicine Northwestern U. Sch. Medicine, Chgo., 1963-68; assoc. prof. Ind. U. Med. Sch., 1968-71, prof., 1971-79; prof. medicine and pharmacology Med. U. S.C., Charleston, 1979—; mem. gen. medicine B study sect. NIH, Bethesda, 1982-86, chmn., 1985-86; bd. dirs. Osteoporosis Found., 1984—. Editorial bd.; Calcified Tissue Internat., 1978-83, Jour. Clin. Endocrinology and Metabolism, 1982-86. Served with USPHS, 1957-63. Recipient Career Devel. USPHS, 1965-68; VA med. investigator, 1979, 81—; recipient Thomas A. Roe Found. award S.C. Med. Assn., 1982, William S. Middleton award VA, 1983. Mem. Am. Soc. Clin. Investigation, Am. Soc. Bone and Mineral Research (sec.-treas. 1978-85, pres. 1986-87), Am. Soc. Pharmacology and Exptl. Therapeutics, Assn. Am. Physicians, Endocrine Soc., Am. Soc. Nephrology, Alpha Omega Alpha. Democrat. Episcopalian. Current work: Physiology and pathophysiology of vitamin D and mineral metabolism. Subspecialties: Internal medicine; Neuroendocrinology. Home: 1 Johnson Rd Charleston SC 29407 Office: VA Med Ctr 109 Bee St Charleston SC 29403

BELL, ROGER ALISTAIR, astronomer, educator; b. Walton-on-Thames, Eng., Sept. 16, 1935; came to U.S., 1963; s. William Ernest and Irene May (Elsley) B.; m. Sylvia Anne Gandine-Stanton, July 16, 1960; children: Alistair M., Andrew C. B.Sc., U. Melbourne, Australia, 1957; Ph.D., Australian Nat. U., 1961; Ph.D. honoris causa, Uppsala U., 1982. Lectr. U. Adelaide, Australia, 1962-63; asst. prof. astronomy U. Md., College Park, 1963-69, assoc. prof., 1969-76, prof., 1976—; program dir. NSF, Washington, 1981-84. Contbr. articles to profl. jours. Mem. Royal Astron. Soc., Am. Astron. Soc., Internat. Astron. Union. Anglican. Current Work: Analysis of stellar spectra and colors. Subspecialties: Theoretical astrophysics; Infrared astronomy. Office: Astronomy Program U Md College Park MD 20742

BELLAN, PAUL MURRAY, applied physics researcher; b. Winnipeg, Man., Can., Apr. 18, 1948; s. Ruben C. and Ruth (Lercher) B.; m. Josette Rosentweig, June 25, 1972. B.S. with honors, U. Man., 1970; M.S., Princeton U., 1972, Ph.D., 1976. Research assoc. Princeton Plasma Physics Lab., N.J., 1976-77; asst. prof. applied physics Calif. Inst. Tech., Pasadena, 1977-83, assoc. prof. 1983—. Contbr. articles to profl. jours. Mem. Am. Phys. Soc. Current work: Plasma physics research experiment and theory. Subspecialties: Nuclear fusion; Plasma (energy science and technology). Office: MS 128-95 Calif Inst Tech Pasadena CA 91125

BELLE ISLE, ALBERT PIERRE, electronics company executive; b. Newburgh, N.Y., Aug. 11, 1943; s. Albert Joseph and Margaret Anna (Durick) Belle Isle; m. Mary Jean Rogers, Aug. 20, 1966; children—Paul Philippe, Nicole Ghislaine. A.A.S., Orange County Community Coll., N.Y., 1963; B.E.E., Rensselaer Poly. Inst., 1965; M.S., Poly. Inst. Bklyn., 1968, Ph.D., 1971. Engring. positions Gen. Electric Co., Pittsfield, Mass., 1965-73, mgr. advanced weapon control devel. engring., 1973-75; mgr. info. and circuit technologies Gen. Electric Electronics Lab., Syracuse, N.Y., 1975-80; dir. corp. tech. Wang Labs., Inc., Lowell, Mass., 1980-81, v.p., 1981-83; pres. Custom Silicon Inc., Lowell, 1983—; adj. prof. Union Coll., Schenectady, 1974, Sch. Engring. Boston U., 1982—; adj. assoc. prof. Syracuse U., 1976-80; non-resident instr. MIT, 1969-74. Author papers on control theory and stability of stochastic systems. Patentee electroniccircuitry, computer architecture. Vice chmn. ward 4 com. Republican Com. Pittsfield, 1972-74. NSF spl. research fellow, 1969. Mem. IEEE (sr., chmn. architecture session, computers in aerospace conf.), N.Y. Acad. Scis., Assn. Computing Machinery, AAAS, Sigma Xi. Current work: computer architectures; logical structures; design methodologies and computer-aided design technology for the cost-effective application of very large scale integrated circuit technology. Subspecialties: Computer architecture; Integrated circuits. Home: 3 Whispering Pines Andover MA 01810 Office: Custom Silicon Inc 600 Suffolk St Lowell MA 01854

BELLER, DAVID I., immunologist, educator; b. N.Y.C., Apr. 24, 1947; s. George J. and Mary R. (Beller) B.; m. Judy J. Bongiorno; 1 son, Aaron J. B.A., Conn. Wesleyan U., 1969; Ph.D., Princeton U., 1975. Research fellow in pathology Harvard U. Med. Sch., Boston, 1975-77, instr., 1977-80, asst. prof., 1980-83, assoc. prof., 1983—. Assoc. editor: Jour. Immunology, 1981—; contbr. articles to sci. jours. Leukemia Soc. Am. spl. fellow, 1978-79. Mem. Am. Assn. Immunologists. Current Work: Research in cell biology of immune function, specifically the regulation of activity of macrophages and T-lymphocytes. Subspecialties: Immunobiology and immunology; Immunology (medicine). Office: Harvard U Med Sch Boston MA 02115

BELLINA, JOSEPH HENRY, obstetrician, gynecologist; b. New Orleans, Jan. 30, 1942; s. Philip Vincent and Sue Bellina; married; children: Shawn, Todd. M.D., La. State U., 1965. Diplomate: Am. Coll. Obstetrics and Gynecology. Intern Charity Hosp., New Orleans, 1965-66, resident, 1966-69; research assoc. Electrosci. and Biophysics Research Lab., Tulane U. Sch. Engring., New Orleans, 1978—; mem. adv. bd. Baromed. Research Inst., JoEllen Smith Hosp., 1982; mem. Internat. Confedn. Advisors Third World Countries for Laser Instrumentation, WHO, 1982; gynecologic and reproductive infertility med. adv. bd. Vet. Laser Inst., 1982; dir. Omega Inst. and Laser Research Found., New Orleans, 1974—; clin. prof. La. State U. Sch. Medicine, 1980—. Contbr. articles to sci. jours. Recipient 1st Prize award Dist VII Jr., Fellow Papers, 1970; Prize award AMA Meeting, 1975; Prize award Am. Coll. Obstetrics and Gynecology, 1979; William B. Mark award Am. Soc. Lasers in Medicine, 1985. Mem. Gynecol. Laser Soc. (founding mem., pres. 1979—), Am. Soc. Laser Medicine and Surgery (pres. 1982), AMA, Am. Coll. Gynecologists, Am. Fertility Soc., Am. Assn. Gynecologic Laparoscopists (prize award 1979), Gynecologic Laser Soc., Am. Soc. Colposcopists and Cervical Pathologists, Jefferson Parish Med. Soc., Orleans Parish Med. Soc. Methodist. Current Work: Lassers in medicine and surgery as applied to tissue interaction, studying wavelength characteristics and tissue effects, laser research in tissue interaction, developing delivery system for laser microsurgery. Subspecialties: Laser medicine; Obstetrics and gynecology. Office: 3439 Kabel Dr Suite 7 New Orleans LA 70114

BELLMER, RUSSELL JOE, marine ecologist, researcher; b. Berkeley, Calif., Nov. 3, 1948; s. Robert Howard and Eleanor Adele (Carter) B.; m. Linda Constance Lee, Feb. 16, 1974; 1 child, Benjamin Russell. B.S., U. Calif.-Irvine, 1971; M.S., Calif. State U.-Dominguez Hills, 1976. Marine biologist Atlantis Sci., Beverly Hills, Calif., 1974-76; sr. marine ecologist C.E., Los Angeles, 1976-83, supr. marine ecologist, Waltham, Mass., 1983—; instr. biology Los Angeles Community Coll., 1976-83; tech. advisor NOAA, San Diego, 1980-81, Calif. State U.-Long Beach, 1981-83; cons. marine biology, Long Beach, 1976-83; tech. advisor Sierra Club, San Francisco, 1976, So. Calif. Marine Biology Methodist Com., Los Angeles, 1977. Contbr. articles to profl. jours. Instr. Am. Heart Assn., Oakland, Calif., 1971, ARC, Oakland, 1969. Grantee U. Calif.-Irvine, 1970, Smithsonian Instn., 1980. Recipient Meritorious Service award Am. Heart Assn., 1980, Meritorious Service award ARC 1981. Mem. So. Calif. Acad. Sci. (chmn. 1982), Western Soc. Naturalists, Ecol. Soc. Am., AAAS, Nat. Assn. Underwater Instrs. Democrat. Methodist. Club: Pacific Divers (Long Beach) (advisor 1978-81). Lodge: DeMolay. Current work: Marine benthic community ecology and population dynamics; ecosystems analysis as related to human induced changes. Subspecialties: Ecology (biology); Ecosystems analysis. Office: Corps of Engrs 424 Trapelo Rd Waltham MA 02254

BELLO-REUSS, ELSA N., physiology and medical educator, researcher; b. La Plata, Buenos Aires, Argentina, May 1, 1939; came to U.S., 1972; d. Jose Fernando and Julia M. (Hiriart) B.; m. Luis Reuss, Apr. 15, 1965; children: Luis F., Alejandro E. B.A., U.Chile, 1957, M.D., 1964. SNS fellow U. Chile, Santiago, 1964-66, instr. exptl. medicine, 1966-72; Fogarty fellow U. N.C., Chapel Hill, 1972-74, Louis Welt fellow, 1975-76; career investigator Am. Heart Assn., 1974-75; asst. prof. physiology and medicine Washington U., St. Louis, 1976—. Contbr. articles to med. jours.; referee: Jour. Lab. and Clin. Medicine, Am. Jour. Physiology. Mem. Internat. Soc. Nephrology, Am. Soc. Nephrology, Am. Fedn. Clin. Research. Current Work: Study of transport properties of isolated perfused renal tubules, electrophysiology of renal tubules. Subspecialties: Physiology (medicine); Nephrology. Office: Sch Medicine Dept Physiology Washington U 660 S Euclid St Louis MO 63110

BELLOWS, ROBERT ALVIN, research physiologist, educator; b. Bozeman, Mont., Aug. 22, 1934; s. Alvin O. and Lucy E. (Norman) B.; m. Laura Mae Pasha, Dec. 27, 1957; children—Donna Kay, William Alvin, Norman Reese, David Scott. B.S. in Animal Sci., Mont. State U., 1956, M.S., 1958; Ph.D. in Endocrinology, U. Wis.-Madison, 1962. Research physiologist Agrl. Research Service, USDA, Miles City, Mont., 1962-67, physiology investigations leader, 1976-71, research physiol. supr., 1971-79, lab. dir., 1979-84, acting research leader, 1984—. Contbr. chpts. to books and articles to profl. jours. Recipient Agrl. Research Service Superior Service award USDA, 1980. Mem. Am. Soc. Animal Sci. (editorial bd. jour. 1972-79, award com. 1973, 80-83), Soc. Study Reprodn., Mont. Beef Performance Assn. (hon.), Sigma Xi, Alpha Zeta. Current work: Improving beef cattle reproductive efficiency, develop methods to predict and prevent dystocia in beef cattle, production of twins and accelerating genetic progress in cattle through embryo manipulation. Subspecialty: Animal breeding and embryo transplants. Office: USDA Agrl Research Service Fort Keogh Livestock and Range Research Sta Route 1 Box 2021 Miles City MT 59301

BELLPORT, BERNARD PHILIP, consulting engineer; b. LaCrosse, Kans., May 25, 1907; s. Bernard P. and Louise H. (Groves) B.; m. Elsy V. Johnson, June 11, 1931 (dec. Mar. 1954); children—Louise Bellport Garcia, Bernard Philip; m. Mabelle W. Kandolin, Sept. 26, 1955. B.S. in Mining Engring, Poly. Coll. Engring., Oakland, Calif., 1927. Registered profl. engr., Colo. Mining engr. Western U.S., 1927-28; engr.-geologist St. Joseph Lead Co., 1928-31; with Phoenix Utility Co., 1931-32, Mont. Hwy. Commn., 1932-35, Bur. Reclamation, 1936-72; regional dir. region 2, Calif., 1957-59, assoc. chief engr., Denver, 1959-63, chief engr., 1963-70, dir. design and constrn., 1970-72, practice as engring. cons., 1972—; arbitrator Constrn. Arbitration Panel, State of Calif. Recipient Distinguished Service award Dept. Interior; Golden Beaver for engring.; named Man of Year Am. Pub. Works Assn., 1970. Mem. Nat. Acad. Engring., U.S. Commn. Large Dams (chmn. 1971-72), Internat. Commn. Irrigation, Drainage and Flood Control, ASCE (pres. Colo. 1966), Am. Arbitration Assn., Rossmoor Engrs. Club, Internat. Water Resources Assn., Hon. Order Ky. Cols., Chi Epsilon (hon.). Episcopalian. Clubs: Masons (32 deg.), Shriners, Round Hill Country. Current Work: Consulting on construction of major heavy structures; improvement of methods and arbitration of contract disputes. Subspecialty: Civil engineering. Address: 855 Terra California Dr Apt 4 Walnut Creek CA 94595

BELMAN, SIDNEY, biochemist; b. Bklyn., May 22, 1926; s. Israel and Sadie (Jacobson) B.; m. Hilda Ann Belman, Apr. 6, 1951; children: Sherry, Vickie. B.S., CCNY, 1948; M.S., Bklyn. Poly. Inst., 1952; Ph.D., N.Y.U., 1958. Research asst. dept. environ. medicine N.Y.U. Med. Ctr., 1949-58, instr., 1958-61, asst. prof., 1961-62, assoc. prof., 1965-76, prof. dept. environ. medicine, 1976—. Mem. AAAS, Am. Soc. Biol. Chemists, Am. Chem. Soc., Environ. Mutagen Soc., N.Y. Acad. Scis., Am. Assn. Cancer Research. Current Work: Mechanisms of carcinogenesis, biochemical effects of tumor promoters, nutritional factors that act to prevent carcinogenesis. Subspecialties: Biochemistry (biology); Cancer research (medicine). Home: 376 Edgewood Ave Teaneck NJ 07666 Office: 550 1st Ave New York NY 10016

BELT, CHARLES BANKS, JR., geology educator, consultant; b. N.Y.C., Dec. 11, 1931; s. Charles Banks and Emily Willard (Keyes) B.; m. Louise McKeon, Feb. 2, 1957; children—Louise, Charles III, Aelred, Emma, Mary, Peggy. B.A., Williams Coll., 1953; M.A., Columbia U., 1955, Ph.D., 1959. Geologist Hanna Co., Belo Horizonte, Brazil, 1958-59, Anaconda, Butte, Mont., 1959; research geologist Bear Creek Mining, Salt Lake City, 1960; research assoc. U. Utah, Salt Lake City, 1960-61; asst. prof. geology St. Louis U., 1961-66, assoc. prof., 1966—; cons. Union Electric, St. Louis, 1982-83; expert Sierra Club, St. Louis, 1970—, Coalition for Environ., St. Louis, 1968—. Contbr. articles to profl. jours. Fellow Geol. Soc. Am.; mem. AIME, Sigma Xi. Republican. Roman Catholic. Current work: Teaching; using statistics to analyse the changes in river channels and flood plains. Subspecialty: Hydrology. Home: 2559 Oak Springs Ln Town and Country MO 63131 Office: Dept Earth and Atmospheric Sci St Louis U 3507 Laclede Ave Saint Louis MO 63103

BELTON, DANIEL JAMES, polymer physicist; b. Yonkers, N.Y., July 20, 1948; s. Harry James and Anne Maureen (Kupko) B.; m. Kyesook Kim, Oct. 23, 1982; 1 child, Alexandra Kye. B.S., Ohio State U., 1971, M.S., 1973; Ph.D., Northwestern U., 1980. Ceramic engr. Myerson Corp., Cambridge, Mass., 1973-76; sr. mem. tech. staff Philips Research Labs., Sunnyvale, Calif., 1980—. Contbr. articles to profl. jours. Ferro Corp. fellow Ohio State U., 1971; Northwestern U. grad. research asst. scholar, 1978. Mem. Am. Chem. Soc. Republican. Roman Catholic. Current work: Adhesion of polyelectrolytes on ionic surfaces; chemical adhesion phenomenon; adhesion of polyamicacids on organosilane modified substrates; positive photoresist adhesion; multilayer photoresist structures; characterization and chemical kinetics of crosslinking in thermosets; structure property relationships in thermosetting polymers. Subspecialties: Polymers (materials science); Polymer physics. Home: 3681 Slopeview Dr San Jose CA 95148 Office: Philips Research Labs 440 Wolfe Rd Sunnyvale CA 94088

BELYTSCHKO, TED B., engineering educator; b. Jan. 13, 1943. B.S. in Engring. Scis., Ill. Inst. Tech., 1965, Ph.D., 1968. NDEA fellow, research asst. dept. mechanics, Ill. Inst. Tech., 1975; vis. assoc. prof. dept. orthopaedic surgery Rush-Presbyn.-St. Luke's Hosp., Chgo., 1975-78; asst. prof. U. Ill.-Chgo., 1968-73, assoc. prof., 1973-76, prof. structural mechanics, 1976-77; prof. civil and nuclear engring. Northwestern U., Evanston, Ill., 1977—; cons. Argonne Nat. Lab., Gen. Motors, Def. Nuclear Agency, John Deere, U.S. Nat. Regulatory Commn., others. Editor Nuclear Engring. and Design Jour., Engring. with Computers Jour.; assoc. editor Jour. Applied Mechanics, others. Recipient Thomas Jaeger prize Internat. Assn. Structural Mechanics in Reactor Tech., 1983. Fellow Am. Acad. Mechanics, ASME (Pi Tau Sigma Gold medal 1975); mem. ASCE (exec. com., chmn. engring. mechanics div., chmn. math. methods com., Walter Huber Research prize 1977), Soc. Engring. Sci. (chmn. computational methods com.), Internat. Soc. Study of Lumbar Spine (charter). Current work: Nonlinear finite element method development; computer-aided engineering. Subspecialties: Theoretical and applied mechanics; Structural engineering. Office: Dept Civil Engring Tech Inst Northwestern U Evanston IL 60201

BENACERRAF, BARUJ, physician, educator; b. Caracas, Venezuela, Oct. 29, 1920; came to U.S., 1939, naturalized, 1943; s. Abraham and Henriette (Lasry) B.; m. Annette Dreyfus, Mar. 24, 1943; 1 dau., Beryl. B. es L., Lycee Janson, 1940; B.S., Columbia U., 1942; M.D., Med. Sch. Va., 1945; M.A., Harvard U., 1970; M.D. (hon.), U. Geneva, 1980; D.Sc. (hon.), NYU 1981, Va. Commonwealth U., 1981, Yeshiva U., 1982, U. Aix-Marseille, 1982, Columbia U., 1985. Intern Queens Gen. Hosp., N.Y.C., 1945-46; research fellow dept. microbiology Columbia U. Med. Sch., 1948-50; charge de recherches Centre National de Recherche Scientique Hospital Broussais, Paris, 1950-56; asst. prof. pathology NYU Sch. Medicine, 1956-58, asso. prof., 1958-60, prof., 1960-68; chief immunology Nat. Inst. Allergy and Infectious Diseases, NIH, Bethesda, Md., 1968-70; Fabyan prof. comparative pathology, chmn. dept. Harvard Med. Sch., 1970—; pres., chief exec. officer Dana-Farber Cancer Inst., 1980; J.S. Blumenthal lectr. in allergy and immunology, 1980; Sci. adviser immunology WHO; mem. immunology study sect. NIH; mem. Am. med. adv. bd. Am. Hosp., Paris; pres. Fedn. Am. Socs. Exptl. Biology, 1974-75; chmn. sci. adv. com. Centre d'Immunologie de Marseille. Editorial bd.: Jour. Immunology. Trustee, mem. sci. adv. bd. Trudeau Found.; mem. sci. adv. com. Children's Hosp. Boston; bd. govs. Weizmann Inst. Medicine; mem. award com. Gen. Motors Cancer Research Found., also chmn. selection com. Sloan prize, 1980. Served to capt. M.C. AUS, 1946-48. Recipient T. Duckett Jones Meml. award Helen Hay Whitney Found., 1976; Rabbi Shai Shacknai lectr. and prize Hebrew U. Jerusalem, 1974; Waterford award for biomed. scis., 1980; Nobel prize for medicine or physiology, 1980. Fellow Am. Acad. Arts and Scis.; mem. Nat. Acad. Scis., Nat. Inst. Medicine, Am. Assn. Immunologists (pres. 1973-74), Am. Assn. Pathologists and Bacteriologists, Am. Soc. Exptl. Pathology, Soc. Exptl. Biology and Medicine, Brit. Assn. Immunology, French Soc. Biol. Chemistry, Harvey Soc., N.Y. Acad. Scis., Scandinavian Immunol. Soc., Internat. Union Immunology Socs. (pres. 1980—), Alpha Omega Alpha. Subspecialties: Immunobiology and immunology; Immunogenetics. Home: 111 Perkins St Boston MA 02130

BENADE, LEONARD EDWARD, virologist, molecular biologist; b. Evansville, Ind., Nov. 13, 1944; s. Leo Edward and Marietta (Taylor) B.; m. Mary Pat Larsen, Nov. 29, 1975; 1 dau.: Tina Marie. B.A. in Biology with high distinction, U. Va., 1966; M.Ph., George Washington U., 1971, Ph.D. in Biochemistry, 1971. Chemist CIA, Washington, 1971-73; sr. biochemist Envirocontrol, Inc., Rockville, Md., 1974-75; sr. analyst JRB Assocs., McLean, Va., 1975-76; postdoctoral fellow Frederick Cancer Reserch Ctr., 1977-79; sr. staff scientist Meloy (Md.) Labs., Springfield, Va., 1979-81; research scientist Lab. Tumor Virus Genetics, Nat Cancer Inst., Bethesda, Md., 1981; head dept. molecular biology and biotech. Microbiol. Assocs., Bethesda, Md., 1982; head dept. virology Am. Type Culture Collection, Rockville, 1982—; lectr. biology No. Va. Community Coll, Alexandria, 1974-77. Contbr. articles to profl. books and jours. NSF trainee, 1963; Miller Scholar, 1965-66; NASA fellow, 1966-68. Mem. Am. Soc. Microbiology; mem. Am. Soc. Virology; Mem. N.Y. Acad. Sci., AAAS, Found. Advanced Edn. in Scis., Phi Beta Kappa, Phi Sigma, Alpha Epsilon Delta. Current Work: Molecular virology, cancer research, regulation of gene expression. Subspecialties: Molecular biology; Cancer research (medicine). Home: 971 Park Ave Herndon VA 22070 Office: 12301 Parklawn Dr Rockville MD 20852

BENBOW, ROBERT MICHAEL, biology educator; b. San Pedro, Calif., Nov. 10, 1943; s. Henry Robertson and Betty Lou (Pederson) B.; m. Lena Camilla Persson, Jan. 5, 1975; children: Wystan, Bronwen, Trefor, Evan, Lovisa. B.S., Yale U., 1967; Ph.D., Calif. Inst. Tech., 1972. Helen Hay Whitney postdoctoral research fellow Lab. Molecular Biology, Med. Research Council, Cambridge, Eng., 1972-75; asst. prof. Johns Hopkins U., Balt., 1975-81, assoc. prof. molecular biology, 1981-85; prof. zoology Iowa State U., Ames, 1985—; mem. cell biology panel NSF, 1980-84, mem. molecular genetics of hypertension study sect., 1985—. Co-author: Biochemistry, 1981. NIH Research Career Devel. awardee, 1976. Mem. Am. Soc. Biol. Chemists, Am. Soc. Cell Biology, Sigma Xi. Republican. Roman Catholic. Clubs: Johns Hopkins (Balt.); Yale (Des Moines). Current Work: Control of DNA replication during embryogenesis in the frog, Xenopus laevis; molecular mechanisms of genetic recombination. Subspecialties: Molecular biology; Developmental biology. Home: 2901 Forest Hills Dr Ames IA 50010 Office: Dept Zoology Iowa State U Ames IA 50011

BENDER, HARVEY ALAN, geneticist, biology educator; b. Cleve., June 5, 1933; s. Oscar and Effie (Goldstein) B.; m. Eileen Teper, June 16, 1956; children: Leslie Carol, Samuel David, Philip Michael. B.A., Case-Western Res. U., 1954; M.S., Northwestern U., 1957, Ph.D., 1959. Diplomate: Am. Bd. Med. Genetics. USPHS fellow U. Calif.-Berkeley, 1959-60; asst. prof. U. Notre Dame, Ind., 1960-64, assoc. prof., 1964-69, prof., 1969—; vis. prof. Yale U., New Haven, 1973-74; adj. prof. Ind. U. Sch. Medicine, Indpls., 1979—; Gosney fellow Calif. Inst. Tech., Pasadena, 1965-66; cons. in field; dir. North Central Ind. Genetics Ctr., South Bend, 1980—; co-chmn. Nat. Genetics Edn. Com., 1978-81. Contbr. articles to profl. jours. Mem. Sickle Cell adv. com. St. Joseph County, Ind., 1981—; chmn. human rights com. No. Ind. State Hosp., 1979—. NIH grantee, 1960-70; Dept. Energy grantee, 1965—; United March of Dimes/Nat. Found. Grantee, 1980—; HHS/Bur. Maternal and Child Health Grantee, 1981—; Health Services grantee, 1966—; NSF grantee, 1978-81; others.; HEW fellow, 1965-67; Soc. for Values in Higher Edn. fellow, 1973-74; others. Fellow AAAS; mem. AAUP, Am. Inst. Biol. Sci., Am. Soc. Human Genetics, Genetics Soc. Am., Radiation Reserach Soc., Soc. for Values in Higher Edn., Soc. for Devel. Biology, Am. Assn. on Mental Deficiency, Sigma Xi (nat. dir.-at-large 1980—, chmn. sci. and soc. com. 1981—). Jewish. Current Work: Developmental genetics; human genetics; biomedical legal ethics. Subspecialties: Genetics and genetic engineering (biology); Genetics and genetic engineering (medicine). Office: Dept Biol Scis Univ Notre Dame Notre Dame IN 46556

BENDER, MYRON LEE, chemist, educator; b. St. Louis, May 20, 1924; s. Averam Burton and Fannie (Leventhal) B.; m. Muriel Blossom Schulman, June 8, 1952; children: Alec Robert, Bruce Michael, Steven Pat. B.S. with highest distinction, Purdue U., 1944, Ph.D., 1948, D.Sc. honoris causae, 1969; postdoctoral student, Harvard, 1948-49; AEC fellow, U. Chgo., 1949-50. Chemist, Eastman Kodak Co., 1944-45; instr. U. Conn., 1950-51; from instr. to asso. prof. Ill. Inst. Tech., 1951-60; mem. faculty Northwstern U., 1960—, prof. chemistry, 1962—, prof. biochemistry, 1975—; cons. to govt. and industry, 1959—; vis. fellow Merton Coll., Oxford U., Eng. 1968; J.S.P.S. vis. lectr., Japan, 1974; vis. prof. U. Queensland, Australia, 1979, Nankai U., China,

1982, univs. Tokyo and Kyoto, Japan, 1982. Recipient Midwest award Am. Chem. Soc., 1972; Sloan fellow, 1959-65; Fulbright Hays disting. prof. Zagreb, Yugoslavia, 1977. Fellow Am. Inst. Chemists; mem. Am. Chem. Soc., AAUP, Chem. Soc. (London), Am. Soc. Biol. Chemists, Assn. Harvard Chemists, AAAS (councilor chemistry sect.), Nat. Acad. Scis., Phi Beta Kappa, Sigma Xi, Phi Lambda Upsilon. Current Work: Mechanisms of enzyme action; mechanisms of action of enzyme models. Subspecialties: Organic chemistry; Biochemistry (biology). Home: 2514 Sheridan Rd Evanston IL 60201

BENDET, IRWIN JACOB, biologist, educator; b. N.Y.C., May 9, 1927; s. Julius and Anna (Feldman) B.; m. Roslyn M. Miller, June 7, 1937; children: David, Elizabeth. B.S., CCNY, 1949; M.A., U. Mich., 1950; Ph.D., U. Calif.-Berkeley, 1954. Faculty U. Pitts., 1954—, prof. biophysics, 1966—. Contbr. articles to profl. publs. Served with USNR, 1945-46. Mem. Biophys. Soc., Electron Microscope Soc. Am., N.Y. Acad. Scis., AAAS, Sigma Xi. Current Work: Virus, protein and nucleic acid structure; electron microscopy. Subspecialty: Biophysics (biology). Home: 1321 Cordova Rd Pittsburgh PA 15206 Office: U Pitts Pittsburgh PA 15260

BENDITT, EARL PHILIP, educator, medical scientist; b. Phila., Apr. 15, 1916; s. Milton and Sarah (Schoenfeld) B.; m. Marcella Wexler, Feb. 18, 1945; children: John, Alan, Joshua, Charles. B.A., Swarthmore Coll., 1937; M.D., Harvard U., 1941. Intern Phila. Gen. Hosp., 1941-43; resident pathology U. Chgo. Clinics, 1944; mem. faculty U. Chgo. Med. Sch., 1945-57, asso. prof. pathology, 1952-57; asst. dir. research LaRabida Children's Sanitarium, Chgo., 1950-56; prof. pathology U. Wash. Sch. Medicine, 1957—, chmn. dept., 1957-81; mem. sci. adv. bd. St. Jude Children's Research Hosp.; cons. USPHS-NIH, 1957-80; Commonwealth Fund fellow, vis. prof. Sir William Dunn Sch. Pathology, U. Oxford, Eng., 1965, Macy faculty scholar, 1979-80, Litchfield lectr., 1980; chmn. bd. sci. counselors adv. com. Nat. Inst. Environ. Health Scis., 1976-79, council mem., 1971-74, 84—. Mem. editorial bds. scis. publs. Recipient Med. Alumni award univ. Chgo., 1968; Rous-Whipple award Am. Assn. Pathologists, 1980; Gold Headed Cane Am. Assn. Pathologists, 1984. Fellow AAAS; mem. Am. Soc. Exptl. Pathology (council 1971-77, sec. treas. 1972-73, pres. 1975-76), Nat. Acad. Scis., Am. Soc. Pathologists and Bacteriologists (council 1972-77), Soc. Exptl. Biology and Medicine, Am. Soc. Cell Biology, Am. Soc. Biol. Chemists, Histochem. Soc. (pres. 1963-64), Phi Beta Kappa, Sigma Xi. Current Work: Atherosclerosis, environmental chemicals and viruses as causes of heart disease; acute responses to injury and toxic substances. Subspecialties: Pathology (medicine); Cell biology (medicine). Home: 3717 E Prospect St Seattle WA 98112

BENDIXEN, HENRIK HOLT, physician; b. Frederiksberg, Denmark, Dec. 2, 1923; came to U.S., 1954, naturalized, 1960; s. Carl Julius and Borghild Nicoline (Holt) B.; m. Karen Skakke, Dec. 20, 1947; children—Nils, Birgitte. C.phil., c.m., c.chir. (laudabilis), U. Copenhagen, 1951. Diplomate: Am. Bd. Anesthesiologists. Postgrad. tng. in surgery and anesthesia in, Denmark and Sweden, 1951-54, also Danish hosp. ship in, Korea; resident in anesthesia Mass. Gen. Hosp., Boston, 1954-57; mem. anesthesia dept. faculty Mass. Gen. Hosp. and Harvard U. Med. Sch., 1957-69; prof. anesthesia, head dept. U. Calif. Med. Sch., San Diego, 1969-73; prof. anesthesiology, chmn. dept. Columbia U. Coll. Phys. and Surg., 1973-85, E. M. Papper prof. anesthesiology, 1984, v.p. health scis. and dean Faculty of Medicine, 1984—; pres. Mass. Soc. Anesthesiologists, 1966; mem. gen. med. research program-project com. NIH, 1967; dir. center research and tng. anesthesiology Harvard U. Med. Sch., 1968; chmn. com. anesthesia NRC, 1970. Author: Respiratory Care, 1965, also articles, revs., abstracts. Mem. Soc. Critical Care Medicine (pres. 1974), Assn. U. Anesthetists, Inst. of Medicine, Am. Soc. Pharmacology and Therapeutics., Am. Physiol. Soc., Assn. Am. Med. Colls., N.Y. Acad. Medicine, N.Y. State, N.Y. County med. socs., AMA, Am. Soc. Anesthesiologists, Am. Heart Assn.; hon. mem. Minn. Surg. Soc., Scandinavian Soc. Anesthesiologists (hon.), Inst. Medicine, Belgian Soc. Anesthesiologists; corr. mem. Danish Soc. Anesthesiologists. Clubs: Harvard (Boston); University (N.Y.C.). Subspecialty: Anesthesiology. Address: Dept Anesthesiology Columbia Univ Coll Phys and Surg 630 W 168th St New York NY 10032

BENEDEK, GEORGE BERNARD, physicist; b. N.Y.C., Dec. 1, 1928; married, 1955; 2 children. B.S., Rensselaer Polytech Inst., 1949; M.A., Harvard U., 1951, Ph.D. in Physics, 1953. Mem. staff Joint Harvard-Lincoln Lab. MIT project, 1953-55; research fellow Harvard U., 1955-57, lectr. solid state physics, 1957-58, asst. prof. applied physics, 1958-61, assoc. prof., 1961-65; prof. physics MIT, Cambridge, Mass., 1965—, A.H. Caspary prof. physics and biol. physics, 1979—. Fellow Guggenheim Found., 1960; Fellow Atomic Energy Research Establishment, Harwell, Eng., 1967. Fellow Am. Acad. Arts and Scis.; mem. Am. Inst. Physics (bd. govs. 1971-74), Am. Phys. Soc., Inst. Medicine, Nat. Acad. Sci. Subspecialty: Biophysics (physics). Office: Dept Physics MIT Cambridge MA 02139

BENEDETTI, LATAYAH MCCLELLAN, veterinarian; b. Nevada City, Calif., Apr. 5, 1949; m. Joseph Francis Benedetti, June 23, 1984. D.V.M., U. Fla., 1981. Staff veterinarian Animal Clinic, Homestead, Fla., 1981-82; resident in vet. surgery U. Fla., Gainesville, 1982-84; veterinarian Genesee Vet. Hosp., Golden, Colo., 1984—. Contbr. articles to profl. jours. U. Fla. faculty fellow, 1981. Mem. AVMA, Colo. Vet. Med. Assn., Am. Animal Hosp. Assn. (award for medicine and surgery), Denver Area Vet. Med. Assn. Republican. Current work: Drug pharmakokinetics in dogs; neurosurgery; mechanics of subarachnoid space puncture in myelography; technique for intramedullary pinning metatarsals and metacarpals; chemotherapy of canine synovial cell sarcoma. Subspecialty: Surgery (veterinary medicine). Office: Genesee Vet Hosp 25958 Genesee Trail Rd Golden CO 80401

BENEDICT, ANTHONY GORMAN, electric connector mfg. cor. exec.; b. Sydney, Australia, Dec. 24, 1920; came to U.S., 1956, naturalized, 1961; s. Ralph Payne and Elsie Lincoln (Vandegrift) B.; m. Shirley Marshall, Mar. 6, 1942; children: Merril Genevieve Benedict Rogers, Leeanna Ruth Benedict Mickelson, Ralph Scott. Student, Calif. Inst. Tech., 1936-37; B.Engring., U. Sydney, 1948. Registered profl. engr., Calif. Local govt. engr., New South Wales, 1952; Instr. radio theory U. Sydney, 1942-43; elec. engr. Brisbane Water County Council, Australia, 1948-52; supervising engr. Rural Electricity Authority New South Wales, 1952-55; elec. engr. Utah Constrn. Co., Australia, 1956; systems engr. So. Calif. Edison Co., 1956-59; chief devel. div. Ordnance Assos. Inc., South Pasadena, Calif., 1959-62; mem. tech. staff Jet Propulsion Lab., Pasadena, 1962-68; pres. Arc Assocs. Inc., Mpls., 1969—. Served to flight lt. Royal Australian Air Force, 1939-44. Mem. IEEE, ASME, Am. Def. Preparedness Assn., Sigma Xi. Current Work: Product development with emphasis on human factors. Subspecialties: Mechanical engineering; Electrical engineering. Home: 8415 Hitsman Ln Maple Plain MN 55359 Office: Arc Assocs Inc 6409 Goodrich Ave Minneapolis MN 55426

BENEDICT, GEORGE FREDERICK, astronomer; b. Los Angeles, Mar. 17, 1945; s. Frederick and Sarah Alice (Guptill) B.; m. Ann Durr, June 24, 1967; children: Michael Robert, Sarah Ann. B.S. in Physics; B.S. in Astronomy, U. Mich., 1967; M.S., Northwestern U., 1970, Ph.D., 1972. Research scientist assoc. U. Tex., Austin, 1972-78, research scientist, 1979—, part-time asst. prof., 1977—; cons. in field; adv. bd. Space Telescope Guide Star Selection System. Contbr. articles to profl. jours. NSF grantee, 1980. Mem. Am. Astron. Soc., Internat. Astron. Union. Current Work: NASA Space telescope astrometry team member. Subspecialties: Optical astronomy; Graphics, image processing, and pattern recognition. Home: 4105 Hycrest Dr Austin TX 78759 Office: McDonald Obs Univ Tex 16.222 RLM Hall Austin TX 78712

BENEDICT, MANSON, chemical engineer, educator; b. Lake Linden, Mich., Oct. 9, 1907; s. C. Harry and Lena I. (Manson) B.; m. Marjorie Oliver Allen, July 6, 1935; children: Mary Hannah (Mrs. Myran C. Sauer, Jr.), Marjorie Alice (Mrs. Martin Cohn). B. Chemistry, Cornell, 1928; M.S., Mass. Inst. Tech., 1932, Ph.D., 1935. NRC fellow chemistry, 1935-36; research asso. geophysics Harvard, 1936-37; research chemist M.W. Kellogg Co., 1938-43; in charge process design gaseous diffusion plant for uranium-235 Kellex Corp., 1943-46; dir. process development Hydrocarbon Research, Inc., 1946-51; tech. asst. to gen. mgr. AEC, 1951-52; prof. nuclear engring. Mass. Inst. Tech., 1951-69, Institute prof., 1969-73, prof. emeritus, 1973—, head dept. nuclear engring., 1958-71; dir. Burns & Roe, Inc., 1979—; sci. adv. Nat. Research Corp., 1951-58, dir., 1962-67; mem. gen. adv. com. AEC, 1958-68, chmn., 1962-64; mem. Mass. Adv. Council on Radiation Protection; dir. Atomic Indsl. Forum, 1966-72; mem. energy research and devel. adv. council Fed. Energy Adminstrn., 1973-75. Co-editor: Engineering Developments in the Gaseous Diffusion Process, 1949; Co-author: Nuclear Chemical Engineering, 1981. Recipient William H. Walker award Am. Inst. Chem. Engrs., 1947, Founders award, 1965; Indsl. and Engring. Chemistry award Am. Chem. Soc., 1962; Perkin medal Soc. Chem. Industry; Robert E. Wilson award in nuclear chem. engring.; Arthur H. Compton award Am. Nuclear Soc.; Fermi award AEC, 1972; John Fritz medal Engring. Founder Socs., 1974; Nat. Medal Sci., 1975; Henry D. Smyth Nuclear Statesman award Atomic Indsl. Forum, 1979; Washington award Western Soc. Engrs., 1982. Fellow Am. Nuclear Soc. (pres. 1962-63), Am. Acad. Arts and Sci., Am. Philos. Soc., Am. Inst. Chem. Engrs.; mem. Nat. Acad. Scis., Nat. Acad. Engring. (Founders award 1976), Sigma Xi. Clubs: Cosmos (Washington); Weston (Mass.) Golf; Country of Naples (Fla.). Current Work: Nuclear fuel cycle, nuclear power safety. Subspecialties: Nuclear fission; Chemical engineering. Home: 2151 Gulf Shore Blvd N Naples FL 33940 Office: Dept Nuclear Engring Mass Inst Tech Cambridge MA 02139

BENENSON, ABRAM SALMON, epidemiologist, educator, retired army officer; b. Napanoch, N.Y., Jan. 22, 1914; s. Jacob and Sonia (Mekler) B.; m. Regina van Aaltenn, May 20, 1939; children—Michael William, Thomas Ralph, James Stevan, Sonia Anne. A.B., Cornell U., 1933; M.D., 1937. Diplomate Am. Bd. Preventive Medicine, Am. Bd. Pathology, Am. Bd. Microbiology. Intern, Queens Gen. Hosp., Jamaica, N.Y., 1937-39; resident in psychiatry Bellevue Hosp., N.Y.C., 1939-40; commd. 1st lt. U.S. Army, 1937, advanced through grades to col., 1960; epidemiologist, commdr. 2d Army Med. Lab., Fort Meade, Md., 1949-52, Tropical Research Med. Lab., San Juan, P.R., 1952-54, dir. exptl. medicine Fort Detrick, Md., 1954-55, dir. div. immunology, 1955-60, dir. div. communicable diseases and immunology Walter Reed Army Inst. Research, Washington, 1960-62; ret., 1962; dir. Pakistan SEATO Cholera Research Lab., Dacca, 1962-66; prof. preventive medicine and epidemiology Jefferson Med. Coll., Phila., 1966-69; prof., chmn. community medicine dept. U. Ky. Med. Coll., Lexington, 1969-77; dir. Gorgas Meml. Lab., Panama, 1977-81; prof. epidemiology Grad. Sch. Pub. Health, San Diego State U., 1982—, head div. epidemiology and biostats., 1982—. Mem. commn. immunization Armed Forces Epidemiol. Bd., Washington, 1956-72, dir., 1967-73, 77-83; mem. cholera panel U.S. Japan Coop. Sci. Program, Washington, 1972-76; mem. expert com. smallpox and cholera WHO, Geneva, 1958-84; mem. sci. adv. bd. Leonard Wood Meml. Am. Leprosy Found., 1981-83. Editor: Control of Communicable Diseases of Man, 1970, 75, 80, 85. Contbr. articles to profl. jours., chpts. to books. Decorated Legion of Merit, 1962; recipient Meritorious Civilian award U.S. Army, 1972, Commdrs. award, 1983, K.F. Meyer Gold Headed Cane award, 1984. Fellow Infectious Disease Soc. Am. (emeritus), Am. Pub. Health Assn. (chmn. com. 1970-75), AAAS; mem. AMA (sec. council preventive medicine 1974-76), Am. Epidemiology Soc. (sec., treas. 1973-76), Internat. Health Soc. (1st v.p. 1973-75), Am. Assn. Immunologists, Am. Soc. Tropical Medicine. Current work: Teaching and research in factors involved in cause and transmission of infectious diseases, emphasis on preventing them; major involvement with smallpox, cholera, typhoid fever, Q fever, and leptospirosis. Subspecialties: Epidemiology; Infectious diseases. Home: 6619 Claremore Ave San Diego CA 92120Office: Grad Sch Pub Health San Diego State U San Diego CA 92182

BENENSON, WALTER, physicist, physics educator; b. N.Y.C., Apr. 27, 1936; s. Charles and Sylvia (Ogush) B.; m. Antje Semsrott, Dec. 4, 1969; children—Arleigh, Tanya. B.S., Yale U., 1957; M.S., U. Wis., 1959, Ph.D., 1962. Fellow U. Strasbourg, France, 1962-63; asst. prof. physics Mich. State U., East Lansing, 1963-68, assoc. prof., 1968-73, prof. physics, 1973—. Fellow Am. Phys. Soc. Clubs: University (East Lansing); Lansing Sailing (vice commodore 1982-83) (Haslett). Current work: Experimental nuclear physics. Subspecialty: Nuclear physics. Home: 6111 Skyline Dr East Lansing MI 48823 Office: Cyclotron Lab Mich State U East Lansing MI 48224

BENERITO, RUTH ROGAN, physical chemist educator, researcher; b. New Orleans, Jan. 12, 1916; d. John Edward and Bernadette (Elizardi) Rogan; m. Frank Henshaw Benerito, Aug. 22, 1950 (dec. 1970). B.S., Newcomb, Coll., 1935; postgrad. Bryn Mawr Coll., 1935-36; M.S., Tulane U., 1938, D.Sc. (hon.), 1981; Ph.D., U. Chgo., 1948. Instr. chemistry Randolph Macon Women's Coll. Lynchburg, Va., 1940-43; asst. prof. chemistry Newcomb Coll., New Orleans, 1943-53; asst. prof. Tulane U., New Orleans, 1945-53, adj. prof. Tulane Sch. Medicine, 1953—; research leader Agrl. Research Service U.S. Dept. Agr., New Orleans, 1953—. Contbr. articles to profl. jours. Patentee in field. Recipient Disting. Service award, 1964, 1970; Gaivan medal, 1970; So. Chemist award, 1968; Southwest Chemist award, 1972; Fed. Woman's award, 1968. Mem. Am. Chem. Soc., Am. Oil Chemists, Am. Assn. Textile Chemists, Research Soc. Am., AAAS, Iota Sigma Pi, Delta Kappa Gamma. Roman Catholic. Subspecialties: Physical chemistry; Polymer chemistry. Home: 4733 Marigny New Orleans LA 70122 Office: So Regional Research Ctr 1100 Robert E Lee St PO Box 19687 New Orleans LA 70179

BENESCH, WILLIAM, molecular physics educator; b. Balt., Apr. 22, 1922; s. Jerome William and Blanche (Koshland) B.; m. Joan Lynn Sagner, June 1, 1946; children—Amy, Sarah, Jane. B.A., Lehigh U., 1942; M.A., Johns Hopkins U., 1950, Ph.D., 1952. Teaching asst. Johns Hopkins U., Balt., 1942-44; Spl. Commn. for Relief of Belgium fellow Institut d'Astrophysique, U. Liege, Belgium, 1952-53; asst. prof. U. Pitts., 1953-60; prof. molecular physics U. Md.-College Park, 1967—, dir. Inst. Molecular Physics, 1973-76; Contbr. articles to prof. jours. Served with U.S. Army, 1944-46. Belgo-Am. Edln. Found. grantee, 1952-53; Weizmann Meml. Fellow Weizmann Inst., Rehovoth, Israel, 1960-62; fellow-by-courtesy Johns Hopkins U., 1977—. Fellow Washington Acad. Sci., Optical Soc. Am., (assoc. editor jour. 1977-83), Am. Phys. Soc. Club: Cosmos (Washington). Current work: Spectroscopy of atmospheric molecules; modeling of auroral energy exchange processes; time-resolved spectra of pulsed electric discharges; emission at metal-plasma interfaces. Subspecialties: Atomic and molecular physics; Aeronomy. Home: 4444 Linnean Ave NW Washington DC 20008 Office: U Md Inst for Phys Sci and Tech IPST Bldg College Park MD 20742

BENET, LESLIE ZACHARY, pharmacology educator; b. Cin. May 17, 1937; s. Jonas J. and Esther R. (Hirschfeld) B.; m. Carol A. Levin, Sept. 8, 1960; children—Reed M., Gilliam V. A.B. in English, U. Mich., 1959, B.S. in Pharmacy, 1960, M.S., 1962; Ph.D., U. Calif.-San Francisco, 1965. Lic. pharmacist, Ohio. Asst. prof. Wash. State U., Pullman, 1965-69, U. Calif.-San Francisco, 1969-71, assoc. prof., 1971-76, prof. pharmacy, 1976—, chmn. dept., 1978—; cons. in field. Editor, founder Jour. Pharmacokinetics and Biopharmaceutics, 1973—; editor: The Effect of Disease States on Drug Pharmacokinetics, 1976; The Pharmacokinetic Basis for Drug Treatment, 1984; Pharmacokinetics: A Modern View, 1984. Chmn. Pharmacology study sect. NIH, 1977-81, mem. pharm. scis. rev. com., 1984—. Recipient Am. Pharm. Assn. Research Achievement award, 1982; Alumnus of Year award U. Mich. Coll. Pharmacy, 1982, A.I. White Lectr. award Coll. Pharmacy Wash. State U., 1981. Fellow Acad. Pharm. Scis. (pres. elect 1984-85, pres. 1985-86); AAAS; mem. Am. Soc. Clin. Pharmacology and Therapeutics, Am. Soc. Pharmacology and Exptl. Therapeutics, Internat. Soc. Immunopharmacology. Current work: Correlation of pharmacokinetics with pharmacodynamics with particular emphasis in immunosuppressive, cardiovascular and diuretic drugs. Subspecialties: Pharmacokinetics; Immunopharmacology. Home: 31 Acacia Ave Belvedere CA 94920 Office: U Calif San Francisco Dept Pharmacy 926 S San Francisco CA 94143

BENEZET, HERMAN JOSEPH, entomologist, pesticide toxicologist; b. Phila., Mar. 12, 1942; s. Herman and Alice (Walters-Tomzak) B.; m. Kuo-Mei Chang, Oct. 25, 1980. B.S., Drexel U., 1964; M.S., Rutgers U., 1966, Ph.D., 1971. Diplomate Am. Bd. Toxicology. Research asst. Rutgers U., 1964-71; research assoc. U. Wis., Madison, 1971-74; postdoctoral fellow U. Mo., Columbia, 1974-75, research assoc. in pesticide chemistry, 1975-81; sr. research and devel. entomologist R.J. Reynolds Tobacco Co., Winston-Salem, N.C., 1981—. Contbr. articles to sci. jours., chpts. to books. Mem. Entomol. Soc. Am., Am. Chem. Soc., Soc. Toxicology, Sigma Xi. Current work: Study all aspects of cigarette beetle biology; develop new methods for control; insecticides, growth regulators, pheromones, biological, etc. Subspecialties: Entomology; Toxicology (agriculture). Office: RJ Reynolds Tobacco Co 611-13W BGTC Winston-Salem NC 27102

BENFIELD, ERNEST FREDERICK, stream ecologist, educator; b. Bangor, Maine, Feb. 1, 1942; s. Ernest Caldwell and Myrtle Jane (Baker) B.; m. Elizabeth Marlene Reary, Dec. 22, 1963; children—Jonathan, Jennifer, Jason. B.S in Biology, Appalachian State U., 1964, M.A., 1965; Ph.D. in Zoology, Va. Poly. Inst. and State U., 1970. Instr., Oak Hill High Sch., Morganton, N.C., 1964; instr. Gordon Mil. Coll., Barnesville, Ga., 1965-67; asst. prof. Va. Poly. Inst. and State U., Blacksburg, Va., 1971-77, assoc. prof., 1977-84, prof. zoology, 1984—. Contbr. articles to profl. jours.; assoc. editor Jour. N.Am. Benthological Soc. Grantee NSF, U.S. Dept. Energy, EPA, ERDA, U.S. Forest Service. Mem. N. Am. Benthological Soc., Ecol. Soc. Am., Assn. Southeastern Biologists, Sigma Xi. Current work: Detritus processing in stream ecosystems. Subspecialty: Stream ecology. Office: Dept Biology Va Poly Inst and State U Blacksburg VA 24061

BENGTSON, ROGER DEAN, physics educator; b. Wausa, Nebr., Apr. 29, 1941; s. Fridolph E. and Edith E. (Pearson) B.; m. Billie A. Spies, May 5, 1963; children—Nissa, Hans. B.S. U. Nebr., 1962; M.S., Va. Poly. Inst., 1964; Ph.D., U. Md., 1968. Aerospace engr. NASA/Langley Research Ctr., Hampton, Va., 1962-67; research assoc. U. Tex., Austin, 1968-70, asst. prof. physics, 1970-75, assoc. prof., 1975-81, prof., 1981—, chmn. dept., 1984—. Mem. Am. Phys. Soc., AAAS, Sigma Xi. Current work: Experimental plasma and atomic physics; spectroscopy; RF heating; turbulence. Home: 411 Honeycomb Ridge Austin TX 78746 Office: Physics Dept U Tex RLM 5.208 Austin TX 78712

BENJAMIN, ROLAND JOHN, optical engineer; b. Williamsfield, Ill, May 18, 1928; s. Harley Wilson and Beulah Isabelle (Doubet) B.; m. Helen Maxine Cadwell, June 25, 1950; 1 dau.: Nancy Anne Benjamin Kwoh. B.S. in Mech. Engring, U. Ill., 1950; M.S. in Theoretical and Applied Mechanics, 1951, Ph.D., 1955. Stress analyst N.Am. Aviation Missile div., Downey, Calif., 1952-56; mgr. aerospace group Cook Research Labs., Morton Grove, Ill., 1956-67; mgr. optical engring. Bell & Howell Co., Lincolnwood, Ill., 1967-71, dir. engring. consumer products group, 1971-74, chief scientist optical div., 1974-83; chief scientist Hughes Optical Products, Inc., Des Plaines, Ill., 1983—. Contbr. articles to profl. jours. Served with AUS, 1945-47. U. Ill. fellow, 1950-52. Mem. Optical Soc. Am., Soc. Photographic and Instrumentation Engrs. Current Work: Developing techniques and application for precision machining nonspherical optical surfaces on non-ferrous metals and infrared transmitting materials using natural diamond tools. Subspecialties: Optical aspheric surfaces; Theoretical and applied mechanics. Office: 7100 McCormick Rd Lincolnwood IL 60645

BENJAMIN, STEPHEN ALFRED, veterinary pathologist; b. N.Y.C., Mar. 27, 1939; s. Frank Joseph and Dorothy (Zweighaft) B.; m. Barbara J. Larson, July 25, 1982; children: Jeffrey, Karen, Susan Douglas, Kristine, Eric. A.B., Brandeis U., 1960; D.V.M., Cornell U., 1964, Ph.D., 1968. Asst. prof. Pa. State U. Sch. Medicine, Hershey, 1967-70; pathologist Inhalation Toxicology Research Inst., Lovelace Found., Albuquerque, 1970-77; assoc. prof. Coll. Vet. Medicine and Biomed. Scis., Colo. State U., 1977-80, prof. pathology and radiation biology, 1981—, dir. Collaborative Radiol. Health Lab., 1977—. Contbr. numerous publs. in field; author profl. reports; contbr. chpts. to books. Mem. AVMA Am. Coll. Vet. Pathologists, Am. Assn. Lab. Animal Sci., Radiation Research Soc., Am. Assn. Pathologists, Internat. Acad. Pathologists, Phi Zeta, Phi Kappa Phi. Current Work: Radiation effects, cancer resarch, immunotoxicology. Subspecialties: Pathology (veterinary medicine); Cancer research (veterinary medicine). Office: Collaborative Radiol Health Lab Coll Vet Medicine and Biomed Sci Foothills Campus Fort Collins CO 80523

BENJAMINI, ELIEZER, immunologist, educator; b. Tel-Aviv, Israel, Feb. 8, 1929; s. Kalman and Anna (Feinman) B.; m. Joyce Barbara Kushner, Sept. 12, 1953; children: Etan Marc, Leora Ann. B.S., U. Calif., Berkeley, 1952, M.S., 1954, Ph.D., 1958. Toxicologist Nat. Canners Assn. Reserach Lab., Berkeley, Calif., 1954-56; jr. specialist Citrus Experiment Sta., U. Calif., Riverside, 1957-58; with Kaiser Found. Research Inst., San Francisco, 1959-70, assoc. research scientist, 1960-64; research scientist, asst. dir. Kaiser Found. Research Inst. (Lab. Med. Entomology), 1964-70; prof. immunology dept. med. microbiology and immunology U. Calif. Sch. Medicine, Davis, 1970—; mem. adv. panel Calif. Cancer Research Coordinating Com., 1976-80, NSF, 1977-80. Contbr. chpts. to books. articles to profl. jours. Mem. Am. Assn. Immunologists, Entomol. Soc. Am., Am. Assn. Cancer Research. Current Work: Research on the immune response and its manipulation; antigenic determinants of protein with emphasis on the relationship between structure and activity; activation of lymphocytes and macrophages. Subspecialties: Immunobiology and immunology; Cell biology. Office: Dept Med Microbiology and Immunology Sch Medicine U Calif Davis CA 95616

BENKOVIC, STEPHEN J., chemist. Prof. dept. chemistry Pa. State U., University Park. Subspecialty: Biophysical chemistry. Office: Pa State U Dept Chemistry University Park PA 16802

BENNETT, BILLY WAYNE, veterinarian; b. Denver, May 31, 1943; s. James Wayne and Billie (Woods) B.; m. Nancy Burr Griffin, June 19, 1965; 1 child, Lisa Erin. B.S. in Vocat. Edn., Colo. State U., 1966, D.V.M., 1975. Extension agt. Colo. State U., Fort Collins, 1966-69, asst. prof. vet. medicine, 1978-83; pvt. practice vet. medicine, La Veta, Colo., 1975-77; veterinarian, feed mgr. Farr Farms Co., Greeley, Colo., 1978; mgr. animal health Monfort of Colo., Inc., Greeley, 1983—; mem. adv. bd. Diamond/Syntex Agribus, 1984—. Mem. research and edn. com. Colo. Cattle Feeders Assn., 1980—. Contbr. articles to profl. jours. Named Top Prof., Colo. State U., 1980. Mem. No. Colo. Sheep Breeders Assn., AVMA (Women's Aux. award 1975), Am. Assn. Bovine Practitioners, Colo. Vet. Med. Assn., Acad. Vet. Cons. (bd. dirs. 1983—, pres.-elect 1985), Phi Zeta. Club: Continental Dorset. Current work: Population dynamics related to epidemiology, control prevention, and or treatment of bovine disease complexes or conditions affecting fed cattle. Subspecialties: Preventive medicine (veterinary medicine); Agricultural administration. Home: 24304 Weld County Rd 74 Eaton CO 80615 Office: Monfort of Colo Inc Feedlots Div PO Box 1876 Greeley CO 80632

BENNETT, CECIL JACKSON, biologist, educator; b. Eau Claire, Wis., Oct. 4, 1927; s. Cecil Hilts and Leah M (Lanam) B.; m. Katherine Wilson, Jan. 22, 1951; children: Scott Jackson, Carroll Anne Bennett Carlson; m. Donna Irene Campbell, June 18, 1974. B. S. in Edn, U. Wis., 1949; Ph.D., 1959; M.A. in Zoology, Washington U., 1953. Asst. prof., then assoc. prof., then prof. biology No. Ill. U., DeKalb, Ill., 1975—; vis. prof. opthalmology Washington U., St. Louis, summers 1964-65. Republican precinct committeeman, 1962-80; adv. bd. DeKalb Airport, 1972-82; comdr. DeKalb Area Composite Squadron, CAP, 1978-81. Served with AUS, 1946. Mem. Soc. Study Evolution, AAAS, Am. Inst. Biol. Scis., Genetics Soc. Am., Am. Genetics Assn., Ill. State Acad. Sci. (past pres., past newsletter editor), Assn. Midwestern Coll. Biology Tchrs (past pres.), Ill. Sci. Tchrs. Assn., AAUP, Am. Fedn. Tchrs. Exptl. Aircraft Assn. Sigma Xi, Phi Sigma. Lodge: Masons. Current Work: Behavior, biochemical, population effects of alleles of white locus in Drosophila melanogaster. Behavior, developmental, population, single gene substitution. Subspecialties: Animal genetics; Gene actions. Home: PO Box 364 DeKalb IL 60115 Office: Biol Scis Dept No Ill U PO Box 364 DeKalb IL 60115

BENNETT, GERALD WILLIAM, physicist, research, consultant; b. Hempstead, N.Y., June 15, 1933; s. William Edward and Mary Cecilia (Hemming) B.; m. Hannelore Helene Knecht, Apr. 19, 1956; children—William, Eric, Mark, James, Paul, Kathleen. B.M.E., Poly. Inst. Tech., Bklyn., 1955; M.A., Hofstra U., 1962; Ph.D., SUNY-Stony Brook, 1968. Diplomate Am. Bd. Sci. in Nuclear Medicine. Devel. engr. Fairchild Engring. Div., Deer Park, N.Y., 1956-59; physicist Brookhaven Nat. Lab., Upton, N.Y., 1959—; cons. VA Med. Ctr., Northport, N.Y.; prof. radiology SUNY-Stony Brook, 1980—. Contbr. numerous articles to profl. jours. Patentee in field. Served to 1st lt. U.S. Army, 1954-56. Mem. Am. Assn. Physicists in Medicine, Am. Coll. Med. Physics, IEEE, Soc. Nuclear Medicine. Current work: Nuclear medicine, physics, instrumentation development; applications of energetic charged particle beams in medicine, therapy. Subspecialties: Medical physics; PET scan. Home: 21 Watchogue Ave East Moriches NY 11940 Office: Brookhaven Nat Lab 490 Medical St Upton NY 11973

BENNETT, JESSE HARLAND, research scientist, cons.; b. Lehi, Utah, June 21, 1936; s. Clifford Crosby and Dorothy (Carr) B.; m. Marily Gubler, Oct. 12, 1938; children: Scott Jesse, Cheryl, Teresa. B.S., Utah State U., Logan, 1961, M.S., 1965; Ph.D. (USPHS grantee), U. Utah, Salt Lake City, 1969; grad. cert. environ. toxicology, Center for Environ. Biology, 1969. Research assoc. Washington U., St. Louis, 1969-70; NIH postdoctoral fellow in biophysics Mo. Bot. Garden, St. Louis, 1969-70; research, teaching assoc. U. Utah, Salt Lake City, 1970-74; research scientist Dept. Agr., Beltsville, Md., 1974—, plant physiologist, toxicologist; cons. in field. Contbr. numerous articles on biol. scis. to profl. jours. Mem. numerous panels and coms. Served with USNG, 1954-59. Named Outstanding Grad. Student in Biol. Scis. U. Utah, 1967; USPHS grantee, 1970-73; ERDA grantee, 1977-80; Dept. Agr.-EPA grantee, 1977. Mem. AAAS., Am. Soc. Plant Physiologists (chmn. stress physiology session annual meeting 1978), Soc. for Environ. Toxicology and Chemistry (panel mem., reviewer). Mormon. Current Work: Physiological/metabolic effects, modes of action and control of toxic stresses due to environmental pollutants. Subspecialties: Plant physiology (biology); Toxicology (agriculture). Home: 12713 Maple St Silver Spring MD 20904

BENNETT, JOE CLAUDE, medical educator; b. Birmingham, Ala., Dec. 12, 1933; s. Claude and Clara Lucille (Clark) B.; m. Nancy Miller Bennett, June 17, 1958; children: Katherine Diane, Miller, Clark Barton. A.B., Samford U., 1954; M.D., Harvard U., 1958. Intern Univ. Hosp., Birmingham, 1958-59, resident, 1959-60; fellow in arthritis and rheumatism Mass. Gen. Hosp., 1960-62; practice medicine specializing in rheumatology; with NIH, 1962-64; sr. research fellow div. biology Calif. Inst. Tech., Pasadena, Calif., 1964-65; asst. prof. dept. medicine, asso. prof. dept. microbiology, asst. dir. div. clin. immunology and rheumatology U. Ala. Med. Sch., Birmingham, 1966-70, dir. div. clin. immunology and rheumatology, prof., chmn. dept. microbiology, 1970-82, prof., chmn. dept. medicine, 1982—, dir. multipurpose arthritis center, 1977-84, disting. faculty lectr., 1979; mem. Nat. Arthritis Adv. Bd., 1977-80; mem. subsplty. bd. rheumatology Am. Bd. Internal Medicine, 1979-83. Author: Vistas in Connective Tissue Diseases, 1968; Editor: Arthritis and Rheumatism, 1975-80. John and Mary R. Markle Found. scholar in acad. medicine, 1965-70; recipient Research Career Devel. award NIH; fellow Arthritis Found. Mem. A.C.P., AAAS, Am. Assn. Immunologists, Am. Fedn. Clin. Research, Am. Rheumatism Assn. (pres. 1981—, Am. Soc. Biol. Chemists), Am. Soc. Clin. Investigation, Am. Soc. Microbiology, Assn. Am. Physicians, Genetics Soc. Am., N.Y. Acad. Sci., Soc. Exptl. Biology and Medicine, So. Soc. Clin. Investigation, Sigma Xi. Current Work: Research in rheumatology and immunology. Subspecialties: Internal medicine; Rheumatology. Home: 3520 River Bend Rd Birmingham AL 35243 Office: U Ala in Birmingham Dept Medicine Univ Station Birmingham AL 35294

BENNETT, JOHN ROSCOE, computer company executive; b. Sparta, N.C., Sept. 14, 1922; s. Walter and Maggie J. (Brooks) B.; 1 son, John Patrick; m. Barbara Wunderle, Sept. 22, 1973. B.S. in Commerce, U. Va., 1949. Nat. accounts mgr. Burroughs Corp., Washington, 1949-58; sales mgr. data systems Collins Radio, Dallas, 1958-65; v.p. mktg. Applied Data Research, Inc., Princeton, N.J., 1965-70, pres., chief exec. officer, 1970—, chmn. bd., 1981—; chmn. bd., dir. ADR Products, Inc., ADR Services, Inc., Mass. Computer Assos., Inc. Served as 1st lt. USAAF, 1943-46. Mem. Assn. Computer Mgmt. Data Processing Mgmt. Assn., Armed Forces Communications and Electronics Assn., Serpentine Club. Clubs: Bedens Brook (Princeton); Pike Brook Country (Belle Mead, N.J.); Crane Creek Country (Stuart, Fla.); Elks. Subspecialty: Computer company management. Office: Applied Data Research Inc Route 206 and Orchard Rd Princeton NJ 08540

BENNETT, LAWRENCE HERMAN, physicist; b. Bklyn., Oct. 17, 1930; s. Harold and Irene (Kamel) B.; m. Devora Mae Spintman, Mar. 22, 1953; children—Claire Ann Bennett Freeland, Charles Leonard, Craig David. B.A., Bklyn. Coll., 1951; M.S., U. Md., 1955; Ph.D., Rutgers U., 1958. Physicist, Naval Ordnance Lab., White Oak, Md., 1950-58, Nat. Bur. Standards, Gaithersburg, Md., 1958—; adj. prof. physics U. Md., 1959—. Author: (with G.C. Carter and D.J. Kahan) Metallic Shifts in NMR, 1977. Editor: Theory of Alloy Phase Formation, 1980. Contbr. numerous articles to profl. jours. Co-discover recognition of cancer in vivo by nuclear magnetic resonance, 1972. Recipient Gold medal U.S. Dept. Commerce, 1971. Fellow Am. Phys. Soc., Am. Soc. Metals (Burgess Meml. award 1964); mem. Metall. Soc. (chmn. com. on alloy phases 1977-80), Materials Research Soc. (fin. com., nominating com.). Current work: Magnetic properties of materials, alloy physics, structure and properties of alloy phases, metallic glasses, nuclear magnetic resonance. Subspecialties: Magnetic physics; Metallurgy. Office: Nat Bur Standards Gaithersburg MD 20899

BENNETT, PETER BRIAN, physiology educator; b. Portsmouth, Hants, Eng., June 12, 1931; s. Charles Risby and Doris Isobel (Peckham) B.; m. Margaret Camellia Rose Warren, July 7, 1956; children: Caroline Susan, Christopher Charles. B.Sc., U. London, 1951; Ph.D., U. Southampton, 1964, D.Sc., 1984. Scientist to dep. dir. R.N. Physiol. Lab., Alverstake, Hants, U.K., 1953-72; head pressure physiology Def. and Civil Inst. for Environ. Research, Toronto, Ont., Can., 1966-68; prof. anesthesiology dept. anesthesiology Duke Med. Ctr., Durham, N.C., 1972—; co-dir. Duke Med. Ctr. (F.G. Hall Lab.), 1972-77, dir., 1977—, Duke Med. Ctr. (Nat. Diving Accident Network), 1980—; chmn. S.E. Consortium Undersea Research, 1982—; advisor U.S./Japan Diving Physiology Panel, NOAA, Washington, 1977—; dir. N.C. Marine Edn. and Resources Found., Raleigh, 1981—. Author: Aetiology of Compressed Air Intoxication, 1966; editor: Physiology and Medicine of Diving, 1969, 75, 82. Served with RAF, 1951-53. Mem. Undersea Med. Soc. (pres. 1975-76, awards 1975, 80, 83), European Undersea Med. Soc., Am. Physiol. Soc., AAAS. Current Work: Laboratory director and research interests in diving physiology and medicine, hypobaric oxygen therapy and mechanisms of general anesthesia, dir. simulated deep 'trimix' research dives to record 2250 feet to study and prevent the high pressure nervous syndrome. Subspecialty: Physiology (medicine). Home: 1921 S Lakeshore Dr Chapel Hill NC 27514 Office: F G Hall Lab Duke Med Center Durham NC 27710

BENNETT, STEPHEN LAWRENCE, materials science, researcher; b. Winnipeg, Can., Oct. 14, 1938; came to U.S., 1966, naturalized, 1973; s. Herbert and Winnifred Mary (McKeown) B.; m. Alice Louise Schupp, May 23, 1970; children—Kevin, Amy. B.S. hons., U. Man., 1960, M.S., 1961; Ph.D., Queens U., Ont., 1966. Research scientist Midwest Research Inst., Kansas City, 1968-70; research assoc. Rockefeller U., N.Y.C., 1970-72, Rice U., Houston, 1972-74; research staff Oak Ridge Nat. Lab., Tenn., 1974-78; materials scientist Kennametal, Inc., Greensburg, Pa., 1978—. Contbr. articles to prof. jours. NRC student scholar 1964-66; A.C. Neish fellow Queen's Univ., 1963-64. Mem. Am. Chem. Soc., Am. Powder Metallurgy Inst., Am. Ceramic Soc. Current work: Carbon control in cemented carbides, advanced cutting tool materials. Subspecialties: High temperature chemistry; Materials processing. Home: 615 Westchester Dr Greensburg PA 15601 Office: Kennametal Inc PO Box 639 Greensburg PA 15601

BENNETT, WILLIAM F., SR., agronomist, college dean; b. Plainview, Ark., Jan. 23, 1927; s. John and Minnie (Winner) B.; children: Linda Kay, William F., Jacqueline S. B.S., Okla. State U., 1950; M.S., Iowa State U., 1952, Ph.D., 1958. Cert. profl. agronomist. Extension soil chemist Tex. A&M U., 1957-63; v.p. and agronomist Elcor Chem. Co., Dimmitt, Tex., 1963-68; agronomist, assoc. dean for resident instrn. Coll. Agrl. Scis., Tex. Tech U., Lubbock, 1968—. Co-author: Food and Fiber for a Changing World, 2d edit., 1982, Crop Science and Food Production, 1983; jr. author: Modern Grain Sorghum Production, in press. Served as cpl. USAF, 1945-47. Mem. Soil Sci. Soc. Am., Am. Soc. Agronomy. Current Work: Soil fertility, fertilizer use and crop management. Subspecialties: Soil science; Plant growth. Home: 9 Brentwood Circle Lubbock TX 79416 Office: Tex Tech U Box 4169 Lubbock TX 79409

BENNETT, WILLIAM RALPH, JR., physicist, educator, university official; b. Jersey City, Jan. 30, 1930; s. William Ralph and Viola Mildred (Schreiber) B.; m. Frances Commins, Dec. 11, 1952; children: Jean, William Robert, Nancy. B.A., Princeton U., 1951; Ph.D., Columbia U., 1957; M.A. (hon), Yale U., 1965; D.Sc. (hon.), U. New Haven. Instr. Yale U., New Haven, 1957-59, assoc. prof. physics and applied sci., 1962-64, prof., 1964-72, C.B. Sawyer prof. engring. and applied sci., 1972—, prof. physics, 1972—, master Silliman Coll., 1981—; mem. tech. staff Bell Telephone Labs., Murray Hill, N.J., 1959-62; cons. Tech. Research Group, Melville, N.Y., 1962-67, Inst. Def. Analyses, 1963-70, Laser Scis. Corp., 1968-71, CBS Labs., 1967-68, AVCO Corp., 1978—; cons. in laser field for numerous indsl. and govt. labs., 1962—. Author: Gas Lasers, 1964, (transl. into Russian) Introduction to Computer Applications, 1976, Scientific and Engineering Problem Solving with the Computer, 1976 (trans. into Japanese), The Physics of Gas Lasers, 1977, Atomic Gas Laser Data; A Critical Evaluation, 1979; mem. editorial adv. bd.: Jour. Quantum Electronics, 1965-69; guest editor: Applied Optics, 1965. Bd. dirs. Friends of WFCR in So. Conn., 1974-78. Recipient Western Electric Fund award for outstanding teaching Am. Assn. Engring. Educator, 1977, Outstanding Patent award Research and Devel. Council N.J., 1977; Sloan Found. Fellow, 1963-65; Guggenheim Found. fellow, 1967. Fellow Am. Phys. Soc., Optical Soc. Am., IEEE (Morris Lieberman prize 1965); mem. Sigma Xi (chmn. New Haven chpt. 1976). Patentee laser field, 1st several gas lasers, helium-neon laser. Current Work: Gas lasers; helium-neon laser; noble gas lasers; ion lasers; metal vapor lasers. Subspecialties: Laser medicine; Atomic and molecular physics. Home: 71 Wall St New Haven CT 06511 Office: Master's Office Silliman College Yale U New Haven CT 06520

BENNINGHOFF, WILLIAM SHIFFER, botany and plant ecology educator; b. Fort Wayne, Ind., Mar. 23, 1918; s. William Nelson and Edith Esther (Shiffer) B.; m. Gladys Helen Kunst, Apr. 19, 1941 (div. 1968); m. Anne Louise Stevenson, June 14, 1969; children—Valerie Anne, Jonathan William. S.B., Harvard U., 1940, M.S., 1942, Ph.D., 1948. Botanist, sect. chief U.S. Geol. Survey, Washington, 1948-57; prof. botany U. Mich., Ann Arbor, 1957—, dir. Matthaei Botany Gardens, 1977—; panel chmn., mem polar research bd. NRC, Washington, 1962-74; mem. sci. com. on Antarctic research Working Group on Biology, 1968-70, chmn., 1976-82. Contbr. articles on bot. and ecol. research to profl. jours. Mem. Mich. Natural Areas Council, Ann Arbor, 1964—. Served to lt. comdr. USNR, 1942-46, ETO, PTO. Recipient Meritorious Service award U.S. Dept. Interior, Washington, 1954, Antarctic Service medal NSF, Washington, 1970, medal for contbn. to nat. sci. Hiroshima U., Japan, 1974. Fellow AAAS, Arctic Inst. N.Am. (bd. govs. 1958-68), Geol. Soc. Am.; mem. Internat. Assn. Aerobiology (hon.; pres. 1974-78), mem. Internat. Vereinigung für Vegetationskunde (v.p. 1968-78), Bot. Soc. Am., Ecol. Soc. Am., Explorers Club. Republican. Lutheran. Club: Cosmos (Washington). Current work: Research on phytogeography of the Quaternary period and investigations of electrostatic influences on growth and distribution of plants. Subspecialties: Ecology (biology); Paleontology, paleoecology. Office: Dept Botany Div Biol Scis U Mich Ann Arbor MI 48109-1048

BENSELER, ROLF WILHELM, forest biologist, educator; b. San Jose, Calif., Sept. 24, 1932; s. William A. and Ella K (Vaeth) B.; m. Donna Alyce Kirk, Dec. 16, 1961; children: William Paul, Mark Christian. Student, San Jose State U., 1951-53; B.S., U. Calif.-Berkeley, 1957; Ph.D., 1968; M.F., Yale U., 1958. Specialist U. Calif. Agrl. Exptl. Sta., Berkeley, 1958-61; instr. Modesto (Calif.) Jr. Coll, 1961-63; asst. prof., then prof. biol. sci. Calif. State U., Hayward, 1968—; mem. ednl. adv. com. East Bay Regional Park Dist., East Bay Mcpl. Utility Dist. Served as petty officer USNR, 1951-58. Mem. Am. Inst. Biol. Scis., Bot. Soc. Am., Am. Soc. Plant Taxonomy, Calif. Bot. Soc., Calif. Acad. Sci., Nat. Wildlife Fedn., N.Am. Versatile Hunting Dog Assn., Wirehaired Pointing Griffon Club Am., Deutschkurzhaar Verband, Nature Conservancy. Lutheran. Subspecialties: Reproductive biology; Evolutionary biology.

BENSON, ANDREW ALM, biochemistry educator; b. Modesto, Calif., Sept. 24, 1917; s. Carl Bennett and Emma Carolina (Alm) B.; m. Dorothy Dorgan, July 31, 1971; children: Claudia Benson Matthews, Linnea, Bonnie Benson Kumar (dec.). B.S., U. Calif., Berkeley, 1939; Ph.D., Calif. Inst. Tech., 1942; Phil.D. (hon.), U. Oslo., 1965. Instr. chemistry U. Calif., Berkeley, 1942-43, asst. dir. bio.-organic group Radiation Lab., 1946-54, assoc. prof. agrl. biol. chemistry, 1955-60; prof. Pa. State U., 1960-61; prof.-in-residence biophys./physiol. chemistry UCLA, 1961-62; prof. Scripps Instn. Oceanography, U. Calif., San Diego, 1962—; research assoc. OSRD dept. chemistry Stanford U., 1944-45. Contbr. articles on biochem. research to profl. jours. Trustee Found. for Ocean Research, San Diego; mem. adv. council The Costeau Soc., 1976—. Recipient Sugar Research Found. award, 1950, Ernest Orlando Lawrence Meml. award, 1962; Sr. Queen's fellow Australia, 1979. Mem. Am. Chem. Soc., Am. Soc. Plant Physiologists (Stephen Hales award 1972), Japan Soc. Plant Physiologists), Am. Soc. Biol. Chemists, Nat. Acad. Sci., Am. Acad. Arts and Scis., Royal Norwegian Soc. Scis. and Letters. Current Work: Symbiotic relationships in marine organisms; wax ester synthesis and utilization; spawning Pacific salmon metabolism; arsenic detoxification in marine algae and higher organisms; arsenic biochemistry, nutrition and pesticides; photosynthesis. Subspecialties: Biochemistry (biology); Marine metabolism. Home: 6044 Folsom Dr La Jolla CA 92037 Office: Scripps Instn Oceanography A-002 La Jolla CA 92093

BENSON, ROYAL HENRY, chemist, researcher; b. Galveston, Tex., Oct. 25, 1925; s. Roy Henry and Kathleen (Bradford) B.; m. Aleta Jo Wooten, Mar. 28, 1970; children: Royal H. III, Tamara K., Melissa A. Sc.B., U. Houston, 1948, M.Sc., 1956. Instr. U. Houston, 1947-48; research chemist M.D. Anderson Inst., Houston, 1948-50; VA, Houston, 1950-56; sr. research chemist Monsanto Co., Texas City, Tex., 1956-65, sr. research specialist, 1965-77, sci. fellow, 1977—. Mem. Am. Chem. Soc. (dir. 1965-70), Am. Nuclear Soc. Democrat. Methodist. Patentee in field. Current Work: Applications of radioisotopes to technical problems in chemical research and chemical manufacturing processes; development of highly sensitive methods of radioassay of wide applicability. Subspecialties: Analytical chemistry; Organic chemistry. Home: 1522 19th Ave N Texas City TX 77590 Office: Monsanto Co 211 Bay St Texas City TX 77590

BENSON, SIDNEY WILLIAM, chemistry educator; b. N.Y.C., Sept. 26, 1918; 2 children. A.B. with honors in Chemistry, Physics and Math, Columbia U., 1938; A.M., Ph.D. in Phys. Chemistry and Chem. Physics, Harvard U., 1941. Postdoctoral research fellow Harvard U., Cambridge, Mass., 1941-42; instr. chemistry CCNY, 1942-43; group leader Manhattan Project, Kellex Corp., 1943; asst. prof. chemistry U. So. Calif., Los Angeles, 1943-48, assoc. prof., 1948-51, prof., 1951-64, 1976—; research assoc. Nat. Def. Research Council, Chem. Warfare Service, 1944-46; chmn. dept. kinetics and thermochemistry Stanford Research Inst., Calif., 1963-76; research assoc. dept. chemistry and chem. engring. Calif. Inst. Tech., Pasadena, 1957-58; vis. prof. UCLA, 1959; vis. prof. chemistry U. Ill.-Champaign, 1959; hon. Glidden lectr. Purdue U., West Lafayette, Ind., 1961; lectr. Phillips Petroleum Co., 1964; vis. prof. dept. chemistry and chem. engring. Stanford U., Calif., 1966-70, 71, 73; hon. vis. prof. chemistry and chem. engring. U. Utah, 1971; vis. prof. chemistry, NSF sr. postdoctoral fellow U. Paris, 1971-72; hon. vis. prof. chemistry U. St. Andrews, Scotland, 1973; sci. dir. Hydrocarbon Research Inst., U. So. Calif., Los Angeles, 1977; hon. vis. prof. chemistry Tex. A&M U., 1978, U. Paris, 1979, U. Lausanne, Switzerland, 1979; hon. James Gucker lectr. U. Ind., 1984; hon. Brotherton Prof. U. Leeds, 1984; dir. Pyrotech N.V. div. KTI, 1980-84; cons. and researcher in chemistry and physics; chmn. com. kinetics of chem. reactions NRC, 1969, 77-80. Author: Syllabus for General College Chemistry, 1948, Chemical Calculations, 1952, The Foundations of Chemical Kinetics, 1960, 1982, Atoms, Molecules and Chemical Reactions: Chemistry from a Molecular Point of View, 1970, Thermo-Chemical Kinetics, 1968, 2d edit., 1976, The Current Contents, 1981; co-author: (with H.E. O'Neal) Kinetic Data on Gas Phase Unimolecular Reactions, 1970; contbr. (with H.E. O'Neal) chpts. to books and articles to profl. jours., to proc. profl. confs., encys.; editorial bd. Elsevier Publishing Co., Amsterdam, 1965—, Combustion and Flame, 1967-71, Combustion and Science Technology, 1973—, Oxidation Communications, 1978—, Reviews of Chemical Intermediates, 1979—, Hydrocarbon Letters, 1980—, Jour. Phys. Chemistry, 1981—; editor-in-chief Internat. Jour. Chem. Kinetics, 1967-84. Recipient cert. of Merit for Contribution to War Effort Nat. Def. Research Council, 1947; faculty award for creativity in research U. S.C., 1984, Polanyi medal Royal Soc. Eng.; hon. lectr. several univs.; Guggenheim fellow, 1950-51; Fulbright fellow France, 1950-51; NSF sr. postdoctoral fellow, 1957-58; Japanese Soc. Promotion of Sci. fellow, 1980. Fellow AAAS (chemistry sect. com. 1978-82), Am. Phys. Soc.; mem. Nat. Acad. Scis., Am. Chem. Soc. (exec. com. 1966-69, 73-77, chmn. 1974-75, award in petroleum chemistry 1977, Tolman award 1978, Irving Langmuir award in chem. physics 1986), Internat. Council Sci. Unions (chmn. task group chem. kinetics 1969-75), Faraday Soc., Phi Beta Kappa, Pi Mu Epsilon, Phi Lambda Upsilon, Sigma Xi, Phi Kappa Phi (hon.). Patentee measurements of concentrations of gaseous phase elements, 1979, conversion of methane, 1980. Current Work: Atmospheric chemistry; free radicals; combustion; theory of solutions; chemical kinetics. Subspecialties: Kinetics; Physical chemistry. Home: 533 Palos Verdes Dr West Palos Verdes Estates CA 90274 Office: U So Calif Los Angeles CA 90089

BENTLEY, ALAN FRANK, astrophysicist, educator; b. Bennington, Vt., Oct. 9, 1932; s. Frank Wilcox and Mildred Irene (Carey) B.; m. Patricia Eileen Manley, Sept. 7, 1952; children—Laura, Rosanna, Brenda, Marcia, Matthew, Carl. B.S. cum laude, U. Vt., 1953; M.S., NYU, 1968; Ph.D., U. Wyo., 1980. Design engr. Block Engring., Cambridge, Mass., 1962-64, sr. systems engr., 1970-76; sr. electro-optical engr. Perkin-Elmer Corp., Norwalk, Conn., 1964-70; research assoc. U. Wyo., Laramie, 1976-80; prof. No. Ky. U., Highland Heights, 1980-82; prof. physics Eastern Mont. Coll., Billings, 1982—. Contbr. articles to profl. jours. USAF fellow, 1984; grantee NSF, U.S. Air Force. Mem. Am. Assron. Soc. (Harlow Shapley lectr. 1984—), Astron. Soc. Pacific, Mont. Acad. Scis, Exptl. Aircraft Assn. (sec., treas., 1984—). Republican. Lodge: Elks. Current work: Study of stellar evolution utilizing infrared techniques for observation of young and old stars; observational and theoretical studies of galaxy formation in the early universe. Subspecialties: Infrared astronomy; Theoretical astrophysics. Home: Route 2 Box 224 Laurel MT 59044 Office: Dept Phys Sci Eastern Mont Coll Billings MT 59101

BENTLEY, CHARLES RAYMOND, geophysicist; b. Rochester, N.Y., Dec. 23, 1929; s. Raymond and Janet Cornelia (Everest) B.; m. Marybelle Goode, July 3, 1964; children: Molly Clare, Raymond Alexander. B.S., Yale U., 1950; Ph.D., Columbia U., 1959. Research geophysicist Columbia U., 1952-56; Antarctic traverse leader and seismologist Arctic Inst. N.Am., 1956-59; project asso. U. Wis., 1959-61, asst. prof., 1961-63, assoc. prof., 1963-68, prof. geophysics, 1968—; mem. council Internat. Antarctic Glaciol. Project; U.S. alt. del. Sci. Com. on Antarctic Research. Chmn. bd. assoc. editors: Am. Geophys. Union Antarctic Research series. Recipient Bellingshausen-Lazarev medal for Antarctic research Acad. Scis. USSR, 1971; NSF sr. postdoctoral fellow, 1968-69; U.S.-U.S.S.R. Acad. Scis. exchange fellow, 1977. Mem. Am. Geophys. Union, Soc. Exploration Geophysicists, AAAS, Internat. Glaciol. Soc., Seismol. Soc. Am., Geol. Soc. Am., Am. Quaternary Assn., Am. Geol. Inst., Am. Polar Soc., AAUP, Phi Beta Kappa, Sigma Xi. Research on Antarctic glaciology and geophysics, seismic refraction measurements at sea, magnetotelluric exploration of earth structure. Current Work: Study of Antarctic ice sheet and subglacial crustal structure; study of past and future extent of the ice. Subspecialty: Geophysics. Home: 5618 Lake Mendota Dr Madison WI 53705

BENTLEY, ORVILLE GEORGE, government official; b. Midland, S.D., Mar. 6, 1918; s. Thomas O. and Ida Marie (Sandal) B.; m. Enolia J. Anderson, Sept. 19, 1942; children: Peter T., Craig E. B.S., S.D. State Coll., 1942, D. Sci. (hon.); M.S. in Biochemistry, U. Wis., 1947, Ph.D., 1950, D.Sc. (hon.), 1984. Asst. prof. animal sci. Ohio Agrl. Expt. Sta.; also mem. dept. animal sci. and dept. agrl. biochemistry Ohio State U., 1950-58; dean Coll. of Agr. and Biol. Scis., S.D. State U., 1958-65, Coll. Agr., U. Ill. at Urbana, 1965-82; asst. sec. agr. for sci. and edn. USDA, Washington, 1982—; Mem. com. animal nutrition NRC-Nat. Acad. Scis., 1958-67; mem. Council U.S. Univs. for Rural Devel. in India, 1967-74; mem. ad hoc adv. com. Ill. Inst. for Environmental Quality, 1971; mem. tech. adv. com. on food and agr. U.S. Dept Agr., Viet Nam, 1966; mem. panel Nat. Acad. Scis. to meet mems. Indonesian Acad. Scis., 1968; co-chmn. Agrl. Research Policy Adv. Com., 1973-77; mem. Bd. for Internat. Food and Agrl. Devel., 1976-80. Editorial bd.: jour. Animal Sci, 1956-59; Contbr. articles to profl. jours. Bd. dirs. Am. U. Beirut, Midwest Univs., Consortium for Internat. Activities, 1966-76; chmn. bd. dirs. Farm Found., 1971-78. Served to maj., chem. warfare service AUS, 1942-45. Named Young Man of Year Wooster Jr. C. of C., 1953; recipient Disting. Alumnus award S.D. State U., 1967; Disting. Service award U. Ill. Alumni Assn., 1985. Fellow Am. Soc. Animal Sci. (v.p. midwestern sect. 1963, Am. Feed Mfrs. award 1958); mem. Am. Chem. Soc., Am. Inst. Nutrition, Am. Soc. Animal Sci., Am. Dairy Sci. Assn., Internat. Union of Nutritional Scis., Farm House (hon.), AAAS (committeeman-at-large 1971-82), Sigma Xi, Phi Kappa Phi. Club: Rotarian. Current Work: Planning coordination and policy guidance for the Agricultural Research Service, Cooperative State Research Service, Extension Service and National Agricultural Library. Subspecialties: Agricultural research administration; Animal nutrition. Home: Concord Ln Rural Route 2 Urbana IL 61801 Office: Dept of Agriculture 14th and Independence Ave SW Washington DC 20250

BENZ, EDWARD JOHN, medical administrator, pathologist; b. Pitts., June 11, 1923; s. Henry John and Gertrude Nora Heffernan B.; m. Verna C. Cuddyre, June 20, 1945; children—Edward J., Thomas J., Gregory P., Mary Louise. B.S., U. Pitts., 1943, M.D., 1946; M.S., U. Minn., 1952. Diplomate Am. Bd. Anatomic Pathology and Clinical Pathology. Fellow in pathology Mayo Found., Rochester, Minn., 1949-53; prof. med. microbiology Lehigh U., Bethlehem, Pa., 1956-64; dir. dept. pathology St. Luke's Hosp., Bethlehem, 1953-84, v.p. in charge med. affairs, 1984—; cons. pathologist Palmerton Hosp., Pa., 1956—, Allentown State U., Pa., 1955—. Contbr. articles to med. jours. Mem. med. adv. com. Miller Meml. Blood Bank, Bethlehem, 1972-84. Served to capt. M.C., AUS, 1947-49. Fellow Am. Soc. Clin. Pathologists, Coll. Am. Pathologists (chmn. anatomic pathology com. 1970-74); mem. Am. Assn. Blood Banks. Republican. Roman Catholic. Current work: Anatomic and clinical pathology with particular emphasis in surgical pathology. Subspecialty: Pathology (medicine). Office: St Lukes Hosp 801 Ostrum St Bethlehem PA 18015

BENZ, EDWARD JOHN, JR., physician, medical educator, researcher; b. Pitts., May 22, 1946; s. Edward John and Verna Marie (Cuddyre) B.; m. Roberta Jean Fiske, Apr. 23, 1947; children: Timothy Edward, Jennifer Kirsten. B.A. cum laude, Princeton U., 1968; M.D. magna cum laude, Harvard U., 1973. Diplomate Am. Bd. Internal Medicine, Am. Bd. Hematology, Nat. Bd. Med. Examiners. Intern internal medicine Peter Bent Brigham Hosp., Boston, 1973-74, resident in internal medicine, 1974-75; research assoc. NIH, Bethesda, Md., 1975-78; fellow in hematology Yale U., 1978-79, asst. prof. medicine, 1979-82, assoc. prof. medicine, 1982—, assoc. prof. human genetics, 1983—, chmn. curriculum com. Sch. Medicine, 1985—; mem. sci. adv. bd. Conn. chpt. ARC, Farmington, Conn., 1982—; cons. dept. reprodn. genetics McGee Women's Hosp., Pitts., 1980—; mem. research rev. panels NIH, Bethesda, 1977—. Mem. editorial bd. Am. Jour. Hematology, 1985—. Contbr. articles to profl. jours., chpts. to books; reviewer, editorialist numerous sci. jours., agys., 1976—. Served with USPHS, 1975-78. Recipient Basil O'Connor award, 1980; NIH Research Career Devel. awardee, 1982; NIH, March of Dimes Cooley Anemia Found. N.J. grantee, 1979—. Mem. Am. Soc. Clin. Investigation, Am. Soc. Hematology (chmn. subcom. 1982-83), Am. Fedn. Clin. Research (councilor Eastern sect.), AAAS. Roman Catholic. Club: Princeton Elm. Current Work: Laboratory research focused on the molecular genetics of hemoglobin diseases and leukemia, utilizing recombinant DNA techniques; clinical care of patients, education. Subspecialties: Genetics and genetic engineering (medicine); Hematology. Home: 57 Cindy Lane Guilford CT 06437 Office: Yale U Sch Medicine 812 LCI Bldg 333 Cedar St New Haven CT 06471

BENZING, WALTER CHARLES, chemical engineer; b. N.Y.C., Aug. 28, 1924; s. Frederick Ludwig and Grace Augusta (Englehart) B.; m. Ruth Elenor McBride, Sept. 11, 1948; children—Steven M., David W., Jeffrey C. B.S., U. Rochester, 1945; M.S., MIT, 1948; Ph.D., Princeton U., 1964. Mgr., chem. engr. research and devel. Merck & Co. Inc., Rahway, N.J., 1952-64; dir. tech. Union Carbide Corp., Mount View, Calif., 1964-68; v.p., dir. tech. Applied Materials, Inc., Santa Clara, Calif., 1985—; dir. Benzing Tech., Santa Clara, XMR Inc., Santa Clara. Contbr. articles to profl. publs. Patentee in field. Served to lt. (j.g.) USNR, 1941-48, PTO. Mem. Electrochem. Soc., Am. Chem. Soc., Am. Assn. Crystal Growth. Republican. Current work: Semiconductor materials, epitaxial silicon film growth, chemical vapor deposition of thin films. Subspecialty: Chemical engineering. Home: 20297 Ljepava Dr Saratoga CA 95070 Office: Applied Materials Inc 3050 Bowers Ave Santa Clara CA 95051

BENZINGER, WILLIAM D(ONALD), research chemist; b. Pitts., Feb. 6, 1940; s. William E. and Philomena (Schnitgen) B.; m. Arlene B. Hando, Sept. 8, 1962; children—Carolyn, William J. B.S. in Chemistry, U. Notre Dame, 1961; Ph.D. in Inorganic Chemistry, Pa. State U., 1967. Sr. research chemist Pennwalt Co., King of Prussia, Pa., 1969-75, project leader, 1975-83; mgr. membrane tech. Culligan Internat. Co., Northbrook, Ill., 1983—. Contbr. articles to profl. jours. Patentee in field. Served to capt. U.S. Army, 1967-68. Mem. Am. Chem. Soc. Current work: development, manufacture and applications of reverse osmosis and ultrafiltration membranes and systems; synthesis and characterization of polymers; coordination chemistry; electrochemistry. Subspecialties: Polymer chemistry; Physical chemistry. Office: Culligan Internat Co 1 Culligan Pkwy Northbrook IL 60062

BENZLEY, STEVEN EDWARD, civil engineer, educator, researcher; b. Pocatello, Idaho, Jan. 26, 1943; s. Owen Waldon and Myrtice (Evans) B.; m. Karen Peterson, June 5, 1964; children—Lance, Kamalyn, Rhonda Lynn, Layne, Caroline. B.S., Brigham Young U., 1966, M.S., 1967; Ph.D., U. Calif.-Davis, 1971. Mem. tech. staff, Sandia Nat. Labs., Albuquerque, 1967-80; assoc. prof. civil engring. Brigham Young U., Provo, Utah, 1980—. Contbr. articles to profl. jours. Mem. ASME, Tau Beta Pi, Phi Eta Sigma, Phi Kappa Phi. Republican. Mormon. Current work: Integration of computer aided engineering tasks, graphical display of engineering analyses, numerical modeling of geotechnical events. Subspecialties: Civil engineering; Computer-aided design. Office: Dept Civil Engring Brigham Young U 368 CB Provo UT 84602

BERAN, GEORGE WESLEY, veterinarian educator; b. Riceville, Iowa, May 22, 1926; s. John and Elizabeth (Buresh) B.; m. Janice Ann Van Zomeren, Dec. 21, 1954; children—Bruce David, Anne Elizabeth, George Stuart, Jr. D.V.M.,

Iowa State U.-Ames, 1954; Ph.D., U. Kans., 1959; L.H.D. (hon.), Silliman U., Dumaguete City, Philippines, 1973. Diplomate Am. Coll. of Vet. Preventive Medicine, Am. Coll. of Epidemiology. Epidemic intelligence officer U.S. Pub. Health Service, 1954-56; prof. microbiology Silliman U., 1960-73; prof. vet. preventive medicine Iowa State U., 1973—; cons. to WHO, India, Laos, Malaysia, Philippines, Jamaica, Ecuador, Surinam; Fulbright prof. Ahmadu Bello U., Zaria, Nigeria. Author or co-author over 105 sci. articles, 10 chpts. in books, 2 monographs. Editor 3 books on zoonoses. Mem. Am. Vet. Med. Assn., Iowa Vet. Med. Assn., Phi Kappa Phi, Phi Zeta, Sigma Xi, Gamma Sigma Delta. Current work: Ecology of dogs in relation to rabies control in the Philippines and Ecuador; pilot control of pseudorabies in Iowa; public health aspects of antibiotic feeding in livestock. Subspecialties: Epidemiology; Preventive medicine (veterinary medicine). Home: 304 24th St Ames IA 50010 Office: Coll of Vet Medicine Iowa State Univ Ames IA 50011

BERARDI, MATTEO P., mech. engr., educator; b. Milford, Mass., July 6, 1935; s. Matteo and Maria (Fantini) B.; m. Marilyn J. Bevere, June 24, 1935; children: Lori A, Susan M. B.S., Northeastern U., 1960, M.S. in Mech. Engring, 1962. Registered profl. engr., Mass. real estate broker, Mass. Notary public. Engr. Am. Sci, & Engring., Inc., Cambridge, Mass., 1962-64; supr. Avco Corp., Wilmington, Mass., 1964-67; engring, mgr. Indsl. Magnetics, Inc., Canton, Mass., 1967-71; cons. Stone & Webster Engring., Inc., Boston, 1971—; sr. lectr. Sch. Engring. Tech., Northeastern U., Boston, 1960—. Contbr. articles to profl. jours. Mem. ASME. Roman Catholic. Current Work: Management, marketing, design, construction and operation of power and processing plants. Subspecialties: Metallurgical engineering; Metallurgy. Home: 15 Putney Ln Lynnfield MA 01940 Office: 245 Summer St Boston MA 02107

BERCI, GEORGE, surgeon, educator, researcher; b. Szeged, Hungary, Mar. 14, 1921; came to U.S., 1969, naturalized, 1975. M.D., U. Szeged, 1950. Cert. gen. surgery Splty. Bd., Budapest, Hungary. Intern in surgery U. Szeged, 1950; resident in surgery Postgrad. Med. Sch., Budapest, 1950-54, asst. in surgery dept. surgery 1954-57; Rockefeller fellow U. Melbourne, Australia, 1957-59, lectr. in exptl. surgery, 1959-62, sr. lectr. in surgery, 1964-66, reader in exptl. surgery, 1966-69; fellow in surgery U. Wash., Seattle, 1962-64; dir. dept. exptl. surgery Cedars-Sinai Med. Ctr., Los Angeles, 1969-73, intern, 1972-73, asst. dir. dept. surgery, 1973-76, assoc. dir. dept. surgery, 1976—; asst. prof., then assoc. prof. surgery UCLA, 1970-79, clin. prof. surgery, 1980—. Author: Endoscopy, 1976; co-author: Operative Biliary Radiology, 1981; Common Bile Duct Exploration, 1984. Grantee Cancer Council (Australia), 1957-62, Am. Cancer Soc., 1973-75, 76-77. Mem. Am. Soc. Gastrointestinal Endoscopy, So. Calif. Endoscopic Soc. (charter), Am. Broncho-Esophagological Assn.; ACS; found. mem. Am. Assn. Gynecol. Laparoscopists, Internat. Biliary Assn. Current work: Biliary surgery, surgical endoscopy, operative radiology, electronic imaging. Office: Cedars-Sinai Med Ctr Dept Surgery 8700 Beverly Blvd Los Angeles CA 90048

BERDAN, JEAN MILTON, paleontologist; b. New Haven, May 9, 1916; d. John Milton and Anna May (Rodgers) B. B.A., Vassar Coll., 1937; M.A., Yale U., 1943, Ph.D., 1949. Geologist, U.S. Geol. Survey, Washington, 1942-46, 49-85; ret., 1985. Contbr. articles, papers and revs. to profl. publs. Fellow Geol. Soc. Am.; mem. Paleontol. Soc., Palaeontol. Assn., Paleontol. Research Instn., Internat. Palaeontol. Assn. Current work: Biostratigraphy and paleoecology of Ordovician through Devonian Ostracoda. Subspecialties: Paleontology; Paleontology, paleoecology. Home: 510 21st St NW Apt 408 Washington DC 20006

BERG, EDUARD, geophysicist, educator; b. Trier, Mosel, Germany, Nov. 9, 1928; s. Matthias and Maria (Gerner) B.; m. Francoise Berg, May 30, 1955; children: Christophe, Frederic. Mathematique/Generales, U. Rennes, France, 1949; Staats Examen, U. Saarlandes, Saarbrucken, W. Ger., 1953, Diplom Physiker, 1953, Dr. rer. nat., 1955. Instr. Physikalisches Institut, U. Saarlandes, 1954-55; chercheur Institut pour la Recherche Scientifique en Afrique Centrale, Lwiro, D.S. Bukavu, Congo, 1955-59; head seismic and volcanic dept. time service IRSAC, 1959-63; instr. U. Bonn, W. Ger., 1957, U. Calif.-Berkeley, 1961; tchr. physics UN in the Congo, Intitut Nat. des Mines, Bukavu, 1962-63; assoc. prof. geophysics Geophys. Inst., U. Alaska, 1963-67, prof., 1967-72; vis. prof. geophysics Hawaii Inst. Geophysics, U. Hawaii, Honolulu, 1971-72, geophysicist, prof. geophysics, 1972—, acting dir., 1980-81, acting chmn. dept. geology and geophysics, 1981, chmn. dept., 1981-84; cons. Dames & Moore, San Francisco, 1969-70; mem. com. on Alaska earthquake, seismological panel Nat. Acad. Scis. Recipient Harry Oscar Wood award Carnegie Instn., Washington, 1963. Mem. Am. Geophys. Union, Seismological Soc. Am., AAAS. Club: Rotary. Current Work: Earthquake seismology, crustal deformation. Subspecialty: Seismology. Home: 661 N Kainalu Dr Kailua HI 96734 Office: Hawaii Inst Geophysics U Hawaii 2525 Correa Rd Honolulu HI 96822

BERG, HENRY CLAY, consulting geologist; b. N.Y.C., Apr. 23, 1929; s. Isidore and Freda (Gottschalk) B.; m. Imogen Jocelyn Siff, Oct. 20, 1951 (div. 1981); 1 dau., Jadine Jocelyn; m. Judith Harriet Graham, June 20, 1982. B.S., Bklyn. Coll., 1951; A.M., Harvard U., 1956. Research geologist Alaskan Geol. Br. U.S. Geol. Survey, Menlo Park, Calif., 1956-82, chief tech. reports unit geol. div., 1965-67, mgr. Alaska Mineral resource assessment program, 1974-80, geologist-in-charge, 1980-82, research geologist, Anchorage, 1982-84; cons. geologist, 1984—. Served with U.S. Army, 1952-54. C. T. Broderick scholar Harvard U., 1956. Fellow Geol. Soc. Am., ; mem. Assn. Earth Sci. Editors, Soc. Tech. Communication, Alaska Geol. Soc. Democrat. Jewish. Current Work: Consultant to coordinate, review, edit, prepare geological reports and related documents for public or private use. Subspecialties: Geology; Tectonics. Home: 115 Malvern Ave Fullerton CA 92632

BERG, HOWARD CURTIS, biology educator; b. Iowa City, Iowa, Mar. 16, 1934; s. Clarence P. and Esther M. (Carlson) B.; m. Mary E. Guyer, Dec. 19, 1964; children: Henry, Alexander, Elena. B.S., Calif. Inst. Tech., 1956; A.M., Harvard U., 1960, Ph.D., 1964. Fulbright fellow Carlsberg Lab., Copenhagen, 1956-57; nat. scholar Harvard Med. Sch., Boston, 1957-59; jr. fellow Harvard Soc. Fellows, Cambridge, Mass., 1963-66; asst. prof., assoc. prof., chmn. bd. tutors in biochem. scis. dept. biochemistry and molecular biology Harvard U., 1966-70; assoc. prof., prof. dept. molecular, cellular and developmental biology U. Colo., Boulder, 1970-79; prof. div. biology Calif. Inst. Tech., Pasadena, 1979—. Recipient Grants NIH, NSF, Am. Heart Assn., Research Corp., 1966—. Fellow AAAS; mem. Am. Phys. Soc., Biophys. Soc., Am. Soc. Biol. Chemists, Am. Soc. Microbiologists, Am. Acad. Arts and Scis., Nat. Acad. Scis., N.Y. Acad. Scis. Current Work: Motility and motile behavior of bacteria, chemotaxis in bacteria, behavior of microorganisms, bacterial flagellar rotation. Subspecialties: Biophysics (biology); Microbiology. Home: 1401 Crest Dr Altadena CA 91001 Office: Div Biology 216-76 Calif Inst Tech Pasadena CA 91125

BERG, KRIS ERIC, health and physical education educator; b. Bremerton, Wash., June 10, 1943; s. Richard and Frederica (Merrell) B.; m. Carolyn May Heard, Oct. 7, 1967; children—Eric, Steven. B.S., U. Kans., 1965, M.S., 1968; Ed.D., U. Mo., 1973. Asst. prof. to full prof. U. Nebr., Omaha, 1971-85, prof. Sch. Health and Phys. Edn., 1985—; tchr. Nallwood Jr. High Sch., Shawnee Mission, Kans., 1965-68; lectr., cons. in field. Contbr. over 50 articles to profl. jours. Mem. exec. bd. Wellness Council Midlands, Omaha, 1981-83, Douglas Sarpy County Am. Heart Assn., 1979-82; med. adv. com. Omaha YMCA, 1978-82. Recipient U. Nebr. Great Tchr. award, 1978, Honor award Nebr. Assn. Health, Phys. Edn. and Recreation, 1977. Mem. Am. Coll. Sports Medicine (state rep. 1982-83), AAHPER (state rep. 1979-81, fellow of research consortium), Phi Epsilon Kappa. Current work: Research in metabolic aspects of exercise, modification of heart disease risk factors and human performance. Office: U Nebr Omaha 6100 Dodge St Omaha NE 68102

BERG, PATRICIA E., molecular biologist; b. Dubuque, Iowa, Sept. 17, 1943; d. Clifford J. and Dorothy R. (McKibben) Emerson; m. Paul S. Lovett, Jan. 5, 1982; 1 dau., Bridget Berg. A.B. (Univ. scholor, Ill. State scholar), U. Chgo., 1965, 1965; Ph.D. (NIH predoctoral fellow), Ill. Inst. Tech., 1973. Postdoctoral fellow U. Chgo., 1973-78; dir. genetic engring. Bethesda (Md.) Research Labs., 1978-80; expert Lab. Molecular Hematology, Nat. Heart, Lung and Blood Inst., NIH, Bethesda, 1980—. Contbr. articles to profl. publs. Mem. AAAS, Am. Soc. Microbiology, Sigma Xi. Club: Chesapeake Masters Swim Team. Current Work: Molecular cloning with goal of gene therapy; studying expression of regulated eucaryotic gene using cloning and transfer into cells in culture and into mice. Subspecialties: Genetics and genetic engineering (biology); Molecular biology. Office: Bldg 10 Room 7D-18 NIH Bethesda MD 20892

BERG, PAUL, biochemist, educator; b. N.Y.C., June 30, 1926; s. Harry and Sarah (Brodsky) B.; m. Mildred Levy, Sept. 13, 1947; 1 son, John. B.S., Pa. State U., 1948; Ph.D. (NIH fellow 1950-52), Western Res. U., 1952; D.Sc. (hon.), U. Rochester, 1978, Yale U., 1978. Postdoctoral fellow Copenhagen (Denmark) U., 1952-53; postdoctoral fellow Sch. Medicine, Washington U., St. Louis, 1953-54, Am. Cancer Soc. scholar cancer research dept. microbiology, 1954-57, from asst. to asso. prof. microbiology, 1955-59; prof. biochemistry Stanford Sch. Medicine, 1959—, Sam, Lula and Jack Willson prof. biochemistry, 1970, chmn. dept., 1969-74; non-resident fellow Salk Inst., 1973; lectr. Weizmann Inst., 1977; disting. lectr. U. Pitts., 1978; Priestly lectr. Pa. State U., 1978; Shell lectr. U. Calif., Davis, 1978; adv. bd. NIH, NSF, M.I.T.; vis. com. dept. biochemistry and molecular biology Harvard U. Contbr. profl. jours.; Editor: Biochem. and Biophys. Research Communications, 1959-68; editorial bd.: Molecular Biology, 1966-69. Served to lt. (j.g.) USNR, 1943-46. Recipient Eli Lilly prize biochemistry, 1959; V.D. Mattia award Roche Inst. Molecular Biology, 1972; Henry J. Kaiser award for excellence in teaching, 1972; Disting. Alumnus award Pa. State U., 1972; Sarasota Med. awards for achievement and excellence, 1979; Gairdner Found. annual award, 1980; Lasker Found. award, 1980; Nobel award in chemistry, 1980; Sci. Freedom and Responsibility award AAAS, 1982; Nat. Medal of Sci., 1985; named Calif. Scientist of Yr. Calif. Museum Sci. and Industry, 1963; Harvey lectr., 1972; Lynen lectr., 1977. Mem. Inst. Medicine, Nat. Acad. Scis. (council 1979), Am. Acad. Arts and Scis., Am. Soc. Biol. Chemists (pres. 1974-75), Am. Soc. Microbiology. Subspecialties: Biophysical chemistry; Biochemistry (biology). Office: Stanford Sch Medicine Stanford CA 94305

BERG, RAISSA LVOVNA, genetics researcher, consultant; b. St. Petersburg (now Leningrad), Russia, Mar. 27, 1913; d. Lev and Paulina (Katlovker) B.; m. Valentin S. Kirpitshnikov, Dec. 20, 1945 (div.); children: Elisabeth, Maria. Diploma, Leningrad U., 1935, Ph.D., 1939; D.Sc., Inst. Cytology and Genetics, Acad. Sci., USSR, 1964. Sr. scientist Inst. Animal Morphology Acad. Sci. USSR, Moscow, 1939-47; assoc. prof. Leningard U., 1954-63; head Lab. Population Genetics, Acad Sci. USSR, Novosibirsk, 1963-68, Inst. Agrophysics, Acad. Agrl. Sci., Leningrad, 1968-70; prof. Hertsen Pedagogical Inst., Leningrad, 1968-74; assoc. scientist U. Wis., Madison, 1976-81; vis. prof. Washington U., St. Louis, 1981—; cons. in field. Contbr. articles to profl. jours. Mem. Genetics Soc. Am.; mem. Genetics Soc. Japan; Mem. AAAS, Nat. Geog. Soc. Current Work: Geography of the spontaneous mutation process in Drosophila populations; mechanisms of mutator gene action; history of genetics USSR. Subspecialties: Gene actions; Evolutionary biology. Home: 5696 Kingsbury 403 St Louis MO 63112 Office: Dept Genetics Box 8031 Washington U Sch Medicine Saint Louis MO 63110

BERG, RICHARD ALAN, clinical neurophychologist; b. Albany, N.Y., Mar. 30, 1953; s. Gunter Alfred and Sylvia (Falkow) B. B.A., SUNY-Buffalo, 1974; M.A., U. Houston, 1976, Ph.D., 1980. Adj. faculty social scis. Houston Community Coll., 1971-77; postdoctoral fellow neuropsychology Nebr. Psychiat. Inst., Omaha, 1979-80; instr. psychiatry U. Tenn. Center for Health Scis., Memphis, 1980—; adj. faculty psychology Memphis State U., 1980—; clin. neuropsychologist St. Jude Children's Research Hosp., Memphis, 1980—; cons. Crisis Center, Memphis, 1981—, Fed. Corrections Inst., Memphis, 1981—. Co-author: Interpretation of Halstead Reitan Neuropsychological Battery, 1981, (with Charles Golden) Interpretation of Luria-Nebraska Neuropsychological Battery, 1982. Mem. Am. Psychol. Assn., Nat. Acad. Neuropsychologists, Internat. Neuropsychol. Soc., Biofeedback Soc. Tenn. Current Work: Neuropsychological effects of leukemia and its treatment. Development of rehabilitation strategies for cerebral dysfunction. Subspecialties: Neuropsychology; Pediatric neuropsychology. Office: St Jude Children's Research Hosp 332 N Lauderdale St Memphis TN 38101

BERG, RICHARD ALAN, biochemist, educator; b. Spokane, Wash., Apr. 17, 1945; s. Norris Herbert and Leta Kathern (Peterson) B.; m. Samantha Francesca Curran, Jan. 5, 1981. B.S., U. Chgo., 1967; Ph.D., U. Pa., 1972. Asst. prof. U. Medicine and Dentistry N.J., Piscataway, 1973-81, assoc. prof. biochemistry, 1981—; staff investigator NIH, Bethesda, Md., 1978-80; cons. in biomaterials. Recipient Sinsheimer Fund award, 1976-79. Mem. Am. Soc. Biol. Chemists, Am. Fedn. Clin. Research, Am. Chem. Soc., AAAS, Soc. Exptl. Biology and Medicine (editorial bd. procs.). Current Work: extracellular matrix; biomaterials; expression of genes for connective tissue proteins; lung injury, inflammation and fibrosis; analytical biochemistry; high pressure liquid chromatography. Subspecialties: Biochemistry (biology); Cell and tissue culture. Home: Route 1 Box 148 Lambertville NJ 08530 Office: U Medicine and Dentistry of NJ Hoes Ln Piscataway NJ 08530

BERGER, BERNARD BEN, environmental engineer, consultant; b. N.Y.C., Aug. 21, 1912; s. Louis and Pauline (Margil) B.; m. Neoma Miller, Nov. 11, 1939; children—Paul S., David R., Susan Beth Berger Atkins. B.S., MIT, 1935; M.S., Harvard U., 1948; Sc.D. (hon.), U. Mass., 1979. Registered profl. engr., Mass.; diplomate Am. Acad. Environ. Engrs. County san. engr. Kent County, Grand Rapids, Mich., 1939-41; commd. asst. san. engr. USPHS, 1941, advanced through grades to san. engring. dir. 1956, ret., 1966; prof. civil engring., dir. water resources research U. Mass., Amherst, 1966-78, emeritus prof. civil engring., 1978—; cons. Amherst and Washington, 1978—. Editor: Removal of Organic Substances from Water and Wastewater, 1980. Contbr. articles to profl. jours. Mem. Mass. Pub. Health Council, 1966-74, Amherst Town Com. on Water Supply, 1972-80. Hon. fellow Inst. Water Pollution Control U.K.; mem. Am. Water Works Assn. (life), ASCE (life), Nat. Acad. Engring., Internat. Assn. Water Pollution Research and Control (hon.), Water Pollution Control Fedn. (hon.), Internat. Water Resources Assn. Current work: Separation of organic solutes from water and wastewater; water resources and pollution control. Subspecialty: Water supply and wastewater treatment. Office: Dept Civil Engring U Mass Amherst MA 01003

BERGER, EDWARD MICHAEL, geneticist; b. N.Y.C., May 2, 1944; s. Benjamin and Sarah (Handelman) B.; m. Barbara Fritsche, Dec. 6, 1981; m. Deirdre Wallace, Dec. 16, 1968; children: Alexander, Nicholas, Tanya, Matthew. B.A., Hunter Coll., 1965; M.S., Syracuse U., 1967, Ph.D., 1969. USPHS postdoctoral fellow Biol. Labs., Harvard U., 1969-70; dept. biology U. Chgo., 1970-71; asst. prof. biology SUNY, Albany, 1971-75; asst. prof. Dartmouth Coll., Hanover, N.H., 1975-77, assoc. prof., 1977-83, prof., 1983—. Contbr. articles to profl. jours. Embo fellow, 1975, 81; NSF grantee, 1975-77, 84—; NIH grantee, 1971—. Mem. Genetics Soc. Am. Current Work: Regulation of gene expression in eucryotic cells. Subspecialties: Gene actions; Genetics and genetic engineering (biology). Office: Dept Biology Dartmouth Coll Hanover NH 03755

BERGER, HARVEY JAMES, physician, medical scientist, cardiac radiologist; b. N.Y.C., June 6, 1950; s. Howard H. and Edith (Muskat) B.; m. Wendy S. Wolk, May 16, 1976; 1 son: Eric Michael. A.B., Colgate U., 1972; M.D., Yale U., 1977. Diplomate: Am. Bd. Nuclear Medicine, Nat. Bd. Med. Examiners. Resident radiology, nuclear medicine Yale-New Haven Hosp., 1977-81; asst. prof. diagnostic radiology and medicine, dir. cardiovascular imaging Yale U. Sch. Medicine, 1981—. Contbr. numerous articles to profl. jours., chpts. to books. Recipient Marc Tetalman Research award Soc. Nuclear Medicine, 1981; Meml. award Assn. U. Radiologists, 1979. Fellow Am. Coll. Cardiology, Am. Coll. Chest Physicians, Council Cardiovascular Radiology, Am. Heart Assn.; mem. N. Am. Soc. Cardiac Radiology, Am. Physiol. Soc., Am. Fedn. Clin. Research, Am. Coll. Radiology, Am. Roentgen Ray Soc., N.Y. Acad. Sci., Soc. Thoracic Radiology, Sigma Xi. Clubs: Yale of N.Y. (New Haven), Mary's Assn. (New Haven). Current Work: Cardiovascular imaging: nuclear, NMR, digital angiography, ultrasound, image processing. Myocardial ischemia, contractivity. Subspecialties: Radiology; Cardiology. Office: Yale U Sch Medicine 333 Cedar St New Haven CT 06510

BERGER, LEV ISAAC, physics educator; b. Rostov, USSR, June 23, 1929, came to U.S., 1978, naturalized, 1985; s. Isaac Mark and Sara (Poltevsker) B.; m. Ninelle Rossine, July 2, 1956; 1 child, Yuri. M.S. in Physics, State U., Moscow, 1955; Ph.D. in Physics, State U., Minsk, USSR, 1959; D. Tech. Sci., U. Steel and Alloys, Moscow, 1968. Lectr. U. Nonferrous Metals, Moscow, 1956-60; docent U. Metallurgy, Moscow, 1960-62; prof. physics Poly. Inst., Moscow, 1962-77; sr. sci. New Eng. Research Ctr., Sudbury Mass., 1979-81; lectr. Calif. State U.-San Diego, 1981—; pres. Calif. Inst. Electronics and Materials Sci., Hemet, 1981—; dir. Inst. Chem. Reagents, Moscow, 1962-71; dir. Introscopy Research Inst., Moscow, 1971-77, Inst. Electronics and Materials Sci., San Diego, 1983—. Contbr. articles to profl. jours.; author 4 books. Patentee in field. San Diego State U. grantee. Mem. Am. Phys. Soc., N.Y. Acad. Scis., Am. Assn. for Crystal Growth, Am. Soc. Engrs. and Architects. Current work: Semiconductor materials; diamond like semiconductors; infrared detectors; crystal growth and epitaxy; non-destructive testing of semiconductor materials and devices. Subspecialties: Electronic materials; Condensed matter physics. Office: Physics Dept San Diego State U San Diego CA 92182

BERGER, PHILIP JEFFREY, educator; b. Newark, June 28, 1943; s. Philip Graham and Jean Bar (Weller) B.; m. Frances Ann Berger, Jan. 9, 1942; children: Sarah Katherine, Philip Calvin. B.S., Delaware Valley Coll., 1965; M.S., Ohio State U., 1967, Ph.D., 1970. Asst. prof. animal sci. Iowa State U., 1972-78, assoc. prof., 1978-82, prof., 1982—; computer cons. animal prodn. div. FAO, UN, Rome; vis. coop. scientist BARD project, Bet Dagan, Israel. Contbr. to profl. jours. Mem. Am. Dairy Sci. Assn., Am. Soc. Animal Sci., Biometrics Soc., Sigma Xi, Delta Tau Alpha, Gamma Sigma Delta. Republican. Methodist. Current Work: Research directed toward developing mixed model techniques for sire and cow evaluation; teaching computer techniques for biol. research; population dynamics in animal breeding; research sire and cow evaluation for production traits; breeding program devel. Subspecialties: Animal breeding and embryo transplants; Statistics.

BERGER, ROBERT LAW, electronic engineer; b. Danville, Ill., May 8, 1922; s. Benton Frederick and Bertha Leona (Law) B.; m. Olga Victoria Fuchs, June 1, 1946 (div. 1973); children—Marquita, Robert, Gregory, Dennis Randolph; m. Audrey Helen Henny, Aug. 30, 1973. B.S. in Elec. Engring., U. Ill., 1947. Registered profl. engr., Mo. Engr., Pub. Service Co., Joliet, Ill., 1947-48; chief engr. Standard Fruit Co., La Ceiba, Honduras, 1948-57; sr. staff engr. Western Electric Co., Lee's Summit, Mo., 1957-83; dir. engring. Signal Systems Inc., Lenexa, Kans., 1983—. Contbr. articles to profl. jours. Patentee logic probe, field effect oscillator, solid state pentode. Served to 1st lt. U.S. Army, 1943-46, ETO. Mem. IEEE (sr.), Internat. Soc. Hybrid Microelectronics. Republican. Baptist. Current work: Satellite TV receiver design; thick film hybrid circuit design. Subspecialties: Microelectronics; Electrical engineering. Home: Route 4 Box 2R Pleasant Hill MO 64080 Office: Signal Systems Inc 12158 Santa Fe Dr Lenexa KS 66215

BERGER, ROBERT LEWIS, researcher, writer, consultant; b. Omaha, Sept. 2, 1925; s. Morris and Ada May (Rayner) B.; m. Margaret Weber, Sept. 1, 1950 (div. Dec. 1980); children—Karen D., Christine E., David L., Kathryn E.; m. Victoria A. Harden, May 23, 1981; stepchildren—C. Durward McDonell III, Emily V. McDonell. B.S. in Physics, Colo. State U., 1950; M.S., Pa. State U., 1953, Ph.D., 1956. Instr. physics Park Coll., Parkville, Mo., 1950-51; grad. asst. in physics, Pa. State U., State Coll., 1951-52, research asst. in physics, 1952-55; asst. prof. physics Utah State U., Logan, 1957-60, assoc. prof., 1960-62; sr. investigator Nat. Heart Inst., NIH, Bethesda, Md., 1962-75; chief sect. on biophys. instrumentation Nat. Heart Lung and Blood Inst., NIH, Bethesda, 1975—. Contbr. chpts. to books, articles to profl. jours. Chmn. bd. Karma House, Inc., Bethesda, 1973-76. Served to lt. (j.g.) U.S. Mcht. Marine, 1943-46, 47-48. Am. Cancer Soc. fellow Pa. State U., 1955-56; Am. Cancer Soc. Brit.-Am. exchange fellow, 1956-57. Fellow AAAS, Am. Phys. Soc. (councilman-at-large div. biol physics); mem. Am. Soc. Biol. Chemists, Soc. Gen. Physiologists, Brit. Biophys. Soc., Biophys. Soc. (chmn. biophys. discussions 1977—), Sigma Xi. Democrat. Episcopalian. Current work: Physical chemistry of hemoglobin; instrument automation and the development of a broad specrum of instruments for the study of macromolecules; special finite element simulation technique for solving heat conduction and kinetic equations used to simulate instrument response and chemical reactions. Subspecialties: Biophysics (physics); Biophysical chemistry. Home: 4503 Avamere St Bethesda MD 20814 Office: Nat Heart Lung Blood Inst NIH Bldg 10 Room 5D20 Bethesda MD 20205

BERGER, STEVEN BARRY, physicist; b. N.Y.C., Dec. 29, 1946; s. Bernard and Sylvia (Reff) B.; S.B., MIT, 1967, Ph.D., 1973. Research physicist dept. physics, MIT, Cambridge, 1974-76; research physicist ITEK Corp., Lexington, Mass., 1976-77; asst. editor Am. Jour. Physics MIT, 1975-78; research physicist TRW, McLean, Va., 1978-80, Redondo Beach, Calif., 1983—; research physicist Naval Research Lab., Washington, 1981-82, lectr. George Washington U., 1981; lectr. Loyola Marymount U., Los Angeles, 1985. Contbr. articles to profl. jours. Edn. counselor MIT Edn. Council, Los Angeles, 1984; mem. leadership group Jewish Fedn. Council, Los Angeles, 1984; mem. Simon Wiesenthal Ctr., Los Angeles, 1983—. Fellow NSF, Sloan Found. Mem. Am. Phys. Soc., Sigma Xi. Jewish. Current work: Math. techniques in astronautics; description of motion of spacecraft. Subspecialties: Theoretical physics; Astronautics. Home: 19009 Laurel Park Rd # 174 Dominguez Hills CA 90220 Office: TRW R5/2031C 1 Space Park Redondo Beach CA 90278

BERGER, THEODORE WILLIAM, neuroscientist; b. Lafayette, Ind., June 11, 1950; s. Arvid William and Marian Hildegard (Beyer) B.; m. Terry Lynn Berger, May 20, 1972. B.S. summa cum laude, Union Coll., Schenectady, 1972; Ph.D., Harvard U., 1976. Postdoctoral research assoc. dept. psychobiology U. Calif., Irvine, 1976-77; asst. research psychobiologist, 1977-78; Alfred P. Sloan Found. fellow Salk Inst. Biol. Studies, LaJolla, 1978-79; asst. prof. psychology and psychiatry U. Pitts., 1979-81, assoc. prof., 1982—. Contbr. articles to profl. jours. Recipient James McKeen Cattell award, 1978, Alfred P. Sloan Found. fellow, 1978, McKnight Found. scholar award, 1980; NIMH research career devel. awardee, 1981. Mem. Soc. Neuroscience, N.Y. Acad. Scis., Psychonomic Soc., AAAS, Phi Beta Kappa, Sigma Xi. Current Work: Neurobiological analysis of associative learning research, neuroscience, electrophysiology, neuroanatomy. Subspecialties: Neurobiology; Neurophysiology. Office: Dept Psycholog Univ Pitts Pittsburgh PA 15260

BERGERON, CLIFTON GEORGE, ceramic engineer, educator; b. Los Angeles, Jan. 5, 1925; s. Lewis G. and Rose C. (Dengel) B.; m. Laura H. Kaario, June 9, 1950; children—Ann Leija, Louis Kaario. B.S., U. Ill., 1950, M.S., 1959, Ph.D., 1961. Sr. ceramic engr. A. O. Smith Corp., Milw., 1950-55; staff engr. Whirlpool Corp., St. Joseph, Mich., 1955-57; research asso. U. Ill., Champaign-Urbana, 1957-61, asst. prof., 1961-63, asso. prof., 1963-67, prof., 1967-78, head dept. ceramic engring., 1978—; cons. A. O. Smith Corp., Whirlpool Corp., Ingraham Richardson, U.S. Steel Corp., Pfaudler Corp., Ferro Corp. Editor, Ann. Conf. on Glass Problems. Served in U.S. Army, 1943-46, ETO. NSF grantee, 1961—. Fellow Am. Ceramic Soc.; mem. AAAS, Nat. Inst. Ceramic Engrs., AAUP, KERAMOS, Am. Soc. Engring. Edn., Sigma Xi. Current work: Research in crystallization kinetics in glass; high temperature reactions. Subspecialties: Ceramic engineering; Ceramics. Home: 208 W Michigan St Urbana IL 61801 Office: 105 S Goodwin St Urbana IL 61801

BERGEY, GREGORY KENT, neurologist, neuroscientist, internist; b. Bryn Mawr, Pa., Nov. 9, 1949; s. Robert Harr and Kathryn Agnes (Schmidt) B.; m. Stefanie Friday Antonakos, Aug. 27, 1972; children: Alyssa Noelle, Alexander Christian. A.B. in Biology, Princeton U., 1971; M.D., U. Pa., 1975. Diplomate Am. Bd. Psychology and Neurology, Am. Bd. Internal Medicine. Intern Yale-New Haven Hosp., 1975-76, resident in internal medicine, 1975-77; research assoc. Lab. Devel. Neurobiology, Nat. Inst. Child Health and Human Devel., NIH, Bethesda, Md., 1977-79, 81-82; resident in neurology, fellow neurology dept. Johns Hopkins U. Sch. Medicine and Hosp., Balt., 1979-83; asst. prof. neurology and physiology U. Md. Sch. Medicine, Balt., 1983—. Served with USPHS, 1977-79, 81-82. Mem. Soc. Neurosci., Am. Soc. Neurol. Investigation, ACP, Am. Acad. Neurology. Current Work: Developmental neurobiology; neuronal cell culture; cellular mechanisms of convulsant and anticonvulsant action; synaptogenesis; clostridial neurotoxins. Subspecialties: Neurophysiology; Neurology. Home: 1219 John St Baltimore MD 21217 Office: Neurology Dept U Md Sch Medicine 22 S Greene St Baltimore MD 21201

BERGMAN, ROBERT GEORGE, chemist; b. Chgo., May 23, 1942; s. Joseph J. and Stella (Horowitz) B.; m. Wendy L. Street, June 17, 1965; children—David R., Michael S. B.A. cum laude in chemistry, Carleton Coll., 1963; Ph.D. (NIH fellow), U. Wis., 1966. NATO fellow in chemistry Columbia U., N.Y.C., 1966-67; Arthur Amos Noyes instr. chemistry Calif. Inst. Tech., Pasadena, 1967-69, asst. prof. chemistry, 1969-71, asso. prof. chemistry, 1971-73, prof., 1973-77; prof. chemistry U. Calif. at Berkeley, 1977—, Miller Research prof., 1982-83; cons. DuPont Co, 1981—; vis. asso. prof. Stanford U., 1972; vis. prof. Iowa State U., 1975; vis. faculty asso. IBM Research Corp., San Jose, 1974; Sherman Fairchild Disting. scholar Calif. Inst. Tech., 1984; Disting. vis. lectr. U. Tex., 1983; Dains Meml. lectr. U. Kans., 1983; Dow lectr. Mich. State U., 1985; Bailar lectr. U. Ill., 1985; mem. panel NIH bioinorganic and metallobiochemistry study sect. NIH, 1977-80. Mem. editorial bd.: Organometallics, Jour.

Organic Chemistry, Chem. Revs.; contbr. articles to profl. jours. Alfred P. Sloan Found. fellow, 1970-72; recipient Camile and Henry Dreyfus Found. Tchr. Scholar award, 1970-75; Excellence in Teaching award Calif. Inst. Tech., 1978; Award in Organometallic Chemistry, Am. Chem. Soc., 1986. Mem. Nat. Acad. Scis., Am. Acad. Arts and Scis., Phi Beta Kappa, Sigma Xi, Phi Lambda Upsilon. Subspecialties: Organometallics; Organic chemistry. Home: 501 Coventry Rd Kensington CA 94707 Office: Dept Chemistry U Calif Berkeley CA 94720

BERGMANN, PETER G(ABRIEL), theoretical physics educator; b. Berlin, Mar. 24, 1915; came to U.S., 1936, naturalized, 1942; s. Max and Emmy Miriam (Grunwald) B.; m. Margot Eisenhardt, May 23, 1936; children—Ernest Eisenhardt, John Eisenhardt. Dr.rer.nat., German U., Prague, Czechoslovakia, 1936; postgrad. Tech. U., Dresden, Germany, 1931-32, Dr.rer.nat.h.c. (hon.), 1979; postgrad. U. Freiburg, Germany, 1932-33. Postdoctoral research asst. to Albert Einstein, Inst. Advanced Study, Princeton, N.J., 1936-41; asst. prof. Black Mountain Coll., N.C., 1941-42, Lehigh U., Bethlehem, Pa., 1942-44; mem. sci. staff Columbia U., N.Y.C., 1944-47; assoc. prof. physics Syracuse U., N.Y., 1947-50, prof., 1950—; research prof. NYU, 1982—; adj. prof. Bklyn. Poly. Inst., 1947-57; vis. prof., chmn. Yeshiva U., N.Y.C., 1959-79, also other vis. positions; chmn. Fedn. Am. Scientists, 1964. Author: Introduction to the Theory of Relativity, 1942, 76; Basic Theories of Physics 2 vols., 1949, 51; The Riddle of Gravitation, 1968; Editor (with others): Cosmology and Gravitation, 1980. Contbr. articles and book revs. to profl. jours. Recipient Pregel award N.Y. Acad. Scis., 1970; NSF grantee, also others, 1948—. Fellow Am. Phys. Soc., AAAS (council 1980-83); mem. Am. Math. Soc., German Phys. Soc., European Phys. Soc., Internat. Soc. Gen Relativity and Gravitation (pres., dep. pres. 1977-83). Current work: Research in general relativity and related fields; author, editor books in field. Subspecialty: Theoretical physics. Office: Dept Physics NYU 4 Washington Pl New York NY 10003

BERGQUIST, JAMES WILLIAM, computer scientist, mathematician; b. Ottumwa, Iowa, Apr. 23, 1928; s. Albin and Lucille (Morrison) B.; m. Madonna T. Dunham, Sept. 15, 1951; children: Catherine, James, Mary, Brian, Thomas, John, Timothy, Joseph, Ann, Robert, Paul. B.S., Iowa State U., 1950; M.S., U. So. Calif., 1955, Ph.D., 1963. Analog computers Lockheed Aircraft, Burbank, Calif., 1951-54; theoretical analyst Gilfillan Bros. (now ITT), Los Angeles, 1955-57; computer scientist IBM, Los Angeles, 1958—; vis. assoc. Calif. Inst. Tech., Pasadena, 1963-67. Chmn, sch. bd. La Canada (Calif.) Unified Sch. Dist., 1971-81; v.p. Catholic Social Service, Los Angeles, 1980-81. Recipient Excellence award IBM, 1970; Pub. Relations award, 1981. Mem. Am. Math. Soc., Math. Assn. Am., Assn. Computing Machinery, Soc. Indsl. and Applied Math. (pres. 1980-81, exec. com. 1979-82). Roman Catholic. Club: Serra (Pasadena) (v.p. 1981-82). Current Work: Application of mathematics and computer science to the understanding of cognition and human consciousness. Subspecialties: Programming languages; Cognition. Home: 4705 Daleridge Rd PO Box 1036 La Canada CA 91011 Office: IBM 3424 Wilshire Blvd Los Angeles CA 90010

BERGSTROM, GARY CARLTON, plant pathologist, educator; b. Chgo., May 12, 1953; s. Robert Carlton and Virginia Mae (Jensen) B. B.S. in Microbiology, Purdue U., 1975, M.S. in Plant Pathology, 1978; Ph.D. in Plant Pathology, U. Ky., 1981. Teaching asst. Purdue U., West Lafayette, Ind., 1975-76, research asst., 1976-77, U. Ky., Lexington, 1978-81; asst. prof. plant pathology Cornell U., Ithaca, N.Y., 1981—; extension pathologist diseases of field crops State of N.Y. Contbr. articles to profl. jours. Mem. Am. Phytopath. Soc., Gamma Sigma Delta. Current Work: Integrated pest management of field crops; interactions of plant pathogenic fungi with insects and other pathogens; physiology of parasitism. Subspecialties: Plant pathology; Integrated pest management. Office: 316 Plant Sci Bldg Cornell U Ithaca NY 14853

BERI, AVINASH CHANDRA, chemical physicist, educator; b. Jullunder, India, Oct. 28, 1949; s. Amrit Lal and Lila (Myer) B. B.Sc. with honors in physics, Delhi U., 1969; M.S. in physics, SUNY, Albany, 1974, Ph.D. in Physics, 1979. Postdoctoral fellow dept. chemistry U. Rochester, 1979-80, research assoc., 1980—. Contbr. articles profl. jours. Mem. Am. Phys. Soc., Am. Assn. Physics Tchrs., Sigma Xi. Current Work: Theory of optical, magnetic and hyperfine properties of ionic solids, theory of laser-stimulated processes at a solid surface. Subspecialties: Laser-induced chemistry; Condensed matter physics. Home: 108 York St Rochester NY 14611 Office: Dept of Chemistry University of Rochester Rochester NY 14627

BERING, EDGAR ANDREW, III, physicist; b. N.Y.C., Jan. 9, 1946; s. Edgar Andrew and Harriet Crocker (Aldrich) B.; m. Stacie Eden Cherniack, June 27, 1971 (div. 1979); m. Barbara Adele Clark, May 11, 1985. B.A., Harvard U., 1967; Ph.D., U. Calif.-Berkeley, 1974. Teaching asst. U. Calif., Berkeley, 1967-69, research assoc., 1969-74; research scientist physics dept. U. Houston, 1974-75, asst. prof., 1975-81, assoc. prof., 1981—; ptnr. I.F.&G. Tech. Cons., Bellaire, Tex., 1984—. Contbr. articles to profl. jours. Pres. Festival Angels, Inc., Houston, 1984, treas., 1983; bd. dirs. Gulf Coast World Affairs Council, Houston, 1982—. Recipient Antarctica Service medal NSF, 1981. Mem. Am. Astron. Soc., Am. Geophys. Union, AAAS, N.Y. Acad. Scis., Sigma Xi. Episcopalian. Current work: Magnetospheric physics, ionospheric physics, auroral physics; astronomy, planetary science, asmospheric electricity. Subspecialty: Aeronomy. Home: 4622 Braeburn Dr Bellaire TX 77401 Office: Dept Physics U Houston University Park Houston TX 77401

BERING, EDGAR ANDREW, JR., neurosurgeon; b. Salt Lake City, Feb. 18, 1917; s. Edgar A. and Ilsa Louise (Billing) B.; m. Harriet Aldrich, Nov. 5, 1944; children: Edgar A., Charles C., Harriet Bering Hoder. A.B., U. Utah, 1927; M.D., Harvard U., 1941. Diplomate: Am. Bd. Neurol. Surgery, Am. Bd. Electroencephalpgraphy. Surg. house officer Boston City Hosp., 1941-42; spl. research assoc. dept. phys. chemistry Harvard U. Med. Sch., 1942; asst. in neurosurgery N.Y. Med. Coll., Flower Fifth Ave Hosp., N.Y.C., 1946-48; Mosely Traveling fellow Harvard U. Med. Sch., Nat. Hosp., London, 1948-49; also clin. clk.; resident in neurosurgery Children's Hosp. and Peter Bent Brigham Hosp., Boston, 1949-50; Harvey Cushing fellow Peter Bent Brigham Hosp., 1950-51, practice medicine specializing in neurosurgery, Boston, 1951-64, Easton, Md., 1973—; dir Neurosurg. Research Lab., Children's Hosp. Med. Center, 1952-63, assoc. neurosurgeon, 1955-64; sr. fellow in poliomyelitis NRC, 1951-52; cons. in surgery of nervous system Lemuel Shattuck Hosp., Jamaica Plain, Mass., 1953-55, sr. cons., 1955-63; clin. assoc. in surgery Harvard U. Med. Sch., 1956-59, asst. clin. prof., 1959-65; attending neurosurgeon West Roxbury (Mass.) VA Hosp., 1954-63; vis. lectr. UCLA Med. Sch., 1958; mem. Conf. on Computer Techniques for Biol. Scientists, M.I.T., 1962; vis. scientist Nat. Inst. Neurol. Disease and Blindness, NIH, 1963-65; spl. asst. to dir. for program analysis Nat. Inst. Neurol. Disease and Stroke, 1965-71, chief spl. programs, 1971-74, spl. cons., 1974—; cons. to adv. com. om coagulation components Commn. on Plasma Fractionation and Related Products, 1954; assoc. clin. prof. neurol. surgery Georgetown U. Med. Sch., Washington, 1968-82; mem. staff Meml. Hosp., Easton, Md., 1974—, vice chief of staff, 1980-83, chief staff, 1983-85; cons. Eastern Shore Hosp. Ctr., Cambridge, Md., 1975—, Johns Hopkins Hosp., Balt., 1975-83. Contbr. numerous articles on neurosurgery to profl. jours. Served to comdr. USN, 1942-46. Mem. Am. Acad. of Neurology, AAAS, Am. Assn. for Neurol. Surgeons, Soc. for Neurosci. (founding mem.), Internat. Soc. for Pediatric Neurosurgery (founding mem.), Soc. of Neurology, Psychiatry and Neurosurgery (Argentina), Chilean Soc. for Neurosurgery and Neurology, D.C. Med. Soc., Neurosurg. Soc. of D.C., Neurosurg. Soc. Am., New Eng. Neurosurg. Soc., N.Y. Acad. Scis., Royal Soc. Medicine (London), Scandinavian Neurosurg. Soc., Research Soc. of Neurosurg. Surgeons (founding mem.), Am. Assn. for Neurol. Surgeons (founding mem. Pediatric sect.), Talbot County Med. Soc., Soc. for Neurosci., Md. Neurosurg. Soc., Sigma Xi. Patentee fibrim foam. Subspecialty: Neurosurgery. Home: Creek House Oxford MD 21654 Office: 4 Talbottown Ln Easton MD 21601

BERKLAND, JAMES OMER, geologist; b. Glendale, Calif., July 31, 1930; s. Joseph Omer and Gertrude Madelyn (Thompson) B.; m. Janice Lark Keirstead, Dec. 19, 1966; children: Krista Lynn, Jay Olin. A.A., Santa Rosa Jr. Coll., 1950; A.B., U. Calif.-Berkeley, 1958; M.S., San Jose State U., 1969; postgrad., U. Calif.-Davis, 1969-72; grad., Bur. Reclamation Soils Sch., Denver, 1967. Registered geologist, cert. engring. geologist, Calif. Phys. sci. technician U.S. Geol. Survey, Menlo Park, Calif., 1958-64; engring. geologist U.S. Bur. Reclamation, Sacramento, 1964-69; cons. geologist, Davis, 1969-72; asst. prof. geology Appalachian State U., Boone, N.C., 1972-73; county geologist Santa Clara County, San Jose, Calif., 1973—; faculty San Jose State U., 1974-75, adj. prof., 1975-76; mem. Earthquake Engring. Research Inst., Berkeley, 1979—, Western Council Engrs., 1980; earthquake watch participant U.S. Geol. Survey/SRI, 1979-82. Advisor Geotech. Adv. Com., San Jose, 1974-76; mem. West Valley Legis. Com., 1980—, Safety Coordinating Com. Santa Clara, 1981—. Doyle scholar, 1949-51. Fellow Geol. Soc. Am.; mem. AAAS, Saber Soc. (co-founder, membership chmn. 1973-75, pres. 1976-77), Assn. Engring. Geologists (vice chmn. sect. 1977-78), Santa Clara County Engring. and Arch. Assn. (v.p. 1981-82), New Weather Observer Soc., Nat. Geog. Soc., Calif. Scholarship Fedn. (life), Peninsula Geol. Soc. (treas. 1978-79), Internat. Platform Assn., West Coast Aquatics Club (pub. relations officer 1981-82), Creekside Homeowners Assn. (treas. 1977-78), San Jose Hist. Mus. Assn., Golden Hills Aquatics Club, San Jose U. Alumni Assn., Sigma Xi. Democrat. Lodges: Sons of Norway, Lions (3d v.p. 1985-86, newsletter editor 1984—). Originator, Earthquake Prediction "Seismic Window Theory", 1974. Current Work: Quaternary geology and geological hazards; lowering risks associated with land development; earthquake history, mitigation and prediction. Subspecialties: Geology; Species interaction. Home: 14927 E Hills Dr San Jose CA 95127 Office: 70 W Hedding St San Jose CA 95110

BERKMAN, HERMAN GERALD, planning educator, consultant information systems; b. Monticello, N.Y., Apr. 29, 1923; s. Isaac and Rebecca (Dorf) B. B.A., NYU, 1945; postgrad. U. of Chgo., 1945-47; M.A., U. Wis., 1954, Ph.D., 1956. Dir. devel. Chgo. Land Commn., 1949-54; prof. econs. U. Wis.-Milw., 1956-61; prof. planning NYU, 1961—; Fulbright prof. geog. info. systems, Massey U., N.Z., 1972; lectr. pub. info. systems, Iceland, 1974; Israel, 1976. Pres., Lake Drive Assn., Stockbridge, Mass., 1985—. Grantee NASA, 1967. Mem. Ops. Research Soc. Am., IEEE, Am. Inst. Cert. Planners. Club: Stockbridge Bowl Assn. (bd. dirs.) (Mass.). Current work: Regional planning, management and development; implications, issues, and impacts of information systems of society and its development; application of computers in management and decision making in state and local government. Subspecialties: Operations research (engineering); Resource management. Home: 100 Bleecker St New York NY 10012 Office: Grad Sch of Pub Adminstrn NYU 40 W 4th St New York NY 10003

BERKSON, HAROLD, biologist; b. Easton, Pa., Oct. 30, 1929; s. Eugene and Lillian (Lukacs) B.; m. Helen Paders Halpern; children—Deborah Ann, Joan Paders. B.A., Rutgers U., 1951; M.A., Amherst Coll., 1953; postgrad. Yale U., 1953-54; Ph.D., Scripps Inst. Oceanography, U. Calif.-San Diego, 1963. Marine biologist USPHS, Portland, Oreg., 1963-66; chief marine ecology sect. Fed. Water Pollution Control Adminstrn., Washington, 1966-69; specialist in environ. policy Library of Congress, Washington, 1969-72; sr. environ. specialist Nuclear Regulatory Commn., Washington, 1972-80, sr. program and planning analyst, br. chief, 1980-83, spl. asst. on environ. policy, 1983—. Contbr. articles to sci. publs., chpts. to books. Mem. Am. Fisheries Soc. (com. chmn. 1968-69), Am. Inst. Fisheries Research Biologists, Washington Acad. Sci., Ecol. Soc. Am., Am. Soc. Limnology and Oceanography, Sigma Xi. Current work: Environmental policy development, environmental impact prediction and mitigation, ecological effects of power generation. Subspecialty: Ecology (environmental science). Office: US Nuclear Regulatory Commn ONRR P-433 Washington DC 20555

BERKWITS, LELAND, physician, engineer; b. Chgo., Jan. 25, 1957; s. Edward and Gloria (Kozin) B. B.S. in Biomed. Engring. magna cum laude, Rensselaer Poly. Inst., 1979; M.S.E.E., U. Ill., 1980; M.D., Northwestern U., 1984. Intern and resident Rehab. Inst. Chgo., 1985—. Contbr. articles to profl. publs. Mem. IEEE, Assn. Computing Machinery, Engring. in Medicine and Biology Soc., Sierra Club, Tau Beta Pi, Eta Kappa Nu. Democrat. Jewish. Current work: Computer applications in clinical medicine; computer simulation and analysis of biological processes; medical image processing; medical information systems. Subspecialties: Physical medicine and rehabilitation; Biomedical engineering. Office: Rehab Inst Chgo 345 E Superior Chicago IL 60611

BERLEKAMP, ELWYN RALPH, computer engineer, educator; b. Dover, Ohio, Sept. 6, 1940; s. Waldo and Loretta (Kimmel) B.; m. Jennifer Wilson, 1966; children: Persis, Bronwen, David. B.S. in Elec. Engring, M.I.T., 1962, M.S., 1962, Ph.D. in Elec. Engring, 1964. Mem. Math. Research Center, Bell Telephone Labs., Murray Hill, N.J., 1967-71; asst. prof. elec. engring. U. Calif., Berkeley, 1964-67, prof. math., elec. engring. and computer sci., 1971—; now pres. Cyclotomics, Inc. Author: Algebraic Coding Theory, 1968, Winning Ways, 1982. Recipient award Eta Kappa Nu, 1972. Fellow IEEE (pres. group on info. theory 1973); mem. Nat. Acad. Engring. Subspecialty: Computer engineering. Office: Cyclotomics 2120 Haste Street Berkeley CA 94704

BERLIN, NATHANIEL ISAAC, physician; b. N.Y.C., July 4, 1920; s. Louis and Gertrude (Sugarman) B.; m. Barbara Ruben, June 14, 1953; children: Deborah Joy, Marc David. B.S., Western Res. U., 1942; M.D., L.I. Coll. Medicine, 1945; Ph.D., U. Calif.-Berkeley, 1949. Intern Kings County Hosp., Bklyn., 1945-46, resident pathologist, 1946-47; Nat. Cancer Inst. postdoctorate research fellow U. Calif., 1948-50, research fellow, 1949-50, research asso., 1950-51, instr., 1951, lectr. and research assoc., 1952-53, lectr., assoc. research med. physicist, 1952-53; Nat. Heart Inst. spl. research fellow Nat. Inst. Med. Research, London, 1953-54; med. officer, analysis br. Effects div. Hdqrs. Armed Forces Spl. Weapons Project, 1954-56; head metabolism service, gen. medicine br. Nat. Cancer Inst., 1956-72, chief gen. medicine br., 1959-61, clin. dir., 1961-71, sci. dir. gen. lab. and clinics, 1969-72, dir. div. cancer biology and diagnosis, 1972-75; dir. Cancer Center, Northwestern U., 1975—, Genevieve B. Teuton prof. medicine, 1975—; vis. scientist Walter Hall Inst. Med. Research, Melbourne, Australia, 1980-81; cons. U.S. Naval Hosp., Bethesda, Md., 1955-65, Armed Forces Spl. Weapons Project, Dept. Def., 1957-59; alumni lectr. Downstate Med. Center, 1966; mem. panel diagnostic applications of radioisotopes in hematology Internat. Com. on Standardization in Hematology, 1964—, chmn., 1974-76; chmn. instnl. rev. bd. Fermi Nat. Lab., 1975—; mem. adv. com. div. blood diseases and resources Nat. Heart, Lung and Blood Diseases Inst., 1975-79; mem. cancer preclin. program project rev. com. Nat. Cancer Inst.; mem. adv. bd. cancer control, State of Ill., 1976—. Editorial adv. bd.: Cancer Letters; mem. editorial bd.: Blood; contbr. articles to med. jours. Mem. med. adv. com. Nat. ARC, 1969-75; trustee Ill. Cancer Council, pres., 1979; bd. dirs. Ill. div. Am. Cancer Soc.; mem. med. adv. bd. Leukemia Research Found., 1976-80; chmn. Leukemia Research Council, 1978-80. Served with AUS., 1943-45; lt. comdr. M.C. USNR, 1954-56; comdr. Res. Recipient Superior Service award HEW; Alumni medal for distinguished service to medicine State U. N.Y. Fellow AAAS, N.Y. Acad. Sci., Internat. Soc. Hematology; mem. Am. Fedn. Clin. Research, Soc. Exptl. Biology and Medicine, Am. Physiol. Soc., Biochem. Soc. (Eng.), Radiation Research Soc., Am. Soc. Hematology (publ. com., pub. issues com.), Assn. Am. Physicians, Am. Soc. Clin. Investigation, Am. Clin. and Climatol. Assn., Western Soc. Clin. Research, Mid-Eastern Soc. Nuclear Medicine (sec.-treas. 1957-60), Am. Soc. Clin. Oncology (legis. liaison com., pub. affairs com.), Am. Soc. Preventive Oncology (pres.), Am. Assn. Cancer Research, Sigma Xi, Alpha Omega Alpha, Zeta Beta Tau, Phi Delta Epsilon. Current Work: Director cancer center. Subspecialties: Cancer research (medicine); Hematology. Home: 1448 N Lake Shore Dr Chicago IL 60611 Office: Cancer Center Northwestern U 303 Chicago Ave Chicago IL 60611

BERLIND, ALLAN, biology educator; b. N.Y.C., Dec. 24, 1942; s. Morris and Ruth (Fischer) B.; m. Wendy Prindle, Aug. 18, 1968; children: Lisa, Andrew. B.A., Swarthmore Coll., 1964; Ph.D., Harvard U., 1969. NIH fellow in zoology U. Calif., Berkeley, 1969-71; asst. prof. dept. biology Wesleyan U., Middletown, Conn., 1971-77, assoc. prof., 1977-84, prof., 1984—; vis. scholar Cambridge (Eng.) U., 1976-77; vis. assoc. prof. U. Hawaii, 1980-81. Mem. Soc. Neurosci., Am. Soc. Zoologists. Current Work: Action of neurohormones on simple neuronal systems. Subspecialties: Neurophysiology; Neuroendocrinology. Office: Dept Biology Wesleyan U Middletown CT 06457

BERLINER, HANS JACK, computer scientist; b. Berlin, Germany, Jan. 27, 1929; came to U.S., 1937, naturalized, 1943; s. Paul and Theodora (Lehfeld) B.; m. Araxie Yacoubian, Aug. 15, 1969. B.A., George Washington U., 1954; Ph.D., Carnegie Mellon U., 1975. Systems analyst U.S. Naval Research Lab., 1954-58; group head systems analysis Martin Co., Denver, 1959-60; adv. systems analyst IBM, Gaithersburg, Md., 1960-69; sr. research scientist Carnegie-Mellon U., Pitts., 1974—. Editorial bd.: Artificial Intelligence, 1976—, Pitman; Research Notes in Artificial Intelligence, 1984—. Served with AUS, 1951-53. Awarded title Internat. Grandmaster Corr. Chess, 1968. Mem. Assn. Computing Machinery, Internat. Joint Conf. Artificial Intelligence, U.S. Chess Fedn., Internat. Computer Chess Assn. Among leading chess players U.S., 1950—, N.Y. State champion, 1953, Southwest Open champion, 1960, So. Open champion, 1949, U.S. Open Corr. Chess champion, 1955, 56, 59, World Corr. Chess champion, 1968-72. Developed 1st computer program to defeat a world champion at his own game (backgammon), 1979; discoverer B* tree search algorithm, 1975, SNAC method of constructing polynomial evaluation functions, 1979. Current Work: Work in artificial intelligence with emphasis on heuristic search, knowledge representation for making judgments, learning. Subspecialty: Artificial intelligence. Home: 657 Ridgefield Ave Pittsburgh PA 15216

BERLINER, MARTHA D., research biologist, educator; b. Antwerp, Belgium, Nov. 18, 1928; came to U.S., 1941; d. A. A. and Frieda (Mandelbaum) Dresner; m. S. Newton Berliner, Sept. 14, 1952; children: Leni Susan, Michael Paul. B.A., Hunter Coll., 1949; M.A., U. Mich., 1950; Ph.D., Columbia U., 1953. Med. microbiologist Lynn Hosp., 1953-60; sr. scientist AVCO Corp., 1958-65; prof. biology Simmons Coll., 1965-82; sr. research assoc. Harvard Sch. Pub. Health, Boston, 1965-74; program mgr., policy analyst NSF, 1980-82; prof., chmn. dept. biology Va. Commonwealth U., Richmond, 1982—; prof. microbiology and immunology, dir. Plant Biotech. Research Lab. Med. Coll. Va., Richmond, 1982—. Contbr. articles to profl. jours.; editorial bd.: Jour. Applied and Environ. Microbiology, 1974-80. Trustee Mary A. Alley Hosp., 1976-80. Fellow Am. Acad. Microbiology, Royal Microscopic Soc. (Oxford). Current Work: Plant tissue culture, plant biotechnology, protoplasts. Subspecialties: Cell and tissue culture; Microbiology. Office: 816 Park Ave Richmond VA 23284

BERLINER, ROBERT WILLIAM, physician, medical educator; b. N.Y.C., Mar. 10, 1915; s. William M. and Anna (Weiner) B.; m. Leah Silver, Dec. 21, 1941; children: Robert William, Alice (Mrs. James L. Hadler), Henry J., Nancy. B.S., Yale, 1936; M.D., Columbia, 1939. Intern Presbyn. Hosp., N.Y.C., 1939-41; resident physician Goldwater Meml. Hosp., N.Y.C., 1942-43, research fellow 3d div. research service, 1943-44, research asst., 1944-47; asst. medicine N.Y.U. Coll. Medicine, N.Y.C., 1943-44, instr., 1944-47; asst. prof. medicine Columbia, research assoc. dept. hosps., N.Y.C., 1947-50; chief lab. kidney and electrolyte metabolism Nat. Heart Inst., NIH, Bethesda, Md., 1950-62, dir. intramural research, 1954-68; dir. lab. and clinics NIH, 1968-69, dep. dir. sci., 1969-73; dean Yale U. Sch. Medicine, New Haven, Conn., 1973-84, prof. physiology and medicine, 1985—, dir. Pew Scholars Program in Biomed. Sci., 1984—; lectr. George Washington U. Sch. Medicine, 1951-73; professorial lectr. Schs. Medicine and Dentistry, Georgetown U., 1964-73. Editorial bd.: Jour. Clin. Investigation, 1954-59, 61-66, Am. Jour. Physiology, 1956-61, Circulation Research, 1958-63, 65-70. Mem. Am. Physiol. Soc. (pres. 1967-68), Soc. Gen. Physiol., Am. Soc. Clin. Investigation (pres. 1959-60), Soc. for Exptl. Biology and Medicine (pres. 1979-81), Am. Acad. Arts and Scis., Washington Acad. Medicine, Philos. Soc. Washington, Assn. Am. Physicians, Nat., Washington acads. scis., Am. Soc. Nephrology (pres. 1968-69), Harvey Soc., Sigma Xi, Alpha Omega Alpha. Subspecialties: Physiology (medicine); Circulatory system. Office: Yale U Sch Medicine New Haven CT 06510

BERLYNE, GEOFFREY MERTON, nephrologist, researcher; b. Manchester, Eng., May 11, 1931; came to U.S., 1976, naturalized, 1981; s. Charles Solomon and Miriam Hannah (Rosenthal) B.; m. Ruth Selbourne, June 7, 1959; children: Jonathan, Benjamin, Suzannah. M.B.Ch.B. with honors, Manchester U., 1954, M.D., 1966. Lectr. U. Manchester, 1961-62, sr. lectr., 1964-68, reader, 1969-70; prof. medicine and life scis. Negev U., Israel, 1970-79; prof. medicine SUNY-Bklyn., 1976—; chief nephrology sect. Brooklyn VA Med. Center, 1976—. Author: Course in Renal Diseases, 1966, Course on Electrolytes and Body Fluids, 1981. Fellow Am. Coll. Physicians, Am. Coll. Nutrition; mem. Japanese Nephrology Soc. (named distinguished nephrologist 1979), Assn. Physicians of G.B., Am. Soc. Trace Element Research (exec. dir.), Am. Fedn. Clin. Research. Current Work: Biology of trace elements; renal disease and physiology; biology of trace elements silicon and aluminum; renal disease and physiology of terminal and preterminal renal failure. Subspecialties: Nephrology; Physiology (medicine). Office: Renal Sect III Bklyn VA Hosp 800 Poly Pl Brooklyn NY 11209

BERMAN, ALAN, physicist; b. Bklyn., Nov. 2, 1925; s. Hyman and Sarah (Levy) B.; m. Charlotte Bernstein, Apr. 28, 1962; children: Julia, Jessica, S. Jonathan, Margaret, James. A.B., Columbia U., 1947, Ph.D., 1952. Research scientist Hudson Labs., Columbia, N.Y.C., 1952-57, assoc. dir., 1957-63, dir., 1963-67; dir. research Naval Research Lab., Washington, 1967-82; dean Sch. Marine and Atmospheric Scis. U. Miami, 1982—; mem. Naval Research Adv. Com., 1982—. Served with AUS, 1944-46. Recipient Superior Civilian Service award Dept. Navy, 1969, Disting. Civilian Service award Dept. Def., 1973, Robert Dexter Conrad award, 1982; named Disting. Sr. Exec. Pres. of U.S., 1980. Fellow Am. Phys. Soc., Acoutical Soc. Am.; mem. Sigma Xi. Subspecialty: Research management. Home: 6645 SW 118th St Miami FL 33156 Office: 4600 Rickenbacker Causeway Miami FL 33149

BERMAN, HERBERT L(AWRENCE), fired heater engineering specialist, consultant; b. Bklyn., Jan. 8., 1931; s. Moses and Bertha (Silverman) B.; m. Pearl M., Mar. 30, 1957; children: Stacey Perri, Marcy Eydie. B.Ch.E., Poly. Inst. Bklyn., 1952; postgrad. in engring, N.Y.U., 1956-57. Lic. profl. engr., N.Y., Tex. Refinery engr. Shell Oil Co., Houston, 1952-53; fired heater proposal engr. Petro-Chem Devel. Co., N.Y.C., 1955-60; sr. fired heater proposal engr. Foster Wheeler Corp., N.Y.C., 1960-62; mgr. fired heater proposal engring. Alcorn Combustion Co., N.Y.C., 1962-72; engring. supr. of heat transfer, energy conservation and cost engring. Caltex Petroleum Corp., Dallas, 1972—. Contbr.: article series on fired heaters to Chem. Engring. mag, 1978. Served with Chem. Corps U.S. Army, 1953-55. Fellow Am. Inst. Chem. Engrs. (organizer and lectr. Fired Heater Engring. continuing edn. course); mem. ASME, Am. Assn. Cost Engrs., Am. Petroleum Inst. (subcom. on heat transfer equipment). U.S. patentee double fired multi-path heater; Can. patentee air cooled fired heater. Current Work: Fired heater engring. Subspecialties: Combustion processes; Chemical engineering. Home: 7310 Blythdale Dr Dallas TX 75248 Office: PO Box 619500 Dallas TX 75261

BERMAN, MARLENE OSCAR, research neuropsychologist, consultant, educator; b. Phila., Nov. 21, 1939; d. Paul and Evelyn (Hess) Oscar; m. Michael Brack Berman, June 22, 1963 (div. Feb. 1980); 1 son, Jesse Michael. B.A., U. Pa., 1961; M.A., Bryn Mawr Coll., 1964; Ph.D., U. Conn., 1968; postgrad., Harvard U., 1968-70. Research assoc., clin. investigator Boston VA Med. Center, 1970-76, research psychologist, 1976—; research assoc. Boston U. Sch. Medicine, 1970-72, asst. prof. dept. neurology, 1972-76, assoc., prof., 1976-81, prof., 1982—; prof. psychiatry, dir. Boston U. Sch. Medicine (Lab. Neuropsychology), 1981—; mem. grant rev. coms. Dept. Health and Human Services; cons. in field. Contbr. articles to profl. jours., chpts. to books. Coordinator Newton (Mass.) Community Schs., 1978-80. Recipient clin. investigator award VA, 1973-76, research scientist devel. awards Nat. Inst. Neurol. Communicative Disorders and Stroke, 1976-81, research scientist devel. awards Nat. Inst. Alcohol Abuse and Alcoholism, 1981—; USPHS grantee, 1964—. Fellow Am. Psychol. Assn. (sec.-treas. div. 6), Mass. Psychol. Assn. (awards com. 1979-80, nominations com. 1982-83); mem. Acad. Aphasia, Soc. for Neurosci., Internat. Neuropsychol. Soc., Psychonomic Soc., Eastern Psychol. Assn., N.Y. Acad. Scis., Huntington's Disease Soc. Am., Sigma Xi (nat. lectr. 1980, 81). Democrat. Jewish. Current Work: Research on mechanisms of human brain function and behavioral abnormalities accompanying brain damage, especially due to alcohol abuse; also research on cerebral laterality and cognitive function in aging. Subspecialties: Neuropsychology; Physiological psychology. Office: Boston VA Med Center 150 S Huntington Ave 14th Floor Boston MA 02130

BERNACKI, RALPH JAMES, pharmacologist, cancer researcher; b. Buffalo, Oct. 9, 1946; s. Roman S. and Emily (Dommer) B.; m. Celeste Agnes, Aug. 16, 1969; children: Rachelle, Gwen. B.S., Rensselaer Poly. Inst., 1968; Ph.D., U. Rochester, 1973. Cancer research scientist I Roswell Park Meml. Inst., Buffalo, from 1972, cancer research scientist V, 1981—; asst. prof. SUNY at Buffalo, 1975-82, assoc. prof., 1982—, dir. pharmacology grad. program, 1982-85. Contbr. numerous articles to profl. jours. Nat. Cancer Inst. grantee, 1977—. Mem. Am. Soc. Pharmacology and Exptl. Therapeutics, Am. Assn. Cancer Research, AAAS, Sigma Xi. Current Work: Design and evaluation of potential antitumor agents. Subspecialties: Pharmacology; Cancer research (medicine). Office: Dept Exptl Therapeutics Roswell Park Meml Inst Buffalo NY 14260

BERNARDIS, LEE LIVIUS, research physiologist, educator; b. Graz, Austria; Sept. 18, 1926; came to U.S., 1961; s. Hannes and Sylvia (von Eyberger) B.; m. Barbara Abbott, May 24, 1958; 1 child, Glenn Allan. Ph.D., U. Graz, 1949, U. Western Ont., Can., 1961. Research assoc. dept. pathology SUNY-Buffalo, 1961-63, research assoc. prof. dept. pathology, 1963-68, research assoc. prof. dept. medicine, 1968-73, research prof., 1973-78, dir. Neuroendo-Neurosci. Lab., dept. surgery, 1973-78; research physiologist VA Med. Ctr., Buffalo, 1978—, dir. Neurovisceral Lab., 1978—. Contbr. articles to profl. jours., chpt. to books. Grantee NSF, 1978-81, NIH, 1971-74. Mem. Am. Physiol. Assn., Am. Inst. Nutrition, Endocrine Soc., Soc. for Neurosci., Internat. Brain Research Orng. Club: Rochester Soaring (N.Y.). Current work: Central nervous elements in food intake, body weight regulation and obesity, body weight set point regulation, metabolic and endocrine changes during set point regulation. Subspecialty: Nutrition (medicine). Office: VA Med Ctr 3495 Bailey Ave Buffalo NY 14226

BERNDT, WILLIAM OSCAR, pharmacologist, toxicologist, university administrator, consultant; b. St. Joseph, Mo., May 11, 1933; s. Oscar Emil and Gertrude Ann (Muthig) B.; m. Bonnie Lou Lampe, Aug. 28, 1954; children: Barbara, Carol, David, Mary, Paul. B.S., Creighton U., 1954; Ph.D., SUNY, Buffalo, 1959. Diplomate Am. Bd. Toxicology. Instr., asst. prof. dept. pharmacology-toxicology Dartmouth Med. Sch., Hanover, N.H., 1959-68, assoc. prof., then prof., 1968-74; prof., chmn. dept. pharmacology-toxicology U. Miss. Med. Center, Jackson, 1974-82; prof. pharmacology, dean for grad. studies and research U. Nebr. Med. Center, Omaha, 1982—, vice chancellor for acad. affairs, 1985—; past mem. pharmacology study sect. NIH; cons. in field. Contbr. chpts. to books, articles to profl. jours. Served to capt. Med. Services Corps U.S. Army, 1962-63. Am. Heart Assn. estblished investigator grantee, 1964-69; recipient fed. grants, 1962—. Mem. Am. Soc. Pharmacology and Exptl. Therapeutics, Soc. Toxicology, Am. Heart Assn., AAAS, Am. Nephrology Soc., Internat. Soc. Study of Xenobiotics. Current Work: Effects of drugs and chemicals on kidney function, specifically studies directed at understanding nephrotoxic events caused by chemicals such as fungal toxins (Mycotoxins)., metals and solvents. Subspecialties: Pharmacology; Nephrology. Office: 5009 Conkling Hall Univ Nebr Med Center 42d and Dewey Ave Omaha NE 86105

BERNE, ROBERT MATTHEW, physiologist, educator; b. Yonkers, N.Y., Apr. 22, 1918; s. Nelson and Julia (Stahl) B.; m. Beth Goldberg, Aug. 18, 1944; children—Julie, Amy, Gordon, Michael. A.B., U. N.C., 1939; M.D., Harvard, 1943; D.Sc., Med. Coll. Ohio, 1973. Intern Mt. Sinai Hosp., N.Y.C., 1943-44, resident, 1946-48; research fellow Western Res. U. Sch. Medicine, Cleve., 1948-49, instr. physiology, 1949-50, sr. instr., 1950-52, asst. prof., 1952-55, assoc. prof., 1955-61, prof., 1961-66; prof., chmn. dept. physiology U. Va. Sch. Medicine, Charlottesville, 1966—; mem. sci. adv. bd. Alfred I. duPont Inst., 1978-82; mem. evaluation com. on post doctoral fellowships in life scis. Nat. Acad. Scis., 1963-65; mem. physiology tng. com. NIH, 1964-65, mem. heart and vascular disease panel, nat. research and devel. demonstration rev. com., 1973-74; mem. tng. com. Nat. Heart Inst., 1966-70; mem. cardio-pulmonary tng. program VA, 1968-71; mem. physiology test Com. Nat. Bd. Med. Examiners, 1969-70; mem. panel on heart and blood vessel diseases, task force Nat. Heart, Lung, and Blood Inst., 1972, mem. heart and lung program project com., 1975-79, mem. hypertension task force, 1976-79; adminstrv. bd., council acad. socs. Assn. Am. Med. Colls., 1975, chmn. council acad. socs., exec. com., 1977-78, disting. service mem., 1982—; Nathanson Meml. lectr. U. So. Calif., 1973; mem. selection com. award for hypertension CIBA Found, 1975-77; Coordinating com. N.Y. State Doctoral Programs rev., 1982—. Author: (with Matthew N. Levy) Cardiovascular Physiology, 1967, 4th edit., 1981; author, editor: textbook Physiology, 1983; Editor: Circulation Research, 1970-75; Sect. editor: Jour. Applied Physiology, 1964-65; mem. editorial bd.: Circulation Research, 1961-70, 75—, Jour. Molecular and Cellular Cardiology, 1969-71, Proc. Soc. Exptl. Biology and Medicine, 1962-64, Am. Jour. Physiology and Applied Physiology, 1964-65; field editor: Pfluegers Achives, 1980—; mem. editorial com.: Annual Rev. of Physiology, 1976—; assoc. editor, 1980-82; editor, 1983—. Trustee Cleve. Area Heart Soc., 1962-65, pres. sci. council, 1964-65; steering com. Circulation Group Physiol. Soc., 1969-71. Served with M.C. AUS, 1944-46. Recipient Carl J. Wiggers award, 1975. Mem. Am. Physiol. Soc. (mem. council 1970-72, mem. finance com. 1966-70, 75—, pres. 1972-73, publs. com. 1976-80, Perkins Meml. Award com. 1977-80), Am. Soc. for Clin. Investigation, Am. Heart Assn. (com. on med. edn. 1963-66, vice chmn. com. on council basic sci., mem. med. adv. bd. council high blood pressure research 1976—, dir. 1979-80, chmn. publs. com. 1981, award of merit 1978, research achievement award 1979), AAAS, Raven Soc. of U. Va., Cardiac Muscle Club, Assn. Chmn. Depts. Physiology (pres. 1970, teaching award 1976), Microcirculatory Soc. (mem. council 1971-72, liaison com. 1973, chmn. Landis award com. 1977-78), Inst. of Medicine, Phi Beta Kappa, Sigma Xi. Current work: Cardiovascular physiology particularly local regulation of blood flow; role of Adenosine. Subspecialties: Physiology (biology); Physiology (medicine). Home: 1851 Wayside Pl Charlottesville VA 22903

BERNEY, CHARLES V., chemical engineering researcher; b. Walla Walla, Wash., July 11, 1931; s. Harry Ulysses and Vera Pauline (Whitney) B.; m. Eleanor Allen Handford, Feb. 10, 1956 (div. Jan. 1967); children—Donald Allen, Susan Elizabeth, Katherine Ann; m. Carole Lynn Smith, July 17, 1976; children—Jennifer Lynn, William Whitney. B.A. in Chemistry, Whitman Coll., 1953; M.S. in Chemistry, MIT, 1954; Ph.D. in Phys. Chemistry, U. Wash., 1962. Research fellow Mellon Inst., Pitts., 1962-65; asst. prof. U. N.H., Durham, 1965-72; sr. research assoc. U.S. Air Force Rocket Propulsion Lab., Edwards, Calif., 1972-73; sr. research assoc. nuclear engring. dept. MIT, Cambridge, 1973-82, dept. chem. engring., 1983—, supr. polymer central facility Ctr. for Materials Sci. and Engring., 1983—; mem. exec. bd. dirs. Nat. Ctr. for Small-Angle Scattering Research, 1979-84. Contbr. articles to profl. jours. Served with U.S. Army, 1954-57, ETO. NSF grantee, 1973, 76, 80, 83. Mem. Am. Phys. Soc., Am. Chem. Soc., Phi Beta Kappa, Sigma Xi. Current work: Characterization of molecular structure of polymeric materials by x-ray and neutron scattering. Subspecialties: Polymer physics; Atomic and molecular physics. Home: 91 Standish Rd Watertown MA 02172 Office: Dept Chem Engring MIT Cambridge MA 02139

BERNEY, STUART ALAN, clin. pharmacologist, pharmacist, educator; b. Albany, N.Y., Aug. 8, 1945; s. Morris and Ester B.; m. Mary Helen, Aug. 28, 1975; children: Elizabeth, Joshua. B.S., Union U., 1969; Ph.D., Vanderbilt U., 1975. Lectr. medicine U. Toronto, Can., 1976-77; research asso. dept. pharmacology Vanderbilt U., 1978, research asst. prof. dept. psychiatry, 1978—. Mem. AAAS, Soc. for Neurosci. Republican. Current Work: Pharm. cons. Subspecialties: Neuropharmacology; Pharmacokinetics. Home: 5562 Ridge Rd Joelton TN 37080 Office: 689 Thompson Ln Nashville TN 37204

BERNHEIM, ROBERT ALLAN, chemistry educator; b. Hackensack, N.J., June 8, 1933; s. Fred and Virginia (White) B.; m. Gloria D. Bernheim, Feb. 14, 1959; 1 dau., Britt; m. Marguerite Yevitz, Aug. 11, 1975; 1 son, Kyle. B.S., Brown U., 1955; M.A., Harvard U., 1957; Ph.D., U. Ill., 1959. Postdoctoral fellow Columbia U., N.Y.C., 1959-61; faculty Pa. State U., University Park, 1961—, now prof. chemistry. NSF fellow, 1967-68; Guggenheim fellow, 1974-75; Joint Inst. for Lab. Astrophysics vis. fellow, 1981-82. Mem. Am. Chem. Soc., Am. Phys. Soc. Current Work: Molecular spectroscopy, Fourier transform spectroscopy, laser spectroscopy. Subspecialty: Physical chemistry. Home: 622 McKee St State College PA 16803 Office: Univ of Pa 152 Davey Lab University Park PA 16802

BERNI, RALPH JOHN, research chemist; b. New Orleans, Nov. 1, 1931; s. Louis J. and Victorie (Parr) B. m. Joan F. McGuire, Oct. 17, 1957; children—Ann L., Ralph H., Erin E. B.S., La. State U., Baton Rouge, 1954; M.S., Tulane U., 1961, Ph.D., 1966. Research chemist So. Regional Research Ctr., Agrl. Research Service USDA, New Orleans, 1955—. Contbr. articles to profl. jours. Patentee in field. Pres. Region 9, Greater New Orleans Sci. and Engring. Fair, New Orleans, 1980-82. Served with M.S.C., U.S. Army, 1955-57. Named Outstanding Civil Servant in Sci. Category, Fed. Bus. Assn. Greater New Orleans, 1976. Fellow Am. Inst. Chemists (pres. 1981—); mem. Am. Chem. Soc. (chmn. 1978), Am. Assn. Textile Chemists (sec. 1984-85), AAAS, Sigma Xi. Roman Catholic. Current work: Cotton fiber, cotton dust, byssinosis, endotoxins, and spectroscopic analysis. Subspecialty: Analytical chemistry. Home: 645 Aris Ave Metairie LA 70005 Office: So Regional Research Ctr PO Box 19687 New Orleans LA 70179

BERNINGER, VIRGINIA WISE, research psychologist, consultant; b. Phila., Oct. 4, 1946; d. Oscar Sharpless and Lucille (Fike) Wise; m. Ronald William Berninger, Aug. 3, 1968. B.A., Elizabethtown Coll., 1967; M.Ed., U. Pitts., 1970; Ph.D., Johns Hopkins U., 1981. Lic. psychologist, Mass. Tchr. Phila. Pub. Schs., 1967-68, Baldwin-Whitehall (Pa.) Pub. Schs., 1969-72, Frederick (Md.) Pub. Schs., 1972-75, Balt. Pub. Schs., 1975-76; research assoc. Children's Hosp., Boston, 1980-83; mem. spl. and sci. staff New Eng. Med. Ctr., Boston, 1983—; instr. psychology Harvard Med. Sch., 1981-83; asst. prof. rehab. medicine Tufts Med. Sch., 1983—, pvt. ednl., pediatric cons., Wellesley, Mass., 1982—; asst. prof. psychology (part-time) Wellesley Coll., 1985; prin. Psychologist Eunice Kennedy Shriver Ctr., 1984-85. Contbr. articles to profl. jours. Md. Psychol. Assn. grantee, 1980. Mem. Am. Psychol. Assn. Current Work: Normal variation and alternative pathways in reading acquisition; cognitive and linguistic development in individuals with severe motor disabilities; microcomputerized procedures for learning written language and diagnosing written language disabilities. Subspecialties: Cognition; Developmental psychology. Home: 6 Northgate Rd Wellesley MA 02181 Office: Box 75K Tufts-New Eng Med Ctr 171 Harrison Ave Boston MA 02111

BERNITSAS, MICHAEL MARINOS, naval architecture and marine engineering educator, offshore engineering researcher; b. Athens, Greece, Jan. 28, 1952; came to U.S., 1975; s. Marinos and Paraskevi (Tsigdemoglou) B.; married. Diploma in mech. engring. and naval architecture, Nat. Tech. U. Athens, 1975; S.M. in Naval Architecture and Marine Engring., MIT, 1977, S.M. in Ocean Engring., 1977, Ph.D. in Ocean Engring., 1979. Research asst. MIT, Cambridge, 1975-79; asst. prof. dept. naval architecture and mech. engring. U. Mich., Ann Arbor, 1979-85, assoc. prof., 1985—; pvt. practice cons., Ann Arbor, 1979—. Author papers, jour. publs. Recipient Disting. Service award Class of 1938E, 1983; faculty research fellow U. Mich., 1980; U. Mich. grantee, 1980-81, Am. Bur. Shipping, 1982-83, Dept. Transp., 1983-85; U. Mich. sea grantee, 1983-84, 85-86. Mem. Am. Acad. Mechanics, Soc. Naval Architects and Marine Engrs. (assoc.), ASME (assoc.), Sigma Xi. Research or work interests: Marine risers, optimal structural redesign, safety of ship towing, mooring systems. Subspecialties: Marine engineering; Ocean engineering. Home: 1120 Bardstown Trail Ann Arbor MI 48105 Office: Dept Naval Architecture and Mech Engring North Campus U Mich 2600 Draper Rd Ann Arbor MI 48109-2145

BERNSTEIN, CAROL, molecular biologist, educator; b. Paterson, N.J., Mar. 20, 1941; d. Benjamin and Mina (Regenbogen) Adelberg; m. Harris Bernstein, June 7, 1962; children: Beryl, Golda, Benjamin. B.S. in Physics, U. Chgo., 1961; M.S. in Biophysics, Yale U., 1963; Ph.D. in Genetics, U. Calif.-Davis, 1967. NIH postdoctoral fellow U. Calif.-Davis, 1967-68; research asso. dept. molecular and med. microbiology Coll. Medicine, U. Ariz., 1968-77, adj. asst. prof., 1977-81, research assoc. prof., 1981—; proposal reviewer NSF; invited speaker Am. Soc. Microbiology Ann. Meeting, 1982. Contbr. articles to profl. jours. NSF grantee, 1975-77, 77-79; Nat. Found. grantee, 1975-76; NIH grantee, 1979—. Mem. Genetics Soc. Am., Biophys. Soc., Am. Soc. Microbiology, Fedn. Am. Scientists, AAUP (pres. U. Ariz. chpt. 1983), Am. Women in Sci. Democrat. Jewish. Current Work: Molecular basis of sex and aging; DNA repair in phage T4; mechanisms of recombinational repair, including enzymes involved and phys. intermediates; recombinationl repair during sex to reverse aging. Subspecialties: Molecular biology; Microbiology. Office: Dept Microbiology and Immunology Coll Medicine U Ariz Tuscon AZ 85724

BERNSTEIN, HARRIS, educator; b. Bklyn., Dec. 12, 1934; s. Benjamin and Hannah (Simonowitz) B.; m. Carol Bernstein, June 7, 1962; children: Beryl, Golda, Benjamin. B.S., Purdue U., 1956; Ph.D., Calif. Inst. Tech., 1961. Postdoctoral fellow Yale U., New Haven, 1961-63; asst. prof. U. Calif., Davis, 1963-68; assoc. prof. U. Ariz, Tucson, 1968-74, prof., 1974—. Contbr. articles to profl. jours. NIH grantee, 1979—. Fellow Am. Acad. Microbiology; mem Am. Soc. Biol. Chemists, Genetics Soc. Am., AAAS. Current Work: Mechanism of DNA replication, DNA repair, recombination and mutation; evolution of sexual reproduction; DNA damage as basis of aging. Subspecialties: Molecular biology; Genetics and genetic engineering (biology). Home: 2639 E 4th St Tucson AZ 85716 Office: Dept Microbiology and Immunology Coll Medicine U Ariz Tucson AZ 85724

BERNSTEIN, I. LEONARD, physician, educator; b. Jersey City, Feb. 17, 1924; s. Sydney and Jean B.; m. Miriam Goldman, Aug. 29, 1948; children—David, Susan, Ellen, Jonathan. Student, St. John's U., Bklyn., 1940-41, George Washington U., 1941-43; M.D., U. Cin., 1949. Diplomate: Am. Bd. Internal Medicine, Am. Bd. Allergy and Clin. Immunology. Intern Cin. Gen. Hosp., 1949-50; jr. resident in internal medicine Jewish Hosp., Cin., 1950-51; resident in chest diseases Bellevue Hosp., N.Y.C., 1953-55; fellow in allergy and immunology Northwestern U. Med. Sch., 1955-56; mem. faculty U. Cin. Med. Center, 1956—, clin. prof. medicine, 1971—, dir. allergy clinic, 1971—, dir. allergy tng. program, 1958—; dir. U. Cin. Med. Center (Allergy Research Lab.), 1958—; now dir. Asthma and Allergy Ctr., Deaconess Hosp.; attending physician Cin. Gen., VA, Jewish hosps. Contbr. articles to med. publs. Served with AUS, 1943-45; as officer M.C. USAF, 1951-53. Grantee Nat. Inst. Allergy and Infectious Disease, 1958—. Fellow Am. Acad. Allergy (pres. 1982—), ACP; mem. Am. Assn. Immunologists, AAAS, Central Soc. Clin. Research, Am. Thoracic Soc., Soc. Occupational and Environ. Health. Current Work: Occupational asthma; food allergy; respiratory allergy due to dust, mites and algae. Subspecialties: Allergy; Immunology (medicine). Home: 3117 Esther Dr Cincinnati OH 45213 Office: 8464 Winton Rd Cincinnati OH 45231

BERNSTEIN, ISADORE ABRAHAM, biochemistry educator, researcher; b. Clarksburg, W.Va., Dec 23, 1919; s. William and Rosa B.; m. Claire Bernstein, Sept. 8, 1942; children: Lynne, Amy. A.B., Johns Hopkins U., 1941; Ph.D., Western Res. U., 1952. Research assoc. Case Western Res. U., Cleve., 1951-52, sr. instr., 1952-53; research assoc. Inst. Indsl. Health, U. Mich., Ann Arbor, 1953-56, 59-70, instr. biol. chemistry, 1954-57, asst. prof., 1957-61, assoc. prof., 1961-68, prof. dept. dermatology, 1968-71, assoc. prof. dept. indsl. health, 1961-67, prof., 1967-70, prof. dept. biochemistry, 1971—, prof. dept. environ. and indsl. health, 1970—; assoc. dir. research Inst. Environ. and Indsl. Health, 1978—; vis. prof. Osaka (Japan) U., 1963-64, Rockefeller U., N.Y.C., 1977-78; vis. scientist Hebrew U. Jerusalem, 1978. Contbr. numerous articles to sci. jours., chpts. to books; author 4 sci. books. Served to capt. U.S. Army, 1941-46. Decorated Bronze Star; co-recipient Internat. Meml. award for Psoriasis, 1959; recipient Stephen Rothman Meml. award Soc. Investigative Dermatology, 1981, Disting. Faculty Achievement award U. Mich., 1981. Fellow AAAS; mem. Am. Soc. Biol. Chemists, Am. Chem. Soc., Am. Soc. Microbiology, Soc. Investigative Dermatology, Am. Soc. Cell Biology, Soc. Toxicology, Am. Pub. Health Assn., Radiation Research Soc., Am. Inst. Biol. Sci., N.Y. Acad. Scis., Sigma Xi. Current Work: Environmental toxicology, cutaneous biochemistry. Subspecialties: Biochemistry (medicine); Toxicology (medicine). Office: U Mich Ann Arbor MI 48109

BERNSTEIN, JERALD J(ACK), neuroscientist; b. Bklyn., Mar. 30, 1934; married; children: Steven, David. B.S., Hunter Coll., 1955; M.S., U. Mich., 1957, Ph.D., 1959. USPHS fellow NIH, Bethesda, Md., 1959; research biologist Lab. Neuroanat. Sci., Nat. Inst Neurol and Communicative Diseases and Stroke, NIH, Bethesda, 1960 -65; asst. prof. anatomy U. Fla. Coll. Medicine, 1965-69, assoc. prof. anat. sci., 1969-70, assoc. prof. neurosci., 1970-76, prof. neurosci. and ophthalmology, 1976-80; prof. neurosurgery and physiology George Washington U. Sch. Medicine, 1980—; chief Lab. Central Nevous System Injury and Regeneration, VA Med. Center, Washington, 1980—; vis. prof. anatomy Hadassah Med. Sch., Jerusalem, 1978; career research scientist VA, 1980. Author numerous articles, abstracts, and book chpts. on spinal cord regeneration. NIH grantee, 1965-82; VA grantee, 1980—; Office Naval Research grantee, 1982. Mem. Soc. Neurosci., Am. Physiol. Soc., Am. Assn. Anatomists, AAAS, Cajal Club. Current Work: Spinal cord injury and regeneration. Subspecialties: Regeneration; Neurobiology.

BERNSTEIN, JERROLD, physician; b. Montreal, Que., Dec. 26, 1936; s. David and Yetta Jacqueline (Hertz) B.; m. Kathleen Marlyn Barber, May 9, 1971; children: Kevin, Patrick, Jennifer. B.Sc., McGill U., 1958, M.D., C.M., 1963; Ph.D., U. Ill., 1967. Pharmacologist, group leader Merck Frosst Labs., Kirkland, Que., 1969-74; dir. clin. investigation Smith Kline Can., St. Laurent, 1974-77; head clin. investigation Ciba Geigy Can., Dorval, 1977-79; sr. dir. anti inflammatory/endocrine sect., Summit, N.J., 1979-82; dir. clin. investigation Lederle Labs., Pearl River, N.Y., 1982-84, dir. internat. clin. research, 1984—. Vice pres. long-range planning, dir. Mixed Media art supply house, Toronto, 1980-84. Contbr. articles to profl. jours. Mem. Soc. Clin. Trials, Am. Chem. Soc., Am. Epilepsy Soc., Can. Assn. Clin. Pharmacology, Internat. Assn. Study Pain, N.Y. Acad. Scis., Soc. Neurosci. Current Work: Clinical trials outside of U.S. Subspecialties: Pharmacology; Neurophysiology. Home: 62 Stanford Ave West Orange NJ 07052 Office: Med Research Div Lederle Labs Pearl River NY 10965

BERNSTEIN, JOEL EDWARD, dermatopharmacologist, educator; b. Chgo., Apr. 8, 1943; s. Jacob and Emma (Roshal) B.; m. Carole Nachman, Sept. 20, 1964; children—Jeffrey, David, Rebecca. B.A., Carleton Coll., 1964; M.D., U. Chgo., 1969. Diplomate Am. Bd. Dermatology. Vice pres. med. affairs Plough, Inc., Memphis, 1973-75; assoc. dir. clin. research Abbott Labs., North Chicago, Ill., 1975-77; sr. clin. fellow U. Chgo. Prizker Sch. Medicine, 1977-79, asst. prof., 1979-82; assoc. prof., dir. sect. dermatopharmacology Northwestern U. Med. Sch., Chgo., 1982-83; pres. Jaye Boern Labs., Northbrook, Ill., 1983—; dir. lab. dermatopharmacology U. Chgo. Hosps., 1979-82. Contbr. articles to profl. jours. and books. Editor various books on dermatology or dermatopharmacology. Mem. Am. Acad. Dermatology, Soc. Investigative Dermatology, Am. Fed. Clin. Research, Am. Soc. Clin. Pharmacology and Therapeutics, Am. Acad. Clin. Pharmacology, Phi Beta Kappa, Sigma Xi, Alpha Omega Alpha. Current work: Development of new pharmacological approaches for treatment of cutaneous diseases. Subspecialties: Dermatology; Pharmacology. Office: Jaye-Boern Labs 425 Huehl Rd Unit 10 Northbrook IL 60062

BERNSTEIN, JOEL M., otolaryngologist; b. Buffalo, July 7, 1935; s. Harold and Blanche (Miller) B.; m. Sheila Jane Jaffe, Sept. 2, 1959; children—David, Jonathan, James. B.A., Harvard U., 1957; M.D., SUNY-Buffalo, 1961, M.A., 1975, Ph.D., 1979. Diplomate Am. Bd. Otolaryngology. Intern, Buffalo Gen. Hosp., 1961-62; resident in Buffalo VA Hosp., 1962-63, Mass. Eye and Ear Infirmary, Boston, 1963-66; teaching fellow Harvard Med. Sch., 1966; attending otolaryngologist Children's Hosp. Buffalo, 1969; clin. assoc. surgery SUNY-Buffalo, 1969-76, clin. asst. prof. otolaryngology, after 1976; cons. ear, nose and throat Mt. View Hosp., Lockport, N.Y., 1971; attending physician otorhinolaryngology Vets. Hosp., Buffalo, 1970; adj. prof. State U. Coll. Buffalo, 1972; cons. clin. staff Roswell Pk. Meml. Inst., Buffalo, 1973; med. staff otolaryngology DeGraff Meml. Hosp, North Tonawanda, N.Y., 1977; clin. asst. prof. otolaryngology and pediatrics Children's Hosp. Buffalo, 1979. Contbr. articles to profl. jours. Recipient Surg. prize SUNY, 1961, Gibson Anatomical Soc. award, 1958; cert. of merit Am. Acad. Ophthalmology and Otology, Mass. Eye and Ear Infirmary, 1966, Service award, 1978; 3rd Internat. award of merit Belgium-Dutch Soc. Allergy and Otolaryngology, 1984; Research Found. grantee, 1972. Fellow Am. Acad. Ophthalmology and Otolaryngology, ACS; mem. Erie County Med. Assn., Med. Soc. State N.Y., AMA, Pan Am. Med. Assn., Am. Audiology Soc., Am. Assn. Clin. Immunology and Allergy (fellow). Subspecialty: Otorhinolaryngology. Office: 910 Maple Rd Williamsville NY 14221

BERNSTEIN, RICHARD BARRY, phys. chemist, educator; b. N.Y.C., Oct. 31, 1923; s. Simon and Stella (Grossman) B.; m. Norma B. Olivier, Dec. 17, 1948; children—Neil David, Minda Dianne, Beth Anne, Julie Lynn. A.B., Columbia, 1943, M.A., 1944, Ph.D., 1948. Mem. research staff SAM Lab., Columbia, 1942-46; asst. prof. chemistry Ill. Inst. Tech., 1948-53, Kilpatrick lectr., 1974; from asst. prof. to prof. chemistry U. Mich., 1953-63; prof. chemistry U. Wis., 1963-66, W.W. Daniells prof., 1966-73, W.T. Doherty prof. chemistry, prof. physics U. Tex., Austin, 1973-77; Higgins prof. natural sci. and chemistry Columbia U., 1977—, chmn. chemistry dept., 1979—; Reilly Centennial lectr. and award honor U. Notre Dame, 1965; Mack lectr. Ohio State U., 1966; FMC lectr. Princeton, 1966; N.Y. State distinguished lectr. Yeshiva U., 1969; Falk-Plaut lectr. Columbia U., 1971; Dreyfus lectr. U. Kans., 1973; vis. prof. Hebrew U., Jerusalem, 1973, Pa. State U., 1974; del. Pontifical Acad. Conf., 1966; mem. adv. bds. chemistry NRC, 1965-69; adv. bd. Army Research Office, 1967-69; Sloan fellow, 1956-60; sr. postdoctoral fellow NSF, 1960-61; Mem. program com. A.P. Sloan Found., 1971-76; mem. ednl. adv. bd. J.S. Guggenheim Found., 1978—; chmn. Office Chemistry and Chem. Tech., NRC, Nat. Acad. Scis., 1974-79. Author books papers in area of chem. physics; editor Chem. Physics Letters, 1978—. Served with C.E. AUS, 1942-44. Fellow Am. Phys. Soc. (chmn. div. chem. physics 1967-68), Am. Acad. Arts and Scis., AAAS; mem. Am. Chem. Soc. (chmn. div. phys. chemistry 1965-66, chmn. div. phys. chemistry Nebr. lectr. award, 1976, Peter Debye award in phys. chemistry, 1981), Nat. Acad. Scis., Sigma Xi. Subspecialty: Physical chemistry. Home: 460 Riverside Dr New York NY 10027 Office: Havemeyer Hall Columbia U New York NY 10027

BERRY, EDWIN X, atmospheric physical scientist, research and development company executive; b. San Francisco, June 2, 1935; s. Edwin F. and Frances A. B.; m. Valerie Stella, Oct. 27, 1973. B.S.E.E., Calif. Inst. Tech., 1957; M.A. in Physics, Dartmouth Coll., 1960; Ph.D. in Atmospheric Physics, U. Nev., Reno, 1965. Research assoc. U. Nev., 1961-72; program mgr. NSF, Washington, 1972-73, Burlingame, Calif., 1973-75; pres. Atmospheric Research & Tech., Inc., Sacramento, 1975—. Contbr. articles, primarily in atmospheric physics, to profl. jours. Mem. Am. Meterol. Soc., Am. Wind Energy Assn. Patentee vibration sensitive valve operating apparatus, vibration/temperature sensitive valve operating apparatus; designer ART800, low powered instrumentation microcomputer, 1981-82. Current Work: Devel. battery-powered computers; wind energy evaluation. Subspecialties: Meteorologic instrumentation; Wind power. Office: 4441 Auburn Blvd Suite O Sacramento CA 95841

BERRY, GUY CURTIS, educator; b. Greene County, Ill., May 11, 1935; s. Charles Curtis and Wilma Francis (Wickes) B.; m. Marilyn Jane Montooth, Jan. 9, 1957; children: Susan Jane, Sandra Jean, Scott Curtis. B.S., U. Mich., 1957, M.S., 1958, Ph.D., 1960. Mellon Inst. fellow, 1960-64, sr. fellow, 1964-73; assoc. prof. Carnegie-Mellon U., Pitts., 1966-73, prof. chemistry and polymer sci., 1973—, acting dean Coll. Sci., 1981-82, acting head dept. chemistry, 1983-84; vis. prof. Tokyo U., 1973, Colo. State U., 1979, Kyoto U., 1983. Contbr. articles to sci. jours. Mem. Am. Chem. Soc., Rheology Soc., AAAS. Current Work: Rheology and light scattering on polymers and their solutions, properties of mesogenic polymers, branched chains, composites. Subspecialties: Polymer chemistry; Polymer physics. Office: 4400 5th Ave Pittsburgh PA 15213

BERRY, JAMES FREDERICK, biology educator, ecology consultant; b. Washington, Dec. 22, 1947; s. James F. and Joyce (Drummond) B.; m. Cynthia Marie Valukas, July 31, 1982. B.S., Fla. State U., 1970, M.S., 1973; Ph.D., U. Utah, 1978. Chmist Fla. Dept. Agr., Tallahassee, 1973-74; teaching fellow U. Utah, Salt Lake City, 1974-78; asst. prof. biology Elmhurst (Ill.) Coll., 1978—; project leader ENCAP, Inc., DeKalb, Ill., 1981-82; research assoc. Carnegie Mus. Natural History, Pitts., 1983—. U.S. Office Endangered Species grantee, 1982. Mem. Am. Soc. Zoologists, Soc. Systematic Biology, Soc. Study of Evolution, Am. Soc. Ichthyologists and Herpetologists, Soc. Study of Amphibians and Reptiles. Democrat. Roman Catholic. Current Work: Evolutionary biology, ecology and systematics of reptiles; particularly turtles of the family Kinosternidae. Subspecialties: Population biology; Ecology (environmental science). Office: Dept Biology Elmhurst Coll 190 Prospect St Elmhurst IL 60126

BERRY, LEE ALLEN, physicist; b. La Junta, Colo., Mar. 18, 1945; s. Harold Lee and Jewel Bertha (Loomis) B.; m. Linda Carol Goff, Jan. 29, 1966; children—Diane Lee, David Allen. B.A., U. Calif.-Riverside, 1966, M.A., 1969, Ph.D., 1970. Research physicist Oak Ridge Nat. Lab., 1970-74, Tokamak sect. head, 1974-77, fusion program dir., 1977-80, dir. Elmo Bumpy Torus program, 1980-84, asst. div. dir. for devel. and tech., 1984—. Recipient Disting. Assoc. award Dept. Energy, 1984. Fellow Am. Phys. Soc.; mem. Phi Beta Kappa, Pi Mu Epsilon. Current work: Magnetic fusion physics and technology. Subspecialty: Fusion. Office: Bldg 9201-2 PO Box Y Oak Ridge National Laboratory Oak Ridge TN 37831

BERRY, MAURICE ROBERT, JR., mechanical engineer; b. Portsmouth, Va., Sept. 10, 1943; s. Maurice R. and Vivian (Harris) B.; m. Diane Lassiter, July 17, 1965; children—Dean Ross, Brian Robert. B.S.M.E., Va. Poly. Inst. and State U., 1966, M.S., 1968, Ph.D., 1970. Aerospace technologist NASA, Langley, Va., 1966; instr. Va. Poly. Inst. and State U., Blacksburg, 1971; food engring. project leader FDA, Cin., 1971—; asst. prof. U. Cin., 1974-81. Contbr. articles to profl. jours. Recipient Commendable Service award FDA, 1984. Mem. ASME, Inst. Food Technologists. Baptist. Current work: Research on sterilization and nutritional quality of foods in cans or unique containers for public health protection. Subspecialty: Food science and technology. Home: 4269 Pinetree Ln Cincinnati OH 45245 Office: Food & Drug Administration 1090 Tusculum Ave Cincinnati OH 45226

BERRY, MICHAEL JAMES, physical chemist; b. Chgo., July 17, 1947; s. Bernie Milton and Irene Barbara (Lentz) B.; m. Julianne Catherine Elward, Apr. 28, 1967; children: Michael James II, Jennifer Anne; m. Patricia Gale Hackerman, July 7, 1984. B.S., U. Mich., Ann Arbor, 1967; Ph.D., U. Calif., Berkeley, 1970. Asst. prof. chemistry U. Wis., Madison, 1970-75, assoc. prof., 1975-76; mgr. proton chem. dept. Allied Chem. Corp., Morristown, N.J.,

1976-79; Robert A. Welch prof. chemistry, dir. Rice Quantum Inst., Rice U., Houston, 1979—; pres. Antropix Corp., Houston, 1982—; acting dir. Laser Applications Research Ctr., Houston Area Research Ctr., 1984—. Contbr. articles to profl. jours. Named to Esquire Register of Best of New Generation: Men and Women under 40 Who are Changing Am., 1984; NSF grantee, 1975—; Air Force Office Sci. Research, 1972-76, 85—; grantee Office Naval Research, 1972-74; recipient Fresenius award Phi Lambda Upsilon, 1982; Alfred P. Sloan Found. research fellow, 1975-76; Camille and Henry Dreyfus Found. fellow, 1974-76; John Simon Guggenheim Meml. Found. fellow, 1981-82. Mem. Am. Chem. Soc. (Pure chemistry award 1983), Am. Phys. Soc., Am. Soc. Photobiology, Optical Soc. Am. Current Work: Chemical, medical and materials science applications of lasers, research and devel. in laser application, anti-entropic applications of sci. and tech. Subspecialties: Laser-induced chemistry; Laser photochemistry. Home: 5627 Innsbruck St Bellaire TX 77401 Office: Dept Chemistry Rice U PO Box 1892 Houston TX 77251

BERRY, RICHARD STEPHEN, chemist; b. Denver, Apr. 9, 1931; s. Morris and Ethel (Alpert) B.; m. Carla Lamport Friedman, Sept. 4, 1955; children—Andrea, Denise, Eric. A.B., Harvard U., 1952, A.M., 1954, Ph.D., 1956. Instr. Harvard U., 1956-57, U. Mich., 1957-60; asst. prof. Yale U., 1960-64; assoc. prof. chemistry U. Chgo., 1964-67, prof. chemistry, 1967—; Arthur D. Little prof. MIT, 1968; Phillips lectr. Haverford Coll., 1968; cons. Avco-Everett Research Labs., 1964-83, Argonne Nat. Lab., 1976—, Oak Ridge Nat. Labs., 1978-81, Los Alamos Sci. Lab., 1975—; mem. adv. com. theory; vis. prof. U. Copenhagen, 1967, 79; mem. adv. panel for chemistry NSF, 1971-73; mem. rev. com. radiol. and environ. research div. Argonne Nat. Lab., 1970-76; mem. evaluation panel measures for air quality Nat. Bur. Standards; chmn. numerical data adv. bd. NRC; mem. steering com. panel on environ. monitoring, mem. com. on atomic and molecular sci., com. on chem. scis. Nat. Acad. Scis.-NRC; mem. adv. panel on health of sci. and tech. enterprise, mem. adv. panel on nat. labs. Office Tech. Assessment; mem. adv. bd. Environ. Health Resource Center; mem. vis. com. div. applied physics Harvard U., 1977-82; mem. adv. panel dept. chemistry Princeton U., 1980-83; Hinshewood lectr. Oxford U., 1980; prof. associé U. Paris, 1979-80; Japan Soc. Promotion of Sci. Fellow, 1984. Co-author: The Total Social Cost of Fossil and Nuclear Power, 1979; co-author: Physical Chemistry, 1980, TOSCA, The Social Cost of Coal and Nuclear Power, 1979; assoc. editor Jour. Chem. Physics, 1971-74, Accounts Chem. Research, 1975—; Revs. Modern Physics, 1983—; bd. dirs. Bull. Atomic Scientists, 1973-83; adv. editor: Resouces and Energy; contbr. articles to profl. jours. Recipient MacArthur Prize fellow, 1983; Alfred P. Sloan fellow, 1962-66; Guggenheim fellow, 1972-73. Fellow Am. Phys. Soc., Am. Acad. Arts and Scis.; mem. Am. Chem. Soc., Nat. Acad. Scis., Royal Danish Acad. Arts and Letters (fgn.), Sigma Xi (nat. lectr. 1976, 77). Current work: Electron correlation; nonrigid molecules, phase changes, especially in finite systems; photoionization; thermodynamics. Subspecialties: Physical chemistry; Atomic and molecular physics. Home: 5317 S University Ave Chicago IL 60615

BERRY, ROBERT WALTER, physical chemist, administrator; b. Atlanta, Oct. 27, 1928; s. Milton Donaldson and Lannes (Morgan) B.; m. Colleen Alice Rudd, June 19, 1954; children—Elizabeth Alice and Robert Walter, Jr. B.S., Clemson U., 1950; Ph.D., Mich. State U., 1956. Mem. tech staff AT&T Bell Labs., Murray Hill, N.J., 1956-61, tech. supr., 1961-63, Allentown, Pa., 1964-66, dept. head, Indpls., 1967-70, Allentown, 1970—; dir. Thin Film div. A.V.S. Author, editor: Thin Film Technologoy, 1968. Inventor in field. Deacon, First Presbyterian Church, Bethlehem, Pa., 1976-78, elder, 1980-83; dir. Monocacy Creek Watershed Assn., Bethlehem, 1978—; mem. Bethlehem Environ. Commn., 1981-85. Served to 1st lt. U.S. Army, 1951-53. Mem. Am. Vacuum Soc., Optical Soc. Am., IEEE, Sigma Xi. Republican. Current work: Integrated optic devices and materials. Subspecialties: Physical chemistry; Fiber optics. Home: 425 Rockhill Circle Bethlehem PA 18017 Office: AT&T Bell Labs 555 Union Blvd Allentown PA 18103

BERRY, WILLIAM BENJAMIN NEWELL, oceanographer, museum director; b. Boston, Sept. 1,1931; s. John King and Margaret Elizabeth (Newell) B.; m. Suzanne Foster Spaulding, June 10, 1961; 1 child, Bradford Brown. A.B., Harvard U., 1953, A.M., 1955; Ph.D., Yale U., 1957. Asst. prof. geology U. Houston, 1957-58; asst. prof. to prof. paleontology U. Calif.-Berkeley, 1958—; curator Mus. of Paleontology U. Calif.-Berkeley, 1960-75, dir., 1975—, chmn. dept. paleontology, 1975—; cons. U.S. Geol. Survey. Author: Growth of a Prehistoric Time Scale, 1968; contbr. numerous articles on stratigraphic and paleontol. subjects to profl. jours.; editor publs. in geol. scis. Guggenheim Found. fellow, 1966-67. Fellow Calif. Acad. Sci; mem. Paleontol. Soc., Geol. Soc. Norway, Internat. Platform Assn., Explorers Club. Current Work: Research currently involves investigation of anoxic ocean waters and sediment. Role of organics in formation of metal sulfides forming under anoxic conditions is one aspect of current research. Another is those conditions under which life may have developed in early stages of development of oceans—a time when oceans were anoxic save for surface layers. Subspecialties: Paleo oceanography; Ocean energy conversion. Home: 1366 Summit Rd Berkeley CA 94708 Office: Dept Paleontology U Calif Berkeley CA 94720

BERRY, WILLIAM BERNARD, electrical engineering educator; b. Shelby, Ohio, July 23, 1931; s. Dorwin and Norma (Laux) B.; m. Lois Georgia Langford, June 25, 1955; children: Elizabeth Mara, William Joseph, Mary Suzanne, Thomas James. B.S.E.E., U. Notre Dame, 1953, M.S.E.E., 1957; Ph.D., Purdue U., 1963. Registered profl. engr., Ind. With Goodyear Atomic Corp., Portsmouth, Ohio, 1953; faculty Marquette U., Milw., 1957-61, Purdue U., West Lafayette, Ind., 1961-63; faculty U. Notre Dame, Ind., 1963—, prof. elec. engring., 1970—, asst. dean for research and grad. study, 1974-85, program mgr. cold weather transit tech., 1980—. Contbr. articles to profl. jours. Active Boy Scouts Am., 1967-72; instl. dir. United Way, 1977. Served with U.S. Army, 1953-55. ASEE/NASA summer faculty fellow, 1965, 66; NRS postdoctoral asso., 1972-73. Mem. Am. Soc. Engring. Edn., IEEE, Electrochem. Soc., Sigma Xi, Sigma Pi Sigma, Eta Kappa Nu. Roman Catholic. Current Work: Electronic properties of materials, electron process in thin films, photovoltaics, thermoelectricity. Subspecialties: Electronic materials; Solar energy. Home: 402 E Pokagon St South Bend IN 46617 Office: Coll of Engring U Notre Dame Notre Dame IN 46556

BERS, LIPMAN, mathematician, educator; b. Riga, Latvia, May 22, 1914; came to U.S., 1940, naturalized, 1949; s. Isaac and Bertha (Weinberg) B.; m. Mary Kagan, May 15, 1938; children: Ruth, Victor. Dr. Rerum Naturalium, U. Prague, 1938; D.Sc. (hon.) SUNY-Stony Brook, 1984. Research instr. Brown U., 1942-45; asst. prof., asso. prof. Syracuse U., 1945-49; mem. Inst. Advanced Study, 1948-50; prof. N.Y. U., 1950-64, chmn. grad. dept. math., 1959-64; prof. Columbia U., 1964-84, chmn. dept. math., 1972-75, Davies prof. math., 1973-82, Davies prof. math. emeritus, 1982, spl. prof., 1982-84; vis. prof. CUNY Grad. Ctr., 1984—. Vis. prof. Stanford U., summer 1955; vis. Miller Research prof. U. Calif. at Berkeley, 1968; chmn. Com. Support on Research on Math. Scis., Nat. Acad. Scis.-NRC, 1966-68; chmn. div. math. scis. NRC, 1969-71; chmn. U.S. Nat. Com. for Math., 1977-81. Author math. books.; Contbr. articles to math. jours. Recipient N.Y. Mayor's award of sci. and tech., 1985; Fulbright fellow, 1959-60; Guggenheim fellow, 1959-60, 79. Fellow Am. Acad. Arts and Scis., AAAS (chmn. math. sect. 1973, 83), Am. Philos. Soc.; mem. Am. Math. Soc. (v.p. 1963-65, Steele prize 1975, pres. 1975-77), Fedn. Am. Scientists (council 1977-79, sponsor 1980—), N.Y. Acad. Scis. (hon. life mem.), London Math. Soc. (hon.), Finnish Acad. Sci. and Letters, Nat. Acad. Scis. (chmn. math. sect. 1967-70, chmn. com. on human rights 1979-84). Current Work: Riemann surfaces, quasicon formal maps, kleinan groups. Home: 111 Hunter Ave New Rochelle NY 10801 Office: Dept Math Columbia U New York NY 10027

BERSOHN, RICHARD, chemist. Prof. dept. chemistry Columbia U., N.Y.C. Recipient Broida prize in atomic and molecular spectroscopy Am. Phys. Soc., 1985. Office: Columbia U Dept Chemistry New York NY 10027

BERSON, JEROME ABRAHAM, chemistry educator; b. Sanford, Fla., May 10, 1924; s. Joseph and Rebecca (Bernicker) B.; m. Bella Zevitovsky, June 30, 1946; children: Ruth, David, Jonathan. B.S. cum laude, Coll. City N.Y., 1944; M.A., Columbia U., 1947; Ph.D., 1949; Ph.D. NRC postdoctoral fellow, Harvard U., 1949-50. Asst. chemist Hoffmann-LaRoche, Inc., Nutley, N.J., 1944; asst. prof. U. So. Calif., 1950-53, asso. prof., 1953-58, prof., 1958-63, U. Wis., 1963-69, Yale U., 1969-79, Irénée du Pont prof., 1979—, chmn. dept. chemistry, 1971-74, dir. div. phys. sci. and engring., 1983—; vis. prof. U. Calif., U. Cologne, U. Western, Ont.; Fairchild Distinguished scholar Calif. Inst. Tech.; cons. Riker Labs., Goodyear Tire & Rubber Co., Am. Cyanamid Co., IBM; mem. adv. panel for chemistry NSF; mem. medicinal chemistry study sect. NIH, 1969-73. Mem. editorial adv. bd.: Jour. Organic Chemistry, 1961-65, Accounts of Chemical Research, 1971-77, Nouveau Journal de Chimie, 1977—, Chem. Revs., 1980-83; contbr. articles to profl. jours. Served with AUS, 1944-46. CBI. Recipient Alexander von Humboldt award, 1980; John Simon Guggenheim fellow, 1980. Fellow Am. Acad. Arts and Scis.; mem. Nat. Acad. Scis., Am. Chem. Soc. (Calif. sect. award 1963, James Flack Norris award 1978, Nichols medal 1985, chmn. div. organic chemistry 1971), Chem. Soc. London, Alumni Assn. of CCNY (Townsend Harris medal 1984), Phi Beta Kappa, Sigma Xi, Phi Lambda Upsilon. Current Work: Reaction mechanism; synthesis of theoretically significant molecules; characterization of reactive intemediates; high-spin systems. Subspecialty: Organic chemistry. Home: 45 Bayberry Rd Hamden CT 06517 Office: Dept Chemistry Yale U PO Box 6666 New Haven CT 06511

BERTALANFFY, FELIX DIONYSIUS, anatomy educator; b. Vienna, Austria, Feb. 20, 1926; emigrated to Can., 1949, naturalized, 1955; s. Ludwig von and Maria (Bauer) B.; m. Gisele D. Lavimodiere, Jan. 20, 1954. Ph.D., Med. Sch., Vienna, 1945; M.Sc., McGill U., 1951, Ph.D., 1954. Asst. prof. anatomy U. Man., Winnipeg, 1955-58, assoc. prof., 1959-63, prof., 1964—. Contbr. articles to profl. jours. Fellow Royal Micros. Soc. London, Pan Am. Cancer Soc.; mem. Am. Assn. Cancer Research, Am. Assn. Anatomists, Can. Assn. Anatomists, Internat. Soc. Stereology, Internat. Soc. Chronobiology, Sigma Xi. Roman Catholic. Current Work: Cancer research; exfoliative cytology; histophysiology of respiratory system, regeneration, cell kinetics, carcinogenesis, histochemistry. Subspecialty: Microscopy. Home: 886 Lindsay St Winnipeg MB R3N 1H8 Canada Office: 750 Bannatyne Ave Winnipeg MB R3E OW3 Canada

BERTANI, GIUSEPPE, research geneticist, educator; b. Como, Italy, Oct. 23, 1923; s. Carlo and Armida (Seveso) B.; m. Lillian E. Teegarden, July 2, 1954; children: Christofer, Niklas. Dr. Sci. Nat., U. Milan, 1945; hon. Dr., Uppsala (Sweden) U., 1982. Various research positions, 1946-54; sr. research fellow in biology Calif. Inst. Tech., Pasadena, 1954-57; assoc. prof. med. microbiology U. So. Calif., Los Angeles, 1957-60; prof. microbial genetics Karolinska Inst., Stockholm, 1960-83; sr. research scientist Jet Propulsion Lab., Calif. Inst. Tech., 1981—. Author articles in microbial and molecular genetics.; Editorial bds. sci. jours. Mem. European Molecular Biology Orgn., Am. Soc. Microbiology, Genetics Soc. Am., AAAS, others. Current Work: Lysogenic bacteria; bacterial viruses; genetic recombination; methanogenic bacteria; applications of genetics to biotechnology. Subspecialties: Genetics and genetic engineering (biology); Microbiology. Office: 4800 Oak Grove Dr Pasadena CA 91109

BERTOZZI, WILLIAM, physicist. Prof. dept physics MIT, Cambridge. Subspecialty: Nuclear physics. Office: MIT Dept Physics Cambridge MA 02139

BERTRAM, TIMOTHY ALLYN, veterinary pathologist, researcher; b. Lemars, Iowa, Aug. 26, 1955; s. James Carl and Gloria Ann (DeVries) B.; m. Julie Ann Hagel, June 3, 1978; children—James Paul, Erin Michelle. D.V.M., Iowa State U., 1979, Ph.D., 1983. Resident, Vet. Diagnostic Lab., Ames, Iowa, 1979-80; vet. med. officer USDA, Ames, 1980-82, research leader, 1982-85; instr. Iowa State U., Ames, 1980; vet. pathologist U. Ill. Coll. Vet. Medicine, Urbana, 1985—. Contbr. chpt. to book, articles to profl. jours. Campaign worker Wis. Democratic Orgn., 1976; Recipient Hawkeye Kennel Club award, 1979, cert. of Merit, USDA, 1984; George Catt Meml. scholar Iowa State U., 1979; Vet. Pathology scholar C.L. Davis Found., 1981; Mem. Council Research Workers Animals' Diseases, AVMA, AAAS, Phi Zeta, Gamma Sigma Delta, Phi Kappa Phi. Mem. Christian Ch. Current work: Immunopathology of lung in domestic animals as related to infectious diseases. Subspecialties: Pathology (veterinary medicine); Animal pathology. Office: Univ Ill Coll Vet Medicine Det Vet Pathology Urbana IL 61801

BERTRAND, JOHN, research and development engineer; b. Athens, Greece, Feb. 6, 1943; came to U.S., 1962, naturalized, 1977; s. Peter and Vasso (Tsoli) B.; m. Daphne Helen Apostoleri, June 30, 1972; 1 dau.: Cleo Vasso. B.E.E., Columbia U., 1966; M.E.E., U. Calif.-Berkeley, 1967; PH.D., Columbia U., 1970. Sr. mem. tech. staff Wavetek Rockland, Inc., Rockleigh, N.J., 1972-81, mgr. software devel., 1981-83, sr, fellow, 1983-84; sr. scientist and voice processing research and devel. coordinator Def. Communications Div. ITT, Nutley, N.J., 1984—; instr. Columbia U., 1973-74, adj. asst. prof., 1974-77, adj. assoc. prof., 1979; group leader digital signal processing group Research Ctr. for Nat. Def., Athens, Greece, 1980-81. Contbr. numerous articles to profl. jours.; Patentee in field. Served with Greek Army, 1970-71. Eugene and Mona Gee fellow, 1966-67. Mem. IEEEE (Sr.), N.Y. Acad. Sci., Assn. Computing Machinery, N.Y. Acad. Sci., Acoustical Soc. Am., Sigma Xi, Tau Beta Pi, Eta Kappa Nu. Current Work: Digital signal processing with applications in spectrum analysis and speech processing. Subspecialties: Computer engineering; Computer architecture. Home: 211 Radcliff Dr Upper Nyack NY 10960 Office: ITT Defense Communications River Rd Nutley NJ 07110

BERTRANDO, BERTRAND ROBERT, aerospace engineer; b. Chgo., May 30, 1927; s. Secondino and Nora (Burlando) B.; m. Virginia Prettyman, Jan. 7, 1952; children: Robert, William, Michael. B.A., U. Ill.-Urbana, 1948; M.S., Ill. Inst. Tech., 1950; M.B.E., Claremont Grad. Sch., 1973. Registered profl. engr., Calif. Research engr. Inst. Gas Tech., Chgo., 1948-50, Worcester Gas Light Co., Mass., 1949, Jet Propulsion Lab., Pasadena, Calif., 1951-53, Douglas Aircraft Co., 1953-57; mgr. propulsion panel Gen. Electric Co., Santa Barbara, Calif., 1957-63; sr. engring. specialist Aerospace Corp., El Segundo, Calif., 1963—. Served with USMC, 1945-46. Fellow AIAA (assoc., pres. central Calif. sect. 1963); mem. System Safety Soc. (sr.). Clubs: La Cumbre Golf and Country (Santa Barbara, Calif.); Antheneum (Pasadena, Calif.). Current Work: Design of satellites, system safety, environmental sciences. Subspecialties: Satellite studies; Aerospace engineering and technology. Home: 4108 Paloma Dr Santa Barbara CA 91310 Office: Aerospace Corp 2350 E El Segundo Blvd El Segundo CA

BESCH, HENRY ROLAND, JR., pharmacologist, educator; b. San Antonio, Sept. 12, 1942; s. Henry Rol and Monette Helen (Kasten) B.; 1 son, Kurt Theodore. B.Sc. in Physiology, Ohio State U., 1964, Ph.D. in Pharmacology (USPHS predoctoral trainee 1964-67), 1967; USPHS postdoctoral trainee, Baylor U. Coll. Medicine, Houston, 1968-70. Instr. Ob-Gyn Ohio State U. Med. Sch., 1967-68; mem. faculty Ind. U. Sch. Medicine, 1971—; prof. pharmacology and medicine, sr. research asso. Krannert Inst. Cardiology, chmn. dept. pharmacology and toxicology, 1977—, Showalter prof. pharmacology, 1980—; Can. Med. Research Council vis. prof., 1979, investigator fed. grants, mem. nat. panels and coms., cons. in field. Contbr. numerous articles pharm. and med. jours.; mem. editorial bds. profl. jours. Fellow Brit. Med. Research Council, 1970-71; Grantee Showalter Trust, 1975—. Fellow Am. Coll. Cardiology; Mem. AAAS, Am. Assn. Clin. Chemistry, Am. Fed. Clin. Research, Am. Heart Assn., Am. Physiol. Soc., Am. Soc. Biol. Chemists, Am. Soc. Pharmacology and Exptl. Therapeutics, Assn. Med. Sch. Pharmacologists, Biochem. Soc., Cardiac Muscle Soc., Internat. Soc. Heart Research (exec. com. Am. sect.), Nat. Acad. Clin. Biochemistry, N.Y. Acad. Scis., Sigma Xi. Subspecialties: Pharmacology; Toxicology (medicine). Office: 1100 W Michigan St Indianapolis IN 46223

BESSMAN, SAMUEL PAUL, pediatrician, educator; b. Newark, Feb. 3, 1921; s. Edward S. and Sara R. (Greenberg) B.; m. Alice Neuman, July 3, 1945; children—Joel David, Ellen. Student, Coll. William and Mary, 1938-41; M.D., Washington U., St. Louis, 1944. Intern. asst. resident St. Louis Children's Hosp., 1944-45; asst. prof. pediatrics George Washington U., 1947-54; dir. research Children's Hosp., Washington, 1947-54; asso. prof. pediatrics U. Md., 1954-59, prof. pediatric research, 1959-68, prof. biochemistry, 1962-68; prof., chmn. dept. pharmacology and nutrition U. So. Calif., 1968—, prof. pediatrics, 1969—; dir. research Rosewood State Hosp., Md., 1962-68, Jewish Home for Retarded Children, Washington, 1962-68. Editor: Biochem. Medicine; editorial bd.: Analytical Biochemistry. Pres. 1st Dist. Community Council, Balt., 1965; trustee Robert Lindner Found. Served with USPHS, 1945-47. Recipient Crawford Long award U. Ga., 1963; Creative Scholar award U. So. Calif., 1978; technion Maimonides award, 1979. Fellow Am. Acad. Pediatrics, AAAS; mem. Am. Soc. Biol. Chemists, Soc. Pediatric Research, Am. Inst. Nutrition, Am. Soc. Pharmacology and Exptl. Therapeutics, Sigma Xi, Alpha Omega Alpha. Research on treatment of lead poisoning, theoretical basis of hepatic coma, mechanism of insulin action chemistry mental retardation, genetic basis of malnutrition, artificial implantable pancreas. Current work: Metabolic diseases; mechanisms of insulin action; chemistry of mental retardation; genetic basis of amino acid malnutrition; artificial self-regulated Beta cell. Subspecialties: Biochemistry (biology); Nutrition (medicine). Home: 7404 Woodrow Wilson Dr Los Angeles CA 90046

BEST, TROY LEE, biologist, natural science educator; b. Fort Summer, N.Mex., Aug. 30, 1945; s. Frank and Nadine L. (Clymer) B.; children—Frank H., Bryan N. B.S., Eastern N.Mex. U., 1967; M.S., U. Okla., 1971; Ph.D., 1976. Preparator U. Okla., Norman, 1968-69, teaching and research asst., 1971-74; asst. prof. Northwestern U., Boston, 1974-76; research prof. Eastern N.Mex. U., Portales, 1976—, asst. prof. biology U. N.Mex., Albuquerque, 1983—; lectr. in field, cons. in field; mem. adv. com. N.Mex. Mus. Natural History, 1983—. Contbr. articles to profl. jours. grantee NSF, 1972-73, HEW, 1975-76, Sandia Nat. Labs., 1977-82. Mem. AAAS, Am. Ornithologists Union, Am. Soc. Mammalogists, Cooper Ornithol. Soc., Ecol. Soc. Am., Herpetologists League, N.Mex. Wildlife Soc., Soc. Systematic Zoology, Southwestern Assn. Naturalists, Tex. Acad. Sci., Wildlife Soc., Phi Sigma, Sigma Xi. Current work: Vertebrate ecology and systematics including population dynamics; reporoduction; food habits, ecosystem analysis, morphologic variation, sexual dimorphism. Subspecialties: Population biology; Systematics. Office: Dept Biology U NMex Albuquerque NM 87131

BETHE, HANS ALBRECHT, physicist, educator; b. Strassburg, Alsace-Lorraine, July 2, 1906; came to U.S., 1935; s. Albrecht Theodore and Anna (Kuhn) B.; m. Rose Ewald, 1939; children: Henry, Monica. Ed. Goethe Gymnasium, Frankfurt on Main, U. Frankfort; Ph.D., U. Munich, 1928; D.Sc., Bklyn. Poly. Inst., 1950, U. Denver, 1952, U. Chgo., 1953, U. Birmingham, 1956, Harvard U., 1958. Instr. in theoretical physics univs. of Frankfort, Stuttgart, Munich and Tubingen, 1928-33; lectr. univs. of Manchester and Bristol, Eng., 1933-35; asst. prof. Cornell U., 1935, prof., 1937-75, prof. emeritus, 1975—; dir. theoretical physics div. Los Alamos Sci. Lab., 1943-46; Mem. Presdl. Study Disarmament, 1958; mem. President's Sci. Adv. Com., 1956-60. Author: Mesons and Fields, 1953, Elementary Nuclear Theory, 1957, Quantum Mechanics of One-and Two-Electron Atoms, 1957, Intermediate Quantum Mechanics, 1964; Contbr. to: books Handbuch der Physik, 1933, Reviews of Modern Physics, 1936-37, Phys. Rev. Recipient A. Cressy Morrison prize N.Y. Acad. Sci., 1938-40; Presdl. Medal of Merit, 1946; Max Planck medal, 1953; Enrico Fermi award AEC, 1961; Nobel Prize in physics, 1967; Nat. Medal of Sci., 1976; Vannever Bush award NSF, 1985. Fgn. mem. Royal Soc. London; mem. Am. Philos. Soc., Nat. Acad. Scis. (Henry Draper medal 1968), Am. Phys. Soc. (pres. 1954), Am. Astron. Soc. Subspecialty: Theoretical physics. Office: Lab Nuclear Studies Cornell U Ithaca NY 14853

BETTELHEIM, FREDERICK ABRAHAM, chemist, educator, researcher, author; b. Gyor, Hungary, June 3, 1923; came to U.S., 1951, naturalized, 1961; s. Anton and Elizabeth (Gyarfas) B.; m. Annabelle Ganz, June 8, 1947; 1 son: Adriel. Student, U. Szeged, Hungary, 1943-44; B.S., Cornell U., 1953; M.S., U. Calif., Davis, 1954, Ph.D., 1956. Chemist Agrl. Expt. Sta., Rehovoth, Israel, 1947-51, Ithaca, N.Y., 1951-53; research instr. U. Mass., 1956-57; asst. prof. chemistry Adelphi U., 1957-60, assoc. prof., 1960-63, prof., chmn. dept., 1963—; Fulbright prof. Weizmann Inst. Israel, 1984; vis. prof. U. Uppsala, Sweden, 1965, Weizmann Inst., 1973, U. Fla., 1981, Nat. Eye Inst., 1985; cons. in field. Author: Experimental Physical Chemistry, 1971, (with J. March) Essentials of Chemistry, Organic Chemistry and Biochemistry, 1983; author: (with J. Lee) Laboratory Manual, 1983; editor: Exptl. Eye Research, 1983—; Author also mongraphs, articles. Served to 2d lt. Israeli Def. Army, 1948-51. Recipient Kiss award U. Szeged, 1944, Lalor award Lalor Found., 1959; recipient Disting. Tchr. award Adelphi U., 1979. Mem. Am. Chem. Soc., Fedn. Am. Scientists for Exptl. Biology, Assn. Research in Vision and Ophthalmology, Internat. Soc. Eye Research (treas.). Jewish. Current Work: Cataract formation in human lens; studying supramolecular changes in cataractogenesis by physical chemical means: light scattering, birefringence, differential scanning calorimetry. Subspecialties: Biophysical chemistry; Ophthalmology. Office: Adelphi U South St Garden City NY 11530

BETTERLEY, DONALD ALAN, research mycologist; b. Colorado Springs, Colo., June 17, 1952; s. Robert Leslie and Joan Madelle (Snavely) B.; m. Margaret Louisa McCollough, Sept. 6, 1975. B.S. in Botany with highest distinction, Colo. State U., 1974; Ph.D. in Botany-Mycology, U. Calif.-Berkeley, 1981. Postdoctoral research botanist U. Calif.-Berkeley, 1980-81; dir. research, research mycologist Spawn Mate, Inc., San Jose, Calif., 1981—; guest lectr. U. Calif.-Berkeley. Mem. Mycol. Soc. Am., Brit. Mycol. Soc., N.Y. Acad. Scis., Internat. Mushroom Soc. Tropics, Bot. Soc. Am., Sierra Club, Sigma Xi, Phi Beta Kappa. Current Work: Fungal genetics, physiology, nutrition and biological control mechanisms as related to mushroom cultivation; scientific photography. Subspecialties: Genome organization; Microbiology. Office: 555 N 1st St San Jose CA 95112

BETTIS, PATRICIA KAREN, geologist; b. Tulsa, Aug. 21, 1953; d. Floyd Earl and Mary Jeanette (Crow) B.; m. John D. Pigott, June 18, 1978; B.A. in Geology, U. Tex., 1975. Geologist, Amoco Internat., Chgo., 1977-78; petroleum geologist Amoco Prodn. Internat., Houston, 1978-81; sr. geologist Kerr-McGee Corp., Oklahoma City, 1981-85; sr. geologist Amoco Prodn. Internat., Houston, 1985—; mem. research com. on sedimentary models Standard Oil of Ind., 1980-81. Mem. Geologic Soc. Am., Soc. Econ. Paleontologists and Mineralogists. Current work: International petroleum exploration and exploitation. Geographic regions of expertise include: Far East, Middle East, North Sea, Trinidad, Columbia, and Gabon. Technical areas of specialty are: seismic stratigraphy and petrophysics. Subspecialties: Geology; Sedimentology.

BETTS, AUSTIN WORTHAM, retired research company executive; b. Westwood, N.J., Nov. 22, 1912; s. Irving Wilcox and Bessie Harris (Boardman) B.; m. Edna Jane Paterson, Dec. 8, 1934; children: Jerry W., Lee W., Lynn P. B.S., U.S. Mil. Acad., 1934; M.S., Mass. Inst. Tech., 1938. Commd. 2d lt. U.S. Army, 1934, advanced through grades to lt. gen., 1966; dist. engr. Bermuda Dist., U.S. Engr. Dept., 1942-43; engr. 14th Air Force, 1944-45; asso. dir. Los Alamos Sci. Lab., 1946-48; chief atomic energy br. G-4, Dept. Army, 1949-52; exec. to chief research and devel. Dept. Army, 1952-54; mil. exec. to spl. asst. of dir. guided missiles Office Sec. Def., 1957-59; dir. Advanced Research Projects Agy., Office Sec. Def., 1959-61; dir. mil. application AEC, 1961-64; dep. chief research and devel. Dept. Army, 1964-66, chief research and devel., 1966-70, retired, 1970; sr. v.p. Southwest Research Inst., San Antonio, 1971-83; cons. corp. mgmt. Mem. Assn. U.S. Army, Nat. Security Indsl. Assn., Inst. Environ. Scis., Soc. Am. Mil. Engrs., AAAS, Am. Inst. Aeros. and Astronautics, Am. Indsl. Preparedness Assn., Sigma Xi. Presbyterian. Clubs: Rotary, Masons. Current Work: Corporate consultant. Subspecialties: Systems engineering; Environmental engineering. Home: 6414 View Point San Antonio TX 78229

BETTS, HENRY BROGNARD, physician, educator; b. New Rochelle, N.Y., May 25, 1928; s. Henry Brognard and Marguerite Meredith (Denise) B.; m. Monika Christine Paul, Apr. 25, 1970. A.B., Princeton, 1950; M.D., U. Va., 1954. Diplomate: Am. Bd. Phys. Medicine and Rehab. Intern Cin. Gen. Hosp., 1954-55; resident, teaching fellow N.Y.U. Med. Center Inst. Rehab. Medicine, N.Y.C., 1958-63; practice medicine, specializing in phys. medicine and rehab., Chgo., 1963—; staff physiatrist Rehab. Inst. Chgo., 1963-64, asso. med. dir., 1964-65, med. dir., 1965-69, v.p., med. dir., 1969-75, exec. v.p., med. dir., 1975—; chmn. dept. rehab. medicine Northwestern U. Med. Sch., 1967—, prof., 1968—; cons. Northwestern Meml. Hosp., Chgo. Contbr. articles to profl. jours. Mem. steering com. United Cerebral Palsy, 1967—; Mem. med. adv. com. Nat. Paraplegia Found., 1969—; bd. dirs. Nat. Com. Arts for Handicapped, 1981—; mem. Gov.'s High Blood Pressure Adv. Bd., 1977—. Served with USNR, 1956-58. Named Physician of Year Ill. Gov.'s Com., 1964; commended by Ill. Gen. Assembly, 1967; cited for meritorious service Pres.'s Com. on Employment of Handicapped, 1965. Mem. Ill. Med. Soc. (chmn. com. on rehab. services), Assn. Acad. Physiatrist (pres. 1968-69), Am. Congress Rehab. Med. (med. adv. com., pres. 1976-77), Mid-m. Soc. Phys. Med. and Rehab. (pres. 1969). Subspecialty: Physical medicine and rehabilitation. Home: 1727 N Orleans Chicago IL 60614 Office: 345 E Superior St Chicago IL 60611

BEUTLER, FREDERICK JOSEPH, information scientist; b. Berlin, Oct. 3, 1926; came to U.S., 1936, naturalized, 1943; s. Alfred David and Kaethe (Italiener) B.; m. Suzanne Armstrong, Jan. 6, 1969; children—Arthur David, Kathryn Ruth, Michael Ernest. S.B., Mass. Inst. Tech., 1949, S.M., 1951; Ph.D., Calif. Inst. Tech., 1957. Mem. faculty U. Mich., Ann Arbor, 1957—, prof. info. and control engring., 1963—, chmn. computer info. and control engring., 1970-71, 77—; vis. prof. Calif. Inst. Tech., 1967-68; vis. scholar U.

Calif. at Berkeley, 1964-65. Editorial cons.: Math. Rev, 1965-67, 75—; contbr. articles to profl. jours. and books. Bd. dirs. Ann Arbor Civic Theatre, 1976-78. Served with AUS, 1945-46. NSF research grantee, 1971-75, 76-81; Air Force Office Sci. Research grantee, 1970-74, 75-80; NASA grantee, 1959-69. Fellow IEEE; mem. Soc. Indsl. and Applied Math (council 1969-74, mng. editor Jour. Applied Math. 1970-75, editor 1984—, editor Rev. 1967-70), Am. Math. Soc., Inst. Math. Statistics, Am. Soc. Engring. Edn. (exec. com. 1967-70), Am. Arbitration Assn., Econ. Club Detroit. Club: Barton Boat. Current Work: Queueing systems; properties, characterizations, estimation,prediction, optimization. Subspecialties: Systems engineering; Probability. Home: 1717 Shadford Rd Ann Arbor MI 48104

BEVAN, THOMAS EDWARD, psychologist; b. Millville, N.J., Mar. 11, 1947; s. Edward George and Fola (Zimmerman) B.; m. Alice Alexander, Sept. 11, 1971; children: Lesley, Cynthia. A.B., Dartmouth Coll., 1969; Ph.D., Princeton U., 1973. Psychologist Sci. Applications Inc., Rosslyn, Va., 1973-76; psychologist Environ. Research Inst. Mich., Rosslyn, Va., 1980—, mgr. systems evaluation group, 1980—. Contbr. articles to profl. jours. Bd. dirs. No. Va. Football Ofcls. Assn., 1981—. Served to capt. U.S. Army, 1973-76. Mem. Soc. Neurosci. Subspecialties: Human factors engineering; Remote sensing (atmospheric science). Home: 1207 N Quantico St Arlington VA 22205 Office: 1501 Wilson Blvd Suite 1105 Arlington VA 22209

BEVELACQUA, JOSEPH JOHN, physicist, researcher; b. Waynesburg, Pa., Mar. 17, 1949; s. Frank and Lucy Ann (Cataneo) B.; m. Terry Sanders, Sept. 4, 1971; children: Anthony, Jeffrey, Megan, Peter, Michael. B.S. in Physics, Calif. State Coll., 1970; postgrad., U. Maine, 1970-72; M.S. in Physics, Fla. State U., 1974, Ph.D. in Physics, 1976. Cert. radiol. shield survey engr., Westinghouse Bettis Atomic Power Lab.; cert. in health physics Am. Bd. Health Physics. Teaching/research asst. U. Maine, 1970-72, Fla. State U., 1973-76; nuclear engr. Bettis Atomic Power Lab., West Mifflin, Pa., 1973, sr. nuclear engr., 1976-78; ops. research analyst U.S. Dept. Energy, Oak Ridge, 1978-80, chief physicist advanced laser isotope separation program, 1980-83; sr. engr. Three Mile Island Sta.-Unit 2, GPU Nuclear Corp. Middletown, Pa., 1983-84, emergency preparedness mgr. Three Mile Island, 1984—; cons. U.S. Dept. Energy's Process Evaluation Bd. of Isotope Separation, Washington, 1981-82; mem. KMC Working Group on Emergency Preparedness, Washington. Contbr. articles to profl. jours. including Physical Rev. Letters. Mem. Republican Presdl. Task Force, Rep. Senatorial Com. NSF research asst., 1975-76. Mem. Am. Nuclear Soc., Am. Phys. Soc., Health Physics Soc., N.Y. Acad. Scis. Republican. Lutheran. Club: Oak Ridge Sportsman's. Current Work: Theoretical studies of light nuclei, few nucleon transfer reactions, radiation shielding, laser isotope separation, neutron nuclei, symmetry violations in nuclei, grand unification theories, quark models of nuclear forces, nuclear fuel cycle, laser fusion and gravitational collapse of stars; nuclear reactor safety. Subspecialties: Nuclear physics; Nuclear engineering. Home: 19 Merion Ln PO Box 166 Hummelstown PA 17036 Office: GPU Nuclear Corp 3 Mile Island Nuclear Generating Sta PO Box 480 Middletown PA 17057

BEVER, BERLINER MICHAEL, materials science educator; b. Germany, Aug. 7, 1911; s. Rudolf and Maria (Bever) Berliner; m. Marion Gordon, Aug. 25, 1936; children: James G., Thomas G., Mary-Ivers B. Witherby. Dr. iur., Heidelberg, 1934; M.B.A., Harvard U., 1937; M.S., MIT, 1942, Sc.D., 1944. Registered profl. engr., Mass. Staff Mem. dept. metallurgy MIT, Cambridge, 1940-44, instr. to prof., 1944-77, prof. emeritus materials sci. and engring., sr. lectr., 1977—; sr. research assoc. Inst. Econ. Analysis, NYU, 1978—; hon. research assoc. Harvard U., 1966-67. Co-editor: Basic Open Hearth Steelmaking, 2d edit, 1951, Metals Handbook Vol. 8, 8th edit, 1973; cons. McGraw-Hill Materials Science and Engring. series, Environ. Impact Assessment Rev.; co-editor: Conservation and Recycling; editor-in-chief: Ency. Materials Sci. and Engring; contbr. articles to profl. jours. Mem. Boston Mus. Sci. corp. Recipient Nat. Assn. Secondary Materials Industries, recycling award, 1972. Fellow Am. Soc. Metals, Am. Acad. Arts and Scis., AAAS; mem. AIME (Mathewson Gold medal 1965), Inst. Metals (London), corr. mem. Berliner Wissenschaftliche Gesellschaft. Clubs: Harvard (Boston), Harvard Musical Assn. Current Work: Physical metallurgy; application of thermodynamics to metallurgy; calorimetry; deformation of metals and intermetallic compounds; alloy theory and metastable phases; surface hardening of metals; characterization of structures; materials engineering; conservation and recycling of materials. Subspecialties: Metallurgy; Materials. Home: 23 Highland St Cambridge MA 02138 Office: MIT Room 13-5026 Cambridge MA 02139

BEYER, KLAUS DIETRICH, research chemist; b. Berlin, W. Ger., Jan 23, 1937; came to U.S., 1966, naturalized, 1975; s. Eduard and Waltraud L. (Eggers) B.; m. Linda Mae Hunt, Aug. 2, 1968; children—Sylvia, Julia. B.S., U. Bonn, W. Ger., 1959, M.S., 1964, Ph.D., 1966. Postdoctoral fellow Ohio State U., Columbus, 1966-68; research chemist IBM, Hopewell Junction, N.Y., 1968—. Patentee in field (8). Contbr. numerous articles to profl. jours. Mem. Am. Chem. Soc. (chmn. Hudson sect. 1973), Electrochem. Soc. Lutheran. Club: Poughkeepsie Tennis) Lodge: Rotary (bd. dirs. 1983-84). Current work: Relationship between electronic and materials characteristics. Development of future, ultrafast semiconductors devices. Subspecialties: Solid state chemistry; Microchip technology (engineering). Home: 3 Tamidan Rd Poughkeepsie NY 12601 Office: IBM Gen Tech Div Rt 52 Hopewell Junction NY 12533

BEYER-MEARS, ANNETTE, physiologist, researcher; b. Madison, Wis., May 26, 1941; d. Karl H. and Annette (Weiss) B.; m. William H. Mears, Jr.; 1 son, Karl. B.S., Vassar Coll., 1963; M.S., Fairleigh Dickinson U., 1973; Ph.D., U. Medicine and Dentistry of N.J., 1977. NIH fellow Cornell U. Med. Sch., N.Y.C., 1963-65; instr. physiology Springside Coll., Phila., 1967-71; teaching asst. dept Physiology U. Medicine and Dentistry N.J.; teaching asst. dept Physiology N.J. Med. Sch., 1974-77, NIH fellow dept. ophthalmology, 1978-80, asst. prof. dept. physiology, 1980—, asst. prof. dept. ophthalmology, 1979—. Contbr. articles in field of diabetic lens and kidney therapy to profl. jours. Chmn. admissions No. N.J. area Vassar Coll., 1974-79; mem. minister search com. St. Bartholomew Episcopal Ch., Ridgewood, N.J., 1978, chmn. fund raising, 1978, 79; del. Epis. Diocesian Conv., 1977, 78. Recipient Nat. Research Service award, 1978-80; Research award NIH, 1980—; Research award Juvenile Diabetes Found., 1985—; Pfizer, 1983—; Research award Found. U. Medicine and Dentistry N.J., 1980; Research award Sigma Xi, 1980. Mem. Am. Physiol. Soc., N.Y. Acad. Scis., Soc. for Neurosci., Assn. for Research in Vision and Ophthalmology, Internat. Soc. for Eye Research, AAAS, Aircraft Owners and Pilots Assn., Sigma Xi. Current Work: Research in diabetic lens and kidney therapy. Subspecialties: Neuroendocrinology; Ophthalmology. Office: Dept Physiology U Medicine and Dentistry NJ 100 Bergen St Newark NJ 07103

BEYSTER, JOHN ROBERT, engineering company executive; b. Detroit, July 26, 1924; s. John Frederick and Lillian Edith (Jondro) B.; m. Betty Jean Brock, Sept. 8, 1955; children—James Frederick, Mark Daneil, Mary Ann. B.S. in Engring., U. Mich., 1945, M.S., 1948, Ph.D., 1950. Registered profl. engr., Calif. Mem. staff Los Alamos Sci. Lab., 1951-56; chmn. dept. accelerated physics Gulf Gen. Atomic Co., San Diego, 1957-69; pres., chmn. bd. Sci. Applications, Inc., La Jolla, Calif., 1969—; mem. Joint Strategic Target Planning Staff, Sci. Adv. Group, Omaha, 1978—; panel mem. Nat. Measurement Lab. Evaluation panel for Radiation Research. Washington, 1983—; dir. Scripps Bancorp, La Jolla, 1983. Co-author: Slow Neutron Scattering and Thermalization, 1970. Served to lt. comdr. USN, 1943-46. Fellow Am. Nuclear Soc., Am. Phys. Soc. Republican. Roman Catholic. Subspecialty: Systems engineering. Home: 9321 La Jolla Farms Rd La Jolla CA 92037 Office: Sci Applications Inc 1200 Prospect St La Jolla CA 92037

BEZDEK, JAMES CHRISTIAN, computer scientist, educator; b. Harrisburg, Pa., Oct. 22, 1939; s. Hugo Frank Bezdek and Louise Kent (Linkins) Seely; m. Linda Rose Perry, May 31, 1963; children—Mark, Kristin, Eric, Tanya. B.S.C.E., U. Nev., 1969; Ph.D., Cornell U., 1973. Asst. prof. SUNY Coll.-Oneonta, 1973-74; asst. prof. Marquette U., Milw., 1974-76; assoc. prof., Utah State U., Logan, 1976-82; research scientist Boeing Aerospace, Seattle, 1982-83; prof., chmn. dept. computer sci. U. S.C., Columbia, 1983—; pres. IJK Sci. Software, Lexington, S.C., 1983—; Author: Pattern Recognition with Fuzzy Algorithms, 1981; editor: The Analysis of Fuzzy Information, 1985; contbr. articles to profl. jours. Served with USN, 1958-62. Mem. IEEE, Assn. Computing Machinery, Pattern Recognition Soc., Classification Soc., N.Am. Fuzzy Info. Processing Soc. (pres. 1983-85). Current work: Numerical analysis; feature selection; classifier design; computer vision; artificially intelligent expert systems, theory and applications. Subspecialties: Artificial intelligence; Graphics, image processing, and pattern recognition. Home: 183 Beechcreek Rd Lexington SC 29072 Office: Computer Sci Dept U SC Columbia SC 29208

BEZKOROVAINY, ANATOLY, biochemist, researcher, educator; b. Riga, Latvia, Feb. 11, 1935; came to U.S., 1951; s. Ignaty and Olga (Solovey) B.; m. Marilyn Grib, June 8, 1964; children—Gregory, Alexander. B.S., U. Chgo., 1956; Ph.D., U. Ill., 1960; J.D., Ill. Inst. Tech.-Chgo. Kent Coll., 1977. Research assoc. Oak Ridge Nat. Lab., Tenn., 1960-61; research chemist U.S. Dept. Agr., Ames, Iowa, 1961-62; from asst. prof. to prof. Rush Presbyn. St. Luke's Med. Ctr., Chgo., 1962—, assoc. chmn. and dir. edn. dept. biochemistry, 1980—. Contbr. articles to profl. jours. Author: Biochemistry of Non-Heme Iron, 1980. Fellow Nat. Acad. Clin. Biochemistry (dir., symposium chmn. 1985); mem. Am. Inst. Nutrition; Am. Soc. Biol. Chemists, Am. Chem. Soc. Eastern Orthodox. Current work: Iron metabolism in mammalian and microbial systems; biochemistry of human and bovine milk. Subspecialties: Biochemistry (medicine); Microbiology (medicine). Home: 6801 N Kilpatrick Lincolnwood IL 60646 Office: Biochemistry Dept Rush Presbyn Saint Lukes Med Ctr Chicago IL 60612

BEZOARI, MASSIMO DANIEL, chemist; b. Glasgow, Scotland, Sept. 11, 1952; came to U.S., 1975; s. Ubaldo Indo and Marta (Agresti) B.; m. Charlotte Ann Pope, May 30, 1980. B.Sc., U. Glasgow, 1974; Ph.D., U. Ala., 1981. Research fellow U. Wis.-Milw., 1980-81; sr. research chemist Dow Chem. Co., Plaquemine, La., 1981-85, project leader, 1985—. Contbr. articles to profl. jours. Contbg. author chpts. in various books. Andrew Carnegie Trust Fund scholar, Scotland, 1970-73; Dean's scholar, U. Ala., 1976-77; Grad. Research Council fellow, U. Ala., 1977-80. Mem. Am. Chem. Soc. Club: Am. Chess Fedn. Chemistry of chlorinated polyolefins, phosphorus-nitrogen compounds and heteroplanes. Subspecialties: Organic chemistry; Polymer chemistry. Office: Dow Chem Co PO Box 400 R&D Plaquemine LA 70764

BHAGAT, PHIROZ MANECK, mechanical engineer, educator; b. Poona, India, Oct. 28, 1948; came to U.S., 1970; s. Maneck Phirozshaw and Khorshed Eduljee (Batliwala) B.; m. Patricia Jane Steckler, Oct. 13, 1979; 1 child, Kay. B.Tech., Indian Inst. Tech.-Bombay, 1970; M.S.E., U. Mich., 1971, Ph.D., 1975. Research fellow in applied mechanics Harvard U., Cambridge, Mass., 1975-77; asst. prof. engring. Columbia U., N.Y.C., 1977-81, adj. asst. prof., 1981-84; staff engr. Exxon Research & Engring. Co., Florham Park, N.J., 1981-83, sr. staff engr., 1983—. Contbr. articles to profl. jours. Named K.C. Mahindra scholar, 1970; J.N. Tata scholar, 1970; Horace Rackham predoctoral fellow, 1973-74, 74-75. Mem. N.Y. Acad. Scis., Am. Inst. Chem. Engrs., ASME, Combustion Inst., AAAS, Tau Beta Pi, Sigma Xi. Current Work: Application of the thermal sciences to model petro-chemical processes; combustion; heat transfer; fluid mechanics; thermodynamics; coal conversion. Subspecialties: Mechanical engineering; Chemical engineering. Home: 252 Sinclair Pl Westfield NJ 07090 Office: Exxon Research & Engring Co Florham Park NJ 07932

BHALLA, VINOD K., endocrinologist, biochemist, educator; b. Lahore, India, Aug. 4, 1940; came to U.S., 1968, naturalized, 1981; s. Lal C. and Shanti (Punga) B.; m. Madhu B. Sarin, May 29, 1966; children: Niti, Jyoti, Varun. B.S., St. John's Coll., Agra, India, 1962, M.S., 1964; Ph.D., Nat. Chem. Lab., Poona, India, 1968. Research assoc. U. Ga., Athens, 1969-72, Emory U., Atlanta, 1972-74; mem. faculty Med. Coll. Ga., Augusta, 1974—, prof. endocrinology, 1982—; mem. endocrinology study sect. NIH, 1985—; speaker in field. Mem. editorial bd.: Biology of Reproduction, 1978-84 reviewer: Endocrinology Jour, 1980, Alcoholism-Clinical and Exptl. Research, 1982—, Andrology Jour, 1982—. NSF grantee, 1976-79; NIH grantee, 1976—. Mem. Am. Soc. Biol. Chemists, Endrocine Soc., Soc. for Study Reprodn., N.Y. Acad. Sci., Am. Fertility Soc., Am. Chem. Soc. Current Work: Polypeptide hormone action at the testicular level: polypeptide hormone receptors, cAMP, mediation and testosterone production. Subspecialties: Receptors; Biochemistry (medicine). Home: 3541 Westlake Dr Augusta GA 30907 Office: Med Coll Ga Endocrinology Dept Augusta GA 30912

BHARAT, RAMASESHA, electronics engineer; b. Thanjavur, Tamilnadu, India, July 2, 1933; s. Somasundaram and Mangalam; m. Trudy Thoeni, June 19, 1964; children—Ashok, Sheila. B.Eng., Govt. Engring. Coll. Jabalpur, India, 1953; M.S., Stanford U., 1957, Ph.D., 1960. Registered profl. engr., Colo. Engr., All India Radio, 1954, Central Electronics Engring. Research Inst., India, 1954-56; engr. RCA, Somerville, N.J., 1960-61; engr. CSF, Puteaux, France, 1961-63; research assoc. Tech. U. Lyngby, Denmark, 1964-65; assoc. prof. Poly. Inst. Bklyn, 1966-69; prof. U. Denver, 1969-73; mem. tech. staff, mgr. Rockwell Internat., Anaheim, Calif., 1974-84, dir. Silicon devices dept., 1984—; adj. prof. U. Calif.-Irvine, 1974-78. Patentee electronic devices; contbr. articles to profl. jours. Stanford U. fellow, 1956-57; Fulbright travel grantee, 1956. Mem. IEEE (sr.), Am. Phys. Soc., Sigma Xi. Current work: Electro-optics; electron devices; visible and infrared imaging; signal processing; microelectronics, radiation hardening; low temperature physics. Subspecialties: Semiconductors; Condensed matter physics. Office: Rockwell Internat 3370 Miraloma Ave Anaheim CA 92803

BHARDWAJ, BRAHM DEV, physicist; b. New Delhi, Mar. 22, 1945; s. Banwari Lal and Lal Wati (Vats) B.; m. Indu Bakhshi, July 2, 1982; children—Rahul, Varun. B.Sc. with honrs, Delhi U., India, 1964, M.Sc., 1966; diploma in solid state physics India Inst. Tech., New Delhi, 1967; M.S. in Physics, U. Lowell, 1969; Ph.D., Rice U., 1972. Postdoctoral fellow Rice U., Houston, 1972; research assoc. Case Western Res. U., Cleve., 1972-73; sr. sci. officer SSPL, Delhi, 1973-78; sr. scientist RMD Inc., Watertown, Mass., 1978-79; prin. engr. EG&G Inc., Salem, Mass., 1979-81; engring. supr. United Detector Tech., Hawthorne, Calif., 1981—. Contbr. articles to profl. jours. Rice U. fellow, 1969-72 Mem. Am. Phys. Soc., Electrochem. Soc., Sigma Xi, Sigma Pi Sigma. Current work: Research and development of solid state semiconductor devices for detection and measurment of light in the ultra-violet, visible and infrared regions of electromagnetic spectrum. Subspecialties: Semiconductors; Solar energy. Home: 5508 W 134th Pl Hawthorne CA 90250 Office: United Detector Tech 12525 Chadron Ave Hawthorne CA 90250

BHATHENA, SAM JEHANGIRJI, research chemist; b. Bombay, India, Sept. 18, 1936; s. Jehangirji and Pirojbai (Mistry) B.; m. Pauruchisty K. Kias, July 13, 1975. B.Sc. with honors, U. Bombay, 1961, M.Sc., 1964, Ph.D., 1970. Vis. fellow NIH. Bethesda, Md., 1971-73, vis. assoc., 1974; research biochemist VA Med. Ctr., Washington, 1975-82; asst. prof. Georgetown U., Washington, 1979-82; research chemist U.S. Dept. Agr., Beltsville, Md., 1983—. Contbr. chtps. to books, articles on biochemistry, nutrition and endocrinology to profl. jours. Treas. Zorastrian Assn. Met. Washington, 1979-82; v.p. Assn. Indians in Am., Washington, 1979-82. Mem. Endocrine Soc., Am. Diabetes Assn., N.Y. Acad. Sci., Soc. for Exptl. Biology and Medicine, Am. Fedn. for Clin. Research, AAAS. Democrat. Current Work: Effects of carbohydrate diets on receptors for insulin, glucagon, somatostatin, endorphins and LDL. Subspecialty: Receptors. Home: 11912 Judson Ct Wheaton MD 20909 Office: Carbohydrate Nutrition Lab Beltsville Human Nutrition Center Barc East Beltsville MD 20705

BHATNAGAR, JAGDISH PRASAD, radiol. physicist; b. Sikandrabad, India, Oct. 4, 1938; came to U.S., 1966, naturalized, 1980; s. Kamta Prasad and Kalvati (Devi) B.; m. Usha Bhatnagar, Nov. 6, 1965; children: Atul, Sonika. Sc.D., Johns Hopkins U., 1973. Diplomate: Am. Bd. Radiology, Radiol. Physics, 1977. Research asst., research officer Bhabha Atomic Research Center, 1959-66; lab. asst. Sch. Hygiene and Public Health, Johns Hopkins U., Balt., 1966-70; radiol. phsyicst Boston City Hosp. U. Med. and Boston U. Med. Center, 1970-75; dir. div. radiol. physics dept. radiology Mercy Hosp., Pitts., 1975—; cons. in field. Contbr. articles to profl. jours. Sec. Hindu Temple Soc. N.Am., Monroeville, 1976-78; sec. Chinmaya Mission (W), Pitts., 1978—. Mem. Am. Assn. Physicists in Medicine, Health Physics Soc., N.Y. Acad. Sci., Am. Coll. Radiology, Pa. Radiol. Soc. Current Work: research in radiation dosimetry. Subspecialty: Radiological physics. Home: 8890 Willoughby Rd Pittsburgh PA 15237 Office: 1400 Locust St Pittsburgh PA 15219

BHATNAGAR, RAVI, chemist, researcher; b. Allahabad, India, Nov. 23, 1950; came to U.S., 1979; s. Ram Ratan and Girija B.; m. Arati Varma, Sept. 12, 1980. Sc.B., U. Saugor, 1968, M.Sc. in Physics, 1970; M. Tech., Indian Inst. Sci., 1972; Ph.D., U. Hull, Eng., 1979. Tech. officer Electronics Corp. India, Hyderabad, 1972-75; faculty intern U. Utah, Salt Lake City, 1979-82, research assoc., 1982—. Contbr. articles to profl. jours. Current Work: Current interests include study of intra and intermolecular energy transfer processes in polyatomic molecules, effect of vibrational excitation of the reactants on the reaction rate and other laser induced processes in molecules. Subspecialty: Laser-induced chemistry. Office: U Utah Box 53 Dept Chemistry Salt Lake City UT 84112

BHATTACHARYA, RABI SANKAR, physicist; b. Silchar, India, Feb. 19, 1948, came to U.S., 1980, naturalized, 1982; s. Ranajit Krishna and Sucharu Bhattacharya; m. Kabita Biswas, Mar. 13, 1979; children—Ratnesh, Debanjana. B.S., Gauhati U., India, 1967; M.S., India Inst. Tech., Kharagpur, 1969; A.S.I.N.P., Saha Inst., Calcutta, 1970; Ph.D., Calcutta U., India, 1975. Postdoctoral fellow Fom-Inst., Amsterdam, The Netherlands, 1975-78; guest sci. Max Planck Inst., Munich, W. Ger., 1978-79; sr. research assoc. McMaster U., Hamilton, Can., 1979-80; sr. research assoc. U. Fla., Gainesville, 1980-81; sr. sci. Universal Energy, Dayton, Ohio, 1981—. Contbr. articles to profl. jours. FOM fellow, The Netherlands; Max Planck fellow, W.Ger. Mem. Am. Phys. Soc., Nat. Assn. Corrosion Engrs. Current work: Synthesis and characterization of new materials for applications in electronics and corrosion protection by using ion beams; ion implantation; amorphous metals; GaAs. Subspecialties: Materials; Condensed matter physics. Office: Universal Energy Systems Inc 4401 Dayton Xenia Rd Dayton OH 45432

BHATTACHARYA, SYAMAL KANTI, biomedical scientist; b. Calcutta, West Bengal, India, Feb. 13, 1949; came to U.S., 1974, naturalized, 1983; s. Sudhir Chandra and Prabhabati B.; m. Keka Ghoshal, Dec. 11, 1969; children: Sumoulindra T., Julie, Syamal Dave. B.Sc. with honors, U. Calcutta, 1968; B.A. in English Lit, 1969; M.S., Murray State U., 1976; A.M., Washington U., St. Louis, 1978; Ph.D., Memphis State U., 1979. Diplomate: Am. Bd. Bioanalysis. Sr. instr. chemistry Bhabanath Instn., Calcutta, India, 1969-70; research and devel. chemist Swastik Household and Indsl. Products Pvt. Ltd., Bombay, India, 1970-74; sr. research technician Washington U. Med. Sch., St. Louis, 1976-77; research assoc. U. Tenn. Med. Ctr., Memphis, 1979-80, instr. medicine, 1980-82, mem. surgery faculty, 1983—; dir. U. Tenn. Med. Ctr. (Surg. Research Lab.), 1982—, U. Tenn. Med. Ctr. (Clin. Chem. Lab.), 1982—; teaching asst. Murray (Ky.) State U., 1974-76; research/teaching fellow Washington U., 1976-78; presdl. research fellow Memphis State U., 1978-79. Indian Nat. scholar Govt. India, New Delhi, 1965-69; Govt. India scholar Bank of India, 1974-75; Muscular Dystrophy Assn. Am. grantee, 1983-84; Am. Heart Assn. research grantee, 1983-84; recipient Nat. Research Service award in medicine NIH, 1979-81. Fellow Am. Instn. Chemists (cert. profl. chemist 1980), Indian Chem. Soc.; mem. Royal Soc. Chemistry (chartered chemist 1981), Am. Fedn. Clin. Research, N.Y. Acad. Sci. Club: U. Tenn. Faculty (Memphis). Current work: Mineral metabolism in muscular dystrophy and other neuromuscular diseases, hypertrophic cardiomyopathy, and acute pancreatitis, application of calcium-channel blocking drugs and surgical procedures to ameliorate these conditions by inhibiting intracellular calcium shift through the leaky membranes, nutritional assessment in critical care patients and those on hyperalimentation and total parenteral nutrition. Subspecialties: Clinical chemistry; Neurophysiology. Home: 3750 Marion Ave Memphis TN 38111 Office: Dept Surgery U Tenn Center Health Scis 956 Court Ave Suite 2GO4 Memphis TN 38163

BHATTACHARYYA, ANJAN, semiconductor physicist; b. Calcutta, India, July 2, 1953; came to U.S., 1977; s. Santiranjan and Malati (Bhattacharyya) B.; m. Sharmila Mukherjee, Aug. 14, 1982; 1 child, Tania. B.Sc. with honors, Gold medalist, U. Calcutta, 1972; B.A. with honors, Cambridge U., 1976, M.A. (hon.), 1979; Ph.D., U. Ill., 1981. Mem. tech. staff Philips Research Lab Sunnyvale, Signetics Corp., Calif., 1981—; vis. scientist Royal Inst. Tech., Stockholm, 1981. Contbr. articles to profl. jours. Brit. Council tuition grantee Cambridge U., Eng., 1974-76; fellow U. Ill.-Urbana-Champaign, 1978. Mem. Am. Phys. Soc., IEEE (sr.), Electrochem. Soc. Hindu. Current work: Semiconductor device physics; ion implantation. Subspecialties: Semiconductors; Condensed matter physics. Office: Philips Research Lab Sunnyvale 811 E Arques Ave Sunnyvale CA 94086

BHATTACHARYYA, SHANKAR, electrical engineering educator, researcher; b. Rangoon, Burma, June 23, 1946; came to U.S., 1967; s. Nil Kantha and Hem Nalini (Mukherji) B.; m. Carole Jeanne Colgate, Feb. 10, 1971; children: Krishna Lee, Mohadev, Sona Lee. B.Tech. with honors, Indian Inst. Tech., Bombay, 1967; M.S.E.E., Rice U., 1969, Ph.D. E.E., 1971. Asst. prof. Fed. U., Rio de Janeiro, Brazil, 1971-72, assoc. prof., 1972-76, prof., 1976-80; research assoc. NASA, Huntsville, Ala., 1974-75; assoc. prof. elec. engring. Tex. A&M U., College Station, 1980-84, prof., 1984—; chmn. elec. engring. dept. Fed. U., Rio de Janerio, 1978-80. Assoc. editor: IEEE Transactions on Automatic Control, 1985—. NRC fellow NASA Marshall Space Flight Ctr., 1974-75. Mem. IEEE, Soc. Indsl. and Applied Math. Current Work: Research in area of control theory and control systems design. Subspecialties: Computer-aided design; Systems engineering. Home: 2803 Normand College Station TX 77840 Office: Texas A&M Univ Elec Engring Dept College Station TX 77843

BHAVANANDAN, VEERASINGHAM P., biochemistry researcher, educator; b. Jaffna, Sri Lanka, Nov. 1, 1936; came to U.S., 1971; s. Ramalingham and Rasam (Chelliah) Veerasingham; m. Esha Charawanamuttu, Jan. 22, 1965; children—Sivakami, Sathy. B.Sc., U. Ceylon, 1958; Ph.D., U. Edinburgh, Scotland, 1962, D.Sc., 1983. Research assoc. Columbia U., 1965-67; agrl. chemist Tea Research Inst., Talawakelle, Sri Lanka, 1967-71; staff scientist Med. Research Found., Oklahoma City, 1971-73; research assoc. M. S. Hershey Med. Ctr., Hershey, Pa., 1973-74, asst. prof., 1975-79, assoc. prof., 1980—. Contbr. numerous articles to sci. jours. NIH Research grantee, 1976—; Eleanor Roosevelt Internat. Cancer fellow Am. Cancer Soc., 1982-83; Sr. Fogarty Internat. fellow NIH, 1982. Fellow Royal Soc. Chemistry, Soc. Complex Carbohydrates; mem. Am. Chem. Soc., Am. Soc. Biol. Chemists, AAAS. Current work: Structure and function of glycoconjugates associated with cancer cells; biochemistry of respiratory mucus; carbohydrate chemistry. Subspecialties: Biochemistry (biology); Cancer research (medicine). Home: 161 Lamp Post Ln Hershey PA 17033 Office: Dept Biol Chemistry Milton S Hershey Med Ctr Box 850 Hershey PA 17033

BIANCO, CELSO, immunologist; b. Sao Paulo, Brazil, May 23, 1941; came to U.S., 1969, naturalized, 1981; s. Jose Antonio and Paulina (Schor) B.; m. Barbara Mei, Sept. 11, 1977; children: Marco, Christina, Julia. M.D., Med. Sch. Sao Paulo, 1966. Diplomate: lic. physician, N.Y. State. Resident in internal medicine Hosp. Sao Paulo, 1968; instr. N.Y. U. Sch. Medicine, 1969-71, asst. prof. pathology, 1971-73; asst. prof. cellular physiology and immunology Rockefeller U., 1974-77; asso. prof. pathology SUNY, Bklyn, 1977-80, prof., 1980-82; investigator Lindsley Friske Kimbal Research Inst., The N.Y. Blood Center, 1982—; dir. research and devel. Greater N.Y. Blood Program, The N.Y. Blood Center, N.Y.C., 1982—; adviser in immunology WHO; mem. sci. adv. com. Trudeau Inst. Med. Research, Saranac Lake, N.Y. Contbr. numerous articles on markers of lymphocyte subpopulations, activation of macrophages, interaction of monocytes and macrophages with plasma proteins to sci. jours. Recipient Research Career Devel. award Nat. Cancer Inst., NIH, 1976-81; named to 1,000 Contemporary Scientist Most Cited, 1965-78, Current Contents, 1981; Leukemia Soc. Am., Inc. scholar, 1975-76. Mem. Am. Soc. Clin. Investigation, Am. Soc. Cell Biology, Am. Assn. Immunologists, Harvey Soc., Sigma Xi. Club: The Douglaston (N.Y.). Current Work: Research on regulation of monocyte function (phagocytosis, adhesion, microbial killing and tumor killing) by proteins of the complement system and of clotting system,including factor B and fibronectin; devel. new areas in blood transfusion. Subspecialties: Immunology (medicine); Cell biology (medicine). Office: 310 E 67th St New York NY 10021

BIBER, MICHAEL PETER, neurologist; b. Newark, Oct. 9, 1941; s. Irving and Hilda (Zuckerman) B.; m. Sharlene Janice Hesse, May 19, 1978; children: Sarah Alexandra, Julia Ariel. A .B. with high honors, Oberlin Coll., 1963; M.D., U. Chgo., 1967. Diplomate: Am. Bd. Internal medicine, Am. Bd. Psychiatry and Neurology. Intern Mt. Sinai Hosp., N.Y.C., 1967-68; resident in medicine Boston City Hosp., 1970-72, resident in Neurology, 1972-74; research asst. Children's Hosp., Boston, 1975-78, research assoc., 1978; assoc. neurologist Beth Israel Hosp., Boston, 1978—, dir. Sleep unit, 1978-83. Served with USPHS, 1968-70. Mem. Am. Acad. Neurology, AAAS. Current Work: Clinical research on sleep-related problems such as sleep apnea, narcolepsy; development of ambulatory monitoring systems. Subspecialties: Neurology; Sleep disorders. Office: 1269 Beacon St Brookline MA 02146

BIBLE, ROY HENDERSON, JR., industrial analytical chemist, nuclear magnetic resonance consultant; b. Roanoke, Va., May 31, 1926; s. Roy Henderson Sr. and Susie Mae (Robertson) B.; m. Harriett Virginia Bertoglio,

June 10, 1951; 1 child, Keith Christopher. B.S., Va. Tech., 1948; M.S., U. Ill., 1949, Ph.D., 1951. Research investigator G.D. Searle and Co., Skokie, Ill., 1951-66, head phys. methodology, 1966-74, asst. dir. analytical resources and methods, 1974-79, research fellow, mgr. phys. methodology, 1979—. Author: Interpretation of NMR Spectra: An Empirical Approach, 1967; A Guide to the Interpretation NMR Spectra, 1976; (with others) (audio visual) Short Course Interpretation of NMR Spectra, 1978. Contbr. articles to profl. jours. Patentee in field. Bd. dirs. Nat. Chem. Exposition, Inc., Chgo., 1968—, pres., 1976-78; sci. fair judge Ill. Jr. Acad. Sci., 1972—. Named to honor scroll Am. Inst. Chemists, 1974. Mem. Am. Chem. Soc. (nat. councilor 1964—, tchr. NMR short course 1967—, com. on coms. 1976-81, nominations and elections com. 1982—, treas. Chgo. sect. 1964-65, chmn. 1967-68, Disting. Service award 1985), Chgo. Assn. Tech. Socs. (acad., Merit award 1973), Soc. Applied Spectroscopy, Sigma Xi, Alpha Chi Sigma, Phi Lambda Upsilon. Club: Chgo. Chemists (pres. 1962-63). Current work: Interpretation and application of nuclear magnetic resonance spectroscopy in organic chemistry; molecular spectroscopy; organic chemistry. Subspecialties: Nuclear magnetic resonance; Analytical chemistry. Home: 9012 Mango Ave Morton Grove IL 60053 Office: G D Searle and Co 4901 Searle Pkwy Skokie IL 60077

BIC, LUBOMIR, computer scientist; b. Iglau, Czechoslovakia, Nov. 28, 1951; s. Lubomir and Olga (Treska) B. M.S. in Computer Sci, Tech. U. Darmstadt, W.Ger., 1976; Ph.D. in Computer Sci, U. Calif.-Irvine, 1979. Cons. DKD, Wiesbaden, W.Ger., 1974-76; research asst. dept. info. and computer sci. U. Calif.-Irvine, 1976-78, lectr., 1978-79; research assoc. computer sci. Siemens AG, Munich, W. Ger., 1979—; asst. prof. info. and computer sci. U. Calif.-Irvine, 1980—. Author: Micos: A Microprogrammable Computer Simulator, 1982. NSF research grantee, 1982-84. Mem. Assn. Computing Machinery, IEEE. Current Work: Highly distributed asynchronous computer architectures, dataflow systems, intelligent data-retrieval systems, database machines. Subspecialties: Computer architecture; Database systems. Office: Dept ICS U Calif Irvine CA 92717

BICE, DAVID E., immunologist; b. Cornville, Ariz., Apr. 8, 1938; s. Virgil J. and Sarah D. (Winona) B.; m. Janet Schmutz, July 1, 1960; children: Cheryl, Patricia, Brent, Robyn, Jon, Brian. B.S., Utah State U., 1962; M.S., U. Ariz., 1964; Ph.D., La. State U. Med. Sch., 1968. Research assoc. La State U. Med. Sch., New Orleans, 1964-69; post doctoral fellow Harvard Med. Sch., Boston, 1969-71; asst. prof. La. State U. Med. Sch., New Orleans, 1971-75; immunologist Inhalation Toxicology Research Inst., Albuquerque, 1975—; mem. lung immunology and immunotoxicology study sects. NIH. Contbr. articles to profl. jours. Am. Cancer Soc. grantee, 1972-1975. Mem. Am. Assn. Immunologists, Am. Thoracic Soc., AAAS. Republican. Mormon. Current Work: Basic research in the development of immune defenses in the lung and how they are affected by inhaled toxic materials. Subspecialties: Immunobiology and immunology; Immunotoxicology. Home: 3101 Alcazar NE Albuquerque NM 87110 Office: PO Box 5890 Albuquerque NM 87185

BICERANO, JOZEF, research scientist; b. Istanbul, Turkey, Oct. 18, 1952; came to U.S., 1971; s. Salamon and Rikocya (Kapeluto) B.; m. Dahlia Grunberg, Oct. 3, 1980 (div. June 1983). B.A., M.S., Northwestern U., 1974; Ph.D., Harvard U., 1979. Teaching fellow Harvard U., 1976-78; postdoctoral research asst. U. Calif.-Berkeley, 1981-82; sr. research scientist Energy Conversion Devices, Inc., Troy, Mich., 1982—; organizer Internat. Conf. on Theory of Structures of Non-Crystalline Solids, 1985, also editor procs. Contbr. articles to profl. jours. Served to lt. Turkish Air Force, 1979-81. Mem. Am. Phys. Soc., Am. Chem. Soc., Sigma Xi, Phi Beta Kappa. Unitarian-Universalist. Clubs: Toastmasters Internat. (Birmingham, Mich.); Orion Art Center (Lake Orion, Mich.). Current work: Use of the techniques of molecular electronic structure theory and theoretical solid state physics to contribute to ongoing research for the development of new synthetic materials. Subspecialties: Theoretical chemistry; Condensed matter physics. Home: 767 Coachman Dr Apt 1 Troy MI 48083 Office: Energy Conversion Devices Inc 1675 W Maple Rd Troy MI 48084

BICHSEL, HANS, physicist; b. Basel, Switzerland, Sept. 2, 1924; came to U.S., 1951, naturalized, 1967; s. Paul and Anna (Blaettler) B.; m. Sue Greenwalt, Sept. 15, 1959; children: Elisabeth Christine, Joseph Oliver. M.A., U. Basel, 1951, Ph.D., 1951. Research asso. Princeton U., 1951-54, Rice Inst., Houston, 1954-57; asst. prof. physics U. Wash., Seattle, 1957-59, from assoc. prof.to prof., 1969-78; from asst. prof. to assoc. prof. U. So. Calif., Los Angeles, 1959-72; assoc. prof. physics U. Calif.-Berkeley, 1969; lectr Aarhus (Denmark) U., 1982; cons. Los Alamos Nat. Lab., 1978-83. Contbr. articles to profl. jours. Served with Swiss Army, 1943-45. Mem. Am. Phys. Soc., Swiss Phys. Soc. Current Work: Interaction of charged particles with matter; dosimetry for charged particle cancer therapy; detection of relativistic charged particles. Subspecialties: Cancer research (medicine); Atomic and molecular physics. Address: 1211 22d Ave E Seattle WA 98112

BICKART, THEODORE ALBERT, engineering educator, consultant; b. N.Y.C., Aug. 25, 1935; s. Theodore Roosevelt and Edna Catherine (Pink) B.; m. Carol Florence Nichols, June 14, 1958 (div. 1972); children: Karl Jeffrey, Lauren Spencer; m. Frani Rudolph, Aug. 14, 1982; 1 stepdau., Jennifer Anne Cumming. B.E.S., Johns Hopkins U., 1957, M.S.E., 1958, D.Eng., 1960. Instr. Johns Hopkins U., 1958-61; asst. prof. elec. and computer engring. Syracuse U., 1963-65, assoc. prof., 1965-70, prof., 1970—, dean engring., 1984—; vis. scholar U. Calif.-Berkeley, 1977; Fulbright lectr. Kiev (USSR) Poly. Inst., spring 1981; vis. lectr. Nanjing (People's Republic of China) Inst. Tech., summer 1981; cons. Deft Labs., East Syracuse, N.Y., 1982-83. Author: (with Norman Balabanian) Electrical Network Theory, 1969, Linear Network Theory, 1981; contbr. articles to profl. publs. Served to 1st lt. U.S. Army, 1961-63. Decorated Army Commendation medal; NSF grantee, 1970, 79. Fellow IEEE (Syracuse Sect. Best Paper award 1969, 70, 73, 74, 77); mem. N.Y. Acad. Scis., Am. Math. Soc., Soc. Indsl. and Applied Maths., Assn. Computing Machinery. Democrat. Current Work: Analysis and design of electrical networks; control systems analysis; design of algorithms and software for analysis of dynamical systems, including retarded systems; logic design of computer systems. Subspecialties: Computer engineering; Mathematical software. Home: 211 Standish Dr Syracuse NY 13224 Office: Office Dean Engring Syracuse U Link Hall Syracuse NY 13210

BICKEL, JOHN HENRY, utility company executive; b. Chgo., June 23, 1950; s. Francis Anthony and Elaine (Broderick) B.; m. Anne Livingston Stuart, June 9, 1973; children: Blake Francis, Catherine Stuart. B.S., U. Vt., 1972, M.S. in Physics, 1974; M.S. in Nuclear Engring, Rensselaer Poly. Inst., 1975, Ph.D., 1980. Nuclear engr. Combustion Engring., Windsor, Conn., 1975-79; fellow, adv. com. reactor safeguards Nuclear Regulatory Commn., Washington, 1979-80; sr. nuclear engr. Northeast Utilities Co., Berlin, Conn., 1980—. Chmn. 10th Dist. Va. Conservative Caucus, Fairfax County, 1980-81. Recipient High Merit award Nuclear Regulatory Commn., 1980. Mem. Am. Nuclear Soc. (Engring. Achievement award 1983). Republican. Roman Catholic. Current Work: Nuclear reactor safety analysis, simulation of reactor core and containment response, hydrogen generation and control, radiolysis and fission product water chemistry; probabilistic risk assessment. Subspecialties: Nuclear engineering; Nuclear fission. Office: Northeast Utilities Co PO Box 270 Selden St Berlin CT 05401

BICKEL, PETER JOHN, university dean, statistician; b. Bucharest, Roumania, Sept. 21, 1940; came to U.S., 1957, naturalized, 1964; s. Eliezer and P. Madeleine (Moscovici) B.; m. Nancy Kramer, Mar. 2, 1964; children: Amanda, Stephen. A.B., U. Calif.-Berkeley, 1960, M.A., 1961, Ph.D., 1963. Asst. prof. stats. U. Calif., Berkeley, 1964-67, assoc. prof., 1967-70, prof., 1970—, chmn. dept., 1976-79, dean phys. scis., 1980—; vis. lectr. math. Imperial Coll., London, 1965-66; fellow J.S. Guggenheim Meml. Found., 1970-71; NATO sr. sci. fellow, 1974; John D. and Catherine T. MacArthur Found. fellow. Author: (with K. Doksum) Mathematical Statistics, 1976; Assoc. editor: Annals of Math. Statistics, 1968-76; contbr. articles to profl. jours. Fellow Inst. Math. Stats. (pres. 1980), Am. Statis. Assn., AAAS; mem. Royal Statis. Soc., Internat. Statis. Inst. Current Work: Asymptotic theory, robust and nonparametric statistics. Subspecialty: Statistics. Office: Dept Statistics Evans Hall Univ of Calif Berkeley CA 94720

BIDELMAN, WILLIAM PENDRY, educator, astronomer; b. Los Angeles, Sept. 25, 1918; s. William Pendry and Dolores (De Remer) B.; m. Verna Pearl Shirk, June 19, 1940; children—Lana Louise Bidelman Stone, Linda Elizabeth Bidelman Holden, Billie Jean Bidelman Little, Barbara Jo Bidelman Talley. Student U. N.D., 1936-37; S.B., Harvard U., 1940; Ph.D., U. Chgo., 1943. Physicist Aberdeen Proving Ground, Md., 1943-45; instr. astronomy, then asst. prof. Yerkes Obs., U. Chgo., 1945-53; asst. astronomer then assoc. Lick Obs. U. Calif., 1953-62; prof. astronomy U. Mich., 1962-69, U. Tex. at Austin, 1969-70, Case Western Res. U., Cleve., 1970—; chmn. dept., dir. Warner and Swasey Obs., 1970-75; mem. adv. panel astronomy NSF, 1959-62; mem. NRC adv. com. astronomy Office Naval Research, 1964-67. Contbr. profl. jours. Mem. Am. Astron. Soc. (councilor 1959-62, participant vis. prof. program 1961-65), Astron. Soc. Pacific (editor publs. 1956-61), Internat. Astron. Union (mem. commns. 5, 29, 45, pres. commn. 45 1964-67), Phi Beta Kappa. Presbyterian. Current work: Observational astrophysics. Subspecialties: Optical astronomy; Spectral classification, astronomical data. Home: 3171 Chelsea Dr Cleveland Heights OH 44118 Office: Dept Astronomy Case Western Res U Cleveland OH 44106

BIDLACK, JEAN MARIE, neurochemist; b. Rochester, N.Y., Dec. 4, 1953; d. William Henry and Mary Louise (Naughton) Bidlack. B.A., Skidmore Coll., 1975; M.S., U. Rochester, 1977, Ph.D., 1979, Postdoctoral fellow U. Rochester, N.Y., 1979-80, sr. instr., 1980-81, asst. prof. neurochemistry, 1981—. Contbr. articles to profl. jours. U. Rochester grad. fellow, 1975-79. Mem. Soc. for Neurosci., Am. Soc. Neurochemistry, Biophys. Soc. Current work: Elucidating the molecular basis of opioid receptor and generating monoclonal antibodies to the opioid receptor; biochem. studies of drug action in nervous system. Subspecialties: Neurochemistry; Neuropharmacology. Home: 61 Roby Dr Rochester NY 14618 Office: Center for Brain Research Univ Rochester Sch Medicine 601 Elmwood Ave Rochester NY 14642

BIEBER, FREDERICK ROBERT, medical educator; b. Regina, Sask., Can., Feb. 9, 1950; came to U.S., 1956, naturalized, 1964; s. Frederick John Andrew and Marjorie Phyllis (Davidson) B.; m. Jane M. McNamara, June 23, 1973. B.A., SUNY-Oswego, 1972; M.S., U. Rochester, 1976; Ph.D., Med. Coll. Va., 1981. Cert. Am. Bd. Med. Genetics. Research fellow Med. Sch., Harvard U., Boston, 1981-83, instr. in pathology, 1983-85, asst. prof., 1985—, vis. instr. in biology Harvard U., Cambridge, Mass., 1982—, tutor in biology, 1982—. Assoc. editor: Birth Defects Atlas, 1985. Contbr. numerous articles to med. jours. Mem. Am. Soc. Human Genetics, Teratology Soc. (Young Investigator award 1982), Soc. Pediatric Pathology, Sigma Xi. Current work: Fetal pathology and spontaneous abortion. Subspecialties: Genetics and genetic engineering (medicine); Teratology. Office: Brigham & Women's Hosp 75 Francis St Boston MA 02115

BIEBER, MARK ALLAN, nutritionist; b. Cleve., Sept. 16, 1946; s. Lester and Ethel (Rubin) B. B.S., U. Pitts., 1968; Ph.D., Mich. State U., 1973. Teaching asst. Mich. State U., East Lansing, 1968-73; Matheson Found. fellow Columbia U., N.Y.C.,1973-77; sr. nutritionist Best Foods, Union, N.J., 1977-80, prin. nutritionist, 1980-83, nutrition research assoc., 1983—. Contbr. articles to profl. jours. Fellow Am. Heart Assn.; mem. Am. Oil Chemists Soc., Inst. Food Technologists, N.J. Nutrition Council, Soc. Nutrition Edn., Phi Eta Sigma. Jewish. Lodge: B'nai B'rith. Current work: Lipid metabolism, essential fatty acids, atherosclerosis, nutrition research; grants administration; advertising and publicity review; insect juvenile hormones and mass spectrometry. Subspecialties: Nutrition (medicine); Biochemistry (biology). Home: 515 Mt Prospect Ave #17E Newark NJ 07104 Office: Best Foods 1120 Commerce Ave Union NJ 07083

BIEDENHARN, LAWRENCE CHRISTIAN, JR., physicist, physics educator; b. Vicksburg, Miss., Nov. 18, 1922; s. Lawrence Christian and Willetta (Lyons) B.; m. Sarah Jeffress Willingham, Mar. 25, 1950; children—John David, Sally Willeta. B.S., MIT, 1944, Ph.D., 1949. Research assoc. MIT, 1949-50; physicist Oak Ridge Nat. Lab., 1950-52; asst. prof. Yale U., 1952-54; assoc. prof. Rice U., 1954-61; prof. physics Duke U., 1961—; cons. in field. Author: (with others) Coulomb Excitation, 1964, Quantum Theory of Angular Momentum, 1965, Quantum Physics: Theory and Application, 1981, The Racah-Wigner Algebra in Quantum Theory, 1981, Relativistics Models of Extended Hadrons Obeying a Mass-Spin Trajectory Constraint, 1982. Assoc. editor Jour. Math. Physics, 1964-68, 70-74, 1979-85, editor, 1985—. Contbr. articles to profl. jours. Served with signal corps AUS, 1943-46, Recipient Alexander von Humboldt Sr. U.S. Scientist award, 1976; Fulbright fellow, 1958, Guggenheim fellow, 1959, NSF sr. postdoctoral fellow, 1964-65. Fellow Am. Phys. Soc. (Jesse Beams award 1979), Inst. Physics. Current work: Topological methods in field theory. Subspecialties: Nuclear physics; Particle physics. Office: Duke Univ Dept Physics Durham NC 27706

BIEMER, THOMAS ANTHONY, chemist, microbiological researcher; b. Paterson, N.J., Jan. 22, 1953; B.S. in Biology, U. Scranton, 1975; B.S. in Chemistry, Fairleigh Dickinson U., 1979 M.S. in Chemistry, Seton Hall U., 1981. Chemist Warner Lambert Co., Morris Plains, N.J., 1979-80, sr. chemist, 1980-81, assoc. scientist, 1981-84, sr. assoc. scientist, 1984—. Mem. Am. Chem. Soc. Current work: Separation of biologically active compounds from complex systems, tissue culturing for production of monoclonal antibodies, analysis of volatile gaseous components present in human mouth and lung air. Subspecialties: Analytical chemistry; Tissue culture. Home: 8 Lakeshore Dr Mine Hill NJ 07801 Office: 170 Tabor Rd Morris Plains NJ 07950

BIER, CHARLES JAMES, chemistry educator, Solar researcher; b. Louisville, June 21, 1945; s. Charles Aloysius and Emilie Julie (Miksik) B.; m. Jerryanne Taber, Aug. 3, 1968; children: Rebecca, Jessica, Jonathan, Sara. B.S. in Chemistry, Providence Coll., 1967; Ph.D., MIT, 1971. Research assoc. Duke U., Durham, N.C., 1971-72; asst. prof. U. North Fla., Jacksonville, 1972-75, Eisenhower Coll., Seneca Falls, N.Y., 1975-76; stockroom curator, instr. chemistry Hollins Coll., Va., 1976-77; assoc., prof. chemistry and environ. studies Ferrum Coll., Va., 1977—. Contbr. articles to profl. jours.; solar inventor. Bd. dirs. Whetstone Br. Living Sch., Ferrum, 1978—. Franklin County Peace fellow. Mem. Internat. Solar Energy Soc. Catholic. Club: Franklin County Organic Gardening. Current Work: Development technology and systems which use minimum of non-renewable resources to support comfortable, productive and full livelihood. Subspecialties: Solar energy; Resource management. Home: Route 2 Box 35 Ferrum VA 24088 Office: Ferrum Coll PO Box 2693 Ferrum VA 24088

BIERENBAUM, RICHARD ELLIOT, research chemist; b. Newark, N.J., Nov. 27, 1953; s. Irving and Shirley (Friedlander) B.; m. Gale Ray Simon; 1 child, Rachel. B.A., Rutgers Coll., 1975; M.S., Northwestern U., 1976, Ph.D., 1979. Research chemist Hooker Chem. Co., Niagara Falls, N.Y., 1979-82, ICI Ams., West Deptford, N.J., 1982—. Contbr. articles to profl. jours. Patentee in field. Dow Chem. Co. fellow, 1976; Northwestern U. fellow, 1977; NSF fellow, 1978. Mem. Am. Chem. Soc. Current work: Process development in MDA (methylene dianiline) synthesis, an MDI precursor. Subspecialty: Organic chemistry. Office: Rubicon Chemicals PO Box 900 Woodbury NJ 08096

BIETZ, JEROLD ALLEN, research executive; b. Mayville, N.D., Feb. 22, 1942; s. Albert Enoch and Mabel Agnes (Skarperud) B.; m. Myrna Elizabeth Blair, June 22, 1963; children—Matthew, Melanie. B.S., Mayville State Coll., 1963; M.S., U. N.D., 1966. Research chemist No. Regional Research Ctr. Agrl. Research Service U.S. Dept. Agr., Peoria, Ill., 1966-83, research leader, 1983—. Contbr. articles to profl. jours. Recipient NDEA fellow, 1963-66. Mem. Am. Chem. Soc., Am. Assn. of Cereal Chemists (chmn. protein div. 1983-84), AAAS. Episcopalian. Current works: Isolation and characterization of cereal proteins. Development of analytical methods for their analysis and for quality prediction. Subspecialties: Biochemistry (biology); Analytical chemistry. Home: 132 Field Grove Court East Peoria IL 61611 Office: No Regional Research Ctr USDA-ARS 1815 N University St Peoria IL 61604

BIGELEISEN, JACOB, educator, chemist; b. Paterson, N.J., May 2, 1919; s. Harry and Ida (Slomowitz) B.; m. Grace Alice Simon, Oct. 21, 1945; children: David M., Ira S., Paul E. A.B., NYU, 1939; M.S., Wash. State U., 1941; Ph.D., U. Calif., Berkeley, 1943. Research scientist Manhattan Dist., Columbia, 1943-45; research asso. Ohio State U., Columbus, 1945-46; fellow Enrico Fermi Inst., U. Chgo., 1946-48; sr. chemist Brookhaven Nat. Lab., Upton, N.Y., 1948-68; prof. chemistry U. Rochester, N.Y., 1968-78, chmn. dept., 1970-75; Tracy H. Harris prof. U. Rochester (Coll. Arts and Scis.), 1973-78; v.p. research, dean grad. studies SUNY, Stony Brook, 1978-80, Leading prof. chemistry, 1978—; vis. prof. Cornell U., 1953; NSF sr. fellow, vis. prof. Eidgen Techn. Hochschule, Switzerland, 1962-63; chmn. Assembly Math. and Phys. Scis., NRC-Nat. Acad. Scis., 1976-80. Mem. editorial bd.: Jour. Phys. Chemistry. Trustee Sayville Jewish Center, 1954-68. Recipient Nuclear award Am. Chem. Soc., 1958, Gilbert N. Lewis lectr., 1963, E.O. Lawrence award, 1964, Disting. Alumnus award Wash. State U., 1983; John Simon Guggenheim fellow, 1974-75. Fellow Am. Phys. Soc., Am. Chem. Soc., AAAS, Am. Acad. Arts and Sci.; mem. Nat. Acad. Scis., Phi Beta Kappa, Sigma Xi, Phi Lambda Upsilon. Research in photochemistry in rigid media, semiquinones, cryogenics, chemistry of isotopes, quantum statistics of gases, liquids and solids. Current Work: Correlation of isotope chemistry with molecular structure; study of molecular motion in condensed media by isotope fractionation. Subspecialties: Physical chemistry; Nuclear engineering. Home: PO Box 217 Saint James NY 11780

BIGGERS, CHARLES JAMES, genetics educator; b. Gastonia, N.C., Feb. 7, 1935; s. Loy Banks and Ruth (Black) B.; m. Shirley Hoover, Aug. 24, 1958; children—Lisa Ellen, Amy Laura, Emily Ann. B.S., Wake Forest U., 1957; M.S., Appalachian U., 1959; Ph.D., U. S.C., 1969. Chmn. dept. biology Orlando Jr. Coll., Fla., 1959-63; prof. biology dept. Memphis State U., 1969—. Contbr. articles on biology to profl. jours. Served to 2d lt. arty., U.S. Army, 1957-58. Recipient Disting. Teaching Service award Memphis State U., 1985; NSF grantee, 1959, 60-61, 62, 63-64. Mem. AAAS, Sigma Xi, Beta Beta Beta, Chi Beta Phi. Baptist. Current work: Biochemical population genetics. Subspecialty: Genetics and genetic engineering (biology). Home: 7250 Abercrombie Ln Memphis TN 38119 Office: Biology Dept Memphis State Univ Memphis TN 38152

BIGIO, IRVING JOSEPH laser physicist, consultant, technical manager; b. Norfolk, Va., Dec. 17, 1946; s. Joseph Isaac and Renee (Kaire) B.; m. Ruth Bosiger, May 18, 1969; children—Aaron J., Erica R. B.S., U. Mich., 1969, M.S., 1979, Ph.D., 1974. Dep. group leader Los Alamos Nat. Lab., N.Mex., 1984-84; cons. Rocketdyne div. Rockwell Internat., Canoga Park, Calif., 1983—, Lambda Physik GmbH, Gottingen, W.Ger., 1982—; cons. in field. Contbr. articles to profl. jours. Bd. dirs. Los Alamos Concert Assn., 1980-84, Los Alamos Jewish Ctr., 1979. Danforth fellow, 1971; Fulbright Sr. scholar, 1976. Mem. Optical Soc. Am., Am. Phys. Soc. Lodge: B'nai B'rith (v.p. local chpt. 1978-79). Current work: General laser physics, general nonlinear optics, excimer lasers, injection locking, harmonic generation, stimulated scattering, laser biophysics, solitons. Subspecialties: Excimers; Nonlinear optics. Office: Los Alamos Nat Lab Mail Stop J566 Los Alamos NM 87545

BIGLER, ERIN DAVID, psychologist, educator; b. Los Angeles, July 9, 1949; s. Erin Boley and Natalie (Webb) B.; m. Janet Beckstrom, June 22, 1971; children: Alicia Suzanne, Erin Daniel. B.S., Brigham Young U., 1971, Ph.D., 1974; postgrad., St. Joseph's Hosp., Phoenix, 1977. Lic. psychologist, Ariz., Tex. Postdoctoral fellow St. Josephs Hosp., Phoenix, 1975-77; psychologist Austin (Tex.) State Hosp, 1977-78; asst. prof. U. Tex., Austin, 1977-82, assoc. prof. psychology, 1982—, pvt. practice psychology, Austin, 1977—. Editor: Clin. Neuropsychology, 1979—; author: Diagnostic Clinical Neuropsychology, 1983; contbr. articles to profl. jours. NIH grantee, 1975-77; Hogg Found. grantee, 1981-82. Mem. Am. Psychol. Assn., Nat. Acad. Neuropsychology (exec. com. 1982-83), N.Y. Acad. Scis., Soc. for Neurosci., Sigma Xi. Democrat. Mormon. Current Work: Brain-behavior relations; neurological diagnostics. Subspecialties: Neuropsychology; Psychobiology. Office: Austin Neurological Clinic 711-F W 38th St Austin TX 78705

BIGLER, RODNEY E., nuclear physicist; b. Pocatello, Idaho, Mar. 15, 1941; s. Vance S. and Mildred (Higham) B.; m. Louise Ann Calabrese, Sept. 17, 1977; children—Ronald, Julie. Student, Multnomah Coll., 1962-63; B.S., Portland State Coll., 1966, postgrad., 1966-67; Ph.D., U. Tex., Austin, 1971. Teaching asst. Portland State Coll., 1966-67; teaching asst. U. Tex., 1967-68, research asst., 1968-71; research assoc. Sloan-Kettering Inst., N.Y.C., 1971-73, assoc., 1973-82, asst. mem., 1982—; research collaborator Brookhaven Nat. Lab., 1973-79, 83—; asst. prof. Cornell U. Grad. Sch. Med. Scis., 1974—, assoc. prof. dept. radiology Cornell U. Med. Coll., 1984—; attending physicist N.Y. Hosp., 1984—. Contbr. numerous articles to sci. jours. Served with AUS, 1959-62. NIH-Nat. Heart Lung and Blood Inst. grantee, 1978—; NIH-Nat. Cancer Inst. grantee, 1983—. Current Work: Medical diagnostic and therapeutic uses of radiation and radioactive materials research; nuclear medicine; nuclear magnetic resonance research. Subspecialties: Biophysics (physics); Nuclear physics. Home: 430 E 63d St Apt 5E New York NY 10021 Office: 1300 York Ave New York NY 10021

BIGLIERI, EDWARD GEORGE, physician; b. San Francisco, Jan. 17, 1925; s. Ned and (Mignacco) B.; m. Beverly A. Bergesen, May 16, 1953; children: Mark, Michael, Gregg. Student, U. San Francisco, 1942-43, Gonzaga U., 1943-44; B.S. in Chemistry summa cum laude, U. San Francisco, 1948, D.Sc. (hon.), 1985; M.D., U. Calif., 1952. Diplomate: Am. Bd. Internal Medicine (endocrine test com. 1971-76). Intern U. Calif., San Francisco Med. Center, also; Intern VA Hosp., San Francisco, 1952-54, resident, 1954-56; clin. assoc. and research physician NIH, 1956-58; also metabolic unit U. Calif., 1958-61, asst. prof. medicine, 1962-65, assoc. prof., 1965-71, prof., 1971—; program dir. gen. clin. research, also chief endocrinology service San Francisco Gen. Hosp., 1962—; vis. prof. Monash U., Melbourne, Australia, 1967; NATO vis. prof., Italy, 1983; cons. Oak Knoll Naval Hosp., Travis AFB; mem. study sect. NIH, 1971-74. Contbr. articles on endocrinology ahd hormones in hypertension to profl. jours. Served to lt. (j.g.) USN, 1944-46. NIH grantee, 1972-73. Mem. Endocrine Soc., A.C.P., Am. Soc. Clin. Investigation, Am. Heart Assn. (council high blood pressure research), Assn. Am. Physicians, Western Assn. Physicians, Am. Fedn. Clin. Research. Current Work: Role of hormones in high blood pressure. Subspecialties: Internal medicine; Endocrinology. Home: 129 Convent Ct San Rafael CA 94901 Office: San Francisco Gen Hosp San Francisco CA 94110

BIKALES, NORBERT M., chemist; b. Berlin, Jan. 7, 1929; s. Solomon and Bertha (Bander) B.; m. Gerda V. Bierzonski, Apr. 28, 1951; children—Marguerite, Edward. B.S., CCNY, 1951; M.S., Poly. Inst. N.Y., 1956, Ph.D., 1961. Research chemist Am. Cyanamid Co., Stamford, Conn., 1951-62; tech. dir. Gaylord Assocs., Newark, 1962-65; chem. cons., Livingston, N.J., 1965-76; prof. chemistry Rutgers U., New Brunswick, N.J., 1973-79; dir. polymers program NSF, Washington, 1976—; vis. scientist Centre de Recherche sur les Macromolecules, Strasbourg, France, 1984; chmn. Gordon Conf. on Polymers, 1985. Exec. editor Ency. Polymer Sci. and Tech., 18 vols., 1962-77, mem. editorial bd. 2d edit., 1982—; editor: Water-Soluble Polymers, 1973; Cellulose and Cellulose Derivatives, 2 vols., 1972. Contbr. numerous articles to profl. publs. Patentee in field. Treas. Livingston Little Theater, 1964-65; pres. Friends of Livingston Library, 1968-72, Livingston Symphony Orch., 1970-76. Recipient Great medal City of Paris, 1985. Fellow N.Y. Acad. Scis.; mem. Am. Chem. Soc. (chmn. div. polymer chemistry 1983), Soc. Plastics Engrs. (div. bd. dirs. 1980), Internat. Union Pure and Applied Chemistry (sec. commn. on macromolecular nomenclature 1978—), AAAS, Am. Phys. Soc. Current work: Synthesis, structure and properties of synthetic polymers; water-soluble polymers; funding of basic polymer research in American universities. Subspecialties: Polymer chemistry; Polymers (materials science). Office: Nat Sci Found 1800 G St NW Washington DC 20550

BILDERBACK, DONALD HEYWOOD, physicist; b. Usumbura, Burundi, Mar. 6, 1947 (parents Am. citizens); s. Allen Heywood and Lillian Alice (Watkins) B.; m. Rebecca B. Belcher, Sept. 16, 1969; 1 child, Douglas Heywood. B.S. in Physics, Seattle Pacific U., 1969; Ph.D. in Physics, Purdue U., 1975. Research mgr. Cornell U., Ithaca, N.Y., 1975-78, staff scientist, 1978—; pres. Multiwire Labs., Ltd., Ithaca, 1981—. Inventor in field. Mem. Am. Phys. Soc., Am. Crystallographic Assn., Soc. for Photo-Optical Instrumentation Engrs., Materials Research Soc. Republican. Current work: Field of synchrotron radiation experimentation, X-ray optics, detectors, and X-ray diffraction. Subspecialty: X-ray physics. Office: Cornell High Energy Synchrotron Source Cornell Univ 231 Clark Hall Ithaca NY 14853

BILITCH, MICHAEL, medical educator, physician; b. Belgrade, Yugoslavia, Feb. 8, 1932; came to U.S., 1949; s. Sasha Alexander and Oona Mary (Ball) B.; m. Mary Jo Ann Minges, June 19, 1956 (dec. 1966); children: Bonnie, Kimberly, David; m. Nancy Ann Neher, Sept. 3, 1967 (div. 1982); children: Kendal Ingram, Dawn, Robert, Susan, Douglas; m. Alexis Donath, June 19, 1983; 1 child, Eric. A.B., San Jose State Coll., 1954; M.A., Miami U., 1956; M.D., U. So. Calif., 1960. Teaching asst. San Jose State Coll., 1952-54; teaching asst. Miami U., Oxford, Ohio, 1954-56; research asst. U. So. Calif., Los Angeles, 1958-60, instr. medicine, 1964-67, asst. prof., 1967-71, assoc. prof., 1971—; dir. U. So. Calif. (Pacemaker ctr.), 1970—; vis. prof. U. Groningen, Netherlands, 1978; cons. Cardiac Pacemakers, St. Paul, 1978—. Author: A Manual of Cardiac Arrhythmias, 1971; co-author: Heart Block, 1972; contbr. articles to profl. jours. Los Angeles County Heart Assn. fellow,

1965-67. Fellow ACP, Am. Coll. Cardiology; mem. Assn. Advancement of Med. Instrumentation (chmn. pacemaker com. 1971-77), N.Am. Soc. Pacing and Electrophysiology (founding mem., exec. com.), Am. Fedn. Clin. Research, AAAS, N.Y. Acad. Scis., Royal Soc. Health. Patentee leadless pacemaker. Current Work: Implantable cardiac pacemakers, development and clinical testing of new devices and systems, evaluating performance standards; cardiac arrhythmias, evaluation by mapping techniques, management by logical schema. Subspecialties: Cardiology; Internal medicine. Home: 1420 San Pablo St Apt C-201 Los Angeles CA 90033 Office: U So Calif Sch Medicine 2025 Zonal Ave Los Angeles CA 90033

BILLEN, DANIEL, radiation biologist, educator; b. N.Y.C., Nov. 27, 1924; s. Morris and Gertrude B.; m. Gertrude Eleanor Berlin; children: Jerome, Rhonda, Robin. B.S., Cornell U., 1948; M.S., U. Tenn., Knoxville, 1949, Ph.D., 1951. Biologist Oak Ridge (Tenn.) Nat. Lab., 1951-57; assoc. prof., staff scientist M.D. Anderson Hosp., Houston, 1957-66; program dir. NSF, Washington., 1961-62; prof. radiation biology U. Fla., Gainesville, 1966-73; dir., prof. biomed. scis. Grad. Sch. Biomed. Scis. U. Tenn., Oak Ridge, 1973-77, prof. biomed. Scis., 1973—. Editor-in-chief: Radiation Research, 1979—; contbr. research papers to profl. publs. Served with USAAF, 1943-44. Mem. Radiation Research Soc., Am. Soc. Microbiologists, Am. Soc. Biol. Chemists. Jewish. Club: Elks. Current Work: Research in DNA damage and repair, radiation and chemical hazards in cells. Subspecialties: Cell biology; Gene actions. Office: Biology Div Oak Ridge Nat Lab Oak Ridge TN 37830

BILLINGSLEY, MELVIN LEE, pharmacology educator, researcher; b. Pitts., Oct. 3, 1953; s. Melvin Leroy and Mary Ann (Niznik) B.; m. Dianne Elaine Dusman, Aug. 20, 1976; 1 child, Tyler Dusman. B.S., U. Pitts., 1974; Ph.D., George Washington U., 1981. Research asst. U. Pitts., 1974-75; pharmacologist Stuart Pharm. Co., Wilmington, Del., 1975-77; postdoctoral fellow Yale U., New Haven, 1981-82; staff fellow Nat. Heart, Lung and Blood Inst., NIH, Bethesda, Md., 1982-84; asst. prof. pharmacology Hershey Med. Ctr., Pa. State U., 1984—; cons. medico-legal field. Contbr. articles to sci. jours. Lectr., Washington Area Council on Drug Abuse, 1979. Recipient Goddard award George Washington U., 1978; PMA Found. fellow, 1980-81. Mem. AAAS, Soc. for Neurosci., Am. Soc. Pharmacology and Exptl. Therapeutics, Sigma Xi. Democrat. Current work: Regulation of tissue-specific gene expression, modification of protein structure in excitable tissue, methyl transferase enzymes. Subspecialties: Molecular pharmacology; Molecular biology. Home: 17 Long Lane Dr RD 2 Hummelstown PA 17036 Office: Dept Pharmacology Hershey Med Ctr Pa State U Hershey PA 17033

BILLINGTON, RANDALL JOHN, psychologist; b. Redding, Calif., Nov. 25, 1951; s. John Austin and Edythe Viola (Carleton) B.; m. Jeri-Lynne Fraser, Nov. 5, 1983; children—Andre Neil, Mara Elizabeth. B.A., U. Calif.-Riverside, 1974; M.S., Yale U., 1981. Research cons. Roper Center, Office for Teaching and Research, Yale U., New Haven, 1979-81; research assoc. in psychology VA Hosp., West Haven, 1982—. Mem. adv. com. on investor responsibility Yale U. Contbr. articles in profl. jours. NSF hon. fellow; Prize teaching fellow Yale U. Mem. Am. Psychol. Assn., AAAS Current work: Psychological research in program evaluation and personality assessment; interrelations among diagnostic categories. Subspecialty: Social psychology. Home: 71 Lake Pl New Haven CT 06511

BILLMEYER, FRED WALLACE, JR., educator, chemist; b. Chattanooga, Aug. 24, 1919; s. Fred W. and Eleanor (Salmon) B.; m. Annette M. Trzcinski, Aug. 4, 1951; children—Fred S., Eleanor A., Dean W., David M. B.S., Cal. Inst. Tech., 1941; Ph.D., Cornell U., 1945. With plastics dept. E.I. du Pont de Nemours & Co., 1945-64; lectr. high polymers dept. chemistry U. Del., 1951-64; Vis. prof. chem. engring. MIT, 1960-61; prof. analytical chemistry Rensselaer Poly. Inst., 1964-85, prof. emeritus, 1984—. Cons. various coms. Internat. Commn. Illumination (CIE), 1964—; mem. U.S. Nat. Com. CIE, 1968—, v.p., 1975-79; Trustee Munsell Color Found., sec., 1975-84. Author: Textbook of Polymer Chemistry, 1957, Textbook of Polymer Science, 1961, 2d edit., 1971, Synthetic Polymers, 1972, (with Max Saltzman) Principles of Color Technology, 1966, 2d edit., 1981, (with E.A. Collins and J. Bares) Experiments in Polymer Science, 1973, (with R. N. Kelley) Entering Industry, 1975; also articles; Editor-in-chief: Color Research and Application, 1976—. Recipient Bruning award Fedn. Socs. Coatings Tech., 1977. Fellow Am. Phys. Soc., Optical Soc. Am., AAAS; mem. Am. Chem. Soc., N.Y. Soc. Coatings Tech., Soc. Plastics Engrs., Inter-Soc. Color Council (pres. 1968-70, sec. 1970-82, Macbeth award 1978, Service award 1983), Council Optical Radiation Measurements (sec. 1979-83), ASTM, Sigma Xi, Phi Kappa Phi. Subspecialty: Polymer chemistry. Home: 2121 Union St Schenectady NY 12309

BILOTTO, GERARDO, neurophysiologist, researcher; b. Benevento, Italy, Sept. 21, 1948; s. Giuseppe and Violetta (DePasquale) B.; m. Sandra Swanson, Sept. 4, 1977. B.S., N.Y. Inst. Tech., 1970; M.S., Columbia U., 1972, M.Phil., 1976, Ph.D., 1978. Dir. independent living research Human Resources Center, Albertson, N.Y., 1978-79; postdoctoral research fellow Rockefeller U., N.Y.C., 1979-81; sr. research assoc. Liberty Mut. Ins. Co. Research Center, 1981-84; research assoc. dept. orthopedic surgery Children's Hosp., Boston, 1981-84, Harvard Med. Sch., Boston, 1981-84; assoc. research scientist Columbia U., 1984—. Contbr. articles to profl. jours. NIH fellow, 1972-77, 79-81. Mem. Soc. Neurosci., IEEE, N.Y. Acad. Scis., AAAS, Sigma Xi. Current Work: Pain physiology; electrophysiology of dental pulp and trigerminal system; signal processing. Subspecialties: Neurophysiology; Biomedical engineering. Home: 508 Van Cortlandt Park Ave Yonkers NY 10705 Office: Columbia U 630 W 168th St New York NY 10032

BINFORD, THOMAS ORIEL, computer scientist, educator, consultant; b. Jefferson Twp., Pa., Apr. 13, 1936; s. Robert J. and Ruth Anna (Sandbach) B.; m. Mira Reym, Apr. 21, 1963 (div. 1968); m. Ione Gargione Junqueira, Dec. 30, 1975. B.S. in Physics, Pa. State Coll., 1957; Ph.D. in Physics, U. Wis. Madison, 1965. Research assoc. MIT, Cambridge, Mass., 1966-70; prof. computer sci. Stanford U., Calif., 1970—. Assoc. editor Internat. Jour. Robotics Research. Current work: Geometric reasoning and artificial intelligence in computer vision and robotics. Subspecialties: Artificial intelligence; Graphics, image processing, and pattern recognition. Office: Computer Sci Dept Stanford U Stanford CA 94305

BING, R.H., educator, mathematician; b. Oakwood, Tex., Oct. 20, 1914; s. Rupert Henry and Lula May (Thompson) B.; m. Mary Blanche Hobbs, Aug. 26, 1938; children—Robert H., Susan Elizabeth, Virginia Gay, Mary Patricia. B.S., S.W. Tex. State Tchrs. Coll., 1935; M.Ed., U. Tex., 1938, Ph.D., 1945. Tchr. high sch., Tex., 1935-42; instr., then asst. prof. math. U. Tex., 1942-47; mem. faculty U. Wis.-Madison, 1947-73, prof. math., 1952-64, research prof., 1964-68, Rudolph E. Langer prof. math., 1968-73, chmn. dept., 1958-60; acting prof. U. Va., 1949-50; vis. prof. U. Tex., 1971-72, prof., 1973—, Ashbel Smith prof. math., 1979-82, Kerr centennial prof., 1982-85, chmn. dept., 1975-77; dir. Summer Inst. on Set Theoretic Topology, Madison, 1955; mem. Inst. Advanced Study, Princeton, 1957-58, 62-63, 67. Mem. Nat. Sci. Bd. (1968-74), Nat. Acad. Scis., NRC (chmn. div. math. 1967-69), Conf. Bd. Math. Sci. (chmn. 1965-66), Nat. Acad. Scis. (chmn. math. sect. 1970-73, councilor 1977-80), Math. Assn. Am. (pres. 1963-64, vis. lectr. 1954-55, 61-62, chmn. Wis. sect. 1952), Am. Math. Soc. (councilor 1952-54, 58-60, v.p. 1967-68, pres. 1977-78), AAAS (v.p., chmn. sect. A 1959), Pi Mu Epsilon (vice dir. gen. 1960-63). Presbyn. (elder). Office: Dept Math U Tex Austin TX 78712

BING, RICHARD JOHN, cardiologist, researcher; b. Nuremberg, Germany, Oct. 12, 1909, came to U.S., 1935, naturalized, s. Bernard H. and Lilli (Aischberg) B.; m. Mary A. Whipple, June 2, 1938; children—John, Julianne, William, Barbara. M.D., U. Munich, Germany, 1934, U. Bern, Switzerland, 1935; hon. M.D., U. Dusseldorf, Germany, 1966. Fellow and resident in organ perfusion Rockefeller Inst., N.Y.C., 1936-37; resident in surgery Columbia U., N.Y.C., 1939-41; instr. physiology NYU, 1941-42; from asst. prof. to assoc. prof. surgery Johns Hopkins Med. Sch., Balt., 1945-51; prof. medicine Wayne State U., Detroit, 1951-69; prof. medicine, dir. cardiology and exptl. devel. Huntington Meml. Hosp., Pasadena, Calif., 1969—; dir. cardiology and exptl. devel. Huntington Med. Research Insts., Pasadena, 1980—; vis. assoc. chemistry Calif. Inst. Tech., Pasadena. Author numerous publs. Served to lt. col. M.C., U.S. Army, 1944-45. Recipient Research Achievement award Am. Heart Assn., 1974, Disting. Scientist award Am. Coll. Cardiology, 1984. Mem. Assn. Am. Physicians, Greek Soc. Cardiology (hon.), Spanish Soc. Cardiology (hon.). Roman Catholic. Current work: Cardiology. Subspecialty: Cardiology. Office: Huntington Meml Hosp 100 Congress St Pasadena CA 91105

BINNS, JACK NEVILLE, engineer; b. Cin., Mar. 20, 1918; s. George W. and Edna Antoinette (Frech) B.; m. Irene Salovaara, Nov. 15, 1940 (div. 1967); children—Jack, Sally, Georgia; m. Michi Choji Binns, July 15, 1970; children—Mitsu, George, Euki. M.E., U. Cin., 1940. Apprentice, Cin. Milacron, 1936-40, field engr., 1940-43; founder Planet Prodn. Corp., Cin., 1947-56, Binns Machinery Products, Cin., 1957—. Patentee in field. Served to lt. (j.g.) USN, 1943-46. Recipient Gold medal ASME 1983. Current work: Designing and manufacturing extremely high production steel mill machinery and machine tools. Subspecialty: Mechanical engineering. Home: 8755 Blome Rd Cincinnati OH 45243 Office: Binns Machinery Products 330 Railroad Ave Cincinnati OH 45217

BIRCKBICHLER, PAUL JOSEPH, biochemist; b. Greenville, Pa., Nov. 13, 1942; s. Paul Joseph and Stella Theresa (Brandt) B.; m. Donna Jean Bowser, July 17, 1965; children: Stacey, Marc. B.S., Duquesne U., 1964, Ph.D., 1969. Instr. chemistry Pa. State U., McKeesport, 1968-69; postdoctoral research fellow Brown U., Providence, R.I., 1969-71; vis. scientist Bergen (Norway) U., 1971-72; research assoc. biomed. div. Noble Found., Ardmore, Okla., 1972-77, asst. scientist, 1977-81, assoc. scientist, 1981—. Mem. Am. Soc. Biol. Chemists, Am. Chem. Soc., Am. Assn. Cancer Research, Tissue Culture Assn., N.Y. Acad. Scis., Okla. Acad. Scis. Current Work: Membranes of normal and transformed human cells, transglutaminase, isopeptide crosslinks. Subspecialties: Membrane biology; Cell and tissue culture. Office: Noble Found Biomedical Div PO Box 2180 Ardmore OK 73402

BIRD, JOHN MALCOLM, geologist; b. Newark, Dec. 27, 1931; s. John Robert and Beryl Elizabeth (Wright) B.; m. Marjorie Ann Kelleher, Apr. 18, 1957 (div. 1982); children: Anne Elizabeth, Marsha Jean. B.S., Union Coll., Schenectady, 1955; M.S., Rensselaer Poly. Inst., Troy, N.Y., 1959, Ph.D., 1961. Grad. asst. Union Coll., 1957-58, Rensselaer Poly. Inst., 1958-61; from instr. to assoc. prof. SUNY-Albany, 1961-70, prof., 1970-72, chmn. dept. geol. scis., 1969-72, vis. research prof., 1972-76; research assoc. Dudley Obs., Albany, 1964-72; sr. research assoc. Lamont-Doherty Geol. Obs., Columbia U., 1970-73; prof. geology Cornell U., Ithaca, N.Y., 1972—; pres., treas. Gamma Prime Corp., 1983—; Nat. Acad. Scis. Vis. scientist, 1967; disting. vis. scientist Am. Geol. Inst., 1971; chmn. Appalachian working group U.S. Geodynamics Com., 1971-73; disting. vis. lectr. Am. Assn. Petroleum Geologists, 1977-78; cons geotech. engring., mineral exploration. Editor: Plate Tectonics, 1981; assoc. editor: Jour. Geophys. Research, 1971-74; contbr. profl. jours. Served with AUS, 1955-57. Research grantee NSF, 1964, 68, 72-84; Nat. Acad. Scis., 1969; Petroleum Research Inst., 1975-77; Office Naval Research, 1978-80; Nat. Geog. Soc., 1977-78, 80. Fellow Geol. Soc. Am. (chmn. N.E. sect. 1975-76), Canadian Geol. Soc., Explorers Club; mem. Am. Geophys. Union, Sigma Xi, Chi Psi. Current Work: Plate tectonics, rock deformation, origin of terrestrial metals, TEM and STEM analysis of minerals, nuclear waste disposal, engring. geology, generation and emplacement of ophiolites, carbon in the earth's mantle, landsat. Subspecialties: Tectonics; Petrology. Home: 1187 Ellis Hollow Rd Ithaca NY 14850 Office: Geol Scis Dept Cornell Univ Ithaca NY 14853

BIRD, ROBERT BYRON, chemical engineering educator, author; b. Bryan, Tex., Feb. 5, 1924; s. Byron and Ethel (Antrim) B. Student, U. Md., 1941-43; B.S. in Chem. Engring, U. Ill., 1947; Ph.D. in Chemistry, U. Wis., 1950; student, U. Amsterdam, 1950-51; D.Eng. (hon.), Lehigh U., 1972, Washington U., 1973, Tech. U. Delft, Holland, 1977; Sc.D. (hon.), Clarkson U., 1980. Asst. prof. chemistry Cornell U., 1952-53, Debye lectr., 1973; mem. faculty U. Wis., 1951-52, 53—, prof. chem. engring., 1957—, C.F. Burgess distinguished prof. chem. engring., 1968-72, John D. MacArthur prof., 1982—, Vilas research prof., 1972—, chmn. dept., 1964-68; vis. prof. U. Calif., Berkeley, 1977; D.L. Katz lectr. U. Mich., 1971; W.N. Lacey lectr. Calif. Inst. Tech., 1974; K. Wohl Meml. lectr. U. Del., 1977; W.K. Lewis lectr. MIT, 1982; lectr. Lectures in Sci. Humble Oil Co., 1959, 61, 64, 66; lecture tour Am. Chem. Soc., 1958, 75, Canadian Inst. Chemistry, 1961, 65; cons. to industry, 1965—; mem. adv. panel engring. sci. div. NSF, 1961-64. Author: (with others) Molecular Theory of Gases and Liquids, 2d printing, 1964, Transport Phenomena, 35th printing, 1982, Spanish edit., 1965, Czech edit., 1966, Italian edit., 1970, Russian edit., 1974, Een Goed Begin: A Contemporary Dutch Reader, 1963, 2d edit., 1971, Comprehending Technical Japanese, 1975, Dynamics of Polymeric Liquids, Vol. 1, Fluid Mechanics, Vol. 2, Kinetic Theory, 1977; Reading Dutch: Fifteen annotated stories from The Low Countries, 1985; also numerous research publs.; Am. editor: (with others) Applied Sci. Research, 1969—; adv. bd.: (with others) Indsl. and Engring. Chemistry, 1970-72; editorial bd.: (with others) Jour. Non-Newtonian Fluid Mechanics, 1975—. Served to 1st lt. AUS, 1943-46. Decorated Bronze Star; Fulbright fellow Holland, 1950; Fulbright lectr., 1958; Guggenheim fellow, 1958; Fulbright lectr. Japan, 1962-63; Fulbright lectr. Sarajevo, Yugoslavia, 1972; recipient Curtis McGraw award Am. Assn. Engring. Edn., 1959, Westinghouse award, 1960. Fellow Am. Phys. Soc. (Otto Laporte lectr. 1980), Am. Inst. Chem. Engrs. (William H. Walker award 1962, Profl. Progress award 1965, Warren K. Lewis award 1974), Am. Acad. Arts and Scis.; mem. Am. Chem. Soc. (chmn. Wis. sect. 1966, unrestricted research grant Petroleum Research Fund 1963), Soc. Rheology (Bingham award 1974), Am. Acad. Mechanics, Brit. Soc. Rheology, Dutch Phys. Soc., Royal Inst. Engrs. (Holland), Nat. Acad. Engring., N.Y. Acad. Scis., Am. Acad. Arts and Scis., Wis. Acad. Scis., Arts and Letters, Phi Beta Kappa, Sigma Xi (v.p. Wis. sect. 1959-60), Tau Beta Pi, Alpha Chi Sigma, Phi Kappa Phi, Omicron Delta Kappa, Sigma Tau. Current Work: Kinetic theory, rheology, and fluid dynamics of polymeric liquids. Transport phenomena and engineering applications. Subspecialty: Fluid mechanics. Office: Chem Engring Dept 3004 Engring Bldg 1415 Johnson Dr U Wis Madison WI 53706

BIRELY, JOHN HORTON, chemist, research executive; b. Glen Ridge, N.J., Oct. 17, 1939; s. Charles W. and Catharine (Horton) B.; m. Laura Mears, Dec. 21, 1969; m. Molly Cooper, June 16, 1982. B.A. in Chemistry, Yale U., 1961; M.S. in Phys. Chemistry, U. Calif.-Berkeley, 1963; Ph.D. in Phys. Chemistry, Harvard U., 1966. Postdoctoral research fellow dept. phys. chemistry Cambridge (Eng.) U., 1966-67; asst. prof. chemistry UCLA, 1967-69; mem. tech. staff Aerospace Corp., 1969-74; mem. staff Los Alamos Nat. Lab., 1974—, assoc. dir. chemistry, earth and life scis., 1981—. Mem. Am. Chem. Soc., Am. Phys. Soc., AAAS, CAP. Current Work: Management of scientific research in chemistry, earth and life sciences. Subspecialties: Physical chemistry; Kinetics. Office: U Calif Los Alamos Nat Lab PO Box 1663 Los Alamos NM 87545

BIRKITT, JOHN CLAIR, defense and aerospace corporation executive; b. Inglewood, Calif., Aug. 20, 1941; S. Clair W. and Helene (Gille) B.; m. Constance E. May, June 4, 1966 (div. July 1980); children: Andra Diane, Robert John; m. Linda A. Aylmer, Sept. 13, 1980; 1 dau., Danielle Laurissa. B.S., Calif. State Poly. U. - Pomona, 1969. Engr. Aerojet Mfg. Co., Placentia, Calif., 1969-74; test condr. TRW-Def. and Space Systems Group, San Clemente, Calif., 1974-79, 1979—; plant mgr. Advanced Ground Systems Engring. Co., Long Beach, Calif., 1979. Treas., engr. Riverside County Fire Dept., Lake Elsinore, Calif., 1978—. Served with USMC, 1959-65. Recipient commendation Minuteman Program Office, Norton AFB, Calif., 1975; commendation Dept. Navy High Energy Laser Project, Washington, 1978; Appreciation for Patriotic Civilian Service cert. Dept. Army, Washington, 1979. Mem. AIAA, Nat. Assn. Watch and Clock Collectors, Music Box Soc. Republican. Current Work: Planning, execution of complex high energy laser tests, reactant storage, delivery systems, mechanical and optical installations, electronic control and data reduction systems and site control and service equipment. Subspecialties: High energy chemical lasers; Aerospace engineering and technology. Home: 32536 Ortega Hwy Lake Elsinore CA 92330 Office: Ford Aerospace and Communications Corp Ford Rd Newport Beach CA 92660

BIRKLE, A(DOLPH) JOHN, metallurgical engr., cons.; b. Chgo., Aug. 26, 1930; s. Adolph and Elizabeth (Lemoch) B.; m. Catherine, Sept. 12, 1957; children: Gregory, Kevin, Eric, Julie. B.S. in Metall. Engring, U. Ill., 1956; M.S. in Metall. Engring, U. Wis., 1958. Sr. research engr. Applied Research Lab., U.S. Steel Corp., Monroeville, Pa., 1958-65; research supr. dept. research Youngstown Sheet & Tube Co., Ohio, 1965-68; mgr. product research and devel. CF&I Steel Corp., Pueblo, Colo., 1968-71; sr. staff engr./sect. head projects, engring. and constrn., project engring. services materials sect. Consumers Power Co., Jackson, Mich., 1971—; mem. NRC and Electric Power Research Inst. Corrosion Adv. Com., Material Property Council Com. on Fracture. Contbr. numerous articles to profl. jours. Served with USAF, 1952-54. Mem. Am. Soc. Metals, Am. Welding Soc., ASTM, ASME (bd. nuclear codes and standards, chmn. subgroup on water-cooled systems, instr. boiler and pressure vessel code), Edison Electric Inst. (chmn. metallurgy and piping task force). Patentee in field; numerous inventions. Current Work: Nuclear power, energy, availability, product research and devel., inspection nuclear power plants, welding, corrosion, cathodic protection. Subspecialty: Metallurgical engineering. Home: 2340 Vaudermere Dr Jackson MI 42901 Office: 1945 Parnall Rd Jackson MI 49201

BIRMINGHAM, BASCOM WAYNE, retired government official; b. Grand Island, Nebr., June 20, 1925; s. James C. and Stella M. (Sorrels) B.; m. Lois Marie Booth, Sept. 3, 1949; children: Steven W., Janet L. Birmingham Chamberlin. S.B., MIT, 1948, S.M., 1951; Sc.D. (hon.), U. Colo., 1983. With Sorrels Supply Co., Poteau, Okla., 1947, Wester Geophys. Soc., Worland, Wyo., 1948, W.R. Holway & Assos., Tulsa, 1948-50; chief processes sect., cryogenics div. Nat. Bur. Standards, Boulder, Colo., 1951-63, chief cryogenics div., 1963-68; dep. dir. Inst. Basic Standards, 1968-77; dir. Boulder Labs., 1977-82; cons. cryogenic engring. Birmingham Assocs., 1982—; Mem. Boulder Zoning Bd., 1964-66; bd. dirs. Community Hosp., 1968-77; v.p. Rocky Mountain Eye Found., 1978—. Author: monograph Technology of Liquid Helium, 1968, Am. editor Cryogenics Jour, 1968-83. Served with USNR, 1944-46. Recipient gold medal service award Commerce Dept., 1953, 71, meritorious service award, 1961, Sci. fellow, 1966-67; Best Paper award Cryogenic Engring. Conf., 1961. Mem. Internat. Inst. Refrigeration (hon.), Boulder C. of C. (bd. dirs. 1979-82). Patentee in field. Current Work: Strategic long range planning in cryogenics and metrology. Subspecialties: Cryogenics; Mechanical engineering. Home: 5440 White Pl Boulder CO 80303

BIRNBAUM, EDWARD R., chemistry educator; b. Bklyn., Oct. 28, 1943; s. David and Sylvia (Deutchman) B.; m. Amy Boule Birnbaum, Apr. 4, 1968; children: David, Eva, Jessica. B.S., Bklyn. Coll., 1964; M.S., U. Ill., 1966, Ph.D., 1968. Asst. prof. chemistry N. Mex. State U., 1968-73, assoc. prof., 1973-78, prof., 1978—. DuPont fellow, 1967. Mem. Am. Chem. Soc., AAAS, Biophysical Soc., Am. Assn. Biol. Chemists, Alpha Chi Sigma. Current Work: Lanthanide spectroscopy in calcium binding proteins, research in the area of lanthanide substitution for calcium in calcium binding biological systems; application of spectroscopic techniques. Subspecialties: Laser spectroscopy; Biophysical chemistry. Office: Department Chemistry New Mexico State University PO Box 3C Las Cruces NM 88003

BIRNBAUM, ZYGMUNT WILLIAM, mathematics educator; b. Lwow, Poland, Oct. 18, 1903; came to U.S., 1937, naturalized, 1943; s. Ignacy and Lina (Nebenzahl) B.; m. Hilde Merzbach, Dec. 20, 1940; children: Ann Miriam, Richard Franklin. LL.M., U. Lwow, 1925, Ph.D. in Math, 1929; postdoctoral research, U. Goettingen, Germany, 1929-31. Math. instr. Gymnasium, Lwow, 1926-29; chief actuary Life Ins. Co. Phoenix in Poland, 1931-36; research biometrician, N.Y.U., 1937-39; mem. faculty U. Wash., Seattle, 1939—, prof. math., 1950—; dir. lab. statis. research, 1948—; vis. prof. Stanford, 1951-52, U. Paris, France, 1960-61, U. Rome, Italy, 1964, Hebrew U., Jerusalem, 1980; cons. Boeing Co., 1956—, HEW, 1963—. Editor: Annals of Math. Statistics, 1967-70. Guggenheim fellow, 1960-61. Fellow Inst. Math. Statistics (pres. 1963-64), Am. Statis. Assn.; mem. Am. Math. Soc., Math. Assn. Am., Soc. Indsl. and Applied Math., Internat. Statis. Inst., AAUP. Current Work: Industrial and biological applications, reliability, life distributions. Subspecialties: Applied mathematics; Statistics. Home: 4540 8th NE Seattle WA 98105 Office: Math Dept Univ Wash Seattle WA 98195

BIRT, DIANE FEICKERT, nutrition educator, reseacher; b. Petaluma, Calif., Oct. 12, 1949; d. Joseph Ernst and Dorothy Beatrice (Cunningham) Feichert; m. Kenneth Allen Birt, June 10, 1973; children—Arlene Lydia, Michelle Dorothy. B.A., Whittier Coll., 1971; Ph.D., Purdue U., 1975. Research asst. Purdue U., West Lafayette, Ind., 1972-75; asst. prof. Iowa State U., Ames, 1975-76; asst. prof. U. Nebr. Med. Ctr., Omaha, 1976-82, assoc. prof., 1982—; cons. NIH, Bethesda, Md., 1984—. Contbr. articles to profl. jours. Mem. profl. edn. com. for Douglas/Sarpy Counties, Am. Cancer Soc., 1982—. NIH grantee Nat. Cancer Inst., 1979—. Mem. Am. Inst. Nutrition, Am. Assn. Cancer Research, Sigma Phi, Phi Kappa Phi. Democrat. Mem. Disciples of Christ Ch. Current work: Dietary aspects of experimental carcinogenesis-dietary fat/-protein and pancreatic cancer; dietary L- tryptophan/vitamin B6 and urinary bladder cancer, cancer inhibition. Subspecialties: Nutrition (medicine); Cancer research (medicine). Home: 2539 Country Club Ave Omaha NE 68104 Office: Eppley Inst Research Cancer Univ Nebr Med Ctr 42nd and Dewey Ave Omaha NE 68105

BISCAYE, PIERRE EGINTON, marine geochemist; b. N.Y.C., Nov. 24, 1935; s. George E. and Ruth E. (Eginston) B.; m. Nedaleine R. Bell, Aug. 23, 1958; children—Timothy, David, Sara, Rachel. B.S., Wheaton Coll., 1957; Ph.D., Yale U., 1964. Research scientist Jersey Prodn. Research Co., Tulsa, 1964-65, Isotopes, Inc., Westwood, N.J., 1965-67; sr. research scientist Lamont-Doherty Geol. Obs., Columbia U., Palisades, N.Y., 1967—. Contbr. articles to profl. jours. Elder Pasack Bible Ch., Hillsdale, N.J., 1972-76, 82-84. Served to 1st lt. Signal Corps., U.S. Army, 1957-59. Fellow Geol. Soc. Am.; mem. AAAS, Am. Geophys. Union. Current work: Oceanographic research on suspended particulate matter; deep sea sedimentation; resuspension and transport by deep ocean currents. Subspecialties: Geochemistry; Oceanography. Home: 120 Berkeley Ave Westwood NJ 07675 Office: Lamont-Doherty Geol Observatory Columbia Univ Palisades NY 10964

BISCHOFF, KENNETH BRUCE, chemical engineer, educator; b. Chgo., Feb. 29, 1936; s. Arthur William and Evelyn Mary (Hansen) B.; m. Joyce Arlene Winterberg, June 6, 1959; children: Kathryn Ann, James Eric. B.S., Ill. Inst. Tech., 1957, Ph.D., 1961. Asst. to assoc. prof. U. Tex., Austin, 1961-67; assoc. prof., then prof. U. Md., 1967-70; Walter R. Read prof. engring. Cornell U., 1970-76, dir. Sch. Chem. Engring., 1970-75; Unidel prof. biomed. and chem. engring. U. Del., 1976—, chmn. dept. chem. engring., 1978-82; cons. Exxon Research and Engring., NIH, Gen. Foods Corp., W. R. Grace Co., Koppers Co. Author: (with D.M. Himmelblau) Process Analysis and Simulation, 1968, (with G.F. Froment) Chemical Reactor Analysis and Design, 1979; editor: (with R.L. Dedrick and E.F. Leonard) The Artificial Kidney; Contbr. articles to research publs.; Editorial bd.: Advances in Chemistry Series, 1973-76, 78-81, Jour. Bioengring, 1976-80, Jour. Pharmacokinetic Biopharm. 1975—; assoc. editor: Advances Chem. Engring., 1982—. Mem. council thrombosis Am. Heart Assn., 1971-81. Recipient Ebert prize Acad. Pharm. Scis., 1972; Profl. Progress award Am. Inst. Chem. Engrs., 1976; Inst. lectr., 1982; Food, Pharm. and Bioengring. award, 1982; Shell Found. fellow, 1959; NSF fellow, 1960; fellow U. Ghent, 1960-61. Fellow AAAS, Am. Inst. Chemists; mem. Am. Inst. Chem. Engrs. (dir. 1972-74, chmn. nat. program com. 1978, chmn. food, pharm. and bioengring. div. 1985), Am. Chem. Soc., Am. Soc. Engring. Edn., Am. Soc. Artificial Internal Organs, Engrs. Council for Profl. Devel. (dir. 1972-78), Council Chem. Research (governing bd. 1981-84, chmn. 1985), Catalysis Soc., AAUP, N.Y. Acad. Scis., Sigma Xi, Tau Beta Pi, Phi Lambda Upsilon, Omega Chi Epsilon, Alpha Chi Sigma. Current Work: Pharmacokinetic basis for quantitative risk assessment in toxicology and cancer chemotheraphy; kinetic modelilng of complex chemical biochemical processes. Subspecialties: Chemical engineering; Biomedical engineering. Home: Box 81A Benge Rd RD 1 Hockessin DE 19707

BISHOP, ALBERT BENTLEY, III, industrial engineering educator; b. Phila., Apr. 7, 1929; s. Albert Bentley and Sara LeCompte (DesPortes) B.; m. Louise Boyd Squire, Nov. 17, 1951; children: John Albert, Suzanne Squire, James DesPortes. B.E.E., Cornell U., 1951; M.S., Ohio State U., 1953, Ph.D., 1957. Mem. tech. staff Bell Telephone Labs., Allentown, Pa., 1954; instr. indsl. and systems engring. Ohio State U., Columbus, 1954-57, asst. prof., 1957-60, asso. prof., 1960-65, prof., 1965—, chmn. dept., 1974-82; vis. scholar in sci., tech. and soc. MIT, 1984; pres. Albert B. Bishop and Assos.; cons. U.S. Army Sci. Adv. Panel, 1975-77. Author: Introduction to Discrete Linear Controls—Theory and Application, 1975; contbr. articles to profl. jours. Mem. Ohio Citizens Council on Health and Welfare, 1973-79; active Cub and Boy Scouts Am., 1965-74; mem. council Cornell U., 1974-80, 81—; trustee Buckeye Boys Ranch, 1976-82, chmn. sci. adv. com., 1982—. Served with USAF, 1951-53. Recipient Tech. Person of Yr. award Columbus Tech. Council, 1983. Fellow Am. Soc. Quality Control, Am. Inst. Indsl. Engrs. (nat. engring. economy research com. 1957-60, chmn. Columbus sect. research com. 1957-59, dir. 1976-78, mem. editorial bd. 1960-67, chmn. council acad. dept. heads 1980-81, dir. acad. affairs 1981-82, 85-86 mem. task force on new technologies 1982—); mem. IEEE, Soc. Mfg. Engrs., Ops. Research Soc. Am., Inst. Mgmt. Sci., Am. Soc. Engring. Edn., Mil. Ops. Research Soc. (dir. 1969-72, co-chmn. edn. com. 1970-71, chmn. prize com. 1971-72), Tau Beta Pi (nat. exec. council 1966-70), Eta Kappa Nu, Alpha Pi Mu, Sigma Xi, Phi Kappa Phi, Pi Mu Epsilon, Sigma Pi. Episcopalian (vestryman 1958-60, 72-75, 77-80, 83-86, jr. warden 1961-63, sr. warden 1963-65, 85-86, mem. diocesan council 1968-72, nat. conv. del. 1973,

76, 79, 82, 85). Patentee in field. Current Work: Industrial and systems engineering engineering educator and consultant. Subspecialties: Systems engineering; Industrial engineering. Home: 1946 W Lane Ave Columbus OH 43221 Office: Ohio State U Dept Indsl and Systems Engring 1971 Neil Ave Columbus OH 43210

BISHOP, BEVERLY P(ETTERSON), neurophysiologist; b. Corning, N.Y., Oct. 19, 1922; d. Elof Bernard and Bonnie (Hungerford) Petterson; m. Charles William Bishop, May 2, 1944; 1 son: Geoffrey Craig. B.A. in Math, Syracuse U., 1944; M.A. in Exptl. Psychology, U. Rochester, 1948; Ph.D. in Physiology, U. Buffalo, 1958. Asst. in physiology U. Glasgow, Scotland, 1956-57; inst. in physiology U. Buffalo, 1958-62; asst. prof. physiology SUNY, Buffalo, 1962-67, assoc. prof., 1967-75, prof., 1975—; cons., lectr. in field; mem. NIH study sect., 1980-84. Author: Basic Neurophysiology, 1982; contbr. numerous articles to profl. jours.; lectr. for: audio-visual series Illustrated Lectures in Neurophysiology, 1980. Recipient Dean's award SUNY, Buffalo, 1969, Chancellor's award, 1975; Golden Pen award Am. Phys. Therapy Assn., 1976. Mem. Am. Physiol. Soc., Soc. Neurosci., Am. Thoracic Soc., Am. Congress Rehab. Medicine, Internat. Soc. Electromyography and Kinesiology, Am. Assn. Electromyography and Electro-diagnosis, Phi Beta Kappa. Current Work: Motor control of respiratory muscles; research to determine organization of neural circuitry controlling respiration, mastication and other rhymical motor activities. Subspecialties: Neurobiology; Physiology (biology). Home: 508 Getzville Rd Buffalo NY 14226 Office: Dept Physiology Sherman Hall SUNY Buffalo NY 14214

BISHOP, JOHN MICHAEL, microbiology educator; b. York, Pa., Feb. 22, 1936; married, 1959. A.B., Gettysburg Coll., 1957; M.D., Harvard U., 1962. Intern in internal medicine Mass. Gen. Hosp., Boston, 1962-63, resident, 1963-64; research assoc. virology NIH, 1964-66, sr. investigator, 1966-68; asst. prof., assoc. prof. Med. Center, U. Calif., San Francisco, 1968-72, prof. microbiology, 1972—, mem. cancer research coordinating com., 1968—; mem. Calif. div. Am. Cancer Soc., 1969—. NIH research grantee, 1968—; recipient Biomed. Research award Am. Assn. Med. Colls., 1981; Lasker award Basic Med. Research, 1982; Gairdner Found. Internat. award, 1984. Mem. Nat. Acad. Sci., AAAS, Am. Soc. Biol. Chemists, Am. Soc. Microbiology, Am. Soc. Cell Biology. Subspecialties: Virology (medicine); Biochemistry (medicine). Office: Dept Microbiology U Calif Med Center San Francisco CA 94143*

BISHOP, RICHARD STEARNS, exploration geologist, researcher; b. Dowagiac, Mich., Apr. 14, 1945; s. Barton Phelps and Margaret (Stearns) B.; m. Edythe Marie White, Jan. 15, 1971; children: Ryan Barclay, Timothy Clinton. B.S., Tex. Christian U., 1967; M.A., U. Mo.-Columbia, 1969; Ph.D., Stanford U., 1977. Devel. geologist Union Oil Co. of California, New Orleans, 1969-71; research geologist Exxon Prodn. Research Co., Houston, 1975-81; exploration geologist Exxon Co. U.S.A., Houston, 1981-82, project leader, 1982-83, sr. supr. prodn. dept., 1983—. Fellow Geol. Soc. Am.; mem. Am. Assn. Petroleum Geologists (Cam Sproule award 1980, edn. com. 1980—, chmn. 1982—), Houston Geol. Soc. (editor Bull. 1981-83), Soc. Petroleum Engrs. Current Work: Assessment of hydrocarbon resources; understanding the accumulation and dispersion of hydrocarbons; diapirism, abnormal pore pressure. Subspecialties: Geology; Geochemistry. Home: 10607 Dunlap St Houston TX 77096 Office: Exxon Co USA PO Box 2180 4550 Dacoma Houston TX 77092

BISTRIAN, BRUCE RYAN, internist, educator; b. Southampton, N.Y., Oct. 22, 1939; s. Peter and Mary Laura (Ryan) B.; m. Eleanor Alice Dix, Sept. 3, 1964; children: Tennille Ryan, Jordan Brooke, Britton Perry. B.A., NYU, 1961; M.D., Cornell U., 1965; M.P.H., Johns Hopkins U., 1971; Ph.D., MIT, 1975. Diplomate: Am. Bd. Internal Medicine. Intern Cornell U., N.Y.C., 1965-66; metabolism fellow U.Vt., Burlington, 1968-69, resident in medicine 1969-70; mem. faculty Harvard U. Med. Sch., Boston, 1975 ; clin. assoc. physician research resources div. NIH, 1975-78; lectr. MIT, 1981 . Contbr. over 120 sci. articles to profl. publs. Served to capt. U.S. Army, 1966-68. Nat. Inst. Gen. Med. Scis. grantee, 1977-80; Nat. Inst. Arthritis, Metabolism and Digestive Disease grantee, 1979-83, 83-87, 85-89; Nat. Cancer Inst. grantee, 1984-87. Fellow Am. Coll. Nutrition, ACP; mem. Fedn. Am. Soc. Exptl. Biologists, Am. Soc. Clin. Nutrition, Am. Fedn. Clin. Research, Am. Soc. Parenteral and Enteral Nutrition, Mass. Med. Soc. Presbyterian. Current Work: Protein calorie malnutrition; total parenteral nutrition; nutrition and infection; treatment of obesity. Subspecialties: Nutrition (medicine); Biochemistry (medicine). Home: Argilla Rd Ipswich MA 01938 Office: New Eng Deaconess Hosp 194 Pilgrim Pr Boston MA 02215

BISWAL, NILAMBAR, molecular virologist; b. Khamar, Orissa, India, Feb. 20, 1934; s. Palau and Jamuna B.; m. Annapurna Biswal, Mar. 7, 1967; children: Sandip, Subrat, Subrina. Ph.D. in Microbiology, Mich. State U., 1965. Asst. research virologist U. Calif., 1965-67; asst. prof. Baylor Coll., 1968-72, assoc. prof., 1972-82; sr. investigator Balt. Cancer Research Program Nat. Cancer Inst. NIH, Balt., 1978-82; head div. molecular biology U. Md. Cancer Center, Balt., 1982—. Contbr. articles in field to profl. jours. Mem. AAAS, Am. Soc. Microbiology, N.Y. Acad. Sci., Am. Assn. Cancer Research, Sigma Xi. Current Work: Isolation and characterization of DNA binding proteins of herpes simplex virus on Viral DNA replication, viral latency and cellular transformation; cloning of transforming genes of HSV. Subspecialties: Virology (biology); Cancer research (medicine). Home: 9704 Kerrigan Ct Randallstown MD 21133 Office: Breseler Research Bldg 655 W Baltimore St Baltimore MD 21201

BISWAS, RANA, physicist; b. Calcutta, India, Sept. 11, 1956; came to U.S., 1978; s. Sukumar and Reba (Bose) B.; m. Sreeparna Mitra, July 14, 1984. B.Sc., Bombay U., 1976; M.Sc., Indian Inst. Tech. (Bombay), 1978; M.S., Cornell U., 1981, Ph.D., 1984. Research asst. Cornell U., Ithaca, N.Y., 1980-84; mem. tech. staff AT&T Bell Labs., Murray Hill, N.J., 1984—. Contbr. articles to profl. jours. Mem. Am. Phys. Soc. Current work: Structural and electronic properties of semiconductor materials and surfaces. Subspecialties: Condensed matter physics; Theoretical physics. Office: AT&T Bell Labs 600 Mountain Ave Murray Hill NJ 07974

BITO, LASZLO Z., ocular physiologist, educator; b. Budapest, Hungary, Sept. 7, 1934; s. Jozsef and Marianna (Bonin) B.; married; children: John, Bucky. B.A. (scholar), Bard Coll., 1959; Ph.D., Columbia U., 1963. Hon. research asst. dept. physiology Univ. Coll. London, 1964-65; instr. ophthalmology Columbia U., N.Y.C., 1965-66, asst. prof., 1967-74, sr. research assoc., 1975-77, assoc. prof. ocular physiology, 1977-80, prof., 1980—. Editorial bd.: Exptl. Eye Research. NIH fellow, 1959-63, 63-65; recipient award Semmelweis Sci. Soc., 1974; NIH grantee, 1964—. Mem. Assn. Research in Vision and Ophthalmology, Internat. Soc. Eye Research, Am. Soc. Pharmacology and Exptl. Therapeutics, Am. Physiol. Soc., N.Y. Acad. Sci. Current Work: Ocular fluid composition; prostaglandins, presbyopia. Subspecialties: Comparative physiology; Pharmacology. Office: 630 W 168th St New York NY 10032

BITRAN, JACOB DAVID, physician, oncologist, researcher; b. Thessaloniki, Greece, Sept. 23, 1947; came to U.S., 1952, naturalized, 1957; s. David Jacob and Martha (Faratzi) B.; m. Linda Sue Androw, Dec. 26, 1970; children: Lauren, Dina. B.S., U. Ill.-Chgo., 1967, M.D., 1971. Diplomate: Am. Bd. Internal Medicine. Intern Michael Reese Med. Ctr., Chgo., 1971-72; resident Rush-Presbyn. St. Luke's Hosp. Chgo., 1972-73, Michael Reese Med. Ctr., 1973-75; fellow hematology-oncology U. Chgo., 1975-77; attending physician Michael Reese Med. Ctr., Chgo., 1977—; clin. asst. prof. medicine U. Chgo., 1977-82, clin. assoc. prof., 1982-84, assoc. prof. medicine, dir. cancer research, 1984—. Fellow ACP.; mem. Am. Soc. Clin. Oncology, Am. Soc. Cancer Research, Am. Fedn. Clin. Research, Am. Soc. Hetamology. Current Work: Lung cancer, chemotherapy. Subspecialties: Oncology; Chemotherapy. Office: Michael Reese Med Ctr 31st and Lake Shore Dr Chicago IL 60616

BITZER, DONALD LESTER, electrical engineering educator, laboratory administrator; b. East St. Louis, Ill., Jan. 1, 1934; s. Jess L. and Marjorie B. (Look) B.; m. Maryann Drost, July 2, 1955; 1 son, David. B.S. in Elec. Engring, U. Ill., 1955, M.S. in Elec. Engring, 1956, Ph.D. in Elec. Engring, 1960. Asst. prof. U. Ill. Coordinated Sci. Lab., Urbana, 1960-63, assoc. prof., 1963-67, dir. computer-based edn. research lab., prof. elec. engring., 1967—; cons. Control Data Corp., Gandalf Ltd.; mem. various coms. Nat. Research Council. Contbr. articles on computer-based edn. to profl. jours. Mem. Regional Health Resource Center Bd., Urbana, Mercy Hosp. Health Care Found., Urbana. Recipient Vladimir K. Zworykin award Nat. Acad. Engring., 1973; Bobby C. Connelly award Miami Valley Computer Assn., 1973; co-recipient Data Processing Mgmt. Assn.'s Computer Scis. Man of Year award, 1975. Fellow IEEE, AAAS; mem. Nat. Acad. Engring., Am. Soc. for Engring. Edn. (Chester F. Carlson award 1981). Patentee in field. Current Work: Computer-based education, communication devices, displays. Subspecialties: Computer engineering; Graphics, image processing, and pattern recognition.

BIZZI, EMILIO, neurophysiologist; b. Rome, Feb. 22, 1933; came to U.S., 1963, naturalized, 1982; s. Vittorio and Anna (Galeazzi) B. M.D. summa cum laude with highest honors, U. Rome, 1958. Postdoctoral tng. Inst. Med. Pathology, U. Siena, Italy, 1958-60, Inst. Physiology, U. Pisa, Italy, 1960-63; research assoc. Neurophysiol. Lab. dept. zoology Washington U., St. Louis, 1963-64; vis. assoc. sect. physiology Lab. Clin. Sci., NIMH, Bethesda, Md., 1964-66; research assoc. dept. psychology MIT, 1966-67, lectr., 1967-68, assoc. prof. psychology, 1969-72, prof. neurophysiology, 1972-80, Eugene McDermott prof. in brain scis. and human behavior, 1980—, dir. Whitaker Coll., 1983—; sr. investigator Istituto di Richerche Cardiovascolari, U. Milan, Italy, 1968-69; mem. NIH Study Sect. Vision B., 1973-77; mem. adv. bd. Biomed. Engring. Center for Clin. Instrumentation; mem. faculty adv. council Whitaker Coll. Contbr. numerous chpts., articles, abstracts to profl. jours.; corr. asso. commentor: Behavorial and Brain Scis, 1980—; mem. editorial staff: Studies of Brain Function, 1980—; editorial bd.: Brain Theory Newsletter, 1980—, Jour. Motor Behavior, 1981—, Jour. Neurobiology, 1981—. Recipient Alden Spencer award Columbia U. Coll. Physicians and Surgeons, 1978, Whitaker Health Scis. award Mass. Inst. Tech., 1978; Found. Fund for Research in Psychiatry fellow, 1978 . Mem. Am. Acad. Arts and Scis., Italian Physiol. Soc., Internat. Brain Research Orgn., AAAS, Am. Physiol. Soc., Soc. Neurosci., Barany Soc. Current Work: Brain mechanisms in motor control. Subspecialties: Neurophysiology; Neurobiology. Office: Whitaker College E25-526 MIT Cambridge MA 02139

BJORNDAHL, DAVID LEE, engineer; b. Rock Island, Ill., June 19, 1927; s. Richard Gideon and Olive Muriel (Winter) B.; m. Clara Mae Buck, Feb. 16, 1952; children—William, Jay, Jan, Jill. B.S.E.E., Purdue U., 1951, M.S.E.E., 1953, Ph.D., 1956. Instr., Purdue U., West Lafayette, Ind., 1953-56; engr. Litton Industries, Beverley Hills and Woodland Hills, Calif., 1956-66, Canoga Park and Moorpark, Calif., 1967—, v.p. engring., Litton Aero Products Div., 1974—. Served with USNR, 1945-46. Mem. IEEE, Inst. Navigation, Sigma Xi. Subspecialty: Electrical engineering. Office: Litton Aero Products 6100 Condor Dr Moorpark CA

BLACHMAN, NELSON M(ERLE), physicist; b. Cleve., Oct. 1923; s. Harry A. and Sarah G. B.; m. Anne Lefkowitz, Nov. 1953; children—Susan J., Nancy R. B.S. in Physics, Case Sch. Applied Sci., 1943; A.M., Harvard U., 1947, Ph.D. in Engring. Scis. and Applied Physics, 1947. Spl. research assoc. underwater sound lab. Harvard U., 1943-45; research assoc. Cruft Lab., 1945-46; assoc. physicist Brookhaven Nat. Lab., Upton, N.Y., 1947-51; physicist math. scis. div. Office Naval Research, 1951-54; sr. engring. specialist electronic def. lab. Sylvania Electric Products, Inc., 1954-58; liaison scientist Office Naval Research, London, 1958-60, 76-78; sr. scientist Sylvania systems group GTE Corp., Mountain View, Calif., 1960-76, 1978—; sr. Fulbright lectr., Madrid, 1964-65; tchr. off-campus programs U. Md., 1951-52, U. Calif., 1961-63, Stanford U., 1967. Author: Noise and Its Effect on Communication, 1966, 2d edit., 1982; also contbr. articles to profl. jours. Recipient Ordance Devel. award U.S. Navy, 1945; John Tyndall fellow, 1946; Gordon McKay scholar, 1946-47. Fellow IEEE (info. theory group gov. 1969-75, v.p. 1970, chmn. com. fellows 1969-73, Communications Soc. prize paper award 1976), AAAS, Instn. Elec. Engrs. London; mem. N.Y. Acad. Scis., Fedn. Am. Scientists, Acoustical Soc. Am., Inst. Math. Stats., Am. Statis. Assn., Soc. Indsl. and Applied Math., Math. Assn. Am., U.S. Nat. Com. of Internat. Union Radio Sci. Current work: Study of effect of random disturbances, such as electrical noise, on electronic communication systems. Subspecialties: Electrical engineering; Statistics. Office: Bldg VI PO Box 7188 GTE Sylvania Systems Group Mountain View CA 94039

BLACK, ARTHUR LEO, physiological chemistry educator, researcher; b. Redlands, Calif., Dec. 1, 1922; s. Leo M. and Marie A. (Burns) B.; m. Trudi E. McCue, Nov. 11, 1945; children—Teresa, Janet, Patricia. A.A., Reed Coll., 1943, Glendale Coll., 1946; B.S., U. Calif.-Davis, 1948; Ph.D., U. Calif.-Berkeley, 1951. Asst. prof. physiol. chemistry U. Calif.-Davis, 1951-57, assoc. prof., 1958-62, prof., 1962—, chmn. dept. physiol. sci., 1967-74; cons. IAEA, Vienna, 1965-72; cons. peer rev. panels NIH, 1970-80. Contbr. articles to profl. jours. Served to 1st lt. USAF, 1943-46. Recipient Outstanding Teaching award U. Calif. Acad. Senate, Davis, 1978. Mem. Am. Soc. Biol. Chemists, Am. Inst. Nutrition (Borden award 1964), Am. Physiol. Soc., Sigma Xi (v.p. 1959), Phi Beta Kappa (v.p. 1974, pres. 1975). Unitarian. Current work: Efficiency of protein utilization in animals; effects of exercise on protein metabolism. Subspecialties: Biochemistry (medicine); Nutrition (medicine). Home: 891 Linden Ln Davis CA 95616 Office: Dept Physiol Scis Univ Calif Sch Vet Medicine Davis CA 95616

BLACK, DAVID JOSEPH, physician, veterinarian; b. Detroit, Jan. 2, 1951; s. Bernard A. and Sarah (Barr) B.; m. Barbara Ann Buttram, Aug. 18, 1977. B.S., Mich. State U., 1971, D.V.M., 1972; M.S. in Physiology, U. Fla., 1975, M.D., 1983. Diplomate Am. Coll. Lab. Animal Medicine. Postdoctoral trainee NIH-USPHS, U. Fla., Gainesville, 1973-75; veterinarian Litton Bionetics, Rockville, Md., 1975-76; asst. prof., zoo veterinarian U. Tenn.-Knoxville, 1976-78; asst. prof. U. Fla., Gainesville, 1978-80, resident community health and family medicine, 1983—, assoc. dir. lab. animal facility, 1978-80. Contbr. articles to profl. jours. Advisor Health Edn. Com. Alachua County Sch. Bd., Gainesville, 1984; active Animal Control Bd., Alachua County, 1984-85. Mem. AMA, Am. Vet. Med. Assn., Wildlife Disease Assn. (wildlife rehab. com. 1982), Am. Acad. Family Physicians, Am. Pub. Health Assn., Phi Kappa Phi, Phi Zeta. Club: Fla. Track. Current work: Public health and public health education; includes health delivery environmental medicine and zoonotic diseases. Subspecialties: Laboratory animal medicine; Family practice. Home: 3301 NW 30th Pl Gainesville FL 32605 Office: Family Practice Med Group 425 SE 4th Ave Gainesville FL 32605

BLACK, EDWARD PARTRIDGE, engineer; b. Tooele, Utah, Jan. 21, 1946; s. Elliot R. and Agnes (Partridge) B.; m. Marybeth Raynes, Feb. 27, 1968 (div. 1977); children—Teriesa, Nathan Jeffery, Sara, Melissa; m. Ardith Lynore Ashpole, Apr. 17, 1980; children—Camille Marie, Emily Jane. B.S., Ariz. State U., 1971; B.S., in Elec. Engring., U. Utah, 1974, Ph.D., 1980. Instrument mgr., dept. chemistry Rice U., Houston, 1977-78; systems engr. Intel Corp., Phoenix, 1978-80; electromagnetic compatability cons. Chris Kendall Cons., Running Springs, Calif., 1980-83; chief engr. Certitech Labs., Inc., Running Springs, 1983—. Contbr. articles to profl. jours. Chmn. Democratic Legis. Dist. Com., Salt Lake City, 1974; mem. State Dem. Central Com., Salt Lake City, 1975-76; operator So. Calif. Emergency Response Radio Net, Colton, 1984—. Served with USAR, 1963—. NSF, grantee 1978. Mem. IEEE, Assn. Computing Machinery, Computer Soc. Mormon. Current work: Design and testing of computer and other electronic equipment to minimize both spurious emissions and susceptability to electrostatic discharge, lighting, and electromagnetic pulse threats. Subspecialty: Systems engineering. Office: Certitech Labs Inc PO Box 300 32765 Hilltop Blvd Running Springs CA 92382

BLACK, FRANKLIN OWEN, physician, med. researcher; b. St. Louis, Aug. 8, 1937; s. Frank and Kathleen Ruth (Scowden) B.; m. Jorita Jenkins, Mar. 30, 1961; children: Owen Brent, Christopher Brian, Jeremy Benjamin. B.A. in Chemistry, S.E. Mo. State U., 1955; M.D., U. Mo., 1963. Diplomate: Am. Bd. Otolaryngology. Intern Mobile (Ala.) Gen. Hosp., 1963-64; resident in surgery Bataan Meml. Hosp. and Loveland Found., Albuquerque, 1964-65; resident in otolaryngology U. Colo. Med. Center, Denver, 1965-68, instr., 1968-69; attending physician in otolaryngology Denver VA Hosp., Denver Gen. Hosp., 1968-69; instr., spl. research fellow dept. surgery U. Colo. Med. Center, 1968-69, asst. prof., 1969, asst. clin. prof., 1970-71; assoc. prof. otolaryngology U. Fla. Coll. Medicine, Gainesville, 1971-74; asso. prof. dept. otolaryngology Eye and Ear Hosp., U. Pitts., 1974-82, dir. div. vestibular disorders, 1974-82, vice chmn. dept. otolaryngology, 1976-81, mem. grad. faculty, 1977-82; mem. med. staff Children's Hosp. Pitts., 1980-82; chief div. neurootology Good Samaritan Hosp. and Med. Center, Portland, Oreg., 1982—; sr. scientist Neurol. Scis. Inst., Portland, 1982—. Contbr. articles to profl. jours. Served to lt. comdr. USNR, 1969-71. Decorated Bronze Star.; NIH fellow, 1968-69; NIH career devel. awardee, 1972-77. Fellow ACS; mem. Assn. Research in Otolaryngology (sec.-treas. 1976-78, pres. 1978-79), Pitts. Neuroscience Soc. (pres. 1977), Am. Acad. Otolaryngology (chmn. com. for research in otolaryngology 1978-82), Pa. Acad. Ophthalmology (program chmn. 1976), Am. Audiology Soc., Am. Council Otolaryngology, AMA, Am. Neurotology Soc., Am. Tinnitus Assn., Am. Nat. Standards Inst., Barany Soc., Internat. Brain Research Orgn., N.Y. Acad. Scis., Otosclerosis Study Group, Pan Am. Assn. Oto-Rhino-Laryngology and Broncho-Esophagology, Pa. Med. Soc., Royal Soc. Medicine, Triological Soc., Soc. Ear, Nose and Throat Advances in Children, Am. Otol. Soc., Soc. Neurosci., Sigma Xi. Current Work: Vestibular physiology, vestibular neurophysiology, sensorimotor integration. Subspecialties: Otorhinolaryngology; Neurophysiology. Office: Good Samaritan Hospital and Medical Center Neurol Scis Ctr 1040 NW 22d Ave Portland OR 97210

BLACK, PETER MCLAREN, neurosurgeon, educator; b. Calgary, Alta., Can., Apr. 3, 1944; s. Thomas Herbert and Elizabeth (Peterson) B.; m. Katharine Cohen, June 15, 1967; children: Winifred, Elizabeth, Katharine, Peter Thomas, Christopher. A.B., Harvard U., 1966; M.D., C.M., McGill U., Montreal, Can., 1970; Ph.D., Georgetown U., 1978. Intern, resident Mass. Gen. Hosp., Boston, 1970-72, resident in neurosurgery, 1975-80; asst. prof. surgery Harvard Med. Sch., Boston, 1980-84, assoc. prof. surgery, 198—. Author numerous sci. articles. NIH tchr. investigator awardee, 1982. Mem. Congress Neurol. Surgeons, Research Soc. Neurol. Surgeons, Soc. Neurosci., Am. Assn. Neurol. Surgeons, Am. Neurol. Assn., Am. Fedn. Clin. Research. Current Work: cerebrospinal fluid physiology, brain peptides, pituitary tumors, higher cortical functions. Subspecialty: Neurosurgery. Office: Mass General Hosp Ambulatory Care Center Suite 312 15 Parkman St Boston MA 02114

BLACKADAR, ALFRED KIMBALL, meteorologist, educator, researcher, consultant; b. Newburyport, Mass., July 6, 1920; s. Walter Lloyd and Harriett Dodge (White) B.; m. Beatrice Fenner, Mar. 23, 1946; children: Bruce E., Russell L., Thomas A. A.B., Princeton U., 1942; Ph.D., NYU, 1950. Cert. cons. meteorologist Am. Meteorol. Soc., 1973. From instr. to assoc. prof. NYU, N.Y.C., 1946-56; from assoc. prof. to prof. Pa. State U., University Park, 1956—, head dept. meteorology, 1967-81; lectr. Columbia U., N.Y.C., 1951-53. Contbr. articles to profl. jours. Served to maj. AC U.S. Army, 1942-46. Alexander von Humboldt Sr. Scientist, 1973. Fellow Am. Meteorol. Soc. (pres. 1971-72, Charles F. Brooks award 1969), Am. Geophys. Union, AAAS; fgn. mem. Deutsche Meteorolgische Gesellschaft. Baptist. Current Work: Turbulent flow and physical processes applied to the atmospheric and oceanic boundary layers. Subspecialties: Micrometeorology; Synoptic meteorology. Home: 805 W Foster Ave State College PA 16801 Office: 503 Walker Bldg University Park PA 16802

BLACKBURN, JACOB FLOYD, computer scientist; b. Newton., N.C., Nov. 27, 1918; s. Julius Walter and Lottie Mae (Lael) B.; m. Beverley England, Mar. 29, 1944; 1 son, Gregg Scott. B.A., Lenoir-Rhyne Coll., 1940; certificate, N.Y.U., 1942; M.A., Duke U., 1947; Ph.D., U. N.C., 1953. Asst. prof. The Citadel, Charleston, S.C., 1947-50; mem. Inst. for Advanced Study, Princeton, N.J., 1953-54; assoc. prof. USAF Acad., 1955-56; various mgmt positions IBM, Cranford, N.J., 1956-77, Geneva, Switzerland, 1956-77, Brussels, Belgium, 1956-77; dir. Office Tech. Policy and Space Affairs, Dept. State, Washington, 1977-79; exec. dir. computer sci. bd. Nat. Acad. Scis., 1980-82; liaison scientist Office Naval Research, London, Eng., 1982-84; industry assessment specialist U.S. Embassy, London, 1984—. Contbr. articles to profl. jours. Pres. Brussels Am. Club, 1974; pres. Brussels Toastmasters, 1972-73, Paris Toastmasters, 1975-76, Dresden Condominium Assn., Washington, 1978-82. Served to capt. USAAF, 1941-46; to lt. col. USAF, 1951-56. Decorated Air medal.; Recipient Computer Pioneer award Nat. Computer Conf., 1975; Alumnus of Yr. award Lenoir-Rhyne Coll., 1981. Mem. Assn. Computing Machinery, Am. Math. Soc. Democrat. Club: Grosvenor Sq. Toastmasters (London) (pres. 1983). Current Work: Reporting on European government and industry policy and technology in computer science and telecommunications. Subspecialties: Numerical analysis (computer science); Applied mathematics. Home: 12A Redcliffe Sq London SW10 England Office: 223 Old Marylebone Rd London NW1 England

BLACKLOW, NEIL RICHARD, medical educator; b. Cambridge, Mass., Feb. 26, 1938; s. Leo Alfred and Clara Edna (Cumenes) B.; m. Margery Lois Brown, June 2, 1963; children: John Andrew, Peter Douglas. B.A., Harvard U., 1959; M.D., Columbia U., 1963. Intern Beth Israel Hosp., Boston, 1963-64, resident, 1964-65; virologist Nat. Inst. Allergy and Infectious Diseases, 1965-68, 69-71; fellow in infectious diseases Mass. Gen. Hosp.-Harvard U., 1968-69; asst. prof. medicine Boston U., 1971-74, assoc. prof., 1974-76; prof. medicine, molecular genetics and microbiology U. Mass., 1976—, dir. div. infectious diseases, 1976—. Mem. editorial bd., Infection and Immunity, 1981—; assoc. editor: Revs. of Infectious Diseases, 1982—; contbr. articles to profl. jours. Served with USPHS, 1965-68. Med. Found. Boston fellow, 1972-74; grantee in field. Mem. Am. Soc. Clin. Investigation, Infectious Diseases Soc. Am., Am. Assn. Immunologists. Current Work: Etiology, diagnosis and treatment of viral diseases, virologist, infectious diseases. Subspecialties: Infectious diseases; Virology (medicine). Office: U Mass Medical School Worcester MA 01605

BLACKWELL, ARLYN NAVET laboratory administrator, mechanical engineer; b. Fyffe, Ala., Dec. 13, 1932; s. Lester Lee and Ruth Isabel (Deal) B.; m. Sharon Jean Ragsdale, May 15, 1970 (div. Sept. 1981); 1 son, John Arlyn. B.S., U. Calif.-Berkeley, 1958, M.S., 1960. Registered profl. engr., Calif. Mem. tech. staff Sandia Nat. Labs., Livermore, Calif., 1959-62, sect. supr., 1962-64, div. supr., 1964-67, dept. mgr., 1967-78, dir. ops., 1978—. Bd. dirs. Valley Meml. Hosp., Livermore, 1984—. Fellow ASME. Republican. Current work: Heat transfer; fluid mechanics; combustion research related to nuclear weapons and energy research and development. Subspecialty: Mechanical engineering. Home: 562 Touriga Ct Pleasanton CA 94566 Office: Sandia Nat Labs PO Box 969 Livermore CA 194550

BLACKWELL, JOHN, polymer science educator; b. Sheffield, Eng., Jan. 15, 1942; came to U.S., 1967, naturalized, 1984; s. Leonard and Vera (Brook) B.; m. Susan Margaret Crawshaw, Aug. 5, 1965; children—Martin Jonathan, Helen Elizabeth. B.Sc. in Chemistry, U. Leeds, Eng., 1963, Ph.D. in Biophysics, 1967. Postdoctoral research assoc. Coll. Forestry, SUNY-Syracuse, 1967-69; vis. asst. prof. dept. macromolecular sci. Case Western Res. U., Cleve., 1969-70, asst. prof., 1970-74, assoc. prof., 1974-77, prof., 1977—, chmn. dept. macromolecular sci., 1985—; vis. prof. Kennedy Inst. Rheumatology, London, 1975, CNRS, U. Grenoble, France, 1977, U. Freiburg, Fed. Republic Germany, 1982. Author: Biopolymers, 1973. Contbr. articles to profl. jours. NIH Research Career Devel. awardee, 1973; grantee NSF, NIH, Dept. Def., Cystic Fibrosis Found. Fellow Am. Phys. Soc.; mem. Biophys. Soc. (chmn. biopolymer group 1975-76), Am. Chem. Soc., Soc. for Complex Carbohydrates, Fiber Soc. (Disting. Achievement award 1981), AAAS. Episcopalian. Current work: Structure and interactions of polymer molecules; structure of liquid crystalline polymers, polyurethanes, cellulose and cellulose derivatives, proteoglycans and glycoproteins. Subspecialties: Polymers (materials science); X-ray crystallography. Home: 16011 Fernway Rd Shaker Heights OH 44120 Office: Case Western Res U Dept Macromolecular Sci Cleveland OH 44106

BLAESE, (ROBERT) MICHAEL, clinical immunologist, pediatrician; b. Mpls., Feb. 16, 1939; s. Robert Marion and Eva Ruth B.; m. Julianne Eleanor Johnson, June 23, 1962; children: Elise, Kristianne. B.S., Gustavus Adolphus Coll., 1961; M.D., U. Minn., 1964. Intern, Parkland Hosp., Dallas, 1964-65; resident in pediatrics U. Minn., Mpls., 1965-66; clin. assoc. metabolism br. Nat. Cancer Inst., Bethesda, Md., 1966-68, sr. investigator, 1968-74, chief cellular immunology sect. metabolism br., 1974—, dep. chief metabolism br., 1985—. Mem. editorial bd.: Jour. Immunology; contbr. chpts. to books, articles to profl. jours. Recipient Mead-Johnson award Am. Acad. Pediatrics, 1980; Wellcome vis. prof. Royal Soc. Medicine, London, 1980. Fellow AAAS; mem. Am. Soc. Clin. Investigation, Am. Assn. Immunologists, Soc. Pediatric Research. Lutheran. Current Work: Immunodeficiency diseases, cellular immunology, development of host defence mechanisms, immunoregulation, tumor immunology. Subspecialties: Immunology (medicine); Pediatrics. Office: NIH Bldg 10 Rm 6B05 Bethesda MD 20205

BLAIR, DONALD GEORGE RALPH, biochemist, educator; b. Lloydminster, Sask., Can., Nov. 5, 1932; s. George Alfred and Ester Pearl (Stromstad) B.; m. Joan Louise Springsteen, June 27, 1959; children: Eric Donald, Karen Jo. B.Sc. with honors, U. Alta., 1955, M.Sc., 1956; Ph.D., U. Wis., 1961. Lect. biochemistry U. Sask., 1963-76, lectr. cancer research, 1961-63, asst. prof., 1963-67, assoc. prof., 1967-76, assoc. prof. biochemistry, 1976—; mem. staff Sask. Research Unit Nat. Cancer Inst. Can., 1961-70, research assoc., 1970-75. Contbr. articles to profl. jours. Robert Tegler Spl. scholar, 1952, 53, 54; recipient Fred H. Irwin prize in organic chemistry, 1955. Mem. Can. Biochem. Soc., Canadian Oncolgy Soc., Am. Assn. Cancer Research, Am. Soc. Biol.

Chemists, AAAS, Sigma Xi. Nazarene. Current Work: Structure and function of RNA polymerases of rodent tissues; teaching biochemistry and cancer research; research on RNA polymerases. Subspecialties: Biochemistry (medicine); Cancer research (medicine). Office: Department Biochemistry University Saskatchewan Saskatoon SK S7N OWO Canada

BLAIR, JOHN, electrical engineer; b. Budapest, Hungary, Dec. 5, 1929; came to U.S., 1950, naturalized, 1955; s. Eugene I. and Helen (Benedek) B.; m. Constance Smith Drown, Sept. 10, 1954; children—David E., Jennifer C. B.S., MIT, 1954, M.S., 1955, Sc.D., 1960. Registered profl. engr., Mass. Faculty dept. elec. engring. MIT, Cambridge, 1957-66, mem. state industry adv. council Sea Grant Program, 1969—; corp. dir. research Raytheon Co., Lexington, Mass., 1966—; cons. Army Sci. Bd., Dept. of Army, Washington, 1978-84; panelist Sea Grant rev. panel NOAA, Dept. Commerce, Washington, 1979-85; mem. dean's adv. council U. Mass., Amherst, 1976—; mem. indsl. adv. group. dept. elec. engring. and computer sci. U. Calif.-Berkeley, 1983—; mem. indsl. affiliates com. dept. elec. engring. U. Ill., Urbana, 1970—. Contbr. articles to profl. jours. Ford Found. fellow, 1961. Mem. IEEE, Indsl. Research Inst., Am. Phys. Soc., Research Mgmt. (bd. editors 1983-85). Club: Cosmos (Washington). Current work: Direct research programs of diversified electronics company. Subspecialties: Semiconductors; Electronic materials. Home: 25 Moore Rd Wayland MA 01778 Office: Raytheon Co 141 Spring St Lexington MA 02173

BLAIR, MICHAEL FRANCIS, research engineer; b. Corry, Pa., Dec. 31, 1942; s. Francis Leon and Mary (Reyda) B.; m. Susan Scanlon, Jan. 14, 1967; children—Patricia Ann, Stephen Michael. B.M.E., Cornell U., 1965, M.M.E., 1966. Research engr. Jet Propulsion Lab., Pasadena, Calif., 1967-68, United Techs. Research Ctr., East Hartford, Conn., 1968—. Contbr. articles to profl. jours. Coach Eastern Conn. Hockey Orgn., Manchester, 1982-84; gen. mgr. Vernon Travel Soccer, Conn., 1984-85. Served to 1st lt. U.S. Army, 1966-68. Mem. ASME (Melville medal 1984). Current work: Experimental investigation of convective heat transfer in boundary layers; current work relates to fundamentals of transport in turbulent and transitional flows and to basic studies of film cooling. Subspecialty: Fluid mechanics. Office: United Techs Research Ctr MS-16 Silver Ln East Hartford CT 06108

BLAIR, ROBERT, animal science administrator, ecucator, researcher; b. Beith, Ayrshire, Scotland, May 29, 1933; s. Samuel and Mary (McBeth) B.; m. Moreen McGhie, Apr. 5, 1958; children—Rosalind M.J., Robert S. B.Sc., U. Glasgow, 1956; Ph.D., U. Aberdeen, 1960; D.Sc., U. Sask., 1983. Prin. sci. officer Agrl. Research Council, Edinburgh, Scotland, 1966-75; dir. nutrition Swift Can. Co. Ltd., Toronto, Ont., 1976-78; prof. animal sci. U. Sask., Saskatoon, Can., 1978-84; prof., head dept animal sci. U. B.C., Vancouver, Can., 1984—; mem. subcom. on vitamin tolerance NRC, Washington, 1984—. Contbr. chpts. to books, articles to profl. jours. Mem. World Assn. Animal Prodn. (council 1983—), Nutrition Soc. U.K., Nutrition Soc. Can., Am. Inst. Nutrition, Am. Soc. Animal Sci., Can. Soc. Animal Sci. (pres. western br. 1985—). Current work: Nutrition of non-ruminant animals. Subspecialty: Animal nutrition. Office: Dept Animal Sci U BC Suite 248 2357 Main Mall Vancouver BC V6T 2A2 Canada

BLAIS, ROGER NATHANIEL, engineering physics educator; b. Duluth, Minn., Oct. 3, 1944; s. Eusebe Joseph and Edith Seldina (Anderson) B.; m. Mary Louise Leclerc, Aug. 2, 1971; children—Christopher Edward, Laura Louise. B.A., U. Minn., 1966; Ph.D., U. Okla., 1971; cert. in programming Tulsa Jr. Coll., 1981. Registered profl. engr., Okla. Instr., Westark Community Coll., Ft. Smith, Ark., 1971-72; asst. prof. Old Dominion U., Norfolk, Va., 1972-77; asst. prof. U. Tulsa, 1977-81, assoc. prof. engring. physics, 1981—, assoc. dir. Artificial Lift Projects, 1983—. Contbr. articles to profl. jours. Mem. Am. Phys. Soc., Nat. Soc. Profl. Engrs., Soc. Petroleum Engrs., Am. Assn. Physics Tchrs., AAUP, AAAS, Instrument Soc. Am., Phi Beta Kappa, Sigma Xi (pres. Tulsa U. club 1981-82), Sigma Pi Sigma, Tau Beta Pi. Unitarian. Current work: Research on petroleum production by artificial lift - gas lift, electric submersible pumping, hydraulic jet pumping, multiphase flow; instrumentation. Subspecialties: Fluid mechanics; Petroleum engineering. Home: 5348 E 30th Pl Tulsa OK 74114-6314 Office: Dept Physics U Tulsa 600 S College Ave Tulsa OK 74104-3189

BLAKE, BRIAN FRANCIS, psychology educator, consultant; b. Jersey City, Aug. 26, 1942; s. Andrew A. and Mary A. (White) B.; m. Ann M. Sicola, Jan. 24, 1965; children: Dristin, Eric, Sean. B.A., St. Peter's Coll., 1964; M.S., Purdue U., 1966, Ph.D., 1969. Asst. prof. St. John's U., N.Y.C., 1969-72, assoc. prof., 1972-73; asst. prof. Purdue U., West Lafayette, Ind., 1973-75, assoc. prof., 1975-79, prof., 1979-81; dir. consumer lindsl. research program and prof. psychology Cleve. State U., 1981—; sr. research cons. Human Affairs Research Center, N.Y.C., 1970-72; market research cons. Pfizer Genetics Land O'Lakes, West Lafayette, Ind., 1977-81, others, 1977-81; program evaluation cons. Fgn. Agr. Services, U.S. Dept. Agr., Washington, 1976-77, AID, Bolivia, 1980; pres. Decision Dynamics, Inc., Cleve., 1982—. Contbr. articles to profl. jours., chpts. to books. Mem. Am. Psychol. Assn., Am. Mktg. Assn., Eastern Psychol. Assn., Midwestern Psychol. Assn., Sigma Xi. Current Work: Consumer psychology, public opinion measurement, market research techniques. Subspecialty: Social psychology. Office: Cleveland State U Cleveland OH 44115

BLAKELY, JOHN MCDONALD, educator; b. Scotland, Apr. 8, 1936; came to U.S., 1961, naturalized, 1967; s. James A. and Elizabeth M. (McDonald) B.; m. Nanette Stewart Irvine, July 1, 1960; children: Robin Mary, Karen Elizabeth. B.Sc., Glasgow U., 1958, Ph.D., 1961. Research fellow Harvard U., Cambridge, Mass., 1961-63; faculty Cornell U., Ithaca, N.Y., 1963—, prof. materials sci. and engring., 1970—; Guggenheim fellow Cambridge (Eng.) U., 1970-71; vis. scientist Argonne (Ill.) Nat. Lab., 1976; NSF fellow, Berkeley, 1977, cons. in field. Author: Introduction to Properties of Crystal Surfaces, 1973, Surface Physics of Materials, vols. I, II, 1975. Recipient Kelvin prize in physics Glasgow U., 1960; NSF grantee, 1970—; Dept. of Energy grantee, 1979—; Sci. and Engring. Research Council (U.K.) fellow York U., Eng., 1984. Fellow Inst. Physics U.K., Am. Phys. Soc.; mem. Am. Vacuum Soc., AIME. Club: Finger Lakes Runners. Current Work: Surface science, oxidation of metals, catalysis, photographic materials. Subspecialties: Materials; Condensed matter physics. Home: 332 Forest Home Dr Ithaca NY 14850 Office: Cornell Univ 312 Bard Hall Ithaca NY 14853

BLAKELY, JOHN PAUL, safety engineer, manager technical publications, chemical engineer, researcher; b. Erie, Pa., Oct. 20, 1922; s. Eugene James, Jr. and Isabelle Marie (Carney) B.; m. Tinque June Spann, Aug. 4, 1944; 1 dau., Carol Tinque Blakely Kaplan. B.S., Washington and Lee U., 1943; M.S., U. Tenn.-Knoxville, 1958. Research chemist Tenn. Eastman Corp., Oak Ridge, 1943-48; research chemist Union Carbide Corp., Oak Ridge, 1948-65, mng. editor, 1965-73, supr. tech. publs., 1973-80, chem. engr., 1980—, editor, author publs. manual, 1982. Editor, author: Nuclear Safety Jour, 1965-73. Pres., bd. Y 12 Fed. Credit Union, Oak Ridge, 1950-73. Mem. Soc. Tech. Communication (sr., outstanding communicator of year E. Tenn. chpt. 1982, dir. 1979-84, chmn. strategic planning com. 1981-84), Am. Nuclear Soc. (chmn. publs. com. 1979-81). Republican. Club: Toastmasters (pres. Knoxville 1951-54). Current Work: Effective technical communication by means of standardized and accepted format, terminology, and usage. Subspecialty: Chemical engineering. Home: 9635 Tunbridge Ln Knoxville TN 37922 Office: Martin Marietta Energy Systems Inc Y-12 9983-58 Nuclear PO Box Y Oak Ridge TN 37831

BLAKESLEE, A. EUGENE, physical chemist; b. Sayre, Pa., June 20, 1928; s. Edwin Stuart and Helen Frances (Bird) B.; m. Marybelle Morrison Capron, May 1, 1954; children—Mark, Bruce. B.S. in Chemistry, Pa. State U., 1950; Ph.D. in Phys. Chemistry, Cornell U., 1955. Investigator N.J. Zinc Co., Palmerton, Pa., 1955-57; mem. tech. staff Bell Telephone Labs., Allentown, Pa., 1957-60; mem. staff Gen. Electric, Syracuse, N.Y., 1960-62; research staff mem. IBM, Yorktown Heights, N.Y., 1962-80; sr. scientist Solar Energy Research Inst., Golden, Co., 1980—. Contbr. articles to profl. jours. Patentee in field. Gen. Electric fellow, 1954. Mem. Electrochem.SSoc., Am. Assn. for Crystal Growth, Democrat. Unitarian. Current work: Semiconductor and photovoltaic materials and devices; crystal growth; multijunction solar cells; government contract administration; grew first strained-layer superlattices. Subspecialties: Semiconductors; Crystal growth. Office: Solar Energy Research Inst Golden CO 80401

BLAKLEY, GEORGE ROBERT, JR., mathematician, computer scientist; b. Chgo., May 6, 1932; s. George Robert and Gladys Margaret (Baechle) B.; m. Virginia Clarke, Sept. 7, 1957; children: George Robert III, Cynthia Ellen, Lydia Anne. A.B., Georgetown U., 1954; M.A., U. Md., 1959, Ph.D., 1960. Asst. prof. math. U. Ill. at Urbana, 1962-66; asso. prof. State U. N.Y. at Buffalo, 1966-70; prof. Tex. A&M U., College Station, 1970—, head dept., 1970-78; Office Naval Research postdoctoral research asso. Cornell U., 1960. Nat. Acad. Scis.-NRC postdoctoral fellow Harvard U., 1961. Mem. IEEE, AAAS, Am. Math. Soc., Assn. Computing Machinery, Math. Assn. Am., Soc. for Indsl. and Applied Math. (vis. lectr. biomath. 1968-70, vis. lectr. applied math. 1979-83), Sigma Xi, Phi Kappa Phi, Pi Mu Epsilon. Current Work: Information theory, computer security, combinatorics. Subspecialties: Cryptography and data security; Information systems, storage, and retrieval (computer science). Home: 1405 Broadmoor St Bryan TX 77802 Office: Dept Math Tex A and M U College Station TX 77843

BLANCHARD, RAY MILTON, psychiatry institute research psychologist; b. Hammonton, N.J., Oct. 9, 1945; s. Ray Milton and Angelina (Celi) Ruggero. A.B., U. Pa., 1967; M.A., U. Ill., 1970, Ph.D., 1973. Cert. psychologist Ont. Bd. Examiners. Psychologist Ont. Correctional Inst., Brampton, Can., 1976-80; research psychologist Gender Identity Clinic, Clarke Inst. Psychiatry, Toronto, Ont., 1980—. Killam fellow Dalhousie U., Halifax, N.S., Can., 1973. Mem. Internat. Acad. Sex Research, Am. Psychol. Assn., Can. Psychol. Assn. Current Work: Taxonomy of gender identity disorders; psychosocial adjustment of transsexuals; phallometric assessment of sexual anomalies. Subspecialty: Gender identity disorders. Home: 32 Shaftesbury Ave Toronto ON M4T 1A1 Canada Office: Gender Identity Clinic Clarke Inst Psychiatry 250 College St Toronto ON M5T 1R8 Canada

BLANCHARD, SUSAN MANNING, biomedical engineer, researcher; b. Knoxville, Tenn., Sept. 15, 1946; d. Frederick Claude and Florence Estelle (Chapin) Manning; m. James Wilson Henderson, Jan. 30, 1968 (div. 1980); children—Paul Manning, Sara Tiers; m. Donald Gray Blanchard, Oct. 11, 1980. A.B., Oberlin Coll., 1968; M.S., Duke U., 1980, Ph.D., 1982. Med. research tech. Duke U. Med. Ctr., Durham, N.C., 1977-78, research assoc., 1983—; mem. tech staff Rockwell Internat., Chapel Hill, N.C., 1982-83. Bd. trustees Eno River Unitarian-Universalist Fellowship, Durham, 1978-80, 83-85. Predoctoral award NIH-NHLBI, 1978-82, postdoctoral, 1983-85. Mem. IEEE Engineers in Medicine and Biology Soc., IEEE Computer Soc., Sigma Xi, Tau Beta Pi. Democrat. Current work: Investigation of informational content of unipolar epicardial electrograms with emphasis on dysrhythmias. Subspecialties: Operations research (engineering); Cardiology. Office: Duke Univ Med Ctr PO Box 3348 Durham NC 27710

BLANCK, A.R., scientist, engineer; b. N.Y.C., Feb. 7, 1925; s. Andrew G. and Anne V. B.; m. Edna H. Ruppert, Nov. 25, 1950; children: Elaine Lois, Evelyn Joyce. B.A., NYU, 1950; M.A., Poly. Inst. Bklyn., 1953; Sc.D., Sussex (Eng.) Inst. Tech., 1959. Project engr. Centro Research Labs., Ossining, N.Y., 1948-53; tech. service engr. Celanese Corp., Summit, N.J., 1953-56; head dielectics lab W.R. Grace, Clifton, N.J., 1956-58; coordinator materials design engring. U.S. Govt., Dover, N.J., 1958-65; pres., tech. dir. Rutherford Research Corp., N.J., 1956—; mem. faculty Sch. Continuing Edn., N.Y.U., 1965—. Contbr. articles to profl. jours. Mem. Am. Council Ind. Labs., Assn. Cons. Chemists and Chem. Engrs., ASTM, AIEE, IEEE. Baptist. Current Work: Electrical insulation; material engineering; plastics and rubbers. Subspecialties: Materials; Electrical engineering. Office: Rutherford Research Drawer 249 Rutherford NJ 07070

BLANCK, EUGENE LOUIS, JR., engineering geologist; b. Mpls., July 4, 1953; s. Eugene Louis and Mary Frances (Brown) B.; m. Doreen Lanora Liberto, Nov. 5, 1983. B.S. in Engring. Geology, UCLA, 1976; M.S. in Geology and Geophysics, Calif. State U.-Los Angeles, 1985. Student asst. UCLA Sch. Engring., 1974; project geologist Rasmussen & Assoc., San Bernadino, Calif., 1976-81; geophysicist Earth Sci. & Engring., Hemet, Calif., 1976—; county geologist San Bernadino County, Calif., 1984—; mem. Lake Arrowhead Erosion Control Ad Hoc Com., 1984—. Mem. Assn. Engring. Geologists, Geol. Soc. Am., Seismol. Soc. Am., Soc. Exploration Geophysicists (assoc.), UCLA Geol. Soc., South Coast Geol. Soc., Grand Canyon Natural History Assn., Am. Geol. Inst., Calif. Scholarship Fedn. Republican. Current work: Microgravity applications to engineering geology. Subspecialties: Engineering geology; Geophysics. Home: 509 Via Vista Dr Redlands CA 92373 Office: San Bernadino County Office Bldg and Safety 385 N Arrowhead Ave San Bernadino CA 92415

BLANFORD, GEORGE EMMANUEL, JR., physicist, educator; b. Lebanon, Ky., Sept. 16, 1940; s. George Emmanuel and Catherine Josephine (Hardesty) B.; m. Julianne Blanford, Aug. 7, 1971 (div.); children: Elizabeth Braznell, Peter Emmanuel. B.A., Cath. U. Am., Washington, 1964; M.S. (NSF summer fellow), U. Louisville, 1967; Ph.D., Washington U., St. Louis, 1971. Maitre de conference associe Universite de Clermont, Clermont-Ferrand, France, 1971-73; research assoc. NASA Johnson Space Ctr., Houston, 1973-75; asst. prof. physics U. Houston, Clear Lake City, 1975-78, assoc. prof., 1978—; visiteur étranger Laboratoire René Bernas, Orsay, France, 1984. Contbr. articles to profl. jours. NRC resident research assoc., 1973-1975. Mem. AAAS, Am. Assn. Physics Tchrs., Am. Geophys. Union, Am. Phys. Soc., Phi Beta Kappa, Sigma Xi, Sigma Pi Sigma. Democrat. Roman Catholic. Club: Johnson Space Ctr. Bicycle (past pres.). Current work: Cosmic ray and solar particle interactions. Subspecialties: Planetary science; Planetology. Office: 2700 Bay Area Blvd B19 Houston TX 77058

BLASINGAME, BENJAMIN PAUL, electronics company executive; b. State College, Pa., Aug. 1, 1918; s. Ralph Upshaw and Sue Mae (Combs) B.; m. Ella Mae Perry, Aug. 29, 1942; children—Nancy J. Blasingame Wambach, James P., Margaret A. Blasingame Kramer, John R. B.S. in Mech. Engring, Pa. State U., 1940; Sc.D. in Aero. Engring, M.I.T., 1950. Head astronautics dept. U.S. Air Force Acad., 1958-59; resigned, 1959; gen. mgr. electronics div. Gen. Motors Corp., 1959-70; mgr. Milw. operation Delco Electronics div., 1970-72; dir. Santa Barbara Bank and Trust. Author: Astronautics, 1964. Mgr. Santa Barbara operation, 1972-79; Bd. dirs. Santa Barbara Cottage Hosp., 1977—; chmn. Santa Barbara Metro, Nat. Alliance Bus., 1972-75. Commd. 2d lt. U.S. Air Force, 1941; advanced through grades to col. 1959. Decorated Legion of Merit; recipient Public Service award NASA, 1969, Public Service medal, 1973. Mem. Nat. Acad. Engring., N.Y. Acad. Scis., Internat. Acad. Astronautics, Santa Barbara C. of C. (bd. dirs. 1977—). Unitarian. Club: La Cumbre Country. Patentee in field. Current Work: Inertial navigation, guidance and control systems. Subspecialties: Aeronautical instrumentation; Aerospace engineering and technology. Home: 517 Carriage Hill Ct Santa Barbara CA 93110

BLAU, LEA, chemist, educator, researcher; b. Arad, Romania, Jan. 30, 1936; came to U.S., 1968, naturalized, 1973; d. Geza-Gershon and Magda (Tuka) Kugel; m. Alfie Blau, Mar. 23, 1969. B.Sc., Technion, Israel Inst. Tech., 1960, M.Sc., 1963; Ph.D., Weizmann Inst. Sci., Israel, 1967. Postdoctoral fellow Rutgers U., New Brunswick, N.J., 1968-69; research assoc., instr. Queens Coll. CUNY, Flushing, 1969-79; asst. prof. chemistry Yeshiva U., N.Y.C., 1979-81, assoc. prof., 1981—. Contbr. articles to profl. jours. Served with Israel Def. Forces, 1955-57. Grantee Office Naval Research, 1982-84; Mellon Found., 1984. Mem. Am. Chem. Soc., Biophys. Soc., N.Y. Acad. Sci., Sigma Xi. Current work: Education in organic chemistry and biochemistry; research in ionophore mediated ion transport across phospholipid bilayers. Subspecialties: Biophysical chemistry; Biochemistry (biology). Office: Yeshiva U 245 Lexington Ave New York NY 10016

BLEACH, RICHARD DAVID, physicist; b. Ft. Riley, Kans., June 7, 1944; s. Norman and Lydia (Corlese) B. B.S., Rensselaer Poly. Inst., 1966; Ph.D., U. Md., 1972. Reseach assoc. U. Md., College Park, 1972-76; cons. Naval Research Lab., Washington, 1976-77, research physicist, 1977-83; staff U.S. Ho. of Reps. Appopriaions Com., 1983-84; asst. dir. program integration/-strategic Def. Iniative Orgn., Office Sec. of Def., 1985—. Contbr. articles to profl. jours. Recipient Superior Performance award Naval Research Lab., 1979, 81. Mem. AAAS, Am. Astron. Soc., Am. Phys. Soc., Am. Vacuum Soc., Sigma Xi. Current Work: Program Integration Office of Secretary of Defense. Subspecialties: Plasma physics; X-ray high energy astrophysics. Home: 6109 Gallery St Bowie MD 20715 Office: SDIO/OSD The Pentagon Washington DC 20301

BLECHNER, MARK J., psychologist; b. N.Y.C., Nov. 6, 1950; s. Norbert and Hannah (Darmstadter) B. B.A., U. Chgo., 1972; M.S., Yale U., 1975, Ph.D., 1977. Lic. psychologist, N.Y. Researcher Haskins Labs., New Haven, 1974-76; researcher Bell Labs., Murray Hill, N.J., 1977-78; asst. clin. prof. Coll. Physicians and Surgeons, Columbia U., N.Y.C., 1981—. Contbr. articles to profl. jours. Mem. AAAS, Am. Psychol. Assn., N.Y. Acad. Sci., Sigma Xi. Current Work: Dreams in borderline personality organization, cognitive development of paranoid perception. Subspecialty: Cognition. Address: 145 Central Park W New York NY 10023

BLEIBERG, MARVIN JAY, pharmacologist, toxicologist; b. Bklyn., Feb. 19, 1928; s. Harold and Rena (Holzer) B.; m. Beulah Matt, Jan. 17, 1960; children: Lawrence, Robert. B.S., Coll. William and Mary, 1949; postgrad., Ohio State U., 1949-50; Ph.D., Med. Coll. Va., 1957. Diplomate: Am. Bd. Toxicology. Postdoctoral trainee in steroid biochemistry Worcester Found. Exptl. Biology, Shrewsbury, Mass., 1957-58; instr., then asst. prof. pharmacology Jefferson Med. Coll., Phila., 1958-61; rev. scientist FDA, Washington, 1961-62; sr. scientist Melpar, Inc., Falls Church, Va., 1962-64; pharmacologist, sect. head Woodard Research Corp., Herndon, Va., 1963-75; interdisciplinary rev. scientist, div. toxicology Bur. Foods, FDA, Washington, 1975—. Contbr. articles to sci. jours. Mem. Am. Soc. Pharmacology and Exptl. Therapeutics, Am. Chem. Soc., Soc. Toxicology, Biometrics Soc., AAAS, N.Y. Acad. Sci., Soc. Exptl. Biology and Medicine (D.C. chpt.), Phi Beta Kappa, Sigma Xi. Current Work: Food additivies; safety evaluation. Subspecialties: Toxicology (medicine); Pharmacology. Home: 3613 Old Post Rd Fairfax VA 22030 Office: 200 C St SW Washington DC 20204

BLESSINGER, MICHAEL ANTHONY, physicist; b. New Albany, Ind., Sept. 14, 1956; s. Claude Martin and Mary Elaine (Henderzahs) B. B.S., Purdue U., 1978; M.S., Calif. Inst. Tech., 1980; postgrad. Calif. State U.-Los Angeles, 1984—. Mem. tech. staff Jet Propulsion Lab., Pasadena, Calif., 1980-84; sr. research specialist Rockwell Sci. Ctr., Thousand Oaks, Calif., 1985—. Fellow Calif. Inst. tech., Pasadena, 1978. Mem. Am. Phys. Soc., IEEE, Soc. Photo-Optical Instrumentation Engrs., Am. Assn. Physics Tchrs., Phi Beta Kappa, Sigma Pi Sigma. Current work: Testing and evaluation of infrared detectors. Subspecialty: Condensed matter physics. Home: 1642 E Hillcrest Apt 105 Thousand Oaks CA 91362 Office: Rockwell Sci Ctr 1049 Camino Dos Rios Thousand Oaks CA 91360

BLEWITT, GEORGE AUGUSTINE, pharmaceutical company executive, physician; b. Pittston, Pa., May 18,1937; s. George Augustus andVirginia (Wills) B.;m. Anne Katherine Mullahy, June 16,1962; children—George,-MaryKatherine,John, Patrick. B.S., King's Coll., Wilkes-Barre, Pa., 1958; M.D., Jefferson Med. Coll., 1962. Diplomate Am. Bd. Internal Medicine. Clin. faculty mem. Stanford U. Sch. Medicine, Stanford, Calif., 1967-75; staff physician Palo Alto Va Hosp., Calif., 1973-75; assoc. dir. clin. services Smith,Kline & French, Phila., 1976-78; med. dir.Menley & James Labs., Phila., 1978, v.p. research and devel., 1978-80; assoc. med. dir. Bristol-Myers Products,N.Y.C., 1980-81, v.p., med. dir., 1981-82, v.p., dir. research and devel., 1982—; clin. prof. medicine Jefferson Med. Coll.-Thomas Jefferson U.,, Phila., 1977-80. Served to maj. U.S. Army Res., 1963-71. Mem. AMA, Am. Soc.Nephrology, Am. Heart Assn., Pa.Med. Soc., The Proprietary Assn., Royal Soc.Medicine. Subspecialty: Internal medicine. Office: Bristol-Myers Products 1350 Liberty Ave Hillside NJ 07207

BLEYMAN, LEA KANNER, biologist, educator; b. Halle, Ger., Nov. 9, 1936; d. Salomon David and Amalia (Azderbal) Kanner; m. Michael Alan Bleyman, June 15, 1958; 1 dau., Anne. B.A. magna cum laude, Brandeis U., 1958; M.A., Columbia U., 1961; Ph.D., Ind. U., 1966. Research assoc. U. Ill., Urbana, 1964-69, U. N.C., Chapel Hill, 1970-72; assoc. prof. biology Baruch Coll., CUNY, 1973-78, prof., 1979—, chairperson dept. natural scis., 1981-83; vis. research scientst Cornell U., Ithaca, N.Y., summers 1975-80; vis. research prof. Albert Einstein Coll. Medicine, Bronx, N.Y., summer 1984, 85. Asst. editor: Protozoological Actualities, 1979; bd. reviewers Jour. Protozoology, 1985—; contbr. articles to sci. jours. Max Planck Inst. fellow Berlin, summer 1974; NIH fellow, 1961-64; CUNY Chancellor's Faculty Fellow, 1985-86. Mem. NOW, AAAS, Am. Assn. Women in Sci., Am. Genetics Assn., Am. Soc. Cell Biology, Genetics Soc. Am., N.Y. Acad. Scis., Soc. Protozoologists (exec. com.), Phi Beta Kappa, Sigma Xi. Current Work: Ciliate genetics; aging and life cycle; nuclear regulation. Subspecialties: Gene actions; Cell biology. Office: 17 Lexington Ave Box 502 New York NY 10010

BLIM, RICHARD DON, pediatrician; b. Kansas City, Mo., Nov. 8, 1927; s. Miles G. and Lutha (Daniels) B.; m. Myrle R. Tingstad; children—Richard David, Carol Blim Kelly, John Miles. A.B., U. Kans., 1949, M.D., 1953. Diplomate Am. Bd. Pediatrics. Intern, U. Kans., Kansas City, 1953-54, resident, 1954-56; practice medicine specializing in pediatrics, Kansas City, Mo., 1956—; mem. staff St. Luke's Hosp., Kansas City, Mo.; pres. Pediatric Assocs., Kansas City, 1970—; pres. Health Plan Mid Am., Kansas City, Mo., 1984—. Mem. editorial bd. Pediatric News, 1980—, Annals of Pediatrics, 1980—. Mem. exec. bd. Crittenton Ctr., Kansas City, Kans., 1981—. Served with U.S. Army, 1946-47, PTO. Named Disting. Med. Alumni, U. Kans., Kansas City, 1978. Fellow Am. Acad. Pediatrics (pres. Mo. chpt. 1965-68, mem. exec. bd. 1973-79, nat. pres. 1980-81, Grulee award 1984), Southwest Pediatric Soc. (pres. Kansas City 1963), Inst. of Medicine of Nat. Acad. Sci., Mo. State Med. Assn., AMA, Alpha Omega Alpha. Republican. Presbyterian. Club: Carriage (Kansas City, Mo.). Current work: Pediatrics; economic aspects of health care delivery. Subspecialty: Pediatrics. Office: Pediatric Assocs 4400 Broadway Kansas City MO 64111

BLINKS, LAWRENCE ROGERS, biologist, educator; b. Michigan City,Ind., Apr. 22, 1900; s. Walter Moulton Blinks and Ella (Little) Blinks Rogers; m. AnneCatherine Hof, July 27, 1928; 1 child, John Rogers. B.S., Harvard U., 1923, A.M., 1925, Ph.D., 1926. Asst. Rockefeller Inst., N.Y.C., 1926-28, assoc., 1928-33; assoc. prof. biology Stanford U., Palo Alto, Calif., 1933-36, prof. 1936-65, dir. Hopkins Marine Sta., Pacific Grove, Calif.; prof. biology U. Calif.-Santa Cruz, 1965-72; asst. dir. NSF, Washington, 1954-55. Editor Jour. Gen. Physiology, 1955-65. Recipient Stephen Hales award Soc. Plant Physiology, 1952. Fellow Am. Acad. Arts and Scis.; mem. Nat. Acad. Scis., Western Soc. Naturalists (pres.). Club: Faculty (Stanford U.). Current work: Photosynthesis of marine algae: electrobiology of giant algal cells. Subspecialties: Plant physiology (biology); Marine biology. Office: Hopkins Marine Station Pacific Grove CA 93950

BLISS, LAWRENCE CARROLL, botany educator; b. Cleve., Nov. 29, 1929; s. Laurence and Ada May (Peterson) B.; m. Gweneth Ruth Jones, Mar. 15, 1952; children: Dwight I., Karen L. B.S., Kent State U., 1951, M.S., 1953; Ph.D., Duke U., 1956. Instr. biology Bowling Green State U., 1956-57; instr. botany U. Ill., 1957-58, asst. prof., 1958-61, assoc. prof., 1961-66, prof., 1966-68; prof. dept. botany U. Alta., 1968-78, dir. controlled environ. facility, 1968-78; prof. botany U. Wash., 1978—, chmn. dept. botany, 1978—; cons. in field. Author: (with M. Balbach) Laboratory Manual for General Botany, 6th edit., 1982; editor: Truelove Lowland, Devon Island, Canada: A High Arctic Ecosystem, 1977, (with others) Tundra Ecosystems: A Comparative Analysis, 1981; contbr. articles to profl. jours. Fulbright scholar, 1963-64. Mem. Ecol. Soc. Am. (v.p. 1976-77, treas. 1977-81, pres.-elect 1981-82, pres. 1982-83), Am. Inst. Biol. Sci.; fellow AAAS, Arctic Inst. N. Am.; mem. Can. Bot. Assn., Sigma Xi. Republican. Presbyterian. Current Work: Plant communities, ecophysiology and ecosystem studies of Arctic and Alpine environments especially Canadian High Arctic, Mount St. Helens. Subspecialties: Ecology (environmental science); Ecosystems analysis. Home: 1226 NW 175th St Seattle WA 98177 Office: Dept Botany U Wash Seattle WA 98195

BLITZ, LEO, astronomer, educator; b. Krakow, Poland, Oct. 21, 1945; s. Abraham and Maria (Salz) B.; m. Judith Ida Klimpl, Aug. 8, 1971; 1 son: Brian Adam. B.S., Cornell U., 1967; M.A., Columbia U., 1975, M.Phil., 1976, Ph.D., 1979. Postgrad. research fellow U. Calif., Berkeley, 1978-81; asst. prof. astronomy program U. Md., College Park, 1981—. Author undergrad. lab. manual; Contbr. articles to profl. jours. Gen. Research Bd. grantee U. Md., 1982; NATO Sci. Affairs grantee, 1983. Mem. Am. Astron. Soc., Internat. Astron. Union. Current Work: Star formation, galactic structure, molecular clouds. Subspecialty: Radio and microwave astronomy. Home: 1530 Red Oak Dr Silver Spring MD 20910 Office: Astronomy Program U Md College Park MD 20742

BLITZER, ANDREW, otolaryngologist; b. Pitts., Apr. 25, 1946; s. Martin Hollander and Lyrene Iris (Lave) B.; m. Patricia Volk, Dec. 21, 1969; children: Peter Morgen, Polly Volk. B.A., Adelphi U., 1967; D.D.S., Columbia U., 1970; M.D., Mt. Sinai Sch. Medicine, 1973. Diplomate: Am. Bd. Otolaryngology. Resident in gen. surgery Beth Israel Hosp., N.Y.C., 1973-74; resident in otolaryngology Mt. Sinai Hosp., N.Y.C., 1974-77; asst. prof. otolaryngology

Coll. Phys. and Surg., Columbia U., N.Y.C., 1977-82, assoc. prof. otolaryngology and oral surgery, 1982-84, clin. prof., 1984—; dir. div. head and neck surgery Columbia-Presbyn. Med. Ctr., N.Y.C., 1980—, dir. residency edn., 1978-84; lectr. dept. otolaryngology Mt. Sinai Sch. Medicine, N.Y.C., 1977—. Co-Author several books; assoc. editor: Oncology Times; contbr. chpts. to books, articles to profl. jours. Recipient award for excellence Am. Assn. Orthodontists, 1970; Nat. Inst. Neurol. Communicative Disorders and Stroke, grantee, 1978—. Fellow A.C.S., N.Y. Acad. Medicine, Am. Soc. for Head and Neck Surgery, Am. Acad. Facial Plastic and Reconstructive Surgery, Am. Laryngol., Rhinol., and Otol. Soc. Current Work: Histopathological and biochemical responses of connective tissue to cancer of the head and neck. Clinical research concerning malignant fibrous histiocytoma and mucormycosis of the paranasal sinuses; electromyography and laryngeal motion disorders. Subspecialties: Otorhinolaryngology; Cancer research (medicine). Home: 1136 Fifth Ave New York NY 10028 Office: Dept Otolaryngology Coll Phys & Surg Columbia U 630 W 168th St New York NY 10032

BLIZNAKOV, EMILE GEORGE, scientist; b. Kamen, Bulgaria, July 28, 1926; came to U.S., 1961, naturalized, 1966; s. George P. and Paraskeva B. M.D. Faculty of Medicine, Sofia, Bulgaria, 1953; Dir. Regional Sta. for Hygiene and Epidemiology, chief dist. dept. health, Pirdop, Bulgaria, 1953-55; staff scientist, microbiologist Research Inst. Epidemiology and Microbiology, Ministry of Public Health, Sofia, 1955-59; vis. scientist Gamaleya Research Inst. Epidemiology and Microbiology, Acad. Med. Scis., Moscow, 1958-59; sr. staff scientist, prof. life scis. New Eng. Inst., Ridgefield, Conn., 1961-81, dir. personnel, 1968-74, v.p., 1974-76, pres., 1976-81; exec. dir. research and devel. Libra Research, 1981—; pres., sci. dir. Lupus Research Inst., Rockville, Md., 1981—; dir. Child Safety Corp.; cons. to indsl., pharm. and public relations firms. Contbr. articles to profl. jours. Fannie E. Rippel Found. grantee, 1972-80; G.M. McDonald Found. grantee, 1972-81; Whitehall Found. grantee, 1971-75; Wallace Genetic Found. grantee, 1972-81. Fellow Royal Soc. Tropical Medicine and Hygiene (London); mem. AMA, Am. Fedn. Clin. Research, Am. Soc. Microbiology, N.Y. Acad. Scis., Am. Coll. Toxicology, Am. Soc. Neurochemistry, Reticuloendothelial Soc., Bioelectromagnetic Soc., AAAS, Internat. Soc. Chronobiology, Interam. Soc. Chemotherapy. Subspecialty: Medical research administration. Home: 189 Ledges Rd Ridgefield CT 06877 Office: Lupus Research Inst 1300 Piccard Dr Rockville MD 20850

BLOCH, ERICH, electrical engineer; b. Sulzburg, Ger., Jan. 9, 1925; came to U.S., 1948, naturalized, 1952; s. Joseph and Tony B.; m. Renee Stern, Mar. 4, 1948; 1 child, Rebecca Bloch Rosen. Student, Fed. Poly. Inst., Zurich, Switzerland, 1945-48; B.S. in Elec. Engring. U. Buffalo, 1952; hon. degrees SUNY-Buffalo, George Washington U., U. Mass., Colo. Sch. Mines. With IBM Corp., 1952-84, v.p. gen. mgr., East Fishkill, N.Y., 1975-80, v.p. tech. personnel devel., Armonk, N.Y., 1980-84; dir. NSF, Washington, 1984—; ; mem. com. computers in automated mfg. NRC, 1980-84. Trustee Marist Coll., Poughkeepsie, N.Y., 1978-82. Author. Fellow IEEE; mem. Nat. Acad. Engring., AAAS, Am. Soc. Mfg. Engrs. (hon.). Patentee in field. Subspecialty: Computer engineering. Office: NSF 1800 G St Washington DC

BLOCH, HERMAN SAMUEL, chemist; b. Chgo., June 15, 1912; s. Aaron and Esther (Broder) B.; m. Elaine J. Kahn, July 4, 1940; children—Aaron N., Janet L. (Mrs. Daniel Martin), Merry D. (Mrs. Dobroslav Valik). B.S., U. Chgo., 1933, Ph.D., 1936. With UOP, Inc., Des Plaines, Ill., 1936-77, asso. dir. research, 1964-73, dir. catalysis research, 1973-77, cons., 1977—; Chmn. com. phys. scis. Ill. Bd. Higher Edn., 1969-71. Author. Commr. Housing Authority Cook County, 1966—, chmn., 1971—; chmn. Skokie (Ill.) Human Relations Commn., 1965-71; pres. bd. edn. Skokie Sch. Dist. 68, 1962-63; trustee Skokie Library Bd., 1981—. Recipient E.V. Murphree award indsl. and engring. chemistry Am. Chem. Soc., 1974; Eugene J. Houdry award Catalysis Soc., 1971; I-R 100 award Indsl. Research mag., 1973. Hon. mem. Am. Inst. Chemists (honor scroll 1957); mem. Am. Chem. Soc. (chmn. bd. 1973-77), AAAS (v.p. for chemistry 1970), Nat. Acad. Scis., Soc. Chem. Industry, Ill. Acad. Sci., N.Y. Acad. Sci., Chemists Club Chgo., Phi Beta Kappa (pres. Chgo. 1968-69), Sigma Xi. Patentee petroleum refining, catalysis, petrochems. Current Work: Catalyst design; interaction of catalyst surfaces with reactants;- mechanisms of catalytic reactions and of catalyst poisoning; processes for petroleum refining and petrochemicals. Subspecialties: Catalysis chemistry; Fuels. Home and Office: 9700 Kedvale Ave Skokie IL 60076

BLOCH, KONRAD, biochemist; b. Neisse, Germany, Jan. 12, 1912; came to U.S., 1936, naturalized, 1944; s. Frederick D. and Hedwig (Steimer) B.; m. Lore Teutsch, Feb. 15, 1941; children—Peter, Susan. Chem.Eng., Technische Hochschule, Munich, Germany, 1934; Ph.D., Columbia, 1938. Asst. prof. biochemistry U. Chgo., 1946-50, prof., 1950-54; Higgins prof. biochemistry Harvard, 1954—. Recipient Nobel prize in physiology and medicine, 1964; Ernest Guenther award in chemistry of essential oils and related products, 1965. Fellow Am. Acad. Scis.; mem. Nat. Acad. Scis., Am. Philos. Soc. Subspecialty: Biochemistry (biology). Office: Dept Biochemistry Harvard U 12 Oxford St Cambridge MA 02138*

BLOCK, DAVID LESTER, energy center executive, engineer, educator; b. Davenport, Iowa, July 10, 1939; s. Albert H. and Florence H. (Rohiser) B.; m. Sharon LaRae Ragan, Dec. 22, 1961; children—Karley A., David A. B.S. in Civil Engring., U. Iowa, 1962; M.S. in Engring., Va. Poly. Inst., 1964, Ph.D. in Engring., 1966. Registered profl engr., Fla., Iowa, Ill. Engr. NASA, Hampton, Va., 1962-66; staff engr. Martin Marietta Corp. Orlando, Fla., 1966-68; prof. engring. U. Central Fla., Orlando, 1977—, assoc. dean engring., 1968-77; dir. Fla. Solar Energy Ctr., Cape Canaveral, 1977—. Fellow Fla. Engring. Soc. (pres. 1975, Engr. of Yr. award 1975, Young Engr. of Yr. award 1973). Current work: Energy policy and research. Subspecialties: Solar energy; Theoretical and applied mechanics. Office: Fla Solar Energy Ctr 300 State Road 401 Cape Canaveral FL 32920

BLOCK, LAWRENCE HOWARD, pharmacist, educator; b. Balt., Nov. 24, 1941; s. Harry C. and Dina (Cooper) B.; m. Sharon Kelson, Aug. 4, 1974; children: Hal Zachary, Dana Elayne. B.S. in Pharmacy, U. Md., 1962, M.S., 1966, Ph.D., 1969. Asst. prof. pharmaceutics U. Pitts., 1966-70; asst. prof. pharm. chemistry, pharmaceutics Duquesne U., Pitts., 1970-71, assoc. prof. pharm. chemistry, pharmaceutics, 1971-75, prof. pharmaceutics, 1975—, chmn. dept. pharm. chemistry and pharmaceutics, 1985—; cons. Thrift Drug Co. div. J.C. Penney Co., Biodecison Lab. Inc., Upsher-Smith Labs., Inc. Author numerous chpts. for sci. books and articles for profl. jours. Fellow Am. Found. Pharm. Edn.; mem. Acad. Pharm. Scis., Am. Pharm. Assn., N.Y. Acad. Sci., Soc. Cosmetic Chemists, Sigma Xi. Current Work: Population pharmacokinetics; individualization of drug therapy; pharmacokinetic-pharmacodynamic correlations; transdermal drug delivery; protein-drug interaction. Subspecialty: Pharmacokinetics. Office: Duquesne U Sch Pharmacy 441 Mellon Hall Sci Pittsburgh PA 15282

BLOCK, ROBERT CHARLES, nuclear engineering educator; b. Newark, Feb. 11, 1929; s. George and Sue (Ehrenkranz) B.; m. Rita Adler, June 28, 1952; children: Keith, Robin. B.S. in Elec. Engring, Newark Coll. Engring., 1950; M.A. in Physics, Columbia U., 1953; Ph.D. in Nuclear Physics, Duke U., 1956. Elec. engr. Nat. Union Radio Corp., W. Orange, N.J., 1950-51, Bendix Aviation Co., Teterboro, N.J., 1951; physicist Oak Ridge Nat. Lab., 1955-66; vis. scientist Atomic Energy Research Establishment, Harwell, Eng., 1962-63; prof. nuclear engring. and sci. Rensselaer Poly. Inst., 1966—; Vis. scientist Am. Inst. Physics, 1961-67; vis. prof. Kyoto (Japan) U., 1973-74; cons. Gen. Electric Co., 1968-79; cons., mem. nuclear cross sect. adv. com. AEC, 1969-72; vis. physicist Brookhaven Nat. Lab., 1975, mem. vis. com. nuclear energy dept., 1982-85; founder, v.p., treas. Becker, Block, & Harris, Inc., 1981—; mem. U.S. Nuclear Data Com., 1972-74, NRC panel on low and medium energy neutrons, 1977; dir. Gaerttner Linac Lab. Co-author chpt. in book. Japanese Ministry Edn. research grantee, 1973-74. Fellow Am. Nuclear Soc.; Mem. AAAS, AAUP, Am. Phys. Soc., Sigma Xi, Sigma Pi Sigma, Phi Beta Tau, Tau Beta Pi. Research on neutron physics. Current Work: Experimental neutron physics; radiation technology for industrial application; nondestructive testing. Subspecialties: Nuclear fission; Nuclear fusion. Home: 114 3d St Troy NY 12180 Office: Rensselaer Poly Inst Troy NY 12181

BLOCK, ROBERT MICHAEL, endodontist, educator, researcher; b. Ann Arbor, Mich., Oct. 15, 1947; s. Walter David and Thelma Violet (Levine) B.; m. Anne Powell Marshall, Sept. 4, 1977. B.A., DePauw U., 1969; D.D.S., U. Mich.-Ann Arbor, 1974; cert. in endodontics, Va. Commonwealth U., 1977, M.S. in Pathology, 1978. Diplomate: Am. Bd. Endodontics. Clin. instr. Va. Commonwealth U., 1975-77, instr. pathology, 1977-78; research assoc. endodontics U. Conn.-Farmington, 1975—; vis. sr. scientist Nat. Med. Research Inst., Bethesda, Md., 1976-78; research assoc. McGuire Vets. Hosp., Richmond, Va., 1975-78; vis. research scientist U. Conn.-Farmington, 1978—; lectr. endodontics Flint Community Schs. Contbr. articles profl. jours., chpt. in book. Exec. mem. campaign com. candidate for U. Mich. Bd. Regents, 1980; candidate for Mich. State Bd. Edn., 1982. HEW and NIH summer research fellow, 1970-71; research grantee McGuire Vets. Hosp., 1976-78. Mem. Internat. Assn. Dental Research (Edward P. Hatton award 1977), Am. Assn. Dental Research, Am. Assn. Endodontists (Meml. Research award 1977), Lapeer Dental Study Club (treas. 1978-82), ADA. Club: Bourben Barrell Hunt (Imlay City, Mich.). Current Work: Biologic responses to endodontic materials. Subspecialty: Endodontics. Home: 1322 Wood Krest Dr Flint MI 48504Office: G 3163 Flushing Rd Suite 212 Flint MI 48504

BLODGETT, JR. ALBERT J., research laboratory administrator. Dir. mfg. research lab. IBM T.J. Watson Research Ctr., Yorktown Heights, N.Y. . Office: IBM T J Watson Research Ctr PO Box 218 Yorktown Heights NY 10598

BLOEMBERGEN, NICOLAAS, physicist, educator; b. Dordrecht, Netherlands, Mar. 11, 1920; came to U.S., 1952, naturalized, 1958; s. Auke and Sophia M. (Quint) B.; m. Huberta D. Brink, June 26, 1950; children: Antonia, Brink, Juliana. B.A., Utrecht U., 1941, M.A., 1943; Ph.D., Leiden U., 1948; M.A. (hon.), Harvard, 1951. Teaching asst. Utrecht U., 1942-45; research fellow Leiden U., 1948; mem. Soc. Fellows Harvard, 1949-51, assoc. prof., 1951-57, Gordon McKay prof. applied physics, 1957—, Rumford prof. physics, 1974, Gerhard Gade univ. prof., 1980; vis. prof. U. Paris, 1957, U. Calif., 1965, Collège de France, Paris, 1980; Lorentz guest prof. U. Leiden, 1973; Raman vis prof. Bangalore, India, 1979; Fairchild disting. scholar Calif. Inst. Tech., 1984. Author: Nuclear Magnetic Relaxation, 1948, Nonlinear Optics, 1965; also articles in profl. jours. Recipient Buckley prize for solid state physics Am. Phys. Soc., 1958, Dirac medal U. New South Wales (Australia), 1983; Stuart Ballantine medal Franklin Inst., 1961; Half Moon trophy Netherlands Club N.Y., 1972; Nat. medal of Sci., 1975; Lorentz medal Royal Dutch Acad., 1978; Frederic Ives medal Optical Soc. Am., 1979; von Humboldt sr. scientist award Munich, 1980; Nobel prize in Physics, 1981; Guggenheim fellow, 1957. Fellow Am. Phys. Soc., Am. Acad. Arts and Scis., IEEE (Morris Liebmann award 1959, Medal of Honor 1983); hon. fellow Indian Acad. Scis.; mem. Optical Soc. Am. (hon.), Nat. Acad. Scis., Nat. Acad. Engring., Am. Philos. Soc., Deutsche Akademie der Naturforscher Leopoldina, Koninklyke Nederlandse Akademie von Wetenschappen (corr.), Paris Acad. Scis. (fgn. assoc.). Current Work: Nonlinear optics and spectroscopy. Subspecialties: Laser spectroscopy; Atomic and molecular physics. Office: Pierce Hall Harvard Univ Cambridge MA 02138

BLOMEKE, JOHN OTIS, nuclear engr.; b. Austin, Tex., Jan. 16, 1923; s. John and Maud (Douglas) B.; m. Margaret Boruff, Aug. 30, 1946; children: Hugh, Linda. B.S. in Chem. Engring, U. Tex. - Austin, 1943, M.S., 1947; Ph.D. in Chem. Engring, Ga. Inst. Tech., Atlanta, 1950. Devel. engr. Clinton Labs., Oak Ridge, 1944-46; sr. research staff mem. Oak Ridge Nat. Lab., 1950—. Served with U.S. Army, 1945-46. Fellow Am. Nuclear Soc. Current Work: Radioactive waste management research, development and applications. Subspecialties: Nuclear fission; Nuclear engineering. Home: Route 3 Sandy Shore Dr Lenoir City TN 37771 Office: Oak Ridge National Laboratory PO Box X Oak Ridge TN 37830

BLOMQUIST, CARL GUNNAR, cardiologist; b. Bararyd, Sweden, Dec. 31, 1931; came to U.S., 1965; s. Arvid Elias and Karin Johanna (Hullman) B.; m. Joan Barre Bakula; children—Mary Jennifer, Peter Carl. B.M., U. Lund, Sweden, 1954, M.D., 1960; Ph.D., Karolinska Inst., Sweden, 1967. Research fellow U. Minn., Mpls., 1960-61; resident in medicine Karolinska Inst., Stockholm, 1962-65; mem. faculty U. Tex. Health Sci. Ctr., Dallas, 1966—, prof. medicine and physiology, 1976—; mem. applied physiology study sect. NIH, 1974-78; research study com. Am. Heart Assn., Dallas, 1970-73. Contbr. articles to profl. jours. Mem. Dallas Symphony Orch. Guild. Recipient Established Investigator award Am. Heart Assn.; grantee NIH, NASA. Fellow Am. Heart Assn. Council Epidemiology, Am. Coll. Cardiology; mem. So. Soc. Clin. Research, Internat. Soc. Cardiology. Current work: Principal investigator for experiment 294 for spacelab life sciences flights 1 and 2 scheduled to fly 1987 (cardiovascular adaption to OG). Subspecialty: Cardiology. Office: U Tex Health Sci Ctr H8 122 5323 Harry Hines Blvd Dallas TX 75235

BLOOM, BARRY MALCOLM, pharmacy company executive; b. Roxbury, Mass., Aug. 12, 1928; s. Morris and Ann (Levine) B.; m. Joan Martha Ensign, June 27, 1956; children—Catherine, Brian, Joanna. S.B., M.I.T., 1948, Ph.D., 1951, postgrad., 1967. Research chemist Pfizer, Inc., Groton, Conn., 1952-63, dir. medicinal chems., research, 1963-71, pres. central research div., 1971—, v.p. research, 1971—, dir., 1973—; mem. mgmt. com. Dekalb-Pfizer Genetics, 1982—; mem. Congl. Commn. on Fed. Drug Approval Process, Commn. on Drugs for Rare Diseases, Pharm. Mgrs. Assn., chmn. research and devel. sect., 1976; cons. Walter Reed Army Inst. Research, 1969, 1975-77, U.S. Congress Office Tech. Assessment, 1976-77; mem. Conn. High Tech. Commn.; mem. vis. commn. U. Conn. Sch. Bus. Adminstrn., Inst. Materials Sci. Mem. editorial bd.; Ann Reports in Medicinal Chemistry, 1968-70. Patentee in field. Trustee Conn. Coll. NRC postdoc. fellow U. Wis., 1952, Poly. Inst. fellow, N.Y.C. Mem. Am. Chem. Soc. (chmn. div. medicinal chemistry 1967), N.Y. Acad. Scis. Subspecialty: Medicinal chemistry. Home: Mackintosh Rd Lyme CT 06371 Office: Pfizer Central Research Eastern Point Rd Groton CT 06340

BLOOM, EDA TERRI, immunologist; b. Los Angeles, May 11, 1945; d. Louis and Lucy (Malin) B. A.B., UCLA, 1966, Ph.D., 1970. Asst. research immunologist UCLA, 1971-1978; asst. prof. U. So. Calif., 1978-80; asst. research immunologist UCLA and VA Wadsworth Med. Center, 1980-81, assoc., 1981—, research biologist, 1983—. Mem. AAAS, Am. Assn. Cancer Research, Am. Assn. Immunologists, N.Y. Acad. Scis., Gerontol. Soc. Am., Transplantation Soc., Sigma Xi. Current Work: Tumor and gerontological immunology. Subspecialties: Immunobiology and immunology; Cancer research (medicine). Office: VA Wadsworth Med Center Los Angeles CA 90073

BLOOM, FLOYD ELLIOTT, physician, research scientist; b. Mpls., Oct. 8, 1936; s. Jack Aaron and Frieda (Shochman) B.; m. D'Nell Bingham, Aug. 30, 1956 (dec. May 1973); children: Fl'Nell, Evan Russell; m. Jody Patricia Corey, Aug. 9, 1980. A.B. cum laude, So. Meth. U., 1956; M.D. cum laude, Washington U., St. Louis, 1960; D.Sc. (hon.), So. Meth. U., 1983, Hahnemann U., 1985, U. Rochester, 1985. Intern Barnes Hosp., St. Louis, 1960-61, resident internal medicine, 1961-62; research asso. NIMH, Washington, 1962-64; fellow depts. pharmacology, psychiatry and anatomy Yale Sch. Medicine, 1964-66, asst. prof., 1966-67, asso. prof., 1968; chief lab. neuropharmacology NIMH, Washington, 1968-75, acting dir. div. spl. mental health, 1973-75; commd. officer USPHS, 1974-75; dir. Arthur Vining Davis Center for Behavorial Neurobiology; prof. Salk Inst., La Jolla, Calif., 1975-83; dir. div. preclin. neurosci. and endocrinology Research Inst. of Scripps Clinic, 1983—; mem. Commn. on Alcoholism, 1980-81, Nat. Adv. Mental Health Council, 1976-80. Author: (with J.R. Cooper and R.H. Roth) Biochemical Basis of Neuropharmacology, 1971; (with A. Lazerson and L. Hofstadter) Brain, Mind and Behavior, 1984; editor: Peptides: Integrators of Cell and Tissue Function, 1980; co-editor: Regulatory Peptides. Recipient A. Cressy Morrison award N.Y. Acad. Scis., 1971; A.E. Bennett award for basic research Soc. Biol. Psychiatry, 1971; Arthur A. Fleming award Science mag., 1973; Mathilde Solowey award, 1973; Biol. Sci. award Washington Acad. Scis., 1975; Alumni Achievement citation Washington U., 1980; McAlpin Research Achievement award Mental Health Assn., 1980; Lectr.'s medal College de France, 1979. Fellow Am. Coll. Neuropsychopharmacology (mem. council 1976-78); mem. Nat. Acad. Sci. (chmn. sect. neurobiology 1979-83), Inst. Medicine, Am. Acad. Arts and Scis., Soc. Neurosci. (sec. 1973-74, pres. 1976), Am. Soc. Pharmacology and Exptl. Therapeutics, Am. Soc. Cell Biology, Am. Physiol. Soc., Am. Assn. Anatomists, Research Soc. Alcoholism. Current Work: Neurotransmitters; identification, characterization, and possible medical and behavioral implications. Subspecialties: Neurobiology; Neuropharmacology. Home: 1145 Pacific Beach Dr Apt B405 San Diego CA 92109 Office: Salk Inst La Jolla CA 92037

BLOOM, JAMES RICHARD, research plant pathologist, educator; b. Clearfield, Pa., Feb., 20, 1924; s. Raymond V. and Rozella G. (Dunlap) B.; m. June Farwell, Sept. 11, 1947; children: James Richard, Heidi L., Gretchen E., Coralie A. B.S. in Botany, Pa. State U., 1950; Ph.D. in Plant Pathology, U. Wis., 1953. Asst. prof. plant pathology Pa. State U., University Park, 1953-59, assoc. prof., 1960-66, prof., 1966—. Contbr. articles to profl. jours. Served to sgt. U.S. Army, 1943-46. Decorated Purple Heart. Mem. Soc. Nematologists, Am. Phytopathol. Soc. Current Work: Interaction of nematodes witn other plant pathogens. Subspecialties: Plant pathology; Nematology. Home: Box 317 Lemont PA 19851 Office: 211 Buckhout Lab University Park PA 16802

BLOOM, RICHARD FREDRIC, behavioral scientist, psychologist; b. Bklyn., Oct. 23, 1931; s. Morris and Mary (Schur) B.; m. Myra R. Thal, Dec. 16, 1956 (div.); children: Laura A.; David T.; m. Susan Davies, Nov. 30, 1981; stepchildren: David Y. Redford II, Hugh T. Redford. B.S., Bklyn Coll., 1953; A.E., Newark Coll. Engring., 1959, M.S., 1962; Ph.D., NYU, 1969. Lic. psychologist, Conn., Fla., Pa. Physicist U.S. Nat. Bur. Standards, Washington, 1953; electronics engr. ITT Fed. Labs., Nutley, N.J., 1955-65; behavioral scientist Dunlap & Assocs. East, Inc., Norwalk, Conn., 1965—; pvt. practice psychologist, New Canaan, Conn., 1970—; co-dir. Psychotherapy & Counseling Assocs., New Canaan, 1981—; dir. Bloom & Witt Assocs., North Haven, Conn., 1985—; bd. dirs. Dunlap & Assocs. East Inc., Norwalk, 1983—; research cons. Silver Hill Found. Hosp., New Canaan, 1972-75. Author tech. reports and research papers. Bd. dirs. Am. Cancer Soc., Darien, Conn., 1981—. Served with U.S. Army, 1953-1955, Korea. Fellow Soc. Clin. and Exptl. Hypnosis; mem. Am. Psychol. Assn., IEEE, Soc. Psychophysiol. Research. Jewish. Current Work: Human-machine interactions; psychophysiological research; human behavior; market research; training and evaluation; psychotherapy services to individuals, couples and families; forensic hypnosis. Subspecialties: Behavioral psychology; Psychotherapy. Home: 45 Silvermine Rd New Canaan CT 06840 Office: Dunlap & Assocs East Inc 17 Washington St Norwalk CT 06854

BLOOMER, RICHARD RODIER, petroleum geologist; b. Norfolk, Va., June 26, 1918; s. Alfred T. and Marie A. (Hefferman) B.; m. Anne Louise Egdorf, June 7, 1948; children: Carol Leigh, Charles Richard. B.S., U. Va., 1940, M.A., 1941; Ph.D., U. Tex., 1949. Instr. geology U. Tex.-Austin, 1941-42, 46-48; research geologist Bur. Econ. Geology, U. Tex., 1948-49; exploration geologist Carter Oil Co., Tulsa, 1949-52; ind. geologist, Abilene, Tex., 1952—; prof. geology Hardin-Simmons U., Abilene, 1967-68; owner R.R. Bloomer & Assocs., Abilene, 1978—; Disting. lectr. Am. Assn. Petroleum Geologists, 1981-82; mem. adv. council U. Tex. Geology Found. Contbr. articles to profl. jours. Served to 1st lt. USAF, 1942-46, CBI. Fellow Geol. Soc. Am.; mem. Am. Assn. Petroleum Geologists (pres. S.W. sect. 1982-83, sec. S.W. sect. 1985-87, Monroe Cheney sci. award for contbns. and service to understanding of petroleum geology in S.W.; mem. found.), Soc. Econ. Paleontologists and Mineralogists (v.p. S.W. sect. 1981), Am. Inst. Profl. Geologists (cert. profl. geologist), Sigma Xi. Current Work: Subsurface channel sandstones. Subspecialties: Sedimentology; Tectonics. Home: 1141 Elmwood Dr Abilene TX 79605 Office: 132 Devonian Bldg 310 N Willis St Abilene TX 79603

BLOOMFIELD, DANIEL KERMIT, college dean, physician; b. Cleve., Dec. 14, 1926; s. Joseph Bernard and Henrietta (Namen) B.; m. Frances Aub, June 10, 1955; children: Louis, Ruth, Anne. B.S., U.S. Naval Acad., 1947, M.S., Western Res. U., 1954, M.D., 1954. Intern Beth Israel Hosp., Boston, 1954-55, resident, 1955-56, Mass. Gen. Hosp., Boston, 1956-67; research fellow chemistry Harvard U., 1957-59; hon. asst. registrar cardiology Nat. Heart Hosp., London, 1959-60; sr. instr. medicine Western Res. U., Cleve., 1960-64, sr. clin. instr. medicine, 1964-70; dir. cardiovascular research Community Health Found., Cleve., 1964-66; assoc. medicine Mt. Sinai Hosp., Cleve., 1966-69; prof. medicine U. Ill. Sch. Medicine, Urbana, 1970—; dean Coll. Medicine U. Ill.-Urbana, 1970-84; Investigator Am. Heart Assn., 1960-64; Bd. dirs. East Central Ill. Health Systems Agy. Served with USN, 1947-50. Recipient citation for contbns. to med. edn. Ohio Heart Assn., 1964. Mem. Am. Profs. Peace in Middle East (vice chmn.); Mem. Alpha Omega Alpha. Current Work: Electrocardiographic screening, ambulatory electrocardiographic monitoring. Subspecialties: Cardiology; Preventive medicine. Home: 103 E Michigan St Urbana IL 61801

BLOOMFIELD, JORDAN JAY, chemist, researcher, chemistry educator; b. South Bend, Ind., Feb. 25, 1930; s. John Jacob and Edith (Gilman) B.; m. Elizabeth Helen Curtis, June 11, 1960 (div. Nov. 1982); children—Jaclyn Louise, Linda Joyce, Janet Lorene; m. Doris Joan Jameson, May 19, 1984. B.S., UCLA, 1952; Ph.D., MIT, 1955. Instr. U. Tex., Austin, 1957-60; postdoctoral fellow U. Ill., Urbana, 1960, U. Ariz., Tucson, 1961; from asst. prof. to assoc. prof. U. Okla., Norman, 1962-66; vis. prof. Monsanto Co., St. Louis, 1966-67, sr. research specialist, 1967-81, fellow, 1981-85; adj. prof. U. Mo.-St. Louis, 1978—; vis. prof. U. Mich., 1985-86. Contbr. articles to profl. jours. Patentee in field. Treas. Chem. Council Greater St. Louis, 1976-79, pres. 1979-80. Mem. Am. Chem. Soc. (chmn. St. Louis 1976, St. Louis award, 1980), Am. Soc. Photobiology, AAAS, Royal Soc. Chemistry. Current work: Small rings, cyclizations, cyclo-additions (photo and thermal). Subspecialties: Organic chemistry; Photochemistry.

BLOOMFIELD, SAUL S., physician, clin. pharmacologist, educator; b. Montreal, June 30, 1925; s. Oscar H. and Tillie S. (Schoilovitch) B.; m. Ellen Steinberg, Jan. 9, 1949; children: Laurence, Patricia, Matthew. B.Sc., McGill U., Montreal, 1946, M.Sc., 1948; M.D., U. Geneva, Switzerland, 1953; M.Sc., U. Montreal, 1965. Practice medicine, Montreal, 1955-63; instr. pharmacology U. Montreal Faculty Medicine, 1963-65; asst. prof. medicine and pharmacology U. Cin. Coll. Medicine, 1965-71, asso. prof., 1971-77, prof., 1977—; vis. scientist Merrell Internat. Research Center, Strasbourg, France, 1972-73; vis. prof. Oxford U., Churchill Hosp., 1980. Contbr. articles to profl. jours. Can. Found. Advancement Therapeutics fellow, 1964-65; NIH fellow, 1966-68; grantee, 1968-72. Mem. Am. Soc. Clin. Pharmacology and Therapeutics, Am. Soc. Pharmacology and Exptl. Therapeutics, Am. Fedn. Clin. Research, AAUP, Can. Med. Assn., N.Y. Acad. Scis., Am. Pain Soc. Current Work: Clinical pharmacology of analgesics; controlled clinical trials of investigational new analgesics in various acute pain models. Subspecialties: Internal medicine; Pharmacology. Home: 57 Carpenter's Ridge Cincinnati OH 45241 Office: University Cincinnati Medical Center 5502 Medical Sciences Bldg Cincinnati OH 452670578

BLOTCKY, ALAN JAY, physicist; b. Omaha, July 5, 1930; s. Paul and Evalyn Sylvia (Meyer) B.; m. Wanda June Richmond, Jan. 20, 1953; children: Steven, Beth. B.S., Carnegie Inst. Tech., 1952; M.S., Creighton U., 1971. Sect. head mass spectrometer maintenance sect. Goodyear Atomic Corp., Portsmouth, Ohio, 1953-55; cons. physicist, mfrs. rep. A.J. Blotcky & Assocs., Omaha, Nebr., 1955-57; reactor supr., research physicist, radiation safety officer VA Med. Ctr., Omaha, 1957—. Contbr. articles to profl. jours. Chief, radiol. def. service Omaha Douglas County Civil Def., 1962—; pres. Operation Bridge, 1972, 77-79. Served with Signal Corps USAR, 1952-77. Recipient VA Chief Med. Dirs. Pub. Service award, 1970. Fellow Am. Nuclear Soc.; mem. Soc. Nuclear Medicine, Health Physics Soc., Am. Assn. Physicists in Medicine, Instrument Soc. Am., Sigma Xi. Lodge: Rotary. Current Work: Use of nuclear reactor for development of elemental and molecular activation analysis techniques, correlation of values in biological tissue. Subspecialties: Analytical chemistry; Nuclear physics. Office: 4101 Woolworth Ave Omaha NE 68105

BLUE, TODD IRWIN, technical educator; b. Carbondale, Colo., July 27, 1939; s. Lloyd G. and June (Kirk) B.; m. Judith Ann Olson, June 17, 1967. B.A., U. N.Mex., 1980, M.A., 1982. Numerous positions in constrn. industry, 1964—; instr. civil and survey tech. Albuquerque Tech. Vocat. Inst., 1968—, coordinator constrn. trades programs, 1969—; ednl. cons. U.S. Air Force, Zia Co. Served with USN, 1960-64. Mem. Am. Tech. Edn. Assn., Am. Vocat. Assn. Roman Catholic. Current Work: Satelite imagery with photogrametric applications to surveying systems and data update, cartographic representations of hypsographic and hydrographic features; solar applications. Subspecialties: Civil engineering; Solar energy. Home: 5700 Aspen NE Albuquerque NM 87110 Office: 525 Buena Vista SE Albuquerque NM 87106

BLUESTEIN, BERNARD R. chemist, research administrator; b. Phila., Oct. 7, 1925; s. Joseph and Minnie (Ravkin) B.: m. Claire S. Kraiman, June 22, 1947; children—Rhona C., Sherrie L., Hazel M., Carol J. B.S. in Chemistry, U. Penn., 1946; M.S., U. Ill., 1947, Ph.D. in Organic Chemistry, 1949; M.B.A., Fairleigh Dickinson U., 1967. Research assoc., postdoctoral fellow Rutgers U., New Brunswick, N.J., 1949-51; instr. Purdue U., West Lafayette, Ind., 1951-52; asst. prof. chemistry Coe Coll., Cedar Rapids, Iowa, 1952-55; dir. research, asst. supt. mfg. Sonneborn Chem. and Refining Corp., Petrolia, Pa., 1955-62; asst. dir. research and devel. Witco Chem. Corp., Oakland, N.J., 1962-76, dir., 1976-83, v.p. Allied Kelite div., New Hudson, Mich., 1983—; continuing edn. prof. Pa. State U.-Butler, 1957-61. Author, editor: Amphoteric Surfactants, 1982. Fellow Royal Soc. Chemistry (London), Am. Inst. Chemistry (N.J. council 1983); mem. Am Chem. Soc. (chmn. North Jersey com. 1977), Am. Oil

Chemists Soc., Assn. Research Dirs. Current work: Developing new materials: compositions to metal plate, both electrolytically and electroless plating, metals and plastics; the analysis of these materials and finished plated surfaces. Subspecialties: Metal Plating and Metal finishing; Organic chemistry. Office: Witco Corp 29111 Milford Rd New Hudson MI 48165

BLUM, BARTON MORRILL, research forester; b. Newark, N.J., May 17, 1932; s. John Morrill and Janet Louise (Smith) B.; m. Marjorie Dawn Pinkham, Aug. 30, 1958; children—Kimberly Louise, Pamela Alice, Jeffrey Lewis. B.S. in Agr., Rutgers U., 1954; M.F., Yale U., 1957; Ph.D., Syracuse U., 1971. Registered forester, Maine. Forester Northeastern Forest Expt. Sta., U.S. Forest Service, USDA, Upper Darby, Pa., 1957-59, research forester, Laconia N.H., 1959-64, Burlington, Vt., 1964-69, staff asst, Upper Darby, 1969-72, project leader, dirs. rep., 1972—; bd. dirs. Maine Forest Products Council, Augusta, Maine Forest and Logging Mus., Bangor. Contbr. articles to profl. jours. Bd. dirs. Holden Sch. Bd., Maine, 1974-78. Served with USAF, 1954-55. Recipient Cert. of Merit, USDA, 1971, 76, Cert. Appreciation, USDA, 1974, 83. Mem. Soc. Am. Foresters, U.S. Power Squadron (treas. 1982-83), Sigma Xi. Republican. Episcopalian. Lodges: Masons, Shriners. Current work: Silvilcultural research; forest management research. Subspecialties: Ecology (environmental science); Silviculture. Office: US Forest Service Northeastern Forest Expt Sta Grove St U Maine Orono ME 04469

BLUM, KENNETH, pharmacology educator; b. Bklyn., Aug. 8, 1939; m. Arlene Schlessel, June 8, 1963; children: Jeffrey H., Seth H. B.S. in Pharmacy, Columbia U., 1961; M.S. in Med. Sci, N.J. Coll. Medicine, 1965; Ph.D. in Pharmacology, N.Y. Med. Coll., 1968. Research pharmacologist U.S. Vitamin & Pharm. Corp., Yonkers, N.Y., 1964-65; postdoctoral research assoc. S.W. Found. Research and Edn., San Antonio, 1968-70, asst. found. scientist, 1970-71; asst. prof. pharmacology U. Tex. Health Scis. Ctr., San Antonio, 1971-75, assoc. prof., 1975-83, prof., 1983—, chief dept., 1975—; fellow U. Colo. Coll. Pharmacy, Boulder, 1977; mem. council Gordon Research Conf., 1979—; mem. sci. adv. com. Internat. Neurotoxicology Congress, 1979; organizer, participant numerous profl. confs.; ad hoc peer reviewer Nat. Council Alcoholism, 1979-80, VA, 1980-81; cons. Tenn. Bd. Edn., 1970-72, Mo. Bd. Edn., 1971-72, U.S. Office Edn., 1972-74, Nat. Drug Abuse Ctr., 1977-79, others; sci. adviser Nat. Alcohol Research Ctr., U. Calif. Sch. Medicine, Irvine, 1981—; mem. Tex. Commn. on Alcoholism, 1979—; v.p., dir. OPOC Corp., 1982—; owner Western Ventures Brokerage Corp., 1982—; lectr. drug abuse; drug abuse expert cons. for health text Scott, Foresman Co., 1985; chief sci. affairs cons. Matrix Techs. Inc., 1985—; adv. med. cons. Unipro Corp., 1985—. Host TV spl. Perspectives of Psychology, 1980-81; editor-in-chief: Substance and Alcohol Actions/Misuses, 1979-85; mem. editorial bd. Jour. Psychoactive Drugs, 1976—, Clin. Toxicology, 1976-83, European Jour. Clin. Toxicology, 1982; mem. editorial adv. bd. Functional Neurology; mem. publ. com. Alcoholism: Clin. and Exptl. Research, 1979—; author: (with others) Pharmacological and Toxicological Perspectives on Commonly Abused Drugs, 1978; (with others) Folk Healing and Herbal Medicine, 1981, (with L. Manzo) Neurotoxicology, 1985, Handbook of Abusable Drugs, 1984; editor: Alcohol and Opiates: Neurochemical and Behavioral Mechanisms, 1977; (with L. Manzo) Clinical Toxicology, 1981, 82; contbr. chpts. to books, articles to sci. jours., World Book Ency.; appearances on local TV shows. Bd. dirs., founder Bexar County Pharm. Speakers Bur., 1969-71; bd. dirs. Agudas Achim Synagogue, 1973-74; bd. dirs. San Antonio Free Clinic, 1971-80, pres., 1973-75; v.p. Drug Inst. San Antonio, 1972-73; chmn. bd., pres. Nat. Found. Addictive Diseases, 1982—, chmn. Hanging Bottle Alcohol Research Fund, San Antonio, 1982-83; bd. dirs. San Antonio Com. Dangerous Drugs, 1972-73; pres. Job Power Now, Inc., 1978-79. Bigelow research fellow Columbia U., 1961; Am. Found. Pharm. Edn. fellow, 1966-68; NSF fellow, summer 1967; recipient citation of honor Nat. Assn. Retail Druggists, 1970; Career Tchrs. award Nat. Inst. Drug Abuse, 1974-77; citation of honor Alamo Area Council Govts., 1979; cert. of Merit St. Mary's U., San Antonio, 1979; Speaking Service award Lions Club, 1979; Gordon Research award, 1979, 82. Fellow Am. Coll. Clin. Pharmacology; mem. Internat. Soc. Substance and Alcohol Abuse (acting pres., co-founder planning phase 1982), Tex. Med. Assn. (ad hoc mem. spl. com. drug and alcohol abuse 1978—), Bexar County Med. Soc. (ad hoc mem. disabled physicians com. 1976—), Italian Drug Abuse Soc., World Fedn. Clin. Toxicology, Internat. Biomed. Research Soc. on Alcoholism (charter), Brain Research Soc. Gt. Britain (hon.), AAAS, AAUP, Am. Soc. Pharmacology and Exptl. Therapeutics, Acad. Med. Educators and Substance Abuse (charter), San Antonio Holistic Health Assn., Neurosci. Soc., Research Soc. Am., Soc. Medicinal Chemistry, Com. of One Thousand, N.Y. Acad. Sci., Research Soc. on Alcoholism (nominating and publ. com. 1978—), Tex. Research Soc. on Alcoholism (charter), Bexar County Pharm. Soc. (hon.), Automobile Club of Italy (Rome). Subspecialty: Neuropharmacology. Home: 3707 Castle Crest San Antonio TX 78230 Office: U Tex Health Sci Center San Antonio TX 78284

BLUMBERG, BARUCH SAMUEL, research physician, research director; b. N.Y.C., July 28, 1925; s. Meyer and Ida (Simonoff) B.; m. Jean Liebesman, Apr. 4, 1954; children: Anne, George, Jane, Noah. B.S., Union Coll., Schenectady, 1946; M.D., Columbia U., 1951; Ph.D., Balliol Coll., Oxford (Eng.) U., 1957; 15 hon. doctoral degrees. Intern, resident Columbia div. Bellevue Hosp., N.Y.C., 1951-53; fellow in medicine Columbia-Presbyn. Med. Center, N.Y.C., 1953-55; chief geog. medicine and genetics sect. NIH, Bethesda, Md., 1957-64; assoc. dir. clin. research Fox Chase Cancer Ctr., Phila., 1964—; Univ. prof. medicine and anthropology U. Pa.; George Eastman vis. prof. Balliol Coll., Oxford U., 1983-84. Contbr. articles to profl. jours. Served to ensign USNR, 1943-46. Recipient Albion O. Berstein, M.D. award Med. Soc. SUNY, 1969; Grand Sci. award Phi Lambda Kappa, 1972; ann. award Eastern Pa. br. Am. Soc. Microbiology, 1972; Passano award Williams & Wilkens Co., 1974; Modern Medicine Disting. Achievement award, 1975; Internat. award Gairdner Found., 1975; Karl Landsteiner Meml. award Am. Assn. Blood Banks, 1975; Nobel prize in physiology or medicine, 1976; Scopus award Am. Friends of Hebrew U., 1977; Strittmatter award Philadelphia County Med. Soc., 1980; Disting. Service award Pa. Med. Soc., 1982. Fellow ACP; mem. Nat. Acad. Scis., Assn. Am. Physicians, Am. Soc. Clin. Investigation, Am. Soc. Human Genetics, Am. Assn. Phys. Anthropologists, John Morgan Soc., Chesapeake and Ohio Canal Soc. Clubs: Atheneum, Provincetown Yacht. Discover causative agt. hepatitis B. Current Work: Research on hepatitis B virus and vaccine against this virus. Our studies contributed to understanding that hepatitis B virus is required for development of primary cancer of the liver, and that this cancer can be prevented. Also, teaching of biomedical anthropology. Subspecialties: Virology (medicine); Genetics and genetic engineering (medicine). Office: Fox Chase Cancer Center 7701 Burholme Ave Philadelphia PA 19111

BLUMBERG, HAROLD, pharmacologist, educator; b. Fairmont, W.Va., June 19, 1909; s. Michael Meyer and Anna (Goodman) B.; m. Dorothy Drasnin, Sept. 1, 1934; 1 son, Mark Allan. Student, Johns Hopkins U., 1926-27, 28-30, W. Va. U., 1927-28; Sc.D., Johns Hopkins U., 1933. Asst., instr. in pediatrics Johns Hopkins Med. Sch., 1933-36; assoc. biochemist USPHS, 1936-38; research biochemist Johns Hopkins U. Sch. Hygiene and Public Health, 1938-42; assoc. toxicologist U.S. Army Indsl. Hygiene Lab., Balt., 1942-44; sr. biologist Sterling-Winthrop Research Inst., Rensselaer, N.Y., 1944-47; assoc. dir. research Endo Labs., Inc., Garden City, N.Y., 1947-74; research prof. pharmacology N.Y. Med. Coll., Valhalla, 1974-81, emeritus, 1981—; cons. in field. Contbr. articles to profl. jours. Mem. AAAS, Am. Inst. Nutrition, Am. Soc. Pharmacology and Exptl. Therapeutics, Eastern Pain Assn., Internat. Narcotic Research Club, N.Y. Acad. Scis., Soc. Exptl. Biology and Medicine, Soc. Toxicology, Parenteral Drug Assn. (hon.). Patentee in field. Current Work: Narcotic antogonists, addiction, analgesics, toxicology. Subspecialties: Pharmacology; Neuropharmacology. Home: 1731 Beacon St Apt 213 Brookline MA 02146

BLUME, JOHN AUGUST, consulting engineer; b. Gonzales, Calif., Apr. 8, 1909; s. Charles August and Vashti (Rankin) B.; m. Ruth Clarissa Reed, Sept. 14, 1942. A.B., Stanford, 1932, C.E., 1934, Ph.D., 1966. Constrn. engr. San Francisco-Oakland Bay Bridge, 1935-36; individual practice civil and structural engring., San Francisco, 1945-57; pres. John A. Blume & Assos. (Engrs.), San Francisco, 1957-81, chmn., sr. cons., 1980—; sr. engr./scientist URS Corp., San Mateo, Calif., 1981—; Mem., past chmn. adv. council Sch. Engring., Stanford U.; chmn. adv. com. Earthquake Engring. Research Center, U. Calif. at Berkeley.; cons. prof. civil engring. Stanford U.; Past chmn. adv. council Sch. Engring. Stanford U.; Adv. com. Earthquake Engring. Research Center. Author: A Machine for Setting Structures and Ground into Forced Vibration, 1935, Structural Dynamics in Earthquake Resistant Design, 1958, A Reserve Energy Technique for the Design and Rating of Structures in the Inelastic Range, 1960, Dynamic Characteristics of Multistory Buildings, 1969; co-author: Design of Multistory Reinforced Concrete Buildings for Earthquake Motions, 1961, An Engineering Intensity Scale for Earthquakes and Other Ground Motion, 1970, The SAM Procedure for Site-Acceleration-Magnitude Relationships, 1977; Contbr. articles to profl. jours. John A. Blume Earthquake Engring. Center at Stanford U. named in his honor. Mem. Nat. Acad. Engring., Structural Engrs. Assn. Calif. (pres. 1949), Cons. Engrs. Assn. Calif. (pres. 1959), ASCE (hon.; pres. San Francisco sect. 1960, Moisseiff award 1953, 61, 69, Ernest E. Howard award 1962), Seismol. Soc. Am., N.Y. Acad. Scis. (hon. life), Soc. Am. Mil. Engrs., Internat. Assn. Earthquake Engring. (hon.), Earthquake Engring. Research Inst. (hon.; pres. 1977-81), Sigma Xi, Tau Beta Pi. Current Work: Structural dynamics; earthquake engineering; earthquake damage: causes, risk of; prevention; evaluation; repair. Subspecialties: Civil engineering; Probability. Home: 85 El Cerrito Ave Hillsborough CA 94010 Office: 130 Jessie St San Francisco CA 94105

BLUME, MARTIN, science administrator, physicist; b. Bklyn., Jan. 13, 1932; s. Julius and Frances (Cohen) B.; m. Sheila Bierman, June 12, 1955; children—Frederick, Janet. A.B. magna cum laude in Physics, Princeton U., 1954; A.M., Harvard U., 1956, Ph.D., 1959. Fulbright fellow Tokyo U., 1959-60; research assoc. AERE, Harwell, Eng., 1960-62; assoc. physicist Brookhaven Nat. Lab., Upton, N.Y., 1962-65, physicist, 1965-70, sr. physicist, 1970—, dep. dir., 1984—; prof. physics SUNY, Stony Brook, 1972—; cons. and lectr. in field. Contbr. chpts. to books, articles to profl. jours. Recipient Kusaka prize in physics Princeton U., E.O. Lawrence award, U.S. Dept. Energy, 1981; Gen. Electric fellow Harvard U., Kennedy travelling fellow; NSF grantee, 1973-77. Fellow Am. Phys. Soc., AAAS, N.Y. Acad. Scis.; mem. Phi Beta Kappa, Sigma Xi. Current work: Theoretical solid state physics; theory of magnetism; phase transitions; slow neutron scattering; synchrotron radiation. Subspecialties: Condensed matter physics; Statistical physics. Office: Brookhaven Nat Lab Bldg 460 Upton NY 11973

BLY, LLOYD GEORGE, JR., engineer; b. Elmira, N.Y., Apr. 20, 1947; s. Lloyd George and Louise Amelia (Heinzman) B.; m. Kathleen Marie Larson, June 14, 1969; 1 child, Daniel. B.S. in Ceramic Engring., Alfred U., 1969. Research engr. Ford Motor Co., Lincoln Park, Mich., 1969, mfg. engr., Tulsa, 1972-79; chief engr. M.H. Detrick Co., Itasca, Ill., 1981—, v.p. engring., also dir. Patentee in field. Served as 1st lt. U.S. Army, 1969-72. Mem. Am. Ceramic Soc., ASTM, Am. Soc. for Metals. Current work: Specify and design furnace linings with high temperature refractory, casting and design structural steel, developing new refractory systems for aluminum, lead, copper, steel and glass furnaces, including coke calciners, incinerators and biomass multi-cells. Subspecialties: Combustion processes; Ceramic engineering. Office: MH Detrick Co 500 Park Blvd Suite 410 Itasca IL 60143

BLYSTONE, ROBERT VERNON, cell biologist, educator; b. El Paso, Tex., July 4, 1943; s. Edward Vernon and Cecilia (Mueller) B.; m. Donna Moore, Mar. 26, 1964; 1 son, Daniel Vernon. B.S., U. Tex., El Paso, 1965; M.A., U. Tex., Austin, 1968, Ph.D., 1971. Instr. U. Tex., El Paso, 1965, teaching asst., Austin, 1965-68, predoctoral fellow, 1968-71; asst. prof. biology Trinity U., San Antonio, 1971-76, assoc. prof., 1976-84, prof., 1984—, dir. electron microscopy labs., 1971—, chmn. biology, 1984—; cons. in field. Contbr. articles to profl. jours. Active Alamo Sci. Fair. NSF fellow, 1976; NSF instrument grantee, 1978. Mem. Am. Inst. Biol. Scis., AAAS, Tex. Soc. Electron Microscopy, Electron Microscopy Soc. Am., Tex. Acad. Sci., Am. Microscopical Soc., AAUP, Am. Soc. Cell Biology. Current Work: The mechanisms leading to the completion of late lung development; the influence of the adrenal pituitary axis on that development. Subspecialties: Cell biology; Developmental biology. Home: 2635 Worldland St San Antonio TX 78217 Office: Dept Biology Trinity U San Antonio TX 78284

BLYTHE, CLEVELAND HENRY, computer scientist, management consultant; b. Ginger Hill, Jamaica, Feb. 19, 1948; came to U.S., 1964, naturalized, 1985; s. Timothy Blythe and Lucy (Buchanan) Blythe Rhoden; m. Joy Clovis Allen, Oct. 31, 1970 (div. 1976); 1 child, David. Diploma in electronics Radio Coll. Can., 1970, Lakehead U., Can., 1975; B.S. in Elec. Engring., Northrop U., 1976, M.B.A., 1978; Ph.D., Internat. Coll., Calif., 1980. Registered profl. engr., Ont., Can. Sr. electronics engr. Litton Systems, Weston, Ont., 1971-73; mktg. mgr. Kratos Corp., Pasadena, Calif., 1978-79; dir. Analog Digital Computing Systems, Reseda, Calif., 1979-81; v.p. Computers and Acctg. Systems, Washington, 1982—; pres. Internat. Strategic Mgmt., Washington, 1982—, also seminar leader. Contbr. articles to profl. jours. Cell leader Plymouth Congl. Ch., Washington, 1983. Mem. IEEE (sec. 1977), Orgn. Black Scientists, Am. Mgmt. Assn., Internat. Hon. Commerce Fraternity (pres. 1978—). Republican. Lutheran. Current work: Conceptualize, design and manufacture of process control instrumentation for oil, gas, petrochemical, nuclear, utility, military and instrumentation industries. Subspecialty: Electronics. Home: 11839 Shire Ct 21A Reston VA 22091

BLYTHE, WILLIAM BREVARD, physician educator, nephrologist; b. Huntersville, N.C., Sept. 23, 1928; s. William LeGette and Esther Emily (Farmer) B.; m. Gloria Eleanor Nassif, Feb. 4, 1956; children: William LeGette II, Anne Dewar, David Samuel Brevard, John Alexander. A.B., U. N.C., 1948, Cert. in Medicine, 1951; M.D., Washington U., St. Louis, 1953. Intern N.C. Meml. Hosp., Chapel Hill, 1953-54, resident, 1954-55; asst. prof. medicine U. N.C. Sch. Medicine, Chapel Hill, 1962-65, assoc. prof. medicine, 1965-70, prof. medicine, 1970—, head div. nephrology, 1973—; assoc. dir. (Clin. Research Unit), 1965-66, dir., 1966-76, editorial bd., 1982—; bd. govs. U. N.C. Press, 1979—; sci. adv. bd. Nat. Kidney Found., 1975-81; cons. NIH, 1968-72. Editor: jour. The Kidney, 1977. Served to capt. M.C. U.S. Army, 1955-57. Fellow ACP; mem. Am. Physiol. Soc., Am. Clin. and Climatalogic Soc., So. Soc. Clin. Investigation, Alpha Omega Alpha. Democrat. Presbyterian. Club: Chapel Hill Tennis. Current Work: Renal disease, renal physiology. Subspecialties: Internal medicine; Nephrology. Home: Hillcrest Circle Chapel Hill NC 27514 Office: Dept Medicine Univ NC Sch Medicine Chapel Hill NC 27514

BOARD, WILLIAM JESSE, JR., chemical engineer; b. Louisville, Dec. 31, 1936; s. William Jesse Board and Helen Marie (Zoeller) Board; m. Marjorie Lee Alexander, Mar. 21, 1958; children—Todd William, Stacey M. B. Chem. Engring., U. Louisville, 1959, M. Chem. Engring, 1960; postgrad., MIT, 1967-68. Mgr. sales Monsanto, Atlanta, 1975-76, dir. mktg. home furnishing, 1976-77, dir. planning, carpet, 1977-78, dir. product mgmt. nylon, 1978-79, dir. tech., nylon and support, Pensacola, Fla., 1980—. Contbr. articles to profl. jours.; patentee in field. Pres. Interfaith Chorale, Gulf Breeze, Fla., 1982-83; corp. sec. Symphony Bd., Pensacola, 1983—. Ford Found. scholar, 1954-59; Monsanto fellow, 1960. Mem. Sigma Xi, Phi Kappa Phi. Republican. Presbyterian. Current work: Nylon fiber process design, control and product development. Subspecialties: Chemical engineering; Materials. Home: 421 Kent Pl Gulf Breeze FL 32561 Office: PO Box 12830 Pensacola FL 32575

BOATENG, KWASI, geologist, consultant; b. Asamankese, Ghana, Apr. 3, 1939; came to U.S., 1979; s. Kwame and Afua (Agyewaa) B.; m. Andrea Antoinette Kinebrew, Mar. 15, 1973; children—Kwame, Kwasi, Jr. B.Sc., State U., Moscow, 1965, M.Sci., 1967. Geologist, Geol. Survey Dept., Ghana, 1967-74; hydrogeologist Water Sewerage Corp., Ghana, 1974-79; sr. hydrogeologist, asst. regional mgr. Ecology Environment Inc., Seattle, 1980-84; sr. hydrogeologist Roy F. Weston Inc., Edison, N.J., 1984—. Ghana Govt. scholar, 1961-67. Mem. Geol. Soc. Ghana (founding), Nat. Water Well Assn., Geol. Soc. Am. Lodge: Rosicrucian. Current work: Site assessment, design and implementation of ground water quality monitoring programs of controlled and uncontrolled hazardous waste sites. Subspecialties: Ground water geology; Hazardous waste disposal. Home: 51 Concord Circle Howell NJ 07731

BOATNER, LYNN ALLEN, research physicist; b. Clarksville, Tex., Aug. 3, 1938; s. Fred L. and Nila (Allen) B.; m. Martha Alice Goodwin, Sept. 5, 1961; children—Mark Jesse, Ivan Aaron, Philip Gordon. B.S. in Physics, Tex. Tech. U., 1960, M.S., 1961; Ph.D. in Physics, Vanderbilt U., 1966. Research asst. Vanderbilt U., Nashville, 1961-66; sr. research scientist LTV Reseaarch Ctr., Dallas, 1966-74; research scientist Ecole Polytechnique Federale de Lausanne, Switzerland, 1975-77; sr. research staff Oak Ridge Nat. Lab., Tenn., 1977—. Patentee in field. Contbr. articles to profl. jours. Vice pres. Anderson County Assn. Retarded Citizens, 1984-85; treas. Oak Ridge Sertoma, 1984-85; ARC rep. Human Rights com. Community Services for Exceptional Citizens. Recipient IR-100 award, 1982; Significant Implications for Energy Tech. in Solid State Physics award Dept. Energy, 1984. Fellow Am. Phys. Soc.; mem. Materials Research Soc., AAAS, AM. Assn. Crystal Growth, Sigma Xi, Phi Eta Sigma, Sigma Pi Sigma. Methodist. Current work: Materials for disposal of nuclear waste, nuclear waste glasses, nuclear waste ceramics, corrosion of nuclear waste forms, growth of single crystals, EPR spectroscopy, optical materials development and characterization, advanced ceramics. Subspecialties: Condensed matter physics; Materials. Office: Oak Ridge Nat Lab PO Box X Oak Ridge TN 37831

BOAZ, NOEL THOMAS, paleoanthropologist, anthropology educator; b. Martinsville, Va., Feb. 8, 1952; s. Thalma Noel and Elena More Anson (Taylor) B.; m. Dorothy Dechant, June 17, 1978. B.A., U. Va., 1973; M.A., U. Calif.-Berkeley, 1974, Ph.D. in Phys. Anthropology, 1977. Sr. mus. scientist (paleoanthropology) U. Calif.-Berkeley, 1975-77; lectr. anthropology UCLA, 1977-78; adj. asst. prof. anatomy N.Y. U. Sch. Medicine, 1978-81, asst. prof. anthropology, 1978—; dir. Internat. Sahabi Research Project, 1976—, Western Rift Research Expdn., 1982—. Contbr. articles to profl. jours. NSF grantee, 1976, 1980-82; Nat. Geog. Soc. grantee, 1978; Presdl. fellow, 1981; Wenner-Gren Found. grantee, 1982. Mem. Am. Assn Phys. Anthropologists, Am. Anthrop. Assn., AAAS, Royal Anthrop. Inst., Soc. Vertebrate Paleontology, Explorers Club. Democrat. Episcopalian. Current Work: Paleoanthropology, hominid evolution, taphonomy, primate paleoecology, biostratigraphy, vertebrate paleontology. Subspecialties: Evolutionary biology; Paleontology. Office: 25 Waverly Pl Paleoanthropology Lab 901 New York NY 10003

BOBER, WILLIAM, mechanical engineering, educator; b. N.Y.C., Mar. 16, 1930; s. Joseph and Bessie Bober; m. Selma S. Silverstein, July 11, 1954; children—Alan, Carolyn, Melanie. B.C.E., CCNY, 1952; M.S. in Engring. Sci., Pratt Inst., 1960; Ph.D. in Engring. Sci., Purdue U., 1964. Registered profl. engr. Fla. Engring. physicist Cornell Labs., Buffalo, 1964-68; vis. prof. Va. Poly. Inst. and State U., Blacksburg, 1968-69; assoc. prof. Rochester Inst. Tech., N.Y., 1969-81, Fla. Atlantic U., Boca Raton, 1981—. Author: (with R.A. Kenyon) Fluid Mechanics, 1980. Contbr. articles to profl. jours. Ford Found. fellow Purdue U., 1960-63. Mem. ASME. Current work: Numerical methods in fluid mechanics and heat transfer. Subspecialties: Fluid mechanics; Numerical analysis (computer science). Office: Fla Atlantic U Dept Mech Engring Boca Raton FL 33431

BOBST, ALBERT MAX, biochemistry educator; b. Zurich, Switzerland, Sept. 10, 1939; came to U.S. 1967, naturalized 1972; s. Max and Paulette (Phily) B.; m. Elisabeth V. Hugi, Mar. 23, 1970; children—Patrick, Cedric, Marcelle. B.S., Zurich State Coll., 1958; Ph.D., U. Zurich, 1965. Postdoctoral fellow U. Calif-Berkeley, 1967-68; research assoc. Princeton U., N.J., 1968-69; prof. biochemistry U. Cin., 1969—; vis. scientist NIH, Washington, 1975-76, 83-84. Contbr. articles to profl. jours. Grantee NIH, NSF. Current work: Nucleic acid chemistry, development of hybridization probes. Subspecialties: Genetics and genetic engineering (agriculture); Biochemistry (biology). Office: Dept Chemistry Univ Cin Cincinnati OH 45221

BOCK, JAN, research and engineering company scientist; b. Phila., Oct. 16, 1944; s. Max M. and Mildred (Ehtridge) B.; m. Linda Ann Pollack, Aug. 19, 1969; children—Jason Benjamin, David Lawrence. B.E.S., Johns Hopkins U., 1966; M.S., U. Rochester, 1968, Ph.D., 1971. Lectr., U. Rochester, N.Y., 1970-71; research engr. Exxon Research & Engring. Co., Linden, N.J., 1971-76, sr. staff engr., group head, Linden, N.J., 1978-80, engring. assoc., group head, 1980-84, sr. engring. assoc., group head, Annandale, N.J., 1984—; staff engr. Exxon Prodn. Research, Houston, 1976-78; mem. indsl. adv. bd. chem. engring. dept. SUNY, Buffalo, 1980-84; mem. adv. bd. Dept. Energy program Columbia U., 1981—. Contbr. articles to profl. jours. Patentee in field. NSF fellow, 1966-70. Mem. Am. Inst. Chem. Engrs., Am. Chem. Soc., AIME, Tau Beta Pi. Subspecialties: Polymer chemistry; Surface chemistry. Home: 500 Juniper Ln Bridgewater NJ 08807 Office: Exxon Research & Engring Co Route 22 E Annandale NJ 08801

BOCK, WALTER J(OSEPH), biology educator, researcher; b. N.Y.C., Nov. 20, 1933; s. Paul Bock and Rose (Kalsch) B.; m. Katherine Lippitt, June 29, 1957; children—Katharine Rose, Susan Ruth, Walter David. B.S., Cornell U., 1955; M.A., Harvard U., 1957, Ph.D., 1959. Asst. prof. zoology U. Ill.-Urbana, after 1961, assoc. prof., to 1965; prof. evolutionary biology Columbia U., 1965—; research assoc. Am. Mus. Natural History, N.Y.C., 1965—. Contbr. articles to profl. jours. Fellow Am. Ornithologists Union (Coues award 1975), AAAS; mem. Internat. Ornithological Com., German Ornithologists Soc., others. Current work: Morphology, classification and evolution of birds; general theory of systematics and evolution. Subspecialties: Evolutionary biology; Morphology. Office: Dept Biol Scis Columbia U New York NY 10027

BOCKHOP, CLARENCE WILLIAM, agrl. engr.; b. Paullina, Iowa, Mar. 28, 1921; s. Fred Henry and Sophie Dorothea (Laue) B.; m. Virginia Buhman, July 9, 1949; children—Barbara Lucille, Nancy Jeanne, Bryan William, Karl David. B.S. in Agrl. Engring, Iowa State U., 1943, M.S. in Agrl. Engring, 1955, Ph.D. in Agr. Engring. and Theoretical and Applied Mechanics, 1957. Service and edn. mgr. Stewart Co., Dallas, 1948-53; mem. faculty Iowa State U., Ames, 1953-57, 60-80, prof. agrl. engring., 1960-80, head dept., 1962-80; head dept. agrl. engring. Internat. Rice Research Inst., Los Banos, Philippines, 1980—; prof., head dept. agrl. engineering U. Tenn., 1957-60; vis. prof. U. Ghana, 1969-70. Gen. reporter, VIth Internat. Congress Agrl. Engring., Lausanne, Switzerland, 1964; Author articles in field. Served to capt. AUS, 1943-48. Fellow Am. Soc. Agrl. Engrs. (chmn. Tenn. sect. 1958-59, chmn. mid-central sect. 1960-61, chmn. Iowa sect. 1963-64, chmn. edn. and research div. 1966-67, dir. 1973-75); mem. Am. Soc. Engring. Edn. (chmn. agrl. engring. div. 1966-67), Sigma Xi, Gamma Sigma Delta, Phi Kappa Phi, Phi Mu Alpha, Tau Beta Pi. Lutheran. Subspecialty: Agricultural engineering. Office: Internat Rice Research Inst Box 933 Manila Philippines

BOCKO, PETER LAWRENCE, industrial chemist; b. Utica, N.Y., Oct. 13, 1953; s. Harold Francis and Marie Louise (Falletta) B.; m. Andrea Patricia Guglielmo, July 10, 1976; children—Andrew Mark, Joseph Peter. B.A., SUNY-Oswego, 1975; M.S., Cornell U., 1977, Ph.D., 1980. Sr. research scientist Corning Glass Works, N.Y., 1979—. Mem. Am. Chem. Soc., Am. Ceramic Soc., Am. Phys. Soc. Current work: New materials for optical waveguide fibers and electrooptics; novel glasses, rare-earth doped silicates via chemical vapor deposition; properties of glass surfaces. Subspecialties: Physical chemistry; Ceramics. Home: 485 S Hamilton St Painted Post NY 14870 Office: Corning Glass Works Sullivan Park DV-25 Corning NY 14831

BOCKSTAHLER, LARRY EARL, radiation biologist, researcher; b. La Junta, Colo., May 13, 1934; s. Harold William and Evangeline (Roath) B.; m. Rotraut Zimmermann, Aug. 27, 1965; 1 child, Katrin Rose. B.S. in Physics, Mich. State U., 1956; M.S. in Biochemistry, U. Wis., 1960, Ph.D. in Biochemistry, 1964. Research assoc. Max Planck Inst., Tubingen, W. Ger., 1964-69; research biophysicist FDA Ctr. for Devices and Radiol. Health, Rockville, Md., 1969—. Contbr. articles to profl. jours. Fellow Alexander von Humboldt Research Found., 1967-69, NIH, 1964-67. Mem. Am. Soc. Virology, Radiation Research Soc., Am. Soc. Photobiology, Biophys. Soc. Republican. Methodist. Current work: Photobiology of mammalian viruses and cells. Subspecialties: Radiation biology; Biochemistry (biology). Office: FDA Ctr for Devices and Radiol Health 5600 Fishers Ln Rockville MD 20867

BODEK, ARIE, physics educator, researcher; b. Tel-Aviv, Israel, May 11, 1947; came to U.S., 1963; naturalized, 1973; s. Moshe and Lea (Braunfeld) B.; m. Yaffa Tatiana Harper, 1970; children—Haim, Esther, Aviva. B.S. in Physics, MIT, 1968, Ph.D., 1972. Research assoc. MIT, Boston, 1972-74; Millikan research fellow Calif. Inst. Tech., Pasadena, 1974-76; asst. prof. U. Rochester, N.Y., 1977-80, assoc. prof., 1980—; spokesman Fermilab Expt. E595, Bativia, Ill., 1977—, dep. spokesman Fermilab Expt. E701, Batavia, 1981—; Co-spokesman SLAC Expt E140, Stanford, Calif., 1984—. Contbr. articles profl. jours. Sloan Found. fellow, 1979-80. Fellow Am. Phys. Soc.; mem. SLAC User Orgn. (inst. rep.), Fer,o;an User Orgn. Jewish. Current work: Experimental high energy physics, neutrino interactions, electron scattering from nuclear targets and quark distributions in Nuclei, Charm Production e+-e minus-reactions. Subspecialties: Particle physics; Nuclear physics. Home: 61 Evandale Rd Rochester NY 14618 Office: Dept Physics and Astronomy U Rochester River Campus Rochester NY 14627

BODEN, RICHARD MARK, organic chemist; b. Bklyn., Mar. 9, 1950; s. Eric Leopold and Greta (Stein) B.; m. Susan Clark, Apr. 18, 1975 (div. 1980); 1 child, Rachel; m. Barbara Adler, Mar. 23, 1982; children—Aaron, Susan. B.S., U. Calif.-Berkeley, 1971; M.A., SUNY-Buffalo, 1974; Ph.D., U. Rochester, 1979. Research chemist Internat. Flavors & Fragrances, Union Beach, N.J., 1978-80, sr. research chemist research and devel., 1980-81, project leader, 1982—. Contbr. articles to profl. jours. Patentee in field. Woodburn award for excellence in teaching, SUNY-Buffalo, 1972. Mem. Am. Chem. Soc. (exec. com. 1980-82), Alpha Chi Sigma. Democrat. Current work: Preparation of new and unusual structures for organoleptic evaluation; structure activity relationships, organic synthesis. Subspecialties: Organic chemistry; Synthetic chemistry. Home: 1116 Darlene Ave Ocean NJ 07712 Office: Internat Flavors and Fragrances 1515 Hwy 36 Union Beach NJ 07735

BODENHEIMER, BERT ARNO, mechanical engineer, consultant; b. Loerrach, Germany, May 22, 1928; came to U.S., 1939, naturalized, 1945; s. Alfred and Martha (Model) B.; m. Ellen Schleicher, Aug. 15, 1954 (dec. Jan. 1981); children—Brenda J., Carol F., Andrew J.; m. Bertha Allen, Oct. 9, 1983. B.M.E., CCNY, 1950; M.S., Columbia U., 1956. Lic. profl. engr., N.Y., Conn. Engr., Slater Electric Co., Queens, N.Y., 1950-55; lectr. CCNY, N.Y.C., 1955-57; mgr. mech. engring. Am. Machine & Foundry Co., Stamford, Conn., 1957-64; mgr. electro-mechs. CBS Labs., Stamford, 1964-68; dir. research and devel. Sea-Land Service, Elizabeth, N.J., 1968-76, Bodenheimer & Co., Stamford, 1976—; chmn. subcom. on refrigeration containers Am. Nat. Standards Com. for Containers, 1968—. Patentee container for handling freight, bulk cargo handling system and method, others. Trustee BiCultural Day Sch., Stamford, 1983—. Served to pfc. Q.M.C., U.S. Army, 1950-52. Recipient John C. Vaaler award Chem. Processing, 1972. Mem. ASME, Transp. Research. Bd. Subspecialties: Mechanical engineering; Systems engineering. Home: 204 Big Oak Rd Stamford CT 06903 Office: B A Bodenheimer & Co Inc 1435 Bedford St Stamford CT 06905

BODIAN, DAVID, neurobiology educator; b. St. Louis, May 15, 1910; s. Harry and Tillie (Franzel) B.; m. Elinor Widmont, June 26, 1944; children—Helen, Marion, Brenda, Alexander, Marc. B.S., U. Chgo., 1931, Ph.D., 1934, M.D., 1937. Asst. in anatomy U. Chgo., 1935-38; NRC fellow medicine U. Mich., 1938; anatomy Johns Hopkins, 1939- 40; asst. prof. anatomy Western Res. U., 1940-41; research on problems poliomyelitis, faculty dept. epidemiology Johns Hopkins, 1942-57; asso. prof. epidemiology Johns Hopkins (Sch. Hygiene and Pub. Health), 1946-57, prof. anatomy, dir. dept., 1957-75, prof. neurobiology dept. otolaryngology, 1975—; tech. com. poliomyelitis vaccine USPHS, 1957-64; vaccine adv. com. Nat. Found., 1956-60; cons. NIH, mem. bd. sci. counselors, div. biol. standards, 1957-59; mem. bd. sci. advisers Nat. Inst. of Neurol. Diseases, 1968—. Author: Neural Mechanisms in Poliomyelitis, 1942; Mng. editor: Am. Jour. Hygiene, 1948-57; mem. editorial bds.: Jour. Comparative Neurology; Contbr. science articles profl. jours. Served as lt. USNR, World War II. Recipient E. Mead Johnson award in pediatrics Am. Acad. Pediatrics, 1941. Mem. Am. Assn. Anatomists (pres. 1971-72), Am. Acad. Arts and Scis., Nat. Acad. Scis., Am. Philos. Soc. (K.S. Lashley award in neurobiology 1985), AAAS, Am. Physiol. Soc., Neurosci. Soc., Assn. Research Nervous and Mental Diseases, Phi Beta Kappa, Sigma Xi. Researcher on structure and diseases of nervous tissue. Current Work: At present making an electron misroscopic analysis of the auditory organ of Cort. Subspecialties: Neurobiology; Cytology and histology. Office: 1721 E Madison St Baltimore MD 21205

BODILY, DAVID MARTIN, chemist, educator; b. Logan, Utah, Dec. 16, 1933; s. Levi Delbert and Norma (Christenson) B.; m. Beth Alene Judy, Aug. 28, 1958; children—Robert David, Rebecca Marie, Timothy Andrew, Christopher Mark. Student, Utah State U., 1952-54; B.A., Brigham Young U., 1959, M.A., 1960; Ph.D., Cornell U., 1964. Postdoctoral fellow Northwestern U., Evanston, Ill., 1964-65; asst. prof. chemistry U. Ariz., Tucson, 1965-67; asst. prof. fuels engring. U. Utah, Salt Lake City, 1967-70, assoc. prof., 1970-77, prof., 1977—, chmn. dept. mining and fuels engring., 1976—, assoc. dean Coll. Mines and Mineral Industries, 1983—. Contbr. articles to profl. jours. Mem. Am. Chem. Soc. (chmn. Salt Lake sect. 1975), Catalysis Soc. N. Am., Am. Inst. Mining and Metall. Engrs., Sigma Xi. Mormon. Current Work: Structure and chemistry of coal synthetic fuels from coal, oil shale and tar sands; coal preparation. Subspecialties: Coal; Fuels. Home: 2651 Cecil St Salt Lake City UT 84117 Office: 320 WBB U Utah Salt Lake City UT 84112

BODINE, RICHARD SHEARON, synthetic organic, chemist, researcher; b. Norman, Okla., Dec. 10, 1946; s. Philip Colby and Lois (Shearon) B. B.S., Phillips U., 1968; M.S., U. N.Mex., 1977, Ph.D., 1978. Instr., Parks Coll., Denver, 1969-70; programmer, analyst McGraw-Hill Inc., Denver, 1970-73; chemist Midwest Research Inst., Kansas City, Mo., 1979-84; team leader Marion Labs. Inc., Kansas City, Mo., 1984—. Author: (with others) Polynuclear Aromatic Hydrocarbons, 1983. Contbr. articles to profl. jours. U. N.Mex. fellow, 1976. Mem. Hist. Kansas City Found., Hyde Park Neighborhood Assn., Am. Chem. Soc., Sigma Xi, Phi Kappa Phi. Republican. Episcopalian. Current work: Synthesis of drugs, drug metabolites, and analytical standards; chemical process development and production; large-scale synthesis; drug recovery operations; radiosynthesis. Subspecialties: Organic chemistry; Synthetic chemistry. Home: 4340 Harrison Kansas City MO 64110 Office: Marion Labs Inc 10236 Marion Park Dr Kansas City MO 64137

BODNAR, RICHARD JULIUS, physiological psychologist, educator, researcher; b. N.Y.C., Feb. 21, 1946; s. Julius and Irene (Monette) B.; m. Carol B. Greenman, July 4, 1981; 1 son, Benjamin P.G. B.A., Manhattan Coll., 1967; M.A., CCNY, 1973; Ph.D. in Psychology, CUNY, 1976. Postdoctoral fellow Columbia U. Coll. Physicians and Surgeons, N.Y.C., 1976-78; research scientist N.Y. State Psychiat. Inst., N.Y.C., 1978-79; asst. prof. Queens Coll., CUNY, 1979-82, asso. prof., 1983-85, prof., 1986—. Contbr. articles to sci. jours. Served to capt. USAF, 1967-71. Decorated Bronze Star.; Sigma Xi nat. lectr., 1983-85; NIH grantee, 1978-82, 84-85. Mem. AAAS, Soc. Neurosci., Eastern Psychol. Assn., Internat. Assn. Study of Pain. Current Work: Mechanisms in central nervous system and endocrine system that inhibit pain. Subspecialties: Neuropsychology; Physiological psychology. Office: Queens Coll Flushing NY 11367

BODOR, NICHOLAS STEPHEN, educator; b. Satu Mare, Transylvania, Romania, Feb. 1, 1939; came to U.S., 1968, naturalized, 1976; s. Miklos Sandor and Berta (Horvath) B.; m. Sheryl Lee Reinmann, Feb. 26, 1971; children: Nicole, Erik; 1 child by previous marriage: Miklos. B.S.-M.S. in Organic Chemistry, Bolyai U., Romania, 1959; Dr. Chemistry, Babes-Bolyai U. and Cluj, Supreme Council of Romanian Acad. Sci., 1965. Prin. investigator, group leader Chem. Pharm. Research Inst., Cluj, Romania, 1961-68, 69-70; R.A. Welch postdoctoral fellow U. Tex., Austin, 1968-69, 70-72; sr. research scientist Alza Co., Lawrence, Kan., 1972-73; dir. medicinal chemistry Interx Research Co., Lawrence, 1973-78; adj. prof. U. Kan., Lawrence, 1974-78; prof., chmn. dept. medicinal chemistry U. Fla., Gainesville, 1979—, grad. research prof., 1983—; cons. Key Pharms., Inc., Miami, 1980—, Schering-Plough, Bloomfield, N.J., 1981—, Warner-Lambert, Ann Arbor, Mich., 1983—; v.p., dir. research Pharmatec, Inc., Arlington Heights, Ill., 1983—. Contbr. articles to profl. jours. Named Fla. Scientist of Yr., 1984. Fellow Acad. Pharm. Scis.; mem. Am. Chem. Soc., Am. Pharm. Assn., Acad. Pharm. Sci., AAAS, N.Y. Acad. Sci. Inventor in field. Current Work: Design of soft (low toxicity) drugs; brain specific drug delivery; computer assisted drug design; neuropharmacology; prodrugs; MO calculations; organic reactions. Subspecialties: Medicinal chemistry; Organic chemistry. Home: 7211 SW 97th Ln Gainesville FL 32608 Office: J H M Health Center Univ Fla Dept Medicinal Chemistry Box J4 Gainesville FL 32610

BOEHM, FELIX HANS, ldgcator, physicist; b. Basel, Switzerland, June 9, 1924; came to U.S., 1952, naturalized, 1964; s. Hans G. and Marquerite (Philippi) B.; m. Ruth Sommerhalder, Nov. 26, 1956; children: Marcus F., Claude N. M.S., Inst. Tech., Zurich, 1948, Ph.D., 1951. Research assoc. Inst. Tech., Zurich, Switzerland, 1949-52; Boese fellow Columbia U., 1952-53; faculty Calif. Inst. Tech., Pasadena, 1953—, prof. physics, 1961—, Sloan fellow, 1962-64, Niels Bohr Inst., Copenhagen, 1965-66, Cern, Geneva, 1971-72, Laue-Langevin Inst., 1980. Recipient Humboldt award, 1980. Fellow Am. Phys. Soc.; mem. Nat. Acad. Scis. Research on nuclear physics, nuclear beta decay, neutrino physics, atomic physics, muonic and pionic atoms, parity and time-reversal. Current Work: Properties of elementary particles and fields. Subspecialties: Particle physics; Nuclear physics. Home: 2510 N Altadena Dr Altadena CA 91001 Office: Calif Inst Tech Pasadena CA 91125

BOEHM, ROBERT FOTY, mechanical engineer, researcher; b. Portland, Oreg., Jan. 16, 1940; s. Charles Frederick and Lufteria (Christie) B.; m. Marcia Kay Pettibone, June 10, 1961; children: Deborah, Robert Christopher. B.S. in Mech. Engring. Wash. State U., Pullman, 1962, M.S., 1964; Ph.D., U. Calif.-Berkeley, 1968. Registered profl. engr., Calif. With Westinghouse Corp., Lima, Ohio, 1961, Lawrence Livermore Lab., Livermore, Calif., 1962, Boeing Aerospace Co., Seattle, 1963, Gen. Electric Co., San Jose, Calif., 1964-66, Jet Propulsion Lab., Pasadena, Calif., 1967, Sandia Labs., Livermore, Calif., 1984-85; mem. faculty U. Utah, Salt Lake City, 1968—, prof. mech. engring., 1976—, chmn. dept., 1981-84; mem. Utah Solar Adv. Com., Utah Energy Conservation and Devel. Council, 1980-84. Author 2 books. Contbr. articles to profl. jours., chpts. to books. Fellow ASME; mem. Am. Soc. Engring. Edn., Internat. Solar Energy Soc., Utah Solar Energy Soc., Bonneville Corvair Club. Congregationalist. Subspecialties: Mechanical engineering; Solar energy. Home: 2217 E Bryan Circle Salt Lake City UT 84108 Office: U Utah Mech Engring Dept Salt Lake City UT 84112

BOEHMER, MATTHEW ANTHONY, chemical engineer, research and development executive; b. Detroit, Aug. 24, 1924; s. Matthew M. and Anna M. (Reuter) B.; m. Yolande Andre, Nov. 25, 1950; children—Matthew A., Mark A., David J., John J., Yolande M. B.S. in Chem. Engring., U. Detroit, 1951. Spl. chemist Revere Copper Co., Detroit, 1942-46; plant mgr., metallurgist Mich. Steel Corp., Detroit, 1950-57; research and devel. supr. BASF-WYANDOTTE, Mich., 1957-80; research and devel. assoc. Diversey-Wyandotte, 1980-84; mgr. new product devel. DETREX Chem. Industries, Inc., Southfield, Mich., 1984—. Patentee automotive fluids. Chmn. Detroit Area council Boy Scouts Am., 1958-63; chmn. CCD edn. program St. Frances Cabrine Catholic Ch., Allen Park, Mich., 1967-69, sec. bd. edn., 1969-71. Served to sgt. U.S. Army, 1944-46. Mem. Am. Chem. Soc., Am. Soc. Lubrication Engrs., Nat. Assn. Corrosion Engrs., ASTM (Daniel H. Green award 1975), Sigma Xi (BASF br. chmn. 1966-67), Tau Beta Pi. Republican. Current work: Inventing and developing new chemical products and processes; market research and commercial development on products for lubrication and corrosion control. Subspecialties: Chemical engineering; Corrosion. Home: 9885 Andrews St Allen Park MI 48101 Office: Detrex Chem Industries Inc PO Box 501 Detroit MI 48232

BOEKELHEIDE, VIRGIL CARL, chemistry educator, consultant; b. Chelsea, S.D., July 28, 1919; s. Charles Frederick and Eleonor Charlotte (Toennies) B.; m. Caroline Ambler Barrett, Sept. 1, 1945; children: Karl, Anne, Erich. A.B., U. Minn., 1939, Ph.D., 1943. Instr. U. Ill., 1943-45; asst. prof. to prof. chemistry U. Rochester (N.Y.), 1946-60; prof. U. Oreg., Eugene, 1960—; cons. Ciba-Geigy Co. Editorial bd.: Organic Reactions and Organic Syntheses; contbr. over 220 articles to sci. jours. Guggenheim fellow, 1953-54; Sloan fellow, 1960-62; Roche fellow, 1962-64; recipient Outstanding Achievement award U. Minn., 1967; Fulbright Disting. prof., 1972; Alexander von Humboldt fellow, 1974-75, 82; Centenary lectr. Royal Soc. Gt. Britain, 1983. Mem. Nat. Acad. Scis., Am. Chem. Soc., Swiss Chem. Soc., German Chem. Soc. Current Work: Syntheses, heterocycles, novel aromatic and organometallics; organic metals and organic electrical conductors. Subspecialty: Organic chemistry. Home: 2017 Elk Dr Eugene OR 97403 Office: U Oreg Eugene OR 97403

BOEKER, ELIZABETH ANNE, biochemist; b. Derby, Conn., Apr. 30, 1941; d. Robert Otto and Anne (Hollmeyer) B.; A.B., Radcliffe Coll., 1962; Ph.D., U. Calif.-Berkeley, 1967. Postdoctoral fellow U. Wash., Seattle, 1967-70; staff fellow NIMH, Bethesda, Md., 1970-72; research asst. prof. U. Wash., Seattle, 1972-75; asst. prof. Utah State U., Logan, 1975-79; assoc. prof. biochemistry Utah State U., Logan, 1979—. Contbr. articles to profl. jours. Bd. dirs. Utah Heart Assn., 1980—. Nat. Merit Scholar Radcliffe Coll., 1958-62; established investigator Am. Heart Assn., 1972-77; hon. fellow U. Birmingham, Eng., 1981-82. Mem. Am. Soc. Biol. Chemists, Biochem. Soc., Biophys. Soc., Am. Chem. Soc., AAAS. Current work: enzyme kinetics using integrated rate equations. Subspecialties: Biochemistry (biology); Biophysics (biology). Home: 3612 S 1200 W Logan UT 84321 Office: Dept Chemistry and Biochemistry UT State U Logan UT 84322

BÖER, KARL WOLFGANG, physicist, engineer, educator; b. Berlin, Mar. 23, 1926; came to U.S., 1961, naturalized, 1972; s. Karl and Charlotte (Gruhlke) B.; m. Renate Schroder, Apr. 18, 1935; children: Ralf-Reinhard, Katarina Karlotta. Dipl. in Physics, Humboldt U., Berlin, 1949, Dr.rer.nat., 1952; Dr.rer.nat. habil., 1955. Asst., docent, prof., chmn. Humboldt U., 1949-61; dir. lab. for dielectric breakdown German Akademie der Wissenschaften, Berlin, 1955-61; prof. physics U. Del., 1962-72; dir. U. Del. (Inst. Energy Conversion), 1972-75, chief scientist, 1975—, prof. physics and engring., 1972—, advisor to pres., 1976—; chmn. SES, Inc., 1972-78, chief scientist, 1978-82. Editor 3 jours.; editor in chief: Advances in Solar Energy, 1982; editor 8 conf. procs.; contbr. numerous articles to profl. jours. Recipient Humboldt medal, 1958; Charles J. Abbott award, 1981. Fellow Am. Phys. Soc.; mem. IEEE (sr.), Electrochem. Soc., Am. Solar Energy Soc. (chmn. 1976 77, sec. 1978). Patentee in field. Current Work: First observer Franz Keldysh effect, light induced modulation of absorption, proposed Bose-Einstein condensation of excitons, conduction mechanism of semiconducting glasses, curve shape factor of jV characteristics, DC electroluminescence, hybrid solar house system, negative differential conductivity effects. Subspecialties: Solar energy; Condensed matter physics. Home: Buck Toe Hills Kennett Square PA 19348 Office: Coll of Engineering U of Del Newark DE 19716

BOERNER, WOLFGANG MARTIN, radar and electronic engineering educator; b. Finschhafen, Morobe, Papua New Guinea, July 26, 1937; came to U.S., 1963, naturalized, 1981; s. Martin Ernst and Ilse Louise (Stoss) B.; m. Eileen A. Hassebrock, Dec. 23, 1967; children: Vaughan W., J. Allan, Joanna E. Dipl. Ing., Tech. U. Munich, Germany, 1963; Ph.D. in E.E, U. Pa., 1967. Research engr. Radiation Lab., U. Mich., Ann Arbor, 1967-68; postdoctoral fellow elec. engring. U. Man. (Can.), Winnipeg, 1968-69, asst. prof. elec. engring., 1969-71, assoc. prof., 1971-75, prof., 1975-78, research prof., 1978—; prof., dir. Elec. Engring. and Computer Sci Lab., U. Ill.-Chgo., 1978—; cons. radar U.S. Dept. Def., Chgo., 1980—; pres. Polarimetrics Inc., Northbrook, Ill., 1982; Dir. Advanced Study Inst., NATO, Bad Windsheim, W.Ger., 1983. Contbr. articles to profl. jours. Fulbright fellow, 1963. Mem. IEEE, AAAS, Humboldt Soc., Soc. Exploration Geophysics, Soc. Engring. Sci., Can. Assn. Physicists, Verein Deutscher Ingenieure, Soc. Photog. Instrumentation Engrs., Optical Soc. Am., Sigma Xi. Current Work: Applied electromagnetics; radar polarimetry; inverse scattering; radar remote sensing; geo-electromagnetics; laser optics, atmospheric optics. Subspecialties: Electrical engineering; Applied magnetics. Home: 1021 Cedar Ln Northbrook IL 60062 Office: Communications Lab Dept Elec Engring and Computer Sci U Ill 851 S Morgan St PO Box 4348 M St SEO-1141 Chicago IL 60680

BOESCH, HAROLD EDWIN, JR., physicist; b. Washington, Mar. 26, 1942; s. Harold Edwin and Lois (Judge) B.; m. Marilyn Pierce, June 19, 1964; children—Stephen, Kathleen, Eric. B.S., Purdue U., 1964. Physicist, Harry Diamond Lab., Washington, 1964—. Contbr. articles to profl. jours. Patentee electronic means for simulating radiation. Mem. IEEE (sr., best paper award Nuclear and Space Radiation Effects Conf. 1976, 79). Presbyterian. Current work: Ionizing radiation effects on semiconductor, dielectric and electronic materials. Subspecialties: Condensed matter physics; Microelectronics. Home: 6315 Leafy Screen Columbia MD 21045 Office: Harry Diamond Labs 2800 Powder Mill Rd Adelphi MD 20783

BOESHAAR, PATRICIA CHIKOTAS, astronomer; b. Butler Twp., Pa., Sept. 25, 1947; d. Joseph S. and Anna (Geritis) Chikotas; m. John Anthony Tyson, Jan. 23, 1981; 1 son, Kristopher Chikotas Tyson. Student, Duquesne U., Pitts, 1965-67; B.S., Northwestern State U., Natchitoches, La., 1969; Ph.D., Ohio State U., 1976. Instr., research assoc. U. Wash., 1975-77; asst. prof. U. Oreg., 1977-80; research assoc U. Ariz., 1980-81; asst. prof. physics Rider Coll., Lawrenceville, N.J., 1981-84, assoc. prof., 1984—. Contbr. articles to profl. jours. NSF grantee, 1978, 79, 84. Mem. Am. Astron. Soc., Astron. Soc. Pacific, Sigma Xi, Sigma Pi Sigma. Current Work: Low luminosity star, spectral classification, stellar distributions. Subspecialty: Optical astronomy. Office: Rider Coll PO Box 6400 Lawrenceville NJ 08648

BOFF, KENNETH RICHARD, research psychologist, consultant; b. Bklyn., Aug. 17, 1947; s. Victor Boff and Ann Yunko; m. Judith Marion Schoer, Aug. 2, 1969; 1 son, Cory Asher. B.A., Hunter Coll., CUNY, 1969, M.A., 1972; M. Phil., Columbia U., 1975, Ph.D., 1978. Research asst. Columbia U., 1976; research psychologist Air Force Human Resources Lab., Wright-Patterson AFB, Ohio, 1977-80, Air Force Aero Med. Research Lab., 1980—; project dir. Integrated perceptual info. for designers project USAF, U.S. Army, USN, NASA, 1980—, program mgr. tactical aircraft cockpit devel. and evaluation program, 1980—, research team leader, 1980—; research dir. Smart Work Stations for Designers: A Designer's Assoc. Project, 1985—. Editor: Handbook of Perception and Human Performance; contbr. articles to profl. jours. Recipient Outstanding Performance award USAF, Wright-Patterson AFB, 1981. Mem. Assn. for Research in Vision and Opthalmology, Am. Psychol. Assn., Human Factors Soc. Current Work: Knowledge-based, information-management systems (artificial intelligence); biocybernetic control; flight simulation; visually coupled systems; information transfer effectiveness of three-dimensional displayed information. Subspecialties: Human factors engineering; Sensory processes. Home: 3114 Village Ct Dayton OH 45432 Office: Air Force Aerospace Med Research Lab Wright-Patterson AFB OH 45433

BOGARD, DONALD DALE, geochemist; b. Fayetteville, Ark., Feb. 6, 1940. B.S., U. Ark., 1962, M.S., 1964, Ph.D. in Isotope Geochemistry, 1966. NSF research fellow geol. sci. Calif. Inst. Tech., 1966-68; staff scientist planetary and earth sci. div. Johnson Space Ctr., NASA, Houston, 1968—, curator Antarctica meteorite collection, 1978-84, discipline scientist, planetary materials program, 1984—. Assoc. editor Jour. Geophys. Research Am. Geophys. Union, 1975-77. Fellow Meteoritical Soc.; mem. Am. Geophys. Union, Geochem. Soc. Subspecialties: Planetology; Meteorites. Office: NASA Johnson Space Ctr Code SN 4 Houston TX 77058

BOGASH, RICHARD, See *Who's Who in America*, 43rd edition.

BOGDONOFF, SEYMOUR MOSES, aeronautical engineer; b. N.Y.C., Jan. 10, 1921; s. Glenn and Kate (Cohen) B.; m. Harriet Eisenberg, Oct. 1, 1944; children: Sondra Sue, Zelda Lynn, Alan Charles. B.S., Rensselaer Poly. Inst., 1942; M.S., Princeton U., 1948. Asst. sect. head fluid and gas dynamics sect. Langley Meml. Aero. Lab., NASA, 1942-46; research assoc. aero. engring. dept. Princeton U., 1946-53, asso. prof., 1953-57, prof., 1957-63, Henry Porter Patterson prof. aero. engring., 1963—, chmn. dept. mech. and aerospace engring., 1974-83; head gas dynamics lab. Princeton U. (James Forrestal Research Campus); cons. aero. engr.; mem. adv. council NASA; mem. sci. adv. bd. Dept. Air Force, 1958-76, 80—. Recipient Exceptional Civilian Service award Dept. Air Force, 1968. Fellow AIAA (dir., Fluid and Plasma Dynamics award 1983); mem. Internat. Acad. Astronautics of Internat. Astronautical Fedn. (corr.), Nat. Acad. Engring., ASME, Am. Phys. Soc., Sigma Xi, Tau Beta Pi. Subspecialty: Aeronautical engineering. Home: 39 Random Rd Princeton NJ 08540

BOGGS, GEORGE JOHNSON, psychophysicist, human factors engineer; b. Beckley, W.Va., Mar. 2, 1949; s. William Arnie and Margaret Pearl (Johnson) B.; m. Hilda Mae Beaver, Aug. 22, 1972 (div. 1977). B.S., Marshall U., Huntington, W.Va., 1972, M.S., 1974; Ph.D., Purdue U., 1981. Psychologist Nicholas County Mental Health Center, Summersville, W.Va., 1974-75; dir. psychology Cabell County Bd. Edn., Huntington, 1975-77; research asst. Purdue U., West Lafayette, Ind., 1977-81; mem. tech. staff GTE Labs., Inc., Waltham, Mass., 1981-84, 85—; sr. Fulbright research fellow U. Nottingham, Eng., 1984-85; cons. U. Md., College Park, 1982. Mem. Am. Inst. Physics, Acoustical Soc. Am., N.Y. Acad. Scis., Am. Psychol. Assn., Sigma Xi. Current Work: Basic and applied research in auditory psychophysics and human factors engineering for telecommunications application. Subspecialties: Psychophysics; Human factors engineering. Home: 78 Jericho Rd Weston MA 02193 Office: GTE Labs Inc 40 Sylvan Rd Waltham MA 02254

BOGGS, JAMES ERNEST, chemistry educator; b. Cleve., June 9, 1921; s. Ernest Beckett and Emily (Reid) B.; m. Ruth Ann Rogers, June 22, 1948; children: Carol, Ann, Lynne. A.B., Oberlin Coll., 1943; M.S. in Chemistry, U. Mich., 1944, Ph.D., 1953. Asst. prof. dept. chemistry Eastern Mich. U., Ypsilanti, 1949-52; instr. U. Mich. at Ann Arbor, 1952-53; mem. faculty dept. chemistry U. Tex. at Austin, 1953—, assoc. prof., 1958-66, prof., 1966—, asst. dean Grad. Sch., 1958-67, dir. Center for Structural Studies, 1969—; acting dir. Inst. Theoretical Chemistry U. Tex. at Austin, 1979-81. Contbr. articles to profl. jours. Mem. Am. Chem. Soc., Am. Phys. Soc., Phi Beta Kappa, Sigma Xi, Phi Lambda Upsilon, Gamma Alpha. Research in structural chemistry, microwave spectroscopy, quantum chemistry. Current Work: Physical and theoretical chemistry. Subspecialties: Physical chemistry; Theoretical chemistry. Home: 4603 Balcones Dr Austin TX 78731

BOGORAD, LAWRENCE, biology educator; b. Tashkent, U.S.S.R., Aug. 29, 1921; came to U.S., 1922; s. Boris and Florence (Bernard) B.; m. Rosalyn G. Sagen, June 29, 1943; children—Leonard Paul, Kiki M. Lee. B.S., U. Chgo., 1942, Ph.D., 1949. Instr. botany U. Chgo., 1948-51, asst. prof. dept. botany, 1953-57, assoc. prof., 1957-61, prof., 1961-67; prof. biology Harvard U., Cambridge, Mass., 1967—, chmn. dept. biology, 1974-76, dir. Maria Moors Cabot Found., Cambridge, Mass., 1976—, Maria Moors Cabot prof. biology, 1980—; vis. investigator Rockefeller Inst., N.Y.C., 1951-53; mem. com. on sci. and public policy Nat. Acad. Scis., 1977-81; mem. Assembly of Life Scis., NRC; mem. joint council on food and agrl. scis. Dept. Agr., 1978-82. Asso. editor: Bot. Gazette, 1958; editoral com.: Annual Rev. Plant Physiology, 1963-67; editorial bd.: Plant Physiology, 1965-66, Biochimica Biophysica Acta, 1967-69, Jour. Cell Biology, 1967-70, Jour. Applied and Molecular Genetics, 1981-85, Plant Molecular Biology, 1981-85, Plant Cell Reports, 1981-85. Served with AUS, 1943-46. Merck fellow, 1951-53; Fulbright fellow, 1960; recipient Career Research award NIH, 1963. Fellow Am. Acad. Arts and Scis.; mem. Am. Soc. Biol. Chemistry, Am. Soc. Cell Biology, Am. Philos. Soc., Nat. Acad. Scis. (chmn. botany sect. 1974-77), Am. Soc. Plant Physiologists (pres. 1968-69, Stephen Hales award 1982), AAAS (bd. dirs. 1982, pres. elect 1985-86), Royal Danish Acad. Scis. and Letters (fgn.), Soc. Developmental Biology (pres. 1984). Subspecialties: Plant physiology (agriculture); Molecular biology. Office: Dept of Biology Harvard Univ 16 Divinity Ave Cambridge MA 02138

BOHME, DIETHARD KURT, chemistry educator; b. Boston, June 20, 1941; s. Kurt Friedrich Wilhelm and Maria Kunigunda (Kiesel) B.; m. Shirley Faith Broadway, Dec. 23, 1966; children: Kurt, Kenneth Diethard, Heidi Claire. B.Sc., McGill U., 1962, Ph.D., 1965. Asst. prof. chemistry York U., Downsview, Ont., Can., 1970-74, assoc. prof., 1974-77, prof., 1977—, dir. grad. program in chemistry, 1979-85, chmn. chemistry, 1985—; sr. scientist, vis. fellow Sci. Research Council, U. Warwick, Eng., 1978; mem. chemistry grant selection com. Nat. Scis. and Engring. Research Council Can., 1983-86. Contbr. chpts. to books, also articles to profl. jours. Recipient Rutherford Meml. medal Royal soc. Can., 1981; Sloan Found. fellow York U., 1974. Fellow Chem. Inst. Can. (exec. phys. chemistry div. 1980-83, Noranda lectr. award 1983); mem. Am. Soc. Mass Spectrometry, Combustion Inst. Current Work: Gas-phase ion chemistry, ion energetics, experimental reaction kinetics, physical organic chemistry, astrochemistry, flame-ion chemistry, ionospheric chemistry. Subspecialties: Physical chemistry; Space chemistry. Home: 28 Colonsay Rd Thornhill ON L3T 3E8 Canada Office: York U Downsview ON M3J 1P3 Canada

BOHN, MARTHA D., neurobiologist, educator; b. Niagara Falls, N.Y., Mar. 30, 1943; d. John W. and Elsie L. (Gregory) Churchill. A.B., Cornell U., 1964; M.S., U. Conn., 1977, Ph.D., 1979. Asst. prof. Cornell U. Med. Coll., N.Y.C., 1980-83, SUNY-Stony Brook, 1983—. Contbr. articles to profl. jours. NIH grantee, 1976-78, 79-81, 82—; NINCDS Research Career Devel. award, 1982. Mem. Soc. Neurosci., AAAS, N.Y. Acad. Scis., Phi Beta Kappa, Phi Kappa Phi. Current Work: Endocrine effects on neuronal and glial cell differentiation; specification and plasticity of neurotransmitter phenotype. Subspecialties: Neurobiology; Developmental biology.

BOIS, PIERRE, medical research organization executive; b. Oka, Que., Can., Mar. 22, 1924; s. Henri and Ethier (Germaine) B.; m. Joyce Casey, Sept. 8, 1953; children: Monique, Marie, Louise. M.D., U. Montreal, Que., 1953, Ph.D., 1957; hon. doctorate, U. Ottawa, Ont., 1982. Research fellow pathology U. Montreal, 1957-58, asst. assoc. prof. dept. pharmacology, 1960-64, prof., head dept. anatomy, 1964-70, dean faculty medicine, 1970-81; pres. Med. Research Council of Can., 1981—; asst. prof. histology, Ottawa, Ont., Can., 1958-60. Contbr. over 130 publs. to profl. jours. Fellow Royal Soc. Can., Royal Coll. Physicians and Surgeons Can.; mem. Am., French Canadian assns. anatomists, N.Y. Acad. Scis., AAAS, Can. Fedn. Biol. Socs., Can. Soc. Clin. Investigation. Research and numerous publs. on morphological effects of hormones, histamine and mast cells in magnesium deficiency, muscular dystrophy, exptl. thymic tumors. Subspecialty: Medical research administration. Office: Med Research Council Can Ottawa ON K1A 0W9 Canada

BOJADZIEV, GEORGE NIKOLOV, mathematics educator; b. Shumen, Bulgaria, July 11, 1927; emigrated to Canada, 1971; s. Nicolas D. and Luba G. (Kodjabanova) B.; m. Maria S. Cekova, Oct. 14, 1956; children: Luba, Nick. Diploma, U. Sofia, Bulgaria, 1950, Ph.D. in Math., 1957. Prof. Math. U. Mech. and Elec. Engring., Sofia, Bulgaria, 1969-70; vis. prof. Simon Fraser U.,

Burnaby, B.C., Can., 1971-75, assoc. prof. dept. math., 1975-79, prof., 1979—. Mem. Can. Applied Math. Soc., Soc. Indsl. and Applied Math. Current Work: Ordinary and partial differential equations and applications; perturbation methods; nonlinear oscillations; population dynamics. Subspecialty: Applied mathematics. Home: 835 Farmleigh Rd West Vancouver BC V7S 1Z8 Canada Office: Simon Fraser U Burnaby BC V5A 1S6 Canada

BOLAND, J. ROBERT, radiological physicist; b. Denver, June 17, 1928; s. Hugh William and Hilda Josephine (Larson) B.; m. Pita Martinez, Feb. 14, 1963; children: Adriana, Nina Marie. B.S., U. Denver, 1952, M.S., 1958. Health physicist Dow Chem. Co., Rocky Flats, Colo., 1952-53; chemist-toxicologist U. Colo. Med. Ctr., Denver, 1953-58; health physicist Dept. Def., White Sands Missile Range, 1959-63; radiation specialist EG & G Inc., Santa Barbara, Calif., 1963-67; health physicist AEC (now U.S. Dept. Energy), Nev. Test Site, 1967—. Contbr. articles to profl. jours. Served with USN, 1946-48. Mem. Am. Chem. Soc., Am. Nuclear Soc., Health Physics Soc., VFW. Club: Rough Riders (trail boss 1981—). Current Work: Developing technology for disposal of high specific activity low-level radioactive waste. Subspecialty: Hazardous waste disposal. Home: 5593 Alfred Dr Las Vegas NV 89108 Office: US Dept Energy PO Box 14100 Las Vegas NV 89114

BOLCH, WILLIAM EMMETT, JR., engineering educator; b. Lenoir, N.C., Oct. 27, 1935; s. William Emmett and Gladys (Hendrix) B.; m. Sandra Lee Talley, Nov. 7, 1959; children: Wesley Emmett, Elizabeth Talley. B.S. in Civil Engring, U. Tex.-Austin, 1959, M.S., 1963; Ph.D., U. Calif.-Berkeley, 1967. Registered profl. engr., Fla. Asst. prof. environ. engring. U. Fla., Gainesville, 1966-70, assoc. prof., 1970-77, prof., 1977—, acting chmn., 1981-82; cons., owner Environ. Radiation Group, Gainesville, Fla., 1981—. Served to 1st lt. USAF, 1959-62. Mem. Am. Nuclear Soc., Health Physics Soc. Democrat. Methodist. Current Work: Health physics, radiation protection, environmental monitoring for radioactivity, radiotracers. Subspecialties: Environmental engineering; Nuclear engineering. Office: Dept Environmental Engring 110 AP Black Hall Gainesville FL 32611

BOLDT, ELIHU A., astrophysicist; b. New Brunswick, N.J., July 15, 1931; s. Joel and Yetta (Miller) B.; m. Yvette, Nov. 25, 1971; children: Adam, Abigail, Jessica. Ph.D., MIT, 1958. Asst. prof. physics dept. Rutgers U., New Brunswick, N.J., 1958-64; astrophysicist Goddard Space Flight Ctr., NASA, Greenbelt, Md., 1964—, also head X-ray astronomy group; adj. prof. physics U. Md., College Park, 1982—. Recipient John C. Lindsay Meml. award Goddard Space Flight Center, 1977; Outstanding Sci Achievement award NASA, 1978. Fellow Am. Phys. Soc.; mem. Am. Astron. Soc., Internat. Astron. Union. Current Work: X-ray astronomy. Subspecialty: X-ray high energy astrophysics. Office: Goddard Space Flight Ct NASA Code 661 Greenbelt MD 20771

BOLE, GILES G., physician, rheumatologist; b. Battle Creek, Mich., July 28, 1928; s. Giles Gerald and Kittie Belle (French) B.; m. Elizabeth Jeanne Dooley, May 11, 1985; children—David Giles, Elizabeth Ann. Grad., U. Mich., 1949, M.D., 1953. Diplomate: Am. Bd. Internal Medicine; cert. rheumatology. Instr. internal medicine U. Mich., 1959-61, asst. prof., 1961-64, assoc. prof., 1964-70, prof., 1970—; assoc. physician Rackham Arthritis Research Unit, 1961-69, acting physician-in-charge, 1969-71, physician-in-charge, 1971—, Rackham Arthritis Research Unit, Rheumatology Div., 1975—; program dir. Multipurpose Arthritis Ctr., NIH, 1977—; sr. investigator Arthritis Found., 1963-68; co-dir. tng. grant in rheumatology USPHS, 1969-76, dir., 1976—; prin. investigator NIH, 1976—; mem. policy adv. com. Centers for Disease Control, 1977-80; mem., chmn. subsplty. bd. rheumatology Am. Bd. Internal Medicine, 1978-84; bd. govs. Am. Bd. Internal Medicine, 1979-83; mem. Nat. Arthritis Adv. Bd., 1980—. Contbr. numerous articles to profl. jours., chpts. in textbooks. Pres. Newport Elem. Sch. Parent-Tchr. Orgn., 1967-68; chmn. spl. citizens com. safety Ann Arbor Pub. Schs., 1968-69, citizen rep. intergovtl. com. student safety, 1969-73; trustee Huron River Heights Property Owners Assn., 1970-73. Served to capt. USAF, 1956-58. Postdoctoral research fellow Arthritis and Rheumatism Found., 1961-63. Fellow A.C.P.; mem. Am. Rheumatism Assn. (exec. com., v.p. 1979-80, pres. 1980-81), AAAS, Am. Fedn. Clin. Research, Central Clin. Research Club, Central Soc. Clin. Research (sec.-treas. 1970-75, v.p. 1975-76, pres. 1976-77), Alpha Omega Alpha, Phi Kappa Phi. Current Work: Biochemistry of osteoarthritis and cartilage; clinical study of rheumatic diseases. Subspecialties: Biochemistry (medicine); Rheumatology. Home: 6015 W Ellsworth Rd Ann Arbor MI 48103 Office: R4633 Kresge Univ Michigan Ann Arbor MI 48109

BOLEY, BRUNO ADRIAN, engineering educator; b. Gorizia, Italy, May 13, 1924; came to U.S., 1939, naturalized, 1945; s. Orville F. and Rita (Luzzatto) B.; m. Sara R. Boley, May 12, 1949; children: Jacqueline, Daniel L. B.C.E., CCNY, 1943, D.Sc. hon., 1982; M.Aero. Engring., Poly. Inst. Bklyn., 1945, D.Sc. in Aero. Engring., 1946. Asst. dir. structural research, aero. engring. dept. Poly. Inst. Bklyn., 1943-48; engring. specialist Goodyear Aircraft Corp., 1948-50; asso. prof. aero. engring. Ohio State U., 1950-52; asso. prof. civil engring. Columbia U., 1952-58, prof., 1958-68; Joseph P. Ripley prof. engring., chmn. theoretical and applied mechanics Cornell U., Ithaca, N.Y., 1968-72; dean Technol. Inst., Walter P. Murphy prof. Northwestern U., Evanston, Ill., 1973—; mem. adv. com. George Washington U., Princeton U., Yale U., FAMU/FSU Inst. Engring.; chmn. Midwest Program for Minorities in Engring., 1975—; bd. govs. Argonne Nat. Lab., 1983—. Author: Theory of Thermal Stresses, 1960, High Temperature Structures and Materials, 1964, Thermoinelasticity, 1970, Crossfire in Professional Education, 1976; also articles, numerous tech. papers.; editor-in-chief: Mechanics Research Communications; bd. editors: Jour. Thermal Stresses, Bull. Mech. Engring. Edn., Internat. Jour. Computers and Structures, Internat. Jour. Engring. Sci., Internat. Jour. Fracture Mechanics, Internat. Jour. Mech. Engring. Scis., Internat. Jour. Solids and Structures, Jour. Applied Mechanics, Jour. Structural Mechanics Software, Letters in Applied and Engring. Sci., Nuclear Engring. and Design. Recipient Disting. Alumnus award Poly. Inst. N.Y., 1974; Townsend Harris medal, 1981; NATO sr. sci. fellow, 1964-65. ; Fellow AIAA; hon. mem. ASME (exec. com., pres. applied mechanics div. 1975, bd. govs. 1984—); fellow Am. Acad. Mechanics (pres. 1974); mem. Nat. Acad. Engring. (chmn. task force engring. edn. 1979-80), Soc. Engring. Scis. (pres. 1975), Assn. Chairmen Depts. Mechanics (founder, pres. 1970-72), Internat. Assn. Structural Mechanics in Reactor Tech. (adv.-gen. 1979—), Internat. Union Theoretical and Applied Mechanics (sec. Congress com. 1976—), N.Y. Acad. Scis. (named Outstanding Educator of Am. 1971), U.S. Nat. Com. Theoretical and Applied Math. (chmn. 1975—), Ill. Council Energy Research and Devel. (chmn. 1979—). Subspecialties: Theoretical and applied mechanics; Applied mathematics. Office: Northwestern U Tech Inst Evanston IL 60201

BOLKER, HENRY IRVING, chemist, research institute director, educator; b. Montreal, Que., Can., Feb. 19, 1926; s. Abraham Isaac and Mary (Ballon) B.; m. Estelle Ruth Samuels, Nov. 22, 1953; 1 dau., Louis Ellen. B.A., Queen's U., Kingston, Ont., Can., 1948, M.A., 1950; Ph.D., Yale U., 1952. Research chemist DuPont of Can., Ltd., Kingston, Ont., 1954-60, Pulp and Paper Research Inst. Can., Pointe Claire, Que., 1960-67; sect. head Pointe Claire, 1967-77; div. dir. Pulp and Paper Research Inst. Can., 1977-80, asst. dir. research, 1980-81, assoc. dir. research, 1981—; research assoc. McGill U., Montreal, 1962—. Author: Natural and Synthetic Polymers, 1974; contbr. articles to profl. jours.; patentee in field. Pres. Youth Sci. Found., Ottawa, 1965-66; sec. Lakeshore Chamber Music Soc. Ste. Anne de Bellevue, Que., 1973-74; pres. Lakeshore Dog Tng. Assn., Pointe Claire, 1975-77; Served with Can. Army, 1944-45. Internat. Acad. Wood Sci. fellow, 1980. Fellow Chem. Inst. Can. (chmn. 1979-81, Montreal medal 1984), Royal Soc. Chemistry; mem. Am. Chem. Soc., Can. Pulp and Paper Assn.; Fellow Sigma Xi. Subspecialty: Wood chemistry. Office: McGill U Dept Chemistry Montreal PQ H3A 2T5 Canada

BOLL, DAVID JACKSON, chemist; b. Pioche, Nev., Sept. 17, 1948; s. Harold Samuel and Kathleen Elizabeth (Steele) B.; m. Sharon Lee Odle, May 22, 1971. B.S. in Chemistry, Westminster Coll., 1971. Research asst. dept. biochemistry U. Utah, Salt Lake City, 1971-77; sr. technician N-L Industries, Salt Lake City, 1977-81; sr. chemist Hercules Aerospace, Bacchus, Utah, 1981—. Contbr. articles to profl. jours. Mem. Am. Chem. Soc., Soc. for Advancement of Materials and Process Engring., U.S. Naval Inst. Current work: Special rheological studies of various polymer and graphite fiber composite systems; surface analysis of graphite fibers; fracture analysis of composite systems. Subspecialties: Aerospace engineering and technology; Surface chemistry. Home: 4562 Jarrah St Salt Lake City UT 84123 Office: Hercules Aerospace Bacchus Works MS 8132 TR Magna UT 84044

BOLLINGER, JOHN GUSTAVE, mechanical engineer; b. Grand Forks, N.D., May 28, 1935; s. Elroy William and Charlotte (Kirchner) B.; m. Heidelore Ladwig, Aug. 16, 1958; children: William, Kristin, Pamela. B.S., U. Wis., Madison, 1957; M.S., Cornell U., 1958; Ph.D., U. Wis., 1961. Asst. prof. U. Wis., Madison, 1961-65, asso. prof. dept. mech. engring., 1965-68, prof., 1968—, Bascom prof., 1973—, chmn. dept., 1975-79, dir. data acquisition and simulation lab., 1972-75; dean Coll. Engring. U. Wis., 1981—; chmn., dir. Unico Inc.; dir. Rexnard Inc., Nicolet Instrn. Corp., Andrew Corp., Kohler Corp., Astronautics Corp. Am. Contbr. articles to profl. jours. Bd. dirs. Madison Gen. Hosp. Fulbright postdoctoral fellow Aachen, Ger., 1962; vis. Fulbright prof. Cranfield (Eng.) Inst. Tech., 1980-81. Fellow ASME (Gustus L. Larson Meml. award 1976, Pi Tau Sigma Gold medal 1965, Donald P. Eckman award 1965, Centennial award 1980); mem. Am. Soc. Engring. Edn., Nat. Acad. Engring., Am. Welding Soc., Wis. Soc. Profl. Engrs., Nat. Soc. Profl. Engrs., Soc. Mfg. Engrs. (Research Medal award 1978), Sigma Xi. Club: Mendota Yacht. Patentee in field. Current Work: Robot intelligence, computer control of machines and processes, manufacturing systems. Subspecialties: Robotics; Systems engineering. Home: 6117 S Highlands Madison WI 53705 Office: 1513 University Ave Madison WI 53706

BOLLON, ARTHUR PETER, molecular geneticist, educator, administrator; b. N.Y.C., Dec. 15, 1942; s. Arthur and Emily B.; m. Rhonda Bollon; children: Marc, Erica. B.A., C.W. Post Coll., 1965; Ph.D., Rutgers U., 1970. Postdoctoral fellow Yale U., New Haven, Conn., 1970-71; asst. prof. U. Tex. Health Sci. Ctr., Dallas, 1972-78; chmn. dept. molecular genetics, dir. genetic engring. Wadley Insts. Molecular Medicine, Dallas, 1979—; adj. prof. U. Tex.-Dallas; adj. faculty U. Tex. Health Sci. Ctr., Dallas; cons. Diamond Shamrock Corp., Dallas, 1981, mem. sci adv. bd. Imuno Modulatory Lab., Houston, Am. Bionuclear, Emeryville, Calif. Editor: Recombinant DNA Products, 1984; assoc. editor Jour. Clin. Hematology and Oncology; contbr. articles to sci. publs. Vice pres. Dallas Chamber Orch.; mem. Dallas Symphony Guild, Dallas Ballet Barre Assn. Research grantee NSF, 1974-79; Research grantee NIH, 1980-85; Research grantee Am. Cancer Soc., 1974-76. Mem. Am. Soc. Biol. Chemists, Genetics Soc. Am., Am. Soc. Microbiologists, N.Y. Acad. Scis., Sigma Xi. Current Work: genetic engineering and analysis of human and yeast genes; gene and chromosome organization and expression; lymphokines—interferon and tumor necrosis factor. Subspecialties: Genetics and genetic engineering (biology); Enzyme technology. Office: Wadley Insts Molecular Medicine 9000 Harry Hines Blvd Dallas TX 75235

BOLT, BRUCE ALAN, seismologist, educator; b. Largs, Australia, Feb. 15, 1930; s. Donald Frederick and Arlene (Stitt) B.; m. Beverley Bentley, Feb. 11, 1956; children: Gillian, Robert, Helen, Margaret. B.S. with honors, New Eng. U. Coll., 1952; M.S., U. Sydney, Australia, 1954, Ph.D., 1959, D.Sc. (hon.), 1972. Math. master Sydney (Australia) Boys' High Sch., 1953; lectr. U. Sydney, 1954-61, sr. lectr., 1961-62; research seismologist Columbia U., 1960; dir. seismographic stas. U. Calif., Berkeley, 1963—, prof. seismology, 1963—, chmn. Grad. Council, 1980-82; Mem. com. on seismology Nat. Acad. Scis., 1966-72, mem. Day Fund Com., 1974-76; also chmn. nat. earthquake obs. com. 1979-81; mem. earthquake and wind forces com. VA, 1971-75; mem. Calif. Seismic Safety Commn., 1978—, chmn., 1984-86; earthquake studies adv. panel U.S. Geol. Survey, 1979-84, U.S. Geodynamics Com., 1979-84. Author, editor textbooks on applied math., earthquakes, geol. hazards and detection of underground nuclear explosions. Recipient H.O. Wood award in seismology, 1967, 72; Fulbright scholar, 1960; Churchill Coll. Cambridge overseas fellow, 1980. Fellow Am. Geophys. Union (mem. geophys. monograph bd. 1971-78, chmn. 1976-78), Geol. Soc. Am., Calif. Acad. Scis. (trustee 1981—, pres. 1982-85), Royal Astron. Soc.; mem. Nat. Acad. Engring., Seismol. Soc. Am. (editor bull. 1965-70, dir. 1973-76, pres. 1974-75), Internat. Assn. Seismology and Physics Earth's Interior (exec. com. 1964-67, v.p. 1975-79, pres. 1980-83), Earthquake Engring. Research Inst., Australian Math. Soc., Sigma Xi. Club: Univ. Research on dynamics, elastic waves, earthquakes, reduction geophys. observations; inferences on structure of earth's interior; cons. on seismic hazards. Subspecialties: Geophysics; Applied mathematics. Home: 1491 Greenwood Terr Berkeley CA 94708

BOLTON, CHARLES THOMAS, astronomer; b. Camp Forrest, Tenn., Apr. 15, 1943; s. Clifford Theordore and Pauline Grace (Voris) B. B.S., U. Ill., 1966; M.S., U. Mich., 1968, Ph.D., 1970. Postdoctoral fellow David Dunlap Obs. U. Toronto, 1970-73, asst. prof. astronomy, 1970-71; instr. astronomy Scarborough Coll., 1971-72; asst. prof. astronomy Erindale Coll., 1972-73; asst. prof. astronomy U. Toronto, 1973-76, assoc. prof., 1976-80; prof., assoc. dir. David Dunlap Obs., 1980—. Contbr. articles to sci. jours. Fellow Royal Soc. Can., mem. Internat. Astron. Union, Can. Astron. Soc., Am. Astron. Soc., Astron. Soc. Pacific, Royal Astron. Soc. Can., Sigma Xi. Current Work: Optical observations of stellar x-ray and radio sources, mass transfer in binary star systems, stellar mass loss, stellar atmospheres and envelopes, variable stars. Subspecialties: Optical astronomy; Ultraviolet high energy astrophysics. Home: 326 Palmer Ave Richmond Hill ON L4C 1P3 Canada Office: David Dunlap Observatory PO Box 360 Richmond Hill ON L4C 4Y6 Canada

BOMBIERI, ENRICO, mathematician; b. Milan, Italy, Nov. 26, 1940; came to U.S., 1977; s. Carlo and Luisa (Cambi) B.; m. Susan Russell, Jan. 21, 1967; 1 dau., Donata. Ph.D., U. Milan, 1963. Prof. U. Cagliari, Italy, 1965, U. Pisa, Italy, 1966-74, Scuola Normale Superiore, Pisa, 1974; prof. math. Inst. Advanced Study, Princeton, N.J., 1977—. Recipient Fields medal Internat. Math. Union, Vancouver, B.C., 1974; Balzan prize Rome, 1981. Mem. Am. Acad. Arts and Scis., Accademia Nazionale Delle Scienze (Italy), Accademia Nazionale dei Lincei (corr. mem., recipient Feltrinelli prize 1976, Balzan prize 1981). Office: Inst Advanced Study Princeton NJ 08540

BONA, CONSTANTIN A(TANASIE), immunologist, microbiologist, educator; b. Turnu, Severin, Rumania, July 5, 1934; came to U.S., 1977; s. Traian and Maria B.; m. Alexandra, Dec., 1968; 1 dau., Monique. M.D., Faculty Medicine Bucharest, Rumania, 1958; Ph.D. in Med. Scis, Postgrad. Sch. Medicine Bucharest, 1965; Docteur es Science Naturelles, Faculty Sci., Paris, 1972. Chief lab. Inst. Cantacuzene, Bucharest, 1961-62; research worker Inserm, Paris, 1967-71; maitre de Recherche Pasteur Inst., Paris, 1971-77; vis. scientist NIH, Bethesda, Md., 1977-79; prof. microbiology Mt. Sinai Med. Center, N.Y.C., 1979—. Author: books, including Lymphocytes and Idiotypes, 1980, Lymphocytic Regulations by Antibodies, 1981; contbr. numerous articles to profl. jours. Greek Orthodox. Patentee in field. Current Work: Immunology. Subspecialty: Immunobiology and immunology. Home: 406 E 73d St 5R New York NY 10021 Office: One Gustave L Levy Pl Microbiology New York NY 10029

BONAVENTURA, CELIA JEAN, biochemist. Assoc. prof. Duke U. Marine Lab., Beaufort, N.C. Subspecialty: Biochemistry (biology). Office: Duke U Marine Lab Beaufort NC 28516*

BONAVENTURA, JOSEPH, biochemist. Assoc. prof. Duke U. Marine Lab., Beaufort, N.C. Subspecialty: Biochemistry (biology). Office: Duke U Marine Lab Beaufort NC 28516*

BOND, CLIFFORD WALTER, virologist; b. Buffalo, Apr. 7, 1937; s. Walter F. and Eva M. B.; m. Pamela Jo Bond, Aug. 12, 1978; 1 dau., Tana E. Student, Cornell U., 1954-55; B.A., SUNY, Buffalo, 1966; postgrad., Case Western Res. U., 1967-69; Ph.D., U. Ky., 1973. Technician Case Western Res. U., 1966-67, research fellow, 1967-69, U. Ky., 1969-73, postdoctoral fellow, 1974; trainee U. Calif., San Diego, 1976-77, asst. research pathologist, 1977-78; asst. prof. microbiology Mont. State U., 1978-84, assoc. prof., 1984—. Contbr. in field. Leukemia Soc. Am. fellow, 1976-78. Mem. Am. Soc. Microbiology; mem. Am. Soc. Virology; Mem. AAAS. Current Work: Molecular biology of pathogenic viruses. Subspecialties: Virology (biology); Molecular biology. Home: 9552 Cougar Dr Bozeman MT 59715 Office: Department Microbiology Montana State University Bozeman MT 59717

BOND, MEREDITH GENE, comparative medicine researcher, educator, consultant; b. Schenectady, Mar. 8, 1940; s. Frank Chester and Margaret (Schaller) B.; m. Mary Rose Crew, Sept. 3, 1972; 1 child, Kathleen Renee. B.S., Ohio State U., 1968, M.S. in Pathology, 1971, M.S. in Anatomy, 1974, Ph.D., 1975. Instr. pathology Ohio State U., Columbus, 1971-75; instr. Bowman Gray Sch. Medicine, Winston-Salem, N.C., 1975-76, asst. prof., 1976-82, assoc. prof. comparative medicine, 1982—; cons. pharm. industries, U.S., S.Am., W.Ger., 1979—. Author: Clinical Diagnosis of Atherosclerosis, 1982. Contbr. numerous articles to profl. jours. Served with AUS, 1958-61. NIH grantee, 1975—. Fellow Arteriosclerosis Council and Stroke Council of Am. Heart Assn. Current work: Atherosclerosis-progression and regression; animal models of atherosclerosis; high-resolution B-mode ultrasonography; morphometry; noninvasive detection; quantification and monitoring of atherosclerosis; clinical trials; drug intervention. Subspecialties: Pathology (medicine); Ultrasound. Office: Dept Comparative Medicine Bowman Gray Sch Medicine 300 S Hawthorne Rd Winston-Salem NC 27103

BOND, WILLIAM HOLMES, scientist; b. Toronto, Ont., Can., Sept. 20, 1916; s. Ernest Albert and Edna Lucille (Haines) B.; m. Virginia King, Jan. 3, 1949 (dec.); children: Roy Alan, James King, Robert Simpson, Linda Jane. B.S., U. Chgo., 1940, M.D., 1942. Diplomate: Am. Bd. Internal Medicine. Intern Vanderbilt U. Hosp., Nashville, 1942-43; resident in internal medicine Ind. U. Med. Ctr., 1948-51; instr. medicine Ind. U., 1952-55, asst. prof., 1955-60, assoc. prof., 1960-67, prof., 1967-85, prof. emeritus, 1985—. Contbr. articles on chemotherapy to med. jours. Served to capt. AUS, 1944-46. Fellow ACP; mem. AMA, Am. Soc. Hematology, Central Soc. Clin. Research, Am. Assn. Cancer Research, Phi Betta Kappa, Sigma Xi, Alpha Omega Alpha. Republican. Roman Catholic. Current Work: Cancer chemotherapy. Subspecialties: Chemotherapy; Hematology. Home: 4525 W 59th St Indianapolis IN 46254 Office: 1828 N Illinois St Indianapolis IN 46202

BONDURANT, BYRON LEE, agricultural engineering educator; b. Lima, Ohio, Nov. 11, 1925; s. Earl Smith and Joyce Koneta (Gesler) B.; m. Lovetta May Alexander, Feb. 28, 1944; children—Connie Jane Jaycox, Richard Thayne, Cindy Lynn Gardino. B.Agr. Eng., Ohio State U., 1949; M.S., U. Conn., 1953; postgrad Purdue U., 1958-59. Registered profl. engr., Maine, Ohio, Kenya, India; registered land surveyor, Maine. Dist. extension agrl. engr. Cornell U., Ithaca, N.Y., 1949-50; instr., ext. agrl. engr. U. Conn., Storrs, 1950-53; assoc. prof., extension agr. engr. U. Del., Newark, 1953-54; prof., head agr. engring. dept. U. Maine, Orono, 1954-64; dean, adviser to dean Punjab Agr. U., Ludhiana, Punjab, India, 1965-72; prof., agrl. engring. Ohio State U., Columbus, 1964—; vis. prof. U. Nairobi, 1974; mgr. UNDP/FAO project Ohio State U., Mogadiscio, Somalia, 1976-78. Author: Agriculture and Forest Hydrology, 1982; contbr. articles to profl. jours. Chmn., Orono PTA, 1959-62; chmn. bd. trustees Nazarene Ch., Bangor, Maine, 1960-64; dep. dir. Civil Def., Orono, 1962-64. Fulbright prof. U. Nairobi, 1979-80. Fellow AAAS, Am. Soc. Agrl. Engrs. (dir. 1980-82; Kishida Internat. award 1983); mem. Am. Soc. Engring. Edn. (chmn. internat. div. 1985-86). Current work: Agricultural engineering administration; international institutional development; appropriate technology. Subspecialties: Agricultural engineering; Civil engineering. Home: 265 Franklin St Dublin OH 43017 Office: Ohio State U 2073 Neil Ave Columbus OH 43210

BONDURANT, STUART, physician, educational administrator; b. Winston-Salem, N.C., Sept. 9, 1929; s. Stuart Osborne B.; m. Margaret Fortescue, Aug. 28, 1954; children—Stuart, Margaret Lynn, Nancy Vance. B.S., Duke U., 1952, M.D., 1953; Sc.D. (hon.), Ind. U., 1980. Intern Duke Hosp., Durham, N.C., 1953-54, resident in internal medicine, 1954-55; resident Peter Bent Brigham Hosp., Boston, 1958-59; asst. prof. medicine Ind. U. Sch. Medicine, Indpls., 1959-61, asso. prof., 1961-66, prof., 1966-67; asso. dir. Ind. U. Cardiovascular Research Center, 1961-67; chief med. br. artificial heart-myocardial infarction program NIH, Bethesda, Md., 1966-67; prof. medicine, chmn. dept., physician in chief Albany Med. Center Hosp., 1967-74; pres., dean Albany (N.Y.) Med. Coll., 1974-79; prof. medicine, dean Sch. Medicine, U. N.C., Chapel Hill., 1979—. Contbr. articles to med. jours. Recipient Disting. Alumnus award Duke U. Sch. Medicine, 1974; Merit award Am. Heart Assn., 1975. Fellow A.C.P. (regent, pres. 1980), Am. Soc. Clin. Investigation (v.p. 1974), Assn. Am. Physicians (treas. 1974), Inst. of Medicine, Assn. Am. Med. Colls. (exec. com. 1977, adminstrv. bd. of council deans). Subspecialty: Medical institution administration. Office: U NC Sch Medicine 125 MacNider Bldg #202H Chapel Hill NC 27514

BONDY, JONATHAN, computer systems engineer; b. Atlanta, Apr. 29, 1951; s. Phillip Kramer and Sarah Berheim (Ernst) B. B.S. in Math., Haverford Coll., 1973. Cons. to dir. advanced devel. orgn. Burroughs Corp., 1973-74; programmer Ketron, Inc., 1974-77; computer systems engr. Gen. Electric Space Div., King of Prussia, Pa., 1977-79, 1982-84; project mgr., computer systems engr. Energy Data Systems, Wayne, Pa., 1979-81; ind. cons., 1984—. Contbr. articles to profl. jours. Mem. IEEE, Assn. Computing Machinery, UCSD p-System Users Soc., Phila. Area Computer Soc. Current Work: Software tools, Modula-2, real-time multi-tasking applications. Subspecialties: Software engineering; Programming languages. Home: Box 148 Ardmore PA 19003

BONDYBEY, VLADIMIR EDMUND, chemist; b. Prague, Czechoslovakia, Jan. 4, 1942; s. Edmund T. and Marie (Kovarikova) B.; m. Dinny R. Burian, June 19, 1965; children—Renee Marie, Andrea Lynn, Frances Caroline. RNDr., Charles U., Prague, 1967; Diplomchemiker, U. Rostock, German Dem. Republic, 1966; Ph.D., U. Calif., Berkeley, 1972. Asst. prof. Charles U., Prague, 1967-69; postdoctoral assoc. Oreg. State U., Corvallis, 1972-73; mem. tech. staff AT&T Bell Labs., Murray Hill N.J., 1973—. Mem. adv. edit. bd. Chem. Physics Letters, 1980—; edit. bd. Jour. Chem. Physics, 1984—; editor: Molecular Ions: Spectroscopy, Structure and Chemistry, 1984; contbr. articles to profl. jours. Patentee in fiber optics. Recipient Disting. Mem. Tech. Staff award Bell Labs., 1984. Fellow Am. Phys. Soc.; mem. Am. Chem. Soc., AAAS, Sigma Xi. Roman Catholic. Current work: Photochemistry; photophysics and spectroscopy of small molecules; molecular ions and free radicals; studies of metal clusters; laser induced chemistry and nonradiative transitions. Subspecialties: Physical chemistry; Atomic and molecular physics. Office: AT&T Bell Labs Rm 1D 348 Murray Hill NJ 07974

BONE, DONALD ROBERT, microbiologist/hybridoma technologist, virologist; b. Minot, N.D., July 13, 1944; s. Lawrence Henry and Ora Marie (Sather) B.; m. Jeri Faye Selleseth, Aug. 27, 1966; children: Aaron, Adam. B.A., Pasadena Coll., 1966; Ph.D. in Microbiology, U. Calif.-Davis, 1971. Postdoctoral fellow Baylor Coll. Medicine, Houston, 1971-74; research virologist Lederle Labs., Pearl River, N.Y., 1974-77; postdoctoral fellow Salk Inst., La Jolla, Calif., 1977-78; asst. prof. U. Okla.-Norman, 1978-81, adj. asst. prof. zoology, 1981—; dir. research and devel. Celtek, Inc., Norman, 1981—; adj. asst. prof. microbiology and immunology U. Okla. Coll. Medicine-Oklahoma City, 1980—. Contbr. articles to profl. jours. Mem. AAAS, Am. Soc. Microbiology. Current Work: The development and characterization of monoclonal antibodies specific for microbial pathogens, hormones, and other molecules of clinical significance. Subspecialties: Hybridoma technology; Cellular engineering. Office: 102 W Eufaula St Norman OK 73069

BONNER, JAMES, educator; b. Ansley, Nebr., Sept. 1, 1910; s. Walter Daniel and Grace (Gaylord) B.; m. Ingelore Silberbach, Nov. 10, 1967; children by previous marriage—Joey, James Jose. A.B., U. Utah, 1931; Ph.D., Calif. Inst. Tech., 1934. NRC fellow Univs. Utrecht, Leiden, Zürich, 1934-35; faculty Calif. Inst. Tech., Pasadena, 1935-81, prof. biology, 1946-81; chmn. bd., chief exec. officer Phytogen, Inc., 1981—. Author: Plant Biochemistry, 1950, 3d edit., 1977, Principles of Plant Physiology, 1952, The Next 100 Years, 1957, The Nucleohistones, 1964, The Molecular Biology of Development, 1965, The Next 90 Years, 1967, The Next 80 Years, 1977. Mem. Nat. Acad. Sci. Current Work: Research in gentic engineering for plants. Subspecialties: Genetics and genetic engineering (agriculture); Molecular biology. Home: 1914 Edgewood Dr South Pasadena CA 91030

BONNER, JAMES JOSE, biology educator; b. Los Angeles, May 1, 1950; s. James Frederick and Harriet (Rees) B.; m. Monica Atkinson, Mar. 16, 1974; 1 child, James Justin. Ph.D., M.I.T., 1976. Am. Cancer Soc. postdoctoral fellow U. Calif.-San Francisco, 1977-78; asst. prof. biology Ind. U., Bloomington, 1979-85, assoc. prof. biology, 1985—. Contbr. articles to profl. jours. Am. Cancer Soc. fellow, 1977-78, 82-85; NIH research grantee, 1979—; NSF research grantee, 1985—. Mem. Genetics Soc. Am., Am. Soc. Cell Biology, Am. Soc. Developmental Biology. Current Work: Molecular and genetic analysis of hyperthermic stress; mechanisms of induction of heat shock-induced proteins and mechanisms whereby these proteins protect cells from lethality at high temperatures. Subspecialties: Molecular biology; Gene actions. Office: Dept Biology Ind U Bloomington IN 47405

BONNER, JOHN TYLER, biology educator; b. N.Y.C., May 12, 1920; s. Paul Hyde and Lilly Marguerite (Stehli) B.; m. Ruth Anna Graham, July 11, 1942; children: Rebecca, Jonathan Graham, Jeremy Tyndall, Andrew Duncan. Grad., Phillips Exeter Acad., 1937; B.Sc., Harvard U., 1941, M.A., 1942, Ph.D. (Jr. fellow 1942, 46-47), 1947; D.Sc. (hon.), Middlebury Coll., 1970. Asst. to asso. prof. Princeton U., 1947-58, prof., 1958—, chmn. dept. biology, 1965-77,

83-84; lectr. embryology Marine Biol. Lab., Woods Hole, Mass., 1951-52; spl. lectr. U. London, 1957; Bklyn. Coll., 1966; trustee Biol. Abstracts, 1958-63; Mem. bd. editors Princeton U. Press, 1965-68, 71, trustee, 1976-82. Author: Morphogenesis, 1952, Cells and Societies, 1955, The Evolution of Development, 1958, The Cellular Slime Molds, 1959, rev. edit. 1967, The Ideas of Biology, 1962, Size and Cycle, 1965, The Scale of Nature, 1969, On Development, 1974, The Evolution of Culture in Animals, 1980, (with T.A. McMahon) On Life and Size, 1983; also scientific papers.; Editor: Growth and Form, 1961, Evolution and Development, 1981; Asso. editor: Am. Scientist, 1961-69; editorial bd.: Am. Naturalist, 1958-60, 66-68, Jour. Gen. Physiology, 1962-69, Growth, 1955—, Differentiation, 1976—. Served from pvt. to 1st lt. USAC, 1942-46; staff aero. med. lab. Wright Field, Dayton, Ohio. Sheldon traveling fellow Panama, 1941; Rockefeller traveling fellow France, 1953; Guggenheim fellow Scotland, 1958, 71-72; recipient Selman A. Waksman award for contbns. to microbiology Theobold Smith Soc.; NSF sr. postdoctoral fellow, 1963. Fellow Am. Acad. Arts and Scis.; mem. Am. Soc. Naturalists, Soc. Growth and Devel., Mycol. Soc. Am., Am. Philos. Soc., Nat. Acad. Scis., Phi Beta Kappa, Sigma Xi. Current Work: Development of cellular slime molds, evolution and development. Subspecialties: Developmental biology; Evolutionary biology.

BONNER, WILLIAM DARRELL, meteorologist; b. rochester, Minn., Apr. 28, 1933; s. Walter E. and Ruth W. (Evesmith) B.; m. Nancy Kay Moore, May 22, 1985; 1 child, Thomas. B.S., U. Chgo., 1952, M.S., 1960, Ph.D., 1965; B.S., Pa. State U., 1954. Asst. prof. meteorology UCLA, 1965-70; research meteorologist Nat. Weather Service, Washington, 1970-76, dir. eastern region, Garden City, N.Y., 1976-79, dep. dir. Nat. Weather Service, Silver Spring, Md., 1979-81, dir. Nat. Meteorol. Ctr., Camp Springs, Md., 1981—. Author: (with others) (textbook) Understanding our Atmospheric Environment, 1973. Served to 1st lt., USAF, 1953-58. Ford Found. fellow, 1960-62; recipient Meritorious Exec. award Fed. Govt., 1982. Fellow Am. Meteorol. Soc. (councilor 1978-80); mem. Am. Oceanic Orgn. Current work: Numerical weather prediction Subspecialty: Meteorology. Office: Nat Meteor Ctr 5200 Auth Rd Camp Springs MD 20233

BONNET, JUAN AMEDEE, nuclear engineer, environmental research administrator; b. Santurce, P.R., Apr. 22, 1939; s. Juan A. and Josefa L. (Diez) B.; m. Wally Vargas, Dec. 27, 1963; children: Juan, Carlos, Antonio, Luis, Gerardo, Gabriel. B.S. in Chem. Engring, U. Mich., 1960, Ph.D. in Nuclear Engring, 1971; M.S. in Nuclear Tech, U. P.R., 1961. Registered profl. engr., P.R. Safety and analysis engr. P.R. Water Resources Authority, 1962-67, head nuclear engring. dept., 1971-73, head environ. protection, quality assurance and nuclear divs., 1972-75, asst. exec. dir. planning and engring., 1975-77; dir. Center for Energy and Environment Research, U. P.R., San Juan, 1977—; mem. adj. faculty P.R. Technol. U., 1973-77; adhonorem prof. Sch. Medicine, San Juan, 1979—; adj. prof. Engring. Sch. Mayaguez, P.R., 1979-80; asst. prof. Bayamon Technol. U. Coll., 1980—; cons. Energy and Environ. Engring., 1971—; pres. Profl. Engrs., Architects and Surveyors Exam. Bd. P.R., 1979—. Contbr. articles on energy and environ. matters to profl. publs. Bd. dirs. Rincon Fund Raising, P.R. Soc. Mentally Retarded Children, 1967; mem. Caribbean Islands Directorate of UNESCO-U.S. Com. Men and the Biosphere, 1979—; bd. dirs. U. P.R., 1978—, So. Solar Energy Center, 1979-82. Named Outstanding Young Scientist of P.R. Jaycees, 1978, Disting. Engr.; Tau Beta Pi, 1978; Sci. award P.R. Mobil Oil, 1981; P.R. chemist award, 1984. Mem. Am. Nuclear Soc., P.R. Inst. Chem. Engrs. (pres. 1977-79), Interam. Confedn. Chem. Engrs. (gen. sec. 1976-78), Internat. Solar Energy Assn., Nat. Soc. Profl. Engrs., P.R. Chemist Soc. (editorial bd. 1979—), Pan Am. Union of Assns. Engrs. (energy com. 1972—), Assn. Energy Engrs. (cert. energy mgr.), Ateneo de P.R., P.R. Acad. Arts and Scis., Assn. Engrs. and Surveyors (dir. 1967-76), Dominican Republic Acad. Sci., N.Y. Acad. Sci., Sigma Xi, Phi Eta Mu. Roman Catholic. Subspecialty: Energy research administration. Home: Calle 1 No H-7 Los Frailes Norte Guaynabo PR 00657 Office: GPO Box 3682 San Juan PR 00936

BONVENTRE, JOSEPH VINCENT, nephrologist, researcher; b. Bklyn., May 13, 1949; s. Vincent and Philomena (Orsino) B.; m. Kristina Cannon; 1 dau., Joanna. B.S. with distinction, Cornell U., 1970; M.D., Harvard U., 1976, Ph.D., 1979. Diplomate: Am. Bd. Internal Medicine. Instr. medicine Harvard Med. Sch., Boston, 1980-81, asst. prof. medicine, 1981—; asst. medicine Mass. Gen. Hosp., Boston, 1981—. Author: Key References in Nephrology, 1982. Recipient NIH new investigator research award, 1980-83. Mem. Am. Soc. Nephrology, Am. Fedn. Clin. Research, Am. Physiol. Soc., Internat. Soc. Nephrology, N.Y. Acad. Scis., Tau Beta Pi, Phi Kappa Phi. Roman Catholic. Current Work: Cellular aspects of anoxic and ischemic injury; renal concentration mechanisms; cell volume regulation; cellular calcium homeostasis. Subspecialties: Nephrology; Cell biology (medicine). Home: 1 Sylvan Way Wayland MA 01778 Office: Mass Gen Hosp Fruit St Boston MA 02114

BOOKER, HENRY GEORGE, educator, scientist; b. Barking, Essex, Eng., Dec. 14, 1910; came to U.S., 1948, naturalized, 1952; s. Charles Henry and Gertrude Mary (Ratcliffe) B.; m. Adelaide Mary McNish, July 9, 1938; children—John Ratcliffe, Robert William, Mary Adelaide, Alice. Student, Palmer's Sch., Grays, Essex, 1921-30; B.A., Christ's Coll., Cambridge, 1933, Ph.D., 1936; Guggenheim fellow, Cambridge U., 1954-55. Fellow Christ's Coll., 1935-48; sci. officer Ministry Aircraft Prodn., London, 1940-45; lectr. Cambridge U., 1945-48; prof. elec. engring. Cornell U., 1948-65, dir. sch. elec. engring., 1959-63; asso. dir. Center Radio Physics and Space Research, IBM; prof. engring. and applied math., 1962-65; prof. applied physics U. Calif. at San Diego, 1965—. Author: An Approach to Electrical Science, 1959; A Vector Approach to Oscillations, 1965; Energy in Electro-magnetism, 1982; Cold Plasma Waves, 1984; also sci. papers on radio wave propagation. Jr. intermediate and sr. county scholarships Essex, Eng., 1920-30; Entrance scholarship Christ's Coll., 1930; Allen scholarship, 1934-35; Smith's prize, 1935; Duddell, Kelvin and instn. premiums Instn. Elec. Engrs., London, 1948-50. Fellow IEEE; mem. Nat. Acad. Scis., Internat. Union Radio Sci. (hon. pres. 1979—), Sigma Xi. Current Work: Electromagnetic theory and radio wave propagation. Subspecialties: Remote sensing (atmospheric science); Plasma physics. Home: 8696 Dunaway Dr La Jolla CA 92037 Office: Dept Electrical Engineering and Computer Sci U Calif at San Diego La Jolla CA 92093

BOOKSTEIN, ABRAHAM, information science educator; b. N.Y.C., Mar. 22, 1940; s. Alex and Doris (Cohen) B.; m. Marguerite Lindley Vickers, June 20, 1968. B.S., C.C.N.Y., 1961; M.S., U. Calif.-Berkeley, 1966; Ph.D., Yeshiva U.-N.Y.C., 1969; M.A., U. Chgo., 1970. Prof. info. sci. and behavioral scis. U. Chgo., 1970—. Editor: Prospects for Change in Bibliographic Control, 1977; editorial bd.: Library Quar., Info. Processing and Mgmt; dir.: ATLA Religion Indexes; contbr. articles in field to profl. jours. NSF grantee, 1981, 85; DFI (Sweden) grantee, 1982. Mem. Am. Soc. Info. Sci., Assn. Computing Machinery. Current Work: Application of probability theory to information retrieval systems; bibliometric distributions. Subspecialties: Information systems, storage, and retrieval (computer science); Operations research (mathematics). Home: 5445 S East View Park Chicago IL 60615 Office: U Chgo Grad Library Sch 1100 E 57th St Chicago IL 60637

BOONE, DONALD H(ERBERT), metallurgical research scientist, consultant, educator; b. Moline, Ill., Aug. 27, 1936; s. W. Donald and E. Eugenia (Duncan) B.; m. Karolin M., Aug. 18, 1956; children: Dana L.; Christina A., Cynthia J. B.S. with high honors, U. Ill., 1957, M.S., 1959, Ph.D., 1962. Supr. Pratt & Whitney Aircraft, East Hartford, Conn., 1961-74; tech. mgr. Airco Temescal, Berkeley, Calif., 1974-78; staff scientist Lawrence Berkeley Lab., U. Calif., Berkeley, 1979-84; cons. Boone & Assocs., Walnut Creek, Calif., 1984—; adj. prof. mech. engring. Naval Postgrad. Sch., 1978—; cons. high temperature materials and coatings. Contbr. numerous articles to profl. jours., confs. Served to 1st lt. C.E. U.S. Army, 1962-63. Mem. Am. Soc. Metals, AIME, ASME, AIEE, Am. Vacuum Soc. Patentee in field. Current Work: High temperature coatings and materials. Subspecialties: Metallurgy; High-temperature materials. Home: 2412 Cascade Dr Walnut Creek CA 94598 Office: Naval Postgrad Sch Dept Mech Engring Code 69 Bl Monterey CA 93943

BOOR, MYRON VERNON, psychologist, researcher; b. Wadena, Minn., Dec. 21, 1942; s. Vernon LeRoy and Rosella Katharine (Eckhoff) B. B.S., U. Iowa, 1945; M.S., So. Ill. U.-Carbondale, 1947, Ph.D., 1970; M.S. in Hygiene, U.Pitts., 1981. Cert. psychologist, Kans. R.I. Clin. psychology intern Galesburg (Ill.) State Research Hosp., 1968-69; research psychologist Milw. County Mental Health Ctr., Milw., 1970-72; asst. prof. psychology Ft. Hays State U., 1972-76, assoc. prof., 1976-79; NIMH postdoctoral fellow U. Pitts., 1979-81; psychologist, asst. prof. R.I. Hosp.-Brown U., 1981-. Contbr. articles to profl. jours. USPHS fellow, 1965-67; NIMH postdoctoral fellow, 1979-81. Mem. Am. Psychol. Assn., Am. Assn. Suicidology, Soc. Psychol. Study Social Issues, AAAS. Current Work: Social networks; psychosocial adjustment; psychiatric epidemiology; suicidology; psychopathology; clinical psychology. Subspecialties: Behavioral psychology; Social psychology. Home: 825 Pontiac Ave Apt 17302 Craston RI 02910 Office: Dept Psychiatry RI Hosp 593 Eddy St Providence RI 02902

BOOTH, JAMES ALBERT, research company executive; b. Salem, Ohio, Dec. 14, 1946; s. Kenneth Bishop and Helen Elizabeth (Kelly) B.; m. Anita Jean, Aug. 10, 1974; children—Jennifer Lynn, Stephen Andrew. B.S., Bowling Green State U., 1968, M.S., 1973; M.S. in Nuclear Engring, Ohio State U., 1974; M.S. in Engring. Mgmt., U. Dayton, 1982. Registered profl. engr., Ohio. Sr. research engr. Monsanto Research Corp., Dayton, Ohio, 1974-81, mgr. engring. research and devel., 1981-84, group leader non-destructive testing, Miamisburg, Ohio, 1984—; cons. in neutron and gamma sources. Contbr.: 18 articles on 19th-20th century physicist to Aca. Am. Ency, 1980. Served to sgt. U.S. Army, 1969-71, Vietnam. Decorated Bronze Star, Army Commendation medal. Mem. Am. Nuclear Soc., Am. Soc. Quality Control (cert. quality engr. 1979), ASME, Am. Soc. for Nondestructive Testing, History of Sci. Soc. Republican. Methodist. Current Work: Non-destructive testing of weapons components. Subspecialties: Nuclear engineering; Nuclear fission. Home: 3141 Westview Dr Xenia OH 45385 Office: Monsanto Research Corp MCR-Mound Miamisburg OH 45342

BOOTZIN, RICHARD RONALD, psychologist, educator; b. Milw., Feb. 25, 1940; s. Arnold and Evelyn (Myslis) B.; m. Maris Kay Pittelman, Dec. 27, 1959; children—Deborah Jeanne, Helaine Beth. B.S., U. Wis., 1963; M.S., Purdue U., 1966, Ph.D., 1968. Ward psychologist Palo Alto (Calif.) VA Hosp., 1967-68; mem. faculty Northwestern U., 1968—, prof. psychology, 1978—, chmn. dept., 1980—; vis. asso. prof. Stanford U., 1977-78; prin. investigator various grants, 1971—. Author books, papers, revs. in field; editorial cons. profl. jours. Fellow Am. Psychol. Assn.; mem. Assn. Advancement Behavior Therapy (dir. 1973-77, chmn. publs. bd. 1975-77), Sleep Research Soc. Jewish. Subspecialty: Behavioral psychology. Office: Dept Psychology Northwestern Univ Evanston IL 60201

BORCH, JENS, chemical engineer; b. Copenhagen, Jan 19, 1941; came to U.S., 1965; s. Kay and Inger (Harbom) B.; m. Dorothy May Jenson, Apr. 5, 1969; children—Susanne Dorothy, Inger Louise. M.S. Chem. Engring., Tech. U. Denmark, 1965; M.S., Forestry and Environ. Sci. Coll. SUNY, 1967, Ph.D., 1970. Fellow, Mellon Inst., Pitts., 1969-70; scientist Pulp and Paper Research Inst., Pointe Claire, Que., Can., 1970-76; tech. specialist, project mgr. Xerox Corp., Webster, N.Y., 1977-79; adv. engr IBM Corp., San Jose, Calif., Tucson and Boulder, Colo., 1979—. Contbr. articles to profl. jours. Mem. Am. Chem. Soc., Am. Phys. Soc., TAPPI. Current work: Natural polymers; synthetic polymers; physical fiber and paper properties. Subspecialties: Polymers (materials science); Polymer physics. Home: 6481 Frying Pan Rd Boulder CO 80301 Office: IBM Corp 55Q/023 PO Box 1900 Boulder CO 80301

BORCHARDT, JOHN KEITH, industrial chemist, petroleum engineer; b. Evanston, Ill., June 2, 1946; s. George Samuel and Martha Annette (Stein) B. B.S. in Chemistry, Ill. Inst. Tech., 1968; Ph.D. in Organic Chemistry, U. Rochester, 1973. Postdoctoral research assoc. U. Notre Dame, 1972-74; research chemist Hercules Inc., Wilmington, Del., 1974-77; devel. chemist Halliburton Services, Duncan, Okla., 1977-84; sr. research chemist Shell Oil Co., Houston, 1984—. Contbr. articles to profl. jours. Patentee in field. Mem. Am. Chem. Soc. (councilor 1983-84, local sect. chmn. 1981-82, coeditor Polymer Edn. Newsletter, 1984—), Soc. Petroleum Engrs., Clay Mineral Soc., Sigma Xi. Current work: Surfactant and foam technology for enhanced oil recovery, polymer technology for enhanced oil recovery and prevention of formation damage. Subspecialties: Organic chemistry; Polymer chemistry. Home: 8010 Vista del Sol Dr Houston TX 77083 Office: Shell Devel Co PO Box 1380 Houston TX 77001

BORDEN, ERNEST CARLETON, physician; b. Norwalk, Conn., July 12, 1939; s. Joseph Carleton and Violet Ernette (Lanneau) B.; m. Louise Dise, June 24, 1967; children: Kristin Louise, Sandra Lanneau. A.B., Harvard U., 1961; M.D., Duke U., 1966. Diplomate: Am. Bd. Internal Medicine. Intern Duke U. Med. Ctr., 1966-67; asst. resident in internal medicine Hosp. of U. Pa., 1967-68; med. officer Viropathology Lab., Nat. Communicable Disease Ctr., USPHS, Atlanta, 1968-70; clin. instr. dept. medicine Emory U. Sch. Medicine also Grady Meml. Hosp., Atlanta, 1968-70; mem. med. attending staff Peachtree Hosp., Atlanta; postdoctoral fellow oncology div. dept. medicine Johns Hopkins U. Sch. Medicine, Balt., 1970-73; asst. prof. div. clin. oncology and depts. human oncology and medicine Wis. Clin. Cancer Ctr., Univ. Hosps. and Sch. Medicine, U. Wis.-Madison, 1973-79, assoc. prof., 1979-83; prof. Wis. Clin. Cancer Ctr., Univ. Hosps. and Sch. Medicine, U. Wis-Madison, 1983—, Am. Cancer Soc. prof. clin. oncology, 1985—; chief div. clin. oncology William S. Middleton VA Hosp., 1977-81; cons. staff Madison Gen. Hosp., 1974—. Contbr. chpts. to books, articles to profl. jours.; editorial bd.: Jour. Interferon Research, 1980—; editorial bd: Cancer Immunology and Immunotherapy, 1981—, Jour. Biologic Response Modifiers, 1982—, Investigational New Drugs, 1982—. Mem. AAAS, ACP, Am. Soc. Microbiology, Am. Assn. Cancer Research, Am. Fedn. Clin. Research, Eastern Coop. Oncology Group, Am. Soc. Clin. Oncology, Am. Assn. Immunologists. Unitarian. Current Work: Mechanism of action and clinical application of immunomodulators, particularly interferons. Subspecialties: Cancer research (medicine); Immunopharmacology. Office: 600 Highland Ave K4/414 CSC Madison WI 53792

BORENSTEIN, JEFFREY MARK, business executive; b. Newton, Mass., June 5, 1946; s. Milton Conrad and D. Anne (Shapiro) R.; m. Margaret Ruth Beller, Dec. 4, 1977; children—Danielle Louise, David Bruce. A.B., Harvard U., 1968, A.M., 1971, Ph.D., 1975. Adj. asst. prof. physics U. N.H., 1975-76; exec. v.p. Sweetheart Paper Products Co., Inc., Chelsea, Mass., 1976-83, pres., 1983-84; mng. ptnr. Concorde Assocs., Boston, 1984—; sec. Md. Baking Co. of Atlanta, 1976-84. Mem. Am. Inst. Physics. Jewish (trustee 1980). Current Work: Gauge field theory. Subspecialty: Particle physics. Home: 200 Highland St West Newton MA 02165 Office: Concorde Assocs One Devonshire Pl Suite 2912 Boston MA 02109

BORES, LEO DANIEL, physician, consultant; b. Detroit, July 1, 1937; s. Leo Daniel and Mary (Gryskevich) B.; m. Sondra Lee Perkins, June 14, 1958 (div. Feb. 1972); children—Scott Frnaklin, Dawn Lynn; m. Leara Anne Madge, Mar. 15, 1972; children—Kelley Ann, Richard Eric. B.S., Wayne State U., 1958, M.D., 1962. Resident in ophthalmology Harper Hosp., Detroit, 1963, 65-68, clinic day chief, 1979-79; asst. clin. prof. Kresge Eye Inst., 1968-70; clinic day chief Children's Hosp. Mich., 1970-79; chief ophthalmology Rehab. Inst., Detroit; dir. Internat. Found. for Ophthalmology Research & Edn., Scottsdale, Ariz., 1979—, Bores Eye Inst., Scottsdale, 1981—; dir. edn. Vision Inst., Santa Anna, Calif., 1985—; cons. in field. Author: Lens Implants in Children, 1979. Contbr. articles to profl. jours. Mem. Pres. Inner Circle, Washington, 1985. Served to lt. U.S. Navy, 1963-65. Recipient award Paleologus Soc., 1980. Fellow Am. Acad. Ophthalmology; mem. Kerato-Rafractive Soc. (chmn. sci. adv. bd.). Current work: Radial keratotomy; refractive surgery Subspecialty: Ophthalmology. Office: Bores Eye Inst 7350 E Stetson Dr Scottsdale AZ 85251

BORGES, LAWRENCE FRANCIS, neurosurgeon, educator; b. N.Y.C., Aug. 8, 1953; B.A., Johns Hopkins U., 1974, M.D., 1977. Asst. prof. neurosurgery Mass. Gen. Hosp., Harvard U., Boston, 1984—. Contbr. articles to profl. jours. Van Wagenen fellow, 1983. Mem. AMA, Soc. for Neurosci., Mass. State Med. Soc., Congress Neurol. Surgeons, Phi Beta Kappa, Alpha Omega Alpha. Current work: Axonal sprouting; axonal transport; neural transplantation; cerebrospinal fluid shunt infections. Subspecialties: Neurosurgery; Regeneration. Office: Mass Gen Hosp Dept Neurosurgery 32 Fruit St Boston MA 02114

BORGMAN, CHRISTINE L., library and information science educator. Asst. prof. UCLA Grad. Sch. Library and Info. Sci. Subspecialty: Information systems (Information science). Office: UCLA Grad Sch Library and Info Sci Los Angeles CA 90024

BORGSTEDT, HAROLD HEINRICH, physician, pharmacologist, toxicologist; b. Hamburg, Germany, Apr. 21, 1929; s. Gustav Johannes and Anna Dorothea (Wulf) B.; m. Agneta D. von Rehren, May 11, 1957; children: Eric, Astrid. M.D., U. Hamburg, 1956. Intern Rochester (N.Y.) Gen. Hosp., 1956-57; fellow in anatomy and pharmacology U. Rochester Med. Center, 1957-60, instr., 1960-63, sr. instr., 1963-66, research sr. instr. in anesthesiology, 1963-66, asst. prof. pharmacology and toxicology. anesthesiology, 1966-83, research asst. prof. anesthesiology; v.p. Health Designs, Inc., 1983—; cons. in field. Contbr. articles to profl. jours., books. Mem. Am. Soc. Pharmacology and Exptl. Therapeutics, Soc. Toxicology, Drug Info. Assn., N.Y. Acad. Scis., Sigma Xi. Republican. Unitarian. Current Work: Clinical drug and device research; mathematical modelling and computer prediction of toxicity. Subspecialties: Pharmacology; Toxicology (medicine). Office: 183 Main St E Rochester NY 14604

BORISON, RICHARD LEWIS, neuropsychiatrist, psychiatry educator; b. Boston, Mar. 4, 1950; s. Melville and Faye (Golub) B. B.A., Boston U., 1972; Ph.D. in Pharmacology, Chgo. Med. Sch., 1975; M.D., U. Ill.-Chgo., 1977. Diplomate: Am. Bd. Nat. Med. Examiners. Asst. prof. pharmacology Chgo. Med. Sch., 1975-81; intern Mt. Sinai Hosp., Chgo., 1977-78; resident in psychiatry Ill. State Psychiat. Inst., Chgo., 1977-81; assoc. prof. psychiatry Med. Coll. Ga., Augusta, 1981—, dir. neuropsychopharmacology program, 1981—. Contbr. numerous sci. and psychiat. articles to profl. publs. Mem. Ill. Psychiatry Soc. (first prize 1975), Am. Psychiat. Assn., Soc. Biol. Psychiatry, Soc. Neuroscis. Current Work: Clinical neuropsychopharmacology and extrapyramidal movement disorders. Research on the therapeutics and side effects of psychoactive medication, and the teaching of the rational use of psychoactive agents in man. Subspecialties: Psychopharmacology; Neuropharmacology. Office: Downtown VA Med Center Psychiatry Service 116A-D Augusta GA 30910

BORKO, HAROLD, information scientist, psychologist, educator; b. N.Y.C., Feb. 4, 1922; s. George and Hilda (Karpel) B.; m. Hannah Levin, June 22, 1947; children: Hilda, Martin. Student, Coll. City N.Y., 1939-41; B.A., U. Calif. at Los Angeles, 1948; M.A., U. So. Calif., 1949, Ph.D. in Psychology, 1952. System tng. specialist Rand Corp., 1956-57; with System Devel. Corp., Santa Monica, Calif., 1957-68, asso. staff head lang. processing and retrieval staff, 1965-68; instr. psychology U. So. Calif., 1957-65; instr. Sch. Library Service U. Calif. at Los Angeles, 1965-68, prof. Grad. Sch. Library and Info. Sci., 1968—. Author: Computer Applications in the Behavioral Sciences, 1962, Automated Language Processing, 1967, Targets for Research in Library Education, 1973, (with H. Sackman) Computers and the Problems of Society, 1972, (with C. Bernier) Abstracting Concepts and Methods, 1975, Indexing Concepts and Methods, 1978; Asso. U.S. editor: Information Processing and Management, 1963—; editor: Academic Press Library and Information Science series, 1970—; book rev. editor: Jour. Ednl. Data Processing, 1963-75. Served with AUS, 1942-46; to capt., Med. Service Corps AUS, 1950-56. Mem. Am. Soc. for Info. Sci. (pres. 1966), Assn. Computing Machinery, Am. Psychol. Assn., Assn. Am. Library Schs., Am. Soc. Indexers, Phi Beta Kappa, Sigma Xi, Phi Gamma Mu. Current Work: Professor, Graduate school of Library information science. Subspecialties: Automated language processing; Information systems (Information science). Home: 11507 National Blvd Los Angeles CA 90064

BORLAUG, NORMAN ERNEST, agricultural scientist; b. Cresco, Iowa, Mar. 25, 1914; s. Henry O. and Clara (Vaala) B.; m. Margaret G. Gibson, Sept. 24, 1937; children: Norma Jean (Mrs. Richard H. Rhoda), William Gibson. B.S. in Forestry, U. Minn., 1937, M.S. in Plant Pathology, 1940, Ph.D. in Plant Pathology, 1941; Sc.D. (honoris causa), Punjab (India) Agrl. U., 1969, Royal Norwegian Agrl. Coll., 1970, Luther Coll., 1970, Uttar Pradesh Agrl. U., India, 1971, Kanpur U., India, 1970, Mich. State U., 1971, Universidad de la Plata, Argentina, 1971, U. Ariz., 1972, U. Fla., 1973; L.H.D., Gustavus Adolphus Coll., 1971; LL.D. (hon.), N.Mex. State U., 1973; D.Agr. (hon.), Tufts U., 1982; others. With U.S. Forest Service, 1935-36, 37, 38; instr. U. Minn., 1941; microbiologist E.I. DuPont de Nemours, 1942-44; research scientist in charge wheat improvement Coop. Mexican Agrl. Program, Mexican Ministry Agr.-Rockefeller Found., Mexico, 1944-60; assoc. dir. assigned to Inter-Am. Food Crop Program, Rockefeller Found., 1960-63; dir. wheat research and prodn. program Internat. Maize and Wheat Improvement Center, Mexico City, 1964-79; assoc. dir. Rockefeller Found., 1964—, cons., 1983—; cons., collaborator Instituto Nacional de Investigationes Agricolas, Mexican Ministry Agr., 1960-64; cons. FAO, North Africa and Asia, 1960; ex-officio cons. wheat research and prodn. problems to govts. in, Latin Am., Africa, Asia.; Mem. Citizen's Commn. on Sci., Law and Food Supply, 1973—, Commn. Critical Choices for Am., 1973—, Council Agr. Sci. and Tech., 1973—; dir. Population Crisis Com., 1971; asesor especial Fundacion para Estudios de la Poblacion A.C., Mexico, 1971—; mem. adv. council Renewable Natural Resources Found., 1973—. Recipient Distinguished Service awards Wheat Producers Assns., and state govts. Mexican States of Guanajuato, Queretaro, Sonora, Tlaxcala and Zacatecas, 1954-60; Recognition award Agrl. Inst. Can., 1966; Recognition award Instituto Nacional de Tecnologia Agropecuaria de Marcos Juarez, Argentina, 1968; Sci. Service award El Colegio de Ingenieros Agronomos de Mexico, 1970; Outstanding Achievement award U. Minn., 1959; E.C. Stakman award, 1961; named Uncle of Paul Bunyan, 1969; recipient Distinguished Citizen award Cresco Centennial Com., 1966; Nat. Distinguished Service award Am. Agrl. Editors Assn., 1967; Genetics and Plant Breeding award Nat. Council Comml. Plant Breeders, 1968; Star of Distinction Govt. of Pakistan, 1968; citation and street named in honor Citizens of Sonora and Rotary Club, 1968; Internat. Agronomy award Am. Soc. Agronomy, 1968; Distinguished Service award Wheat Farmers of Punjab, Haryana and Himachal Pradesh, 1969; Nobel Peace prize, 1970; Diploma de Merito El Instituto Tecnologico y de Estudios Superiores de Monterrey, Mexico, 1971; medalla y Diploma de Merito Antonio Narro Escuela Superior de Agricultura de la U. de Coahuila, Mexico, 1971; Diploma de Merito Escuela Superior de Agricultura Hermanos Escobar, Mexico, 1973; award for service to agr. Am. Farm Bur. Fedn., 1971; Outstanding Agrl. Achievement award World Farm Found., 1971; Medal of Merit Italian Wheat Scientists, 1971; Service award for outstanding contbn. to alleviation of world hunger 8th Latin Am. Food Prodn. Conf., 1972; named to Oreg. State U. Agrl. Hall of Fame, 1981; numerous other honors and awards from govts., ednl. instns., citizens groups. Hon. fellow Indian Soc. Genetics and Plant Breeding; mem. Nat. Acad. Sci., Am. Soc. Agronomy (1st Internat. Service award 1960, 1st hon. life mem.), Am. Assn. Cereal Chemists (hon. life mem., Meritorious Service award 1969), Crop Sci. Soc. Am. (hon. life mem.), Soil Sci. Soc. Am. (hon. life mem.), Sociedad de Agronomia do Rio Grande do Sul Brazil (hon.), India Nat. Sci. Acad. (fgn.), Royal Agrl. Soc. Eng. (hon.), Royal Soc. Edinburgh (hon.), Hungarian Acad. Sci. (hon.), Royal Swedish Acad. Agr. and Forestry (fgn.), Academia Nacional de Agronomia y Veterinaria (Argentina); hon. academician N.I. Vavilov Acad. Agrl. Scis. Lenin Order (USSR.). Address: Centro Internacional de Mejoramiento del Maiz y del Trigo Apartado Postal 6-641 Londres 40 Mexico City 6 Mexico

BORNS, DAVID JAMES, geologist, researcher; b. Phila., Feb. 10, 1950; s. William Joseph and Patricia (Flint) B. B.A., Dartmouth Coll., 1972; M.Sc., U. Otago, Dunedin, N.Z., 1975; Ph.D., U. Wash., 1980. Research asst. U. Wash., Seattle, 1976-79, research assoc., 1979-81; mem. tech. staff Sandia Nat. Labs., Albuquerque, 1981—. Contbr. articles to profl. jours. Counselor U. N.Mex. Crisis Ctr., Albuquerque, 1983—. Fellow NSF, 1972, AMOCO Found., 1978; Fullbright grantee U.S.-N.Z. Ednl. Found., 1972-75. Mem. Geol. Soc. Am. (research grantee 1978). Democrat. Unitarian. Current work: Geologic characterization of sites for nuclear waste disposal, the role of fluids in deformation. Subspecialties: Geology; Hazardous waste disposal. Home: 3615 Mackland NE Albuquerque NM 87110 Office: Earth Sci Div Sandia Nat Labs (6331) Albuquerque NM 87185

BORNSTEIN, JOSEPH, agricultural engineer, consultant; b. Boston, June 24, 1921; s. Julius and Minnie (Greenberg) B.; children—Lise, Benjamin J. B.S., U. Mass.-Amherst, 1947; M.S., Mich. State U., 1949. Registered profl. engr., Vt., N.H. Agrl. engr. U.S. Soil Conservation Service, Waltham and Chelmsford, Mass., 1949-52, Plattsburg, N.Y., 1953, civil engr. design, Upper Darby, Pa., 1954-57; agrl. engr. U.S. Agrl. Research Service, Burlington, Vt., and Orono, Maine, 1957-85; asst, prof. agrl. engring. U. Vt.-Burlington, 1961-71, adj. assoc. prof., 1971-75, faculty assoc., 1975-85; cons. agrl. engr., 1985—. Contbr. articles to tech. jours. Served with USAAF, 1942-45. Fellow Soil Conservation Soc. Am.; mem. Am. Soc. Agrl. Engrs. (chmn. North Atlantic region 1970-71), Nat. Soc. Profl. Engrs., Boston Soc. Civil Engrs., Can. Soc. Agrl. Engring., Sigma Xi. Current work: Drainage research of sloping fragipan soils and of clay soils forage and feed production in cool climates. Subspecialty: Agricultural engineering. Office: 465 North St Burlington VT 05401

BOROCHOFF, ROBERT M., research computer scientist; b. Tulsa, Jan. 24, 1956; s. Stan J. and Jean (Halff) B. B.S. Computer Sci, U.S.C., 1978; M.S.C.S., U. Md., 1980. Computer specialist Nat. Library Medicine, Bethesda, Md.,

1982; research computer scientist Fed. Jud. Center, Washington, 1982—. Adv. council Internat. Policy Inst., Washington, 1981—; co-chmn. Human Rights, Internat., 1982—. Exec. bd. Unicorn, fed. govt. Unix users group, 1983—. Recipient Burroughs Corp. scholarship, 1976. Mem. ACM, IEEE, IEEE Soc. for Social Implications of Tech. (sec. Washington chpt. 1985—), AAAS, Software Psychology Soc. Democrat. Jewish. Current Work: Current research and work interests: design and implementation of computerized court management systems for the fed. judiciary. Areas of work include distributed systems, networks, databases and human factors. Subspecialties: Information systems, storage, and retrieval (computer science); Distributed systems and networks. Home: 4615 North Park Ave Apt 1114 Chevy Chase MD 20815 Office: Fed Jud Ctr 1520 H St NW Washington DC 20005

BORON, DAVID JOHN, chemist, energy researcher; b. Shadyside, Ohio, Mar. 10, 1953; s. Manuel John and Sophia Cecilia (Wonsik) B.; m. Audrey Marie Slimak, Nov. 24, 1979. B.A., Miami U., Oxford, Ohio, 1975; M.S., Duquesne U., 1983. With Wheeling-Pitts. Steel Co., W.Va., 1976; research chemist U.S. Dept. Energy, Pitts., 1977-83; sr. project mgr. N.Y. State Energy Research and Devel. Authority, Albany, 1983—, environ. coordinator, 1983—. Contbr. articles to profl. jours. Program vice chmn. United Way-State Employees Federated Appeal, Albany, 1984-85; active Cerebral Palsy Ctr. for Disabled, Albany, 1984—; judge N.Y. State Student Energy Research Competition, 1984—. Recipient Outstanding Performance awards U.S. Dept. Energy, Pitts., 1982, 83. Mem. Am. Chem. Soc. (session chmn. nat. meeting 1985, editor conf. proc. 1985), Soc. Analytical Chemists, Soc. Mining Engrs. of AIME, AAAS, Nat. Geog. Soc. Roman Catholic. Club: Century 21 (Albany). Current work: Physical, chemical and microbial methods of cleaning coal to provide low-sulfur, low-ash and high-BTU fuel; acid rain formation - causes, mitigation and mechanism of formation. Subspecialties: Coal; Atmospheric chemistry. Office: New York State Energy Research and Devel Authority Two Rockefeller Plaza Albany NY 12223

BOROS, EUGENE JOSEPH, See *Who's Who in America*, 43rd edition. .

BOROWITZ, GRACE BURCHMAN, chemistry educator, researcher; b. N.Y.C., Dec. 7, 1934; d. Hyman and Edith (Cohen) Burchman; m. Irving J. Borowitz, Nov. 26, 1959; children: Susan Debra, Lisa Naomi. B.S., CCNY, 1956; M.S., Yale U., 1958, Ph.D. in Organic Chemistry, 1960. Research chemist Am. Cyanamid, Stamford, Conn., 1960-62; lectr. Yeshiva Coll., N.Y.C., 1967; asst. prof. chemistry Upsala Coll., East Orange, N.J., 1967-73; asst. prof. Ramapo Coll. of N.J., Mahwah, 1973-75, assoc. prof., 1975-80, prof., 1980—. Contbr. articles on chemistry to profl. jours. NSF grantee, 1971, 85; Ramapo Faculty Devel. research grantee, 1975-85; recipient Florence Thomas Faculty Research award Ramapo Coll., 1981. Fellow AAAS; mem. Am. Chem. Soc., N.Y. Acad. Scis. (award 1976), N.J. Acad. Scis., Sigma Xi. Democrat. Jewish. Current Work: Synthesis and complexing of ionophores with cations. Subspecialty: Organic chemistry.

BORRA, ERMANNO FRANCO, physicist, researcher; b. Gattinara, Vercelli, Italy, Mar. 23, 1943; came to Can., 1968; s. Paolo and Mary (Beretta) B.; m. Rosa Maria Rivera, July 19, 1978. B.Sc./D.Sc. in Physics, U. Torino, 1967; Ph.D. in Astronomy, U. Western Ont., 1972. Carnegie fellow Hale Obs., Pasadena, Calif., 1972-75; prof. physics Laval U., Quebec City, Que., 1975-81, prof., 1982—; vis. scientist Steward Obs., Tucson, 1981-82. Current work: Cosmology-deep sky surveys-instrumentation. Subspecialties: Cosmology; Theoretical astrophysics. Office: Laval U Dept Physics Quebec PQ G1K 7P4 Canada

BORRESEN, C. ROBERT, psychology educator; b. Chgo., July 12, 1926; s. Kristen and Dagny (Mathiesen) B.; m. Thelma Jasper, Dec. 28, 1966; 1 stepson, Mike Meacham. B.A., Northwestern U., 1953; M.A., U.Mo., 1958, Ph.D., 1968. Lic. psychologist, Kans. Instr. psychology U. Mo., Columbia, 1962-63; asst. prof. psychology Memphis State U., 1964-65; asst. prof. Wichita (Kans.) State U., 1965-73, assoc. prof., 1974—, chmn. dept. psychology, 1978-83; Mem. continuing edn. com. Behavioral Scis. Regulatory Bd. Kans., 1984—. expert witness perception and human factors various law firms. Contbr. articles to profl. jours. Treas. Re-election Com. Republican Meacham, Wichita, 1976, 78, 80, 82; advisor Behavioral Sci. Bd., Topeka, Kans., 1980-82. Served with USN, 1944-46. Wichita State U. grantee, 1976, 78, 80. Mem. Am. Psychol. Assn., Southwestern Psychol. Assn., Midwestern Psychol. Assn., Kans. Psychol. Assn. (mem. practices and ethics com. 1984—), Wichita Area Psychol. Assn., Internat. Sci. Soc. for Polit. Psychology. Current Work: Empirical research on locus of control; research in political behavior. Subspecialties: Psychophysics; Behavioral psychology. Home: 2215 Hathway Cir Wichita KS 67226 Office: Dept Psychology Wichita State U Wichita KS 67208

BORZELLECA, JOSEPH FRANCIS, pharmacologist, toxicologist, educator, cons.; b. Norristown, Pa., Oct. 3, 1930; s. Peter and Madeline (Fiorillo) B.; m. Mary Elizabeth Ford, Aug. 9, 1931; children: Joseph F., Paul, David, Michael, Therese Marie, Mark. B.S., St. Joseph U., Phila., 1952; M.S., Thomas Jefferson U., 1954, Ph.D., 1956. Instr., assoc. dept. pharmacology Med. Coll. Pa., Phila., 1956-59; asst. prof. pharmacology Med. Coll. Va., Richmond, 1959-62, assoc. prof., 1962-67, prof., 1967—, head div. toxicology, 1972—; pres. Toxicology and Pharmacology, Inc.; cons. FDA, NIMH, EPA, U.S. Army; chmn. carcinogens standards com. OSHA, Dept. Labor. Mem. editorial bd.: Toxicology and Applied Pharmacology, 1975-78, Jour. Environ. Pathology and Toxicology, 1977—, Pharmacology, 1978—, Jour. Environ. Sci. and Health, 1979—, Pharmacology and Drug Devel, 1980—, Jour. Cutaneous and Ocular Toxicology, 1981—; contbr. articles to profl. jours. Mem. AAAS, Am. Chem. Soc., Am. Coll. Toxicology, Am. Soc. Pharmacology and Exptl. Therapeutics, Soc. Exptl. Biology and Medicine (councilor, program chmn. Southeastern sect.), Soc. Toxicology (chmn. edn. com., sec. 1967-71, councilor 1971-72, pres. 1973-74, chmn. numerous coms.), Va. Acad. Sci. (chmn. med. scis. div.), Sigma Xi. Club: Cosmos (Washington). Current Work: Toxicology, safety evaluation, water contaminants, food safety. Subspecialties: Toxicology (medicine); Pharmacology. Home: 8718 September Dr Richmond VA 23229 Office: Med Coll Virginia Box 613 Richmond VA 23298

BOSHKOV, STEFAN HRISTOV, educator, mining engr.; b. Sofia, Bulgaria, Sept. 29, 1918; came to U.S., 1938, naturalized, 1944; s. Hristo and Karla (Lubich) B.; m. Bianca G. Amaducci, Aug 28, 1943; children—Lynn Karla, Stefan Robert. Diploma, Am. Coll., Sofia, Bulgaria, 1938; B.S., Columbia U., 1941, E.M., 1942. Mem. faculty Columbia, 1946—; prof. Henry Krumb Sch. Mines, 1951—, chmn., 1967—, Henry Krumb prof., 1980—; disting. prof., sr. scientist (Fulbright program), Yugoslavia, 1969, guest lectr., Taiwan, China, 1972, 76; guest lectr. OAS, Chile, 1972, USSR, 1974, Poland, 1976, Bulgaria, 1976, Bolivia, 1977, People's Republic of China, 1980, 81; cons. engr., 1950—; mem. internat. organizing com. World Mining Congress, 1962—; chmn. 4th Internat. Conf. Strata Control and Rock Mechanics, N.Y.C.; 1964; mem. adv. com. metal and nonmetallic health and safety standards Dept. Labor, 1978. Mem. editorial bd.: Internat. Jour. Rock Mechanics and Mining Scis, 1964-76. Pres. Benedict Found., 1973—, Harrison (N.Y.) No. 7 Sch. Bd., 1954-63. Served to lst lt. AUS, 1943-46, CBI. Recipient Boleslaw Krupinski medal State Mining Council Poland, 1980. Mem. AIME (Mineral Industry Edn. award 1980), Am. Arbitration Assn., Sigma Xi. Presbyterian. (trustee 1965-69). Club: Masons. Current Work: Strata control and rock mechanics; mine economics; consulting; school administration. Subspecialty: Coal. Home: 119 White Plains Ave White Plains NY 10604 Office: Mudd Bldg Columbia Univ New York NY 10027

BOSIN, TALMAGE RAYMOND, pharmacologist, educator, researcher; b. Fond du Lac, Wis., Mar. 6, 1941; s. Raymond W. and Edna S. B.; m. Elizabeth W. Witler, July 18, 1971; children: Sara, Catherine. B.S. in Chemistry, Wheaton (Ill.) Coll., 1963; Ph.D. in Organic Chemistry (NIH fellow), Ind. U., 1967. Mem. faculty Ind. U. Sch. Medicine, Bloomington, 1969—, assoc. prof. pharmacology, 1973-78, prof., 1978—. Contbr. articles to profl. jours. NIH postdoctoral fellow, 1967-69; sr. internat. fellow, 1977-78. Mem. Am. Soc. Pharmacology and Exptl. Therapeutics, Soc. Toxicology. Evangelical. Current Work: Effects of toxicants on vasoactive agent handling by the pulmonary microvasculature. Subspecialties: Pharmacology; Cellular pharmacology. Home: 1300 Valley Forge Bloomington IN 47401 Office: Ind U Myers Hall Bloomington IN 47405

BOSS, ALAN PAUL, astrophysicist; b. Lakewood, Ohio, July 20, 1951; s. Paul and Marguerite May (Gehringer) B.; m. Barbara Carol Woltz, Sept. 8, 1973; m. Catherine Ann Starkie, Aug. 4, 1979. B.S., U. South Fla., 1973; M.A., U. Calif.-Santa Barbara, 1975, Ph.D., 1979. Research asst. U. Calif.-Santa Barbara, 1974-79; resident research assoc. Nat. Acad. Scis./NRC, Ames Research Center, Calif., 1979-81; staff assoc. Carnegie Instn. Washington, 1981-83, staff mem., 1983—. Contbr. articles to profl. jours. Mem. Am. Astron. Soc., Am. Geophys. Union, AAAS. Democrat. Current Work: Theory of stellar and planetary system formation. Subspecialties: Theoretical astrophysics; Planetary science. Office: 5241 Broad Branch Rd NW Washington DC 20015

BOSSART, GREGORY DANA, veterinary pathologist, consultant; b. Pitts., May 5, 1951; s. Charles Dana and Lois Claire (Gregory-Capuder) B. B.A., U. Pitts., 1973, B.S. in Biology, 1973; V.M.D., U. Pa., 1978. Veterinarian exotic small animals Shank Animal Hosp., Ft. Lauderdale, Fla., 1978-81; cons. marine mammals Ocean World, Ft. Lauderdale, 1980—, Ocean Reef, Key Largo, 1979—; cons. sea turtle research U. Miami, 1981—, postdoctoral NIH fellow Div. Comparative Pathology, Sch. Medicine, 1981—; med. dir. Wildlife Vet. Ctr., Mus. Sci., Miami, 1980—; instr. U. Miami Marine Labs., 1983; adj. asst. prof. Sch. Marine and Atmospheric Sci., U. Miami, 1985—; adj. asst. prof. Sch. Medicine, 1985—. Contbr. articles to sci. jours. NIH fellow, 1983-85; recipient Dept. Interior Minerals Mgmt. Service Contract award, 1983—. Mem. Internat. Assn. Aquatic Animal Medicine, Am. Vet. Med. Assn., Soc. Marine Mammalogy, Am. Assn. Wildlife Veterinarians, Am. Assn. Vet. Labs. Diagnosticians, Broward Audubon Soc. (lectr. 1982-83), Tropical Audubon Soc. (lectr. 1982, 84). Presbyterian. Current work: Medicine of captive marine mammals and pathology of stranded cetaceans and sea turtles; avian medicine. Subspecialties: Pathology (veterinary medicine); Diseases of aquatic animals. Office: U Miami Sch Medicine Div Comparative Pathology (R-46) PO Box 016960 Miami FL 33101

BOSTON, JOHN ROBERT, medical computing researcher; b. Evanston, Ill., Oct. 16, 1942; s. John Robert and Elizabeth Louise (Olmstead) B.; m. Carol Lee Dillon, Oct. 23, 1971; children: Christopher, Patrick. B.S.E.E., Stanford U., 1964, M.S.E.E., 1966; Ph.D., Northwestern U., Chgo., 1971. Research assoc. Northwestern U., 1971-72; asst. prof. U. Md., College Park, 1972-75, Carnegie-Mellon U., Pitts., 1975-80; research assoc. prof. dept. anesthesiology and critical care medicine U. Pitts., 1980—. Contbr. articles to profl. jours., chpts. in books. Mem. AAAS, IEEE, Soc. Neurosci., Sigma Xi. Current Work: Acquisition and analysis of sensory evoked potentials. Subspecialties: Biomedical engineering; Neurophysiology. Home: 307 High Oaks Ct Wexford PA 15090 Office: U of Pitts 1060 J Scaife Hall Pittsburgh PA 15261

BOSTON, PENELOPE JANE ASHLEY, microbiologist, microbiol ecologist; b. St. Petersburg, Fla., Jan. 14, 1954; d. William Ashley and Eilene Elizabeth Moore (Marshall) B. B.S., Fla. Atlantic U., 1976; B.S., U. Colo., 1979, Ph.D., 1984. Researcher, Lab. for Atmospheric and Space Physics, Boulder, Colo., 1978-79; tchr. U. Colo., Boulder, 1980-82; researcher Nat. Ctr. Atmospheric Research, Boulder, 1982—; treas., Boulder Ctr. for Sci. and Policy, 1980—. Contbr. articles to profl. jours. Program producer Sta. KGNU Pub. Radio, Boulder, 1984. NASA biology fellow, 1980-81; Nat. Ctr. for Atmospheric Research fellow, 1982—; recipient Space Found. award, Houston, 1982; Fellow Phi Sigma Tau; mem. Am. Soc. Microbiology, Boulder Ctr. for Sci. and Policy, (bd. dirs. 1980—), Mars Inst. Planetary Soc. (adv. bd. 1982—), Am. Astron. Soc., Sigma Xi (research award). Current work: Global biogeochemical cycling especially the nitrogen cycle. Precambrian biology and its effects on the atmosphere and biogeochemistry of the period. Life support for Mars research base, spacecraft life support. Exobiology and planetary contamination issues. Subspecialty: Microbiology. Office: Nat Ctr Atmospheric Research Box 3000 Boulder CO 80307-3000

BOTEZ, DAN, semiconductor-device physicist; b. Bucharest, Romania, May 22, 1948; came to U.S. 1968, naturalized 1981; s. Emil and Ecaterina (Iacob) B.; m. Lynda Diane Arnold, Sept. 25, 1976; children—Anca, Adrian. B.E.E. with highest honors, U. Calif.-Berkeley, 1971, M.E.E., 1972, Ph.D. in Elect. Engring., 1976. Postdoctoral fellow IBM Labs., Yorktown Heights, N.Y., 1976-77; mem. tech. staff RCA Labs., Princeton, N.J., 1977-82, research leader, 1982-84; dir. device devel. Lytel Inc., Somerville, N.J., 1984—. Author: Electro-Optical Communications Dictionary, 1983. Patentee in field. Contbr. articles to profl. jours. Recipient RCA Outstanding Achievement award RCA Labs, 1979. Mem. IEEE (sr.; named Outstanding Young Engr., Centennial Key to Future award 1984), Optical Soc. Am., Phi Beta Kappa. Republican. Eastern Orthodox. Current work: High-power semiconductor diode lasers, phase-locked arrays of diode lasers, components for fiber-optical communications. Subspecialties: Semiconductor lasers; Electronic materials. Home: 44 Springhill Rd Randolph NJ 07869 Office: Lytel Inc 61 Chubb Way Somerville NJ 08876

BOTTARO, JEFFREY CHARLES, synthetic chemist; b. Buffalo, June 3, 1954; s. Andrew and Josephine (Gianoni) B.; m. Lisbeth M. Holley, June 12, 1980. B.S. in Medicinal Chemistry, SUNY-Buffalo, 1976; Ph.D., MIT, 1980. Research assoc., Northeastern U., Boston, 1980-81, Oxford U., Eng., 1981-83, Sacramento State U., Calif., 1983-84, SRI Internat., Menlo Park, Calif., 1984—. Mem. Am. Chem. Soc. Libertarian. Current work: Refining the methodology of chemical synthesis beyond existing boundaries. Home: 720 Coleman Ave Menlo Park CA 94025 Office: SRI Internat 333 Ravenswood St Menlo Park CA 94025

BOTTEMA, MURK, optical physicist; b. Velsen, Netherlands, May 23, 1923; came to U.S., 1958; s. Fokke and Eatske (Wijbenga) B.; m. Willy Tielrooy, Mar. 3, 1950; children: Frank, Murk Jan, Nicolaas. Ph.D. in Physics, U. Groningen, Netherlands, 1957. Research assoc. physics dept. U. Groningen, 1957-58, 60-62, Lab. for Astrophysics, Johns Hopkins U., Balt., 1958-60, 62-68; staff scientist, later staff cons. space systems div. Ball Aerospace Systems Div., Boulder, Colo., 1968—. Contbr. articles to profl. jours. Fellow Optical Soc. Am.; mem. Am. Astron. Soc., Soc. Photo-optical Instrumentation Engrs., Current Work: Conceptual design and performance analysis of optical instruments for space research/space astronomy. Subspecialties: Aerospace engineering and technology; Optical design. Home: 2525 Table Mesa Dr Boulder CO 80303 Office: Ball Aerospace Systems Div PO Box 1062 Boulder CO 80306

BOUBEL, RICHARD WILLIAM, engineering educator, cons., inventor; b. Portland, Oreg., Aug. 1, 1927; s. William Francis and Cleo Adeen (Link) B.; m. Ruth Abbey, Mar. 28, 1952; children: Jane A., Thomas R., William W., Elizabeth Boubel Nutter. B.S. in Mech. Engring, Oreg. State U., 1953, M.S. M.E., 1954; Ph.D. in Environ. Engring, U. N.C., 1963. Diplomate Am. Acad. Environ. Engrs., 1970; registered profl. engr., Oreg. Instr. Oreg. State U., Corvallis, 1954-57, asst. prof., 1957-63, assoc. prof., 1963-67, prof., 1967—; engr. Engring. Expt. Sta., Oreg. State U., 1957-58; dir. Oreg. State U. Air Resources Center, 1979-82; engr. CH2M Hill, Corvallis, 1955-57, U.S. Dept. Def., 1984—; statistician U.S. Bur. Mines, Albany, Oreg., 1963-73; cons. in field. Author: Fundamentals of Air Pollution, 1973, 2d edit., 1984, also articles. Mem. Corvallis Airport Commn., 1970-73; edler First United Presbyterian Ch., Corvallis, 1966—. Served in USNR, 1944-46. USPHS fellow, 1960; named Eminent Engr. Tau Beta Pi, 1979. Mem. Air Pollution Control Assn. (Pres. 1978-79), ASME (sect. dir. 1977-78, chmn. 1983, membership chmn. 1981—), Am. Acad. Enviro. Engrs., Oreg. Pilots Assn. (pres. 1958-59), Pi Tau Sigma. Republican. Patentee energy systems and air pollution samplers (5). Current Work: Gas turbine and jet engine air pollution emission control; biomass utilization with atmospheric emissions; hydrogen/oxgen direct steam production-combustion and cycle analysis. Subspecialties: Environmental engineering; Biomass (energy science and technology). Home: 2111 Jefferson Davis Hwy Apt 318S Arlington VA 22202 Office: 1717 H St NW Washington DC 20006

BOUDART, MICHEL, chemical engineering educator; b. Belgium, June 18, 1924; came to U.S., 1947, naturalized, 1957; s. Francois and Marguerite (Swolfs) B.; m. Marina D'Haese, Dec. 27, 1948; children: Mark, Baudouin, Iris, Philip. B.S., U. Louvain, Belgium, 1944, M.S., 1947; Ph.D., Princeton U., 1950. Research asso. James Forrestal Research Center, Princeton, 1950-54; mem. faculty Princeton U., 1954-61; prof. chem. engring. U. Calif. - Berkeley, 1961-64; prof. chem. engring. and chemistry Stanford U., 1964-80, William J. Keck prof. chem. engring., 1980—; cons. to industry, 1955—; dir. Catalytica Assos., Inc.; Humble Oil Co. lectr., 1958, Am. Inst. Chem. Engrs. lectr., 1961, Sigma Xi nat. lectr., 1965; chmn. Gordon Research Conf. Catalysis, 1962. Author: Kinetics of Chemical Processes, 1968, (with G. Djéga-Mariadassov) Kinetics of Heterogeneous Catalytic Reactions, 1983; editor: (with J.R. Anderson) Catalysis: Science and Technology, 1981; adv. editorial bd.: Jour. Catalysis, 1964—, Internat. Chem. Engring., 1964—, Advances in Catalysis, 1968—, Catalysis Rev., 1968—, Accounts Chem. Research, 1978—. Belgium-Am. Ednl. Found. fellow, 1948; Procter fellow, 1949; Recipient Curtis-McGraw research award Am. Soc. Engring. Edn., 1962, R.H. Wilhelm award in chem. reaction engring., 1974. Fellow AAAS; mem. Am. Chem. Soc. (Kendall award 1977; Murphree award 1985), Catalysis Soc., Am. Inst. Chem. Engrs., Chem. Soc., Nat. Acad. Sci., Nat. Acad. Engring.; fgn. assoc. Académie Royale de Belgique. Current Work: Synthesis, characterization and testing of new catalytic matrerials. Subspecialty: Surface chemistry. Home: 512 Gerona Rd Stanford CA 94305 Office: Dept Chem Engring Stanford Univ Stanford CA 94305

BOUDOULAS, HARISIOS, cardiologist, educator, researcher; b. Velvendo-Kozani, Greece, Nov. 3, 1935; came to U.S., 1975; s. Konstantinos and Sophia (Manolas) B.; m. Olga Paspati, Feb. 27, 1976; children—Shophia, Konstantinos. M.D. diploma, Aristoteliam U., 1959, U. Thessaloniri, 1967. Intern Red Cross Hosp.-Athens, Greece, 1960; resident in medicine and cardiology U. Thessaloniki, 1962-66; sr. lectr. U. Thessaloniri, Greece, 1973-75; resident Ohio State U., 1970-73, asst. prof. cardiology, 1975-78, assoc. prof. cardiology, 1978-80, prof. pharmacy, 1984—, dir. cardiovascular research, 1983; prof. cardiology Wayne State U., Detroit, 1980-82, dir. cardiovascular research, 1980-82, adj. chief cardiology, 1982; chief diagnostic and tng. cardiovascular ctr. VA Med. Ctr., Allen Park, Mich., 1980-82. Contbr. numerous articles to profl. jours. Recipient disting. research investigator award Am. Heart Assn., 1982. Fellow Am. Coll. Cardiology, Am. Coll. Clin. Pharmacology, Council Clin. Cardiology of Am. Heart Assn., ACP; mem. Central Soc. Clin. Research. Greek Orthodox. Club: President's (Columbus). Current Work: My research interests covers a side spectrum of cardiovascular medicine. Subspecialties: Cardiology; Internal medicine. Home: 4185 Mumford Ct Columbus OH 43220 Office: Ohio State U Dept Cardiology 466 W 10th Ave Columbus OH 43210

BOUDRIE, RICHARD LYNN, physicist; b. Monroe, Mich., July 17, 1947; s. Harold D. and Doris E. (Halleen) B.; m. Nancy Jane Winkelman, July 19, 1969; children—Michelle, Ryan. B.A., Western Mich. U., 1969; Ph.D., U. Kans., 1976. Research assoc. U. Colo., Boulder, 1976-79; staff Los Alamos Nat. Lab., 1979-80, group leader, 1980—. Fellow Am. Phys. Soc. Republican. Lutheran. Current work: Basic research in nuclear structure physics; design and develop magnet spectrometer facilities. Subspecialty: Nuclear physics. Home: 2565 36th St Los Alamos NM 87544 Office: MP10 MSH841 Los Alamos Nat Lab Los Alamos NM 87545

BOUILLANT, ALAIN MARCEL, virologist; b. Gisors, France, Aug. 13, 1928; came to Can., 1953; s. Marcel and Madeleine (Tripier) B.; m. Marie-Andrée Pouliot, July 1, 1965; 1 child, Valérie. Ingénieur d' Agriculture, Ecole Supérieure d'Ingénieurs et Techniciens, Paris, 1950; D.M.V., U. Montreal, 1958; M.S., U. Wis., 1953; Ph.D., U. Laval, 1967. Lic. veterinarian, Que., Man. Pvt. practice vet. medicine, Swan River, Man., Can., 1959-60; research asst. U. Wis., Madison, 1960-63; lab. asst. U. Laval, Quebec City, Que., Can., 1964-67; research scientist Animal Disease Research Inst., Nepean, Ont., Can., 1967—; mem. rev. com. for research grants Conseil des Recherches et services Agricoles du Que., Dept. Agr., 1980—. Contbr. articles to profl. jours. Served with French Army, 1948-49. Med. Research Council Can. grantee, 1964-67; Mink Research Found. grantee, 1960-63. Mem. Can. Vet. Med. Assn., AVMA, AAAS, Tissue Culture Assn., N.Y. Acad. Scis., Am. Soc. Virology, Sigma Xi. Roman Catholic. Current work: Host cell virus relationships; latent viral infections; study of events occuring in malignant cell transformation; retroviridae; practical usage of malignant transformed cells. Subspecialties: Meteorologic instrumentation; Genome organization. Office: Animal Disease Research Inst 801 Fallowfield Rd PO Box 11300 Station H Nepean ON K2H 8P9 Canada

BOULGER, FRANCIS WILLIAM, metallurgical engineer; b. Mpls., June 19, 1913; s. Francis J. and Mary (Armstrong) B. Metall. Engr., U. Minn., 1934; M.S. (Battelle fellow), Ohio State U., 1937. With A.P., 1929-34; engr. Minn. Dept. Hwys., 1935-36; metallurgist Republic Steel Corp., Cleve., 1937; research metallurgist Battelle Meml. Inst., Columbus, Ohio, 1938-45, div. chief, 1945-67, sr. tech. adviser, 1967—; cons. USAF; Materials Adv. Bd. OECD. Author: (with others) Forging Materials and Practices, 1968, Tri-Lingual Dictionary of Production Engineering, 1969, Forging Equipment, Materials and Practices, 1973; also numerous articles. Named Man of Yr. Columbus Tech. Council, 1966; Gold medalist Soc. Mfg. Engrs., 1967; recipient Am. Machinist award, 1975. Fellow Am. Soc. Metals, ASME; mem. AIME (Hunt medal 1955), Soc. Mfg. Engrs., Nat. Acad. Engring., Internat. Inst. for Prodn. Research (pres., hon. mem.), Internat. Cold Forging Group (founder), North Am. Mfg. Inst. Roman Catholic. Current Work: Computerized planning and control of manufacturing processes, particularly metalworking operations. Subspecialties: Materials processing; Mechanical engineering. Home: 1816 Harwich Rd Columbus OH 43221 Office: 505 King Ave Columbus OH 43201

BOULTON, ALAN ARTHUR, neuropsychopharmacologist,educator; b. Buxworth, Derbyshire, Eng., Mar. 14, 1936; immigrated to Can., 1968; s. Clifford and Mabel (Barber) B.; m. Anne McCall, Mar. 28, 1969; children—Adrian, Alistair, Anneli, Alana. B.SC. with honors, U. Manchester, 1958, Ph.D., 1962, D.Sc., 1976. Mem. sci. staff chem. pathology of mental disorders unit Med. Research Council, U. Birmingham, Eng., 1962-68, fellow dept. physiology, 1962-68; assoc. prof. psychiatry U. Sask., Saskatoon, 1971-76, prof., 1976—; dir. biochemistry research Psychiat. Research div. Dept. Health Govt. Sask., Saskatoon, 1971—. Editor: (series) Neuromethods, 1984—. Contbr. articles to profl. jours. Pres. Sask. Amateur Diving Assn., 1982; pres. Sask. Freestyle Skiing Discipline, 1982; v.p. Sask. Ski Assn., 1982. Recipient Clark prize U. Toronto, 1970. Mem. Canadian Coll. Neuropsychopharmacology (pres. 1984—), Internat. Soc. Neurochemistry (treas. 1981-85, chmn. 1985—). Club: U. Sask. Faculty. Current work: The neurobiology of the trace amines and their relationship to psychiatric and neurological disorders Subspecialties: Neurobiology; Psychopharmacology. Office: Phychiat Research Div CMR Bldg U Sask Saskatoon SK S7N 0W0 Canada

BOUNDY, RAY HAROLD, chemical engineer; b. Brave, Pa., Jan. 10, 1903; s. George W. and Anetta (Cather) B.; m. Geraldine McCurdy, Nov. 27, 1926; children: Richard Ray, Lois Cather. B.S. in Chemistry, Grove City Coll., Pa., 1924; B.S., Case Western Res. U., 1926, M.S. in Chem. Engring, 1930; D.Sc. in Chemistry (hon.), Grove City (Pa.) Coll., 1961. With Dow Chem. Co., Midland, Mich., 1926-68, v.p., dir. research, corp. dir., 1951-68, cons. mgmt. of research, 1968—; vol. Internat. Exec. Service Corps., Taiwan and Iran, 1968—. Co-editor: Styrene, Its Polymers and Copolymers, 1951; Contbr. articles to profl. jours. Bd. dirs. Grove City Coll., Saginaw Valley State Coll. Recipient Gold medal Indsl. Research Inst., 1967; Alumni Achievement award Case Western Res. U., 1967; Alumni Achievement award Grove City Coll., 1968. Mem. NAM, Modern Pioneers in Creative Industry, Nat. Acad. Engring., Am. Chem. Soc., Am. Inst. Chem. Engrs. Clubs: Kiwanis, Torch, Midland Country. Patentee in field. Subspecialties: Chemical engineering; International research management. Address: 600 S Ocean Blvd Apt 1503 Boca Raton FL 33432

BOURGEOIS, JOANNE, geological educator, sedimentary geologist; b. Hartford, Conn., July 2, 1950; d. Louis Edward and Miriam Priscilla (Smith) B. B.A., Barnard Coll., 1972; Ph.D., U. Wis., 1980. Instr. Barnard Coll., N.Y.C., 1972-76; asst. prof. geology U. Wash., Seattle, 1980—; cons. archaeol. excavations Am. Acad. in Rome, 1974. Author: (with others) The Portus Cosanus (in press). Editor: Ency. of Sedimentology, 1973-78. Contbr. articles to profl. jours. Shell Merit scholar Barnard Coll., 1968-72; Van Hise fellow U. Wis., 1976-78; M.C. Kohler fellow U. Wis., 1978-80; research grantee. Mem. AAAS, Geol. Soc. Am. (assoc. editor 1984—), Internat. Assn. Sedimentologists, Soc. Econ. Paleontologists and Mineralogists (co-chmn., chmn. bed forms and bedding structures research group 1982-84), Sigma Xi. Current work: Sedimentary facies and analysis, basin analysis and tectonics, hydrodynamic interpretation of sedimentary structures, history of geology. Subspecialties: Sedimentology; Geology. Office: Dept Geol Scis Univ Wash AJ-20 Seattle WA 98195

BOURGEOIS, SIDNEY V., JR., chemical engineer; b. Thibodaux, La., July 29, 1946; s. Sidney V. and Juanita Marie (Use) B.; m. Loraine Faye Sear; children—Angelle, Aimee. B.S. in Chem. Engring., La. State U., 1968, M.S. in Chem. Engring., 1970, Ph.D. in Chem. Engring., 1971; cert. Santa Clara U., 1983. Registered profl. engr., Wis. Asst. process engr. Shell Oil Co., Norco, La., 1967-68, Esso Research Labs., Baton Rouge, 1969; devel. engr. Ethyl Corp., Baton Rouge, 1970; grad. asst. La. State U., Baton Rouge, 1970-71; research engr. Lockheed Missiles & Space Co., Inc., Huntsville, Ala., 1971-79, mgr., 1979-82, resident dir. engring. ctr., 1982—. Contbr. articles to profl. jours. Bd.

dirs. fund drive United Way, Huntsville, 1984, Huntsville Hosp. Found., 1985. Mem. Am. Def. Preparedness Assn. (v.p., 1983-85), Assn. U.S. Army, AIAA. Lodge: Rotary. Subspecialty: Aerospace engineering and technology. Office: Lockheed Missiles & Space Co Inc 4800 Bradford Dr Huntsville AL 35805

BOUSHEY, HOMER ASTLEY, JR., physician, educator; b. Washington, Aug. 10, 1942; s. Homer Astley and Eleanor Sprott (Boyd) B.; m. Virginia Regan Thomson, Aug. 8, 1964; children—Sarah Thomison, Geiffrey Alexander, Graeme Thomison. A.B. in Biology, Stanford U., 1964; M.D., U. Calif.-San Francisco, 1968. Diplomate Am. Bd. Internal Medicine. Intern, then resident U. Calif.-San Francisco, 1968-70, asst. prof., 1974-81, assoc. prof., 1981—; resident in medicine Beth Israel Hosp., Boston, 1970-71. U. Calif. fellow. Mem. Western Soc. Clin. Investigation, Am. Fedn. Clin. Research, Am. Physiology Soc., Am. Thoracic Soc., Calif. Thoracic Soc. (pres. 1983-84). Episcopalian. Current work: Study of causes and treatments of asthsma; study effects on lung of air pollutants. Subspecialty: Pulmonary medicine. Home: 35 El Verano Way San Francisco CA 94127 Office: U Calif 1315-M CVRI San Francisco CA 94143

BOUWER, HERMAN, laboratory executive; b. Haarlem, Netherlands, July 11, 1927; came to U.S., 1952, naturalized, 1959; s. Eduard and Trinette (Dusschoten) B.; m. Agnes N. Temminck, Mar. 29, 1952; children: Edward John, Herman (Archie) Gerard, Annette Nancy. B.S., Nat. Agr. U., Wageningen, Netherlands, 1949, M.S., 1952; Ph.D., Cornell U., 1955. Asso. agr. engr. Auburn U., 1955-59; research hydraulic engr. U.S. Water Conservation Lab., Phoenix, 1959-72, dir., 1972—; lectr. groundwater hydrology Ariz. State U.; cons. in field. Author: Groundwater Hydrology, 1978; Contbr. articles in field to profl. jours. OECD fellow, 1964; recipient Superior Service awards U.S. Dept., Agr., 1963, 73. Mem. ASCE (Walter Huber Research prize 1966, Royce J. Tipton award 1984), Am. Soc. Agr. Engrs., Am. Soc. Agronomy, Nat. Water Well Assn., Dutch Inst. Agr. Engrs. Club: Tempe Racquet and Swim. Current Work: Water conservation, sewage treatment by filtration through soils and aquifers via groundwater recharge, groundwater pollution, irrigation, drainage. Subspecialties: Agricultural engineering; Water supply and wastewater treatment. Home: 338 La Diosa St Tempe AZ 85282 Office: 4331 E Broadway St Phoenix AZ 85040

BOVAY, HARRY ELMO, JR., utilities executive, retired engineering company executive; b. Big Rapids, Mich., Sept. 4, 1914; s. Harry E. and Addibelle (Bentley) B.; m. Sue Goldston, Feb. 1, 1977; children—Mark Benson, Susan Stone. C.E., Cornell U., 1936. Jr. engring. aide U.S. C.E., 1936-37; jr. metal insp., project engr. Humble Oil & Refining Co., Baytown, Tex., 1937-45; cons. engr., Houston, 1946-62; pres. Bovay Engrs., Inc., Houston, 1962-73, chmn., bd. chief exec. officer, 1974-83; pres. Mid-South Telephone Co., Rienzi, Miss., 1959—, Lamar Telephone Co., Millport, Ala., 1975—, Mid-South Cablevision Co., Inc.; owner Bovista Farms, Somerville, Tenn., 1963—; Mem. Houston Adv. Council Naval Affairs, 1959; mem. Tex. Water Resources Research Adv. Com., 1968-71; mem. adv. com. Coastal Engring. Lab., Tex. A. and M. U., 1969; mem. engring. adv. com. Miss. State U., 1974, 77. Editor: Mechanical and Electrical Systems for Buildings. Pres. Sam Houston Area council Boy Scouts Am., 1963-64; exec. com. South Central region, 1973-76, bd. dirs., 1975-79, v.p., 1980-81, pres., 1981-82, mem. nat. exec. bd., 1981-85, chmn. camping/outdoor com., 1983-85, chmn. audit com., 1982—; chmn. Houston Commn. Zoning, 1959-60, 1982-83, bd. dirs. Vis. Nurse Assn. Houston, 1970-75; active United Fund Houston and Harris County. Named Disting. Engr. Tex. Engring. Found. Fellow ASCE, ASHRAE (ASHRAE-ALCO award); mem. Nat. Soc. Profl. Engrs. (pres. 1976), Tex. Soc. Profl. Engrs. (pres. 1967-68), Am. Inst. Cons. Engrs. (past pres. Tex. chpt.), Houston Engring. and Sci. Soc. (past 2d v.p.), Am. Rd. Builders Assn. (mem. exec. com.), Am. Concrete Inst., Am. Wood Preservers Assn., ASTM (councilor 1960-64), Forest Products Research Soc., Tex. Forest Products Mfrs. Assn., ASME (Toulmin medal), Pres.' Assn., Newcomen Soc. N.Am., Nat. Acad. Engring. Episcopalian. Clubs: Houston, Kiwanis, Cosmos, Houston Country, Warwick, Petroleum. Subspecialties: Civil engineering; Industrial engineering. Home: 2200 Willowick Dr Apt 12-H Houston TX 77027 Office: 5251 Westheimer Suite 1025 Houston TX 77056

BOVEY, FRANK ALDEN, research chemist; b. Mpls., June 4, 1918; s. John Alden and Margaret Eugenia (Jackson) B.; m. Shirley June Elfman, June 19, 1941 (div. 1980); children: Margaret Bovey Glassman, Peter, Victoria A. B.S., Harvard U., 1940; Ph.D., U. Minn., 1948. With 3M Co., 1942, 48-62, Nat. Synthetic Rubber Corp., Louisville, 1942-45; with Bell Telephone Labs., Murray Hill, N.J., 1962—, head polymer chemistry research dept., 1967—; v.p., dir. Bodel Corp., Mpls.; adj. prof. Stevens Inst. Tech., 1965-67, Rutgers U., 1971—, MIT, 1981, Princeton U., 1985. Author: Effects of Ionizing Radiation on Polymers, 1958, Nuclear Magnetic Resonance, 1969, Polymer Conformation and Configuration, 1969, High Resolution NMR of Macromolecules, 1972, Chain Structure and Conformation of Macromolecules, 1982; also articles.; Asso. editor: Macromolecules, 1968—; editorial bd.: Accounts of Chem. Research, 1968-74, Biopolymers, 1972—. Recipient Outstanding Achievement award U. Minn. Fellow N.Y. Acad. Scis.; mem. Nat. Acad. Scis., Am. Chem. Soc. (Union Carbide award 1958, Minn. award 1962, Witco award polymer chemistry 1969, Nichols medal 1978, Phillips award 1983), Am. Phys. Soc. (High Polymer Physics prize 1974), Am. Soc. Biol. Chemists, Sigma Xi, Phi Lambda Upsilon. Current Work: Structure and dynamics of polymer molecules; application of nuclear magnetic resonance spectroscopy to these areas. Subspecialties: Polymer chemistry; Nuclear magnetic resonance. Home: 9C Dorado Dr Morristown NJ 07960 Office: AT&T Bell Laboratories Murray Hill NJ 07974

BOVEY, RODNEY WILLIAM, research agronomist; b. Craigmont, Idaho, July 17, 1934; s. William August and Elnora Lucile (Click) B.; m. Shirley Ellen Deffenbaugh, Mar. 3, 1956; children—Seth Ivan, Todd Evin, Shawn Erin, Cary Lane. B.S., U. Idaho, 1956, M.S., 1959; Ph.D., U. Nebr., 1964. Instr. agronomy U. Nebr.-Lincoln, 1959-64; research agronomist Agr. Research Service, College Station, Tex., 1964-84, research leader, 1968-84. Author: (with H.L.Young) The Science of 2, 4,5-T, 1980; contbr. numerous articles to profl. jours. Mem. Weed Sci. Soc. Am., Am. Soc. Range Mgmt., Am. Soc. Agronomy, Council for Agr. Sci. and Tech., Plant Growth Regulator Soc. Am., Sigma Xi, Gamma Sigma Delta, Phi Kappa Phi. Current work: Weed and brush control on pastures and rangeland. Subspecialties: Agronomy; Plant physiology (agriculture). Office: Tex A&M U Dept Range Sci College Station TX 77843

BOWDEN, BRYANT BAIRD, mechanical engineer; b. Knoxville, Tenn., Sept. 20, 1945; s. Andrew Jackson and Calberta Ethel (Baird) B.; m. Patricia Tuck, June 11, 1966; children: Elisabeth Ann, David Aaron. B.S. in Mech. Engring, U. Tenn., Knoxville, 1968. Registered profl. engr., Tenn. With Nuclear div. Union Carbide Corp., Oak Ridge, 1968-84, head dept. gas centrifuge mech. engring. Oak Ridge Gaseous Diffusion Plant, 1977-82, mgr. mech. engring., 1982-84; mgr. mech. engring. Y-12 Plant, Martin Marietta Energy Systems, Oak Ridge, 1984—. Chmn. deacons, minister of music Bible Bap. Ch., Lenoir City, Tenn. Mem. ASME, Tenn. Soc. Profl. Engrs., Nat. Soc. Profl. Engrs. Republican. Club: Gideons Internat. Patentee gas centrifuge products. Current Work: Mechanical design engineering of equipment and facilities for Y-12 weapons plant. Subspecialties: Mechanical engineering; Fuels and sources. Home: Route 1 Box 290 Mountain View Dr Lenoir City TN 37771 Office: Bldg 9111 M/S 1 Oak Ridge TN 37831

BOWDEN, DAVID MERLE, research station administrator; b. Hedley, B.C., Can., Sept. 2, 1929; s. Frederick Oswald and Golda Ann Bowden; m. Margaret Ann Booth, Dec. 27, 1952; children—John David, Graeme Campbell. B.S. in Agr., U. B.C., 1952, M.S. in Agr., 1957; Ph.D., Oreg. State U., 1961. Research scientist Agr. Can. Research Sta., Agassiz, B.C., 1952-67, research scientist, Lethbridge, Alta., 1969-80, regional program specialist, Saskatoon, Sask., 1980-83, dir. research sta., Swift Current, Sask., 1983—; animal nutritionist FAO, Heyderabad, Iran, 1967-69. Contbr. articles to profl. jours. Mem. Agrl. Inst. Can., Sask. Inst. Agrologists, Am. Soc. Animal Sci., Can. Soc. Animal Sci. (pres. 1965). Roman Catholic. Lodge: Kiwanis. Current work: research administration Subspecialty: Agricultural research administration. Office: Agr Can Research Sta PO Box 1030 Swift Current SK S9H 3X2 Canada

BOWEN, JEFFREY LOUIS, dental materials researcher; b. Wooster, Ohio, July 1, 1960; s. Edward Brooks and Ruth (Sanderson) B. B.S. in Geology, Mary Washington Coll., 1982. Researcher, Arlington, Va., 1982—. Recipient Eagle Scout award Boy Scouts Am., 1976. Mem. Geol. Soc. Am., Sigma Gamma Epsilon. Current work: Determined that tooth-like material and a laser may be used to restore teeth. Subspecialty: Dental materials. Home and office: 1602 N Rhodes St Apt A3 Arlington VA 22209

BOWEN, JOHN METCALF, pharmacologist, college dean; b. Quincy, Mass., Mar. 23, 1933; s. Loy John and Marjorie Alice (Metcalf) B.; m. Jean Schmidt, Dec. 27, 1956; children: Mark John, Richard Kelley. D.V.M., U. Ga., 1957; Ph.D., Cornell U., 1960. Asst., then assoc. prof. Kans. State U., Manhattan, 1960-63; assoc. prof. U. Ga., 1963-69, prof., 1969—; assoc. dean research and grad. affairs, dir. U. Ga. (Vet. Med. Expt. Sta.), 1976—. Mem. AVMA (council biologic and therapeutic agts., drug availability com.), Soc. Neurosci., Am. Soc. Pharmacology and Exptl. Therapeutics, AAAS, Sigma Xi. Current Work: Pharmacologic and toxicologic studies of excitable cells in culture. Subspecialties: Cellular pharmacology; Neurophysiology. Office: Coll Vet Medicine Athens GA 30602

BOWEN, LAWRENCE HOFFMAN, chemistry educator; b. Lynchburg, Va., Dec. 20, 1934; s. Charles Wesley, Jr. and Eleanor (Hoffman) B. B.S., Va. Mil. Inst., 1956; Ph.D., MIT, 1961. Asst. prof. chemistry dept. N.C. State U., Raleigh, 1961-65, assoc. prof., 1965-70, prof. chemistry, 1970—. Contbr. articles in field to sci. jour. Served to 1st lt. Chem. Corps, U.S. Army, 1961. Recipient Jackson-Hope medal Va. Mil. Inst., 1956. Mem. Am. Chem. Soc., Am. Phys. Soc., Sigma Xi (young scientist research award 1970). Current Work: Mossbauer spectroscopy of iron oxides in synthetic systems and environmental samples, magnetic properties of small particles, solid state chemistry. Subspecialties: Physical chemistry; Solid state chemistry. Office: Dept Chemistry Box 8204 NC State U Raleigh NC 27695

BOWER, JAMES MASON, neurophysiologist; b. Northampton, Mass., Feb. 17, 1954; s. Mason James and Dorothe (Gule) B.; m. Markrid Izquierdo, Nov. 10, 1976; children—Katherine, John. Student Antioch Coll., Yellow Springs, Ohio, 1972-75; B.S., Mont. State U., 1977; Ph.D., U. Wis.-Madison, 1981. Research asst. U. Wis.-Madison, 1978-81, research assoc., 1983; assoc. research scientist NYU Med Ctr., N.Y.C., 1982-83; asst. prof. neurophysiology Calif. Inst. Tech., Pasadena, 1984—. Contbr. articles to profl. jours. Recipient 1st Jerzy E. Rose award U. Wis., 1981. Mem. Soc. Neurosci., AAAS. Current work: Information processing within local neural circuitry, especially cerebral and cerebellar cortices using both experimental and theoretical approaches. Subspecialties: Neurophysiology; Neurobiology.

BOWER, ROBERT WILLIAM, applied physicist, inventor; b. Santa Monica, Calif., June 12, 1936; s. Sidney W. and Sarah T. (Walker) B.; children—Christine, Rob, Tom, Mike; m. Linda Lou Reinemer, Feb. 27, 1982. A.B. in Physics with honors, U. Calif.-Berkeley, 1962; M.S.E.E., Calif. inst. Tech., 1963; Ph.D. in Applied Physics, 1973. Physicist, dept. mgr. Hughes Research Labs., Malibu, Calif., 1965-69; asst. div. mgr. Hughes Aircraft Co., Newport Beach, Calif., 1969-70; pres. Mnemonics, Inc., San Antonio, 1974-77; assoc. prof. UCLA, 1977-79; mgr. research and devel., sr. mem. tech. staff Advanced Micro Devices, Sunnyvale, Calif., 1979—; cons. in field, 1971-79. Author: Ion Implantation Semiconductors, 1970; Vascular Access Surgery, 1980; also articles on semicondr. tech. and devices. Patentee including on self-aligned ion implanted mosfet. Mem. IEEE (sr., sec. local chpt. 1977), Am. Phys. Soc., Bohmische Physikalische Gesellschaft, Phi Beta Kappa, Sigma Xi. Current work: Research and development of high performance, high density integrated circuit techologies and devices. Subspecialties: Microchip technology (engineering); Microelectronics. Home: 23064 Evergreen Ln Los Gatos CA 95030 Office: Advanced Micro Devices 901 Thompson Pl Sunnyvale CA 94086

BOWERS, PHILLIP FREDERICK, radio astronomer; b. Huntington, Ind., Dec. 14, 1947; s. Frederick Wallace and Frances Maxine (Everett) B.; m. Katherine Lorimer Woolley, June 27, 1970. B.S. in Astrophysics, Ind. U., 1969; Ph.D. in Astronomy, U. Md., 1977. Research assoc. U. Md., 1977; research assoc. Nat. Radio Astronomy Obs., Charlottesville, Va., 1977-80; research astronomer U. Md. and Naval Research Lab., Washington, 1980-82, Sachs/-Freeman Assoc. and Naval Research Lab., Washington, 1983—. Contbr. articles to profl. jours. E.O. Hulburt fellow, 1981—. Mem. Internat. Astron. Union, Am. Astron. Soc., Sigma Pi Sigma. Current Work: Interferometric studies of radio emission from stars. Subspecialty: Radio and microwave astronomy. Office: EO Hulburt Ctr Space Research Naval Research Lab Code 4134-5 Washington DC 20375

BOWES, GEORGE ERNEST, botanist, educator, consultant; b. London, May 22, 1942; came to U.S., 1968; s. George and Ivy Primrose (Haynes) B.; m. Helen Clifford, Sept. 12, 1970; children: George Edward Aden, Joel Asher. B.Sc., Queen Mary Coll., U. London, 1963, Ph.D., 1967; M.I.Biol. (hon.), Inst. Biology, London, 1968. Lectr. in biology Regents St. Poly., London, 1966-68; high sch. tchr. Inner London Edn. Authority, 1968; vis. research assoc. agronomy dept. agr. U. Ill., 1968-71; Carnegie Instn. research fellow dept. plant biology Stanford (Calif.) U., 1971-72; asst. prof. botany U. Fla., Gainesville, 1973-78, assoc. prof., 1978-84, prof., 1984—, prof. agronomy, 1984—. Mem. editorial bd. Editor: Aquatic Botany, 1982—, What's New in Plant Physiology, 1978-82; contbr. articles on photosynthesis research to profl. jours. Bd. elders Community Evang. Free Ch. Fla. Dept. Natural Resources grantee, 1976-83; Dept. Agr. Sci. and Edn. Adminstrn. grantee, 1978-86; Gas Research Inst. grantee, 1981-85; NSF grantee, 1982-87. Mem. Am. Soc. Plant Physiologists, Soc. Exptl. Biology, Inst. Biology London, Aquatic Plant Mgmt. Soc., Sigma Xi. Current Work: Pioneer in ribulose bisphosphate carboxylase-oxygenase enzyme and its role in photorespiration; aquatic plant photosynthetic pathways, research use of aquatic plants as alternative energy (biomass) source; biology of aquatic weeds. Subspecialties: Photosynthesis; Biomass (agriculture). Office: 3157 McCarty Hall U Fla Photosynthesis Research Lab Gainesville FL 32611

BOWHILL, SIDNEY ALLAN, electrical engineering educator; b. Dover, Kent, Eng., Aug. 6, 1927; came to U.S., 1955, naturalized, 1962; s. Sidney Allan and Violet (Clarke) B.; m. Margaret M. McLaughlin, Aug. 22, 1959; children: Allan J.C., Amanda M. B.A., Cambridge (Eng.) U., 1948, M.A., 1950, Ph.D., 1954. Research engr. Marconi's Wireless Telegraph Co. Ltd., Chelmsford, Essex, Eng., 1953-55; assoc. prof. elec. engring. Pa. State U., University Park, 1955-62; prof. elec. engring. U. Ill., Urbana, 1962—; Pres. Aeronomy Corp., Champaign, Ill., 1969—; Chmn. U.S.A. Comm. 3, Internat. Sci. Radio Union; assoc. editor Radio Sci., 1964-67, editor, 1968-72; vice chmn. Internat. Commn. 3, 1969-72, chmn., 1972-75; vice chmn. U.S.A. Nat. Com., 1985—; mem. working group 4 Inter-Union Com. Space Research, 1966-79, co-chmn. panel interactions neutral and ionized atmospheres, 1966-79, chmn. sci. commn. C, 1979—; mem. panel sci. ballooning Inter-Union Com. Space Research (commn. C), 1979-82; convenor, program chmn. Symposium (9th meeting), Vienna, Austria, 1966, Symposium (14th meeting), Seattle, 1971, Solar-Terrestrial Physics Symposium, São Paulo, Brazil, 1974, Innsbruck, Austria, 1978; mem. com. data interchange and data centers Nat. Acad. Scis., 1967-82, potential contamination and interference from space expts., 1963—, com. polar research, 1967-70, chmn. panel upper atmospheric phys., 1967-70, com. on solar terrestrial research, 1969-79; mem. panel on Jicamarca Radio Obs., 1969-83, chmn. panel, 1976-78; mem. Inter-Union Sci. Com. on Solar-Terrestrial Physics, 1967—, chmn. working group II, 1968-73; chmn. atmospheric phys. programs com. Inter-Union Sci. Com. on Solar-Terrestrial Physics (Working Group 11), 1974-80; chmn. steering com. for middle atmosphere program, 1977—; editorial adv. bd. Jour. Atmospheric and Terrestrial Physics, 1965-81. Contbr. numerous articles to profl. jours. Fellow IEEE (procs. bd. cons., procs. editorial bd. 1965-68), AAAS, Am. Geophys. Union, Am. Astron. Soc., Am. Meteorol. Soc.; mem. Am. Soc. Engring. Edn., Nat. Acad. Engring., Sigma Xi, Sigma Tau, Eta Kappa Nu. Club: Cosmos (Washington). Current Work: Middle-atmosphere physics and chemistry; rocket studies of the D region; meteor radar and MST radar studies of atmospheric dynamics; small-signal processing and detection; computer language development. Subspecialties: Aeronomy; Remote sensing (atmospheric science). Home: 2203 Anderson St Urbana IL 61801

BOWMAN, JAMES EDWARD, physician, educator; b. Washington, Feb. 5, 1923; s. James Edward and Dorothy (Peterson) B.; m. Barbara Taylor, June 17, 1950; 1 dau., Valerie June. B.S., Howard U., 1943, M.D., 1946. Intern Freedmen's Hosp., Washington, 1946-47; resident pathology St. Lukes Hosp., Chgo., 1947-50; chmn. dept. pathology Provident Hosp., 1950-53, Shiraz (Iran) Med. Center, Nemazee Hosp., 1955-61; vis. prof., chmn. dept. pathology Faculty of Medicine, U. Shiraz, 1959-61; dir. labs. U. Chgo., 1971—, prof. dept. pathology, medicine, com. on genetics and biol. scis., collegiate div., 1972—; dir. U. Chgo. (Comprehensive Sickle Cell Center), 1973—; cons. pathology, div. hosp. and med. facilities HEW, USPHS; mem. USPHS (Sci. Adv. Com. for Sci. Collaboration between U.S. and Iran), 1968, (Health and Hosps. Governing Commn. Cook County), 1969-72; mem. exec. com. hemalytic anemia study group NHLI, NIH, Bethesda, Md., 1973-75; Sabbatical fellow Center for Advanced Study in Behavioral Scis., Stanford U., 1981-82. Contbr. articles profl. jours. Served to capt. M.C. AUS, 1953-55. Spl. research fellow NIH Galton Lab., Univ. Coll., London, 1961-62. Mem. Coll. Am. Pathologists, Am. Soc. Clin. Pathologists, Am. Soc. Human Genetics, Central Soc. Clin. Research, Am. Soc. Hematology, Am. Assn. Phys. Anthropologists, Acad. Clin. Lab. Physicians and Scientists. Current Work: Population distribution of abnormal hemoglobins; ethical and legal issues in genetics programs. Subspecialties: Pathology (medicine); Genetics and genetic engineering (medicine). Home: 4929 S Greenwood St Chicago IL 60615 Office: 950 E 59th St Chicago IL 60637

BOWMAN, TERESA ANN, laboratory animal veterinarian, researcher; b. Walla Walla, Wash., Apr. 4, 1954; d. John Anderson and Opal Bell (Lamb) B. B.S. in Animal Sci., Wash. State U., 1976, B.S. in Vet Sci., 1977, D.V.M., 1980; M.S. in Lab. Animal Medicine, Pa. State U., 1983. Veterinarian Spring Glen Vet. Hosp., Renton, Wash., 1980; resident dept. comparative medicine Coll. Medicine, Pa. State U., Hershey, 1981-83, asst. prof. lab. animal medicine, 1983—; cons. ZooAmerica, Hershey, 1982—. Contbr. articles to profl. jours. Mem. AVMA, Am. Assn. for Lab. Animal Sci., Assn. Women Vets., Am. Soc. for Lab. Animal Practitioners, Nat. Audubon Soc. Current work: Studying effects of stress on the immune function and corticosterone levels in rodents used for research. Subspecialty: Laboratory animal medicine. Office: Dept Comparative Medicine Hershey Med Ctr Hershey PA 17033

BOWYER, ALLEN FRANK, cardiologist, administrator; b. Milw., Aug. 9, 1932; s. Charles Maynard and Mildred Berniece (Haagensen) B.; m. Carolyn Isabel Gramlich, June 5, 1954; children: Sylvia Renee, Susan Rayleen. B.A., Pacific Union Coll., 1955; M.D., Loma Linda U., 1959. Diplomate: Am. Bd. Cardiology. Resident in medicine Rush-Presbyn., St. Luke's Hosp., Chgo., 1960-63, fellow in cardiology, 1963-66; extramural fellow Nat. Heart Inst., Bethesda, Md., 1963-66; instr. in medicine U. Ill. Sch. Medicine, Chgo., 1960-65; asst. prof. Loma Linda (Calif.) U., 1966-72, assoc. prof., 1972-73; prof. medicine W. Va. U., Morgantown, 1973-78, East Carolina U., Greenville, 1978—; research physician Rush-Presbyn. Hosp., 1965-66; dir. cardiovascular research lab. Loma Linda U., 1970-73; dir. cardiac catheterization lab. W.Va. U. Sch. Medicine, 1973-78; dir. cardiac labs. East Carolina U.Sch. Medicine, 1975-81. Author and producer: Computer Graphics Film, Heart Motion by Computer Graphics, 1968 (1st prize for research at Internat. Film Festival 1970), Teaching Heart Function by Computer Graphics, (sci. film award Australia, New Zealand Sci. Film Festival 1970). Pres. Monoghalia County Heart Assn., Morgantown, 1974, 75; trustee Columbia Union Coll., Takoma Park, Md., 1976-78; pres. Pitt County Unit Am. Heart Assn., Greenville, N.C., 1983; dir. W. Va. Heart Assn., Charleston, 1974, 75. Recipient Golden Eagle ward Council on Internat. Non-theatrical Events, 1969, 1970; MacNeal award for Med. Research Rush-Presbyn. Hosp., 1963. Mem. IEEE, Instrument Soc. Am., Am. Fedn. for Clin. Research, Assn. for Computing Machinery, Sigma Xi. Democrat. Adventist. Current Work: Applications of computer graphics to clinical medicine and cardiology, development of computer graphics programs to describe cardiac valve and chamber motion and development of information theory methods to medical diagnosis, development of new approaches to artificial intelligence. Subspecialties: Cardiology; Graphics, image processing, and pattern recognition. Home: 315 King George Rd Greenville NC 27834 Office: East Carolina U Sch Medicine Sect Cardiology Dept Medicine Greenville NC 27834

BOX, GEORGE EDWARD PEHHEM, statistician; b. Gravesend, Eng., Oct. 18, 1919; s. Harry and Helen (Martin) B.; m. Joan Gunnhild Fisher, Dec. 12, 1959; children—Helen Elizabeth, Harry Christopher. B.Sc., U. Coll., U. London, Eng., 1947, Ph.D., 1952, Sc.D., 1961; Sc.D. (hon.), U. Rochester, 1975. Statistician, head statis. techniques research sect. Imperial Chems. Industries, Blackley, Manchester, Eng., 1948-56; dir. statis. techniques research group Princeton U., 1957-59; prof. stats. U. Wis.-Madison, 1960—, William F. Vilas prof., 1980; vis. research prof. U. N.C., 1952-53; Ford Found. vis. prof. Harvard Bus. Sch., 1965-66, U. Essex, Eng., 1970-71. Author: (with others) Statistical Methods in Research and Production, 1957; Design and Analysis of Industrial Experiments, 1959; Evolutionary Operation: A Statistical Method for Process Improvement, 1969; Time Series, Forecasting and Control, 1970; Bayesian Inference in Statistical Analysis, 1973; Statistics for Experimenters, 1978. Contbr. articles to profl. jours. Served with Brit. Army, 1939-45. Decorated Brit. Empire medal; recipient Profl. Progress award Am. Inst. Chem. Engrs., 1963; Benjamin Smith Reynolds award for teaching excellence, 1972. Fellow Am.AAcad. Arts and Scis., Royal Statis. Soc. (Guy medal 1964), Am. Statis. Assn. (Wilks Meml. medal 1972, pres. 1978), Inst. Math. Statistics (pres. 1979), Am. soc. Quality Control (Shewhart medal 1968), AAAS (past v.p.); mem. Internat. Statis. Inst., Biometrics Soc. Subspecialty: Statistics. Office: U Wis Dept Math Madison WI 53706*

BOXER, LAURENCE ALAN, physician, pediatric hematologist; b. Denver, May 17, 1940; s. Sam and Tillie (Belstock) B.; m. Grace Jordison, Aug. 23, 1969; 1 son; David E.K. B.A., U. Colo., 1961; M.D., Stanford U., 1966. Diplomate: Am. Bd. Pediatrics. Intern, resident in pediatrics Yale New Haven Hosp., 1966-68; resident in pediatrics Stanford (Calif.) U., 1966-68; fellow in hematology Childrens Hosp. Med. Center, Boston, 1972-74; instr. pediatrics Harvard Med. Sch., 1974-75; asst. prof. Ind. U. Med. Sch., Indpls., 1975-82, assoc. prof., 1978-82, prof., 1982; prof., dir. pediatric hematology, oncology U. Mich. Med. Sch., Ann Arbor, 1982—. Contbr. numerous articles to med. jours. Served to maj. AUS, 1969-72. Established investigator Am. Heart Assn., 1978—. Fellow A.C.P.; mem. Am. Soc. Clin. Investigation, Am. Soc. Pathologists, Am. Assn. Immunologists, Soc. Pediatric Research, Am. Pediatric Soc., Am. Soc. Pediatric Research, Am. Soc. Hematology, Phi Beta Kappa, Sigma Xi. Republican. Jewish. Current Work: Mechanisms of phagocytic cell function, host defense. Subspecialties: Pediatrics; Hematology.

BOYAN, BARBARA DALE, biochemistry educator; b. Boise, Idaho, Sept. 20, 1948; d. Jack R. and Berniece Alice (Elling) B.; m. Gregory Allen Salyers, May 17, 1975 (div. Dec. 1981); m. Don Mauldin Ranly, Apr. 24, 1982; children: Elizabeth Melva, Edmund Don. B.A., Rice U., 1970, M.A., 1974, Ph.D., 1975. Postdoctoral fellow Health Sci. Center, U. Tex.-Houston, 1974-75, research assoc., 1975-77, asst. prof. dept. microbiology, 1977-81; assoc. prof. dept. periodontics, biochemistry and orthopedics Health Sci. Center, U. Tex.-San Antonio, 1981—; cons. in field. Contbr. articles to profl. jours. Religious edn. adviser Temple Emanu El, Houston, 1979-81. NIH postdoctoral fellow, 1974-77; Nat. Acad. Sci.-NRC research assoc., 1974; NIH Research Career Devel. awardee, 1977-82; NIH research grantee, 1974—. Mem. Am. Assn. for Dental Research, Internat. Assn. for Dental Research, Am. Soc. for Bone and Mineral Research, Electron Microscopy Soc. Am., Tex. Soc. Electron Microscopy, Alpha Omega. Jewish. Current Work: Study of the mechanisms of mineral formation in normal bones and teeth; study of regulation of mineralization by vitamin D; analysis of how pathologic calcification occurs; bone induction. Subspecialties: Oral biology; Biochemistry (medicine). Office: Department Periodontics University of Texas Health Science Center 7703 Floyd Curl Dr San Antonio TX 78284

BOYCE, JOSEPH MICHEAL, space science researcher, government official; b. Mesa, Ariz., July 30, 1946. B.S., No. Ariz. U., 1969, M.S., 1972. Geologist Br. Astrogeology, U.S. Geol. Survey, Flagstaff, Ariz., 1969-77; staff scientist NASA Planetary Geology Program, Washington, 1977-79, discipline chief, 1979-83, discipline chief planetary Geoscis. Programs, 1983—. Contbr. writings to sci. publs., Smithsonian Press, 1982—. Mem. Am. Geophys. Union, Geol. Soc. Am., Am. Astron. Union, Meteoritical Soc. Current Work: Management of science programs, research planetary stratigraphy, impact cratering, surface processes. Subspecialty: Planetology. Office: NASA Hdqrs Code EL-4 Washington DC 20546

BOYD, ANN LEWIS, viral oncologist, researcher, educator; b. Shreveport, La., Nov. 15, 1944; d. Fletcher Willard and Bess Juanita (Sherman) Lewis; m. James Pierce Boyd, June 4, 1964 (div.); 1 dau., Kathryn Ann. B.S., Northwestern State U., Natchitoches, La., 1965, M.S., 1968; Ph.D., La. State U., 1971. Postdoctoral researcher Baylor U. Sch. Medicine, 1971-73; prin. scientist Nat. Cancer Inst.-Frederick (Md.) Cancer Research Facility, Litton Bionetics, Inc., 1973—; asso. prof. biology Hood Coll., 1981—. Contbr. articles, chpts. to profl. publs. Bd. dirs. Penn Laurel council Girl Scouts Am.; mem. vestry, jr. warden Harriet Chapel Episcopal Ch., Frederick. Grantee Nat. Cancer Inst. Mem. Am. Soc. Microbiology, Am. Tissue Culture Assn., AAAS, N.Y. Acad. Scis., Sigma Xi, Phi Kappa Phi. Republican. Current Work: Manual microinjectin of mammalian cells with DNA, RNA or protein, using glass capillary micropipettes to study gene expression. Subspecialties: Cancer research (medicine); Virology (medicine). Home: 8821 Indian Springs Rd Frederick MD 21701 Office: Nat Cancer Inst-FCRF Bldg 560 PO Box B Frederick MD 21701

BOYD, EDWARD LEE, physicist, computer scientist; b. Mexico, Mo., Nov. 27, 1932; s. Lee Moore Boyd and Billy (Richter) Boyd Falk; m. Irene Howe Crossman, July 26, 1969; children—Sloane Victoria, Ashton Lee. B.A. in Physics, Lehigh U., 1954; D.S. in Materials Sci., Kyoto U., Japan, 1967. Engr. Beva Labs., Trenton, 1953-54, Associated Enrs., Poughkeepsie, N.Y., 1954-55; physicist in research IBM, Yorktown Heights, N.Y., 1955-66, physicist in components, Poughkeepsie, N.Y., 1966-76, sr. staff mem. corp. hdqrs., Armonk, N.Y., 1976-79, sr. engr. gen. tech. div., East Fishkill, N.Y., 1979—. Contbr. chpt., articles on physics of magnetism to profl. publs. Patentee in field. Bd. dirs. various cultural orgns. Served as pfc. USAR, 1957-69. Mem. Am. Phys. Soc., Am. Assn. Physics Tchrs., AAAS. Episcopalian. Current work: Study of the interaction of technology (semiconductor/materials) with computer architecture. Subspecialties: Computer architecture; Materials. Home: PO Box 450 Hughsonville NY 12537 Office: IBM Route 52 Hopewell Junction NY 12533

BOYD, JAMES, consulting geologist; b. Kanowna, West Australia, Dec. 20, 1904; s. Julian and Mary (Innes) Cane; m. Ruth Ragland Brown, Aug. 17, 1932 (dec. 1979); children: James Brown, Harry Bruce, Douglas Cane, Hudson; m. Clemence D. Jandrey, 1980. B.S., Calif. Inst. Tech., 1927; M.Sc., Colo. Sch. Mines, 1932, D.Sc., 1934. Instr. geology Colo. Sch. Mines, Golden, 1929-34, asst. prof. mineralogy, 1934-37, asso. prof. econ. geology, 1938-41, dean faculty, 1946-47; asst. to sec. interior chmn. interdeptl. com. (Resources for Marshall Plan), 1947; dir. Bur. Mines, 1947-51, Def. Minerals Adminstrn., 1950-51; exploration mgr. Kennecott Copper Corp., 1951-55, v.p. exploration, 1955-60; pres. Copper Range Co., 1960-70, chmn. bd. dirs., 1970-71; exec. dir. Nat. Commn. on Materials Policy, Washington, 1971-73; pres. Materials Assos., 1974-78; geologist U.S. Geol. Survey, 1933-34; cons. geology, mining and geophysics, 1935-40; pres., gen. mgr. Goldcrest Mining Co., 1939-40; dir. engrs. Joint Council and United Engring.; Trustees, 1969-71; chmn. com. on mineral research NSF, 1952-57; vice chmn. Engrs. Commn. on Air Resources, 1970-71; chmn. sec. interior's adv. com. on non-coal mine safety, 1971-74; exec. dir. Nat. Commn. Materials Policy; chmn. materials com. Office Tech. Assessment, 1974-79; mem. nat. materials adv. bd. NRC, 1975-77, mem. mineral and energy resources bd., 1977-80, mem. mineral resources bd., 1973-75, chmn. com. on surface mining and reclamation, 1978-79; mem. tech. adv. com. Office of Nuclear Waste Isolation, 1979-82; Bd. dirs. Watergate S. Corp., 1972-79, pres., 1976-77. First reader Carmel Christian Sci. Ch., 1983-85. Served from capt. to col. AUS, 1941-46. Decorated Legion of Merit with oak leaf cluster; recipient Distinguished Service medal Colo. Sch. Mines, 1949; Distinguished Alumni award Calif. Inst. Tech., 1967; Hoover medal, 1975. Mem. Mining and Metall. Soc. Am. (pres. 1960-63), Am. Inst. Mining Engrs. (Rand gold medal 1963, pres. 1969), Nat. Acad. Engring., Am. Soc. Econ. Geologists, Geol. Soc. Am., Am. Inst. Profl. Geologists (Parker Meml. medal 1973, v.p. 1965-66), Soc. Exploration Geophysicists, Australasia Inst. Mining and Metallurgy (hon.), Acad. Polit. Sci. Clubs: Cosmos (Washington); Burning Tree. Subspecialties: Hazardous waste disposal; Resource management. Home and Office: 228 Del Mesa Carmel Carmel CA 93921

BOYD, JOHN PHILIP, geophysl fluid dynamicist; b. Winchester, Mass., Feb. 21, 1951; s. Hugh Robert and Marjorie Frances (Markham) B. A.B., Harvard U., 1973, S.M., 1975, Ph.D., 1976. Postdoctoral fellow Nat. Center Atomospheric Research, 1976; postdoctoral scholar U. Mich., 1977, asst. prof. atmospheric sci., 1977-82, assoc. prof., 1982—. Contbr. articles to profl. jours.; author sci. fiction stories. Mem. Am. Meteorol. Soc. Roman Catholic. Current Work: Fluid dynamics of the atmosphere and ocean; math. and numerical methods. Subspecialties: Meteorology; Oceanography. Home: 3385 Burbank Ann Arbor MI 48105 Office: 2455 Hayward Room 2215 Ann Arbor MI 48109

BOYD, LANDIS LEE, agricultural research administrator; b. Orient, Iowa; s. Harold Everett and Edith Elizabeth (Lauer) B.; m. Lila Mae Hummel, Sept. 7, 1946; children—Susan Lee, Barabara Edith, Shirley Rae, Carl Steven, Philip Wayne. B.S., Iowa State Coll., 1947, M.S., 1948; Ph.D., Iowa State U., 1959. Asst. prof. agrl. research Cornell U., 1948-53, assoc. prof., 1953-60, prof., 1960-64; head agrl. engring. U. Minn.-St. Paul, 1964-72, asst. dir. agrl. research, 1972-78; dir. agrl. research, assoc. dean Wash. State U., Pullman, 1978—; engring. design analyst Allis-Chalmers Co., West Allis, Wis., 1962-63; postdoctoral fellow U. Mich., Ann Arbor, 1968; CSRS fellow Fed. Exec. Inst., Charlottesville, Va., 1975. Served to lt. (j.g.) USNR, 1943-45. Paul Harris Fellow Rotary Found., 1984. Fellow Am. Soc. Agrl. Engrs. (v.p. region 1970-73); mem. Am. Soc. Engring. Edn., AAAS. Republican. Methodist. Lodge: Rotary. Current work: Research administration; perishable crops storage. Subspecialties: Agricultural engineering; Theoretical and applied mechanics. Home: SE 520 Spring St Pullman WA 99163 Office: 403 Agrl Sci II Wash State Univ Pullman WA 99164-6240

BOYD, WILLIAM EDWARD, remote sensing applications scientist; b. Pasadena, Tex., May 17, 1950; s. Butler Edward and Emma (Fortune) B. B.S., Tex. A&M U., 1972, Ph.D., 1984; M.S., Tex. Tech. U., 1976. Research assoc. Remote Sensing Ctr., College Station, Tex., 1978-83; pres. Remote Sensing Internat., College Station, 1984—; mktg. coordinator Aerial Survey's Inc., College Station, 1981-83; ecol. cons. Remote Sensing Ctr., S.D. State U., Brookings, 1981-82. Contbr. articles to profl. jours. Mem. Soc. Range Mgmt., Sigma Xi. Current work: Applications of remote sensing technology to agriculture and petroleum exploration. Subspecialties: Remote sensing (geoscience); Resource management. Home: 2112 Randolph Rd 204 Silver Spring MD 20902

BOYER, HERBERT WAYNE, biochemist; b. Pitts., July 10, 1936. B.A., St. Vincent Coll., Latrobe, Pa., 1958; Ph.D., U. Pitts., 1963; D.Sc. (hon.), St. Vincent Coll., 1981. Mem. faculty U. Calif., San Francisco, 1966—, prof. biochemistry, 1976—; investigator Howard Hughes Med. Inst., 1976—; co-founder, dir. Genentech, Inc., South San Francisco, Calif. Mem. editorial bd.: Biochemistry. Recipient V.D. Mattai award Roche Inst., 1977; Albert and Mary Lasker award for basic med. research, 1980; USPHS postdoctoral fellow, 1963-66. Mem. Am. Soc. Microbiology, Am. Acad. Arts and Scis., Nat. Acad. Scis. Subspecialty: Biochemistry (biology). Address: Dept Biochemistry HSE 1504 Univ Calif San Francisco CA 94143*

BOYER, PAUL D., biochemist, educator; b. Provo, Utah, July 31, 1918; s. Dell Delos and Grace (Guymon) B.; m. Lyda Mae Whicker, Aug. 31, 1939; children: Gail Anne (Mrs. Denis Hayes), Marjorie Lynne (Mrs. Lukman Clark), Douglas. B.S., Brigham Young U., 1939; M.S., U. Wis., 1941, Ph.D., 1943; D.Sc. (hon.), U. Stockholm, 1974. Instr., research asso. Stanford, 1943-45; asst. prof. to prof. biochemistry U. Minn., 1946-55; Hill research prof. U. Minn. (Med. Sch.), 1955-63; prof. chemistry U. Calif. at Los Angeles, 1963—, dir. Molecular Biology Inst., 1965—, dir. Biotech. Program, 1985—; chmn. biochemistry study sect. USPHS, 1962-67; mem. U.S. Nat. Com. for Biochemistry, 1965-71. Editor: Ann. Rev. of Biochemistry, 1965-70, Biochemical and Biophysical Research Communications, 1968-80, The Enzymes, 1970—; Mem. editorial bd.: Biochemistry, 1969-76, Jour. Biol. Chemistry, 1978-83; Contbr. articles to profl. jours. Recipient Am. Chem. Soc. award in enzyme chemistry, 1955, Tolman award, 1982; Guggenheim fellow, 1955. Fellow Am. Acad. Arts and Sci. (council, v.p. biol. scis. 1985—); mem. Nat. Acad. Sci., Am. Soc. Biol. Chemists (past pres., council mem.), Am. Chem. Soc. (past div. chmn.), Biophys. Soc. Current Work: Enzyme mechanisms, biological energy transductions, oxidative phosphorylation, photophosphorylation, active transport. Subspecialty: Biochemistry (biology). Home: 1033 Somera Rd Los Angeles CA 90024

BOYER, RAYMOND FOSTER, physicist; b. Feb. 1910. B.S. in Physics, Case Western Res. U., 1933, M.S. in Physics, 1935, D.Sc. (hon.), 1955. With Dow Chem. Co., Midland, Mich., 1935—, asst. dir. phys. research lab., 1945-48, dir. phys. research lab., 1948-52, dir. plastics research, 1952-68, asst. dir. corporate research for polymer sci., 1968-72, research fellow, 1972-75; partner Boyer and Boyer, Midland, 1975—; research affiliate Mich. Molecular Inst., 1975—; Vis. prof. Case Western Res. U., 1974, adj. prof., 1979; adj. prof. Central Mich. U., 1980; guest Russian Acad. Scis., 1972, 78, 80, Polish Acad. Scis., 1973; Past chmn. Gordon Conf. on Polymers. Contbr. numerous articles to profl. jours. Recipient Swinburne award Plastics Inst., London, 1972. Mem. Am. Chem. Soc. (past chmn. high polymer div., Borden award in chemistry of plastics and coatings 1970), Am. Phys. Soc. (past chmn. high polymer div.), Soc. Plastics Engrs. (Internat. award in polymer engring. and sci. 1968), Nat. Acad. Engring. Research on physics and physical chemistry of high polymers with emphasis on transitions and relaxations in polymers. Current Work: Multiple transitions and relaxations in polymers with emphasis on thermal and dynamic mechanical properties and statistical data analysis. Subspecialties: Polymer physics; Polymers (materials science). Office: 1910 W St Andrews Rd Midland MI 48640

BOYER, ROBERT ERNST, geologist, educator; b. Palmerton, Pa., Aug. 3, 1929; s. Merritt Ernst and Lizzie Venetta (Reinard) B.; m. Elizabeth Estella Bakos, Sept. 1, 1951; children—Robert M., Janice E., Gary K. B.A., Colgate U., 1951; M.A., Ind. U., 1954; Ph.D., U. Mich., 1959. Instr. geology U. Tex., Austin, 1957-59, asst. prof., 1959-62, asso. prof., 1962-67, prof., 1967—, chmn. dept. geol. scis., 1971-80; dean U. Tex. (Coll. Natural Scis.), 1980—; exec. dir. Natural Scis. Found., 1980—; chmn. exec. com. Geology Found., 1971-80. Author: Activities and Demonstrations for Earth Science, 1970, Geology Fact Book, 1972, Oceanography Fact Book, 1974, The Story of Oceanography, 1975, Solo-Learn in the Earth Sciences, 1975, GEO-Logic, 1976, GEO-VUE, 1978; editor: Tex. Jour. of Sci, 1962-65, Jour. of Geol. Edn, 1965-68. Fellow Geol. Soc. Am., AAAS; mem. Tex. Acad. Sci. (hon. life, pres. 1968), Nat. Assn. Geology Tchrs. (pres. 1974-75), Am. Geol. Inst. (pres. 1983), Am. Assn. Petroleum Geologists, Austin Geol. Soc. (pres. 1975), Gulf Coast Assn. Geol. Soc. (pres. 1977). Subspecialty: Geology. Home: 7644 Parkview Circle Austin TX 78731

BOYLE, BRIAN JOHN, medical information scientist, consultant artificial intelligence; b. Monmouth, Ill., Aug. 5, 1945; s. Brian Edward and Frances Virginia (Hickman) B. B.S., Harvey Mudd Coll., 1967; Ph.D., U. Calif.-San Francisco, 1976. Sr. systems researcher Berkeley Sci. Labs., Calif., 1969-72; mgr. Varian Instrument Data Systems, Walnut Creek and Palo Alto, Calif., 1972-75; pres., dir. Clin. Systems of Calif., Berkeley, 1975—; dir. Integral Systems Internat., San Francisco, Novon, Inc., San Francisco; cons., vis. prof., lectr. U. Calif.-Berkeley, Stanford U. Alt. mem. Berkeley City Council, 1969-70; mem. Community Coll. Bd., 1971-72; bd. govs. Harvey Mudd Coll., 1974-77. Served with USNR, 1966-69. Decorated Purple Heart medal, Bronze Star medal. Mem. Am. Mgmt. Assn., Assn. Computing Machinery, IEEE, Am. Soc. Math., Assn. Advancement Med. Instrumentation, Software Underground Club. Democrat. Patentee high speed continuously variable transmission. Current Work: Artificial intelligence; cognitive science and human factors applied to medical research and genetic engineering. Subspecialties: Biomedical engineering; Artificial intelligence. Office: 222 Downey St San Francisco CA 94117

BOYLE, MICHAEL DERMOT, immunochemist, educator; b. Belfast, No. Ireland, Jan. 4, 1949; came to U.S., 1974; s. Dermot P. and Joan M. (West) B.; m. Carla E. Boyle, Jan. 27, 1973; children: Kieron, Sarah. B.Sc., U. Glasgow, 1971; Ph.D., U. London, 1974. Expert Nat. Cancer Inst., Bethesda, Md., 1976-80, vis. scientist, 1980; assoc. prof. dept. immunology and med. microbiology dept. pediatrics U. Fla., Gainesville, 1981-85, prof. immunology, med. microbiology and pediatrics, 1985—. Contbr. articles in field to profl. jours. Mem. Am. Assn. Immunology, Am. Assn. Cancer Research, Fedn. Advancement of Edn. in the Scis. Current Work: Immunochemistry of complement system; cytotoxic action on complement of tumor cells; bacterial Fc-reactive proteins. Subspecialties: Immunology (medicine); Microbiology (medicine). Home: Box 532 Route 2 Alachua FL 32615 Office: U Fla PO Box J266 JHMHC Gainesville FL 32610

BOYNTON, ROBERT MERRILL, psychology educator; b. Evanston, Ill., Oct. 28, 1924; s. Merrill Holmes and Eleanor (Matthews) B.; m. Alice Neiley, Apr. 9, 1947; children: Sherry, Michael, Neiley, Geoffrey. Student, Antioch Coll., 1942-43, U. Ill., 1943-45; A.B., Amherst Coll., 1948; Ph.D., Brown U., 1952. Asst. prof. psychology and optics U. Rochester, N.Y., 1952-57, asso. prof., 1957-61, prof., 1961-74, dir. Center for Visual Sci., 1963-71, chmn. dept. psychology, 1971-74; prof. psychology U. Calif., San Diego, 1974—; guest researcher Nat. Phys. Lab., Teddington, Eng., 1960-61; vis. prof. physiology U. Calif. Med. Center, San Francisco, 1969-70. Author: Human Color Vision, 1979. Chmn. editorial bd. Vision Research, 1980-85. Contbr. articles to profl. jours. Served with USNR, 1943-45. Fellow AAAS, Optical Soc. Am. (dir. at large 1966-69), Am. Psychol. Assn., Nat. Acad. Scis., Assn. Research in Vision and Ophthalmology (trustee 1984—). Current Work: Visual science, especially human color vision. Subspecialties: Psychophysics; Sensory processes. Home: 376 Bellaire St Del Mar CA 92014

BRAATZ, JAMES ANTHONY, research biochemist; b. Balt., July 17, 1943; s. James Anthony and Janet Barbara (Klosek) B.; m. Geraldine Lee Waldecker, May 9, 1964; children: James Anthony III, Ronald Chester, Mary Janet. B.S., Johns Hopkins U., 1968, Ph.D., 1973. Sr. research technician W. R. Grace & Co., Clarksville, Md., 1963-68; postdoctoral fellow Nat. Inst. Arthritis, Metabolism and Digestive Diseases, NIH, Bethseda, Md., 1973-75; sr. investigator Nat. Inst. Arthritis, Metabolism and Digestive Diseases, NIH (Nat. Cancer Inst.), 1975-81; head biochemistry sect. Nat. Inst. Arthritis, Metabolism and Digestive Diseases, NIH (Biol. Response Modifiers Program), Frederick, Md., 1981—; tech. cons. Abbott Labs., Chgo., 1981—, Hoffmann-LaRoche, Nutley, NJ, 1983—. Editorial adv. bd.: Jour. Biol. Response Modifiers, 1982—. Mem. Am. Chem. Soc., AAAS, Internat. Soc. Oncodevel. Biology and Medicine, Am. Soc. Biol. Chemists. Democrat. Roman Catholic. Patentee in field. Current Work: Biochemical studies on human lung tumor-associated proteins, evaluation of these proteins as serum markers for lung cancer. Subspecialty: Biochemistry (biology). Home: 4510 Yates Rd Beltsville MD 20705 Office: NIH Nat Cancer Inst Frederick Cancer Research Facility Bldg 560 Room 31-93 Frederick MD 21701

BRABB, EARL EDWARD, geologist; b. Detroit, May 27, 1929; s. John Hudson and Grace Elizabeth (Seldon) B.; m. Gisela Marianne Reichel, Sept. 14, 1957; children—Robin Elizabeth, Kristin Anne. A.B., Dartmouth Coll., 1951; M.S., U. Mich., 1952; student Sorbonne, Paris, 1955-56; Ph.D., Stanford U., 1960. Registered profl. geologist, Calif. Research geologist U.S. Geol. Survey, Menlo Park, Calif., 1959-65, 67-83, dep. asst. chief, Washington, 1965-67, chief landslide group, Menlo Park, 1983—. Author: books, maps and articles. Geotech. advisor cities and counties in the San Francisco Bay region, 1972—. Served to lt. USNR, 1952-55. Recipient Meritorious service award U.S. Dept. Interior, 1983. Fellow Geol. Soc. Am.; mem. Internat. Assn. Engring. Geologists, Assn. Geologues de Bassin de Paris. Current work: An assessment of the extent and expense of landsliding in the U.S.; an evaluation of world methods for preparing landslide hazard and risk maps. Subspecialties: Engineering geology; Geology. Home: 3262 Ross Rd Palo Alto CA 94303 Office: US Geol Survey 345 Middlefield Rd MS977 Menlo Park CA 94025

BRACIALE, VIVIAN LAM, immunologist, educator; b. N.Y.C., June 6, 1948; d. Wing Ching and Wai Ching (Li) Lam; m. Thomas Joseph Braciale, Jr., Aug. 5, 1972; children: Kara, Michael Stephen, Laura. A.B., Cornell U., 1969; Ph.D., U. Pa., 1973. Postdoctoral fellow U. Pa., Phila., 1974-75; postdoctoral fellow Washington U., St. Louis, 1975-76; research instr. pathology Washington U. Sch. Medicine, 1978-83, research asst. prof. pathology, 1983—; vis. fellow Australian Nat. U., Canberra, 1976-78; mem. clin. scis. study sect. NIH, 1985—. Contbr. articles on immunology to profl. jours. N.Y. State regent scholar, 1965-69; recipient Nat. Research Service award NIH, 1976-78. Mem. Am. Assn. Immunologists, Am. Diabetes Assn. Lutheran. Current Work: Study of the role of T lymphocytes in the immune response and events in their induction and differentiation, using cloned cell populations. Subspecialty: Immunobiology and immunology. Office: Washington U Sch Medicine 660 S Euclid Ave St Louis MO 63110

BRACK, KARL, chemist, polymer development executive; b. Kuttigen, Switzerland, Nov. 22, 1928; came to U.S., 1953; s. Karl and Emma (Wehrli) B.; m. June Collins, Apr. 16, 1983; children by a previous marriage—Karl Edward, Hans Peter. Ph.D., Swiss Fed. Inst. Tech., 1952. Research chemist Hercules Inc., Wilmington, Del., 1953-71; research assoc. Dennison Mfg. Co., Framingham, Mass., 1971-78; group leader Polymer Industries, Stamford, Conn., 1979-82; mgr. polymer devel. UPACO Adhesives, Nashua, N.H., 1983—; v.p. Brack Constrn. Co., Holliston, Mass., 1982—. Contbr. articles to profl. jours.; patentee in field. Mem. Am. Chem. Soc., Soc. Mfg. Engrs., TAPPI. Current work: Polymers for water-based adhesives, coatings polymers for radiation-curable coatings and adhesives, polymers for 100% reactive coatings and adhesive systems. Subspecialties: Polymer chemistry; Laser photochemistry. Home: 21 New Boston Rd Amherst NH 03031 Office: UPACO Adhesive Inc 3 E Spit Brook Nashua NH 03060

BRADDOCK, PETER SAMUEL, electrical engineer; b. Paterson, N.J., Aug. 26, 1931; s. John C.T. and Henrietta T. (Stapert) B.; m. Josephine Tiritilli, Nov. 12, 1955; children—Peter John, Paul Carmine. B.E.E., Newark Coll., 1970. Test tech. Bogue Elec. Co., Paterson, 1953-57; lab tech. Nat. T.V. Tube Inc., Saddlebrook, N.J., 1957-58; sr. project engr. Regulators Inc., Allendale, N.J., 1958-70; chief engr. White Metal Mfg., Co., Hawthorne, N.J., 1970-80; project engr. Trilectron Industry, Inc., Hawthorne, 1980—; cons. Dynastat Inc., Midland Park, N.J., 1971-81, Wilco Elec., Hackensack, N.J., 1978-82. Served with U.S. Army, 1949-52. Mem. IEEE, Am. Soc. Metals, Nat. Soc. Profl. Engrs. (assoc.), N.J. Inst. Tech. Alumni Assn. Subspecialties: Applied magnetics; Computer engineering. Home: 24 New Read St Pequannock NJ 07440 Office: Trilectron Industries Inc 300 Ninth Ave Hawthorne NJ 07506

BRADEN, CHARLES HOSEA, physics educator; b. Chgo., Mar. 21, 1926; s. Charles Eugene and Rachel Irene (Atchison) B.; m. Sara Caroline McKinley, Sept. 7, 1952; children—Patsy Irene, Jack David. B.S. in Engring., Columbia U., 1946; Ph.D. in Physics, Washington U., 1951. From asst. prof. to regents; prof. physics Ga. Inst. Tech., Atlanta, 1951—, assoc. dir. sch. physics, 1975-80, interim dir. sch. physics, 1980-81; assoc. dir. physics NSF, Washington, 1959-60. Contbr. articles to profl. jours. Served to lt. (j.g.) USNR, 1943-47. Fellow Am. Phys. Soc.; mem. System Dynamics Soc. Episcopalian. Current work: Computer aided modeling of non-linear systems with particular applications to socio-economic systems. Subspecialties: Nuclear physics; Systems engineering. Home: 1645 Berkeley Ln NE Atlanta GA 30329 Office: Ga Inst Tech Sch Physics Atlanta GA 30332

BRADFORD, BERT LARUE, programmer; b. Alton, Ill., May 4, 1954; s. Paul C. and Norma J. (LaRue) B.; m. Kerri C. Cobb, Aug. 14, 1976; children—Jessica L., Jeremy S. B.A., North Tex. State U., 1976; M.A., U. Tex.-Austin, 1979. Staff programmer IBM, Houston, 1979—. Recipient Silver Snoopy award NASA, 1984. Mem. Soc. Indsl. and Applied Math., Am. Astron. Soc., Phi Kappa Phi. Current work: Research in new algorithm for solving ordinary differential equations. Subspecialties: Mathematical software; Numerical analysis (mathematics). Home: 302 Oak Harbor Houston TX 77062 Office: IBM 1322 Space Pk Dr Houston TX 77058

BRADFORD, MARION MCKINLEY, biochemist; b. Rome, Ga., Oct. 28, 1946; s. Adrian LeRoy and Ollie Mae (McCurry) B.; m. Janet Cornelia Holliday, June 12, 1971; children—Shawn Elizabeth, Jennifer Leigh. B.A., Shorter Coll., 1967; M.S., U. Ga., 1974, Ph.D., 1975. Postdoctoral, U. Ga., 1975-77, asst. biochemist, 1979-81; research biochemist AE Staley Mfg. Co., Decatur, Ill., 1981-83, sr. research biochemist, 1983—. Contbr. articles to profl. jours. Patentee in field. Mem. Athens Symphony, Ga., 1980-81; Decatur Millikin Symphony, 1981—; charter mem Messien String Quartet, 1982—. Mem. Am. Chem. Soc., Sigma Xi. Mem. Christian Ch. Current work: Protein chemistry, enzymology, renewable resources utilization, nutrition. Subspecialty: Biochemistry (biology). Office: AE Staley Mfg Co 2200 E Eldorado St Decatur IL 62525

BRADFORD, WESLEY LAMONT, hydrologist, geochemist; b. Morgantown, W.Va., May 9, 1944; s. Ralph Miller and Martha Ward (Ogilvie) B.; m. Pamela Lynn Jones, Mar. 17, 1968; children—Zachary Roberts, Emily Kuxhaus. B.S. in Chemistry, W.Va. U., 1966; M.S. in Chem. Oceanography, Oreg. State U., 1968; Ph.D. in Earth Sci., Johns Hopkins U., 1972. Postdoctoral fellow U.S. Geol. Survey, Menlo Park, Calif., 1972-73; environ. cons. URS Research Co., San Mateo, Calif., 1973-75; hydrologist water quality U.S. Geol. Survey, Menlo Park, 1975-80, hydrologist, geochemist, Reston, Va., 1980—. Contbr. articles to profl. jours. Recipient Spl. Achievement award U.S. Geol. Survey, Reston, 1981, Superior Performance award, 1984. Mem. Water Pollution Control Fedn. (reviewer), Internat. Assn. Water Pollution Research, Am. Chem. Soc., Internat. Assn. Applied Limnology, AAAS. Current work: Movement of hazardous man made organic substances in stream water and sediment. Subspecialties: Environmental chemistry; Hydrology. Office: 6850 Versar Inc PO Box 1549 Springfield VA 22151

BRADLEY, A. FREEMAN, JR., research and development laboratory director, cardiovascular-anesthesia researcher; b. Tuskegee Institute, Ala., Jan. 14, 1932; s. Arthur Freeman and Marion (Davis) B.; m. Dorothy Shamwell, Oct. 31, 1953; children: Lynn, Karen, Freeman. B.A., Lincoln U., 1953; student, Howard U., 1953-54. Biologist, Nat. Heart Inst., Bethesda, Md., 1954-58; staff research assoc. U. Calif.-San Francisco, 1958-68; specialist Cardiovascular Research Inst., 1968-77, dir. research and devel. lab., 1977—; pres., owner Med. Research Specialties, San Francisco, 1961-69. Co-designer: Po_2 and Pco_2 Electrodes, 1958. Chmn., mem. steering com. U. Calif.-San Francisco Black Caucus, 1968—; bd. dirs. Bay Area Men United, 1980—. Mem. Am. Physiol. Soc., AAAS, N.Y. Acad. Sci., Assn. Advancement Med. Instrumentation, Instrument Soc. Am. (sr.). Democrat. Episcopalian. Current Work: Cardiovascular and anesthesia research with emphasis on respiratory physiology and neuroanatomy, design of biomedical apparatus. Subspecialties: Bioinstrumentation; Biomedical engineering. Home: 59 Topaz Way San Francisco CA 94131 Office: U Calif San Francisco Research and Devel Lab 4th and Parnassus Ave San Francisco CA 94143

BRADLEY, JOHN MICHAEL, reading educator; b. Los Angeles, Mar. 5, 1940; s. Earl Chase and Angela Grace (McNamee) B.; m. Nancy Joyce Donaldson, Aug. 11, 1962; children: Christopher Michael, Gia Laverne. A.A., Am. River Coll.-Calif., 1960; B.A., San Jose State Coll., 1962; M.A., Calif. State U.-Sacramento, 1967; Ed.D., U. Pa., 1973. Lectr. edn. U. Pa., Phila., 1968-69; asst. prof. tchr edn. U. Sacramento, Calif., 1969-73; assoc. prof. dept. reading U. Ariz., Tucson, 1973-79, assoc. prof., 1979—. Pres. Foothills Homeowners Assn., Tucson, 1982. Mem. Am. Psychol. Assn., Internat. Reading Assn., Nat. Assn. Sch. Psychologists, Phi Delta Kappa, Kapp Delta Pi, Psi Chi. Democrat. Roman Catholic. Current Work: Coordinating a reading clinic and researching text readability, comprehension and interest. Subspecialty: Reading-related cognition and perception. Home: 3219 E Table Mountain Rd Tucson AZ 85718 Office: Dept Reading U Ariz Tuscon AZ 85721

BRADLEY, KATHARINE TRYON, arboretum director emeritus; b. Washington, Oct. 13, 1920; d. Henry Harrington and Margaret (Ramsay) Tryon; m. Joseph Crane Bradley, June 29, 1956; children: James Watrous, Margaret Bradley Timmerman. A.B. (75th Anniversary scholar, Nancy Skinner Clark fellow), Vassar Coll., 1943; M.S., U. Minn., 1944; Ph.D. (Phoenix fellow), U. Mich., 1953. Instr. biology Bowling Green (Ohio) State U., 1946-48; instr. botany Wellesley (Mass.) Coll., 1951-54; instr. U. Wis.-Madison, 1956-57, dir. univ. arboretum, 1974-83, ret., 1983. Author profl. papers. Vice-pres. 1st Unitarian Soc., 1973-74, pres., 1977-79; pres. Friends of Madison Pub. Library, 1968-71. Am. Cancer Soc. research fellow, 1954-56. Mem. Am. Assn. Bot. Gardens and Arboreta (dir. 1979-82, chmn. awards com. 1979-82), Am. Inst. Biol. Scis., Nature Conservancy, Wilderness Soc. Current Work: Subspecialties: Resource management; Resource conservation. Home: 3102 Bluff St Madison WI 53705

BRADLEY, MICHAEL DOUGLAS, hydrology and water resources educator; b. Wichita, Kans., May 20, 1938; s. Lincoln P. and Nora Belle (Stultz) B.; m. Dorotha M. Bradley, Dec. 23, 1961. B.A., U. N.Mex., 1967; M.P.A., U. Mich., 1968, Ph.D., 1971. Postdoctoral fellow Scripps Instn. Oceanography, La Jolla, Calif., 1971-72; asst. prof. hydrology and water resources U. Ariz., Tucson, 1972-76, assoc. prof., 1976—; vis. prof. Grad. Sch. Architecture and Urban Planning, UCLA, 1980-81; cons. U.S. Army C.E., 1981-82, Hydrogeochem, Inc., 1982-83. Author: The Scientist and Engineer in Court, 1983. Bd. govs. U. Mich. Sch. Natural Resources. Served with USMC, 1956-60. Mem. AAAS, Geoscientists for Internat. Devel., Am. Water Resources Assn. Democrat. Current Work: Water resources policy; water law and rights; Indian water rights; use of scientific information in public decision-making, law and science. Subspecialties: Water resources policy; Resource management. Home: 3301 N Christmas Ave Tucson AZ 85716 Office: Dept Hydrology and Water Resources U Ariz Tucson AZ 85721

BRADLEY, RONALD JAMES, neuroscientist, educator, researcher; b. Enniskillen, No. Ireland, Feb. 17, 1943; came to U.S., 1967; s. Samuel John and Mary Elizabeth (Irvine) B.; m. Doris Maud Brown, Mar. 5, 1966; children—Nicola, Jason. B.Sc., Queens U., Belfast, No. Ireland, 1964; Ph.D., U. Edinburgh, Scotland, 1967. Postdoctoral fellow Yale U., 1967-69; sr. research assoc. U. N.Mex., Albuquerque, 1969-71; asst. prof. neurosci. U. Ala.-Birmingham, 1972-74, assoc. prof., 1974-76, prof., 1976—. Co-editor: Internat. Rev. Neurobiology, 1975—. Mgr., cellist Red Mountain Chamber Orch., 1983—.

Mem. Soc. Biol. Psychiatry, Biophys. Soc., Soc. for Neurosci. Current work: The study of membrane receptors for hormones and drugs in the nervous system, also in the immune system. Subspecialties: Neurobiology; Membrane biology. Home: 2644 Butte Woods Dr Birmingham AL 35243 Office: Neuroscis Program U Ala PO Box 190 University Sta Birmingham AL 35294

BRADLEY, WILLIAM GUERIN, JR., radiologist; b. Los Angeles, July 30, 1948; s. William Guerin and Shirley Ann (Premack) B.; m. Sara Jane Smith, Nov. 6, 1976; children—David, Kristin. B.S., Calif. Inst. Tech., 1970; M.A., Princeton U., 1973, Ph.D., 1973; M.D., U. Calif.-San Francisco, 1977. Intern U. Calif.-San Francisco, 1977-78, resident in radiology, 1978-81; radiologist San Jose Hosp., Calif., 1981-82, Huntington Meml. Hosp., Pasadena, Calif., 1982—; dir. Magnet Resonance Imaging Lab., Huntington Med. Research Insts., Pasadena, 1982—; asst. clin. prof. U. Calif.-San Francisco, 1981—, U. Calif.-San Diego, 1983—, UCLA, 1983—, U. Calif.-Irvine, 1985—; vis. assoc. Calif. Inst. Tech., 1983—. Author: MRI of Head, Neck, and Brain: A Text-Atlas, 1985. Contbr. articles to profl. jours. Mem. Am. Coll. Radiology, Radiol. Soc. N.Am., Am. Roentgen Ray Soc., Los Angeles Radiol. Soc. Republican. Presbyterian. Club: Twilight (Pasadena). Current work: Clinical and research in medical magnetic resonance imaging. Subspecialty: Magnetic resonance imaging. Office: Medical Resonance Imaging Lab Huntington Med Research Insts 10 Pico St Pasadena CA 91105

BRADNER, WILLIAM TURNBULL, research scientist; b. Short Hills, N.J., Aug. 16, 1924; s. Palmer and Emily (Turnbull) B.; m. Ruth Marie Snyder, June 3, 1951; children: Terry Ellen, Tymm, Philip Russell. B.A., Lehigh U., 1948, M.S., 1949, Ph.D., 1952. Research assoc. Brown U., Providence, 1953-55; research assoc. Cornell U. Med. Sch., N.Y.C., 1956-58, asst. prof., 1958; asst. mem. Sloan Kettering Inst., N.Y.C., 1955-58; sr. research scientist Bristol Labs., Inc., Syracuse, N.Y., 1958-65, asst. dir. pharmacology, 1965-73, asst. dir. microbiology, 1973-77, dir. antitumor biology dept., 1977-84, dir. administrn. preclin. anticancer research. Bd. dirs. Am. Cancer Soc. (Onondaga County unit), Syracuse, 1977-81, v.p., 1980. Contbr. over 100 sci. articles to profl. publs. Served with U.S. Army, 1943-45. Decorated Purple Heart. Mem. Am. Assn. Cancer Research, AAAS, Am. Soc. Microbiology, N.Y. Acad. Scis. Republican. Episcopalian. Patentee in field. Current Work: Discovery and evaluation of new cancer chemotherapeutic agents from fermentation, natural, and synthetic sources. Subspecialties: Cancer research (medicine); Microbiology (medicine). Home: 4903 Briarwood Circle Manlius NY 13104 Office: Box 4755 Syracuse NY 13221-4755

BRADSHAW, HOWARD HOLT, management consultant; b. Phila., Feb. 28, 1937; s. Howard Holt and Emojeane (Campbell) B.; m. Loretta Warren Sites, Aug. 13, 1982; children by previous marriage: Elaine Allen, Howard Holt. B.A., Yale U., 1958; postgrad., Duke U., 1958-60. Cert. mgmt. cons. With Western Electric Co., various locations, 1960-68; head behavioral scis. cons. Celanese Fibers Co., Charlotte, N.C., 1968-71; pres. Orgn. Cons., Inc., Charlotte, 1972—; cons. in field. Author: Personal Power, Self Esteem and Performance, 1983, The Management of Self Esteem, 1981; Contbr. articles to profl. jours. Regional chmn. Constl. Party of Pa., Harrisburg, 1964-66; pres. Coordinated Planning League, Inc., Charlotte, 1972-74. Recipient cert. of appreciation Charlotte Police Dept., 1969, cert. of appreciation Mecklenburg County Com., 1970. Mem. Inst. Mgmt. Cons., Am. Psychol. Assn., Soc. Indsl. and Orgn. Psychology, Am. Soc. Tng. and Devel., Orgnl Devel. Network. Republican. Presbyterian. Current Work: Research and application of general system theory to improve individual and group performance within hi-tech and other organizations. Design of psychosocial systems to facilitate the effective introduction of robotics, CAD/CAM and other technologies. Subspecialty: Behavioral psychology. Home: 3031 Arundel Dr Charlotte NC 28209 Office: 1913 Charlotte Dr Charlotte NC 28203

BRADT, HALE VAN DORN, physicist, x-ray astronomer, educator; b. Colfax, Wash., Dec. 7, 1930; s. Wilber Elmore and Norma (Sparlin) B.; m. Dorothy Ann Haughey, July 19, 1958; children—Elizabeth, Dorothy Ann. A.B., Princeton U., 1952; Ph.D. in Physics, M.I.T., 1961. Mem. dept. physics M.I.T., 1961—, prof., 1972—; sci. investigator Small Astronomy Satellite, NASA, 1975-79, High Energy Astronomy Obs., 1977-79. Co-editor: X and Gamma Ray Astronomy, 1973; asso. editor: Astrophys. Jour. Letters, 1974-77. Served with USNR, 1952-54. Recipient Exceptional Sci. achievement medal NASA, 1978. Mem. Am. Astron. Soc. (sec.-treas. high energy astrophysics div. 1973-75, chmn. 1981), Am. Phys. Soc., Sigma Xi. Current Work: Galactic x-ray source; optical counterparts of x-ray sources. Subspecialties: X-ray high energy astrophysics; Optical astronomy. Home: Belmont MA Office: 37-581 MIT Dept Physics Cambridge MA 02139

BRADY, LUTHER W., JR., physician; b. Rocky Mount, N.C., Oct. 20, 1925; s. Luther W. and Gladys B. A.A., George Washington U., 1944, A.B., 1946, M.D., 1948. Diplomate Am. Bd. Radiology (treas. 1980-82, pres. 1984—). Intern Jefferson Med. Coll. Hosp., Phila., 1948-50, resident in radiology, 1954-55; resident radiology Hosp. U. Pa., Phila., 1955-56; fellow Nat. Cancer Inst., 1953-57, 1957-59, practice medicine, specializing in radiation therapy and oncology, Phila.; asst. instr. radiology Jefferson Med. Coll. Hosp., 1954-55, U. Pa., Phila., 1955, instr., 1956-57, asso. radiology, 1957-59; asst. prof. radiology Coll. of Physicians and Surgeons, Columbia U., N.Y.C., summer, 1959; assoc. prof. radiology Hahnemann Med. Coll. and Hosp., Phila., 1959-62, prof., 1963—, chmn. dept. radiation therapy, 1970—; asst. prof. radiology Harvard Med. Sch., Boston, 1962-63; mem. med. radiation adv. com. Bur. Radiation Health, HEW, 1971-74; cons. radiation therapy various hosps.; mem. U.S. del. to Interam. Congress Radiology, 1975, Internat. Congress on Radiology, 1981; sec. gen. Internat. Congress Radiology, 1985; med. adv. radiation therapy, dir. Pa. Blue Shield, Camp Hill. Author: Tumors of the Nervous System, 1975, Cancer of the Lung, Clinical Applications of the Electron Beam; editor: Cancer Clin. Trials (Am. Jour. Clin. Oncology); editorial bd. Cancer; assoc. editor: Am. Jour. Roentgenology; sr. editor Internat. Jour. Radiol. Oncology; assoc. editor Gynecologic Oncology; contbr. articles on radiation therapy to profl. jours. Bd. dirs. Assn. Artists Equity of Phila., Welcome House, 1974—, Settlement Music Sch., 1973—, Phila. Art Alliance, 1977—; trustee Phila. Mus. Art, also mem. oriental art com., 1974—, chmn. exec. com., 1968-72, mem. print, contemporary art and Indian art coms., 1974—. Served to lt. M.C. USN, 1950-54. Recipient Grubbe award Chgo. Radiol. Soc., 1977, Soil and Gold medal U. So. Calif., 1985. Fellow Am. Coll. Radiology (chmn. commn. radiation therapy 1975-81, bd. chancellors 1975-81, Gold medal 1983), Deutsches Roentgen Gesellschaft (hon.), Royal Coll. Radiologists London (hon); mem. Radiol. Soc. N.Am. (bd. dirs. 1977-84, pres. 1984—, chmn. bd. dirs. 1982-83, chmn. refresher course com. com. 1971-75, Erskine lectr. 1979), Pa. Radiol. Soc. (dir. 1970-77, councilor to Am. Coll. Radiology 1971-77), Am. Radium Soc. (pres. 1976-77, dir., Janeway lectr. 1980), Am. Cancer Soc. (pres. Phila. div. 1976-78, dir. 1968—, exec. com. 1976-78, mem. breast cancer task force 1974—), Am. Soc. Therapeutic Radiologists (pres. 1971-72), Assn. U. Radiologists, Am. Roentgen Ray Soc., Am. Assn. for Cancer Research, Radiation Research Soc., Am. Fedn. Clin. Oncologic Soc. (exec. com.), Am. Soc. Clin. Oncology, Phila. Roentgen Ray Soc. (pres. 1976-77, mem. exec. com. 1976-78), Am. Fedn. Clin. Research, Coll. Physicians Phila., James Ewing Soc., Assn. Pendergrass Fellows, Philadelphia County Med. Soc., AMA, Med. Soc. State Pa., Internat. Skeletal Soc., Council Acad. Socs., Soc. Chairmen Acad. Radiation Oncology Programs (pres. 1977), Soc. Chairmen Acad. Radiology Depts. (pres. 1974-75), Gynecologic Oncology Group (exec. com. 1971—, assoc. chmn. 1971—), Radiation Therapy Oncology Group (chmn. 1980—), Internat. Club Radiotherapists, Nat. Cancer Inst. (bd. sci. counselors, com. for radiation therapy studies 1971—, chmn. cancer clin. trails com.), Smith-Reed-Russell Soc., Alpha Omega Alpha, Phi Lambda Kappa. Clubs: Merion Cricket, Racquet of Phila, Union League of Phila. Current Work: Monoclonal antibodies, tumor research (radiation synthesizers, combined modality treatment.). Subspecialties: Cancer research (medicine); Radiology. Office: 230 N Broad St Philadelphia PA 19102

BRADY, LYNN ROBERT, pharmacognosist, educator; b. Shelton, Nebr., Nov. 15, 1933; s. Connie E. and Laura M. (Vohland) B.; m. Geraldine Ann Walcott, June 23, 1957. B.S., U. Nebr., 1955, M.S., 1957; Ph.D., U. Wash., 1959. Asst. prof. pharmacognosy U. Wash., 1959-63, assoc. prof., 1963-67, prof., 1967—, chmn. dept., 1972-80, asst. dean, 1982—; Chmn. conf. Tchrs. Am. Assn. Colls. Pharmacy, 1966-67. Author: (with others) Pharmacognosy, 6th edit., 1970, 7th edit., 1976, 8th edit., 1981. Fellow Acad. Pharm. Scis. (chmn. sect. pharmacognosy and natural products 1969-70); mem. Am. Pharm. Assn., Am. Soc. Pharmacognosy (pres. 1970-71), Sigma Xi, Rho Chi, Kappa Psi. Research in fungal constituents, alkaloid biosynthesis, chemotaxonomy Current Work: Identification of fungal constituents, plant poisonings and chemotaxonomy. Subspecialty: Pharmacognosy. Home: 5815 NE 57th St Seattle WA 98105

BRADY, ROSCOE O., physician; b. Phila., Oct. 11, 1923; s. Roscoe O. and Martha (Roberts) B.; m. Bennett Carden Manning, 1972; 2 sons. Student, Pa. State U., 1941-43; M.D., Harvard, 1947; postgrad., U. Pa., 1948-49. NRC fellow U. Pa., 1948-50, USPHS spl. fellow, 1950-52; sect. chief Nat. Inst. Neurol. Diseases and Blindness, NIH, 1954-67, acting lab. chief neurochemistry, Bethesda, Md., 1967; chief developmental and metabolic neurology br. Nat. Inst. Neurol. and Communicative Disorders and Stroke, 1972—; professorial lectr. George Washington Sch. Medicine, 1963—; faculty Georgetown U. Sch. Medicine, 1967—. Author: (with Donald B. Tower) Neurochemistry of Nucleotides and Amino Acids, 1960, Basic Neurosciences, 1975, (with John A. Barranger) Molecular Basis of Lysosomal Storage Disorders, 1984, also numerous articles. Mem. Am. Soc. Biol. Chemists, Am. Chem. Soc., Am. Acad. Neurology, Am. Acad. Mental Retardation, Soc. Exptl. Biology and Medicine, Am. Soc. Clin. Investigation, Inst. Medicine, Nat. Acad. Sci. First demonstration of enzyme system for fatty acid synthesis; biosynthesis of myelin sheath lipids, nature of metabolic defects in Gaucher's disease, Niemann-Pick disease, Fabry's diseases and Tay-Sachs disease; diagnostic tests for Gaucher's Niemann-Pick, Fabry's diseases; control and therapy of lipid storage diseases; metabolism of sphingolipids in neoplastic diseases. Current Work: Therapy of inherited metabolic disorders; molecular basis of metabolic diseases in humans; role of glycoproteins in myelination and demyelinating diseases. Subspecialties: Biochemistry (medicine); Genetics and genetic engineering (medicine). Home: 9501 Kingsley Ave Bethesda MD 20814 Office: NIH 9000 Rockville Pike Bethesda MD 20892

BRAGG, DARRELL BRENT, nutrition educator, researcher; b. Sutton, W.Va., May 24, 1933; s. William Harvey and Gertrude (Perrine) B.; m. Elizabeth Hoose, Dec. 28, 1957; children—Roger, Larry, Teresa. B.Sc., W.Va. U., 1959, M.Sc., 1960; Ph.D., U. Ark., 1966. Research assoc., U. Ark., Fayetteville, 1963-67; asst. prof. U. Man., Winnipeg, 1967-68, assoc. prof., 1968-70; assoc. prof. U. B.C., Vancouver, 1970-74, prof., 1974—, head dept. poultry sci., 1977—; research cons. El Dorado BioTechnology Co., Richardson, Tex., RaiwGrow Industries Inc., Surrey, B.C. Author: Canadian Grain for Poultry, 1975, Poultry Production in Western Canada, 1980. Contbr. numerous articles to profl. jours. Grantee in field. Mem. Poultry Sci. Assn. (pres. 1983-84), World's Poultry Sci. (v.p. Can. br. 1980-84), Can. Soc. Nutritional Sci., others. Current work: Animal nutrition, protein (amino acids), energy, minerals; poultry management and production technology Subspecialty: Animal nutrition. Office: Univ British Columbia Dept Poultry Sci 2357 Main Mall Vancouver BC V6T 2A2 Canada

BRAGG, ROBERT HENRY, engineering educator; b. Jacksonville, Fla., Aug. 11, 1919; s. Robert Henry and Lilly Camille (McFarland) B.; m. Violette Mattie McDonald, June 14, 1947; children: Robert Henry, Pamela. B.S., Ill. Inst. Tech., 1949, M.S., 1951, Ph.D., 1960. Asso. physicist research lab. Portland Cement Assn., Skokie, Ill., 1951-56; sr. physicist physics div. Armour Research Found., Ill. Inst. Tech., Chgo., 1956-61; sr. mem., mgr. phys. metallurgy dept. Lockheed Palo Alto Research Lab., Calif., 1961-69; prof. materials sci. U. Calif., Berkeley, 1969—, chmn. dept. materials sci. and mineral engring., 1978-81; faculty sr. scientist Lawrence Berkeley Lab., 1969—; cons. NASA, IBM, NIH., NSF; mem. adv. com. div. materials research NSF, 1981—. Contbr. articles to profl. jours. Pres. Palo Alto NAACP, 1967-68. Served with U.S. Army, 1943-46. Decorated Bronze star (2); Recipient Disting. awards No. Calif. sect. Am. Inst. Mining and Metall. Engrs., 1970, No. Calif. sect. Am. Ceramic Soc., 1980. Mem. Am. Phys. Soc., Am. Ceramic Soc. (chmn. No. Calif. sect. 1980), AIME (chmn. No. Calif. sect. 1970), Am. Carbon Soc., Am. Soc. Metals, AAUP, No. Calif. Council Black Profl. Engrs., Sigma Xi, Tau Beta Pi, Sigma Pi Sigma., Am. Crystallography Assn. Democrat. Current Work: Structure and physical properties of carbon materials, graphitization in hard and soft carbons. Home: 2 Admiral Dr 373 Emeryville CA 94608 Office: Dept Materials Sci and Mineral Engring Univ of Calif Berkeley CA 94720

BRAGGIO, JOHN THOMAS, research psychologist, educator; n. Bergamasco, Alessandria, Italy, July 31, 1947; came to U.S., 1956; s. Battista and Joanne (Prandini) B.; m. Sherryll Morris, Mar. 15, 1973, B.S., Coe Coll., 1969; M.A., Ga. State U., 1973, Ph.D., 1975. Research asst. Lockheed Aircraft Co., Marietta, Ga., 1969-70, Yerkes PRC of Emory U., Atlanta, 1970-72; instr. Ga. State U., Atlanta, 1972-74; instr. U. N.C., Asheville, 1974-75, asst. prof., 1975-82; sr. research asst. U. Okla., Oklahoma City, 1983-84; research health scientist Behavioral Scis. Labs., VA Med Ctr., Oklahoma City, 1985—; adj. faculty dept. psychology and personnel services Central State U., Edmond, Okla., 1983—. Contbr. articles to profl. jours. Bd. dirs. Asheville Assn. for Children With Learning Disabilities, 1979; vol. Boys Club Am., Asheville, 1974-76. Grantee State of N.C., 1979, NSF, 1979, 1980; NIH fellow, 1982. Mem. Am. Psychol. Assn., Okla. Psychol. Assn. (exec. com. div. acad. and research psychologists 1985—), AAAS, N.Y. Acad. Sci., Soc. for Neurosci., Soc. for Psychophysiol. Research. Democrat. Unitarian. Current work: The degree of influence which is exerted by the fastigial nucleus of the cerebellum on behavior, arterial pressure, and heart rate in freely moving dogs. Subspecialties: Physiological psychology; Neuropsychology. Home: 504 N W 138th St Edmond OK 73034 Office: 921 NE 13th St Oklahoma City OK 73104

BRAKEFIELD, JAMES CHARLES, research engineer, scientist; b. Janesville, Wis., Nov. 28, 1944; s. John Henry and Edith Gertrude (Thompson) B.; m. Irene Lopez Casiano, June 10, 1978. B.S., U. Wis., 1966, M.S.E.E., M.S. in Computer Sci, 1972. Teaching asst. Engring. Computing Lab., U. Wis.-Madison, 1963-66; programmer analyst Control Data Corp., Arden Hills, Minn., 1968-70; systems. analyst Tex. Instruments, Austin, Tex., 1973-74; research engr. Tech. Inc., San Antonio, 1975—. Contbr. articles to tech jours. Served with AUS, 1966-68. Mem. IEEE, Assn. Computing Machinery. Current Work: Computer architectures, computer tools and languages; software engineering for biomedical experiments, image processing, simulation and modeling, computer instruction set design. Subspecialties: Computer engineering; Theoretical computer science. Home: 5803 Cayuga St San Antonio TX 78228 Office: 300 Breesport St San Antonio TX 78216

BRAKKE, MYRON KENDALL, research chemist; b. Fillmore County, Minn., Oct. 23, 1921; s. John T. and Hulda Christina (Marburger) B.; m. Betty-Jean Einbecker, Aug. 16, 1947; children—Kenneth Allen, Thomas Warren, Joan Patricia, Karen Elizabeth. B.S., U. Minn., 1943, Ph.D., 1947. Research asso. Bklyn. Bot. Garden, 1947-52; research asso. U. Ill., 1952-55; research chemist U.S. Dept. Agr., Lincoln, Nebr., 1955—; prof. plant pathology U. Nebr., Lincoln, 1955—. Editor: Virology, 1960-66. Contbr. articles to profl. jours. Fellow AAAS, Am. Phytopath. Soc.; mem. Am. Chem. Soc., Electron Microscope Soc., Nat. Acad. Scis., Am. Soc. Microbiology, Sigma Xi, Phi Lambda Upsilon, Gamma Sigma Delta, Alpha Zeta. Current Work: Purification and characterization of plant viruses, nucleic acids and proteins; formation of mosaics, virus-induced mutations in maize; cereal viruses. Subspecialties: Plant virology; Biochemistry (biology). Office: Room 406 Plant Science Bldg 8-K U Nebr Lincoln NE 68583

BRAMBLE, JAMES HENRY, mathematics educator; b. Annapolis, Md., Dec. 1, 1930; s. Charles Clinton and Edith (Rinker) B.; m. Margaret H., June 25, 1977; children—Margot, Tamara, Mary, James; 1 stepson, Myron Alan Hayes. A.B., Brown U., 1953; M.A., U. Md., 1955, Ph.D., 1958; D.Sc. (hon.), Chalmers U., Tech., Gothenburg, Sweden, 1985. Mathematician Gen. Electric Co., Cin., 1957-59, Naval Ordnance Lab., White Oak, Md., 1959-60; asst. prof., asso. prof., prof. U. Md., 1960-68; prof. Cornell U., Ithaca, N.Y., 1968—; dir. Center Applied Math., 1974-80, assoc. chmn. math., 1979-84; cons. Brookhaven Nat. Lab., 1976—; vis. prof. Chalmers U. Tech., Göteborg, 1970, 72, 73, 76, U. Rome, 1966-67, Ecole Poly., Paris, 1978, Lausanne, Switzerland, 1979; vis. prof. U. Paris, 1981; lectr. in field. Chmn. editorial bd.: Mathematics of Computation, 1975-84; contbr. articles profl. jours. Mem. Am. Math. Soc. (council), Soc. Indsl. and Applied Math. Subspecialties: Applied mathematics; Numerical analysis (computer science). Address: 220 Berkshire Rd Ithaca NY 14850

BRAMLAGE, LAWRENCE ROBERT, veterinary surgeon, educator; b. Marysville, Kans., July 12, 1951; s. Bernard Wesley and Geraldine Louise (Lierz) B.; m. Marilyn Sue Burns, May 25, 1974; children: Joey Marie, Matthew Bernard. D.V.M., Kans. State U., 1975; M.S., Ohio State U., 1978. Vet. intern Colo. State U., Ft. Collins, 1975-76; resident Ohio State U., Columbus, 1976-78, asst. prof. vet. surgery, 1978-82, 83—; equine surgery cons. Mem. AVMA, Am. Assn. Equine Practitioners. Democrat. Roman Catholic. Current Work: Orthopedic surgery in horses. Subspecialty: Surgery (veterinary medicine). Office: 1935 Coffey Rd Columbus OH 43210

BRAMWELL, FITZGERALD BURTON, chemist; b. Bklyn., May 16, 1945; s. Fitzgerald and Lula (Burton) B.; m. Charlott Burns Bramwell, Aug. 12, 1973; children: Fitzgerald T., Elizabeth B., Jill B. B.A., Columbia U., 1966; M.S., U. Mich., 1967, Ph.D., 1970. Research chemist Esso Research & Engring., Linden, N.J., 1970-71; asst. prof. chemistry Bklyn. Coll., CUNY, 1971-75, assoc. prof., 1975-80, prof., 1980—, Bklyn. Coll., CUNY (Grad. Sch. Univ. Ctr.), 1980—; mem. grad. fellowship evaluation panel NRC, 1981-82, chmn., 1983, cons. in field. Author: (with G. Wieder, C.J. Shahani, C.R. Dillard) General Chemistry 2 Laboratory Manual, 1975, (with C.J. Shahani, C.R. Dillard) General Chemistry 1 Laboratory Manual, 1975, (with C.R. Dillard, C.J. Shahani, G.M. Wieder) Investigations in General Chemistry Quantitative Techniques and Basic Principles, 1977, Instructor's Guide for Investigations in General Chemistry Quantitative Techniques and Basic Principles, 1978; contbr. (with C.R. Dillard, C.J. Shahani, G.M. Wieder) book reviews and articles to prof. jours. NSF grantee, 1977-78; Bell Telephone Labs. Equipment grantee, 1977; NIH grantee, 1985—. Mem. N.Y. Acad. Sci., Am. Phys. Soc., Am. Chem. Soc. (dir.-at-large N.Y. sect. 1985—), Sigma Xi, Phi Lambda Upsilon. Current Work: Structure and properties of organic semiconductors, structures and properties of group IV organometallics electron spin resonance spectroscopy. Subspecialties: Physical chemistry; Solid state chemistry. Office: Dept Chemistry Brooklyn Coll Bedford Ave and Ave H Brooklyn NY 11210

BRANCH, LAURENCE GEORGE, health policy researcher, educator, gerontologist; b. Cleve., Oct. 31, 1944; s. John Howard and Mercedes (Brachle) B.; m. Patricia Mary Skalski, June 24, 1967; children: Kathryn Helen, Carolyn Mercedes, Daniel Laurence. B.A., Marquette U., 1967; M.A., Loyola U., Chgo., 1969, Ph.D., 1971. Program dir. Ctr. Survey Research, Boston, 1973-79; Assoc. prof. Harvard Med. Sch., 1978—, Harvard Sch. Pub. Health, 1980—; exec. com. div. aging Harvard Med. Sch., 1979—; assoc. dir. Geriartric Research, Edn. and Clin. Center Brockton/West VA Outpatient Clinic, 1982—; trustee, pres. North Hill Life Care Community, Needham, Mass., 1980—; mem. profl. staff Brigham & Women's Hosp., Boston, 1981—; cons. Robert Wood Johnson Found., Princeton, N.J. Mem. editorial bd.: Jour. Gerontology, 1981, Jour. Community Health, 1980, Gerontologist, 1982. Served to maj. USAR, 1968—. Fellow Gerontol. Soc. Am.; Mem. Am. Pub. Health Assn. (sect. chmn. 1983—), Am. Psychol. Assn., AAAS. Current Work: Epidemiology of disability, normal aging, gerontology, research health policy, population survey research, evaluation research. Subspecialties: Health services research; Gerontology. Home: 20 Hammondswood Rd Chestnut Hill MA 02167 Office: Harvard Medical School 643 Huntington Ave Boston MA 02115

BRANCH, WILLIAM DEAN, plant breeder, agronomist, researcher; b. Duncan, Okla., Sept. 14, 1950; s. William M. and Effie M. (Holbrook) B.; m. Milla J. Pruitt, July 31, 1972; children—Joshua W., Mia J. B.S., Okla. State U., 1972, M.S., 1974, Ph.D., 1976. Research assoc. Auburn U., Ala., 1977-78; asst. geneticist U. Ga., Tifton, 1978-84, assoc. prof., 1985—. Contbr. articles to profl. jours. Collaborative Research Support Program grantee, 1982—. Mem. Am. Soc. Agronomy, Crop Sci. Soc. Am., Am. Peanut Research Edn. Soc., Am. Genetic Assn., Council Agr. Sci. Tech., Sigma Xi. Club: Tifton Lions. Current work: Peanut genetics, breeding and evaluation. Subspecialties: Plant genetics; Agronomy. Office: U Ga Dept Agronomy Coastal Plain Exptl Sta Tifton GA 31793

BRANCO, MARIA DOS MILAGRES, nuclear engineer; b. Almada, Portugal, Feb. 5, 1955; came to U.S., 1970; d. Jose Vieira and Herminia (Torrado) B.; m. George Leo Rorke, Oct. 6, 1979; children—Evan Daniel, Catrina Ann. B.S. in Mech. Engring., Newark Coll., 1974; M.S. in Nuclear Engring., Cornell U., 1975. Cert. profl. engr., N.J. Asst. engr. L.I. Lighting Co., Hicksville, N.Y., 1975-78, engr., 1978 82, prin. engr., 1982-84, engring. supr., 1985—; officer Met. Nuclear Fuel Group, N.Y.C., 1977. Contbr. articles to profl. jours. Mem. Am. Nuclear Soc. (best paper award winter meeting 1983). Current Work: Computerized 3D core follow and predictive methodology and reload design. Subspecialties: Nuclear engineering; Numerical analysis (computer science). Office: Shoreham Nuclear Power Sta North Country Rd Wading River NY 11792

BRANDINGER, JAY JEROME, electronics company executive; b. N.Y.C., Jan. 2, 1927; s. Abraham and Lillian (Newman) B.; m. Alice Levite, Dec. 23, 1949; children—Paul, Donna, Norman. B.S. in Elec. Engring., Cooper Union, 1951; M.S. in Elec. Engring., Rutgers U., 1962, Ph.D. in Elec. Engring., 1968. Registered profl. engr., Ind. Mem. tech. staff RCA Labs., Riverhead, N.Y., 1951-59; head communications systems research, Princeton, N.J., 1959-66, group head display systems research, 1966-70, TV systems research, 1970-74; div. v.p., TV engr. RCA Consumer Elec. div., Indpls., 1974-79, div. v.p., gen. mgr. SelectaVision VideoDisc Ops., 1979-84, staff v.p., systems engr. electronics products and labs., 1984—; mem. communications tech. group Ind. Corp. Sci. and Tech., Indpls., 1984—; mem. dean's indsl. adv. bd. Purdue U., Indpls., 1983—. Patentee (4). Active Boy Scouts Am., N.J./Washington council; del.-at-large Ind. Congress Edn., Indpls., 1983. Recipient RCA Achievement awards, 1952, 70, 73. Fellow Soc. Info. Display; mem. N.Y. Acad. Sics., Inst. Math. Statis., IEEE, Sigma Xi, Eta Kappa Nu. Current work: Consumer electronics, TV, VideoDiscs, computers. Subspecialty: Electronics. Office: RCA Electronic Products and Labs 7900 Rockville Rd Indianapolis IN 46291

BRANDT, CARL DAVID, virologist, researcher; b. Bridgeport, Conn., Jan. 19, 1928; s. Carl August and Hildur (Wedberg) B.; m. Elsa Lund Erickson, Apr. 25, 1964; children: Karen, Erik. B.S., U. Conn., 1949; M.S., U. Mass., 1951; Ph.D., Harvard U., 1958. Research instr. dept. vet. sci. U. Mass., 1949-52, 54; research virologist Charles Pfizer and Co., Ind. and Conn., 1958-62; assoc. dept. epidemiology Public Health Research Inst., N.Y.C., 1962-66; research assoc. virology sect. Children's Hosp., Washington, 1966-79; sr. research assoc. virology sect. Children's Hosp. Nat. Med. Center, 1979—; instr. in pediatrics Georgetown U. Sch. Medicine, 1966-69; asst. prof. child health and devel. George Washington U. Sch. Medicine, 1969-74, asso. prof., 1974—. Contbr. numerous articles, chpts. to profl. publs. Served to 1st lt. USAF, 1952-54. Fellow Am. Acad. Microbiology, Infectious Diseases Soc. Am., Am. Coll. Epidemiology; mem. AAAS, Am. Soc. Microbiology, Soc. Epidemiologic Research, Pan Am. Group for Rapid Viral Diagnosis, Sigma Xi. Current Work: Diagnosis and epidemiology of viral gastroenteritis, viral respiratory disease, rapid viral diagnosis, electron microscopy. Subspecialties: Virology (medicine); Epidemiology. Home: 819 E Franklin Ave Silver Spring MD 20901 Office: Virology Sect Children's Hosp 111 Michigan Ave NW Washington DC 20010

BRANDT, EDWARD NEWMAN, JR., university administrator, epidemiologist; b. Oklahoma City, July 3, 1933; s. Edward Newman and Myrtle Frances (Brazil) B.; m. Patricia Lawson, Aug. 29, 1953; children—Patrick James, Edward Newman III, Rex Carlin. B.S., U. Okla., 1954, M.D., 1960, Ph.D. in Biostats., 1963; M.S., Okla. State U., 1955; L.H.D. (hon.), Med. U. S.C., 1984; D.Sc. (hon.), N.Y. Inst. Tech., 1984; L.H.D. (hon.), Rush U., 1985. Intern VA Hosp., Oklahoma City, 1960-61; resident U. Okla. Med. Ctr., Oklahoma City, 1961-62, from instr. to assoc. prof., dept. preventive medicine, also from instr. to asst. prof., dept. medicine Sch. Medicine, 1961-67, prof., chmn. dept. biostats. and epidemiology Sch. Health, 1967-68, prof. dept. preventive medicine, assoc. prof. dept. medicine Sch. Medicine, prof. dept. biostats. and epidemiology Sch. Health, 1967-70, assoc. dir. Med. Ctr., assoc. dean Sch. Medicine, 1968-70; prof. dept. preventive medicine and community health Sch. Medicine, U. Tex.-Galveston, 1970-84, prof. dept. family medicine, 1973-84, dean Grad. Sch., 1970-74, dean of medicine, 1974-76, exec. dean, 1976-77; vice chancellor for health affairs U. Tex. System Adminstrn., Austin, 1977-81; asst. sec. for health HHS, Washington, 1981-84; prof. dept. epidemiology and preventive medicine U. Md.-Balt., 1985—, prof. dept. family medicine, 1985—, chancellor, 1985—. Contbr. articles to profl. jours. Bd. govs. ARC, 1981-84. Served as asst. surgeon gen. USPHS, 1981-84. Recipient numerous awards. Hon. fellow Am. Coll. Cardiology; mem. AAAS, Am. Fedn. Clin. Research, AMA (chmn. sect. on med. schs. 1979-81), Md. Med. Assn., Am. Acad. Family Physicians, Md. Acad. Family Physicians, Sigma Xi (sec. Galveston chpt. 1973-74), Alpha Omega Alpha (pres. Tex. Alpha chpt. 1974-75), Phi Eta Sigma, Alpha Epsilon Delta, Phi Kappa Phi, Phi Sigma, Pi Mu Upsilon. Current work: academic administration; public policy in health. Subspecialties: Biostatistics; Public policy in health. Office: U Md at Baltimore 520 W Lombard St Baltimore MD 21201

BRANNIGAN, GARY G(EORGE), clinical psychologist, consultant; b. Bridgeport, Conn., Mar. 22, 1947; s. George Tierney and Anna (Chisarik) B.; m. Linda Ann Baker, Sept. 7, 1969; children: Marc, Michael. B.A., Fairfield U., 1969; M.A., U. Del., 1973, Ph.D., 1973. Lic. clin. psychologist, N.Y. cert. sch. psychologist, N.Y. Panel psychologist Office Vocat. Rehab.; Asst. prof. psychology SUNY-Plattsburgh, 1973-76, assoc. prof. psychology, 1976-82, prof. psychology, 1982; cons. No. N.Y. Center, Plattsburgh, 1974-77, Early Infant Intervention Program, Plattsburgh, 1977—, Essex County Head Start, Elizabethtown, N.Y., 1981—; dir. Psychol. Services Clinic, Plattsburgh, 1975-80; cons. editor Exceptional People Quar., 1981-84, Jour. Genetic Psychology, 1984—, Genetic Psychology Monographs, 1984—. Co-author: Research and Clinical Applications of the Bender Gestalt Test, 1980; test Preschool and Primary Visual Motor Gestalt Screening Instrument, 1982; editor: test Psychoeducational Perspectives: Reading in Educational Psychology, 1982; contbr. articles to profl. jours., chpts. to books, articles to newspapers. Bd. dirs. Plattsburgh Little League, 1980-82; coordinator YMCA Youth Basketball Program, 1981-85; coach Plattsburgh Grasshopper Baseball Program, 1980—. Grantee State Conn., 1971-73; Grantee SUNY, 1974; Grantee HEW, 1976-79. Fellow Soc. for Personality Assessment; mem. Am. Psychol. Assn., Clinton County Assn. for Retarded Children, Clinton County Mental Health Assn. Lodge: Elks. Current Work: Psychological assessment of infants and children; development of intervention strategies for handicapped and high-risk infants and children. Subspecialties: Developmental psychology; Learning. Home: 53 Leonard Ave Plattsburgh NY 12901 Office: SUNY Plattsburgh NY 12901

BRANNON, H(EZZIE) RAYMOND, JR., oil co. scientist; b. Midland, Ala., Jan. 23, 1926; s. Hezzie Raymond and Cora Mae B.; m. Rita Alice Newville, Oct. 19, 1957; 1 dau., Sarah Elaine. B. Engring. Physics, Auburn (Ala.) U., 1950, M.S., 1951. Research asso. Auburn Research Found., 1951-52; engr. Exxon Prodn. Research Co., Houston, 1952—, research scientist, 1973—. Contbr. articles to profl. jours. Served with USNR, 1943-46. Mem. Am. Phys. Soc., Soc. Petroleum Engrs. of AIME (Disting. Lectr. 1976-77), Soc. Exploration Geophysicists, NRC (marine bd.), Nat. Acad. Engring., Sigma Xi, Phi Kappa Phi, Tau Beta Pi, Sigma Pi Sigma. Republican. Patentee in field. Current Work: Offshore petroleum production systems and drilling vessels; design and operation of offshore structures. Subspecialties: Petroleum engineering; Civil engineering. Home: 5807 Queensloch St Houston TX 77096 Office: PO Box 2189 Houston TX 77001

BRANSCOMB, LEWIS MCADORY, physicist; b. Asheville, N.C., Aug. 17, 1926; s. Bennett Harvie and Margaret (Vaughan) B.; m. Margaret Anne Wells, Oct. 13, 1951; children—Harvie Hammond, Katharine Capers. A.B. summa cum laude, Duke U., 1945, D.Sc. (hon.); M.S., Harvard U., 1947, Ph.D., 1949; D.Sc. (hon.), Poly. Inst. N.Y., Clarkson Coll., Rochester U., U. Colo., Western Mich. U., Lycoming Coll., U. Ala., Pratt Inst., Rutgers U., Lehigh U.; L.H.D. (hon.), Pace U. Instr. physics Harvard U., 1950-51; lectr. physics U. Md., 1952-54; vis. staff mem. Univ. Coll., London, 1957-58; chief atomic physics sect. Nat. Bur. Standards, Washington, 1954-60, chief atomic physics div., 1960-62; chmn. Joint Inst. Lab. Astrophysics, U. Colo., 1962-65, 68-69; chief lab. astrophysics div. Nat. Bur. Standards, Boulder, Colo., 1962-69; prof. physics U. Colo., 1962-69; dir. Nat. Bur. Standards, 1969-72; chief scientist, v.p. IBM Corp., Armonk, N.Y., 1972—; mem. JASON div. Inst. Def. Analyses, 1962-69; U.S. rep. to CODATA com. Internat. Council Sci. Unions, 1970-73; mem.-at-large Def. Sci. Bd., 1969-72; mem. high level policy group sci. and tech. info. Orgn. Econ. Coop. and Devel., 1968-70; mem. Pres.'s Sci. Adv. Com., 1965-68, chmn. panel space sci. and tech., 1967-68; mem. Nat. Sci. Bd., 1978-84, chmn., 1980-84; mem. Pres.'s Nat. Productivity Adv. Com., 1981-82; mem. standing com. controlled thermonuclear research AEC, 1966-68; mem. adv. com. on sci. and fgn. affairs Dept. State, 1973-74; mem. U.S.-USSR Joint Commn. on Sci. and Tech., 1977-80; chmn. Com. on Scholarly Communications with the People's Republic of China, 1977-80; dir. Gen. Foods Corp., Mobil Corp., IBM World Trade/Europe/Middle East/Africa Corp., Mem. pres.'s bd. visitors U. Okla., 1968-70; mem. astronomy and applied physics vis. coms. Harvard U., 1969-83; Harvard bd. overseers, 1984—; mem. physics vis. com. M.I.T., 1974-79; mem. Pres.'s Com. Nat. Medal Scis., 1970-72; Bd. dirs. Am. Nat. Standards Inst., 1969-72; trustee Carnegie Instn., 1973—, Poly. Inst. N.Y., 1974-78, Vanderbilt U., 1980—, Nat. Geog. Soc., 1984—. Editor Rev. Modern Physics, 1968-73. Served to lt. (j.g.) USNR, 1945-46. USPHS fellow, 1948-49; Jr. fellow Harvard Soc. Fellows, 1949-51; recipient Rockefeller Pub. Service award, 1957-58, Gold medal exceptional service Dept. Commerce, 1961, Arthur Flemming award D.C. Jr. C. of C., 1962, Samuel Wesley Stratton award Dept. Commerce, 1966, Career Service award Nat. Civil Service League, 1968, Proctor prize Research Soc. Am., 1972. Fellow Am. Phys. Soc. (chmn. div. electron physics 1961-68, pres. 1979), AAAS (dir. 1969-73), Am. Acad. Arts and Scis.; mem. IEEE (sr.), Nat. Acad. Scis. (council 1972-75), Nat. Acad. Engring., Washington Acad. Scis. (Outstanding Sci. Achievement award 1959), Nat. Acad. Public Adminstrn., Internat. Astron. Union, Am. Geophys. Union, Am. Astron. Soc., Internat. Union Geodesy and Geophysics, Am. Philos. Soc., Phi Beta Kappa, Sigma Xi (pres. 1985—). Club: American Yacht (Rye, N.Y.). Current Work: National science and technology policy, information science and technology, experimental atomic physics. Subspecialties: Information systems, storage, and retrieval (computer science); Computer engineering. Office: Old Orchard Rd Armonk NY 10504

BRANSOME, EDWIN DAGOBERT, JR., endocrinologist, educator; b. N.Y.C., Oct. 27, 1933; s. Edwin D. and Margaretta (Homans) B.; m. Janet Grace Williams, June 27, 1959; children: Edwin D., April Grace. A.B., Yale U., 1954; M.D., Columbia U., 1958. Resident internal medicine Peter Bent Brigham Hosp. and Harvard Med. Sch., Boston, 1958-62, research fellow endocrinology, 1959-61; research assoc. biochemistry Columbia U., N.Y.C., 1962-64; assoc. in endocrinology Scripps Clinic, La Jolla, Calif., 1964-66; asst. to assoc. prof. MIT, Cambridge, 1966-70; prof. medicine Med. Coll. Ga., Augusta, 1970—; cons. in field; med. advisor Social Security Administrn., Bur. Hearings & Appeals, 1983-—; chmn. endocrinology adv. com. U.S. Pharmacopeia and mem. com. of rev., 1976—. Author: Self Assessment of Current Knowledge in Clinical Endocrinology, Metabolism and Diabetes, 1975, The Current Status of Liquid Scintillation Counting, 1970; contbr. articles to profl. jours. Chmn. bd. Am. Diabetes Assn., Ga., 1980-82. Am. Cancer Soc. Faculty Research asso. award, 1965-70; various research grants, 1964—. Mem. Endocrine Soc., Am. Diabetes Assn. (bd. dirs.), Am. Chem. Soc., Am. Physiol. Soc., Am. Clin. and Climatol. Soc. Clubs: Golf, Palmetto Golf. Patentee in field. Current Work: Research on the potential interaction of drugs and hormones with DNA, prediction of activity of drugs or homones using molecular models. Subspecialties: Endocrinology; Drug design. Home: 621 Magnolia Ln Aiken SC 29801 Office: Med Coll Ga Augusta GA 30912

BRANT, RUSSELL ALAN, geologist; b. Bklyn., Mar. 18, 1919; s. Ray Basil and Mary Beulah (Weber) B.; m. Elizabeth Frances Rae Dewey, May 29, 1945; children—Wanda Phyllis Lys Burden, Robert Alan, Duane James, Daniel Paul. Student U. Akron, 1939-43; B.S., U. Mich., 1948, M.S. in Geology, 1949. Asst. chemist Monarch Rubber Co., Hartville, Ohio, 1937-43; geologist U.S. Geol. Survey, Washington, 1949-52; asst. state geologist Ohio Geol. Survey, Columbus, 1952-68; staff geologist River Valley Sanitation Commn., Cin., 1969-76; research geologist Ky. Geol. Survey, Lexington, 1976—. Contbr. articles to profl. jours. Served to s/sgt. USAAF, 1943-45. Fellow Geol. Soc. Am. (coal div. chmn. 1981-82), Ohio Acad. Sci.; mem. Am. Inst. Profl. Geologists (certificant), Geol. Soc. Washington, Ky. Geol. Soc. Democrat. Unitarian. Clubs: U.S. Power Squadron (Lexington), Wilderness Trail Amateur Radio. Current work: Coal resources assessments, geology of coal, mine drainage and control, underground injection of waste water and hazardous materials. Subspecialty: Resource management. Home: 309 Pasadena Dr Lexington KY 40503 Office: Ky Geol Survey U Ky Lexington KY 40506

BRASHER, JOHN ODUS, JR., mechanical engineer; b. Bruce, Miss., Sept. 4, 1945; s. John Odus and Catherine (Cooper) B.; m. Lynnie Jean Williams, Sept. 30, 1966; children—James Odus, Steven Odus. B.S.M.E., Miss. State U., 1968; M.B.A., Miss. Coll., 1977. Registered profl. engr., Miss. With Entex, Inc., Miss. and Tex., 1968—, div. chief engr., Jackson, Miss., 1975-77, dist. mgr., Gulfport, Miss., 1977-84, div. chief engr., Houston, 1984—. Mem. ASME, Nat. Soc. Profl. Engrs., So. Gas Assn., Miss. Natural Gas Assn. (co-founder 1977). Subspecialty: Mechanical engineering. Home: 2507 Anniston Houston TX 77080Office: Entex Inc PO Box 2628 Houston TX 77252

BRATTAIN, MICHAEL G., biochemistry educator; b. Ponca City, Okla., Oct. 31, 1947; s. Harold G. and June M. (Oxford) B.; m. Diane E. Roche, Sept. 11, 1966; children: Kathleen A., Michael A. B.S., Rutgers U., 1970, Ph.D., 1974. Teaching asst. Rutgers U., New Brunswick, N.J., 1970-72, NSF research intern, 1972-74; research assoc. U. Ala., Birmingham, 1974-75, instr., 1976-77; assoc. scientist U. Ala. (Cancer Research and Tng. Ctr.), 1976-81, asst. prof. dept. biochemistry and pathology, 1977-81; adj. assoc. prof. dept. biochemistry U. Tex. System Cancer Ctr., M.D. Anderson Hosp. and Tumor Inst., Houston, 1982—; adj. assoc. prof. dept. pharmocology, dir. Bristol-Baylor Lab., Baylor coll. Medicine, Houston, 1982—; asst. dir. sci. ops. Nat. Large Bowel Cancer Project, 1982-84. Contbr. numerous articles to sci. publs. Nat. Cancer Inst. Am. Cancer Soc. grantee, 1978—. Mem. Am. Assn. Cancer Researchers, Am. Assn. Pathologists. Current Work: cancer research; cell biology. Subspecialties: Cancer research (medicine); Cell biology (medicine). Home: 1002 Willowvale Dr Taylor Lake Village TX 77586 Office: Bristol-Baylor Lab 1200 Moursund Ave Houston TX 77030

BRATTER, THOMAS EDWARD, psychotherapist, educator; b. N.Y.C., May 18, 1939; s. Edward Maurice and Marjorie (Lowell) B.; m. Carole Jaffe, Aug. 25, 1963; children: Edward Philip, Barbara Ilyse. B.A., Columbia Coll., 1961, M.A., 1963, Ed.M., 1964, Ed.D, Columbia U., 1974. Cons. N.Y.C. Probation Dept., 1976-79, Pelham (N.Y.) Guidance Council, 1973-79, North Castle Police Dept., Armonk, N.Y., 1978—; founder, pres. John Dewey Acad., Great Barrington, Mass., 1984. Author: (with A. Bassin, R.L. Rachin) The Reality Therapy Reader, 1976, (with R. and N. Kolodny) How to Survive Your Adolescent's Adolescence, 1984; (with G.G. Forrest) Alcoholism and Substance Abuse, 1985; (with R. and N. Kolodny) The Teenager's Official Survival Manual, 1986; mem. editorial bd. Jour. for Specialists in Group Work, 1975-78, Jour. Drug Issues, 1970-78, Corrective and Social Psychiatry, 1971-76, Jour. Reality Therapy, 1980—, Addiction Therapist, 1975—, Jour. Counseling and Devel., 1983—. Mem. Am. Group Psychotherapy Assn. (history com. 1974—), Am. Psychol. Assn. (substance abuse com. 1972—), Am. Acad. Family Therapy, Am. Acad. Psychotherapists. Current Work: Individual, family and group psychotherapy with adolescent substance abusers and their families. Subspecialties: Behavioral psychology; Learning. Home: 88 Spier Rd Scarsdale NY 10583

BRAUER, BETH-ELLEN, chemist, researcher; b. Chgo., Jan. 16, 1957. B.A., Northwestern U., 1978; M.S., U. Ill., 1981, Ph.D., 1984. Research and teaching asst. U. Ill., Urbana, 1978-84; contract scientist Naval Research Lab., Washington, 1984-85. Ill. State scholar, 1974; NSF researcher, 1977. Mem. Am. Chem. Soc., Am. Phys. Soc., Sigma Xi, Iota Sigma Pi. Current work: Study of reactive intermediates by various methods including laser spectroscopy. Subspecialties: Physical chemistry; Laser spectroscopy. Home: 524 N Nelson St Arlington VA 22203

BRAUER, GERHARD MAX, chemist, material scientist; b. Berlin, Ger., Feb. 5, 1919; came to U.S., 1939; s. Ernst Moritz and Alice Therese B.; m. Inge Wolf, June 1, 1969. B. in Chemistry, U. Minn., 1941; M.A., U. N.C., 1948, Ph.D. 1950. Research fellow U. N.C., Chapel Hill, 1947-49; research chemist Nat. Bur. Standards, Gaithersburg, Md., 1950—; U.S. sr. scientist awardee Humboldt Found. Freie U. of Berlin, 1974-75. Contbr. revs. to books and numerous articles to profl. jours. Patentee in field. Served with U.S. Army, 1942-46. Recipient Silver medal U.S. Dept. Commerce, 1964; Gold medal U.S. Dept. Commerce, 1976. Mem. Am. Chem. Soc., Chem. Soc. Washington (Chmn. 1969; Charles Gordon award 1974), Internat. Assn. Dental Research (pres. dental material group 1971, Souder award 1968), ASTM (chmn. polymeric materials sect.), Washington Acad. Scis. (v.p. 1959-63), Adhesion Soc., Am. Coll. Dentists (hon.), Deutsche Gesellschaft für Zahnärztliche Prothetik and Werkstoffkunde (corr.), Sigma Xi (sec. 1967-68), Alpha Chi Sigma (chpt. pres. 1966). Current work: Biomaterials. Subspecialties: Dental materials; Polymer chemistry. Home: 7609 Maryknoll Ave Bethesda MD 20817 Office: Nat Bur Standards Room 143 Bldg 224 Gaithersburg MD 20899

BRAUGHLER, J(OHN) MARK, biochemical pharmacologist, researcher; b. Pitts., Dec. 29, 1950; s. John Thomas and Dorothy Jean (Ament) B.; m. Elisabeth Christine Headrick, June 17, 1972; children—Jason, Timothy. B.S. in Biology, Point Park Coll., 1972; Ph.D. in Pharmacology, U. Pitts., 1977. Research asst. dept. pharmacology U. Pitts. Sch. Medicine, 1977; fellow in clin. pharmacology U. Va., Charlottesville, 1977-79; asst. prof. pharmacology Northeastern Ohio Univs. Coll. Medicine, Rootstown, 1979-83, assoc. prof. pharmacology, 1983; research scientist The Upjohn Co., Kalamazoo, 1983-84, sr. research scientist, 1985—. Contbr. numerous articles to profl. publs. Mem. N.Y. Acad Sci., Am. Soc. Pharmacology and Exptl. Therapeutics, Soc. Neurosci. Lutheran. Current work: Central nervous system trauma and ischemia therapy and pathophysiology; oxygen radicals and lipid peroxidation in disease. Subspecialties: Pharmacology; Biochemistry (medicine). Office: Upjohn Co CNS Diseases Research Unit Kalamazoo MI 49002

BRAUMAN, JOHN I., chemist, educator; b. Pitts., Sept. 7, 1937; s. Milton and Freda E. (Schlitt) B.; m. Sharon Lea Kruse, Aug. 22, 1964; 1 dau., Kate Andrea. B.S., Mass. Inst. Tech., 1959; Ph.D. (NSF fellow), U. Calif., Berkeley, 1963. NSF postdoctoral fellow U. Calif., Los Angeles, 1962-63; asst. prof. chemistry Stanford (Calif.) U., 1963-69, asso. prof., 1969-72, prof., 1972-80, J.G. Jackson-C.J. Wood prof. chemistry, 1980—, chmn. dept., 1979-83; cons. in phys. organic chemistry; adv. panel chemistry div. NSF, 1974-78; adv. panel NASA, AEC, ERDA, Research Corp., Office Chemistry and Chem. Tech., NRC. Mem. editorial adv. bd.: Jour. Am. Chem. Soc, 1976-83, Jour. Organic Chemistry, 1974-78, Nouveau Jour. de Chimie, 1977—, Chem. Revs, 1978-80, Chem. Physics Letters, 1982—, Jour. Phys. Chemistry, 1985—; dep. editor Sci., 1985—. Alfred P. Sloan fellow, 1968-70; Guggenheim fellow, 1978-79. Fellow AAAS; mem. Nat. Acad. Scis., Am. Acad. Arts Scis., Am. Chem. Soc. (award in pure chemistry 1973, Harrison Howe award 1976, James Flack Norris award 1986, Arthur C. Cope scholar award 1986, exec. com. phys. chemistry div.), Brit. Chem. Soc., Sigma Xi, Phi Lambda Upsilon. Current Work: Structure, reactivity, photochemistry and spectroscopy of gas-phase ions. Electron photodetachment spectroscopy. Reaction mechanisms. Subspecialties: Organic chemistry; Physical chemistry. Home: 849 Tolman Dr Stanford CA 94305 Office: Dept Chemistry Stanford U Stanford CA 94305

BRAUMILLER, ALLEN SPOONER, exploration geologist, executive; b. Texarkana, Tex. Feb.1, 1934; s. Jack and Jenny (Spooner) B.; m. Patsy McCoy, Dec. 23, 1955; children—Allen S., Dana Braumiller Nance, Adrienne Brevard B., Colin M. Student Tulane U., 1952-53; B.S., U. Miss., 1955; M.S., U. Ill., 1957. Exploration geologist Carter Oil Co. (merged into Humble Oil and Research Co., then Exxon Corp.), various locations, 1957-69; v.p. exploration Helmerich & Payne, Inc., Tulsa, 1969—. Contbr. articles to profl. jours. Exec. v.p. Windsor Betterment Assn., Oklahoma City, 1967-69. Mem. Am. Assn. Petroleum Geologists, Geol. Soc. Am., Ill. Geol. Soc. (qualified prof. geologist), Oklahoma City Geol. Soc., Tulsa Geol. Soc. (treas. 1978-79), Tulsa C. of C. Republican. Presbyterian (ruling elder). Club: Petroleum (Tulsa). Current work: Exploration for oil and gas, concentrating in mid-continent area. Subspecialties: Geology; Sedimentology. Home: 4979 E 113th St S Tulsa OK 74137 Office: Helmerich & Payne Inc Utica and 21st Tulsa OK 74114

BRAUN, CHARLES LOUIS, chemist, educator; b. Webster, S.D., June 4, 1937; s. Louis F. and Myrene C. B.; m. Kathleen L. Brickel; children: Sarah K., David C. B.S. in Chemistry, S.D. Sch. Mines and Tech., 1959; Ph.D. in Phys. Chemistry, U. Minn., 1963. Successively instr., asst. prof., assoc. prof. chemistry Dartmouth Coll., Hanover, N.H., 1965-77, prof. chemistry, 1977—, chmn. dept. chemistry, 1982-85; cons. Exxon Research and Engring. Lab., Eastman Kodak Corp. Contbr. articles to profl. publs. Served to 1st lt. U.S. Army, 1963-65. Co-recipient Eastman Kodak prize, 1963; NSF grad. fellow, 1961-63; NSF grantee, 1966-81; Dartmouth Coll. faculty fellow, 1969-70; Dept. Energy grantee, 1983—. Mem. Am. Chem. Soc., Am. Phys. Soc. Current Work: Photophysics of organic molecules; luminescence, photoionization and photoconductivity of organic liquids and solids. Conformational dynamics of chain molecules. Subspecialties: Physical chemistry; Kinetics. Office: Dept Chemistry Dartmouth Coll Hanover NH 03755

BRAUN, RICHARD, chemist; b. New Brunswick, N.J., May 12, 1951; s. Alfred and Alice (Hermann) B.; m. Eileen Sue Greene, June 25, 1972; children—Stephanie, Lauren. B.S. in Chemistry, MIT, 1972; M.S. in Phys. Chemistry, Ind. U., 1974. Research chemist Signal Research ctr., Des Plaines, Ill., 1974-76, sr. research chemist, 1976-80, contract adminstr., 1980-84, supr. analytical devel., 1984—. 1984. Mem. Am. Chem. Soc. Current work: Analytical developmental, chromotography, amino acid analysis, robotics. petroleum refining, fouling of heart transfer surfaces. Subspecialties: Physical chemistry; Surface chemistry. Office: Signal Research Center Box 5016 Des Plaines IL 60017

BRAUN, STEPHEN HUGHES, consulting and clinical psychologist, educator; b. St. Louis, Nov. 20, 1942; s. William Lafon and Jayne Louise (Shellabarger) B.; m. Penny Lee Prada, Aug. 28, 1965; 1 son, Damian Hughes. B.A., Washington U., St. Louis, 1964, M.A., 1965; Ph.D., U. Mo.-Columbia, 1970. Asst. prof. psychology Calif. State U.-Chico, 1970-71; dir. social learning div. Ariz. State Hosp., Phoenix, 1971-74; chief planning and evaluation Ariz. Dept. Health Services, Phoenix, 1974-79; pres. Braun and Assocs., Scottsdale, Ariz., 1979—; asst. prof. psychology Ariz. State U., 1971-79, asst. prof. criminal justice, 1974-79, asst. prof. public affairs, 1979-82. Contbr. articles, chpts. to profl. publs.; author clin. evaluation system: Behavioral Health Treatment Outcome Evaluation System, 1981 and subsequent revisions; editorial cons. to profl. jours., 1971—. Recipient Research award State of Calif., 1971; USPHS fellow, 1967-70; NIMH grantee, 1971-74. Mem. Am. Psychol. Assn., Sigma Xi. Current Work: Development of systems for planning and managing human service programs (e.g., mental health, drug abuse, alcoholism, corrections, social services, physical health); development of systems for evaluating the efficiency and effectiveness of human service programs; development of microcomputer software to facilitate the planning, management and evaluation of human service programs. Subspecialties: Clinical psychology; Information systems, storage, and retrieval (computer science). Home: 6122 E Calle Tuberia Scottsdale AZ 85251 Office: Braun and Assocs 7125 E Second St Suite 110 Scottsdale AZ 85251

BRAUN-MUNZINGER, PETER, physicist, educator; b. Heidelberg, Ger., Aug. 26, 1946; s. Theodor and Brigitte (Föhrenbach) Braun-M.; m. Gabriele Huys, July 21, 1973; children: Lena, Karen. Diploma, U. Heidelberg, 1970, Ph.D. in Physics, 1972. Research assoc. Max-Planck Inst., Heidelberg, 1973-76; vis. asst. prof. SUNY-Stony Brook, 1976-78, asst. prof., 1978-80, assoc. prof., 1980-82, prof., 1982—. Conbtr. articles to sci. jours. Mem. Am. Phys. Soc. Current Work: Study of nuclear reactions and structure of complex nuclei. Subspecialty: Nuclear physics. Office: SUNY Stony Brook NY 11794

BRAUNWALD, EUGENE, physician; b. Aug. 15, 1929; s. William and Clare (Wallach) B.; m. Nina Starr, May 23, 1952; children—Karen, Allison, Jill. A.B., NYU, 1949, M.D., 1952; M.A. (hon.), Harvard U., 1972, M.D. (hon.), 1984. Diplomate: Am. Bd. Internal Medicine and Cardiovascular Diseases. Tng. internal medicine Mt. Sinai, Johns Hopkins hosps., also Columbia, 1952-58; commd. USPHS, 1954, med. dir., 1963; research cardiology and physiology Nat. Heart Inst., 1955-68, chief cardiology dept., 1960-67, clin. dir. inst., 1966-68; clin. prof. medicine Georgetown U., 1966-68; prof., chmn. dept. medicine U. Calif. at San Diego Sch. Medicine, La Jolla, 1968-72; Hersey prof., Blumgart prof., chmn. dept. medicine Peter Bent Brigham Hosp., Beth Israel Hosp., Harvard Med. Sch., Boston, 1972—; Mem. Nat. Heart and Lung Adv. Council, 1975-79. Author: Heart Disease, A Textbook of Cardiovascular Medicine, 2d edit. Editorial bd.: Yearbook of Medicine; editor: Principles of Internal Medicine; contbr. numerous sci. articles. Recipient John Abel award research pharmacology; Arthur Fleming award for outstanding fed. service; Outstanding Service award USPHS, 1967; Nylin award Swedish Med. Soc., 1970; Einthoven medal, 1970; Research Achievement award Am. Heart Assn., 1972; Lilly medal Royal Coll. Physicians, 1979. Fellow Am. Coll. Chest Physicians (hon.), A.C.P. (master), Am. Coll. Cardiology (v.p., gov., trustee), Am. Acad. Arts and Scis.; mem. Am. Heart Assn. (v.p., dir. chmn. publs. 1965—, Research Achievement award 1972, chmn. council on clin. cardiology; Herrick award 1981), Nat. Acad. Scis., Am. Fedn. for Clin. Research (pres. 1969-70), Soc. Clin. Investigation (pres. 1974-75), Western Soc. for Clin. Research (pres. 1971-72), Am. Physiol. Soc., Am. Pharmacology Soc., Assn. Am. Physicians, Assn. Profs. Medicine (pres. 1974-75). Subspecialties: Internal medicine; Cardiology. Home: 75 Scotch Pine Rd Weston MA 02193

BRAUTBAR, NACHMAN, pharmacology, nutrition and medicine educator, researcher; b. Haifa, Israel, Oct. 22, 1943; came to U.S., 1975, naturalized, 1980; s. Pinhas and Sabina (Lohite) B.; children—Sigalit, Shirly, Jacques. M.D., Hebrew U., 1969. Intern Rambam Hosp., Haifa U., Israel, 1969-70; resident in internal medicine Rothschild Med. Ctr., Haifa, 1971-73; chief resident dept. medicine Hadassah U. Hosp., Jerusalem, 1974-75; intern Wadsworth VA Med. Ctr., Los Angeles, 1976-77; nephrology fellow, 1977-78; asst. chief hemodialysis unit, 1978; asst. prof. medicine U. So. Calif., Los Angeles, 1978-81, asst. prof. pharmacology, 1981-82, assoc. prof. medicine and pharmacology, 1982—; chmn. research com Kidney Found., Los Angeles, 1980—; head nephrology sect. Hollywood Presbyterian Hosp., 1980—; mem. study sect. Am. Heart Assn., Los Angeles, 1982—; guest speaker, vis. prof. numerous instns.; cons. in field. Author over 150 articles, book chpts., revs., abstracts to med. and sci. publs. Named hon. citizen City of Los Angeles, 1984; recipient award for outstanding orgn. of 2nd Internat. Congress on Myocardial and Cellular Bioenergetics, U. So. Calif., 1984; grantee Am. Heart Assn., 1979-83, NIH, 1984—. Mem. European Dialysis and Transplantation Assn., Am. Fedn. for Clin. Research, Internat. Soc. for Nephrology, Israel Nephrology Soc., Am. Soc. for Nephrology, Am. Soc. Artificial Internal Organs, Am. Coll. Emergency Medicine, Am. Soc. Bone and Mineral Metabolism, Western Soc. for Clin. Investigation, Am. Physiol. Soc., Am. Endocrine Soc., Biophys. Soc., Biochem. Soc., Am. Chem. Soc., Am. Coll. Nutrition, Am. Soc. for Neurosci., Am. Soc. Exptl. Biology and Medicine, Am. Soc. for Renal Biochemistry, Internat. Soc. for Alcohol Research. Current work: Mineral metabolism, effects of alcoholism on mineral metabolism, osteoporosis and metabolic bone disease; nutrition, vitamin D metabolism, magnesium and phosperous metabolism. Subspecialties: Nephrology; Nutrition (medicine). Office: 2105 Beverly Blvd Los Angeles CA 90057

BRAY, PHILIP JAMES, physicist; b. Kansas City, Mo., Aug. 25, 1925; s. Harry James and Ruth (Moerdyke) B.; children—Carolyn, Philip James, Katherine. Sc.B. in Physics, Brown U., 1948; A.M., Harvard U., 1949, Ph.D., 1953. Asst. prof. physics Rensselaer Poly. Inst., 1952-55; asso. prof. physics Brown U., Providence, 1955-58, prof., 1958-85, Hazard prof. physics, 1985—, chmn. dept., 1963-68; vis. prof. dept. glass tech. U. Sheffield, Eng., 1961-62, 68-69; vis. prof. dept. chemistry U. Exeter, Eng., 1975-76. Asso. editor: Revs. Modern Physics, 1963-65; editorial bd.: Jour. Non-Crystalline Solids, 1968-71; Jour. Nonmetals, 1971-77, Jour. Biol. Physics, 1973-77, Magnetic Resonance in Chemistry, 1985—. NSF fellow, 1961-62; Guggenheim fellow, 1968-69; Winston Churchill overseas fellow, 1984-85. Fellow Am. Phys. Soc. (chmn. New Eng. sect. 1965-67), Soc. Glass Tech., Korean Phys. Soc., Am. Acad. Arts and Scis., AAAS, Sigma Xi (nat. lectr. 1969-70), Am. Ceramic Soc. (George W. Morey award for outstanding contributions to glass sci. and tech. 1970); mem. Internat. Soc. Magnetic Resonance, N.Y. Acad. Scis., Am. Assn. Physics Tchrs., Groupement Ampere, Assn. Koreans of R.I. (hon.). Congregationalist. Current work: Nuclear magnetic resonance (NMR) studies of the structure of glasses. Subspecialties: Condensed matter physics; Ceramics. Home: 133 Power St Providence RI 02906 Office: Dept Physics Brown U Providence RI 02912

BREAKIRON, LEE ALLEN, astronomer; b. Arlington, Va., July 26, 1948; s. Philip Lewis and Margaret Elizabeth (Jensen) B.; m. Patricia Joy McDonough, June 14, 1975 (div. Aug. 1985); 1 son, Jason Lance. B.A. in Astronomy, U. Va., Charlottesville, 1970; M.S. in Astronomy, U. Pitts., 1973, Ph.D. in Astronomy (Zaccheus Daniel fellow), 1977. Grad. teaching asst., researcher U. Pitts., 1971-76; postdoctoral research fellow Wesleyan U., Middletown, Conn., 1976-80; spl. asst. to dir. div. astron. scis. NSF, Washington, 1980-85; research assoc. U. Pitts., 1985—. Contbr. articles to profl. jours. Mem. Am. Astron. Soc., Sigma Xi. Current Work: Astrometry. Subspecialty: Optical astronomy. Home: 1350 Steuben St Pittsburgh PA 15220 Office: Allegheny Observatory Pittsburgh PA 15214

BRECHER, AVIVA, applied physicist, technical consultant; b. Bucarest, Romania, July 4, 1945; came to U.S., 1965; d. Radu and Melita (Hecht) Schwartz; m. Kenneth Brecher, Aug. 18, 1965; children—Karen Iris, Daniel Isaac. B.S. in Physics, MIT, 1968, M.S. in Physics, 1968; Ph.D. in Applied Physics, U. Calif.-San Diego, 1972. Research assoc. Earth and Planetary Scis. MIT, Cambridge, 1972-77, vis. research scientist, 1977-80, lectr. in physics, 1979-80; asst. prof. physics Wellesley Coll., Mass., 1977-79; sr. cons. Geotech. and nuclear systems safety, also space systems and sci. policy, A.D. Little, Inc., Cambridge, 1980-85; dir. Office Acad.-Corp. Relations, Boston U., 1985—; Congl. Sci. fellow Am. Phys. Soc., 1983-84. Assoc. editor procs. Lunar and Planetary Sci. Conf., 1974-76. Bd. dirs. Profl. Council, Mass., 1980-82. Japan Soc. for Promotion of Sci. fellow, 1980; recipient Spl. Recognition award NASA, 1979. Mem. Am. Phys. Soc., Am. Geophys. Union (nat. chmn. Women in Geoscis. 1980-82), Am. Astron. Soc., Internat. Astron. Union, Assn. MIT Alumnae (bd. mem., program chmn. 1977-80). Democrat. Jewish. Current work: Risk assessment for nuclear waste (disposal, processing facilities, transportation) and for mining operations; space systems. Subspecialties:

Planetary science; Applied physics. Home: 35 Madison St Belmont MA 02178 Office: Boston U 145 Bay State Rd Boston MA 02215

BRECHER, KENNETH, astronomer, physicist, educator; b. N.Y.C., Dec. 7, 1943; s. Irving and Edythe (Grossman) B.; m. Aviva Schwartz, Aug. 18, 1965; children: Karen, Daniel. B.S. in Physics, MIT, 1969, Ph.D. in Physics, 1969. Research physicist U. Calif., San Diego, 1969-72; asst., then assoc. prof. physics M.I.T., Cambridge, Mass., 1972-79; assoc. prof. astronomy and physics Boston U., 1979-81, prof., 1981—. Co-author/co-editor: (with G. Setti) High Energy Astrophysics and Its Relation to Elementary Particles Physics, 1974, (with M. Feirtag) Astronomy of the Ancients, 1979; also numerous articles. Recipient 2d prize Gravity Research Found., 1969; grantee NATO, 1972; grantee NSF, 1974—; grantee NASA, 1981-82; Guggenheim meml. fellow, 1979-80. Mem. Am. Astron. Soc. (sec.-treas. hist. astronomy div.), Am. Phys. Soc., Internat. Astron. Union. Current Work: Theoretical high energy astrophysics, relativity, cosmology. Theoretical research aimed at applying and testing the know laws of physics in astrophysical objects of extreme conditions of density, gravitational field. Subspecialties: High energy astrophysics; General relativity.

BRECHER, LEE EDWARD, engineering and consulting company executive; b. Pekin, Ill., June 20, 1941; m. Phyllis Walker, Nov. 21, 1984. B.S. in Chem. Engring., U. Ill. 1963; M.S. in Chem. Engring., Carnegie-Mellon U., 1966, Ph.D., 1967. Fellow engr. chem. engring. dept. Energy Systems div. Westinghouse Electric Corp., Pitts., 1966-76; dep. dir. Inst. Mining and Minerals Research, U. Ky., 1976-84; dir. Ky. Ctr. for Energy Research, Lexington, 1976-84; v.p. tech. devel. Ky. Found. for Energy Tech. Devel. Inc., Lexington, 1984—; pres. Brecher Engring. and Cons. Co., Lexington, 1984—. Contbr. articles to tech. jours. Patentee in field. Dow scholar, 1962; recipient Agnes Sloan Larson award, 1960, NASA Traineeship award, 1963; DuPont fellow, 1966. Mem. Am. Inst. Chem. Engrs., Am. Chem. Soc., Am. Mgmt. Assn. Current work: Coal-fired locomotives. Subspecialties: Coal; Oil shale. Office: Brecher Engring and Cons Co 3476 Belvoir Dr Lexington KY 40502 Also: Ky Found Energy Techn Devel Inc PO Box 12858 Lexington KY 40583

BREEDLOVE, STEPHEN MARC, psychology educator, neuroscience researcher; b. Springfield, Mo., June 20, 1954; s. John Thomas and Lula (Collins) B.; m. Susan M. Mort, Aug. 21, 1976; children—Benjamin Drew, Nicholas James. B.A. in Psychology, Yale U., 1976; M.A. in Psychology, UCLA, 1978, Ph.D. in Psychology, 1982. Asst. prof. U. Calif.-Berkeley, 1982—. Recipient presdl. young investigator award NSF, 1985; research grantee NIH, 1983, Basil O'Connor grantee March of Dimes, 1984. Mem. Soc. Neurosci. (Lindsley award 1982), Am. Psychol. Assn., AAAS. Current work: Development of the nervous system, specifically the ontogeny of sex differences in neuroanatomy in rodents, permanent and transient effects of hormones on neurons and behavior. Subspecialties: Psychobiology; Neurobiology. Office: Dept Psychology U Calif Berkeley CA 94720

BREEN, JOHN EDWARD, civil engineer, educator; b. Buffalo, May 1, 1932; s. Timothy J. and Alice C. (Keenan) B.; m. Marian T. Killian, June 20, 1953; children: Mary L., Michael T., Dennis P., Sheila A., Sean E., Kerry T., Christopher D. B.C.E., Marquette U., Milw., 1953; M.S. in Civil Engring, U. Mo., 1957; Ph.D., U. Tex., Austin, 1962. Registered profl. engr., Tex., Mo. Structural designer Harnischfeger Corp., Milw., 1952-53; asst. prof. U. Mo., Columbia, 1957-59; mem. faculty U. Tex., Austin, 1959—, prof. civil engring., 1969—, J.J. McKetta prof. engring., 1977-81, Carol Cockrell Curran chair in engring., 1981-84, Nasser I. Al-Rashid chair in civil engring., 1984—; dir. P.M. Ferguson Structural Engring. Lab., Balcones Research Center, 1967-85; cons. in field. Contbr. articles to profl. jours. Served to lt. USNR, 1953-56. Recipient Teaching Excellence award Gen. Dynamics Corp., 1971, Teaching Excellence award U. Tex. Student Assn., 1963, Teaching Excellence award Standard Oil Found. Ind., 1968. Fellow Am. Concrete Inst. (bd. direction 1974-77, Wason medal 1972, 83, Raymond C. Reese Research medal 1972, 79, Kelly medal 1981, Raymond Davis lectr. 1978), ASCE (T.Y. Lin medal 1985); mem. Nat. Acad. Engring., Sigma Xi, Chi Epsilon, Tau Beta Pi. Democrat. Roman Catholic. Club: Austin Yacht (commodore 1977). Current Work: Research and development in design and construction of reinforced and prestressed concrete structures. engineering; structural engineering. Subspecialty: Civil engineering. Home: 8603 Azalea Trail Austin TX 78759 Office: Dept Civil Engring Univ Texas Austin TX 78712

BREGMAN, ALLYN AARON, educator; b. Bklyn., Apr. 29, 1941; s. Irving and Rose (Balmages) B.; m. Sybil Oakley Brewster, Jan. 2, 1943; children: Susannah, Naomi. B.S. magna cum laude, Bklyn Coll., 1962; M.S., U. Rochester, 1964, Ph.D., 1968. Asst. prof. biology SUNY-New Paltz, 1967-71, assoc. prof., 1971-85, prof., 1985—. Author: Laboratory Investigations in Cell Biology, 1983; Contbr. articles in field to profl. jours. Mem. Am. Soc. for Cell Biology, AAAS, Genetics Soc. Am. Current Work: Teacher, writer in area of cell biology. Subspecialties: Cell biology; Genome organization. Home: 11 Prospect St New Paltz NY 12561 Office: State University of New York Dept Biology New Paltz NY 12561

BREGMAN, JACOB ISRAEL, corporate executive; b. Hartford, Conn., Sept. 17, 1923; s. Aaron and Jennie (Katzoff) B.; m. Mona Madan, June 27, 1948; children: Janet, Marcia, Barbara. B.S., Providence Coll., 1943; M.S., Poly. Inst. Bklyn., 1948, Ph.D., 1951. Research chemist Fels & Co., 1947-48; head phys. chem. labs. Nalco Chem. Co., Chgo., 1950-59; supr. phys. chemistry research sect. Armour Research Found., Chgo., 1959-63; asst. dir. chemistry research Ill. Inst. Tech. Research Inst., Chgo., 1963-65, dir. chem. scis., 1965-67; dep. asst. sec. U.S. Dept. Interior, 1967-69; pres. Wapora Inc., 1969-82; v.p. Dynamac Corp., 1983-84; pres. Bregman and Co., 1984—. Chmn. N.E. Ill. Met. Area Air Pollution Control Bd., 1962-63; chmn. Ill. Air Pollution Control Bd., 1963-67; chmn. adv. bd. on saline water conversion NATO Parliamentarians Conf., 1963; chmn. Water Resources Research Council, 1964-67. Author: Corrosion Inhibitors, 1963, Surface Effects in Detection, 1965, The Pollution Paradox, 1966, Handbook of Water Resources and Pollution Control, 1976; contbr. articles to profl. jours. Mem. plan commn., Park Forest, Ill., 1956-58, trustee, 1958-62; Mem. Md. Democratic State Central Com., 1974-78; treas. Montgomery Dem. Central Com., 1974-76; del. Dem. Conv., 1976. Served with AUS, 1943-46, ETO. Fellow Am. Inst. Chemists; mem. Am. Chem. Soc., Sigma Xi, Phi Lambda Upsilon. Current Work: Environmental activities—air, water hazardous and toxic wastes, environmental impact. Subspecialties: Environmental engineering; Water supply and wastewater treatment. Home: 5630 Old Chester Rd Bethesda MD 20814 Office: 6900 Wisconsin Ave Chevy Chase MD 20815

BREININGER, DAVID ROBERT, wildlife biologist, environmental consultant; b. Allentown, Pa., Nov. 21, 1956; s. Robert R. and Mamie E. (Hausmann) B.; m. Kathy S. Milner (div. 1983). B.S. in Marine Biology, Fla. Inst. Tech., 1978, M.S. in Ecology, 1981. Grad. teaching asst. Fla. Inst. Tech., Melbourne, 1978-81; researcher Tech. Inc., Kennedy Space Center, Fla., 1981; environ. engr. Planning Research Corp., Kennedy Space Center, 1982-83; wildlife ecologist Bionetics Corp., Kennedy Space Center, 1983—; environ. cons., Indian Harbor Beach, Fla., 1984—. Mem. Ecol. Soc. Am., Wildlife Soc., Colonial Waterbird Group, Fla. Acad. Sci. Democrat. Lutheran. Current work: Research on wildlife/habitat relationships; environmental assessment and monitoring of impacts to endangered and potentially endangered species. Subspecialty: Ecology (environmental science). Home: 1101 Ashley Indian Harbour Beach FL 32937 Office: Bio-2 Kennedy Space Center FL 32899

BREITBART, YURI JACOB, computer scientist; b. Moscow, Nov. 7, 1940; came to U.S., 1975, naturalized, 1983; s. Jacob and Pesia B. B.A., Moscow Pedagogical Inst., 1963, M.S., 1968; D.Sc., Technion, Haifa, Israel, 1973. Lectr. Technion, 1972-75; asst. prof. SUNY-Albany, 1975-78; assoc. prof. U. Wis.-Milw., 1978-79; mgr. data base evaluation ITT Programming Tech. Center, Stratford, Conn., 1979-81; data base group supr. Amoco Prodn. Research, Tulsa, 1981—; cons. IBM Sci. Center Israel, Haifa, 1973-74, Astronautic Corp. Am., Milw., 1978-79. Israel Acad. Sci., Bat-Sheba grantee, 1974; NSF grantee, 1976-78. Mem. IEEE, Computer Soc. IEEE, Assn. Computing Machinery, Spl. Interest Group on Mgmt. of Data. Current work: Distributed heterogeneous database management systems; logical database design for engineering and scientific databases. Subspecialties: Database systems; Distributed systems and networks. Office: Amoco Prodn Research PO Box 3385 Tulsa OK 74102

BREITMAN, THEODORE RONALD, biochemist; b. N.Y.C., Feb. 25, 1931; s. Sol and Bertha (Morell) B.; children: Sara, Linda. B.S., CCNY, 1948; M.S., Ohio State U., 1955, Ph.D., 1958. Postdoctoral fellow Brandeis U., 1958-61; research biochemist Lederle Labs., Pearl River, N.Y., 1961-63, Nat. Cancer Inst., Bethesda, Md., 1963—. Mem. Am. Soc. Biol. Chemists, Am. Assn. Cancer Research, AAAS. Current Work: Terminal differentiation of human leukemic cells promoted by physiological substances such as retinoic acid, prostaglandins and lymphokines. Subspecialties: Cell and tissue culture; Cell study oncology. Home: 8194 Inverness Ridge Rd Potomac MD 20854 Office: NIH Bldg 37 Room 5B14 Bethesda MD 20892

BREITSCHWERDT, EDWARD BEALMEAR, veterinarian, educator; b. Balt., Oct. 25, 1948; s. Edward Paul and Sarah Ester (Bealmear) B.; m. Anne Shepherd, May 23, 1981; children—Edward Brett, Kyle Thomas. B.S., U. Md., 1970; D.V.M., U. Ga., 1974. Diplomate: Am. Coll. Vet. Internal Medicine, 1979. Intern U. Mo., Columbia, 1974-75, resident, 1975-77; asst. prof. medicine La. State U., Baton Rouge, 1977-82, asso. prof., 1982; sect. chief Small Animal Clinic, 1979-82; assoc. prof. medicine N.C. State U., Raleigh, 1982—. Contbr. articles to profl. jours. Mem. AVMA, Am. Assn. Vet. Med. Colls., Am. Animal Hosp. Assn. Episcopalian. Current Work: Canine Rocky Mountain Spotted Fever, Immunoproliperative enteropathy, identification of animal diseases and animal models of human disease. Subspecialty: Internal medicine (veterinary medicine). Home: Route 3 Box 342A Fuguay Varina NC 27526 Office: Sch Veterinary Medicine NC State U 4700 Hillsborough St Raleigh NC 27606

BREMNER, JOHN MCCOLL, agronomy and biochemistry educator; b. Dumbarton, Scotland, Jan. 18, 1922; came to U.S., 1959; s. Archibald Donaldson and Sarah Kennedy (McColl) B.; m. Eleanor Mary Williams, Sept. 30, 1950; children—Stuart, Carol. B.S., Glasgow U., 1944; Ph.D., U. London, 1948, Sc.D., 1959. With chemistry dept. Rothamsted Exptl. Sta., Harpenden, Eng., 1945-59; assoc. prof. Iowa State U., Ames, 1959-61, prof. agronomy and biochemistry, 1961—, C.F. Curtiss Disting. prof. agriculture, prof. agronomy, biochemistry, 1975—; tech. expert Internat. Atomic Energy Agy., Austria, 1964-65, Yugoslavia, 1964-65. Recipient Alexander Von Humboldt award Alexander Von Humboldt Found., W.Germany, 1982, Outstanding Research award First Miss. Corp., 1979; Harvey Wiley award U.S. Assn. Ofcl. Analytical Chemists, 1984. Rockefeller fellow, 1957; Guggenheim fellow, 1968; recipient Gov.'s Sci. medal State of Iowa, 1983. Fellow Am. Soc. Agronomy (Soil Sci. Achievement award 1967, Bouyoucos Soil Sci. Disting. Career award 1982, Agronomic Research award 1985), Iowa Acad. Sci. (Disting.), Am. Chem. Soc., AAAS, Soil Sci. Soc. Am.; mem. Nat. Acad. Scis., Brit. Soc. Soil Sci., Internat. Soil Sci. Soc., Phi Kappa Phi, Sigma Xi, Gamma Sigma Delta. Current work: Biological transformations of nitrogen in soils, and methods for control of these transformations; air and water pollution problems related to agriculture. Subspecialties: Agronomy; Soil science. Home: 2028 Pinehurst Dr Ames IA 50010 Office: Iowa State U Dept Agronomy Ames IA 50011

BRENCHLEY, JEAN ELNORA, microbiologist, research exec.; b. Towanda, Pa., Mar. 6, 1944; d. J. Edward and Elizabeth (Jefferson) B. B.S., Mansfield (Pa.) U., 1965; M.S., U. Calif.-San. Diego, 1967; Ph.D., U. Calif.-Davis, 1970. Research assoc. MIT, Cambridge, 1970; asst. prof., then assoc. prof. Pa. State U., 1971-77, head dept. molecular cell biology, dir. biotech., 1984—; prof. biology Purdue U., Lafayette, Ind., 1977-81; research dir. Genex Corp., Gaithersburg, Md., 1981-84; dir. biotech., head dept. Pa. State U., 1984—; cons., lectr. Editor: Applied and Environ. Microbiology, 1982—; Contbr. chpts. to books, articles to sci. jours. Vol. Crisis Center, Pals Program. Recipient alumni award Mansfield U., 1984, Waksman award, 1985. NSF and NIH grantee, 1971-81; Becton & Dickinson lectr., 1979; Am. Soc. Microbiology Found. lectr., 1973. Mem. NOW, Assn. Women in Sci., Am. Soc. Microbiology (pres. elect), Am. Chem. Soc., Am. Soc. Biol. Chemists, Am. Genetics Soc. Current Work: Microbial genetics; biotechnology. Subspecialties: Microbiology; Genetics and genetic engineering (biology). Office: 108 Althouse Pa State U University Park PA 16802

BRENNAN, EILEEN G., plant pathologist, educator; b. Jersey City, N.J., Dec. 21, 1922; s. John J. and Mary (Gallagher) B. B.S., Rutgers U., 1944, M.S., 1946, Ph.D., 1975. Research asst. Cook Coll., Rutgers U., 1946-56, asst. prof., 1956-74, prof., 1974—. Contbr. numerous articles to profl. jours. Mem. Am. Phytopathol. Soc., Air Pollution Control Assn. (recipient Reuben W. Wasser award Mid-Atlantic States sect. 1981, Lyman A. Ripperton award 1985), Internat. Soc. Arboriculture, Sigma Xi. Current Work: Effect of air pollutants and heavy metals on vegetation. Subspecialty: Plant pathology. Home: 120 Cleveland Ave Colonia NJ 07067 Office: Cook Coll Dept Plant Pathology Rutgers Coll Agr Box 231 New Brunswick NJ 08903

BRENNER, BARRY MORTON, physician; b. Bklyn., Oct. 4, 1937; s. Louis and Sally (Lamm) B.; m. Jane P. Deutsch, June 12, 1960; children: Robert, Jennifer. B.S., L.I. U.; M.D., U. Pitts.; M.A., Harvard U. Asst. prof. medicine U. Calif., San Francisco, 1969-72, asso. prof. medicine and physiology, 1972-75, prof. medicine, 1975-76; Samuel A. Levine prof. medicine Harvard U. Med. Sch., Boston; with Peter Bent Brigham Hosp., Boston, 1976—; dir. renal div. Brigham and Women's Hosp., Boston, 1979—; cons. NIH. Contbr. numerous articles to various publs. Recipient research award NIH, Homer W. Smith award N.Y. Heart Assn., George E. Brown award Am. Heart Assn. Mem. Am. Physiol. Soc., Assn. Am. Physicians, Western Assn. Physicians, Am. Soc. Nephrology (councillor), Am. Soc. Clin. Investigation (councillor, v.p.), Salt and Water Club, Interurban Clin. Club, Alpha Omega Alpha, Phi Sigma. Subspecialties: Physiology (biology); Nephrology. Office: 75 Francis St Boston MA 02115*

BRENNER, HOWARD, chemical engineer; b. N.Y.C., Mar. 16, 1929; s. Max and Margaret (Wechsler) B.; children: Leslie, Joyce, Suzanne. B.Ch.E., Pratt Inst., 1950; M.Ch.E., NYU, 1954, Eng.Sc.D., 1957. Instr. chem. engring. NYU, 1955-57, asst. prof. chem. engring., 1957-61, assoc. prof., 1961-65, prof., 1965-66, Carnegie-Mellon U., 1966-77; prof., chmn. dept. chem. engring. U. Rochester, 1977-81; Willard Henry Dow prof. chem. engring. MIT, Cambridge, 1981—; sr. vis. fellow Sci. Research Council, Gt. Britain, 1974. Author: (with J. Happel) Low Reynolds Number Hydrodynamics, 1965, 2d edit., 1973, Russian edit., 1976; contbr. (with J. Happel) numerous articles to profl. jours.; assoc. editor: Internat. Jour. Multiphase Flow, 1973—, Internat. Jour. PhysicoChem. Hydrodynamics, 1979—. Fairchild Disting. scholar Calif. Inst. Tech., 1975-76; Named to 11th Ann. Honor Scroll Indsl. Engring. Chemistry div. Am. Chem. Soc., 1961. Fellow Am. Inst. Chem. Engrs., Am. Acad. Mechanics, AAAS, Am. Inst. Chem. Engrs. (Alpha Chi Sigma award 1976, William H. Walker award 1985); mem. Nat. Acad. Engring., Soc. Indsl. and Applied Math., Internat. Assn. Colloid and Interface Scientists, Am. Inst. Civil Engrs., Soc. Rheology (Bingham medal 1980), Soc. Nat. Philosophy, Soc. Engring. Sci. (bd. dirs. 1982—), Physico-Chem. Hydrodynamics Internat. Assn. (bd. dirs. 1983—), Am. Chem. Soc. Subspecialty: Chemical engineering. Office: Dept Chem Engring MIT Cambridge MA 02139

BRESLOW, JAN LESLIE, physician, scientist, educator; b. N.Y.C., Feb. 28, 1943; s. Frank and Pearl (Feit) B.; m. Marilyn Ganon, June 27, 1965; children—Noah, Nicholas. A.B., Columbia Coll., 1963; M.A., Columbia U., 1964; M.D., Harvard Med. Sch., 1968. Diplomate Am. Bd. Pediatrics. Intern in pediatrics Children's Hosp., Boston, 1968-69; jr. asst. resident, 1969-70; staff assoc. Molecular Disease br. Nat. Heart, Lung and Blood Inst., Bethesda, Md., 1970-73; instr. Harvard Med. Sch.-Children's Hosp., Boston, 1973-74, asst. prof., 1974-80, assoc. prof., 1980-84; prof. and dir. lab. biochem. genetics and metabolism Rockefeller U., N.Y.C., 1984—. Mem. editorial bd. Jour. Lipid Research, 1983—, Arteriosclerosis Jour., 1984—; sr. physician Rockefeller U. Hosp., 1984—. Contbr. articles to profl. jours. Served with USPHS, 1970-73. Recipient E. Mead Johnson award Am. Acad. Pediatrics, Established Investigator award Am. Heart Assn. Mem. Am. Heart Assn. (council on arteriosclerosis), AAAS, Am. Acad. Pediatrics, N.Y. Heart Assn. (research council), Soc. for Pediatric Research, Am. Soc. for Clin. Investigation. Current work: Studies of genetic susceptibility to atherosclerosis. Isolation and characterization of genes controlling lipoprotein metabolism, and indentification of defects in patients with premature coronary artery disease. Subspecialties: Genetics and genetic engineering (medicine); Biochemistry (medicine). Office: Rockefeller U 1230 York Ave New York NY 10021

BRESLOW, LESTER, physician, educator; b. Bismarck, N.D., Mar. 17, 1915; s. Joseph and Mayme (Danziger) B.; children: Norman, Jack, Stephen; m. Devra J.R. Miller, 1967. B.A., U. Minn., 1935, M.D., 1938, M.P.H., 1941. Diplomate: Am. Bd. Preventive Medicine and Public Health. Intern USPHS Hosp., Stapleton, N.Y., 1938-40; dist. health officer Minn. Dept. Health, 1941-43; chief bur. chronic diseases Calif. Dept. Public Health, Berkeley, 1946-60, chief div. preventive medicine, 1960-65, dir. dept., 1965-68; lectr. U. Calif. Sch. Pub. Health, Berkeley, 1950-68, prof. pub. health, 1968—, chmn. dept. preventive medicine and social medicine, 1969-72; dean Sch. Pub. Health, UCLA, 1972-80, co-dir. div. cancer control Jonsson Comprehensive Cancer Ctr., 1982—; dir. study Pres.'s Commn. Health Needs of Nation, 1952; cons. Nat. Cancer Inst., 1981—. Author med. publs.; editor: Ann. Rev. Pub. Health, 1979—; editorial cons.: Jour. Preventive Medicine. Served to capt. U.S. Army, 1943-45. Decorated Bronze Star; recipient Lasker award; Sedgwick medal Am. Pub. Health Assn.; Outstanding Achievement award U. Minn. Fellow Am. Coll. Preventive Medicine (Disting. service award 1976), ACP; fellow AAAS; mem. Am. Heart Assn. (fellow epidemiology sect.), Am. Public Health Assn. (past pres.), Public Health Cancer Assn. (past pres.), Am. Epidemiol. Soc., Internat. Epidemiol. Assn. (past pres.), Am. Cancer Soc. (nat. dir., Calif. dir., chmn. adv. com. on research etiology), Assn. Schs. Public Health (pres. 1973-74), Inst. Medicine, Nat. Acad. Scis. (council 1978-80, chmn. bd. health promotion and disease prevention 1981—). Current Work: Measurement of health and factors influencing it; public health. Subspecialties: Preventive medicine; Epidemiology. Home: 10926 Verano Rd Los Angeles CA 90024

BRESLOW, RONALD CHARLES, chemist, educator; b. Rahway, N.J., Mar. 14, 1931; s. Alexander E. and Gladys (Fellows) B.; m. Esther Greenberg, Sept. 7, 1955; children: Stephanie, Karen. A.B. summa cum laude, Harvard, 1952, M.A., 1953, Ph.D., 1955. NRC fellow Cambridge (Eng.) U., 1955-56; mem. faculty Columbia, 1956—, prof. chemistry, 1962-66, S.L. Mitchill prof., 1966—; cons. to industry, 1958—; Mem. medicinal chemistry panel NIH, 1964—; mem. adv. panel on chemistry NSF, 1971—. Editor: Benjamin, Inc, 1962—; Author: Organic Reaction Mechanisms, 1965, 2d edit., 1969; also articles. Mem. editorial bd.: Organic Syntheses, 1964—, Jour. Organic Chemistry, 1969—, Jour. Bio-organic Chemistry, 1972—, Tetrahedron, 1975—, Tetrahedron Letters, 1975—, Procs. Nat. Acad. Sci., 1983—. Recipient Fresenius award Phi Lambda Upsilon, 1966; Mark Van Doren award Columbia, 1969; Roussel prize, 1978; Centenary lectr. London Chem. Soc., 1972. Fellow Am. Acad. Arts and Scis.; mem. Am. Philos. Soc., Nat. Acad. Scis. (chmn. chemistry div. 1974-77), Am. Chem. Soc. (Pure Chemistry award 1966, Baekeland medal 1969, chmn. div. organic chemistry 1970, Harrison Howe award 1974, Remsen award 1977, J. F. Norris award 1980, Richards medal 1984), Phi Beta Kappa (first marshall 1952). Current Work: Artificial enzymes; bio-mimetic chemistry; anti-aromatic compounds; enzyme mechanisms. Subspecialty: Organic chemistry. Home: 275 Broad Ave Englewood NJ 07631 Office: Dept Chemistry Columbia Univ New York NY 10027

BRETT, ROBIN, geologist, researcher; b. Adelaide, Australia, Jan. 30, 1935; came to U.S. 1957, naturalized 1973; s. Alan Gore and Sheila Mary (MacCabe) B.; m. Abigail Trafford, Aug. 10, 1963 (div. Mar. 14, 1983); children—Abigail, Victoria. B.Sc. (hons.), U. Adelaide, Australia, 1956; A.M., Harvard U., 1960, Ph.D., 1963. Postdoctoral fellow Carnegie Inst. Washington, 1963-64; geologist U.S. Geol. Survey, Washington, 1964-69, Reston, Va., 1974-78, 82—; chief geochem. br. NASA, Houston, 1969-74; dir. div. earth scis. NSF, Washington, 1978-82; hon. fellow Australian Nat. U., Canberra, 1967-68; mem. bd. earth scis. Nat. Acad. Sci. NRC, Washington, 1984—. Assoc. editor Geochim. Cosmochim. Acta, 1970-85, Jour. Geophys. Research, 1972-74, 83-85, Geochem. Jour., 1975—. Served to acting cpl. Royal Australian Air Force, 1953-55. Recipient Exceptional Sci. Achievement medal NASA, 1973. Mem. Geochem. Soc. (councillor 1977-79), Am. Geophys. Union (council 1984—), Soc. Econ. Geols. (Lindgren award 1964. Meteoritical Soc. (pres. 1973-74), Geol. Soc. Am. (chmn. planetary geology div. 1984), Geol. Soc. Washington (pres. elect 1985). Club: Cosmos (Washington). Current work: Composition of planetary cores, geochemistry and petrology of meteorites, petrology of sulfide ore deposits and submarine "black smokers."Subspecialties: Petrology; Planetology. Home: 2314 44th St NW Washington DC 20007 Office: US Geological Survey 959 Reston VA 22092

BREUER, CHARLES BENEDICT, medical products company executive; b. Bklyn., Aug. 7, 1931; s. Michael and Anne (Hirsch) B.; m. Elisabeth Charlotte Lang, June 30, 1962; 1 child, Lloyd Michael. B.A., NYU, 1953; M.S., Rutgers U., 1959, Ph.D., 1963. Research scientist E.R. Squibb & Sons, New Brunswick, N.J., 1959-62; group leader Lederle div. Am. Cyanamid Co., Pearl River, N.Y., 1966-69, head dept. research and devel., 1969-71, dir. research and devel., 1972-76; dir. tech. ops. Allied-Fisher Sci. Co., Orangeburg, N.Y., 1977—. Pres. pvt. sector Grace Commn., Washington, 1982. Served with U.S. Army, 1953-55. Mem. Am. Soc. Biol. Chemists, AAAS, Am. Chem. Soc., N.J. Acad. Sci. Republican. Episcopalian. Current work: Medical diagnostic products. Subspecialty: Medical products research and development management. Office: Fisher Sci Co 526 Route 303 Orangeburg NY 10962

BREWER, RICHARD GEORGE, physicist; b. Los Angeles, Dec. 8, 1928; s. Louis Ludwig and Elise B.; m. Lillian Magidow, Sept. 23, 1954; children: Laurence R., Emily S., Catherine. B.S., Calif. Inst. Tech., Pasadena, 1951; Ph.D., U. Calif., Berkeley, 1958. Instr. Harvard U., 1958-60; asst. prof. UCLA, 1960-63; mem. research staff IBM Corp. Research Lab., San Jose, Calif., 1963-73, IBM fellow, 1973—; cons. prof. applied physics Stanford U., 1977—; adj. prof. Nat. Inst. Optics, Florence, Italy, 1977—; vis. prof. M.I.T., 1968-69, U. Tokyo, spring 1975, U. Calif., Santa Cruz, fall 1976; mem. Calif. Scientist of Year Awards Jury, 1980, 81; mem. com. atomic and molecular physics Nat. Acad. Scis.-NRC, 1974-77; mem. bd. on physics and astronomy Commn. on Phys. Scis., Math. and Resources, Nat. Acad. Scis.-NRC, 1983-86; mem. rev. panel for Nat. Bur. Standards, 1981—; mem. com. on recommendations U.S. Army Basic Sci. Research, 1982-85; rev. com. San Francisco Laser Center, 1980-83, AEC-Lawrence Berkeley Lab., 1974. Asso. editor: Optics Letters, 1977-80, Jour. Optical Soc. Am, 1980—. Served with AUS, 1955-57. Recipient Albert A. Michelson Gold medal Franklin Inst., 1979. Fellow Am Phys. Soc. (Joint Council Quantum Electronics 1982-83 O.E. Buckley prize com.), Optical Soc. Am. (chmn. optical physics tech. council 1978-80, com. on fellows and hon. mems. 1981, W.F. Meggers award com. 1981); mem. Nat. Acad. Scis. Current Work: Laser spectroscopy; quantum optics. Subspecialties: Atomic and molecular physics; Condensed matter physics. Office: IBM Research Lab 5600 Cottle Rd San Jose CA 95193

BREY, WALLACE SIEGFRIED, chemist, educator; b. Schwenksville, Pa., June 6, 1922; s. Wallace S. and Roxie (Lichty) B.; m. Mary Louise Van Natta, Apr. 7, 1955; children: William W., Paul D. B.S., Ursinus Coll., 1942; Ph.D., U. Pa., 1948. With Warner Co., Phila., 1942-44; faculty DePauw U., Greencastle, Ind., 1948-49, St. Joseph Coll., Phila., 1949-52; faculty U. Fla., Gainesville, 1952—, now prof. chemistry. Author books and tech. papers.; Editor: Jour. Magnetic Resonance. Mem. Am. Chem. Soc. (Fla. award 1981), Am. Phys. Soc., Royal Soc. Chemistry, N.Y. Acad. Scis. Current Work: Nuclear magnetic resonance spectroscopy in study of molecular structure and molecular interactions. Subspecialties: Nuclear magnetic resonance; Surface chemistry. Office: Dept Chemistry U Fla Gainesville FL 32611

BRICK, DONALD BERNARD, engineering consultant; b. Bklyn., Oct. 1, 1927; s. Maxwell Bert and Edna (Newman) B.; m. Phyllis Madeline Hahn, Oct. 19, 1952; children—James L., Susan C. Brick Weinbaum, Howard A. A.B. cum laude, Harvard U., 1950, S.M., 1951, Ph.D., 1954. Registered profl. engr., Mass. Sr. scientist, sci. dir. GTE, Waltham, Mass., 1955-65; pres., chmn. Infoton, Inc., Burlington, Mass., 1965-71; v.p. A.M. Internat., Cambridge, Mass., 1971-72; owner, cons. D.B. Brick & Co., Inc., Lexington, Mass., 1972-75, 83—; tech. dir. U.S. Air Force, Bedford, Mass., 1975-83. Contbr. articles to profl. jours. Trustee Combined Jewish Philantropies of Greater Boston, 1975—, bd. dirs., 1981—, chmn. high tech. team, 1984—; v.p., bd. dirs. Temple Bmunah, Lexington, 1970. Fellow IEEE; mem. AAAS, N.Y. Acad. Sci., Harvard Soc. Engrs. and Physicists, Armed Forces Communications and Electronics Assn., AIAA, Sigma Xi. Current work: Local area networks, especially fiber optics, systems science, pattern recognition and artificial intelligence. Subspecialties: Computer engineering; Electronics. Home: 4 Blueberry Ln Lexington MA 02173 Office: Donald B Brick and Co Inc 4 Blueberry Ln Lexington MA 02173

BRICK, JOHN, biopsychologist, researcher, educator; b. N.Y.C., Mar. 18, 1950; s. H. C. and V.A. (Carmella) B.; m. Laurie Stockton Krulish, May 1, 1976. B.A., Queens Coll., CUNY, 1973; M.A. in Psychology, SUNY, Binghamton, 1979, Ph.D. in Psychology, 1981. Research asst. Rockefeller U., 1973-76; research asso. Center Alcohol Studies Rutgers U., 1980-82, research specialist, asst. prof., 1982—; lab. dir., research coordinator Alcohol Behavior Research Lab., 1984—; cons. dept. medicine and surgery VA, Washington, 1982—. Editor: Stress and Alcohol Use; co-author Biological Psychology; contbr. over 20 articles to profl. jours. Mem. Soc. Neurosci., AAAS, N.Y. Acad. Sci., Brit. Brain Research Assn., European Brain and Behavior, Sigma Xi. Current Work: Physiological and behavioral effects of alcohol; interaction between stress and to alcohol. Subspecialty: Psychobiology. Office: Alcohol Behavior Research Lab Bldg 3530 Rutgers U New Brunswick NJ 08903

BRICKMAN, EUGENE, geologist; b. N.Y.C., Oct. 29, 1954; s. Alan Murray and Judith (Grabel) B. Student NYU, 1971-73; B.S., CCNY, 1975; M.S., U. Del., 1978. Cert. profl. geologist Ind. Instr. U. Del., Newark, 1976; geologist Jenny Geotech. Co., South Orange, N.J., 1979; geologist U.S. Army C.E., Waltham, Mass., 1979-83; div. geologist, N.Y.C., 1983—; cons., 1979—. U. Del. fellow 1975. Mem. Geol. Soc. Am., Assn. Engring. Geologists, Smithsonian Instn. Current work: Geotechnical aspects of rock-tunnel design; coastal processes and stratigraphy. Subspecialties: Engineering geology; Coastal zones. Home: 26-20 Bayside Ln Queens NY 11358 Office: US Army Corps Engrs 90 Church St New York NY 10007

BRIDGE, CHARLES SOMMERS, electronics company executive. Vice pres., chief scientist Litton Industries, Inc., Beverly Hills, Calif. Subspecialty: Electronics. Office: Litton Industries Inc 360 N Crescent Dr Beverly Hills CA 90210*

BRIDGE, HERBERT SAGE, space physics educator; b. Berkeley, Calif., May 23, 1919; married, 1941; 3 children. B.S., U. Md., 1941; Ph.D. in Physics, MIT, 1950. Mem. research staff Los Alamos Sci. Lab., 1943-46; research assoc. cosmic ray research MIT, Cambridge, 1946-50, mem. research staff, 1950-55, research physicist, 1955-65, assoc. dir. ctr. space research, 1965-78, dir. ctr., 1978-84, prof. physics, 1965-85, prof. emeritus, sr. lectr., 1985—; vis. scientist European Orgn. Nuclear Research, Geneva, 1957-58. Fellow Am. Geophysical Union, Am. Acad. Arts and Scis., AAAS. Subspecialty: High energy astrophysics. Office: Ctr Space Research MIT Rm 37-241 Cambridge MA 02139*

BRIDGES, ALAN LYNN, computer scientist; b. Knoxville, Tenn., Oct. 10, 1950; s. Elijah Paul and Beuna Flynn B. B.S., Ga. Inst. Tech., 1972, M.S., 1974, postgrad., 1975-78. Asst. research scientist Engring Expt. Sta., Ga. Inst. Tech., Atlanta, 1975-78; asst. product mgr. Humphrey Instrs., San Leandro, Calif., 1978-79; pres., founder ETC West Ltd. dba VeXP Research/Systems, Atlanta, 1978-82; new tech. trg. dir. Gen. Motors Assembly Div., Warren, Mich., 1979-80; product mgr. picture processing systems Via Video, Inc., Cupertino, Calif., 1982; lead engr., prin. investigator electronics research and devel. dept. Lockheed - Ga. Co., Marietta, Ga., 1982—. Contbg. editor: Computer Tech. Rev.; Contbr. articles in field to profl. jours. Sr. mem. IEEE; mem. Optical Soc. Am., Soc. Photo-optical Instrumentation Engrs., AIAA, Assn. Computing Machinery, Atlanta Computer Soc., Computer Press Assn., Nat. Mgmt. Assn., Pi. Sigma. Democrat. Clubs: Radio (Atlanta) (editor 1975-76); Kennehoochee Amateur Radio (Marietta, Ga.) (bd. dirs. 1976-79). Current Work: Man-machine interface, speech recognition/synthesis, computer-generated imagery for flight simulation and battle management, VLSI/VASIC, optical memory systems, cockpit display technology, automatic test equipment. Subspecialties: Graphics, image processing, and pattern recognition; Information systems, storage, and retrieval (computer science). Home: 2007 Variations Dr Atlanta GA 30329 Office: Lockheed-Ga Co Electronices Research and Devel Dept 72-95 Zone 316 86 S Cobb Dr Marietta GA 30063

BRIDGES, JACK E(DGAR), electronic engineer; b. Denver, Jan. 1 1925; s. Byron Edgar and Edith Katherin (Kimmel) B.; m. Martha Ernest, Dec. 22, 1951; children—Victoria, Amelia, Cynthia. B.S.E.E., U. Colo., 1945, M.S.E.E., 1947. Antenna-design engr., Andrew Corp., Chgo., 1948-49; research engr. Zenith Radio Corp., Chgo., 1949-55; head color TV research Magnavox, Fort Wayne, Ind., 1955-56; chief electronics engr. Warwick Mfg. subs. Sears-Roebuck & Co., Niles, Ill., 1956-61; sr. sci. adviser Ill. Inst. Tech. Research Inst., Chgo., 1961—. Author: DNA Electromagnetic Pulse Awareness, 1971; EMP: Radiation and Protection, 1976; also numerous research papers, 1950—. Patentee, inventor in TV, electromagnetics. Served to ensign USN, 1943-46, PTO. Recipient Disting. Alumnus award U. Colo., 1983. Fellow IEEE (chmn. standards com. group on electromagnetic compatibility 1970-78, chmn. confs. 1960-61, 62-63, Browder J. Thompson Meml. prize 1956, certs. of appreciation 1972, 76); mem. IEEE Power Engring. Soc. (Prize Paper award 1981). Current work: High level electromagnetic effects from nuclear weapons; radio frequency and microwave heating; biological effects of electromagnetic fields; electric shock, subscription television systems; below threshold receivers and sensors. Subspecialty: Electronics. Home: 1937 Fenton Ln Park Ridge IL 60068 Office: IIT Research Inst 10 W 35th Chicago IL 60616

BRIDGES, WILLIAM BRUCE, research electrical engineer, educator; b. Inglewood, Calif., Nov. 29, 1934; s. Newman K. and Doris L. (Brown) B.; m. Carol Ann French, Aug. 24, 1957; children: Ann Marjorie, Bruce Kendall, Michael Alan. B.E.E., U. Calif. at Berkeley, 1956, M.E.E. (Gen. Electric Rice fellow), 1957, Ph.D. in Elec. Engring. (NSF fellow), 1962. Asso. elec. engring. U. Calif., Berkeley, 1957-59, grad. research engr., 1959-61; mem. tech. staff Hughes Research Labs. div. Hughes Aircraft Co., Malibu, Calif., 1960-77, sr. scientist, 1968-77, mgr. laser dept., 1969-70; prof. elec. engring. and applied physics Calif. Inst. Tech., Pasadena, 1977—, Carl F Braun prof. engring., 1983—, exec. officer elec. engring., 1978-81; lectr. elec. engring. U. So. Calif., Los Angeles, 1962-64; Sherman Fairchild Distinguished scholar Calif. Inst. Tech., 1974-75; chmn. Conf. on Laser Engring. and Applications, Washington, 1971. Author: (with C.K. Birdsall) Electron Dynamics of Diode Regions, 1966; contbr. articles on gas lasers, optical systems and microwave tube to profl. jours.; asso. editor: IEEE Jour. Quantum Electronics, 1977-82, Jour. Optical Soc. Am, 1978-83. Active Boy Scouts Am., 1968-82; bd. dirs. Ventura County Campfire Girls, 1973-76. Recipient L.A. Hyland Patent award, 1969. Fellow IEEE (chmn. Los Angeles chpt. Quantum Electronics and Applications Soc. 1979-81), Optical Soc. Am. (chmn. lasers and electro-optics tech. group 1974-75, bd. dirs. 1982-84); mem. Nat. Acad. Engring., Nat. Acad. Scis., Am. Radio Relay League, Phi Beta Kappa, Sigma Xi, Tau Beta Pi, Eta Kappa Nu (One of Outstanding Young Elec. Engrs. for 1966). Lutheran. Inventor noble gas ion laser, patentee in field. Current Work: Laser device physics; microwave device physics. Subspecialties: Physics research; Microwaves. Home: 413 W Walnut St Pasadena CA 91003 Office: Calif Inst Tech 128-95 Pasadena CA 91125

BRIDGEWATER, ALBERT LOUIS, physicist, government official; b. Houston, Nov. 22, 1941; s. Albert Louis and Rita (Narcisse) B.; m. Juanita Edington, June 11, 1967 (div. July 1984); children—Ramesi, Akin. B.A. in Physics, U. Calif.-Berkeley, 1963; postgrad. Columbia U., 1972. Postdoctoral fellow Lawrence Berkeley Lab., Berkeley, Calif., 1970-73; staff asst. physics NSF, Washington, 1973-76, spl. exec. asst., 1976-81, dep. asst. dir. AAEO, 1981—, acting asst. dir. AAEO, 1983—; adj. asst. prof. Howard U., Washington, 1975-76. Mem. Am. Geophys. Union. Current work: science policy; science management. Subspecialty: Particle physics. Office: Dep Asst Dir AAEO NSF 1800 G St NW Washington DC 20550

BRIDGMAN, CHARLES JAMES, engineering educator; b. Toledo, May 6, 1930; s. Charles D. and Wilhhelmina EstherBelle (O'Neill) B.; m. Lucy Hull, May 15, 1954; children: Kathleen Bridgman McFadden, Stephanie Bridgman Danahy, Charles J., Paula J., Kenneth M., Thomas A. B.S., U.S. Naval Acad., 1952; M.S., N.C. State U., 1958, Ph.D., 1963. Commd. 2d lt. U.S. Air Force, 1952, advanced through grades to capt., 1958, resigned, 1963; asst. prof. Air Force Inst. Tech., Dayton, Ohio, 1963-64, assoc. prof. engring., 1964-68, prof., chmn. com. nuclear engring., 1968—. Contbr. articles to sci. jours. Recipient awards Air Force Inst. Tech. Mem. Am. Nuclear Soc., Am. Assn. Engring. Edn., Health Physics Soc., AAUP, Sigma Xi. Republican. Roman Catholic. Current Work: Nuclear weapon effects, neutral particle transport; computational physics. Subspecialty: Nuclear engineering. Home: 7362 Natoma Pl Huber Heights OH 45424 Office: Air Force Inst Tech Wright Patterson AFB OH 45433

BRIGGS, ARTHUR BRAILSFORD, JR., computer systems engineering official, artificial intelligence official; b. Hamlet, N.C., Jan. 11, 1944; s. Arthur Brailsford and Margaret Louise (Poston) B.; m. Annesley Rembert Stuckey, Mar. 12, 1966; children: Catherine Margaret, Nancy Annesley. B.S. in Math, Wofford Coll., 1965; M.S. in Ops. Research, Air Force Inst. Tech., Dayton, Ohio, 1975. Computer maintenance officer Offutt AFB, Nebr., 1967-70; computer systems analyst Wright-Patterson AFB, Ohio, 1970-77; resigned, 1977; computer systems engr. Tex. Instruments, Inc., Dallas, 1977, mgr. engring. tng. and edn., Dallas and Lewisville, Tex., 1978-82, mgr. artificial intelligence br., 1983—. Commd. 2d lt. U.S. Air Force, 1966; advanced through grades to capt. 1969. Mem. Ops. Research Soc. Am. (assoc.), Assn. Computing Machinery, Air Force Assn. Republican. Lutheran. Current Work: Expert systems logic programming, knowledge based systems, natural language processing, development of software engineering methodology. Subspecialties: Artificial intelligence; Software engineering. Office: Texas Instruments Inc PO Box 405 MS 3407 Lewisville TX 75067

BRIGGS, ARTHUR HAROLD, pharmacologist; b. East Orange, N.J., Nov. 3, 1930; s. Arthur H. and Marie (Schoepf) B.; m. Elizabeth Jensen, June 6, 1953; children: Kimberlee, Norman Arthur. B.A., Johns Hopkins U., 1952, M.D., 1956. Diplomate: Am. Bd. Internal Medicine. Intern, then resident in internal medicine Vanderbilt U. Hosp., 1956-58; postdoctoral fellow dept. pharmacology Vanderbilt U. Hosp. (Med. Sch.), 1959; asst. prof. pharmacology and medicine U. Miss. Med. Center, 1959-68; prof., chmn. dept. pharmacology U. Tex. Health Sci. Center, San Antonio, 1968—. Author books and sci. articles. USPHS spl. fellow, 1967-68. Mem. Am. Soc. Pharmacology and Exptl. Therapeutics, Soc. Exptl. Biology and Medicine, Sigma Xi. Current Work: Pharmacology of alcohol and drugs of abuse. Teacher, researcher, chairman department of pharmacology. Subspecialties: Molecular pharmacology; Internal medicine. Home: 707 Serenade St San Antonio TX 78216 Office: 7703 Floyd Curl Dr San Antonio TX 78284

BRIGGS, ROBERT WILBUR, geneticist; b. Delevan, Ill., Mar. 27, 1934; s. Charles Wilbur and Hazel Berneice (Hymbaugh) B.; m. Gail Ann Chelmo, Mar. 31, 1962; children—David Robert, Sarah Ann. B.S., U. Ill., 1956, M.S., 1958; Ph.D., U. Minn., 1963. Asst. geneticist Brookhaven Nat. Lab., Upton, N.Y., 1965-68, assoc. geneticist, 1968-69; research scientist Funk Seeds Internat., Bloomington, Ill., 1969-75, prin. research scientist, 1975—; adj. prof. Adelphi U., Garden City, N.Y., 1963-65, Ill. State U., Normal, 1984—. Contbr. articles to profl. jours. Chmn. membership Corn Belt dist. Boy Scouts Am., 1982-84, chmn. advancement com., 1984—; project leader 4-H, 1984—; mem. adminstrv. bd. United Meth. Ch., 1984—. Served with U.S. Army, 1958-63. Mem. Crop Sci. Soc., Am. Soc. Agronomy, Am. Genetic Assn., Sigma Xi. Republican. Methodist. Current work: Application of biotechnology to plant breeding. Subspecialties: Plant genetics; Cell and tissue culture. Home: Rural Route 1 Box 30 Towanda IL 61776 Office: Funk Seeds Internat 1300 W Washington St Bloomington IL 61701

BRIGGS, WINSLOW RUSSELL, plant physiologist; b. St. Paul, Apr. 29, 1928; s. John DeQuedville and Marjorie (Winslow) B.; m. Ann Morrill, June 30, 1955; children: Caroline, Lucia, Marion. B.A., Harvard U., 1951, M.A., 1952, Ph.D., 1956. Instr. biol. scis. Stanford (Calif.) U., 1955-57, asst. prof., 1957-62, asso. prof., 1962-66, prof., 1966-67; prof. biology Harvard U., 1967-73; dir. dept. plant biology Carnegie Instn. of Washington, Stanford, 1973—. Author: (with others) Life on Earth, 1973; Asso. editor: (with others) Annual Review of Plant Physiology, 1961-72; editor (with others), 1972—; Contbr. (with others) articles on plant growth and devel. and photbiology to profl. jours. John Simon Guggenheim fellow, 1973-74; Alexander von Humboldt sr. scientist awardee, 1984-85. Fellow AAAS; mem. Am. Soc. Plant Physiologists (pres. 1975-76), Calif. Bot. Soc. (pres. 1976-77), Nat. Acad. Scis., Am. Acad. Arts and Scis., Am. Inst. Biol. Scis. (pres. 1980-81), Am. Soc. Photbiology, Bot. Soc. Am., Nature Conservancy, Sigma Xi. Current Work: Role of light in plant development, interaction of light reactions with hormones in plant development, molecular consequences of photoexcitation of pertinent plant photoreceptor molecules in light-regulated development. Subspecialties: Plant physiology (biology); Photobiology. Home: 480 Hale St Palo Alto CA 94301 Office: Dept of Plant Biology Carnegie Institution of Washington 290 Panama St Stanford CA 94305

BRIGHT, HAROLD JOHN, biochemistry and biophysics educator; b. Salisbury, Eng., Aug. 25, 1935; s. Leonard George and Kathleen Rosemund (Greenhall) B.; m. Janice Watson; children: Deborah, Leslie, Christopher. B.A. with honors, Cambridge (Eng.) U., 1957; Ph.D., U. Calif.-Davis, 1961. Mem. Faculty Sch. Medicine, U. Pa., Phila., 1962—, prof. biochemistry and biophysics, 1975—; vis. prof. U. Coll. London, 1971, Oxford (Eng.) U., 1971, Bristol (Eng.) U., Eng., 1971, 79; cons. in field. Editorial bd.: Jour. Biol. Chemistry; contbr. over 80 sci. articles to profl. publs. Rector's warden St. Mary's Episcopal Ch., Phila. USPHS Research Career Devel. grantee, 1967-71; NIH Research grantee, 1963—; NSF Research grantee, 1971-74; Guggenheim fellow, 1971; Fogarty Sr. Internat. fellow, 1979. Home: 689 Meadowbrook Ln Media PA 19063 Office: U Pa Sch Medicine Biochemistry and Biophysics Dept Philadelphia PA 19104

BRIGHTON, JOHN AUSTIN, mechanical engineer, educator; b. Gosport, Ind., July 9, 1934; s. John William and Esther Pauline B.; m. Charlotte L. McCarty, Mar. 20, 1953; children: Jill, Kurt, Eric. B.S., Purdue U., 1959, M.S., 1960, Ph.D., 1963. Draftsman Switzer Corp., Indpls., 1952-56; instr. Purdue U., 1960-63; asst. prof. mech. engring. Carnegie-Mellon U., 1963-65; asst. prof. Pa. State U., 1965-67, asso. prof., 1967-70, prof., 1970-77, Mich. State U., 1977-82, chmn. dept. mech. engring., 1977-82; dir. Sch. Mech. Engring. Ga. Inst. Tech., 1982—; Chmn. Community Sponsors Inc., State College, Pa., 1976-77; chmn. Pre-Trial Alts. Program for First Offenders, State College, 1976-77; bd. dirs. Impression 5. Author: (with Hughes) Fluid Dynamics, 1966. NSF grantee, 1975-77; NIH grantee, 1974-78. Mem. ASME (Engr. of Yr. award for Central Pa. 1977, tech. editor Jour. Biomech. Engring. 1976-79), Am. Soc. Engring. Edn., Am. Soc. Artificial Internal Organs. Current Work: Biofluid mechanics, artificial heart, engineering education and administration. Subspecialties: Mechanical engineering; Biomedical engineering. Home: 525 Kenbrook Dr Atlanta GA 30327 Office: Ga Inst Tech Atlanta GA 30332

BRILLIANT, HOWARD MICHAEL, air force engineering officer; b. Balt., Aug. 15, 1945; s. Benjamin and Anne Gertrude (Grodnitzky) B.; m. Arleen H. Blatt, Oct. 22, 1978; children—Rachelle Idena, Amy Alinda. B.S. in Mech. Engring, U. Pitts., 1966; M.S.Engring., U. Mich., 1967, Ph.D., 1971. Registered profl. engr., Colo. Commd. 2d lt. U.S. Air Force, 1966, advanced through grades to lt. col., 1985; project officer (Air Force Aero. Propulsion Lab.), Wright-Patterson AFB, Ohio, 1970-75; faculty mem. (U.S. Air Force Acad.), Colo., 1975-80, assoc. prof. aeros., 1978-80; chief laser tech. group (Air Force Weapons Lab.), Kirtland AFB, N.Mex., 1980-82, chief new laser concepts br., 1982, chief laser systems devel. sect., 1982-84, chief fluid mechanics br., 1984, mgr. F-16/F100 European engine program, 1984-85, dep. dir. Directorate of Acquisition Support, 1985—; cons. NASA Dryden Flight Research Ctr., Edwards AFB, Calif., 1976-78. Recipient Sci. Achievement award U.S. Air Force Systems Command, 1973, Commendation medal U.S. Air Force, 1974, Meritorious Service medal, 1979, 84. Mem. AIAA, Sigma Xi. Club: Sierra (Colorado Springs, Colo.) (chmn. group 1978). Current Work: Transonic and supersonic aerodynamics, propulsion, kinetics, thermodynamics, physics of chemical lasers, chemical laser systems. Subspecialties: Aeronautical engineering; Fluid mechanics. Home: 3643 Mecca Dr Dayton OH 45431 Office: ASD/YZW Wright-Patterson AFB OH 45433

BRILLINGER, DAVID ROSS, statistician; b. Toronto, Oct. 27, 1937; s. Austin Carlyle and Winnifred Elsie (Simpson) B.; m. Lorie Silber, Dec. 17, 1960; children: Jef Austin, Matthew David. B.A., U. Toronto, 1959; M.A., Princeton U., 1960, Ph.D., 1961. Lectr. math Princeton U. and; mem. tech. staff Bell Labs., 1962-64; lectr. stats. London Sch. Econs., 1964-66, reader, 1966-69; prof. stats. U. Calif., Berkeley, 1970—, chmn. dept., 1979-81. Author: Time Series: Data Analysis and Theory, 1975. Woodrow Wilson fellow, 1959; Bell Telephone Labs. fellow, 1960; Social Sci. Research Council postdoctoral fellow, 1961; Miller prof., 1973; Guggenheim fellow, 1975-76, 82-83. Fellow Am. Statis. Assn., Inst. Math. Stats., AAAS, Royal Soc. Can.; mem. Internat. Statis. Inst., Royal Statis. Soc., Can. Statis. Soc., Seismol. Soc. Am., Bernoulli Soc. Current Work: Mainstream statistics, but especially applications in seismology and neurophysiology. Subspecialty: Statistics. Office: Dept Stats U Calif Berkeley CA 94720

BRIMHALL, GEORGE H., geology educator, researcher; b. Santa Monica, Calif., Aug. 24, 1947; s. George and Alice (Traver) B.; m. Mary Jane Patroan, June 19, 1971; children: Lara Claire, Hilary Alyse. Project geologist Anaconda Co., Butte, Mont., 1972-76; asst. prof. Johns Hopkins U., Balt., 1976-78; asst. prof. geology U. Calif.-Berkeley, 1978-80, assoc. prof., 1980-82, prof., 1982—; mem. panel on mineral resources NRC, 1981—. Contbr. articles on econ. geology to profl. jours. Mem. Soc. Econ. Geologists (Lindgren award 1980, mem. research com. 1981—, nominating com. 1982—), Geochem. Soc., Mineral Soc. Am., AIME, Geol. Soc. Am. Current Work: Geological, geochemical and petrological study of the origin of economic metals in the crust; ore deposits, and economic geology. Subspecialties: Petrology; Geochemistry. Office: Dept Geology and Geophysics U Calif Berkeley CA 94720

BRINK, GILBERT O., physicist, educator; b. Los Angeles, May 26, 1929; s. Oscar C. and Leoti (Gilbert) B.; m. Lois M. Fredstrom, Mar. 2, 1957; children: Janet L., David R. B.A., Coll. Pacific, Stockton, Calif., 1953; Ph.D., U. Calif., Berkeley, 1957. Asst. research prof. U. Calif., Berkeley, 1957-59; research physicist Lawrence Radiation Lab., Livermore, Calif., 1959-63; vis. asst. research prof. U. Pitts., 1962-63; prin. physicist Cornell Aero. Lab., Buffalo, 1963-68; assoc. prof. physics SUNY-Buffalo, 1968-80, chmn. dept. physics and astronomy, 1972-74, prof. physics, 1980—; vis. McDonnell Disting. prof. Washington U., St. Louis, summer 1981. Contbr. numerous articles to profl. jours. Mem. Am. Phys. Soc., Optical Soc. Am., N.Y. Acad. Sci., Sigma Xi. Current Work: Laser spectroscopy of atoms and molecules, laboratory astrophysics. Subspecialties: Atomic and molecular physics; Laser spectroscopy. Home: 79 Buttonwood Ct East Amherst NY 14051 Office: Dept Physics and Astronomy SUNY at Buffalo Amherst NY 14260

BRINK, PETER RICHARDS, physiologist, educator; b. Wellsley, Mass., Oct. 24, 1946; s. Raymond and Mary (Richards) B.; m. Nancy Ann Brink, Sept. 17, 1969; 1 dau., Stephanie. B.A., Quinnipiac Coll., 1969; M.S., So. Conn. State Coll., 1971; Ph.D., U. Ill., 1976. Postdoctoral fellow SUNY at Stony Brook, 1975-77, research asst. prof., 1977-80, asst. prof. anat. scis., 1980—. Author: (with Dewey) Diffusions of Substances Inside Cells, 1981; Effects of Deuterian Oxide on Junctional Membrane Conductance and Permeability, 1985. Contbr. articles to profl. jours. NIH research grantee. Mem. Biophys. Soc., Gen. Physiology Soc., Soc. Neurosci. Current Work: Mechanism of gap junctional membrane transport. Effects of heavy water, acclimation or junctional membrane resistance. Subspecialties: Biophysics (biology); Neurophysiology. Office: Anatomical Sci HSC SUNY at Stony Brook Stony Brook NY 11794

BRINKHOUS, KENNETH MERLE, pathologist, emeritus educator; b. Clayton County, Iowa, May 29, 1908; s. William and Ida (Voss) B.; m. Frances E. Benton, Sept. 5, 1936; children: William Kenneth, John Robert. Student, U.S. Mil. Acad., 1925; A.B., State U. Iowa, 1929, M.D., 1932; D.Sc., U. Chgo., 1967. Asst. in pathology State U. Iowa, 1932-33, instr., 1933-35, asso. in pathology, 1935-37, asst. prof., 1937-45, assoc. prof., 1945-46; prof. pathology U. N.C., Chapel Hill, 1946-61, alumni disting. prof., 1961-80, emeritus, 1980—; Mem. Nat. Adv. Heart and Lung Council, 1969-74; chmn. med. adv. council Nat. Hemophilia Found., 1954-73; sec. gen. Internat. Com. Hemostasis and Thrombosis, 1966-78. Bd. editors: Perspectives in Biol. Medicine, 1968—; editor: Archives Pathology and Lab. Medicine, 1974-83, Yearbook Pathology Clin. Pathology, 1980—. Served from capt. to lt. col. M.C. U.S. Army, 1941-46; col. Med. Res. Corps 1946—. Co-recipient Ward Burdick award Am. Soc. Clin. Pathologists, 1941; recipient same, 1963, O. Max Gardner award, 1961; N.C. award, 1969; Internat. Heart Research award, 1969; Murray Thelin award Nat. Hemophilia Found., 1972; Distinguished Achievement award Modern Medicine, 1973; Maude Adams internat. pathology award, 1985; Robert P. Grant internat. thrombosis medal, 1985; H.P. Smith lectr., 1974. Mem. Nat. Acad. Scis. Inst. of Medicine, Am. Acad. Arts and Scis., Assn. Am. Physicians, Internat. Soc. Thrombosis and Haemostasis (pres. 1971), Am. Assn. Pathologists and Bacteriologists (sec., treas. 1968-71, pres. 1973), Am. Soc. Exptl. Pathology (pres. 1965-66), Fedn. Am. Socs. Exptl. Biology (pres. 1966-67), Univs. Asso. Research and Edn. Pathology (pres. 1964-68). Current Work: Blood coagulation and platelets; Thrombosis. Subspecialties: Hematology; Pathology (medicine). Home: 524 Dogwood Dr Chapel Hill NC 27514

BRINSON, DONALD EDWARD, data processing executive; b. Ponca City, Okla., Sept. 6, 1953; s. Merwyn Glen and Mildred Colleen (Good) B. B.S., U. Okla., Norman, 1980. Computer programmer Oscar Rose Jr. Coll., Midwest City, Okla., 1974-78, dir. computing services, 1980-85; systems specialist Hertz Corp., Oklahoma City, 1985—; systems programmer Okla. Tax Commn., Oklahoma City, 1978-80. Mem. Assn. for Computing Machinery, Hewlett-Packard Internat. Users Group (program dir. Central Okla. Regional chpt. 1981-82, pres. 1982-83). Democrat. Methodist. Club: Internat. Order Foresters. Current Work: Operating systems, software engineering, distributed systems and networks. Subspecialties: Information systems, storage, and retrieval (computer science); Operating systems. Home: 308 Draper Dr Midwest City OK 73110 Office: Hertz Corp 5601 Northwest Expressway Oklahoma City OK 73132

BRION, CHRISTOPHER EDWARD, chemist, educator; b. U.K., May 5, 1937; emigrated to Can., 1961, naturalized, 1971; s. Joseph Richard and Bessie May (Carter) B.; m. Elizabeth Mary Rogers, Apr. 15, 1961; children—Cathy, Peter, Susan. B.Sc., U. Bristol, Eng., 1958, Ph.D., 1961. Asst. prof. chemistry U. B.C., Can., Vancouver, 1964-69, asso. prof., 1969-77, prof., 1977—. Contbr. numerous articles to profl. jours. Recipient Noranda award Chem. Inst. Can., 1977, Herzberg award Spectroscopy Soc. Can., 1983; NRC Can. sr. fellow, 1969-70; John Simon Guggenheim Meml. fellow, 1978-79; Can. Council Killan research fellow, 1984-86. Fellow Chem. Inst. Can., Royal Soc. Can. Mem. Christian Ch. Current work: Electron spectroscopy, electron energy loss spectroscopy, photoionization. Subspecialties: Physical chemistry; Atomic and molecular physics. Home: 4097 W 15th Ave Vancouver BC V6R 3A2 Canada Office: Dept Chemistry U BC Vancouver BC V6T 1W5 Canada

BRIOTTA, DANIEL A., JR., astronomer, computer cons.; b. Springfield, Mass., Nov. 24, 1947; s. Daniel A. and Frances T. (Bruno) B. B.S., M.I.T., 1969; M.S., Cornell U., 1973, Ph.D., 1976. Lect., planetarium dir. U. Wyo., 1975-77; research assoc. Cornell U., Ithaca, N.Y., 1977-82; asst. prof. Ithaca (N.Y.) Coll., 1982—. Mem. Am. Astron. Soc., Astron. Soc. Pacific, Sigma Xi. Current Work: Teaching, laboratory microcomputing, infrared spectroscopy. Subspecialties: Infrared astronomy; Laboratory microcomputing. Office: Dept Physics Ithaca Coll Ithaca NY 14850

BRISKIN, MADELEINE, geology educator; b. Paris, Sept. 4, 1932; came to U.S., 1951, naturalized, 1956; d. Michael and Mina (Blevinal) B. B.S., CCNY, 1965; M.S., U. Conn., 1967; Ph.D., Brown U., 1973. Asst.prof. geology U. Cin., 1973-79, assoc. prof., 1979—. Mem. Am. Geophys. Union, N.Y. Acad. Scis., Paleontol. Soc., AAAS, Soc. Econ. Paleontologists and Mineralogists, Engring. Soc. Cin., Sigma Xi. Current Work: Past circulation of ocean and atmosphere, paleoclimatic study (mechanism of climate), new identification of astronomical quasi-periodicity of 413,000 to 430,000 years in deep sea sediments. Subspecialties: Geology; Oceanography. Office: Dept Geology U Cin Mail Location 13 Cincinnati OH 45221

BRITO, GILBERTO OTTONI, neuroscientist, physician; b. Rio de Janeiro, Brazil, May 24, 1951; s. Ney P. and Herbene I. (Ottoni) B.; children: Alexandre, Bianca. M.D., State U. Rio de Janeiro, 1974; Ph.D., U. Rochester. Postdoctoral fellow Center for Brain Research, U. Rochester Med. Center, 1981; asst. prof. Center for Brain Research U. Rochester Med. Center, 1982—. Contbr. articles to profl. publs. Co-investigator NIH. Mem. AAAS, Soc. Neurosci., N.Y. Acad. Scis., Assn. Child Psychology and Psychiatry, Sigma Xi. Current Work: Neuropsychology of memory; hormones and behavior. Supervising students' theses and performing own research. Subspecialties: Neuropsychology; Neuroendocrinology. Home: 27 Mountain Rd Rochester NY 14625 Office: 27 Mountain Rd Rochester NY 14625

BRITTAIN, ROBERT DAMERON, chemist; b. Birmingham, Ala., Jan. 11, 1949; s. George Marshall and Bettysu (Bozeman) B.; m. Cynthia Jane Elsberry, Dec. 18, 1971. B.S., Furman U., 1971, M.S., 1974; Ph.D., U. Fla., 1979. Phys. chemist SRI Internat., Menlo Park, Calif., 1979—. Contbr. articles to profl. jours. Mem. Am. Chem. Soc., AIME, Am. Ceramic Soc., Electrochem. Soc., Sierra Club. Current work: Characterization by mass spectrometry or thermogravimetry of vaporization processes in high temperature ceramic, metallurgical or energy related processes. Subspecialties: Physical chemistry; High temperature chemistry. Home: 10451 Lansdale Ave Cupertino CA 95014 Office: SRI Internat 333 Ravenswood Ave AG-221 Menlo Park CA 94025

BROACH, ROBERT WILLIAM, chemistry researcher; b. Fayetteville, Ark., May 19, 1949; s. Wilson James and Billie Ellena (Godbey) B.; m. Mary Jeannine Halverson; children—Christopher, Riley. B.S., U. Ark.-Fayetteville, 1971; Ph.D., U. Wis.-Madison, 1977. Research asst. Argonne Nat. Lab., Ill., 1977-78; assoc. research scientist Signal Research Ctr., Des Plaines, Ill., 1978—. Contbr. articles to profl. jours. Mem. Am. Chem. Soc., Am. Crystallographic Assn., Materials Research Soc., Catalysis Club Chgo. Current work: Research in x-ray diffraction and EXAFS characterization of catalysts and other materials. Subspecialties: Inorganic chemistry; X-ray crystallography. Home: 330 Arizona Blvd Hoffman Estates IL 60194 Office: Signal Research Ctr 50 E Algonquin Rd Box 5016 Des Plaines IL 60017

BROADBENT, DONALD CLARENCE, optics scientist; b. Detroit, Sept. 3, 1929; s. Clarence Coleman and Josephine (Janiga) B.; m. Rose Marie Morasky, May 20, 1950. Pres., Westech Devel. Lab., Inc., Mountain View, Calif., 1978-81; owner, mgr. Broadbent Devel. Lab., Mountain View, Calif., 1981—. Served with USMC, 1952-54. Mem. Optical Soc. Am., Soc. Photo-Optical Instrumentation Engring., VFW. Current work: Holographic optical elements - HOE to use in solar concentrating systems, heads up displays. Subspecialties: Holography; Solar energy. Address: 2439 Whitney Ct Mountain View CA 94043

BROADHURST, JOHN HENRY, physics educator; b. Stoke-on-Trent, Eng., Apr. 27, 1935; came to U.S., 1968; s. Leonard B. and Clarice L. (Robinson) B.; m. L. Jaeger, July 25, 1959; children: Nina Louise, Denise Joan. B.Sc., U. Birmingham (Eng.), 1956, Ph.D., 1959. Grad. researcher minerals engring. U. Birmingham, 1956-59, postgrad. in physics, 1959-61, staff fellow physics, 1962-68; assoc. prof. physics U. Minn., Mpls., 1968-78, prof. physics, 1979—; cons. in field. Contbr. articles to profl. jours. Mem. Am. Phys. Soc. Current Work: Research in applied nuclear physics, in physiology of contractile tissue. Subspecialties: Nuclear physics; Cell and tissue culture. Office: U Minn 324 Physics Dept 116 Church St SE Minneapolis MN 55455

BROADWELL, RICHARD DOW, neurocytologist, cell biologist, neuropathologist, consultant, researcher, educator; b. Oak Park, Ill., Nov. 4, 1945; s. Robert and Dorothy Jane (Dow) B. B.A., Knox Coll., 1967; M.S., U. Wis., 1971, D. Phil., 1974. Staff fellow in neurocytology/neuropathology Nat. Inst. Neurol. and Communicable Diseases and Stroke, NIH, Bethesda, Md., 1974-80; assoc. prof. pathology and neurol. surgery, head Lab. Exptl. Neuropathology, dir. Labs. Neuro-oncology and Cerebrovascular studies, U. Md. Sch. Medicine, 1980—, cons. in field. Contbr. numerous articles, chpts. on brain and neurocytology to profl. publs. Recipient Undergrad. Research award NSF, 1966-67; Japanese Soc. for Promotion of Sci. fellow, 1980-81; NIH Nat. Inst. Neurol. and Communicable Diseases and Stroke grantee, 1982-86. Mem. Neurosci. Soc., Am. Soc. Cell Biology, Histochem. Soc., Washington Electron Microscopy Soc. Republican. Presbyterian. Subspecialties: Neurobiology; Cell biology (medicine). Home: 10401 Grosvenor Pl Unit 1010 Rockville MD 20852 Office: U Md Dept Pathology 10 S Pine St Baltimore MD 21201

BROBECK, JOHN RAYMOND, physiology educator; b. Steamboat Springs, Colo., Apr. 12, 1914; s. James Alexander and Ella (Johnson) B.; m. Dorothy Winifred Kellogg, Aug. 24, 1940; children: Stephen James, Priscilla Kimball, Elizabeth Martha, John Thomas. B.S., Wheaton Coll., 1936, LL.D., 1960; M.S., Northwestern U., 1937, Ph.D., 1939; M.D., Yale U., 1943. Instr. physiology Yale, 1943-45, asst. prof., 1945-48, asso. prof. physiology, 1948-52; prof. physiology, chmn. dept. U. Pa., Phila., 1952-70, Herbert C. Rorer prof. med. scis., 1970-82, prof. emeritus, 1982—. Editor: Yale Jour. Biology and Medicine, 1949-52; chmn. editorial bd.: Physiol. Revs, 1963-72. Fellow Am. Acad. Arts and Scis.; mem. Am. Physiol. Soc. (pres. 1971-72), Am. Inst. Nutrition, Nat. Acad. Scis., Am. Soc. Clin. Investigation, Halsted Soc., Phila. Coll. Physicians, Sigma Xi, Alpha Omega Alpha. Current Work: Control of food intake, energy balance, temperature regulation. Subspecialties: Physiology (medicine); Neurophysiology. Home: 224 Vassar Ave Swarthmore PA 19081 Office: U Pa G/3 Philadelphia PA 19104

BROBST, DUANE FRANKLIN, pathologist, educator; b. Medicine Lake, Mont., Oct. 8, 1923; s. Herbert Franklin and Inez (Bell) B.; m. Janice Dean, Nov. 26, 1970; children: Clay, Todd, Amy; married; 1 stepson, Bill Wasson. A.B., U. So. Calif., Los Angeles, 1949; D.V.M., Wash. State U., Pullman, 1954; Ph.D., U. Wis., Madison, 1962. Asst. prof. to prof. Purdue U., West Lafayette, Ind., 1960-70; prof. vet. pathology Wash. State U., 1970—. Author: (with D.J. Blackmore) Biochemical Values in Equine Medicine, 1981; contbr. chpt. in book. Served with USN, 1943-46. Mem. Am. Coll. Vet Pathologists, Am. Soc. Vet. Clin. Pathologists. Republican. Methodist. Current Work: Acid-base balance and renal disease. Subspecialty: Pathology (veterinary medicine). Office: McCoy Hall Washington State University Pullman WA 99164

BROCKA, BRUCE, software engineering educator; b. Davenport, Iowa, Nov. 1, 1959; s. Donald H. and Daisy A. (Robertson) B.; m. Mary St. Ledger, Mar. 17, 1984. B.S. in Physics, St. Ambrose Coll., 1981; M.S.E.E., U. Iowa, 1984. Research asst. U. Iowa, 1983-84; mem. faculty Army Mgmt. Engring. Tng. Activity, Rock Island, Ill., 1984—; pres. Kattor Research, Davenport, 1984—. Contbr. articles to profl. jours. Mem. Am. Astron. Soc. (jr.), IEEE (sec.). Republican. Roman Catholic. Current work: Data flow graphs; software development; planetary nebulae; unusual binary stars; software and computer engineering training. Subspecialties: Software engineering; Radio and microwave astronomy. Home: 1005 Mississippi Davenport IA 52803 Office: US AMETA Rock Island Arsenal Rock Island IL 61299-7040

BROCKMEYER, JERRY W., ceramic engineer; b. Peoria, Ill., Apr. 16, 1949; s. Frank O. and Agnes H. (Kennedy) B.; m. Jeanette M. Adams, June 9, 1973; children—Justin W., Jennifer M. B.S. in Ceramic Engring., U. Ill., 1971, postgrad., 1971-73. Ceramic engr. Universal Oil Products, Des Plaines, Ill., 1973-77; research engr. Consol. Aluminum Corp., St. Louis, 1977-79, supr. product and process devel., Hendersonville, N.C., 1979—; bd. dirs. Mfrs. of Emissions Controls Assn., Washington, 1984—. Patentee in molten metals filtration. Contbr. articles to tech. publs. Corning research fellow, 1971. Mem. Soc. Automotive Engrs., Am. Ceramic Soc. Current work: Molten metals filters and filtrations; open-pore ceramics and applications; automotive emissions controls. Subspecialties: Ceramic engineering; Ceramics. Home: 3032 Laurel Park Hwy Hendersonville NC 28739 Office: Consol Aluminum Corp PO Box 747 Hendersonville NC 28793

BRODE, JOHN, mathematician; b. Cambridge, Mass., Mar. 17, 1932; s. Robert Bigham and Bernice (Bidwell) B.; m. Joanne Dolgin, Dec. 24, 1963; children—Michel, David, Dina. A.B., Ecole Nationale des Langues Orientales Vivantes, Paris, 1957; A.M., U. Paris, 1958; Ph.D., Harvard U., 1980. IBM fellow Harvard U., Cambridge, 1964-67; sr. research assoc. MIT/Harvard U., Cambridge, 1968-74; prof. ISCAE, Casablanca, Morocco, 1980-81; lectr. U. Mass., Boston, 1981-82; asst. prof. math. U. Lowell, Mass., 1982-85; mem. tech. staff Alphatech, Burlington, Mass., 1985—; cons. ABT Assocs., Cambridge, 1974-76, others, 1976—. Author: Process of Modernization, 1969; TSP/DATATRAN, 1974. Contbr. articles to profl. jours. Pres. Neighborhood 10 Assn., Cambridge, 1984—; chmn. Community Schs. Council, Cambridge, 1976-79, Cambridge Democratic City Com., 1972-73, Mass. PAX, Cambridge, 1970-71. Mem. Time Series Analysis and Forecasting Soc., Am. Math. Assn., Inst. Math. Stats., Ops. Research Soc. Am., Soc. Indsl. and Applied Math., Societé Mathématique de France. Jewish. Current work: Non-Gaussian Feller diffusions; interfacing statistical computing and data base management. Subspecialties: Stochastic processes; Artificial intelligence. Home: 23 Berkeley St Cambridge MA 02138 Office: Alphatech 111 Burlington Turnpike Burlington MA 01803

BRODIE, HARLOW KEITH HAMMOND, university president; b. Stamford, Conn., Aug. 24, 1939; s. Lawrence Sheldon and Elizabeth White (Hammond) B.; m. Brenda Ann Barrowclough, Jan. 26, 1967; children: Melissa Verduin, Cameron Keith, Tyler Hammond, Bryson Barrowclough. A.B., Princeton U., 1961; M.D., Columbia U., 1965. Diplomate: Am. Bd. Psychiatry and Neurology. Intern Ochsner Found. Hosp., New Orleans, 1965-66; resident in psychiatry Columbia-Presbyn. Med. Center, N.Y.C., 1966-68; clin. assoc. intramural research program NIMH, 1968-70; asst. prof. psychiatry, dir. gen. clin. research center Stanford U. Med. Sch., 1970-74; prof. psychiatry, chmn. dept. Duke U. Med. Sch., 1974-82, prof. law, adj. prof. psychology, 1981—; psychiatrist-in-chief Duke U. Med. Center, 1974-82; chancellor Duke U., 1982-85, pres., 1985—. Co-author: The Importance of Mental Health Services to General Health Care, 1979, Modern Clinical Psychiatry, 1981; co-editor: American Handbook of Psychiatry, vols. 6 and 7, 1975, 81, Controversy in Psychiatry, 1978; asso. editor: Am. Jour. Psychiatry, 1973-81. Chmn. Durham Area Mental Health, Mental Retardation and Substance Abuse Bd., 1981-82; pres. bd. trustees. Durham Acad., 1985—. Recipient Strecker award Inst. of Pa. Hosp., 1980, Disting. Alumnus award Ochsner Med. Found., 1984, Columbia U. Coll. Physicians and Surgeons, 1985; Gold medal Alumni Assn., 1985. Mem. Am. Psychiat. Assn. (sec. 1977-81, pres. 1982-83), Inst. Medicine, Royal Coll. Psychiatrists, Soc. Biol. Psychiatry (A.E. Bennet research award 1970), Am. Psychosomatic Soc. Subspecialties: Pharmacology; Neuropsychology. Home: 63 Beverly Dr Durham NC 27707 Office: 207 Allen Bldg Duke U Durham NC 27706

BRODNER, ROBERT ALBERT, neurosurgeion, researcher; b. New Haven, Aug. 15, 1946; s. Albert Abraham and Louise Margaret (DeStefano) B.; m. Stephanie Margaret, Mar. 20, 1970; children: David C., John J., Christina L. B.S., Fordham U., 1968; M.D., Loyola U. of Chgo. Stritch Sch. Medicine, 1972. Diplomate: Nat. Bd. Med. Examiners. Intern in surgery Mt. Sinai Hosp. N.Y., N.Y.C., 1972-73, resident in neurosurgery, 1973-74, 76-78; research fellow in neurosurgery Yale U., 1975-76; sr. instr. in neurosurgery and staff attending neurosurgeon Hahnemann Med. Coll. and Hosp., 1981—. Contbr. articles to profl. jours. Served to lt. comdr. M.C. USN, 1978-80. Recipient First Place prize N.Y. Soc. Neurosurgery; Resident's Research Award, 1976, 78. Mem. Congress Neurosurgery, Soc. Neurosci., Am. Fedn. Clin. Research, Pa. Neurosurg. Soc., Pa. Med. Soc. Roman Catholic. Club: Waynesborough Country (Paoli, Pa.). Inventor fetal ventriculo-amniotic shunt. Current Work: Microneurosurgery; fetal intracranial surgery; experimental fetal hydrocephalus; spinal cord injury. Subspecialties: Fetal surgery; Neurosurgery. Office: Dept Neurosurger Hahnemann Med Coll and Hosp Philadelphia PA 19102

BRODY, BURTON ALAN, physicist, researcher, educator; b. N.Y.C., June 8, 1942; s. Jules and Shirley (Nudriv) B.; m. Susan Simon, Aug. 3, 1980. B.A., Columbia U., 1963; Ph.D., U. Mich., Ann Arbor, 1970. Computer programmer, systems analyst, mgr. OLI Systems and SBM, Inc., N.Y.C., 1978-79; prof. physics Bard Coll., Annandale-on-Hudson, 1970—; vis. scholar in physics Columbia U., 1981—. Author: Electronics from the Ground Up; contbr. articles to profl. jours. Active ACLU, Union Concerned Scientists, Fedn. Atomic Scientists. Mem. Am. Phys. Soc. Subspecialties: Atomic and molecular physics; Low temperature physics. Office: Physics Dept Bard College Annandale on Hudson NY 12504

BRODY, JEROME SAUL, physician, medical educator; b. Chgo., Dec. 6, 1934; s. Louis J. and Esther (Snyder) B.; m. Ann Frankel, Sept. 4, 1955; children—Lisa, Karen, Marion. B.S., U. Ill., 1955, M.D., 1959. Intern Michael Reese Hosp., Chgo., 1959-60, resident in medicine, 1960-62; resident in medicine U. Okla., Oklahoma City, 1964-65; NIH postdoctoral fellow U. Pa., Phila., 1965-67, asst. prof. medicine and physiology, 1967-72; assoc. prof. medicine and biochemistry Boston U. Sch. Medicine, 1973-78, prof. medicine, 1978—; chief pulmonary medicine Univ. and Boston City Hosps., 1977—; mem. study sect. NIH, 1983—. Editor: Current Topics Management Respiratory Diseases, Vol. 1, 1981, Vol. 2, 1984; mem. editorial bd. New Eng. Jour. Medicine, 1977-80, Am. Rev. Respiratory Disease, 1984—. Contbr. chpts. to books, sci. articles to profl. jours. NIH grantee, 1968—. Fellow ACP; mem. Am. Soc. Cell Biology, Am. Physiol. Soc., Am. Soc. Clin. Investigation, Am. Thoracic Soc. Current work: Lung development and repair-regulation of cell differentiation. Subspecialties: Pulmonary medicine; Cell biology (medicine). Office: Pulmonary Ctr K-602 Boston Univ Sch Medicine 80 E Concord St Boston MA 02118

BRODY, STEVEN, physicist, engineer; b. Phila., Apr. 16, 1952; s. Bernard Irving and Eleanor (Albert) B. B.S. in Physics, Drexel U., 1974; M.S., MIT, 1977. Intelligence analyst/phys. scientist trainee CIA, Washington, 1970-73; study participant space colonies NASA/Ames Research Center, summer 1975; research asst. MIT Earth & Planetary Sci. Dept., 1975-77; avionics systems engr. Intermetrics, Inc., Cambridge, Mass., 1977-80, program mgr. space shuttle test, Huntington Beach, Calif., 1980—. Recipient award for acad. excellence in sci. Drexel U., 1970, others. Mem. AIAA (chmn. sect. tech. com. for guidance, control, and dynamics), Aircraft Owners and Pilots Assn., The L-5 Soc., Planetary Soc. Club: Long Beach Rowing Assn. Current Work: Space Shuttle checkout and operation, space sta. devel., space exploration and industrialization, artificial intelligence, civil air traffic control improvements. Subspecialties: Aerospace engineering and technology; Software engineering. Office: 5392 Bolsa Ave Huntington Beach CA 92649

BRODY, STUART MARTIN, analytical chemist, research scientist; b. Bklyn., June 25, 1936; m. Helene Levine, Feb. 8, 1958; children—Russell S., Elyse K. B.S. in chemistry, Queens Coll., 1958. Sr. research scientist pharmaceuticals div. Ciba-Geigy Corp., Summit, N.J., 1958—. Contbr. articles, primarily on separation and purification of pharmaceuticals, to profl. jours. Designer, developer automate O distillation instrument for purification of chemicals and pharm. intermediates. Mem. Am. Chem. Soc. (div. analytical chemistry, lab. automation/computers div., chromatography and separation chemistry div., Assn. Ofcl. Analytical Chemists, Am. Inst. Chemists, N.J. Chromatography Discussion group, chromatography Forum of Del. Valley, N.Y. Acad. Scis. Current work: Chromatographic and distillation techniques as applied to the separation and purification of pharmaceutical intermediates. Subspecialties: Analytical chemistry; Distributed systems and networks. Home: 8 Timberlane Dr Colonia NJ 07067 Office: Ciba-Geigy Corp 556 Morris Ave Summit NJ 07901

BRODY, THEODORE MEYER, educator, pharmacologist; b. Newark, May 10, 1920; s. Samuel and Lena (Hammer) B.; m. Ethel Vivian Drelich, Sept. 7, 1947; children—Steven Lewis, Debra Jane, Laura Kate, Elizabeth. B.S., Rutgers U., 1943; M.S., U. Ill., 1949, Ph.D., 1952. Mem. faculty U. Mich. Med. Sch., Ann Arbor, 1952-66; prof. pharmacology, chmn. dept. Coll. Medicine, Mich. State U., East Lansing, 1966—; cons. NIH, 1969-73, NIDA, 1975—, Internat. Soc. Heart Research, 1973—; mem. sci. adv. com. Pharm. Mfrs. Assn. Found., 1973—; U.S. rep. Internat. Union Pharmacology, 1973-76; mem. bd. Fedn. Am. Socs. for Exptl. Biology, 1973-76; mem. Com. Sci. Soc. Presidents; NSF Distinguished scholar lectr. U. Hawaii, 1974. Mem. editorial bd.: Jour. Pharmacology and Exptl. Therapeutics, 1965—; specific field editor, 1981; editorial bd.: Research Communications in Chem. Pathology and Pharmacology, Molecular Pharmacology, 1972—. Served with AUS, 1943-46. Recipient Disting. Faculty award Mich. State U., 1984. Mem. Soc. Pharmacology and Exptl. Therapeutics (John Jacob Abel award 1955, chmn. Abel award com. 1966, mem. council 1969-72, sec.-treas. 1970, pres. elect 1973, pres. 1974), Internat. Soc. Biochem. Pharmacology, Am. Coll. Clin. Pharmacology, Assn. Med. Sch. Pharmacologists (sec. 1984-86), Soc. Toxicology, Am. Soc. Pharmacology and Exptl. Therapeutics (pres. 1974-75, awards com. 1977, chmn. 1978), Soc. Neurosci., Japanese Pharmacology Soc., AAUP, Sigma Xi, Rho Chi, Phi Kappa Phi. Subspecialty: Pharmacology. Home: 842 Longfellow Dr East Lansing MI 48823 Office: Dept of Pharmacology and Toxicology Mich State Univ East Lansing MI 48824

BROERSMA, SYBRAND, physics educator; b. Harlingen, Friesland, The Netherlands, Sept. 20, 1919; came to U.S., 1947; s. Jacob and Johanna (Zwanenburg) B. Student in Physics, Leiden U., 1939, Doctorate, 1941; D.Sc. cum laude in Physics, Delft Inst. Tech., 1947. Research assoc. Columbia U., 1947; instr. U. Toronto, 1948; prof. physics U. Indonesia, Bandung, 1949-51; asst. prof. physics Northwestern U., 1952-58; prof. physics U. Okla., Norman, 1959—; adj. prof. materials research U. Tex., Dallas, 1967-70. Author: Magnetic Measurements on Organic Compounds, 1947; Elementary Physics Laboratory Manual, 1963. Contbr. articles to profl. jours. Internat. exchange fellow Northwestern U., 1947; NSF grantee, 1956-68. Mem. Am. Phys. Soc., Netherlands Phys. Soc., European Phys. Soc., AAUP, Sigma Xi. Current work: Calculation of the viscous force constants of irregularly shaped objects (macromolecules); calculation of the absorptance of a spectrum of infrared absorption lines. Subspecialties: Fluid mechanics; Magnetic physics. Home: PO Box 524 Norman OK 73070 Office: Dept Physics Univ Okla Norman OK 73019

BROMBERG, YURY, engineer, researcher; b. Moscow, May 22, 1937; came to U.S., 1980, naturalized, 1984; s. Abraham and Klarissa (Lirtsman) B.; married, Nov. 5, 1958; 1 child, Sonia. M.A. in Mech. Engring., Moscow Road Inst., 1959, Ph.D. in Mech. Engring., 1964. Project engr. Design Office, Moscow, 1959-61; postdoctoral Research Inst., Moscow, 1962-64, sr. researcher, 1964-67; asst. prof. Ry. Inst., Moscow, 1967-73; sr. researcher Technion Inst. Tech., Haifa, Israel, 1974-79; project engr. dept. research and devel. Mark Industries, Long Beach, Calif., 1980-85; cons. engr. B&K Engring., Fountain Valley, Calif., 1980—. Author: Bridges Mounting Equipment, 1968; Road Construction Equipment, 1971; Hydraulic Systems of Construction Equipment, 1971. Contbr. articles to profl. publs., chpts. to Big Soviet Ency. Patentee in field. Mem. Fluid Power Soc. Current work: Development of hydraulic systems for construction equipment. Subspecialties: Mechanical engineering; Fluid mechanics.

BROMLEY, DAVID ALLAN, physicist, educator; b. Westmeath, Ont., Can., May 4, 1926; s. Milton Escott and Susan Anne (Anderson) B.; m. Patricia Jane Brassor, Aug. 30, 1949; children—David John, Karen Lynn. B.S. in Engring. and Physics, Queen's U., Kingston, Ont., 1948; M.S. in Physics, 1950; Ph.D. in Nuclear Physics, U. Rochester, 1952; M.A. (hon.) Yale U., 1961; Dr. Nat. Phil. (hon.), U. Frankfurt, 1978; Docteur Physique (hon.), U. Strasbourg, 1980; D.Sc. (hon.), Queen's U., 1981; Litt.D. (hon.), U. Bridgeport, 1981; Sc.D. (hon.), U. Witwatersrand, 1981; D.Sc. (hon.), U. Notre Dame, 1982, others. Operating engr. Hydro Electric Power Commn., Ont., 1947-48; research officer Nat. Research Council Can., 1948; instr., then asst. prof. physics U. Rochester, 1952-55; sr. research officer, sect. head Atomic Energy Can., Ltd., 1955-60; assoc. prof. physics, assoc. dir. heavy ion accelerator lab. Yale, U., 1960-61, prof. physics, dir. A.W. Wright Nuclear Structure Lab., 1961—, chmn. dept. physics, 1970-77, Henry Ford II prof., 1972—; dir. United Nuclear Corp., N.E. Bancorp Inc., Union Trust Co., United Illuminating Corp., Gen. Ionex Co., Barnes Engring. Co., cons. Brookhaven, Argonne, Berkley and Oak Ridge nat. labs., Bell Telephone Labs., IBM, G.T.E. Mem. panel nuclear physics Nat. Acad. Scis., 1964, chmn. physics survey, 1969-74; mem. U.S. Nat. Com. Internat. Union Pure and Applied Physics, 1969, chmn., 1975, v.p., 1975-81, pres. 1984—; mem. naval sci. bd. NRC, 1974-78; mem. high energy physics adv. panel ERDA, 1974-78; mem. nuclear sci. adv. panel NSF and Dept. Energy, 1980—; mem. White House Sci. Council, 1981—; bd. dirs. Oak Ridge Assoc. Univs., 1977-80, U., Bridgeport, 1981; mem. adv. bd. Inst. Nuclear Power Ops., 1983-85, Electric Power Research Inst., 1984—, Southeastern Univs. Research Assn., 1985—. Editor: Physics in Perspective, 5 vols., 1972; Large Electrostatic Accelerators, 1974; Nuclear Detectors, 1978; Heavy Ion Science, 7 vols., 1984; co-editor Procs. Kingston Internat. Conf. on Nuclear Structure, 1960; Facets of Physics, 1970; Nuclear Science in China, 1979; assoc. editor Annals of Physics, 1968, Am. Scientist, 1969-81, Il Nuovo Cimento, 1970—, Nuclear Instruments and Methods, 1974—, Sci. Tech. and the Humanities, 1978—, Jour. Physics, 1978—, Nuclear Sci. Applications, 1978—, Tech. in Soc., 1981—, Physics Today, 1984—; cons. editor McGraw Hill Series in Fundamentals of Physics, 1967, McGraw Hill Ency. Sci. and Tech. Recipient medal Gov. Gen. Can., 1948; NRC fellow, 1952; fellow Branford Coll., Guggenheim fellow, 1977-78; Humboldt fellow, 1978-82-84; Benjamin Franklin fellow Royal Soc. Arts, London, 1979. Fellow Am. Phys. Soc. (mem. council 1967-71), AAAS (chmn. physics sect. 1977-78, pres. 1981, chmn. bd. 1982), Am. Acad. Arts and Scis.; mem. Can. Assn. Physicists, European Phys. Soc. Conn. Acad. Arts and Scis., Conn. Acad. Sci. and Engring. (council 1976-78), Sigma Xi. Subspecialty: Nuclear physics. Home: 35 Toneneke Dr Hamden CT 06518 Office: Wright Nuclear Structure Lab Yale U 272 Witney Ave New Haven CT 06520

BRONSON, DAVID LEE, cell biologist/virologist, educator; b. Holland, Mich., Oct. 29, 1936; s. John and Dorothy (Tilden) B.; m. Judith Gunn, Apr. 23, 1970. B.A., Hope Coll., 1963; M.S., Iowa State U., 1966, Ph.D., 1969. Postdoctoral fellow dept. virology and epidemiology Baylor Coll. Medicine, 1969-71; research assoc. dept. microbiology U. Miami-Coral Gables, Fla., 1971-72; with dept. urologic surgery U. Minn., Mpls., 1972-83, asst. prof. urologic surgery, 1974-83; assoc. scientist Southwest Found. for Edn. and Research, San Antonio, 1984—. Contbr. articles to sci. jours. Served with USAF, 1954-57. Mem. AAAS. Current Work: Control of cell differentiation in human embroyonal carcinoma cells. Subspecialties: Cancer research (medicine); Cell and tissue culture. Office: Southwest Found PO Box 28147 San Antonio TX 78284

BROOK, ADRIAN GIBBS, chemistry educator; b. Toronto, Ont., Can., May 21, 1924; s. Frank Adrian and Beatrice Maud (Wellington) B.; m. Margaret Ellen Dunn, Dec. 18, 1954; children—Michael A., Katherine M., David L. B.A., U. Toronto, 1947, Ph.D., 1950. Lectr. U. Toronto, 1953-56, asst. prof., 1956-60, assoc. prof., 1960-62, prof. chemistry, 1962—, acting chmn. dept., 1968-71, chmn. dept. chemistry, 1971-74. Contbr. to publs. in field. Served with Royal Can. Naval Res., 1943-45. Fellow Royal Soc., Can., Chem. Inst. Can. (CIC medal 1985); mem. Am. Chem. Soc. (Frederick Stanley Kipping award 1973). Mem. United Ch. of Can. Current work: Organosilicon or organometalloid chemistry Subspecialty: Organic chemistry. Office: Dept Chemistry U Toronto 80 St George St Toronto ON M5S 1A1 Canada

BROOK, MARX, physics educator, academic administrator, researcher; b. N.Y.C., July 12, 1920; s. Abraham and Esther B.; m. Dorothy; children: Janet, Jimmy, Georgia. B.S., U. N. Mex., 1944; Ph.D., UCLA, 1953. Asst. U. N. Mex., 1943-46; research physicist UCLA, 1947-53; research physicist N. Mex. Inst. Mining and Tech., 1954-58, assoc. prof. physics, 1958-60, prof., 1960—, chmn. dept. physics, 1960-68, dir. research and devel. div., 1978—; trustee N. Mex. Tech. Research Found.; mem. N. Mex. Gov.'s Com. on Tech. Excellence; mem. steering com. Sen Dominicis Rio Grande Communications Network. Contbr. numerous articles to profl. publs. Recipient Vis. Scientist award Japan Soc. Promotion Sci., Japan, 1976, Disting. Scientist award N. Mex. Acad. Sci., 1981. Fellow Am. Phys. Soc., Am. Meteorol. Soc., Am. Geophys. Union, AAAS; mem. Am. Assn. Physics Tchrs., Royal Meteorol. Soc., Sigma Xi. Patentee fast-scanning meteorol. radar, means and method for removing airborne particulates from aerosol stream. Current Work: Scrubbers; electrostatic dischargers for helicopters; weather radar; air quality; cloud physics; lightning. Subspecialties: Remote sensing (atmospheric science); Gas cleaning systems. Home: 1216 North Dr Socorro NM 87801 Office: Research and Devel Div Campus Sta N Mex Inst Mining and Tech Socorro NM 87801

BROOKE, MICHAEL HOWARD, neurologist; b. Leeds, Eng., Mar. 4, 1938; came to U.S., 1959, naturalized, 1966; s. Vincent Howard and Margaret (Craven) B.; m. Sara Vesper; children: Jennifer, Brenda, Mark. B.A., Cambridge U., 1955; M.B., B.Ch., Guy's Hosp., London, 1955. Intern San Francisco Children's Hosp., 1959-60; resident in neurology U. Calif. Med. Center, San Francisco, 1960-64; clin. and research fellow NIH, 1964-68; asso. prof. neurology U. Colo. Med. Center, 1968-75; prof. neurology Washington U. Med. Sch., St. Louis, 1975—, prof. preventive medicine, 1979—; dir. Jerry Lewis Neuromuscular Research Center, 1975—; med. dir. I.W.J. Rehab. Inst., 1979—; rehabilitationist-in-chief Barnes Hosp., St. Louis, 1979—. Author: A Clinician's View of Neuromuscular Diseases, 1977; co-author: Muscle Biopsy: A Modern Approach, 1973; editorial bd.: Muscle and Nerve. Served with USPHS, 1966-68. Fellow Am. Acad. Neurology; mem. Am. Neurol. Assn., Amateur Radio Club. Current Work: Basic biochemical mechanisms in normal and diseased muscle; treatment of muscular diseases by exercise; medication and orthoses. Subspecialty: Neurology. Office: Dept Neurology Washington Univ Med Sch Saint Louis MO 63110

BROOKER, ALAN EDWARD, clinical neuropsychologist; b. Madison, Wis., Jan. 26, 1949; s. Russell Alan and Margaret Theresa (Gorman) B.; m. Mary Elizabeth Naglee, Apr. 15, 1972; children: Jeffrey Alan, Jarrod Russell. A.A., Yuba Coll., 1969; B.A., Chapman Coll., 1971; M.S., Calif. State U., 1975; Ph.D., Kans. State U., 1977. Diplomate in clin. neuropsychology Am. Bd. Profl. Psychology, in profl. psychotherapy Internat. Acad. Profl. Counseling and Psychotherapy. Commd. officer U.S. Air Force, 1968, advanced thorugh grades to maj.; social actions officer, Malmstrom AFB, Mont., 1972-73; rehab. counselor State Dept. Rehab., Auburn, Calif., 1973-77, clin. psychologist, Wiebaden, W.Ger., 1977-81, clin. neuropsychologist, Travis AFB, Calif., 1982—; fellow in neuropsychology U. Oreg. Med. Sch., Portland, 1981-82; vocat. expert Bur. Hearings and Appeals, Sacramento, 1975-77; neuropsychology cons. State Dept. Rehab., 1981—. Vice pres. Calif. Human Services Orgn., Auburn, 1974-75, Voluntary Action Ctr., South Lake Tahoe, Calif., 1976-77; European mem.-at-large Soc. Air Force Clin. Psychologists, Wiesbaden, 1978-81. Recipient Proclamation of Appreciation City of South Lake Tahoe, 1977; Calif. Human Services award, 1977; Mil. Psychology award Am. Psychol. Assn., 1981; Cert. of Appreciation U.S. State Dept., 1981; award of merit Calif. Dept. Rehab., 1984. Fellow Soc. Air Force Clin. Psychologists, Pa. Psychol. Assn.; mem. Am. Psychol. Assn., Internat. Neuropsychol. Assn. Democrat. Roman Catholic. Current Work: Neuropathology; autism; memory; behavioral treatment for psychiatric disorders; teaching in psychology. Subspecialties: Behavioral psychology; Neuropsychology. Home: 206 Emory Dr Vacaville CA 95688 Office: David Grant USAF Med Ctr Bldg 121 Travis AFB CA 4535

BROOKS, CHANDLER MCCUSKEY, physiology educator; b. Waverly, W.Va., Dec. 18, 1905; s. Earle Amos and Mary (McCuskey) B.; m. Nelle Irene Graham, June 25, 1932. A.B., Oberlin Coll., 1928; M.A., Princeton U., 1929, Ph.D., 1931; D.Sc. (hon.), Berea Coll., 1970. NRC fellow, teaching fellow Harvard Med. Sch., 1931-33; instr., then assoc. prof. physiology Johns Hopkins Med. Sch., 1933-48; prof. physiology and pharmacology, chmn. dept. L.I. Coll. Medicine, 1948-50; prof. physiology, chmn. dept. State U. N.Y. Downstate Med. Center, Bklyn., 1950-72, dir. grad. edn., 1956-66; dean State U. N.Y. Downstate Med. Center (Grad. Sch.), 1966-72, State U. N.Y. Downstate Med. Center (Med. Sch.); acting pres. State U. N.Y. Downstate Med. Center (Med.

Center), 1969-71, distinguished prof., 1971—; vis. prof. Tokyo and Kobe (Japan) med. schs., 1961-62, U. Otago, Dunedin, New Zealand, 1975; vis. scholar U. Aberdeen, Scotland, 1973-74; hon. mem. faculty Catholic U., Santiago, Chile.; Mem. study sects. NIH, 1949-69. Author: (with others) Excitability of the Heart, 1955, Humors, Hormones and Neurosecretions, 1962, (with Kiyomi Koizumi) Japanese Physiology, Past and Present, 1965; Editor: (with P.F. Cranefield) The Historical Development of Physiological Thought, 1959, (with others) Cerebrosphinal Fluid and the Regulation of Ventilation, 1965, The Changing World and Man, 1970, (with H.H. Liu) The Sinoatrial Pacemaker of the Heart, 1972, (with K.K. Koizumi) Integrations of Autonomic Reactions, 1972, Jour. of Autonomic Nervous System, 1978—. Trustee Internat. Found., 1972—, chmn. grants com., 1973—. Decorated Order of Rising Sun 3d class Japan; cited Internat. Physiol. Congress, 1965; Guggenheim fellow, 1946-48; Rockefeller fellow, 1950; China Med. Bd. N.Y. fellow, 1961-62. Mem. Nat. Acad. Scis., Harvey Soc. (pres. 1965), AAAS (council 1950—), N.Y. Heart Assn. (council 1965—), Am. Soc. Pharmacology and Exptl. Therapeutics, Internat. Brain Research Orgn., Nat. Soc. Med. Research, Royal Soc. Medicine, N.Y. Acad. Scis., Soc. Exptl. Biology and Medicine, Soc. Study Internal Secretions, Soc. Study Nervous and Mental Diseases, Am. Coll. Cardiology, Am. Coll. Pharmacology and Chemotherapy, Am. Inst. Biol. Scis., AMA (spl. affiliate), Am. Physiology Soc., Phi Beta Kappa, Sigma Xi, Alpha Omega Alpha; hon. mem. Nat. Acad. Medicine Buenos Aires, Cardiology Soc. Argentina, biol. socs. Montevideo, Uruguay, Inst. Hist. Medicine and Med. Research New Delhi, Alumni Assn., Coll. Medicine Downstate Med. Center. Research, publns. central control autonomic system, function of hypothalamus, motor cortex function in regulation of posture, activity in heart and nerve cells. Current Work: Nutritional, medical, educational philanthropy, functions of the autonomic nervous system. Subspecialties: Physiology (medicine); Neurophysiology. Home: 623 2d St Brooklyn NY 11215

BROOKS, DAVID PATRICK, physiology researcher and educator; b. London, May 31, 1952; came to U.S., 1979; m. Jane Renie Brunton, Nov. 18, 1978; 1 child, David Christopher. B.Sc. in Physiology and Chemistry, Queen Elizabeth Coll./U. London, 1974; M.Sc. in Biochem. Pharmacology, U. Southampton, Eng., 1976, Ph.D. in Physiology, 1979. Postdoctoral teaching fellow U. Southampton, 1978-79; postdoctoral research fellow U. Hawaii, Honolulu, 1979-81; asst. prof. physiology U. Tenn.-Memphis, 1981—. Contbr. articles to sci. jours. Vestryman St. George's Episcopal Ch., Germantown, Tenn., 1984-86. Sci. Research Council M.Sc. studentship, 1976; Med. Research Council Ph.D. studentship, 1976-79. Mem. Am. Physiol. Soc., Endocrine Soc. Current work: Studies on the control of vasopressin (antidiuretic hormone) re secretion, its cardiovascular actions and its role in the pathogenesis of hypertension. Subspecialties: Physiology (medicine); Neuroendocrinology. Office: Dept Physiology and Biophysics U Tenn Ctr for Health Scis 894 Union Ave Memphis TN 38163

BROOKS, DONALD LEE, hydrologist, researcher; b. Boston, July 25, 1956; s. Douglas Lee and Elizabeth (Thatcher) B. B.A. in Biology, Earlham Coll., 1979; M.S. in Watershed Mgmt., U. Ariz., 1985. Research biologist, Ariz. State U., Tempe, 1980-81; research asst. U. Ariz., Tucson, 1982-84; prin. engring. technician (hydrology) Pima County Flood Control, Tucson, 1984—. Contbr. articles to profl. jours. Mem. Ecol. Soc. Am., Soil Conservation Soc. Am., Internat. Ecol. Soc., Am. Water Resources Assn. Democrat. Quaker. Club: Cliffhangers (v.p. 1984, Tucson). Current work: Arid ecosystem management, hydrology, flood control, simulation, watershed management, linear programming, riparian habitat management, revegetation/reforestation/afforestation. Subspecialties: Integrated systems modelling and engineering; Ecology (biology). Home: 2459 N Santa Rita Ave Tucson AZ 85719 Office: Dept Watershed Mgmt Univ Ariz Tucson AZ 85721

BROOKS, FRANK PICKERING, physiology educator; b. Portsmouth, N.H., Jan. 2, 1920; s. Frank Edwin and Florence Isabel (Towle) B.; m. Emily Elizabeth Marden, July 5, 1942; children—William B., Sally E., Robert P. A.B., Dartmouth Coll., 1941; M.D., U. Pa., 1943, Sc.D. in Medicine, 1951. Diplomate Am. Bd. Radiology; diplomate Am. Bd. Internal Medicine, Am. Bd. Gastroenterology. Intern Hosp. U. of Pa., Phila., 1944; postdoctoral fellow dept. physiology Jefferson Med. Coll., Phila., 1951-52; instr. to assoc. dept. physiology U. Pa., Phila., 1952-54, asst. prof., 1954-59, assoc. prof., 1958-70, prof., 1970—; cons. Merck, Sharpe & Dohme, West Point, Pa., 1960-66, NIH, Bethesda, Md., 1966—, FDA, Rockville, Md., 1975-79. Author: Control GI Function, 1970; Editor: Digestive Disease and Science, 1982. Pres., Christian Assoc. U. Pa., 1968. Served to lt. (j.g.) USN, 1946-48. Recipient Research Career Devel. award Nat. Inst. Arthritis and Metabolic Disease, NIH, 1963. Mem. Am. Physiol. Soc. (chmn. gastrointestinal sect. 1965), Am. Gastroent. Assn. (pres. 1980-81), The Physiol. Soc., Brit. Soc. Gastroenterology (hon. mem.), Am. Pancreatic Assn. (pres. 1980-81). Republican. Episcopalian. Club: Union League (Phila.). Current work: Nervous control of gastrointestinal function. Subspecialties: Physiology (medicine); Gastroenterology. Home: 206 Almur Ln Wynnewood PA Office: Hosp U Pa 3400 Spruce St Philadelphia PA 19104

BROOKS, FREDERICK PHILLIPS, JR., computer science educator; b. Durham, N.C., Apr. 19, 1931; s. Frederick Philips and Octavia Hooker (Broome) B.; m. Nancy Lee Greenwood, June 16, 1956; children: Kenneth Phillips, Roger Greenwood, Barbara Suzanne. B.A., Duke U., 1953; S.M., Harvard U., 1955, Ph.D., 1956. Engr. IBM Corp., Poughkeepsie, N.Y., 1956-59, Yorktown Heights, N.Y., 1959-60; corp. processor devel. system/360 computer IBM Corp. (System/360), Poughkeepsie, 1960-64; mgr. devel. IBM Corp. (Operating System/360), 1964-65; prof. U. N.C. at Chapel Hill, 1964-75, Kenan prof., 1975—; bd. dirs. Triangle Univ. Computation Center, 1966-83, chmn., 1975-77; bd. dirs. N.C. Ednl. Computing Service, from 1965. Author: The Mythical Man-Month-Essays on Software Engineering, 1975, (with K.E. Iverson) Automatic Data Processing, 1963, Automatic Data Processing, System/360 Edition, 1969; Contbr. articles to profl. jours. Chmn. com. Central Carolina Billy Graham Crusade, 1972-73; trustee Durham Acad., pres., 1977-80; mem. corp. Inter-Varsity Christian Fellowship, 1968-77. Recipient McDowell award IEEE Computer Soc., 1970, Computer Pioneer award IEEE Computer Soc., 1982, Man of Year award Data Processing Mgmt. Assn., 1970; NSF grantee; AEC grantee; NIH grantee; Guggenheim fellow, 1975. Fellow IEEE, Am. Acad. Arts and Scis.; mem. Assn. Computing Machinery (council mem.-at-large 1966-70), Nat. Acad. Engring., NRC (computer sci. and tech. bd. 1977-80). Methodist. Inventor (with D.W. Sweeney) Program Interruption System, Alphabetical Read-Out Device. Current Work: Man-machine interfaces; computer graphics for interactive molecular modeling. Subspecialties: Graphics, image processing, and pattern recognition; Computer architecture. Office: Dept Computer Sci U NC Chapel Hill NC 27514

BROOKS, HAROLD KELLY, geologist, educator, consultant; b. Winfield, Kans., Nov. 27, 1924; s. Daniel Jackson and Ina Bessie (Courtney) B.; m. Susan Robison, Nov. 16, 1962; children—Richard D., Jennifer B., Philip D., Ellen B. B.S., Kans. State U., 1947; M.A., Harvard U., 1950, Ph.D., 1962. Instr. Brown U., Providence, 1950-51, Oberlin Coll., Ohio, 1951-52; asst. prof. U. Tenn.-Knoxville, 1952-54, U. Cin., 1954-56; from asst. prof. to prof. U. Fla., Gainesville, 1956-80, prof. emeritus, 1980—; cons. geologist, 1952-81; pres. Earth Resources Devel. Corp., Gainesville, 1976-81. Author sci. papers. Served with USN, 1942-45. Grantee NSF, 1950-52, 71-72, Fla. Dept. Transp., 1976, NASA, 1977-80; Antarctic Service medal, 1980. Fellow Geol. Soc. Am. Clubs: Exchange (Gainesville); Am. Orchid Soc. (Palm Beach, Fla.); Am. Hibiscus Soc. (Pompano Beach). Current work: Application of aerial photography and satellite imagery to geological interpretation and engineering practice. Subspecialties: Geology; Remote sensing (geoscience). Home: PO Box 937 Patillas PR 00723

BROOKS, HAROLD LLOYD, investigative cardiologist; b. Durban, South Africa, July 26, 1932; s. John and Erna (Holt) B.; m. Carolyn M. Brooks, Aug. 26, 1932; children: Mark D., Pamela J. B.A., Oklahoma City U., 1955; M.D., Okla. U., 1963. Med. resident U. Tex. Southwestern Med. Sch., Dallas, 1964-67; research fellow in cardiology Harvard U. Med. Sch., Boston, 1967-69; instr. in medicine, 1969-71; dir. cardiac catheterization and Hecht Research Labs., U. Chgo., 1971-76; Northwestern Mut. Chair in Cardiology prof. medicine and pharmacology, dir. cardiology, dir. Heath Exptl. Labs., Med. Coll. Wis., Milw., 1977—; chief of staff Milw. County Med. Complex, 1982-84; pres. Milw. Heart Inst., 1985—; attending County Gen. Hosp., Wood VA Hosp., Froedtert Meml. Luth. Hosp. Editor: (with J. S. Soin) Nuclear Cardiology for Clinicians, 1980, (with L. Bonchek) Management of Patients with Operable Heart Disease, 1981; Electrocardiography; Basic Diagnostic Criteria, 1985; contbr. numerous articles to profl. jours.; co-dir.: film Nuclear Imaging of the Heart, 1980. Raymund J. Thompson scholar, 1959-60; NIH grantee, 1967, 71-76, 83—; recipient Research award Mead Johnson Labs., 1967-69; Louis Block Research award U. Chgo., 1971-76; numerous others. Fellow Am. Coll. Cardiology, Am. Heart Assn. Circulation Council, Am. Coll. Geriatrics, Am. Coll. Clin. Pharmacology; mem. Am. Fedn. Clin. Research, AAAS, Am. Soc. Pharmacology and Exptl. Therapeutics, Am. Physiol. Soc., Central Soc. Clin. Research, Am. Coll. Sports Medicine, Nat. Assn. VA Physicians, Wis. Heart Assn. (bd. govs. 1980-86), Smithsonian Instn., Milw. C. of C. Club: University (Milw.). Current Work: Investigative cardiology involving experimental myocardial infarction; right ventricular response to stress; response of normal and ischemic myocardium to experimental pharmacologic intervention, including beta adrenergic blockers, calcium antagonists. Subspecialties: Cardiology; Pharmacology. Office: 8700 W Wisconsin Ave Milwaukee WI 53226

BROOKS, HOWARD CLAUDE, geologist; b. Twin Falls, Idaho, Dec. 3, 1928; s. Claude Cecil and Gladys Marie (Fretwell) B.; m. Colleen Stewart, Nov. 23, 1952. B.S. in Geology, Idaho State Coll., 1953; M.S. in Geology, U. Nev., 1956. Geologist, Westvaco, Pocatello, Idaho, 1953-54, Oreg. Dept. Geology & Mineral Industries, Baker, 1956—. Contbr. articles to profl. jours. Mem. Geol. Soc. Am., Northwest Mining Assn. Republican. Current work: Geology and mineral deposits of northeastern Oregon, regional geologic mapping. Subspecialty: Geology. Office: Dept Geology & Mineral Ind 1831 1st St Baker OR 97814

BROOKS, JAMES ELWOOD, educator; b. Salem, Ind., May 31, 1925; s. Elwood Edwin and Helen Mary (May) B.; m. Eleanore June Nystrom, June 18, 1949; children: Nancy, Kathryn, Carolyn. A.B., DePauw U., 1948; M.S., Northwestern U., 1950; Ph.D., U. Wash., 1954. Research assoc. Ill. Geol. Survey, 1950; geologist Gulf Oil Corp., Salt Lake City, summers 1951-53; instr. geol. scis. So. Meth. U., Dallas, 1952-55, asst. prof., 1955-59, assoc. prof., 1959-62, prof., 1962—, chmn. dept., 1961-70, dean, assoc. provost univ., 1970-72, provost, v.p., 1972-80, pres. ad int, 1980-81; pres. Inst. for Study Earth and Man, Dallas, 1981—; cons. geologist firm DeGolyer & MacNaughton, Dallas, 1954-59. Contbr. articles to profl. jours. Trustee Inst. Study Earth and Man, Dallas; trustee Hockaday Sch.; exec. bd. Circle Ten council Boy Scouts Am.; bd. vistors DePauw U., 1979-83; bd. dirs. Rangaire Corp. Served with USNR, 1943-46. Fellow Geol. Soc. Am., AAAS, Tex. Acad. Sci.; mem. Am. Assn. Petroleum Geologists, Dallas Geol. Soc., Sigma Xi, Sigma Gamma Epsilon, Sigma Phi. Current Work: Geomorphology and stratigraphy of the Qattara Depression, N.W. Egypt leading to an understanding of the origin of the Depression. Subspecialties: Geology; Sedimentology. Home: 7055 Arboreal Dr Dallas TX 75231 Office: Inst Study Earth and Man Box 274 Dallas TX 75275

BROOKS, JOHN BILL, research chemist; b. Hyatt, Tenn., Aug. 9, 1929; s. Walter Markey and Cosbie (Amburn) B.; m. Mary Jane Hushes; children—Greer W., Mark H. Degree in Chemistry, Western Carolina U., 1961; Ph.D., Va. Poly. Inst. and U., 1970. Chemist Tenn. Copper Co., Copperhill, 1959; U.S. Govt., Chamblee, Ga., 1961-66; research chemist Ctr. Disease Control, Atlanta, 1966—, research dir., 1976—. Contbr. articles to profl. jours. Served to pfc. U.S. Army, 1954-56. Mem. Am. Soc. Microbiology, Research Soc. Am., Am. Chem. Soc. Lodge: Masons. Current work: Use of modern chemical technology such as gas chromatography, mass spectrometry and computers to diagnose and study the physiological changes in the disease state. Office: Ctr Disease Control 1600 Chifton Rd Atlanta GA 30333

BROOKS, MARVIN ALAN, chemist; b. Trenton, N.J., Jan. 28, 1945; s. Hyman and Miriam (Lipshutz) B.; m. Susan Gail Pristoop, June 16, 1968; children—Paul Benjamin, Cheryl Elizabeth. B.S., Lafayette Coll., 1966; Ph.D., U. Md., 1971. Sr. scientist Hoffmann LaRoche, Nutley, N.J., 1971-76, research group chief, 1976-81, sr. research group chief, 1981-85; sr. research fellow dept. pharm. research and devel. Merck Sharpe and Dohme Research Lab., West Point, Pa., 1985—. Contbr. articles to profl. jours. Mem. Am. Chem. Soc., Am. Pharm. Assn., Sigma Xi. Current work: Analysis of drugs and quality assurance. Subspecialty: Analytical chemistry. Home: 1718 Benjamin Dr Ambler PA 19002 Office: Merck Sharpe and Dohme Research Lab West Point PA 19486

BROOKS, NORMAN HERRICK, environmental and civil engineer; b. Worcester, Mass., July 2, 1928; s. Charles Franklin and Eleanor Merritt (Stabler) B.; m. Frederika Nelson, Dec. 22, 1948; children: Diana, Alexander, Laura. A.B. magna cum laude, Harvard U., 1949, M.S. in Civil Engring, 1950; Ph.D. summa cum laude in Civil Engring. and Physics, Calif. Inst. Tech., 1954. With Calif. Inst. Tech., Pasadena, 1953—, prof., 1962—, James Irvine prof., 1976—, dir. environ. quality lab., 1974-84, 85—, exec. officer for engring. sci. dept., 1985—; vis. asso. prof. SEATO Grad. Sch. Engring., Bangkok, 1959-60; vis. prof. M.I.T., 1962-63; vis. environ. scientist Scripps Instn. Oceanography, fall 1971; guest prof. Swiss Fed. Inst. Tech., Zurich, 1984-85; cons. in hydraulics and ocean pollution control; mem. assembly sci. and tech. advisory com. Calif. State Legislature, 1970-73; mem. environ. studies bd. Nat. Acad. Scis., 1973-76. Co-author: Mixing in Inland and Coastal Waters, 1979; contbr. articles to profl. jours. Chmn. Altadena-Pasadena Human Relations Com.; mem. Altadena Planning Adv. Com. Fellow ASCE (chmn. com. on hydrologic transport processes 1975-76, Huber research prize 1959, Collingwood prize 1959, J.C. Stevens award 1959, Rudolph Hering medal 1957, 62, Hilgard hydraulics prize 1970); mem. Nat. Acad. Engring., Nat. Acad. Scis., Am. Geophys. Union, Internat. Assn. Hydraulic Research, Univ. Council on Water Resources, AAAS, Water Pollution Control Fedn., Sigma Xi. Current Work: Turbulant diffusion of sewage effluents and sewage sludge in the ocean; design of outfall pipes for ocean discharge; transport of sediments by rivers and oceans; sedimentation. Subspecialties: Water supply and wastewater treatment; Fluid mechanics. Home: 2521 N Santa Anita Ave Altadena CA 91001 Office: Keck Labs Calif Inst Tech Pasadena CA 91125

BROOKS, PHILIP RUSSELL, chemistry educator; b. Chgo., Dec. 31, 1938; s. John Russell and Louise Jane (Seyler) B.; children: Scott, Robin, Christopher, Steven. B.S., Calif. Inst. Tech., 1960; Ph.D., U. Calif., Berkeley, 1964. Research assoc. U. Chgo., 1964; asst. prof. Rice U., 1964-70, assoc. prof., 1970-75, prof., 1975—. Contbr. articles to profl. jours. Active Boys Scouts Am. NSF gellow, 1960-63, 64; Alfred P. Sloan Found. fellow, 1970-74; Guggenheim fellow, 1975-76; Robert A. Welch Found. grantee, 1966—; USAF grantee, 1975-79. Mem. AAAS, Am. Chem. Soc., Am. Phys. Soc. Current Work: Reactions of state selected molecules. Subspecialties: Physical chemistry; Laser-induced chemistry. Office: Dept Chemistry Rice U Houston TX 77251

BROOKS, RICHARD CAVETT, electrical engineer; b. Phila., Aug. 31, 1945; s. James Gilbert and Dana Louise (Cavett) B.; m. Catherine Marie Thomas, May 20, 1972; children—Richard Cavett Jr., James Gilbert III. B.E.E. with honors, U. Va., 1967; M.S.E.E., Johns Hopkins U., Balt., 1970; Ph.D., U. Mo.-Columbia, 1973; M.B.A., Va. Polytech. Inst., 1978. Registered profl. engr., Va. Mem. tech. staff Analytic Services, Inc., Arlington, Va., 1973-78; ops. research analyst FDA, Bethesda, Md., 1978-80, Dept. of Transp., Washington, 1980-82; computer systems analyst Dept. of Treasury, 1982-84; chief tech. support div. Joint Data Systems Support Ctr., Def. Communications Agy., Washington, 1984—. Contbr. articles to profl. jours. Co-pres. Arlington Sch. PTA, 1981. Served to lt. USPHS, 1968-70. Mem. IEEE (sr.), Sigma Xi, Tau Beta Pi, Eta Kappa Nu. Mem. Christian Ch. Subspecialties: Graphics, image processing, and pattern recognition; Wind power. Home: 6221 N 12th St Arlington VA 22205 Office: Joint Data Systems Support Ctr C130 Def Communications Agy Washington DC 20305-2000

BROOKS, WALTER FANGER, aerospace engineer; b. Phila., Mar. 25, 1949; s. Wharton Hillman and Mary Louise (Fanger) B.; m. Bernadette Evelyn Hayek, Aug. 4, 1948; children—Sarah, Vanessa. B.A., Rutgers U., 1970; M.S., Stevens Inst. Tech., 1972, Ph.D., 1977. Research assoc. Brookhaven Nat. Lab., Upton, N.Y., 1973-77; cryogenics researcher NASA/Ames Research Ctr., Moffett Field, Calif., 1977-79, IRAS Cryogenic engr., 1979-81, PACE project mgr. 1981-82, SIRTF telescope mgr., 1982—. Contbr. articles to profl. publs. Recipient innovative contbns. award NASA, 1983, 84, IRAS Cryogenics award, 1984, IRAS Achievement award, 1984. Mem. Am. Phys. Soc., AIAA (tech. com. 1983—), Soc. Photo-Optical Instrumentation Engrs., Calif. Bluegrass Soc., Sigma Xi. Current work: Development of space infrared telescopes employing state of the art cryogenic, pointing and optics systems. Subspecialties: Aerospace engineering and technology; Low temperature physics. Office: NASA/Ames Research Ctr MS 244-15 Moffett Field CA 94035

BROOM, ARTHUR DAVIS, chemistry educator; b. Panama Canal Zone, Republic Panama, July 26, 1937; s. Thomas Selwyn and Georgia Mae (Stallings) B.; m. Mary Jo Duffin, June 13, 1960, children—Thomas, Carol, Laura. B.S. in Chemistry, U. Tex., 1957; Ph.D., Ariz. State U., 1965. Research assoc. Johns Hopkins U., Balt., 1965-66; asst. then assoc. prof. U. Utah, Salt Lake City, 1966-75, prof., 1975—; chmn. dept. medicinal chemistry, U. Utah, 1978—, study sect. NIH, 1980-84. Contbr. articles to profl. jours. Lctr. Am. Cancer Soc., 1980-82; chmn., bd. dirs. United Methodist Ch., Salt Lake City, 1978-83. Recipient John R. Park award, 1979; Fullbright Sr. fellow, 1983; NIH grantee, Am. Cancer Soc., 1968—. Mem. Am. Assn. Colls. Pharmacy (chmn. sect. 1984—), Acad. Pharmacol. Scis., Am. Chem. Soc., AAAS, Am. Assn. Cancer Research. Current work: Design and synthesis potent specific inhibitors key enzymes as antitumor and antiviral agents. Subspecialties: Medicinal chemistry; Organic chemistry. Home: 2718 Parleys Way Salt Lake City UT 84109 Office: Dept Medicinal Chemistry Coll Pharmacy U Utah Salt Lake City UT 84112

BROPHY, GERALD PATRICK, geology educator; b. Kansas City, Mo., Sept. 11, 1926; s. William Edward and Dorothy Ann (Johnson) B.; m. Joanne Young, Apr. 29, 1951; children—William, James, Thomas. A.B., Columbia U., 1951, M.A., 1953, Ph.D., 1954; M.A. (hon.). Amherst Coll., 1968. Lectr. Amherst Coll., Mass., 1954-56; asst. prof., 1956-61, assoc. prof., 1961-68, prof. geology, mus. dir., 1968—; cons. geologist in field, 1954—; research geologist U. Baghdad, Iraq, 1965-66; mgr. geothermal program U.S. Dept. Energy, Washington, 1978-80. Contbr. articles to profl. jours. Mem. Fin. Com., Amherst, 1962, 63. Served to lt. (j.g.) USNR, 1943-46. Grantee NIH, 1962-67, NSF, 1967-77, Dept. Energy, 1980-82; Fulbright fellow, 1965. Fellow Geol. Soc. Am. (chmn. membership com. 1975-77); mem. Soc. Econ. Geologists, Am. Geophys. Union, Mineral Soc. Am., Yellowstone-Bighorn Research Assn. (councillor 1962—, pres. 1974-75). Roman Catholic. Subspecialties: Geology; Mineralogy. Home: 70 Red Gate Ln Amherst MA 01002 Office: Amherst Coll Dept Geology Amherst MA 01002

BROSNIHAN, K. BRIDGET, physiologist, researcher; b. Omaha, June 3, 1941; d. Thomas Timothy and Anna Marie (Evon) B.; m. Tony William Simmons, May 30, 1975; children: Joshua, Jonathan. B.S., Coll. St. Mary, Omaha, 1965; M.S., Creighton U., 1970; Ph.D., Case Western Res. U., 1974. Instr. biology Coll. St. Mary, 1967-68; instr. sci. St. Albert High Sch., Council Blufs, Iowa, 1969-70; postdoctoral fellow Cleve. Clinic, 1974-76, asso. staff, then staff, 1976—; adj. asst. prof. dept. physiology Case Western Res. U., Cleve., 1981—. Contbr. articles to profl. jours., chpts. to books. Heart Assn. N.E. Ohio grantee, 1974-79; NIH grantee, 1978—. Mem. Am. Heart Assn., Am. Physiol. Soc., Soc. Neurosci. Endocrine Soc., Sigma Xi, Am. Women in Sci. Democrat. Roman Catholic. Current Work: Neurohormones in hypertension. Subspecialties: Endocrinology; Neuroendocrinology. Office: 9500 Euclid Ave Cleveland OH 44106

BROUWER, MARIUS, biochemist; b. Leeuwarden, Friesland, Netherlands, Jan. 3, 1942; came to U.S., 1976; s. Tjeerd and Sophia (Dragstra) B.; m. Theodora Minke Hoexum, Mar. 12, 1965; children—Jeroen Tjeerd, Marieke Joanne. M.A., U. Groningen, Netherlands, 1966, Drs., 1969, Ph.D., 1975. Staff scientist U. Groningen, 1969-75, 79-81; research assoc. Duke U. Marine Lab., Beaufort, N.C., 1976-78, research assoc., 1981-83, research assoc. prof., 1984—. Mem. Am. Soc. Biol. Chemists, N.Y. Acad. Scis., AAAS. Current work: Structure and function of synthetic and biological oxygen carriers; role of metallothionein in trace metal metabolism and detoxification with special emphasis on the potential role of Cu (I) metallothioenein as a CU(I) donor to O2 binding site of hemocyanin; molecular mechanisms of trace metal toxicity. Subspecialties: Biochemistry (biology); Biophysical chemistry. Home: 124 Charles St Beaufort NC 28516 Office: Duke U Marine Lab Pivers Island Beaufort NC 28516

BROWDER, FELIX EARL, mathematician, educator; b. Moscow, July 31, 1927; s. Earl and Raissa (Berkmann) B.; m. Eva Tislowitz, Oct. 5, 1949; children: Thomas, William. S.B., MIT, 1946; Ph.D., Princeton U., 1948. C.L.E. Moore instr. math. MIT, 1948-51, vis. assoc. prof., 1961-62, vis. prof., 1977-78; instr. math. Boston U., 1951-53; asst. prof. Brandeis U., 1955-56; from asst. prof. to prof. math. Yale U., 1956-63; prof. math. U. Chgo., 1963-72, Louis Block prof. math., 1972-82, Max Mason Disting. Service prof. math., 1982—, chmn. dept., 1972-77, 80-85; vis. mem. Inst. Advanced Study, Princeton U., 1953-54, 63-64; vis. prof. Instituto de Matematica Pura e Aplicada, Rio de Janeiro, 1960, Princeton U., 1968; Fairchild disting. visitor Calif. Inst. Tech., 1967, 78; sr. research fellow U. Sussex, Eng., 1970, 76; vis. prof. U. Paris, 1973, 75, 78. Served with AUS, 1953-55. Guggenheim fellow, 1953-54, 66-67; Sloan Found. fellow, 1959-63; NSF sr. postdoctoral fellow, 1957-58. Fellow Am. Acad. Arts and Scis.; mem. Nat. Acad. Scis., Am. Math. Soc. (editor bull. 1959-68, 78-83, council mem. 1959-72, 78-83, mng. editor 1964-68, 80, exec. com. council 1979-80), Math. Assn. Am., AAAS (chmn. sect. A 1983), Sigma Xi. Home: 5505 S Kimbark Ave Chicago IL 60637

BROWDER, WILLIAM, mathematician, educator; b. N.Y.C., Jan. 6, 1934; s. Earl and Raissa (Berkmann) B.; m. Nancy O'Brien, Jan. 30, 1960; children: Julia, Risa, Daniel. B.S., MIT, 1954; Ph.D., Princeton U., 1958. Instr. U. Rochester, 1957-58; from instr. to assoc. prof. math. Cornell U., 1958-63; prof. math. Princeton U., 1964—, chmn. dept., 1971-73, vis. mem. Inst. for Advanced Studies, 1963-64, 83; vis. fellow Math. Inst. and Magdalen Coll., Oxford U. (Eng.), 1978-79; chmn. office Math. Scis. NAS-NRC, 1978-83. Guggenheim fellow, 1974-75; NSF postdoctoral fellow, 1959-60; vis. fellow Inst. Advanced Study, 1963-64, 83. Mem. Am. Acad. Arts and Scis., Am. Math. Soc. (v.p. 1977-78), Am. Acad. Arts and Scis., Nat. Acad. Scis. Office: Fine Hall 16 Washington Rd Princeton NJ 08544

BROWER, JOSEPH GILBERT, computer systems programmer, writer, educator; b. Point Pleasant, N.J., Jan 31, 1949; s. Gilbert Joel and Bertha Sarah (Halmuth) B. B.S., Monmouth Coll., West Long Branch, N.J.; M.S., Rutgers U., 1973. Mem. programming staff AT&T Communications, Piscataway, N.J., 1977—. Author-editor: tech. manual VM/CMS Programmer's Guide, 1983; author: slide-tape VM/CMS Introduction for Users, 1982. Mem. Ocean County Rep. Com., Toms River, N.J., 1980-83. Research intern Rutgers U., 1971; Monmouth Coll. Trustee scholar, 1967-71. Mem. AAAS, Am. Math. Soc., Soc. Indsl. and Applied Math., World Boxing Historians Assn., Rochester Boxing Assn., Monmouth Scholars, Lambda Sigma Tau (life 1971). Republican. Baptist. Current Work: Design, coding, testing, implementation of software subsystems in VM/CMS operating systems: VM/CMS technical training and education, coordination of release and distribution of software components to the VM Standard Operating Environment. Subspecialties: Operating systems; Software engineering. Home: 1029 Kerwin St Piscataway NJ 08854 Office: AT&T 30 Knightsbridge Rd Piscataway NJ 08854

BROWN, ARNOLD LANEHART, JR., pathologist, educator, univ. dean; b. Wooster, Ohio, Jan. 26, 1926; s. Arnold Lanehart and Wilda (Woods) B.; m. Betty Jane Simpson, Oct. 2, 1949; children—children—III, Anthony, Allen, Fletcher, Lisa. Student, U. Richmond, 1943-45; M.D., Med. Coll. Va., 1949. Diplomate: Am. Bd. Pathology. Intern Presbyn.-St. Luke's Hosp., Chgo., 1949-50, resident, 1950-51, 53-56, asst. attending pathologist, 1957-59, practice medicine specializing in pathology, Rochester, Minn., 1959-78; cons. exptl. pathology, anatomy Mayo Clinic, Rochester, 1959-78, also prof., chmn. dept., 1968-78; prof. pathology U. Wis. Med. Sch., Madison, 1978—, dean, 1978—; mem. nat. cancer adv. council NIH, 1971-72; nat. cancer advisory bd. NIH, HEW, 1972-74; chmn. clearing house on environ. carcinogens Nat. Cancer Inst., 1976-80, chmn. com. to study carcinogenicity of cyclamate, 1975-76; mem. Nat. Com. on Heart Disease, Cancer and Stroke, 1975-79; mem. com. on safe drinking water NRC, 1976-77; mem. award assembly Gen. Motors Cancer Research Found., 1978-84, vice chmn., 1983-84. Contbr. articles to profl. jours. Served with USNR, 1943-45, 51-53. Nat. Heart Inst. postdoctoral fellow, 1956-59. Mem. Am. Soc. Exptl. Pathology, Internat. Acad. Pathology, Am. Assn. Pathologists, Am. Gastroent. Assn., Assn. Am. Med. Colls. (chmn. council of deans 1984-85), Electron Microscope Soc. Am., AMA. Subspecialty: Pathology (medicine). Home: 1705 Camelot Dr Madison WI 53705 Office: 1300 University Ave Madison WI 53706

BROWN, CHARLES ERIC, biochemistry educator; b. Spangler, Pa., Nov. 23, 1946; s. Charles E. and Dorothy R. (Riddle) B.; m. Kathy Louise Houck, July 24, 1971; 1 child, Eric Nathaniel. B.A. in Chemistry, SUNY-Buffalo, 1968; Ph.D., Northwestern U., 1973. Instr./postdoctoral fellow Northwestern U., Evanston, Ill., 1973-75; research fellow Roche Inst. Molecular Biology, Nutley, N.J., 1975-77; asst. prof. biochemistry Med. Coll. Wis., Milw., 1977-83, assoc.

prof., 1983—; cons. in field. Contbr. articles to profl. jours., chpts. to books. Patentee in field. NIH fellow, 1968-72; Cottrell Research grantee, 1979-82; Arthritis Found. grantee, 1984. Mem. Am. Soc. Pharmacology and Exptl. Therapeutics, Internat. Soc. Magnetic Resonance, Soc. Neurosci., AAAS, Am. Chem. Soc., Sigma Xi, Phi Lambda Upsilon. Current work: Characterization of polymers and bone with cross polarization/magic angle sample spinning nuclear magnetic resonance and laser desorption/Fourier transform mass spectroscopies. Subspecialties: Polymers (materials science); Bioinstrumentation. Office: Med Coll Wis 8701 Watertown Plank Rd Milwaukee WI 53226

BROWN, CONNELL J., animal science educator; b. Everton, Ark., Mar. 6, 1924; s. Clarence Jackson and Winnie Dee (Trammell) B.; m. Erma Dexter, May 19, 1946; children: Craig Jay, Mark Allen. B.S.A., U. Ark., 1948; M.S., Okla. State U., 1950, Ph.D., 1956. Asst. prof. dept. animal sci. U. Ark., Fayetteville, 1950-57, assoc. prof., 1957-62, prof., 1962—; lectr. Internat. Stockmans Short course, 1980—. Contbr. articles to profl. jours. Served with USAAF, 1943-46, PTO. Recipient Research award Performance Registry Internat., 1977, U. Ark. Coll. Agr. research award, 1981. Fellow AAAS; mem. Am. Soc. Animal Sci. (pres. So. sect. 1975, leadership award So. sect. 1975), Am. Genetics Assn., N.Y. Acad. Sci., So. Assn. Agrl. Scientists (dir.), Sigma Xi, Gamma Sigma Delta. Lodge: Kiwanis. Current Work: Genetic and phenotypic relationships among size, shape and performance traits of beef cattle and other farm animals. Subspecialty: Animal genetics. Home: 2583 Elizabeth St Fayetteville AR 72703 Office: Dept Animal Sci Univ Ark Fayetteville AR 72703

BROWN, DONALD DAVID, biology educator; b. Cin., Dec. 30, 1931; s. Albert Louis and Louise (Rauh) B.; m. Linda Jane Weil, July 2, 1957; children: Deborah Lin, Christopher Charles, Sharon Elizabeth. M.S., U. Chgo., 1956, M.D., 1956, D.Sc. (hon.), 1976; D.Sc. (hon.), U. Md., 1983. Staff mem. dept. embryology Carnegie Instn. of Washington, Balt., 1963-76, dir., 1976—; prof. dept. biology Johns Hopkins U., 1968—. Served with USPHS, 1957-59. Recipient U.S. Steel Found. award for molecular biology, 1973; V.D. Mattia award Roche Inst., 1975; Boris Pregel award for biology N.Y. Acad. Scis., 1976; Ross G. Harrison award Internat. Soc. Developmental Biology, 1981; Bertner Found. award, 1982; Rosensteil award basic biomed. sci. Brandeis U., 1985; Louisa Gross Horwitz prize Columbia U., 1985. Fellow Am. Acad. Arts and Scis., AAAS; mem. Nat. Acad. Scis., Soc. Developmental Biology (pres. 1975), Am. Soc. Biol. Chemists, Am. Soc. Cell Biology, Am. Philos. Soc. Subspecialty: Developmental biology. Home: 5721 Oakshire Rd Baltimore MD 21209 Office: Carnegie Instn of Washington 115 W University Pkwy Baltimore MD 21210

BROWN, ELLEN RUTH, theoretical physicist, engineer; b. N.Y.C., June 15, 1947; d. Aaron Joseph and Grace (Presser) B. B.S., Mary Washington Coll., 1969; M.S., Pa. State U., 1971; Ph.D. in Theoretical Atomic Physics, U. Va., 1981. Physicist, Naval Weapons Lab., Dahlgren, Va., 1969; instr. physics Lord Fairfax Community Coll., Middletown, Va., 1971-74; fellow NASA, Langley, Va., 1974-75; engr. EG&G Washington Analytical Services Center, Dahlgren, 1979—, head dept. analysis and evaluation, Va., 1982—; v.p. Windy Knoll Enterprises, Inc., Magnolia, Tex., 1981—. First violinist, Coll. and Community Orch., Fredericksburg, Va., 1979—; Contbr. articles to profl. jours. NSF fellow, 1973; Gov.'s fellow U. Va., 1975-78; Physics Dept. fellow U. Va., 1978-79. Mem. Am. Phys. Soc., Sierra Club, Sigma Xi. Club: Barry Lee Bressler Sci. (Fredericksburg) (pres. 1979—). Current Work: Photoionization calculations, optical ray tracing in the atmosphere, meteorological effects on reentry bodies, technical assessment, semiconductor physics. Subspecialties: Atomic and molecular physics; Theoretical physics. Home: PO Box 1397 Fredericksburg VA 22402 Office: PO Box 552 Dahlgren VA 22448

BROWN, ERIC REEDER, immunologist, educator; b. Cortland, N.Y., Mar. 16, 1925; s. Harold McDaniel and Helen (Seitz) B.; m. Chloe Cassandra Ledbetter, May 11, 1961; children—Carl F., Christopher H.A., Amy Elizabeth French; children by previous marriage—Eric Reeder II, Christine Virginia, Dianne Mary, Daniel K. B.A., Syracuse U., 1949, M.S., 1951; Ph.D. (Nat. Cancer Inst. Fellow), U. Kan., 1957; D.Sc., Quincy Coll., 1966. Instr. U. Ill. Med. Sch., 1957-58; asst. prof. U. Ala., 1958-60, U. Minn. Sch. Medicine, 1960-61; sr. research assoc. Hektoen Inst., Chgo., 1961-67; assoc. prof. Northwestern U. Med. Sch., 1964-68; chmn. dept. microbiology Chgo. Med. Sch., 1967-82; cons. Newport Pharms., Inc., Strategic Med. Research Corp., U. Ill.; med. adviser to Ill. dir. SSS; dir. Lake Bluff Labs., Inc., Chesterton, Ind.; reviewer grants NSF, 1978—, Am. Cancer Soc. fellow, 1960-63, Leukemia Soc. scholar, 1965—; mem. med. adv. bd. Leukemia Research Found. Co-author: Cancer Disemination and Therapy, 1961; author: Textbook of Micromolecular Biology, 1974, Immunobiological Characteristics of Leukemia, 1975, Sailing Made Easy, 1978; contbr. articles to profl. jours. Served with USCGR, 1942-46; served to col. USAF, 1951-55; col. Res. Fellow Am. Inst. Chemists, Am. Acad. Microbiology, Chgo. Inst. Medicine; mem. Royal Soc. Medicine, Histochem. Soc., Internat. Soc. Lymphology, AAUP, Am. Mus. Natural History, Med. Mycol. Soc. of Ams., Soc. Exptl. Biology and Medicine, Res. Officers Assn., Phi Beta Kappa, Sigma Xi, Psi Chi, Phi Sigma. Research on virus etiology of cancer and leukemia. Current Work: Epidemiology of cancer; gynecological microbiology; tumor virology. Subspecialties: Oncology; Immunology (medicine). Home: PO Box 335 7704 Camellia Chicago IL 60097 Office: Chicago Med Sch 3333 Greenbay Rd North Chicago IL 60064 *

BROWN, GEORGE HAROLD, radio engineer; b. North Milwaukee, Wis., Oct. 14, 1908; s. James Clifford and Ida Louise (Siegert) B.; m. Julia Elizabeth Ward, Dec. 26, 1932; children: James Ward and George H. (twins). B.S., U. Wis., 1930, M.S., 1931, Ph.D., 1933, E.E., 1942; Dr.Eng. (hon.), U. R.I., 1968. With RCA, 1933-37, 38-73, successively research engr., Camden, Princeton, N.J., dir. Systems Research Lab., chief engr. Comml. Electronic Products div., Camden, chief engr. indsl. electronic products, 1933-59, v.p. engring., 1959-61, v.p. research and engring., 1961-65, exec. v.p. research and engring., 1965-68, exec. v.p. patents and licensing, 1968-72; dir. Trane Co., 1967-79, cons. engr., 1937—; dir. RCA Global Communications, 1962-71, RCA, 1965-72, RCA Internat., Ltd., 1968-72; Shoenberg Meml. lectr. Royal Instn., 1972; Marconi Centenary lectr. AAAS, 1974. Author: (with R.A. Bierwirth and C.N. Hoyler) Radio Frequency Heating, 1947, And Part of Which I Was, 1982; contbr. articles to sci. jours. Exec. bd. George Washington council Boy Scouts Am.; bd. govs. Hamilton Hosp. Recipient Silver Beaver and Silver Antelope awards Boy Scouts Am.; citation Internat. TV Symposium, Montreux, Switzerland, 1965; DeForest Audion award, 1968; David Sarnoff award for outstanding achievements in radio and TV U. Ariz., 1980, Modern Pioneer award NAM, 1940. Fellow IEEE (Edison medal 1967, Centennial medal 1984), AAAS, Royal TV Soc.; mem. Nat. Acad. Engring., Am. Mgmt. Assn., Sigma Xi, Tau Beta Pi, Eta Kappa Nu (eminent mem.). Clubs: Nassau, Springdale. Patentee in field. Current Work: History of electrical engineering and electronics. Subspecialties: Electrical engineering; Electronics. Home: 117 Hunt Dr Princeton NJ 08540

BROWN, GERALD LAVONNE, medical scientist, psychiatrist, psychoanalyst; b. Athens, Georgia, Mar. 8, 1940; s. Coile Frank and Lillie Rice (Spratlin) B.; m. Margaret Stadler, Mar. 25, 1966; children: Klara, Suzanne, Stefanie, Kristine. A.B., Duke U., 1963, M.D., 1967; postgrad., Washington Psychoanalytic Inst., 1970-83. Intern Queens Med. Center, Honolulu, 1967-68; resident Duke U. Med. Center, Durham, N.C., 1968-71, fellow in research, 1971-72; staff scientist intramural research program NIMH, Bethesda, Md., 1974—, pvt. practice child and adult psychiatry and psychoanalysis, McLean, Va., 1972—. Contbr. over 50 med. articles to profl. pubs. Served with USMC, 1961-63; with USN, 1963-74; with USPHS, 1974—. Recipient Residency Achievement award Duke U., 1970; Psychobiol. Research Tng. fellow, 1971-72. Mem. Am. Psychiat. Assn., Am. Acad. Child Psychiatry, Am. Psychoanalytic Assn. Baptist. Current Work: Psychobiology of aggression and suicide; psychobiology of childhood mental illness and sequelae; child and adult psychoanalysis. Subspecialties: Psychopharmacology; Neuropharmacology. Office: NIMH Clin Center Room 3N234 Bldg 10 Bethesda MD 20205

BROWN, GLENN HALSTEAD, chemist, educator; b. Logan, Ohio, Sept. 10, 1915; s. James E. and Nancy J. (Mohler) B.; m. Jessie Adcock, May 27, 1943; children—Larry H., Nancy K., Donald S., Barbara J. B.S., Ohio U., 1939; M.S., Ohio State U., 1941; Ph.D., Iowa State U., 1951; D.Sc. (hon.), Bowling Green State U., 1972. Asst. prof. U. Miss., 1941-46, 49-50; instr. Iowa State U., 1946-49; asst. prof. U. Vt., 1950-52; assoc. prof. U. Cin., 1952-60; with Kent (Ohio) State U., 1960—, prof. chemistry, head dept., 1960-65; dir. Liquid Crystal Inst., 1965-83, fellow, 1983—, dean for research, 1963-69, Regents prof. chemistry, 1968—; Bikerman lectr., 1981. Author: (with F.A. Anderson) Fundamentals of Chemistry, 1944, (with Wollett and Fogelsong) Laboratory Manual for Organic Chemistry, 1944, Record Book for Quantitative Analysis, 1954, (with E. M. Sallee) Quantitative Chemistry, 1963, (with others) Liquid Crystals, 1967, Review of the Structure and Properties of Liquid Crystals, 1970, (with J.J. Wolken) Liquid Crystals and Biological Structures; contbr. articles to sci. jours.; editor: Liquid Crystals 2, Parts I and II, 1969, Photochromism, 1971, Liquid Crystals 3, parts I and II, 1972, Advances in Liquid Crystals, vol. I, 1975, vol. II, 1976, vol. III, 1978, vol. IV, 1979, vol. V, 1982, vol. VI, 1983; editor-in-chief: Jour. Molecular Crystals and Liquid Crystals, 1968-84, cons. editor, 1984—. Recipient Morley award in chemistry, 1977; Pres.'s award Kent State U., 1980; 8th Internat. Liquid Crystal Conf. dedicated in his hon. Tokyo, 1980; citation of honor 9th Internat. Liquid Crystal Conf., Bangalore, India, 1982. Fellow Ohio Acad. Sci. (pres. 1960, Distinguished Service award 1966); mem. Am. Chem. Soc. (chmn. Akron sect. 1965, nat. councilor Akron sect., chmn. regional meeting planning com. 1968, Distinguished Service award Akron sect. 1971), Am. Inst. Chemists (chmn. Ohio 1969-71), Am. Crystallographic Assn., AAAS, N.Y. Acad. Scis., Sigma Xi (nat. lectureship 1970), Alpha Chi Sigma, Phi Lambda Upsilon, Omicron Delta Kappa. Methodist. Spl. research X-ray structural studies liquids, concentrated salt solutions, photochromism, liquid crystals. Subspecialty: Liquid crystals. Home: 470 Harvey Ave Kent OH 44240

BROWN, GLENN ROBBINS, JR., oil company executive; b. Greensburg, Pa., June 1, 1930; s. Glen Robbins and Hazel Virginia (Kramer) B.; m. Joanne E. Barnett, June 2, 1952 (dec. Nov. 1972); children—Robyn L. Brown Boebinger, Eric R. B.S. in Chem. Engring., Pa. State U., 1952; M.S. in Chem. Engring, Case Inst. Tech., 1954, Ph.D., 1958. Engr., Standard Oil Co. (Ohio), Cleve., 1953-63, mgmt. positions, 1963-70, mgr. research, 1970-75, v.p. research and engring., 1975-78, v.p. research, engring. and corp. planning, 1978-79, sr. v.p. tech. and planning, 1979—, also dir.; dir. Centran Corp., Cleve., Central Nat. Bank, Cleve. Contbr. articles to profl. jours. Trustee Cleve. Playhouse Sq. Found., 1980—; bd. advisers Notre Dame Coll., 1982—. Recipient Disting. Service award Cleve. Tech. Soc. Council, 1984; Disting. Alumnus award Pa. State U., 1984. Mem. Am. Chem. Soc. (chem. Cleve. sect. 1976, trustee, 1980), Am. Inst. Chem. Engrs., Soc. Automotive Engrs., Soc. Chem. Industry. Clubs: Union, Pepper Pike (Cleve.). Current work: Research management. Subspecialty: Chemical engineering. Office: The Standard Oil Co (Ohio) Midland Bldg Cleveland OH 44115

BROWN, GORDON M(ARSHALL), research optical engineer, consultant; b. Detroit, Feb. 17, 1934; s. Everett J. and Agnes E. (Craig) B.; m. Sharla A. Smith, Aug. 15, 1958; children: Gordon C., Julie Marie. Student in math. (Coll. scholar), Greenville Coll., 1952-54; B.S.M.E., Gen. Motors Inst., 1958; M.S. in Nuclear Engring. (Gen. Motors fellow), U. Mich., 1961. Project engr. Bendix Aerospace Systems, Ann Arbor, Mich., 1961-67; dir. engring. GCO, Inc., Ann Arbor, 1967-71, dir. mfg., 1971-73; prin. research engr., physics dept. Ford Motor Co., Dearborn, Mich., 1973—; cons. optical/digital systems engring. Contbr. articles to profl. publs. Mem. Optical Soc. Am., Am. Soc. Nondestructive Testing (Achievement award 1970), Soc. Photo-Optical Instrumentation Engrs., Internat. Soc. Optical Engring. Republican. Methodist. Inventor holographic tire tester. Current Work: Holographic interferometry, image processing, optical metrology; development holographic methods and apparatus for vibration analysis of large automotive structures; devel. noncontact distance measurement instruments. Subspecialties: Optical engineering; Holography. Home: 3191 Bluett St Ann Arbor MI 48105 Office: Room S-1024 SRL PO Box 2053 Dearborn MI 48121

BROWN, GREGORY GAYNOR, biochemist, educator; b. Englewood, N.J., Aug. 17, 1948; s. Norbert Hugh and Edith Mary (Krabach) B.; m. Sheila Marie Sullivan, Nov. 19, 1977; 1 dau., Meghan Anne. B.S., U. Notre Dame, 1970; Ph.D., Mt. Sinai Sch. Medicine CUNY, 1977. Postdoctoral fellow SUNY-Stony Brook, 1977-81; asst. prof. biology McGill U., Montreal, Que., Can., 1981—, mem. genetic manipulation research group, 1981—. Contbr. articles to profl. jours. NIH fellow, 1979-81; Natural Scis. and Engring. Research Council Can. grantee, 1981—. Mem. Am. Soc. Cell. Biology, Genetics Soc. Am. Current Work: Organization and evolution of mitochondrial genetic system; regulation of mitochondrial gene activity and replication. Subspecialties: Genetics and genetic engineering (biology); Molecular biology. Home: 4836 Westmore Ave Montreal PQ H4V 1Z3 Canada Office: Dept. Biology McGill U 1205 Ave Dr Penfield Montreal PQ H3A 1B1 Canada

BROWN, HANNAH R(EEVA), virologist, electron microscopist; b. Bklyn., Apr. 23, 1934; d. Samuel and Fanny (Cumings) Sussman; m. Morris Brown, July 11, 1954; children: Ilene, Eric, Jess. B.A. in Biology (N.Y. State Regents scholar), Hunter Coll., 1954; M.S. in Microbiology, Rutgers U., 1981. Fellow Hunter Coll., 1955; technician dept. virology N.Y. State Inst. for Basic Research in Devel. Disabilities, S.I., 1968-69, asst. research scientist, 1969-73, research scientist I, 1973-79, research scientist II, 1979-84; research scientist III, 1984—. Contbr. articles to profl. jours., 1973—. NIH grantee, 1981-82. Mem. N.Y. Acad. Scis., N.Y. Soc. Electron Microscopists, Electron Microscope Soc. Am., Am. Soc. Microbiology, AAAS, Council Research Scientists, Phi Beta Kappa, Phi Sigma. Current Work: Use of immunocytochemistry and in situ hybridization to locate virus in CNS. Subspecialty: Immunocytochemistry. Home: 199 Ardmore Ave Staten Island NY 10314 Office: 1050 Forest Hill Rd Staten Island NY 10314

BROWN, HAROLD, scientist, educator, corporate director, consultant, secretary defense; b. N.Y.C., Sept., 19, 1927; s. A.H. and Gertrude (Cohen) B.; m. Colene Dunning McDowell, Oct. 29, 1953; children: Deborah Ruth, Ellen Dunning. A.B., Columbia U., 1945, A.M., 1946, Ph.D. in Physics (Lydig fellow 1948-49), 1949; D.Eng. (hon.), Stevens Inst. Tech., 1964; LL.D., L.I. U., 1966, Gettysburg Coll., 1967, Occidental Coll., 1980, U. Calif., 1969; Sc.D., U. Rochester, 1975, Brown U., 1977, U. of the Pacific, San Francisco, 1978, U. S.C., 1979, Franklin and Marsall Coll., 1982, Chung-Ang U., Seoul, Korea, 1983. Research scientist Columbia U., 1945-50, lectr. physics, 1947-48, Stevens Inst. Tech., 1949-50; research scientist Radiation Lab., U. Calif. at Berkeley, 1950-52, lectr. physics, 1951-52; various positions from group leader to dir. Radiation Lab. at Livermore, 1952-61; dir. def. research and engring. Dept. Def., 1961-65; sec. of air force, 1965-69; pres. Calif. Inst. Tech., Pasadena, 1969-77; sec. Def., Washington, 1977-81; Disting. vis. prof. nat. security Sch. Advanced Internat. Studies, Johns Hopkins U., Washington, 1981-84; chmn. Johns Hopkins Fgn. Policy Inst., 1984—; cons., 1981—; dir. AMAX, CBS, IBM, Philip Morris, Inc., Cummins Engine Co., Synergen, Inc.; mem. Polaris Steering Com., 1956-58; cons., mem. Air Force Sci. Adv. Bd., 1956-61, Pres.'s Sci. Adv. Com., 1958-61; sr. sci. adviser Conf. Discontinuance Nuclear Tests, 1958-59; U.S. del. SALT, Helsinki, Vienna and; Geneva, 1969-77; chmn. Tech. Assessment Adv. Council to U.S. Congress, 1974-77; mem. exec. com. Trilateral Commn., 1973-76. Decorated Medal of Freedom; named One of 10 Outstanding Young Men U.S. Jaycees, 1961; recipient Medal of Excellence Columbia U., 1963; Joseph C. Wilson award in internat. affairs, 1976; award for disting. contbns. to higher edn. Stony Brook Found., 1979. Mem. Nat. Acad. Engring., Am. Phys. Soc., Am. Acad. Arts and Scis., Nat. Acad. Scis., Council on Fgn. Relations, N.Y.C. (dir. 1983—), Phi Beta Kappa, Sigma Xi. Clubs: Bohemian (San Francisco); California (Los Angeles); Athenaeum (London). Subspecialty: National security policy. Office: Johns Hopkins U Sch Advanced Internat Studies 1740 Massachusetts Ave NW Washington DC 20036

BROWN, HARRISON SCOTT, research scientist, writer; b. Sheridan, Wyo., Sept. 26, 1917; s. Harrison H. and Agatha (Scott) B.; m. Rudd Owen, Nov. 11, 1949; 1 son, Eric Scott; m. Theresa Tellez, 1975. B.S., U. Calif., 1938, LL.D., 1970; Ph.D., Johns Hopkins U., 1941; LL.D., U. Alta., 1961; Sc.D., Rutgers U., 1964, Amherst Coll., 1966, Cambridge U., 1969. Instr. chemistry Johns Hopkins U., 1941-42; asst. dir. chemistry Clinton Labs., Oak Ridge, 1943-46; research asso. plutonium project U. Chgo., 1942-43; asst. prof. Inst. Nuclear Studies, 1946-48, asso. prof., 1948-51; prof. geochemistry Calif. Inst. Tech., 1951-77, prof. sci. and govt., 1967-77; dir. Resource Systems Inst., East-West Center, Honolulu, from 1977; editor-in-chief Bull. Atomic Scientists, 1985—. Author: Must Destruction Be Our Destiny? , 1946, The Challenge of Man's Future, 1954, The Next Hundred Years, 1957, The Cassiopeia Affair, 1968, The Human Future Revisited, 1978, Learning How To Live in a Technological Society (Ishizaka lectures, Japan), 1979. Recipient Lasker Found. award, 1958, N.Y. Acad. Scis. award, 1978. Mem. Nat. Acad. Scis. (fgn. sec. 1962-74, chmn. world food and nutrition study 1975-77), Internat. Council Sci. Unions (pres. 1974-76), Am. Chem. Soc. (award in pure chemistry 1952), Geol. Soc. Am., AAAS (ann. award 1947), Am. Geophys. Union, Phi Beta Kappa, Sigma Xi. Current Work: Demand for and availability of natural resources. Subspecialty: Geochemistry. Office: Bull Atomic Scientists 5801 S Kenwood Ave Chicago IL 60637

BROWN, HERBERT CHARLES, chemist; b. London, May 22, 1912; came to U.S., 1914; s. Charles and Pearl (Gorinstein) B.; m. Sarah Baylen, Feb. 6, 1937; 1 son, Charles Allan. A.S., Wright Jr. Coll., Chgo., 1935; B.S., U. Chgo., 1936, Ph.D., 1938, D.Sc., 1968, hon. doctorates, 1968; hon. doctorates, Wayne State U., 1980, Lebanon Valley Coll., 1980, L.I. U., 1980, Hebrew U. Jerusalem, 1980, Pontificia Universidad de Chile, 1980, Purdue U., 1980, U. Wales, 1981. Asst. chemistry U. Chgo., 1936-38, Eli Lilly post-doctorate research fellow, 1938-39, instr., 1939-43; asst. prof. chemistry Wayne U., 1943-46, asso. prof., 1946-47; prof. inorganic chemistry Purdue U., 1947-59, Richard B. Wetherill prof. chemistry, 1959, Richard B. Wetherill research prof., 1960-78, emeritus, 1978—; vis. prof. U. Calif. at Los Angeles, 1951, Ohio State U., 1952, U. Mexico, 1954, U. Calif. at Berkeley, 1957, U. Colo., 1958, U. Heidelberg, 1963, State U. N.Y. at Stonybrook, 1966, U. Calif. at Santa Barbara, 1967, Hebrew U., Jerusalem, 1969, U. Wales, Swansea, 1973, U. Cape Town, S. Africa, 1974, U. Calif., San Diego, 1979; Harrison Howe lectr., 1953, Friend E. Clark lectr., 1953, Freud-McCormack lectr., 1954, Centenary lectr., Eng., 1955, Thomas W. Talley lectr., 1956, Falk-Plaut lectr., 1957, Julius Stieglitz lectr., 1958, Max Tishler lectr., 1958, Kekule-Couper Centenary lectr., 1958, E. C. Franklin lectr., 1960, Ira Remsen lectr., 1961, Edgar Fahs Smith lectr., 1962, Seydel-Wooley lectr., 1966, Baker lectr., 1969, Benjamin Rush lectr., 1971, Chem. Soc. lectr., Australia, 1972, Armes lectr., 1973, Henry Gilman lectr., 1975, others; chem. cons. to indsl. corps. Author: Hydroboration, 1962, Boranes in Organic Chemistry, 1972, Organic Synthesis via Boranes, 1975, The Nonclassical Ion Problem, 1977; Contbr. articles to chem. jours. Bd. govs. Hebrew U., 1969—. Served as co-dir. war research projects U. Chgo. for U.S. Army, Nat. Def. Research Com., Manhattan Project, 1940-43. Recipient Purdue Sigma Xi research award, 1951; Nichols medal, 1959; award Am. Chem. Soc., 1960; S.O.C.M.A. medal, 1960; H.N. McCoy award, 1965; Linus Pauling medal, 1968; Nat. Medal of Sci., 1969; Roger Adams medal, 1971; Charles Frederick Chandler medal, 1973; Chem. Pioneer award, 1975; C.U.N.Y. medal for sci. achievement, 1976; Elliott Cresson medal, 1978; C.K. Ingold medal, 1978; Nobel prize for chemistry, 1979; Gold medal Am. Inst. Chemists, 1985; Priestley medal, 1981; Perkin medal, 1982; others. Fellow Royal Soc. Chemistry (hon.), AAAS, Indian Nat. Sci. Acad. (fgn.); mem. Am. Acad. Arts and Scis., Nat. Acad. Scis., Chem. Soc. Japan (hon.), Pharm. Soc. Japan (hon.), Am. Chem. Soc. (chmn. Purdue sect. 1955-56), Ind. Acad. Sci., Phi Beta Kappa, Sigma Xi, Alpha Chi Sigma, Phi Lambda Upsilon (hon.). Research in phys., organic, inorganic chemistry relating chem. behavior to molecular structure; selective reductions; hydroboration; chemistry of organoboranes Research in phys., organic, inorganic chemistry relating chem. behavior to molecular structure; selective reductions; hydroboration; chemistry of organoboranes. Current Work: Development of new hydridereagents for selective reductions, hydroboration-kinetics and mechanism,new hydroboration agents, organoboranes, syntheses via organoboranes. Subspecialties: Organic chemistry; Synthetic chemistry. Office: Dept Chemistry Purdue U West Lafayette IN 47907

BROWN, JAY CLARK, microbiologist; b. Jersey City, June 23, 1942; s. John Robert and Vonna Lee (Lamme) B.; m. Sallie Dietrich, June 26, 1965; children: Jeffrey, Norman, Michael. B.A. with honors, John Hopkins U., 1964; Ph.D. in Biochemistry and Molecular Biology, Harvard U., 1969. Postdoctoral researcher Med. Research Council Lab. of Molecular Biology, Cambridge, Eng., 1969-71; asso. prof. microbiology U. Va. Sch. Medicine, 1971—; mem. adv. com. for personnel in research Am. Cancer Soc. Mem. Am. Soc. Biol. Chemists, Am. Soc. Microbiology. Current Work: Research on membrane structure and virus structure. Subspecialties: Microbiology (medicine); Cancer research (medicine). Office: Dept Microbiology U VA Med Center Charlottesville VA 22908

BROWN, JIM MCCASLIN, consultant engineering geologist; b. Mpls., Sept. 29, 1938; s. James McCaslin and Alvi Vieno (Ojennus) B.; m. Dean Naomi Alexander, Sept. 1, 1963; children: Robin, Shelly. B.S., U. Alaska, 1960, M.S., 1963; Ph.D., U. Wis.-Madison, 1968. Cert. profl. geologist, Alaska registered profl. geologist, cert. engring. geologist, Oreg. Jr. geologist Pan Am. Petroleum Corp., Anchorage, 1960; geologist U.S. Geol. Survey, Fairbanks, Alaska, 1962; sr. asst. geologist Ont. Dept. Mines, Toronto, Can., 1964; asst. prof. geology St. Louis U., 1968-69, Ind. U.-Indpls., 1969-74; sr. engring. geologist R&M Cons., Inc., Anchorage, 1974-83; pres. Arctic Geo-Terrain Cons., Wasilla, Alaska, 1983—. Mem. Valdez (Alaska) City Sch. Bd., 1975-76, treas., 1975-76. Fellow Geol. Soc. Am.; mem. Alaska Geol. Soc., AIME, Soc. Mining Engrs., Am. Inst. Profl. Geologists (pres. Alaska sect. 1981-82), U. Alaska Alumni Assn. (bd. dirs. 1980—). Republican. Current Work: Geology of Arctic regions including permafrost and the development of resource extraction infrastructures; remote sensing and terrain analysis for resource management and design/construction purposes; geologic hazards including seismic analysis and rock slope stability. Subspecialties: Remote sensing (geoscience); Geology. Office: Arctic Geo-Terrain Cons PO Box 870366 Wasilla AK 99687

BROWN, JOHN EROS, structural engineer; b. Budapest, Hungary, Feb.12, 1917; came to U.S., 1936, naturalized, 1943; s. Cornelius and Serena (Brown) E.; m. Florence Olga Brown, May 11, 1942; children—Serena-Lynn, Eric Andrew, Jonathan Davis. Student CCNY, 1937-1942, Ga. Inst. Tech., 1943; B.S. in Civil Engring., Columbia U., 1949. Registered profl. engr., Calif. Joined U.S. Army, 1942, advanced through grades to 1st lt., 1951; pres., prin. engr. John E. Brown Assocs., San Francisco, 1953—, Brown and Lindsey, San Francisco, 1982—; assoc. prof. San Francisco State U., 1959-72, chmn. adv. bd. to Div. Engring., 1969-72; lectr. in field; arbitrator Am. Arbitration Assn., San Francisco; mem. Bldg. Safety Bd., State of Calif.; chmn. structural survey and damage engring. com. Calif. Gov.'s Earthquake Task Force. Recipient 14 awards AIA, various mags., 1954-75. Fellow ASCE (past pres., com. on manpower tng.); mem. Structural Engrs., Assn. No. Calif. (bd. dirs.), Nat. Soc. Profl. Engrs., Bay Area Engring. Soc. Jewish. Current work: Wood diaphragms; seismic performance of low-rise buildings. Subspecialties: Structural engineering; Civil engineering. Home: 1002 Rhode Island St San Franciso CA 94107 Office: Brown and Lindsey 2722 Hyde St San Francisco CA 94109

BROWN, KEITH IRWIN, educator, researcher; b. Hunter, Kans., Sept. 28, 1925; s. Fabius L. and Antonette P. (Lawson) B.; m. Dorothy J. Johnson, Feb. 4, 1951; children: Phyllis, Roger, Ann, Jane. B.S. in Zoology, Kans. State Coll., 1949, M.S., 1950; Ph.D. in Zoology, U.Wis., 1956. Asst. prof. physiology Okla. State U., 1955-57; asst. prof. poultry sci. Ohio Agrl. Research and Devel.Ctr., Ohio State U., 1957-61, assoc. prof., 1961-64, prof., 1964—, chmn. dept., 1964—. Pres. Wooster Fish, 1970-74; pres. Wooster Interfaith Housing Co., 1973-78; mem. Zoning Bd. Apls. Wooster, 1974-78; pres. Wooster Community Residents Inc., 1978-81. Served with USN. Recipient Nat. Turkey Fedn. Research award, 1965; Laymans award merit Wooster Kiwanis, 1974. Mem. Soc. Study Reproduction, Poultry Sci. Assn., Worlds Poultry Sci. Assn., AAAS, Sigma Xi, Gamma Alpha Sigma. Democrat. Presbyterian. Current Work: Reproductive physiology in birds, stress physiology in birds, animal welfare with emphasis on fitness traits in modern production systems. Subspecialties: Animal physiology; Endocrinology. Office: Dept Poultry Sci Ohio Agrl Research and Devel Ctr Wooster OH 44691

BROWN, KENNETH LAWRENCE, chemist, educator; b. Phila., July 6, 1946; s. S. Robert and Lillian (Tentzer) B.; m. Kathleen Thompson, Dec. 21, 1968; children: Elizabeth L., Dana Marin. B.S., U. Chgo., 1968; Ph.D., U. Pa., 1971. NIH postdoctoral trainee U. Pa., 1972-73; NIH postdoctoral fellow U. Calif.-Davis, 1973-75; asst. prof. U. Tex., Arlington, 1975-80, assoc. prof. chemistry, 1980—. Contbr. articles to profl. jours. Woodrow Wilson fellow; NSF fellow; grantee NIH, 1976-79; grantee Petroleum Research Fund, 1976-79; grantee Robert A. Welch Found., 1979-82, 82-85, 85—. Mem. AAAS, Am. Chem. Soc., Am. Soc. Biol. Chemists, Sigma Xi, Phi Beta Kappa. Democrat. Current Work: Bioinorganic chemistry of vitamin B-12, organocobalt chemistry.; teaching biochemistry, organic chemistry; research in kinetics, thermodynamics, organocobalt synthesis, nuclear magnetic resonance. Subspecialties: Biochemistry (biology); Organometallics. Office: Dept Chemistry Box 19065 U Tex at Arlington TX 76019

BROWN, LESTER RUSSELL, association executive; b. Bridgeton, N.J., Mar. 28, 1934; s. Calvin C. and Delia (Smith) B.; m. Shirley Ann Woolington, June 12, 1960 (div.); children—Brian, Brenda. B.S. in Agrl. Sci., Rutgers U., 1955; M.A. in Agrl. Econs., U. Md., 1959; M.P.A., Harvard U., 1962; hon. degrees from numerous instns. including Dickinson Coll., U. Md., Franklin Coll., Williams Coll., Rutgers U., Glassboro State Coll., Tufts U. With USDA,

1959-69, adminstr. internat. agrl. devel. service, 1966-69; sr. fellow Overseas Devel. Council, 1969-74; pres. Worldwatch Inst., Washington, 1974—; faculty mem. Salzburg Seminar in Am. Studies, summer 1971, 74; guest scholar Aspen Inst., summers 1972-74; project dir. State of the World, 1984, 85. Author: Man, Land and Food, 1963; Increasing World Food Output, 1965; Seeds of Change, 1970; World Without Borders, 1972; In the Human Interest, 1974; (with Erik Eckholm) By Bread Alone, 1974 (Christopher award); The Twenty-Ninth Day, 1978 (Ecologia Fierenza award); Building a Sustainable Society, 1981; numerous others, also articles. Mem. U.S. com. for UNICEF; mem. Planning Commn. for New Directions; bd. dirs. Overseas Devel. Council. Recipient Superior Service award USDA, 1965; Arthur S. Flemming award, 1965; named One of 10 Outstanding Young Men in Am., U.S. Jr. C. of C., 1966. Mem. Am. Farm Econs. Assn., Soc. Internat. Devel., Internat. Assn. Agrl. Economists, Am. Acad. Arts and Scis. (working group on year 2000), Am. Econs. Assn., Council of Fgn. Relations, Zero Popluation Growth, Common Cause, World Future Soc., AAU. Club: Cosmos. Subspecialties: Agronomy; Ecosystems analysis. Office: 1776 Massachusetts Ave NW Washington DC 20036

BROWN, LOREN DENNIS, physician; b. Des Moines, Feb. 21, 1949; s. Wendell James and Vivian Rose (Young) B.; m. Debra Dee Winders, Feb. 27, 1971; children: Marcus Loren, Melissa Lynn, Katherine Megan. B.A., U. Iowa, 1971; D.O., Coll. Osteopathic Medicine and Surgery, Des Moines, 1974. Diplomate: Nat. Bd. Examiners for Osteopathic Physicians and Surgeons, Am. Coll. Osteo. Internists. Intern, Des Moines Gen. Hosp., 1974-75; resident internal medicine Chgo. Osteopathic Hosp., 1975-76, Youngstown Osteopathic Hosp., 1976-77; fellow hematology/med. oncology Cleve. Clinic Found., 1977-79; practice medicine specializing in hematology/med. oncology Assoc. Med.Clinic, Des Moines, 1979—; assoc. prof. medicine U. Osteopathic Medicine and Health Scis., Des Moines, 1979—; assoc. investigator North Central Cancer Treatment Group/Iowa Oncology Research Assn., Des Moines, 1980—; co-prin. investigator Iowa Oncology Research Assn. Mem. Am. Osteopathic Assn., Am. Coll. Osteo. Internists, Am. Soc. Clin. Oncology, Ia. Soc. Osteopathic Physicians and Surgeons. Roman Catholic. Club: Golf and Country (Des Moines). Current Work: Private practice in hematology and medical oncology, part-time teaching faculty, participate in National Clinical Cancer Research Trials, investigation of new methods in chemotherapy delivery. Subspecialties: Oncology; Hematology. Home: 401 S 28th St W Des Moines IA 50265 Office: 1440 E Grand Ave Suite 2E Des Moines IA 50316

BROWN, MICHAEL GREGORY, materials scientist; b. Rockville Center, N.Y., Oct. 2, 1951; s. Edward J. and Eileen (Conway) B.; m. Janice C. Stapley, Apr. 20, 1980. B.S., Siena Coll., 1973; M.S., Rensselaer Poly. Tech., 1977, Ph.D., 1980. Mem. tech. staff AT&T Bell Labs., Murray Hill, N.J., 1980—. Mem. Am. Phys. Soc., AAAS, IEEE. Current work: Research and development in optoelectronic devices for fiberoptic systems. Past work on long wave length photodetectors and lasers. Subspecialties: Electronic materials; Microelectronics. Office: AT&T Bell Labs 600 Mountain Ave Murray Hill NJ 07974

BROWN, MICHAEL STUART, geneticist; b. N.Y.C., Apr. 13, 1941; s. Harvey and Evelyn (Katz) B.; m. Alice Lapin, June 21, 1964; children: Elizabeth Jane, Sara Ellen. B.A., U. Pa., 1962, M.D., 1966. Intern, then resident in medicine Mass. Gen. Hosp., Boston, 1966-68; served with USPHS, 1968-70; clin. assoc. NIH, 1968-71; asst. prof. U. Tex. Southwestern Med. Sch., Dallas, 1971-74; Paul J. Thomas prof. genetics, dir. Center Genetic Diseases, 1977—. Recipient Pfizer award Am. Chem. Soc., 1976, Passano award Passano Found., 1978, Lounsbery award U.S. Nat. Acad. Scis., 1979; Lita Annenberg Hazen award, 1982; Louisa Gross Horwitz prize Columbia U., 1984; Nobel prize, 1985. Mem. Nat. Acad. Scis., Am. Soc. Clin. Investigation, Assn. Am. Physicians, Harvey Soc. Subspecialty: Genetics and genetic engineering (medicine). Office: U Tex Southwestern Med Sch 5323 Harry Hines Blvd Dallas TX 75235

BROWN, NEAL BOYD, geophysicist, educator; b. Moscow, Idaho, Dec. 13, 1938; s. Kenneth Wayne and Ruth Alvina (Boyd) B.; m. Frances Claire Tannian, Aug. 23, 1980; children: Steven Ross Sweet, Kris David, Melody Jo, Michael Scott Sweet, Nathaniel Scott. B.S., Wash. State U.-Pullman, 1961; M.S., U. Alaska, 1966. Research engr. NASA Ames, Moffeit Field, Calif., 1961-62; research scientist Am. Geophys. Soc., Thule, Greenland, 1962-63; asst. engr. Geophys. Inst., U. Alaska, Fairbanks, 1968-69; dir. asst. prof. Poker Flat Research Range, 1971—. Mem. Am. Assn. Physics Tchrs., Am. Geophys. Union, AIAA, Air Force Assn., AAAS, Alaska Assn. Computers in Edn., Pacific Planetarium Assn., Alaska Geographic Soc., Alaska Acad. Engring. and Scis. Current Work: Implementing coordinated studies of atmospheric phenomena using earthbased, aircraft, balloon, rocket and spacecraft-borne sensors. Subspecialties: Aeronomy; Meteorology. Home: 1569 La Rue Ln Fairbanks AK 99775 Office: Geophys Inst U Alaska Fairbanks AK 99701

BROWN, PAUL BURTON, physiologist; b. Panama City, Panama, Nov. 29, 1942; s. Harold E. and Nina E. (Wetzler) B.; m. Sally Ann Brown, Dec. 23, 1942. B.S., M.I.T., 1964; Ph.D., U. Chgo., 1968. Research assoc. Cornell U., 1969-72; neurophysiologist Boston State Hosp., 1972-74; asst. prof. physiology W. Va. U., Morgantown, 1974-78, assoc. prof., 1978-82, prof., 1982 . Editor-in-chief: Jour. Electrophysiol. Techniques; Contbr. articles to profl. lit.; Author: Electronics for the Modern Scientist. Recipient Gellhorn prize for grad. research, 1968; grantee NIH; grantee NSF; Fogarty sr. internat. fellow, 1980-81. Mem. AAAS, N.Y. Acad. Scis., Am. Physiol. Soc., Soc. Neurosci. Current Work: Somatosensory system. Electrophysiology, neuroanatomy of spinal cord neurons responding to low threshold mechano-receptor input. Subspecialties: Neurobiology; Physiology (biology). Office: Physiology Dept W Va U Med Center Morgantown WV 26506

BROWN, PAUL EDMUND, physical and radiation chemist, educator; b. Schuyler County, Ill., Oct. 17, 1916; s. James Edmund and Bertha Ann (Haney) B.; m. Patricia Wilson Cochran, Oct. 18, 1952; children—James Dixon, Patricia Cochran. B.Ed., Western Ill. U., 1943; Ph.D., Purdue U., 1949. Engr. Bettis plant Westinghouse Corp., Pitts., 1949-54, fellow in engring., 1954-59, supr., Idaho Falls, 1959-62, Pitts., 1962-71, adv. scientist, 1971—; instr. Carnegie Mellon U., Pitts., 1962-65. Author: Corrosion Handbook, 1955. Patentee in field. Served with USNR, 1945-46. Fellow AAAS; mem. Am. Chem. Soc., Sigma Xi, Sigma Zeta, Sigma Pi Sigma, Phi Lambda Upsilon. Republican. Episcopalian. Current work: Power plant primary and secondary water chemistry. Subspecialties: High temperature chemistry; Inorganic chemistry. Home: 1531 Redfern Dr Pittsburgh PA 15241 Office: Westinghouse Bettis PO Box 79 West Mifflin PA 15122

BROWN, R. MALCOLM, JR., plant scientist. Prof. dept. botany U. Tex., Austin, holder Johnson and Johnson Centennial Chair in plant cell biology. Subspecialty: Cell biology. Office: U Tex Dept Botany Austin TX 78712

BROWN, RICHARD EDWARD, animal nutrition consultant; b. Swarthmore, Pa., Oct. 21, 1923; s. James Paul and Blanche (Wheelock) B.; m. Ada Wells, June 19, 1943; children—Richard Edward, Paul H., Stephen W., Scott W. B.S., U. Md., 1947, M.S., 1951, Ph.D., 1954. From asst. prof. to prof. nutrition U. Ill., Urbana, 1954-70; mgr. research and devel. Smith Kline Corp., West Chester, Pa., 1971-73; v.p. E.S. Erwin & Assocs., Phoenix, 1973-79; pres. Erwin & Assocs. of Colo., Lamar, 1974-79; animal nutrition cons., St. Michaels, Md., 1979—. Contbr. articles to profl. jours. Commr., Town of St. Michaels, Md., 1982—. Served to 1st lt. USAAF, 1943-45. Mem. Am. Inst. Nutrition, AAAS, Am. Soc. Animal Sci., Am. Dairy Sci. Assn. Republican. Current work: Research and development of new animal drugs; consultant to beef cattle feedlots in nutrition and mgmt. Subspecialties: Animal nutrition; Animal physiology. Home and Office: 406 Water St PO Box 5 St Michaels MD 21663

BROWN, RICHARD HART, engineer, researcher; b. N.Y.C., June 15, 1941; s. Raymond Edward and Helen Marie (Fenton) B.; m. Frances B. Dazio; children—Erika, Edward, Carolyn. B.E.E., Poly. Inst. Bklyn, 1967; M.B.E., Case Western Res. U., 1972, Ph.D., 1977. Project engr., dir. Gait Lab. Biomechanics Lab. Case Western Res. U., Cleve., 1967-68, instr. orthopaedic surgery (engring.), 1968-72, dir. implant telemetry devel. orthopaedic engring. lab., 1969—, sr. instr. orthopaedic surgery (biomed. engring.), 1972-77, sr. researcher orthpaedic engring. lab., 1972—; engring. dir. Univ. Youth Spine Ctr., Cleve., 1973-78; dir. Orthopaedic Research Computer Ctr., 1976-82; chief Spinal Cord Monitoring Service Univ. Hosps. of Cleve., 1977-82; asst. prof. orthopaedic engring., 1977—; research dir. Univ. Youth Spine Ctr., also co-dir. Orthopaedic Spine Research Lab., 1978-82; chief spinal cord monitoring service St. Luke's Hosp., Cleve., 1982—, research dir. Spine Ctr., 1982—, co-dir. div. surg. research, 1982—; chmn. several spinal cord monitoring workshops; co-chmn. Joint Japanese/Am. Com. on Spinal Cord Monitoring Terminology, 1981—; mem. clin. and research applications organizing com. for 1984 meeting Internat. Conf. Com. on Spinal Cord Monitoring, chmn. 1986 meeting; presenter numerous profl. meetings; mem. dean's com., research and devel. merit rev. com. VA. Contbr. articles to profl. jours. and books. Served with USN, 1958-62. Grantee NIH 1977-84, VA 1978-84. Mem. Orthopaedic Research Soc., Scoliosis Research Soc. (data retrieval com. 1976-78), ASTM, AAAS, IEEE, N.Y. Acad. Scis., Rehabilitative Engring. Soc. N.Am. Current work: Spinal cord monitoring during surgery, three dimensional analysis of the morphology of spinal deformity. Subspecialties: Biomedical engineering; Orthopedics. Office: Div Surg Research St Luke's Hosp 11311 Shaker Blvd Cleveland OH 44104

BROWN, ROBERT MICHAEL, psychology educator; b. Seattle, Jan. 17, 1945; s. Robert Bruce and Katherine Elizabeth (Schneider) B.; m. Norma Lynn Andersen, Nov. 12, 1966; children: Stephanie Lynn, Michelle Terese. B.A., Seattle U., 1967; M.Sc., U. Calgary, 1972; Ph.D., U. N.C., 1974. Asst. prof. Seattle U., 1974-77; asst. prof. No. Mich. U., Marquette, 1977-78, U. Wash, Seattle, 1978-82; asst. prof. psychology Pacific Luth. U., Tacoma, 1982—. Cons. reviewer: Prentice Hall, 1982, Dorsey Press, 1980-81, Little Brown Press, 1976, Child Devel, Chgo., 1979; Sr. author: Psychology, 1984; contbr. articles to profl. jours.; internat. editorial bd., Carfax Pub. Co., Oxford, Eng., 1982—. Summer camp adminstr. Cath. Youth Orgn., Seattle, 1962-67. Teaching fellow U. N.C., 1972-73; Seattle U. grantee, 1976; U. Wash. grantee, 1979, 80; Pacific Luth. U. grantee, 1982. Mem. AAUP, Am. Psychol. Assn., Soc. Research in Child Devel. Current Work: Development of cognitive processes in children. Subspecialties: Developmental psychology; Cognition. Office: Dept Psychology Pacific Luth Univ Tacoma WA 98447

BROWN, ROGER WILLIAM, psychologist, educator; b. Detroit, Apr. 14, 1925; s. Frank Herbert and Muriel Louise (Graham) B. A.B., U. Mich., 1948, Ph.D., 1952; M.A. (hon.), Harvard, 1962; D. Univ. (hon.), U. York, Eng.; D.Sc., Bucknell U., 1980; D.Sci., Northwestern U., 1983. Asst. prof. psychology Harvard, Cambridge, Mass., 1952-57, prof. social psychology, 1962—, John Lindsley prof. psychology in memory William James, 1974—, chmn. dept. social relations, 1967-70; asso. prof. psychology Mass. Inst. Tech., Cambridge, 1957-61, prof. social psychology, 1961-62; Chmn. behavioral scis. study sect. NIH, 1961-63. Author: Words and Things, 1958, (with others) New Directions in Psychology, 1962, The Acquisition of Language, 1964, Social Psychology, 1965, Psycholinguistics, 1970, A First Language, 1973, (with R. Herrnstein) Psychology, 1975; Social Psychology, 2d edit, 1985. Recipient Distinguished Research award Nat. Council Tchrs. English, 1974; Fyssen internat. prize in cognitive sciences, 1984. Mem. Am. (Disting. Sci. Contbn. award 1971, G. Stanley Hall award), New Eng. Psychol. Assn. (pres. 1965-66), Eastern Psychol. Assn. (pres. 1971-72), Linguistic Soc. Am., Am. Acad. Arts and Scis., Nat. Acad. Scis. Current Work: Psychological causality and language. Subspecialties: Cognition; Social psychology. Home: 100 Memorial Dr Cambridge MA 02142

BROWN, R(OY) LEONARD, computer science educator, scientific computing consultant; b. Montgomery, Ala., Aug. 30, 1949; s. Roy Leonard and Mary Emma (Clark) B. B.S. Cum Laude, Tulane U., 1971; M.S., U. Ill.-Urbana, 1973, Ph.D., 1975. Asst. prof. applied math U. Va., Charlottesville, 1974-79; asst. prof. Drexel U., 1979—; vis. researcher Inst. Computer Applications in Sci. and Engring., Hampton, Va., 1975; cons. in field. Trustee Unitarian Ch., Cherry Hill, N.J., 1982. NASA grantee, 1976-79; Air Force Office Sci. Research grantee, 1979-80. Mem. Assn. Computing Machinery, Soc. Indsl. and Applied Math., Am. Math. Soc., Sigma Xi, Alpha Sigma Phi. Current Work: Development of interactive software to allow engineers to describe a system of differential equations in mathematical language and let the computer determine and display the appropriate numerical solution. Subspecialties: Mathematical software; Algorithms. Office: Department of Mathematical Sciences Drexel University Philadelphia PA 19104

BROWN, STEPHEN JAMES, parasitology educator, researcher; b. Santa Monica, Calif., July 4, 1951; s. Walter Jerome and Beverly Maureen (Petri) B.; m. Kathleen Marie Flynn, Aug. 24, 1979; 1 child, Joshua Patrick. B.S., Loyola U., 1974; M.S., San Diego State U., 1977; Ph.D., U. Ky., 1979. Postdoctoral fellow Yale U., New Haven, 1979-81, research scientist, 1981-83, asst. prof., 1983-84; asst. prof. parasitology U. Ill., Urbana, 1984—; mem. editorial bd. Vet. Parasitology, Amsterdam, Netherlands, 1984—; grant reviewer NIH, Bethesda, Md., 1981, NSF, Washington, 1983. Contbr. chpts. to books, over 40 research papers. Research grantee NIH, 1981, 82, 84, Rockefeller Found, 1982, Sigma Xi, 1979. Mem. Am. Assn. Immunologists, Am. Soc. Parasitologists, Entomol. Soc. Am., Acarological Soc. Am., Sigma Xi. Current work: Host immune responses to infestation by ectoparasites. Subspecialties: Parasitology; Immunobiology and immunology. Office: Coll Vet Medicine 2001 Lincoln Ave Urbana IL 61801

BROWN, STEPHEN WOODY, psychologist; b. Cleve., Aug. 3, 1939; s. Joe and Enid (Hirsch) B.; m. Malinda Slugocki, July 27, 1975; children: Kimberly M., David M. B.A., Calif. State U.-Los Angeles, 1962; Ph.D., U. So. Calif., 1966. Asst. prof. Calif. State U.-Dominquez Hills, 1968; asst. prof. U. So. Calif. Med. Sch., Los Angeles, 1972-76; prof. Calif. Sch. Profl. Psychology, Fresno, 1976-80; assoc. prof. Pepperdine U., Los Angeles, 1980—; clin. psychologist Fresno Community Hosp., 1978-80; cons. pub. schs., Los Angeles, Orange, Riverside County, 1968—. Author: Schools and Microcomputers, 1982; Contbr. articles to profl. jours. USPHS postdoctoral fellow, 1969. Fellow Am. Geriatrics Soc.; mem. Am. Psychol. Assn. Current Work: Educational applications of computers; research in clinical psychology. Subspecialties: Clinical psychology; Computer applications in education and psychology. Home: 23391 Devonshire St El Toro CA 92630 Office: Dept Psychology Pepperdine U Los Angeles CA 90044

BROWN, STEVEN HARRY, corporation health physicist, consultant; b. Phila., Sept. 16, 1948; s. Robert Martin and Vera Ethel (Lipovsky) B.; m. Kathryn Helena Vassie, May 24, 1970; children—Chad, Joshua, Sean. A.B.S., Temple U., 1970, B.S., 1971; M.A., West Chester (Pa.) U., 1974. Cert. Am. Bd. Health Physics. Health physicist Temple U., Phila., 1969-71; tchr. phys. sci. Phila. Sch. Dist., 1971-76; mgr. radiation protection Westinghouse Electric Corp., Lakewood, Colo., 1976-80; mgr. western regional office Radiation Mgmt. Corp., Phila., 1980-82; prin. safety analysis engr. Rockwell Internat., Golden, Colo., 1982-83, program mgr. waste isolation pilot project, 1983-85; sr. project mgr. West Valley Nuclear Project, Dames and Moore, West Valley, N.Y., 1985—; cons. Westinghouse Electric Corp., Lakewood, Colo., 1981, Earth Scis. Inc., Golden, 1982, Radiation Mgmt. Corp., Chgo., 1982. Mem. Nat. Health Physics Soc. (pres. Rocky Mountain chpt. 1982-83), Am. Nuclear Soc., Nat. Mgmt. Assn. Current Work: Radiological safety and environment assessment for high level radioactive waste vitrification and management. Subspecialties: Nuclear engineering; Environmental toxicology. Home: 49 Tanglewood W Orchard Park NY 14127 Office: West Valley Nuclear Services PO Box 191 West Valley NY 14171

BROWN, THOMAS HUNTINGTON, neuroscientist; b. N.Y.C., June 13, 1945; s. Thomas H. and Elvira Ruth (Crandall) B.; m. Patricia Ann Carson, Aug. 10, 1968. B.A. in Molecular Biology, Calif. State U., 1972, M.A. in Psychology, 1972; Ph.D. in Neurosci., Stanford U., 1977. Postdoctoral fellow Stanford U. (Calif.), 1977-79; asst. research scientist Beckman Research Inst. of City of Hope, Duarte, Calif., 1979-82, assoc. research scientist, 1982—; advisor study sects. NIH, NIMH, 1982-83. Contbr. articles to sci. jours. Recipient award Epilepsy Found. Am., 1980; scholar's award McKnight Found., 1981, career devel. award, 1984; Muscular Dystrophy Found. fellow, 1978; NIH fellow, 1979; U.S. Govt. grantee. Mem. Soc. for Neurosci., AAAS. Current work: Brain mechanisms involved in learning and memory and causes of neurological diseases such as Alzheimer's and epilepsy. Subspecialties: Neurophysiology; Neuropsychology. Office: Beckman Research Inst of the City of Hope 201 Familian Bldg 1450 E Duarte Rd Duarte CA 91010

BROWN, WILLIAM LACY, genetic supply company executive; b. Arbovale, W.Va., July 16, 1913; s. Tilden L. and Mamie Hudson (Orndoff) B.; m. Alice Hevener Hannah, Aug. 17, 1941; children: Alicia Anne, William Tilden. B.A., Bridgewater Coll., Va., 1936; M.S., Washington U., St. Louis, 1939, Ph.D., 1941. Cytogeneticist Dept. Agr., Washington, 1941-42; dir. maize breeding Rogers Bros. Co., Olivia, Minn., 1942-45; with Pioneer Hi-Bred Internat., Inc., 1945—, v.p., dir. corp. research, Des Moines, 1965-75, pres., 1975-79, chief exec. officer, 1975-81, chmn., dir., 1979-83; dir. Am. Farmland Trust; extra-mural prof. botany Washington U., 1957-65; mem. Gov. Iowa Sci. Adv. Council, 1977—; chmn. Bd. on Agr. NRC-Nat. Acad. Scis., 1981—. Author papers maize cytogenetics, evolution, germplasm conservation. Bd. regents Nat. Colonial Farm. Trustee Accokeek Found., Washington; bd. regents Bridgewater (Va.) Coll. Fulbright advanced research scholar Imperial Coll. Tropical Agr., Trinidad, 1952-53; Univ. fellow Drake U., 1981—. Fellow Am. Soc. Agronomy, Iowa Acad. Sci. (dir.); mem. AAAS, Nat. Acad. Scis., Am., Can. genetics socs., Am. Genetics Assn., Am. Inst. Biol. Scis., Bot. Soc. Am., Soc. Econ. Botany (Disting. Econ. Botanist award 1980), Phi Beta Kappa, Sigma Xi. Quaker. Clubs: Hyperion Field, Des Moines. Subspecialty: Plant genetics. Home: 5770 Linden Ct Johnston IA 50131 Office: 6800 Pioneer Pkwy Johnston IA 50131

BROWN, WILLIAM MILTON, electrical engineer; b. Wheeling, W.Va., Feb. 14, 1932; s. John David and Marjorie Jennie (Walter) B.; m. Norma Jean Hulett, Aug. 24, 1963; children—Cherryl Lynn, Mark William, Jennifer Christine. B.S. in Elec. Engring, W.Va., U., 1952; M.S., Johns Hopkins U., 1955, D.Engring., 1957. Registered profl. engr. Asst. instr. physics, W.Va. U., 1950-52; engr. Air Arm div. Westinghouse Electric Corp., Balt., 1952-54; project supr. countermeasures group radiation lab. Johns Hopkins U., Balt., 1954-57; also part-time lectr.; mem. tech. staff Inst. Def. Analysis, Weapons Systems Evaluation Group, The Pentagon, 1957-58; mem. faculty U. Mich., Ann Arbor, 1958—, prof. elec. engring., 1963-73, adj. prof., 1975—, head radar and optics lab., 1960-68; pres. Environ. Research Inst. Mich., 1972—; cons. in field. Author: Analysis of Time-Invariant Systems, 1963, Random Processes; co-author: Communications and Radar, 1969; Asso. editor: Trans. Aerospace and Electronic Systems, 1965-74; editor-in-chief, 1974—; Contbr. articles to profl. jours. Recipient Rufus A. West prize W.Va. U., 1952. Mich. Fellow IEEE; mem. Aerospace and Electronic Systems Soc. (gov. 1978-82). Club: Rotary. Home: 525 Huntington Dr Ann Arbor MI 48104 Office: PO Box 8618 3300 Plymouth Rd Ann Arbor MI 48107

BROWN, WILLIAM TED, medical researcher, physician; b. Missoula, Mont., Feb. 18, 1946; s. C. W. and H. F. B.; m. Barbara Blegen, Mar. 31, 1967 (div. Jan. 1982); 1 child, Vanessa. B.A., Johns Hopkins U., 1967, M.A., 1969, Ph.D., 1973; M.D. cum laude, Harvard U., 1974. Diplomate: Am. Bd. Internal Medicine, Am. Bd. Clin. Genetics. Intern Roosevelt Hosp., N.Y.C., 1974-75, resident in medicine, 1975-77; Nat. Inst. on Aging postdoctoral fellow in genetics Cornell U. Med. Sch., N.Y.C., 1977-78, asst. prof., 1978-82; chmn. dept. human genetics N.Y. State Inst. Basic Research in Developmental Diseases, N.Y.C., 1982—; asst. attending physician N.Y. Hosp., N.Y.C., 1981—; adj. asst. prof. Rockefeller U., N.Y.C., 1981—; mem. Nat. Inst. Aging Research Resources Adv. Panel. Contbr. chpts., articles on aging, genetics, mental retardation to profl. jours.; editorial bd.: Trisory 21. Recipient Andrew W. Mellon Tchr.-Scientist award, 1979; NSF research fellow Johns Hopkins U., 1967-69. Mem. Am. Soc. Human Genetics, Gerontol. Soc., Am. Fedn. Clin. Research, Harvey Soc., N.Y. Acad. Scis. Current Work: Genetic diseases affecting aging, mental retardation, fragile x syndrome, and Downs syndrome. Subspecialties: Genetics and genetic engineering (medicine); Gerontology. Office: NY State Inst Basic Research in Developmental Disabilities 1050 Forest Hill Rd Staten Island NY 10314

BROWNE, RONALD GREGORY, biomedical scientist, educator; b. San Diego, Mar. 15, 1948; s. Berle Eldon and Shirley Reed (Mathews) B. B.A. in Psychology; B.A. in Biology, U. Calif., San Diego, 1971; M.S. in Biomed. Sci, Health Sci. Center, U. Tex., Houston, 1973, Ph.D. in Biomed, Sci, 1975. Predoctoral fellow Tex. Research Inst. Mental Sci., Houston, 1971-75; NIH postdoctoral research fellow U. Calif., San Diego, La Jolla, 1975-77; instr. in psychology Miramar Coll., 1977-78; Nat. Inst. Drug Abuse postdoctoral research fellow dept. psychiatry U. Calif. San Diego Sch. Medicine, La Jolla, 1977-78; research scientist Pfizer, Inc., Groton, Conn., 1978-81, sr. research and scientist, 1982—; adj. assoc. prof. psychology U. R.I., 1982—; vis. assoc. prof. psychology Conn. Coll., 1983-84. Contbr. articles, abstracts, chpts. to profl. publs. Current Work: Drug discovery; neuropeptides and behavior; drug discrimination. Subspecialty: Neuropharmacology. Office: Central Research Pfizer Inc Groton CT 06340

BROWNELL, GORDON LEE, physicist; b. Duncan, Okla., Apr. 8, 1922; s. Roscoe David and Mabel (Gourley) B.; divorced; children—Wendy L., Peter G., David L., James K. B.S., Bucknell U., Lewisburg, Pa., 1944; Ph.D., Mass. Inst. Tech., 1950. Mem. faculty Mass. Inst. Tech., 1950—, prof., 1970—; dir. Physics Research Lab. Mass. Gen. Hosp., Boston, 1950—; trustee Retina Found.; bd. dirs. Boston Biomed. Found., Neuroresearch Fund. Served to lt. (j.g.) USNR, 1944-46. Fellow Am. Phys. Soc., Am. Nuclear Soc.; mem. Am. Assn. Physicists in Medicine, Soc. Nuclear Medicine (Paul C. Aebersold award 1975), European Soc. Nuclear Medicine (de Hevesy medal 1979). Clubs: Union Boat (Boston); Cambridge (Mass.); Tennis. Current Work: Positron tomography, medical imaging. Subspecialties: Biophysics (physics); PET scan. Home: 100 Memorial Dr Apt 8-2B Cambridge MA 02142 Office: Physics Research Lab Mass Gen Hosp Boston MA 02114 Office: Whitaker Coll Mass Inst Tech Cambridge MA 02139

BROWNING, CHARLES BENTON, university dean; b. Houston, Sept. 16, 1931; s. Earl William and Emma B.; m. Magda L. Luest, Jan. 14, 1956; children: Charles, Susan, Steve, Karen, Heidi, Gary. B.S., Tex. Tech. U., 1955; M.S., Kans. State U., 1956, Ph.D., 1958. Asst. to full prof. Miss. State U., 1958-66; head dept. dairy sci. U. Fla., Gainesville, 1966-69; dean (Coll. of Agr.), 1969-79, Coll. of Agr., Okla. State U., Stillwater, 1979—; dir. Agrl. Expt. Sta., and Coop. Extension Service. Subspecialty: Animal nutrition. Home: 1002 W Will Rogers St Stillwater OK 74074 Office: 139 Ag Hall Okla State U Stillwater OK 74078

BROWNING, STERLING EDWIN, II., analytical chemist, consultant; b. Ardmore, Okla, Aug. 27, 1933; s. Sterling Edwin and Viola Mae (Jones) B.; m. Merlene Fox, Sept. 29, 1962; children—Melissa Anne, Sterling Edwin III., Jonathan Brian. Student Okla. A&M U., 1951-56, U. Tulsa, 1960-62; B.A., Okla State U., 1967. Ptnr., Browning's Carpet Co., Tulsa, 1957-61; research asst. chemistry Dowell div. Dow Chem. Co., Tulsa, 1961-63; tech. corr. Fisher Sci. Co., St. Louis, 1963-65; lab. technician Okla. State U., Stillwater, 1965-67; analytic chemist Sci. Assocs., St. Louis, 1967-68; chief chemist Sherwood Med. Inds., St. Louis, 1968-74; sr. analytical chemist Sigma Chem. Co., St. Louis, 1974—; applied sci. cons., St. Louis, 1972—. Trustee Greemar Subdiv., Mo., 1972-73; active Boy Scouts Am., Girl Scouts U.S.A., 1974—. Mem. Am. Chem. Soc., St. Louis Soc. Analysts, Soc. for Applied Spectroscopy, Coblentz Soc., St. Louis Chromatography Discussion Group, Sigma Study Group, Sigma Alpha Epsilon. Republican. Presbyterian. Subspecialties: Analytical chemistry; Nuclear magnetic resonance. Home: 664 Greenbrae Ct Fenton MO 63026

BRUBAKER, BURTON DALE, materials researcher, ceramic engineer; b. Tiffin, Ohio, June 15, 1935; s. Lester Leroy and Ruth Eleanor (Cook) B.; m. Nancy Jean Wittman, June 14, 1959; children—Debra Ann, Andrew David. B.S. in Ceramic Engring., Ohio State U., 1958, M.S., 1958, Ph.D., 1962. Registered profl. engr. Ohio. Research assoc. Ohio State U., 1960-62; research engr. Dow Chem. Co., Midland, Mich., 1962-68, sr. research engr., 1968-72, sr. research specialist, 1972-76, Sr. research specialist, Granville, Ohio, 1976-80, research assoc. Granville, 1980—. Patentee in field. Mem. Am. Ceramic Soc., Nat. Inst. Ceramic Engrs., Ceramic Ednl. Council, Soc. Plastic Engrs. (sr.), Sigma Xi. Current work: Electron microscopy of polymer foams, advanced engineering ceramics. Subspecialties: Ceramic engineering; Polymers (materials science). Home: 44 Shady Ln Granville OH 43023 Office: Dow Chem USA Box 515 Granville OH 43023

BRUCE, CLEMONT HUGHES, geologist, consultant; b. Central City, Ky., Sept. 5, 1921; s. Ezra Clemont and Nancy (Woodson) B.; m. Bettie J. Kemp, June 11, 1949; children—Lynette, Byron. B.S., U. Ky., 1948, M.S., 1949. Exploration and prodn. geologist Mobil Oil Corp., Mount Vernon, Ill., 1949-53, regional and exploration geologist, Dallas and Jackson, Miss., 1953-65, geol. specialist Gulf Coast, Corpus Christi, Tex., 1965-72, staff geologist Alaska and Gulf Coast, Denver, Houston, 1972-76, spl. projects and research geologist, Dallas, 1976-84, ret., 1984; cons. geology, Carrollton, Tex., 1985—. Contbr. articles to profl. jours. Served to sgt. USAAF, 1942-45, ETO. Mem. Am. Assn. Petroleum Geologists (disting. lectr. 1973-74, v.p. exec. com. 1985-86, George C. Matson award 1983), Geol. Soc. Am., Dallas Geol. Soc., Sigma Xi, Sigma Gamma Epsilon. Current work: Role of smectite clay minerals in hydrocarbon generation, migration and accumulation; relation of clay minerals to structural deformation. Subspecialties: Geology; Tectonics. Home and Office: 1912 Chesham Dr Carrollton TX 75007

BRUCE, THOMAS ALLEN, educator, physician; b. Mountain Home, Ark., Dec. 22, 1930; s. Rex Floyd and Dora Madeline (Fee) B.; m. Dolores Fay Montgomery, May 28, 1960; children: T.K. Montgomery, Dana Fee. B.S.M., M.D., U. Ark., 1955. Intern Duke Hosp., 1956-57; resident medicine Bellevue Hosp., N.Y.C., 1957, Meml. Center Cancer and Allied Diseases, N.Y.C., 1958, Parkland Meml. Hosp., Dallas, 1958-59; cardiopulmonary trainee Southwestern Med. Sch. of U. Tex., 1959-60; cardiac research fellow Hammersmith Hosp. and U. London Postgrad. Med. Sch., London, 1960-61, Harvard Bus. Sch., 1974; instr. to prof. medicine Wayne State U., 1961-68; also asst. dean Wayne State U. (Sch. of Medicine); prof., head cardiovascular sect. U. Okla. Med. Center, 1968-74; prof. medicine, dean Coll. Medicine, U. Ark. Med. Scis., 1974—; med. dir. Barton Research Inst.; coordinator Sino-Am. Med. Exchange Program; mem. ednl. adv. com. Nat. Fund Med. Edn., 1982—; mem. research support rev. com. NIH, 1983—. Dir. Comml. Nat. Bank.; Mem. Ark. Commn. on Health Cost Containment; active Friends of the Zoo, Partners of the Ams., Ark. Symphony Assn., Ark. Opera Theater, Ark. Art Center, Ark. Chamber Music Soc., Friends of Library. Recipient Ark. Gov.'s Meritorious Achievement award. Fellow A.C.P., Am. Coll. Cardiology, Internat. Coll. Angiology, Council Clin. Cardiology, Council Arteriosclerosis; mem. Assn. Univ. Cardiologists, Assn. Am. Med. Colls. Council Deans (chmn. so. council deans 1977-78, com. on payment physician services in teaching hosps. 1983—), Central Soc. Clin. Research, Am. Fedn. Clin. Research, Ark. Heart Assn., Internat. Soc. Heart Research, Soc. for Human Values in Medicine, Am. Rural Health Assn. (nat. cabinet), Ark. Caduceus Club, Old Statehouse Founders Soc., Ark. Med. Soc., Pulaski County Med. Soc. (exec. com.), Ark. Hist. Assn., Ark. Geneal. Soc. (bd. dirs. 1983—), Pulaski County Hist. Soc., Smithsonian Inst. Assocs., Sigma Xi, Alpha Omega Alpha. Clubs: Rotary (Washington), Cosmos (Washington). Bruce Soc. Am. Research and publs. on cardiovascular disease including left ventricular function in cardiac denervation, coronary heart disease, myocardial metabolism relating to phospholipids in graded cardiac ischemia, med. edn. with particular reference to rural health care. Subspecialty: Cardiology. Home: 4 Hillandale Robinwood Little Rock AR 72207 Office: 4301 W Markham Little Rock AR 72201

BRUCH, REINHARD FRANK, physicist, educator, researcher; b. Berlin, Nov. 28, 1941; came to U.S. Jan. 15, 1984; s. Walter Heinz and Ruth Hildegard (Jeskulke) B.; m. Karin Siglinde Falge, Aug. 1, 1980 (div. Dec. 20, 1983); 1 child, Jan Frederik. Vordiplom, Technische U., Hannover, Fed. Republic Germany, 1966, Diplom, 1970; Dr. Rer. Nat., Freie U., Berlin, 1976. Lectr. Medizinische Hochschule, Hannover, 1969-70; research assoc. Freie U., Berlin, 1970-76; research scientist U. Arhus, Denmark, 1976-77, Argonne Nat. Lab., Ill. 1982; sr. group leader U. Freiburg, Fed. Republic Germany, 1978-83; assoc. prof. U. Nev., Reno, 1984—; mem. Sonderforschungs-Bereich, 161 (hyperfine Interaction), 1972-76. Contbr. numerous articles to tech. jours. Research grantee Deutsche Forschungsgemeinschaft, Land Baden-Württemberg, 1978-83, Wissenschaftliche Gesellschaft Freiburg. Mem. Am. Phys. Soc., Deutsche Physikalische Gesellschaft. Current work: Electron and photon spectroscopy, Auger effect, autoionization, hyperfine structure, relativistic interactions, ion-atom collisions, charge transfer, EUV lasers, synchrotron radiation. Subspecialties: Atomic and molecular physics; Plasma physics. Home: 401 College Dr Apt 239 Reno NV 89503 Office: Dept Physics Univ Nevada Virginia St Reno NV 89557

BRUGAM, RICHARD BLAIR, biology educator, ecology researcher; b. Phila., Dec. 23, 1946; s. Richard J. and Margaret S. (Blair) B.; m. Ella Suzanne Oren, Aug. 1, 1970; children—Amy, Matthew. B.A., Lehigh U., 1968; M.Phil., Yale U., 1974, Ph.D., 1975. Teaching asst. Yale U., New Haven, 1974-75; research assoc. U. Minn., Mpls., 1975-78; asst. prof. biology So. Ill. U., Edwardsville, 1978-83, assoc. prof., 1983—; vis. scholar U. Wash., Seattle, 1984-85. Served with U.S. Army, 1969-72. Mem. Ecol. Soc. Am., Am. Quaternary Assn., Am. Soc. Limnology and Oceanography, AAAS. Current work: Paleolimnology, historical development of lakes, neutralization of acidic surface mine lakes, eutrophication of lakes, influence of postglacial climatic change on lakes. Subspecialties: Limnology; Ecology (environmental science). Home: 205 Franklin Ave Edwardsville IL 62025 Office: Dept Biol Scis So Ill Univ Box 656 Edwardsville IL 62026

BRUGEL, EDWARD WILLIAM, astrophysicist; b. N.Y.C., Nov. 29, 1948; s. Edward William and Muriel Ellen (Flanly) B.; m. Kanistra Woointranant, July 25, 1974 (div.); 1 child, Narinton Woointranont. B.S., SUNY, Stony Brook, 1970; M.S., U. Wash., 1978, Ph.D., 1980. Teaching/research asst. U. Wash., Seattle, 1974-80; research asso., dir. Regional Data Analysis Facility, Internat. Ultraviolet Explorer satellite, Lab. Atmospheric and Space Physics, U. Colo., Boulder, 1981—. Contbr. articles to profl. jours. Served with U.S. Army, 1970-74. NASA grantee, 1980, 81, 83. Mem. Am. Astron. Soc., Astron. Soc. Pacific. Current Work: Research, interstellar medium in regions of recent star formation, ejecta from young objects (Herbig-Haro objects); shock waves in interstellar clouds, symbiotic stars. Subspecialties: Ultraviolet high energy astrophysics; Optical astronomy. Office: Lab Atmospheric and Space Physics Campus Box 392 U Colo Boulder CO 80309 Office: Lab Atmospheric and Space Physics Campus Box 392 U Colo Boulder CO 80309

BRUHN, ARNOLD RAHN, JR., clinical psychologist; b. Bklyn., Dec. 30, 1941; s. Arnold Rahn and Paula (Muich) B.; m. Arlene C. Palmer, June 23, 1967; children: Alexis, Erika. B.A., U. Portland, 1963, M.A., 1966; M.S., Portland State U., 1972; Ph.D., Duke U., 1976. Psychologist Dorothea Dix Hosp., Raleigh, N.C., 1973-76; psychology intern Duke U Med. Center, Durham, N.C., 1975-76; asst. prof. psychology George Washington U., Washington, 1976-82; staff psychologist Alexandria (Va.) Community Mental Health Center, 1977-85; asst. research prof. psychiatry and behavioral scis. George Washington Med. Center, Washington, 1980-83. Cons. editor: Jour. Personality Assessment, 1976—; author articles. USPSH fellow, 1972-76. Fellow Soc. for Personality Assessment; mem. Am. Psychol. Assn. Current Work: Personality theory and personality assessment. Earliest memories. Subspecialties: Clinical psychology; Cognition. Home: 7820 Glenbrook Rd Bethesda MD 20814 Office: 7910 Woodmont Ave Suite 906 Bethesda MD 20814

BRUMBERGER, HARRY, physical chemist, educator, researcher, consultant; b. Vienna, Austria, Aug. 28, 1926; came to U.S., 1940, naturalized, 1948; s. Leon and Rose (Kraft) B.; m. Vilma, June 21, 1950; children: Jesse, Eva. B.S. in Chemistry, Poly. Inst. Bklyn., 1949, M.S., 1952, Ph.D., 1955. Teaching asst. Poly. Inst. Bklyn., 1951-54; research asso. dept. chemistry Cornell U., 1954-57; asst. prof. phys. chemistry Syracuse U., 1957-62, asso. prof., 1962-69, prof., 1969—, dir. grad. biophysics progrm, 1977-83. Contbr. numerous articles to profl. publs. Served with U.S. Army, 1946-47. Research Corp. grantee, 1959-60; NSF grantee, 1959-61, 61-63, 64-66, 64-65, 72-74, 80-81, 80-85; Army Research Office grantee, 1964-65; Am. Chem. Soc. Petroleum Research Fund grantee, 1965-69; Office Naval Research grantee, 1964-69; Oak Ridge Assoc. Univs. grantee, 1977-78; Syracuse U. grantee, 1979-81. Mem. AAAS, Am. Crystallographic Assn. Current Work: Small-angle x-ray scattering and its applications to study of supported-metal catalysts; biol. macromolecules; others. Subspecialties: Physical chemistry; Catalysis chemistry. Office: Dept Chemistry Syracuse U Syracuse NY 13210

BRUMER, PAUL WILLIAM, chemistry educator, chemical physicist; b. N.Y.C., June 8, 1945; arrived in Can., 1975; s. Abraham and Barbara (Feldman) B.; m. Abbey Pohrille, Aug. 18, 1968; children—Debbie, Jeremy, Eric, Sharon. B.Sc., Bklyn. Coll., 1966; Ph.D., Harvard U., 1972. Lectr. astronomy Harvard U., Cambridge, Mass., 1974-75; asst. prof. chemistry U. Toronto, Ont., Can., 1975-80, assoc. prof. chemistry, 1980-83, prof. chemistry, 1983—. Contbr. articles to profl. jours. Woodrow Wilson fellow, 1966-67; NSF grad. fellow, 1966-71; Weizmann Inst. fellow, 1972-73; A.B. Sloan fellow, 1977-81; Killam Research fellow, 1981-83; recipient Noranda award Chem. Inst. Can., 1985. Mem. Am. Phys. Soc. Jewish. Current work: Theories of intramolecular and intermolecular processes; nonlinear mechanics and chemical dynamics. Subspecialties: Theoretical chemistry; Atomic and molecular physics. Home: 37 Fisherville Rd Toronto ON M2R 3B8 Canada Office: U Toronto Dept Chemistry 80 St George St Toronto ON M5S 1A1 Canada

BRUMM, DOUGLAS BRUCE, electrical engineer, educator, consultant, researcher; b. Barry County, Mich., Aug. 4, 1940; s. Bruce Dwight and Dorotha Clarice (Green) B.; m. Phyllis Jean Orthner, Aug. 14, 1965; children: Bruce Douglas, Dawn Marie. B.S.E.E., Mich. Technol. U., 1962; M.S.E., U. Mich., 1964, Ph.D., 1970. Registered profl. engr., Mich. Assoc. engr. Raytheon Co., Wayland, Mass., 1962-63; Research assoc. U. Mich., Ann Arbor, 1963-70; assoc. prof. elec. engring. Mich. Technol. U., Houghton, 1970—. Contbr. articles to profl. jours. Mem. IEEE, IEEE Computer Soc., Optical Soc. Am., Sigma Xi. Baptist. Current Work: Fiber optic communication systems, microprocessor-controlled instruments, laser applications, holography. Subspecialties: Electronics; Fiber optics. Home: 1140 Rockhouse Rd Calumet MI 49913 Office: Elec Engring Dept Mich Technol U Houghton MI 49931

BRUN, MILIVOJ KONSTANTIN, ceramist; b. Novi Sad, Yugoslavia, Jan. 8, 1948; came to U.S., 1967; s. Konstantin Leonid and Nada (Pecic) B.; m. Cathiie-Jo Master, May 31, 1980; 1 child, Christina. B.S., Pa. State U., 1970, Ph.D., 1974. Postdoctoral fellow Tech. U. of Norway, Trandheim, Norway, 1975-76; research fellow Pa. State U., University Park, 1976-79; staff ceramist General Electric Corp. Research and Devel., Schenectady, N.Y., 1979—. Contbr. articles to prof. jours. Mem. Am. Ceramic Soc., AAAS, Keramos-Ceramic Nat. Orgn. Current work: Hard and refractory materials, processing of ceramics, hipping, high temperature chemistry and thermodynamics, composites. Subspecialties: Ceramics; High-temperature materials. Home: RD3 Jockey St Ballston Lake NY 12019 Office: General Electric Corp Research and Devel Box 8 Schenectady NY 12301

BRUNDA, MICHAEL JOHN, immunologist; b. Passaic, N.J., Dec. 16, 1950; s. John and Helena (Gawronski) B.; m. Patricia Katherine Ann Mongini, July 28, 1979; 1 dau., Nicole Anna. A.B., U. Rochester, 1971; Ph.D., Stanford U., 1975. Postdoctoral fellow Nat. Jewish Hosp. and Research Center, Denver, 1975-78; immunologist Nat. Cancer Inst., Bethesda, Md., 1978-82; sr. scientist dept. exptl. oncology and virology Hoffmann LaRoche, Nutley, N.J. Contbr. articles to profl. jours. Nat. Cancer Inst. postdoctoral fellow, 1977; AAI Travel grantee, 1980. Mem. Am. Assn. Immunologists, Am. Assn. Cancer Research, AAAS. Democrat. Orthodox Christian. Current Work: Study of interferons, interleukins and other immunomodulators on natural killer cell activity and macrophage function as antitumor defense mechanism. Subspecialties: Immunobiology and immunology; Immunopharmacology. Office: Dept Exptl Oncology and Virology Hoffman La Roche Nutley NJ 07110

BRUNDAGE, BRUCE HOWARD, cardiology educator, physician; b. Blakely, Pa., Sept. 19, 1938; s. J. Arthur and Dorothy Mae (MacConnell) B.; m. Rita Doreen Mitchell, June 27, 1959; children—Pamela Ann, Lisa Marie, Todd Mitchell. A.B., Lafayette Coll., 1960; M.D., U. Medicine and Dentistry N.J.-Newark, 1965. Diplomate Am. Bd. Internal Medicine. Intern Tripler Army Med. Ctr., Honolulu, 1965-66; resident in internal medicine Fitzsimons Army Med. Ctr., Denver, asst. chief cardiology, 1974-76; resident in cardiology Letterman Army Med. Ctr., San Francisco; chief cardiac catheter lab. Walter Reed Hosp., Washington, 1971-74; dir. cardiac catheter labs. U. Calif., San Francisco, 1976-83; chief cardiology U. Ill., Chgo., 1983—; cons. Westside VA Hosp., Chgo., 1983—. Served to lt. col. M.C., U.S. Army, 1964-76. Fellow ACP, Am. Coll. Cardiology, Am. Heart Assn. Council on Clin. Cardiology. Current work: Evaluation of myocardial infarction and myocardial blood flow by ultrafast computed tomography. Subspecialties: CAT scan; Cardiology. Office: Dept Medicine U Ill-Chgo PO Box 6998 Chicago IL 60680

BRUNELLE, DANIEL JOSEPH, organic chemist, researcher; b. Woonsocket, R.I., Apr. 3, 1949; s. Horace Leo and Anna Julia (Stoklosa) B.; m. Bette Agnes Smith, July 27, 1968; children—Lara Anne, Nora Katherine. B.S., Emory U., 1970; M.A., Johns Hopkins U., 1972, Ph.D., 1974. Postdoctoral fellow Harvard U., Cambridge, Mass., 1975-77; staff chemist Gen. Electric Co., Schenectady, 1977-85, mgr. reactive intermediates project, 1985—. Contbr. articles to profl. jours. Patentee in field. Served to 1st lt. USAF, 1974-75. Mem. Am. Chem. Soc. (cert.), AAAS, Sigma Xi, Phi Lambda Upsilon (v.p. 1972-74.) Current work: Design and development of novel reactions and chemical reagents, investigation of new methods and intermediates for synthesis of engineering themoplastics, chemical methods for destruction of chemical wastes, phase transfer catalysis. Subspecialties: Organic chemistry; Synthetic chemistry. Office: Gen Electric Corp Research and Development PO Box 8 Schenectady NY 12345

BRUNER, RALPH CLAYBURN, testing services company executive, metallurgist; b. Oklahoma City, Apr. 22, 1921; s. Ralph Sylvester and Macil Gladys (Stroup) B.; m. Cicely Louise Fidler, July 3, 1954; children: Martha Ellen, David Ralph. B.A. in Chemistry, Calif. State U. - Fullerton, 1965. Registered profl. engr., Okla. Research engr. N.Am. Aviation, Inc., Los Angeles, 1947-52, supr. metallurgy, Columbus, Ohio, 1952-56; chief chem. lab. Autonetics, Anaheim, Calif., 1956-65; mgr. labs. Rockwell Internat., Tulsa, 1965-76; pres. Metlab Testing Services, Inc., Tulsa, 1976—. Contbr. articles to profl. meetings. Mem. Am. Soc. Metals, ASME, Am. Welding Soc., Am. Foundrymen's Soc. Automotive Engrs., Nat. Assn. Corrossion Engrs. Republican. Roman Catholic. Patentee in field. Current Work: Metallurgical forensic analysis. Subspecialty: Metallurgy. Office: 6825 E 38th St Tulsa OK

BRUNISH, WENDEE M., astronomer; b. Los Angeles, Dec. 31, 1953; d. Robert and Virginia Florence (Hughes) B.; m. Stephen A. Becker, May 30, 1980. A.B., Vassar Coll., 1975; M.S., U. Ill., 1977, Ph.D., 1981. Teaching and research asst. U. Ill., 1975-81; research assoc. astronomy U. So. Calif., Los Angeles, 1981-83; vis. staff mem. Los Alamos Nat. Lab., 1983-84, staff mem., 1984—. Mem. Am. Astron. Soc. Current Work: Stress waves in rock; evolution of massive stars. Subspecialties: Theoretical astrophysics; Solar physics. Office: LANL PO Box 1663 MS F665 Los Alamos NM 87545

BRUNK, WILLIAM EDWARD, astronomer; b. Cleve., Nov. 24, 1928; s. Edgar Rea and Mabel Mowbray (Pearson) B.; 1 dau., Anna Kathryn. B.S., Case Inst. Tech., 1952, M.S., 1954, Ph.D., 1963. Aero. research scientist Lewis Flight Propulsion Lab., NACA, Cleve., 1954-58; aerospace engr. Lewis Research Center, NASA, Cleve., 1958-64; staff scientist for planetary astronomy NASA Hdqrs., Washington, 1964-65, program chief planetary astronomy, 1965-77, discipline scientist planetary astronomy, 1977-82, chief planetary sci. br., 1982—. Fellow AAAS; mem. Am. Astron. Soc., Internat. Astron. Union; Mem. Sigma Xi. Subspecialty: Planetary science. Home: PO Box 3466 Annapolis MD 21403 Office: Code EL-4 NASA Hdqrs Washington DC 20546

BRUNS, DAVID EUGENE, clinical pathologist, researcher; b. St. Louis, Dec. 12, 1941; s. Eugene H. and Ellen E. (Johnson) B.; m. Elizabeth Hirst; children: Elizabeth P., David H. B.S. Chem.E., Washington U., St. Louis, 1963, A.B., 1965; M.D., St. Louis U., 1973. Diplomate: Nat. Bd. Med. Examiners, Va. State Bd. Medicine. Intern lab. medicine Barnes Hosp., St. Louis, 1973-74; fellow exptl. pathology Washington U., St. Louis, 1974-75, instr. pathology, 1973-77; resident lab. medicine Barnes Hosp., St. Louis, 1975-77; asst. prof. pathology U. Va., Charlottesville, 1977-81, assoc. prof., 1981—, assoc. dir. clin. chemistry, 1977—. NIH grantee, 1978—; Am. Cancer Soc. grantee, 1982—. Mem. Assn. Clin. Scientists, Am. Assn. Clin. Chemistry, Am. Assn. Pathologists, Nat. Acad. Clin. Biochemistry, Acad. Clin. Lab. Physicians and Scientists. Roman Catholic. Current Work: Research in clinical enzymology, toxicology of polyethylene glycol, tumor markers, and subcellular calcium metabolism. Subspecialties: Clinical chemistry; Pathology (medicine). Home: 2516 Woodhurst Rd Carlottesville VA 22901 Office: Dept Pathology U Va Sch Medicine Charlottesville VA 22908

BRUNSON, BRADFORD IRA, psychologist; b. Sioux City, Iowa, Sept. 4, 1949; s. Ira Wandel and Shirley A. (Branch) B.; m. Cheryl A. Hollenshead, Aug. 25, 1980. B.A., Rutgers U., 1977; M.S., Kans. State U., 1979, Ph.D., 1982. Lic. profl. counselor, Tex.; lic. psychologist, Tex.; cert. clin. mental health counselor. Instr. Kans. State U., Manhattan, 1979-81; counseling psychologist Tex. A&M U., College Station, 1981-82; dir. counseling center St. Mary's U., San Antonio, 1982—; dir. Commn. II Am. Coll. Personnel Assn., Falls Church, Va., 1980—. Contbr. articles to profl. jours. Active Boy Scounts Am., Montebello, Calif., 1964. Served with USMC, 1979-81. Mem. Am. Psychol. Assn., Am. Personnel and Guidance Assn., Internat. Acad. Profl. Counseling and Psychotherapy, Am. Coll. Personnel Assn., Am. Mental Health Counselors Assn., Psi Chi, Phi Delta Kappa, Alpha Sigma Lambda. Lutheran. Current Work: Type A coronary-prone behavior pattern; depression and learned helplessness; social influence in counseling. Subspecialties: Counseling psychology; Social psychology. Home: 5414 Timberhurst St San Antonio TX 78250 Office: Saint Marys U 1 Camino Santa Maria San Antonio TX 78284

BRUSSARD, PETER FRANS, evolutionary biologist; b. Reno, June 20, 1938; s. William and Evelyn (Anderson) B.; m. Janet E. McDonald, 1962 (div. 1969); 1 child, William R.; m. Trudy Elizabeth Byers, Dec. 20, 1969; 1 child, Peter H. A.B., Stanford U., 1960, Ph.D., 1969; M.S., U. Nev., 1966. Asst. prof. ecology Cornell U., Ithaca, N.Y., 1969-75, assoc. prof., 1975-85; prof., head dept. biology Mont. State U., Bozeman, 1985—; dir. Rocky Mountain Biol. Lab., Crested Butte, Colo., 1979-83. Editor: Ecological Genetics, 1978. Assoc. editor jour. The Biologist, 1977—, Jour. Soc. for Sci. Exploration, 1983—. Served to lt. USNR, 1960-65. Grantee NSF, 1970—, NIH, 1970-73. Mem. Soc. Study Evolution (mem. council 1980-82), Am. Soc. Naturalists (treas. 1981-83), Soc. Sci. Exploration (mem. council 1983—), Genetics Soc. Am., Ecol. Soc. Am. Democrat. Episcopalian. Current work: Relations between distribution, abundance, and variation in plant and animal species, speciation. Subspecialties: Evolutionary biology; Genetics and genetic engineering (biology). Home: 3408 Wagon Wheel Rd Bozeman MT 59715 Office: Mont State U Lewis Hall Bozeman MT 59717

BRYAN, DAVID A., physicist; b. Austin, Tex., July 29, 1946; s. William C. and Virginia S. (Vedder) B.; m. JoAnn Grossman, Aug. 3, 1974; children: Kenna, Kimberlee, Benjamin, Joshua. B.A., Rice U., 1968; M.S., U. Mo.-Rolla, 1973, Ph.D., 1976. Research asst. U. Mo.-Rolla, 1971-76; tech. specialist electro-optics dept. McDonnell Douglas Astronautics Co., St. Louis, 1976—. Contbr. articles to profl. jours. Patentee in field. Mem. Grace World Outreach Ctr. Served to lt. USNR, 1968-71. Mem. Optical Soc. Am., Internat. Soc. Optical Engrs. Current Work: Holographic and other optical studies of non-linear optical materials; photorefractive effect of laser-frequency-doubler materials and electro-optic modulator materials. Subspecialties: Holography; Optical signal processing. Home: 3044 Westminister Saint Charles MO 63301 Office: McDonnell Douglas Astronautics Co PO Box 516 Saint Louis MO 63166

BRYAN, JAMES THOMAS, JR., state government accountant, observational astronomer; b. Fort Worth, Tex., Mar. 27, 1951; s. James Thomas and Julia Clarissa (Wilson) B.; m. Nancy Beth Lavender, Jan. 12, 1985. B.A., U. Tex., 1973, M. in Profl. Acctg., 1980. Chief asst. State of Tex., Austin, 1980—; adminstr. Consortium for Extragalactic Astronomy, Austin, 1984—; mem. com. AAVSO Nova/Supernova Search Com., Cambridge, Mass., 1983—. Author: The Visual Supernova Search Charts, 1985. Contbr. articles to profl. jours. Served to 2d lt. USAF, 1973-75. NASA grantee, 1984. Mem. Am. Astron. Soc., Astron. Soc. Pacific (bd. dirs. 1984—), Austin Astron. Soc. (pres. 1984). Christian Scientist. Current work: Survey of galaxies to discover supernovae; survey of the Andromeda Galaxy to detect common novae. Subspecialties: Optical astronomy; Supernovae. Office: Consortium for Extragalactic Astronomy PO Box 5934 Austin TX 78763

BRYAN, JOHN HENRY DONALD, biologist, educator, researcher; b. London, Sept. 18, 1926; s. John and Mary (Barnes) B.; m. Janet Goff, Aug. 23, 1952; children: Mary E., Melissa L. B.Sc., U. Sheffield, Eng., 1947; M.A., Columbia U., 1949, Ph.D., 1952. Lectr. zoology Columbia U., N.Y.C., 1949-50; instr. biology M.I.T., Cambridge, 1951-54; asst. prof. Iowa State U., Ames, 1954-62, assoc. prof., 1962-67; prof. zoology U. Ga., Athens, 1967—; cons. AID, 1968-69. Contbr. articles to profl. jours. McCallum Found. fellow, 1950-52. Fellow AAAS; mem. Am. Soc. Naturalists, AAAS, Am. Soc. Cell Biology, Genetics Soc. Am., Soc. Devel. Biology, Internat. Assn. Torch Clubs (chpt. dir. 1974-77, chpt. pres. 1975-76), Sigma Xi. Current Work: Use of mutants as probes to study normal processes in production of male reproductive cells, and in development of the nervous system; relationship between ultrastructural makeup and functional specializations of cells. Subspecialties: Cell biology; Gene actions. Office: U Ga Athens GA 30602

BRYANT, CHARLES THOMAS, science administrator, hydrologist; b. Paragould, Ark., Sept. 4, 1931; s. Harvey Allen and Florence Ruby (Cameron) B.; m. Elizabeth Virginia Rice, Dec. 22, 1956; children—Charles Thomas, Jr., Angela Rice Langley. B/S., Harding U., 1959. Analytical chemist U.S. Geol. Survey, Portland, Oreg., 1959-63, lab. chief, Little Rock, 1963-72, project chief, 1972-76, chief tech. services, 1976-81, chief hydrologic investigations, 1981—. Author numerous publs. in field of hydrology. Recipient Unit citation U.S. Geol. Survey, 1970, Sustained Performance award, 1979. Mem. Am. Chem. Soc., Ark. Acad. Sci., Am. Water Works Assn. Club: Toastmasters Internat. (lt. gov. 1974, disting. toastmaster 1981). Current work: Ground-water contamination. Subspecialty: Hydrology. Home: 305 Lanehart Rd Little Rock AR 72204 Office: U S Geol Survey 2301 Fed Office Bldg Little Rock AR 72201

BRYANT, JAMES WINSTON, JR., clinical psychologist; b. Oklahoma City, Feb. 26, 1949; s. James Winston and Elly Elizabeth (Geissler) B.; m. Martha Rosa Moroyoqui, Apr. 10, 1982. M.S., Calif. State U., 1973; M.A., Palo Alto Sch. Profl. Psychology, 1979, Ph.D., 1980. Lic. psychologist, Calif. Chem. dependency therapist Pathways Soc., Inc., Santa Clara, Calif., 1980—; psychiat. asst. Hugh Kohn, Ph.D., San Jose, Calif., 1979-81, O'Connor Hosp., Campbell, Calif., 1981-82; clin. psychologist Palomares Group Homes, Inc., San Jose, 1982—, El Dorado Guidance Ctr., San Jose, 1982—, pvt. practice clin. psychology, Los Gatos, Calif., 1980—; mem. psychologist panel Dept. Vocational Rehab., San Jose, 1982—; provider W. Bay Health Systems Agy., San Mateo Subarea Adv. Council, 1979-81; examiner San Mateo County Oral Commrs. Bd. Mental Health Services, 1979-81. Contbr. articles to profl. jours. Mem. Am. Psychol. Assn. (assoc.), Calif. Psychol. Assn., Calif. Soc. Clin. Hypnosis (bd. govs. 1981-83), San Jose Soc. Clin. Hypnosis, Santa Clara County Psychol. Assn. Democrat. Current Work: L-facility with a chronically-impaired schizophrenic population. Subspecialty: Neuropsychology.

BRYANT, MICHAEL DAVID, engineering educator, researcher; b. Danville, Ill., Feb. 8, 1951; s. David Kinley and Helen (Jacobs) B.; m. Eugenia Sturino, Sept. 9, 1978; children—David Ercole, Daniella Helene, Christina Frances. B.S. in Info. Elec. Engring., U. Ill.-Chgo., 1972, postgrad., 1972-74; M.S. in Mech. Engring., Northwestern U. 1980, Ph.D., 1981. Asst. prof. N.C. State U., Raleigh, 1981-85, assoc. prof., 1985—; design coordinator, 1984. Contbr. articles to profl. jours. Panel reviewer NSF, 1984. NSF grantee, 1982, 84, Presdl. Young Investigator, 1985. Mem. IEEE, Soc. Indsl. and Applied Math., Soc. Mfg. Engring., Sigma Xi; assoc. mem. ASME. Current work: Contact mechanics and tribology-wear in electrical and frictional contacts; precision engineering-dynamics and control of 10 nanometer phenomena; nonlinear mechanics-solutions of nonlinear differential equations. Subspecialties: Theoretical and applied mechanics; Applied mathematics. Office: NC State U Campus Box 7910 Raleigh NC 27695

BRYDEN, MARK PHILIP, psychologist; b. Boston, Nov. 14, 1934; s. Samuel David and Ellen Agnes (Sibley) B.; m. Patricia Mabel Rowe, Nov. 2, 1962; children—Penny Elizabeth, Pamela Joanna. S.B., MIT, 1956; M.Sc., McGill U., 1958, Ph.D., 1961. Research assoc. McGill U., Montreal, 1960-63; asst. prof. psychology U. Waterloo, Ont., 1963-64, assoc. prof., 1964-67, prof., 1967—; vis. prof. Monash U., 1985. Author: Laterality, 1982; editor: Can. Jour. Psychology, 1981-85. NRC Can. sr. scientist, 1969-70; Can. Council fellow, 1975-76. Fellow Can. Psychol. Assn. (dir. 1981-83), Am. Psychol. Assn.; mem. Internat. Neuropsychology Soc., Psychonomic Soc. Current Work: Brain lateralization, handedness, sex hormones and behavior. Subspecialties: Neuropsychology; Cognition.

BRYNES, PAUL JEFFREY, bio-organic chemist, clinical chemist; b. Balt., Nov. 30, 1947; s. Kermit and Lore Brynes; m. Inge Strarup, June 28, 1978. B.S., Brandeis U., 1969; M.S., Cornell U., Ithaca, N.Y., 1970, Ph.D., 1975. Postdoctoral fellow Rockefeller U., N.Y.C., 1975-77; asst. prof. SUNY-Stony Brook, 1977-81; sr. scientist Abbott Labs., North Chicago, Ill., 1981-85, chmn. tech. adv. bd. diagnostics div., 1984—. Recipient Snyder award Brandeis Univ., 1969. Mem. Am. Chem. Soc., Am. Assn. Clin. Chemistry. Subspecialties: Synthetic chemistry; Clinical chemistry. Office: Abbott Labs D-9OU/AP-8B Abbott Park IL 60064

BRYNJOLFSSON, ARI, nuclear physicist; b. Akureyri, Iceland, Dec. 7, 1926; came to U.S., 1965, naturalized, 1970; s. Brynjolfur and Gudrun (Rosinkarsdottir) Sigtryggsson; m. Marguerite Reman, Dec. 22, 1950; children: Ariane, Olaf, Erik, John, Alan. Cand. Phil., U. Copenhagen, 1949, Cand. Mag., 1954, Mag. Scien., 1954; D.Phil., Niels Bohr Institut Theoretical and Exptl. Nuclear Physics, 1973; post grad., Advanced Mgmt. Program, Harvard U., 1971. Dir. radiation research Danish Atomic Energy Research Establishment, Roskilde, 1957-65; chief radiation research U.S. Army Natick (Mass.) Lab., 1965-72, dir. food irradiation program, 1972-80, spl. asst. for physics, 1980—; lectr. M.I.T., 1980—. Contbr. articles to profl. jours. Recipient Mollers Found. award for exceptional service to Danish industry, 1965. Mem. Am. Physi Soc., Radiation Research Soc., Am. Nuclear Soc., Am. Soc. Physicists in Medicine, Inst. Food Technologists. Current Work: Astrophysics, theoretical physics, general theory of relativity. Biological effects of radiation. Subspecialties: Nuclear physics; Population biology. Home: 7 Bridle Path Wayland MA 01778 Office: 6 Kansas St Natick MA 01760

BRYSON, ARTHUR EARL, JR., engring. educator; b. Evanston, Ill., Oct. 7, 1925; s. Arthur Earl and Helen Elizabeth (Decker) B.; m. Helen Marie Layton, Aug. 31, 1946; children—Thomas Layton, Stephen Decker, Janet Elizabeth, Susan Mary. Student, Haverford Coll., 1942-44; B.S., Iowa State U., 1946; M.S., Calif. Inst. Tech., 1949, Ph.D. in Aeros, 1951; M.A. (hon.), Harvard., 1956. With Container Corp. Am., 1947-48, United Aircraft Corp., 1948; research asst. aero. Calif. Inst. Tech., 1949-50; mem. tech. staff Hughes Research & Devel. Labs., 1950-53; mem. faculty Harvard, 1953-68, Gordon McKay prof. mech. engring., 1961-68; mem. faculty Stanford, 1968—, chmn. dept. applied mechanics, 1969-71, chmn. dept. aeros. and astronautics, 1971-79, Paul Pigott prof. engring., 1972—; Hunsaker prof. Mass. Inst. Tech., 1965-66; Mem. nat. com. Fluid Mechanics Films, 1961-68. Author: (with Y.C. Ho) Applied Optimal Control, 1969. Served as ensign USNR, 1944-46. Recipient Rufus Oldenberger medal ASME, 1980. Fellow AIAA (asso. editor Jour. 1963-65, bd. dirs. 1965-68, Pendray Award 1968, mechanics and control of flight award 1980, Dryden award 1984); mem. Am. Acad. Arts and Scis., Am. Soc. Engring. Edn. (Westinghouse award 1969), Nat. Acad. Engring. (aero. and space engring. bd. 1970-79), Nat. Acad. Scis., Sigma Xi, Tau Beta Pi. Conglist. Subspecialty: Theoretical and applied mechanics. Office: Dept Aeros and Astronautics Stanford U Stanford CA 94305

BRYSON, GEORGE GARDNER, physiologist/psychologist; b. Santa Barbara, Calif., Dec. 16, 1935; s. George Omar and Mary Dewey (Gardner) B. A.B. in Zoology, U. Calif.- Santa Barbara, 1957, Ph.D., 1981; M.A. in Psychology, San Francisco State Coll., 1971. Zoologist Santa Barbara Cottage Hosp. Research Inst., 1957-71, physiologist, 1971-82, physiologist-psychologist, 1982—; teaching asst. dept. psychology U. Calif., Santa Barbara, 1976; rev. cons. Nat. Inst. Child Health and Human Devel., 1977. Contbr. articles to profl. jours. Mem. Am. MENSA Selection Assn. Mem. Am. Assn. Cancer Research. Current Work: Steroid hormones and behavior; neuropharmacology of biogenic amines; basic research on metabolism and on carcinogenesis. Subspecialties: Neuroendocrinology; Neuropsychology. Home: 2412 Chapala St Santa Barbara CA 93105 Office: PO Box 689 Santa Barbara CA 93102

BRYSON, REID ALLEN, educator; b. Detroit, June 7, 1920; s. William Riley and Elma (Turner) B.; m. Frances Edith Williamson, June, 13, 1942; children—Anne, William, Robert, Thomas. A.B., Denison U., 1941, D.Sc. (honoris causa), 1971; postgrad., U. Wis., 1941, 46; Ph.D., U. Chgo., 1948. Asst. prof. meteorology and geology U. Wis., 1946-48, asst. prof. meteorology, 1948-50, asso. prof., 1950-56, chmn. dept., 1948-50, 52-54, prof., 1957—; dir. Inst. for Environ. Studies, 1970-85; prof. U. Ariz., 1956-57; Mem. various coms. Nat. Acad. Sci.-NRC, 1958—, mem. remote sensing com., 1964-67, mem. com. on mil. geography, 1966-69; mem. (Smithsonian Council), 1976-79; sr. cons. (UN Environ. Programme), 1975-78; Trustee Univ. Corp. for Atmospheric Research. Author: Atlas of 500 mb Wind Characteristics for the Northern Hemisphere, 1958, Atlas of Five-Day Normal Sea-Level Pressure Charts for the Northern Hemisphere, 1958, Atlas of 300 mb Wind Characteristics, 1959; Editor: (with F.K. Hare) Climates of North America, 1974, Climates of Hunger, 1977 (Banta medal 1978); Contbr. articles to profl. jours. Cited by Denison U., 1966. Fellow Am. Meteorol. Soc., Explorers Clubs, Wis. Acad. Scis., Arts and Letters (past pres.); mem. Wis. Phenological Soc. (past pres.), Soc. Am. Archaeology, Assn. Am. Geographers, Arts and Letters (pres. 1981), Phi Beta Kappa, Sigma Xi, Phi Kappa Phi (hon.). Application of climatology to archaeol. problems; regional and global climatic modification; climatic changes and world food supply; interdisciplinary environmental studies. Current Work: Year-or-more-in-advance climate forecasting; paleo climatology. Subspecialty: Climatology. Home: 11 Rosewood Circle Madison WI 53711

BUBE, RICHARD HOWARD, materials scientist; b. Providence, Aug. 10, 1927; s. Edward Neser and Ella Elvira (Baltteim) B.; m. Betty Jane Meeker, Oct. 9, 1948; children: Mark Timothy, Kenneth Paul, Sharon Elizabeth, Meryl Lee. Sc.B., Brown U., 1946; M.A., Princeton U., 1948, Ph.D., 1950. Mem. sr. research staff RCA Labs., Princeton, N.J., 1948-62; prof. materials sci. and elec. engring. Stanford U., 1962—, chmn. dept., 1975—; cons. to industry and govt. Author: A Textbook of Christian Doctrine, 1955, Photoconductivity of Solids, 1960, The Encounter Between Christianity and Science, 1968, The Human Quest: A New Look at Science and Christian Faith, 1971, Electronic Properties of Crystalline Solids, 1974, Electrons in Solids, 1981, Fundamentals of Solar Cells, 1983, Science and the Whole Person, 1985; also articles; editor: Jour. Am. Sci. Affiliation, 1969-83; editorial bd.: Solid State Electronics; asso. editor: Ann. Rev. Materials Sci., 1969-83, Materials Letters. Fellow Am. Phys. Soc., AAAS, Am. Sci. Affiliation; mem. Am. Soc. Engring. Edn., Internat. Solar Energy Soc., Sigma Xi. Evangelical. Current Work: Solid state physics; photo electronic materials and devices with particular attention to semiconductor junction conversion of solar energy into electricity. Subspecialties: Semiconductors; Electronic materials. Home: 753 Mayfield Ave Stanford CA 94305 Office: Dept Materials Sci and Engring Stanford Univ Stanford CA 94305

BUBENZER, GARY DEAN, agricultural engineering educator; b. Bicknell, Ind., Aug. 21, 1940; s. Ernest and Nelda (Tellingman) B.; m. Sandra Lee Capehart, June 10, 1962; children—Nathan E., Brian P. A.B., Vincinnes U., 1960; B.S., Purdue U., 1962, M.S., 1964; Ph.D., U. Ill., 1970. Registered profl. engr., Wis. Instr., U. Ill., Urbana, 1964-69; asst. prof. agrl. engring. U. Wis., Madison, 1969-74, assoc. prof., 1974-79, prof., 1979—, chmn. agrl. engring., 1983—. Contbr. articles to profl. jours. Japan Soc. Promotion Sci. vis. scholar, 1981; recipient Alumni citation Vincennes U., 1984, Outstanding Instr. award Coll. Agrl. and Life Scis. U. Wis., 1983. Mem. Am. Soc. Agrl. Engrs. (chmn. soil and water div. 1983-84), Am. Soc. Engring. Edn. Methodist. Current work: Soil and water conservation engineering. Subspecialty: Agricultural engineering. Home: 5105 Sherwood Rd Madison WI 53711 Office: Dept Agrl Engring U Wis Madison WI 53706

BUCHANAN, JUDITH ANN, dentist, educator; b. Akron, Ohio, Aug. 19, 1946; d. Henry and Geraldine Elizabeth (Telford) Musch; m. Minor Ferris Buchanan, Feb. 5, 1983; 1 dau., Holly Dean. B.S., Ga. So. U., 1970; M.S., U. Tex.-Houston, 1973, Ph.D., 1975; D.M.D., U. Fla., 1980. Postdoctoral fellow U. Fla., Gainesville, 1975-77; asst. prof. restorative dentistry U. Miss., Jackson, 1981—. Capt., Army N.G., 1982—. NIH fellow U. Fla., 1977; NIH grantee U. Miss., 1983. Mem. ADA, Assn. Mil. Surgeons U.S., Omicron Kappa Upsilon (sec. 1981-84). Current work: Phenytoin-induced gingival overgrowth. Subspecialties: Periodontics; Cell and tissue culture. Home: 1806 Hillview Dr Jackson MS 39211 Office: U Miss 2500 N State Jackson MS 39216

BUCHANAN, PAUL, physician. Head biomed. office John F. Kennedy Space Ctr., Fla. Recipient Jeffries Med. Research award AIAA, 1983. Subspecialty: Space medicine. Office: John F Kennedy Space Ctr Biomed Office FL 32899

BUCHANAN, ROBERT ALEXANDER, pediatrician, clinical researcher; b. Detroit, Sept. 8, 1932; s. Alexander Duncan and Genevieve (Hodgson) B.; m. Jeannine Duffell, Jan. 6, 1962; children—Lawrence, Elizabeth Gregory. M.D., U. Mich., 1957. Diplomate Am. Bd. Pediatrics. Intern, Phila. Gen. Hosp., 1957-58; resident in pediatrics U. Mich. Med. Ctr., 1960-62; practice medicine specializing in pediatrics, Ann Arbor, Mich., 1962-66; med. investigator dept. clin. investigation Parke, Davis & Co. subs Warner-Lambert Co., Ann Arbor, 1966-67, asst. dir. clin. therapeutics dept. clin. investigation, 1967-68, assoc. dir., 1969-74, dir., 1974-83, v.p. clin. research, 1983—; dir. Guthrie Clinic Research Found., 1968-79. Contbr. articles to profl. publs. Mem. bd. ushers First Presbyn. Ch., Ann Arbor, 1969—, elder, 1980—; mem. exec. council Wolverine council Boy Scouts Am., 1976—; mem. com. Young Life of Ann Arbor, 1982—; past pres. Bader Sch. PTO. Served to capt. USAF, 1958-60. Mem. Washtenaw County Med. Soc., Mich. State Med. Soc., AMA, Am. Acad. Pediatrics, Am. Therapeutic Soc., Alpha Omega Alpha. Republican. Clubs: Barton Boat (Ann Arbor), Racquet of Ann Arbor. Lodge: Rotary. Current work: Conduct human testing of new drugs with special interest in infectious diseases; responsible for introducing antiviral chemotherapy to medical practice. Subspecialties: Clinical research; Pharmacology. Home: 3045 Foxcroft Ann Arbor MI 48104 Office: Warner Lambert Co 2800 Plymouth Rd Ann Arbor MI 48105

BUCHHOLZ, DONNA MARIE, microbiologist, immunologist; b. Chgo., May 27, 1950; d. Arthur George and Doris Hedwig (Lewis) B.; m. William E. Hourigan, Oct. 12, 1974. B.S., Quincy (Ill.) Coll., 1972; M.S. in Microbiology-Immunology, U. Ill.-Chgo., 1975, Ph.D. in Microbiology-Immunology, 1978. Postdoctoral research scientist div. biol. and med. research Argonne (Ill.) Nat. Lab., 1978-80; research info. scientist pharm. products div. Abbott Labs., Abbott Park, Ill., 1980-82, project mgr. research mgmt. and devel., 1980—; mem. faculty Northeastern Ill. U., Chgo., 1985-86. Contbr. articles to profl. jours. Mem. nat. sci. and engring. exploring com., exploring div. Boy Scouts Am. Recipient research award Sigma Xi, 1978. Mem. Soc. Indsl. Microbiology, Ill. Soc. Microbiology (councilor exec. com.), AAAS, Am. Soc. Microbiology, Am. Assn. Immunologists, Sigma Xi. Current Work: New drug discovery and development; microbiology, infectious diseases, immunology, health services, environl Toxicology, hematology. Subspecialties: Allergy; Immunology (medicine). Home: 451 Highland Ave West Chicago IL 60185 Office: Abbott Labs Abbott Park IL 60064

BUCHMAN, RUSSELL, chemist; b. N.Y.C., Dec. 19, 1947; s. Charles Joseph and Pauline Diana (Bernstein) B.; m. Diane Ellen Dorfman, June 28, 1970; children—Joshua Paul, Matthew Scott. B.A., SUNY-Buffalo, 1969; Ph.D., Purdue U., 1973. Research assoc. U. Kans., Lawrence, 1973-75; research chemist Diamond Shamrock Corp., Painesville, Ohio, 1975-78, sr. research chemist, 1978-79, research supr., 1979-82, group leader, 1982-83; group leader SDS Biotech Corp., Painesville, 1983—. Patentee in field. Am. Found. Pharm. Edn. fellow, 1971-72, Purdue U. Research Found. fellow, 1972-73. Mem. Am. Chem. Soc. (sec. Northeast Ohio sect. 1978-80), Phi Lambda Upsilon, Rho Chi. Current work: Analytical services for agricultural chemical and animal health care products, including liquid chromatography, gas chromatography, and spectroscopy (nuclear magnetic resonance, mass spectrometry, infra-red and ultra-violet). Subspecialties: Organic chemistry; Synthetic chemistry. Home: 178 Willobend Dr Madison OH 44057 Office: SDS Biotech Corp PO Box 348 Painesville OH 44077

BUCHSBAUM, DONALD JAY, cancer immunology researcher, educator; b. N.Y.C., Mar. 27, 1945; s. Milton Buchsbaum and Estelle (Cherkos) Rapoport; children—Donelle, Lisa. B.S., Carnegie Inst. Tech., 1967; M.S., U. Rochester, 1970, Ph.D., 1972. Tchg. asst. U. Rochester, N.Y., 1967-69; research asst. U. Minn., Mpls., 1972-74, instr., 1972-75, asst. prof., 1975—, admin. asst., 1975—; adj. asst. prof. Emory U., Atlanta, 1983—; cons. Med. Research Found., Inc., Atlanta, 1983—. Grantee NIH Nat. Cancer Inst. Mem. AAAS, Soc. Nuclear Medicine, Am. Assn. Cancer Research, N.Y. Acad. Scis., Soc. Exptl. Biology and Medicine. Jewish. Current work: Radiolabeled antibody tumor localization and therapy. Subspecialties: Cancer research (medicine); Nuclear medicine. Home: 6016 Eden Prairie Rd Minnetonka MN 55345 Office: Univ Minn Box 494 Univ Hosps 420 Deleware St SE Minneapolis MN 55455

BUCHTEL, HENRY AUGUSTUS, IV, psychologist, researcher; b. Denver, Nov. 29, 1942; s. Henry Augustus III and Kathrina Holland (Van Wagenen) B.; m. Evelyn Margaret Evans, Aug. 29, 1975; children—Emma Ellen Kathrina, Henry Augustus V. B.A., Dartmouth Coll., 1964; M.A., McGill U., 1965, Ph.D., 1969. Research fellow U. Pisa, Italy, 1969-72; neuropsychologist Nat. Hosp. for Neurological Diseases, London, 1972-75; research fellow U. Parma, Italy, 1975-78, Montreal Neurological Inst., Que., Can., 1978-80; assoc. prof. psychology U. Mich., Ann Arbor, 1981—; psychologist VA Med. Ctr., Ann Arbor, 1980—. Editor: The Conceptual Nervous System, 1982; mem. editorial bd. Cortex jour., 1983—; contbr. sci. articles to profl. jours. Mem. Am. Psychol. Assn., Neurosci. Soc., Internat. Neuropsychology Symposium, Internat. Brain Research Orgn., Sigma Xi. Current work: Biological basis of mind, especially localization of mental functions. Subspecialties: Neuropsychology; Psychobiology. Office: VA Med Ctr 2215 Fuller Rd Ann Arbor MI 48105

BUCHWALD, HENRY, surgeon, educator; b. June 21, 1932; m. Emilie D. Bix, June 6, 1954; children: Jane Nicole, Amy Elizabeth, Claire Gretchen, Dana Alexandra. B.A. summa cum laude, Columbia U., 1954, M.D., 1957; M.S., U. Minn., 1966, Ph.D. in Surgery, 1966. Diplomate: Am. Bd. Surgery. Intern in surgery Columbia Presbyn. Med. Ctr., N.Y.C., 1957-58; resident in surgery U. Minn. Hosp., 1960-66; instr. in surgery U. Minn. Med. Sch., 1966-67, asst. prof. surgery, 1967-70, assoc. prof. surgery, 1970-77, prof. surgery, 1977—, prof. biomed. engring., 1977—; established investigator Am. Heart Assn., 1964-69. Mem. editorial bd.: Jour. Clin. Surgery. Served to capt. SAC USAF, 1958-60. Helen Hay Whitney fellow, 1962-64; Found. for Allergic Diseases fellow, 1956; recipient Essay prize Am. Coll. Chest Physicians, 1957; Shering award, 1957; 1st Clin. Research award Minn. Surg. Soc., 1965; 1st prize research forum Am. Coll. Chest Physicians, 1966; Samuel D. Gross award, 1969; Disting. Service award Am. Assn. Acad. Surgery, 1976. Fellow Am. Surg. Assn., ACS, Soc. Univ. Surgeons, Central Surg. Assn. (chmn. program com.), Assn. for Acad. Surgery, Am. Heart Assn., Am. Coll. Cardiology, Soc. for Surgery of Alimentary Tract, Am. Therapeutic Assn.; mem. Minn. Surg. Assn., Mpls. Surg. Assn., Minn. Heart Assn., Am. Assn. History of Medicine, Saint Paul Surg. Soc. (hon.), AAAS, Paleopathology Club, Hennepin County Med. Assn., Minn. State Med. Assn., Am. Coll. Nutrition (chmn. surgery council), Am. Soc. Artificial Internal Organs (program com.), Internat. Study Group on Diabetes Treatment with Implantable Insulin Delivery Devices (sec.-gen.), Phi Beta Kappa, Alpha Omega Alpha, Phi Lambda Upsilon. Current Work: Implantable infusion devices; lipid metabolism; obesity surgery. Subspecialties: Surgery; Biomedical engineering. Office: Minn Sch Medicine Minneapolis MN 55455

BUCHWALD, JENNIFER SULLIVAN, neurophysiologist, neuroscience educator; b. Okla., Oct. 20, 1930; A.B., Lindenwood Coll., 1951; Ph.D., Tulane U., 1959; LL.D. (hon.) Lindenwood Coll., 1970. Prof. physiology Univ. Calif. Med. Center, Los Angeles, 1973—, assoc. dir. brain research inst., 1978—; mem. programs adv. com. NIH, 1982—, bd. sci. counselors NIH, 1977-81. Contbr. articles to profl. jours. Mem. Neuroscience Soc. (treas. 1975-77), Physiology Soc., Assn. Acad. Women (pres. 1983-84). Current work: Auditory information processing in CNS, auditory evoked potentials, vocalization in infants. Subspecialties: Neurophysiology; Electrophysiology. Office: Univ Calif Med Ctr Dept Physiology Los Angeles CA 90024

BUCK, OTTO, materials science and engineering educator; b. Stuttgart, Fed. Republic Germany, May 14, 1933; came to U.S., 1964, naturalized, 1983; s. Otto and Klara (Haeberlein) B.; married; children—Bettina, Stefanie. B.S., U. Stuttgart, 1956, M.S., 1959, Ph.D., 1961. Research fellow Max-Planck Inst., Stuttgart, 1961-64; mem. tech. staff Rockwell Internat., Thousand Oaks, Calif., 1964-66, Siemens, Munich, Fed. Republic Germany, 1966-68; group mgr. Rockwell Internat., 1968-80; prof., sr. scientist Iowa State U., Ames, 1980—. Editor: Electron and Positron Spectroscopy, 1979; Nondestructive Evaluation, 1981; Ultrasonic Fatigue, 1982; Nondestructive Evaluation, 1984. Mem. Am. Phys. Soc., AIME, ASTM, Materials Research Soc. Republican. Lodge: Lions (bd. dirs. 1984). Current work: Mechanical metallurgy and nondestructive evaluation for materials reliability. Subspecialties: Metallurgy; Acoustical engineering. Home: 1315 Big Bluestem Ct Ames IA 50010 Office: Iowa State U Ames Lab Ames IA 50011

BUCK, ROSS WORKMAN, communication sciences and psychology educator; b. Sewickley, Pa., Aug. 16, 1941; s. Ross Workman and Ruth (Hadley) B.; m. Marianne Jenney, Dec. 28, 1963; children; William, Maria, Jenney, Theodore. B.A., Allegheny Coll., 1963; M.A., U. Wis., Madison, 1965; Ph.D., U. Pitts., 1970. Research assoc. U. Pitts. Med. Sch., 1967-70; asst. prof. Carnegie-Mellon U., Pitts., 1970-74; asst. prof. U. Conn., Storrs, 1974-76, assoc. prof., 1976-81, prof. communication sciences and psychology, 1981—; vis. scholar dept. psychology Harvard U., Cambridge, Mass., 1980-81; vis. scholar aphasia research unit Boston VA Hosp., 1980-81. Author: Human Motivation and Emotion, 1976, The Communication of Emotion, 1984; editor: (with P. Blanck and R. Rosenthal) Nonverbal Communication in the Clinical Context, 1985; mem. editorial bd.: Jour. Personal and Social Psychology, 1981—, Jour. Nonverbal Behavior, 1978—, Brit. Jour. Social Psychology, 1984—. Chmn. social action community of reconciliation University and City Ministries, Pitts., 1970-74. NIMH grantee, 1972, 85. Mem. Am. Psychol. Assn., Internat. Communication Assn., Eastern Psychol. Assn., Midwestern Psychol. Assn., Internat. Soc. Research on Emotion, Internat. Soc. Research on Aggression, Soc. Exptl. Social Psychology. Democrat. Current Work: Neural bases of the communication of emotion; social learning and temperament in emotional development and education, emotion, communication, stress and disease; cross-cultural nonverbal communication. Subspecialties: Social psychology; Neuropsychology. Home: 64 Cedar Swamp Rd Storrs CT 06268 Office: Department Communication Sciences U-85 University of Connecticut Storrs CT 06268

BUCKLEY, JOSEPH JOHN, analytical chemist; b. Saginaw, Mich., Sept. 26, 1956; s. Albert Francis and Mary Louise (Bloom) B. B.S., Central Mich. U., 1980. Analytical chemist Total Petroleum Inc., Alma, Mich., 1979-83; analytical chemist, cons. Core Labs., Long Beach, Calif., 1984—. Contbr. articles to profl. jours. Mem. Am. Chem. Soc. Current work: Mass spectrometry; characterization of resids in the petroleum industry. Home: 9743 Glasgow Pl #7 Los Angeles CA 90045 Office: Core Labs Inc 3700 Cherry Ave Long Beach CA 90807

BUCKLEY, JOSEPH PAUL, pharmacologist, educator, univ. dean; b. Bridgeport, Conn., Jan. 12, 1924; m. Shirley Elizabeth Shipman, Aug. 16, 1947. B.S., U. Conn., 1949; M.S., Purdue U., 1951, Ph.D., 1952. Asst. prof. pharmacology U. Pitts., 1952-55, assoc. prof., 1955-58, prof., chmn. dept., 1958-73, assoc. dean Sch. Pharmacy, 1969-73; prof. pharmacology U. Houston, 1973—, dean Coll. Pharmacy, 1973—; dir. U. Houston Inst. for Cardiovascular Studies, 1973—; hon. prof. San Carlos U., Guatemala City, Guatemala, 1967; trustee U.S. Pharmacopeial Conv., 1985—. Author: (with Ferrario) Central Actions of Angiotensin and Related Hormones, 1977, Central Nervous System Mechanisms in Hypertension, 1981; contbr. over 200 articles to sci. publs. Served to 2d lt. USAAF, 1943-45. Decorated Air medal with oak leaf clusters; recipient honors achievement award Angiology Research Found., 1965, Disting. Alumnus award Purdue U. Sch. Pharmacy, 1984; Am. Found. for Pharm. Edn. fellow, 1950-52; numerous grants NIH, Dept. Def., pharm. industry, 1955—. Mem. Am. Heart Assn. (council for high blood pressure research), Soc. Exptl. Biology and Medicine, Acad. Pharm. Scis., Am. Pharm. Assn. (Eli Lilly award in pharmacodynamics 1966), Am. Soc. Pharmacology and Exptl. Therapeutics, N.Y. Acad. Scis., Sigma Xi. Methodist. Clubs: University (Pitts.); Warwick (Houston). Current Work: Central nervous system actions of angiotensin with emphasis on relationship to hypertension; mechanisms of action of antihypertensive compounds, vasodilators and antiarrhythmic compounds. Subspecialty: Pharmacology. Home: 13714 Pebble Brook Houston TX 77079 Office: Coll Pharmacy U Houston 139 SR-2 Houston TX 77004

BUCKMAN, A(LVIN) BRUCE, electrical engineering educator, optical electronics consultant; b. Omaha, Dec. 7, 1941; s. Alvin J. and Clara (Lauritsen) B.; m. Carole M. Duncan, June 11, 1966; children—Jacqueline, Jill. B.S., MIT, 1964; M.S., U. Nebr., 1966, Ph.D., 1968. Assoc. prof. elec. engring., U. Nebr., Lincoln, 1973-74; U. Tex., Austin, 1974—. Contbr. articles to profl. jours. Grantee NSF, Office Naval Research, Dept. Defense, 1962-82. Mem. Am. Phys. Soc., Optical Soc. Am. Current work: Simulation and modeling of guided-wave optical devices and systems for sensors and communications. Subspecialties: Fiber optics; Semiconductors. Home: 1800 Brookhaven Dr Austin TX 78704 Office: Elec Engring Dept U Tex Austin TX 78712

BUCKMAN, MAIRE TULTS, medical educator, researcher, physician; b. Tartu, Estonia, Sept. 25, 1939; came to U.S., 1949, naturalized, 1954; d. Harald and Kate (Gaag) T.; div.; children: James Harold, Sabrina Ellen. M.D., U. Wash., 1966. Diplomate: Nat. Bd. Med. Examiners; lic. physician, N. Mex. Rotating intern Santa Clara Hosp., San Jose, Calif., 1966-67; resident in endocrinology and metabolism Sch. Medicine, U. N. Mex., Albuquerque, 1971-72, NIH spl. fellow, 1972-74, instr. medicine, 1973-74, asst. prof., 1974-80, assoc. prof., 1980—; chief endocrinology and metabolism, dir. Radioimmunoassay Lab., VA Med. C., Albuquerque, 1980—. Contbr. articles to med. jours. Mem., active speaker Physicians for Social Responsibility, Albuquerque, 1982—. Served as capt. M.C. U.S. Army, 1966-68. Irwin Collison scholar, 1965; VA Career Devel. Program awardee, 1974-80; VA Merit Rev. awardee, 1980-82. Mem. ACP, Am. Fedn. Clin. Research (counselor 1977-80), Endocrine Soc., Western Soc. Clin. Research, Pacific Coast Fertility Soc., West Coast Endocrine Club (chmn. Carmel, Calif. 1978). Current Work: Prolactin physiology and pathophysiology with special interest in prolactin role in regulation of blood pressure and renal function and its effect on psychological well-being in humans. Subspecialties: Neuroendocrinology; Psychopharmacology. Home: 2415 Vista Larga Albuquerque NM 87106 Office: University of New Mexico School of Medicine 2211 Lomas St NE Albuquerque NM 87106

BUCKMAN, ROBERT WILLIAM, clinical pharmacologist; b. Detroit, Dec. 23, 1939; s. Raymond Roy and Mary (Lega) B.; m. Mary Anne Schubert, Aug. 5, 1967; children—Kenneth Robert, Thomas Robert. B.S. in Chemistry, B.S. in Biology, U. Detroit, 1961; Ph.D., Loyola U., Chgo., 1974. Predoctoral fellow USPHS, Chgo., 1970-72; med. scholar U.S. Navy, Chgo., 1972-74; fellow in perinatal medicine Mead Johnson, Chgo., 1974-75; corp. clin. pharmacologist Sieber & McIntyre, Chgo., 1975—, dir. med. affairs, 1978—, sr. v.p., dir. med. affairs, 1982—; health officer Dept. Health, Bellwood, Ill., 1968-72; clin. pharmacology trainee Loyola U. Stritch Sch. Medicine, Chgo., 1972-74; cons. FDA, Chgo., 1972—; vis. clin. faculty Northwestern U., Chgo., 1977—. Editor Medicine Illustrated, 1983; contbr. articles to profl. jours. Mem. tech. adv. council State of Ill. Div. Food and Drugs, Springfield, 1980—; chmn. clin. pharmacology adv. panel Ill. Dept. Pub. Aid, Springfield, 1980—; mem. scholars selection com. Evans Scholars Found. Western Golf Assn. Served to lt. comdr. USN, 1975-77. Schmidt Scholar Loyola Stritch Sch. Medicine, Chgo., 1971-72; fellow Loyola U., 1972-74. Mem. Am. Soc. Clin. Pharmacology and Therapeutics, Am. Soc. Clin. Oncology, Am. Fedn. Clin. Research, N.Y. Acad. Scis., Sigma Xi. Roman Catholic. Club: Cress Creek Country (Naperville, Ill.). Current work: Clinical pharmacology as it pertains to research and development and marketing as applied to the pharmaceutical industry Subspecialties: Pharmacology; Chemotherapy.

BUCOVAZ, EDSEL T., biochemist; b. Eldorado, Ill., May 8, 1928; s. Antonio and Ardell (Wilson) B.; m. Alma Ruth Hankla, Aug. 8, 1953; children—Tona Dee, Joseph Owen. B.A., So. Ill. U., 1955, M.A., 1957; Ph.D., St. Louis U., 1962. Prof. biochemistry U. Tenn. Ctr. Health Sci., Memphis, 1975—. Mem. editorial bd. Chemico-biol. Interactions, 1969-74; patentee various assays for detection of cancer. Recipient Research award Central Assn. Ob-Gyn, 1977; Alumni Achievement award So. Ill. U., 1978. Mem. AAAS, Am. Assn. Cancer Research, Am. Chem. Soc., Southeast Regional Cancer Soc., Am. Assn. Cancer Research, Sigma Xi. Current work: Cancer detection, causation and metastasis; fatty acid metabolism. Subspecialties: Biochemistry (medicine); Cancer research (medicine). Home: 4929 Mockingbird Ln Memphis TN 38117 Office: U Tenn Ctr Health Scis 984 Union Ave Memphis TN 38163

BUDDINGTON, PATRICIA ARRINGTON, aerospace engineer; b. Takoma Park, Md., Dec. 25, 1950; d. Warren and Elsie (Miller) B. B.S. in Aerospace Engring, Northop Inst. Tech., 1973; postgrad space technology, Flas. Inst. Tech., 1982—. With Air Force Systems Command Rocket Propulsion Lab., Edwards AFB, Calif., 1973-78, facility design engr., 1974-76, primary test engr. magneto-plasma-dynamic electric propulsion thrustor-pulsed plasma, 1976-78; with Boeing Aerospace Co., 1979—; test engr. reaction control system, inertial upper stage Cape Canaveral Air Force Sta., Cocoa Beach, Fla., 1981—. Mem. AIAA, Inst. Environ. Scis. (treas. Pacific N.W. chpt. 1981). Current Work: Advanced propulsion/space applications of technology: space industrialization. Subspecialty: Aerospace engineering and technology. Home: 4010 Monterey St Cocoa FL 32927 Office: Boeing Aerospace Co PO Box 220 M/S FC-51 Cocoa Beach FL 32931

BUEHLER, ROBERT JOHN, biochemist; b. Schenectady, Dec. 4, 1947; s. Frederick P. and Frederica R. (Wickert) B.; married; children: Sandra, Robyn. B.S. in Biology, Boston Coll., 1969; M.A. in Biochemistry, Boston U., 1970; Ph.D., 1975. Research asst. Wellesley (Mass.) Coll., 1973-75; cons. toxicologist Leary Clinic Lab., Boston, 1973-75; dir. research and devel. Damon Diagnostics, Needham Heights, Mass., 1975-82; project leader Corning Med. and Sci., East Walpole, Mass., 1982—. Contbr. articles in field to profl. jours. Served with U.S. Army, 1970-72. USPHS fellow, 1969-70. Mem. Am. Assn. Clin. Chemistry, Clin. Ligand Assay Soc., AAAS. Roman Catholic. Current Work: Development of in vitro diagnostic test procedures for use in thyroid and oncological medicine; devel. of hybridoma cell lines for production ofmonoclonal antibodies and cell growth factors. Subspecialties: Immunology (medicine); Cancer research (medicine). Office: 333 Coney St East Walpole MA 02032

BUELOW, FREDERICK HENRY, educator; b. Minot, N.D., Mar. 13, 1929; s. Albert Wilhelm Gustav and Frieda Alvina Adele (Hass) B.; m. Selma Lois Ione Eia, July 21, 1954; children—David Frederick, Diane Louise, Darci Jo, Darin Martin. B.S., N.D. Agrl. Coll., 1951; M.S.E., Purdue U., 1952; Ph.D., Mich. State U., 1956. Faculty agrl. engring. Mich. State U., 1956-66, prof., 1965-66; prof., chmn. dept. agrl. engring. U. Wis.-Madison, 1966-83, prof., 1983—. Served to lt. USAF, 1952-54. NSF grantee, 1963, 69, 70. Fellow Am. Soc. Agrl. Engrs. (Jour. Paper award 1957, dir. 1972-74, 77-79, 85-87), Am. Soc. for Engring. Edn., Sigma Xi, Gamma Sigma Delta. Lutheran. Club:

Kiwanis. Subspecialty: Agricultural engineering. Home: 6401 Landfall Dr Madison WI 53705

BUERGELT, CLAUS DIETMAR, veterinary pathology educator; b. Schmiedeberg, Germany, Sept. 16, 1939; came to U.S., 1972; s. Wilhelm and Elsa (Langer) B.; m. Nancy Kordak, Apr. 12, 1968. D.V.M., Vet. Coll., Hannover, W.Ger., 1965; Ph.D., Cornell U., 1976. Diplomate: Am. Coll. Vet. Pathology. Asst. prof. Yale U., New Haven, 1976-77; assoc. prof. vet. pathology U. Fla., Gainesville, 1978—. Mem. German Vet. Assn., AMVA, Am. Coll. Vet. Pathologists, Internat. Acad. Pathologists, Soc. Environ. Pathologists. Lutheran. Current Work: Bovine paratuberculosis; macrophage phagocytosis and digestion. Subspecialty: Pathology (veterinary medicine).

BUFE, CHARLES GLENN, geophysicist, researcher; b. Duluth, Minn., Jan. 2, 1938; s. Bancroft Washington and Margaret (Lesperance) B.; m. Jacquelyn Claire Abbott, Nov. 18, 1967; children—Glennica, Sierra, Nathaniel. B.S. in Engring., Mich. Technol. U., 1960, M.S. in Geophysics, 1962; Ph.D. in Geology, U. Mich., 1969. Registered geophysicist, Calif. Assoc. research geophysicist U. Mich., Ann Arbor, 1967-69; research geophysicist NOAA Earthquake Lab., San Francisco, 1969-72; vis. asst. prof. U. Wis.-Milw., 1973; geophysicist (seismology) U.S. Geol. Survey, Menlo Park, Calif., 1973-80, Reston, Va., 1980-85, Golden, Colo., 1985—; geothermal liaison to Dept. Energy, Washington, 1980-83; earthquake liaison to Fed. Emergency Mgmt. Agy., Washington, 1983-84. Contbr. articles to profl. jours. Served to lt. NOAA Corps., 1964-66. NSF fellow, 1960-63. Mem. Am. Geophys. Union, Seismol. Soc. Am., Soc. Exploration Geophysicists, Geothermal Resources Council, Earthquake Engring. Research Inst. Current work: Earthquake recurrence and prediction; triggering of earthquakes and volcanic eruptions; seismic risk. Subspecialties: Seismology; Geophysics. Home: 11697 Coal Creek Hts Dr Golden CO 80403 Office: Box 25046 MS 966 Denver Fed Center Denver CO 80225

BUFF, JAMES STEVE, research scientist; b. Lincolnton, N.C., Nov. 2, 1947; s. Clee Howard and Pauline Susan (Hovis) B.; m. Margaret Anne LeClair, Jan. 2, 1982. B.S. in Physics, U.N.C., Chapel Hill, 1969; Ph.D. in Physics, U. colo., Boulder, 1974. Research scientist Mass. Inst. Tech., 1974-76; research scientist IBM Watson Research Center, Yorktown Heights, N.Y., 1976-78; vis. asst. prof. Dartmouth Coll., 1978-80; research scientist Mission Research Corp., Albuquerque, 1980—. Contbr. articles to sci. jours. Mem. Am. Astronom. Soc., Am. Phys. Soc., Internat. Astronom. Union, Phi Beta Kappa. Current Work: Inertial fusion. Subspecialties: Plasma physics; X-ray high energy astrophysics. Office: 1720 Randolph Rd SE Albuquerque NM 87106

BUFFINGTON, JOHN DOUGLAS, research and development administrator, ecologist; b. Jersey City, Nov. 26, 1941; s. John Franklin and Rosemary Eileen (Snowdy) B.; m. Mary Elizabeth Coughlin, Jan. 15, 1965; children—Jill Anne, John Matthew. B.S., St. Peter's Coll., 1963; M.S., U. Ill., 1965, Ph.D., 1967. Cert. Am. Registry Profl. Entomologists. Asst. prof. Ill. State U., Normal, 1969-72; mem. staff, asst. div. dir. Argonne Nat. Lab., Ill., 1972-77; sr. staff, staff Council on Environ. Quality, Washington, 1977-80; chief Office of Biol. Services U.S. Fish & Wildlife Service, Washington, 1980-82, dept. assoc. dir. research and devel., 1982—; dir. WAEPA, Falls Church, Va., 1983—. Served to capt. U.S. Army, 1967-69. Mem. Ecol. Soc. Am. (chmn. applied ecology sect. 1983-85, chmn. Washington chpt. 1984-85. Roman Catholic. Current work: Management of a research organization dealing with the nations' fish and wildlife resources. Subspecialties: Resource management; Ecology (environmental science). Home: 6009 Dewey Dr Alexandria VA 22310 Office: DDR/US Fish and Wildlife Service/Dept Interior Washington DC 20240

BUFFORD, RODGER KEITH, psychology educator, clinical psychologist; b. Santa Rosa, Calif., Dec. 23, 1944; s. John Samuel and Evelyn (Rude) B.; m. Kathleen A. Parson, Aug 17, 1968; children: Heather, Brett. B.A., King's Coll., 1966; M.A., U. Ill.-Urbana, 1970, Ph.D., 1971. Lic. psychologist, Va., Oreg. Asst. prof. Am. U., 1971-76; asst. prof. chmn. dept. psychology Huntington Coll., 1976-77; assoc. prof., dir. clin. tng. Psychol. Studies Inst., 1977-81; psychologist Atlanta Counseling Center, 1980-82; assoc. prof. psychology, chmn. dept. psychology Western Sem., 1982—; allied health profl. Portland Adventist Med. Ctr., 1984—, Cedar Hills Hosp., 1984—; bd. dirs. Mental Health Assn., Huntington, Ind., 1976-77. Author: The Human Relfex: Behavioral Psychology in Biblical Perspective, 1981; contbr. articles to profl. jours.; contbr. Baker's Ency. of Psychology, 1985; contbg. editor: Jour. Psychology and Christianity, 1979—; cons. reviewer: Jour. Psychology and Theology, 1974-81; contbg. editor, 1982—; cons. reviewer jours., pubs., Elder Chapel Woods Presbyterian Ch., Decatur, Ga., 1982-83. USPHS trainee, 1967-68, 70-71; Am. U. Faculty research grantee, 1972. Mem. Christian Assn. Psychol. Studies (program chmn. 1982), Am. PSychol. Assn., Am. Sci. Affiliation, Midwestern Psychol. Assn., Western Psychol. Assn. Republican. Current Work: Behavioral psychology and biblical principles; psychology of religion; measurement of religious variables; training in psychology and religious perspectives. Subspecialties: Behavioral psychology; Psychology and religion. Home: 19504 Hidden Springs Rd West Linn OR 97068 Office: Dept Psychology Western Sem 5511 SE Hawthorne Blvd Portland OR 97215

BUJTAS, MARK STEVEN, mechanical engineer; b. Princeton, N.J., Aug. 24, 1952; s. Andrew E. and Anneliese (Kindler) B.; m. Cornelia E., Sept. 7, 1980. B.S.M.E., Newark Coll. Engring., 1974. Asst. engr. U.S. Machine Co., Cedar Grove, N.J., 1974-75; project engr. Fluorocarbon, Pine Brook, N.J., 1975-77, chief engr., 1977-83; v.p. Bermag Corp. Internat., 1983—. Mem. ASME (asso.), Soc. Mfg. Engrs. (cert. mfg. engr.), Am. Concrete Inst. (bearing systems com.), ASTM (subcom. on bridges and structures, bridge-bearing com.). Current Work: Low-friction structural expansion bearings using resin teflon and woven teflon, particularly for use in pot bearings, spherical bearings, and elastomeric backed slide bearings; full computerization for design and manufacture of structural bearings. Subspecialties: Mechanical engineering; Materials. Office: 18 Commerce Rd Fairfield NJ 07006

BUKOVAC, MARTIN J., horticulture educator; b. Johnson City, Ill., Nov. 12, 1929; m. Judith Ann Kelley; 1 child, Janice Louise. B.S. with honors, Mich. State U., 1951, M.S., 1954, Ph.D., 1957; postdoctoral, Oxford and Bristol Univs., 1965-66. Asst. prof. horticulture Mich. State U., East Lansing, 1957-61, assoc. prof., 1961-63, prof., 1963—; cons., lectr., examiner and researcher in field. Contbr. articles to profl. jours. Patentee in field. Served with U.S. Army, 1951-53. William and Sarah E. Hinman scholar, 1950; NSF sr. postdoctoral fellow, 1965; recipient numerous awards for excellence in horticulture. Fellow AAAS, Am. Soc. Hort. Sci. (pres. 1974-75); mem. Nat. Acad. Scis., Am. Hort. Soc., Am. Soc. Plant Physiologists, Botanical Soc. Am., Soc. Exptl. Biology, Internat. Soc. Hort. Sci., Scandinavian Soc. Plant Physiology, Japanaese Soc. Plant Physiologists, Sigma Xi (past pres.), Phi Kappa Phi. Subspecialty: Horticulture. Office: Dept Horticulture Mich State U East Lansing MI 48823

BUKRY, J(OHN) DAVID, geologist; b. Balt., May 17, 1941; s. Howard Leroy and Irene Evelyn (Davis) Snyder. Student, Colo. Sch. Mines, 1959-60; B.A., Johns Hopkins U., 1963; M.A., Princeton U., 1965, Ph.D., 1967; postgrad., U. Ill., 1965-66. Geologist U.S. Army Corp. Engrs., Balt., 1963; research asst. Mobil Oil Co., Dallas, 1965; geologist U.S. Geol. Survey, La Jolla, Calif., 1967-84; geologist U.S. Minerals Mgmt. Service, La Jolla, Calif., 1984—; research assoc. dept. geol. research div. U. Calif.-San Diego, 1970—; cons. Deep Sea Drilling Project, La Jolla, 1967—. Author: Leg I of the Cruises of the Drilling Vessel Glomar Challenger, 1969, Coccoliths from Texas and Europe, 1969, Leg LXIII of the Cruises of the Drilling Vessel Glomar Challenger, 1981; editor: Marine Micropaleontology, 1976-83; mem. editorial bd. Micropaleontology, 1985—. Mobil Oil, Princeton U. fellow, 1965-67; Am. Chem. Soc., Princeton U. fellow, 1966-67. Fellow AAAS, Geol.Soc. Am., Explorer's Club; mem. Paleontol. Research Inst. (assoc.), Am. Assn. Petroleum Geologists, Sigma Xi. Club: San Diego Shell. Current Work: Defining new species of phytoplankton for chronologic and paleoecologic analysis of ocean strata. Subspecialties: Oceanography, biochronology; Paleontology, paleoecology. Home: 675 S Sierra Ave Solana Beach CA 92075 Office: US Minerals Mgmt Service A015 Scripps Inst Oceanography La Jolla CA 92093

BULGER, ROGER JAMES, university president, physician; b. Bklyn., May 18, 1933; s. William Joseph and Florence Dorothy (Poggi) B.; m. Ruth Ellen Grouse, June 8, 1960; children: Faith Anne, Grace Ellen. A.B., Harvard U., 1955, M.D., 1960; postgrad., Emmanuel Coll., Cambridge (Eng.) U., 1955-56. Intern, resident internal medicine U. Wash. Hosps., 1960-62, 64-65; postgrad. trainee infectious disease and microbiology U. Wash., 1962-63, 65-66; renal and metabolic diseases Boston U., 1963-64; asst. prof., then assoc. prof. medicine U. Wash. Med. Sch., Seattle, 1966-70; med. dir. Univ. Hosp., Seattle, 1967-70; prof. community health scis., asso. dean allied health Duke U. Med. Center, 1970-72; exec. officer Inst. Medicine, Nat. Acad. Scis., 1972-76; prof. internal medicine George Washington U. Sch. Medicine, 1972-76; prof. internal medicine, family and community medicine, dean Med. Sch., chancellor Worcester campus U. Mass., 1976-78; pres. U. Tex. Health Sci. Center, Houston, 1978—; mem. report rev. com. Nat. Acad. Scis.; adv. panel nat. health ins. com., ways and means com. U.S. Ho. Reps., 1975-76. Author: Hippocrates Revisited, 1973, also articles, chpts. in books.; Mem. editorial bds. various jours. Bd. dirs. Georgetown U. Lionel de Jersey Harvard fellow, 1955-56. Fellow A.C.P.; mem. Inst. Medicine, Am. Soc. Microbiology, Infectious Disease Soc. Am., Am. Fedn. Clin. Research, Soc. Tchrs. Preventive Medicine, Am. Soc. Nephrology, Soc. Health and Human Values. Subspecialty: Internal medicine. Office: Office of Pres U Tex Health Sci Center at Houston PO Box 20036 Houston TX 77225

BULKLEY, BERNARDINE HEALY, physician, government executive. Dep. dir. Office of the Sci. Advisor to the Pres., Washington. Subspecialty: Cardiology. Office: Sci Advisor to Pres Old Exec Office Bldg Washington DC 20500*

BULKLEY, GREGORY BARTLETT, general surgeon, scientist, medical educator; b. Spokane, Wash., Apr. 28, 1943; s. George J. and Patricia (Bartlett) B.; m. Bernadine Healy, Aug. 13, 1967 (div. 1982); 1 child, Bartlett Anne. A.B., Princeton U., 1965; M.D., Harvard U., 1970. Diplomate: Am. Bd. Surgery. Intern Johns Hopkins U. Hosp., Balt., 1970-72, resident in surgery, 1974-77, staff, 1978—; mem. faculty Johns Hopkins U. Sch. Medicine, Balt., 1977—, assoc. prof. surgery, 1982—, dir. surgical research, 1982—. Author, editor: Measurement of Blood Flow, 1982; contbr. numerous sci. articles to profl. pubs. Served in USPHS, 1972-74. NSF fellow, 1963; Am. Heart Assn. grantee, 1979; gen. surgeon, scientist, Sadie Hyman Found. grantee, 1979; NIH grantee, 1982—. Fellow ACS; mem. Assn. Acad. Surgery (mem. membership com. 1981-83), Am. Physiol. Assn., Am. Gastroenterol. Assn., Soc. Univ. Surgeons. Current Work: Control of the splanchnic circulation; pathophysiology; diagnosis and treatment of intestinal ischemic disease; conduct primary original research in these conditions - both basic laboratory work and clinical applications and clinical trials; fundamental mechanisms of ischemic tissue injury, free radical chemistry. Subspecialties: Surgery; Physiology (medicine). Office: Johns Hopkins Univ Sch Medicine 600 N Wolfe St Baltimore MD 21205

BULL, BRIAN STANLEY, physician, educator; b. Watford, Hertfordshire, Eng., Sept. 14, 1937; came to U.S., 1954, naturalized, 1960; s. Stanley and Agnes Mary (Murdoch) B.; m. Maureen Hannah Huse, June 3, 1963; children: Beverly Velda, Beryl Heather. B.S. in Zoology, Walla Walla Coll., 1957; M.D., Loma Linda (Calif.) U., 1961. Diplomate: Am. Bd. Pathology. Intern Yale U., 1961-62, resident in anat. pathology, 1962-63; resident in clin. pathology NIH, Bethesda, Md., 1963-65, fellow in hematology and electron microscopy, 1965-66, staff hematologist, 1966-67; research asst. dept. anatomy Loma Linda U., 1958, dept. microbiology, 1959, asst. prof. pathology, 1968-71, assoc. prof., 1971-73, prof., 1973—, chmn. dept. pathology, 1973—; vis. prof. Institut de Pathologie Cellulaire, Paris, 1972, 74, Royal Postgrad. Med. Sch., London, 1972, U. Wis.-Madison, 1973, U. Ohio, Columbus, 1974, U. Minn., Mpls., 1979, U. Hawaii, 1981, St. Thomas Hosp. and Med. Sch., 1981. Bd. editors: Jour. Clin. Lab. Haematology, U.K., Blood, U.S. Editor-in-chief Blood Cells, U.S.; contbr. chpts. to books and numerous articles to med. jours. Served with USPHS, 1963-67. Nat. Inst. Arthritis and Metabolic Diseases fellow, 1967-68; recipient Daniel D. Comstock Meml. award Loma Linda U., 1961, Merck Manual award, 1961, Mosby Scholarship Book award, 1961; Ernest B. Cotlove Meml. lectr. Acad. Clin. Lab. Physicians and Scientists, 1972. Fellow Am. Soc. Clin. Pathologists, Am. Soc. Hematology, Coll. Am. Pathologists, N.Y. Acad. Scis.; mem. AMA, Assn. Pathology Chmn., Calif. Soc. Pathologists, San Bernardino County Med. Soc., Acad. Clin. Lab. Physicians and Scientists, Am. Assn. Pathologists, Sigma Xi, Alpha Omega Alpha. Seventh-day Adventist. Patentee in field. Current Work: Researcher, inventor devices for med. analysis, devel. math. algorithms for quality control, red cell modelling, antocoagulant control and thrombosis prevention. Subspecialties: Hematology; Pathology (medicine). Home: 24489 Barton Rd Loma Linda CA 92354 Office: Department of Pathology and Laboratory Medicine Loma Linda University School of Medicine Loma Linda CA 92350

BULL, COLIN BRUCE BRADLEY, geology educator; b. Birmingham, Eng., June 13, 1928; s. George Ernest and Alice Matilda (Collier) B.; m. Diana Gillian Garrett, June 16, 1956; children—Nicholas, Rebecca, Andrew. B.Sc., Birmingham U., 1948, Ph.D., 1951. Geophysicist later chief scientist Brit. N. Greenland Expdn., 1952-56; sr. lectr. physics Victoria U., Wellington, New Zealand, 1956-61; assoc. prof. geology Ohio State U., Columbus, 1962-65; prof., dir. Inst. Polar Studies, 1965-69, chmn. dept. geology, 1969-72; dean Coll. Math. and Phys. Scis., 1972-85, dean emeritus, 1985—. Vis. fellow geophysics Australian Nat. U., Canberra, 1960; vis. scholar Cambridge (Eng.) U., 1969; vis. prof. Nat. Inst. Polar Research, Tokyo, Japan, 1983; U.S. rep. working group on glaciology Sci. Com. Antarctic Research, 1974—, sec., 1978—. Contbr. articles to profl. jours. Recipient Polar medal Queen Elizabeth, 1954; U.S. Antarctic Service medal, 1974. Fellow Arctic Inst. N. Am. (bd. govs. 1966-72); Fellow Geol. Soc. Am., Royal Soc. Arts; mem. Internat. Glaciology Soc. (council 1974-78), Am. Geophys. Union, Phi Beta Kappa (hon.). Current Work: Stability and dynamics of ice sheets, Antarctica and Greenland. Subspecialties: Geophysics; Glaciology. Home: 9219 SE 33d Pl Mercer Island WA 98040

BULL, LEONARD SETH, animal nutrition educator, researcher; b. Westfield, Mass., Jan. 31, 1941; s. Floyd Milton and Erna Magdaline (Preissler) B.; m. Deborah Carol Stevens, May 22, 1971; 1 child, Seth Tyler. B.S., Okla. State U., 1963, M.S., 1964; Ph.D., Cornell U., 1969. Cert. animal scientist Am. Soc. Animal Sci., 1978. Fellow med. physiology U. Va., 1968-70; asst. prof. nutrition U. Md., 1970-74, assoc. prof., 1974-75; assoc. prof. nutrition U. Ky., 1975-79; prof. U. Maine, 1979-81; prof. animal sci. U. Vt., 1981-, also chmn. dept.; mem. subcoms. Nat. Acad. Scis.; cons. in field. Contbr. numerous articles to profl. jours. Recipient Moorman Internat. Travel award, 1979. Mem. Am. Dairy Sci. Assn., Am. Soc. Animal Sci., Am. Inst. Nutrition. Republican. Methodist. Current Work: Research on nutritional energetics and protein metabolism; teaching in animal sci.; adminstrn. of animal scis. academic program. Subspecialties: Animal nutrition; Nutrition (medicine). Home: 23 Tanglewood Dr Essex Junction VT 05452 Office: 220 Carrigan Hall Vt Burlington VT 05405

BULL, STANLEY RAYMOND, engineer, research administrator; b. Montezuma, Iowa, May 15, 1941; s. Raymond W. and Neola A. B.; m. Diana Lee Maxwell, Sept. 7, 1963; children: Melanie J., Julia D., Jeffrey D. B.S. in Chem. Engring, U. Mo., 1963; M.S., Stanford U., 1964; Ph.D. in Mech. Engring, 1967. Registered profl. engr., Mo. Successively asst. prof., assoc. prof., prof. Coll. Engring., U. Mo., Columbia, 1967-80; Solar Energy Research Inst., Golden, Colo., 1980-81, sr. sci. adviser, 1981-82, mgr. planning and research devel., 1982-84, dep. dir. solar fuels research div., 1984—; Fulbright-Hays prof. Centre d'Etudes, Grenoble, France, 1973-74. Contbr. articles to tech. jours. Mem. Am. Inst. Chem. Engrs., Internat. Am. Solar Energy Soc., Am. Phys. Soc. Current Work: Energy systems and resources; renewable fuel options and processes; evaluation renewable energy technology. Subspecialties: Engineering physics; Solar energy. Office: 1617 Cole Blvd Golden CO 80401

BULLA, LEE AUSTIN, JR., science educator and administrator, industrial consultant and researcher; b. Oklahoma City, May 1, 1941; s. Lee Austin and Ruthie (Pearce) B.; m. Betty Lee Harvison, Sept. 29, 1962; children: Stephen, Susan, Stacey. B.S. in Biology and Math, Midwestern U., 1965; Ph.D. in Microbiology and Biochemistry, Oreg. State U., 1968. Microbiologist and project leader No. Regional Research Lab., Agr. Research Service, U.S. Dept. Agr., Peoria, Ill., 1968-73; microbiologist Kans. State U., Manhattan, 1973-81, prof. div. biology, 1973-81; prof. dept. bacteriology and biochemistry U. Idaho, Moscow, 1981-84; assoc. dean Coll. Agr. and dir. Idaho Agr. Expt. Sta., 1981-84; dir. Inst. Molecular and Agr. Genetic Engring., Idaho, 1981-84; dean Coll. Agr., U. Wyo., 1984—, prof. dept. microbiology and biochemistry, 1984—. Contbr. numerous articles to profl. jours. Bd. dirs. Idaho Research Fdn., 1983. Mem. Am. Soc. Microbiology, AAAS. Lodges: Kiwanis, Rotary. Current Work: Genetic characterization of insecticidal proteins of Bacillus thuringiensis and regulation of protein synthesis in gram-positive bacilli. Subspecialties: Microbiology; Genetics and genetic engineering (agriculture). Home: 3610 Reynolds St Laramie WY 82070 Office: Office of Dean Coll Agr U Wyo Laramie WY 82071

BULLAS, LEONARD RAYMOND, microbiologist, educator, researcher; b. Lismore, New South Wales, Australia, Dec. 8, 1929; s. Raymond and Arum Adelaide (Semmens) B.; m. Rosemary Grace Ekdahl, Nov. 30, 1958; (dec. Feb. 1985); children: Roslyn Mary, Graham Leonard. B.S., U. Adelaide, Australia, 1953, M.S., 1958; Ph.D., Mont. State U., 1962. Teaching asst. U. Adelaide, Australia, 1953-58; research asst. Mont. State U., Bozeman, 1958-62; instr. Loma Linda (Calif.) U., 1962-64, asst. prof., 1964-70, assoc. prof., 1970-80, prof. microbiology, 1980—; vis. prof. European Molecular Biology Lab., Heidelberg, W. Ger., 1981-82; researcher in field; research contract Office Naval Research, 1965-69. Contbr.: articles to profl. publs. including Jour. of General Microbiology. Basic sci. fellow Loma Linda U. Med. Sch. Alumni Assn., 1981; named basic sci. investigator of year, 1975, 81. Mem. Am. Soc. Microbiology, Genetics Soc. Am., Sigma Xi. Seventh-day Adventist. Current Work: Genetics and molecular biology of genes for Salmonella restriction endonucleases. Subspecialties: Genetics and genetic engineering (biology); Genome organization. Office: Dept Microbiology Loma Linda Univ Loma Linda CA 92350

BULLOCK, KEVIN EDWARD, analytical chemist; b. Clifton, N.J., Sept. 16, 1951; s. Edward Fitzgerald and Joan Valerie (Batura) B.; m. Lea Doerr, July 22, 1978. B.S. in Chemistry, Memphis State U., 1973; Ph.D., U. New Orleans, 1978. Sr. analytical chemist Monsanto Research Corp., Dayton, Ohio, 1978-81; research specialist Monsanto Ind. Chem., St. Louis, 1981-82, Monsanto Nutrition Chem., St. Louis, 1982—. Author of more than 70 proprietary analytical methods, 1981—. Mem. Am. Chem. Soc., N.Y. Acad. Scis. Roman Catholic. Current work: The comml. devel. recombinent DNA products, process control through chromatography, raw materials quality control, good lab. practice, good mfg. practice. Subspecialty: Analytical chemistry. Home: 239 Aspen Village Dr Ballwin MO 63011 Office: Monsanto Nutrition Chemicals Div 800 N Lindberch Blvd St Louis MO 63167

BUMP, FREDERICK H., physics and astronomy educator; b. Cambridge, Mass., Aug. 28, 1946; s. William Nelson and Catharine (Richardson) B. B.S., Kenyon Coll., 1969; M.S. in Edn., Colgate U., 1970; postgrad. in Physics, U. Conn. 1983—. Tchr. sci. and math. Bedford Jr. High Sch., Westport, Conn., 1970-81; tchr. physics, astronomy and earth sci. Staples High Sch., Westport, Conn., 1981—; dir. Rolnick Obs., Westport, 1974—; Mem. Am. Assn. Physics Tchrs., Am. Astron. Soc., Am. Astron. League, Westport Astron. Soc. (pres. 1974-79, 81-83). Republican. Current work: Astrophotography of nebulae. Subspecialty: Optical astronomy. Home: 52 Sawyer Rd Fairfield Ct CT 06430

BUNCEL, ERWIN, chemistry educator; b. Presov, Czechoslovakia, May 31, 1931; came to Can., 1962, naturalized, 1971; s. Ignacz and Irene (Sharman) B.; m. Henny Bienenfeld, Dec. 16, 1956; children—Irene, Jacqueline. B.Sc., London U., 1954, Ph.D., 1957, D.Sc., 1970. Research assoc. U. N.C. Chapel Hill, 1957-58; postdoctoral fellow McMaster U., Ont., Can., 1958-60; research chemist Am. Cyanamid Corp., Stamford, Conn., 1960-62; asst. prof. chemistry Queen's U., Kingston, Ont., 1962-66, assoc. prof., 1966-70, prof., 1970—. Author: Carbanions: Mechanisms, 1975; Electron Deficient Aromatics, 1984. Editor: Isotopes in Organic Chemistry, 6 vols., 1975-84. Contbr. numerous articles to sci. jours. Grantee Am. Chem. Soc., 1965, NATO, 1976, Nat. Research Council Can., 1979, Natural Sics. and Engring. Research Council Can., 1985. Fellow Chem. Soc. U.K., Chem. Inst. Can. (treas. 1984—, vice chmn. organic div. 1985, Syntex award 1985); mem. Am. Chem. Soc. Current work: Dynamic organic chemistry, isotope effects, structure and mechanism. Subspecialties: Organic chemistry; Organometallics. Office: Queen's U Chemistry Dept Kingston ON K7L 3N6 Canada

BUNDY, HALLIE FLOWERS, biochemist, educator; b. Santa Monica, Calif., Apr. 2, 1965; d. Douglas and Phyllis (Flowers) B. B.A., Mt. St. Mary's Coll., 1947; M.S., U. So. Calif., 1955, Ph.D. in Biochemistry, 1958. Instr. U. So. Calif. Sch.Medicine, 1959-60; asst. program dir. undergrad. research program NSF, Washington, 1965-66; from asst. prof. to assoc. prof. Mt. St. Mary's Coll., Los Angeles, 1960-65, prof. biochemistry, 1966—. Contbr. articles to profl. jours. USPHS fellow, 1955-58; NSF faculty fellow, 1969; Grad. Women in Sci. Grant-in-Aid awardee, 1974. Mem. Am. Chem. Soc., Pacific Slope Biochem. Conf., AAAS, Grad. Women in Sci., Sigma Xi. Current Work: Comparative biochemistry of algal, higher plant and animal carbonic anhydrases. Subspecialties: Biochemistry (biology); Enzymology. Office: 12001 Chalon Rd Los Angeles CA 90049

BUNDY, WAYNE MILEY, mineralogist; b. Anderson, Ind., Jan. 10, 1924; s. Ernest Frank and Flossie (Miley) B.; m. Lorraine Jerabek, May 7, 1945; children—Mark, Janet, Michael. A.B., Ind. U., 1950, M.A., 1954, Ph.D. in Clay Mineralogy, 1957. Registered profl. geologist, Ga. Geologist, N.Mex. Bur. Mines, Socorro, 1951-53; petrographer Ind. Geol. Survey, Bloomington, Ind., 1953-57; chief mineralogist Ga. Kaolin Co., Elizabeth, N.J., 1957-67, dir. research, 1967-74, v.p. research, Union, N.J., 1974—. Contbr. articles to profl. jours. Patentee in field. Served with USMC, 1943-45. Mem. Clay Minerals Soc. (pres. 1984-85), Am. Mineral. Soc., Am. Chem. Soc., TAPPI. Current work: Clay mineral technology, surface chemistry, rheology. Subspecialty: Mineralogy. Office: Ga Kaolin Research 25 Route 22 E Springfield NJ 07081

BUNGE, CARLOS FEDERICO, physicist, educator; b. Buenos Aires, Mar. 27, 1941; s. Mario Augusto and Julia Delfina (Molina y Vedia) B.; m. Ana Maria Vivier, May 28, 1962; children: Pablo, Veronica, Lucia, Diego. B.Sc. in Chemistry, U. Buenos Aires, 1962; Ph.D. in Chemistry, U. Fla., 1966. Asst. prof. Central U. Venezuela, Caracas, 1968-70; prof. U. Sao Paulo, Sao Carlos, Brazil, 1971-76; sr. theoretical physicist, prof. Nat. U. Mex., 1976—. Guggenheim Meml. fellow, 1981-82. Mem. Am. Phys. Soc., Optical Soc. Am. Patentee in field. Current Work: Computer programs for atomic and molecular electronic structure calculations, atomic spectroscopy, laser physics, chemical structure. Subspecialties: Atomic and molecular physics; Theoretical chemistry. Home: Edificio 29 104 Villa Olimpica Mexico DF 14020 Mexico Office: Instituto de Fisica Apdo 20 364 Mexico 01000 Mexico

BUNGER, ROLF, physiology educator; b. Hamburg, Fed. Republic Germany, Oct. 19, 1941; s. Heinz and Helga (Franz) B.; m. Margriet Akkerman, Dec. 14, 1973; children—Nils, Frank. Dr. Med., U. Heidelberg, 1970, M.D., 1971; Dr. Med. Habil, U. Munich, 1979. Sci. asst. in physiology U. Aachen, Fed. Republic Germany, 1970-74, U. Munich, 1974-79; asst. prof. physiology Uniformed Services U., Bethesda, Md., 1979-82, assoc. prof., 1982—; reviewer sci. manuscripts European Jour. Physiology, 1978—, Am. Jour. Physiol., 1981—, also others. Contbr. articles to profl. jours. Served to capt. Med. Service, Fed. Republic Germany Air Force. Grantee Deutsche Forschungsgemeinschaft, 1978, Uniformed Services U., 1979—, NIH, 1982—, NRC, 1983. Mem. Deutsche Physiologische Gesellschaft, Internat. Study Group for Heart Research, Am. Physiol. Soc., Am. Heart Assn., AAAS. Current work: Regulation of coronary flow in relation to compartments of cardiac adenine nucleotides; regulation of energy-metabolism in oxygen deficient heart; regulation of pyruvate metabolism in physiologically and pathophysiologically performing heart. Subspecialties: Physiology (medicine); Bioenergetics of heart. Home: 2237 Whitcomb Pl Falls Church VA 22046 Office: Dept Physiology Uniformed Services Univ 4301 Jones Bridge Rd Bethesda MD 20814

BUNN, PAUL AXTELL, JR., oncologist; b. N.Y.C., Mar. 16, 1945; s. Paul Axtell and Elizabeth (Maxwell) B.; m. Camille Ann Bunn, Aug. 17, 1968; children: Rebecca, Kristen, Paul. B.S., Amherst (Mass.) Coll., 1967; M.D., Cornell U., 1971. Diplomate: Am. Bd. Internal Medicine, Nat. Bd. Med. Examiners; Lic. physician, Md. Intern U. Calif., San Francisco, 1971-72, resident in medicine, 1972-73; with USPHS, 1973—; clin. assoc. Nat. Cancer Inst., NIH, Bethesda, Md., 1973-76; sr. investigator med. oncology br. Washington VA Hosp., Nat. Cancer Inst., 1976-81; asst. prof. medicine Georgetown U., 1978-81; chief cellular kinetic sect. navy med. oncology br. Nat. Naval Med. Center, Nat. Cancer Inst., Bethesda, 1981-84; assoc. prof. medicine Uniformed Services U. Health Scis., Bethesda, 1981-84; head div. med. oncology, prof. medicine U. Colo. Health Scis. Ctr., 1984—. Assoc. editor Cancer Treatment Reports, 1976-80, Medical and Pediatric Oncology, 1984—; contbr. articles and abstracts to profl. jours. Recipient Howard Hill Mossman award Amherst Coll., 1967, Sondra Lee Shaw Research award Cornell U. Md. Coll., 1971, medal of commendation USPHS, 1984. Mem. Am. Soc. Hematology, Am. Assn. Cancer Research, Am. Soc. Clin. Oncology, Cell Kinetic Soc., Am. Fedn. Clin. Research, Internat. Assn. Study of Lung Cancer, Alpha Omega Alpha. Current Work: T cell lymphomas, T cell biology, lung cancer, cell kinetics. Subspecialties: Oncology; Cancer research (medicine). Home: 560 Sundown Ln Evergreen CO 80439 Office: Div Med Oncology Box B171U Colo Health Scis Ctr 4200 E 9th Ave Denver CO 80262

BUNNETT, JOSEPH FREDERICK, chemist, educator; b. Portland, Oreg., Nov. 26, 1921; s. Joseph and Louise Helen (Boulan) B.; m. Sara Anne Telfer, Aug. 22, 1942; children—Alfred Boulan, David Telfer, Peter Sylvester (dec. Sept. 1972). B.A., Reed Coll., 1942; Ph.D., U. Rochester, 1945. Mem. faculty Reed Coll., 1946-52, U. N.C., 1952-58; mem. faculty Brown U., 1958-66, prof. chemistry, 1959-66, chmn. dept., 1961-64; prof. chemistry U. Calif. at Santa Cruz, 1966—; Erskine vis. fellow U. Canterbury, New Zealand, 1967; vis. prof. U. Wash., 1956, U. Würzburg, Germany, 1974; research fellow Japan Soc. for Promotion of Sci., 1979; Lady Davis vis. prof. Hebrew U., Jerusalem, Israel, 1981. Contbr. articles to profl. jours. Trustee Reed Coll., Societá Chimica Italiana (hon.). Fulbright scholar Univ. Coll., London, Eng., 1949-50; Guggenheim fellow, Fulbright scholar U. Munich, Germany, 1960-61. Fellow AAAS; mem. Am. Acad. Arts and Scis., Am. Chem. Soc. (editor jour. Accounts of Chem. Research), Chem. Soc. (London), Internat. Union Pure and Applied Chemistry (chmn. commn. on phys. organic chemistry 1978—; sec. organic chemistry div. 1981-83, v.p. 1983-85, pres. 1985-87). Subspecialty: Organic chemistry. Home: 608 Arroyo Seco Santa Cruz CA 95060 Office: U of California Santa Cruz CA 95064

BURBIDGE, E. MARGARET, astronomy educator; b. Davenport, Eng., Aug. 12, 1919; m. Geoffrey Burbridge. B.Sc., U. London, 1939, Ph.D. in Astrophysics, 1943; D.Sc. (hon.), Smith Coll., 1963, U. Sussex, 1970, U. Bristol, 1972, U. Leicester, 1972, City U. London, 1974, U. Mich., 1978, U. Mass., 1978. Acting. dir. U. London Obs., 1943-51; research assoc. astronomy Yerkes Obs., 1951-53; Shirley Farr fellow in astronomy, 1957-59; research fellow in astrophysics Calif. Inst. Tech., Pasadena, 1955-57; assoc. prof. U. Chgo., 1959-62; research assoc. in astrophysics U. Calif., San Diego, La Jolla, Calif., 1962-64, prof. astronomy, 1964—; Abby Mauze Rockefeller prof. MIT, Cambridge, 1968; mem. Space Sci. Bd., Nat. Acad. Sci.; mem. NRC, 1971-74, mem. astronomy com., 1973-75, mem. NSF astronomy adv. panel, 1972-74; mem. steering group Large Space Telescope, 1973-77; mem. Associated Univs. for Research Astronomy Bd., 1974—; Virginia Gildersleeve prof. Barnard Coll., N.Y.C., 1974. Mem. AAAS (pres. 1982-83), Nat. Acad. Sci., Am. Astron. Soc. (Warner prize 1959, pres. 1976-78), Royal Astron. Soc., Am. Acad. Arts and Scis., Internat. Astron. Union. Subspecialty: Optical astronomy. Office: Dept Physics U Calif San Diego La Jolla CA 92093

BURBIDGE, GEOFFREY, astrophysicist, educator; b. Chipping Norton, Oxon, Eng., Sept. 24, 1925; s. Leslie and Eveline B.; m. Margaret Peachey, 1948; 1 dau. B.Sc. with spl. honors in Physics, Bristol U., 1946; Ph.D., U. Coll., London, 1951. Asst. lectr. U. Coll., London, 1950-51; Agassiz fellow Harvard, 1951-52; research fellow U. Chgo., 1952-53, Cavendish Lab., Cambridge, Eng., 1953-55; Carnegie fellow Mt. Wilson and Palomar Obs., Calif. Inst. Tech., 1955-57; asst. prof. dept. astronomy U. Chgo., 1957-58, assoc. prof., 1958-62, U. Calif.-San Diego, La Jolla, 1962-63, prof. physics, 1963-83, now faculty; dir. Kitt Peak Nat. Obs., Tucson, 1978-84; Phillips vis. prof. Harvard U., 1968; bd. dirs. Associated Univs. Research in Astronomy, 1971-74; trustee Associated Univs., Inc., 1973-82. Author: (with Margaret Burbidge) Quasi-Stellar Objects, 1967; Contbr. (with Margaret Burbidge) articles to sci. jours. Fellow Royal Soc. London, Am. Acad. Arts and Scis., Royal Astron. Soc.; mem. Am. Phys. Soc., Am. Astron. Soc., Internat. Astron. Union, Astron. Soc. of Pacific (pres. 1974-76). Subspecialties: High energy astrophysics; Cosmology. Office: U Calif-San Diego La Jolla CA 92093

BURD, ROBERT M., physician, educator; b. N.Y.C., Aug. 25, 1937; s. David and Ann (Popkin) B.; m. Alice E. Stoller, May 30, 1964; children: Russell J., Stephen J. B.A., Columbia U., 1959, M.D., 1963. Diplomate: Am. Bd. Internal Medicine, (subspecialty in hematology, oncology). Med. intern Albert Einstein Med. Coll., N.Y.C., 1963-64, resident in medicine, 1964-66; fellow in hematology Montefiore Hosp., N.Y.C., 1966-67; physician in pvt. practice, Fairfield, Conn., 1969—; chief hematology/oncology St. Vincents Med. Center, Bridgeport, Conn., 1980—; assoc. prof. clin. medicine Yale U. Med. Center, New Haven, 1981—; program dir. Yale-St. Vincents Oncology Program, New Haven, 1980—. Editor: St. Vincent Med. Bull, 1972—; mem. editorial bd.: Conn. Medicine, 1972-76; contbr. articles to profl. jours. Chmn. profl. edn. Am. Cancer Soc., Bridgeport, 1983, bd. dirs., 1983—; vice pres. Leukemia Soc. Am., Fairfield County, Conn., 1973-75. Served to lt. comdr. U.S. Navy, 1967-69. Ettinger fellow Am. Cancer Soc., 1983. Fellow ACP; mem. Am. Soc. Hematology, Am. Soc. Clin. Oncology, N.Y. Acad. Sci., AAAS, Am. Soc. Internal Medicine, AMA. Jewish. Current Work: Cooperative protocols in therapy of lung cancer. Subspecialties: Hematology; Oncology. Office: 1305 Post Rd Fairfield CT 06430

BURDETTE, WALTER JAMES, surgeon, educator; b. Hillsboro, Tex., Feb. 5, 1915; s. James S. and Ovazene (Weatherred) B.; m. Kathryn Lynch, Apr. 9, 1947; children: Susan, William J. A.B., Baylor U., 1935; A.M., U. Tex., 1936, Ph.D., 1938; M.D., Yale, 1942. Diplomate: Am. Bd. Surgery, Am. Bd. Thoracic Surgery. Intern Johns Hopkins Hosp., 1942-43; Harvey Cushing fellow surgery Yale, 1943-44; resident staff surgery New Haven Hosp., 1944-46; instr., asst., assoc. prof. surgery La. State U., 1946-55; vis. surgeon Charity Hosp. of La., 1946-55; cons. Touro Infirmary and So. Baptist Hosp., 1952-55, Oak Ridge Inst. Nuclear Studies Hosp., 1953-59; vis. investigator Chester Beatty Inst. Cancer Research, Brompton, and Royal Cancer Hosp., London, 1953, Max Planck Institut Fuer Biochemie, Tuebingen, Germany, summer 1955; prof., chmn. dept. surgery U. Mo., 1955-56; prof. clin. surgery St. Louis U. Sch. Medicine, 1956-57; prof., head dept. surgery U. Utah, 1957-65; dir. lab. clin. biology, surgeon-in-chief Salt Lake Gen. Hosp., 1957-65; chief surg. cons. VA Hosps., Salt Lake City, 1957-65; prof. surgery, assoc. dir. U. Tex-M.D. Anderson Hosp. and Tumor Inst., Houston, 1965-72; prof. surgery U. Tex. Sch. Medicine at Houston, 1971-79; adj. prof. pharmacology U. Houston, 1975—; pres. Nat. Biomed. Found., 1972—; cons. St. Luke's Hosp., 1975—, Park Plaza Hosp., 1976—, Meth. Hosp., 1976—; Gibson lectr. advanced surgery Oxford U., 1966; vis. prof. U. Oxford, spring 1965; ofcl. U. Congo, summer 1968. Editor, author: Etiology, Treatment of Leukemia, 1958, Methodology in Human Genetics, 1962, Methodology in Mammalian Genetics, 1962, Methodology in Basic Genetics, 1963, Primary Hepatoma, 1965, Carcinoma of the Alimentary Tract, 1965, Viruses Inducing Cancer, 1966, Carcinoma of the Colon and Antecedent Epithelium, 1970, Planning and Analysis of Clinical Studies, 1970, Invertebrate Endocrinology and Hormonal Heterophylly, 1974; mem. editorial bd.: Surg. Rounds; contbr. articles to med. and sci. jours. Chmn. genetics study sect., mem. morphology study sect. NIH; cons. Nat. Cancer Inst.; mem. Nat. Adv. Cancer Council, Nat. Adv. Heart Council, Surgeon General's Com. on Smoking and Health; chmn. U.S.A. nat. com. Internat. Union Against Cancer; mem. transplantation com. Nat. Acad. Scis.; chmn. working Cadre on cancer large intestine Nat. Cancer Inst.; elder, deacon Christian Ch. Alpha Epsilon Delta Disting. Alumni award Baylor U., 1983; Rockefeller travel fellow, summer 1957. Fellow A.C.S.; mem. Soc. Surgery Alimentary Tract, Am. Assn. Cancer Research (dir.), Am. Cancer Soc. (chmn. research adv. council, mem. council on analysis and projection), Am. Surg. Assn., Soc. Clin. Surgery (treas.), Soc. U. Surgeons, A.M.A., Soc. Exptl. Biology and Medicine, Genetics Soc. Am., AAAS, Western Soc. Clin. Research, Am. Assn. Thoracic Surgery, Transplantation Soc., N.Y. Acad. Sci., Soc. Am. Naturalists, New Orleans, St. Louis, Salt Lake City, Houston surg. socs., Tex. Med. Soc., Harris County Med. Soc., So., Western surg. assns., So. Thoracic Surg. Soc., Peruvian Cancer Soc. (hon.), Am. Assn. for Cancer Research, Soc. for Surgery Alimentary Tract, Am. Soc. Clin. Oncology, Am. Soc. for Cancer Edn., Tex. Surg. Soc., Assn. Yale Alumni in Medicine (exec. com. 1977), Soc. Internat. de Chirurg., Phi Beta Kappa, Sigma Xi, Alpha Omega Alpha. Current Work: Gene action and modifications for cancer therapy; general and thoracic surgery; genetic research. Subspecialties: Genetics and genetic engineering (medicine); Cancer research (medicine). Home: 239 Chimney Rock Rd Houston TX 77024 Office: Plaza Med. Center 1200 Binz St Suite 740 Houston TX 77004

BURDICK, GLENN ARTHUR, university dean, electrical engineer; b. Pavilion, Wyo., Sept. 9, 1932; s. Stephen Arthur and Mary Elizabeth (McClerg) B.; m. Joyce Mae Huggett, July 14, 1951; children: Stephen Arthur, Randy Glenn. B.S., Ga. Inst. Tech., 1958, M.S., 1959; Ph.D., MIT, 1961. Reg. profl. engr., Fla. Office mgr. Statewide Contractors, Las Vegas, Nev., 1955-56; spl. tool designer Ga. Inst. Tech., Atlanta, 1954-55, instr., 1956-59; sr. mem. research staff Sperry Microwave, Oldsmar, Fla., 1961-65; prof. elec. engring. U. So. Fla., Tampa, 1965—, dean Coll. Engring., 1979—. Invented underground pipeline leak detector, 1956, sail boat mast insulation, 1981. Mem. Tampa Bay Fgn. Affairs Com., 1981—, Pinellas County (Fla.) High Speed Rail Task Force, 1982—, Gov. of State of Fla. Energy Task Force, 1980—; vice chmn. Fla. Task Force for Sci, Energy and Tech. Service to Industry, 1981-82; mem. Tampa Mayor's Internat. Trade Com., 1982—; mem. Fla. Gov.'s program com. World Trade Conf., 1985. Tex. Gulf scholar, 1957-58; NSF fellow, 1958-61; Woodrow Wilson fellow, 1958-59. Mem. Fla. Engring. Soc. (Engr. of Yr. award 1981), Internat. Soc. Hybrid Microelectronics (nat. pres. 1974), IEEE (sr. mem., Engr. of Yr. award 1980), Am. Ry. Engring. Assn., N.Y. Acad. Sci., Am. Soc. Engring. Edn. Clubs: Clearwater Tennis (pres. Fla. chpt. 1965, 69), Downtown. Lodge: Rotary. Current Work: Engineering education; accident reconstruction. Subspecialties: Theoretical physics; Electrical engineering. Home: 1000 County Rd 80 Tarpon Springs FL 33589 Office: Univ So Fla Coll Engring Tampa FL 33620

BURFORD, HUGH JONATHAN, pharmacologist, educator; b. Memphis, Aug. 5, 1931; s. Tolbert Hugh and Margaret Elizabeth (Henderson) B.; m. Dorothy Marie Moffett, Dec. 26, 1957; children: Jonathan Mark, Jennifer Lynn. B.S., Millsaps Coll., 1954; M.S., U. Miss., 1956; Ph.D. in Pharmacology, U. Kans., 1962. USPHS fellow in pharmacology Tulane U., New Orleans, 1962-63; asst. Bowman Gray Sch. Medicine, 1963-68; assoc. prof. pharmacology and pharmacy, teaching assoc. in basic med. sci. U. N.C., Chapel Hill, 1971—; cons. for pharmacology teaching materials Health Scis. Consortium; cons. Audio Visual (Computer Search) Line; liaison mem. Computer Assisted Teaching System Consortium. Author: HEALER programs and data base for student self-assessment in med. pharmacology, 1978—, also articles. Democratic precinct worker. Served with U.S. Army, 1956-57. Recipient Sloan Faculty Facilitator award U.N.C., 1973-74. Mem. Am. Soc. Pharmacology and Exptl. Therapeutics, Assn. Multi-Discipline Edn. Health Scis. (founding 1968), Spl. Interest Group in Health Profl. Edn., Am. Edn. Research Assn. (founding 1969), Sigma Xi. Democrat. Baptist. Current Work: Research in cognitive learning styles and computer instruction in pharmacology for health profession students. Subspecialties: Pharmacology; Information systems, storage, and retrieval (computer science).

BURGE, CHARLES ARTHUR, management information systems engineer; b. Honolulu, Feb. 25, 1948; s. Carlos and Mary Chieko (Koyama) B.; m. Rebecca Lynn Johnson, Sept. 7, 1971 (div. Jan. 1978); m. Deborah Simon, Oct. 9, 1982. Student Widener U., 1985—. Engr. ops. dept. Pub. Service Elec. & Gas Co., Salem Generating Sta., Hancocks Bridge, N.J., 1977-78, engr. licensing hdqrs., Newark, 1978-79; engr. emergency plan Pub. Service Elec. & Gas Co., Salem Generating Sta. (Artificial Island), Hancocks Bridge, 1979-82, lead engr, emergency planning, 1982-84, sr. methods analyst methods and systems, 1984—. Mem. nat. com. Republican Com., Washington, 1981. Served with USN, 1969-77. Mem. Am. Nuclear Soc., N.Y. Acad. Scis., AAAS, Phi Kappa Phi, Alpha Pi Mu. Republican. Episcopalian. Current Work: Development of management information systems to reduce radiation dose and provide improved radiological information for health physics managers and supervisors. Subspecialties: Nuclear fission; Industrial engineering. Home: 13 N Main St Mullica Hill NJ 08062 Office: Pub Service Elec and Gas Co PO Box 236 Hancocks Bridge NJ 08038

BURGESS, ERIC, high technology company executive, writer; b. Stockport, Cheshire, Eng., May 30, 1920; came to U.S., 1956, naturalized, 1962; s. William and Lily B.; m. Lilian Slater, Aug. 9, 1947; children: Janis, Marie, Stephen Roy, Howard John. B.A., Coll. Commerce, Manchester, Eng., 1940; B.Sc., Coll. Tech., Manchester, 1950. Vice-pres. Mellonics Inc., Tucson and Northridge, La., 1959-62; sr. tech. staff mem. Informatics Inc., Sherman Oaks, Calif., 1962-65; dep. dir. Wolf Research & Develop Co., Encino, Calif., 1965-68; sci. correspondent The Christian Sci. Monitor, Boston, 1968-71; pvt. practice cons. space mission, high tech., satellite communications, Santa Rosa and Los Angeles, 1971-81; sr. v.p. corp. devel. Space Microwave Labs. Inc., Santa Rosa, Calif., 1981—; pres. Am. Only, Inc., Sebastopol, Calif., 1983—. Author: Rocket Propulsion, 1952, Frontier to Space, 1954, Rockets & Spaceflight, 1956, Guided Weapons, 1957, Long-Range Ballistic Missiles, 1961, Assault on the Moon, 1966; Author with Bruce Murray: Flight to Mercury, 1977; Author: (with James Dunn) To The Red Planet, 1978, The Voyage of Mariner 10, 1978, (with R.O. Fimmel, James A Van Allen) First to Jupiter, Saturn and Beyond, 1981, By Jupiter, 1982, Celestial Basic, 1982, Pioneer Venus, 1983, (with H.J. Burgess) Timex, Sinclair 1000: Astronomy, 1983; Venus, The Errant Twin, 1985; contbr. numerous articles to profl. jours. Fellow Royal Astron. Soc., Brit. Interplanetary Soc. (chmn. 1946-47), AIAA; mem. Nat. Assn. Sci. Writers. Current Work: Planetology, military radar and electronic warfare. Subspecialties: Software engineering; Planetary science. Home: 13361 Frati Ln Sebastopol CA 95472 Office: Space Microwave Labs Inc 396 Tesconi Ct Santa Rosa CA 95401

BURGESS, JOSEPH WESLEY, JR., research neurobiologist, medical educator; b. Dumas, Tex., Mar. 5, 1952; s. Joseph Wesley and Dorothea Inez (Nelson) B. B.S., Purdue U., 1974; Ph.D., N.C. State U., 1979. Teaching asst. N.C. State U., Raleigh, 1975; research asst. N.C. Dept. Mental Health-Dix Hosp., Raleigh, 1976-78; researcher Stanford U., Calif., 1979; research assoc., lectr. U. Calif.-Davis, 1979-81, co-prin. investigator NSF, 1980-81; assoc. research neurobiologist UCLA Med. Sch., 1981—; research cons. Caribbean Primate Research Ctr., La Parguera, P.R., 1977. Contbg. author: Spider Communication: Mechanisms and Evolutionary Significance, 1982; Animal Societies and Evolution, 1982; Behavioral Biology of Early Brain Damage, 1984. Contbr. numerous articles to profl. jours. Mem. Calif. Children's Lobby, 1979—. Mem. N.Y. Acad. Scis., Am. Assn. Anatomists, Soc. for Neurosci. (N.C. state council 1977-78), Amyotrophic Lateral Sclerosis Soc. Am., Animal Behavior Soc. (research ethics com. 1978), Sigma Xi. Current work: Research on neural and behavioral processes of recovery from nervous system disorders; instinctive behavior in humans and animals; neurobehavioral mechanisms and function. Subspecialties: Ethology; Neurobiology. Home: 748 Flower Ave Venice CA 90291 Office: Neuropsychiat Inst UCLA Med Sch 760 Westwood Ave Room 58-177 Los Angeles CA 90024

BURGGREN, WARREN WILLIAM, zoology educator; b. Edmonton, Alta., Can., Aug. 14, 1951; came to U.S., 1978; s. William Arthur Ora and Ella Maureen (Hill) B.; m. Ann Tracy Goodman, Jan. 12. 1985; 1 dau., Kimberly Alison; m. Ann Tracy Goodman, Jan. 12, 1985. B.Sc. with 1st class honors, U. Calgary, 1973; Ph.D., U. East Anglia, Norwich, Eng., 1976. Postdoctoral assoc. U. B.C., Vancouver, 1976-78; asst. prof. zoology U. Mass., Amherst, 1978-82, assoc. prof., 1982—. Author: (with others) Evolution of Air Breathing in Vertebrates, 1981; contbr. (with others) articles to profl. jours. NSF grantee, 1980, 83, 85. Mem. Am. Soc. Zoologists (program officer div. physiology and biochemistry), Can. Soc. Zoologists, Soc. Exptl. Biology. Current Work: Comparative and environmental animal physiology; physiological adaptations associated with evolution of terrestrial animal life, especially respiration, circulation, osmoregulation. Subspecialties: Comparative physiology; Evolutionary biology. Office: Dept Zoology U Mass Amherst MA 01003-0027

BURGHARD, RONALD ALBERT, integrated circuit researcher, surface analysis researcher; b. Spokane, Wash., Mar. 11, 1946; s. Fred Albert and Gladys Irene (Whitman) B.; m. Sharon Louise Laws, June 24, 1967; children—John, Melody. B.S.E.E., Mont. State U., 1968, Ph.D. in Physics, 1977; M.S.E.E., Stanford U., 1969. Mem. tech. staff Sandia Labs., Albuquerque, 1968-74; sr. scientist Tektronix, Inc., Beaverton, Oreg., 1977-79; sr. engr. Intel Corp., Aloha, Oreg., 1979—. Contbr. articles to profl. jours. Mem. IEEE. Current work: integrated circuit development and characterization utilizing electrical and beam surface analysis techniques. Subspecialties: Integrated circuits; Microchip technology (materials science). Home: Route 4 Box 1020 Hillsboro OR 97123

BURGOYNE, WILLIAM FRANKLIN, JR., organic chemist; b. Salem, Ohio, June 1, 1953; s. William Franklin and Marilyn Elizabeth (Hogg) B.; m. Cathleen Mary Openhowski, Mar. 20, 1976; children—William Franklin III, Benjamin Joseph, Michael Adam, Rebecca Claire. B.S., Drexel U., 1976; Ph.D., U. Ill., 1981. Sr. research chemist Air Products and Chems. Inc., Allentown, Pa., 1980-83, prin. research chemist, 1983—. Contbr. articles to profl. jours. Mem. Am. Chem. Soc., Phila. Organic Chemist Club, Sigma Xi. Current work: Development of new synthetic methods utilizing non-homogeneous media; synthesis of novel organic structures for commercial application; studies in organonitrogen chemistry. Subspecialties: Organic chemistry; Synthetic chemistry. Home: 1950 Potomac St Allentown PA 18103 Office: Air Products Chems Inc PO Box 538 Allentown PA 18105

BURKE, JERRY ALAN, chemist; b. Elkins, W.Va., June 30, 1937; s. John Albert and Iyone Dell (Robinson) B.; m. Janet Helen Berg, Apr. 15, 1962; children—John, James. B.S. in Chemistry, W.Va. Wesleyan Coll., 1959. Chemist FDA, Washington,, 1959-65, head halogenated compounds sect., 1965-72, chief pesticides and indsl. chems. br., 1972-78, assoc. dir. div. chemistry and physics, 1978-80, dir. div. chem. tech., 1980—. Contbr. articles to profl. jours. Recipient FDA award of merit, 1965, 75. Fellow Assn. Ofcl. Analytical Chemists (gen. referee chlorinated pesticides 1965-80, methods com. 1980—), Trout Unltd., Nat. Wild Turkey Fedn., Nat. Rifle Assn. Lutheran. Current work: Development and validation of analytical methodology, especially multiresidue methodology, for pesticide and industrial chemical contaminants in foods; acquiring food-residue data for the protection and promotion of public health. Subspecialty: Analytical chemistry. Office: FDA Div Chem Tech 200 C ST SW Washington DC 20204

BURKE, KEVIN CHARLES ANTONY, geologist; b. London, Nov. 13, 1929; U.S., 1973; s. Charles Henry and Kathleen (Daly) B.; m. Angela Marion Phipps, Jan. 23, 1960; children—Nicholas, Matthew, Jane. B.Sc., Univ. Coll., London, 1951, Ph.D., 1953. Lectr. U. Ghana, 1953-56; geologist Brit. Geol. Survey, 1956-61; head geology, dept. U. West Indies, Kingston, Jamaica, 1961-65; prof. geology U. Ibadan, Nigeria, 1963-71, SUNY-Albany, 1973-83; prof. U. Houston, 1983—; dir. Lunar and Planetary Inst. NASA, 1983—; vis. prof. U. Toronto, 1971-73, Calif. Inst. Tech., 1976, U. Minn., 1977, U. Calgary, 1979; cons. in field. NSF grantee, 1976—. Fellow Geol. Soc. Am.; mem. Am. Geophys. Union, Nigerian Mining, Geol. and Metall. Soc. Research in plate tectonics. Current work: The history of the Earth from the earliest times related to the Wilson Cycle of the opening and closing of oceans. Subspecialties: Geology; Tectonics. Office: Lunar and Planetary Inst 3303 NASA Rd 1 Houston TX 77058

BURKE, LUKE ANTHONY, chemistry educator, researcher; b. N.Y.C., Feb. 18, 1948; s. Luke A. and Virginia (Kelly) B.; m. Bernadette Otte, July 24, 1976; 1 dau., Catheryn. B.S., Fordham U., 1969; M.S., NYU, 1973; D.Sc., Universite de Louvain, Belgium, 1978. NATO postdoctoral fellow Facultes de Namur, Belgium, 1978-79, SUNY-Stony Brook, 1979-80; asst. prof. chemistry Rutgers U., 1980—. NASA faculty fellow, 1982, 83; recipient Jean Stas prize Royal Acad. Arts and Scis., Belgium, 1978. Mem. Am. Chem. Soc., AAAS, N.Y. Acad. Scis., Societe Chimique de Belgique. Club: Chemists (N.Y.C.). Current Work: Theoretical description of reaction mechanisms; electronic properties of polymers and molecules of biological interest. Subspecialties: Theoretical chemistry; Organic chemistry. Home: 40 Lincoln Dr PO Laurel Springs NJ 08021 Office: Rutgers University Department of Chemistry 406 Penn St Camden NJ 08102

BURKE, ROBERT EMMETT, neurophysiologist; b. N.Y.C., July 26, 1934; s. N. Thomas and Margaret K. (Meudt) B.; m. Patricia Donovan, July 16, 1960; children: Mary Kay, David W., Jean E., Christina E. B.S., St. Bonaventure U., 1956; M.D., U. Rochester, 1961. Katherine Whipple postdoctoral scholar U. Rochester Sch. Medicine, 1961; intern Mass. Gen. Hosp., Boston, 1961-62, asst. resident in medicine, 1962-63, asst. resident in neurology, 1963-64; med. officer Lab. Neural Control, Nat. Inst. Neurol, and Communicative Disorders and Stroke, NIH, 1964-76; chief Lab. Neural Control, 1975—. Contbr. numerous articles, revs. essays to profl. jours. Recipient Borden prize U. Rochester Sch. Medicine, 1961; Superior Service award HEW, 1972. Mem. Am. Physiol. Soc., Soc. Neurosci., Internat. Brain Research Orgn., AAAS, Alpha Omega Alpha. Current Work: Structure and function of spinal cord, spinal cord, physiology, anatomy, neurobiology of motor units, synaptic transmission, dendrites. Subspecialties: Physiology (biology); Neurophysiology. Office: NIH Bldg 36 Room 5A29 Bethesda MD 20205

BURKET, GEORGE EDWARD, JR., family physician; b. Kingman, Kans., Dec. 10, 1912; s. George Edward and Jessie May (Talbert) B.; m. Mary Elizabeth Wallace, Nov. 12, 1938; children: George Edward III, Carol Sue, Elizabeth Christine. Student pre-med. Wichita State U., 1930-33; M.D., U. Kans., 1937. Diplomate: Am. Bd. Family Practice (pres. 1976-78). Intern Santa Barbara (Calif.) Gen. Hosp., 1937-38, resident, 1938-39; grad. asst. in surgery Mass. Gen. Hosp., Boston, 1956-57; practice medicine, Kingman, 1939-73; preceptor in medicine U. Kans. Med. Sch., 1950-73, asso. prof., 1973-78, clin. prof., 1978—. Contbr. articles to profl. jours. Mem. Kingman Bd. Edn., 1946-58; mem. Kans. State Bd. Health, 1960-66. Mem. Kans. Med. Soc. (pres. 1966-67), Am. Acad. Family Physicians (pres. 1967-68, John Walsh Founders award 1979), inst. Medicine, AMA, Assn. Am. Med. Colls., Soc. Tchrs. Family Medicine, Alpha Omega Alpha. Republican. Episcopalian. Clubs: Garden of Gods (Colorado Springs, Colo.); Wichita Country, Wichita. Lodges: Masons, Shriners. Subspecialty: Family practice. Home: Spring Lake Route 1 Kingman KS 67068 Office: Rainbow Blvd at 39th St Kansas City KS 66103

BURKHART, JAMES NELSON, JR., electronics engineer administrator, pastor; b. Indpls., Feb. 27, 1928; s. James Nelson and Louise Elizabeth (Bradley) B.; m. Alma Jean Long, Apr. 10, 1955; 1 child, David Eugene. Student U. Okla., 1980-86. Electronics engr. Def. Electronics Supply Ctr., Dayton, Ohio, 1962-79, supervisory electronic engr., 1979—. Pastor Apostolic Ch. Jesus Christ, Tipp City, Ohio, 1967—; pres. Ch. Corp., Tipp City, Served with U.S. Army, 1946-47. Mem. IEEE (chmn. chpt. 1966), ASTM (subcom. performance award 1983). Current work: Reliability and quality control; instrumental in incorporation of Weibull and log-normal distributions for lot-by-lot life tests in military specifications for capacitors. Subspecialty: Electronics. Home: 4125 Tipp-Cowlesville Rd Tipp City OH 45371 Office: Def Electronics Supply Ctr 1507 Wilmington Pike Dayton OH 45444

BURKMAN, ALLAN MAURICE, pharmacology educator, researcher, drug evaluation cons.; b. Waterbury, Conn., Apr. 23, 1932; s. Leon Oscar and Ann (Deitcher) B.; m. Katherine Horween, Aug. 8, 1965; children: David Eric, Deborah Rae. B.Sc., U. Conn., 1954; M.Sc., Ohio State U., 1955, Ph.D., 1958. Registered pharmacist, Conn. Asst. prof. pharmacology U. Ill.-Chgo., 1958-63; assoc. prof. pharmacology Butler U., Indpls., 1963-66; assoc. prof. pharmacology Ohio State U., Columbus, 1966-71, prof., 1971—, chmn. div. pharmacology, 1978—; vis. prof. pharmacology U. Utah, Salt Lake City, 1981-82. Mem. editorial rev. bd., referee various profl. and sci. jours.; contbr. numerous articles to profl. and sci. jours., chpts. to books. Recipient R. B. Allen Instructorship award U. Ill., 1963; Mead Johnson Research award, 1965; Am. Found. for Pharm. Edn. fellow, 1957-58; NIH, Office Naval Research, pharm. industry grantee, 1959—. Mem. Am. Soc. Pharmacology and Exptl. Therapeutics, Soc. for Exptl. Biology and Medicine, Am. Pharm. Assn., AAUP. Current Work: Characterization of drugs acting on the central nervous and cardiovascular systems; emetic and anti-emetic drug evaluation; drug effects on anterior pituitary function. Subspecialties: Pharmacology; Neuropharmacology. Office: Div Pharmacology Coll Pharmac Ohio State U 500 W 12th Ave Columbus OH 43210

BURLEIGH, BRUCE DANIEL, biochemist researcher; b. Augusta, Ga., June 23, 1942; s. Bruce Daniel and Billie Ann (Carter) B.; m. Dorothy Jean Roskos, Sept. 4, 1962; 1 son, Michael Eugene. B.S. in Chemistry, Carnegie-Mellon U., 1964; M.S. in Biochemistry, U. Mich., 1967, Ph.D., 1970. Post-doctoral fellow MRC Lab. Molecular Biology, Cambridge, Eng., 1970-72, sci. staff, 1972-73; asst. prof. biochemistry M.D. Anderson Hosp., Houston, 1973-78, assoc. biochemist, 1978-81; research biochemist research and devel. div. Internat. Minerals and Chem. Corp., Terre Haute, Ind. and Northbrook, Ill., 1981-83, sr. research scientist, 1983—; cons. biochemist, endocrinologist, molecular naturalist, 1981—. Contbr. book chpts., articles to profl. jours. Robert A. Welch Found. grantee Houston, 1979. Mem. Am. Chem. Soc., Am. Soc. Biol. Chemists, Endocrine Soc., N.Y. Acad. Scis., Union Concerned Scientist, AAAS, Tau Beta Pi, Phi Lambda Upsilon, Sigma Xi. Episcopalian. Current Work: Peptide and protein chemistry; endocrinology and mechanics of peptide hormone action; molecular and cellular endocrinology; recombinant DNA technology; industrial production of protein and peptide hormones; regulation of animal growth. Subspecialties: Biochemistry (biology); Cell and tissue culture. Home: Northbrook IL 60062 Office: IMC Corp Research and Devel Ctr 1810 Frontage Rd Northbrook IL 60062

BURNET, GEORGE, JR., educator; b. Ft. Dodge, Iowa, Jan. 30, 1924; s. George and Myrtle Violet (Hutchinson) B.; m. Betty Arlene Riggs, Oct. 8, 1944; children—Kathryn Ann, Betty Jo, Dolores Unalee, Joan Marie, Elaine Kaye, George VI. B.S. in Chem. Engring, Iowa State U., 1948, M.S., 1949, Ph.D., 1951. Registered profl. engr., Iowa. Mem. faculty Iowa State U., 1949-51, 56—, prof. chem. engring., 1958—, head dept., 1961-78, chmn. dept. nuclear engring., 1978-83, coordinator engring. edn. projects office, 1978—, Anson Marston distinguished prof., 1975—; process design engr. Comml. Solvents Corp., 1952-56; successively engr., sr. engr., div. chief Ames Lab., U.S. Dept. Energy, 1956—; Phillips lectr. Okla. State U., 1970; Dir. for planning Iowa State U., Civil Def. Orgn., 1961-69; AID cons. in higher edn. to, India, 1967; mem. pres.'s task force on energy research and devel. U.S. AEC, 1973; mem. adv. com. Sci. and Engring. Edn. Directorate NSF, 1984-86. Contbr.

articles. Active Boy Scouts Am.; Trustee Iowa State U. Alumni Achievement Fund, chmn. bd., 1973-74; mem. Nat. Sci. Bd. Commn. Pre-coll. Edn., 1982-83. Served to lt. col. AUS, 1944-48. Recipient Faculty citation Iowa State U., 1969; Iowa Citizen Chem. Engr. award, 1970. Fellow Am. Soc. Engring. Edn. (chmn. chem. engring. div. 1964, nat. dir. 1972-74, pres. 1976, Lamme medal 1982); mem. Am. Inst. Chem. Engrs. (chmn. Terre Haute sect. 1956, chmn. Iowa sect. 1967, nat. rep. to Engrs.' Council for Profl. Devel. 1969—, chmn. nat. com. on chem. engring. mem., 1969-70, Founders award 1981), div. 1964, nat. dir. 1972-74, pres. 1976, Lamme medal 1982), Am. Chem. Soc. (chmn. div. fertilizer and soil chemistry 1969), Accrediation Bd. Engring. and Tech. (chmn. engring. edn. and accreditation com. 1975-77, dir. 1977-83, exec. com. 1981-83, Grinter award 1984), Am. Assn. Engring. Socs. (chmn. ednl. affairs council 1980-81), Sigma Xi, Tau Beta Pi, Phi Lambda Upsilon, Phi Kappa Phi, Alpha Chi Sigma, Tau Kappa Epsilon, Omega Chi Epsilon (nat. pres. 1970). Methodist (chmn. ofcl. bd., bd. trustees). Club: Cardinal Key. Patentee in field. Current work: Resource recovery from coal solids wastes; carbothermal processing. Subspecialties: Chemical engineering; Resource management. Home: 4813 Dover Dr Ames IA 50010

BURNETT, JAMES ROBERT, electronics company executive, consultant; b. Eldorado, Ill., Nov. 27, 1925; s. James Lawrence and Edith Lillian (Bramlett) B.; m. Betty Anne Knox, Aug. 18, 1949; children—James William, Karen Jean, Susan Anne, Janice Leigh. B.S. in Elec. Engring., Purdue U., 1946, M.S. in Elec. Engring., 1947, Ph.D., 1949, hon. Dr. Engring., 1969. Assoc. prof. elec. engring. Purdue U., Lafayette, Ind., 1946-56; dir. electromech. lab. TRW Systems Group, Redondo Beach, Calif., 1956-61, minuteman program mgr., San Bernardino, Calif., 1961-66, mgr. San Bernardino ops., 1966-69, v.p., asst. gen. mgr., Redondo Beach, 1969-70, v.p., gen. mgr. systems engring. and integration div., 1970-74, sr. v.p., 1974-77, asst. gen. mgr. def. and space systems group, 1977-82, v.p., gen. mgr., 1982—; bd. dirs. OEA, Inc., Denver, 1977—. Served to 1st lt. USMC, 1943-50. Recipient Charles A. Coffin fellow; Air Force Systems Command award. Fellow AIAA; mem. IEEE, Nat. Acad. Engring. Republican. Current work: Group general manager. Office: TRW Def Systems Group 1 Space Pk Redondo Beach CA 90278

BURNHAM, ALAN KENT, chemist; b. Deocrah, Iowa, Oct. 10, 1950; s. Francis Harvey and Julia Genevieve (Branstad) B.; m. Mary Elizabeth Focht, Nov. 21, 1970; children—Amy Hope, Emily Beth, Aaron Alan. B.S., Iowa State U., 1972; Ph.D., U. Ill., 1977. Researcher Lawrence Livermore Lab., Calif., 1977-83, group leader in chemistry, 1983—. Contbr. articles to profl. jours. U. Ill. fellow, 1972; NIH fellow, 1974. Mem. Am. Chem. Soc., Am. Phys. Soc. Current work: Chemistry of oil shale pyrolysis and petroleum formation; devel. targets for laser fusion energy. Subspecialties: Fuels; Laser fusion. Home: 862 Adams Ave Livermore CA 94550 Office: Lawrence Livermore Nat Lab PO Box 808 Livermore CA 94550

BURNHAM, DONALD CLEMENS, manufacturing company executive; b. Athol, Mass., Jan. 28, 1915; s. Charles Richardson and Freda (Clemens) B.; m. Virginia Gobble, May 29, 1937; children: David Charles, Joan (Mrs. Robert Graham), John Carl, William Lawrence, Mary Barbara (Mrs. F. David Throop). B.S. in Mech. Engring, Purdue U., 1936, D.Eng. (hon.), 1959; D.Eng. (hon.), Ind. Inst. Tech., 1963, Drexel Inst. Tech., 1964, Poly. Inst. Bklyn., 1967. With Gen. Motors Corp., 1936-54; asst. chief engr. Gen. Motors Corp. (Oldsmobile div.), 1953-54; with Westinghouse Electric Corp., 1954—, group v.p., 1962-63, pres., chief exec. officer, 1963-68, chmn., chief exec. officer, 1969-75, dir.-officer, 1975-80; adv. bd. Mellon Bank (N.A.). Mem. The Bus. Council; emeritus trustee Carnegie-Mellon U., Carnegie Inst.; bd. dirs. Am. Wind Symphony Orch., Logistics Mgmt. Inst.; chmn. bd. dirs. Goodwill Industries of Pitts. Served to maj. AUS, World War II. Recipient Outstanding Achievement in Mgmt. award Am. Inst. Indsl. Engrs., 1964. Mem. ASME, Soc. Mfg. Engr. (Hoover Medal award 1978), Soc. Automotive Engrs., IEEE, Nat. Acad. Engring., Am. Assn. Engring. Socs. (Nat. Engring. award 1981). Club: Duquesne (Pitts.). Current Work: Productivity improvement. Subspecialties: Industrial engineering; Systems engineering. Home: 615 Osage Rd Pittsburgh PA 15243 Office: Westinghouse Bldg Gateway Center Pittsburgh PA 15222

BURNS, JACK O'NEAL, JR., astrophysicist; b. Ayer, Mass., Jan. 2, 1953; s. Jack O'Neal and Irene Blanche (Gendron) B.; m. Cathleen Spalding, Nov. 8, 1980; 2 children. B.S., U. Mass., 1974; M.A., Ind. U., 1976, Ph.D., 1978. Postdoctoral research asso. Nat. Radio Astronomy Obs. (VLA Project), Socorro, N.Mex., 1978-80; asst. prof. astronomy U. N.Mex., Albuquerque, 1980-84, assoc. prof., 1984—; cons. computer image processing Sandia Nat. Labs., Albuquerque, 1980 . Contbr. Articles to profl. jours. Sandia Nat. Labs. grantee, 1980-82; NASA grantee, 1980-83; Ind. U. Found. fellow, 1977-78; NSF grantee, 1984—. Mem. Internat. Astron. Union, Internat. Union Radio Sci., Am. Astron. Soc., Royal Astron. Soc. Eng. Democrat. Current Work: Radio, X-ray, optical studies of clusters of galaxies, research on extragalactic radio sources, radio jets, optical spectra of radio galaxies for distance determinations, large-scale structure (superclusters and voids), optical and radioimaging. Subspecialties: Radio and microwave astronomy; High energy astrophysics. Home: 12208 La Charles Ave NE Albuquerque NM 87111 Office: Dept Physics and Astronomy U NMex Albuquerque NM 87131

BURNS, JAY, III, physicist and space scientist, educator; b. Lake Wales, Fla., Mar. 22, 1924; s. Jay, Jr. and Harlan (Sheafe) B.; m. Dulcie Evans, Sept. 18, 1948; children: Jay, Wendy, William Scott. B.S., Northwestern U., 1947; M.S., U. Chgo., 1951, Ph.D., 1959. Dir. Chgo. Midway Labs., U. Chgo., 1962-65; assoc. prof. astrophysics Northwe. U., 1965-72; assoc. dir. research Rauland div. Zenith Radio Corp., 1967-68, sr. research cons., 1968-78; dir. Lakeside Labs., Chgo., 1972-75; prof., head dept. physics and space scis. Fla. Inst. Tech., Melbourne, 1976—; cons. U.S. Navy. Contbr. articles sci. jours. Served with USNR, 1944-46. Research grantee U.S. Air Force; Research grantee U.S. Navy; Research grantee U. S. Army; Research grantee NSF. Mem. Am. Phys. Soc. Club: East Coast Cruising Assn. (Indian Harbour Beach, Fla.). Current Work: Electron emission from solids, surface physics. Subspecialties: Atomic and molecular physics; Condensed matter physics. Home: 226 Sand Pine Rd North Indialantic FL 32903 Office: Dept Physics and Space Sciences Fla Inst Tech Melbourne FL 32901

BURNS, JOSEPH ARTHUR, Astronomer, educator; b. N.Y.C., Mar. 22, 1941; s. John Driscoll and Genevieve Mary (McCarthy) B.; m. Judith Ann Klein, July 1, 1967; 1 son, Patrick Matthew. B.S., Webb Inst., Glen Cove, N.Y., 1962; Ph.D., Cornell U., 1966. Asst. prof. Cornell U., 1966-67, 68-73, asso. prof., 1974-81, prof. space mechanics, 1981—; NRC postdoctoral fellow NASA-Goddard Space Flight Center, Greenbelt, Md., 1967-68; U.S. exchange fellow Schmidt Inst., Moscow, 1973; sr. scientist NASA Ames, Moffett Field, Calif., 1975-76; astronom titular Paris Obs., Meudon, France, 1979; vis. prof. U. Calif., Berkeley, 1982-83. Contbr. numerous articles to profl. jours. Grantee N.Y. Arts Council, 1973; Grantee NSF, 1973, 83-84, NASA, 1975-85. . Mem. Internat. Astron. Union, AAAS, Am. Astron. Soc., Am. Geophys. Union, Sigma Xi. Current Work: Solar system dynamics. Subspecialties: Planetary science; Theoretical and applied mechanics. Office: Cornell U 237 Thurston Hall Ithaca NY 14853

BUROKER, NORMAN EVERETT, population and molecular geneticist, researcher; b. Portland, Oreg., Mar. 27, 1943; s. Joseph Martin and Usona Sadene (Ary) B.; m. Linda Marie Brekke, Sept. 3, 1966; 1 child, Lindsay Ann. B.S., Miss. State U., 1968; M.S., U. Wash., 1975, Ph.D., 1978. Research asst. Dept. Interior, Seattle, 1970-72; post-doctoral fellow U. Md., Horn Point, 1978-80; post-doctoral Busch fellow Rutgers U., Piscataway, N.J., 1981-83; research assoc., dept. biochemistry Sch. Medicine, Oreg. Health Scis. U., Portland, 1983—. Contbr. articles to sci. jours. Regional scholar Miss. State U., 1967-68; Sea Grant awardee NOAA, 1978; Fisheries grantee Nat. Marine Fisheries Service, 1979. Mem. Soc. Study Evolution, Nat. Shell-fisheries Assn., Molecular Biology and Evolution Assn. Current work: Population genetic and evolutionary biological studies in family Ostreidae. Subspecialties: Evolutionary biology; Marine biology. Home: 11340 SE Pine Ct Portland OR 97220 Office: Dept Biochemistry Sch of Medicine Oreg Health Scis Univ 3181 SW Sam Jackson Park Rd Portland OR 97201

BUROW, DUANE FRUEH, chemist, educator; b. San Antonio, June 12, 1940; s. Martin and Hermine Elizabeth (Frueh) B.; m. Janice M. Bockstahler, Aug. 3, 1969; children: Nathan Allan, Bethanie Kristin. B.A., U. Tex., 1961, Ph.D., 1966. Instr. chemistry St. Edwards U., Austin, Tex., 1964-65; research phys. chemist engring. physics lab. E.I. DuPont de Nemours, Inc., Wilmington, Del., 1966-67; asst. prof. chemistry Mich. State U., 1967-69; asst. prof. chemistry U. Toledo, 1969-73, assoc. prof., 1973-78, prof. chemistry, 1978—. Contbr. chpts. to books, articles to profl. jours. Mem. Sylvania Schs. Com. on Gifted Edn., 1979—. NSF grantee, 1974, 77; Dept. Energy grantee, 1978; Ohio Coal Research Labs. Assn. grantee, 1980. Mem. Am. Chem. Soc., Royal Soc. Chemistry (U.K.), Coblentz Soc., Optical Soc. Am., Soc. Applied Spectroscopy, Sigma Xi. Current Work: Chemistry of sulfur dioxide, solution chemistry, application to fossil fuels and minerals processing; molecular spectroscopy, modeling of moleculaoptical properties, application to bio and geochemical systems. Subspecialties: Physical chemistry; Inorganic chemistry. Office: Dept Chemistry U Toledo Toledo OH 43606

BURR, ALEXANDER FULLER, physicist, educator; b. Cambridge, Mass., July 18, 1931; s. A.C. and Lily (Fuller) B.; m. Marjorie McKinstry, Aug. 18, 1962; children: Margaret, Catherine, Susan. B.S., Jamestown Coll., 1953; M.A., U. Edinburgh, Scotland, 1958; Ph.D., Johns Hopkins U., 1967. Solid state physicist U.S. Naval Research Lab., Washington, 1965-66; sr. vis. fellow U. Strathclyde, Glasgow, Scotland, 1973; chief research scientist Duntech Industries, Las Cruces, N.Mex., 1979-80; instrumentation expert IAEA, Vienna, 1981, 83; prof. physics N.Mex. State U., Las Cruces, 1966—. Author book, also papers and articles. Served with U.S. Army, 1954-56. Grantee Am. Assn. Physics Tchrs. Mem. Am. Phys. Soc., Am. Assn. Physics Tchrs., AAAS. Subspecialty: Atomic and molecular physics. Home: 2025 O'Donnell Dr Las Cruces NM 88001 Office: Physics Dept Box 3 NMex State U Las Cruces NM 88003

BURR, BALDWIN GWYNNE, energy cons. firm exec.; b. Columbus, Ohio, Dec. 29, 1945; s. Baldwin Gwynne and Edna Mae (Tracey) B.; m. Katherine Moore Harvey, May 27, 1972; 1 dau., Katherine Alexandra. B.A., U. N.Mex., 1969, M.A., 1977. Cert. energy auditor, N. Mex., Ariz., Colo., Fla. Asst. dir. So. Vt. Art Center, Manchester, 1969-70; prin. Godbold Burr and Burr, Albuquerque, 1975-; cons. N.Mex. Energy Inst., Albuquerque, 1978-80; pres. Energy Mgmt. Co., Tome, N.Mex., 1978—; guest lectr. U. N.Mex., Valencia. Author manuals in field of energy conservation. Served with U.S. Army, 1969-71. Mem. Profl. Energy Auditors Assn. N.Mex., Solar Lobby, Greater Albuquerque C. of C., Phi Gamma Delta. Current Work: Development of microcomputer software for sophisticated energy analysis of buildings. Subspecialties: Solar energy; Mathematical software. Home: Route 2 Box 816 Los Lunas NM 87031 Office: Box 362 Tome NM 87060

BURRELL, CHARLES FREDERICK, physicist; b. Danville, Pa., Sept. 26, 1942; s. Charles Earl and Helen Gertrude (Conrad) B. B.S., Lehigh U., 1964; M.S., Cornell U., 1967; Ph.D. in Physics, U. Md., 1974. Postdoctoral trainee U. Md., College Park, 1975; physicist Lawrence Berkeley Lab., Berkeley, Calif., 1976—. Contbr. articles to profl. jours. Mem. Am. Phys. Soc., AAAS. Current Work: Research and development of neutral beam injectors for plasma heating in magnetic fusion energy experiments; especially neutral beam diagnostics by optical spectroscopy and laser induced fluorescence. Subspecialties: Fusion; Plasma physics. Home: 6526 Kensington Ave Richmond CA 94805 Office: Lawrence Berkeley Lab Berkeley CA 94720

BURRELL, CRAIG DONALD, physician; b. Gravesend, Kent, Eng., July 5, 1926; came to U.S., 1960, naturalized, 1968; m. Mary Elizabeth Granger, 1960; children—Catherine, Sarah, Craig, Walter, David. M.B., B.Surgery, U. N.Z., 1951; D.Sc. (hon.), Ricker Coll., 1975, LL.D., (hon.), Union Coll., 1975. Rotating intern Wellington (N.Z.) Hosp., 1951-52; locum sr. house officer pediatrics Nottingham (Eng.) Children's Hosp., 1953; house physician gen. medicine and endocrinology Hammersmith Hosp. and Royal Postgrad. Med. Sch. Gt. Britain, London, 1954, sr. house officer endocrinology, 1954-56; registrar gen. medicine Royal Infirmary and Welsh Nat. Sch. Medicine, Cardiff, Wales, 1957-60; asst. prof. medicine and medicine in psychiatry Cornell U. Med. Sch., 1960-61; dir. clin. labs. Payne Whitney Psychiat. Clinic, 1960-61; with Sandoz Pharms., Inc., East Hanover, N.J., 1961-72, v.p. med. affairs, 1969-72; v.p., dir. external affairs Sandoz, Inc., East Hanover, 1973-85, v.p. external affairs, 1985—; asst. attending physician Cornell 2d Div., Bellevue Hosp., 1966-68; clin. asso. prof. medicine Coll. Medicine and Dentistry N.J., Newark, 1968—; clin. prof. dept. community and family medicine U. Calif.-San Diego Sch. Medicine, 1982—; participant numerous internat. profl. confs.; mem. tech. com. White House Conf. on Aging, 1980-81. Mem. editorial bd.; Internat. Jour. on Addictions; editor: Drug Assessment in Ferment, 1976, Primary Health Care in Industrialized Nations, 1978; contbr. articles profl. jours. Vice pres. Sandoz Found.; v.p., trustee Playfair Found., Kessler Inst. for Rehab., West Orange, N.J. Fellow Am. Sch. Health Assn. (hon.), N.Y. Acad. Scis. (pres. elect 1983), Royal Soc. Medicine, Am. Sch. Health Assn. (hon.); N.Y. Acad. Sci.; mem. AAAS, Am. Coll. Clin. Pharmacology and Therapeutics, AMA, Endocrine Soc., European Soc. for Study Drug Toxicity, Sierra Club, Delaware County (N.Y.). Conservation Assn. Presbyterian (elder). Subspecialties: Endocrinology; Internal medicine. Office: Sandoz Corp East Hanover NJ 07639

BURRELL, MORTON I, diagnostic radiologist, educator, researcher; b. Phila., May 20, 1941; s. Louis and Susan Burrell; m. Barbara Marie McCann, June 7, 1970; children—Lynn Meredith, Mark Francis. B.S., Bklyn. Coll., 1962; M.D., SUNY Downstate Med. Ctr., 1966; M.A. (hon.), Yale U., 1980. Diplomate Nat. Bd. Med. Examiners. Intern Kings County Hosp., Bklyn., 1966-67, resident in internal medicine, 1967-68; resident in radiology Yale-New Haven Hosp., 1970-73; asst. prof. Yale U. Sch. Medicine, New Haven, 1973-76, assoc. prof., 1976-80, prof. radiology, 1980—; chief gastrointestinal radiology dept. Yale New Haven Hosp., 1973—; cons. West Haven VA Hosp., Conn., 1973—; St. Vincent's Hosp., Bridgeport, Conn., 1976—. Served to lt. comd. USNR, 1968-70. Fellow ACP, Am. Coll. Radiology,; mem. Am. Gastroent. Assn., Soc. Gastrointestinal Radiologists, Radiol. Soc. N.Am., Am. Roentgen Ray Soc., New Eng. Roentgen Ray Soc. Current work: Abdominal imaging, radiology of gastrointestinal disease, biliary tract imaging. Subspecialty: Diagnostic radiology. Office: Yale U Sch Medicine 333 Cedar St New Haven CT 06510

BURRIDGE, MICHAEL JOHN, epidemiologist; b. St. Albans, Eng., Apr. 27, 1942; s. Arthur Bailey and Georgina Augusta (Davis) B.; m. Karen Maureen Bengtsson, Jan. 1, 1983; 1 child, Christina Michelle; m. Desree Margaret Wiggins, Aug. 11, 1973 (div. Sept. 1981). B.V.M. & S., U. Edinburgh, 1966; M.P.V.M., U. Calif.-Davis, 1974, Ph.D, 1976. Research scientist, East African Trypanosomiasis Research Orgn., Tororo, Uganda, 1966; practice veterinary medicine, Woking, Eng., 1967-68; animal health officer FAO, Muguga, Kenya, 1968-73; assoc. prof. epidemiology U. Fla., Gainesville, 1976-82, prof., 1982—; cons. FAO, 1978, World Bank, Bunia, Zaire, 1982; dir. ctr. for tropical animal health U. Fla., Gainesville, 1982—, chmn. dept. infectious diseases, 1984—. Editor: Impact of Diseases on Livestock Production in the Tropics, 1984; contbr. articles to profl. jours. Grantee U.S. Dept. Agrl. Fellow Am. Coll. Epidemiology; mem. Royal Coll. Vet. Surgeons, AVMA, U.S. Animal Health Assn., Phi Kappa Phi. Epidemiology and control of animal diseases that form constraints to food animal production, and that are of significance to human health, especially those of relevance to tropical regions. Subspecialties: Epidemiology; Preventive medicine (veterinary medicine). Office: Box J-137 JHMHC U Fla Gainesville FL 32610

BURRILL, MELINDA JANE, genetics educator; b. Washington, Mar. 31, 1947; d. Richard William and Virginia (Jones) B. B.S., U. Ariz., 1969; Ph.D., Oreg. State U., 1974. Cert. animal geneticist. Postdoctoral fellow U. Minn., St. Paul, 1975-76; asst. prof. Calif. State Poly. U., Pomona, 1976-80, assoc. prof. genetics, dept. animal sci., 1980-85, prof., 1985—; cons. to various cos., 1977—. Contbr. research articles to profl. jours. Active Granada Villas Homeowners Assn., Upland, Calif., 1979-82. Women in Devel. fellow U.S. AID, 1984; research fellow Centre Nat. de Recherches Zootechniques, France, 1980. Mem. Am. Soc. Animal Sci., Brit. Soc. Animal Prodn., Can. Soc. Animal Sci., Am. Genetics Assn., Internat. Soc. for Gen. Sumantics, Richard III Soc., Phi Beta Kappa, Sigma Xi, Phi Kappa Phi, others. Republican. Methodist. Current work: Breed characterization; quantitative genetics; rare breed preservation; factorial genetics; reproductive physiology of sheep/goats. Subspecialties: Animal genetics; Animal breeding and embryo transplants. Office: Dept Animal Sci Calif State Polytechnic Univ 3801 W Temple Ave Pomona CA 91768

BURRINGTON, JAMES DAVID, chemist; b. Cleve., June 27, 1951; s. James Douglas and Josephine (Santella) B.; m. Cynthia Ann Ross, Aug. 2, 1975; children—John David, David Joseph. B.S. in Chemistry, John Carroll U., 1973; Ph.D. in Organic Chemistry, MIT, 1977. Sr. research chemist Sohio Research, Cleve., 1977-79, project leader, 1979-82, research assoc., 1982-84, research supr., 1984—. Contbr. articles to profl. jours., chpts. to books. Patentee in field. Served to capt. U.S. Army, 1975. Recipient Chemistry award Chemical Rubber Co., 1970, award in chemistry Lubrizol Corp., 1973, Am. Inst. Chemistry award, 1973. Mem. Am. Chem. Soc. (petroleum div. sec. 1983—), N. Am. Catalysis Soc. (orgn. reactions sec.), Pitts.-Cleve. Catalysis Soc. (pres. 1983-84), Am. Assn., Sigma Xi. Republican. Roman Catholic. Current work: Supervisor for professionals in areas of molecular catalysis and biotechnology. Subspecialties: Catalysis chemistry; Organic chemistry. Home: 23860 Harms Rd Richmond Heights OH 44143 Office: Sohio Research 4440 Warrensville Center Rd Cleveland OH 44128

BURRIS, ROBERT HARZA, biochemist, educator; b. Brookings, S.D., Apr. 13, 1914; s. Edward T. and Mable C. (Harza) B.; m. Katherine Irene Brusse, Sept. 12, 1945; children: Jean Carol, John Edward, Ellen Louise. B.S., S.D. State Coll., 1936, D.Sc., 1966; M.S., U. Wis., 1938, Ph.D., 1940. NRC fellow Columbia U., 1940-41; faculty U. Wis., Madison, 1941—, prof., 1951—; chmn. biochemistry Coll. Agr., 1958-70, W.H. Peterson prof. biochemistry, 1976—. Recipient Charles Thom award Soc. Indsl. Microbiology, 1977; Nat. Medal of Sci., 1980; Guggenheim fellow Cambridge U., 1954. Mem. Am. Chem. Soc., Am. Soc. Biol. Chemistry, Am., Am. Soc. Plant Physiologists (Stephen Hales award 1968, Charles Reid Barnes award 1977, pres. 1960), Japanese Soc. Plant Physiology, Biochem. Soc., AAAS, Am. Soc. Microbiology, Nat. Acad. Scis., Am. Acad. Arts and Scis., Am. Philos. Soc. Current Work: Biochemical mechanism of biological nitrogen fixation; role of hydrogenase in nitrogen fixation; associative nitrogen fixation; blue-green algae. Subspecialties: Nitrogen fixation; Biochemistry (biology). Home: 1015 University Bay Dr Madison WI 53705

BURROUGHS, MARK SCOTT, lightwave device engineer; b. Ravena, Ohio, May 24, 1955; s. Paul Brian and Pamela Ann (Beeler) B.; m. Mary Lou Gurney, May 3, 1980. B.S.E.E., Bucknell U., 1978, B.A. in Physics, 1978; M.S.E.E., U. Ill. Champaign-Urbana, 1981. Engr., Western Electric, Reading, Pa., 1978-79, devel. engr. lightwave, 1979-80; devel. engr. lightwave Bell Labs., Murray Hill, N.J., 1981-83; devel. engr. lightwave AT&T Tech., Reading, 1983-84, dept. chief light wave wafer fabrication, Reading, 1984—. Patentee bi-modal temperature controller; contbr. articles to profl. jours. Mem. IEEE, Quantum Electronics Applications Soc., Optical Soc. Am., Am. Inst. Physics. Current work: Semiconductor devices for lightwave technology (fiber optics) such as lasers, LEDs, photodetectors, etc. Subspecialties: Semiconductor lasers; Fiber optics. Office: AT&T Technology Systems 2525 N 12th St Reading PA 19604

BURROUGHS, RICHARD H., III, oceanographer, geologist, educator; b. New Haven, July 5, 1946; s. Richard H., Jr. and Mary Drummond (Page) B. A.B. with honors, Princeton U., 1969; Ph.D. (grad. research fellow), M.I.T. Woods Hole Oceanographic Inst., 1975. Staff officer Nat. Acad. Scis-NRC, 1974-77; sr. fellow Ecosystems Center, Marine Biol. Lab., Woods Hole, Mass., 1977-79, 81; vis. lectr. Sch. Forestry and Environ. Studies, Yale U., 1979; sci. advisor to dir. Bur. Land Mgmt., Dept. Interior, Washington, 1979-81; research scientist John Gray Inst., Lamar U., Beaumont, Tex., 1982-83; asst. prof. grad. program in marine affairs U. R.I., Kingston, 1983—. Contbr. articles to profl. jours. Mem. AAAS, Am. Geophys. Union, Geol. Soc. Am., Sigma Xi. Current Work: Management of natural resources. Subspecialties: Resource management; Oceanography. Office: Grad Program in Marine Affairs Washburn Hall U RI Kingston RI 02881

BURROWS, ADAM SETH, astrophysicist; b. Salt Lake City, Nov. 11, 1953; s. Reynold Zachary and Diane Marion (Axelrad) B. A.B. summa cum laude, Princeton U., 1975; Ph.D., MIT, 1979. Postdoctoral assoc. physics U. Mich., Ann Arbor, 1979-80; postdoctoral assoc. physics SUNY-Stony Brook, 1980-83, asst. prof. physics, 1983—. Contbr. articles to profl. publs. NSF fellow, 1975-78, Alfred P. Sloan fellow, 1985-85; recipient Dudley award Dudley Obs., 1983. Mem. Am. Astron. Soc., Internat. Astron. Union, N.Y. Acad. Scis., Am. Physical Soc. Current work: Supernova theory, neutrino astrophysics, neutron star physics. Subspecialties: Theoretical astrophysics; High energy astrophysics.

BURROWS, DAVID NELSON, astrophysicist; b. Abilene, Tex., May 5, 1953; s. Robert Nelson and Marion Elsie (Jauch) B.; m. Nancy Jane Willis, June 28, 1975; children—Daniel Nelson, Susannah Marie, Michael Christopher. B.A. in Physics, Music, Beloit Coll., 1975; M.S. in Physics, U. Wis., 1976, Ph.D. in Physics, 1982. Research assoc. U. Wis., Madison, 1982-83, Pa. State U., University Park, 1983—. Mem. Am. Astron. Soc., Sigma Xi, Phi Beta Kappa. Current work: Study of diffuse soft X-ray background and local interstellar medium. Subspecialty: X-ray high energy astrophysics. Home: 1132 S Garner St State College PA 16801 Office: Dept Astronomy 525 Davey Lab Pa State U University Park PA 16802

BURROWS, ELIZABETH PARKER, research chemist; b. Pitts., Nov. 5, 1930; d. William Wilson and Elizabeth (Lockwood) Parker; m. W. Dickinson Burrows, Mar. 8, 1958. B.A., Middlebury Coll., 1952; M.S., Stanford U., 1954, Ph.D., 1957. Mem. research faculty M.I.T., Cambridge, 1958-66; Vanderbilt U., Nashville, 1971-76, John's Hopkins U., Balt., 1976-78; staff scientist Worcester Found., Shrewsbury, Mass., 1967-68; lectr. U. Md., College Park, 1977-80; research chemist U.S. Army Fort Detrick, Frederick, Md., 1980—. Contbr. articles to profl. jours. Recipient Research and Devel. Achievement award U.S. Army, 1982. Fellow Am. Inst. Chemists; mem. Am. Chem. Soc., Sigma Xi. Current work: Organic mass spectrometry, especially environmental and health effects applications; structural and mechanistic organic chemistry. Subspecialties: Organic chemistry; Analytical chemistry. Home: 5111 Valley Pine Ct Frederick MD 21701 Office: U S Army Med Bioengineering Research and Devel Lab Fort Detrick Frederick MD 21701

BURROWS, JAMES H., computer science government program administrator. Dir., Inst. for Computer Scis. and Tech., Nat. Bur. Standards, Gaithersburg, Md. . Office: Nat Bur of Standards Inst for Computer Scis and Tech Gaithersburg MD 20234

BURROWS, THOMAS WESLEY, physicist; b. Janesville, Wis., May 17, 1943; s. Martin Harry and Esther Marie (Hugget) B.; m. Lucy Marion Grant, Aug. 31, 1968; children—Laura Lee, Sean Nicholas Grant. B.S., U. Wis.-Madison, 1965, Ph.D., 1972. Nuclear info. research assoc. U. Ky., Lexington, 1972-74; asst. physicist Brookhaven Nat. Lab., Upton, N.Y., 1974-76, assoc. physicist, 1976-79, physicist, 1979—; sec. Panel on Reference Nuclear Data, Upton, 1977-82. Editor: NEANDC Specialists Meeting on Yields and Decay Data of Fission Product Nuclides, 1984. Contbr. articles to profl. jours. Mem. The Inst. of Physics, Am. Phys. Soc., Am. Chem. Soc. (nuclear chemistry and tech. div.). Fast neutron physics; light-ion charged-particle reactions; nuclear structure and decay data. Subspecialty: Nuclear physics. Office: Brookhaven Nat Lab Bldg 197D Upton NY 11973

BURRUS, CHARLES ANDREW, JR., research physicist; b. Shelby, N.C., July 16, 1927; s. Charles Andrew and Velma (Martin) B.; m. Barbara Ione Dunlevy, May 4, 1957; children: Charles Andrew III, Barbara Jean, John Alan. B.S. cum laude in Physics, Davidson Coll., 1950; M.S. in Physics, Emory U., 1951; Ph.D. in Physics (Tex. Co. fellow, Shell Co. fellow), Duke U., 1955. Research assoc. dept. physics Duke U., Durham, N.C., 1954-55; mem. tech. staff AT&T Bell Labs., Holmdel, N.J., 1955—. Contbr. articles on millimeter and submillimeter-wave spectroscopy, techniques and semicondr. devices for lightwave communications, long-wavelength photoemitters and photodetectors for lightwave communications to tech. jours. Served with USNR, 1945-46. Named Disting. Mem. Tech. Staff Bell Telephone Labs., 1982. Fellow AAAS, Am. Phys. Soc., IEEE, Optical Soc. Am. (David Richardson medal 1982). Methodist. Current Work: Research on devices and technology for lightwave (optical fiber) communications. Subspecialties: Semiconductors; Fiber optics. Home: 62 Highland Ave Fair Haven NJ 07701 Office: AT&T Bell Labs Crawford Hill Lab Holmdel NJ 07733

BURSTEIN, ELIAS, physicist, educator; b. N.Y.C., Sept. 30, 1917; s. Samuel and Sarah (Plotkin) B.; m. Rena Ruth Benson, Sept. 19, 1943; children—Joanna Bliss, Sandra Joy, Miriam Stephanie. A.B., Bklyn. Coll., 1938, D.Sc. (hon.), 1985; A.M., U. Kans., 1941; postgrad. MIT, 1941-43, Cath. U., 1946-48; D. Tech. (hon.), Chalmers U. Tech., Göteborg, Sweden, 1982; D.Sc. (hon.), Bklyn. Coll., 1985. Asst. instr. U. Kans., 1939-41; research asst. M.I.T., 1941-43, research asso., 1943-44; project engr. White Research Assos., Boston, 1944-45; physicist Crystal br. U.S. Naval Research Lab., 1945-58, head semiconductor br., 1958; prof. physics U. Pa., Phila., 1958—, Mary Amanda Wood prof. physics, 1982—; Jubilee vis. prof. physics Chalmers U. Tech., Göteborg, 1981. Editor-in-chief: Solid State Communications, 1969—; co-editor: Comments on Solid State Physics, 1971—. Recipient John Price Wetherill medal Franklin Inst., 1979; Guggenheim fellow, 1980. Fellow Am. Phys. Soc., Optical Soc. Am.; mem. Nat. Acad. Scis., AAAS, Sigma Xi. Club: Cosmos (Washington). Patentee in field. Current work: Linear and nonlinear electromagnetic phenomena at metal and semiconductor surfaces with and without associates. Subspecialty: Solid state physics. Office: Dept Physics U Pa Philadelphia PA 19104

BURSTEIN, PAUL HARRIS, physicist; b. Chelsea, Mass., Aug. 28, 1948; s. Sol and Esther (Levine) B.; m. Dorothy P. Peavy, Dec. 7, 1946. B.S., MIT, 1970; Ph.D., U. Wis., 1976. Postdoctoral fellow U. Wis., Madison, 1976; sr. staff scientist Am. Sci. & Engring., Inc., Cambridge, Mass., 1976—. Contbr. articles to profl. jours. Mem. Am. Phys. Soc., Am. Astron. Soc., Optical Soc. Am. Patentee in field. Current Work: Non destructive testing applications of x-rays; high energy x-ray inspection; computed tomography; science management. Subspecialty: X-Ray applications. Home: 19 Glengarry Rd Winchester MA 01890 Office: Fort Washington Cambridge MA

BURT, MICHAEL EDWARD, physician, surgeon; b. Newark, Jan. 3, 1948; s. Edward and Shirlee (Muzzio) B.; m. Jacqueline JoAnn Panlone, July 9, 1970; children: Bryan Michael, Lauren Gail. A.B., Rutgers U., 1970; M.D., St. Louis U., 1975; Ph.D., George Washington U., 1981. Diplomate Am. Bd. Surgery. Intern dept. surgery U. Wash. Affiliated Hosps., Seattle, 1975-76; jr. asst. resident N.Y. Hosp.-Cornell Med. Center, N.Y.C., 1976-77, resident, 1981-83; clin. assoc. Nat. Cancer Inst. NIH, Bethesda, Md., 1977-79, investigator, 1979-80, cancer expert, 1980-81; fellow in cardio-thoracic surgery N.Y. Hosp.-Cornell Med. Ctr., Meml. Sloan-Kettering Cancer Ctr., N.Y.C. Contbr. articles to profl. jours. Served with USPHS, 1977-80. Recipient James Ewing research award Soc. Surg. Oncology, 1980, 81; research award Assn. Acad. Surgery, 1981. Mem. N.Y. Acad. Scis., Am. Fedn. Clin. Research, Am. Assn. Cancer Research, Am. Physiol. Soc., Fedn. Am. Soc. Exptl. Biology. Current Work: Evaluating metabolic host-tumor interactions at the substrate level. Subspecialties: Surgery; Cancer research (medicine). Office: NY Hosp-Cornell Med Center 525 E 68th St Dept Surgery New York NY 10021

BURT, PHILIP BARNES, physicist, educator; b. Memphis, July 1, 1934; s. Louie Einsinger and Bess Maud (Bolton) B.; m. Harriet Grace Clack, June 18, 1954; children—Elizabeth Lynn, Constance Harris, Sydney Faith, Timothy Clack. A.B., U. Tenn., 1956, M.S., 1968, Ph.D., 1961. Sr. scientist Calif. Inst. Tech., Pasadena, 1961-65; vis. prof. U. So. Calif., Los Angeles, 1963; cons. Oak Ridge Nat. Lab., 1966-71; asst. prof. physics Clemson U., S.C., 1965-69, assoc. prof., 1969-73, prof., 1973—, head dept., 1982—; cons. in field. Author: Quantum Mechanics and Nonlinear Waves, 1981. Contbr. articles to profl. jours., chpts. to books. NSF fellow, 1960-61; NATO grantee, 1983-84. Mem. Am. Phys. Soc., Am. Math. Soc., Sigma Xi, Omicron Delta Kappa, Kappa Sigma (pres. 1956). Baptist. Current work: Nonlinear field theories, nonlinear waves in quantum theory; nonlinear partial differential equations; high energy physics. Subspecialty: Theoretical physics. Home: 210 Wyatt Ave Clemson SC 29631 Office: Dept Physics Clemson U Clemson SC 29631

BURTON, DONALD JOSEPH, chemistry educator; b. Balt., July 16, 1934; s. Lawrence Andrew and Dorothy Wilhelmina (Koehler) B.; m. Margaret Anna Billing, June 21, 1958; children—Andrew, Jennifer, David, Julie, Elizabeth. B.S., Loyola Coll.-Balt., 1956; Ph.D., Cornell U., 1961; postgrad., Purdue U., 1961-62. Asst. prof.chemistry U. Iowa, Iowa City, 1962-67, assoc. prof., 1967-70, prof., 1970—. Mem. Am. Chem Soc. (Creative Work award 1984), Chem. Soc. London, Sigma Xi, Alpha Chi Sigma. Roman Catholic. Current work: Fluorine and phosphorus chemistry, organometallics chemistry. Subspecialties: Organic chemistry; Synthetic chemistry. Home: RR2 Box 72 Iowa City IA 52240 Office: U Iowa Chemistry Dept Iowa City IA 52242

BURTON, GLENN WILLARD, geneticist; b. Clatonia, Nebr., May 5, 1910; s. Joseph Fearn and Nellie (Rittenburg) B.; m. Helen Maurine Jeffryes, Dec. 16, 1934; children: Elizabeth Ann (Mrs. John Edward Fowler), Robert Glenn, Thomas Jeffryes, Joseph William, Richard Bennett. B.Sc., U. Nebr., 1932, D.Sc. (hon.), 1962; M.Sc., Rutgers U., 1933, Ph.D., 1936, D.Sc. (hon.), 1955. With U.S. Dept. Agr. and U. Ga. at Tifton Expt. Sta., 1936—, prin. geneticist, 1952—, chmn. div. agronomy, 1950-64; Univ. Found. prof. U. Ga., 1957. Mem. Tift County Bd. Edn., 1953-58. Recipient 1st ann. agrl. award So. Seedsmen Assn., 1950; Sears-Roebuck research award, 1953, 60; Superior Service award Dept. Agr., 1955; Disting. Service award, 1980; 1st Ford Almanac Crops and Soils Research award, 1962; Pres.'s award for Disting. Fed. Civilian Service, 1981; Nat. Medal of Sci., 1983; named Man of Year in So. Agr. Progressive Farmer, 1954; numerous other awards and citations. Fellow Am. Soc. Agronomy (Stevenson award 1949, John Scott award 1957, v.p. 1961, pres. 1962); mem. Am. Genetic Assn., Am. Soc. Range Mgmt., Nat. Acad. Sci., Sigma Xi, Alpha Zeta, Gamma Sigma Delta. Current Work: Genetic improvement and germplasm management of Cynodon spp; Paspalum spp. developing superior genetic and physiology research methods. Subspecialties: Plant genetics; Plant physiology (agriculture). Home: 421 W 10th St Tifton GA 31794

BURTON, HOWARD ALAN, neuropsychologist, computer company executive; b. Bklyn., May 9, 1951; s. Lawrence and Esther P. (Scondutto) B. B.A., SUNY, Stony Brook, 1973, M.A., 1974; Ph.D., St. Louis U., 1978. Lectr. Dowling Coll., Oakdale, N.Y., 1974; data processing cons. Immunology Researching Found., Great Neck, N.Y., 1975; research asst. sleep lab. St. Louis U., 1976; research asso. Md. Psychiat. Research Center, Balt., 1978-81; pres. Synclastic Communications, Inc., Syncom, Inc., Richmond Heights, Mo., 1982—. Contbr. articles to profl. jours. Active Boy Scouts Am., Eagle Scout. Recipient Order of Arrow. Mem. Soc. Neurosci., N.Y. Acad. Sci, Brit. Brain Research Assn., European Brain and Behavior Soc. Current Work: Neural correlates of behavior/information processing and real time data capture and analysis. Subspecialties: Neuropsychology; Numerical analysis (computer science).

BURTON, KAREN POLINER, physiologist, educator; b. Albuquerque, Feb. 18, 1952; d. Saul and Mary (With) P.; m. Michael David Burton, June 29, 1974; B.S., So. Meth. U., 1974; Ph.D., U. Tex. Health Sci. Ctr., 1978. Faculty assoc. U. Tex. Health Sci. Ctr., Dallas, 1979, instr., 1979-81; asst. prof. U. South Ala., Mobile, 1981-82; asst. prof. physiology U. Tex. Health Sci. Ctr., Dallas, 1983—. Contbr. articles to profl. jours. Grantee NIH, 1982-85, Am. Heart Assn. of Tex. 1980-81, 83-85, Am. Heart Assn. of Ala., 1982-83, U. Tex. Health Sci. Ctr. fellow, 1978-79. Mem. Am. Physiol. Soc., Am. Heart Assn., Internat. Soc. Heart Research, Electron Microscopy Soc. Am., AAAS. Democratic. Roman Catholic. Current work: Cardiovascular physiology; membrane pathophysiology, electron microscopy, electron probe x-ray microanalysis. Subspecialties: Physiology (medicine); Cardiology. Home: 4004 Bobbin Ln Addison TX 75244 Office: U Tex Health Sci Ctr Dept Physiology 5323 Harry Hines Dallas TX 75235

BURTON, WILLIAM BUTLER, astronomer; b. Richmond, Va., July 13, 1940; s. Joseph Ashby and Denison (Laws) B.; m. Judy Marie Johnson, Mar. 26, 1972; children: Hannah Marie, Benjamin Joseph, Molly Catherine. B.A., Swarthmore Coll., 1962; postgrad. (Fulbright scholar 1962-63, 63-64, Kovalenko scholar 1964), U. Leiden, Netherlands, 1965, Ph.D., 1970. Research asso. Nat. Radio Astromomy Obs., 1971-73, asst. scientist, then scientist, 1973-78; prof. astronomy, chmn. dept. U. Minn., 1978-81; prof. astronomy U. Leiden, 1981—. Mem. Am. Astron. Soc., Internat. Astron. Union, Netherlands Astron. Soc., Sigma Xi. Current Work: Observation radio astronomy with interest focussed on problems relating to galactie structure and the interstellar medium. Subspecialty: Radio and microwave astronomy. Address: Sterrewacht U Leiden PO Box 9513 Leiden The Netherlands

BURWELL, EDWARD LANGDON, physician; b. Seattle, Dec. 7, 1919; s. Edward Langdon and Lucretia (Owings) B.; m. Barbara Gates, June 13, 1943; children—Langdon Gates, David Gates, Beverly Burwell Lacey. B.S., Harvard U., 1941, M.D., 1944. Diplomate Am. Bd. Internal Medicine. Intern in medicine Peter Brent Brigham Hosp., Boston, 1944-45, asst. resident in medicine, 1947-48; asst. in pathology Pathology Inst., U. Zurich, 1948-49; research fellow hematology U. Wash. Med. Sch., Seattle, 1949-50; sr. resident in medicine U. Wash. Hosp., Seattle, 1950-51; pvt. practice internal medicine, Falmouth, Mass., 1954—; mem. staff Falmouth Hosp., clin. instr. Harvard U., Med. Sch., 1973—; bd. dirs. Mass. Blue Shield, 1969-73. Served with AUS, 1945-47, USPHS, 1951-53. Mem. ACP, Am. Assn. Founds. Med. Care (bd. dirs. 1973—), Commonwealth Inst. Medicine (bd. dirs. 1972—), Inst. Medicine, AMA, Mass. Med. Soc., Barnstable Med. Soc., Pilgrim Found. Med. Care., Mass. Soc. Internal Medicine, Am. Soc. Internal Medicine, Assn. Preservation Cape Cod. Subspecialty: Internal medicine. Office: Falmouth Med Assocs 4 Bramblebush Park Falmouth MA 02540

BURZYNSKI, STANISLAW RAJMUND, internist, cancer researcher; b. Lublin, Poland, Jan. 23, 1943; came to U.S., 1970, naturalized, 1977; s. Grzegorz and Zofia Miroslawa (Radzikowski) B.; m. Barbara Burzynski, Feb. 8, 1979; 1 son, Grzegorz Stanislaw. M.D. with distinction, Med. Acad., Lublin, 1967, Ph.D., 1968. Lic. Tex. State Bd. Med. Examiners, 1973. Teaching asst. Med. Acad., Lublin, 1962-67, intern, 1967-68, resident, 1969-70; research asso. Baylor Coll. Medicine, 1970-72, asst. prof., 1972-77, practice medicine specializing in internal medicine, Houston, 1977—; pres. Burzynski Research Inst., Houston, 1977—. Contbr. articles in field to profl. jours. Nat. Cancer Inst. grantee, 1974-77; West Found. grantee, 1975. Mem. AMA, AAAS, Am. Assn. Cancer Research, Harris County Med. Soc., Polish Nat. Alliance (pres. Houston chpt. 1974-75), Soc. Neuroscience, Tex. Med. Assn., Sigma Xi. Current Work: Antineoplastons and their role in the treatment of neoplastic disease. Subspecialties: Internal medicine; Cancer research (medicine).

BUSBY, JOHN CARROLL, pharmaceutical company executive; b. Salisbury, N.C., Sept. 24, 1920; s. John C. and Florence (Fransioli) B.; m. Helen McGill, June 10, 1951; children—John III, Florence E., Helen K., Virginia L. B.S., U.N.C., 1940; M.S., Lowell U., 1947. Commd. ensign U.S. Navy, 1942, advanced through grades to capt.; ret., 1965; v.p. S.F. Durst & Co., Inc., Phila., 1966-70; pres. Am. Biologics Corp., N.Y.C., 1971-73; chmn. Phila. Biologics Ctr., 1974—. Editor Pacific Supply Letter, 1955-57; assoc. editor Naval Research Logistics Quar., 1959-69. Contbr. articles to profl. jours. Inventor apparatus and method for drafting fibers. Decorated Navy Commendation medal. Mem. AAAS, Am. Chem. Soc., N.Y. Acad. Scis., Smithsonian Instn., Mensa Edn. and Research Found. (bd. dirs. 1979—), Phi Beta Kappa, Beta Gamma Sigma. Episcopalian. Club: N.Y. Yacht (N.Y.C.). Subspecialty: Biotechnology administration. Office: Philadelphia Biologics Ctr 1015 Chestnut St Philadelphia PA 19107

BUSCH, ALLEN CYRIL, research analyst, educator; b. Cin., Aug. 21, 1931; s. Walter A. and Lillian (Voegtle) B.; m. Patricia Burr, Mar. 23, 1957; children—Michael, Melany, Eric, Craig. B.A., Miami U., 1955, M.A., 1958. Suggestion investigator Gen. Motors, Dayton, Ohio, 1955-57; personnel research specialist Korger Co., Cin., 1958-60; human factors bd. chief Avco Research & Devel. Corp., Wilmington, Mass., 1960-63; human factors bd. chief HRB Singer, State Coll., Pa., 1964-65; research psychologist USAF Cambridge Research Lab., Bedford, Mass., 1965-67; branch mgr. FAA Tech. Ctr., Atlantic City, N.J., 1967—; adj. prof. North Eastern U., Boston, 1966-67; adj. prof., Embry Riddle U., Atlantic City, 1982. Contbr. articles to profl. jours. Mem. regional sch. bd., N.J., 1978-79. Served to cpl. USMC, 1951-52. Decorated U.S. Naval Midshipman award, 1952; recipient N.Y. Acad. Sci. award, Sec. Silver medal award, Dept. Transp., 1982. Mem. IEEE (sr., chmn., treas., sec. 1975-78), Am. Phychol. Assn., Human Factor Soc., System Safety Soc., AAAS. Current work: Study air traffic control system safety and collision risk; advisor to panels and work groups Internat. Civil Aviation Organization. Subspecialties: Systems engineering; Statistics. Home: 1014 Richard Dr Linwood NJ 08221 Office: FAA Tech Ctr Act 220 Atlantic City NJ 08405

BUSCH, DANIEL ADOLPH, consulting petroleum geologist; b. St. Paul, May 31, 1912; s. Karl George Adolph and Lulu E. (Snapp) B.; m. Emilie Louise Finch, Dec. 22, 1939; children—Daniel Andrew, David Arthur. B.S., Capital U., 1934, D.Sc. (hon.), 1960; M.A., Ohio State U., 1936, Ph.D., 1939. Instr., U. Pitts., 1938-42; petroleum geologist Pa. Geol. Survey, Pitts., 1942-43; cons. geologist Huntley & Huntley, Pitts., 1943-46; sr. research geologist Carter Research Lab., Tulsa, 1946-49; staff geologist Carter Oil Co., Tulsa, 1949-51; mgr. exploration Zephyr Petroleum Co., Tulsa, 1951-54; cons. geologist, Tulsa, 1954—; vis. prof. U. Okla., Norman, 1964-74; lectr. Oil and Gas Cons. Internat., Inc., Tulsa, 1969—. Author: Stratigraphic Traps in Sandstones-Exploration Techniques, 1973 (Pres.'s award 1975); Exploration Methods for Sandstone Reservoirs, 1985; contbr. articles to profl. jours. Recipient Orton award Ohio State U., 1960. Fellow Geol. Soc. Am., Sigma Xi; mem. Am. Assn. Petroleum Geologists (hon.; v.p. 1966-67, pres. 1973-74, Matson award 1959, A.I. Levorsen award 1971, Sidney Powers Meml. medal 1982), Tulsa Geol. Soc. Methodist. Club: Petroleum of Tulsa. Current work: Consulting geology (petroleum) and world-wide lecturing on exploration methods for sandstone reservoirs. Home: 3757 S Wheeling Ave Tulsa OK 74105

BUSCH, HARRIS, pharmacologist; b. Chgo., May 23, 1923; s. Maurice Ralph and Rose Lillian (Feigenholtz) B.; m. Rose Klora, June 16, 1945; children: Daniel Avery, Laura Anne Busch Smolkin, Gerald Irwin, Fredric Neal. B.S., U. Ill., 1944, M.D. with honors, 1946; M.S., U. Wis., 1950, Ph.D., 1952. Intern Cook County Hosp., Chgo., 1946-47; asst. surgeon, sr. asst. surgeon USPHS, 1947-49; postdoctoral fellow Nat. Cancer Inst., 1950-52; asst. prof. biochemistry, internal medicine Yale U., 1952-55; asso. prof., prof. pharmacology U. Ill., 1955-60; prof. biochemistry, chmn. dept. Baylor U. Coll. Medicine, 1960-62, prof. pharmacology, chmn. dept., 1960—, disting. service prof., 1978—, chmn. student promotions com., 1969—, mem. policy planning com., 1972—, dir. Cancer Research Center; vis. prof. U. Chgo., 1968, 71, Northwestern U., 1968, Ga. Med. Coll., 1971, Washington U., St. Louis, 1972, U. Ala., Birmingham, 1972, Ind. U., Indpls., 1972, U. Nev., Reno, 1978, U. Colo., Denver, 1980; cons. lectr. U. Tenn., U. Tex., San Antonio, 1971; disting. lectr. SUNY, Buffalo, 1977; Centennial lectr. U. Ill. Coll. Medicine, 1981; cons. VA, Meth. hosps., both Houston, Bristol-Myers.; mem. adv. com. cell and devel. biology Am. Cancer Soc., 1978—; cancer chemotherapy study sect. USPHS; mem. Nat. Cancer Planning Com., 1971; mem. bd. sci. counselors to div. cancer treatment Nat. Cancer Inst., 1975. Author: Chemistry of Pancreatic Diseases, 1959, An Introduction to the Biochemistry of the Cancer Cell, 1962, Histones and Other Nuclear Proteins, 1965; co-author: Chemotherapy, 1966, The Nucleolus, 1970; editor: Frontiers in Medical Biochemistry, 1962, The Nucleus of the Cancer Cell, 1963, Jour. Phys. Chemistry and Physics, Methods in Cancer Research, vol. I, 1966, vols. II and III, 1967, vol. IV, 1968, Methods in Cancer Research, vol. V, 1970, vol.VI, 1971, vols. VII-IX, 1973, vol. X, 1973, Methods in Cancer Research, vol. XI, 1975, vols. XII and XIII, 1976, Methods in Cancer Research, vols. XIV, XV, 1978, Molecular Biology of Cancer, 1974, Cell Nucleus, Vols. I-III, 1974, IV-VII, 1978, VIII-IX, 1980; editorial bd.: Jour. Cancer Research and Clin. Oncology, Jour. Biol. Chemistry, Cancer Investigation, New Drugs, Physiol. Chemistry, Phys. Life Scis. Recipient Outstanding Alumnus award for service to edn. and research U. Ill., 1977, Disting. Faculty award Baylor U. Coll. Medicine, 1982; Baldwin scholar oncology Yale U. Sch. Medicine, 1952-55; scholar cancer research Am. Cancer Soc., 1955. Mem. Am. Soc. Biol. Chemists, Am. Assn. Cancer Research (public issues com. 1977), Am. Chem. Soc., Soc. Pharmacology and Exptl. Therapeutics, Soc. Exptl. Biology and Medicine, Sigma Xi, Alpha Omega Alpha. Current Work: The nucleus of the cancer cell. Subspecialties: Cell study oncology; Pharmacology. Home: 4966 Dumfries Dr Houston TX 77096

BUSECK, PETER R., geochemistry educator; b. Sept. 30, 1935; s. Paul M. and Edith G. (Stern) B.; m. Alice E. Buseck, June 20, 1960; children: Lori, David, Susan, Paul. A.B., Antioch Coll., 1957; M.A., Columbia U., 1959, Ph.D., 1962. Fellow geophys. Lab. Carnegle Inst., Washington, 1961-63; with depts. chemistry and geology Ariz. State U., 1963—; now prof., vis. prof. dept. geology Oxford U., 1970-71, Stanford U., 1979-80. Contbr. articles to profl. jours. NSF fellow, 1970-71; Overseas fellow Churchill Coll., Cambridge U., 1979-80; recipient Corning award, 1975; JEOL award Microbeam Analysis Soc., 1981. Fellow AAAS, Geol. Soc. Am., Mineral. Soc. Am.; mem. Am. Geophys. Union, Geochem. Soc., Microbeam Soc., Soc. Econ. Geologists, Can. Mineral Soc., Air Pollution Control Assn., Am. Assn. Aerosol Research, Electron Microscope Soc. Am. Current Work: Solid state geochemistry, mineralogy, electron microscopy, meteoritics, atmospheric chemistry environmental geochemistry/air pollution, geochemical monitoring of active volcanism and geothermal activity. Subspecialties: Geochemistry; Mineralogy. Office: Dept Chemistry Arizona State Tempe AZ 85287

BUSH, DAVID FREDERIC, psychology educator, researcher, consultant; b. Watertown, N.Y., July 12, 1942; s. Frederic R. and Charlotte M. (Ellingworth) B. B.A., U. South Fla., 1965; M.A., U. Wyo., 1968; Ph.D., Purdue U., 1972. Mgmt. trainee Pan Am. World Airways, Cocoa Beach, Fla., 1964-65; instr. Hiram Scott Coll., Scottsbluff, Nebr., 1967-69; assoc. dir. human orgn. sci. Villanova (Pa.) U., 1981—, assoc. prof. psychoogy, 1972—; cons. Delaware Valley Transplant, Phila., 1979—; dir. Bush Assocs., Broomall, Pa., 1980—, Life Guidance Services, Broomall, 1977—; cons. MidAtlantic Research Inst., Bethesda, Md., 1975-78. Co-editor: Straight Talk, 1975, Communication in the Consultation, 1982; editor: Human Development, 1975; assoc. editor: Social Sci. Rev, 1977—. Mem. Phila. Orch. Assn., 1976—, People's Light & Theater Co., Malvern, Pa., 1982, Am. Lung Assn., Norristown, Pa., 1982. Recipient Disting. Service award Hiram Scott Coll., 1969; David Ross fellow, 1972; NDEA fellow, 1969-71; E-SU grantee Oxford U., summer 1980. Mem. Internat. Communication Assn. (div. membership chmn. 1980—), Am. Psychol. Assn., Acad. Mgmt., Internat. Assn. Applied Psychology, Midwestern Psychol. Assn. (local rep. 1981—), Phi Kappa Phi (chpt. pres. 1982-83), English-Speaking Union. Club: Phila. Masters Track. Current Work: Gender differences in nonverbal communication; effects of gender differences in speaker on listener's ability to recall information; influences on memory for medical information and health-related decision making. Subspecialties: Social psychology; Health psychology. Home: 53 S Greenhill Rd Broomall PA 19008 Office: Villanova U Villanova PA 19085

BUSH, GEORGE EDWARD, physicist, cons.; B.S. in Physics, Purdue U., West Lafayette, Ind., 1960; M.S. in Cybernetic Systems, San Jose (Calif.) State Coll., 1975. Physicist Midwestern Univs. Research Assn., Madison, 1960-66, Lawrence Livermore (Calif.) Nat. Lab., 1966—; founder Solar Systems, Inc. Contbr. to: Solar Technology Handbook, 1980. Mem. AAAS, Internat. Solar Energy Soc. Current Work: Man-machine interface, small computers, data acquisition systems, instrumentation development, work station development, graphics applications, databases. Subspecialties: Solar energy; Computer engineering. Office: Box 931 Livermore CA 94550

BUSH, JAMES HASTINGS, chemist; b. Marion, Ohio, Sept. 18, 1951; s. Robert Roy and Anna Marie (Hastings) B.; m. Phyllis Louise Miller, June 7, 1974; 1 child, Jered Hastings. B.S., Findlay Coll. (Ohio), 1973; M.S., Xavier U., 1975; Ph.D., U. Wyo-Laramie, 1980. Research chemist, Cities Services, Tulsa, Okla., 1980-82; research chemist Minerec Mining Chems., Tucson, 1982-84, dir. research, 1984—. Contbr. articles to profl. jours. Mem. Am. Chem. Soc. Current work: Synthesis of low ph collectors for froth flotation. Subspecialties: Organic chemistry; Metallurgy. Home: 3861 W Sunny Hills Pl Tucson AZ 85741 Office: Minerec Mining Chems 2420 N Hunchuca St Tucson AZ 85745

BUSH, SPENCER HARRISON, metallurgist; b. Flint, Mich., Apr. 4, 1920; s. Edward Charles and Rachel Beatrice (Roser) B.; m. Roberta Lee Warren, Aug. 28, 1948; children: David Spencer, Carl Edward. Student, Flint Jr. Coll., 1938-40, Ohio State U., 1943-44, U. Mich., 1946-53. Registered profl. engr., Calif. Asst. chemist Dow Chem. Co., 1940-42, 46; asso. Engring. Research Inst., U. Mich., 1947-53; research asst. Office Naval Research, 1950-53, instr. dental materials, 1951-53; metallurgist Hanford Atomic Products Operation, Gen. Electric Co., 1953-54, supr. phys. metallurgy, 1954-57, supr. fuels fabrication devel., 1957-60, metall. specialist, 1960-63, cons. metallurgist, 1963-65; cons. to dir. Battelle N.W. Labs., Richland, Wash., 1965-70, sr. staff cons., 1970-83; pres. Rev. & Synthesis Assocs., cons., 1983—; lectr. metall. engring. Center for Grad. Study, U. Wash., 1953-67, affiliate prof., 1967—; chmn., com. study group on pressure vessel materials Electric Power Research Inst., 1974-78; cons. U. Calif. Lawrence Berkeley Labs., 1975-79; chmn. com. on reactor safeguards U.S. AEC, 1971; mem. Wash. Bd. Boiler Rules, 1972-85; Gillett lectr. ASTM, 1975; Mehl lectr., 1981, mem. Bd. Nuclear Codes and Standards, 1983—. Contbr. tech. articles to profl. jours. Served with U.S. Army, 1942-46. Recipient Silver Beaver award Boy Scouts Am.; Am. Foundrymens Soc. fellow, 1948-50; Regents prof. U. Calif., Berkeley, 1973-74. Fellow Am. Nuclear Soc. (adv. editorial bd. nuclear applications 1965-77, bd. dirs. 1984—), Am. Soc. Metals (chmn. program council 1966-67, trustee 1967-69, chmn. fellow com. 1968), ASME (mem. editorial bd. Jour. Pressure Vessel Tech., chmn. sect. XI 1985—, Langer award 1983); mem. AIME (chmn. ann. seminar com. 1967-68), ASTM, Nat. Acad. Engring., Sigma Xi, Tau Beta Pi, Phi Kappa Phi. Current Work: Reactor safety, pressure boundary codes and standards, nondestructive examination, fracture mechanics. Subspecialties: Metallurgical engineering; Nuclear engineering. Home: 630 Cedar Ave Richland WA 99352 Office: PO Box 999 Richland WA 99352

BUSHAW, THOMAS HENRY, chemist; b. Pullman, Wash., Sept. 9, 1953; s. Donald Wayne and Sylvia Ruth (Lybecker) B. B.A., Carleton Coll., 1975; Ph.D., Purdue U., 1979. With Dallas Research Lab., Mobil Research & Devel. Corp., 1979—, research chemist, 1982-84, sr. research chemist, 1984—. Contbr. articles to profl. jours. Mem. Am. Chem. Soc. Democrat. Current Work: Inductively coupled plasma emission spectroscopy; fluorescence spectroscopy; laboratory automation and computer applications to chemistry. Subspecialty: Analytical chemistry.

BUSHNELL, ROBERT HEMPSTEAD, solar energy consultant, engineer; b. Wooster, Ohio, May 11, 1924; s. John and Dyllone (Hempstead) B.; m. Martha W. Dicks, Oct. 2, 1965; children: Helen, Orson. B.Sc. in Engring. Physics, Ohio State U., 1946, M.Sc. in Physics, 1947; Ph.D. in Meteorology (Univ. Corp. Atmospheric Research fellow), U. Wis., 1962. Registered profl. engr., Colo. Physicist Hoover Co., Ohio, 1948-50; engr. Goodyear Aircraft Corp., Ohio, 1950-56, RCA, N.J., 1957-58; research meteorologist Nat. Center Atmospheric Research, Boulder, Colo., 1962-74, cons. solar energy, 1974—. Contbr. articles to profl. jours. Served with USNR, 1944-46. Mem. Am. Meteorol. Soc., ASHRAE, Internat. Solar Energy Soc., AAAS, U.S. Metric Assn. (treas. 1975-79). Current Work: Climatology of solar irradiation and temperature, response of bldgs. to climate, distbn. of intensity of solar irradiation. Subspecialties: Climatology; Solar energy. Home and Office: 502 Ord Dr Boulder CO 80303

BUSHNELL, WILLIAM RODGERS, plant physiologist, educator; b. Wooster, Ohio, Aug. 19, 1931; s. John and Dyllone (Hempstead) B.; m. Ann Holcomb, Sept. 20, 1952; children: Thomas, John, Mary. B.A., U. Chgo., 1951; B.S., Ohio State U., 1953, M.S., 1955; Ph.D., U. Wis., 1960. Research plant physiologist Agrl. Research Service, U.S. Dept. Agr., St. Paul, 1960—; asst. prof. dept. plant pathology U. Minn., 1966-72, assoc. prof., 1972-73, adj. prof., 1973—. Contbr. articles in field to profl. jours. NSF fellow, 1957-60; NSF grantee, 1964, 66; Dept. Agr. grantee, 1980, 82, 85; Alexander Von Humboldt Found. award, 1984; Fellow Am. Phytopath. Soc.; mem. Am. Soc. Plant Physiologists, AAAS. Current Work: Research on physiology of rust and powdery mildew diseases of cereal plants. Subspecialties: Plant physiology (agriculture); Plant pathology. Office: University of Minnesota Cereal Rust Lab Saint Paul MN 55108

BUSIS, NEIL AMDUR, neurologist, neurobiologist; b. Pitts., Mar. 4, 1951; s. Sidney Nahum and Sylvia (Amdur) B.; m. Cynthia Dickter, May 24, 1981. B.A. summa cum laude (Nat. Merit scholar), Yale Coll., 1973; M.D., U. Pa., 1977. Diplomate: Nat. Bd. Med. Examiners. Student researcher Lab. Neuropharmacology, NIMH, Washington, summers 1974, 75, Mar. 1976; intern and asst. resident in medicine Johns Hopkins Hosp., Balt., 1977-79; research assoc. Lab. Biochem. Genetics, Nat. Heart, Lung and Blood Inst., NIH, 1979-81; resident dept. neurology Mass. Gen. Hosp., Boston, 1981—. Contbr. articles to profl. jours. Served with USPHS, 1979-81. Recipient Mosby Book award U. Pa. Sch. Medicine. Mem. Am. Acad. Neurology, AAAS, Soc. Neurosci., Amyotrophic Lateral Sclerosis Soc. Am., Phi Beta Kappa, Alpha Omega Alpha. Current Work: Nervous system development and neuronal communication. Subspecialties: Neurobiology; Neurology. Office: Mass Gen Hosp Dept Neurology Boston MA 02114

BUSKE, NORMAN L., consulting scientist, energy researcher; b. Milw., Oct. 11, 1943; s. Gilbert and Genevieve (Strutt) B.; m. Patricia Teller, June 10, 1965; children: Heather, Alisyn, Robin; m. Linda S. Josephson, Aug. 25, 1980. B.A. in Physics, U. Conn., 1964, M.A., 1965; M.S. in Oceanography, Johns Hopkins U., 1967. Oceanographer Ocean Sci. & Engring., Inc., Rockville, Md., 1968-71; prin. Sea-Test Co., Laie, Hawaii, 1972-76; sr. scientist/engr. Van Gulik & Assocs., Lake Oswego, Oreg., 1976-77; dir. research Pacific Engring. Corp., Portland, Oreg., 1977-78; prin. Search Technical Services, Davenport, Wash., 1978—; sci. adviser Greenpeace. Inventor reciprocating and rotary, nonlinear engines. Author: Physical Reality, 1985. Mem. ASME, ASTM, IEEE, N.Y. Acad. Scis., Soc. Automotive Engrs. Current Work: Development of methodologies for fire investigations; energy and nuclear weapons policy. Subspecialties: Relativity and gravitation; Theoretical and applied mechanics. Home and Office: Star Route Box 17 Davenport WA 99122

BUSKIRK, ELSWORTH ROBERT, applied physiology educator; b. Beloit, Wis., Aug. 11, 1925; s. Ellsworth Fred and Laura (Parman) B.; m. Mable Heen, Aug. 28, 1948; children—Laurel Ann, Kristine Janet. B.A., St. Olaf Coll., 1950; M.A., U. Minn.-Mpls., 1951, Ph.D., 1954. Research assoc. U. Minn.-Mpls.,

1954; physiologist Quartermaster Research & Devel. Ctr., Natick, Mass., 1954-57, NIAMD, NIH, Bethesda, Md., 1957-63; prof. applied physiology Pa. State U., 1963—; mem. nutritional panel gen. com. Dept. Def. Food Program, Nat. Acad. Scis., Nat. Research Council, 1980—. Assoc. editor: Jour. Applied Physiology, 1976-84, Jour. Cardiac Rehab., 1980—, Am. Jour. Clin. Nutrition, 1982—, Jour. Gerontology, 1982—; guest reviewer Jour. Clin. Nutrition, Clin. Investigation, Research Quar., Metabolism, Diabetes, Circulation Research, and Sci., editor-in-chief, Medicine and Sci. in Sports and Exercise, 1985—; contbr. numerous articles to sci. jours., chpts. to books. Trustee, Centre Community Hosp., State College, Pa., 1966-74, pres., 1972-74; bd. dirs. Centre chpt. Am. Heart Assn., 1976—. Served with AUS, 1943-46. NATO Sr. Fellow in Sci. award, NSF, 1977. Mem. Aerospace Med. Assn., Am. Acad. Phys. Edn., Am. Assn. Health, Phys. Edn. and Recreation, AAAS, Am. Coll. Sports Medicine (Honor award, 1984), Am. Soc. Clin. Nutrition, Am. Inst. Nutrition, Am. Physiol. Soc., Am. Soc. Heating, Refrigerating and Air Conditioning Engrs., Assn. Chmn. Depts. Physiology, Nat. Insts. Health Alumni Assn., N.Y. Acad. Scis., Nutrition Today Soc., Pa. Assn. Health, Phys. Edn. and Recreation, N. Am. Assn. Study of Obesity. Lutheran. Club: Centre Hills Country (greens chmn. 1970-76). Current work: Physiology of exercise; environmental physiology; calorimetry; metabolism and nutrition; epidemiology of coronary heart disease; physiology of aging. Subspecialties: Physiology (biology); Nutrition (biology). Home: 216 Hunter Ave State College PA 16801 Office: Pa State U 119 Noll Lab University Park PA 16802

BUSS, EDWARD GEORGE, geneticist; b. Concordia, Kans., Aug. 28, 1921; s. George Edward and Kathryn (Luginsl) B.; m. Dorothy Ruth; children: Ellen, Norman. B.S., Kans. State Coll., 1943; M.S., Purdue U., 1949, Ph.D., 1956. Research asst. Purdue U., West Lafayette, Ind., 1946-49, instr. poultry sci., 1955-56; asst. prof. Colo. State U., Fort Collins, 1949-55; acting head dept., 1950-55; assoc. prof. poultry sci. Pa State U., State College, 1956-65, prof., 1965—. Served to capt. inf. U.S. Army, 1943-46. NIH research grantee, 1960-79. Mem. AAAS, Am. Inst. Biol. Scis., Am. Genetic Assn., Am. Soc. Zoologists, Genetics Soc. Am., Poultry Sci. Assn., Soc. for Study Reproduction, Phi Eta Sigma. Democrat. Unitarian. Current Work: Parthenogenesis in turkeys, biochem. nature of difference between normal and mutant individuals and between desired and undesired individuals for quantitative traits. Subspecialties: Animal genetics; Reproductive biology. Home: 1420 S Garner St State College PA 16801 Office: Pennsylvania State University 2 Agrl Engring Bldg University Park PA 16802

BUSSARD, ROBERT WILLIAM, physicist; b. Washington, Aug. 11, 1928; s. Marcel Julian and Elsa Mathilda (Griesser) B.; m. Dolly H. Gray, 1981; children: Elise Marie Bussard Bright, William Julian, Robert Lee, Virginia Lesley. B.S. in Engring., UCLA, 1950, M.S. in Engring., 1952; A.M. in Physics, Princeton U., 1959, Ph.D. in Physics, 1961. Design engr. Falcon program Hughes Aircraft Co., 1949-51; mech. engr. aircraft nuclear propulsion project Oak Ridge Nat. Lab., 1952-55; alt. group leader nuclear rocket program Los Alamos Sci. Lab., 1955-62, alt. leader laser div., 1971-73; dir. nuclear systems staff, asst. dir. mechanics div. Space Tech. Labs., Thompson-Ramo-Wooldridge, Inc., Redondo Beach, Calif., 1962-64; assoc. mgr. research and engring., corp. chief scientist Electro-Optical Systems div. Xerox Corp., Pasadena, Calif., 1964-69; with CSI Corp., Los Angeles, 1969-70; mgr. Cherokee Assos., Pasadena, Md., 1970-74; asst. dir. div. controlled thermonuclear research U.S. AEC, Washington, 1973-74; founder, pres., chmn. Energy Resources Group, (ERG), Inc., La Jolla, Calif., Alexandria, Va., 1974, Internat. Nuclear Energy Systems Co. (INESCO), Inc., La Jolla and McLean, 1976—; cons. NATO, 1960-64, U.S. Dept. Energy, 1974-78; lectr. UCLA, 1960-69, U. Fla., 1962-64. Author: (with R.D. DeLauer) Nuclear Rocket Propulsion, 1958, Fundamentals of Nuclear Flight, 1965; editor: Nuclear Thermal and Electric Rocket Propulsion, 1967; contbr. articles to profl. jours. Fellow AIAA; mem. Am. Phys. Soc., Internat. Acad. Astronautics. Clubs: Princeton (N.Y.C.); Cosmos (Washington), Capitol Hill (Washington). Patentee space nuclear propulsion, power generation, fusion and fission power, solar power systems. Current Work: Fusion power development; space, propulsion; space weapons. Subspecialties: Fusion; Aerospace engineering and technology. Office: 11077 N Torrey Pines Rd La Jolla CA 92037

BUSSGANG, JULIAN JAKOB, electronic engineer; b. Lwow, Poland, Mar. 26, 1925; came to U.S., 1949, naturalized, 1954; s. Joseph and Stephanie (Philipp) B.; m. Fay Rita Vogel, Aug. 14, 1960; children: Jessica Edith, Julia Claire, Jeffrey Joseph. B.Sc., U. London, 1949; S.M. in Elec. Engring., MIT, 1951; Ph.D. in Applied Physics, Harvard U., 1955. Registered profl. engr., Mass. Mem. tech. staff Lincoln Lab., M.I.T., Lexington, 1951-55; mgr. applied research RCA, Burlington, Mass., 1955-62; pres. Signatron, Inc., Lexington, 1962—; vis. lectr. Harvard U., 1964; lectr. Northeastern U., Boston, 1962-65; mem. Mass. del. White House Conf. on Small Bus., 1980. Assoc. editor: Radio Sci., 1976-78; contbr. chpts. to books, also articles. Mem. Town Meeting, Lexington, 1975—; mem. alumni council M.I.T., 1965-72. Served with Free Polish Forces, 1942-46. Fellow IEEE; mem. Research Mgmt. Assn., Smaller Bus. Assn. New Eng., Am. Assn. Small Research Cos. Patentee in field. Current Work: Communication theory; information theory. Subspecialties: Electronics; Systems engineering. Office: 110 Hartwell Ave Lexington MA 02173

BUSTIN, MICHAEL, biochemist; b. Bukarest, Romania, Apr. 19, 1937; came to U.S. 1961, naturalized, 1982; s. Elmer M. and Lea (Nemesh) B.; m. Penelope E. Phipps, June 10, 1967; children—Ari, Ruth. B.S., U. Denver, 1964; Ph.D., U. Calif.-Berkeley, 1968. Assoc. prof. Weizman Inst., Israel, 1969-75; research chemist NIH, Bethesda, Md., 1975—. Current work: Gene structure and function; chromatin structure; chromosomol protiens; immunochemistry. Subspecialties: Biochemistry (biology); Cell biology. Office: Nat Cancer Inst Bldg 37 Room 3D-20 NIH Bethesda MD 20205

BUTCHER, HARVEY RAYMOND, III, astronomer; b. Salem, Mass., Aug. 3, 1947; s. Harvey Raymond, Jr. and Marilyn (Corning) B.; m. Phillipa Ruth Newton, Dec. 30, 1971; children: Jeremy Robert, Christopher Thomas. B.S., Calif. Inst. Tech., 1969; Ph.D., Australian Nat. U., Canberra, 1974. Research asst. infrared astronomy group Calif. Inst. Tech., Pasadena, 1967-69; research scholar Mt. Stromlo Obs., Australian Nat. U., Canberra, 1970-74; Bart Bok fellow Steward Obs., U. Ariz., Tucson, 1975-76; asst. astronomer Kitt Peak Nat. Obs., Tucson, 1976-79, asso. astronomer, 1979-81, astronomer, 1981-83; prof., dir. Kapteyn Obs. U. Groningen (Netherlands), 1983—. Mem. Am. Astron. Soc., Royal Astron. Soc. Current Work: Observational research on evolution of galaxies and on physics of non-thermal radio sources; devel. of advanced instrumental techs. Subspecialty: Optical astronomy. Office: Postbus 800 9700 AV Groningen Netherlands

BUTCHER, JAMES WALTER, biologist; b. Pa., Feb. 14, 1917; s. Louis and Mary B.; m. Mary Katharine Culley, June 18, 1944; children: Craig, Mary Helen. B.S., U. Pitts., 1943; M.S., U. Minn., 1949, Ph.D., 1951. With Gulf Research Devel. Corp., 1948, Dept. Agr., 1950-52, Minn. Dept. Agr., 1952-57; mem. faculty Mich. State U., East Lansing, 1957—, prof. biology, 1965—, asst., asso. dean research, 1969-74, chmn. dept. zoology, 1974-81, prof., chmn. emeritus, 1981—; acting dean Mich. State U. (Coll. Natural Sci.), 1973; cons. in field. Author papers in field, rev. articles. Served with USAAF, 1943-47. Fulbright sr. research scholar U. Vienna, 1966-67; grantee fed. and state govts., also industry. Mem. Ecol. Soc. Am., Am. Zool. Soc., Entomol. Soc. Am., Phi Beta Kappa, Sigma Xi. Subspecialty: Entomology. Home: 1002 Aragon Saint Augustine FL 32086 Office: 203 Natural Sci Bldg Mich State Univ East Lansing MI 48824

BUTCHER, JOHN EDWARD, animal scientist, educator, researcher; b. Belle Fourche, S.D., Aug. 4, 1923; s. James E. and Eva L. (Kirk) B.; m. Virginia O. Butcher, Apr. 28, 1951; children: Joan, Jean, James. B.S., Mont. State U., 1950, M.S., 1952; Ph.D., Utah State U., 1956. Ranch mgr. Mont. State U., 1949-50, mem. coop. extension staff, 1952, mem. range mgmt. faculty, 1952-53; mem. faculty Utah State U., 1955—, asst. prof. animal, dairy and vet. sci., 1955-59, assoc. prof., 1959-67, prof., 1967—; cons. Office Internat. Cooperation and Devel. Contbr. articles on beef cattle and sheep nutrition to profl. jours., 1953—. Mem. Nat. Land Adv. Council, 1982-85. Served with U.S. Army, 1946, 51. Named Utah Citizen of Yr. Utah Cattlemen's Assn., 1972; NSF fellow, 1954-55, 63; Rockefeller Found. fellow Mexico, 1965, 72. Fellow Am. Soc. Animal Sci., AAAS; mem. Am. Soc. Farm Mgrs. and Rural Appraisers, Am. Registry Profl. Animal Scientists, Soc. Range Mgmt., Am. Inst. Biol. Scis., Council Agrl. Sci. and Tech. Presbyterian. Lodge: Masons. Current Work: Beef cattle and sheep, from production to consumption; dietary phosphorus requirements of cows; (nutrition and management range and feed lot) beef and sheep. Subspecialties: Animal nutrition; Integrated systems modelling and engineering. Home: 1703 E 1030 N Logan UT 84321 Office: Utah State Logan UT 84322

BUTKUS, DONALD EUGENE, physician, army officer; b. Binghamton, N.Y., Oct. 9, 1934; s. John Geddy and Mary Margaret (Koval) B.; m. Nancy E. Whorton, Sept. 14, 1984; children—Allison M. Cunningham, Brian G., Christine E. B.S., Cornell U., 1956; M.D., Albany Med. Coll., 1960. Commd. 2d lt. U.S. Army, 1959, advanced through grades to col., 1975; intern Brooke Army Med. Ctr., San Antonio, 1960-61; resident Madigan Army Med. Ctr., Tacoma, 1961-64; chief gen. medicine Fitzsimons Army Hosp., Aurora, Colo., 1968-70; nephrology fellow U. Colo. Med. Ctr., Denver, 1970-72; chief nephrology service Fitzsimons Army Hosp., 1972-76; chief nephrology service Walter Reed Army Med. Ctr., Washington, 1976-77; chief dept. nephrology Walter Reed Army Inst. Research, Washington, 1977-81, dir. div. medicine, 1979—; nephrology cons. to U.S. Army surg. gen., Washington, 1976—. Contbr. articles to med. jours., chpts. to med. books. Decorated Bronze star. Fellow ACP; mem. Am. Fedn. Clin. Research, Am. Soc. Nephrology, Internat. Soc. Nephrology, Am. Physiol. Soc., Theta Chi. Club: Cornell of Washington. Current work: Pathophysiology of renal failure, mechanisms of vasopressin action. Subspecialties: Nephrology; Physiology (medicine). Office: Walter Reed Army Inst Research Washington DC 20307

BUTLER, JACK FAIRCHILD, electronics engineer; b. El Centro, Calif., July 18, 1933; s. Jack O. and Dorothy (Marsh) B.; m. Colette Guerard, Sept. 6, 1959; children—Alice, Jack, Michael, Patricia. B.S., U. Calif.-Berkeley, 1959, M.S., 1960, Ph.D., 1963. Staff sci. MIT Lincoln Lab., Lexington, Mass., 1962-68; staff sci. Gen. Dynamics Corp., Pomona, Calif., 1968-71; research dir. Arthur D. Little Inc., Cambridge, Mass., 1971-74; pres., founder Laser Analytics Inc., Bedford, Mass., 1974-80; pres., founder, Butler Research and Engring. Inc., Lexington, Mass., 1980—. Patentee CdS Ultraviolet Detector, and others. Served to sgt. USMC, 1954-57, Korea. Mem. IEEE (sr.), Am. Phys. Soc., AAAS. Current work: Semiconductor device research optoelectronic applications. Subspecialties: Semiconductors; Semiconductor lasers.

BUTLER, JAMES EHRICH, research chem. physicist; b. Tenafly, N.J., Nov. 29, 1944; m. Shahla Amoukhteh Agah. S.B., MIT, 1966; Ph.D., U. Chgo., 1972. Research chem. physicist Naval Research Lab., Washington, 1975—. NASA trainee, 1969-71; NIH fellow, 1972-74. Mem. Am. Phys. Soc., Optical Soc. Am., Sigma Xi. Current Work: Reaction dynamics and kinetics, spectroscopy, photochemistry, molecular interaction at surfaces. Subspecialties: Physical chemistry; Laser photochemistry. Office: Code 6110 US Naval Research Lab Washington DC 20375

BUTLER, JAMES PRESTON, physicist, physiologist; b. Boston, Aug. 19, 1945; s. Clay Preston and Delilah Graham (Barber) B.; m. Susan Nowers, Aug. 18, 1973; children: Matthew Preston, Aaron Joseph. B.A., Pomona Coll., 1967; M.A., Harvard U., 1968, Ph.D., 1974. Research assoc. Los Angeles County-U. So. Calif. Med. Ctr., 1969-71; research assoc. Harvard U., Boston, 1971-74, 75-78, asst. prof. dept. physiology, 1978—; vis. scholar Henry Luce Found., Sendai, Japan, 1974-75; cons. Adage, Inc., Billerica, Mass., 1982, Mass. Gen. Hosp., Boston, 1982—. Contbr. articles to profl. jours. Mem. Back Bay Water Table Com., Boston, 1981—. Recipient Young Investigator Pulmonary Research award NIH, 1976, Light Scattering Stereology award, 1982. Mem. Math. Assn. Am. Episcopalian. Current Work: Mathematics and physics of lung gas exchange and mechanics, optical dynamic stereology with lasers, mathematics of ill-posed inverse problems, oscillatory continuum mechanics. Subspecialties: Biophysics (physics); Physiology (biology). Home: 176 Coolidge St Brookline MA 02146 Office: Dept Physiolog Harvard Sch Pub Health 665 Huntington Ave Boston MA 02115

BUTLER, ROBERT NEIL, gerontologist, psychiatrist, writer, educator; b. N.Y.C., Jan. 21, 1927; s. Fred and Easter (Dikeman) B.; m. Diane McLaughlin, Sept. 2, 1950; children: Ann Christine, Carole Melissa, Cynthia Lee; m. Myrna I. Lewis, May 19, 1975; 1 dau., Alexandra Nicole. B.A., Columbia U., 1949, M.D., 1953. Intern St. Lukes Hosp., N.Y.C., 1953-54; resident U. Calif. Langley Porter Clinic, 1954-55; resident NIMH, 1955-56, research psychiatrist, 1955-62; founder geriatric unit Chestnut Lodge, 1958, adminstr., 1958-59; research psychiatrist Washington Sch. Psychiatry, 1962-76; dir. Nat. Inst. on Aging, NIH, 1976-82; Brookdale prof. geriatics and adult devel. Mt. Sinai Sch. Medicine, N.Y.C., 1982; mem. faculty George Washington U. Med. Sch., Washington, 1962—, Howard U. Sch. Medicine; cons. NIMH, 1967-76, U.S. Senate Spl. Com. on Aging. (Recipient Pulitzer prize for gen. nonfiction 1976); Author: (with others) Human Aging, 1963, (with Myrna I. Lewis) Aging and Mental Health, 1973, Why Survive? Being Old in America, 1975, Sex After Sixty, 1976; Mem. editorial bd.: (with Myrna I. Lewis) Jour. Geriatric Psychiatry, Aging and Human Development; Contbr. (with Myrna I. Lewis) articles to publs. Sec. Nat. Ballet of Washington, 1962-75; chmn. D.C. Advisory Commn. on Aging, 1969-72; bd. dirs. Nat. Council on Aging. Served with U.S. Maritime Service, 1945-47. Leo Laks award, 1976; McIntyre award, 1977; others. Fellow Am. Psychiat. Assn., Am. Geriatrics Soc. (founding mem.); mem. Group for Advancement Psychiatry (trustee 1974-76), Gerontol. Soc., Forum for Profls. and Execs. (founding). Club: Cosmos (Washington). Current Work: Senile dementia; aging processes: geriatrics. Subspecialties: Gerontology; Psychiatry. Home: 211 Central Park W New York NY 10024 Office: Mt Sinai 100th St and Fifth Ave New York NY 10029

BUTLER, WILLIAM HILL, physicist; b. Tallassee, Ala., Aug. 13, 1943; s. Jack Scott and Phyllis Maxine (Hill) B.; m. Jamie Frances Galloway, Mar. 12, 1967; children—William Stephen, Susanna Frances B.S., Auburn U., 1964; Ph.D, U. Calif.-San Diego, 1969. Asst. prof. physics Auburn U., 1969-72; research staff Oak Ridge Nat. Lab., 1972—, mgr. computer planning, 1984—. Contbr. articles to profl. jours. Recipient Outstanding Sustained Materials Sci. Research award Dept. Energy, 1982. Mem. Am. Phys. Soc., AAAS. Club: Oak Ridge Gymnastic (pres. 1983—). Current work: Theory of Alloys; theory and occurence of superconductivity, transport in metals and alloys. Subspecialty: Condensed matter physics. Home: 152 Cumberland View Dr Oak Ridge TN 37830 Office: Oak Ridge Nat Lab Bldg 4500 N Box X Oak Ridge TN 37830

BUTT, JOHN B., chemical engineering educator; b. Norfolk, Va., Sept. 10, 1935; m. Regina E. Roche, June 29, 1963; 1 child, John Jr. B.S. in Chem. Engring., Clemson U., 1956; M.S., Yale U., 1958, Ph.D., 1960. Registered profl. engr., Conn. Instr. Yale U., New Haven, 1950-60, asst. prof., 1960-63; assoc. prof., 1964-69; engr. Chevron Research Co., Richmond, Calif., 1963-65; vis. prof. U. Calif.-Davis, 1967; prof. chem. engring. Northwestern U., 1969-81, Walter P. Murphy prof., 1981—; vis. prof. U. Libre de Bruxelles, 1971, U. Calif.-Berkeley, 1979; engr. Exxon Research & Engring. Co., Baton Rouge, summer 1978; cons. Argonne Nat. Lab., Exxon Research & Devel. Lab. Assoc. editor Catalysis and Chem. Reaction Engring. Revs., Indsl. and Engring. Chemistry Process Design and Devel.; mem. editorial bd. Jour. Catalysis. Author: Reaction Kinetics and Reactor Design, 1980. Contbr. articles to profl. jours. Recipient Alexander von Humboldt sr. scientist award, 1985. Patentee enhancing reaction rates. Mem. Am. Inst. Chem. Engrs. (chmn. Chgo. sect. 1974-75, nat. dir. 1975-78; Allan P. Colburn award 1968, Profl. Progress award 1978), Am. Chem. Soc. (petroleum research fund adv. bd.), AAAS, Catalysis Soc. (pres. Chgo. sect. 1973-74), Va. Hist. Soc. Current work: Chemical reaction engineering catalysis. Subspecialties: Chemical engineering; Catalysis chemistry. Office: Dept Chem Engring Northwestern U Evanston IL 60201

BUTTERY, CHRISTOPHER M. G., public health administrator, physician; b. Yorkshire, England, July 1, 1934; m. E. Rosemary MacGowan; M.B. B.S., 1955; M.D. Johns Hopkins U., M.P.H., 1968. Diplomate Am. Bd. Preventive Medicine, Am. Bd. Pub. Health. Intern Montreal Gen. Hosp., P.Q., Can., 1955-57; practice medicine specializing in family medicine, Franklin County, Va., 1957-66; asst. dir. pub. health Fairfax County, Va., 1966-68; dir. pub. health City of Portsmouth, Va., 1968-75, Corpus Christi-Nueces County, Tex.; asst. prof. family medicine Ea. Va. Med. Sch., 1973-75, assoc. prof., dir. div. community medicine, dept. family medicine, 1975-80; adj. assoc. prof. U. Tex., 1981—; mem. mental health services com. Regional Health Services Council, 1968-75; mem. health systems com. Va. State Health Dept., 1969-75; vis. lectr. Sch. Soc. Work, O.D.U., 1972-80, Sch. Nursing, Med. Coll. Va., 1973-80. Contbr. articles to profl. jours., chpts. to books. Appointed mem. State Bd. Sanitatian Examiners, Va., 1971-75; mem. Portsmouth Mental Health and Retardation Services Bd., 1968-74; mem. tuberculosis adv. com. Va. Lung Assn., 1972-80, mem. program planning com., 1977-80; mem. Portsmouth Commn. on Emergency Med. Services, 1973-80, pres., 1974-76; bd. dirs. Flynn Christian Home for Alcoholics, 1974-80, Health, Welfare, Recreation Planning Council, 1975-80; mem. State Adv. Com. on Health Stats., Va., to 1980; mem. Portsmouth Sch. Com. for Devel. Disabilities, 1975-77, Portsmouth Human Resources Adv. Council, 1975-77. Served with USAR 1974—. Recipient Best Sci. Exhibit award Va. Acad. Family Physicians, 1964, 65, Outstanding Pub. Official's award Tidewater Homebuilders Assn., 1971, Outstanding Environ. award Va. Environ. Health Assn., 1971. Fellow Am. Col. Preventive Medicine; mem. AMA (residency review com. for preventive medicine, occupational health 1978-84), Am. Pub. Health Assn. (governing council 1971-79), Am. Assn. Pub. Health Physicians (immediate past pres.), Assn. Mil. Surgeons U.S., Assn. Tchrs. Preventive Medicine, Am. Acad. Family Physicians (chmn. sci. program Va. chpt. 1978), Med. Soc. Va., Tex. Med. Assn., So. Health Assn. (exec. com. 1976—), Am. Assn. Pub. Health Physicians (bd. dirs. 1974—, pres. elect. 1979-80, pres. 1980-82), Va. Pub. Health Assn. (exec. com. 1970-76). Subspecialties: Epidemiology; Preventive medicine. Office: Corpus Christi-Nueces County Dept Pub Health PO Box 7927 Corpus Christi TX 78408

BUTTON, KENNETH J(OHN), physicist; b. Rochester, N.Y., Oct. 11, 1922; s. Kenneth P. and Ruth C. (Wagner) B.; m. Margaret Jane Wells, Dec. 22, 1952. B.S., U. Rochester, 1950, M.S. in Physics, 1952; Sc.D., Tokyo Inst. Tech., 1985. Research physicist MIT, 1952-62, research group leader, 1962-72, sr. scientist, 1972—; organizer, program chmn. Ann. Internat. Conf. on Infrared and Millimeter Waves, 1974-84. Author: Microwave Ferrites and Ferrimagnetics, 1962; Editor: Infrared and Millimeter Waves, vols. 1-12, 1979-84; editor: Internat. Jour. Infrared and Millimeter Waves, 1980-84. Served to sgt. U.S. Army, 1942-46. Decorated Bronze Star with oak leaf cluster.; Recipient Disting. Service award IEEE Microwave Theory and Techniques Soc., 1980, cert. merit, 1981. Fellow IEEE, Am. Phys. Soc. Current Work: Experimental semiconductor physics, millimeter and submillimeter wave propagation; semmicondrs; millimeter and submillimeter wave propagation in semiconductors, magnetic materials, ceramics, glasses and liquids. Subspecialties: Condensed matter physics; Electronics. Office: MIT PO Box 72 MIT B Cambridge MA 02139

BUZEN, JEFFREY PETER, software company executive, computer scientist; b. Bklyn., May 28, 1943. Sc.B., Brown U., 1965; Sc.M., Harvard U., 1966, Ph.D., 1971. Computer specialist NIH, Bethesda, Md., 1967-69; prin. engr. Honeywell Co., Waltham, Mass., 1971-75; sr. v.p. BGS Systems, Inc., Waltham, 1975—; lectr. Harvard U., Cambridge, Mass., 1971-77, Brown U., Providence, 1976-77, Tech. Transfer Inst., Santa Monica, Calif., 1979-85. Inventor in field. Served with USPHS, 1967-69. Mem. Computer Measurement Group (bd. dirs. 1978-84, A.A. Michelson award 1979), Assn. Computing Machinery (bd. dirs Sigmetrics 1976-84), Ops. Research Soc. Am. Current work: Computer performance; queueing models; capacity planning, system architecture Subspecialty: Computer performance. Office: BGS Systems Inc 1 University Office Park Waltham MA 02254

BYERS, BRECK EDWARD, cell biologist, educator; b. St. Louis, July 4, 1939; s. F. Donald and Melba Constance (Boothman) B.; m. Margaret Read, Nov. 26, 1964; children: Mark Andrew, Carl Bradford. Research fellow dept. biology Harvard U., 1967 68; charge des researches Inst. Molecular Biology, U. Geneva, Switzerland, 1968-70; asst. prof. dept. genetics U. Wash., Seattle, 1970-76, assoc. prof., 1976-80, prof., 1980—. Mem. editorial bd.: Molecular and Cellular Biology; contbr. articles to sci. jours. Recipient NIH career devel. award, 1971-76, research grantee, 1971—. Mem. Genetics Soc. Am., Am. Soc. for Cell Biology. Current Work: Yeast cell division and meiotic recombination. Subspecialties: Cell biology; Genetics and genetic engineering (biology). Office: Dept Genetics SK-50 U Wash Seattle WA 98195

BYERS, HORACE ROBERT, meteorology educator; b. Seattle, Mar. 12, 1906; m. Frances Clark; 1 child, Henrietta Louise Bilhorn. A.B., U. Calif.-Berkeley, 1929; S.M., MIT, 1932, Sc.D., 1935. Mem. meteorology staff TWA, 1933-35; research meteorologist U.S. Weather Bur., 1935-40; assoc. prof. dept. meteorology U. Chgo., 1940-45, prof., 1945-65, chmn. dept., 1948-60; Disting. prof. meteorology Tex. A&M U., College Station, 1965-74, Disting. prof. meteorology emeritus, 1974—, dean Coll. of Geoscis., 1965-68, acad. v.p., 1968-71; vis. prof. U. Clermont-Ferrand, France, 1975; dir. U.S. Govt. Thunderstorm Research Project, 1945-50; chmn. bd. trustees Univ. Corp. for Atmospheric Research, 1962-65; chmn. bd. dirs. Gulf Univs. Research Consortium, 1967-69; chmn. adv. com. weather modification Tex. Water Devel. Bd., 1967-74; cons. to various univs., state and nat. agys.; mem. various nat. and internat. sci. and advt. coms. Author: General Meteorology, 1937, latest rev. edit., 1974; (with R.R. Braham, Jr.) The Thunderstorm, 1949; Element of Cloud Physics, 1965. Editor, contbr.: Thunderstorm Electricity, 1953; editorial adviser Ency Brit.; assoc. editor various jours. Contbr. articles to profl. jours. Fellow Am. Meteorol. Soc. (pres. 1952-53, Charles F. Brooks award 1960, cert. of recognition 1972, Cleveland Abbe award 1978); mem. Am. Geophys. Soc. (sect. pres. 1947-48), Internat. Assn. Meteorology and Atmospheric Physics (pres. 1960-63), Nat. Acad. Scis. (chmn. sect. of geophysics 1966-69), Royal Meteorol. Soc., Am. Geog. Soc., AAAS, Sigma Xi (pres. Chgo. chpt. 1958-60), Phi Kappa Phi. Current work: Consulting, lecturing Subspecialty: Meteorology.

BYKOWSKY, MICHAEL JOHN, immunologist; b. Jersey City, Jan. 14, 1955; s. Michael and Margaret (Zagrod) B.; m. Kathryn Hunter, Dec. 11, 1982. B.S., Tufts U., 1977; Ph.D., Brandeis U., 1983. Fellow, Meml. Sloan-Kettering Inst., N.Y.C., 1982—. Contbr. articles to Jour. Immunology, 1983, Fedn. Proceedings, 1982, 85, Cellular Immunology, 1982. Recipient Citation award Hewlett-Packard, 1972. Mem. AAAS, Am. Assn. Immunologists, Soc. Analytical Cytology. Current work: Function and distribution of natural killer cells; cell interactions in immune responses. Subspecialty: Immunobiology and immunology. Home: 658 Valley Rd Upper Montclair NJ 07043 Office: Sloan-Kettering Inst 1275 York Ave Section 6105 New York NY 10021

BYLANDER, ERNEST GERALD, physicist, educator; b. Farmington, Ark., May 22, 1931; s. Robert Joseph and Mary Esther (Rouse) B.; m. Mary Lamar, Mar. 15, 1953 (div. Aug. 1967); children—Mary Katherine, Steve Kenneth, Elizabeth Karen, Robert Joseph, Sharon Rhoda; m. Jane Temple Estes, Mar. 23, 1975. Student Ga. Inst. Tech., 1949-53; B.S., U. Ark., 1955, M.S., 1961. Sr. engr. Convair, Fort Worth, 1955-59; sr. engr. Texas Instruments, Dallas, 1959-62, mem. tech. staff, 1966—; sr. physicist Melpar, Falls Church, Va., 1962-63; research physicist, solid state Naval Ordnance Lab., Silver Springs, Md., 1963-66; adj. instr. Austin Coll., Sherman, Tex., Grayson Community Coll., Sherman, Montgomery Community Jr. Coll., Takoma Park, Md. Author: Electronic Displays, 1979; patentee in field. Elder, Grand Ave. Presbyterian Ch., Sherman, 1977. Served as pvt. USAF, 1950-51. Decorated Superior Performance award; recipient joint research grant Tex. Instruments, Tex. Tech., NSF, 1981. Mem. IEEE (sr.), Am. Phys. Soc., Electrochem. Soc., Sigma Pi Sigma (v.p. 1955). Club: Outdoor (Sherman) (v.p. 1980-81). Current work: Metal-insulator-semiconductor device stability (particularly mercury cadmium telluride); defects in semiconductors. Subspecialties: Semiconductors; Electronic materials. Home: 1501 Ridgeway St Sherman TX 75090 Office: Tex Instruments Inc MS270 Box 226015 Dallas TX 75266

BYLUND, DAVID B., pharmacologist; b. Spanish Fork, Utah, Apr. 16, 1946; s. H. Bruce and Rhea (Bowen) B.; m. Elaine C. Thurman, May 27, 1970; children: Carma, Eric, Michelle, Kevin, Kristen, Jennifer. Student, Calif. Inst. Tech., 1966-68; B.S., Brigham Young U., 1970; Ph.D., U. Calif., Davis, 1974. Postdoctoral fellow Johns Hopkins U. Med. Sch., Balt., 1975-77; asst. prof. pharmacology U. Mo., Columbia, 1977-82, assoc. prof., 1982—. Contbr. articles to profl. jours. Scoutmaster Boy Scouts Am., 1980-81. Mem. Am. Soc. Pharmacology and Exptl. Therapeutics, Soc. Neurosci., AAAS. Mormon. Current Work: Adrenergic receptors; adenylate cyclase and radioligand binding studies; smooth muscle; hypertension; receptor purification. Subspecialties: Neuropharmacology; Molecular pharmacology. Office: U Mo Columbia MO 65212

BYRD, LARRY DONALD, research scientist, pharmacologist; b. Salisbury, N.C., July 14, 1936; s. Donald Thomas and Mildren Alexina (Gardner) B.; m. Vivian Corrinne Williams, Dec. 23, 1961; children: Kay, Lynn, Renee, Andrew. A.B., East Carolina U., 1962, M.A., 1964; Ph.D., U. N.C., Chapel Hill, 1968; Ph.D. postdoctoral fellow, Harvard U. Med. Sch., 1967-70. Assoc. scientist New Eng. Regional Primate Research Center, Southborough, Mass., 1969-74; instr. psychobiology Harvard U., Boston, 1970-73, prin. assoc. in psychiatry, 1973-74; psychobiologist, chmn. div. primate behavior Yerkes Regional Primate Research Center, Emory U., Atlanta, 1974-79, assoc. researchprof., chmn., 1979-80, assoc. research prof., 1980-82, chief div. behavioral biology, 1980—, research prof., 1982—, adj. prof psychology, 1982—, assoc. prof.pharmacology, 1981—; lectr. psychology Ga. Inst. Tech., 1974—; cons. Nat. Center Toxicol. Research, FDA, Jefferson, Ark., 1976-77, Naval Aerospace Med. Research Lab., Pensacola, Fla., 1977, Addiction Research Center, Lexington, Ky., 1979, S.W. Found. Research and Edn., San Antonio, 1977, MIT Press, Cambridge, Mass., 1975, Nat. Inst. Drug Abuse, Rockville, Md., 1979—. Editorial bd.: Jour. Exptl. Analysis of Behavior, 1969-79; assoc. editor, 1970-76; editor: Psychopharmacology Newsletter, 1976-82; cons. editor: Am. Jour. Primatology, 1980—; editorial advisor: Jour. Pharmacology and Exptl. Therapeutics, 1973—, Psychopharmacology, 1976—, Sci, 1973—, Physiology and Behavior, 1980—, Behavioral and Neural Biology, 1981—. Served with AUS, 1954-57. Recipient Outstanding Alumnus award East Carolina U., 1977. Fellow Am. Psychol. Assn. (pres. div. psychopharmacology 1982-83); mem. Am. Soc. Pharmacology and Exptl. Theapeutics, Behavioral Pharmacology Soc., Soc. Exptl. Analysis of Behavior, AAAS, Soc. Neurosci., Ea. Psychol. Assn., Southea. Psychol. Assn., Phi Sigma Pi. Current Work: Behavioral pharmacology and behavioral physiology. Subspecialties: Psychopharmacology; Psychobiology. Home: 1026 Viking Dr Stone Mountain GA 30083 Office: Yerkes Regional Primate Research Center Emory University Atlanta GA 30322

BYRNE, GEORGE DENNIS, mathematician, consultant; b. Earlham, Iowa, June 15, 1933; s. Alphonsus Dennis and Mary Maurine (Bricker) B.; m. Laura Joan Brindle, May 30, 1960; children—Elizabeth Mary Hensley, Margaret Ann, Stephen Alphonsus, Dennis William (dec. 1985), Michael Robert, Karen Frances, David George, Mark John. B.S., Creighton U., 1955; M.S., Iowa State U., 1961, Ph.D., 1963. Mathematician, White Sands Proving Ground, N.Mex., 1955-56; mem. staff Sandia Corp., Albuquerque, 1956-58; grad. asst. Iowa State U., Ames, 1958-63; asst. prof. U. Pitts., 1963-67, assoc. prof., 1967-80; sr. staff mathematician Exxon Research and Engring. Co., Linden, N.J., 1980-82, research assoc., Annandale, N.J., 1982—; asst. physics lab. instr. Creighton U., Omaha, 1954-55; mem. vis. faculty Lawrence Livermore Lab., Calif., 1973; vis. scientist Argonne Nat. Lab., Ill.; cons. in field. 1974-80. Co-editor: Numerical Solution of Systems of Nonlinear Algebraic Equations, 1973. Editor Applied Numerical Math., 1984—. Contbr. articles to profl. jours. and books. Served as 2d lt. U.S. Army, 1956, to capt. USAR, 1956-66. NSF grantee, 1979. Mem. Am. Inst. Chem. Engrs. (profl. devel. cert.), Assn. Computing Machinery (assoc. editor Trans. on Math. Software 1976-78), Nat. Speakers Assn., Soc. for Indsl. and Applied Math. (pres. eastern Ohio-western Pa. sect. 1979-80, pres. N.J. sect. 1984—). Republican. Roman Catholic. Clubs: Toastmasters Internat. (Westfield, N.J.)(treas. 1982, area gov. 1985-86) (Florham Park, N.J.)(co-founder 1982, pres. 1983); White Sands Pioneer Group (N.Mex.), N.J. Advanced Speakers Club. Current work: Numerical analysis and related software and their application to problems in science and engineering; especially differential equations and nonlinear systems. Subspecialties: Numerical analysis (mathematics); Applied mathematics. Home: 820 Nancy Way Westfield NJ 07090 Office: Exxon Research and Engring Co Clinton Twp Route 22 E Annandale NJ 08801

BYRNE, JOHN MAXWELL, biological sciences educator; b. Gassaway, W.Va., May 7, 1933; s. George Coble and Margret Cathering (Heater) B.; m. Garnet Ruth Boblett, July 8, 1960; 1 dau. Kimberly Ann. B.A., Glenville State U., 1960; M.A., Miami U., Oxford, Ohio, 1964, Ph.D., 1969. Asst. prof. Va. Poly. Inst. and State U., Blacksburg, 1969-75; asso. prof. biol. Scis. Kent (Ohio) State U., 1975—. Contbr. articles on biol. scis. to profl. jours. Served with USMC, 1954-57. Mem. Bot. Soc. Am., Am. Inst. Biol. Sci., AAAS, Sigma Xi. Current Work: Developmental plant anatomy, root development. Subspecialty: Morphology. Office: Dept Biol Scis Kent State U Kent OH 44242

BYRNE, JOHN VINCENT, oceanographer, university president. Pres., Oreg. State U.; former adminstr. NOAA. Subspecialty: Oceanography. Office: Oreg State U Corvallis OR 97331*

BYSTRYN, JEAN-CLAUDE, dermatologist; b. Paris, May 8, 1938; m. Marcia Bystryn, Dec. 17, 1947; 1 dau. Anne. B.S., U. Chgo., 1958; M.D., N.Y.U., 1962. Diplomate: Am. Bd. Dermatology. Intern Montefiore Hosp., N.Y.C., 1962-63, resident in medicine, 1973-64; resident in dermatology N.Y.U., 1966-69, USPHS fellow dermatology, 1966-72, mem. faculty, 1970—, assoc. prof. dermatology, 1976-84, prof., 1984—, dir. immunofluroescence lab., 1972—; co dir. Bullous Disease Clinic, Skin and Cancer Clinic, 1974—; dir. melanoma program and melanoma immunotherapy clinic Kaplan Cancer Ctr., 1984—; attending physician N.Y.U. Hosp. Contbr. articles to profl. jours. Served with USPHS, 1964-66. Ford Found. fellow, 1954; recipient Irma T. Hirschl Career Scientist award, 1979. Mem. Am. Assn. Immunologists, Am. Assn. Cancer Research, Soc. Investigative Dermtology, Am. Acad. Dermatology, Am. Dermatol. Assn., Am. Soc. Cell Biology, Task Force on Immunofluorescence Internat. Soc. Tropical Dermatology, Am. Fedn. Clin. Research, N.Y. Dermatol. Soc., Dermatology Found., Skin Cancer Found. (chmn. grant rev. com. 1980—), Dystrophic Epidermolysic Bullosa Found. (adv. bd. 1980-81). Current Work: Melanoma immunology, immunology of blistering diseases of the skin and vitiligo. Subspecialties: Dermatology; Immunology (medicine). Office: 530 1st Ave Suite 7F New York NY 10016

CABANILLAS, FERNANDO, medical oncologist, internist, medical educator; b. San Juan, P.R., Nov. 20, 1945; s. Jose and Antonia E. (Escalona) C.; m. Myrta Narvaez-Ochoa, July 14, 1967; children—Maria Antonia, Maria Eugenia. B.A., U. P.R., 1966, M.D., 1970. Diplomate Am. Bd. Internal Medicine. Intern, resident Univ. Dist. Hosp., P.R., 1970-73; clin. instr. U. P.R., San Juan, 1973-74; faculty assoc. M.D. Anderson Hosp., Houston, 1976-77, asst. internist, asst. prof. medicine, 1977-78, assoc. internist, asst. prof. medicine, 1978-80, assoc. internist, assoc. prof., 1980-83, internist, assoc. prof., 1983—, chief, sect. lymphoma, 1984—. Fellow ACP, 1981. Recipient 2d prize P.R. Med. Assn., 1973, M.D. Anderson Hosp., 1976; Pfizer scholar, 1968-69. Mem. Am. Assn. Cancer Research, Am. Soc. Clin. Oncology, Tex. Med. Assn., AAAS, N.Y. Acad. Sci., Harris County Med. Assn. Current work: Therapeutic trials in patients with lymphoma. Subspecialties: Oncology; Chemotherapy. Office: M D Anderson Hosp 6723 Bertner Houston TX 77030

CABRERA, BLAS, physicist, educator, researcher; b. Paris, Sept. 21, 1946; s. Nicolas and Carmen (Navarro) C.; m. JoAnn Nelson, Apr. 1 1972; children: Nicolas, Joseph, Blas Jacob. B.S. in Physics, U. Va., 1968; Ph.D. in Physics, Stanford U., 1974. Research assoc. Stanford U., 1975-78, sr. research assoc., 1979, acting asst. prof., 1980, asst. prof., 1980—. Contbr. articles to sci. publs. Woodrow Wilson fellow, 1968; Churchill fellow Cambridge (Eng.) U., 1968; NSF fellow, 1968-72; Nat. Bur. Standards grantee, 1978-81. Mem. Am. Phys. Soc., Sigma Xi, Sigma Pi Sigma. Current Work: Application of cryogenic techniques and devices to study of fundamental physics: e.g., search for magnetic monopoles, determination of Planck's constant divided by the electron mass, and test of general relativity with orbiting gyroscope. Subspecialty: Low temperature physics. Office: Dept Physics Stanford U Stanford CA 94305

CABRERA, EDELBERTO JOSE, immunologist; b. Pinar del Rio, Cuba, Nov. 5, 1944; s. Baltazar Edelberto and Maria Paulina (Chirino) C.; m. Lourdes Elena Rodriguez, Aug. 13, 1944; children: Edward, Michelle. Ph.D., U. Ill., 1972. Research assoc. U. N.Mex., 1972-77; research scientist Norwich Eaton Pharms Inc., N.Y., 1977-84, immunology group leader, 1984—; faculty SUNY, Binghamton, 1978-79. Contbr. articles to profl. jours. Mem. Am. Assn. Immunologists, N.Y. Acad. Sci. Roman Catholic. Club: Peaks and Trail Ski. Current Work: Immune regulation, immunomodulators. Subspecialties: Immunopharmacology; Infectious diseases. Home: RD 4 Gibbon Rd Norwich NY 13815 Office: Norwich Eaton Pharms Inc Procter & Gamble Co Norwich NY 13815

CACIOPPO, JOHN TERRANCE, psychologist, educator, researcher; b. Marshall, Tex., June 12, 1951; s. Cyrus Joseph and Mary Katherine (Kazimour) C.; m. Barbara Lee Andersen, May 17, 1981. B.S., U. Mo.-Columbia, 1973; M.A., Ohio State U., 1975; Ph.D., 1977. Grad. fellow Ohio State U., 1973-77; asst. prof. psychology U. Notre Dame, 1977-79; asst. prof. psychology U. Iowa, 1979-81, assoc. prof. psychology, 1981-85, prof., 1985—. Author: (with R. Petty) Attitudes and Persuasion, 1981; Editor: (with R. Petty) Perspectives in Cardiovascular Psychophysiology, 1982, Social Psychophysiology: A Sourcebook, 1983; Communication and Persuasion, 1985. Contbr. articles to profl. jours. Old Gold fellow U. Iowa, 1980; NSF grantee, 1979—; NIH grantee, 1980-81; U. Iowa faculty scholar, 1980-83; Early Career contbn. to Psychophysiology recipient, 1981. Mem. Am. Psychol. Assn., 500. Soc. for Psychophysiol. Research, Midwestern Psychol. Assn., AAAS, Soc. for Exptl. Social Psychology, Sigma Xi, Phi Kappa Phi. Current Work: Investigating the elementary operations underlying social influence and attitudinal processes using verbal, behavioral, chronometric, and psychophysiological procedures. Subspecialties: Social psychology; Psychophysiology. Home: 15 Woodland Heights Iowa City IA 52240 Office: Dept Psychology U Iowa Iowa City IA 52242

CACUCI, DAN GABRIEL, applied physicist, researcher; b. Cluj, Romania, May 16, 1948; s. Gabriel D. and Malvina (Preda) C. M.S., Columbia U., N.Y.C., 1973, M. Philosophy, 1977, Ph.D., 1978. Nuclear engring. assoc. III, Brookhaven Nat. Lab., Upton, N.Y., 1975-76; lead engr. Ebasco Services, Inc., N.Y.C., 1976-77; group leader, sr. scientist Oak Ridge (Tenn.) Nat. Lab., 1977-84, sect. head, sr. scientist, 1984—; assoc. prof. U. Tenn., Knoxville, 1983-85, prof., 1985—. Assoc. editor Nuclear Sci. & Engring., 1984—. Contbr. sci. articles to profl. publs. Recipient Merriman Meml. award Columbia Univ., 1977; Spl. Recognition award Oak Ridge Nat. Lab., 1982. Mem. AAAS, Am. Nuclear Soc. (sec., nat. planning com. 1983—), N.Y. Acad. Scis., Sigma Xi. Current Work: Sensitivity and uncertainty analysis; radiation and particle transport phenomena; regular and chaotic motion of dynamical systems; intelligent control systems; A-bomb dose reassessment. Subspecialties: Applied mathematics; Nuclear fission. Office: Oak Ridge Nat Lab PO Box X Oak Ridge TN 37830

CADDELL, ROBERT MACORMAC, mechanical engineer, consultant, researcher, educator; b. Paterson, N.J., Nov. 13, 1925; s. David and Louise (Coutts) C.; m. Doris Louise Nash, June 25, 1954; children: Steven, David, Gary. B.S., Newark Coll. Engring., 1948; M.S., U. Mich., 1951, Ph.D. (NSF sci. faculty fellow 1962, DuPont grantee-in-aid, 1963, Ford Found. faculty devel. grantee 1963), 1963. Registered profl. engr., Mich. Instr. U. Mich., 1952-55, asst. prof. prodn. engring., 1955-56, asst. prof. mech. engring. and applied mechanics, 1956-63, asso. prof. mech. engring. and applied mechanics, 1963-71, prof., 1971—, cons. materials and mfg. processes, mech. behavior solids, fracture. Author: Deformationand Fracture of Solids, 1980, (with W.F. Hosford) Metal Forming: Mechanics and Metallurgy, 1982; contbr. numerous articles to profl. jours. Served with inf. U.S. Army, 1944-46. Decorated Bronze Star; named hon. editorial adv. bd. mem. Internat. Jour. Mech. Scis., 1981—; recipient Outstanding Tchr. award Coll. Engring., U. Mich., 1982. Mem. ASME, Am. Soc. Metals, ASTM, Research Club U. Mich., Sigma Xi, Tau Beta Pi, Pi Tau Sigma (Outstanding Mech. Engring. Prof. 1981). Club: Ann Arbor (Mich.) Golf and Outing. Current Work: Mech. behavior of solids (deformation and fracture) and sheet metal forming. Subspecialties: Solid mechanics; Fracture mechanics. Home: 1840 Mershon Ann Arbor MI 48103 Office: Dept Mech Engring U Mich 2020 GGBL North Campus Ann Arbor MI 48109

CADIEUX, R. D., chemical company executive; b. 1937; married. B.S. in Econs. and Acctg., Ill. Inst. Tech.; M.B.A., U. Chgo. Former div. controller internat. ops. Standard Oil Co (Ind.); v.p. adminstrn. and planning Amoco Chems. Corp., Chgo., 1975-81, exec. v.p., dir., 1981-83, pres., 1983—. Office: Amoco Chems Corp 200 E Randolph Dr Chicago IL 60601

CADUFF, NORALYNN JO, industrial analytical chemist; b. Pueblo, Colo., Jan. 28, 1957; d. Gerald Frank and Marilyn Jo (Mankle) C. A.A., U. So. Colo., 1977; B.A., U. Colo., 1980, B.S. in Chem. Engring., 1980; M.A., Washington U., St. Louis, 1982. Phys. sci. aid NOAA, Boulder, Colo., 1978-80; chemist Rockwell Internat., Golden, Colo., 1982-83, analytical chemist, 1983—; NSF undergrad. research program participant, 1977. Mem. Am. Chem. Soc., Geol. Soc. Am., Am. Inst. Chem. Engrs., Tau Beta Pi. Republican. Mem. Evangelical Covenant Ch. Clubs: St. Andrew Soc., City of Denver Pipe Band. Current work: Development of analytical techniques and separation techniques for radio isotopic analysis. Subspecialties: Analytical chemistry; Radiochemistry. Office: Rockwell Internat Rocky Flats Plant Golden CO 80020

CADUTO, RALPH, chemist; b. Providence, Aug. 20, 1927; s. Ralph and Anna (Durante) C.; m. Esther Martone, Apr. 11, 1953; children—Linda, Michael, Nancy, Mary. B.Sc., U. R.I., 1952; M.Sc., R.I. Coll., 1977. Chief chemist Hosp., Providence, 1952-57; analytical chemist CIBA-GEIGY, Cranstom, R.I., 1957, supt. pharm. prodn., 1977-79, ret., 1979; chemist nuclear medicine VA Med Ctr., Providence, 1979—; cons. water waste chemistry, Cranston, 1972-77. Contbr. articles to profl. jours. Pres., PTA, Warwick, R.I., 1967-68. Mem. Am. Chem. Soc., Clin. Ligand Assay Soc., Theta Delta Chi, Beta Psi Alpha, Psi Sigma, Sigma Xi. Roman Catholic. Clubs: VFW, ITAM, Cranston Garden (pres. 1975-76), Squaredance (pres. 1968-73). Current work: Presently involved in RIA assay, research, experimental evaluation. Subspecialties: Kinetics; Analytical chemistry. Office: VA Med Ctr Davis Park Providence RI

CADY, WAYNE ALLEN, chemist; b. Denver, Dec. 18, 1944; s. Wilifred Marion and Wilma C.; m. Susan Anne Strow, Dec. 28, 1968. B.S., Calvin Coll., 1966; Ph.D., U. Ill., 1972. Assoc. prof. Purdue U., Indpls., 1972-78; research assoc. Oxy-Catalyst Co., Westchester Pa., 1978-79; scientist Baker Chem. Co., Phillipsburg, N.J., 1979-83, sr. scientist, 1983—. NDEA fellow, U. Ill., 1966-69; grantee Am. Chem. Soc., Indpls., 1973-77. Mem. Am. Chem. Soc., Am. Physical Soc.; Soc. Photo-Optical Instrumental Engrs., Sigma Xi, Phi Lambda Upsilon. Current work: Photolithography; intergrated circuit manufacturing processes. Subspecialties: Physical chemistry; Microchip technology (materials science). Home: 3507 Glen Ave Easton PA 18042 Office: JT Baker Chem Co 222 Red Sch Ln Phillipsburg NJ 08865

CAHILL, DAVID WOODING, academic neurosurgeon; b. Danville, Va., Sept. 18, 1951; s. Herbert Astor and Elsie Gilliam (Wooding) C.; m. Sandra Green, Aug. 30, 1974; children—Erin Elizabeth, Austin Patrick. B.A., U. Va., 1973; M.D., 1976. Diplomate Am. Bd. Psychiatry and Neurology, Am. Bd. Neurological Surgery. Intern in surgery Med. Coll. Va., Richmond, 1976-77, resident in neurology, 1977-78; resident in neurosurgery U. Md., Balt., 1978-83, resident in neurology, 1980-82, chief resident in neurosurgery, 1982—; fellow Md. Inst. for Emergency Med. Services, Balt., 1983. Contbr. numerous articles to profl. jours. Echols scholar. Fellow Stroke Council for Am. Heart Assn.; mem. AMA, Am. Acad. Neurology, AAAS, N.Y. Acad. Sci., Am. Soc. Neurological Investigation, Soc. for Neuroscience, Am. Fed. Clin. Research, Congress of Neurological Surgeons, Md. Neurological Soc., Fla. Med. Assn., Phi Beta Kappa, Alpha Epsilon Delta, Phi Eta Sigma. Subspecialties: Neurosurgery; Neurology. Office: U So Fla Dept Surgery Box 16 Coll Medicine 12901 N 30th St Tampa FL 33612

CAHILL, GEORGE FRANCIS, JR., physician, educator; b. N.Y.C., July 7, 1927; s. George Francis and Eva Marion (Wagner) C.; m. Sarah Townsend duPont, Dec. 20, 1949; children: Colleen (Mrs. Thomas P. Remley), Peter duPont, George F. III, Sarah Rhett, Eva Wagner, Elizabeth Anglin. B.S., Yale, 1949; M.D., Columbia U., 1953; M.A., Harvard U., 1966. Intern Peter Bent Brigham Hosp., Boston, 1953-54, resident, 1954-55, 57-58, asso. in medicine, 1962-65, sr. physician, 1983—; research fellow biol. chemistry Harvard U., 1955-57, prof. medicine, 1970—, practice medicine specializing in metabolism, Boston, 1965-78; Prin. cons. endocrinology, metabolism VA, 1972-75; investigator Howard Hughes Med. Inst., 1962-68, dir. research, 1978-85, v.p. sci. tng. and devel., 1985—; mem. research tng. coms. NIH. Contbr. articles to profl. jours. Served with USNR, 1945-47. Recipient Banting medal U.S., 1971, Banting medal Eng., 1974, J.P. Hoet award Belgium, 1973. Mem. Am. Diabetes Assn. (pres. 1975, Lilly award 1965), Endocrine Soc. (Oppenheimer award 1963, Gairdner Internat. award 1979), Nat. Commn. on Diabetes, Am. Soc. Clin. Investigation, Assn. Am. Physicians, Am. Clin. Climatol. Assn., Am. Physiol. Soc., Am. Acad. Arts and Scis. Club: Wellesley Country. Subspecialties: Endocrinology; Physiology (medicine). Home: Upton Pond Stoddard NH 03464 Office: 398 Brookline Ave Boston MA 02215

CAHILL, LAURENCE JAMES, JR., physicist, educator; b. Frankfort, Maine, Sept. 21, 1924; s. Laurence J. and Wilma (Lord) C.; m. Alice Adeline Krieger, Sept. 10, 1949; children: Laurence James III, Thomas G., Daniel A. Student, U. Maine, 1942-43; B.S., U.S. Mil. Acad., 1946, U. Chgo., 1950; M.S., U. Iowa, 1956, Ph.D., 1959. Staff U. Iowa, 1954-59, research asso., 1959; mem. faculty U. N.H., 1959-68, prof. physics, 1965-69; dir. Space Scis. Center, 1966-68; prof. physics U. Minn., Mpls., 1968—, asso. head physics, 1974-77; dir. Space Sci. Center, 1968-74; chief physics NASA Hdqrs., Washington, 1962-63, cons., 1962—; vis. prof. U. Calif. at San Diego, 1965-66; cons. NSF, 1965—. Recipient NASA award for sustained superior performance, 1963; NATO sr. fellow, 1974; vis. scientist Max Planck Inst. Extraterrestrial Physics, W. Ger., 1977-78. Fellow Am. Geophys. Union, Am. Phys. Soc.; mem. AAAS, Sigma Xi. Research and publs. on measurement by rocket-borne magnetometer of elec. currents in ionosphere, measurement boundary between earth's magnetic field and interplanetary medium, ring current of charged particles encircling earth and causing magnetic storms, hydromagnetic waves. Current Work: Rocket studies of auroral phenomena; hydromagnetic waves in magnetosphere. Subspecialties: Space physics; Satellite studies. Home: Afton MN 55001 Office: U Minn Dept Physics 116 Church St SE Minneapolis MN 55455

CAHILL, MARY-CAROL, psychologist, consultant; b. N.Y.C.; d. Harold Daniel and Mildred Eva (Gessler) C. A.B., Coll. of New Rochelle; A.M., Fordham U., Ph.D., 1967. Lic. psychologist, N.Y. Human factors engr. Grumman Aerospace Corp., Bethpage, N.Y., 1967-70; asst. prof. psychology Rensselaer Poly. Inst., Troy, N.Y., 1970-74; asst. prof. Fordham U., Bronx, N.Y., 1974-76, assoc. prof., 1976-78; pvt. human factors engring. and environ. design cons., Bronx, 1967—. Contbr. articles to sci. and profl. jours.; editorial cons. various textbooks. Regents scholar State of N.Y.; Regents fellow State of N.Y.; NSF fellow. Mem. Human Factors Soc. (pres. met. chpt. 1979), Soc. Info. Display (vice chmn. Mid-Atlantic chpt. 1976, 77, Cert. of Recognition 1976, 77), Am. Psychol. Assn., N.Y. State Psychol. Assn., Eastern Psychol. Assn., N.Y. Acad. Scis., Assn. Women in Sci., Sigma Xi. Current work: Visual display systems evaluation; perceptual information coding; pictorial symbol interpretation; rotary motion illusions; environmental influences on behavior; privacy; creativity; pain and analgesia. Subspecialties: Cognition; Human factors engineering. Office: PO Box 418 Riverdale Sta Bronx NY 10471

CAHILL, VERN RICHARD, meat scientist, educator, researcher; b. Tiro, Ohio, May 5, 1918; s. Verrill W. and Marie A. (Galehr) C.; m. Ruth Alice Huber, June 23, 1946; children: Nancy Cahill Haar, Donna Cahill Solovay, Kenneth. B.Sc., Ohio State U., 1941, M.S., 1942, Ph.D., 1955. Mem. faculty Ohio State U., 1946—, asst. prof. meat sci., 1955-56, assoc. prof., 1956-61, prof., 1961—, coordinator meat sci., 1972—, acting chmn. animal sci., 1983-84. Author: Processing, rev. edit, 1980; contbr. numerous articles to profl. jours. Served to lt. col. U.S. Army. Recipient Educators award Nat. Assn. Meat Purveyors, 1972. Mem. Am. Meat Sci. Assn. (Disting. Teaching award 1967, Signal Service award 1979), Am. Assn. Animal Sci., Inst. Food Technologists, Ohio Meat Processors Assn. (dir.), Ohio Meat Industries Assn. (trustee). Lutheran. Current Work: Meat quality, comminuted meat processing. Subspecialty: Food science and technology. Home: 133 Aldrich Rd Columbus OH 43214 Office: 2029 Fyffe Rd Columbus OH 43210

CAIMI, FRANK MICHAEL, optical scientist, electrical engineer; b. Brookville, Pa., Aug. 11, 1948; s. Frank B. and Ann (Palenski) C.; m. Pamela June Luther, July 10, 1976; children—Brian, Leanna. B.S., Carnegie Mellon U., 1970, M.S., 1971, Ph.D., 1976. Research scientist, assoc. prof. Carnegie Mellon U., Pitts., 1976-82; sr. elec. engr. Harbor Branch Found., Fort Pierce, Fla., 1982-83, head elec. engring. dept., scientist, 1983—; cons. Lockheed Missiles & Space Co., 1980, Westinghouse Co., 1980-82, Mine Safety Appliances, Pitts., 1981—. Contbr. articles to profl. jours. Mem. Optical Soc. Am. (pres. Pitts. 1980-81), IEEE (spl. service award 1979), Soc. Photo-optical Instrumentation Engrs., Sigma Xi. Current work: Acousto and electro-optic systems, spectroscopy, ocean optics, holographic methods. Subspecialties: Optical engineering; Electrical engineering. Home: PO Box 650163 Vero Beach FL 32965 Office: Harbor Branch Found Fort Pierce FL 33450

CAIN, BRYAN EDMUND, mathematics educator; b. Libertyville, Ill., Mar. 12, 1941; s. Milburn C. and Katherine (Crocker) C. B.S., MIT, 1963; M.S., U. Wis.-Madison, 1964, Ph.D., 1968. Instr., U. Wis.-Madison, 1968, MIT, Cambridge, 1968-70; mem. faculty Iowa State U., Ames, 1970—, prof. math., since 1981—; vis. prof. Technische Universität München, Federal Republic Germany, 1974-75, 79, U. Montreal, Can., 1977, Universidade de Coimbra, 1978-79, Technion, Israel, 1981, U. Paris VII, 1981-82, Ceskoslovenska Akademie Ved, Prague, 1984, Magyar Tudomanyos Akademia, Budapest, Hungary, 1984. Assoc. editor Linear Algebra and Its Applications, 1984—. Contbr. articles to profl. jours. Mem. Am. Math. Soc., Math. Assn. Am., Soc. Indsl. and Applied Math. Current work: Linear operators; Hilbert space; matrices; inertia; types of stability Subspecialty: Analysis. Office: Math Dept Iowa State U Ames IA 50011

CAIN, LAURENCE SUTHERLAND, physics educator; b. Washington, Feb. 4, 1946; s. Leighton Aubrey and Beatrice (Sutherland) C.; m. Jane Dimmock, Aug. 21, 1971; 1 child, Rebecca Anne, Peter Laurence. B.S., Wake Forest U., 1968; M.S., U. Va., 1970, Ph.D., 1973. Research assoc. U. N.C., Chapel Hill, 1973-76, lectr., 1976-78; asst. prof. Davidson Coll., N.C., 1978-85, assoc. prof., 1985—; cons. dept. materials engring. N.C. State, Raleigh, 1982-83. Contbr. articles to profl. jours. Treas. North Mecklenburg Child Dev. Assn., Davidson, N.C., 1979—; session Davidson Coll. Presbyn. Ch., N.C., 1982—. Atlantic Coast Conf. scholar, 1968; grantee NSF, 1981, Research Corp., 1981-83. Mem. Am. Phys. Soc., Am. Assn. Physics Tchrs., AAAS, AAUP, Phi Beta Kappa, Sigma Xi. Democrat. Current work: Elastic, mechanical and electrical properties of solids. Subspecialty: Condensed matter physics. Office: Davidson Coll Dept Physics Davidson NC 28036

CAIN, WILLIAM S., psychology educator, researcher; b. N.Y.C., Sept. 7, 1941; s. William H. and June (Stanley) C.; m. Eileen M. Nugent, Jan. 25, 1964; children: Justin, Alison. B.S., Fordham U., 1963; S.M., Brown U., 1966, Ph.D., 1968. Asst. fellow to fellow Pierce Found., New Haven, 1967—; instr. to. assoc. prof. epidemiology and psychology Yale U., 1969—; v.p. Fragrance Research Fund N.Y.C., 1981—. Contbr. numerous articles to profl. publs.; co-editor: Stimulus and Sensation, 1971, Evaluation, Utilization, and Control, 1974. Fellow N.Y. Acad. Scis. (pres.-elect 1985, pres. 1986), Am. Psychol. Assn.; recipient Javits Neuroscience Investigator award NIH, 1984; Crosby Field Award Am. Soc. Hearing, Refrigerating, and Air Conditioning Engrs., 1984; mem. Assn. for Chemoreception Scis. (exec. chmn. 1983-84). Current Work: Chemoreception, i.e. smell, taste, irritation; sensory reactions to indoor and outdoor air contaminants; disorders of sense of smell. Subspecialties: Sensory processes; Environmental health. Home: 79 Colony Rd New Haven CT 06511 Office: John B Pierce Found 290 Congress Ave New Haven CT 06519

CAIRD, JOHN ALLYN, physicist; b. Bklyn., Dec. 24, 1947; s. William John and Ethel (Fountain) C. B.S., Rutgers U., 1969; M.S., UCLA, 1971; Ph.D., U. So. Calif., 1975. Reliability analyst Consol. Edison, N.Y.C., 1968; staff mem., masters fellow, doctoral fellow, staff physicist Hughes Aircraft Co., Culver City, Calif., 1969-76; NSF postdoctoral fellow, Argonne postdoctoral fellow Argonne Nat. Lab., Ill., 1976-78; engring. specialist, sr. scientist Bechtel Group, Inc., San Francisco, 1978-81; staff mem. Los Alamos Nat. Lab., 1981—. Contbr. articles to profl. jours. Mem. IEEE, Am. Phys. Soc., Optical Soc. Am. Club: Ski (Santa Fe). Current Work: Laser-induced chemistry and spectroscopy, energy-related tech., primarily nuclear fission, currently performing experiments to demonstrate feasibility of molecular laser isotope separation. Subspecialties: Laser-induced chemistry; Atomic and molecular physics. Office: Los Alamos Nat Lab Mail Stop J-565 Los Alamos NM 87545

CAIRE, WILLIAM, biology educator, researcher; b. Savannah, Ga., Nov. 3, 1946; s. James Andrew and Anna (Rahn) C.; m. Ruth Wooldridge, Aug. 30, 1969; children—William James, Jacob Wooldridge, Samuel Rahn. A.A., Howard County Coll., 1966; B.S., Tex. Tech. U., 1969; M.S., N. Tex. State U., 1972; Ph.D., U. N.Mex., 1978. Field biologist U.S. Fish and Wildlife Service, Ft. Collins, Colo., 1975; research analyst U. Mo., Columbia, 1976; assoc. prof. biology Central State U., Edmond, Okla., 1976—. Co-author: Mammal Species of the World, 1982; contbr. articles to sci. jours. Mem. Cub Scouts Am., Boy Scouts Am., Edmond, 1984, Eagle Scouts Am., Edmond, 1984. Served to ensign USN, 1968-69. Named Disting. scholar AAUP, 1983. Mem. Am. Soc. Mammalogists, Okla. Acad. Sci., Assn. Southwestern Naturalists, Systematic Zoologist Soc., Sigma Xi (pres. chpt. 1983-84, Outstanding Researcher of Yr. 1982). Mem. Church of Christ. Current work: Physiology of bats, bat hibernation ecology, ecology, behavior and genetics of bat flyes, rodent systemtics and ecology. Subspecialties: Comparative physiology; Behavioral ecology. Office: Central State U Edmond OK 73034

CAIRNS, JOHN, JR., environmental studies educator; b. Conshokocken, Pa., 1923. A.B., Swarthmore Coll., 1947; M.S., U. Pa., 1949, Ph.D., 1953. With Va. Poly. Inst. and State U., Blacksburg, 1968—, now Univ. Disting. prof. environ. studies. Recipient Charles B. Dudley award ASTM, 1978; Superior Achievement award EPA, 1980; Morrison medal U.S. Dept. Agr.-Agrl. Research Service, 1984. Fellow AAAS; mem. Am. Coll. Toxicology, AAUP, Am. Fisheries Soc., Am. Inst. Biol. Scis. (mem. governing bd. 1976-78), Am. Microscopical Soc. (v.p. 1968-69, pres. 1980), ASTM (chmn. biol. assessment com. 1981), Am. Water Resources Assn. (mem. editorial bd. 1975-81, Icko Iben award 1984), Assn. Southeastern Biologists, Ecol. Soc. Am. (program chmn.

aquatic ecology sect. 1978-79), Inst. Ecology (Founder), Internat. Assn. Ecology, Internat. Assn. Water Pollution Research, Soc. Environ. Toxicology and Chemistry (Founders award 1981), Soc. Protozoologists, Va. Acad. Sci., Water Pollution Control Fedn. (chmn. com. on toxic chems. 1978-80), Sigma Xi. . Office: Va Poly Inst and State Univ Univ Ctr for Environ Studies 1020 Derring Hall Blacksburg VA 24061

CAIRNS, THEODORE LESUEUR, chemist; b. Edmonton, Alta., Can., July 20, 1914; came to U.S., 1936, naturalized, 1945; s. Albert William and Theodora (MacNaughton) C.; m. Margaret Jean McDonald, Aug. 17, 1940; children: John Albert, Margaret Eleanor (Mrs. William L. Etter), Elizabeth Theodora (Mrs. Ernest I. Reveal III), James Richard. B.S., U. Alta., 1936, LL.D., 1970; Ph.D., U. Ill., 1939. Instr. organic chemistry U. Rochester, 1939-41; research chemist central research dept. E.I. duPont de Nemours & Co., Wilmington, Del., 1941-45, research supr., 1945-51, lab. dir., 1951-63, dir. basic scis., 1963-66, dir. research, 1966-67, asst. dir. central research and devel. dept., 1967-71, dir., 1971-79; Regents prof. UCLA, 1965-66; mem. adv. bd. Organic Syntheses, 1958—; mem. Pres.'s Sci. Adv. Com., 1970-73, Pres.'s Com. Nat. Medal Sci., 1974-75; chmn. Office of Chemistry and Chem. Tech., NRC, 1979-81. Editorial bd.: Organic Reactions, 1959—, Jour. Organic Chemistry, 1965-69. Recipient award for creative work in synthetic organic chemistry Am. Chem. Soc., 1968; Perkin medal, 1973; Cresson medal Franklin Inst., 1974. Mem. Nat. Acad. Scis., Am. Chem. Soc. (chmn. organic div. 1964-65), AAAS, Sigma Xi, Phi Lambda Upsilon, Alpha Chi Sigma, Phi Lambda Upsilon (hon.). Subspecialty: Organic chemistry. Home: 2 Ridge Run Rd Chadds Ford PA 19317

CALABI, EUGENIO, mathematics educator; b. Milan, Italy, May 11, 1923; came to U.S., 1939, naturalized, 1943; s. Giuseppe and Maria (Bassani) C.; m. Giuliana Segre, Sept. 3, 1952; children—Nora J., Joseph A. B.S. in Chem. Engring., MIT, 1946; M.A. in Math., U. Ill., 1947; Ph.D., Princeton U., 1950. Asst. prof. math. La. State U., Baton Rouge, 1951-54; vis. asst. prof. Calif. Inst. Tech., Pasadena, 1954-55; asst. prof., prof. math. U. Minn., 1955-66; prof. math. U. Pa., 1964-67, T.A. Scott prof. math., 1967—. Contbr. articles to profl. jours. Served with U.S. Army, 1943-46, ETO. Guggenheim fellow, 1962-63. Mem. Nat. Acad. Sci. Current work: Differential geometry; complex manifolds; geometric extremal problems. Office: Math Dept E-1 U Pa Philadelphia PA 19104

CALABRESE, VINCENT PAUL, physician; b. Jamaica, N.Y., Sept. 23, 1939; s. Giuseppe O. and Florence (Verderese) C.; m. Linda Metzger, June 24, 1966; children: Gregory Paul, Dana Lynn. A.B., Columbia U., 1961; M.D., Downstate SUNY, 1965. Diplomate: Am. Bd. Psychiatry and Neurology. Intern U. Pitts., 1965-66, resident in internal medicine, 1966-67; resident in neurology Albert Einstein Coll. Med., N.Y.C., 1967-70; asst. prof. neurology Med. Coll. Va., Richmond, 1972-78, assoc. prof., 1978—; staff physician McGuire VA Hosp., Richmond, 1974—, dir. neurochemistry lab., 1972—. Contbr. articles to profl. jours. Served to maj USAF, 1970-72. Fellow NIH, 1979-80. Mem. Am. Acad. Neurology, Soc. Neurosci., Am. Soc. Neurochemistry, Internat. Soc. Neurochemistry, AAAS, N.Y. Acad. Sci., Sigma Xi. Current Work: Myelin and axolemma interactions, isolation of specific proteins from axolemma and interspecies differences; neuroimmunology—demyelinating disease, determination of antigens for abnormal IgA, IgM, IgG produced. Subspecialties: Neurochemistry; Neuroimmunology. Office: Dept Neurology Med Coll Va Box 599 Richmond VA 23298

CALAME, KATHRYN LEE, molecular biology educator, researcher; b. Leavenworth, Kans., Apr. 23, 1940; d. Jay O. and Marjorie (Musick) Boehm; m. Byron Edward Calame, June 9, 1962; children—Christine Lee, Jonathan David. B.S. with honors, U. Mo., 1962; M.S., George Washington U., 1965, Ph.D., 1975. Postdoctoral fellow U. Pitts., 1975-77, research asst. prof., 1977-78; research assoc. Calif. Inst. Tech., Pasadena, 1978-80; asst. prof. biol. chemistry UCLA Sch. Medicine, 1980—. Contbr. articles to sci. jours., chpts. to books. Recipient Scholar award Leukemia Soc., 1984-89; Nat. Inst. Gen. Med. Sci. fellow, 1975-78, grantee, 1980—; Am. Cancer Soc. grantee, 1985-87. Mem. Am. Assn. Biol. Chemists, AAAS, Am. Assn. Microbiology, Phi Beta Kappa, Sigma Xi. Democrat. Presbyterian. Current work: Research on regulation of gene expression with special interest in oncogenes and antibody genes, teaching medical students and graduate students. Subspecialties: Immunogenetics; Molecular biology. Home: 132 N Norton Los Angeles CA 90004 Office: Dept Biol Chemistry UCLA Sch Medicine Los Angeles CA 90024

CALDER, CLARENCE ANDREW, mech. engr., educator, cons., researcher; b. Baker, Oreg., Oct. 30, 1937; s. Clarence Leroy and Viola Mary (Lucas) C.; m. Judy Lee Wood, Dec. 15, 1961; children: Brian, Gregory, Kaylene, Chad, Jared. B.S.M.E., Oreg. State U., 1960; M.S., Brigham Young U., 1962; Ph.D. in Engring. Sci, U. Calif., Berkeley, 1969. Registered profl. engr., Calif., Oreg. Design engr. Boise Cascade Corp., Emmett, Idaho, 1960-61; project engr. Sandia Labs., Albuquerque, 1962-64; research assoc. U. Calif., Berkeley, 1966-69; asst. prof. Wash. State U., 1969-74; research engr. Lawrence Livermore (Calif.) Nat. Labs., 1974-78; assoc. prof. mech. engring. Oreg. State U., 1978—, cons. laser applications in engring., athletic shoe performance. Contbr. articles on exptl. mechanics, laser applications in engring., instrumentation, stress waves in materials, athletic shoe performance to profl. jours. Recipient Best Paper award of recognition Am. Nuclear Soc., 1978. Mem. Soc. Exptl. Stress Analysis (F. G. Tatnal award 1982), ASME, Soc. Engring. Edn. Republican. Mormon. Current Work: Research and applications using lasers as sensors and as ultrasonic stress wave generators in non-destructive testing; noncontact material testing using lasers; athletic shoe performance testing and analysis. Subspecialties: Mechanical engineering; Solid mechanics. Home: 2015 Wooded Knolls Dr Philomath OR 97370 Office: Dept Mech Engring Oreg State U Corvallis OR 97331

CALDWELL, DAVID ORVILLE, physicist, educator; b. Los Angeles, Jan. 5, 1925; s. Orville Robert and Audrey Norton (Anderson) C.; divorced (div.); children: Bruce David, Diana Miriam. B.S., Calif. Inst. Tech., 1947; postgrad., Stanford U., 1947-48; M.A., UCLA, 1949, Ph.D., 1953. Instr. dept. physics MIT, 1954-56, asst. prof., 1956-58, assoc. prof., 1958-63; vis. assoc. prof. Princeton U., 1963-64; lectr. U. Calif.-Berkeley, 1964-65; prof. physics U. Calif.-Santa Barbara, 1965—; cons. Lawrence Radiation Lab., U. Calif., 1950-51, 65-70, Am. Sci. and Engring., Cambridge, Mass., 1959-60, Inst. Def. Analyses, 1960-67, Dept. Def., 1966-70; assoc. dir Intercampus Inst. Research at Particle Accelerators. Contbr. chpts. to books, articles to profl jours. Served to 2d lt. USAAF, 1943-46. AEC predoctoral fellow, 1950-52; NSF postdoctoral fellow, 1953-54; NSF sr. postdoctoral fellow, 1960-61; Ford Found. fellow, 1961-62; Guggenheim Found. fellow, 1971-72; research grantee AEC, Energy Research and Devel. Agy., Dept. of Energy, 1966—. Fellow Am. Phys. Soc. Current Work: Teaching and research; research generally seeking the fundamental laws of nature; current experiments in two-photon annihilation and double-beta decay. Subspecialties: Particle physics; Nuclear physics. Office: Dept Physics U Calif Santa Barbara CA 93106

CALDWELL, ELWOOD FLEMING, food science educator, researcher; b. Gladstone, Man., Can., Apr. 3, 1923; s. Charles Fleming and Frances Marion (Ridd) C.; m. Irene Margaret Sebille, June 13, 1949; children: John Fleming, Keith Allan; m. Florence Annette Zar, June 23, 1979. B.Sc., U. Man., 1943; M.A. in food chemistry, U. Toronto, 1949, Ph.D. in nutrition, 1953; M.B.A., U. Chgo., 1956. Chemist Lake of the Woods Milling Co., Can., 1943-47; research chemist Can. Breweries Ltd., Toronto, Ont., 1948-49; chief chemist Christie, Brown & Co. (Nabisco), Toronto, 1949-51; research assoc. in nutrition U. Toronto, 1951-53; with Quaker Oats Co., Barrington, Ill., 1953-72, dir. research and devel., until 1972; prof., head dept. food sci. and nutrition U. Minn., St. Paul, 1972—; chmn. bd. Dairy Quality Control Inst., Inc., St. Paul, 1972—, R.& D. Assocs. for Mil. Food & Packaging, Inc., San Antonio, 1970-71; chmn. evening programing food sci. Ill. Inst. Tech., Chgo., 1965-69. Contbr. articles to sci. jours. Chmn. North Barrington (Ill.) Bd. Appeals, 1966-69, mayor, 1969-72; vice-chmn. Barrington Area Council Govts., 1972; bd. dirs. Family Guidance Barrington, 1971-72. Recipient cert. of appreciation for civilian service U.S. Army Materiel Command, 1970. Fellow Inst. Food Technologists (Chmn.'s Service award Chgo. sect. 1975); mem. Am. Assn. Cereal Chemists, Am. Home Econs. Assn., Phi Tau Sigma, Sigma Xi, Gamma Sigma Delta. Republican. Lutheran. Club: Minnesota Alumni (Mpls.). Current Work: Administration of teaching, research and extension in food science and nutrition; direct undergraduate and graduate instruction and graduate research in food science, food technology, nutrition, dietetics, consumer studies. Subspecialties: Food science and technology; Nutrition (biology). Office: 1334 Eckles Ave U Minn Saint Paul MN 55108

CALDWELL, GLYN GORDON, physician, epidemiologist, virologist, government administrator; b. St. Louis, Jan. 14, 1934; s. Cecil Gordon and Zelma Mae (Peeler) C.; m. Mary Jean Pandolfo, Aug. 13, 1960; children: Michael, Elizabeth, Thomas. B.S. (Univ. scholar), St. Louis U., 1960; M.S., U. Mo., 1962, M.D., 1966. Intern USPHS Hosp., Brighton, Mass., 1966-67; resident in internal medicine Cleve. Met. Gen. Hosp., 1969-71; commd. sr. asst. surgeon USPHS, 1966, advanced through grades to dir., 1979; with Center for Disease Control, Atlanta, 1967-85, Chief field investigations sect. cancer research, 1974-77, chief cancer br., chronic diseases div., 1977-82, dep. dir. epidemiology and environ. service div., 1982-85; asst. dir. Ariz. Dept. Health Services, Div. Disease Control Services, 1985—. Contbr. articles to profl. publs. Served to sgt. Signal Corps U.S. Army, 1954-62. Recipient Commendation medal USPHS, 1980. Mem. Am. Soc. Microbiology, Soc. Epidemiologic Research, Am. Soc. Preventive Oncology, USPHS Commd. Officers Assn. Roman Catholic. Lodge: KC. Current Work: General public health; cancer epidemiology, including radiation, viral, chem. and genetic oncology. Subspecialties: Epidemiology; Internal medicine. Home: 4341 N 24th St #118 Phoenix AZ 85016 Office: Ariz Dept Health Services 431 N 24th St Phoenix AZ 85008

CALDWELL, KARIN MARIA ELISABET, biochemist; b. Stockholm, June 4, 1940; d. Tore and Ester (Sigrid Arrhenius) Dahlgren; m. Dennis James Caldwell, Oct. 3, 1970. B.S., U. Uppsala, 1964, Ph.D., 1968, Fil, Doktor, 1976. Teaching asst. ENSCM, Montpellier, France, 1964-65; postdoctoral research assoc. U. Utah, Salt Lake City, 1968-73; research asst. U. Uppsala, 1973-76; postdoctoral research assoc. U. Utah, 1976-79; asst. research prof., 1979-82, assoc. research prof., 1982—, dir. ctr. for biopolymers at interfaces, 1985—. Edit. bd. Separation Sci. & Tech., 1977—; contbr. articles to profl. jours. Pres., Swedish Heritage Soc. Utah, 1983-84; bd. dirs. Utah Symphony Guild, 1981-84; trustee Wasatch Mountain Club, 1981-84. Mem. Am. Soc. Biol. Chemists, Am. Chem. Soc., AAAS. Lutheran. Current work: Fractionation and characterization of macromolecules and particles. Subspecialties: Biophysical chemistry; Analytical chemistry. Home: 3645 Golden Hills Ave Salt Lake City UT 84121

CALEDONIA, GEORGE ERNEST, research scientist; b. Boston, Nov. 9, 1941; s. George F. and Gilda (Cimmino) C.; m. Diane M., Nov. 6, 1965; children: Karen, Julie, Elizabeth. A.B., Northeastern U., 1965, M.S., 1967. Prin. scientist Avco Everett Research Lab., Mass., 1967-73; prin. scientist Phys. Scis. Inc., Andover, Mass., 1973-80, v.p. research, 1980—, also dir. Contbr. articles to profl. jours. Recipient Marcus O'Day Meml. award USAF Geophysics Lab. Mem. Am. Phys. Soc., Am. Geophys. Union, Am. Chem. Soc. Current Work: Upper atmospheric radiative and kinetic phenomena, high temperature gas radiation properties, electron excitation of gases, kinetic analysis. Subspecialties: Aeronomy; Atomic and molecular physics. Office: Research Park Andover MA 01810

CALESNICK, BENJAMIN, physician, clinical pharmacologist; b. Phila., Dec. 27, 1915; s. Samuel and Ida (Lichtenstein) C.; m. Sophie Adele Brenner, Dec. 27, 1921; 1 son, Jay Lee. B.S., St. Joseph's Coll., 1938; M.A., Temple U., 1941; M.D., Hahnemann Med. Coll., 1944. Intern Phila. Gen. Hosp., 1944-45; faculty Hahnemann U., Phila., 1946—; prof. pharmacology and medicine Hahnemann Med. Coll., 1971—. Served to lt. comdr. USN, 1945-54. Current Work: Teaching and research in clin. pharmacology. Subspecialties: Internal medicine; Pharmacology. Home: 646 W Springfield Rd Springfield PA 19064 Office: Hahnemann U Dept Pharmacology and Medicine 230 N Broad St Philadelphia PA 19102

CALIFANO, JOSEPH MICHAEL, quality engr.; b. Bklyn., Jan. 1, 1951; s. Joseph Frank and Ann (Ruscitto) C.; m. Theresa Ann Marie Swartout, June 16, 1978; 1 son. Eric Michael. B.A. in Physics, Hunter Coll., CUNY, 1972. Asst. mgr. research and devel. lab. Pall Corp., Glen Cove, N.Y., 1974-75, mgr. biomed. quality control, 1975-77; mgr. quality control Amicon Corp., Lexington, Mass., 1978-79, Gelman Scis. Co., Ann Arbor, Mich., 1979-81, quality engr., 1981—. Mem. Am. Soc. for Quality Control (cert. quality engr.), High I.Q. Soc. San Francisco. Democrat. Roman Catholic. Current Work: Design, review and validation of products and processes for filtration membranes; statistical analysis of product and process data; design of experiments; establish test methods. Subspecialties: Statistics; Filtration membranes.

CALKIN, PARKER EMERSON, geology educator; b. Syracuse, N.Y., Apr. 27, 1933; s. Frank G. and Georgia (Spencer) C.; m. Joan A. Chace, Sept. 15, 1955 (div. 1978); children: Mark, Lisa; m. Harriet R. Simons, Feb. 19, 1979. B.S., Tufts U., 1955; M.Sc., U. B.C., 1959; Ph.D., Ohio State U.-Columbus, 1963. Asst. prof. geology Coll. at SUNY-Buffalo, 1963-65; asst. prof. SUNY-Buffalo, 1965-68, assoc. prof., 1968-75, prof. geology, 1975—; dir. Tech. Systems Research, Inc., N.Y., 1981—. Editor, author: series Great Lakes Coastal Geology, 1981, 82. Served to lt. (j.g.) USN, 1955-57. NSF grantee, 1960-64, 66-72, 76-83; SUNY faculty research fellow, 1973; NOAA sea grantee, 1974-80. Fellow Geol. Soc. Am.; mem. Glaciological Soc., N.Y. State Geol. Assn. (pres. 1982), Am. Quaternary Assn., Sigma Xi. Current Work: Polar geology, particularly geomorphology and glacial geology in Antarctica, Greenland and Alaska. Subspecialty: Geology. Home: 49 Blossom Heath Williamsville NY 14221 Office: Dept Geol Scis SUNY 4240 Ridge Lea Rd Buffalo NY 14226

CALKINS, EVAN, physician, educator; b. Newton, Mass., July 15, 1920; s. Grosvenor and Patty (Phillips) C.; m. Virginia McC. Brady, Sept. 9, 1946; children: Sarah Calkins Oxnard, Stephen, Lucy McCormick, Joan Calkins Bender, Benjamin, Hugh, Ellen Rountree, Geoffrey, Timothy. Grad., Milton Acad., 1939; A.B., Harvard U., 1942, M.D., 1945. Intern, asst. resident medicine Johns Hopkins, 1946-47, 48-50; chief resident physician Mass. Gen. Hosp., 1951-52, mem. arthritis unit, 1952-61; NRC fellow med. scis. Harvard, 1950-51, instr., asst. prof. medicine, 1952-61, practice medicine, specializing in rheumatology, Boston, 1951-61, Buffalo, 1961—; prof. medicine SUNY, Buffalo, 1961—, chmn. dept., 1965-77, head div. geriatrics and gerontology, 1978—; head dept. medicine Buffalo Gen. Hosp., 1961-68; dir. medicine E.J. Meyer Meml. Hosp., 1968-78; head geriatrics service Buffalo VA Med. Center, 1978—; head dir. geriatrics/gerontology SUNY-Buffalo, 1978—; founder, pres. Network in Aging of Western N.Y., Inc., 1980-83; cons. Nat. Inst. Arthritis and Metabolic Diseases Tng. Grants Com., 1958-62, Program Project Com., 1964-68, Nat. Insts. Spl. Study Sect. for Health Manpower, 1969-77, for Behavioral Medicine, 1978-79; mem. acad. awards com. Nat. Inst. on Aging, 1979-80; dir. Western N.Y. Geriatrics Edn. Center, 1983—. Editor: Handbook of Medical Emergencies, 1945, Practice of Geriatric Medicine, 1983; Contbr. articles to profl. jours. Served to capt., M.C. AUS, 1943-45, 46-48. Recipient Presdl. citation for Community Service, 1983. Fellow A.C.P.; mem. Am. Assn. Pathologists, Gerontol. Assn., Am. Geriatrics Soc., Am. Rheumatism Assn. (pres.), Am. Clin. and Climatological Assn., Am. Soc. Clin. Investigation, Assn. Am. Physicians, Central Soc. for Clin. Research, Soc. Medicine Argentina (hon.), Alpha Omega Alpha. Current Work: Research on clinical aspects of geriatrics and rheumatology, amyloidosis and curriculum development in geriatric medicine. Subspecialties: Internal medicine; Gerontology. Home: 3799 Windover Hamburg NY 14075 Office: VA Med Center 3495 Bailey Ave Buffalo NY 14215

CALLAWAY, JOSEPH, educator, physicist; b. Hackensack, N.J., July 1, 1931; s. Joseph and Sybil Leigh (Mock) C.; m. Mary Morrison, July 30, 1949; children: Joseph A., Paul E., Jessie S. B.S., Coll. William and Mary, 1951; M.A., Princeton U., 1953, Ph.D., 1956. Asst. prof. physics U. Miami, 1954-60; asso. prof. physics U. Calif.-Riverside, 1960-64, prof., 1964-67; prof. physics and astronomy La. State U., 1967-76, Boyd prof. physics and astronomy, 1976—. Author: Quantum Theory of the Solid State, 1974; contbr. articles to sci. jours. Fellow Am. Phys. Soc.; fellow Inst. Physics U.K.; mem. AAAS, European Phys. Soc., Phi Beta Kappa. Democrat. Current Work: Theoretical solid state and atomic physics; band theory of solids; theory of ferromagnetism; theory of electron scattering by atoms. Subspecialties: Condensed matter physics; Atomic and molecular physics. Office: Dept Physics La State U Baton Rouge LA 70803

CALLEN, JEFFREY PHILLIP, dermatologist, educator; b. Chgo., May 30, 1947; s. Irwin R. and Rose P. (Cohen) C.; m. Susan M. Manis, Dec. 21, 1968; children: Amy, David. B.S., U. Wis., 1969; M.D., U. Mich., 1972. Diplomate: Am. Bd. Internal Medicine, 1975, Am. Bd. Dermatology, 1977. Intern/resident in internal medicine U. Mich., 1972-75, in dermatology, 1975-77; asst. clin. prof. U. Louisville Sch. Medicine, 1977-81, assoc. clin. prof., 1982-83, assoc. prof., 1984—, dir. Residency Program, 1984—. Author: Manual of Dermatology, 1980, Cutaneous Aspects of Internal Disease, 1981; editor: Clinics in Rheumatic Disease, 1982, others. editor-in-chief Dermavision video program; editorial cons. Dialogues in Dermatology audio tape program, 1981-84. Chief Shawnee Indian Guides, Louisville, 1983-84; bd. dirs. Louisville Jewish Community Ctr., 1982-84, Actor Theatre of Louisville. Fellow ACP, Am. Acad. Dermatology (chmn. audio/visual edn. com. 1981-84, task force therapeutic agts. 1981-84, internal medicine symposium 1978-83, Cutaneous Oncology Symposium 1984—); mem. Am. Fedn. Clin. Research, AMA, Am. Rheumatism Assn., Dermatology Found. (chmn. corp fund raising com.). Current Work: condition in which systemic disease has cutaneous manifestations. Subspecialties: Dermatology; Internal medicine. Office: Dept Dermatology U Louisville 310 E Broadway Suite 200 Louisville KY 40202

CALLEWAERT, DENIS MARC, chemist, educator; b. Detroit, Feb. 20, 1947; s. Marcel August and Mary Theresa (Lams) C.; m. Karen Margaret Koehn, Sept. 25, 1971; children: Amy Marlene, Megan Elizabeth. B.S. in Chemistry, U. Detroit, 1969; Ph.D. in Biochemistry, Wayne State U., 1973. Research assoc. Wayne State U., Detroit, 1969-73, postdoctoral assoc., 1973-74; asst. prof. chemistry Oakland U., Rochester, Mich., 1974-80, assoc. prof., 1980-85, prof., 1985—, chmn. interdepartmental biochemistry program, 1980—; pres. Oxford Biomedical Research, Inc.; cons. in field. Author: (with J. Genyea) Basic Chemistry: General Organic, Biological, 1980; contbr. articles to profl. jours. Leukemia Soc. Am. fellow, 1975-77; Nat. Cancer Inst. awardee, 1980-85. Mem. Am. Chem. Soc., Am. Assn. Immunologists, AAAS, Sigma Xi. Current Work: Function and biochemistry of human natural killer cells; modulation of human immune function; enzyme evolution. Subspecialties: Biochemistry (biology); Immunobiology and immunology. Home: 1600 Hosner Rd Oxford MI 48051 Office: Dept Chemistry Oakland U Rochester MI 48063

CALLOWAY, DORIS HOWES, nutrition educator; b. Canton, Ohio, Feb. 14, 1923; married, 1981; 2 children. B.S., Ohio State U., 1943; Ph.D. in Nutrition, U. Chgo., 1947. Diplomate: Am. Bd. Nutrition, 1951. Intern dietetics Johns Hopkins Univ. Hosp., Balt., 1944; research dietitian dept. medicine U. Ill., 1945; cons. Med. Assocs., Chgo., 1948-51; nutritionist OM Food and Container Inst., 1951-58, head metabolism lab., 1958-59, chief nutrition br., 1959-61; chmn. dept. food sci. and nutrition Stanford Research Inst., Calif., 1961-64; prof. nutrition U. Calif.-Berkeley, 1963—; provost U. Calif.-Berkeley (Profl. Schs. and Colls.), 1981—; Bd. dirs. Am. Bd. Nutrition, 1968-71; mem. panel White House Conf. on Food, Nutrition and Health, 1969; trustee Nat. Council Hunger and Malnutrition in U.S., 1969-71; mem. food and nutrition bd. Nat. Acad. Sci.-NRC, 1972-75; mem. vis. com. MIT, 1972-74; mem. expert adv. panel on nutrition WHO, 1972—; mem. adv. council Nat. Inst. Arthritis and Metabolism and Digestive Diseases, NIH, 1974-77; cons. nutrition div. FAO, 1974-75; mem. adv. council, Nat. Inst. Aging, NIH, 1977-81. Assoc. editor: Nutrition Rev, 1962-68; editorial bd.: Jour. Nutrition, 1967-72, Environ. Biology and Medicine, 1969—, Jour. Am. Dietetic Assn, 1974-77, Interdisciplinary Sci. Rev, 1975—. Mem. Am. Inst. Nutrition (pres. 1982-83), Am. Dietetic Assn. Subspecialty: Nutrition (biology). Office: U Calif Berkeley CA 94720

CALTER, PAUL, mechanical engineer, educator, author; b. N.Y.C., June 18, 1934; s. Arthur and Frances (Bankowitz) Calcaterra; m. Margaret Jolind Carey, May 13, 1959; children—Amy, Michael. B.S. in Engring., The Cooper Union, 1962; M.M.E., Columbia U., 1965. Sr. research asst. Columbia U., N.Y.C., 1952-60; engr. Kollsman Instrument Co., N.Y.C., 1960-65; sr. project engr. Intertype Co., N.Y.C., 1965-68; prof. math. Vt. Tech. Coll., Randolph, 1968—; cons. engr. in optical design, Randolph, 1968-72; pres. Med. Computation Service, Randolph, 1973-76. Author: Problem Solving with Computers, 1973; Solution of Differential Equations, 1975; Magic Squares, 1976; Outline of Technical Mathematics, 1978; Fundamentos De Matematica, 1980; Technical Mathematics, 1983; Practical Math Handbook for the Building Trades, 1983; Mathematics for Electricity and Electronics, 1983; Technical Mathematics with Calculus, 1984. Steel sculpture Focus. Served with U.S. Army, 1957-59. Recipient Ralph Horton Meml. award in sci., 1952. Mem. ASME, Author's Guild, Am. Assn. Two-Yr. Colls. (del.), Vols. in Tech. Assistance. Democrat. Club: University (Randolph) (pres. 1984—). Current work: Author in fields of mathematics and computer programming. Subspecialties: Applied mathematics; Numerical analysis (mathematics). Home: 33 S Pleasant St Randolph VT 05060 Office: Vt Tech Coll Randolph Center VT 05061

CALVERT, DAVID VICTOR, agriculture educator; b. Chaplin, Ky., Feb. 26, 1934; s. Stanford Byron and Willia (Neal) C.; m. Joyce Faye LeMay, July 27, 1957; children—Victor neal, Yvonne Carole. B.S., U. Ky., 1956, M.S., 1958; Ph.D., Iowa State U., 1962. Cert. profl. soil scientist, cert. profl. agronomist. Grad. research asst. U. Ky., Lexington, 1956-58, Iowa State U., Ames, 1958-62; asst. prof. agriculture U. Fla., Gainesville, 1962-68, assoc. prof., 1968-76, prof., 1976—, research ctr. dir., 1978—; official collaborator U.S. Dept. Agr. agr. research service, southeastern U.S., 1968—; cons. Jamaican Sch. Agr., Kingston, 1970. Contbr. articles to profl. jours. Scoutmaster, Boy Scouts Am., 1963-70; pres. Baptist Mens' Brotherhood, First Bapt. Ch., Fort Pierce, Fla., 1972-73. Recipient annual research award Fla. Fruit and Vegetable Assn., 1979; named Dist. Conservationist of Yr. Soil Conservation Service U.S. Dept. Agr., 1983. Mem. Am. soc. Agronomy, Soic Sci. Soc. Am., Internat. Soc. Soil Sci., AAAS, Internat. Soc. Citriculture, Council of Agrl. Sci. and Tech., So. Assn. Agrl. Scientists, Am. Forestry Assn., Soil and Crop Sci. Soc. Fla. (bd. dirs. 1981-84), Fla. State Hort. Soc., Sigma Xi, Gamma Sigma Delta, Alpha Zeta (sec.-treas. 1956—). Lodge: Kiwanis (pres. Fort Pierce 1968-69). Republican. Current work: Soil chemistry, soil fertility, soil and water management as related to citrus industry of U.S. and world. Subspecialty: Soil science. Office: U Fla Agrl Research and Edn Ctr PO Box 248 Fort Pierce FL 33454

CALVERT, GLENN SPENCER, mechanical engineer; b. Memphis, May 6, 1934; s. Glenn Spencer and Martha Lee (Wolf) C.; m. Patricia Lee, June 20, 1964; 1 child, Caron Lee. A.A., Christian Bros. Coll., 1954; B.S. in M.E., U. Miss., 1957; M.S. in M.E., U. Mo.-Columbia, 1962. Registered Profl. Engr., Fla. Exptl. engr. Pratt & Whitney Aircraft, West Palm Beach, Fla., 1962-63, sr. exptl. engrs., 1963-65, asst. project engr., 1965-79, project engr., 1979—. Contbr. articles to tech. jours. Served with USNR, 1958-62. Mem. ASME. Democrat. Roman Catholic. Current work: Gas turbine airfoil design and manufacture. Subspecialties: Mechanical engineering; Aerospace engineering and technology. Home: 80 Yacht Club Pl Tequesta FL 33458 Office: Pratt & Whitney Aircraft Box 2691 West Palm Beach FL 33403

CALVERT, JACK GEORGE, atmospheric chemist, educator; b. Inglewood, Calif., May 9, 1923; s. John George and Emma (Eschstruth) C.; m. Doris Arlene Breimon, Nov. 8, 1946; children—Richard John, Mark Steven. B.S. in Chemistry, UCLA, 1944, Ph.D., 1949. Mem. faculty Ohio State U., 1950-81, prof. chemistry, 1960-81, Kimberly prof. chemistry, 1974-81, prof. emeritus, 1981—, chmn. dept., 1964-68; sr. scientist Nat. Center Atmospheric Research, Boulder, Colo., 1981—; Cons. air pollution tng. com. USPHS, 1964-66; mem. Nat. Air Pollution Control Manpower Devel. Com., 1966-69, chmn., 1968-69; bd. dirs. Gordon Research Confs., 1969-71; mem. air pollution control research grants com. EPA, 1970-72, chmn., 1971-72, mem. chemistry and physics adv. com., 1973-75; chmn. air pollution com. Conservation Found., 1968-70; mem. air conservation commn. Am. Lung Assn., 1973-75; chmn. EPA environ. chemistry/physics grants rev. panel, 1979-83. Author: (with J.N. Pitts, Jr.) Photochemistry, 1966; (with J.N. Pitts and G.H. Dorion) Graduate School in the Sciences, 1972; also articles. Served to ensign USNR, 1944-46. Named Honor Prof. of Year Coll. Arts and Scis., Ohio State U., 1957; recipient Alumni award for disting. teaching, 1961, Disting. Research award, 1981; Fellow NRC Can., 1949; Guggenheim fellow, 1977-78. Fellow Ohio Acad. Sci., Am. Inst. Chemists, AAAS; mem. Am. Chem. Soc. (award for creative research in environ. sci. and tech. 1981, Columbus sect. award 1981), Air Pollution Control Assn., Phi Beta Kappa, Sigma Xi, Pi Mu Epsilon, Phi Lambda Upsilon, Alpha Chi Sigma. Current work: Study of chemical mechanics of transient molecules involved in atmospheric processes. Subspecialties: Kinetics; Photochemistry. Office: NCAR Atmospheric Chemistry Div PO Box 3000 Boulder CO 80307

CALVIN, MELVIN, chemist, educator; b. St. Paul, Apr. 8, 1911; s. Elias and Rose I. (Hervitz) C.; m. Marie G. Jemtegaard, 1942; children: Elin, Karole, Noel. B.S., Mich. Coll. Mining and Tech., 1931, D.Sc., 1955; Ph.D., U. Minn., 1935, D.Sc., 1969; hon research fellow, U. Manchester, Eng., 1935-37; Guggenheim fellow, 1967; D.Sc., Nottingham U., 1958, Oxford (Eng.) U.,

1959, Northwestern U., 1961, Wayne State U., 1962, Gustavus Adolphus Coll., 1963, Poly. Inst. Bklyn., 1962, U. Notre Dame, 1965, U. Gent, Belgium, 1970, Whittier Coll., 1971, Clarkson Coll., 1976, U. Paris Val-de-Marne, 1977, Columbia U., 1979. With U. Calif., Berkeley, 1937—, successively instr. chemistry, asst. prof., prof., Univ. prof., dir. Lab. Chem. Biodynamics, 1963-80, assoc. dir. Lawrence Berkeley Lab., 1967-80; Peter Reilly lectr. U. Notre Dame, 1949; Harvey lectr. N.Y. Acad. Medicine, 1951; Harrison Howe lectr. Rochester sect. Am. Chem. Soc., 1954; Falk-Plaut lectr. Columbia U., 1954; Edgar Fahs Smith Meml. lectr. U. Pa. and Phila. sect. Am. Chem. Soc., 1955; Donegani Found. lectr. Italian Nat. Acad. Sci., 1955; Max Tishler lectr. Harvard U., 1956; Karl Folkers lectr. U. Wis., 1956; Baker lectr. Cornell U., 1958; London lectr., 1961, Willard lectr., 1982; Vanuxem lectr. Princeton U., 1969; Disting. lectr. Mich. State U., 1977; Prather lectr. Harvard U., 1980; Dreyfus lectr. Dartmouth Coll., 1981, Berea Coll., 1982; Barnes lectr. Colo. Coll., 1982; Nobel lectr. U. Md., 1982; Abbott lectr. U. N.D., 1983; Gunning lectr. U. Alta., 1983; O'Leary disting. lectr. Gonzaga U., 1984, other lectureships; Eastman prof. Oxford (Eng.) U., 1967-68. Author: (with G. E. K. Branch) The Theory of Organic Chemistry, 1940, Isotopic Carbon, (with others), 1949, Chemistry of Metal Chelate Compounds, (with Martell), 1952, Path of Carbon in Photosynthesis, (with Bassham), 1957, Photosynthesis of Carbon Compounds, 1962, Chemical Evolution, 1969; contbr. articles to chem. and sci. jours. Recipient prize Sugar Research Found., 1950, Flintoff medal prize Brit. Chem. Soc., 1953, Stephen Hales award Am. Soc. Plant Physiologists, 1956, Nobel prize in chemistry, 1961; Davy medal Royal Soc., 1964; Virtanen medal, 1975; Priestley medal, 1978; Am. Inst. Chemists medal, 1979; Feodor Lynen medal, 1983; Sterling B. Hendricks medal, 1983; Oesper award Cin. sect. Am. Chem. Soc., 1981. Mem. Britain's Royal Soc. London (fgn. mem.), Am. Chem. Soc. (Richards medal N.E. sect. 1956, Chem. Soc. Nichols medal N.Y. sect. 1958, award for nuclear applications in chemistry, pres. 1971, Gibbs medal Chgo. sect. 1977, Priestley medal 1978), Am. Acad. Arts and Scis., Nat. Acad. Scis., Royal Dutch Acad. Scis., Japan Acad., Am. Philos. Soc., Sigma Xi, Tau Beta Pi, Phi Lambda Upsilon. Current Work: Hydrocarbon-biomass; photochemical decomposition of water 1) with H_2 product or cO_2 red 2) with O_2 or organic oxide. Subspecialty: Photochemistry. Home: 2683 Buena Vista Berkeley CA 94708

CAMERMAN, ARTHUR, chemist, pharmacologist, educator, researcher; b. Vancouver, B.C., Can., Apr. 12, 1939; came to U.S., 1967; s. Philip and Dora (Charkow) C. B.Sc. with honors, U. B.C., 1961, Ph.D. in Chemistry, 1964. NRC of Can. overseas postdoctoral fellow Royal Instn. Gt. Brit., London, 1964-66; research asso. depts. biol. structure and pharmacy U. Wash., Seattle, 1967-71, research asst. prof. depts. medicine and pharmacology, 1971-75, research asso. prof., 1975-81, research prof., 1981—; vis. investigator Howard Hughes Med. Inst., 1971-72. Contbr. numerous articles and abstracts to sci jours. NIH research career devel. awardee, 1974-79; Klingenstein sr. fellow in the neuroscis., 1983-86; Internat. League Against Epilepsy research award, 1983; numerous research grants NIH; numerous research grants NSF. Mem. AAAS, Am. Chem. Soc., Am. Crystallographic Assn., Am. Soc. for Neurochemistry, Am. Soc. Pharmacology and Exptl. Therapeutics, Fedn. Am. Scientists. Current Work: Structure-activity relationships in drugs and biol. molecules; antiepileptic drugs; neurochemistry; anti-cancer drugs. Subspecialties: Crystallography; Molecular pharmacology. Office: U Wash Neurology Dept RG-20 Seattle WA 98195

CAMERON, ALASTAIR GRAHAM WALTER, astrophysicist; b. Winnipeg, Can., June 21, 1925; came to U.S., 1959, naturalized, 1963; s. Alexander Thomas and Airdrie Edna (Bell) C.; m. Elizabeth Aston MacMillan, June 11, 1955. B.Sc., U. Man., 1947; Ph.D., U. Sask., 1952, D.Sc. (hon.), 1977; A.M. (hon.), Harvard U., 1973. Asst. prof. physics Iowa State Coll., Ames, 1952-54; asst. asso. and sr. research officer Atomic Energy Can., Ltd., Chalk River, Ont., 1954-61; sr. research fellow Calif. Inst. Tech., Pasadena, 1959-60; sr. scientist Goddard Inst. Space Studies, N.Y., 1961-66; prof. space physics Yeshiva U., 1966-73; prof. astronomy Harvard U., Cambridge, Mass., 1973—; chmn. Space Sci. Bd., 1976-82, Nat. Acad. Scis. Contbr. articles to profl. jours. Mem. Nat. Acad. Scis., Am. Acad. Arts and Scis., World Acad. Art and Sci., Royal Soc. Can., AAAS, Am. Phys. Soc., Am. Geophys. Union, Am. Astron. Soc., Royal Astron. Soc., Internat. Astron. Union, Internat. Assn. Geochemistry and Cosmochemistry, Meteoritical Soc. Club: Cosmos. Subspecialties: Theoretical astrophysics; Planetary science. Office: 60 Garden St Cambridge MA 02138

CAMERON, H. RONALD, educator; b. Oakland, Calif., June 30, 1929; s. Sidney H. and Violet N. (Mecklenberg) C.; m. Barbara L. Snook, June 23, 1956; children: William S., Kathryn L. B.S., U. Calif., Davis, 1951; Ph.D., U. Wis., 1955. Faculty plant pathology Oreg. State U., Corvallis, 1955—. Contbr. articles to profl. jours. NSF fellow, 1962; NATO fellow, 1972. Mem. Am. Phytopath. Soc. (treas. 1982—), Sigma Xi. Current Work: Researcher in isolation and identification of previously unidentified virus-like diseases. Subspecialties: Plant virology; Plant pathology. Office: Oregon State University Dept Botany and Plant Pathology Corvllis OR 97331

CAMIOLO, SARAH MAY, cancer researcher; b. Enna, Italy, May 18, 1924; came to U.S., 1924; d. Stephen and Mary (Incardona) C. B.A., Seton Hill Coll., 1946; M.S., Canisius Coll., 1949; Ph.D., American U., 1971. Research chemist surg. research lab. E. J. Meyer Meml. Hosp., Buffalo, 1950-52; silicones div. Union Carbide Corp., Tonawanda, N.Y., 1952-63; chemistry educator Peace Corps, Cameroon, West Africa, 1963-66; research assoc. J. F. Mitchell Med. Inst., Washington, 1967-72; asst. research prof. SUNY-Buffalo dept pharmacology, 1974-76; sr. cancer research scientist Roswell Park Meml. Inst., Buffalo, 1976—; cons. AID, Kerala, India, 1967, Madras, India, 1968. Mem. pastoral council Diocese of Buffalo, 1982-85. Michael Reese Blood Center fellow, 1972; United Way of Western N.Y. fellow, 1973. Mem. Am. Chem. Soc., Am. Soc. Biol. Chemists, Internat. Soc. on Thrombosis and Haemostasis, Am. Women in Sci., N.Y. Acad. Scis., Iota Sigma Pi. Current Work: Plasminogen activators and the role of these fibrinolytic enzymes in cancers. Subspecialties: Cancer research (medicine); Molecular biology. Home: 120 Lakewood Pkwy Buffalo NY 14226 Office: Roswell Park Meml Inst 666 Elm St Buffalo NY 14263

CAMPBELL, ALLAN MCCULLOCH, educator; b. Berkeley, Calif., Apr. 27, 1929; s. Lindsay and Virginia Margaret (Henning) C.; m. Alice Del Campillo, Sept. 5, 1958; children—Wendy, Joseph. B.S. in Chemistry, U. Calif.-Berkeley, 1950; M.S. in Bacteriology, U. Ill., 1951; Ph.D., 1953; Sc.D. (hon.), U. Chgo., 1978, U. Rochester, 1981. Instr. bacteriology U. Mich., 1953-57; research assoc. Carnegie Inst., Cold Spring Harbor, N.Y., 1957-58; asst. prof. biology U. Rochester, N.Y., 1958-61, assoc. prof., 1961-63, prof., 1963-68; prof. biol. sci. Stanford, 1968—; mem. genetics study sect. NIH, 1964-69, mem. DNA recombinant adv. com., 1977-81; mem. genetics panel NSF, 1973-76. Author: Episomes, 1969; co-author: General Virology, 1978; Editor: Gene, 1980—, Ann. Rev. Genetics, 1984—; assoc. editor: Virology, 1963-69, Ann. Rev. Genetics, 1969-84; editorial bd.: Jour. Bacteriology, 1966-72, Jour. Virology, 1967-75. Served with AUS, 1953-55. Recipient Research Career award USPHS, 1962-68. Mem. Nat. Acad. Scis., Am. Acad. Arts and Scis., Am. Soc. Microbiology, Soc. Am. Naturalists, AAAS. Democrat. Current Work: Lysogeny in bacteriophage; biotin biosynthesis in E. coli. Subspecialties: Genome organization; Virology (biology). Home: 947 Mears Ct Stanford CA 94305 Office: Dept Biol Scis Stanford U Stanford CA 94305

CAMPBELL, CARLOS BOYD GODFREY, physician, army officer; b. Chgo., July 27, 1934; s. Joseph G. Bumzahem and Ruby V. Brown-Campbell; m. Deborah E. Stephens, June 28, 1958 (div.); children: Ellen, Gowan, Kenneth; m. Nydia Haydee Gonzalez, Feb. 3, 1979; 1 child, Christopher; 1 stepdau., Zinnia. B.S., M.S., M.D., Ph.D., U. Ill. Neuroanatomist Walter Reed Army Inst. Research, Washington, 1964-67, research neurologist, 1979—; asst. to assoc. prof. neural scis., anatomy, and physiology Ind. U., Bloomington, 1967-74; asso. clin. prof. anatomy U. Calif., Irvine, 1975-77; vis. assoc. in biology Calif. Inst. Tech., Pasadena, 1976-77; prof., head dept. anatomy U. P.R., Rio Piedras, 1977-79; research prof. neurology Uniformed Services U. Health Scis., Bethesda, Md. 1983—, adj. prof. anatomy Georgetown U. Schs. Medicine and Dentistry, Washington, 1980—; lectr. psychology U. Md., College Park, 1982—; commd. lt. col. M.C. U.S. Army, 1979, advanced through grades to col., 1984. Editor: (with others) Evolution of Brain and Behavior in Vertebrates, 1976; Contbr. (with others) articles, abstracts, papers, book revs., forewords to profl. lit. Served to capt. M.C. U.S. Army, 1964-67. NIH, NSF grantee. Mem. AAAS, Cajal Club, Am. Soc. Primatologists, Internat. Primatological Soc., Am. Assn. Anatomists, Soc. Neurosci., Am. Soc. Zoologists, J.B. Johnston Club, Sigma Xi, Phi Rho Sigma. Episcopalian. Current Work: Research currently involves central nervous system regulation of respiration. Other areas of interest are comparative neurology and evolutionary biology. Subspecialties: Evolutionary biology; Neurobiology. Home: 6003 McKinley St Bethesda MD 20817 Office: Walter Reed Army Inst Research Washington DC 20307

CAMPBELL, CHARLES JOHN, ophthalmologist; b. Steubenville, Ohio, June 24, 1926; m. Mary Catherine McGuigan, July 2, 1955; children—Catherine Mary, Barbara Irene, Charles Arbuthnot III. B.S., Muskingum Coll., 1949; M.D., George Washington U., 1948; M.S. in Optics, U. Rochester, 1951; Med.Sc.D., Columbia U., 1957. Intern George Washington U. Hosp., 1948-49; resident Edward S. Harkness Eye Inst., 1954-57; practice medicine specializing in ophthalmology, N.Y.C., 1957—; dir. Edward S. Harkness Eye Inst., Ophthalmology Service of Columbia-Presbyn. Med. Center, N.Y.C., 1974—, Knapp Meml. Lab. of Physiol. Optics, 1957—; prof., chmn. dept. ophthalmology Columbia U., 1974—. Served with USAF, 1952-54. Mem. Am. Ophthal. Soc., Am. Acad. Ophthalmology and Otolaryngology, A.C.S., Optical Soc. Am., Assn. U. Profs. Ophthalmology, AMA, N.Y. Ophthal. Soc., Assn. for Research in Vision and Ophthalmology, N.Y. State Med. Soc., N.Y. Acad. Scis. Current Work: Clinical studies on vitreous and retina. Subspecialty: Ophthalmology. Office: 635 W 165th St New York NY 10032

CAMPBELL, COLIN KYDD, electrical and computer engineering educator; researcher; b. St. Andrews, Fife, Scotland, May 3, 1927; came to Can., 1960; s. David Walker and Jean (Bell) C.; m. Vivian Gwyn Norval, Apr. 17, 1954; children—Barry Norval, Gwyn Elizabeth, Ian Harris. B.Sc. with honors in Engring., St. Andrews U., Scotland, 1952; S.M., MIT, 1953; Ph.D., St. Andrews U., 1960; D.Sc., U. Dundee, Scotland, 1984. Registered profl. engr., Ont., Can. Communications engr. Fgn. Office, London, Eng., 1946-47, Brit. Embassy, Washington, 1947-48; electronics engr. Atomic Instrument Co., Cambridge, Mass., 1954-57; cons. engr. A. Kusko Inc., Cambridge, 1957; prof. elec., computer engring. McMaster U., Hamilton, Ont., Can., 1960—. Contbr. articles to profl. jours. Served with Brit. Army, 1944-46. Recipient Mass. Golf scholar Mass. Golf Assn., 1952, Teaching citation Ont. Confedn. Univ. Faculty Assn., 1976, Inventor Insignia Can. Patents Devel. Ltd., 1973. Fellow Royal Soc. Can. (Thomas W. Eadie medal 1983), Engring. Inst. Can., Royal Soc. Arts; mem. IEEE (sr.), Royal Can. Mil. Inst. Mem. Ch. Eng. Current work: Surface acoustic wave devices, VLSI, solid-state devices, microwave and millimeter wave instrumentation, superconductivity, giant pulse lasers, electromagnetics. Subspecialties: Acoustical engineering; Superconductors. Office: Dept Elec Computer Engring McMaster U 1280 Main St W Hamilton ON L8S 4L7 Canada

CAMPBELL, DONALD BRUCE, astronomer; b. Wollongong, N.S.W., Australia, May 19, 1942; came to U.S. 1965; permanent resident; s. John Herbert and Helen Elizabeth (Davis) C. B.S., U. Sydney, 1963, M.S., 1965; Ph.D., Cornell U., 1971. Research assoc. Cornell U., Ithaca, N.Y., 1971-73; staff Haystack Obs., MIT, Westford, Mass., 1973-74; research assoc. Arecibo Obs., Cornell U., P.R., 1974-79, assoc. dir., 1979-82, dir. ops., 1982—. Mem. Am. Astron. Soc., Am. Geophys. Union, AAAS. Subspecialty: Optical astronomy. Address: Nat Astronomy and Ionosphere Ctr Box 995 Arecibo PR 00613

CAMPBELL, GILBERT SADLER, medical educator; b. Toronto, Ont., Can., Jan. 4, 1924; came to U.S., 1926; s. Gilbert S. and Ellen (Thorson) C.; m. Dorothy Jean Nugent, Sept. 18, 1947 (div. 1960); children: Kathryn, Rebecca, Thomas, William; m. Joan Louise Hancock, Sept. 28, 1961; children: Susan, John. Student, Hampden-Sydney Coll., 1939-40; B.A., U. Va., 1943, M.D., 1946; M.S., U. Minn., 1949, Ph.D., 1954. Diplomate: Am. Bd. Surgery. Asst. prof. surgery U. Minn., Mpls., 1954-58; prof. surgery U. Okla., Oklahoma City, 1958-65; prof., head dept.surgery U. Ark. Med. Sch., Little Rock, 1965-83, prof., 1983—. Contbr. over 150 articles to med. jours. Served to capt. U.S. Army, 1949-51, Korea. Decorated Silver Star (2), Bronze Star (2), Purple Heart; Markle scholar, 1954-59. Mem. Am. Surg. Assn., So. Surg. Assn. (v.p. 1980-81), Internat. Cardiovascular Soc. (v.p. 1973), Southwestern Surg. Congress (pres. 1980), So. Thoracic Surg. Assn. (v.p. 1982). Current Work: Cardiovascular and thoracic surgery. Subspecialty: Surgery. Home: 66 River Ridge Rd Little Rock AR 72207 Office: 4301 W Markham Little Rock AR 72205

CAMPBELL, JAMES NORMAN, neurosurgeon, neurophysiologist, educator; b. Royal Oak, Mich., Aug. 5, 1948; s. James Stewart and Lilla Cleo (Upton) C.; m. Regina Helen Anderson, July 31, 1982. B.A., U. Mich., 1969; M.D., Yale U., 1973. Diplomate: Am. Bd. Neurol. Surgery. Resident dept. neurosurgery Johns Hopkins U., Balt., 1973-79, postdoctoral fellow in neurophysiology, 1975-77, asst. prof. neurosurgery, 1979—; neurosurgeon Johns Hopkins Hosp., 1979—. Contbr. articles and abstracts to profl. jours. Recipient research fellowship award NIH, 1975, tchr. investigator award, 1980. Mem. Soc. for Neurosci., Internat. Assn. for Study of Pain, Am. Assn. Neurol. Surgeons, AAAS, Research Soc. for Neurol. Surgery, Phi Beta Kappa. Current Work: Pain physiology, microneurosurgery, psychophysics; investigation of mechanisms of pain sensation, pain secondary to nerve injury, and also performance of vascular and peripheral nerve neurosurg. procedures. Subspecialties: Neurophysiology; Neurosurgery. Home: 15 St Georges Rd Baltimore MD 21210 Office: Dept Neurosurgery Johns Hopkins Hosp Baltimore MD 21205

CAMPBELL, JOHN HYDE, physical chemist. Sr. research scientist chemistry dept. Lawrence Livermore Lab., U. Calif. Subspecialty: Physical chemistry. Office: Lawrence Livermore Lab Livermore CA 94550

CAMPBELL, JUDITH LYNN, molecular biology educator; b. New Haven, Mar. 24, 1943; d. John and Marjorie (Hutt) C. B.A., Wellesley Coll., 1965; Ph.D., Harvard U., 1974. Postgrad. Harvard U., 1969-74, research assoc., 1974-77; asst. prof. Calif. Inst. Tech., Pasadena, 1977-82, assoc. prof., 1982—; biochemistry study sect. NIH, Bethesda, Md., 1982—. Research Career Devel. awardee NIH, 1979-84. Mem. Fedn. Am. Socs. Exptl. Biology. Current Work: Genetic and biochemical analysis of DNA replication, recombination and repair in microorganisms. Subspecialties: Molecular biology; Genetics and genetic engineering (biology). Office: Calif Inst Tech 1201 E California Blvd Pasadena CA 91125

CAMPBELL, PHILIP MONTGOMERY, JR., physicist; b. Wichita, Kans., Feb. 17, 1936; s. Philip Montgomery and Dorothy Louise (Lynch) C.; m. Virginia Gail Wiley, July 6, 1957; children—Diana Daphne Malcolm Bradford. B.A., U. Colo., 1958, M.S., 1960, Ph.D., 1963; M.B.A., U. Mich., 1982. Research scientist Lawrence Radiation Lab., Livermore, Calif., 1962-66; asst. prof. U. N.Mex., Albuquerque, 1966-69; research scientist Systems Sci. and Software, LaJolla, Calif., 1969-70, Sci. Applications, Inc., LaJolla, 1970-72; dir. theory div. KMS Fusion Inc., Ann Arbor, Mich., 1972-83, primary scientist, 1983—; cons. Argonne Nat. Lab., 1979-80. Contbr. articles to profl. jours. NSF fellow, 1961-62; grantee Dept. Def., NSF, others. Mem. Am. Phys. Soc., Am. Assn. Physics Tchrs., Soaring Soc. Am., Sierra Club. Current work: Laser fusion physics, specifically energy transport anomalies in laser heated plasmas. Subspecialties: Theoretical physics; Fusion. Office: KMS Fusion Inc PO Box 1567 Ann Arbor MI 48106

CAMPBELL, RUSSELL BRUCE, educator; b. Hartford, Conn., Sept. 18, 1952; s. Andrew Burr and Marian Priscilla (Champlin) C. Sc.B., Brown U., 1974, Sc.M., 1974; Ph.D., Stanford U., 1979. Asst. prof. math. Purdue U., West Lafayette, Ind., 1979-83, U. No. Iowa, Cedar Falls, 1983—. Contbr. articles to profl. jours. Mem. Am. Math. Soc., Genetics Soc. Am., Am. Soc. Naturalists, Sigma Xi. Current Work: Selection-migration interaction; cost of inbreeding, sources of genetic variation, phenotypic selection and genetic change. Subspecialties: Evolutionary biology; Applied mathematics. Home: 7 Waterside Ln West Hartford CT 06107 Office: Dept Math and Computer Sci U No Iowa Cedar Falls IA 50614

CAMPBELL, RUSSELL HARPER, geologist; b. Bakersfield, Calif., Apr. 20, 1928; s. James Douglas and Esther Augusta (Peake) C.; m. Marilee Drake, Feb. 14, 1953; children—Marlissa Anne, Ian Andrew. B.A. in Geology, U. Calif.-Berkeley, 1951. Geologist U.S. Geol. Survey, Denver, 1951-57, Menlo Park, Calif., 1957-76, Reston, Va., 1976—; chmn. com. on methodologies for predicting mud flow areas NRC, Washington, 1981-82. Author: (with others) Geology and Uranium Deposits, Elk Ridge Utah, 1965; Area Geology of the Chariot Site North West Alaska, 1967; Soil Slips, Debris Flows and Rainstorms, Santa Monica Mountains, 1975. Served with USNR, 1945-46. Recipient Meritorious Service award Dept. Interior, 1981. Fellow Geol. Soc. Am.; mem. Am. Geophys. Union, Soc. Econ. Paleontologists and Mineralogists, Internat. Assn. Engring. Geology. Current work: Research on active earth processes especially methods for predicting landslide probability and risk. Subspecialties: Geology; Engineering geology. Office: US Geol Survey 922 Nat Ctr Reston VA 22092

CAMPBELL, WILBUR HAROLD, research plant biochemist, educator; b. Santa Ana, Calif., Apr. 23, 1945; s. Russell Carton and Vivian (Yates) C.; m. Ellen Roth, June 6, 1981. A.A., Santa Ana Coll., 1965; B.A., Pomona Coll., 1967; Ph.D., U. Wis., 1972. Postdoctoral U. Ga., Athens, 1972-73, Mayo Clinic, Rochester, Minn., 1973-74, Mich. State U., E. Lansing, 1974-75; asst. prof. Coll. Environmental Sci. and Forestry SUNY, Syracuse, 1975-80, assoc. prof., 1980-85; assoc. prof. Mich. Tech. U., 1985—. Mem. editorial bd. Plant Physiology, 1982-88. Contbr. numerous articles to profl. jours. Guest prof. Botanisches Inst., U. Bayreuth, Fed. Republic Germany, 1982. Mem. Am. Chem. Soc., Am. Soc. of Plant Physiologists, AAAS, Am. Soc. Agronomy/-Crop Sci. Soc. Am., Japanese Soc. Plant Physiologists, Plant Growth Regulator Soc. Am., N.Y. Acad. Sci., Internat. Soc. for Plant Molecular Biology, Sigma Xi. Current work: Biochemistry and immunochemistry of higher plant nitrate reductase. Subspecialties: Biochemistry (biology); Plant physiology (agriculture). Home: 334 Hecla St Lake Linden MI 49945 Office: Dept Biological Scis Michigan Tech U Houghton MI 49931

CAMPBELL-SMITH, ROSEMARY GILLES, dental science educator; b. Rapid City, S.D., Mar. 16, 1939; d. Albert Peter and Anna (Schmitz) Gilles; m. Richard Lee Smith, Aug. 6, 1978; 1 child, by previous marriage, Christina Lynn Campbell. Cert., Eastman Sch. Dental Hygiene, 1960; B.S.H.E. with high honors, U. Fla., 1964; M.S., U. Miami, 1968, Dr.Arts, 1976. Registered dental hygienist, Fla. Dental hygienist in pvt. practice, Palm Beach County, Fla., 1960-63; chief lab. technician dept. physiology U. Fla., Gainesville, 1965-66; instr. dept. biology U. Miami, Coral Gables, 1968-70; asst. prof. dept. dental hygiene Miami-Dade Community Coll., 1974-77; lead instr. Dental Aux. Programs, Santa Fe Community Coll., 1977-81; cons. Campbell-Smith Cons., Gainesville, 1982—. Author: Head and Neck: What's It All About, 1976; editor: Prophyways/Prophygram, 1982—. Recipient Albert E. Sevenson award for art. sci. and service N.Y. Dental Soc., 1960; Sci. award Eastman Sch. Dental Hygiene, 1960; J. Hillis Miller award U. Fla., 1964; Cancer Assn. award, 1964; Merit Citation Am. Dental Assn. Commn. on Accreditation Report, 1979; named Outstanding Young Leader in Allied Health for the S.E. Region. Mem. Am. Dental Hygienists Assn. (student liaison Dist. IV 1981-84, sec. Dist. IV 1984—, jour. manuscript rev. bd. 1984—), Internat. Assn. Dental Research, AAAS, Sigma Xi, Phi Kappa Phi, Phi Lambda Pi. Current Work: Endagenous pain control/pain control/pain/endorphins/dental anxiety reduction. Subspecialties: Dental practice consulting; Neuropsychology. Office: 3609 NW 30 Blvd Gainesville FL 32605

CAMPION, DENNIS ROBERT, research physiologist; b. Janesville, Wis., Oct. 28, 1945; s. Robert E. and Marie (Wilbur) C.; m. Rita Ann Fish, July 5, 1969; children: Anna, Sara, Carrie, Andrea, Amy. B.S., U. Wis.-Madison, 1969, M.S., 1971, Ph.D., 1973. Postdoctoral assoc. Iowa State U., Ames, 1973-74; research biochemist U.S. Meat Animal Research Ctr., Clay Center, Nebr., 1974-76; research physiologist R. B. Russell Research Ctr.,/U.S. Dept. Agr., Athens, Ga., 1976—; Editorial bd. Jour. Animal Sci., 1979-81. vis. scientist Monsanto Co., St. Louis, 1984-85; adj. prof. U. Ga., 1976—. Mem. Ga. Nutrition Council (publicity chmn. 1982-83, sec. 1983-84), Am. Meat Sci. Assn. (research priorities com. 1979-84, dir. 1984-85), Am. Soc. Animal Sci., Am. Inst. Nutrition, Sigma Xi. Current Work: Growth and development of skeletal muscle of meat animals; factors that regulate myofiber nuclear proliferation and muscle metabolism are identified and their physiological function determined. Subspecialty: Animal physiology. Office: USDA RB Russell Research Ctr College Station Rd Athens GA 30613

CANDIA, OSCAR A., ophthalmologist, medical educator; b. Buenos Aires, Argentina, Apr. 30; came to U.S.;; s. Jose F. and Luisa (Mitri) C.; m. Blanca F.; children: Roberto, Leticia, Silvina. M.D., U. Buenos Aires, 1959. Prof. U. Louisville, 1965-68; assoc. prof. biophysics and physiology Mt. Sinai Sch. Medicine, N.Y.C., 1977-78, prof., 1984—, prof. ophthalmology, 1978—, dir. small group, 1976—; mem. vision research program com. Nat. Eye Inst., Bethesda, Md., 1979—, cons. cataracts, 1980—. Recipient Alcon award 1985; U. Buenos Aires postdoctoral fellow, 1961-63; USPHS career devel. award, 1966-68. Current Work: Mechanisms of ultralaser infrascopy in ophthalmology. Subspecialties: Membrane biology; Ophthalmology. Home: 17 Sunny Ridge Rd New Rochelle NY 10804 Office: Mount Sinai Sch Medicine One Gustave Levy Pl New York NY 10029

CANGIALOSI, CHARLES PHILIP, podiatrist, editor. B.S., John Carroll U., 1970; Dr. Podiatric Medicine with acad. honors, Ohio Coll. Podiatric Medicine, 1975. Diplomate Am. Bd. Podiatric Surgery, Nat. Bd. Podiatry Examiners. Resident, Foot Clinic of Youngstown, Ohio, 1975-76; then mem. dept. podiatric medicine and surgery Community Hosp. Warren, Ohio; mem. dept. surgery Sharon Gen. Hosp., Pa.; mem. podistry sect. No. Community Hosp., Oradell, N.J., Barnert Meml. Hosp. Med. Ctr., Paterson, N.J., Bergen Pines Hosp., Ridgewood, N.J., Saddle Brook Gen. Hosp., N.J., S. Bergen Community Hosp., Hasbrouck Heights, N.J., Roseland Ambulatory Surg. Ctr., Roseland, N.J.; editor-in-chief Current Podiatry Publs., Inc., Waldwick, N.J., 1983—; former instr. dept. med. scis. Cuyahoga Community Coll., Cleve.; field researcher innovative products Spenco Med. Corp., Waco, Tex.; participating physician clin. clerkship program Ohio Coll. Podiatric Medicine; former mem. credential com. S. Bergen Community Hosp.; adj. clin. prof. dept. podiatric medicine, clin. externship program Osteopathic Coll. Medicine and Health Scis., Des Moines; pres., chmn. bd. Blackbox Images Photography, Inc., Waldwick, 1982; mem. sci. com. Saddle Brook Gen. Hosp. Surg. Seminar, 1982-83; sci. chmn. Current Podiatry Annual Podiatric Med. Seminar, Orlando, Fla., 1983; mem. candidate interview credentials com., residency tng. and interview com. dept. podiatric medicine Saddle Brook Gen. Hosp., 1982; attending podiatric surgeon Port of Newark div. Internat. Longshoremen's Assn., 1982; participant radiographic div. Poloroid Film Corp., 1983-84; disting. lectr. N.Y. Coll. Podiatric Medicine, 1984-85. Contbg. editor: Yearbook of Podiatric Medicine and Surgery, 1984; contbg. editor dept. podiatric medicine Current Podiatry Jour., contbg. editor dept. podiatric neurology, 1977-80, editor-at-large, 1982; gen. editor Jour. Am. Podiatry Assn., 1981-82; gen. editor Jour. Am. Podiatry Assn., 1981-82, gen. rev. editor, 1982-83; program cons., exec. editor Podiatry Newsletter, 1982—; assoc. editor Hosp. Podiatrist, 1983; mem. editorial rev. bd. Hershey Surg. Sem., 1984. Contbr. articles to profl. jours. Former co-chmn. Waldwick Lions Juvenile Diabetes Found.; Fellow Am. Soc. Podiatric Medicine (sci. co-chmn. 1981-82, trustee, soc./treas., sci. chmn. annual spring surg. sem. 1982-83, credential com. 1983, v.p. 1984-85, named Man of Yr. 1983), Am. Assn. Hosp. Podiatrists, Am. Soc. Podiatric Dermatology, Acad. Ambulatory Foot Surgery (editor-in-chief 1982, dir. N.J. state div. 1982), Am. Coll. Foot Surgeons, Am. Acad. Podiatric Microsurgery, Alph Epsilon Delta; mem. N.J. Acad. Sci., Ohio Acad. Sci., AAAS, Am. Writers Assn., Aircraft Owners and Pilots Assn., U.S. Seaplane Pilots Assn., N.J. Podiatry Soc. (no. div., legis com. 1983-84), Am. Soc. Podopediatrics, Acad. Ambulatory Foot Surgery (grievance bd. 1984), Am. Soc. Podiatric Angiology (profl. assoc.), Roseland Ambulatory Surg. Ctr. (credentials com. 1983-84), Inst. Cert. Photographers, Inc., U.S. Trotting Assn., Pi Delta (past pres.), Alpha Gamma Kappa. Subspecialty: Podiatry; podiatric surgery. Office: 22 Wycoff Ave Waldwick NJ 07463

CANIZARES, CLAUDE ROGER, physicist, educator; b. Tucson, June 14, 1945; s. Orlando and Stephanie (Bolan) C.; m. Jennifer Wilder, Aug. 31, 1968; children: Kristen Elizabeth, Alexander Orlando. B.A., Harvard U., 1967, M.A., 1968, Ph.D., 1972. Staff scientist MIT, 1971-74, asst. prof. physics, 1974-78, assoc. prof. physics, 1978-84, prof., 1984—; vis. fellow Inst. Astronomy, U. Cambridge, 1981-82. Contbr. numerous articles to profl. jours. Alfred P. Sloan Research fellow, 1980-84. Mem. Am. Astron. Soc., Am. Phys. Soc., Internat. Astron. Union, Phi Beta Kappa, Sigma Xi. Current Work: X-ray astronomy, satellite experiments, x-ray spectroscopy, plasma diagnostics, extragalactic astrophysics, optical telescopes and instrumentation. Subspecialties: X-ray high energy astrophysics; Optical astronomy. Office: MIT 37-501 Cambridge MA 02139

CANNON, JOHN JOSEPH, biochemical engineer, biochemist; b. Chgo., Oct. 3, 1952; s. John J. and Helen S. (Maloney) C.; m. Margaret Anne Hickner, Dec. 26, 1981; 1 child, Kathleen Megan. B.S., Ill. Benedictine Coll., 1974; M.S., Purdue U., 1977, Ph.D., 1980. Research asst. Daubert Research, Chgo., 1974-75; teaching asst. Purdue U., West Lafayette, Ind., 1975-78; sr. research scientist Pfizer Central Research, Groton, Conn., 1980—; lectr. in field. Contbr.

articles to profl. jours. State of Ill. scholar, 1970-74; Ill. Benedictine Coll. scholar, 1970. Mem. Am. Chem. Soc., Phi Lambda Upsilon. Current work: Development of purification techniques for fermentation products; including cloned gene products, antibiotics, and specialty chemicals; immobilized enzyme technology and bio-reactor design. Subspecialties: Chemical engineering; Enzyme technology. Office: Pfizer Central Research Eastern Point Rd Groton CT 06340

CANO, ELMER RAUL, radiotherapist, educator; b. Trujillo, Peru, Feb. 23, 1946; came to U.S., 1974, naturalized, 1985; s. Justo Roman Cano and Zoila Rosa Iglesias; married; children: Malina Dianah, David Raul. B.S., U. Trujillo (Peru), 1971, M.D., 1972. Intern St. John Hosp., Detroit, 1974-75, resident in therapeutic radiology, 1976-79; fellow in radiotherapy M.D. Anderson Hosp., U. Tex., Houston, 1979-80; assoc. radiotherapist St. Joseph Hosp., Elgin, Ill., 1980-81; asst. prof. radiotherapy Duke U., Durham, N.C., 1981-83 U. Pitts., 1983—; radio therapist St. Francis Hosp., Memphis, 1983—. Mem. AMA., Am. Soc. Therapeutic Radiology, Radiol. Soc. N.Am., Am. Coll. Radiology, Fletcher's Soc. Roman Catholic. Current Work: Head and neck tumors; gynecologic malignancies research. Subspecialty: Radiology. Home: 162 Fairfax Rd Forest Hills PA 15221 Office: Univ Health Ctr of Pitts Joint Radiation Oncology Ctr Presbyn Hosp Pittsburgh PA 15213

CANONICO, DOMENIC ANDREW, engring. co. exec., lectr., cons., researcher; b. Chgo., Jan. 18, 1930; s. Angelo Anthony and Anna (Contratto) C.; m. Colleen Margaret Jennings, Aug. 27, 1955; children: Judith Canonico Asreen, Mary Carol, Angelo Edward, Domenic Michael, Catherine Ann. B.S. in Metall Engring, Mich. Tech. U., 1951; M.S. in Metall. Engring, Lehigh U., 1961, Ph.D. in Metall. Engring, 1963. Group leader Pressure Vessel Tech. Lab. div. metals and ceramics Union Carbide Corp. at Oak Ridge Nat. Lab., 1965-81; dir. Metall. and Materials Lab., Combustion Engring., Inc., Chattanooga, 1981—; mem. adv. bd. Coll. Engring. U. Tenn., Knoxville. Served with USAF, 1952-53. Fellow Am. Soc. Metals; mem. ASME (main com. boiler and pressure vessel code), Am. Welding Soc. (Rene D. Wasserman award 1977, N.E. Sect. Disting. Service award 1978, nat. Lincoln Gold medal 1980), Sigma Xi. Roman Catholic. Club: Walden (Chattanooga). Current Work: Research and devel. for current and advanced energy systems. Subspecialty: Metallurgical engineering. Home: 3 Big Rock Rd Signal Mountain TN 37377 Office: 911 W Main St Chattanooga TN 37402

CANOVA-DAVIS, ELEANOR, biochemist; b. San Francisco, Jan. 18, 1938; d. Gaudenzio Enzio and Catherine (Bordisso) C.; m. Kenneth Roy Davis, Feb. 10, 1957; children—Kenneth Roy Jr., Jeffrey Stephen. B.A., San Francisco State U., 1968, M.S., 1971; Ph.D., U. Calif.-San Francisco, 1977. Lab. asst. Frederick Burk Found. for Edn., San Francisco, 1969-71; teaching asst. U. Calif., San Francisco, 1972-74, research asst., 1974-77; NIH postdoctoral fellow, U. Calif., Berkeley, 1977-80; asst. research biochemist U. Calif., San Francisco, 1980-84; sci. Liposome Tech., Menlo Pk., Calif., 1984—. Contbr. articles to profl. jours. Mem. AAAS, Am. Chem. Soc., Calif. scholarship Fedn. Roman Catholic. Club: Sequoia Woods Country (Arnold, Calif.). Current work: Dev. homogeneous liposome immunoassays; preparation of lipid vesicles containing a hapten covalently-linked to their surface; antibody. complement mediated lysis of these vesicles release encapsulated enzyme reporter. Subspecialties: Drug delivery systems; Clinical chemistry. Office: Liposome Tech Inc 1050 Hamilton Ct Menlo Pk CA 94025

CANTOR, BENJAMIN BORUCH, medical and dental educator; b. Winnipeg, Man., Can. Dec. 31, 1909; s. David Cantor and Hodel Ada (Isenberg) C.; m. Brena Lois Druxerman, Sept. 2, 1938; children—Gail Fox, Bonnie Klass, Robin Shore, Paul David. B.Sc., U. Man., 1930; M.Sc., U. Sask., 1931; D.D.S., U. Toronto, 1935; D.D.C., Dominion Dental Council, 1935; M.D., Hyogo Coll. Medicine, Japan, Ph.D., 1985; D.Sc., Osaka State Dental Sch.-Japan, 1948 F.R.S.H., Eng., 1965. Prof. orthodontics Northwestern Dental Sch., Chgo., 1959-61; chief prof. craniofacial anomalies U. Kansas City Sch. Dentistry, 1961-66; cons. in research Hyogo Coll. Medicine, Japan, 1980-81, 84-85. Author: Craniofacial Anomalies, 1985. Editor Internat. Jour. Orthodontics, 1958-65. Pres., Congregation Shaarey Zedek, Winnipeg, Can., 1965-66; chmn. Shaary Zedek Cemetery, 1935-66. Fulbright scholar, 1962-63; Kennedy Presdl. award, 1948. Mem. Can. Sch. Assn. (pres. 1940-41), Am. Assn. Cleft Palate and Craniofacial Anomalies, Am. Dental Assn., Chgo. Dental Assn., Am. Orthodontic Assn., Can. Orthodontic Assn. Jewish. Clubs: Pacemaker (pres. 1925-30), Glendale Golf. Lodge: B'nai B'rith (pres. 1932-33, life). Current work: Cleft palate rehabilitation and craniofacial anomalies. Subspecialty: Orthodontics. Address: 411-555 Lanark Winnipeg MB R3N 1L9 Canada

CANTOR, CHARLES R., molecular biology educator, researcher; b. Bklyn., Aug. 26, 1942; s. Louis and Ida Dianne (Banks) C.; m. Linda Beth Newmark, Feb. 2, 1964 (div. July 1976). A.B., Columbia Coll., 1963; Ph.D., U. Calif.-Berkeley, 1966. Asst. prof. chemistry Columbia U., N.Y.C., 1966-69, assoc. prof., 1969-72, prof., 1972-81, prof., chmn. dept. human genetics and devel., 1981—; cons. Syntex Med. Diagnostics, 1983—; Actagen, Inc., 1984-85, Molecular Biophysics Tech. Inc., 1985—, Gene Labs., Inc., 1985—; mem. adv. council dept. molecular biology, Princeton U., 1984—; mem. sci. adv. bd. Am. Cyanamid Co., 1984—; chmn. proposal rev. panel Stanford Synchrotron Radiation Lab., 1980—; mem. com. on causes and effects of changes in stratospheric ozone NRC, 1983-84; mem. study sect. biophysics and biophys. chemistry NIH, 1971-75; trustee Cold Spring Harbor Lab., 1978-83. Author: Biophysical Chemistry I, II, III, 1980. Editor: (book series) Springer-Verlag Advanced Chemistry Texts, 1976. Mem. editorial bd. Archives of Biochemistry and Biophysics, 1972—, Jour. Molecular Biology, 1972—, Nucleic Acids Research, 1973—, Biochemistry, 1978-83, Biopolymers, 1980-83, Jour. Biol. Chemistry, 1981—; mem. editorial bd. Jour. Molecular Evolution, 1972-81, assoc. editor, 1983—; assoc. editor Ann. Rev. Biophysics, 1982—. Patentee in field. Fellow A.P. Sloan Found., 1969, Guggenheim Found., 1973. Fellow Am. Acad. Arts and Scis.; mem. Biophys. Soc. (council 1978-81), Am. Inst. Chemists (Fresenius award 1974), Am. Chem. Soc. (nominating com. div. biol. chemistry 1979-81, Eli Lilly award 1978), Am. Soc. Biol. Chemists (nominating com. 1982-84). Current work: Genome organization and rearrangements, nucleic acid structure and assembly into nucleoprotein complexes. Subspecialties: Genome organization; Molecular biology. Home: 560 Riverside Dr New York NY 10027 Office: Columbia U Dept Human Genetics and Devel 701 W 168th St New York NY 10032

CANTOR, MURRAY ROBERT, applied mathematician, exploration geophysicist; b. Mpls., July 6, 1947; s. Joel Malcom and Muriel Esther (Goldsman) C.; m. Ann Rochelle Metzelaar, June 20, 1969 (div. 1978); 1 child, Scott Benjamin; m., Judi Taylor, Aug. 11, 1979; 1 child, Michael Taylor. B.A., U. Calif.-Berkeley, 1969, M.A., 1970, Ph.D., 1973. Asst. prof. Duke U., Durham, N.C., 1973-77; asst. prof. U. Tex.-Austin, 1977-82, cons. applied research lab., 1981-82; research mathematician Shell Devel. Co., Houston, 1982—. Contbr. articles to profl. jours. NSF grantee, 1979, 81. Mem. Soc. Indsl. and Applied Math., Am. Math. Soc., AAAS, Sigma Xi, Soc. Exploratory Geophysics (assoc.). Democrat. Jewish. Current work: Seismic imaging; seismic migration and inversion. Subspecialties: Applied mathematics; Geophysics. Home: 20731 Prince Creek Katy TX 77450 Office: Shell Devel Co PO Box 481 Houston TX 77001

CANTRELL, CYRUS DUNCAN, III, physicist; b. Bartlesville, Okla., Oct. 4, 1940; s. Cyrus Duncan and Janet Ewing (Robinson) C.; m. Mary Lynn Marple, Nov. 18, 1972. B.A., Harvard U., 1962; Ph.D., Princeton U., 1968. Asst., then assoc. prof. physics Swarthmore Coll., 1967-73; staff mem. Los Alamos Sci. Lab., 1973-79; professeur associe Universite Paris-Nord, 1980; prof. physics, dir. Center Quantum Electronics and Applications, U. Tex. at Dallas, 1980-85, dir. Ctr. for Applied Optics, 1985—; cons. in field. Editor: Laser Induced Fusion and X-Ray Laser Studies, 1976; contbr. articles to profl. jours. Fellow Optical Soc. Am., Am. Physic Soc.; mem. Am. Phys. Soc., Optical Soc. Am., IEEE, Am. Chem. Soc. Patentee in field. Current Work: Laser separation of isotopes; infrared multiphoton molecular excitation; coherent laser propagation effects. Subspecialties: Laser-induced chemistry; Laser spectroscopy. Home: 2409 Lawnmeadow Dr Richardson TX 75080 Office: U Tex at Dallas PO Box 688 Richardson TX 75080

CAPANZANO, CHARLES THOMAS, clinical psychologist, mental health administrator; b. N.Y.C., Aug. 2, 1949; s. Salvatore and Josephine Marguerite (Lupo) C. B.A. with honors in Psychology, Dartmouth Coll., 1971; M.A. in Clin. Psychology, U. Windsor, Ont., 1973, Ph.D. in Clin. Psychology, 1976. Registered psychologist, N.Y. Cons. Children's Aid Soc., Windsor, 1975-76; project research dir., parental counselor U. Windsor, 1975-76; dir. profl. services Heartline, Inc., Detroit, 1975-76; dir. continuing edn., Twin Tiers br. N.Y.Sch. Psychiatry, Elmira, 1976-78; dir. community services Schuyler and Yates Counties, N.Y., 1978-79, Cortland County, N.Y., 1979—; sec. exec. com. Conf. Mental Hygiene Dirs., Albany, 1978—; chmn. Central N.Y. Mental Health Dirs., 1980-81, Cortland Area council Central N.Y. Health Systems Agy., Syracuse, 1981—. Chmn. govt. div. United Way of Cortland County, 1981—; treas. Hitchcock Hose Co.-Cortland Fire Dept., 1981—; adv. council Central N.Y. Div. of Youth, 1982—. Regents scholar, 1967; Laidlaw Found. grantee, 1975-76. Mem. Am. Psychol. Assn. Lodge: Rotary. Current Work: Parent counseling; cognitive behavior modification; forensic mental health, mental health administration. Subspecialty: Clinical psychology. Home: 11/2 Broadway Cortland NY 13045 Office: Cortland County Community Services 60 Central Ave Cortland NY 13045

CAPE, ROBERT E., university administrator, consultant; b. Schenectady, Aug. 31, 1943; s. Edward F. and Hazel D. (Finehout) C.; m. Barbara A. Tilley, Sept. 3, 1966; children—Amanda E., Laura. B.S., Hartwick Coll., 1964; M.S., Rensselaer Poly. Inst., 1966, Ph.D., 1972. Cons. Research and Devel. Ctr. Gen. Electric, Schenectady, 1969-71; asst. prof. computer sci. U. Va., Charlottesville, 1971-75, assoc. prof., 1975-82, dir. academic computing, 1975-82; dir. academic computing Carnegie Mellon U., Pitts., 1982-84, dir. telecommunications, 1984—; cons. in field. Mem. Assn. Computing Machinery. Current work: Computer networks, campus/building wiring. Subspecialties: Telecommunications; Distributed systems and networks. Office: Carnegie Mellon Univ UCC Bldg Pittsburgh PA 15213

CAPLAN, DANIEL BENNETT, pediatrician, gastroenterology researcher; b. Boston, Sept. 14, 1937; children from previous marriage—Phyllis Diane, Lloyd Howard, Andrew Russell. A.B., Brandeis U., 1958; M.D., Tufts U., 1962. Intern, Boston City Hosp., 1962-63, resident in pediatrics, 1963-64; resident in pediatrics Boston Floating Hosp., 1964-65; fellow in pediatric gastroenterology Yale U. Med. Sch., 1967-68; asst. prof. pediatrics Emory U., Atlanta, 1968-72, assoc. prof., 1972-78, prof., 1978—, dir. Cystic Fibrosis Ctr., 1968—, dir. div. pediatric gastroenterology, 1968—; mem. med. staff Emory U. Hosp., Henrietta Egleston Hosp. for Children, Grady Meml. Hosp.; practice medicine specializing in pediatrics, Atlanta; collaborative scientist Yerkes Regional Primate Research Ctr., 1980—; chmn. med. adv. bd. Ga. chpt. Cystic Fibrosis Found., 1968—; mem. med. adv. bd. Ga. chpt. Am. Liver Found., 1974-78; camp pediatrician Cystic Fibrosis Camp Ga., Camp Barney Mednitz. Contbr. articles to profl. jours. Grantee Ortho Pharm. Co., 1977-79, Smith, Kline & French, 1978-81, Searle Med. products, 1980-81, Abbott Labs., 1981—. Diplomate Am. Bd. Pediatrics. Fellow Am. Acad. Pediatrics, Am. Coll. Gastroenterology, Am. Coll. Nutrition; mem. AMA, Med. Assn. Atlanta, Med. Assn. Ga., N. Am. Soc. Pediatric Gastroenterology, So. Soc. Peiatric Research, So. Med. Assn., Ga. Gastroenterol. Soc., Am. Acad. Pediatrics, Am. Celiac Soc., Ga. Gastroenterol. Soc. (sec. treas. 1973-75), Am. Gastroenterol. Assn., N. Am. Soc. Pediatric Gastroenterology (sec. treas. 1975-81), Digestive Disease Found., Am. Soc. Parenteral and Enteral Medicine, Am. Soc. Gastrointestinal Endocscopy. Served with AUS, 1965-67. Subspecialties: Pediatrics; Gastroenterology. Office: Cystic Fibrosis Research Ctr Emory U 69 Butler St SE Atlanta GA 30303

CAPLAN, JOHN DAVID, industrial research company executive; b. Weiser, Idaho, Mar. 5, 1926; s. Manley Maurice and Kathleen Malaby (Coldwell) C.; m. Loris Elizabeth Green, June 21, 1952; children: Barbara E., Carole E., Nancy B. Student, Stanford U., 1943-44; B.S. in Chem. Engring, Oreg. State U., 1949; M.S. in Mech. engring, Wayne State U., 1955; grad. advanced mgmt. program, Harvard U., 1976. With Gen Motors Research Labs., Warren, Mich., 1949—, dept head, 1963-67, tech. dir. basic and applied scis., 1967-69, exec. dir., 1969—; bd. dirs. Coordinating Research Council, 1970—, pres., 1975-77. Research publs. in field. Served to staff sgt. U.S. Army, 1943-46. Recipient Crompton-Lanchester medal INstn. Mech. Engrs., 1964. Fellow AAAS, Am. Inst. Chem. Engrs.; mem. Am. Chem. Soc., Am. Mgmt. Assn., Indsl. Research Inst. (bd. dirs. 1985—), Soc. Automotive Engrs., Nat. Acad. Engring, Dirs. Indsl. Research (sec. 1980, chmn. 1981). Current Work: Engine fuels and combustion; automotive air pollution; research administration. Subspecialties: Chemical engineering; Mechanical engineering. Office: GEN Motors Research Labs Warren MI 48090-9055

CAPPUCCINO, CARLETON C., endodontist, educator, researcher; b. Boston, Apr. 24, 1947; s. Anthony and Gertrude (Rogers) C.; m. Noreen Coughlan, Aug. 1, 1970. B.A. magna cum laude, Tufts U., Medford, Mass., 1969; D.M.D. cum laude, Harvard U., 1973; cert. in endodontics, Harvard U. and Forsyth Dental Center, Boston, 1975. Diplomate: Am. Bd. Endodontics. Endodontist Thomas, Mellion & Cappuccino, Inc., Warwick, R.I., 1975—; staff assoc. dept. endodontics Forsyth Dental Center, Boston, 1975-78, asst. clin. prof. endodontics, 1978-82, staff assoc., dept. endodontics, 1982—; clin. instr. in endodontics Harvard Sch. Dental Medicine, 1978-82, asst. clin. prof., 1982—. Author, editor: Textbook of Oral Biology, 1978; Contbr. articles to profl. jours. Mem. U.S. Olympic Com., Boston, 1982—. Recipient cert. of merit Harvard U. Odontological Soc., 1973. Fellow Am. Coll. Stomatologic Surgeons; mem. Am. Assn. Endodontists (editorial bd. jour. 1981—), Am. Dental Assn., Internat. Assn. for Dental Research, R.I. Dental Assn., Boston Cancer Research Assn. Current Work: Patient care; clinical and basic science teaching; histochemistry of the human dental pulp; evaluation of new materials. Subspecialties: Endodontics; Oral biology. Office: Thomas Mellion & Cappuccino Inc 265 Jefferson Blvd Warwick RI 02888

CAPRILES, VICTOR ANTONIO, biology educator, marine ecology researcher; b. San Germán, P.R., July 10, 1936; s. Antonio and Leandra (Anglero) C. B.A., Inter-Am. U., 1957; M.Sc., NYU, 1968. Lectr., NSF Program Sci. Lectures for P.R., V.I., U. P.R., 1961-66; asst. prof. biology Inter-Am. U., San Germán, 1967-71, assoc. prof. biology, chmn. dept., 1971-76, assoc. prof. biology, 1976—, dir. NSF Program in Marine Biology, 1978-80, 81; dir. Health Careers Opportunity Program Coll. Students, Dept. Health and Human Welfare, 1984—; mem. council Internat. Sci. and Engring. Fair, 1980-83; dir. sci. fair Western P.R. Regional Sci. Fairs, 1971—. Grantee NSF, 1978, 79, 80, 81, 82, Dept. Edn., 1982, 84. Contbr. articles to profl. jours. Mem. Nat. Assn. Biology Tchrs., Assn. Tropical Biology, N.Y. Acad. Scis., Ecol. Soc. Am., Nat. Sci. Tchrs. Assn., AAAS, Am. Mus. Natural History, P.R. Sci. Tchrs. Assn., AAUP, Internat. Oceanographic Found., Am. Inst. Biol. Scis., Animal Behavior Soc., Crustacean Soc., Beta Beta Beta, Lambda Iota Tau. Democrat. Roman Catholic. Current work: Symbiotic associations in animals inhabiting the littoral zone. Subspecialties: Marine biology; Behavioral ecology. Home: H-6 Santa Marta Devel San German PR 00753 Office: Inter American Univ Dept Biology San German PR 00753

CARAKOSTAS, MICHAEL CHARLES, veterinary clinical pathologist, researcher; b. Detroit, Sept. 28, 1952; s. Kenneth and Margaret Elizabeth (Stephenson) C.; m. Barabara Jean Sherman, Sept. 7, 1974. B.S., Mich. State U., 1974, D.V.M., 1975; Ph.D., Kans. State U., 1980. Diplomate Am. Coll. Vet. Pathologists. Instr. Kans. State U., Manhattan, 1977-80; asst. prof. La. State U., Baton Rouge, 1980-82, assoc. prof., 1982-83; assoc. prof. Tufts U., Boston, 1983-85; staff pathologist DuPont Co., Newark, Del., 1985—. Contbr. articles to profl. jours. Mem. Am. Soc. Vet. Clin. Pathology, AVMA, Phi Zeta. Current work: Evaluation of hematologic and clinical biochemistry alterations in laboratory animals in experimental toxicology work. Subspecialties: Pathology (veterinary medicine); Clinical chemistry. Office: DuPont Co Haskell Lab PO Box 50 Elkton Rd Newark DE 19711

CARASSO, ALFRED SAM, mathematician; b. Alexandria, Egypt, Apr. 9, 1939; came to U.S., 1962; s. Samuel and Renee (Ades) C.; m. Beatrice Kozak, June 12, 1964; children: Adam, Rachel. B.S. in Physics, U. Adelaide, Australia, 1960; M.S. in Meteorology, U. Wis.-Madison, 1964, Ph.D. in Math, 1968. Asst. prof. math. Mich. State U., East Lansing, 1968-69; asst. prof. math. U. N.Mex., Albuquerque, 1969-72, assoc. prof. math., 1972-76, prof. math., 1976-81; mathematician Nat. Bur. Standards, math. analysis div. Center for Applied Math., Washington, 1982—; cons. Los Alamos Nat. Lab., 1972-81. Mem. Soc. for Indsl. and Applied Math. Current Work: Mathematical and computational analysis of inverse problems and their application in heat conduction, seismology, acoustics, image processing, and electromagnetics. Subspecialties: Applied mathematics; Numerical analysis (computer science). Office: Nat Bur Standards Adminstrn A-302 Washington DC 20234

CARBERRY, JAMES JOSEPH, operations research analyst, consultant; b. Newark, Aug. 8, 1953; s. James Joseph and Alice Reeves (Camp) C. B.S., Stevens Inst. Tech., 1975; M.S., Am. U., 1979. Water analyst N.J. Med. Labs., Bricktown, 1973-74; ops. research analyst Naval Facilities Engring. Command, Alexandria, Va., 1975—. Author: Economic Analysis Handbook, 1980. Mem. Ops. Research Soc. Am., Mil. Ops. Research Soc., Nat. Computer Graphics Assn., Washington Ops. Research/Mgmt. Sci. Council, Pi Lambda Phi. Current Work: Developing computer-aided graphics planning system for master planning and natural resource management applications. Subspecialties: Operations research (engineering); Graphics, image processing, and pattern recognition. Home: 2421 Byrd Ln Alexandria VA 22303 Office: Naval Facilities Engring Command 200 Stovall St Alexandria VA 22332

CARBONE, PAUL PETER, cancer researcher; b. White Plains, N.Y., May 2, 1931; s. Antonio and Grace (Cappelieri) C.; m. Mary Iamurri, Aug. 20, 1954; children—David, Kathryn, Karen, Kim, Paul J., Mary Beth, Matthew. Student, Union Coll., Schenectady, 1949-52; M.D., Albany (N.Y.). Med. Coll., 1956. Diplomate: Am. Bd. Internal Medicine. Joined USPHS, 1956; intern USPHS Hosp., Balt., 1956-57, resident in internal medicine, San Francisco, 1958-60; mem. staff Nat. Cancer Inst., NIH, Bethesda, Md., 1960-76, chief medicine br., 1968-72, asso. dir. for med. oncology, div. cancer treatment, 1972-76, dep. clin. dir., 1972-76; clin. prof. Georgetown U. Med. Sch., 1971-76; lectr. hematology Walter Reed Army Inst. Research, 1962-76; prof. medicine and human oncology U. Wis., Madison, 1976—, dir. div. clin. oncology, 1976—, chmn. dept. human oncology, 1977—; dir. Wis. Clin. Cancer Center, 1978—. Contbr. articles to profl. jours. Decorated USPHS Commendation medal; recipient Trimble Lecture award Md. Chirurgical Faculty, 1968; Lasker award clin. cancer chemotherapy, 1972; Rosenthal award for improvement in clin. cancer care, 1977. Fellow ACP; mem. Exptl. Hematology Soc., Am. Soc. Clin. Investigation, Am. Soc. Clin. Oncology (pres. 1972-73), Am. Soc. Clin. Investigation, Am. Soc. Hematology, Am. Assn. Cancer Research (pres. 1978-79), Am. Fedn. Clin. Research, AMA, Alpha Omega Alpha. Current Work: Breast cancer, lynmphomas, clinical trials. Subspecialties: Internal medicine; Oncology. Home: 6115 N Highlands Ave Madison WI 53705 Office: Univ Hosps 600 Highland Ave Madison WI 53792

CARD, DARRELL HOLDER, consultant radioactive waste management; b. Salem, Utah, Nov. 8, 1926; s. Earl F. and Louise (Holder) C.; m. Wynnette Kartchner, Sept. 1, 1950; children: Darelyn, Dyann, William, Miriam, David, Michael. B.S., Brigham Young U., 1950; M.Engring. Adminstrn., U. Utah, 1967. Chemist U.S. Bur. Mines, Salt Lake City, 1950-52; shift supr. E.I. DuPont de Nemours & Co., Inc., Martinsburg, W.Va., 1952-54; shift supt. Phillips Petroleum Co., Idaho Falls, Idaho, 1954-61; sr. process engr. Thiokel Chem. Corp., Brigham City, Utah, 1961-67; supr. rocket mfg. Northrup Aircraft Co., North Edwards AFB, Calif., 1967-68; mfg. project engr. Lockheed Propulsion Co., Redlands, Calif, 1968-74; project mgr. E.G.&G Idaho Inc., Idaho Falls, 1974-77; program mgr. Ford, Bacon & Davis, Salt Lake City, 1977—. Served with USNR, 1945-46. Mem. Am. Nuclear Soc. Mormon. Lodge: Lions. Current Work: Development of new concepts in radioactive waste management and disposal techniques. Subspecialty: Nuclear engineering. Home: 454 N Main St Alpine UT 84003 Office: Ford Bacon & Davis 375 Chipeta Way Salt Lake City UT 84108

CARD, ROGER JOHN, industrial chemist; b. Grand Rapids, Mich. Oct. 31, 1947; s. Lester and Jessica Gertrude (Machiela) C.; m. Shirley Ann Noyes, Sept. 13, 1984. B.A. in Chemistry, Hope Coll., 1969; M.S. in Chemistry, Iowa State U., 1972, Ph.D. in Chemistry, 1975. Lectr. Nat. Univ. Malaysia, Petaling, Jaya, 1975-77; postdoctoral Bowling Green State U., Ohio, 1977-78; sr. research chemist Am. Cyanamid, Stamford, Conn., 1978—. Contbr. articles to profl. jours. Patentee in field. Advisor Jr. Achievement, Stamford, Conn., 1983. Mem. Am. Chem. Soc., Am. Ceramic Soc. Current work: Design of improved materials for ceramics applications; technical evaluation of new business opportunities. Subspecialties: Organometallics; Ceramics. Office: Am Cyanamid 1937 W Main St Stamford CT 06904-0060

CARDIFF, ROBERT DARRELL, pathologist, educator; b. San Francisco, Dec. 5, 1935; s. George Darrell and Helen (Kohfield) C.; m. Sally Bounds, June 23, 1962; children: Darrell, Todd Trevor, Shelley Lynn. B.S., U. Calif.-Berkeley, 1958; Ph.D., 1968; M.D., U. Calif.-San Francisco, 1962. Diplomate: Am. Bd. Anatomical Pathology, 1968. Intern Kings County Hosp., Bklyn., 1962-63; resident in pathology U. Oreg., Portland, 1963-66; NIH spl. fellow U. Calif.-Berkeley, 1966-68; mem. faculty U. Calif. Med. Sch.-Davis, 1971—, prof. pathology, 1977—, vice chmn. dept. pathology, 1982—. Contbr. articles to profl. jours. Served to lt. col. M.C. U.S. Army, 1968-71. Recipient Disting. teaching award U. Calif., 1985, Triton Research award, 1985; grantee NIH, Am. Cancer Soc. Mem. AAAS, Internat. Acad. Pathology, Am. Soc. Pathology Bacteriologists, Internat. Assn. Breast Cancer Research (bd. dirs. 1985—), Internat. Assn. Comparative Research Leukemia, N.Y. Acad. Scis., Am. Assn. Cancer Research. Current Work: Research in tumor biology, breast cancer, molecular biology-genetics. Subspecialties: Cancer research (medicine); Pathology (medicine). Office: Dept Pathology U Calif Med Sch Davis CA 95616

CARDUCCI, BERNARDO JOSEPH, psychology educator; b. Detroit, May 20, 1952; s. Edward and Mary (Bosco) C.; 1 child, Rozana. A.A., Mt. San Antonio Coll., 1972; B.A., Calif. State U., Fullerton, 1974, M.A., 1976; Ph.D., Kans. State U., 1981. Asst. prof. psychology Ind. U., New Albany, 1979—; textbook reviewer Holt, Rinehart and Winston, 1981—. Author: Instructor's Manual to Accompany Mehr's Abnormal Psychology, 1983; contbr. articles to profl. jours. Ind. U. S.E. instructional devel. grantee, 1980; Ind. U. S.E. summer faculty fellow, 1981. Mem. Am. Psychol. Assn., Soc. for Personality and Social Psychology, Midwestern Psychol. Assn., Council of Undergrad. Psychology Depts., Southeastern Psychol. Assn., Soc. for Psychol. Study of Social Issues, Psi Chi. Current Work: The role of cognitive factors in the attribution of responsibility for domestic and sexual violence and psychophysiological responses to interpersonal stressors; cross-generational perceptions of sexuality and interpersonal attraction. Subspecialties: Social psychology; Personality. Home: 4002 Summer Pl New Albany IN 47150Office: Department of Psycholog Indiana University Southeast New Alban IN 47150

CARELLI, MARIO DOMENICO, nuclear engineer; b. Taggia, Imperia, Italy, Feb. 6, 1942; came to U.S., 1969, naturalized, 1982; s. Giuseppe and Rosa (Cichero) C.; m. Maria Sabina Viti, Mar. 29, 1969; children: Eric Viti, Eliana Jennifer. B.Sc., U. Florence, Italy, 1962; Ph.D. in Nuclear Engring. summa cum laude, U. Pisa, Italy, 1966. Registered profl. engr. Italy, Pa. With Westinghouse Advanced Energy Systems Div., Madison, Pa., 1969—, prin. engr., 1974-77, engring. fellow, 1977—; adj. faculty prof. U. Pitts., 1975—, mem. faculty adv. com. energy resources, 1982—. Contbr. over 60 nuclear engring. articles to profl. pubis. Recipient Engring. Achievement award Westinghouse, 1983; Research fellow U. Pisa, 1966-67. Mem. Am. Nuclear Soc., Internat. Assn. Hydraulic Research (mem. exec. com. 1979—), ASME. Roman Catholic. Patentee flow orificing of breeder core assemblies, 1975, blanket management method for breeder reactors, 1982. Current Work: Nuclear breeder reactors core design; heat transfer and fluid flow research and design; academic teaching on nuclear technology. Subspecialties: Nuclear engineering; Fluid mechanics. Home: 652 Buckingham Circle Greensburg PA 15601 Office: Westinghouse Advanced Energy Systems Div PO Box 158 Madison PA 15663

CAREW, LYNDON BELMONT, JR., nutritionist, educator; b. Lynn, Mass., Nov. 27, 1932; s. Lyndon Belmont and Myrtle Louella (Woodworth) C.; m. Lynn Harrington, July 9, 1960; children: Leslie, Audre. B.S., U. Mass., 1955; Ph.D., Cornell U., 1961. Research asst. and assoc. in animal nutrition Cornell U., Ithaca, N.Y., 1955-61, 65; dir. Colombian Nat. Poultry Program and Animal Nutrition Lab., Rockefeller Found., Bogota, 1961-65; dir. poultry research div. Hess and Clark, Ashland, Ohio, 1966-69; sci. program mgr. Internat. Nutrition Project, U. Vt., Burlington, 1980-82, prof. animal scis., prof. human nutrition and foods, 1969—. Contbr. articles to profl. jours. Pres. Vt. Nutrition Council, 1976-81, 83—; mem. Vt. Gov.'s Council Phys. Fitness; vice chmn. Shelburne (Vt.) Conservation Com., 1970-73. Recipient Carrigan Outstanding Teaching award U. Vt., 1981, George V. Kidder Outstanding Faculty award U. Vt., 1983; grantee NSF; grantee U.S. Dept. Agr.; grantee Bur. Internat. Food and Agr. Devel.; grantee U. Vt.; grantee Agway Inc.; grantee Muscular Dystrophy Assn.; grantee others. Mem. Am. Inst. Nutrition, Soc. Exptl. Biology and Medicine, Endocrine Soc., Poultry Sci. Assn., World Poultry Sci. Assn., Animal Nutrition Research Council (chmn. bd. trustees 1984-85), Nutrition Edn. Soc., N.Y. Acad. Scis., Am. Inst. Biol. Scis., AAAS, Nat. Assn. Coll. Tchrs. of Agr., Sigma Xi, Gamma Alpha, Phi Kappa Phi. Current Work: Radioimmunoassay, nutrition, thyroid, energy metabolism, growth hormone thyroid receptors, unusualffeedstuffs, poultry nutrition. Nutrition in Latin America, poultry science in Latin America, computer assisted instruction, computers in diet analysis. Subspecialties: Animal nutrition; Endocrinology. Home: 57 Collamer Circle Shelburne VT 05482 Office: Bioresearch Lab 655 Spear St South Burlington VT 05401

CAREY, CYNTHIA, biology educator, physiologist; b. Denver, July 17, 1947; d. Raymond Giddens and Faye (Kingsbury) C.; A.B., Occidental Coll., 1969, M.A., 1970; Ph.D., U. Mich., 1976. Teaching fellow U. Mich., Ann Arbor, 1970-74, research asst., 1974-76; asst. prof. biology U. Colo., Boulder, 1976-82, assoc. prof., 1982—; mem. adv. panel NSF, Washington, 1982-85, NASA Workshop, Washington, 1984. Editor Am. Zoologist Avian Egg, 1980. Contbr. articles to profl. jours. Recipient Disting. Teaching award U. Colo., 1983; AAAS fellow, 1981. Mem. Am. Ornithologists Union (Marcia Brady Tucker award 1973), Cooper Ornithol. Soc. (bd. dirs. 1982—), Am. Physiol. Soc., Am. Soc. Zoologists, Sigma Xi. Current work: Physiological adaptation of animals to cold temperatures, fluctuating temperatures, high altitudes and deserts. Subspecialty: Comparative physiology. Home: 3335 Chisholm Trail Apt 301 Boulder CO 80301 Office: Dept EPO Biology U Colo Boulder CO 80309

CAREY, GRAHAM FRANCIS, researcher, engineering science and mechanics, applied mathematics educator; b. Cairns, Queensland, Australia, Nov. 14, 1944; came to U.S., 1968; s. Lionel Dudley and Alma Lilian (Courtice) C.; m. Kira Iljins, Jan. 13, 1968; children—Varis, Tija. B.S., U. Queensland, 1965, B.S. with honors, 1966; M.S., U. Wash., 1970, Ph.D., 1974. Research faculty U. Queensland, 1966-68; research engr. Boeing Co., Seattle, 1968-70; research prof. U. Wash., 1974-76; prof. U. Tex., Austin, 1977—; lectr. Summer Research Inst., Australia, 1984. Author: Introduction to Finite Element Method (Japanese and Hungarian transl.), 1974; Finite Element Series Vols. I-VI, 1980-85; Finite Elements in Fluids, 1984, 85. Editor Internat. Jour. Communications in Applied Numerical Methods, 1984—. Contbr. articles to profl. jours., books, proc. vols. U.S. rep. Fenomech Conf., Germany, 1978, U.S.-Europe Conf., Germany, 1981; keynote lectr. confs., Australia, 1979, 84. Mem. Nat. Com. Undergraduate Math. and Applications, Soc. Indsl. and Applied Math., Internat. Assn. Math. and Computers in Simulation, Am. Acad. Mechanics, Soc. Engring. Sci. (computer methods com.). Current work: Development and analysis of computational methods for problems in engineering and applied science. Subspecialties: Theoretical and applied mechanics; Applied mathematics.

CAREY, MARTIN CONRAD, gastroenterologist, molecular biophysicist, educator; b. Clonmel, County Tipperary, Ireland, June 18, 1939; came to U.S., 1967; s. John Joseph and Alice (Broderick) C.; m. Gracia Antonieta Fernández, July 1, 1972; children—Julian Albert, Dermot Martin. M.B., B.Ch., B.A.O. with 1st class honors, Nat. U. Ireland, 1962, M.D., 1981, D.Sc., 1984. Intern, St. Vincent's Hosp., Dublin, Ireland, 1962-63, resident, 1965-67; resident Nat. Maternity Hosp., Dublin, 1963, St. Luke's Hosp., Dublin, 1964, Queen Charlotte's Hosp., London, 1964; postdoctoral fellow, research assoc. Boston U. Sch. Medicine, 1968-73, asst. prof. medicine, 1973-75; asst. prof. medicine Harvard U. Med. Sch., Boston, 1975-79, assoc. prof., 1979—, assoc. prof. physiology and biophys. cs, 1983—; Lawrence J. Henderson assoc. prof. health sci. and tech., 1979—; mem. staff Brigham and Women's Hosp., Boston, 1976—; cons. West Roxbury VA Hosp., Boston, 1976—, Calif. Biotech. Inc., Palo Alto, 1983—. Author: Bile Salts and Gallstones, 1974; Hepatic Excretory Function, 1975; contbr. numerous articles to med. and sci. jours.; assoc. editor Jour. Lipid Research, 1978-81; mem. editorial bds. Am. Jour. Physiology, 1976-81, Gastroenterology, 1983—, Hepatology, 1981-84. Recipient Acad. Career Devel. award NIH, 1976; Adolf Windaus prize Falk Found., 1984; Guggenheim Found. fellow, 1974; Fogarty internat. fellow NIH, 1968. Fellow Royal Coll. Physicians Ireland; mem. Gastroenterology Research Group (vice chmn., steering coms.), Am. Soc. Clin. Investigation, Am. Gastroent. Assn., Am. Oil Chemists Soc., Biophys. Soc. Democrat. Roman Catholic. Club: Babson (Wellesley, Mass.). Current work: Phase transitions and equilibria in biologically relevant and classical lipid systems; physical-chemistry and pathophysiology of bile; biochemistry and biophysics of gallstone formation and dissolution and of lipid absorption and malabsorption; lipid-protein interactions; chemistry and physics of micelles, liquid crystals and emulsions. Subspecialties: Gastroenterology; Biophysics (physics). Home: 94 Westgate Rd Wellesley MA 02181 Office: Brigham and Women's Hosp Div Gastroenterology 75 Francis St Boston MA 02115

CARINO, FELIPE, JR., computer scientist, tech. cons.; b. Bronx, N.Y., Feb. 5, 1956; s. Felipe and Manuela (Rios) C. B.A. in Computer Sci. and Math, N.Y.U., 1977, M.S. in Computer Sci, 1979. Mem. tech. staff Bell Labs., Piscataway, N.J., 1977-80; sr. systems programmer Fairchild Test Systems, San Jose, Calif., 1980-81; staff engr. Ampex Corp., Redwood City, Calif., 1981; sr. software engr. Britton-Lee, Berkeley, Calif., 1981, Ford Aerospace and Communications Corp., Palo Alto, Calif., 1982—. Mem. Assn. for Computing Machinery, IEEE, Robot Inst. Am. Democrat. Current Work: Research into data base theory and machines, especially as applied to pictorial data base management system. Subspecialties: Database systems; Graphics, image processing, and pattern recognition. Home: 655 S Fairoaks Ave N103 Sunnyvale CA 94086 Office: 3939 Fabian Way Palo Alto CA 94303

CARLEY, JOHN WESLEY, III, industrial psychology consultant; b. Dallas, Dec. 15, 1942; s. John Wesley and Velma Ruth (Miller) C.; m. Pamela A. Reynolds, Jan. 26, 1978. B.S., N. Tex. State U., Denton, 1965, Ph.D., 1970; postgrad., Harvard U., 1979. Dir. Tex. Dept Mental Health and Mental Retardation, Austin, 1964-76, asst. commr., 1976-78, dep. commr., 1978-82, self-employed indsl. cons., Austin, 1982—; pres. Tex. Showdown Games, Austin, 1982—, Greater Southwest Devel. Corp., 1981—. Author: Transportation and Mental Retardation, 1980; Contbr. articles to profl. jours. Fellow Am. Assn. Mental Deficiency; mem. Am. Psychol. Assn., Tex. Assn. Mental Deficiency (pres. 1977-78). Republican. Methodist. Current Work: Management, personnel turnover, employee safety. Subspecialty: Human factors engineering. Home: 8140 Greenslope Austin TX 78759 Office: PO Box 5877 Austin TX 78763

CARLIN, RICHARD LEWIS, chemist. Prof. dept. chemistry U. Ill., Chgo. Subspecialty: Inorganic chemistry. Office: U Ill Dept Chemistry Chicago IL 60680

CARLO, JAIME RAFAEL, immunomicroscopist, immunologist; b. Utuado, P.R., Sept. 15, 1943; s. Rafael and Carmen Aida (Casellas) C.; m. Judith B. Bragg, Dec. 19, 1964; children: Judson Dupree, Tyler Bragg. B.S., Med. Coll. Ga., 1967; M.S., U. Ga., 1968; Ph.D., U. Md., 1976. Research immunologist Becton-Dickinson, Cockeysville, Md., 1972-73; pres. Immunodiagnostics, Inc., Houston, 1973-74; asst. prof. pathology U. Md., Balt., 1973-76; asst. prof. pathology/medicine Med. Coll. Va., Richmond, 1976-82; asst. prof. med. lab. sci. Northeastern U., Boston, 1982—. Contbr. articles in field to profl. jours. Advisor AIDS (Aquired Immune Deficiency Syndrome) Action Com., Boston, 1982-83. Served to lt. comdr. USN, 1968-72. Med. Coll. Va. grantee-in-aid, 1977; Dept. Health and Human Services grantee, 1977-79; NIH grantee, 1982; recipient Research and Scholarship Devel. award Northeastern U., 1983. Fellow Arthritis Found.; mem. Am. Assn. Immunologists, Am. Soc. Microbiology (pres. Va. br. 1979-81), Am. Soc. Clin. Pathologists, Am. Fedn. Clin. Research, N.Y. Acad. Scis. Democrat. Roman Catholic. Current Work: The characterization of the catabolism of the third component of complement in immunologically mediated tissue injury by immunocytochemical methods. Subspecialties: Immunocytochemistry; Immunobiology and immunology. Home: 39 Middlesex Ave Swampscott MA 01907 Office: Northeastern U 360 Huntington Ave Boston MA 02026

CARLSON, DAVID EMIL, physicist; b. Weymouth, Mass., Mar. 5, 1942; s. Emil Algot and Anne Alice (Salomaa) C.; m. Mary Ann Lewinski, June, 1966; children—Eric, Darcey. B.S. in Physics, Rensselaer Poly. Inst., 1963, Ph.D., Rutgers U., 1968. Research scientist U.S. Army Nuclear Effects Lab., Edgewood Arsenal, Md., 1968-69; head photovoltaic device research RCA Labs., Princeton, N.J., 1970-83; dep. gen. mgr., dir. research Solarex Thin Film Div., Newtown, Pa., 1983—. Contbr. articles to profl. jours. Served to capt. Signal Corps U.S. Army, 1968-70; Vietnam. Decorated Bronze Star medal; recipient Ross Coffin Purdy award Am. Ceramic Soc., 1976, Outstanding Achievement award RCA Labs., 1973, 1976. Mem. Am. Phys. Soc., Electrochem. Soc., IEEE (co-recipient Morris N. Liebmann award 1984), Am. Vacuum Soc., Sigma Xi. Patentee in field; inventor amorphous silicon solar cell, 1974. Current work: Direct research on thin film, amorphous silicon solar cells. Subspecialties: Solar energy; Condensed matter physics. Home: 514 Nancy Rd Yardley PA 19067 Office: Solarex Thin Film Div Newtown PA 18940

CARLSON, GEORGE ALFRED, JR., immunogeneticist; b. Phila., June 29, 1947; s. George Alfred and Aldona (Kukcinovich) C.; m. Frances Isabel Lee, Sept. 7, 1974; 1 child, G. Benjamin. A.B., U. Pa.-Phila., 1969; Ph.D., Tufts U., 1976. Tchr., Berkshire Sch., Sheffield, Mass., 1969-70; postdoctoral fellow immunology U. Alta., Can., 1975-77; asst. prof. immunology, 1977-80; assoc. staff scientist The Jackson Lab., Bar Harbor, Maine, 1980-84, staff scientist, 1984—; mem. grants com. on immunology, transplantation Med. Research Council Can., 1981-83; mem. clin. scis. study sect. NIH, USPHS, 1984—. Contbr. articles to sci. jours. Leukemia Soc. Am. Postdoctoral fellowship, 1975-77; Nat. Cancer Inst. Can. Scholar, 1978-80. Mem. Am. Assn. Immunologists, Reticuloendothelial Soc., Internat. Soc. Comparative and Developmental Immunology. Current work: Natural resistance to malignancy; nonimmunological functions of the major histocompatibility complex. Subspecialties: Immunobiology and immunology; Immunogenetics. Office: The Jackson Lab Bar Harbor ME 04609

CARLSON, HAROLD ERNEST, physician, medical educator; b. S.I., May 17, 1943; s. Clarence Herbert and Edith Amelia (Anderson) C.; m. Gabrielle Arakelian, July 2, 1966. B.S. in Chemistry, Rensselaer Poly. Inst., 1964; M.D., Cornell U. Med. Coll., 1968. Diplomate: Am. Bd. Internal Medicine. Intern Barnes Hosp., St. Louis, 1968-69, resident, 1969-70; fellow in metabolism Washington U. Sch. Medicine, St. Louis, 1972-74; asst. chief endocrinology Wadsworth VA Hosp., Los Angeles, 1974-82; asst. prof. medicine UCLA, 1974-79, assoc. prof., 1979-82; chief endocrinology sect. Harry Truman VA Hosp., Columbia, Mo., 1982-85; assoc. dir. endocrinology div. , assoc. prof. medicine U. Mo.-Columbia, 1982-85; acting chief endocrinology sect. Northport VA Hosp., N.Y., 1985—; Contbr. numerous articles, abstracts to profl. publs.; contbg. author, editor: Endocrinology, 1983; editorial bd.: Jour. Clin. Endocrinology and Metabolism, 1979-82. Served to lt. comdr. USPHS, 1970-72. VA Merit Rev. research grantee, 1974—. Prof. medicine SUNY-Stony Brook, 1985—. Mem. Am. Fedn. Clin. Research (sec.-treas. Western sect. 1982-83), Endocrine Soc., Western Soc. Clin. Investigation, Central Soc. Clin. Research. Current Work: Regulation of pituitary and parathyroid gland function. Subspecialty: Endocrinology. Office: Med Service Northport VA Hosp Northport NY 11768

CARLSON, JOHN B., astronomer, anthropologist; b. Joliet, Ill., June 22, 1945; s. Bernard C. and Mary W. (West) C. B.A. in Physics, Oberlin Coll, 1967; M.S. in Astronomy, U. Md., College Park, 1971, Ph.D. in Astronomy, 1977. Tinker Found. postdoctoral fellow Yale U., 1977-79; dir., founder Center for Archaeoastronomy, U. Md., 1978—; vis. asst. prof., research assoc. Inst. Phys. Sci. and Tech., U. Md., 1977-81; lectr. Smithsonian Instn. Resident Assoc. Program, 1977—; affiliate asst. prof. astronomy program, adj. asst. prof. anthropology U. Md. Editor-in-chief, founder: Archaeoastronomy, 1977—; assoc. editor: Current Anthropology, 1979—; adv. editor: Jour. History of Astronomy, 1979; contbr. articles profl. jours. Dumbarton Oaks summer research fellow, 1982. Fellow Royal Astron. Soc.; mem. Am. Astron. Soc. (council hist. astronomy div.), Internat. Astron. Union, Soc. Am. Archaeology, AAAS. Current Work: Archaeoastronomy, native Am. Astronomy, pre-Columbian studies, Maya hieroglyphic writing, history of astronomy, extragalactic astronomy. Subspecialty: Archaeoastronomy; Extragalactic astronomy. Office: Center for Archaeoastronomy U M College Park MD 20742

CARLSON, KENNETH T., chemist, educator; b. Douglas, N.D., June 18, 1921; s. Torkel and Clara A. (Jorgens) C.; m. Sylvia G. Aafedt, June 12, 1949; children: Sandra Whitney, David Carlson, Cartor C. B.S., Minot State Coll., 1947; M.A., U. No. Colo., 1953; postgrad., Oreg. State U., 1963-64. Tchr. math. Harvey (N.D.) High Sch., 1947-48; tchr. sci. Carrington (N.D.) High Sch., 1948-50; prin. high sch., Cando, N.D., 1950-54; prof. sci. Mayville (N.D.) State Coll., 1954—. Treas. Mayville Vol. Dept., 1956-63. Served with USAAF, 1942-46. Recipient Service award Mayville State Coll., 1978. Mem. Nat. Sci. Tchrs., Am. Chem. Soc., World Future Soc., N.D. Acad. Sci., Red River Valley Chem. Soc., N.D. Edn. Soc., NEA, Lambda Sigma Tau. Republican. Lutheran. Lodge: Elks. Current Work: Science education, environment, energy and the future. Subspecialty: Organic chemistry. Office: Mayville State Coll Mayville ND 58257

CARLSON, MARIAN BILLE, molecular genetics educator, researcher; b. Princeton, N.J., Oct. 19, 1952; d. B.C. and Louise G. (Winston) C.; m. Stephen P. Goff, Oct. 15, 1977; 1 child, Sarah. A.B., Radcliffe Coll., Cambridge, Mass., 1973; Ph.D., Stanford U., 1978. Fellow dept. biology M.I.T., Cambridge, 1978-81; asst. prof. human genetics and devel. Coll. Physicians and Surgeons Columbia U., N.Y.C., 1981—. Jane Coffin Childs fellow, 1978-81; recipient Irma T. Hirschl Career Scientist award, 1982. Mem. Genetics Soc. Am. Current Work: Molecular genetics of yeast. Subspecialties: Genetics and genetic engineering (biology); Molecular biology. Office: 701 W 168th St New York NY 10032

CARLSON, ROGER DAVID, psychologist, educator; b. Berkeley, Calif., Nov. 19, 1946; s. George Clarence and Elizabeth (Norris) C.; m. Ema Teresa Paviolo, June 11, 1977; children—Erik Andres Paviolo, Lucas Sven Paviolo, Justin Nikolaus Paviolo. B.A., Calif. State U., 1968, M.A., 1969; Ph.D., U. Oreg., 1972. Lic. psychologist, Pa., Calif. Grad. asst. Calif. State U., Sacramento, 1969-70; grad. tchng. fellow U. Oreg., Eugene, 1971-72; asst., then assoc. prof. psychology Lebanon Valley Coll., Annville, Pa., 1972—; cons. Wellness Assocs., Campbelltown, Pa., 1983-84, Assocs. Bus. Cons., Schafferstown, Pa., 1984—; cons. psychologist, Annville Family Practice, Pa., 1984—; Contbr. articles to profl. jours. Sustaining mem. Democratic Nat. Com., 1984—; bd. dirs. Lebanon County chpt. ARC, 1983-84, chmn. water safety, 1983-84. Fellow Am. Coll. Psychology (charter); mem. Am. Psychol. Assn., Eastern Psychol. Assn., AAUP (pres. chpt. 1982—), Psi Chi. Methodist. Current work: Development in infancy; psycholinguistics and cognitive processing, developmental and intelligence tests, philosophical psychology. Subspecialties: Cognition; Developmental psychology. Home: 332 W Main St Annville PA 17003 Office: Dept Psychology Lebanon Valley Coll Annville PA 17003

CARLTON, DONALD MORRILL, research and development company executive; b. Houston, July 20, 1937; s. Spencer William and Ruth (Morrill) C.; m. Elaine Yvonne Smith, Jan. 28, 1961; children: Donna Kay, Spencer Frank, Monica Elaine. B.A., U. St. Thomas, Houston, 1958; Ph.D., U. Tex., Austin, 1962. Mem. staff, then group leader Sandia Corp., Albuquerque, 1962-65; with Tracor, Inc., Austin, 1965-69, asst. dir. research, 1968-69; pres., chmn. bd. Radian Corp., Austin, 1969—; dir. Hartford Steam Boiler Insp. and Ins. Co., Interfirst Bank, Austin, Ecolaire, Inc. Mem. Gov.'s Task Force on Hazardous Waste Disposal, 1984. Mem. Nat. Coal Council, Am. Chem. Soc., Austin C. of C. (past dir.). Current Work: Environmental aspects of coal gasification; sulfur dioxide control; toxic and hazardous waste disposal. Subspecialties: Coal; Gas cleaning systems. Home: 4601 Cat Mountain Dr Austin TX 78731 Office: PO Box 9948 Austin TX 78766

CARLTON-FOSS, JOHN ANDREW, psychology and technical company executive; b. Appleton, Minn., May 4, 1945; s. Harvey J. and Camilla A. (Person) Foss; m. Elizabeth J. Dennison, June 21, 1972; m. Rhona Newcomb Carlton, Aug. 15, 1980. S.B., M.I.T., 1967; S.M., 1969; Ed.M., Harvard U., 1973; Ph.D. in Psychology, Saybrook Inst., 1981. Ind. research and devel. and orgnl. cons., Lincoln, Mass., 1971-75; lead project researcher, adminstr. M.I.T., 1975-77; lead engr., action researcher Energy Investment, Inc., Boston, 1978; pres. Human-Tech. Energy Systems, Inc., Lincoln Center and Weston, Mass., 1978—; instr. physics and energy U. Mass., 1980-81; mgr. Energy Edn. Project, Dept. Energy/Mass. Energy Office, 1980-81; Mem. local congl. energy task force Program Task Force for Suffolk County Project for Reliable and Affordable energy; energy adv. com. Weston Pub. Schs.; com. for ednl. policy M.I.T. Contbr. articles to profl. jours. Recipient William L. Steward, Jr., award M.I.T.; NDEA fellow. Mem. Am. Psychol. Assn., AAAS, ASHRAE (standards com. on ventilation for acceptable air quality, chmn. com. on ventilation effectiveness), IEEE, Human Factors Soc. Episcopalian. Club: M.I.T. of Boston. Current Work: Organizational consulting on human-organizational-technical factors in analysis, design, and implementation of energy and computer-based systems; research on human and organizational factors associated with technology; personal and situational stresses in relation to burnout and preventive medicine; technical inventions in these areas. Subspecialty: Systems engineering. Office: Box 151 Lincoln Center MA 01773 99 School St Weston MA 02193

CARNEY, BRUCE WILLIAM, astronomer; b. Guam, Mariana Islands, Nov. 30, 1946; s. William Robert and Anne Elizabeth (Skow) C.; m. Lynn Christopher, Dec. 18, 1971. B.A., U. Calif.-Berkeley, 1969; A.M., Harvard U., 1971, Ph.D., 1978. Carnegie fellow dept. terrestrial magnetism, Washington, 1978-80; asst. prof. astronomy U. N.C., Chapel Hill, 1980-85, assoc. prof., 1985—; mem. Kitt Peak Nat. Obs. Users Com., 1980-85, chmn., 1983-85; mem. astronomy adv. com. NSF, 1984-87. Contbr. articles in field to profl. jours. Served with U.S. Army, 1971-74. NSF trainee, 1969-70; Harvard fellow, 1970-71. Mem. Internat. Astron. Union, Am. Astron. Soc. (Shapley lectr.), Astron. Soc. Pacific., Audubon Soc., Sierra Club. Democrat. Current Work: Optical photometry, imagery and spectroscopy, studies aimed at stars and clusters of our galaxy's oldest stars. Subspecialties: Optical astronomy; Infrared astronomy. Home: Woodbridge Apts B-10 Carrboro NC 27510 Office: U NC Dept Physics and Astronomy Phillips Hall 039A Chapel Hill NC 27514

CARNEY, LEROY LLOYD, chemist, consultant; b. Hammond, La., Sept. 4, 1931; s. Thomas Isiah and Mae Emma (Benett) C.; m. Dorothy Lou Cammack, Feb. 6, 1971; children—Mary, Rene, Richard. B.S. in Phys. Chemistry, Southeastern La. U., 1953; M.S. in Phys. Chemistry, La. State U., 1956. Supr. x-ray lab Dresser Magcobar, Inc., Houston, 1956-65; plant mgr., dir. research Dixie Chemical, Houston, 1965-69; supr. product devel. IMC Drilling Mud, Houston, 1969-72; drilling fluid sect. supr. Halliburton Services, Duncan, Okla., 1972-76; mgr. fluid service and devel. IMCO Services, Houston, 1976-79; cons. Exxon Chem. Americas, Houston, 1984—, fed. govt. contract on geothermal research Sandia Lab., Albuquerque, 1982—; pres. Concentrated Mud Chems., Houston, 1979-80, Carney Oilfield Chems., Inc., Houston, 1980—, Carney Mud Cons., Houston, 1980—; invited lectr. La. State U., Okla. State U., Tex. Tech. U., Mining Acad., Clausthal Zellerfeld, Germany, Mediterranean Oil Prodn. Seminar, Porec, Yugoslavia, Halliburton's Energy Inst., Houston; Patentee in field. Mem. Am. Chem. Soc., Am. Petroleum Inst. (chmn. standardization of drilling fluids com. 1975-77), Clay Minerals Soc., Soc. Petroleum Engrs. of AIME, TAPPI. Current work: President of Carney Mud Consultants and consultant to Exxon Chemical Americas. Home: 2055 W FM 1488 Magnolia TX 77355 Office: Carney Mud Cons 16800 Greenspoint Park N Atrium Suite 224 Houston TX 77060

CARNEY, RICHARD EDWARD, research psychologist, educator, consultant; b. Miami, Fla., Feb. 5, 1929; s. Clifford R. and Johnie Ora (Des Roches) C.; m. Jane Rima Wallace, June 20, 1953; children: Cathleen Jane, Daniel Richard, Bonnie Ann. Student, Fla. State U., 1947-48; 1B.S., U. Wash., 1954, M.S., 1956; Ph.D. in Psychology, U. Mich., 1961. Research asst. U. Wash., Seattle, 1954-55, teaching asst., 1955-58; asst. prof. psychology Drake U., Des Moines, 1958-62, Ind. U.-Gary, 1962-64; assoc. prof. psychology Calif. Western U. (later U.S. Internat. U.), San Diego, 1964-70; founder, pres. Carney Enterprises, Inc., San Diego, 1969—; prof. psychology Eastern Ky. U., Richmond, 1970-72; contract and core faculty Calif. Sch. Profl. Psychology, San Diego, 1972-79; co-founder, v.p. Timao Found. For Research and Devel., San Diego, 1972-80, pres., 1980—; research scientist System Devel. Corp., Santa Monica, Calif., 1974-75; assoc. dir. South San Diego Area Health Edn. Ctr., 1980-82; summer lectr. U. Mich. Extension Service, Flint and Saginaw, 1961; lectr. Roosevelt U., Chgo., 1962-63; summer assessment officer two Peace Corps tng. programs, 1966; cons. Non-Linear Systems, Inc., Solano Beach, Calif., 1967, Educator's Assistance Inst., 1972-74; evaluation cons. Title IX U.S. Office of Edn., 1977-78, cons. various sch. systems and orgns.; speaker profl. confs. Editor/author: Risk Taking Behavior, 1961; co-author: How to Reach Your Goals, 1981; author, co-author psychol. tests, 1976-81; contbr. articles, book revs., chpts. to publs. in field. Active ACLU, Planned Parenthood, Zero Population Growth; bd. dirs. San Diego Hypertension Program, Neighborhood House, Head Start; speaker polit., civic, religious groups. Served with U.S. Army, 1949-52. Grantee Ind. U., 1963; Grantee Methodist Ch., 1965; Grantee Calif. Western U., 1967; Grantee Dept. Def., 1974-75; Grantee Title IX U.S. Dept. Edn., 1977-78; Grantee USPHS, 1980-82, Pritikin Research Found., 1983-84. Mem. Am. Psychol. Assn., Western Psychol. Assn., San Diego Psychol. Assn. (pres. 1967-68), AAAS, AAUP (chpt pres. 1966-67), Soc. Psychologists in Substance Abuse (founding), Sigma Xi, Psi Chi (faculty advisor 1964-70). Democrat. Unitarian. Inventor Digi-Tutor, 1968. Current Work: Psychophysiological bases of substance abuse and health application of learning-motivation. Subspecialties: Physiological psychology; Learning. Office: Timao Found for Research and Devel 2223 El Cajon Blvd #307 San Diego CA 92104

CAROZZI, ALBERT VICTOR, geology educator; b. Geneva, Switzerland, Apr. 26, 1925; came to U.S., 1955, naturalized, 1963; s. Luigi and Anna-Maria (Ferrario) C.; m. Marguerite Peier, July 23, 1949; children: Viviane Marrocco, Nadine B. M.S., U. Geneva, 1947, Dr.Sc. summa cum laude, 1948. Lectr. geology U. Geneva, 1953-57; asst. vis. prof. U. Ill.-Urbana, 1955-56, assoc. prof geology, 1957-59, prof. geology, 1959—; invited prof. Geol. Fed. U. of Ouro Preto, Minas Gerais, Brazil, 1983-85; cons. Petroleo Brasileiro, 1969—, Yacimientos Petroliferos Fiscales, 1978—, Philippine Oil Devel. Co., 1970—. Author: Microscopic Sedimentary Petrography, 1972, Carbonate Depositional Models, 1983, Geology Emerging, 1984; editor: Sedimentary Rocks, 1975. Davy award U. Geneva, 1949, 54; Disting. Lectr. Am. Assn. Petroleum Geologists, 1959. Fellow Geol. Soc. Am.; mem. Soc. Econ. Paleontolgists and Mineralogists (councillor), Internat. Com. History Geol. Scis., U.S. Com. History of Geology, History of Earth Scis. Soc. (pres. 1984). Current Work: Devel. of depositional models for carbonates with computer and microfacies techniques; experimental simulation of generation of porosity and permeability at depth in major basins; analysis of historical development of geological concepts. Subspecialty: Sedimentology. Home: 709 W Delaware St Urbana IL 61801 Office: Dept Geology NHB 245 U Ill 1301 W Green St Urbana IL 61801

CARPENTER, CHARLES BERNARD, medical educator; b. Melrose, Mass., Sept. 11, 1933; s. Seymour Charles and Pauline Annette (Freeman) C.; m. Sandra Davis, Aug. 4, 1956; children: Bradford, Scott. A.B., Dartmouth Coll., 1955; M.D., Harvard U., 1958. Diplomate: Am. Bd. Internal Medicine, 1966. Research fellow, assoc., instr. Harvard U., 1962-70, asst. prof., 1970-73; assoc. prof. medicine Peter Bent Brigham Hosp., 1975-80, prof. medicine, 1980—; dir. Immunogenetics Lab., Brigham and Women's Hosp., Harvard U., 1980—; investigator Howard Hughes Med. Inst., 1973-80; mem. exec. com. New Eng. Organ Bank. Contbr. articles to profl. jours.; mem. editorial bd.: Am. Jour. Kidney Diseases, Jour. Human Immunology. Served to lt. USN, 1960-62. NIH research career devel. awardee, 1968-73. Mem. Assn. Am. Physicians, Am. Soc. Clin. Investigation, Transplantation Soc., Am. Soc. Transplant physicians, Am. Assn. Immunologists, Am. Soc. Nephrology, Am. Soc. Histocompatibility and Immunogenetics. Baptist. Current Work: Immunogenetics and transplanation. Subspecialties: Immunogenetics; Transplantation. Office: 75 Francis St Boston MA 02115

CARPENTER, CHARLES COLCOCK JONES, physician, educator; b. Savannah, Ga., Jan. 5, 1931; s. Charles Colcock Jones and Alexandra (Morrison) C.; m. Sally R. Fisher, Nov. 29, 1958; children—Charles Morrison, Murray Douglas, Andrew Fisher. A.B., Princeton, 1952; M.D., Johns Hopkins, 1956. Diplomate: Am. Bd. Internal Medicine (mem. bd. 1976—, exec. com. 1980—, chmn. 1983-84). Intern Johns Hopkins Hosp., 1956-57, resident, 1957-59, 61-62, practice medicine, specializing in infectious disease, Balt., 1962-73; asst. prof. medicine Johns Hopkins, 1962-67, asso. prof., 1967-69, prof., 1969-73; physician-in-chief Balt. City Hosps., 1969-73; prof., chmn. dept. medicine Case Western Res. Sch. Medicine, 1973—; physician-in-chief Case Western Res. Univ. Hosp., 1973—; dir. Cholera Research Program, Johns Hopkins Center Med. Research and Tng., Calcutta, India, 1962-64; chmn. cholera panel U.S.-Japan Coop. Med. Sci. Program, 1965-72; mem. U.S.-Japan Coop. Med. Sci. Program (U.S. del.), 1973—; mem. adv. com. Sch. Medicine Johns Hopkins U., 1982—; mem. Am. Bd. Med. Spltys., 1982—; mem. nat. adv. com. Allergy and Infectious Diseases Council, NIH. Trustee Internat. Center for Infectious Disease Research, Bangladesh, 1979. Served as sr. asst. surgeon USPHS, 1959-61. Fellow ACP; mem. Am. Soc. Clin. Investigation, Assn. Am. Physicians (sec. 1975-81, councillor 1981-86), Infectious Diseases Soc. Am., Johns Hopkins Soc. Scholars. Current Work: Chairman of department of medicine, with active involvement in clinical investigation, patient care and teaching; major research interest is immune mechanisms in enteric infections. Subspecialties: Infectious diseases; Internal medicine. Home: 2720 Dryden Rd Shaker Heights OH 44121

CARPENTER, JAMES MICHAEL, entomologist, educator; b. Youngstown, Ohio, Jan. 24, 1956; s. James Willard and Rose Ellen (Levitsky) C. B.S., Mich. State U., 1977; Ph.D., Cornell U., 1983. Fellow Smithsonian Instn., Washington, 1983-84; asst. prof. biology, asst. curator entomology Harvard U., Cambridge, Mass., 1984—. Contbr. articles to sci. publs. NSF fellow 1977; grantee NSF, 1982, 85, Sigma Xi, 1982; Fulbright Fellow, 1985. Fellow Willi

Hennig Soc.; mem. Soc. Systematic Zoology, Soc. Study of Evolution, Sigma Xi. Current work: Phylogenetic systematics of aculeate Hymenoptera, especially Vespidae; zoogeography; quantitative phyletic methods. Subspecialties: Systematics; Taxonomy. Office: Harvard U 26 Oxford St Cambridge MA 02138

CARPENTER, JOSEPH ANDREW, JR., research scientist; b. Washington, July 8, 1941; s. Joseph Andrew and Kathleen Adair (Moore) C.; m. Susan Ann Compton, June 20, 1964; children—Keri Adette, Timothy Benjamin. B.S. in Metall. Engring. with honors, Va. Poly. Inst., 1963; Ph.D. in Materials Engring. Sci., 1970, postgrad., 1970-71. Research scientist in automotive emissions catalysts Chrysler Corp., Highland Park, Mich., 1971-75; research scientist nuclear fuels and environ. impacts Oak Ridge Nat. Lab., 1975-79, mem. lab. program planning and analysis staff in analyses of energy-related research needs, 1979-80, tech. mgr. materials and tribology projects Energy Conversion and Utilization Techs. program Dept. Energy, 1981—. Contbr. to Barnwell Nuclear Fuel Plant Applicability Study, 1978. Active Oak Ridge PTA. Mem. Am. Soc. Metals (chmn. local chpt. 1982-83), Am. Ceramic Soc., Tau Beta Pi, Sigma Xi. Episcopalian. Club: Oak Ridge Country. Current work: Materials research for energy conservation. Subspecialty: Materials (engineering). Home: 145 Greystone Dr Oak Ridge TN 37830 Office: Oak Ridge Nat Lab PO Box X Oak Ridge TN 37831

CARPENTER, RICHARD AMON, chemist; b. Kansas City, Mo., Aug. 22, 1926; s. Harry Russell and Ina Marie (Garver) C.; m. Joanne Fisher, Aug. 14, 1948; children: Stephen Russell, Lynne, Wendy. B.S., U. Mo., 1948, M.A., 1949. Chemist Shell Oil Co., Wood River, Ill., 1949-51; asst. mgr. Midwest Research Inst., Kansas City, 1951-58, trustee, 1964-69, 75-79; mgr. Washington office Callery Chem. Co., 1958-64; sr. specialist in sci. and tech. Congl. Research Service, Library of Congress, Washington, 1964-69, chief environmental policy div., 1969-72; exec. dir. Commn. on Natural Resources, NRC, Nat. Acad. Scis., Washington, 1972-77; research asso. East-West Center, Honolulu, 1977—; vis. prof. environ. studies, Dartmouth, 1976. Editor: Assessing Tropical Forest Lands: Their Suitability for Sustainable Uses, 1981, Natural Systems for Development: What Planners Need to Know, 1983; Contbr. articles to profl. jours. Trustee Inst. Ecology, 1979-83; Mem. corp. vis. com. dept. civil engring. M.I.T., 1974-84; mem. internat. environ. programs com. NRC-Nat. Acad. Scis., 1980-83. Served with USAAF, 1945. Fellow Am. Inst. Chemists, AAAS; mem. Am. Chem. Soc., Ecol. Soc. Am., Internat. Council Sci. Unions (U.S. nat. com. for sci. on problems of environment 1984—), Sigma Xi, Sigma Chi. Presbyn. Club: Cosmos (Washington). Patentee in field. Current Work: Methods for acquiring and analyzing information about natural systems to be used in economic development planning and management. Subspecialties: Resource management; Ecosystems analysis. Home: 2419 Halekoa Dr Honolulu HI 96821 Office: 1777 East West Rd Honolulu HI 96848

CARR, DANIEL BARRY, endocrinologist, medical researcher; b. N.Y.C., Apr. 6, 1948; s. Andrew Joseph and Florence (Glassman) C.; m. Justine M. Meehan, Nov. 11, 1978; children: Nora, Rebecca. B.A., Columbia U., 1968, M.A., 1970, M.D., 1976. Diplomate Am. Bd. Internal Medicine (subsplty. Bd. Endocrinology and Metabolism). Intern Columbia-Presbyn. Med. Ctr., N.Y.C., 1976-78; resident med. service Mass. Gen. Hosp., Boston, 1978-79, endocrine fellow, 1979-82, staff physician endocrine unit, 1982—, clin. assoc. physician, clin. research ctr., 1982-84, clin. fellow anesthesia dept., 1984—, clin. asst. in medicine, 1983—; cons. internal medicine Mass. Eye and Ear Infirmary, 1980-82; instr. medicine Harvard U. Med. Sch., 1982-84, asst. prof., 1984—. Contbr. articles, research reports, essays, revs. to profl. lit. Daland fellow Am. Philos. Soc., 1980-82. Mem. AAAS, Am. Fedn. for Clin. Research, Soc. Neurosci., Internat. Anesthesia Research Soc. Alpha Omega Alpha. Club: Corinthians. Current Work: Clinical neuroendocrinology of opioid peptides with emphasis on implications for anesthesiology. Subspecialties: Neuroendocrinology; Anesthesiology. Office: Mass Gen Hosp Fruit St Boston MA 02114

CARR, EDWARD GARY, psychology educator and consultant; b. Toronto, Ont., Aug. 20, 1947; s. Saul and Anne (Goldsmith) C. B.A., U. Toronto, 1969; M.A., U. Calif.-San Diego, 1970, Ph.D., 1973. Adj. asst. prof. UCLA, 1973-76; asst. prof. SUNY-Stony Brook, 1976-81, assoc. prof., 1981-85, prof., 1985—; cons. psychologist Suffolk Child Devel. Ctr., Smithtown, N.Y., 1976—, Lega del Filo d'Oro, Ancona, Italy, 1984—; adv. bd. May Inst., Chatham, Mass., 1980—; bd. cons. Children's Treatment Program, Binghamton, 1980—; faculty sponsor Fulbright Program, Washington, 1980-82. Author: In Response to Aggression, 1981, How to Teach Sign Languange, 1982; contbr. articles to profl. jours. W.W. Found. fellow, 1969; Regents fellow U. Calif.-San Diego, 1969-73; UCLA fellow, 1973-76; recipient Cert. of Commendation Nat. Soc. Autistic Children, 1981. Mem. Am. Psychol. Assn., Assn. for Advancement Behavior Therapy, Soc. Research Child Devel., Nat. Soc. Autistic Children. Current Work: Research in experimental child psychopathology including studies of language disorders and analysis and remediation of severe behavior problems. Subspecialties: Behavioral psychology; Clinical psychology. Home: 28 Rolling Rd PO Box 851 Miller Place NY 11764Office: SUNY Dept Psychology Stony Brook NY 11794

CARR, GERALD PAUL, aerospace consultant, retired astronaut; b. Denver, Aug. 22, 1932; s. Thomas Ernest and Freda (Wright) C.; m. JoAnn Petrie, June 20, 1954 (div. 1977); children—Jennifer, Jamee, Jeffrey, John, Jessica, Joshua; m. Patricia Musick, Sept. 14, 1979. B.S. in Mech. Engring., U. Southern Calif., 1954, B.S. in Aero. Engring., U.S. Naval Postgrad. Sch., 1961; M.S. in Aero. Engring., Princeton U., 1962; D.Sc. (hon.) in Aero. Engring., Parks Coll., St. Louis U., 1976. Registered profl. engr., Tex. Commd. 2d lt. USMC, 1954, advanced through grades to col., 1973, ret., 1975; jet fighter pilot, U.S., Mediterranean, Far East, 1956-65; astronaut NASA, Houston, 1966-77; comdr. 3d Skylab Manned Mission, 1973-74; sr. v.p. Bovay Engrs., Inc., Houston, 1977-82; cons. Applied Research, Inc., Houston, 1980, sr. cons., 1982-84; project mgr., 300 in. telescope MacDonald Obs., U. Tex., Austin, 1983—; v.p. CAMUS, Inc., Houston, 1984—. Editor: (with others) Aerospace Crew Sta. Design, 1984. Bd. dirs. Houston POPS Orch., Sunsat Energy Council, Space Found. Recipient Group Achievement award NASA, 1971, Disting. Service medal NASA, 1974, Gold medal City of Chgo., 1974, Gold medal City of N.Y., 1974, Alumni Merit award U. Southern Calif., 1974, Disting. Eagle Scout award Boy Scouts Am., 1974, Robert J. Collier trophy, 1974, Robert H. Goddard Meml. trophy, 1975, FAI Gold Space medal, others. Fellow Am. Astronautical Soc. (Flight Achievement award 1975); mem. Marine Corps Assn., Marine Corps Aviation Assn., Nat. Soc. Profl. Engrs., Soc. Exptl. Test Pilots, Soc. Profl. Engrs., Nat. Space Inst., U. So. Calif. Alumni Assn., Tau Kappa Epsilon. Presbyterian. Current work: Space station design and development. Subspecialties: Aerospace engineering and technology; Human factors engineering.

CARR, RALPH W., mathematics educator; b. St. Paul, Apr. 19, 1946; s. Charles W. and Betty J. (Westman) C.; m. Linda M. Berscheid, June 3, 1979. B.A., Carleton Coll., 1968; Ph.D., U. Wis.-Madison. Asst. prof. math. St. Cloud (Minn.) State U., 1977—. Served with U.S. Army, 1969-72, Vietnam. NSF grad fellow U. Wis., 1968. Mem. Am. Math. Soc., Math. Assn. Am., Soc. Indsl. and Applied Math., AAAS, N.Y. Acad. Scis. Unitarian/Universalist. Current Work: Director of computer science. Subspecialties: Applied mathematics; Differential and integral equations. Home: 1821 11th Ave S Saint Cloud MN 56301 Office: Dept Math and Computer Sc St Cloud State Saint Cloud MN 56301

CARR, STEVEN MCEWIN, geneticist; b. San Jose, Calif., Sept. 13, 1953; s. Paul Francis and Hazel Bernice (McEwin) C. B.S., Calif. Poly. State U., 1975; Ph.D., U. Calif.-Berkeley, 1983. Research technologist Northwestern U., Chgo., 1975-76; teaching and research asst. U. Calif.-Berkeley, 1977-83, research biochemist, 1983; research scientist Tex. A&M U., College Station, 1984—. NIH biomed. grantee, 1984. Mem. Soc. for Study Evolution, Am. Soc. Mammalogists, ACLU. Current work: Genetic analysis of evolutionary phenomena, molecular genetic analysis of hybridization zones between species, use of mitochondrial DNA as probe in vertebrate population studies. Subspecialties: Evolutionary biology; Genetics and genetic engineering (biology). Office: Dept Wildlife and Fisheries Scis Tex A&M College Station TX 77843

CARR, THOMAS MICHAEL, spectroscopist; b. Shamokin, Pa., Mar. 5, 1953; s. Thomas Edward and Mary Irene (Novosel) C.; m. Debra Lorraine Sugar, June 22, 1985. B.S. in Chemistry, Elizabethtown Coll., 1975; M.S. in Chemistry, Case Western Res. U., 1977, Ph.D. in Chemistry, 1980. Research asst. U. Nijmegen, Netherlands, 1979-80; project chemist Dow Corning Corp., Midland, Mich., 1980-83, analytical specialist, 1983—; adj. instr. Saginaw Valley State Coll., Mich., 1983—. Contbr. articles to Spectroscopy Letters. Recipient Walt Brown Speech award Mich. Jaycees, 1982. Mem. Am. Chem. Soc., Soc. for Applied Spectroscopy, Midland Jaycees (bd. dirs. 1982-83, v.p. 1983-84), Sigma Xi. Republican. Roman Catholic. Current work: Characterization of organosilicon chemistry through the use of multi-nuclear NMR spectroscopy. Subspecialties: Nuclear magnetic resonance; Organometallics. Home: 4645 Orchard Manor Blvd Bay City MI 48706 Office: Analytical Research Dept Dow Corning Corp 026 3901 S Saginaw Rd Midland MI 48640

CARR, WILLIAM HOGE, JR., chemical engineering and nuclear fuel processing consultant; b. Princeton, W.Va., Jan. 31, 1921; s. William H. and Bertalee (Sackett) C.; m. Joy Hammitt, 1940 (div.); children: Melissa Carr Sullivan, Anne Carr Wackeen; m. Florence Louise Smith, Mar. 28, 1948; children: Robert A., William W. B.S. in Chem Engring, Va. Tech., 1943. Registered profl. engr., Tenn., S.C. Jr. engr. SAM Lab, Columbia U., N.Y.C., 1943-44; prodn. supr. Oak Ridge Gaseous Diffusion Plant, 1944-46; pilot plant engr. Oak Ridge Nat. Lab., 1946-49; devel. engr., 1954-70; research engr. and lab. comdg. office U.S. Army Chem. Corps, Md., Utah, Korea and Japan, 1949-53; devel. engr. Allied Gen. Nuclear Services, Barnwell, S.C., 1970-83; pvt. practice cons. engr., 1983—. Contbr. articles in field to profl. jours. Pres., chmn. bd. trustees Oak Ridge Hosp., 1964-70; vice chmn., bd. assocs. Hiwassee Coll., Tenn., 1968-70; bd. dirs. ORNL Credit Union, 1963-70; trustee Barnwell County Hosp., 1983—; pres. S.C. Lions Sight Conservation Assn., 1984—. Served to capt. U.S. Army, 1949-53. Mem. Am. Chem. Soc., Am. Inst. Chem Engrs., Nat. Soc. Profl. Engrs., Am. Nuclear Soc. Republican. Methodist. Lodges: Masons; Lions. Patentee diaphragm pumping system. Current Work: Nuclear fuel reprocessing; primary emphasis on safety analysis and on radioactive waste processing, storage, and disposal. Subspecialties: Chemical engineering; Hazardous waste disposal. Office: 1071 Donna St Williston SC 29853

CARRANO, ANTHONY VITO, cytogeneticist, researcher; b. N.Y.C., Mar. 22, 1942; s. Anthony and Geraldine Agnes (Salerno) C.; m. Elizabeth Patricia Hnatow, June 20, 1964; children: Christopher, Scott. B.S. in Chemistry, Rensselaer Poly. Inst., 1964; M.Bioradiology, U. Calif., Berkeley, 1970, Ph.D. in Biophysics, 1972. Postdoctoral fellow Argonne Nat. Lab., Ill., 1972-73; biomed. scientist Lawrence Livermore Nat. Lab., Calif., 1973—, sect. leader cell biology and mutagenesis, biomed. scis. div., 1980—; adj. prof. San Jose (Calif.) State U., 1980—. Mem. editorial bd. Radiation Research, 1977-80, Mutation Research, 1979—, Environ. Mutagenesis, 1979—, Cytogenetics and Cell Genetics, 1981—. Contbr. 100 articles to profl. publs. Served to capt. USMC, 1964-68. Mem. Environ. Mutagen Soc. (treas. 1983—), Am. Soc. Human Genetics, Am. Soc. Cell Biology, Radiation Research Soc., AAAS, Genetics Soc. Am., Genetic and Environ. Toxicology Assn. of No. Calif. (pres. 1979-80). Current Work: Mechanisms and significance of cytogenetic damage; organization and structure of the mammalian chromosome; relation between mutation/cytogenetic damage and cancer. Subspecialties: Genome organization; Cancer research (medicine). Office: PO Box 5507 Livermore CA 94550

CARRICK, WAYNE LEE, chemical company executive; b. Benton, Ark., Feb. 23, 1927; s. Dewell A. and Mabel (Coyle) C.; m. Bobbie R. Browning, June 19, 1949; children—David, Beverly, Kathryn, Patricia, Kevin. B.S., U. Ark., 1952, M.S., 1953, Ph.D., 1956. Research chemist Union Carbide, Bloomfield, N.J., 1954-56, group leader, 1956-65, major group leader, Bound Brook, N.J., 1965, assoc. dir., 1965-77, sr. research fellow, 1975-77; v.p. Chemplex, Rolling Meadows, Ill., 1977-85, Norchem, Rolling Meadows, 1985—. Patentee (12); author tech. papers. Served with USN, 1944-45. Mem. Am. Chem. Soc., Sigma Xi. Current work: Research management. Subspecialties: Polymer chemistry; Catalysis chemistry. Office: Norchem 3100 Golf Rd Rolling Meadows IL 60008

CARRIER, E. BERNARD, microbiologist, university dean; b. Ferriday, La., Dec. 26, 1929; s. Dewey H. and Ella L. (Bunch) C.; m. Pauline Erma Peak, Jan. 31, 1951; children: Ernest Bernard, Gail Christine Carrier Mason. B.S., Southeastern La. U, 1953; M.S., La. State U., 1961, Ph.D., 1963. Cert. specialist in pub. health bacteriology, Am. Soc. Microbiology. Med. lab. technologist Baton Rouge Gen. Hosp., 1953-60; mem. faculty Southeastern La. U., Hammond, 1961-74; dir. La. Office Fed. Affairs, Baton Rouge, 1974-77; asst. sec. La. Dept. Culture, Baton Rouge, 1977-80; dean Grad. Sch., Southeastern La. U., 1980—. Served in USAF, 1950-54. Mem. Am. Soc. Microbiology, La. Acad. Scis., Sigma Xi. Democrat. Baptist. Current Work: Medical microbiology, immunology and general microbiology. Subspecialties: Microbiology; Immunobiology and immunology. Office: 100 W Dakota St Hammond LA 70402

CARRIER, GEORGE FRANCIS, applied mathematics educator; b. Millinocket, Maine, May 4, 1918; s. Charles Mosher and Mary (Marcaux) C.; m. Mary Casey, June 30, 1946; children: Kenneth, Robert, Mark. M.E., Cornell U., 1939, Ph.D., 1944. From asst. prof. to prof. Brown U., 1946-52; Gordon McKay prof. mech. engring. Harvard U., 1952-72, T. Jefferson Coolidge prof. applied math., 1972—; mem. council Engring. Coll., Cornell U. Co-author: Functions of a Complex Variable, 1966, Ordinary Differential Equations, 1968, Partial Differential Equations, 1976; assoc. editor: Quar. Applied Math., Jour. Fluid Mechanics. Former trustee Rensselaer Poly. Inst., Troy. N.Y. Recipient Von Karman prize ASCE, 1977. Fellow Am. Acad. Arts and Scis.; hon. fellow Brit. Inst. Math. and Its Applications; hon. mem. ASME (Timoshenko medal 1978, Centennial medal 1980); mem. Nat. Acad. Scis. (award applied math. and mumerical analysis 1980), Soc. Indsl. and Applied Math. (Von Karman prize 1979), Am. Phys. Soc. (Fluid Dynamics prize 1984), Nat. Acad. Engring., Am. Philos. Soc. Current Work: Dynamics of Tsunamis and atmospheric vortices; growth and propagation of large fires; phenomena in internal combustion engines; centrifuge phenomena. Subspecialties: Fluid mechanics; Combustion processes. Office: Pierce Hall 311 Harvard Univ Cambridge MA 02138

CARRIGAN, CHARLES ROGER, research geophysicist; b. Pasadena, Calif., Sept. 7, 1949; s. Charles Francis and Alyce (Krosley) C.; m. Suzann Lundin, Feb. 21, 1976; 1 dau., Alisa Lynn. B.A., UCLA, 1971, M.S., 1973, Ph.D., 1977. Research fellow dept. geodesy and geophysics Cambridge U., 1977-78, 79; NATO fellow, 1978-79; research geophysicist Inst. Geophysics and Planetary Physics, UCLA, 1979-80; mem. tech. staff (Geophysics Research Div. 1541, Sandia Nat. Labs.), Albuquerque, 1980—; Chancellor's intern fellow UCLA, 1971, Chancellor's dissertation fellow, 1975; NATO postdoctoral fellow, 1977. Mem. Am. Geophys. Union, Sigma Xi. Club: Bible Study Fellowship (Albuquerque). Current Work: Natural convection in geophysical systems, laboratory studies of convective stability, fluid mechanics of volcanism, geophysical fluid dynamics, crustal volcanism, thermal convection. Subspecialties: Geophysics; Fluid mechanics. Office: Sandia Nat Labs PO Box 5800 Geophysics Research Div (1541) Albuquerque NM 87185

CARROLL, BARBARA ANNE, radiology educator; b. Beaumont, Tex., Oct. 20, 1945; s. Theron Demp and Annette Ione (Anderson) C. B.A., U. Tex.-Austin, 1967; M.D., Stanford U., 1972. Intern Stanford U., 1972-73, resident in radiology, 1973-76, fellow in ultrasound, 1974-76, instr. radiology, 1976-78, asst. prof., 1978-84, assoc. prof., 1984-85; assoc. prof. Duke U., 1985—; cons. NIH, Acuson, Mountain View, Calif., Diasonics, Inc., Fremont, Calif. Nat. Cancer Inst. awardee, 1981-83. Mem. Am. Inst. Ultrasound in Medicine, Am. Coll. Radiology, Soc. Radiologists in Ultrasound. Current Work: Development of ultrasound contrast agent; development of new, high frequency ultrasound equipment. Subspecialties: Diagnostic radiology; Imaging technology. Office: Dept Radiology Duke U Durham NC 27710

CARROLL, DANA, biochemist, educator; b. Palm Springs, Calif., Sept. 2, 1943; s. William Robert and Harriet (Dana) C.; m. Susan Slade, June 25, 1966; children: Adam Slade, Jessica Ann. B.A. in Chemistry, Swarthmore Coll., 1965; Ph.D., U. Calif.-Berkeley, 1970. Postdoctoral fellow Beatson Inst. Cancer Research, Glasgow, Scotland, 1970-72, Carnegie Instn. of Washington, Balt., 1972-75; asst. prof. microbiology, adj. asst. prof. biology U. Utah, Salt Lake City, 1975-81; assoc. prof. cellular, viral, and molecular biology U. Utah (Med. Sch.), adj. assoc. prof. biology, 1981—. Contbr. articles to profl. jours. Recipient Ivy award Swarthmore Coll., 1965; Jane Coffin Childs postdoctoral fellow, 1970-72; USPHS fellow, 1966-70, 73-75; Am. Cancer Soc. scholar, 1983. Mem. Am. Soc. Microbiology, AAAS, Sigma Xi, Phi Beta Kappa. Current Work: Eukaryotic gene structure and function; mechanisms of genetic recombination; recombinant DNA technology. Subspecialties: Genetics and genetic engineering (biology); Molecular biology. Office: Dept CVMB U Utah Med Sch Salt Lake City UT 84132

CARROLL, DYER EDMUND, mechanical engineer; b. Boston, June 4, 1921; s. Jeremiah Charles and Grace Mildred (Rice) C.; m. Betty Wilder, Nov. 23, 1921; children: Dyer Edmund, Nancy Wilder Carroll Doran. Cert. M.E., Lowell Inst., 1942; M.E., Northeastern U., 1953, B.A. in Engring. and Mgmt, 1963. Registered profl. engr., Mass. Supr. research Mut. Boiler and Machine Ins. Co., Boston, 1948-51, 54-65; chief metall. engr. Factory Mut. Engring. Corp., Norwood, Mass., 1965-68; pres. Carroll Engrs., Inc., Andover, Mass., 1968—. Chmn. Bd. of Appeal, Stoneham, Mass., 1962-64; mem. Stoneham Park Commn., 1953-56; active Little League, Boy Scouts Am. Served with USN, 1942-46. Mem. ASME, Am. Soc. for Non-destructive Testing, ASTM, Am. Soc. for Metals, Am. Legion. Republican. Roman Catholic. Current Work: Consulting engineering, design materials, testing and evaluation; failure analysis. Boiler, pressure vessel failures and explosions. Accident investigation and reconstruction: industrial, aircraft, automotive, marine. Subspecialties: Metallurgical engineering; Mechanical engineering. Home: 89 Spring St Stoneham MA 02180 Office: 200 Andover St Ballardvale MA 01810

CARROLL, FELIX ALVIN, JR., chemistry educator; b. High Point, N.C., Aug. 17, 1947; s. Felix Alvin and Addie R. (Doss) C.; m. L. Carol Crutchfield, July 15, 1972; children—Heather Elaine, Brandon Russell. B.S. with highest honors in Chemistry, U. N.C., 1969; Ph.D. in Organic Chemistry, Calif. Inst. Tech., 1973. Polymer synthesis chemist Burlington Industries Research Center, Greensboro, N.C., summers, 1968,69; asst. prof. chemistry Davidson (N.C.) Coll., 1972—80, assoc. prof., 1980—. Contbr. articles on chemistry to profl. jours. Mem. Am. Chem. Soc., Inter-Am. Photochem. Soc., AAAS, N.C. Acad. Sci. Club: Wildcat Investment (Davidson). Current Work: Kinetics and mechanisms of photochemical reactions, applications of heavy atom effects, chemical conversion and storage of solar energy, photochemical control of pH. Subspecialties: Photochemistry; Organic chemistry. Office: Chemistry Dept Davidson Coll Davidson NC 28036

CARROLL, JOHN STEPHEN, psychology educator, researcher; b. Bklyn., Nov. 5, 1948; s. Hyman Benjamin and Estelle (Silverman) C.; m. Helaine Dankner, June 13, 1970; children: Michael David, Deborah Ann. S.B. in Physics, M.I.T., 1970; M.A. in Social Psychology, Harvard U., 1972, Ph.D., 1973. Asst. prof. psychology Carnegie Mellon U., 1973-78; assoc. prof. Loyola U., Chgo., 1978-83; assoc. prof. Sloan Sch. Mgmt. MIT, Cambridge, 1983—; vis. assoc. prof. Grad. Sch. Bus. U. Chgo., 1981-82; cons. Decision Assocs., Chgo., 1982—. Editor: (with J.W. Payne) Cognition & Social Behavior, 1976, (with Frieze and Bar-Tal) New Approaches to Social Problems, 1979. NSF fellow, 1970-72; NSF grantee, 1975-77, 85-87; NIMH grantee, 1978-84. Fellow Am. Psychol. Assn.; mem. Soc. Exptl. Social Psychology, Am. Psychology Law Soc. (dir. 1982—). Current Work: Research on decision processes of criminal justice personnel (judges, parole boards), attribution theory, decision sciences. Subspecialties: Social psychology; Cognition. Office: Sloan Sch Mgmt MIT 50 Memorial Dr Cambridge MA 02139

CARROLL, KENNETH KITCHENER, biochemist, nutrition researcher; b. Carrolls, N.B., Can., Mar. 9, 1923; s. Lawrence and Sarah Della (Estey) C.; m. Margaret Aileen Ronson, Aug. 26, 1950; children—Douglas, Stephen, James. B.Sc., U. N.B. (Can.), 1943, M.Sc., 1946; M.A., U. Toronto (Can.), 1946; Ph.D., U. Western Ont. (Can.), 1949. Postdoctoral fellow U. Western Ont., London, 1949-52; Cambridge U., Eng., 1952-54; asst. prof. U. Western Ont., 1954-57, assoc. prof. med. research, 1957-65, prof., acting head dept. med. research, 1965-68, prof. biochemistry, 1968—. Contbr. chpts. to books, articles to profl. jours. Leader Scouts Can., London, 1963-70, exec. com., 1971—. Recipient Postdoctoral fellow Merck & Co., 1952-53; postdoctoral fellow Agrl. Research Council, 1953-54; Chem. Inst. Can. fellow; Royal Soc. Can. fellow, 1982; Career Investigator grantee Med. Research Council Can., 1963. Mem. Can. Biochem. Soc., Can. Soc. Nutritional Sci. (sec. 1965-67, pres. 1978-79) Can. Fedn. Biol. Soc. (hon. sec. 1967-71), Am. Oil Chemists Soc., Internat. Union Nutritional Scis. (chmn. commn. on nutrition and cancer). Baptist. Current work: Role of nutrition in cancer and heart disease; distribution and metabolism of fatty compounds. Subspecialties: Biochemistry (medicine); Nutrition (medicine). Home: 561 St George St London ON N6A 3B9 Canada Office: Dept Biochemistry U Western Ontario London ON N6A 5C1 Canada

CARROLL, LEE FRANCIS, elec. engr., cons.; b. Berlin, N.H., Oct. 14, 1937; s. Alton Francis and Mary Elizabeth (Cushing) C.; m. Judith A. Magoun, Apr. 9, 1960; children: Shawn, Pamela, Bruce. B.S.E.E., Northeastern U., 1960. Registered profl. engr., Maine, N.H., Vt., Mass., N.Y., Pa., Va., La., Tex. Maintenance engr. Am. Optical Co., Southbridge, Mass., 1964-65; elec. engr. Ga. Pacific Corp., Lyons Falls, N.Y., 1965-66; chief elec. engr. Brown Co., Berlin, N.H., 1966-70, Wright Pierce Barnes & Wyman, Topsham, Maine, 1970-73; propr. L.F. Carroll, P.E. Elec. Cons., Gorham, N.H., 1973—. Commr. Water and Sewer Dept., Gorham; pres. Gorham Devel. Corp. Mem. Nat. Soc. Profl. Engrs., IEEE, Illumination Engring. Soc., Nat. Fire Protection Assn. Current Work: Co-generation electrical design-utility interface coordination; alternate fuel (wood chip-waste) power plants. Subspecialty: Electrical engineering. Office: 1 Exchange St Gorham NH 03581

CARROLL, WILLIAM FINCH, engineering educator, army officer; b. Rochester, N.Y., June 6, 1935; s. Francis Lee and Frieda Elisabeth (Finch) C.; m. Susan Dean Epley, May 28, 1960 (dec. 1977); children—Jeffrey L., Dorothy J., Petra A., Daniel W.; m. Kathleen Therese Kern, Nov. 20, 1982. B.S., U.S. Mil. Acad., 1957; M.S. in Engring., U. Ill., 1961, Ph.D. in Civil Engring., 1963; postdoctoral student U. Tex., Austin, 1981-82. Registered profl. engr. Ill., N.Y., Calif. Commd. 2d lt. U.S. Army, 1957, advanced through grades to col.; served with C.E. in Korea, Vietnam, Fed. Republic Germany; prof. mechanics U.S. Mil. Acad., West Point, N.Y., 1976—, head dept. mechanics, 1984—. Decorated Legion of Merit. Mem. ASCE, Earthquake Engring. Research Inst. Democrat. Current work: Wave propagation in solid materials as applied to geotechnical prospecting. Subspecialties: Structural engineering; Solid mechanics. Office: Dept Mechanics US Mil Acad West Point NY 10996

CARRUTHERS, PETER AMBLER, physicist, educator; b. Lafayette, Ind., Oct. 7, 1935; s. Maurice Earl and Nila (Ambler) C.; m. Jean Ann Breitenbecher, Feb. 26, 1955; children—Peter, Debra, Kathryn; m. Lucy J. Marston, July 10, 1969; m. Cornelia B. Dobrovolsky, June 20, 1981. B.S., Carnegie Inst. Tech., 1957, M.S., 1957; Ph.D., Cornell U., 1960. Asst. prof. Cornell U., 1961-63, asso. prof., 1963-67, prof. physics, atomic and solid state physics, nuclear studies, 1967-73; div. leader, theoretical div. Los Alamos Sci. Lab., 1973-80, sr. fellow, 1980—; vis. asso. prof. Calif. Inst. Tech., 1965, vis. prof., 1969-70, 77-78; mem. physics adv. panel NSF, 1975-80, chmn. 1978-80; Trustee Aspen Center for Physics, 1976—, chmn. exec. com., 1977-79, chmn. bd. trustees, 1979-82; mem. High Energy Physics Adv. Panel, 1978—; mem. com. on U.S.-USSR cooperation in physics Nat. Acad. Scis., 1978-82. Author: (with R. Brout) Lectures on the Many-Electron Problem, 1963, Introduction to Unitary Symmetry, 1966, Spin and Isospin in Particle Physics, 1971. Recipient Merit award Carnegie Mellon U., 1980; Alfred P. Sloan research fellow, 1963-65; NSF sr. postdoctoral fellow U. Rome, 1967-68. Fellow Am. Phys. Soc., AAAS. Current work: Elementary particle physics; statistical physics. Subspecialties: Statistical physics; Theoretical physics. Home: 1459 46th St Los Alamos NM 87544 Office: T-DO MS B285 Los Alamos Nat Lab Los Alamos NM 87545

CARSON, DAVID BROOKS, petroleum geologist; b. Dayton, Ohio, Mar. 29, 1953; s. L. Turner and Mary M. (Wening) C.; m. Patricia Ann Boehm, Apr. 17, 1981. B.S. in Geology, U. Dayton, 1975; M.S., N.E. La. U., 1977. Registered profl. geologist. Teaching asst. N.E. La. U., Monroe, 1975-77; geologist Law Engring., Atlanta, 1977-78; field office mgr., Hattiesburg, Miss., 1978-80; chief geologist Kepco, Inc., Pitts., 1980—; lectr. in field. Grantee N.E. La. U., 1976-77, Ark. Geol. Survey, 1977. Mem. Geol. Soc. Am., Am. Assn. Petroleum Geologists, N.Y. Acad. Sci., Soc. Engring. Geologists, Pitts. Soc. Petroleum Geologists. Current work: Petroleum geology—Appalachian basin; nuclear waste disposal—Gulf Coast Salt Domes, 1977-80. Subspecialties: Petroleum engineering; Geophysics. Office: Kepco Inc 436 Blvd Allies Pittsburgh PA 15219

CARSON, GEORGE STEPHEN, computer scientist; b. Lakewood, Ohio, Dec. 7, 1948; s. Sylvester and Madelyn Frances (Melson) C.; m. Brenda Geraldine Whaley, Feb. 7, 1969; children: Stephen, Elizabeth. B.S., U. Tenn., 1970; Ph.D., U. Calif.-Riverside, 1975. Mem. tech. staff B-1 Div. Rockwell Co., 1976-77, GTE Labs., Northlake, Ill., 1977-78; sr. assoc. prin. engr. Harris Govt. Electronics Systems Div., 1978-81; pres. GSC Assocs., Hawthorne, Calif., 1981—; tchr. UCLA Extension, 1981—. Served to capt. U.S. Army, 1974-75. Mem. IEEE (assoc. editor), IEEE Computer Soc., Am. Math. Soc., Assn. Computing Machinery, Math. Assn. Am., AAAS, Am. Nat. Standards

Inst. (mem. computer graphics standards com.), Sigma Xi. Current Work: Computer systems engring., graphics, databases, distributed systems, real-time systems. Subspecialties: Distributed systems and networks; Graphics, image processing, and pattern recognition. Office: 13663 Prairie Ave Suite B Hawthorne CA 90250

CARSON, HAMPTON LAWRENCE, genetics educator; b. Phila., Nov. 5, 1914; s. Joseph and Edith (Bruen) C.; m. Meredith Shelton, Aug. 14, 1937; children: Joseph II, Edward Bruen. A.B., U. Pa., 1936, Ph.D., 1943. Instr. dept. zoology U. Pa., Phila., 1938-42; mem. faculty dept. biology Washington U., St. Louis, 1943-70, prof. biology, 1956-70; prof. genetics U. Hawaii, Honolulu, 1970—; vis. prof. biology U. Sao Paulo, Brazil, 1951, 77. Author: Heredity and Human Life, 1963; contbr. articles to profl. jours. Trustee B.P. Bishop Mus., Honolulu. Fulbright research scholar zoology U. Melbourne, Australia, 1961. Mem. Nat. Acad. Scis., Am. Acad. Arts and Scis., Genetics Soc. (pres. 1982), Soc. Study of Evolution (pres. 1971), Am. Soc. Naturalists (pres. 1973), AAAS, Phi Beta Kappa, Sigma Xi. Current Work: Genetics and evolution. Subspecialties: Evolutionary biology; Genetics and genetic engineering (biology). Home: 2001 Ualakaa St Honolulu HI 96822 Office: U Hawaii Honolulu HI 96822

CARSON, JAMES MATTHEW, mech. engr.; b. Camden, N.J., Feb. 14, 1944. B.S., U.S. Air Force Acad., 1966; M.S., Drexel U., 1972, Ph.D., 1978. Registered profl. engr., Colo. Commd. 2d lt. USAF, 1966, advanced through grades to capt., 1969; engr. (Air Force Materials Lab.), Wright-Patterson AFB, Ohio, 1966-70; asst. prof. (U.S. Air Force Acad.), 1972-76; ret. active duty, 1976; now lt. col. USAFR; research engr. DuPont, Seaford, Del., 1978-80; sr. research engr. N. Mex. Engring. Research Inst., U. N. Mex., 1980—. Contbr. articles to profl. jours., confs. Mem. ASME, Sigma Xi, Tau Beta Pi, Pi Tau Sigma, Sigma Xi. Current Work: Applications of applied mechanics techniques to solve civil engring. research problems; current techniques include pattern analysis, pattern recognition, stats. and exptl. methods. Subspecialties: Theoretical and applied mechanics; Materials. Home: 902 Ganado Ct SE Albuquerque NM 87123 Office: U N Mex N Mex Engring Research Inst Box 25 Albuquerque NM 87131

CARSON, PAUL LANGFORD, radiological physicist, educator. B.S., Colo. Coll., 1965; Ph.D., U. Ariz., 1972. Diplomate: Am. Bd. Radiology. Instr. dept. radiology U. Colo. Sch. Medicine, Denver, 1972—, asst. prof., 1973-78, assoc. prof., 1978-81; dir. radiol. physics and engring. dept. radiology U. Mich. Hosps., Ann Arbor, 1981—, assoc. prof., 1981-84, prof., 1984—. Current Work: Physics of Diagnostic ultrasound, new technology, nuclear magnetic resonance imaging, general radiological physics. Subspecialty: Imaging technology.

CARSON, STEVEN, educator, toxicologist, pharmacologist, cons., researcher; b. Bklyn., Oct. 17, 1925; s. David and Rebecca (Kraiewicz) C.; married Aug. 22, 1948; children: Ellen J., Susan L. Carson Friedman. B.S., Washington U., St. Louis, 1948; M.S. in Sci. Edn, N.Y.U., 1950, Ph.D., 1958. With Pub. Health Research Inst., N.Y.C., 1948; with Endo Labs., Inc., N.Y.C., 1950-58, Food & Drug Research Labs., Inc., N.Y.C., 1958-72, Biometrics Testing, Inc., Englewood Cliffs, N.J., 1972-75, Toxi Con Assocs., N.Y.C., 1975-79; assoc. prof. St. John's U. Coll. Pharmacy and Allied Professions, N.Y.C., 1979—. Served with U.S. Army, 1942-46. Fellow Am. Inst. Chemists, Royal Soc. Health, Soc. Cosmetic Chemists (Lit. award 1964); mem. Am. Soc. Pharmacology and Exptl. Therapeutics, Clin. Soc. Exptl. Therapeutics, Harvey Soc., Internat. Soc. Immunopharmacology, Soc. Toxicology, European Soc. Toxicology. Club: Chemists (N.Y.C.). Current Work: Effects of drugs, foods, cosmetics, and chemicals on behavioural responses of tissues, organs, and organisms; relevance to ultimate safe use in/by man. Subspecialties: Toxicology (medicine); Pharmacology. Home: PO Box 373 Ryder Sta Brooklyn NY 11234 Office: St John's U Coll Pharmacy Jamaica NY 11439

CARSON, VIRGINIA ROSALIE GOTTSCHALL, biologist; b. Pitts., Jan. 22, 1936; d. Walter Carl and Rosalie Madelaide (Paulin) G.; m. John Richard Carson, June 12, 1960; children: Margaret Rosalie, Kenneth Robert. Student, Swarthmore Coll., 1953-57; B.A., Calif. State U., Los Angeles, 1960, M.A., 1965; Ph.D., UCLA, 1970. Research aide Calif. Inst. Tech., Pasadena, 1958-60; asst. clin. research chemist Magaw Labs., Glendale, Calif., 1960-64; mental health trainee Brain Research Inst. UCLA, 1965-69; NIH postdoctoral trainee, 1972-74; asst. prof. biology Chapman Coll., Orange, Calif., 1971-77, assoc. prof., 1977-83, prof., 1983—, chairperson div. natural scis., 1983—; assoc. prof. So. Calif. Coll. Optometry, Fullerton, 1979-83; assoc. research pharmacologist U. Calif., Irvine, 1981—, asst. research pharmacologist, 1972-81. Contbr. articles to profl. jours. Recipient Outstanding Faculty Mem. award Chapman Coll., 1979-80; Chapman Coll. research fellow, 1983—. Mem. AAAS, Am. Pharmacol. Assn., Am. Soc. Pharmacology and Exptl. Therapeutics, IEEE, Soc. Neuroscience, Iota Sigma Pi. Republican. Presbyterian. Current Work: Physiological behavioral and neurochemical effects of alcohol and aging. Subspecialties: Physiology (biology); Neuropharmacology.

CARSRUD, ALAN LEE, consulting research psychologist; b. Denver, July 23, 1946; s. George Edward and Clara Lee (Jones) C.; 1 son, Nichel David Victor. Asst. prof. psychology SUNY-Brockport, 1973-75; asst. prof. Tex. A&M U., 1975-77; coordinator psychol. services and research Travis State Sch., Tex. Dept. Mental Health/Mental Retardation, Austin, 1977-79; research assoc., cons. psychologist Robert Helmreich, Inc. (indsl. psychologists), Austin, 1980-83; research assoc. dept. psychology U. Tex.-Austin, 1981-83, lectr. dept. mgmt., 1982—; cons. in field, 1978—; mem. adv. com. on supervision standards Tex. Bd. Examiners Psychologists, 1979-80, mem. adv. com. on profl. and ethical exams., 1981-82. Author: (with others) Study Guide and Instructor's Manual for Lindzey,Hall, and Thompson: Psychology, 2d edit, 1978; contbr. (with others) articles to profl. publs. NDFA fellow, 1968-72; Eastern Psychol. Assn. grantee, 1971; U. N.H. Teaching and Learning Council grantee, 1972; grantee Am. Psychol. Assn. and Nat. Council Psi Chi, 1973-77; Research Found. SUNY grantee-in-aid, 1974; faculty research fellow, 1974; Research Found. Tex. A&M U. mini-grantee, 1977; Tex. Dept. Mental Health and Mental Retardation grantee, 1979; IBM-Inst. Assn. Mgmt. Cos. grantee, 1984. Mem. Am. Psychol. Assn. (grantee 1979), Eastern Psychol. Assn., Southeastern Psychol. Assn., Acad. Mgmt., Sigma Xi, Alpha Kappa Delta. Current Work: Effects of competition and personality traits on complex task performance; relationship of group think to personality characteristics of decision makers, or achievement motivation, scholastic aptitude and personality to academic performance; social, psychological and environmental variables affecting outcome of psychotherapeutic treatment; analysis of complex organizational behavior and its relationship to personality factors. Subspecialties: Social psychology; Applied social/personality psychology. Home: 4702 Sinclaire St Austin TX 78758Office: Dept Mgmt U Tex Austin TX 78712

CARSTEN, MARY E., biochemist, physiologist, educator; b. Berlin, Mar. 2, 1926; d. Paul and Frida (Born) Carsten; m. Don Marlin, Apr. 23, 1964 (dec. 1981). A.B., NYU, 1946, M.S., 1948, Ph.D., 1951. Instr., NYU, 1952-53; research assoc. Columbia U., N.Y.C., 1953-55; asst. research biochemist UCLA, 1956-61, assoc. research biochemist, 1961-63, assoc. prof. physiology, 1963-70, prof. Ob-gyn, 1970—; mem. Com. Vis. Scholars, Los Angeles, 1960-63, Chancellor's Adv. Com. on Status of Women, Los Angeles, 1981-83, Status of Women in Medicine, Los Angeles, 1981—. Contbg. author to med. books. Fellow, Am. Cancer Soc., 1955-57, Nat. Found. Infantile Paralysis fellow 1954-55; recipient Established investigator award Los Angeles County Heart Assn., 1961-64, Disting. Service award 1963-65; Research Devel. award USPHS, 1964-74. Mem. Am. Soc. Biol. Chemists, Am. Physiol. Soc., Soc. for Gynecol. Investigation, Sigma Xi. Current work: Research, publications on calcium transport in smooth muscle; regulation of uterine contractility; prostaglandins; teaching of endocrinology of pregnancy and parturition. Subspecialties: Biochemistry (medicine); Reproductive endocrinology. Home: 624 N Highland Ave Los Angeles CA 90036 Office: UCLA Dept ob-Gyn Sch Medicine Los Angeles CA 90024

CARSTENSEN, EDWIN LORENZ, biophysicist, biomedical engineer, engineering educator; b. Oakdale, Nebr., Dec. 8, 1919; s. August Hans and Opal Lois (Norwood) C.; m. Pam McDonald, 1947; children—Richard L., Allen B., Laura L., Loretta D., Christina M. B.S., Nebr. State Tchrs. Coll., 1941; M.S., Case Inst. Tech., 1947; Ph.D., U. Pa.-Phila., 1955. Mem. sci. staff Columbia U. Div. of War Research, Orlando, Fla., 1942-45; head lab. sect. U.S. Naval-Underwater Sound Ref. Lab., Orlando, 1945-48; research assoc., prof. elec. engring. U. Pa.-Phila., 1948-55; prin. investigator U.S. Army Biol. Labs., Frederick, Md., 1956-61; assoc. prof. elec. engring. U. Rochester, 1961-73, prof. 1973—, prof. radiol. biology and biophysics, 1981—; cons. in field. Contbr. numerous articles to sci. jours. Fellow Acoust. Soc. Am., IEEE, Am. Inst. Ultrasound Medicine; mem. Biophys. Soc., Biomed. Engring. Soc. Democrat. Current work: Ultrasonic and dielectric properties of biological materials; effects of electric and ultrasonic fields on living things. Subspecialties: Biophysics (biology); Biomedical engineering. Home: 103 Eastland Ave Rochester NY 14618 Office: Dept Elec Engring U Rochester Rochester NY 14627

CARSWELL, ALLAN IAN, physics educator; b. Toronto, Ont., Can., Oct. 4, 1933; s. Duncan and Margaret (McAskill) C.; m. Helen Alexandra Aird, June 2, 1956; children—Donald, Ruth, Diane. B. Applied Sci., U. Toronto, 1956, M.A., 1957, Ph.D., 1960. NRC fellow U. Amsterdam, Netherlands, 1960-61; dir. optical physics RCA Research Labs., Montreal, P.Q., 1961-68; prof. physics York U., Toronto, Ont., 1968—; founder, pres. Optech Inc., Toronto, 1974—; mem. Internat. Radiation Commn., 1984—. Contbr. articles to sci. and tech. jours. Fellow Royal Soc.Can., Can. Aeronautics and Space Inst.; mem. Can. Assn. Physicists (dir. corp. mems. 1982-84, pres. 1985—), Am. Meteorol. Soc., Optical Soc. Am., Assn. Profl. Engrs. Ont. Current work: Laser radar (lidar) studies of the atmosphere; atmospheric optics; laser systems; remote sensing. Subspecialties: Laser radar; Atmospheric physics. Office: York U Dept Physics 4700 Keele St Downsview ON M3J 1P3 Canada

CARTER, BENJAMIN DUDLEY, nuclear engineer; b. Lake Wales, Fla., Apr. 16, 1952; s. Bobby and Shirley (Cresse) C.; m. Sandra D. Earl, June 15, 1974; 1 son, Brian Dudley. B.S., U. Fla., 1974, M.E. Nuclear, 1977. Research asst. U. Fla., Gainesville, 1974-79, 8081; sr. research engr. RTS Labs., Inc., Gainesville, 1979-80; sr. resident startup engr. Combustion Engring., Windsor, Conn., 1981—. Inventor nuclear pumped helium-neon laser, ENRAD device. Van Dorn scholar, 1973. Mem. Am. Nuclear Soc., Tau Beta Pi. Democrat. Current Work: Startup, low power physics and power acention testing-nuclear power plants. Subspecialty: Nuclear engineering. Office: 1000 Prospect Hill Rd Windsor CT 06095

CARTER, JEFF CROSSETT, computer scientist; b. Washington, Apr. 12, 1952; s. William Allen and Jean (Crossett) C.; m. Harriet Haynes, Jan. 2, 1955; 1 son: David. Student, Clarkson Coll. Tech., 1974-77; B.S. in Elec. and Computer Engring, Rochester Inst. Tech., postgrad., 1978—. Tech. specialist Xerox Corp., Rochester, N.Y., 1977—. Mem. IEEE, Computer Soc., Assn. for Computing Machinery. Current Work: Development of O.S. for distributed computer controls. Engaged in development of high level language, architecture and communications of the O.S. environment for distributed computer based control systems. Subspecialties: Distributed systems and networks; Operating systems. Office: Xerox Corp 800 Phillips Rd Webster NY 14580

CARTER, JOHN PAUL, corrosion scientist, electrochemist; b. Pitts., Sept. 26, 1930; s. George Regis and Ethel (Hughes) C. B.S. in Chemistry, U. Pitts., 1953. Cert. corrosion specialist. Asst. technologist U.S. Steel, Pitts., 1955-61; research chemist U.S. Bur. Mines, Avondale, Md., 1961—. Editor and contbg. author: Solving Corrosion and Scaling Problems in Geothermal Systems, 1984; also articles. Served with U.S. Army, 1953-55, Korea. Mem. Am. Chem. Soc., Am. Soc. Metals (chpt. treas. 1970-72), ASTM, Electrochem. Soc., Nat. Assn. Corrosion Engrs. (chmn. sect. T-2E 1979-85, sec. sect. T-2 1984—), Soc. Am. Mil. Engrs., Res. Officers Assn. (dept. pres. 1981-82), VFW (jr. vice comdr. post 1968-69). Roman Catholic. Current work: Effects of acid rain on materials; corrosion mechanisms of stainless steels during acid pickling; high temperature corrosion; corrosion in fluids at their critical temperatures. Subspecialties: Corrosion; Inorganic chemistry. Home: 3366 Toledo Terr Apt A Hyattsville MD 20782 Office: US Bur Mines 4900 La Salle Rd Avondale MD 20782

CARTER, LELAND LAVELLE, nuclear engineer, physicist; b. Oberlin, Kans., Nov. 27, 1937; s. LaVelle Wilford and Della Belle (Kathka) C.; m. Gerry L. Lindley, June 7, 1958; children: Carol Lynn, Michael Lee, Linda Marie, Wayne Mark. B.A., N.W. Nazarene Coll., Nampa, Idaho, 1961; M.S., U. Wash., Seattle, 1964, Ph.D., 1969. Scientist Battelle Nat. Lab., Richland, Wash., 1962-65; nuclear engr. Los Alamos Nat. Lab., 1969-77, alt. group leader, 1973-77, cons., 1978—; fellow engr. Hanford Engring. Devel. Lab., Richland, Wash., 1977—. Author: Particle-Transport Simulation with the Monte Carlo Method, 1975. AEC trainee, 1965-69. Mem. Am. Nuclear Soc. (mem. exec. com. 1980-84). Republican. Nazarene. Current Work: Neutronics and shielding for fusion facilities and fast breeder reactors and the development and application of the Monte Carlo method; previously was alternate group leader of the Monte Carlo Group at Los Alamos National Laboratory. Subspecialties: Nuclear engineering; Numerical analysis (computer science). Home: 2417 Michael Ave Richland WA 99352 Office: Hanford Engineering Development Laboratory PO Box 1970 Richland WA 99352

CARTER, MARY KATHLEEN, retired pharmacologist; b. Franklinton, La., July 11, 1922; d. Elijah Augustus and Ora Victoria (Kemp) C. B.A., Newcomb Coll. Tulane U., 1949, M.S., 1953; Ph.D., Vanderbilt U., 1955. Postdoctoral fellow U. Kans., 1955-57; instr. Tulane Med. Sch., 1957-59, asst., then assoc. prof., 1959-73, prof., 1973-84, prof. emeritus, 1985—. Contbr. articles to profl. jours. USPHS postdoctoral awardee, 1955-57; sr. research career awardee, 1957-61. Mem. Am. Soc. Pharmacology and Exptl. Therapeutics, Soc. Exptl. Biology and Medicine, Am. Soc. Nephrology. Democrat. Baptist. Current Work: Renal function studies related to effects of autonomic nervous system agents on electrolyte excretion. Subspecialties: Pharmacology; Nephrology. Home: Route 3 Box 724 Kentwood LA 70444

CARTER, ROBERT LAWRENCE, chemistry educator, administrator; b. Cleve., July 31, 1944; s. James Harwood and Helen (Borth) C.; m. Penelope A. Woods, July 9, 1966; 1 child, Geoffrey Woods. B.A., Coll. Wooster, 1966; Ph.D., U. Kans., 1970. Asst. prof. chemistry U. Mass.-Boston, 1970-76, assoc. prof., 1976—, assoc. provost, 1983—; vis. prof. Dartmouth Coll., Hanover, N.H., 1971-73. Contbr. articles to sci. publs., chpt. to book. Faculty devel. grantee, U. Mass., 1979, 82, computer devel. Title III grantee, 1982-83. Mem. Am. Chem. Soc., AAAS, Boston Computer Soc., Sigma Xi, Phi Lambda Upsilon. Mem. United Ch. of Christ. Current work: Structural investigations of phases changes in ionic compunds; Raman spectroscopy; ferroelectrics; applications of group therapy. Subspecialties: Inorganic chemistry; Laser spectroscopy. Office: U Mass Harbor Campus Boston MA 02125

CARTER, ROBERT LEROY, engineer, educator; b. Leavenworth, Kans., Aug. 22, 1918; s. Joseph LeRoy and Viola Elizabeth (Hayner) C.; m. Jewell M. Long, June 3, 1941; children: Roberta, Benjamin, Judy Meadows, Frederick, Camille Ronchetto. B.S. in Engring. Physics, U. Okla., Norman, 1941; Ph.D., Duke U., 1949. Registered profl. engr., Mo. Tesing technician Eastman Kodak Co., Rochester, N.Y., 1940-42; physicist Tenn. Eastman Co., Oak Ridge, 1945-46; engring. group leader, research specialist Atomics Internat., Canoga Park, Calif., 1949-63; vis. scientist Los Alamos Sci. Lab., 1968-69; prof. elec. engring. and nuclear engring. U. Mo., Columbia, 1962—; commr. Gov.'s Low Level Radioactive Waste Task Force, Jefferson City, Mo., 1981—. Contbr. articles to profl. jours. Trustee Mo. Soc. Profl. Engrs. Edn. Found., Jefferson City, 1982—. Served with AUS, 1942-45, PTO. Mem. Am. Phys. Soc., Nat. Soc. Profl. Engrs., Mo. Soc. Profl. Engrs. (pres. chpt. 1977-78, state dir. 1978-80), Am. Nuclear Soc. (mem. nat. program com. 1973-77), Am. Soc. Engring. Edn. Republican. Methodist. Current Work: Examining variety of applications of cryogenic techniques to engineering practice. Subspecialties: Nuclear fission; Nuclear fusion. Home: 1311 Parkridge Dr Columbia MO 65201 Office: Dept Elec Engring U Mo Columbia MO 65211

CARTER, TIMOTHY HOWARD, microbiologist, educator; b. Los Angeles, Nov. 6, 1944; s. Everett and Cecile (Doudna) C.; m. Jocklyn Armstrong, Dec. 31, 1976; children—Benjamin, Jonathan. A.B., Harvard Coll., 1966; Ph.D., Princeton U., 1972. Postdoctoral fellow Pa. Plan to Develop Scientists in Med. Research, U. Pa., Phila., 1972-73; postdoctoral fellow Mattheson Found., 1973-74, Nat. Cancer Inst., 1974-75, Columbia U. Coll. Physicians and Surgeons, N.Y.C., 1973-75; asst. prof. Pa. State U. Med. Sch., Hershey, 1975-78; asst. prof. dept. biol. scis. St. John's U., N.Y.C., 1978-81, assoc. prof., 1981—, cons. in field; sci. adv. bd. Nuclear and Genetic Tech., Inc., 1982—. Contbr. chpts. to books, articles to jours.; also musician. Research grantee Nat. Cancer Inst., NIH, 1978-82, 84—, NOAA, 1984—. Mem. Am. Soc. Microbiology; mem. Am. Soc. Biol. Chemists; Mem. Am. Soc. Virology, N.Y. Acad. Scis., Sigma Xi. Current Work: Regulation of gene expression and action; molecular biology of adenovirus replication; mechanism of viral oncogenesis; interaction of viruses with carcinogens, growth regulators, tumor promoters. Subspecialties: Molecular biology; Virology (biology). Office: Dept Biol Scis St John's Univ New York NY 11439

CARTER, WILLIAM CASWELL, computer scientist; b. Waterville, Maine, Jan. 16, 1917; s. Benjamin Edward and Mary Helen (Caswell) C.; m. Virginia Lee Davis, Aug. 14, 1957; children—Benjamin Everett, Candace, Clark Thomas. B.A. magna cum laude, Colby Coll., 1938; postgrad., Oxford U., 1938-39, U. Chgo., 1939-42; Ph.D. in Math., Harvard U., 1947. Mathematician, Aberdeen Proving Ground, Md., 1947-52; computer scientist Raytheon Corp., Waltham, Mass., 1952-55, Honeywell Computer Div., 1955-59, IBM T.J. Watson Research Center, Yorktown Heights, N.Y., 1959—; mem. adv. com. systems tech. NASA, 1982—. Contbr. chpts. to books, articles to profl. jours. Mem. Woodbury (Conn.) Charter Revision Com., 1977; mem. Woodbury Democratic Town Com., 1976-77. Served to lt. USNR, 1942-45; PTO. Rhodes scholar, 1938. Fellow IEEE; mem. Assn. Computing Machinery, Phi Beta Kappa., Sigma Xi. Democrat. Episcopalian. Patentee in field. Current work: Analysis and design of available/fault/tolerant reliable complex systems that contain computers. Subspecialty: Computer architecture. Home: 3 Shagbark Ln Woodbury CT 06798 Office: IBM TJ Watson Research Center PO Box 218 Yorktown Heights NY 10598

CARTER, WILLIAM DOUGLAS, geologist, consultant; b. Keene, N.H., Apr. 24, 1926; s. William Ambrose and Laura (Tuckerman) C.; m. Mary Jane Shannon, Sept. 10, 1950; children: Cindy Jean, Judy Lynn, Katherine Ann, William Douglas. A.B., Dartmouth Coll., 1949; postgrad., Johns Hopkins U., 1951, U. Colo., 1956. Geol. field asst. U.S. Geol. Survey, Fairbanks, Alaska, 1948-50, geologist, Grand Junction, Colo., 1951-57, mining geologist, Santiago, Chile, 1957-62, commodity geologist, Washington, 1962-65, remote sensing geologist, 1965-71, asst. program mgr. research, Reston, Va., 1972-82; geol. adv. AID, Santiago, 1957-62, remote sensing advisor, Washington and Costa Rica, 1975; remote sensing advisor InterAm. Devel. Bank, Washington, UN, 1982, China, 1982; co-leader internat. geol. program on remote sensing and mineral exploration, 1976-82; pres. Globex Inc., 1983. Contbr. articles to profl. jours. Active Boy Scouts Am., Reston, 1978. Served to cpl. USAAF, 1944-45. Fellow Geol. Soc. Am.; mem. Geol. Soc. Washington (sec. 1968), Am. Assn. Petroleum Geologists (lectr. continuing edn. program 1975-82), Soc. Econ. Geologists, Soc. Exploration Geophysicists. Club: Fairfax (Va.) Jubilaires. Current Work: Mapping geologic structures and spectral discrimination of rock types, ore deposits, and energy resources from space platforms. Subspecialties: Geology; Remote sensing (geoscience).

CARTER, WILLIAM EUGENE, research geodesist; b. Steubenville, Ohio, Oct. 16, 1939; s. Donald W. and Helen (Martin) C.; m. Marilyn Johnson, Jan. 16, 1960; children: Terri Lynn, Merri Sue, Pamela. B.S., U. Pitts., 1961; M.S., Ohio State U., 1965; Ph.D., U. Ariz., 1973. Commd. 2d lt. USAF, 1961, advanced through grades to capt., 1965, geodetic officer, 1961-69; research geodesist (USAF Cambridge Research Labs), 1969-72; research assoc. U. Hawaii, 1972-76; chief gravity astronomy and satellite div. (Nat. Geodetic Survey), 1977-81; chief advanced tech. br. (Geodetic Research and Devel. Lab.), 1981—. Contbr. 50 articles to profl. jours. Mem. Am. Astron. Soc., Internat. Astron. Union, Am. Geophys. Union, Internat. Union Geodesy and Geophysics. Current Work: Research and development of advanced techniques for geodesy. Subspecialties: Geodesy; Radio and microwave astronomy. Home: 19004 Oxcart Pl Gaithersburg MD 20879 Office: Nat Geodetic Survey N/CG114 Rockville MD 20852

CARTER, WILLIAM HAROLD, research physicist; b. Houston, Nov. 17, 1938; s. William Henry and Fannie Augusta (Simpson) C.; children: William Harold, Elizabeth Lee. B.S.E.E., U. Tex., Austin, 1962, M.S.E.E., 1963, Ph.D., 1966. Instr. elec. engring. U. Tex.-Austin, 1966; research assoc. in physics U. Rochester, 1969-70; research physicist Naval Research Lab., Washington, 1971—; vis. research fellow U. Reading, Eng., 1976-77; prof. elec. engring. U. Nebr., Lincoln, 1981-82. Assoc. editor: Jour. Optical Soc. Am, 1980-83; contbr. articles to profl. jours. Served to capt. U.S. Army, 1967-69. Fellow Optical Soc. Am.; fellow Internat. Soc. Optical Engring.; mem. Am. Phys. Soc., Sigma Xi, Tau Beta Pi, Eta Kappa Nu. Club: Cosmos (Washington). Lodge: Masons. Current Work: Optical communications systems design; developing theoretical models for describing the effects of interference phenomena on radiometry and radiative transfer by use of coherence theory. Subspecialties: Laser research; Optics research. Office: Naval Research Lab Code 7740 Washington DC 20375

CARTLIDGE, EDWARD SUTTERLEY, mech. engr.; b. Trenton, N.J., Feb. 5, 1945; s. Leon James and Agnes Jean (Cinkay) C.; m. Marilyn Spinuzza, July 21, 1979. B.S. in Marine Engring, U.S. Mcht. Marine Acad., 1968; M.S. in M.E, N.J. Inst. Tech., 1971; M.B.A., Temple U., 1982. Registered profl. engr., Pa., Ill., Wis., Minn., Calif. Marine engr. Seatrain Lines, 1968-69; performance engr. Foster Wheeler Corp., Livingston, N.J., 1969-71; cons. engr. Fluor, Sargent & Lundy, and Kuljian Corp., 1971-75; chief engr. Gimpel Corp., Langhorne, Pa., 1976-79; sr. research and devel. engr. Yarway Corp., Bluebell, Pa., 1976-79; sr. project engr. Merck, Sharp & Dohme, West Point, Pa., 1982—. Served to lt. comdr. USNR, 1968—. Mem. Nat. Soc. Profl. Engrs. (chpt. pres.), Pa. Soc. Profl. Engrs. (Young Engr. of Yr. 1980), ASME, Instruments Soc. Am., Soc. Mfg. Engrs., Am. Soc. Metals, Soc. Naval Architects and Marine Engrs. Christian. Patentee in field. Current Work: State-of-the-art pharmaceutical tablet manufacturing plant. Subspecialty: Fluid mechanics.

CARTNER, JOHN AUBREY, maritime consulting company executive; b. Jacksonville, N.C., Nov. 6, 1947; s. John Alexander and Anna Gertrude (Hardison) C.; m. Tanya Lynn Morris, Feb. 18, 1978; children: Christian W. J., Natalie V. O. B.S., U.S. Merchant Marine Acad., 1969; M.Sc., U. Ga., 1974, Ph.D., 1975; M.B.A., Ga. State U., 1979. Research scientist U.S. Army Research Inst., Alexandria, Va., 1976-78; asst. prof. bus. administrn. U. Ga. System-Columbus, 1978-79; dir. marine transp. cons. Grumman Data Systems, Bethpage, N.Y., 1979-81; v.p. IMA Resources, Inc., Washington, 1981; prin. Phillips Cartner & Co., Inc., Washington, 1981—, mng. prin., 1981—; mem. Supts.'s Council, U.S. Merchant Marine Acad., 1982—. Contbr. articles to profl. jours., 1975—; author various monographs, reports, 1974—. Adv. U.S. Merchant Marine Acad. Found., 1980—, Christ Ch. Found., Alexandria, Va., 1982—. Served to lt. USNR, 1965-73. Recipient Supt.'s trophy U.S. Merchant Marine Acad., 1982. Mem. Soc. Naval Architects and Marine Engrs., Am. Psychol. Assn., Inst. Navigation, N.Y. Acad. Scis., Sigma Xi. Republican. Episcopalian. Clubs: Downtown Athletic (N.Y.C.), Whitehall (N.Y.C.). Current Work: Applications of state-of-the-art technology in computers and information processing to command, control and communications in maritime settings; applications of creative paradigms to engineering solutions in the maritime environment; transfer of commercial maritime technology to military applications offshore. Subspecialties: Naval architecture and marine engineering; Offshore technology. Office: Phillips Cartner & Co Inc 1629 K St NW Washington DC 20006

CARTON, JAMES ALFRED, oceanographer; b. Highland Park, Ill., July 10, 1954; s. Robert Wells and Jean (Keating) C.; m. Allison Joan Mankin, Aug. 7, 1983. B.S.E. in Elec. Engring., Princeton U., 1976, Ph.D., 1983; M.S. in Oceanography, U. Wash., 1979. Postdoctoral fellow in theoretical oceanography Harvard U., Cambridge, Mass., 1982—. Contbg. author sci. articles. Recipient Manfred Pika Physics prize Princeton U., 1973. Mem. Am. Geophys. Union, IEEE, Am. Meteorol. Soc., Sigma Xi. Current work: Dynamics of coastal circulation and the interaction of currents on the continental shelf with the open ocean. Subspecialty: Oceanography. Office: Pierce Hall Harvard Univ 29 Oxford St Cambridge MA 02138

CARTWRIGHT, DAVID CHAPMAN, technical manager, researcher; b. Mpls., Dec. 2, 1937; s. Arvid Chapman and Elizabeth (Swain) C.; m. Carole Roth, July 10, 1965; children: Scott, Alison. B.S. in Physics, Hamline U., 1962; M.S. in Applied Mechanics, Calif. Inst. Tech., Pasadena, 1964, Ph.D. in Chem. Physics and Physics, 1968. Staff mem. Space Scis. Lab. The Aerospace Corp., El Segundo, Calif., 1969-74; staff mem., group leader Los Alamos Nat. Lab., 1975-80, dep. div. leader, 1980-84, prin. inertial confinement fusion (ICF) program mgr., 1984—. Contbr. articles in field to profl. jours. Served with U.S. Navy, 1955-58. NSF fellow, 1961-62; NATO fellow, 1967-68. Mem. Am. Phys. Soc., Am .Geophys. Union. Republican. Current Work: Electron impact processes; spectral properties of atoms and molecules; atmospheric processes. Subspecialties: Atomic and molecular physics; Aeronomy. Office: PO Box 1663 MS E527 Los Alamos NM 87545

CARUBELLI, RAOUL, biochemistry educator, researcher; b. Cordoba, Argentina, June 17, 1929; came to U.S., 1956; naturalized, 1966; s. Pedro Juan Pablo and Josefina Paulina (Aghem) C.; m. Barbara Rose Waken, Jan. 24, 1959; children—Michael Lawrence, Cecilia Maria. Student in Pharmacy, U. Cordoba, 1953, in Biochemistry, 1955, D. Pharmacy and Biochemistry, 1960. Lab.

instr. U. Cordoba, 1953-56; research biochemist Okla. Med. Research Found., Oklahoma City, Okla., 1957—; prof. biochemistry and molecular biology U. Okla., Oklahoma City, 1963—. Contbr. articles to sci. jours. Patentee in field. Served as subteniente Argentinian Army, 1949. NIH grantee, 1962—; recipient Research Career Devel. award NIH, 1968. Mem. Am. Soc. Biol. Chemists, Am. Chem. Soc., AAAS, Acad. Med. Scis. (Argentina), Sigma Xi. Democrat. Roman Catholic. Current work: Biochemistry of carbohydrates and glycoproteins, chemical carcinogenesis. Subspecialties: Biochemistry (biology); Cancer research (medicine). Home: 3626 NW 53 Oklahoma City OK 73112 Office: Okla Med research Found 825 NE 13 Oklahoma City OK 73104

CARUOLO, EDWARD VITANGELO, animal physiology educator, researcher; b. Providence, Nov. 1, 1931; s. Antonio and Emma (Baldoni) C.; m. Alice Elenor Villanis; children—Douglas, Gary, Edward, Paul. B.S., U.R.I., 1953; M.S., U. Conn., 1955; Ph.D., U. Minn., 1962. Research asst. U. Conn., Storrs, 1953-55; research asst. U. Minn., St. Paul, 1955-60, instr., 1960-63; asst. prof. N.C. State U., Raleigh, 1963-68, assoc. prof., 1968-83, prof., 1983—. Contbr. articles to profl. jours. Mem. Am. Physiology Soc., Am. Dairy Sci. Assn., Nat. Mastitis Council (research com. 1964—, bd. dirs. 1967-71). Episcopalian. Current work: Lactational physiology of lab animals and farm animals; physiological aspects of milk ejection; milking machine function as related to mammary function and disease. Subspecialties: Animal physiology; Bioinstrumentation. Home: 6412 Brandywine Dr Raleigh NC 27607 Office: NC State U 1147 Grinnells Animal Health Lab Raleigh NC 27695-7626

CARUSO, JOHN HOWARD, zoological curator, ichthyologist; b. Hackensack, N.J., June 1, 1947; s. Paul F. and Gilda (Liva) C.; m. Pamela M. Conway, May 3, 1975. A.B., Lafayette Coll., 1969; M.S., Tulane U., 1971, Ph.D., 1977. Asst. prof. Lafayette Coll., Easton, Pa., 1975-83; curator fishes and reptiles Audubon Zool. Garden, New Orleans, 1983—; adj. prof. biology Tulane U., New Orleans, 1983—; research assoc. U. New Orleans, 1983—. Contbr. papers and articles to jours. and books. Recipient Superior Teaching awards Lafayette Coll. Student Body, 1979, 83; NSF grantee, 1973, 81. Mem. Am. Soc. Ichthyologists and Herpetologists, Soc. Systematic Zoology, Am. Assn. Zool. Parks and Aquariums. Current work: Systematics of marine fishes. Subspecialties: Systematics; Marine biology. Office: Audubon Zool Garden PO Box 4327 New Orleans LA 70178

CARY, JOHN ROBERT, physicist, educator; b. Livermore, Calif., Mar. 15, 1953; s. John Robert and Helen Cramer (Harris) C.; m. Christine Lettie Graham, June 12, 1971; children—Jeremy Robert, Colleen Lettie, Cathryn Lorinda. B.A. cum laude in Math. and Physics, U. Calif.-Irvine, 1973; M.A. in Physics, U. Calif.-Berkeley, 1975, Ph.D. in Physics, 1979. Mem. staff Los Alamos Nat. Lab. (N.Mex.), 1978-80; research scientist U. Tex., Austin, 1980-84; assoc. prof. physics U. Colo., Boulder, 1984—; vis. scientist Culham Lab., London, Eng., 1984. Contbr. articles to profl. publs. Mem. Am. Phys. Soc. Current work: Nonlinear dynamics, 3-dimensional MHD equilibrium, plasma waves, free-electron lasers. Subspecialties: Plasma physics; Fusion. Home: 7741 Essex Pl Boulder CO 80301 Office: APAS Dept U Colorado Boulder CO 80309

CASASENT, DAVID PAUL, elec. engring. educator, cons.; b. Washington, Dec. 8, 1942; s. Harold Kane and Delta (Fletchal) C.; m. Paula T. Timko, Feb. 14, 1977; children: Candace, Erin, Tod, Jon, Maureen. B.S. in Elec. Engring, U. Ill., 1964, M.S. in Elec. Engring, 1965, Ph.D. in Elec. Engring, 1969. Research asst. Digital Computer Lab., U. Ill., 1965-69; prof. elec. engring. Carnegie-Mellon U., Pitts., 1969—, George Westinghouse prof. elec. engring., 1980—, dir. Ctr. for Excellence in Optical Data Processing, 1983—; tchr. numerous short courses on signal and image processing; cons. to numerous indsl. and govt. agys., including task force on automatic target recognition Def. Sci. Bd., 1982. Author 3 books on electronics and data processing; contbr. chpts. to 12 books, over 200 articles to profl. jours. Active Mt. Lebanon Civic League. Recipient best paper award AIAA, 1979. Fellow IEEE (pres. Pitts. electron devices chpt. 1971-72, best paper award 1976), Optical Soc. Am. (pres. Pitts. chpt. 1975-77), Soc. Photo-Optical Instrumentation Engrs. (numerous coms.). Democrat. Roman Catholic. Patentee in field. Current Work: Real-time hybrid optical/digital data processing. Subspecialties: Optical image processing; Optical signal processing. Office: Dept Elec Engring Carnegie-Mellon U Pittsburgh PA 15213

CASE, DELVYN CAEDREN, JR., hematologist, clin. researcher; b. Brownwood, Tex., Jan. 15, 1945; s. Delvyn Caedren and Dorothy Nellie (Dul) C.; m. Carole Ann Case, Aug. 1, 1970; children: Delvyn Caedren III, Wendy Nadia, Keith William. A.B. cum laude, Brown U., 1967; M.D., Jefferson Med. Coll., 1971. Diplomate: Am. Bd. Internal Medicine, Am. Bd. Hematology, Am. Bd. Oncology. Intern, resident in internal medicine Cornell U., N.Y.C., 1971-74; fellow in hematology and oncology Meml. Sloan-Kettering Cancer Center, N.Y.C., 1974-76; attending physician Maine Med. Center, Portland, 1976—; clin. researcher Found. for Blood Research, 1979—; assoc. Sidney Farber Cancer Inst., 1978—; instr. Tufts U., 1976-77; sr. clin. instr. U. Vt., 1978-80, clin. asst. prof., 1980-84, assoc. prof., 1984—; prin. investigator Cancer and Leukemia Group B, 1984—; cons. hematologist Ventrex Corp., Portland, 1980—; bd. dirs. Found. Blood Research, Scarborough, Maine, 1979—. Contbr. articles on hematology and immunology to profl. jours. Recipient 2d prize for cancer research Meml. Sloan-Kettering Cancer Center, 1976. Fellow ACP; mem. Am. Soc. Hematology, Am. Soc. Clin. Oncology, Am. Assn. Cancer Research, Sigma Xi. Current Work: Myeloma, Waldenstrom's macroglobucinemia, leukemia, lymphoma, M-components, chemotherapy. Subspecialties: Hematology; Oncology. Office: 180 Park Ave Portland ME 04102

CASE, GEORGE DAVID, biophysical chemist, researcher; b. Newark, Ohio, Aug. 10, 1947; s. George C. and Adelaide Eastman (Crane) C.; m. Diana Jeanne Mayville, Apr. 26, 1968; children—Heather Renee, Jason Michael, Ryan Matthew, Trevor Mayville, Alison Jacqueline. B.S. in Chemistry, U. Mich., 1968; Ph.D., U. Wash., 1972. Postdoctoral fellow U.Pa., Phila., 1972-74; lectr. chemistry Swarthmore Coll., Pa., 1973-74; biochemist Lawrence Berkeley Lab., U. Calif., 1974-76; research chemist U.S. Dept. Energy, Morgantown, W.Va., 1976-79; v.p., dir. research Resource Tech. Group, Inc., Morgantown, 1979—; adj. assoc. prof. W.Va. U., Morgantown, 1981—; cons. environ. and forensic sci. industries, 1975-76, 79—. Author: Preval, 1982 (award of excellence Soc. Tech. Communications 1983). Contbr. articles to profl. jours. Patentee in field. Eli Lilly fellow U. Wash., Seattle, 1971. Mem. Biophys. Soc., N.Y. Acad. Scis., Phi Lambda Upsilon. Current work: Nitrogenous pollutant metabolism, biophysics of electron transport reactions, mechanisms of heterogeneous environmental reactions, coal waste conversion to liquid fuels and waste gas cleanup and processing. Subspecialties: Environmental toxicology; Biophysical chemistry. Office: Resource Technologies Group Inc 400 Mississippi St Morgantown WV 26505

CASE, MARVIN THEODORE, medical research manager, veterinary pathologist; b. Anna, Ill., Dec. 20, 1934; s. Lester B. and Viola L. (Heisner) C.; m. Beverly Ann Meyer, June 14, 1958; children—Stephen, Lori. D.V.M., U. Ill., 1959, M.S., 1964, Ph.D., 1968. Diplomate Am. Bd. Toxicology. Veterinarian, Ill. Dept. Agr., Urbana, 1961-62; instr. Coll. Vet. Medicine, U. Ill., Urbana, 1962-68, asst. prof., 1968-69; research vet. pathologist Riker Labs., Northridge, Calif., 1969-71; mgr. pathology-toxicology Riker Labs.-3M Co., St. Paul, 1971-84; mgr. clin. devel., apheresis program 3M Co., 1984—; assoc. clin. prof. pathology Sch. Medicine, U. So. Calif., Los Angeles, 1969-71; cons. vet. pathology to Los Angeles County Veterinarian, 1969-71. Contbr. articles to sci. jours. Served as 1st lt. U.S. Army, 1959-61. Recipient Outstanding Tchr. award Coll. Vet. Medicine, U. Ill., 1966. Mem. AVMA, AAAS, Soc. Toxicologic Pathologists, Soc. Toxicology, Phi Zeta. Current work: Pathology, carcinogenesis, autoimmune diseases, toxicology, aphersis, medical research management. Subspecialties: Pathology (veterinary medicine); Maternal and fetal medicine. Office: 3 M Co 3 M Ctr Bldg 270-25-06 Saint Paul MN 55144

CASE, MARY ELIZABETH, educator; b. Crawfordsville, Ind., Dec. 10, 1925; d. Ralph Thomas and Leila Luckenbill (Sharar) C. B.A., Maryville Coll., 1947; M.S., U. Tenn., 1950; Ph.D., Yale U., 1957. Research asso. Yale U., New Haven, Conn., 1957-72, lectr., 1965-72; assoc. prof. genetics U. Ga., Athens, 1972—. Contbr. articles in field to profl. jours. Current Work: Neurospace molecular genetics. Subspecialty: Genetics and genetic engineering (biology). Office: University of Georgia Molecular and Population Genetics Dept Athens GA 30602

CASEY, H. CRAIG, JR., electrical engineering educator; b. Houston, Dec. 4, 1934; s. Horace Craig and Mae (Walls) C.; m. Jean Anne Merritt, June 11, 1960 (div. Jan. 1983); m. Jacqueline Joan Lucas, Jan. 23, 1983; children—Anne Elizabeth, Michael Alley. B.S., Okla. State U., 1957; M.S., Stanford U., 1959, PH.D., 1964. Devel. engr. Hewlett-Packard, Palo Alto, Calif., 1957-62; mem. tech. staff Bell Labs., Murray Hills, N.J., 1964-79; prof. chmn. elec. engring. Duke U., 1979—; dir. Acme Electric, Olean, N.Y.; cons. IBM, Raleigh, N.C. Author: Heterostructure Lasers, 1978. Contbr. articles to profl. jours. Patentee in field. Fellow IEEE; mem. Am. Phys. Soc., Electrochem. Soc., Am. Vacuum Soc. Current work: Compund semiconductor, material and devices, optoelectronics, semiconductor lasers, heteroepitaxial devices Subspecialties: Semiconductor lasers; Semiconductors. Office: Duke U Dept Elec Engring Durham NC 27906

CASEY, LESLIE ANNE, nuclear waste engineer; b. Evanston, Wyo., June 13, 1952; d. Ernest Raymond and Katherine Louise (Hanley) C. A.A., U. Fla.-Gainesville, 1972; B.S. in Chemistry, SUNY-Brockport, 1974; M.S. in Nuclear Engring., UCLA, 1976. Engr., mgr. U.S. Nuclear Regulatory Commn., Washington, 1976-80, U.S. Dept. Energy, Columbus, Ohio, 1980—. Mem. Am. Nuclear Soc., Am. Chem. Soc., Soc. Women Engrs. Democrat. Current work: Disposal of high level nuclear waste from commercial nuclear power plants. Subspecialty: Nuclear engineering. Home: 1035 Highland St Columbus OH 43201 Office: US Dept Energy 505 King Ave Columbus OH 43201

CASH, DEREK JOHN, neuroscientist, educator; b. Sutton, Eng., Sept. 13, 1938, came to U.S. 1961; s. Wilfrid Ernest and Marjorie (Heron Smith) C. B.Sc., Imperial Coll., London U., Eng., 1961; M.A., Duke U., 1963, Ph.D., 1965. Research assoc. Columbia U., N.Y.C., 1964-66; jr. research fellow Bristol U., Eng., 1966-67; sr. sci. 3M Research, Harlow, Eng., 1967-77; research assoc. Cornell U., Ithaca, N.Y., 1977-82; asst. prof. biochemistry U. Mo., Columbia, 1982—. Contbr. articles to profl. jours. Fellow Royal Soc. Chemistry; mem. Am. Chem. Soc., Soc. for Neuroscience, Am. Soc. for Neurochemistry, AAAS. Current work: Chemistry in synapses; acetylcholine receptor; GABA receptor; ligand induced changes in protein structure and function; molecular mechanism of neurotransmitter-receptor interaction and its modulation. Subspecialties: Neurochemistry; Biochemistry (medicine). Home: 720 E Swon Ave Saint Louis MO 63119 Office: Missouri Inst Psychiatry Neurochemistry Unit 5400 Arsenal St Saint Louis MO 63139

CASLAVSKA, VERA BARBARA, chemistry researcher; b. Chrudim, Czechoslovakia; came to U.S., 1966; d. Vilem and Vera (Kudrnkova) Novak; m. Jaroslav L. Caslavsky, Dec. 25, 1952; 1 dau., Veronika. M.S., Charles U., Prague, 1957, C.Sc., 1965. Research asst. Czech Acad. Sci., Prague, 1957-61; research assoc. Mining Inst., Prague, 1962-65, Pa. State U., 1966-69; asst. staff mem. Forsyth Dental Ctr., Boston, 1969—. Recipient award Czech Acad. Sci., 1961. Mem. Internat. Assn. Dental Research, Sigma Delta Epsilon. Patentee in field. Current Work: Chemistry of fluoride interactions with human enamel, topical fluoridation to effect caries prevention, crystal growth, structure and properties of glasses, reduction processes of iron ores. Subspecialties: Preventive dentistry; Inorganic chemistry. Office: Forsyth Dental Center 140 The Fenway Boston MA 02115

CASLER, LAWRENCE, psychology educator, researcher; b. Portland, Oreg., Jan. 26, 1932; s. David H. and Fyrne (Levinson) C. B.A., Harvard U., 1953, M.A., 1954; Ph.D., Columbia U., 1962. Staff editor for psychology Internat. Ency. Social Scis., N.Y.C., 1962-63; asst. prof. CCNY, 1963-66; lectr. L.I.U., Bklyn., 1965; research assoc. S.I. Mental Health Soc., N.Y., 1965-66; assoc. prof. SUNY-Geneseo, 1966-68, prof. psychology, 1968—; cons. Theleme exptl. community, Akron, N.Y., 1971-72; scholar-in-residence U. Del., Newark, 1976; mem. postdoctoral fellowship evaluation panel NRC, 1976. Editorial bd.: Developmental Psychlogy, 1970-75; author: Is Marriage Necessary? , 1974; contbr. articles to profl. jours. Mem. ACLU. Served in U.S. Army, 1955-56. Grantee in field; recipient Chancellor's award SUNY-Albany, 1975; sr. exchange scholar SUNY-Moscow State U., 1980. Mem. Am. Psychol. Assn., Parapsychol. Assn., AAUP, Com. for Elimination of Death (adv. council 1968-78), Com. for Extended Lifespan, Soc. Advancement of Good English (founder, pres. 1978-85). Current Work: Alternatives to marriage; relationships between hypnosis and parapsychology; psychological approaches to healthy logevity. Subspecialties: Behavioral psychology; Social psychology. Office: SUNY Geneseo NY 14454

CASPAR, DONALD LOUIS DVORAK, biophysics educator, researcher; b. Ithaca, N.Y., Jan. 8, 1927; s. Caspar V. and Blanche (Dvorak) C.; m. Gwladys Williams, Dec. 20, 1962; children—Emma, David. B.A., Cornell U., 1950; Ph.D. in Biophysics, Yale U., 1955. Postdoctoral fellow Calif. Inst. Tech., Pasadena, 1954-55, MRC Lab. of Molecular Biology, Cambridge, Eng., 1955-56, vis. assoc., 1965, 68; instr. biophysics Yale U., New Haven, 1956-58, asst. prof., 1958-59; research assoc. in biophysics Harvard U. Med. Sch., Boston, 1962-63; lectr. biophysics Children's Cancer Research Found., Harvard Med. Sch., 1963-73; prof. physics, research prof. structural biology Brandeis U., Waltham, Mass., 1972—; research assoc. in pathology Children's Hosp. Med. Ctr., 1959-73; mem. biophysics and biophys. chemistry study sect. NIH, 1970-73; guest research assoc. in biology Brookhaven Nat. Lab., Upton, N.Y., 1972—, chmn. vis. com. dept. biology, 1974-77, neutron users adv. group, 1980-81, adv. com. scanning transmission electron microscope facility, 1983—; mem. sci. adv. com. European Molecular Biology Lab., Heidelberg, Fed. Republic Germany, 1976-81; mem. nat. laser users facility steering com. Lab. for Laser Energetics, U. Rochester, N.Y., 1981-83. Contbr. numerous articles to profl. jours. Grantee NIH, 1959—, NSF, 1974-82, 83—. Fellow Am. Acad. Arts and Scis.; mem. Biophys. Soc. (nat. lectr. 1985), Am. Crystallographic Assn. Current work: Structural biology of viruses, membranes and tissue assemblies. Subspecialty: Biophysics (biology). Home: 9 Hyslop Rd Brookline MA 02146 Office: Rosenstiel Basic Med Scis Research Ctr Brandeis U Waltham MA 02254

CASPARI, ERNEST W(OLFGANG), biologist, educator; b. Berlin, Germany, Oct. 24, 1909; s. Wilhelm and Gertrud (Gerschel) C.; m. Hermine Bertha Abraham, Aug. 16, 1938. Ph.D., U. Gottingen, Ger., 1933; M.A., Wesleyan U., 1951; Dr. rer. nat. (hon.), U. Giessen, Ger., 1982. Asst. U. Gottingen, 1933-35; asst. in microbiology U. Istanbul Med. Sch., 1935-38; fellow, later asst. prof. Lafayette Coll., 1938-44; asst. prof. U. Rochester, 1944-46, prof., 1960-75, prof. emeritus, 1975—, chmn. dept., 1960-65; assoc. prof. Wesleyan U., 1946-47, prof., 1949-60; mem. staff dept. genetics Carnegie Instn., 1947-49. Author: (with W.A. Ravin) Genetic Organization, 1969; editor: Advances in Genetics, Vols. 10-21, 1961-82, Genetics, 1968-72. Fellow Center Advanced Study in Behavioral Sci., 1956-57, 65-66; recipient Sr. U.S. Scientist award A. von Humboldt Found., 1981. Fellow AAAS, Am. Acad.; mem. Genetics Soc. Am. (pres. 1966), Am. Soc. Naturalists (v.p. 1961, hon. mem.), Am. Soc. Zoologist, Behavior Genetics Soc. Current Work: Genetic basis of learning ability in fish. Subspecialties: Genetics and genetic engineering (biology); Gene actions. Office: Dept Biology U Rochester Rochester NY 14627

CASPARY, DONALD MICHEL, neuropharmacologist; b. N.Y.C., Sept. 1, 1943; s. Ernst C. and Helene R. (Lauchheimer) C.; m. Sonya E. Ginsberg, Jan. 22, 1966; children—Steven, Eric. B.A., U. Wisc.-Madison, 1965; M.S., Syracuse U., 1968; Ph.D., NYU, 1971. Nat. Inst. Neurological Clin. Disorders postdoctoral fellow SUNY, Albany, 1971-73; asst. prof. So. Ill. U., Sch. Medicine, Springfield, 1973-76, assoc. prof., 1976—, also dir. lab.; advisor Commn. Hearing and Bioacoustics Nat. Acad. Sci. Deafness Research Found. grantee, 1978-82; recipient Founders award NYU, 1971, various NIH awards, 1979—. Mem. Acoustical Soc. Am., AAAS, Assn. Research in Otolaryngology, Soc. Neurosci., Sigma Xi (v.p., sec.-treas. 1975-77). Current work: Auditory neurobiology, pharmacology of auditory system. Subspecialties: Neuropharmacology; Neurobiology. Home: 3109 Norwood Dr Springfield IL 62704 Office: So Ill U Sch Medicine 801 N Rutledge Springfield IL 62702

CASPE, MARC S., civil engineer, consultant. Pres. M.S. Caspe, San Mateo, Calif. Subspecialty: Civil engineering. Office: M S Caspe 1640 Oakwood Dr San Mateo CA 94403

CASPERSON, RICHARD L., engineering software company executive, consultant; b. McKeesport, Pa., Apr. 9, 1940; s. Robert E. and Beulah B. (Overturf) C.; married, June 10, 1967; children: Mylee M., Lea G. B.S. in Civil Engring. with honors, Colo. State U., 1963; M.S. in Mechanics, U. Colo., 1966. Sr. engr., lead engr. Martin-Marietta Aerospace, Denver, 1965-67, 71-72; scientist amd project mgr. Aerojet Nuclear Co., Idaho Nat. Engring. Lab., Idaho Falls, 1972-76; pres. Energy Engring. Group, Inc., Golden, Colo., 1977-85, Systems Internat., Inc., Lakewood, Colo., 1985—; vis. faculty U. Colo., cons. nuclear and alternative energy areas and computer applications in engring. scis. Contbr. articles in field of aerospace, nuclear safety and solar energy articles to profl. jours. Pres. Clear Lake County Bd. Edn. Colo. Energy Research Inst. fellow, 1977-78; recipient Outstanding Faculty award U. Colo., 1980, 83; U.S. Dept. Energy grantee, 1977-82. Mem. AAAS, ASCE, Internat. Solar Energy Soc., ASHRAE, Wilderness Soc., Audubon Soc., Sigma Tau, Chi Epsilon. Democrat. Club: Sierra. Current Work: Mathematical optimization in building energy design; solar energy applications; numerical and computer methods in engineering analysis and design. Subspecialties: Solar energy; Theoretical and applied mechanics. Home: PO Box 3159 Miner St Idaho Springs CO 80452 Office: Systems Internat Inc 143 Union Blvd Suite 410 Lakewood CO 80228

CASSIDY, MARTIN MACDERMOTT, oil company executive, geologist; b. N.Y.C., Mar. 29, 1933; s. George Livingston and Mary-Light (Schaeffer) C.; m. Jo Reesor, June 10, 1955; children: Cathy-Jo, Brandt, Caroline. B.A. cum laude, Harvard U., 1955, postgrad., 1960-62; M.S., U. Okla., 1962. Cert. petroleum geologist. Gordon McKay teaching fellow Harvard U., Cambridge, Mass., 1960-62; geologist Amoco Prodn. Co., Corpus Christi-Houston, Tex., 1962-69; chief geologist Amoco Libya Oil Co., Tripoli, 1969-73; staff geology div. ops supr. Amoco Prodn. Internat. Co., Chgo. and Houston, 1973-82; div. ops. supr. Amoco UK Exploration Co., London, 1982-84, exploration mgr., 1984—. Served to 1st lt. USAF, 1956-58, Korea. Mem. Am. Assn. Petroleum Geologists, Houston Geol. Soc. (treas. 1968, 2d v.p. 1969). Republican. Episcopalian. Current Work: Exploration for oil and gas. Subspecialties: Fuels; Geology. Home: Expatriate London UK PO Box 4381 Houston TX 77210 Office: Amoco UK Exploration 1 Stephen St Tottenhmm Court Rd London WIP IPJ United Kingdom

CASSITY, C. R., mathematician; b. Orange, N.J., Mar. 19, 1908; s. Leonard H. and Eola Ellen (McIntosh) C. A.B., Millikin U., 1929; M.A., U. Ill., 1931, Ph.D., 1938. Fellow, mem. faculty various ednl. instns., 1929-42; analyst Army Security Agy., Arlington, Va., 1942-46; asst. prof. math. N.Mex. Inst. Mining and Tech., Socorro, 1946-47, sr. mathematician, 1947-59; shock hydrodynamicist Gen. Electric Co., King of Prussia, Pa., 1959-62, mathematician, Huntsville, Ala., 1962-65; mem. tech. staff Environ. Research Corp., Alexandria, Va., 1965-70; cons. Scope Electronics, Reston, Va., 1972-74; adj. prof. math. Millikin U., Decatur, Ill., 1984—. Contbr. articles to profl. jours. Pres., bd. dirs. Community Concert Assn., Soccoro, 1956-58. Recipient Alumni Merit award Millikin U., 1967. Mem. Am. Math. Soc., Soc. Indsl. and Applied Math. Presbyterian. Lodge: Masons. Current work: Solution of higher order Runge-Kutta equations. Subspecialty: Numerical analysis (mathematics). Home: PO Box 264 Alexandria VA 22313

CASTELLINO, FRANCIS JOSEPH, univ. dean; b. Pittston, Pa., Mar. 7, 1943; s. Joseph Samuel and Evelyn Bonita C.; m. Mary Margaret Fabiny, June 5, 1965; children—Kimberly Ann, Michael Joseph, Anthony Francis. B.S., U. Scranton, 1964; M.S., U. Iowa, 1966, Ph.D. in Biochemistry, 1968. Postdoctoral fellow Duke U., Durham, N.C., 1968-70; mem. faculty dept. chemistry U. Notre Dame, Ind., 1970—, prof., 1977—; dean U. Notre Dame (Coll. Sci.), 1979—. Contbr. articles to profl. jours. NIH fellow, 395201968-70. Fellow N.Y. Acad. Scis.; mem. AAAS, Am. Heart Assn., Am. Chem. Soc., Am. Soc. Biol. Chemistry. Roman Catholic. Current Work: Structure and function of components of the blood coagulation and fibrinolytic systems. Subspecialties: Biochemistry (biology); Biophysical chemistry. Office: College of Science University of Notre Dame Notre Dame IN 46556

CASTELLO, JOHN DONALD, biology educator; b. Paterson, N.J., May 1, 1952; s. Dominick and Catherine (Ackaway) C.; m. Jody Lynn, May 22, 1982. B.A., Montclair State Coll., 1973; M.S., Wash. State U., 1975; Ph.D., U. Wisc., 1978. Assoc. prof. dept. environ. and forest biology SUNY, Syracuse, 1978—, Mem. Am. Phytopath. Soc., Sigma Xi, Phi Kappa Phi. Current Work: Researcher in enzyme linked immunosorbent assay techniques for use in detecting and characterizing viruses and mycoplasmas infecting woody perennials. Subspecialties: Plant pathology; Immunology (agriculture). Office: State University of New York Dept Environ Forest Biology Syracuse NY 13210

CASTELLUCCI, VINCENT FRANCOIS, neurobiology educator; b. Montreal, Que., Can., July 26, 1940; came to U.S., 1964, naturalized, 1979; s. Vincenzo Daniele and Evangeline (Cardinal) C.; m. Lise M. Bernier, May 12, 1965; children—Christine, Laurent. B.A., U. Laval, Quebec City, 1960, B.Sc., 1964; Ph.D., Wash. U.-St. Louis, 1968. Trainee physiology NYU, 1968-70, asst. prof., 1971-75; assoc. prof. neurobiology Columbia U. and N.Y. Psychiatric Inst., 1975—. Contbr. articles to profl. jours. Mem. AAAS, Am. Physiol. Soc., Am. Soc. Zoologists, Soc. for Neurosci. Democrat. Current work: Neurobiology and behavior, cellular neurophysiology. Subspecialty: Neurobiology. Home: 267 W 256th St New York NY 10471 Office: NY Psychiatric Inst Ctr of Neurobiology and Behavior 722 W 168th St New York NY 10032

CASTELVECCHI, JOHN PATRICK, mechanical engineer; b. Richmond, Va., July 10, 1959; s. Francis Garrett and Anne Shearer (Robertson) C.; m. Jane Anne Shonts, Aug. 26, 1978; children—John Patrick, Michael Scott. B.S., Va. Poly. Inst. & State U., 1981. Mech. engr. Hankins & Anderson, Inc., Richmond, 1981—. Mem. ASHRAE. Current work: Design and analysis of heating, ventilating and air conditioning systems, solar heating systems. Subspecialty: Mechanical engineering. Office: Hankins & Anderson Inc 1604 Santa Rosa Rd Richmond VA 23288

CASTLE, CHARLES HILMON, physician, educator; b. Eupora, Miss., Feb. 15, 1928; s. Hays D. and Ruby Ward (Bowen) C.; m. Carol Mae Losee, July 16, 1954 (div. Aug. 1981); children: Cy, Chris, Candace; m. Elaine Marie Litton, Sept. 19, 1981. B.S., U. Miss., 1948; M.D., Duke U., 1951. Instr. medicine Sch. Medicine, U. Utah, Salt Lake City, 1959-61, asst. prof., 1961-65, assoc. prof., 1965-70, prof., 1970—. Served to maj. USAF, 1954-56. Fellow ACP, Am. Coll. Cardiology, Am. Heart Assn. (council clin. cardiology). Methodist. Current Work: Cardiology; echocardiography. Subspecialties: Internal medicine; Cardiology.

CASTRO, ALBERTO, medical educator; b. San Salvador, Nov. 15, 1933; came to U.S., 1952; s. Alberto Lemus and Maria Emma (de la Cotera) C.; m. Jeris Adelle Goldsmith, Oct. 19, 1956; children: Stewart, Sandra, Albert, Richard, Juan. B.S., U. Houston, 1958; M.T., Jeff Davis Hosp.-Baylor U., 1958; Ph.D., U. El Salvador, 1962; M.D., U. Santo Domingo, Dominican Republic, 1982. Prof., head basic scis. dept. U. El Salvador, San Salvador, 1958-66; NIH sr. research fellow U. Oreg. Med. Sch., Portland, 1966-70, asst. prof. pediatrics, 1969-73; sr. scientist Papanicolaou Cancer Research Inst., Miami, Fla., 1973-75; assoc. prof. dept. pathology, dept. medicine U. Miami Sch. Medicine, 1975-77, prof., 1977—, dir. hormone research lab., 1974—, dir. researchLatin Am. program, 1981—; coordinator exec. program com. internat. tech. transfer and tng. program U. Miami Sch. Medicine (Latin Am. program), 1979—. Contbr. chpts. to books, more than 200 articles to profl. jours. Fellow Acad. Clin. Lab. Physicians and Scientist, Am. Inst. Chemists, Acad. Biochemistry (charter), Royal Soc. Health; mem. N.Y. Acad. Scis. Democrat. Roman Catholic. Current Work: Research in biotechnology, immunology (hybrodomas, immunochemistry), hormone mechanisms and receptors. Subspecialties: Immunobiology and immunology; Endocrinology. Home: 6275 SW 123d Terr Miami FL 33156 Office: Dept Pathology U Miami Sch Medicine Miami FL 33101

CASTRO, JOSEPH RONALD, physician, oncology researcher; b. Chgo., Apr. 9, 1934; m. Barbara Ann Kauth, Oct. 12, 1957. B.S. in Natural Sci., Loyola U.-Chgo., 1956, M.D., 1958. Diplomate: Am. Bd. Radiology, 1964. Intern Rockford (Ill.) Meml. Hosp.; resident U.S. Naval Hosp., San Diego; assoc. radiotherapist and assoc. prof. U. Tex.-M.D. Anderson Hosp. and Tumor Inst., 1967-71; prof. radiology/radiation oncology U. Calif. Sch. Medicine, San Francisco, 1971—, vice-chmn. dept. radiation oncology, 1980—; dir. particle radiotherapy Lawrence Berkeley Lab., Calif., 1975—; mem. program project rev. com. NIH/Nat. Cancer Inst. Cancer Program, 1982-85. Author sci. articles. Past pres., chmn. bd. trustees No. Calif. Cancer Program, 1980-83. Served to lt. comdr., M.C. USN, 1956-66. Recipient Teaching award Mt. Zion Hosp. and Med. Center, San Francisco, 1972. Fellow Am. Coll. Radiology; mem. Rocky Mountain Radiol. Soc. (hon.), Am. Soc. Therapeutic Radiology. Current Work: Clinical research in radiation oncology. Subspecialties: Oncology; Cancer research (medicine). Office: Bldg 55 Lawrence Berkeley Lab Berkeley CA 94720

CASTRONOVO, FRANK PAUL, JR., radiopharmacologist, pharmacist, health physicist, radiation safety officer; b. Newark, Jan. 2; s. Frank Paul and Edna Viola (Weingartner) C.; m. Judith Anne Belli, Apr. 3, 1977; children: Jessica Belli, Elizabeth Frances. Pharmacy B.S., Rutgers U., Newark, 1962; M.S. in Health Physics, Rutgers U., New Brunswick, N.J., 1963-64; Ph.D., Johns Hopkins U., 1970. Diplomate: (Radiopharms./Radiochem. Sci.) Am. Bd. Sci. in Nuclear Medicine, 1979; registered pharmacist, 1965 cert. Med. Nuclear Physics Am. Bd. Radiology, 1978 Nuclear Med. Scientist, 1979. Staff pharmacist Terry's Drug, Verona, N.J., 1962-63; health physics trainee Brookhaven Nat. Lab., Upton, N.Y., 1964; research scientist in radiopharms. Squibb Inst. for Med. Research, New Brunswick, 1964-65; part time staff pharmacist Johns Hopkins Hosp., Balt., 1965-70, part time radiopharmacy technologist, 1965-70; asst. physicist in radiology Mass. Gen. Hosp., Boston, 1970-80, radiopharmacy supr. in radiology, 1970-75, asso. radiopharmacologist in radiology, 1980—, health physicist, 1980, radiation safety officer, 1980—; vis. scientist M.I.T., 1975—, adj. asso. prof. radiopharmacology, 1975-77; adj. clin. asso. prof. radiopharmacology Mass. Coll. Pharmacy, 1977—; asst. prof. radiology Harvard U. Med. Sch.; radiopharmacy radiation safety cons. various regional hosps.; dir., lectr. hosp. courses in field. Contbr. chpts. to books, articles to profl. publs. Recipient Anthony De Rosa Meml. Award Rutgers Coll. Pharmacy, 1959, parenteral research award Parenteral Drug Assn., 1969. Mem. Am. Pharm. Assn., Health Physics Soc., Soc. Nuclear Medicine, Am. Assn. Physicists in Medicine, AAAS, Am. Soc. Hosp. Pharmacists, Internat. Radiation Protection Assn., Ethnopharmacology Soc., Radiopharm. Sci. Council (bd. dirs. 1977-80, chmn. quality control com. 1978), Am. Coll. Radiology, N.Y. Acad. Scis., Soc. for Risk Analysis. Inventor 125I Phenylphosphonic Acid. Current Work: Radiopharmacology, devel. new radiopharms., med. health physics (patient and personnel radiation doses), ethnopharmacy. Subspecialties: Radiology in nuclear medicine; Pharmacology. Home: 36 Gedlick Rd Burlington MA 01803 Office: Mass Gen Hosp Radiology Boston MA 02114

CATACOSINOS, PAUL ANTHONY, geologist; b. N.Y.C., Sept. 29, 1933; s. Anthony and Elpeniki (Cocotos) C.; m. Joan Diane Cook, Jan. 16, 1958; children: Alice E., Andrew C., Diana N. B.A., U. N.Mex., 1957; M.S., 1962; Ph.D., Mich. State U., 1972. Petroleum exploration geologist Mt. Fuel Supply Co., Salt Lake City, 1962-66, Consumers Power Co., Jackson, Mich., 1967-69; prof. geology Delta Coll., Univ. Center, Mich., 1969—; v.p. exploration Oil and Gas Corp., Birmingham, Mich., 1982-83. Contbr. articles to profl. jours. Served to lt. (j.g.) USNR, 1956-60. Recipient Bergstein award Delta Coll., 1972. Mem. Am. Assn. Petroleum Geologists, Geol. Soc. Am., Am. Astron. Soc., Sigma Xi. Current Work: Oil and gas exploration in the Mich. Basin; origin of the Mich. Basin. Subspecialty: Stratigraphy. Office: Dept Geology Delta Coll University Center MI 48710

CATENA, ROBERT JOHN, chemist; b. Montclair, N.J., Mar. 14, 1956; s. Fernando and Yolanda Jane (Folli) C. B.S. in Chemistry, Seton Hall U., 1978; M.S. in Organic Chemistry, Poly. Inst. N.Y., 1981, Ph.D. in Organic Chemistry, 1982. Research fellow Poly. Inst. N.Y., Bklyn., 1979-80, teaching fellow, 1981-82; research chemist Sun Chem. Corp., Carlstadt, N.J., 1982-84; sr. research chemist, 1985—. Contbr. articles to profl. publs. Recipient Seymour L. Shapiro award Poly. Inst. N.Y., Bklyn., 1981. Mem. Am. Chem. Soc., N.Y. Acad. Scis. Current work: Synthesis and characterization of condensation type resins (amides, esters, urethanes) for use in water-borne and solvent-borne systems for liquid inks, chemistry and structure modification of block and graft polymers via free radical polymerization routes. Subspecialties: Polymer chemistry; Organic chemistry. Home: 224 Baldwin Terr Orange NJ 07050 Office: Sun Chem Corp 631 Central Ave Carlstadt NJ 07072

CATES, LINDLEY ADDISON, JR., medicinal chemist, educator, pharm. cons. and researcher; b. Chgo., Nov. 20, 1932; s. Lindley Addison and Alice Jewett (Gilbert) C.; m. Ruth Elizabeth Cates, Oct. 27, 1932; children: Catherine, Douglas. B.S. in Pharmacy, U. Minn., 1954; M.S., U. Colo., 1958, Ph.D., 1961. Lic. pharmacist, Tex. Commd. 2d lt. U.S. Air Force, 1954; advanced through grades to capt. U.S. Air Force (M.S.C.), 1956; ret., 1965; instr. in pharmacy U. Colo, 1958-61; asst. to prof. pharmacy U. Houston, 1961—, chmn. dept. medicinal chemistry and pharmacognosy, 1973-83, assoc. dean for grad. studies and research, 1985—; vis. prof. Baylor U., Houston, 1970-72, U. London, 1972; pres. Syncates Assocs., Inc.; v.p. Gt. So. Labs., Inc. Contbr. articles profl. jours. Research grantee NIH; Research grantee USPHS; Research grantee Robert A. Welch Found. Mem. Am. Pharm. Assn., Am. Assn. Cancer Research, Acad. Pharm. Scis., Am. Chem. Soc., Am. Assn. Colls.of Pharmacy. Methodist. Lodge: Masons. Patentee in field. Current Work: Design and synthesis of potential anticancer, anticonvulsant and anti-fertility agts. Subspecialty: Medicinal chemistry.

CATES, REX GORDON, plant ecologist; b. Vernon, Tex., Aug. 30, 1943; s. George A. and Evelyn (Gordon) C.; m. Kay Roberts, Aug. 5, 1965; children: Todd, Michele, Brian, Tanya, Shawn, Sharee. B.S., Utah State U., 1965, M.S., 1968; Ph.D., U. Wash., 1971. Research assoc. U. Wash., Seattle, 1972-75; asst. prof. biology U. N.M., Albuquerque, 1975-78, assoc. prof., 1978-85; prof. botany and range sci., Brigham Young U., 1985—; mem. ecology adv. panel NSF, Washington, 1978-81, mem. ecosystem adv. panel, 1978-81. Exec. officer Boy Scouts Am., Albuquerque, 1978-80. NSF grantee, 1976—. Mem. Am. Soc. Naturalists, Ecol. Soc. Am. Democrat. Mormon. Current Work: Research in plant-herbivore interactions, stress physiology of trees, outbreaks of forest insects, and defensive natural product chemistry of plants. Subspecialties: Ecology (environmental science); Species interaction. Office: Botany & Range Sci Dept Brigham Young U 401 WIDB Provo UT 84602

CATHOU, RENATA EGONE, scientist, consultant; b. Milan, Italy, June 21, 1935; d. Egon and Stella Mary Egone; m. Pierre-Yves Cathou, June 21, 1959. B.S., MIT, 1957, Ph.D., 1963. Postdoctoral fellow, research assoc. in chemistry MIT, Cambridge, Mass., 1962-65; research assoc. Harvard Med. Sch., 1965-69, instr., 1969-70; research assoc. Mass. Gen. Hosp., 1965-69, instr., 1969-70; asst. prof. dept. biochemistry Tufts U. Sch. Medicine, 1970-73, assoc. prof., 1973-78, prof., 1978-81; vis. prof. dept. chemistry UCLA, 1976-1977; ind. cons., writer, from 1981; now pres. Tech. Evaluations, mgmt. cons. in biotech.; mem. adv. panel NSF, 1974-75; mem. bd. sci. counselors Nat. Cancer Inst., 1979-83. Mem. editorial bd.: Immunochemistry, 1972-75; contbr. chpts. to books, articles to profl. jours. NIH predoctoral fellow, 1958-62; sr. investigator Arthritis Found., 1970-75; grantee Am. Heart Assn., 1969-81; grantee USPHS, 1970-81. Mem. Am. Soc. Biol. Chemists, Am. Assn. Immunologists, AAAS, Biophys. Soc., N.Y. Acad. Sci. Current Work: consulting in biotechnology. Subspecialties: Biochemistry (biology); Immunobiology and immunology. Home: PO Box 23 Lexington MA 02173 Office: 430 Marrett Rd Lexington MA 02173

CATLIN, B. WESLEY, microbiologist, educator, researcher; b. Mt. Vernon, N.Y., June 26, 1917; s. Harold Burd and Abby Faber (Dunning) C.; m. Lew S. Cunningham, Feb. 15, 1954. M.A., UCLA, 1943, Ph.D., 1947. Postdoctoral fellow Carnegie Instn. Washington, Cold Spring Harbor, N.Y., 1948-50; mem. faculty Med. Coll. Wis. (name formerly Marquette U. Sch. Medicine), Milw., 1950—, assoc. prof. microbiology, 1955-65, prof., 1965—; mem. bd. sci. counselors Nat. Inst. Allergy and Infectious Diseases, Bethesda, Md., 1977-80; mem. Neisseriaceae subcom. Internat. Com. on Systematic Bacteriology, 1964—, sec., 1966-78. Mem. editorial bd.: Jour. Bacteriology, 1972-75; contbr. articles to sci. jours., 9 chpts. to books. Recipient ann. citation Nat. Bd. Med. Coll. Pa., 1978, Disting. Service award Med. Coll. Wis., 1980, Pasteur award Ill. Soc. Microbiology, 1983; NIH grantee, 1954—. Mem. Am. Soc. for Microbiology, Genetics Soc. Am., Soc. for Study Evolution, AAAS, Soc. for Gen. Microbiology (London). Current Work: Genetics and physiology of Neisseria; microbiology teaching and research. Subspecialties: Microbiology; Genome organization.

CATT, JOHN DAVID, organic chemist; b. Decker, Ind., Sept. 30, 1942; s. John Willard and Fern Alma (Marchino) C.; m. Dianna Lucille Snyder, Dec. 20, 1964; children—Kathey Lynn, John David. B.A., Ind. State U., 1964. Gas analyst U.S. Steel, Gary, Ind., 1965; research chemist Mead Johnson Co., Evansville, Ind., 1966—. Contbr. articles to profl. jours, chpt. to book. Patentee in field. Asst. leader Buffalo Trace council Boy Scouts Am., 1984. Mem. Internat. Soc. Hetrocyclic Chemistry, AAAS, Am. Chem. Soc. (medicinal chemistry div., organic div.). Lutheran. Subspecialties: Organic chemistry; Synthetic chemistry. Home: 418 Holly Hill Dr Evansville IN 47710 Office: Mead Johnson Co 2404 Pennsylvania Ave Evansville IN 47721

CATTERALL, WILLIAM A., pharmacologist. Chmn. dept. of pharmacology U. Wash. Sch. of Medicine, Seattle. Subspecialty: Pharmacology. Office: Univ of Washington Sch of Medicine Dept of Pharmacology Seattle WA 98195

CATTOI, ROBERT LOUIS, See *Who's Who in America*, 43rd edition.

CATTON, IVAN, mechanical engineering educator, consultant; b. Vancouver, B.C., Can., June 29, 1934; came to U.S., 1943, naturalized, 1959; s. John Arthur and Amy (Bowcock) C.; m. Susan Ann Layton, Oct. 1, 1961; children—Mark Douglas, Michael Scott, Craig Mitchel. B.Sc., UCLA, 1959, Ph.D., 1966. Lic. mech. engr., Calif., nuclear engr., Calif. Sr. scientist Douglas Aircraft Co., Santa Monica, Calif., 1959-66; mech. engring. faculty UCLA, 1967—, prof. 1977—; cons. McDonnel Douglas Astronautics, Huntington Beach, Calif., 1967—, U.S. Nuclear Regulatory Commn., Washington, 1974—, Brookhaven Nat. Lab., Long Island, N.Y., 1978—. Editor Jour. Heat Transfer, 1982—; mem. editorial bd. Jour. Nuclear Engring. and Design, 1983. Contbr. articles on heat transfer and fluid mechanics to profl. jours. Served to cpl. U.S. Army, 1954-56. Mem. Am. Nuclear Soc., Am. Phys. Soc., ASME (chmn. honors and awards com. heat transfer div., heat transfer meml. award 1982). Republican. Current work: Heat transfer and fluid mechanics. Subspecialty: Heat transfer. Home: 22436 Galilee St Woodland Hills CA 91364 Office: Univ California 405 Hilgarde Ave Los Angeles CA 90024

CAUGHEY, DAVID ALAN, engineering educator; b. Grand Rapids, Mich., Mar. 5, 1944; s. Carl William and Margaret (Arman) C.; m. Linda Criss Jones, June 28, 1969; children: Elizabeth Roma, Amanda MeeAe. B.S.E., U. Mich., 1965; M.A., Princeton U., 1967, Ph.D., 1969. Research scientist McDonnell Douglas Research Labs., St. Louis, 1971-75; asst. prof. Cornell U., Ithaca, N.Y., 1975-80, assoc. prof., 1980—; cons. McDonnell Douglas Corp., St. Louis, 1975—. Recipient Excellence in Teaching award Cornell Soc. Engrs., 1976-77. Mem. AIAA (Lawrence Sperry award 1979). Current Work: Development of computational techniques to predict aerodynamic forces on flight vehicles. Subspecialties: Aeronautical engineering; Fluid mechanics. Home: 125 Pearl St Ithaca NY 14850 Office: Dept Aero Engring Cornell U Ithaca NY 14853

CAULK, DAVID ALLEN, mechanical engineer; b. Mpls., Sept. 24, 1950; m. Sharon F., June 10, 1972; children: Rebecca, Sarah, Deborah. B.S., Rensselaer Poly. Inst., 1972; M.S. (NSF fellow), U. Calif., Berkeley, 1974, Ph.D. (NSF fellow), 1976. Sr. staff research engr. Gen. Motors Research Labs., Warren, Mich., 1976—. Contbr. numerous articles to profl. jours. Mem. ASME, Sigma Xi. Current Work: Fluid mechanics, polymer processing, metal plasticity, industrial research in composites processing and manufacturing. Subspecialties: Theoretical and applied mechanics; Fluid mechanics. Home: 4332 Cahill Dr Troy MI 48098

CAVALLARO, JOSEPH JOHN, microbiologist, educator, cons.; b. Lawrence, Mass., Mar. 18, 1932; s. John and Salvatrice (Zappala) C.; m. Kathleen Frances Kraus, Dec. 2, 1972; children: Theresa Margaret, Sandra Marie, Elizabeth Camille, Danielle Kay, Gina Kathleen. Student, Merrimack Coll., 1948-50; B.S., Tufts Coll., 1952; M.S., U. Mass., 1954; Ph.D., U. Mich., 1966. Pub. health sanitarian Hartford (Conn.) Health Dept., 1954-55, 57-61; teaching assoc. in microbiology U. Mass., 1961-62; research virologist Med. Research Labs. Charles Pfizer & Co., Groton, Conn., 1966-67; research assoc. in epidemiology U. Mich., 1967-70; microbiologist diagnostic immunology tng. br. Center Diseases Control, Atlanta, 1971—; cons. Pan Am. Health Orgn., Colombia, 1976, 77, Brazil 1977; asst. prof. dept pathology. Emory U. Med. Sch., Atlanta, 1985—; asst. prof. Morehouse Sch. Medicine, 1982—. Author: (with others) Serodiagnosis of Mycotic Diseases, 1977; author, co-author (with others) lab. manuals, 1971—; contbr. (with others) articles, chpts. to profl. publs. Served with Med. Service Corps U.S. Army, 1955-57. Fellow Am. Acad. Microbiology; mem. Am. Soc. Microbiology, Am. Assn. Immunologists, N.Y. Acad. Sci., Sigma Xi. Democrat. Roman Catholic. Current Work: Diagnostic immunology; teaching, training of laboratory personnel in diagnostic immunology. Subspecialties: Immunology (medicine); Infectious diseases. Home: 1325 Balsam Dr Decatur GA 30033 Office: 1600 Clifton Rd 1-B-206 Atlanta GA 30333

CAVALLI-SFORZA, LUIGI LUCA, geneticist; b. Genova, Italy, Jan. 25, 1922; s. Pio and Attilia Manacorda; m. Alba Maria Ramazzotti, Jan. 12, 1946; children: Matteo, Francisco, Tomaso, Violetta. Degree in medicine, U. Pavia, Italy, 1944; M.A., U. Cambridge, Eng., 1950. Asst. in research U. Cambridge, 1948-50; dir. research in microbiology Istituto Sieroterapico Milanese, 1950-57; prof. genetics U. Parma, Italy, 1958-62; prof., chmn. genetics dept. U. Pavia, 1962-71; prof. genetics Stanford U., Calif., 1970—. Author: Statistical Methods in Biology, 1958, (with W. Bodmer) The Genetics of Human Populations, 1971, Genetics Evolution and Man, 1976, other books on human genetics and cultural evolution, also numerous articles. Fgn. assoc. Nat. Acad. Scis. Subspecialty: Genetics and genetic engineering (biology). Office: Dept Genetics Stanford Univ Med Ctr Stanford CA 94305

CAVALLO, TITO, pathology educator; b. São Paulo, Brazil, Feb. 9, 1936; came to U.S., 1968, naturalized, 1977; s. Fiore and Carmen (Martins) C.; m. Anita Hahn, Jan. 28, 1966; children: Alexander L., Charles A. Student, Oswaldo Cruz Coll., Sao Paulo, 1953-55; M.D., U. Sao Paulo, 1963; postgrad., Harvard U., 1968-71. Intern Hospital das Clinicas, U. São Paulo Sch. Medicine, 1963; resident Peter Bent Brigham Hosp., Boston, 1968-69, Mallory Inst. Pathology, Boston, 1969-72; instr. pathology U. Sao Paulo (Brazil) Sch. Medicine, 1964-68, Harvard U. Med. Sch., Boston, 1971-72; assoc. prof. pathology U. Pitts. Sch. Medicine, 1972-77; prof. pathology U. Tex. Med. Br., Galveston, 1977—, dir. renal immunopathology div.; cons. U. Pitts. Health Ctr. Hosps., Pitts., 1972-77. Recipient Dr. Menotti Sainati award U. São Paulo Sch. Medicine, 1963; Golden Apple award Student AMA, 1975. Mem. Internat. Acad. Pathology, Am. Soc. Nephrology, Am. Assn. Pathologists, AAAS, Internat. Soc. Nephrology. Current Work: Immunologic renal disease, glomerular permeability, inflammation. Subspecialties: Pathology (medicine); Nephrology. Office: U Tex Med Br 201 Keiller Bldg Galveston TX 77550

CAVE, WILLIAM THOMPSON, JR., medical educator and researcher; b. Washington, Oct. 17, 1942; s. William Thompson and Dorothy Mae (Cleary) C.; m. Jacqueline Clarice Cave, May 4, 1968; children: Catherine, John, Christopher. B.A. cum laude, Kenyon Coll., Gambier, Ohio, 1963; M.D., Yale U., 1967. Diplomate: Am. Bd. Internal Medicine. Intern U. Va. Hosp., 1967-68; resident in internal medicine U. Va., 1968-69, fellow in endocrinology, 1972-75; instr. U. VA., 1975-77, asst. prof., 1977; asst. prof. dept. internal medicine and cancer center U. Rochester, N.Y., 1977-83, assoc. prof., 1983—; assoc. chmn. dept. internal medicine St. Mary's Hosp., Rochester, 1979—. Contbr. in field. Bd. dirs. Rochester Regional Am. Diabetes Assn. Served to maj. USAR, 1969-72. NIH fellow, 1974-75; NIH grantee, 1978-79, 81—. Mem. Endocrine Soc., Am. Thyroid Assn., Am. Assn. Cancer Research, Soc. Exptl. Biology and Medicine, A.C.P., Am. Fedn. Clin. Research, Am. Diabetes Assn., N.Y. Acad. Scis., Sigma Xi. Current Work: Nutritional and hormonal factors that influence mammary tumor growth, medical researcher, consulting endocrinologist. Subspecialties: Endocrinology; Cancer research (medicine). Office: Endocrine Unit Saint Mary's Hosp 89 Genesee St Rochester NY 14611

CAVINESS, VERNE STRUDWICK, JR., neurologist; b. Raleigh, N.C., July 25, 1934; s. Verne Strudwick and Alice Hill (Webb) C.; m. Madeline Viva Harrison, June 2, 1962; children: Gwendoline Angela, Alison Chantal. B.A., Duke U., 1956; D.Phil., Oxford U., 1960; M.D., Harvard U., 1962. Diplomate: Am. Bd. Neurology and Psychiatry. Intern Mass. Gen. Hosp., Boston, 1962-63, resident in medicine, 1963-64, resident in neurology, 1964-67, staff, Boston, 1969—, neurologist, 1982—; mem. faculty Harvard Med. Sch., 1969—, assoc. prof., 1976-82, prof., 1982—; dir. Southard Lab., Eunice Kennedy Shriver Center, Waltham, Mass. Served with USAF, 1967-69. NIH fellow, 1969-71; Joseph P. Kennedy Meml. Found. fellow, 1971-74. Mem. Am. Neurol. Assn., Am. Acad. Neurology, AAAS, Soc. Neurosci. Current Work: Anatomic studies of developing cerebral cortex. Subspecialties: Neurology; Neurobiology.

CAVINS, JOHN ALEXANDER, physician, research scientist; b. Terre Haute, Ind., Feb. 18, 1929; s. Alexander W. and Grace Lillian (Erickson) C.; m. Myrtle I, McCleod, June 24, 1961; children: Scott A., Bonnie H., Susie G. A.B., Amherst Coll., 1950; M.D., Johns Hopkins U., 1954. Intern Univ. Hosp., Columbus, Ohio, 1954-55, resident in medicine and hematology, 1955-59; research assoc. Harvard U. Med. Sch., Cambridge, Mass., 1963-70; assoc. prof. Ind. U. Sch. Medicine, Indpls., 1970-72, clin. assoc. prof. medicine, 1975—; chief oncology and hematology dept. St. Vincent Hosp., Indpls., 1974—, dir. cancer research, 1974—, pvt. practice medicine specializing in oncology and hematology, Indpls., 1972—; cons. Beta Med. Pharm. Co., Indpls., 1982—. Contbr. sci. articles to profl. publs. Served to lt. comdr. USN, 1955-62. Mem. Internat. Soc. Hematology, Am. Soc. Hematology, Am. Assn. for Cancer Research, AAAS, Am. Soc. Clin. Pharmacology and Therapeutics. Republican. Presbyterian. Current Work: Cancer immunology and immunotherapy, cancer research, cancer medicine, and clinical trials. Subspecialties: Cancer research (medicine); Hematology. Home: 6202 N Sherman Dr Indianapolis IN 46220 Office: 8220 Naab Rd Indianapolis IN 46260

CAWLEY, WILLIAM ARTHUR, government research administrator; b. N.Y.C., Dec. 11, 1925; s. John Martin and Anna Catherine (Winters) C.; m. Virginia Mary Harris, Oct. 6, 1951; children—Susan, Virginia, William Arthur, Daniel, Margaret, Marieanne. A.B., Harvard U., 1946; B.S. in Civil Engring., Tufts Coll., 1950; M.S. in San. Engring., MIT, 1955. Registered prof. engr., Maine; diplomate Am. Acad. Environ. Engrs. With Mass. Dept. Pub. Health, 1950, 52-54, Rayonier, Inc., 1955-58, Scranton Pub. Co., 1959; with Mead Corp., Chillicothe, Ohio, 1959-63, staff cons. research dept., 1961-63; mgr. engring. waste treatment Crane Co., King of Prussia, Pa., 1963-66; chief pollution control tech. br., div. research Fed. Water Pollution Control Adminstrn., Washington, 1966-68; dir. div. process research and devel. Fed. Water Quality Adminstrn., EPA, 1968-72, dep. dir. Office Program Mgmt., Office Research and Devel., 1972-75, dir. tech. support div. Office Research and Devel., 1975-78, dep. dir. indsl. environ. research lab. Office Research and Devel., 1978-84, dep. dir. hazardous waste engring. research lab. Office Research and Devel., 1984—. Served to lt. USNR, 1943-46, 50-52. Recipient Performance award EPA, 1980, Bronze medal EPA, 1983, 84. Fellow ASCE; mem. Water Pollution Control Fedn., Sigma XI. Current work: Control technology; destruction/detoxification methods for hazardous waste and industrial wastes. Subspecialties: Water supply and wastewater treatment; Hazardous waste disposal. Office: EPA AW Breidenbach Environ Research Ctr Cincinnati OH 45687

CAZES, ALBERT N., computer specialist, educator; b. Cairo, July 30, 1942; came to U.S., 1961; s. Nessim B. and Julia J. (Chaky) C.; m. Rose V. Chimchirian, Aug. 20, 1972; children: Caroline,Annabelle. B.S., CUNY, 1969; M.A., Hunter Coll., 1975; Ph.D., Poly. Inst., 1982. Computer specialist N.Y.C.-D.S.S.-O.D.P., 1970-83; staff programmer IBM, Yorktown Heights, N.Y., 1983—. Served with U.S. Army, 1965-67. Mem. Am. Math. Soc. Democrat. Jewish. Current Work: Videotex, inverse boundary problems, Hill's equations, computer assisted education. Subspecialties: Information systems, storage, and retrieval (computer science); Applied mathematics.

CEDARBAUM, JESSE MICHAEL, neurologist, neuropharmacology researcher; b. Chgo., July 6, 1951; s. David I. and Sophia Ann (Nahamkin) C.; m. Caryn L. Balaban, July 1, 1973 (div. Oct. 1977); m. Shari Kolodny, Nov. 18, 1979. B.A. in Human Biology, Stanford U., 1973, M.A. in Biology, 1973; M.D., Yale U., 1978. Intern, Univ. Chgo. Hosps. and Clinics, 1978-79, resident in medicine, 1979-80; resident in neurology New York Hosp., 1980-83; asst. prof. neurology Cornell U. Med. Coll., 1983—; guest investigator Rockefeller U., 1983—; asst. attending neurologist New York Hosp., 1983—; attending physician Burke Rehab. Ctr., White Plains, N.Y., 1983—. Mem. Soc. Neurosci., Am. Soc. Neurol. Investigation, Am. Acad. Neurology. Current work: Development of drugs for treatment of neurological illnesses. Subspecialties: Neurology; Neuropharmacology. Office: Burke Rehab Ctr 785 Mamaroneck Ave White Plains NY 10021

CEMEN, IBRAHIM, structural geologist, educator; b. Bursa, Turkey, July 23, 1951; came to U.S., 1975; s. Rahmi and Hikmet (Bollu) C.; m. Pamala Byrd, Aug. 20, 1983. B.S in Geology, Istanbul U., Turkey, 1974; M.S. in Geology, Ohio U., 1977; Ph.D., PA. State U., 1983. Geologist, Minning Exploration and Research Inst., Ankara, Turkey, 1974-75; asst. prof. Ohio U., Athens, 1982-83, Okla. State U., Stillwater, 1984—. Contbr. articles to profl. jours. Dean's Starter grantee Okla. State U., 1984. Mem. Am. Assn. Petroleum Geologists., Geol. Soc. of Am., Am. Geophys. Union. Current work: Structural geology and tectonics of the southwestern great basin; structural geology and tectonics of southern Oklahoma. Home: 807 Dryden Circle Stillwater OK 74075 Office: Okla State U 148 Phys Scis Stillwater OK 74078

CENSOR, YAIR, educator, researcher; b. Rehovot, Israel, Nov. 29, 1943; s. Emanuel and Else (Simon) C.; m. Erga Goldfinger, Aug. 21, 1966; children: Aviv, Nitzan, Keren. B.S., Technion, Haifa, Israel, 1967, M.S., 1969, D.Sc., 1975. Research fellow Technion, Haifa, 1975-76; lectr. U. Haifa, 1976-77, sr. lectr., 1979—; research asst. prof. SUNY-Buffalo, 1977-79; research assoc. Med. Image Processing Group, Buffalo, 1977-79; vis. assoc. prof. U. Pa., Phila., 1982-83. Mem. Israeli Union of Math., Soc. Indsl. and Applied Math. Current Work: Mathematical optimization theory; numerical analysis; optimization theory techniques in image reconstruction from projections. Subspecialties: Applied mathematics; Imaging technology. Home: 25 Gilboa St Haifa 32716 Israel Office: Dept Radiology U Pa Hosp 3400 Spruce St G1 Philadelphia PA 19104 Office: Univ Haifa Dept Math Mount Carmel Haifa 31999 Israel

CENZER, DOUGLAS ALFRED, mathematics educator; b. Detroit, Nov. 15, 1947; s. Alfred V. and Hattie (Czaczkowski) C.; m. Pamela Scharstein, May 21, 1970; 1 son, Michael. B.S. in Math., Mich. State U., 1968; Ph.D. in Math., U. Mich., 1972. Research asst. Nat. Security Adminstrn., Ft. Meade, Md., 1967; asst. prof. U. Fla., Gainesville, 1972-77, assoc. prof., 1977—; vis. assoc. prof. North Tex. State U., Denton, 1981-82; referee NSF, Washington, 1978—, Trans. Am. Math. Soc., Providence, 1982—. Reviewer: Math. Revs, 1976—, Jour. Symbolic Logic, 1981—; contbr. articles on math. to profl. jours. Mem. exec. com. United Faculty of Fla., Gainesville, 1977-79. Ford scholar, 1966-68; NSF fellow, 1968-72; grantee, 1974-76; U.Fla. grantee, 1978. Mem. Am. Math. Soc., Assn. for Symbolic Logic, Soc. for Indsl. and Applied Math., Phi Beta Kappa, Pi Mu Epsilon. Democrat. Current Work: Analytic sets, computational complexity, game theory, inductive definability. Subspecialty: Theoretical computer science. Home: 2439 NW 12th Pl Gainesville FL 32605 Office: U Fla Dept Math 201 Walker Hall Gainesville FL 32611

CERA, LEE MARIE, veterinarian; b. Chgo., June 24, 1950; d. Ernest J. and Gloria E. (Bonet) C. B.A., St. Xavier U., 1971; B.S., U. Ill, 1973, D.V.M., 1975; postgrad., U. Chgo., 1975—. Vet. asst. BevLab Vet. Hosp., Blue Island, Ill., 1974-75, emergency clinician, 1975-77; equine cons. Pine Bluff Animal Hosp., Joliet, Ill., 1975-77; instr. St. Xavier Coll., 1975-77; resident, trainee in comparative pathology U. Chgo.-Lincoln Park Zoo, 1975-77; resident in comparative medicine and pathology A.J. Carlson Animal Research Facility, Pritzker Sch. Medicine; resident in comparative medicine and pathology U. Chgo., 1975-78, chief clin. and lab. services biol. scis. div., 1978-80; acting dir. U. Chgo. (A.J. Carlson div.), 1980-81, dir. animal care, 1981—; course asst. comparative pathophysiology and med. histology U. Chgo., 1977-80; asst. program dir. Charles Louis Davis D.V.M. Found. for Vet. Pathology, 1977-82, program dir., 1982—. Contbr. articles to profl. jours. Mem. med. adv. bd. Lincoln Park Zoo.; mem. med. adv. bd. Wyler Children's Hosp. Recipient award Lake County Humane Soc., 1975, award Pfizer Co., 1974. Mem. Avma, Midwest Vet. Pathology Assn., Wildlife Disease Assn., Am. Assn. for Lab. Animal Sci., Am. Animal Hosp. Assn., Am. Soc. for Lab. Animal Practitioners, Ill. Soc. Med. Research (v.p. 1981—), Sigma Xi. Roman Catholic. Current Work: Laboratory animal science, burn rehabilitation. Subspecialty: Pathology (veterinary medicine). Office: Box 144 Chicago IL 60637

CERCEO, JOHN MICHAEL, physicist, scientific company executive; b. Washington, July 1, 1933; s. John G. and Marie L. C.; m. Aline V. Cook; children: Michael, Andrea, Alyssa, Michelle, Anthony. B.S. cum laude, Cath. U., 1957, M.S. in Physics, 1961; Ph.D. in Physics, Pacific Western U., 1981. Scientist, advanced research div. AMF, 1961-64, Gen. Techs. Corp., 1964-65; tech. group leader TRACOR Labs., 1965-70; sr. scientist VERTEX Corp., 1970-72; sr. scientist, pres. ISC, Inc., 1972-75, v.p., partner, 1977—, also dir.; ind. cons., 1975-77. Contbr. tech. papers and articles to profl. lit. Served with U.S. Army, 1954-55. Mem. AAAS, IEEE, Optical Soc. Am., Philos. Soc. of Washington, Acoustical Soc. Am., Am. Inst. Physics, AIAA. Current Work: Computer systems/weapons system research; analyses/applications; executive technical director, programs mgr. Subspecialties: Acoustics; Applied mathematics. Home: 13305 Moran Dr Travilah MD 20878 Office: 8478 Tyco Rd Vienna VA 22180

CERINI, COSTANTINO PETER, virologist, researcher; b. Phila., Nov. 19, 1931; s. Joseph and Rita Lillian (Cruciani) C.; m. Lydia G. De Angelis, June 18, 1960; children: Angela, Christina. B.A., LaSalle Coll., Phila., 1953; M.S.,

Lehigh U., 1960, Ph.D., 1964. Research virologist Am. Cyanamid Corp., Pearl River, N.Y., 1964-70; group leader Lederle Labs., Pearl River, 1970-75, sr. research virologist, 1975—. Contbr. articles to profl. publs. Served with U.S. Army, 1955-57. Mem. N.Y. Acad. Scis., Am. Soc. Microbiology, AAAS, Sigma Xi. Roman Catholic. Patentee in field. Current Work: Development of vaccines for infectious diseases. Subspecialties: Virology (biology); Immunobiology and immunology. Office: Lederle Labs Pearl River NY 10965

CERMAK, IVAN ANTHONY, research and development executive; b. Povazska Bystrica, Czechoslovakia, Dec. 23, 1940; s. Anton Josef and Maria (Lysa) C.; m. Joan Elizabeth Hinch, Aug. 15, 1964. B.Eng. (E.E.), McGill U., 1963, M.Eng., 1967, Ph.D. (E.E.), 1969. Mem. tech. staff Bell Labs., Holmdel, N.J., 1969-70, tech. supr., 1970-78, tech. dept. head, Denver, 1978-81; corp. v.p., dir. Advanced Tech. Center, ITT, Shelton, Conn., 1981-84; pres. ITT Telecom Network Systems Div., Raleigh, N.C., 1984—; cons. Contbr. articles to sci.-tech. jours. Served to capt. RCAF, 1959-66. Mem. IEEE (editorial bd. Spectrum), U.S. C. of C. Current Work: Systems, particularly telecommunications and office systems. Subspecialties: Electrical engineering; Computer engineering. Office: ITT Telecom Network Systems Div 3128 Smoketree Ct Raleigh NC 27604

CERMAK, JACK EDWARD, engineer, educator; b. Hastings, Colo., Sept. 8, 1922; s. Joseph and Helen (Herman) C.; m. Helen Jane Carlson, Dec. 17, 1949; children: Douglas Karl, Jonathan Joel. B.S., Colo. State U., 1947, M.S., 1948; Ph.D., Cornell U., 1959; NATO postdoctoral fellow, Cambridge (Eng.) U., 1961-62. Mem. faculty Colo. State U., Ft. Collins, 1948—, prof. charge fluid mechanics and wind engring. program, also dir. Fluid Dynamics and Diffusion Lab., 1960—, chmn. engring. sci., 1963-72; pres., dir. Colo. State U. (Research Found.), 1965-72; pres. Cermak/Peterka and Assocs, Inc., 1982—; cons. in field. Mem. bd. mems. Univ. Corp. Atmospheric Research, 1966-67; pres., chmn. 10th Midwestern Mechanics Conf., 1966-67; dir. summer inst. fluid mechanics NSF, 1963, 65, 68, 72; chmn. 2d U.S. Nat. Conf. Wind Engring. Research, 1975, 5th Internat. Conf. Wind Engring., 1979; pres. Wind Engring. Research Council, Inc., 1979-85; co-chmn. U.S.-Japan Seminar Lab. Simulation of Stratified Shear Flows; mem. Colo. Gov.'s Sci. and Tech. Adv. Council, Com. on Army Basic Research, NRC, 1979-82. Mem. editorial adv. bd. Indsl. Aerodynamics Abstracts, Mechanics Research Communications; Archives for Meteorology, Bioclimatology and Geophysics, Series A; regional editor U.S., Internat. Jour. Wind Engring. Contbr. articles to profl. jours. Fellow ASCE, Am. Acad. Mechanics; asso. fellow AIAA; mem. Am. Soc. Engring. Edn. (chmn. mechanics div.), Nat. Acad. Engring. (chmn. com. natural disasters, chmn. panel on wind engring. research), Internat. Assn. Wind Engring. (chmn. bd. 1975-79, regional sec. North and S.Am. 1983—), Am. Meteorol. Soc., Am. Geophys. Union, ASME, AAAS, ASHRAE (mem. com. flow around bldgs.), Air Pollution Control Assn., N.Y. Acad. Scis., Sigma Xi (nat. lectr. 1976-77). Current Work: Physical modeling of natural wind and atmospheric diffusion; boundary-layer wind tunnels; wind engineering-wind forces on buildings and structures, control of wind blown sand and snow, dispersion of air pollutants. Subspecialties: Fluid mechanics; Civil engineering. Home: 407 E Prospect Rd Fort Collins CO 80525

CERNI, TODD ANDREW, atmospheric scientist, educator; b. Milw., Apr. 28, 1947; s. Andrew J. and Margaret L. C. B.S. in Physics, Marquette U., Milw., 1969; M.S. in Physics, Ind. U., 1971; Ph.D. in Atmospheric Sci, U. Ariz., Tucson, 1976. Research assoc. U. Wyo., Laramie, 1976-79, asst. prof. dept. atmospheric sci., 1979—. Contbr. articles to profl. jours. Mem. Am. Phys. Soc., Am. Meteorol. Soc. Patentee in field. Current Work: Research in cloud physics, instrumentation, radiative transfer. Subspecialties: Meteorology; Meteorologic instrumentation. Office: Atmospheric Sci Dept U Wyo Laramie WY 82071

CESARI, LAMBERTO, mathematician. Prof. emeritus dept. math. U. Mich., Ann Arbor. Subspecialty: Analysis. Office: U Mich Dept Math Ann Arbor MI 48109*

CETAS, THOMAS CHARLES, physicist, educator; b. Petoskey, Mich., Aug. 25, 1941; s. Carl N. and Rae L. (Jolls) C.; m. Betty Lou Schultz, June 15, 1963; children: Amanda, Justin, Melissa. Student, Cedarville (Ohio) Coll., 1959-61; A.B. cum laude, Hope Coll., 1963; Ph.D., Iowa State U., Ames, 1970. Fellow Nat. Measurement Lab., Sydney, New South Wales, Australia, 1970-73; physicist Nat. Bur. Standards, Gaithersburg, Md., 1973-75, Bur. Radiol. Health, Rockville, Md., 1975; research assoc. radiology U. Ariz., Tucson, 1975-78, asst. prof. radiation oncology and elec. engring., 1978-82, assoc. prof., 1982—. Recipient Research Grants Nat. Cancer Inst., 1976—, Research Grants Technicon Corp., 1979—, Research Grants Bur. Radiol. Health, 1976, 78. Mem. Radiation Research Soc., Am. Phys. Soc., Am. Assn. Physicists in Medicine, Bioelectromagnetics Soc., Sigma Xi. Baptist. Patentee in field. Current Work: Phys. apsects of hyperthermia for cancer therapy, hyperthermia, thermometry, thermal dosimetry, microwave heating, radiofrequency, ultrasound. Subspecialties: Medical physics; Biomedical engineering. Home: 7520 N San Lorenzo St Tucson AZ 85704 Office: Radiation Oncology Dept Health Sci Center Tucson AZ 85724

CEZAIRLIYAN, ARED, physicist; b. Istanbul, Turkey, May 9, 1934; came to U.S., 1957, naturalized, 1971; s. Onnik and Valantin (Mangassarian) C.; m. Sylvia Papazian, May 24, 1970; 1 son, Brent. B.S.M.E., Robert Coll., Istanbul, 1957; M.S.M.E., Purdue U., 1960, Ph.D., 1963. Research engr. Purdue U., West Lafayette, Ind., 1960-63; research physicist Nat. Bur. Standards, Washington, 1963—; cons. CINDAS/Purdue U., 1968—. Founding editor: Internat. Jour. Thermophysics, 1980—; contbr. articles to profl. jours. Recipient Silver medal Dept. Commerce, 1975, Gold medal, 1980, Engr. of Yr. award Nat. Soc. Profl. Engrs., 1982; Gold medal French High Temperature Soc., 1982; Indsl. Research-100 award, 1983; named Disting. Engring. Alumnus Purdue U., 1978. Mem. Am. Phys. Soc., ASME (Heat Transfer Meml. award 1981), ASTM, Internat. Thermophysics Congress (chmn.), Washington Philos. Soc. Current Work: Research in developing advanced techniques for measurement of properties of substances at high temperatures by rapid dynamic pulse-heating techniques of millisecond and microsecond resolution. Subspecialties: High-temperature materials; Condensed matter physics. Home: 12 Tapiola St Rockville MD 20850 Office: Nat Bur Standards Washington DC 20234

CHA, CHARLES YOUNG, research chemist; b. Seoul, Republic Korea, Aug. 8, 1931; came to U.S., 1954, naturalized, 1970; s. Jae Sup and Yung Duk (Kang) C.; m. Catherine Chonghi Kim, June 6, 1960; children—Millie, Sue, Felix. B.A., Lincoln U., 1957; M.S., Cornell U., 1959, Ph.D., 1964. Research chemist Goodyear Tire & Rubber Co., Akron, Ohio, 1963-67; sr. research chemist Dow Badische Co., Williamsburg, Va., 1967-69; group leader Borg-Warner Corp., Des Plaines, Ill., 1969-73; head materials research & devel. div. Agency Def. Devel., Seoul, 1973-77; sr. research assoc. Calgon Corp., Pitts., 1977—. Contbr. articles to profl. jours. Patentee in field. Mem. Am. Chem. Soc. Current work: Research in the chemical treatment technology of industrial cooling water systems; investigation on dispersion and flocculation phenomena of colloid in cooling water system; polymer structure versus performance for industrial water treatment. Subspecialties: Physical chemistry; Polymer chemistry. Home: 123 Druid Dr McMurray PA 15317 Office: Calgon Corp Research and Devel PO Box 1346 Pittsburgh PA 15230

CHA, SE DO, physician; b. Seoul, Korea, Dec. 17, 1942; came to U.S., 1966, naturalized, 1977; s. Young Sun and Hee Joo (Chang) C.; m. Elsa Jane Greene, Dec. 21, 1974. M.D., Yon Sei U., 1966. Diplomate: Am. Bd. Internal Medicine. Cardiologist Roger Williams Gen. Hosp., Providence, 1973-75; cardiologist Deborah Heart and Lung Center, Browns Mills, N.J., 1975—, asst. dir. adult cardiac catheterization lab., 1975—; instr. Brown U., Providence, 1973-75. Contbr. articles to profl. jours. Fellow Am. Coll. Angiology, Soc. for Cardiac Angiography, ACP; mem. AMA, Fedn. Clin. Research, Internat. Soc. Heart Transplantation, Am. Heart Assn. Current Work: Valvular heart disease, especially tricuspid valve disease. Intracardiac phonocardiography, primary pulmonary hypertension. Subspecialties: Cardiology; Internal medicine. Home: 71 Hartford Rd Medford NJ 08055 Office: Deborah Heart and Lung Center Trenton Rd Bronws Mills NJ 08015

CHABAL, YVES JEAN, physicist; b. Pau, Basses-Pyrenees, France, Aug. 5, 1952; came to U.S., 1970, permanent resident, 1981; s. Eric Henri and Josette Alice (Mondain) C.; m. Linda Elisabeth Aristondo, Oct. 16, 1984. A.B., Princeton U., 1974; M.S., Cornell U., 1976, Ph.D., 1980. Postdoctoral fellow Bell Labs., Murray Hill, N.J., 1980-81; mem. tech. staff AT&T Bell Labs., Murray Hill, 1981—; advisor Ph.D. students Princeton U., 1982-85. Contbr. articles to profl. jours. Mem. Union Concerned Scientists, Am. Phys. Soc., Optical Soc. Am., Sigma Xi. Current work: Surface infrared spectroscopy of semiconductor and metal surfaces; development of new surface spectroscopic techniques; basic research in surface science. Subspecialty: Condensed matter physics. Home: 288 Barrow St Apt 1 Jersey City NJ 07302 Office: AT&T Bell Labs MH1C-333 600 Mountain Ave Murray Hill NJ 07974

CHACKO, GEORGE KUTTY, biochemist, educator; b. Kottarakkara, Kerala, India, Feb. 15, 1933; came to U.S., 1962, naturalized, 1967; s. Kurian and Sosamma (Abraham) C.; m. Thankamma Joseph, Jan. 11, 1962; children: Jacob, Joseph, George. B.Sc., U. Kerala, 1956, M.Sc., 1958; Ph.D., U. Ill., 1966. Postdoctoral research assoc. U. Wash., Seattle, 1966-67, U. Ariz., Tucson, 1967-68; asst. prof. biochemistry Med. Coll. Pa., Phila., 1968-74, assoc. prof., 1974—. Wright fellow, 1963. Mem. Am. Chem. Soc., Am. Physiol. Sco., AAAS, Soc. Exptl. Biology and Medicine., Am. Soc. Biol. Chemists. Current Work: Metabolism of lipids and lipoproteins; lipoprotein-membrane interactions; membrane structure and function. Subspecialties: Biochemistry (medicine); Membrane biology. Home: 1131 Cleveland Rd Blue Bell PA 19422 Office: Med Coll Pa Philadelphia PA 19129

CHACKO, JACOB, veterinarian, government agency official; b. Kerala, India, Aug. 15, 1947; came to U.S., 1972, naturalized, 1978; s. Pulimoottil and Saramma (Chummar) C.; m. Cerine Jacob, Nov. 8, 1976; children—Ron, Reena. D.V.M., Kerala, India, 1971; postdoctoral tng., U. Wis., 1983. Research veterinarian U. Md., Balt., 1973-78; veterinarian Guil-Rand Vet. Hosp., High Point, N.C., 1979-81; vet. med. officer U.S. Dept. Agr., Memphis, 1983—. Author: Serotonin and Pulmonary Circulation, 1982. Contbr. articles to profl. jours. Mem. Soc. Prevention of Cruelty to Animals, Am. Assn. Lab. Animal Sci., AVMA, Am. Assn. Lab. Animal Medicine, Animal Sci. Assn. Baptist. Current work: Veterinary regulatory and public health. Subspecialties: Pathology (veterinary medicine); Laboratory animal medicine. Home: 4825 Berry Dale Ave Memphis TN 38118 Office: USDA Office 1400 Warford Rd Memphis TN 38118

CHADDOCK, JACK BARTLEY, See *Who's Who in America,* 43rd edition.

CHADWICK, ROBERT WILLIAM, toxicologist, researcher; b. Buffalo, N.Y., Mar. 16, 1930; s. Elihu Clair and Helen (Murray) C.; m. Claire Jeannette Crisp, Aug. 20, 1966; 1 child, Natanya Laurel. B.A., Case Western Res. U., 1957; M.S., 1962; Ph.D., Utah State U., 1967. Cert. Am. Bd. Toxicology. Chemist, Republic Steel Research Ctr., Cleve., 1957-62; toxicologist Primate and Pest Effects Lab EPA, Berrine, Fla., 1966-73, Environ. Research Ctr., Research Triangle Park, N.C., 1973—. Editor: Gables Chess Notes newsletter, 1969-73. Contbr. numerous articles to profl. jours. Served with U.S. Army, 1951-53. NIH fellow, 1964. Mem. Soc. toxicology, Am. Chem. Soc., Internat. Soc. Study Xenobiotics, N.Y. Acad. Scis., Sigma Xi, Pi Delta Epsilon. Clubs: Coral Gables Chess Club (pres. 1969-73), Fla. Chess Assn., U.S. Chess Fedn. Current work: Investigate dynamics of absorption, distribution, biotransformation and excretion of environmental toxicants; interactions of chemicals with detoxification in developing animal. Subspecialties: Toxicology (medicine); Analytical chemistry. Home: Route 2 Box 56A Apex NC 27502 Office: US EPA Environ Research Ctr MD#67 HERL Research Triangle Park NC 27711

CHAET, ALFRED B., biology educator, administrator; b. Boston, June 7, 1927; m. Shirley Rice, Sept. 2, 1950; children—Douglas Lee, Mark Steven, Judi Elise. B.S. in Zoology, U. Mass., 1949, M.S. in Comparative-Marine Physiology, 1950; Ph.D. in Gen.-Cellular Physiology, U. Pa., 1953; postgrad. Oak Ridge Inst. Nuclear Studies, 1961. Research asst. in zoology U. Pa., Phila., 1950-53, teaching asst. Sch. Medicine, 1953; instr. zoology U. Maine, Orono, 1953-56; research Boston City Hosp., 1956-59; asst. prof. physiology Sch. Medicine, Boston U., 1956-58; sr. investigator Marine Biol. Lab., Woods Hole, Mass., summers 1955-63; assoc. prof. biology Am. U., Washington, 1958-61; prof. biology, 1961-66; vis. scholar Scripps Inst. Oceanography, U. Calif., San Diego, 1964-66; assoc. dean scis., math. and tech. U. W. Fla., Pensacola, 1966, prof. biology provost Gamma Coll., 1966-76, prof. biology, assoc. v.p. research and sponsored programs, 1976—; lectr. med. physiology for residents and interns Sibley Meml. Hosp., Washington, 1960-62; mem. reviewing panels on undergrad. programs NSF, 1959-69; asst. program chmn. XVI Internat. Congress Zoology; mem. planning com. Two Plus, Two Plus/The Upper-Level Univ. Internat. Conf., 1970; sea grant coordinator U. W. Fla., 1971—; sec., treas., chmn. exec. com. NW Fla. Comprehensive Health Planning Council, 1971-75; chmn. Task Force on Environ. Health Planning, 1972-73; mem. NW Fla. Regional Med. Program, 1972-74; mem. task force on coll. credit through exam. State of Fla., 1972-78; U. West Fla. rep. to Fla. Inst. Oceanography, 1966-78; participant Inst. Acad. Deans, Am. Council on Edn., 1972; mem. adv. com. trustees Univ. Hosp., 1976; com. chmn. several So. Assns. of colls. and schs. accreditation teams to assist in evaluating various univs. for accreditation, 1969-81; bd. dirs. Pensajcola Found. for Med. Edn. and Research, 1976—; mem. Health Systems Agy. Com. on Univ. Hosp., 1976-77; chmn. Pensacola Med. Edn. Program on Univ. Hosp., 1977-78; vice-chmn., chmn. and exec. com. 18 County Health Systems Agy., 1977-82; mem. clin. investigation bd. Sacred Heart Hosp., 1978—. Contbr. articles, and abstracts to profl. publs. Com. mem. Boy Scouts Am., 1972-76; sec.-treas. Panhandle Health Systems Agy., 1975-76; vice chmn. Blue Ribbon Com. for Univ. Hosp., 1976; mem. human rights com. W. Fla. Hosp., 1980—; mem. adv. bd. Cross Creek Nursing Home, 1983. Served with U.S. Army, 1944-46. Spl. fellow NIH, Nat. Inst. Neurol. Diseases and Blindness, 1964-66; research grantee NIH, 1956-58, 60-67; tng. grantee NSF, 1959-67; equipment grantee AEC, 1961, 62, NSF, 1963. Mem. Soc. Research Adminstrs. (chmn. edn. com. 1979—, chmn. nominating com. 1981, mem. editorial bd., internat. com. 1983), Am. Soc. Oceanography, Fla. Acad. Scis., Am. Inst. Biol. Scis. (rep. to AAAS coop. com. for teaching sci. and math. 1962-68, speaker vis. biologists program 1964-72), AAAS, Soc. Gen. Physiology, Soc. Cell Biology, Marine Biol. Lab. (corp.), Am. Physiol. Soc., Am. Zool. Soc., Sigma Xi, Tri Beta, Phi Kappa Phi. Current work: Neural hormones in starfish, the shedding substance and shedhibin; amino acid uptake by starfish tube feet; mechanism of adhesion in invertebrates; toxic factor theory in burns. Office: Univ West Florida Research and Sponsored Programs Pensacola FL 32514

CHAFFEE, FREDERIC H., astronomer. Dir. Multiple Mirror Telescope Obs., U. Ariz.; astronomer optical and infrared astronomy div. Harvard Smithsonian Ctr. for Astrophysics, Cambridge, Mass. Subspecialty: Optical astronomy. Office: U Arizona MMT Observatory Tucson AZ 85721*

CHAHINE, MOUSTAFA TOUFIC, atmospheric scinetist; b. Beirut, Jan. 1, 1935; s. Toufic M. and Hind S. (Tabbara) C.; m. Marina Bandak, Dec. 9, 1960; children—Tony T., Steve S. B.S., U. Wash., 1956, M.S., 1957; Ph.D., U. Calif., Berkeley, 1960. With Jet Propulsion Lab., Calif. Inst. Tech., Pasadena, 1960—, mgr. planetary atmospheres sect. 1975-78, sr. research scientist, mgr. earth and space scis. div., 1978-85, chief scientist, 1985—; vis. scientist MIT, 1969-70; vis. prof. Am. U., Beirut, 1971-72; mem. NASA Space and Earth Sci. Adv. Com., 1982—; cons. U.S. Navy, 1972-76. Contbr. articles on atmospheric scis. to profl. jours. Recipient medal for exceptional sci. achievements NASA, 1969. Fellow Am. Phys. Soc.; mem. Am. Meteorol. Soc., Sigma Xi. Subspecialty: Physics of fluids. Office: Jet Propulsion Lab 4800 Oak Grove Dr Pasadena CA 91109

CHAISSON, ERIC JOSEPH, astrophysicist, educator; b. Lowell, Mass., Oct. 26, 1946; s. Louis Joseph and Marion Loretta (Brennan) C.; m. Lola Judith Eachus, May 1, 1976; children—Megan Lyra, Paul Cygnus. B.S., U. Lowell, 1968; M.A., Harvard U., 1969, Ph.D., 1972. Postdoctoral fellow Nat. Acad. Scis., Smithsonian Astrophys. Obs., 1972-74; asst. prof. Harvard U., 1974-79, assoc. prof., 1979-82; prof. astrophysics Haverford (Pa.) Coll., 1982—; mem. NASA Working Group on Extraterrestrial Intelligence; Shapley vis. prof. Am. Astron. Soc.; mem. sci. adv. com. Boston Mus. Scis., Hayden Planetarium; sci. adv. com. Public Broadcasting System series Search for Solutions; chmn. com. on public edn. Harvard-Smithsonian Obs. Author: Cosmic Dawn: The Origins of Matter and Life, 1981; La Relativita, 1983; The Invisible Universe, 1985. Mem. editorial adv. bd. Zygon: Jour. Religion and Sci. Contbr. numerous articles to profl. jours. Served to capt. USAF, 1969-70. Sloan fellow, 1977; recipient Bok prize Harvard U., 1977, Smith prize, 1978; Phi Beta Kappa Writing prize, 1981. Mem. AAAS, Am. Astron. Soc., Am. Assn. Physics Tchrs., Fedn. Am. Scientists, Internat. Union Radio Sci., Internat. Astron. Union, Authors Guild, Am. Inst. Physics. (sci. writing award 1981), Sigma Xi. Current work: Synthesis of Astrophysics and biochemistry to form new subject of cosmic evolution. Subspecialties: Radio and microwave astronomy; Cosmology. Home: 803 Stoke Rd Villanova PA 19085 Office: Haverford Coll Haverford PA 19041

CHAIT, EDWARD MARTIN, chemical executive, research scientist; b. N.Y.C., May 8, 1942; s. William and Beatrice Lillian (Faigelman) C.; m. Carol Eileen Werner, June 19, 1966; children—Lisa, Steven. A.B., Cornell U., 1964; Ph.D., Purdue U., 1968. Research chemist DuPont Corp., Wilmington, Del., 1968-71, lab supr., Monrovia, Calif., 1971-76, product mgr., Wilmington, 1976-83, program mgr., 1983—; chmn. adv. panel Nat. Bur. of Standards, 1980—. Mem. AAAS, Am. Chem. Soc. Current work: Tech. transfer and new venture devel. in analytical and clinical chem. and biotech. Subspecialties: Analytical chemistry; Bioinstrumentation. Home: 1019 Oriente Ave Wilmington DE 19807 Office: DuPont Biomedical Products Barley Mill Plaza P24-1260 Wilmington DE 19898

CHAKRABARTY, ANANDA MOHAN, microbiologist; b. Sainthia, India, Apr. 4, 1938; s. Satya Dos and Sasthi Bala (Mukherjee) C.; m. Krishna Chakraverty, May 26, 1965; children—Kaberi, Asit. B.Sc., St. Xavier's Coll., 1958; M.Sc., U. Calcutta, 1960, Ph.D., 1965. Sr. research officer U. Calcutta, 1964-65; research asso. in biochemistry U. Ill., Urbana, 1965-71; mem. staff Gen. Electric Research and Devel. Center, Schenectady, 1971-79; prof. dept. microbiology U. Ill. Med. Center, 1979—. Editor: Genetic Engineering, 1977. Named Scientist of Year Indsl. Research Mag., 1975. Mem. Am. Soc. Microbiology, Soc. Indsl. Microbiology, Am. Soc. Biol. Chemists. Current Work: Toxic chemical pollution, genetically engineered microorganism for secondary oil recovery. Subspecialties: Genetics and genetic engineering (biology); Microbiology. Home: 206 Julia Dr Villa Park IL 60181 Office: Dept Microbiology U Ill Med Center 835 S Wolcott St Chicago IL 60612

CHAKRAVARTY, INDRANIL, research scientist; b. New Delhi, India, Jan. 7, 1954; came to U.S., 1971; s. Sunil Kumar and Monica (Bagchi) C. B.S.E.E., NYU, 1974; M.Eng., Rensselaer Poly. Inst., 1976, Ph.D., 1982. Research asst. Image Processing Lab., Rensselaer Poly. Inst., 1975-80, instr. dept. elec. and systems engring., 1980-81; mem. profl. staff Schlumerger-Doll Research Ctr., Ridgefield, Conn., 1981—. Mem. IEEE, Assn. for Computing Machinery (editor Computing Revs.), Spl. Interest Group Computer Graphics, N.Y. Acad. Scis., Sigma Xi. Current Work: 3D image synthesis, image realism, computer vision and robotics, computer aided design. Subspecialties: Graphics, image processing, and pattern recognition; Computer engineering. Home: 19-37 Hudson St Bethel CT 06801 Office: Schlumberger-Doll Research Ctr Old Quarry Rd Ridgefield CT 06877

CHALILPOYIL, PURUSH, chemistry research scientist; b. Calicut, India, May 18, 1947, came to U.S., 1972; s. P.K. Krishnan Nair and Narayani Amma Chalilpoyil. B.Sc. and M.Sc., Kerala U., India, 1968; Ph.D., Georgetown U., 1976. Postdoctoral fellow Calif. Inst. Tech., Pasadena, 1976-77; research assoc. Johns Hopkins U., Balt., 1977; sr. scientist Duracell, Inc., Burlington, Mass., 1979-82, program mgr., Needham, Mass., 1982—. Author: (with others) Organic Chemistry, 1975. Translator: Chemical Background for Biological Sciences, 1974. Fulbright fellow, 1972-76. Mem. Am. Chem. Soc., Electrochemical Soc., Sigma Xi. Subspecialty: Inorganic chemistry. Home: RFD #2 Box 235 Lincoln MA 01773 Office: Duracell Inc Needham MA 02194

CHALLINOR, DAVID, scientific institute administrator; b. N.Y.C., July 11, 1920; s. David and Mercedes (Crimmins) C.; m. Joan Ridder, Nov. 22, 1952; children—Julia M., Mary E., Sarah L., D. Thompson. B.A., Harvard U., 1943; M.F., Yale U., 1959, Ph.D., 1966. With Offerman-Anderson, Clayton & Co., Houston, 1947-51; cotton farmer, Culberson County, Tex., 1951-53; asst. sec. First Mortgage Co., Houston, 1953-57; research asst. Conn. Agr. Expt. Sta., New Haven, 1959-60; dep. dir. Yale Peabody Mus., New Haven, 1960-65, acting dir., 1965-66; spl. asst. in tropical biology Smithsonian Instn., Washington, 1966-67, dep. dir. office internat. activities, 1967-68, dir. office internat. activities, 1968-70, asst. sec. sci., 1971—; Am. adminstrv. sec. Charles Darwin Found., 1971—. Contbr. articles to sci. jours. Trustee Manhattanville Coll., 1964-70, Environ. Law Inst., 1975-84; bd. dirs. Environ Def. Fund, 1982—, African Wildlife Found., 1980—. Served with USNR, 1943-46. Fellow AAAS; mem. Sigma Xi. Subspecialty: Administration. Office: Smithsonian Inst 1000 Jefferson Dr SW Washington DC 20560

CHALLONER, DAVID REYNOLDS, university health affairs administrator; b. Appleton, Wis., Jan. 31, 1935; s. Reynolds R. and Marion (Below) C.; m. Jacklyn Anderson, Aug. 30, 1958; children: David H., Laura R., Britt D. B.S., Lawrence U., 1956; M.D., Harvard U., 1961. Diplomate: Am. Bd. Internal Medicine. Intern Presbyn. Hosp., N.Y.C., 1961-62; resident in internal medicine U. Wash., Seattle, 1965-67; prof. medicine Ind. U., Indpls., 1967-74; dean sch. medicine St. Louis U., 1974-82; v.p. health affairs U. Fla., Gainesville, 1982—; cons. Eli Lilly and Co., Indpls., 1968-80. Recipient alumni award Harvard Med. Sch., 1961; Dr. William Beaumont award AMA, 1982. Mem. Am. Fedn. Clin. Research (pres. 1975-76), Assn. Am. Physicians, Inst. Medicine (membership com. 1982-86), Am. Soc. Clin. Investigation. Clubs: Cosmos, Washington. Subspecialties: Endocrinology; Internal medicine. Office: U Fla PO Box J-14 JHMHC Gainesville FL 32610

CHALMERS, JOHN H., JR., educator; b. St. Paul, Minn., Mar. 5, 1940; s. John H. and Jane Amelia (Bedson) C. A.B., Stanford U., 1962; Ph.D., U. Calif.-San Diego, 1968. Postdoctoral fellow U. Wash.-Seattle, 1968-71; postdoctoral fellow U. Calif.-Berkeley, 1971-73; research fellow Merck Sharpe & Dohme Research Labs., Rahway, N.J., 1973-75; asst. prof. Baylor Coll. Medicine, Houston, 1976—. NIH Predoctoral and Postdoctoral fellowships, 1966-67, 69-71; NSF fellowship, 1963-67. Mem. AAAS, Computer Music Assn., Loglan Inst., Sigma Xi. Patentee in field. Current Work: Molecular biology of genetic engineering, biotechnology. Subspecialties: Molecular biology; Biochemistry (biology). Office: Biosyne Corp 2210 Maroneal Suite 302 Houston TX 77030

CHALMERS, THOMAS CLARK, physician, educational and research adminstrator; b. Forest Hills, N.Y., Dec. 8, 1917; s. Thomas Clark and Elizabeth (Ducat) C.; m. Frances Crawford Talcott, Aug. 31, 1942; children: Elizabeth Ducat (Mrs. Daniel G. Wright), Frances Talcott, Thomas Clark, Richard Matthew. Student, Yale U., 1936-39; M.D., Columbia U., 1943. Diplomate: Am. Bd. Internal Medicine. Intern Presbyn. Hosp., N.Y.C., 1943-44; research fellow NYU Malaria Research Unit, Goldwater Meml. Hosp., N.Y.C., 1944-45; resident Harvard Med. Services of Boston City Hosp., 1945-47; asst. physician Thorndike Meml. Lab., 1947-53; chief med. services Lemuel Shattuck Hosp., Boston, 1955-68; asst. chief med. dir. for research and edn. VA, Washington, 1968-70; asso. dir. clin. care NIH, also dir. clin. center NIH, Bethesda, Md., 1970-73; pres. (Mt. Sinai Med. Center), 1973-83; prof. medicine, dean Mt. Sinai Sch. Medicine, N.Y.C., 1973-83, Disting. Service prof., dir. clin. trials unit, 1983—, pres. emeritus, dean emeritus, 1983—; lectr. medicine Harvard; vis. prof. dept. health policy and mgmt. Harvard Sch. Pub. Health, 1983—; prof. medicine Tufts U., 1961-68, George Washington U., 1970-73; vis. prof. Harvard Sch. Pub. Health, 1983; chmn. bd. trustees Dartmouth-Hitchcock Med. Ctr., 1983—. Contbr. numerous articles profl. jours. Bd. dirs. New Eng. Home for Little Wanderers, 1960-65; bd. regents Nat. Library Medicine, 1978-79. Served as capt., M.C. AUS, 1953-55. Mem. Am. Assn. Study Liver Diseases (pres. 1959), Am. Clin. and Climatol. Assn., ACP, Am. Fedn. Clin. Research, Am. Gastroent. Assn. (pres. 1969), Am. Soc. Clin. Investigation, Assn. Am. Physicians, N.Y. Acad. Medicine, Inst. Medicine of Nat. Acad. Scis.; mem. Internat. Physicians for the prevention of Nuclear War, Soc. Clin. Trials (pres. 1985), Eastern Gut Club., Physicians for Social Responsibility, Am. Acad. Arts and Scis. Current Work: Methodology of clinical trials. Subspecialty: Gastroenterology. Office: Mt Sinai Med Center One Gustave L Levy Pl New York NY 10029

CHALOVICH, JOSEPH MICHAEL, biochemist, educator; b. Pitts., July 5, 1952; s. Joseph Michael and Magdeline (Stojhovic) C.; m. Patricia Edith Blackburn, Aug. 9, 1975. B.S., Pa. State U., 1974; M.S., Va. Poly. Inst., 1976; Ph.D., U. Ill. Med. Sch.-Chgo., 1978. Research assoc. U. Ill. Med. Sch., Chgo., 1978-79; staff fellow NIH, Bethesda, Md., 1979-84; asst. prof. biochemistry, East Carolina U., Greenville N.C., 1984—. Contbr. articles to profl. jours. Mem. Biophysical Soc., Am. Chem. Soc., AAAS, Am. Assn. Biochemists, Sigma Xi (cert. recognition 1977-78), Phi Sigma (award 1976). Democrat. Roman Catholic. Current work: Regulation of muscle contraction and cell motility; role of actin binding protiens in modulating the actomyosin ATPase activity. Subspecialties: Biochemistry (biology); Cell biology. Home: 207 Westhaven Rd Greenville NC 27834 Office: E Carolina U Sch Medicine Dept Biochemistry 5W-56 Brody Bldg Greenville NC 27834

CHAMBERLAIN, CHARLES FRANKLIN, marine geologist, consultant; b. Columbus, Ohio, Sept. 7, 1946; s. George Victor and Margaret Lytle C.; m. Janet A. Mathers, Aug. 7, 1970; 1 dau., Circe Ann. B.S., St. Joseph's Coll., 1970; M.S., Boston Coll., 1976. Research assoc. Skidaway Inst. Oceanography, Savannah, Ga., 1973-78; instr. Calif. State U., Northridge, Calif., 1978-79; sr. oceanographer Interstate Electronic, Anaheim, Calif., 1979-80; marine geologist Ertec Western, Inc., Long Beach, Calif., 1980-81; mgr. offshore ops. Mesa, Inc., Northridge, Calif., 1981—; lectr. Marymount; Los Angeles. Contbr. articles in field to marine geologic jours. Mem. Marine Tech. Soc. (bd. dirs. 1982—), Soc. Exploration Geophysicists, Soc. Econ. Paleontologists and Mineralogists, Am. Geophys. Union, Sigma Xi. Current Work: Direct offshore geophysical data acquisition. Subspecialties: Sedimentology; Offshore technology. Office: Mesa 2 Inc 4250 Pennsylvania Ave La Crescenta CA 91214

CHAMBERLAIN, OWEN, nuclear physicist; b. San Francisco, July 10, 1920; 4 children from previous marriage; m. June Steingart, 1980. A.B. (Cramer fellow), Dartmouth Coll., 1941; Ph.D., U. Chgo., 1949. Instr. physics U. Calif., Berkeley, 1948-50, asst. prof., 1950-54, assoc. prof., 1954-58, prof., 1958—, civilian physicist, Manhattan Dist., Berkeley, Los Alamos, 1942-46. Guggenheim fellow, 1957-58; Loeb lectr. at Harvard U., 1959; Recipient Nobel prize (with Emilio Segré) for physics, for discovery anti-proton, 1959. Fellow Am. Phys. Soc., Am. Acad. Arts and Scis.; mem. Nat. Acad. Scis. Subspecialty: Nuclear physics. Address: Physics Dept U Calif Berkeley CA 94720*

CHAMBERLAIN, STEVEN CRAIG, neuroanatomist, bioengineer, mineralogist, educator; b. Everett, Pa., Dec. 13, 1946; s. Carl Eugene and D. Suzanne (Rearick) C.; m. Helen Haritou, Apr. 29, 1972. B.S. in Elec. Engring., MIT, 1968; Ph.D. in Sensory Sci., Syracuse U., 1978. Instr., Inst. Sensory Research, Syracuse U., N.Y., 1977-78, asst. prof., 1978-82, assoc. prof. neurosci. and bioengring., 1982—, assoc. dir. Inst. Sensory Research, 1985—; curator minerals Hamilton Coll., Clinton, N.Y., 1981—; lectr. in field. Cons. editor Rocks and Minerals, 1980—. Contbr. articles, book chpts. and abstracts to profl. lit. Served with U.S. Army, 1970-73, W.Ger. Recipient Presdl. award for teaching by sharing Eastern Fedn. Mineral Lapidary Soc., 1978; Grass Found. fellow, 1977. Mem. Assn. Research in Vision and Ophthalmology, Soc. Neurosci., Sigma Xi. Democrat. Lutheran. Current work: Neuroanatomy—role of efferent feedback to sensory organs; structure and function of eye and ear; mineralogy—bacterial origins of minerals; metamorphic paragenesis. Subspecialties: Neurobiology; Mineralogy. Home: 113 Brooklea Dr Syracuse NY 13207 Office: Inst Sensory Research Syracuse U Syracuse NY 13210

CHAMBERS, JAMES VERNON, food science educator, consultant; b. Pekin, Ill., Mar. 12, 1935; s. Hershel O. and Clela Belle (Stoops) C.; m. Shirley Ann Clarke, Sept. 1, 1957; 1 dau., Deborah Evelyn. B.Sc., Ohio State U., 1961, M.Sc. in Dairy Tech, 1966, Ph.D. in Food Sci, 1972. Corp. microbiologist Ross Labs., Columbus, Ohio, 1961-69; lab. dir. div. foods, dairy and drugs Ohio Dept. Agr., 1969-71; asst. prof. food sci. U. Wis.-River Falls, 1972-74; assoc. prof., extension specialist Purdue U., West Lafayette, Ind., 1974—, cons. indsl. wastewater mgmt. Contbr. articles to sci. jours.; co-author extension manual series on water and wastewater mgmt. Served in USN, 1953-58. Recipient award Nat. Ice Cream Retailers Assn., 1979; award Linder Dairy Ctrs., 1979. Mem. Internat. Assn. Milk, Food and Environ. Sanitarians, Am. Dairy Sci. Assn., N.Y. Acad. Scis., Water Pollution Control Fedn., Am. Soc. Microbiology, Inst. Food Technologists. Current Work: Medical microbiology in mastitis; food by-product utilization; environmental microbiology. Subspecialties: Food science and technology; Water supply and wastewater treatment. Office: Purdue U West Lafayette IN 47907

CHAMBERS, KENTON LEE, botanist, educator, researcher; b. Los Angeles, Sept. 27, 1929; s. Maynard Macy and Edna Georgia (Miller) C.; m. Henrietta Laing, June 21, 1958; children: Elaine Patricia, David Macy. A.B. with highest honors, Whittier Coll., 1950; Ph.D., Stanford U., 1955. NSF postdoctoral fellow UCLA, 1955-56; instr. botany Yale U., New Haven, 1956-58; asst. prof., 1958-60; assoc. prof. botany Oreg. State U., Corvallis, 1960-65, prof., 1965—, curator herbarium, 1960—; program dir. systematic biology NSF, Wahington, 1967-68. Contbr. articles to sci. jours. Mem. Bot. Soc. Am., Am. Soc. Plant Taxonomists, Soc. Study of Evolution, AAAS, Am. Inst. Biol. Scis., Calif. Bot. Soc., Soc. Systematic Zoology, Assn. Tropical Biology. Current Work: Evolutionary genetics and chromosome cytology of higher plants; quantitative DNA variation in natural populations of annual species of plants; polyploidy and hybridization in natural populations of annual plants. Subspecialties: Evolutionary biology; Systematics. Home: 3220 NW Lynwood Circle Corvallis OR 97330 Office: Oreg State U Corvallis OR 97331

CHAMBLISS, CARLSON ROLLIN, astronomy educator; b. Boston, July 17, 1941; s. Rollin James and Amy Christine (Carlson) C. A.B., Harvard U., 1962; M.S., U. Pa., 1964, Ph.D., 1968. Asst. prof. Georgetown U., Washington, 1968-70; faculty Kutztown U., Pa., 1970—, assoc. prof., 1975-79, prof. astronomy, 1979—. Contbr. articles to profl. jours. Pawling fellow, 1964-65, Spl. Harrison fellow, 1965-66; Fulbright grantee, 1966-67, Am. Astron. Soc. grantee, 1981. Mem. Internat. Astron. Union (commn. close binary stars), Am. Astron. Soc. Current work: Eclipsing binary stars; stellar photometry. Subspecialty: Optical astronomy. Office: Dept Physical Scis Kutztown Univ Kutztown PA 19530

CHAMIS, CHRISTOS CONSTANTINOS, research engineer; b. Sotira, Greece, May 16, 1930; came to U.S., 1948; s. Constantinos and Anastasia (Kyriakos) C.; m. Alice Yanosko, Aug. 20, 1966; children—Chrysantie, Anna-Lisa, Constantinos. B.S. in Civil Engring., Cleve. State U., 1960; M.S., Case Western Res. U., 1962, Ph.D., 1967. Draftsman, designer Cons. Engring., Cleve., 1955-60; research asst. Case Western Res. U., Cleve., 1960-62, research assoc., 1964-68; research mathematician B. F. Goodrich, Brecksville, Ohio, 1962-64; aerospace engr. Lewis Research Ctr., NASA, Cleve., 1968-84, sr. research engr., 1984—; cons. Lawrence Livermore Labs., Calif., 1974-79; adj. prof. Cleve. State U., 1968—, Akron U., 1980—. Editor: Composites Analytical Design, 1975. Contbr. numerous articles to sci. jours. Patentee in field. Served with USMCR, 1953-54. Fellow AIAA (assoc.); mem. ASCE, ASME, ASTM, Sigma Xi. Clubs: Dodoni, Hellenic U. Current work: Composite mechanics; aerospace structures and computational structural mechanics; non-linear analysis and optimization methodology development. Subspecialties: Theoretical and applied mechanics; Software engineering. Home: 24534 Framingham Dr Westlake OH 44145 Office: NASA Lewis Research Ctr 21000 Brookpark Rd Cleveland OH 44135

CHAMPE, SEWELL PRESTON, microbiologist, educator; b. Montgomery, W.Va., Nov. 24, 1932; s. Sewell J. and Janice M.; m. Gertrud G. Graubart, Aug. 3, 1959 (div. 1968); children: Mark, Peter; m. Pamela Chambers, June 28, 1969. B.S., M.I.T., 1954; Ph.D., Purdue U., 1959. Asst. prof. biology Purdue U., West Lafayette, Ind., 1962-66, assoc. prof. biology, 1966-69; prof. microbiology Rutgers U., New Brunswick, N.J., 1969—. Contbr. articles to sci. jours. NIH grantee, 1963—. Mem. Am. Soc. Microbiology, Am. Soc. Biol. Chemists. Current Work: Genetics of fungal development; gene expression during development. Subspecialties: Microbiology; Gene actions. Home: 17 Beech Ln Edison NJ 08820 Office: Waksman Inst Microbiology Rutgers U New Brunswick NJ 08903

CHAN, ALBERT SUN CHI, chemist; b. Canton, China, Oct. 30, 1950; came to U.S. 1975; s. Kwong Fook and Woon Nam (Yan) C.; m. Mabel Wong, Apr. 13, 1977; 1 child, Alan Ken. A.B., Internatl. Christian U., Tokyo, 1975; M.S., U. Chgo., 1976, Ph.D., 1979. Sr. research chemist Monsanto Co., St. Louis, 1979-82, research specialist, 1982-83, sr. research specialist, 1983—. Patentee in field, Sir Graham scholar Hong Kong gov., 1971, United Bd. for Christian Higher Educ. in Asia scholar, 1971-75, Internatl. Christian U. Merit scholar, 1973-75. Mem. Am. Chem. Soc., Sigma Xi. Current work: Organometallic chemical and homogeneous catalysis, chemical synthesis and reaction mechanisms, new products and process research. Subspecialties: Catalysis chemistry; Inorganic chemistry. Home: 1522 Lynndale Dr Saint Charles MO 63303 Office: Monsanto Co 800 N Lindbergh Blvd Saint Louis MO 63167

CHAN, ARTHUR WING KAY, research scientist, educator; b. Hong Kong, June 24, 1941; came to U.S., 1969, naturalized, 1976; s. Yut-Fat and Shin-Yee (Yung) C.; m. Shirley Pou, Feb. 27, 1967; 1 son, Alvin Mark. B.Sc. with 1st class honors, Australian Nat. U., 1966, Ph.D., 1969. Postdoctoral fellow chemistry dept. Washington U., St. Louis, 1969-71, postdoctoral research asso. pharmacology dept., 1971-73; research scientist III Research Inst. on Alcoholism, Buffalo, 1974-76, research scientist IV, 1976-79, research scientist V, 1979—; research asst. prof. pharmacology SUNY, Buffalo, 1974-81, research asso. prof., 1982—. Contbr. articles to profl. jours. Nat. Inst. Alcohol Abuse and Alcoholism research grantee, 1975-77, 84-86; N.Y. State Health Research Council grantee, 1976-77, 78-80; Nat. Inst. Drug Abuse grantee, 1980-81. Mem. Am. Soc. for Pharmacology and Exptl. Therapeutics, Research Soc. on Alcoholism, Sigma Xi. Current Work: Biochemical and pharmacological effects of alcohol and other drugs, as well as their interactions. Subspecialties: Pharmacology; Psychopharmacology. Office: 1021 Main St Buffalo NY 14203

CHAN, DONALD PIN KWAN, orthopaedic surgery educator; b. Rangoon, Burma, Jan. 21, 1937; came to U.S., 1968; s. Charles Y.C. and Josephine (Golamco) C.; m. Dorothy S. Lau, July 31, 1966; children: Joanne, Elaine. M.B., B.S., U. Rangoon, 1960. Diplomate: Am. Bd. Orthopaedic Surgery. Intern U. Hong Kong, 1960-61, surg. trainee, 1961-68; resident in orthopedic surgery U. Vt. Hosps., 1968-71; Scoliosis Research Soc. traveling fellow, 1971-72; asst. prof. orthopedics U. Rochester, 1972-80, assoc. prof., 1980—, chief sect. spine surgery, 1983. Contbr. chpts. in books; designer spine instruments for surgery. Recipient Moire Topography award Easter Seals Soc., 1979, Phase Locked Interferometry award Scoliosis Research Soc., 1979, award for spinal cord injury model system HEW, 1981, 82, 83. Fellow ACS, Scoliosis Research Soc., Am. Acad. Orthopedic Surgeons; mem. Eastern Orthopaedic Assn., AMA. Roman Catholic. Current Work: Spine surgery and research related to disorders of spine. Subspecialty: Orthopedics. Office: School of Medicine and Dentistry University of Rochester Rochester NY 14642

CHAN, IU-YAM, chemistry educator; b. Hong Kong, Apr. 1, 1940; came to U.S., 1962; s. Shu Kwan and Choi Gee (Chow) C.; m. Sophia R. Su, Aug. 18, 1973; 1 son: Raymond. B.Sc., Cheng Kung U., Tainan, Taiwan, 1961; Ph.D., U. Chgo., 1969. Research asst. U. Leiden, The Netherlands, 1968-71; asst. prof. Brandeis U., 1971-77, assoc. prof., 1977-85, prof., 1985—; vis. scientist IBM Research Lab., Yorktown Heights, N.Y., 1977-78. Contbr. articles to sci. jours. Union Carbide Fellowship awardee, 1964; Gustavus F. Swift Fellowship awardee, 1965; William Rainey Harper Fellowship awardee, 1966; recipient numerous research grants. Mem. Am. Phys. Soc., Am. Chem. Soc., Sigma Xi. Current Work: Utilization of the fluorescence line-narrowing technique in studying phonon-assisted energy transfer; interaction of an electronically excited molecule with phonons in molecular crystals; supersonic jet spectroscopy of large molecules; spectroscopy and magnetic resonance under high pressure. Subspecialty: Condensed matter physics. Home: 100 Hickory Rd Weston MA 02193 Office: Dept Chemistry Brandeis U 415 South St Waltham MA 02254

CHAN, JAMES CHIU MING, pediatrician, nephrology researcher, educator; b. Hong Kong, Dec. 27, 1937; came to U.S., 1965, naturalized, 1974; m. Winnie Man Yee Chou, June 15, 1968; 1 child. Med. Degree, McGill U., Montreal, Can., 1964. Diplomate Am. Bd. Pediatrics. Asst. prof. pediatrics U. So. Calif., 1970-73; assoc. prof. child health George Washington U., 1973-76; prof. pediatrics Med. Coll. Va., Richmond, 1977—, vice chmn. dept., 1982—, also dir. pediatric nephrology; vis. scientist Nat. Heart, Lung and Blood Inst., Bethesda, Md., 1976-77; cons. NIH, 1978-82, 84—; chmn. med. adv. bd. Va. div. Nat. Kidney Found., Richmond, 1983—. Recipient Best Tchr. award Med. Coll. Va., 1978-79. Mem. Am. Soc. Pediatric Nephrology, Am. Inst. Nutrition, Am. Acad. Pediatrics, Am. Pediatric Soc., Richmond Pediatric Soc. Current work: Principal investigator of NIH grant. Office: Med Coll of VA Va Commonwealth Univ MCV Sta Box 498 Richmond VA 23298

CHAN, KAM HANG, electrical engineer, technology company executive; b. Macau South China, Feb. 20, 1949; came to U.S., 1968, naturalized, 1984; s. Yau and Mong H. (Wong) S.; m. Shao Ying Lee, Feb. 4, 1959. B.S., Calif. State U.-Fresno, 1972; M.S., U. Calif.-Berkeley, 1974, Ph.D., 1977. Devel. engr. Motorolo, Pheonix, 1974, Hewlett Packard, Palo Alto, Calif., 1977-80; research asst. U. Calif.-Berkeley, 1973-77, acting instr., 1977; tech. devel. engr. Advanced Micro Device, Sunnyvale, Calif., 1980-82; pres. Tatung Sci. & Tech., Inc., Sunnyvale, 1982—. Mem. IEEE. Current work: System products as well as the development of MOS technology and I.C.s. Subspecialties: Integrated circuits; Computer engineering. Office: Tatung Sci & Tech Inc 1050F E Duane Ave Sunnyvale CA 94086

CHAN, KWAN MING, geology educator, consultant; b. Hong Kong, July 30, 1935; s. Cheuk Fai and Sau Ying C.; m. Karen Kung-Mei, July 9, 1965; children: Karl, Ken, Kim. B.Sc. with spl. honors, U. Hong Kong, 1960; Ph.D., U. Liverpool, Eng., 1966. Research officer Hong Kong Dept. Agr. and Fisheries, 1961-68; asst. scientist Woods Hole Oceanographic Instn., Mass., 1968-69; prof. Calif. State U.-Long Beach, 1969—; vis. scientist Commonwealth Sci. Indsl. Research Orgn., Sydney, Australia, 1961; vis. scientist Maritime Safety Agy., Tokyo, 1967; vis. prof. Nat. Taiwan U., Taipei, 1975. Pres. Huntington Beach (Calif.) Chinese Sch., 1977; treas. Chinese Am. Faculty Assn., 1979. Rotary Club scholar, 1959; UNESCO fellow Paris, 1967. Mem. AM. Soc. Limnology and Oceanography, Am. Chem. Soc., Royal Inst. Chemistry (assoc.). Democrat. Current Work: Oceanography, chemistry, education, Chinese culture. Subspecialties: Oceanography; Analytical chemistry. Home: Box 605 Westminster CA 92684 Office: 1250 Bellflower Blvd Long Beach CA 90840

CHAN, PAK HOO, biochemist, researcher; b. Canton, Kwangtong, China, Apr. 11, 1942; came to U.S., 1968, naturalized, 1979; s. Sik-Kee and Hong-King (Leung) C.; m. Helen Shang Chu, Mar. 17, 1974; children: Tammy Yuen-Wah, Olivia Yee-Wah, Goldie Yan-Wah. B.S., Chinese U., Hong Kong, 1964; M.A., UCLA, 1970, Ph.D., 1972. Postdoctoral fellow U. Calif.-Berkeley, 1972-74, Stanford U., 1974-75; asst. research biochemist U. Calif.-San Francisco, 1975-80, assoc. research biochemist, 1980-83, adj. assoc. prof., 1983—; cons. clin. fellow, 1975—; mem. NIH-NINCDS Spl. Rev. Com., 1984—; ad hoc mem. neurology study sect. NIH, 1985—. Author: Symposium Brain Edema, 1982, 85; Symposium Neural Membranes, 1982; Symposium Sendi 1984; Handbook of Neurochemistry, 1985; Symposium Cerebrovascular Disease, 1985. Recipient Yale-New Haven Scholarship award, 1964; NIH grantee, 1978—. Mem. Am. Soc. Neurochemistry, Soc. Neurosci., Internat. Soc. Neurochemistry, Am. Soc. Brol. Chemists, Soc. Free Radical Research, N.Y. Acad. Scis., Am. Fedn. Clin. Research. Current Work: Biochemistry and molecular aspects of neurological disorders, e.g., brain edema, stroke; biochemical mechanisms. Subspecialties: Neurochemistry; Biochemistry (medicine). Home: 635 Jackson St Albany CA 94706 Office: U Calif Sch Medicine Dept Neurology San Francisco CA 94143

CHAN, PHILLIP C., biochemistry educator; b. Amoy, Fujian, China, June 14, 1928; came to U.S., 1949, naturalized, 1965; s. Hwa-Liong and Kim-Luan (Tan) C.; m. Joan Mildred Pon, June 2, 1965; 1 dau., Melinda. B.S., Monmouth Coll., 1952; M.A., Columbia U., 1953, Ph.D., 1957. Postdoctoral fellow Johns Hopkins U., Balt., 1957-59; med. research fellow Max-Planck Inst. for Cell Chemistry, Munich, W.Ger., 1959-60; from asst. prof. to prof. biochemistry SUNY Downstate Med. Ctr., Bklyn., 1960—. Contbr. articles to profl. jours. Mem. Am. Soc. Biol. Chemists, Am. Chem. Soc., N.Y. Acad. Scis. Current Work: Biochemical reactions involving reactive oxygen species including oxygen free radicals, excited states of molecular oxygen, ozone, peroxides and metal oxygen complexes. Subspecialty: Biochemistry (biology). Office: SUNY Downstate Med Ctr 450 Clarkson Ave Brooklyn NY 11203

CHAN, PO CHUEN, cell biologist, cancer research scientist; b. Ichong, Hupeh, China, May 13, 1935; came to U.S., 1960, naturalized, 1975; s. Tin Wa and Pui Wa (Ho) C.; m. Lillian Mak, Oct. 16, 1961; children: Yola, Vella. B.A., Internat. Christian U., Tokyo, 1960; M.A., Columbia U., 1963; Ph.D., N.Y.U., 1967. Research assoc. Sloan-Kettering Inst. Cancer Research, N.Y.C., 1967-70; assoc. mem. Am. Health Found., Valhalla, N.Y., 1971-78; cancer research scientist IV Roswell Park Meml. Inst., Buffalo, 1978-83; chem. mgr. nat. toxicology program Nat. Inst. Environ. Health Scis., Research Triangle Park, N.C., 1983—. Contbr. articles to profl. jours. Nat. Cancer Inst. grantee, 1980-81. Fellow AAAS; mem. Am. Assn. Cancer Research, N.Y. Acad. Sci., Am. Physiol. Soc., Tissue Culture Assn., Am. Soc. Zoologists. Current Work: Carcinogenesis, relationship between dietary fat and mammary carcinogenesis. Subspecialty: Cancer research (medicine). Home: 7909 Hollander Pl Raleigh NC 27606

CHAN, SHIH HUNG, mech. engr., cons. and researcher; b. Chang-hwa, Taiwan, Nov. 8, 1943; came to U.S., 1964, naturalized, 1976; s. Chan Ping and Liao (Fu) Zon; m. Shirley Shih, Apr. 15, 1944; children: Bryan, Erick. M.S. in Mech. Engring, U. N.H., 1966; Ph.D. (Ehrman fellow), U. Calif., Berkeley, 1969. Registered profl. engr., Wis. Asst. to assoc. prof. N.Y.U., 1969-73; assoc. prof. Poly. Inst. N.Y., 1973-74; mem. research staff Argonne Nat. Lab., 1974-75; prof., chmn. dept. mech. engring. U. Wis.-Milw., 1975—, cons. Contbr. heat transfer and nuclear reactor safety articles to tech. jours. NSF grantee, 1970-82. Mem. Am. Nuclear Soc., ASME. Current Work: Radiative heat transfer, thermal hydraulic of nuclear reactor safety, fouling and scale in heat exchange. Subspecialties: Fluid mechanics; Nuclear fission. Home: 3416 W Meadowview Ct Mequon WI 53092 Office: Dept Mech Engring U Wis PO Box 784 Wilwaukee WI 53201

CHAN, W. Y., pharmacologist, educator; b. Shanghai, China, Dec. 1, 1932; came to U.S., 1952, naturalized, 1968; m. Beatrice Ho Chan, June 11, 1961; children: Mina, Jennifer. B.A., U. Wis., Madison, 1956; Ph.D. in Pharmacology, Columbia, U., 1961. Research asso. to asst. prof. biochemistry Cornell U. Med. Coll., N.Y.C., 1960-67, asst. prof. to asso. prof. pharmacology, 1966-76, prof., 1976—, acting chmn., 1982—; mem. basic pharmacology adv. com. Pharm. Mfrs. Assn. Found., 1973-80; mem. study sect. NIH, 1977, cons., 1981. Contbr. articles to profl. jours. Recipient NIH research career devel. award, 1968-73; Irma T. Hirschl Career Scientist, 1973-77; NIH grantee, 1965—. Mem. Am. Soc. Pharmacology and Exptl. Therapeutics, Soc. Study of Reprodn., Soc. Exptl. Biology and Medicine, Harvey Soc., N.Y. Acad. Sci., AAAS. Current Work: Pharmacology of neurohypophys hormones and polypeptides; uterine and renal actions of oxytocin and prostaglandins; pathophysiology and pharmacology of dysmenorrhea. Subspecialties: Pharmacology; Endocrinology. Office: Cornell U Med Coll New York NY 10021

CHAN, WAI-YEE, molecular geneticist, laboratory administrator, educator; b. Kwangzhou, China, Apr. 28, 1950; came to U.S., 1974; s. Kui and Fung-Hing (Wong) C.; m. May-Fong Sheung, Sept. 3, 1976; children: Connie Hai-Yee, Joanne Hai-Wei, Victor Hai-Yue. B.Sc. (1st hons.), Chinese Univ. Hong Kong, 1974; Ph.D., U. Fla., 1977. Teaching asst U. Fla., 1974-77; fellow U. Okla., Oklahoma City, 1977-78, research assoc., 1978-79, asst. prof., 1979-82, assoc. prof., 1982—; staff affiliate Okla. Children's Meml. Hosp., Oklahoma City, 1979—; vis. scientist U. Wash., Seattle, 1982; sci. dir. trace metals lab. State Okla. Teaching Hosp., Oklahoma City, 1982—; affiliate assoc. mem. Okla. Med. Research Found., 1984—; cons. VA Med. Ctr., Oklahoma City, 1982—. Editor: Metabolism of Trace Metals in Man: Developmental Biology and Genetic Implications, Volume I and II, 1983; consulting editor: Jour of Am. Coll. Nutrtion, 1982—; contbr. articles to profl. jours. NATO fellow, 1979; recipient Tak Shing prize for biochemistry Chinese U. Hong Kong, 1973; NIH grantee, 1983. Mem. Am. Soc. Biol. Chemists, Soc. Pediatric Research, Am. Inst. Nutrition, N.Y. Acad. Sci., Biochemical Soc. Eng., Am. Soc. Human Genetics, Nutrition Soc. Eng. Lodge: Rotary. Current Work: Molecular biology of genetic diseases; cellular polyamine metabolism and biochemical nutrition and metabolism of trace metals. Subspecialties: Genetics and genetic engineering (medicine); Nutrition (medicine). Home: 8725 Raven Ave Oklahoma City OK 73132 Office: University of Oklahoma Health Sciences Center Oklahoma City OK 73190

CHAN, YUN LAI, medical educator, physiologist; b. Taichung, Taiwan, China, Dec. 3, 1941; came to U.S. 1968, naturalized, 1977; s. Yunn-Perng and Tsai-Mei C.; m. Vicky Chiu, June 18, 1968; children—Jason, Grace. B.S., Kaohsiung Med. Coll., 1965; M.S., Nat. Taiwan U., 1967; Ph.D., U. Louisville, 1971. Instr. U. Louisville, 1971, 73; fellow Max Planck Inst., Frankfurt, Germany, 1972-73; instr. Yale U., New Haven, 1974-76; asst. prof. U. Ill.-Chgo., 1976-81, assoc. prof., 1981—; vis. prof. Nat. Yang Ming Med. Coll., Taipei, Taiwan, 1982, 84; vis. specialist Nat. Sci. Council, Taipei, 1982-84; prin. investigator NIH, Bethesda, Md., 1981—. Contbr. articles to profl. jours. Active Chgo. Heart Assn. Recipient Golden Apple award U. Ill., 1980; grantee Pharm. Mfrs. Assn., 1972, Am. and Chgo. Heart Assn., 1977. Mem. Am. Physiol. Soc., Am. Soc. Nephrology, Internat. Soc. Nephrology, Am. Fedn. Clin. Research, Am. Heart Assn. (mem. council). Current work: Cellular mechanism underlying hormonal control on renal tubular function. Subspecialties: Physiology (medicine); Nephrology. Office: Ill Coll Medicine 835 S Wolcott E202 MSA Chicago IL 60612

CHANANA, ARJUN DEV, biomedical researcher; b. LyallPur, Punjab, India, Nov. 6, 1930; came to U.S., 1963, naturalized, 1975; s. Bhagat R. and Vidya V. (Sachdev) C.; m. Judith Taylor, Sept. 6, 1963; children: Arun Paul, Nina Lee. M.D., Swai Man Singh Med. Coll., Jaipur, Rajasthan, 1955. Intern Irwin Hosp., New Delhi, India, 1955-57; resident in surgery Bolton (Eng.) Dist. Gen. Hosp., 1960-63; with Brookhaven Nat. Lab., Upton, N.Y., 1963—, sr. scientist, 1979—; cons. researcher Nassau County Med. Ctr., East Meadow, N.Y., 1974—; guest prof. immunopathology U. Berne, Switzerland, 1971-72; Mem. NIH study sect. U.S. Dept. HHS, Bethesda, Md., 1974-79. Contbr. over 100 sci. articles to profl. publs. Fellow Royal Coll. Surgeons London, Royal Coll. Surgeons Edinburgh; mem. Transplantation Soc., Am. Soc. Hematology, Am. Assn. Pathologists, Soc. Exptl. Biology and Medicine, AAAS, Radiation Research Soc. Current Work: Pulmonary immunobiology; hemopoletic cell proliferation; transplantation immunology. Subspecialties: Environmental toxicology; Hematology. Office: Brookhaven Nat Lab Bldg 490 Upton NY 11973

CHANCE, BRITTON, educator; b. Wilkes Barre, Pa., July 24, 1913; s. Edwin M. and Eleanor (Kent) C.; m. Jane Earle, Mar. 4, 1938 (div.); children: Eleanor, Britton, Jan, Peter; m. Lilian Streeter Lucas, Nov. 1956; children: Margaret, Lilian, Benjamin, Samuel; stepchildren—Ann Lucas, Gerald B. Lucas, A. Brooke Lucas, William C. Lucas. B.S. and M.S., U. Pa., 1936, Ph.D. (E.R. Johnson Found. fellow), 1940; Ph.D., U. Cambridge, 1942, D.Sc., 1952; M.D. (hon.), Karolinska Inst., Stockholm, 1962, Semmel Weis U., Budapest, 1976; D.Sc., Med. Coll. Ohio, 1974; D.Sc. (hon.), Hahnemann Coll. and Hosp., 1977. Asst. prof. biophysics U. Pa., 1940-48, prof., 1949—, acting dir. Johnson Found., 1940-41, dir. Johnson Found., 1949-83, emeritus prof. biophysics and biochemistry; dir. Inst. Structural and Functional Studies, 1982—; staff MIT, 1941-46; Cons. NSF, 1952-55; mem. Pres.'s Sci. Adv. Com., 1959-60; mem. adv. council Nat. Inst. Alcohol Abuse and Alcoholism, 1971-75; mem. molecular control working group Nat. Cancer Inst., from 1973. Author: (with F.C. Williams, V. Hughes, E.F. McNichol, David Sayre) Waveforms, 1949, (with R.I. Hulsizer, E.F. McNichol, F.C. Williams) Electronic Time Measurements, 1949, Energy-linked Functions of Mitochondria, 1964, (with Q.H. Gibson, R. Eisenhardt, K.K. Lonberg-Holm) Rapid Mixing and Sampling Techniques in Biochemistry, 1964, (with R.W. Estabrook, J.R. Williamson) Control of Energy Metabolism, 1965, (with R.W. Estabrook, T. Yonetani) Hemes and Hemoproteins, 1966, (with others) Probes of Structure and Function of Macromolecules and Enzymes, 1971, Alcohol and Aldehyde, Vol. I, 1974, II, III, 1977, Tunneling in Biological System, 1979; rev. articles Advances in Enzymology, Vo. 12, 1951, Vol. 17, 1956, Ann. Rev. of Biochemistry, 1952, 70, 76, The Enzymes, Vol. II. Part 1, 1952, Vol. XIII, 1976, Ann. Rev. Plant Physiology, 1958, 68; Bd. editors: Physiol. Revs, 1951-54, FEBS Letters, 1973-75, BBA Reviews, from 1972, Photobiochemistry and Photobiophysics, from 1979. Contbr. articles to Am., Brit., Swedish, German and Japanese Jours. Presdl. lectr. U. Pa., 1975; Julius L. Jackson Meml. lectr. Wayne State U., 1976; Da Costa oration Phila. County Med. Coll., 1976; Recipient Paul Lewis award for enzyme chemistry, 1950; Pres.'s Certificate of Merit for services, 1941-45, as staff mem. Radiation Lab. of M.I.T., 1950; Guggenheim fellow Stockholm, 1946-48; Harvey lectr., 1954; Phillips lectr., 1955, 65; Pepper lectr., 1957; Exchange scholar to USSR, 1963; Genootschapps medal Dutch Acad. Scis., 1965; Heineken medal, 1970; Keilin medal Brit. Biochem. Soc., 1966; Harrison Howe award, 1966; Franklin medal, 1966; Overseas fellow Churchill Coll., 1966; Herter lectr. NYU, 1968; Pa. award for excellence in life scis., 1968; Nichols award N.Y. sect. Am. Chem. Soc., 1970; Phila. sect. award, 1969; Redfearn lectr., 1970; Gairdner award, 1972; Post-Congress Festschrift Stockholm, 1974; Semmelweis medal, 1974; Nat. medal Sci., 1974; Troy C. Daniels lectr. U. Calif.-San Francisco, 1984. Fellow Am. Phys. Soc., IEEE (Morlock award 1961, Phila. sect. award 1984), AAAS, Am. Inst. Chemists; mem. Internat. Union Pure and Applied Biophysics (pres. 1972-75), Chem. Soc., Royal Soc. Arts, Biochem. Soc. Eng., Am. Soc. Biol. Chemists (Sober lectr. 1984), Am. Philos. Soc., Am. Acad. Arts and Sci., Nat. Acad. Sci., Am. Physiol. Soc., Soc. Gen. Physiologists (council 1957-60), Am. Inst. Physics, Soc. for Neurosci., Biophys. Soc. (council 1959-62), Swedish Biochem. Soc., Royal Swedish Acad. Scis., Royal Acad. Arts and Scis., Sweden, Bavarian Acad. Scis., Acad. Leopoldina DDR, Max-Planck Gesellschaft für Forerung der Wissenschaften (fgn.), Argentine Nat. Acad. Sci., Royal Soc. London (fgn.), Harvey Soc., Sigma Xi, Tau Beta Pi. Clubs: Corinthian Yacht (Phila.); St. Anthony. Holder numerous patents on automatic steering devices, also spectrophotometric devices, radar circuitry. Gold medal winner (yachting) 1952 Olympics. Current Work: Structure of metalloenzymes and proteins by x-ray techniques; reaction kinetics of unstable intermediates at low temperatures; tunneling phenomena; 31-P NMR of animal models and humans. Subspecialties: Biophysics (biology); Magnetic resonance imaging. Office: U Pa Med Sch Philadelphia PA 19104

CHANDLER, EDWARD WILLIAM, engineering educator; b. Milw., Oct. 10, 1953; s. Donald Harold and Helen Aliedia (Wonders) C. B.S., U. Wis.-Milw., 1975; M.S., Ill. Inst. Tech., 1978; Ph.D., Purdue U., 1985. Registered profl. engr., Wis. Elec. engr. Motorola Communications, Schaumburg, Ill., 1976-77; mem. faculty Milw. Sch. Engring., 1977-80; grad. instr. research Purdue U., 1980-82; assoc. prof. Milw. Sch. Engring., 1982-84; asst. prof. Marquette U., Milw., 1984—; sec. Elec. Engring. Communications Research Group, Marquette U., 1985—. Contbr. articles to profl. jours. Mem. IEEE, Am. Soc. Engring. Edn., Tau Beta Pi, Eta Kappa Nu, Triangle Frat. (sec. 1984—). Current work: Optimization of low probability of intercept and anti-jam communication systems, spread spectrum communications, performance of error correction codes, communication networking. Subspecialties: Electrical engineering; Telecommunications. Home: 4155 W Rivers Edge Circle 18 Brown Deer WI 53209 Office: Marquette Univ EECS Dept 1515 W Wisconsin Ave Milwaukee WI 53233

CHANDLER, HUBERT THOMAS, See *Who's Who in America,* 43rd edition.

CHANDLER, JERRY LEROY, biochemical geneticist, toxicologist, sci. policy advisor; b. Little Falls, Minn., Sept. 14, 1940; s. Bert Emery and Blanche Anastasia (Drellack) C.; m. Donna Kay Fitzgerald, June 7, 1969; children: Bert, Jerry-David. A.A., Brainerd Jr. Coll., 1960; B.S., Okla. State U., 1963, Ph.D. in Biochemistry, 1968. Instr. biochemistry dept. Okla. State U., Stillwater, 1969, research assoc., 1973-74; chemistry group leader Central Lab. for Mutagenicity, Freiburg, W.Ger., 1969-72; scientist Nat. Inst. for Occupational Safety and Health, Rockville, Md., 1975-76, sr. scientist, 1976-82, sr. sci. advisor office of dir., 1982—, criteria documentation sect. chief, 1977-79, sci. advisor div. criteria documentation, 1980; faculty Found. for Advanced Edn. in Scis., NIH; lectr. in field. Contbr. articles in field to profl. publs. Chmn. Cub Scouts troop Nat. Capital Area Council Boy Scouts Am. Served as commd. officer USPHS, 1975—. NSF research grantee, 1973. Mem. Am. Indsl. Hygiene Assn., Am. Statis. Assn., Inst. for Theol. Encounter with Sci. and Tech., Soc. for Risk Analysis, USPHS Commd. Officers Assn. Roman Catholic. Club: Langley (Va.). Current Work: Quantitative molecular origins of health and disease; government health policy science advisor, quantitative risk assessment, molecular dynamics of health and disease processes, occupational health standards. Subspecialties: Environmental toxicology; Genetics and genetic engineering (medicine). Home: 7412 Churchill Rd McLean VA 22101 Office: 5600 Fishers Ln Rockville MD 20857

CHANDLER, JOHN CHRISTOPHER, nuclear engineer; b. Gulfport, Miss., Oct. 31, 1946; s. Thomas Alfred and Jo Beth (Majure) C., Jr.; m. Lynne Blair Bratcher, Aug. 1, 1967 (div. 1976); 1 dau., Gwendolyn Amy; m. Jean Marie Vaz, June 29, 1980. B.S., Miss. State U., 1968; M.S. in Nuclear Engring, U. Wash., 1980. Nuclear engr. Ingalls Nuclear Ships Co., Pascagoula, Miss., 1968; advanced engr. Westinghouse Hanford Co., Richland, Wash., 1973-79; nuclear engr. Middle South Services, New Orleans, 1979-80; sr. engr. Exxon Nuclear Co., Inc., Richland, 1980—. Contbr. articles to profl. jours. Advisor CAP, Richland, 1973-76. Served to capt. USAF, 1968-73. Mem. Am. Nuclear Soc. Current Work: Determination of safety requirements for nuclear reactor operations; establishment of operating limits to assure reactor safety; analytical determination of accident results. Subspecialties: Nuclear engineering; Nuclear fission. Office: Exxon Nuclear Co Inc 2101 Horn Rapids Rd Richland WA 99352

CHANDLER, THOMAS CLINTON, research engineer, designer; b. York, S.C., Jan. 3, 1952; s. Thomas Clinton, Sr. and Frances (Mitchell) C.; m. Katrina Pipkins, Aug. 24, 1975; 1 child, Thomas C. Chandler III. B.S. in Elec. Engring., U. S.C., 1974, M.S., 1976; student U. Cin., 1981-82. Research assoc. U. S.C., Columbia, 1974-76; with infrared research dept. Air Force Materials Lab, Dayton, Ohio, 1977-81; research instr. U. Cin., 1981-82; with quality assurance dept. Monsanto Co., Spartanburg, S.C., 1983—. Contbr. articles to tech. jours. Patentee in field. Served as capt. USAF, 1977-81. Recipient U.S. Air Force/Navy Sci. Achievement award, 1979. Mem. IEEE (recipient service award 1974; chmn. U. S.C. br. 1973-74), Electrochem. Soc., Sigma Xi. Current work: Silicon crystal growth by Czochralski method, solid solutions, intrinsic gettering, infrared spectroscopy, ESCA and auger spectroscopy, CV characterization of silicon and semiconductor process modeling. Subspecialties: Electronic materials; Microchip technology (materials science). Home: Box 87 Roebuck SC 29376 Office: Monsanto Electronic Materials Co PO Box 5397 Spartanburg SC 29304

CHANDRA, ASHOK KUMAR, computer scientist; b. Allahabad, India, July 30, 1948; s. Harish and Sushila C.; m. Mala, Sept. 17, 1974; children: Ankur, Anuj. B.Tech., Indian Inst. Tech., 1969; M.S., U. Calif.-Berkeley, 1970; Ph.D., Stanford U., 1973. Mem. research staff IBM Thomas J. Watson Research Center, Yorktown Heights, N.Y., 1973-83, mgr. theoretical computer sci., 1981-83; tech. adv. office of v.p. and chief scientist IBM, Armonk, N.Y., 1983—. Editor: Jour. Computing Soc. Indsl. and Applied Math, 1982; contbr. articles to profl. jours. Recipient Pres.'s Gold medal Indian Inst. Tech., 1969; recipient IBM Outstanding Innovation award, 1980, Invention Achievement award, 1977, 81. Mem. ACM, Soc. Indsl. and Applied Math. Patentee magnetic bubble tech. (2). Current Work: Theoretical computer science, VLSI testing, magnetic bubbles. Subspecialties: Theoretical computer science; Algorithms. Office: PO Box 218 Yorktown Heights NY 10598

CHANDRA, SATISH, cancer biophysicist; b. Ghazipur, India, May 6, 1927; came to U.S., 1958, naturalized, 1973; s. Shyamlal and Lilawati (Srivastava) Vidyarthi; m. Shimmi P. Chandra, Mar. 9, 1953; children: Arun, Piyush, Arti. B.S., U. Allahabad, India, 1947, M.S., 1949; Ph.D., U. Toronto, 1958. Lectr. physics U. Allahabad, India, 1950-55; research fellow Ont. Cancer Inst., Toronto, 1957-58, Sloan Kettering Inst., N.Y.C., 1958-61; sr. research assoc. U. Buffalo, 1961-63; asst. prof. biophysics Post Grad. Inst. of Med. Edn. Research, Chandigarh, India, 1963-65; research biologist John L. Smith Meml. Center for Cancer, Maywood, N.J., 1966-71; viral oncologist Mercy Hosp., Chgo., 1971-75; assoc. prof. microbiology Abraham Lincoln Sch. Medicine, Chgo., 1973-78; cancer biophysicist in therapeutic radiology VA Hosp., Hines, 1976—; prof. anatomy Loyola U. Stritch Sch. Medicine, 1978—; cons. in field of hyperthermia; cons. UN Devel. program, 1982. Bd. dirs. Am. Cancer Soc., Bergen County, N.J., 1968-71. McGee-Gilchrist Fund fellow U. Toronto, 1956-57; Damon Runyon Fund for Cancer fellow, 1958-61; recipient quality award VA, 1978. Mem. Assn. of Indians in Am., Am. Assn. for Cancer Research, AAAS, Radiation Research Soc. Current Work: Cancer research, radiation biology, hyperthermia. Subspecialties: Cancer research (medicine); Cell biology (medicine). Office: VA Edward Hines Jr Hosp Hines IL 60141

CHANDRAN, KRISHNAN B., engineering educator, researcher, consultant; b. Madurai, India, May 16, 1944; came to U.S. 1967, naturalized 1982; s. Krishna and Meenambal (Subramanian) A.; m. Vanaja Murthy, June 22, 1972; children—Aruna, Anjana. B.Tech., Indian Inst. Tech., Madras, India, 1966; M.S., Wash. U., 1969, D.Sc., 1972. Research assoc. Tulane U., New Orleans, 1972-74, asst. prof., 1974-78; assoc. prof. U. Iowa., Iowa City, 1978-84, prof., 1984—; research engr. Bendix Corp., Davenport, Iowa, 1980. Mem. ASME, Biomed. Engring. Soc., Am. Soc. Biomechanics, AM. Soc. Engring. Educ., Am. Heart Assn. Current work: Flow characteristics past heart valve prostesis, left ventricular mechanics, laser and pulsed doppler anemometry, finite element analysis. Subspecialties: Biomedical engineering; Artificial organs and prostheses. Office: Dept Biomedical Engring U Iowa Iowa City IA 52242

CHANDRASEKARAN, BALAKRISHNAN, computer science educator, consultant; b. Lalgudi, India, June 20, 1942; came to U.S., 1963, naturalized, 1977; s. T.S. and Nagamani Balakrishnan. B. Engring. with honors, Madras U., India, 1963; Ph.D., U. Pa., 1967. Research scientist Philco-Ford Corp., Phila., 1967-69; from asst. prof. to prof. dept. computer sci. Ohio State U., Columbus, 1969—. Editor: Computer Program Testing, 1981. Contbr. articles to profl. jours. Recipient award Govt. India, 1957-63; Moore fellow U. Pa., 1964-67; Outstanding Paper citation Pattern Recognition Soc., 1976; Morton Disting. Visitor award Ohio U., 1982; Sr. Research award Coll. Engring. Ohio State U., 1983. Sr. mem. IEEE; mem. Assn. Computing Machinery, Am. Assn. Artificial Intelligence. Democrat. Current work: Understanding how computers can understand and solve problems intelligently; perception and cognition via computational models. Subspecialties: Artificial intelligence; Graphics, image processing, and pattern recognition. Home: 2053 Iuka Ave Columbus OH 43201 Office: Dept Computer and Info Sci Ohio State U Columbus OH 43210

CHANDRASEKHAR, SUBRAHMANYAN, theoretical astrophysicist; b. Lahore, India, Oct. 19, 1910; came to U.S., 1936, naturalized, 1953; m. Lalitha, Madras, India, Sept. 1936. M.A., Presidency Coll., Madras, 1930; Ph.D., Trinity Coll., Cambridge, 1933, Sc.D., 1942; Sc.D., U. Mysore, India, 1961, Northwestern U., 1962, U. Newcastle Upon Tyne, Eng., 1965, Ind. Inst. Tech., 1966, U. Mich., 1967, U. Liege, Belgium, 1967, Oxford (Eng.) U., 1972, U. Delhi, 1973, Carleton U., Can., 1978, Harvard U., 1979. Govt. India scholar in theoretical physics Cambridge, 1930-34; fellow Trinity Coll., Cambridge, 1933-37; research asso. Yerkes Obs., Williams Bay and U. Chgo., 1937, asst. prof., 1938-41, assoc. prof., 1942-43, prof., 1944-47, Disting. Service prof., 1947-52, Morton D. Hull Disting. Service prof., 1952—; Nehru Meml. lectr., Padma Vibhushan, India, 1968. Author: An Introduction to the Study of Stellar Structure, 1939, Principles of Stellar Dynamics, 1942, Radiative Transfer, 1950, Hydrodynamic and Hydromagnetic Stability, 1961, Ellipsoidal Figures of Equilibrium, 1969, The Mathematical Theory of Black Holes, 1983; Eddington: The Most Distinguished Astrophysicist of His Time, 1983; Mng. editor: The Astrophysical Jour, 1952-71; Contbr. various sci. periodicals. Recipient Bruce medal Astron. Soc. Pacific, 1952, gold medal Royal Astron. Soc., London, 1953; Rumford medal Am. Acad. Arts and Scis., 1957; Nat. Medal of Sci., 1966; Nobel Prize in Physics, 1983; R. D. Birla Meml. award Indian Physics Assn., 1984. Fellow Royal Soc. (London) (Royal medal 1962, Copley medal 1984); mem. Nat. Acad. Scis. (Henry Draper medal 1971), Am. Phys. Soc. (Dannie Heineman prize 1974), Am. Philos. Soc., Cambridge Philos. Soc., Am. Astron. Soc., Royal Astron. Soc. Club: Quadrangle (U. Chgo.). Subspecialties: General relativity; Theoretical astrophysics. Address: Lab for Astrophysics and Space Research 933 E 56th St Chicago IL 60637

CHANG, ALBERT FUWU, computing analyst, educator; b. Pingtung, Taiwan, Dec. 30, 1934; came to U.S., 1960; s. Ming and Fei-chi (Lin) C.; m. Joan R. Yang, Dec. 30, 1964. B.S., Nat. Taiwan U., 1957; M.S., U. Houston, 1963, Calif. Inst. Tech., 1964; Ph.D., U. So. Calif., 1979. Mem. profl. staff Calif. Inst. Tech., Pasadena, 1965—; cons. Dr. Maxwell C. Cheung & Assocs., Irvine, Calif., 1977—. Mem. Soc. Indsl. and Applied Math., Assn. Computing Machinery. Current Work: Mathematical software development, microcomputer application, numerical analysis. Subspecialties: Mathematical software; Numerical analysis (computer science). Office: California Institute Technology 1201 E California Blvd Pasadena CA 91125

CHANG, B(YUNG) JIN, optical systems engring. co. exec., elec. engr.; b. Danyang, Korea, Sept. 26, 1941; came to U.S., 1968, naturalized, 1974; s. Yung S. and Ahzie (Chon) C.; m. Sharon O. Hong, Dec. 27, 1969; children: Jane Y., Michael. Ph.D. in Elec. Engring, U. Mich., 1974. Research engr. ERIM, Ann Arbor, Mich., 1971-79; v.p., chief scientist Kaiser Optical Systems, Inc. subs. Kaiser Aerospace & Electronics Corp., Ann Arbor, 1979—. Contbr. articles to profl. jours. Mem. IEEE, Optical Soc. Am., Soc. Info. Display, Soc. Photo-optical Instrumentation Engrs. Methodist. Lodge: Ann Arbor Rotary. Patentee in field. Current Work: Holographic optical elements, dichromated gelatin, interferometry, optical systems design, optical signal processing. Subspecialties: Holography; Optical signal processing. Home: 1495 Folkstone Ct Ann Arbor MI 48105 Office: 6087 Jackson Rd Ann Arbor MI 48106

CHANG, CHOONG-SEOCK, plasma physicist, researcher; b. Yechon, Korea, Nov. 12, 1951; s. Ki-Oh and Oh-Young (Kim) C.; m. Inja Byun, July 2, 1975; children—Andrew Han, Celene Hyunju. B.S., Seoul Nat. U., 1974; Ph.D., U. Tex., 1979. Teaching asst. Seoul Nat. U., Korea, 1975; research asst. U. Tex., Austin, 1975-79; sr. scientist Ga. Techs., La Jolla, Calif., 1979-82; staff scientist AMPC, Inc., Encinitas, Calif., 1982—; cons. TRW, Los Angeles, 1984. Contbr. articles to physics jours. Mem. Korean Born Plasma Physicist Assn. U.S.A. (sec. 1984), Am. Phys. Soc., Sigma Xi. Current work: Study of particle and energy confinement in various magnetic fusion devices; study of plasma instabilities. Subspecialties: Plasma physics; Nuclear fusion. Home: 1627 Valleda Ln Encinitas CA 29024 Office: AMPC Inc 2210-P Encinitas Blvd Encinitas CA 92024

CHANG, ERNEST SUN-MEI, endocrinologist, educator; b. Berkeley, Calif., Dec. 7, 1950; s. Shu Chi and Helen (Fong) C. A.B., U. Calif., Berkeley, 1973; Ph.D., UCLA, 1978. Postdoctoral fellow dept. biochemistry U. Chgo., 1978; asst. prof. animal sci. U. Calif., Davis, 1978-85; Asst. prof. Bodega Marine Lab., Bodega Bay, Calif., 1978-85, assoc. prof., 1985—. Am. Cancer Soc. grantee, 1979-82; Calif. Sea Grant Coll. Program grantee, 1981-87. Mem. AAAS, Am. Soc. Zoologists, Tissue Culture Assn., World Mariculture Soc., Crustacean Soc. Current Work: Effects of hormones on crustacean and insect development. Subspecialties: Endocrinology; Developmental biology. Office: Bodega Marine Lab PO Box 247 Bodega Bay CA 94923

CHANG, JAE CHAN, physician, educator, clinical scientist; b. Chong An, Korea, Aug. 29, 1941; came to U.S., 1965, naturalized, 1976; s. Tae Whan and Kap Hee (Lee) C.; m. Sue Young Chung, Dec. 4, 1965; children: Sung-Jin, Sung-Ju, Sung-Hoon. M.D., Seoul Nat. U., 1965. Diplomate: Am. Bd. Internal Medicine, Am. Bd. Pathology. Intern Ellis Hosp., Schenectady, 1965-66; resident in medicine Harrisburg (Pa.) Hosp., 1966-69; fellow hematology and oncology U. Rochester (N.Y.) Med. Ctr., 1970-72; chief hematology sect. VA Hosp., Dayton, Ohio, 1972-75; dir. oncology unit, chief hematology and oncology sect. Good Samaritan Hosp. and Health Ctr., Dayton, 1975—; clin. prof. medicine Wright State U. Sch. Medicine, Dayton, 1980—. Trustee Montgomery County Soc. Cancer Control, 1976-84, Dayton Area Cancer Assn., 1984—, Community Blood Ctr., 1982—; mem. med. adv. com. Leukemia Soc. Am., Dayton chpt., 1977. Recipient Outstanding Tchr. award Good Samaritan Hosp., 1979; Profl. Excellence award Wright State U. Acad. Medicine, 1985, Faculty Tchr. of Yr. award Wright State U. Sch. Medicine, 1985, others; NIH grantee, 1970-72. Fellow ACP; mem. Am. Fedn. Clin. Research, Am. Soc. Hematology; mem. Am. Soc. Clin. Oncology; Mem. Am. Assn. Cancer Research. Roman Catholic. Current Work: Neoplastic fever; biochemical behavior of cancer and malignant cells and chemotherapy of hematologic malignancy and solid tumors. Subspecialties: Hematology; Oncology. Home: 1122 Wycliffe Pl Dayton OH 45459 Office: 2222 Philadelphia Dr Dayton OH 45406

CHANG, JAMES C., chemistry educator; b. Shanghai, China, Aug. 8, 1930. B.S., Mt. Union Coll., 1957; Ph.D., UCLA, 1964. Mem. faculty dept. chemistry U. No. Iowa, Cedar Falls, 1964—, prof., 1974—. Fellow Iowa Acad. Sci.; mem. Am. Chem. Soc., Chinese Am. Chem. Soc., Sigma Xi. Current Work: Nucleophilic substitution reactions of transition-metal complexes. Subspecialty: Inorganic chemistry. Office: Dept Chemistry U No Iowa Cedar Falls IA 50614

CHANG, JI YOUNG, metallurgist; b. Sudongmyon Hamyang Kun, Kyungnam, South Korea, Apr. 18, 1932; came to U.S., 1958, naturalized, 1972; s. Jae Bouk Chang and Kyung Douk (Ieshil) Lee; m. Ki Chung, Apr. 3, 1965; children: Grace Saechung, Gloria Younchung, Gail Hyochung. B.S., Seoul (Korea) Nat. U., 1955; M.S., U. Tenn.-Knoxville, 1964, postgrad., 1965-69; Ph.D., Inha U., Inchun, Korea, 19. Registered profl. engr., Pa. Research engr. Sci. Research Inst., Seoul, 1955-58; sr. engr. Atomic Energy Research Inst., Seoul, 1959-63; cons. Oak Ridge Nat. Lab., 1963-67, devel. engr., 1967-70; sr. and prin. engr. Westinghouse Advanced Reactors Div., Madison, Pa., 1970-81, fellow engr., 1981—. Contbr. articles to profl. publs. Mem. Am. Soc. Metals, Am. Nuclear Soc., Korean Nuclear Soc., Internat. Metall. Soc., Korean Engrs. and Scientists Assn. (pres. chpt. 1976-77). Republican. Presbyterian. U.S., Korean patentee in field. Current Work: Thermal fatigue and self-welding behavior of high-temperature materials in liquid metals. Subspecialties: Metallurgical engineering; High-temperature materials. Home: 3308 Hermar Dr Murrysville PA 15668 Office: Westinghouse Advanced Energy Systems Div PO Box 158 Madison PA 15663

CHANG, KWEN-JEN, biochemist, pharmacologist, educator; b. Taiwan, Oct. 21, 1943; s. Hwa-chi and Hsing-Mei (Chou) C.; m. Lan Yui Chiang, July 25, 1969; children: Linie, Emily. B.S., Nat. Taiwan U., 1966; PH.D., SUNY-Buffalo, 1972. Postdoctoral fellow Johns Hopkins U., 1972-75; research scientist Burroughs Wellcome Co., Research Triangle Park, N.C., 1975-84, group leader, 1984—; adj. prof. Duke U. Med. Ctr., 1980—. Contbr. articles to profl. jours. NIH postdoctoral fellow, 1972-74; research fellow Am. Heart Assn., 1974-75. Mem. Am. Soc. Pharmacology and Exptl. Therapeutics, Am. Soc. Biol. Chemists, Soc. Neurosci., N.Y. Acad. Scis. Current Work: Opiates, endorphins, neuropeptides, hormones, biochemistry and pharmacology of receptors. Subspecialties: Neurobiology; Biochemistry (biology).

CHANG, MING JEN WU, analytical chemist, genetic toxicologist; b. Shwatow, Kwangtung, Republic of China, Feb. 15, 1943, came to U.S., 1969, naturalized, 1980; s. Lin-Kun and Huey (Hsu) Wu; m. Yat Shu, July 17, 1964; children—Daniel C., Judy S. B.S., Nat. Normal Taiwan U., China, 1964; M.S., Ohio State U., 1972; Ph.D., 1978. Research sci. Ohio State U., Columbus, 1978-80; staff fellow Nat. Ctr. Toxicological Research, Jefferson, Ark., 1980-82; prin. research sci. Battelle Columbus Labs., Ohio, 1982—; adj. asst. prof. Ohio State U., Columbus, 1982—. Contbr. numerous articles to profl. jours. Recipient Ann T.A. Edison Meml. award for Outstanding Youth in Sci., Taiwan, Republic of China, 1960. Mem. Am. Chem. Soc., Soc. Neuroscience, Am. Soc. Neurochemistry, Am. Coll. Toxicology, Sigma Delta Epsilon. Current work: In vitro toxicology; organ and tissue culture; molecular mechanism in carcinogenesis. Subspecialties: Cancer research (veterinary medicine); Toxicology (medicine). Home: 1086 Stanhope Dr Columbus OH 43221 Office: Battelle Columbus Labs 505 King Ave Columbus OH 43201

CHANG, RICHARD LI-CHAI, research biochemist; b. Hupei, China, Jan. 23, 1932; s. Kaitsen and K.F. C.; m. Tsailing Chang, Feb. 8, 1961; children: Wan B., Ben Y. B.S. in Agrl. Chemistry, Nat. Taiwan Chung Hsing U., 1957; M.S. in Biochemistry and Nutrition, Utah State U., 1964. Research asst. dept. pharmacology Sch. Medicine, N.Y. U., N.Y.C., 1964-67; research biochemist Burroughs Wellcome and Co. (U.S.A.), Inc., Tuckahoe, N.Y., 1967-70; scientist dept. biochemistry Schering Corp., Bloomfield, N.J., 1970-74; scientist dept. biochemistry and drug metabolism Hoffmann-La Roche, Inc., Nutley, N.J., 1974-79, sr. scientist, 1979-85; sr. scientist Lab. of Exptl. Carcinogenesis and Metabolism, Roche Inst. Molecular Biology, Nutley, 1985—. . Contbr. numerous articles to sci. jours. Mem. Am. Soc. Pharmacology and Exptl. Therapeutics. Current Work: Chemical carcinogenesis by polycyclic aromatic hydrocarbons. Subspecialties: Cancer research (veterinary medicine); Pharmacology. Home: 107 Konner Ave Pine Brook NJ 07058 Office: Kingsland St Nutley NJ 07110

CHANG, SHI-KUO, engineering educator; b. Chun-King, China, July 17, 1944; came to U.S., 1966, naturalized, 1977; s. Yen-Tang Chang and Ming (Chu) C.; m. Judy C.C. Pan, Mar. 15, 1969; 2 children. B.S., Nat. Taiwan U., 1965; M.S., U. Calif., 1967, Ph.D., 1969. Research asst. electronics research lab., dept. elec. engring. and computer scis. U. Calif.-Berkeley, 1967-69; research mem. T.J. Watson Research Ctr., IBM, Yorktown Heights, N.Y., 1969-70, 71-72, 73-75; asst. prof. Cornell U. Sch. Elec. Engring., Ithaca, N.Y., 1970-71; vis. prof. dept. computer sci. Nat. Chiao-Tung U., Hsing-Chu, Taiwan, 1972-73; cons. Nat. Electronic Data Processing Ctr., Taipei, Taiwan, 1972-73; assoc. prof., dir. info. systems research lab. U. Ill., Chgo., 1975-78, prof. dept. info. engring., dir. lab., cons. Bell Telephone Labs., 1978-82; prof., chmn. dept. elec. and computer engring. Ill. Inst. Tech., dir. info. systems lab., 1982—; cons. various cos. including Computing Ctr., Tan-Run Steel Inc., Kaoshiung, Taiwan, 1978-79, Naval Research Lab., Washington, 1980—, Standard Oil Co., Ind., 1982-83, IMB Quality Inst., Danbury, N.J., Bell Labs., Holmdel, N.J., Honeywell Corp., Mpls., summer 1984. Author various fiction works including: Water of Yellow River, 1979, Nebula Suite, 1980, Five Jade Discs, 1983, Heroes Have No Tears, 1984, Serenade, 1985; tech. works: Intelligent Database Systems, 1978, Management and Office Information Systems, 1984, Languages for Automation, 1985, (with T. Ichikawa) Visual Languages, 1986. Translator from Chinese various fiction, sci. works. Co-editor Pictorial Information Systems, 1980, Fuzzy Sets-Theory and Applications to Policy Analysis and Information Systems, 1980. Contbr. chpt. to book, numerous articles and papers to profl. lit. Named Outstanding New Citizen of 1977-78, Citizenship Council Met. Chgo., 1978; U. Calif. fellow, 1967-69; grantee NSF, 1971-72, 78-86, U.S. Army, 1978-80, Office Naval Research, 1980-83, Yosin Found., 1983-85, AT&T Found., 1985-86. Mem. IEEE (sr., Appreciation cert. Computer Group 1978, chmn. various workshop, coms.), Assn. Computing Machinery, Chinese Inst. Elec. Engring., Chinese Lang. Computer Soc. (council 1974-85), Republic China Acad. Sinica (Inst. Info. Sci. research fellow 1972-85). Current work: Research on picture reconstruction from projections providing theoretical foundation for computerized tomography; application of relational database to pictorial information management systems; picture grammars for Chinese language computers; iconic languages. Subspecialties: Graphics, image processing, and pattern recognition; Information systems (Information science). Office: Dept Elec and Computer Engring Info Systems Lab Ill Inst Tech 410 Greenleaf Ave Glencoe IL 60022

CHANG, TE-WEN, microbiologist, researcher, educator; b. Nanchang, Kiangsi, China, Oct. 12, 1920; came to U.S., 1949, naturalized, 1960; m. Diana Tan, June 22, 1952; children. M.D., Nat. Central U. Med. Coll., Chengdu, China, 1945. Intern Gen. Hosp. Chengdu, 1944-45; resident in internal medicine Univ. Hosp., Nanking, 1946-49; researcher in virology U. Kans. Med. Ctr., 1951-52; asst. in medicine Boston U. Sch. Medicine, 1952-54, instr., 1954-57; sr. instr. Tufts U. Sch. Medicine, 1957-59, asst. prof. medicine and microbiology, 1959-67, assoc. prof., 1968—; cons. in field. Contbr. chpts., numerous articles, abstracts to profl. publs. Served to capt. Chinese Army, 1944-46. Mem. AAAS, Am. Fedn. Clin. Research, N.Y. Acad. Scis., Am. Soc. Microbiology, Am. Acad. Microbiology, Infectious Disease Soc. Am. Current Work: Bacterial toxins, herpes virus and chemotherapy. Subspecialties: Microbiology; Infectious diseases. Home: 50 Longwood Ave Brookline MA 02146 Office: 171 Harrison Ave Boston MA 02111

CHANG, THOMAS MING SWI, physician, medical scientist, biotechnologist; b. Swatow, Kwantang, China, Apr. 8, 1933; s. Henry Sue-Yue and Frances Hue-Soo (Lim) C.; m. Lancy Yuk Lan, June 21, 1958; children: Harvey, Victor, Christine, Sandra. B.Sc., McGill U., 1957, M.D., C.M., 1961, Ph.D., 1965, F.R.C.P.(C), 1972. Intern Montreal (Que.) Gen. Hosp., 1961-62; research fellow McGill U., Montreal, 1962-65, lectr. dept. physiology, 1965, asst. prof., 1966-69, assoc. prof., 1969-72, prof. physiology, 1972—, prof. medicine, 1975—, dir. artificial organs research unit, 1975-79, dir. artificial cells and organs research center, 1979—, specializing in med. scis. and biotech., Montreal, 1962—; staff Royal Victoria Hosp.; hon. cons. Montreal Chinese Hosp., 1970—; cons. Montreal Children's Hosp., 1979—; Med. Research Council fellow, 1962-65, scholar, 1965-68, career investigator, 1968—. Inventor artificial cells; Author: Artificial Cells, 1972, Biomedical Application of Immobilized Enzymes and Protiens, Vols. I and II, 1977, Artificial Kidney, Artificial Liver and Artificial Cells, 1978, Hemoperfusion-Kidney and Liver Supports and Detoxification, 1980, Hemoperfusion, 1981, Past Present and Future of Artificial Organs, 1983, Microencapsulation Including Artificial Cells, 1984, Hemopertusion and Artificial Organs, 1985; sect. editor: Internat. Jour. Artificial Organs, 1977—; assoc. editor: Jour. Artificial Organs, 1977—; editorial bd.: Jour. Biomaterial Med. Devel. and Orgn, 1972—, Jour. Membrane Soc, 1975—, Jour. Bioengring, 1975-79, Jour. Enzyme and Microbial Tech, 1978—, Jour. Microencapsulation, 1984—. Fellow Royal Coll. Physicians Can.; mem. Biophysic Soc., Am., Physiology Soc., Internat. Soc. Artificial Organs (trustee), Can. Soc. Artificial Organs (pres. 1980-82), Canadian Med. Assn. Current Work: Research (laboratory and clinical), teaching, consulting, and administration; artificial cells, artificial organs, micro encapsulation, immobilised enzymes, immobilised cells, absorbents, detoxification, blood substitutes, artificial blood, artificial liver, artificial kidney, biotechnology. Subspecialties: Artificial organs and prostheses; Enzyme technology. Office: Artificial Cells and Organs Research Centre McGill U 3655 Drummond St Montreal PQ H3G 1Y6 Canada

CHANG, TIANG-SHING, biopolymer chemist, dental researcher; b. China; came to U.S., 1967; s. Hao and Pavan (Yu) C.; m. Wan-Shun Huang, Sept. 4, 1971; 1 child, Wandy. B.S., Tankang Coll., Taipei, 1964; M.S., U. Calif.-Irvine, 1969; Ph.D., St. John's U., 1973. Group leader Block Drug Co., Jersey City, 1973-77, sect. chief, 1977-83, mgr., 1983—. Contbr. articles to profl. jours. Patentee in field. Mem. Am. Chem. Soc., AAAS, Internat. Assn. Dental Research, N.Y. Acad. Scis. Current work: Biomedical and dental applications of polymers, chemical adhesive of dental materials, especially dental composites and cements. Subspecialties: Dental materials; Polymer chemistry. Office: Block Drug Co 257 Cornelison Ave Jersey City NJ 07302

CHANG, TU-NAN, physics educator; b. Hangzhou, China, Apr. 20, 1945; came to U.S., 1967, naturalized, 1979; s. Hao and Pe-ven (Yu) C.; m. Hsiao-lin Chang, Nov. 1, 1945; children: Amy Chia-Mae, Angela Chia-Loh. B.S., Tunghai U., Taiwan, 1966; M.S., U. Calif.-Riverside, 1969, Ph.D., 1972. Research assoc. U. Chgo., 1973-75; asst. prof. physics U. So. Calif., Los Angeles, 1975-81, assoc. prof., 1981—. Contbr. articles to profl. jours. NSF research grantee, 1978—. Mem. Am. Phys. Soc. Current Work: Atomic and molecular physics, many-body interactions in atomic transitions, photon-atom interactions. Subspecialties: Atomic and molecular physics; Theoretical physics. Office: Physics Dept U So Calif Los Angeles CA 90089

CHANG, WEI, med. nuclear physicist, researcher; b. Szechun, China, Oct. 20, 1945; came to U.S., 1969, naturalized, 1982; s. Cheng-Jen and Hui-Yin (Chueh) C.; m. Ching Lin, Jan. 5, 1974; children—Brian Lin, Amanda Yi Peng. B.S., Nat. Taiwan U., Taipei, 1968; Ph.D., SUNY-Buffalo, 1976. Diplomate: Am. Bd. Sci. in Nuclear Medicine, Am. Bd. Radiology (Physics). Physicist Miriam Hosp., Providence, 1975-76; med. nuclear physicist Loyola U. Med. Center, Maywood, Ill., 1977-82, assoc. prof. radiology, 1981-82; med. physicist, assoc. prof. radiology U. Md. Med. Sch., Balt., 1983-84; assoc. prof. radiology U. Iowa, Iowa City, 1984—. Mem. Soc. Nuclear Medicine, Am. Assn. Physicist in Medicine. Current Work: Computer processing of medical images, emissions computed tomography; collimator tomographic techniques. Subspecialties: Imaging technology; Bioinstrumentation. Home: 2300 Jessup Circle Iowa City IA 52240 Office: Dept Radiology U Iowa Iowa City IA 52242

CHANG, WILLIAM SHEN CHIE, electrical engineering educator; b. Nantung, Kiangsu, China, Apr. 4, 1931; s. Tung Wu and Phoebe Y.S. (Chow) C.; m. Margaret Huachen Kwei, Nov. 26, 1955; children: Helen Nai-yee, Hugh Nai-han, Hedy Nai-lin. B.S.E., U. Mich., 1952, M.S.E., 1953; Ph.D., Brown U., 1957. Lectr., research asso. elec. engring. Stanford, 1957-59; asst. prof. elec. engring. Ohio State U., 1959-62, asso. prof., 1962-65; prof. dept. elec. engring. Washington U., St. Louis, 1965-76, chmn. dept., 1965-71; dir. Applied Electronic Scis. Lab., 1971-79, Samuel Sachs prof. elec. engring., 1976-79; prof. dept. elec. engring. and computer scis. U. Calif., San Diego, 1979—. Author: Principles of Quantum Electronics, 1969; Contbr. articles to profl. jours. Mem. Am. Optical Soc., Am. Phys. Soc., AAUP, IEEE. Research on quantum electronics and optics. Subspecialty: Electrical engineering. Home: 763 Santa Olivia Solana Beach CA 92075

CHANMUGAM, GANESAR, physicist, astronomer, educator, researcher; b. Colombo, Sri Lanka, Oct. 24, 1939; s. Paul K. and Savundramanie (Canapathipillai) C.; m. Prithiva S. Kanagasundram, Aug. 22, 1966; children: Ravi, Suresh. B.Sc. in Math. with honors, U. Ceylon, Colombo, 1961; B.A. in Math. with honors, Cambridge U. (Eng.), 1963; Ph.D. in Physics, Brandeis U., 1970. Instr. physics U. Mass., Amherst, 1963-64; research fellow Institut d'Astrophysique, Université de Liège, Belgium, 1969-71; research assoc. dept. physics and astronomy La. State U., Baton Rouge, 1971-72, asst. prof., 1972-78, assoc. prof., 1978-83, prof., 1983—; vis. fellow Joint Inst. Lab. Astrophysics, U. Colo., Boulder, 1979-80. Contbr. writings to publs. in field. Grantee NSF, 1976, 77-85; Grantee NASA, 1981-82, 82-83; recipient award So. Regional Edn. Bd., 1982. Fellow Royal Astron. Soc. (U.K.); mem. Am. Phys. Soc., Am. Astron. Soc., Internat. Astron. Union. Current Work: Theoretical astrophysics, magnetic degenerate stars (white dwarfs and neutron stars). Subspecialty: Theoretical astrophysics. Office: Dept Physics and Astronomy La State U Baton Rouge LA 70803

CHANNELL, JAMES ESSEX TREVELYAN, geology educator; b. Peterborough, United Kingdom, Feb. 6, 1950; came to U.S., 1981; s. Essex Trevelyan and Mary (Minns) C. B.S., Leeds U. (U.K.), 1971; M.S., Durham U. (U.K.), 1972; Ph.D., Newcastle Upon Tyne U. (U.K.), 1975. Research ETH, Zurich, Switzerland, 1976-81; research fellow Columbia U., N.Y.C., 1981-82; prof. U. Fla., Gainesville, 1982—. Contbr. articles to profl. jours.; editor book. Fellow Geol. Soc. London; mem. Geol. Soc. Am., Am. Geophys. Union. Current work: Paleomagnetism, magnetic stratigraphy, rock magnetism, tectonics, structural geology. Subspecialties: Geophysics; Tectonics. Home: 400 NE 13 Ave Gainesville FL 32601

CHAO, BEI TSE, mechanical engineering educator; b. Soochow, China, Dec. 18, 1918; came to U.S., 1948, naturalized, 1962; s. Tse Yu and Yin T. (Yao) C.; m. May Kiang, Feb. 7, 1948; children: Clara, Fred Roberto. B.S. in Elec. Engring. with highest honor, Nat. Chiao-Tung U., China, 1939; Ph.D. (Boxer Indemnity scholar), Victoria U., Manchester, Eng., 1947. Asst. engr. tool and gage div. Central Machine Works, Kunming, China, 1939-41, asso. engr., 1941-43, mgr. tool and gage div., 1943-45; research asst. U. Ill., Urbana, 1948-50, asst. prof. dept. mech. engring., 1951-53, asso. prof., 1953-55, prof., 1955—, head thermal sci. div., 1971-75, head dept. mech. and indsl. engring., 1975—; assoc. mem. U. Ill. (Center for Advanced Study), 1963-64; cons. to industry and govtl. agys., 1950—; Russell S. Springer prof. mech. engring. U. Calif.-Berkeley, 1973; mem. reviewing staff Zentralblatt für Mathematik, Berlin, 1970-82; mem. U.S. Engring. Edn. Del. to Visit People's Republic of China, 1978; mem. adv. screening com. in engring. Fulbright-Hays Awards Program, 1979-81, chmn., 1980, 81; mem. com. U.S. Army basic sci. research NRC, 1980-83; Prince disting. lectr. Ariz. State U., 1984. Author: Advanced Heat Transfer, 1969; contbr. numerous articles on mech. engring. to profl. jours.; tech. editor: Jour. Heat Transfer, 1975-81; mem. adv. editorial bd.: Numerical Heat Transfer, 1977—. Recipient Outstanding Tchr. award Ill. Mech. Engring. Alumni, 1978, Max Jakob Meml. award ASME/Am. Inst. Chem. Engrs. 1983, Outstanding Achievement award Am. Acad. Higher Edn., 1984, Tau Beta Pi-Daniel C. Drucker Eminent Faculty award U. Ill., 1985. Fellow ASME (Blackall award 1957, Heat Transfer award 1971), AAAS; mem. Am. Soc. Engring. Edn. (Outstanding Tchr. award. 1975, Western Electric Fund award 1973), Nat. Acad. Engring., Am. Soc. Engring. Edn. (Benjamin Garver Lamme award 1984), Soc. Engring. Sci., Chiao-Tung U. Alumni Assn. (pres. Mid-West sect. 1975-76), Sigma Xi, Tau Beta Pi, Pi Tau Sigma. Current Work: Thermal hydraulics in nuclear reactors; multiphase flows; particlate removal from engine exhaust and fluidized bed dynamics. Subspecialties: Mechanical engineering; Fluid mechanics. Home: 704 Brighton Dr Urbana IL 61801 Office: 148 Mechanical Engineering Bldg Univ Ill Urbana IL 61801

CHAO, JIATSONG JASON, nuclear engineer, research project manager; b. Venden, Shanton, China, Dec. 15, 1948; came to U.S., 1972; s. Gwei-Hai and Chui-Yun Tsoong C.; m. Lily Ni, May 26, 1974; 1 son, Neal. B.S., FuJen Catholic U., Taipei, Taiwan, 1971; M.A., U. Tex.-Austin, 1974; Ph.D., M.I.T., 1979. Research assoc. M.I.T., 1976-79; sr. scientist Sci. Applications Inc., Oak Brook, Ill., 1979-81; project mgr. Electric Power Research Inst., Palo Alto, Calif., 1981—, Argonne (Ill.) Nat. Lab., 1981—, Gen. Electric, Sunnyvale, Calif., 1981—, Energy, Inc., Idaho Falls, 1981—. Contbr. articles to profl. jours. Mem. Am. Nuclear Soc., ASME. Patentee fusion blanket design. Current Work: Thermal hydraulic and neutronic design of fusion reactor blanket magnetohydrodynamics, two-phase heat transfer nuclear plant analyses for pressurized thermal shock and steam generator tube break events. Subspecialties: Nuclear fission; Nuclear fusion. Home: 1841 Newcastle Dr Los Altos CA 94022 Office: Electric Power Research Institute 3412 Hillview Ave Palo Alto CA 94303

CHAO, MOU SHU, chemist; b. Changsha, Hunan, China, Nov. 20, 1924; came to U.S., 1955; s. Heng-ti and Hwei-ying Chao; m. Patricia Hu, July 20, 1968; 1 child, Anita. B.S., Nat. Central U., Nanking, China, 1947; M.S., U. Ill., 1958, Pd.D., 1961. Teaching asst. Nat. Central U., 1947-49; tech. asst. Taiwan Fertilizer Co., Taipei, 1947-55; research chemist Dow Chem. Co., Midland, Mich., 1960-72, research specialist, 1973-80, research leader, 1980—. Author: Taiwan Fertilizers, 1951. Contbr. articles to profl. jours. Deacon 1st Baptist Ch., Midland, 1974-76. Fellow Am. Inst. Chemists; mem. Electrochem. Soc. (sect. chmn. 1973-74, 83-84, councillor 1974-76, 85—), Am. Chem. Soc. N.Y. Acad. Sci., Mensa, Sigma Xi, Phi Lambda Upsilon. Club: Midland Chinese. Current work: Electrochemical synthesis, electrochemical analysis, electrochemical instrumentation. Subspecialties: Physical chemistry; Analytical chemistry. Home: 1206 Evamar Dr Midland MI 48640 Office: Dow Chem Co 1776 Bldg Midland MI 48640

CHAPIN, CHARLES EDWARD, geologist; b. Porterville, Calif., Oct. 25, 1932; s. William Frank and Gladys Lillian (Mitchell) C.; m. Carol Ruth Giles, June 11, 1958; children: Giles Mathew, John Edward, Laura Ann. B.Geol.Engring., Colo. Sch. Mines, 1954, D. Sc., 1965. Exploration geologist J.M. Huber Corp., Borger, Tex., 1955-58; devel. geologist Lucky Mc Uranium Corp., Riverton, Wyo., 1958-59; asst. prof. U. Tulsa, 1964-65; asst. and assoc. prof. N.Mex. Inst. Mining & Tech., Socorro, 1965-70, head geosci. dept., 1968-70; sr. geologist N. Mex. Bur. Mines, Socorro, 1970—; cons. Western Nuclear Inc., 1967-69, Rampart Exploration, 1978—; chmn. exec. com. Rio Grande Rift Consortium, 1982—; chmn. program com. Internat. Symposium on Rio Grande Rift, 1977-78. Author, co-editor: Field Guide... Datil-Mogollon Volcanic Field, N.Mex, 1978, Ash-Flow Tuffs, 1979; contbr. articles to profl. jours. Cubmaster Boy Scouts Am., Socorro, 1968-70. Served with U.S. Army, 1955-57. Recipient Van Diest Gold medal Colo. Sch. Mines, 1980. Fellow Geol. Soc. Am.; mem. N.Mex. Geol. Soc., Am. Geophys. Union, Soc. Exploration Paleontologists and Mineralogists, Rocky Mountain Assn. Geologists. Current Work: Tectonics of Southern Rocky Mountain-Rio Grande rift area; volcanic geology of the N.E. Datil-Mogollon volcanic field, N.Mex.; Tallahassee Creek uranium dist., Colo. Subspecialty: Tectonics. Home: 204 Grant Ave Socorro NM 87801 Office: New Mex Bur Mines Campus Station Socorro NM 87801

CHAPLINE, GEORGE FREDERICK, JR., physicist; b. Teaneck, N.J., May 6, 1942; s. George Frederick and Ferne Louise (Copeland) C.; m. Marie Jeanne Hjort, Mar. 5, 1968; 1 child, Michael. Ph.D., Calif. Inst. Tech., 1967. Asst. prof. U. Calif.-Santa Cruz, 1967-69; physicist Lawrence Livermore Nat. Lab., Calif., 1969—. Recipient Lawrence award Dept. Energy, 1983. Patentee X-ray laser, x-ray holography system. Current work: X-ray lasers, unified string theories. Subspecialties: Theoretical physics; X-ray lasers. Office: Lawrence Livermore Nat Lab Livermore CA 94550

CHAPMAN, ORVILLE LAMAR, chemist, educator; b. New London, Conn., June 6, 1932; s. Orville Carmen and Mabel Elnora (Tyree) C.; m. Faye Newton Morrow, Aug. 20, 1955 (div. 1980); children: Kenneth, Kevin; m. Susan Elizabeth Parker, June 15, 1981. B.S., Va. Poly. Inst., 1954; Ph.D., Cornell U., 1957. Prof. chemistry Iowa State U., 1957-74; prof. chemistry UCLA, 1974—; Cons. Mobil Chem. Co. Recipient John Wilkinson Teaching award Iowa State U., 1968; award Nat. Acad. Scis., 1974; Founders prize Tex. Instruments; George and Freda Halpern award in photochemistry N.Y. Acad. Scis., 1978; McCoy award UCLA, 1984. Mem. Am. Chem. Soc. (award in pure chemistry 1968, Arthur C. Cope award 1978, Midwest award 1978, Havinga medal 1982). Subspecialty: Organic chemistry. Home: 1213 Roscomare Rd Los Angeles CA 90077 Office: Dept Chemistry U Calif 405 Hilgard Ave Los Angeles CA 90024

CHAPMAN, RUSSELL LEONARD, phycologist, cytologist, educational administrator; b. Bklyn., May 30, 1946; s. Russell Hood and Helen Theresa (Egnotas) C.; m. Melanie Ripperton, June 28, 1969; children: Christopher John, Timothy Sean. A.B., Dartmouth Coll., 1968; M.S., U. Calif., Davis, 1970, Ph.D. (NSF fellow), 1973. Asst. prof. dept. botany La. State U., Baton Rouge, 1973-77, assoc. prof., 1977-83, prof., 1983—, assoc. dean Coll. Arts and Scis., 1979-83, assoc. dean Coll. Basic Scis., 1983-84; vis. prof. dept. molecular, cellular and devel. biology U. Colo., 1984. Contbr. numerous articles on phycology and cytology to profl. jours. Active Found. for Hist. La. Recipient Amoco Found. Outstanding Undergrad. Teaching award, 1978; La. State U. Alumni Fedn. Disting. Faculty award, 1981. Mem. Phycological Soc. Am., Brit. Phycological Soc., Internat. Phycological Soc., Bot. Soc. Am., Am. Soc. Cell Biology, Electron Microscopy Soc. Am., Sigma Xi, Phi Kappa Phi. Republican. Episcopalian. Current Work: Ultrastructure and phylogeny green algae, cellular research, ultrastructure, phycology. Subspecialties: Cell biology; Evolutionary biology. Home: Route 2 Box 167 Iberville LA 70746 Office: Dept Botany La State U Baton Rouge LA 70803

CHAPPELL, GARY ALAN, software designer; b. Independence, Mo., Jan. 24, 1954; s. Jesse Earl and Eunice Mildred (Ralston) C. B.S. in Computer Sci, U. Mo.-Rolla, 1976; B.S. in Chemistry, 1976. Grad. teaching asst. Stanford U., 1976-77; graphics programmer Lawrence Livermore Lab., Calif., 1977-79; prin. investigator research and devel. Def. and Space Systems Group TRW, Redondo Beach, Calif., 1979; product mgr. Comtal Image Processing, Inc., Pasadena, Calif., 1979-80; mgr. user interface devel. Tymshare, Inc., Cupertino, Calif., 1980-82; software mgr.-graphics Qubix Graphic Systems, Saratoga, Calif., 1982-84; sr. software engr. Suntek Tech. Internat., Sunnyvale, Calif., 1984—. Mem. Assn. Computing Machinery, Spl. Interest Group for Graphics, Spl. Interest Group for Computer-Human Interaction, Soc. Info. Display, Am. Chem. Soc., Mensa. Current Work: Design and implementation of interactive, graphics-oriented human-computer interfaces for non-technical computer system users; research into software and hardware components of highly interactive graphics systems. Subspecialties: Graphics, image processing, and pattern recognition; Cognition. Home: 2220 Homestead Ct Apt 204 Los Altos CA 94022 Office: 720 Lucerne Dr Sunnyvale CA 94086

CHAPPELL, ROBERT PAUL, dental educator; b. Des Moines, Iowa, Nov. 28, 1918; s. William and Nellie Margaret (Florer) C.; m. Penelope Alyce Nelson, Apr. 20, 1979. B.S., U. Ill.-Chgo., 1948; D.D.S., 1950. Lic. dentist, Mo. Commd. 2d lt. U.S. Army, 1941, advanced through grades to lt. col., 1964, served, U.S. and E.T.O., 1941-46, dental officer, U.S.A., France, Eng., 1952-67; asst. prof. U. Mo., Kansas City, 1967-70, assoc. prof., 1970-80, prof., 1980—, chmn. dept. dental materials, 1974—. Contbr. articles to profl. jours. Mem.(life) Retired Officers Assn., Alexandria, Va., Mil. Order of World Wars., Washington. Univ. Mo. faculty grantee, 1972, 74. Fellow Internat. Coll. Oral Implantology; mem. Internat. Assn. Dental Research, Am. Assn. Dental Schs. Republican. Current Work: oral implantology, endosteal, biomaterials. Subspecialties: Implantology; Biomaterials. Office: School of Dentistry Univ Mo 650 E 25th St Kansas City MO 64108

CHARACKLIS, WILLIAM GREGORY, microbial chemical process and environmental engineering researcher, consultant; b. Annapolis, Md., Aug. 21, 1941; s. Gregory Arthur and Artemis (Batayannis) C.; m. Nancy Crowley, Aug. 30, 1964; children: Gregory William, Erin Elizabeth. B.E.S., Johns Hopkins U., 1964, Ph.D., 1970; M.S.Ch.E., U. Toledo, 1967. Lic profl. engr., Tex. Research engr. Olin-Mathieson Chem. Corp., New Haven, 1964-65; grad. research asst. U. Toledo, 1965-67, Johns Hopkins U., 1967-70; asst. prof. Rice U., 1970-74, assoc. prof., 1974-78, prof., 1978-79; prof. environ. engring. Mont. State U., 1979—, dir. Inst. Biol. and Chem. Process Analysis, 1983—; prin. W. G. Characklis Cons. Engrs., Inc., Bozeman, Mont., 1981—. Merck fellow, 1972; NSF fellow, 1977-78. Mem. Am. Inst. Chem. Engrs., Am. Soc. Microbiology, Internat. Assn. Water Pollution Research, Water Pollution Control Fedn., Cooling Tower Inst. Club: Karl Marx Athletic and Social (Bozeman). Inventor in field. Current Work: Microbial and chemical process engineering. Subspecialties: Chemical engineering; Water supply and wastewater treatment. Home: 516 W Cleveland Bozeman MT 59715 Office: Mont State U Coll Engring Bozeman MT 59717

CHARAN, NIRMAL BISWAS, physician, researcher; b. Ranikhet, India, Dec. 7, 1946; came to U.S., 1977; s. Isaac Albert and Salomi (Singh) C.; m. Lalita Clive, June 20, 1973; children: Ankur, Neev. B.Sc., Hindu Coll., Moradabad, India, 1964; M.B.B.S., Christian Med. Coll., Ludhiana, India, 1969. Intern Christian Med. Coll. Hosp., Ludhiana, India, house physician, 1970, resident in internal medicine, 1970-74; registrar in internal medicine Auckland (New Zealand) Hosp., 1974-77; fellow in pulmonary U. Wash., Seattle, 1977-80, asst. prof., 1981—; staff physician VA Med. Ctr., Boise, 1980—; dir. VA Med. Ctr. (Respiratory-Therapy and Pulmonary Function Lab.), 1980—. Author: Drug Therapy in Elderly, 1983; cons editor: Jour. Chest, 1982; contbr. articles to profl. jours. NIH fellow, 1979-80; VA grantee, 1981—. Fellow A.C.P., Am. Coll. Chest Physicians; mem. Am. Thoracic Soc., Am. Physiol. Soc., Am. Fedn. Clin. Research. Methodist. Current Work: Lung fluid balance, lung mechanics and role of bronchial circulation in health and disease. Subspecialties: Internal medicine; Pulmonary medicine. Home: 722 Harcourt Rd Boise ID 83702

CHARGAFF, ERWIN, biochemistry educator; b. Austria, Aug. 11, 1905; came to U.S., 1928, naturalized, 1940; s. Hermann and Rosa C.; m. Vera Broido; 1 child, Thomas. Dr. Phil., U. Vienna, 1928; Dr. phil. h.c, U. Basel, 1976; Sc.D. (hon.), Columbia U., 1976. Research fellow Yale U., 1928-30; asst. U. Berlin, Germany, 1930-33; research assoc. Inst. Pasteur, Paris, France, 1933-34; faculty Columbia U., 1935—, prof. biochemistry, 1952-74, prof. emeritus, 1974—, chmn. dept. biochemistry, 1970-74; vis. prof., Sweden, 1949, Japan, 1958, Brazil, 1959; vis. prof. Coll. de France, 1965, Naples, Palermo, Cornell, 1966, Stazione biologica, Naples, 1969. Author: Essays on Nucleic Acids, 1963, Voices in the Labyrinth, 1977, Heraclitean Fire, 1978, Das Feuer des Heraklit, 1979, Unbegreifliches Geheimnis, 1980, Bemerkungen, 1981, Warnungstafeln, 1982, Kritik der Zukunft, 1983; Zeugenschaft, 1985; numerous articles in field, other lit. work in English and German.; Editor: The Nucleic Acids, 3 vols, 1955, 60. Guggenheim fellow, 1949, 58; recipient Pasteur medal Soc. Biol. Chemistry, Paris, 1949; Neuberg medal Am. Soc. European Chemists, 1958; Bertner Found. award Houston, 1965; C.L. Mayer prize French Acad. Scis., 1963; Dr. H.P. Heineken prize Netherlands Acad. Scis., 1964; Gregor Mendel medal German Acad. Scis. Leopoldina, 1973; Nat. Medal of Sci., 1975; medal N.Y. Acad. Medicine, 1980; Disting. Service award Columbia U., 1982; Johann-Heinrich-Merck prize German Acad. Lang. and Lit., 1984. Fellow Am. Acad. Arts and Scis.; mem. Nat. Acad. Scis., Am. Philos. Soc.; fgn. mem. Royal Swedish Physiographic Soc., German Acad. Scis. Leopoldina. Subspecialty: Biochemistry (medicine). Home: 350 Central Park W New York NY 10025

CHARLESWORTH, EDWARD ALLISON, clinical psychologist, author, publishing corporation executive; b. New Orleans, AMar. 23, 1949; s. Albert Ernest and Wilma Nadine (Wright) C.; m. Robin Elaine Rupley, Dec. 7, 1974. B.S., U. Houston, 1974, M.S., 1978, Ph.D., 1980. Diplomate: Am. Acad. Behavioral Medicine; lic. psychologist, Tex. Pres. Stress Mgmt. Research Assos., Inc., Houston, 1977—; research assoc. Baylor Coll. Medicine, Houston, 1970-81, psychologist, instr., 1981-82; dir. Willowbrook Psychol. Assos., Houston, 1982—; chmn., chief editor Biobehavioral Press, Houston, 1980—. Author: recordings Stress Management Trng. Program, 1977, Stress Mgmt. and Relaxation Program, 1981; co-author: recordings Stress Management: A Conceptual and Procedural Guide, 1980, Stress Management: A Comprehensive Guide to Wellness, 1982. Founder, sponsor Forest Lake Teens in Action, Houston, 1978-80; instr. Cypress Fairbank Sch. Dist. Wellness Program, 1982. Trainee NIMH, 1976-78; Trainee VA. Hosp, 1978. Mem. Am. Psychol. Assn., Tex. Psychol. Assn., Harris County Biofeedback Soc., Am. Soc. Biofeedback Clinicians, Houston Psychol. Assn. (bd. dirs.). Democrat. Presbyterian. Club: Mensa. Lodge: Rotary (bd. dirs.). Current Work: Research: behavioral treatments for hypertension, addictive disorders and stress related problems; clinical work, psychotherapy, hypnotherapy, biofeedback. Subspecialties: Behavioral psychology; Preventive medicine. Home: 11803 Moorcreek Houston TX 77070 Office: Willowbrook Psychological Assos 9725 Louedd Houston TX 77070

CHARNEY, ELLIOT, biophysicist; b. N.Y.C., June 1, 1922; s. David and Etta (Ginsburg) C.; m. Gloria Kamen, June 22, 1941; children—Tina, Ruth, Juliet. B.S., CCNY, 1942; Ph.D., Columbia U., 1956. Research chemist Manhattan Project, N.Y., 1942-45; tech. adv. Carbide Carbon Chem. Corp., 1945-48; staff cons. U.S. AEC, Vitro Corp., 1948-54; research phys. chemist NIH, 1956-72, chief sect. spectroscopy, structure, 1972—; vis. scholar Oxford U., 1962-63, U. Oreg., 1965, Dartmouth Coll., 1973, 83. Author chpts. in sci. monographs, two books. DuPont Teaching fellow 1951; recipient USPHS superior service award, 1979. Mem. Am. Phys. Soc., N.Y. Acad. Scis., Fedn. Am. Scientists, World Federalists Assn. Current work: Structure and physical properties of nucleic acids; polyelectrolyte theory; optical rotatory dispension; electric linear dichroism and birefringence studies of nucleic acids and biological structure, DNA. Subspecialties: Biophysics (physics); Physical chemistry. Office: NIH Bldg 2 Room B1-03 Bethesda MD 20205

CHARNIAK, EUGENE, computer scientist. Assoc. prof. computer sci. Brown U., Providence, R.I. Subspecialty: Automated language processing. Office: Brown U Dept Computer Sci Providence RI 02912

CHARPIE, ROBERT ALAN, physicist; b. Cleve., Sept. 9, 1925; s. Leonard Asbury and Dorothy (McLean) C.; m. Elizabeth Downs, July 12, 1947; children: Richard Alan, Carol Elizabeth, David Wayne, John Robert. B.S. with honors, Carnegie Inst. Tech., 1948, M.S., 1949, D.Sc. in Theoretical Physics, 1950; D.H.L., Denison U., 1965; D.Sc., Alderson-Broaddus Coll., 1967; LL.D., Marietta Coll., 1975; D.Sc., Boston Coll., 1982. With Westinghouse Electric Corp., 1947-50; with Oak Ridge Nat. Lab., 1950-51, tech. asst. to research dir., 1952-54, asst. research dir., 1954-58, dir. reactor div., 1958-61; mgr. adv. devel. Union Carbide Corp., 1961-63, gen. mgr. devel. dept., 1963-64, dir. tech., 1964-66, pres. electronics div., 1966-68; pres. Bell & Howell Co., Chgo., 1968-69; pres., dir. Cabot Corp., Boston, 1969—; trustee Mitre Corp., Boston, 1966-82, chmn., 1972-82; dir. Federated Dept. Stores, Inc., Champion Internat. Corp., Schlumberger Ltd., Northwest Airlines, Inc.; sec. gen. adv. com. AEC, 1959-63; mem. Nat. Sci. Bd., 1969-76; sci. sec., editor-in-chief proc., also asst. U.S. mem. 7 nation adv. com. 1st Internat. Conf. Peaceful Uses Atomic Energy, 1955; coordinator U.S. fusion research exhibit, 2d Conf., 1958; chmn. invention and innovation panel U.S. Dept. Commerce, 1965-67. Gen. editor: Internat. Monograph Series on Nuclear Energy, 1955-60; editor: Progress Series in Nuclear Energy, 1955-60, Jour. Nuclear Energy, 1955-60. Mem. Oak Ridge Bd. Edn., 1957-61; pres. Byram Hills Central Sch. Dist., 1966-68; trustee Carnegie Inst. Tech., 1962—. Recipient Alumni Merit award Carnegie Inst. Tech., 1957. Fellow Am. Phys. Soc., Am. Nuclear Soc. (dir.); mem. N.Y. Acad. Sci., Nat. Acad. Engring., Sci. Research Soc. Am., Sigma Xi, Tau Beta Pi, Phi Mu Epsilon. Subspecialty: Theoretical physics. Home: 45 Ridgeway Rd Weston MA 02193 Office: 125 High St Boston MA 02110

CHARYK, JOSEPH VINCENT, satellite telecommunications company executive; b. Canmore, Alta., Can., Sept. 9, 1920; came to U.S., 1942, naturalized, 1948; s. John and Anna (Dorosh) C.; m. Edwina Elizabeth Rhodes, Aug. 18, 1945; children: William R., J. John, Christopher E., Diane E. B.Sc. in Engring. Physics, U. Alta., 1942, LL.D., 1964; M.S., Calif. Inst. Tech., 1943, Ph.D., 1946; D.Engring. (hon.), U. Bologna, 1974. Sect. chief Jet Propulsion Lab., Calif. Inst. Tech., 1945-46, instr. aeros., 1945-46; asst. prof. aeros. Princeton U., 1946-49, assoc. prof., 1949-55; dir. aerophysics and chemistry lab., missile systems div. Lockheed Aircraft Corp., 1955-56; dir. aero. lab. Aeronutronic Systems, Inc. subs. Ford Motor Co., 1956-58, gen. mgr. space tech. div., 1958-59; asst. sec. Air Force (for research and devel.), 1959; undersec. Air Force, 1960-63; pres., dir. Communications Satellite Corp., from 1963, chief exec. officer, 1979-85, chmn., 1983-85; chmn. bd. Comsat Gen. Corp., Environ. Research and Tech., Inc., Satellite TV Corp.; mem. partners' com. Satellite Bus. Systems; dir. Am. Security Corp., Abbott Labs.; mem. corp. C. S. Draper Lab., Inc. Fellow AIAA, IEEE; mem. Nat. Acad. Engring., Internat. Acad. Astronautics, Nat. Inst. Social Scis., Nat. Space Club, Sigma Xi. Clubs: 1925 F Street, Chevy Chase, Burning Tree, Met. Subspecialty: Telecommunications. Home: 5126 Tilden St NW Washington DC 20016

CHASE, JOHN DAVID, physician, university dean; b. Detroit, Sept. 24, 1920; s. Clyde Harrison and Bonnie Lucille (Fogas) C.; m. Margaret Julia Chamberlain, July 25, 1942; 1 child, Robert Winslow. A.B., Wabash (Ind.) Coll., 1942; M.D., Western Res. U., 1945. Diplomate: Am. Bd. Internal Medicine. Intern Detroit Receiving Hosp., 1945-46; resident in internal medicine Wayne State U. Hosp., 1948-52; teaching fellow Nat. Heart Inst., 1952; with VA, 1952-78, dep. asso. chief med. dir. academic affairs, Washington, 1970-73; chief med. service VA Hosp., Tacoma, 1973-74; chief med. dir. VA Central Office, Washington, 1974-78; assoc. dean clin. affairs U. Wash. Sch. Med., Seattle, 1978—, dean Sch. Medicine, 1981-82; mem. nat. adv. council Heart and Lung Inst., 1968-70, Regional Med. Programs, 1970-73, Nat. Library Medicine, 1972-73; mem. Nat. Adv. Council VA Edn., 1973, Nat. Adv. Council Health Services Planning and Resources, 1976, Fed. Coordinating Council Sci., Engring. and Tech., 1976-78, Nat. Adv. Council Health Planning and Devel., 1976—; bd. govs. Armed Forces Inst. Pathology, 1976-78. Trustee Chgo. Med. Sch., 1978—. Served with M.C. USNR, 1946-48. Recipient Disting. Service award Wayne State U. Med. Sch., 1976. Fellow ACP, Am. Coll. Chest Physicians; mem. Assn. Mil. Surgeons U.S., AMA (ho. dels.), Am. Hosp. Assn. (trustee 1976-78). Current work: Medical institution administration. Subspecialties: Internal medicine; Medical institution administration. Home: 3700 Soundview Dr W Tacoma WA 98466 Office: U Wash AA316 Health Sci Bldg Seattle WA 98195

CHASE, JOHN WILLIAM, molecular biologist, educator; b. Balt., May 30, 1944; s. John Webster and Ethel Adele (Mewshaw) C.; m. Anne Christine Wright, July 1, 1967; children: Kristen Lynnette, Kimberly Anne. A.B., Drew U., Madison, N.J., 1966; Ph.D., Johns Hopkins U., 1971. NIH fellow Harvard U. Med. Sch., Boston, 1971-75, Am. Cancer Soc. fellow, 1972-73; asst. prof. Albert Einstein Coll. Medicine, Bronx, N.Y., 1975-81, assoc. prof. molecular biology, 1981—; cons. NIH, Bethesda, Md., 1978—; established investigator Am. Heart Assn., Dallas, 1978-83. Contbr. numerous sci. articles to profl. publs. NIH grantee, 1976—; Am. Cancer Soc. grantee, 1977-78. Mem. Am. Soc. Biol. Chemists, Am. Soc. Microbiologists. Current Work: Biochemical and genetic studies of DNA replication; recombination; repair mechanisms. Subspecialties: Biochemistry (biology); Enzyme technology. Home: 90 Perth Ave New Rochelle NY 10804 Office: Albert Einstein Coll Medicine 1300 Morris Park Ave Bronx NY 10461

CHASE, ROBERT ARTHUR, surgeon, educator; b. Keene, N.H., Jan. 6, 1923; s. Albert Henry and Georgia Beulah (Bump) C.; m. Ann Crosby Parker, Feb. 3, 1946; children: Deborah Lee, Nancy Jo, Robert N. B.S. cum laude, U. N.H., 1945; M.D., Yale, 1947. Diplomate: Am. Bd. Surgery, Am. Bd. Plastic Surgery. Intern New Haven Hosp., 1947-48, asst. resident, 1949-50, sr. resident surgery, 1952-53, chief resident surgeon, 1953-54; mem. faculty Yale Sch. Medicine, 1948-54, 59-62, asst. prof. surgery, 1959-62; mem. faculty U. Pitts., 1957-59, resident plastic surgeon, also teaching fellow, 1957-59; attending surgeon VA Hosp., W. Haven, Conn., 1959-62, Grace New Haven Community Hosp., 1959-63; prof., chmn. dept. surgery Stanford Sch. Medicine, 1963-74, Emile Holman prof. surgery, 1972—; prof. surgery U. Pa., 1974-77; attending surgeon Pa. Hosp., Hosp. U. Pa., Grad. Hosp., Phila., 1974-77; pres., dir. Nat. Bd. Med. Examiners, Phila., 1974-77; prof. anatomy Stanford (Calif.) U., 1977—; Cons. plastic surgery Christian Med. Coll. and Hosp., Vellore, S. India, 1962; cons. to surgeon gen. USAF, 1970—; Benjamin K. Rank prof. Australasian Coll. Surgeons, 1974. Author: Atlas of Hand Surgery; Editor: Videosurgery, 1974—; editorial bd.: Med. Alert Communication; Contbr. articles to profl. jours. Served to maj. M.C. AUS, 1949-57. Recipient Francis Gilman Blake award Yale Sch. Medicine, 1962, Henry J. Kaiser award Stanford U. Sch. Medicine, 1978-79. Fellow A.C.S., Australasian Coll. Surgeons (hon.); mem. Am. Soc. Plastic Surgery, Calif. Acad. Medicine (pres.), San Francisco Surg. Soc., Am. Surg. Assn., Santa Clara County, Conn. med. socs., Am. Soc. Surgery Hand (pres.), Am. Soc. Cleft Palate Rehab., Am. Assn. Surgery Trauma, Plastic Surgery Research Council, AMA, Soc. Clin. Surgery, Western Surg. Assn., Pacific Coast Surg. Soc., Am. Assn. Plastic Surgery, James IV Assn. Surgeons, Am. Cancer Soc. (clin. fellowship com.), Found. Am. Soc. Plastic and Reconstructive Surgery (dir.), Soc. Univ. Surgeons, Inst. Med. (exec. com. 1976), Nat. Acad. Scis., Am. Soc. Most Venerable Order Hosp., St. John of Jerusalem, Halsted Soc., South African Soc. Surgery Hand (hon.), South African Soc. Plastic and Reconstructive Surgery (hon.), Sigma Xi. Current Work: Medical director man-made interface; computer-imaging interest. Subspecialties: Computers in Medicine; Surgery. Home: 797 N Tolman Ln Stanford CA 94305 Office: Dept Surgery Stanford U Stanford CA 94305

CHASIN, MARK, pharm. co. exec.; b. N.Y.C., Feb. 20, 1942; s. Philip J. and Florence (Friedman) C.; m. Rena Bleiweiss, June 19, 1963; children: Jeffrey, Larry, Marni. A.B. in Chemistry, Cornell U., 1963; Ph.D. in Biochemistry (Am. Cancer Soc. fellow), Mich. State U., 1967. NIH trainee, 1964-67; sr. research investigator Squibb Inst., Princeton, N.J., 1967-74; dir. biochem. research Ortho Pharm. Corp., Raritan, N.J., 1974-78, dir. intercorp. new product devel., 1978-80, dir. clin. devel., 1980-81, dir. research info. services, 1981—. Editor: Methods in Cyclic Nucleotide Research, 1972; contbr. articles to profl. jours. Mem. Am. Soc. Biol. Chemists, Am. Soc. for Pharmacology and Exptl. Therapeutics, Am. Soc. Clin. Pharmacology and Therapeutics. Current Work: Cyclic nucleotides, control of hormonal action. Subspecialties: Biochemistry (medicine); Pharmacology.

CHASSON, ROBERT LEE, physics educator; b. Cin., May 30, 1919; s. Mayer Leon and Fanny (Kondritzer) C.; m. Frances Jean Bray, Nov. 20, 1971; children by previous marriage: Barbara, William. A.B., U. Calif.-Berkeley, 1940, M.A., 1950, Ph.D., 1951. Asst. prof. physics U. Nebr., Lincoln, 1951-56, assoc. prof., 1956-59, prof., 1959-62, chmn. dept., 1956-62; prof. physics U. Denver, 1962-85, prof. emeritus, 1985—, chmn. dept. physics, div. head research inst., 1962-76; mem. adv. panel atmospheric sci. NSF, 1968-70; trustee Univ. Corp. Atmospheric Research, Boulder, Colo., 1970-79; mem. geophysics research bd. Nat. Acad. Scis., 1973-76. Author, editor works in field. Served with AUS, 1943-45. Guggenheim Found. fellow, 1962-63; Rockefeller Found. fellow, 1978-79. Fellow Am. Phys. Soc., AAAS; mem. Am. Geophys. Union, AAUP (chpt. pres. 1960-61), Sigma Xi. Democrat. Current Work: Cosmic rays and geophysics, solar-terrestrial relationships, interplanetary fields and particles, high energy astrophysics. Subspecialties: Cosmic ray high energy astrophysics; Solar physics. Home: 3255 S Albion St Denver CO 80222 Office: Dept Physics U Denver Denver CO 80208

CHASTAIN, CLAUD BLANKENHORN, veterinary medicine educator; b. Stamford, Tex., Oct. 12, 1945; s. Claud H. and Jean (Blankenhorn) C.; m. Joyce L. Busche, June 25, 1977; children—Andrea Lee, Danielle Renee. B.S., U. Mo., 1967, D.V.M., 1969; M.S., Iowa State U., 1972. Asst. prof. Iowa State U., Ames, 1972-75, 76-77, assoc. prof., 1977-81, prof., 1981-82; asst. prof. La. State U., Baton Rouge, 1975-76; assoc. prof. vet. medicine U. Mo., Columbia, 1982—, chief small animal medicine, 1982—; cons. Canine Practice Jour., Feline Practice Jour. Contbr. chpts. to texts, articles to profl. jours. Leader, Methodist Youth Fellowship, Ames, 1981; tchr. Sunday sch. Meth. Ch., Columbia, 1982. Served to capt. USAF, 1969-71. Recipient Curator's award U. Mo., 1963. Diplomate Am. Coll. Vet. Internal Medicine. Mem. Am. Acad. Vet. Dermatology, AVMA, Am. Assn. Vet. Clinicians. Democrat. Current work: Clincal endocrinology of companion animals. Subspecialty: Internal medicine (veterinary medicine). Home: 300 DeFoe Dr Columbia MO 65203 Office: U Mo Coll Vet Med Columbia MO 65211

CHASTAIN, GARVIN, psychology educator; b. Ft. Worth, Tex., Feb. 23, 1945; s. Garvin Dunn and Bertha Pearl (Parrish) C.; m. Gloria Jean Pollard, Nov. 21, 1975; 1 child by previous marriage, Ross Calvert. Ph.D. in Human Exptl. Psychology, U. Tex.-Austin, 1976. Head computer instruction Durhams Coll, Austin, Tex., 1976-77; research scientist Human Resources Research Orgn., Ft. Hood, Tex., 1977-78; asst. prof. Boise (Idaho) State U., 1978-82, assoc. prof. psychology, 1982—. Contbr. articles to profl. jours. Bd. dirs. Univ. Scholastic Assn., Boise, 1982—; mem. Idaho Com. of Creation/Evolution, Boise, 1982—; v.p. Rockies, Freedom From Religion Found., Madison, Wis., 1980-82. Faculty research grantee Boise State U., 1982. Mem. Psychonomic Soc., Am. Psychol. Assn., Rocky Mt. Psychol. Assn., Phi Kappa Phi, Psi Chi. Libertarian. Current Work: Human exptl. psychology; visual info. processing; pattern recognition; spatial attention; reading; visual signal detection. Subspecialties: Cognition; Psychophysics. Home: 3500 Tulara Dr Boise ID 83704 Office: Boise State Univ 1910 University Dr Boise ID 83725

CHATEAU, GEORGES MICHEL, engineer; b. St. Leonard de Noblat, France, May 13, 1934; came to U.S., 1981; s. Jean Roger and Marcelle M. (Lachaise) C.; m. Ruth M. Loeffler, June 12, 1964. Engr., Ecole Nationale Superieure de Mecanique de Nantes, France, 1957, Ecole Nationale Superieure des Petroles, Rueil-Malmaison, France, 1959. Drilling engr. S.N. Repal, Algiers, Algeria, 1962-65; offshore engr. Elf Aquitaine, Pau-Paris-Bordeaux, France, 1965-81, Port-Gentil, Gabon, 1968; frontiers arctic and offshore studies and ops. staff Elf Aquitaine Petroleum, Houston, 1981—. Contbr. articles to profl. publs. Patentee in field. Served with French Armed Forces, 1959-62. Mem. Soc. Petroleum Engrs., ASME, Assn. Francaise des Techniciens du Petrole. Current work: Deep sea and Arctic engineering for oil and gas production facilities, design and on-site full scale live tests. Subspecialties: Petroleum engineering; Mechanical engineering. Home: 5000 Montrose Blvd Apt 13B Houston TX 77006 Office: Elf Aquitaine Petroleum 1000 Louisiana Suite 3800 Houston TX 77002

CHATTERJEE, SATYA NARAYAN, medical educator, surgeon; b. Calcutta, India, Dec. 31, 1934; came to U.S., 1973; s. R. N. and J. C.; m. Patricia Sheppard, Sept. 26, 1964; children: Sharmila, Shalini, Arun. Inter.Sci., Scottish Ch. Coll., Calcutta, 1951; M.B.B.S., R.G. Kar Med. Coll., Calcutta, 1957. Diplomate: Brit. Bd. Surgery. Registrar dept. surgery North Staff Royal Infirmary, Stoke, Eng., 1963-64; med. supt. A.R.T. Co., Margherita, India, 1965-69; registrar transplant unit U. Edinburgh, Scotland, 1970-73; clin. and research fellow U. So. Calif. Med. Sch., Los Angeles, 1973-75; asst. prof. surgery UCLA, 1975-77; assoc. prof. surgery U. Calif.-Davis, Sacramento, 1977-84, prof. surgery, 1984—; cons. surgeon Martin Luther King Gen. Hosp., Los Angeles, 1975-77; dir. renal transplant unit No. Calif. Tissue Bank, San Jose, 1977-78. Editor: Surgical Clinics of North America, 1978, Manual of Renal Transplantation, 1979, Renal Transplantation: A Multidisciplinary Approach, 1980, Organ Transplantation, 1982, Monoclonal Antibodies, 1985. R.G. Kar Med. Coll. scholar, 1954. Fellow ACS; mem. Am. Soc. Transplant Surgeons, Assn. Acad. Surgery, Transplantation Soc., Royal Soc. Medicine, Western Assn. Transplant Surgeons (pres. 1979-80). Hindu. Club: Tennis (Davis). Current Work: Transplantation immunology, clinical renal transplantation, infectious complications of transplantation, viral infections in transplantation, immunologic monitoring, and tissue typing. Subspecialties: Transplant surgery; Transplantation. Home: PO Box 3102 El Macero CA 95618 Office: 4301 X St Sacramento CA 95817

CHATTERJEE, SUNIL KUMAR, cancer research scientist; b. Calcutta, India, Aug. 7, 1940; came to U.S., 1966, naturalized, 1981; s. Bhupendra Nath and Parimal Bala (Banerjee) C.; m. Malaya Chatterjee, Oct. 25, 1972; children: Indranil, Sumana. B.S., U. Calcutta, 1959, M.S., 1961, Ph.D., 1966. With U. Pa., 1966-68, Inst. Cancer Research, Phila., 1968-70; research assoc. U. Calcutta, 1970-71; asst. research officer Max-Planck Institut, Gottingen, W. Ger., 1972-73; sr. cancer research scientist Roswell Park Meml. Inst., Buffalo, 1973—. Contbr. articles and abstracts to profl. jours. Mem. AAAS, Am. Assn. Cancer Research, N.Y. Acad. Scis. Democrat. Hindu. Current Work: Biochemistry of cancer cell, glycoprotein biosynthesis, membrane changes in malignacy, markers for cancers, cancer metastasis. Subspecialties: Biochemistry (biology); Oncology. Home: 152 Telfair Dr Williamsville NY 14221 Office: 666 Elm St Buffalo NY 14263

CHATTERTON, ROBERT TREAT, JR., endocrinologist; b. Catskill, N.Y., Aug. 9, 1935; s. Robert T. and Irene (Spoor) C.; m. Patricia A. Holland, June 4, 1956 (div. 1965); children—Ruth Ellen, William Matthew, James Daniel; m. Astrida J. Vanags, June 25, 1966 (div. 1977); 1 child, Derek Scott. B.S., Cornell U., 1958; M.S., U. Conn., 1960; Ph.D., Cornell U., 1963; postdoctoral fellow Harvard U., 1963-65. Research assoc. Inst. Steroid Research, N.Y.C., 1965-70; asst. prof. U. Ill. Med. Sch., Chgo., 1970-72, assoc. prof. 1972-79; prof. Northwestern Med. Sch., Chgo., 1979—; mem. sci. adv. com. AID, Washington, 1972-83; dir. reproductive endocrinology lab. Northwestern U. Med. Sch., Chgo., 1979—. Author: Biochemical Mammalian Reproduction, 1982; patentee detection of ovulation in women and method of totally suppressing ovarian follicular devel.; contbr. articles to profl. jours. Deacon, Presbyterian Ch., River Forest, Ill., 1980—. Grantee: NIH, AID, NSF. Mem. Soc. Gynecol. Investigation, Endocrine Soc., Am. Physiol. Soc., AAAS, Am. Chem. Soc., Sigma Xi, Phi Kappa Phi, Gamma Sigma Delta. Current work: Biosynthesis; mechanism of action and metabolism of steroid hormones; contraceptive development. Subspecialty: Reproductive endocrinology. Home: 5018 W Agatite St Chicago IL 60630 Office: Dept Ob Gyn Northwestern U Med Sch 333 E Superior St Chicago IL 60611

CHATTOPADHYAY, SOMNATH, mechanical engineer, researcher, educator; b. Howrah, West Bengal, India, Feb. 25, 1946; came to U.S., 1969, naturalized, 1981; s. Bireswar and Shakti C.; m. Mandira, July 2, 1971; children: Somak, Parama, Prince. Ph.D. in Mechanics, Princeton U., 1974. Registered profl. engr., Pa. Research asst. Princeton U., 1969-71, instr., 1971-73; postdoctoral fellow Purdue U., 1973-74; sr. engr. Westinghouse Electric Corp., Pitts., 1974-78, lead engr., steam generator, 1979-85; mem. faculty dept. mech. engring. Villanova U., 1985—; cons. Princeton U., 1974; mem. adj. faculty Pa. State U. Contbr. articles to profl. jours. Govt. India nat. scholar, 1962-67. Mem. ASME, Soc. Engring. Sci., Am. Acad. Mechanics, ASTM. Current Work: Dynamics, structural stability, composites, electromagnetic interaction, structural mechanics in reactor technology, fatigue design of structures. Subspecialties: Mechanical engineering; Theoretical and applied mechanics. Home: 1005 Crestwood Dr North Huntingdon PA 15642

CHATURVEDI, ARVIND KUMAR, toxicologist, pharmacologist; b. Azamgarh, India, July 29, 1947; s. Vijai Narain and Sursari Devi (Pandey) C.; m. Mira Shukla, June 14, 1970; children: Priyanka, Vivek. B.S., Gorakhpur U., 1966; M.S., Banaras Hindu U., 1968; Ph.D., Lucknow U., 1972. Research fellow Lucknow U., India, 1968-74; research assoc. Vanderbilt U., Nashville, 1974-77, research instr., 1977-78; acting state toxicologist N.D. State U., Fargo, 1980, asst. prof. toxicology, 1978-82, assoc. prof., 1982—; asst. toxicologist Office N.D. State Toxicologist, 1978—. Am. Cancer Soc. grantee, 1979—; NIH grantee, 1980-82. Mem. Indian Pharmacol. Soc. (life); mem. Indian Acad. Neurosci. (life); Mem. Internat. Soc. Biochem. Pharmacology, Am. Soc. Pharmacology and Exptl. Therapeutics, Soc. Environ. Toxicology and Chemistry, Internat. Soc. Study Xenobiotics, Soc. Toxicology, Soc. Neurosci., Soc. Exptl. Biology and Medicine, Soc. Neurosci., Soc. Toxicology, Internat. Union Pharmacology (sec. toxicology), Rho Chi. Current Work: Drug toxicity on male reproductive system, influence of toxic agents on calcium transport, devel. of choline acetyltransferase inhibitors, analytical toxicology, pesticidalinteraction. Subspecialties: Toxicology (medicine); Pharmacology. Office: Dept Toxicology ND State U Coll Pharmacy PO Box 5195 Farg ND 58105

CHAUDHURI, SIDDHESWAR, physicist, researcher; b. Madhupur, India, May 21, 1953; s. Kamala K. and Karuna M. (Biswas) C.; m. Anita Datta, Aug. 16, 1979; 1 child, Ilina. B.S., Presidency Coll., 1973; M.S., Calcutta U., 1976; M.S., U. Pitts., 1978, Ph.D., 1981. Research physicist Wright State U., Dayton, Ohio, 1981-84; mem. tech. staff AT&T Bell Labs, Holmdel, N.J., 1984—. Contbr. numerous articles to tech. jours. Andrew W. Mellon Found. fellow, 1978-81. Mem. Am. Phys. Soc. Current works: Electronic and optical properties of semiconductor quantum well structures. Subspecialties: Condensed matter physics; Telecommunications. Office: AT&T Bell Labs Holmdel NJ 07733

CHAUDHURI, TAPAN KUMAR, physician; b. Calcutta, West Bengal, India, Nov. 25, 1944; came to U.S., 1967, naturalized, 1978; s. Taposh K. and Bulu R. Chowdbury; m. Chhanda Sen, Mar. 4, 1980; children: Lakshmi, Madhu, Krishna, Deboki. I.Sc., U. Calcutta, 1961, M.D., 1966. Intern NRS Med. Coll. Hosp., Calcutta, 1966-67, South Side Hosp., Pitts., 1968-69; NRS Med. Coll. Hosp., 1967, W. Va. U. Hosp., Morgantown, 1970-71; chief nuclear medicine VA Med. Center, Hampton, Va., 1974—; prof. nuclear medicine Eastern Va. Med. Sch., Norfolk, 1979—. Recipient Gold and Silver medals U. Calcutta, 1961-66. Fellow ACP, Am. Coll. Gastroenterology; mem. Soc. Nuclear Medicine. Current Work: Medical research, administrator, educator. Subspecialty: Nuclear medicine. Home: 304 Rudisill Rd Hampton VA 23669 Office: VA Med Center Hampton VA 23667

CHAUDRY, IRSHAD HUSSAIN, medical biochemist; b. Jalander-Musaibpur, Punjab, India, May 2, 1945; came to U.S., 1971; s. Noor Mohammed and Anayat (Bagam) C.; m. Micheline Denise Laperle, Mar. 22, 1974; children—Khalil, Jameel, Sabiha. B.S., Sind U., Pakistan, 1965, M.S., 1966; Ph.D., Monash U., Australia, 1970. Asst. prof. Washington U., St. Louis, 1971-75; assoc. prof. Yale U., New Haven, 1976-83, prof., 1983—; research cons. U. Toronto, Ont., Can., 1971-72, Monash U., Clayton, Australia, 1978; ad hoc cons. NIH, Bethesda, Md., 1982-85, mem. site visit team, 1983-85. Mem. editorial bd. Am. Jour. Physiology, 1982—, Circulatory Chock, 1981—. Contbr. chpts. to books. Mem. Shock Soc. (exec. council 1983—, publ. com., 1982—, session chmn. 1983-85), Am. Physiol. Soc., Am. Coll. Nutrition, Surg. Infection Soc., Reticuloendothelial Soc., Soc. Exptl. Biology and Medicine, Sigma Xi. Republican. Muslim. Current work: Metabolic, hormonal, reticuloendothelial function and cation metabolism in shock, sepsis and ischemia, organ preservation, cancer chemotherapeutic agents. Subspecialties: Biochemistry (medicine); Cellular pharmacology. Office: Dept Surgery Yale U 333 Cedar St New Haven CT 06510

CHAUNDHARI, PUNDLIK KASHIRAM, electrophysicist, engineer; b. Nanded, Maha, India, Apr. 15, 1930; came to U.S., 1961, naturalized, 1982; s. Kashiram S. and Ganga K. C.; m. Malati Pundlik, May 30, 1955; children—Shobhana, Chandra. B.Sc., Poona U., India, 1953; B.E., Gujarat U., A'dabad, India, 1957; M.S.E.E., Toledo U., 1962; Ph.D., U. Fla., 1970. Assst. elec. engr. Owens-Ill., Toledo U., 1962-63; research asst. Syracuse U., N.Y., 1963-66; adv. engr. IBM Corp., East Fishkill, N.Y., 1966—; advisor to world trade IBM-Essones, Paris, 1980-81. Contbr. articles to profl. jours. Patentee in field. Mem. IEEE (sr.), Electrochem. Soc., N.Y. Acad. Scis., Sigma Xi, Phi Kappa Phi. Current work: CMOS, advanced biopolar technology and process development device diagnostic. Subspecialties: Semiconductors; Microelectronics. Home: 10 Plaza Rd Wappingers Falls NY 12590

CHAVIN, WALTER, biologist, educator; b. N.Y.C., Dec. 6, 1925; s. Isidor and Fanny (Kesch) C. B.S., CCNY, 1946; M.S., NYC, 1949; Ph.D., NYU, 1954. Instr. biology CCNY, 1946-47, U. Ariz., 1949-51; research specialist Am. Mus. Natural History, N.Y.C., 1951-53; asst. prof. Wayne State U., Detroit, 1953-60, assoc. prof., 1960-65, prof. dept. biol. scis., 1965—, prof. radiobiology Sch. Medicine, 1975-80; research assoc. Argonne Nat. Lab., 1955-58; NSF sr. postdoctoral fellow Sorbonne, Paris, 1960-61; cons. AEC, 1955-58, Dept. Interior, 1963-68. Author: Responses of Fish to Environmental Changes, 1973. Fellow AAAS, N.Y. Acad. Sci.; mem. Sigma Xi (research award 1968). Current Work: Control mechanisms in cells and changes producing abnormal growth or function, the impact of hormones upon cellular control mechanisms and the effects of environmentally induced hormone alterations on cellular control mechanisms. Subspecialties: Endocrinology; Cancer research (medicine). Home: 1368 Joliet Pl Detroit MI 48207 Office: Wayne State U 5104 Gullen Mall Detroit MI 48202

CHAWLA, TARA (TILAK), nuclear engineer; b. Punjab, India, July 1, 1938; s. Sunder Das and Luxmi Devi C.; m. Carolyn Clare Mackay, June 12, 1968. B.S., Banaras Hindu U., India, 1960; M.S., U. N.S.W., 1962; Ph.D., Pa. State U., 1969. Asst. nuclear engr. Argonne Nat. Lab., Ill., 1969-72, assoc. nuclear engr., 1972, nuclear engr., 1973—. Bd. editors Numerical Heat Transfer Jour., 1982—; editor: Ann. Rev.in Numerical Fluid Mechanics and Heat Transfer, 1985—; chmn., mem. adv. group dept. nuclear engring. Pa. State U., 1976-78. Contbr. articles to sci. jours. Mem. ASME, Am. Nuclear Soc., Sigma Xi. Current work: Development of numerical methods and research into fluid flow; heat transfer nuclear reactor safety and engineering. Subspecialties: Fluid mechanics; Nuclear engineering. Office: Argonne Nat Lab 9700 Cass Ave Argonne IL 60439

CHEAL, MARYLOU, psychobiologist; b. St. Clair County, Mich.; d. Marion Louis and Leda Eleanor Shaw (Martin) Fast; m. James Cheal, Mar. 13, 1946; children: Thomas James, Catheryn Leda, Robert David. B.A. with honors, Oakland U., Rochester, Mich., 1969; Ph.D. in Psychology, U. Mich., Ann Arbor, 1973. Research investigator dept. zoology U. Mich., 1973-75; dept. oral biology U. Mich. (Sch. Dentistry), 1975-76; postdoctoral fellow McLean Hosp., Belmont, Mass., 1976-77, asst. psychologist, 1977-81; assoc. psychologist Neuropsychology Lab., 1981-83; mem. research faculty dept. psychology Ariz. State U., Tempe, 1983—; lectr. psychology Harvard U. Med. Sch., also mem. summer sch. faculty. Contbr. articles and revs. to profl. jours.; invited referee sci. jours. Charles A. King fellow, 1976-77; Howard U. and Rockefeller Found. award, 1980; grantee McLean Hosp., 1976-78; grantee NIMH, 1977-78; grantee Scottish Rite Schizophrenia Research Program, 1977-79; grantee McLean Hosp., 1979-81. Mem. AAAS, Am. Psychol. Assn., Internat. Soc. Comparative Psychology, Southwestern Comparative Psychology Assn. (governing bd.), Women in Neurosci. (com.), Eastern Psychol. Assn., Soc. Neurosci., Assn. Chemoreception Sci., Sigma Xi. Current Work: Neural mechanisms of attention and habituation, aging development, psychopharmacology, gerbils, brain, olfactory, sex differences, reprodn., dopamine, acetylcholine scopolamine, apomorphine, catecholamines, odor preferences, norepinephrine, clonidine. Subspecialties: Psychobiology; Physiological psychology. Home: 127 E Loma Vista Tempe AZ 85282 Office: Dept Psychology Ariz State U Tempe AZ 85287

CHECHIK, BORIS E., immunologist, leukemia researcher; b. Kislovodsk, USSR, Mar. 31, 1931; emigrated to Can., 1973, naturalized, 1977; s. Eber L. and Eva (Grinberg) C.; m. Batia Jurbinski, Nov. 21, 1956; 1 dau., Miriam Sternberg. M.D., 2d Moscow Med. Sch., 1956; Ph.D., Acad. Med. Sci., P.A. Gertzen Oncol. Inst., Moscow, 1963. Gen. practice medicine, Moscow, 1956-59; scientist, then sr. scientist P.A. Gertzen Oncological Inst., 1959-71; scientist Hebrew U., Jerusalem, Israel, 1971-73; research assoc. Hosp. for Sick Children, Toronto, Ont., Can., 1974-76; research investigator Mt. Sinai Hosp., Toronto, 1977-80, sr. scientist, 1981—; assoc. prof. immunology U. Toronto, 1981—. Contbr. articles to profl. jours. Nat. Cancer Inst. Can. grantee, 1977—; Leukemia Research Fund grantee, 1977—. Mem. Internat. Assn. Comparative Research on Leukemia and Related Diseases, Am. Assn. Cancer Research, Can. Soc. Immunology. Discovered 1st human thymus-leukemia-assoc. antigen, 1967-68, established enzymatic nature, 1980, developed detection methods, 1979-81. Current Work: Cancer research, hematology, immunochemistry, immunomorphology, leukemia-associated antigens, differentiation of lymphoid cells. Subspecialties: Cancer research (medicine); Immunology (medicine). Office: Research Inst Mt Sinai Hosp 600 University Ave Toronto ON M5G 1X5 Canada

CHEDID, ANTONIO, pathologist, educator, researcher; b. Barranquilla, Colombia, May 5, 1939; came to U.S., 1966; s. Aziz Antonio and Maria (Turbay) C.; m. Hoda Abi-Rached, Sept. 14, 1974; children: Anthony John, Marie-Claude, Erica Houda. B.S., Coll. of Barranquilla, 1954; M.D., U. Madrid, 1962. Diplomate: Am. Bd. Pathology. Intern Columbus Hosp., Chgo., 1967-68; resident in pathology Michael Reese Hosp., Chgo., 1968-72; instr. pathology Pritzker Sch. Medicine, U. Chgo., 1972-73; asst. prof. pathology U. Cin. Coll. Medicine, 1973-76; assoc. prof. pathology Chgo. Med. Sch., North Chicago, Ill., 1976-85, prof., 1985—; pathol. cons. coop. study of alcoholic hepatitis VA, 1979—, primary reviewer liver cancer Eastern coop. oncology group. Am. Cancer Soc. grantee, 1974; NIH grantee, 1985—. Mem. Am. Assn. Pathologists, Fedn. Am. Socs. Exptl. Biology, Internat. Acad. Pathology, Am. Assn. for Study of Liver Diseases. Current Work: Cell enzyme markers during differentiation and experimental carcinogenesis as well as chronobiology; cardiomyopathy and congestive heart failure. Subspecialties: Pathology (medicine); Hepatology.

CHEESEMAN, RAY, consultant; b. Saint John's Nfld., Can., Mar. 27, 1947; came to U.S., 1949; s. Joseph Samuel and Lillian Mary (Singleton) C.; m. Valerie Christine McGowan, July 31, 1971. B.A. in Geology, CUNY, 1970; diploma in Prospecting U. Alaska, Fairbanks, 1968; M.S. in Geology, No. Ariz. U., 1975. Field geologist Gen. Mining & Fin. & Union Corp., Africa, 1970-71; geologist U.S. Geol. Survey, Roswell, N.Mex., 1975-77, Denver, 1977-78, Reston, Va. and Washington, 1978-80; geologist, chief geologist, exploration mgr. Peabody Coal and Peabody Devel. Co., various locations, 1980-84; pres. Cheeseman Exploration Co. Inc., Albuquerque, 1983—; cons. in field. Author articles and maps. Served with U.S. Army, 1967-69. Recipient Appreciation award U.S. Govt.-Asst. Sec. Interior, 1978. Mem. Denver Regional Exploration Geologists, Geol. Soc. Am. Current work: Exploration for new energy mineral deposits-coal, oil, oil shale, gas; occasionally explore for precious metals and base metals. Subspecialties: Geology; Coal. Home: 2608 Virginia St NE Albuquerque NM 87110 Office: Cheeseman Exploration Co Inc 3003 Adams NE Suite J-11 Albuquerque NM 87110

CHEN, CHIH PING, engineer; b. Kwangtung, China, June 12, 1938; s. Thai and Kieu (Mach) Tran; m. Virginia Wu-jen Wu, June 15, 1968; 1 dau., Christine. B.S., Cheng-Kung U., Taiwan, 1961; M.S., Pa. State U., 1965; Ph.D., Carnegie-Mellon U., Pitts., 1970. Registered profl. engr., Pa., N.J. Project engr. Carnegie Inst. Tech., Pitts., 1965-70; lead engr. Gibbs & Hill, Inc., N.Y.C., 1970-73; sr. staff engr. Pub. Service Electric & Gas Co., Newark, N.J., 1973-77; staff nuclear engr. Power Authority of State N.Y., N.Y.C., 1977-79; project mgr. Battelle Meml. Inst., Columbus, Ohio, 1979—; dir. Pinsan Enterprises, Inc., Columbus; cons. Inst. Nuclear Energy Research, Taiwan, 1978. Contbr. articles to profl. jours. Treas. Columbus Chinese Sch., 1980-81. NSF grantee, 1965; NDEA fellow, 1970. Mem. Am. Nuclear Soc. (mem. standards com.), ASME, N.Y. Acad. Sci., Nat. Soc. Profl. Engrs., Project Mgmt. Inst., Internat. Platform Assn., AAAS, Sigma Xi. Current Work: Managed projects to develop and license a deep geologic repository for disposal of high-level nuclear wastes. Experience in nuclear power which includes engineering and design, operations supports, licensing, safety and engineering analyses. Research in magnetohydrodynamics. Subspecialties: Mechanical engineering; Nuclear engineering. Home: 254 Chinkapin Way Westerville OH 43081 Office: Battelle Meml Inst 505 King Ave Columbus OH 43201

CHEN, CHIN, earth science educator, oceanography researcher; b. Foochow, Fukien, China, Apr. 15, 1927; came to U.S., 1955, naturalized, 1969; s. Y.C. and N.M. (Lin) C.; m. Concordia Chao, July 2, 1960; children: Marie H.M., Albert C. B.S., Nat. Taiwan U., China, 1952; M.S., Wayne State U., 1957; Ph.D., Boston U., 1962. Jr. geologist Taiwan (China) Geol. Survey, 1952-55; adj. staff Boston Coll., 1961-62; research assoc. Lamont-Doherty Geol. Observatory, Columbia U., 1962-69; prof. earch sci. Western Conn. State U., 1969—; cons. Dobex Internat. Ltd., W. Nyack, N.Y., summer, 1981; Lamont-Doherty Geol. Observatory, summer 1980. Co-author: Economic Geology and Mineral Resource of China, 1986. Recipient Sohio Scholarship award, 1958. Fellow Geol. Soc. Am.; mem. Paleontol. Research Inst. Roman Cath. Current Work: Pteropod-globigerina ooze of deep sea sediments and stratigraphy; sea level change in South China Sea; petroleum geology and energy resources in People's Republic of China. Subspecialties: Paleontology, paleoecology; Deep-sea biology. Home: Mountain Pass Box 34 RD 6 Hopewell Junction NY 12533 Office: Western Conn State U 181 White St Danbury CT 06810

CHEN, CHING JEN, engineering educator, administrator, research scientist, consultant; b. Taipei, Taiwan, July 6, 1936; s. I. Sung and T. (Yen) C.; m. Ruei Man, Aug. 14, 1965; children: Sandra, Anthony. Diploma, Taipei Inst. Tech., 1957; M.S. in Mech. Engring., Kans. State U., 1962; Ph.D., Case Western Res. U., 1967. Design engr. Ta-Tung Grinding Co., Taipei, Taiwan, 1959-60; asst. prof. U. Iowa, Iowa City, 1967-70, assoc. prof., 1970-77, prof., 1977-82, chmn., prof. energy div., 1982—, chmn. dept. mech. engring., 1982—; sr. research scientist Iowa Inst. Hydraulic Research, 1970—; sci. advisor U.S. Army Weapons Command, Rock Island, Ill., 1973; cons. Westinghouse Research Lab., Pitts., 1973-79, Jet Propulsion Lab., Pasadena, Calif., 1973, Argonne (Ill.) Nat. Lab., 1979—. Author: Vertical Turbulent Buoyant Jets, 1979; contbr. monograph to profl. publ. Old Gold fellow U. Iowa, Iowa Found., 1968; recipient sr. U.S. scientist award Alexander von Humboldt Fund., W.Ger., 1974. Mem. ASME, AIAA, Am. Phys. Soc., ASCE, Sigma Xi. Current Work: Heat transfer, computational fluid mechanics, turbulent flows, numerical analysis. Subspecialties: Fluid mechanics; Heat transfer processes. Home: 7 Heather Dr Iowa City IA 52240 Office: Univ Iow EB 2216 Iowa City IA 52242

CHEN, CHING-NIEN, government health institution chemist; b. Checkiang, China, Jan. 22, 1945; came to U.S., 1973, naturalized, 1980; s. Ko-Fei and Ju-Chuen (Ma) C. B.S., Nat. Taiwan U., 1967; M.S., Nat. Tsing-Hua U., 1969; Ph.D., SUNY-Stony Brook, 1980. Instr. Fu-jen U., Taipei, Taiwan, 1968-70, Nat. Tsing-Hua U., Hsin-chu, Taiwan, 1969-73; vis. fellow NIH, Bethesda, Md., 1980-81, expert chemist, 1981—. Mem. Soc. Magnetic Resonance in Medicine, Sigma Xi (assoc.). Current Work: Nuclear magnetic resonance imaging (zeugmatography) to obtain 3D NMR signal distribution in objects - one application is to image the internal structure of human body as in CT, but with added dimension of physiologically related chemical information. Subspecialties: Nuclear magnetic resonance; Biomedical engineering. Office: NIH Bldg 13 3W-13 Bethesda MD 20205

CHEN, DANIEL RAY, electronic company executive, physicist; b. Peking, China, Jan. 31, 1938; came to U.S., 1948, naturalized 1959; s. S. Y. and Ruth (P.) C.; m. Chi Li, Nov. 30, 1974; children—Irene Alexander. B.A. in Physics, U. Oregon, 1960; Ph.D. in Physics, U. Calif.-Berkeley, 1969. Sr. scientist research and devel. lab. Avantek, Inc., Santa Clara, Calif., 1973-76; mgr. Rockwell Internat., Thousand Oaks, Calif., 1976-81; pres. DRC Assoc., Thousand Oaks, 1981-82; pres. Microwave Monolithics, Inc., Simi Valley, Calif., 1982—; dir. editorial rev. Microwave Systems News, Palo Alto, Calif., 1983—. Contbr. articles to profl. jours. Mem. IEEE, Electron Devices Soc., Am. Phys. Soc., MTT Soc. Republican. Congregationalist. Current work: Microwave devices and integrated circuits. Subspecialties: Condensed matter physics; Semiconductors. Office: Microwave Monolithics Inc 465 E Easy St Simi Valley CA 93065

CHEN, ENG MING, environmental chemist; b. Keeliing, Republic of China, Feb. 3, 1938; came to U.S., 1963, naturalized, 1977; s. Sue-yuan and Pin(Lin) C.; m. Shirley S. M. Cheng, Jan. 4, 1969; children—Waynea, Weldon. B.S., Nat. Taiwan U., Taipei, 1960, M.S., 1963; M.S., U. Calif.-Davis, 1967; Ph.D., U. Nev., 1972. Researcher Desert Research Inst., U. Nev., Reno, 1967-76; water pollution chemist Nev. State Health Lab., Reno, 1978—. Contbr. articles to profl. jours. Mem. Am. Chem. Soc. Subspecialties: Photochemistry; Environmental chemistry. Home: 7485 Hillview Dr Reno NV 89503 Office: Nev State Health Lab 1660 N Virginia St Reno NV 89503

CHEN, ER-PING, research engineer; b. Ping-Liang, Kansu, China, May 19, 1944; came to U.S., 1967, naturalized, 1977; s. Shen-Huang and Tze-Yu (Chou) C.; m. Regina Chi Chen, Mar. 31, 1973; children: Candice, Benjamin. B.S., Nat. Chung-Hsing U., Taichung, Taiwan, 1966; M.S., Lehigh U., 1969, Ph.D., 1972. Asst. prof. Lehigh U., Bethlehem, Pa., 1972-77, assoc. prof., 1977-78; mem. tech. staff Sandia Nat. Labs., Albuquerque, 1978—. Author: Cracks in Composites, 1981; contbr. articles in field to profl. jours. Mem. ASME, Soc. Exptl. Stress Analysis, Soc. Engring. Sci., Chinese Inst. Engrs., Sigma Xi. Current Work: Fracture of composites analysis, nuclear power plant safety analysis, fracture and fragmentation in rock. Subspecialties: Fracture mechanics; Solid mechanics. Home: 1128 Bernalillo St SE Albuquerque NM 87123 Office: Div 1523 Sandia Nat Labs Albuquerque NM 87185

CHEN, GLORIA CHAO, chemist; b. Foochow, China, Sept. 3, 1935; came to U.S., 1961, naturalized, 1971; d. Tsan-Tang and Siu-ping (Li) C. B.S. in Chem. Engring., Cheng-Kung U., Republic of China, 1957; M.A. in Chemistry, Temple U., 1965; Ph.D., Rutgers U., 1982. Cert. acupuncture edn. Asst. instr. Taipei Inst. Tech., Republic of China, 1959-61; chem. engr. Hoeganaes Sponge Iron Corp., Riverton, N.J., 1962-63; research assoc. Albert Einstein Coll. Medicine, Bronx, N.Y., 1965-67; chemist Hoffmann La Roche, Nutley, N.J., 1967-81, sr. chemist, 1981—; mem. com. North Jersey Chromatography Discussion Group, 1983-84. Editor: Basic Gas Chromatography in Chinese, 1970; High Performance Liquid Chromatographic Separation of Nucleic Acids in Chinese, 1973. Reviewer, Jour. Agr. and Food Chemistry, 1984—. Founder, mem. St. Joseph's Lakota Devel. Council, Chamberlain, S.D., 1984. Mem. Sigma Xi (Roche Research chpt. com. 1984—). Republican. Current work: Develop and validate new and existing chemical and microbiological methodology for assay of trace level drugs in different matrixes to provide data for NADA/FDA submission and to support in human food safety and in chronic toxicity studies. Subspecialties: Analytical chemistry; Environmental chemistry. Home: #5 Renaissance Dr Clifton NJ 07013 Office: Hoffmann La Roche 340 Kingsland St Nutley NJ 07110

CHEN, HOFFMAN HOR-FU, chemistry educator; b. Hualien, Taiwan, Aug. 5, 1941; came to U.S., 1969; s. Sing-Wong and Youg-Mei (Ray) C.; m. Ay-Ming Yuan, May 5, 1973; children—Jeffrey, Jennifer, Justin. B.S., Tamkang U., 1963; Ph.D., U. Tex., 1976. Research scientist U. Tex., Austin, 1976; research asso. Okla. State U., Stillwater, 1977-78; assoc. prof. chemistry Grambling State U., La., 1979—. Robert Welch Found. fellow, 1972-76; NIH fellow, 1980. Mem. Am. Chem. Soc., AAAS, Beta Kappa Chi. Presbyterian. Current Work: Researcher in homogeneous and heterogeneous catalysis especially as applied to new Friedel-crafts and Fischer-Tropsch chemistry. Subspecialties: Organic chemistry; Catalysis chemistry. Home: 707 Tarreyton Dr Ruston LA 71270 Office: Grambling State University Dept Chemistry Grambling LA 71245

CHEN, HOLLIS CHING, electrical engineer, educator, researcher; b. Chekiang, China, Nov. 17, 1935; came to U.S., 1960, naturalized, 1971; s. Yu-Chao and Shui-tan C.; m. Donna Liu, Sept. 3, 1961; children: Desiree, Hollis Tao. B.S., Nat. Taiwan U., 1957; M.S., Ohio U., 1961; Ph.D., Syracuse U., 1965. Asst. prof. Syracuse (N.Y.) U., 1965-67; asst. prof. elec. engring. Ohio U., Athens, 1967-69, assoc. prof., 1969-74, prof., 1975—, acting chmn., 1984—; mem. Commn. B., U.S. Nat. Com., Internat. Union Radio Sci. Contbr. numerous articles to profl. jours. Mem. AAAS, IEEE (sr., best paper and best corr. awards 1967), Soc. Indsl. and Applied Math., Math. Assn. Am., Optical Soc. Am., Am. Soc. for Engring. Edn., Sigma Xi, Eta Kappa Nu. Current Work: Electromagnetic wave propagation and excitation, mocrowave, antennas, applied mathematics. Subspecialties: Computer engineering; Plasma (energy science and technology). Home: 1 Ball Dr Athens OH 45701 Office: Elec and Computer Engring Dept Ohio U Athens OH 45701

CHEN, HOLLY HO, chemistry educator, research chemist; b. Taiwan, China, July 25, 1939; came to U.S., 1963, naturalized, 1974; d. Chiu and Tan (Tai) Cheng; m. Wen-Yuan Wilbur Chen, Jan 31, 1965; children—Wilbur H., Anita Emily. B.S. in Chem. Engring., Nat. Taiwan U., 1962; M.S. in Inorganic Chemistry, U. So. Calif., 1966; Ph.D., in Phys. Chemistry, U. Calif.-San Diego, 1969. Asst. prof. Christopher Newport Coll., Newport News, Va., 1970-73; research assoc., Princeton U., N.J., 1973-75; research chemist NIH, Bethesda, Md., 1975—; asst. prof. chemistry George Mason U., Fairfax, Va., 1980—. Mem. Am. Chem. Soc., Chinese-Am. Chem. Assn., N.Am. Taiwanese Profs. Assn. (treas. 1983-84). Current work: Teaching in physical chemistry and general chemistry; research in structure and dynamics of DNA by electric dichroism. Subspecialties: Physical chemistry; Biophysical chemistry. Home: 10525 Farnham Dr Bethesda MD 20814 Office: Dept Chemistry George Mason U 4400 University Dr Fairfax VA 22030

CHEN, HSIANG TSUN, physicist; b. Taiwan, Oct. 10, 1947; came to U.S., 1973; s. Chin Fa and Pan C.; m. Ching-Min Chen, Mar. 18, 1973; children: Hong Hsiang, Kaivin Hong, Anchie. Ph.D., U. Ga., 1980. Sr. scientist Machlett Labs., Inc., Stamford, Conn., 1979-82, Ortho Diagnostic Systems, Inc., Raritan, N.J., 1982-84; research physicist EMR photoelectric, Princeton, N.J., 1984—. Served to 2d lt. China Air Force, 1971-72. Mem. IEEE, Internat. Soc. Optical Engring. Current Work: Application of experience in physics, optics, electronics, computer engineering to design and build microprocessor based diagnostic equipment of high temperature, rugged photomultipliers. Subspecialties: Optical signal processing; Computer engineering. Home: 114 Devonshire Ct Somerville NJ 08876 Office: EMR Photoelectric PO Box 44 Princeton NJ 08542

CHEN, JESSE HSIANG, chemical engineer; b. Fuzhou, China, Oct. 10, 1943; came to U.S., 1966; s. T.K. and T.Y. (Hsu) C.; m. Wendy Chung-yu Liu, June 14, 1969; children—Christine, Jonathan, David, Grace. B.S. in Chem. Engring., Tunghai U. (China), 1965; M.S. in Chem. Engring., Mich. State U., 1968; Ph.D. in Chem. Engring., SUNY-Buffalo, 1973; postgrad. Northwestern U., 1981. Registered profl. engr., Pa. Research engr. Chgo. Bridge and Iron Co., Oak Brook, Ill., 1967-69; research asst. SUNY-Buffalo, 1969-73; group leader Cabot Corp., Kokomo, Ind., 1973-81, assoc. dir. tech., Boyertown, Pa., 1981-83, dir. tech., 1983—. Contbr. articles to profl. jours. Bd. dirs. Chinese Community Ch., Indpls., 1977-81; pres. Mainline Chinese Christian Ch. Bd., Berwyn, Ill., 1985—. Served to 2d lt. Chinese Army, 1965-66. Mem. Am. Inst. Chem. Engrs., Instrument Soc. Am. (dir. metal div. 1979-81), Am. Soc. Metals (chmn. electronic materials div. 1985—). Current work: Tantalum powder manufacture, electro ceramics, extractive metallurgy of rare metals, process modelling and control, technical management. Subspecialty: Materials (engineering). Office: Cabot Corp County Line Rd Boyertown PA 19512

CHEN, KIRK CHING SHYONG, biochemistry educator; b. Taichung, Taiwan, Nov. 30, 1941; came to U.S., 1968; s. Chi-Nan and Yen-Yang (Pang) C.; m. Cindy C.Y. Wang, Mar. 18, 1972; children: Lucy, Megan. B.S. in Agrl. Chemistry, Nat. Taiwan U., 1965, M.S. in Biochemistry, 1968; Ph.D. in Biochemistry, U. Okla., 1972. Postdoctoral fellow Rockefeller U., 1972-75, Lab. of Molecular Biology, Med. Research Council, Cambridge, Eng., 1975-76; asst. prof. pathobiology U. Wash., 1976-80, assoc. prof., 1980—. Served to 2d lt. Chinese Army, 1965-66. Helen Hay Whitney Found. postdoctoral fellow, 1973-76. Mem. Harvey Soc., Am. Soc. Biol. Chemists. Current Work: Structural and functional studies on surface antigens from pathogenic microorganisms, degradation of beta-lactam antibiotics by microorganisms. Subspecialties: Biochemistry (medicine); Microbiology (medicine). Home: 543 NE 79th St Seattle WA 98115 Office: Dept of Pathobiolog University of Washington Seattl WA 98195

CHEN, KON SWEE, chemist; b. Kuala Lumpur, Malaysia, Dec. 24, 1943; s. Soo and Kwee Yin (Lee) Ch.; m. Linda Susan Culver, July 31, 1971; children—Kim Foong, Karen Kim-Lian. B.A., Ill. Wesleyan U.; Ph.D., U. Kans., 1973. Research chemist Alrac Corp., Stamford, Conn., 1973-74, Stauffer Chem. Co., Dobbs Ferry, N.Y., 1974-77; tech. dir. Barson Corp., Stamford, 1977—. Contbr. articles to profl. jours. Patentee in field. Mem. adminstrv. bd. United Methodist Ch., Norwalk, Conn., 1974-77; founding mem., pres. Chinese Assn. Fairfield County, Westport, Conn., 1973—; chmn. bd. Chinese Lang. Sch., Stamford; bd. visitors Ill. Wesleyan U., Bloomington, Ill., 1978—. Recipient 10th Yr. Ann. award Chinese Assn. of Fairfield County, 1984. Mem. Am. Chem. Soc., Sigma Xi, Phi Lambda Upsilon. Current work: Developing a commercial process to manufacture polypyrrolidone (nylon 4) and to find specialty uses for this hydrophilic polymer. Eventual use as a textile fiber that bridges the synthetic with the natural fiber. Subspecialties: Organometallics; Polymer chemistry. Home: 76 Maple St Norwalk CT 06850

CHEN, KUAN, mechanical engineering educator; b. Tai Chung, Taiwan, Mar. 1, 1953; s. James T.R. and Jye-Fen (Han) C. B.S., Chung Yuan U., 1974; M.S., Nat. Taiwan U., 1976; Ph.D., U. Ill., 1981. Asst. prof. mech. engring. U. Utah, Salt Lake City, 1981—. Contbr. articles to profl. jours. Mem. ASME (assoc.); mem. Sigma Xi, Phi Kappa Phi. Current work: Heat/mass transfer in materials processing; thermal and hydrodynamical stability analysis; fiber-optics laser velocimetry. Subspecialties: Mechanical engineering; Fluid mechanics. Home: 1415 E 4045 S Salt Lake City UT 84117 Office: Dept Mech Engring Univ Utah Salt Lake City UT 84112

CHEN, KUN-MU, electrical engineering educator, electromagnetics researcher; b. Taipei, Republic of China, Feb. 3, 1933; came to U.S., 1957, naturalized, 1969; s. Tsa-mo and Che (Wu) C.; m. Shun-shun Yu, Feb. 22, 1962; children—Maggie, Kathy, Kenny, George. B.S., Nat. Taiwan U., 1955; M.S., Harvard U., 1958, Ph.D., 1960. Teaching asst. Nat. Taiwan U., 1956-57; research asst. Harvard U., Cambridge, Mass., 1958-60; research assoc. U. Mich., Ann Arbor, 1960-64; assoc. prof. elec. engr. Mich. State U., East Lansing, 1964-67, prof., 1967—, grad. program dir., 1968-72. Contbr. articles to profl. jours. Patentee in field. Faculty advisor Taiwanese Student Assn. Mich. State U., 1966—. Recipient Disting. Faculty award Mich. State U., 1976, Achievement award in sci. and engring. Taiwanese Am. Found., 1984. Fellow IEEE, AAAS; mem. Internat. Union Radio Sci., Taiwanese Assn. in Am. (pres. Lansing chpt., 1975-78), Sigma Xi, Phi Kappa Phi, Tau Beta Pi. Current work: Electromagnetic radiation, radar technology, bioelectromagnetics, plasma physics. Subspecialties: Electrical engineering; Electronics. Home: 4608 Tacoma Blvd Okemos MI 48864 Office: Dept Electrical Engring Mich State Univ East Lansing MI 48828

CHEN, MICHAEL MING, biomedical engineer, educator; b. Hankow, China, Mar. 10, 1933; came to U.S., 1953, naturalized, 1965; s. Kwang Tzu and Hwei Chuing (Deng) C.; m. Ruth Hsu, Oct. 15, 1961; children—Brigitte (dec.), Derek, Melinda. B.S., U. Ill., 1955; S.M., M.I.T., 1957, Ph.D., 1961. Sr. staff scientist research and devel. Avco Corp., Wilmington, Mass., 1960-63; asst. prof. engring. and applied sci. Yale U., 1963-69; asso. prof. mech. engring. NYU, 1969-73; prof. mech. engring. and bioengring. U. Ill., Urbana-Champaign, 1973—; cons. A.D. Little Co., NIH, Argonne Nat. Lab. Assoc. editor: Applied Mechanics Revs. Contbr. to profl. publs. Mem. ASME, Am. Phys. Soc., Sigma Xi, Phi Kappa Phi, Tau Beta Pi, Pi Tau Sigma. Subspecialties: Biomedical engineering; Mechanical engineering. Home: 311 Eliot Dr Urbana IL 61801 Office: 140 MEB Univ Ill 1206 W Green St Urbana IL 61801

CHEN, RICHARD YUAN ZIN, anesthesiologist, educator; b. Chia-Yi, Taiwan, Feb. 7, 1947; came to U.S., 1972, naturalized, 1977; s. L.C. and Elizabeth (Pi-Aru) C.; m. Chang Chiu, July 14, 1972; children: Jason T.S., Gregory T.M. M.D., Nat. Taiwan U.-Taipei, 1971. Diplomate: Am. Bd. Anesthesiology. Intern in surgery Maimonides Med. Center, Bklyn., 1972-73; resident in anesthesiology Albert Einstein Coll. Medicine, Bronx, N.Y., 1973-74, Columbia-Presbyterian Med. Center, N.Y.C., 1974-75; NIH research fellow Coll. of Physicians and Suregons, Columbia U., N.Y.C., 1975-76, asst. prof. anesthesiology, 1976-85; assoc. prof. anesthesiology UCLA, 1985—. Fellow Am. Coll. Anesthesiologists; mem. Am. Physiol. Soc., Am. Soc. Anesthesiologists, N.Y. Acad. Scis., Internat. Anesthesia Research Soc. Current Work: Circulatory physiology; blood volume, blood rheology; cerebral circulation; hypothermia; circulatory effects of anesthetics; anesthetic actions; neurohumoral control of circulation. Subspecialties: Anesthesiology; Psychophysiology. Office: Dept Anesthesiology UCLA Med Ctr Wadsworth VA Hosp Los Angeles CA 90073

CHEN, SHUENN-TZONG, chemist, researcher; b. Chun-Hua, Republic of China, May 27, 1948; came to U.S., 1972, naturalized, 1985; s. Chin-Tong and Chu-Shei (Lin) C.; m. Ray-Mei Su, Jan. 22, 1976; children—Jeffrey, Crystal. B.A. in Agrl. Chemistry, Nat. Taiwan U., 1971; Ph.D. in Chem., SUNY-Stony Brook, 1978. Sr. assoc. research scientist Miles Lab., Inc., Elkhart, Ind., 1978-79, research scientist, 1979-80, sr. research scientist, 1980-81, supr. research and devel., 1981-83; dir. research and devel. Orange Med. Instruments, Costa Mesa, Calif., 1983—. Patentee in field. Mem. Am. Chem. Soc., Am. Assn. Clin. Chemistry, Am. Diabetes Assn., Sigma Xi. Current work: Research and development of solid-phase reagent chemistry test devices, especially related to home blood glucose monitoring tests for diabetic and any other self testing devices for home health care. Subspecialties: Solid state chemistry; Clinical chemistry. Home: 2 Tory Irvine CA 92714 Office: 3183-F Airway Ave Costa Mesa CA 92626

CHEN, STEVE S., computer scientist. Vice pres. new product devel Cray Research, Inc., Mpls. Chief designer Cray X-MP computer. Subspecialty: Computer architecture. Office: Cray Research Inc 608 2d Ave S Minneapolis MN 55402

CHEN, TAO-SENG, physicist, educator; b. Hunan, China, July 25, 1938; s. Yeh-Chieu and Zu-chuan (Yang) C.; m. Yun-Jane Dai, Apr. 20, 1967; 1 son, David. B.S., Taiwan Cheng Kung U., 1962; M.S., Nat. Tsing Hua U., 1965; Ph.D., U. Tex., 1971; postdoctoral, Harvard U. Med. Sch., 1978-80. Research assoc. physicist U. Tex., Austin, 1972-76, instr., 1976-78; med. physicist Harvard U. Med. Sch., Boston, 1978-80; asst. prof. radiology W.Va. U., 1980-81; chief med. physicist, asst. prof. dept. radiation oncology Vanderbilt U., Nashville, 1981—. Contbr. articles to profl. jours. Recipient Robert Welch Found. award, 1971-73; NIH research grantee, 1978-80. Mem. Am. Phys. Soc., Am. Assn. Physicists in Medicine, Sigma Xi. Current Work: High energy photon and electron radiation oncology. Subspecialties: Radiology; Condensed matter physics. Home: 144 Cottonwood Dr Franklin TN 37064 Office: Dept Radiation Oncology Vanderbilt U Nashville TN 37232

CHEN, TEH-YI JAMES, electrical engineer, physicist; b. Taipei, Taiwan, Rep. of China, Nov. 13, 1949; came to U.S. 1976; s. Sen-Po and Yi-Mei (Chang) C.; m. Yue-Wen Chen, Jan. 13, 1982. B.S., Nat. Taiwan U., 1972; M.S. SUNY-Stony Brook, 1977; Ph.D., U. Pa., 1980. Mem. tech. staff Advanced Tech. Ctr., Signetics Corp., Sunnyvale, Calif., 1981-82; sr. mem. tech. staff Philips Research Labs., Sunnyvale, 1982—. Patentee in field. Mem. IEEE, The Electrochemical Soc. Current work: To develop one micron or submicron CMOS tech. and related device physics study; future silicon devices such as 3D devices or other alternatives to silicon devices. Subspecialties: Microchip technology (engineering); Microelectronics. Home: 4241 Atlantic Ct Santa Clara CA 95054 Office: Philips Research Labs Sunnyvale MS 2165 811 E Arques Ave Sunnyvale CA 94086

CHEN, TUNG-SHAN, food science educator; b. Chungking, China, Apr. 17, 1939; came to U.S., 1962, naturalized, 1976; s. Sze-Chen and Mary M. (Chen) Lin; m. Yolanda Chu Chen, Dec. 26, 1964; children: Andy, Lynn. B.S., Nat. Taiwan U., 1960; M.S., U. Calif., Berkeley, 1964, Ph.D., 1969. Research asst. U. Calif., Berkeley, 1962-69; asst. prof. food sci. and tech. Calif. State U., Northridge, 1969-73, assoc. prof., 1973-78, prof., 1978—; vis. assoc. prof. UCLA, 1974; food engring. specialist Chinese univ. devel. project Nat. Acad. Scis., 1985. Contbr. articles to profl. jours. Pres. San Fernando Valley Chinese Cultural Assn., 1974-75; bd; dirs. Greater Los Angeles Nutrition Council, 1978-81. Sr. research fellow Ctr. Cancer and Developmental Biology, Calif. State U., Northridge; Joseph Drown Found. research grantee, 1983. Mem. AAAS, Am. Chem. Soc., Am. Dietetic Assn. (Plan IV rep. 1980—), Am. Inst. Chemists (fellow), Inst. Food Technologists. Current Work: Improving and developing methodology for vitamin analysis and assessing stability of nutrients during food processing. Subspecialties: Food science and technology; Nutrition (biology). Office: Calif State Univ 18111 Nordhoff St Northridge CA 91330

CHEN, WAI-FAH, civil engrineer, researcher, consultant, educator; b. Chekiang, China, Dec. 23,1936; came to U.S., 1961, naturalized, 1972; s. Yu-Chao and Shui-Da (Hsia) C.; m. Lily Lin-Lin Hsuan, June 11, 1966; children: Eric, Arnold, Brian. B.S.C.E., Cheng-Kung U., Tainan, Taiwan, 1959; M.S.C.E., Lehigh U., 1963; Ph.D., Brown U., 1966. Profl. engr., Taiwan, 1959. Asst. prof. civil engring. Lehigh U., 1966-71, assoc. prof., 1971-75, prof., 1975-76; prof. structural engring. Sch. Civil Engring., Purdue U., West Lafayette, Ind., 1976-80, head structural engring., prof., 1980—, cons. to oil co. Author: books, the most recent being Plasticity in Reinforced Concrete, 1982, Constitutive Equations for Engineering Materials, vol. 1, 1982, vol. 2, 1985, Tubular Members in Offshore Structures, 1985, Soil Plasticity-Theory and Implementation, 1985. Co-recipient James F. Lincoln Arc Welding Found. award, 1972, 74, 81; U.S. Sr. Scientist award Alexander von Humboldt Found., 1985; T. R. Higgins lectr. award Am. Inst. Steel Constrn., 1985. Am. Iron and Steel Inst. grantee, 1966-76; NSF grantee, 1968—; Nat. Coop. Hwy. Research Program grantee, 1972-75; Can. Steel Industries Constrn. Council grantee, 1973-74; Am. Petroleum Inst. grantee, 1973-75; Dept. Energy grantee, 1974-76; Naval Constrn. Bn. Center grantee, 1977-79; Bechtel Group grantee, 1983-86; T.R. Higgins lectureship award, 1984-85; U.S. sr. scientist award Alexander von Humboldt Found., 1985. Mem. ASCE (Raymond C. Reese research prize 1985), Internat. Assn. Bridge and Structural Engrs., Am. Acad. Mechanics, Structural Stability Research Council, Earthquake Engring. Research Inst., Am. Concrete Inst., ASME. Current Work: Structural engineering and structural mechanics-inelastic behavior of structures and mathematical modeling of materials; plasticity and elasticity theories applying to metal, soil, concrete and rock mechanics; computer analysis of structures. Subspecialties: Civil engineering; Solid mechanics. Home: 1021 Vine St West Lafayette IN 47906 Office: Sch Civil Engring Purdue U West Lafayette IN 47907

CHEN, WAI-KAI, electrical engineering and computer science educator, consultant; b. Nanking, China, Dec. 23, 1936; came to U.S., 1959; s. You-Chao and Shui-Tan (Shen) C.; m. Shirley Shiao-Ling, Jan. 13, 1939; children: Jerome, Melissa. B.S., Ohio U., 1960, M.S., 1961; Ph.D, U. Ill.-Urbana, 1964. Asst. prof. Ohio U., 1964-67, assoc. prof., 1967-71, prof., 1971-78, disting. prof., 1978-81; prof., head dept. elec. engring. and computer sci. U. Ill.-Chgo., 1981—; vis. assoc. prof. Purdue U., 1970-71; vis. prof. U. Hawaii-Manoa, 1979. Author: Applied Graph Theory, 1970, Theory and Design of Broadband Matching Networks, 1976, Applied Graph Theory: Graphs and Electrical Networks, 1976, Active Network and Feedback Amplifier Theory, 1980, Linear Networks and Systems, 1983; editor: Brooks/Cole Series in Electrical Engineering, 1982-84; assoc. editor: Jour. Circuits, Systems and Signal Processing, 1981-86. Recipient Lester R. Ford award Math. Assn. Am., 1967; Disting. Accomplishment award Chinese Acad. and Profl. Assn. Mid-Am., 1985; Alexander von Humboldt award, 1985; Hon. Prof. award Nanking Inst. Tech., Peoples Republic of China, 1985; others; Research Inst. fellow Ohio U., 1972. Fellow IEEE, AAAS; mem. Soc. Indsl. and Applied Math., Assn. Computing Machinery, Tensor Soc. Gt. Britain, Sigma Xi, Phi Kappa Phi, Pi Mu Epsilon, Eta Kappa Nu. Current Work: Electrical circuits, filters, signal processing; applied graph theory, broadband matching, feedback amplifier design. Subspecialties: Electrical engineering; Integrated circuits. Office: Dept of Electrical Engineering and Computer Science University of Illinois PO Box 4348 Chicago IL 60680

CHEN, YI-HSIANG (ALAN), medical educator, researcher; b. Taipei, Taiwan, Feb. 20, 1939; s. Chi-Tsan and Yueh-Kwei (Chang) C.; m. Yu-Hsi (Judy) Chang, Oct. 21, 1967; children: Jennie, Josephine, Jacqueline. M.D., Nat. Taiwan U., 1964; Ph.D., U. Colo., 1970. Diplomate: Am. Bd. Internal Medicine, 1975, Hematology, 1976, Med. Oncology, 1981. Intern U. Miss. Med. Center, Jackson, 1970-71; resident U. Ill. Hosp., Chgo., 1971-72, fellow, 1972-74; asst. prof. U. Ill. Coll. Medicine, Chgo., 1974-80, assoc. prof., 1980—; vis. prof. Taipei Med. Coll., 1982. Contbr. articles to sci. and med. jours. Served to 2d lt. Chinese Army Med. Corps, 1964-65. Fellow ACP.; Mem. Am Soc. Hematology, Am. Assn. Immunologists, Central Soc. Clin. Research, Am. Soc. Clin. Oncology, Nat. Taiwan U. Med. Coll. Alumni Assn. N.Am. (treas. 1982), N.Am. Taiwanese Profs. Assn. Current Work: Immunological dysfunctions and tumor immunity in lymphoid neoplasia, and the proliferation and differentiation of cancer cells. Subspecialties: Immunology (medicine); Cell study oncology. Home: 528 Hunter Ct Wilmette IL 60091 Office: 840 S Wood Chicago IL 60612

CHEN, YU MIN, research biochemist; b. I-shing, Kiangsu, China, Dec. 23, 1922; came to U.S., 1954, naturalized, 1976; s. Mu Fan and Yueh Wah (Pan) C.; m. Jia-chun Nei, July 11, 1964; children: Peter P.T., Plato P.T. B.S. in Agrl. Chemistry, Nat. Chekiang U. China, 1946; M.S. in Biochemistry, Nat. Taiwan U., 1950; Ph.D. in Biochemistry and Nutrition, U. So. Calif., 1960. Assoc. prof. biochemistry Nat. Taiwan U., 1960-63; fellow Inst. Chemistry Academia Sinica, Taiwan, 1962-63; research scientist Wayne State U., 1963-68, Mich. Cancer Found., Detroit, 1968-73; prin. investigator Wayne State U., 1973-80; sr. research biochemist Providence Hosp., Southfield, Mich., 1981—. Contbr. articles in field to profl. jours. NIH grantee, 1971-74, 75-78. Mem. Am. Assn. Cancer Research, China Chem. Soc., Chinese Assn. Agrl. Chemistry, Sigma Xi. Current Work: Tyrosinase isozymes and inhibitors in vertebrate melanogenesis; serum tyrosinase in malignant disease, its immunological aspects and their applications for early detection in certain cancers; methodology in hormone receptor assay; endogenous activation and inhibition of hormone-receptor binding reaction. Subspecialties: Biochemistry (medicine); Immunology (medicine). Home: 30105 High Valley Rd Farmington Hills MI 48018

CHENETTE, DAVID LOUIS, physicist; b. Chgo., June 25, 1952; s. Louis Fred and Emily Louise (Scanlan) C.; m. Sara Jane Brewer, Sept. 8, 1973; children—Elizabeth, Emily, Susanna. A.B. with honors in Physics, U. Chgo., 1974, M.S., 1975, Ph.D. in Physics, 1979. Research assoc. U. Chgo., 1979-80; research fellow Calif. Inst. Tech., Pasadena, Calif., 1980-82, vis. fellow, 1982-83; mem. tech. staff Aerospace Corp., Los Angeles, 1982—. Contbr. articles to sci. jours. Recipient Marc Perry Galler award U. Chgo., 1980. Mem. AAAS, Am. Phys. Soc., Am. Geophys. Union, Sigma Xi. Current work: Physics of planetary magnetospheres; earth, Jupiter, Saturn; interplanetary charged particle transport; energetic solar flare ions; single-event upsets in microelectronics. Subspecialties: Cosmic ray high energy astrophysics; Satellite studies. Office: Aerospace Corp M2-259 PO Box 92957 Los Angeles CA 90009

CHENEY, BRIGHAM VERNON, physical chemist; b. Salt Lake City, June 11, 1936; s. Silas Lavelle and Klara (Young) C.; m. Marsali McAllister, Aug. 20, 1964; children—Jill, Mark Vernon, Heather, Karin, Brigham McAllister, John David. B.A., U. Utah, 1961, Ph.D., 1966. Research asst. U. Utah, Salt Lake City, 1964-66; research scientist Upjohn Co., Kalamazoo, 1966-71, scientist, 1971-75, sr. research scientist, 1975—. Contbr. articles to profl. jours. Mem. Am. Chem. Soc., AAAS, Internat. Soc. Quantum Biology, N.Y. Acad. Scis., Sigma Xi. Mem. Ch. of Jesus Christ of Latter-day Saints. Current work: Determination of relationships between molecular structure and biological activity in drugs, toxic agents and naturally occurring substances. Subspecialties: Physical chemistry; Drug design. Home: 3507 Runnymede Dr Kalamazoo MI 49007 Office: Upjohn Co Kalamazoo MI 49001

CHENG, ANDREW FRANCIS, physicist; b. Princeton, N.J., Oct. 15, 1951; s. Sin I. and Jean (Sing) C.; m. Linda Sun Hu, Nov. 24, 1979. A.B., Princeton U., 1971; Ph.D., Columbia U., 1977. Postdoctoral fellow Bell Labs., Murray Hill, N.J., 1976-78; asst. prof. physics Rutgers U., Piscataway, N.J., 1978-83; mem. sr. staff Applied Physics Lab., Johns Hopkins U., Laurel, Md., 1983—. Mem. Am. Phys. Soc., Am. Astron. Soc., Am. Geophys. Union, N.Y. Acad. Sci. Current Work: Theoretical studies on physics of magnetospheres. Subspecialty: Theoretical astrophysics. Office: Applied Physics Lab Johns Hopkins U. Laurel MD 20707

CHENG, CHIA-CHUNG, chemist, researcher, educator; b. Tientsin, China, May 5, 1925; s. Kuo-Liang and Chui-yuen (Chien) C.; m. Katherine Cheng, May 30, 1953; children: Amy Yuwei, Anna Yumin, Alice Yuray, Audrey Yuhui. B.S., Nat. U. Chekiang, China, 1948; M.A., U. Tex, Austin, 1951, Ph.D. in Organic Chemistry, 1954. Chemist, munitions plant, Chungking, China, 1944-45; research assoc. N.Mex. Highlands U., 1954-57; research assoc. dept. chemistry Princeton U., 1957-59; head medicinal chemistry sect., prin.adv. in chemistry Midwest Research Inst., Kansas City, Mo., 1959-78; dir. Mid-Am. Cancer Center, Kansas City, 1978-81; prof. pharmacology, toxicology and therapeutics U. Kans. Med. Center, Kansas City, 1978—, dir. drug devel. lab., 1978—. Contbr. articles to profl. jours. NIH grantee. Mem. Am. Chem. Soc., Am. Assn. Cancer Research, Internat. Soc. Heterocyclic Chemistry, Sigma Xi, Phi Lambda Upsilon. Club: Chinese Club of Greater Kansas City (1st pres.). Patentee in field. Current Work: Design and synthesis of anticancer and antimalarial agents. Subspecialties: Synthetic chemistry; Medicinal chemistry. Office: U Kans Med Center Kansas City KS 66103

CHENG, EDWARD TEH-CHANG, nuclear engineer, researcher; b. Ping Tung, Taiwan, Nov. 23, 1946; came to U.S., 1972; s. Sui Ping and Tsai Yin (Li) C.; m. Shu-Ching Lai, June 4, 1973; children: Eric, Wendy. B.S., Nat. Tsing Hua U., 1969, M.S., 1971; M.S., U. Wis., 1974, Ph.D., 1976. Research assoc. U. Wis., Madison, 1976-78; staff engr. GA Techs. Inc., San Diego, 1978—. Mem. Am. Nuclear Soc. (sec./treas. fusion energy div. 1980-82). Current Work: Fusion neutronics, fusion blanket engineering and technology, fusion-fission hybrid, nuclear data. Subspecialties: Nuclear engineering; Nuclear fusion. Home: 14090 Recuerdo Dr Del Mar CA 92014 Office: GA Techs Inc PO Box 85608 San Diego CA 92138

CHENG, H. S., mechanical engineering educator; b. Shanghai, Peoples Republic China, Nov. 15, 1929, came to U.S.; married; 4 children. B.S.M.E., U. Mich., 1952; M.S.M.E., Ill. Inst. Tech., 1957; Ph.D., U. Pa., 1961. Registered profl. engr. Jr. mech. engr. Internat. Harvester Co., 1952-53; project engr. Machine Engring. Co., 1953-56; instr. Ill. Inst. Tech., Chgo., 1956-57, U. Pa., 1957-61; asst. prof. Syracuse U., N.Y., 1961-62; research engr. Mech. Tech. Inc., 1962-68; assoc. prof. Northwestern U., Evanston, Ill., 1968-74, prof. mech. engring., 1974—; cons. numerous orgns. Contbr. numerous articles to profl. jours. Grantee NASA NSF, Alcoa, Mobil, Ford. Mem. ASME (chmn. research com. lubrication, fluid film and bearings com., adv. com. design tech. transfer conf., Best Paper award 1971), Am. Gear Mfg. Assn., Am. Soc. Lubrication Engrs., Gear Research Ins. (v.p.), Sigma Xi, Pi Tau Sigma, Tau Beta Pi. Home: 2746 Bernard Pl Evanston IL 60201 Office: Northwestern U Dept Chem Engring Evanston IL 60201

CHENG, H(WEI)-H (SIEN), soil science educator; b. Shanghai, China, Aug. 13, 1932; came to U.S., 1951, naturalized, 1961; s. Chi-Pao and Anna (Lan) C.; m. Jo Yuan, Dec. 15, 1962; children—Edwin, Antony. B.A., Berea Coll., 1956; M.S., U. Ill., 1958, Ph.D., 1961. Cert. profl. soil scientist. Research assoc. Iowa State U., Ames, 1962-64, asst. prof., 1964-65; asst. prof. dept. agronomy and soils Wash. State U., Pullman, 1965-71, assoc. prof., 1971-77, prof., 1977—; assoc. dean Wash. State U. (Grad. Sch.), 1982—; vis. scientist Julich Nuclear Research Ctr., W. Ger., 1972-73, 79-80, Academia Sinica, Taipei, Republic of China, 1978, Fed. Agrl. Research Center, Braunschweig, W.Ger., 1980. Fulbright scholar, 1962-63. Fellow Am. Soc. Agronomy, Soil Sci. Soc. Am.; Mem. AAAS, Am. Chem. Soc., Soc. Environ. Toxicology and Chemistry. Methodist. Current Work: Transformation of nitrogen, pesticides, and organic matter in the soil-water environment; impact of organics on enviromental quality; development of 15N and 14C tracer methodology for soils research; nitrogen availability and fertilization. Subspecialties: Soil science; Environmental toxicology. Home: NW 305 Joe St Pullman WA 99163 Office: Dept Agronomy and Soils Wash State U Pullman WA 99164

CHENG, KEVIN K. T., prosthodontist, artificial organs investigator. Pvt. practice, Tempe, Ariz. Subspecialties: Prosthodontics; Artificial organs and prostheses. Office: 6000 S McClintock Dr Tempe AZ 85283*

CHENG, KWOK-TSANG, physicist; b. Hong Kong, May 5, 1950; came to U.S., 1972; s. Sau-Mou and Kam-Mui (Chan) C.; m. Guang-Meei Doris, Aug. 30, 1975. B.Sc. (Hong Kong Govt. scholar), Chinese U. of Hong Kong, 1971; Ph.D., Notre Dame U., 1977. Postdoctoral employee Argonne (Ill.) Nat. Lab., 1977-80, asst. physicist, 1980-84; physicist Lawrence Livermore Nat. Lab., 1985—. Contbr. articles to physics jours. Mem. Am. Phys. Soc. Current Work: Theoretical atomic physics, atomic structure calculations, relativistic many-body theory. Subspecialties: Atomic and molecular physics; Theoretical physics. Home: 3262 Curtis Circle Pleasanton CA 94566 Office: Lawrence Livermore Nat Lab PO Box 808 Livermore CA 94550

CHENG, LANNA, biologist; b. Singapore, Apr. 27, 1941; came to U.S., 1969, naturalized, 1980; d. Ao-Lun and Fu-Huang Cheng; m. Ralph A. Lewin, June 3, 1969. B.Sc., U. Singapore, 1963, B.Sc. with honors, 1964, M.Sc., 1966; Ph.D. Oxford U. (Eng.), 1969. Postdoctoral fellow U. Waterloo (Ont., Can.), 1969-70; research assoc. Scripps Inst. Ocenaogrophy, U. Calif.-San Diego, La Jolla, 1971-72, asst. research biologist, 1972-77, assoc. research biologist, 1977—. Author: (cook book) Chinese Cookery Made Easy, 1975. Editor: Marine Insects, 1976. Contbr. articles to sci. publs. Fellow Royal Entomol. Soc., AAUW; mem. Oxford U. Malaysia-Singapore Assn. (pres. 1967-68), Western Soc. Naturalists (pres. 1985—). Current work: Ecology of the ocean-dwelling insect Halobates and other marine insects, production of polysaccharides by algae for soil improvements. Subspecialty: Marine biology. Home: 8481 Paseo del Ocaso La Jolla CA 92037 Office: U Calif A-002 La Jolla CA 92093

CHENG, MEI-FANG HSIEH, psychobiology educator; b. Keelung, Taiwan, Nov. 24, 1938; d. Chao-Chin and Ai Chu Hsieh; m. Wen-Kwei Cheng, 1963; children: Suzanne, Po-Yuan, Julie. B.S., Nat. Taiwan U., 1958; M.A., U. Oreg., 1961; Ph.D., Bryn Mawr Coll., 1965. Postdoctoral and research assoc. U. Pa., 1965-68; asst. research prof. Inst. Animal Behavior, Rutgers U., Newark, 1969-72, assoc. prof., 1973-78, prof., 1979—; mem. edn. and research rev. com. NIMH; mem. ad hoc rev. com. NSF. Contbr. chpts. to books, articles to profl. jours. Fulbright scholar, 1959-63; NIMH research scientist devel. awardee, 1974-79, 79-84. Mem. Soc. Animal Behavior, Soc. Neuroscience, N.Y. Acad. Scis., Internat. Soc. Psychoneuroendocrinology, AAAS. Current Work: Hormonal and neural mechanisms of reproductive behavior. Subspecialties: Neuroendocrinology; Neurobiology. Office: Inst Animal Behavior Rutgers U 101 Warren St Newark NJ 07102

CHENG, PETER YU-HUNG, design engineer; b. Hong Kong, Feb. 4, 1952, came to U.S., 1970, naturalized, 1984; s. Yuk Kwan and Sussy Shui-wan (Kao) C.; m. Pearl Po-Yee Li, Mar. 21, 1981. B.S. in Elec. Engring., Wash. State U., 1974; M.S. in Elec. Engring., U. Pa., 1976; postgrad. in engring. mgmt. Stanford U., 1982—. Design engr. Tex. Instruments, Houston, 1977-78; design engr. Intel, Santa Clara, Calif., 1978-79, sr. design engr. 1980-81; sr. design engr. Intersil, Cupertino, Calif., 1979-80; devel. engr. Hewlett-Packard Co., Cupertino, 1981-82, project mgr., 1982—, conf. chmn. Hewlett-Packard Design Tech. Conf., 1983—. Contbr. to profl. publs. U. Pa. fellow, 1974-76. Mem. IEEE, Am. Assn. for Artificial Intelligence, Tau Beta Pi, Phi Kappa Phi. Republican. Club: Stanford Alumni. Current work: Very large scale integrated circuits, standard and application specific, full custom and semicustom design methodologies research and development. Subspecialties: Integrated circuits; Computer engineering. Office: Hewlett-Packard 10900 Wolfe Rd Cupertino CA 95014

CHENGAPPA, MUCKATIRA MADAIAH, microbiologist, researcher; b. Virajpet, India, June 5, 1947; s. Muckatira Devaiah Madaiah and Muckatira Madaiah (Ponnaki) Ponnava; m. Muthu Muckatira Muthurani, Aug. 18, 1978; children—Tina, Tanya. D.V.M., Mysore Vet. Coll., Bangalore, India, 1970; M.Vet. Sci., 1973; M.S. Mich. State U., 1977, Ph.D., 1981. Diplomate Am. Coll. Vet. Microbiologists. Microbiologist Bangalore Agrl. U., India, 1972-73; lectr. Mysore U., 1973-74; research asst. Mich. State U., East Lansing, 1975-76, 79-81, research assoc., 1977-79; head microbiology dept. Murray State U., Hopkinsville, Ky., 1981-83, head microbiology and serology dept., 1985—; asst. prof. Kans. State U., Manhattan, 1983-85; cons. Custom Biologics, Hopkinsville, 1983—. Author numerous research papers and abstracts. Mem. Am. Vet. Microbiology Assn., Am. Assn. Vet. Lab. Diagnosticians, AVMA. Hindu. Current work: Pathogenic mechanism of Pasteurella species pathogenic bacteriology in general; serology and immunology of Pasteurella species diagnostic microbiology; teaching. Subspecialties: Microbiology; Immunobiology and immunology. Home: 939 Hurst Dr Hopkinsville KY 42240 Office: Breathitt Veterinary Ctr Murray State U Hopkinsville KY 42240

CHENNAULT, MADELYN JOANNE, psychology educator, reseacher; b. Atlanta, July 15, 1934; d. Benjamin Quillion and and Othello (Jones) C.; married; children: Eugene Chaires Majaied, Bennel Mosby, Lyssa Sampson. B.S., Morris Brown Coll., Atlanta, 1957; M.A., U. Mich., 1961; Ed. S, Ind. U.-Bloomington, 1965, Ed.D., 1966; postgrad., U. Ga., 1970-72. Tchr. 3d grade R.L. Craddock Sch., Atlanta, 1957-59, Caldwell Sch., Fontana, Calif., 1959-60; asst. prof. psychology Albany (Ga.) State Coll., 1962-64, Atlanta U., 1966-67; prof. edn. and psychology Ft. Valley State Coll., Ga., 1967—; B.E. Mayes prof. psychology Morehouse Coll., Atlanta, 1979—, chairperson dept. psychology, 1979—; cons., mgr. O & M Properties, Atlanta, 1974-85. Mem. Am. Psychol. Assn., Southeastern Psychol. Assn., Am. Pub. Health Assn., Council Exceptional Children, Am. Acad. Behavioral Medicine, Alpha Kappa Alpha. Club: Link's Inc. Current Work: Principal investigator Middle Georgia Community Hypertension Intervention Program. Subspecialties: Psychobiology; Social psychology. Home: 1930 Honeysuckle Ln SW Apt 32 Atlanta GA 30311 Office: Fort Valley State College State College Dr Fort Valley GA 31030

CHENOWETH, PHILIP ANDREW, consulting geologist; b. Chgo., Aug. 21, 1919; s. Joseph Gayne and Helen (Burton) C.; m. Marilyn Myers, Apr. 11, 1952; children: Kathryn, Amelia. B.A., Columbia Coll., 1946; M.A., Columbia U., 1947, Ph.D., 1949. Cert. Am. Inst. Profl. Geologists. Instr. Amherst (Mass.) Coll., 1949-51; asst. dist. geologist Sinclair Oil and Gas Co., Ardmore, Okla., 1951-54; assoc. prof. U. Okla., Norman, 1954-60; research assoc. Sinclair Research Labs., Tulsa, 1960-68, cons., 1968—. Contbr. articles to profl. jours. Chmn. Higher Edn. Subcom., Goals for Tulsa. Served with U.S. Army, 1941-45. Recipient Best Tchr. award U. Okla., 1956. Fellow Geol. Soc. Am.; mem. Am. Assn. Petroleum Geologists, Oklahoma City Geol. Soc., Rocky Mountain Assn. Geologists; hon. mem. Tulsa Geol. Soc. Inventor oil spill removal method. Subspecialty: Geology. Home: 5828 62d Pl Tulsa OK 74136 Office: 1000 Petroleum Club Bldg Tulsa OK 74119

CHEO, PEN CHING, plant virologist; b. Ho-fei, Anhwei, China, Mar. 28, 1919; came to U.S., 1947, naturalized, 1965; s. Hsiu Cheng and Yee (Dah) C.; m. Helen Chen, Aug. 16, 1949. Ph.D., U. Wis., 1951. Research assoc. U. R.I., Kingston, 1952-53; research fellow Calif. Inst. Tech., Pasadena, 1957-61; asst. prof. U. Wash., Wenatchee, 1961-66; plant pathologist Los Angeles State and County Arboretum, Arcadia, 1966-67, chief research div., 1967-83. Contbr. articles to profl. jours. Mem. Am. Phytopathology Soc., Sigma Xi. Current Work: Physiology of viral resistance in plant, virus degradation in soil. Subspecialties: Plant virology; Plant pathology. Home: 144 S Catalina Apt 9 Pasadena CA 91106 Office: 301 N Baldwin St Arcadia CA 91006

CHEREMISINOFF, PAUL NICHOLAS, environmental engineering educator, researcher, consultant; b. N.Y.C., Feb. 20, 1929; s. Nicholas P. and Luba N. (Meonikov) C.; m. Louise M. Nappi, Aug. 25, 1951; children—Nicholas, Peter. B. Chem. Engring., Pratt Inst., 1949; M.S., Stevens Inst. Tech., 1952. Registered profl. engr., N.J. Tech. dir. Joseph Turner Co., Ridgefield, N.J., 1949-56; plant mgr. Am. Polyglas-Alsynite, Carlstadt, N.J., 1956-60; sr. chem. engr. Celanese Corp., Newark, 1960-63, Tenneco Corp., Garfield, N.J., 1963-67; mgr. environ. services Engelhard Industries Inc., Newark, 1967-73; prof. environ. engring. N.J. Inst. Tech., Newark, 1973—; cons. engr. maj. cos., utilities, govt. agys. Author numerous books on engring., environ. scis. Editor: Pollution Engineering Technology Series (30 vols.). Editor Pollution Engring. Mag., Engring. Edn. Water and Sewage Works. Contbr. numerous articles to tech. jours. Fellow N.Y. Acad. Scis. (chmn. engring. 1973-76); mem. Am. Chem. Soc., Sigma Xi (sr.). Current work: Physical treatment for hazardous and toxis substances. Subspecialties: Hazardous waste disposal; Chemical engineering. Home: 230 Terrace Ave Hasbrouck Heights NJ 07604 Office: New Jersey Inst Tech 323 High St Newark NJ 07102

CHERKASKY, MARTIN, physician; b. Phila., Oct. 6, 1911; s. Samuel and Sarah (Kosharsky) C.; m. Sarah Griffin, Feb. 3, 1941; children—Marny, Michael. M.D., Temple U., 1936. Pvt. med. practice, Phila., 1939-40; exec. home care dept. Montefiore Hosp., 1947; dir. Med. Group, 1948-51, chief div. social medicine, 1950; dir. Montefiore Hosp. and Med. Center, 1951-75, pres., 1975-81, cons. to hosp. and to bd. trustees, 1981—; Atran prof. dept. community health Albert Einstein Coll. Medicine, 1967-77; cons. N.Y. State Joint Hosp. Rev. and Planning Council; cons. to commr. hosps. N.Y.C. Dept. Hosps., 1961-62; exec. com. Health Research Council of N.Y.C., 1968-74; regional health adv. bd. Region II, Dept. Health, Edn. and Welfare, 1970-72; chmn. profl. adv. com. Joint Distbn. Com., N.Y.C., 1969-78; com. of 100 for Nat. Health Ins., 1969—; dir. Asso. Hosp. Service, 1969—; mem. Commn. Yr. 2000, City of N.Y., 1984—; mem. bd. profl. med. conduct N.Y. State Dept. Health, 1983—; mem. med. adv. bd. Hadassah, 1981—; spl. advisor to mayor for health affairs, N.Y.C., 1978-79. mem. Gov.'s Steering Com. Social Problems, 1970-72. Editorial bd. jour.: Chronic Diseases, 1956-57, Commonwealth and Internat. Library Sic. Tech. and Engring; Contbr. articles to various publs.; Lectr. Served as lt. col. M.C. AUS, 1940-46. Fellow N.Y. Acad. Medicine; mem. Am. Pub. Health Assn., Am. Hosp. Assn., Greater N.Y. Hosp. Assn. (past pres.), Nat. Acad. Scis. (sr. mem. inst. medicine 1971—, mem. council of inst. 1972-74, program com. 1984—), Assn. Am. Med. Colls. Current work: Consultant in public health and professional organization to hospitals and other health care related bodies. Subspecialties: Internal medicine; Preventive medicine. Office: 111 E 210th St Bronx NY 10467

CHERMOL, BRIAN HAMILTON, psychologist; b. Bryn Mawr, Pa., June 24, 1944; s. John Thomas and Esther Louise (Hamilton) C.; m. Judy S. Williams, July 7, 1965 (div. 1972); 1 dau., Sherry L.; m. Jackie L. Burroughs, Feb. 7, 1975 (dec. 1975); m. Annie L. Mahone, Jan. 8, 1983; 1 dau., Laurie A. B.A., Park Coll., 1970; M.A., U. Mo., 1972; Ph.D., U. S.C., 1978. Lic. psychologist, Tex., Ala. Psychologist Ga. VA Hosp., Augusta, 1974; commd. 2d lt. U.S. Army, 1962, advanced through grades to lt. col., 1981—; staff psychologist Psychology Service, Walter Reed Army Med. Ctr., Washington, 1976-78; staff psychologist Community Mental Health, Ft. Rucker, Ala., 1978-80, chief psychiatry dept., 1980-81; chief behavioral sci. specialty br. Acad. Health Sci., Ft. Sam Houston, Tex., 1981-83; dep. chief Med. Tng. Team, El Salvador, 1984—; comdr. 142d Med. Bn., Panama, 1985—; cons. White House Staff, 1977-78, Washington Police Dept., 1976-78, U.S. Helicopter Team, 1981, Army Safety Ctr., 1981. Contbr. articles to profl. jours. Decorated Silver Star, Bronze Star medal; named Man of the Yr. Columbus C. of C., 1963. Mem. Am. Psychol. Assn., Assn. for Advancement Psychology, Am. Soc. Clin. Hypnosis. Republican. Current Work: Determine best methods for identifying and treating casualties generated by nuclear war; assess new teaching formats and procedures, aviation psychological research. Subspecialties: Behavioral psychology; Social psychology. Home: 76 Muir Fort Clayton Panama Office: Hdqrs 142d Med Bn (Panama) APO Miami FL 34004

CHERN, SHIING-SHEN, mathematician; b. Kashing, Chekiang, China, Oct. 26, 1911; s. Lien Ching and Mei (Han) C.; m. Shih-ning Chern, July 28, 1939; 1 child, Paul May. B.S., Nankai U., Tientsin, China, 1930; M.S., Tsing Hua U., 1934; D.Sc., U. Hamburg, Germany, 1936, 1972; LL.D. (hon.), Chinese U., Hong Kong, 1969; Sc.D. (hon.) U. Chgo., 1969; D.Math., Eidgenossische Technische Hochschule, Zurich, Switzerland, 1982. Prof. math. Nat. Tsing Hua U., China, 1937-43; mem Inst. Advanced Study, Princeton, N.J., 1943-45; acting dir. Inst. Math. Academia Sinica, China, 1946-48; prof. math U. Chgo., 1949-60; prof. U. Calif.-Berkeley, 1960-79, prof. emeritus, 1979—; dir. Math. Scis. Research Inst., 1981—. Hon. prof. various fgn. univs.; recipient Chauvenet prize Math. Assn. Am., 1970, Nat. Medal of Sci., 1975, Wolf prize in Math., 1984. Mem. Am. Math. Soc. (Steele prize 1983), Nat. Acad. Scis., Am. Acad. Arts and Scis., Indian Math., Royal Soc. London, Soc. (hon.), Brazilian Acad. Scis. (corr.), Academia Sinica. Subspecialty: Differential geometry. Office: U Calif Dept Math Berkeley CA 94720*

CHERNICK, MICHAEL ROSS, mathematical statistician; b. Havre de Grace, Md., Mar. 11, 1947; s. Jack and Norma Leonia (Weiner) C. B.S., SUNY-Stony Brook, 1969; M.A., U. Md., 1973; M.S., Stanford U., 1976, Ph.D., 1978. Mathematician U.S. Army, Aberdeen Proving Ground, Md., 1969-74; math. statistician Oak Ridge Nat. Lab., 1978-80, Aerospace Corp., Los Angeles, 1980—; adj. prof. Calif. State U.-Fullerton, 1982—; vis. lectr. U. Calif.-Santa Barbara, 1981. Referee: Annals of Probability, 1981, Zeitschrift Wahrscheinlichkeit Theorie, 1982; reviewer: Math. Reviews, 1982. Stanford U. fellow, 1974. Recipient Jacob Wolfowitz prize 1983. Mem. Am. Statis. Assn., Bernoulli Soc., Inst. Math. Statistics, Soc. Indsl. and Applied Math. Democrat. Jewish. Current Work: Develop statistical procedures for detecting outliers in multivariate and time series data. Statistical methods and probability models for satellite and other space systems. Subspecialties: Statistics; Probability. Home: 20920 Anza Ave Apt 208 Torrance CA 90503 Office: Aerospace Corp PO Box 92957 M4-955 Los Angeles CA 90009

CHERNICOFF, DAVID PAUL, hematologist, oncologist, educator; b. N.Y.C., Aug. 3, 1947; s. Harry and Lillian (Dobkin) C.; m. Jean Bogart, June 20, 1970; children; William, Jacki. A.B., U. Rochester, 1969; D.O., Phila. Coll. Osteopathic Medicine, 1973. Cert. internal medicine, hematology/oncology Nat. Bd. Osteopathic Examiners cert. Am. Osteopathic Bd. Internal Medicine. Intern Rocky Mountain Hosp., Denver, 1973-74; resident Community Gen. Osteopathic Hosp., Harrisburg, PA., 1974-76; fellow Cleve. Clinic, 1976-78; asst. prof. medicine Chgo. Coll. Osteopathic Medicine, 1978-82, assoc. prof., 1982—; staff physician hematology-oncology Chgo. Osteopathic Med. Ctr., 1978-82, dir. sect. hematology oncology, 1982—; staff Olympia Fields Osteopathic Med. Ctr., Ill., 1982—; sr. investigator Eastern Coop. Oncology Group, Chgo., 1980-83. Suburban South, Contbr., articles to profl. jours. Trustee Ill. Cancer Council, Chgo.; bd. dirs. Chgo. unit Am. Cancer Soc. Mem. Am. Soc. Clin. Oncology, Am. Osteopathic Assn., AMA. Current Work: Cancer treatment (chemotherapy) and clinical cancer research protocols. Subspecialties: Oncology; Cancer research (medicine). Office: Chicago Osteopathic Medical Center 5200 S Ellis Ave Chicago IL 60615

CHERNOFF, AMOZ IMMANUEL, hematologist, government health research institute administrator; b. Malden, Mass., Mar. 17, 1923; s. Isaiah and Celia (Margolin) C.; m. Renate R. Fisher, Jan. 25, 1953; children—David F., Susan N., Judith A. B.S. in Chemistry with honors, Yale U., 1944, M.D. cum laude, 1947. Diplomate: Am. Bd. Internal Medicine. Med. intern Mass. Gen. Hosp., Boston, 1947-48; asst. resident in medicine Barnes Hosp., St. Louis, 1948-49; fellow in hematology Michael Reese Hosp., Chgo., 1949-51, asst. dir. hematology research lab., 1950-51; A.C.P. fellow Washington U. Sch. Medicine, St. Louis, 1951-52, USPHS spl. research fellow, 1952-53, instr. in medicine, 1952-54, asst. prof., 1954-56; assoc. prof. medicine Duke U., 1956-58; chief sect. hematology VA Hosp., Durham, N.C., 1956-58; research prof. U. Tenn. Meml. Research Center, Knoxville, 1958-79, dir., 1964-77; assoc. vice chancellor for acad. affairs Center Health Scis., 1977-79; prof. medicine Coll. Medicine, Memphis, 1966-79; med. dir. Cystic Fibrosis Found., Atlanta, 1975-77; dir. div. blood diseases and resources Nat. Heart Lung and Blood Inst., NIH, Bethesda, Md., 1979—; cons. med. program devel. Contbr. articles to profl. jours. Served with U.S. Army, 1943-45. Recipient Campbell award Yale U. Sch. Medicine, 1947, Research Career award USPHS, 1962-77. Fellow A.C.P.; mem. Am. Soc. Clin. Investigation, Am. Soc. Hematology, Internat. Soc. Hematology, Central Soc. Clin. Research, So. Soc. Clin. Investigation, Soc. Exptl. Biology and Medicine, Am. Fedn. Clin. Research, Sigma Xi, Alpha Omega Alpha. Current Work: Director of NIH's extramural programs of support of hematologic research, particulary in red cell, hemoglobin area, in thrombosis and hemostasis, and in blood banking. Subspecialties: Internal medicine; Hematology. Home: 9417 Copenhaver Dr Potomac MD 20854 Office: NIH Fed Bldg Room 518 Bethesda MD 20205

CHERRY, JOE H., plant physiologist, biochemist; b. Newbern, Tenn., June 3, 1934; s. Howard F. and Rosa Lee (Parnell) C.; married, June 4, 1983; children—Michael, Richard, Kandy. B.S. U. Tenn.-Martin, 1957; M.S., U. Ill., 1959, Ph.D., 1961. Biochemist, USDA, New Orleans, 1961-62; mem. faculty Purdue U., West Lafayette, 1962—, assoc. prof. plant physiology, 1964-67, prof., 1967—; asst. dir. Purdue Research Found. div. Sponsored Research Purdue U., 1981-83; vis. lectr. U. Ill., summer 1965, 66; vis. prof. U. So. Calif., 1969, Oxford U., 1969; cons. Gen. Foods Corp., Atlantic Richfield, UN Ednl. Sci and Cultural Orgn. Edit. bd. Plant Physiology, 1967-69; contbr. articles to profl. jours. Fulbright scholar Aristotelian U., Thessaloniki, Greece, 1975; recipient Sigma Xi research award, 1979. Fellow AAAS; mem. Am. Soc. Plant Physiologists (pres. 1971, 84), Am. Soc. Biol. Chemists, Phi Tau Sigma. Office: Dept Horticulture Purdue U West Lafayette IN 47907

CHERRY, JOHN THOMAS, ceramic engineer, glass engineer; b. East Orange, N.J., Jan. 17, 1951; s. Sidney John and Doris Elizabeth (McGarry) C.; m. Cynthia Annette Ingham, Mar. 25, 1972. B.S., Alfred U., 1974. Engr., Thatcher Glass, Elmira, N.Y., 1974-76, supr., 1976-78; research engr. Ferro Corp., Cleve., 1978-80; head dept. ceramic and materials engring. Sterling China, Wellsville, Ohio, 1980—. Mem. Soc. Glass and Ceramic Decorators, Am. Ceramic Soc., Am. Ceramic Soc. (Whitewares div., Glass div.). Roman Catholic. Current work: Automated ceramic decorating; new shades and tints of ceramic color and improved ceramic body formulations. Subspecialties: Ceramic engineering; Ceramics. Home: 8060 Thomas Rd Lisbon OH 44432 Office: Sterling China Co 12th and Commerce St Wellsville OH 43968

CHERYAN, MUNIR, food engineer, biotechnologist, consultant; b. Cochin, Kerala, India, May 7, 1946; came to U.S., 1968; s. Parathuparambil C. and Aley (Mathulla) C.; m. Leela S. Sundararajan, Jan. 26, 1972; children: Sapna, Anura. B.Tech. with honors, Indian Inst. Tech, Kharagpur, West Bengal, 1968; M.S., U. Wis., 1970, Ph.D., 1974. Research asst. chem. engr. U. Wis., Madison, 1969-70, research asst. food sci., 1970-74, postdoctoral fellow food sci., 1974-75; research assoc. INTSOY, U.Ill.-Urbana, 1975-76, asst. prof. engring., 1976-80, assoc. prof., 1980-85, prof. food and biochem. engring., 1985—; Ill. Soybean Program Operating Bd. grantee, 1977-80; U.S. Dept. Agr. grantee, 1976—. Mem. Inst. Food Technologists, Am. Inst. Chem. Engrs., Am. Chem. Soc., Soc. Indsl. Microbiology, Am. Assn. Agrl. Engrs., Indian Inst. Chem. Engrs., Indian Dairy Assn., Assn. Food and Sci. Tech. Inventor protein hydrolyzats. Current Work: Membrane processing, enzyme technology, heat transfer and thermal process design, biochemical reactor engineering, functional properties and interactions of food constituents, enzyme technology, dairy technology, vegetable protein technology. Subspecialties: Food science and technology; Enzyme technology. Office: U Ill Dept Food Scis 382D Agrl Engring Scis Bldg 1302 W Pennsylvania Ave Urbana IL 61801

CHESIRE, REBECCA MARTHA, neuroscientist, researcher; b. Grand Island, Nebr., Nov. 25, 1949; d. Matthew Nelson and Simmy (Deitch) C. B.A., Incarnate Word Coll., 1972; M.A., St. Mary's U., San Antonio, 1974; Ph.D., U. Nebr., 1979. Postdoctoral fellow U. Ill., Champaign, 1979-80, research assoc., 1980-82; asst. prof. psychology U. Hawaii, Honolulu, 1982—. Contbr. articles to profl. jours. Fellow NSF, 1979, Am. Coll. Neuropsychopharmacology, 1982. Mem. Soc. Neurosci., Am. Psychol. Assn., AAAS, Internat. Brain Research Orgn., World Fedn. Neuroscientists, N.Y. Acad. Scis., Nat. Soc. Med. Research. Current work: Neuropharmacology of neurologically-induced movement disorders; recovery of function from brain damage, psychopharmacology of substances of abuse. Subspecialties: Neuropharmacology; Physiological psychology. Office: U Hawaii at Manoa 2430 Campus Rd Honolulu HI 96822

CHESKY, JEFFREY ALAN, biogerontologist, educator; b. Lynn, Mass., May 11, 1946; s. Harold Lester Chesky and Elizabeth (Joseph) Chesky Balter; m. Annette Sternberg, Aug. 19, 1970; 1 child, Barry. A.B., Cornell U., 1967; Ph.D., U. Miami, 1974. Asst. prof. biogerontology Sangamon State U., Springfield, Ill., 1977-83, assoc. prof., 1983—; adj. assoc. prof. Sch. Medicine, So. Ill. U., Springfield, 1978—. Editor: Theoretical Aspects of Aging, 1974. Vice pres. Ill. Sr. Olympics, Springfield, 1979-83. Served with U.S. Army, 1969-71. Research grantee Ill. Heart Assn., 1979-81, 83, NIH, 1983-85. Mem. Gerontol. Soc. Am., Am. Aging Assn., AAAS, Am. Physiol. Soc. (assoc.). Current work: Effects of exercise on modifying age changes in muscle. Subspecialties: Gerontology; Physiology (medicine). Home: 700 S Durkin Dr Apt 359 Springfield IL 62704 Office: Dept Gerontology Sangamon State U Springfield IL 62708

CHESLER, STEPHEN NORMAN, analytical chemist; b. Los Angeles, Apr. 16, 1944; s. Morris and Sarah (Ship) C.; m. Ruth Ann Chalupny, Jan. 10, 1970; children—Charles William, Katherine Courtney. B.S., UCLA, 1966; M.S., U. Ill., 1969, Ph.D., 1971. Postdoctoral, U. Fla., 1971-72; supervisory research chemist Nat. Bur. Standards, Gaithersburg, Md., 1972—. Editor: Trace Organic Analysis, 1978. Mem. Am. Chem. Soc., Sigma Xi. Subspecialty:

Analytical chemistry. Office: Nat Bur Standards A113 Chemistry Gaithersburg MD 20899

CHESNEY, CHARLES FREDERIC, industrial pathologist, toxicologist; b. Kew Gardens, L.I., N.Y., Oct. 16, 1942; s. Morris H. and Esther S. (Storch) C.; m. Patricia Ann Staffeld, June 12, 1965; children—Holly Beth, Jason Alan, Amy Marie. B.S. in Biology, Chemistry, U. Wis.-Madison, 1965; B.S. cum laude in Med. Scis., U. Minn., 1968; D.V.M., U. Minn.-St. Paul, 1970; Ph.D. in Med. Pathology, Toxicology, U. Wis.-Madison, 1973. Postdoctoral research fellow pathology U. Wis., Madison, 1970-73; research assoc., 1973-74; assoc. dir. drug safety Hoechst-Roussel Pharma.; Somerville, N.J., 1974-77; dept. head toxicology research Lederle Labs./Am. Cyanamid Co., Pearl River, N.Y., 1977-79; v.p., tech. dir. Xybion Med. Systems Corp., Cedar Knolls, N.J., 1979-83; cons. pathology, toxicology Path/Tox Assocs., Inc., Bridgewater, N.J., 1978-84, biomed. research cons., 1978-84; mgr. pathology, toxicology Riker Labs/3M Co., St. Paul, 1984—. Contbr. articles to profl. jours. Troop committeeman Watchung council Boy Scouts Am., 1981-84. Regents Achievement scholar U. Minn., 1967-69. Mem. Soc. Toxicology, Am. Coll. Toxicology, Am. Assn. Pathologist, Am. Soc. Clin. Pathologists, Soc. Toxicologic Pathologists, Am. Assn. Lab. Animal Sci., Am. Vet. Med. Assn., Am. Assn. Indsl. veterinarians, Am. Acad. Vet. and Comparative Toxicology, Internat. Acad. Pathology. Current work: Pharmaceutical research and development; industrial toxicologic pathology; drug safety evaluation; drug/chemical risk assessment. Subspecialties: Toxicology (medicine); Pathology (veterinary medicine). Home: 5 Acorn Dr Sunfish Lake MN 55075 Office: Riker Labs/3M Co Bldg 270-3S-05 3M Ctr Saint Paul MN 55144-1000

CHESNEY, ROBERT HAROLD, microbiologist, educator; b. Paterson, N.J.; s. David Martin and Goldie (Heiman) C.; m. Ellen Lucas, Aug. 19, 1972; 1 dau., Dana Llewellyn. B.A., U. Va., Charlottesville, 1968, Ph.D., 1974. Postdoctoral fellow Emory U., Atlanta, 1974-77; research assoc. U. Ga., Athens, 1977-78; asst. prof. microbiology Rutgers U., Newark, 1978—. Contbr. articles to jours. NIH postdoctoral fellow, 1975-77. Mem. AAAS, Am. Soc. Microbiology, Sigma Xi, Phi Sigma. Jewish. Current Work: Asparaginase genetics, gene mapping, gene cloning, Bacteriophages P1 and P7, Agrobacterium tumefaciens, tumorigenesis. Subspecialties: Genetics and genetic engineering (biology); Microbiology. Office: Dept Zoology and Physiology Rutgers U Newark NJ 07102

CHESSER, NANCY JEAN, physics consultant; b. Albany, N.Y., Aug. 31, 1946; d. Owen Francis and Sylvia Alice (Tefft) Chesser; m. J. Michael Rowe, Jan. 1, 1975. A.B. in Physics, Cornell U., 1967; Ph.D. in Physics, SUNY-Stony Brook, 1972. Asst. prof. Iowa State U./Ames Lab. U.S. AEC, 1972-76; research assoc. NRC of Nat. Acad. Sci., Nat. Bur. Standards, Gaithersburg, Md., 1975-77; prin. scientist B-K Dynamics Inc., Rockville, Md., 1977-83; Directed Technologies Inc., McLean, Va., 1983—. Pres., Potomac Springs Civic Assn., Rockville, 1984. Mem. Am. Phys. Soc., Sigma Xi. Current work: Systems important to national defense in year 2000. Subspecialty: Operations research (engineering). Home: 2516 Oakenshield Dr Rockville MD 20854 Office: Directed Technologies Inc 1226 Potomac Sch Rd McLean VA 22101

CHESSON, EUGENE, JR., civil engineering educator, consultant; b. Sao Paulo, Brazil, Dec. 1, 1928; s. Eugene and Mary Josie (Foy) C.; m. Marilyn Ryder Hershey, Aug. 21, 1954; children: Christopher Eugene, David Anson. B.S.C.E., Duke U., 1950; M.S., U. Ill.-Urbana, 1956, Ph.D., 1959. Registered profl. engr. Refinery engr. Standard Oil Ind., Whiting, 1953; research asst., research assoc. civil engring. dept. U. Ill.-Urbana, 1953-59, asst. prof., 1959-62, assoc. prof., 1962-66; prof. civil engring. U.Del., Newark, 1966—, chmn. dept., 1966-75; pres. Chesson Engring., Inc., Newark, 1981—. Contbr. articles in field to profl. jours. Served to lt. (j.g.), C.E. USN, 1950-53. Named Outstanding Young Faculty Mem. dept. Civil Engring. U. Ill., 1962, Del. Outstanding Engr. Del. Soc. Profl. Engrs., 1981. Fellow ASCE (pres. local sect. 1982-83); mem. Am. Soc. Engring. Edn. (W. E. Wickenden award 1981), Am. Inst. Steel Constrn., Nat. Soc. Profl. Engrs. Republican. Presbyterian. Current Work: Structural steel design, application of minicomputers to engineering design, forensic engineering and failure analysis. Subspecialty: Civil engineering. Home: 30 Bridle Brook Ln Newark DE 19711 Office: U Del 130 DuPont Hall Newark DE 19716

CHESTNUT, HAROLD, foundation executive, electrical engineer; b. Albany, N.Y., Nov. 25, 1917; s. Harry and Dorothy (Schulman) C.; m. Erma Ruth Callaway, Aug. 24, 1944; children: Peter Callaway, H. Thomas, Andrew T. B.S. in Elec. Engring, Mass. Inst. Tech., 1939, M.S., 1940; D.E. (hon.), Case Western Res. U., 1966, Villanova U., 1972. With Gen. Electric Co., 1940-83; cons. systems engr., aeros. and ordnance dept. Advanced Tech. Lab., Schenectady, 1956-66; mgr. Research and Devel. Center, 1966-71; cons. systems engr., 1972-83; pres. SWIIS Found., Inc., 1983—. Editor: Systems Engring. and Analysis, John Wiley and Sons, 1965-85; author: Servomechanisms and Regulating Systems Design, Vol. I, 1951, Vol. II, 1955, Systems Engineering Tools, 1965, Systems Engineering Methods, 1967; editor: Jour. Automatica, 1961-67. Mem. commn. sociotech. systems NRC, 1975-78. Case Western Res. U. Centennial scholar, 1980. Fellow IEEE (v.p. tech. activities 1970-71, v.p. regional activities 1972, pres. 1973, exec. com. 1967-75), AAAS, Instrument Soc. Am.; mem. Nat. Acad. Engring., Internat. Fedn. Automatic Control (pres. 1957-58), World Federalists Assn. (bd. dirs. 1980—), Am. Automatic Control Council (pres. 1962-63, Honda prize 1981, IEEE Centennial award 1984, Bellman Control Heritage award 1985), Nat. Soc. Profl. Engrs. Current Work: Improving international stability; presently president SWIIS Foundation, Inc. involves systems engineering. Subspecialty: Systems engineering. Home: 1226 Waverly Pl Schenectady NY 12308

CHEUNG, HERBERT CHIU-CHING, biochemistry educator, researcher; b. Canton, China, Dec. 19, 1933; came to U.S., 1950, naturalized, 1965; s. Kun Hui and Tak Woo (Yuen) C.; m. Daisy S. Lee, Feb 12, 1966; children: Sharon, Melissa. A.B., Rutgers U., 1954, Ph.D., 1961; M.S., Cornell U., 1956. Research chemist FMC Corp., Marcus Hook, Pa., 1960-63, Allied Chem. Corp., Morristown, N.J., 1963-66; sr. fellow U. Calif. Med. Ctr.-San Francisco, 1966-69; assoc. prof. biophysics U. Ala.-Birmingham, 1969-75, prof., 1975-82, prof. biochemistry, 1982—; mem. phys. biochemistry rev. group NIH, 1980-81, mem. phys. biochemistry study sect., 1981-84; mem. rev. com. Ala. Heart Assn., 1981-83. Recipient Research Career Devel. award NIH, 1972-77; NIH grantee, 1970—; NSF grantee, 1974, 78-80, 85—. Mem. Am. Soc. Biol. Chemists, Biophys. Soc., Am. Chem. Soc., Sigma Xi. Current Work: Molecular mechanism of energy transduction in muscle, structure-function relationship of proteins, particularly calcium binding proteins; fluorescence; physical studies of biomembranes; transporting ATPases. Subspecialties: Biophysics (biology); Biophysical chemistry. Office: U Ala at Birmingham 520 CHSB Birmingham AL 35294

CHEUNG, JOHN YAN-POON, educator; b. Hong Kong, Oct. 13, 1950; came to U.S., 1965, naturalized, 1983; s. Paul To-Kwong and Mei-Shin (Lau) C.; m. Rose Kwan-Fun, Aug. 6, 1977; children—Christina Phoebe, Jonathan Paul. B.S. in Math, Oreg. State U., 1969; Ph.D. in E.E, U. Wash., 1975. Sr. engr. Boeing Computer Service, Seattle, 1977-78; asst. prof. U. Okla., Norman, 1978-83, assoc. prof., 1983—; reviewer IEEE, Choice, Brooks/Cole Pub. Co. Contbr. articles to profl. jours. NSF grantee, 1981-83; United Engring. Trustees, Inc. grantee, 1981-82. Mem. Acoustical Soc. Am., IEEE, Assn. Computing Machinery, Eta Kappa Nu. Mem. Christian Ch. Current Work: Computer applications in signal processing, biomedical instrumentation, parallel processing as applied to algorithms, computer arch. and very large scale integration (VLSI) designs. Subspecialties: Computer engineering; Computer architecture. Home: 11909 Autumn Leaves Oklahoma City OK 73170 Office: 202 W Boyd St Room 219 Norman OK 73019

CHEUNG, JOSEPH YAT-SING, physician; b. Hong Kong, June 21, 1950; came to U.S., 1972; m. Barbara Ann Miller, June 14, 1975. B.Sc. with honors, McGill U., 1972; M.S., Pa. State U., 1974, Ph.D., 1976; M.D., Duke U., 1978. Diplomate Am. Bd. Internal Medicine, Nat. Bd. Med. Examiners. Intern, Duke U. Med. Ctr., Durham, N.C., 1978-79, asst. resident, 1979-80; clin. and research fellow Mass. Gen. Hosp., Boston, 1980-83; instr. medicine Harvard U. Med. Sch., Boston, 1983-84, asst. prof., 1984—. Contbr. articles to profl. jours. Recipient Nat. Research Services award Nat. Heart, Lung and Blood Inst., 1981-84; Mem. Internat. Soc. Nephrology, Am. Soc. Nephrology, Am. Physiol. Soc., Am. Fedn. Clin. Research, Am. Heart Assn. (Clinician Scientist award 1984—). Republican. Current work: Cell calcium homeostasis; hormonal effects on cell calcium metabolism; intracellular calcium and PH; regulation of glucose transport. Subspecialties: Internal medicine; Physiology (medicine). Office: Renal Unit Mass Gen Hosp Fruit St Boston MA 02114

CHEUNG, SAU WAI, cytogeneticist, researcher; b. Shanghai, China, Sept. 20, 1944; came to U.S., 1967; naturalized, 1978; d. Un-lin and Tessie (Wong) C.; m. Ching Po Ko, July 31, 1972 (div. 1979); 1 child, Lester Ko. B.S., Chinese U. of Hong Kong, 1966; M.S., U. Louisville, 1969; Ph.D., Ind. U., 1975. Prefect of studies St. Margaret's Girls' Coll., Hong Kong, 1966-67; NIH predoctoral traineeship in med. genetics Ind. U. Sch. Med., 1970-74; research fellow in medicine Harvard Med. Sch., Boston, 1975-77, instr., 1977-79; assoc. dir. Kleberg Cytogenetics Lab., Baylor Coll. Medicine, Houston, 1979-80; research asst. prof. Wash. U. Sch. Med., St. Louis, 1980—; assoc. in medicine Peter Bent Bringham Hosp. and Affiliated Hosps. Ctr., Boston, 1977-79; dir. cytogenetics lab. Wash. U. Sch. Med., St. Louis, 1980—. Contbr. articles to profl. jours. NIH fellow, 1976-78; grantee Harvard U. Med. Sch., grants, 1977-78. Mem. Am. Soc. Human Genetics, AAAS, Assn. Women in Sci., Sigma Xi. . Home: 8528 Douglas Ct Saint Louis MO 63144 Office: Dept Ob-Gyn Washington U Sch Medicine 4911 Barnes Hosp Plaza Saint Louis MO 63110

CHEUNG, W(AH-KWAN) STEPHEN, physicist; b. Hong Kong, Sept. 12, 1953; came to U.S., 1974, naturalized, 1983; m. Annette Yung Teng, Dec. 27, 1982. B.S., in Physics, U. Wis.-Stevens Point, 1976; M.S. in Physics, U. Va., 1978, Ph.D., in Physics, 1982. Research scientist Hansen Labs., Stanford U., Calif., 1981—; dir. acad. devel. Microwave Tng. Inst., Mountain View, Calif., 1983—; consultant in microwave field. Editor: Microwaves Made Simple, 1985. Contbr. articles to profl. jours. Mem. IEEE, Soc. Mfg. Engrs., Instrument Soc. Am., Sigma Xi. Current work: Work on NASA-Gravity Probe B Program, electrical breakdown of thin films, homogeneity of quartz crystals, quartz gyroscope fabrication, UV photolithography, monolithic microwave integrated circuits. Subspecialties: Relativity and gravitation; Microelectronics. Home: 1037 Campbell Ave Los Altos CA 94022 Office: Hansen Labs Stanford U Stanford CA 94305

CHEVALIER, ROBERT LOUIS, pediatrics educator and researcher; b. Chgo., Oct. 25, 1946; s. Frank Charles and Marion Helen (Jahnke) C.; m. Janis Julia Slezak, Dec. 23, 1970; 1 dau., Juline Ariane. B.S. in Zoology, U. Chgo., 1968, M.D., 1972. Diplomate: Am. Bd. Pediatrics (subcert. in pediatric nephrology). Intern, residence in pediatrics N.C. Meml. Hops., Chapel Hill, 1972-75; asst. prof. pediatrics U. Va., Charlottesville, 1978-83, assoc. prof., 1983—, chief div. pediatric nephrology, 1978—. Louis Welt scholar U. N.C., Chapel Hill, 1975; research grantee NIH, 1979; established investigator Am. Heart Assn., 1983. Mem. Am.Soc. Nephrology, Internat. Soc. Nephrology, Am. Fedn. Clin. Research, Nat. Kidney Found., Am. Soc. Pediatric Nephrology. Current Work: Investigation of developmental renal physiology using micropuncture techniques. Subspecialties: Pediatrics; Nephrology. Home: 113 Wildflower Dr Charlottesville VA 22901 Office: U Va Dept Pediatrics Box 386 Charlottesville VA 22908

CHEVILLE, NORMAN FREDERICK, pathologist, researcher; b. Iowa, Sept. 30, 1934; s. Fred M. and Lucille H. C.; m. Beth M. Clark, June 22, 1958; children. D.V.M., Iowa State U., 1959; Ph.D., U. Wis., 1964. Research assoc. U. Wis., 1961-63; with Nat. Animal Disease Center, Ames, Iowa, 1963—, vet. med. officer, 1963-65; chief Pathology Research lab., 1965—; prof. pathology Iowa State U., 1966—. Research numerous publs. in field; author: Cytopathology of Viral Diseases, 1975, Cell Pathology, 1976. Pres. Assn. Handicapped Children, Ames; bd. dirs. First United Methodist Ch. Served to capt. U.S. Army, 1959-61. Recipient Outstanding Achievement award; Alumni Merit award Iowa State U., 1980. Mem. Am. Coll. Vet. Pathologists, Internat. Acad. Pathology, AAAS, Sigma Xi, Phi Zeta, Phi Kappa Phi. Current Work: Infectious diseases of domestic animals. Subspecialty: Pathology (veterinary medicine). Office: Pathology Research Lab Nat Animal Disease Center PO Box 70 Ames IA 50010

CHEW, CATHERINE STRONG, physiology educator; b. Savannah, Ga., July 6, 1942; d. William Harmon and Pegge Catherine (Bradley) Strong; m. Frank Ellis Chew, Sept. 25, 1969; 1 son, Frank Ellis. B.S., Armstrong State Coll., Savannah, 1970; Ph.D., Emory U., Atlanta, 1970-77. Horse trainer, instr. Sa-Hi Stables, Savannah, 1960-65; research technician Emory U., 1970-74, research assoc., 1977-78, NIH postdoctoral fellow, 1979-80; asst. prof. physiology Morehouse Sch. Medicine, Atlanta, 1980—; lectr. Internat. Congress of Physiol. Sci., Budapest, Hungary, 1980, Montpellier, France, 1979; lectr. Porter Found., Atlanta, 1978, 80, 82, 83; instr. Ga. Heart Assn., 1975. Author: Hormone Receptors in Digestion and Nutrition, 1969, Advances in Physiological Sciences, 1980; Contbr. articles to profl. jours. Mem. ednl. policy com. Paideia Sch., Atlanta, 1981—; mem. Candler Park Neighborhood Orgn., 1977—, CAUTION, 1982—. Mem. AAUP, Am. Physiol. Soc., N.Y. Acad. Scis., Am. Women in Sci., AAAS. Democrat. Episcopalian. Current Work: Gastrointestinal physiologist studying cellular mechanism of action of neural, hormonal and paracrine factors controlling gastric (parietal cell) acid secretion and chief cell pepsinogen secretion. Subspecialties: Physiology (medicine); Cell biology (medicine). Home: 607 Page Ave NE Atlanta GA 30307 Office: Morehouse Sch Medicine 720 Westview Dr SW Atlanta GA 30310

CHEW, WENG CHO, research company executive, researcher; b. Kuantan, Pahang, Malaysia, June 9, 1953; came to U.S., 1973; s. Fatt Sim and Toh Lan (Goh) C.; m. Chew-Chin Phua, Dec. 21, 1977; children—Huibin Amelia, Shinen Ethan. B.S. E.E., MIT, 1976, M.S. E.E., 1978, E.E., 1978, Ph.D. in E.E., 1980. Research assoc. MIT, Cambridge, Mass., 1980-81; mem. profl. staff Schlumberger-Doll Research, Ridgefield, Conn., 1981-82, program leader electromagnetics, 1982-84, head dept. electromagnetics, 1984—. Contbr. numerous articles to profl. jours. Mem. IEEE (assoc. editor Geosci. and Remote Sensing 1984—), Union Radio Sci. Internat., Sigma Xi, Tau Beta Pi, Eta Kappa Nu. Current work: Electromagnetic theory; inverse scattering; applied mathematics. Subspecialty: Applied magnetics.

CHEWNING, JUNE SPANGLER, energy labor force specialist; b. Atlanta, July 27, 1925; d. George McClannahan and Esther (Ward) Spangler; m. Bernard P. Chewning, June 25, 1955; children: B. Peter, Pamela A. B.A., Am. U., 1950; A.A., McNeese State U., 1946; cert. Ga. Inst. Tech., 1982. Editor/writer Dept. Navy, Washington, 1949-52; econ. analyst Library of Congress, Washington, 1952-63, Dept. Def., Arlington, Va., 1963-66; edn. and tng. analyst U.S. AEC, Germantown, Md., 1966-72; sr. manpower analyst Dept. Energy, Washington, 1972—; cons. numerous career guide publs., 1971—; cons. IAEA, Vienna, 1979-80. Editor: Industrial Noise Control, 1963; author govt. publs.; contbr. articles to profl. jours. Co-founder Federally Employed Women, Inc., 1968, CHANGE, 1980; dept. chmn., deacon National City Christian Ch., Washington, 1979-82, elder, 1983—; bd. dirs. various civic and nat. women's orgns. Recipient Superior Performance award Library of Congress, 1950; Spl. Achievement award ERDA, 1976, Fed. Exec. Women, 1984. Mem. Am. Nuclear Soc., Atomic Indsl. Forum, AAAS, Nuclear Energy Women, Women in Energy, Am. U. Alumni Assn. (v.p. 1974-75), Women's Equity Action League, FEW, Phi Theta Kappa. Democrat. Mem. Disciples of Christ Ch. Current Work: Projections of needs for and supply of nuclear-trained personnel, adequacy of training, evaluation of education and training delivery modes. Transfer of nuclear technology to developing nations. Subspecialties: Employment aspects of energy production; Nuclear fission. Home: 3637 Appleton St NW Washington DC 20008 Office: US Dept Energy 1000 Independence Ave SW Washington DC 20585

CHI, CHAO SHU, computer storage scientist; b. Nanking, China, Sept. 12, 1936, came to U.S.; naturalized, 1966; s. Yuan Pau and Lien Hsian (Ken) C.; m. Kitty H. Hsu, Dec. 20, 1962; children—Clive, Andrew, Theodore. B.S. in Elec. Engring., Cheng Kung U., Taiwan, Republic of China, 1961; M.S. in Elec. Engring., Worcester Poly. Inst., Mass., 1964, Ph.D., 1974. Registered profl. engr., N.J., Conn. Engr. Northeast Utilities, Hartford, Conn., 1964-67; prin. mem. tech. staff RCA, Marlboro, Mass., 1967-71; prin. engr. Digital Equipment Corp., Maynard, Mass., 1971-77; mgr. Sperry Research Ctr., Sudbury, Mass., 1977-84; group mgr. Optical Storage Internat., Santa Clara, Calif., 1984-85; sr. lab. head Kodak Research Labs., San Diego, 1985—. Contbr. articles to profl. jours.; patentee electronics systems and apparatus. Recipient Tech. Excellence award Control Data Corp., 1984, Spl. Achievement award Digital Equipment Corp., 1974; Worcester Poly. Inst. scholar, 1962. Mem. IEEE (sr.), IEEE Hybrid Soc. (edn. chmn.), IEEE Boston Magnetic Soc. (sect. chmn.), IEEE Magnetic Transactions Soc. (tech. reviewer). Current work: Optical and magnetic recording, coding, signal processing, signal detection; recording head tech.; circuit tech.; computer simulation. Subspecialties: Information systems, storage, and retrieval (computer science); Applied magnetics.

CHI, DAVID S., immunologist, educator, researcher; b. Taiwan, July 7, 1943; s Ching Hsing and Ah Chu (Chen) C. B.S., Nat. Chung-Hsing U., Taiwan, 1965; M.A., U. Tex., Galveston, 1974, Ph.D., 1977. Cert. clin. lab. dir. Am. Bd. Bioanalysis, 1981. Farm dir. Taiwan Sugar Corp., 1968-69; asst. mgr. Chai-Tai Enterprise Co., Ltd., Taiwan, 1969-70; postdoctoral fellow and research scientist N.Y.U. Med. Ctr., N.Y.C., 1977-80; assoc. prof. and clin. lab. dir. E. Tenn. State U., Johnson City, 1980—, chief div. biomed. research, 1981—. Contbr. articles to sci. jours. Recipient New Investigator Research award Nat. Cancer Inst., 1980. Mem. Am. Soc. Microbiology, Reticuloendothelial Soc., Am. Assn. Immunologists, Soc. Exptl. Biology and Medicine, N.Y. Acad. Scis., Am. Soc. Zoologists, Harvey Soc., Internat. Soc. Developmental and Comparative Immunology, Sigma Xi. Current Work: Research in cellular immunology, tumor immunology and clinical immunology. Subspecialties: Immunobiology and immunology; Immunology (medicine). Home: 419 W Locust St Johnson City TN 37601 Office: E Tenn StateU Johnson City TN 37614

CHIANG, CHIN LONG, biostatistician, educator; b. Chekiang, China, Nov. 12, 1916; came to U.S., 1946, naturalized, 1963; s. Tse Shang and (Chen) C.; m. Fu Chen Shiao, Jan. 21, 1945; children: William S., Robert S., Harriet W. B.A. in Econs, Tsing Hwa U., 1940; M.A., U. Calif.-Berkeley, 1948; Ph.D. in Stats, U. Calif., Berkeley, 1953. Teaching asst. U. Calif., Berkeley, 1948, research asst., 1950-51, asso., 1951-53, instr., 1953-55, asst. prof. biostatistics, 1955-60, assoc. prof., 1960-65, prof., 1965—, chmn. div. measurement scis., 1970-75, chmn. faculty Sch. Public Health, 1975-76; chmn. U. Calif. (Program in Biostats.), 1970—, co-chmn. group in biostats., 1971—; vis. prof. U. Mich., 1959, U. Minn., 1960, 61, Yale U., 1965-66, Emory U., 1967, U. Pitts., 1968, U. Wash., 1969, U. N.C., 1969, 70, U. Tex., 1973, Vanderbilt U., 1975, Harvard U., 1977; cons. WHO, HEW, NIH, others. Author: Introduction to Stochastic Processes in Biostatistics, 1968, Life Table and Mortality Analysis, 1978, An Introduction to Stochastic Processes and Their Applications, 1979, The Life Table and its, Applications, 1984; Assoc. editor: Biometrics, 1972-75; Asso. editor: Math. Biosciences, 1976—; editorial bd.: WHO World Health Statis. Quar, 1979—. Nat. Heart Inst. fellow, 1959-60; Fulbright sr. lectr., 1964. Fellow Am. Statis. Assn., Inst. Math. Stats., Am. Public Health Assn., Royal Statis. Soc. London; mem. Internat. Statis. Inst., Biometric Soc. Democrat. Subspecialty: Statistics. Home: 844 Spruce St Berkeley CA 94707 Office: School Public Health U Calif Berkeley CA 94720

CHIANG, FU-PEN, mechanical engineering educator; b. Checkiang, China, Oct. 10, 1936; s. Chien-lo and Lien-yin (Mao) C.; m. Charlotte Chen-yi Chen, June1, 1963; children: Brian (dec.), Ted, Michelle. B.S. in Civil Engring, Nat. Taiwan U., 1953-57; M.S., U. Fla., 1963; Ph.D. in Engring. Sci. and Mechanics, 1966. Civil engr., 1958-62; asst. prof. mech. engring. SUNY-Stony Brook, 1967-70, assoc. prof., 1970-73, prof., 1974—, dir. Lab for Exptl. Mechanics Research, 1984—; vis. prof. Swiss Fed. Inst. Tech., Lausanne, 1973-74; sr. vis. fellow dept. physics Cavendish Lab., U. Cambridge, Eng., 1980-81; cons. Army Material and Mechanics Research Ctr., Army Missile Command, Grumann Aerospace Corp., and; others. Contbr. articles to profl. jours. Postdoctoral fellow Cath. U. Am.; NSF grantee, 1968-73, 76-83, 84-86; Office Naval Research grantee, 1982-86. Fellow Soc. Exptl. Stress Analysis; mem. Optical Soc. Am., Soc. Photo-Optical Instrumentation Engrs., Am. Acad. Mechanics, N.Y. Acad. Scis., AAAS, ASME. Current Work: Development of optical stress analysis techniques such as laser speckles techniques, holographic interferometry, white light speckle techniques, moire methods, electron speckle and acoustic speckle techniques. Subspecialties: Stress analysis; Solid mechanics. Office: Dept Mech SUNY Stony Brook NY 11794

CHIANG, JOHN YOUNG LING, biochemistry educator, researcher; b. Hangchew, CheKiang, China, July 29, 1947; came to U.S., 1970, naturalized, 1980; s. Ming-ming and Ya-Jung (Huang) C.; m. Lisa H. Kang, Aug. 3, 1973; children: Eric, David. B.S., Chung-Hsing U., Taichung, Taiwan, 1969; M.S., SUNY-Albany, 1973, Ph.D., 1976. Postdoctoral scholar U. Mich. Med. Sch., Ann Arbor, 1976-78; asst. prof. biochemistry Northeastern Ohio U. Coll. Medicine Rootstown, 1978-83, assoc. prof., 1983—. Contbr. articles to profl. jours. NIH fellow, 1977-78; Pharm. Mfrs. Assn. Found. grantee, 1982-83; Am. Heart Assn. grantee, 1980-82; NIH grantee, 1983—. Mem. AAAS, Am. Soc. Biol. Chemists. Current Work: Basic biochemical research in studying the induction and regulation of liver detoxication enzymes; regulation and metabolism of cholesterol and bile acids. Subspecialty: Biochemistry (medicine). Home: 1173 Erin Dr Kent OH 44240 Office: Northeastern Ohio University College of Medicine 4209 State Route 44 Rootstown OH 44272

CHIANG, JOSEPH FEI, chemist, educator, researcher; b. Hunan, China, Feb. 22, 1938; s. K. K. and W. S. (Ma) C.; m. Nancy S. Chang; children: Calvin, Amy. B.S., Tunghai U., 1960; M.S., Cornell U., 1965, Ph.D., 1967. Research fellow Cornell U., Ithaca, N.Y., 1967-68; prof. chemistry SUNY at Oneonta, 1968—; vis. prof. U. Chgo., 1983. Contbr. articles on chemistry to profl. jours. Nat. Acad. Scis. exchange scholar to Hungarian Acad. Scis., 1980; NIH fellow, 1975-76; research fellow Harvard U., 1978. Mem. Am. Chem. Soc., Am. Phys. Soc., Sigma Xi. Republican. Roman Catholic. Current Work: Molecular structure by spectroscopic techniques, X-ray cyrstallography, van der waals molecules, molecular quantum mechanics. Subspecialties: Physical chemistry; Biophysical chemistry. Home: 16 Suncrest Terr Oneonta NY 13820 Office: Dept Chemistry SUNY Oneonta NY 13820

CHIBUCOS, THOMAS ROBERT, family and child studies educator, researcher, writer; b. Chgo., Apr. 14, 1946; s. Gus and Jennie (Lalla) C.; m. Pamela Elizabeth Perry, May 15, 1982; m. Mary Clare Gilbert, Jan. 21, 1967 (div. Feb. 1976); children: Thomas, Marcus, Elise. B.A. in Psychology, No. Ill. U., 1969, M.A., 1970; Ph.D. in Developmental Psychology, Mich. State U., 1974. Research assoc. Nat. Inst. Edn., Washington, 1973-75; asst. prof. psychology No. Ill. U., 1975-76, asst. prof. child devel., 1976-80, assoc. prof., coordinator div. family and child studies, 1981—; day care cons. Growing Place Day Care, DeKalb, 1979-81; expert witness Kane County States Atty., Wheaton, Ill., 1982. Guest editor: spl. issue Infant Mental Health Jour, 1980; contbr. chpt. to book, articles to profl. jours. Coach Am. Youth Socer Orgn., DeKalb, Little League; mem. DeKalb Human Relations Commn., 1982. Mich. Office Edn. grantee, 1972-83; Ill. Office Edn. grantee, 1977. Mem. Am. Psychol. Assn., Soc. Research in Child Devel., Ill. Assn. Infant Mental Health (co-founder, dir. 1981—), Internat. Assn. Infant Mental Health. Current Work: Social policy, children and families, child mistreatment, fathers and infants, life span development, family violence, research methodology. Subspecialties: Developmental psychology; Child development and family studies. Office: No Ill U 209 Wirtz Hall DeKalb IL 60115

CHIGNELL, COLIN FRANCIS, pharmacologist; b. London, Apr. 7, 1938; s. Francis George and Elsie Mary (Lee) C.; m. Anke K. Kreienbring, Nov. 19, 1966; children: Kimberly, Kevin. B.Pharm. with honours, U. London, 1959, Ph.D., 1962. Vis. fellow Lab. Chemistry, Nat. Inst. Arthritis and Metabolic Disease, NIH, Bethesda, Md., 1962-64; vis. assoc. Lab. Chem. Pharmacology, Nat. Heart, Lung and Blood Inst., 1964-69, research pharmacologist, 1969-74, research pharmacologist pulmonary br., 1974-77; chief Lab. Environ. Biophysics Nat. Inst. Environ. Health Scis., Research Triangle Park, N.C., 1977—; adj. prof. pharmacology U. N.C., Chapel Hill, 1978—. Editor: Methods in Pharmacology Vol. 2, 1972; mng. editor: Jour. Biochem. and Biophys. Methods; contbr. numerous articles to sci. and tech. jours. Mem. Am. Soc. Pharmacology and Exptl. Therapeutics (J.J. Abel award 1973), Am. Soc. Biol. Chemists, Biophys. Soc., Am. Soc. Photobiology, AAAS, Pharm. Soc. Gt. Britain. Lutheran. Current Work: Molecular mechanisms of chemical toxicity, toxicology, spectroscopy, biochemical pharmacology, molecular pharmacology. Subspecialties: Molecular pharmacology; Medicinal chemistry. Home: 128 Bruce Dr Cary NC 27511 Office: Lab Environ Biophysics Nat Inst Environ Health Scis PO Box 12233 Research Triangle Park NC 27709

CHILCOAT, ROBERT TALMADGE, biomedical engineer, physicist, researcher; b. Lancaster, Calif., May 21, 1944; s. Jesse Green and Mildred Elizabeth (Bates) C.; m. Susan Adele McBride, Nov. 19, 1966; children—Gareth Robert, Gwyneth Marie, Gethyn McBride. B.S., Indiana U. of Pa., 1967; M.Sc., Welsh Nat. Sch. Med., 1975, Ph.D., 1983. Cert. secondary tchr., Pa. Tchr. physics Churchill Area High Sch., Pitts., 1967-70; research asst. Welsh Nat. Sch. Med., Cardiff, U.K., 1970-79; asst. prof. SUNY-Upstate Med. Ctr., Syracuse, N.Y., 1979—. Co-author computer teaching program: Simulation of Swan-Ganz Catheter Placement, 1980. Contbr. articles to profl. jours. Recipient 1st prize for sci. exhibit N.Y. state Soc. Anesthesiologists, 1980;

grantee computer application in anesthesiology Am. Edwards Labs., 1981, Med. Gas Sensors Sensors, Inc., 1984. Mem. Am. Soc. Anesthesiologists (affiliate, 1st prize for sci. exhibit 1980), Internat. Anesthesia Research Soc. (1st prize for sci. exhibit 1980), Anaesthetic Research Soc. (Gr. Britain), IEEE, Assoc. for Advancement Med. Instrumentation. Club: Willow Bank Yacht (Cazenovia NY) (fleet capt. 1981-83). Current work: Automatic control of anesthesia, sensor technology, computer applications in anesthesia, computer modelling, various engineering research in anesthesia. Subspecialties: Anesthesiology; Bioinstrumentation. Home: 4858 Candy Ln Manlius NY 13104 Office: Dept Anesthesiology SUNY Upstate Med Ctr 750 East Adams St Syracuse NY 13210

CHILDERS, JOHN STEPHEN, psychologist, psychological educator; b. Elizabeth City, N.C., Aug. 10, 1946; s. Earl Stephen and Norma (Houchin) C.; m. Beth Austin, Feb. 13, 1966; children: John Stephen, Amy Suzanne. B.A., E. Carolina U., 1968, M.A., 1972; Ed. D., N. C. State U., 1983. Lic. psychol. assoc., N.C. Psychologist adult services Coastal Plain Mental Health Center, Greenville, N.C., 1969-71; acting chmn. Inst. Mental Health, Pitt Tech. Inst., Greenville, 1971-72; dir. testing, asst. prof. psychology E. Carolina U., 1972—; cons. numerous pub. sch. systems, N.C. area, 1970—; vice-chmn. N.C. State Dept. Pub. Instrn., 1978-81; area coordinator various test developing cos., N.C., 1972—. Contbr. articles to profl. jours. Mem. Greenville Mayor's Adv. Council on Leisure Activities, 1980-81; mem. Domiciliary Home Community Adv. Com., Pitt County, N.C., 1982—; adv. Real Crisis Intervention Center, Greenville, 1971—. Am. Guidance Services Inc. grantee, 1979—; N.C. Mental Health Authority grantee, 1973-74. Mem. Am. Psychol. Assn., Southeastern Psychol. Assn. Republican. Methodist. Clubs: Civitan, Greenville Sports. Current Work: Research projects include reliability and validity research on the Kaufman-Assessment Battery for Children; the Vineland Adaptive Behavior Scales and Child Behavior Checklist; researching social networks inpact on elderly. Subspecialties: Developmental psychology; Social psychology. Home: 1101 Johnston St Greenville NC 27834 Office: Psychology Dept East Carolina U Greenville NC 27834

CHILDS, JEFFREY JOHN, computer engr.; b. Des Moines, Oct. 11, 1956; s. John Edwin and Dorothy Louise (Graham) C.; m. Debbie Banwart, June 24, 1978. B.S.E.E., Iowa State U., 1978; postgrad., U. Minn., 1981—. Machinist Hull Industries, Iowa, 1974-76; computer technician Cyclone Computer Lab., Iowa State U., Ames, 1976-78; software design engr., computer systems div. Hewlett Packard, Cupertino, Calif., 1978-80; hardware design engr. Def. Systems div. Sperry Univac, St. Paul, 1980-83, Star Techs., Inc., Brooklyn Park, Minn., 1983—. Mem. IEEE, Assn. for Computing Machinery, Eta Kappa Nu, Tau Beta Pi. Presbyterian. Club: Apple Computer (St. Paul). Current Work: Design and implementation of array processor architectures for real-time processing. Subspecialties: Computer engineering; Computer architecture. Home: 1272 Easter Ln Eagan MN 55123 Office: 7101 Northland Circle Suite 102 Brooklyn Park MN 55428

CHILDS, MARIAN TOLBERT, nutrition educator; b. Twin Falls, Idaho, Nov. 18, 1925; d. Ed and Helen (Mills) Tolbert; m. Morris E. Childs, Nov. 25, 1952; children—Robert, Mary, Ruth, Amy. B.S., U. Calif.-Berkeley, 1946, Ph.D., 1950. Asst. prof. U. Ill., Urbana, 1950-54; asst. prof., acting prof., prof. U. Wash., Seattle, 1968-70, 1973-81; assoc. prof. nutrition, 1981—. Contbr. articles to profl. jours. NIH fellow, 1976-78. Mem. Am. Inst. Nutrition, Fedn. Am. Soc. Experimental Biology. Current work: Lipid and lipoprotein metabolism as affected by diet; omega-3 fatty acids; shellfish sterols. Subspecialty: Nutrition (medicine). Home: 7857 56th Pl NE Seattle WA 98195 Office: U Wash NutriScience DL10 Seattle WA 98195

CHILDS, WENDELL ARTHUR, physics educator, army officer; b. Cullman, Ala., Sept. 12, 1933; s. Charlie F. and Myrtle I. (Young) C.; m. Carol J. Poole, Apr. 21, 1956; children—Cristy A. Childs Edwards, Richard L., Scott D. B.S. in Engring. Physics, Auburn U., 1955; M.S. in Physics, Stevens Inst. Tech., 1963; Ph.D. in Physics, U. Va., 1971. Commd. 2d lt. U.S. Army, 1955, advanced through grades to col., 1976; served in Germany, 1957-60, Korea, 1964-65; asst. prof. physics U.S. Mil. Acad., West Point, N.Y., 1965-68, prof., 1970—, dep. head dept., 1971-84, head dept., 1984—. Mem. Am. Phys. Soc., Am. Assn. Physics Tchrs., Am. Soc. Engring. Edn. Current work: Gamma ray spectroscopy. Subspecialties: Physics education; Nuclear physics. Home: 32-B Thayer Rd West Point NY 10996 Office: Dept Physics US Mil Acad West Point NY 10996

CHILDS, WILLIAM JEFFRIES, physicist; b. Boston, Nov. 9, 1926; s. Paul Dudley and Clemence d'Espaigne (Jeffries) C.; m. Jean Mallory, June 17, 1951; children: Linton Jeffries, Lee Tracy. A.B., Harvard U., Cambridge, Mass., 1948; M.S., U. Mich., Ann Arbor, 1949, Ph.D., 1956. Physicist Argonne (Ill.) Nat. Labs., 1956—, sr. physicist, 1980—; vis. prof. U. Bonn., W. Ger., 1972-73. Contbr. articles to profl. jours. Served with AUS, 1944-46. Mem. Am. Phys. Soc., Am. Optical Soc. Current Work: Laser and radiofrequency spectroscopy of atomic and molecular beams, fine and hyperfine structure. Subspecialty: Atomic and molecular physics. Home: 539 Fairview Ave Glen Ellyn IL 60137 Office: 9700 S Cass Ave Argonne IL 60439

CHILINGARIAN, GEORGE VAROS, educator; b. Tbilisi, Ga., July 22, 1929; s. Varos and Klavdia (Gorchakova) C.; m. Yelba Maria Salmeron, June 12, 1953; children: Modesto George, Eleanore Elizabeth, Mark Steven. B.E., U. So. Calif., 1949, M.S., 1950, Ph.D., 1954; Dr. Honoris Causa, Kensington U., 1977, Pacific Western U., 1978, Pepperdine U., 1979, Academiya Studiorum, Italy, 1960. With Wright-Patterson AFB, Dayton, 1954-56; faculty U. So. Calif., Los Angeles, 1956—, prof. petroleum engring., 1970—. Contbr. numerous articles to profl. jours.; author 32 books on petroleum engring. and geology. Served to col. USAFR, 1954—. Recipient numerous profl. awards. Republican. Subspecialties: Petroleum engineering; Geology. Home: 101 S Windsor Blvd Los Angeles CA 90004 Office: Dept Petroleum Engring Univ So Calif Los Angeles CA 90007

CHILTON, MARY-DELL, molecular biologist. Exec. dir. biotech. div. Ciba-Geigy Corp., Research Triangle Park, N.C. Subspecialty: Biotechnology research and development. Office: Ciba-Geigy Corp Biotech Div PO Box 12257 Research Triangle Park NC 27709

CHILTON, NEAL W(ARWICK), dental biostatistician, consultant; b. N.Y.C., June 24, 1921; s. Benjamin Bernard and Bertha (Warich) C.; m. Naomi Lilian Alexander, Dec. 28, 1947; children: Peninah, Jonathan, Abigail, Seth, Miriam. B.S., CCNY, 1939; D.D.S., NYU, 1943; M.P.H., Columbia U., 1946. Diplomate: Am. Bd. Periodontology, Am. Bd. Endodontics. Asst. prof. pharmacology NYU, N.Y.C., 1944-46; adj. prof. Columbia U., N.Y.C., 1948-56, sr. research assoc., 1960-84, sr. research scientist, 1984—; clin. prof. periodontics Temple U., Phila., 1957-75; research prof. oral medicine U. Pa., Phila., 1975-79, research cons., 1979-84, prof. clin. research, 1984—; Lady Davis prof. preventive dentistry Hebrew U., Jerusalem, Israel, 1977. Author: Design and Analysis in Dental and Oral Research, 2nd edit, 1982; contbr. articles to profl. publs. Served to maj. U.S. Army, 1953-55. NIH grantee, 1963—; contract, 1966, 81; Office Naval Research grantee, 1947. Fellow Am. Coll. Dentists; mem. Am. Acad. Periodontology, Am. Acad. Endodontics, Am. Acad. Oral Pathology, European Orgn. for Caries Research, Internat. Assn. Dental Research, Phi Beta Kappa, Sigma Xi, Omicron Kappa Upsilon. Democrat. Current Work: Clinical trials of oral preventive and therapeutic agents; dental biostatistics; research consultant; epidemiology. Subspecialties: Periodontics; Statistics. Home: 2975 Princeton Pike Lawrenceville NJ 08648 Office: Univ Pennsylvania 4001 Spruce St Philadelphia PA 19104

CHIMNEY, MICHAEL JOHN, aquatic biologist, consultant; b. Cleve., Dec. 19, 1951; s. Florian Frank and Lucille Colleta (Moenich) C. B.S., U. Dayton, 1974; M.S., Miami U., 1976; Ph.D., So. Ill. U., 1981. Research project dir. Coop. Wildlife Research Lab., So. Ill. U., Carbondale, 1980-83, vis. asst. prof. zoology, 1981-82; project mgr. ECS, Inc., Aiken, S.C., 1984—. Contbr. articles to profl. jours. Research fellow So. Ill. U., 1979-80; Sigma Xi grantee, 1979; Ill. Mining and Mineral Resources Inst. grantee, 1981. Mem. AAAS, Am. Soc. Limnology and Oceanography, Ecol. Soc. Am., Ill. State Acad. Sci., Internat. Assn. Theoretical and Applied Limnology, N. Am. Benthological Soc., Sigma Xi. Roman Catholic. Current work: Limnology, ecology; structure and functioning of strip mine lakes and cooling reservoirs, ecology of freshwater zooplankton communities. Subspecialties: Limnology; Ecology (biology). Office: ECS Inc PO Box 1393 Aiken SC 29801

CHIN, GILBERT YUKYU, metallurgist; b. Kwangtung, China, Sept. 21, 1934; s. George Shee Ng and Liawah (Gee) C.; m. Ginie Wong, June 26, 1960; children—Patrick Ken, Michael Philip, Grace Fay, Karen Jean. S.B., MIT, 1959, Sc.D., 1963. Mem. tech. staff Bell Telephone Labs, Murray Hill, N.J., 1962—, head phys. metallurgy and crystal growth research dept., 1973-75, head phys. metallurgy and ceramics research and devel. dept., 1975-84, dir. materials research lab., 1984—. Author. Recipient Achievement award Chinese Inst. Engrs. of U.S.A., 1980, Chinese Engrs. and Scientists Assn. So. Calif., 83. Fellow Metall. Soc. AIME (Mathewson Gold medal 1974), Am. Soc. Metals, Am. Soc. Metals, mem. Nat. Acad. Engring., Metall. Soc. Am., Am. Ceramics Soc., Magnetics Soc. of IEEE, AAAS, Sigma Xi, Tau Beta Pi, Phi Lambda Upsilon. Episcopalian. Patentee in field. Current Work: Metallurgy of magnetic alloys and development of magnetically soft, semi-hard and hard alloys; mechanical properties of materials; management of research and development program on electronic materials including metals, ceramics and semiconductors. Subspecialties: Metallurgy; Materials (engineering). Office: AT&T Bell Labs Mountain Ave Murray Hill NJ 07974

CHIN, HONG W., radiation oncologist, educator, clinical researcher; b. Seoul, Korea, May 14, 1935; came to U.S., 1974; s. Jik H. and Woon K. (Park) C.; m. Soo J. Cheung, Dec. 27, 1965; children: Richard, Helen, Ki. M.D., Seoul Nat U., 1962, Ph.D., 1974. Diplomate: Am. Bd. Radiology. Radiation oncologist, asst. prof. dept. radiation medicine U. Ky. Med. Ctr., Lexington, 1979—. Contbr. med. articles to profl. jours.; author 2 monographs. Mem. AMA, Am. Coll. Radiology, Am. Soc. Therapeutic Radiologists, AAAS, Can. Assn. Radiologists, N.Y. Acad. Scis., Radiation Research Soc., Radiol. Soc. N.Am., Pan-Am. Med. Assn. (council), Sigma Xi. Current Work: Researcher in cancer treatment, especially brain tumors. Subspecialties: Oncology; Cancer research (medicine). Office: U Ky 800 Rose St Lexington KY 40536

CHINCARINI, GUIDO LUDOVICO, educator, astronomer; b. Venice, Italy, Jan. 24, 1938; came to U.S., 1965; s. Ludovico and Maria-Luisa (Bonaldi) C.; m. Ioanna Manousoyannaki, Mar. 27, 1980; children: Ludwig Boris, Wolfgang Maximillian. M.S., Lyceum of Sci., Venice, 1956; Ph.D., U. Padua, Italy, 1960. Astronomer U. Padua, 1961-68, Lick Obs. U. Calif., 1964-67, U. Bonn., Ger., 1968-69; research assoc. NASA, Houston, 1969-71, Wesleyan U., Conn., 1969-71; research scientist McDonald Obs., Austin, Tex., 1971-74; vis. asst. prof. astronomy U. Okla., 1975, vis. assoc. prof., 1976-77, assoc. prof., 1977-79, prof., 1979—; chmn. astrophysics U. Naples, Italy, 1976; chmn. astronomy U. Bologna, 1976; assoc. European So. Obs., Garching bei Munchen, W.Ger., 1978—. Contbr. articles in field to profl. jours. Served with Nat. Def., 1967-68. NASA grantee, 1980-83; NSF grantee, 1983-84. Mem. Internat. Astron. Union, Am. Astron. Soc., Italian Astron. Soc., Sigma Xi. Current Work: Study of the large scale distribution of matter in the universe; interaction between the interstellar medium of galaxies and intracluster Galaxies. Subspecialties: Cosmology; Optical astronomy. Home: 1223 Cruce St Norman OK 73069 Office: Physics and Astronomy University of Oklahoma Norman OK 73019

CHING, WAI-YIM, physics educator, researcher; b. Shaoshing, China, Oct. 18, 1945; came to U.S., 1969, naturalized, 1980; s. Di-son Ching and Hung-Wong Sung; m. Mon Yin Lung, Dec. 27, 1975; 1 child, Tianyu. B.S., U. Hong Kong, 1969; M.S., La. State U., 1971, Ph.D., 1974. Research assoc., lectr. U. Wis., Madison, 1974-78; asst. prof. to assoc. prof. U. Mo., Kans. City, 1978-84, prof., 1984—; cons. Argonne Nat. Lab., Ill., 1978-82; vis. prof. U. Sci. and Tech. of China, 1983. Contbr. articles to profl. jours. Mem. Am. Phys. Soc., Am. Vacuum Soc., AAAS, Sigma Xi, Sigma Pi Sigma. Current work: Structural, electronic and magnetic properties of crystalline and non-crystalline solids; theoretical condensed matter physics. Subspecialties: Condensed matter physics; Theoretical physics. Home: 1207 W 85th Terrace Kansas City MO 64114 Office: Dept Physics U Mo Kansas City MO 64110

CHINN, KENNETH SAI-KEUNG, research chemist; b. Hong Kong, Dec. 20, 1935; came to U.S., 1951; s. Edward K. and Sinn-tai (Zan) C.; m. Marie L. Leung, Aug. 22, 1964; 1 son, Stephen A. B.S., Washington U., St. Louis, 1957, postgrad., 1957-59. Research chemist U.S. Army Med. Research Ctr., Denver, 1959-68; research biol. Chemist U.S. Naval Med. Research Ctr., Taipei, Taiwan, 1968-74; research chemist U.S. Army, Dugway, Utah., 1974—; cons. in field. Served with U. S. Army, 1959-61. Mem. Am. Nutrition Soc., Colo.-Wyo. Acad. Sci., S.E. Asian Ministers of Edn. Orgn. Current Work: Effects of nutrition regarding nutrient utilization, growth, neurometer development, resistance to infectious disease as well as various aspects of biochemical, clinical and nutritional interaction, various aspects of chemical and biological warfare agents (worldwide). Subspecialties: Biochemistry (medicine); Nutrition (medicine). Home: 499 Country Club Dr Stansbury Park UT 84074 Office: US Army Dugway Proving Ground Dugway UT 84022

CHIODO, LOUIS ANTHONY, neurobiologist, neurophysiologist, educator; b. Detroit, July 13, 1954; s. Louis John and Joann Marie (Weberski) C.; m. Kathleen Ann Cahill, Aug. 31, 1973; 1 child, Louis Michael. B.S. in Psychology, Wayne State U., 1977; M.S. in Neurosci., U. Pitts., 1979, Ph.D. in Neurosci., 1981. NIH postdoctoral fellow in pharmacology Yale U., 1981-82, NIMH postdoctoral fellow in psychiatry, 1982-84; dir. research psychiatry Sinai Hosp., Detroit, 1984—, lab. chief neurophysiology, 1984—; assoc. prof. psychiatry Wayne State U., Detroit, 1984—; dir. Activational Systems, Inc., Warren, Mich. Contbr. articles to profl. jours., chpts. to books. Mem. Soc. for Neurosci., N.Y. Acad. Scis., Internat. Brain Research Orgn., AAAS. Democrat. Current work: Electrophysiological investigation of physiology of mammalian catecholamine-containing neurons and the mode of action of psychoactive substances on them. Subspecialties: Neurophysiology; Neuropharmacology. Home: 867 Lincoln Rd Grosse Pointe MI 48230 Office: Ctr for Cell Biology Sinai Hosp of Detroit 6767 W Outer Dr Detroit MI 48235

CHIORAZZI, NICHOLAS, physician; b. Weehawken, N.J., Oct. 2, 1945; s. Joseph P. and Mary L. (Ippolito) C.; m. Mary Lorraine Dziadowicz, June 19, 1971; children: Anne, Michael. B.A., Coll. Holy Cross, 1966; M.D., Georgetown U., 1970. Diplomate Am. Bd. Internal Medicine. Intern, resident Cornell Cooperating Hosps., N.Y.C., 1970-74; postdoctoral fellow in immunology dept. pathology Harvard U. Med. Sch., Boston, 1974-76; postdoctoral fellow in immunology Rockefeller U., N.Y.C., 1976-77, asst. prof., assoc. physician, 1977-82, assoc. prof., physician, 1982—. Mem. ACP, Am. Assn. Immunologists, Am. Fedn. Clin. Research. Current Work: Clinical investigator of medical problems relating to immunology. Subspecialties: Immunology (medicine); Internal medicine. Home: 18 Bliss Ave Tenafly NJ 07670 Office: Rockefeller U 1230 York Ave New York NY 10021

CHIRLIAN, PAUL M., electrical engineering educator, consultant, author; b. N.Y.C., Apr. 29, 1930; s. Gustave and Leonora (Morrison) C.; m. Barbara E. Schein, Aug. 21, 1961; children—Lisa, Peter. B.E.E., NYU, 1950, M.E.E., 1956, Sc.D. in Engring. Registered profl. engr., N.J., N.Y. Instr. NYU, 1952-56, asst. prof. elec. engring., 1956-60; assoc. prof. elec. engring., Stevens Inst. Tech., Hoboken, N.J., 1960-64, prof. elec. engring., 1964—; cons. in field. Author: Analysis & Design of Integrated Electronic Circuits, 1981; Digital Circuits, 1982; Beginners FORTH, 1983; Introduction to Modula-Z, 1984; Introduction to ADA, 1984; Introduction to C, 1984; and others. Mem. IEEE (fellow), Am. Soc. Elec. Engrs., Nat. Soc. Profl. Engrs. Current work: Digital and analog signal processing, effective band width, transient response. Subspecialties: Electrical engineering; Programming languages. Office: Stevens Inst Tech Hoboken NJ 07030

CHIRNSIDE, ANASTASIA ELIZABETH MCHUGH, agronomist; b. Kansas City, Mo., Oct. 9, 1955; d. George Francis and Claire Jeanne (Baldwin) McHugh; m. Robert Laurence Chirnside, Aug. 13, 1977. B.S., U. Del., 1977, M.S., 1981. Cert. profl. agronomist. Greenhouse asst. Heritage Gardens, Hamorton, Pa., 1978; research asst. U. Del., Newark, 1978, grad. teaching asst., 1978-80, instr., 1981, research assoc., 1980—. Editor: (with others) Graduate Student Handbook, 1979. Contbr. articles to profl. jours. Rep. Citizens Party Del., 1984. Mem. Am. Soc. Agronomy, Northeast Weed Sci. Soc., AAAS, Del. Field Hockey Assn. Current work: Investigation of the effect of agronomic practices, irrigation management practices and animal waste management practices on the quality of ground and surface water. Subspecialty: Agronomy. Home: 1820 Old Newport Rd Wilmington DE 19808 Office: Agrl Engring Dept U Del Newark DE 19717-1303

CHISHOLM, MALCOLM HAROLD, chemistry educator, researcher; b. Bombay, India, Oct. 15, 1945; came to Eng., 1946; s. Angus MacPhail and Gweneth (Robey) C.; m. Cynthia Ann Brown, May 1, 1982; m. Susan Patricia Sage, Oct. 1968 (div. Apr. 1978); children—Calum, Selby, Derek. B.Sc. with spl. honors, London U., 1966, Ph.D. in Inorganic Chemistry, 1969, D.Sc. (hon.), 1980. Session lectr. U. Western Ont., Can., London, 1970-72; asst. prof. Princeton (N.J.) U., 1972-78; assoc. prof. Ind. U., Bloomington, 1978-80, prof. chemistry, 1980-85, disting. prof., 1985—; cons. to industry; sci. councilor to Sen. Birch Bayh of Ind., 1979-80; editorial cons. Inorganic Reactions, 1980—. Am. Editor: Polyhedron Reports, 1982—; editor/author: Reactivity of Metal-Metal Bonds, 1981, Inorganic Chemistry: Toward the 21st Century, 1983; contbr. over 200 articles to sci. jours. Sci. Research Council Eng. fellow, 1966-69; Alfred P. Sloan Found. fellow, 1976-78; Dreyfus Found. Tchr.-scholar, 1979-84; recipient Corday-Morgan medal Royal Soc. Chemistry, Eng., 1979. Mem. Am. Chem. Soc. (Akron sect. award 1981, sec.-treas. Princeton sect. div. inorganic chemistry 1976, alt. councilor So. Ind. sect. 1979—). Club: Ind. Univ. Current Work: Transition metal chemistry; metal-metal bonds; catalysis. Subspecialties: Inorganic chemistry; Organometallics. Home: 900 S High St Bloomington IN 47401 Office: Ind U Dept Chemistry Bloomington IN 47405

CHISHOLM, WILLIAM PRESTON, physical chemist, researcher; b. Fayetteville, Ark., July 29, 1951; s. William Preston and Allie Dupre (Pickell) C. B.S. in Chemistry, U. Ark., 1977; Ph.D., Washington U., 1981. Research assoc. U. Tex., Austin, 1981-82, U. Pitts., 1982-83, U.S. Dept. Energy, Pitts., 1984—. Mem. Am. Chem. Soc., Am. Phys. Soc. Analytical Chemists Pitts., Spectroscopy Soc. Pitts. Current work: Application of ESR to coal chemistry and pollution control, laser and time-resolved spectroscopy, raman spectrosopy, laser photochemistry. Subspecialties: Laser spectroscopy; Electron spin resonance. Office: US Dept Energy PO Box 10940 Pittsburgh PA 15236

CHITSAZ, SIRUS, computer engineer, communications center administrator; b. Tehran, Iran, Oct. 4, 1945; came to U.S., 1963, naturalized, 1975; s. Gholamali and Parvin Dokht (Hendizadeh) C.; m. Kaye Edwards, June 8, 1968; children—Amanda, Jacob. B.S.E.E., U. Mo., 1969; M.S.E.E., N.C. State U., 1975. Sr. engr. ITT Telecom, Raleigh, N.C., 1974-77, tech. staff engr., 1977-78, project mgr., 1978-80, mgr. signal processing group, 1980-81, mgr. engring., 1981-83, cons., 1984—; prof. elec. and computer engring. N.C. State U., 1980—, dir. Ctr. for Communications and Signal Processing, 1983—; cons. Rockwell, Dallas, 1984—, Silicon Gen., Concord, Calif., 1984—, Telco Systems, 1984—, others; mgr. key tech. group ITT, Shelton, Conn., 1981-83; lectr. in field. Contbr. articles to profl. jours. Patentee in field. Lay minister Asbury United Methodist Ch., Raleigh, 1982—. Served to 2d lt., Iranian Air Force, 1969-71. U. Mo., scholar, 1964-69. Mem. IEEE, Tau Beta Pi, Eta Kappa Nu, Pi Mu Epsilon. Current work: Analog and digital communications, architecture and implementation of digital signal processing systems, management and technology planning, technology and information exchanges. Subspecialties: Computer engineering; Telecommunications. Office: NC State U Ctr for Communication and Signal Processing Box 7914 Raleigh NC 27695-7914

CHITTENDEN, MARK EUSTACE, JR., aquatic biologist, educator; b. Jersey City, N.J., July 30, 1939; s. Mark Eustace and Margaret Beaumont (Neil) C.; m. Susan Rae Morrison, Jan. 20, 1968; children: Laura Lynne, Julie Anne. B.A., Hobart Coll., 1960; M.S., Rutgers U., 1965, Ph.D. in Aquatic Biology, 1969. Fisheries biologist N.J. Div. Fish and Game, 1960-64; research fellow dept. environ. sci. Rutgers U., 1964-67, research asst., 1967-68, research assoc. fisheries, 1968-69; asst. prof. marine fisheries Coll. William and Mary and U. Va., 1969-72; assoc. marine scientist Va. Inst. Marine Sci., Gloucester Point, 1969-72; asst. prof. dept. wildlife and fisheries sci. Tex. A&M U., College Station, 1973-77, assoc. prof., 1977-84, prof., 1984—; prof. Va. Inst. Marine Sci., Coll. William and Mary, Gloucester Point, 1984—. Contbr. articles to profl. jours. Mem. Am. Fisheries Soc., Am. Soc. Ichthyologists and Herpetologists, AAAS, Gulf and Caribbean Fisheries Inst., Am. Inst. Fishery Research Biologists. Current Work: Research and teaching in marine fish and fisheries ecology and population dynamics. Subspecialties: Ecology (environmental science); Oceanography. Office: Va Inst Marine Sci Gloucester Point VA 23062

CHITTINENI, CHITTIBABU, research scientist; b. Chinaogirala, India, Oct. 5, 1943; came to U.S., 1972, naturalized, 1981; s. Bapaiah and Seshamma (Paladugu) C.; m. Sreedhana Seshamamba Surapaneni, Feb. 10, 1971; children—Bharati, Sreedevi. B.S. in Elec. Engring. Mysore U., 1966; M.S., Indian Inst. Sci., 1968; Ph.D., U. Calgary, 1970. Researcher, U. Calif., Irvine, 1972-73; sr. engr. Minn. Mining & Mfg. Co., St. Paul, 1974-78; prin. scientist Lockheed Electronics Co., Houston, 1978-81; sr. engring. scientist Conoco, Inc., Ponca City, Okla., 1981—. Contbr. articles to profl. jours. Mem. IEEE, (sr.), Soc. Exploration Geophysicists. Republican. Hindu. Current work: Research in signal processing. Subspecialties: Graphics, image processing, and pattern recognition; Remote sensing (geoscience). Home: 2721 Homestead Ponca City OK 74604 Office: Conoco Inc PO Box 1267 Ponca City OK 74602

CHIU, JEN-FU, biochemist, educator; b. Tungshi, Taiwan, China, Sept. 30, 1940; came to U.S., 1972, naturalized, 1979; s. Kuo-Fun and Chien-Leon (Yu) C.; m. Lucia Chi-Kai, May 30, 1970; children: Rosaleen I-Hsuen, Cynthia I-Tyng. B.Pharm., Taipei Med. Coll., 1964; M.Sc. in Biochemistry, Nat. Taiwan U., 1967; Ph.D., U. B.C., Can., 1972. Project investigator M.D. Anderson Hosp. and Tumor Inst., Houston, 1972-74; asst. biochemist, 1974-75; asst. prof. biochemistry Vanderbilt U., Nashville, 1975-78; assoc. prof. biochemistry U. Vt., Burlington, 1978—, dir. biochemistry grad. studies, 1982—. Contbr. articles to profl. jours. Can. Med. Research Council student, 1968-72; Rosalie B. Hite fellow, 1972-73; NIH grantee, 1975—. Mem. Am. Soc. for Cell Biology, Am. Assn. Cancer Research, Can. Biochem. Soc., Biophys. Soc., Am. Soc. Biol. Chemists, Sigma Xi. Current Work: Biochemistry of chromatin and gene regulation; biochemistry of cancer. To study the alteration of genome organization and gene expression in cells during neoplastic transformation by using hybridoma and recombinant DNA techniques. Subspecialties: Gene actions; Cancer research (medicine). Home: 65 East Terr South Burlington VT 05401 Office: Dept Biochemistry U Vt Coll Medicin Burlington VT 05405

CHIU, KAO DING, civil engineer; b. Berlin, Oct. 24, 1935; s. Chin Chuen and Swei King (Yeh) C.; came to U.S., 1960, naturalized, 1971; m. Yu Shih, Nov. 11, 1962; children—Christopher S.H., Angela S.C. B.S., Nat. Taiwan U., Taipei, Republic of China, 1958; M.S., U. Minn., 1961; postgrad. Columbia U., 1963-66, U. Wash., 1967-68. Registered profl. engr., N.Y., Taiwan. Design engr. Weiskopf & Pickworth, N.Y.C., 1961-62; design engr. Ebasco Services, Inc., N.Y.C., 1962-66, assoc. cons. engr., 1970—; sr. engr. Boeing Co., Seattle, 1966-70. Contbr. articles to tech. jours. Mem. Earthquake Engring. Research Inst., Chinese Civil Engrs. Assn. Current work: Structural research in static and dynamic behavior, composite materials, earthquake related topics. Subspecialties: Structural engineering; Theoretical and applied mechanics. Home: 42 Adams St Edison NJ 08820 Office: Ebasco Services Inc 2 World Trade Ctr New York NY 10048

CHIU, KUANG-YI, electrical engineer, researcher; b. Kaohsiung, Taiwan, Nov. 3, 1943; came to U.S., 1969; s. Chi-Chou and Jung (Meh) C.; m. Janet Chen-Yuan, Feb. 20, 1972; children—Tina Ju, Andrew Ting. B.E.E., Nat. Cheng Kung U., Republic of China, 1966; M.E.E., Nat. Chiao Tung U., Hsinchu, Republic of China, 1968; Ph.D. in Materials Sci., U. So. Calif., 1974. Engr., Northrop Co., Los Angeles, 1973-77, project leader, 1977-79; engr. Hewlett Packard Labs, Palo Alto, Calif., 1979-82, mgr., 1982—; cons. IEEE Electron Device Soc., Santa Clara, Calif. Mem. IEEE, Eta Kappa Nu. Current work: Very large scale integration process develoment. Home: 609 Arastradero Rd Palo Alto CA 94306 Office: Hewlett Packard Labs 3500 Deer Creek Rd Palo Alto CA 94304

CHIUTEN, DELIA FUNG SHE, internist, med. educator; b. Philippines, Apr. 24, 1943; came to U.S., 1972; d. Juan and Constancia (Fungshe) C. B.S., U. San Carlos, Philippines, 1966; M.D., U. Philippines, 1971. Resident in surgery Victoria (B.C., Can.) Vets. Hosp., 1972; rotating intern Mt. Sinai Hosp. Services, City Hosp. at Elmhurst, N.Y., 1972-73, resident in medicine, 1973-75, chief resident in medicine, 1975; fellow in hematology Montefiore Hosp. and Med. Center, Bronx, N.Y., 1975-76; fellow in oncology Balt. Cancer Research Center, Nat. Cancer Inst., U. Md. Hosp., 1976-77; vis. asso. Nat. Cancer Inst., NIH, Bethesda, Md., 1977-79; faculty asso. and instr. in devel. therapeutics U. Tex. System Cancer Center M.D. Anderson Hosp. and Tumor Inst., Houston, 1979-80, asst. internist, asst. prof. medicine, 1980—; cons. Office Health Resources Opportunity Program, USPHS, HEW, 1981-82. Mem. Pan Asian Women's Orgn., Am. Soc. Clin. Oncology, Am. Assn. Cancer Research, Internat. Assn. Study Lung Cancer, Am. Fedn. Cancer Research, AAAS, Am. Soc. Internal Medicine, Am. Soc. Microbiology, Tex. Soc. Internal Medicine.

Current Work: Evaluation of new antitumor drugs in lung cancer and other tumors in man. Subspecialties: Cancer research (medicine); Chemotherapy. Office: 6723 Bertner Ave Houston TX 77030

CHO, ARTHUR KENJI, pharmacologist, educator; b. Oakland, Calif, Nov. 7, 1928; s. Iwao and Mary Yoshiko (Takata) C.; m. Sachiko Yoshida, Aug. 16, 1953; children: David, Nancy. B.S., U. Calif., Berkeley, 1952; M.S., Oreg. State U., 1953; Ph.D., UCLA, 1958. Research chemist Don Baxter Inc., Glendale, Calif., 1961-65; research pharmacologist Nat. Heart Inst., Bethesda, Md., 1965-70; from asso. to prof. dept. pharmacology UCLA, 1970—. Author abstracts, articles and book chpts. on drug metabolism, neurochemistry and medicinal chemistry. Mem. Am. Chem. Soc., Am. Soc. Pharmacology and Exptl. Therapeutics, Soc. Toxicology. Current Work: Drug metabolism, mechanisms of nitrogen oxidation, adrenergic mechanisms. Subspecialties: Molecular pharmacology; Medicinal chemistry. Home: 3393 Colbert Ave Los Angeles CA 90066 Office: Dept Pharmacology U Calif Los Angeles CA 90024

CHO, SOUNG MOO, energy company executive, engineering educator; b. Seoul, Korea, Oct. 1, 1937; came to U.S., 1962, naturalized, 1975; s. Song-Nyung and Mi-Ok (Lee) C.; m. Ki Sun Kim, Mar. 6, 1965; children: Rose, Richard, Karen, Grace, Christopher, Andrew. B.S., Seoul Nat. U., 1960; M.S., U. Calif.-Berkeley, 1964, Ph.D., 1967. Registered profl. engr., N.J. Researcher Korean Atomic Energy Research inst., Seoul, 1960-61; research asst./specialist U. Calif.-Berkeley, 1962-67; engring. specialist Garrett Corp., Los Angeles, 1967-69; staff cons. Energy Tech. Engring. Ctr. div. Rockwell Internat., Canoga Park, Calif., 1969-73; engring. mgr. Foster Wheeler Energy Corp., Livingston, N.J., 1973-80; dir. engring. Foster Wheeler Energy Applications, Inc., 1980—; adj. prof. Stevens Inst. Tech., Hoboken, N.J., 1978—, Fairleigh Dickinson U., Teaneck, N.J., 1975—; cons. lectr. to various univs., utilities, profl. socs., 1975—. Assoc. editor Applied Mechanics Revs. Contbr. articles to profl. jours.; reviewer various jours. Recipient Republic Korea Presdl. award, 1960; Fulbright travel scholar, 1962. Mem. ASME (exec. com. nuclear engring. div. 1982—, chmn. nuclear heat exchanger com. 1980-82), Am. Nuclear Soc. Current Work: Liquid metal fast breeder reactor engineering, advanced heat transfer device design, thermal/fluid science education. Subspecialties: Mechanical engineering; Nuclear engineering. Home: 1051 Vail Rd Parsippany NJ 07054 Office: Foster Wheeler Energy Applications Inc 110 S Orange Ave Livingston NJ 07039

CHOATE, JERRY RONALD, zoologist, museum director, educator; b. Bartlesville, Okla., Mar. 21, 1943; s. C.W. and Alice Joyce (Cox) Marks; m. Rosemary Fidelis Walker, Apr. 13, 1963; 1 son, Judd Randolph. B.A. in Biology, Pittsburg (Kans.) State U., 1965; Ph.D. in Zoology, U. Kans.-Lawrence, 1969. Cert. wildlife biologist. Asst. prof. U. Conn.-Storrs, 1969-71; lectr. Yale U., New Haven, 1970; asst. prof. Ft. Hays State U., Hays, Kans., 1971-76, assoc. prof., 1976-80, prof. dept. zoology, 1980—, dir. museums, 1980—; cons. Kans. Fish and Game, 1975—, Assn. Systematics Collections, Lawrence, 1976—, Sunflower Electric Coop., Hays, 1980. Contbr. articles to sci. jours. Coach Little League baseball, Hays, 1980, Jr. League football, 1979, 80. NSF grantee, 1967-82; recipient grants, research contracts various orgns. and agencies. Mem. Am. Soc. Mammalogists (rec. sec. 1974-85), Assn. Systematics Collections (sec. 1976-78), Southwestern Assn. Naturalists (pres. 1979-80), other profl. assns. Republican. Current Work: Systematics, evolution, biogeography of mammals. Subspecialties: Systematics; Evolutionary biology. Home: Route 1 Victoria KS 67671 Office: Fort Hays State Univ 600 Park St Hays KS 67601

CHOI, MICHAEL KAM-WAH, mechanical engineer; b. Baoan, Quangdong, China, Aug. 16, 1952; came to U.S., 1972; s. Ying-Loi and Kan-Hau (Yuen) C. Sc.B. with honors, magna cum laude, Brown U., 1976; M.S.M.E., MIT, 1978, Engr., 1979. Research asst. MIT, Cambridge, Mass., 1977-79; sr. research engr. Sci. Applications Internat. Corp., McLean, Va., 1979—. Contbr. articles to profl. jours. Reviewer Solar Energy Jour., 1983—. Mem. ASME, Am. Solar Energy Soc., Sigma Xi, Tau Beta Pi. Current work: Computer modeling, simulation and systems analysis of active solar heating and cooling systems. Subspecialties: Solar energy; Mechanical engineering. Home: 11309 Gatesborough Ln Reston VA 22091 Office: Sci Applications Internat Corp 1710 Goodridge Dr McLean VA 22102

CHOI, SEUNG HOON, nuclear engineer, consultant; b. Korea, Aug. 12, 1943; came to U.S., 1973, naturalized, 1981; s. Maeng Soon and Hwa Jin (Lee) C.; m. Carol Changsoon Kim, Nov. 28, 1970; children: Tina Eunhye, Joanne Mindulla, Brian Myongwon. B.S., Han Yang U., Seoul, Korea, 1969; cert., Westinghouse Nuclear Tng. Sch., Zion, Ill., 1974; postgrad., Northwestern U., 1974-78. Registered profl. engr., Mich., N.H. Nuclear engr. Korea Electric Power Corp., Seoul, 1969-73; nuclear process engr. Sargent & Lundy Engrs., Chgo., 1974-77; nuclear systems engr. Gilbert/Commonwealth Co., Jackson, Mich., 1977-79; sr. engr. Yankee Atomic Electric Co., Framingham, Mass., 1979—. Served with Korean Army, 1964-65. Mem. ASME, Am. Nuclear Soc. Current Work: Nuclear power plant engring., design and operation. Subspecialties: Nuclear engineering; Hazardous waste disposal. Home: 13 Kristyn Dr Northboro MA 01532 Office: 1671 Worcester Rd Framingham MA 01701

CHOI, SUNG CHIL, biostatistics educator; b. Seoul, Korea, Dec. 26, 1931; came to U.S., 1955, naturalized, 1962; m. Elizabeth P. Park, Aug. 17, 1967; 1 child, Tina. B.S., U. Wash., 1957, M.S., 1960; Ph.D., UCLA, 1966. Engr. Boeing Co., Seattle, 1959-62; asst. prof. biostats. Calif. State U.-Long Beach, 1964-66, Wash. U., St. Louis, 1967-71, assoc. prof., 1971-78, prof., 1978, Med. Coll. Va., Richmond, 1978—; cons. Eli Lilly and Co., Indpls., 1976—, NIH, 1978—, ACS, Chgo., 1984—. Author: Applied Statistics in Science, 1978. Contbr. articles to profl. jours. NIH grantee, 1978—, 84—. Mem. Am. Statis. Assn., Biometric Soc., Sigma Xi. Current work: Teaching, research and consulting in biostatistics. Subspecialties: Biostatistics; Statistics.

CHOLVIN, NEAL ROBERT, educator; b. Chippewa Falls, Wis., Sept. 8, 1928; s. Elmer Frank and Olympia (Elkow) C.; m. Valerie Perkins, June 25, 1957; children—Brooke Diane, Craig Steven, Mark Douglas. B.S., Wayne State U., 1949; D.V.M., Mich. State U., 1954, M.S., 1958; Ph.D., Iowa State U., 1961. From instr. to asso. prof. dept. vet. surgery and medicine Mich. State U., 1955-63; mem. faculty Iowa State U., 1959—, USPHS postdoctoral research fellow, 1960-61, prof. vet. physiology and pharmacology, 1963—, prof. biomed. engring., 1963—, chmn. biomed. engring. program, 1963-74, 80—, chmn. dept. vet. anatomy, pharmacology and physiology, 1974-79; USPHS spl. research fellow U. Wash., 1971-72. Asso. editor: Lab. Animal Sci, 1967-75. Mem. Am. Physiol. Soc., Soc., AAAS, Am. Heart Assn. (pres. Iowa affiliate 1978-80), Am. Vet. Med. Assn., Sigma Xi. Research in cardiopulmonary control mechanisms, hemodynamics, vascular dynamics. Current Work: Surgical efficay studies on experimental animals to support applications to FDA for markering approval of surgical devices; biomechanics research on wound healing and fastening. Subspecialties: Biomedical engineering; Surgery (veterinary medicine). Home: 1167 Delaware Dr Bridgewater NJ 08807

CHOMA, JOHN, JR., electrical engineering educator, consultant; b. Sewickley, Pa., Nov. 6, 1941; s. John and Katherine (Nelick) C.; m. Lorraine Mary Stante, Sept. 22, 1976. B.S.E.E. magna cum laude, U. Pitts., 1963, M.S.E.E., 1965, Ph.D. in Elec. Engring., 1969. Teaching asst. elec. engring. U. Pitts., 1963-65, asst. instr., 1965-67, instr., 1967-69; assoc. prof. elec. engring. Calif. State U.-Sacramento, 1969-71; Ill. Inst. Tech., Chgo., 1971-72; mem. tech. staff Santa Clara div. Hewlett-Packard Co., Calif., 1972-75; assoc. prof. U. Pa., Phila., 1975-76; sect. head vulnerability and hardness lab. TRW, Redondo Beach, Calif., 1976-78, sr. staff engr. Microelectronics Ctr., 1978-82; lectr. U. So. Calif., Los Angeles, 1980-81, vis. assoc. prof., 1981-83, assoc. prof., 1983—; lectr. U. Santa Clara, 1972-75, UCLA, 1977-81; sr. lectr. Calif. Inst. tech., 1978-81; cons. microelectronics; active profl. confs.; presentations in field. Author: Electrical Networks: Theory and Analysis, 1985; also numerous articles, papers. Recipient Teaching award U. Pa., 1976, Teaching award UCLA, 1980, 81, Students' award UCLA, 1982, Teaching award U. So. Calif. chpt. Tau-Beta Pi, 1983, Teaching award TRW/U. So. Calif., 1984, Mortar Bd. Teaching award U. So. Calif., 1984. Mem. IEEE (sr., mem. cirs. and systems, solid-state cirs. and electron devices groups, assoc. editor Cirs. and Systems 1974-75, editor 1975-77), N.Y. Acad. Sci., Sigma Xi, Phi Eta Sigma, Eta Kappa Nu. Current work: Metallization parasitics in high-speed integrated circuits; programmable analog arrays; CMOS/MOS modeling; high-speed custom IC design; radiation hardening of integrated circuits. Subspecialties: Integrated circuits; Microelectronics. Office: U So Calif Univ Park Los Angeles CA 90089-0271

CHOPPIN, GREGORY ROBERT, chemist; b. Eagle Lake, Tex., Nov. 9, 1927; s. Gilbert P. and Nellie M. C.; m. Ann Mary Warner, June 9, 1951; children: Denise, Suzanne, Paul, Nadine. B.S. maxima cum laude, Loyola U., New Orleans, 1949, D.Sc. (hon.), 1969; Ph.D., U. Tex., Austin, 1953; D.Tc. (hon.), Chalmers Inst. Tech., Goteborg, Sweden, 1985. Research scientist Radiation Lab., U. Calif., Berkeley, 1956-59; prof. chemistry Fla. State U., Tallahassee, 1956—, chmn. dept., 1968-77; research scientist Centre d'Etude Nucleaire, Mol, Belgium, 1962-63; vis. scientist European Transuranium Inst., Karlsruhe, W.Ger., 1979-80. Author: Experimental Nuclear Chemistry, 1961, Nuclei and Radioactivity, 1964, (with B. Jaffe) Chemistry, 1965, 3d edit., 1973, (with L. Summerlin), 1978, 2d edit., 1982, (with R. Johnson) Introductory Chemistry, 1972, (with R. Rydberg) Nuclear Chemistry, 1980; contbr. articles in field to physics and chemistry jours. Served with U.S. Army, 1946-48. Recipient Mfg. Chemist Nat. award, 1979; Alexander von Humboldt Stiftung U.S. sr. sci. award, 1979. Mem. Am. Chem. Soc. (Fla. sect. award 1973, So. Chemist award Memphis sect. 1971, award in nuclear chemistry 1985), AAAS, Sigma Xi. Current Work: The behavior of the lanthanide and actinide elements in aqueous systems, the complexation and separation of these elements and their behavior in the environment. Subspecialties: Inorganic chemistry; Nuclear fission. Home: 3290 Longleaf Dr Tallahassee FL 32304 Office: Dept Chemistry Fla State U Tallahassee FL 32306

CHOPPIN, PURNELL WHITTINGTON, virologist, physician; b. Baton Rouge, July 4, 1929; s. Arthur Richard and Eunice (Bolin) C.; m. Joan Harriet Macdonald, Oct. 17, 1959; 1 dau., Kathleen Marie. Student, La. State U., 1946-53, M.D., 1953. Cert. Am. Bd. Internal Medicine. Intern Barnes Hosp., St. Louis, 1953-54, resident in medicine, 1957-58; fellow Rockefeller U., N.Y.C., 1957-59, research assoc., 1959-60, asst. prof., 1960-62, 1962-64, assoc. prof., 1964-70, prof., 1970—, Leon Hess prof., 1980—, v.p. acad. programs, 1983—, dean grad. studies, 1985—, assoc. physician, 1960-62; assoc. physician, 1962-64, physician, 1964-70, sr. physician, 1970-85, vice pres. acad. programs, 1983-85, dean grad. studies, 1985; v.p., chief sci. officer Howard Hughes Med. Inst., 1985—; chmn. virology study sect. NIH; mem. nat. adv. council Nat. Inst. Allergy and Infectious Diseases, NIH; mem. bd. sci. cons. Meml. Sloan Kettering Cancer Center. Contbr. articles in field to profl. jours. Served with USAF, 1954-56. Nat. Found. fellow, 1954-56; grantee in field; recipient Howard Taylor Ricketts award U. Chgo., 1978, Waksman award Nat. Acad. Scis., 1984. Mem. Nat. Acad. Scis. (Waksman award for excellence in microbiology 1984), Assn. Am. Physicians, Am. Clin. Research, Am. Soc. Microbiology, Am. Soc. Cell Biology, Am. Assn. Immunologists, Soc. Exptl. Biology Medicine, Harvey Soc., Infectious Diseases Soc. Am., Royal Soc. Medicine Found. (dir. 1979—), Am. Soc. Virology (pres. 1985-86), Club: Century (N.Y.C.). Current Work: Virus structure, replication, and mechanisms of pathogenesis virology, infectious diseases, membrane biology. Subspecialties: Virology (biology); Infectious diseases. Home: 530 E 72d St Apt 7G New York NY 10021 Office: The Rockefeller University 1230 York Ave New York NY 10021

CHOPRA, DHARAM PAL, cell biologist researcher; b. Punjab, India, Feb. 2, 1944; came to U.S., 1971; s. Madan Lal and Kaushlya A. C.; m. Pearl Gurnani, Dec. 8, 1968; 1 child, Paul. B.Sc., U. Delhi, India, 1963; M.Sc., U. London, 1967; Ph.D., Univ. Newcastle, Eng., 1971. Asst. prof. Temple U., Phila., 1971-74; sr. scientist So. Research Inst., Birmingham, Ala., 1974-81, sect. head, 1981—; cons. Am. Tissue Type Culture Collection, Bethesda, Md., 1980—. Mem. AAAS, Am. Assn. Cancer Research, Tissue Culture Assn., Am. Assn. Cell Biology. Subspecialties: Cell biology (medicine); Cell and tissue culture. Office: Southern Research Inst 2000 9th Ave S Birmingham AL 35255

CHOU, ALBERT CHUNG-HO, biochemistry educator; b. Hunan, China, Mar. 14, 1944; came to U.S., 1967; s. Cheng-chin and Liang (Chou) C.; m. Iris Ching-ho-Lee, Dec. 19, 1970; 1 dau.: Lynne. B.S., Nat. Taiwan U., 1966; M.S., W.Va. U., 1969; Ph.D., Mich. State U., 1973. Research assoc. St. Louis U., 1975-78, asst. research prof., 1978-80; asst. prof. nutrition Tulane U., New Orleans, 1980—; asst. dir. research Touro Infirmary, New Orleans, 1980—. Mem. Am. Soc. Biol. Chemists, Am. Fedn. Clin. Research, Sigma Xi. Current Work: Role of ferriheme in hemolytic anemias; vitamin E and iron metabolism; hormone and drug receptors; purification and characterization of enzyme. Subspecialties: Biochemistry (medicine); Hematology. Home: 7254 Cornell Ave Saint Louis MO 63130 Office: Tulane Univ Dept Nutrition 1430 Tulane Ave New Orleans LA 70112

CHOU, IIH-NAN, cell biologist, biochemist; b. Taiwan, China, Apr. 12, 1943; came to U.S., 1967, naturalized, 1979; s. Chou Ming-Ho and Yeh Hwang-Chiao; m. Denise Kuo-Howere, Sept. 8, 1968; children: Jerome, Wendy. B.S., Nat. Taiwan U., 1966; Ph.D., U. Ill., 1971. Instr. Harvard Med. Sch., Boston, 1975-77, asst. prof., 1977-80; asst. biochemist Mass. Gen. Hosp., Boston, 1977-80; asst. prof. Boston U. Sch. Medicine, 1980-82, assoc. prof., 1982—; also mem. Hubert H. Humphrey Cancer Research Ctr. Contbr. articles to sci. jours. Recipient Nat. Research Service award NIH, 1974-75; NIH postdoctoral fellow, 1972-74; Am. Cancer Soc. scholar, 1977-80. Mem. Am. Soc. Cell Biology, Am. Soc. Microbiology, N.Y. Acad. Scis., AAAS. Current Work: Laboratory research in cell biology and environmental toxicology; role of the cytoskeleton in growth control and mechanisms of toxicity of environmental hazardous agents. Teaching graduate course in cell biology and medical microbiology laboratory. Subspecialties: Cell and tissue culture; Cancer research (medicine). Home: 151 Albemarle Rd Newton MA 02160 Office: Dept Microbiology Boston U Sch Medicine Boston MA 02118

CHOU, SHELLEY NIEN-CHUN, neurosurgeon, medical educator; b. Chekiang, China, Feb. 6, 1924; s. Shelley P. and Tse-tsun (Chao) C.; m. Jolene Johnson, Nov. 24, 1956 (div. 1977); children: Shelley T., Dana, Kerry; m. remarried, 1979. B.S., St. John's U., Shanghai, China, 1946; M.D., U. Utah, 1949; M.S., U. Minn., 1954, Ph.D., 1964. Diplomate: Am. Bd. Neurol. Surgery (mem. bd.). Resident U. Minn. Hosps., 1950-55, practice medicine, specializing in neurosurgery, Salt Lake City, 1955-58, Bethesda, Md., 1959, Mpls., 1960—; clin. asst. Coll. Medicine U. Utah, 1956-58; vis. scientist Nat. Insts. Neurol. Diseases and Blindness NIH, 1959; mem. faculty U. Minn., 1960—, asso. prof. neurosurgery, 1965-68, prof. neurosurgery, 1968—, head dept. neurosurgery, 1974—; mem. resident rev. com. for neurosurgery Am. Bd. Neurol. Surgery, 1984. Contbr. numerous articles to profl. jours.; Publs. on studies of intracranial lesions using radioactive angiography techniques; malformations of cerebral vasculature; neurol. dysfunctions of urinary bladder. Mem. AMA, ACS (adv. council for neurosurgery 1981—), Congress Neurol. Surgery, Soc. Neurol. Surgeons (pres. 1978-79), Am. Acad. Neurol. Surgery, Soc. Nuclear Medicine, Am. Assn. Neurol. Surgeons (bd. dirs. 1980-83, v.p. 1984-85), Neurosurg. Soc. N.Am. (pres. 1977-78), N.Y. Acad. Medicine, Forum Univ. Neurosurgeons (pres. 1968-69), AAAS, Phi Rho Sigma. Current Work: Cerebrovasospasn, cerebral andeurysms, cerebral A-V malformation,spinal deformity, bladder physiology. Subspecialties: Neurosurgery; Neurophysiology. Home: 12 S Long Lake Trail North Oaks MN 55110 Office: B-590 Mayo Meml 420 SE Delaware St Minneapolis MN 55455

CHOU, SHYAN-YIH, nephrologist, internist, researcher; b. Taipei, Taiwan, Aug. 7, 1941; came to U.S., 1968, naturalized, 1980; s. En-Truen and Lin-Oh (Lin) C.; m. Wanda Louie, Dec. 7, 1974; children: Janet, Denise. M.D., Nat. Taiwan U., Taipei, 1966. Diplomate: Am. Bd. Internal Medicine. Intern Brookdale Hosp. Med. Center, Bklyn., 1968-69, resident in Medicine, 1969-70, Nat. Kidney Found. fellow, 1970-73, asst. attending physician, 1973-74, assoc. attending physician, 1974-77, attending physician, 1977—; physician-in-charge (Nephrology Lab.), 1977—; asst. prof. medicine SUNY-Downstate Med. Center, Bklyn., 1978-84, assoc. prof. medicine, 1984—. Contbr. sci. articles to profl. publs. Fellow ACP; mem. Am. Soc. Nephrology, Internat. Soc. Nephrology, Am. Fedn. Clin. Research, Am. Heart Assn., AAAS, Am. Physiol. Soc. Current Work: Hormonal factors regulating medullary blood flow; role of medullary hemodynamics in regulating renal sodium excretion. Subspecialties: Nephrology; Comparative physiology. Office: Brookdale Hosp Med Center Nephrology Div Linden Blvd and Brookdale Plaza Brooklyn NY 11212

CHOU, TING-CHAO, biochemical pharmacologist, theoretical biologist; b. Hsin-Chu, Hu-Ko, Taiwan, China, Sept. 9, 1938; came to U.S., 1965, naturalized, 1976; s. Chao-Yun and Sheng-Mei (Chen) C.; m. Dorothy Tsui-Shin Tseng, June 26, 1965; children: Joseph Hsin-I; Julia Hsin-Ya. B.S., Kaoshiung Med. Coll, Taiwan, 1961; M.S., Nat. Taiwan U., Taipei, 1965; Ph.D., Yale U., 1970. Postdoctoral fellow Johns Hopkins U. Sch. Medicine, Balt., 1969-72; asst. prof. biology Cornell U. Grad. Sch. Med. Scis., N.Y.C., 1972-77, asst. prof. pharmacology, 1977-79, assoc. prof. pharmacology and therapeutics, 1979—; assoc. mem. Sloan-Kettering Inst. Cancer Research, Meml. Sloan-Kettering Cancer Center, N.Y.C., 1979—, assoc., 1972-78; research asst. pharmacology Yale U. Sch. Medicine, New Haven, 1969; teaching asst. pharmacology Nat. Taiwan U. Coll. Medicine, Taipei, 1964-65. Nat. Cancer Inst. research grantee NIH, USPHS, 1975-78, 80-83, 83—; cancer research grantee Am. Cancer Soc., 1976-80. Mem. AAAS, Am. Assn. Cancer Research, Am. Soc. Pharmacology and Exptl. Therapeutics, Am. Soc. Preventive Oncology, Am. Soc. Biol. Chemists, Sigma Xi. Club: Yale (Princeton, N.J.). Current Work: Pharmacology of cancer chemotherapeutic agents, metabolism of drugs, mechanism of action of drugs, evaluation of selective effects and toxicity of drugs, theoretical biology of dose-effect relationships, receptor theory, evaluation of synergism, antagonism and additivism of multiple drugs, and low-dose risk assessment of toxic substances and carcinogens. Subspecialties: Molecular pharmacology; Cancer research (medicine). Office: Sloan-Kettering Inst Cancer Research 1275 York Ave New York NY 10021

CHOUDARY, PRABHAKARA VELAGAPUDI, molecular geneticist; b. Guntur, India, Dec. 20, 1948; came to U.S., 1976; s. Venkata Narasimha Velagapudi and Annapurna (Jampala) Rao; m. Kothapalli Durgesh Nandini, Aug. 9, 1978; 1 child, Vikram. B.Sc., Andhra U., Waltair, India, 1966; M.Sc., U. Bombay, India, 1969, D.Sc. candidate, Ph.D., Indian Inst. of Sci., Bangalore, 1975. Research scholar Indian Inst. Sci., 1970-75, DST project assoc., 1975-76; postdoctoral fellow Pa. State U., University Park, 1976-77; research assoc. Yale U., New Haven, 1977-80; vis. scientist U. Wis., Madison, 1980-81; sr. staff fellow, prin. investigator NIH, Bethesda, Md., 1981—; cons. Agrigenetics Corp., Denver, 1981, Intersearch Corp., Phila., 1984. Recipient Disting. Scientist award Telugu Assn. N. Am., 1985. Patentee in field, Fellow Sigma Xi; mem. Am. Soc. Human Genetics, AAAS, Am. Soc. Microbiology, Am. Soc. Biol. Chemists. Current work: Gene cloning transfer and expression, gene therapy, DNA polymorphisms, recombinant DNA products. Subspecialties: Genetics and genetic engineering (biology); Genetics and genetic engineering (medicine). Home: 1901 Winexburg Ct Silver Spring MD 20906 Office: NIH-10/4N 248 Bethesda MD 20205

CHOUDHURY, ABDUL LATIF, physics educator; b. Dhaka, Bangaldesh, Jan. 1, 1933; came to U.S., 1966, naturalized, 1975; s. Abdur Rub and Arefa Khatun C.; m. Jutta Kausch, Nov. 4, 1960; children—Kadjol, Marcel. B.Sc., Dhaka U., 1953, M.Sc., 1954; Dr. rer. nat., Freie U., Berlin, 1960. Sr. lectr. Dhaka U., 1961-66; assoc. prof. Elizabeth City State Coll., (N.C.), 1966-68, assoc. prof., 1969-73, prof., 1973—; sr. lectr. Dacca U., 1968, reader, 1969; cons. Nat Bur. Standards, Washington, 1963-65. Contbr. articles to profl. jours. East Bengal Govt. Merit scholar, 1950-53; W. German Govt. exchange scholar, 1955-58; Fritz Haber Inst. research fellow, 1960; Imperial Coll. research fellow London, 1960-61. Mem. Am. Phys. Soc., Bangladesh Phys. Soc. (life), AAUP (v.p. 1984—). Current work: Fermion mass determination from gravity induces super symmetric potentials; symmetry breaking mechanism for GUT theories. Subspecialties: Theoretical physics; Particle physics. Home: 605 Forest Park Rd Elizabeth City NC 27909 Office: Dept Physics Elizabeth City State U Parkview Dr Elizabeth City NC 27909

CHOUDHURY, DEO CHAND, physicist; b. Darbhanga, India, Feb.1, 1926, came to U.S., 1955, s. Kapleshwar and Gutainya (Choudhury) C.; m. Annette Patricia DuBois, Aug. 3, 1963; 1 child, Raj. B.Sc., U. Calcutta, India, 1944, M.Sc., 1946; Ph.D., UCLA, 1959. Research fellow Niels Bohr Inst., Copenhagen, 1952-55; research asst. physics U. Rochester, N.Y., 1955-56; research teaching asst. physics UCLA, 1956-59; asst. prof. U. Conn., Storrs, 1959-62; assoc. prof. Poly. Inst. N.Y., Bklyn., 1962-67, prof. physics, 1967—; vis. asst. physicistBrookHaven Nat. Lab., summer 1960; vis. physicist Oak Ridge Nat. Lab., summer 1962; Niels Bohr Inst., Copenhagen, 1978-79. Contbr. articles to profl. jours., chpt. to book. Govt. India Council Sci. and Indsl. Research scholar U. Calcutta Coll. Sci., 1947-52. Mem. Am. Phys. Soc., N.Y. Acad. Scis., AAAS, Indian Phys. Soc., Sigma Xi, Sigma Pi Sigma. Current work: Research on problems of nuclear structure, nuclear reactions, high energy scattering. Subspecialties: Nuclear physics; Theoretical physics. Home: 90 Gold St New York NY 10038 Office: Poly Inst NY Dept Physics 333 Jay St Brooklyn NY 11201

CHOVNICK, ARTHUR, geneticist; b. N.Y.C., Aug. 2, 1927; s. Herman and Fannie (Hutkin) C.; m. Elinor Joy Mosher, June 7, 1949; children: Lisa, Benjamin. A.B., Ind. U., 1949, M.A., 1950; Ph.D., Ohio State U., 1953. Instr. zoology U. Conn., 1953-57, asst. prof., 1957-59; asst. dir. Biol. Lab., Cold Spring Harbor, N.Y., 1959-60, lab. dir., 1960-62; prof. genetics and cell biology U.Conn., 1962—; mem. genetics study sect. NIH, 1972-76. Assoc. editor Genetics, 1972—, Genetical Research, 1981—. Mem. Genetics Soc. Am. (treas., bd. dirs. 1981-83). Current Work: Research in organization and control of gene expression during development in higher organisms. Subspecialties: Intragenic recombination; Gene conversion. Office: Dept Molecular and Cell Biology U Conn Storrs CT 06268

CHOW, CHUEN-YEN, aerospace engineering educator; b. Nanchang, Kiangsi, China, Dec. 5, 1932; came to U.S., 1956, naturalized, 1972; s. Pan-Tao and Huey-Ching (Yang) C.; m. Julianna H.S. Chen, June 26, 1960; children: Chi Hui, Chi Tu, Chi An. B.S.M.E., Nat. Taiwan U., Taipei, 1954; M.S.A.E., Purdue U., 1958; S.M. in Aeros. and Astros, M.I.T., 1961; Ph.D., U. Mich., 1964. Asst. prof. U. Notre Dame, 1965-67, assoc. prof., 1967-68; assoc. prof. aerospace engring. scis. U. Colo., Boulder, 1968-76, prof., 1976—; Disting. Vis. prof. U.S. Air Force Acad., 1979-80. Author: (with A.M. Kuethe) Foundations of Aerodynamics, 3d edit, 1976, An Introduction to Computational Fluid Mechanics, 1979; contbr. articles to profl. jours. USAF grantee, 1980—; NASA grantee, 1982—; NSF grantee, 1967-68, 71-73. Mem. AIAA, Sigma Xi, Sigma Gamma Tau. Current Work: Fluid dynamics, computational fluid mechanics, unsteady aerodynamics. Subspecialty: Aeronautical engineering. Home: 345 Seminole Dr Boulder CO 80303 Office: Dept Aerospace Engring Sci U Colo Campus Box 429 Boulder CO 80309

CHOW, PAO-LIU, mathematics educator, researcher; b. Fujian, China, Nov. 28, 1936; came to U.S., 1962; s. Fa-cheng and Tse-jung (Lin) C.; m. Chien-Jen Huo, June 19, 1965; children: Lawrence, Lily. B.S., Nat. Cheng-Kung U., Taiwan, 1959; M.S., Rensselaer Poly. Inst., 1964, Ph.D., 1967. Asst. prof. Rensselaer Poly. Inst., 1967-68; asst. prof. N.Y. U., 1968-72; assoc. prof. math. Wayne State U., 1972-77, prof., 1977—; vis. scholar U. Calif.-Berkeley, 1978; vis. prof. Nat. Inst. Research Computer and Automation, Le Chesnay, France, 1979. Editor: Multiple Scattering and Wave Propagation in Random Media, 1981; assoc. editor: Jour. Stochastic Analysis and Applications, 1982—. NSF grantee, 1970; NASA grantee, 1974—; U.S. Army Research Office grantee, 1976—; Acad. Applied Sci. grantee, 1981—. Mem. Am. Math. Soc., Soc. Indsl. and Applied Math. Current Work: Stochastic partial differential equations, differential equations, probability, wave propagation, turbulence, stability theory, filtering and control theory, fluid dynamics, inverse problems, methods in applied mathematics. Subspecialties: Applied mathematics; Theoretical and applied mechanics. Home: 19621 Hickory Leaf Ln Southfield MI 48076 Office: Wayne State University Detroit MI 48202

CHOW, TSU SEN, scientist; b. China, Nov. 8, 1939; came to U.S., 1964, naturalized, 1974; s. Kong and Helen (Chen) C.; m. Shang Mei Tang, June 10, 1967; 1 son, Albert. B.Sc., Nat. Cheng Kung U., Taiwan, 1962; M.E., Rensselaer Poly. Inst., 1966; Ph.D., Carnegie-Mellon U., 1968. Teaching asst. Nat. Cheng Kung U., 1963-64; research assoc. chemistry U. N.C.-Chapel Hill, 1968-72; sr. scientist, mem. research staff Xerox Corp., Webster, N.Y., 1972—. Contbr. articles sci. jours., chpts. in books. Served to 2d lt. Chinese Army, 1962-63. Recipient Spl. Merit award Xerox Corp., 1981. Mem. Am. Phys. Soc., Am. Chem. Soc., Soc. Rheology, Am. Acad. Mechanics. Democrat. Current Work: Basic and applied research in physical properties of polymers and composites, thin film surface and adhesion, photoreceptors. Subspecialties: Polymer physics; Composite materials. Home: 1608 Brattleboro Dr Webster NY 14580 Office: Xerox Webster Research Center 800 Phillips Rd W 114 Webster NY 14580

CHOWDHURY, PARIMAL, physiologist, educator; b. Chittagong, Bangladesh, Dec. 31, 1940; s. Paresh Nath and Kiranbala C.; m. Pranati, Nov. 14, 1971; children: Parag, Pritam. B.S., Chittagong Govt. Coll., Bangladesh, 1960; M.S., Dacca U., Bangladesh, 1962; Ph.D., McGill U., Montreal, Can., 1970. Lectr. in biochemistry Calcutta (India) Med. Coll., 1965-67; instr. medicine U. Medicine and Dentistry, Newark, 1970-76, asst. prof. medicine, 1976-80; asst. prof. physiology U. Ark., Little Rock, 1980—, asst. prof. toxicology, 1981—, assoc. prof. physiology, 1984—; chemist Standard Chem Corp., Chittagong,

Bangladesh, 1964; lect. Bipra Das Pal Chowdhury Inst. Tech., West Bengal, India, 1964-65. Author: Structure and Function of Biopolymers, 1968; contbr. articles to profl. publs. Mem. Kallol N.J. Inc., Friends of India, Ark. (exec.). NIH grantee, 1975-80, 78-81, 1980-82, 82-87. Mem. AAAS, Am. Chem. Soc., AAUP, Am. Physiol. Soc., Sigma Xi. Current Work: Pulmonary toxicology (mechanism of lung injury); effect of smoking and environmental pollutants on gastrointestinal distribution, secretion and release of gastrointestinal hormones. Subspecialties: Environmental toxicology; Physiology (biology). Home: 5 New Haven Ct Little Rock AR 72207 Office: Dept Physiology U Ark Med Scis 4301 W Markham Little Rock AR 72205

CHOY, DANIEL SHU JEN, internist; b. Shanghai, China, May 29, 1926 (parents Am. citizens); s. Jun Ke and Jessie Pei (Tsung) C.; children: Martha, Danny. B.A., Columbia Coll., 1944, M.D., 1949. Diplomate Am. Bd. Internal Medicine. Intern Meadowbrook Hosp., Hempstead, L.I., 1949-50; resident Francis Delafield Hosp., Columbia Presbyn. Med. Ctr., N.Y.C., 1952-54; practice medicine, specializing in internal medicine, N.Y.C., 1955—; attending physician Lenox Hill Hosp., N.Y.C., 1955—; research scientist investigative cardiology lab. St. Luke's Hosp., N.Y.C., 1983—. Contbr. articles to profl. jours. Inventor aeroplast, 1950, laser catheter for vascular recanalization, 1980. Served to capt. USAF, 1950-51. Fellow ACP, Am. Soc. Laser Medicine and Surgery; mem. Am. Soc. Clin. Oncology (founding mem.). Club: Explorers. Current work: initiated concept of using laser energy to recanalize arteries blocked by arteriosclerotic plaques and/or thrombi. Subspecialties: Laser medicine; Surgery. Office: 170 E 77th St New York NY 10021

CHRETIEN, MICHEL, scientific institute administrator, medical researcher; b. Shawinigan, Que., Can., Mar. 26, 1936; s. Willie and Marie (Boisvert) C.; m. Micheline Ruel, July 9, 1960; children—Marie, Lyne. M.D., U. Montreal, 1960; M.Sc., U. McGill, 1962; D.Sc. (hon.), U. Liège, 1981. Intern, St. Justine Hosp., Montreal, 1959-60, Maisonneuve Hosp., Montreal, 1959-60, Notre-Dame Hosp., Montreal, 1959-60; research fellow Hotel-Dieu de Montreal Hosp., 1960-62; resident in medicine Peter Bent Brigham Hosp., Boston, 1962-64; asst. biochemist Hormone Research Lab. U. Calif., Berkeley, 1964-67; sr. investigator Clin. Research Inst. Montreal, 1967—, chief exec. officer, scientific dir., 1984—; lectr. and speaker in field. Contbr. numerous articles to profl. jours. Recipient Gen. Gov. of Can. award, 1955; Fundamental Research award Assn. des Medecine de Lanque Francaise du Can., 1971; award Clarke Inst. Psychiatry, Toronto, 1977; Michel Sarrazin award Club de Recherches Cliniques du Que., 1977; Queen Elizabeth's 25th Anniversary of Reign medal, 1978; Archambault medal Assn. Canadienne-Francaise pour l'Avancement des Scis., 1978; Marcel Piche award Clin. Research Inst. Montreal, 1978; faculty scholar Josiah Macy Jr. Found., 1979-80. Mem. Am. Fedn. Clin. Research, Can. Soc. Clin. Investigation, AAAS, Club de Recherches Cliniques Que., Am. Soc. Exptl. Biology and Medicine, Can. Soc. Biochemistry, Endocrine Soc., N.Y. Acad. Scis., Can. Soc. Endocrinology and Metabolism, Peripatetic Club, Can. for Health Research, Am. Soc. Clin., Investigation, Am. Clin. and Climatological Assn., Sigma Xi. Subspecialty: Neuroendocrinology. Office: Clin Research Inst Montreal 110 Pine Ave W Montreal PQ H2W 1R7 Canada

CHRIST, DUANE MARLAND, systems engineer; b. Lakota, Iowa, Jan. 5, 1932; s. George Andrew and Esther Gertrude (Franke) C.; m. Lily Esther Shih, Sept. 14, 1963; 1 son, Wesley Anzo. B.S., Iowa State U.-Ames, 1953; M.A., U. Minn., 1960. Sci. programmer United Aircraft Corp., Hartford, Conn., 1960-63; sr. assoc. programmer IBM Corp., N.Y.C., 1964-68, staff programmer, 1968-72, staff instr., 1973-76, adv. systems engr., 1976-82, sr. systems engr., 1982—. Served to 1st lt. USAF, 1953-56. IBM resident study fellow, 1966-68. Mem. Assn. Computing Machinery, Soc. Indsl. and Applied Math., Math. Assn. Am. Lutheran. Current Work: Network architecture. Subspecialties: Systems engineering; Distributed systems and networks. Office: IBM Corp 77 Water St New York NY 10005

CHRISTEN, ARDEN GALE, dental educator and researcher; b. Lemmon, S.D., Jan. 25, 1932; s. Harold John and Dorothy Elizabeth (Taylor) Deering; m. Joan Ardell Akre, Sept. 10, 1955; children: Barbara, Penny, Rebecca, Sarah. B.S., U. Minn.-Mpls., 1954, D.D.S., 1956; M.S.D., Ind. U.-Indpls., 1965; M.A., Ball State U., 1973. Lic. dentist, S.D., Minn., Ind. Chief oral diagnosis, tng. officer Lackland AFB, Tex., 1965-70; base dental surgeon Zaragoza Air Base, Spain, 1970-73, Bentwaters Air Base, Eng., 1973-75; Air Force preventive dentistry officer Sch. Aerospace Medicine, Brooks AFB, Tex., 1975-78, chief dental research, 1978-80; chmn. dept. preventive dentistry Ind. U.-Indpls., 1981—; mil. cons USAF, 1973-75; sr. med. service cons. Surgeon Gen. USAF, 1974-80; spl. cons. preventive dentistry asst. Surgeon Gen. for Dental Services, Washington, 1975-80; dental cons. Dow Chem. Co., Indpls., 1982—. Author: (with others) Primary Preventive Dentistry, 1982, 2d edit., 1986; contbr. numerous articles to profl. jours. Bd. dirs. Bexar County chpt. Am. Cancer Soc., 1976-80; mem. Ind. div. Pub. Edn. Standing Com., Indpls., 1980; bd. dirs. Marion County chpt. Am. Cancer Soc., 1980—. Served to col. USAF, 1956-80. Decorated Meritorious Service Medal with 2 oak leaf clusters, Legion of Merit. Fellow Am. Coll. Dentists; mem. ADA, Am. Acad. Oral Pathology, Internat. Assn. Dental Research, Am. Acad. History of Dentistry. Lutheran. Current Work: Preventive dentistry, motivation, psychology, clinical oral pathology, dental history, quit-smoking programs, tobacco effects on the mouth, smokeless tobacco, nicotine. Subspecialty: Preventive dentistry. Home: 7112 Sylvan Ridge Rd Indianapolis IN 46240 Office: Oral Health Research Institute Indiana University School of Dentistry 415 Lansing St Indianapolis IN 46202-2876

CHRISTENSEN, MARY LUCAS, virologist, lab. adminstr., researcher; b. St. Louis, Oct. 18, 1937; d. Kermit and Margaret Isabelle (Lucas) C. B.A. in Bacteriology, U. Iowa, 1959, M.S. in Bacteriology, 1961; Ph.D. in Microbiology, Northwestern U., 1974. Research virologist Wyeth Labs., Phila., 1961-65, Abbott Labs., North Chicago, Ill., 1965-68; chief clin. virology lab. Northwestern U., 1969-71; research fellow Nat. Cancer Inst., Northwestern U., 1974-78, asst. prof. pathology and pediatrics, 1978—; dir. virology lab. Children's Meml. Hosp., 1978—; guest lectr. in field. Author: Basic Laboratory Procedures in Diagnostic Virology, 1977, Microbiology for Nursing and Allied Health Students, 1982; contbr. articles in field to profl. jours. Mem. Am. Soc. Microbiology, Ill. Soc. Microbiology (pres. elect 1985-86), AAAS, U. Iowa Alumni Assn., Northwestern U. Alumni Assn., Iota Sigma Pi, Gamma Phi Beta. Episcopalian. Current Work: Biochemical virology; rapid lab. diagnosis of virus infections; author books in microbiology and related health fields. Subspecialties: Virology (medicine); Biochemistry (medicine). Home: 900 N Lake Shore Dr Apt 1905 Chicago IL 60611 Office: 2300 Children's Plaza Chicago IL 60614

CHRISTENSEN, VERN LEE, poultry science and physiology educator; b. Moroni, Utah, June 25, 1945; s. Charles W. and Mary R. (Christensen) C. B.S., Utah State U., 1971; M.S., Brigham Young U., 1974; Ph.D., U. Mo., 1978. Research asst. Brigham Young U., 1973-75, U. Mo., 1975-78; assoc. prof. poultry sci. and physiology N.C. State U., 1978—. Served to capt. U.S. Army, 1971-73. Mem. Poultry Sci. Assn., AAAS, Am. Soc. Zoologists, Sigma Xi. Mormon. Current Work: Embryonic respiration of avian species and reproductive physiology of avian species; incubation, fertility, hatchability, reproduction. Subspecialties: Animal physiology; Animal breeding and embryo transplants. Home: 7415 Post Oak Rd Raleigh NC 27609 Office: NC State U Dept Poultry Science PO Box 5307 Raleigh NC 27650

CHRISTIAN, BARRY THEODORE, clinical child psychologist, behavioral scientist; b. Erie, Pa., Sept. 11, 1951; s. Archie Theodore and Alma Jean (Bundy) C.; m. Lillian Schwartz, Aug. 10, 1974. B.A. in Psychology, Edinboro State Coll., 1973; M.A. in Psychology, Austin Peay State U., 1975; Ed.S. in Counseling, U. Mo., 1977, Ph.D. in Psychology, 1981. Cert. psychologist, cert. examiner in sch. psychology, cert. psychol. counselor, approved spl. edn. mediator and impartial hearing authority, N. Mex. Psychol. technician Harriet Cohn Mental Health Ctr., Clarksville, Tenn., 1973-75; psychology intern U. Mo. Med. Ctr., Columbia, 1978-79; trng. cons.-lectr. emergency med. services, 1978-79; instr. ednl. psychology U. Mo., 1979-80; pvt. practice psychol. counseling Columbia, 1980-81; child clin. psychologist Coop. Edn. Services of N.Mex., Albuquerque, 1981—; research cons. Big Bros. Am., Columbia, 1975-76; behavior modification cons. Woodhaven Learning Ctr., Columbia, 1977-78. Contbr. articles to profl. jours. Mem. Am. Psychol. Assn., N.Mex. Counseling and Devel., Nat. Rifle Assn., N. Mex. Hist. Research Assn., Am. Congress on Real Estate. Republican. Mem. Ch. of Nazarene. Current Work: Applied behavior analysis in family and educational settings; learning theory applications in psychotherapy; cognitive behavior therapy research; behavior modification in the classroom. Subspecialties: Behavioral psychology; Learning. Office: Cooperative Ednl Services of NMex 208 Carlisle St NE Albuquerque NM 87108

CHRISTIAN, JOHN JERMYN, biologist, educator; b. Scranton, Pa., Apr. 12, 1917; s. John Oren and Margaret Adams (Jermyn) C.; m. Constance Koons, June 26, 1944 (div. 1958); children: John Jermyn, Patricia E.; m. Patricia Hart, Nov. 6, 1958. A.B., Princeton U., 1939; Sc.D., Johns Hopkins U., 1954. Exptl. med. physiologist Naval Med. Research Inst., Bethesda, Md., 1951-59; assoc. dir. Lab. Comparative Pathology, Phila. Zool. Soc., 1959-62; mem. Albert Einstein Med. Center Research Labs., Phila., 1962-70; prof. biology SUNY, Binghamton, 1970—. Author articles. Served with U.S. Navy, 1944-46. Recipient Merrer award Ecol. Soc., 1957. Mem. Endocrine Soc., Am. Soc. Mammalogists, Am. Ornithol. Union., Am. Soc. Exptl. Biology and Medicine, Am. Assn. Pathologists, N.Y. Acad. Scis., Wildlife Soc. Current Work: Population endocrinology, population regulation. Subspecialties: Behavioral ecology; Population biology. Home: Box 24 Starlight PA 18461 Office: SUNY Binghamton NY 13901

CHRISTIAN, JOHN THOMAS, consulting civil engineer; b. N.Y.C., Nov. 2, 1936; s. Thomas Douglas and Evelyn Catherine (Maestri) C.; m. Lynda Ballou Gregorian, June 8, 1960; children: Douglas Arthur, Shirin Lynda. B.S., MIT, 1958, M.S., 1959, Ph.D., 1966. Registered profl. engr., Mass., Maine. Pvt. geotech. engring. cons., Cambridge, Mass., 1966-73; asst. prof. civil engring. MIT, Cambridge, 1966-70, assoc. prof., 1970-73; geotech. cons. Stone & Webster Engring. Corp., Boston, 1973-76, cons. engr., 1976-79, sr. cons. engr., 1979—; mem. com. on mechanics of layered media Univs. Council for Earthquake Engring. Research, Transp. Research Bd., 1978-80. Co-author, editor: (with C. S. Desai) Numberical Methods in Geotechnical Engineering, 1977. Served to 1st lt. USAF, 1959-63. Fellow ASCE (exec. com. geotech. engring. div. 1981—, also numerous other coms., tech. council on computer practices 1974—, named outstanding news corr. 1979); mem. Boston Soc. Civil Engrs. (recipient Desmond Fitzgerald medal 1974), Internat. Soc. Soil Mechanics (Found. Engring.), Earthquake Engring. Research Inst. (mem. research com. 1975-79), Seismol, Soc. Am., Brit. Geotech. Soc., Assn. for Computing Machinery. Club: Boston Racquet. Current Work: Applications of computer and numerical methods to geotechnical and earthquake engineering; offshore structures; design and construction of energy facilities including dams, nuclear power plants, petrochemical facilities; development of production computer software. Subspecialties: Civil engineering; Software engineering. Home: 23 Fredana Rd Waban MA 02168 Office: Stone & Webster Engring Corp PO Box 2325 Boston MA 02107

CHRISTIANSEN, MERYL NAEVE, plant physiologist; b. Gooselake, Iowa, Sept. 5, 1925; s. Charles Carl and Louise Christine (Schroeder) C.; m. Shearin Ann Duldt, June 13, 1983. B.S., U. Ark., 1950, M.S., 1955; Ph.D., N.C. State U., 1960. Tech. asst. U. Ark., Fayetteville, 1951-55; plant physiologist, Stoneville, Miss., 1955-63, plant physiologist, Beltsville, Md., 1963—. Editor: Breeding Plants for Less Favorable Environments, 1982. Contbr. articles to plant sci. jours. Served with U.S. Army, 1943-46, 1950-51. Grantee: Dept. Agr., Nat. Cottonseed Assn., Am. Soybean Assn. Fellow Washington Acad. Sci.; mem. Am. Soc. Plant Physiology, N.Y. Acad. Sci., Am. Soc. Agronomy, Sigma Xi, Gamma Sigma Delta. Current work: Molecular biology; plant stress; plant hormones; photobiology; nitrogen fixation. Subspecialty: Plant physiology (agriculture). Office: US Dept Agr Agrl Research Service Agrl Research Ctr Beltsville MD 20705

CHRISTIANSON, KEITH ALAN, electrical engineering educator; b. Columbus, Ohio, Apr. 12, 1957; s. Halvor Samuel and Nell Marie (Hespenheide) C.; m. Carol Diane Chaney, Oct. 15, 1982; 1 child, Christina Ann. B.S. in E.E., Ohio State U., 1980, B.S. in Metall. Engring., 1980; Ph.D. in Materials Sci. and Engring., Northwestern U., 1984. Asst. prof. elec. engring. U. Maine-Orono, 1984—. Mem. Am. Soc. Metals, Am. Inst. Mining, Metall. and Petroleum Engrs., Electrochem. Soc., Optical Soc. Am., Inst. Elec. Electronics Engrs. Current work: Growth and characterization of compound semiconductors. Subspecialties: Semiconductors; Electronic materials. Office: Univ Maine Elec Engring Dept Orono ME 04469

CHRISTMAN, ARTHUR CASTNER, JR., scientific advisor; b. North Wales, Pa., May 11, 1922; s. Arthur Castner and Hazel Ivy (Schirmer) C.; m. Marina Ilia Diterichs, Apr. 17, 1945; children: Candace Lee Cupps, Tatiana Marina Harvey, Deborah Ann Clark, Arthur C. III, Keith Ilia, Cynthia Ellen. B.S. in Physics, Pa. State U., 1944, M.S., 1950. Teaching asst. dept. physics Pa. State U., State College, 1943-44, grad. asst., 1946-48; instr. dept. physics George Washington U., Washington, 1948-51; cons. U.S. Navy, 1950-51; physicist ops. research office Johns Hopkins U., Chevy Chase, Md., 1951-58; sr. physicist Stanford Research Inst., Menlo Park, Calif., 1958-62, head ops. research group, 1962-64, dept. mgr., 1965-67, dir. dept., 1968-71, dir. tactical weapons systems, 1971-75; sci. advisor to comdg. gen. and dep. chief staff Tng. and Doctrine Command, Ft. Monroe, Va., 1975—; cons. in field. Author or co-author classified papers on tactical systems and weapons effectiveness. Fellow AAAS; mem. Am. Phys. Soc., Ops. Research Soc. Am., Sigma Xi, Sigma Pi Sigma. Republican. Am. Baptist. Current Work: Advisor on technical quality and analytical soundness of research in support of decisions by Training and Doctrine Command. Subspecialty: Operations research (mathematics). Home: 102 Sherwood Dr Williamsburg VA 23185 Office: Sci Advisor HQTRADOC Fort Monroe VA 23651

CHRISTMAN, JUDITH KERSHAW, biochemistry educator; b. Teaneck, N.J., Apr. 8, 1941; d. James and Ruth (Niederer) Kershaw; m. Donald A. Christman, June 6, 1959. A.B., NYU, 1962; Ph.D. in Biochemistry, Columbia U., 1967. Postdoctoral fellow N.Y. Blood Ctr., 1967-71; asst. mem. Inst. Muscle Disease, N.Y.C., 1971-74; asst. prof. pediatrics Mt. Sinai Sch. Medicine, N.Y.C., 1974-75, assoc. prof. pediatrics, 1975-80, research prof. pediatrics, 1980—, assoc. prof. biochemistry, 1977-82, prof., 1982—. Contbr. articles to profl. jours.; assoc. editor: Cancer Research, 1981—. N.Y. Heart Assn. grantee, 1977-81; NIH grantee. Mem. Harvey Soc., Am. Soc. Cell Biology, Am. Soc. Biol. Chemists, Am. Assn. Cancer Research, Sigma Xi. Current Work: DNA methylation and regulation of gene expression, regulation of cloned hepatitis genes in mammalian cells, effects of tumor promoters on differentiation of cultured leukemic cells. Subspecialties: Biochemistry (biology); Genetics and genetic engineering (biology). Office: Dept Biochemistry 1 Gustave Levy Pl New York NY 10029

CHRISTY, JAMES WALTER, physicist, astronomer; b. Milw., Sept. 15, 1938; s. Walter Witald and Mary (Nistor) C.; m. Charlene Mary Crockett, Nov. 22, 1975; children—James Randolph, Nola Marie; children—David James, Teresa Elizabeth. B.S., U. Ariz., 1967. Astronomer, U.S. Naval Obs., Flagstaff, Ariz., 1962-71, Washington, 1971-82; physicist Hughes Aircraft Co., Tucson, 1982—; astronomer U. Ariz., Tucson, 1983—. Contbr. articles to profl. jours.; discovered, named Charon, moon of planet Pluto, 1978. Mem. Internat. Astronom. Union, Am. Astronom. Soc., Astronom. Soc. Pacific. Explorers Club N.Y. Subspecialties: Infrared astronomy; Planetary science. Home: 1720 W Niona Pl Tucson AZ 95704 Office: Hughes Aircraft Co Bldg 802-2 Tucson AZ 85734

CHRONIC, BYRON JOHN, geologist, educator; b. Tulsa, June 3, 1921; s. Byron John Chronic and Pansy Lee (Whitehead) Yarbrough; m. Halka Pattison, Aug. 21, 1948 (div. 1981); children—Emily Ann, Felicie Jane, Lucy Marylka, Susan Elizabeth; m. 2d, Carol A. Williams, June 18, 1981. B.S. in Petroleum Engring. with honors, U. Tulsa, 1942; prof. cert. in meteorology, U. Chgo., 1943; M.S. in Geology, U. Kans., 1947; Ph.D. in Geology, Columbia U., 1949. Mem. faculty dept. geology U. Colo., 1950-80, prof. emeritus, 1980—; prof., chmn. dept. geology Haile Sellassie U., Addis Ababa, Ethiopia, 1965-66; lectr. Edinburgh U. (Scotland), 1958-59; prof. U. P.R., Mayaguez, 1978-79; sr. geologist Keplinger & Assocs., Houston, 1981-83; cons. geologist Sirle Oil Co., Libya, 1984, Tenneco, Houston, 1984—; cons. U.S. Geol. Survey, Denver, 1970-78, U.S. Nat. Park Service, Denver, 1975-78, Win-Eldrich Mines, Inc., Toronto, Ont., Can., 1984. Author: Prarie, Peak and Plateau, 1972; Upper Paleozoic of Peru, 1952; editor Bibliography of Geology Theses, 1960-65. Served to 1st lt. USAAF, 1942-46; ETO; PTO. Recipient Disting. Service award Rocky Mt. Assn. Geologists, 1973; Woods Hole Oceanographic Inst. faculty fellow, 1956. Fellow Geol. Soc. Am., AAAS, Geol. Soc. of London; mem. Am. Assn. Petroleum Geologists (assoc. editor, del.), Houston Geol. Soc. Democrat. Club: Explorers (N.Y.C.; editor jour.). Current work: Surveying west coast of Africa for hydrocarbon potential areas, fossils of Colorado, ms. in prepin, locating hydrocarbon prospects in North America in progress. Subspecialties: Paleontology; Fuels. Home: 5943 Spellman St Houston TX 77096 Office: Sastex Exploration Inc Houston TX 77096

CHU, BENJAMIN, chemist, educator; b. Shanghai, China, Mar. 3, 1932; came to U.S., 1953, naturalized, 1967; s. Charles and Gladys (Chen) C.; m. Louisa King, Mar. 30, 1959; children: Peter, Joanne, Laurence. B.S. magna cum laude, St. Norbert Coll., 1955; Ph.D., Cornell U., 1959. Vis. scientist Brookhaven Nat. Lab., summer 1957; research assoc. Cornell U., 1958-62; asst. prof. chemistry U. Kans., 1962-65, asso. prof., 1965-68; prof. chemistry SUNY, Stony Brook, 1968—, chmn. dept., 1978—. Contbr. articles to profl. jours. Recipient Humboldt award for sr. U.S. scientists, 1976-77; Disting. Achievement award in natural sci. St. Norbert Coll., 1981; Alfred P. Sloan research fellow, 1966-68; John Simon Guggenheim fellow, 1968-69. Fellow Am. Inst. Chemists; mem. Am. Chem. Soc., Am. Phys. Soc., AAAS, N.Y. Acad. Scis., Sigma Xi, Phi Lambda Upsilon. Roman Catholic. Current Work: Rayleigh, Brillouin and Raman scattering; small angle x-ray scattering and small angle neutron scattering; static and dynamical properties of macromolecular solutions and colloidal suspensions; critical opalescence and spinodal decomposition. Subspecialties: Physical chemistry; Polymer physics. Home: 27 View Rd Setauket NY 11733 Office: Dept Chemistry SUNY Stony Brook NY 11794

CHU, NAI-SHIN, medical educator, neurologist, neuroscience researcher; b. Taiwan, Apr. 28, 1937; came to U.S., 1964; s. Han-Yau and Ping-Yi C.; m. Shiu-Yuan, Dec. 23, 1967; children: Eric, Curran. M.D., Nat. Taiwan U., 1963; Ph.D., U. Mich., 1969. Diplomate: Am. Bd. Psychiatry and Neurology. Intern U. Colo., Denver, 1972-73, resident in neurology, 1973-76; vis. scientist NIMH, Bethesda, Md., 1970-73; asst. prof. neurology U. Calif.-Irvine, 1976-80, assoc. prof., 1980—, dir. seizure clinic, 1976—; mem. profl. adv. bd. Orange County (Calif.) Epilepsy Soc., 1976—. Rackham fellow, 1966-69; NIH Fogarty fellow, 1970-73; also recipient research career devel award, 1980-85. Mem Am. Acad. Neurology, Am. Epilepsy Soc., Internat. Soc. Biochem. Research on Alcoholism. Current Work: Effects of alcohol on the brain, epilepsy and clinical neurology. Current efforts are concentrated on the actions of alcohol on the single brain cells and the damaging effects of chronic alcoholism on the brain stem. Subspecialties: Neurology; Neuropharmacology. Home: 32 Sycamore Creek Irvine CA 92715 Office: Univ of California Irvine Medical Center 101 City Drive South Orange CA 92668

CHU, TING L., elec. engr., educator; b. Beijing, China, Dec. 26, 1924; m. Shirley S. Yu, Sept. 6, 1954; children: Dennis, Dora, Daniel. B.S., Cath. U. Peking, 1945, M.S., 1948; Ph.D., Washington U., 1952. Asst. prof. Duquesne U., Pitts., 1952-55, assoc. prof., 1955-56; research scientist, fellow scientist, mgr. electronic materials Westinghouse Research Labs., Pitts., 1956-67; prof. elec. engring. So. Meth. U., Dallas, 1967—; cons. Poly Solar, Inc., Garland, Tex. Contbr. articles to profl. jours. NSF, NASA, Dept. Energy grantee. Mem. Electrochem. Soc., IEEE, Am. Soc. Engring. Edn., AAUP. Patentee in field. Current Work: Electronic materials and devices, including photovoltaic solar energy conversion, growth and characterization of crystals and films and fabrication and characterization of junction devices, dielectric-semiconductor devices. Subspecialties: Electronic materials; Semiconductors. Home: 12 Duncannon Ct Dallas TX 75225 Office: So Meth U Dallas TX 75275

CHU, WEI-KAN, physicist; b. Kunming, China, Apr. 1, 1940; came to U.S., 1963; s. Din-Yuan and Ya-Chung (Wong) C.; m. Agnes Kuen, May 28, 1966; 1 child; Lawrence Dalpon. B.S., Cheng-Kung U., 1962; M.S., Baylor U., 1965, Ph.D., 1969. Postdoctoral fellow Baylor U., Waco, Tex., 1969-72; sr. research fellow Calif. Inst. Tech., Pasadena, 1972-75; sr. engr. IBM, East Fishkill, N.Y., 1975-81; prof. physics U. N.C., Chapel Hill, 1981—; chief scientist Modern Sci. Tech., Chapel Hill, 1984—. Edit. bd. Jur. Nuclear Instruments and Methods, 1984—; contbr. articles to profl. jours.; patentee in electronic material processing, ion beams; author: (with J.W. Mayer and M-A. Nicolet) Backscattering Spectrometry, 1978. Pres., Chinese Am. Soc., 1984. Mem. Am. Phys. Soc., Electrochem. Soc., Materials Research Soc. (pres. N.C. sect 1984-85). Subspecialties: Condensed matter physics; Electronic materials. Home: 6 Whisper Ln Chapel Hill NC 27514 Office: Dept Physics and Astronomy Univ NC Chapel Hill NC 27514

CHU, WILLIAM TONGIL, physicist; b. Seoul, Korea, Apr. 16, 1934; came to U.S., 1953, naturalized, 1968; s. Yohan and Sunbok (Choi) C.; m. Insoo La, June 16, 1962; children: Joan Inyul, Jean Suyul. B.S., Carnegie Inst. Tech., 1957, M.S., 1959, Ph.D., 1963. Research asso. Brookhaven Nat. Lab., 1963-64; asst. prof. physics Ohio State U., Columbus, 1964-70; asso. prof. radiation scis. Loma Linda (Calif.) U. Sch. Medicine, 1975-78, prof., 1978-79; scientist III div. accelerators and fusion research Lawrence Berkeley Lab., U. Calif., 1979—. Contbr. articles in field to profl. jours. Mem. Am. Phys. Soc., Radiation Research Soc., Am. Assn. Physicists in Medicine, Assn. Korean Scientists and Engrs. Am. (pres. 1986), Sigma Xi, Tau Beta Pi. Republican. Current Work: Radiation physics, heavy-ion applications in biomed. research. Subspecialties: Particle physics; Biophysics (physics). Home: 3282 Ameno Dr Lafayette CA 94549 Office: 64-230 Lawrence Berkeley Lab Berkeley CA 94720

CHUA, LEON ONG, electrical engineering and computer science educator; b. Tarlac, Philippines, June 28, 1936; came to U.S., 1959, naturalized, 1969; s. Te and Yan-King C.; m. Dec. 24, 1960; children—Amy Lynn, Michelle Ann, Katrin Faye, Cynthia Mae. M.S.E.E., MIT, 1962; Ph.D., U. Ill., 1964; D. (hon. causa), Ecole Polytechnique, Lausanne, Switzerland, 1983; D. (hon.), Tokushima U., Japan, 1984. From asst. prof. to assoc. prof. Purdue U., 1964-71; prof. elec. engring. and computer sci. U. Calif.-Berkeley, 1973—; vis. U.S. scientist of Japan Soc. for Promotion Sci. at Waseda U., Tokyo, 1983-84. Author: Introduction to Nonlinear Network Theory, 1969; Computer-Aided Analysis of Electronic Circuits, 1975; also numerous research papers on nonlinear networks and systems. Patentee in field. Recipient Frederick Emmons Terman award Am. Soc. Elec. Engrs., 1974, Miller research professorship Miller Inst., 1976; sr. vis. fellow Cambridge U., Eng., 1982, Waseda U., Tokyo, 1985-86; Alexander Humboldt sr. U.S. scientist award Tech. U. Munich, Federal Republic Germany, 1982-83. Mem. IEEE (guest editor Transactions on Edn. 1971, Browder J. Thompson Meml. prize 1967, W.R.G. Baker prize 1973, Centennial medal 1984), IEEE Cirs. and Systems Soc. (adminstrv. com. 1971-74, pres. 1971-78, editor transactions 1974-75, Best Paper award 1973, Guillemin-Cauer prize paper award 1985), Sigma Xi, Eta Kappa Nu, Tau Beta Pi. Subspecialties: Electrical engineering; Computer-aided design. Home: 955 Galvin Dr El Cerrito CA 94530 Office: U Calif Dept Elec Engring and Computer Sci Berkeley CA 94720

CHUAN, RAYMOND LU-PO, science-technology consultant, atmospheric aerosol researcher; b. Shanghai, China, Mar. 4, 1924; came to U.S., 1941; s. Peter Shao-wu and Katherine (Tao) C.; m. Norma Nicoloff, Dec. 22, 1951 (dec. 1973); children: Jason, Alexander; m. Eugenia Nishimine Sevilla, Apr. 23, 1982. B.A., Pomona Coll., 1944; M.S., Calif. Inst. Tech., 1945, Ph.D., 1953. Dir. engring. center U. So. Calif., Los Angeles, 1957-64; pres. Celesco, South Pasadena, Calif., 1964-68; mgr. advanced tech. Atlantic Research Corp., Costa Mesa, Calif., 1968-72; staff scientist Celesco Industries, Costa Mesa, 1972-76; Brunswick Corp., Costa Mesa, 1976—; trustee Sequoyah Sch., Pasadena, 1958-71; cons. NASA, Hampton, Va., 1978—. Assoc. fellow AIAA (Minta Martin Award 1953); mem. Am. Phys. Soc. Inventor high speed ground transp. fire detection system. Current Work: Gas detection, fire detection, acoustic arrays (underwater), characterization and transport of stratospheric aerosols. Subspecialty: Aerospace engineering and technology. Home: 19471 Sandcastle Ln Huntington Beach CA 92648 Office: Brunswick Corp Costa Mesa CA 92626

CHUANG, HANSON YII-KUAN, pathology educator; b. Nanking, China, Sept. 24, 1935; came to U.S., 1963, naturalized, 1972; s. Wai-Ching and Yah-Fang (Chang) C.; m. Lucy Wen-Hwa Tai, Apr. 2, 1966; children: Philip Duen-Ho, Helen Duen-Fang. B.S., Nat. Taiwan U., Taipei, 1958; Ph.D., U. N.C., Chapel Hill, 1968. Postdoctoral fellow Johns Hopkins U., Balt., 1968-71; instr. U. N.C., Chapel Hill, 1972-73, asst. prof., 1973-75, Brown U., Providence, 1975-77, U. South Fla., Tampa, 1977-79; research assoc. prof. U. Utah, Salt Lake City, 1979—. Author: Replacement of Renal Function by Dialysis, 1978, 83, Textbook of Hemostasis and Thrombosis, 1982. NIH grantee, 1978—. Mem. Am. Chem. Soc., Am. Assn. Pathology, Internat. Soc. Artificial Organs, N.Y. Acad. Sci. Current Work: Thrombosis and hemostasis, blood-biomaterial interaction, blood coagulation, blood banking, platelet biochemistry and function, artificial organs. Subspecialties: Biochemistry (medicine); Biomaterials. Home: 3427 E Brockbank Dr Salt Lake City UT 84124 Office: U Utah 50 N Medical Dr Salt Lake City UT 84132

CHUANG, RONALD Y(AN-LI), pharmacologist, biochemist; b. Feb. 12, 1940; s. Linda F.; m. Ching Wha C., July 8, 1967; children: Ann, Katherine, Teddy. M.S., U. Calif.-Davis, 1966, Ph.D., 1970. Asst. prof. pharmacology Duke U., 1972-76; asst. biochemist Calif. Primate Research Center, U. Calif.-Davis, 1976-78, asst. prof. pharmacology, 1981-85, assoc. prof., 1985—; asst. prof. biochemistry Oral Roberts U., 1978-81. Contbr. articles to profl. jours.; editorial bd., mem. adv. bd.: Jour. Molecular Pharmacology, 1979—. NIH postdoctoral fellow, 1971-72; NIH grantee, 1974-78, 82-88. Mem. Am. Soc. Biol. Chemists, Am. Assn. Cancer Research, Am. Soc. Pharmacology and Exptl. Therapeutics. Current Work: Control mechanism of gene expression in eukaryotic cells; mechanism of mode of action of cancer chemotherapeutic agts; recombinant DNA researh in animal virus. Subspecialties: Biochemistry (biology); Enzyme technology. Home: 1521 Brown Dr Davis CA 95616 Office: Dept Pharmacology U Calif Davis CA 95616

CHUBB, WALSTON, nuclear engineer, consultant; b. Washington, July 23, 1923; s. Robert Walston and Irene (Sylvester) C.; m. Carolyn Elizabeth Carpenter, June 16, 1951; children: Walston, Catherine Louise. B.A., Harvard U., 1944; B.S., U. Mo.-Rolla, 1948, M.S., 1949. Asst. engr. Brush Beryllium Corp., Luckey, Ohio, 1949-51; research fellow Batelle Meml. Inst., Columbus, 1951-72; prin. engr. Westinghouse Electric Corp., Monroeville, Pa., 1972—. Contbr. articles to profl. jours. Served with USNR, 1944-46. Ludlow-Saylor Wire Co. fellow, 1948-49. Mem. Am. Soc. Metals, Am. Nuclear Soc., Nat. Soc. Profl. Engrs., Sigma Xi. Patentee in field. Current Work: Application of high temperature material science to the design of fuels for nuclear reactors; design of mathematical codes to describe the behavior of fuels in reactors, interpretation of radiochemical content of primary reactor water as an indicator of the condition of the reactor core. Subspecialties: Materials (engineering); High-temperature materials. Home: 3450 MacArthur Dr Murrysville PA 15668 Office: Westinghouse Electric Corp PO Box 3912 Monroeville PA 15230

CHUGHTAI, GUL MUHAMMAD, medical physicist; b. Khanewal, Multan, Pakistan, May 10, 1943; came to U.S., 1971, naturalized, 1977; s. Bahadur Khan and Noorjehan (Bahadur) C.; m. Sarwat Gul, Mar. 1, 1970; children: Tabinda, Farhan. M.S. in Physics, Punjab U., Pakistan, 1967; Ph.D., Pacific W.U. Calif., 1982. Radiation physicist Georgetown U., Washington, 1975-77; sr. med. physicist Pakistan Atomic Commn., Islamabad, 1977-80; commd. capt. U.S. Air Force, 1980; chief med. physicist Malcolm Grow USAF Med. Ctr., Andrews AFB, Washington, 1980—; asst. prof. Uniformed Services U. of Health Sci., Bethesda, Md., 1985—; prof. physics Prince George Coll., Largo, Md., 1985—. Mem. Am. Assn. Physicists in Medicine, Health Physics Soc. Current Work: Study of thermoluminescent dosimetry; ionizing radiation for treatment cancer; treatment plg. with computer for external interstitial and intra cavitory radiation therapy treatment; nuclear medicine and diagnostic radiology physicist. Home: 10130 Walnutwood Ct Burke VA Office: Dept Radiology MGMC Andrews AFB Washington DC 20331

CHUNG, CHIEN, nuclear science educator, consultant; b. Tokyo, Sept. 7, 1950; s. Han-Po and Wing-Jing (Fan) C.; m. Ching Ling Lee, June 22, 1974; children: Martin, Brian. B.Sc., Nat. Tsing Hua U., Hsinchu, Taiwan, 1972; Ph.D., McGill U., Can., 1980. Teaching asst. McGill U., Montreal, Que., 1975-79, postdoctoral fellow, 1980; guest research assoc. Brookhaven Nat. Lab., Upton, N.Y., 1980-83; research assoc. U. Md., College Park, 1980-83; assoc. prof. Nat. Tsing Hua U., Hsinchu, 1983—, dir. Inst. Nuclear Sci., 1985—. Contbr. articles to profl. publs. Recipient Winkler award McGill U., 1982; McGill U. scholar, 1975-80. Mem. Am. Nuclear Soc., Am. Phys. Soc., Am. Chem. Soc. Current Work: Front-line research on basic and applied nuclear science: analytical, nuclear medicine, nuclear reaction, fission and structure. Subspecialties: Nuclear fission; Nuclear engineering. Office: Inst Nuclear Sci Nat Tsing Hua U Hsinchu 300 Taiwan

CHUNG, CHUNG-TAIK, medical educator, physician; b. Tae-Gue, Korea, Jan. 11, 1942; came to U.S., 1970, naturalized, 1977; s. Woon Yong and Boon-Jo (Kim) C.; m. Nam Sook Chung, May 10, 1969; children: Michael, Robert, Terrine. M.D., Yonsei U., Seoul, Korea, 1967. Diplomate: Am. Bd. Radiology; lic. physician, N.Y., Pa., Calif. Intern H.S. Martland Hosp., Newark, 1970-71; resident in radiation therapy SUNY Upstate Med. Center-Syracuse, 1971-74, instr. radiology, 1974-75, asst. prof., 1976-81, assoc. prof., 1981—, assoc. prof. otolaryngology, 1982—; staff radiotherapist Wilkes-Barre (Pa.) Gen. Hosp., 1975-76; cons. radiotherapist Crouse Irving Meml. Hosp., VA Hosp., Community Gen. Hosp., St. Joseph's Hosp. Contbr. articles to med. jours. Served with Republic of Korea Air Force, 1967-70. Mem. Am. Coll. Radiology, Am. Soc. Therapeutic Radiologists, Radiol. Soc. N.Am., Central N.Y. Radiol. Soc., N.Y. State Med. Soc., Korean Soc. Central N.Y. (pres. 1974-75), Yonsei U. Coll. Medicine Alumni Assn. Central N.Y. (sec. 1973-80). Club: Pompey (Pompey, N.Y.). Current Work: Radiation oncology. Subspecialty: Oncology. Home: 7329 Barberry Ln Manlius NY 13104 Office: SUNY Upstate Medical Center 750 E Adams St Syracuse NY 13210

CHUNG, HEE MOK, nuclear engr., material scientist; b. Okchun, Chungbuk, Korea, Jan. 26, 1941; came to U.S., 1966; s. Chin Wook and In Hah (Choi) C.; m. Haijung W. Lee, Sept. 9, 1972; children: Gina, Joanne. B.S., Seoul Nat. U., 1963; Ph.D., U. Pa., 1972. Research assoc. Yale U., New Haven, 1972-74; asst. metallurgist Argonne (Ill.) Nat. Lab., 1974-78, project mgr., 1980-82, prin. investigator metallurgist, 1978—; cons. Dept. Energy, 1979-82, U.S. Nuclear Regulatory Commn., 1977-80. Recipient cert. of award U.S. Dept. Energy, 1979; Best Paper award material sci. and tech. div. Am. Nuclear Soc., 1983. Mem. AIME, Am. Nuclear Soc. ASTM. Methodist. Developer Chung-Kassner Criterion in reactor safety, 1979, Chung-Thomas effect for reactor accident fuel behavior, 1982. Current Work: Nuclear reactor fuel behavior and performance, related safety aspects, advanced alloy design and performances in energy systems, materials corrosion, surface phenomena, irradiation effects. Subspecialties: Metallurgy; Nuclear fission. Home: 1709 Warbler Dr Naperville IL 60540 Office: Argonne Nat Lab 9700 S Cass Ave Argonne IL 60439

CHUNG, HO, pharmacologist, toxicologist; b. Canton, China, Aug. 15, 1938; came to U.S., 1959; s. Park-Shek and Hunline (Chan) C.; m. MaryAnn Sell, Mar. 26, 1965; children—Kai, Gai. B.S. in Chemistry, U. Wis.-Oshkosh, 1962; M.S. in Pharmacology, Toxicology, U. Md.-Balt., 1973, Ph.D., 1974. Nuclear medicine technologist Straub Clinic, Honolulu, 1962-63; chemist quality control Western Foam Co., Phoenix, 1963-69; research pharmacologist Walter Reed Army Inst. Research, Washington, 1974-76, asst. chief Drug Metabolism Br., 1976-81, chief, Biochem. Pharmacology and Toxicology Br., 1981—, contract monitor, 1975—; IND project dir., 1976—; cons. CNS Corp., 1980—. Recipient Walter Reed Army Inst. Research Exceptional Performance award, 1981, 82, 84, Achievement award, 1984. Fellow Am. Coll. Clin. Pharmacology; mem. Soc. Toxicology (mem. placement com.), Am. Soc. Pharmacology and Exptl. Therapeutics, Am. Acad. Clin. Toxicology, Am. Coll. Toxicology, Rho Chi, Sigma Xi, Assn. Govt. Toxicologists, Am.-Chinese Toxicology Soc. (v.p.). Current work: Drug development, drug and chemical toxicology, preclinical and clinical pharmacokinetics and toxicokinetics, drug interactions. Subspecialties: Pharmacology; Toxicology (medicine). Office: Walter Reed Army Inst Research Walter Reed Army Med Ctr Washington DC 20307-5100

CHUNG, MELVIN CHUNG-HING, anatomist, educator; b. Honolulu, Feb. 11, 1935; s. Harry Su-Lung and Rosaline Tam (Tom) C.; m. Jane Ching-An Hsia, Aug. 21, 1965; children: Mark K. S., Mona M.-L. B.A., U. Nebr., Lincoln, 1957, M.S., 1960; Ph.D. in Anatomy, U. Calif., Berkeley, 1971. Instr. life scis. San Francisco City Coll., 1964-66; instr. U. Rochester, 1971-73, asst. prof. anatomy, 1973-78; assoc. prof. anatomy Med. Coll. Va., Va. Commonwealth U., 1978—. Contbr. articles to profl. jours. Human Growth Found. grantee, 1976-78; NIH grantee, 1976-77, 77-80. Mem. Am. Soc. Anatomy, Endocrine Soc., Neurosci. Soc., N.Y. Acad. Sci., Va. Acad. Sci., So. Soc. Anatomy, AAAS, Sigma Xi. Current Work: Hypothalamic release of neuropeptides influencing pituitary gonadotrophic and thyrotrophic function and growth; target hormone feedback on pituitary and hypothalamic activity. Subspecialties: Neuroendocrinology; Reproductive biology. Home: 12301 Roaring Brook Ct Richmond VA 23233

CHUNG, SUH-URK, physicist; b. Korea, Nov. 11, 1936; came to U.S., 1959; s. Dall-Bin and Sung-Sil (Yu) C.; m. Kristin D. Deurloo, June 8, 1963 (div. 1983); children—Edward, James; m. Marie-Christine Mifsud, Sept. 22, 1984. Ph.D., U. Calif.-Berkeley, 1966. Physicist, Brookhaven Nat. Lab., Upton, N.Y., 1966—; vis. scientist CERN, Geneva, 1969-71, 81-83. Democrat. Methodist. Current work: Hadron spectroscopy. Subspecialty: Particle physics. Home: 6 Amherst Ct Setauket NY 11733 Office: Brookhaven Nat Lab Bldg 510A Upton NY 11973

CHUPP, TIMOTHY EDWARD, physics educator; b. Berkeley, Calif., Nov. 30, 1954; s. Edward Lowell and Mary Christine (Miklos) C. A.B., Princeton U., 1977; M.Sc., U. Wash., 1978, Ph.D., 1983. Asst. prof. physics Princeton U., (N.J.), 1983-85, Harvard U., Cambridge, Mass., 1985—. Contbr. articles to profl. jours. Bd. dirs. Am. Youth Hostels, Wash. State Council Inc., Seattle, 1980-83. Mem. Am. Physical Soc., Sigma Xi (assoc.). Current work: Application of atomic and nuclear physics systems and techniques to the study of the fundamental forces of the weak interaction, gravity and electrodynamics. Subspecialties: Atomic and molecular physics; Relativity and gravitation. Home: 1 Fort Washington Pl Cambridge MA 02139 Office: Jefferson Lab Physics Harvard U Cambridge MA 02138

CHURCH, ALLEN CHARLES, neuroscientist; b. Binghamton, N.Y., Aug. 1, 1950; s. William Allen and Margaret Eletheare C.; m. Jennifer Lindsay, Oct. 30, 1976; 1 son, Joel. B.A., Harpur Coll., 1972; M.A., SUNY, Binghamton, 1974, Ph.D., 1976. Fellow Jackson Lab., Bar Harbor, Maine, 1976-78; fellow dept. psychiatry and pharmacology U. Pa., Phila., 1978-80, asst. prof. anatomy, 1980; sr. staff fellow NIMH, St. Elizabeth's Hosp., Washington, 1980—. Mem. AAAS, Soc. for Neurosci., N.Y. Acad. Sci. Current Work: Researcher in interactions of neurotransmitters and their receptors. Subspecialties: Neurobiology; Neuropharmacology. Office: NIMH St Elizabeth's Hospital Adult Psychiatry Branch Washington DC 20032

CHURCH, DAVID ARTHUR, physicist; b. Berlin, N.H., Apr. 3, 1939; s. Andrew Ivan and Barbara Brown (Holmes) C.; m. Diane Claire Burnham, Sept. 15, 1963; children: Kirin Alene, Aran Holmes. A.B., Dartmouth Coll., 1961; M.S., U. Wash., 1963, Ph.D., 1969. Research assoc. U. Bonn, W. Ger., 1969, U. Mainz, W.Ger., 1969-71, U. Ariz., Tucson, 1971-72; physicist Lawrence Berkeley (Calif.) Lab., 1972-75; asst. prof. to prof. physics Tex. A&M U., College Station, 1975—. Contbr. articles profl. jours., chpts. in books. Recipient Precision Measurement Grant award Nat. Bur. Standards, 1981; research grantee Dept. Energy; research grantee Research Corp.; research grantee NSF. Mem. Am. Phys. Soc. Presbyterian. Current Work: Coherence spectroscopy and anistropic excitation of fast ions, slow ion storage and spectroscopy, multi-charged ion charge transfer, antimatter confinement, photoionization of ions. Subspecialty: Atomic and molecular physics. Home: 1810 Langford St College Station TX 77840 Office: Physics Dept Texas A&M University College Station TX 77843

CHURCH, EUGENE LENT, research physicist; b. Yonkers, N.Y., July 30, 1925; s. Wallace L. and Wilhelmina L. (Binger) C.; m. Anne Richardson Meirs, May 15, 1948; children: Rebecca Meirs, David Lent. A.B., Princeton U., 1948; Ph.D., Harvard U., 1953. With Dept. Def., 1952—; sr. physicist Frankford Arsenal, Phila., 1971-77; sr. research physicist U.S. Armament Research and Devel. Ctr., Dover, N.J., 1977—; guest physicist Argonne Nat. Lab., 1952-55, Brookhaven Nat. Lab., 1955-59; vis. scientist Niels Bohr Inst., Copenhagen, 1959-61; guest physicist Brookhaven Nat. Lab., 1961-71. Contbr. articles to profl. jours. Served with USN, 1944-46. Fellow Am. Phys. Soc., AAAS, Soc. Photo-Optical, Instrumentation Engrs.; mem. Am. Optical Soc., IEEE. Republican. Presbyterian. Club: Princeton (N.Y.C.). Current Work: Properties and metrology of high performance optical surfaces; precision machining; digital signal processing. Subspecialty: Optical engineering. Office: US Armament Research and Devel Ctr Bldg 1 Dover NJ 07801

CHURCHILL, STUART WINSTON, chemical engineering educator; b. Imlay City, Mich., June 13, 1920; s. Howard Heenan and Faye Erma (Shurte) C.; m. Donna Belle Lewis, Feb. 22, 1946 (div.); children: Stuart Lewis, Diana Gail, Cathy Marie, Emily Elizabeth; m. Renate Ursula Treibmann, Aug. 3, 1974. B.S. in Math, U. Mich., 1942, B.S. in Chem. Engring, 1942, M.S., 1948, Ph.D., 1952; M.A. honoris causa, U. Pa., 1972. Technologist Shell Oil Co., 1942-46; tech. supr. Frontier Chem. Co., 1946-47; mem. faculty U. Mich., 1949-67, prof. chem. engring., 1957-67, chmn. dept. chem. and metall. engring., 1962-67; Carl V.S. Patterson prof. chem. engring. U. Pa., 1967—; chmn. region 2 edn. and accreditation com. Engrs. Council Profl. Devel., 1961-65, mem. nat. council, 1965-71, exec. com., 1968-71; cons. heat transfer and combustion. Recipient S. Reid Warren, Jr. award for distinguished teaching U. Pa., 1976; Max Jakob Meml. award for heat transfer ASME/Am. Inst. Chem. Engrs., 1979; Japan Soc. for Promotion of Sci. grantee, 1977. Fellow Am. Inst. Chem. Engrs. (nat. council 1962-64, pres. 1966, Profl. Progress award 1964, William H. Walker award 1969, Warren K. Lewis award 1978, Founders award 1980); mem. Nat. Acad. Engring., Combustion Inst., Am. Chem. Soc., Verein Deutscher Ingenieure (Corr. mem.), Sigma Xi, Phi Kappa Phi, Phi Lambda Upsilon (award U. Mich. chpt. 1961), Tau Beta Pi. Unitarian. Current Work: Interpretation and use of rate data, correlation, natural convection in enclosures, combustion in a refractory tube, reaction kinectics, pollution control. Subspecialties: Chemical engineering; Combustion processes. Home: 137 Pole Cat Rd Glen Mills PA 19342

CHURNET, HABTE GIORGIS, geology educator, researcher; b. Shewa, Ethiopia, May 9, 1946; came to U.S., 1975; s. Churnet Argaw and Yeshewa (Mebrat) Tilahun; m. Enat Negussie, Jan. 17, 1983; children—Dargay H., Bethlehem H. B.Sc., Haile Selassie I U., Addis Ababa, Ethiopia, 1969; M.Sc., Leeds (Eng.) U., 1972; Ph.D., U. Tenn., 1979. Tchr. Ras Abate Boyalew High Sch., Hossana, Ethiopia, 1967-68; lectr. Haile Selassie I U., 1971-75; asst. prof. geology U. Tenn.-Chattanooga, 1980-83, assoc. prof. geoscis., 1983—; research-investigator dept. geoscis. U.S. Geol. Survey, Chattanooga, 1980-85. Author: (in Ethiopian): Techet, 1974. Brit. Council scholar, 1970. Mem. AAAS, Geol. Soc. Am. Current Work: Ore deposition, sedimentary processes. Subspecialties: Geology; Petrology. Home: 731-M Mansion Circle Chattanooga TN 37405 Office: Dept Geoscis 615 McCallie Ave Chattanooga TN 37402

CHUSED, THOMAS M., immunologist, physician; b. St. Louis, Mar. 29, 1940; s. Joseph J. and Marie Irene (Steinberg) C.; m. Judith A. Chused, June 28, 1965; children: Amy Elizabeth, Nicholas Fingert. B.A., Harvard U., 1962, M.D., 1967. Diplomate: Am. Bd. Internal Medicine. Intern Cleve. Met. Gen. Hosp., 1967-68, resident, 1968-69; clin. assoc. Nat. Inst. Arthritis and Metabolic Diseases, NIH, Bethesda, Md., 1969-72; sr. investigator Nat. Inst. Dental Research, 1972-79, Nat. Inst. Allergy and Infectious Diseases, NIH, Bethesda, 1979—. Contbr. articles to profl. jours. Served to lt. comdr. USPHS, 1969-72. Mem. Am. Assn. Immunologists, Am. Rheumatism Assn. Current Work: Pathogenesis of autoimmune disease, lymphocyte physiology, flow cytometry, immunoregulation. Subspecialties: Immunobiology and immunology; Immunology (medicine). Home: 1805 Randolph St NW Washington DC 20011 Office: NIH Bldg 5 Bethesda MD 20205

CHUTE, DOUGLAS LAWRENCE, psychologist, educator; b. Toronto, Ont., Aug. 22, 1947; s. Andrew L. and Helen (Reid) C.; married; children: Jesse Robert, Deborah Evans, Andrew Lawrence. B.A., U. Western Ont., 1969; M.A., U. Mo., 1971, Ph.D., 1973. Lic. psychologist, Ont., Pa. Research fellow NASA, Columbia, Md., 1972-73; asst. prof. U. Houston, 1973-77; lectr. U., Otago, Dunedin, N.Z., 1977-80; assoc. clin. prof. McMaster U., Hamilton, Ont., from 1980; supr. neuroscis. U. Toronto, Scarborough, Ont., from 1980; now dir. neuropsychology Drexel U., Phila. Editorial bd. Clin. Neuropsychology, 1978—; author, editor: Drug Discrimination and State Dependent Learning, 1978; author: Introduction to Surgery in Neuroscience, 1974, General Experimental Psychology, 2d edit, 1977, Mac Laboratory for Psychology, 1985. Group com. chmn. Boy Scouts, Can., 1981—. Mem. Am. Psychol. Assn., Canadian Psychol. Assn., Soc. for Neursci., Canadian Assn. Neursci., Sigma Xi. Current Work: Role of cyclic nucleotides and protein phosphorylation in memory rehab. in severe neurotrauma. Subspecialties: Neuropharmacology; Neuropsychology. Office: Drexel U Philadelphia PA 19104

CHWEH, ANDREW YOUNG CHUL, biochemical pharmacology researcher, educator; b. Korea, Feb. 12, 1944; m. Joanne H. Cho, June 7, 1969; children—Caroline, Thomas, Andrew Y. B.S., Seoul Nat. U., Korea, 1969; Ph.D., U.Pitts., 1977. Postdoctoral research assoc., dept. medicinal chemistry Sch. Pharmacy, U. Pitts., 1977-78, U. Tex.-Austin, 1979-80; postdoctoral fellow dept. pharmacology U. Ala., Birmingham, 1980-82; research asst. prof. dept. biochem. pharmacology and toxicology U. Utah, Salt Lake City, 1982—, also sr. scientist anticonvulsant drug devel. program. Contbr. articles to sci. jours. Mem. Soc. Neurosci., N.Y. Acad. Scis. Lutheran. Current work: Mechanisms of action of anticonvulsant drug and development of neurochemical models for the identification of substances with antiepileptic potential. Subspecialty: Neuropharmacology. Home: 2661 E 3300 S Salt Lake City UT 84109 Office: U Utah Coll Pharmacy Salt Lake City UT 84112

CHYNOWETH, ALAN GERALD, research executive; b. Harrow Middlesex, Eng., Nov. 18, 1927; came to U.S., 1953; s. James Charles and Marjorie (Fairhurst) C.; m. Betty Freda Edith Boyce, 1950; children—Trevor, Kevin. B.S. in Physics, U. London, Kings College, U.K., 1948, Ph.D. in Physics, 1950. Postdoctoral fellow NRC, Ottawa, Can., 1950-52; with tech. staff Bell Labs., Murray Hill, N.J., 1953-60, head crystal electronics dept., 1960-65, asst. dir. metall. research lab., 1965-73, dir. materials research lab., 1973-76, exec. dir. electronic and photonic devices div., 1976-83, exec. dir. applied research planning div., 1983; v.p. applied research Bell Communications Research, Inc., Morristown, N.J., 1984—. Current work: Semiconductors; dielectrics; solid state plasmas; material science; solid state electronics; photonics; telecommunications systems. Subspecialties: Condensed matter physics; Electronics. Office: Bell Communications Research Inc 435 S St Morristown NJ 07960

CHYTIL, FRANK, biochemist; b. Prague, Czechoslovakia, Aug. 28, 1924; came to U.S., 1965, naturalized, 1971; s. Frantisek and Ruzena (Vitouskova) C.; m. Lucie Scheinost, Nov. 26, 1949; children: Frank, Anna, Helena. M.S., Sch. Chem. Tech., Prague, 1949, Ph.D., 1952; C.Sc., Czechoslovak Acad. Sci., Prague, 1956. Research biochemist Charles U., Prague, 1949-51; research fellow Inst. Human Research, Prague, 1952-63; sr. scientist Czechoslovak Acad. Sci., Prague, 1956-64; sr. research fellow Brandeis U., Waltham, Mass., 1964—, sr. research assoc., 1965-66; head sect. enzymology S.W. Found. Research and Edn., San Antonio, 1966-69; mem. faculty Vanderbilt U., 1969—, prof. biochemistry, from 1975, Gen. Foods Disting. prof. nutrition, 1984—; adj. assoc. prof. U. Tex., San Antonio, 1968-69. Editor: Vitamins and Hormones, 1983; mem. editorial bd.: Analytical Biochemistry, 1980—, Jour. Biol. Chemistry, 1982—; contbr. profl. jours. Recipient Osborne-Mendel award; USPHS grantee, 1967—. Mem. Am. Chem. Soc., Am. Soc. Biol. Chemists, Am. Inst. Nutrition (chmn. (nomenclature) 1982, 83 Osborne Mendel award), Endocrine Soc., Sigma Xi. Current Work: Mechanism of vitamin A action in nonvisual tissues. Subspecialties: Biochemistry (biology); Animal nutrition. Address: 914 Lynnwood Blvd Nashville TN 37205 Office: Vanderbilt U Sch Medicine Nashville TN 37232

CIANCIO, SEBASTIAN GENE, pharmacology and periodontology educator; b. Jamestown, N.Y., June 21, 1937; married, 1963; 2 children. D.D.S., U. Buffalo, 1961. Diplomate: Am. Bd. Periodontology. Fellow in pharmacology and periodontology SUNY Sch. Dentistry, Buffalo, 1963-65, from asst. prof. to assoc. prof. periodontology, chmn. dept., 1965-74; assoc. prof. pharmacology SUNY Sch. Dentistry (Sch. Medicine), 1965-73; prof. periodontology and chmn. dept. SUNY Sch. Dentistry (Sch. Dentistry), 1973—; clin. prof. pharmacology SUNY Sch. Dentistry (Sch. Medicine), 1973—; cons. VA Hosp., Buffalo, 1970—, U.S. Pharmacopeae, 1975—, ADA, 1978—; dir. Chautauqua Dental Congress, 1979—. Grantee United Health Found., Western N.Y., 1965-66, 70-71, Nat. Inst. Dental Research, 1967-69, Merrill Nat. Labs., 1973-82, Warner Lambert Co., 1983-85. Fellow Internat. Coll. Dentists; mem. ADA (chmn. council dental therapeutics 1976-78), Internat. Assn. Dental Research, Am. Assn. Dental Research (pres. pharmacology, toxicology and therapeutics group 1979), Am. Acad. Periodontology (exec. council 1981—), Nat. Soc. Med. Research (dir. 1979-83). Subspecialties: Periodontics; Dental materials. Office: SUNY Dental Sch Buffalo NY 14214*

CIARLONE, ALFRED EDWARD, pharmacologist, educator, consultant; b. Reading, Pa., May 2, 1932; s. Jack and Minnie (D'Agostino) C.; m. Jo Ann Nina Zuccaro, July 18, 1959; children: Lisa Anne, Mark David. Student, Kutztown State Coll., 1953-55, Albright Coll., Reading, Pa., 1954; D.D.S., U. Pitts., 1959, Ph.D., 1973. Lic. dentist, Pa. Gen. practice dental resident VA Hosp., Pitts., 1959-60; pvt. practice gen. dentistry, Reading, Pa., 1960-69; Nat. Inst. Dental Research trainee U. Pitts., 1969-73; asst. prof. oral biology Sch. Dentistry, Med. Coll. Ga., 1973-77, assoc. prof., 1977-82, 1982—; asst. prof. pharmacology Sch. Medicine, Med. Coll. Ga., 1973-79, assoc. prof. pharmacology, 1979—; prof. oral biology and pharmacology Sch. Grad. Studies, Med. Coll. Ga., 1982—; also cons.; pharmacology test preparer Nat. Bd. Dental Examiners. Author: (with L.P. Gangarosa Sr. and A.H. Jeske) Pharmacotherapeutics in Dentistry; textbook, 1983, also numerous articles, abstracts and book revs.; Cons., adv. editorial bd.: Jour. of ADA. Served with USAF, 1951-52; to maj. USAFR, 1963-69. Nat. Inst. Dental Research grantee, 1978-81. Mem. Am. Soc. Pharmacology and Exptl. Therapeutics, Internat. Assn. Dental Research (pres.-elect. pharmacology, toxicology, and therapeutics group 1984-85, Am. Assn. Dental Schs. (sec. pharmacology and therapeutics sect. 1983-84), Ga. Acad. Sci. Current Work: Neuropharmacology of CNS; mineralization of oral hard tissues. Fluorometry, dopamine, norepinephrine, serotonin; calcium, phosphorus, fluoride, enamel, dentin. Subspecialties: Neuropharmacology; Oral biology. Home: 25 Plantation Hills Dr Evans GA 30809 Office: Med Coll Ga Sch Dentistry Dept Oral Biology-Pharmacology 1120 15th St Augusta GA 30912

CIBOSKY, WILLIAM, ocean engineer, aerospace engineer; b. Haverhill, Mass., June 25, 1933; s. Edward and Mary (DiPucchio) C.; m. Beverlee Johnson, June 7, 1958 (div. 1978); children: Stephen, Stacia, Dawn, John Courtney, Thomas; m. Marlene Lois Johnson, Feb. 14, 1980. B.S., U.S. Mil. Acad., 1958; M.S., Stevens Inst. Tech., 1964; postgrad. student, Northwestern U., 1967-69. Commd. 2d lt. U.S. Army, 1951, advanced through grades to capt.; project engr., Kwajalein, Mich., 1964-66, ret., 1966; sr. project engr. (Avco Missile Systems Div.), Wilmington, Mass., 1966-72; project mgr. ocean surveillance (Raytheon Submarine Systems Div.), Portsmouth, R.I., 1972-75; mgr. bus. devel. Rockwell Internat., Anaheim, Calif., 1975-77; progrm mgr. Fiber Optics, ITT, Roanoke, Va., 1977-78; project mgr. TRW, Ocean and Energy Systems, Redondo Beach, Calif., 1978-80, project engr. reentry tech. project, San Bernadino, Calif., 1980-81, project engr. undersea surveillance program, McLean, Va., 1982—. Mem. Air Force Assn., Marine Tech. Soc., Soc. Naval Architects and Marine Engrs., U. S. Mil. Acad. Alumni Assn. Club: Harbor View Recreation Assn. (bd dirs. 1982). Patentee deep ocean, multi-leg non-rotating moors. Current Work: Ocean engineering; hydrodynamics; marine design; ocean testing; aerospace engineering; advanced reentry concepts and missile systems. Subspecialties: Ocean engineering; Aerospace engineering and technology. Home: 10725 Greene Dr Lorton VA 22079 Office: TRW 7600 Colshire Dr McLean VA 22102

CIHANGIR, SELCUK, physicist; b. Ankara, Turkey, Jan. 27, 1951; came to U.S., 1975; s. Adnan and Nezihe (Kocer) C.; m. Diane Carol Murphy, Apr. 16, 1984. B.S. in Physics, Middle East Tech. U., Ankara, 1974; M.A. in Physics, U. Rochester, 1978, Ph.D. in Physics, 1981. Research assoc. U. Rochester, 1981-82, U. Ill., Urbana, 1982-85, Tex. A&M U., College Station, 1985—. Contbr. articles to sci. jours. Mem. Am. Phys. Soc. Muslim. Current work: Fundamental forces and interaction of the universe. Subspecialty: Particle physics. Office: Dept Physics Tex A&M U College Station TX 77843

CINADER, BERNHARD, scientist, immunologist, educator; b. Vienna, Austria, Mar. 30, 1919; s. Leon and Adele (Schwarz) C.; 1 dau., Agatha. B.Sc., U. London, 1945, Ph.D., 1948, D.Sc., 1958. Research asst. Jenner Meml. student Lister Inst. Preventive Medicine, London, 1945-46, Beit Meml. fellow, 1949-53; fellow immunochemistry Inst. Pathology, Western Res. U., Cleve., 1948-49; prin. sci. officer, dept. exptl. pathology Inst. Animal Physiology, Babraham Hall, Cambridge; also hon. lectr. biochemistry dept. U. Coll., London, 1955-58; head subdiv. immunochemistry, div. biol. research Ont. (Can.) Cancer Inst., Toronto, 1958-69; assoc. prof. depts. med. biophysics and pathol. chemistry U. Toronto, 1958-67, prof. dept. med. biophysics, 1967—, prof. dept. med. cell biology, 1969—; dir. Inst. Immunology, 1971-81; mem. governing body U. Toronto, 1980—; vis. prof. U. Man., 1967, U. Alta., 1968, U. Sask, 1970, U. Western Ont., 1972, U. Bombay, 1981, Mahidd U., Bangkok, 1982; chmn. immunology con. Biol. Council Can., 1967—; mem. WHO Expert Adv. Panel on Immunology, 1970—; chmn. adv. bd. Internat. Immunology Tng. and Research Center, Amsterdam, 1975-80; mem. adv. bd. dept. basic and clin. immunology Med. U. S.C., 1974; mem. adv. bd. Research in Immunology and Immunobiology, 1972-74; chmn. nomenclature com. WHO/Internat. Union Immunol. Socs., 1980-84; lectr. numerous instns., profl. meetings, confs. and seminars. Editor: Antibody to Enzymes - A Three Component System, 1964, Antibodies to Biologically Active Molecules, 1967, Regulation of the Antibody Response, 1968, Immunological Response of the Female Reproductive Tract, 1976, Immunology of Receptors, 1976-77; Series editor: Receptors and Ligands in Intercellular Communication, 1983—; editorial bd.: Immunochemistry, 1965-70; editorial bd. Immunology, Serology, Transplantation sect., Excerpta Medica Found., 1966—; editorial bd.: Can. Jour. Biochemistry, 1967-71, Immunol. Methods, 1970-74, Bolletino dell-istituto sieroterapico Milanese, 1972—, Immunol. Communication, 1973-85, Jour. Immunogenetics, 1973—, Immunology Letters, 1978—, Jour. Receptor Research, 1979—, Asian

Pacific Jour. Allergy and Immunology, 1983—, Immunol. Investigations, 1985—; contbr. articles to numerous profl. publs.; also catalogues and articles on Canadian Indian art. Decorated Order of Can.; recipient Old Student prize London, 1944; medal Société de Chimie Biologique, Paris, 1954; Pfizer fellow Institut de Recherches Cliniques de Montreal, 1972; Jubilee medal Ottawa, 1977; Ignac Semmelweis medal Budapest, 1978; decorated officer Order of Can. Fellow Royal Inst. Chemistry (U.K.), Royal Soc. Can. (Thomas W. Eadie medal 1982), N.Y. Acad. Scis.; mem. Internat. Union Immunol. Socs. (chmn. 1970—, pres. 1969-74), Can. Soc. Immunology (pres. 1967-69, 79-81), Nat. Com. Immunology (chmn. 1981—), Can. Fedn. Biol. Socs. (chmn. 1976-77), Internat. Council of Sci. Unions (mem. council and assembly 1980—). Current Work: Cellular immunology, immunigenetics and gerontology. Subspecialty: Immunology (agriculture). Home: 73 Langley Ave Toronto ON M4K 1B4 Canada Office: Dept Immunology Rm 4366 Med Scis Bldg U Toronto Toronto ON M5S 1A8 Canada

CIPOLLA, SAM JOSEPH, physics educator; b. Chgo., July 24, 1940; s. Joseph and Florence M. (Mistretta) C.; m. F. Virginia Stover, Jan. 12, 1939; children: Mark, Karen. B.S., Loyola U., Chgo., 1962; M.S., Purude U., 1965, Ph.D., 1969. Adminstrv. asst. Purdue U., West Lafayette, Ind., 1968-69, research assoc., 1969; asst. prof. Creighton U., Omaha, 1969-73, assoc. prof., 1973-83, prof., 1983—; vis. prof. U. Nebr., 1982-83; cons. in field. Contbr. articles to profl. jours. NSF grantee, 1970, 82; Research Corp. grantee, 1972, 74, 79, 80, 81. Mem. Am. Phys. Soc., Am. Assn. Physics Tchr., Nebr. Acad. Sci. Democrat. Roman Catholic. Current Work: Heavy ion-atom collision studies at low energies in solids; efficiency response determinations of semiconductor radiation detectors. Subspecialty: Radiation physics and radiation dosimetry. Home: 2917 S 116 Ave Omaha NE 68144

CIPRIANO, LEONARD FRANCIS, physiologist, space shuttle projects manager; b. N.Y.C., Feb. 26, 1938; s. Angelo and Doris (Silverstein) C.; m. Brenda Leslie Alenick, Aug. 12, 1962; 1 child, Adam David. B.S., CCNY, 1959; Ph.D. in Physiology, U. Calif.-Berkeley, 1970. Group leader U.S. Army Research Inst. Environ. Medicine Natick, Mass., 1970-72; dir. cardiopulmonary lab. Lovelace Found. Med. Edn. Research, Edwards, Calif., 1972-76; asst. prof. Baylor U. Coll. Medicine, Houston, 1976-77; spacelab 4 payload scientist Gen. Electric Co., Mountain View, Calif., 1979-83, mgr., 1983—; adj. prof. Calif. State U.-Bakersfield, 1972-75, Antelope Valley Coll., Lancaster, Calif., 1977-79; cons. Tech. Inc., Dayton, Ohio, 1978-79. Author: Winetasters Choice, 1982. Contbr. articles to profl. jours. Sec. Framingham Conservation Commn., Mass., 1971-72. Mem. Am. Physiol. Soc., Sierra Club, Sigma Xi. Current work: Planning, scheduling, assembling, testing and integrating life sciences payload equipment into space shuttle, negotiating international agreements. Subspecialties: Aerospace engineering and technology; Gravitational biology. Home: 1460 Middlefield Rd Palo Alto CA 94301 Office: Gen Electric Co PO Box 138 Mountain View CA 94035

CISNE, JOHN LUTHER, biostratigrapher, paleontologist, researcher, educator; b. Summit, N.J., Apr. 27, 1947; s. Luther Elmore and Georgia Lee (Johnson) C.; m. Robin Hope Fisher, July 22, 1978; children—Joel Edwin, Nathaniel Robinson. B.S., Yale U., 1969; Ph.D., U. Chgo., 1973. Asst. prof. dept. geol. scis. and div. biol. scis. Cornell U.-Ithaca, 1973-79, assoc. prof., 1979—; trustee Paleontol. Research Instn., Ithaca, 1976—, asst. sec., treas., 1980—. Contbr. articles to profl. jours. NSF grantee, 1975—. Fellow AAAS; mem. Geol. Soc. Am., Internat. Paleontol. Assn., Paleontol. Soc., Soc. Econ. Paleontologists and Mineralogists. Current Work: Gradient analysis of fossil assemblages as applied to paleobathymetry, stratigraphic correlation by sea level curve and paleobathymetric mapping; Morphometric study of evolution. Subspecialties: Stratigraphy; Paleontology. Home: 115 Oak Hill Rd Ithaca NY 14850 Office: Dept Geol Scis Cornell U Ithaca NY 14853

CIVJAN, SIMON, dental educator, researcher, consultant; b. Linkuva, Lithuania, May 25, 1920; came to U.S., 1940, naturalized, 1945; s. Haim and Sonia Rebecca (Blumberg) C.; m. Velta Lilia Jansons, Nov. 6, 1946; children: Ralph Haime, Neal Gabriel. B.Chem. Engring. with honors, U Fla., 1944; D.D.S., U. Md., 1954; M.S. in Dental Materials, Georgetown U., 1963. Enlisted in U.S. Army, 1944, advanced through grades to col., 1971, dental officer, chief clinician various locations, 1954-63; chief div. dental materials U.S. Army Inst. Dental Research, Washington, 1963-73, dir., 1973-74; comdr. 464th Med. Detachment, Vogelweh, W.Ger., 1974-75; dep. comdr. for dental activities U.S. Army Med. Dept. Activity, Landstuhl, W.Ger., 1975-77, Ft. Leonard Wood., Mo., 1977-80, ret., 1980; prof. U. Tex. Dental Br., Houston, 1980—; U.S. Army cons. standards com. on dental materials and devices ADA, Chgo., 1969-74. Contbr. to: Improving Dental Practice through Preventive Measures, 1975; contbr. articles to profl. jours. Decorated Legion of Merit with oak leaf cluster. Fellow Am. Coll. Dentists, Internat. Coll. Dentists, Acad. Dental Materials; mem. ADA, Am. Assn. Dental Schs., Federation Dentaire Internationale, Assn. Mil. Surgeons U.S., Internat. Assn. Dental Research. Jewish. Current Work: Teaching dental students, undergraduate and graduates; dental materials science and research methodology; research in physical, chemical and manipulative properties of dental materials; and act as consultant to individual dentists and dental organizations or groups. Subspecialties: Dental materials; Biomaterials. Home: 5734 Indigo St Houston TX 77096 Office: U Tex Health Sci Center at Houston Dental Br 6516 John Freeman Ave Houston TX 77030

CLAASSEN, RICHARD STRONG, physicist; b. Ithaca, N.Y., May 10, 1922; s. Peter Walter and Evelyn (Strong) C.; m. Ruth Louise Leonard, Aug. 4, 1945; children—Peter Walter, Ann Claassen, Sarah Darlington. B.A., Cornell U., 1944; M.A. in Physics, Columbia U., 1947; Ph.D. in Physics, U. Minn., 1950. Research asst. Substitute Alloy Material Lab., Manhattan Engring. Dist., N.Y.C., 1944-46, U. Minn., Mpls., 1947-50l; staff mem., physicist Sandia Nat. Labs., Albuquerque, 1951-53, div. supr., 1953-57, dept. mgr., 1957-60, dir., 1960-82, v.p., Livermore, Calif, 1982—; chmn. solid state scis. com. Nat. Acad. Scis., 1974, chmn. ad hoc com. on critical materials problems in energy program, 1974; mem. nat. material adv. bd. NRC, 1973-76. Bd. dirs. Bernalillo County Planned Parenthood, Albuquerque, 1979-82. Named Disting. Scientist, N.Mex. Acad. Sci., 1967. Fellow Am. Phys. Soc. Republican. Current work: Materials, energy and adminstrn. of science and technology. Subspecialty: Condensed matter physics. Home: 80 Castlewood Dr Pleasanton CA 94566 Office: Sandia Nat Labs Orgn 8000 Livermore CA 94550

CLAFLIN, ROBERT MALDEN, educator; b. Flint, Mich., Nov. 11, 1921; s. Robert Hugh and Kathryn Elizabeth (Ruhl) C.; m. Barbara Ellen Garrison, June 21, 1957; children—Deborah Ann, Blair Lawrence, Kathryn Elizabeth. D.V.M., Mich. State U., 1952; M.S., Purdue U., 1956, Ph.D., 1958. Faculty Purdue U., Lafayette, Ind., 1952—; prof. vet. pathology Purdue U. (Sch. Vet. Sci. and Medicine), 1959—, head dept. vet. microbiology, pathology and pub. health, 1959—. Mem. AVMA, Internat. Acad. Pathology, Conf. Research Workers Animal Diseases N.A., Sigma Xi, Phi Zeta, Phi Kappa Phi. Current Work: Pathology and academic administration. Subspecialties: Microbiology (veterinary medicine); Solar physics. Home: 706 Carrolton Blvd West Lafayette IN 47906 Office: Purdue U Lafayette IN 47907

CLAIBORNE, C. CLAIR, polymer materials scientist; b. Fredonia, Kans., May 30, 1952; s. Sylvester Oty and Edna Claire (Cummings) C. B.A., U. Kans., 1973; Ph.D., Northwestern U., 1984. Chemotechnician Sued Chemie A.G., Moosburg, W.Ger., 1973-75; engr. Janes Mfg. Inc., Fort Scott, Kans., 1975-76; research asst. Northwestern U., 1976-80; research chemist Phillips Petroleum, Bartlesville, Okla., 1980-84; materials engr. Westinghouse Electric, Sharon, Pa., 1984—. Author: Working with Metals, 1981; Working with Non-Metals, 1981. Contbr. articles to profl. jours. Achievement Rewards for Coll. Scientists Found. fellow, 1980. Mem. Am. Chem. Soc., Alpha Kappa Lambda. Current work: Structure-property relationships in polymer science, polymer composite development, combustion products of polymers and dielectric materials. Subspecialties: Polymers (materials science); Polymer chemistry. Home: 44 S 6th St Sharpsville PA 16150 Office: Westinghouse Electric Corp 469 Sharpsville Ave Sharon PA 16146

CLANTON, JEFFREY ALAN, nuclear pharmacist, educator, researcher; b. Evansville, Ind., Nov. 3, 1953; s. Esly Arthur and Gladys Marie (Seaton) C.; m. Pamela Bean, Aug. 28, 1976; 1 dau., Jennifer Leigh. B.S. in Pharmacy, Samford U., 1976; M.S. in Radio-pharmacy, U. So. Calif., 1977. Lic. pharmacist, Nev., Tenn. Teaching asst. U. So. Calif., 1976-77; intern in radiopharmacy U. Utah, 1977-78; research instr. Vanderbilt U., 1978-79, assoc. in radiology, 1979—; chief radiopharmacy services Vanderbilt U. Med. Ctr., 1981—. Mem. CAP, Birmingham, Ala., 1976, Los Angeles, 1977. Mem. Am. Pharm. Assn. (chmn. communications com. nuclear pharmacy sect.), Soc. Nuclear Medicine, Soc. Magnetic Resonance Imaging, Internat. Aerobatic Club (pres. Springfield, Tenn. chpt. 1980-82), Omicron Delta Kappa. Co-inventor paramagnetic metal compounds for physiol. use as Nuclear Magnetic Resonance contrast agts. Current Work: Developing and testing radiopharmaceuticals and nuclear magnetic resonance imaging contrast agents. Subspecialties: Nuclear medicine; Imaging technology. Office: Div Nuclear Medicine Vanderbilt U Med Center Nashville TN 37232

CLAPHAM, WENTWORTH BEGGS, JR., environmental geology educator, author; b. N.Y.C., Mar. 20, 1942; s. Wentworth B. Sr. and Mittie McGaw (Boardman) C.; m. Anita K. Stoll, June 2, 1973; children—Matthews, Stephen A. B.A., Amherst Coll., 1963; Ph.D., U. Chgo., 1968. Asst. prof. geology Case Western Res. U., Cleve., 1968-74, sr. research assoc., assoc. prof. systems research, 1974-77; research scientist Internat. Inst. Applied Systems Analysis, Laxenburg, Austria, 1977-79; cons. Clapham Assocs., Cleve., 1979-82; assoc. prof. environ. geology Cleve. State U., 1982—. Author: Human Ecosystems, 1981; Natural Esosystems, 1973, 82. Mem. Ohio Hazardous Waste Facility Bd., Columbus, 1984—. Grantee George Gund Found. 1984, Ohio Office Litter Control 1982. Mem. AAAS, Assn. Am. Geographers, Ecol. Soc. Am., Water Pollution Control Fedn., Soc. Computer Simulation, Sierra Club (hazardous waste issue com., 1982-84, Ohio state govt. liaison steering com. chmn. 1982-84), Sigma Xi. Democrat. Unitarian. Current work: Hazardous waste management systems, acid rain, computer simulation. Subspecialties: Hazardous waste disposal; Resource management. Home: 2081 Lamberton Rd Cleveland OH 44118 Office: Cleve State U Dept Geol Scis Cleveland OH 44115

CLAPP, NEAL KEITH, pathologist; b. Waldron, Ind., Oct. 14, 1928; s. Worril G. and Dora (Hurst) C.; m. Dorothy Louise Stockwell, Dec. 19, 1953; children—Cheryl Lynne, Mark Allen, Stephen Neal. B.S., Purdue U., 1950; D.V.M., Ohio State U., 1960, Ph.D., 1964. NIH postdoctoral fellow Colo. State U., Fort Collins, 1961-64; exptl. pathologist Oak Ridge Nat. Lab., Tenn., 1964-81, Oak Ridge Assoc. Univs., 1981—, dir. marmoset research program, 1983—. Contbr. articles to profl. jours., chpts. to books. Bd. dirs. Clinton Little League, Tenn., 1970-83; minister Clinton Christian Ch., 1972—; Mem. Am. Assn. Cancer Research, Am. Vet. Med. Assn., Radiation Research Soc., Am. Primatology Soc., Am. Assn. Lab. Animal Sci. Republican. Lodges: Masons, Optimists. Current work: Chemical and physical carcinogenesis, mechanisms, modification with dietary additives (antioxidants and fiber), primatology, colon cancer models and inflammatory bowel disease. Subspecialties: Pathology (veterinary medicine); Cancer research (medicine). Home: 628 River Bend Rd PO Box 88 Clinton TN 37716 Office: Oak Ridge Assoc Univs PO Box 117 Oak Ridge TN 37831

CLARK, ALAN LEE, research engineer; b. Vicksburg, Mich., Aug. 15, 1951; s. Loren Herbert and Anne Eleanor (Bishop) C. B.S., U. Mich.-Ann Arbor, 1979. Programmer U. Mich.-Ann Arbor, 1972-74; sr. systems analyst MIS Internat., Inc., Southfield, Mich., 1974-81; research engr. Ford Motor Co., Dearborn, Mich., 1981—; vis. sr. engr. P.A.P., U. Rochester, N.Y., 1982. Bd. dirs. Ann Arbor Comic Opera Guild. Mem. Assn. Computing Machinery. Current Work: Evaluation/enhancement of state-of-the-art solid modelling systems and applications, evaluation/enhancement of user interfaces to solid modelling systems. Subspecialties: Graphics, image processing, and pattern recognition; Geometric modelling of solids. Home: 3155 Dolph St Ann Arbor MI 48103 Office: Ford Motor Co SCI Research Lab MS E-1142 PO Box 2053 Dearborn MI 48121

CLARK, ANDREW GALEN, geneticist, researcher; educator; b. Urbana, Ill., July 4, 1954; s. Carl C. and Elizabeth (Taylor) C.; m. Barbara Ghilotti Andersen, Sept. 1, 1979. B.S., Brown U., 1976; Ph.D., Stanford U., 1980. Research asst. Oak Ridge Nat. Lab. (Tenn.), 1976; teaching asst. Stanford U. Dept. Biol. Scis., Calif., 1976-78, instr., 1979-80; postdoctoral assoc. dept. zoology Ariz. State U., Tempe, 1980-81, instr., 1981; vis. researcher Inst. Ecology and Genetics, U. Aarhus (Denmark), 1982-83; asst. prof. biology Pa. State U.-University Park, 1983—. Contbr. articles to profl. publs. Mem. Genetics Soc. Am., Soc. Study Evolution, Am. Genetics Assn. (life), Am. Soc. Naturalists, AAAS, Am. Soc. Genetics. Subspecialties: Plant genetics; Evolutionary biology. Office: Dept Biology Pa State U 208 Mueller Lab University Park PA 16802

CLARK, BILL PAT, physicist, researcher, analyst; b. Bartlesville, Okla., May 15, 1939; s. Lloyd A. and Ruby L. (Holcomb) C. B.S. in Physics, Okla. State U., 1961, M.S. in Physics, 1964, Ph.D. in Physics, 1968. Postdoctoral fellow theoretical physics U. Warwick, Coventry, Eng., 1968, 69; sr. staff Booz Allen Applied Research, Kansas City, Mo., Albuquerque, Ft. Monmouth, N.J., 1969-70; sr. staff Computer Sci. Corp., Ft. Leavenworth ops., 1970-74, Langley ops., 1974-76, ops. staff image processing ops. Goddard Space Flight Ctr., 1976-81, ops. staff sci. and applications project, 1981-83, tech. advisor Landsat Project, 1983—. Author tech. papers. Recipient Am. Legion scholarship, 1957-58; Okla. State U. Instnl. scholarship, 1957-58; Phillips Petroleum Co. scholarship, 1957-60. Mem. IEEE, Am. Phys. Soc., N.Y. Acad. Scis., AAAS, Soc. Photooptical Instrumentation Engrs. Democrat. Current work: Research and development for remote sensors, landsat instrument calibration; ground system design and evaluation for worldwide landsat data production systems; interface with technical representatives from worldwide landsat data production systems. Subspecialties: Remote sensing (geoscience); Condensed matter physics. Home: 5811 Barnwood Pl Columbia MD 21044 Office: Computer Scis Corp Silver Spring MD 20910

CLARK, CLIFTON BOB, physics educator; b. near Fort Smith, Ark., July 8, 1927; s. Clifton Breckenridge and Coly Elizabeth (Stroud) C.; m. Helen Louise Magruder, Sept. 1, 1950; children—Jane Clark Lindle, Charles Brian, Richard Thomas. B.A., U. Ark., 1949, M.A., 1950; Ph.D., U. Md., 1957. Asst. prof. sci. Florence State Tchrs. Coll., Ala., 1950-51; asst. prof. physics U.S. Naval Acad., Annapolis, Md., 1951-55; physicist U.S. Naval Research Lab., Washington, 1955-56; assoc. prof. U.S. Naval Acad., 1956-57; assoc. prof. physics So. Methodist U., 1957-61, prof., 1961-65, head dept., 1962-65; prof. physics U. N.C., Greensboro, 1965—, head dept., 1965-75; cons. Oak Ridge Nat. Lab., 1967, 69, 73, 74, 82. Contbr. articles to profl. jours. Bd. dirs. Wesley Found., Greensboro, 1977-82, 84—. Served with USNR, 1945-46. Recipient Teaching Excellence award U. N.C., Greensboro, 1983. Mem. Am. Assn. Physics Tchrs. (pres. So. Atlantic Coast sect. 1974-75, 77-78), Am. Phys. Soc. (treas. Southeastern sect. 1974—), AAAS, Sigma Xi. Methodist. Current work: Molecular lattice dynamics theory. Subspecialty: Condensed matter physics. Home: 800 Montrose Dr Greensboro NC 27410 Office: Dept Physics Univ NC Greensboro NC 27412-5001

CLARK, DONALD RAY, JR., wildlife biologist, research administrator; b. Garrett, Ind., Jan. 20, 1940; s. Donald Ray and Virginia Ruth (Davison) C.; m. Judith Ruth Fletcher, Aug. 16, 1958 (div. June 20, 1984); children—Diana Lynne, Bryan Stewart, Jill Marie. B.S., U. Ill., 1961; M.S., Tex. A&M U., 1964; Ph.D., Univ. Kans., 1968. Asst. prof. Tex. A&M U., College Station, 1968-72; biologist U.S. Fish and Wildlife, Laurel, Md., 1972-75, biologist, sect. leader, 1975—. Contbr. articles to profl. jours. Recipient stipend Organ. Tropical Studies, 1967, Special Achievement award U.S. Fish and Wildlife Service, 1981. Mem. AAAS, Am. Soc. Mammalogists, Ecol. Soc. Am., Am. Soc. Ichthyologists and Herpetologists, southwestern Assn. Naturalists. Current work: Effects of environmental contaminants on wild mammals and reptiles. Subspecialty: Environmental toxicology. Office: Patuxent Wildlife Research Ctr Laurel MD 20708

CLARK, EDWARD ALAN, immunogeneticist, educator; b. Long Beach, Calif., Sept. 3, 1947; s. Elliott Goss and Iris Evelyn (Price) C.; m. Yukika Tanaka, July 14, 1975; children: Tomas Dylan, Sashya Sabina Tanaka. B.S., UCLA, 1969, Ph.D., 1977. Staff research asso., renal transplant coordinator UCLA, 1970-74, postgrad. research asst., 1974-77; hon. staff research asst. Univ. Coll., London, 1977-79; asst. prof. genetics Primate Center, U. Wash., Seattle, 1979-84, core staff immunologist, 1979-82, 84—; assoc. prof. microbiology and immunology, 1984—, sr. scientist Genetic Systems Corp., Seattle, 1981-84; affiliate Fred Hutchinson Cancer Center, Seattle, 1980—. Contbr. articles to profl. jours. Univ. Regents scholar, 1965-69; Inter-Sci. Research Found. prize, 1977; Edna A. Old Meml. fellow Cancer Research Inst. N.Y., 1977-79. Mem. AAAS, Physicians for Social Responsibility, Zero Population Growth., Am. Assn. Immunologists. Current Work: Human B cell growth and differentiation; monoclonal antibody therapy; immunologic diseases; immunogenetics and evolution. Subspecialties: Immunobiology and immunology; Immunogenetics. Office: Dept Microbiology and Immunology SC-42 U Wash Seattle WA 98195

CLARK, GARY EDWIN, scientist, administrator; b. Lee's Summit, Mo., Jan. 5, 1939; s. Charles Edwin and Mattie Ruth (Galloway) C. B.A., Park Coll., 1961; M.S., Kans. State U., 1966; Ph.D., Iowa State U., 1972. Asst. prof. Central Mo. State Coll., Warrensburg, 1966-68; presdl. intern Nat. Bur. Standards, Gaithersburg, Md., 1972; staff dir. Nat. Acad. Scis., Washington, 1972—. Contbr. articles to profl. jours. Mem. Am. Phys. Soc., AAAS, Sigma Xi. Subspecialties: Nuclear physics; Foundations of computer science. Home: 7505 Democracy Blvd A-123 Bethesda MD 20817 Office: Nat Acad Scis 2101 Constitution Ave NW Washington DC 20418

CLARK, GEORGE ALFRED, JR., biology educator; b. Camden, N.J., May 6, 1936; s. George Alfred and Emily Elizabeth (Fox) C.; m. Nancy Barnes, June 17, 1961; 1 son, Kevin Douglas. B.A., Amherst Coll., 1957; Ph.D., Yale U., 1964. Acting instr. U. Wash., Seattle, 1964-65; asst. prof. U. Conn., Storrs, 1965-70, assoc. prof., 1970-82, prof. biology, 1982—; state ornithologist State of Conn., 1981—. Mem. Northeastern Bird Banding Assn. (pres. 1981—). Current Work: Research on integumental structure in relation to behavior in birds. Subspecialties: Morphology; Ethology. Office: Biol Scis Group U Conn Storrs CT 06268

CLARK, GEORGE WHIPPLE, educator, physicist; b. Evanston, Ill., Aug. 31, 1928; s. Robert Keep and Margaret (Whipple) C.; m. Elizabeth Kister, Dec. 18, 1954; children—Katherine, Jacqueline. B.A., Harvard, 1949; Ph.D., Mass. Inst. Tech., 1952. Instr. physics Mass. Inst. Tech., 1952-54, asst. prof., 1954-60, asso. prof., 1960-65, prof., 1965—; bd. dirs., past mem. vis. com., mem. space telescope inst. council Asso. Univs. for Research in Astronomy. Mem. Nat. Acad. Scis., Am. Acad. Arts and Scis., Internat. Astron. Union (nat. com.), Am. Astron. Soc., Am. Phys. Soc. Research on high energy astronomy. Subspecialty: X-ray high energy astrophysics. Home: 177 Gardner Rd Brookline MA 02146 Office: Mass Inst Tech Cambridge MA 02139

CLARK, HOWARD GARMANY, chemist, center director. Dir. Ctr. for Biomed. Engring. Duke U., Durham, N.C. Subspecialty: Biomedical engineering. Office: Duke U Ctr for Biomed Engring Durham NC 27706

CLARK, JAMES HENRY, biology educator; b. Earlington, Ky., June 17, 1932; s. Henry H. and Emma Louise (Peyton) C.; m. Janis L. Hendrix, Sept. 18, 1957; children: James Gregory, Tricia Lynn. B.S., Western Ky. U., 1959; M.S., Purdue U., 1966, Ph.D., 1968. Asst. prof. Purdue U., Lafayette, Ind., 1970-73; assoc. prof. Baylor U. Coll. Medicine, Houston, 1973, prof. cell biology, 1973—; cons. in field. Author: (With E.J. Peck Jr.) Female Sex Steriods: Receptor and Function, 1979; contbr. (With E.J. Peck Jr.) articles to profl. publs. NIH grantee, 1970—; Am. Cancer Soc. grantee, 1972-78. Mem. AAAS, Endocrine Soc., Soc. Study of Reprodn., Sigma Xi. Subspecialties: Receptors; Cell biology (medicine).

CLARK, JOHN HAMILTON, chemist, educator; b. San Gabriel, Calif., Nov. 22, 1949; s. Charles Warren and Nellie May (Hamilton) C.; m. Piyanud Ruth Hussey, June 12, 1971; 1 child, Cynthia Alison. A.B. in Chemistry and Physics with highest honors, U. Calif., Santa Barbara, 1971; Ph.D. in Chemistry, U. Calif., Berkeley, 1976. J. Robert Oppenheimer research fellow Los Alamos Sci. Lab., 1976-79, asst. group leader laser photochemistry, 1979; asst. prof. chemistry U. Calif.-Berkeley, 1979-85; research supr. photon processes group Amoco Research Ctr., Naperville, Ill., 1985—. Contbr. numerous articles to sci. jours. Nat. Merit scholar, 1967-71; Regents' scholar, 1967-71; Bank of Am. scholar, 1967; President's Undergrad. fellow, 1970-71; NSF Summer fellow, 1970; Chancellor's Sci. fellow, 1971-72; Charles Kofoid Eugenics fellow, 1972-73; Camille and Henry Dreyfus tchr.-scholar, 1981—; Alfred P. Sloan Research fellow, 1982—. Mem. Am. Chem. Soc., Am. Phys. Soc., AAAS, Soc. Applied Spectroscopy, Optical Soc. Am., Phi Beta Kappa, Sigma Xi. Patentee in field. Current Work: Picosecond laser spectroscopy, ultrafast reaction kinetics, chemical dynamics of reactions in solution, laser photochemistry. Subspecialty: Laser-induced chemistry.

CLARK, MERVIN LESLIE, educator, physician, clinical pharmacologist; b. Balt., May 18, 1921; s. Harry and Kate (Simons) C.; m. Lenore Meyers, Aug. 20, 1949; children: Lawrence, Ellen, Andrew, Kathryn. B.S. in Chemistry, Va. Poly. Inst., 1942; M.D., Northwestern U., 1948. Intern Wesley Meml. Hosp., Chgo., 1948-49; resident in medicine City Receiving Hosp., Detroit, 1949-51, VA Hosp., Oklahoma City, 1953-55; gen. practice medicine, mem. Exptl. Therapeutics Unit, U. Okla. Sch. Medicine, Norman, 1955-56, asst. prof. dept. medicine, 1956-62, assoc. prof., 1962-69, prof., 1969—, adj. prof. dept. psychiatry and behavioral scis., 1979—, sect. head clin. pharmacology dept. medicine, 1970-75; prof. medicine Health Scis. Center; chief medicine, dep. supr. med. services Central State Griffin Meml. Hosp., Hayden H. Donahue Mental Health Inst., Norman, 1980—; cons., mem. staff VA Hosp., Oklahoma City, part-time, 1971—. Contbr. articles on pharmacology to profl. jours; mem. editorial bd.: Psychopharmacology Communications, 1977-81. Served to capt. U.S. Army, 1944-45, 1951-53. NIMH grantee, 1957-77; Okla. Dept. Mental Health, 1981. Fellow Am. Coll. Neuropsychopharmacology; mem. Central Soc. for Clin. Research, So. Soc. for Clin. Investigation, Am. Soc. for Pharmacology and Exptl. Therapeutics, Am. Soc. for Clin. Pharmacology and Therapeutics, N.Y. Acad. Scis., AAAS, Sigma Xi, Alpha Omega Alpha. Current Work: Schizophrenia, drug and other treatments, clinical evaluation and experimental design, pharmacokinetics mechanisms. Subspecialties: Internal medicine; Psychopharmacology. Home: 1019 Mockingbird Ln Norman OK 73071 Office: PO Box 151 Norman OK 73070

CLARK, OMER P., laser and electrical engineer; b. Sabula, Iowa, Feb. 25, 1918; s. John P. and Rosa W. (Henrichs) C.; m. Agnes C. Hanna, May 25, 1943; children—Roseanne, Richard O. B.E.E., State U. Iowa, 1941; postgrad. Stevens Inst. Tech., 1957, Northeastern U., 1961, U. Ariz., 1983, 84. Lic. profl. engr., N.J. Mem. tech. staff AT&T Bell Labs., Murray Hill, N.J., 1941-83,, communications cons., 1960-83; pres. Clark Engring. Labs., Inc., Tucson, Ariz., 1979—; laser engring. cons. Clark Engring Lab., Inc., 1983—. Contbr. articles to profl. jours. Patentee transistor binary counters. Designed radar systems for Army, Navy and Air Force, and long-distance communication systems for AT&T long lines. Mem. IEEE (life sr.), AAAS, Eta Kappa Nu. Current work: Designing and building own laser research laboratory, and writing textbook entitled Laser Telecommunications Engineering. Home and Office: 3783 N Forgeus Ave Tucson AZ 85716

CLARK, PAMELA ELIZABETH, planetary geoscientist, educator; b. Troy, N.Y., Apr. 26, 1951; s. Frederick Earl and Elizabeth Smyth C. B.A., St. Joseph Coll. for Women, 1973; Ph.D., U. Md., 1979. Lab. asst./instr. biochem./geochem. chromatography, organizer/editor newspaper, coordinator/biology subgroup dir./field studies investigator NSF project St. Joseph Coll. for Women, West Hartford, Conn., 1970-73; teaching asst. U. Md., College Park, 1973-74; research asst. lunar geochemistry geology Goddard Space Flight Center, Greenbelt, Md., 1974-79; geologist remote sensing sci. U.S. Geol. Survey Astrogeol. Br., Flagstaff, Ariz., 1977-78; resident research assoc. planetary geochemistry/geophysics Nat. Acad. Scis., Jet Propulsion Lab., NASA, Pasadena, Calif., 1980-82; asst. prof geoscis. Murray State U., Ky., 1982-84; prin. investigator Planetary Geoscis. Program NASA, 1983—; cons. planetary radar NASA-Jet Propulsion Lab., 1983-84, NASA/ASEE Faculty research fellow, 1983-84, mem. tech. staff, 1984—. Conbtr. articles in field to profl. jours. Mem. Am. Geophys. Union, AAAS, Geol Soc. Am., Los Angeles Fedn. Scientists, Sierra Club, Wilderness Soc., Sigma Xi. Current Work: Geochem. classification of planetary terrains, planetary radar data analysis, devel. correlation techniques for related remote sensing of different resolutions and wavelengths, devel. text on planetary applications remote sensing, synthesis geol. data for comparison major terrains of terrestrial planets. Subspecialties: Remote sensing (geoscience); Planetology.

CLARK, RICHARD JAMES, electrical company executive, engineer, consultant; b. Cortland, N.Y., June 10, 1925; s. Elwin Emmet and Marjorie Aileen (Snow) C.; m. Anita Frances Rutherford, Aug. 30, 1947; children—Sharon Lynn, Richard James, Jr. B.E.E., Syracuse U., 1950. Engr. Gen. Electric Co., Syracuse N.Y., 1950-61, sr. engr., 1961-70, cons. engr., 1970-82, mgr. design review, 1982—. Author: Handbook of Thick Film Technology. Contbr. articles to profl. jours. Patentee in field. Trustee, deacon N. Syracuse Baptist Ch., 1960-76. Served with USN, 1943-46, PTO. Recipient citation Internat. Electric Packaging Soc., Glen Ellyn, Ill., 1980. Mem. Internat. Electric Packaging Soc. (founder 1977, pres. 1979-82), IEEE, Internat. Soc. Hybrid Microelectronics.

Baptist. Current work: Developing state of the art electronics packaging and interconnection techniques; performing trade studies. Subspecialties: Electronics; Microelectronics. Home: 106 David Dr North Syracuse NY 13212

CLARK, ROBERT WILSON, See *Who's Who in America,* 43rd edition.

CLARK, ROY, optical design engineer, research chemist; b. Brighton, Eng., May 7, 1950; came to U.S., 1976; s. Roy Douglass and Renee (Gardener) C.; m. Laura Marie Ayala, June 28, 1979. M.A. in Chemistry, Jesus Coll., Oxford U., 1973; D.Phil. in Chem. Physics, Sussex U., Eng., 1976. Postdoctoral fellow U. So. Calif., Los Angeles, 1976-79; mem. tech. staff Rockwell Internat., Newbury Park, Calif., 1979-82; devel. chemist Am. Hoechst, Camarillo, Calif., 1982-83; sr. design engr. Sundstrand Optical Techs., Newbury Park, 1983—. Contbr. articles to profl. publs. Patentee visibility monitoring device, 1983. Mem. Am. Optical Soc., Am. Chem. Soc., Soc. Photooptical Instrumentation, Engrs., Soc. Applied Spectroscopy. Current work: Interactions of polarized light with matter in both classical optics, lasers and molecular and atomic spectroscopy; current emphasis on ring lasers and thin film characterization. Home: 561 Westminster St Thousand Oaks CA 91360 Office: Sundstrand Optical Techs 2495 Teller Rd Newbury Park CA 91320

CLARK, ROY WHITE, chemistry educator; b. Oak Park, Ill., Nov. 11, 1930; s. Roy E. and Clara W. (Moore) C.; m. Suma Jane Maupin, Mar. 19, 1955; children: Stephen (dec.), Kathy, Samuel. B.S., Middle Tenn. State Coll., 1957; M.S., La. State U., 1959, Ph.D., 1966. Instr. Middle Tenn. State U., Murfreesboro, 1955-56, prof., 1963—; instr. La. Tech. U., Ruston, 1959-61, La. State U., Baton Rouge, 1962-63. Co-author: Concepts of General Chemistry, 1967. Mem. exec. com. Rutherford County Democratic Party, Murfreesboro, 1976—. Served with USAF, 1948-52. Mem. Am. Chem. Soc., Am. Assn. Physics Tchrs. (chmn. Tenn. sect. 1981-82), AAAS, AAUP, Tenn. Acad. Sci. Current Work: Applications of continuous wave n.m.r.; physics and chemistry of modern weapons. Subspecialty: Physical chemistry. Home: 1315 Lakeshore Dr Murfreesboro TN 37130 Office: Dept Chemistry and Physics Middle Tenn State U Murfreesboro TN 37132

CLARK, SANDRA HELEN BECKER, geologist, researcher; b. Kansas City, Mo., July 27, 1938; d. LuVern John and Mildred (File) Becker; m. Allen LeRoy Clark, Sept. 29, 1955 (div. 1977); children: Brett Harlan, Holly Lin. Student, Iowa State U., 1956-60; B.S., U. Idaho, 1963, M.S., 1964, Ph.D., 1968. Field and teaching asst. Coll. Mines, U. Idaho, 1963-66; geologist Cominco Am., Inc., Spokane, Wash., 1966-67; geologist Alaska br. U.S. Geol. Survey, Menlo Park, Calif., 1967-72, staff geologist, office mineral resources, Washington, 1972-75, equal opportunity officer, Reston, Va., 1976-80, geologist, eastern mineral resources, 1980—; coordination staff mem. Dept. Interior Arctic Gas Systems Project, Washington, 1974-75; chmn. women geoscientists com. Am. Geol. Inst., 1979. Contbr. articles to profl. publs.; author maps. Fellow Geol. Soc. Am.; mem. Geol. Soc. Washington, Sigma Xi, Phi Kappa Phi. Current Work: Geology and resources of barite; Mississippi-Valley-type lead and zinc deposits; geology of Chugach Mountains, Alaska. Subspecialty: Geology. Office: US Geol Survey Nat Center MS 954 Reston VA 22092

CLARK, THOMAS ALAN, astronomer, educator; b. Coalville, Leicestershire, Eng., Mar. 14, 1938; s. Walter Joseph and May (Neale) C.; m. Jean Dennis, Aug. 11, 1960; children: Gillian Anne, David Andrew. B.Sc. in Physics, U. Leeds, Eng., 1959, Ph.D. in Cosmic Ray Physics, 1963. NRC postdoctoral fellow U. Calgary, Alta., Can., 1962-64, sessional lectr., 1965, asst. prof., 1970-71, assoc. prof., 1971-81, prof., 1981—, co-dir. Rothney Astrophys. Obs., 1981—; Killam resident fellow, 1979; lectr. in physics, tutor Univ. Coll., London, 1965-69. Contbr. sci. articles to profl. jours. Fellow Inst. Physics, Explorers Club; mem. Can. Astron. Soc., Am. Astron. Soc., Can. Assn. Physicists. Anglican. Current Work: Infra-red solar studies from balloon altitudes; stratospheric constituent measurement; infra-red astronomy; fourier transform spectroscopy; balloon astronomy. Subspecialties: Infrared astronomy; Solar physics. Office: Dept Physics U Calgary 2500 University Dr NW Calgary AB T2N 1K4 Canada

CLARKE, FRANK H., mathematician; b. Montreal, Que., Can., July 30, 1948; s. Frank H. and Rita M. (Tourville) C. B.Sc. summa cum laude, McGill U., 1969, M.S., 1970; Ph.D., U. Wash., 1973. Prof. math. U. B.C., Vancouver, 1973-84; dir. Centre de Recherches Mathématiques, U. Montréal, 1984—. Author: Optimization and Nonsmooth Analysis, 1983. Assoc. editor Jour. Math. Analysis and Applications, 1985—, Can. Jour. Math., 1985—, Can. Math. Bull., 1985—. Contbr. research articles to profl. jours. Killam fellow Can. Council, 1979, 80. Fellow Royal Soc. Can.; mem. Can. Math. Soc. (v.p. 1985—), Soc. for Indsl. and Applied Math., Am. Math. Soc., Math. Assn. Am. Current work: Optimal control calculus of variations optimization. Subspecialty: Applied mathematics. Office: Centre de Recherches Mathématiques Université de Montréal CP 6128 Succ A Montréal PQ H3C 3J7 Canada

CLARKE, GEORGE LEE, veterinary pathologist; b. Seattle, July 4, 1934; s. Montgomery H. and Jean B. (Cook) C.; m. Carol A. Rogers, Oct. 26, 1968; children—Andrew J.M., Sarah A. D.V.M., Wash. State U., 1958; M.S., Tex. A&M U., 1967; Ph.D., U. Calif.-Davis, 1974. Diplomate Am. Coll. Vet. Pathologists, Am. Coll. Lab. Animal Medicine. Pvt. practice Blue Cross Vet. Hosp., Honolulu, 1958-59, Saratoga Pet Clinic, Calif., 1962-63; research vet. officer USPHS, Bethesda, Md., 1963-80; vet. pathologist and assoc. dir. Upjohn Co., Kalamazoo, Mich., 1980—. Contbr. articles to profl. jours. Served with USAF, 1959-62. Mem. Am. Coll. Vet. Pathologists, Am. Coll. Lab. Animal Medicine (bd. dirs. 1971-73), Am. Vet. Med. Assn. Current work: CNS research, neuropathology, toxicology, drug development. Subspecialties: Pathology (veterinary medicine); Laboratory animal medicine. Home: 9057 34th St N Richland MI 49083 Office: Upjohn Co Pathology and Toxicology Research 301 Henrietta St 7263-209-2 Kalamazoo MI 49001

CLARKE, LARRY DENMAN, aerospace company executive; b. Eng., 1925. Degree, Osgoode Hall Law Sch., 1949. Mem. staff DeHavilland Aircraft; founder, chmn., chief exec officer Spar Aerospace, Toronto, 1967—. Served with Royal Navy. Subspecialty: Aerospace engineering and technology. Office: Spar Aerospace Ltd Royal Bank Plaza Toronto ON M5J 2J2 Canada*

CLARKE, ROBERT FRANCIS, nuclear physics educator, consultant; b. Mpls., Mar. 20, 1915; s. Charles Patrick and Maurine Elizabeth (Clark) C.; m. Charlotte Adele Radwill, July 24, 1966; children: Robert, Carol, David. B.S., U. Fla., 1948; M.S., U. Ariz., 1971; grad., USAF Air Tactical Sch., Air Command and Staff Coll., Air War Coll., U.S. Army Command and Gen. Staff Coll., Indsl. Coll. Armed Forces. Meteorologist U.S. Weather Bur., Washington, 1940-42, 52-58; supervisory electronics engr. Dept. Army, Fort Huachuca, Ariz., 1956-58, nuclear physicist, 1958-62; aerospace engr. NASA, Lewis Research Center, Cleve., 1962-66; physicist optics Hughes Aircraft Co., Tucson, Ariz., 1966-68; instr. math. Am. Internat. Sch., Kabul, Afghanistan, 1976-79; cons., dir. North Star Internat. Metals, Tucson, 1973-75, 79—; radiol. defense officer Fed. Emergency Mgmt. Agy., Tucson, 1980—. Staff officer sr. programs and aerospace edn. CAP, Tucson, Ariz., 1978—, Patriotic and Civic Coordinating Council Tucson, 1982—. Served to col. USAF, 1942-75, PTO. Recipient Grad. Scholarship NSF, 1969; Freedoms Found. of Valley Forge cert. merit; Disting. and Outstanding Service awards Mil. Order World Wars, 1982; Scholarships U. Chgo., 1932; Scholarships U. Minn., 1934. Mem. IEEE (sr.), AIAA, AAUP, Am. Meteorol. Soc. (pres. So. Ariz. chpt. 1982-83), Am. Nuclear Soc., N.Y. Acad. Scis., Ariz.-Nev. Acad. Scis., Soc. Photo-Optical Instrument Engrs., Space Studies Inst., Scientists and Engrs. for Secure Energy, Nat. Trust Historic Preservation; Fusion Power Assocs., Am. Soc. Photogrammetry and Remote Sensing, Assn. Unmanned Vehicle Systems, Acad. Polit. Sci., Arctic Inst. N.Am., Assn. Former Intelligence Officers, Ret. Officers Assn. (n.p. Tucson chpt.), Assn. U.S. Army (pres. 1980-81), Mil. Order World Wars (dir. 1981-83). Lodges: Kiwanis; Elks; Odd Fellows. Current Work: Consultant, physical processes involved in metallic ore extraction and processing using new technology, conducting public education programs relative to nuclear fission and fusion power generation. Subspecialty: Nuclear physics. Home: 5846 E Wilshire Dr Tucson AZ 85711 Office: North Star Internat Metals Inc 35 N Camino Espanol Tucson AZ 85716

CLARKE, STEVEN GERARD, biochemist, educator; b. Los Angeles, Nov. 19, 1949; s. Gerard Theodore and Ann (Rose) C.; m. Catherine Freitag, Dec. 19, 1982. B.A., Pomona Coll., 1970; Ph.D., Harvard U., 1976. Miller fellow dept. biochemistry U. Calif.-Berkeley, 1976-78; asst. prof. chemistry and biochemistry UCLA, 1978-83, assoc. prof., 1983—. A.E. Sloan Found. fellow, 1982-84. Mem. Am. Soc. Biol. Chemists. Current Work: Protein chemistry, role of protein methylation reactions in cell function, protein-lipid interactions. Subspecialty: Biochemistry (biology). Office: Dept Chemistry and Biochemistry UCLA Los Angeles CA 90024

CLARKSON, THOMAS WILLIAM, toxicologist, educator; b. Eng., Aug. 1, 1932; came to U.S., 1957; s. William and Olive (Jackson) C.; m. Winifred Browne, Mar. 4, 1957; children: Ian, Jean, Ann. B.Sc., U. Manchester, 1953, Ph.D., 1956. Sci. officer tox research unit Med. Research Council U.K., Carshalton, Surrey, 1962-64; sr. fellow polymer sci. Weizmann Inst. Sci., Rehovot, Israel, 1964-65; mem. faculty U. Rochester (N.Y.) Med. Sch., 1958—, prof. toxicology, 1971—, head div., 1980—; mem. Inst. Medicine-Nat. Acad. Sci., 1980—. Mem. editorial bds. profl. jours.; author articles in field. Mem. Internat. Assn. Occupational Health, Soc. Toxicology, AAAS, Brit. Pharm. Soc., La Academia Nacional de Medicina de Buenos Aires. Current Work: Toxicology of metals. Subspecialties: Toxicology (agriculture); Environmental toxicology. Address: Div Toxicology U Rochester Med Sch Rochester NY 14642

CLARY, WARREN POWELL, research project leader; b. Lewellen, Nebr., Sept. 8, 1936; s. Oren Vernon and Naome (Riggs) C.; m. Jeanne Carlholm, Aug. 18, 1957; children—David Warren, Douglas Oren, Diane Jeanne. B.S., U. Nebr., 1958; M.S., Colo. State U., 1961, Ph.D., 1972. Rangeland scientist U.S. Forest Service Research, USDA, Flagstaff, Ariz., 1960-76, project leader, Pineville, La., 1976-77, rangeland scientist, Ogden, Utah, 1977-79, project leader, Provo, Utah, 1979-84, Boise Idaho, 1984—. Contbr. articles to profl. jours. Mem. Soc. Range Mgmt., Northwest Sci. Assn. (assoc. editor 1984—), Sigma Xi, Xi Sigma Pi, Gamma Sigma Delta, Alpha Zeta. Methodist. Current work: Ecology of rangelands including grazing effects, understory-overstory relationships, and production relationships. Subspecialty: Ecology (biology). Home: 9615 Ramsgate Dr Boise ID 83704 Office: Forestry Scis Lab 316 E Myrtle St Boise ID 83702

CLASS, JAY BERNARD, chemist; b. Balt., Apr. 14, 1928; s. Morton and Sonia (Smordin) C.; m. Marion Frances Schwartz, Nov. 1, 1958; children—Julia, David. B.S. in Chemistry, U. Md., 1949; Ph.D. in Organic Chemistry, Pa. State U., 1952. Research chemist Hercules Inc., Wilmington, Del., 1952-66, research supr. resins, 1966-69, group leader rubber lab., 1969-80, group leader adhesives lab., 1978-82, research scientist polymer sci. div., 1982—. Mem. editorial adv. bd. Adhesives Age mag., 1984—. Contbr. articles to profl. jours. Served with Chem. Corps, U.S. Army, 1953-55. Mem. Am. Chem. Soc., Adhesion Soc., ASTM, TAPPI, Sigma Xi. Current work: Viscoelastic properties and rheology of polymers and polymer systems; pressure sensitive and hot melt adhesives. Subspecialties: Polymer chemistry; Polymers (materials science). Office: Hercules Inc Hercules Research Ctr Wilmington DE 19894

CLAUSING, ARTHUR MARVIN, engring. educator, cons., researcher; b. Palatine, Ill., Aug. 17, 1936; s. Arthur Henry Fred and Emma Marie Sophia (Opfer) C.; m. Willa Louise Spence, Dec. 19, 1964; children: Erin, Kimberly. B.S., Valparaiso (Ind.) U., 1958; M.S., U. Ill., Urbana, 1960, Ph.D., 1963. Prof. mech. engring., dir. solar energy program U. Ill., Urbana, 1979—; cons. Electric Power Research Inst., Office Energy Related Inventions, Machinenfabrik Angsburg-Nurmberg Neue Technologies. Contbr. articles to profl. jours. Recipient Standard Oil award for heat transfer lab. devel., 1968, disting. alumnus award Valparaiso U., 1985; Fulbright scholar, 1983. Mem. ASME, Am. Solar Energy Soc., Internat. Solar Energy Soc., ASHRAE. Lutheran. Club: Ill. Track. Current Work: Heat transfer, cryogenic modeling, solar energy, numerical methods, performance monitoring. Subspecialties: Mechanical engineering; Solar energy. Home: 613 Hessel Blvd Champaign IL 61820 Office: 1206 W Green St Urbana IL 61801

CLAXTON, LARRY DAVIS, genetic toxicologist; b. Chattanooga, June 17, 1946; s. Carl Woods and Margaret Jane (Davis) C.; m. Betty Reed, May 29, 1971; children: Meredith, Matthew. B.S., Middle Tenn. State U., 1967; M.S., Memphis State U., 1971; Ph.D., N.C. State U., 1980. Asst. Oak Ridge (Tenn.) Nat. Lab., 1971-72; biologist Nat. Inst. Environ. Health Sci., Mutagenesis Br., Research Triangle Park, N.C., 1972-77; research biologist Genetic Toxicology Div., EPA, Research Triangle Park, 1977—. Editorial bd.: Environ. Mutagenesis; Contbr. articles to profl. jours. Recipient Bronze medal EPA, 1980, Sci. and Tech. achievement award, 1983. Mem. Environ. Mutagen Soc. (councilor 1985-87), Genotoxicity and Environ. Mutagen Soc. (pres. 1983-84), AAAS, Genetic Soc. Am., Am. Soc. Risk Analysis, Genetic Toxicology Assn., Beta Beta Beta, Gamma Beta Phi. Mem. Ch. of Christ. Current Work: Development genetic systems for detecting mutagenic/carcinogenic effects of environmental substances, their mechanism of action and statistical methods. Subspecialties: Environmental toxicology; Genetics and genetic engineering (biology). Home: 5121 Huntingdon Dr Raleigh NC 27606 Office: EPA MD 68 Research Triangle Park NC 27711

CLAY, CHARLES GEORGE, JR., computer scientist; b. Kingston, N.Y., Oct. 8, 1954; s. Charles George and Evelyn Bernice (Miller) C. B.Engring., Stevens Inst. Tech., 1976; M.S. in Computer Scis, 1976. Student assoc. IBM, Kingston, 1974; computer systems engr. Space div. Gen. Electric Co., King of Prussia, Pa., 1976-81, Software project engr., Lanham, Md., 1981—. Recipient Batchelor award Stevens Inst. Tech., 1976; Gen. Electric Profl. Recognition award, 1979, 83. Mem. Assn. for Computing Machinery, SIGACT, SIGARCH, SIGPLAN, SIGNUM. Current Work: Image processing, numeric processing methods. Bulk image processing software engineering management. Subspecialties: Software engineering; Mathematical software. Home: 8201 Mandan Ct Greenbelt MD 20770 Office: 4701 Forbes Blvd Lanham MD 20706

CLAY, KEITH ANDREW, botany educator; b. Banbury, Eng., June 29, 1954 (parents Am. citizens); s. John E. and Jane R. (Brown) C.; m. J. Caroline Lee, Oct. 17, 1982; 1 child, Zachary. B.S., Rutgers U., 1977; Ph.D., Duke U., 1982. Research assoc. U. Tex.-Austin, 1982-83; asst. prof. botany La. State U., Baton Rouge, 1983—. Contbr. articles to sci. jours. NSF grantee, 1984. Mem. Soc. Study Evolution, Botanical Soc. Am., Ecol. Soc. Am., Am. Soc. Naturalists, Phi Beta Kappa, Sigma Xi. Methodist. Current work: Symbiotic interactions between grasses and fungi. Subspecialties: Ecology (biology); Population biology. Office: La State U Dept Botany Baton Rouge LA 70803

CLAY, VICKIE LYNN, Quaternary geologist, researcher; b. Long Beach, Calif., July 7, 1955; d. Alfred Levoid and Mettie Lee (Caldwell) C. B.S. in Geology, Idaho State U., 1977; M.S. in Quaternary Studies, U. Maine, 1983. Asst., Idaho State U. Mus., Pocatello, 1973-75; field geologist U.S. Bur. Reclamation, Boise, 1977-78; grad. researcher U. Maine, Orono, 1980; project geologist Dolores Archaeol. Project-Colo. U., 1979—; mus. asst. Anasazi Heritage Ctr., Dolores, Colo., 1984—. Contbr. articles to profl. jours. Mem. Am. Quaternary Assn., Geol. Soc. Am., Idaho Archaeol. Soc. Democrat. Current work: Eolian deposits and soils of the Four Corners Region; including Pleistocene muskox find and agricultural potential of these soils for the prehistoric inhabitants of the area. Subspecialty: Geology. Home: 16662 CR 26 Dolores CO 81323 Office: Dolores Archaeol Project 17219 CR 26 Dolores CO 81323

CLAYMAN, LEWIS, oral and maxillofacial surgeon, educator; b. Bklyn., Sept. 3, 1947; s. Irwin and Esther (Small) C.; m. Minou Rouhani, July 3, 1976; children: Eric Harald, Lara Marie. B.S., Bklyn. Coll., 1968; D.M.D., Harvard Sch. Dental Medicine, 1972; M.S., Wayne State U., 1978; M.D., Hahnemann Med. Coll., 1978. Diplomate: Am. Bd. Oral and Maxillofacial Surgery. Resident oral and maxillofacial surgery Sinai Hosp., Detroit, 1972-76; resident anesthesiology U. Pa., Phila., 1978-79; asst. prof. surgery, chief div. oral and maxillofacial surgery Marshall U. Sch. Medicine, Huntington, W. Va., 1979—; clin. assoc. prof. oral and maxillofacial surgery W.Va. U. Sch. Dentistry, 1985—; examiner sect. on Oral and Maxillofacial Surgery, Oral Surgery Licensing Sect. W. Va. Bd. Dental Examiners, 1981-82. Contbr. articles to profl. publs. Huntington Clin. Found. grantee, 1981-83. Fellow Am. Assn. Oral and Maxillofacial Surgeons (W.Va. alt. del.), Am. Dental Soc. of Anesthesiology, Internat. Assn. Oral Surgeons; mem. Chalmers Lyons Acad. Oral Surgeons, N.Y. Acad. Scis. Democrat. Jewish. Club: Harvard. Lodge: Rotary. Current Work: Application of lasers in bone surgery, microsurgical transfers of bone. Subspecialties: Oral and maxillofacial surgery; Laser medicine. Home: 1427 5th St Huntington WV 25701 Office: 2828 1st Ave Huntington WV 25701

CLAYTON, DAVID LAWRENCE, laboratory director, ocean engineer; b. Santa Monica, Calif., Sept. 23, 1952; s. Robert Ashton and Marion (Mackie) C.; m. Theresa Garvey, Aug. 21, 1982. B.S., U. So. Calif., 1975; M.S. in Ocean Engring., Fla. Inst. Tech., 1977. Technician mech. Harbor Br. Found., Inc., Fort Pierce, Fla., 1976-77, mech. engr., 1977-79, program mgr., 1979-80, research and devel. mgr., 1980-81; dir. Link Engring. Lab., 1981—. Dist. commr. Indian River dist. Boy Scouts Am., 1977-79; dist. chmn. Gulf Stream council, 1979—, mem. exec. com., 1979—. Served with USN, 1970-73. Recipient Dist. award of merit Gulf Stream council Boy Scouts Am., 1981. Mem. AIAA, Soc. Naval Architects and Marine Engrs. (com. mem. 1980—), ASME (com. mem. 1982-87), IEEE, AAAS, N.Y. Acad. Scis., Sigma Xi. Clubs: Pelican Yacht (Fort Pierce, Fla.); Westside Tennis (Vero Beach, Fla.) (1977—). Current Work: Submersible technology, oceanographic instrumentation, remotely-operated vehicles (design and operation), computer-aided design, engineering management. Subspecialties: Ocean engineering; Computer-aided design. Home: 4351 Second Sq SW Vero Beach FL 32960 Office: Harbor Branch Found Inc Rural Route 1 Box 196 Fort Pierce FL 33450

CLEELAND, CHARLES SAMUEL, clinical psychologist, researcher, educator; b. Jacksonville, Ill., Sept. 23, 1938; s. Joseph C. and Charlotte S. (Swanson) C.; m. Lynne Mary Schultheiss, Dec. 31, 1981; children—Sarah, Travis. B.A., Wesleyan U., 1960; Ph.D., Washington U., St. Louis, 1966. Instr. U. Wis. Med. Sch.-Madison, 1966-67, asst. prof. neurology, 1967-72, assoc. prof. neurology, 1972-84, prof. neurology, 1984—. Contbr. articles to profl. jours. NIH grantee, 1980—; Nat. Cancer Inst. grantee, 1979—; Robert Wood Johnson grantee, 1982—. Fellow Am. Psychol. Asns.; mem. Am. Acad. Neurology. Current Work: Pain research and treatment, behavioral treatment in chronic disease, neuropsychology. Subspecialties: Behavioral psychology; Neuropsychology.

CLELAND, CHARLES CARR, psychologist, educator; b. Murphysboro, Ill., May 15, 1924; s. Homer W. and Stella (Carr) C.; m. Betty Lou Woodburn, July 18, 1948. B.S., So. Ill. U., 1950, M.S., 1951; Ph.D., U. Tex.-Austin, 1957. Lic. psychologist, Tex. Chief psychologist Lincoln (Ill.) State Sch., 1956-57, Austin State Sch., 1957-59; supt. Abilene (Tex.) State Sch., 1959-63; prof. spl. edn. and ednl. psychology U. Tex.-Austin, 1963—. Author: Mental Retardation, 1969, 2d edit., 1978, Profound Retardation, 1979, Exceptionalities, 1982; contbr. articles to profl. jours. Bd. dirs. Child Guidance Center, Austin, 1966-67. Served with USAAF, 1943-46, PTO. Recipient Disting. Psychologist award Tex. Psychol. Assn., 1980; Edn. award Am. Assn. Mental Deficiency, 1978. Fellow AAAS, Am. Psychol. Assn., Am. Assn. for Mental Deficiency (v.p. psychology div. 1973); mem. Tex. Psychol. Assn. (pres. 1962-63). Republican. Presbyterian. Club: Headliners (Austin). Patentee in field. Current Work: Creativity, origins of; non-verbal communication; mental retardation (profound). Subspecialty: Developmental psychology. Home: 3427 Monte Vista Austin TX 78731 Office: Univ Texas EDB408A Austin TX 78712

CLELAND, W(ILLIAM) WALLACE, biochemistry educator; b. Balt., Jan. 6, 1930; s. Ralph E. and Elizabeth P. (Shoyer) C.; m. Joan K. Hookanson, June 18, 1967; children: Elsa E., Erica E. A.B. summa cum laude, Oberlin Coll., 1950; M.S., U.Wis.-Madison, 1953, Ph.D., 1955. Postdoctoral fellow U. Chgo., 1957-59; asst. prof. U. Wis.-Madison, 1959-62, assoc. prof., 1962-66, prof., 1966, M. J. Johnson prof. biochemistry, 1978, Steenbock prof. chem. sci., 1982. Contbr. numerous articles on biochemistry to profl. jours. Served with M.C. U.S. Army, 1955-57. NIH, NSF grantee, 1960—. Mem. Am. Acad. Arts and Scis., Nat. Acad. Scis., Am. Soc. Biol. Chemists, Am. Chem. Soc., Sigma Xi. Current Work: The use of enzyme kinetic studies to determine enzyme mechanisms. Subspecialty: Biochemistry. Office: U Wis Dept Biochemistry Madison WI 53706

CLEMENS, GEORGE RONALD, teratologist; b. Albany, N.Y., Nov. 8, 1946; s. George Casper and Helen Ann (Pagargus) C.; m. Barbara Teresa Stoliker, Feb. 9, 1968; children—George Scott, Joseph Garrett, Melissa Ann. B.S., Coll. Santa Fe, 1968; M.S., Coll. St. Rose, 1973; doctoral candidate U. Notre Dame. Research biologist Sterling Winthrop, Rensselaer, N.Y., 1968-79; sr. research scientist Miles Labs., Elkhart, Ind., 1979—, study dir., sect. head teratology and reproductive toxicology, 1979—. Contbr. articles to profl. jours. Mem. Teratology Soc., Behavioral Teratology Soc., Midwest Teratology Soc., Mid. Atlantic Reproductive and Teratology Assn., Midwest Regional Soc. Toxicology. Roman Catholic. Current work: Screening chem. agts. for potential deleterious effects on male and female fertility and embryonic, fetal and neonatal growth and devel. Subspecialty: Toxicology (agriculture). Home: 22561 Briarhill Dr Goshen IN 46526 Office: Miles Labs PO Box 40 Elkhart IN 46515

CLEMENS, WILLIAM JENKINS, psychology educator, researcher; b. Leesburg, Va., Feb. 11, 1947; s. John William and Mary Morton (Riddle) C.; children: Carolyn, Jennifer. A.B., U. N.C., 1968; Ph.D., U. Tenn., 1972. Asst. prof. psychology Coll. of Cape Breton, Sydney, N.S., Can., 1971-77, assoc. prof. psychology, 1978—, chmn. dept. psychology, 1979—; asst. research psychologist, dept. psychiatry UCLA, 1977; vis. research fellow U. Hull, Eng., 1977-78; mem. exec. N.S. Confedn. Univ. Faculty Assns., 1975-77, 81—. Contbr. articles, abstracts in field to publs.; editorial cons. publs. in field. Grantee St. Francis Xavier U., 1971-74; Grantee Nat. Research Council Can., 1975-79; Grantee Natural Sci. and Engring. Research Council, 1979—. Mem. Am. Psychol. Assn., Can. Psychol. Assn., AAAS, Soc. for Psychophysiol. Research, Internat. Orgn. Psychophysiology, N.Y. Acad. Scis. Episcopalian. Current Work: Autonomic self-control, biofeedback, visceral perception. Subspecialties: Learning; Physiological psychology. Office: Univ Coll of Cape Breton PO Box 5300 Sydney NS B1P 6L2 Canada

CLEMENTE, FRANK MASSIMINO, JR., civil engineer; b. N.Y.C., Nov. 3, 1941; s. Frank F. and Catherine (Monaco) C. B.E., Cooper Union, 1966; M.S. in Civil Engring., NYU, 1967; Ph.D., Tulane U., 1984. Registered profl. engr., N.Y., Hawaii, La. Profl. assoc. Parsons Brinckerhoff Quade & Douglas, Inc., Honolulu and N.Y.C., 1967-84; ind. cons. engr., New Orleans, 1984—; adj. instr. Cooper Union, N.Y.C., 1967; lectr. U. Hawaii, 1982; expert reviewer NSF, 1982. Contbr. articles to tech. jours. Mem. Honolulu Transit Coalition, 1980-81. Fellow, Tulane U., 1982-83. Mem. ASCE (Outstanding Tech. Chmn. award Hawaii sect. 1975, pres. Hawaii sect. 1979-80), Nat. Soc. Profl. Engrs., Earthquake Engring. Research Inst., Deep Founds. Inst., Internat. Soc. Soil Mechanics and Found. Engrs., Am. Soc. Engring. Edn. Current work: Field testing and quality assurance of prestressed concrete piles, downdrag, bitumen coatings, pile splices, embankment stability, stabilization of softcompressible soils, construction monitoring. Subspecialties: Civil engineering; Structural engineering. Address: 6062 Chestnut St New Orleans LA 70118

CLEMENTI, ENRICO, theoretical chemist; b. Trento, Italy, Nov. 19, 1931; s. Ambrogio and Laura (Marzari) C.; m. Hildegard Cornelius, 1956 (div. 1972). Ph.D., U. Pavia, Italy, 1954; Postdoctal student, Politecnic Inst. Milano, Fla. State U., Tallahassee, U. Calif., Berkeley, U. Chgo. Mem. staff IBM Research, San Jose, Calif., 1961-65, mgr. research, 1965-69, IBM fellow, 1961-74; mgr. Calcolo Chimico-Montedison, Italy, 1974-79, IBM fellow, mgr. Dept. D55, tech. advisor sci., engring. computation, Poughkeepsie, N.Y., 1979—. Contbr. numerous articles to sci. jours. Mem. Am. Phys. Soc., Am. Chem. Soc., N.Y. Acad. Sci. Current Work: Computational methods to solve biophysical and biochemical problems; use of quantum theory, statistical mechanics, fluid dynamics. Subspecialties: Theoretical chemistry; Biophysical chemistry. Home: 104 Beechwood Ave Poughkeepsie NY 12601 Office: IBM PO Box 390 Bldg 701 Dept D5 Poughkeepsie NY 12602

CLEMENTS, GREGORY LELAND, physics educator, microcomputer programmer, astronomer; b. Lincoln, Nebr., Apr. 5, 1949; s. Dwight L. and Marjory R. (Horstman) C.; m. Pamela A. Clements, Jan. 5, 1974; children: Christina, James, John, Brian. B.A. in Physics, U. Iowa, 1971, M.S. in Astronomy, 1976, Ph.D. in Physics, 1978. Asst. prof. Dickinson Coll., 1978-82; systems mgr. Softec Inc., Iowa City, 1982-83; asst. prof. Midland Lutheran Coll., Fremont, Nebr., 1983—. Mem. Am. Assn. Physics Tchrs. Current Work: College teaching. Subspecialties: Optical astronomy; Software engineering. Home: 749 N Clarkson Fremont NE 68025 Office: Midland Coll Fremont NE 68025

CLEMENTS, JOHN ALLEN, physiologist; b. Auburn, N.Y., Mar. 16, 1923; s. Harry Vernon and May (Porter) C.; m. Margot Sloan Power, Nov. 19, 1949; children—Christine, Carolyn. M.D., Cornell U., 1947. Research asst. dept. physiology Cornell U. Med. Coll. N.Y., 1947-49; commd. 1st lt. U.S. Army, 1941, advanced through grades to capt., 1951; asst. chief clin. investigation br. (Army Chem. Center), 1951-61; asso. research physiologist U. Calif. at San Francisco, 1961-64, prof. pediatrics, 1964—; mem. staff U. Calif. at San Francisco (Cardiovascular Research Inst.), 1961—; career investigator Am. Heart Assn., 1964—; mem. group in biophysics and med. physics U. Calif. at Berkeley, 1969—; cons. Surgeon Gen. USPHS, 1964-68, Surgeon Gen. U.S.

Army, 1972-79; sci. counselor Nat. Heart and Lung Inst., 1972-75; Bowditch lectr. Am. Physiol. Soc., 1961; 2d ann. lectr. Neonatal Soc., London, 1965; Distinguished lectr. Can. Soc. Clin. Investigation, 1973. Mem. editorial bd.: Jour. Applied Physiology, 1961-65, Am. Jour. Physiology, 1965-72, Physiol. Reviews, 1973—, Jour. Developmental Physiology, 1979-85; assoc. editor: Am. Rev. Respiratory Diseases, 1973-79; chmn. publs. policy com.: Am. Thoracic Soc., 1982-86. Recipient Dept. Army Research and Devel. Achievement award, 1961; Modern Medicine Distinguished Achievement award, 1973; Howard Taylor Ricketts medal and award U. Chgo., 1975; Mellon award U. Pitts., 1976; Calif. medal Am. Lung Assn. of Calif., 1981; Trudeau medal Am. Lung Assn., 1982; Internat. award Gairdner Found., 1983. Hon. fellow Am. Coll. Chest Physicians; mem. N.Y. Acad. Scis., Western Assn. Physicians, Western Soc. Clin. Research, Perinatal Research Soc. (councillor 1973-75), Nat. Acad. Scis., Am. Lung Assn. (hon., life). Current Work: Pulmonary surfactont respiratory distress syndrome. Subspecialties: Physiology (medicine); Neonatology. Office: U Calif Sch Medicine Cardiovascular Research Inst 3d and Parnassus Ave San Francisco CA 94143

CLEVELAND, SIDNEY EARL, psychologist, clinical psychology educator; b. Boston, Jan. 22, 1919; s. Herbert C. and Edith (Willey) C.; m. Marjorie Spacht, Nov. 27, 1942; children: John A., Carol T., Mark E., Sarah D. A.B., Brown U., 1941; M.A., U. Nebr., 1942; Ph.D., U. Mich., 1950. Lic. psychologist, Tex. Staff psychologist VA Med. Center, Houston, 1950-57, asst. chief psychologist, 1957-62, chief psychology service, 1962—; clin. prof. psychology Baylor Coll. Medicine, 1957—, pvt. practice psychology, Houston, 1961—; cons. Houston Police Dept., 1967-68, U.S. Surgeon Gen., Washington, 1965, NIMH, 1962, NYU Postgrad. Sch. Medicine, 1966. Co-author: Body Image and Personality, 1958, 68; contbr. numerous articles to profl. jours. Served to comdr. USNR, 1942-46. Fellow Am. Psychol. Assn.; mem. Assn. VA Chief Psychologists, Houston Psychol. Assn. (pres. 1955-56), Southwest Psychol. Assn. Current Work: Medical psychology; psychosomatic medicine; body image; cardiac rehabilitation. Subspecialty: Clinical psychology. Home: 12021 Tall Oaks Houston TX 77024 Office: VA Med Center Houston TX 77211

CLEVELAND, WILLIAM LOUIS, microbiology educator, immunologist; b. Murf, N.C., Nov. 30, 1941; s. Alfred Eugene and Marjorie Jeter (Pipkin) C.; m. Fay Ray Hallen, Mar. 2, 1973; children—Jonathan Hallegua. B.S., Columbia U., 1967; Ph.D., Rutgers U., 1975. Postdoctoral fellow Columbia U., N.Y.C., 1974-79, sr. staff assoc. in microbiology, 1980-81, asst. prof., 1982—. Contbr. articles to profl. jours. Mem. Am. Assn. Immunologists, N.Y. Acad. Scis., Sigma Xi. Current work: Basic aspects of immune regulation, including idiotype networks, acetylcholine receptor immunochem., suppressor T cells, and mechanistic basis of T-cell antigen recognition. Subspecialties: Immunobiology and immunology; Tissue culture. Office: Dept Microbiology Columbia U 701 W 168 St New York NY 10032

CLEWELL, DAYTON HARRIS, research and engineering consultant; b. Berwick, Pa., Dec. 15, 1912; s. H. Bert and Emma Marilla (Kile) C.; m. Vesta Jean Rapp, June 25, 1938; children—Don Bert, Nancy Hartzell Clewell Forsdick. B.S. in Physics, MIT, 1933, Ph.D. in Physics, 1936. Research physicist C.K. Williams Co., Easton, Pa., 1935-38; dir. research Magnolia Petroleum Co., Dallas, 1938-56; gen. mgr. research Mobil Oil Corp., N.Y.C., 1956-62, gen. mgr. research and engring., 1962-64, sr. v.p., 1964-77; ind. cons., Darien, Conn., 1977—; dir. Cordis Corp., Miami, Fla., 1977—, Dynecology, Inc., N.Y.C., 1980—. Patentee (30); contbr. articles to profl. jours. Active Nat. Adv. Com. Oceans and Atmosphere, Washington, 1971-73, Navy Oceanographic Adv. Com., Washington, 1975-77, Nat. Exec. Service Corps., N.Y.C., 1981—. Recipient Environ. Conservation Dist. Service award Mining, Metall. and Petroleum Engrs., 1974. Fellow AAAS, IEEE; mem. Am. Assn. Petroleum Geologists, Soc. Exploration Geophysicists, Nat. Acad. Engring. Clubs: Wee Burn Country (Darien); Cosmos (Washington). Current work: Member executive committee Bermuda Biological Station. Subspecialty: Petroleum research management.

CLEWS, HENRY MADSION, aircraft engr.; b. Phila., Nov. 19, 1944; s. M. Madison and Margaret (Strawbridge) C.; m. Henrietta Thompson, Aug. 20, 1966; children: Alex, Margaret, Leta, Charlotte. B.S.M.E., U. Pa., 1967; postgrad. in areo. engring, N.C. State U., 1968-69. Project engr., chief engr. Bensen Aircraft Corp., Raleigh, N.C., 1967-70; project engr., test pilot Thurston Aircraft Corp., Sanford, Maine, 1970-72; founder, pres. Solar Wind, Inc., East Holden, Maine, 1972-76; chief design engr. Enertech Corp., Norwich, Vt., 1976—. Author: Electric Power from the Wind, 1972. Current Work: Design of state of the art wind energy conversion devices. Designed the Enertech 1500, 1800, 4000, also the Enertech 44, wind generators. Subspecialty: Wind power. Office: Entertech Corp PO Box 420 Norwich VT 05055

CLIFFORD, MARGARET LOUISE, health center administrator, counselor; b. Lakeland, Fla., Dec. 13, 1920; d. Thomas Saxon and Beatrice (Tillie) C.; m. Charles Robert Davis, Apr. 4, 1950 (div. June 1983); children: Daniel Thomas Davis (dec. 1984), Kelly Owen Davis. B.A., Chapman Coll., 1950; M.S., San Diego State U., 1972; Ph.D., Union Grad. Sch., Cin., 1976. Cert. sch. psychologist, Calif., Fla. lic. mental health counselor, Fla. Tchr. elem. schs., Hanford, Cuyama and Blythe, Calif., 1950-68; columnist Daily Midway Driller, Taft, Calif., 1955; owner, operator Marge Davis Sch. Dance, Blythe, 1961-64; psychologist, dance inst. Peace Corps, Kingston, Jamaica, W.I., 1973-76; psychologist Apalachee Community Mental Health Center, Quincy, Fla., 1977-80; coordinator elderly services Ben Johnson Community Mental Health Center, Orlando, Fla., 1980—, pvt. practice counseling; guest speaker Fla. So. Coll., 1981-82, Rollins Coll., 1982. Contbr.: articles to La Femme Newspaper. Organizer, pres. Widowed Person Service of Orange County, Fla., 1981—. Served with USN WAVES, 1943-45. Mem. Fla. Council for Community Mental Health (pres. chpt. 1979-80), Orange County Citizens Adv. Council on Aging (sec. 1982-83), Am. Psychol. Assn., Fla. Council on Aging, Am. Personnel and Guidance Assn., Am. Assn. Ret. Persons, Art Therapy Assn. Democrat. Current Work: Counseling services to elderly. Subspecialties: Developmental psychology; Behavioral psychology. Home: 223 N Central St Winter Garden FL 32808 Office: Beth Johnson Community Mental Health Center 2804 Belcoe Dr Orlando FL 32808

CLIFTON, DAVID GEYER, research chemist; b. Pomeroy, Ohio, Mar. 20, 1924; s. A.R. and Helen (Geyer) C.; m. Anna Marie. B.A., Miami U., Oxford, Ohio, 1948, M.S., 1950; Ph.D., Ohio State U., 1955. Research chemist E.I. duPont de Nemours & Co., Del., 1955-56; postdoctoral fellow Ohio State U., Columbus, 1956-57; research chemist Los Alamos Nat. Lab., 1957-63, Gen. Motors Def. Research Lab., Santa Barbara, Calif., 1963-68, Los Alamos Nat. Lab., 1968—. Contbr. articles to sci. jours. Served to 1st lt. USAF, 1943-46, PTO. Mem. Am. Chem. Soc., Am. Phys. Soc., Am. Nuclear Soc., AAAS. Current Work: Plutonium chemistry. Subspecialties: Physical chemistry; Thermodynamics. Home: 352 Cheryl Ave Los Alamos NM 87544 Office: PO Box 1663 Los Alamos NM 87545

CLINE, JAMES GERARD, engineering and environmental consulting firm executive; b. Yonkers, N.Y., Feb. 18, 1933; s. Barrymore Francis and Mary Frances (Keefe) C.; m. Rose Marie Koeppel; children—Denise, Michelle, James, Christopher, Candace. B.S. in Elec. Engring., Marquette U., 1955; M.S. in Nuclear Engring., NYU, 1960; M.B.A., Columbia U., 1977. Registered profl. engr., N.Y., N.J. Engr. AEC, N.Y.C., 1959-62; gen. mgr. N.Y. State Atomic and Space Devel., N.Y.C., 1962-70; chmn., chief exec. Energy Resource and Devel. Authority, N.Y.C., 1970-76, energy cons., 1976-78; free lance cons., Nanuet, N.Y., 1978-82; engring. cons. Dames and Moore, White Plains, N.Y., 1980—; cons. N.Y. State Legis. Coms., 1976-80. Co-author monograph: Nuclear Power Waste Management, 1965. Served to lt. USN, 1955-58. Fellow N.Y. Acad. Scis.; mem. N.Y. State Energy Research and Devel. Authority, N.Y. State Adv. Council Advancement Indsl. Research and Devel. Republican. Roman Catholic. Club: N.Y. Yacht (social chmn. 1972—). Current work: Energy policy, radioactive waste management, hazardous materials cleanup and control, disposal facilities siting and design. Subspecialties: Environmental engineering; Hazardous waste disposal. Office: Dames and Moore 1 Blue Hill Plaza Pearl River NY 10603

CLINE, MARTIN JAY, physician, educator; b. Phila., Jan. 12, 1934; s. David and Rose C.; m. Evelyn Helen Cohen, June 19, 1955; children—Eric, Avril, David. Student, U. Pa., 1951-54; M.D., Harvard U., 1958. Intern Peter Bent Brigham Hosp., Boston, 1958-59, resident in medicine, 1959-60; asst. prof. medicine U. Calif. Sch. Medicine, San Francisco, 1964-67, assoc. prof., 1968-73; asso. dir. Cancer Research Inst., 1968-73; Bowyer prof. med. oncology UCLA, 1973—, chief div. hematology-oncology dept. medicine, 1973-81; Wright Meml. lectr. Ohio State U., 1980; 1st Dameshek lectr. Tufts U., 1981. Author 4 books in field; contbr. articles to profl. jours. Served with USPHS, 1960-62. Mem. Assn. Am. Physicians, Am. Soc. Clin. Investigation, AAAS, Am. Soc. Hematology, ACP, Internat. Soc. Exptl. Hematology. Republican. Current work: Genetic modification. Subspecialties: Genetics and genetic engineering (medicine); Hematology. Office: Div Hematology and Oncology Dept Medicine UCLA Center Health Scis Los Angeles CA 90024

CLINE, THOMAS LYTTON, astrophysicist; b. Peking, China, May 14, 1932; s. Warren Williams and Helen (Thomas) C.; m. Marjorie Hart, Aug. 7, 1954; children: Judith L., Karen B., Marcia V. B.A. in Math, Hiram Coll., 1954; Ph.D. in Physics, M.I.T., 1961. Astrophysicist, sr. scientist NASA Goddard Space Flight Center, Greenbelt, Md., 1961—. Contbr. articles to profl. jours. Recipient John Lindsay Meml. award Goddard Space Flight Center, 1980, medal for exceptional sci. achievement NASA, 1981. Fellow Am. Phys. Soc.; mem. Am. Astron. Soc., Washington Acad. Scis., Washington Philos. Soc., Exptl. Aviation Assn. Current Work: Cosmic gamma ray bursts, research in astrophysics of gamma ray transients. Subspecialty: Gamma ray high energy astrophysics. Home: 13708 Sherwood Forest Dr Silver Spring MD 20904 Office: Laboratory for High Energy Astrophysics Code 661 Goddard Space Flight Center Greenbelt MD 20771

CLINTON, JAMES MICHAEL, quality assurance scientist; b. Framingham, Mass., May 30, 1950; s. J. Earl and Dorothea Ann (Keller) C.; m. Diane Reazin, Oct. 2, 1976; children: Patricia, Stephanie. Student, Bryan & Stratton Sch. Bus., Boston, 1969-70, Quinsigamond Community Coll., 1971-72; B.A., U. Mass., 1974; M.S., Ind. U., 1977. Cert. quality engr. Research technician, asst. Ind. U., 1976-78; supr. microbiology, immunology quality assurance, radiation safety officer Bio-Dynamics div. Boehringer Mannheim Diagnostics, Indpls., 1978-81; quality assurance devel. scientist Ames Div. Miles Labs., Elkhart, Ind., 1981—. Contbr. article to profl. jours. Active St. Vincent de Paul Soc. Mem. Am. Soc. Microbiology, Am. Soc. Quality Control, Clin. Ligand Assay Soc. Democrat. Roman Catholic. Club: YMCA. Current Work: Devel. quality assurance systems for new immunoassay products. Subspecialties: Immunology (medicine); Microbiology (medicine). Home: 10 Manchester Ln Elkhart IN 46514 Office: 1127 Myrtle St Elkhart IN 46515

CLIPPINGER, EVERETT, research chemist; b. Buffalo, July 18, 1923; s. Grover Cleveland and Joanna (Purcell) C.; m. Delphine M. Marlinski, Sept. 27, 1946 (div. 1974); children—Mark S., Karen S.; m. Mary Elizabeth Borrowe, June 19, 1976; children—Bonnie, Beverley. Research chemist chem. products Chevron Research, Richmond, Calif., 1955-60, sr. research chemist, 1960-63, research assoc., 1963-68, mgr. product devel., 1968-74, sr. research assoc. Chevron Oil Field Research, La Habra, Calif., 1974—; instr. engring. and sci. ext. U. Calif.-Berkeley, 1958-73. Contbr. articles to sci. jours. Served with USNR, 1943-46. Mem. Soc. Petroleum Engrs., Am. Chem. Soc. (chmn. continuing edn. 1956-73, chmn. symposium on olefins 1970). Current work: Chemicals for oil recovery, synthesis and study of detergents. Subspecialties: Enhanced oil recovery; Surface chemistry. Home: 924 Ave Presidio San Clemente CA 92672

CLOPINE, GORDON ALAN, consulting geologist, educator; b. Los Angeles, Nov. 28, 1936; s. Walter Gordon and Sara Elizabeth (Donahue) C.; m. Sara Rose Lapinski, Mar. 2, 1979; children: William, Susan, Russell, Cynthia. B.S., U. Redlands, Calif., 1958; M.S., U. Houston, 1960. Registered geologist, Calif. cert. profl. geol. scientist, Calif. Pres. Clopine Geol. Services (cons. geologists), Redlands, 1961—; prof. San Bernardino Community Coll. Dist., Calif., 1961—, dean instrn., 1978-81; lectr. U. Redlands, 1961—; mem. extension faculty U. Calif.-Riverside, 1965—, field leader geol. field studies and natural environment series. Author numerous reports and studies on geol. hazards in So. Calif. and San Andreas Fault Zone. Pres. San Bernardino County Mus. Assn., 1972. Fellow Geol. Soc. Am.; mem. Soc. Mining Engrs., Am. Inst. Profl. Geologists (cert. profl. geol. scientist). Republican. Current Work: Geologic field studies; lecturer and researcher on San Andreas fault zone in Southern California; geologic hazards investigation. Subspecialties: Geology; Sedimentology. Home: 13093 Burns Ln Redlands CA 92373 Office: Crafton Hills Coll 11711 Sand Canyon Rd Yucaipa CA 92399

CLOUD, JAMES DOUGLAS, electrical engineer; b. Dover, Ohio, Mar. 29, 1928; s. Joseph Douglas and Vieleta (Stiffler) C.; m. Virginia Jane, Aug. 9, 1946; children: Joy, Jay Lee, Paul Franklin, Dayne Bryan, Blake Darron. B.E.E., Purdue U., 1951, M.E.E., 1952; cert., UCLA, 1973. Mgr. systems engring., analysis lab Hughes Aircraft Co., El Segundo, Calif., 1965-67, 70-73, asst. program. mgr. engring., mfg., 1967-68, assoc. mgr. systems labs., 1968-69, advanced systems labs, 1969-70, defense systems div., 1973-76, mgr. tech. div., 1976-79, group v.p., div. mgr. electro-optical, data systems group, 1979—; chmn. bd. Santa Barbara Research Ctr., 1979—. Served with USN, 1946-48. Recipient Surveyor V spl. award Hughes Aircraft Co., 1966. Assoc. fellow AIAA; sr. mem. IEEE; mem. Eta Kappa Nu, Tau Beta Pi, Sigma Pi Sigma. Current Work: engineering management. Subspecialty: Aerospace engineering and technology. Office: Hughes Aircraft Co 2000 E El Segundo St El Segundo CA 90245

CLOUD, PRESTON, geologist, author, consultant; b. West Upton, Mass., Sept. 26, 1912; s. Preston E. and Pauline L. (Wiedemann) C.; m. Janice Gibson, 1972; children by previous marriage: Karen, Lisa, Kevin. B.S., George Washington U., 1938; Ph.D., Yale U., 1940. Instr. Mo. Sch. Mines and Metallurgy, 1940-41; research fellow Yale U., 1941-42; geologist U.S. Geol. Survey, 1942-46, 48-61, 74-79, chief paleontology and stratigraphy br., 1949-59, research geologist, 1959-61, 74-79; asst. prof., curator invertebrate paleontology Harvard U., 1946-48; prof. dept. geology and geophysics U. Minn., 1961-65, chmn., 1961-63; faculty geology dept. UCLA, 1965-68; prof. biogeology and environ. studies dept. geol. scis. U. Calif., Santa Barbara, 1968-74, prof. emeritus, 1974—; vis. prof. U. Tex., 1962, 78; H.R. Luce prof. cosmology Mt. Holyoke Coll., 1979-80; Sr. Queens fellow Baas-Becking Geobiology Lab., Canberra, Australia, 1981; internat exchange scholar Research Council Can., 1982; hon. vis. prof. U. Ottawa (Ont. Can.), 1982; Nat. Sigma Xi lectr., 1967; Emmons lectr. Colo. Sci. Soc.; Bownocker lectr. Ohio State U.; French lectr. Pomona Coll.; Dumaresq-Smith lectr. Acadia Coll., N.B., Can.; A.L. DuToit Meml. lectr. Royal Soc. and Geol. Soc. of South Africa; mem. governing bd. NRC, 1972-75; mem. Pacific Sci. Bd., 1952-56, 62-65; del. internat. sci. congresses; cons. to govt., industry, founds. and agys. Author: Terebratuloid Brachiopoda of the Silurian and Devonian, 1942, (with Virgil E. Barnes) The Ellenburger Group of Central Texas, 1948, (with others) Geology of Saipan, Mariana Islands, 1957, Environment of Calcium Carbonate Deposition West of Andros Island, Bahamas, 1962, Resources and Man, 1969, Cosmos, Earth and Man, 1978; editor and co-author: (with others) Adventures in Earth History, 1970; Author articles. Recipient A. Cressey Morrison prize natural history, 1941; Rockefeller Pub. Service award, 1956; U.S. Dept. Interior Distinguished Service award and gold medal, 1959; medal Paleontol Soc. Am., 1971; Lucius W. Cross medal Yale U., 1973; Penrose medal Geol. Soc. Am., 1976; J.S. Güggenheim fellow, 1982-83. Fellow Am. Acad. Arts and Scis. (com. on membership 1978-80, council 1980-83); mem. Am. Philos. Soc., Nat. Acad. Scis. (com. on sci. and pub. policy 1965-69, mem. council 1972-75, exec. com. 1973-75, chmn. com. on resources and man 1965-69, chmn. ad hoc com. nat. materials policy 1972, chmn. study group on uses of underground space 1972, chmn. com. mineral resources and environment 1972-73, chmn. com. geology and climate 1977, chmn. sect. geology 1976-79, mem. assembly math. and phys. scis. 1976-79, C.D. Walcott medal 1977), Polish Acad. Scis. (fgn. assoc.), Geol. Soc. Am. (council 1972-75), Paleontol. Soc. Am., Paleontol. Soc. India (hon.), AAAS, Geol. Soc. Belgium (hon. fgn. corr.), Phi Beta Kappa, Sigma Xi, Sigma Gamma Epsilon. Field work 6 continents and 2 oceans. Current Work: Biological, sedimentological, geochemical and atmospheric processes in earth history; crustal evolution. Subspecialty: Sedimentology. Home: 400 Mountain Dr Santa Barbara CA 93103 Office: Dept Geol Scis U Calif Santa Barbara CA 93106

CLOUGH, DAVID WILLIAM, molecular geneticist; b. Schenectady, Dec. 27, 1952; s. David W. and Constance Marie (Patnaude) C. B.S., U. Ariz., 1974; Ph.D., Med. Coll. Wis., 1979. Research fellow Eye Inst. of Med. Coll. Wis., 1979; fellow in microbiology and molecular genetics and dept. medicine Harvard U., Harvard Med Sch., Boston, 1979-81; asst. prof. genetics Ctr. for Genetics, U. Ill. Coll. Medicine, Chgo., 1981—. Contbr. articles to profl. jours.; referee profl. jours. Mem. AAAS, Am. Soc. Microbiology. Current Work: Investigations concerning regulation of expression of viral and cellular genes in mammalian cells. Subspecialties: Genetics and genetic engineering (biology); Gene actions. Office: 808 S Wood St Chicago IL 60612

CLOUGH, RAY WILLIAM, JR., educator; b. Seattle, July 23, 1920; s. Ray William and Mildred (Nelson) C.; m. Shirley Claire Potter, Oct. 30, 1942; children—Douglas Potter, Allison Justine, Meredith Anne. B.S. in Civil Engring, U. Wash., 1942; M.S., Calif. Inst. Tech., 1943; S.M., Mass. Inst. Tech., 1947; Sc.D., MIT, 1949; D.Tech. (hon.), Chalmers U. (Sweden), 1979, U. Trondheim, (Norway), 1982. Registered profl. engr., Wash. Faculty U. Calif.-Berkeley, 1949—, prof. civil engring., 1959—, chmn. div. structural engrng. and structural mechanics, 1967-70; dir. U. Calif.-Berkeley (Earthquake Engring. Research Center), 1973-76; Nishkian prof. structural engr. U. Calif.-Berkeley, 1983—; Cons. in field, 1953—; Mem. Nat. Acad. Scis.-Nat. Acad. Engring. adv. com. Environmental Sci. Services Adminstrn., 1967-70; mem. dynamics panel Nat. Acad. Scis. adv. bd. on hardened electric power system, 1964-70; mem. U.S. C.E. Structural Design Adv. Bd., 1967—. Served to capt. USAAF, 1942-46. Fulbright fellow Ship Research Inst., Trondheim, Norway, 1956-57; Overseas fellow Churchill Coll., Cambridge (Eng.) U., 1963-64; hon. researcher Laboratorio Nacional de Engenharia Civil, Lisbon, Portugal, 1972; Fulbright fellow Tech. U. Norway, Trondheim, 1972-73. Fellow ASCE (chmn. engring. mechanics div. 1964-65, Research award 1960, Howard award 1970, Newmark medal 1979, Moissieff medal 1980); mem. Structural Engrs. Assn. No. Calif. (dir. 1967-70), Earthquake Engring. Research Inst. (dir. 1957-60, 70-73), Seismol. Soc. Am. (dir. 1970-73), Nat. Acad. Scis., Nat. Acad. Engring., Det Kongelige Norske Videnskabers Selskab. Current Work: Research in methods of analysis of dynamic structural response to earthquakes; shaking table study of nonlinear structural dynamic behavior. Subspecialty: Civil engineering. Home: 576 Vistamont Ave Berkeley CA 94708

CLOUTIER, PAUL ANDREW, space physicist, educator, research and development executive; b. Opelousas, La., Feb. 7, 1943; s. Andrew Hyams and Carmena Madeline (Mizzi) C.; m. Sybil Ann Camel, June 6, 1964; children—Niki Monique, Andrew Michael. B.S. in Physics, U. Southwestern La., 1964; Ph.D. in Space Sci., Rice U., 1967. Asst. prof. Rice U., Houston, 1967-72, assoc. prof., 1972-77, prof. space physics and astronomy, 1977—; pres., chmn. Innovatum, Inc., Houston, 1979—, also dir.; pres., dir. Hatteras, Inc., Rio Hondo, Tex., 1976—; cons. Office Space Sci., NASA, Washington, 1967—. Contbr. chpt. to textbook, articles to profl. jours. Patentee magnetic location invention. Co-discoverer historic shipwreck USS Hatteras. NASA fellow, 1965-67; research grantee NSF, 1968-78, NASA, 1967—. Republican. Current work: Solar wind interaction with planetary atmospheres, computer models of magnetic sources, design of remote sensing equipment in magnetics, electrostatics, optics, acoustics. Subspecialties: Planetary atmospheres; Plasma physics. Office: Rice Univ Dept Space Physics and Astronomy Main St Houston TX 77001

CLOWES, ALEXANDER WHITEHILL, vascular surgeon, researcher; b. Boston, Oct. 9, 1946; s. George H.A. (Sr.) and Margaret (Jackson) C.; m. Monika Meyer, May 4, 1980. A.B., Harvard U., 1968, M.D., 1972. Diplomate: Am. Bd. Surgery. Resident in surgery Case Western Res. U., Cleve., 1972-74, 76-79; research fellow in pathology Harvard Med. Sch., Boston, 1974-76; fellow in vascular surgery Peter Bent Brigham Hosp., Boston, 1979-80; asst. prof. surgery U. Wash., Seattle, 1980-85, assoc. prof. surgery, 1985—; attending surgeon Seattle hosps., Pacific Med. Ctr., Harborview Med. Center, Univ. Hosp., Seattle VA Hosp., 1980—. NIH Research Career Devel. awardee, 1983. Mem. Assn. for Acad. Surgery, Soc. Univ. Surgeons, ACS, Assn. Am. Pathologists, Am. Soc. Cell Biology, Internat. Soc. Cardiovascular Surgery, Henry Harkins Soc. Current Work: Atherosclerosis, arterial injury, and repair, arterial endothelial and smooth muscle cell proliferation, mechanisms of arterial graft failure. Subspecialties: Surgery; Cell biology (medicine). Home: 702 Fullerton Ave Seattle WA 98122 Office: Univ Wash Sch Medicine RF-25 Seattle WA 98195

CLUFF, LEIGHTON EGGERTSEN, physician, foundation executive; b. Salt Lake City, June 10, 1923; s. Lehi Eggertsen and Lottie (Brain) C.; m. Beth Allen, Aug. 19, 1944; children: Claudia Beth, Patricia Leigh. B.S., U. Utah, 1944; M.D. with distinction, George Washington U., 1949; Sc.D. (hon.), Hahnemann Med. Sch., 1979. Intern Johns Hopkins Hosp., 1949-50, asst. resident, 1951-52; asst. resident physician Duke Hosp., 1950- 51; vis. investigator, asst. physician Rockefeller Inst. Med. Research, 1952-54; fellow Nat. Found. Infantile Paralysis, 1952-54; mem. faculty Johns Hopkins Sch. Medicine; staff Johns Hopkins Hosp., 1954-66, prof. medicine, 1964-66, physician, head div. clin. immunology, allergy and infectious diseases, 1958-66; prof., chmn. dept. medicine U. Fla., 1966-76; exec. v.p. Robert Wood Johnson Found., 1976—; U.S. del. U.S.-Japan Coop. Med. Sci. Program, 1972-81; mem. council drugs A.M.A., 1965-67; mem. NRC-Nat. Acad. Sci. Drug Research Bd., 1965-71; mem. expert adv. panel bacterial diseases (coccal infection) WHO; mem. council Nat. Inst. Allergy and Infectious Diseases, 1968-72; cons. FDA; tng. grant com. NIH, 1964-68. Author, editor books on internal medicine, infectious diseases, clin. pharmacology.; Contbr. articles to profl. jours. Markle scholar med. scis., 1955-62; recipient Career Research award NIH, 1962; named to Johns Hopkins U. Soc. Scholars, 1985. Mem. Inst. Medicine-Nat. Acad. Scis., Am. Soc. Clin. Investigation, Assn. Life Scis.-Nat. Acad. Scis., Assn. Am. Physicians, Soc. Exptl. Biology and Medicine, Am. Assn. Immunologists, Am. Fedn. Clin. Research, Harvey Soc., N.Y. Acad. Sci., Infectious Disease Soc. Am. (pres. 1973), So. Soc. Clin. Investigation, A.C.P. (Fla. gov. 1975-76, Mead-Johnson postgrad. scholar 1954-55, Ordronaux award med. scholarship 1949), Am. Clin. and Climatological Assn., Alpha Omega Alpha. Subspecialties: Internal medicine; Pharmacology. Home: 7 Beechtree Ln Princeton NJ 08540

COAKLEY, STELLA MELUGIN, plant pathologist, educator; b. Modesto, Calif., Sept. 1, 1947; d. John Bannister and Alice Dora (Caulkins) Melugin; m. James Alexander Coakley, Sept. 18, 1971; children: Sarah Christine, Miriam Alice, Martha Vey. A.A., Modesto Jr. Coll., 1967; B.S., U. Calif., Davis, 1969, M.S., 1970, Ph.D., 1973. Instr. dept. biol. scis. U. Denver, 1973; vis. asst. prof. Instr. dept. biol. scis., 1973-75; adj. asst. prof. U. Denver, 1977-81, assoc. research prof., 1981—; postdoctoral fellow advanced study program Nat. Ctr. Atmospheric Research, Boulder, Colo., 1975-76. Contbr. articles to profl. jours. NSF trainee, 1969-72; NSF grantee. Mem. Am. Phytopath. Soc., AAAS, Am. Meteorol Soc. Current Work: Investigation of the effect of climatic variation on the occurrence of plant diseases; emphasis on fungal diseases on wheat. Subspecialties: Plant pathology; Climatology. Office: Nat Ctr Atmospheric Research PO Box 3000 Boulder CO 80307

COATE, BARRIE DOUGLAS, horticulturist, consultant; b. Juneau, Alaska; s. Carl Douglas and Ruth (Carmichael) C.; m. Bernice Frances Gryba, 1962; children: Richard D., Wesley D.; m. Carol Ann Riehl. Student, San Jose State Coll., 1952-53, San Jose City Coll., 1954-56. Supt. Saratoga Hort. Found., 1956-63; br. mgr. Pacific Nurseries, Inc., Colma, Calif., 1963-69; mgr. Western Tree Nurseries, Inc., Gilroy, Calif., 1969-71; v.p., gen. mgr. Barrier's Trees & Shrubs, Aptos, Calif., 1971-78; dir. hort. Saratoga (Calif.) Hort. Found., 1978—. Author: Selected Native Plants in Color, 1980, A Success List of Water Conserving Plants, 1982, Selected California Native Plants with Commercial Sources, 1979. Mem. Calif. Water Conservation Com. Served with inf. U.S. Army, 1952-54. Mem. Internat. Plant Propagators Soc., Internat. Soc. Arboriculture, Soc. Cons. Arborists. Club: Midori Bonsai (San Jose, Calif.). Current Work: Search, evaluation for introduction of new ornamental, drought-tolerant plants for mid-California. Subspecialties: Resource conservation; Plant growth. Office: PO Box 308 Saratoga CA 95070

COATE, LESTER EDWIN, environmental engineer, government official; b. Albany, Oreg., Jan. 21, 1936; s. Lester and Mildred Roxanne (Clark) C.; m. Cheryl Mizer, Dec. 22, 1973; children—Steven Allen, David Scott, Carol Maureen. B.S., Oreg. State U., 1959; M.A., Calif. State U.,-San Diego, 1969; Ph.D., U.S. Internat. U., 1973. Diplomate Am. Acad. Environ. Engrs.; registered profl. engr., Calif., Wash., Oreg., Alaska. Civil engring. asst. Los Angeles County Flood Control Dist., 1959-61; gen. mgr., ptnr. Robinson & Coate, Valley Ctr., Calif., 1961-64; gen. mgr., chief engr. Valley Ctr. Mcpl. Water Dist., 1964-70; White House fellow, special asst. to chmn. Council on Environ. Quality, Exec. Office Pres., Washington, 1970-71, staff asst. to Pres. for environ. affairs, 1971; dir. Integrated Regional Environ. Mgmt. Project, San Diego, 1971-73; dep. regional adminstr. EPA, Seattle, 1973—; affiliate assoc. prof. environ. studies U. Wash., Seattle, 1974—. Author: A Case Study in Implementation of Environmental Impact Report Requirement, 1973; Regional Environmental Management, Selected Proceedings of National Conference, 1975; Acid Rain in the Northwest, 1984. Served to 1st lt. AUS, 1959-60.

Recipient John Murdoch State and Nat. Advancement award Am. Water Works Assn., 1966, Bronze medal EPA, 1975, Outstanding Young Civil Engr. award ASCE, 1966, Silver medal EPA, 1977. Mem. Calif. C. of C. (v.p. 1965-67). Lodge: Rotary (pres.). Current work: Supervision of resource protection; serve on national task forces concerning employee and polluter behavior; field coordinator for national lake survey to assess acid deposition problem. Subspecialties: Resource management; Environmental engineering. Office: 1200 6th Ave Seattle WA 98101

COBB, CAROLUS MELVILLE, science and engineering corporation executive, industrial chemist; b. Lynn, Mass., Jan. 22, 1922; s. Carolus Melville and Estelle Cecillia (Snow) C.; 1 child, Carolus Melville. S.B., MIT, 1944, PH.D., 1951. Chemist, Tenn. Eastman Co., Oak Ridge, 1944-46; sr. chemist Ionics Inc., Cambridge, Mass., 1951-55, Allied Research Inc., Boston, 1955-60; chief chemist, v.p., dir. Am. Sci. & Engring. Inc., Cambridge, 1960—. Contbr. articles to profl. jours. Patentee in field. Mem. Am. Chem. Soc., Am. Phys. Soc., AAAS. Club: Maugas (Wellesley, Mass.). Current work: Medical research, advanced material problems. Subspecialty: Chemistry research management. Office: Am Sci & Engring Inc Fort Washington Cambridge MA 02139

COBB, R(AYMOND) LYNN, chemist, researcher; b. Ochelata, Okla., Dec. 10, 1929; s. Wilmer Raymond and Tura Bee (Harman) C.; m. Frances Anne Ohlendorf, Mar. 5, 1966; 1 child, Jonathan. B.S., Ottawa U. (Kans.), 1951; Ph.D., U. Kans.-Lawrence, 1955. Research chemist Phillips Petroleum, Bartlesville, Okla., 1955-66, sr. research chemist, 1966-80, research assoc., 1980—. Author: Cycloaddition Reactions, 1965. Contbr. articles to profl. jours. Patentee in field. Mem. Am. Chem. Soc. Republican. Baptist. Subspecialties: Organic chemistry; Synthetic chemistry. Home: 2806 Staats St Bartlesville OK 74006 Office: Phillips Petroleum Co 88F PRC Bartlesville OK 74004

COBB, WILLIAM THOMPSON, research scientist; b. Spokane, Wash., Nov. 10, 1942; s. Elmer Jean and Martha Ella (Napier) C.; m. Sandra L. Hodgson, Aug. 30, 1964; children: Michael R., Melanie S. Cobb Kaye, Megan A., William Thompson. B.A., Eastern Wash. U., 1964; Ph.D., Oreg. State U., 1973. Cert. profl. agronomist. Mgr./agronomist Sun Royal Co., Royal City, Wash., 1970-74; sr. scientist Lilly Research Labs., Kennewick, Wash., 1974-78, research scientist, 1978—; instr. plant pathology Columbia Basin Coll., 1971, 73, 75, 77. Mem. Royal City (Wash.) Sch. Bd., 1973-74, scoutmaster, 1972-73. Served to 1st lt. AC U.S. Army, 1964-66. Mem. Am. Soc. Agronomy, Weed Sci. Soc. Am., Am. Phytopath. Soc., Sigma Xi. Current Work: Pesticide research and development. Subspecialties: Plant pathology; Weed science. Home: 815 S Kellogg Kennewick WA 99336

COBURN, HERBERT DIGHTMAN, JR., mech. design engr.; b. N.Y.C., Nov. 5, 1919; s. Herbert Dightman and Miriam (Ware) C.; m. Julia Mae Ledbetter, July 29, 1944; children: Herbert Bryant, Randall Nye. Student, Friends Sem., N.Y.C., 1936-39, Newark Coll. Engring., 1939-42; B.S.M.E., So. Meth. U., 1947. Chem. lab. asst. Philip Stroughton & Co., N.Y.C., 1936-39; plate grainer Photoplate Co., Newark, 1939-42; results engr. Southwestern Electric Service Co., Jacksonville, Tex., 1947-50, Tex. Electric Service Co., Monahans, 1950-52; mech. design engr., geophys. exploration equipment Tex. Instruments Inc., Dallas, 1952—. Active Circle Ten council Boy Scouts Am., 1958-75; active Southwood Meth. Ch., Dallas, 1958-82, including chmn. bd., 1959-60. Served with U.S. Army, 1942-45. Recipient Order of Arrow award Boy Scouts Am., 1962. Mem. ASME. Patentee in field. Current Work: Design, development, prototype construction and evaluation of geophysical exploration equipment. Subspecialties: Mechanical engineering; Petroleum engineering. Home: 3427 S Ravinia Dallas TX 75233 Office: PO Box 225621 M/S 3904 Dallas TX 75265

COBURN, TIMOTHY CRAIG, statistician, engineering consultant; b. Houston, May 10, 1951; s. Robert Reeves and Doris Madeline (Gardner) C. B.S., B.S.Ed., Abilene Christian U., 1973; M.S., Okla. State U., 1975, Ph.D., 1980. Research asst. stats. Okla. State U., Stillwater, 1973-76; regional statistician Food and Nutrition Service, USDA, Dallas, 1976-78; asst. cons. statistician Okla. Agr. Exptl. Sta., Stillwater, 1978-80; statistician Phillips Petroleum Co., Bartlesville, Okla., 1980-83, research statistician, Denver, from 1983; now with Marathon Oil Co., Littleton, Colo.; cons. statistician Carson & Tratner, Oklahoma City, 1975, dept. gen. sci. Jackson State U., Miss., 1981—; expert witness Mobil Oil, Phillips Petroleum, Chevron USA, Seattle, 1983-84; mem. vis. com., math. dept. Abilene Christian U., Tex., 1985—. Referee Jour. Communications in Stats., 1984-85. Contbr. articles to profl. jours. Lectr. secondary sch. lecture program Math. Assn. Am. (Dallas sect.), 1977. Grantee USDA, 1979. Mem. Am. Statis. Assn. (pres. Okla. chpt. 1983-84), Internat. Assn. Math. Geologists, AAAS, Am. Soc. Quality Control, Internat. Biometric Soc., Sigma Xi. Democrat. Mem. Church of Christ. Current work: Statistical calibration techniques; design of experiments; sample survey design; systematic sampling techniques; as applies to petroleum production and drilling research problems. Subspecialties: Statistics; Petroleum engineering. Office: Marathon Oil Co PO Box 269 Littleton CO 80160

COCHÉ, ERICH HENRY ERNST, psychologist; b. Nijmegen, Netherlands, June 24, 1941; came to U.S., 1968; s. Erich Johannes Maximilian and Frieda Sophie (Moellmann) C.; m. Judith Abbe Milner, Oct. 16, 1966; children: Raymond Erich, Juliette Laura. Ph.D., U. Bonn, 1968. Diplomate: Am. Bd. Profl. Psychology. Teaching asst. Tchrs. Coll., Bonn, Ger., 1966-68; clin. psychologist Friends Hosp., Phila., 1968-74, dir. psychol. services and research, 1974—; pvt. practice psychology, Phila. Contbr. articles to profl. jours. Vice pres. Mental Health Assn. Southeastern Pa., 1982-84. Fellow Pa. Psychol. Assn., Soc. Personality Assessment; mem. Am. Psychol. Assn., Phila. Soc. Clin. Psychologists (pres. 1977-78). Current Work: Psychotherapy outcome and process research. Subspecialties: Clinical psychology; Behavioral psychology. Address: 2037 Delancey Pl Philadelphia PA 19103

COCKERHAM, COLUMBUS CLARK, geneticist, educator; b. Mountain Park, N.C., Dec. 12, 1921; s. Corbett C. and Nellie Bruce (McCann) C.; m. Joyce Evelyn Allen, Feb. 26, 1944; children: Columbus Clark Jr., Jean Allen, Bruce Allen. B.S., N.C. State Coll., 1943, M.S., 1949; Ph.D., Iowa State Coll., 1952. Asst. prof. biostats. U. N.C., Chapel Hill, 1952-53; mem. faculty N.C. State U., Raleigh, 1953—, prof. stats., 1959-72, William Neal Reynolds prof. stats. and genetics, 1972—; mem. genetics study sect. NIH, 1965-69; cons. adv. com. protocols for safety evaluation FDA, 1967-69. Author papers population and quantitative genetics, plant and animal breeding.; Editor, assoc. editor: Theoretical Population Biology, 1975—; editorial bd.: Genetics, 1969-72, Genetic Epidemiology, 1984—; asso. editor: Am. Jour. Human Genetics, 1978-80. Served with USMCR, 1943-46. Recipient N.C. award in sci., 1976, Oliver Max Gardner award, 1980, D.D. Mason faculty award, 1983; grantee Nat. Inst. Gen. Med. Scis., 1960—. Fellow Am. Soc. Agronomy; mem. Nat. Acad. Scis., AAAS, Am. Soc. Animal Sci., Am. Soc. Naturalists, Biometric Soc., Genetics Soc. Am., Am. Soc. Human Genetics, Genetics Soc. Japan (foreign hon. mem. 1984), Sigma Xi, Gamma Sigma Delta (award merit 1964), Phi Kappa Phi. Subspecialties: Animal genetics; Plant genetics. Home: 2110 Coley Forest Pl Raleigh NC 27607 Office: Dept Statistics Box 8203 NC State Univ Raleigh NC 27695

COCKERHAM, LORRIS G., air force officer, scientist; b. Denham Springs, La., Sept. 27, 1935; s. Warren Conrad and Frances Leda (Scivicque) C.; m. Patricia Ann Stagg, Aug. 16, 1957; children—Michael B., Richard L., Ann E., Joseph D. B.A., La. Coll., 1957; M.S., Colo. State U., 1973, Ph.D., 1979. Instr. U.S. Air Force Acad., Colorado Springs, Colo., 1973-75, asst. prof., div. dir., 1975-77; wing elec. warfare officer Griffiss AFB, N.Y., 1977-78, squadron comdr., 1978-80; chief div. Armed Forces Radiobiology Research Inst., Bethesda, Md., 1980—; cons. Biomed. Cons. Inc., Arlington, Va., 1984—, Triangle Research and Devel. Corp., N.C., 1983—. Contbg. author various books. Contbr. articles to profl. jours. Chmn. bd. deacons 1st Baptist Ch., Rockville, Md., 1984; chmn. coms. Iroquois council Boy Scouts Am., 1978-80. Mem. Aerospace Med. Assn., Am. Physiol. Soc., N.Y. Acad. Scis., Soc. for Neurosci., Soc. Toxicology, Sigma Xi, Alpha Epsilon Delta, Phi Kappa Phi. Republican. Current work: Effects of radiation on the central nervous system. Subspecialties: Neurophysiology; Radiation biology. Home: 11613 Silent Valley Ln Gaithersburg MD 20878 Office: Armed Forces Radiobiolgy Research Inst Bethesda MD 20814-5145

COCKSHUTT, ERIC PHILIP, research scientist; b. Brantford, Ont., Can., May 30, 1929; s. Eric Morton and Kathleen Isobel (Buck) C.; m. Julia Ann Fink, Sept. 11, 1954; children—Martha Jane, Catherine Margaret, Eric William, Amanda Mary, Paul Edmund. B.A.Sc in Mech. Engring. U. Toronto, 1950; M.S., M.I.T., 1951, Sc.D., 1954. Research officer Engine Lab., NRC, Ottawa, Ont., 1953-67, sect. head, 1967-75, dir. energy research, 1975—; sessional lectr. Carleton U., Ottawa, 1959-73. Ethyl Corp. fellow, 1952-54. Fellow Can. Aero. and Space Inst. (Casey Baldwin award 1960, 64); mem. Can. Soc. Mech. Engring. Anglican. Current work: Direct extramural programs in solar, wind, biomass, heat pumps, hydrogen and energy storage. Subspecialty: Solar energy. Home: 120 Dorothea Dr Ottawa ON K1V 7C7 Canada Office: Nat Research Council Ottawa ON K1A 0R6 Canada

CODD, EDGAR FRANK, computer scientist, consultant; b. Portland, Eng., Aug. 19, 1923; came to U.S., 1948; s. Edgar and Katherine Jane (Adcock) C.; m. Elizabeth Shannon Forbes, Sept. 14, 1952 (div. June 1978); children—Katherine Susan, Ronald Edgar, Frank Lawrence, David Fairfield. B.A., U.Oxford, Eng., M.A.; M.S., U. Mich., Ph.D. Mathematician, IBM Corp., N.Y.C. and Washington, 1949-53, research/scientist, Poughkeepsie, N.Y., after 1957, Ann Arbor, Mich., San Jose, Calif., to 1984; applied scientist Computing Devices of Can., Ottawa, Ont., 1953-57; pres. The Relational Inst., San Jose, 1984—; cons. to numerous U.S. and fgn. companies. Author: Cellular Automata, 1968. Served to capt. RAF, 1942-45. IBM Corp. fellow, 1976. Fellow Brit. Computer Soc.; mem. Assn. for Computing Machinery (Turing award 1981), Nat. Acad. Engring. Republican. Current work: Multiprogramming; relational approach to database management. Subspecialty: Foundations of computer science. Office: The Relational Inst 6472 Camden Ave Suite 206 San Jose CA 95120

COE, JOHN EMMONS, research immunologist; b. Evanston, Ill., Sept. 1, 1931; s. Emmons Sylvester and Lillian Elizabeth (Beckman) C.; m. Nancy Rowland, June 18, 1954; children: Kristine Wing Coe Sutton, Anne Lindstrom, Paul Rowland. B.A., Oberlin Coll., 1953; M.D., Hahnemann Med. Coll., 1957. Intern U. Ill. Research and Ednl. Hosp., Chgo., 1957-58; resident in medicine U. Colo. Med. Ctr., Denver, 1958-60; surgeon USPHS, NIH, Rocky Mountain Lab., Hamilton, Mont., 1960-63; fellow dept. pathology Scripps Clinic and Research Found., LaJolla, Calif., 1963-65; med. officer Nat. Inst. Allergy and Infectious Diseases, NIH, Rocky Mountain Lab., Hamilton, 1965—; affiliate prof. dept. microbiology U. Mont., Missoula, 1966—. Bd. dirs. Mill Lake Irrigation Dist. Mem. Am. Assn. Immunologists, Alpha Omega Alpha. Clubs: Hamilton (Mont.) Lacrosse, Handball. Current Work: Selective induction of antibody production in immunoglobulin classes of rodents; immunochemistry and pathophysiology of pentraxins. Subspecialties: Immunology (medicine); Infectious diseases. Home: NW 986 Orchard Dr Hamilton MT 59840 Office: Rocky Mountain Lab Hamilton MT 59840

COFFEY, TIMOTHY, physicist; b. Washington, June 27, 1941; s. Timothy and Helen (Stevens) C.; m. Paula Marie Smith, Aug. 24, 1963; children: Timothy, Donna, Marie. B.S. in Elec. Engring. (Cambridge scholar 1958), MIT, 1962; M.S. in Physics, U. Mich., 1963, Evening News Assn. fellow, 1964, Ph.D., 1967. Research physicist Air Force Cambridge Research Lab., 1964; theoretical physicist EGG, Inc., Boston, 1966-71; head plasma dynamics br., then supt. plasma physics div. Naval Research Lab., Washington, 1971-80, asso. dir. research for gen. sci. and tech., 1980-83, dir. research, 1983—. Recipient award Naval Research Lab., 1974, 75. Fellow Am. Phys. Soc., Washington Acad. Scis.; mem. Am. Inst. Physics, AAAS, N.Y. Acad. Scis., Internat. Union Radio Sci. Office: 4555 Overlook Ave SW Washington DC 20375

COFFIN, LOUIS FUSSELL, JR., mech. engr.; b. Schenectady, Aug. 30, 1917; s. Louis Fussell and Laura C. (Glen) C.; m. Mary Elizabeth McCarthy, Apr. 24, 1943; children—John, Sarah (Mrs. Joseph Fitzgerald), Laura (Mrs. Thomas Koch), Robert, Patricia (Mrs. Jeffrey Mullen), Deborah (Mrs. Patrick Higgins), Louis Fussell III, Margaret. B.S., Swarthmore (Pa.) Coll., 1939; Sc.D., Mass. Inst. Tech., 1949. From asst. to asst. prof. mech. engring. Mass. Inst. Tech., 1939-49; research asso., then supr. mech. metallurgy Knolls Atomic Power Lab., Gen. Electric Co., 1949-54, mech. engr. corporate research and devel., Schenectady, 1954—; adj. prof. mech. engring. Rensselaer Poly. Inst., Troy, N.Y., 1955-60, Union Coll., Schenectady, 1965—; vis. fellow Clare Hall Cambridge U., 1976. Author. Recipient Alfred E. Hunt award Am. Soc. Lubrication Engrs., 1958; award excellence Carborundum Co., 1974; Clamer medal Franklin Inst.; Clayton lectr. Inst. Mech. Engrs., London, 1974; Coolidge fellow, 1974. Fellow ASME (Nadai award 1979), Am. Soc. Metals (Albert Sauveur Achievement award 1980), ASTM (chmn. E9 com. on fatigue 1974—, Dudley award 1975, award of merit 1978); mem. Nat. Acad. Engring., Am. Inst. Metall. Engrs. (Disting. Career award 1978), Sigma Xi, Pi Tau Sigma, Sigma Tau. Patentee in field. Current Work: Mechanism, materials and environmental aspects of fracture of structural materials under cyclic and static loadings, especially fatigue and stress corrosion. Subspecialties: Fracture mechanics; High-temperature materials. Home: 1178 Lowell Rd Schenectady NY 12308 Office: Corporate Research and Devel Gen Electric Co PO Box 8 Schenectady NY 12301

COFFMAN, JAY DENTON, medical educator, researcher; b. Quincy, Mass., Nov. 17, 1928; s. Frank David and Etta (Kline) C.; m. Louise G. Peters, June 29, 1955; children—Geoffrey, Joanne, Linda, Robert. B.A., Harvard Coll., 1950; M.D., Boston U., 1954. Diplomate Am. Bd. Internal Medicine. Intern, Univ. Hosp., Boston, 1954-55, resident, 1955-58, chief perpheral vascular sect., 1960—, assoc. dir. med. service, 1972—; asst. prof. medicine Boston U., 1960-68, assoc. prof., 1968-72, prof., 1972—. Author: Ischemic Limbs, 1973; contbr. numerous articles to med. jours. Bd. dirs. Solomon Carter Fuller Mental Health Ctr., Boston, 1978-82. Served to capt. USAR, 1958-60. NIH grantee, 1960—. Mem. Am. Heart Assn., Council on Circulation (Am. Heart Assn.; chmn. 1978-80), Am. Soc. Clin. Investigation, Am. Physiol. Soc. Current work: Study of physiology and pathophysiology of the peripheral circulation. Subspecialty: Cardiology. Office: University Hosp 75 E Newton St Boston MA 02021

COGBILL, CHARLES LIPSCOMB, III, nuclear engineer; b. Rochester, N.Y., Nov. 25, 1946; s. Charles Lipscomb and Elton Francis (Mills) C.; m. Hortensia Martin Sanchez, Mar. 28, 1981. B.A.S., Troy State U., 1980. Registered profl. engr., N.H. Engr./sr. engr. B Westinghouse Electric Co., Zion, Ill., 1974-78, sr. engr. B., Dothan, Ala., 1978-80, sr. engr., Almaraz, Spain, 1980-82, Seabrook, N.H., 1982—. Contbr. articles in field to profl. jours. Served with USN, 1965-74. Mem. Am. Nuclear Soc. Republican. Current Work: Mechanical engineering (startup) work at nuclear power plants. Subspecialties: Nuclear engineering; Human factors engineering. Office: Seabrook Sta Startup Dept PO Box 700 Seabrook NH 03874

COGGESHALL, IVAN STODDARD, telecommunication engineer; b. Newport, R.I., Sept. 30, 1896; s. Benjamin Bateman and Minnie Louise (Stoddard) C.; m. Ada Louise Crowe, Oct. 23, 1920; children—Lynette, Coggeshall Crandall Miller. Student Worcester Poly. Inst., 1917, D. Engring. (hon.), 1951. Registered profl. engr., N.Y. Gen. insp. Western Union Telegraph Co., N.Y.C., 1920-27, cable system mgr., 1927-52, dir. planning, 1952-57, asst. v.p., 1957-59; mgr. tech. ops. Am. Inst. Elec. Engrs., N.Y.C., 1960-62, ret., 1963; U.S. Navy liaison Western Union Telegraph Co., Washington, 1942-48; bd. war communication FCC, Washington, 1942-45. Editor: Electrical Engineering, 1966-72. Contbr. articles to profl. jours. Served to comdr. U.S. Navy, 1917-57. Recipient Harry Houck award Antique Wireless Assn., 1979. Fellow IEEE (Haraden Pratt award 1978, Centennial medal 1984), Radio Club Am. Current work: genealogy, telecommunication, electrical. Subspecialty: Telecommunications.

COHEN, AARON, aerospace engineering manager. Dir. research and engring. Lyndon B. Johnson Space Ctr., Houston. Recipient Engrs. medal ASME, 1984. Subspecialty: Aerospace engineering and technology. Office: NASA Lyndon B. Johnson Space Ctr Research and Engring Houston TX 77058

COHEN, ARTHUR DAVID, geologist, consultant; b. Wilmington, Del., Feb. 26, 1942; s. Herman and Anna Mary (Stein) C.; m. Mary Jo Purcell, June 7, 1970; children: Benjamin, Jonathan. B.S., U. Del., 1964; Ph.D., Pa. State U.-State College, 1968. Assoc. prof. So. Ill. U., Carbondale, 1969-74; geologist U.S. Geol. Survey, Reston, Va., 1974-75; prof. U. S.C., Columbia, 1975-82; staff mem. Los Alamos Nat. Lab., 1982—; dir. Organic Sediments Research Center, U. S.C., Columbia, 1975-82; cons. U.S. Dept. Justice, Dept. Energy, 1979-82. Contbr. articles to profl. jours. Research grantee NSF, 1969-82; Research grantee Dept. Energy, 1979-82; Research grantee Nat. Geographic Soc., 1980-81; Research grantee Sea Grant Consortium, 1980. Fellow Geol. Soc. Am. (chmn. coal div. 1976); mem. ASTM (chmn. peat classification com. 1979-85), Sigma Xi, Phi Beta Kappa, Phi Kappa Phi. Current Work: Origin of coal, development of models to aid in coal mining and coal quality evaluation, peat resource evaluation, geology and paleoecology of modern and ancient swamps. Subspecialties: Coal; Geology. Home: 76 Barcelona Ave Los Alamos NM 87544 Office: Los Alamos Nat Lab MS D 462 Los Alamo NM 87545

COHEN, CURTIS RAE, petroleum exploration geophysicist; b. Chgo., Jan. 11, 1954; s. Louis and Emili (Chappie) C.; m. Margaret Christine Jeanne Fischer, Mar. 24, 1975; children—Naomi Sarah, Jennifer Rebecca, Emili Helène, Pierre Andrew Chaim. B.A. in Geology, Lawrence Coll., 1975; M.A. in Geology, Columbia U., 1979. Geophysicist, Gulf Research and Devel. Co., Houston and New Orleans, 1979-81; sr. petroleum geophysicist Esso Exploration Inc., Walton-on-Thames, Surrey, England, 1981-83, exploration geophysicist, Houston, 1983-84; exploration geophysicist Esso Exploration and Prodn., Stavanger, Norway, 1985—. Contbr. articles to prof. jours. Campaign chmn. United Way Esso Exploration Inc., Houston, 1983. Faculty fellow Columbia U., 1977-79; Penrose grant-in-aid Sigma Xi, 1978. Mem. Am. Assn. Petroleum Geologists, Geol. Soc. Am. (Penrose grantee 1978), Am. Geophys. Union. Jewish. Current work: Exploration for petroleum in little-known, frontier regions of the world; application of existing technology and development of new technology to discover untapped reserves. Subspecialties: Geophysics; Tectonics. Home: 19 Hannasdalsgate Stavanger 4000 Norway Office: Esso Exploration and Prodn Norway PO Box 560 4001 Stavanger/Forus Norway

COHEN, DAVID HARRIS, neuroscientist; b. Springfield, Mass., Aug. 26, 1938; s. Nathan Edward and Sylvia (Golden) C.; m. Anne Helena Remmes, Jan. 17, 1981; 1 child, Kaitlin; children from previous marriage: Bonnie, Daniel, Ian. B.A., Harvard U., 1960; Ph.D., U. Calif., Berkeley, 1963. Postdoctoral fellow in physiology UCLA, 1963-64; asst. prof. physiology Western Res. U., Cleve., 1964-68; asso. prof. physiology U. Va., 1968-71, prof. physiology, dir. neurosci., 1971-79; leading prof., chmn. neurobiology and behavior SUNY, Stony Brook, 1979—; mem. study sects. and spl. rev. group NIH; mem. adv. groups NSF; vis. prof. numerous univs. Author books, articles in field of neurosci. Mem. Soc. Neurosci. (pres. 1981-82), Am. Physiol. Soc., Nat. Soc. Med. Research (dir.), Pavlovian Soc. (pres. 1978-79), Am. Assn. Anatomists. Jewish. Current Work: Cellular basis of memory; neural control of the cardiovascular system. Subspecialties: Neurobiology; Neurophysiology. Office: Dept Neurobiology SUNY Stony Brook NY 11794

COHEN, DAVID MARSHALL, computer scientist, researcher; b. N.Y.C., June 7, 1951; s. Morton Louis and Ruth (Baum) C.; m. Marlene Zichi, Mar. 5, 1978. B.A. in Chemistry cum laude, Case Western Res. U., 1974; M.S. in Computer and Communication Scis., U. Mich., 1978, Ph.D., 1981. Asst. prof. U. Mich., Flint, 1981-83; sr. software engr. Applied Dynamics Internat., Ann Arbor, Mich., 1983—. Contbr. articles to profl. jours. Mem. AAAS, Am. Assn. Artificial Intelligence, Assn. Computing Machinery, IEEE, Soc. Computer Simulation, Phi Beta Kappa. Jewish. Current work: Compiler optimization; biomedical computing; automata theory; complexity theory; code generation for multiprocessors. Subspecialties: Theoretical computer science; Programming languages. Home: 1210 Saunders Crescent Ann Arbor MI 48103 Office: Applied Dynamics Internat 3800 Stone School Rd Ann Arbor MI 48104

COHEN, DAVID WALTER, periodontist, educator. Prof., former dean Sch. Dental Medicine, U. Pa., Phila. Subspecialty: Periodontics. Office: U Pa Sch Dental Medicine 4001 Spruce St Philadelphia PA 19104*

COHEN, DONALD SUSSMAN, mathematician. Prof. applied math. Calif. Inst. Tech., Pasadena. Subspecialty: Applied mathematics. Office: Calif Inst Tech Pasadena CA 91125*

COHEN, EDGAR ALLAN, JR., mathematician; b. Charleston, S.C., Aug. 29, 1938; s. Edgar Allan and Elizabeth (Sternberger) C.; m. Joy Anne Bashlow, Nov. 23, 1975. A.B., Duke U., 1960; M.S., U. Cin., 1964, Ph.D., 1968. Applied mathematician Naval Surface Weapons Center, Silver Spring, Md., 1968—. Asst. scoutmaster Nat. Capital Area council Boy Scouts Am., Silver Spring, 1969-74. Served U.S. Army, 1961-62. Mem. Soc. for Indsl. and Applied Math., Assn. for Computing Machinery, Md. Entomol. Soc., Bot. Soc. Washington, Md. Ornithol. Soc. Democrat. Jewish. Current Work: Signal processing as applied to target detection, stochastic modeling for minefield theory, pattern recognition and image processing as applied to target detection. Subspecialties: Probability; Graphics, image processing, and pattern recognition. Home: 5454 Marsh Hawk Way Columbia MD 21045 Office: Naval Surface Weapons Center New Hampshire Ave White Oak Silver Spring MD 20910

COHEN, EDWARD, consulting engineer; b. Glastonbury, Conn., Jan. 6, 1921; s. Samuel and Ida (Tanewitz) C.; m. Elizabeth Belle Cohen, Dec. 19, 1948 (dec. June 1979); children—Samuel, Libby, James; m. Carol Simon Kalb, Jan. 11, 1981. B.S. in Engring, Columbia U., 1945; M.S. in Civil Engring, Columbia, 1954. Registered profl. engr., N.Y., Conn., Fla., Ga., Md., N.J., Pa., D.C., Okla., Va., Wis., Del., La., Nat. Council Engring. Examiners. Engring. aide Conn. Hwy. Dept., 1940-41; asst. engr. East Hartford Dept. Pub. Works, 1942-44; structural engr. Hardesty & Hanover, N.Y.C., 1945-47, Sanderson & Porter, N.Y.C., 1947-49; lectr. architecture Columbia, 1948-51; with Ammann & Whitney (cons. engr.), N.Y.C., 1949—, ptnr., 1963-74, sr. ptnr., 1974-76, mng. ptnr., 1977—; exec. v.p. in charge bldg., transp., communications, mil. projects Ammann & Whitney, Inc., 1963-77, chmn., chief exec. officer, 1977—; v.p. Ammann & Whitney Internat. Ltd., 1963-73; pres. Safeguard Constrn. Mgmt. Corp., 1973-77, chmn., 1977; cons. to govt. and industry.; Stanton Walker lectr. U. Md., 1973; adv. com. Urban and Civil Engring. U. Pa., 1974-84; mem. engring. council Columbia U., 1975—, vice chmn., 1984—; dir. Concrete Industry Bd., 1976—, pres., 1978-79; concrete specialist European Concrete Com. Contbr. manuals to profl. assns., articles to profl. jours.; Co-editor Structural Concrete Handbook, 1983. Bd. dirs. Cejwin Youth Camps, 1972—; trustee Hall of Sci., N.Y.C., 1976—; mem. Bklyn. Bridge Centennial Commn., 1981-83. Recipient Illig medal Columbia, 1946, Egleston medal Columbia U., 1981; Patriotic Civilian Service award Dept. of Army, 1973. Fellow ASCE (Ridgway award 1946, Civil Engring. State of the Art award 1974, Raymond Reese award 1976, Earnest Howard award 1983, v.p. Met. sect. 1978-79, pres. 1980, chmn. reinforced concrete research council 1980—), N.Y. Acad. Scis. (hon. life, Laskowitz Aerospace research award 1970, vice chmn. engring. sect. 1975-77, chmn. 1977-79), Am. Concrete Inst. (hon. mem., dir. 1966-76, v.p. 1970-72, pres. 1972-73, chmn. bldg. code requirements for reinforced concrete 1963-71, Wason medal 1956, Delmar Bloem award 1973), Am. Cons. Engring. Council; mem. N.Y. Assn. Cons. Engrs. (dir. 1981-85), Nat. Acad. Engring., Am. Welding Soc., Am. Nat. Standards Inst. (chmn. minimum design loads for bldgs. and other structures 1968—), ASCE Performance of Structures Research Council (chmn. com. long term observations 1972-76), N.Y. Concrete Constrn. Inst. (pres. tall bldg. council 1975-77), Am. Ordnance Assn., Internat. Assn. Bridge and Structural Engrs., Internat. Bridge and Turnpike Assn., Moles, Sigma Xi, Chi Epsilon (hon.), Tau Beta Pi. Jewish religion. Clubs: Engineers (dir. 1974-75); Wings, Century Assn. (N.Y.C.). Current Work: Development of seismic building codes,dynamic response of structures advancing knowledge of reinforced concrete, wind force evaluation antenna structures. Subspecialties: Civil engineering; Aerospace engineering and technology. Home: 56 Chestnut Hill Roslyn NY 11576 Office: 2 World Trade Center New York NY 10048

COHEN, EDWIN, psychologist; b. N.Y.C., Aug. 26, 1924; s. Paul and Clara (Lobel) C.; m. Myrna Skalovsky, Aug. 22, 1949 (div. 1951); 1 dau., Kaye Suzanne Kramer; m. Judith Barnett, Aug. 21, 1958 (dec. 1984); children: Rebecca, Deborah. A.B., Cornell U., 1944; M.S., U. Okla., 1949, Ph.D., 1955. Lic. psychologist, N.Y. State cert. Soc. Automotive Engrs. Project dir. Psychol. Research Assocs., Washington, 1953-55; tng. specialst The RAND Corp., Santa Monica, Calif., 1955-56; project dir. Ednl. Research Corp., Cambridge, Mass., 1956-58; staff scientist link flight simulation div. The Singer Co., Binghamton, N.Y., 1958—; adj. faculty Simmons Coll., Boston, 1957-58, SUNY-Binghamton, 1968-74; mem. N.Y. State Bd. Psychology, 1977—. Contbr. articles to tech. jours. Officer, trustee Temple Concord, Binghamton, 1970-73. Served with USN, 1944-46. Mem. Am. Psychol. Assn., Human Factors Soc. Republican. Jewish. Inventor. Current Work: Training, simulation and training equipment, visual perception as related to visual simulation, control/display optimization, human performance measurement, safety. Subspecialties: Human factors engineering; Systems engineering. Home: 5 Crestmont Rd Binghamton NY 13905 Office: Singer Co Link Flight Simulation Div Binghamton NY 13902

COHEN, HAGGAI, electrical engineer; b. Balt., Jan. 12, 1924; s. Meyer Samson and Gilla (Kitinick) C.; m. Anita Krieger, May 11, 1950; children—P-'nina M., Bronna T. B.S. in Elec. Engring., U. Man., 1949; M.S. in Elec.

Engring., Case Inst. Tech., 1950. Supr. prodn. engring. Crosley div. Avco Corp., Cin., 1950-55; mgr. quality and reliability Martin-Marietta Corp., Balt., 1955-66; dir. reliability, quality and safety NASA Hdqrs., Washington, 1966-84, dep. chief engr., 1984—. Contbr. articles to trade jours. Served with USAAF, 1942-45, ETO. Recipient Exceptional Service medal NASA, 1973, Outstanding Leadership medal NASA, 1981. Democrat. Jewish. Current work: Management of NASA research and development engineering and product assurance functions. Subspecialties: Electrical engineering; Aerospace engineering and technology. Office: NASA Hdqrs 600 Independence Ave SW Washington DC 20546

COHEN, HARLEY, civil engineering educator, researcher; b. Winnipeg, Man., Can., May 12, 1933; s. Joseph and Ettie (Gilman) C.; m. Estelle Brodsky, Dec. 25, 1956; children: Brent, Murray, Carla. B.Sc. with honors, U. Man., Winnipeg, 1956; Sc.M., Brown U., 1958; Ph.D., U. Minn.-Mpls., 1964. Research engr. Boeing Co., Seattle, 1958-60; prin. scientist Honeywell Inc., Mpls., 1960-64; asst. prof. aero. and engring. mechanics U. Minn., 1964-65; prof. civil engring. U. Man., 1965-83, Univ. disting. prof., 1983—; James L. Record prof. U. Minn.-Mpls., 1979; Killam vis. scholar U. Calgary, Alta., Can., 1982. Mem. editorial bd.: Utilitas Mathematics, 1975—, Iran Jour. Sci. Tech, 1975—; contbr. numerous articles to profl. jours. Mem. Acad. Mechanics, Soc. Engring. Sci., Soc. Natural Philosophy. Current Work: Nonlinear wave propagation in rods, shells and membranes. Subspecialties: Theoretical and applied mechanics; Applied mathematics. Home: 55 Tanoak Park Dr Winnipeg MB R2V 2W6 Canada Office: Department Civil Engineering University Manitoba Winnipeg MB R3T 2N2 Canada

COHEN, IRA LARRY, psychologist, therapist, researcher; b. Phila., Nov. 15, 1947; s. Meyer and Pauline (Smogar) C.; m. Chaya Frohman, June 7, 1970; children: Micole, Mirit. B.A., Temple U., 1969; M.S., Rutgers U., 1972, Ph.D., 1974; postgrad., NYU Med. Ctr., 1975-77. Adj. asst. prof. Lehman Coll., CUNY, 1974; instr. Seton Hall U., 1974, Kean Coll., 1974-77; instr. NYU Med. Ctr., N.Y.C., 1975-80, research asst. prof. psychiatry, 1981-83; research scientist Inst. Basic Research, S.I., N.Y., 1981—; dir. div. behavioral assessment and research Inst. Basic Research, 1984—; behavior therapist Ctr. Counseling & Behavior Therapy, N.Y.C., 1977-78, Group for Psychol. Counseling, N.Y.C., 1978-79; consulting psychologist Assn. Advancement Blind and Retarded, St. Albans, N.Y., 1980—. Contbr. chpts. to books and articles to profl. jours. NIMH fellow, 1975. Mem. Am. Psychol. Assn., AAAS, Am. Assn. Mental Deficiency, N.Y. State Psychol. Assn. Current Work: Behavioral and learning characteristics of autistic and other developmentally disabled persons; behavior therapy with these same populations; psychopharmacological treatment with same populations. Subspecialties: Behavioral psychology; Developmental psychology. Office: Inst Basic Research 1050 Forest Hill R Staten Island NY 10314

COHEN, IRWIN, chemistry educator; b. Cleve., Feb. 28, 1924; s. Louis M. and Sadie (Dorsky) C.; m. Beatrice Lewin, Dec. 30, 1945; children: Martin, Richard, David. A.B., Western Res. U., 1944, M.S., 1948, Ph.D., 1950. Asst. prof. chemistry Youngstown (Ohio) State U., 1949-53, asso. prof., 1953-58, prof., 1958—, dir. individualized curriculum program, 1971-73; coordinator Youngstown B.S./M.D. program (Ohio) State U., 1974-77; coordinator non-traditional programs, 1978-81. Contbr. articles on chemistry to profl. jours. Served with USN, 1944-46. Recipient Disting. Prof. award Youngstown State U, 1965, 79; NSF grantee, 1967, 1967,68. Mem. Am. Chem. Soc., AAUP, Ohio Edn. Assn., Sigma Xi, Alpha Epsilon Delta, Phi Beta Kappa, Phi Kappa Phi. Jewish. Current Work: Relation of molecular orbital calculations to chemical covalent bond order and charge distribution, using density differences, localized orbitals and population analysis. Subspecialties: Organic chemistry; Theoretical chemistry. Home: 45 Melrose Ave Youngstown OH 44512 Office: Youngstown State U Youngstown OH 44555

COHEN, JAMES SAMUEL, physicist; b. Houston, July 29, 1946; s. Herman and Jimmie Ruth (Harrington) C.; m. Marion Fay Daniel, Dec. 28, 1968; children: Stephen James, Christy Lynn. B.A., Rice U., 1968, M.A., 1970, Ph.D., 1973. Staff mem. Los Alamos (N.Mex.) Nat. Lab., 1972—; vis. asso. prof. Rice U., Houston, 1979-80. Contbr. articles in field to profl. jours. Recipient H. A. Wilson Prize Rice U., 1973. Mem. Am. Phys. Soc., Phi Beta Kappa, Sigma Xi. Current Work: Research in basic atomic and molecular physics, laser kinetics and muon physics. Subspecialties: Atomic and molecular physics; Theoretical physics. Home: 330 Valle del Sol Los Alamos NM 87544 Office: Los Alamos Nat Lab T-12 MS-J569 Los Alamos NM 87545

COHEN, JEFFREY M., physicist, educator; b. Elizabeth, N.J., Aug. 30, 1940; s. Isadore M. and Hilda (Pollack) C.; m. Marion Deutsche, Aug. 9, 1964; children—Marielle, Arin, Bret. B.E.E., N.J. Inst. Tech., 1962; M.S., Yale U., 1963, Ph.D., 1966; M.A. (hon.) U. Pa., 1973. NSF fellow Yale U., New Haven, 1962-66, AEC fellow, 1966-67; research assoc. Inst. Space Studies, N.Y.C., 1967-69; mem. staff Inst. Advanced Study, Princeton, N.J., 1969-71; prof. physics U. Pa., Phila., 1971—; dir. Acad. Scis., Phila.; vis. scholar Max Planck Inst., Munich, Fed. Republic Germany, 1971; sr. research assoc. High Energy Astrophysics Lab., NASA, Greenbelt, Md., 1972-74. Contbr. articles to profl. jours. Patentee in field. Communications specialist N.J. Civil Def., Elizabeth, 1954-58. Recipient Achievement Honor Roll award N.J. Inst. Tech., 1984. Fellow N.Y. Acad. Scis., Am. Phys. Soc.; mem. Internat. Astron. Union, Internat. Soc. Gen. Relativity and Gravitation, Acad. Scis. (bd. dirs. 1980—). Current work: Specialize in Einstein's general theory of gravitation and have recently proved Einstein's conjecture; other interests are astrophysics, cosmology, and mathemetical physics. Subspecialties: Relativity and gravitation; Theoretical astrophysics. Office: Physics Dept U Pa Philadelphia PA 19103

COHEN, JEROME BERNARD, materials science educator; b. Bklyn., July 16, 1932; s. David I. and Shirley Anne C.; m. Lois Nesson, Sept. 15, 1957; children: Elissa Diane, Andrew Neil. B.S., Mass. Inst. Tech., 1954, Sc.D., 1957. Sr. scientist materials AVCO Corp., Wilmington, Mass., 1958-59; mem. faculty Northwestern U., 1959—, prof. materials sci. and engring., 1965—, chmn. dept. materials sci. and engring., 1973-78, Frank C. Engelhart prof., 1974—, fellow Center Teaching Professions, 1971—, prof. Technol. Inst., 1983—; sci. liaison officer Office Naval Research, London, 1966-67; cons. to govt. and industry. Mem. bd. Author: Diffraction Methods in Materials Science, 1966; co-author: Diffraction from Materials, 1978; Co-editor: Local Atomic Arrangements Studied by X-Ray Diffraction, 1967, Jour. Applied Crystallography, Modulated Structures, 1979. All-Star coach Glencoe (Ill.) Hockey Assn., 1974-77. Served as 1st lt. AUS, 1959. Fulbright fellow U. Paris, 1957-58; recipient Tech. Inst. Teaching award Northwestern U., 1976. Fellow Am. Inst. Metall., Mining and Petroleum Engring. (Hardy Gold medal 1960), Am. Soc. Metals (Henry Marion Howe medal 1981); mem. Am. Soc. Engring. Edn. (George C. Westinghouse award 1976), Am. Ceramic Soc., Am. Crystallographic Assn., Royal Instn. Gt. Britain, AAUP, Sigma Xi, Tau Beta Pi, Alpha Sigma Mu, Phi Lambda Upsilon. Jewish. Patentee in field. Subspecialties: Ceramics; Materials. Home: 362 Jackson Ave Glencoe IL 60022 Office: 2145 Sheridan Rd Evanston IL 60201

COHEN, JERRY DAVID, plant biochemist; b. San Mateo, Calif., Nov. 19, 1949; s. Herman Charles and Evadna Fern (Tull) C.; m. Susan Dey Anderson, Aug. 18, 1972; 1 son, Aaron Ethan. B.S. in Biology, U. Calif.-Riverside, 1972; M.S. in Plant Physiology, San Diego State U., 1974; Ph.D. in Plant Biochemistry, Mich. State U., 1979. Research assoc. Mich. State U., East Lansing, 1979-81; vis. scientist Volcani Ctr., ARO Bet Dagan, Israel, 1980; plant physiologist, research chemist U.S. Dept. Agr., Agrl. Research Service, Plant Hormone Lab., Beltsville, Md., 1981—. Contbr. articles to sci. jours. Recipient Ernst A. Bessey Research award Mich. State U., 1979. Mem. AAAS, Am. Soc. Plant Physiologists, Am. Inst. Biol. Scis., Union Concerned Scientists. Democrat. Current work: Mechanisms by which plants control the in vivo level of the plant hormone indole-3-acetic acid. Subspecialties: Plant physiology (agriculture); Analytical chemistry. Home: 14P Laurel Hill Rd Greenbelt MD 20770 Office: US Dept Agr Agrl Research Service Plant Hormone Lab BO50 HH4 Barc-West Beltsville MD 20705

COHEN, JOEL RALPH, microbiologist, biology educator; b. Chelsea, Mass., Oct. 20, 1926; s. Julius Meyer and Pearl (Mankin) C.; m. Marilyn Roberta Lezar, Sept. 7, 1947; children: Robert Neil, Deborah Ellen, Peter Alan. B.S., U. Mass., 1949, M.S., 1950, Ph.D., 1975. Specialist, registered microbiologist Nat. Registry of Microbiology cert. clin. lab. specialist Nat. Cert. Agy. for Med. Lab. Personnel. Microbiologist Baystate Med. Ctr., Springfield, Mass., 1950-68, chief clin. labs., 1960-68; assoc. prof. biol. sci. Springfield Coll., 1968-75, chmn. biology dept., 1969-81, prof. biol. sci., 1975-83, prof. biol. and health scis., 1983—; cons. VA Med. Ctr., Springfield Mcpl. Hosp., Springfield Dept. Pub. Health, Baystate Med. Ctr. Contbr. articles to profl. jours. Served to col. USAR, 1943-80. Fellow AAAS, Am. Pub. Health Assn. (sec. lab. sect. 1979-82), Royal Soc. Health, Am. Acad. Microbiology; mem. N.Y. Acad. Scis, Am. Soc. Microbiology, Am. Assn. Blood Banks, Sigma Xi. Current Work: History of development of public health laboratory methods. Subspecialty: Microbiology. Home: 14 Inglewood Ave Springfield MA 01119 Office: Springfield College 263 Alden St Springfield MA 01109

COHEN, KARL PALEY, nuclear energy consultant; b. N.Y.C., Feb. 5, 1913; s. Joseph M. and Ray (Paley) C.; m. Marthe-H. Malartre, Sept. 20, 1938; children: Martine-Claude Lebouc, Elisabeth M. Brown, Beatrix Josephine Cashmore. A.B., Columbia U., 1933, M.A., 1934, Ph.D., 1937; postgrad., U. Paris, 1936-37. Research asst. to Prof. H. C. Urey Columbia U., 1937-40, dir. theoretical div., SAM Manhattan project, 1940-44; physicist Standard Oil Devel. Co., 1944-48; tech. dir. H.K. Ferguson Co., 1948-52; v.p. Walter Kidde Nuclear Lab., 1952-55; cons. AEC, sr. sci. Columbia U., 1955; mgr. advance engring. atomic power equipment dept. Gen. Electric Co., 1955-65, gen. mgr. breeder reactor devel. dept., 1965-71, mgr. strategic planning, nuclear energy div., 1971-73, chief scientist, nuclear energy group, 1973-78; cons. prof. Stanford U., 1978-81. Author: The Theory of Isotope Separation as Applied to Large Scale Production of U-235, 1951; contbr. articles to profl. jours. Recipient Energy Research prize Alfried Krupp Found., 1977; Chem. Pioneer award Am. Inst. Chemists, 1979. Fellow Am. Nuclear Soc. (pres. 1968-69, dir.), AAAS; mem. Nat. Acad. Engring., Am. Phys. Soc., Cactus and Succulent Soc., Phi Beta Kappa, Sigma Xi, Phi Lambda Upsilon. Current Work: Reactor safety and nuclear power economics and their interaction. Subspecialties: Nuclear engineering; Nuclear fission. Office: 928 N California Ave Palo Alto CA 94303

COHEN, MARLENE LOIS, research scientist, educator; b. New Haven, May 5, 1945; d. Abraham David and Jeanette (Bader) C.; m. Jerome Herbert Fleisch, August 8, 1976; children: Abby Faye, Sheryl Brynne. B.S. in Pharmacy, U. Conn., 1968; Ph.D. in Pharmacology, U. Calif., San Francisco, 1973. Registered pharmacist, Conn., Calif. Postdoctoral fellow Roche Inst. Molecular Biology, Nutley, N.J., 1973-75; sr. pharmacologist Lilly Research Labs., Eli Lilly and Co., Indpls., 1975-80, research scientist, 1980-85, research assoc., 1985—; adj. asst. prof. pharmacology Ind. U. Sch. Medicine, Indpls., 1976-82, adj. assoc. prof., 1982—; ad hoc reviewer for sci. jours. Mem. editorial bd.: Jour. Clin. and Exptl. Hypertension, 1978—, Procs. Soc. Exptl. Biology and Medicine, 1979—; Life Sci., 1984—; contbr. articles, revs. and abstracts to profl. jours., also chpts. to books. Mem. Soc. for Exptl. Biology and Medicine, Am. Soc. Pharmacology and Exptl. Therapeutics, Indpls. Children's Mus., Alpha Lambda Delta, Phi Kappa Phi, Rho Chi. Current Work: Smooth muscle function with emphasis on treatment of hypertension; role of neuronal innervation, serotonin receptors, enkephalins and angiotensin converting enzyme in smooth muscle function. Subspecialties: Pharmacology; Neuropharmacology. Office: Cardiovascular Pharmacology Dept Lilly Research Labs Indianapolis IN 46285

COHEN, MICHAEL PAUL, mathematical statistician; b. San Mateo, Calif., July 8, 1947; s. Herman Charles and Evadna Fern (Tull) C. B.A., U. Calif.-San Diego, 1969; M.A., UCLA, 1971, Ph.D., 1978. Statistician, Office Prices and Living Conditions, Bur. Labor, Stats., U.S. Dept. Labor, Washington, 1979—. Mem. Am. Statis. Assn., Inst. Math. Stats., Am. Math. Soc., Soc. Indsl. and Applied Math., Am. Assn. Pub. Opinion Research. Club: Calif. State Soc. (Washington). Current Work: Variance estimation for the U.S. Consumer Price Index, composite estimation for small areas, applied survey design research, properties of finite population estimators. Subspecialties: Statistics; Applied mathematics. Office: Office Prices Bur Labor Statistics 600 E St NW Room 5217 Washington DC 20212

COHEN, MORREL HERMAN, physicist, biologist, educator; b. Boston, Sept. 10, 1927; s. David and Rose (Kemler) C.; m. Sylvia Zwein, June 18, 1950; children: Julie, Robert, Daniel, Lisa. B.S. in Physics, Worcester Poly. Inst., 1947, D.Sc. (hon.), 1973; M.A. in Physics, Dartmouth Coll., 1948; Ph.D. in Physics, U. Calif.-Berkeley, 1952. Mem. faculty U. Chgo., 1952-81, assoc. prof. physics, 1957-60, prof., 1960-81, prof. theoretical biology, 1968—, Louis Block prof. physics and theoretical biology, 1972-81, mem. com. developmental biology, 1973-74, publs. bd., 1969-70; acting dir. James Franck Inst., 1965-66, dir., 1968-71; dir. materials research lab. NSF, 1977-81; sr. sci. advisor corp. research scis. lab. Exxon Research and Engring. Co., 1981—; cons. govt. and industry, 1953—; vis. scientist NRC, Can., 1960, Xerox Corp., 1978; Shrum lectr. Simon Fraser U., 1973; assoc. Clare Hall U. Cambridge, Eng., 1973—; vis. prof. U. Va., 1976, Kyoto U., 1979; mem. adv. panel electrophysics NASA, 1962-66; mem. adv. com. Nat. Magnet Lab., 1963-66; mem. rev. com. solid state sci. and metallurgy div. Argonne Nat. Lab., 1964-67, chmn., 1966, bd. govs., 1982—; chmn. Gordon Conf., 1968, 4th Internat. Conf. Armorphous and Liquid Semicondrs., 1971; mem. adv. com. Inst. Amorphous Studies, 1982—; mem. Army Basic Research Com., 1979—, mem. steering com., 1980—; mem. adv. com. dept. physics U. Tex., Austin, 1982—. Author articles physics of solids, liquids, gases, theoretical and developmental biology.; assoc. editor: Jour. Chem. Physics, 1960-63; mem. editorial bd.: advanced physics monograph series McGraw-Hill Co., 1963-70; editorial bd.: The Physics of Condensed Matter, 1962-74; publs. bd., U. Chgo., 1969-70; bd. editors: Jour. Statis. Physics, 1970-75. AEC fellow, 1951-52; Guggenheim fellow, 1957-58; NSF sr. postdoctoral fellow Rome, 1964-65; NIH spl. fellow, 1972-73. Fellow Am. Phys. Soc. (council 1978-82, chmn. solid state physics div. 1970, div. councillor 1978-82); mem. AAAS, Am. Inst. Physics, Nat. Acad. Scis., Sigma Xi (nat. lectr. 1966). Subspecialties: Biophysics (physics); Condensed matter physics. Home: 1100 Crim Rd Bridgewater NJ 08807 Office: Route 22E Clinton Twp Annandale NJ 08801

COHEN, MORRIS, materials science and engineering educator; b. Chelsea, Mass., Nov. 27, 1911; s. Julius Harry and Alice (Ovson) C.; m. Ruth Krentzman, Jan. 24, 1937 (dec.); children—Barbara (Mrs. Willy Nordwind), Joel Alan. S.B., MIT, 1933, Sc.D., 1936; D.Tekn. (hon.), Royal Inst. Tech., Stockholm, 1977; D.Tech. (hon.), Israel Inst. Tech., 1979; D.Eng. (hon.), Col. Sch. Mines, 1985. Asst. prof. MIT, 1937-42, assoc. prof., 1942-46, prof., 1946-62, Ford prof. materials sci. and engring., 1962-74, Inst. prof., 1974—; hon. prof. Beijing U. Iron and Steel Tech., 1980—, Beijing Inst. Aeros. and Astronautics, 1980—; metall. cons.; dir. Addison-Wesley Pub. Co., Reading, Mass. Recipient Mathewson Gold medal Am. Inst. Mining and Metall. Engrs., 1953, Inst. Metals award Am. Inst. Mining, Metall. Engrs., Robert F. Mehl award, 1953, Clamer medal Franklin Inst., 1959, Gold medal Japan Inst. Metals, 1970, Chevenard medal French Metall. Soc., 1971, Killian faculty achievement award MIT, 1974, Procter prize Research Soc. North Am., 1976, Nat. Medal of Sci., 1977, Joseph R. Vilella award ASTM, 1979, Gold Medal Acta Metallurgica, 1981. Fellow Metall. Soc. of AIME, Am. Acad. Arts and Scis., N.Y. Acad. Scis., Am. Soc. Metals (hon., past pres., trustee, Howe medal 1945, 49, 60, Gold medal 1968, Sauveur achievement award 1977), Indian Nat. Sci. Acad. (fgn. fellow); mem. Nat. Acad. Scis., Nat. Acad. Engring., Korean Inst. Metals (hon.), Indian Inst. Metals (hon., Kamani Gold medal 1953), Iron and Steel Inst. Japan, Japan Inst. Metals, Metals Soc. London. Current work: Materials science and engineering; materials policy and education; physical metallurgy; phase transformations; strengthening mechanisms; mechanical behavior of metals. Subspecialties: Metallurgy; Materials. Office: MIT Cambridge MA 02139

COHEN, NICHOLAS, immunologist, educator, consultant; b. N.Y.C., Nov. 20, 1938; s. Saris and Frances Edith (Pakett) C.; m. Jayne Sevin, July 1, 1962; children: Jaime, Jessica; m. Catharina Johanna, Oct. 23, 1974; children: Misha, Mark. A.B., Princeton U., 1959; Ph.D., U. Rochester, 1966; postdoctoral scholar, UCLA, 1965-67. Asst. prof. microbiology (immunology) U. Rochester (N.Y.) Sch. Medicine and Dentistry, 1967-73, assoc. prof., 1973-80, prof., 1980—, dir. div. immunology, 1980—; mem. Basel (Switzerland) Inst. Immunology, 1975-76; vis. prof. Agrl. U. Wageningen (Netherlands); mem. peer rev. panels and study sects. NIH and NSF; cons. Mem. editorial bds. profl. jours.; also editor books; contbr. articles to profl. jours. NIH grantee, 1967—; recipient Donald R. Charles Meml. award U. Rochester Dept. Biology, 1966; Fulbright scholar, 1982-83. Mem. Am. Soc. Zoologists, Transplantation Soc., Am. Assn. Immunologists, Internat. Soc. Developmental and Comparative Immunology, ACLU, Sigma Xi. Current Work: Evolution of immunity, ontogeny of immunity, transplantation immunology, psychoneuroimmunology. Subspecialties: Immunogenetics; Neuroimmunology. Office: U Rochester Med Center Box 672 Rochester NY 14642

COHEN, NOAL, chemist; b. Rochester, N.Y., Dec. 29, 1937; s. Hymen David and Sabina (Diamond) C.; m. Ann Bryce, Sept. 3, 1960; children—Ruth Miriam, Claire Amy. B.S., U. Rochester, 1959; Ph.D., Northwestern U., 1965. Prodn. chemist Eastman Kodak, Rochester, 1959-61; sr. scientist Hoffmann-LaRoche, Nutley, N.J., 1967-75, research fellow, 1975-80, research group chief, 1980-84, research sect. chief, 1984-85, research leader, 1985—; adj. prof. Rutgers U., Newark, 1983. Editorial adv. bd. Jour. Organic Chemistry, 1984—. Contbr. articles to profl. jours. NSF fellow, 1965-67. Mem. Am. Chem. Soc. (topical group chmn. 1985—), AAAS, N.Y. Acad. Scis., Internat. Soc. Heterocyclic Chemistry, Sigma Xi. Current work: Synthesis of organic compounds of biological interest. Subspecialties: Organic chemistry; Synthetic chemistry. Home: 19 Euclid Pl Montclair NJ 07042 Office: Hoffmann-LaRoche Inc Nutley NJ 07110

COHEN, PHILIP, hydrogeologist; b. N.Y.C., Dec. 13, 1931; s. Isadore and Anna (Katz) C.; m. Barbara Sandler, Dec. 26, 1954; 1 son, Jeffery. B.S. cum laude, CCNY, 1954; M.S., U. Rochester, 1956. Cert. profl. geologist, Va. With U.S. Geol. Survey, 1956—, asso. chief land info. and analysis office, Reston, Va., 1975-78, asst. chief hydrologist water resources div., 1978-79, chief hydrologist water resources div., 1979—. Contbr. numerous articles on geology and hydrology to profl. jours. Recipient Ward medal Coll. City, N.Y., 1954; Meritorious Ser. award Dept. Interior, 1975, Disting. Ser. award, 1979. Fellow Geol. Soc. Am.; mem. Am. Water Resources Assn., Internat. Assn. Hydrologists, Am. Geophys. Union, Am. Inst. Profl. Geologists, Sigma Xi. Current Work: Science manager. Subspecialty: Hydrology. Office: 709 Geol Survey Reston VA 22092

COHEN, ROBERT EDWARD, chemical engineering educator, consultant; b. Oil City, Pa., Jan. 21, 1947; s. David M. and Minnie (Magdovitz) C.; m. Jane Woodman, Nov. 18, 1978; 1 dau., Genevieve E. B.S., Cornell U., 1968; M.S., Calif. Inst. Tech., 1970, Ph.D., 1972; postdoctoral student, Oxford (Eng.) U., 1972-73. Asst. prof. chem. engring. M.I.T., 1973-77, assoc. prof., 1977-82, prof., 1982—; cons. Hercules Inc., Wilmington, Del., 1980—, Xerox Corp., Webster, N.Y., 1980—. Named Dreyfus Found. Tchr.-Scholar, 1977. Mem. Am. Inst. Chem. Engring., Am. Chem. Soc., Soc. Rheology, British Soc. Rheology, N.Y. Acad. Scis. Co-patentee polymer blends; process for fluorinating polymers surfaces. Current Work: Physics and chemistry of polymers. Subspecialties: Polymer engineering; Chemical engineering. Office: Dept Chem Engring Mass Inst Tech Bldg 66 Room 554 Cambridge MA 02139

COHEN, RONALD ALEX, dentist; b. Flushing, N.Y., Sept. 16, 1944; s. Joseph Nathan and Rose (Rutkay) C.; m. Anita Sharon Liedarson, Oct. 26, 1969; children-Jill Stacie, Jodi Nicole. A.A., Queensborough Community Coll., 1964; B.A., Qunnipiac Coll., 1968; M.S., Adelphi U., 1970; D.D.S., N.Y.U., 1974. Tchr., N.Y.C., 1968-71; dentist Am. Dental Assn., Chgo., 1971—; instr Coll. Dentistry N.Y.U., 1978-80; lectr., U.S., 1979—. Sec. Bayside (N.Y.) Democratic Club, 1966. Fellow 11th Dist. Dental Soc., Acad. Gen. Dentistry; mem. Queens Acad. Gen. Dentistry (v.p. 1979-80), Am. Acad. Oral Medicine, Am. Acad. Periodontics, Coral Springs C. of C., Alpha Omega, Alpha Epsilon Pi. Current Work: preventive dentistry, periodontics, iatrogenic dentistry lectrs. Subspecialties: Periodontics; Prosthodontics. Home: 10717 NW 19th St Coral Springs FL 33065 Office: 7305 W Sample Rd Coral Springs FL 33065

COHEN, SAMUEL M., pathologist; b. Milw., Sept. 24, 1946; s. David A. and Harriett (Goldman) C.; m. Janet L. Olson, Jan. 27, 1968; children—Sheri Lyn, Benjamin Aaron, Daniel Eric, Erica Ann. B.S., U. Wis.-Madison, 1967, M.D., 1972, Ph.D., 1972. Diplomate: Am. Bd. Pathology, 1976. Resident in pathology St. Vincent Hosp., Worcester, Mass., 1972-75, staff pathologist, Mass., 1975-81; asso. prof. U. Mass. Med. Sch., Worcester, 1977-81; prof., vice chmn. dept. pathology and microbiology U. Nebr. Med. Ctr., Omaha, 1981—; vis. prof. Nagoya (Japan) City U. Med. Sch., 1976-77; mem. chem. pathology study sect. Nat. Cancer Inst. Assoc. editor: Cancer Research, 1982—; contbr. articles to profl. jours. Mem. Am. Assn. Cancer Research, Am. Assn. Pathologists, Japanese Cancer Assn., AAAS. Current Work: Chemical carcinogenesis, urinary bladder carcinogenesis, carcinogen metabolism, computer modeling, diagnostic electron microscopy. Subspecialties: Pathology (medicine); Cancer research (medicine). Home: 2721 S 101 St Omaha NE 68124 Office: U Nebr Med Ctr 42d and Dewey Ave Omaha NE 68105

COHEN, SEYMOUR STANLEY, biochemist; b. N.Y.C., Apr. 30, 1917; s. Herman and Lena (Tanz) C.; m. Elaine Pear, July 12, 1940; children: Michael, Sara. B.S., CCNY, 1936; Ph.D. in Biol. Chemistry, Columbia U., 1941; Dr.h.c., U. Louvain, Belgium, 1972, U. Kuopio, Finland, 1982. NRC fellow Rockefeller Inst., 1941-42; mem. faculty U. Pa., 1943-71, prof. biochemistry in pediatrics, 1954-71, Charles Hayden-Am. Cancer Soc. prof. biochemistry, 1957-71, Hartzell prof., chmn. dept. therapeutic research Sch. Medicine, 1963-71; Am. Cancer Soc. prof. microbiology U. Colo. Sch. Medicine, Denver, 1971-76; disting. prof., Am. Cancer Soc. prof. pharm. scis. SUNY, Stony Brook, 1976-85, emeritus, 1985—; chmn. council analysis and projection Am. Cancer Soc., 1972-74, adviser research, 1974-76; Guggenheim fellow Pasteur Inst., Paris, 1947-48; Jesup lectr. Columbia U., 1974-77), Phi Beta Kappa. guest investigator Institut du Radium, Paris, 1967-68; vis. prof. Collège de France, Paris, 1970; vis. fellow Smithsonian Instn., 1973-74; vis. prof. U. Tokyo, 1974, Hadassah Med. Sch., 1974, Zuckerman lectr. tropical disease, 1979; Guggenheim and Lady Davis fellow Faculty Agr., Israel, 1983; fellow Nat. Humanities Ctr., N.C., 1982-83, 85. Trustee emeritus Marine Biol. Lab., Woods Hole, Mass.; bd. sci. cons. Sloan-Kettering Inst. Author: Virus-Induced Enzymes, 1968, Introduction to the Polyamines, 1971; editorial bd.: Virology, 1954-59, Jour. Biol. Chemistry, 1959-65, Jour. Cell Physiology, 1966-71, Bacteriological Revs, 1969-73. Recipient certificate war research OSRD, 1945, War Manpower Commn., 1945; War Research medal Columbia U., 1943; Eli Lily award and medal Am. Soc. Bacteriology, Immunology and Pathology, 1951; 1st Mead Johnson award Am. Acad. Pediatrics, 1952; medal Soc. de Chimie Biologique France, 1964; Borden award Am. Assn. Med. Colls., 1967; Passano award, 1974; Townsend Harris medal CCNY Alumni Assn., 1978; Forster award German Acad. Sci. and Letters, Mainz, 1978; Fogarty scholar NIH, 1973-74. Fellow AAAS (Newcomb Cleveland award 1955); mem. Am. Acad. Arts and Scis., Soc. Gen. Physiologists (councilor, pres. 1967-68), Nat. Acad. Scis., Serbian Acad. Scis. and Art, Inst. Medicine, Am. Assn. Cancer Research (dir. 1974-77), Phi Beta Kappa. Subspecialty: Biochemistry (biology).

COHEN, SHELDON AVERY, research psychologist, consultant, educator; b. Detroit, Oct. 11, 1947; s. Harry F. and Ruth (Shapiro) C. Ph.B., Monteith Coll., Wayne State U., 1969; Ph.D., N.Y.U., 1973. Asst. prof. U. Oreg., 1973-78; assoc. prof., 1978-82; prof. psychology Carnegie-Mellon U., Pitts., 1982—. Co-Author: Behavior, Health and Environmental Stress, 1986; contbr. chpts., articles to profl. publs.; editor: (with S.L. Syme) Social Support and Health, 1985. NIMH trainee, 1969-73; grantee NSF, 1974-77, 77-80, 80-83; grantee Nat. Inst. Environ. Health Scis., 1978-80; grantee Nat. Heart, Lung and Blood Inst., 1982-84, Nat. Cancer Inst., 1984—. Fellow Am. Psychol. Assn., Soc. Behavioral Medicine; mem. Acad. Behavioral Medicine, Internat. Commn. on Biol. Effects of Noise (exec. com. 1978—), Soc. Exptl. Social Psychology, Soc. Psychol. Study Social Issues, Environ. Design Research Assn. Current Work: Effects of environmental and psychological stresses on health and behavior; role of social support systems in protecting people from stress-induced illness. Subspecialty: Social psychology. Office: Dept Psychology Carnegie-Mellon U Pittsburgh PA 15213

COHEN, STANLEY NORMAN, educator, geneticist; b. Perth Amboy, N.J., Feb. 17, 1935; s. Bernard and Ida (Stolz) C.; m. Joanna Lucy Wolter, June 27, 1961; children: Anne, Geoffrey. B.A., Rutgers U., 1956; M.D., U. Pa., 1960. Intern, Mt. Sinai Hosp., N.Y.C., 1960-61; resident Univ. Hosp., Ann Arbor, Mich., 1961-62; clin. asso. arthritis and rheumatism br. Nat. Inst. Arthritis and Metabolic Diseases, Bethesda, Md., 1962-64; sr. resident in medicine Duke U. Hosp., Durham, N.C., 1964-65; Am. Cancer Soc. postdoctoral research fellow Albert Einstin Coll. Medicine, Bronx, 1965-67, asst. prof. devel. biology and cancer, 1967-68; mem. faculty Stanford (Calif.) U., 1968—, prof. medicine, 1975—, prof. genetics, 1977, chmn. dept. genetics, 1978—; mem. com. recombinant DNA molecules Nat. Acad. Sci.-NRC, 1974; mem. com. on genetic experimentation Internat. Council Sci. Unions, 1977—. Mem. editorial bd.: Jour. Bacteriology, 1973-79; asso. editor: Plasmid, 1977—. Served with USPHS, 1962-64. Recipient Burroughs Wellcome Scholar award, 1970; V.D. Mattia award Roche Inst. Molecular Biology, 1977; Albert Lasker basic med. research award, 1980; Wolf prize, 1981; Marvin J. Johnson award Am. Chem. Soc., 1981; Josiah Macy Jr. Found. faculty scholar, 1975-76; Guggenheim fellow, 1975. Mem. Nat. Acad. Sci., Am. Acad. Arts and Sci., Am. Soc. Biol. Chemists, Genetics Soc. Am., Am. Soc. Microbiology, Am. Soc. Pharmacology and Exptl. Therapeutics, Am. Soc. Clin. Investigation, Phi Beta Kappa, Sigma Xi. Subspecialties: Gene actions; Genome organization. Office: Dept Genetics S-337 Stanford U Sch Medicine Stanford CA 94305

COHEN, WAYNE ROY, medical educator; b. N.Y.C., Apr. 27, 1946; s. Eugene Mark and Helen (Paul) C.; m. Sharon Rose Ominski, Aug. 24, 1980; children—Aaron, Daniel Paul. A.B., U. Rochester, 1967; M.D., Boston U., 1971. Diplomate: Am. Bd. Ob-Gyn. Asst. prof. Harvard Med. Sch., Boston, 1978-82; assoc. prof. ob-gyn Albert Einstein Coll. Medicine, N.Y.C., 1983—. Co-editor: Management of Labor, 1983; contbr. articles to profl. jours. Fellow Am. Coll. Ob-Gyn; mem. Am. Fedn. Clin. research, Soc. for Exptl. Biology and Medicine. Jewish. Current Work: Fetal sympathoadrenal function; management of parturition. Subspecialties: Maternal and fetal medicine; Reproductive biology (medicine). Home: 146 Cedar Hill Rd Bedford NY 10506 Office: Bronx Mcpl Hosp Ctr Pelham Pkwy S Bronx NY 10461

COHN, DAVID V(ALOR), biological chemistry educator, research consultant; b. N.Y.C., Nov. 11, 1926; s. Ralph and Clara (Schenkman) C.; married, 1947; children: Robert Warren, Emily. B.S., CCNY, 1948; Ph.D., Duke U., 1952; postgrad., Western Res. U., 1953. Mem. faculty U. Kans. Sch. Medicine, Kansas City, 1953-83, assoc. dean research, 1974-82; assoc. chief staff for research devel. VA Med. Ctr., Kansas City, Mo., 1953-82; prof. biochemistry U. Mo.-Kansas City, 1971-82; v.p. research and devel. Immuno Nuclear Corp., Stillwater, Minn., 1982, sci. cons., 1983; research prof. oral biology and biochemistry U. Louisville Sch. Medicine, Sch. Dentistry, 1984—; pres. Internat. Conf. on Calcium Regulating Hormones; mem. bd. sci. counselors Nat. Inst. Dental Research, Bethesda, Md., 1980-84, chmn., 1984. Editor: Hormonal Regulation of Calcium Metabolism, 1981-86; editor-in-chief Bone and Mineral, 1985—; contbr. articles to profl. jours. Served with USN, 1945-46. USPHS grantee, 1957—; VA grantee, 1975-82; Am. Cancer Soc. grantee, 1959-60. Mem. Am. Soc. Biol. Chemists, Am. Chem. Soc., AAAS, Gordon Research Conf. Chem. and Biol. of Bones and Teeth (chmn. 1974). Jewish. Current Work: Calcium metabolism, parathyroid gland biosynthesis and secretion, bone cell growth, differentiation and hormone responsivity. Subspecialties: Endocrinology; Biochemistry (medicine). Home: 5709 Apache Rd Louisville KY 40207 Office: Dept Oral Biology Health Scis Ctr U Louisville Louisville KY 40292

COHN, MAJOR LLOYD, neurologist, clinic adminstr., researcher, cons. toxicology; b. N.Y.C., Oct. 29, 1927; s. Isidore and Pauline (Bustein) C.; m. Marthe Hoffnung, Feb. 9, 1958; children—Stephan Jacques, Remi Benjamin. M.D., U. Geneva, Switzerland, 1956; Ph.D. (Am. Cancer Soc. fellow) in Biochemistry and intermediate Metabolism, U. Pitts., 1969. Intern Bklyn. Jewish Hosp., 1956-57; resident Washington U., St. Louis, 1957-58, Cornell U. Med. Sch. - Mem. Hosp. Cancer and Allied Diseases, 1959-60; Am. Cancer Soc. fellow asso. attending in medicine Montefore Hosp., N.Y.C., 1961-62; asst. prof. Sloan-Kettering Inst. and Meml. Hosp. for Cancer, 1960-61; U. Pitts. Sch. Medicine, 1969-79; asso. prof. UCLA Charles R. Drew Med. Sch., 1979—; dir. anesthesiology research UCLA Charles R. Drew Med. Sch. (Pain Clinic, Martin Luther King, Jr./Charles R. Drew Med. Center.). Contbr. articles on neuropharmacology to profl. jours. Served with USN, 1945-46. Recipient Henry L. Moses award, 1978. Fellow Royal Soc. Medicine; mem. Soc. for Neurosci., Internat. Assn. for Study of Pain, Internat. Soc. Psychoneuroendocrinology, Am. Soc. for Pharmacology and Exptl. Therapeutics, Am. Coll. Toxicology. Current Work: Neurochemistry, neuropharmacology, neurotoxicology, biochemistry, neuroendocrinology. Subspecialties: Internal medicine; Neurochemistry. Home: 4015 Exultant Dr Rancho Palos Verdes CA 90274 Office: Charles R Drew Med Sch 1621 E 120th St Los Angeles CA 90059

COHN, MILDRED, biochemist; b. N.Y.C., July 12, 1913; d. Isidore M. and Bertha (Klein) C.; m. Henry Primakoff, May 31, 1938; children—Nina, Paul, Laura. B.A., Hunter Coll., 1931; M.A., Columbia, 1932, Ph.D., 1938; Sc.D. (hon.), Med. Coll. Pa., 1966, Radcliffe Coll., 1978, Washington U., St. Louis, 1981, Brandeis U., 1984, U. Pa., 1984, Hunter Coll., 1984, U. N.C., 1985. Research asst. biochemistry George Washington U. Sch. Medicine, 1937-38; research asso. Cornell U., 1938-46; research asso. Washington U., 1946-50, 51-58, asso. prof. biol. chemistry, 1958-60; asso. prof. biophysics and phys. biochemistry U. Pa. Med. Sch., 1960-61, prof., 1961-78, Benjamin Rush prof. physiol. chemistry, 1978-82, prof. emerita, 1982; sr. mem. Inst. Cancer Research U. Pa., 1982—. Editorial bd.: Jour. Biol. Chemistry, 1958-63, 67-72. Established investigator Am. Heart Assn., 1953-59, career investigator, 1964-78. Recipient Garvan medal, Cresson medal., Nat. medal of sci. Am. Acad. of Achievement. Mem. Am. Philos. Soc., Nat. Acad. Scis., Am. Chem. Soc., Harvey Soc., Am. Soc. Biol. Chemists (pres. 1978), Am. Biophys. Soc., Am. Acad. Arts and Scis., Phi Beta Kappa, Sigma Xi. Current Work: Nuclear magnetic resonance of enzyme mechanisms and in vivo phosphate metabolism. Subspecialties: Biophysical chemistry; Nuclear magnetic resonance. Office: Inst Cancer Research 7701 Burholme Ave Philadelphia PA 19111

COHN, NATHAN, consultant, former engineering company executive; b. Hartford, Conn., Jan. 2, 1907; s. Harris and Dora Leah (Levin) C.; m. Marjorie Kurtzon, June 30, 1940; children: Theodore Elliot, David Leslie, Anne Harris, Amy Elizabeth, Julie Archer. S.B., M.I.T., 1927; D.Eng. (hon.), Rennsalear Poly. Inst., 1976. With Leeds & Northrup Co., Phila., 1927-72, mgr. market devel. div., 1955-58, v.p. tech. affairs, 1958-65, sr. v.p. tech. affair, 1965-67, exec. v.p. research and corp. devel., 1967-72, dir., 1963-75, cons. mgmt. and tech. of measurement and control, Jenkintown, Pa., 1972—; dir. AEL Industries Inc., Alkco Mfg. Co., Weinschel Engring. Co.; dir. Milton Roy Co., Modular Comptar Systems, Parlex Corp.; gen. partner Network Systems Devel. Assos.; pres. Nat. Electronics Conf., 1950; mem. NRC; exec. bd. Found. Instrumentation, Edn. and Research, 1962-64; del. congress Internat. Fedn. Automatic Control, 1960, 63, 66, 69, 72, 75, 78, 81, 84, advisor for life, 1984, chmn. tech. com. on applications, 1969-72; chmn. U.S. organizing com. 1975 World Congress, mem. tech. coms. on computers, systems, mem. com. on social effects of automation, 1975—; mem. vis. com. libraries M.I.T., 1964-69, mem. vis. com. philosophy, 1972-74. Contbr. articles to profl. jours., chpts. to books, textbook. Bd. dirs., v.p. Eagleville (Pa.) Hosp. and Rehab. Center. Fellow IEEE (life, Lamme medal 1968, Edison medal 1982, chmn. fellow com. 1974-76, chmn. awards bd. 1977-78, mem. Centennial com. 1979-84); chmn. Intersoc. Hoover Medal (Bd. of Award 1978-81); mem. Instrument Soc. Am. (v.p. industries and scis. 1960-61, sec. 1962, pres. 1963, Sperry medalist 1968, hon. mem. award 1976), AAAS, Franklin Inst. (life, Wetherill medalist 1968, mem. bd. mgrs. 1971—, chmn. bd. mgrs. 1971-75), Nat. Acad. Engring., Engrs. Joint Council (exec. bd. 1975-78, commn. on internat. relations 1978-79), Am. Assn. Engring. Socs. (council for internat. affairs 1980-81), Indsl. Research Inst., Engrs. Council Profl. Devel. (vis. com. curriculum accreditation), Sci. Apparatus Makers Assn. (exec. bd. 1961-62, 66-73, pres. 1969-71, SAMA award 1978), Nat. Soc. Profl. Engrs. (Engr. of Yr. Delaware Valley 1968, State of Pa. 1969), Sigma Xi, Tau Beta Pi, Eta Kappa Nu, Pi Lambda Phi. Jewish. Club: Rydal (Phila.). Patentee electric power systems controls. Current Work: Automatic control and control performance evaluation of interconnected electric power systems. Subspecialties: Electrical engineering; Systems engineering.

COHN, ZANVIL A., physician; b. N.Y.C., Nov. 16, 1926; s. David and Esther (Schwartz) C.; m. Fern R. Dworkin, Dec. 19, 1949; children: David, Ellen. B.S., Bates Coll., 1949; M.D. summa cum laude, Harvard U., 1953. Mem. staff Rockefeller Inst. (now Rockefeller U.), N.Y.C., 1958—, prof., sr. physician, 1966—; Co-dir. Joint Rockefeller U.-Cornell U. Med. Coll. M.D.-Ph.D. program, 1973-78; adj. prof. medicine Cornell U., 1977—. Contbr. articles to profl. jours. Mem. Commn. on Radiation and Infection, Armed Forces Epidemiology Bd.; mem. study sect. on immunology NIH; cons. Nat. Cancer Inst. Recipient Boylston Medal Harvard U., 1961; Basic Sci. award Am. Soc. Cytology, 1970; Fifth Ann. Squibb award Am. Soc. Infectious Diseases, 1972; 7th Ann. Research award Samuel Noble Found., 1982. Mem. Nat. Acad. Sci. Current Work: Cellular physiology and immunology. Subspecialties: Cell biology (medicine); Infectious diseases. Office: Rockefeller U 1230 York Ave New York NY 10021

COKELET, GILES ROY, biophysics educator, researcher; b. N.Y.C., Jan. 7, 1932; s. Roy Sylvester and Anna Mary (Trippel) C.; m. Sarah Drew, June 15, 1963; children: Becky, Bradford Roy. A.A., Pasadena City Coll., 1953; B.S., Calif. Inst. Tech., 1957, M.S., 1958; Sc.D., M.I.T., 1963. Research Engr. Dow Chem. Co., Williamsburg, Va., 1958-61; asst. prof. M.I.T., Cambridge, 1963-64, Calif. Inst. Tech., Pasadena, 1964-68; assoc. prof. Mont. State U., Bozeman, 1968-76, prof., 1976-78; prof. radiation biology and biophysics U. Rochester, N.Y., 1978—; ad hoc cons. NIH, 1970—; cons. Cordis-Dow Co., 1977. Assoc. editor: Advances in Chemical Engineering, 1969-81; editor: Erythrocyte Mechanics and Blood Flow, 1980; contbr. articles to profl. jours. Served with U.S. Army, 1954-55. Recipient Sr. U.S. Scientist award A. von Humboldt-Stiftung, Cologne, W.Ger., 1981-82. Fellow AAAS; mem. Am. Inst. Chem. Engrs., Mirocirculatory Soc. (council 1981-85), Soc. Rheology, European Microcirculatory Soc. Current Work: Blood rheology and hemodynamics; microcirculatory blood flow; mass transport phenomena in biological systems, including the microcirculation. Subspecialties: Biomedical engineering; Biophysics (physics). Home: 62 Burrows Hills Dr Rochester NY 14625 Office: U Rochester 601 Elmwood Ave Rochester NY 14642

COLAHAN, PATRICK TIMOTHY, veterinary surgeon; b. Klamath Falls, Oreg., May 31, 1948; s. Robert Martin and Maggie A. (Lovelady) C.; m. Carlye Ann Baker, July 28, 1973. B.S., U. Calif.-Davis, 1970, D.V.M., 1974. Diplomate: Am. Coll. Vet. Surgeons. Intern N.Y. Vet. Coll., Ithaca, 1974-75; resident U. Calif. Sch. Vet. Medicine, Davis, 1975-77, lectr., 1977-78; asst. prof. vet. surgery U. Fla. Coll. Vet. Medicine, Gainesville, 1978-84, assoc. prof., 1984—; chief large animal surgery service U. Fla. Coll. Vet. Medicine (Vet. Med. Teaching Hosp.), 1979-84, chief Large Animal Hosp., 1984—. Mem. League Conservation Voters, Gainesville, 1982—. Recipient award for proficiency in vet. clin. medicine Upjohn Co., 1974. Mem. Am. Assn. Equine Practitioners, Vet. Orthopedic Soc., Orthopedic Research Soc., Internation Vet. Radiology Soc., AVMA, Am. Forestry Assn., Phi Zeta. Democrat. Roman Catholic. Club: Commonwealth of Calif. (San Francisco). Current Work: General and orthopedic surgery; biomechanical analysis of equine musculoskeletal and respiratory systems. Subspecialties: Surgery (veterinary medicine); Biomedical engineering. Home: 7716 SW 53d Pl Gainesville FL 32608 Office: Dept Surg Scis Coll Vet Medicine U Fla Box J-116 JHMHC Gainesville FL 32610

COLASANTI, BRENDA KAREN, pharmacologist, educator; b. Charleston, W.Va., Dec 5, 1945; d. Harry Gordon and Mary Louise (Moore) Frame; m. Louis Colasanti, Jr., Sept. 21, 1968. B.A. in Zoology, W.Va. U., 1966, Ph.D. in Pharmacology, 1970. NIMH postdoctoral fellow in neuropsychopharmacology Mt. Sinai Sch. Medicine, N.Y.C., 1970-72; asst. prof. ophthalmology and pharmacology W.Va. U., Morgantown, 1972-76, asso. prof., 1976-80, prof., 1980—. Contbr. articles to sci. jours.; contbr.: (Craig and Stitzel) 8 chpts. to Modern Pharmacology, 1982. NIH grantee, 1974-80, 82—; acad. investigator award, 1977-80. Mem. Am. Soc. Pharmacology and Exptl. Therapeutics, Assn. for Psychophysiol. Study of Sleep, Am. Soc. for Neurochemistry, Assn. for Research in Vision and Ophthalmology, AAAS, Sigma Xi. Current Work: Neurochem. mechanisms of psychotropic drug action; role of autonomic input in the intraocular pressure lowering effects of drugs. Subspecialties: Ophthalmology; Neuropharmacology. Office: Dept Pharmacology and Toxicolog WVa U Med Cente Morgantown WV 26506

COLBERG, MAGDA, research psychologist; b. San Juan, P.R., July 25, 1936; d. Carlos and Maria I. (Colberg) Munoz-Santaella. A.B., Colegio Universitario del Sagrado Corazon, San Juan, 1957; Ph.D., Georgetown U., 1965; postgrad. Princeton U., 1969-71. Asst. liaison officer OAS, Washington, 1965-69; research psychologist U.S. Office Personnel Mgmt., Washington, 1974—. Contbr. articles to profl. jours. Recipient award for Superior Accomplishment U.S. Office Personnel Mgmt., 1981. Mem. Am. Philos. Assn., Assn. Symbolic Logic, Am. Psychol. Assn., Am. Math. Soc., Internat. Assn. Applied Psychology. Club: Princeton. Current Work: Special interest logic-based ability measurement and event predictive induction in psychometrics. Subspecialty: Probability. Home: 3101 New Mexico Ave NW Washington DC 20016 Office: 1900 E St NW Washington DC 20405

COLBERT, EDWIN H., paleontologist, museum curator; b. Clarinda, Iowa, Sept. 28, 1905; s. George Harris and Mary (Adamson) C.; m. Margaret Mary Matthew, July 8, 1933; children: George Matthew, David William, Philip Valentine, Daniel Lee, Charles Diller. Student, N.W. Mo. State Tchrs. Coll., 1923-26; B.A., U. Nebr., 1928, Sc.D., 1973; A.M., Columbia U., 1930, Ph.D., 1935; Sc.D., U. Ariz., 1976, Wilmington Coll., 1984. Student asst. Univ. Museum, U. Nebr., 1926-29; univ. fellow Columbia U., 1929-30, lectr. dept. zoology, 1938-39, prof. vertebrate paleontology, 1945-69, prof. emeritus, 1969—; research asst. Am. Museum Natural History, 1930-32, asst. curator, 1933-42, acting curator, 1942, curator, 1943, chmn. dept. amphibians and reptiles, 1943-44, curator of fossil reptiles and amphibians, 1945-70, chmn. dept. geology and paleontology, 1958-60, chmn. dept. vertebrate paleontology, 1960-66, curator emeritus, 1970—; curator vertebrate paleontology Mus. No. Ariz., Flagstaff, 1970—. Author: Evolution of the Vertebrates, 1955, 69, 80, Millions of Years Ago, 1958, Dinosaurs, 1961, (with M. Kay) Stratigraphy and Life History, 1965, The Age of Reptiles, 1965, Men and Dinosaurs, 1968, Wandering Lands and Animals, 1973, The Year of the Dinosaur, 1977, A Fossil Hunter's Notebook, 1980, Dinosaurs: An Illustrated History, 1983; also sci. papers and monographs. Recipient John Strong Newberry prize Columbia U., 1931; Daniel Giraud Elliot medal Nat. Acad. Sci., 1935; medal Am. Mus. Natural History, 1970. Fellow AAAS, Geol. Soc. Am., Paleontol. Soc. (v.p. 1963), N.Y. Zool. Soc.; mem. Soc. Vertebrate Paleontology (sec.-treas. 1944-46, pres. 1946-47), Soc. Mammalogy, Soc. Ichthyology and Herpetology, Soc. for Study Evolution (editor 1950-52, v.p. 1957, pres. 1958), Nat. Acad. Sci., Sigma Xi. Current Work: Vertebrate paleontology: evolution and distribution of vertebrates; evolution: morphological evolution in vertebrates, especially reptiles. Subspecialties: Paleobiology; Evolutionary biology. Office: Museum of No Arizona Route 4 Box 720 Flagstaff AZ 86001

COLBY, LEWIS JAMES, JR., See *Who's Who in America,* 43rd edition.

COLBY, NATHANIEL FRED, nuclear engineer; b. Bennington, Vt., July 5, 1936; s. Nathaniel Henry and Ruth Marjorie (Dudley) C.; m. Mary Louise Grenfell, June 6, 1959; children: Susan, Nathaniel R., Lindsey, Robert J.D. B.S., U.S. Mil. Acad., 1959; M.S. in Nuclear Engring., U. Mo.-Rolla, 1972; M.B.A., Fairleigh Dickinson U., 1983. Commd. 2d lt. U.S. Army, 1959; advanced through grades to lt. col.; research coordinator Def. Nuclear Agy., 1973-74; exec. asst. to dep. dir. for sci. and tech. Def. Nuclear Agy., 1975, ret., 1981; engring. planning mgr. GPU Nuclear Corp., Parsippany, N.J., 1981—. Decorated Silver Star medal, Bronze Star medal with cluster, Legion of Merit; Cross of Gallantry. Mem. Am. Nuclear Soc. Republican. Episcopalian. Subspecialty: Nuclear engineering. Home: 12 Baker Ave Dover NJ 07801 Office: GPU Nuclear Corp 100 Interpace Pkwy Parsippany NJ 07054

COLE, IRAD DEAN, computer systems specialist; b. Blair, Nebr., Mar. 14, 1930; s. Oliver and Mabel Louise (Reel) C.; m. Patricia Ann DeWitt, Nov. 12, 1950; 1 child, Steven Robert. B.A. in Math. and Physics, Omaha U., 1959; M.A. in Econs., U. Nebr.-Omaha, 1970. Computer programmer Lawrence Radiation Lab., Livermore, Calif., 1959-60; statistician Dow Chem. Co., Denver, 1960-61; programmer analyst System Devel. Corp., Santa Monica, Calif., 1961-71, project head, McLean, Va., 1973—; computer systems analyst U.S. Govt., Omaha, 1971-73. Contbr. papers to profl. confs. Co-chmn. Citizens for Goldwater Com., Sarpy County, Nebr., 1964. Served with U.S. Army, 1954-56. Mem. IEEE, Computer Soc. of IEEE, Systems, Man and Cybernetics Soc. of IEEE, Austrian Soc. for Cybernetic Studies (fgn. affiliate). Lutheran. Lodge: Moose. Current work: Relationships between rhetoric and computer programs. Subspecialties: Software engineering; Information systems, storage, and retrieval (computer science). Home: 9014 Jersey Dr Fairfax VA 22031 Office: System Devel Corp 7929 Westpark Dr McLean VA 22102

COLE, JACK WESTLEY, physician; b. Portland, Oreg., Aug. 28, 1920; s. Alva Warren and Louise (Shafer) C.; m. Ruth Adele Kraft, Dec. 22, 1943; children—Deborah, Linda, Douglas, John. A.B., U. Oreg., 1941; M.D., Wash. U., 1944; M.A., Yale, 1966. Mem. faculty Western Res. U. Sch. Medicine, 1952-63; prof., chmn. dept. surgery Hahnemann Med. Coll. and Hosp., 1963-66; Ensign prof. surgery Yale U. Sch. Medicine, 1966—, chmn. dept. surgery, 1966-74, Josiah Macy Jr. faculty scholar, 1974-75, dir. div. oncology and cancer center, 1975-84, vice chmn. dept. surgery, 1984—; cons. various hosps. Eleanor Roosevelt Internat. Cancer Research fellow, 1962. Mem. Am. Surg. Assn., Halsted Soc., Soc. Surgery of Alimentary Tract, Am. Soc. Cell Biology, Soc. Cryobiology. Research and publs. on histochemistry, cytochemistry, carcinogenesis; studies dealing with cellular kinetics in normal and abnormal intestinal epithelium. Subspecialty: Oncology. Home: Prospect Ct Woodbridge CT 06525 Office: 333 Cedar St New Haven CT 06510

COLE, JONATHAN JAY, aquatic ecologist; b. N.Y.C., Jan. 14, 1953; s. Leonard and Selma Ruth (Greenblatt) C.; m. Nina Caraco, Nov. 25, 1980; 1 child, Aaska Puccoon. B.A. magna cum laude, Amherst Coll., 1975; Ph.D., Cornell U., 1981. Postdoctoral fellow Woods Hole Oceanographic Inst., Mass., 1981-82, Marine Biol. Lab., 1982-83; asst. scientist Inst. Ecosystem Studies, Millbrook, N.Y., 1983—; assoc. site coordinator Hubbard Brook Exptl. Forest, Thornton, N.H., 1983—. Contbr. sci. articles to profl. jours. NSF grantee NSF. Mem. Am. Soc. Limnology and Oceanography, Am. Soc. Microbiology, Sigma Xi (assoc.). Current work: Biogeochemistry, microbial interactions, aquatic ecosystems, decomposition processes. Subspecialties: Ecosystems analysis; Limnology. Home: Gifford Toad House Box 276 Millbrook NY 12545 Office: Inst Ecosystem Studies Cary Arboretum Millbrook NY 12545

COLE, KENNETH DEAN, designer, consultant; b. Peoria, Ill., July 3, 1951; s. Don R. and Emma Jayne C.; m. Jeanette Eileen O'Brien, May 2, 1975. Student, Sacramento City Coll., 1968-69, Am. River Coll., 1970. With Bechtel Corp., 1969-73, 76-78, Fluor M & M, 1973-76; ind. cons. to Detroit Edison Co., Pacific Gas & Electric Co. and Chevron Chem. Co., 1978-81; owner, operator Interim Tech. Assocs., Pinole, Calif., 1981—. Mem. John Anderson Presdl. Campaign, 1980. Mem. ASME (affiliate). Subspecialty: Mechanical engineering.

COLE, LEE ARTHUR, solid state physicist, program administrator; b. Pitts., May 2, 1953; s. Basil Lee and Virginia Ruth (Smyers) C. B.S., Indiana U. Pa.-Indiana, Pa., 1975; Ph.D., Dartmouth Coll., 1979. Fellow in physics Tulane U., 1979-81; vis. asst. prof. Dartmouth Coll., 1980; physicist Ames Lab., Iowa State U., 1980; program mgr. SERI, Dept. Energy, Golden, Colo., 1981-85; program mgr. Solid State Electronics div. Honeywell Inc., Colorado Springs, Colo., 1985—. Contbr. articles to sci. jours. Active, Operation Up-Lift, Indiana, Pa., 1971-75. Dartmouth Coll. fellow, 1975-79, Tulane Univ. fellow, 1979-81. Mem. Am. Phys. Soc., Internat. Assn. Math. Modelling. Republican. Roman Catholic. Current work: Research management in advanced semiconductor crystal growth; Gallium arsenide and related materials (GaAs, AlGaAs, GaAsP, GaAsSb, GaAsIn). Subspecialties: Semiconductors; Theoretical physics. Home: 812 S Vance St Lakewood CO 80226 Office: Solid State Electronics Div Honeywell Inc 1150 Cheyenne Mountain Blvd Colorado Springs CO 80906

COLE, MICHAEL, psychologist, educator; b. Los Angeles, Apr. 13, 1938. B.A. with highest honors in Psychology, UCLA, 1959; Ph.D. in Psychology (Woodrow Wilson fellow 1959-60, Ford Found. fellow 1960-62), Ind. U., 1962. Research asst. UCLA, 1958-59, Ind. U., 1959-62; exchange scholar, State Dept. grantee Moscow U., 1962-63; research asso. Inst. Math. Studies in Social Scis., lectr. Stanford U., 1963-64; asst. prof. Yale U., 1964-66; asso. prof. U. Calif., Irvine, 1966-69; asso. prof. Rockefeller U., 1969-75, prof., 1975-78; prof. psychology, communications U. Calif., San Diego, 1978—, also dir. lab. comparative human cognition; mem. for psychology Joint Soviet-Am. Commn. in Social Scis. Author: (with others) The Cultural Context of Learning and Thinking, 1971, (with S. Scribner) Psychology of Literacy, 1981; others; author introductions, forewords; contbr. (with S. Scribner) articles to profl. publs.; editor: (with others) Developing Child Series, Soviet Psychology, 1969—; guest editor spl. issue: (with others) Am. Psychologist, 1977; cons. editor to (with others) jours. Recipient Research Scientist Devel. award USPHS, 1969-74 (hon. 1970-74); Behavioral Sci. award N.Y. Acad. Sci., 1978; Van Leer-Jerusalem Found. fellow, 1975—. Mem. AAAS, Am. Psychol. Assn., Psychonomic Soc., Am. Anthrop. Assn., Librarian Research Assn., Council on Anthropology and Edn., Social Sci. Research Council, Soc. Research in Child Devel., Am. Acad. Arts and Sci., Nat. Acad. Edn., Phi Beta Kappa, Sigma Xi. Subspecialty: Cognition. Office: U Calif at San Diego Lab Comparative Human Cognition X003 La Jolla CA 92093

COLE, TERRY, chemist; b. Albion, N.Y., Mar. 28, 1931; s. Marc Wheeler and Florence (Terry) C.; m. Margaret Campbell, July 16, 1955; children—Vallance, Catherine, Sarah. B.S., U. Minn., 1954; Ph.D., Calif. Inst. Tech., 1958. Research scientist Ford Motor Co., Dearborn, Mich., 1959-70, mgr. chem. dept., 1970-80; chief technologist Jet Propulsion Lab., Pasadena, Calif., 1980—; sr. research assoc. Calif. Inst. Tech., Pasadena; adj. prof. U. Mich., Dearborn, 1968-72. Fairchild Disting. scholar, 1976-77. Mem. Am. Chem. Soc., Am. Phys. Soc. Subspecialties: Physical chemistry; Aerospace engineering and technology. Home: 5246 Gould Ave La Canada CA 91011 Office: Calif Inst Tech Pasadena CA 91125

COLE, THOMAS EARLE, nuclear engineer; b. Winter Park, Fla., Dec. 13, 1922; s. Henry Earle and Lizzie Bell (Perrine) C.; m. Jean Holden, Feb. 24, 1944; children: Henry Earle, Edmund Platt. B.S., Rollins Coll., 1946. Various staff assignment Oak Ridge Nat. Lab., 1946-73; spl. assignment Oak Ridge Nat. Lab. (AEC Reactor Safety Study), 1973-74; mgr. Oak Ridge Nat. Lab. (HTGR safety program), 1974-77, group leader various programs, 1977-81; mgr. Oak Ridge Nat. Lab. (LWR tech. program), 1980—, group leader reactor systems analysis, 1981—; cons. in field of nuclear research reactors to various U.S. and fgn. cos., 1955-65. Contbg. author: Ann. Rev. of Nuclear Science-Technology of Research Reactors, 1963. Served to lt. j.g. USNR, 1943-46, PTO. Mem. Am. Nuclear Soc. (charter), Am. Phys. Soc., Sigma Xi. Current Work: Nuclear reactor systems analysis and safety studies; studies of the role of nuclear reactor electric power plants in the U.S. electric utility industry, e.g., energy parks, advanced concepts, etc. Subspecialties: Nuclear engineering; Nuclear fission. Home: 103 Disston Rd Oak Ridge TN 37830

COLEMAN, C. NORMAN, physician, educator, researcher; b. N.Y.C., Jan. 24, 1945; s. Samuel A. and Minna (Kramer) C.; m. Karolynn Forsburg, May 25, 1970; children: Gabrielle, Keith. B.A. summa cum laude, U. Vt., 1966; M.D., Yale U., 1970. Intern and resident U. Calif.-San Francisco, 1970-72; fellow in med. oncology Nat. Cancer Inst., Bethesda, Md., 1972-74; resident in radiation therapy Stanford (Calif.) U. Med. Sch., 1975-78, asst. prof. radiology and medicine, 1978-83, assoc. prof. radiology and medicine, 1983-85; prof., dir. Joint Ctr. for Radiation Therapy, Harvard Med. Sch.; prin. investigator NIH grants Stanford-No. Calif. Oncology Group, 1978-85, Stanford-Radiation Therapy Oncology Group, 1980-85, Joint Ctr. for Radiation Therapy, 1985—, Chem. Modifiers of Radiation Therapy, 1984—. Served to lt. comdr. USPHS, 1972-74. Recipient Newell award Stanford U., 1978; Am. Cancer Soc. jr. faculty clin. fellow, 1979-82; Moule fellow Stanford U., 1980-83. Fellow ACP; mem. Am. Coll. Radiology, Am. Assn. Cancer Research, Am. Soc. Therapeutic Radiologists, Am. Soc. Clin. Oncology, Radiation Research Soc., Phi Beta Kappa, Alpha Omega Alpha. Current Work: Study of late effects of cancer treatment, e.g. secondary cancers; study of chemical modifiers of chemotherapy and radiotherapy, sensitizers of cancer to therapy and protectors of normal tissues; cancer treatment. Subspecialties: Cancer research (medicine); Oncology. Home: 115 Cherry Brook Rd Weston MA 02193

COLEMAN, CHARLES CLYDE, physics educator; b. York, Eng., July 31, 1937; came to U.S. 1939; s. Jesse C. and Geraldine C. (Doherty) C.; m. Lynne Barbara Smiley, Sept. 29, 1967 (div.); m. Sharon Ruth Slutsky, Sept. 12, 1976; children—Jeffrey Andrew, Matthew Casey. B.A., UCLA, 1959, M.A., 1961, Ph.D., 1968. Assoc. prof. Calif. State U., Los Angeles, 1971-76; sr. research fellow U. Cambridge, Eng., 1975-76, 83-84; prof. physics Calif. State U., Los Angeles, 1976—; exec. dir. Applied Physcis Inst., Los Angeles, 1981—; dir. CSULA Accelerator Lab., Los Angeles, 1980—; trustee CSULA Found. Contbr. articles to profl. jours. Fellow British Internat. Soc., Am. Phys. Soc. Current work: Optical properties of solids, interfacos, intercalation, backscuttering spectroscopy. Subspecialty: Condensed matter physics.

COLEMAN, CHARLES F(RANKLIN), chemist; b. Burley, Idaho, Dec. 30, 1917; s. Arthur Enos and Orpha Mary (Cauthorn) C.; m. E(mma) Virginia Spivey, Apr. 5, 1952; children—Franklin Cauthorn, Nancy Lee, Arthur Wheless. B.S. in Chem. Engring., U. Utah, 1941; M.S., Purdue U., 1943, Ph.D. in Phys. Chemistry, 1948. Chemist, Manhattan Project, Columbia U., 1944, Tenn. Eastman Co., Oak Ridge, Tenn., 1944-46; chemist ORNL, Union Carbide, Oak Ridge, Tenn., 1948-67, asst. sect. chief, 1967-76, sect. mgr. separations, 1976-83, cons., 1984—. Mem. editorial bd. Hydrometallurgy, 1975-79; contbr. chpts. to tech. jours.; patentee in field. Vol. reader Recording for the Blind, 1961—. Mem. Am. Chem. Soc., AAAS, Sigma Xi, Tau Beta Pi, Phi Kappa Phi. Clubs: Smoky Mountain Hiking, Marin Marietta Camera. Current work: Separations chemistry; solvent extraction and ion exchange; separations reagents, equilibria, kinetics; actinide-lanthanide chemistry; phase equilibria; process development. Subspecialties: Physical chemistry; Nuclear chemistry. Home: 106 Elliott Circle Oak Ridge TN 37830 Office: Oak Ridge Nat Lab Bldg 4501 PO Box X Oak Ridge TN 37831

COLEMAN, COURTNEY STAFFORD, mathematics educator, analyst; b. Ventura, Calif., July 19, 1930; s. Courtney Clemon and Una (Stafford) C.; m. Julia Alva Louise Wellnitz, June 26, 1954; children—David, Margaret, Diane. B.A., U. Calif.-Berkeley, 1951; M.A., Princeton U., 1953, Ph.D., 1955. Lectr.

Princeton U., N.J., 1954-55; asst. prof. Wesleyan U., Middletown, Conn., 1955-58; asst. prof., prof. math. Harvey Mudd Coll., Claremont, Calif., 1959—; research scientist RIAS, Balt., 1958-59, 63-64; NSF sci. faculty fellow Oxford U., Eng., 1979-80. Editor: Differential Equations Models, 1983. Contbr. articles to profl. jours. Mem. Am. Math. Soc., Math. Assn. Am., Soc. for Indsl. and Applied Math., AAUP. Presbyterian. Current work: Teaching undergraduate mathematics; carrying out research on topological and algebraic characterizations of the orbital structure of differential equations. Subspecialties: Analysis; Applied mathematics. Home: 675 Northwestern Dr Claremont CA 91711 Office: Harvey Mudd Coll Claremont CA 91711

COLEMAN, JAMES MALCOM, marine geology educator; b. Vinton, La., Nov. 19, 1935; s. Leo George and Clara (Gaudet) C.; m. Travis Lucille Alexander, July 28, 1958; children—Thomas M., Sarah E. B.S. in Geology, La. State U., 1958; M.S., 1962, Ph.D., 1966. Asst. prof. coastal studies inst. La. State U., Baton Rouge, 1966-69, assoc. prof., 1969-74, asst. dir., 1971-73, prof. geology, acting dir., 1974-75, prof., dir., 1975-80, Boyd prof., dir., 1980-85, head Sch. Geosci., chmn. dept. geology, 1985—; disting. lectr. Shell Oil Co., 1979; mem. devel. council Gulf Univ. Research Council, 1980; cons. numerous oil cos. Contbr. articles to profl jours. Cons. editor: Royal Soc. Edinburgh, Scotland, 1984. Mem. Am. Assn. Petroleum Geologists, Geol. Soc. Am., Gulf Coast Soc. Soc. Econ. Paleontologists and Mineralogists (Shepard award 1980). Democrat. Methodist. Lodge: Rotary Internat. (Baton Rouge) (Internat. Fellowship com.). Current work: Deltaic sedimentation; riverine processes; shallow structure shelf sediments; deep sea fans. Subspecialties: Geology; Sedimentology. Home: 667 Castle Kirk Ave Baton Rouge LA 70808 Office: Coastal Studies Inst La State U Baton Rouge LA 70803-7527

COLEMAN, JAMES MARK, ecologist, climatologist, consultant; b. Chgo., Apr. 9, 1946; s. James Daniel and Matilda Frances (Matic) C.; m. Lynda Lee Lundberg, May 6, 1970. B.A., Loyola U., New Orleans, 1969; M.S., U. Tenn., 1975; Ph.D., U. Fla., 1979. Research supr. Environ. Quality Lab., Inc., Port Charlotte, Fla., 1977-79; prin. engr. Planning Research Corp., Kennedy Space Ctr., Fla., 1979-81; dir. field ops. Bionetics Corp., Kennedy Space Ctr., 1981-82; pres. Environ. Mgmt., Inc., Cape Canaveral, Fla., 1982—, also dir. Contbr. articles to profl. jours. Recipient Austin award Fla. State Mus. and U. Fla., 1979; Aerospace Awareness award NASA, 1980; grad. fellow C.E., U.S. Army, 1974-75. Mem. Ecol. Soc. Am. (cert. sr. ecologist), AAAS, Planetary Soc. Current work: Limnological nutrient dynamics; pre-industrial phosphorous budgets; southeastern U.S. climatology. Subspecialties: Ecology (biology); Limnology. Home: 5003 Riveredge Dr Titusville FL 32780 Office: Environ Mgmt Inc PO Box 125 Cape Canaveral FL 32920

COLEMAN, JAMES R., psychologist, neuroscientist; b. Kansas City, Mo., Oct. 12, 1946; s. James D. and Marion (Rice) C.; m. Yolanda G. Salitrero, Dec. 18, 1971. B.A. in Zoology, UCLA, 1969, Ph.D. in Psychology, 1974. Postdoctoral trainee Duke U., Durham, N.C., 1974-76; asst. prof. psychology U. S.C., Columbia, 1977-81, assoc. prof., 1981—; adj. asst. prof. physiology U. S.C. Sch. Medicine, 1978-81, adj. assoc. prof., 1981—. Contbr. articles to profl. jours. NIH grantee, 1979-82, 85—; Deafness Research Found. grantee, 1979-85. Mem. AAAS, Am. Assn. Anatomists, Assn. Research in Otolaryngology, Internat. Soc. Developmental Psychobiology, Soc. Neuroscience. Current Work: Developmental neuroscience; development of central auditory systems; aging of central auditory systems. Subspecialties: Neurophysiology; Developmental neuroscience. Office: Dept Psychology U SC Columbia SC 29208

COLEMAN, JAMES STAFFORD, government energy research administrator; b. Cleelum, Wash., May 8, 1928. B.S., Wash. State U., 1950; Ph.D. in Phys. Chemistry, MIT, 1953. Mem. staff Los Alamos Nat. Lab., 1953-67; chemist div. Research, AEC, 1967-69; tech. advisor Office of Gen. Mgr., 1969-75; asst. div. dir. Div. Phys. Research, Energy Research & Devel. Adminstrn., 1975-77; div. dir. Office of Energy Research, Dept. Energy, Germantown, Md., 1977—. Mem. AAAS, Sigma Xi. Subspecialty: Energy research management. Office: Engring Math & Geoscis Div Dept of Energy Route 270 Germantown MD 20545

COLEMAN, JEFFREY OWEN, electrical engineer; b. Louisville, Ky., Oct. 1, 1953; s. Everett Shannon Coleman and Rose-Marie Fain; m. Teresa Gae Dame; 1 child, David Jason. S.B.E.E., MIT, 1975; M.S.E.E., Johns Hopkins U., 1979; cert. in computer programming Inst. for Cert. of Computer Profls., 1979. Mem. tech. staff Watkins-Johnson Co., Gaithersburg, Md., 1975-76, Digital Communications Corp., Gaithersburg, 1976-77; sr. design engr. Penril Corp., Rockville, Md., 1977-78; electronics engr. radar div. Naval Research Lab., Washington, 1978-85. Author articles in profl. jours., conf. papers, tech. reports. Mem. IEEE, Assn. Computing Machinery, Sigma Xi, Tau Beta Pi, Eta Kappa Nu. Current work: Research in digital communications. Subspecialties: Telecommunications; Aerospace engineering and technology. Home: PO Box 95680 Seattle WA 98145-2680 Office: Univ Wash Dept Elec Engring FT-10 Seattle WA 98195

COLEMAN, JOHN HOWARD, physicist; b. Danville, Va., Aug. 21, 1925; m. Virginia Manwaring Robertson, 1964; children—Caroline, Struan, Alexander, David; 1 child by previous marriage, John W.M. B.E.E., U.Va., 1946; postgrad. physics Princeton U., 1946-50. With RCA, Princeton, N.J., 1946-52; pres. Radiation Research Corp., Westbury, N.Y., 1952-67, Plasma Physics Corp., Locust Valley, N.Y., 1967—. Contbr. articles to profl. publs. Patentee in field. Served to lt. USNR, 1943-46. Mem. Am. Vacuum Soc., IEEE, Soc. Photographic Scientists and Engrs., Materials Research Soc., Am. Nuclear Soc., Soc. Applied Spectroscopy, AAAS, Am. Solar Energy Soc., Am. Inst. Mech. Engrs. Clubs: Piping Rock (Locust Valley); Princeton (N.Y.); Boodles (London). Current work: A-Si solar cells, a-Si reprography, research and manufacture of plasma CVD equipment. Subspecialties: Superconductors; Plasma physics. Office: Plasma Physics Corp PO Box 548 Locust Valley NY 11560

COLEMAN, MARILYN RUTH ADAMS, poultry science educator, consultant; b. Lancaster, S.C., Mar. 27, 1946; d. Coyte and Jill J.D. (Lyon) Adams; m. George Edward Coleman, III, Jan. 27, 1968; children: Jill Ann Marie, George Edward. Student, S.C. Med. Coll., 1967; B.S. in Biology, U. S.C., 1968; postgrad., U. Va., 1971, 72, Va. Poly. Inst., 1972; Ph.D. in Physiology, Auburn U., 1976. Teaching asst. U. S.C., 1967-68; research technician in animal sci. Va. Poly. Inst. and State U., Blacksburg, 1968, teaching asst. in biology, 1970-72; biology tchr., basketball coach Brunswick County Schs., 1968-69; research asst. in poultry sci. Auburn U., 1973-76; asst. prof. poultry sci. Ohio Agrl. Research and Devel. Ctr., Ohio State U., Columbus, 1977-82; owner MAC Assocs., Upper Arlington, Ohio, 1974—; Resource person in scis. Upper Arlington Schs., 1977—; cons. Bird House, Cin. Zoo, 1978, other clients in 49 states and over 60 fgn. countries; mem. research com. Columbus Zoo, 1979—; welcome chmn. Upper Arlington French Exchange Program, 1979—. Grantee NSF, 1967, 71, 72. Mem. Poultry Sci. Assn. (session chmn. Southeastern sect. 1980), World Poultry Sci. Assn. (life), Am. Physiol. Soc., Chem. Biomed. Environ. Research Group (chmn. seminar series), Auburn U. Alumni Assn. (life), Va. Poly. Inst. Alumni Assn., U. S.C. Alumni Assn., Sigma Xi, Phi Sigma, Gamma Sigma Delta. Republican. Baptist. Current Work: Incubation and reproductive problems of poultry; effect of environment and management on reproductive performance and hatchability of poultry. Subspecialties: Animal physiology; Reproductive biology. Home and Office: 2532 Zollinger Rd Columbus OH 43221

COLEMAN, MICHAEL MURRAY, polymer science educator; b. Herne Bay, Eng., Jan. 24, 1938. B.Sc., Borough Poly., Eng., 1968; M.S., Case Western Res. U., 1971, Ph.D. in Polymer Sci., 1973. Assayer, Rhokana Corp. Ltd., Zambia, 1955-61; analytical chemist Johnson Mathey Ltd., Eng., 1963-64; research chemist polymers Revertex Ltd., Eng., 1968-69, E.I. du Pont deNemours & Co., 1973-75; asst. prof. Pa. State U., University Park, 1975-78, assoc. prof. polymers, 1978-82, prof., 1982—, program chmn. polymer sci., 1976-84, head dept. materials sci. and engring., 1983—. Mem. Am. Chem. Soc., Royal Inst. Chemistry, Am. Phys. Soc. Subspecialty: Polymer chemistry. Office: Dept Materials Sci Pa State U University Park PA 16802

COLEMAN, PAUL D., neurobiologist; b. N.Y.C., Dec. 2, 1927; s. Aaron Barnett and Martha (Michaels) C.; married; children from previous marriage: Laura, Paul. A.B. magna cum laude, Tufts U., 1948; Ph.D., U. Rochester, 1953. Asst. prof. Tufts U., Medford, Mass., 1956-59; computer ctr. assoc. M.I.T., Cambridge, Mass., 1957-59; spl. fellow Johns Hopkins U. Med. Sch., Balt., 1959-62; assoc. prof. physiology U. Md. Med. Sch., Balt., 1962-67; prof. anatomy U. Rochester (N.Y.) Med. Sch., 1967—. Contbr. articles to profl. jours. Served to 1st lt. U.S. Army Res., 1953-56. NIH spl. fellow, 1959-62; NSF grantee, 1957-67; NIH grantee, 1962—. Mem. Soc. Neuroscience, Am. Assn. Anatomy, Am. Psychol. Assn. Club: Rochester Yacht. Current Work: Quantitative neuroanatomical studies of aging brain. Subspecialty: Neurobiology. Office: Univ Rochester Med Ctr Box 603 Rochester NY 14642

COLEMAN, RONALD L., toxicology educator; b. Wellington, Tex., Aug. 20, 1934; s. J. Leon and Mary Emalyne (Blevins) C.; married; children: Christy, John Edward, Dennis. B.S., Abilene Christian Coll., 1956; postgrad., Tex. A&M U., 1958; Ph.D. in Biochemistry, U. Okla., 1963. Asst. prof. biochemistry U. Okla., Oklahoma City, 1964-69, assoc. prof. environ. health, 1969-73, prof. environ. health, 1975—, chmn. dept., 1982—; owner, lab. dir. Environ. Cons., Oklahoma City, 1970—. Served with U.S. Army, 1958-60. Mem. Am. Coll. Toxicologists, Am. Indsl. Hygiene Assn., Am. Conf. Govt. Indsl. Hygienists, Soc. Environ. Geochemistry and Health, Am. Chem. Soc. Current Work: Toxicology of metals/biological monitoring; water and wastewater; occupational health. Subspecialties: Environmental toxicology; Toxicology (medicine). Office: Dept Environ Health U Okla Health Scis Ctr PO Box 26901 Oklahoma City OK 73190

COLEMAN, SIDNEY RICHARD, physicist, educator; b. Chgo., Mar. 7, 1937; s. Harold Albert and Sadie (Shanas) C. B.S., Ill. Inst. Tech., 1957; Ph.D., Calif. Inst. Tech., 1962. Research fellow dept. physics Harvard U., 1961-63, asst. prof., 1963-66, assoc. prof., 1966-69, prof., 1969—; vis. prof. U. Rome, Italy, 1968, Princeton U., 1973, Stanford U., 1979-80; partner Advent Pubs. Author: Aspects of Symmetry, 1985. Recipient prize for physics lectures Ettore Majorana Centre Sci. Culture; Boris Pregel award N.Y. Acad. Scis. Fellow Am. Phys. Soc., Am. Acad. Arts and Sci., Nat. Acad. Sci.; mem. LILAPA. Current Work: Quantum field theory, symmetry principles, magnetic monopoles. Subspecialties: Particle physics; Theoretical physics. Home: Unit 12 1 Richdale Ave Cambridge MA 02140 Office: Lyman Lab Harvard U Cambridge MA 02138

COLEMAN, WALDEN EMILE, research chemist, mass spectroscopist; b. Mobile, Ala., May 11, 1934; s. Richard Durette and Jessie Mae (Gibbs) C.; m. Altitia Valencia Dean, Dec. 30, 1957; children—Terrence, Tira, Craig. Student, Iona Coll., 1952-53; B.S. in Chemistry, Xavier U. of La., 1956. Electronics instr. Dept. Def., Keesler AFB, Miss., 1959-63; chemist USPHS, Cin., 1963-68, research chemist, 1968-70; research chemist, analytical team leader EPA, Cin., 1970—, project officer, 1970—. Peer reviewer Jour. Environ. Sci. and Tech., 1978—, Archives of Environ. Contamination and Toxicology, 1980—. Contbr. articles to profl. jours., chpts. to books. Patentee in field. Mentor, High Sch. Research Apprentice Program, Cin., 1979-84. Served with U.S. Army, 1956-58. Recipient Sustained Superior Performance award EPA, 1975, Outstanding Performance award EPA, 1980, 81. Mem. Am. Chem. Soc. (best paper 1975), Am. Indsl. Hygiene Assn., Am. Conf. Govt. Indsl. Hygienists, Nat. Orgn. Black Chemists and Chem. Engrs., Xavier U. Alumni Assn. (v.p. 1985-86). Roman Catholic. Club: Magnificents (pres. 1979-80) (Cin.). Current work: Trace analysis of organic contaminants in drinking water using gas chromatography/mass spectrometry; identification of biologically active substances for health effect studies. Subspecialties: Analytical chemistry; Environmental chemistry. Home: 7657 Ginnala Ct Cincinnati OH 45243

COLES, DONALD EARL, aeronautics educator; b. St. Paul, Feb. 8, 1924; s. Courtney J. and Lorna (Addison) C.; m. Ellen Searight, Sept. 11, 1947; children—Christopher Lee, Elizabeth Anne, Kenneth Spencer, Janet Jacqueline. B.Aero. Engring., U. Minn., 1947; M.S., Calif. Inst. Tech., 1948, Ph.D., 1953. Research engr. Jet Propulsion Lab., Pasadena, Calif., 1950-53; research fellow Calif. Inst. Tech., 1953-56, mem. faculty, 1953, prof. aeros., 1964—; Cons. to industry, 1954—; mem. Nat. Com. Fluid Mechs. Films, 1960. Producer; ednl. film Channel Flow of a Compressible Fluid, 1966. Served with AUS, 1943-46. Fellow AIAA (Lawrence Sperry award 1954, Dryden medal 1985), Am. Phys. Soc.; mem. Nat. Acad. Engring., Sigma Xi. Subspecialties: Aeronautical engineering; Fluid mechanics. Office: 1201 E California Blvd Pasadena CA 91125

COLGATE, STIRLING A., physicist; b. N.Y.C., Nov. 14, 1925; m. Rosemary Williamson; children: Henry, Sarah, Arthur. B.A. in Physics, Cornell U., Ithaca, N.Y., 1948, Ph.D., 1952. With Lawrence Radiation Lab., Berkeley, Calif., 1951-52, Livermore, Calif., 1952-64, electron and accelerator physicist; physicist nuclear weapons and tests, 1955; staff Controlled Thermonuclear Fusion project, 1955-64; tech. adviser Conf. Discontinuance Nuclear Weapons Tests, Geneva, 1959; pres. N.Mex. Inst. Mining and Tech., Socorro, 1965-74; sr. fellow, physicist, spl. research on controlled thermonuclear fusion, astrophysics, atmospheric physics Los Alamos Nat. Lab., 1976—; partner Richard M. Colgate (patent devel.), 1958—; Mem. nuclear panel Sci. Adv. Bd., 1959-61; adv. com. fluid mechanics NASA, 1960-62; cons. ballistic missile div. USAF, 1960-62; cons. Def. Atomic Support Agy., 1962-64; mem. adv. com. environ. scis. NSF, 1967; mem. Nat. Acad. Sci. panel on space plasma physics, 1977-79, panel on physics of sun, 1979—; chmn. panel on physics of sun Space Sci. Bd., 1980-81. Trustee-at-large Associated Univs., 1970-73, Aura-Kitt Peak, 1973-78, Space Sci. Bd., 1976-79. Fellow Am. Phys. Soc.; mem. Am. Astron. Soc., Nat. Acad. Scis., Sigma Xi. Subspecialty: High energy astrophysics. Home: 4616 Ridgeway Los Alamos NM 87544 Office: MS 275 Los Alamos Nat Lab Los Alamos NM 87545

COLIGAN, JOHN ERNEST, biochemist, chemist, consultant; b. Canonsburg, Pa., July 3, 1944; s. John Baptist and Rose (Koval) C.; m. Nelda Olivia Clodfelter, Apr. 13, 1968. B.A., Wabash Coll., 1966; M.S., Ind. U. Med. Sch., Indpls., 1968, Ph.D., 1971. Jr. research scientist City of Hope Nat. Med. Center, Duarte, Calif., 1971-73, asst. research scientist, 1973-75; asst. prof. Rockefeller U., 1975-77; research chemist Nat. Inst. Allergy and Infectious Disease, Bethesda, Md., 1977—. Editor: Surveys in Immunologic Research, 1981—; assoc. editor: Jour. Immunology. Recipient NIH Dir.'s award, 1985. Mem. Am. Assn. Immunologists, Am. Assn. Cancer Research, Fedn. Am. Socs. for Exptl. Biology, Phi Beta Kappa, Sigma Xi. Current Work: Structure-function relationships of membrane proteins. Subspecialties: Biochemistry (biology); Immunobiology and immunology. Home: 10913 Broad Green Terr Potomac MD 20854 Office: Nat Inst Allergy and Infectious Disease 9000 Rockville Pike Bethesda MD 20205

COLINVAUX, PAUL ALFRED, ecologist, author; b. St. Albans, Eng., Sept. 22, 1930; came to U.S., 1959; m. L. Hillis, July 10, 1961. B.A., Cambridge U., 1956, M.A., 1960, cert. agr., 1956; Ph.D., Duke U., 1962. Research biologist Yale U., New Haven, 1963-64; faculty Ohio State U.-Columbus, 1964—, prof. ecology, 1972—; mem. ecology adv. com. NSF, Washington, 1979-82; chmn. sponsors Inst. Ecology, Indpls., 1977-79; mem. U.S. Internat. Quateternary Assn. Nat. Commn., Washington, 1977—. Author: Introduction to Ecology, 1973, Why Big Fierce Animals are Rare, 1978 (Award 1978), The Fates of Nations, 1980; actor/narrator/writer: TV series What Ecology Really Says, 1973. Concilor Charles Darwin Found. for Galapagos Isles, 1972—. Served to lt. Brit. Army, 1951. NSF research grantee, 1963—; Guggenheim fellow, 1972; NATO fellow, 1963; Tansley lectr British Ecol. Soc., 1981. Fellow Explorers Club, Arctic Inst. N.Am.; mem. Ecol. Soc. Am., Am. Soc. Limnology and Oceanography, Am. Soc. Naturalists. Current Work: Environment of ice age earth using sediments of ancient lakes in Amazonia, Andes, Galapagos, Alaska, Siberia, China, and Ohio, ecological causes of war and history of human populations. Subspecialties: Ecology (environmental science); Evolutionary biology. Home: 319 S Columbia Ave Columbus OH 43209 Office: Ohio State U 484 W 12th Ave Columbus OH 43210

COLLEN, MORRIS FRANK, physician; b. St. Paul, Nov. 12, 1913; s. Frank Morris and Rose (Finkelstein) C.; m. Frances B. Diner, Sept. 24, 1937; children—Arnold Roy, Barry Joel, Roberta Joy, Randal Harry. B.E.E., U. Minn., 1934, M.B. with distinction, 1938, M.D., 1939. Diplomate: Am. Bd. Internal Medicine. Intern Michael Reese Hosp., Chgo., 1939-40; resident Los Angeles County Hosp., 1940-42; chief med. service Kaiser Found. Hosp., Oakland, Calif., 1942-53, chief of staff, San Francisco, 1953-61; med. dir. Permanente Med. Group (West Bay Div.), 1953-79; dir. Med. Methods Research, 1962-79, Tech. Assessment, 1979-83; cons. med. methods research, 1983—; chmn. exec. com. Permanente Med. Group, Oakland, Calif., 1953-73; dir. Permanente Services, Inc., Oakland, 1958-73; lectr. Sch. Public Health, U. Calif., Berkeley, 1966-78; lectr. info. sci. U. Calif., San Francisco, 1970—; lectr. U. London, 1972, Harvard U., 1974, Stanford Med. Center, 1973, 75, 84, 85, Johns Hopkins U., 1976, others; fellow Ctr. for Advanced Study in Behavorial Scis., Stanford, Calif., 1985-86; cons. Bur. Health Services, USPHS, 1965-68, chmn. health care systems study sect., 1968-72, adv. com. demonstration grants, 1967; adv. U.S. VA, 1968; cons. European region WHO, 1968-72, USAF Med. Fitness Program, 1968, Pres.'s Biomed. Research Panel, 1975; adv. com. Automated Multiphasic Health Testing, 1970; mem. Pres.'s Ad Hoc Panel on Prevention and Personal Health Care, 1971; discussant Nat. Conf. Preventive Medicine, Bethesda, Md., 1975; mem. com. on tech. in health care Nat. Acad. Sci., 1976; mem. adv. group Nat. Commn. on Digestive Diseases, U.S. Congress, 1978; mem. adv. panel to U.S. Congress Office of Tech. Assessment, 1980-85; mem. peer rev. adv. group Dept. Def. program, 1978-85; program chmn. Internat. Conf. Med. Informatics, Tokyo, 1980, mem. organizing com. 5th Internat. Conf. Med. Informatics, Washington, 1986; Author: Treatment of Pneumococcic Pneumonia, 1948, Hospital Computer Systems, 1974, Multiphasic Health Testing Systems, 1977; editor: Permanente Med. Bull, 1943-53, Lecture Notes in Med. Informatics, 1943-53; mem. editorial bd.: Diagnostic Medicine; contbr. articles to med. jours., chpts. to med. books. Johns Hopkins U. Centennial Scholar, 1976. Fellow ACP, Am. Coll. Cardiology, Am. Coll. Chest Physicians; mem. Pan Am. Med. Assn. (council mem.), Internat. Fedn. Med. Electronics, AMA, Am. Fedn. Clin. Research, Inst. Medicine Nat. Acad. Sci., Nat. Acad. Practice in Medicine (chmn. 1983—), Am. Coll. Med. Informatics (pres. 1986-87), IEEE, Soc. Biomed. Computing, Salutis Unitas (v.p. 1972), Soc. Advanced Med. Systems (pres. 1973), Ops. Research Soc. Am., Nat. Acad. Practioners in Am., Alpha Omega Alpha, Eta Kappa Nu, Tau Beta Pi. Subspecialty: Medical research administration. Home: 4155 Walnut Blvd Walnut Creek CA 94596 Office: 3451 Piedmont Ave Oakland CA 94611

COLLIER, JOHN WALTER, mechanical engineer, chemical company inspection and testing administrator; b. Ocala, Fla., Jan. 8, 1941; s. Jessie Wilburn and Blanche Adelia (East) C.; m. Shirley Ann Moore, July 27, 1963; children: Leslie Dawn, Michael Shawn. Student in math. (Univ. football scholar), Harding U., 1959-62; B.S. in Tech. (Dow Loan scholar), U. Houston, 1978. Cert. engring. technician Inst. Cert. Engring. Technicians,1974. Test technician Engring. Test Services, Inc., Houston, 1963-66; devel. engr. Magnaflux Corp., Houston, 1966-68; v.p. NDT Services, Inc., Houston, 1968-71; pres. Inspection Engrs. Inc., Houston, 1971-73; supr. Tex. div. Dow Chem. U.S.A., Freeport, 1973—. Contbr. articles to profl. jours. Vice pres. Brazosport sect. S.W. Basketball Ofcls. Assn., Freeport, Tex., 1974—; sec. Brazosport Affiliated Bd. Ofcls., 1978—; mem. City of West Columbia (Tex.) Parks Bd., 1981-83. Served with U.S. N.G., 1958-66. Named Outstanding Student student sect. Soc. Mfg. Engrs., 1978. Mem. Am. Soc. Nondestructive Testing, ASME, Instrument Soc. Am. Republican. Mem. Ch. of Christ. Current Work: Development of predictive/preventive maintenance programs utilizing nondestructive testing. Home: 601 Kirby West Columbia TX 77486 Office: Dow Chem USA Tex Div B-2615 Freeport TX 77541

COLLIN, ARTHUR EDWIN, Canadian government science advisor; b. Collingwood, Ont., July 16, 1929; s. William Edwin, and Louis Viola (Leggott) C.; m. Christa Herbert Dedering, 1963; children—David, Andrew, Christiane. B.Sc., U. Western Ont., 1953, M.Sc., 1955; Ph.D., McGill U., 1962; postdoctorate Nat. Def. Coll., 1969-70. Scientist, Fisheries REsearch Bd. Can., 1955; Oceanographer U.S. IGY Program Ice Island T-3, 1958 and Polar cont. Shelf Project, 1959-62; vis. research instr. U. Wash., 1962-63; oceanographer in charge of Artctic research Bedford Inst. Oceanography, Dartmouth, N.S., 1963-65; sr. oceanographer Dept. Nat. def. Can. Forces Hdqrs., Ottawa, 1965-68; Dom. Hydrographer, Can. Hydrog. Service, 1968-71; dir.-gen. marine sci. directorate 1971-73, and gir. gen. fisheries research, 1972-73, asst. dep. min. ocean and aquatic scis., 1974-77; asst. dept minister atmospheric environ. service Dept. of Environ., 1977-80; assoc. dep. minister Dept. Energy, Mines and Resources, 1980-85; sec. Ministry of State for Sci. and Tech., chief sci. advisor to Govt. of Can., 1985—. Fellow Arctic Inst. N.Am. Subspecialties: Oceanography; Arctic studies.*

COLLIN, ROBERT EMANUEL, electrical engineering educator; b. Donalda, Alta., Can., Oct. 24, 1928; came to U.S., 1958, naturalized, 1964; s. Knute Emanuel and Hannah (Hanson) C.; m. Kathleen Patricia Smith, Sept. 15, 1952; children: Patricia Ann, Linda Marie, David Robert. B.S. in Engring. Physics, U. Sask., Can., 1951; Ph.D., Imperial Coll., U. London, Eng., 1954. Sci. officer Canadian Def. Research Bd., 1954-58; faculty Case Western Res. U., 1958—, prof. elec. engring., 1965—, chmn. elec. engring. and applied physics dept., 1978-82. Author: Field Theory of Guided Waves, 1960, (with R. Plonsey) Principles and Applications of Electromagnetic Fields, 1961, Foundations for Microwave Engineering, 1966; contbr., editor: (with F.J Zucker) Antenna Theory, 2 vols., 1969. Recipient Jr. Achievement award Cleve. Tech. Socs. Council, 1964. Fellow IEEE (sr. mem., chmn. Que. subsect. 1956-57); mem. Sigma Xi (v.p. Case Inst. Tech. chpt. 1966-67), Eta Kappa Nu. Current Work: Antennas, microwave devices. Subspecialties: Electrical engineering; Electronics. Home: 1041 West Mill Dr Highland Heights OH 44143 Office: 10900 Euclid Ave Cleveland OH 44106

COLLINS, ANITA MARGUERITE, research geneticist; b. Allentown, Pa., Nov. 8, 1947; d. Edmund and Virginia (Hunsicker) C. B.S., Pa. State U., 1969; M.Sc., Ohio State U., 1972, Ph.D., 1976. Instr. biology Mercyhurst Coll., Erie, Pa., 1975-76; research geneticist Agrl. Research Service, U.S. Dept. Agr., Bee Breeding and Stock Ctr. Lab., Baton Rouge, 1976—. Mem. Assn. Women in Sci. (chpt. pres. 1981), Am. Genetic Assn., Entomol. Soc. Am., Animal Behavior Soc., Sigma Xi. Current Work: Behavior genetics of defensive behavior of the honey bee, especially africanized bee. Subspecialties: Animal genetics; Animal breeding and embryo transplants. Office: 1157 Ben Hur Rd Baton Rouge LA 70820

COLLINS, BOBBY RAY, veterinarian, immunologist; b. Durham, N.C., May 7, 1946; s. Dewey William and Mary Lee (Boone) C.; m. Docia Mae Outlaw, Feb. 5, 1967; children—Michael Raymond, Matthew Robert. Student U. S.C., 1966-68, Frederick Community Coll., 1977; B.S. with honors in Poultry Sci., N.C. State U., 1977; D.V.M. cum laude, U. Ga., 1974; M.S. in Exptl. Pathology, U. Fla., 1983. Diplomate Am. Coll. Lab. Animal Medicine. NIH postdoctoral fellow in comparative medicine, dept. spl. clin. sci. Coll. Vet. Medicine, U. Fla., Gainesville, 1977-80, asst. prof., 1981—, assoc. dir. health ctr. resources dept. J. Hillis Miller Health Ctr., 1981—; dir. lab. animal services sect., project leader, toxicology sect. Ill. Inst. Tech. Research Inst., Chgo., 1980-81; mem. cons. pathology group Lincoln Park Zoo, Chgo., 1980-81; cons. Am. Assn. Lab. Animal Sci., Joliet, Ill., 1984—. Co-author: (videotape) The Procedure for Castration of Male Stumptail Monkey, 1979; contbr. articles to profl. jours., chpt. to book. Served to capt. U.S. Army, 1973-77. Mem. AVMA, Am. Assn. Lab. Animal Sci., Am. Vet. Dental Soc., Alachua County Vet. Med. Assn., Eastern States Vet. Conf. (mem. organizing com. 1983—). Democrat. Mormon. Current work: Animal models of human diseases, pathology of animal diseases, comparative immunology, veterinary dentistry, periodontal diseases. Subspecialties: Laboratory animal medicine; Immunobiology and immunology. Home: 3331 NW 45th Ave Gainesville FL 32605 Office: J Hillis Miller Health Ctr U Fla Box J-6 Gainesville FL 32610

COLLINS, FRANK GIBSON, mechanical engineering educator; b. Chgo., Feb. 20, 1938; s. Forrest Gibson and Elizabeth (Freeman) C.; m. Sarah Ruth Knight, May 13, 1960; children: James Forrest, Pamela Ruth. B.S.C.E., Northwestern U., 1961; Ph.D.M.E., U. Calif.-Berkeley, 1968. Registered profl. engr., Tex. Asst. prof. aerospace engring. U. Tex., Austin, 1968-74; assoc. prof. aerospace engring. U. Tenn. Space Inst., Tullahoma, 1974-81, prof., 1981—; cons. to industry. Contbr. articles to scholarly jours. Bd. deacons 1st Christian Ch., 1978-81; treas. N.W. Austin Civic Assn., 1973-74. NSF fellow, 1961-63; NSF grantee, 1974-75; recipient award for paper ASCE, 1961. Fellow. AIAA (sec. 1981-92) (assoc.); mem. Am. Phys. Soc., Sigma Xi, Tau Beta Pi, Pi Mu Epsilon, Order of Engr., Sigma Gamma Tau. Lodge: Kiwanis. Current Work: Wind tunnel testing, viscous interactions, flow instability, space processing of materials, computational fluid mechanics. Subspecialties: Fluid mechanics; Aerospace engineering and technology. Home: 1703 Country Club Dr Tullahoma TN 37388 Office: University of Tennessee Space Institute Tullahoma TN 37388

COLLINS, FRANK MILES, microbiologist, researcher; b. Adelaide, South Australia, Mar. 30, 1928; s. Frank Vernon and Ethelwyn Rollison (Littler) C.; m. Lorna Fay Hannaford, May 24, 1952; children: William Mark, Michael James. M.Sc., U. Adelaide, 1952, Ph.D., 1960, D.Sc., 1976. Lectr. bacteriology U. Adelaide, 1954-60, asst. prof. microbiology, 1961-65; assoc. mem. Trudeau Inst., Saranac Lake, N.Y., 1965-68, mem., 1969—; mem. study sects. NIH, 1976-80, 81—. Fellow Am. Acad. Microbiologists; mem. Soc. Gen Microbiology (U.K.), Am. Soc. Microbiology, Reticuloendothelial Soc. (hon. life), Am. Assn. Immunologists. Republican. Presbyterian. Lodge: Rotary. Current

Work: Cellular mechanisms of antibacterial immunity to facultative intracellular parasites; antituberculous and antityphoid immunity; role of T-cells in DTH and CMI. Subspecialties: Infectious diseases; Microbiology (medicine). Office: Trudeau Inst Algonquin Ave Saranac Lake NY 12983

COLLINS, JAMES FRANCIS, biochemist, educator; b. Balt., Jan. 26, 1942; s. James M. and Mary M. (Dolan) C.; m. Barbara J. Betka, June 15, 1969; children—Chris, Cavan. B.S., Loyola Coll., 1963; Ph.D., U. N.C., 1968. Postdoctoral fellow Nat. Inst. Arthritis, Diabetes, Digestive and Kidney Diseases, NIH, 1968-70; sr. staff fellow Nat. Heart, Lung and Blood Inst., NIH, Bethesda, Md., 1973-75; mem. faculty U. Tex. Health Sci. Ctr., San Antonio, 1975—; research chemist VA Hosp., San Antonio, 1975—; lectr. U. Tex., San Antonio, 1983—; asst. found. scientist S.W. Fed. Biomed. Research, San Antonio, 1980—; mem. adv. bd. Minority Biol. Sci. Research Program, San Antonio, 1976-78, research preceptor, 1976-81; instr. NIH Upward Mobility Coll., Bethesda, Md., 1972. Contbr. articles to profl. jours. and books. Corr. sec. Terra-Genesis, San Antonio, 1984—; mem. St. Matthew's Athletic Assn., San Antonio, 1977—. NIH fellow U. N.C., 1966-67. Mem. Am. Soc. Biol. Chemists, Am. Chem. Soc., Am. Thoracic Soc., AAAS, Sigma Xi. Democrat. Roman Catholic. Subspecialties: Biochemistry (biology); Pulmonary medicine. Home: 10435 Applegate San Antonio TX 78230 Office: U Tex Health Sci Ctr 7703 Floyd Curl San Antonio TX 78284

COLLINS, JAMES JOSEPH, electronics company executive; b. N.Y.C., June 16, 1936; s. Maurice Joseph and Ellen Mary (Kiely) C.; m. Eileen Mary Murphy, Sept. 2, 1961; children—Patricia, James Joseph, Kevin, Kathleen. B.E.E., Manhattan Coll., 1957; postgrad. NYU, 1964-66, Adelphi U., 1966-68; M.B.A., Adelphi U., 1973. Registered profl. engr., N.H. Project engr. Airborne Instruments, Deer Park, N.Y., 1957-62; staff cons. Kollsman Instruments, Syosset, N.Y., 1963-74, program mgr., 1974-75, engring. mgr., 1975-79, dept. head mfg. engring., 1979-80, dir. mfg. engring., 1980-84, dir. avionics engring., 1984—; electronic cons. Silicon Transitor, N.Y.C., 1968. Contbr. articles to profl. jours. Patentee in field. Head coach Nashua Soccer League, 1975-77; bd. dirs. Mt. St. Mary Assocs., Nashua, 1981-82; mem. adv. com. N.H. Vocat.-Tech. Sch., Nashua, 1982; engring. adv. com. Daniel Webster Coll., Nashua, 1982. Mem. Soc. Mfg. Engrs. (sr.), IEEE, Am. Mgmt. Assn., Assn. U.S. Army, Soc. for Info. Displays, Army Aviation Soc. Republican. Club: Nashua Fish and Game (publicity chmn. 1976-80). Current work: Avionics research and development of sensors, instrumentation. Subspecialties: Electrical engineering; Electronics. Home: 27 Deerhaven Dr Nashua NH 03060 Office: Kollsman Instrument Co 220 Daniel Webster Hwy S Merrimack NH 03054

COLLINS, JOHN H., biochemistry educator; b. Peabody, Mass., Sept. 6, 1942. A.B. in Chemistry, Northeastern U., 1965; Ph.D. in Biochemistry, Boston U., 1970. Research assoc. Boston Biomed. Research Inst., 1969-74, staff scientist, 1974-76; asst. prof. Baylor Coll. Medicine, Houston, 1976-77; asst. prof. U. Cin., 1977-79, assoc. prof., 1979—. Grantee in field. Mem. Am. Soc. Biol. Chemists, Biophys. Soc., Am. Chem. Soc., N.Y. Acad. Scis., AAAS. Current Work: Protein structure, contractile and membrane proteins. Subspecialties: Biochemistry (medicine); Pharmacology. Office: Dept Biology Clarson Univ Potsdam NY 13676

COLLINS, MARGARET STRICKLAND, zoology educator; b. Institute, W.Va., Sept. 4, 1922; d. Rollins Walter and Luella (Bowling) James; m. Bernard E. Strickland, July 5, 1942 (div. 1949); m. Herbert L. Collins, Aug. 1951 (div. 1963); children: Herbert Louis Jr., James Joseph. B.S., W.Va. State Coll., 1943; Ph.D., U. Chgo., 1949. Instr. zoology Howard U., Washington, 1947-50, asst. prof., 1950-51, prof., from, 1978—, now ret; prof., zoology Fla. A&M U., Tallahassee, 1951-63; prof. biology Fed. City Coll., Washington, 1969-78. Editor: Science and the Question of Human Equality, 1981. Bd. dirs. Nat. Assn. So. Poor, Norfolk, Va., 1979—. Mem. Entomol. Soc. Washington (pres. 1982—), Ecol.Soc. Am., N.Y. Acad. Scis., Earthwatch. Democrat. Current Work: Defensive behavior in South American termites; termite ecology; species abundance in virgin and disturbed tropical rain forests. Subspecialties: Behavioral ecology; Entomology. Home: 1642 Promrose Rd NW Washington DC 20012 Office: Dept Entomology Smithsonian Inst NHB Washington DC

COLLINS, MICHAEL THOMAS, microbiology educator; b. St. Paul, Jan. 2, 1949; s. Thomas Wellington and June Claire (Anderson) C.; m. Jeannette McDonald, June 6, 1981; children: Christopher, David, Katrina. B.S., U. Minn., 1970, D.V.M., 1972; Ph.D., U. Ga., 1976. Asst. prof. dept. microbiology Colo. State U., Ft. Collins, 1976-81, assoc. prof., 1981-83; assoc. prof. dept. pathobiol. scis. U. Wis.-Madison, 1983—; mem. faculty aquavet program Woods Oceanographic Instn., 1979—; cons. Colo. Assn. Continuing Med. Lab. Edn., 1979. Contbr. articles to profl. jours. NIH fellow, 1974; Marshall Found. fellow, 1981. Mem. AVMA, Am. Soc. Microbiology, Am. Coll. Vet. Microbiology, Conf. Research Workers in Animal Diseases, Wildlife Disease Assn. Roman Catholic. Current Work: Pathogenesis of bacterial infections of food producing animals on Pasteurella; immunology, serology and antigenic structure of Legionella. Subspecialties: Microbiology (veterinary medicine); Microbiology (medicine).

COLLINS, WILLIAM EDWARD, aviation psychology research administrator, researcher; b. Bklyn., May 16, 1932; s. William Edward and Loretta Agnes (Brasier) C.; m. Corliss Jean Barnes, June 20, 1970; 1 dau. Corliss Adora. B.S., St. Peter's Coll., 1954; M.A., Fordham U., 1956, Ph.D., 1959. Lic. psychologist, Okla. Psychol. research asst. Fordham U., 1954-56, teaching fellow, 1958, research asst., 1958-59; research psychologist Aviation Psychology Lab., FAA Civil Aeromed. Inst., Oklahoma City, 1961-63, chief sensory integration sect., 1963-65; supr. Aviation Psychology Lab., FAA Civil Aeromed. Inst. (Aviation Psychology Lab.), 1965—; adj. assoc. prof. psychology U. Okla.-Norman, 1963-70, adj. prof., 1970—; adj. assoc. prof. research psychology dept. psychiatry and behavioral scis. U. Okla. Health Scis. Center, Oklahoma City, 1965-70; adj. prof., 1970—; mem. Nat. Acad. Sci.-NRC Com. on Vision, 1963—, mem. exec. council, 1973-81; mem. Nat. Acad. sci.-NRC Com. on Hearing, Bioacoustics and Biomechanics, 1963—; appearances before House Sub-Com. on Pub. Health and Environ., 1971, House Sub-Com. on Investigations and Oversight, 1984; mem. rating panel Interagy Bd., U.S. Civil Service Examiners for State Okla., 1967—; judge Okla. State Sci. and Engring. Fair, Ada, 1980, 81, 82; mem. Okla. Bd. Examiners Psychologists, 1981-84, chmn., 1982-84; evaluator proposals NSF, 1968—, HeW, 1971—; lectr. in field. Contbr. chpts., numerous articles to profl. publs.; research numerous prsentations in field. Served to 1st lt. Med. Services Corps U.S. Army, 1959-61; capt. USAR. Recipient award for employee invention FAA, 1966, Sustained Superior Performance award, 1966, 67, Spl. Achievement award, 1971, 83, Quality Performance award, 1964, 69, 70, 74, Outstanding Performance rating, 1966-71, 74, 81, 83-85, Spl. Group Act award, 1985, Fed. Employee of Yr. award Okla. City Area Fed. Exec. Council. Fellow AAAS, N.Y. Acad. Scis., Am. Psychol. Assn. (abstractor Psychol. Abstracts 1962—, citation 1973), Aerospace Med. Assn. (assoc., Raymond F. Longacre award 1971, presdl. exec. com. 1982-84, exec. council 1982-85, editorial bd. Aviation, Space and Envir. Medicine 1974—, assoc. editor 1980—); mem. Assn. Aviation Psychologists (pres. 1974-75), Barany Soc., Okla. acad. Sci. (vis. scientist program 1966), Okla. Psychol. Assn. (vice chmn. awards com. 1980, 82, chmn. sci. program com. ann. meeting 1977, disting. psychologist award 1984). Current Work: Effects of motion on perceptual and motor skills; vestibular-visual interactions; alcohol and drug effects on orientation; personnel selection and training. Subspecialties: Behavioral psychology; Sensory processes. Home: 8900 Sheringham Dr Oklahoma City OK 73132 Office: FAA Civil Aeromed Inst AAC-118 PO Box 25082 Oklahoma City OK 73125

COLLISON, BETTY CHRISTINE, researcher; b. Balt., July 17, 1952. B.S., Towson State U., Balt., 1974; M.A.S., Johns Hopkins U., 1979; postgrad., U. Md. Dental Sch., 1983—. Research asst. psychology Johns Hopkins U., 1975-77, research asst. immunology, 1977-79; commd. officers summer tng. extern in immunology Nat. Inst. Dental Research, NIH, Bethesda, 1980-81; research assoc. U. Md. Dental Sch., Balt., 1982—. Contbr. articles to profl. publs. Research scholar U. Md., 1982. Mem. Acad. Gen. Dentistry, Am. Assn. Dental Research, ADA (student clinician). Current Work: Dental student conducting research investigating neutrophil dysfunction and abnormalities in juvenile periodontitis and other periodontitis patients. Subspecialty: Immunology (medicine). Home: 3321 Chestnut Ave Baltimore MD 21211 Office: University of Maryland Dental School 666 W Baltimore St Baltimore MD 21201

COLMENARES, NARSES JOSE, electrical engineer; b. Caracas, Venezuela, Apr. 29, 1945; came to U.S., 1977; s. Jose and Isabel (Guevara) C. Communications Engr., Escoelfa, Venezuela, 1974; Elec. Engr., Met. U., Caracas, 1976; M.Sc. in Engring., Princeton U., 1980. Communications engr. Navy Hdqrs., Caracas, 1974-75; asst. prof. Simon Bolivar U., Caracas, 1975-77; systems engr. CSEE, Paris and Sumatelco, Caracas, 1981-82; telecommunication engr. CE-Lummus, Bloomfield, N.J., 1982-83; staff engr. Ram Broadcasting Corp., Avenel, N.J., 1983-85; systems engr. Metromedia Inc., Englewood Cliffs, N.J., 1985—; cons. Thevenin S.A., Caracas, 1974-77, 82; asst. researcher Princeton U., 1978-79. Author: Commanders' Code, 1970. Contbr. articles to profl. jours. Served to lt. Venezuelan Navy, 1965-75. Princeton U. scholar, 1977-80; Venezuela Communication Sch. scholar, 1972-74, recipient Meritory Acts in Peace Time, 1969, Merit Communications Bar, 1975. Mem. IEEE, Venezuelan Assn. Elec. and Mech. Engrs. (exec. dir. 1976-77), Princeton U. Alumni Assn. Club: Princeton. Current work: Statistical analysis of language; telecommunications analysis of networks and systems. Subspecialties: Telecommunications; Statistics. Office: Metromedia Telecommunications 5A Joanna Ct East Brunswick NJ 08816

COLOTLA, VICTOR ADOLFO, psychologist, educator; b. Mexico City, May 8, 1944; s. Adolfo and Josefina (Espinosa) C.; m. Xochitl Gallegos, Sept. 18, 1967; children: Ian Rolando, Eileen Vivian. Grad. in psychology, Nat. U. Mex., 1966; M.A., U. Toronto, 1969; Ph.D., York U., Toronto, 1973. Registered psychologist, Ont. Prof. psychology Nat. U. Mexico, Mexico City, 1973-74; psychologist Toronto Western Hosp., 1974-75; coordinator program on behavioral pharmacology Nat. U. Mex., 1976-80; chief dept. psychophysiology Nat. U. Mex. (Faculty of Psychology), 1980-81, head grad. studies, 1981—. Co-editor: Modificacion de Conducta: Applicaciones a la Biomedicina, 1980; author articles. Recipient various scholarships and grants. Mem. Sociedad Mexicana de Analisis de la Conducta (pres. 1977-78), Sociedad Mexicana de Psicologia (sec. sci. events 1979—), Am. Psychol. Assn., Eastern Psychol. Assn., N.Y. Acad. Scis. Club: Terranova (Mexico City). Current Work: Effects of organic solvents on behavior; biofeedback; history of psychology in Mexico. Subspecialties: Behavioral toxicology; Learning. Home: Zaragoza 3 Chimalcoyotl Mexico City 14630 Mexico Office: Nat U Mex Ciudad Universitaria Mexico City 04510 Mexico

COLSON, ELIZABETH FLORENCE, anthropologist; b. Hewitt, Minn., June 15, 1917; d. Louis H. and Metta (Damon) C. B.A., U. Minn., 1938, M.A., 1940; M.A., Radcliffe Coll., 1941; Ph.D. (A.A.U.W. Traveling fellow), 1945; Ph.D. hon. doctorate, Brown U., 1978; D.Sc., Rochester U., 1985. Asst. social sci. analyst War Relocation Authority, 1942-43; research asst. Harvard, 1944-45; research officer Rhodes-Livingstone Inst., 1946-47, dir., 1948-51; sr. lectr. Manchester U., 1951-53; asso. prof. Goucher Coll., 1954-55; research asso. African Research Program, Boston U., 1955-59, part-time, 1959-63; prof. anthropology Brandeis U., 1959-63, U. Calif. at Berkeley, 1964-84, ret.; Lewis Henry Morgan lectr. U. Rochester, 1973. Author: The Makah, 1953, Marriage and the Family Among The Plateau Tonga, 1958, Social Organization of the Gwembe Tonga, 1960, The Plateau Tonga, 1962, The Social Consequences of Resettlement, 1971, Tradition and Contract, 1974; Jr. Author (Secondary Education and the Formation of an Elite), 1980; Sr. editor: Seven Tribes of British Central Africa, 1951. Fellow Center Advanced Study Behavioral Scis., 1967-68; Fairchild fellow Calif. Inst. Tech., 1975-76. Fellow Am. Anthrop. Assn., Brit. Assn. Social Anthropologists, Royal Anthrop. Inst. (hon.); mem. Nat. Acad. Sci., Am. Acad. Arts and Scis., Phi Beta Kappa. Current Work: Longitudinal study of changing adaptation in Gwembe District, Zambia. Subspecialty: Behavioral ecology. Office: Dept Anthropology U Calif Berkeley CA 94720

COLVIN, BURTON HOUSTON, mathematician, government administrator; b. West Warwick, R.I., July 12, 1916; s. Asa Burton and Sara Elsie (Houston) C.; m. Lois Ann Scholes, Dec. 22, 1947; children: Daniel Burton, David Walter, Thomas Alan. A.B., Brown U., 1938, A.M. in Math. (Grand Army of Republic fellow), 1939; Ph.D. in Math. (Univ. fellow), U. Wis., 1943. Instr. math. and mechanics, dept. math. U. Wis., Madison, 1943, instr. math., and asst. prof. math., 1946-51; tech. aide nat. def. research com. Office Sci. Research and Devel., 1944-45; cons. applied mathematician phys. research staff Boeing Co., Seattle, 1951-55, supr. math. analysis group, 1955-58; with Boeing Sci. Research Labs., Seattle, 1958-72, head math. research lab., 1958-70, acting head info. scis. lab., 1966-70, head math. and info. scis. lab., 1970-72; chief div. applied math. Nat. Bur. Standards, Dept. Commerce, Washington, 1972-78; dir. Center for Applied Math., 1978—; NSF lectr., 1957; mem. council Conf. Bd. Math. Scis., 1964, 70-77, chmn., 1975-77; adv. bd. Sch. Math. Study Group, 1963-71, chmn., 1965-66; chmn. computer sci. adv. com. Stanford U., 1970-71. Recipient Silver Medal award Dept. Commerce, 1978, Gold medal award Dept. Commerce, 1981, Presdl. Meritorious Rank award Dept. Commerce, 1980. Fellow AAAS (council 1965-67, vice-chmn. commn. on sci. edn. 1968-72, chmn. task force on tech. edn. 1968-69); mem. Soc. Indsl. and Applied Math. (vis. scientist lectr. 1962-63, trustee 1962-65, 67-70, 78-80, pres. 1971-72), AAAS (council 1965-67, vice-chmn. commn. on sci. edn. 1968-72, chmn. task force on tech. edn. 1968-69), Math. Assn. Am. (vis. lectr. 1963-65), Am. Math. Soc., NEA, Inst. Math. Stats., Assn. Women in Math., Nat. Council Tchrs. Math, Phi Beta Kappa, Sigma Xi. Subspecialty: Applied mathematics. Office: Nat Bur Standards Center for Applied Math Gaithersburg MD 20899

COLVIN, LONNIE BENARD, mariculture technical executive, consultant; b. Port Arthur, Tex., Apr. 15, 1938; s. Lonnie Boyd and Margaret Arlene (Merideth) C.; m. Joyce Kathryn Smith, July 29, 1958, (dec. Dec. 1970); children—Deborah Karen, Michael Benard, Joel Boyd, Rachael Arlene; m. Kathleen Elsie Day, Mar. 17, 1982; 1 child, Meredith Grace Kaiulani. B.S. Tex. A&M U., 1960, M.S., 1962; Ph.D., 1966. Scientist, Salisbury Lab., Charles City, Iowa, 1966-69, sr. research chemist Monsanto Co., St. Louis, 1969-74; sect. head, nutrition U. Ariz., Tucson, 1974-82, assoc. research prof., 1974-82, head Fleischmann Lab., 1978-82; mgr. cons. and contract research and devel. CSCI, Los Fresnos, Tex., 1982-83; tchr. dir, gen. mgr., Worldwide Protein (Bahamas) Ltd., Long Island, 1983—; cons.-Aquaculture Coca-Cola Corp., Tucson, Ariz., 1974-82; ind. cons. nutrition devel. Aquaculture 1982—. Contbr. articles to sci. jours. Mem. AAAS, Am. Chem. Soc., Crustacean Soc., World Mariculture Soc., Sigma Xi. Democrat Unitarian Club: Associated Students (Tex. A&M U.). Current work: Nutrition; aquaculture Subspecialties: Animal nutrition; Aquaculture. Home and Office: Worldwide Protein (Bahamas) Ltd Diamond Roads Long Island Bahamas

COMBES, RICHARD WILLARD, physician; b. Cleve., July 2, 1926; s. Willard Wetmore and Vivian C. (Kepler) C.; m. Angela Katryn Wright, Aug. 26, 1949; children—Carol K., Holly V., Willard W., Pamela W. A.B., Oberlin Coll., 1947; M.D., Case Western Res. U., 1951. Intern, St. Luke's Hosp., Cleve., 1951-52, resident, 1957-58, staff anesthesiologist, 1958-60; chief anesthesiologist Booth Meml.-Salvation Army Hosp., 1961-70, St. Anthony's Hosp., Rock Island, Ill., 1970-73, Rutland Hosp., Vt., 1973—; owner Oak Research Lab., Rutland, 1961—. Served to lt. USNR, 1944-45, 52-54. Fellow Royal Micros. Soc., Am. Inst. Chemistry; mem. Royal Soc. Chemistry, AAAS, AMA, Am. Chem. Assn., N.Y. Acad. Scis., SAR. Current work: Theoretical chemistry design and synthesis of bioreactive stains and compounds for microscopy, recently for plant pathology; design of polyphase vacuum azeotropic compound mixtures for use in physical chemistry. Subspecialties: Microbiology; Organic chemistry. Home: 3 Robinwood Ln Rutland VT 05701 Office: Oak Research Lab Rutland VT 05701

COMBS, CLAUD STEVE, health industry co. exec.; b. Macon, Ga., June 12, 1952; s. Claud L. and Virginia (Cheatham) C.; m. Cynthia Ham, Nov. 4, 1952; children: Joshua, Matthew. B. Elec. Engring. Tech., So. Tech. Inst., Marietta, Ga., 1975. Engr. Carolina Med. Electronics, Inc., King, N.C., 1976-79; dir. customer support Healthdyne, Inc., Marietta, from 1979. Subspecialties: Bioinstrumentation; Anesthesiology. Office: 2253 Northwest Pkwy Marietta GA 30067

COMBS, LEON LAMAR, chemistry educator; b. Meridian, Miss., Sept. 19, 1938; s. Leon Lamar and Roberta (Weems) C.; m. Martha Carol Bunch, Feb. 17, 1962; 1 son, Jeffrey Lamar. B.S., Miss. State U., 1961; Ph.D., La. State U., 1968. Polymer chemist Devoe and Reynolds, Louisville, 1961-64; asst. prof. chemistry and physics Miss. State U., 1967-71, asso. prof., 1971-75, prof., 1975—, head dept. chemistry, 1981—; vis. prof. quantum chemistry U. Uppsala, Sweden, 1977-78. Contbr. articles to profl. jours. Tchr. Sunday sch. United Methodist Ch., 1978-81, Faith Baptist Ch., 1981—. Esso fellow, 1965-66. Mem. Am. Chem. Soc., Am. Phys. Soc., Sigma Xi, Phi Kappa Phi, Phi Lambda Upsilon. Current Work: Quantum and statistical mechanics of molecular interactions. Subspecialty: Theoretical chemistry. Office: Miss State U Drawer CH Mississippi State MS 39762

COMINS, NEIL FRANCIS, astronomer; b. N.Y.C., May 11, 1951; s. Francis Malcolm and Pearl Murian (Finkelstein) C.; m. Suzanne Rodrique; 1 child, James Aaron. B.S., Cornell U., 1972; M.S., U. Md., 1975; Ph.D. in Astronomy, Univ. Coll., Cardiff, Wales, 1978. Registered Emergency Med. Technician. Research technician La. State U., 1975; asst. prof. physics and astronomy U. Maine, Orono, 1978-84, assoc. prof., 1984—; cons. Am. Coll. Testing Service. Contbr. articles to profl. astron. papers, proceedings. Recipient Rotary Internat. fellowship, 1976; NASA-ASEE Summer Faculty fellowship, 1980, 81. Fellow Royal Astronom. Soc.; mem. Am. Astronom. Soc., Mt. Desert Island Astronom. Assn. (acting pres., v.p.), Canadian Astronom. Soc., Nat. Wildlife Fedn., Sigma Xi. Holder copyright Stellar 28 constellation games. Current Work: Modeling of galaxy dynamics and evolution galaxies, computer simulations, N-Body programs, stochastic self-propagating star formation, galactic evolution. Subspecialty: Theoretical astrophysics. Home: 95 Silver Rd Bangor ME 04401 Office: U Maine 314 Bennett Hall Orono ME 04469

COMISO, JOSEFINO CACAS, physical scientist; b. Narvacan, Philippines, Sept. 21, 1940; came to U.S., 1964, naturalized, 1976; s. Severino Cabot and Silvestra Cacho (Cacas) C.; m. Diana Parenas Jiminez, June 27, 1970; children—Glen Arnold, David Arnel, Melissa Jane. B.S. in physics, U. Philippines, Diliman, 1962; M.S., Fla. State U., 1966; Ph.D., UCLA, 1972. Scientist Philippines Atomic Research Ctr., Diliman, 1963; instr. U. Philippines, 1963-64; research physicist UCLA, 1972-73; research assoc. U. Va., Charlottsville, 1973-77; sr. mem. tech. staff C.S.C., Silver Spring, Md., 1977-79; phys. scientist NASA Goddard Space Flight Ctr., Greenbelt, Md., 1979—. Author: (with others) Antarctic Sea Ice, 1983 (NASA award 1983). Contbr. articles to profl. jours. Coll. scholar U. Philippines, 1962. Mem. Am. Geophys. Union, Am. Phys. Soc., Internat. Glaciological Soc., Philippine-Am. Acad. Sci. Current work: Remote sensing of geophysical earth parameters in the microwave and infrared region; radiative transfer modeling of microwave radiation from sea ice and ice sheets; cluster analysis and use of artificial intelligence in parameter retrievals; polar oceanography. Subspecialties: Remote sensing (geoscience); Arctic studies. Home: 11013 Elon Dr Bowie MD 20715 Office: NASA Goddard Space Flight Ctr Code 671 Greenbelt MD 20771

COMMISSO, FRANKLYN W., biologist, educator, curator; b. White Plains, N.Y., July 14, 1948; s. Frank R. and Elsie M. (Rowe) C.; m. Mary Elizabeth Jerry, Aug. 14, 1976. B.A., Pace U., 1970; M.A., Queens Coll., 1973; Ph.D., Fordham U., 1981. Teaching asst. U. Conn., Storrs, 1970-71; lab. technician Pace U., Pleasantville, N.Y., 1966-70, lab. supr., 1971-75, adj. prof., 1971—; curator Natural History Mus., 1974—; adj. asst. prof. Coll. New Rochelle, N.Y., 1980—, Marymount Coll., 1982—, Manhattanville Coll., 1983—; researcher dept. ornithology Am. Mus. Natural History, 1971—. Contbr. chpts. to books. Mem. Am. Ornithologists Union, Am. Mus. Natural History, Nat. Wildlife Fedn., Moravian Music Found., Sigma Xi, Tri Beta. Democrat. Lutheran. Current Work: Analysis of myology and osteology of avian hindlimb with associated functional aspects correlated to niche utilization, species interaction, taxonomy and evolution. Subspecialties: Evolutionary biology; Morphology. Home: 78 Elmore Ave Croton-on-Hudson NY 10520 Office: 861 Bedford Rd Pleasantville NY 10570

COMPAAN, ALVIN DELL, physics educator, researcher; b. Hull, N.D., June 11, 1943; s. William and Dena (DeJong) C.; m. Mary Han, Oct. 6, 1946; children: Timothy, Kristina, Deanne, David. A.B., Calvin Coll., 1965; M.S., U. Chgo., 1966, Ph.D., 1971. Assoc. research scientist N.Y.U., 1971-73; asst. prof. physics Kans. State U., 1973-77, assoc. prof., 1977-81, prof., 1981—. Contbr. articles to profl. jours. NDEA fellow, 1967-68; NSF trainee, 1968-70; Humboldt fellow, 1982-83. Mem. Am. Phys. Soc., AAAS, Materials Research So., Optical Soc. Am., Sigma Xi. Current Work: Laser interactions with semiconductors, coherent Raman spectroscopy. Subspecialties: Condensed matter physics; Laser spectroscopy. Office: Department Physics Kansas State University Manhattan KS 66506

COMPERE, CLINTON LEE, physician; b. Greenville, Tex., Feb. 17, 1911; s. Edward L. and Clara (Davison) C.; m. Katharine Gram, Mar. 31, 1949; children: Clinton Lee, Mary Katherine. B.S., U. Chgo., 1936, M.D., 1937. Diplomate: Am. Bd. Orthopaedic Surgery. Intern Henry Ford Hosp., Detroit, 1938-39; resident Blodgett Meml. Hosp., Grand Rapids, Mich., 1939-40; practice medicine specializing in orthopaedic surgery, Chgo., 1946—; mem. sr. attending staff Chgo. Wesley Meml. Hosp., 1949—, chief staff, 1964-66; acad. dir. Prosthetic Research Center, Chgo., 1955—, Prosthetic-Orthotic Edn., Chgo., 1958—; dir. Rehab. Engring. Center, 1972—; cons. 5th Army Hdqrs., 1947—; cons. amputee clinics Regional Office VA, 1947—; assoc. prof. orthopaedic surgery Northwestern U. Med. Sch., 1954-65, prof., 1965—, Edwin Ryerson prof., chmn. dept. orthopaedic surgery, 1978-80; vice chmn. bd. Rehab. Inst., Chgo.; mem. med. adv. com. Ill. Div. Vocational Rehab.; sec.-treas. Orthopedic Research and Edn. Found., 1972-78; med. dir. Ill. State Med. Drs. Services, 1980—. Co-author: Fracture Treatment, 1937, also articles. Served to lt. col., M.C. AUS, 1940-46. Recipient citation Pres.'s Com. Employment Physically Handicapped, 1959; Profl. Achievement award U. Chgo., 1979. Mem. Am. Acad. Orthopaedic Surgeons (sec. 1959-62, pres. 1963-64), Ill., Chgo. med. socs., A.M.A., A.C.S., Am., 20th Century orthopaedic assns., Chgo. Orthopaedic Soc., Clin. Orthopaedic Soc., Ill. Soc. Med. Research, Internat. Soc. Orthopaedic Surgery and Traumatology, Alpha Omega Alpha. Subspecialties: Orthopedics; Physical medicine and rehabilitation. Home: 2011 McMullen Dr Dunedin FL 33528 Office: 233 E Erie St Chicago IL 60611

COMPTON, WILLIAM AVERA, agronomy educator; b. Richmond, Va., Aug. 2, 1927; s. Ruel Keith and Charlotte (Avera) C.; div.; children—William J., Clinton K.; m. Mary Alice Thomas, Aug. 9, 1980. B.S., N.C. State U., 1958, M.S., 1960; Ph.D., U. Nebr., 1963. Asst. prof. N.C. State U., Raleigh, 1963-65, U. Minn., St. Paul, 1965-67; instr. U. Nebr., 1962-63, assoc. prof., 1967-75, prof., 1975—; cons. in field. Author: Conceptos Basicos di la Genetica Estadistica, 1965. Served with USN, 1950-53. Mem. Crop Sci. Soc. Am., Am. Soc. Agronomy, AAAS. Democrat. Current work: Corn breeding; corn genetics; quantitative genetics. Subspecialties: Plant genetics; Genetics and genetic engineering (agriculture). Home: William A Compton 1300 N 41st St Lincoln NE 68503 Office: Dept Agronomy U Nebr Lincoln NE 68523

CONCANNON, JAMES THOMAS, psychopharmacologist, educator; b. Shamokin, Pa., Apr. 18, 1951; s. Theodore Patrick and Mary Dolores (Sokoloskie) C. B.S., St. Joseph's Coll., Phila., 1973; M.A., SUNY, Binghamton, 1975, Ph.D., 1977. USPHS fellow, postdoctoral research asso. Kent (Ohio) State U., 1977-79; asst. prof. psychology U. R.I., Providence, 1979-80; research instr. dept. pharmacology Northeastern Ohio Univs. Coll. Medicine, Rootstown, 1980-82, research asst. prof., 1982-84; asst. prof. pharmacology Southeastern Coll. Osteo. Medicine, North Miami Beach, Fla., 1984—. Contbr. articles to profl. jours. Nat. Inst Alcohol Abuse and Alcoholism fellow, 1976-77; NIH grantee, 1980-81; Occupational Health grantee, 1982-84. Mem. Soc. for Neurosci., Am. Psychol. Assn. Internat. Soc. for Developmental Psychobiology, Soc. for Stimulus Properties of Drugs, AAAS, Eastern Psychol. Assn., Midwestern Psychol. Assn., Sigma Xi. Current Work: Animal models of psychiatric and neurological problems; behavioral pharmacology. Subspecialties: Neuropharmacology; Pharmacology. Home: 3211 SW 44th St Apt 207 Fort Lauderdale FL 33312 Office: Southeastern Coll Osteo Medicine 1750 NE 168th St North Miami Beach FL 33312

CONCORDIA, CHARLES, electrical, mechanical engineer, consultant; b. Schenectady, June 20, 1908; s. Francis G. and Susie Elizabeth (Decker) C.; m. Frances Butler, Dec. 18, 1948. Sc.D. (hon.), Union Coll., 1971. With Gen. Electric Co., Schenectady, 1926-73, in electric utility systems engring., 1936-73, applications engr., 1936-49, in aircraft devel., 1941-45, cons. engr., 1949-73, cons. electric power systems engring., Venice, Fla., 1973—; lectr. various univs. Author: Synchronous Machines, 1951; contbr. 120 articles to profl. jours. Recipient Lamme medal Am. Inst. Elec. Engrs., 1961; Coffin award Gen. Electric Co., 1942; Steinmetz award, 1973; named Engr. of Yr. Profl. Engrs. Soc., 1963. Fellow IEEE, ASME, AAAS; mem. Assn. Computing Machinery (founding mem.), Conf. Internationale des Grands Reseaux Electriques a Haute Tension, Nat. Acad. Engring., Nat. Soc. Profl. Engrs., Sigma Xi, Tau Beta Pi. Republican. Presbyterian. Clubs: Venice Yacht, Mohawk Golf. Patentee in field (6). Current Work: Electric power system dynamic performance and control: system modeling, reliability, operating problems, major breakdowns (blackouts), stability improvement, design and planning. Subspecialties: Systems engineering; Numerical analysis (computer science). Home and Office: 702 Bird Bay Dr W Venice FL 33595

CONE, RIC IAN, biochemist; b. Chgo., Jan. 8, 1947; s. Gilbert George and Frances (Mided) C.; m. Susan Marie Jones, Aug. 14, 1976; 1 child, Ambria Michelle. Student U. Ill.-Chgo., 1965; B.A. in Biochemistry U. Calif.-Berkeley, 1971; postgrad. U. Ill. Med. Ctr., Chgo., 1972-74; Ph.D., in Neurosci., U. Wis.-Madison, 1980; postdoctorate in Pharmacology, Stanford U., 1980-83. Technician, U. Calif.-Berkeley, 1968-70; predoctoral candidate U. Ill.-Chgo., 1972-74, Rush-Presbyn. St. Luke's Hosp., Chgo., 1974-75, U. Wis., 1975-79; postdoctoral fellow Stanford U. Med. Ctr., Calif., 1980-83; instr. biochemistry So. Calif. Coll. Optometry, Fullerton, 1983; research biochemist Monoclonal Antibodies, Inc., Mountain View, Calif., 1983-85, U. Tex. Health Sci. Ctr., Dallas, 1985—. Contbr. articles to profl. jours. Referee NSF, 1981—, Life Scis. Jour., 1983—, Brain Research Bull., 1984—. Recipient Nat. Research Services award Nat. Inst. Drug Abuse, 1980. Mem. Soc. for Neurosci., AAAS, N.Y. Acad. Scis., Fitness U.S.A. (exec. bd. 1984—). Club: Alfred William Harris Faculty (Dallas). Current work: Neuroendocrine effects of opioid peptides. Subspecialties: Neurochemistry; Neuroendocrinology.

CONE, ROBERT EDWARD, immunologist, educator; b. Bklyn., Aug. 18, 1943; s. Joseph and Ruth C.; m. Michele Joy Nash, Aug. 21, 1966; children: Jennifer, Laura. B.S., Bklyn Coll., 1964; M.S., Fla. State U., 1967; Ph.D., U. Mich., 1970. Postdoctoral fellow Walter and Eliza Hall Inst. for Med. Research, Melbourne, Australia, 1971-73, Basel (Switzerland) Inst. for Immunology, 1973-74; asst. prof. depts. surgery and pathology Yale U., 1974-80, assoc. prof., 1980-84; prof. dept. pathology U. Conn. Health Ctr., 1984—; mem. histocompatibility com. New Eng. Organ Bank. Author articles. F.G. Novy fellow, 1968; Horace Rackham fellow, 1969-70; Damon Runyon postdoctoral fellow, 1971-73; Upjohn Co. grantee, 1979, 80. Mem. AAAS, Am. Assn. Immunologists, Internat. Cell Research Orgn. Current Work: Structure and function of lymphocyte membranes and receptors. Subspecialties: Transplantation; Membrane biology.

CONE, RUFUS LESTER, physicist, educator; b. Statesboro, Ga., Apr. 28, 1944; s. Rufus Lester and Louise (Lipford) C.; m. Margaret Nelson Van Horn, Aug. 12, 1967. B.S., Ga. Inst. Tech., 1966, M.S., 1967; M.Phil., Yale U., 1968, Ph.D., 1971. Asst. prof. physics U. Ga., Athens, 1971-74; asst. prof. physics Mont. State U., Bozeman, 1974-77, assoc. prof., 1977—; cons. coherent laser spectroscopy Bell Labs., Murray Hill, N.J., 1980—; vis. fellow Clarendon Lab., U. Oxford, Eng., 1983. Contbr. articles to profl. jours. NSF grantee, 1974—; Research Corp. grantee, 1974-75; Mont. State U. Research/Creativity grantee, 1980-82. Mem. Am. Phys. Soc., Optical Soc. Am., IEEE, Yale Sci. and Engring. Assn., Nat. Rail Hist. Current Work: Nonlinear optics and laser spectroscopy. Laser spectroscopy of condensed matter, nonlinear optical processes, interionic interactions, rare earth insulators. Subspecialties: Laser spectroscopy; Condensed matter physics. JOffice: Dept Physic Mont State U Bozeman MT 59717

CONEY, CHARLES CLIFTON, malacologist; b. Kingsport, Tenn., Aug. 24, 1949; s. Charles Herbert and Emma Sue (Snell) C.; 1 child, Sonia Lorraine. B.S., East Tenn. State U., 1977, M.S., 1980. Research asst. East Tenn. State U., Johnson City, 1977-79, teaching asst., 1979-80; instr. biology U. S.C., Conway, 1980-83; collection mgr. malacology sect. Natural History Mus., Los Angeles, 1983—. Contbr. articles to profl. jours. Mem. Paleontological Research Inst., Am. Malacological Union, Conchological Club So. Calif., Pacific Shell Club, Western Soc. Malacologists. Current Work: Ontogeny and phylogeny of molluscan bivalve gill, with emphasis on comparative microanatomy of bivalve gill structure, leading to an understanding of mode and tempo of bivalve gill devel. and speciation among convergent bivalve shell homeomorphs. Subspecialties: Evolutionary biology; Ecology (environmental science). Office: Malacology Sect Natural History Mus 900 Exposition Blvd Los Angeles CA 90007

CONN, JEROME W., medical educator, internist; b. N.Y.C., Sept. 24, 1907; married; 2 children. M.D., U. Mich., 1932; D.Sc. (hon.), Rutgers U., 1964; M.D. (hon.), U. Turin, 1975. From instr. to prof. Med. Sch., U. Mich., Ann Arbor, 1935-68, Louis Harry Newburgh Univ. prof. medicine, 1968-74, emeritus Disting. Univ. prof. internal medicine, 1974—, cons. clin. investigation, dept. internal medicine, 1974-76; disting. physician VA, 1973-76. Recipient Bernard medal U. Montreal, 1957; HenryRussell Lectr. award U. Mich., 1961; Wilson medal Am. Clin. and Climatological Assn., 1962; Gairdner Found. Internat. prize, 1965; Phillips Meml. award ACP, 1965; Howard Taylor award Am. Therapeutic Soc., 1967, Ruth Gray Meml. medal Evanston Hosp., 1968; Stouffer Internat. prize, 1969; gold medal Internat. Soc. Progress in Internal Medicine, 1969; Heath Med. award and meda. U. Tex.-Houston, 1971; award Am. Coll. Nutrition, 1973. Hon. fellow ACS; mem. Nat. Acad. Sci., Assn. Am. Physicians, Am. Diabetes Assn. (pres. 1962-63, Banting medal 1958, Banting Meml. award 1963). Subspecialty: Internal medicine.

CONN, REX BOLAND, JR., physician, educator; b. Marengo, Iowa, Aug. 3, 1927; s. Rex Boland and Helena Dorothea (Schoenfelder) C.; m. Victoria Grace Sellens, Dec. 28, 1950; children: Elizabeth Marian, Victoria Anne, Mary Catherine. B.S., Iowa State U., 1949; M.D., Yale U., 1953; B.Sc., U. Oxford, Eng., 1955; M.S., U. Minn., 1960. Prof. pathology, dir. clin. labs. W.Va. Med. Center, Morgantown, 1960-68; prof. lab. medicine, dir. dept. Johns Hopkins Med. Instns., Balt., 1968-77; prof. pathology and lab. medicine, dir. clin labs. Emory U., Atlanta, 1977—; mem. pathology tng. com. NIH, 1972-73, mem. pathology study sect., 1968-72; cons. Walter Reed Army Med. Center, 1972-77, VA Pathology Adv. Com., 1984—, Armed Forces Inst. Pathology, 1984—. Editor: Current Diagnosis, 1985, 7th edit., 1984; co-editor Yearbook of Pathology and Clinical Pathology, 1980. Served with USNR, 1945-46. Mem. Coll. Am. Pathologists, Am. Soc. Clin. Pathologists (dir. 1975-81), Acad. Clin. Lab. Physicians and Scientists (pres. 1972—). Current Work: Diagnostic laboratory medicine, clinical enzymology, medical instrumentation, medical computing. Subspecialties: Pathology (medicine); Biochemistry (medicine). Home: 2505 Greenglade Rd Atlanta GA 30345 Office: 1364 Clifton Rd Atlanta GA 30322

CONNELLY, JOHN PETER, pediatrician; b. Boston, May 12, 1926; s. Thomas Joseph and Bridget T. (Finnigan) C.; m. Martha T. Cronin, June 24, 1950; children: Maureen, Marie, Eileen, Martha, Cathleen, John, Michael. B.S., Boston Coll., 1951; M.D., Georgetown U., 1955. Diplomate: Am. Bd. Pediatrics. Intern Royal Victoria Hosp., Montreal, Que., Can., 1955-56; resident in pediatrics Johns Hopkins Hosp., 1957-58; resident Mass. Gen. Hosp., Boston, 1956-68, 61-62, asst. pediatrician, 1961-64; chief Mass. Gen. Hosp. (Children's Ambulatory Clinic), 1963-64, chief ambulatory div., 1964-69, pediatrician to children;s service, 1967-73; exec. dir. Bunker Hill Health Ctr., 1967-73; vis. physician Boston Hosp. for Women, 1961-73; chief of pediatrics Foster G. McGaw Hosp., Loyola U., Chgo., 1972-76; cons. dir. Regional Center for Study of Sudden Infant Death Syndrome, 1976-81; dir. div. health services research and devel. Am. Acad. Pediatrics, Evanston, Ill., 1976-83; chief staff, assoc. dean for profl. affairs, prof. community and family health Loyola U. Med. Ctr., 1983—; mem. faculty Harvard Med. Sch., 1957-73, assoc. prof. pediatrics, 1969-73; vis. lectr. Harvard U. Sch. Pub. Health, Harvard Ctr. Community Health and Med. Care; prof., chmn. dept. pediatrics Loyola U.-Stritch Sch. Medicine, Chgo., 1972-76; sr. lectr. U. Chgo. Sch. Social Service Adminstrn. and Policy, 1979—; prof. community health scis. U. Ill. Sch. Pub. Health, 1980—; vis. scholar Northwestern U. Ctr. Health Services Policy Research, 1981—. Contbr. chpts. to books, articles to profl. jours. Trustee Nat. Sudden Infant Death Syndrome Found., 1975—; bd. dirs. Mass. Soc. Prevention of Cruelty to Children, 1966-73; mem. Ill. Sudden Infant Death Syndrome Study Commn., 1975—. Served to rear adm. M.C. USNR, 1944—. Decorated Naval Commendation medal, others; recipient Cahill medal Georgetown U.; citation for humanitarianism Commonwealth of Mass., 1973; numerous others. Mem. Soc. Med. Cons. to Armed Forces, Naval Res. Assn. (life), Am. Fedn. Clin. Research, Assn. Ambulatory Pediatric Services, Irish and Am. Pediatric Soc. (pres. 1977-78), Royal Coll. Medicine, Am. Irish Found., AMA, Chgo. Med. Soc., Ill. Med. Soc., Mass. Med. Soc. Res. Officers Assn. U.S., Harvard Med. Alumni Assn. (assoc.), Riverside C. of C. Roman Catholic. Club: St. Mary's Holy Name Soc. (Riverside). Lodge: Lions. Current Work: Health services research on maternal and child health related projects; i.e., sudden infant death syndrome. Subspecialties: Health services research; Pediatrics. Home: 147 Herrick Rd Riverside IL 60546 Office: Loyola U Med Ctr Maywood IL 60153

CONNERS, RICHARD WILLIAM, computer engineering educator; b. St. Joseph, Mo., Jan. 26, 1946; s. Beuron Alexander and Blanche Anna (Crow) C.; m. Jeanette McDowell, Jan. 20, 1979. B.A. in Math., U. Mo., 1968, M.A. in Math., 1973, Ph.D. in Elec. Engring., 1976. Intelligence analyst CIA, Washington, 1969-72; asst. prof. U. Mo., Columbia, 1977-78; asst. prof. computer engring. La. State U., Baton Rouge, 1978-82, assoc. prof., 1982—. Contbr. articles to profl. jours. Mem. IEEE, Internat. Soc. Optical Engring., Am. Assn. for Artificial Intelligence, Soc. Mfg. Engrs., Sigma Xi. Methodist. Current work: Theoretical development of general purpose early vision operators for computer vision systems; development and analysis of control strategics for computer vision systems; analysis of object models and knowledge representation in vision systems. Subspecialties: Graphics, image processing, and pattern recognition; Artificial intelligence. Home: 6336 Esplanade Ave Baton Rouge LA 70806 Office: Elec and Computer Engring Dept La State U Baton Rouge LA 70803

CONNEY, ALLAN HOWARD, pharmacologist; b. Chgo., Mar. 23, 1930; s. Leo Younkers and Celia (Gasway) C.; m. Diana Locke, Sept. 5, 1954; children: Michael Raymond, Steven Herbert. B.S. in Pharmacy, U. Wis., 1952, M.S. in Oncology, 1954, Ph.D. in Oncology, 1956. Registered pharmacist, Ill. Research asst. McArdle Lab., Madison, Wis., 1952-56; guest investigator Nat. Heart Inst., Bethesda, Md., 1957-58, pharmacologist, 1958-60; head dept. biochem.-pharmacology Burroughs Wellcome & Co., Tuckahoe, N.Y., 1960-70; dir. dept. biochemistry Hoffman-LaRoche, Inc., Nutley, N.J., 1970-71, dir. dept. biochemistry and drug metabolism, 1971-83, assoc. dir. exptl. therapeutics, 1979-83, dir. dept. exptl. carcinogenesis and metabolism, 1983-85, head lab. exptl. carcinogenesis and metabolism, 1985—; pres. Roche Inst. Molecular Biology, Nutley; adj. prof. Rockefeller U.; adj. prof. Columbia U.; vis. disting. prof. Rutgers U. Contbr. numerous articles to profl. jours. Mem. Am. Soc. Biol. Chemists, Nat. Acad. Scis., Am. Soc. Pharmacology and Exptl. Therapeutics, Am. Assn. Cancer Research (G.H.A. Clowes award lectr. 1981), Soc. Toxicology, Inc., Acad. Pharm. Scis., Am. Pharm. Assn., AAAS, N.Y. Acad Scis. Current Work: Chemical Carcinogenesis, factors influencing metabolism and action of drugs, steroids and chemical carcinogens. Subspecialties: Cancer research (medicine); Biochemistry (medicine). Office: 340 Kingsland St Bldg 86 Nutley NJ 07110

CONNOLLY, JOHN WILLIAM, physicist, government official; b. South Porcupine, Ont., Can., July 18, 1938; came to U.S., 1960, naturalized, 1972; m. Stuart Mackay and Mary Isabel (Roe) C.; m. Charlotte Bernier, Mar. 1, 1962 (div. July 1976); children—Michele, Julie; m. Helene Margaretta Steene, May 20, 1977; 1 child, Stuart. B.A., U. Toronto, 1960; Ph.D., U. Fla. 1966. Research scientist United Aircraft Co., East Hartford, Conn., 1967-70; prof. physics U. Fla., Gainesville, 1970-76; adminstr. NSF, Washington, 1976—, dir. advanced sci. computing, 1984—. Contbr. articles on solid state and molecular theory to profl. jours. Fellow Am. Phys. Soc.; mem. Phi Beta Kappa, Sigma Xi. Current work: Theoretical solid state physics. Subspecialty: Condensed matter physics. Office: NSF 1800 G St NW Washington DC 20550

CONNOLLY, LEO PAUL, astronomer, educator; b. Sebastopol, Calif., Jan. 1, 1947; s. Leo F. and Virginia U. (Trigeiro) C.; m. Jacqueline B. Bonanno, July 14, 1973; 1 son: Richard. B.A., U. Calif.-Berkeley, 1969; Ph.D. in Astronomy, U. Ariz., 1975. Astronomy and physics instr., dir. MacLean Obs., Sierra Nevada Coll., Incline Village, Nev., 1973-78; assoc. prof. astronomy Southeast Mo. State U., Cape Girardeau, 1978—, also researcher. Contbr. numerous articles to sci. publs. NSF Sci. Faculty Profl. Devel. awardee, 1979. Mem. Am. Astron. Soc., Astron. Soc. of Pacific. Current Work: Photometry of pulsating stars. Subspecialty: Optical astronomy. Home: 913 N Missouri Ave Cape Girardeau MO 63701 Office: Dept Physics Southeast Mo State U Cape Girardeau MO 63701

CONOMY, JOHN PAUL, neurologist, health cons., researcher; b. Cleve., July 31, 1938; s. John Paul and Marie Elizabeth (Bimbea) C.; m. Jeannette Melchior, Oct. 19, 1963; children: John, Lisa, Christopher. B.S. cum laude, John Carroll U., 1960; M.D., St. Louis U., 1964. Diplomate: Am. Bd. Psychiatry and Neurology (examiner). Intern, house officer St. Louis U., 1964-65; resident in neurology Univ. Hosps., Cleve., 1965-68; fellow in neuropathology Cleve. Met. Gen. Hosp., 1968; research fellow neuroanatomy U. Pa., 1970-71; staff neurologist Scott and White Found., 1971-72; asst. prof. neurology Case Western Res. U., 1972-75; chmn. dept. neurology Cleve. Clinic Found., 1975—; cons. health care allocation; attending physician Univ. Hosps., Cleve., 1968; Highland View Hosp., Cleve., 1968; assoc. neurologist Hosp. U. Pa., 1970; sr. staff neurologist Scott and White Clinic and Hosp., Temple, Tex., 1971-72; clin. attending neurologist Parkland Hosp., Dallas, 1971-72; clin. instr. neurology U. Tex. Southwestern Med. Sch., Dallas, 1971-72; attending neurologist Univ. Hosps., Cleve., 1972—; dir. Mellen Ctr. for Multiple Sclerosis Treatment and Research, 1984—; cons. neurologist VA Center, Temple, 1971, VA Hosp., Cleve., 1972; examiner Am. Bd. Neurol. Surgery, 1976—; cons. NSF, 1977; mem. physician evaluation bd. Whittaker Corp., 1980—; sci. adv. bd. Communicative Disorders Found; vis. prof. various univs.; lectr. Reviewer, NIH, 1978, Postgrad. Medicine, 1975—, Neurology, 1977—, Cleve. Clinic Quar, 1977, Neurosurgery, 1979—, Am. Jour Physiology, 1980-81; contbr. articles and abstracts to profl. jours. Served to capt. M.C. USAF, 1968-70. Decorated Air Force Commendation medal; recipient Frances Grogan prize in psychiatry, 1964; Reinberger Found. grantee, 1978—; NIH grantee. Fellow Am. Acad. Neurology, ACP; mem. Am. Neurol. Assn., Soc. Neurosci., AAAS, Am. EEG Soc., Soc. Neurosci. (past pres. Cleve. chpt.), Am. Assn. History of Medicine, Ohio Med. Assn., Cleve. Acad. Medicine, No. Ohio Neurol. Soc., Assn. Research in Nervous and Mental Diseases, Soc. Clin. Neurologists, Assn. Univ. Profs. Neurology, Internat. Assn. Study of Pain, AMA, Am. Assn. Neurol. Surgeons, AAAS, Royal Soc. Medicine, Cleve. Med. Library Assn. (trustee). Roman Catholic. Current Work: Behavorial aspects of neurology and neurophysiology related to hypertension, stroke, multiple sclerosis and peripheral nerve illness. Subspecialty: Neurology.

CONRAD, HANS, educator, metallurgical engineer; b. Konradstahl, Germany, Apr. 19, 1922; came to U.S., 1926, naturalized, 1944; s. Henry K. and Martha Ann (Bader) C.; m. Emma Ann Bort, June 10, 1944; children—Sandra Joy, Roberta Lee, Gary Richard. Student, Washington and Jefferson Coll., 1940-42; B.S. in Metall. Engring, Carnegie Inst. Tech., 1943; M.Eng., Yale, 1951, D.Eng., 1956. Research metallurgist Chase Copper & Brass Co., Waterbury, Conn., 1953-55; supervisory engr. Westinghouse Research Labs., Churchill Boro, Pa., 1955-59; sr. research specialist Atomics Internat., Canoga Park, Calif., 1959-61; head dept. physics Aerospace Corp., El Segundo, Calif., 1961-64; tech. dir. Franklin Inst. Research Labs., Phila., 1964-67; prof., chmn. dept. metall. engring. and materials sci., asso. dir. Inst. Mining and Minerals Research, U. Ky., Lexington, 1967-80; prof., head dept. materials engring., dir. minerals and materials research programs N.C. State U., 1981—; disting. vis. prof. Am. U., Cairo, Egypt, 1983, Soviet Acad. Scis., 1984. Contbr. articles to profl. jours. and books. Recipient U. Ky. Research award, 1971; U.S. Sr. Scientist award Alexander von Humboldt-Stiftung, 1974; Japan Soc. Promotion Sci. vis. prof., 1976; Alcoa Research award N.C. State U., 1985. Fellow Am. Soc. Metallurgy; mem. Am. Inst. M.E., Am. Soc. Metals, Am. Soc. Testing and Materials, Sigma Xi, Tau Beta Pi. Subspecialty: Metallurgy. Home: 205 Glasgow Rd Cary NC 27511 Office: Materials Engring Dept NC State U Raleigh NC 27695

CONRAD, MARCEL EDWARD, physician, educator; b. N.Y.C., Aug. 15, 1928; s. Marcel Edward and Lulu Marie (Geraghty) C.; children—Marcel E. III, Mark E., Carol J., Erin E., Julia P. B.S., Georgetown U., 1949, M.D. cum laude, 1953. Diplomate Am. Bd. Internal Medicine, Am. Bd. Hematology. Intern, then resident Walter Reed Army Med. Ctr., Washington, 1953-58; prof. medicine U. Ala., Birmingham 1974-83; prof. U. South Ala., Mobile, 1983—; lectr. in field. Contbr. articles to profl. jours. Served to col. U.S. Army, 1953-74. Decorated Legion of Merit with oak leaf cluster; recipient John Shaw Billings award, 1968; William Beaumont award, 1972; Walter Reed award, 1974. Mem. ACP, Assn. Am. Physicians, Am. Soc. Clin. Investigation, Am. Fed. Clin. Research, So. Soc. Clin. Research, Am. Physiol. Soc., Internat. Soc. Hematology, Am. Soc. Hematology, Internat. Soc. Blood Transfusion, Am. Soc. Clin. Oncology, AAAS, Soc. Exptl. Biology Medicine, Am. Assn. Blood Banks, Soc. Med. Consultants to Mil. Services, Assn. Hematology and Oncology Program Dirs., Med. Assn. State Ala., Mobile County Med. Assn. Roman Catholic. Subspecialties: Hematology; Oncology. Home: 1314 Dauphin St Mobile AL 36604 Office: Univ South Ala Cancer Ctr Mobile AL 36688

CONRAD, MICHAEL, computer scientist, educator. Prof. dept. computer sci. Wayne State U., Detroit. Subspecialty: Computers and biological systems. Office: Wayne State U Dept of Computer Sci Detroit MI 48202

CONROW, EDMUND HENRY, aerospace engineer; b. N.Y.C., Aug. 1, 1949; s. Edmund Charles and Statia Henrietta (Kaminski) C. B.S. in Nuclear Engring., U. Ariz., 1971, M.S., 1973; Ph.D., Okla. State U., 1976; Ph.D. candidate Rand Grad. Inst., Santa Monica, Calif., 1983—. Instr., Okla. State U., Stillwater, part-time, 1974-76; engring. specialist Gen. Dynamics, San Diego, 1977-79; project engr. Aerospace Corp., Los Angeles, 1979—; cons. Rand Corp., Santa Monica, 1981-83, U.S. Arms Control and Disarmament Agy., Washington, 1980-85; tech. advisor Civilian and Service Dirs. U.S. Cruise Missile Program, Washington, 1980-82. Contbr. articles to sci. jours. Rand Corp. Grad. Inst. fellow, 1981-83; The Aerospace Corp. fellow, 1981-83. Mem. Am. Soc. Photogrammetry, AIAA (sr. mem.; missile systems tech. com. 1980-85), IEEE. Current work: Evaluation of operational utility, acquisition strategies and cost, schedule and technical risk associated with U.S. military and space programs. Subspecialties: Aerospace engineering and technology; Remote sensing (geoscience). Home: PO Box 2973 Culver City CA 90230

CONROY, GLENN C., anatomist. Prof. anatomy, anthropology Washington U. Sch. Medicine, St. Louis. Subspecialties: Paleobiology; Anatomy and embryology. Office: Washington U Sch Medicine Dept Anatomy and Neurobiology Saint Louis MO 63110

CONSIGLI, RICHARD ALBERT, virologist; b. Bklyn., Mar. 2, 1931; s. Benjamin M. and Maria (Corchia) C.; m. Barbara J. Seel, Jan. 29, 1938; children: Linda, Joanne, Maria. B.S., Bklyn. Coll., 1954; M.A., U. Kans., 1956, Ph.D., 1960; postdoctoral, U. Pa., 1960-63. Instr. U. Kans., 1959-60; prof. Kans. State U., 1963—, Univ. disting. prof. biology, 1985—. Contbr. numerous articles to profl. jours. NIH career devel. awardee, 1968-73; recipient Grad. Faculty award Kans. State U., 1976. Fellow Am. Acad. Microbiology; mem. Am. Soc. Microbiology, AAAS, Am. Assn. Cancer Research, Soc. Exptl. Biology and Medicine, Am. Soc. Virology. Roman Catholic. Current Work: Tumor virology, biochemistry of virus proteins. Subspecialty: Microbiology (medicine). Office: Kans State U Manhattan KS 66506

CONTI, PETER SELBY, astronomy educator; b. N.Y.C., Sept. 5, 1934; s. Attilio and Marie (Selby) C.; m. Carolyn Safford, Aug. 26, 1961; children—Michael, Karen, Kathe. B.S., Rensselaer Poly. Inst., 1956; Ph.D., U Calif.-Berkeley, 1963. Research fellow Calif. Inst. Tech., Pasadena, 1963-66; asst. prof. astronomer U. Calif., Santa Cruz, 1966-71; prof., fellow Joint Inst. Lab. Astrophysics, U. Colo., Boulder, 1971—, chmn. dept. astrophys., planetary and atmospheric scis., 1980—; chmn. bd. Assoc. Univs. for Research in Astronomy, Inc., Tucson, 1983—; Co-editor: Mass Loss and Evolution of O-type Stars, 1979. Contbr. articles to profl. jours. Served to lt. (j.g.) USNR, 1956-59. Fulbright fellow, 1969-70; recipient Gold medal U. Liege, Beligum, 1975. Fellow AAAS. (chmn. sect. D astronomy 1980); mem. Am. Astronom. Soc. (councillor 1983—), Astronom. Soc. Pacific. Current work: Spectroscopy of hot luminous stars and their winds, to understand their evolution and role in star formation. Subspecialty: Optical astronomy. Office: Box 391 Astrophys Planetary and Atmospheric Scis Dept U Colo Boulder CO 80329

CONTI, SAMUEL FRANCIS, educational administrator, microbiologist; b. Bklyn., Dec. 24, 1931; s. John and Sabina Conti; m. Judith Rosenberg, Jan. 27, 1954; children—Deborah, Scott, Suzanne. B.S., Bklyn. Coll., 1952; M.S., U. Conn., 1956; Ph.D., Cornell U., 1959. Research assoc. Brookhaven Nat. Lab., Upton, N.Y., 1959-61; instr., Dartmouth Med. Sch., Hanover, N.H., 1961-62, asst. prof. microbiology, 1962-63, assoc. prof., assoc. dean arts and scis., and dir. T.H. Morgan Sch. Biol. Scis., U. Ky., Lexington, 1966-80; dean Grad. Studies and Research U. Mass., Amherst, 1980-84, acting dean engring., 1981-82, acting vice chancellor for acad. affairs, provost, 1983-84, vice chancellor for research and dean Grad. Sch., 1984—; chmn. com. on govtl. and assn. relations, Council of Grad. Schs., 1982—; mem. nat. adv. council, allergy and infections NIH, 1982—; dir. Ctr. for Molecular Medicine and Immunology, Inc., N.J., 1984—; Found. microbiology lectr. McDowell Cancer Network, 1967-68, 79-80, chmn. basic sci. com., 1976-80; mem. Ky. Gov.'s Commn. on Endangered Species, 1977-80. Mem. editorial bd. Jour. Bacteriology, 1965-80, Biology Digest, 1973—. Contbr. articles to profl. jours. Served with U.S. Army, 1953-55. Recipient Career Devel. award NIH, 1963-66, W.B. Sturgill award U. Ky., 1978, Chancellor's medal U. Mass., 1984. Mem. Am. Acad. Microbiology, Am. Soc. Microbiology (chmn. gen. microbiology div. 1974-75, vice chmn. 1972-74), Am. Soc. Biol. Chemistry, AAAS, Phi Kappa Phi. Subspecialty: Microbiology. Home: 40 Harris Mountain Rd Amherst MA 01002 Office: A217 Grad Research Ctr U Mass Amherst MA 01003

CONWAY, JOHN G., physicist; b. Pitts., May 16, 1922; s. John George and Irene M. (Clifford) C.; m. Florence M. Bittner, May 10, 1922; children: John George III, Jane M., Michael F., Ann S., Kathleen M., Patrick K., Caroline M. B.S. in Physics and Engring, U. Pitts., 1944. Mem. staff Los Alamos Sci. Lab., 1944-46; research assoc. U. Pitts., 1946-47, CNRS, Orsay, France, 1973-74, 79-80; with Lawrence Berkeley Lab., 1947—, sr. staff scientist, 1950—. Contbr. articles to profl. jours. Mem. El Cerrito (Calif.) City Council, 1958-63, mayor of, El Cerrito, 1961. Named Outstanding Man of Yr. El Cerrito Jaycees, 1959; recipient Louis A. Strait award No. Calif. Soc. for Spectroscopy, 1978. Fellow Optical Soc. Am. (Wm. F. Meggers award 1980); mem. Am. Phys. Soc., Soc. for Applied Spectroscopy, AAAS. Roman Catholic. Current Work: Optical spectroscopy of the actinide elements, both free ion and crystals. Subspecialties: Atomic and molecular physics; Condensed matter physics. Home: 1153 King Dr El Cerrito CA 94530 Office: Lawrence Berkeley Lab 1 Cyclotron Rd Berkeley CA 94720

CONWAY, LYNN ANN, computer scientist, electrical engineer; b. Mount Vernon, N.Y., Jan. 2, 1938. B.S., Columbia U., 1962, M.S.E.E., 1963. Mem. research staff IBM Corp., 1964-69; sr. staff engr. Memorex Corp., 1969-73, mem. research staff, 1973-77; mgr. LSI Systems Area, 1977-80; research fellow, mgr. VLSI Systems Design Area, Xerox Palo Alto Research Center, 1980-1983; chief scientist, asst. dir. strategic computing applications Def. Advanced Research Projects Agency, 1983-85; prof. elec. engring. and computer sci., assoc. dean Coll. Engring., U. Mich., 1985—; cons. Systems Industries, 1973-74; vis. assoc. prof. elec. engring. and computer sci. MIT, 1978-79. Co-author: Introduction to VLSI Systems; also articles. Cons. editor VLSI Systems Series. Recipient 1981 Electronics Award for Achievement; Harold Pender award U. Pa.; Sec. of Def. Meritorious Civilian Service award; Wetherill medal Franklin Inst. Fellow IEEE; mem. Assn. Computing Machinery, AAAS. Current work: Machine intelligence technology; artificial intelligence; computer architecture; microelectronic design. Subspecialties: Artificial intelligence; Computer architecture. Home: 2427 Londonderry Rd Ann Arbor MI 48104 Office: Chrysler Center University of Michigan Ann Arbor MI 48109-2092

CONWAY, THOMAS PATRICK, immunologist; b. Chgo., Dec. 31, 1941; s. Thomas John and Nora (McWalter) C.; m. Patricia Ann Walsh, Oct. 26, 1974; children: Felicia Yvonne, Erin Colleen. B.S., Loyola U., Chgo., 1963; M.S., U. Ill., 1966, Ph.D., 1969. USPHS fellow Scripps Clinic and Research Found., La Jolla, Calif., 1971-75; research assoc. Willian Beaumont Hosp., Royal Oak, Mich., 1975-77; assoc. prof. dept. biol. scis. No Ill. U., DeKalb, 1978—; adj. asst. prof. dept. microbiology Wayne State U., Detroit, 1975-77. Contbr. articles to sci. jours. Served to capt., M.S.C. U.S. Army, 1969-71. USPHS trainee, 1967-69; Am. Cancer Soc. fellow, 1979-80. Mem. AAAS, Am. Soc. Microbiology, Am. Assn. Immunologists, Sigma Xi. Current Work: Expression, synthesis and degradation of membrane proteins, especially B2 microglobulin in normal, activated and transformed lymphocytes, production of monoclonal antibodies. Subspecialties: Immunobiology and immunology; Membrane biology. Office: Dept Biol Scis No Ill U DeKalb IL 60115

CONWAY DE MACARIO, EVERLY, research scientist; b. Buenos Aires, Argentina, Apr. 20, 1939; d. Delfin E. and Maria G. (Benatuil) C.; m. Alberto J. L. Macario, Mar. 16, 1963; children: Alex, Everly. Ph.D. in Pharmacy, Nat. U. Buenos Aires, 1960, Ph.D. in Biochemistry, 1962. Research fellow Nat. Acad. Medicine Argentina, Buenos Aires, 1962-63; head lab. oncology and immunology Argentinian Assn. Against Cancer, Buenos Aires, 1966-77; chief immunology Sch. Medicine, U. Buenos Aires, 1967-68; research fellow dept. tumor biology Karolinska Inst., Stockholm, 1969-71; sr. research scientist lab. cell biology NRC Italy, Rome, 1971-73; vis. scientist Internat. Agy. Research on Cancer, WHO, Lyon, France, 1973-74, Brown U., Providence, 1974-76; research scientist Lab. Medicine Inst., N.Y. State Dept. Health, Albany, 1976—, supr. pregnancy test proficiency testing program, 1978-80; grant reviewer nat. and internat. agys. Contbr. chpts. to books, articles to profl. jours. Recipient Prof. J. M. Mezzadra award Nat. U. Buenos Aires, 1969; travel grantee French Soc. Immunology, 1974; travel grantee Am. Assn. Immunologists, 1977; Gold medal Argentinian Soc. Biochemistry, 1980; Hans Osterman Found. grantee Sweden, 1969; Sir Samuel Scott of Yews Trust grantee Sweden, 1970; Winifred Cullis grantee Internat. Fedn. Univ. Women, 1972; NATO grantee, 1975-81; U.S. Dept. Energy grantee, 1981. Mem. Argentinian Soc. Biochemistry, Scandinavian Soc. Immunology, Italian Assn. Immunologists, French Soc. Immunology, Am. Assn. Immunologists, Am. Soc. Microbiology. Current Work: Immunology of methanogenic bacteria; methanogenic bacteria, monoclonal antibodies, bacterial surface immunochemistry. Subspecialties: Immunobiology and immunology; Immunology (medicine). Home: 18 Carriage Rd Delmar NY 12054 Office: Empire State Plaza E-225 Albany NY 12201

CONWELL, ESTHER MARLY, physicist; b. N.Y.C., May 23, 1922; d. Charles and Ida (Korn) C.; m. Abraham A. Rothberg, Sept. 30, 1945; 1 son, Lewis J. B.A., Bklyn. Coll., 1942; M.S., U. Rochester, N.Y., 1945; Ph.D., U. Chgo., 1948. Lectr. Bklyn. Coll., 1946-51; mem. tech. staff Bell Telephone Labs., 1951-52; physicist GTE Labs., Bayside, N.Y., 1952-61, mgr. physics dept., 1961-72; vis. prof. U. Paris, 1962-63; Abby Rockefeller Mauze prof. M.I.T., 1972; prin. scientist Xerox Corp., Webster, N.Y., 1972-80, research fellow, 1981—; cons., mem. adv. com. engring. NSF, 1978-81. Author: High Field Transport in Semiconductors, 1967, also research papers; editorial bd.: Jour. Applied Physics; proc.: IEEE. Fellow IEEE, Am. Phys. Soc. (sec.-treas. div. condensed matter physics 1977-82); mem. Soc. Women Engrs. (Achievement award 1960), Nat. Acad. Engring. Patentee in field. Current Work: Basic research in condensed matter physics, electrical engineering, semiconductors. Subspecialties: Condensed matter physics; Semiconductors. Office: 800 Phillips Rd Webster NY 14580

CONZETT, HOMER EUGENE, nuclear physicist; b. Dubuque, Iowa, Oct. 16, 1920; s. Andrew and Christina (Accola) C.; m. Nancy Carolyn Tapscott, Apr. 30, 1960. B.A. in Physics and Math. magna cum laude, U. Dubuque, 1942; Ph.D. in Physics, U. Calif.-Berkeley, 1956. Degaussing physicist U.S. Navy, Key West, Fla., 1942-44, Japan, Korea, 1951-53, electronics officer, 1944-46; research physicist Lawrence Berkeley Lab., U. Calif.-Berkeley, 1956-64, dir. 88 inch cyclotron, 1964-71, sr. scientist, dir. research, 1964—. Editor Hadronic Jour., 1985—, editorial council, 1983—, procs. conf. on reactions between complex nuclei, 1963. Contbr. articles to profl. jours. Served to comdr. USNR, 1944-46, 51-53. Fulbright lectr., 1957; U. Dubuque fellow, 1938-42. Fellow Am. Phys. Soc.; mem. Fedn. Am. Scientists. Democrat. Current work: Spin polarization phenomena in nuclear and particle physics. Subspecialty: Nuclear physics. Office: Lawrence Berkeley Lab U Calif Berkeley CA 94720

COOK, CLARENCE EDGAR, chemist; b. Jefferson City, Tenn., Apr. 27, 1936; s. Edgar M. and Lillie G. (Hodge) C.; m. Gail O'Connor McKee, June 1, 1957; children: David Grey, Lisa O'Connor, Kevin McKee. B.S., Carson-Newman Coll., 1957; Ph.D. in Organic Chemistry, U. N.C., 1961; postdoctoral, Cambridge (Eng.) U., 1961. Chemist, Research Triangle Inst., Research Triangle Park, N.C., 1962-64, sr. chemist, 1964-78, group leader, 1968-71, asst. dir., 1971-75, dir. life scis. and bioorganic chemistry, 1975-80, dir. bioorganic chemistry, 1980-85, v.p. chemistry and life scis., 1983—. Contbr. articles to profl. jours. Am. Chem. Soc. Petroleum Research Fund fellow, 1961. Mem. Am. Soc. Pharmacology and Exptl. Therapeutics, Am. Chem. Soc., AAAS; fellow N.Y. Acad. Scis. Current Work: Development of immunoassay methodology—enantioselective antibodies; metabolism of xenobiotics, especially drugs of abuse; synthesis of steroids as contraceptives. Subspecialties: Organic chemistry; Pharmacology. Office: PO Box 12194 Research Triangle Park NC 27709

COOK, ELTON STRAUS, educator; b. Oberlin, Ohio, Dec. 24, 1909; s. Edward Monroe and Bertha (Straus) C.; m. Adelaide Elizabeth Luck, June 1, 1935; children—Edward Mark, David Charles. B.A., Oberlin Coll., 1930; Ph.D., Yale U., 1933. Cert. profl. chemist. Postdoctoral fellow Yale U., New Haven, 1933-34; head dept. organic prodn. William S. Merrell Co., Cin., 1934-37; prof. chemistry and biochemistry St. Thomas Inst., Cin., 1937—, dean, 1945—; cons. in field; chmn. Chief Acad. Officers, Greater Cin. Consortium of Colls. and U., Cin., 1977-79. Contbr. articles to profl. jours. Patentee in field. Co-discoverer pressed disc technique for infrared spectroscopy. Bd. dirs. Mariemont Town Meeting, Ohio, 1955-58; mem. Oberlin Coll. Alumni Bd., 1958-59. Recipient Diploma of Honor, First Pan Am. Cancer Cytology Congress, 1967; award, Gordon Research Conf., 1959. Mem. Am. Chem. Soc. (Cin. Chemist award 1964), Am. Inst. Chemists (hon. fellow), Ohio Inst. Chemists (pres. 1973-75), Sigma Xi, Phi Beta Kappa. Current work: Cellular growth and metabolism; antimicrobiol and antifibrinolytic compounds; antineoplastic agents. Subspecialties: Biochemistry (biology); Organic chemistry. Home: 6503 Park Ln Cincinnati OH 45206 Office: Saint Thomas Inst 1842 Madison Rd Cincinnati OH 45206

COOK, GERALD, electrical engineering educator; b. Hazard, Ky., Oct. 31, 1937; s. Rudolph Harry and Rose Irebe (Boyer) C.; m. Nancy Ann Gillispie, June 9, 1962; children—Gerald Boyer, Allan Binford. B.S., Va. Poly. Inst. & State U., 1961; M.S., MIT, 1962, Sc.D., 1965. Lectr. U. Colo., Colo. Springs, 1965-68; research assoc. and asst. prof. Air Force Acad., Colo. Springs, 1965-68; assoc. prof. U. Va., Charlottesville, 1968-73, prof., 1973-81; prof., chmn. dept. elec. engring. Vanderbilt U., Nashville, 1981-85; Earle C. Williams prof. elec. engring. George Mason U., Fairfax, Va., 1985—; cons. Melpar, Babcock & Wilcox, Philip Morris, Sverdrup, Performance Measurements Assoc. Contbr. articles to profl. jours. Served to 1st lt. USAF, 1965-68. Fellow IEEE (Centennial medal, 1984), Indsl. Electronics Soc. IEEE (sec., 1974-79, v.p., 1979-81, pres., 1981-83, editor, 1984—). Presbyterian. Current work: Modern control; automation and robotics; digital simulation. Subspecialty: Electrical engineering. Home: 10855 Weisigee Ln Oakton VA 22124 Office: George Mason Univ Computer Engring Fairfax VA 22030

COOK, JAMES HOWELL, JR., engineer, consultant; b. Anderson, S.C., Oct. 28, 1937; s. James Howell and Louise (Goss) C.; m. Gail Eugenia Baker, Mar. 28, 1960; children—Pamela Leigh, Sheri Gail, Michelle Anne. B.S.E.E., Ga. Inst. Tech., 1961; M.S.E.E., 1970. Engr. Bendix Radio, Towson, Mo., 1961-64; sr. engr. Scientific-Atlanta, Inc., 1964-68, engring. mgr., 1968-70, product line mgr., 1970-77, tech. dir. of telecommunications, 1979-80, prin. engr., 1977-84, corporate tech. staff, 1985—; cons. Ga. Tech. Research Inst., Atlanta, 1980-84 Chmn. earth sta. working group FCC Adv. Com. on Reduced Satellite Spacing, 1985. Author: (with others) Microwave Antenna Measurements, 1970, Antenna Engineering Handbook, 1984, Electronic Communications Applications Handbook, 1985. Contbr. articles to profl. jours. Mem. IEEE (sr. mem.), Old Crows Assn., Am. Inst. of Aero. and Astronautics. Methodist. Current work: Design of antennas, satellite communication system design and analysis, radar subsystem design, microwave circuitry, millimeter wave antennas, antomatic tracking system design and analysis, electronic warfare systems. Subspecialty: Telecommunications. Home: 4641 Westhampton Dr Tucker GA 30084 Office: Scientific-Atlanta 3845 Pleasantdale Rd Atlanta GA 30340

COOK, JOHN W., research astrophysicist; b. Selma, Ala., Oct. 25, 1946; s. John W. and Veda Ray (McInturff) C. B.S., M.I.T., 1967; M.A., CCNY, 1970; Ph.D., Dartmouth Coll., 1976. Skylab Workshop postdoctoral astrophysicist High Altitude Obs., Washington, 1976-78; resident Naval Research Lab., Washington, 1976-78; research astrophysicist solar physics br. Space Sci. Div. Naval Research Lab., 1978—. Contbr. writings in field to profl. publs. Served with U.S. Army, 1969-71. Mem. Am. Phys. Soc., Am. Astron. Soc. (and solar div.), Internat. Astron. Union. Current Work: Physics of solar atmosphere; analysis of high spatial and spectral resolution ultraviolet spectra; solar UV variability; cool stars. Subspecialty: Solar physics. Office: Code 4163 Naval Research Lab Washington DC 20375

COOK, JOSEPH MARION, mathematician; b. Oak Park, Ill., Feb. 18, 1924; s. Morris Henry and Francis Lillian (Lynch) C.; m. Beryl Smith, Sept. 5, 1955; children—Karen Jo, Marian Francis, Gregory John. B.S., U. Ill., 1947, M.S., 1948; Ph.D., U. Chgo., 1951. Instr., Johns Hopkins U., 1951-52; postdoctoral fellow Harvard U., 1952-53; assoc. mathematician Argonne Nat. Lab., Ill., 1953-60; lectr. U. Calif.-Berkeley, 1960-61; sr. mathematician Argonne Nat. Lab, 1961—; tchr. Ill. Inst. Tech., Chgo., 1984—; cons. in field. Contbr. article to profl. jours. and chpts. to books. Served to 1st lt. USAF, 1943-46, ETO. Decorated Air medal with one oak leaf cluster. Mem. Am. Math. Soc., Soc. Indsl. and Applied Math. Current work: Research mathematical physics and engineering systems analysis. Subspecialties: Applied mathematics; Software engineering. Home: 5929 Osage Ave Downers Grove IL 60516 Office: Argonne Nat Lab 9700 S Cass Ave Argonne IL 60439

COOK, LEE MELBOURNE, research scientist; b. Cheyenne, Wyo., July 10, 1952; s. Thomas Melbourne and Arlene (Huss) C. B.A., Grinnell Coll., 1974. Research technician Georgetown U. Med. Sch., Washington, 1974-75, vitreous state lab. Catholic U., Washington, 1975-77; chemist Canstar Communications Ltd., Montreal, Can., 1977-79; lab. engr. Schott Glass Techs., Inc., Duryea, Pa., 1978-80, research scientist, 1980—. Contbr. articles to profl. jours. Patentee in field. Bd. trustees West Pittston Free Library, 1984. Mem. Am. Ceramic Soc. Current work: Glass corrosion, surface chemistry, design of optical glasses, active and passive laser component development, phosphate glasses, fluorophosphate glasses. Subspecialties: Ceramics; Ceramic engineering. Office: Schott Glass Technologies Inc 400 York Ave Duryea PA 18642

COOK, MAURICE GAYLE, conservation educator; b. Frankfort, Ky., Dec. 26, 1931; s. Price Cash and Evelyn (Moore) C.; m. Eva Nancy Blalock, Aug. 27, 1966; 1 child, Stephen Price. B.S., U. Ky., 1957, M.S., 1959; Ph.D., Va. Poly. Inst., 1961. Asst. prof. N.C. State U., Raleigh, 1961-65, assoc. prof., 1965-70, prof. resource conservation, 1970—; cons. Fgn. Mission Bd. So. Bapt. Conv., Richmond, Va., 1975—; dir. Div. Soil and Water Conservation, N.C. Dept. Natural Resources, Raleigh, 1982-84. Author: Concepts in Soil Science, 1974; also articles. Recipient Alumni Disting. Prof. award N.C. State U., 1975, Disting. Service award Soil Sci. Soc. N.C., 1981. Fellow Nat. Assn. Colls. and Tchrs. Agr. (Regional award 1979, Disting. Tchr. award 1980); mem. Soil Conservation Soc. Am. (v.p. 1984, pres. elect 1985, Outstanding Service award 1983). Democrat. Baptist. Current work: Promotion soil and water conservation programs in N.C.; development and execution programs in non-point source pollution; watershed planning. Subspecialties: Resource conservation; Resource management. Home: 3458 Leonard St Raleigh NC 27607 Office: Dept Soil Sci NC State Univ Box 7619 Raleigh NC 27695-7619

COOK, STEPHEN ARTHUR, computer science educator; b. Buffalo, Dec. 14, 1939; s. Gerhard Albert and Lura Harriet (Lincoln) C.; m. Linda Marie Craddock, Mar. 5, 1968; children—Gordon James, James Alexander. B.S., U. Mich., 1961; S.M., Harvard U., 1962, Ph.D., 1966. Asst. prof. U. Calif.-Berkeley, 1970; assoc. prof. U. Toronto, Ont., Can., 1970-75, prof., 1975—. E.W.R. Staecie Meml. fellow, 1977-78; Killam Found. fellow, 1982-83. Recipient A.M. Turing award Assn. for Computing Machinery, 1982. Fellow Royal Soc. Can.; mem. Nat. Acad. Scis., Assn. for Symbolic Logic (exec. com. 1984—). Current work: Research in computational complexity and theory of parallel computation. Subspecialty: Theoretical computer science. Office: Dept Computer Sci U Toronto Toronto ON M5S 1A4 Canada

COOK, STUART DONALD, physician, educator; b. Boston, Oct. 23, 1936; s. Martius and Nina (Schwartzman) C.; m. Josepha Emdin, June 26, 1960; children—Andrew, Peter, Jonathan. A.B., Brandeis U., 1957; M.S., U. Vt., 1959, M.D., 1962. Diplomate: Am. Bd. Psychiatry and Neurology. Intern Upstate Med. Center, Syracuse, N.Y., 1962-63, resident in neurology, 1965-67, chief resident, 1967-68; instr. dept. neurology Albert Einstein Coll. Medicine, Bronx, N.Y., 1968-69; asst. prof. neurology Coll. Physician and Surgeons, Columbia U., 1969-71; prof. medicine N.J. Med. Sch., Newark, 1971—, chmn. dept. neuroscis., 1972—; chief neurology service VA Med. Center, East Orange, N.J., 1971—; vis. scientist div. virology Nat. Inst. Med. Research, London, 1977-78; cons. HEW. Contbr. articles to profl. jours. Served with USN, 1963-65. Mem. Am. Acad. Neurology (S. Weir Mitchell award 1968), Am. Assn. Neuropathologists, AAUP, Am. Fedn. Clin. Research, Assn. Univ Profs. Neurology, Harvey Soc., N.Y. Acad. Sci., Sigma Xi, Alpha Omega Alpha. Current Work: Epidemiology, virology, immunology of multiple sclerosis, inflammatory neuropathics. Subspecialties: Neurology; Neuroimmunology. Home: 26 Dogwood Dr Morristown NJ 07960 Office: VA Med Center East Orange NJ 07019

COOKSON, ALBERT ERNEST, telecommunications co. exec.; b. Needham, Mass., Oct. 30, 1921; s. Willard B. and Sarah Jane (Jack) C.; m. Constance J. Buckley, Sept. 10, 1949; children—Constance J., William B. B.E.E., Northeastern U., 1943; M.E.E., Mass. Inst. Tech., 1951; Sc.D., Gordon Coll., 1974. Group leader Research Lab. Electronics, Mass. Inst. Tech., 1947-51; lab. dir. ITT Fed. Labs., Nutley, N.J., 1951-59; v.p., dir. operations ITT Fed. Labs. (Internat. Elec. Corp. div.), Paramus, N.J., 1959-62; pres. ITT Intelcom, Falls Church, Va., 1962-65; dep. gen. tech. dir. Internat. Tel. and Tel. Corp., N.Y.C., 1965-66, v.p., tech. dir., 1966-68, sr. v.p., gen. tech. dir., 1968—; chmn. bd. ITT Interplan; dir. Internat. Standard Electric, ITT Industries.; Mem. Def. Communications Satellite Panel; adviser research and engring. on def. communications satellite systems Dept. Def.; mem. indsl. panel sci. and tech. NSF.; Mem. Fairfax County Econ. and Indsl. Devel. Com., 1962-65; mem. nat. council Northeastern U.; mem. pride com. U. Hartford, 1973-76; elec. engring./computer adv. bd. Mass. Inst. Tech., 1977—. Served with USNR, 1943-46. Fellow IEEE; mem. Armed Forces Communications and Electronics Assn., Am. Mgmt. Assn., Am. Inst. Aeros. and Astronautics, Electronic Industries Assn., Sigma Xi, Tau Beta Pi. Patentee frequency search and track system. Subspecialty: Electrical engineering. Home: 2 Baywater Dr Darien CT 06820 Office: 320 Park Ave New York NY 10022

COOL, RODNEY LEE, physicist, educator; b. Platte, S.D., Mar. 8, 1920; s. George E. and Muriel (Post) C.; m. Margaret E. MacMillan, June 21, 1949; children: Ellen, John, Mary Lee, Adrienne. B.S., U. S.D., 1942; M.A., Harvard U., 1947, Ph.D., 1949. Research physicist Brookhaven Nat. Lab., Upton, L.I., N.Y., 1949-59, dep. chmn. high energy physics, 1960-64, asst. dir. high energy physics, 1964-66, asso. dir., 1966-70, sec. high energy adv. com., 1960-67, chmn., 1967-70; prof. exptl. high energy physics Rockefeller U., N.Y.C., 1970—; Mem. policy com. Stanford Linear Accelerator Center, 1962-67, 76-80; mem. Asso. Univs. High Energy Panel, Asso. Univs., Inc., 1963-70; mem. Walker panel, com. on sci. and pub. policy Nat. Acad. Sci., 1964; mem. Princeton-Pa. Accelerator Sci. Com., 1966-68; mem. high energy physics adv. panel AEC, 1967-70; chmn. physics adv. com. Nat. Accelerator Lab., 1967-70; mem. adv. panel for physics NSF, 1970-73; sci. asso. European Center Nuclear Research, 1973—; trustee Univs. Research Assn., 1977-83; mem. rev. com. Argonne Univs. Assn., 1978-80. Co-editor: Advances in Particle Physics, vols. I and II, 1968; contbr. articles to profl. jours. Served to maj., Signal Corps AUS, 1942-46. Decorated Bronze Star medal. Fellow Am. Phys. Soc. (program cons. div. particles and fields 1968-70); mem. Nat. Acad. Scis., Phi Beta Kappa, Sigma Xi. Current Work: Research in experimental high energy particle physics. Subspecialty: Particle physics. Home: 450 E 63d St New York NY 10021 Office: Rockefeller University New York NY 10021

COOLEY, DONALD WAYNE, electrical engineer, researcher, physicist; b. Kirksville, Mo., July 28, 1952; s. Elmo Franklin and Deloris Coleen (Bowers) C.; m. Yolanda A. Florencio, Feb. 28, 1985. B.A. in Physics, U. Colo., 1974, M.S., 1976, M.E.E., 1981. Sr. research engr., SRI Internat., Menlo Park, Calif., 1981—. Gates Rubber Co. scholar, 1970-74. Mem. Am. Phys. Soc., IEEE, Soc. Indsl. and Applied Math., Phi Beta Kappa, Sigma Pi Sigma. Current work: Digital signal processing, modern spectral analysis, adaptive filters, mathematical modeling, numerical analysis. Subspecialties: Electrical engineering; Numerical analysis (computer science). Home: 1730 Halford Ave #154 Santa Clara CA 95051 Office: SRI Internat 333 Ravenswood Ave Menlo Park CA 94025

COOMBE, JOHN RAYMOND, engineering executive; b. Trenton, N.J., Sept. 26, 1926; s. John Raymond and Elizabeth (Tholander) C.; m. Kathleen Marie Jennings, Feb. 22, 1958; children: John, Mary, Elizabeth, James. B.A., Washington and Jefferson U., 1951. Engr. Gen. Electric Co., Schenectady, 1951-59; physicist Tech. Ops., Burlington, Mass., 1959-60; supr. Alco Products, Schenectady, 1960-62; mgr. Westinghouse Co., Pitts., 1962-72; asst. chief licensing Stone & Webster, Boston, 1972—. Mem. Am. Nuclear Soc. (nat. program com., standards com.); gen. chmn. internat. meeting on severe accident eval., tech. program chmn. nat. meeting, tech. program com. internat. meeting reactor safety). Patentee in field. Current Work: Power plant and advanced concept licensing activities. Subspecialties: Nuclear engineering; Cryogenics. Office: Stone & Webster 245 Summer St Boston MA 02107

COOMBS, CLYDE HAMILTON, psychologist, educator; b. Paterson, N.J., July 22, 1912; s. Clyde and Mildred (Horandt) C.; m. Lolagene Convis, Sept. 1, 1939; children: Steven, Douglas. A.B., U. Calif., Berkeley, 1935, M.A., 1937; Ph.D., U. Chgo., 1941; D.S.S. (hon.), U. Leiden, Netherlands, 1975. Instr. psychology U. Chgo., 1939-41, research asso. biophysics, 1939-41; research psychologist Adj. Gen.'s Office, War Dept., 1941-43; mem. faculty dept. psychology U. Mich., Ann Arbor, 1947—, Disting. Univ. prof., 1978—; vis. prof. Harvard U., Boston, 1948-49; vis. research prof. U. Amsterdam, Netherlands, 1955-56; cons. Dept. Army, 1957-59; lecture tour various univs. in, Europe, 1964-65; vis. prof. U. Colo., Boulder, 1965, U. Wash., Seattle, 1967; cons. VA Hosp., Ann Arbor, 1968-69; vis. prof. U. Western Australia, 1969, Central U. Venezuela, 1970, Inst. Psychology, Academia Sinica, Beijing, China, 1981; mem. U.S.-USSR Interacad. seminar math. psychology, Tbilisi, Russia, 1979; vis. research scholar U. London, 1978; mem. com. biometry and epidemiology NIH, 1971. Author: (with R.M. Thrall and R.C. Davis) Decision Processes, 1954, (with R.C. Kao) Nonmetric Factor Analysis, 1955, A Theory of Data, 1964, (with R.M. Dawes and A. Tversky) Mathematical Psychology: An Elementary Introduction, 1970; cons. editor: Psychol. Rev, 1953-58; book rev. editor: Psychometrics, 1951-54. Served from capt. to maj. U.S. Army, 1943-46. Decorated Legion of Merit; recipient Fulbright award, 1955-56, Fulbright-Hayes award, 1975; named Disting. Sr. Faculty lectr. U. Mich., 1980. Fellow Am. Psychol. Assn. (pres. div. 5 1958-59, chmn. bd. sci. affairs 1960-62), Am. Acad. Arts and Scis., Am. Statis. Assn. (hon.); mem. Soc. Math. Psychology (pres. 1977-78), Psychometric Soc. (pres. 1955-56), Nat. Acad. Scis., Psychol. Assn. Spain (hon.). Home: 3419 Daleview Dr Ann Arbor MI 48103 Office: 580 Union Dr Dept Psychology Univ Mich Ann Arbor MI 48109

COONEY, MARION KATHLEEN, educator; b. Mercedes, Tex., Feb. 2, 1920; d. Albert John and Marie (Jansen) C. B.A., Coll. St. Benedict, 1939; M.S., U. Minn., 1953, Ph.D., 1962. Med. technologist Fairview Hosp., Mpls., 1940-43; bacteriologist Minn. Dept. Health, Mpls., 1943-45, bacteriologist-/virologist, 1945-53, chief, lab. sect. of virus and rickettsial diseases, 1953-65; asst. prof. dept. preventive medicine U. Wash., Seattle, 1966-70, asst. prof. dept. pathobiology, 1970-72, asso. prof., 1972-78, prof., 1978-83, prof. emeritus, 1983—. Contbr. articles in field to profl. jours. Mem. Am. Soc. Microbiology, Am. Assn. Immunologists, Soc. Exptl. Biology and Medicine, Am. Public Health Assn., N.Y. Acad. Sci. Democrat. Roman Catholic. Current Work: Researcher, tchr. med. virology, infectious disease epidemiology and methodology. Subspecialties: Virology (medicine); Infectious diseases. Office: University of Washington F262C Health Sciences Bldg Seattle WA 98195

COONS, WILLIAM RAY, JR., research laboratories administrator, chemical engineer; b. Gonzalez, Tex., Sept. 1, 1930; s. Willie Ray and Gehla Adelaid (Heye) C.; m. Ola Lee Currie, June 29, 1957; children—Lynda Lee, Edward Ray (dec.). B.S., U. Tex.-Austin, 1952. Registered profl. engr., Tex. Chem. engr. Port Arthur Research Labs., Texaco Inc., Tex., 1955—, sr. project chem. engr., 1967, asst. supr., 1968, supr., 1969-81, asst. mgr., 1981-83, mgr., 1983—. Patentee grease manufacture and refinery fuels processing. Precinct chmn. Republican Party Tex., Port Arthur, 1960-69; Served to lt. (j.g.) USN, 1952-55, comdr. Res. ret. Mem. Am. Inst. Chem. Engrs. Methodist. Club: Port Arthur Rotary. Current work: Manage petroleum research facility involved in process and product development. Subspecialty: Petroleum engineering. Office: Texaco USA PO Box 1608 Port Arthur TX 77641

COONTS, HARVEY LEE, petroleum engr.; b. Weslaco, Tex., Mar. 8, 1934; s. Charles Francis and Ruth Jean (Smith) C.; m. Rosa Lee Knowles, Apr. 26, 1955; children: Diana, Joy, Elaine, Janice. B.S. in Petroleum and Natural Gas Engring, Tex. A&I U., 1958. Registered profl. engr., Colo., Tex., Calif. Petroleum engr. Findlay Engring., Alice, Tex., 1958-59; state petroleum engr. State of Utah, Salt Lake City, 1959-64; sr. petroleum engr. Sunset Internat., Beverly Hills, Calif., 1964-66; staff petroleum engr. Union Pacific R.R., Wilmington, Calif., 1966-70; pres. Coonts Petroleum Engring., Inc., Littleton, Colo., 1970—. Contbr. articles to profl. jours. Mem. Soc. Petroleum Engrs., AIME. Current Work: Consulting in petroleum engineering. Subspecialty: Petroleum engineering.

COOPER, ALAN DOUGLAS, chemist, educator; b. Lynn, Mass., Apr. 4, 1942; s. Everett James and Helen Eunice (Marble) C.; m. Susan Marie Brown, Sept. 10, 1967; children: Deborah, Stephen, Christina. B.S. in Chemistry, Tufts U., 1964; A.M., Boston U., 1966, Ph.D., 1968. Postdoctoral fellow in biochemistry Johns Hopkins U., Balt., 1968-70; vis. scientist Worcester Found. for Exptl. Biology, 1980; assoc. prof. chemistry Worcester (Mass.) State Coll., 1970-83, prof. chemistry, 1983—. Contbr. articles on chemistry to profl. jours. Mem. Town Meeting, Auburn, Mass., 1974-84. NSF grantee, 1979-80. Mem. Am. Chem. Soc. (past chmn. central Mass. sect.), AAAS, New Eng. Assn. Chemistry Tchrs., Beta Beta Beta. Democrat. Roman Catholic. Current Work: Nucleotide sequences of actin genes, recombinant DNA, evolution of actin genes, origins of life, synthesis and characterization of proteinoids, eukaryotic DNA replication. Subspecialties: Biochemistry (biology); Biophysical chemistry. Office: Worcester State Coll Worcester MA 01602

COOPER, ARTHUR WELLS, forester, educator, researcher; b. Washington, Aug. 15, 1931; s. Gustav Arthur and Josephine Phelps (Wells) C.; m. Jean Farnsworth, Aug. 30, 1953; children: Paul Arthur, Roy Alan. B.A., Colgate U., 1953, M.A., 1955; Ph.D., U. Mich., 1958. Asst. prof. N.C. State U., Raleigh, 1958-63, assoc. prof., 1963-68, prof. botany, 1968-71, prof. forestry, 1976-80, head dept. forestry, 1980—; dep. dir. Dept. Conservation and Devel. State of N.C., Raleigh, 1971; asst. sec. Dept. Natural and Econ. Resources, 1971-76; trustee N.C. Nature Conservancy, 1977—; chmn. bd. trustees Inst. Ecology, Washington, 1982-84. Mem. N.C. Coastal Resources Commn., Raleigh, 1976—; chmn. com. scientists U.S. Forest Service, Washington, 1977-79, 82. Recipient Conservation award Am. Motors, 1972; Environ. award Sol Feinstone, Syracuse, N.Y., 1982. Fellow AAAS; mem. Ecol. Soc. Am. (pres. 1981, Disting. Service award 1984), N.C. Acad. Sci. (pres. 1978-79), Soc. Am. Foresters (chmn. N.C. div. 1983-84). Democrat. Current Work: Forest ecology, application of ecol principles to renewable resource mgmt. Subspecialties: Forestry; Ecology (environmental science). Home: 719 Runnymede Rd Raleigh NC 27607 Office: Dept Forestry NC State U Raleigh NC 27695-8002

COOPER, CHARLES DEWEY, physics educator; b. Whittier, N.C., Jan. 11, 1924; s. Grady T. and Mary L. (Howell) C.; m. Corrie W. Johnson, Dec. 21, 1946; children: Norma, Claire, Edward. B.S., Berry Coll., 1944; M.A., Duke U., 1948, Ph.D., 1950. Asst. prof. physics U. Ga., 1950-56, assoc. prof., 1956-61, prof., 1961—; research fellow Harvard U., 1954-55; cons. Oak Ridge Nat. Lab. Contbr. articles to profl. pubs. Served with USN, 1944-46. Recipient Micheal research award U. Ga., 1958, IR 100 award, 1983. Mem. Am. Phys. Soc., Am. Assn. Physics Tchrs., Sigma Xi. Current Work: Multiphoton ionization and angular distribution of photoelectrons resulting from laser light interaction with matter. Subspecialties: Atomic and molecular physics; Laser spectroscopy. Home: 4235 Barnett Shoals Rd Athens GA 30605 Office: Physics Dept U G Athens GA 30602

COOPER, DAVID YOUNG, biochemist, pharmacologist, science historian; b. Henderson, N.C., Aug. 14, 1924; s. James and Frances (Chatham) C.; m. Cynthia Laughlin, Aug. 6, 1955; children: Lucy, Allison. B.S., U. N.C., 1946; M.D., U. Pa., 1948. Diplomate: Am. Bd. Surgery. Intern Hosp. U. Pa., Phila., 1948-49, resident in surgery, 1952-57; asst. prof. U. Pa. Med. Sch., Phila., 1957-60, assoc. prof., 1960-68, prof., 1968—. Contbr. articles to profl. jours. Served in USN, 1943-46, 49-51. Mem. Am. Physiol. Soc., Am. Soc. Pharmacology and Exptl. Therapeutics, Am. Soc. Biol. Chemistry, Endocrine Soc., Phila. Coll. Physicians, Sigma Xi, others. Episcopalian. Club: Racquet (Phila.). Current Work: Biochemical pharmacology; chemical carcinogenesis; experimental microsurgery. Subspecialties: Biochemistry (medicine); Toxicology (medicine). Office: U Pa Med Sch 36th and Spruce Sts Philadelphia PA 19104

COOPER, EDWARD SAWYER, internal medicine educator, consultant; b. Columbia, S.C., Dec. 11, 1926; s. Henry Howard and Ada Crosland (Sawyer) C.; m. Jean Marie Wilder, Dec. 2, 1951; children: Lisa Marie Cooper Hudgins, Edward Sawyer, Jan Ada, Charles Wilder. A.B., Lincoln U., Pa., 1946; M.D., Meharry Med. Coll., Nashville, 1949; M.S., U. Pa., 1972. Diplomate: Nat. Bd. Med. Examiners, Am. Bd. Internal Medicine. Intern Phila. Gen. Hosp., 1949-51, resident in medicine, 1951-54, NIH fellow in cardiology, 1956-57, pres. med. staff, 1969-71; co-dir. Phila. Gen. Hosp. (Stroke Research Ctr.), 1968-74, chief of med. service, 1973-76; prof. medicine U. Pa., 1973—; dir. Blue Cross of Greater Phila., 1975—; adv. bd. Hypertension Detection and Followup Program, NIH, 1974—. Trustee Am. Found. Negro Affairs, 1969—. Served to capt. USAF, 1954-56. Fellow ACP (govs. adv. bd.), Phila. Coll. Physicians (mem. council), Am. Coll. Chest Physicians; mem. Am. Heart Assn. (chmn., dir.), Alpha Omega Alpha. Democrat. Methodist. Current Work: Stroke and hypertension. Subspecialty: Internal medicine. Home: 6710 Lincoln Dr Philadelphia PA 19119 Office: University of Pennsylvania Hospital 3400 Spruce St Philadelphia PA 19119

COOPER, FRANKLIN SEANEY, speech scientist; b. Robinson, Ill., Apr. 29, 1908; s. Frank A. and Myrtle Alma (Seaney) C.; m. Frances Edith Clem, Feb. 14, 1935; children: Robert Craig, Alan Kent. B.S. in Engring. Physics, U. Ill., 1931; Ph.D. in Physics, Mass. Inst. Tech., 1936; D.Sc. (hon.), Yale U., 1976. Teaching and research asst. U. Ill., 1931-34, Mass. Inst. Tech., 1934-36; research engr. Gen. Electric Research Labs., 1936-39; asso. research dir. Haskins Labs., New Haven, 1939-55, 75—, pres., research dir., 1955-75; liaison officer, then sr. liaison officer OSRD, 1941-46; vis. com. dept. modern langs. Mass. Inst. Tech., 1949-65; adv. com. research div. Coll. Engring., N.Y. U., 1949-65; bd. dirs. Center Applied Linguistics, 1968-74; adj. prof. phonetics Columbia U., 1955-65; adj. prof. linguistics U. Conn., 1969-80, vis. prof., 1980—; sr. research asso. linguistics Yale U., 1970-76; fellow Calhoun Coll., 1971-80, asso. fellow, 1980—; adv. panel on White House tapes U.S. Dist. Ct. D.C., 1973-74; chmn. communicative scis. interdisciplinary cluster President's Biomed. Research Panel, 1975; mem. adv. council Nat. Inst. for Neurol. and Communicative Disorders and Stroke, NIH, 1978-81. Author papers, book chpts. speech processing, perception and prodn., aids for blind and deaf, biophysics, high-voltage/high vacuum engring. Recipient Presdl. Certificate of Merit, 1948; honors of assn. Am. Speech and Hearing Assn., 1966; Warren medal Soc. Exptl. Psychology, 1975; Fletcher-Stevens award Brigham Young U., 1977. Fellow IEEE (Pioneer award speech communication 1972), Acoustical Soc. Am. (Silver medal speech communication 1975); mem. Nat. Acad. Engring., Sigma Xi. Congregationalist. Club: Cosmos (Washington). Current Work: Speech science; production and perception of speech; speech analysis and synthesis by computer; experimental linguistics. Subspecialties: Psychophysics; Automated language processing. Home: 5 Parsell Ln Westport CT 06880 Office: 270 Crown St New Haven CT 06511

COOPER, GEOFFREY MITCHELL, molecular biologist; b. Los Angeles, June 16, 1948; B.S., MIT, 1969; Ph.D., U. Miami, 1973. Fellow in virology McArdle Lab. Cancer Research, U. Wis.-Madison, 1973-75; asst. prof., assoc. prof. prof. Harvard U. Med. Sch., 1975—. Recipient U.S. Stell award Nat. Acad. Scis., 1984. Subspecialty: Molecular biology. Office: Dana-Farber Cancer Inst Harvard U Med Sch 44 Binney St Boston MA 02115*

COOPER, HERBERT ASEL, medical educator, pediatric hematologist, experimental pathologist; b. Grand Junction, Colo., Feb. 21, 1938; s. Herbert I. and Inez F. (Samples) C.; m. Karen R. Groe, June 7, 1963; children: Christopher Scott, Kevin Andrew. B.A. in Chemistry, U. Kans., 1960, M.D., 1964. Diplomate: Am. Bd. Pediatrics. Intern Charles T. Miller Hosp., also Children's Hosp., St. Paul, 1965; resident in pediatrics, 1965-67; in pediatric hematology/oncology Mayo Clinic, Rochester, Minn., 1969-71; postdoctoral fellow U. N.C., Chapel Hill, 1971-74, asst. prof. pathology and pediatrics, 1974-78, assoc. prof., 1978-85, prof., 1985—; vis. research prof. Theodor Kocher Inst., Bern, Switzerland, 1977-78; asst. med. dir. clin. coagulation lab. dept. hosp. labs. N.C. Meml. Hosp., Chapel Hill, 1974-78, assoc. dir. share lab. service, 1980-84; mem. exec. com. Specialized Center for Research Hemostasis and Thrombosis, Chapel Hill, 1980-84, dir. div. pediatric hematology/oncology, 1985—; sci. advisor Comprehensive Hemophilia Diagnostic and Treatment Center, Chapel Hill, 1975—; cons. Chapel Hill Bd. Edn. Contbr. to numerous publs. in field. Mem. and sec. exec. bd. Chapel Hill United Fund. NIH Research Career Devel. awardee, 1975-80. Mem. Am. Assn. Pathologists, Soc. for Pediatric Research, Am. Soc. Hematology, Internat. Soc. Hemostasis and Thrombosis, Orange County Med. Soc. Lutheran. Current Work: Hemostasis and thrombosis; structure function of Factor VIII; Hemophilia A and von Willebrand's disease; biochemistry of blood coagulation; platelets, platelet membrane receptors. Subspecialties: Biochemistry (medicine); Hematology. Home: 111 Springhill Forest Chapel Hill NC 27514Office: Department Pediatrics UNC Sch of Medicine 509 Clin Scis Bldg 229-H Chapel Hill NC 27514

COOPER, (HOWARD) GORDON, computer peripheral co. exec., researcher; b. Joliet, Ill., Feb. 16, 1927; s. Howard Gordon and Jennie (Paalberg) C.; m. Lacy Ellen Underwood, June 2, 1953; children: Mary, John. Student, Ill. Inst. Tech., 1943-45; B.S., U. Ill., 1949, M.S., 1950, Ph.D., 1954. Mem. tech. staff Bell Telephone Labs., Murray Hill, N.J., 1954-62, Whippany, N.J., 1962-70; mgr. corp. research Recognition Equipment Inc., Dallas, 1970—. Contbr. articles to profl. jours. Mem. U.S. Senatorial Bus. Adv. Com., 1980—; mem. Republican Presdl. Task Force, 1981. Served with USN, 1945-46. Mem. Optical Soc. Am., Pattern Recognition Soc., Am. Phys. Soc., IEEE, World Future Soc., Optical Soc. Tex., Sigma Xi, Tau Beta Pi, Sigma Tau. Methodist. Club: Brookhaven. Patentee in field. Current Work: Optical scanning, image processing, pattern recognition, image displays, info. processing, electronic printing, computer systems, robotics. Subspecialties: Graphics, image processing, and pattern recognition; Computer engineering. Home: 1005 Sierra Pl Richardson TX 75080 Office: PO Box 222307 Dallas TX 75222

COOPER, JACK ROSS, pharmacologist; b. Ottawa, Ont., Can., July 26, 1924; s. Harry and Jean (Levine) C.; m. Helen Achbar, Aug. 14, 1951; children: Marilyn, Sheila, Nancy. B.A., Queen's U., 1948; M.A., George Washington U., 1952, Ph.D., 1954. Asst. prof. pharmacology Yale U. Sch. Medicine, 1958-63, asso. prof., 1963-71, prof., 1971—; Mem. adv. bd. U.S.-Israel Binat. Sci. Found. Editorial bd.: Jour. Neurochemistry. Served with RCAF, 1945. Mem. Am. Soc. Pharmacology and Exptl. Therapeutics, Internat. Soc. Neurochemistry., Soc. Neurosci. Current Work: Cholinergic mechanisms; thiamin in nervous tissue. Subspecialties: Molecular pharmacology; Neurochemistry. Home: 11 Jenick Ln Woodbridge CT 06525 Office: 333 Cedar St New Haven CT 06510

COOPER, JAMES DANIEL, civil engineer, consultant; b. San Francisco, Mar. 19, 1942; s. James Waite and Zebulon (Ballard) C.; m. Susan Sauvan Low, June 25, 1966; children—James John, Karen Dorthea. B.S. in Civil Engring., Syracuse U., 1965, M.S. in Civil Engring., 1968. Registered profl. engr., D.C. Instr., Syracuse U., N.Y., 1971-72; Presdl. intern NSF/FHWA, McLean, Va., 1972-73; structural research engr. Fed. Hwy Adminstrn. McLean, 1973-82, supervisory structural engr., 1982-84; civil engr. Def. Nuclear Agy., Alexandria, Va., 1984—; cons. UN, Geneva, 1983—, orgns. on earthquake design transp. structures, 1976—. Editor: Lifeline Earthquake Engineering: Performance, Design and Construction, 1984; contbr. articles to engring. jours. Mem. editorial bd. Jour. Civil Engring. Design, 1978-81. Recipient Superior Achievement award Fed. Hwy. Adminstrn., 1981, Spl. Commendations and Outstanding Performance awards. Mem. ASCE, Earthquake Engring. Research Inst., Sigma Xi. Club: Difficult Run Pony (Herndon, Va.) (treas. 1982—). Current work: Responsible for managing U.S. research program, conducting research and developing current national specification on earthquake design of highway bridges; pursuing topics in lifeline earthquake engineering and structural dynamics. Subspecialties: Structural engineering; Civil engineering. Home: 116 N Johnson Rd Sterling VA 22170

COOPER, LEON N., physicist, educator; b. N.Y.C., Feb. 28, 1930; s. Irving and Anna (Zola) C.; m. Kay Anne Allard, May 18, 1969; children: Kathleen Ann, Coralie Lauren. A.B., Columbia U., 1951, A.M., 1953, Ph.D., 1954, D.Sc., 1973; D.Sc. hon. degrees; D.Sc., U. Sussex, Eng., 1973, U. Ill., 1974, Brown U., 1974, Gustavus Adolphus Coll., 1975, Ohio State U., 1976, U. Pierre et Marie Curie, Paris, 1977. NSF postdoctoral fellow, mem. Inst. for Advanced Study, 1954-55; research assoc. U. Ill., 1955-57; asst. prof. Ohio State U., 1957-58; assoc. prof. Brown U., Providence, 1958-62, prof., 1962-66, Henry Ledyard Goddard U. prof., 1966-74, Thomas J. Watson Sr. prof. sci., 1974—; co-dir. Center for Neural Sci.; lectr. Summer Sch., Varenna, Italy, 1955; vis. prof. Brandeis Summer Inst., 1959, Bergen Internat. Sch. Physics, Norway, 1961, Scuola Internatzionali Di Fisica, Erice, Italy, 1965, L'Ecole Normal Supèrieure, Centre Universitaire Internationale, Paris, 1966, Cargèse Summer Sch., 1966; cons. indsl., ednl. orgns. Author: Introduction to The Meaning and Structure of Phsyics, 1968; Contbr. articles to profl. jours. Alfred P. Sloan Found. research fellow, 1959-66; John Simon Guggenheim Meml. Found. fellow, 1965-66; Recipient Comstock prize Nat. Acad. Scis., 1968, Nobel prize, 1972. Fellow Am. Phys. Soc., Am. Acad. Arts and Scis.; mem. Am. Philos. Soc., Nat. Acad. Scis., Phi Beta Kappa, Sigma Xi. Subspecialty: Theoretical physics. Office: Brown U Providence RI 02912*

COOPER, LOUIS ZUCKER, physician, virologist; b. Albany, Ga., Dec. 25, 1931; s. Jacob Harrison and Cecile (Berman) C.; m. Janet Clissold, Aug. 27, 1955 (div.); children—Edward, Cecile, Jacob, Elizabeth; m. Madeline Winegar, June 18, 1976. B.S., Yale U., 1954, M.D., 1957. Intern, Mass. Meml. Hosp. and Boston VA Hosp., 1957-58, resident, 1958-59, fellow, 1961-64; instr. medicine Tufts-New Eng. Med. Ctr., Boston, 1964; instr. medicine NYU, N.Y.C., 1964-65, asst. prof. pediatrics, 1965-66, assoc. prof. pediatrics, 1969-73; prof. pediatrics Coll. Physicians and Surgeons of Columbia U., N.Y.C., 1973—; dir. rubella project NYU-Bellevue Hosp. Ctr., N.Y.C., 1964-73; dir. pediatrics Roosevelt Hosp., N.Y.C., 1973-80, St. Luke's-Roosevelt Hosp. Ctr., 1980—. Contbr. chpts. to books and articles to profl. jours. Served to capt. USAF, 1959-61. Fellow Am. Acad. Pediatrics; mem. Am. Pediatric Soc., Am. Soc. Virology, Infectious Disease Soc. Am., Soc. Pediatric Research. Democrat. Jewish. Current work: AIDS, virology, vaccines, rubella, congenital infections. Subspecialties: Pediatrics; Virology (medicine). Office: St Luke's Roosevelt Hosp Ctr Amsterdam Ave at 114th St New York NY 10025

COOPER, REGINALD RUDYARD, orthopaedic surgeon, educator; b. Elkins, W.Va., Jan. 6, 1932; s. Eston H. and Kathryn (Wyatt) C.; m. Jacqueline Smith, Aug. 22, 1954; children—Pamela Ann, Douglas Mark, Christopher Scott, Jeffrey Michael. B.A. with honors, W.Va. U., 1952, B.S., 1953; M.D., Med. Coll. Va., 1955; M.S., U. Iowa, 1960. Diplomate: Am. Bd. Orthopedic Surgeons (examiner 1968—). Orthopedic surgeon U.S. Naval Hosp., Pensacola, Fla., 1960-62; assoc. in orthopedics U. Iowa Coll. Medicine, Iowa City, 1962-65, asst. prof. orthopaedics, 1965-68, assoc. prof. orthopedics, 1968-71, prof. orthopedics, 1971—, chmn. orthopedics, 1973—; research fellow orthopedic surgery Johns Hopkins Hosp., Balt., 1964-65; exchange fellow to Britain for Am. Orthopedic Assn., 1969. Trustee Nat. Easter Seals Research Found., 1977-81, chmn., 1979-81. Served to lt. comdr. USNR, 1960-62. Mem. Iowa, Johnson County med. socs., Orthopedic Research Soc. (sec.-treas. 1970-73, pres. 1974-75), Am. Acad. Orthopedic Surgeons (Kappa Delta award for outstanding research in orthopedics 1971), Canadian, Am. Orthopedic assns., Am. Acad. Orthopedic Surgeons (dir. 1973-74), N.Y. Acad. Sci., Assn. Bone and Joint Surgeons, AMA, Am. Rheumatism Assn., Am. Fedn. Clin. Research, Am. Acad. Cerebral Palsy, Am. Acad. Orthopedic Surgeons (chmn. exams. com. 1978-82, sec. 1982, v.p. 1985-86). Current Work: Ultrastructure of musculoskeletal system. Subspecialty: Orthopedics. Home: 201 Ridgeview Ave Iowa City IA 52240

COOPER, RICHARD ALAN, hematologist; b. Milw., Sept. 23, 1936; s. Peter and Annabelle (Schlomovitz) C.; m. Jaclyn Koppel, June 22, 1958; children: Stephanie, Jonathan. B.S., U. Wis., 1957; M.D., Washington U., St. Louis, 1961. Intern Harvard U. Med. Services, Boston City Hosp., 1961-63, resident in medicine, 1965-66; fellow in hematology Thorndike Meml. Lab., Boston City Hosp., 1966-69; asst. prof. medicine Harvard Med. Sch., 1969-71; chief hematology div. Thorndike Meml. Lab. and Harvard Med. Services, Boston City Hosp., 1969-71; prof. medicine, dir. Cancer Center, chief hematology-oncology sect. U. Pa., Phila., 1971-85; dean Med. Coll. Wis., Milw., 1985—. Mem. editorial bd.: Blood, 1979-84, Lipid Research, 1983-84. Served with USPHS, 1963-65. NIH grantee. Mem. Am. Soc. Hematology, Am. Soc. Clin. Oncology, Am. Fedn. Clin. Research, Am. Soc. Clin. Investigation, Assn. Am. Physicians, Phi Beta Kappa, Alpha Omega Alpha. Current Work: Cell membrane structure; membrane lipids; cellular differentiation. Subspecialty: Hematology. Office: 8701 Watertown Plank Rd Milwaukee WI 53226

COOPER, ROBERT ARTHUR, JR., pathologist, educator; b. St. Paul, Aug. 27, 1932; s. Robert Arthur and Theodora (Yarborough) C.; children: Robert Arthur, III, Timothy Rychner, Theodore Thomas. A.B., U. Pa., 1954; M.D., Jefferson Med. Coll., Phila., 1958. Intern Moffitt Hosp., U. Calif., 1958-59, resident in pathology, 1959-62; chief resident in pathology Women's Free Hosp. and Boston Lying-in Hosp., Harvard, 1962-63; teaching fellow Harvard Med. Sch., 1962-63; from asst. prof. to prof. pathology U. Oreg. Med. Sch., 1963-69; mem. faculty U. Rochester (N.Y.) Med. Sch., 1969—, assoc. dean curricular affairs, assoc. prof. pathology, 1969-72, prof. pathology, dir. surg. pathology, 1972-75, prof. oncology in pathology, dir. cancer center, 1974—; cons. subcom. on comprehensive cancer centers Nat. Cancer Adv. Bd., Nat. Cancer Inst., 1976-78, mem. breast cancer treatment com. (breast cancer task force), div. cancer biology, 1974-77, mem. cancer center support grant rev. com., 1978-82, chmn., 1981-82; bd. sci. counsellors div. Nat. Cancer Inst., 1983-85; mem. spl. study sect. cancer epidemiology NIH, 1972; bd. dirs. United Cancer Council, Inc., v.p., 1981—; bd. dirs. Monroe County unit Am. Cancer Soc., 1976-80, mem. profl. edn. com. N.Y. State div., 1974-78; cons. Population Council, Rockefeller U., 1972—; mem. Lasker award jury Lasker Found., 1977. Author articles, chpts. in books.; Asso. editor: Internat. Jour. Radiation Oncology, Biology and Physics, 1974-81; mem. editorial bd.: Cancer Clin. Trials, 1977—. Bd. dirs. Brighton Little League, 1973-77, vice commnr., 1975-76; bd. dirs. Wilmot Found., 1981—. Recipient Allan J. Hill Teaching award U. Oreg. Med. Sch., 1966, 67, 69; named 2d Year Tchr. of Year U. Rochester Med. Sch., 1973; Lester P. Slade civic achievement award Real Estate Bd. of Rochester, 1980; research fellow Am. Cancer Soc., 1960-61; grantee Nat. Cancer Inst., 1975—. Mem. Alpha Omega Alpha. Current Work: Radiation pathology-toxicology/ultrastructure. Subspecialties: Pathology (medicine); Cancer research (medicine). Home: 212 Gregory Park Rochester NY 14620 Office: U Rochester Cancer Center 601 Elmwood Ave Box 704 Rochester NY 14642

COOPER, ROBERT CARL, JR., veterinary educator; b. Macon, Miss., Aug. 11, 1950; s. Robert Carl and Kathryn Emma (Woodcock) C.; m. Deborah Anne Roach, Aug. 26, 1972; children—Ben, Adam, Elizabeth. Student Miss. State U., 1968-71; M.S., Auburn U., 1979, D.V.M., 1975. Assoc. veterinarian West Broward Animal Hosp., Ft. Lauderdale, Fla., 1975-76; instr. anatomy Auburn U., Ala., 1976-79; asst. prof. Coll. Vet. Medicine, Miss. State U., Starkville, 1979—, coordinator surg. services, 1984—. Deacon First Presbyterian Ch., Opelika, Ala., 1979, chmn. bldg. and grounds, 1979, youth group leader, 1979. Recipient Deans Pegasus award Coll. Vet. Medicine, Miss. State U., 1984, Faculty award Sr. Class, Coll. Vet. Medicine, Miss. State U., 1983; named one of Outstanding Young Men Am., 1983. Mem. Am. Vet. Med. Assn., Am. Assn. Vet. Anatomists, Am. Assn. Vet. Med. Colls., Miss. Vet. Med. Assn., Phi Kappa Phi, Phi Zeta. Current work: Clinical surgery. Subspecialty: Surgery (veterinary medicine). Home: 110 Kirk Side Starkville MS 39759 Office: Coll Vet Medicine Miss State U Drawer V Mississippi State MS 39762

COOPER, ROBERT SHANKLIN, government official; b. Kansas City, Mo., Feb. 8, 1932; s. Robert S. and Edna A. (Pobanz) C.; m. Margaret Niven Shipman, Apr. 15, 1956; children—Jonathan A., James G. B.S. in Elec. Engring., U. Iowa, 1954; M.S., Ohio State U., 1958; Sc.D., Mass. Inst. Tech., 1963, 1963-65. Mem. staff elec. engring. dept. Mass. Inst. Tech., 1958-65; mem. staff Lincoln Lab., 1965-72; asst. dir. def. research and engring. Dept. Def., 1972-75; dep. dir. Goddard Space Flight Center, Greenbelt, Md., 1975-76, dir., 1976-79; v.p. engring. Satellite Bus. Systems, McLean, Va., 1979-81; dir. Def. Adv. Research Projects Agy., Arlington, Va., 1981—. Served with USAF, 1954-56. Westinghouse fellow, 1958; recipient Sec. Def. Meritorious Civilian Service award, 1975. Mem. AAAS, IEEE, Sigma Xi, Tau Beta Pi, Eta Kappa Nu. Subspecialty: Electrical engineering. Office: 1400 Wilson Blvd Arlington VA 22209

COOPER, THEODORE, pharmaceutical company executive, physician; b. Trenton, N.J., Dec. 28, 1928; s. Victor and Dora (Popkin) C.; m. Vivian Cecilia Evans, June 16, 1956; children—Michael Harris, Mary Katherine, Victoria Susan, Frank Victor. B.S., Georgetown U., 1949; M.D., St. Louis U., 1954, Ph.D., 1956. USPHS fellow St. Louis U. Dept. Physiology, 1955-56; clin. asso. surgery br. Nat. Heart Inst., Bethesda, Md., 1956-58; faculty St. Louis U., 1960-66, prof. surgery, 1964-66; prof., chmn. dept. pharmacology U. N.Mex., Albuquerque, 1966-68, on leave, 1967-69; assoc. dir. artificial heart, myocardial infarction programs Nat. Heart Inst., Bethesda, 1967-68; dir. Nat. Heart and Lung Inst., 1968-74; dep. asst. sec. for health HEW, 1974-75, asst. sec. health, 1975-77; dean Med. Coll., Cornell U., N.Y.C., 1977-80; provost for med. affairs Cornell U., 1977-80; exec. v.p. Upjohn Co., Kalamazoo, 1980—, vice chmn. bd., 1984—; mem. USPHS Pharmacology and Exptl. Therapeutics Study Sect., 1964-67; Bd. overseers Meml. Sloan-Kettering Cancer Center. Author: (with others) Nervous Control of the Heart, 1965, Heart Substitutes, 1966, The Baboon in Medical Research, Vol. II, 1967, Factors Influencing Myocardial Contractility, 1967, Acute Myocardial Infarction, 1968, Advance in Transplantation, Prosthetic Heart Valves, 1969, Depressed Metabolism, 1969; Editorial bd.: Jour. Pharmacology and Exptl. Therapeutics, 1965-77, 77—, Circulation Research, 1966-71; editor: Supplements to Circulation, 1966-71; sect. co-editor for: Jour. Applied Physiology, 1967-73; Contbr. numerous articles med. jours. Recipient Borden award, 1954; Albert Lasker Spl. Public Service award, 1978; Ellen Browning Scripps medal, 1980. Mem. Am. Soc. Pharmacology and Exptl. Therapeutics, Am. Physiol. Soc., Soc. Exptl. Biology and Medicine, Am. Soc. Clin. Investigation, Am. Fedn. Clin. Research, Am. Soc. Artificial Internal Organs, Internat. Cardiovascular Soc., Am. Coll. Chest Physicians, AAUP, Am. Coll. Cardiology, AAAS, Sigma Xi. Discoverer new techniques of denervating heart which have helped delineate role of nerves in heart, on its ability to function under a wide variety of circumstances, and on its ability to respond to drugs. Current Work: Pharmaceutical business executive. Subspecialties: Pharmacology; Cardiology. Home: 3656 Woodcliff Dr Kalamazoo MI 49008 Office: Upjohn Co 7000 Portage Rd Kalamazoo MI 49001

COOPER, WILLIAM WAGER, educator; b. Birmingham, Ala., July 23, 1914; s. William Wager and Rae (Rossman) C.; m. Ruth Fay West, Sept. 11, 1944. A.B., U. Chgo., 1938; postgrad., Columbia U., 1940-42; D.Sc. (hon.), Ohio State U., 1969, M.A., Harvard U., 1976, D.Sc., Carnegie-Mellon U., 1982. Asst. to comptroller TVA, 1938-40; prin. economist Bur. Budget, 1942-44; asst. prof. econs. U. Chgo., 1944-46; asst. prof. to prof. Carnegie-Mellon U., 1946-68, dean, 1968-75. Univ. prof. mgmt. sci. and pub. affairs, 1975-76, research prof. mgmt. sci. and pub. policy, 1976-80; Arthur Lowes Dickinson prof. accounting Grad. Sch. Bus. Adminstrn., Harvard U., 1976-80; Foster Parker prof. fin. mgmt. and acctg. Grad. Sch. Bus. Adminstrn. U. Tex., Austin, 1980—; Author: (with A. Charnes) Management Models and Industrial Applications of Linear Programming, (with H. Leavitt, M.W. Shelly) New Perspectives in Organization Research, (with others) Studies in Budgeting, (with A. Charnes and R. Niehaus) Studies in Manpower Planning, (with Y. Ijiri) Eric Louis Kohler: Accounting's Man of Principles; (with A. Warner) Creative and Innovative Management: Essays in Honor of George Kozmetshu; (with Y. Ijiri) Kohler's Dictionary for Accountants, 6th edit.; Editorial bd.: Auditing: A Jour. Practice and Theory, 1978-82; contbr. articles to profl. jours. Co-recipient John Von Neumann Theory prize, 1982; Disting. Internat. vis. lectr. Am. Acctg. Assn., 1986. Fellow Econometric Soc., AAAS, Inst. Constructive Capitalism; mem. Inst. Mgmt. Sci. (past pres.), Ops. Research Soc. Am. (editorial bd. 1957-68). Current work: Modeling Management and Social Processes. Subspecialties: Operations research (engineering); Operations research (mathematics). Home: 4 Hillside Ct Austin TX 78746

COOVER, HARRY WESLEY, chemist, former manufacturing company executive; b. Newark, Del., Mar. 6, 1919; s. Harry Wesley and Anna (Rohm) C.; m. Muriel Zumbach, Sept. 17, 1941; children—Harry Wesley, Stephen R., Melinda Coover Paul. B.S. in Chemistry (Southerland prize 1941), Hobart Coll., Geneva, N.Y., 1941; M.S., Cornell U., 1942, Ph.D., 1944. Research chemist Eastman Kodak Co., Rochester, N.Y., 1944-49; sr. research chemist Tenn. Eastman Co., Kingsport, 1949-54, research asso., 1954-63, head polymers div., 1963-65, dir. research, 1965-73, v.p., 1970-73, exec. v.p., 1973-81; v.p. Eastman Kodak Co., from 1981. Author. Recipient Indsl. Research Inst. medal, 1984. Mem. Internat. Union Pure and Applied Chemistry, Am. Chem. Soc. (So. Chemist award 1960, Speaker of Year award N.E. Tenn. sect. 1962), AAAS, Am. Assn. Textile Tech., Am. Inst. Chemists, Assn. Research Dirs., Dirs. Indsl. Research, Indsl. Research Inst. (pres. 1981-82), Soc. Chem. Industry, Soc. Plastics Industry, Textile Research Inst. (trustee), N.Y. Acad. Scis. Presbyterian. Clubs: Lions, Masons. Patentee in field. Subspecialty: Organic chemistry. Office: care Kodak Research Labs 1669 Lake Ave Rochester NY 14650

COPELAND, JAMES CLINTON, enzyme manufacturing company executive, microbial geneticist; b. Chgo., Nov. 15, 1937; s. Wallace J. and Ann T. (Tuka) C.; m. Ella Grace Greene, Apr. 30, 1960; children: Catherine, Carolmarie, Christina, James C., Jeffrey. B.S., U. Ill.-Urbana, 1959; M.S., U. Tenn.-Knoxville, 1962; Ph.D. (NIH fellow), Rutgers U.-New Brunswick, N.J., 1965; M.B.A., U. Chgo., 1981. Sci. asst. biology div. Oak Ridge Nat. Labs., 1960-62; Am. Cancer Soc. postdoctoral fellow Albert Einstein Coll. Medicine, 1965-67; assoc. geneticist Div. Biology and Medicine, Argonne (Ill.) Nat. Lab., 1967-72; assoc. prof. microbiology Ohio State U., 1972-77; dir. biotech. CPC Internat., Argo, Ill., 1977-81; founder, pres. Enzyme Tech. Corp., Ashland, Ohio, 1981—, also dir.; dir. Genon Corp. Contbr.: articles to profl. jours. Ency. Brit. Book of Yr., 1968-71; editor: articles to profl. jours. Microbiol. Genetics Bull., 1973-77. Recipient Career Devel. award NIH, 1973-78; Oak Ridge Inst. Nuclear Studies fellow, 1961. Mem. AAAS, Ohio Acad. Sci., Sigma Xi. Clubs: Torch (Chgo.); Country of Ashland. Current Work: Microbiology, genetic engineering, germentation, enzymes, biotechnical process development. Subspecialties: Genetics and genetic engineering (biology); Enzyme technology. Office: 783 US 250 E Route 2 Ashland OH 44805

COPELAND, JOHN ALEXANDER, III, instrumentation company executive, electrical engineer; b. Atlanta, Feb. 6, 1941; s. John Alexander Jr. and Gay Elise (Stafford) C.; m. Sandra Chandler, June 22, 1960; children—Brian C., Kathleen. B.S., Ga. Inst. Tech., 1962, M.S., 1963, Ph.D. in Physics, 1965. Research physicist Ga. Inst. Tech., Atlanta, 1958-65; dept. head Bell Telephone Labs., Murray Hills, N.J., 1965-82; v.p. engring. tech. Sangamo Weston, Inc., Atlanta, 1983—; trustee Ga. Tech. Research Inst., Atlanta, 1983—. Contbr. articles to profl. jours. Patentee electronic devices. Fellow IEEE (editor Transactions on Electron Devices 1967—; Morris Liebmann award 1970); mem. Am. Phys. Soc. Current work: Design of electronic instruments and data communications systems that use microcomputers and integrated circuits (microchips). Subspecialties: Computer engineering; Microchip technology (engineering). Home: 1070 Green Way Dunwoody GA 30338 Office: Sangamo Weston Inc/Schlumberger 180 Technology Pkwy Norcross GA 30092

COPES, JOHN CARSON, III, consulting mechanical engineer; b. Baton Rouge, Sept. 6, 1923; s. John Carson and Beatrix (Lyons) C.; m. Edith Estelle Givens, Mar. 4, 1944; 1 son, John Carson IV. B.S., La. State U., 1947. Registered profl. engr. La. Mech. design engr. Esso Research Labs., 1947-50; design engr. Ethyl Corp., 1950-56; head mech. sect. Frederic R. Harris, Inc, 1956-61; chief engr. Arthur G. Keller Inc., 1961-65; prin. John C. Copes, Cons. Engrs., Baton Rouge, 1965—. Chmn. Livingston parish dist. Boy Scouts Am., 1951-52. Served with U.S. Army, 1943-45. Decorated Purple Heart., Bronze Star. Fellow ASME; mem. La. Engring. Soc. (James M. Todd Tech. Accomplishment medal 1977), Nat. Soc. Profl. Engrs., SAR. Democrat. Episcopalian. Lodges: Masons; Shriners. Patentee split mech. seals, mech. seal inserts. Current Work: Mechanical products development. Subspecialty: Mechanical engineering. Home: 2750 McConnell Dr Baton Rouge LA 70809 Office: 1956 Wooddale Ct Baton Rouge LA 70806

CORAN, ARNOLD GERALD, pediatric surgeon, educator; b. Boston, Apr. 16, 1938; s. Charles and Anne (Cohen) C.; m. Susan Williams, Nov. 17, 1960; children: Michael, David, Randi Beth. B.A. cum laude, Harvard U., 1959, M.D. cum laude, 1963. Diplomate: Am. Bd. Surgery, Am. Bd. Thoracic Surgery. Intern Peter Bent Brigham Hosp., Boston, 1963-64, resident in surgery, 1964-68, chief surg. resident, 1969; resident in surgery Children's Hosp. Med. Center, Boston, 1965-66, sr. surg. resident, 1966, chief surg. resident, 1968; instr. surgery Harvard, Cambridge, Mass., 1967-69; asst. clin. prof. surgery George Washington U., 1970-72; head physician pediatric surgery Los Angeles County-U. So. Calif. Med. Center, 1972-74; asst. prof. surgery U. So. Calif., 1972-73, assoc. prof., 1973-74; prof. surgery U. Mich., Ann Arbor, 1974—; head sect. pediatric surgery U. Mich. Hosp., 1974—; Surgeon-in-chief Mott Children's Hosp. Contbr. numerous articles in field to profl. jours. Served to lt. comdr. MC AUS. Fellow ACS; mem. Am. Acad. Pediatrics, Am. Surg. Assn., Soc. Univ. Surgeons, Am. Pediatric Surg. Assn., Western, Central surg. assns. Current Work: Neonatal and pediatric metabolism; shock and nutrition. Subspecialty: Surgery. Home: 3450 Vintage Valley Rd Ann Arbor MI 48105 Office: Mott Children's Hosp Room F7516 Box 66 Ann Arbor MI 48109

CORBASCIO, NICOLA ALDO, physician, pharmaceutical company executive; b. Castellana, Italy, Mar. 21, 1928; came to U.S., 1954, naturalized, 1961; s. Vincenzo and Caterina (Zinza) C.; m. Elise Margareta Holgerson, Nov. 5, 1965; children: Sebastian, Matthias, Catherine. B.A., Horatius Flaccus Lycee, 1947; M.D., U. Bari, 1953; D.Sc., U. Pa., 1958. Intern U. Bari Med. Clinic, 1953-54; Fulbright scholar U. Pa. Med. Sch., 1954-55; fellow therapeutic research U. Hosp. U. Pa.-Phila., 1954-56; instr. pharmacology U. Pa. Med. Sch., 1956-59; asst. research pharmacologist U. Calif. Med. Ctr., 1959-65; assoc. med. dir. Miles Labs., Westhaven, Conn., 1982—; prof. pharmacology Coll. Physicians and Surgeons, U. Pacific, 1963-68; prof., chmn. dept. pharmacology Coll. Physicians and Surgeons, U. Pacific (Sch. Dentistry), 1968-76; dir. med. affairs Nordic countries Rhone Poulenc A/S Neuropharmacologist Napa State Hosp., Imola, Calif., 1980—. Contbr. articles to sci. jours.; Co-author: Interactions of Drugs and Anesthetics, 1981. Mem. Am. Soc. Clin. Pharmacology, Western Pharmacol. Soc., AMA, Calif. Med. Assn., Alameda-Contra Costa Med. Soc. Patentee cardiovascular pharmacology. Current Work: Cardiovascular pharmacology; psychopharmacology. Subspecialty: Molecular pharmacology. Office: Miles Labs 400 Morgan Ln West Haven CT 06516

CORDELL, BRUCE MONTEITH, geophysicist, space scientist, geophysicist; b. Shelby, Mich., Sept. 10, 1949; s. Carl C. and Ruth M. C.; m. Lee Clark, Aug. 3, 1977. B.S., Mich. State U., East Lansing, 1971; M.S., UCLA, 1973; Ph.D.,

U. Ariz., 1977. Weizmann research fellow Calif. Inst. Tech., Pasadena, 1977-78; asst. prof. physics and earth scis. Central Conn. State U., New Britain, 1978-80; asst. prof. physics and geology Calif. State U., Bakersfield, 1980-84; sr. engr. Space Systems div. Gen. Dynamics, San Diego, 1984—. Contbr. articles to profl. jours. Mem. Am. Geophys Union, Am. Astron. Soc., Brit. Interplanetary Soc. Republican. Current Work: Space exploration and utilization, extraterrestrial resources, planetary physics. Subspecialties: Geophysics; Planetary science. Office: Space Systems Div General Dynamics PO Box 85990 CI-9530 San Diego CA 92138

CORDER, MICHAEL PAUL, physician, educator; b. Zanesville, Ohio, Jan. 20, 1940; s. Thurman Edward and Dorothy (Shipps) C.; m. Sue Tawney, June 20, 1962; m. Dorothy M. Smith, Aug. 6, 1970; children: Anita, Wendy, Jennifer. B.S., Capital U., 1961; M.D., Ohio State U., 1965. Diplomate: Am. Bd. Internal Medicine, subcert. in med. oncology. Resident in internal medicine Letterman Army Med. Center, 1965-69, fellow in oncology, 1971-75; asst. prof. U. Iowa Hosps., 1975-78, assoc. prof., 1978-83; chmn., dir. oncology/-hematology Kern Med. Center, Bakersfield, Calif., 1983—; adj. prof. medicine, UCLA, 1984—; cons. in field. Contbr. articles to profl. jours., chpts. to books. Served with M.C., U.S. Army, 1964-75; to col. Res. 1980—. Fellow in oncology Nat. Cancer Inst., NIH, 1969-71. Fellow ACP, Internat. Soc. Hematology; mem. Am. Soc. Hematology, Am. Assn. Cancer Research, Am. Soc. Clin. Oncology, Western Soc. Clin. Investigation, Am. Soc. Preventive Oncology. Current Work: Med. decision making, cancer clin. trials. Subspecialties: Oncology; Algorithms. Home: 12430 Cattle King Bakersfield CA 93306 Office: Dept Medicine U Kern Med Center Bakersfield CA 93305

CORDERO, JULIO, systems engineer; b. San Jose, Costa Rica, Jan. 10, 1923; came to U.S., 1944, naturalized, 1961; s. Julio R. and Maria C. (Fonseca) C.; m. Claire Cox, Oct. 26, 1963; 1 child, Astrid Cox Cordero. B.S. in Meteorology, Inter-Am. Meteorol. Inst., Colombia, 1943; B.S.A.E., Wayne State U., 1948; M.S. in Aerodynamics, U. Minn., 1951. Meteorologist Pan-Am. World Airways, 1944; scientist U. Minn., Mpls., 1951-53; sr. scientist Fluidyne Engring. Corp., Mpls., 1953-61, AVCO Research and Devel., Wilmington, Mass., 1961-68; sr. systems analyst ANSER, Falls Church, Va., 1969-75; chief engr. magnetohydrodynamics MIT, Cambridge, 1975-81; tech. staff AVCO SD, Wilmington, Mass., 1981-83; sr. staff AVCO Everett Research Lab., Everett, Mass., 1983—; cons. Mobil Oil Corp., N.Y.C., 1970. U.S. Weather Bur. scholar, 1943; Kales scholar, 1976. Mem. Am. Phys Soc., AIAA, AAAS, Sigma Xi. Club: MIT Faculty. Current Work: Large laser systems integration. Subspecialties: Systems engineering; Excimers. Home: 23 Mohawk St Danvers MA 01923 Office: 2385 Revere Beach Pkwy Everett MA 02149

CORDOVA, FRANCE ANNE-DOMINIC, astrophysicist; b. Paris, France, Aug. 5, 1947; d. Frederick Ben and Joan Frances (McGuinness) C. B.A. magna cum laude, Stanford U., 1969; Ph.D., Calif. Inst. Tech., 1979. Postdoctoral research asst. Calif. Inst. Tech., Pasadena, 1979; staff scientist, project leader Los Alamos (N.Mex.) Nat. Lab., 1979—, mem. earth and space sci. research council, 1985—; cons. Lawrence Berkeley Radiation Lab., Calif., 1979-80; mem. adv. council NSF, 1981-83. Contbr. articles to various sci. books, mags., sci. jours. and popular sci. jours. U. Calif. Regents scholar, 1965; Ford Found. research grantee, 1968-69; NATO postdoctoral fellow, 1982; named one of top brightest scientists under 40 Sci. Digest, 1984. Mem. Am. Astron. Soc., Internat. Astron. Union, New Mexicans for Space Exploration. Current Work: Observational astronomy: X-ray, ultraviolet, optical, infrared, and radio measurements of high energy sources using satellites and ground-based telescopes. Subspecialties: Ultraviolet high energy astrophysics; X-ray high energy astrophysics. Office: Los Alamos Nat Lab M S D436 Los Alamos NM 87545

CORDOVA-SALINAS, MARIA ASUNCION, physiology educator; b. Punta Arenas, Magallanes, Chile, May 14, 1941; came to U.S., 1972; d. Miguel and Maria Asuncion (Requena Aizcorbe) Cordova-Santana; m. Carlos Francisco Salinas, July 27, 1963; children: Carlos Miguel, Claudio Andres, Maria Asuncion. B.S., U. Chile, 1958, D.D.S., 1965; cert., Johns Hopkins U., 1974. Faculty U. Chile, Valparaiso, 1965-74; postdoctoral fellow Johns Hopkins U., Balt., 1972-74; vis. scientist N.Y. Med. Coll., N.Y.C., 1974; faculty dept. pharmacology Med. U. S.C., Charleston, 1975-79, asst. prof. physiology, 1980—; pvt. practice dentistry, Valparaiso, 1965-72. Coordinator Circulo Hispanoamericano, Charleston, 1978—; bd. dir. Iglesia Hispanica, 1983; chmn. Amnesty Internat., Charleston, 1984. Pan Am. Health Orgn./WHO fellow, 1972-74; named Guest of Honor City of Mayaguez, P.R., 1979. Mem. Am. Physiol. Soc. Current Work: Oral physiology and oral diagnosis. Subspecialty: Physiology (medicine). Office: Dept Physiology Med Univ SC 171 Ashley Ave Charleston SC 29425

CORDUNEANU, CONSTANTIN C., mathematics educator, researcher; b. Iasi, Moladvia, Romania, July 26, 1928; came to U.S., 1978; s. Costache and Aglaia (Anitoaie) C.; m. Alice Olga Vultur, July 23, 1949. Diploma in Math, U. Iasi, 1951, D.Math., 1956. Instr. U. Iasi, Romania, 1949-55, asst. prof., 1955-62, assoc. prof., 1962-67, prof., 1968-78; prof. dept. math. U. Tex.-Arlington, 1979—; vis. prof. U. R.I.- Kingston, 1967-68, 73-74, 80, U. Tenn.-Knoxville, 1978-79. Author: Almost Periodic Functions, 1968, Principles of Differential and Integral Equations, 1971, 77, Integral Equations and Stability of Feedback Systems, 1973; assoc. editor: jours. including Math. System Theory, 1967-75, Revue Roumaine Pure Applied Math, 1973-78, Nonlinear Analysis, 1977-85, Jour. Integral Equations, 1979—, Libertas Mathematica, 1981—. Served with Romanian Army, 1952. Recipient research prizes Romanian Acad., Bucharest, 1963, research prizes Ministry of Edn., Bucharest, 1965; research fellow Inst. Math. Romanian Acad., Iasi, 1954-59, 63-67. Mem. Am. Math. Soc., Math. Assn. Am., Soc. Indsl. and Applied Math., Am. Romanian Acad. Arts and Scis. Christian Orthodox. Current Work: Differential and related equations. Subspecialty: Applied mathematics. Home: 812 S Collins Ave Arlington TX 76010Office: Univ Tex-Arlington S Cooper St Arlington TX 76019

COREY, DAVID PAUL, neurobiologist, educator; b. Boston, May 9, 1951; s. E. Raymond and Joan Castleton (Danner) C.; m. Xandra O. Breakefield; children—Susanna M.B. Giller, Sarah J.C. B.A., Amherst Coll., 1974; Ph.D., Calif. Inst. Tech., 1980. Asst. prof., Yale Med. Sch., 1983-84; asst. prof. Harvard Med. Sch., 1984—; asst. physiologist dept. neurology Mass. Gen. Hosp., Boston, 1984—; assoc. investigator Howard Hughes Med. Inst., Boston, 1984—. Contbr. articles to sci. jours. Sloan research fellow, 1984; recipient Intra-Sci. Research Found. prize, 1978. Mem. Soc. Neurosci. (mem. program com. 1984—), Soc. Gen. Physiologists, Biophys. Soc., Sigma Xi. Current work: Sensory transduction by the auditory system and by mechanosensitive systems; mechanisms of activation of ion channel proteins in cell membranes. Subspecialties: Neurobiology; Biophysics (biology). Home: 127 Homer St Newton Center MA 02159 Office: Dept Neurology Mass Gen Hosp Fruit St Boston MA 02114

COREY, ELIAS JAMES, chemistry educator; b. Methuen, Mass., July 12, 1928; s. Elias and Tina (Hashem) C.; m. Claire Highham, Sept. 14, 1961; children—David, John, Susan. S.B., MIT, 1948, Ph.D., 1951; A.M. (hon.), Harvard U., 1959, D.Sc., U. Chgo., 1968, Hofstra U., 1974, contd., Colby Coll., 1977. From instr. to asst. prof. U. Ill., Champaign-Urbana, 1951-55, prof., 1955-59; prof. chemistry Harvard U., Cambridge, Mass., 1959—, Sheldon Emory prof., 1968—. Contbr. articles to profl. jours. Bd. dirs. phys. sci. Alfred P. Sloan Found., 1967-72; mem. sci. adv. bd. dirs. Robert A. Welch Found. Recipient Intrasci. Found. award, 1968, Ernest Guenther award in chemistry of essentials oils and related products, 1968, Harrison Howe award, 1971, Ciba Found. medal, 1972, Evans award Ohio State U., 1972, Linus Pauling award, 1973, Dickson prize in sci. Carnegie Mellon U., 1973, George Ledlie prize in sci. Harvard U., 1973, Nichols medal, 1977, Buchman award Calif. Inst. Tech., 1978, Franklin medal in sci. Franklin Inst., 1978, Sci. Achievement award CCNY, 1979; fellow Swiss-Am. exchange, 1957, Guggenheim Found., 1957-58, 68-69, Alfred P. Sloan Found., 1956-59. Mem. Am. Acad. Arts and Scis., AAAS, Am. Chem. Soc. (award in synthetic chemistry 1971, Pure Chemistry award 1960, Fritzche award 1968, Md. sect. Remsen award 1974, Arthur C. Cope award 1976), Nat. Acad. Sci., Sigma Xi. Home: Avon Hill St Cambridge MA 02140 Office: Dept Chemistry Harvard U Cambridge MA 02138

CORFF, NICHOLAS J., architect, consulting computer systems developer; b. Oklahoma City, June 30, 1942; s. Nicholas C. and Barbara E. (Geirk) C. B.Arch., Stanford U., 1966, M.Arch., 1972. Dir., Workshops on Polit. and Social Issues Stanford U., 1970-72, instr. Micronesia seminar, 1971-72, founder Stanford Oceania Ctr., 1972; cons. Campbell & Assocs., Menlo Park, Calif., 1972-73; dir. planning div. Parsell Yeager, Inc., Seattle, 1973-74; pres. chief exec. officer Corff & Shapiro, Inc., Seattle, 1974-77; pres., chief exec. officer CDS Assocs., Ltd., Seattle, 1977-81; pres., chief exec. officer Corgraphics Corp., Seattle, 1981-82, chmn. bd., 1983, cons., 1983—. Author works in field. Vol. Peace Corps, Palau, Micronesia, 1966-67. Served as officer C.E., U.S. Army, 1968-69. Mem. Inst. Island Research and Assistance (pres. 1977—), Assn. Computing Machinery, Nat. Computer Graphics Assn., Northwest Computer-Aided Mapping Assn. (vice chmn. 1982—), Palau Forum. Current Work: Computer aided design, computer based graphics analysis, graphic-based language design, island research; founder, key concept developer of computer graphics systems corporation; consulting, writing, architecture. Subspecialties: Graphics, image processing, and pattern recognition; Artificial intelligence. Home: 511 Malden Ave E Seattle WA 98112

CORNATZER, WILLIAM EUGENE, biochemist, consultant, researcher; b. Mocksville, N.C., Sept. 23, 1918; s. William P. and Stella Agusta (Vogler) C.; m. Margaret Virginia Freeman, Mar. 30, 1946; children—Nancy Freeman, William E. B.S. in Chemistry, Wake Forest U., 1939; M.S. in Biochemistry, U. N.C., 1941, Ph.D., 1944; M.D., Bowman Gray Sch. Medicine, 1951. Asst. prof. biochemistry Bowman Gray Sch. Medicine, Winston-Salem, N.C., 1946-51; prof., head dept. biochemistry U. N.D. Med. Sch., Grand Forks, 1951-83, Chester Fritz Disting. prof., 1973, emeritus prof., 1983—, dir. Ireland Research Lab., 1953-84; dir. clin. chem. lab. Grand Forks Clinic, 1969—. Bd. editors Jour. Clin. Chemistry, 1971-81, Jour. Nutrition, 1975-79. Contbr. articles to profl. jours. Frank Billing Original Investigator AMA, 1951; recipient Outstanding Sci. Research award Sigma Xi, 1970; Disting. Service award U. N.C. Sch. Medicine, 1970; Disting. Alumni award Bowman Gray Medicine, 1976. Fellow AAAS, ACP, N.Y. Acad. Sci., Nat. Acad. Clin. chemistry, Am. Bd. Clin. Chemistry (dir. 1960-66); mem. Am. Chem. Soc., Am. Soc. Biol. Chemists, Am. Inst. Nutrition, Am. Assn. Clin. Chemists, Am. Assn. Study Liver Disease, Am. Assn. Cancer Research, Am. Oil Chemists Soc., Soc. Exptl. Biology and Medicine, Radiation Research Soc., Sigma Xi, Alpha Omega Alpha. Republican. Methodist. Current work: Liver disease; cancer research; phospholipids metabolism; phospholipid synthesis in membranes in health and disease, nutrition. Subspecialties: Biochemistry (medicine); Clinical chemistry. Home: 307 Park Ave Grand Forks ND 58201 Office: Biochemistry Dept U ND Med Sch Grand Forks ND 58202

CORNELL, ROBERT WITHERSPOON, mechanical engineer, consultant; b. Orange, N.J., Aug. 16, 1925; s. Edward S. and Helen L. (Lawrence) C.; m. Patricia Delight Plummer, June 24, 1950; children: Richard W., Delight W., Elizabeth P., Roberta S. B.E. in M.E. with high honors, Yale U., 1945, M.E., 1947, D.Eng. in M.E, 1950; grad., U.S. Naval acad., 1945. Registered profl. engr., N.Y. State, Conn. With Naval Research Lab., Washington, 1945-46; instr. math. New Haven Jr. Coll., 1947-48; Engr. Pratt & Whitney Aircraft, East Hartford, Conn., 1947; with Hamilton Standard div. United Techologies Corp., Windsor Locks, Conn., 1948—, now chief applied mechanics and aerodynamics; instr. engring. Hillyer Coll., Hartford, Conn., 1955; prin. Cornell Cons., West Hartford, 1973—, Cornell Enterprises, 1984—; adj. prof. Yale U., 1985. Contbr. articles to tech. jours. Republican dist. committeeman; bd. dirs., past pres. West Hartford Taxpayers Assn.; bd. dirs. Conn. Taxpayers Assn.; mem. coms. West Hartford Sch. Task Force. Served in USNR, 1943-46. Mem. Yale Sci. and Engring. Assn. (award 1969, dir., treas.), ASME, Sigma Xi, Tau Beta Pi. Congregationalist. Clubs: Hartford Golf, Yale (Hartford and N.Y.C.). Patentee in field (8), including space suit joint and prop-fan multi-bladed propeller. Current Work: Manage technical group specializing in aerodynamics, acoustics, applied mechanics, vibrations and structure; advanced work on gear dynamics, stressing and strength. Subspecialties: Mechanical engineering; Aerospace engineering and technology. Home: 40 Belknap Rd West Hartford CT 06117 Office: Hamilton Standard Bradley Field Rd Windsor Locks CT 06096

CORNETT, JAMES BRYCE, research microbiologist; b. Orange, Calif., Apr. 30, 1945; s. Royce Wesley and Margaret Lititia (Glenn) C. B.A., U. Calif., Riverside, 1967; M.S., U. Calif.-Davis, 1969; Ph.D., U. Ariz., 1973. NIH postdoctoral fellow Temple U. Sch. Medicine, Phila., 1973-75, research asst. prof., 1977-78; sr. research biologist Sterling-Winthrop Research Inst., Rensselaer, N.Y., 1978-81, group leader microbiology dept., 1981-83, sect. head, 1981—. Contbr. articles to profl. jours. Mem. Am. Soc. Microbiology (nat. councillor 1980-82). Current Work: The development of antimicrobial agents for clinical use; drug development. Subspecialty: Microbiology (medicine). Office: Sterling Winthrop Research Inst Columbia Turnpike Rensseslaer NY 12144

CORRADINO, ROBERT A., biomedical researcher, educator; b. Lancaster, Pa., Aug. 6, 1938; s. Nicholas and Minnie M. C.; divorced; 1 child, Tony R. B.S., State Coll., Millersville, Pa., 1960; M.S., Purdue U., 1962; Ph.D., Cornell U., 1966. Research assoc. Wyeth Labs., Radnor, Pa., 1962-64; research assoc. Cornell U., Ithaca, N.Y., 1966-72, sr. research assoc., 1972-80, asso. prof. physiology, 1980—. Editor: Functional Regulation at the Cellular and Molecular Level, 1983; contbr. 70 articles to profl. jours. Served with USMC, 1958-64. Recipient Research Career Devel. award NIH, 1975-80. Mem. Am. Physiol. Soc., Am. Inst. Nutrition, Endocrine Soc., Soc. Exptl. Biology and Medicine, AAAS, Sigma Xi. Current Work: Study of the regulation of induction of a specific intestinal calcium-binding protein and the role of this protein in the cholecalciferol (vitamin D030)-stimulated calcium transport. Subspecialties: Physiology (biology); Endocrinology. Home: 61 Lois Ln Ithaca NY 14850 Office: Cornell U 720 VRT Ithaca NY 14853

CORRY, ANDREW FRANCIS, utility co. exec.; b. Lynn, Mass., Oct. 28, 1922; s. Andrew Francis and Julia Agnes (Gaynor) C.; m. Mildred M. Dunn, Sept. 16, 1950 (dec. 1977); children—Andrea, Janice, James. B.S. in E.E, M.I.T., 1947; postgrad, Advanced Mgmt. program Harvard U., 1966. Registered profl. engr., Mass. With Boston Edison Co., 1947-84, asst. to exec. v.p., 1969-72, dir. engring., planning, nuclear and systems ops., 1972-75, v.p. engring. and distbn., 1975-79, sr. v.p., 1979—. Served with Signal Corps U.S. Army, 1942-46. Fellow IEEE (Habirshaw award 1983), Nat. Acad. Engring. Roman Catholic. Club: Ancient Order of Hibernians. Subspecialty: Electrical engineering.

CORSINI, ALFIO, analytical chemist. Prof. chemistry McMaster U., Recipient Fisher Sci. award Chem. Inst. Can., 1985. Subspecialty: Analytical chemistry. Office: McMaster U Dept Chemistry Hamilton ON L8S 4L8 Canada

CORSO, JOHN FIERMONTE, psychologist, consultant; b. Oswego, N.Y., Dec. 1, 1919; m. Josephine A. Solazzo, Feb. 8, 1943; children: Gregory Michael, Douglas Jerome, Christine Ann. B.Ed., SUNY-Oswego, 1942; M.A., U. Iowa, Iowa City, 1948, Ph.D., 1950. Lic. psychologist, N.Y. Chief sound and vibration sect. Psychology Br. Army Med. Research lab., Ft. Knox, Ky., 1950-51; chief human factors office Rome Air Devel. Center, Griffiss AFB, Rome, N.Y., 1951-52; prof., dir. human factors research program Pa. State U., 1952-62; prof., dir. dept. psychology St. Louis U., 1962-63; prof., chmn. dept. psychology SUNY-Cortland, 1963-80, Disting. prof., 1973—; engring. psychology cons. HRB-Singer, State College, Pa., 1952-62; staff psychologist U.S. Naval Tng. Device Ctr., Port Washington, N.Y., 1959. Author: The Experimental Psychology of Sensory Behavior, 1967, Aging Sensory Systems and Perception, 1981; contbr. chpts. to books. Served to capt. U.S. Army, 1942-46. NSF grantee, 1955-58; Pa. State U. grantee, 1956-61; Nat. Inst. Neurol. Diseases and Blindness grantee, 1960-63; SUNY grantee, 1965-80; Nat. Inst. Child Health and Human Devel. fellow, 1969-70. Fellow Am. Psychol. Assn., AAAS, Human Factors Soc.; mem. Eastern Psychol. Assn., Midwestern Psychol. Assn., Acoustical Soc. Am., N.Y. State Psychol. Assn., Pa. Psychol. Assn., AAUP, Pa. Acad. Sci., N.Y. Acad. Sci., Internt. Soc. Cybernetic Medicine, Internat. Soc. Audiology, Psychonomic Soc., Sigma Xi, Psi Chi. Roman Catholic. Current Work: Research in experimental psychology, especially sensory processes, psychophysics, and perception in older adults; psychoacoustics; audiology; musical acoustics; human factors; research design and administration. Subspecialties: Sensory processes; Aging. Home: Cosmos Hill Rd RD #4 Cortland NY 13045 Office: Department of Psychology State Univeristy of New York Cortland NY 13045

CORVIN, WAYNE CLAY, power electronics engineer, consultant; b. Richmond, Va., July 25, 1946; s. Julian Paris and Jane Elizabeth (Clay) C.; m. Kim Patrice Gay, May 2, 1981; 1 child, Kinsey Justin. B.S. in Elec. Engring., Va. Poly. Inst. and State U., 1968. Registered profl. engr., Calif. Assoc. engr. Va. Electric and Power Co., Norfolk, 1965-70; indsl. electrician Coca Cola Co. Foods div., Hightstown, N.J., 1974-76; power engr. Princeton Plasma Physics Lab., N.J., 1976-78; elec. engr. Lawrence Livermore Lab., Livermore, Calif., 1978-83; dept. head Stanford Linear Accelerator, Calif., 1983—. Patentee heating tubes for cable, synthetic fault measurement. Served with U.S. Army, 1970-71. Mem. IEEE, Nat. Soc. Profl. Engrs., Calif. Profl. Engrs. Republican. Unitarian. Current work: Power system harmonic analysis, transient analysis, and solid state control. Subspecialties: Particle physics; Fusion. Home: 427 Embarcadero Rd Palo Alto CA 94301 Office: Stanford Linear Accelerator PO Box 4349 B-22 Stanford CA 94305

CORWIN, HAROLD GLENN, JR., astronomer; b. Pasadena, Calif., June 5, 1943; s. Harold Glenn and Eleanor Aida (Burbank) C.; m. Kathleen Chaloner Castellini, Dec. 21; 1977. B.A., U. Kans., 1965, M.A., 1967; Ph.D., U. Edinburgh, Scotland, 1981. Research scientist assoc. dept. astronomy U. Tex., Austin, 1971-76; research astronomer dept. astronomy U. Edinburgh, Scotland, 1976-81; research scientist assoc. dept. astronomy U. Tex., Austin, 1981-85, research scientist dept. astronomy, 1985—; cons., 1977-81, lectr., 1982, 84, 85; cons. dept. astronomy UCLA, 1977-81. Author: (with others) Second Reference Catalogue of Bright Galaxies, 1976; Southern Galaxy Catalogue, 1985. Served to capt. USAF, 1967-71. NSF grantee, 1982. Mem. Internat. Astron. Union, Royal Astron. Soc., Am. Astron. Soc., Astron. Soc. Pacific, Sigma Xi. Current Work: Galaxy catalogues, galaxy photometry, photometric standard stars. Subspecialty: Optical astronomy. Office: Dept Astronomy U Tex Austin TX 78712

COSCINA, DONALD VICTOR, psychiatric institute administrator, researcher, educator; b. New Britain, Conn., Oct. 11, 1943; emigrated to Can., 1970; s. Victor Joseph and Edna Agnes (Prills) C.; m. Elizabeth Deen Bridgen, June 25, 1966; children: David Victor, Lynn Elizabeth. B.A., U. Vt., 1965; M.A., Bucknell U., 1967; Ph.D., U. Chgo., 1971. Registered psychologist, Ont. Vis. scientist in neurochemistry Clarke Inst. Psychiatry, Toronto, Ont., Can., 1970-71, research scientist in neurochemistry, 1971-77, head biopsychology, 1977—; assoc. prof. psychology U. Toronto, 1977—, assoc. prof. psychiatry, 1980—; mem. initial rev. group in neuropsychology NIMH, Washington, 1982-85. Editor: Anorexia Nervosa, Recent Developments in Research, 1983; editor: Pharmacological Biochem. Behavior, 1973—, Neurosci. and Biobehavior Rev, 1977—, Nutrition And Behavior, 1981—. Recipient Research Fund award Clarke Inst. Psychiatry, 1974; Bucknell Univ. scholar, 1965-67; USPHS trainee U. Chgo., 1967-70. Mem. AAAS, Can. Coll. Neuropsychopharmacology, Can. Assn. Neurosci., Soc. Neurosci., Eastern Psychol. Assn. Roman Catholic. Current Work: Neuroanatomical and neurochemical determinants of behavior; abnormal feeding and body weight in humans and animals (e.g., obesity, anorexia nervosa); recovery of function in central nervous system. Subspecialties: Physiological psychology; Neurochemistry. Home: 3075 Council Ring Rd Mississauga ON L5L 1N7 Canada Office: Clarke Inst Psychiatry 250 College St Toronto ON M5T 1R8 Canada

COSMAN, BARD, plastic surgeon, sculptor; b. Bklyn., Nov. 10, 1930; s. Max and Cornelia (Kaps) C.; m. Madeleine Pelner, Sept. 7, 1958; children: Marin, Bard Clifford. A.B., Columbia U., 1952, M.D., 1955. Diplomate: Am. Bd. Plastic Surgery. Intern Roosevelt Hosp., N.Y.C., 1955-59; resident Presbyn. Hosp., N.Y.C., 1959-61; instr. in surgery Columbia U., 1963-67, asst. clin. prof. surgery, 1967-70, assoc. clin. prof. surgery, 1970-73, assoc. prof. surgery, 1973-77, prof. clin. surgery, 1977-82, prof. clin. surgery in anatomy and cell biology, 1982—; pres., exec. bd. N.Y. Physicians Art Assn., 1979—. Abstracts editor, contbr.: articles Cleft Palate Jour; contbr.: articles Plastic and Reconstructive Surgery Jour; sculptor: articles Madeleine (first prize AMA Physicians Art Show 1961). Served to lt. comdr. USN, 1961-63. Recipient Curtis Gold Medal Columbia U., 1947, Janeway Prize, 1955. Fellow Am. Assn. Plastic Surgeons; mem. N.Y. Regional Soc. Plastic and Reconstructive Surgery (pres. 1979-80), N.Y. State Med. Soc. (chmn. Sect. on Plastic and Reconstructive Surgery 1973), Am. Cleft Palate Assn., Am. Soc. Plastic and Reconstructive Surgeons, Am. Soc. for Laser Medicine and Surgery (founding). Democrat. Jewish. Current Work: Argon laser treatment of port-tine stain hemangiomas. Subspecialties: Surgery; Laser medicine. Home: 32 Knickerbocker Rd Tenafly NJ 07670 Office: Columbia Univ Med School 630 W 168th St New York NY 10032

COSMIDES, GEORGE JAMES, pharmacologist/toxicologist, consultant; b. Pitts., July 23, 1926; s. James and Catherine (Palogaris) C.; m. Nasia Murlas, Sept. 12, 1948; 1 dau., Leda. B.S., U. Pitts., 1952; M.S., Purdue U., 1954, Ph.D. in Pharmacology, 1956. Registered pharmacist, Pa. Sr. scientist Smith Kline & French Labs., Phila., 1956-57; asst. prof. pharmacology U. R.I., Kingston, 1957-59; pharmacologist NIMH, Bethesda, MD., 1959-63; dir. pharmacology-toxicology Nat. Inst. Gen. Med. Scis., Bethesda, 1963-74; dep. dir. div. specialized info. services Nat. Library of Medicine, Bethesda, 1974—; cons. Contbr. articles to profl. jours. Mem. Citizens for Good Govt., Rockville, Md., 1962—; pres. Montgomery County (Md.) PTA, 1963-74; mem. parish council St. George's Ch., 1970-80. Served with inf. U.S. Army, 1944-46. Decorated Bronze Star; recipient Disting. Alumunus award U. Pitts., 1966; Disting. lectr. AAAS, 1971; others. Mem. Am. Soc. Pharmacology and Exptl. Therapeutics, Soc. Toxicology, Am. Soc. Info. Sci. Current Work: Online handling of specialized info. in med. scis.; toxicology info.; database systems; distributed systems and networks; info. systems, storage and retrieval; environ. health/toxicology. Subspecialties: Pharmacology; Toxicology (medicine). Home: 639 Crocus Dr Rockville MD 20850 Office: NIH 8600 Rockville Pike Bethesda MD 20209

COSTA, MAX, toxicologist/pharmacologist, researcher; b. Cagliari, Italy, Jan. 10, 1952; came to U.S., 1957, naturalized, 1962; s. Erminio and Anna (Marazzi) C.; m. Elizabeth R. Costa, June 15, 1974. B.S. in Biology, Georgetown U., 1974; Ph.D. in Pharmacology, U. Ariz., 1976. Asst. prof. lab medicine U. Conn., 1977-79; asst. prof. pharmacology U. Tex., Houston, 1980-81, assoc. prof., 1981—; speaker, community cons. toxicol. problems; cons. EPA, AMAX, Inc., Nickel Producers Environ Research Assn. Reviewer profl. jours.; contbr. abstracts, articles and revs. to profl. jours. Recipient Young Envrion. Scientist award NIH, 1977-81; EPA grantee; Nat. Cancer Inst. grantee; Nat. Inst. Environ. Health Scis. grantee. Mem. Am. Soc. Biol. Chemists, Am. Soc. Pharmacology and Exptl. Therapeutics, Am. Soc. Cell Biology, AAAS, N.Y. Acad. Scis., Soc. Toxicology, Am. Assn. Cancer Research. Current Work: Mechanisms of metal carcinogenesis. Subspecialties: Biochemistry (biology); Gene actions. Office: Dept Pharmacology U Tex Med Sch Houston TX 77025

COSTANZA, MARY E., physician; b. Quincy, Mass., Feb. 21, 1937; d. Fred P. and Clara (Zottoli) C. A.B. magna cum laude, Radcliffe Coll., 1958; M.A., U. Calif., Berkeley, 1963; M.D., U. Rochester, 1968. Diplomate: Am. Bd. Internal Medicine, 1972. Resident in medicine Tufts-New Eng. Med. Ctr., Boston, 1968-70, fellow in med. oncology, 1970-72, instr. medicine, 1972-74, asst. prof., 1974-79; assoc. prof. medicine U. Mass. Med. Sch., Worcester, 1979—, dir. div. oncology, 1980—. Contbr. numerous articles to profl. jours. Woodrow Wilson fellow, 1961-63; recipient Lange book award, 1968. Fellow ACP; mem. Am. Assn. Clin. Oncologists, Am. Assn. Cancer Research, Am. Fedn. Clin. Research, Am. Assn. Edn. Current Work: Oncology chemotherapy, cancer research, clinical cancer education. Subspecialties: Internal medicine; Oncology. Office: 55 Lake Ave N Worcester MA 01605

COSTANZO, RICHARD MICHAEL, physiologist, educator, researcher; b. Bklyn., July 18, 1947; s. William H. and Agatha (Maraventano) C.; m. Linda N. Schupper, July 3, 1971; children: Daniel, Rebecca. B.S. in Biology, SUNY, Stony Brook, 1969; Ph.D. in Physiology, SUNY Upstate Med. Sch., Syracuse, 1975. NIH postdoctoral fellow Rockefeller U., N.Y.C., 1975-77; research asso. dept. physiology N.Y.U. Sch. Medicine, N.Y.C., 1977-78, instr., 1978-79; asst. prof. dept. physiology Med. Coll. Va., Richmond, 1979-85, assoc. prof., 1985—. Contbr. articles to profl. jours. Served with USAF Res., 1971-77. Nat. Inst. Neurol. Communicative Disease and Stroke grantee, 1981—; research career devel. award 1984—. Mem. Physiol. Soc., Soc. for Neurosci., Assn. for Chemoreception Scis., N.Y. Acad. Scis., Sigma Xi. Current Work: Research on olfaction. Subspecialty: Neurophysiology.

COSTEA, NICOLAS VINCENT, physician, researcher; b. Bucharest, Romania, Nov. 10, 1927; came to U.S., 1957; s. Nicolas and Florica (Ionescu) C.; m. Ileana Paunescu, Apr. 20, 1973. B.A., Nat. Coll., Bucharest, 1946; M.S., U. Paris, 1949; M.D., 1956. Intern St. Francis Hosp., N.Y.C., 1956-57; resident L.I. Jewish Hosp., 1957-59; fellow in hematology Tufts U., 1959-62; dir. clinic Pratt Clinic, Boston, 1962-63; clin. investigator VA West Side Med. Ctr., Chgo., 1963-68; chief hematology U. Ill., Chgo., 1968-70, prof. medicine, Chgo, 1970-72; chief hematology-oncology UCLA-VA Hosp., Sepulveda, 1972—;

prof. UCLA, 1972—; vis. prof. Nat. Acad. Scis., 1972. Contbr. numerous chpts., articles to profl. publs. Recipient Lederle award Lederle Industries, 1966. Mem. Am. Soc. Hematology, Am. Soc. Immunology, N.Y. Acad. Scis., Western Soc. Clin. Research. Current Work: Antibody mediated hemolysis; biochemistry of immune competent cells. Subspecialties: Immunology (agriculture); Hematology. Home: 3651 Terrace View Encino CA 91436 Office: VA Med Center-UCLA Sepulveda CA 91343

COSTELLO, RICHARD JAMES, engineer, industrial hygienist; b. Newton, Mass., Apr. 19, 1945; s. Richard E. and Phyllis Ruth (Burton) C. B.S. in Civil Engring., U. Ariz., 1968; M.S. in Environ. Health Engring., U. Tex., 1973. Registered profl. engr., Tex.; cert. Bd. Cert. Safety Profls., Am. Bd. Indsl. Hygiene. Sr. research indsl. engr. Nat. Inst. for Occupational Safety and Health, Cin., 1977-85, Morgantown, W.Va., 1985—; lectr. in field. Contbr. articles to profl. jours. Served to capt. USAF, 1964-76. Decorated Commendation medals. Mem. Am. Indsl. Hygiene Assn., Am. Acad. Indsl. Hygiene (diplomate), Air Pollution Control Assn., Am. Chem. Soc., Am. Soc. Safety Engrs., Am. Acad. Environ. Engrs. (diplomate). Current work: Performs industrial hygiene and ambient air monitoring studies to assess the effect of hazardous waste sites and Superfund sites on workers. Subspecialties: Health services research; Hazardous waste disposal. Home: PO Box 4198 Star City WV 26504 Office: Nat Inst Occupational Safety and Health Appalachian Lab 944 Chosnut Ridge Rd Morgantown WV 26505

COSTLOW, JOHN DEFOREST, marine biologist. Dir., Duke U. Marine Lab., Beaufort, N.C. Subspecialty: Marine biology. Office: Duke U Marine Lab Beaufort NC 28516*

COTTER, WILLIAM BRYAN, JR., anatomist, educator, researcher; b. Hartford, Conn., May 8, 1926; s. William Bryan and Johanna (Sumeriva) C.; m. Alice Wadsworth Wendt, Sept. 11, 1948; children: William B. III, Daniel T., Ellen L., Elizabeth W., Sarah D., Andrew R. Student, New Britain (Conn.) Tchrs. Coll., 1946-47; B.A. with honors, Wesleyan U., 1949, M.A., 1951; Ph.D., Yale U., 1956. Postdoctoral teaching fellow Med. Coll. S.C., 1959-60; Asst. prof. biology Coll. Charleston, S.C., 1955-56, asst. prof., 1957-59; asst. prof. biology Wesleyan U., 1956-57; asst. prof. anatomy U. Ky., Lexington, 1960-66, asso. prof., 1967-73, prof., 1974—. Served in USAAF, 1943-45. Mem. Am. Assn. Anatomists, Am. Soc. Zoologists, Soc. Study of Evolution, Genetics Soc. Am., Am. Soc. Human Genetics, Sigma Xi. Current Work: Physiological genetics; specifically, behavorial modification, courtship behavior, melanism, pleiotropy, polymorphic population maintenance. Subspecialties: Evolutionary biology; Anatomy and embryology. Home: 1005 Lane Allen Rd Lexington KY 40504 Office: Rose St The Medical Center Lexington KY 40536

COTTON, FRANK ALBERT, chemist, educator; b. Phila., Apr. 9, 1930; s. Albert and Helen (Taylor) C.; m. Diane Dornacher, June 13, 1959; children: Jennifer Helen, Jane Myrna. Student, Drexel Inst. Tech., 1947-49; A.B., Temple U., 1951, D.Sc. (hon.), 1963; Ph.D., Harvard U., 1955; Dr. rer. Nat. (hon.), Bielefeld U., 1979; D.Sc. (hon.), Columbia U., 1980, Northwestern U., 1981, U. Bordeaux, 1981, St. Joseph's U., 1982, U. Louis Pasteur, 1982, U. Valencia, 1983, Kenyon Coll., 1983, Technion-Israel Inst. Tech., 1983. Instr. chemistry M.I.T., 1955-57, asst. prof., 1957-60, assoc. prof., 1960-61, prof., 1961-71; Robert A. Welch Distinguished prof. chemistry Tex. A&M U., 1971—; Cons. Am. Cyanamid, Stamford, Conn., 1958-67, Union Carbide, N.Y.C., from 1964. Author: (with G. Wilkinson) Advanced Inorganic Chemistry, 4th edit, 1980, Basic Inorganic Chemistry, 1976, Chemical Applications of Group Theory, 2d edit, 1970, (with L. Lynch and C. Darlington) Chemistry, An Investigative Approach; Editor: (with L. Lynch and C. Darlington) Progress in Inorganic Chemistry, Vols. 1-10, 1959-68, Inorganic Syntheses, Vol. 13, 1971, (with L.M. Jackman) Dynamic Nuclear Magnetic Resonance Spectroscopy, (with R.A. Walton) Multiple Bonds between Metal Atoms. Recipient Michelson-Morley award Case Western Res. U., 1980, Nat. Medal of Sci., 1982. Mem. Nat Acad. Scis., Am. Soc. Biol. Chemists, Am. Chem. Soc. (awards 1962, 74, Baekland medal N.J. sect. 1963, Nichols medal N.Y. sect. 1975, Pauling medal Oreg. and Puget Sound sect. 1976, Kirkwood medal N.Y. sect. 1978, Gibbs medal Chgo. sect. 1980), Am. Acad. Arts and Scis., Royal Danish Acad. Scis. and Letters (hon.), N.Y. Acad. Scis. (hon. life), Göttingen Acad. Scis. (corr.), Royal Soc. Chemistry (hon.), Societa Chimica Italiana (hon.). Subspecialties: Inorganic chemistry; X-ray crystallography. Office: Tex A and M U College Station TX 77843

COTTON, JOHN M., computer and switching systems architect; b. Murree, India, Oct. 9, 1931; s. Geoffrey and Mary Z. (Barwell) C.; m. Valerie Cheshire, Oct. 11, 1979; children—Simon G., Christopher T., Dominic M. B.Sc. in Physics, U. London, 1954. With G.E.C., Stanmore, Middlesex, Eng., 1954-57, Computer Devel. Ltd., Kenton, Middlesex, 1957-62; engr. ICL' Harrow, Middlesex, 1962-64; sr. engr. Plessey Telecom Research, 1964-72, mgr. Poole, Dorset, 1972-74; sr. mgr. Bell No. Research, Ottawa, Can., 1974-76; dir. advanced systems architecture ITT Advanced Tech. Ctr., Shelton, Conn., 1977—. Patentee in field; contbr. articles to profl. jours. Fellow Brit. Computer Soc.; mem. IEEE. Club: Cedar Point Yacht (Westport, Conn.). Current work: Research and development of S.I.M.D., parallel processing architecture and applications; research and devel. of M.I.M.D. distributed computer systems. Subspecialties: Computer architecture; Telecommunications. Office: ITT Advanced Tech Ctr Research Dr Shelton CT 06484

COULSON, KINSELL LEROY, meteorologist; b. Hatfield, Mo., Oct. 7, 1916; s. Charles Samuel and Nora Madge (Swank) C.; m. Vera Vivien Vainer, Mar. 23, 1947. B.S., Northwest Mo. State Tchrs. Coll., 1942; M.A., UCLA, 1952, Ph.D., 1959. Jr. meteorologist U.S. Weather Bur., Chgo., 1942; meteorologist UN, Shanghai, China, 1946-47, Naval Civil Service, China Lake, Calif., 1950-51; assoc. research meteorologist UCLA, 1951-59; meteorologist Stanford Research Inst., Menlo Park, Calif., 1959-60; mgr. geophysics Gen. Electric Space Scis. Lab., Phila., 1960-65; prof. meteorology U. Calif.-Davis, 1965-79, prof. emeritus, 1983—; dir. Mauna Loa Obs., Hilo, Hawaii, 1979-83; cons. NASA, Lawrence Livermore Nat. Lab.; cons., lectr. Author: Solar and Terrestrial Radiation: Methods and Measurements, 1975, (with J.V. Dave and Z. Sekera) Tables Related to Radiation Emerging, From a Planetary Atmosphere with Rayleigh Scattering, 1960; contbr. articles to profl. jours.; patentee atmospheric density calculator. Served with USN, 1943-46. Recipient numerous research grants. Mem. Am. Meterol. Soc., Am. Geophys. Union, Am. Solar Energy Soc., AAAS, No. Calif. Energy Assn., Planetary Soc., Mauna Kea Astron. Soc., Sigma Xi. Current work: Remote sensing. Subspecialties: Meteorology; Remote sensing (atmospheric science). Home: 119 Bryce Way Vacaville CA 95688

COUNCIL, EDWARD LATIMER, software engineer; b. Princeton, Ill., Mar. 12, 1956; s. Harold Edward and Sarah Latimer (Skinner) C. B.S.E.E., Bradley U., 1978, postgrad., 1979-80; postgrad. Ariz. State U., 1985. Assoc. engr. Midwest Engring., Creve Coeur, Ill., 1981; software engr. Motorola Microsystems, Phoenix, 1981-84; sr. software engr. K-TRON Internat., Scottsdale, Ariz., 1984-85; sr. engr. Northrop Corp. Electro-Mech. Div., Anaheim, Calif., 1985—. Contbr. articles in field. Sound designer, tech. dir., bd. dirs., treas. Scottsdale Community Players (Stagebrush Theatre), 1981-85. Mem. IEEE, (past sec., and chmn. Phoenix chpt. computer soc.), Assn. Computing Machinery. Club: Motorola Computer (v.p., pres.), Sagurao Astronomy, Jazz in Ariz. Current Work: Software development, testing and quality assurance, software engineering; real-time systems; programming language development; microprocessor applications. Subspecialties: Software engineering; Programming languages.

COUNSELMAN, CLARENCE JAMES, agricultural research corporation administrator; b. West Palm Beach, Fla., July 4, 1925; s. Clifford and Victoria C.; m. Marion Helseth, July 9, 1949; children: Michael, Jenine, Lynn C. Garriott, Steven. B.S., Auburn U., 1952, M.S., 1953. Prodn. mgr. Big Springs Hatchery, Albertville, Ala., 1953-55; project leader State of Fla., Vero Beach, 1955-57; asst. mgr. Mobay (then Vero Beach Labs.), Vero Beach, 1957-63; mgr. CIBA-GEIGY Corp., Vero Beach, 1963—. Contbr. to profl. confs. Served with USN, 1942-46. Decorated Purple Heart. Mem. Am. Inst. Biol. Sci., Am. Phytopath. Soc., Am. Soc. Photogrammetry, Entomol. Soc. Am. (cert. entomologist), Fla. Hort. Soc., Internat. Platform Assn., N.Y. Acad. Scis., Soc. Nematology, Phi Kappa Phi. Democrat. Patentee chlordimeform with organophosphate compounds. Current Work: Administration and research. Subspecialties: Biochemistry (biology); Polymer chemistry. Office: PO Box 1090 Vero Beach FL 32960

COUNTS, WAYNE BOYD, chemist, educator, consultant; b. Prosperity, S.C., Oct. 27, 1936; s. Clarence Boyd and Nell (Long) C.; m. Mary Grace Stansbury, Sept. 29, 1962; children: Wayne Boyd, Alicia Anne, Cynthia Lynn. B.S., Furman U., 1958; Ph.D., U. N.C., Chapel Hill, 1963. NIH fellow, Bethesda, Md., 1966-69; prof. Lincoln Meml. U., Harrogate, Tenn., 1969; assoc. prof. chemistry Ga. Southwestern Coll., 1969-79, prof., 1979—. Mem. Am. Chem. Soc., Sigma Xi. Baptist. Current Work: Synthesis of hetrocyclic and novel organic compounds. Subspecialties: Organic chemistry; Synthetic chemistry. Home: 402 Sharon Dr Americus GA 31709 Office: Ga Southwestern Coll Americus GA 31709

COUPER, JAMES RILEY, chemical engineer, educator; b. St. Louis, Dec. 10, 1925; s. James G. and Annetta (Riley) C.; m. Fanny D. Collins, Sept. 5, 1953 (div.); children: Geoffrey, Kathleen; m. Maribelle Wyton, Aug. 12, 1979. B.S.Ch.E., Washington U., St. Louis, 1949, M.S. Ch.E., 1950, D.Sc., 1957. Registered profl. engr., Mo., Ark. Research engr. Mo. Portland Cement, St. Louis, 1951-52; sr. engr. Organic Chem. Engring. dept. Monsanto, St. Louis, 1952-58; prodn. supr. J.F. Queeny plant, St. Louis, 1958-59; assoc. prof. U. Ark., Fayetteville, 1959-65, prof. dept. chem. engring., 1965—, chmn. dept., 1968-79, also cons. Contbr. articles to profl. publs. Served to lt. USNR, 1944-62. Mem. Am. Inst. Chem. Engrs., Am. Chem. Soc., Am. Soc. Engring. Edn., Soc. Rheology, Tau Beta Pi, Omega Chi Epsilon, Alpha Chi Sigma, Sigma Chi. Episcopalian. Current Work: Process economics and process design, polymer rheology. Subspecialty: Chemical engineering. Office: U Ark E-227 Dept Chem Engring Fayetteville AR 72703

COURNAND, ANDRE F., physiologist; b. Paris, France, Sept. 24, 1895; came to U.S., 1930, naturalized, 1941; s. Jules and Marguerite (Weber) C.; m. Sibylle Blumer (dec. 1959); children: Muriel, Marie-Eve, Marie Claire; m. Ruth Fabian, 1963 (dec. 1973); m. Beatrice Bishop Berle, 1975. B.A., Sorbonne U., Paris, 1913, P.C.B. in Sci, 1914; M.D., U. Paris, 1930; Dr. h.c., U. Strasbourg, 1957, U. Lyon, 1958, U. Brussels, 1959, U. Pisa, 1960, Columbia U., 1965, U. Brazil, 1965, U. Nancy, 1969; D.Sc., U. Birmingham, 1961, Gustavus Adolphus Coll., 1963. Prof. emeritus medicine Coll. Phys. & Surg., Columbia. Served with French Army, 1915-19. Decorated Croix de Guerre (France); recipient Laureate (silver medal), faculty medicine U. Paris; Andrea Retzius silver medal Swedish Soc. Internal Medicine; Lasker award USPHS; winner (with Dr. Dickinson W. Richards and Dr. Werner Forssman) of 1956 Nobel Prize in medicine and physiology; recipient Jiminez Diaz prize, 1970. Fellow Royal Soc. Medicine; mem. Nat. Acad. Scis. U.S.A., de l'Academie Nationale de Medecine (fgn.) (France), Academie Royale de Medecine de Belgique, Am. Physiol. Soc., Assn. Am. Physicians, Brit. Cardiac Soc., Swedish Soc., Internal Medicine, Soc. Medicale Hopitaux de Paris, Academie des Sciences, Institut de France (fgn. mem.). Clubs: Century Assn, Am. Alpine. Current Work: Since retirement, I have published on history of science and on ethics and psychology of scientists. Subspecialty: Physiology (medicine). Home: 142 E 19th St New York NY 10003

COURTNEY, JOHN VINCENT, physician, radiologist; b. Belfast, Ireland, Aug. 4, 1948; came to U.S., 1975; s. John Vincent and Catherine Patricia (Rogers) C.; m. Ann Margaret Kieran, Oct. 5, 1973; 1 dau., Rachel Melanie. M.B., B.Ch., BAO, Univ. Coll., Dublin, 1974. Intern St. Lawrence's Hosp., Dublin, 1974-75; resident in radiology U. Chgo., 1976-79, asst. prof. radiology, 1979-83, clin. asst. prof., 1983—; staff radiologist, dir. dept. nuclear medicine Oak Park Hosp., Ill. Mem. Chgo. Med. Soc., Ill. Med. Soc., AMA, Radiol. Soc. N. Am. Roman Catholic. Current Work: Cancer of esophagus, lung cancer, mammography. Subspecialty: Diagnostic radiology. Office: Dept Radiolog Univ Chicago Chicago IL 60637

COURTNEY, CHARLES HILL, III, veterinary parasitologist, researcher; b. Balt., Jan. 1, 1947; s. Charles Hill, Jr. and Pansy Blanche (Howell) C.; m. Deborah Louise Gotwalt, May 31, 1969; children—Elizabeth Ashley, Matthew Avery. B.S., Clemson U., 1969; M.S., U. Fla., 1973; D.V.M., Auburn U., 1977; Ph.D., Ohio State U., 1982. Pvt. vet. practice, New Port Richey, Fla., 1977-78; instr. Ohio State U., Columbus, 1978-82; asst. prof., dept. infectious diseases Coll. Vet. Medicine, U. Fla., Gainesville, 1982—. Editor 3 books; contbr. articles to profl. jours. Served as lt. USNR, 1969-71. Mem. AVMA, Am. Assn. Vet. Parasitologists, Am. Soc. Parasitologists, Am. Heartworm Soc. (charter). Republican. Current work: Epidemiology and control of ruminant helminths, genetic parasite resistance in sheep, canine heartworm disease. Subspecialties: Parasitology; Preventive medicine (veterinary medicine). Home: 9216 SW 19th Ave Gainesville FL 32607 Office: Dept Infectious Diseases Coll Vet Medicine Box J-137 JHMHC Univ of Fla Gainesville FL 32610

COUSE, NANCY LEE, geneticist; b. Syracuse, May 3, 1941; d. Charles Richard and Rosa Elizabeth (Saupe) C.; m. George Albert Desborough, Aug. 10, 1966. B.S., Cornell U., 1962; Ph.D., U. Wis., Madison, 1966. Research assoc. U. Wis., 1966; staff fellow NIH, Bethesda, Md., 1966-67; postdoctoral fellow U. Colo. Med. Ctr., Denver, 1967-69; asst. prof. biol. scis. U. Denver, 1969—; cons. Denver Research Inst. Contbr. articles to profl. jours. NSF grantee, 1979-81; EPA grantee, 1977-79; Research Corp. grantee, 1970. Mem. Am. Genetic Assn., Genetics Soc. Am., AAAS, Am. Inst. Biol. Scis., Am. Soc. Microbiology, Soc. Coll. Sci. Tchrs., Sigma Xi. Patentee in improved grid for use in counting colonies of bacteria present in discrete areas of a spiral deposition pattern. Current Work: Researcher in physiology of higher fungi, enzymological responses of microbes to environmental chemicals. Subspecialties: Gene actions; Environmental toxicology. Home: 2164 Zang St Golden CO 80401 Office: Dept Biology U Denver Denver CO 80208

COUTTS, ROBERT LAROY, psychologist; b. Royal, Nebr., Nov. 5, 1928; s. Hazen Coutts and Anita (Morrison) Coutts Cernik; m. Sue Webb, Feb. 17, 1952 (div. Oct. 1973); children: Robert LaRoy, William C., Candila S., R. Christopher; m. Mary E. Reutinger, Jan. 13, 1974. B.S., Fla. State U., 1951, M.S., 1954, Ph.D., 1962. Asst. prof. guidance Western Ill. U., Macomb, 1962-64; prof. psychology SUNY, Oswego, 1964-66; assoc. prof. psychology Parsons Coll., Fairfield, Iowa, 1966-73; psychologist Mesa County Mental Health Center, Grand Junction, Colo., 1973-78, pvt. practice, Colorado Springs, 1979—. Author: Love and Intimacy: A Psychological Approach, 1973. Mem. Am. Psychol. Assn., Colo. Psychol. Assn., El Paso County Psychol. Assn. (dir. 1981-83), Phi Delta Kappa. Lodge: Lions. Current Work: Obtaining baseline data regarding brain dysfunction; assessment of specific response to psychotropic medications. Subspecialty: Neuropsychology. Home: 3752 Quiet Circle Colorado Springs CO 80917 Office: Colorado Springs Psychol Center 308 W Fillmore St #200 Colorado Springs CO 80907

COVERT, EUGENE EDZARDS, educator, engineer; b. Rapid City, S.D., Feb. 6, 1926; s. Perry and Eda (Edzards) C.; m. Mary Solveig Rutford, Feb. 22, 1946; children: David H., Christine J., Pamela M., Steven P. B.S., U. Minn., 1946, M.S., 1948; Sc.D., MIT, 1958. Registered profl. engr., Mass.; chartered engr., U.K. Preliminary design group USNADS, Johnsville, Pa., 1948-52; mem. staff MIT Aerophysics Lab., 1952—, asso. dir. aerophysics lab., 1963—, asso. prof. aeronautics and astronautics, 1963-68, prof., 1968—, head dept., 1985—; cons. Bolt, Beranek & Newman, Inc., Hercules, Inc., MIT Lincoln Lab., U.S. Army Research Office, Sverdrup Tech. Inc.; chief scientist USAF, 1972-73; mem. panel Naval Aeroballistic Adv. Com., 1965-75; mem., chmn. USAF Sci. Adv. Bd.; chmn. Power, Energetics and Propulsion panel Adv. Group for Aerospace Research and Devel. NATO, 1976-83; dir. Megatech Inc., Billerica, Mass., Sverdrup ARO Inc., Tullahoma, Tenn. Served with USNR, 1943-47. Recipient Exceptional Civilian Service award USAF, 1973, Univ. Educator of Yr. award Am. Soc. Aerospace Edn., 1980, Pub. Service award NASA, 1980. Fellow AIAA, Royal Aero. Soc.; mem. AAAS, N.Y. Acad. Sci., Nat. Acad. Engring., Sigma Xi. Current Work: Unsteady fluid mechanics, in particular as relates to turbulence, separation characteristics for application to stability, turbines and compressors. Subspecialties: Fluid mechanics; Aeronautical engineering. Office: Mass Inst Tech 77 Massachusetts Ave Cambridge MA 02139

COVINGTON, EDWARD ROYALS, chemistry educator, consultant; b. Meridian, Miss., Jan. 6, 1925; s. James Howard and Lolah Lillian (Lucius) C.; m. Dorothy Louise Warnack, Oct. 17, 1944 (div. 1969); 1 son, James Edward; m. Janet Elaine Ferguson, Mar. 22, 1975; 1 son, Andrew Royals. A.B. in Chemistry, Emory U., 1948, M.A. in Chemistry, 1951, Ph.D. in Organic Chemistry, 1954. Research chemist, staff scientist, film dept. DuPont Co., Old Hickory, Tenn., 1953-58, Richmond, Va., 1953-63, staff chemist fabrics and finishes dept., Old Hickory, 1968-70; research assoc. Ethyl Corp., Baton Rouge, 1963-64; sr. chemist So. Research Inst., Birmingham, Ala., 1964-68; prof. chemistry U. Tenn., Nashville, 1970-79, Tenn. State U., Nashville, 1979—; cons. polymer and organic chemistry. Served to 2d lt. USAAF, 1943-45, ETO. Recipient Outstanding Tchr. award U. Tenn. Gen. Alumni Assn., 1973. Republican. Presbyterian. Inventor/co-inventor coatings and copolymers. Current Work: Teaching organic and polymer chemistry; establishment of polymer research program. Subspecialties: Organic chemistry; Polymer chemistry. Office: Tennessee State University 10th and Charlotte Sts Nashville TN 37203

COVIT, ANDREW B., internist; b. Mineola, N.Y., Mar. 30, 1954; s. Harold and Gertrude (Lindenbaum) C.; m. Michelle Masarsky, July 3, 1978. B.A. in Biology, Hofstra U., 1975; M.D. magna cum laude, SUNY Downstate Med. Ctr., 1979. Diplomate: Am Bd. Internal Medicine. Intern N.Y. Hosp., Cornell U. Med Ctr., N.Y.C., 1979-80, asst. jr. and sr. physician, 1980-82, fellow in nephrology, 1982-1984. Contbr. articles to sci. publs. Cornell U. Cardiovascular Ctr. Research assoc., 1983-84. Mem. Am. Fedn. Clin. Research, ACP (assoc.), Alpha Omega Alpha. Current Work: Neuro-humoral factors in congestive heart failure; hemodynamics and renal function in hypertension. Subspecialties: Nephrology; Cardiology. Home: 445 E. 68th St New York NY 10021 Office: Cornell U Med Ctr Box 205 525 E 68th St New York NY

COWAN, DALE HARVEY, consultant; b. Cleve., Jan. 25, 1938; s. Milton Jerome and Clara (Umans) C.; m. Deborah Wolowitz, Jan. 28, 1967; children—Rachel, Morris Benjamin, William Ezra. A.B., Harvard U., 1959, M.D., 1963; J.D., Case Western Res. U., 1981. Diplomate Am. Bd. Internal Medicine. Intern, Cleve. Met. Gen. Hosp., 1963-64, resident, 1964-65, 67-70; asst. prof. medicine Case Western Res. U., Cleve., 1970-75, assoc. prof., 1975-83, clin. prof. epidemiology and community health, 1983-84, clin. prof. environ. health scis., 1985—; dir. hematology and oncology Marymount Hosp., Cleve., 1982—; of counsel Burke, Haber & Berick, Cleve., 1984—; bd. dirs. Physicians Peer Rev. Orgn., Cleve., 1981-83; spl. cons. Pres.'s Commn. on Bioethics, Washington, 1981—; mem. nat. adv. council Nat. Heart, Lung and Blood Inst., Bethesda, Md., 1982—. Author: Preferred Provider Organizations, 1984. Contbr. articles to profl. jours., chpts. to books. Bd. dirs. Bur. Jewish Edn., Cleve., 1977—, N.E. Ohio affiliate Am. Heart Assn., Cleve., 1982—. Served to lt. comdr. USPHS, 1965-67. NIH grantee, 1970-82. Fellow ACP, Am. Coll. Legal Medicine; mem. Am. Soc. Hematology, Am. Soc. Clin. Oncology, Am. Assn. Cancer Research, Am. Soc. Law and Medicine, others. Current work: Effect of growth factors on tumor cells, carcinogenesis, new treatments of cancer, cancer chemotherapy. Subspecialties: Hematology; Chemotherapy. Home: 19600 Shaker Blvd Shaker Heights OH 44122 Office: Marymount Hosp 12300 McCracken Rd Garfield Heights OH 44125

COWAN, JOHN JAMES, astronomy educator; b. Washington, Apr. 3, 1948; s. John Robert and Anna Wise (Vick) C.; m. Linda Demetry Cowan, May 29, 1971. B.A. in physics, George Washington U., 1970; M.S., Case Inst. Tech., Cleve., 1972; Ph.D. in astronomy, U. Md., College Park, 1976. Teaching asst. U. Md., 1971-74; research asst. NASA Goddard Space Flight Center, 1972-75; instr. U. Md., 1975, research asst., 1976; fellow Center for Astrophysics Harvard U., 1976-79; asst. prof. astronomy U. Okla., 1979-84, assoc. prof., 1984—. Contbr. articles to profl. jours. Am. Astron. Soc.-NASA grantee, 1980; NSF grantee, 1982—. Mem. Am. Astron. Soc., Internat. Astron. Union, Sigma Xi, Phi Beta Kappa, Sigma Pi Sigma, Pi Mu Epsilon. Current Work: Theoretical astrophysics; stellar evolution and nucleosynthesis, computer modeling, cometary physics; radio observations of supernovae astron. observations; optical spectropotometry and spectroscopy. Subspecialties: Theoretical astrophysics; Radio and microwave astronomy. Home: 2813 Meadow Ave Norman OK 73069 Office: Department of Physics and Astronomy Norman OK 73019

COWAN, ROBERT DUANE, research physicist; b. Lincoln, Nebr., Nov. 24, 1919; s. Ralph Ellis and Florence Athey (Eller) C.; m. Dorothy Mabel Martinson, July 6, 1944; children: Nancy Jean Cowan Lemons, Charles Eller, Gerald Stanley, Marjorie Sue Cowan Larson. B.A., Friends U., Wichita, Kans., 1942; Ph.D., Johns Hopkins U., 1946; Ph.D. (hon.), U. Lund, Sweden, 1982. NRC fellow U. Chgo., 1946-47, research assoc., 1947-48; prof. physics Friends U., 1948-51; staff mem. Los Alamos Nat. Lab., 1951-82, fellow, 1982—; adj. prof. U. N.Mex., 1958, 64, 72; vis. prof. Purdue U., 1971; Fulbright lectr., Lima, Peru, 1958-59; cons. Appleton Lab., Eng., 1977, Internat. Astron. Union, 1968—. Author: The Theory of Atomic Structure and Spectra, 1981; contbr. articles profl. jours. Fellow Am. Phys. Soc., Optical Soc. Am. Current Work: Theory of atomic structure and spectra, computer calculation of atomic spectra. Subspecialties: Atomic and molecular physics; Theoretical physics. Home: 4493 Trinity Dr Los Alamos NM 87544 Office: Los Alamos National Laboratory PO Box 1663 Los Alamos NM 87545

COWAN, WILLIAM MAXWELL, neurobiologist; b. Johannesburg, South Africa, Sept. 27, 1931; s. Adam and Jessie Sloan (Maxwell) C.; m. Margaret Sherlock, Mar. 31, 1956; children: Ruth Cowan Eadon, Stephen Maxwell, David Maxwell. B.Sc., Witwatersrand U., Johannesburg, 1951, B.Sc. (Hons.), 1952; D.Phil., Oxford U., 1956, B.M., B.Ch., 1958, M.A., 1959. From demonstrator to lectr. anatomy Oxford U., 1953-66; fellow Pembroke Coll., 1958-66; vis. prof. anatomy Washington U. Med. Sch., St. Louis, 1964-65, prof., chmn. dept., 1968-80; asso. prof. U. Wis. Med. Sch., Madison, 1966-68; research prof., dir. Weingart Lab. Devel. Neurobiology, Salk Inst. Biol. Studies, La Jolla, Calif., 1980; mem. Inst. Medicine, Nat. Acad. Scis., 1978; fgn. asso. Nat. Acad. Scis., 1981. Editor-in-chief: Jour. Neurosci.; editor: Ann. Revs. Neurosci. Fellow Am. Acad. Arts and Scis., Royal Soc. (London); mem. Internat. Brain Research Orgn. (exec. council), AAAS, Anat. Soc. Gt. Britain and Ireland, Royal Micros. Soc., Am. Assn. Anatomists, Soc. Neurosci. (pres. 1977-78), Sigma Xi, Alpha Omega Alpha. Current Work: The development of the brain and the organization of the visual system. Subspecialty: Neurobiology. Home: 1230 Avocet Ct Cardiff CA 92007 Office: Salk Inst PO Box 85800 San Diego CA 92138

COWARD, DAVID HAND, experimental physicist; b. Buffalo, Nov. 16, 1934; m. Doris Dickerson, June 4, 1960; 3 children. B. Engring. Physics, Cornell U., 1957; M.S. in Physics, Stanford U., 1958, Ph.D., 1963. Exptl. physicist Stanford Linear Accelerator Ctr. (Calif.), 1963—; sci. assoc. European Ctr. for Nuclear Research, Geneva, 1976-77; cons. MITRE Corp., McLean, Va., 1976. Fellow Am. Phys. Soc. Current work: High energy physics involving (a) electron-positron and electron-proton colliding beams, and (b) electron and photon beams on stationary targets. Subspecialty: Particle physics. Office: Stanford Linear Accelerator Ctr PO Box 4349 Stanford CA 94305

COWIE, LENNOX LAUCHLAN, educator; b. Jedburgh, Scotland, Oct. 18, 1950; came to U.S., 1970; s. James Reid C. B.Sc., Edinburgh U., 1970; postgrad., Glasgow U., 1970-71; Ph.D., Harvard U., 1976. Research assoc. Princeton (N.J.) U., 1976-78, research staff mem., 1978-79, research astronomer, assoc. prof. astrophys. sci., 1979-81; assoc. prof. physics MIT, Cambridge, 1980-84; astronomer Space Telescope Sci. Inst., 1983—; prof. physics and astronomy John Hopkins U., 1984—. Assoc. editor: Astrophys. Jour. Letters; Contbr. articles to profl. jours. Kennedy scholar, 1971-73; Fairchild Disting. scholar, 1980; Alfred P. Sloan fellow, 1983-85; recipient Bok prize Harvard U., 1984. Mem. Internat. Astron. Union, Royal Astron. Soc., Am. Astron. Soc. Warner prize 1985 Am. Phys. Soc. Current Work: Gas dynamics of interstellar and intergalactic gas. Subspecialties: Theoretical astrophysics; Optical astronomy. Home: 310 Linkwood Rd Apt 7 Baltimore MD

COX, ARTHUR NELSON, astrophysicist; b. Van Nuys, Calif., Oct. 12, 1927; s. Arthur Hildreth and Sarah (Nelson) C.; m. Joan Frances Ellis, Oct. 21, 1973; children by previous marriage: Bryan, Kay, Sally, Charles, Edward. B.S., Calif. Inst. Tech., 1948; M.A., Ind. U., 1952, Ph.D., 1953, D.Sc. (hon.), 1973. Staff Los Alamos (N. Mex.) Sci. Lab., summer, 1947, 48, 49, astrophysicist on staff, 1953—; lab. fellow Los Alamos (N.Mex.) Nat. Lab., 1983—; program dir. adviser NSF, 1973-74; vis. prof. UCLA, 1966; staff Avco-Everett Research Lab., 1960-61. Contbr. articles to profl. jours. NSF fellow, 1952-53; Harvard U. fellow, summer 1952; NATO sr. fellow in sci., 1968; Fulbright research scholar Belgium, 1968-69. Mem. Am. Astron. Soc., AAAS, Internat. Astron. Union, Sigma Xi. Current Work: Stellar opacities, stellar structure, evolution, stability, pulsation, atmospheres. Subspecialties: Theoretical astrophysics; Atomic and molecular physics. Home: 1700 Camino Redondo Los Alamos NM 87544 Office: MS B288 PO Box 1663 Los Alamos NM 87545

COX, DONALD STEPHEN, periodontist, immunologist, educator; b. Buffalo, Dec. 24, 1948; s. John Cecil and Ann (Cherup) C.; m. Molly Joslyn Gushue, July 17, 1971. B.S., Syracuse U., 1971; D.D.S., SUNY-Buffalo, 1975; D.M.Sc., Harvard U., 1980. Research assoc. Forsyth Dental Center, Boston,

1979-80; asst. prof. SUNY-Stony Brook, 1980—. Recipient Univ. award N.Y. State, 1980-82; Nat. Research award NIH, 1975-80; Am. Fund for Dental Health grantee, 1979-81; NIH grantee, 1983—; Office Naval Research grantee, 1985—. Mem. AAAS, N.Y. Acad. Sci., Internat. Assn. for Dental Research, Northeast Soc. Periodontists, Am. Acad. Periodondology, Am. Assn. Immunologists, Sigma Xi. Current Work: Immune mechanisms of tissue destruction, Interleukin-2, immune function in stress, Immunochemistry of IgA. Subspecialties: Immunology (medicine); Periodontics. Office: Dept Periodontics Sch Dental Medicine SUNY Stony Brook NY 11794

COX, HOLLACE LAWTON, JR., physical chemist; b. Oak Park, Ill., Nov. 17, 1935; s. Hollace Lawton and Frances Marian (Murray) C.; m. Sue Burdon, June 25, 1983. A.B., U. Rochester, 1959; Ph.D., Ind. U., 1967. Mem. tech. staff Tex. Instruments, Inc., Dallas, 1967-70; Robert A. Welch postdoctoral fellow Baylor U. dept. chemistry, Waco, Tex., 1970-73; Robert A. Welch postdoctoral fellow dept. pathology M.D. Anderson Hosp. and Tumor Inst., Houston, 1973-75, postdoctoral fellow med. physics tng. program, 1975-76; instr. Washington U. Sch. Medicine, St. Louis, 1976-77; asst. prof. U. Kans. Med. Sch., Kansas City, 1977-80; assoc. prof. U. Louisville Sch. Medicine, 1980-83; lectr. elec. engring. U. Louisville, 1983-85, asst. prof. elec. engring., 1985—. Robert A. Welch fellow, 1973-75; NSF grantee, 1980-82. Mem. Am. Phys. Soc., Optical Soc. Am., Am. Assn. Physicists in Medicine, N.Y. Acad. Sci., Sigma Xi, Sigma Pi Sigma, Phi Lamba Upsilon. Epsicopalian. Current Work: Laser-induced phase conjugation and other nonlinear optical interactions using thin film and optical waveguide technology. Applications in integrated optical devices, fiber optics, and optical communications. Subspecialties: Physical chemistry; Laser-induced chemistry. Office: Dept Elec Engring WS Speed Bldg U Louisville Louisville KY 40292

COX, JAMES CARL, JR., chemist, researcher, consultant; b. Wolf Summit, W.Va., June 17, 1919; s. James Carl and Maggie Lillian (Merrells) C.; m. Alma Lee Tenney, Sept. 8, 1945; children—James Carl III, Joseph Merrells, Alma Lee, Elizabeth Susan Cox Unger, Albert John. B.S. summa cum laude, W.Va. Wesleyan Coll., 1940; M.S. in Organic Chemistry, U. Del., 1947, Ph.D. in Phys. Organic Chemistry, 1949; postgrad. in law Am. U., summer 1953, George Washington U., summer 1954; J.D. with honors, U. Md., 1955. Bar: Md. 1955. Registered profl. sanitarian, Tex. Research chemist E.I. duPont de Nemours, Belle, W.Va., 1940-43; grad. instr. chemistry U. Del., Newark, 1946-49; prof. chemistry, head dept. chemistry Wesleyan Coll., Mason, Ga., 1949-51; prof. U.S. Naval Acad., Annapolis, Md., 1951-55; prof., research dir. Lamar U., Beaumont, Tex., 1955-65; prof., head dept. chemistry, dir. div. sci. and math. Oral Roberts U. Tulsa, 1965-68; prof., head dept. chemistry Wayland Baptist U., Plainview, Tex., 1968-76; v.p., research dir. Agrl. & Indsl. Devel., Inc., Plainview, 1976-79; environ. health expert Tex. Dept. Health, Plainview, 1979-84; cons. in field; vis. prof. organic chemistry Middle Tenn. State U., Murfreesboro, summer 1950, U. Baghdad, Iraq, 1956-57. Author books, the most recent being: Lives of Splendor, 1970; Patterson's German-English Chemical Dictionary, rev. edit., 1985, contbr. articles to profl. jours., also abstracts. Editor The Condenser, 1957-65. Hale County Republican precinct chmn., Plainview, 1983-84; bd. dirs. Plainview chpt. ARC, 1969-73, United Way, Plainview, 1972-75. Served to cpl. Combat Engrs., U.S. Army, 1943-45, ETO. Named Outstanding Prof., Lamar U., 1963-64, Wayland Bapt. U., 1971-74; fellow DuPont Endowment Found., 1947-49, Carnegie Found., 1949-51, State of Tex., 1957-59. Fellow Tex. Acad. Sci.; mem. Am. Chem. Soc., AAAS, AAUP, Tex. Pub. Health Assn., Tex. Environ. Health Assn. (governing council 1982-84). Methodist. Lodge: Rotary (pub. relations officer 1969-84). Current work: Novel fuels for industry; agricultural chemicals. Subspecialties: Organic chemistry; Polymer chemistry. Home: 804 Portland St Plainview TX 79072

COX, JEROME ROCKHOLD, JR., electrical engineer, educator; b. Washington, May 24, 1925; s. Jerome R. and Jane (Mills) C.; m. Barbara Jane Lueders, Sept. 2,1951; children—Nancy Jane Cox Battersby, Jerome Mills, Randall Allen. S.B., Mass. Inst. Tech., 1947, S.M., 1949, Sc.D., 1954. Mem. faculty Washington U., St. Louis, 1955—, prof. elec. engring., 1961—, prof. biomed. engring. in physiology and biophysics Sch. Medicine, 1965—; dir. Washington U. (Biomed. Computer Lab.), 1964-75, chmn. computer labs., 1967—, program dir. tng. program tech. in health care, 1970-78, chmn. dept. computer sci., 1975—; co-chmn. computers in cardiology conf. Inst. Medicine, Nat. Acad. Scis., 1974—; cardiology adv. com. Nat. Heart and Lung Inst., 1975-78; mem. epidemiology biostatistics and bioengring. cluster President's Biomed. Research Panel, 1975. Editorial bd.: Computers and Biomed. Research, 1967—; asso. editor, IEEE, trans. biomed. engring., 1969-71. Served with U.S. Army, 1943-44. Fellow Acoustical Soc. Am., IEEE; mem. Biomed. Engring. Soc., Biophys. Soc., Assn. Computing Machinery, Sigma Xi, Eta Kappa Nu, Tau Beta Pi. Author, patentee air traffic control, computerized tomography. Subspecialties: Computer architecture; Biomedical engineering. Office: Dept Computer Sci Box 1045 Washington Univ Saint Louis MO 63130

COX, LAWRENCE HENRY, mathematician; b. Yonkers, N.Y., Feb. 19, 1947; s. Ernest Fields and Ursula Madeline (Lynch) C.; m. Jane C. Haarsgaard, May 30, 1970; 1 child, Timothy. B.Sc., Manhattan Coll., 1968; Ph.D., Brown U., 1973. Research assoc. IBM Corp., Yorktown Heights, N.Y., 1968; asst. prof. U. Md., College Park, 1973-74; adj. faculty U. Md., 1979—; researcher Bur. of Census, Washington, 1974-80, asst. chief statis. research, 1980-83, sr. math. statistician, 1983—. Contbr. articles to profl. jours. Recipient Coll. Math. medal Mahattan Coll., 1968; Deptl. medal U.S. Dept. Commerce, 1981. Mem. Am. Statis. Assn. (chmn. com. on privacy and confidentiality), Nat. Computer Graphics Assn. (chmn. statis. graphics program), Am. Math. Soc., Ops. Research Soc. Am. Current work: Statistical confidentiality, applications of mathematical theory in statistics. Subspecialty: Statistics. Office: Bur of the Census FOB 3-3065 Washington DC 20233

COX, STEPHEN KENT, atmospheric sciences educator; b. Galesburg, Ill., Sept. 2, 1940; s. Joseph E. and Ruth B. (Burroughs) C.; m. Phyllis A. Cox, Dec. 23, 1961; children: Mark, Joseph, Elizabeth. B.A., Knox Coll., Galesburg, Ill., 1961; M.S., Ph.D., U. Wis.-Madison, 1967. Research meteorologist ESSA, Madison, Wis., 1965-67; research scientist Space Sci. and Engring. Ctr., U. Wis.-Madison, 1967-69; mem. faculty Colo. State U., Ft. Collins, 1969—, prof. atmospheric scis., 1977—. Editor Jour. Atmospheric Scis., 1982—. Contbr. over 100 sci. articles to profl. publs. Mem. Am. Meteorol. Soc. (spl. award for contbns. to GATE 1975). Subspecialties: Meteorology; Remote sensing (atmospheric science). Office: Atmospheric Scis Dept Colo State U Fort Collins CO 80523

COX, STEVEN WILLARD, mining geologist, mining engineer; b. Denver, Apr. 18, 1951; s. Robert West and Dorothy Dee (Wright) C.; m. Connie Lynn Rion, Oct. 8, 1971 (div. 1979); m. Emily Kay Mackender, Sept. 5, 1981; 1 child, Sara Louise. B.S., Western Wash. U., 1975. Grade control supr. Exxon, Casper, Wyo., 1976-78, geol. technician, 1978-79; mine geologist Phillips Petroleum Co., Grants, N.Mex., 1979-80; geol. engr. Union Oil Co. of Calif., Tucson, Ariz., 1980-81, Casper, 1981-82, mine engr., Parachute, Colo., 1982—. Mem. Geol. Soc. Am., Wyo. Geol. Assn. Congregationalist. Subspecialties: Geology; Database systems. Home: 560 Princess St Grand Junction CO 81501 Office: Union Oil Co of Calif PO Box 76 Parachute CO 81635

COZZARELLI, NICHOLAS ROBERT, biochemist. Prof. dept. molecular biology U. Calif., Berkeley. Subspecialty: Molecular biology. Office: U Calif Dept Molecular Biology Berkeley CA 94720

CRABTREE, GERALD WINSTON, biochemical pharmacologist; b. Denton, Lancashire, Eng., June 29, 1941; came to U.S., 1970; s. Emmanuel Cox and Sarah Ann (Craig) C.; m. Gloria Ferne Pilfrey, May 31, 1965; children—Lisa, Jill, Beth. B.S.A., Ont. Agrl. Coll., Guelph Ont., Can., 1963; M.S., U. Guelph, Can., 1965; Ph.D., U. Alberta, Can., 1970; M.A. (hon.), Brown U., Providence, 1980. Research assoc. Brown Univ., Providence, 1970-72, instr. biochem. pharmacology, 1972-74, asst. prof. biochem. pharmacology, 1974-78, assoc. prof. biochem. pharmacology, 1978-83; assoc. prof. medicine Roger Williams Gen. Hosp. & Brown U., Providence, 1983—; mem. chemotherapy and hematology adv. com. Am. Cancer Soc., N.Y.C., 1982-85. Recipient Nat. Cancer Inst. of Canada Research fellow, 1968-70. Mem. Can. Biochem. Soc., Am. Assn. for Cancer Research. Baptist. Current works: Clinical pharmacology of antieoplastic agents; biochemical pharmacology of new purine and pyrimdidine antineoplastic and antiparasitic agents; development of new treatment modalities (combinations of agents) for cancer. Subspecialties: Cancer research (medicine); Chemotherapy. Office: Roger Williams Gen Hosp 825 Chalkstone Ave Providence RI 02908

CRABTREE, JEROME OTTO, metallurgist; b. Coker, Ala., Sept. 26, 1921; s. J. Otto and Minnie Lee (Findley) C.; m. Hilda Ann Dunagan, May 21, 1948; children—Fred, Charlotte, Mimi. B.S. in Chemistry, U. Ala., 1943; postgrad. Case Inst. Tech., 1946. With Thompson Products (now TRW Corp.), Cleve., 1945-46, Redstone Arsenal, Huntsville, Ala., 1952-55, Reynolds Metals, Sheffield, Ala., 1955-56, Brown Engring., Huntsville, 1956-57, So. Research Inst., Birmingham, Ala., 1957-58; metallurgist U.S. Bur. Mines, University, Ala., 1963—. Mem. Am. Soc. Metals (com. chair 1977-78), Ala. Soc. Profl. Engrs. (sec.-treas. 1984-85), Am. Ceramic Soc., Materials Research Soc., Nat. Soc. Profl. Engrs. Democrat. Methodist. Clubs: University, Toastmasters (pres. 1980) (Tuscaloosa). Subspecialties: Metallurgy; Ceramics. Home: 1101 13th St Tuscaloosa AL 35401 Office: PO Box L University AL 35486

CRADDOCK, CAMPBELL, geologist, educator; b. Chgo., Apr. 3, 1930; s. John and Bernice (Campbell) C.; m. Dorothy Dunkelberg, June 13, 1953; children—Susan Elizabeth, John Paul, Carol Jean. B.A., DePauw U., 1951; M.A., Columbia U., 1953, Ph.D., 1954. Geologist Shell Oil Co., N.Mex., Tex., Colo., Wyo., 1954-56; asst. prof. U. Minn., Mpls., 1956-60, asso. prof., 1960-67; prof. geology U. Wis., Madison, 1967—, chmn. dept., 1977-80; leader Antarctic geologic field research programs, 1959-69, 80, Alaskan geologic field research programs, 1968-81, Svalbard field programs, 1977—; cons. C.E., AUS, 1957-58, N. Star Research Inst., 1965-68, Dept. State, 1976; vis. scientist N.Z. Geol. Survey, 1962-63; lectr. Nanjing and Beijing univs., China, 1981; chmn. panel geology and geophysics NRC, 1967-71, mem. polar research bd., 1978—; U.S. mem. working group on geology Sci. Com. on Antarctic Research, 1967—, chmn. group, 1973-80; co-chief scientist Leg 35, Deep Sea Drilling Project, Antarctica, 1974; chmn. Antarctic panel Circum-Pacific Map Project, 1979—; cons. Phillips Petroleum Co., 1980. Editor: Antarctic Geoscience, 1982; Co-editor: Geologic Maps of Antarctica, Folio 12, Antarctic Map Folio Series, Am. Geog. Soc., 1970, Initial Reports of the Deep Sea Drilling Project, Vol. 35, 1976; Contbr. articles sci. jours. Higgins fellow, 1951-52; NSF fellow, 1952-53; research grantee, 1957—; recipient U.S. Antarctic Service medal, 1968; Bellingshausen-Lazarev medal Soviet Acad. Scis., 1970; Alumni citation DePauw U., 1976. Fellow Geol. Soc. Am. (chmn. sect. 1982-83, books editor 1982—); mem. Internat. Union Geol. Scis. (mem. commn. on structural geology 1968-76, mem. com. on tectonics 1976—, del. Sci. Com. on Antarctic Research 1974—, mem. com. on geologic map of world 1974—), Polar Research Bd. (1978-82), Internat. Union Geol. Scis. (v.p. for Antarctica 1979—), Am. Geophys. Union, Am. Assn. Petroleum Geologists, Phi Beta Kappa, Sigma Xi. Subspecialty: Geology. Mailing Address: 1109 Winston Dr Madison WI 53711 Office: Dept Geology and Geophysics U Wis Madison WI 53706

CRAFT, CHARLES DOUGLAS, research chemist; b. Pensacola, Fla., Oct. 4, 1953; s. Manuel Charles and Betty Odell (Boyd) C.; m. Audrey Jeanne Daniels, Nov. 15, 1981. B.S. in Chemistry, U. West Fla., 1975. Biol. aide EPA, Gulf Breeze, Fla., 1974-75; research chemist U.S. Bur. Reclamation, Denver, 1976—, prin. investigator research projects, 1978—. Contbr. articles to profl. jours. Recipient Spl. Achievement award U.S. Bur. Reclamation, 1981, 84. Mem. Am. Chem. Soc., Soc. Environ. Toxicology and Chemistry. Mem. Christian Ch. Current work: Bioavailability of toxic metals using chemical techniques; acid precipitation effects on aquatic ecosystems; multivariate statistics applied to environmental data. Subspecialties: Environmental chemistry; Analytical chemistry. Office: US Bur Reclamation PO Box 25007 D-1523A Denver CO 80225

CRAGON, HARVEY GEORGE, See *Who's Who in America,* 43rd edition.

CRAIG, BURTON MACKAY, chemist; b. Vermilion, Alta., Can., May 29, 1918; s. Walter Alexander and Mary Jessie (Baillie) C.; m. Inez Gladys Guttormson, July 5, 1945; children—Wayne Keith, Cheryl Lynne. B.Sc.A., U. Sask., 1944, M.Sc., 1946; Ph.D., U. Minn., 1950. Research officer Prairie Regional Lab., Saskatoon, Sask., 1950-69, assoc. dir., 1969-70, dir., 1970-83. Fellow Chem. Inst. Can.; mem. Am. Oil Chemists Soc., AAAS, Research Mgrs. Assn. Can., Sigma Xi; hon. life mem. Agrl. Inst. Can. Lutheran. Current Work: Plantcell, plant tissue culture; cryopreservation; nitrogen fixation, photosynthesis; cell biology; mutagenesis. Subspecialties: Plant cell and tissue culture; Nitrogen fixation. Home: 423 Lake Crescent Saskatoon SK S7H 3A3 Canada

CRAIG, CHARLES ROBERT, pharmacologist, educator; b. Buckhannon, W.Va., Jan. 24, 1936; s. Thorne C. and Martha (Blakeslee) C.; m. Margaret A. Craig, June 12, 1960; 1 child, Gary Lynn. B.S., Glenville State Coll., 1959; Ph.D., U. Wis., 1964. Sr. investigator GD Searle & Co., Chgo., 1964-65; asst. prof. pharmacology W.Va. U., Morgantown, 1966-71, assoc. prof., 1971-75, prof., 1975—. Editor: (with others) Modern Pharmacology, 1982; Contbr. (with others) articles, abstracts to profl. jours. Served with U.S. Army, 1954-57. Mem. Am. Soc. Pharmacology and Exptl. Therapeutics, Soc. Neurosci., Am. Soc. Neurochemistry, Sigma Xi. Democrat. Methodist. Current Work: Pharmacological and morphological studies of experimental epilepsy. Cobalt-induced epilepsy, transmitters, amino acids, anticonvulsants. Subspecialties: Neuropharmacology; Neurochemistry. Home: 1315 Cherry Ln Morgantown WV 26505 Office: Dept Pharmacology and Toxicology WVa U Med Center Morgantown WV 26506

CRAIG, RICHARD G., geology educator; b. Wilmington, Del., June 3, 1949; s. Murray Breeze and Elinore Mary (Russell) C.; married, 1982; 1 dau., Lara. B.A., Dickinson Coll., 1971; M.S., Pa. State U., 1976, Ph.D., 1979. Asst. prof. dept. geology Kent (Ohio) State U., 1978-82, assoc. prof., 1982—; cons. in field. Contbr. articles to profl. jours.; editor: Future Trends in Geomathematics, 1982, Applied Geomorphology, 1982. Mem. AAAS, Am. Geophys. Union, Geol. Soc. Am. Current Work: Computer simulations of geologic processes in landform evolution. Subspecialties: Geology; Mathematical software. Home: 955 Meloy Rd Kent OH 44240 Office: Dept Geology Kent State U 116A McGilvery Hall Kent OH 44242

CRAIGHEAD, HAROLD G., physicist, researcher; b. Elizabethtown, Pa., Sept. 21, 1952; s. Mayer and Esta Craighead; m. Teresa Miller. B.S., U. Md., 1974; M.S., Cornell U., 1978, Ph.D., 1980. Mem. tech. staff Bell Labs., Holmdel, N.J., 1979-84; research mgr. Bell Communications Research, Holmdel, 1984—. Contbr. articles to profl. jours. Patentee in field. Mem. Am. Phys. Soc., Am. Vacuum Soc., Electron Microscope Soc. Am., Optical Soc. Am. Current work: Electron microscopy; electron beam lithography; microfabrication; solid state experimental physics. Subspecialties: Condensed matter physics; Microchip technology (materials science). Office: Bell Communications Research Crawfords Corner Rd Holmdel NJ 07733

CRAIK, GARY C., SR., project engineer; b. Birmingham, Ala., Mar. 20, 1949; s. David Warren and Eva Lee (Young) C.; m. Susan Ann Quanstrom Finley, Apr. 29, 1972 (div. 1980); 1 child, Tiffany Nicole; m. Kathy Paige Harrell, Jan. 2, 1982. B.S. in Physics, North Tex. State U., 1970, M.S. in Physics, 1972. Vice pres. Plasmatronics, Inc., Albuquerque, 1976-78; sr. staff mem. BDM Corp., Albuquerque, 1978-81; sr. project engr. Dresser Atlas, Houston, 1981—. Author, editor test plans and reports. Served to capt. USAF, 1972-76. Mem. Soc. Profl. Well Log Analysts (assoc.), Soc. Petroleum Engrs. of AIME (assoc.), Am. Inst. Physics, Am. Vacuum Soc., Sigma Pi Sigma. Research or work interests: pulsed neutron tube engineering, vacuum flask engineering, cryogenic system design, pulsed neutron capture logging. Subspecialties: Nuclear physics; Carbon dioxide lasers. Home: 10219 Greentree Houston TX 77042 Office: Dresser Atlas 10201 Westheimer Bldg 14 Houston TX 77042

CRAIN, BARBARA JEAN, physician, neuroscientist, educator; b. Long Beach, Calif., Sept. 18, 1950; d. Gerald Clough and Reva Jean (Dahms) C.; m. Michael Joseph Borowitz, Dec. 29, 1978. B.S., U. Calif.-Irvine, 1972; Ph.D., Duke U., 1978, M.D., 1979. Diplomate Am. Bd. Pathology. Resident in pathology Duke U. Med. Ctr., Durham, N.C., 1979-82, asst. prof. pathology and anatomy, 1983—; staff physician, research assoc. VA Hosp., Durham, 1983—; cons. John Umstead State Hosp., Butner, N.C., 1983—. M.D.-Ph.D. trainee Nat. Inst. Gen. Med. Sci., Bethesda, Md., 1972-79; pharmacology-morphology fellow Pharm. Mfrs. Assn., Washington, 1982; mem. research career devel. program VA, Washington, 1983-85. Mem. Internat. Acad. Pathology, Soc. for Neurosci., N.Y. Acad. Sci., AAAS, AMA. Current work: Anatomic and neuropathology with emphasis on reorganization of the brain after experimental lesions in animals and spontaneous disease states in humans. Subspecialties: Pathology (medicine); Neurobiology. Home: 2327 Anthony Dr Durham NC 27705 Office: Dept Pathology Duke U Med Ctr Box 3712 Durham NC 27710

CRAIN, CHESTER RAYMOND, statistician; b. St. Louis, Apr. 17, 1944; s. Chester and Mary Louise (Landers) C.; m. Barbara Hope Fagnan, Sept. 2, 1967; 1 dau., Michelle C. Pidot. A.B., Knox Coll., 1965; M.A., U. Calif.-Riverside, 1967; Ph.D., U. N. Mex., 1974. Biostatistician Inhalation Toxicology Research Inst., Albuquerque, 1974-76; research statistician Schering Research Ctr., Bloomfield, N.J., 1976-80; statistician Knoll Pharm., Whippany, N.J., 1980; sr. statistician McNeil Pharm., Spring House, Pa., 1980-81; sr. biostatistician Miles Pharm., West Haven, Conn., 1982-83; dir. statis. services Boots Pharms., Shreveport, La., 1983—. Contbr. articles to profl. jours. Mem. Am. Statis. Assn., East Coast Pharm. Stats. Soc. (pres. 1980-81), Am. Soc. Quality Control, Biometric Soc., Math. Assn. Am., Soc. Clin. Trials, Phi Beta Kappa, Pi Mu Epsilon. Unitarian. Subspecialty: Statistics. Office: 3003 Knight St Suite 222 Shreveport LA 71105

CRAINE, ERIC RICHARD, research scientist; b. Harlan, Ky., June 21, 1946; s. Eugene Richard and Carol Dawn (Ward) C.; m. Margaret Helen Zavala, Sept. 18, 1976; children: Patrick Richard, Jennifer Carol. B.S. in Math., Physics, Astronomy, U. Okla., Norman, 1968; Ph.D. in Astronomy, Ohio State U., 1973. Research fellow Ohio State U. Radio Obs., Columbus, 1973-74; project scientist Steward Obs. U. Ariz., Tucson, 1975—; sr. scientist Energy/Environ. Research Group, Inc., Tucson, 1980—; dir. Electro-Optical Test Facility, Bell Aerospace, Tucson. Author: Quasistellar and BL Lacertae Objects, 1977, Near Infrared Photographic Sky Survey, 1980; contbr. numerous articles to profl. jours. Grantee in field. Mem. Am. Astron. Soc., Internat. Astron. Union, Soc. Photo-Optical Instrumentation Engrs. Republican. Presbyterian. Club: Tucson Sailing. Current Work: Optical infrared sky survey astronomy; electro-optical instrumentation, infrared sources, molecular clouds and BL Lacertae objects. Subspecialties: Infrared astronomy; Solar energy. Office: Steward Observatory University of Arizona Tucson AZ 85721

CRALL, JAMES MONROE, plant pathologist, plant breeder; b. Monongahela, Pa., July 13, 1914; s. James Shelby and Margaret Bureau (Rabe) C.; m. Duronda Stanberry, Dec. 22, 1943; children: Cynthia Ann Crall Smith, James Stanberry. Student, Washington and Jefferson Coll., 1934-35; B.S., Purdue U., 1939; M.A., U. Mo., 1941, Ph.D., 1948. Asst. prof. dept. botany and plant pathology Iowa State U., Ames, 1948-52; prof., dir. Agrl. Research Center, Inst. Food and Agrl. Scis., U. Fla., Leesburg, 1952-77, prof., plant pathologist, 1977—. Bd. dirs. United Appeal, Leesburg, 1960-69, v.p., 1965, pres., 1966. Served with USAAF, 1942-46, CBI. Mem. AAAS, Council Agrl. Sci. and Tech., Am. Phytopath. Soc., Mycological Soc. Am., Am. Soc. Hort. Scis., Sigma Xi, Gamma Sigma Delta, Gamma Alpha. Democrat. Episcopalian. Lodge: Kiwanis. Current Work: Development of new watermelon cultivars. Watermelon breeding, with particular emphasis on disease resistance in high quality shipping-type watermelons. Subspecialties: Plant genetics; Plant pathology. Home: PO Box 321 Leesburg FL 32748 Office: PO Box 388 Leesburg FL 32748

CRAM, DONALD JAMES, chemistry educator; b. Chester, Vt., April 22, 1919; s. William Moffet and Joanna (Shelley) C.; m. Jane Maxwell, Nov. 25, 1969. B.S., Rollins Coll., 1941; M.S., U. Nebr., 1942; Ph.D. (Nat. Research fellow), Harvard, 1947; Ph.D. (hon.), U. Uppsala, 1977; D.Sci. (hon.), U. So. Calif., 1983. Research chemist Merck and Co., 1942-45; asst. prof. chemistry UCLA, 1947-50, assoc. prof., 1950-56, prof., 1956, S. Winstein prof., 1985—; chem. cons. Upjohn Co., 1952—, Union Carbide Co., 1960-81, Eastman Kodak Co., 1981—, Technicon Co., 1984—; State Dept. exchange fellow to Inst. de Quimica, Nat. U. Mex., summer 1956; guest prof. U. Heidelberg, Germany, summer 1958; guest lectr., South Africa, 1967; Centenary lectr. Chem. Soc. London, 1976. Author: (with S.H. Pine, J.B. Hendrickson and G.S. Hammond) Organic Chemistry, 1960, 4th edit., 1980, Fundamentals of Carbanion Chemistry, 1965, (with John H. Richards and G.S. Hammond) Elements of Organic Chemistry, 1967, (with J.M. Cram) Essence of Organic Chemistry, 1977; Contbr.: chpts. to Applications of Biochemical Systems in Organic Chemistry; also articles in field of host-guest complexation chemistry, carbonium ions, stereochemistry, mold metabolites, large ring chemistry. Named Young Man of Yr. Calif. Jr. C. of C., 1954, Calif. Scientist of Yr., 1974; recipient award for creative work in synthetic organic chemistry Am. Chem. Soc., 1965, Arthur C. Cope award, 1974, Roger Adams award, 1985, Willard Gibbs Medal, 1985, William Tolman medal, 1985; Herbert Newby McCoy award, 1965, 75; award for creative research organic chemistry Synthetic Organic Chem. Mfrs. Assn., 1965; Am. Chem. Soc. fellow, 1947-48; Guggenheim fellow, 1954-55. Mem. Am. Chem. Soc., Nat. Acad. Scis., Am. Acad. Arts and Scis., Royal Soc. Chemistry, Sigma Xi, Lambda Chi Alpha. Club: San Onofre Surfing. Current Work: Host-guest complexation chemistry; biomimetic chemistry; designed ionosphere chemistry; chiral regocnition chemistry. Subspecialty: Organic chemistry. Home: 1250 Roscomare Rd Los Angeles CA 90077

CRAMBLETT, HENRY GAYLORD, pediatrician, virologist, educator; b. Scio, Ohio, Feb. 8, 1929; s. Carl Smith and Olive (Fulton) C.; m. Donna Jean Reese, June 16, 1960; children: Deborah Kaye, Betsy Diane. B.S., Mt. Union Coll., 1950; M.D., U. Cin., 1953. Diplomate: Am. Bd. Pediatrics, Am. Bd. Microbiology. Clin. research asso. Nat. Inst. Allergy and Infectious Diseases, Clin. Center, Bethesda, Md., 1955-57; faculty State U. Iowa, 1957-60, asst. prof., 1958-60; faculty Bowman Gray Sch. Medicine, 1960-64, prof. pediatrics, 1963-64, dir. virology lab., 1960-64; prof. pediatrics Ohio State U., Columbus, 1964—, prof. med. microbiology, 1966—, exec. dir. Children's Hosp. Research Found., 1964-73, chmn. dept. med. microbiology, 1966-73, dean Coll. Medicine, 1973-80, acting v.p. for med. affairs, 1974-80, v.p. health scis., 1980-83, Warner M. and Lora Kays Pomerene chair in medicine, 1982—, assoc. to v.p. for health services, 1984—; dir. med. and postgrad med. edn. King Faisal Specialist Hosp., Riyadh, Saudi Arabia, 1983-84; Mem. Ohio Med. Bd.; chmn. FLEX Bd., 1985-86; Mem. Nat. Bd. Med. Examiners, 1978—, mem. exec. bd., 1981—; mem. com. on cert., subcert. and recert. Am. Bd. Med. Specialists, 1979-83; mem. coms. on written exam., comprehensive qualifying evaluation program Nat. Bd. Med. Examiners; chmn. Accreditation Council Continuing Med. Edn.; mem. Fedn. State Med. Bds., 1976-82, pres., 1980; bd. dirs. Ohio State U. Hosp., 1979-80. Recipient Hoffheimer prize U. Cin., 1953, Eben J. Carey award in anatomy, 1950. Fellow Am. Acad. Microbiology, AAAS; mem. Infectious Diseases Soc. Am., So. Soc. Pediatric Research (past pres.), Soc. Pediatric Research, Am. Pediatric Soc., Am. Acad. Pediatrics, Midwest Soc. Pediatric Research, Soc. Exptl. Biology and Medicine, Am. Soc. Microbiology, Alpha Omega Alpha. Research, publs. on etiologic assn. virus infections in illnesses of infants and children, estimation of importance of various viruses in morbidity and mortality in pediatric age group. Subspecialties: Pediatrics; Infectious diseases. Home: 2480 Sheringham Rd Columbus OH 43220 Office: 200 Adminstrn Center 370 W 9th Ave Ohio State U Columbus OH 43210

CRAMER, HARRISON EMERY, air pollution meteorologist; b. Johnstown, Pa., May 27, 1919; s. Frank Wilson and Ella Field (Emery) C.; m. Virginia Myrtle Viets, Dec. 22, 1942; children—Anne Cramer Tupker, Dorothy Cramer Kitchen, Nancy Cramer Donoghue, William H. A.B., Amherst Coll., 1941; M.S., MIT, 1943, Sc.D., 1948. Lab. instr. MIT, Cambridge, Mass., 1942-44, research assoc., 1946-49, research meteorologist, 1949-65; dir. environ. scis. lab. GCA Corp. Tech. Div., Bedford, Mass., 1965-72; pres. H.E. Cramer Co., Inc., Salt Lake City, 1972—. Contbr. articles to profl. jours. Served with USNR, 1944-46 PTO. Amherst Meml. fellow, 1941-42. Fellow Am. Meteorol. Soc., AAAS, Royal Meteorol. Soc.; mem. Air Pollution Control Assn., N.Y. Acad. Sci., Am. Geophys. Union, Phi Beta Kappa, Sigma Xi. Current work: Implementation of full-automated procedures for calculating the impact of all types of sources including the space shuttle and air discharges from hazardous waste sites. Subspecialty: Aerospace engineering and technology. Home: 1581 Millbrook Rd Salt Lake City UT 84106 Office: 540 Arapeen Dr Salt Lake City UT 84108

CRAMER, HOWARD ROSS, geology educator; b. Chgo., Sept. 17, 1925; s. Don William and Esther (Johnson) C.; m. Ardis Lahann, Dec. 15, 1950 (dec. 1980); m. Themis Poulos, Dec. 5, 1982. B.S., U. Ill., 1949, M.S., 1950; Ph.D., Northwestern U. 1954. Instr. to asst. prof. Franklin & Marshall Coll., Lancaster, Penn., 1953-58; asst. prof. to assoc. prof. Emory U., Atlanta, 1958-76, prof. geology, 1976—, chairman dept. geology, 1981—; cons., pvt. practice, 1953—. Author numerous books. Contbr. articles to profl. jours. Served to 2nd lt. U.S. Army, 1943-46, 48-53, ETO and PTO. Recipient Cert. Commendation, Am. Soc. State and Local History, 1974. Fellow Geol. Soc. Am.; mem. Am. Assn. Petroleum Geologists, Nat. Assn. Geology Tchrs. (concillor 1982-84). Greek Orthodox. Club: St. Catherine Soc. (Atlanta), AHEPA. Current work: Subsurface coastal plain; bibliography. Subspecialties:

Geology; Paleontology. Home: 2047 Deborah Dr Atlanta GA 30345 Office: Emory U Geology Dept Atlanta GA 30322

CRAMPTON, GEORGE HARRIS, psychologist, educator; b. Spokane, Wash., Nov. 20, 1926. B.S., Wash. State U., 1949, M.S., 1950; Ph.D., U. Rochester, 1954. Prof. psychology Wright State U., Dayton, Ohio, 1971—. Served to col. U.S. Army; ret. Mem. Soc. Neurosci., Barany Soc., Aerospace Med. Assn. Current Work: Vestibular system. Subspecialties: Neurophysiology; Sensory processes. Office: Dept Psychology Wright State U Dayton OH 45435

CRANE, HORACE RICHARD, educator, physicist; b. Turlock, Calif., Nov. 4, 1907; s. Horace Stephen and Mary Alice (Roselle) C.; m. Florence Rohmer LeBaron, Dec. 30, 1934; children—Carol Ann, Janet (dec.), George Richard. B.S., Calif. Inst. Tech., 1930, Ph.D., 1934. Research fellow Calif. Inst. Tech., 1934-35; mem. faculty U. Mich., Ann Arbor, 1935—, prof. physics, 1946—, chmn. dept. physics, 1965-72, George P. Williams Univ. prof., 1972-78, emeritus, 1978—; Research asso. (radar) Mass. Inst. Tech., 1940-41; physicist Carnegie Inst. Washington, 1941; project dir., proximity fuze project U. Mich., 1941-43, atomic energy project, 1943-45; cons. NDRC, 1941-45; mem. standing com. on controlled thermonuclear research AEC, 1969-72; Vice pres. Midwestern Univs. Research Assn., 1956-57, pres., 1957-60; mem. policy bd. Argonne Nat. Lab., 1957-67; Bd. govs. Am. Inst. Physics, 1964-71, chmn., 1971-75; mem. Commn. on Human Resources, 1977-80, Council for Internat. Exchange of Scholars, 1977-80. Contbr. sci. articles to profl. mags. Recipient Davisson-Germer prize, 1967; Henry Russel lectr., 1967; Distinguished Alumni medal Cal. Inst. Tech., 1968; Distinguished Service award U. Mich., 1957. Fellow Am. Phys. Soc., AAAS, Am. Acad. Arts and Scis.; mem. Nat. Acad. Scis., Am. Assn. Physics Tchrs. (pres. 1965, Oersted medal 1977), Sigma Xi. Clubs: Research Univ. of Mich. (pres. 1956-57); Science Research (U. Mich.) (v.p. 1946-47, pres. 1947-48). Inventor of Race Track, a modified form of synchrotron for nuclear studies, 1946; made early discoveries in field of artificially produced radioactive atoms, 1934-39; measurements of magnetic moment of free electron, 1950. Subspecialty: Nuclear physics. Home: 830 Avon Rd Ann Arbor MI 48104

CRANE, PETER R., paleobotanist. Assoc. curator dept. geology, Field Mus. Natural History, Chgo. Recipient Bicentenary Med. Linnean Soc. of London, 1984. Subspecialty: Paleobiology. Office: Field Mus Natural History Dept Geology S Lake Shore Dr Chicago IL 60605

CRANE, ROBERT, clinical researcher; b. Atlantic City, N.J., Mar. 11, 1928; s. William James and Luba (Davidson) C.; m. Louise Marion Novack, July 23, 1950 (div. Sept. 1982); children—Randall L., Kendall T.; m. Joan Marie Scott, Nov. 21, 1982. B.S., MIT, 1948, M.S., 1949; Ph.D., Polytechnic Inst. of N.Y., 1974; M.D., U. Autónoma de Ciudad Juárez, Chihuahua, Mex., 1979. Project engr. Sperry Gyroscope Co., Great Neck, N.Y., 1949-53; pres. Crane and Egert Corp., Elmont, N.Y., 1953-65; pres. Crane Bio-Med. Inst., Elmont, 1965-73; co-dir., lung transplant lab. Montefiore Hosp. and Med. Ctr., Bronx, N.Y., 1973-77; house staff officer Bronx-Lebanon Hosp. Ctr., 1979-81; dir. clin. research Sterling Internat. Group, N.Y.C., 1981—. Inventor: Automated Body Plethysmograph, 1971. Contbr. articles to med. jours. Chmn. Bd. Edn., Plainview, N.Y., 1957-63; v.p., trustee Universalist Ch., N.Y.C., 1983—, Unitarian Ch., Old Bethpage, N.J., 1966-67. Mem. AMA, N.Y. Acad. of Scis., Inst. of Elec. and Electronic Engrs., AAAS, Biomed. Engring. Soc., Assn. for the Advancement of Med. Instrumentation, Eta Kappa Nu, Sigma Xi, Mensa. Democrat. Current work: Clinical research on new compounds, internal medicine. Subspecialties: Biomedical engineering; Internal medicine. Home: 301 W 53rd St #9B New York NY 10019 Office: Sterling Internat Group 90 Park Ave New York NY 10016

CRANEFIELD, PAUL FREDERIC, educator, physician; b. Madison, Wis., Apr. 28, 1925; s. Paul Frederic and Edna (Rothnick) C. Ph.B., U. Wis., 1946, Ph.D., 1951; M.D., Albert Einstein Coll. Medicine, 1964. Fellow biophysics Johns Hopkins U., 1951-53; from instr. to assoc. prof. physiology State U. N.Y. Downstate Med. Center, N.Y.C., 1953-62; research fellow psychiatry Albert Einstein Coll. Medicine, 1960-64; exec. sec. com. publs. and med. information, editor bull. N.Y. Acad. Medicine, 1963-66; adj. assoc. prof. pharmacology Columbia Coll. Physicians and Surgeons, 1964-75, adj. prof., 1975—; assoc. prof. Rockefeller U., 1966-75, prof., 1975—. Author: (with Hoffman) The Electrophysiology of the Heart, 1960, Paired Pulse Stimulation of the Heart, 1968, (with C. McC. Brooks) The Historical Development of Physiological Thought, 1959, The Way In and the Way Out, 1974, The Conduction of the Cardiac Impulse, 1975, Claude Bernard's Revised Edition of his Introduction a L'Etude de la Médicine Expérimentale, 1976; also numerous articles.; Editor: Jour. Gen. Physiology, 1966—; mem. editorial bd.: Circulation Research, Spl. Collections, other jours.; cons. editor: Internat. Microform Jour. Legal Medicine, 1969-77. Chmn. bd. dirs. LaMama Exptl. Theatre Club, 1965-69; chmn. bd. dirs. Circle Repertory Co., 1970-76, The Working Theatre; trustee Milton Helpern Library Legal Medicine. Recipient Einthoven medal U. Leiden, 1983. Fellow N.Y. Acad. Medicine, Internat. Acad. History of Medicine; mem. Am. Physiol. Soc., Biophys. Soc., Am. Assn. History Medicine, Episcopal Actors Guild. Clubs: Century, Players, Nat. Arts, Coffee House, Grolier, (N.Y.C.); Cosmos (Washington); Savile (London). Current Work: Electrophysiology of heart, electrophysiological basis of cardic arhythmias. Subspecialties: Biophysics (biology); Electrophysiology. Home: 310 E 9th St New York NY 10003 Office: 1230 York Ave New York NY 10021

CRANG, RICHARD FRANCIS EARL, botanist, research center adminstr.; b. Clinton, Ill., Dec. 2, 1936; s. Richard Francis and Clara Esther (Cummins) C.; m. Linda L., Aug. 10, 1958 (div.); children: Steven E., Douglas E. B.S., Eastern Ill. U., 1958; M.A., U. S.D., 1962; Ph.D., U. Iowa, 1965. Asst. prof. biology Wittenberg U., 1965-69; assoc. prof. biol. sci. Bowling Green State U., 1969-74, prof., 1974-80; prof. plant biology U. Ill., Urbana-Champaign, 1980—; dir. U. Ill. (Center Electron Microscopy), 1980—; adj. prof. anatomy Med. Coll. Ohio, 1974-80; vis. scientist, botany Cambridge (Eng.) U., 1978-79. Research, numerous publs. in field, 1967—. Mem. Statewide Democratic Support Group, Ill. Recipient Outstanding Faculty Research Recognition award Bowling Green State U., 1973, 75; Paint Research Inst. grantee, 1976-83; NSF grantee, 1981-83. Mem. AAAS, Bot. Soc. Am. Mem. Christian Ch. (Disciples of Christ). Current Work: Inhibitation of biodegredational fungi involving studies with electron microscopy; air pollution studies. Subspecialties: Cell and tissue culture; Microbiology. Home: 2903 Deske Ct Champaign IL 61821 Office: 905 S Goodwin Av 74A Bevier Hall Urbana IL 61801

CRANIN, ABRAHAM NORMAN, oral surgeon, researcher; b. Bklyn., June 17, 1927; s. Samuel Leonard and Henrietta C.; m. Marilyn Sunners, June 14, 1953; children: Jonathan, Andrew, Elizabeth. A.B., Swarthmore Coll., 1947; D.D.S., NYU, 1951; cert., Mt. Sinai Hosp., 1952, 53. Assoc. attending oral surgeon Mt. Sinai Hosp., N.Y.C., 1961—; practice dentistry specializing in oral surgery; chief oral surgery Greenpoint Hosp., Bklyn., 1961-63; attending oral surgeon Community Hosp., Bklyn., 1962-72; assoc. clin. prof. Mt. Sinai Sch. Medicine, N.Y.C., 1974—; clin. prof. oral and maxillofacial surgery NYU, 1975—; dir. dental and oral surgery Brookdale Hosp. Med. Ctr., Bklyn., 1965—; cons. Nat. Patent Devel. Corp., N.Y.C., 1964-70; dir. Soc. for Biomaterials, San Antonio, 1973—; cons. oral surgeon Bklyn. Devel. Ctr., 1973—. Editor-in-chief: Jour. Oral Implantaology Quar, 1973 (Gold Key 1974), Jour. Biomed. Materials and Research, 1978 (cert. 1981). Pres. Informed Citizens Com. Hewlett Bay Park, N.Y., 1976. Served to ensign USN, 1950-51. Named Man of Yr. Fedn. of Jewish Philanthropies, Bklyn., 1973; honoree United Jewish Appeal, Brookdale Hosp., 1980; recipient award Soc. for Biomaterials, 1978; award of honor Met. Conf. Hosp. Dentists, 1982. Fellow Am. Acad. Implant Dentistry (pres. 1971), Am. Dental Soc. Anesthesiology, Royal Soc. Health, Internat. Coll. Dentistry, Brazilian Soc. Oral and Maxilofacial Surgery (hon., Rene Lefort medal 1980); hon. mem. Japanese Soc. Implant Dentistry (medal and plaque 1980). Clubs: Woodmere Bay (Bay Park, N.Y.); Woodmere (N.Y.). Current Work: Basic and clinical research, dental, oral and maxillofacial implants, sintered titanium, hydroxyapatite, chrome-alloy anchors, Brookdale bar implant. Subspecialties: Implantology; Oral and maxillofacial surgery. Home: Copper Top Hewlett Bay Park NY 11557 Office: Brookdale Hosp Med Center Brookdale Plaza Brooklyn NY 11212

CRASEMANN, BERND, physicist, educator; b. Hamburg, Germany, Jan. 23, 1922; came to U.S., 1946, naturalized, 1955; s. Pablo Joaquin and Hildegard Carlota (Vorwerk) C.; m. Jean Millicent McEown, June 7, 1952. A.B., UCLA, 1948; Ph.D., U. Calif. at Berkeley, 1953. With Lavadora de Lanas S.A., Viña del Mar, Chile, 1941-46; asst. prof. physics U. Oreg., Eugene, 1953-58, assoc. prof., 1958-63, prof., 1963—, chmn. dept. 1976-84, dir. Chem. Physics Inst., 1984—; guest assoc. physicist Brookhaven Nat. Lab., Upton, N.Y., 1961-62; vis. prof. U. Calif. at Berkeley, 1968-69, Université Pierre et Marie Curie, Paris, 1977; cons. Lawrence Radiation Lab., 1954-68, physicist, 1968-69; mem. com. on atomic and molecular sci. NRC/Nat. Acad. Scis., 1976-82; vis. scholar Stanford U., 1983; vis. scientist NASA Ames Research Center, 1975-76; vis. scholar Stanford U., 1983. Author: (with J.L. Powell) Quantum Mechanics, 1961; Editor: Atomic Inner-Shell Processes, 1975; Atomic Inner-Shell Physics, 1985; mem. editorial bd.: Phys. Rev. C, 1978, Atomic Data and Nuclear Data Tables, 1982—. Contbr. articles to sci. jours. Mem. region XIV selection com. Woodrow Wilson Nat. Fellowship Found., 1959-61, 62-68. Recipient Ersted award for disting. teaching U. Oreg., 1959; NSF research grantee, 1954-64; U.S. AEC grantee, 1964-72; NASA grantee, 1972-79; AFOSR grantee, 1979—. Fellow Am. Phys. Soc. (chmn. div. electron and atomic physics 1981-82, councillor 1983-86); mem. Am. Assn. Physics Tchrs. (pres. Oreg. sect. 1956-57), Sierra Club, ACLU, Phi Beta Kappa. Current Work: Atomic inner-shell processes; applications of synchrotron radiation to atomic physics; interface of atomic and nuclear physics. Subspecialty: Atomic and molecular physics. Office: Dept Physics U Oreg Eugene OR 97403

CRATTY, LELAND EARL, JR., chemist; b. Oregon, Ill., June 3, 1930; s. Leland E. and Kathryn E. (Prugh) C.; m. Carol R. Gardiner, June 9, 1956 (dec.); children: Paul Donald, Sarah Louise, Susan; m. Margaret B. Mason, May 28, 1982. Sc.B., Beloit Coll., 1952; Ph.D., Brown U., 1957. Research chemist Linde Air Products, Buffalo, 1956-58; vis. fellow Mellon Inst., Pitts., 1964-65, Ames (Iowa) Lab., 1969-70; faculty Hamilton Coll., Clinton, N.Y., 1958—, prof. chemistry, 1973—; vis research faculty U. Pa., 1982-83. Pres. Clinton (N.Y.) A Better Chance Program, 1976-77, Hamilton Coll. Sewer Commn., 1978—. Mem. Am. Chem. Soc., AAAS, Phi Beta Kappa, Sigma Xi. Current Work: Fast ion conduction in solids, cluster metal catalysis. Subspecialties: Inorganic chemistry; Catalysis chemistry. Office: Hamilton Coll Clinton NY 13323

CRAVEN, DONALD EDWARD, physician, educator; b. Omaha, Jan. 13, 1944; s. Orvin William and Florence Elizabeth (Waite) C.; m. Margaret Anne McClave, Aug. 27, 1966; m. Dianne Munson, Sept. 10, 1983. B.A., Wesleyan U., 1966; M.D., Albany Med. Coll., 1970. Med. intern Albany (N.Y.) Med. Ctr., 1971; med. resident McGill U., Montreal, Can., 1971-74; infectious disease fellow Boston U., 1974-76; research assoc. Bur. Biologics, /FDA/NIH, Bethesda, Md., 1976-79; asst. prof. medicine Boston U., 1979—, assoc. prof., 1983—; assoc. prof. epidemiology and stats. Boston U. Sch. Pub. Health, 1983—; epidemiologist Boston City Hosp., 1979—; cons. Merck Sharpe & Dohme, West Point, Pa., 1982-83. Author: Internal Medicine, 1983; contbr. articles to sci. jours. Served to sr. surgeon USPHS, 1976-79. Fellow ACP, Royal Coll. Physicians; mem. Infectious Diseases Soc., Am. Soc. Microbiology, Am. Fedn. Clin. Research. Current Work: nosocomial infections; gram negative sepsis, bacterial adherence; meningococcal vaccines; hospital epidemiology. Subspecialties: Infectious diseases; Epidemiology. Home: 17 Ellery Sq Cambridge MA 02138 Office: Boston City Hosp 818 Harrison Ave Boston MA 02118

CRAWFORD, BRYCE LOW, JR., chemist, educator; b. New Orleans, Nov. 27, 1914; s. Bryce Low and Clara Hall (Crawford) C.; m. Ruth Raney, Dec. 21, 1940; children: Bryce, Craig, Sherry Ann. A.B., Stanford U., 1934, M.A., 1935, Ph.D., 1937; Nat. Research fellow, Harvard U., 1937-39. Instr. chemistry Yale U., 1939-40; asst. prof. U. Minn., Mpls., 1940-43, assoc. prof., 1943-46, prof. phys. chemistry, 1946-82, Regents' prof. chemistry, 1982-85, chmn. dept., 1955-60, dean grad. sch., 1960-72; Mem. Grad. Record Exam. Bd., 1968-72; chmn. Council Grad Schs. in U.S., 1962-63; pres. Assn. Grad. Schs., 1970; dir. research on rocket propellants under Div. 3 Nat. Def. Research Com., 1942-45. Editor: Jour. Phys. Chemistry, 1970-80. Trustee Midwest Research Inst., 1963—. Guggenheim fellow, 1950-51, 72-73; Fulbright grantee Oxford, 1951; Fulbright grantee Oxford, Tokyo, 1966; recipient Presdl. Cert. of Merit. Mem. Am. Chem. Soc. (dir. 1969-77, Priestley medal 1982, Pitts. Spectroscopy award, Ellis Lippincott award), Optical Soc. Am., AAAS, AAUP, Am. Phys. Soc., Nat. Acad. Scis. (council 1975-78, home. sec. 1979—), Coblentz Soc., Am. Philos. Soc., Am. Acad. Arts and Scis., Phi Beta Kappa, Sigma Xi, Phi Lambda Upsilon, Alpha Chi Sigma. Episcopalian. Clubs: Campus, Cosmos. Specialist in molecular structure and molecular spectra. Subspecialties: Physical chemistry; Molecular spectroscopy. Home: 1545 Branston St Saint Paul MN 55108 Office: Molecular Spectroscopy Lab U Minn 207 Pleasant St SE Minneapolis MN 55455

CRAWFORD, DAVID LIVINGSTON, astronomer; b. Tarentum, Pa., Mar. 2, 1931; s. William L. and A. Blanche (Livingston) C.; m. Mary Louise Mueller, Apr. 4, 1962; children: Christine Bayze, Deborah, Lisa. Ph.D., U. Chgo., 1958. Asst. prof. Vanderbilt U., 1958-59; astronomer Kitt Peak Nat. Observatory, Tucson, 1960—; project mgr. 4-meter Telescopes, 1962-72, assoc. dir., 1970-73. Contbr. numerous articles to sci., tech. jours. Chmn. Outdoor Lighting Com., City of Tucson, 1980—. Mem. Am. Astron. Soc. (chmn. light pollution com.), Internat. Astron. Union, Astron. Soc. Pacific, Soc. Illuminating Engrs. Current Work: Large telescope design, astronomy instrumentation, photoelectric photometry, galactic structure, star clusters, roadway lighting and light trespass. Subspecialties: Optical astronomy; Optical engineering. Home: 3545 N Stewart St Tucson AZ 85716 Office: KPNO Box 26732 Tucson AZ 85726

CRAWFORD, LESTER MILLS, JR., veterinarian; b. Demopolis, Ala., Mar. 13, 1938; s. Lester Mills and Susan Doris (Mitchell) C.; m. Catherine Walker, July 27, 1963; children—Catherine Leigh, Mary Stuart. D.V.M., Auburn U., 1963; Ph.D., U. Ga., 1969. Pvt. practice vet. medicine, Meridian, Miss. and Birmingham, Ala., 1963-64; research and devel. staff Agrl. div. Am. Cyanamid Co., Princeton, N.J., 1964-66; also cons.; assoc. prof. pharmacology, assoc. dean Coll. Vet. Medicine, U. Ga., 1970-75; dir. Bur. Vet. Medicine, FDA, HEW, Rockville, Md., 1978-80, 82—; head dept. physiology-pharmacology U. Ga., 1981-82; cons. pharm. industry, agribus. FDA. Contbr. sci. articles to profl. jours. Lay speaker Methodist Ch., 1970—; bd. dirs.; Ga. div. Am. Cancer Soc. U. Ga. Faculty Club, Athens Acad. Recipient Alpha Psi Nat. Council award Am. Coll. Vet. Pharmacology and Therapeutics, 1977; A.M. Mills award; K.F. Meyer award; named Outstanding Sr. Auburn U. Sch. Vet. Medicine, 1963; Commr.'s spl. citation FDA. Mem. AVMA (Aux. award), Ga. Vet. Med. Assn., D.C. Vet. Med. Assn., AAAS, Sigma Xi, Phi Zeta, Phi Kappa Phi. Republican. Club: Athens (Ga.) Country. Current work: Direct center for veterinary medicine. Subspecialties: Pharmacology; Physiology (medicine). Home: 11925 Gainsborough Rd Potomac MD 20854 Office: Bur Vet Medicine FDA 5600 Fishers Ln Rockville MD 20857

CRAWLEY, PAUL F., nuclear engineer; b. Carthage, N.Y., Nov. 23, 1943; s. Richard F. and Alice M. (Franks) C.; m. Lorraine J. Campbell, Jan. 28, 1967; children: Kevin, Sean. J.T. A.B. cum laude, Kenyon Coll., 1965; M.S., Carnegie-Mellon U., 1967. Scientist, Bettis Atomic Power Lab., West Mifflin, Pa., 1967-72; nuclear engr. Middle South Services, New Orleans, 1972; scientist Bettis Atomic Power Lab., 1972-74; sr. nuclear engr. Boston Edison Co., 1974-78; nuclear supr. Ariz. Pub. Service, Phoenix, 1978-83, mgr. nuclear fuel mgmt., 1983—. Chmn. Litchfield Little League, 1981-82. Mem. Am. Nuclear Soc. Republican. Roman Catholic. Current Work: Optimization of nuclear fuel management strategies consistent with commercial nuclear power plant reactor engineering operational needs. Subspecialties: Nuclear fission; Nuclear engineering. Home: 300 W Llano Dr Litchfield Park AZ 85340 Office: Ariz Pub Service Co PO Box 21666 Phoenix AZ 85036

CRAWSHAW, RALPH, psychiatrist; b. N.Y.C., July 3, 1921. A.B., Middlebury (Vt.) Coll., 1943; M.D., N.Y. U., 1947. Diplomate: Nat. Bd. Med. Examiners, Am. Bd. Psychiatry and Neurology. Intern Lenox Hill Hosp., N.Y.C., 1947-48; resident Menninger Sch. Psychiatry, Topeka, 1948-50, Oreg. State Hosp., Salem, 1950-51; practice medicine specializing in psychiatry, Washington, 1954; staff psychiatrist C.F. Menninger Meml. Hosp., Topeka, 1954-57; asst. chief VA Mental Hygiene Clinic, Topeka, 1957-60; staff psychiatrist Community Child Guidance Clinic, Portland, Oreg., 1960-63; founder, clinic dir. Tualatin Valley Guidance Clinic, Beaverton, Oreg., 1961-67; pvt. practice medicine, specializing in psychiatry, Portland, 1960—; mem. staff Holladay Park Hosp., 1961—; lectr. dept. child psychiatry U. Oreg. Med. Sch., 1961-63, clin. prof. dept. psychiatry, 1976; lectr. Sch. Social Work, Portland State U., 1964-67; founder Benjamin Rush Found., 1968, pres., 1968—; founder Friends of Medicine, 1969, Ct. of Man, 1970, Club of Kos, 1974. Contbr. editor: AMA Jour. of Socio-Econs, 1972-75; Columnist: Prism mag, 1972-76, The Pharos, 1972—, Portland Physician, 1975; Contbr. articles to med. jours. Cons. Bur. Hearings and Appeals, HEW, 1964—; cons. Albina Child Devel. Center, Portland, 1965-75, HEW Region 8 Health Planning, 1979; mem. Inst. Medicine, Nat. Acad. Sci., 1978, Oreg. Health Coordinating Council, 1979; Mem. Gov.'s Adv. Com. on Mental Health, 1966-72; ad hoc com. Nat. Leadership Conf. on Am. Health Policy, 1976, Gov.'s Adv. Com. on Med. Care to Indigent, 1976—; trustee Millicent Found., 1964-67, Multnomah Found. for Med. Care, 1977; vis. scholar Center for Study Democratic Instns., 1969, Jack Murdock Charitable Trust, 1977, U.S.-USSR exchange scholar, 1973. Served with AUS, 1943-46; to lt., M.C. USN, 1951-54. Named Oreg. Dr./Citizen of Yr., 1978; U.S.-USSR exchange scholar, 1973, 79. Fellow Am. Psychiat. Assn.; mem. AMA, Nat. Med. Assn., Oreg. Med. Assn. (trustee 1972—), Multnomah County Med. Soc. (pres. 1975), Royal Soc. Medicine, Inst. of Medicine of Nat. Acad. Sci., Am. Psychol. Assn., N.Pacific Soc. Neurology and Psychiatry, Soc. for Psychol. Study Social Issues, Western European Assn. Aviation Psychology, Am. Med. Writers Assn., AAAS, Portland Psychiatrists in Pvt. Practice (pres. 1971), Alpha Omega. Current Work: Health services research; impaired physician; allocation of health resources. Subspecialty: Psychiatry. Address: 2525 NW Lovejoy St Suite 404 Portland OR 97210

CRAY, SEYMOUR R., computer designer; b. Chippewa Falls, Wis., 1925. B.S.E.E., U. Minn., 1950; B.S. in Math, 1950. Computer scientist Engring. Research Assocs., later Remington Rand, Sperry Rand Univac div., St. Paul, until 1957; co-founder Control Data Corp., 1957, computer scientist, 1957-72; founder Cray Research Inc., Mendota Heights, Minn., 1972, now cons., dir. Designer first computer made with transistors, Cray-1, Cray-2, other computer systems. Subspecialty: Computer architecture. Office: Cray Research Inc 1440 Northland Dr Mendota Heights MN 55120

CREAGAN, ROBERT JOSEPH, energy scientific consultant; b. Rockford, Ill., Aug. 24, 1919; s. Paul Thomas and Mary (Sulivan) C.; m. Irene Marie Tkacs, Aug. 21, 1948; children: Susan, Robert II, Mary, Tim. B.S. in Engring, Ill. Inst. Tech., Chgo., 1942; M.S. in Physics, Yale U., 1943; Ph.D., 1948. Mgr. nuclear engring. Westinghouse Electric Corp., Pitts., 1949-57, asst. tech. dir. nuclear engring., 1961-69, project mgr., 1969-74, dir. tech. assessment, 1974-79, cons. Research and Devel. Ctr., 1978-84, ret., 1984; tchr. sci. Boyce Coll., 1984—, Chatham Coll., 1985—; dir. nuclear program Bendix Corp., Detroit, 1957-61; dir. Atomic Power Devel. Assocs., Detroit, 1958-61; cons. Power Reactor Devel. Corp., Detroit, 1961-65, Yankee Atomic Electric Corp., Rowe, Mass., 1965-68. Author: Nuclear Engineering, 1948; Contbr. articles to profl. jours. Served as lt. USNR, 1943-46, PTO. Fellow Am. Nuclear Soc. (chmn. power div. 1965-66); mem. Nat. Acad. Engring. Club: Gateway Heights (Monroeville, Pa.) (pres. 1976-81). Current Work: Nuclear power development; advanced energy development energy, power and fuel economics. Subspecialty: Fuels. Home: 2305 Haymaker Rd Monroeville PA 15146

CREAGER, JOE SCOTT, geology and oceanography educator; b. Vernon, Tex., Aug. 30, 1929; s. Earl Litton and Irene Eugenia (Keller) C.; m. Barbara Clark, Aug. 30, 1951; children: Kenneth Clark, Vanessa Irene. B.S., Colo. Coll., 1951; postgrad., Columbia U., 1952-53; M.S., Tex. A&M U., 1953, Ph.D., 1958. Asst. prof. Sch. Oceanography, U. Wash., Seattle, 1958-61, assoc. prof., 1962-66, asst. chmn., 1964-65, prof. oceanography, 1966—, prof. geol. sci., 1981—, assoc. dean arts and scis. for earth and planetary scis., assoc. dean research, 1966—; program dir. oceanography NSF, 1965-66; chief scientist numerous oceanographic expdns. to Arctic and sub-arctic including Leg XIX of Deep Sea Drilling project, 1959—; vis. geol. scientist Am. Geol. Inst., 1962, 63, 65; U.S. Nat. coordinator Internat. Indian Ocean Expedition, 1965-66; vis. scientist, program lectr. Am. Geophys. Union, 1965-72; Battelle cons., advanced waste mgmt., 1974; cons. U.S. Army C.E., 1976, U.S. Depts. Interiors and Commerce, 1975; exec. sec., exec. com., chmn. planning com. Joint Oceanographic Insts. Deep Earth Sampling, 1970-72, 76-78. Editorial bd.: Internat. Jour. Marine Geology, 1964—; assoc. editor: Jour. Sedimentary Petrology, 1963-67; asst. editor: Quaternary Research, 1970-82; contbr. articles in field to profl. jours. Skipper, Sea Scout Ship Boy Scouts Am., Bryan, Tex., 1957; coach Little League Baseball, Seattle, 1964-71, sec., 1971; cons. sci. curriculum Northshore Sch. Dist., 1970; mem. Seattle Citizens Shoreline Com., 1973-74, King County Shoreline Com., 1980. Served with U.S. Army, 1953-55. Colo. Coll. scholar, 1949-51; NSF grantee, 1962-82; ERDA grantee, 1962-64; U.S. Army C.E. Grantee, 1975-82; Office Naval Research grantee; U.S. Dept. Commerce grantee; U.S. Geol. Survey grantee. Fellow Geol. Soc. Am., AAAS; mem. Internat. Assn. Quaternary Research, Am. Geophys. Union, Internat. Assn. Math. Geologists, Internat. Assn. Sedimentology, Soc. Econ. Paleontologists and Mineralists, Marine Tech. Soc. (sec.-treas. 1972-75), Sigma Xi, Beta Theta Pi, Delta Epsilon. Club: Explorers. Current Work: Shallow-water marine sediment transport mechanics; sea-level changes; recent marine sedimentary stratigraphy. Subspecialties: Oceanography; Sedimentology. Home: 6320 NE 157th St Bothell WA 98011 Office: U Wash Sch Oceanography WB-10 Seattle WA 98195

CREECH, RICHARD HEARNE, physician; b. Boston, Apr. 6, 1940; s. Hugh J. and E. Marie (Hearne) C.; m. Charlotte E. Goetz, Dec. 28, 1963; children: Susan Marie, Nancy Elizabeth. A.B., Johns Hopkins U., 1961; M.D., U. Pa., 1965. Diplomate: Am. Bd. Internal Medicine (Subspecialty in med. oncology, hematology). Intern, resident in medicine Hosp. of U. Pa., 1965-67; clin. assoc. lab. molecular pharmacology Nat. Cancer Inst., Bethesda, Md., 1967-70; fellow in hematology and immunology Hosp. of U. Pa., 1970-71; chief med. oncology service Phila. Gen. Hosp., U. Pa. Service, 1971-72; assoc. attending physician Am. Oncologic Hosp., Fox Chase Cancer Ctr., Phila., 1972—. Contbr. articles to profl. jours. Served with USPHS, 1967-70. Fellow ACP; mem. Am. Soc. Clin. Oncology, Am. Assn. Cancer Research, AMA, Coll. Physicians Phila. Republican. Episcopalian. Current Work: Development of minimally toxic but maximally active chemotherapy regimens for patients with breast cancer; determination of respective roles of multi-drug chemotherapy and radiation therapy in treatment of localized small cell lung cancer. Subspecialties: Cancer research (medicine); Oncology. Office: Physicians' Office Bldg 7500 Central Ave Suite 203 Philadelphia PA 19111

CREESE, IAN NIGEL RICHARD, psychopharmacologist, educator; b. Bristol, Eng., Apr. 4, 1949; s. Douglas Ernest and Marjorie Florence Creese; m. Paula Anne Tallal, July 21, 1972. B.A., Queens' Coll., Cambridge (Eng.) U., 1970, M.A., 1972, Ph.D., 1973. Postdoctoral fellow Johns Hopkins Med. Sch., 1973-79; asst. prof. U. Calif.-San Diego, 1978-81, assoc. prof., 1981-84, prof., 1984—; mem. study sect. NIMH, 1979-84; cons. in field. A.P. Sloan fellow, 1978-82; NIMH research award, 1978-85. Mem. Soc. Neurosci., AAAS, European Soc. Neurosci., Am. Soc. Pharmacology and Exptl. Therapeutics, Am. Soc. Neurochemistry; mem. Am. Coll. Neuropsychopharmacology; Mem. Internat. Narcotics Research Club. Current Work: Psychopharmacology, drug and neurotransmitter receptors. Subspecialties: Neuropharmacology; Regeneration.

CREGGER, BARTON BENTLEY, electrical engineer; b. Roanoke, Va., Mar. 14, 1958; s. Frank Albert and Susan (Bentley) C. B.S.E.E., U. Va., 1980, M.S.E.E., 1982. Design engr. Tex. Instruments, Inc., Dallas, 1982—. Mem. IEEE. Republican. Methodist. Club: Virginia of Dallas. Lodge: Masons. Current work: Gallium arsenide monolithic microwave integrated circuit design, processing, characterization, testing, and subsequent applications. Subspecialties: Semiconductors; Microelectronics. Home: 9236 Church Rd #1041 Dallas TX 75231 Office: Tex Instruments Inc 13500 N Central Expressway Dallas TX 75266

CREIGHTON, DONALD JOHN, biochemist, educator; b. Stockton, Calif., Jan. 25, 1946; s. William H. and Helen K. (Norberg) C.; m. Arlene G. Keh, Aug. 16, 1969; children: Diane K., Christine Gail. B.S. magna cum laude, Calif. State U.-Fresno, 1968; Ph.D. in Biol. chemistry, UCLA, 1972. Postdoctoral fellow in biochemistry Inst. Cancer Research, Phila., 1972-75; assoc. prof. chemistry U. Md., Balt., 1975—. Contbr. articles to profl. jours. Grantee Am. Cancer Soc., 1980, 82; Grantee Research Corp., 1976; Grantee Petroleum Research Fund, 1976; Grantee NIH, 1979, 83, 85. Mem. Am. Chem. Soc., Sigma Xi. Democrat. Current Work: Protein structure and enzyme mechanisms. Subspecialty: Biochemistry (medicine). Office: U Md Baltimore County 5401 Wilkens Ave Catonsville MD 21228

CRELLING, JOHN CRAWFORD, geology educator; b. Phila., June 13, 1941; s. Gerard Pearce and Margaret Emily (Fisher) C.; m. Elizabeth Carol Anne Matheson, Aug. 26, 1967; children—James Alexander Crawford, Ian Matheson Pearce. B.A. in Geology, U. Del., 1964; M.S., Pa. State U., 1967, Ph.D., 1973. Research geologist Bethlehem Steel Corp., Pa., 1972-77; asst. prof.

geology So. Ill. U., Carbondale, 1977-81, assoc. prof., 1981—; sr. vis. research fellow No. Carbon Research Labs., Newcastle-Upon-Tyne, Eng., 1981; vis. prof. fuels engring. U. Utah, Salt Lake City, 1984. Served as capt. U.S. Army, 1968-70. Fellow Geol. Soc. Am.; mem. Soc. Organic Petrology (v.p. 1985—), Am. Chem. Soc., AIME, Internat. Commn. Coal Petrology. Anglican. Current work: Coal petrology, coal geology, fluorescence and photoacoustic microscopy of coal and organic material. Subspecialties: Geology; Coal. Office: So Ill U Dept Geology Carbondale IL 62901

CRENNER, JAMES CHARLES, electrical engineer; b. Pitts., July 1, 1948; s. August Francis and Patricia Ann (Vidler) C.; m. Susan Marie Kopsho, Apr. 11, 1970; children—Julie Louise, Jennifer Sue. Student Riverside City Coll., 1975-76, Fullerton Coll., 1975-76; A.S., W. Coast U., 1980, B.S.E.E. magna cum laude, 1983. Enlisted man U.S. Marine Corps, 1966-75; air traffic controller, Camp Pendleton, Calif., 1966-75; resigned, 1975; quality assurance technician Edwards Pacemaker Systems, Irvine, Calif., 1976-68; sr. technician Sperry Univac Corp., Irvine, 1978-81; sr. engr. Coopervision Systems, Irvine, 1981-83; devel. engr. Cilco, Inc., Pomona, Calif., 1983-84; product engr. Gen. Cable Co., Westminster, Colo., 1984—. Co-designer irrigation aspiration unit for opthalmic surgery; project engr./mgr. phacoemulsifier unit for opthalmic surgery. Recipient Eagle Scout award Boy Scouts Am., 1966. Mem. IEEE. Republican. Episcopalian. Current work: Transducer design. Subspecialties: Electrical engineering; Ophthalmology. Home: 9512 Garland Ct Westminster CO 80020 Office: Gen Cable Corp PO Box 666 5600 W 88th Ave Westminster CO 80030

CRENSHAW, DAVID BROOKS, educator, animal scientist; b. Columbia, Mo., May 15, 1945; s. Joe Perry and A. Karleen (Brooks) C.; m. Sherry Gail Quisenberry, Mar. 26, 1966; children: Denise Renee, David Keith, Joe Perry. B.S. in Agr. U. Mo., Columbia, 1968, M.S. in Animal Husbandry, 1969, Ph.D. in Animal Genetics, 1972. Asst. prof. animal sci. Tex. A&I U., Kingsville, 1972-76, assoc. prof., 1976-82, prof., 1982-84; prof., head dept. agr. East Tex. State U., Commerce, 1984—. Contbr. articles to profl. jours. Named Outstanding Prof., Coll. Agr. Tex. A&I U., 1982, 83; recipient numerous research grants. Mem. Am. Soc. Animal Sci. Democrat. Mem. Disciples of Christ. Lodge: Kiwanis of Commerce. Current Work: manipulation of postpartum estrus period in range beef cow and heifer, cytogenetic effects of drugs and feed additives on chromosomes in domestic animals. Subspecialties: Animal breeding and embryo transplants; Animal genetics. Home: Route 2 Box 14 Campbell TX 75422 Office: Box 156 Kingsville TX 78363

CREUTZ, EDWARD CHESTER, physicist, science administrator; b. Beaver Dam, Wis., Jan. 23, 1913; s. Lester Raymond and Grace (Smith) C.; m. Lela Marie Rollefson, Sept. 13, 1957 (dec. Feb. 1972); children—Michael, Carl, Ann Jo; m. Elisabeth Butler Cordle, Oct. 5, 1974. B.S., U. Wis.-Madison, 1936, Ph.D. in Physics, 1939. Group leader Los Alamos Sci. Lab., 1944-46; head dept. physics Carnegie Inst. Tech., Pitts., 1946-55; v.p. research and devel., Gen. Atomic Co., San Diego, 1955-70; asst. dir. NSF, Washington, 1970-77; dir. Bishop Mus., Honolulu, 1977-84, ret., 1984. Inventor energy devices. Vice pres. Industry-Edn. Council, San Diego, 1955-70, Hall of Sci. and Planetarium, San Diego, 1965-70. Recipient Disting. Service award NSF, 1977. Fellow Am. Phys. Soc., Am. Nuclear Soc., AAAS; mem. Nat. Acad. Scis., Social Sci. Assn. Honolulu, Explorers Club Washington, Phi Beta Kappa, Tau Beta Pi. Current work: Nuclear physics; allocation of funds among science disciplines; museum management. Subspecialty: Nuclear physics.

CREVELING, CYRUS ROBBINS, pharmacologist, educator; b. Washington, May 30, 1930; s. Cyrus Robbins and Edith Lois (Hill) C.; m. Cornelia Mills Rector, Aug. 6, 1935; children: Victoria, Diana. A.A., George Washington U., 1952, B.S., 1954, M.S., 1955; Ph.D. (Am. Diabetes fellow), Harvard U., 1964. Instr. George Washington U., 1954-58; Nat. Heart Inst. grantee, 1958-62; research assoc. Harvard Sch. Medicine, Mass. Gen. Hosp., 1962-64; pharmacologist Nat. Inst. Arthritis Metabolics Digestive Kidney Diseases, Lab. Bioorganic chemistry, NIH, Bethesda, Md., 1980—; adj. prof. Howard U. Med. Sch., Washington, 1969—; prof. Med. Coll. Va., Richmond, 1985—; mem. div. research grants, study sect. A Pharmacology and Exptl. Therapeutics; mem. NSF neurobiology rev. adv.; mem. project adv. group FDA div. nutrition; spl. examiner Bd. Civil Service Examiners; Wash. Acad. Scis. fellow, 1977; chmn. awards com. Found. for Advanced Edn. in the Scis., 1979—. Contbr. articles on pharmacology to profl. jours.; editor: Transmethylation, 1978, Biochemistry of S-Adeno-syl Methionine and Related Compounds, 1982; Biochemistry of S-Adenosylmethionine as a Basis for Drug Design, 1984. Active BCC-YMCA, 1964—; mem. Pres.'s Club, Howard U., 1979—. Mem. Soc. Exptl. Biology and Medicine (pres. D. C. Chpt. 1978-79, recipient disting. scientist award 1979), AAAS, Am. Soc. Pharmacology and Exptl. Therapeutics, Am. Chem. Soc., Chem. Soc. Washington, Gordon Conf. on Cylic Nucleotides and Catecholamines, Soc. Neurosci. Republican. Methodist. Clubs: Howard U. Century (Washington); Catecholamine (pres. 1980-81). Current Work: Pharmacology of biogenic amines; biosynthesis and degradation of biogenic amines; immunolocalization of biogenic amines and related biosynthesis and degredative enzymes. Subspecialties: Molecular pharmacology; Neuropharmacology. Office: Lab Bioorganic Chemistr NIADDK NIH Bethesda MD 20205

CREWE, ALBERT VICTOR, physicist, research adminstr.; b. Bradford, Yorkshire, Eng., Feb. 18, 1927; came to U.S., 1955, naturalized, 1961; s. Wilfred and Edith Fish (Lawrence) C.; m. Doreen Blunsdon, Apr. 9, 1949; children—Jennifer, Sarah, Elizabeth, David. B.S. in Physics, U. Liverpool, Eng., 1947, Ph.D., 1951; hon. degrees, Lake Forest Coll., 1972, U. Mo., 1972, Elmhurst Coll., 1972. Asst. lectr. U. Liverpool, Eng., 1950-52, lectr., 1952-55; research asso. U. Chgo., 1955-56, asst. prof., 1956-58, asso. prof., 1958-63; prof. dept. physics and Enrico Fermi Inst., 1963-71, dean phys. scis. div., 1971-81; now William Wrather Disting. Service prof. physics and biophysics; dir. particle accelerator div. Argonne Nat. Lab., 1958-61, dir., 1961-66. Chmn. Chgo. Area Research and Devel. Council. Recipient Outstanding Local Citizen in Field of Sci. award Chgo. Jr. Assn. Commerce and Industry, 1961; Outstanding New Citizen of Year award Citizenship Council Chgo., 1962; award for outstanding achievement in field of sci. Immigrant's Service League, 1962; Man of Year in Research award Indsl. Research, Inc., 1970; Michelson medal Franklin Inst., 1977; Duddell medal Inst. of Physics, 1980. Fellow Am. Phys. Soc., Am. Nuclear Soc.; mem. Sci. Research Soc. Am., Electron Microscopy Soc. Am. (Disting. Service award 1976), N.Y. Microscope Soc. (Abbe award 1979), Am. Acad. Arts and Scis., Nat. Acad. Scis. Subspecialty: Nuclear physics. Office: Dept Physics U Chgo Chicago IL 60637

CREWS, DAVID P., behavorial endocrinologist; b. Jacksonville, Fla., Apr. 18, 1947; s. Sidney Walker and Anne (Pafford) C. B.A., U. Md., 1969; Ph.D., Rutgers U., 1973. Research asst. Bur. Social Sci. Research, Washington, 1968-69; NIMH predoctoral trainee Inst. Animal Behavior, Rutgers U., 1969-73; research zoologist dept. zoology U. Calif., Berkeley, 1973-75; assoc. Mus. Comparative Zoology, Harvard U., Cambridge, Mass., 1975-81, lectr. biology and psychology, 1975-76, asst. prof. biology and psychology, 1976-78, assoc. prof. biology and psychology, 1978-81; sr. assoc. prof. zoology and psychology U. Tex., Austin, 1982-84, prof. zoology and psychology, 1984—. Contbr. numerous articles to sci. jours. NIMH research scientist devel. awardee, 1977—; Sloan fellow, 1978-80. Fellow AAAS; Mem. Am. Soc. Zoologists, Soc. Study of Reprodn., Soc. Neurosci., Animal Behavoir Soc., Endocrine Soc., Sigma Xi, Psi Chi. Current Work: Psychoneuroendocrinology; comparative endocrinology; reproductive biology of lower vertebrates. Subspecialties: Ethology; Evolutionary biology. Office: Dept Zoology U Tex Austin TX 78712

CREWS, HAROLD RICHARDSON, clinical chemist, researcher; b. Sylvania, Ga., Aug. 31, 1934; s. George Mills and Eva Marie (Scott) C.; m. Barbara McFarlane, Feb. 27, 1970; children—Karen Hope, Mark Richardson. A.A., South Ga. Coll., Douglas, 1960; B.S., Ga. Southwestern U., 1962; postgrad. U. Miami, 1966-67; Ph.D., Walden U., Mpls., 1984. Research assoc. dept. biochemistry Timken Mercy Hosp., Canton, Ohio, 1962-64; research assoc. cardiovascular research, lipid metabolism Med. Coll. S.C., Charleston, 1964-66; research assoc., asst. dir. research, cardiovascular medicine Miami Heart Inst., Miami Beach, Fla., 1966-68; dir. clin. automated systems, research and devel. Coulter Electronics, Inc., Hialeah, Fla., 1971-75, dir. spl. projects, applied research and biomed. systems, 1976-80; dir. research and devel. Coulter Diagnostics, Hialeah, 1980-82, gen. mgr., 1982—. Contbr. articles to profl. jours. Patentee multi-purpose blood diluent, differential lymphoid-myeloid determination of leukocytes in whole blood, multi-purpose blood diluent and lysing agent for differential determination of lymphoid-myeloid population of leukocytes, 1982, others. Mem. ch. council Bethany Lutheran Ch., Miami, also mem. mng. commn. and chmn. call com. Served with U.S. Navy, 1953-57; Far East. Mem. AAAS, N.Y. Acad. Sci., Am. Assn. Clin. Chemistry, Can. Soc. Clin. Chemistry, Am. Chem. Soc., Am. Mgmt. Assn. Dmocrat. Current work: Research and clinical investigation on the development and use of monoclonal antibodies in cancer therapy. Subspecialties: Cell biology (medicine); Hematology. Home: 8960 NW 11th St Pembroke Pines FL 33023 Office: Coulter Diagnostics 740 NW 83d St Hialeah FL 33014

CRIBB, WALTER RAYMOND, metallurgist; b. Columbia, S.C., Aug. 29, 1949; s. Paul and Hildegard (Ulbrich) C.; m. Katherine Morlock, Sept. 4, 1971; children—Suzanne Michelle, Alan Michael. B.S. in Engring. Sci., U. Fla., 1971, M.S. in Materials Sci. and Engring., 1973, Ph.D. in Materials Sci. and Engring., 1975. Registered profl. engr. Sr. research metallurgist Republic Steel Corp., Independence, Ohio, 1975-79; supr. research and devel. Brush Wellman, Inc., Elmore, Ohio, 1979-80, mgr. mfg. engring., 1980-82, dir. research and devel., Cleve., 1982—. Contbr. articles to profl. jours. Patentee in field. Served to capt., USAF, 1972-73. Mem. AIME, Am. Soc. for Metals. Current work: Metals development and processing. Subspecialty: Metallurgical engineering. Office: Brush Wellman Inc Research and Devel Lab 17876 Saint Clair Ave Cleveland OH 44110

CRICK, FRANCIS HARRY COMPTON, biologist, educator; b. June 8, 1916; s. Harry and Annie Elizabeth (Wilkins) C.; m. Ruth Doreen Dodd, 1940 (div. 1947); 1 son; m. Odile Speed, 1949; 2 daus. B.Sc., Univ. Coll., London; Ph.D, Cambridge U., Eng. Scientist Brit. Admiralty, 1940-47, Strangeways Lab., Cambridge, Eng., 1947-49; biologist Med. Research Council Lab. of Molecular Biology, Cambridge, 1949-77; Kieckhefer Disting. prof. Salk Inst. for Biol. Studies, San Diego, 1977—, non-resident fellow, 1962-73; vis. lectr. Rockefeller Inst., N.Y.C., 1959; vis. prof. chemistry dept. Harvard U., 1959, vis. prof. biophysics, 1962; fellow Churchill Coll., Cambridge, 1960-61, UCLA, 1962; Warren Triennial prize lectr. (with J.D. Watson), Boston, 1959; Korkes Meml. lectr. Duke U., 1960; Henry Sedgewick Meml. lectr. Cambridge U., 1963; Graham Young lectr., Glasgow, 1963; Robert Boyle lectr. Oxford U., 1963; Vanuxem lectr. Princeton U., 1964; Willaim T. Sedgwick Meml. lectr. MIT, 1965; Cherwell-Simon Meml. lectr. Oxford U., 1966; Shell lectr. Stanford U., 1969; Paul Lund lectr. Northwestern U., 1977; Dupont lectr. Harvard U., 1979. Author: Of Molecules and Men, 1966, Life Itself, 1981; contbr. papers and articles on molecular and cell biology to sci. jours. Recipient Prix Charles Leopold Mayer, French Academies des Sciences, 1961; Research Corp. award, 1961; (with J.D. Watson) Nobel Prize for medicine, 1962; Gairdner Found. award, 1962; Royal Medal Royal Soc., 1972; Copley Medal, 1976; Michelson-Morley award, 1981. Fellow AAAS, Royal Soc.; mem. Am. Acad. Arts and Scis. (fgn hon.), Am. Soc. Biol. Chemistry (hon.), U.S. Nat. Acad. Scis. (fgn. assoc.), German Acad. Sci., Am. Philos. Soc. (fgn. mem.), French Acad. Scis. (assoc. fgn. mem.). Subspecialties: Cell biology; Neurobiology. Office: Salk Inst Biol Studies PO Box 85800 San Diego CA 92138

CRIM, GARY ALLEN, dental educator, researcher; b. Louisville, July 13,1949; s. John William and Ruby Mae (Willis) C. Student, Ind. U., 1967-69; student, U. Ky., 1969-70, D.M.D., 1974; M.S.D., Ind. U. Sch. Dentistry-Indpls., 1981. Practice gen. dentistry, Milton, Ky., 1974-77; assoc. prof. restorative dentistry U. Louisville Sch. Dentistry, 1977—. Recipient Nat. Research Service award Nat. Inst. Dental Research, 1980. Mem. Internat. Assn. Dental Research, ADA, Acad. Dental Materials, Acad. Operative Dentistry, Acad. Internat. Dental Studies, Am. Assn. Dental Schs., Omicron Kappa Upsilon. Democrat. Baptist. Club: Gideons (Clarksville, Ind.) (v.p. club 1982—). Current Work: Microleakage of composite restorative resins; cavity preparations for Class II posterior composite resins. Subspecialties: Biomaterials; Operative dentistry. Home: 200 La Fontenay Ct Louisville KY 40223 Office: U Louisville Sch Dentistry 501 S Preston Louisville KY 40292

CRIMINALE, WILLIAM OLIVER, JR., applied mathematics educator; b. Mobile, Ala., Nov. 29, 1933; s. William Oliver and Vivian Gertrude (Sketoe) C.; m. Ulrike Irmgard Wegner, June 7, 1962; children: Martin Oliver, Lucca. B.S., U. Ala., 1955; Ph.D., Johns Hopkins U., 1960. Asst. prof. Princeton (N.J.) U., 1962-68; assoc. prof. U. Wash., Seattle, 1968-73, prof. oceanography, geophysics, applied math., 1973—, chmn. dept. applied math., 1976-84; cons. Aerospace Corp., 1962-65, Boeing Corp., 1968-72, AGARD, 1967-68, Lennox Hill Hosp., 1967-68; guest prof., Can., 1965, France, 1967-68, Germany, 1973-74, Sweden, 1973-74, Scotland, 1985; Nat. Acad. exchange scientist, USSR, 1969, 72. Author: Stability of Parallel Flows, 1967; Contbr. articles to profl. jours. Served with U.S. Army, 1961-62. Boris A. Bakmeteff Meml. fellow, 1957-58; NATO Postdoctoral fellow, 1960-61; Alexander von Humboldt Sr. fellow, 1973-74. Mem. AAAS, Am. Phys. Soc., Am. Geophys. Union, Fedn. Am. Scientists, Soc. Indsl. and Applied Math. Subspecialty: Fluid mechanics. Home: 1635 Peach Court E Seattle WA 98112 Office: Applied Math FS-20 U Wash Seattle WA 98195

CRIPPS, DEREK J., physician; b. London, Sept. 17, 1928; married, 1963; 4 children. M.B., B.S., U. London, 1953, M.D., 1965; M.S., U. Mich., 1961. Diplomate: Am. Bd. Dermatology. Intern in medicine London Hosps., 1953-54; resident dermatology Med. Center U. Mich., 1959-62; sr. registrar Inst. Dermatology Eng., 1962-65; asst. prof. medicine U. Wis., Madison, 1965-68, assoc. prof. dermatology, 1968-72; prof. dermatology, chmn. dept. U. Wis. (Med. Center), 1972—; mem. study com. NIH, 1969—. NIH grantee, 1966—. Mem. British Dermatol. Assn., Am. Acad. Dermatology, Am. Fedn. Clin. Research, Soc. Investigative Dermatology, ACP. Subspecialty: Dermatology. Office: Med Center U Wis 600 Highland Ave Madison WI 53792

CRISS, CECIL M., chemist; b. Wheeling, W.Va., Apr. 22, 1934; s. Cecil M. and Anna V. (Reece) C.; m. Laura A. Criss, Aug. 18, 1958; children: Cecil M. III, Laura A. M. A.B., Kenyon Coll., 1956; Ph.D., Purdue U., 1961. Research assoc. Purdue U., 1961; asst. prof. U. Vt., Burlington, 1961-65; asst. prof. U. Miami, Coral Gables, 1965-70, assoc. prof., 1970-76, prof. chemistry, 1976—, dept. chmn., 1984—; vis. scientist U. Lund, Sweden, 1977-78; vis. research prof. San Diego State U., 1978-79; program officer chem-div. NSF, 1982-83. Mem. Am. Chem. Soc. (award Fla. 1977), Chem. Soc. (London), AAAS, Calorimetry Conf., Sigma Xi, Phi Lambda Upsilon. Episcopalian. Current Work: Thermodynamic properties of aqueous and nonaqueous electrolytic solutions, especially ionic entropies, volumes, heat capacities, and compressibilities. Subspecialties: Physical chemistry; Thermodynamics. Home: 4910 San Amaro Dr Coral Gables FL 33146 Office: Dept Chemistry U Miami Coral Gables FL 33124

CRISTOL, STANLEY JEROME, chemistry educator; b. Chgo., June 14, 1916; s. Myer J. and Lillian (Young) C.; m. Barbara Wright Swingle, June 1957; children: Marjorie Jo, Jeffrey Tod. B.S., Northwestern U., 1937; M.A., UCLA, 1939, Ph.D., 1943. Research chemist Standard Oil Co., Calif., 1938-41; research fellow U. Ill., 1943-44; research chemist U.S. Dept. Agr., 1944-46; asst. prof., then asso. prof. U. Colo., 1946-55, prof., 1955—, Joseph Sewall disting. prof., 1979—, chmn. dept. chemistry, 1960-62, grad. dean, 1980-81; vis. prof. Stanford U., summer 1961, U. Geneva, 1975, U. Lausanne, Switzerland, 1981; with OSRD, 1944-46; adv. panels NSF, 1957-63, 69-73, NIH, 1969-72. Author: (with L.O. Smith, Jr.) Organic Chemistry, 1966; editorial bd., Chem. Revs., 1957-59, Jour. Organic Chemistry, 1964-68; contbr. research articles to sci. jours. Guggenheim fellow, 1955-56, 81, 82; recipient James Flack Norris award in phys.-organic chemistry, 1972. Fellow AAAS, Chem. Soc. London; mem. Am. Chem. Soc. (chmn. organic chemistry div. 1961-62, adv. bd. petroleum research fund 1963-66, council policy com. 1968-73), AAUP, Colo.-Wyo. Acad. Sci., Nat. Acad. Scis., Phi Beta Kappa, Sigma Xi, Phi Lambda Upsilon. Current Work: Organic reaction mechanisms; reaction of excited states; energy and electron transfer; stereochemistry of excited state reactions. Subspecialties: Organic chemistry; Photochemistry. Home: 2918 3d St Boulder CO 80302 Office: U Colo Dept Chemistry Box 215 Boulder CO 80309

CRITCHLOW, B(URTIS) VAUGHN, foundation administrator, researcher; b. Hotchkiss, Colo., Mar. 5, 1927; s. Arthur Burtis and Nancy Gertrude (Lynch) C.; children—Christopher, Eric, Jan, Carey. A.A., Glendale Coll., 1949; B.A., Occidental Coll., 1951; Ph.D., U. Calif., 1957. Tchr. life sci. Marshall High Sch., Los Angeles, 1952-53; inst. anatomy Baylor U. Coll. Medicine, Houston, 1957-58, asst. prof., assoc. prof., prof., acting chmn. anatomy, 1958-72; chmn. anatomy Oreg. Health Sci. U., Portland, 1972-82; dir. Oreg. Regional Primate Research Ctr., Beaverton, 1982—, mem. sci. adv. com., 1973-82; trustee Med. Research Found. Oreg., 1982—. Contbr. articles to profl. jours. Vis. investigator Nobel Inst. Neurophysiology, Karolinska Inst., Stockholm, Sweden, 1961-62; recipient Research Career Devel. award NIH, 1959-69. Teaching award Oreg. Health Scis. U., 1978-79, Baylor Coll. Medicine, 1969-72. Mem. Am. Assoc. Anatomists, Endocrine Soc., Am. Physiol. Soc., Internat. Brain Research Orgn., Soc. for Neurosci., Internat. Soc. Neuroendocrinology. Subspecialty: Neuroendocrinology. Office: Oregon Regional Primate Research Ctr 505 NW 185th Ave Beaverton OR 97006

CRITOPH, EUGENE, laboratory executive, consultant; b. Vancouver, C., Can., Mar. 29, 1929; m. Mary Elizabeth Ivens, Feb. 9, 1952; children: Christopher M., S. Bard, E. Mark, Boyd. B.A.Sc., U. B.C., 1951, M.A.Sc., 1957. Research officer Atomic Energy Can. Ltd. Chalk River Nat. Lab., Chalk River, Ont., Can., 1953-67, br. head, 1967-75, div. head, 1975-79, v.p., gen. mgr., 1979—. Mem. Am. Nuclear Soc., Can. Nuclear Soc., Can. Assn. Physicists. Current Work: Research and development in nuclear power; particularly in nuclear engineering and reactor physics. Subspecialty: Nuclear fission. Home: 4 Darwin Crescent Deep River ON K0J 1P0 Canada Office: Atomic Energy Can Ltd Chalk River ON K0J 1J0 Canada

CRNIC, LINDA SUE SMITH, psychobiology educator; b. Ft. Wayne, Ind., Mar. 29, 1948; d. Herman Edward and Patricia Ellen (Leeth) Smith; m. David Michael Crnic, June 21, 1969 (div. 1976). A.B., U. Chgo., 1970; M.A., U. Ill.-Chgo., 1972, Ph.D., 1975. Postdoctoral fellow U. Colo. Sch. Medicine, Denver, 1975-77, instr., 1977-78, asst. prof. psychobiology, 1979—; chmn. Rocky Mountain region Neurosci. Group, Denver, 1983-85. Contbr. articles to profl. jours., chpts. to books. Nat. Merit scholar, Ill. State scholar; State of Ill. fellow NIH; recipient various federal grants. Mem. Internat. Soc. Developmental Psychology (sec., treas. 1983—), Soc. for Neurosci., Western Soc. for Pediatric Research, Internat. Soc. for Developmental Neurosci., Animal Behavior Soc. Clubs: Denver Bicycle Touring, Colo. Mountain. Current work: Research on environmental influences on brain development and behavior, including nutrition, environment, stimulation, altitude and viral effects. Subspecialty: Nutrition (biology). Home: 1811 S Quebec Way Apt 187 Denver CO 80231 Office: U Colo Sch Medicine 4200 E 9th Ave C233 Denver CO 80262

CROCE, CARLO MARIA, molecular geneticist; b. Milan, Italy, Dec. 17, 1944. 1 child. M.D., U. Rome, 1969. Scientist Wistar Inst. Anatomy and Biology, Phila., 1970-71, research assoc., 1971-74, assoc. mem., 1974-76, prof., 1976-80, assoc. dir., inst. prof., 1980—; also Wistar prof. human genetics Sch. Medicine, U. Pa., Phila.; vis. scientist Carnegie Inst., 1978-79; mem. Mammalian Genetics Study Sect., NIH, Bethesda, Md., 1979-83. Mem. adv. com. Am. Cancer Soc. Recipient Outstanding Investigator award Nat. Cancer Inst. Subspecialties: Genetics and genetic engineering (biology); Molecular biology. Office: Wistar Inst Anatomy and Biology 36th St at Spruce Philadelphia PA 19104

CROFT, BARBARA YODER, physicist; b. Port Chester, N.Y., Aug. 11, 1940; d. Paul Henry and Harriet French (Postle) Yoder; m. Joseph Edward Croft, Dec. 15,1977. B.A., Swarthmore Coll., 1962; M.A., Johns Hopkins U., 1964, Ph.D., 1967. Sr. scientist Johnston Labs., Inc., Balt., 1967-69; instr. radiology U. Va., Charlottesville, 1969-72, asst. prof., 1972—; cons. radiopharm. adv. com. FDA. Co-author: Basics of Radiopharmacy, 1978; author: Single-Photon Emission Computed Tomography, 1985. Mem. Am. Chem. Soc., Am. Assn. Physicists in Medicine, Soc. Nuclear Medicine, Am. Coll. Nuclear Physicians, Pattern Research Soc., Sigma Xi. Episcopalian. Current Work: Single photon emission computed tomography; computerized radiology. Subspecialty: Radiology in nuclear medicine. Home: Route 2 Box 565 Scottsville VA 24590 Office: U Va Dept Radiology Box 170 Charlottesville VA 22908

CROFT, BRIAN A., entomology educator, biochemist; b. Sugar City, Idaho, Mar. 3, 1941; s. Arnold Douglas and Cathryn (McKay) C.; m. Candace E. Babbel, Sept. 6, 1964; children—Marnie, Mark, Timothy, Erin, Laurin, Christopher, Brett. B.S., M.S., Brigham Young U.; Ph.D., U. Calif.-Riverside. Postdoctoral fellow U. Calif.-Riverside, 1969-70; prof. entomology Mich. State U., East Lansing, 1970-82, Oreg. State U., Corvallis, 1982—; dir. research E.T. Benson Food Inst., Provo, Utah, 1976-77. Author: Integrated Management of Insect Pests of Pome and Stone Fruits, 1981. Contbr. articles to profl. jours. Bishop Mormon Ch., Lansing, Mich., 1980-82, br. pres., 1971-75. Kellogg Found. nat. fellow, 1980-83. Mem. Entomol. Soc. (Bussart Meml. award 1974, Ciba-Geigy award 1978), Can. Entomol. Soc., Sigma Xi. Republican. Current work: Pest management, systems modelling, mite ecology, population dynamics, international agriculture, resistance to pesticides. Subspecialties: Integrated pest management; Integrated systems modelling and engineering. Home: 2895 NW Duchess Corvallis OR 97331 Office: Oreg State U Dept Entomology Corvallis OR 97330

CROFT, THOMAS A(RTHUR), research executive; b. Denver, Feb. 15, 1931; s. Edwin T. and Pearl M. (Jordan) C.; m. Rachel Marie Whitman, Apr. 3, 1965; children: Andrew A., Steven T., Rachel E. B.A., Dartmouth Coll., 1953, M.S., 1954; Ph.D. in Elec. Engring, Stanford U., 1964. Elec. engr. Convair/Astronautics, Gen. Dynamics Corp., 1957-59; research assoc. radio propagation Radiosci. Lab. Stanford U., 1959-68; adj. prof. Stanford U. (Ctr. Radar Astronomy), 1968-75; cons. Stanford U. (Stanford Research Inst.), 1965—; dir. research Tech. for Communications Internat., Sunnyvale, Calif., 1982-85; cons. Applied Tech. Inc., 1965—, Barry Research Corp., 1968—, ESSA, 1969—. Served to lt. USN, 1954-57. Mem. Internat. Sci. Radio Union (assoc. mem. commn. 3 1966—, assoc. editor Radio Sci.), Am. Geophys. Union, AAAS (div. planetary scis.), IEEE (sr.), Soc. Motion Picture and TV Engrs. Current Work: Ionospheric simulation of performance of complex high frequency radar systems by means of digital computer wave propagation analysis and synthesis; use of artificial intelligence methods to control HF skywave communication. Subspecialties: Electronics; Graphics, image processing, and pattern recognition. Office: SRI Internat Menlo Park CA 94025

CROMBIE, DOUGLASS DARNILL, govt. ofcl.; b. Alexandra, N.Z., Sept. 14, 1924; came to U.S., 1962, naturalized, 1967; s. Colin Lindsay and Ruth (Datnill) C.; m. Pa uline L.A. Morrison, Mar. 3, 1952. B.Sc., Otago U., Dunedin, N.Z., 1947, M.Sc., 1949. N.Z. nat. research fellow Cavendish Lab., Cambridge, Eng., 1958-59; head radio physics div. N.Z. Dept. Sci. and Industry Research, 1961-62; chief spectrum utilization div., chief low frequency group Inst. Telecommunications Scis., Dept. Commerce, Boulder, Colo., 1962-71, dir. inst., 1971-76; dir. Inst. Telecommunication Scis., Nat. Telecommunications and Info. Adminstrn., 1976-80; chief scientist Nat. Telecommunication and Info. Agy., 1980—. Served with N.Z. Air Force, 1943-44. Recipient Gold medal Dept. Commerce, 1970, citation, 1972. Mem. IEEE, Nat. Acad Engring., Union Radio Sci. Internat. Current Work: Efficiency of radio frequency spectrum use by communication systems. Propagation of medium frequency radio signals to great distances. Selective fading of microwave signals. Subspecialties: Telecommunications; Electromagnetic wave propagation. Home: 1441 Mariposa Ave Boulder CO 80302 Office: 325 S Broadway Boulder CO 80302

CROMWELL, NORMAN H, emeritus chemistry educator, consultant; b. Terre Haute, Ind., Nov. 22, 1913; s. Henry and Ethyl Lee (Harkelroad) C.; m. Grace Newell, Jan. 29, 1955; children—Christopher Newell, Richard Earl. B.S. with honors, Rose-Hulman Inst., 1935; Ph.D., U. Minn., 1939. From instr. to prof. chemistry U. Nebr., Lincoln, 1939-60, chmn. dept. chemistry, 1964-70, v.p., dean grad. studies and research, 1970-73, regents' prof. chemistry, 1960-83, regents' prof. emeritus, 1983—; dir. Eppley Inst. Cancer Research, Med. Ctr., Omaha, 1981-83; cons. Parke Davis & Co., Detroit, 1943-46, Smith Kline & French, Phila., 1946-51, Philip Morris, Inc., Richmond, Va., 1964-69. Co-author: New Trends in Heterocyclic Chemistry, 1979. Contbr. articles to profl. jours. Trustee Nebr. Art Assn., Lincoln, 1958-70, v.p., 1971. Fulbright Research scholar, 1950-51; Guggenheim fellow, 1950, 58; recipient Outstanding Alumnus award U. Minn., 1975, Outstanding Research and Creativity award U. Nebr., 1978. Mem. Am. Chem. Soc. (40th Midwest award 1984), Internat. Soc. Heterocyclic Chemistry (pres. 2d internat. congress 1969), Chem. Soc. London. Club: Round Table of Lincoln. Current work: Synthesis of new anti-cancer drugs and potential immunity inducing agents. Subspecialties: Cancer research (medicine); Medicinal chemistry. Home: 2417 S 70th St Lincoln NE 68506 Office: Hamilton Hall U Nebr Lincoln NE 68588

CRONAUER, DONALD CHARLES, chemical engineer, researcher; b. Sewickley, Pa., Nov. 4, 1936; s. Andrew Vincent and Marie Frances (Scherpf) C. m. Mary Ann Cleary, Aug. 19, 1961; children—Elaine L., David F., Stephen A. B.S., Carnegie-Mellon U., 1958, M.S., 1959, Ph.D., 1962. Sr. chem. engr. Amoco Research and Devel., Whiting, Ind., 1962-65; sr. engr., research assoc. Marbon Chems. Co., Parkersburg, W.Va., 1965-70; staff engr. Gulf Research and Devel., Pitts., 1970—. Contbr. articles to profl. jours. Patentee in field. Bd.

dirs. Parkersburg Community Concert Assn., 1968-70. Served to 1st lt. U.S. Army, 1962-64. Mem. Am. Inst. Chem. Engrs., Am. Chem. Soc., AAAS, Sigma Xi. Club: Square Dance (pres. 1979-81). Current work: Combination of process engineering and chemistry in the conversion of heavy species (coal, shale, etc.) to useful fuels, reaction fundamentals, hydrogenations, catalysis, ion exchange. Subspecialty: Chemical engineering. Home: 525 Edge Hill Dr Gibsonia PA 15044Office: Gulf Research and Devel Co PO Drawer 2038 Pittsburgh PA 15230

CRONHOLM, LOIS S., college dean, biology educator; b. St. Louis, Aug. 15, 1930; s. Fred and Emma (Tobias) Kisslinger; m. Stuart E. Neff, Apr. 11, 1975; children: Judith Frances, Peter Foster; m. James Norman Cronholm, Aug. 11, 1964 (div. 1973). B.A., U. Louisville, 1962, Ph.D., 1966. Asst. prof. U. Louisville, 1973-76, assoc. prof., 1976-80, prof. biology, 1980—; dean U. Louisville (Coll. Arts and Scis.), 1979—. Chmn. Jefferson County-Louisville Human Relations Commn., 1968-73; mem. nominating com. Met. United Way, Louisville, 1981—; chmn. Econ. Devel. Council, Jefferson County, Ky., 1982-83; mem. Leadership Louisville, 1982-83. HEW fellow, 1963-66, 66-69; recipient Research award Dept. Interior, 1975-78, Research award NOAA, 1976-77, Research award Dept. Interior, 1977-82. Current Work: Efficiency of package plants in wastewater treatment, ecology of Histoplasma capsulatum and its relationships to roosting birds. Subspecialties: Microbiology; Water supply and wastewater treatment. Home: 9811 Gandy Rd Louisville KY 40272 Office: Coll Arts and Scis U Louisville Louisville KY 40292

CRONIN, JAMES WATSON, educator, physicist; b. Chgo., Sept. 29, 1931; s. James Farley and Dorothy (Watson) C.; m. Annette Martin, Sept. 11, 1954; children: Cathryn, Emily, Daniel Watson. A.B., So. Methodist U. (1951); Ph.D., U. Chgo. Asso. Brookhaven Nat. Lab., 1955-58; mem. faculty Princeton, 1958-71, prof. physics, 1965-71, U. Chgo., 1971—; Loeb lectr. physics Harvard U., 1967. Recipient Research Corp. Am. award, 1967; John Price Wetherill medal Franklin Inst., 1976; E.O. Lawrence award ERDA, 1977; Nobel prize for physics, 1980; Sloan fellow, 1964-66; Guggenheim fellow, 1970-71, 82-83. Mem. Am. Acad. Arts and Scis., Nat. Acad. Sci. Participant early devel. spark chambers; co-discover CP-violation, 1964. Subspecialty: Particle physics. Home: 5825 S Dorchester St Chicago IL 60637

CRONKHITE, LEONARD WOLSEY, JR., research foundation executive; b. Newton, Mass., May 4, 1919; s. Leonard Wolsey and Orpah Glencor (Brewster) C.; m. Joan Dunn, July 2, 1955 (div. 1976); children—Judith, Marcia, Janice, Wendy; m. Linda M. Marchky, Aug. 14, 1976. B.S., Bowdoin Coll., 1941; M.D., Harvard U., 1950; LL.D. (hon.), Northeastern U., 1970; L.H.D. (hon.), Curry Coll., 1977; LL.D. (hon.), Bowdoin U., 1979. Gen. dir. Children's Hosp. Med. Ctr., Boston, 1962-71, exec. v.p., 1971-73, pres., 1973-77; pres. Med. Coll. of Wis., Milw., 1977-84, MCW Research Found., Milw., 1984—; trustee Northwestern Mut. Ins. Co., Milw.; dir. Am. Med. Bldgs., Milw., Universal Health Service, King of Prussia, Pa. Contbr. articles on medicine and med. edn. to profl. jours. Trustee Bowdoin Coll., Brunswick, Maine; mem. Wis. Alcohol and Drug Abuse Research Adv. Com.; mem. Bd. on Army Sci. and Tech., Washington, Inst. of Medicine, Nat. Acad. Scis., Washington. Recipient Bowdoin prize Bowdoin Coll., 1973; named hon. alumnus Med. Coll. Wis., 1984. Mem. Soc. Med. Adminstrs. (pres.), Assn. Am. Med. Colls. (chmn. 1975-76), Council of Teaching Hosps. (chmn. 1972-73). Clubs: University (Milw.); Harvard (Boston); Army and Navy (Washington). Current work: Transfer of technology from academic institution to the marketplace. Subspecialty: Medical institution administration. Office: MCW Research Found 8701 Watertown Plank Rd Milwaukee WI 53226

CRONKITE, EUGENE PITCHER, physician; b. Los Angeles, Dec. 11, 1914; s. Clarence Edgar and Anita (Pitcher) C.; m. Elizabeth Erna Kaitschuk, Aug. 17, 1940; 1 dau., Christina Elizabeth. A.B., Stanford U., 1936, M.D., 1940; D.Sc. (hon.), L.I. U., 1962. Intern Stanford U. Hosps., San Francisco, 1939-40, resident in medicine, 1941-42; commd. lt. (s.g.) U.S. Navy, 1942, advanced through grades to rear adm., 1969, ret., 1954; head hematology Naval Med. Research Inst., Bethesda, Md., 1945-54; sr. scientist med. dept. Brookhaven Nat. Lab., 1954—, chmn., 1967-79; prof. medicine Health Sci. Center, SUNY, Stony Brook, 1979—. Contbr. articles to med. jours. Recipient Alfred Benzon award Denmark, 1969; Ludwig Heilmeyer medal W.Ger., 1974; Semmelweiss award Hungary, 1975; Alexander von Humboldt sr. scientist award W.Ger., 1977. Mem. Am. Soc. Hematology (pres. 1970), Internat. Soc. Exptl. Hematology (pres. 1976), U.S. Nat. Acad. Scis., Am. Soc. Clin. Investigation, Assn. Am. Physicians, Am. Soc. Hematology, Am. Assn. Physiologists. Current Work: Regulation of blood cell production, effects of radiation on man and mammals. Subspecialties: Hematology; Radiation biology. Office: Med Dept Brookhaven Nat Lab Upton NY 11973

CRONQUIST, BRIAN EDWARD, semiconductor process engineer; b. Roanoke, Va., Aug. 22, 1957; s. William Edward and Roberta Ann (Huston) C.; m. Jaymelynn Green, June 16, 1979; children—Lucannus Edward, Paul Michael. B.S. in Chemistry, U. Santa Clara, 1979. Process devel. engr. Synertek, Inc., Santa Clara, Calif., 1979-83; staff process research and devel. engr. Am. Microsystems Inc., Santa Clara, 1983-84; sr. process engr. Sierra Semiconductor Co., Sunnyvale, Calif., 1984—. Mem. Am. Chem. Soc., IEEE, Electrochem. Soc. Republican. Baptist. Current work: Growth conditions and quality factors associated with high temperature growth of silicon dioxide; analytical measurement of submicron structures, CMOS process architecture, latchup prevention. Subspecialties: Microchip technology (materials science); Microchip technology (engineering). Home: 6315 Cessna Ct San Jose CA 95123 Office: Sierra Semiconductor Corp 2075 N Capitol Ave San Jose CA 95132

CRONSHAW, JAMES, cell biologist, educator; b. Lancashire, Eng., Mar. 11, 1933; came to U.S., 1962; s. William and Edith (Wilkinson) C.; m. Patricia Birwhistle, Sept. 1, 1956; 1 dau., Caroline Anne. B.S. in Botany, U. Leeds, (Eng.), 1954, Ph.D., 1957, D.Sc., 1973. Demonstrator dept. botany U. Leeds, 1955-57; research officer, div. forest products Commonwealth Sci. and Indsl. Research Orgn., Melbourne, Australia, 1957-62; demonstrator dept. botany U. Melbourne, 1957-62; asst. prof. dept. biology Yale U., 1962-65; assoc. prof. dept. biol. scis. U. Calif-Santa Barbara, 1965-71, prof., 1971—. Contbr. articles to profl. jours. NSF grantee, 1962-64, 65-66, 67-69, 69-72, 75-78, 80-86; NIH grantee, 1962-67; Santa Barbara Med. Found. Clinic grantee, 1974-76; Dickson Blanchard Pathology Group grantee, 1978; U.S. Dept. Interior grantee, 1976-80. Mem. Am. Soc. Cell Biology, Bot. Soc. Am., Electron Microscopy Soc. Am., So. Calif. Soc. for Electron Microscopy, AAAS, Soc. Exptl. Biology, Sigma Xi. Current Work: Enzyme cytochemistry of phloem and electron microscopy of the adrenal cortex. Subspecialty: Cell and tissue culture. Office: Dept Biol Scis U Calif Santa Barbara CA 93106

CROOKE, STANLEY THOMAS, pharmacologist, pharmaceutical company executive, educator; b. Indpls., Mar. 28, 1945; s. Robert Ellison and Catherine Elizabeth C.; m. Nancy Ann Alder, Aug. 29, 1964 (dec.); 1 son, Evan. B.S., Butler U., 1966; Ph.D., Baylor U. Coll. Medicine, 1971, M.D., 1974. Postdoctoral fellow Baylor Coll. Medicine, Houston, 1971-72, intern, 1974-75, dir. Bristol-Baylor Molecular Pharmacology Lab., 1976-80, asst. prof. dept. pharmacology, 1976-79, assoc. prof., 1979-82, prof., 1982—; asst. dir. med. research Bristol Labs., Syracuse, N.Y., 1975-76, assoc. dir. med. research, 1976-77, assoc. dir. research and devel., 1977-79, v.p., assoc. dir. research and devel., 1979-80; clin. instr. dept. medicine Upstate Med. Center, Syracuse, 1976-77, clin. asst. prof., 1977-79, clin. assoc. prof., 1979-80; v.p. research and devel. Smith Kline & French Labs., Phila., 1980-82, pres. research and devel., 1982—. Contbr. articles to profl. jours. Recipient Research award So. Med. Assn., 1973-74; Julius W. Sturmer Meml. Lecture award Rho Chi, 1981; USPHS fellow, 1968-71, 71-72; Nat. Cancer Inst. awardee, 1973-74; named Outstanding Faculty Mem. Baylor U. Coll. Medicine; other awards. Mem. AAAS, Am. Assn. Cancer Research, Am. Soc. Microbiology, Cancer and Acute Leukemia Group B, Am. Soc. Clin. Pharmacology and Therapeutics, Am. Soc. Pharmacology and Exptl. Therapeutics, Am. Soc. Clin. Oncology, Coll. Physicians Phila. Current Work: Molecular pharmacology, antitumor biology, clinical research, anticancer and other drug development. Subspecialty: Molecular biology. Office: PO Box 7929 L-320 Philadelphia PA 19101

CROSBY, LON OWEN, nutritionist; b. Webster City, Iowa, Aug. 6, 1945; s. Owen S. and Viola F. (Short) C.; m. Ann E. Sonerholm, Aug. 5, 1967; children—Brian L., Teresa A. B.S., Iowa State U., 1967; Ph.D., Purdue U., 1971. Cert. animal scientist. Research asst. Purdue U., Lafayette, Ind., 1967-71; research assoc. Cornell U., Ithaca, N.Y., 1971-73; head monogast physiology Syntex Corp., Palo Alto, Calif., 1973-75; sr. scientist Enviro Control Inc., Rockville, Md., 1975-79; dir. Central Lab. 221, VA, Phila., 1982—; research assoc., research asst. prof. U. Pa., Phila., 1979—; cons., Rosemont, Pa., 1979—. Editor: Surgical Nutrition, Vol. 61, 1981; asst. editor Cancer and Nutrition, 1979—. Fellow Am. Coll. Nutrition; mem. Am. Soc. Parenteral and Enteral Nutrition, Am. Soc. Animal Sci. Current work: Clinical nutrition, nutrition and disease prevention, body composition, disease effect on nutrient requirements. Subspecialties: Nutrition (medicine); Physiology (medicine). Home: 430 Hollybush Rd Rosemont PA 19010 Office: Room A405R Surgical Research PVAMC University and Woodland Aves Philadelphia PA 19104

CROSS, RALPH EMERSON, mechanical engineer; b. Detroit, June 3, 1910; s. Milton Osgood and Helen (Heim) C.; m. Eloise Florence Fountain, June 18, 1932; children: Ralph Emerson, Carol (Mrs. Peter G. Wodtke), Dennis W. Student, MIT, 1933; D.Eng. (hon.), Lawrence Inst. Tech., 1977. Vice pres. Cross Co., Fraser, Mich., 1932-67, pres., gen. mgr., 1967-79, chmn., 1979-82; chmn. bd. Cross & Trecker, Bloomfield Hills, Mich., 1979-82, chmn. emeritus, dir., 1982—; chmn. bd., chief exec. officer Intelitec Corp., Bloomfield Hills, Mich., 1982—; chmn. bd., pres. Cross Internat. A.G., Fribourg, Switzerland, 1965-68; pres. Cross Export Corp., 1972-80; dir. Axiomatic Inc., Peter G. Wodtke Inc.; spl. cons. to asst. sec. Air Force for Material, 1955-59; Mem. corp. Econ. Devel. Corp. Greater Detroit, 1968-73, Mich. Blue Shield, 1969-74; mem. corp. devel. com. Mass. Inst. Tech., 1970—; mem. Am. Iranian Joint Bus. Council, 1975-76; trustee Lawrence Inst. Tech., 1979—; pres. SME Edn. Found., 1979—. Recipient Engring. citation Am. Soc. Tool Engrs., 1956; Corp. Leadership award Mass. Inst. Tech., 1976. Mem. Nat. Acad. Engring., Nat. Machine Tool Builders Assn. (pres. 1975), Soc. Automotive Engrs., Soc. Mfg. Engrs. (hon.), Engring. Soc. Detroit. Clubs: Detroit Athletic, Lochmoor; Quail Ridge Country. Current Work: Machine tools. Subspecialty: Mechanical engineering. Home: 22 Windemere Dr Grosse Pointe Farms MI 48236 Home: 4120 Shelldrake Ln Boynton Beach FL 33436 Office: 505 N Woodward Ave Bloomfield Hills MI 48013

CROSSAN, DONALD FRANKLIN, research station administrator, plant pathology educator; b. Wilmington, Del., Apr. 8, 1926; s. Samuel Davis and Anna Bertha (Spinken) C.; m. Ruth Swanson; children—Connie, Donna, Eric. B.S. with distinction, U. Del., Newark, 1950; M.S., N.C. State U., 1952; Ph.D., 1954. Asst. prof. U. Del., Newark, 1954-60, assoc. prof., 1960-65, prof., 1965—, dir. Del. Agrl. Exptl. Sta., 1977—, dean Coll. Agr. Sci., 1977—. Chmn. State of Del. Coastal Zone Indsl. Control Bd., Dover, 1971—; trustee Longwood Gardens, Kenneth Square, Pa., 1973—; chmn. State Del. Farmland Assessment Adv. Council, Dover, 1978—. Served with USAF, 1944-46. Recipient Lindback award for excellence in teaching U. Del., 1969. Mem. Am. Phytopath. Soc. Current work: Control of plant diseases. Subspecialty: Plant pathology. Office: Univ Del 132 Townsend Hall Newark DE 19717

CROSSLEY, IAN, physicist; b. Huddersfield, Yorkshire, Eng., Mar. 21, 1947; came to U.S., 1977, naturalized, 1984; s. Harold and Joan (Ramsden) C.; m. Rita B. Haigh, Mar. 23, 1968. B.Sc. in Applied Physics, Brighton Poly., 1969, Ph.D., 1972. Sr. prin. scientist Plessey Co., Towcester, Eng., 1972-77; engring. mgr. Alpha Industries, Inc., Woburn, Mass., 1977-83, asst. div. mgr., 1983—. Contbr. articles to profl. jours. Mem. IEEE. Current work: Monolithic microwave integrated circuits of gallium arsenide. Subspecialties: Semiconductors; Microelectronics. Office: Alpha Industries Inc 20 Sylvan Rd Woburn MA 01801

CROWE, DENNIS TIMOTHY, JR., veterinary surgeon, researcher; b. Milw., Nov. 21, 1946; s. Dennis Timothy and Anna Mae (Persen) C.; m. Deborah Gene Coulson, Jan. 2, 1971; children: Michael, Kristin. D.V.M., Iowa State U., 1972. Diplomate: Am. Coll. Veterinary Surgeons. Intern Colo. State U., 1972-73; resident in surgery Ohio State U., 1973-76; chief surgery Westcott Hosp. and Animal Emergency Room, Detroit, 1976-78; asst. prof. surgery Kans. State U., Manhattan, 1978-80, U. Ga., Athens, 1980—; dir. Shock Trauma team U. Ga. (Veterinary Teaching Hosp.), 1981—, co-dir. intensive care unit, 1981—, asst. chief gen. surgery, 1982—; clin. cons. emergency med. services Athens Gen. Hosp.; chmn. quality assurance com. Emergency Med. Services Council, Ga. Dept. Health and Human Services; lectr. in field. Contbr. numerous articles to profl. jours. Veterinary Med. Experiments Sta. grantee, 1981-83; recipient G.G. Graham award in clin. veterinary medicine Iowa State U., 1972. Mem. AVMA, Am. Coll. Veterinary Surgeons, Am. Animal Hosp. Assn., Veterinary Emergency and Critical Care Soc. (pres.). Methodist. Current Work: Research in shock (hemorrhagic, septic) abdominal counterpressure, cardiopulmonary rescuscitation; primarily involved in the teaching and training of students, residents, and interns in the field of small animal general surgery and emergency and critical care and in related research. Subspecialties: Surgery (veterinary medicine); Critical care. Home: 630 Sandstone Dr Athens GA 30605 Office: U Ga H316 Veterinary Teaching Hospital Department of Small Animal Medicine and Surgery College of Veterinary Medicine Athens GA 30602

CROWE, DEVON GEORGE, physicist, researcher; b. Portland, Oreg., Mar. 11, 1948; s. Frank I. and Jeannie (Scott) C.; m. Bonnie Jean McPherson, June 7, 1974 (div. Aug. 1984). B.S., U. Ariz., 1971, M.B.A., 1977, M.S., 1980. Sr. research asst. Kitt Peak Nat. Obs., Tucson, 1975-76; chief systems devel. and ops. Bell Tech. Ops., Textron, Tucson, 1977-80; sr. scientist, mgr. advanced concepts br. Sci. Applications Internat. Corp., Tucson, 1980—. Author: Optical Radiation Detectors, 1984. Contbr. articles to profl. jours. Served to 1st lt. USAF, 1971-74. Mem. IEEE (sr.), Am. Astron. Soc., Optical Soc. Am., Soc. Photo-optical Instrumentation Engrs. Current work: Research and development of optical, infrared, and synthetic aperture radar systems including the associated image processing functions. Subspecialties: Optical engineering; Graphics, image processing, and pattern recognition. Home: PO Box 11755 Tucson AZ 85734 Office: Sci Applications Internat Corp 5151 E Broadway Suite 1100 Tucson AZ 85711

CROWL, DANIEL A., chemical engineer. Mem. dept. chem. and metall. engring. Wayne State U., Detroit. Subspecialty: Oil shale technology. Office: Wayne State U Dept Chem and Metall Engring Detroit MI 48202

CROWLE, ALFRED JOHN, immunologist; b. Mexico City, Apr. 15, 1930; s. Alfred C. and Hazel Araminta (Mason) C.; m. Clarice Marjorie Futrelle, Oct. 22, 1954; children: Nelson Frederick, Cynthia Nanette. A.B., San Jose State Coll., 1951; Ph.D., Stanford U., 1954. Instr., U. Colo. Sch. Medicine, Denver, 1956-59, asst. prof., 1959-65, asso. prof., 1965-75, prof., 1974—; research microbiologist Webb-Waring Lung Inst., Denver, 1956-59, head div. immunology, 1965—; cons. U.S. Army, NSF, others. Author: Immunodiffusion, 2d edit., 1973, Delayed Hypersensitivity in Health and Disease, 1962; also articles. Active Boy Scouts Am., 1966-7l. Nat. Tb Assn. fellow, 1953-55; Nat. Acad. Scis.-NSF postdoctoral fellow, 1955; James Alexander Miller fellow N.Y. Tb and Health Assn., 1960-61; grantee NIH; grantee NSF; grantee others. Mem. Reticuloendothelial Soc., Am. Assn. Immunologists, AAAS, AAUP, Am. Soc. Microbiology, Soc. Exptl. Biology and Medicine. Clubs: Cherry Creek Gun (pres. 1967-70), Colorado Mountain (head rock climbing sch. Denver group 1977-82, dir.). Current Work: Immunodiffusion and crossed immunoelectrophoresis; applications in clinical medicine; bacteria, macrophages, lymphokines, lymphocytes: tests and mechanisms of cellular immunities to infectious diseases; tuberculosis and immunization: mechanisms and control of tuberculoimmunity in man and animals. Subspecialties: Immunology (medicine); Infectious diseases. Office: B-122 E 9th Ave Denver CO 80262

CROWLEY, MICHAEL SUMMERS, ceramic engineer, consultant; b. Chgo., Dec. 24, 1928; s. John Laurance and Roslyn (Summers) C.; m. Elaine A. Reynolds, June 17, 1950; children—Veronica Elaine, Michael Reynolds. B.S. in Ceramic Engring., Iowa State U., 1953; Ph.D. in Geochemistry, Pa. State U., 1959. Registered profl. engr., Ill., Tex., Calif. Research assoc. Standard Oil Co. (Ind.), Naperville, Ill., 1953—; mem. chem. task force refractories Metals Property Council, Chgo., 1972-77. Contbr. articles to tech. jours.; patentee in field. Fellow Am. Ceramic Soc.; mem. Nat. Inst. Ceramic Engrs., ASTM, Nat. Soc. Profl. Engrs. Current work: Materials research in refractories, insulation, fireproofing for refining and petrochemical plants; engineering design, inspection and repairs of refractory linings; teaching materials technology. Subspecialties: Ceramic engineering; High-temperature materials. Home: 114 Mildred Ln Chicago Heights IL 60411 Office: Standard Oil Co (Ind) PO Box 400 Naperville IL 60566

CROWN, BARRY MICHAEL, psychologist, educator; b. Waukegan, Ill., June 23, 1943; s. Frank Edward and Sara (Babel) C.; m. Sheryl Joyce Lowenthal, Oct. 31, 1982. B.A., U. Miami, 1965; M.Ed., Fla. Atlantic U., 1966; Ph.D., Fla. State U., 1969. Research coordinator Fla. Gov.'s Office, Tallahassee, 1967-69; fellow in psychiatry Mass. Gen. Hosp., Boston, 1969-70; asst. prof. psychology U. Ill. Med. Sch., Chgo., 1970-71; asst. prof. psychiatry U. Miami Med. Sch., 1971-73; assoc. prof. psychology Fla. Internat. U., Miami, 1973-78, courtesy prof., 1978—; assoc. dir. Nat. Council Drug Abuse, Chgo., 1972—; clin. dir. NIMH Nat. Drug Abuse Tng. Ctr., Miami, 1972-74. Recipient award for disting. contrbns. Am. Ontoanalytic Assn., 1976; Sci. Achievement award Nat. Council Drug Abuse, 1975; NIMH fellow, 1969. Fellow Royal Soc. Health; mem. Am. Psychol. Assn., Soc. Behavioral Medicine, Am. Psychology and Law Soc., Southeastern Psychol. Assn. Democrat. Jewish. Club: Tiger Bay. Current Work: Developing diagnostic instruments in neuropsychology; applying behavioral concepts in psychosomatic medicine. Subspecialties: Neuropsychology; Behavioral psychology. Office: 7800 Red Rd Suite 310 South Miami FL 33143

CRUESS, RICHARD LEIGH, surgeon, university dean; b. London, Ont., Can., Dec. 17, 1929; s. Leigh S. and Martha A. (Peever) C.; m. Sylvia Crane Robinson, May 30, 1953; children: Leigh S., Andrew C. B.A., Princeton U., 1951; M.D., Columbia U., 1955. Diplomate: Am. Bd. Orthopedic Surgery. Intern Royal Victoria Hosp., Montreal, Que., 1955-56, resident surgery, 1956-57, N.Y. Orthopedic Hosp., 1959-60, asst. resident orthopedic surgery, 1960-61, resident orthopedic surgery, 1961-62, Annie C. Kane fellow orthopedic surgery, 1961-62; research asso. depts. orthopedic surgery and biochemistry Columbia U., N.Y.C., 1962-63, John Armour Travelling fellow, 1962-63, Am.-Brit.-Can. Travelling fellow, 1967, practice medicine specializing in orthopedic surgery, Montreal, 1963—; orthopedic surgeon Royal Victoria Hosp., orthopedic surgeon-in-charge, 1968-81, asst. surgeon-in-chief, 1970-81; chief surgeon Shriner's Hosp. for Crippled Children, Montreal, 1970-82; prof. surgery McGill U., Montreal, 1970—, chmn. div. orthopedic surgery, 1976-81, dean faculty medicine, 1981—; hon. cons. orthopedic surgery Queen Elizabeth Hosp., 1972—; mem. clin. grants com. Med. Research Council, 1972-75. Contbr. articles on surgery to profl. jours.; editorial bd.: Jour. Internat. Orthopedics, 1976—, Jour. Bone and Joint Surgery, 1977—, Current Problems in Orthopedics, 1977—. Served to lt. M.C., USN, 1957-59. Fellow Royal Soc. Can., Royal Coll. Physicians and Surgeons Can. (chief examiner orthopedic surgery 1970-72), ACS, Am. Acad. Orthopedic Surgeons; mem. Can. Orthopedic Assn. (sec. 1971-76, pres. 1977-78), Can. Orthopedic Research Soc. (pres. 1971-72), Am. Orthopedic Research Soc. (pres. 1975-76), Am. Orthopedic Assn., Assn. Orthopedic Surgeons Province Que. (treas. 1971-72), Société Française de Chirurgie Orthopedique, McGill Osler Reporting Soc. Subspecialty: Orthopedics. Home: 526 Mount Pleasant Ave Montreal PQ H3Y 3H5 Canada Office: 3655 Drummond St Montreal PQ H3G 1Y6 Canada

CRUZ, JOSE BEJAR, engineering educator; b. Bacolod City, Philippines, Sept. 17, 1932; came to U.S., 1954, naturalized, 1969; s. Jose P. and Felicidad (Bejar) C.; m. Patria Cunanan, June 23, 1953; children: Fe E., Ricardo A., Rene L., Sylvia C., Loretta C. B.S. in Elec. Engring. summa cum laude, U. Philippines, 1953; M.S., MIT, 1956; Ph.D., U. Ill., 1959. Registered profl. engr., Ill. Instr. elec. engring. U. Philippines, Quezon City, 1953-54; research asst. MIT, 1954-56, vis. prof., 1973; instr. U. Ill., Urbana-Champaign, 1956-59, asst. prof., 1959-61, assoc. prof., 1961-65, prof. elec. engring., 1965—, research prof. Coordinated Sci. Lab., 1965—; assoc. mem. Center Advanced Study, 1967-68; vis. assoc. prof. U. Calif.-Berkeley, 1964-65; vis. prof. Harvard U., 1973; pres. Dynamic Systems; mem. theory com. Am. Automatic Control Council, 1967; gen. chmn. Conf. on Decision and Control, 1975; mem. Ill. Profl. Engring. Exam. Com., 1984—. Author: (with M.E. Van Valkenburg) Introductory Signals and Circuits, 1967, (with W.R. Perkins) Engineering of Dynamic Systems, 1969, Feedback Systems, 1972, System Sensitivity Analysis, 1973, (with M.E. Van Valkenburg) Signals in Linear Circuits, 1974. Assoc. editor Jour. Franklin Inst, 1976-82, Jour. Optimization Theory and Applications, 1981-85; series editor: Advances in Large Scale Systems Theory and Applications. Contbr. articles fields network theory, automatic control systems, system theory, sensitivity theory of dynamical systems, large scale systems and dynamic games to sci., tech. jours. Recipient Purple Tower award Beta Epsilon U., Philippines, 1969, Curtis W. McGraw Research award Am. Soc. for Engring. Edn., 1972, Halliburton Engring. Edn. Leadership award, 1981. Fellow IEEE (chmn. linear systems com., group on automatic control 1966-68, assoc. editor Trans. on Circuit Theory 1962-64); mem. Control Systems Soc. (adminstrv. com. 1966-75, 78-80, pres. 1979, chmn. awards com. 1973-75, ednl. activities bd. 1973-75, editor Trans. on Automatic Control 1971-73, mem. tech. activities bd. 1979-81, chmn., v.p. tech. activities 1981-83, edn. med. com. 1977-79, v.p. publs. activities 1984-85, chmn. TAB periodicals com. 1981, chmn. PUB Soc. publs. com. 1981), Philippine Engrs. and Scientists Orgn. (pres. 1982), Soc. Indsl. and Applied Math., AAUP, AAAS, Nat. Soc. Profl. Engrs. U.S. Nat. Acad. Engring., Philippine-Am. Acad. Sci. and Engring. (founding), Internat. Fedn. Automatic Control (theory com. 1981-84, vice chmn. tech. bd. 1984-87), Sigma Xi, Phi Kappa Phi, Eta Kappa Nu. Current Work: Control systems, sensitivity analysis, decentralized and theoretical decision-making. Subspecialties: Systems engineering; Electrical engineering. Home: 2014 Silver Ct W Urbana IL 61801 Office: Coordinated Sci Lab U Ill Urbana IL 61801

CSERMELY, THOMAS JOHN, electrical and computer engineer; b. Szombathely, Hungary, June 25, 1931; came to U.S., 1957; s. Janos and Maria (Szarvas) C.; m. Tiiu Vaharu, June 17, 1961; 1 child, Erik Thomas. Diploma Ing., Polytech. U., Budapest, Hungary, 1953; Ph.D., Syracuse U., 1968. Instr. Inst. for Thearetical physics, Polytech U., Budapest, 1953-56; research engr. Carrier Corp., Syracuse, N.Y., 1957-67; research assoc. physics dept. Syracuse U., 1967-68; asst. prof. physiology dept. SUNY Upstate Med. Ctr., Syracuse, 1968-76; asst. prof. dept. physics LeMoyne Coll., Syracuse, 1976-77; assoc. prof. dept. elec. computer engring. Syracuse U., 1977—; cons. Design Bur. for Power Stations, Budapest, 1956. Contbr. articles to tech. jours. Bd. dirs. Assn. for Retarded Citizens, Syracuse, 1984—. Recipient Wolverine - ASHRAE Diamond Key award, 1965. Mem. IEEE, Biophys. Soc., Am. Phys. Soc., AAAS, N.Y. Acad. Scis. Roman Catholic. Club: Technology. Computer simulation of the dynamic behavior of physiological systems; computer applications in medicine. Subspecialties: Computer engineering; Biomedical engineering. Home: 149 Humbert Ave Syracuse NY 13224 Office: Elec and Computer Engring Dept Syracuse U Syracuse NY 13210

CSERR, HELEN FITZGERALD, physiologist, educator; b. Boston, June 23, 1937; d. Joseph Harold and Ruth Knowles (Milliken) FitzGerald; m. Robert Cserr, May 28, 1962; 1 child, Ruth. B.A., Middlebury Coll., 1959; Ph.D., Harvard U., 1965. Fellow in physiology Harvard U., 1965-67, instr. physiology, 1967-70; lectr. in med. sci. Brown U., Providence (R.I.), 1970-71, asst. prof. med. sci., 1971-76, assoc. prof. med. sci., 1976-82, prof. med. sci., 1982—; mem. study group Physiology Study sect. NIH, 1975-79; trustee Mount Desert Island Biol. Lab., Salsbury Cove, Maine, 1971-73, 83—. Author: Fluid Environment of the Brain, 1975; contbr. articles to profl. jours., chpts. to books. United Cerebral Palsy Research and Ednl. Found. Postdoctoral fellow in brain research, 1964-67; recipient NIH Research Career Devel. award, 1973-78. Mem. Am. Physiol. Soc., Soc. Gen. Physiologists, Royal Soc. Medicine. Current work: Physiology of brain extracellular fluids; teaching. Subspecialty: Physiology (medicine). Home: Green Acres North Dighton MA 02764 Office: Dept Physiology & Biophysics Brown U Providence RI 02912

CSINOS, ALEXANDER STEPHEN, plant pathology educator; b. Tillsonburg, Ont., Can., Jan. 28, 1948; s. Alexander Joseph and Elizabeth (Ribar) C.; m. Lucia Veronica Csinos, June 23, 1973; 1 dau., Alexa Nicole. B.S. in Agr, U. Guelph, 1972; Ph.D., U. Ky., 1977. Vis. asst. prof. Coastal Plain Expt. Sta., U. Ga.-Tifton, 1977-78, asst. prof., 1978-81, assoc. prof., 1981—. Contbr. articles to profl. jours. Mem. Ga. Assn. Plant Pathologists, Am. Phytopathol. Soc., Am. Peanut Research and Edn. Assn., Ga. Vegetable Growers Assn., Tobacco Disease Council, Gamma Sigma Delta. Current Work: Investigative research on control of soil-borne diseases of tobacco and peanuts. Subspecialty: Plant pathology. Office: Dept Plant Pathology Coastal Plain Experiment Station PO Box 748 Tifton GA 31793

CUADRA, CARLOS ALBERT, information scientist, management consultant; b. San Francisco, Dec. 21, 1925; s. Gregorio and Amanda (Mendoza) C.; m. Gloria Nathalie Adams, May 3, 1947; children: Mary Susan Cuadra Nielsen, Neil Gregory, Dean Arthur. A.B. with highest honors in Psychology, U. Calif., Berkeley, 1949, Ph.D. in Psychology, 1953. Staff psychologist VA, Downey, Ill., 1953-56; with System Devel. Corp., Santa Monica, Calif., 1957-78, mgr. library and documentation systems dept., 1968-70, mgr. edn. and library systems dept., 1971-74; gen. mgr. SDC Search Service, 1974-78; founder Cuadra Assos., Santa Monica, 1978—. Contbr. articles to profl. jours.; Editor: Ann. Rev. of Info. Sci. and Tech, 1964-75. Mem. Nat. Commn. Libraries and

Info. Sci., 1971-84. Served with USN, 1944-46. Recipient Merit award Am. Soc. Info. Sci., 1968, Best Info. Sci. Book award, 1969; named Disting. Lectr. of Year, 1970; received Miles Conrad award Nat. Fedn. Abstracting and Indexing Services, 1980. Mem. Info. Industry Assn. (bd. dirs., Hall of Fame award 1980). Home: 13213 Warren Ave Los Angeles CA 90066 Office: 2001 Wilshire Blvd Suite 305 Santa Monica CA 90403

CUATRECASAS, PEDRO MARTIN, research pharmacologist; b. Madrid, Sept. 27, 1936; came to U.S., 1947, naturalized, 1955; s. Jose and Martha C.; m. Carol Zies, Aug. 15, 1959; children: Paul, Lisa, Diane, Julia. A.B., Washington U., St. Louis, 1958, M.D., 1962; D.Sc. (hon.), U. Barcelona, 1984, Mt. Sinai Sch. Medicine, CUNY, 1985. Intern, then resident in internal medicine Osler Service, Johns Hopkins Hosp., 1962-64, asst. physician, 1972-75; clin. asso., clin. endocrinology br. Nat. Inst. Arthritis and Metabolic Diseases, NIH, 1964-66; spl. USPHS postdoctoral fellow Lab. Chem. Biology, 1966-67, med. officer, 1967-70; professorial lectr. biochemistry George Washington U. Med. Sch., 1967-70; asso. prof. pharmacology and exptl. therapeutics, asso. prof. medicine, dir. div. clin. pharmacology, Burroughs Wellcome prof. clin. pharmacology Johns Hopkins U. Med. Sch., 1970-72, prof. pharmacology and exptl. therapeutics, asso. prof. medicine, 1972-75; v.p. research, devel. and med. Wellcome Research Labs.; dir. Burroughs Wellcome Co., Research Triangle Park, N.C., 1975—; adj. prof. Duke U. Med. Sch., 1975—; adj. prof., mem. adv. com. cancer research program U. N.C. Med. Sch., 1975—; bd. dirs. Burroughs Wellcome Fund. Editor: Receptors and Recognition Series, 1975, Jour. Solid-Phase Biochemistry, 1975-80; editorial bd.: Jour. Membrane Biology, 1973, Internat. Jour. Biochemistry, 1973, Molecular and Cellular Endocrinology, 1973-77, Biochimica Biophysica Acta, 1973-79, Life Scis., 1978—, Neuropeptides, 1979—, Jour. Applied Biochemistry, 1978—, Cancer Research, 1980-81, Jour. Applied Biochemistry and Biotech., 1980—, Toxin Revs., 1981—, Biochem. Biophys. Research Communications, 1981—; contbr. articles to profl. jours. Recipient John Jacob Abel prize in pharmacology, 1972, Laude prize Pharm. World, 1975, Beerman award, 1981, Isco award, 1985. Mem. Am. Soc. Biol. Chemists, Nat. Acad. Scis., Inst. Medicine of Nat. Acad. Scis., Am. Soc. Pharmacology and Exptl. Therapeutics (Goodman and Gilman award 1982), Am. Soc. Clin. Investigation, Am. Soc. Clin. Research, Spanish Biochem. Soc., Md. Acad. Scis. (Outstanding Young Scientist of Year 1970), Am. Cancer Soc., Endocrine Soc., Am. Chem. Soc., Am. Diabetes Assn. (Eli Lilly award 1975), Sigma Xi. Subspecialties: Cell biology (medicine); Molecular pharmacology. Home: 626 Kensington Dr Chapel Hill NC 27514 Office: 3030 Cornwallis Rd Research Triangle Park NC 27709

CUDABACK, DAVID DILL, astronomer, lecturer, consultant; b. Napa, Calif., Jan. 18, 1929; s. Walter Harold and Luella Matilda (Dill) C.; m. Dorothea Jean, Aug. 16, 1953; 1 dau.: Cynthia Nova. B.A. in Physics, U. Calif., Berkeley, 1951, Ph.D. in Astronomy, 1962. Physicist Lawrence Berkeley Lab., 1950-53, 54-58; Los Alamos Sci. Lab., 1953-54; research assoc. Stanford Electronics Lab., 1958-62; research astronomer U. Calif., Berkeley, 1962—; assoc. dir. White Mountain Research Sta., 1972-80. Contbr. articles to profl. pubs., (with Richard o'Hanlon) astron. sculptures; installed, San Raphael, Palo Alto, Berkeley, Calif. Mem. Am. Astron. Soc., Astron. Soc. of the Pacific, Internat. Astron. Union, Internat. Sci. Radio Union, AAAS. Current Work: Studies of interstellar dust and star formation with radio and infrared techniques, development novel instruments for these studies, development high altitude observatories. Subspecialties: Infrared astronomy; Radio and microwave astronomy. Home: 6639 Longwalk Dr Oakland CA 94611 Office: Astronomy Dept Univ Calif Berkeley CA 94720

CUDKOWICZ, LEON, physician, medical educator, physiology educator; b. Lodz, Poland, Jan. 18, 1923; came to U.S., 1969, naturalized, 1978; s. Maurice and Masza (Malinska) C.; divorced (div.); children: Alexander, Penelope. M.B.B.S., U. London, 1946, M.D., 1951. Intern King's Coll. Hosp., U. London; resident St. Thomas Hosp., U.London; assoc. prof. medicine and physiology Dalhousie U., Halifax, N.S., 1960-69; prof. medicine Jefferson Med. Coll., 1969-72; prof. medicine, physiology Hahnemann Med. Coll., 1973-75; prof. dept. medicine, chmn. Wright State U., 1975-77; prof. dept. medicine, chmn. dept. King Faisal U., Dammam, Saudi Arabia, 1978-81; prof. medicine U. Cin. Med. Center, 1981—. Author: Human Bronchial Circulation in Health and Disease, 1968; Contbr. numerous articles to profl. jours., chpts. to books. Served to capt. Royal Army Med. Corps, 1948-49. Canadian Soc. Clin. Investigation Schering awardee, 1973; sr. internat. fellow Fogarty Ctr. NIH, 1974; Orgn. Am. States Fellowship awardee, 1982. Fellow Am. Coll. Cardiology, Am. Coll. Physicians, Royal Coll. Physicians, Royal Soc. Medicine. Current Work: High altitude physiology. Subspecialties: Cardiology; Pulmonary medicine. Office: U Cin Bethesda Ave Cincinnati OH 45267

CUDWORTH, KYLE MCCABE, astronomer, educator; b. Mpls., June 7, 1947; s. Kyle Gilmore and Jane McCabe (Irvine) C. B. Physics, U. Minn., 1969; Ph.D., U. Calif., Santa Cruz, 1974. Asst. prof. U. Chgo. (Yerkes Obs.), Williams Bay, Wis., 1974-81, asso. prof., 1981—. Contbr. articles to profl. jours. Alfred P. Sloan Found. fellow, 1980. Mem. Am. Astron. Soc., Astron. Soc. Pacific, Internat. Astron. Union, Am. Sci. Affiliation. Mem. Calvary Community Ch. Club: Quadrangle (Chgo.). Current Work: Stellar motions, distances, and photometry; star clusters; planetary nebulae. Subspecialty: Optical astronomy. Office: Yerkes Obs Box 258 Williams Bay WI 53191

CUGINI, EDWARD THOMAS, mech. engr.; b. Pitts., Aug. 28, 1930; s. Addison Gregory and Antonette Pearl (Misivich) C.; m. Martha Jean Peacher, Nov. 5, 1953; children: Gregory, Thomas, Joel, Matthew. B.S., Calif. U.-Long Beach, 1963. Project engr. Shaffer Tool Works, Brea, Calif., 1965-67, chief engr., 1967-69; engr. Grant Oil Tool, Los Angeles, 1969-75; chief engr. Shafco Industries Inc., Anaheim, Calif., 1975—. Served with USN, 1951-55, Korea. Mem. ASME, Am. Soc. Metals. Lutheran. Patentee in field. Current Work: Design pressure vessels used during drilling and production of oil, gas and steam wells. Subspecialty: Mechanical engineering. Home: 429 Catalpa Ave Brea CA 92621 Office: 2850 E Coronado St Anaheim CA 92806

CUKOR, GEORGE, medical microbiologist, researcher, educator; b. Szolnok, Hungary, Mar. 16, 1946; came to U.S., 1957, naturalized, 1962; s. Andor and Lili (Vamos) C.; m. Adrienne G., Aug. 2, 1969; children: Michael, Daniel. B.A. (N.Y. State Regents scholar), Bklyn. Coll., 1968; Ph.D. (USPHS tng. grantee), Rutgers U., 1973. Postdoctoral fellow Boston U. Sch. Medicine, 1973-76; instr. U. Mass. Med. Sch., 1976-77, asst. prof., 1977-80, assoc. prof. medicine and molecular genetics and microbiology, 1980-84; research supr. E.I. DuPont de Nemours & Co., 1984—; dir. Hosp. Diagnostic Virology Lab., U. Mass. Med. Center, 1978-83. Contbr. numerous articles, abstracts to profl. publs.; editorial bd.: Jour. Clin. Microbiology, 1982—. Nat. Cancer Inst. postdoctoral research fellow, 1974-76. Mem. Am. Soc. Microbiology, Am. Assn. Immunologists, AAAS, N.Y. Acad. Scis., Am. Soc. Virology. Current Work: Immunology, pathogenesis and rapid diagnosis of infectious disease; research on gastroenteritis viruses, sexually transmitted diseases, immunoassays, monoclonal antibodies, bacterial toxins. Subspecialties: Infectious diseases; Virology (medicine). Home: 7 Kensington Heights Worcester MA 01602 Office: DuPont de Nemours & Co 331 Treble Cove Rd North Billerica MA 01862

CULLARI, SALVATORE SANTINO, psychologist, researcher; b. Caroniti, Catanzaro, Italy, Apr. 1, 1952; came to U.S., 1955, naturalized, 1968; s. Carmelo and Carmela (Cullari) C.; m. Kathryn A. Plesce, Apr. 27, 1985. Lic. psychologist, W.Va. B.A., Kean Coll., 1974; M.A. with honors, Western Mich. U., 1976, Ph.D., 1981. Lic. psychologist (ltd.), Mich. lic. psychologist, Pa. Assoc. dir. Kalamazoo Learning Village, 1976-77; cons. Lansing (Mich.) Dept. Mental Health, 1978-79; staff psychologist Coldwater (Mich.) Regional Center, 1979-80; research psychologist Anova Research Assn., Kalamazoo, 1980-82; psychol. services coordinator White Haven (Pa.) Center, 1982-83; clin. psychologist Danville State Hosp., 1983-85; coordinator psychol. services Harrisburg State Hosp., 1985—. Co-author booklet on bulimia, 1982; Effective Consultation. Contbr. articles to profl. jours. Mich. Dept. Mental Health grantee, 1981. Mem. Am. Psychol. Assn., Am. Assn. Mental Deficiency, Assn. Advancement Behavior Therapy, Assn. Behavior Analysis, Mich. Mental Health Assn., Kalamazoo Inst. Arts, AAAS. Current Work: Eating disorders (bulimarexia); radical behaviorism; eastern religions; psychopharmacology; artificial intelligence; communal living, primary prevention; quantum theory and psychology. Subspecialties: Behavioral psychology; Clinical psychology. Home: PO Box 595 Hershey PA 17033 Office: Harrisburg State Hosp Harrisburg PA 17105

CULLEN, DONALD LEE, rapidly solidified metals co. exec., physicist; b. Shortcreek Twp., Ohio, Dec. 28, 1940; s. James and Grace Virginia (Huffman) C.; m. Hedy Louise, June 24, 1943; children: Michelle Lynn, Christine Kelley. B.S.E.P., Ohio State U., 1970, M.B.A., 1980. Project engr. instrument div. Reliance Electric Co., Columbus, Ohio, 1963-69; engring. mgr. Autech Corp., Columbus, 1969-74, exec. v.p., 1974-76, pres., 1976-81, Transmet Corp., Columbus, 1981—; cons. electro-optics, lasers; dir. Harrison Enterprises, Morrison Electronics, Digitronics; speaker. Contbr. articles on application of low powered lasers to profl. jours. Mem. Brookside Civic Assn. Served with USN, 1959-63. Mem. Instrument Soc. Am., Optical Soc. Am., IEEE, Am. Phys. Soc., Soc. Mfg. Engrs. Republican. Patentee in field. Current Work: Electro-optics and rapidly quenched metals; devel. of product and markets of rapidly solidified metals. Subspecialties: Materials processing; Systems engineering. Office: 4290 Perimeter Dr Columbus OH 43228

CULLER, FLOYD LEROY, JR., chemical engineer; b. Washington, Jan. 5, 1923; s. Floyd LeRoy Culler; m. Della Hopper, 1946; 1 son, Floyd LeRoy III. B. Chem. Engring. cum laude, Johns Hopkins, 1943. With Eastman Kodak and Tenn. Eastman at Y-12, Oak Ridge, 1943-47; design engr. Oak Ridge Nat. Lab., 1947-53, dir. chem. tech. div., 1953-64, asst. lab. dir., 1965-70, dep. dir., 1970-77; pres. Electric Power Research Inst., Palo Alto, Calif., 1978—; research design chem. engring. applied to atomic energy program, chem. processing nuclear reactor plants, energy research. Mem. sci. adv. com. Internat. Atomic Energy Agy., 1974—; mem. energy research adv. com. Dept. Energy, 1981—. Recipient Ernest Orlando Lawrence award, 1964; Atoms for Peace award, 1969; Robert E. Wilson award in nuclear chem. engring., 1972; Engring. Achievement award E. Tenn. Engrs. Joint Council, 1974. Fellow Am. Nuclear Soc. (dir. 1973-80, spl. award 1977), Am. Inst. Chemists, AAAS, Inst. Chem. Engrs.; mem. Am. Chem. Soc., Nat. Acad. Engring. Subspecialty: Nuclear fission. Home: 1385 Corinne Ln Menlo Park CA 94025 Office: 3412 Hillview Ave Palo Alto CA 94303

CULLINGFORD, HATICE S(ADAN), chemical engineer, consultant; b. Konya, Turkey, June 10, 1945; d. Ahmet and Emine (Kadayifcioglu) Harmanci. B.S. with high honors, N.C. State U., 1969, engring. cert., 1969, Ph.D., 1974. Registered profl. engr., Tex. Reactor engr. AEC, Washington, 1973-75, spl. asst., 1975; mech. engr. Dept. Energy, Washington, 1975-78; mem. staff Los Alamos Nat. Lab., 1978-82; mem. Fusion Power Assocs., Gaithersburg, Md., 1981—; organizing mem. 3d, 4th, 5th, 6th Alt. Energy Sources Confs., Miami, Fla., 1979-83; sci. cons., Houston, 1982-84. Contbr. articles to profl. jours. Mem. Tex. Round Table on Hazardous Waste, Houston, 1982—; Vol. income tax asst. ARC and IRS, 1983. Recipient Spl. Achievement award ERDA, 1976, Inventor award Los Alamos Nat. Lab., 1982, Women's badge Tau Beta Pi, 1968; Cities Service fellow, 1969-72. Mem. Am. Nuclear Soc. (sec.-treas. fusion energy div. 1982-84, vice chmn. South Tex. sect. 1984-85), Am. Inst. Chem. Engrs. (chmn. low pressure processes and tech. 1981—, rep. to Engrs.' Council Houston 1983—), Am. Chem. Soc., Am. Vacuum Soc., Internat. Assn. Hydrogen Energy (hon.), Phi Kappa Phi, Pi Mu Epsilon. Clubs: No. N. Mex. Chem. Engrs. (chmn./organizer 1980-82), Sierra Co-inventor method and apparatus for storing hydrogen isotopes. Current work: Environmental control and life support engineering; fluid flow. Subspecialties: Nuclear fission; Nuclear fusion. Home: 404 Oak Harbor Dr Houston TX 77062

CULP, LLOYD ANTHONY, cell biologist, educator, researcher; b. Elkhart, Ind., Dec. 23, 1942; s. Robert Eugene and Genevieve (Murdock) C.; m. Margaret Mary, July 17, 1965; children: Robert Joseph, Catherine Anne. B.S. in Chemistry, Case Inst. Tech., 1964; Ph.D. in Biochemistry, MIT, 1969. Postdoctoral trainee in virology Harvard U. Med. Sch., Boston, 1969-71; asst. prof. microbiology Case Western Res. U. Sch. Medicine, 1972-77, assoc. prof., 1977-83, prof. molecular biology, 1983—; cons., lectr. in field. Contbr. numerous articles to profl. jours., texts, 1969—. Recipient Career Devel. award Nat. Cancer Inst., 1974-79; Pinney scholar, 1973-75; NIH grantee, 1972—; Am. Cancer Soc. grantee, 1974-80. Mem. AAAS, Am. Soc. Cell Biology, N.Y. Acad. Scis., Soc. Complex Carbohydrates, Sigma Xi. Current Work: Adhesion of normal or malignant fibroblasts or neuronal cells to extracellular matrices. Subspecialties: Cell and tissue culture; Cell study oncology. Office: Dept Microbiology Case Western Res U Sch Medicine Cleveland OH 44106

CULVER, CHARLES GEORGE, civil engineer, government official; b. Bethlehem, Pa., Dec. 4, 1937; s. Charles-Herman and RuthRose (Showers) C.; m. R. Bernice Johnston, Apr. 3, 1964; 1 child, Bruce. B.S. in Civil Engring., Lehigh U., 1959, M.S. in Civil Engring., 1961, Ph.D., 1965. Research engr. U.S. Navy Marine Lab., Annapolis, Md., 1963-65; assoc. prof. Carnegie-Mellon U., Pitts., 1966-72; chief structures div. Nat. Bur. Standards, Gaithersburg, Md., 1972—; cons., Pitts., 1966-72. Contbr. articles to tech. jours. Recipient silver medal Dept. Commerce, 1976. Mem. ASCE (research prize 1973), Am. Arbitration Assn. Current work: Manage engineering research program related to building technology. Subspecialties: Structural engineering; Civil engineering. Office: Nat Bur Standards Bldg 226 Room B268 Gaithersburg MD 20899

CUMMIN, ALFRED S(AMUEL), chemist; b. London, Sept. 5, 1924; U.S., 1940, naturalized, 1948; s. Jack and Lottie (Hainesdorff) C.; m. Sylvia E. Smolok, Mar. 24, 1945; 1 dau., Cynthia Katherine. B.S., Poly. Inst. Bklyn., 1943, Ph.D. in Chemistry, 1946; M.B.A., U. Buffalo, 1959. Research chemist S.A.M. labs, Manhattan Project, Columbia U., 1943-44; plant supr. Metal & Plastic Processing Co., Bklyn., 1946-51; research chemist Gen. Chem. div. Allied Chem. & Dye Corp., N.Y.C., 1951-53; sr. chemist Congoleum Nairn, Kearny, N.J., 1953-54; supr. dielecs-advance devel. Gen. Elec. Co., Hudson Falls, N.Y., 1954-56; mgr. indsl. products research dept. Spencer Kellogg & Sons, Inc. (Textron), Buffalo, 1956-59; mgr. plastics div. Trancoa Chem. Corp; Reading, Mass., 1959-62; asso. dir. product devel. service labs. chem. div. Merck & Co., Inc., Rahway, N.J., 1962-69; dir. product devel. Borden Chem. div. Borden Inc., N.Y.C., 1969-72, tech. dir., 1972-73, Borden Inc., 1973-78, v.p. product safety and quality, 1978-81, v.p. sci. and tech., 1981—; mem. exec. com. Food Safety Council, 1976-81, trustee, chmn. membership com., 1976-81; bd. dirs. Formaldehyde Inst., 1977—, vice chmn., 1982—, mem. exec. com., 1981—, mem. med. com., 1977—, steering com., 1977-81;' instr. Poly. Inst. Bklyn., 1946-47; asst. prof. Adelphi Coll., 1952-54; prof. math. sci. U.S. Merchant Marine Acad., 1954; seminar leader Am. Mgmt. Assn.; prof. mgmt. N.Y. U. Sch. Mgmt., 1968—. Contbr. articles to profl. jours. Recipient cert. award Fedn. Socs. Paint Tech., 1965. Mem. Am. Chem. Soc. Fedn. Coatings Tech., Synthetic Organic Chem. Specialties Assn. (bd. govs. 1981-84), Inst. Food Tech., ASTM, Synthetic Organic Chems. Mfg. Assn. (dir. 1977—), Paint Research Inst., Delta Sigma Pi, Gamma Sigma Epsilon, Beta Gamma Sigma, Phi Lamba Upsilon. Research in polymers, electrochemistry, food packaging. Patentee in field. Current work: Administration, research development, quality assurance, regulatory affairs, industrial health. Subspecialties: Polymer chemistry; Food science and technology. Office: 960 Kings Mill Pkwy Columbus OH 43229

CUMMINGS, CHARLES WILLIAM, physician, educator; b. Boston, Nov. 16, 1935; s. Harry Blanchard and Madge (Frey) C.; m. Jane E. Drake, July 1, 1983; children—Charles William, Lee Blanchard, Evelyn Howard. A.B., Dartmouth Coll., 1957; M.D., U. Va., 1961. Intern Mary Hitchcock Meml. Hosp., Hanover, N.H., 1961-62; resident otolaryngology Harvard U. Med. Sch., 1965-68; practice medicine specializing in otolaryngology, Seattle, 1978—; asso. prof. otolaryngology Upstate Med. Sch., SUNY, Syracuse, 1976-78; prof., chmn. dept. otolaryngology U. Wash. Med. Sch., Seattle, 1978—. Contbr. sci. articles to profl. jours. Served to capt., M.C. USAF, 1963-65. Mem. A.C.S., Soc. Head and Neck Surgeons, Am. Soc. for Head and Neck Surgery, Soc. U. Otolaryngologists, Assn. Acad. Depts. Otolaryngology, Triological Soc., Laryngological Soc., Bronchoesophagological Soc. Episcopalian. Current Work: Head and neck surgical reconstruction. Subspecialty: Otorhinolaryngology. Office: RL-30 Dept Otolaryngology U Wash Med Sch Seattle WA 98195

CUMMINGS, EDWARD MARK, psychologist; b. Honolulu, May 19, 1950; s. Edward Mark and Miriam (Gilchrist) C.; m. Mary Lorraine Cummings, Mar. 25, 1972. B.A., Johns Hopkins U., 1972; M.A., UCLA, 1973, Ph.D., 1977. Lectr. UCLA, 1977-79; sr. staff assoc. NIMH, Bethesda, Md., 1979—; cons. NBC-TV, N.Y.C., 1978, Alfred Pub., Los Angeles, 1977. Author, editor: Development of Aggression and Altruism. Johns Hopkins U. scholar, 1968-72; NIMH grantee, 1972-76; U. Calif. Regents grantee, 1976-79; Soc. for Research in Child Devel. grantee, 1982; Fellow Internat. Soc. for Research on Aggression. Mem. Am. Psychol. Assn., Soc. for Research in Child Devel., Johns Hopkins U. Alumni Assn., MacArthur Found. Network, AAAS, Internat. Soc. Research in Behavioral Devel. Republican. Roman Catholic. Current Work: Aggression in young children, the impact of stress on devel. of aggression, parental psychopathology and aggression, anger in the home and aggression, day care and emotional devel. Subspecialty: Developmental psychology. Home: 6009 67th Ave Apt 4 Riverdal MD 20737 Office: Lab Developmental Psychology NIMH Bldg 15K 9000 Rockville Pike Bethesda MD 20205

CUMMINGS, GARTH ELLIS, nuclear engineer; b. Oakland, Calif., Jan. 31, 1934; s. Ellis N. and Dorothy M. (Boyd) C.; m. Shirley E. Wolfe, Nov. 10, 1956; children: Gregg A., Jill L. B.S. in Mech. Engring., U. Calif.-Berkeley, 1956, M.S. in Engring. Sci., 1959; Ph.D., U. Calif.-Davis, 1978. Registered profl. engr., Calif. Nuclear/mech. engr. Lawrence Livermore Lab., Livermore, Calif., 1956—, chief reactor ops. Livermore PoolType Reactor, 1963-67, leader nuclear systems group, 1974-79, leader engring. mechanics sect., 1979-81, dep. program leader nuclear systems safety program, 1981-84, program leader, 1984—; systems analyst AEC reactor safety study Lawrence Livermore Lab./AEC, 1972-74. Chmn. com. Boy Scouts Am., Danville, Calif., 1977-80; adviser De Molay, Walnut Creek Calif., 1979-81. Mem. Am. Nuclear Soc. (sect. chmn. 1971-72), AAAS, Soc. Risk Analysis. Current Work: Nuclear reactor safety research and technical application with specialization in probabilistic risk assessment, seismic safety, project and general management. Subspecialties: Nuclear engineering; Mechanical engineering. Home: 1551 Harlan Dr Danville CA 94526 Office: Lawrence Livermore National Laboratory PO Box 808 Livermore CA 94550

CUMMINGS, MARTIN MARC, physician, scientific administrator; b. Camden, N.J., Sept. 7, 1920; s. Samuel and Cecelia (Silverman) C.; m. Arlene Sally Avrutine, Sept. 27, 1942; children: Marc Steven, Lee Bernard, Stuart Lewis. B.S., Bucknell U., 1941, D.Sc. (hon.), 1969; M.D., Duke U., 1944, D.Sc. (hon.), 1985; D.Sc. (hon.), U. Nebr., Emory U.; L.H.D. (hon.), Georgetown U., 1971; M.D. (hon.), Karolinska Inst., 1972. Diplomate: Am. Bd. Microbiology. Intern, resident Boston Marine Hosp., 1944-46; resident Tb Grasslands Hosp., Valhalla, N.Y., 1946-47; dir. Tb evaluation lab. Communicable Disease Center, USPHS, Atlanta, 1947-49; instr. medicine Emory U. Sch. Medicine, 1948-50, assoc. medicine, 1950-52, asst. prof., 1953; chief Tb sect., also dir. Tb research lab. VA Hosp., Atlanta, 1949-53; dir. research services VA Central Office, Washington, 1953-59; spl. lectr. microbiology George Washington U. Sch. Medicine, 1953-59; prof. microbiology, chmn. dept. Okla. U. Sch. Medicine, 1959-61; chief Office Internat. Research, NIH, USPHS, 1961-63; dir. Nat. Library of Medicine, 1964-84, dir. emeritus, 1984—; assoc. dir. for research grants NIH, 1963-64; chmn. com. med. research Nat. Tb Assn., 1958-59; chmn. panel Sarcoidosis NRC-Nat. Acad. Scis., 1958-60. Author: (with Dr. H.S. Willis) Diagnostic and Experimental Methods in Tuberculosis, 1952; Contbr. chpt. on: (with Dr. H.S. Willis) Tubercle Bacilli, Diagnostic Procedures and Reagents, 1950. Served with AUS, 1943-44. Recipient Exceptional Service award VA, 1959; Distinguished Service award HEW, 1968; Rockefeller Pub. Service award, 1973; Disting. Achievement award Modern Medicine, 1976; Disting. Service award Am. Coll. Cardiology, 1978; John C. Leonard award Assn. Hosp. Med. Edn., 1979. Fellow AAAS (dir.); Sr. mem. Am. Soc. Clin. Investigation, Am. Fedn. Clin. Research; mem. Am. Clin. and Climatol. Assn. Current Work: Library consultant. Subspecialties: Information systems (Information science); Information systems, storage, and retrieval (computer science). Home: 11317 Rolling House Rd Rockville MD 20852 Office: Nat Library Medicine Bethesda MD 20209

CUMMINGS, RICHARD DALE, biochemist; b. Clanton, Ala., Nov. 2, 1951; s. William Joseph and Fannie Lee (LeCroy) C.; m. Sandra Fay Felkenhein, May 7, 1983. B.S., U. Montevallo, 1974; Ph.D., Johns Hopkins U., 1980. Postdoctoral fellow Washington U. Sch. Medicine, St. Louis, 1980-83; asst. prof. U. Ga., Athens, 1983—. Author numerous research articles. Recipient Nat. Research Service award NIH, 1980-83; Nat. Cancer Inst. grantee, 1984—. Mem. Am. Chem. Soc., AAAS, Am. Soc. Cell Biology, Soc. Complex Carbohydrates. Current work: Structure and function of cell surface glycoproteins, biosynthesis of cell surface glycoproteins; changes in surface glycoproteins upon neoplastic transformation and differentiation. Subspecialties: Biochemistry (biology); Cancer research (medicine). Office: U Ga Dept Biochem Athens GA 30602

CUNNINGHAM, BRUCE ARTHUR, biochemist; b. Winnebago, Ill., Jan. 18, 1940; s. Wallace Calvin and Margaret Wright (Clinite) C.; m. Katrina Sue Susdorf, Feb. 27, 1965; children—Jennifer Ruth, Douglas James. B.S., U. Dubuque, 1962; Ph.D., Yale U., 1966. NSF postdoctoral fellow Rockefeller U., N.Y.C., 1966-68, asst. prof. biochemistry, 1968-71, assoc. prof., 1971-77, prof. developmental and molecular biology, 1978—. Editorial bd. Jour. Biol. Chemistry, 1978-82. Camille and Henry Dreyfus Found. grantee, 1970-75; recipient Career Scientist award Irma T. Hirschl Trust, 1975. Mem. Am. Soc. Biol. Chemists, Am. Assn. Immunologists, Am. Chem. Soc., Harvey Soc. (councillor 1976-79), Am. Soc. Cell Biology, AAAS, Sigma Xi. Democrat. Lutheran. Research on structure and function of molecules on cell surfaces. Subspecialties: Developmental biology; Molecular biology. Office: 1230 York Ave New York NY 10021

CUNNINGHAM, CLARENCE MARION, chemistry educator, computer programming consultant; b. Cooper, Tex., July 24, 1920; s. Willie Lee and Naoma Mae (Stokes) C.; m. Janet Ruth Kohl, Sept. 16, 1951; children: Elizabeth Jane, Daniel Marvin, Steven Charles, Margaret Helen. B.S., Tex. A&M U., 1942; M.S., U. Calif.-Berkeley, 1948; Ph.D., Ohio State U., 1954. Teaching asst. U. Calif., 1946-48; instr. chemistry Calif. State Poly. Inst., 1948-49; research asst. Ohio State U., 1949-51; cryogenic engr. AEC program H. L. Johnston, Columbus, Ohio, 1951-54; asst. prof. chemistry Okla. State U., 1954-59, assoc. prof., from 1959, now prof.; cons. Author: (with Jones) Electrolytic Conductance of Lithium Bromide in Acetone and Acetone-Bromosuccinic Acid Solutions, 1976, (with More) A Student's Guide to Independent Study for Petrucci's General Chemistry, 1977. Sec. Payne County (Okla.) Democratic Com., 1962-65, 75-77; scoutmaster Will Rogers council Boy Scouts Am., 1967-83, dist. commn., 1983—; bd. dirs. Stillwater (Okla.) Neighborhood Nursery, 1967-85. Served with U.S. Army, 1942-46; to col. USAR, 1946-72. Recipient Silver Beaver award Boy Scouts Am., 1977; Petroleum Research grantee, 1955-60; NASA grantee, 1964-70. Mem. Am. Chem. Soc., Am. Phys. Soc., AAAS, AAAUP. Quaker. Lodge: Kiwanis. Current Work: Association constants from the chemical shift in the nuclear magnetic resonance spectrum of solutions. Subspecialties: Physical chemistry; Nuclear magnetic resonance. Home: 924 Lakeridge Ave Stillwater OK 74074 Office: Dept Chemistry Okla State U Stillwater OK 74078

CUNNINGHAM, EARLENE BROWN, biochemistry educator; b. Cleve., Aug. 27, 1930. B.S., U. Ill., 1949; M.S., UCLA, 1951; Ph.D., U.S.C., 1954. Research assoc. Ind. U. Sch. Medicine, Indpls., 1954-59; asst. prof. Howard U. Coll. Medicine, Washington, 1959-63, assoc. prof., 1963-64; research fellow U. Calif.-Berkeley, 1964-68; lectr. U. S.C., Columbia, 1968-71; assoc. prof. Med. U. S.C., Charleston, 1971-78, U. Medicine and Dentistry N.J.-N.J. Med. Sch., Newark, 1978—. Recipient Lederle Med. Faculty award Howard U. Coll. Medicine, 1961-63; NIH fellow, 1964-68. Mem. Sigma Xi. Current Work: Receptor-mediated regulation of cell proliferation and cell growth; emphasis upon mechanisms involving covalent modification of membrane proteins and phospholipids. Subspecialty: Biochemistry (medicine). Office: Dept Biochemistr U Medicine and Dentistry NJ-NJ Med Sch 100 Bergen St Newark NJ 07103

CUNNINGHAM, JAMES THOMAS, mechanical engineer; b. Yonkers, N.Y., Aug. 9, 1922; s. James Thomas and Grace Agnes (Weed) C.; m. Ellen Conover Erickson, June 17, 1950; children—Christopher James, Mark Robert. B.A., Rutgers U., 1956. Project engr. feeder design Merrick Scale Mfg. Co., Passaic, N.J., 1962-66; mech. engr. Austin Co., Roselle, N.J., 1966; sr. systems engr. Robins Engrs. & Constructors, Totowa, N.J., 1966-70; product mgr., mine dept. Hewitt-Robins, Inc., Passaic, N.J., 1970-74; mgr. engineered systems Orba Corp., Fairfield, N.J., 1974-77, Robins Engrs. & Constructors, Totowa, 1977—. Inventor device for loading Great Lakes ore boats. Served with U.S. Army, 1943-45, ETO. Mem. Soc. Mining Engrs. of AIME, ASME, ASTM, Nautical Research Guild, Steamship Hist. Soc. Am. Lodge: Vasa. Subspecialties: Mechanical engineering; Structural engineering. Home: 14 Francis Pl Caldwell NJ 07006 Office: Robins Engrs and Constructors 711 Union Blvd Totowa NJ 07511

CUNNINGHAM, JOHN FRANCIS, computer company executive; b. Boston, Mar. 5, 1943; s. William J. and Rose L. (Mulhern) C.; m. Ellen M. Condon, June 25, 1966; children—Christopher, Erin, Trisha. B.A., Boston Coll., 1964; M.B.A., Amos Tuck Sch., Dartmouth Coll., 1966. V.p. mktg. Wang Labs.,

Inc., Lowell, Mass., 1972-76, sr. v.p., 1976-83, pres., chief operating officer, 1983—, dir.; dir. Bank of Boston Corp., First Nat. Bank of Boston; trustee Wang Inst. Grad. Studies, Lowell; bd. dirs. Comml. Club, Boston. Bd. dirs. Boys & Girls Club Boston; bd. overseers Amos Tuck Sch., Dartmouth Coll., Hanover, N.Y.; trustee Boston Coll. Roman Catholic. Club: Weston Golf (Mass.). Office: Wang Labs Inc One Industrial Ave Lowell MA 01851

CUNNINGHAM, RAYMOND LEO, research chemist; b. Easton, Ill., Jan. 5, 1934; s. Raymond J. and Minnie G. (Vaughn) C. B.A., St. Ambrose Coll., 1955; postgrad. U. Ill., 1955-56, Bradley U., Peoria, Ill. Phys. sci. aid in chemistry Northern Regional Research Ctr. Agrl. Research Service U.S. Dept. Agr., Peoria, 1957-61, chemist, 1961-78, research chemist, 1978—. Contbr. articles to profl. jours. Served with USAR, 1958. Mem. Am. Chem. Soc., Ill. Acad. Sci., TAPPI. Democrat. Roman Catholic. Lodge: K.C. Current work: Modifications of annual plant lignocellulose; delignifications; separation, hydrolysis, and utilization of hemicellulose; hydrolysis of cellulose. Subspecialties: Biomass (agriculture); Fuels and sources. Home: 1108 W MacQueen Ave Peoria IL 61604 Office: Northern Regional Research Ctr Agrl Research Service US Dept Agr 1815 N University St Peoria IL 61604

CUOMO, FRANK WILLIAM, physics educator, consultant; b. Providence, Jan. 29, 1928; s. William Frank and Imperia (Palazzo) C.; m. Evelyn J. Charves, July 14, 1956; children—Ann, William, Teresa, Deborah. Assoc. in Engring., Roger Williams Coll., 1951; B.S. in Physics, U. R.I., 1959, M.S. in Physics, 1961. Instr. physics U. R.I., Kingston, 1959-62, asst. prof., 1963-74, assoc. prof., 1975-82, prof., 1983—; cons. Naval Underwater Systems Ctr., Newport, R.I., 1961—. Contbr. articles to profl. jours.; patentee in field. NSF faculty fellow Brown U., 1965-66; grantee NASA, Naval Underwater Systems Ctr., 1984-85; recipient several achievement awards for papers and patents Naval Underwater Systems Ctr., 1970-85. Mem. Optical Soc. Am., Acoustical Soc. Am. (vice chmn. Narragansett chpt. 1976-77, chmn. 1977-78, award 1978), Sigma Xi, Tau Beta Pi, Sigma Pi Sigma. Roman Catholic. Current work: Fiber optic sensors; underwater sound; transducers; Schlieren imaging; materials science. Subspecialties: Fiber optics; Acoustics. Home: 108 Wannamoisett Rd East Providence RI 02914 Office: U RI 312 E Hall-Physics Kingston RI 02881

CUPCHIK, WILLIAM, psychologist; b. Montreal, June 5, 1940; s. David and Chana (Trifskin) C.; m. Gila Gladys Holtzman, Aug. 20, 1961 (div. 1972); 1 son, Jeffrey Wayne. B.Engring., McGill U., 1961; B.A., Carleton U., 1963; M.Ed., U. Toronto, 1970, Ph.D., 1979. Registered psychologist, Ont. Navigational systems design engr. Computing Devices of Can., Bells Corners, Ont., 1961-62; tchr., guidance counselor Ottawa Bd. Edn., 1963-66, North York Bd. Edn., 1966-69; attendance counselor Etobicoke Bd. Edn., Ont., 1969-72; psychologist in charge forensic outpatient psychol. service Clarke Inst. Psychiatry, Toronto, Ont., 1979—; guest faculty Order of Mt. Mary Immaculate, Lafayette, Calif., 1977-82; lectr. Sch. Continuing Studies, U. Toronto, 1980-85; cons., group leader career counseling Sun Oil Co. Can., 1980-83. Originator, author psychotherapeutic procedure, reintrojection therapy, 1983; author: Clinical Uses of Mental Imagery, 1983; originator, inventor: navigational guidance system Map Display Unit and Vector Adder, 1962. Mem. Am. Group Psychotherapy Assn., Ont. Group Psychotherapy Assn. (treas. 1980-81), Internat. Transactional Analysis Assn., Am. Psychol. Assn., Ont. Psychol. Assn., Internat. Council Psychologists. Jewish. Current Work: Clinical uses of mental imagery procedures; reintrojection therapy development; criminal activities of middle and upper class ethical majority; researcher atypical theft offenders. Subspecialty: Psychotherapy. Home: 321 Chaplin Crescent Apt 709 Toronto ON M5P 1B2 Canada Office: 250 College St Toronto ON M5T 1R8 Canada

CURD, JOHN GARY, physician, rheumatology, immunologist, researcher; b. Grand Junction, Colo., July 2, 1945; s. H. Ronald and Edna (Hegsted) C.; m. Karen Wendel, June 12, 1971; children: Alison, Jonathan, Edward. B.A. magna cum laude, Princeton U., 1967; M.D. cum laude (Univ. nat. scholar), Harvard U., 1971. Diplomate Am. Bd. Internal Medicine, Am. Bd. Rheumatology, Am. Bd. Allergy and Immunology, Am. Bd. Lab. Med. Immunology. Intern Med. Service, Mass. Gen. Hosp., Harvard U. Med. Sch., Boston, 1971-72, asst. resident, 1972-73; research assoc. Lab. Chem. Biology, Nat. Inst. Arthritis, Metabolism and Digestive Diseases, NIH, Bethesda, Md., 1973-75; postdoctoral fellow div. rheumatology Sch. Medicine, U. Calif.-San Diego, La Jolla, 1975-77; postdoctoral fellow dept. molecular immunology Research Inst., Scripps Clinic, La Jolla, 1977-78, asst. mem. II dept. molecular immunology and dept. clin. research, 1978-84, assoc. adj. mem. dept. basic clin. research, 1985—; assoc. dir. Gen. Clin. Research Ctr., Scripps Clinic and Research Found., La Jolla, 1981-83; asst. clin. prof. U. Calif.-San Diego, La Jolla, 1980—; active San Diego Rheumatism Soc.; established investigator Am. Heart Assn., 1983-85. Research numerous publs. in field. Served with USPHS, 1973-75. Helen Hay Whitney fellow, 1975-78; NIH clin. investigator, 1978-81. Mem. Am. Acad. Allergy, Am. Rheumatism Assn., Am. Assn. Immunologists. Republican. Methodist. Current Work: Complement research; arthritis research. Subspecialties: Internal medicine; Rheumatology. Office: Div Rheumatology Scripps Clinic and Research Found 10666 N Torrey Pines Rd La Jolla CA 92037

CURELARU, IRINA MARIANA, physics educator, researcher; b. Iasi, Romania, Sept. 29, 1935; came to U.S., 1981; d. Dumitru and Maria (Agarici) Marinescu; m. Ioan Curelaru, Dec. 22, 1960 (div. Mar. 1978); children—Maria, John. B.S., Bucharest U., 1957; Ph.D., Chalmers U. Tech., 1980. Research assoc. Inst. Atomic Physics, Bucharest, Romania, 1957-62, 64-74, Joint Inst. Nuclear Research, Dubna, USSR, 1962-64, Chalmers U. Tech., Gothenburg, Sweden, 1974-80, research assoc., asst. prof., 1980-81; assoc. prof. materials sci. U. Utah, Salt Lake City, 1981—. Author: Elementary Particles-Strong Interactions, 1970. Contbr. articles to profl. jours. IAEA fellow, 1972, 74. Mem. Am. Phys. Soc., Am. Ceramic Soc., Nat. Inst. Ceramic Engrs., Ceramic Ednl. Council, European Phys. Soc., AAAS. Current work: Experimental electronic structure and surface/interface properties of solids; characterization of electronic ceramics, luminophors, catalysts, one-dimensional conductors, intermetallics. Subspecialties: Condensed matter physics; Electronic materials. Home: 6249 S 44 East Murray UT 84107 Office: Dept Materials Sci and Engring U Utah Salt Lake City UT 84112

CURL, ROBERT FLOYD, JR., educator; b. Alice, Tex., Aug. 23, 1933; s. Robert Floyd and Lessie (Merritt) C.; m. Jonel Whipple, Dec. 21, 1955; children—Michael, David. B.A., Rice U., 1954; Ph.D. (NSF fellow), U. Cal. at Berkeley, 1957. Research fellow Harvard, 1957-58; asst. prof. chemistry Rice U., Houston, 1958-63, asso. prof., 1963-67, prof., 1967—; master Lovett Coll., 1968-72; Vis. research officer NRC Can., 1972-73; vis. prof. Inst. for Molecular Sc., Okazaki, Japan, 1977. Contbr. articles profl. jours. Alfred P. Sloan fellow, 1961-63; NATO postdoctoral fellow, 1964; recipient Clayton prize Instn. Mech. Engrs., London, 1958. Mem. Am. Chem. Soc., Phi Beta Kappa, Sigma Xi. Methodist. Current Work: Laser spectroscopy of transient molecules. Subspecialties: Physical chemistry; Laser spectroscopy. Home: 1824 Bolsover St Houston TX 77005

CURNUTTE, BASIL, JR., physicist, educator, researcher; b. Portsmouth, Ohio, Mar. 1, 1923; s. Basil and Lula Alafair (Cooper) C.; m. Mary Leete Lukemire, June 10, 1945; children: William Basil, Gregory Mark. B.S., U.S. Naval Acad., 1945; Ph.D. (NSF fellow), Ohio State U., 1953. Grad. asst. Ohio State U., 1950-51, Univ. research scholar, 1951, research assoc., 1953; asst. prof. physics Kans. State U., 1954-55, assoc. prof., 1956-64, prof., 1964—; physicist Lawrence Radiation Lab., 1961; vis. scientist Am. Inst. Physics, 1965-71; vis. prof. Ariz. U., 1968. Research, publs. in atomic and molecular spectroscopy. Served to lt. USN, 1945-49. Fellow Am. Phys. Soc., Optical Soc. Am.; mem. AAAS, Am. Assn. Physics Tchrs., Kans. Acad. Sci. Current Work: Research in atomic spectroscopy on fast ion beams, Mossbauer Spectroscopy, applied x-ray spectroscopy. Subspecialties: Atomic and molecular physics; Infrared spectroscopy. Home: 1607 Wood Crest Dr Manhattan KS 66502 Office: Dept Physics Kans State U Manhattan KS 66506

CURRAN, BRUCE HOWLETT, medical physicist; b. New Haven, Oct. 26, 1951; s. Lawrence T. and Barbara (Howlett) C. A.B., Dartmouth Coll., 1973, M.E., 1982. Sr. programmer Mary Hitchcock Meml. Hosp., Hanover, N.H., 1973-74, sr. engring. analyst, 1974-78; med. physicist Tufts New Eng. Med. Center, Boston, 1978—, instr., 1978-84, asst. prof., 1984—. Contbr. articles to profl. jours. Mem. Am. Assn. Physicists in Medicine, Assn. Computing Machinery, IEEE, Health Physics Soc. Current Work: Hyperthermia, computers in radiology; radiation therapy, ultrasound, digital radiography, cardiology, nuclear medicine. Subspecialties: Medical physics; Biomedical engineering. Office: 171 Harrison Ave Boston MA 02111

CURRENT, STEVEN PAUL, chemist; b. Downers Grove, Ill., May 20, 1950; s. Harlan P. and Margaret (Risser) C.; m. Karen Trumble, Aug. 24, 1973; 1 child, Kimberly Mae. B.S. in Chemistry, U. Chgo., 1972; Ph.D. in Chemistry, Stanford U., 1975. Research assoc. Case Western Res. U., Cleve., 1975, MIT, Cambridge, 1976-77; research chemist Chevron Research Co., Richmond, Calif., 1977-83, sr. research chemist, 1983—; research cons. Chevron Chem. Co., San Francisco, 1984-85. Subspecialties: Organic chemistry; Catalysis chemistry. Office: Chevron Research Co PO Box 1627 Richmond CA 94802

CURRIE, BRUCE LAMONTE, chemistry educator, researcher; b. Pasadena, Calif., Mar. 1, 1945; s. Paul Quentin Currie and Ellen Irene (Gifford) Currie Cloyd; m. Lynda Marc Thompson, July 2, 1965; children—Paul Bryan, Charles David, Kathren Lynda. B.S., Ariz. State U., 1966; Ph.D. in Organic Chemistry, U. Utah, 1969. Postdoctoral fellow Inst. Biomed. Research-U. Tex.-Austin, 1969-74; research assoc. Inst. Biomed. Research, asst. prof. dept. medicinal chemistry Coll. Pharmacy, U. Ill.-Chgo., 1974-81, assoc. prof., 1981—. Author jour. articles and abstracts. Patentee in field. Mem. sch. bd. Community Consol. Sch. Dist. 59, Elk Grove Twp., Ill., 1978-79; bd. dirs. NW Suburban Spl. Edn. Orgn., No. Cook County, Ill., 1978-79. Mem. Am. Chem. Soc., Internat. Soc. Heterocyclic Chemistry, Endocrine Soc., Am. Assn. Colls. Pharmacy. Baptist. Current work: Peptide hormones and neurotransmitters: structure activity relationships; synthesis of conformationally rigid analogs. Peptide antigelation agents of HbS. High performance liquid chromatography. Subspecialties: Medicinal chemistry; Organic chemistry. Office: Dept Medicinal Chemistry and Pharmacognosy Coll Pharmacy U Ill Chicago IL 60612 Also: PO Box 6998 Chicago IL 60680

CURRIE, MALCOLM RODERICK, scientist, aerospace executive; b. Spokane, Wash., Mar. 13, 1927; s. Erwin Casper and Genevieve (Hauenstein) C.; m. Sunya Lofsky, June 24, 1951; children—Deborah, David, Diana; m. Barbara L. Dyer, Mar. 5, 1977. A.B., U. Calif. at Berkeley, 1949, M.S., 1951, Ph.D., 1954. Research engr. Microwave Lab., U. Calif. at Berkeley, 1949-52, elec. engring. faculty, 1953-54; lectr. U. Calif. at Los Angeles, 1955-57; research engr. Hughes Aircraft Co., 1954-57, v.p., 1965-66; head electron dynamics dept. Hughes Research Labs., Culver City, Calif., 1957-60, dir. physics lab., Malibu, Calif., 1960-61, asso. dir., 1961-63, v.p., dir. research labs., 1963-65, v.p., mgr. research and devel. div., 1965-69; v.p. research and devel. Beckman Instruments, Inc., 1969-73; dir. def. research and engring. Office Sec. Def., Washington, 1973-77; v.p. missile systems group Hughes Aircraft Co., Canoga Park, Calif., 1977-83, exec. v.p., 1983—; mem. Def. Sci. Bd. Author articles. Served with USNR, 1944-47. Decorated comdr. Legion of Honor France; named nation's outstanding young elec. engr. Eta Kappa Nu, 1958, one of 5 outstanding young men of Calif. Calif. Jr. C. of C., 1960. Fellow IEEE, AIAA; mem. Nat. Acad. Engring., Am. Phys. Soc., Phi Beta Kappa, Sigma Xi, Lambda Chi Alpha. Patentee in field. Subspecialty: Aerospace engineering and technology. Home: 28780 Wagon Rd Agoura CA 91301 Office: Hughes Aircraft Co 200 N Sepulveda Blvd Mail Sta C2/A103 El Segundo CA 90245*

CURRIER, WILLIAM WESLEY, biochemist, educator, researcher; b. Seattle, Sept. 18, 1947; s. Walter S. and Angeline B. (Clarke) C.; m. Janice K. Cameron, Mar. 22, 1969; 1 son, Reid B. B.S. in Chemistry, U. Wash., 1969; Ph.D. in Biochemistry, Purdue U., West Lafayette, Ind., 1974. Postdoctoral fellow dept. plant pathology Mont. State U., 1974-77; asst. prof. biochemistry, dept. microbiology and biochemistry U. Vt., 1977-82, assoc. prof., 1982—. Contbr. numerous articles to profl. jours. Mem. AAAS, Am. Soc. Plant Physiologists, Sigma Xi (pres. Vt. chpt. 1982-83). Mem. Chs. of Christ. Subspecialties: Nitrogen fixation; Plant pathology. Office: Dept Microbiology and Biochemistry U Vt 115 Hills Bldg Burlington VT 05405

CURRY, JAMES REGNALD, physicist, weapons scientist; b. Memphis, Tex., Apr. 20, 1943; s. Herbert Regnald and Opal Evelina (Hill) C.; m. Carolyn Trail, June 4, 1965; 1 child, Klay Regnald. B.S. in Physics, U. Tex.-Austin, 1965, Ph.D. in Nuclear Physics, 1969. Sr. physicist Kaman Scis. Corp., Colorado Springs, 1969-76, Ga. Inst. Tech., Atlanta, 1976-77; tech. staff Sandia Labs., Albuquerque, 1977-80; sr. scientist/group leader Mission Research Corp., Colorado Springs, 1980—; med. physics cons. Author: MIL-Handbook 760, Radiated Susceptibility Investigative Methodology, Vol. I and II, 1978; Compendium of Long-Line SREMP Transients, 1984; also articles. Elder, deacon Acad. Christian Ch. and Security Christian Ch., Colorado Springs, 1975-80. AEC Spl. Fellow in Nuclear Sci. and Engring., 1965; recipient Kaman Scis. Corp. Performance award, 1971; Med. Physics Research grantee NIH, 1979. Mem. IEEE, Am. Assn. Physicists in Medicine, Phi Beta Kappa, Sigma Pi Sigma, Phi Kappa Phi. Club: Ent Gun. Current work: Weapons (nuclear) effects, especially nuclear electromagnetic pulse and source region EMP research. Subspecialties: Nuclear physics; Electrical engineering. Home: 2811 Country Club Circle Colorado Springs CO 80909 Office: Mission Research Corp 4935 N 30th St Colorado Springs CO 80919

CURRY, MARY GRACE, environmental scientist; b. New Orleans, June 16, 1947; d. Clyde Lalio and Gladys Ruth (Ehret) C. B.S., U. New Orleans, 1969, M.S., 1971; Ph.D., La. State U., 1973. Cert. environ. profl., La. Vis. asst. prof. botany La. State U., Baton Rouge, 1974; environ. scientist VTN La., Inc., Metairie, 1974-79; environ. impact officer Parish of Jefferson, Metairie, 1979—. Contbr. articles to profl. jours. Mem. La. Acad. Scis., La. Environ. Profls. Assn. (pres. 1979, exec. council 1977—), Am. Inst. Biol. Scis., Bot. Soc. Am., Assn. Southeastern Biologists, Ecol. Soc. Am., So. Appalachian Bot. Soc., Coastal Soc., Gretna Hist. Soc., Jefferson Histo. Soc. La., D.A.R., U.D.C., Sigma Xi. Democrat. Roman Catholic. Current Work: Taxonomy, ecology and distbr. of freshwater leeches; vascular plant taxonomy and ecology; coastal zone and wetland mgmt. Subspecialties: Ecology (environmental science); Taxonomy. Home: 3404 Tolmas Dr Metairie LA 70002 Office: 3330 N Causeway Blvd Room 303 Metairie LA 70002

CURRY, STEPHEN MARTINDALE, physicist, laser engineer; b. Dallas; s. Duncan Ford and Frances Janella (Martindale) C. B.S., So. Meth. U., 1967; M.S., Stanford U., 1969, Ph.D., 1972. Asst. prof. U. Tex., Dallas, 1973-78; research scientist Vought Corp., Dallas, 1978-79, cons., 1979-81; sr. laser engr. Cooper LaserSonics, Santa Clara, Calif., 1981-85, cons., 1985—; research assoc. Stanford U., Calif., 1972-73. Contbr. articles to profl. jours. Fellow NSF, 1967-71, Sloan Found., 1977-78. Mem. Optical Soc. Am., Am. Phys. Soc., Phi Beta Kappa, Phi Eta Sigma, Democrat. Current work: Consultant in the physical sciences and computer technology. Subspecialties: Laser spectroscopy; Laser medicine. Home: 520 Fern Ridge Ct Sunnyvale CA 94087 Office: Sound Decisions 19925 Stevens Creek Blvd Suite 164 Cupertino CA 95014*

CURTIS, DAVID CARLETON, hydrologist; b. Jamestown, N.Y., Apr. 28, 1950; s. David Fayette and Mary Margret (Woodburn) C.; m. Kathleen Ann Miscik, July 1, 1972; children—Brendon Jarod, Carleton John. B.S. in Agrl. Engring., Pa. State U., 1972; M.S. in Civil Engring., U. Md., 1975; Ph.D. in Water Resources, MIT, 1982. Research hydrologist Nat. Weather Service, Silver Spring, Md., 1975-79, flash flood hydrologist, Bloomfield, Conn., 1979-83; pres. Internat. Hydrological Services, Bloomfield, Conn., 1983—; dir. Sierra-Misco, Inc., Berkeley, Calif. Contbr. articles to profl. jours. Legal asst. adv. com. Manchester Community Coll., Conn., 1983-84; bd. dirs. Frederick County Civic Fedn., Md., 1973-74. Recipient Spl. Achievement award NOAA, 1981, 83; unit citation Nat. Weather Service, 1984; Bronze medal U.S. Dept. Commerce, 1984. Mem. ASCE, Am. Geophys. Union, Assn. State Flood Plain Mgrs., Internat. Water Resources Assn., Research Soc. N.Am., Sigma Xi. Current work: Automated environmental monitoring and control systems; principal applications in flood forecasting, reservoir management, agricultural, fireweather and water quality. Home: 13 Westbrook Rd Bloomfield CT 06002

CURTIS, LORENZO JAN, physics educator; b. St. Johns, Mich., Nov. 4, 1935; s. Lorenzo F. and Grace C.; m. Maj R. Curtis, Nov. 29, 1971. B.S., U. Toledo, 1958; M.S., U. Mich., 1961, Ph.D., 1963. Registered profl. engr., Ohio. Faculty U. Toledo, 1963—, prof. physics and astronomy, 1973—; docent U. Lund, Sweden, 1976-79. Contbr. articles to profl. jours. Mem. Am. Phys. Soc., Am. Assn. Physics Tchrs., Optical Soc. Am., European Phys. Soc., Swedish Phys. Soc. Current Work: Teaching and research in the atomic structure of heavy and highly ionized systems. Subspecialty: Atomic and molecular physics. Office: U Toledo Dept Physics and Astronomy Toledo OH 43606

CURTIS, RONALD SANGER, computer scientist, educator; b. Claremont, N.H., Nov. 1, 1950; s. Harding Sanger and Dorothy (Therrien) C. B.A. in Math, Keene State Coll., 1972; M.S. in Math, U. N.H., 1974. Tchr. sci. Windsor (Vt.) High Sch., 1974-76; research asst. SUNY, Buffalo, 1976-79; chmn. dept. computer sci. Canisius Coll., Buffalo, 1979-83, asst. prof., 1984—. Contbr. articles to profl. jours. Mem. Assn. Computing Machinery, IEEE, Kappa Delta Pi. Current Work: Distributed systems, microcomputer networks, network computers, debugging environments. Subspecialties: Distributed systems and networks; Programming languages. Home: PO Box 51 Buffalo NY 14216 Office: Canisus Coll 2001 Main St Buffalo NY 14205

CURTISS, ROY, III, biology educator; b. May 27, 1934; m. Josephine Clark, Dec. 28, 1976; children: Brian, Wayne, Roy IV, Lynn, Gregory Clark, Eric Garth, Megan Kimberly. B.S. in Agr., Cornell U., 1956; Ph.D. in Microbiology, U. Chgo., 1962. Instr., research asst. Cornell U., 1955-56; jr. tech. specialist Brookhaven Nat. Lab., 1956-58; fellow microbiology U. Chgo., 1958-60, USPHS fellow, 1960-62; biologist Oak Ridge Nat. Lab., 1963-72; lectr. microbiology U. Tenn., 1965-72, lectr. Grad. Sch. Biomed. Scis., Oak Ridge, 1967-69; prof. U. Tenn. (Sch. Biomed. Scis.), 1969-72; assoc. dir. U. Tenn. (Grad. Sch. Biomed. Scis.), 1970-71, interim dir., 1971-72; Charles H. McCauley prof. microbiology U. Ala., Birmingham, 1972—83; sr. scientist Inst. Dental Research, 1972—83, Comprehensive Cancer Center, 1972—83; dir. molecular cell biology grad. program, 1973-82, vice chmn., 1980-81, acting chmn. dept. microbiology, 1981—82; dir. Cystic Fibrosis Research Center, 1981-83; prof. cellular and molecular biology Sch. Dental Medicine Washington U., St. Louis, 1983, George William and Irene Koechig Freiberg prof. biology, 1984—; v.p., bd. dirs. Molecular Engring. Assocs., Inc., 1982—; sci. advisor Protis Biologics, Inc., 1984—; vis. prof. Instituto Venezolana de Investigaciones Cientificas, 1969, U. P.R., 1972, U. Católica de Chile, 1973, U. Okla., 1983; adj. prof. dept. microbiology U. Ala., Birmingham, 1983—; mem. NIH Recombinant DNA Molecule Program Adv. Com., 1974-77, NSF Genetic Biology Com., 1975-78; mem. NIH Genetic Basis of Disease Rev. Com., 1979-83, chmn. 1981-83; chmn. WHO Immunology of Tb steering com., 1984—, Therapy of Leprosy steering com., 1984—. Contbr. articles to profl. jours.; Editor: Jour. Bacteriology, 1970-76, Infection and Immunity, 1985—. Mem. Oak Ridge City Council, 1969-72. Recipient Kreshover award Nat. Inst. Dental Research, 1984. Fellow Am. Acad. Microbiology; mem. Genetics Soc. Am., Soc. Gen. Microbiology, Am. Soc. Microbiology (parliamentarian 1970-75, dir. 1977-80), N.Y. Acad. Scis., AAAS, Council Advancement Sci. Writing (dir. 1976—82, v.p. 1978—82), Sigma Xi. Current Work: Genetic and biochemical mechanisms of bacterial pathogenicity. Subspecialties: Genetics and genetic engineering (biology); Microbiology. Home: 6065 Lindell Blvd Saint Louis MO 63112 Office: Dept Biology Washington University Saint Louis MO 63130

CUSHMAN, DAVID WAYNE, research biochemist; b. Indpls., Nov. 15, 1939; s. Wayne B. and Mildred M. (Coffin) C.; m. Linda L. Kranch, July 31, 1964; children: Michael, Laura. B.A., Wabash Coll., 1961; Ph.D., U. Ill., 1966. Research investigator Squibb Inst. for Med. Research, Princeton, N.J., 1966-69, sr. research investigator, 1969-73, research fellow, 1973-78, sr. research fellow, 1978-83, asst. dept. dir., 1983—. Recipient CIBA award, 1983; NSF fellow, 1961-63. Mem. Am. Soc. Pharmacology and Exptl. Therapeutics, Am. Chem. Soc. (Alfred Burger award in medicinal chemistry 1982), AAAS, N.Y. Acad. Sci., Am. Soc. Biol. Chemists, Phi Beta Kappa, Delta Phi Alpha, Sigma Xi. Current Work: Design of drugs acting via inhibition of pathophyiologically important enzyme systems; renin-angiotensin system and blood pressure control; opiate peptides and analgesia. Subspecialties: Biochemistry (biology); Molecular pharmacology. Home: RD 6 20 Lake Shore Dr Lawrenceville NJ 08648 Office: Squibb Inst for Med Research PO Box 4000 Princeton NJ 08540

CUTLER, CASSIUS CHAPIN, See *Who's Who in America,* 43rd edition.

CUTTLER, JERRY MILTON, nuclear physicist-engineer; b. Toronto, Ont., Can., Feb. 11, 1942; s. Sam and Annie (Weiner) C.; m. Vera Nikolic, June 5, 1967; children: Sandra, Shai. B.A.Sc., U. Toronto, 1964; M.Sc., Technion-Israel Inst. Tech., 1968, D.Sc., 1971. Research and devel. engr. Israel AEC Soreq Nuclear Research Ctr., Yavne, Israel, 1964-67; research and devel. engr., lab. mgr. dept. nuclear sci. Technion, Haifa, Israel, 1967-71; tech. mgr. Seforad-Applied Radiation Ltd., Jordan Valley, Israel, 1971-74; supr. reactor control Atomic Energy of Can. Ltd., Mississauga, Ont., 1974-78; mgr. Atomic Energy of Can. Ltd. (Nuclear Instn. br.), 1979-82; asst. to v.p. engring. Atomic Energy of Can. Ltd. (Nuclear Inst. br.), 1982; engring. mgr. Bruce B, 1983-85; resident engring. mgr. Cernovoda Romania, 1985—; Contbr. to profl. lit. Mem. Assn. Profl. Engrs. Province Ont., Am. Nuclear Soc., Can. Nuclear Soc. Patentee fast neutron spectrometer, self-powered neutron and gamma-ray flux detector. Current Work: Technical management of nuclear engineering, design and development in control and instrumentation for nuclear power plants. Subspecialties: Nuclear engineering; Nuclear physics. Home: 1188 Vanier Dr Mississauga ON L5H 3X1 Canada Office: Atomic Energy of Can Ltd Sheridan Park Mississauga ON L5K 1B2 Canada

CWYCYSHYN, WALTER, mechanical engineer, consultant; b. Detroit, Aug. 10, 1927; s. John and Julia (Bush) C.; m. Rebecca J., July 25, 1933; children: Bradley, David. B.M.E., U. Detroit, 1951. Registered profl. engr., Mich. Supr. Gen. Motors Tech. Ctr., Warren, Mich., then devel. engr., staff engr., now supr. devel. Served with USAAF, 1945-47. Mem. Soc. Mfg. Engrs. Patentee in fields of mechanics and control. Current Work: Robotics, development engineering, systems, manufacturing engineering. Subspecialties: Robotics; Mechanical engineering. Office: Advanced Engring Staff Gen Motors Tech Ctr 30300 Mound Rd Warren MI 48090*

CYR, REGINALD JOHN, electronics engineering executive; b. Caribou, Maine, Dec. 24, 1933; s. Dennis Merchant and Regina Agnes (Trusty) C.; m. Clare Marie Tardif, Dec. 26, 1953; children: Roxanne M., Philip Dennis, Scott M., Krista M. B.S. in E.E., magna cum laude, U. Maine, 1959; postgrad., UCLA, 1962, 66. Design engr. Bendix Electrodynamics Div., Sylmar, Calif., 1959-63; v.p., dir. engring. Aquasonics Engrs., 1963-65; staff engr. to chief engr. Bendix Corp., Sylmar, 1966-68; dir. engring. EMS div. Marine Resources, Inc., Northridge, Calif., 1968-73; pres. Sonatech Inc., Goleta, Calif., 1973—, also dir. Served with USN, 1951-54. Recipient IR 100 award, 1971. Mem. Acoustical Soc. Am., Inst. Navigation. Democrat. Roman Catholic. Patentee in field. Current Work: Development of acoustic navigation systems, command and control, acoustic telemetry, acoustic sensors—for government, offshore petroleum and deep sea mining. Subspecialties: Electronics; Acoustical engineering. Home: 1442 Crestline Dr Santa Barbara CA 93117 Office: Sonatech Inc 449 Kellogg Way Goleta CA 93117

CZARNECKI, CAROLINE MARY ANNE, veterinary anatomy educator; b. Detroit, Aug. 3, 1929; s. Daniel and Pauline (Panas) C. B.S., Bemidji State U., 1950; M.A., U. No. Iowa, 1960; Ph.D., U. Minn., 1967. Instr. high schs., Eagle Bend, Minn., 1950-51, Williams, Minn., 1951-53, 54-59, Warroad, Minn., 1953-54, Robbinsdale, Minn., 1960-62; asst. prof. vet. anatomy U. Minn., 1967-71, assoc. prof., 1971-76, prof., 1976—. Contbr. to profl. jours. NIH-USPHS trainee, 1962-67; recipient Norden Disting. Teaching award, 1971. Mem. AAAS, AAUP, Am. Assn. Vet. Anatomy, World Assn. Veterinary Anatomy, Am. Assn. Anatomy, Conf. Research Workers in Animal Diseases, Am. Heart Assn. (Basic Scis. Council). Current Work: Investigation of drug induced cardiomyopathy using an avian model; teaching the microanatomy of domestic animals to veterinary students. Subspecialty: Veterinary anatomy. Home: 2159 S Rosewood Ln Roseville MN 55113 Office: Dept Vet Biology 1988 Fitch Ave Saint Paul MN 55108

CZERNIK, DANIEL EDWARD, mechanical engineer; b. Chgo., July 7, 1936; s. Edward Albert and Frances Alvina (Stanek) C.; m. Christina Cecilia Barry, July 30, 1963; children: Michele, Brian, Bradley. B.S. in Mech. Engring, U. Ill., 1959, M.S. in Mech. Engring, 1960; M.B.A., Northwestern U., 1972. Registered profl. engr., Ill. Product engr. Argonne Nat. Lab., Ill., 1960-63; asst. chief engr. Victor Mfg. & Gasket Co., Chgo., 1963-69; dir. product engring. Fel-Pro Inc., Skokie, Ill., 1969—. Contbr. numerous sci. articles to profl. publs. Sec. Timberlake Civic Assn., Hinsdale, Ill., 1981-83. Served with USMC, 1963. Mem. ASME, Soc. Automotive Engrs., Nat. Soc. Profl. Engrs. Republican. Roman Catholic. Patentee in field. Current Work: Gasket engineering; director of product engineering of gaskets for engines and equipment. Subspecialties: Mechanical engineering; Theoretical and applied mechanics. Office: 7450 N McCormick Blvd Skokie IL 60076

CZITROM, ANDREI ALEXANDER, immunology educator, consultant orthopaedic surgery; b. Brasov, Rumania, June 3, 1946; came to Can., 1972, naturalized, 1983; s. Ladislau and Cecilia (Siegler) C.; m. Patricia E. Bell, Nov. 28, 1976; children—Jacqueline, Alec. Dr.Med., Justus Liebig U., 1972; Ph.D., U. London, 1982. Intern St. Michael's Hosp., Toronto, 1972-73; resident in orthopedic surgery U. Toronto, 1973-78, asst. prof. immunology, 1982—; staff orthopaedic surgeon Mount Sinai Hosp., Toronto Gen. Hosp., 1982—. Contbr. sci. articles to profl. jours. Centennial fellow Med. Research Council, 1979-82, scholar, 1982-87. Fellow Royal Coll. Physicians and Surgeons; mem. Can. Orthopaedic Assn. (ABC fellow 1985), Brit. Soc. for Immunology, Am. Assn. Immunologists. Current work: Transplantation immunology, hand surgery. Subspecialty: Transplant surgery. Office: Suite 441 Mount Sinai Hosp 600 University Ave Toronto ON M5G 1X5 Canada

DABKOWSKI, JOHN, electrical engineer, consultant, researcher; b. Chgo., Feb. 15, 1933; s. John and Harriet (Sierakowski) D.; m. Cecilia Klonowski, June 26, 1976. B.S.E.E., Ill. Inst. Tech., 1955, M.S.E.E., 1960, Ph.D. in Elec. Engring., 1969. Sr. research engr. Ill. Inst. Tech. Research Inst., Chgo., 1957-79; ops. mgr. Sci. Applications Internat. Corp., Hoffman Estates, Ill., 1979-85, dir. EM effects research, 1985—; instr. Grad. Sch., Ill. Inst. Tech., Chgo., 1962-79. Research, publs. in field. Served with U.S. Army, 1955-57. Mem. IEEE, Nat. Assn. Corrosion Engrs., Sigma Xi. Roman Catholic. Current work: Corrosion engineering and inductive interference from electrical power lines upon railroad and cross-country buried pipelines. Subspecialties: Electrical engineering; Corrosion. Home: 7021 Foxfire Dr Crystal Lake IL 60014 Office: Sci Applications Internat Corp 2401 W Hassell Rd Suite 1570 Hoffman Estates IL 60195

DACEY, GEORGE CLEMENT, laboratory administrator; b. Chgo., Jan. 23, 1921; s. Clement Anthony Dacey and Helyn MacLachan; m. Anne Zeamer, June 20, 1954; children: Donna Lynn, John Clement, Sarah Anne. B.S. in E.E, U. Ill., 1942; Ph.D. in Physics, Calif. Inst. Tech., 1951. Research engr. Westinghouse Research Labs, East Pittsburgh, 1942-45; mem. tech. staff transistor research Bell Telephone Labs, 1952-55, head transistor devel., 1955-58, dir. solid state electronics research, 1958-61, exec. dir. telephones div., 1963-68, v.p. customer equipment devel., 1968-70, v.p. transmission systems, 1970-79, v.p. ops. systems, 1979-81; pres. Sandia Nat. Labs., 1981—; v.p. research Sandia Corp., Albuquerque, 1961-63; dir. Perkin-Elmer Corp., Norwalk, Conn., 1st N.Mex. Bankshare Corp. Contbr. articles on transistor physics, lasers to tech. jours. Mem. exec. bd. Monmouth council Boy Scouts Am., 1970-75; bd. dirs. Monmouth Mus., from 1972. Recipient distinguished alumnus award U. Ill. Elec. Engring. Alumni Assn., 1970. Fellow IEEE, Am. Phys. Soc.; mem. Nat. Acad. Engring., Sigma Xi, Phi Kappa Phi, Tau Beta Pi, Eta Kappa Nu. Patentee transistors. Subspecialties: Semiconductors; Condensed matter physics. Home: 1201 Cuatro Cerros TR SE Albuquerque NM 87123 Office: Sandia National Laboratories Albuquerque NM 87185

DAEHLER, MARK, research physicist; b. Cedar Rapids, Iowa, Mar. 21, 1934; s. Max and Mary Gertrude (Bingham) D. B.A., Coe Coll., 1955; M.A., U. Wis., Madison, 1957, Ph.D., 1966. Mem. Staff Los Alamos Sci. Lab., 1966-68; guest scientist Max Planck Inst. for Plasma Physics, Garching, W.Ger., 1968-71; research physicist Naval Research Lab., Washington, 1971—. Contbr. articles to profl. jours. Mem. IEEE, Optical Soc. Am., Am. Astron. Soc., Am. Phys. Soc. Current Work: Prediction of ionospheric properties relevant to high frequency communications; establishment of global HF frequency management systems. Subspecialties: Infrared astronomy; Optical astronomy. Home: 900 Massachusetts Ave NE Washington DC 20002 Office: Naval Research Lab Code 4180 Washington DC 20375 Office: Naval Research Lab Code 4181 Washington DC 20375

DAEHNICK, WILFRIED WOLFGANG, physics educator, consultant; b. Berlin, Dec. 30, 1928; came to U.S., 1955, naturalized; s. Adolf F.W. and Adelheid E. (Janke) D.; m. Claire A. Fullerton, Jan. 30, 1960; children—Christian, Michael, Karen. B.S., Tech. Univ. Munich, Fed. Republic Germany, 1951; M.A. in Physics and Math., U. Hamburg, Fed. Republic Germany, 1955; Ph.D. in Physics, Washington U., St. Louis, 1958. Instr. Princeton U., 1959-62; asst. prof. U. Pitts., 1962-65, assoc. prof., 1965-69, prof. physics, 1969—; cons. various comml. orgns., St. Louis, 1957-75, NSF, Washington, 1976-79. Contbr. articles to profl. jours. NSF grantee, 1964—. Fellow Am. Physical Soc.; mem. Nuclear Physics div. of Am. Physical Soc. Current work: Nuclear structure; weak interactions; nuclear instrumentation; computers reaction theories; medium energy physics. Subspecialty: Nuclear physics. Office: Dept Physics U Pitts Pittsburgh PA 15260

DAFERMOS, CONSTANTINE MICHAEL, educator, researcher; b. Athens, Greece, May 26, 1941; came to U.S., 1964, naturalized, 1979; s. Michael Constantine and Sophia (Raptarchis) D.; m. Stella Theodoracopoulos, Sept. 6, 1964; children—Thalia, Michael. Diploma in Civil Engring., Nat. Tech. U., 1964; Ph.D., Johns Hopkins U., 1967. Postdoctoral fellow Johns Hopkins U., Balt., 1967-68; asst. prof. Cornell U., Ithaca, N.Y., 1968-71; assoc. prof. Brown U., Providence, 1971-76, prof., 1976—. Contbr. articles to profl. jours. Mem. Am. Math. Soc., Soc. Indsl. and Applied Math., Soc. Natural Philosophy (chmn. 1977-78), Soc. Internat. Math. and Mechanics (sec. 1983—). Current work: Applied analysis, partial differential equations, continuum mechanics. Subspecialties: Applied mathematics; Theoretical and applied mechanics. Office: Box F Brown U Providence RI 02912

DAFNY, NACHUM FRENKEL, neuroscientist, educator; b. Tel Aviv, Mar. 5, 1934; came to U.S., 1969, naturalized, 1974; s. Nathan and Zelda Frenkel; m. Dita Mirkin Dafny, June 15, 1969; children: Galit, Leemore, Hadar. B.Sc., Hebrew U., Jerusalem, 1964, M.Sc., 1965, Ph.D., 1968. Fellow Calif. Inst. Tech., Pasadena, 1969, Brain Research Inst., UCLA, 1970, Coll. Physicians and Surgeons, Columbia U., N.Y.C., 1971-72; prof. neurobiology and anatomy U. Tex. Med. Sch., Houston, 1972—. Contbr. over 100 articles to sci. publs. Mem. Soc. for Neurosci., Am. Physiol. Soc., Am. Soc. Pharmacology and Exptl. Therapeutics, Am. Assn. Anatomy, Internat. Neuroendocrinology Soc. Current Work: Neurophysiology, neuropharmacology and neuroendocrinology of drug addiction, pain and peptides. Subspecialties: Neurobiology; Neuroimmunology. Office: Dept Neurobiology and Anatomy U Tex Medical School Houston TX 77030

DAHL, J(OHN) ROBERT, radiochemist, consultant; b. Jacksonville, Dec. 13, 1934; s. John Edgar and Frances Louise (Marjenhoff) D.; m. Loretta M. VanDeMark, Aug. 25, 1962 (div. Jan. 1977); children—John Joseph, Ingrid Kirsten, John Eric; m. Janice Eloise Aber, Jan. 1, 1978. B.A. in Chemistry, Marist Coll. 1968; M.S. in Chem. Physics, Poly. Inst. N.Y., 1983. Prodn. mgr. Medi-Physics Inc., Emeryville, Calif., 1971-73; research radiochemist Biophysics Lab. Sloan Kettering Inst., N.Y.C., 1973—; cons. in field. Contbr. chpts. to books and articles to profl. jours. Served with USAF, 1954-58. Mem. AAAS, Am. Chem. Soc., N.Y. Acad. Sci., Internat. Nuclear Target Devel. Soc., Am. Nuclear Soc. Current work: Application of cyclotron-produced radioisotopes to medical diagnosis and positron emission tomography. Subspecialties: Nuclear chemistry; Medical physics. Home: 234 Mountain Rd Pleasantville NY 10021 Office: Biophysics Lab Sloan Kettering Inst 1275 York Ave New York NY 10021

DAHLBERG, JAMES ERIC, physiological chemistry educator; b. Chgo., May 30, 1940; m. Elsebet Lund, Jan. 6, 1978; children—Caroline, Maria. B.A., Haverford Coll., 1962; Ph.D., U. Chgo., 1966. Postdoctoral fellow Med. Research Council Lab. Molecular Biology, Cambridge, Eng., 1966-68; postdoctorial fellow U. Geneva, 1968-69; prof. U. Wis.-Madison, 1969—; cons. Cambridge Bioscience Corp., Hopkinton, Mass., 1981—; cons. Agracetus Corp., Middleton, Wis., 1984—. Josiah Macy Found. fellow, 1979; recipient Eli Lilly award Am. Chem. Soc., 1974. Fellow AAAS; mem. Am. Soc. Biol. Chemistry, Am. Soc. Microbiologists, Am. Chem. Soc. Current work: Synthesis and function small nuclear RNAs; RNA processing; control gene expression. Subspecialties: Genetics and genetic engineering (medicine); Molecular biology. Home: 1119 Merrill Springs Rd Madison WI 53705 Office: 551 Med Sci Bldg U Wis 1300 University Ave Madison WI 53706

DAHLGRAN, JAMES ROBERT, research chemist; b. Nebraska City, Nebr., Dec. 4, 1950; s. Harold Robert and Mary Elizabeth (Henly) D.; m. Dava Lynne Rolf, Jan. 2, 1977; children—Christine Ann, Kelly Reid, Emily Elizabeth. B.S., Iowa Sate U., 1973. Forensic chemist Iowa Crime Lab, Des Moines, 1973-78; research chemist Finnigan Corp., Cin., 1978-79, Borg-Warner Chems., Washington, W. Va, 1983—; lab. mgr. O.H. Materials Co., Findlay, Ohio, 1979-83. Contbr. articles to profl. jours. Mem. Am. Chem. Soc., Am. Soc. Mass Spectroscopists, Assn. of Official Analytical Chemists. Methodists. Lodge: Masons. Current work: The use of gas chromatography and/or mass spectroscopy in new areas which have not been explored or are currently being developed. Subspecialty: Analytical chemistry. Office: Borg-Warner Chems Box 68 Washington WV 26181

DAHLSTEN, DONALD LEE, entomologist, educator; b. Clay Ctr., Nebr., Dec. 8, 1933; s. Leonard Harold and Shirley B. (Courtwright) D.; m. Reva D. Wilson, Sept. 19, 1959; children—Dia Lee, Andrea; Janet Clair Winner, Aug. 7, 1965; stepchildren—Karen Rae, Michael Allen. B.S., U. Calif.-Davis, 1956, M.S., U. Calif.-Berkeley, 1960, Ph.D., 1962. Asst. prof. Los Angeles State Coll., 1962-63; asst. entomologist U. Calif., Berkeley, 1963-65, lectr., 1965-68, asst. then assoc. prof. 1968-74; prof., 1974—, chmn. div. Biol. Control, 1980—; Mellon vis. lectr. Yale U., New Haven, 1980; vis. prof. Am. Inst. Biol. Scis., 1970-71, 71-72. Editor, Environment Mag., D.C., Vice chmn. Scientists Inst. Pub. Info., N.Y.C., 1974-79. Mem. AAAS, Ecol. Soc. Am., Entomological Soc. Am., Soc. Am. Foresters. Current work: Ecological pest management forest and urban tree insect pests; effect of human disruption on insects; role insectivoneous birds in forests. Subspecialties: Ecology (environmental science); Population biology. Office: Div Biol Control U Calif 1050 San Pablo Ave Albany CA 94706

DAHLSTROM, DONALD ALBERT, research educator; b. Mpls., Jan. 16, 1920; s. Raymond Estin and Dora Adina (Bloomgren) D.; m. Betty Cordelia Robertson, Dec. 4, 1942; children: Mary Elizabeth, Donald Raymond, Christine Dora, Stephanie Lou, Michael Jeffrey. Student, Macalester Coll., 1937-39; B.S. in Chem. Engring, U. Minn., 1942; Ph.D., Northwestern U., 1949. Petroleum engr. Internat. Petroleum Co., Ltd., Negritos, Peru, 1942-45; from instr. to asso. prof. chem. engring. Northwestern U., 1946-56; with Eimco Corp., Palatine, Ill., 1952-69, v.p., dir. research and devel., 1960-75, also dir.; v.p. research and devel. Envirotech Corp., Salt Lake City, 1969-81; v.p., dir. Erco-Environtech, 1974-81; sr. v.p. research and devel. Eimco Process Equipment Co., 1981-84; dir. Process Engrs., Inc.; Am. mem. internat. sci. com. 6th Internat. Mineral Processing Congress, 1963; mem. adv. council on engring. NSF. Contbr. to handbooks. Mem. State Air Conservation Com. State Utah, 1971-78, vice chmn., 1977-78, Mem. sch. bd. dist. 110, Deerfield, Ill., 1959-61; pres. Riverwoods Residents Assn., 1962-63; chmn. bd. Northwestern YMCA, 1950-52; trustee Village of Riverwoods, 1966-69. Served with USNR, 1945-46. Recipient Merit award Northwestern U., 1965. Mem. Am. Inst. Chem. Engrs. (dir. 1960-62, v.p. 1963, pres. 1964-65, chmn. environ. div. 1971, Founders award 1972, Environ. award 1977, named 1 of 30 eminent chem. engrs. 1983), Am. Inst. Mining, Metall. and Petroleum Engrs. (chmn. minerals benefication div. 1963-64, bd. dirs. soc. mining engrs. 1965-67, pres. soc. mining engrs. 1974-75, dir. 1973-75, Rossiter W. Raymond award 1952, Richards award 1976, Krumb lectr. 1980, Taggart award 1983), Am. Chem. Soc., Nat. Acad. Engring., Water Pollution Control Fedn., Canadian Inst. Mining and Metallurgy, The Filtration Soc. (London), Mining and Metall. Soc. Am. (dir. Engrs. Council Profl. Devel.), Nat. Acad. Engrs., Sigma Xi (Holgate award Northwestern U. chpt. 1949), Phi Lambda Upsilon, Tau Beta Pi (nat. pres. 1958-62). Presbyterian. Current Work: Development of improved and new types of equipment and processes in liquid-solid separation and mineral processing. Subspecialties: Chemical engineering; Metallurgical engineering. Home: 5340 Cottonwood Ln Salt Lake City UT 84117 Office: U Utah Dept Chem Engring Salt Lake City UT 84112

DAHMS, ARTHUR STEPHEN, chemist, educator; b. Mankato, Minn., Sept. 12, 1943; s. Arthur Edwin and Janet Helen (Bassett) D.; m. Judith Claire Dahms, Dec. 31, 1966; children—Jacquelyne Kristin, Geoffrey Marc. B.S. in Chemistry, Coll. St. Thomas, 1965; Ph.D. in Biochemistry, Mich. State U., 1969. Chemist, Minn. Mining & Mfg., St. Paul, 1963-65; NIH predoctoral fellow Mich. State U., 1965-69; NSF and AEC postdoctoral fellow UCLA, 1969-72; asst. prof. San Diego State U., 1972-75, assoc. prof., 1975-79, prof. chemistry, 1979—, dir. Molecular Biology Inst., 1979—. Contbr. articles to profl. jours. Alexander von Humboldt sr. fellow, Munich, Fed. Republic Germany, 1979-80; NSF/NIH grantee, 1972—. Mem. Am. Soc. Biol. Chemists. Republican. Roman Catholic. Current work: Hormone regulation of membrane function; bioenergetics; membrane structure and function; phototoxicology. Subspecialties: Biochemistry (medicine); Molecular biology. Home: 5444 New Mills Rd San Diego CA 92182 Office: Dept Chemistry Molecular Biology Inst San Diego State Univ San Diego CA 92182-0328

DAI, HAI-LUNG, chemistry educator, researcher; b. Feb. 25, 1954; b. Taiwan, Republic of China; came to U.S., 1976; s. Chuang-Yen and Chung Hwa (Liu) D. BS., Nat. Taiwan U., 1974; Ph.D., U. Calif.-Berkeley, 1981. Postdoctoral fellow MIT, Cambridge, 1981-84; asst. prof. chemistry U. Pa., Phila., 1984—. Contbr. articles to profl. jours. Served to 2nd lt. Armed Services Taiwan, 1974-76. Predoctoral fellow U. Calif.-Berkeley, 1976-78; Camille and Henry Dreyfus new faculty award, 1985. Mem. Am. Physical Soc., Am. Chem. Soc. Current work: Laser spectroscopy and photochemistry of molecules in gas phase and on surfaces. Subspecialties: Physical chemistry; Laser-induced chemistry. Office: U Pa Dept Chemistry Philadelphia PA 19104

DAILY, FAY KENOYER, research botanist; b. Indpls., Feb. 17, 1911; d. Fredrick and Camellia Thea (Neal) Kenoyer; m. William A. Daily, June 24, 1937. A.B., Butler U., 1935, M.S., 1952. Lab. technician Eli Lilly & Co., Indpls., 1935-37, Abbott Labs., North Chicago, Ill., 1939, William S. Merrell Co., Reading, Ohio, 1940-41; lubrication chemist Indpls. propellor plant Curtiss Wright Corp., 1945; lectr. botany Butler U., Indpls., 1947-49, instr. immunology and microbiology, 1957-58, lectr. microbiology, 1962-63, mem. herbarium staff, 1949—. Contbr. articles to profl. jours. Ind. Acad. Sci. grantee. Mem. Am. Inst. Biol. Sci., Phycol. Soc. Am., Bot. Soc. Am., Internat. Phycol. Soc., Ind. Acad. Sci., Torrey Bot. Club, Sigma Xi, Phi Kappa Phi, Sigma Delta Epsilon. Methodist. Patentee in field. Current Work: Charophytes, extant and fossil research. Subspecialties: Morphology; Taxonomy. Home: 5884 Compton St Indianapolis IN 46220

DAILY, JAMES WALLACE, engineering educator, consultant; b. Columbia, Mo., Mar. 19, 1913; s. Wallace Edgar and Marjory Isabel (McGrath) D.; m. Sarah Vanderlip Atwood, Sept. 10, 1938; children: John Wallace, Sarah Anne Vanderlip (Mrs. Charles Rosenberg). A.B., Stanford U., 1935; M.S., Calif. Inst. Tech., 1937, Ph.D., 1945. Registered profl. engr. Test engr. Byron Jackson Co., Berkeley, Calif., 1935; research asst. hydraulics Calif. Inst. Tech., 1936-37, research fellow, mgr. hydraulic machinery lab., 1937-40, instr. mech. engring., 1940-46; hydraulic engr. OSRD, Navy Research Projects, 1941-46; asst. prof. hydraulics M.I.T., 1946-49, asso. prof., 1949-55, prof., 1955-64; prof. engring. mechanics, chmn. dept. U. Mich., 1964-72, prof. fluid mechanics and hydraulic engring., 1972-81, prof. emeritus, 1981—; vis. prof. Tech. U. of Delft, Netherlands, 1971; vis. scientist Electricite de France Centre de Recherches et d'Essais, Paris, 1971; mem. U.S. del. water resources specialists to, People's Republic of China, 1974; vis. prof. East China Coll. Hydraulic Engring., Nanking, 1979; domestic and internat. cons. various firms. Author: (with D.R.F. Harleman) Fluid Dynamics, (with R.T. Knapp and F.G. Hammitt) Cavitation; Contbr. tech. articles Am., fgn. jours. Mem. sch. com. Town of Arlington, Mass., 1959-65. Recipient Naval Ordnance Devel. award, 1945. Mem. Nat. Acad. Engring., Internat. Assn. Hydraulic Research (hon. mem., pres. 1967-71, mem. Council 1963-65, 71-77), ASCE, ASME (hon.), Japan Soc. C.E. (hon.), Internat. House of Japan, Sigma Xi, Tau Beta Pi, Chi Epsilon. Congregationalist. Club: Cosmos (Washington). Current Work: Hydraulic engineering: pumps and turbines. Subspecialties: Mechanical engineering; Fluid mechanics. Home: 2968 San Pasqual St Pasadena CA 91107

DAI-SHU-HO, chemical machinery educator; b. Beijing, China, May 16, 1923; s. Ming-Zheng Dai and Wei-Xin Xu; m. Jia-Zhen Chu, Oct., 1947; children: Dai, Qi. B.S., Nat. Central U., Chungking, China, 1946. Mem. faculty Nat. Central U., Nanjing, China, 1947-49, U. Nanjing, 1950-52; lectr. Nanjing Inst. Tech., 1953-58; sr. lectr. Nanjing Inst. Chem. Tech., 1959-77, prof. chem. machinery, 1978—, vice chmn. dept. chem. machinery, 1958-77, chmn. dept., 1978—; cons. Xerox Co., Rochester, N.Y., 1981-82; vis. prof. U. Rochester, 1980-82. Author: (with others) Silicate Industrial Equipment, 1958, Cement Product Euipment, 1959, Process Equipment Design, 1961,65, 80. Mem. Chinese Soc. Chem. Engring. (councilor 1978—), Chinese Soc. Chem. Machinery (councilor 1979—), Jiangsu Province Br. Chinese Soc. Chem. engring. (councilor 1978—), Am. Soc. Engring. sci. Current Work: Research on dynamics generation of dislocations from a crack tip and on reliability of process equipment. Subspecialties: Materials (engineering); Mechanical engineering. Office: Nanjing Inst Chem Tech 5 New Model Rd Nanjing 210009 People's Republic of China

DAKSS, MARK LUDMER, applied physicist; b. N.Y.C., Mar. 1, 1940; s. Joseph Walter and Rose (Ludmer) D.; m. Sheryl Judith (Cooper), Nov. 4, 1973; children: Jonathan, Alison. B.E.E., Cooper Union, N.Y.C., 1960; A.M. in Physics, Columbia U., 1962, Ph.D. in Physics, 1966. Research asst. Columbia U., N.Y.C., 1962-66; research staff mem. IBM Research Ctr., Yorktown Heights, N.Y., 1966-71; mem. tech. staff GTE Labs., Inc., Waltham, Mass., 1971—; lectr. State-of-the-Arts engring. program Northeastern U., Boston, 1974—. Contbr. articles to profl. jours. Eugene Higgins fellow, 1966-67; Columbia U. Pres. fellow, 1968-69, 70-71; Raytheon fellow, 1969-70. Mem. Optical Soc. Am., IEEE Quantum Electronics and Applications Soc. Patentee in field. Current Work: Raman light amplification in fibers. Subspecialty: Fiber optics. Office: 40 Sylvan Rd Waltham MA 02254

DALBEC, PAUL EUCLIDE, physics educator, researcher; b. New Bedford, Mass., June 26, 1935; s. Euclide and Alice Marie (Sicard) D.; m. Rosa Dolores Schwaiger, Dec. 28, 1963; 1 son, John Paul. B.S. in Physics, Boston Coll., 1957; M.S., U. Notre Dame, 1959; Ph.D., Georgetown U., 1966. Physicist, Melpar, Inc., Falls Church, Va., 1959-60; head thin films Gen. Instrument Co., Newark, 1960-61; asst. prof. Am. U., Washington, 1966-68; asst. prof. physics Youngstown State U. (Ohio), 1968-71, assoc. prof., 1971-78, prof., 1978—. Contbr. articles to physics jours. Chmn. troop com. Boy Scouts Am., Youngstown, 1983—. Fellow: NASA, 1964-66, Georgetown U., 1961-64, U. Notre Dame, 1957-59. Mem. ASTM, Am. Vacuum Soc., Am. Phys. Soc., Am. Assn. Physics Tchrs., Ohio Ednl. Assn. (exec. com. 1980—). Clubs: Alliance Franco-Am. du Midwest (bd. dirs. 1984—), LeCercle Francais (pres. 1984—) (Youngstown). Current work: Electron spectroscopy, electronic properties of semiconductor and metallic thin films, vacuum ultraviolet spectroscopy. Subspecialties: Condensed matter physics; Electronic materials. Home: 1984 Innwood Dr Youngstown OH 44515 Office: Youngstown State U 410 Wick Ave Youngstown OH 44555

DALBY, (JOHN) THOMAS, psychologist; b. Oshawa, Ont., Can., Feb. 25, 1953; s. John Thomas and Marion Cecelia (Kinlin) D.; m. Deborah Lynn Dutton, Nov. 19, 1971; children: Krista Faith, Meagan Carmel, Brittany Nicole. B.A. with honors, York U., 1975; M.A., U. Guelph, 1976; Ph.D., U. Calgary, 1979. Diplomate: Am. Acad. Behavioral Medicine, Am. Bd. Profl. Neuropsychology, Nat. Register of Health Service Providers in Psychology.; Cert. psychologist, Alta. Fellow Hosp. for Sick Children, Toronto, Ont., Can., 1976-77; research assoc. U. Calgary (Alta., Can.) Med. Sch., 1979-82, asst. clin. prof. psychiatry, lectr. psychology, 1984—; clin. psychologist Calgary Gen. Hosp., 1982—; research coordinator, neurology Alta. Children's Hosp., Calgary, 1979-82. Contbg. editor: Alberta Psychology, 1981-82; cons. editor: Jour. Pediatric Psychology, 1979; author: Introduction to Learning Disabilities: Student Handbook, 1983; contbr. articles to profl. publs. in field. Bd. Assn. for Children with Learning Disabilities, 1978. Can. Council doctoral fellow Calgary, 1978; Social Scis. and Humanities Research Council Can. doctoral fellow Calgary, 1979. Mem. Am. Psychol. Assn., N.Y. Acad. Scis., Can. Psychol. Assn., Psychologist's Assn. Alta., Nat. Acad. Neuropsychologists. Roman Catholic. Current work: Brain dysfunction in children and adults, forensic psychology, behavioral medicine, learning disorders. Subspecialties: Neuropsychology; Behavioral psychology. Home: 4 Varshaven Pl NW Calgary AB T3A 0E1 Canada Office: Calgary Gen Hosp 841 Centre Ave E Calgary AB T2E 0A1 Canada

DALEY, MICHAEL LEO, biomedical engineer, educator; b. Brighton, Mass., May 16, 1942; s. James Joseph Daley and Agnes Elizabeth (Hallasey) Walton; m. Carol Donna Place, Dec. 28, 1968; 1 child, Leah Diana. B.S. in Elec. Engring., U. Mass., 1968; M.S. in Elec. Engring., U. Rochester, 1970, Ph.D., 1973. Registered profl. engr., Oreg. Dept. fellow, instr. U. Rochester, N.Y., 1970-72; postdoctoral fellow Good Samaritan Hosp., Portland, Oreg., 1973; research assoc., instr., asst. prof. Oreg. Health Sci. U., Portland, 1974-84, asst. prof., 1984—. Contbr. articles to profl. jours. Patentee method and apparatus for testing flicker fusion frequency. Mem. Community Planning Orgn., Cedar Hill, Cedar Mill, Oreg., 1981-84. Served with USAF, 1960-64. Mem. IEEE (sec. Portland soc. Engring. Biology and Medicine, 1983-84, v.p., 1984-85), British Photobiology Soc., Tau Beta Pi, Eta Kappa Nu. Republican. Roman Catholic. Subspecialties: Biomedical engineering; Electrical engineering. Home: 9345 SW Westhaven Dr Portland OR 97225 Office: Oreg Health Sci U Engr Lab L-350 SW Sam Jackson Park Rd Portland OR 97201

DALGARNO, ALEXANDER, astronomy educator; b. London, Eng., Jan. 5, 1928; s. William and Margaret (Murray) D.; m. Barbara W.F. Kane, Oct. 31, 1957 (div.); children: Penelope, Rebecca, Piers, Fergus; m. Emily K. Izsak, June 23, 1972. B.Sc., U. London, 1947, Ph.D., 1951; M.A. (hon.), Harvard U., 1967; D.Sc. (hon.), Queen's U. Belfast, 1980. Lectr., Queen's U., Belfast, No. Ireland, 1951-56, reader, 1956-61, prof. math. physics, 1961-67, dir. computation lab., 1961-66; prof. astronomy Harvard U., 1967—, Phillips prof., 1977—, chmn. dept., 1971-76; asso. dir. Center for Astrophysics Harvard U., 1973-80; acting dir. Harvard Coll. Obs., 1971-73; research scientist Smithsonian Astrophys. Obs., Cambridge, Mass., 1967—. Editor: Astrophys. Jour. Letters, 1973—; contbr. articles to profl. jours. Recipient Hodgkins medal Smithsonian Instn., 1977. Fellow Royal Soc., Phys. Soc. (London), Am. Phys. Soc. (Davisson-Germer award 1980), Am. Geophys. Union; mem. Am. Acad. Arts and Scis., Royal Astron. Soc., Internat. Acad. Astronautics (corr. mem.). Current Work: Study of atomic and molecular phenomena in astrophysical, atmospheric and laboratory plasmas. Subspecialties: Theoretical astrophysics; Metallurgical engineering. Home: 27 Robinson St Cambridge MA 02138

DALLA-FAVERA, RICCARDO, medical scientist; b. Legnano, Italy, Dec. 30, 1951; came to U.S., 1978; s. Luciano and Leda (Perissinotto) Dalla-F. M.D., U. Milan, Italy, 1976. Cert. Italian Bd. Hematology. Vis. fellow Nat. Cancer Inst., Bethesda, Md., 1978-81, vis. assoc., 1981-82; asst. prof. pathology, assoc. mem. Kaplan Cancer Ctr., NYU Sch. Medicine, N.Y.C., 1982—. Contbr. articles to profl. jours. Leukemia Soc. Am. spl. fellow, 1982—. Mem. N.Y. Acad. Scis., AAAS, Am. Assn. Microbiology. Current Work: Cancer research, cancer genetics, oncogenes and leukemia. Subspecialties: Cancer research (medicine); Hematology. Home: 300 E 33d St Apt 18D New York NY 10016 Office: Dept Pathology NYU Med Ctr 550 1st Ave New York NY 10016

DALLMAN, JOHN CLAY, research engineer; b. Chgo., Oct. 19, 1947; s. Herman H. and Marie Barbara (Westermeir) D.; m. Patricia Roberts, Apr. 10, 1976; 1 child, Alexis Rae. B.S. in Math. and Physics, St. Procopius Coll., Lisle, Ill., 1965-69; M.S. in Nuclear Engring, U. Ill., 1972-72; Ph.D. in Nuclear Engring, 1978. Nuclear steam supply engr. Combustion Engring., Inc., Windsor, Conn., 1972-73; mem. staff Los Alamos Nat. Lab., N.Mex., 1978—. Author: Investigation of Separated Flow Model, 1979. Pres., bd. dirs. Los Alamos YMCA, 1982-83. Mem. Soc. Physics Students, Am. Phys. Soc., AAAS, Sigma Pi Sigma. Inventor application of ultrasonics to measurement of flowing liquid films. Current Work: Application of Spectroscopic techniques to reaction Kinetics in shocked media; detonation physics. Subspecialties: Fluid mechanics; Laser spectroscopy. Office: Los Alamos Nat Lab Box 1663 Los Alamos NM 87545

DALLOS, PETER, neurobiology educator; b. Budapest, Hungary, Nov. 26, 1934; came to U.S., 1956, naturalized, 1962; s. Ernest and Maria (Klein) D.; m. Joan Usis, Aug. 18, 1977; 1 child, Christopher. Student Tech. U., Budapest, 1953-56; B.S., Ill. Inst. Tech., 1958; M.S., Northwestern U., 1959, Ph.D., 1962. From asst. to assoc. prof. audiology and elect. engring. Northwestern U., Evanston, Ill., 1962-69, prof., 1969—, founding chmn. neurobiology and physiology, 1980-84, prof., 1980—, assoc. dean Coll. Arts and Scis., 1984-85; mem. nat. adv. council Neurol. and Communicative Disorders and Stroke Council, NIH, Bethesda, Md., 1983—. Author: The Auditory Periphery, 1973. Mem. editorial bd. Hearing Research, 1981—. Contbr. numerous articles to profl. jours. Assoc. editor: Jour. Nurosci., 1985—. Recipient Beltone award Beltone Inst., 1977, Jacob Javits Neurosci. award NIH, 1984—, Amplifon Internat. prize, 1984; Guggenheim fellow, 1977-78. Fellow Acoustical Soc. Am., IEEE; mem. Soc. Neurosci., Internat. Audiology Soc. (exec. com. 1974-81), Am. Speech, Hearing and Lang. Assn. Current work: Neurobiology of hearing, specifically the physiology and biophysics of the mammalian cochlea. Subspecialty: Comparative neurobiology. Office: Northwestern Univ Frances Searle Bldg 2299 Sheridan Rd Evanston IL 60201

DALVI, RAMESH R., toxicologist, educator, consultant; b. Bombay, India, Nov. 8, 1938; s. Rajaram S. and Sumitra R. (Sawant) D.; m. Rekha B. Jadhav, Jan. 22, 1969; children: Rajan, Samir. B.Sc. with honors, U. Bombay, 1962, B.Sc.Tech., 1964, M.Sc., 1967; Ph.D., Utah State U., Logan, 1972. Diplomate Am. Bd. Toxicology. Research fellow Univ. Grants Commn., New Delhi,

1964-67; biochemist Hindustan Lever, Ltd., Bombay, 1967; sci. research officer Bhabha Atomic Research Ctr., Bombay, 1967-69; grad- research fellow Utah State U., 1969-72; postdoctoral fellow Vanderbilt U., Nashville, 1972-74; asst. prof. to prof. toxicology Tuskegee U., Ala., 1974—; cons. Nat. Acad. Scis. Editorial bd., internat. adv. bd.: Tropical Veterinarian, 1982—; contbr. articles to profl. jours., chpt. in book. Recipient award So. Regional Edn. Bd., 1975, numerous research grants, 1975—. Mem. Soc. Toxicology, Am. Coll. Vet. Toxicologists, Am. Chem. Soc., Am. Soc. Vet. Physiol. Pharmacology, AAAS, Inst. Food Tech., Internat. Soc. Study of Xenobiotics, Am. Assn. Vet. Med. Colls., Pharm. Soc. Japan, Sigma Xi. Current Work: Analytical and diagnostic toxicologic service to veterinarians, toxicologic research, especially cytochrome P-450 mediated metabolism of toxic substances. Subspecialties: Toxicology (medicine); Environmental toxicology. Home: 1243 Ferndale Dr Auburn AL 36830 Office: School of Vet Medicine Tuskegee U Tuskegee AL 36088

DALY, FRANCIS PATRICK, chemist; b. Providence, Apr. 7, 1946; s. Francis Patrick and Mary (Wallis) D.; m. Barbara Elizabeth Hunt, July 5, 1975; children—Nathan Hunt, Caitlin Hunt. B.S., Lowell Tech. Inst., 1968; Ph.D., U. R.I., 1975. Research chemist Hydrocarbon Research, Inc., Lawrenceville, N.J., 1976-79; group leader Air Products & Chems., Marcus Hook, Pa., 1979-82; prin. research chemist Am. Cyanamid Co., Stamford, Conn., 1982—. Contbr. articles to profl. jours. Patentee in field. Served with U.S. Army, 1970-72. Gold medalist Am. Inst. Chemists, 1968; NDEA fellow, 1972-74; U.S. Dept. Energy postdoctoral research assoc., 1975. Mem. The Catalysis Soc., Am. Chem. Soc., Am. Inst. Chem. Engrs. Roman Catholic. Current work: Preparation, characterization and evaluation of heterogeneous catalysists in areas relating to hydrotreating, oxidation and CO/H2 reactions. Subspecialties: Catalysis chemistry; Kinetics. Office: Am Cyanamid Co 1937 W Main St Stamford CT 06904

DALY, JOHN ANTHONY, research administrator; b. N.Y.C., Oct. 7, 1937; s. Anthony C. and Ethel E. (Braunton) D.; m. Patricia Ann Cross, Oct. 7, 1966; 1 son, John P. B.S., UCLA, 1959; M.S.E.E., U. Calif.-Berkeley, 1962; Ph.D., U. Calif.-Irvine, 1975. Vol. Peace Corps, Chile, 1965-67; sr. research engr. McDonnell Douglas Corp., Newport Beach, Calif., 1962-65, 68-70; dep. dir. research project WHO, Cali, Colombia, 1970-73; dir. health sector analysis Office Internat. Health, HEW, Rockville, Md., 1973-76; dir. sci. and tech. policy AID, Washington, 1976-82, Nat. Acad. Scis. program coordinator, office sci. adv., 1982—; tutor U. Md., 1982—; adj. prof. U. Valle, Cali, Colombia, 1971-73; instr. U. Calif.-Irvine, 1968; cons. Ford Found., 1967. Coordinator: book series Syncrisis: The Dynamics of Health, 1974-76. Mem. AAAS, Am. Pub. Health Assn., Ops. Research Soc. Am., Inst. Mgmt. Sci., Tau Beta Pi, Phi Eta Sigma. Democrat. Current Work: Manage international, small-grants, innovative-research program stressing underutilized technologies of potential economic value. Subspecialties: Operations research (mathematics); Artificial intelligence. Home: 14205 Bauer Dr Rockville MD 20853 Office: AID Washington DC 20523

D'AMBROSIO, STEVEN MARIO, pharmacologist, educator, researcher; b. Phila., May 7, 1949; s. Mario and Louise (Cerino) D'A.; m. Ruth Elaine Gibson, Mar. 21, 1981. B.S., St. Joseph's U., Phila., 1971; Ph.D., Tex. A&M U., 1975. Research assoc. Brookhaven Nat. Lab., Upton, N.Y., 1975-78; asst. prof. Ohio State U., Columbus, 1978-81, assoc. prof. depts. radiology and pharmacology, 1981-85, prof., 1985—, dir. div. radiobiology, dept. radiology, 1980—; cons. in field. Contbr. articles to profl. jours. EPA and NIH grantee, 1978—. Mem. AAAS, Am. Soc. Photobiology, Am. Soc. Pharmacology and Exptl. Therapeutics, Ohio Fedn. Aging Research, Am. Assn. Cancer Research, N.Y. Acad. Scis. Current Work: DNA damage, repair and replication as related to cancer, aging and degenerative disease process. Molecular mechnanisms and ways to alter these processes through molecular biology and genetic enegineering. Subspecialties: Toxicology (medicine); Genetics and genetic engineering (medicine). Office: Div Radiobiology 450 W 10th Ave Columbus OH 43210

DAMIANOV, VLADIMIR BLAGOI, mechanical engineer, researcher; b. Sofia, Bulgaria, Sept. 19, 1938; came to U.S., 1971, naturalized, 1976; s. Blagoi Petrov and Bona Krasteva D.; m. Millie Melanoff, Sept. 16, 1972; 1 son: William. B.S., U. Sofia, Bulgaria, 1961, M.S., 1967. Dept. mgr. research and devel. dept. Ctr. Lift Trucks, Sofia, Bulgaria, 1961-70; project engr. Modern Tool & Die Products Inc., Cleve., 1972-74; chief engr., prodn. mgr. Canton Stoker Corp., Canton, Ohio, 1974-77; sr. project engr. McNeil Akron Inc., Akron, Ohio, 1977-81; sr. devel. engr. Goodyear Aerospace Corp., Akron, Ohio, 1981—. Mem. ASME, ASTM. Eastern Orthodox. Clubs: Businessmen (v.p. 1980, 81), Fort Island Swim (bd. dirs. 1980-82). Patentee field lift trucks. Current Work: Mechanical engineering; gas centrifugeuranium enrichment. Subspecialties: Mechanical engineering; Fluid mechanics. Home: 3021 Morewood Rd Fairlawn OH 44313

DAMJANOV, IVAN, pathologist, educator; b. Subotica, Yugoslavia, Mar. 31, 1941; s. Milenko and Ana (Pavkovic) D.; m. Andrea Zivanovic, 1964; children: Nevena, Ivana, Milena. M.D., U. Zagreb, Yugoslavia, 1964, Ph.D., 1970. Asst. in pathology U. Zagreb, 1969-73; asst. prof. U. Conn., 1973-77; prof. pathology Hahnemann U. Sch. Medicine, Phila., 1977—. Contbr. articles to profl. jours. Mem. Am. Assn. Pathologists, Am. Assn. Cancer Research. Current Work: Experimental pathology; developmental biology; teratology. Subspecialties: Pathology (medicine); Teratology.

DAMON, RICHARD WINSLOW, physicist; b. Concord, Mass., May 14, 1923; s. Winslow Johnson and Florence Mabel (Smith) D.; m. Anna Trotter, Aug. 4, 1946; children—Laura, Louise, Paul Trotter. B.S. cum laude, Harvard U., 1944, M.A., 1947, Ph.D., 1952. Engr., Raytheon Co., Waltham, Mass., 1948-49; research assoc. Gen. Electric Co., Schenectady, N.Y., 1951-60; dept. head Microwave Assocs., Burlington, Mass., 1960-62; dir. applied physics Sperry Research Ctr., Sudbury, Mass., 1962-83; dir. tech. Sperry Corp., Waltham, Mass., 1983—; dir. Matec Corp.; trustee United Engring.; mem. various adv. coms. NASA, Nat. Bur. Standards, Dept. Def., 1964-80. Mem. Marconi Internat. Fellowship Selection Com., N.Y.C., 1984—; Trustee, West Concord Union Ch., 1964-67; mem. Spl. Sch. Salary Practices Com., 1965, Comprehensive Town Plans Com., 1968-70. Patentee in field; contbr. articles to profl. jours. Served to lt. (j.g.) USNR, 1943-46. Recipient Appreciation cert. Dept. Def., 1980. Fellow IEEE, (internat. pres. 1981, internat. bd. dirs. 1977-78, 81-83) Am. Phys. Soc., AAAS; mem. Internat. Union Radio Scis. (U.S. com.), Sigma Xi. Republican. Lodges: Corinthian, Masons. Current work: Corporate long range, technical program planning; special interests in materials, electronic devices, optics and electromagnetics. Subspecialty: Electronics. Home: 1623 Main St Concord MA 01742 Office: Sperry Corp 1601 Trapelo Rd Waltham MA 02154

DANAHER, BRIAN GRAYSON, health behavior change consultant, media education specialist; b. Atlanta, June 16, 1949; s. Eugene Ignacious and Betty LaVerne (Kefauver) D.; m. Kathleen Ellen Horrall, Sept. 8, 1973. B.A., Stanford U., 1971; M.S., U. Oreg., 1974, Ph.D., 1976. Postdoctoral researcher Stanford U., 1976-78; asst. prof. UCLA, 1978-80; pres. B.G. Danaher & Assocs., Inc., Pasadena, Calif., 1980—; cons. U.S. Army Med. Corps, Ft. Sam Houston, Tex., 1982—; mgr. Am. Healthway Systems, Inc., Menlo Park, Calif., 1985—. Author: Become an Ex-Smoker, 1978; contbr. articles profl. jours. Fellow Am. Heart Assn. Council on Epidemiology; mem. Am. Psychol. Assn., Assn. Advancement Behavior Therapy, Am. Pub. Health Assn., Phi Beta Kappa. Current Work: Search for cost-effective delivery systems for health behavior change technology including mass media (television), self-help methods and computer-based and managed instructional approaches. Subspecialties: Behavioral psychology; Computer-based instruction. Home and office: 159 Glen Summer Rd Pasadena CA 91105

DANBY, J(OHN) M(ICHAEL) ANTHONY, mathematics educator; b. London, Aug. 5, 1929; came to U.S., 1957; m. Phyllis Creighton, 1958; children—Colin, Arthur, Michael, Dinah, Winifred. B.A., Oxford U., 1950, M.A., 1954; Ph.D., U. Manchester, 1953. Prin. oboist London Philharm. Orch., 1956-57; asst. prof. astronomy U., Minn., Mpls., 1957-61; assoc. prof. astronomy Yale U., New Haven, 1961-67; prof. math and physics N.C. State U., Raleigh, 1967—. Mem. edit. com. Celestial Mechanics, 1970-72, 75-78; author: Fundamentals of Celestial Mechanics, 1962; Qualitative Methods in Celestial Mechanics, 1971; Computing Applications to Differential Equations, 1985; contbr. articles to profl. jours. Pres., Wake County chpt. N.C. Symphony, 1973-75. Mem. Internat. Astronom. Union, Am. Astronom. Assn. (chmn. div. dynamical astronomy 1978-79), Celestial Mechanics Inst. (pres. 1975—). Current work: numerical methods; celestial mechanics. Subspecialty: Astronautics. Office: Dept Math NC State U Raleigh NC 27607

DANCIK, BRUCE PAUL, forest geneticist; b. Chgo., Dec. 27, 1943; s. Charles John and Sophie Marie (Zaleske) D.; m. Deborah Bloomfield, Mar. 5, 1947. B.S., U. Mich., 1965, M.F., 1967, Ph.D., 1972. Asst. prof. Saginaw (Mich.) Valley Coll., 1972-73; asst. prof. U. Alta., Edmonton, Can., 1973-77, assoc. prof., 1977-84, prof., 1984—; chmn. Forestry panel Environ. Council of Alta., 1977-81. Editor: Canadian Jour. Forest Research, 1981—; assoc. editor: Forestry Chronicle, 1976-83; Contbr. articles to profl. jours. Recipient Forestry Achievement award Canadian Inst. Forestry, 1979. Mem. Canadian Inst. Forestry, Soc. Am. Foresters. Club: Flyfishers. Current Work: Population genetics, differentiation, molecular genetics, evolution of trees. Subspecialties: Plant genetics; Evolutionary biology. Office: Dept Forest Sci Univ Alta Edmonton AB T6G 2G6 Canada

DANDAPANI, BALA SUBRAMANIAM, researcher, consultant; b. Madras, Tamilnadu, India, Nov. 28, 1936; came to U.S., 1983; s. Pasupathy and Swarnambal (Muthuswamy) Balasubramaniam; m. Vijayalakshmi Ramchandran, Aug. 27, 1972. B.Sc., St. Joseph's Coll., Tiruchirapalli, India, 1957; M.Sc., Banararas Hindu U., Varanasi, India, 1966; Ph.D., Southampton U., Eng., 1969. Researcher, Electrochem. Research Inst., Karaikudi, India, 1960-69, U. Ottawa, Ont., Can., 1970-74, Meml. U., St. John's, Nfld., Can., 1974-77; sr. research assoc. Laval U., Que., Can., 1977-81, cons., 1981—; research chemist Ballard Research Inc., North Vancouver, B.C., Can., 1981-83; research scientist Tex. A&M U., College Station, 1983—. Contbr. chpts. to books and articles to profl. jours. Patentee in field. Mem. Electrochem. Soc., Metall. Soc., Nat. Assn. Corrosion Engrs., Am. Chem. Soc., Can. Chem. Engring. Inst. Current work: Production of hydrogen from non-fossil sources in industrial quantities and from pollutants like hydrogen sulphide. Subspecialties: Corrosion; Materials. Home: 2808 700 Dominik Dr College Station TX 77840 Office: Hydrogen Research Ctr Dept Chemistry Texas A&M U College Station TX 77843

DANDO, WILLIAM ARTHUR, educator; b. Newell, Pa., June 13, 1934; s. Carl Frederick and Myrtle Jane (Foster) D.; m. Caroline Zaporowsky, July 19, 1958; children: Christina Elizabeth, Lara Margaret, William Arthur. B.S., Calif. State U., 1959; M.A., U. Minn., 1960, Ph.D., 1969. Vis. instr. U. Man. (Can.), Winnipeg, summer 1961; instr. to asst. prof. U. Md., College Park, 1965-75; asso. prof. to prof. U. N.D., Grand Forks, 1975—, chmn. dept. geography, 1977-82; hon. prof. The Chinese U. of Hong Kong, 1981-82; dir. China Remote Sensing Project, 1980-84, Columbian Remote Sensing Project, 1980-84; dir. Am. Indians and the Natural Scis. project NSF, 1981-82, dir. Meteorology-Climatology project, 1985—; Seminaro Conjuncto CIAF and UNDIRS, 1981; dir. N.D. Drought Project, 1980-81, Cyclic Water Levels and Land Use Problems in the Devils Lake Basin project, 1977-78. Contbr. articles to profl. jours. Chmn. bd. Univ. Luth. Ch., 1979-80, Christus Rex Campus Ministry, 1974-81; v.p. N.D. Luth. Campus Ministry Assn., 1982-83, pres., 1983—. Served with USAF, 1954-56. United Bd. grantee Hong-Kong-Phillipines-China, 1981-82; Fulbright-Hays research fellow Romania, 1972-73; Tozer fellow, 1963; named Illustrious Alumni Calif. State U., 1976; Danforth Assos., 1970; Excellance in Teaching award U. Md., 1969. Mem. Assn. Am. Geographers (chmn. div. 1978-79), Nat. Council for Geog. Edn. (disting. teaching award 1984), Great Plains Rocky Mt. Div. Am. Assn. Geographers, N.D. Acad. Sci., Sigma Xi. Club: Jefferson-Lafayette Hunting. Lodge: Moose. Current Work: Agroclimatology, natural and cultural hazards, land use applications of modern tech. to studies of drought and famine; climate and food prodn.; remote sensing - computer applications to world food problems. Subspecialties: Climatology; Remote sensing (atmospheric science). Home: 2602 5th Ave N Grand Forks ND 58201 Office: Dept Geography Remote Sensing Univ ND Grand Forks ND 58202

DANES, ZDENKO FRANKENBERGER, physicist, educator, cons.; b. Prague, Czechoslovakia, Aug. 25, 1920; s. Zdenko and Eleonora (Rebensteiger von Blankenfeld) Frankenberger; m. Marie V. Hankova, Jan. 20, 1945; children: Peter, Ellen. Ph.D. in Math./Physics, Charles U., Prague, 1949. Designer Vilnes Electronics, Prague, 1942-45; with Czechoslovak Nat. Geophys. Servey, Prague, 1945-47; asst. prof. Charles U., 1948-50; geophysicist Gulf Research & Devel. Co., Pitts., 1952-59, Boeing Co., Seattle, 1959-62; prof. physics U. Puget Sound, Tacoma, 1962-84; pres. Danes Research Assocs., Tacoma, 1978—. Contbr. articles to sci. jours. Served in Czechoslovak Army, 1947-48. Mem. Am. Geophys. Union, Soc. Exploration Geophysicists, Czechoslovak Soc. Arts and Scis. in Am. Current Work: Gravimetric exploration. Subspecialties: Geophysics; Applied mathematics. Office: U Puget Sound Tacoma WA 98416

DANG, RICHARD KAOYU, scientist; b. Nanking, China, Aug. 6, 1948; came to U.S., 1972, naturalized, 1978; s. Peter H. C. and Ay-Fang (Huang) D. B.S., Chung-Yuan Coll., Taiwan, 1970; M.S., N.Y.U., 1974, Ph.D., 1979. Research asst. dept. physics N.Y.U., 1975-79; research assoc. Joint Inst. for Lab. Astrophysics, Boulder, Colo., 1979-81; project engr. EMR Photoelectric, Princeton, N.J., 1981—. Mem. Am. Phys. Soc. Current Work: Applied research and engineering ; computer computation and modeling; electron optics system design; laser and optics system. Subspecialty: Atomic and molecular physics. Home: 2-04 Fox Fun Dr Plainsboro NJ 08536 Office: PO Box 44 Princeton NJ 08540

DANIEL, ALEX VAN, electronics engineer; b. Marietta, Ga., Mar. 25, 1958; s. Thomas Jerrel and Ruby Wylene (Brown) D. B.E.E.T., So. Tech. Inst., Marietta, 1983. Quality control technician OECO Corp., Portland, Oreg., 1976; quality control insp. G.J. Aigner Co., Marietta, 1977-78; biomed. electronics technician Emory U. Hosp., Atlanta, 1981-82; field service engr. Life Services, Marietta, 1983—. Mem. Engring. in Medicine and Biology Soc. of IEEE, Oceanic Engring. Soc. of IEEE. Current work: Installation and service of biomedical instrumentation. Subspecialties: Biomedical engineering; Ocean engineering. Home: 1730 Cedar Grove Dr Marietta GA 30066

DANIEL, MICHAEL ANDREW, microbiologist, cons., researcher; b. Austin, Tex., Mar. 11, 1952; s. Wayne Alvin and Peggy Jane Daniel. B.S. in Microbiology and Psychology, Mich. State U., 1974; M.S. in Biology, Ill. Inst. Tech., 1980. Lab. dir. Windsor Med. Assocs. S.C., Riverside, Ill., 1975-77; supr. Baxter Travenol Labs., Round Lake, Ill., 1977-78, supt., 1978-80, systems analyst, Deerfield, Ill., 1980-82, program mgr., 1982; mgr. quality assurance Novacor Med. Corp., Oakland, Calif., 1982-84, program mgr., 1984—; cons. on fin. systems, microbiology and med. products. Contbr. articles to sci. jours. Mem. Am. Soc. for Quality Control (cert. quality engr.), Am. Soc. Microbiology, Am. Acad. Microbiology (registered microbiologist). Current Work: Behavorial teratology, gen. toxicology, immunochemistry, computer information systems, management information and analysis systems, inplantable medical device engineering, microbiology and good manufacturing practice consulting. Subspecialties: Artificial organs and prostheses; Teratology. Office: Novacor Med Corp 7799 Pardee Ln Oakland CA 94621

DANIEL, SAMUEL HENDERSON, III, utility company executive, chemist; b. Dublin, Tex., Jan. 7, 1945; s. Samuel Henderson and Bebe Joyce (Barnett) D.; m. Carol Lyn Wright, Dec. 28, 1982. B.S., Tarleton State U., 1967; Ph.D., Tex. A&M U., 1971. Mem. staff chemistry Va. Tech. Inst., Blacksburg, Va., 1971-73; mgr. tech. services Radiation Mgmt. Corp., Phila., 1973-76; mem. staff Scott & White Clinic, Temple, Tex., 1976-78; radiochemist, engr., chemist Tex. Utilities Generating Co., Glen Rose, Tex., 1978—. Contbr. papers to profl. lit. Stage mgr. Temple Civic Theater, 1978. Fellow Am. Inst. Chemists; mem. Am. Chem. Soc. (chmn. 1977-78), ASME (utility subcom. N.Y.C. 1981—), Soc. Nuclear Medicine, Health Physics Soc. (steering com. 1982—, pres. Northeast Tex. chpt. 1982-83), Nat. Assn. Corrosion Engrs., Am. Nuclear Soc. Current Work: Control of corrosion and minimization of radioactive contamination. Subspecialties: Nuclear power plant chemistry; Corrosion. Home: 1303 3d St Granbury TX 76048

DANIELLI, JAMES FREDERIC, scientist, educator, editor; b. Wembley, Eng., Nov. 13, 1911; s. James Frederic and Helena (Hollins) D.; m. Mary Guy, Jan. 4, 1937; children—Richard, Corinne. Ph.D., London (Eng.) U., 1933, Cambridge (Eng.) U., 1942; D.Sc., London U., 1938, Gent (Belgium) U., 1956, Med. Coll. Pa., 1970, Worcester Poly. Inst., 1972. Fellow Princeton, 1933-35, St. John's Coll., Cambridge (Eng.) U., 1942-45; physiologist Marine Biol. Assn., 1946; reader cell physiology Royal Cancer Hosp., 1946-49; prof. zoology, chmn. dept. King's Coll., London, Eng., 1949-61; prof. medicinal chemistry and biochem. pharmacology State U. N.Y. at, Buffalo, 1962-65, chmn. dept. biochem. pharmacology, 1962-65; prof. theoretical biology, dir. Center for Theoretical Biology, 1965-74, provost faculty natural sci. and math., 1967-69, asst. to pres., 1969-74; prof. Worcester (Mass.) Poly. Inst., 1974-80, emeritus prof., 1980—; vis. research prof. Salk Inst., 1973-75; cons. various indsl. firms, pubs., govt. orgns. Author: Permeability of Natural Membranes, 1942, Cell Physiology and Pharmacology, 1952, Cytochemistry, 1953; Editor: Symposia Soc. for Exptl. Biology, 1946-56, Symposia Internat. Soc. for Cell Biology, 1950-60, Internat. Rev. Cytology, 1951—, Jour. Theoretical Biology, 1960—, Gen. Cytochem. Methods, 1958-65, Progress in Surface and Membrane Sci, 1962-79, Jour. Social and Biol. Structures, 1978—; Contbr. articles to profl. jours. Fellow Royal Soc.; mem. Inst. Biology (past sec.), Biochem. Soc., Physiol. Soc., Soc. for Exptl. Biology (past sec.), Am. Soc. Cell Biology, Internat. Soc. for Cell Biology (past sec.), Am. Inst. Biol. Scis., Internat. Soc. for Study of Origin of Life. Subspecialty: Cell biology. Office: Danielli Assos Inc 185 Highland St Worcester MA 01609

DANOS, MICHAEL, physicist, researcher; b. Riga, Latvia, Jan. 10, 1922; came to U.S., 1951; s. Arpad and Olga (Viksne) D.; m. Victoria Nieroda, Aug. 1969; children—Johanna, Tamara, Arpad. Student U. Riga, 1941-44, U. Dresden (W.Ger.), 1944-45; M.S., U. Hannover (W.Ger.), 1948; Ph.D., U. Heidelberg (W.Ger.), 1950. Jr. asst. U. Dresden, 1944-45; asst. U. Heidelberg, 1948-52; research assoc. Columbia U., N.Y.C., 1952-54; physicist Nat. Bur. Standards, Gaithersburg, Md., 1954—. Co-author: Relativistic Many-Body Bound Systems, 1975; Methods in Relativistic Physics, 1984; contbr. numerous articles to sci. jours.; patentee in medical instrumentation and electronics. Recipient Silver medal Dept. Commerce, 1966, Gold medal, 1984; Alexander V. Humboldt Sr. U.S. Scientist award, 1973; fellow Guggenheim Found., 1959, Sir Thomas Lyle Found., 1970, Nat. Bur. Standards, 1983. Fellow Am. Phys. Soc.; mem. AAAS, Fedn. Atomic Scientists. Current work: Understanding of the nuclear forces and of the structure of the elementary particles on the basis of quantum chromo-dynamics, quantum field theory. Subspecialties: Nuclear physics; Imaging technology. Office: Nat Bur Standards Bldg 245 Room B106 Gaithersburg MD 20899

DAOUST, DONALD ROGER, pharmaceutical and toiletries company executive; b. Worcester, Mass., Aug. 13, 1935; s. G. Arthur and Alice Anne (Lavallee) D.; m. Johanna K. Kalinoski, May 30, 1959; children: Donna Jean, Stephen Michael, Sandra Marie. B.A., U. Conn., 1957; M.S., U. Mass., 1959, Ph.D., 1962. Sr. research microbiologist Merck Sharp & Dohme Research Labs., Rahway, N.J., 1962-70, research fellow, 1970-72; mgr. biol. quality control Merck Sharp & Dohme, West Point, Pa., 1972-75; dir. quality control Armour Pharm. Co., Kankakee, Ill., 1975-76, v.p. quality assurance-regulatory compliance, Phoenix, 1976-78; corp. v.p. quality control Carter-Wallace Inc., Cranbury, N.J., 1978—. Contbr. articles to sci. jours., chpt. to book. Bd. dirs. South Plainfield (N.J.) Jaycees, 1968-69, pres., 1969-70; mem. South Plainfield Boro Council, 1970-72; v.p. programs George Washington council Boy Scouts Am., 1981, v.p., treas., 1982, pres., 1984—. Recipient Disting. Service award South Plainfield Jaycees, 1969; named Outstanding Young Man of N.J. N.J. Jaycees, 1970. Mem. Am. Soc. Microbiology, AAAS, Parenteral Drug Assn., Proprietary Assn., Am. Soc. Quality Control, Pharm. Mfrs. Assn. Roman Catholic. Lodge: Lions. Patentee on fermentation process for producing physostigmine. Subspecialty: Microbiology. Home: 8 Fairway Dr Cranbury NJ 08512 Office: PO Box 1 Cranbury NJ 08512

D'APPOLONIA, BERT LUIGI, cereal chemist educator; b. Sudbury, Ont., Can., Nov. 6, 1939; came to U.S., 1963, naturalized, 1983; s. Luigi and Tarcisia (Marcuzzi) D. B.S., Laurentian U., 1962; M.S., N.D. State U., 1966, Ph.D., 1968. Research asst. N.D. State U., Fargo, 1963-68, asst. prof. dept. cereal chemistry and tech., 1968-73, assoc. prof., 1973-78, prof., 1978—, chmn. dept., 1985—. Contbr. articles to profl. jours. Mem. Am. Assn. Cereal Chemists (pres. 1984-85), Am. Soc. Bakery Engrs., Inst. Food Technologists, Sigma Xi. Roman Catholic. Current work: Cereal carbohydrates and baking research, leader of a wheat quality breeding team as far as quality testing. Office: ND State U Chmn Dept Cereal Sci and Food Tech Fargo ND 58105

D'APPOLONIA, ELIO, civil engineer; b. Coleman, Alta., Can., Apr. 14, 1918; came to U.S., 1946, naturalized, 1959; s. Joseph S. and Constance (Piccinni) D'A.; m. Violet Mary D'Apollonia, May 2, 1942; children: David, Kenneth, Michael, Linda, Mark. B.S., U. Alta., 1942, M.S., 1946; Ph.D., U. Ill., 1948; D. Engring. (hon.), Carnegie-Mellon U., 1983. Cons. U.S. Army C.E., Alaska/No. Can., 1942-45; research asso. U. Ill., 1946-48; asst. prof. civil engring. Carnegie-Mellon U., 1948-56; pres., chmn. bd. D'Appolonia Cons. Engrs., Inc., Pitts., 1956-84; sr. prin. cons. STS D'Appolonia Ltd., Monroeville, Pa., 1984—. Contbr. tech. articles to profl. jours. Recipient Keefer medal Engring. Inst. Can., 1948; William Metcalf award for outstanding engring. achievement Engrs. Soc. Western Pa., 1981; Disting. Alumnus award U. Ill., 1981; Disting. Service award Deep Founds. Inst., 1983. Mem. ASCE (Middlebrooks award 1969, Civil Engr. of Year, Pitts. sect. 1972), Nat. Acad. Engring., ASTM, Nat., Pa. socs. profl. engrs., Internat. Soc. Rock Mechanics, Internat. Assn. Bridge and Structural Engrs., Am. Underground Assn., Internat. Soc. Soil Mechanics and Found. Engrs., U.S. Nat. Com. Tunneling Tech., Deep Foundations Inst., Internat. Commn. Large Dams, Am. Inst. Cons. Engrs., Am. Water Resources Assn., Assn. Engring. Geologists. Republican. Roman Catholic. Club: Edgewood Country. Subspecialty: Civil engineering. Office: STS D'Appolonia Ltd 1 Monroeville Ctr Monroeville PA 15146

DARBY, WILLIAM JEFFERSON, JR., physician; b. Gattoway, Ark., Nov. 6, 1913; s. William J. and Ruth (Douglass) D.; m. Elva Louise Mayo, June 12, 1935; children—William J., James Richard, Thomas Douglass. B.S., U. Ark., 1936, M.D., 1937; M.S. (Univ. Sigma Xi fellow 1939-40, Horace H. Rackham fellow 1940-41), U. Mich., 1941, Ph.D., 1942, D.Sc. (hon.), 1966; D.Sc., Utah State U., 1973. Instr. phys. chemistry U. Ark. Sch. Medicine, 1937-39; asst. prof. biochemistry, also asst. prof. medicine Vanderbilt U. Sch. Medicine, 1944-46, assoc. prof. biochemistry, 1946-48, prof. biochemistry, chmn. dept., dir. div. nutrition, 1949-71, prof. nutrition, 1964-59, prof. medicine in nutrition, 1965-79, prof. biochem. in nutrition, 1972-79, prof. emeritus, 1979—; pres. Nutrition Found., Inc., 1972-82; mem. study sect. biochemistry and nutrition, div. research grants and fellowships USPHS, 1948-53, chmn. study sect. on gen. medicine, 1956-59, mem. com. on selection sr. research fellowships, 1956-59, chmn. study sect. nutrition, 1959-61; mem. food and nutrition bd. NRC, 1949-71, mem. adv. bd. Inst. Nutrition Central Am. and Panama, 1950-64; mem. WHO Expert Adv. Panel on nutrition, 1950—; mem. FAO and WHO Joint Noble Found., 1953-63, 78, chmn., 1955, 58, 61, 66; sci. adv. com. Samuel R. Noble Found., 1953-63, 78, chmn., 1955, 58, 61, 78; chmn. Joint FAO-WHO Expert com. on Food Additives, 1956; cons. Interdeptl. Com. on Nutrition for Nat. Def., 1955-66; co-ordinator WHO Protein adv. group, 1956-60; mem. FAO/Who/UNICEF Protein Adv. Group, 1960-62; mem. sci. adv. com. Nutrition Found., 1958-65, 67-71, Sci. Adv. Com. Nat. Vitamin Found., 1950-64; Kempner lectr. Va. Acad. Sci., 1975; W.O. Atwater lectr. Med. Coll. Va., 1972, Underwood-Prescott Meml. Lectr., 1979; chmn. adv. com. United Health Found., 1962-70; tech. adv. com. Inst. Nutrition Scis., Columbia U., 1966-70; vis. com. dept. nutrition and food sci. MIT, 1963-68, 74-76; nat. cons. USAF Surgeon Gen., 1967-72; mem. council on foods and nutrition AMA, 1948-62, 65-73, chmn., 1967-70; mem. commn. on pesticides sec. HEW, 1969-71; mem. long range planning com. FASEB, 1969-70; mem. Tenn. Gov.'s Adv. Commn. on Consumer Protection, 1969-70; vis. prof. U. Calif.-Davis, 1967; adv. com. on personnel for research Am. Cancer Soc., 1962-65; pub. trustee Food Law Inst., 1962—; mem. bd. basic sci. examiners State of Tenn., 1961-72, pres., 1962-72; mem. bd. commrs. Navajo Health Authority, 1972-77; adv. task force world hunger Presbyn. Ch. U.S., 1972-76; mem. Tenn. Gov.'s Commn. Aging, 1972-76; co-chmn. Hazardous materials adv. com. EPA, 1971-74, environ. health adv. com., 1974-79. Co-author: Nutrition and Diet in Health and Disease; the State of Nutrition in the Arab Middle East; Food: The Gift of Osiris; Fermented Food Beverages in Nutrition; assoc. editor Nutrition Revs., 1944-50, Jour. Clin. Investigation, 1950-54. Co-discoverer Vitamin M and of activity of pteroylglutamic acid in sprue. Decorated Order Rudolf Robles (Guatemala); Star of Jordan, 1963; Order Cedars of Lebanon, 1972; recipient Mead-Johnson B-Complex award, 1947; Joseph Goldberger award, AMA, 1964; Thomas Jefferson award Vanderbilt U., 1969; Charles Franklin Craig lectr. Am. Soc. Tropical Medicine, 1950; Roberts Meml. lectr. U. P.R., 1966; Phi Beta Kappa scholar, 1966-67; Forty-Niner award, 1975. Fellow ACP (master 1973). mem. Nat. Acad. Scis., Am. Chem. Soc. (Spencer award 1972), Am. Inst. Nutrition (pres. 1958; Elvehjem award 1972; Osborne Mendel award 1962, Robert Hermann award 1982), Am. Pub. Health Assn., AMA (chmn. council foods and nutrition 1960-62, 67-70), Am. Soc. Biol. Chemists, Soc. Exptl. Biology and Medicine, Nutrition Soc. (U.K.), So. Soc. Clin. Research (v.p. 1948), Am. Fedn. Clin. Research, Am. Soc. Clin. Investigation, Assn. Am. Physicians, Austrian Pub. Health Assn. (hon.), Nat. Med. Assn. Panama, Am., Servian (hon.) acads. scis., Phillippine Dietetic Assn. (hon.), L'Institute d'Egypte (assoc.). Current work: History of nutrition. Subspecialties: Nutrition (medicine); Biochemistry (medicine). Office: Dept Biochemistry Vancerbilt Sch of Medicine Nashville TN 37232

DARDEN, CHRISTINE MANN, aerospace engineer; b. Monroe, N.C., Sept. 10, 1942; d. Noah Horace, Sr. and Desma (Chaney) Mann; m. Walter Lee Darden, Jr., June 13, 1963; children: Jeanne Oletia, Janet Christine. B.S., Hampton Inst., 1962; M.S., Va. State Coll., 1967; D.Sc., George Washington U., 1983—. Math. tchr. Brunswick County Schs., Lawrenceville, Va., 1962-63, Portsmouth (Va.) City Schs., 1964-65; instr. math. Va. State Coll., Petersburg, 1966-67; data analyst Langley Research Ctr., Hampton, Va., 1967-73, aerospace engr., 1973—. Contbr. articles to publs. Ordained elder Carver Meml. Presbyterian Ch., Newport News, Va., 1980—; program chmn. Nat. Tech. Assn. Student Symposium, Langley Research Center, 1980, 82. HEW research grantee, 1965-66; named Outstanding Alumna Hampton Inst., 1982. Mem. Nat. Tech. Assn. (v.p. 1978-82), AIAA, Alpha Kappa Alpha (treas. 1980-81). Current Work: Basic research in analytic methods used to design and analyze wing-body configurations for supersonic flight. Subspecialties: Fluid mechanics; Applied mathematics. Home: 1028 Barry Ct Hampton VA 23666 Office: NASA Langley Research Center Hampton VA 23665

DARDIRI, AHMED HAMED, veterinarian, government official, educator; b. Cairo, Egypt, Mar. 10, 1919; came to U.S., 1946, naturalized, 1958; s. Hamed Ahmed and Ameena (Reedy) D.; m. Lucille B., April 7, 1951. D.V.M., U. Cairo, 1940, M.V.Sc., 1946; M.Sc., Mich. State U., 1947, Ph.D. in Microbiology, 1950. Dir. Poultry Research Experiment Sta., Cairo, 1940-46; mem. Egyptian Edn. Mission to U.S., 1946-50; sr. lectr. Cairo U., 1950-55; research assoc. in animal pathology U. R.I., 1955-56, asst. prof., 1956-59, assoc. prof., 1959-61; prin. research veterinarian Plum Island Animal Disease Center, Dept. Agr., Greenport, N.Y., 1961—, also lab. dir. diagnostic investigations; cons. Am. Tech. Aid to Egypt, Cairo, 1951-55; adj. prof. U. R.I. and U. Pa., Phila. Contbr. numerous articles to U.S., fgn. profl. jours. Merck and Shope Research grantee, 1950. Mem. AVMA, N.Y. Acad. Assn. Avian Diseases, U.S. Animal Health Assn., Internat. Soc. Micoplasmology, Wildlife Diseases, Am. Soc. Microbiology. Lodge: Rotary. Current Work: Veterinary science, microbiology, immunology, foreign animal disease research and diagnosis. Subspecialties: Microbiology (veterinary medicine); Animal virology.

DARLINGTON, SIDNEY, educator, electrical engineer; b. Pitts., July 18, 1906; s. Philip Jackson and Rebecca Taylor (Mattson) D.; m. Joan Gilmer Raysor, Apr. 24, 1965; children: Ellen Sewall, Rebecca Mattson. B.S. magna cum laude, Harvard U., 1928; B.S. in Elec. Engring, MIT, 1929; Ph.D. in Physics, Columbia U., 1940. Mem. tech. staff Bell Telephone Labs., Murray Hill, N.J., 1929-71, head dept., 1960-71, ret., 1971; adj. prof. elec. engring. U. N.H., Durham, 1971—; cons. in field, 1971—; Mem. U.S. commn. VI Internat. Sci. Radio Union, 1959-75, del. gen. assemblies, 1960, 63, 66, 69. Author. Recipient Medal of Freedom U.S. Army. Fellow IEEE (Edison medal 1975, Medal of Honor 1981), AIAA; mem. Nat. Acad. Engring., Nat. Acad. Scis., Phi Beta Kappa. Club: Appalachian Mountain. Patentee in field. Current Work: Design techniques for digiltal filters. Subspecialties: Electrical engineering; Systems engineering. Home: 8 Fogg Dr Durham NH 03824

DARRAH, MARK IRWIN, biomedical engineer; b. Springfield, Mass., Nov. 9, 1953; s. Irwin Adamson and May Louise (McCreanor) D.; m. Peggy Suzanne Neppel, Aug. 16, 1979 (dec. Oct. 1981); m. Lyn Dee Yoder, Apr. 23, 1983; 1 child, James Erick. B.S., Delaware Valley Coll., 1975; M.S., Iowa State U., 1979, Ph.D., 1982. Research asst. Iowa State U., Ames, 1976-82; prin. scientist Tech. Inc., San Antonio, 1982-84; sr. engr. McDonnell Douglas Co., St. Louis, 1984—. Contbr. articles to profl. jours. Bd. dirs. Episcopal Youth Group, Ames, 1979-81; coach soccer N.E. Youth Assn., San Antonio, 1983-84. Iowa State U. grantee, 1979-81. Mem. IEEE, Aerospace Med. Assn., Lifescis. and Biomed. Engrs., Safety and Flight Equipment. Republican. Current work: Biomedical engineer working within aerospace medicine; life support; biodynamic modeling; design in fighter/attack aircraft. Subspecialties: Space medicine; Biomedical engineering. Home: 1727 Country Acres Dr Saint Peters MO 63376 Office: McDonnell Douglas Astronautics 270A/E423/3/MS94 Saint Louis MO 63166

D'ARRIGO, JOSEPH SALVATORE, surface chemist; b. N.Y.C., Apr. 4, 1946; s. Joseph Richard and Elizabeth (Medici) D'A.; m. Sachie Aoki, July 28, 1977; 1 son, Paul Sakichi. B.A., Queens Coll., 1967; Ph.D., UCLA, 1972. Postdoctoral fellow U. Utah, Salt Lake City, 1972-73, research instr., 1973-75; asst. prof. physiology U. Hawaii, Honolulu, 1975-77, assoc. prof., 1977-84; vis. fellow Australian Nat. U., Canberra, 1982-83; cons. Cavitation-Control Tech., Kaneohe, 1979-84; research mgr. AMF Inc., Stamford, Conn., 1985; sr. research scientist Bio-Polymers, Inc., Farmington, 1985—. Author: Stable Gas-in-Liquid Emulsions: Production in Natural Waters and Artificial Media, 1985. Contbr. articles to profl. jours. NIH fellow, 1972; NSF grantee, 1975; NASA grantee, 1980. Mem. Biophys. Soc., Am. Physiol. Soc., AAUP, Am. Chem. Soc., AAAS. Inventor bubble monitor, 1976, surfactant-stabilized gas-in-liquid emulsions, 1985. Current Work: Research on surfactant stabilization of gas microbubbles in aqueous media by naturally occurring surfactants and in oil-based media by various analogues of biological surfactants. Industrial applications of this research are also being pursued. Subspecialties: Surface chemistry; Biophysics (biology). Home: 23A Brickyard Rd Farmington CT 06032 Office: Bio-Polymers Inc 309 Farmington Ave Farmington CT 06032

DARSEY, JEROME ANTHONY, research scientist; b. Houma, La., Aug. 26, 1946; s. Elmer Joseph and Arline (Houghton) D. B.S., La. State U., 1970, Ph.D., 1982. Tchr. Terrebonne High Sch., Houma, La., 1970-74; grad. teaching asst. La. State U., Baton Rouge, 1974-81, postdoctoral research assoc., 1982—. Mem. Am. Phys. Soc., Am. Chem. Soc., AAAS, Am.Soc. Physics Tchrs., Planetary Soc., Phi Lambda Upsilon. Republican. Roman Catholic. Club: First Day Cover Soc. (Cheyenne, Wyo.). Current Work: Conformational characterization of macromolecules especially biopolymers and structural, conductive and magnetic properties of conductive polymers, chemistry and physics of liquid crystals. Subspecialties: Polymer chemistry; Polymer physics. Office: Chemistry Dept La State U Baton Rouge LA 70803

DAS, ASHOK KUMAR, physics educator, researcher; b. Puri, Orissa, India, Mar. 23, 1953; came to U.S., 1974; s. Braja Kishore and Jayantarani D.; m. Nandita Patnaik, June 6, 1983. B.S. in Physics, U. Delhi, India, 1972, M.S., 1974; Ph.D., SUNY-Stony Brook, 1977. Research assoc. CCNY, N.Y.C., 1977-79, U. Md., College Park, 1979-81, Rutgers U., Piscataway, N.J., 1981-82; asst. prof. physics U. Rochester, N.Y., 1982—. Contbr. articles to profl. jours. Recipient Outstanding Jr. Investigator award U.S. Dept. Energy, 1983. Mem. Am. Phys. Soc. Current work: Studies of lattice theories of supersymmetry, chiral symmetry breaking through Nambu-Jona Lasinio mechanism and effects of curved space-time on quantum field theories. Subspecialties: Particle physics; Theoretical physics. Home: 7 Dawn Valley Dr Rochester NY 14623 Office: Dept of Physics and Astronomy Univ Rochester NY 14627

DAS, PANKAJ K., scientist, educator; b. Calcutta, W. Bengal, India, June 15, 1937; came to U.S., 1964, naturalized, 1975; s. Upendra N. and Susama (Paul) D.; m. Virginia Van Kirk, July 29, 1967; children: Andrea, Joshua. B.Sc., U. Calcutta, 1957, M.Sc., 1960, Ph.D., 1964. Instr. Poly. Inst. Bklyn., 1964-65, asst. prof., 1965-68; assoc. prof. U. Rochester, 1968-74; assoc. prof. Rensselaer Poly. Inst., 1974-77, prof., 1977—; vis. prof. elec. engring. OAS, Mexico City, 1972-73. Contbr. numerous articles to profl. jours. NSF grantee, 1975—. Mem. Am. Phys. Soc., IEEE, Optical Soc. Am., Am. Soc. Non-destructive Testing, Acoustical Soc. Am. Current Work: Signal processing devices such as SAW and CCD, acousto-optic devices, non-destructive testing using elastic waves and ultrasonic imaging. Subspecialties: Semiconductors; Integrated circuits. Home: 15 Johnson Rd Latham NY 12110 Office: Rensselaer Poly Inst Troy NY 12181

DAS, PANKAJ KUMAR, pharmaceutical chemist; b. Dakadakshin, India, May 3, 1944; s. Promothonath and Khela (Chowdhury) D.; m. Keya Dutta, Aug. 13, 1973; children—Proloy K., Bohnnee. B.S., Jadavpur U., Calcutta, India, 1968; M.S., U. Mich., 1973, Ph.D., 1977. Lectr. chemistry U. Conn., Storrs, 1976-77, postdoctoral fellow, 1977-78; polymer chemist Brand-Rex., Willimantic, Conn., 1978-79, sr. polymer chemist, 1979-80, mgr. to tech. and research, 1980-82, mgr., cons., 1982—. Patentee in field. Mem. Am. Chem. Soc., Soc. Plastic Engrs., Sigma Xi, Rho Chi. Lodge: Lions. Current work: Working with different polymers to improve properties and performance to meet specific applications. Subspecialties: Drug delivery systems; Polymer chemistry. Home: 37 Storrs Heights Rd Storrs CT 06268 Office: Brand Rex 1600 W Main St Willimantic CT 06226

DAS, SAJAL, polymer chemist, material scientist; b. Ranchi, India, Jan. 2, 1951; came to U.S., 1980, naturalized, 1983; s. Dhirendra Nath and Surama Das. B.S. with honors, Ranchi U., India, 1972, M.S., 1975; Ph.D., Indian Inst. Tech., Kharagpur, 1980. Vis. asst. prof. N.C. State U., Raleigh, 1980-82; research assoc. Wright State U., Dayton, 1982-83, U. Akron, Ohio, 1984; research scientist Allied Corp., Morristown, N.J., 1984—. Contbr. articles to profl. jours. and chpts. to books. Fellow Allied Resins and Chemical Ltd., Calcutta, India, 1977. Mem. Am. Chem. Soc. (polymer chemistry and polymeric material divs.). Current work: High temperature polymer for aerospace and microelectronics application; crystalline polyimide for composite resin; binding resine for brake system. Subspecialties: Polymer chemistry; Polymers (materials science). Home: H-143 Hinoo Ranchi Bihar India 834002 Office: Allied Corp Columbia Rd and Park Ave Morristown NJ 07960

DASCH, JEAN MUHLBAIER, chemist; b. Woodbury, N.J., Jan. 1, 1950; d. Louis Edward and Pearl (Richards) Muhlbaier; m. Cameron John Dasch, May 15, 1982. B.A., Cath. U. Am., 1972; Ph.D., U. Md., 1978. Postdoctoral asst. Argonne Nat. Lab., Ill., 1978-79; staff research scientist Gen. Motors Research Labs., Warren, Mich., 1979—. Mem. Am. Chem. Soc., Air Pollution Control Assn., Phi Beta Kappa, Sigma Xi. Current work: Acid rain research, local effects and dry deposition, emissions from woodburning. Subspecialty: Environmental chemistry. Home: 10765 Vernon Huntington Woods MI 48070 Office: Gen Motors Research Lab Warren MI 48090

DASGUPTA, AARON, mechanical engineer, researcher; b. Calcutta, India, Nov. 20, 1943; came to U.S., 1965, naturalized, 1969; s. Krishna Prosad and Amita (Sen) D.; m. Runu Biswas, Mar. 9, 1972; children: Elora, Debraj. B.Tech. with honors, Indian Inst. Tech., Kharagpur, 1963; M.Eng., Tech. U. N.S. (Can.), Halifax, 1968; Ph.D., Va. Poly. Inst., 1975. Registered profl. engr., Ill., Va., Tenn., N.Mex. Assoc. engr. Heavy Engring. Corp., Dhurwa, Bihar, India, 1963-65; electronics engr. Can. Marconi Corp., Montreal, Que., 1967-69; prodn. engr. Whittaker AMTD Corp., Gardena, Calif., 1969-70; design engr. Kingsport Press Inc., Tenn., 1973-75; stress analyst Sundstrand Aviation, Rockford, Ill., 1975; sr. mech. engr. Ballistic Research Lab., Aberdeen, Md., 1975—; environ. cons. El Paso Electric Co., Tex., 1971-72; design cons. Comml. Fabrication Co., Mt. Airy, N.C., 1972-73; cons. Ministry of Def., Harwell, Eng., 1980-81, U.S. Army C.E., Balt., 1980-82, Harry Diamond Lab., Adelphi, Md., 1979-80; systems cons. U.S. Army, 1976—. Contbr. articles to tech. jours.; editor: Dynamics of Ballistic Impact, 1980. State adv. U.S. Congressional Adv. Bd., Washington, 1982. Mem. Soc. Engring. Sci. (co-chmn. 1981-82), N.Y. Acad. Sci., Am. Acad. Mechanics (reviewer 1978-81, Quality Performance award 1982), Sigma Xi. Hindu. Club: Cosmopolitan (treas. 1967-68). Current Work: Structural dynamics; penetration mechanics; fracture mechanics; blast damage on structures; nuclear effects; numerical analysis and simulation; containment design. Subspecialties: Mechanical engineering; Theoretical and applied mechanics. Home: 104 John St Perryville MD 21903 Office: U S Army Ballistic Research Lab Terminal Ballistic Div Aberdeen Proving Ground Aberdeen MD 21005

DATTA, BISWA NATH, mathematics educator, computer scientist; b. Bighira, India, July 1, 1941; came to U.S., 1980; s. Nirmal Kumar and Sudha (Rani) D.; m. Karabi Sarkar, June 16, 1972; children—Rajarshi, Rakhi. B.Sc., U. Calcutta, 1960, M.Sc., 1962; M.Sc., McMaster U., Can., 1970; Ph.D., U. Ottawa, Can., 1972. Lectr. math. U. Ottawa, 1972-73, Ahmadu Bello U., Zaria, Nigeria, 1973-75; assoc. prof. U. Estadual De Campinas, Brazil, 1975-80; vis. assoc. prof. Pa. State U., University Park, 1980-81; prof. No. Ill. U., DeKalb, 1981—; vis. scientist Gas Turbine Research Establishment, Bangalore, India, 1973-74; vis. prof. U. Ill., Urbana, 1985; leader del., liaison from U.S. to Internat. Conf. on Math. Theory of Networks and Systems, Stockholm, 1985; lectr. in field. Author: Advanced Numerical Linearal Algebra (in Portuguese), 1984. Editor: Contemporary Mathematics, 1985. Contbr. articles, revs. to profl. jours. Grantee, Air Force, 1983—, NSF, No. Ill. U., 1981. Mem. Am. Math. Soc. (chmn. summer research conf. 1984), Soc. Indsl. Applied Math. (chmn. linear algebra in signals, systems and control 1986), Calcutta Math. Soc. Hindu. Current work: Solving mathematical problems arising in electrical engineering (control and systems theory) using computers, developing algorithms for super computers. Subspecialties: Algorithms; Numerical analysis (mathematics). Home: 7 Cari Ct DeKalb IL 60115 Office: No Ill U DeKalb IL 60115

DATTA, RATHIN, chemical engineer, researcher; b. Calcutta, India, Nov. 11, 1948; s. Amulya Narayan and Karuna (Basu) D.; m. Alicia Reyes, Sept. 14, 1974. B.Tech., India Inst. Tech., Kanpur, 1970; M.A., Princeton U., 1971, Ph.D., 1974. Engring. assoc., Merck & Co., Rahway, N.J., 1974-78; sr. engr. Exxon Research & Engring. Co., Linden, N.J., 1978-82; research engr., sect. leader CPC Internat., Summit, Ill., 1982—. Contbr. articles to profl. jours. Patentee in field. Recipient Dir.'s medal Govt. of India, 1970. Mem. Soc. Indsl. Microbiology (symposium chmn. 1982), Am. Inst. Chem. Engrs., Am. Chem. Soc., AAAS. Current work: Seperation process technology, enzyme technology, biomass conversion, chemical catalysis, microbial physiology and metabolism. Subspecialties: Chemical engineering; Fermentation technology. Home: 442 W Melrose St Chicago IL 60657 Office: CornProducts-CPC Moffett Tech Ctr PO Box 345 Summit-Argo IL 60501

DATTA, RATNA, medical/health physicist; b. Jamshedpur, India, Oct. 10, 1943; came to U.S., 1973, naturalized, 1978; d. Birendranath and Basanti (Roy) Sarkar; m. Sobhendranath Datta, Jan. 23, 1973. B.S. (Gold medalist), Ranchi U., India, 1963; M.S. in Nuclear Physics, Calcutta U., 1966; Ph.D. in Nuclear Physics, Saha Inst. Nuclear Physics, Calcutta U., 1971. Research assoc. fellow Bonner Lab., Rice U., Houston, 1973-74; NIH sr. postdoctoral fellow M.D. Anderson Hosp., Houston, 1974-76; asst. prof. U. Tex. Health Sci. Center, San Antonio, 1976-78; chief radiol. physicist, asst. prof. dept. radiology, head dept. radiation safety La. State U., Shreveport, 1978-82, assoc. prof. radiology, chief radiol. physics sect., head radiol. safety, 1982—. Contbr. articles to profl. jours. Ranchi U. scholar, 1961-63; Atomic Energy scholar Govt. of India, 1963-66; Saha Inst. fellow, 1966-71, 71-73; Sr. NIH fellow, 1974-76; others. Mem. Am. Assn. Physicists in Medicine, Am. Soc. Therapeutic Radiology and Oncology, Health Physics Soc., Assn. Med. Physicists of India. Current Work: Research on effect of radiation on bone healing; comparative study of different dosimetry devices, electron beam treatment planning using CT scan, treatment planning with split beam technique. Subspecialty: Medical physics. Office: 1541 Kings Hwy Dept Radiology Shreveport LA 71130

DATTA, SUBHENDU K(UMAR), mechanical engineering educator, consultant; b. Calcutta, India, Jan. 15, 1936; came to U.S., 1968; s. Srish Chandra and Prabhabati (Ghosh) D.; m. Bishakha Roy, May 10, 1966; 1 child, Kinshuk. B.S., Presidency Coll., Calcutta, 1954; M.S., Calcutta U., 1956; Ph.D., Jadavpur U., Calcutta, 1962. Asst. prof. Indian Inst. Tech., Kanpur, 1965-67; asst. prof. U. Colo., Boulder, 1968-69, assoc. prof., 1969-73, prof. mech. engring., 1973—; cons. NBS, Boulder, 1979—. Editor: Earthquake Ground Motion and Its Effects on Structures, 1982; Earthquake Source Modeling, Ground Motion, and Structural Response, 1984; Procs. U.S. Nat. Congress Applied Mechanics, 1974; contbr. articles to publs. in field. Fulbright fellow, 1962; faculty fellow U. Colo., 1972; NSF grantee, 1970—. Fellow ASME; mem. Soc. Indsl. and Applied Math., Am. Acad. Mechanics, Soc. Engring. Sci. Current Work: Elastic wave scattering and ultrasonic nondestructive evaluation, earthquake engineering, mechanics of composite materials. Subspecialties: Theoretical and applied mechanics; Applied mathematics. Home: 6252 Old Stage Rd Boulder CO 80302 Office: Univ Colo ECOT 4-6 Campus Box 427 Boulder CO 80309

DATTA, SURJIT KUMAR, immunologist; b. Adampur Doaba, Punjab, India, Jan. 1, 1935; s. Jagdish Chander and Jaswanti Devi (Sharma) D.; m. Evelyn B. Dochy, Dec. 17, 1971. B. V. Sc. and A.H., Punjab U., 1957; M.V.Sc., Agra U., 1963; Ph.D., U. Louvain, Belgium, 1970. Assoc., then asst. prof. Coll. Vet. Medicine, Hissar, India, 1963-73; research fellow microbiology U. Brisbane, Australia, 1973-74; inst., research assoc. div. exptl. biology Baylor Coll. Medicine, 1974-78, research asst. prof., 1978—; NIH co-investigator, 1978—. Contbr. articles to profl. jours. Mem. Am. Assn. Cancer Research, Am. Assn. Immunology, Am.Soc. Microbiology, Internat. Soc. Exptl. Hematology. Current Work: Natural and immune resistance to cancer, natural resistance to marrow and lymphona grafts. Subspecialties: Cancer research (medicine); Transplantation. Office: Lab Immunogenetics Dept Surgery MD Anderson Hosp and Tumor Inst Houston TX 77030

DATTA, SYAMAL KUMAR, immunologist, medical educator; b. Cuttack, Orissa, India, Sept. 21, 1943; came to U.S., 1967, naturalized, 1976; s. Jitendra Nath and Kalyani (Hazra) Dutt; m. Tapati Choudhury, Nov. 17, 1976; 1 child, Ronjon. B.S., U. Calcutta, 1960, M.B., B.S., 1966. Diplomate Am. Bd. Internal Medicine. Intern, Mt. Sinai Hosp. Service, Elmhurst, N.Y., 1968-69; resident in medicine Cook County Hosp.-U. Ill., Chgo., 1969-72; research assoc. hematology New Eng. Med. Ctr., Boston, 1972-74, instr. medicine, 1974-76; asst. prof. Tufts U. and New Eng. Med. Ctr., 1976-79, assoc. prof. medicine, staff physician, scientist, 1979-85, prof. medicine, 1985—, faculty mem. immunology grad. program, 1976—, staff scientist Cancer Research Ctr., 1978—; reviewer research grants, site visitor, cons. NSF, NIH, 1977—; prin. investigator NIH-Nat. Cancer Inst., 1976—. Contbr. over 40 sci. articles to profl. jours. Research fellow Leukemia Soc. Am., 1972-74; research scholar Am. Cancer Soc. div. Mass., 1975-78, Am. Cancer Soc. Faculty Research award, 1978-83. Mem. Am. Assn. Immunologists (assoc. editor Jour. Immunology 1984—), AAAS, N.Y. Acad. Scis., Democrat. Hindu. Current work: Immunologic, virologic and genetic studies to define the fundamental mechanisms of autoimmune disease (systemic Lupus Erythematosus); studies on retroviruses, thymic epithelium and thymocyte differentiation in T cell Leukemia development. Subspecialties: Immunogenetics; Virology (medicine). Office: New Eng Med Ctr 171 Harrison Ave Boston MA 02111

DATZ, SHELDON, physicist; b. N.Y.C., July 21, 1927; s. Jacob and Clara (Green) D.; m. Roslyn Gordon, Aug. 25, 1948; children: William Lawrence, Joan Ellen; m. Jonna Holm, Jan. 23, 1973. B.S., Columbia U., 1950, M.A., 1951; Ph.D., U. Tenn., 1960. Technician SAM Labs., Columbia U., Manhattan Project, 1943-45; physics dept. Columbia U., 1946-51; research chemist Oak Ridge (Tenn.) Nat. Lab., 1951-60, assoc. dir. chemistry div., 1965-75, group leader chem. dynamics, 1960-81, sect. chief atomic physics, physics div., 1981—; cons. Gen. Atomics, 1958-62, Republic Aviation Plasma Propulsion Lab., 1959-62. Author: Atomic Collisions in Solids, 1975, Electronic and Atomic Collisions, 1982; Applied Atomic Collision Physics, 1984; contbr. articles to profl. jours. Served with USN, 1945-46. Fulbright sr. research fellow, 1962-63; Union Carbide Corporate research fellow, 1980—. Fellow Am. Phys. Soc.; mem. Am. Chem. Soc., AAAS. Current Work: High energy atomic collision physics, particle solid interactions. Subspecialties: Atomic and molecular physics; Kinetics. Office: Oak Ridge Nat Lab PO Box X Oak Ridge TN 37830

DAUBEN, WILLIAM GARFIELD, chemist, educator; b. Columbus, Ohio, Nov. 6, 1919; s. Hyp J. and Leilah (Stump) D.; m. Carol Hyatt, Aug. 8, 1947; children—Barbara, Ann. A.B., Ohio State U., 1941; A.M., Harvard, 1942; Ph.D., 1944; Ph.D. hon. degree, U. Bordeaux, France, 1980. Edwara Austin fellow Harvard, 1941-42, teaching fellow, 1942-43, research asst., 1943-45; instr. U. Calif. at Berkeley, 1945-47, asst. prof. chemistry, 1947-52, asso. prof., 1952-57, prof., 1957—; lectr. Am.-Swiss Found., 1962; pres. Organic Reactions, Inc., 1967; mem. med. chem. study sect. USPHS, 1959-64; mem. chemistry panel NSF, 1964-67; mem. Am.-Sino Sci. Cooperation Com., 1973-76; mem. assembly math. and phys. scis. NRC, 1977-80. Mem. bd. editors: Jour. of Organic Chemistry, 1957-62; bd. editors: Organic Syntheses, 1959-67; bd. dirs., 1971—; editor-in-chief: Organic Reactions, 1967—; Contbr. articles profl. jours. Recipient award Calif. sect. Am. Chem. Soc., 1959; Guggenheim fellow, 1951, 66; sr. fellow NSF, 1957-58; Alexander von Humboldt Found. Fellow, 1980. Fellow London, Swiss chem. socs.; mem. Am. Chem. Soc. (chmn. div. organic chemistry 1962-63, councilor organic div. 1964-70, mem. council publ. com. 1965-70, mem. adv. com. Petroleum Research Fund 1974-77, Ernest Guenther award 1973), Nat. Acad. Scis. (chmn. chemistry sect. 1977-80), Am. Acad. Arts and Scis., Phi Beta Kappa, Sigma Xi, Phi Lambda Upsilon, Phi Eta Sigma, Sigma Chi. Club: Bohemian. Current Work: Photochemistry, lasers; synthetic chemistry. Subspecialties: Organic chemistry; Photochemistry. Home: 20 Eagle Hill Berkeley CA 94707

DAUGHERTY, JACK D., energy and aerospace company executive. Vice pres. strategic def. programs, Avco Everett Research Lab., Everett, Mass. Subspecialty: Research and development management. Office: Arco Everett Research Lab Inc 2385 Revere Beach Pkwy Everett MA 02149

DAVENPORT, ARTHUR K., engineer; b. St. Albans, N.Y., Oct. 24, 1940; s. Earl K. and Ruth (Croft) D.; m. Wendy Sue Thompson, Nov. 23, 1963; children—Meril Lynn, Christopher Scott, Tyler Croft. Mech. Engr., Stevens Inst. Tech., 1962; M.S.M.E., Rensselaer Poly. Inst., 1977. Registered profl. engr., Conn. Mech. engr. Hamilton Standard Co., Windsor Locks, Conn., 1965—. Contbr. articles to profl. jours. and book. Patentee in field. Served to 1st lt. USAF, 1962-65. Recipient Apollo Achievement award, Silver Snoopy award, Manned Flight Awareness award NASA, 1969-71. Republican. Christian Scientist. Current work: Design of space, naval and ground based environmental control systems. Subspecialty: Aeronautical engineering. Home: Jennifer Lane Box 317 East Hartland CT 06027 Office: Hamilton Standard Div UTC Windsor Locks CT 06096

DAVENPORT, WILLIAM DANIEL, JR., oral pathology and anatomy educator, research laboratories administrator; b. Corinth, Miss., Apr. 19, 1947; s. William Daniel and Flora Louise (Phillips) D. B.S., U. Miss., 1969, M.S., 1971; Ph.D., Med. Coll. Ga., 1976. Instr. Ark. State U., 1971-72; instr. U. Miss. Med. Center, Jackson, 1975-77, asst. prof., 1977-82; asst. prof. oral pathology and anatomy La. State U. Sch. Dentistry, 1982-85, assoc. prof., 1985—, dir. research Labs., 1982—. Named Basic Sci. Tchrs. of Yr. U. Miss. Sch. Dentistry, 1980; Nat. Endowment for Humanities fellow U. Calif.-San Francisco, 1979. Mem. Am. Assn. Anatomists, Electron Microscopy Soc. Am., History of Medicine Soc., Am. Assn. Dental Schs., Internat. Assn. Dental Research, Eastern Soc. Tchrs. Oral Pathology. Republican. Baptist. Current Work: Surface ultrastructural changes in endothelial cells in diet/environment induced cardiovascular diseases; cell surface changes in metastatic/non-metastatic cancer cells after chemotherapy in vitro as diagnostic aid in prognosis; osteoinduction and osteogenesis. Subspecialties: Oral biology; Anatomy and embryology. Home: 3409 Severn Ave Apt 204 Metairie LA 70002 Office: Dept Oral Pathology La State U Med Center Sch Dentistry 1100 Florida Ave New Orleans LA 70119

DAVID, EDWARD EMIL, JR., electrical engineer, business executive; b. Wilmington, N.C., Jan. 25, 1925; s. Edward Emil and Beatrice (Liebman) D.; m. Ann Hirshberg, Dec. 23, 1950; 1 dau., Nancy. B.S., Ga. Inst. Tech., 1945; M.S., Mass. Inst. Tech., 1947, Sc.D., 1950; D.Engring. (hon.), Stevens Inst. Tech., 1971, Poly. Inst. Bklyn., 1971, U. Mich., 1971, Carnegie-Mellon, 1972, Lehigh U., 1973, U. Ill. at Chgo., 1973, Rose-Hulman Inst. Tech., 1978, U. Fla., 1982, Rensselaer Poly. Inst., 1982, Rutgers U., 1984, N.J. Inst. Tech., 1985. Exec. dir. research Bell Telephone Labs., Murray Hill, N.J., 1950-70; sci. adviser to Pres. Nixon; dir. Office Sci. and Tech., Washington, 1970-72; exec. v.p. Gould, Inc., 1973-77; ind. cons., 1977; v.p. Exxon Corp., N.Y.C., 1978-80; pres. Exxon Research and Engring. Co., Florham Park, N.J., 1977—; dir. Materials Research Corp., Orangeburg, N.Y.; cons. Nat. Security Council, 1974-77; mem. def. sci. bd. Dept. of Def., 1974-75; U.S. rep. to NATO Sci. Com.; mem. N.J. Gov.'s Commn. on Sci. and Tech., N.Y. Mayor's Comm. on Sci. and Tech.; life mem., mem. exec. com. and energy adv. bd. M.I.T., trustee John Simon Guggenheim Meml. Found., Twentieth Century Fund. Author: (with Dr. J.R. Pierce) Man's World of Sound, 1958, (with Dr. J.R. Pierce and W.A. van Bergeijk) Waves and the Ear, 1960, (with Dr. J.G. Truxal) The Man-Made World, 1969 (Lanchester prize Operations Research Soc. Am. 1971); Contbr. articles to profl. jours. Mem. Bicentennial adv. com. Chgo. Mus. Sci. and Industry, 1974-75; mem. adv. bd. Office of Phys. Scis., NRC, 1976—; mem. Pres.'s Commn. on Nat. Medal of Sci., 1975-78; mem. vis. com. to div. phys. scis. U. Chgo., 1976—; mem. adv. council Humanities Inst., 1976—; trustee Aerospace Corp., 1974-81, chmn. bd. trustees, 1975-81; mem. corp. MIT, 1974—, life mem., 1984—, also mem. exec. com., energy adv. bd.; bd. dirs. Summit (N.J.) Speech Sch., 1967-70; mem. Marshall Scholarships Adv. Council., mem. nat. selection com., 1980-84; mem. adv. and resource council Princeton U.; mem. cons. sci. com. Chateaubriand Scholarships; trustee Carnegie Instn. of Washington. Served with USNR, 1943-46. Recipient George W. McCarty award Ga. Inst. Tech., 1958, award Summit Jr. C. of C., 1959; ASME award merit, 1971; Harold Pender award Moore Sch. U. Pa., 1972; N.C. award, 1972; award for disting. contbn. Soc. Research Adminstrs., 1980; N.J. Sci. and Tech. medal, 1982; Fahaney medal, 1985. Fellow IEEE, Acoustical Soc. Am., Am. Acad. Arts and Scis., AAAS (dir. 1974-75, 77-80, 80—, pres. 1977-78, chmn. bd. dirs. 1979-80), Audio Engring. Soc.; mem. Nat. Acad. Sci., Assn. Computing Machinery, Engring. Soc. Detroit, Nat. Acad. Engring. (Bueche medal 1984), Nat. Acad. Pub. Adminstrn. Patentee in field. Subspecialty: Electrical engineering. Office: Exxon Research and Engring Co Route 22 E Clinton Twp Annandale NJ 08801

DAVID, GARY SAMUEL, immunologist; b. Aurora, Ill., Oct. 2, 1942; s. Samuel Matthew and Elizabeth Irene (Youngen) D.; m. Denise Nakamura, June 14, 1979. B.S., U. Ill., 1964, Ph.D., 1968. Postdoctoral fellow City of Hope Med. Ctr., Duarte, Calif., 1968-69; research assoc. Salk Inst. Biol. Studies, San Diego, 1970-71; research fellow Scripps Clinic and Research Found., LaJolla, Calif., 1971-77; dir. immunochemistry, prin. scientist Hybritech Inc., San Diego, 1978—. Contbr. articles to profl. jours. NIH grantee, 1974-78. Mem. Am. Assn. Immunologists, Tissue Culture Soc., Clin. Ligand Assay Soc., Soc. Nuclear Medicine, AAAS. Democrat. Current Work: Immunology, protein chemistry, cancer research, cell biology; director immunochemistry research, hybridoma technology and monclonal antibody manipulation. Subspecialties: Immunobiology and immunology; Hybridoma technology. Office: 11085 Torreyana Rd San Diego CA 92121

DAVID, HERBERT ARON, statistics educator; b. Germany, Dec. 19, 1925. B.Sc., U. Sydney, 1947; Ph.D. in Stats, U. London, 1953. Sr. lectr. stats. U. Melbourne, Australia, 1955-57; prof. Va. Polytech. Inst., 1957-64, Sch. Pub.Health, U. N.C., Chapel Hill, 1964-72; dir., head statis. lab., dept. stats. Iowa State U., Ames, 1972-84, disting. prof., 1980—. Editor: Jour. Biometrics, 1967-72. Fellow Am. Statis. Assn., Inst. Math. Stats.; mem. Internat. Statis. Inst., Biometric Soc. (pres. 1982-83). Subspecialty: Statistics. Office: Dept Stats Iowa State U Ames IA 50011

DAVID, YADIN, biomedical engineer, health care consultant; b. Haifa, Israel, Nov. 25, 1946; came to U.S. 1972, naturalized 1979; s. Bezalel and Ziona (Kovalsky) D.; m. Becky Lask, Jan. 23, 1968; children—Tal, Daniel. B.S., W.Va. U., 1974, M.S., 1975, Ph.D., 1983. Cert. profl. biomed. engr. Dir. biomed. engring. W.Va. U. Hosp., Morgantown, 1976-82, research asst. prof., 1979-82; pres. TALDAN Cons., Houston, 1976—; adj. prof. anesthesiology U. Tex. Health Sci. Ctr., 1984—; dir., biomed. instr. St. Luke's Hosp., Tex. Children's Hosp., Tex. Heart Inst., Houston, 1982—. Contbr. articles to profl. jours. Advisor, B'nai B'rith Youth Orgn., Morgantown, W.Va., 1981. Research grantee W.Va. U., 1976. Mem. IEEE (rep. to NFPA and standards com. 1979—), Engring. in Medicine and Biology (com. chmn. 1984—), Assn. Advancement Med. Instrumentation. Jewish. Current work: Biochemical sensors for use in continuous percutaneous bedside monitoring, electrical nerve stimulators for clinical and home based pain relief systems. Subspecialties: Biomedical engineering; Bioinstrumentation. Office: St Luke's Episcopal Hosp Biomed Instrumentation Dept PO Box 20269 Houston TX 77225

DAVIDSEN, ARTHUR FALNES, astrophysicist, educator, researcher; b. Freeport, N.Y., May 26, 1944; s. Andrew and Anna (Falnes) D.; m. Anita Clare Saltz, June 4, 1966; children: Andrew, Austin. A.B., Princeton U., 1966; M.A., U. Calif., Berkeley, 1972, Ph.D., 1975. Asst. prof. physics Johns Hopkins U., 1975-78, assoc. prof., 1978-80, prof., 1980—, dir. Ctr. Astrophys. Scis., 1985—; mem. AXAF Sci. Working Group, 1977-83; dir. Assn. Univs. for Research in Astronomy, Inc., 1979—; mem. Space Telescope Inst. Council, 1981—, Space Scis. Working Group, 1984—; mem. Mgmt. and Ops. Working Group in Space Astronomy, NASA, 1980-83. Contbr. articles to profl. jours. Served to lt. (j.g.) USNR, 1968-71. Alfred P. Sloan Found. research fellow, 1976-80. Fellow AAAS; mem. Am. Astron. Soc. (councilor 1981-84, Helen B. Warner Prize 1979), Royal Astron. Soc., Internat. Astron. Union (U.S. nat. com. 1982—; chmn. local organizing com. 20th Gen. Assembly 1984—). Club: Explorers (N.Y.C.). Subspecialty: Ultraviolet high energy astrophysics. Home: 424 Dunkirk Rd Baltimore MD 21212 Office: Ctr Astrophys Scis Johns Hopkins U Baltimore MD 21218

DAVIDSON, ERIC HARRIS, developmental and molecular biologist; b. N.Y.C., Apr. 13, 1937; s. Morris and Anne D. B.A., U. Pa., 1958; Ph.D., Rockefeller U., 1963. Research asso. Rockefeller U., 1963-65, asst. prof., 1965-71; assoc. prof. devel. molecular biology Calif. Inst. Tech., Pasadena, 1971-74, prof., 1974-81, Norman Chandler prof. cell biology, 1981—. Author: Gene Activity in Early Development, 2d edit, 1976. NIH grantee, 1965—; NSF grantee, 1972—. Research, numerous publs. on DNA sequence orgn., gene expression during embryonic devel., gene regulation. Mem. Nat. Acad. Sci. Subspecialties: Developmental biology; Molecular biology. Office: Div Biology Calif Inst Tech Pasadena CA 91125

DAVIDSON, GILBERT, research and devel. exec.; b. Omaha, June 10, 1934; s. Mike and Reva (Plotkin) D.; m. Barbara Berger, June 8, 1958; children: Amy, Marc, Sharra. Ph.D., M.I.T., 1959. Research asso. Ecole Polytechnique, Paris, 1959-60; v.p. Am. Sci. and Engring., Cambridge, Mass., 1960-72, Infrared Industries, Waltham, Mass., 1972-77, Photometrics, Woburn, Mass., 1977—. Contbr. articles to profl. jours. Fulbright scholar, 1959-60. Mem. Am. Phys. Soc., Am. Vacuum Soc., Optical Soc. Am., Am. Geophys. Union. Patentee in field. Current Work: Remote sensing of atmosphere under a variety of meterol. conditions. Subspecialties: Remote sensing (atmospheric science); Atomic and molecular physics. Home: 23 Exmoor Rd Newton Centre MA 02159 Office: 4 Arrow Dr Woburn MA 01801

DAVIDSON, NORMAN RALPH, biochemistry educator; b. Chgo., Apr. 5, 1916; s. Bernard Ralph and Rose (Lefstein) D.; m. Annemarie Behrendt, July 11, 1942; children—Terence Mark, Laureen Reitman Davidson Agee, Jeffrey Norman, Brian Lee. B.S., U. Chgo., 1937; B.Sc., Oxford U., 1939; Ph.D. in Chemistry, U. Chgo., 1941. Research scientist Manhattan Project, U. Chgo., 1942-46; instr. chemistry Calif. Inst. Tech., Pasadena, 1946-49, asst. prof., 1949-52, assoc. prof., 1952-57, prof. biochemistry, 1957-82, Chandler prof. chem. biology, 1982—; mem. sci. adv. bd. Amgen, Thousands Oaks, Calif., 1981—; chmn. biophys. and biophys. chem. study sect. NIH, Bethesda, Md., 1964-68. Author: Statistical Mechanics, 1962. Named Calif. Scientist of Yr. award Calif. Mus. of Sci. and History, 1980; Rhodes scholar, 1938-39. Mem. Nat. Acad. Scis., Am. Soc. Biol. Chemists, Am. Soc. Microbiology, Am. Chem. Soc. (Calif. sect. award 1954, Peter Debye award in phys. chemistry 1971). Current work: Research in gene structure and expression. Subspecialties: Molecular biology; Gene actions. Office: Calif Inst Tech 164-30 Pasadena CA 91125

DAVIDSON, RONALD CROSBY, physicist, educator; b. Norwich, Ont., Can., July 3, 1941; s. William Crosby and Annie Beatrice (Caley) D.; m. Jean Farncombe, May 18, 1963; children: Cynthia Christine, Ronald Crosby. B.Sc., McMaster U., 1963; Ph.D., Princeton U., 1966. Mem. faculty dept. physics U. Md., 1968-78; vis. scientist Los Alamos Sci. Lab., 1974-75; asst. dir. for applied plasma physics Office of Fusion Energy Dept. Energy, Washington, 1976-78; prof. physics, dir. Plasma Fusion Center MIT, Cambridge, Mass., 1978—; cons. Sci. Applications, Inc. Author: Methods in Nonlinear Plasma Theory, 1972, Physics of Nonneutral Plasmas, 1974. Ford Found. fellow, 1963-64; Imperial Oil fellow, 1963-66; Sloan Research Found. fellow, 1970-72. Fellow Am. Phys. Soc. (chmn. div. plasma physics); mem. Fusion Power Assn. (dir.), Sigma Xi. Subspecialty: Plasma physics. Home: 179 Morse Rd Sudbury MA 01776 Office: 167 Albany St Cambridge MA 02139

DAVIES, DAVID KEITH, geologist; b. Barry, Eng., Oct. 10, 1940; came to U.S., 1966, naturalized, 1973; s. Buller T. and Muriel G. (Champ) D.; m. Ruth Margaret Mary Gilbertson, Dec. 12, 1964; children: Mark James, John Phillip. B.S., U. Wales, 1962, Ph.D., 1966; M.S., La. State U., 1964. Asst. prof. Tex. A. and M. U., College Station, 1966-68, asso. prof., 1968-70, asst. dean, 1968-70; prof. U. Mo., Columbia, 1970-77; chmn. dept. geoscis., dir. Reservoir Studies Inst., Tex. Technol. U., Lubbock, 1977-80; pres. David K. Davies & Assocs., Inc., Houston, 1980—; dir. Tex. Commerce Bank, Kingwood. Contbr. articles to profl. jours. Mem. Planning and Zoning Commn. Columbia, Mo., 1979-80. Recipient A. I. Levorsen Meml. award Am. Assn. Petroleum Geologists, 1978. Fellow Geol. Soc. Am.; mem. Am. Assn. Petroleum Geologists, Soc. Econ. Paleontologists and Mineralogists, Soc. Petroleum Engrs. of AIME (Disting. lectr. 1984-85), Phi Kappa Phi. Current Work: Development of new techniques for well stimulation and electric log interpretation to optimize oil and gas prodn. Subspecialties: Sedimentology; Mineralogy. Home: 2210 Long Valley Kingwood TX 77345 Office: 1410 Stonehollow Dr Kingwood TX 77339

DAVIES, GEOFFREY, Chemistry educator, cons., researcher; b. Stoke-on-Trent, Eng., Feb. 6, 1942; s. Frank and Alice Ada (Boulton) D.; m. Elizabeth Florence Gardiner, Jan. 8, 1965; children: Warwick Harvey, Russell Howard, Claire Elizabeth. B.S., U. Birmingham, Eng., 1963, Ph.D., 1966. Postdoctoral fellow Brandeis U., 1966-68; research assoc. Brookhaven Nat. Lab., 1968-69; I.C.I. fellow U. Kent, Eng., 1969-71; asst. prof. chemistry Northeastern U., Boston, 1971-77, assoc. prof., 1977-81, prof., 1981—. Contbr. numerous articles on chemistry to profl. jours. Ringing master Ch. of the Advent Episcopal Ch., 1971-83; mgr. Bell Restoration Project Old North Ch., Boston, 1981-83. Recipient Excellence in Teaching award Northeastern U., 1981; Dreyfus Found. grantee, 1978. Mem. Am. Chem. Soc. Republican. Lodge: Masons. Current Work: Mechanisms of metal-catalyzed reactions of small, abundant molecules, especially dioxygen. Subspecialties: Catalysis chemistry; Inorganic chemistry. Office: Chemistry Dept Northeastern U Boston MA 02115

DAVIES, IVOR KEVIN, psychologist, consultant; b. Birmingham, Warwichshire, Eng., Dec. 19, 1930; came to U.S., 1970; s. Howard and Selina (Stockton) D.; m. Shirley Diana Winyard, Feb. 24, 1966; children: Simon Winyard, Michelle Winyard. B.A., U. Birmingham, Eng., 1952, M.A., 1953, Dip.Edn., 1955; M.S., U. Ill., 1954; Ph.D., U. Nottingham, 1967. Sr. lectr., chmn. dept. behavioral sci. RAF U., Cranwell, 1968-72; prof. edn. Ind. U., Bloomington, 1972—. Author: Programmed Learning in Perspective, 1962, What is Programmed Learning, 1965, The Management of Learning, 1971,82, Competency Based Learning, 1972, Objectives in Curriculum Design, 1976, 81, Contributions to an Educational Technology, vols. 1 and 2, 1978, Instructional Technique, 1981. Served to lt. col. RAF, 1955-71. Fellow Brit. Psychol. Soc., Coll. Preceptors (Eng.); mem. Am. Ednl. Research Assn., Am. Soc. Tng. and Devel., Nat. Soc. Performance and Instrn. Club: RAF (London). Current Work: Analysis of human performance, with special emphasis to the reduction of error in work situations. Subspecialties: Cognition; Human factors engineering. Home: 2447 Rock Creek Dr Bloomington IN 47401 Office: Ind U Bloomington IN 47405

DAVIES, MERTON EDWARD, planetary scientist; b. St. Paul, Sept. 13, 1917; s. Albert Daniel and Lucile Francis (McCabe) D.; m. Margaret Louise Darling, Feb. 10, 1946; children: Deidra Louise Davies Stauff, Albert Karl, Merton Randel. A.B., Stanford U., 1938. Group leader math. lofting Douglas Aircraft Co., El Segundo, Calif., 1940-48; mem. sr. staff The Rand Corp., Santa Monica, Calif., 1948, U.S. observer inspected stas. under terms of Antarctic Treaty. Author: (with Bruce Murray) The View from Space, 1971, (With others) Atlas of Mercury, 1978; contbr. (With others) articles to tech. jours. Recipient Antarctic Service medal U.S. Navy, 1967, George W. Goddard award Soc. Photo-Optical Instrumentation Engrs., 1966. Asso. fellow AIAA; mem. Am. Astron. Soc., Am. Soc. Photogrammetry (hon. mention Talbert Abrams award 1973), Am. Geophys. Union, AAAS. Patentee spinning panoramic camera. Current Work: Geodetic control on planets and satellites, photogrammetry, coordinate systems of planets and satellites. Subspecialties: Planetary science; Remote sensing (geoscience). Home: 1414 San Remo Dr Pacific Palisades CA 90272 Office: 1700 Main St Santa Monica CA 90406

DAVIES, PATRICK HANLON, aquatic toxicologist, chemist, researcher; b. Santa Fe, N.Mex., Sept. 4, 1938; s. Gerald Leo and Helen (Burritt) D.; m. Laurin C. Walter, Oct. 8, 1964 (div.); children—Kathleen, Kerry, Edward; m. R. Edith Lyttle, Jan. 21, 1972; 1 child, Jien-Ai. B.S., N.Mex. State U., 1964; M.S., Colo. State U., 1972, Ph.D., 1985. Aquatic biologist N.Mex. Game and Fish Dept., Santa Fe, 1964-67; researcher asst. Colo. Game, Fish and Parks, Ft. Collins, 1967-71; wildlife researcher Colo. Div. Wildlife, Ft. Collins, 1972—; mem. faculty Colo. State U., Ft. Collins, 1972—; mem. water quality standards com. Colo. Water Quality Control Commn., Denver, 1975-77, 85. Author chpt. in book. Contbr. articles to profl. jours. Mem. Am. Chem. Soc., Soc. Environ. Toxicology and Chemistry, Am. Fisheries Soc. (award of excellence 1983), ASTM, Am. Sci. Affiliation. Current work: Investigating analytical chemical methodologies for measuring the toxic (bio-available) fractions of metals in natural waters and the effects of chemical kinetics on metal toxicities to aquatic life and developing water quality standards. Subspecialties: Environmental chemistry; Environmental toxicology. Home: 4725 Venturi Ln Fort Collins CO 80525 Office: 317 West Prospect Fort Collins CO 80526

DAVILA, ENRIQUE, medical educator, physician; b. Bogota, Colombia, Dec. 28, 1948; came to U.S., 1974; s. Enrique Patricio Davila and Elvira (Davila) D. Bachiller, Gimnasio Campestre, Bogota, 1965; M.D., Nat. U. Colombia, Bogota, 1973. Diplomate: Am. Bd. Internal Medicine, Am. Bd. Hematology and Oncology. Intern Nassau Hosp., Mineola, N.Y., 1974-75; resident in medicine U. Miami, Fla., 1975-78, chief med. resident, 1980-81, asst. prof. medicine, 1981—, asst. prof. oncology, 1982—; fellow in hematology/oncology U. Pa., Phila., 1978-80; cons. Pan Am. Health Orgn., 1982—. Mem. Am. Fedn. for Clin. Research, ACP, Sociedad Colombiana de Hematologia, Am. Soc. Clin. Oncology, Southeastern Cancer Study Group. Current Work: Phase I trials of chemotherapy; continuous infusion chemotherapy; primary and secondary cancer of liver; biochemical modulators; esophageal cancer. Subspecialties: Chemotherapy; Hematology. Home: 575 Crandon Blvd Apt 512 Key Biscayne FL 33149 Office: Department of Oncology University of Miami 1475 NW 12th Ave Miami FL 33136

DAVIS, ALAN LYNN, computer architect, consultant; b. Salt Lake City, Nov. 17, 1946; s. H. Lynn and Mary Jean (Holt) D. S.B., MIT, 1969; Ph.D., U. Utah, 1972. Asst. prof. U. Waterloo, Ont., Can., 1972-73; computer scientist Burroughs IRC, LaJolla, Calif., 1973-77; assoc. prof. U. Utah, Salt Lake City, 1977-82; mgr. artificial intelligence architecture Schlumberger Palo Alto Research, Calif., 1982—; cons. Burroughs Corp., Detroit, 1973-82, Rand Corp., Santa Monica Calif., 1983—, Evans & Sutherland, Salt Lake City, 1983—. Contbr. articles to profl. jours. Patentee in field. Mem. IEEE. Current work: Computer architecture for concurrent AI machines, VLSI design, Parallel Programming Systems. Subspecialty: Computer architecture.

DAVIS, BRIAN KEITH, biologist; b. Sydney, New South Wales, Aus., May 15, 1937; came to U.S., 1962; S. and Ruby (Constance) D.; m. Nelida Rodrigo Villanueva, Aug. 3, 1963. B.Sc., U. New South Wales, 1958, Ph.D., 1962, D.Sc., 1982. Teaching fellow Sch. Wool and Pastoral Sci. U. New South Wales, Sydney, Aus., 1958-61; Ford Found. fellow Worcester Found. Exptl. Biology, Shrewsbury, Mass., 1962-63; research fellow Harvard U., Cambridge, Mass., 1963-65; sci. officer MRC Lab. Molecular Biology, Cambridge, U.K., 1965-66; research fellow McGill U., Montreal, Can., 1966-69; scientist Worcester Found. Exptl. Biology, Shrewsbury, Mass., 1970-78; research prof. SUNY-Stony Brook, 1978-82; dir. Research Found. So. Calif., San Diego, 1983—. Contbr. articles in field to profl jours. Served with Australian Armed Forces, 1955-57. Australian Atomic Energy Commn. grantee, 1961; AID grantee, 1974-75; Nat. Inst. Child Health & Devel. grantee, 1973—. Mem. Am. Physiol.Soc., Biophys. Soc., Soc. Exptl. Biology & Medicine, N.Y. Acad. Sci., Am. Soc. Cell Biology, Fedn. Am. Scientists. Current Work: The biochemistry of fertilization, especially concerning the molecular mechanism of sperm capacitation and decapacitation; biophysics of template-directed polymerization, especially concerning kinetics complexity and far from equilibrium thermodynamics; polymer gel drug delivery systems. Subspecialties: Reproductive biology; Biophysics (biology). Home: PO Box 2135 Del Mar CA 92014 Office: Research Found So. Calif PO Box 2504 La Jolla CA 92038

DAVIS, BRIAN KENT, geneticist; b. Laramie, Wyo., Dec. 2, 1939; s. Preston John Colver and Myrtle Ann (Barrett) D.; m. Janet Anne Pettingill, June 2, 1962; children: Christopher M., Catherine M., Casandra N. B.A., U. Wis., 1962, M.A. (NSF grad. fellow), 1963; Ph.D., U. Wash., 1970. NIH tng. grantee, 1966-70; research fellow U. Calif., San Diego, La Jolla, 1970-72; asst. prof. Va. Poly. Inst. and State U., Blacksburg, 1973-80, Coll. Medicine, King Faisal U., Saudi Arabia, 1980-81; research assoc. Allied Corp., Morristown, N.J., 1981—. Contbr.: articles to sci. jours., chpt. to Dermatoglyphics-50 Years Later, 1980. Am. Cancer Soc. grantee, 1970-72. Mem. Environ. Mutagen Soc., Genetics Soc. Am., Am. Genetic Assn., Internat. Dermatoglyphics Assn. Current Work: Genetic toxicology, recombinant DNA. Subspecialties: Toxicology (agriculture); Genetics and genetic engineering (biology). Office: Allied Corp PO Box 1021R Morristown NJ 07960

DAVIS, CHARLES HARGIS, information scientist, university dean; b. Tell City, Ind., Sept. 23, 1938; s. Charles Alban and Ruth Elizabeth (Hargis) D. B.S. (State Merit scholar), Ind. U., 1960, A.M., 1966, Ph.D., 1969; postgrad. (German Govt. Fellow), U. Munich, W. Ger., 1960-61. Asst. editor Chem. Abstracts Service, Columbus, Ohio, 1962-65; chem. info. specialist Ind. U. Aerospace Research Applications Center, 1965-66; dir. systems Ind. U. ERIC Clearinghouse on Reading, 1967-69; asst. prof. library sci. Drexel U., 1969-71; assoc. prof. U. Mich., 1971-76; prof., dean Faculty of Library Sci., U. Alta. (Can.), Edmonton, 1976-79, Grad. Sch. Library and Info. Sci., U. Ill., Urbana-Champaign, 1979—; speaker and condr. workshops and seminars in field; cons. in field; cons. editor Greenwood Press, Westport, Conn., 1974-79; pres. Can. Council Library Schs., 1978-79. Author: Illustrative Computer Programming for Libraries: Selected Examples for Information Specialists, 1974, 2d edit. (with Gerald W. Lundeen), 1981, (with James E. Rush) Information Retrieval and Documentation in Chemistry, 1974, Guide to Information Science, 1979; contbr. numerous articles, revs., bibliographies and columns to profl. publs. NSF research grantee, 1959-60. Mem. AAAS, Am. Chem. Soc., ALA (chmn. Library Research Round Table 1978-79), Am. Soc. Info. Sci. (chmn. Ind. U. student chpt. 1967-68, chmn. Ind. chpt. 1968-69, treas. Delaware Valley chpt. 1971, chmn. Mich. chpt. 1974-75, chmn. Western Can. chpt. 1978-79, pres. 1982-83), Assn. Computing Machinery, Assn. Am. Library Schs. (chmn. research com. 1976-78), Phi Lambda Upsilon, Beta Phi Mu. Subspecialty: Library and information science education administration. Office: Grad Sch Library and Info Sci 410 DKH U Ill at Urbana-Champaign 1407 Gregory Dr Urbana IL 61801

DAVIS, DEAN EARL, aerospace engineer, systems engineering consultant; b. Cheyenne, Wyo., Sept. 13, 1952; s. Vernon Lewis and Myrtle Elizabeth (Cary) D. M.S. in Astrogeophysics and Aerospace Engring., U. Colo., 1977; B.S. in Aeros. and Astronautics, U. Wash., 1979; B.S. in Computer and Mgmt. Sci., Denver Metro State Coll., 1981; B.S. in Astronomy, San Diego State U., 1982. Assoc. engr. Boeing Mil. Airplane Co., Wichita, Kans., 1978; engr. Boeing Aerospace Co., Seattle, 1978-79, Martin Marietta Aerospace Co., Denver, 1979-82; sr. engr. Convair div. Gen. Dynamics, San Diego, 1982-83; sr. advanced systems specialist Lockheed Missiles & Space Co., Sunnyvale, Calif., 1983-85; pres., gen. mgr. Star Tech Corp., Sunnyvale, 1984-85; sr. staff engr. Ultra Systems Def. & Space Systems Inc., Sunnyvale, 1985—. Author: Military Spacecraft Survivability Enhancement, 1981; CONUS Defense Study—Strategic Threats, 1982; also articles. Winner space essay contest Nat. Space Inst., 1982. Mem. AIAA (local chmn. 1974-75), Am. Astronautical Soc., Mil. Ops. Research Soc., Soc. Am. Mil. Engrs. (local pres. 1973-75), Air Force Assn., Arnold Air Soc. Republican. Methodist. Current work: Signature technology, space sensor and directed energy weapon technology, computer modeling and simulation of antisatellite engagements, nuclear and laser hardening, artificial intelligence and spacecraft autonomy, manned space systems. Subspecialties: Aerospace engineering and technology; Systems engineering. Home: 555 E El Camino Real Apt 410 Sunnyvale CA 94087 Office: Star Tech Corp 555 E El Camino Real Apt 410 Sunnyvale CA 94087

DAVIS, ELIZABETH EMILY LOUISE THORPE, psychophysicist, researcher; b. Grosse Pointe Farms, Mich., Aug. 11, 1948; d. Jack and Mary Alvina (McCarron) Thorpe; m. Ronald Wilson Davis, May 16, 1969. Student U. Calif.-Irvine, 1966-69; B.S., U. Ala., 1972; M.A., Columbia U., 1975, M.Phil., 1976, Ph.D., 1979. Research asst. U. Ala., University, 1972, Columbia U., N.Y.C., 1973-77; research assoc. NYU, 1979-81, adj. asst. prof., 1981; asst. prof. Oberlin Coll., Ohio, 1981-82; research asst. prof. Inst. Vision Research, SUNY-N.Y.C., 1983—. Ad hoc reviewer Perception mag., N.Y.C.; contbr. articles to profl. jours. Grantee NIH, 1979-81, 84—. Mem. Assn. Research in Vision and Ophthalmology, Optical Soc. Am. (ad hoc reviewer jour., San Diego session chairperson 1984), Soc. Neuroscis., N.Y. Acad. Scis., Am. Psychol. Assn., AAAS, Sierra Club, Pi Mu Epsilon, Sigma Xi. Current work: Spatial and temporal information processing by human and other mammalian visual systems, computer vision. Subspecialties: Psychophysics; Sensory processes. Office: State Coll Optometry SUNY 100 E 24th St New York NY 10010

DAVIS, GUY DONALD, physicist; b. Newport News, Va., June 15, 1952; s. Donald Arthur and Elinor Wilson (Ware) D.; B.S. in Physics, Rensselaer Poly. Inst., 1974; M.S. in Physics, U. Wis.-Madison, 1975, M.S. in Materials Sci., 1979, Ph.D. in Materials Sci., 1982. Scientist Martin Marietta Labs., Balt., 1980—. Contbr. chpt. to book: Surface and Interfacial Analysis, 1983. Contbr. articles to profl. publs. Recipient Outstanding Achievement award Martin Marietta Labs., 1984. Mem. Am. Vacuum Soc., Am. Phys. Soc., ASTM, Sigma Xi. Current work: Development of surface behavior diagrams to study surface and interfacial reactions; metal-polymer adhesive bonds, especially durability of aluminum structures in humid environments; interactions between compound semiconductors and thin metallic overlayers. Subspecialties: Materials; Condensed matter physics. Home: 5830 Alderleaf Pl Columbia MD 21045 Office: Martin Marietta Labs 1450 S Rolling Rd Baltimore MD 21227

DAVIS, HOWARD TED, chemical engineering educator; b. Hendersonville, N.C., Aug. 2, 1937; s. William Howard and Gladys Isabell (Rhodes) D.; m. Eugenia Asimakopoulos, Sept. 18, 1960; children: William Howard III, Maria Katherine. B.S., Furman U., 1959; Ph.D., U. Chgo., 1962. NSF postdoctoral fellow Free U. Brussels, 1962-63; asst. prof. U. Minn., Mpls., 1963-65, asso. prof., 1965-68, prof. chem. engring. and chemistry, 1968—, head dept. chem. engring. and materials sci., 1980—, chmn. exec. com. Microelectronic and Info. Scis. Ctr., 1982-85. Editor books.; Contbr. articles to tech. jours. indsl. cons. NSF fellow, 1959-62; NSF postdoctoral fellow, 1962-63; Sloan Found. fellow, 1968-70; Guggenheim fellow, 1969-70. Mem. Am. Inst. Chem. Engring., Am. Chem. Soc., Am. Phys. Soc., Soc. Petroleum Engrs., Phi Beta Kappa, Sigma Xi, Tau Beta Pi. Current Work: Teaching, research and administration. Subspecialties: Chemical engineering; Physical chemistry. Home: 1822 Mt Curve Ave Minneapolis MN 55403

DAVIS, JAMES NORMAN, neurologist, pharmacology researcher; b. Dallas, Oct. 24, 1939; s. Moses and Ruth (Grossman) D.; m. Frances Isabel Cantor, May 1, 1965; children: Amanda, Adam, Joanna. B.A., Cornell U., 1961, M.D., 1965. Diplomate: Am. Bd. Neurology and Psychiatry. Intern Bellevue Hosp., N.Y.C., 1965-66; research assoc. Lab. Chem. Pharmacology, Nat. Heart Inst., NIH, Bethesda, 1966-68; resident Duke U., 1968-69, asst. prof., 1972-77, assoc. prof. medicine and pharmacology, 1977-80, prof., 1980—; resident in neurology Cornell U.-N.Y. Hosp., 1969-72, North Shore Hosp., 1971; instr. neurology Cornell U., 1969-71. Contbr. articles to profl. jours. Served with USPHS, 1966-68. Mem. Am. Neurol. Assn., Soc. Clin. Investigation, Am. Soc. Pharmacology and Exptl. Therapeutics, Am. Acad. Neurology, Soc. Neurosci. Democrat. Jewish. Current Work: Catecholamine neuronal plasticity; catecholamine neuronal responses to brain injury and adrenergic cholinergic interactions. Subspecialties: Neurology; Regeneration. Home: 6 Harvey Pl Durham NC 27705 Office: Duke University PO Box 2900 Durham NC 27710

DAVIS, JAMES (OTHELLO), physician, educator; b. Tahlequah, Okla., July 12, 1916; s. Zemry and Villa (Hunter) D.; m. Florrilla Louise Sides, Dec. 27, 1941; children: Janet Ruth, James Lawrence. M.A. in Zoology, U. Mo., 1939, Ph.D., 1942, B.S. in Medicine, 1943; M.D., Washington U., 1945. Intern Barnes Hosp., St. Louis, 1945-46; investigator Lab. Kidney and Electrolyte Metabolism, Nat. Heart Inst., Bethesda, Md., 1949-57, chief sect. on exptl. cardiovascular disease, 1957-66; asso. prof. physiology Temple U. Sch. Medicine, Phila., 1955-56; vis. asso. prof. physiology Johns Hopkins Sch. Medicine, 1961-64; vis. prof. physiology U. Va. Sch. Medicine, 1964; prof., chmn. dept. physiology U. Mo. Sch. Medicine, Columbia, 1966-82, prof. emeritus, 1982—. Mem. editorial bd.: Am. Jour. Physiology, 1961-63, 66-69, Endocrinology, 1962-65, Circulation Research, 1962-66, 71-76, 78-81, Hypertension, 1979-80. Served with AUS, 1943-45; Served with USPHS, 1946-66. Recipient AMA Golden Apple award for teaching U. Mo., 1968; Sigma Xi Research award U. Mo., 1971; Modern Medicine Distinguished Achievement award, 1973; Alumni gold medal U. Mo., 1973; Volhard award, 1974; CIBA award for hypertension research, 1975; Carl T. Wiggers award, 1976; citation of merit U. Mo. Sch. Medicine, 1981. Mem. Am. Heart Assn. (mem. med. adv. council, vice chmn. council for high blood pressure research 1970-72, chmn. council 1972-74), Am. Physiology Soc. (council 1974-78, steering com. circulation group 1978-81, pres. circulation sect. 1981), Endocrine Soc., Soc. Exptl. Biology and Medicine, Nat. Inst. Health Extramural Program, Assn. Physiology Dept. Chairmen (council 1971-74), Inter-Am. Soc. Hypertension (council 1978-80), Internat. Soc. Hypertension (pres. 1980-82), Nat. Acad. Scis., Sigma Xi, Alpha Omega Alpha. Current Work: Roles of kidney and adrenal cortex in pathogenesis of hypertension and heart failure. Subspecialties: Physiology (biology); Nephrology. Home: 612 Maplewood Dr Columbia MO 65203

DAVIS, JAY CLARENCE, physicist; b. Haskell, Tex., July 12, 1942; s. J.C. and Mary Emma (Whitaker) D.; m. Mary Jean McIntyre, June 8, 1963; children—Mary Kathleen, Robert Kenneth. B.A., U. Tex., 1963, M.A., 1964; Ph.D., U. Wis.-Madison, 1969. AEC postdoctoral fellow U. Wis.-Madison, 1969-71; sr. physicist Lawrence Livermore Nat. Lab., Calif., 1971-74, project and ops. mgr., 1974-84, dep. assoc. dir., 1984—. Contbr. articles to profl. jours. Mem. Am. Phys. Soc., AAAS, Phi Beta Kappa. Democrat. Unitarian. Current work: Accelerator research facility design and construction. Subspecialties: Particle physics; Nuclear fusion. Office: Lawrence Livermore Nat Lab PO Box 808 Livermore CA 94550

DAVIS, JOHN MIHRAN, surgeon, educator; b. N.Y.C., Aug. 13, 1946; s. Drought Delaney and Ruth Radcliff (Kalaidjian) D.; m. Marlene Morgan, Oct. 13, 1973; children—Nicholas Mihran, Elizabeth Whitfield. B.A., Columbia Coll., N.Y.C., 1968; M.D., Wayne State U., Detroit, 1972. Diplomate: Am. Bd. Surgery. Resident in surgery N.Y. Hosp., 1972-77; fellow NIH, Bethesda, Md., 1977-79; asst. prof. surgery Cornell U. Med. Coll., 1979—; prin. investigator NIH, 1981. Mem. soccer adv. com. Columbia Coll., 1977—; mem. alumni council Collegiate Sch., N.Y.C., 1981—. Mem. Surg. Infection Soc. (charter), Am. Burn. Assn., Soc. Univ. Surgeons, Am. Fedn. Clin. Research, N.Y. Cancer Soc., Soc. Univ. Surgeons, N.Y. Surg. Soc., N.Y. State Med. Soc. Current Work: Neutrophil function in burn patients and patients with abdominal sepsis. Subspecialties: Surgery; Immunology (medicine). Office: Cornell Univ Med Coll 1300 York Ave New York NY 10021

DAVIS, JOHN MOULTON, physicist; b. Nottingham, Eng., Aug. 28, 1938; s. John Henry and Gladys Winifred (Moulton) D.; m. Margery Grady, July 10, 1976. B.Sc. with 1st class honors, U. Leeds, 1960, Ph.D., 1964. Research assoc. M.I.T., 1964-70; sr. scientist Am. Sci. & Engring. Inc., Cambridge, Mass., 1970-72, staff scientist, 1972-74, sr. staff scientist, 1974-85, dir. space research, 1985—. Contbr. articles to profl. jours. Mem. Republican Town Com., Lexington, Mass., 1972-76. Recipient Skylab Achievement award NASA, 1974, Sounding Rocket award, 1977, two certs. of Recognition for Tech. Innovation, NASA, 1983. Mem. Am. Geophys. Union, Am. Astron. Soc. Current Work: Study of solar corona through analysis of X-ray observations. Subspecialties: Solar physics; X-ray high energy astrophysics. Home: 386 Winchester St Newton MA 02161 Office: Am Sci & Engring Inc Fort Washington Cambridge MA 02139

DAVIS, JOHN ROWLAND, research adminstrator; b. Mpls., Dec. 19, 1927; s. Roland Owen and Dorothy (Norman) D.; m. Lois Marie Falk, Sept. 4, 1947; children—Joel C., Jacque L., Michele M., Robin E. B.S., U. Minn., 1949, M.S., 1951; postgrad., Purdue U., 1955-57; Ph.D., Mich. State U., 1959. Registered profl. engr., Calif., Oreg. Hydraulic engr. U.S. Geol. Survey, Lincoln, Nebr., 1950-51; instr. Mich. State U., 1951-55; asst. prof. Purdue U., 1955-57; lectr. U. Calif. at Davis, 1957-62; hydraulic engr. Stanford Research Inst., South Pasadena, Calif., 1962-64; prof. U. Nebr., Lincoln, 1964-65; dean U. Nebr. (Coll. Engring. and Architecture), 1965-71; prof., head dept. agrl. engring. Oreg. State U., Corvallis, 1971-75, dir. Agrl. Expt. Sta., assoc. dean Sch. Agr., 1975-85, dir. spl. programs in agr., 1985—; instl. athletic rep. Oreg. State U., 1972—; cons. Stanford Research Inst., Dept. Agr.; dir. Engrs. Council Profl. Devel., 1966-72; pres. Pacific-10 Conf., 1978-79. Contbr. articles to profl. jours. Served with USNR, 1945-46. Fellow Am. Soc. Agrl. Engrs. (dir. 1971-73, agrl. engr. of year award Pacific Northwest region 1974); mem. Nat. Coll. Athletic Assn. (v.p. 1979-83, sec.-treas. 1983-85, pres. 1985—). Current work: Irrigation engineering; soil erosion control Subspecialties: Agricultural engineering; Resource conservation. Home: 2940 NW Aspen St Corvallis OR 97330

DAVIS, LEONARD GEORGE, research neurochemist; b. Chgo., Nov. 23, 1946; s. Willard George and Mildred Ann (Poole) D.; m. Penny Suzanne Barber, Aug. 30, 1969; 1 dau., Robin. B.S., U. Ill., 1969; M.S. (scholar), Northwestern U., 1974; Ph.D., U. Ill. Med. Sch., Chgo., 1977. Mem. research staff med. research div. William Beaumont Army Hosp., El Paso, Tex., 1975-76; mem. research staff neurochemistry unit Mo. Inst. Psychiatry, St. Louis, 1976-80; group leader, research scientist central research dept. E.I. du Pont de Nemours & Co., Wilmington, Del., 1980—, group leader cellular and molecular neurobiology, 1984—. Contbr. numerous articles to sci. jours. Bd. dirs. New Castle County Mental Health Assn., 1982-83. NIMH scholar, 1975-76; Nat. Inst. Drug and Alcohol grantee, 1980; NIHM grantee, 1980; Nat. Inst. Aging grantee, 1979-81. Mem. Soc. for Neurosci. (pres. local chpt. 1983), Am. Soc. Neurochemistry, N.Y. Acad. Scis. Current Work: Understanding the regulation of neuropeptides and their genes in brain function, their genetic regulation, and their molecular mechanisms of action. Subspecialties: Neurochemistry; Neurobiology. Office: EI du Pont de Nemours & C Exptl Sta E400 Wilmington DE 19898

DAVIS, LEROY WELLINGTON, Metallurgical and chemical engineer, engineering technical company executive; b. Cleve., May 29, 1901; s. George Embury and Jessie Eunice (Wellington) D.; m. Ruth Miller Durbs, Oct. 4, 1950 (dec. 1970); children: Gilbert George (dec.) Linda Elaine. B.Sc. in Chem. Engring, Case Inst. Tech., Cleve., 1922, Metall. Engr., 1931. Metallurgist Aluminum Co. of Am., Cleve., 1926-42, asst. div. chief. metallurgist, Pitts., 1942-52; tech. supt. Kaiser Aluminum, Halethrope, Md., 1952-55, Erie, Pa., 1952-55; div. mgr. Harvey Aluminum, Torrance, Calif., 1955-57, asst. dir. research and devel. div., 1958-70; pres. Nev. Engring. and Tech. Corp., Long Beach, Calif., 1971-80, chmn. bd., 1980—. Author: (with S.W. Bardstreet) Metal and Ceramic Matrix Composites, 1971; contbr. numerous articles to profl. publs. Active Heritage Found.; mem. Republican Congressional Com., 1978-82. Recipient Commendation Am. Ceramic Soc., 1982. Fellow Am. Soc. Metals, Am. Ceramic Soc.; mem. ASTM, Am. Soc. Nondestructive Testing, Nat. Assn. Corrosion Engrs., Am. Def. Preparedness Assn., AIME. Baptist. Club: Univ. (Erie). Patentee in field. Current Work: Metal matrix composites information center; composites technology development and evaluation, and non-destructive testing. Subspecialties: Composite materials; Metallurgy. Home: 21462 Pacific Coast Hwy 58 Huntington Beach CA 92646 Office: 2225 E 28th St Bldg 511 Long Beach CA 90806

DAVIS, LEWIS BERKLEY, JR., mechanical engineer; b. Owensboro, Kent., Mar. 3, 1944; s. Lewis Berkley and Elizabeth (Miller) D. B.S. in Mech. Engring., U. Kent., 1966, M.S., 1970, Ph.D., 1972. Combustion devel. engr. gasturbine div. Gen. Electric Co., Schenectady, N.Y., 1972-79, mgr. advanced combustor design, 1979-81, mgr. spl. combustion projects, 1981, mgr. advanced combustion design, 1982—. Contbr. articles to profl. jours. Patentee in field. NASA fellow U. Kent., 1967-70. Mem. ASME (vis. accreditation bd. engring. and tech. 1980—), AIAA, Sigma Xi. Current work: Development of combustion systems and design technology for advanced gas turbines. Subspecialties: Mechanical engineering; Combustion processes. Home: 24 Ray St Schenectady NY 12309 Office: Gen Electric Co 1 River Rd Schenectady NY 12345

DAVIS, LLOYD EDWARD, veterinarian, educator, researcher; b. Akron, Ohio, Aug. 23, 1929; s. Roger Q. and Myrtle Elva (Burke) D.; m. Thelma L. Brunty, June 4, 1953; m. Carol A. Neff, Sept. 25, 1972; children: Mark E., Kimberly A. D.V.M., Ohio State U., 1959; Ph.D. in Pharmacology, U. Mo., 1963. Lic. veterinarian, Ill., Mo. Instr. then asst. prof., assoc. prof. U. Mo., Columbia, 1959-69; prof. Ohio State U., Columbus, 1969-72; vis. prof. U. Nairobi, Kenya, 1972-74; prof. Colo. State U., Ft. Collins, 1974-78; prof. clin. pharmacology U. Ill., Urbana, 1978—; mem. U.S. Pharmacopeia Gen. Com. Revision; sci. adv. Mercenene Med. Corp.; spl. cons. FDA. Contbr. numerous articles in field of clin. pharmacology to profl. jours. Served with USN, 1950-53. Recipient Disting. Teaching award U. Mo., 1968. Mem. Am. Soc. Pharmacology and Exptl. Therapeutics, Am. Acad. Vet. Pharmacology and Therapeutics (pres. 1976-78), Am. Soc. Clin. Pharmacology and Therapeutics, Soc. Exptl. Biol. Medicine, Sigma Xi, Phi Zeta (pres. 1982). Current Work: Clinical evaluation of drugs, drug therapy, influence of disease on disposition and fate of drugs in animal patients. Subspecialties: Pharmacology; Internal medicine (veterinary medicine). Home: 621 W Hill St Champaign IL 61820 Office: 1102 W Hazelwood Dr Urbana IL 61801

DAVIS, L(LOYD) WAYNE, scientific consultant; b. Medicine Lodge, Kans., July 16, 1929; s. Lloyd and Edith Elda (Furnas) D.; m. Betty Louise Pyke, Sept. 7, 1963; 1 child, William W.; children by previous marriage—Robert L., Cheryl S. B.S. in Engring. Physics, U.Kans., 1952; M.S. in Elec. Engring., U. N.Mex., 1959. Staff mem. systems analysis dept. Sandia Corp., Albuquerque, 1952-56, cons., 1956-57; research physicist Dikewood Corp., Albuquerque, 1957-60, sr. research physicist, 1960-64, head weapons effects div., 1964-67, dep. tech. dir., 1967-69, asst. v.p., 1969-72, sec., 1970-80, dir., 1971-82, v.p., 1972-77, sr. v.p., 1977-80, pres., chmn. bd., 1980-82; v.p. Kaman Scis. Corp., gen. mgr. Dikewood div., Albuquerque, 1982-83; sci. cons., 1983—. Trustee Christian Ch., 1970-73. Summerfield scholar U. Kans., 1948-52; U. N.Mex. fellow, 1958-59. Mem. IEEE (sr.), Am. Phys. Soc. (S.E. sect.), Sigma Xi, Phi Kappa Phi, Tau Beta Pi, Sigma Tau, Sigma Pi Sigma, Kappa Mu Epsilon, Beta Gamma Sigma, Delta Sigma Pi, Sigma Chi. Republican. Current work: Developer urban nuclear-casualty prediction model for high-yield nuclear burst from Japanese data-base over many years. Subspecialty: Nuclear weapons effects. Home: 4411 Altura Ave NE Albuquerque NM 87110

DAVIS, MARK HEZEKIAH, JR., electrical engineer; b. Knoxville, Tenn., Oct. 5, 1948; s. Mark Hezekiah and Grace Carson (Owens) D.; m. Susan Nakamura, July 14, 1977; 1 dau.: Michelle Grace. B.S. in E.E, U. Tenn., 1972, M.S., 1973. Devel. engr. Westinghouse Electric Corp.-U.S. AEC, Pitts. and Oakridge, 1969-76; sr. research engr. N.L. Petroleum Service, Houston, 1977-79; mgr. research and devel. Advanced Ocean Systems div. Hydril Corp., Houston, 1980-81; engring. mgr. Schlumberger Corp., Sugarland, Tex., 1981-82; dir. electronics devel. Tech. for Energy Corp., Knoxville, Tenn., 1982-84; mgr. digital signal processing N.E.C. Electronics, Mountain View, Calif., 1984—. Pres. N.W. Houston United Civic Assn., 1980-81. Robert Miller scholar, 1971; U. Tenn. Nat. Alumni scholar, 1972; U.S. AEC grantee, 1973. Mem. IEEE (sr.), Am. Soc. Engring. Edn., Optical Soc. Am., Electro-Chem. Soc., Marine Tech. Soc., Soc. Photo-Optical Instrumentation Engrs. Current Work: Fiber optic sensors and communications systems and high temperature electronics in geosci. Subspecialties: Ocean engineering; Fiber optics. Home: PO Box 118 Knoxville TN 37901 Office: NEC Electronics Mountain View CA

DAVIS, MICHAEL, psychopharmacologist, educator, researcher; b. Bronxville, N.Y., Nov. 14, 1942; s. Pearce and Lucia Banks (Bates) D.; m. Linda Shaffer, Dec. 30, 1967; children: Nathaniel, Alexander. B.A., Northwestern U., 1965; Ph.D., Yale U., 1969. Research assoc. dept. psychiatry Yale U., New Haven, 1969-70, asst. prof., 1970-75, assoc. prof., 1975—. Contbr. numerous articles to sci. jours. NIMH career devel. award, 1975—. Mem. Am. Psychol. Assn., Soc. for Neurosci., Soc. for Psychophysiol. Research. Current Work: Measure how drugs affect the brain and behavior. Subspecialties: Neuropharmacology; Neuropsychology.

DAVIS, MICHAEL JAY, plant pathologist, educator; b. Denver, Mar. 9, 1947; s. Jay Edward and Joan Roberta (Dirmeyer) D.; m. Carol Ann Freeman, June 21, 1980; 1 son, Christopher Michael. B.S., Colo. State U., 1973, M.S., 1975; Ph.D., U. Calif., Berkeley, 1978. Asst. prof. dept. pathology Rutgers U., New Brunswick, N.J., 1979-81; asst. prof. plant pathology Agrl. Research and Edn. Center, U. Fla., Ft. Lauderdale, 1981—. Contbr. articles to sci. jours. U.S. Dept. Agr. grantee, 1980, 82. Mem. Am. Phytopath. Soc., Am. Soc. Microbiology, U.S. Fedn. Culture Collections, Sigma Xi, Gamma Sigma Delta. Current Work: Etiology, epidemiology and control of plant disease caused by bacteria; plant pathology, phytobacteriology, fastidious vascular plant pathogens of plants, plant disease resistance, genetic engineering. Subspecialties: Plant pathology; Genetics and genetic engineering (agriculture). Home: 10121 NW 21st Ct Pembroke Pines FL 33023 Office: 3205 SW College Ave Fort Lauderdale FL 33314

DAVIS, RAYMOND, JR., nuclear chemist; b. Washington, Oct. 14, 1914; s. Raymond and Ida Rogers (Younger) D.; m. Anna Marsh Torrey, Dec. 4, 1948; children: Andrew Morgan, Martha Safford, Nancy Elizabeth, Roger Warren, Alan Paul. B.S., U. Md., 1937, M.S., 1939; Ph.D., Yale U., 1942. Chemist Dow Chem. Co., Midland, Mich., 1938-39, Monsanto Chem. Co., Dayton, Ohio, 1946-48; with Brookhaven Nat. Lab., Upton, N.Y., 1948-84; research prof. dept. astronomy U. Pa., Phila., 1984—. Contbr. articles to profl. jours. Served with USAAF, 1942-46. Recipient Boris Prejel prize N.Y. Acad. Scis., 1955; Comstock prize Nat. Acad. Scis., 1978; award for nuclear applications in chemistry Am. Chem. Soc., 1979. Mem. Am. Phys. Soc., Am. Geophys. Union, Am. Acad. Arts and Scis., Am. Astron. Soc., AAAS, Meteoritical Soc., Nat. Acad. Scis. Current Work: Studying the neutrino radiation from the sun, cosmic radiation, and particle physics. Subspecialties: Cosmic ray high energy astrophysics; Planetary science. Office: Dept Astronomy Univ Pa Philadelphia PA 19104

DAVIS, ROBERT EDGAR, analytical chemist, surface scientist; b. Raleigh, N.C., Jan. 6, 1949; s. Bryan Glenn and Eloise (Furr) D.; m. Bette Meyer-Davis. B.S., U. N.C., 1975; Ph.D., U. Ill., 1981. Staff engr. IBM, Tucson, 1981-85, project mgr., 1985—. Contbr. articles to profl. jours. Served to 2d class petty officer USCG, 1969-71. Mem. Am. Chem. Soc., Am. Phys. Soc., Am. Vacuum Soc., Electrochem. Soc., Sigma Xi. Democrat. Methodist. Current work: Materials characterization using Auger electron spectroscopy, x-ray photoelectron spectroscopy, Rutherford backscattering spectrometry and electron microscopy. Subspecialties: Analytical chemistry; Surface chemistry. Home: 2541 N Shannon Rd Tucson AZ 85745 Office: IBM Corp D/68V/061-1 9000S Rita Rd Tucson AZ 85744

DAVIS, ROBERT GENE, plant scientist; b. Doddsville, Miss., Mar. 2, 1932; s. Robert Jeff and Osa (McCarty) D.; m. Dorothy Hobart, Jan. 29, 1954; children: Sondra, Elizabeth, Carl, David. B.S. in Agr, Miss. State U., 1953, M.S. in Plant Pathology, 1968; Ph.D. in Plant Pathology, La. State U., 1970. Research plant pathologist Miss. Agr. and Forest Expt. Sta., Stoneville, 1971-82; prof. dept. plant pathology and weed sci. Miss. State U., 1981-82; owner Davis Research Co. (cons. and agrl. research, mfr. of bacterial inoculants), Avon, 1982—. Served with U.S. Army, 1955-57. Mem. Am. Phytopath. Soc., Sigma Xi, Phi Kappa Phi. Subspecialty: Plant pathology. Address: PO Box 359 Avon MS 38723

DAVIS, ROBERT JAMES, astronomer; b. Omaha, Oct. 26, 1929; s. Harry Cleve and Margaret Louise (Homan) D.; m. Ruth Cinnamon, May 16, 1953; children: Carolyn (Mrs. Norman Hargis), Deborah (Mrs. Thomas Mossberg), Paul, Elizabeth. A.B., Harvard U., 1951, M.A., 1956, Ph.D., 1960. With Smithsonian Astrophys. Obs., 1955—, physicist, 1958—. Served with USNR, 1951-54. Recipient Smithsonian Sustained Outstanding Service award, 1968. Mem. Internat. Soc. Philos. Enquiry (historian 1975-84, trustee 1984—), Am. Astron. Soc., Internat. Astron. Union, Sigma Xi. Congregationalist. (sr. deacon 1972-75, moderator 1980-81). Current Work: Stellar and extragalactic spectroscopy; astrophysical data files stars; galaxies, galaxy clusters; spectroscopy; data management. Subspecialties: Optical astronomy; Ultraviolet high energy astrophysics. Home: 307 Pleasant St Belmont MA 02178 Office: 60 Garden St Cambridge MA 02138

DAVIS, STEPHEN HOWARD, engineering educator; b. N.Y.C., Sept. 7, 1939. B.E.E., Rensselaer Poly. Inst., 1960, M.S. in Math., 1962, Ph.D. in Math., 1964. Mathematician, Rand Corp., Santa Monica, Calif.,1964-66; lectr. dept. math. Imperial Coll., U. London, 1966-68; asst. prof. Johns Hopkins U., Balt., 1968-70, assoc. prof., 1970-75, prof. mech. and materials sci., 1975-79; prof. mech. and nuclear engring. Northwestern U., Evanston, Ill., 1978—, prof. engring. scis. and applied math., 1978—; mem. Environ. Research Guidance Com. to State Md., 1975-78; vis. prof. Monash U., Melbourne, Australia, 1973, U. Ariz., Tucson, 1977, 82; lectr. U. So. Calif., 1966, UCLA, 1965, Johns Hopkins Evening Coll., 1971-78. Asst. editor: Jour. Fluid Mech., 1969-75, assoc. editor, 1975—. Contbr. articles to profl. jours. Fellow Am. Phys. Soc.; mem. Sigma Xi, Pi Mu Epsilon. Current work: Research on hyrodynamic stability theory, thermal convection, interfacial phenomena, solidification. Subspecialties: Fluid mechanics; Applied mathematics. Office: Northwestern U Dept Engring Scis and Applied Math Evanston IL 60201

DAVIS, THOMAS EDWARD, medical oncologist; b. Ft. Monroe, Va., July 21, 1943; s. Thomas O. and Marlynn D.; m. Amy Gibson, June 7, 1969; children: Matthew, Sarah. B.A., Johns Hopkins U., 1965, M.D., 1969. Diplomate: Am. Bd. Internal Medicine, also Sub-Bd. Med. oncology. Intern Osler med. service Johns Hopkins U., Balt., 1969-70, resident, 1970-72, fellow in med. oncology, 1972-74; mem. faculty U. Wis. Med. Sch., Madison, 1974-85, assoc. prof. human oncology and medicine, 1980-85; assoc. dir. clin. programs Wis. Clin. Cancer Center, 1982-85; prof. medicine Stanford U. Med. Sch., 1985—; dir. No. Calif. Cancer Program, 1985—; exec. officer Eastern Coop. Oncology Group, 1977-85. Author 60 papers on cancer diagnosis and treatment. Mem. Am. Soc. Clin. Oncology, Am. Assn. Cancer Research, ACP. Current Work: Cancer chemotherapy. Subspecialties: Oncology; Chemotherapy. Office: No Calif Cancer Program PO Box 10144 Palo Alto CA 94303

DAVIS, THOMAS PAUL, pharmacology educator; b. Los Angeles, Jan. 13, 1951; s. Joseph Jefferson and Margaret (Moran) D.; m. Alecia Anne Kiehn, June 17, 1971; children: Melissa Catherine, Rebecca Marie, Ryan Thomas. B.S., Loyola U.-Los Angeles, 1973; M.S., U. Nev., 1975; Ph.D., U. Mo., 1978. Grad. research asst. physiology U. Mo., Columbia, 1975-78; analytical chemist Abbott Diagnostics Div., Abbott Labs., North Chgo., 1978-80; adj. asst. prof. pharmacology U. Ariz., Tucson, 1980-81, asst. prof., 1981—, dir. analytical chemistry, mass spectrometry, lab., 1980—; cons. Hansen's Natural Foods Inc., Los Angeles, 1983—, Gibson-Stephens Neuropharmaceuticals, Tucson, 1984—. Contbr. chpts. to books and articles in field to profl. jours. Recipient D.B. Dill award U. Nev., 1974-75. Mem. Soc. Neurosci., Am. Physiol. Soc., Am. Chem. Soc., Assn. Ofcl. Analytical Chemists, Am. Soc. Pharmacology and Exptl. Therapeutics, Sigma Xi. Democrat. Roman Catholic. Current Work: Teaching and research in peptide biochemistry and neuropharmacology; biochemical pharmacology of drugs and metabolites; neuropharmacology of opioid peptides in gut and brain. Subspecialties: Analytical chemistry; Neuropharmacology. Home: 7701 N Lundberg Tucson AZ 85741 Office: U Ariz Coll Medicine Tucson AZ 85724

DAVIS, THOMPSON ELDER, JR., psychologist; b. Calhoun, Ga., Sept. 4, 1940; s. Thompson Elder and Anna May (Carper) D.; m. Margaret Louise Campbell, Sept. 7, 1963 (div. 1983); 1 son, Thompson Elder III. Student, King Coll., Bristol, Tenn., 1958-61; B.S., E. Tenn. State Coll., 1962; M.S., U. Ga., 1973, Ph.D., 1974. Tchr., librarian Habersham County Bd. Edn., Alto, Ga., 1962-64; auditor Fed. Res. Bank, Atlanta, 1964-66, So. Services, Inc., Atlanta, 1966-67; asst. dir. internat. auditing div. U. Ga., Athens, 1967-68; mgmt. cons., Athens, 1968-69; clin. psychology intern Johns Hopkins U. Med. Sch., Balt., 1971-72, pub. psychology pilot intern, 1971-72; dir. psychol. services Glass Mental Health Ctr., Balt., 1974-81; v.p. ops. Behavioral Cons. Service, Inc., Balt., 1974-81; pres. Med. Data Fin. Corp. Inc., Balt., 1979-81; dir. psychol. research Glass Mental Health Found., Inc., Balt., 1977-81, pvt. practice clin. psychology, Lutherville, Md., 1979—; Bd. dirs. Friends Med. Sci. Research Ctr., Inc., 1978-80. King Coll. scholar, 1958-59; USPHS grantee, 1972-73; William Cooper Walker scholar, 1971-72. Mem. Am. Psychol. Assn., Md. Psychol. Assn., AAAS, Balt. Assn. Cons. Psychologists, Nat. Register Health Service Providers in Psychology, Psi Chi. Republican. Presbyterian. Current Work: Cognitive behavior therapy. Subspecialty: Clinical psychology. Home: Left Bank 10220 Davis Ave Woodstock MD 21163 Office: York Pl 1204 York Rd Suite 14 Lutherville MD 21163

DAVIS, WILBUR MARVIN, pharmacology and toxicology educator, researcher; b. Calumet City, Ill., Apr. 13, 1931; s. Lester and Gladys (Cyphers) D.; m. Sandra Smith, Nov. 23, 1956; children: Brian Lee, Catherine Lee. B.S. in Pharmacy, Purdue U., 1952, M.S., 1953, Ph.D., 1955. From asst. prof. to prof. Coll. Pharmacy, U. Okla., Norman, 1955-64; prof. pharmacology U. Miss. Sch. Pharmacy, Oxford, 1964—, chmn. dept., 1964-83; cons. NIH. Contbr. articles on pharmacology to profl. jours. Recipient Borden award, 1951; Lalor Found. Research award, 1958. Mem. Am. Soc. for Pharmacology and Exptl. Therapeutics, Soc. Toxicology, Soc. for Neurosci., AAAS, Am. Pharm. Assn., Acad. Pharm. Scis., Am. Assn. Colls. Pharmacy. Baptist. Current Work: Behavioral mechanisms and toxicologic actions of abuse drugs; teaching and research in toxicology and pharmacology. Subspecialties: Neuropharmacology; Toxicology (medicine). Home: 308 Lewis Ln Oxford MS 38655 Office: Sch Pharmacy U Miss 309 Faser Hall University MS 38677

DAVISON, KENNETH LEWIS, scientist; b. Hopkins, Mo., Dec. 27, 1935; s. Harlan R. and Hilda E. (Mendenhall) D.; m. Joyce Yvonne Schmitt, Sept. 8, 1957; children: Jeanette, Kenneth, Kathryn. B.S., U. Mo., 1957; M.S., Iowa State U., 1959, Ph.D., 1961. Research specialist in plant and animal nutrition Cornell U., 1961-65; research physiologist U.S. Dept. Agr.-Agrl. Research Service Metabolism and Radiation Research Lab., Fargo, N.D., 1965—. Mem. AAAS, Am. Inst. Nutrition, Am. Soc. Animal Sci., Am. Dairy Sci. Assn. Methodist. Current Work: Metabolism of agricultural chemicals by animals. Subspecialties: Animal nutrition; Animal physiology. Home: 2860 N 2d St Fargo ND 58102 Office: 1605 W College St Fargo ND 58105

DAVISON, SYDNEY GEORGE, educator; b. Stockport, Eng., Sept. 6, 1934; s. Wilfrid and Sara H. (Warrington) D.; m. Prudence G. Allonby, Mar. 28, 1959; children: Terry, Symon, Timothy Scott. B.Sc., U. Manchester, Eng., 1958, M.Sc., 1962, Ph.D., 1964, D.Sc., 1982. Prof. physics Clarkson Coll., Potsdam, N.Y., 1970-72, Bartol Research Found., Swarthmore, Pa., 1972-74; prof. applied math. U. Waterloo, Ont., 1974—, prof. physics, 1982—; dir. Guelph-Waterloo Surface Sci. and Tech. Group. Editor: Progress in Surface Science; Contbr. articles to nat. and internat. jours. Nat. Sci. and Engring. Research Council Can. grantee, 1965-73, 75—. Fellow Am. Phys. Soc., Inst. Physics (U.K.). Anglican. Current Work: Quantum theory of solid surfaces; chemisorption, surface states, disordered systems; quantum electrochemistry. Subspecialties: Surface chemistry; Condensed matter physics. Home: 313 Hiawatha Dr Waterloo ON N2L 2V9 Canada Office: Applied Math Dept U Waterloo Waterloo ON N2L 3G1 Canada

DAVY, PHILIP SHERIDAN, consulting engineer; b. Madison, Wis., July 12, 1915; s. Francis Joseph and Mathilda Sara (Femrite) D.; m. Caecilia Magdalen Thiemann, Jan. 12, 1916; children—Katherine Davy Bathurst, Patricia Davy Sciborski, Michael, Barbara Davy Salassa, Thomas, Margaret Davy Claeys. Student U. Wis.-La Crosse, 1932-33; B.S. in Civil Engring., U. Wis.-Madison, 1937, M.S. in Environ. Engring., 1938. Registered profl. engr., Wis., Minn., Iowa, Ill., Ind., Mich. Research fellow U. Wis.-Madison, 1937-38; engr. Frank J. Davy & Son, La Crosse, 1938-40, Permutit Co., N.Y.C., 1946; v.p. Davy Engring. Co., La Crosse, 1946-56, pres., 1956—; lectr. U. Wis.-Madison, 1965-75; instr. State Bd. Health, 1965-75, State Dept. Natural Resources, 1975-80. Bd. dirs., pres. United Fund of La Crosse, 1962-65; pres. Gateway Area council Boy Scouts Am., 19-75, v.p. region 1, 1979-81, nat. and regional council rep., 1976—; v.p., pres., bd. dirs. Riverside U.S.A., La Crosse, 1980-85. Served to lt. col. U.S. Army Engrs., 1941-45. Decorated Army Commendation medal with oak leaf cluster; knight comdr. with star Equestrian Order of Holy Sepulchre; recipient George Warren Fuller award Am. Water Works Assn., 1984. Fellow ASCE (Outstanding Service award 1979); mem. Water Pollution Control Fedn., AAAS, Am. Acad. Environ. Engrs. (diplomate), Nat. Soc. Profl. Engrs. (bd. dirs. 1966-69), Wis. Soc. Profl. Engrs. (pres. 1974-75, Engr. of Yr. 1970), La Crosse County Hist. Soc. (bd. dirs. 1979-81, pres. 1982). Republican. Roman Catholic. Clubs: La Crosse, La Crosse Country. Lodges: Rotary (bd. dirs. 1984—), Elks, K.C. Current work: Design of water supply and distribution systems, design of waste water treatment plants. Subspecialties: Civil engineering; Water supply and wastewater treatment. Home: 1230 King St La Crosse WI 54601 Office: Davy Engring Co 115 S 6th St La Crosse WI 54601

DAWID, IGOR BERT, biologist; b. Czernowitz, Romania, Feb. 26, 1935; came to U.S., 1960, naturalized, 1977; s. Josef and Pepi (Druckmann) D.; m. Keiko Naito Ozato, Apr. 5, 1976. Ph.D., U. Vienna, 1960. Fellow dept. biology MIT, 1960-62; fellow dept. embryology Carnegie Instn. of Washington, Balt., 1962-66, mem. staff, 1966-78; chief devel. biochemistry sect. Lab. Biochemistry, Nat. Cancer Inst., Bethesda, Md., 1978-82; chief lab. molecular genetics Nat. Inst. Child Health and Human Devel. (NIH), Bethesda, 1982—; vis. scientist Max Planck Inst. for Biology, 1964-67; asst. prof. to prof. dept. biology Johns Hopkins U., 1967-78. Editor: Devel. Biology, 1971-75, Cell, 1977—; editor-in-chief: Devel. Biology, 1975-80, adv. editor, 1980—. Mem. Am. Soc. Biol. Chemists, Am. Soc. Cell Biology, Soc. Devel. Biology, Internat. Soc. Devel. Biologists, AAAS, Nat. Acad. Sci. Subspecialties: Developmental biology; Molecular biology. Office: 9000 Rockville Pike Bethesda MD 20205

DAWKINS, BARRY GILBERT, veterinarian, editor; b. Meridian, Miss., June 15, 1952; s. Gilbert Lee and Betty Jean (Cheatham) D.; m. Karie Elizabeth Kueven, Mar. 12, 1977; children—Lauryn, Elizabeth, Gilbert James. A.A., Meridian Jr. Coll., 1972; D.M.V., Auburn U., 1977. Vet. clinician Gurley's Small Animal Hosp., Durham, N.C., 1977-78; emergency practice vet. medicine Charlotte Emergency Vet. Clinic, Charlotte, N.C., 1977-78; scientist, vet., asst. to dir., of lab. animal medicine dept., dir. controlled substances Hazleton Lab., Am., Vienna, Va., 1978-84; asst. editor Am. Vet. Med. Assn., Schaumburg, Ill., 1984—. Mem. AVMA, Phi Theta Kappa. Mem. Christian Bible Ch. Current work: All biomedical disciplines, including toxicology, immunology, pharmacology, genetics, teratology, chemotherapy, oncology, pathology, reproduction, metabolism, laboratory animal medicine, surgery, radiology, neurology, cardiology and ophthalmology. Subspecialties: Ophthalmology; Laboratory animal medicine. Home: 4103 Wildwood Dr Crystal Lake IL 60014 Office: Am Vet Med Assn 930 N Meacham Rd Schaumburg IL 60196

DAWSON, EARL BLISS, biochemist, consultant; b. Perry, Fla., Feb. 1, 1930; s. Bliss and Linnie Estella (Calliham) D.; m. Winnie Ruth Isbell, Apr. 10, 1951; children: Barbara Gail, Patricia Ann, Robert Earl, Diana Lynn. B.A., U. Kans., 1955; M.A., U. Mo.-Columbia, 1960; Ph.D., Tex. A. and M. U., 1964. Instr. U. Tex. Med. Br., Galveston, 1963-65, asst. prof., 1965-68, assoc. prof. biochemistry, 1968—; cons. NIH/State Dept., Guatamala City, Guatamala, 1965, NIH, Tex. Health Dept., 1968-71, NIH, Nat. Inst. Childhood Diseases, 1970-76, NIH/EPA, 1974-76. Author: Nutritional Evaluation of Population of Central America and Panama, 1969, Ten State Nutrition Survey, 1974, Effect of Water Borne Nitrates on the Environment of Man, 1977, Effect of Water Borne Fluoride on the Environment of Man, 1977; contbr. articles to profl.

jours. Scoutmaster Boy Scouts Am., LaMarque, Tex., 1968—. Served with USNR, 1947-52. NSF scholar, 1962; NIH grantee, 1963; Moody Found. grantee, 1964. Mem. Am. Inst. Nutrition, Am. Soc. Clin. Nutrition, Am. Soc. Exptl. Biology and Medicine, N.Y. Acad. Sci. Baptist. Lodge: Masons. Current Work: Trace metal and vitamin metabolism. Subspecialties: Nutrition (medicine); Biochemistry (medicine). Home: 15 Chimney Corners LaMarque TX 77568 Office: Dept Obstetrics and Gynecology U Tex Med Br Galveston TX 77550

DAWSON, JOHN MYRICK, plasma physics educator; b. Champaign, Ill., Sept. 30, 1930; s. Walker Myrick and Wilhelmina Emily (Stephan) D.; m. Nancy Louise Wildes, Dec. 28, 1957; children: Arthur Walker, Margaret Louise. B.S., U. Md., 1952, M.S., 1954, Ph.D., 1957. Research physicist Plasma Physics Lab. Princeton U., 1956-73, head theoretical group, 1965-73; prof. plasma physics UCLA, 1973—; dir. Center for Plasma Physics & Fusion Engring., 1976; cons. in field; John Danz lectr. U. Wash., 1974; guest Russian Acad. Scis., 1971; invited lectr. Inst. Plasma Physics, Nagoya, Japan, 1972. Contbr. articles in field to profl. jours. Recipient Exceptional Sci. Achievement award TRW Systems, 1977; James Clerk Maxwell prize in Plasma Physics, 1977; named Calif. Scientist of the Year, 1978; Fulbright fellow, Nagoya, Japan, 1964-65. Fellow AAAS, Am. Phys. Soc. (chmn. plasma div. 1970-71); mem. Nat. Acad. Scis., N.Y. Acad. Scis., N.J. Acad. Scis., Sigma Pi Sigma, Phi Kappa Phi, Sigma Xi. Unitarian. Patentee in field. Subspecialty: Plasma physics. Home: 359 Arno Way Pacific Palisades CA 90272 Office: University of California 405 Hilgard Ave Los Angeles CA 90024

DAWSON, LIONEL JAMES, veterinarian, educator, researcher; b. Rangoon, Burma, Nov. 22, 1955; came to U.S., 1978, naturalized, 1978; s. Samuel and Lily D. B.V.Sc., Madras Vet. Coll., India, 1978; M.S., Iowa State U., 1980. Diplomate Am. Coll. Theriogenologists. Research assoc. Iowa State U., Ames, 1979-80, resident in theriogenology U. Mo., Columbia, 1980-82; instr. Okla. State U., Stillwater, 1982-83, asst. prof., 1983—; adviser student chpt. Am. Assn. Bovine Practitioners, 1983—. Contbr. articles to profl. publs. Mem. Soc. Theriogenology, Okla. Vet. Med. Assn., AVMA, Phi Zeta. Democrat. Methodist. Current work: Embryo transfer in domestic animals; herd health management in domestic animals. Subspecialty: Theriogenology. Office: Dept Vet Medicine and Surgery Okla State U Stillwater OK 74078

DAY, CALVIN LEE, JR., dermatologist, cancer researcher; b. Karnes City, Tex., July 4, 1951; s. Calvin Lee and Theresa Louise (Hoffman) D.; m. Regina Carroll, Jan. 8, 1972; 1 dau., Berica. B.S. summa cum laude, Tex. A&M U., 1973; M.D. with honors, U. Tex. Southwestern Med. Sch., 1976. Diplomate: Am. Bd. Dermatology. Research fellow in phys. chemistry Tex. A&M U., 1971; research fellow in biochemistry U. Tex. Southwestern Med. Sch., Dallas, 1973; intern in medicine Mass. Gen. Hosp., Boston, 1976-77, resident in medicine, 1977-78, resident in dermatology, 1978-79, 79-80, clin. fellow in dermatology, 1980-81, clin. and research fellow in dermatology, 1981-82; clin. fellow in medicine Harvard U., 1976-77, 77-78, clin. fellow in dermatology, 1978-79, 79-80, 80-81, research fellow in dermatology, 1981-82; fellow in chemosurgery dept. dermatology N.Y.U., 1982-83; clin. asst. prof., dir. skin cancer surgery div. dermatology U. Tex. Med. Sch., San Antonio, 1983—. Contbr. articles, chpts. to profl. publs.; editor: Melanoma Letter, Skin Cancer Found., 1982—. Pres. Tex. Skin Cancer Found., 1983—. Southwestern Med. Found. scholar, 1972-73; Robert Wood Johnson scholar, 1975-76; Tex. Merit scholar, 1975-76; Julia Ball Lee fellow, 1970-71; NIH research grantee, 1978, 80-82. Fellow N.Y. Acad. Scis.; mem. Am. Fedn. Clin. Research, AMA, Alpha Omega Alpha, Phi Kappa Phi, Phi Eta Sigma. Current Work: Malignant melanoma; microscopically controlled surgery for skin cancers. Subspecialties: Cancer research (medicine); Dermatology.

DAY, EUGENE DAVIS, immunologist, educator; b. Cobleskill, N.Y., June 24, 1925; s. Emmons Davis and Alice Dorothy (McCartey) D.; m. Shirley Warner, Sept. 14, 1946; 1 son, Eugene Davis. B.S., Union Coll., 1949; Ph.D., U. Del., 1952. Research assoc. Jackson Meml. Lab., Bar Harbor, Maine, 1952-54; sr., then assoc. cancer research scientist Roswell Park Meml. Inst., Buffalo, 1954-62; assoc. prof. Duke U. Med. Ctr., 1962-64, prof., 1964—. Author books; contbr. articles to profl. jours. Served with AUS, 1943-46. Recipient Jacob Javits Neurosci. Investigator award NIH, 1984-91. Fellow An. Acad. Microbiology; Mem. Am. Assn. Immunologists, Am. Soc. Neurochemistry, Am. Soc. Microbiology, AAUP, Am. Assn. Cancer Research, Sigma Xi. Current Work: Immunochemistry of myelin basic protein. Subspecialties: Neuroimmunology; Immunobiology and immunology. Home: 2727 McDowell St Durham NC 27705 Office: Duke U Med Center Box 3045 Durham NC 27710

DAY, RICHARD ALLEN, chemistry educator; b. Kellogg, Iowa, Apr. 4, 1931; s. Clarence Hodson and Della (Mendenhall) D.; m. Lyn Tibbits, Aug. 19, 1956; children—Eric, Sylvia. B.S., Iowa State U., 1953; Ph.D., MIT, 1958. Research assoc. div. biochemistry MIT, Cambridge, 1957-59; asst. prof. chemistry U. Cin., 1959-63, assoc. prof., 1963-68, prof., 1968—; dir. Datachem Inc., Indpls. Contbr. articles to profl. jours. Recipient USPHS Career Devel. award U. Cin., 1969-74; U. Cin. fellow, 1979. Fellow AAAS; mem. Am. Chem. Soc. (chmn. Cin. sect. 1982-83), Sigma Xi (pres. U. Cin. chpt. 1978-81). Democrat. Mem. Soc. of Friends. Current work: Protein structure, mass spectrometry, enzymes. Subspecialties: Biochemistry (biology); Biophysical chemistry. Home: 7415 Silver Creek Rd Cleves OH 45002 Office: Dept Chemistry U Cin Cincinnati OH 45221

DAY, STACEY BISWAS, physician, educator, health tech. and info. sci. cons.; b. London, Dec. 31, 1927; s. Satis B. and Emma L. (Camp) D.; m. Ivana Podvalova, Oct. 18, 1973; 2 children. M.D., Dublin, Ireland, 1955; Ph.D. in Exptl. Surgery, McGill U., 1964; D.Sc., U. Cin., 1970. Med. educator various univs., 1955-66; research dir. phase I and II Hoechst Inc., Cin., 1966-67; regional med. dir. for New Eng. Hoffman La Roche Co., 1967-69; educator, cons., 1969—; v.p. Mario Negri Found. (sci. research), 1975-80, Internat. Found. Biosocial Devel. and Human Health, 1979—; cons. in health tech. and informatics; tech. control, communications, behaviorism and social/community control; prof. N.Y. Med. Coll.; cons. health communications U.S.-USSR Exchange, Nat. Cancer Inst., NIH; cons. to dean 4th Med. Coll., Abha, Saudi Arabia; cons. Cross River State, Nigeria, WHO, Pan Am. Health Orgn.; adj. prof. family medicine and community health U. Ariz., Tuscon; vis. prof. internat. health Meharry Med. Coll., Nashville; prof., chmn. dept. community health U. Calabar, Nigeria, 1982-84. Author, editor 50 books; founder: Bioscis. Communications, 1974, Monograph Publs. in Health Communications and Biospychosocial Health; contbr. numerous articles to profl. jours. Hon. chmn., bd. dirs. Am. Friends of Lambo Found. Served with Brit. Army, 1946-49. Recipient medals and prizes Royal Coll. Surgeons, Ireland, medals and prizes Royal Coll. Surgeons, Eng.; Ciba fellow, 1964. Fellow Japan Soc. BioPsycho Soc. Health (most disting. fellow), Zool. Soc. London; mem. AMA, Harvey Soc., numerous others. Mem. Ch. of England. Current Work: Technology; information; culture and high technology control; biopsychosocial control; behaviorism and technocracy; technology and transition; parasympathetic way; international health. Subspecialties: Behaviorism; Information systems (Information science). Home: 6 Lomond Ave Spring Valley NY 10977 Office: Lambo Found 27 Chemin des Chataigniers 1292 Chambesy Geneva Switzerland

DE, BIBHAS RANJAN, physicist, researcher; b. Silchar, India, Jan. 22, 1946; came to U.S., 1968; s. Binod Bihari and Lila (Rakshit) D.; m. Gopa Sarkar, Jan. 16, 1971. B.S. with honors, U. Calcutta, 1967; M.S., U. Mich., 1970; Ph.D., U. Calif.-La Jolla, 1973. Research asst. U. Mich., Ann Arbor, 1969-71; asst. research physicist U. Calif.-La Jolla, 1974-75; vis. scientist Lunar and Planetary Inst., Houston, 1976-79; sr. physicist Sci.-Atlanta Inc., Atlanta, 1979-80; sr. research physicist Exxon, Houston, 1980-81, Chevron, La Habra, Calif., 1981—. Guest editor Astrophysics and Space Sci., 1979. Contbr. articles to profl. jours. Patentee in field. Nat. scholar Govt. of India, 1967; UNESCO fellow, 1968. Mem. Am. Phys. Soc., IEEE, N.Y. Acad. Scis., Phi Kappa Phi. Hindu. Current work: Apply electromagnetic theory and radiofrequency techniques to minimize risk in exploring for and evaluating petroleum reservoirs. Subspecialties: Aerospace engineering and technology; Composite materials. Office: Chevron Oil Field Research Co PO Box 446 La Habra CA 90631

DEAN, ANTHONY MARION, research chemist; b. Savannah, Ga., Aug. 26, 1944; s. Anthony David and Anne (Mylod) D.; m. Linda Eunice Nicks, Aug. 27, 1966; children—Paul, Dianne, Melanie, David. B.S., Spring Hill Coll., 1966; A.M., Harvard U., 1967, Ph.D., 1970. Asst. prof. U. Mo., Columbia, 1970-75; assoc. prof., 1975-79; sr. staff chemist Exxon Research and Engring., Linden, N.J., 1979-82; research assoc. Exxon Research and Engring., Annandale, N.J., 1982—. Contbr. articles to profl. jours. Patentee in field. NSF fellow, 1966-70. Mem. Am. Chem. Soc., Am. Phys. Soc., Combustion Inst., Sigma Xi. Current work: Kinetic characterization of complex chemical systems; oxidation and pyrolysis reactions; laser diagnostics; flame kinetics; laser perturbation of flames. Subspecialties: Physical chemistry; High temperature chemistry. Home: 67 Country Acres Dr Hampton NJ 08827 Office: Exxon Research and Engring Co Route 22 E Annandale NJ 08801

DEAN, DAVID DEVEREAUX, biochemist; b. Cin., Oct. 24, 1952; s. Omer Stanley and Betty Lee (Phillips) D.; m. Mary Nell Fleming, June 18, 1977; 1 child, Betty Ruth. B.S., Randolph Macon Coll., 1975; Ph.D., U. N.C., 1981. Research assoc. U. Miami Sch. Medicine, Fla., 1981-83, postdoctoral assoc., 1983—. Author: A Biochemical Approach to Cell Biology, 1979. Contbr. articles to profl. jours. Mem. Am. Chem. Soc., AAAS, Sigma Xi. Republican. Baptist. Current work: Enzymology of connective tissue degrading enzymes; role of enzymes in arthritis; inhibitors of proteases involved in connective tissue degratation. Subspecialties: Biochemistry (biology); Biochemistry (medicine). Home: 8475 SW 94th St #215E Miami FL 33156 Office: U Miami Sch of Medicine PO Box 016960 Dept Biochemistry Miami FL 33101

DEAN, EDWIN BECTON, lead cost analyst; b. Danville, Va., Feb. 7, 1940; s. Edwin Becton and Lois Pearl (Campbell) D.; m. Deirdre Anne Jacovides, Aug. 16, 1964; chilren: Jennifer, Kristin, Brian. B.S. in Physics, Va. Poly. Inst., 1963, M.S. in Math, 1965; postgrad., George Washington U., 1974-77. Assoc. engr., technician Applied Physics Lab., Johns Hopkins U., Laurel, Md., 1959-63; mathematician, physicist, elec. engr., ops. research analyst Naval Surface Weapons Ctr., Silver Spring, Md., 1964-79; rep. First Investors Corp., Arlington, Va., 1971-85; bus. counselor Gen. Bus. Services, Virginia Beach, Va., 1979-84; computer security specialist NAVSUP, Norfolk, Va., 1982-83; head cost modeling and control sect. NASA Langley Research Ctr., Hampton, Va., 1983—. NASA fellow, 1963-65. Mem. IEEE, Assn. Computing Machinery, Internat. Soc. Parametric Analysts, Inst. Mgmt. Soc., AIAA, Phi Kappa Phi, Sigma Pi Sigma, Pi Mu Epsilon. Club: Tidewater Apple Worms (Virginia Beach). Current Work: Applying differential geometry to optimization, graphics, image processing, pattern recognition, artificial intelligence, business forecasting, economics, numerical analysis and system measurement, cost estimating. Subspecialties: Operations research (mathematics); Graphics, image processing, and pattern recognition. Home: 2412 Whaler Ct Virginia Beach VA 23451 Office: NASA Langley Research Ctr Hampton VA 23665

DEAN, JOHN DAVID, geologist, geological consultant; b. Shreveport, La., Nov. 18, 1953; s. William Richard and Peggy Jane (Hooper) D.; m. Terry Lynn Hastings, Apr. 21, 1984. B.A., Washington and Lee U., B.S. in Geology, 1978. Asst. geologist Intercoastal Operating, Houston, 1978-80; geologist and geophysicist IOC Prodn., Inc., Houston, 1980-83; head geol. dept., ptnr. Rockbridge Oil and Gas Co., Houston, 1983—; cons. IOC Prodn., Inc., 1983-84. Contbg. author: Typical Oil and Gas Fields. Mem. Am. Assn. Petroleum Geologists, Geol. Soc. Am., Houston; Geol. Soc. Republican. Episcopalian. Current work: Researcher program that produces oil and gas from bypassed zones in supposedly depleted fields. Subspecialty: Geology. Home: 1112 Bering #39 Houston TX 77057 Office: Rockbridge Oil and Gas Co 2807 Buffalo Speedway Houston TX 77098

DEAN, JUDITH CAROL HICKMAN, medical research; b. Baton Rouge, Oct. 19, 1943; d. Cecil Lamar and Johnnie Louise (Efferson) Hickman. B.S., Northwestern State U., La., 1965; M.S., U. Central Ark., 1973; doctoral candidate, U. Ariz., 1980—. Registered nurse, La., Ariz. Psychiat. nurse Mercy Hosp., Urbana, Ill., 1966-67; chief nurse rehab. and extended care Central La. State Hosp., Pineville, 1967-69; instr. nursing U. Ark., Little Rock, 1970-73; asst. dir. nursing for medicine U. Ariz. Health Sci. Ctr., Tucson, 1974; clin. specialist in oncology VA Med. Ctr., Tucson, 1975-81; research assoc. internal medicine U. Ariz. Cancer Ctr., Tucson, 1981—; mem. council collegiate edn. for nursing So. Regionl Edn. Bd., 1972-73; vol. abstractor Am. Nurses Found., 1972-74. Author, lectr., cons. Mem. profl. edn. com. Ariz. div. Am. Cancer Soc., 1978—; mem. tumor registry adv. bd. Ariz. Dept. Health Services, 1980—. Walter Teagle Fond. scholar, 1961-65. Mem. Am. Soc. Clin. Oncology, Am. Psychol. Assn. Am. Personnel and Guidance Assn., Oncology Nursing Soc. (charter), Sigma Theta Tau, Kappa Delta Pi. Current Work: Psychological impact of cancer and cancer treatment(s), special interest areas sexuality issues for the cancer patient, family dynamics, and prevention of alopecia. Subspecialties: Cancer research (medicine); Oncology counseling psychology. Office: 1501 N Campbell Ave Tucson AZ 85724

DEAN, NATHAN WESLEY, educational administrator, physicist; b. Johnson City, Tenn., Dec. 10, 1941; s. Everett Francis and Mary Ethel (Garvin) D.; m. Mary Dugger Fetzer, Apr. 11, 1963; 1 child, Mary Ellen. B.S. in Physics with honors, U. of N.C., 1963; Ph.D. in Element Particle Physics, U. Cambridge, 1968. Instr., asst. prof. physics Vanderbilt U., Nashville, 1968-69; asst., assoc., prof. physics Iowa State U., Ames, 1970-80, asst. dean sci.-humanities, 1974-80; physicist Ames Lab U.S. Dept. Energy, Iowa, 1970-80; asst. v.p. research U. of Ga., Athens, 1980—, acting v.p. research, 1984—; univ. system rep. Ga. High Tech. Adv. Council, Atlanta, 1983—; dir. indsl. interface program, biol. resources and biotechnology program U. Ga., 1984—; mem. Athens C. of C. Author: Introduction to Strong Interactions, 1976. Contbr. articles to profl. jours. Pres. cedar Creek Civic Assn., Athens, 1982. Grantee U.S. Dept. Energy, NIH, U.S. Army, NSF, NEH, USPHS; mem. Am. Physics Soc., AAAS, Nat. Council Univ. Research Adminstrs. (chmn. region III, 1984—), Sigma Xi, Phi Beta Kappa. Current work: Leadership and administration of $90,000,000 research program, with special emphasis in biotechnology and supercomputers. Subspecialties: Research administration; Biotechnology administration. Home: 270 Skyline Pkwy Athens GA 30606 Office: Office of VP Research Univ Ga 609 Grad Studies Athens GA 30602

DEAN, REGINALD LANGWORTHY, III, research scientist; b. New Haven, Aug. 20, 1953; s. Reginald Langworthy and Mary Ellen (Keenan) D.; m. Luan Kulof, May 9, 1975; children—Courtney Meghan, Ashley Erin. B.A., Denison U., 1976; M.A., Western Mich. U., 1978. Asst. scientist Warner Lambert-/Park-Davis, Ann Arbor, Mich., 1978-79; research scientist med. research div. Am. Cyanamid Co. Lederle Labs., Pearl River, N.Y., 1979—. Contbr. articles to profl. jours. Mem. Soc. Neurosci., Am. Aging Assn., AAAS. Roman Catholic. Current Work: Development of animal models to accurately mimic age-related memory impairments. Subspecialties: Neuropharmacology; Gerontology. Home: 4 Beatrice Ln New City NY 10956 Office: Lederle Labs/Bldg 56B Room 119 Pearl River NY 10965

DEAN, RICHARD H., surgery educator; b. Radford, Va., June 16, 1942; s. Howard Lee and Minnie (Yates) D.; children: Richard Lancaster, Harrison Blaylock, Howard Lee Alexander. B.A., Va. Mil. Inst., 1964; M.D., Med. Coll. Va., Richmond, 1968. Intern Vanderbilt Hosp., 1968-69, resident in surgery, 1969-73, chief surg. resident, 1973-74, dir. surg. intensive care unit, 1975—, head div. vascular surgery, 1978—, prof. surgery, 1981—, co-clin. dir. hypertension ctr., 1981—, chmn. profl. program, 1982—; fellow in vascular surgery Northwestern U., 1974-75. Author, editor: (with others) Vascular Disease of Childhood, 1983. NIH grantee, 1976-86; Fellow ACS Southeastern Surg. Congress. Mem. So. Surg. Assn., Halsted Soc., Soc. Vascular Surgery, Soc. Univ. Surgeons, Internat. Cardiovascular Soc., Assn. Acad. Surgery, So. Assn. Vascular Surgery, Internat. Soc. Surgery, Pan-Pacific Surg. Assn., So. Med. Assn., Nashville Surg. Soc., Tenn. Med. Assn., Nashville Acad. Medicine, AMA, H. William Scott Jr. Soc. Episcopalian. Current Work: Hypertension, atherosclerosis, renal function, cerebrovascular disease, liver failure. Subspecialty: Vascular surgery. Home: Old Natchez Trace Franklin TN 37064 Office: Vanderbilt University Hospital T-2104 21st Ave at Garland St Nashville TN 38232

DEAN, ROBERT CHARLES, JR., mechanical engineer, business executive, educator; b. Atlanta, Apr. 13, 1928; s. Robert C. and Ruth (Andrew) D.; m. E. Nancy Hayes, Sept. 22, 1951; children: Margaret S., James C., Elizabeth S., Martha A., Charles E. B.S., M.S., MIT, 1949, Sc.D., 1954. Project engr. Ultrasonic Corp., 1949-51; head advanced engring. dept. Ingersoll-Rand Co., 1956-60; dir. research Thermal Dynamics Cor., 1960-61; dir. Ecol. Sci. Corp., 1968-70; co-founder, pres. Creare Inc., 1961-75; Ecol. Research Corp., 1968-70; co-founder, chmn. bd., prin. engr. Creare Innovations Co., 1976-79; founder Verax Corp., Hanover, N.H., 1979, pres., 1979-83, chmn. bd., dir. sci. and tech., 1983—; asst. prof. mech. engring. MIT, 1951-56; prof. engring. Thayer Sch. Engring., Dartmouth Coll., 1960—; mem. turbine and compressor subcom. NACA, 1954-55. Author numerous articles and patentee in field; editor: Jour. Fluid Engring., 1973-79. Recipient Gold medal Pi Tau Sigma, 1953, Master Designer award Product Engring. mag., 1967. Fellow ASME (chmn. hydraulics div. 1962-63, dir. Turbomachinery Inst. 1968—, Thurston lectr. 1977, Fluids Engring. award 1979); mem. Nat. Acad. Engring., Tau Beta Pi. Current Work: Research and development of advanced bioprocessing for manufacture of biochemicals. Subspecialties: Biomedical engineering; Mechanical engineering. Home: Hawk Pine Hill Norwich VT 05055 Office: PO Box B-1170 Hanover NH 03755

DEAN, THOMAS SCOTT, architect, engineering educator, consultant; b. Sherman, Tex., July 6, 1924; s. Lura Cecil and Lucille (Scott) D.; m. Jan Marie Irvine, June 1, 1945; 1 son, Thomas Scott. B.S., N. Tex. State U., Denton, 1947, M.S., 1949; Ph.D., U. Tex., Austin, 1963. Registered architect. Registered profl. engr., Tex., 1963. With Thomas Scott Dean AIA, Dallas, 1950-60; guest lectr. U. Tex., Austin, 1960-64; from assoc. prof. to prof. Okla. State U., Stillwater, 1964-76; prof. architecture and engring. U. Kans., Lawrence, 1976—; vis. prin. lectr. N.E. London Poly., 1973. Author: Engineering Education, 1975, Thermal Storage, 1979, Accumulation de Chaleur, 1980, How to Solarize Your House, 1981; contbr. articles profl. jours.; works include 2000 houses, chs., sci. bldgs. Served with C.E. AUS, 1942-43. Recipient 3 awards of merit House and Home, 1954, 55; NASA-Stanford fellow Am. Soc. Engring. Edn., 1974; award for design Kans. Soc. Architects. Mem. AIA, ASHRAE, Internat. Solar Energy Soc. Current Work: Solar heat assistance small buildings, teaching, research, energy conserving buildings consultant. Subspecialties: Solar energy; Energy conservation. Home: 1304 Raintree Pl Lawrence KS 66044 Office: 335 Art and Design Kans Lawrence KS 66045

DEAN, WILLIAM DENNIS, chemist; b. Memphis, Jan. 4, 1952; s. William Newton and Marilyn (Deane) D.; m. Valerie Clare Looney, Aug. 6, 1977; 1 child, Sierra Renee. B.S., U. Ark.-Fayetteville, 1975; M.S., U. N.Mex.-Albuquerque, 1978, Ph.D., 1981. Research chemist Dow Chem. Co., Midland, Mich., 1981-82, Lederle Labs., Pearl River, N.Y., 1982—. Contbr. articles to profl. jours. Mem. Am. Chem. Soc. Democrat. Current work: Heterocyclic synthesis, steroid chemistry, asymmetric syntheses, process development; development of novel and improvement of existing methodology; condensation reactions of arylactonitriles, isothiocyanate chemistry. Subspecialties: Organic chemistry; Synthetic chemistry. Office: Lederle Labs N Middletown Rd Pearl River NY 10965

DEAN, WILLIAM EVANS, aerospace, electronics, energy company executive; b. Greenville, Miss., July 6, 1930; s. George Thomas Dean and Martha Myrtle (Evans) Dean Carlton; m. Dorothy Sue Hamilton, Oct. 14, 1953; children—Janet Lea, Jody Anne, Justin Hamilton. B. Aero. Engring., Ga. Inst. Tech., 1952; M.B.A., Pepperdine U., 1970. Commd. officer U.S. Air Force, 1952, advanced through grades to maj., 1962, resigned, 1962; div. mgr., dir. Rockwell Internat., Los Angeles, 1962-67, v.p., div. gen. mgr., 1967-80; exec. v.p. Acurex Corp., Mountain View, Calif., 1981, pres., chief operating officer, 1982, pres., chief exec. officer, 1983—, also dir.; dir. Acurex Solar Corp., Mountain View, Acurex Waste Tech. Inc., Mountain View. Contbr. articles to profl. jours. Bd. dirs. NCCJ, San Jose, Calif., Saddleback Community Coll., Mission Viejo, Calif., 1976, United Fund, Orange County, Calif., 1971. Decorated Air Force Commendation medal with oak leaf cluster; recipient cert. of Achievement NASA, 1972; Silver Knight award Nat. Mgmt. Assn., 1978. Assoc. fellow AIAA (bd. dirs. 1979—, space shuttle award 1984); fellow Am. Astron. Soc.; mem. Am. Electronics Assn., Aircraft Owners and Pilots Assn., Santa Clara County Mfg. Group (bd. dirs.). Republican. Baptist. Club: Rockwell Flying. Current work: Aeronautics/astronautics; aerothermodynamics; composite materials; command, control and intelligence electronics; combustion energy and solar energy research; management science. Subspecialties: Aerospace engineering and technology; Energy research administration. Office: Acurex Corp 555 Clyde Ave Mountain View CA 94039

DEARBORN, DORR GELLATLY, medical scientist, pediatric pumonologist; b. Ontario, Oreg., Nov. 14, 1939; s. Oris Daniel Dearborn and Margaret Emma (Gellatly) Osborn; m. Betty Smallmon, June 10, 1963 (div. 1974); children—John G., Ulyssa M., D. Perkins, Natalie A., Nathan W.; m. Joyce Protiva, Sept. 24, 1976. B.A., Willamette U., 1961; Ph.D., U. Minn., 1969, M.D., 1970. Pediatric intern U. Minn. Hosps., Mpls., 1970-71; staff assoc. NIH, Bethesda, Md., 1971-74; asst. prof. pediatrics and biochem. Case Western Res. U., Cleve., 1974-81, assoc. chief pediatric pulmonologist div., 1985—; research dir. Cystic Fibrosis Research Inst., Cleve., 1979—. Author: (with others): Cystic Fibrosis: Future Prospectives, 1976—, Pulmonary Disease and Disorders, 1980, Methods of Enzymology, vol. 91, 1983, Cystic Fibrosis, 1984. Bd. trustees Cystic Fibrosis Found., Rainbow Chpt., Cleve., 1979—. Served to sr. surgeon, USPHS, 1971-74. Mem. Biophysical Soc., Cystic Fibrosis Found., "CF Club" (pres. 1983-84), Am. Chem. Soc., Am. Soc. Biological Chemist Soc. for Complex Carbohydrates, Sigma Xi, Alpha Omega Alpha, Phi Lambda Upsilon. Republican. Methodist. Current work: Role of amino groups in protein structure and function; intracellular calcium homeostasis; pathogenesis and pathophysiology of Cystic Fibrosis. Subspecialties: Biochemistry (medicine); Pediatrics. Office: Dept Pediatrics Case Western Research U 2101 Adelbert Rd Cleveland OH 44106

DEARING, WILLIAM HILL, physician, educator, researcher; b. Memphis, Dec. 3, 1908; s. William H. and Theresa Irene (Trenham) D.; m. Laura Edith Wintersteen, Aug. 29, 1936; children: Jane Dearing Kearney, John Charles (dec.), Carl Baylor. B.A., U. Pa., 1930, M.D., 1934, M.A., 1934; Ph.D., U. Minn., 1941. Diplomate: Am. Bd. Internal Medicine. Intern Geisinger Meml. Hosp., Danville, Pa., 1934-35, assoc. in medicine, 1935-36; cons. in medicine Mayo Clinic, Rochester, Minn., 1936-76, head med. sect., 1955-67, bd. govs., 1955-60, emeritus cons. in medicine, 1977—; prof. medicine Mayo Grad. Sch. Medicine, U. Minn., 1962-76; prof. medicine Mayo Med. Sch., Rochester, 1973-76, prof. medicine emeritus, 1977—. Contbr. articles to profl. jours. Recipient Cert. of Merit U. Minn., 1977. Fellow ACP; mem. AMA (chmn. sect. gastroenterology 1952-73, ho. of dels. 1963-73), Am. Gastroenterology Assn. (officer, bd. govs. 1962-67), Am. Fedn. Clin. Research, Central Soc. Clin. Research, Central Clin. Research Club, AAAS, N.Y. Acad. Sci. Presbyterian. Current Work: Research in gatroenterology. Subspecialties: Internal medicine; Gastroenterology. Home: 4505 S Ocean Blvd Apt 808 Highland Beach FL 33431

DEB, KRISHNA K., physicist; b. Calcutta, India, Sept. 1, 1936; came to U.S., 1972; naturalized, 1977; m. Lily Ghosh, Feb. 9, 1963; children—Subrato, Rina. B.Sc., Calcutta U., 1954, M.Sc., 1956, Ph.D., 1964. Analytical chemist Litton Bionetics, Fredrick, Md., 1973-75; assoc. chemist U. Ariz., Tucson, 1976-78, U. Hawaii, Honolulu, 1978-79; research chemist Belvoir Research and Devel. Ctr., Fort Belvoir, Va., 1979-80, research physicist U.S. Army Night Vision Lab., 1980—. Contbr. chpts. to books in field; also articles to profl. jours. Mem. N.Y. Acad. Scis., Xi Research Soc., Optical Soc. Am., Am. Chem. Soc., Am. Physical Soc. Republican. Roman Catholic. Current work: Gas lasers; solid state lasers, nonlinear phasematching; electronic materials; coatings development; spectroscopy. Subspecialty: Electronic materials.

DE BAKEY, MICHAEL ELLIS, surgeon; b. Lake Charles, La., Sept. 7, 1908; s. Shaker Morris and Raheeja (Zorba) DeB.; m. Diana Cooper, Oct. 15, 1936; children—Michael Maurice, Ernest Ochsner, Barry Edward, Denis Alton, Olga Katerina; m. Katrin Fehlhaber, July 1975. B.S., Tulane U., 1930, M.D., 1932, M.S., 1935, LL.D., 1965; Docteur Honoris Causa, U. Lyon, France, 1961, U. Brussels, 1962, U. Ghent, Belgium, 1964, U. Athens, 1964; D.H.C., U. Turin, Italy, 1965, U. Belgrade, Yugoslavia, 1967; LL.D., Lafayette Coll., 1965; M.D. (hon.), Aristotelean U. of Thessaloniki, Greece, 1972; D.Sc., Hahnemann Med. Coll., 1973, numerous others. Diplomate: Nat. Bd. Med. Examiners, Am. Bd. Surgery, Am. Bd. Thoracic Surgery. Intern Charity Hosp., New Orleans, 1932-33, asst. surgery, 1933-35, U. Strasbourg, France, 1935-36, U. Heidelberg, Germany, 1936, instr. surgery, Tulane U., 1937-40, asst. prof., 1940-46, assoc. prof., 1946-48; prof. surgery, chmn. dept. Baylor U., 1948—, v.p. med. affairs, from 1968; chief exec. officer Baylor Coll. Medicine, 1968-69, pres., from 1969, chancellor, 1979—; dir. Nat. Heart and Blood Vessel Research and Demonstration Center, Baylor Coll. Medicine, 1975—; surgeon-in-chief Ben Taub Gen. Hosp., 1963—; sr. attending surgeon Meth. Hosp.; cons. surgery VA, St. Elizabeth's, M.D. Anderson, St. Luke's, Tex. Children's Hosps.; clin. prof. surgery U. Tex. Dental Br., Houston; cons. Tex. Inst. Rehab. and Research, Brooke Gen. Hosp., Brooke Army Med. Center, Ft. Sam Houston, Tex.; cons. surgery Walter Reed Army Hosp., Washington.; mem. med. adv. com. sec. def., 1948-50; chmn. com. surgery NRC, 1953, mem. exec. com., 1953; mem. com. med. services Hoover Commn.; chmn. bd. regents Nat. Library Medicine, 1959; past mem. nat. adv. heart council NIH; mem. Nat. Adv. Health Council,

1961-65, Nat. Adv. Council Regional Med. Programs, from 1965, Nat. Adv. Gen. Med. Scis. Council, 1965, Program Planning Com., Com. Tng., Nat. Heart Inst., from 1961; mem. civilian health and med. adv. council Office Asst. Sec. Def.; chmn. Pres.'s Commn. Heart Disease, Cancer and Stroke, 1964. Author: (with Robert A. Kilduffe) Blood Transfusion, 1942, (with Gilbert W. Beebe) Battle Casualties, 1952, (with Alton Ochsner) Textbook of Minor Surgery, 1955, (with T. Whayne) Cold Injury, Ground Type, 1958, A Surgeon's Visit to China, 1974, (with A.M. Gotto) The Living Heart, 1977; editor: (with A.M. Gotto) Yearbook of Surgery, 1958-70; chmn. adv. editorial bd.: (with A.M. Gotto) Medical History of World War II. Mem. Tex. Constl. Revision Commn., 1973. Served as col. Office Surgeon Gen. AUS, 1942-46; now col. Res.; cons. to Surgeon Gen. from 1946. Decorated Legion of Merit, 1946; Rudolph Matas award, 1954; Independence of Jordan medal 1st class; Merit Order of Republic 1st class Egypt; comdr. Cross of Merit Pro Utiliate Hominum Sovereign Order Knights of Hosp. of St. John of Jerusalem in Denmark; Hektoen gold medal AMA; Internat. Soc. Surgery Distinguished Service award, 1957; recipient Modern Medicine award, 1957, Roswell Park medal, 1959; A.M.A. Distinguished Service award, 1959; Leriche award Internat. Soc. Surgery, 1959; Great medallion U. Ghent, 1961; Grand Cross of Order Leopold Belgium, 1962; Albert Lasker award for clin. research, 1963; Order of Merit Chile, 1964; St. Vincent prize med. scis. U. Turin, 1965; Orden del Libertador Gen. San Martin Argentina, 1965; Centennial medal Albert Einstein Med. Center, 1966; Gold Scalpel award Internat. Cardiology Found., 1966; Distinguished Service prof. Baylor U., 1968; Distinguished Faculty award, 1973; Eleanor Roosevelt Humanities award, 1969; Civilian Service medal sec. def., 1970; USSR Acad. Sci. 50th Anniversary Jubilee medal, 1973; Phi Delta Epsilon Disting. Service award, 1974; La Madonnina award, 1974; 30 Yr. Service award Harris County Hosp. Dist., 1978; Knights Humanity award honoris causa Internat. Register Chivalry, Milan, 1978; Diploma de Merito Caja Costarricense de Seguro Social, San Jose, Costa Rica, 1979; Disting. Service plaque Tex. Bd. Edn., 1979; Britannica Achievement in Life award, 1979; Medal of Freedom with Distinction Presdl. award, 1969; Disting. Service award Internat. Soc. Atherosclerosis, 1979; Centennial award ASME, 1980; Marian Health Care award St. Mary's U., 1981; numerous others; named Dr. of Year Med. World News, 1965, Med. Man of Year, 1966, Humanitarian Father of Year award, 1974, Tulane U. Alumnus of Year, 1974, Tex. Scientist of Yr., Tex. Acad. Sci., 1979. Fellow A.C.S. (Ann. award Southwestern Pa. chpt. 1973), Inst. of Medicine Chgo. (hon.); mem. Am. Coll. Cardiology (hon. fellow), Royal Soc. Medicine, Halsted Soc., Am. Heart Assn., So. Soc. Clin. Research, AAAS, Southwestern Surg. Congress (pres. 1952), Soc. Vascular Surgery (pres. 1953), AMA, Am. Surg. Assn. (Disting. Service award 1981), So. Surg. Assn., Western Surg. Assn., Am. Assn. Thoracic Surgery (pres. 1959), Internat. Cardiovascular Soc. (pres. 1958, pres. N.Am chpt 1964), Mexican Acad. Surgery, (hon.), Soc. Clin. Surg., Soc. Univ. Surgeons, Internat. Soc. Surgery, Soc. Exptl. Biology and Medicine, Hellenic Surg. Soc. (hon.), Bio-med. Engring. Soc. (dir. 1968), Houston Heart Assn. (mem. adv. council 1968-69), Sociedad Nacional de Cirugia (Cuba), C. of C., Sigma Xi, Alpha Omega Alpha. Democrat. Episcopalian. Club: University (Washington). Current Work: Cardiovascular disease. Subspecialties: Surgery; Cardiac surgery. Office: Baylor Coll Medicine 1200 Moursund Ave Houston TX 77030

DEBARI, VINCENT ANTHONY, research chemist, research laboratory administrator, educator; b. Jersey City, Feb. 1, 1946; s. Vincent and Josephine (Buzzanco) DeB.; m. Margaret A. Danning, Feb. 28, 1970; children: Michele, Christopher, Jillanne. B.S. in Chemistry, Fordham U., 1967; M.S. in Chemistry, Newark Coll. Engring. (now N.J. Inst. Tech.), 1970; Ph.D. in Biochemistry, Rutgers U.-Newark, 1981. Research chemist Witco Chem. Corp., Oakland, N.J., 1967-73; research chemist Renal Lab., St. Joseph's Hosp. and Med. Center, Paterson, N.J., 1973-81, dir. renal lab., 1981—, mem. affiliate med. staff in medicine and pathology, 1981—; chmn. blood cells sect. 5th Internat. Conf. Histochemistry and Cytochemistry, Bucharest, Romania, 1976; cons. Rutgers U.; adj. faculty Seton Hall U., St. Peter's Coll.; grad. faculty assoc. Rutgers U. Contbr. articles to profl. publs. Founder, mem. research and grants com. Lupus Erythematosus Found. N.J., 1979-83, first chmn., 1979-81, bd. dirs., 1983—1983—. Recipient Clin. Chemists Recognition award, 1984; Lions Charitable Found. grantee, 1978—; Lupus Erythematosus Found. grantee, 1978-84. Mem. Am. Chem. Soc., Am. Assn. Clin. Chemistry (charter mem.; edn. chmn. clin. and diagnostic immunology div. 1984—), Am. Fedn. Clin. Research, Biophys. Soc., N.Y. Acad. Scis., AAAS, Am. Soc. Clin. Pathology, Sigma Xi. Roman Catholic. Current Work: Immunochemistry, specifically characterization of auto-antibodies and biochemistry of phagocytic cells; other interests are cation-polyanion interactions and metabolic regulation. Subspecialties: Biochemistry (biology); Clinical chemistry. Home: 32 Jacksonville Rd Pompton Plains NJ 07444 Office: Renal Lab St Joseph's Hosp and Med Center 703 Main St Paterson NJ 07503

DE BLAS, ANGEL LUIS, neurobiology educator, researcher; b. Madrid, Spain, Jan. 31, 1950; came to U.S., 1974; s. Cemente De Blas and Mercedes Ortega; 1 child, Celia Aurora. M.S. in Biochemistry, U. Madrid, 1972; Ph.D. in Biochemistry, Ind. U., 1978. Postdoctoral fellow NIH, Bethesda, Md., 1978-81; asst. prof. neurobiology SUNY-Stony Brook, 1981—; mem. study sect. NIH, 1985—. Contbr. articles to sci. publs. Grantee NIH, 1981—, Nat. Found. March of Dimes, 1982—, NSF, 1984—, others; Esther A. and Joseph Klingenstein fellow in neurosci., 1985—; Epilepsy Found. award; Ctr. Biotech. SUNY, 1985—. Mem. Soc. Neurosci., Am. Soc. Neurochemistry, Spanish Biochem. Soc., N.Y. Acad. Scis., Am. Soc. Biol. Chemists. Current work: GABA and benzodiazepine receptors; endogenous benzodiazepines; monoclonal antibodies to synaptic molecules; benzodiazepine. Subspecialties: Comparative neurobiology; Neurochemistry. Office: Dept Neurobiology and Behavior SUNY Stony Brook NY 11794

DEBLASIO, RICHARD, research engineer; b. Norristown, Pa., Nov. 29, 1941; s. Anthony and Louise (Boccarro) DeB.; m. Olivia Ann Crouch, Apr. 6, 1968; children: Richard Andrew, Olivia Catherine. B.S. in Elec. Engring, U. Santa Clara, 1968-72; cert., MIT, 1977. Researcher, technician Stanford U., 1965-72; project engr. Underwriters Lab., Santa Clara, Calif., 1972-74; nuclear engr. U.S. AEC, Washington, 1974-78; group mgr. advanced systems research Solar Energy Research Inst., Golden, Colo., 1978—; cons. Teledyne Isotopes Corp., Palo Alto, Calif., 1967-70, Nat. Nuclear Corp., Palo Alto, 1968, Custom Nuclear Corp., Palo Alto, 1968; project acceptance testing leader U.S./Saudi Solar Projects, Golden, Colo., 1981, Saudi Arabia, 1981. Served with USAF, 1961-65. Decorated Air Force Commendation medal. Mem. IEEE (chmn. photovoltaic systems com. 1980—, mem. standards photovoltaic coordinating com. 1980—), Am. Nuclear Soc. Roman Catholic. Current Work: Manager for advanced photovoltaic systems research which includes conceptual systems research on thin film solar cells, modules and systems including economic analysis and field testing. Subspecialties: Solar energy; Electrical engineering. Home: 2581 Scorpio Dr Colorado Springs CO 80906 Office: Solar Energy Research Inst 1617 Cole Blvd Golden CO 80401

DEBOER, BARRY GOODWIN, chemist, crystallographer; b. Black River Falls, Wis., Aug. 18, 1942; s. Stanley Goodwin and Norma Mae (Prell) DeB.; m. Barbara Ann Varsik, Aug. 22, 1964. B.S. in Chemistry with honors, U. Wis.-Madison, 1964; Ph.D., U. Calif.-Berkeley, 1968. Research assoc. MIT, Cambridge, 1968-71, U. Ill.-Chgo., 1971-75; vis. asst. prof. U. Ill.-Chgo. Circle, 1975-76; research assoc. Northwestern U., Evanston, Ill., 1976-79; engring. specialist GTE Products Corp., Salem, Mass., 1979—. Contbr. articles to profl. jours. NSF fellow U. Calif., Berkeley, 1964-67. Mem. Am. Inst. Physics, Am. Chem. Soc., AAAS, Electrochem. Soc. Current work: Synthesis and characterization of luminescent materials for lighting applications; other ceramic materials. Subspecialties: Inorganic chemistry; X-ray crystallography. Home: 4 Emily Lane Georgetown MA 01833 Office: GTE Products Corp 60 Boston St Salem MA 01970

DEBOER, EDWARD DALE, research chemist; b. Hammond, Ind., May 24, 1955; s. Edward and Ann (Kruizenga) D.; m. Carol Ann Fennema, Dec. 2, 1977; children—David Peter, Sara Jean, Ruth Ann. B.S., Calvin Coll., 1977. Jr. chemist Am. Maize-Products Co., Hammond, 1977, scientist, 1977-84, project leader, 1984—. Mem. Am. Chem. Soc. (Chgo. sect.). Christian Reformed. Current work: Derivitization of starch and other polysaccharides; use of starch derivatives in textile warp sizing, high temperature oil well drilling, paper sizing and paper coating. Subspecialties: Organic chemistry; Polymer chemistry. Home: 21911 Merrill Ave Sauk Village IL 60411 Office: 1100 Indianapolis Blvd Hammond IN 46320-1094

DE BRANGES, LOUIS, mathematician. Prof. dept. math. Purdue U., West Lafayette, Ind. . Office: Purdue U Dept Math West Lafayette IN 47907*

DECAPRIO, ANTHONY PAUL, toxicologist; b. New Haven, Apr. 22, 1953; s. Fred Carl and Antoinette (Casciello) DeC.; m. Patricia Radigan, June 21, 1975. B.S. in Biology, Rensselaer Poly. Inst., 1975; Ph.D. in Toxicology, Albany Med. Coll., 1981. Postdoctoral research fellow Albany Med. Coll., N.Y., 1981; research toxicologist N.Y. State Dept. Health, Albany, 1981—; adj. asst. prof. pharmacology and toxicology Albany Med. Coll., 1985—. Contbr. articles to profl. jours. NIOSH research grantee, 1984-87. Mem. Am. Chem. Soc., Am. Coll. Toxicology, Soc. of Toxicology (Mid-Atlantic chpt.). Roman Catholic. Current work: Molecular mechanisms of action of neurotoxic chemicals; toxicology of chlorinated dioxins; toxicological assessment of complex environmental mixtures. Subspecialties: Toxicology (agriculture); Environmental toxicology. Office: New York State Dept Health Wadsworth Ctr for Labs and Research Empire State Plaza Albany NY 12201

DECI, EUGENE CLARK, physicist, educator; b. Clifton Springs, N.Y., May 9, 1942; s. Fredrick Theodore and Florence Helen (Ashman) D.; m. Mary Frances DePauw, May 26, 1967; children—Todd John, Benjamin Theodore. B.A., Hamilton Coll., 1964; Ph.D., SUNY-Binghamton, 1972. Asst. prof. physics Bklyn. Coll., 1972-78; assoc. prof. Alma Coll., Mich., 1978—; vis. assoc. prof. Nat. Superconducting Cyclotron lab., East Lansing, Mich., 1984-85. Contbr. articles to profl. jours. Mem. Am. Phys. Soc., Sigma Xi. Republican. Presbyterian. Current work: Heavy ion physics. Subspecialty: Nuclear physics. Home: 1021 Falkirk Ct Alma MI 48801 Office: Alma Coll Alma MI 48801

DECKER, BRUCE MICHAEL, electrical engineer, systems specialist; b. Waterbury, Conn., June 9, 1955; s. Lloyd S. and Erma B. (Miller) D.; m. Holly Jean Hatch, May 28, 1977; children: Stephen Paul, Mark Timothy. B.S. in engring, U. Conn.-Storrs, 1977, M.S., 1979. Engr. in tng., Conn. Mfg. engr. DuPont, Newtown, Conn., 1979-82; research engr. U. N.H., 1982; mem. tech. staff RCA, Burlington, Mass., 1983—. Mem. IEEE, Sigma Xi. Republican. Current Work: Robotics; automation; productivity improvement; testing. Subspecialties: Artificial intelligence; Computer engineering. Office: RCA Government Systems Division PO Box 588 Burlington MA 01803

DECKER, CHARLES DAVID, physicist, research laboratory administrator; b. Oxnard, Calif., Feb. 12, 1945; s. Charles Smith and Lois Maxine (Myers) D.; m. Penelope Grace Corcoran, Mar. 30, 1968; children—Elizabeth, Christopher, Andrew. A.B., Wabash Coll., 1967; A.M., Harvard U., 1969; Ph.D., Rice U., 1974. Physicist, Arthur D. Little Co., Cambridge, Mass., 1968-69; mgr. research and devel. dept. GTE Sylvania, Mountain View, Calif., 1973-79; research mgr. GTE Labs., Waltham, Mass., 1979-81, research lab. dir., 1983—; dir. tech. labs. RCA, Camden, N.J., 1982. Contbr. articles to profl. jours. Mem. vestry St. Elizabeth's Episcopal Ch., Sudbury, Mass., 1984. Served to 1st lt. U.S. Army, 1969-71, Vietnam. Woodrow Wilson fellow, 1967. Mem. Am. Phys. Soc., IEEE, Optical Soc. Am., Am. Chem. Soc., Am. Assn. for Artificial Intelligence, Phi Beta Kappa. Current work: Nonlinear optics; laser physics; optical properties of materials. Subspecialty: Atomic and molecular physics. Office: GTE Labs 40 Sylvan Rd Waltham MA 02254

DECKER, DAVID ARNOLD, oncology researcher; b. Wyandotte, Mich., June 14, 1948; s. James Edward and Viola (Cordes) D.; m. Veronica Decker, Mar. 25, 1952; children: Brian David, Paul David, Marc David, Anne Veronica Decker. Student, Eastern Mich. U., 1966-70; M.D., Wayne State U., 1973. Diplomate: Am. Bd. Internal Medicine. Intern Mayo Clinic, Rochester, Minn., 1974, resident, 1975-77; instr medicine Mayo Med. Sch., 1978; asst. prof. medicine Mich. State U., 1979-81, dir. fellowship program hematology and oncology, 1979-81; head hematology, oncology sect. Ingham County Hosp., 1979-81; asst. prof. oncology Wayne State U., 1982-83, assoc. prof. medicine, 1983-84; vice chief oncology Harper Hosp., Detroit, 1983-84. Contbr. articles to profl. jours. Bd. dirs. Ingham County unit Am. Cancer Soc. Fellow ACP; mem. Am. Fedn. Clin. Research, Am. Soc. Clin. Oncology, Am. Assn. Cancer Research, ACP. Home: 3825 Burkoff St Troy MI 48084 Office: 1777 W Big Beaver Rd Troy MI 48084

DECKER, JAMES FREDERICK, physicist, technical program administrator; b. Albany, N.Y., Aug. 5, 1940; s. Foster Oliver and Calista (Gifford) D.; m. Anne Eleanor Romig, July 1964; children—John Sperry, David Foster. B.S., Union Coll., 1962; M.S., Yale U., 1963, Ph.D., 1967. Mem. tech. staff Bell Labs., Murray Hill, N.J., 1967-73; physicist U.S. AEC, Washington, 1973-74; chief exptl. plasma research Dept. Energy, Washington, 1974-78, dir. applied plasma physics, 1978-84; dir. sci. computing, 1984-85, dep. dir. Office of Energy Research, 1985—; chmn. supercomputer com. U.S. Govt., Washington, 1983—; mem. Parallel Processing Research Council, 1984—. Contbr. articles to profl. jours. Recipient Meritorious Service award Dept. Energy, 1984. Mem. IEEE (mem. supercomputer com. 1983—), Am. Phys. Soc. Current work: Management of research programs in high energy and nuclear physics, basic energy sciences, magnetic fusion energy, large-scale scientific computing. Subspecialties: Algorithms; Computer architecture. Office: Dept Energy 1000 Independence Ave SW Washington DC 20585

DECKER, RICHARD HENRY, biochemist; b. Grand Rapids, Mich., Aug. 12, 1934; s. Dennis H. and Helen L. (Schwalm) D.; m. Mary E. Burris, Aug. 5, 1960; children—Stephen H., Richard J., Stephanie S. A.B., Hope Coll., 1956; M.S., U. Ill., 1958; Ph.D., Okla. State U., 1961. Postdoctoral fellow U. Wis.-Madison, 1960-62; research assoc., tchr. Mayo Clinic, Rochester, Minn., 1962-66, career devel. fellow, 1966-71; research scientist Abbott Labs., N. Chgo., Ill., 1971-81, mgr. research, 1981—; mem. com. Hepatitus Test Nat. Commn. Clin. Lab. Standards, Villanova, Pa., 1983—. Contbr. articles to profl. jours. Elder, Reformed Church, Rochester, Minn., 1965-71. Served with USN, 1952-60. Abbott Labs. fellow, 1981—. Mem. Soc. Exptl. Pathology, AAAS, Fedn. Am. Socs. Exptl. Biology. Presbyterian. Subspecialties: Biochemistry (biology); Infectious diseases. Home: 924 Castlewood Deerfield IL 60015 Office: Abbott Labs 14th and Sheridan North Chicago IL 60064

DECKER, ROBERT WAYNE, geophysicist, educator; b. Williamsport, Pa., Mar. 11, 1927; s. P. Harold and Catherine T. (Sullivan) D.; married; 4 children. B.S., MIT, 1949, M.S., 1951; D.Sc. (Sinclair fellow), Colo. Sch. Mines, 1953. Asst. geologist Bethlehem Steel Co., Venezuela, 1949; geophysicist New World Exploration Co., Reno, 1952-54; asst. prof. Dartmouth, 1954-61, asso. prof., 1961-67, chmn. dept. geology, 1963-65, 74-77, prof., 1967-79, adj. prof., 1979—; geophysicist U.S. Geol. Survey, 1957—; scientist-in-charge Hawaiian Volcano Obs., 1979-84; asso. prof. Inst. Tech., Bandung, Indonesia, 1959-60; Mem. adv. panel for earth scis. NSF, 1971-74, chmn., 1972-73; chmn. geoscis. adv. panel Los Alamos Sci. Lab. Research affiliate Hawaii Inst. Geophysics, U. Hawaii, 1964—; participant Internat. Symposium on Volcanology, Japan, 1962, New Zealand, 1965; vis. scientist U.S. Geol. Survey Nat. Center for Earthquake Research, 1969-70; lectr. various colls., univs. Editor: Catalog of Active Volcanoes of the World, 1968-80; Am. editor: Bull. Volcanologique, 1967-75; author with Barbara Decker books on volcanoes; Contbr. articles to profl. jours. NSF grantee, 1968-71, 72-73. Fellow Geol. Soc. Am. (chmn. div.), Am. Geophys. Union (sect. v.p.); mem. Internat. Assn. Volcanology and Chemistry of Earth's Interior (pres. 1976-80), AAAS, Sigma Xi. Seismic and geodetic research on volcanism and tectonism of Hawaii, Iceland and Cascades; research on geothermal power. Subspecialties: Geophysics; Volcanology. Home: 4087 Silver Bar Rd Mariposa CA 95338

DECKER, WALTER JOHNS, toxicologist, consultant, researcher, educator; b. Tannersville, N.Y., June 13, 1933; s. H. Russell and Leola (Coons) D.; m. Barbara Allan Hart, Aug. 19, 1961; children: Karl Hart, Reid Johns, Sam Travis. A.B., SUNY, Albany, 1954, M.A., 1955; Ph.D., George Washington U., 1966. Commd. 2d lt. U.S. Army, 1955, advanced through grades to lt. col., 1970; research asst. Walter Reed Army Inst. Research, Washington, 1955-56, research biochemist, 1957-60; chief indsl. hygiene U.S. Army Med. Lab., Japan, 1956-57; asst. chief clin. research William Beaumont Army Med. Center, El Paso, 1965-71; chief chemistry dept. U.S. Army Med. Lab., San Antonio, 1971-75; ret., 1975; assoc. prof. pharmacology and toxicology, also dept. pediatrics U. Tex. Med. Br., Galveston, 1976-83, cons. in toxicology, 1983—. Assoc. editor: Clin. Toxicology; mem. editorial bd.: Jour. Toxicology and Environ. Health; contbr. articles to profl. jours. Decorated Legion of Merit, others; recipient Aesculapius award Tex. Med. Assn., 1977. Fellow Am. Acad. Clin. Toxicology. Mem. Am. Chem. Soc., Soc. Toxicology, Sigma Xi. Episcopalian. Current Work: Methods of detection and treatment of poisoning. Subspecialty: Toxicology (medicine). Home: 10741 Lemonade El Paso TX 79924 Office: 9220 McCombs Suite A El Paso TX 79924

DECKER, WAYNE LEROY, meteorologist, educator; b. Patterson, Iowa, Jan. 24, 1922; s. Albert Henry and Effie (Holmes) D.; m. Martha Jane Livingston, Dec. 29, 1943; 1 dau., Susan Jane. B.S., Central Coll., Pella, Iowa, 1943; postgrad., UCLA, 1943-44; M.S., Iowa State U., 1947, Ph.D., 1955. Meteorologist U.S. Weather Bur., Washington and Des Moines, 1947-49; mem. faculty U. Mo. at Columbia, 1949—, prof. meteorology, 1958-67, prof., chmn. dept. atmospheric sci., 1967—; chmn. com. climatic fluctuations and agrl. prodn. NRC, 1975-76; bd. dirs. Council for Agrl. Sci. and Tech., 1978—, mem. exec. com., 1981—. Mem. Am. Meteorol. Soc., Internat. Soc. Biometeorology, Am. Geophys. Union, Am. Agronomy Soc., Sigma Xi, Gamma Sigma Delta. Current Work: Graduate education and research on the impacts of weather and climate variabilities on agricultural production. Subspecialty: Climatology. Home: 1007 Hulen Dr Columbia MO 65201 Office: 701 Hitt St Columbia MO 65211

DEDIU, MIHAI MICHAEL, computer scientist; b. Iasi, Romania, Nov. 6, 1943; came to U.S., 1978, naturalized, 1983; s. Virgil and Ana (Condurache) D.; m. Sofia Scarlat, July 22, 1964; children: Ovidiu, Horatiu. M.S., U. Bucharest, 1966; Ph.D., Inst. Math., Bucharest, 1972. Researcher Inst. Math., Bucharest, 1967-75; asst. prof. U. Bucharest, 1973-74; researcher Inst. Physics, Bucharest, 1976-76, U. Turin, Italy, 1977-78, Case Western Res. U., Cleve., 1979-82; pres. Dr. Dediu Research Inst., Medford, Mass., 1981—. Author: Mathematical Software, 1984; Graphics, 1985. Mem. Republican Presdl. Task Force, Washington, 1981. Mem. Soc. Indsl. and Applied Math., Am. Math. Soc., Math. Assn. Am., Math. Modelling Assn., N.Y. Acad. Scis., Library Computer and Info. Scis., IEEE Computer Soc. Current Work: Mathematical software, programming languages, graphics systems analysis, applied numerical analysis, algorithms, artificial intelligence, database systems, information systems, operating systems. Subspecialties: Mathematical software; Programming languages. Home: 43 Lawler Rd Medford MA 02155 Office: Encode Tech Inc Nashua NH

DE DUVE, CHRISTIAN RENE, educator, scientist; b. Thames-Ditton, Eng., Oct. 2, 1917; s. Alphonse and Madeleine (Pungs) de D.; m. Janine Herman, Sept. 30, 1943; children: Thierry, Anne, Francoise, Alain. M.D., U. Louvain, Belgium, 1941, Ph.D., 1945, M.Sc., 1946; Dr. honoris causa, U. Turin, U. Leiden, U., Lille, U. Sherbrooke, U. Ghent, U. Liége, Catholic U. Chile, Université René Descartes, Paris, Gustavus Adolphus Coll., St. Peter, Minn., U. Rosario, Argentina, U. Aix-M eille II, U. Keele, Katholieke U. Leuven. Prof. physiol. chemistry U. Louvain Med. Sch., 1947—; prof. biochem. cytology Rockefeller U., N.Y.C., 1962-74, Andrew W. Mellon prof., 1974—. Recipient Prix des Alumni, 1949, Prix Pfizer, 1957, Prix Francqui, 1960, Prix Quinquennal Belge des Sciences Médicales, 1967; Belgium; Gairdner Found. Internat. award merit Can., 1967; Dr. H.P. Heineken Prijs Netherlands, 1973; Nobel Prize in Physiology or Medicine, 1974. Mem. Royal Acad. Medicine, Royal Acad. Belgium, Am. Chem. Soc., Biochem. Soc., Am. Soc. Biol. Chemists, Pontf Acad. Sci., Am. Soc. Cell Biology, Deutsche Akademie der Naturforscher Leopoldina, Soc. Chim. Biol., Soc. Belge Biochim., Sigma Xi; fgn. mem. Am. Acad. Arts and Scis.; fgn. assoc. Nat. Acad. Scis., Académie des Scis. de Paris, Académie des Sciences d'Athenes. Current Work: Basic cellular and molecular biology and its applications in medicine, therapeutics and biotechnology. Subspecialties: Biochemistry (biology); Cell biology. Home: 80 Central Park W New York NY 10023 Office: Rockefeller U York Ave and 66th St New York NY 10021

DEEDWANIA, PRAKASH CHANDRA, cardiologist, educator; b. Ajmer, India, Aug. 28, 1948; came to U.S., naturalized, 1971; s. Gokul C. and Paras D. (Garg) D.; m. Catherine E. Deedwania, June 26, 1977. M.B.B.S., U. Rajasthan, India, 1969. Diplomate: Am. Bd. Internal Medicine, Am. Bd. Cardiology, Am. Bd. Pulmonary Disease. Intern Coney Island Hosp.-Downstate Med. Ctr., 1971-72; resident in medicine VA Hosp., Mt. Sinai, N.Y., 1972-74; fellow in cardiology U. Ill., 1975-77; chief cardiology VA Med. Ctr. U. Calif.-San Francisco, 1980—, dir. med. intensive care unit/CCU, 1980—, chmn. critical care com., 1982—, assoc. clin. prof. medicine, 1980—. Research grantee Merck Sharpe and Dohme, West Pitts., Pa., 1982—; Research grantee Marion Labs., Kansas City, Mo., 1982—; Research grantee Miles Labs., West Haven, Conn., 1982—. Fellow Am. Coll. Cardiology, Am. Heart Assn., ACP, Am. Coll. Chest Physicians; mem. Am. Fedn. Clin. Research, Central Valley Heart Assn. Current Work: Role of myocardial imaging techniques in diagnosis of cardiac patients; newer agents in heart failure and myocardial ischemia; treatment of hypertension; coronary risk factors and prevention of coronary disease. Subspecialties: Cardiology; Internal medicine. Office: VA Medical Center 2615 E Clinton Ave Fresno CA 93711

DEFIEBRE, CONRAD WILLIAM, microbiologist; b. Bklyn., Jan. 19, 1924; s. Conrad William and Barbara (Benisch) deF.; m. Harriet M. Hamm, Oct. 26, 1946; children—Conrad, Henry, Jeremy, Timothy, David, Christopher. B.S., Rensselaer Poly. Inst., 1949; M.S., U. Wis., 1950, Ph.D., 1952. Asst. bacteriologist U. Wis., 1949-52; research microbiologist duPont, Wilmington, Del., 1952-61; research dir. Wilson Labs. div. Wilson Pharm. & Chem. Corp., Chgo., 1961-67, v.p. research, 1967-69; with Ross Labs. div. Abbott Labs., Columbus, Ohio, 1969—, v.p. research and devel., 1971-85, ret., 1985, chmn. bd. infant formula council, 1976-77, 81-85; 2d vice chmn. Central Ohio Rehab. Ctr., Goodwill Industries, 1980, chmn., 1985—; acting dir. Food Industries Ctr. of Ohio State U., 1985—. Served with AUS, 1943-46. Recipient award of merit Ohio State U., 1981. Fellow Am. Inst. Chemists; mem. Am. Chem. Soc., Am. Soc. Microbiology, Am. Inst. Biol. Scis., Sigma Xi. Roman Catholic. Clubs: Worthington Hills Country, Businessmen's Athletic. Subspecialty: Microbiology. Home: 8000 Fairway Dr Worthington OH 43085

DEFRANK, JOSEPH JOHN, biotechnologist, researcher; b. Rochester, N.Y., Nov. 3, 1946; s. Frank James and Christine Virginia (Ciraulo) DeF.; m. Linda Diane Koser, Aug. 1, 1981. B.S. in Biology, St. John Fisher Coll., 1968, Ph.D. in Biochemistry, U. Miami, 1975. Dir. microbiology Bio-Tech. Resources, Inc., Manitowoc, Wis., 1977-81; sr. research chemist PPG Industries, Inc., Pitts., 1981-83; research chemist U.S. Army Chem. Research and Devel. Ctr., Aberdeen Proving Ground, Md., 1984—. Served with U.S. Army, 1969-70; Vietnam. Mem. AAAS, Am. Chem. Soc., Am. Soc. for Microbiology, N.Y. Acad. Scis. Soc. for Ind. Microbiology. Current work: Devel. biomicrosensors for use in detection of chemical agents, toxins and biologicals. Subspecialties: Enzyme technology; Biochemistry (biology). Home: 619 Aspen Ln Edgewood MD 21040 Office: US Army Chem Research and Devel Ctr Biotech Div Research Directorate SMCCR-RSB Aberdeen Proving Ground MD 21010

DEGNAN, JAMES HENRY, physicist; b. Norristown, Pa., July 18, 1947; s. James H and Madeleine Mary (Bennis) D.; m. Elizabeth Teresa Castillo, Aug. 8, 1970 (div. May 1984); children—James, Michelle. B.S., St. Josephs Coll., Phila., 1969; M.S., U. Pitt., 1972, Ph.D., 1973. Physicist, Air Force Weapons Lab., Albuquerque, 1978—; adj. prof. U. N.Mex., Albuquerque, 1981, 83. Contbr. articles to profl. jours. Served to capt. USAF, 1973-78. Mem. Am. Phys. Soc., Planetary Soc., Air Force Assn. Republican. Roman Catholic. Club: Albuquerque Astronomers. Current work: Plasma liner implosion; radiation measurements; explosive magnetic compression generators; inductive storage; multi mega amp opening switches; coaxial guns. Subspecialties: Plasma physics; Nuclear physics. Office: Air Force Weapons Lab Kirtland AFB Albuquerque NM 87117

DEGNAN, JOHN JAMES, III, physicist; b. Phila., Dec. 10, 1945; s. John James and Ruth Deloris (Vece) D.; m. Adele Susan Henry, June 27, 1969; children: Adam John, Andrew Paul. B.S., Drexel U., 1968; M.S., U. Md., 1970, Ph.D., 1979. Student trainee NASA Goddard Space Flight Center, Greenbelt, Md., 1964-68, research physicist, 1968-72, sr. physicist, 1972-79, head advanced electro-optical instrument sect., 1979—; assoc. mem. Adv. Group on Electron Devices, Working Group D, 1980. Trustee Scholarship Drexel U., 1963. Recipient Quality Increase award NASA, 1974, Spl. Achievement award, 1976. Mem. Optical Soc. Am., Am. Inst. Physics, Sigma Pi Sigma, Sigma Pi. Roman Catholic. Current Work: Laser ranging and altimetry, infrared heterodyne spectroscopy dye lasers, ultrashort pulse Nd: YAG lasers, waveguide carbon dioxide lasers, laser communications. Subspecialty: Infrared spectroscopy. Office: Code 723 NASA Goddard Space Flight Center Greenbelt MD 20771

DEGOOYER, WILLIAM JAY, chemist; b. Denver, Nov. 26, 1956; s. Allison Jay and Arline Jozina (Jagerink) DeG. B.S. in Chemistry, Colo. Sch. Mines, 1978; M.S. in Organic Chemistry, U. Wis.-Madison, 1980. Chemist, Celanese Splty. Resins, Louisville, 1980—. Patentee epoxy curing agts., 1984. Recipient

Max I. Silber award Colo. Sch. Mines, 1975, Robert Baxter award, 1978. Mem. Am. Chem. Soc. Current work: Synthesis of curing agents for epoxy resins both waterborne and solventborne; synthesis of high solids resins; synthesis of epoxy ester resins. Subspecialties: Organic chemistry; Polymer chemistry. Home: 7701 H Royalty Ave Louisville KY 40222 Office: Celanese Specialty Resins 9800 Bluegrass Pkwy Jeffersontown KY 40299

DEGUCHI, SHUJI, physics educator; b. Nagoya, Japan, Feb. 7, 1948; came to U.S., 1979; s. Minoru and Kaoru (Yamauchi) D.; m. Yukie Masuda, June 10, 1977; children—Fumi, Gaku. B.Sc., U. Kyoto (Japan), 1970; M.Sc., U. Tokyo, 1973, Ph.D., 1977. Lectr. Sophia U., Tokyo, 1977-78, Keio U., Tokyo, 1978-79; research fellow Calif. Inst. Tech., Pasadena, 1979-80; research assoc. U. Mass., Amherst. 1980-81; chief researcher Pacific Aerosurvey, Tokyo, 1982-83, vis. asst. prof. physics, U. Ill., Urbana, 1983—; enseignant associe Observatoire de Paris, Meudon, France, 1982; research assoc. Nobeyama Radio Obs., Nagano-ken, Japan, 1982. Author: Futatabi Kitt-Peak e, 1982. Mem. Am. Astron. Soc., Japan Astron. Soc. Radiative transfer of astrophysical masers, mass loss from rate-type stars related to the grain formation in circumstellar envelopes, radio observations of complex molecules in interstellar clouds. Subspecialty: Radio and microwave astronomy. Home: 1944A Orchard St Urbana IL 61801 Office: U Ill Physics Dept 1110 W Green St Urbana IL 61801

DE HAAN, HENRY JOHN, research psychologist; b. St. Clair County, Ill., Nov. 23, 1920; s. Henry John and Fanny (Haislip) de H.; m. Mary J. Farrell, Oct. 22, 1943. A.B., Washington U., St. Louis, 1942, A.M., 1949; Ph.D. in Psychology, U. Pitts., 1960. Postdoctoral trainee in physiol. psychology VA Hosp., Coatesville, Pa., 1960-62; research scientist George Washington U., 1962-64; research psychologist Armed Forces Radiobiology Research Inst., Bethesda, Md., 1965-69, Dept. Army, U.S. Army Research Inst., Alexandria, Va., 1969—; faculty mem. Dept. Agr. Grad. Sch., 1967-77. Contbr. articles on research psychology to profl. jours. Served with USN, 1942-44. Mem. AAAS, Am. Psychol. Assn., Internat. Neuropsychology Soc., Internat. Primatological Soc., Psychonomic Soc., Soc. for Neurosci., Sigma Xi. Current Work: Speech perception, analysis, and synthesis; time-compressed speech; machine recognition of speech, visual perception, biological factors in perception and behavior. Subspecialties: Perception; Psychobiology. Home: 5403 Yorkshire St Springfield VA 22151 Office: 5001 Eisenhower Ave Alexandria VA 22333

DE HERTOGH, AUGUST ALBERT, horticultural science educator, administrator, researcher; b. Chgo., Aug. 24, 1935; s. Frank Joseph and Marie Louise (Van Cauwenbergh) De H.; m. Faye Kipp, June 5, 1957 (div. Apr. 1985); children—Christopher Mark, Michelle Louise, Jennifer Leigh. B.S., N.C. State U., 1957, M.S., 1961; Ph.D., Oreg. State U., 1963. Asst. plant physiologist, Boyce Thompson Inst., Yonkers, N.Y., 1964-65; asst. prof. horticultural sci. Mich. State U., East Lansing, 1965-69, assoc. prof., 1969-72, prof., 1972-78; prof., head dept. horticultural sci. N.C. State U., Raleigh, 1978—; tech. advisor Dutch Bulb Exporters Assoc., Hillegom, The Netherlands, 1965—. Author: Holland Bulb Garden Guide, 1982; Holland Bulb Forcers Guide, 1985. Served to 1st lt. U.S. Army, 1957-59. Recipient Meritorious Service award Mich. State Florist Assn., 1969; Medal of Honor, Netherlands Ministry of Agr. and Fisheries, 1985. Fellow Am. Soc. Horticulture Sci. (Research award 1976, cross commodity dir. 1980-81), Internat. Soc. Horticulture Sci., Weed Soc. N.C., Sigma Xi. Democrat. Roman Catholic. Subspecialty: Plant physiology (agriculture). Office: NC State U Dept Horticulture Sci Raleigh NC 27695

DEHGAN, BIJAN, horticulture educator, researcher; b. Shiraz, Iran, Mar. 4, 1939; came to U.S., 1961, naturalized, 1981; s. Kamal and Arfaa (Hamidi) D.; m. Nancy Dumars, Feb. 2, 1964; children: Ramine, Michael, Daria. B.S., Pahlavi U., 1960; cert. Am. lang, Columbia U., 1962; B.S., U. Calif.-Davis, 1965, M.S., 1972, Ph.D., 1976. Staff research assoc. dept. botany U. Calif.-Davis, 1965-71, lectr. environ. horticulture, 1972-78; asst. prof. dept. ornamental horticulture U. Fla., Gainesville, 1978—; researcher, mem. U. Fla. (Center for Environ. Programs), 1980—. Contbr. articles on horticulture and botany to profl. jours. Mem. Bot. Soc. Am., Am. Soc. Plant Taxonomists, Internat. Assn. Plant Taxonomists, Linnean Soc. London, Am. Hort. Soc., Sigma Xi. Current Work: Energy farming-production of hydrocarbons from plant biomass, taxonomy of the genus Jatropha L. (Euphoribiaceae) and Cycadales. Subspecialties: Biomass (agriculture); Taxonomy. Home: 5720 NW 57th Way Gainesville FL 32606 Office: U Fla 2519 HS/PP Bldg Gainesville FL 32611

DEHMELT, HANS GEORG, physics educator; b. Germany, Sept. 9, 1922; came to U.S., 1952, naturalized, 1962; s. Georg Karl and Asta Ella (Klemmt) D.; 1 son, Gerd. Grad., Graues Kloster, Abitur, 1940; Ph.D. summa cum laude, U. Goettingen, 1950. Postdoctoral fellow U. Goettingen, Germany, 1950-52, Duke U., Durham, N.C., 1952-55; vis. asst. prof. U. Wash., Seattle, 1955, asst. prof. physics, 1956, asso. prof., 1957-61, prof., 1961—; cons. Varian Assos., Palo Alto, Calif., 1956-76. Contbr. articles to profl. jours. Recipient Humboldt prize, 1974; award in basic research Internat. Soc. Magnetic Resonance, 1980; NSF grantee, 1958—. Fellow Am. Phys. Soc. (Davisson-Germer prize 1970); mem. Am. Acad. Arts and Scis., Nat. Acad. Scis. Current Work: Single elementary/atomic particle at rest in space, mass, magnetic moment and radius of electron/positron, ultimate laser frequency standard, particle identity. Subspecialties: Atomic and molecular physics; Particle physics. Home: 1600 43d Ave E Seattle WA 98112 Office: Physics Dept FM 15 U Wash Seattle WA 98195

DE HODGINS, OFELIA CANALES, materials scientist, engineer; b. Mexico City, Oct. 25, 1943; came to U.S., 1974, naturalized, 1978; s. Fernando and Leana (Del Olmo) Canales Rocha; m. Garry Hodgins, Aug. 24, 1974; 1 child, Alfonso Sidarta. B.S. in physics, U. Mexico, 1972; M.S. in Physics and Materials Sci., 1977, Ph.D., 1985. Jr. researcher Lab. Ultracentrifuges Nuclear Inst. Mexico, 1971-73, sr. researcher, 1973-76; vis. research fellow U. Va., 1973; prof. math. Physics and Lab. Physics High Sch. Instituto Freinet de Mexico, Mexico City, 1971-72; asst. prof. thermodynamics U. Mexico, 1972-73; asst. prof. math. Instituto Politecnico Nacional, Mexico City, 1973-74; grad. research asst. dept. physics U. Va., 1974-75, grad. research asst. dept. materials sci., 1976-79, grad. research asst. dept. nuclear engring. and engring. physics, 1979—; staff negr. Internat. Bus. Machines Corp., Poughkeepsie, N.Y., 1981—. Contbr. articles to profl. jours. Dorothea Buck fellow, 1975-76; recipient Nat. Prize of Sci. Mexico, 1974. Mem. Mexican Soc. Physics, Am. Soc. Metals, Am. Nuclear Soc., Electron Microscopy Soc. Am., Soc. Exptl. Stress Analysis, Sigma Xi. Current Work: Solid state physics, metallurgy, polymers, electronics integrated circuits, reactor pressure vessel steels. Subspecialty: Microchip technology (materials science).

DE HOFFMANN, FREDERIC, See *Who's Who in America,* 43rd edition. .

DEHORITY, BURK ALLYN, rumen microbiologist, educator; b. Peoria, Ill., Sept. 3, 1930; s. Harry A. and Marie B. D.; m. Barbara June, July 5, 1953; children: Katherine, Christine, Sue Ellen, Burk Joel. B.A., Blackburn Coll., 1952; M.S., U. Maine, 1954; Ph.D., Ohio State U., 1957. Asst. prof. dept. animal scis. U. Conn., 1957-59; with Ohio Agr. Research and Devel. Ctr., Ohio State U., 1959—, prof. dept. animal sci., 1970—, assoc. chmn. dept., 1981—. Contbr. to profl. jours. Mem. Am. Soc. Animal Sci., Am. Soc. Microbiology, Am. Dairy Sci. Assn. Lutheran. Current Work: Rumen microbiology, studies on the rumen bacteria responsible for breakdown of forages, types and their isolation and classification, synergism between bacterial species; rumen protozoa. Subspecialties: Animal nutrition; Microbiology. Home: 708 Kieffer St Wooster OH 44691 Office: Dept Animal Science Ohio Agr Research and Devel Center Wooster OH 44691

DEIBEL, MARTIN ROBERT, JR., biochemist; b. Columbus, Ohio, Apr. 21, 1949; s. Martin R. and Edith (Marolt) D.; m. Megan Gower, May 19, 1979. B.S., Ohio State U., 1971, Ph.D., 1977. Postdoctoral fellow U. Ky., Lexington, 1977-79, sr. research assoc., 1979-80, research asst. prof. biochemistry, 1980—; researcher Ohio State U., Columbus, 1971-77. Contbr. articles to profl. jours. NIH grantee, 1982. Mem. Am. Soc. Biol. Chemists, AAAS, Phi Beta Kappa. Current Work: Biochemical studies of terminal deoxynucleotidyl transferase; an enzyme found in lymphoid tissues and in the blood of some leukemic patients; active site and enzymatic studies of the enzyme; physical biochemistry. Subspecialty: Biochemistry (medicine). Office: Dept Biochemistry U Ky Sch Medicine 800 Rose St Lexington KY 40536

DEIBEL, RUDOLF, medical virologist; b. Berlin, Apr. 27, 1924; came to U.S., 1962, naturalized, 1968; s. Rudolf and Margarete (Bernhoft) D.; m. Waltraut Rosenbrock, Oct. 4, 1957; children: Rudolf, Stephan, Christiane. Cand. med., Humboldt U., Berlin, 1946-51; Dr. med., Albert Ludwigs U., Freiburg, Ger., 1953; Bd. in Pediatrics, Landes Aerztekammer Baden-Wuerttemberg, Ger., 1961. Intern Stadt, Wenckebach Krankenhaus, Berlin-Tempelhof, Ger., 1953-54; resident Inst. Pathology, U. Freiburg, 1955-56, Children's Hosp., Freiburg, 1956-61; assoc. med. virologist Div. Labs. and Research, N.Y. State Dept. Health, Albany, 1962-67; dir. Virus Labs., Wadsworth Ctr. for Labs. and Research, 1967—; prof. microbiology and pediatrics Albany Med. Coll. of Union U. 1977—. Mem. Am. Pub. Health Assn., Am. Soc. Microbiology, Am. Assn. Immunologists, Capital dist. Pediatric Soc., Am. Soc. Tropical Medicine and Hygiene, N.Y. State Assn. Pub. Health Labs., Am. Soc. Virology., N.Y. Acad. Sci. Current Work: Pathology and immunology of virus infections. Subspecialties: Virology (medicine); Pediatrics.

DEISSLER, ROBERT GEORGE, fluid dynamacist; b. Greenville, Pa., Aug. 1, 1921; s. Victor Girard and Helen Stella (Fisher) D.; m. June Marie Gallagher, Oct. 7, 1950; children: Robert Joseph, Mary Beth, Ellen Ann, Ann Marie. B.S., Carnegie Inst. Tech., 1943; M.S., Case Inst. Tech., 1948. Research engr. Goodyear Aircraft Corp., Akron, Ohio, 1943-44; aero. research scientist NASA Lewis Research Ctr., Cleve., 1947-52, chief fundamental heat transfer br., 1952-70, staff scientist, sci. cons. fluid physics, 1970—. Contbr. articles to profl. jours. Served to lt. (j.g.) USNR, 1944-46. Recipient Max Jacob Meml. award ASME/Am. Inst. Chem. Engrs., 1975; NACA/NASA Exceptional Service award, 1957; Outstanding Publ. award, 1978. Fellow AIAA (tech. achievement award 1981), ASME (Heat Transfer Meml. award 1964, award 1977); mem. Am. Phys. Soc., Soc. Natural Philosophy, Sigma Xi. Roman Catholic. Current Work: Theoretical turbulence incl. numerical solutions, turbulent heat transfer, vortex flows, atmospheric and astrophys. flows, thermal radiation, heat transfer in powders. Subspecialties: Fluid mechanics; Heat transfer. Home: 4540 W 213 St Fairview Park OH 44126 Office: NASA Lewis Research Center 21000 Brookpark Rd Cleveland OH 44135

DEJOHN, CHARLES SAMUEL, psychiatrist; b. Houston, Nov. 26, 1940; s. Sam and Theresa (Rizzo) DeJ.; m. Tania Mena D'Alessandro, June, 1976; children—Alicia, Carla, Samuel. B.S., St. Thomas U., 1962; M.S., U. Houston, 1965, Ph.D., 1968; M.D., U. Tex., 1976. Diplomate Nat. Bd. Med. Examiners; cert. nat. Bd. Psychiatry and Neurology. Research physicist Shell Devel. Co., Houston, 1968-72; intern Baylor Coll. Medicine, Houston, 1976-79, resident in psychiatry, 1976-79; practice medicine specializing in psychiatry, Houston, 1979—; clin. instr. Baylor Coll. Medicine, Houston, 1979—, U. Tex., Houston, 1979—. Contbr. articles to profl. jours. Jesse H. Jones scholar, Health Profl. scholar, Dr. Walter Julius Hildebrand scholar; grantee U. Houston; fellow NASA, NSF; cert. Tex. Commn. on Fire Protection. Mem. Am. Phys. Soc., Am. Med. Soc., Am. Psychiatric Assn., Harris County Med. Soc., Tex. Psychiatric Assn., Houston Psychiatric Soc., Harris County Bio-Feedback Soc., Am. Assn. Geriatric Psychiatry, Sigma Pi Sigma, Phi Kappa Phi, Mu Delta. Office: Psychiatric Clinic of Houston 7580 Fannin Suite 315 Houston TX 77054

DE JONG, GERALD, computer engineer. Assoc. prof. dept. elec. and computer engring. U. Ill., Urbana. Subspecialty: Artificial intelligence. Office: Dept Elec and Computer Engring U Ill Urbana IL 61801

DE KEYSER, THOMAS LEE, geologist; b. Green Bay, Wis., Nov. 30, 1945; s. Alphonse William and Frances Mildred (Nihil) Bohm; m. Lorraine Marie La Freniere, Jan. 20, 1970; div. Oct. 12, 1973. B.S. in Geology U. Wis., 1972, M.S. in Geology, 1974; Ph.D. in Geology, Oreg. State U., 1979. Project asst. U. Wis. Geol. Mus., Madison, 1971-74; research scientist Amoco Prodn. Co. Research Ctr., Tulsa, summers 1972-76; geology instr. Oreg. State U., Corvallis, 1976-79; field geologist Chromalloy Mineral and Metals, Elko, Nev., 1979; asst. prof. Tex. Tech. U., Lubbock, 1979-82; sr. geologist Marathon Oil Co., Houston, 1982—. Contbr. articles to profl. jours. Served with USN, 1967-71. Mem. Am. Assn. Petroleum Geologists, Geol. Soc. Am., Paleontol. Soc., Soc. Econ. Paleontologists and Mineralogists, Sigma Xi. Current work: Computer integrated basin analysis in support of hydrocarbon exploration in U.S. Gulf and Atlantic coast. Subspecialties: Sedimentology; Paleontology, paleoecology. Home: 2607 Stoney Brook Dr Houston TX 77063 Office: Marathon Oil Co PO Box 3128 Houston TX 77253

DE LAGUNA, FREDERICA, anthropology educator; b. Ann Arbor, Mich., Oct. 3, 1906; s. Theodore de Laguna and Grace (Mead) Andrus. A.B., Bryn Mawr Coll., 1927; Ph.D., Columbia U., 1933; LL.D. (hon.), U. Alaska, 1982. Asst., field dir. U. Pa. Mus., Phila., 1931-33, cataloguer, 1933-34; assoc. soil conservationist U.S. Dept. Agr., Altuquerque, 1935-36; lectr. Bryn Mawr Coll., Pa., 1938-41, asst. prof., 1941-42, 46-49; prof. emeritus, 1975—. Author: Archeology of Cook Inlet, 1934, 75; Prehistory of Northern North America, 1947; Under Mount St. Elias, 1972; Voyage to Greenland, 1977. Served to lt. comdr. USNR, 1942-45. Fellow AAAS, Am. Anthropol. Assn. (assoc. editor 1947-48, mem. exec. bd. 1955-58, pres. 1965-67); mem. Nat. Acad. Scis., LWV. Democrat. Current work: Cultural anthropology, combining archeology and ethnology, history of anthropology, cultures of Alaskan Eskimos and Indians and of Greenlanders. Home: 830 Montgomery Ave #510 Bryn Mawr PA 19010 Office: Dept Anthropology Bryn Mawr Coll Bryn Mawr PA 19010

DE LANEROLLE, NIHAL CHANDRA, neuroanatomy and neuroethology researcher, educator; b. Colombo, Sri Lanka, Apr. 16, 1945; came to U.S., 1974; s. Leslie Barnes and May Adelaide (Jayawardena) de L. B.Sc., U. Ceylon, 1967; D.Phila., U. Sussex, Eng., 1972; B.A., U. Cambridge, Eng., 1974, M.A., 1981. Asst. lectr. zoology U. Ceylon, 1967-69; postdoctoral research fellow in behavioral physiology and psychopharmacology U. Minn., St. Paul, 1975-78; research fellow in biol. psychiatry Yale U. Sch. Medicine, 1978-79, research asso., 1979-82, asst. prof. neurosurgery and neuroanatomy, 1982—; vis. asst. prof. psychology Wesleyan U., Middletown, Conn., 1981-82. Contbr. articles to profl. jours. Amyotrophic Lateral Sclerosis Soc. Am. grantee, 1982. Mem. Soc. for Neurisci., Assn. for Study Animal Behavior, Animal Behavior Soc., N.Y. Acad. Sci., AAAS. Episcopalian. Current Work: Chemically defined neural circuits in brainstem and neocortex of mammals; neural basis of vocalization and emotion in birds and mammals. Subspecialties: Neurobiology; Ethology. Office: Sect Neurosurgery Yale U Sch Medicine 333 Cedar St New Haven CT 06510

DE LA NOUE, JOEL JEAN-LOUIS, biologist, university administrator, researcher; b. Ferryville, Tunisia, Mar. 18, 1938; s. Jean and Genevieve (Adelus) de la N.; m. Christiane Laboissonniere, Dec. 26, 1959; children: Eric, Philippe; m. Helene Raymond, July 16, 1980; 1 dau., Marie-Eve. B.Sc., U. Laval., Can., 1960, D.Sc., 1968; postgrad., U. Sheffield, Eng., 1968-69, U. Wash., 1969-70. Asst. prof. biology dept. U. Laval, Que., 1964-70, adj. prof., 1970-72, assoc. prof., 1972-78, prof., 1978—; dir. U. Laval (Nutrition Research Centre), 1978—, founding pres. Aquaculture inst., 1973-77. Contbr. articles to profl. jours. Recipient medal Vice-Gov. Province Que., 1960; Natural Scis. and Engring. Research Council Can. grantee, 1970—; Ministry Edn. Que. grantee, 1972—. Mem. AAAS, Assn. canadienne-francaise pour l'advancement des sciences, Assn. des biologistes du Que., Que. Assn. Aquaculture (founding pres.), Aquaculture Assn. Can. (v.p. 1985-86), Canadian Inst. Food Sci. and Tech. Co-inventor automatic particle collector for material in suspension in water. Current Work: Biotechnological recycling with integrated food chains, aquaculture, research, teaching, administration, consulting. Subspecialties: Water supply and wastewater treatment; Biomass (agriculture). Home: 1082 Dijon St Ste-Foy PQ G1W 4M4 Canada Office: Local 1312 Pavillon Comtois U Laval Ste-Foy PQ G1K 7P4 Canada

DELAP, JAMES HARVE, chemist; b. Carbondale, Ill., Feb. 6, 1930; s. Harve Eugene and Adena Rosetta (Harriss) D.; m. Clara Prudence Todd, Mar. 29, 1959; children: Carolyn Adena, Mary Amelia, Margaret Jane, James Todd. B.A., So. Ill. U., Carbondale, 1952; postgrad., U. Calif.-Berkeley, 1954-55; M.A., Duke U., 1959, Ph.D., 1960. Research chemist Chemstrand Corp., Durham, N.C., 1960-62; asst. prof. Stetson U., Deland, Fla., 1962-68, assoc. prof., 1968-71, prof. chemistry, 1971—. Served with U.S. Army, 1952-54. Recipient McEniry award Stetson U., 1982; James B. Duke Fellow, Duke U., 1957-60; Fulbright lectr., 1970-71, 78-79. Mem. Union Concerned Scientists, Am. Chem. Soc., Gamma Sigma Epsilon. Democrat. Presbyterian. Current Work: Photochemistry, photodegradation; luminescence. Subspecialties: Physical chemistry; Laser photochemistry. Home: 1103 N Boston Ave Deland FL 32724 Office: Stetson U Box 8277 Deland FL 32720

DELASHMIT, WALTER HOWARD, JR., engineering researcher; b. Memphis, Dec. 14, 1944; s. Walter Howard and Gertrude Marie (Scott) D.; m. Linda Fay Vaught, Aug. 20, 1967; children—Mark Robert, Rick Alan. B.S. in Elec. Engring., Christian Bros. Coll., 1966; M.S., U. Tenn., 1968. Registered profl. engr., Pa. Mem. tech. staff TRW Systems, Houston, 1969-72; sr. engr. Martin Marietta, Orlando, Fla., 1972-76; research engr. Pa. State U., State College, 1976-82; sr. engr. specialist LTV Aerospace and Def. Co., Dallas, 1982—; contbg. mem. Automatic Target Recognizer Working Group, Dayton, Ohio, 1984—. Contbr. articles to sci. jours. Youth basketball coach YMCA, Bellefonte, Pa., also Arlington, Tex., 1981, 83, 84; youth baseball coach Little League and Optimist Club, State College, also Arlington, 1980-83; youth soccer coach Centre Region Parks and Recreation Dept., State Coll., 1980-81; active Longhorn council Boy Scouts Am., Arlington, 1982-84. Mem. IEEE (sr.; chmn. Orlando sect. aerospace and electronic systems group), Am. Statis. Assn. Republican. Baptist. Clubs: Optimist; Toastmasters Internat.; Arlington Runners. Current work: Developing image processing and artificial intelligence techniques to synergistically combine sensor imagery for automatic target recognition. Subspecialties: Graphics, image processing, and pattern recognition; Algorithms. Home: 3409 Woodside Dr Arlington TX 76016 Office: LTV Aerospace and Defense Co M/S TH-61 PO Box 650003 Dallas TX 75265

DE LA TORRE, JACK CARLOS, physician, brain researcher; b. Paris, France; s. Rafael and Maria C. (Parodi) de la T.; m. Florinda Bayod, June 30, 1962. B.S., Am. U., Washington, 1961; Ph.D. in Anatomy, U. Geneva, 1968; M.D., U. Mex., Juarez, 1979. Asst. prof. neurosurgery and psychiatry U. Chgo. Sch. Medicine, 1969-75, assoc. prof., 1975-79; assoc. prof. neurosurgery U. Miami Sch. Medicine, 1979-82, dir. research, 1979-82; assoc. prof. neurosurgery, dir. neurosurgery research Northwestern U. Med. Sch., Chgo., 1982-83; assoc. prof. neurosurgery, head exptl. surgery U. Ottawa Health Scis., (Ont. Can.), 1983—. Author: Dynamics of Brain Monoamines, 1972; editor-in-chief: Biological Actions and Medical Applications of Dimethyl Sulfoxide, 1983; translator: Histology of the Nervous System (Ramon y Cajal), vol. I, 1983; contbr. articles to profl. jours. Grantee NIH, 1970-73; Grantee U. Chgo., 1970-72; Grantee Purer Found., 1979-80; Grantee Paralysis Cure Research Found., 1981-82; Grantee Am. Paralysis Assn., 1983-84. Mem. Internat. Brain Research Orgn., Am. Acad. Neurology, Soc. Neurosci., AAUP, N.Y. Acad. Scis., AAAS, Cajal Club. Patentee in control of bacteria. Current Work: Regeneration of central nervous system; pathophysiology of head and spinal cord trauma and cerebral stroke; therapy of brain ischemia/trauma; stress and brain neurotransmitters. Subspecialties: Neurobiology; Neurophysiology. Office: 451 Smyth Rd Ottawa ON K1H 8M5 Canada

DELAUBENFELS, DAVID JOHN, geography educator; b. Pasadena, Calif., Dec. 5, 1925; s. Max Walker and Beth (Jones) de L.; m. Gudrun Josephine Erickson, Dec. 21, 1954; children: Eric Arthur, Lucia Beth de Laubenfels Sweetland, Evelyn Jo, Marion Jean; m. Linda Elaine Price, Dec. 27, 1973. A.A., Pasadena Jr. Coll., 1947; A.B., Colgate U., 1949; A.M., U. Ill., 1950; Ph.D., 1953. Postdoctoral fellow Johns Hopkins U., Balt., 1955-56; asst. prof. U. Ga., Athens, 1953-58, assoc. prof., 1958-59, Syracuse (N.Y.) U., 1959-71, prof., 1971—. Author: Mapping the World's Vegetation, 1975, Gymnospermes, Fasc. 4-Flore de la Nouvelle Caledonie et Dependancies, 1972, A Geography of Plants and Animals, 1970; contbr. articles on geography of plants and animals to profl. jours. Served with AUS, 1944-46. Travel grantee in field. Mem. Assn. Am. Geographers, Am. Geography Soc., Ecol. Soc. Am., Bot. Soc. Am., Internat. Soc. Plant Morphologists, Sigma Xi. Current Work: Geographic differentiation of vegetation systems, taxonomy and ecology of tropical conifers. Subspecialties: Biogeography; Taxonomy. Office: Dept Geography Syracuse U Syracuse NY 13210

DE LAUER, RICHARD D., aerospace consultant; b. Oakland, Calif., Sept. 23, 1918; s. Michael and Matilda (Giambruno) DeL.; m. Ann Carmichael, Dec. 6, 1940; 1 son, Richard Daniel. A.B., Stanford U., 1940; B.S., U.S. Naval Postgrad. Sch., 1949; Aero. Engr., Calif. Inst. Tech., 1950, Ph.D., 1953. Structrual designer Glenn L. Martin Co., Balt., 1940-42; design engr. Northrop Co., Hawthorne, Calif., 1942; commd. ensign USN, 1942, advanced through grades to comdr., 1958, assignments in, U.S., 1943-58, ret., 1966; lab. dir. Space Tech. Labs., El Segundo, Calif., 1958-60, Titan Program dir., 1960-62, v.p., dir. ballistic missile program mgmt., 1962-66; v.p., gen. mgr. systems engring. and integration div. TRW Systems Group, Redondo Beach, Calif., 1966-68, v.p., gen. mgr., 1968-70; exec. v.p. TRW, Inc., Redondo Beach, 1970-81; also dir.; undersec. for research and engring. Dept. Def., Washington, 1981-84; pres. The Orion Group, 1985—; dir. Ducommen, Inc., Los Angeles, Cordura, Inc., Chgo.; vis. lectr. UCLA, Chmn. Nat. Alliance Businessman, 1968-69; chmn. Region IX, 1970; mem. Def. Sci. Bd., Dept. Def. Author: (with R.W. Bussard) Nuclear Rocket Propulsion, 1958, Fundamentals of Nuclear Flight, 1965. Trustee U. Redlands. Fellow Am. Inst. Aeros. and Astronautics, Am. Astron. Soc.; mem. Nat. Acad. Engring., AAAS, Aerospace Industries Assn. (gov.), Sigma Xi. Subspecialty: Research engineering administration. Home: 1101 S Arlington Ridge Rd Arlington VA 22202 Office: The Orion Group Ltd 1215 Jefferson Davis Hwy Suite 1203 Arlington VA 22202

DE LA ZERDA, ALBERTO, physicist; b. Bogota, Colombia, Mar. 24, 1955; came to U.S., 1980; s. Rafael and Selma (Lerner) de la Z. Physicist, Universidad Nacional de Colombia, 1980; Ph.D., NYU. Tchr., Colegio San Patricio, Bogota, Colombia, S.A., 1979-80; physicist Dept. Energy, N.Y.C., 1982—. Mem. Am. Phys. Soc., Am. Geophys. Union. Democrat. Club: Canterbury Choral Soc. Current work: Interaction of charged particles of galactic and solar origin with the earth's atmosphere and the effects of the solar wind and geomagnetic field on those —primary particles—. Subspecialties: Cosmic rays; Solar physics. Home: 10 Cooper St Apt 5L New York NY 10034 Office: Environ Measurements Lab DOE 376 Hudson St New York NY 10014

DEL BENE, JANET ELAINE, chemist, educator; b. Youngstown, Ohio, June 3, 1939; d. Anthony Joseph and Elizabeth Josephine (Pastier) Del B. B.S. summa cum laude, Youngstown State U., 1963, A.B. summa cum laude, 1965; Ph.D., U. Cin., 1968. Postdoctoral fellow Theoretical Chemistry Inst., U. Wis., 1968-69; NIH postdoctoral fellow Mellon Inst., 1969-70; asst. prof. chemistry Youngstown State U., 1970-73, assoc. prof., 1973-76, prof., 1976—; research prof. molecular pathology and biology Northeastern Ohio Univs. Coll Medicine, 1977—; mem. grad. faculty Kent State U. Mem. Girard (Ohio) Bd. Health, 1982—. Research numerous publs. in field. Am. Chem. Soc.-Petroleum Research Fund starter grantee, 1971-74; Camille and Henry Dreyfus Found. tchr-scholar grantee, 1974-79; NIH grantee, 1974-77, 80-83, 85—. Fellow AAAS; mem. Am. Chem. Soc., N.Y. Acad. Scis., Sigma Xi, Phi Kappa Phi, Iota Sigma Pi (Agnes Fay Morgan Research award 1972). Roman Catholic. Current Work: Molecular orbital studies of hydrogen bonding, protonation, and lithium ion assn. Subspecialty: Theoretical chemistry. Home: 871 N Ward Ave Girard OH 44420 Office: Dept Chemistry Youngstown State U Youngstown OH 44555

DEL CERRO, MANUEL, physician, educator; b. Buenos Aires, Argentina, Aug. 20, 1931; came to U.S., 1964; s. Manuel and Julia (Caceres) del C.; m. Constancia Clotilde Nunez, May 17, 1958; children: Alicia, Marilu. B.A., Nat. Coll., Buenos Aires, 1951, B.S., 1951; med. diploma, U. Buenos Aires, 1958. Sr. instr. histology U. Rochester, N.Y., 1958-61, assoc. prof., 1961-64, research assoc., 1965-69, sr. research assoc., 1969-71; assoc. prof. U. Rochester (Ctr. for Brain Research and Neurology), 1971-79, assoc. prof. dept. anatomy, 1976—, dept. ophthalmology, 1980—; cons. in field. Contbr. articles to profl. jours. Mem. N.Y. State Health Research Council, 1981-84. Served with Argentine Army, 1952. Nat. Eye Inst. grantee, 1978-81, 81—; N.Y. State Health Research Council grantee, 1980-81. Mem. Internat. Brain Research Orgn., Assn. Research in Vision and Ophthalmology, Am. Assn. Neuropathologists. Roman Catholic. Current Work: Research in experimental ophthalmology, dealing with eye neuroimmunology and neuropathology. Interest in developmental neurobiology and retinal transplants. Subspecialties: Neuroimmunology; Ophthalmology. Home: 14 Tall Acres Dr Pittsford NY 14534 Office: University of Rochester Medical School PO Box 605 Rochester NY 14642

DELEVORYAS, THEODORE, botanist, educator; b. Chicopee Falls, Mass., July 22, 1929; s. Basil John and Sophie (John) Dulchinos D.; m. Nancy Lou Foster, June 23, 1956 (div. Dec. 1978); children: Matthew Torrey, Christopher Theodore; m. Cecilia Ann Dean, Aug. 14, 1981. B.S., U. Mass., 1950; M.S., U. Ill., 1951, Ph.D., 1954; M.A. (hon.), Yale, 1968. Postdoctoral fellow NRC, U. Mich., Ann Arbor, 1954-55; asst. prof. botany Mich. State U., East Lansing, 1955-56; instr. botany Yale, New Haven, 1956-58, asst. prof., 1958-60, asso. prof. biology, 1962-68, prof. biology, 1968-72; asso. prof. botany U. Ill., Urbana, 1960-62; prof. botany U. Tex., Austin, 1972—, chmn. dept. botany, 1974—, chmn. dir. biol. scis., 1982—. Author: Morphology and Evolution of Fossil Plants, 1962, Plant Diversification, 1966, (with others) Morphology of Plants and Fungi, 1980; Contbr. (with others) numerous articles to profl. jours.

Fellow Linnean Soc. London; mem. Bot. Soc. Am. (treas. 1967-72, v.p. 1973, pres. 1974), Paleontol. Soc., Palaeontol. Assn., Am. Inst. Biol. Scis., Internat. Assn. Plant Taxonomy, Internat. Soc. Plant Morphologists, Torrey Bot. Club, Am. Inst. Biol. Scis. (mem. bd. govs. 1975-77), Internat. Orgn. Paleobotany (pres. 1978-81), Phi Beta Kappa, Phi Kappa Phi. Club: Austin Yacht. Current Work: Morphology and evolution of mesozoic plants, especially cycadophytes and conifers. Subspecialties: Botany; Paleontology. Home: 4204 Zuni Dr Austin TX 78759

DELFINO, MICHELANGELO, research scientist; b. Bronx, N.Y., June 19, 1950; s. Cosimo and Mary (Nicolosi) D.; m. Joan Marie Tolomer, Dec. 26, 1971; children—Michel John, Janine Marie, Robert Jon. B.S., St. Johns U., 1972; M.S., Fordham U., 1977, Ph.D., 1979. Assoc. profl. Philips Labs., Briarcliff Manor, N.Y., 1973-78; assoc. scientist Optical Info. Systems, Elmsford, N.Y., 1978-79; sr. mem. staff Fairchild Research Ctr., Palo Alto, Calif., 1979-83, Philips Research Labs., Sunnyvale, Calif., 1983—. Patentee in field. Mem. IEEE (sr. mem.), Materials Research Soc., Electrochem. Soc., Am. Assn. for Crystal Growth. Current work: Ion-beam modification of materials for fabrication VLSI devices; laser annealing semiconductors; optical characterization techniques. Subspecialties: Electronic materials; Condensed matter physics. Home: 2141 Deodara Dr Los Altos CA 94022 Office: Philips Research Labs 811 E Arques Ave Sunnyvale CA 94088

DEL GUERCIO, LOUIS RICHARD MAURICE, surgeon, educator; b. N.Y.C., Jan. 15, 1929; s. Louis and Hortense (Ardengo) Del G.; m. Paula Marie Helene de Vautibault, May 18, 1957; children: Louis, Francsca, Paul, Catherine, Maria, Michelle, Christopher Anthony. B.S., Fordham U., 1949; M.D., Yale U., 1953. Diplomate: Am. Bd. Surgery, Am. Bd. Thoracic Surgery. Intern Columbia-Presbyn. Med. Center, N.Y.C., 1953-54; resident St Vincent's Hosp., N.Y.C., 1954-58, Cleve. City Hosp., 1958-60; practice medicine specializing in thoracic surgery, 1960—; mem. faculty Albert Einstein Coll. Medicine, N.Y.C., 1960-71, assoc. prof., 1966-70, prof. surgery, 1970-71, dir. Clin. Research Center-Acute, 1967-71, dir.; clin. prof. surgery N.J. Coll. Medicine, Newark, 1971-76; prof. surgery N.Y. Med. Coll., N.Y.C., 1976—, chmn. dept., 1976—; chief surgery Westchester County Med. Center, 1976—; cons. surgeon other hosps.; mem. surg. study sect. NIH, 1970-74; mem. com. on shock NRC-Nat. Acad. Scis., 1969-71; mem. merit rev. bd. VA, 1971-74; mem. health care tech. study sect. Dept. Health and Human Services, 1980—; cons. Nat. Center Health Services Research, 1980—; chmn. bd. dirs. Daltex Med. Scis., Inc. Author: (with B.G. Clarke) Urology, 1956, The Multilingual Manual for Medical History Taking, 1972, (with S.G. Hershey, R. McConn) Septic Shock in Man, 1971; editor-in-chief: Critical Care Monitor, 1980—; contbr. articles to med. jours. Served with Mcht. Marine, 1946-47; served with AUS, 1949-50. Recipient award in medicine Fordham U. Alumni Assn., 1974; recipient award in medicine Gold award Am. Acad. Pediatrics, 1973, Alpha Omega Alpha Faculty award N.Y. Med. Coll., 1982; Am. Thoracic Soc fellow, 1959-60; grantee Health Research Council N.Y., 1965-71; grantee NIH, 1962-71. Fellow ACS; mem. Am. Trauma Soc. (founding mem.), Soc. Critical Care Medicine (founding mem., pres. 1976), Am. Surg. Assn., Am. Physiol. Soc., Soc. Univ. Surgeons, Equestrian Order of Holy Sepulchre of Jerusalem. Patentee in field. Current Work: Surgical physiology;physiological assessment and mointoring of high-risk and critically ill or injured patient. Subspecialties: Bioinstrumentation; Biomedical engineering. Home: 14 Pryer Ln Larchmont NY 10538 Office: NY Medical College Munger Pavilion Valhalla NY 10595

DELISI, CHARLES, biophysicist; b. N.Y.C., Dec. 9, 1941; s. Jack and Phyllis (Colameo) DeL.; m. Lynn E. Moskowitz, Aug. 11, 1968; children: Jacqueline, Daniel. B.A., CCNY, 1963; Ph.D. in Physics, N.Y.U., 1969. Postdoctoral fellow in chemistry and biophysics Yale U., 1969-72; sr. lectr. engring. and applied sci., 1971-72; elec. engr. Sperry Gyroscope, 1963-65; physicist theoretical div. Los Alamos Nat. Lab.-U. Calif., 1972-77; chief theoretical immunology NIH, Bethesda, Md., 1977—, spl. asst. Office of Dir., 1978-79, chief lab. math. biology, 1982-84; dir. Office Health and Environ. Research, Dept. Energy, 1985—. Author 5 books in field; contbr. numerous articles to profl. jours. Recipient Gordon Research Conf. award, 1979. Mem. AAAS, Am. Assn. Immunologists, Biophysics Soc. Current Work: Immunology, structural biology, mathematical biology. Subspecialties: Biophysics (biology); Cell biology. Home: 7700 Persimmon Tree Ln Bethesda MD 20817 Office: NIH Bethesda MD

DELLIOSSO, LOUIS FRANK, med. scientist, educator; b. Bklyn., Mar. 16, 1941; s. Frank and Rose (Perrone) Dellio. B.S. in Elec. Engring, Bklyn. Poly. Inst., 1961; Ph.D., U. Wyo., 1968. Bioengring. cons. Westinghouse Research and Devel. Labs., Pitts., 1966-67, sr. bioengr., 1967-70; asst. prof. biomed. engring. and surgery U. Miami, Fla., 1970-72, asst. prof. neurology, 1972-75, assoc. prof. neurology, 1975-79, prof. neurology, 1979-80; co-dir. ocular motor neurophysiology lab. VA Med. Ctr., Miami, 1972-80; prof. neurology and biomed. engring. Case Wetern Res. U., Cleve., 1980—; dir. ocular motor neurophysiology lab. VA Med. Ctr., Cleve., 1980—. Contbr. articles on neurology and biomed. engring. to profl. jours. Bd. dirs. Vineland Galloway Civic Assn., 1973-76. Mem. IEEE (sr.), Profl. Group on Engring. in Medicine and Biology (chmn. Miami chpt.), AAAS, Assn. Research in Vision and Ophthalmology. Current Work: Study of normal and abnormal human ocular motor control. Computer modeling of brainstems control systems involved in normal and pathological eye movements. Disease diagnosis. Subspecialties: Biomedical engineering; Neuro-ophthalmology. Home: 2356 Tudor Dr Cleveland Heights OH 44106 Office: VA Med Ctr Ocular-Motility Cleveland OH 44106

DELONG, LANCE ERIC, physics educator; b. Denver, Nov. 12, 1946; s. Robert Earl and Svea Virginia (Selander) DeL.; m. Michele Denise Arranaga, Dec. 30, 1977 (div. 1983); m. Mary Jane Gorham, Sept. 16, 1983; children—Kristin Ann, Rebecca Jane. B.A., U. Colo., Boulder, 1968; M.S., U. Calif.-San Diego, 1970, Ph.D., 1977. Asst. prof. physics U. Va., Charlottesville, 1977-79; asst. prof. U. Ky., Lexington, 1979-83, assoc. prof., 1983—; scientist in residence Argonne Nat. Lab., 1985-86. Cottrell research grantee Research Corp., 1982; NSF internat. travel grantee, 1982; recipient research contract U.S. Dept. Energy, 1981-84. Mem. Am. Phys. Soc., Am. Assn. Physics Tchrs. Current Work: Electronic and magnetic properties of solids at low temperatures, high pressures and high magnetic fields, especially the superconducting and magnetic properties of metals. Subspecialties: Condensed matter physics; Low temperature physics. Office: Dept Physics and Astronomy U Ky Lexington KY 40506

DELOS, JOHN BERNARD, chem. physicist, educator; b. Ann Arbor, Mich., Mar. 24, 1944; s. John S. and Katherine (Petruccione) D.; m. Sue Ellen Steere, May 29, 1965; children: Peter, Gregory, Rebecca. B.S. in Chemistry, U. Mich., 1965; Ph.D. in Phys. Chemistry, MIT, 1970. Research assoc. U. Alta., 1970, U. B.C., 1970-71; asst. prof. physics Coll. of William and Mary, 1971-77, assoc. prof., 1977-83, prof., 1983—; vis. scientist FOM (Netherlands) Inst. Atomic and Molecular Physics, 1979-80; cons. Naval Surface Weapons Lab., 1981; vis. scientist Oak Ridge Nat. Lab., 1982. Contbr. articles to profl. jours. NSF research grantee, 1976—. Mem. Am. Phys. Soc., Soc. Natural Philosophy, Fedn. Am. Scientists. Current Work: Atoms, molecules and their collisions; theoretical research on electronic transitions in atomic collisions; atoms in fields; dynamics of molecular vibrations. Subspecialties: Atomic and molecular physics; Theoretical chemistry. Home: 251 Tyler Brooks Dr Williamsburg VA 23185

DEL REGATO, JUAN ANGEL, radio-therapeutist and oncologist, educator; b. Camaguey, Cuba, Mar. 1, 1909; came to U.S., 1937, naturalized, 1941; s. Juan and Damiana (Manzano) del R.; m. Inez Johnson, May 1, 1939; children: Ann Cynthia del Regato Jaeger, Juanita Inez del Regato Peters. John Carl. Student, U. Havana, Cuba, 1930; M.D., U. Paris, France, 1937, Laureat, 1937; Dr.S. (honoris causa), Colo. Coll., 1969; D.Sc. (honoris causa, ad gradum), Hahnemann Med. Coll., 1977; D.Sc. (honoris causa), Med. Coll. Wis., 1981. Diplomate: Am. Bd. Radiology (trustee 1975-85, historian 1976-85). Asst. Radium Inst., U. Paris, 1934-37, Chgo. Tumor Inst., 1938; radiotherapeutist Warwick Cancer Clinic, Washington, 1939-40; research Nat. Cancer Inst., Balt., 1941-43; chief dept. radiotherapy Ellis Fischel State Cancer Hosp., Columbia, Mo., 1943-48; dir. Penrose Cancer Hosp., Colorado Springs, Colo., 1949-73; prof. clin. radiology U. Colo. Med. Sch., 1950-74; prof. radiology U. South Fla., 1974—; David Gould lectr. Johns Hopkins U., 1983. Author: (with L.V. Ackerman, M.D.) Cancer: Diagnosis Treatment and Prognosis, 1947, 54, 62, 70, (with H.J. Spjut), 1977, (with H.J. Spjut and J.O. Cox), 1985. Editor: Cancer Seminar, 1950-81; Radiological Physicists, 1985. Contbr. articles to profl. jours. Inventor lighting devices used in clin. radiotherapy (prototypes now on display at Smithsonian Instn. Decorated Order of Carlos Finlay of Cuba; Order Francisco de Miranda Republic of Venezuela; Béclère medal à titre exceptionnel, 1980; recipient Gold medal Radiol. Soc. North Am., 1967; Gold medal Inter-Am. Coll. Radiology, 1967; Gold medal Am. Coll. Radiology, 1968; Gold plaque, 1975; Grubbe gold medal Ill. Radiol. Soc., 1973; Prix Bruninghaus French Acad. Medicine, 1979; Disting. Scientist award U. South Fla. Coll. Medicine, 1980, Am. Cancer Soc., 1983; named Disting. Physician VA, 1974. Mem. Nat. Adv. Cancer Council, Bethesda, Md. (1967-71); mem. med. adv. com. Milheim Found., Denver. Fellow Am. Coll. Radiology (bd. chancellors; chmn. commn. radiation therapy, com. awards and honors); mem. AMA Nat. Acad. Medicine of France (Laureat 1948), Radiol. Soc. N.Am. (v.p. 1959-60, Arthur Erskine lectr. 1978), Am. Roentgen Ray Soc., Am. Radium Soc. (v.p. 1963-64, treas. 1966-68, pres. 1968-69, chmn. exec. com. 1971-72, historian 1969—, Janeway gold medal 1973), Assn. Am. Med. Colls., Internat. Club Radiotherapists (pres. 1962-65), Inter-Am. Coll. Radiology (pres. 1967-71, U.S. counselor 1971-79), Am. Soc. Therapeutic Radiologists (sec. 1958-68, historian 1968—, pres. 1974-75, chmn. bd. dirs. 1975-76, gold medal 1977), Fedn. Clin. Oncologic Socs. (pres. bd. dirs. 1976-77); hon. mem. Rocky Mountain, Pacific N.W., Tex., Oreg., Minn. radiol. socs., radiol. socs. Cuba, Mex., Panama, Ecuador, Peru, Paraguay, Can., Argentina, Buenos Aires (Argentina), Am. Inst. Radiology (historian 1978—). Current Work: Radiophysiology; clinical radio therapy; cancer. Subspecialties: Radiology; Psychophysiology. Home: 3101 Cocos Rd Carrollwood Tampa FL 33618 Office: Dept Radiology U South Florida Coll Medicine Tampa FL 33618 also VA Med Center 13000 N 30th St Tampa FL 33612

DE LUCA, CARLO JOHN, biomedical engineer, researcher; b. Bagnoli del Trigno, Italy, Oct. 12, 1943; came to U.S., 1973, naturalized, 1982; s. John and Josephine De L.; m. Christine M. Rafferty, June 11,1982. B.A.Sc., U. B.C. (Can.), Vancouver, 1966; M.Sc. in Biomed. Engring, U. N.B., Can., 1968; Ph.D. (Ont. Govt. fellow), Queen's U., Kingston, Ont., Can., 1972. Lab. instr. in elec. engring. U. N.B., 1967-68, lectr. in computing sci., 1968-69; lectr. in biomed. engring. Queen's U., 1969-70, lab. instr. in anatomy, 1970-71, lectr. in anatomy, 1971-72, asst. prof. anatomy, 1972-73; research assoc. in orthopedic surgery Harvard U. Med. Sch., Boston, 1973-79, prin. research assoc. in orthopedic surgery, 1979-84; lectr. in mech. engring. M.I.T., 1973-84; research assoc. in orthopedic surgery Children's Hosp. Med. Ctr., Boston, 1973-84; dir. Children's Hosp. Med. Ctr. (NeuroMuscular Research Lab.), 1980-84; adj. assoc. prof. biomed. engring. Boston U., 1977-84, prof., 1984—, dir. Neuromuscular Research Ctr., 1984—; project dir. Liberty Mut. Research Ctr., Hopkinton, Mass., 1973—; affiliated scientist New Eng. Regional Primate Ctr., Southboro, Mass., 1977—; research mem. Harvard-M.I.T. Div. Health Sci. and Tech., 1978—. Co-author: Muscles Alive, 5th edit. Contbr. chpts., numerous articles to profl. publs.; editor: Procs. of the Fourth Congress of I.S.E.K, 1979; editorial bd.: Jour. Rehab. Research and Devel., 1978—, Jour. Motor Behavior, 1981—, Orthopedics, 1985—. Mem. IEEE (sr.), Internat. Soc. Electrophysiol. Kinesiology (sec. gen. 1976-70, sec. 1980-84), Can. Med. and Biol. Engring. Soc. (sr.), AAAS, Soc. Neurosci., Orthopaedic Research Soc., Biomed. Engring. Soc., Rehab. Engring. Soc. N.Am., Sigma Xi. Club: Harvard (Boston). Patentee apparatus for interfacing to anatomic signal sources, method and apparatus for interfacing to anatomic signal sources; co-patentee methods and apparatus for interfacing to nerves, monitoring myoelectric signals. Current Work: Motor control of normal and abnormal muscles; motor unit properties of muscles; control of electro-mech. prostheses; objective evaluation of muscle fatigue in humans; myoelectric biofeedback; interaction of sensory and motor systems in muscle spasticity. Subspecialties: Biomedical engineering; Neurophysiology.

DE LUCA, LUIGI MARIA, research biochemist; b. Maglie, Lecce, Italy, Feb. 25, 1941; s. Antonio and Elena (Toma) De L.; m. Silvana Matilde Mendola, June 30, 1965; children: Nicholas, Mara. Dr. Organic Chemistry, U. Pavia, Italy, 1964. Cert. Italian Bd. Chemists. Dir. clin. lab. U. Milan Poly. Hosps., 1965; research assoc. M.I.T., 1965-69, instr., 1969-71; research chemist lung cancer br. Nat. Cancer Inst., Bethesda, Md., 1971-73, chief differentiation control sect., 1972-75, chief differentiation control sect. lab. exptl. pathology, 1975-81, chief differentiation control sect. lab. cellular carcinogenesis and tumors promotion, 1981—; chmn. program com. Am. Inst. Nutrition. Contbr. numerous articles to profl. jours. Recipient Mead Johnson award, 1978; award Japan Soc. Promotion Sci.; Lions Club award City of Maglie. Mem. Am. Soc. Biol. Chemists, AAAS, Fedn. Am. Sosientists, Soc. Complex Carbohydrates, N.Y. Acad. Scis. Current Work: Prevention of carcinogenesis by nutrients. Subspecialty: Biochemistry (biology).

DE LUQUE, ORLANDO RAFAEL, biochemistry educator, researcher; b. Riohacha, Colombia, Mar. 18, 1933; came to U.S., 1961; s. Alfredo De Luque and Maria Francisca Rosado; m. Edith Andrade, Dec. 16, 1958; children—Mabel, Orlando, Ivette, Sandra. B.S., Nat. U., 1959; M.A., So. Ill. U., 1964; Ph.D., U. R.I., 1969. Research asst. So. Ill. U., Carbondale, 1961-62; postdoctoral fellow U. Conn., Farmington, 1969-71; vis. prof. CIEA Poly. Inst., Mexico City, 1973-74; prof. Zulia U., Maraciabo, Venezuela, 1978-84; prof. biochemistry Inter Am. U., Arecibo, P.R., 1984—, cons., 1983—. Contbr. articles to profl. jours. Fellow Rockefeller Found., 1962-64, Conn. Heart Assn., 1969; Nat. U. scholar, 1955, U. R.I. scholar, 1967. Mem. Am. Chem. Soc., AAAS, Phi Sigma. Roman Catholic. Current work: Chemistry and functions of proteins from snake venoms, molecular assembly of collagen fibrils and enzyme production. Subspecialties: Biochemistry (biology); Artificial organs and prostheses. Office: Inter Am U of PR PO Box UI Arecibo PR 00613

DEL VALLE, FRANCISCO RAFAEL, food science researcher, educator, consultant; b. Laredo, Tex., Oct. 19, 1933; s. Roberto and Margarita (Canseco) Del V.; m. Estela Alicia Urrutia, Aug. 6, 1961; children: Estela Margarita, Francisco Roberto. S.B. in Chemistry, MIT, 1954, M.S. in Biochem. Engring., 1956, S.M. in Chem. Engring., 1957, Ph.D. in Food Sci. and Tech., 1965. Prof. chem. engring. and food sci. Instituto Tecnologico y de Estudios Superiores de Monterrey, Mex.; Guaymas, 1961-77; dir. Instituto Chihuahuense de Investigacion y Desarollo de la Nutricion, Chihuahua, Mex., 1970-80; prof. Universidad Autonoma de Chihuahua, 1977—; pres. Fundacion de Investigaciones en Ciencias Alimentarios y Nutricianoles, 1980—; adj. prof. U. Tex.-El Paso, 1984—; cons. to industry. Contbr. articles to tech. jours. Recipient Nat. Prize in Technology Pres. Mex., 1977; recipient Nat. prize in Sci. and Tech. Banco Nacional de Mex., 1970, 81; Tomas Valles Vivar prize in sci. and tech., Mex., 1983. Mem. Academia de la Investigacion Cientifica, Academia Nacional de Ingenieria, Asociacion de Tecnicos en Alimentos de Mex., Inst. Food Technologists, Sociedad Latinoamericana de Nutricion. Developed processes for prodn. of quick-salted fish cakes, soy-oats infant formula, other soy-oats high-nutrition, low-cost foods. Current Work: Research, development, evaluation and industrial-commercial production of high-nutrition, low-cost foods from plant, marine and fresh-water fish sources. Subspecialties: Food science and technology; Nutrition (biology). Office: Apartado Postal 1545 Sucursal C Chihuahua Chihuahua Mexico

DELVILLANO, BERT C., JR., Immunologist; b. Phila., Apr. 9, 1943; s. Bert C. and Beulah A. DelV.; m. Anne M., Nov. 16, 1963; 1 dau., Diane M. B.A., Lehigh U., 1965; Ph.D., U. Pa., 1971. Postdoctoral fellow Scripps Clinic, La Jolla, Calif., 1971-73, asst., 1973-75; mem. staff Cleve. Clinic, 1975-80; dir. product devel. Centocor, Malvern, Pa., 1980—. Contr. articles in field to profl. jours. Basic O'Connor grantee, 1973-75; Nat. Cancer Inst. grantee, 1975-80. Mem. Am. soc. Microbiology, Am. Assn. Immunology. Current Work: Developed CA 19-9 RIA for detection of pancreatic and other GI cancers. Subspecialties: Cancer research (medicine); Immunology (medicine).

DEMAIN, ARNOLD LESTER, industrial microbiology educator; b. Bklyn., Apr. 26, 1927. B.S., Mich. State U., 1949, M.S., 1950; Ph.D. in Microbiology, U. Calif., 1954. Asst. yeast physiologist U. Calif., 1952-54; research microbiologist Merck, Sharp & Dohme Research Labs., 1954-64, head fermentation research, 1964-69; prof. indsl. microbiology MIT, 1969—; Labatt lectr. U. Western Ont., Can., 1977. Recipient Waksman award Am. Soc. Microbiology, 1975, Charles Thom award Soc. Indsl. Microbiology, 1978. Subspecialty: Microbiology. Office: Dept Applied Biol Scis MIT room 56-123 Cambridge MA 02139

DE MARCO, THOMAS JOSEPH, periodontist, dean; b. Farmingdale, N.Y., Feb. 12, 1942; s. Joseph Louis and Mildred Nora (Cifarelli) De M.; children: Todd Gordon, Kristin Alice, Lisa Anne. B.S., U. Pitts., 1962; D.D.S., 1965; Ph.D., certificate in Periodontology, Boston U., 1968; cert. in fin. planning, Coll. Fin. Planning, Denver, 1976. Certificate in clin. hypnosis. Practice dentistry specializing in periodontics, Cleve., 1968—; mem. staff Met. Gen. Hosp., Cleve., Univ. Hosp., Cleve., VA Hosp., Cleve.; asst. prof. periodontics and pharmacology Case-Western Res. U., 1968-70, asso. prof., 1970-73, prof., 1973—; asso. dean Case-Western Res. U. (Sch. Dentistry), 1972-76, dean, 1976-84. Author review books in dentistry, book on fin. planning, also articles on periodontology, pharmacology, fin. planning. Grantee Air Force Office Sci. Research, 1969; Grantee Upjohn Co., 1970; Grantee Columbus Dental Mfg. Co., 1971. Mem. Am. Acad. Periodontology, Internat. Assn. Dental Research, Am. Soc. for Preventive Dentistry (past pres. Ohio chpt.). Subspecialty: Periodontics. Home: 12208 Fox Run Rd Chesterland OH 44026 Office: 5 Severance Circle 507 Cleveland Heights OH 44118

DE MARIA, ANTHONY J., electrical engineer; b. Santa Croce, Italy, Oct. 30, 1931; came to U.S., 1935; s. Joseph and Nicolina (Daddona) De M.; m. Katherine M. Waybright, Aug. 29, 1953; 1 dau., Karla Kay. B.S. in Elec. Engring, U. Conn., 1956, Ph.D. in Elec. Engring, 1965; M.S., Rensselaer Poly. Inst., 1960. Acoustic research engr. Anderson Lab., West Hartford, Conn., 1956-57; magnetic research engr. Hamilton Standard Div. United Techs. Corp., Windsor Locks, Conn., 1957-58; scientist United Techs. Research Center, East Hartford, Conn., 1958—; instr. in electronics U. Hartford, 1959-60; adj. prof. physics Rensselaer Poly. Inst. Grad. Center, Hartford, 1970-77; lectr. in lasers UCLA, 1974-79; mem. Dept. Def. Adv. Group on Electronic Devices, 1977—, chmn., 1980-83; mem. evaluation com. on electromagnetic tech. Nat. Bur. Standards, 1978-79; mem. Center Elec. and Electronic Engring., 1979-83; mem. Air Force Sci. Adv. Com., 1982—; mem. U. Ill. Microelectronic Bd. Overseers, 1984—. Author: Lasers, Vol. III, 1975, Vol. IV, 1976; Contbr. articles to profl. jours. Mem. Air Force Sci. Adv. Bd., 1981—. Recipient Disting. Alumnus award U. Conn., 1978, Disting. Engring. award U. Conn., 1983, Davies medal and award Rensselaer Poly. Inst., 1980; Sherman Fairchild Disting. Scholar fellow, 1982-83. Fellow IEEE (editor Jour. Quantum Electronics, Morris N. Liebman meml. award 1980, Centennial medal 1984), Optical Soc. Am. (v.p. 1979, pres. 1981); mem. Am. Phys. Soc., Nat. Acad. Engring., Conn. Acad. Scis. and Engring. Subspecialty: Laser physics. Office: United Techs Research Center 400 Main St East Hartford CT 06108

DE MAYO, PAUL, chemistry educator; b. London, Eng., Aug. 8, 1924; m. Mary Turnbull, May 28, 1949; children—Ann, Philip. B.Sc., U. London, 1944, Ph.D., 1954; D.es-Sc., U. Paris, 1970. Asst. lectr. Birkbeck Coll., London, 1954-55; lectr. U. Glasgow, Scotland, 1955-57, Imperial Coll., London, 1957-59; prof. chemistry U. Western Ont., Can., London, 1959—, dir. photochemistry unit, 1969-72. Author: Mono and Sesquiterpenoids, 1959, The Higher Terpenoids, 1959, numerous publs. in chem. lit.; editor: Molecular Rearrangements, vol. 1, 1963, vol. II, 1964, Rearrangements in Ground and Excited States, Vol. 1-3, 1980; editorial bd.: Nouveau Journal de Chimie. Recipient Centennial medal Govt. Can., 1967; Merck, Sharp & Dohme Lecture award Chem. Inst. Can., 1966, Palladium medal, 1982, E.W.R. Steacie award in photochemistry, 1985. Fellow Royal Soc. Can., Royal Soc. (London). Current Work: Photochemistry of adsorbed molecules; surface photochemistry; organic chemistry of semi-conductors . Subspecialties: Photochemistry; Organic chemistry. Office: Chemistry Dept U Western Ont London ON N6A 5B7 Canada

DEMELLO, AUSTIN EASTWOOD, science writer, principal research investigator, cosmologist; b. New Bedford, Mass., Oct. 15, 1939. B.A. in English, UCLA, 1974; M.S. in Physics and Astronomy, Met. Coll. Inst., London, 1977, Sc.D. in Theoretical Astrophysics, 1981. Engring. writer Raytheon Co., Santa Barbara, Calif., 1982; dir. research Cosmosci. Research Inst., Ventura, Calif., 1983—. Author: The Metagalactic System, 1969; Theory of Cosmodynamics, 1983; Early Development of the Scientific Mind, 1981; The Four States of Man, 1971; Mem. N.Y. Acad. Sci., Am. Astronautical Soc., AIAA, AAAS, Mensa Internat. Current work: Investigation of theoretical cosmotorsional forces related to helical structure of rotating electrodynamic metagalaxy. Home: PO Box 461 Moss Landing CA 95039 Office: Cosmosci Research Inst 3639 Harbor Blvd Ventura CA 93001

DEMEO, EDGAR ANTHONY, research institute executive; b. Yonkers, N.Y., Jan. 14, 1942; s. Peter C. and Lucia (Goldthorp) DeM.; m. Linda Loring Whitney, May 4, 1968; children—Tracy, Jonathan. B.E.E., Rensselaer Poly. Inst., 1963; Sc.M., Brown U., 1965, Ph.D., 1968. Asst. prof. Brown U., Providence, 1969-74, assoc. prof. research, 1974-76; cons. Electric Power Research Inst., Palo Alto, Calif., 1974-76, project mgr., 1976-80, program mgr., 1980—; cons. Naval Research Lab., Washington, 1974. Editorial bd. mem. Solar Cells jour., 1981—. Contbr. articles to profl. jours. Patentee optical sensor. Active Friends of Chamber Music, Providence, 1973-76; bd. dirs. Girls Softball League, Palo Alto; mem. Palo Alto Sch. Dist. Com., 1984—. Served to lt. USNR, 1967-69. C.L. Fortescue fellow IEEE, 1963. Mem. AAAS. Current work: Research and development management - solar and wind energy for bulk electric power applications. Subspecialties: Solar energy; Wind power. Office: Electric Power Research Inst PO Box 10412 Palo Alto CA 94303

DEMERSON, CHRISTOPHER ALEX, research chemist; b. St. John, N.B., Can., May 16, 1942; came to U.S., 1984; s. Alexander and Jennie (Jouris) D.; m. Helen Vatsis, July 8, 1972; children—Dimitra, Paula, Alexander. B.S., U. N.B., 1964, Ph.D., 1968. Sr. scientist Ayerst Laboratories, Montreal, Que., Can., 1968-72, research assoc., 1972-80, sect. head, 1980-84; sect. head Ayerst Research, Inc., Princeton, N.J., 1984—. Contbr. articles to profl. jours. Patentee in field. Mem. Chem. Inst. Can., (chmn. Montreal sect. 1978), Am. Chem. Soc. Current work: Medicinal chemistry especially in the anti-inflammatory field and synthesis of novel ring systems. Subspecialties: Medicinal chemistry; Drug design. Home: 19 Franklin Dr Plainsboro NJ 08536 Office: Ayerst Labs Research Inc CN 8000 Princeton NJ 08540

DEMET, EDWARD MICHAEL, neurochemist, educator, consultant; b. Elmhurst, Ill., July 27, 1949; s. Michael Constantine and Elvira Linnea (Franson) DeM.; m. Virginia Lynn Dietz, Aug. 27, 1971 (div. Aug. 1972); m. Aleksandra Chicz, Oct. 22, 1983. Student Ill. Inst. Tech., Chgo., 1963-66; A.S., Harper Coll., Palatine, Ill., 1969; B.S., U. Ill., 1971; Ph.D., Ill. Inst. Tech., 1976. Research asst. prof. U. Chgo., 1976-80; research chemist VA Med. Ctr., West Los Angeles, Calif., 1980-83; asst. prof. dept. psychiatry UCLA, 1980—, U. Calif., Irvine, 1983—; cons. VA Med. Ctr., West Los Angeles, 1983—. Contbr. articles to profl. jours. USPHS fellow, 1976-78. Mem. Soc. Neurosci., Am. Chem. Soc., AAAS, N.Y. Acad. Sci., West Coast Coll. Biol. Psychiatry. Current work: Biochemistry and physiology of psychiatric disorders; laboratory instrumentation, software and automation. Subspecialties: Psychopharmacology; Neurochemistry. Home: 2775 Mesa Verde Dr E #R-103 Costa Mesa CA 92626 Office: Univ Calif Dept Psychiatry Irvine CA 92717

DEMETER, STEVEN, neurologist; b. Budapest, Hungary, Jan. 12, 1947; came to U.S., 1957, naturalized, 1965; s. Arpad and Ilona (Wiesner) D. B.S., Bklyn. Coll., 1969; M.D., N.Y. Med. Coll., 1973. Diplomate: Am. Bd. Neurology and Psychiatry, 1979. Intern Beth Israel Med. Center, N.Y.C., 1973-74; resident in neurology Albert Einstein Coll. Medicine, Bronx, 1974-77; instr. neurology N.Y. Med. Coll., N.Y.C., 1977-79; fellow asso. in behavioral neurology U. Iowa, Iowa City, 1979-81; fellow Center for Brain Research, U. Rochester, N.Y., 1981-84, asst. prof., 1984—; instr. neurology U. Rochester, N.Y., 1981—, instr. neurology and psychiatry, 1984—. Mem. Am. Acad. Neurology, Nat. Soc. Med Research, AAAS, N.Y. Acad. Scis., Soc. for Neurosci. Current Work: Investigation of anatomical, functional and clinical aspects of higher brain function in primates including man. Subspecialties: Neurology; Neurobiology. Office: University of Rochester Medical Center PO Box 605 Rochester NY 14642

DEMING, WILLIAM EDWARDS, physics educator, statistician, consultant. B.S., U. Wyo., 1921, LL.D. (hon.), 1958; M.S., U. Colo., 1924; Ph.D., Yale U., 1928; Sc.D. (hon.), River Coll., 1981, Ohio State U., 1982, Md. U., 1983, Clarkson U., 1983; Ph.D. in Engring.(hon.), Miami U., 1985. Instr. engring. U. Wyo., 1921-22; asst. prof. physics Colo. Sch. of Mines, 1922-24; asst. prof. physics U. Colo., 1924-25; instr. Yale U., 1925-27; math. physicist Dept. Agr., 1927-39; adviser in sampling Bur. of the Census, 1939-45; prof. stats. Grad. Sch. Bus. Adminstrn. NYU, 1946—; cons. to industry, research, 1946—; statistician Allied Mission to Observe the Greek Elections, 1946; cons. in sampling Govt. of India, 1947, 51, 71; del. AAAS to Indian Sci. Congress, New Delhi, 1947; adviser in sampling techniques Supreme Command of the Allied Powers, Tokyo, 1947, 50; tchr., cons. to Japanese industry, 1950, 51, 52, 55, 60, 65; adviser in sampling techniques High Commn. for Germany, 1952, 53, exchange scholar Germany, 1952, 53; mem. UN Sub-Commn. on Statis. Sampling, 1947-52; cons. Census of Mexico, Bank of Mexico, Ministry of Economy, 1954, 55, Statistisches Bundesamt, Wiesbaden, 1953, Central Statis. Office of Turkey, 1959—, China Productivity Ctr., Taiwan, Republic of China, 1970-71; lectr.

London Sch. Econs., 1964, Inst. de Statistique de l'Université de Paris, 1964, Inter-Am. Statis. Inst., Santiago Cordoba, Argentina, Buenos Aires, 1971. Named Most Disting. Grad. U. Wyo., 1972; recipient Shewhart medal Am. Soc. Quality Control, 1955; 2d Order Medal of the Sacred Treasure Emperor of Japan, 1960; Deming Prize established by Union of Japanese Scientists and Engrs. in his honor; recipient Taylor Key award Am. Mgmt. Assn., 1983. Fellow Am. Statis. Assn., Inst. Math. Stats., Royal Statis. Soc. (hon.); mem. Am. Soc. Quality Control (hon. life mem.), Internat. Statis. Inst., Philosophical Soc. Washington, World Assn. for Public Opinion Research, Market Research Council, Biometric Soc. (hon. life), ASTM (hon.), Union of Japanese Scientists and Engrs. (hon. life), Japanese Statis. Assn., Deutsche Statistische Gesellschaft (hon. life), Ops. Research Soc. Am. Author: Statistical Adjustment of Data, 1943, 1964; Some Theory of Sampling, 1950; Elementary Principles of the Statistical Control of Quality, (in Japanese), 1950, (in English) 1952; Sample Design in Business Research, 1960; Quality, Productivity, and Competitive Position, 1982; Out of the Crisis, 1985; contbr. chpts. to brochures, more than 150 papers to profl. publs. Subspecialty: Statistics.

DEMMERLE, ALAN MICHAEL, electronic engineer; b. Port Jefferson, N.Y., Nov. 4, 1933. B.S., Carnegie Inst. Tech., 1955; M.S., Columbia U., 1958. Engr. circuit design Westinghouse Electric, 1955-56; engr. U.S. Naval Research Lab., 1957-60; engr. telemetry procesing Goddard Space Flight Ctr., NASA, 1960-66; chief computer systems lab. NIH, Bethesda, Md., 1966—; dir. Aspin Research Inst., 1981—. Subspecialty: Information systems, storage, and retrieval (computer science). Office: NIH Room 2035 Bldg 12 A Bethesda MD 20205*

DEMONSABERT, WINSTON RUSSEL, JR., environmental engineer; b. New Orleans, Apr. 22, 1957; s. Winston Russel and Eleanor Ray (Ranson) deM.; m. Sharon Mishler, July 11, 1981. B.S., U. Md., 1979; M.S., Purdue U., 1982. Research environ. engr. Naval Civil Engring. Lab., Port Hueneme, Calif., 1982—. Patentee oily waste pyrolysis system (pending). Mem. ASCE, Am. Chem. Soc., Soc. Am. Mil. Engrs., Sigma Xi, Alpha Chi Sigma. Industrial and hazardous waste treatment, water quality and supply, pesticide detoxification, oil recovery systems, environmental chemistry. Subspecialties: Environmental engineering; Water supply and wastewater treatment. Home: 3240 Landen St Camarillo CA 93010 Office: Naval Civil Engring Lab Code L71 Port Hueneme CA 93043

DEMOTT, DIANA L(YNN), nuclear engineer; b. Coffeyville, Kans., June 18, 1952; d. Marion Dean and Sharylon Joan (O'Brien) DeM. B.S. in Nuclear Engring, Tex. A&M U., 1974. Field engr. Gen. Electric Co., Atlanta, 1974-76; quality assurance engr. Westinghouse Hanford, Richland, Wash., 1976-79, systems engr., 1979-81, licensing engr. Clinch River breeder reactor project, Oak Ridge, 1981-83, system engr., 1983—. Contbr. tech. paper to profl. publ. Mem. Soc. Women Engrs. (sr.), Am. Nuclear Soc., ASME, Instrument Soc. Am. (standard com.). Methodist. Subspecialty: Nuclear engineering. Office: Westinghouse 120 S Jefferson Circle Oak Ridge TN 37830

DENHARDT, DAVID TILTON, molecular biologist, educator; b. Sacramento, Feb. 25, 1939; s. David Burton Denhardt and Edith Elura (Tilton) Denhardt Penrose; m. Georgetta Louise Harrar, July 2, 1961; children—Laura Jean, Kristin Ann, David Harrar. B.A., Swarthmore Coll., 1960; Ph.D., Calif. Inst. Tech., 1965. Asst. prof. Harvard U., Cambridge, Mass., 1965-70; assoc. prof. McGill U., Montreal, Que., Can., 1970-77, prof. biochemistry, 1977-80; prof. biochemistry, prof. microbiology and immunology, dir. cancer research lab. U. Western Ont., London, Can., 1980—. Editor: The Single-Stranded DNA Phages, 1978. Contbr. articles to profl. jours. Mem. Am. Soc. Biol. Chemists, Am. Soc. Microbiologists, Am. Cancer Soc., Am. Chem. Soc., Can. Biochem. Soc. Current work: Cloning, identification, characterization, expression of low abundance mammalian mRNA; DNA replication and repair in mammalian cells; 0X174 replication; E coli rep gene. Subspecialties: Molecular biology; Genetics and genetic engineering (biology). Home: 96 Nathaniel Ct London ON N5X 2N6 Canada Office: U Western Ont Cancer Research Lab London ON N6A 5B7 Canada

DEN HARTOG, JACOB PIETER, consulting mechanical engineer; b. Java, East Indies, July 23, 1901; came to U.S., 1924, naturalized, 1930; s. Marten and Elisabeth (Schol) Den H.; m. Elisabeth Stolker, July 29, 1926; children—Maarten Dirk, Stephen Ludwig. E.E., U. Delft, Holland, 1924, Dr. Tech. Sci. (hon.), 1967; Ph.D., U. Pitts., 1929; A.M. (hon.), Harvard, 1942, D.Eng., Carnegie Inst. Tech., 1962; D.Sc., U. Ghent, Belgium, 1966, Salford U., 1970, U. Newcastle/Tyne, 1975. Engr. Westinghouse Research Labs., Pitts., 1924-32; asst. prof. mech. engring. Harvard, 1932-36, asso. prof., 1936-41; prof. Mass. Inst. Tech., 1945-67, emeritus, 1967—, head dept. mech. engring., 1954-58. Author: Mechanical Vibrations, 1934, 41, 46, 54, Mechanics, 1948, Strength of Materials, 1949, Advanced Strength of Materials, 1952. Served with USN, 1941-45; now capt. USNR; ret. Fellow Am. Inst. Aeros. and Astronautics, Am. Cons. Engrs. Council, Brit. Inst. M.E.; hon. mem. ASME, Japan Soc. M.E.; mem. Nat. Acad. Sci., Nat. Acad. Engring., Dutch Acad. Arts and Scis. Subspecialty: Theoretical and applied mechanics. Home: Rural Route 1 Box 429 Lebanon NH 03766 Office: Mass Inst Tech Cambridge MA 02139

DENIO, ALLEN A(LBERT), phys. chemist, educator; b. Lowell, Mass., June 6, 1934; s. Albert A. and Ethel (Lawson) D.; m. Valerie S., June 20, 1959; children: Thomas, Susan, Richard. B.S., Lowell Technol. Inst., 1956, M.S. in Textile Chemistry, 1957; M.S. in Phys. Chemistry, U. N.H., 1960, Ph.D. in Phys. Chemistry, 1962. Chemist Dow Chem. Co., Midland, Mich., summer 1956; chemist dept. textile fibers E. I. duPont de Nemours & Co., Inc., Wilmington, Del., 1957-58, research chemist, 1962-64; mem. faculty U. Wis., Eau Claire, 1964—, asst. prof. phys. chemistry, 1964-68, assoc. prof., 1968-73, prof., 1973—; vis. prof. U. Wis.-Madison, 1969-70, U. Del., Newark, 1978-79; cons. to industry, pubs. Active Wis. Democratic party. Served with USAFR, 1957-63. Mem. Am. Chem. Soc., AAAS, Sigma Xi. Club: Indianhead Track (Eau Claire). Current Work: Properties of polymer films containing metal atoms; revision phys. chemistry textbook. Subspecialties: Physical chemistry; Polymer chemistry. Home: 433 McKinley Ave Eau Claire WI 54701 Office: Dept Chemistry U Wis Eau Claire WI 54701

DENNING, DOROTHY ELIZABETH, computer science educator, researcher; b. Grand Rapids, Mich., Aug. 12, 1945; d. Cornelius Lowell and Helen Dorothy (Watson) Robling; m. Peter James Denning, Jan. 24, 1974. B.A., U. Mich., 1967, M.A., 1969; Ph.D., Purdue U., 1975. Asst. research mathematician Radio Astronomy Obs., U. Mich., 1967-69; systems programmer Computer Center, U. Rochester, 1969-72, instr. in elec. engring., 1971-72; asst. prof. computer scis. Purdue U., 1975-81, assoc. prof., 1981-83. Author: Cryptography and Data Security, 1982. IBM fellow, 1974-75; NSF grantee, 1981-83. Mem. Assn. Computing Machinery, IEEE Computer Soc., Internat. Assn. Cryptologic Research, Sigma Xi, Phi Kappa Phi. Current Work: Study methods of protecting sensitive data stored in computer systems. Subspecialty: Cryptography and data security. Office: SRI Internat 333 Ravenswood Ave Menlo Park CA 94025

DENNING, PETER JAMES, computer scientist; b. N.Y.C., Jan. 6, 1942; s. James Edwin and Catherine M. (Manton) D.; m. Dorothy Elizabeth Robling, Jan. 24, 1974; children—Anne, Diana. B.E.E., Manhattan Coll., 1964; M.S. in Elec. Enging. (NSF fellow 1964-67), MIT, 1965, Ph.D., 1968; LL.D. (hon.), Concordia U., 1984. Asst. prof. elec. enging. Princeton U., 1968-72; assoc. prof. computer scis. Purdue U., 1972-75, prof., 1975-84, head dept., 1979-83; dir. Research Inst. Advanced Computer Sci., NASA Ames Research Center, Mountain View, Calif., 1983; lectr. Author: Profl. Devel. Seminars, 1968—; Author textbooks, also numerous research papers. Recipient Outstanding Faculty award Princeton U. Engring. Assn., 1971, Best Paper award Am. Fedn. Info. Processing Socs., 1972. Fellow IEEE, AAAS; mem. Assn. Computing Machinery (pres. 1980-82, editor-in-chief Computing Surveys 1977-79, Best Paper award 1968, editor communications of ACM 1983—, Recognition of Service award 1974), N.Y. Acad. Scis., Sigma Xi, Eta Kappa Nu, Tau Beta Pi. Subspecialty: Computer architecture. Home: 30 Bear Gulch Dr Portola Valley CA 94025 Office: Research Inst Advanced Computer Sci Mail Stop 230-5 NASA Ames Research Center Moffett Field CA 94035

DENNIS, KENT SEDDENS, polymer chemist; b. Monongahela, Pa., June 25, 1928; s. William Warren and Mabel Gladys (Seddens) D.; B.S., Grove City Coll., 1950; M.S., Case WR U, 1953, Ph.D., 1954. Polymer chemist Dow Chem. Co., Midland, Mich., 1956—. Contbr. articles to profl. jours.; patentee in field. Bd. dirs. Midland Symphony Orchestra Assn., 1961-64 (pres. 1962-64); Midland Ctr. for the Arts, 1964-71, Midland Interlochen Arts Acad., 1975-81 (pres. 1979-81). Served to cpl. U.S. Army, 1954-56. Recipient Alumni Achievement award Grove City Coll., 1977. Fellow Am. Inst. Chemists; mem. Am. Chem. Soc., N.Y. Acad. Sci., Am. Guild of Organists (dean Saginaw Valley chpt. 1961-62, 1974), Sigma Xi. Current work: Anionic polymerization; block polymers; polymer blends; impact and flame retardant polymers. Subspecialties: Physical chemistry; Polymer chemistry. Home: 5800 Highland Dr Midland MI 48640 Office: Dow Chem Co Bldg 1702 Midland MI 48640

DENNY, FLOYD WOLFE, JR., pediatrician; b. Hartsville, S.C., Oct. 22, 1923; s. Floyd Wolfe and Marion Elizabeth (Porter) D.; m. Barbara H. Denny, Apr. 27, 1946; children: Rebecca E., Mark W., Timothy P. B.S., Wofford Coll., 1944; M.D., Vanderbilt U., 1946. Diplomate: Am. Bd. Pediatrics. Intern Vanderbilt Hosp., Nashville, 1946-47, resident in pediatrics, 1947-48; instr. pediatrics U. Minn., 1951-52, asst. prof., 1952-53; asst. prof. pediatrics Vanderbilt U. Sch. Medicine, 1953-55; asst. prof. preventive medicine and pediatrics Western Res. U. Sch. Medicine, 1955-60, asso. prof. preventive medicine, 1960; prof. Sch. Medicine, U. N.C., Chapel Hill, 1960—, chmn. dept. pediatrics, 1960-81; vis. scholar dept. epidemiology Sch. Pub. Health and Child Devel. Inst., 1977-78; vis. worker Med. Research Council Clin. Research Centre, London, 1970-71; mem. Commn. on Streptococcal and Staphylococcal Diseases Armed Forces Epidemiol. Bd., 1954-72, dep. dir., 1959-63; mem. Commn. on Acute Respiratory Diseases Armed Forces Epidemiol. Bd., 1960-73, dep. dir., 1963-67, dir., 1967-73; mem. Inst. Medicine, Nat. Acad. Scis., 1981-86. Mem. editorial bd.: Am. Rev. Respiratory Diseases, 1971-74; mem. publs. com.: Jour. Infectious Diseases, 1973-78; Contbr. articles to med. jours. Served to maj. M.C. U.S. Army, 1948-51. Mem. Am. Acad. Pediatrics, Am. Assn. Immunologists, Am. Epidemiology Soc., Am. Fedn. Clin. Research, Am. Pediatric Soc. (pres. 1980-81), Am. Soc. Clin. Investigation, Am. Soc. Microbiology, Am. Thoracic Soc., Assn. Am. Physicians, Infectious Diseases Soc. Am. (pres. 1979-80), Soc. Exptl. Biology and Medicine, Soc. Pediatric Research (pres. 1968-69), So. Soc. Clin. Research, So. Soc. Pediatric Research, Phi Beta Kappa, Alpha Omega Alpha. Current Work: Epidemiology of acute respiratory tract infections. Subspecialties: Pediatrics; Epidemiology. Home: Route 10 Box 56 Chapel Hill NC 27514 Office: Dept Pediatrics Box 3 Wing D 208H U NC Sch of Medicine Chapel Hill NC 27514

DENSEN, PAUL MAXIMILLIAN, retired health administrator; b. N.Y.C., Aug. 1, 1913; s. Charles Edwin and Carrie (Weinberg) D.; m. Elizabeth A. Reed, Dec. 19, 1939; children—Rebecca E. (Mrs. John Rothfuss), Peter. A.B., Bklyn.Coll., 1934; D.Sc., Johns Hopkins, 1939; M.A. (hon.), Harvard, 1968. From instr. to asso. prof. preventive medicine Vanderbilt U. Med. Sch., 1939-46; chief div. med. research statistics VA, Washington, 1946-49; asso. prof., then prof. biometry Grad. Sch. Pub. Health, U. Pitts., 1949-54; dir. div. research and statistics Health Ins. Plan Greater N.Y., 1954-59; dept. commr. N.Y.C. Dept. Health, 1959-66; dept. adminstr. N.Y.C. Health Services Adminstrn., 1966-68; dir. Harvard Center Community Health and Med. Care, 1968—; prof. community health emeritus Harvard Sch. Pub. Health, 1968—. Fellow Am. Statis. Assn., Am. Pub. Health Assn., AAAS; mem. Am. Epidemiol. Soc., Inst. Medicine. Subspecialties: Epidemiology; Health services research. Home: PO Box 405 Sandown NH 03873

DENTON, ARNOLD EUGENE, soup company executive; b. Remington, Ind., Mar. 18, 1925; s. Alvin J. and Gertrude M. Denton; m. Catherine Maxine Bruner, Sept. 6, 1950; children—James, Gregory, David. B.S., Purdue U., 1949; M.S., U. Wis., 1950, Ph.D., 1953. Head Pet Food div. Swift & Co., Chgo., 1953-56, head biochemistry, 1956-68; dir. basic research Campbell Inst. for Food Research, Camden, N.J., 1966-70, v.p. basic research, 1966-70; with Campbell Soup Co., Camden, N.J., 1970-83, sr. v.p., 1983—; trustee Food Processing Inst., Washington, 1982—. Contbr. articles to profl. jours. Pres. United Fund, Moorestown, N.J.; mem. Zoning Bd., Moorestown. Served to 1st lt. USAF, 1943-46. Mem. Nat. Food Processing Assn. (chmn. sci. affairs council), Am. Chem. Soc., Am. Council Sci. and Health, U.S. Figure Skating Assn. Presbyterian. Subspecialties: Food science and technology; Biochemistry (biology). Home: 6 Walnut Ct Moorestown NJ 08057 Office: Campbell Soup Co Campbell Pl Camden NJ 08101

DENTON, RICHARD ANDREW, civil engineering educator; b. Levin, N.Z., Feb. 14, 1951; s. Richard Becket and Pamela Vivienne Denton. B.Engring., U. Canterbury, Christchurch, N.Z., 1971, Ph.D., 1978. Phys. oceanographer N.Z. Oceanographic Inst., Wellington, 1978; research engr. Sonderforschungsbereich 80, U. Karlsruhe, W.Ger., 1978-81; asst. prof. civil engring. U. Calif.-Berkeley, 1981—. Contbr. sci. articles to profl. jours. Travelling fellow Alexander von Humboldt Found., Karlsruhe, 1978-81. Mem. Internat. Assn. for Hydraulic Research, ASCE, Am. Geophys. Union, Am. Soc. Limnology and Oceanography. Current work: Mixing in stratified flow over fjord sills; dispersion processes in rivers and estuaries; density current inflows to stratified reservoirs; surfaces water hydrology. Subspecialty: Civil engineering. Office: Dept Hydraulic and Coastal Engring Room 412 O'Brien Hall U Calif Berkeley CA 94720

D'ENTREMONT, EDWARD JOSEPH, software engineer; b. Lynn, Mass., June 25, 1954; s. Joseph Albenie and Gertrude Grace (Flattery) D'E. B.A., Salem State Coll., 1976; M.S., Northeastern U., 1982. Head salesman Jordan Marsh Co., Peabody, Mass., 1972-76; sci. programmer Electronic Corp. Am., Burlington, Mass., 1977; sci. programmer Sulivan & Cogliano, Waltham, Mass., 1977; software engr. Raytheon Service Co. Burlington, 1977—; instr. Fitchburg State Coll., 1983—. Campaign worker Dukakis for Gov., various presdl. campaigns. Mem. Soc. Indsl. and Applied Math., IEEE, IEEE Computer Soc., Assn. Computing Machinery, N.Y. Acad. Scis., Math. Assn. Am., Am. Math. Assn. Democrat. Roman Catholic. Club: Lexington Racquet and Swim (Mass.). Current work: Operating systems and compiler design. Subspecialties: Software engineering; Applied mathematics. Home: 151 Bowler St Lynn MA 01904 Office: Raytheon Missile Systems Div Hartwell Rd Bedford MA 01730

DENYSYK, BOHDAN, computer company executive, international trade consultant; b. Kornberg, W. Germany, Feb. 13, 1947; came to U.S., 1949; s. John and Maria (Zelenewich) D.; m. Halina B. Bubela, June 28, 1969; children: Maria H., Danya L., Adrienne Y., Alexis M. B.S., Manhattan Coll., 1968; M.S., Cath. U. Am., Washington, 1973; Ph.D., Union Exptl. Colls. and Univs., 1981. Physicist Naval Weapons Lab., Dahlgren, Va., 1968-72; biophysicist Naval Medicine Research Inst., Bethesda, Md., 1972-75; physicist, group mgr. Naval Surface Weapons Ctr., White Oak, Md., 1975-78; physicist, dept. head. E G & G, Inc., Rockville, Md., 1978-81; dep. asst. sec. U.S. Dept. Commerce, Washington, 1981-83; exec. IBM Corp., Gaithersburg, Md., 1983—; internat. trade cons., 1983—; pres. DLR Assocs., Arlington, Va., 1972-81; cons. Republican Nat. Com., 1980-81, NSF, 1982. Dir. pub. relations Ukrainian Nat. Info. Service, 1978-81. Navy fellow, 1969-71; N.Y. Regents scholar, 1964-68. Mem. AIAA, Am. Def. Preparedness Assn., Am. Phys. Soc. Current Work: Flow field for vehicles reentering into atmosphere from space flight, with special emphasis on computational techniques. Subspecialty: Fluid mechanics. Home: 1301 19th Rd S Arlington VA 22202 Office: IBM Corp 708 Quince Orchard Rd Gaithersburg MD 20878

DEPALMA, ROBERT ANTHONY, endodontist; b. Orange, N.J., July 2, 1941; s. Germano Frederick and A. Lily (Rende) DeP.; m. Mary Lynn McNair, Feb. 7, 1981; 1 son, Robert Anthony II; married; 1 stepdau., Melissa Ann Mauriell. A.B. in Sci, Villanova U., 1963; D.D.S., W.Va. U., 1968; cert. in endodontics, N.J. Dental Sch., 1972. Diplomate: Am. Bd. Endodontics. Practice gen. denistry, Livingston, N.J., 1968-72, practice specializing in endodontics, Boca Raton, Fla., 1972—; cons. endodontics St. Mary's S. Barnabas, Orange Meml., Newark Beth Israel hosps., N.J., 1968-72, Boca Raton Community Hosp., 1972—; lectr. seminars. Contbr. articles sci. jours. Pres. Boca Raton Fraternal Order Police, 1976-78. Fellow Am. Coll. Dentists, Am. Acad. Oral Medicine; mem. ADA, N.J. Acad. Medicine, Fla. Dental Soc., Am. Hosp. Assn., Am. Assn. Hosp. Dentists, Am. Assn. Endodontics, South Palm Beach County Dental Soc., Cath. Hosp. Assn., Internat. Hosp. Assn., Am. Assn. Dental Radiology, Am. Assn. Clin. Oral Pathology, Internat. Assn. Dental Research, Brit. Endodontic Soc. Lodge: Kiwanis. Current Work: Oral pathology, immunology and microbiology, bone pathology. Subspecialty: Endodontics. Office: 2351 N Federal Hwy Boca Raton FL 33432

DEPAULO, JOSEPH RAYMOND, JR., psychiatrist; b. Charleston, W.Va., May 21, 1946; s. Joseph Raymond and Mary Catherine (Wilson) DeP.; m. Elizabeth Ratterman, June 8, 1970; children: Marianne, Margaret. B.S. magna cum laude, Xavier U., Cin., 1968; M.D., John Hopkins U., 1972. Diplomate: Am. Bd. Psychiatry and Neurology. Intern dept. medicine Johns Hopkins Hosp., 1972-73; resident in psychiatry Balt. City Hosps., 1973-74, Henry Phipps Psychiat Clinic and Johns Hopkins Hosp., 1974-76; Maudsley exchange resident, London, 1975; chief resident in psychiatry Henry Phipps Psychiat. Clinic and Johns Hopkins Hosp., 1976-77; asst. prof. psychiatry Johns Hopkins U., 1977-82, assoc. prof., 1983—, dir. edn. dept. psychiatry and behavioral scis.; dir. Affective Disorders Clinic, Johns Hopkins Hosp., 1977—; Contbr. abstracts and articles to profl. jours., chpts. in books. Mem. Am. Psychiat. Assn., Md. Psychiat. Soc., Am. Psychopath. Assn., Johns Hopkins Med. and Surg. Soc., Alpha Sigma Nu. Roman Catholic. Current Work: Clinical psychopharmacology of affective disorders, clinical effects of lithium carbonate. Subspecialties: Psychopharmacology; Psychiatry. Home: 504 Overbrook Rd Baltimore MD 21212 Office: Dept of Psychiatry Meyer 4-181 Johns Hopkins Hosp Baltimore MD 21205

DEPOMPEI, MICHAEL FREDERICK, chemistry educator, consultant, researcher; b. Warren, Ohio, Dec. 28, 1947; s. Frederick and Marie (Ramicone) DeP.; m. Barbara Jean Rini, July 28, 1973; children—Amanda, Andrew. B.S. in Chemistry, Ohio U., 1970; Ph.D. in Chemistry, U. Ala., 1976. Research chemist, Diamond Shamrock, Concord, Ohio, 1976-79, sr. chemist, 1979-83; sr. chemist SDS Biotech, Concord, 1983-84; asst. prof. chemistry Lake Erie Coll., Painesville, Ohio, 1984—; tech. coordinator Mooney Chem. Co., Cleve., 1984—. Mem. Am. Chem. Soc. Roman Catholic. Current work: Synthetic heterocyclic chemistry. Subspecialty: Organic chemistry. Office: Lake Erie Coll Painesville OH 44077

DERDERIAN, GEORGE, physicist, research consultant; b. Rochester, N.Y., Nov. 19, 1922; s. Sirkes G. and Sogoma (Bogoshian) D.; m. Alice Joan Kenney, May 30, 1953; children: Gregory, Jeanne, Susan, Elizabeth. B.S. in Physics, Queens Coll., 1947; M.S. in Physics, N.Y. U., 1951. Instr. Pratt Inst., Bklyn, 1947-50; physicist Evans Signal Lab., Belmar, N.J., 1950-55, Republic Aviation, Farmingdale, N.Y., 1955-59; adj. prof. Hofstra U., 1956-67; research engr. Sperry, Great Neck, N.Y., 1960-64; head phys. sci. lab. Naval Tng. Equipment Ctr., Orlando, Fla., 1964-80, cons. electro-optics and visual simulation tech., Maitland, Fla., 1980—; bd. dirs. Laser Inst. Am., 1978-80; mem. Army Laser Adv. Group. Contbr. numerous articles to profl. jours. Served with U.S. Army, 1943-46. Decorated Bronze Star medal; recipient Chemistry Tchr.'s award Am. Chem. Soc., 1941, Rockefeller Service award State of N.Y., 1959, Ten. Yrs. Outstanding Tchr. plaque Hofstra U., 1967, Outstanding Service award Laser Inst. Am., 1978. Fellow AAAS, Brit. Interplanetary Soc.; mem. Am. Optical Soc., Navy Laser Group, Sigma Xi (exec. com. chpt. 1969-78, v.p. chpt. 1968-69, pres. chpt. 1969-72, 77-78), Sigma Pi Sigma. Patentees in electro-optics tech. Current Work: Electro-optical systems; applications of optics and lasaers to training systems. Subspecialties: Optical image processing; Laser data storage and reproduction. Home and Office: 921 Gillis Ct Maitland FL 32751

DERGARABEDIAN, PAUL, systems engineer, applied mathematics consultant; b. Racine, Wis., Jan. 19, 1922; s. John and Mary (Hirmizian) D.; m. Mary Anna Jansouzian, Dec. 27, 1947; children—Celeste, Claudia, Clarice, Paul Jr. B.S. in Math., U. Wis., 1948, M.S. in Math., 1949; Ph.D. in Mech. Engring. and Physics, Calif. Inst. Tech., 1952. Br. head Naval Ordnance, Pasadena, Calif., 1952-55; lab. dir. TRW, Redondo Beach, Calif., 1955-80, cons., 1980—; sr. engr. Aerospace Corp., El Segundo, Calif., 1980—; vis. prof. Calif. Inst. Tech., 1971-72. Contbr. articles to tech. jours. Served with USAF, 1943-46. Fellow Am. Astronautical Soc. (pres. 1968-70); mem. Am. Meteorol. Soc., Phi Beta Kappa, Sigma Xi. Current work: Severe storms research, space technology (economics and productivity). Subspecialties: Applied mathematics; Aerospace engineering and technology. Home: 18 Poppy Trail Rolling Hills CA 90274 Office: Aerospace Corp M3/371 PO Box 92957 Los Angeles CA 90009

DE RICHEMOND, ALBERT LEO, engineering mechanics specialist; b. Bryn Mawr, Pa., Oct. 17, 1950; s. John Francis and Joan Marie (Lappin) de R.; m. Jean Ann Rollo, Dec. 30, 1972; children: Annelise Rollo, Jeannine Rollo. B.S., Pa. State U., 1972; M.S., Va. Poly. Inst., 1974; postgrad., Drexel U., 1976-79, 85—. Registered profl. engr. Pa. Structural analysis engr. Re-Entry and Environ. Systems div. Gen. Electric, Phila., 1974-75; lab. supr. Pa. Crusher Corp., Broomall, 1976-79; sr. devel. engr. Fuller Co., Bethlehem, Pa., 1980-84; project engr. Robinson-Halpern Co., 1984—. Mem. Am. Acad. Mechanics, ASME, Am. Soc. for Metals, Mensa. Current Work: Pressure transducer design, strain gauge design and use, thin film technology; failure analysis. Subspecialties: Theoretical and applied mechanics; Solid mechanics. Home: 41 Blythewood Rd Doylestown PA 18901 Office: 1 Apollo Rd Plymouth Meeting PA 19462

D'ERRICO, ALBERT PASQUALE, JR., psychologist; b. Dallas, Feb. 27, 1941; s. Albert and Carol (Whitney) D'E. A.B., Southwestern at Memphis, 1965; M.A., Whittier Coll., 1969; Ph.D., U. Ga., 1976. Lic. psychologist, Tenn. Psychologist Northeastern La. U., Monroe, 1974-76; diagnostic adminstr. Shelby County and State of Tenn., Memphis, 1976—; cons. in field. Author: On the State of Inerrancy, 1982; contbr. articles to profl jours. Law Enforcement Assistance Adminstrn. grantee, 1976; State of Tenn. and Shelby County grantee, 1977-80. Mem. Am. Psychol. Assn. Current Work: Cognition; formal operations intelligence and achievement behavioral psychology; psychological assessment and prediction of behavior by computer. Subspecialties: Cognition; Behavioral psychology. Address: PO Box 1 Elberton GA 30635

DERTOUZOS, MICHAEL LEONIDAS, computer scientist, electrical engineer; b. Athens, Greece, Nov. 5, 1936; came to U.S., 1954, naturalized, 1965; s. Leonidas Michael and Rosana G. (Maris) D.; m. Hadwig Gofferje, Nov. 21, 1961; children—Alexandra, Leonidas. B.S. in E.E, U. Ark., 1957, M.S. in E.E, 1959; Ph.D., MIT, 1964. Head research and devel. Baldwin Electronics, Inc., 1958-60; research asst. MIT, Cambridge, 1960-64, asst. prof., 1964-68, assoc. prof., 1968-73, prof., 1973—; dir. MIT (Lab. for Computer Sci.), 1974—; founder, chmn. bd. Computek, Inc., 1968-74; cons. in computers to industry. Author: Threshold Logic: a Synthesis Approach, 1966, (with Athens, Spann and Mason) Systems, Networks and Computation: Multivariable Methods, 1974, Systems, Networks and Computation: Basic Concepts, 1972, (with Clark, Halle, Pool and Wiesner) The Telephone's First Century—and Beyond, 1977, The Computer Age; A Twenty Year View, 1979; Contbr. articles profl. jours. Trustee Athens Coll., Greece, 1973—; chmn. bd. Boston Camerata, 1976—; dir. Cambridge Soc. Early Music, 1974-75. Recipient Terman Internat. Edn. award Am. Soc. Engring. Edn., 1975; Ford postdoctoral fellow, 1964-66; Fulbright scholar, 1954. Fellow IEEE (Thompson best paper prize 1968); mem. Sigma Xi, Tau Beta Pi, Pi Mu Epsilon. Greek Orthodox. Patentee in field. Current Work: Personal computers, graphics. Subspecialties: Graphics, image processing, and pattern recognition; Personal computers. Office: Mass Inst Tech Cambridge MA 02139

DERUDDER, JAMES LOUIS, plastics engineer, researcher; b. Blue Island, Ill., Apr. 9, 1951; s. John Russel DeRudder and Geraldine (Reedy) Wohlgemuth; m. Dinah Susan Mullins, May 5, 1973; children—Jennifer, David, Heather, Daniel. B.S.E., U. Mich., 1972, M.S.E., 1973, Ph.D., 1977. Teaching asst. U. Mich., Ann Arbor, 1974-77; researcher B.F. Goodrich, Brecksville, Ohio, 1977-84, Gen. Electric Co., Mt. Vernon, Ind., 1984—. Contbr. articles to profl. jours. Mem. Am. Phys. Soc., Am. Chem. Soc., Alpha Sigma Mu. Current work: Research and development of new polymer alloys and blends; failure analysis and non-destructive testing of polymer alloys and composites. Subspecialties: Polymers (materials science); Composite materials. Office: Gen Electric Co Hwy 69 S Mount Vernon IN 47620

DESAI, KIRIT NAVNITRAI, polymer chemist; b. Bilimora, Gujarat, India, Feb. 9, 1949; came to U.S., 1971; s. Navnitrai R. and Vinaben (Vina) D.; m. Kailash Ratilal Desai, Mar. 21, 1975; children—Nirav, Kirit, Desai. B.Sc. in Chemistry, Gujarat U., India, 1968; M.Sc., 1970; M.S. in Chemistry, St. Joseph's U., 1974, M.B.A., 1984. Research specialist U. Pa., Phila., 1974—. Contbr. articles to profl. jours. M.G. Sci. Inst.-India merit scholar, 1964-68; Indian Rys. fellow, 1968-70. Mem. Am. Chem. Soc. (polymer div.), Internat. Confedn. Thermal Analysis, N.Am. Thermal Analysis Soc., Del. Valley Thermal Analysis Forum. Current work: Synthetic chemistry of heterocyclic charge transfer complexes, diacetylenes, monomers and polymers, crystal growth, kinetic studies, polymerization, current interest in molecular and liquid crystals for optical and electronic applications. Subspecialties: Polymer chemistry; Electronic materials. Home: 740 Providence Rd Aldan PA 19018 Office: 412 LRSM U Pa 3231 Walnut St Philadelphia PA 19104

DESAI, RASHMI C., physics educator; b. Amod, India, Nov. 21, 1938; came to U.S., 1962, naturalized, 1968; s. Chimanlal P. and Savita (Vakil) D.; m.

Kalpakam Shanker, May 2, 1963; children—Anuj, Aparna. B.Sc. with honors, Bombay U., India, 1957; Ph.D., Cornell U., 1966. Sci. officer Bhabha Atomic Research Ctr., Bombay, India, 1957-62; research assoc. MIT, Cambridge, 1966-68; asst. prof. U. Toronto, Ont., Can., 1968-71, assoc. prof., 1971-78, prof., 1978-83, prof. physics and coordinator grad. studies, 1983—; vis. assoc. Calif. Inst. Tech., 1975; vis. scientist IBM, San Jose, Calif., 1981-82. Author: (with others) Advances in Chemical Physics, Vol. 46, 1981; Interfacial Dynamics, 1985. Contbr. articles to profl. jours. Chmn., trustee Nirvan Bhavan, Toronto, 1979-81; trustee Indo-Can. Cultural Ctr., Toronto, 1981—. Nat. Sci. and Engring. Research Council Can. grantee, 1968—. Mem. Can. Assn. Physicists (sec. 1970-71), Am. Phys. Soc., Am. Assn. Physics Tchrs., Personal Computer Club Toronto. Current work: Statistical physics, phase transitions; molecular structure and transport in fluids; fluid interfaces and fractal lattices; kinetic theory and hydrodynamics of fluids; computer simulation. Subspecialties: Statistical physics; Statistical mechanics. Office: Dept Physics U Toronto Toronto ON M5S 1A7 Canada

DESAIAH, DURISALA, neuropharmacologist, neurotoxicologist, educator, researcher, cons.; b. Gowravaram, India, Nov. 22, 1944; came to U.S., 1970, naturalized citizen; d. Durisala and Veeramma D. (Kasineni) Hanumaiah; m. Nirmala D. Desaiah, June 14, 1964; 1 son: Rao V.H. B.Sc., Osmania U., India, 1962, M.Sc., 1964, Ph.D., 1969. Research fellow U. Minn., 1970-73, Miss. State U., 1973-75; research assoc. U. Miss. Med. Center, Jackson, 1975-77, instr. dept. pharmacology, 1977-78, asst. prof. dept. neurology, 1978-81, assoc. prof., 1981-85, prof., 1985—. Contbr. numerous articles and abstracts to profl. publs. Nizam Trust travel grantee to U.S., 1970; NIH research grantee, 1980—; FASEB Vis. Scientist, 1980—. Mem. Am. Soc. Pharmacoloy and Exptl. Therapeutics, Soc. Toxicology, Soc. for Neurisci., N.Y. Acad. Scis., Sigma Xi. Current work: Membrane pharmacology, neuropharmacology, neurotoxicology, neuromuscular and neurological disorders. Subspecialties: Neuropharmacology; Toxicology (medicine). Office: Dept Neurology U Miss Med Center Jackson MS 39216

DE SALVA, SALVATORE JOSEPH, pharmacologist, toxicologist; b. N.Y.C., Jan. 14, 1924; s. Nicola Carlo and Frances Agnes (Caldarella) De S.; m. Elaine Mae Radloff, June 14, 1948; children: Salaine Claire De Salva Bonanne, Christopher Joseph, Stephanie De Salva Farrelly, Steven William, Gregory Vincent, Peter Nicholas, Philip Anthony, Deirdre De Salva Berry. B.S., Marquette U., 1947, M.S., 1949; postgrad., U. Ill., Chgo., 1951-53; Ph.D., Stritch Sch. Medicine, Loyala U., Chgo., 1958. Research and teaching asst. Marquette U., Milw., 1947-49; research biochemist Milwaukee County Gen. Hosp., 1954; instr. U. Ill., 1951-52; asst. prof. Chgo. Coll. Optometry, 1951-53; pharmacologist Armour Pharm. Lab., 1953-59; sect. head Colgate Palmolive Co., Piscataway, N.J., 1959-66, sr. research assoc., 1966-72, mgr., 1972-76, assoc. dir. research for pharmacology and toxicology, 1976-83, dir. research for pharmacology and toxicology, 1983—; lectr. Loyola U., 1957-59. Editor: Symposium for Bio Medical Electronic Instrumentation, 1965; contbr. articles to profl. jours. Mem. Park Forest (Ill.) Mosquito Abatement Program, 1952-55, Franklin Twp. (N.J.) Sch. Bd., 1969-70, Somerset (N.J.) Bd. Health, 1965-67, Cath. Youth Orgn., Somerset, 1960-67; v.p. Cedar Hill Swim Club; active Boy Scouts Am., 1965-67; trustee Franklin Twp. Day Care Center, 1969; mem. technician tng. com. N.J. Council for Research and Devel., Rutgers U., 1969-72. Served with USN, 1942-46. Mem. AAAS, Soc. Exptl. Biology and Medicine, Am. Soc. Pharmacology and Exptl. Therapeutics, Soc. Toxicology, Internat. Union Pharmacology (toxicology sect.), Soc. Xenbiotics, Soc. Regulatory Pharmacology and Toxicology, N.Y. Acad. Scis., Sigma Xi. Roman Catholic. Patentee in field. Current Work: Pharmaco-toxicology of fluorides, sequestering agents and surfactants. Subspecialties: Pharmacology; Toxicology (medicine). Office: 909 River Rd Piscataway NJ 08854

DESCHNER, ELEANOR ELIZABETH, biologist; b. Jersey City, Oct. 18, 1928; d. Fred and Anna (Sichler) D. B.A., Notre Dame Coll. of S.I., 1949; M.S., Fordham U., 1951, Ph.D., 1954. Head lab. digestive tract carcinogenesis Meml. Sloan-Kettering Cancer Center, N.Y.C., 1980—; assoc. prof. medicine/radiology Cornell U. Med. Coll., N.Y.C., 1976—; assoc. radiobiologist dept medicine Meml. Hosp., N.Y.C., 1978—. Contbr. articles to profl. jours. Nat. Cancer Inst. grantee; Am. Cancer Soc. grantee; NIH grantee. Mem. Am. Assn. Cancer Research, Am. Gastroent. Assn., Royal Soc. Medicine, Am. Soc. Cell Biology, Cell Kinetics Soc., Genetics Soc. Am., Am. Inst. Biol. Sci., AAAS, Sigma Xi, Kappa Gamma Pi. Republican. Roman Catholic. Club: Bus./Profl. Women's. Current Work: Cell proliferation in human/animal gastrointestinal cancer. Subspecialties: Cell study oncology; Gastroenterology. Address: 1275 York Ave New York NY 10021

DESER, STANLEY, physicist, educator; b. Poland, Mar. 19, 1931. B.S. summa cum laude Bklyn. Coll., 1949; M.A., Harvard U., 1950, Ph.D., 1953; D.S.C. (hon.), U. Stockholm, 1978. NSF postdoctoral fellow Inst. for Advanced Study, Princeton, N.J., 1953-55, Niels Bohr Inst., Copenhagen, 1955-57; lectr. Harvard U., Cambridge, Mass., 1957-58, Loeb lectr., 1975; prof. physics Brandeis U., Waltham, Mass., 1958—. Recipient Disting. Alumni award Bklyn. Coll.; Guggenheim fellow, Sorbonne, Paris, 1966-67; Fulbright fellow, 1966, 71. Fellow Am. Acad. Arts and Scis., Am. Phys. Soc. Subspecialties: Relativity and gravitation; Particle physics. Office: Brandeis U Dept Physics Waltham MA 02254

DESHMUKH, VINOD DHUNDIRAJ, neurologist, neurophysiologist, surgeon, educator; b. Wani, Dist. Yeotmal, India, July 31, 1938; came to U.S., 1974, naturalized, 1982; s. Dhundiraj Govind and Leela Keshav (Shekdar) D.; m. Sunanda Vasant Deodhar, May 8, 1940; children: Abhijit, Asvin, Rahul. I.Sc., Sir Parashurambhau Coll. U. Poona, India, 1957, M.B.B.S., 1962; M. Surgery, U. Bombay, 1966; Ph.D., U. Glasgow, 1972. Intern Civil Hosp., Thana, Bombay, India, 1962; resident J. J. Hosp., Bombay, 1963-66, Nat. Hosp. Neurol. Diseases, London, 1967-68, Inst. Neuroscis., U. Glasgow, Scotland, 1969-72; cons. clin.neurophysiology Central Middlesex Hosp., London, 1973-74; asst. prof. neurology Baylor Coll. Medicine, Houston, 1974-76; dir. Baylor Coll. Medicine (Cerebral Blood Flow and Cerebral Evoked Potentials Lab.), 1974-76; asst. prof. U. Tex., Houston, 1976-78; clin. asst. prof. U. Fla., 1978—; dir. edn. U. Fla. (Sch. EEG Tech.), 1981—, practice medicine specializing in neurology, Jacksonville, Fla., 1978—; mem., tchr. Vedant Edn. Soc., Jacksonville, 1982. Contbr. articles to profl. jours. Local rep. Krishnamurtl Info. Ctr., Jacksonville, 1981-82. Recipient B.J. Med. Coll. Poona 1st prize in physiology, 1958; St. Georges Hosp. Bombay P.W. Shikhare prize, 1964-65. Mem. Soc. Neuroscis. Am. Acad. Neurology, Am. Med. EEG Assn., Am. Assn. Electromyography and Electrodiagnosis, AMA, Duval County Med. Soc., Jacksonville C. of C. Current Work: Study of attentional energy and its modulations; two distinct modes of attention: mnemic and free modes, its theoretical implications and practical applications in human life; integrative models of observer, observed and the ultimate universal energy. Subspecialties: Neurophysiology; Neurology. Home: 3600 Rustic Ln Jacksonville FL 32217 Office: 3599 University Blvd S #601 Jacksonville FL 32216

DESNICK, ROBERT JOHN, medical geneticist; b. Mpls., July 12, 1943; s. Theodore David and Celia Janice (Marcus) D. B.A., U. Minn., 1965, Ph.D. in Genetics, 1970, M.D., 1971. Diplomate Am. Bd. Med. Genetics, Nat. Bd. Med. Examiners. Research assoc. dept. pediatrics U. Minn., Mpls., 1970-72, intern, then resident dept. pediatrics, 1971-73, asst. prof. pediatrics, 1973-75, assoc. prof., 1976-77, prof., 1977, asst. prof. lab. medicine and pathology, 1973-75, asst. prof. Dight Inst. Human Genetics, 1973-75, assoc. prof., 1975-77, assoc. prof. genetics and cell biology Coll. Biologic Scis., 1975-77; Arthur J. and Nellie Z. Cohen prof. pediatrics and genetics, chief div. med. genetics Mt. Sinai Sch. Medicine, N.Y.C., 1977—; attending physician pediatrics Mt. Sinai Hosp., N.Y.C.; cons. physician pediatric genetics Beth Israel Hosp., N.Y.C., City Hosp. Ctr. at Elmhurst, N.Y., Hosp. for Joint Diseases, N.Y.C.; City Univ. N.Y., 1977—; mem. med. adv. bd. Nat. Tay-Sachs and Allied Diseases Assn., 1975—, Nat. Neurofibromatosis Found., 1978-81, Nat. Found. for Jewish Genetic Diseases, 1981—, Am. Porphyria Found., 1984—; mem. Gov.'s State Adv. Com. on Genetics, 1982—. Mem. editorial bd. Enzyme, 1979—, Clinica Chimica Acta, 1984—; assoc. editor Am. Jour. Human Genetics, 1980-84; editor several books. Contbr. articles to profl. jours. Recipient Ross award in Pediatric Research, 1972; C.J. Watson award 1973, NIH Research Ctr. Devel. award, 1975-80; E. Mead Johnson award, 1981; USPHS fellow in genetics, 1968-70. Mem. Am. Soc. Human Genetics (chmn. nominating com. 1982, program com. 1982-85), Soc. Inherited Metabolic Diseases (bd. dirs.), Genetics Soc. Am., Cyrus P. Barnum Soc., Behavior Genetics Assn., Soc. Complex Carbohydrates, Am. Fedn. Clin. Research, AAAS, Midwest Soc. Pediatric Research, Soc. Pediatric Research, Soc. Exptl. Biology and Medicine, Am. Soc. Exptl. Pathology, Central Soc. Clin. Research, Soc. Study Social Biology, N.Y. Acad. Scis., European Soc. Human Genetics, Am. Soc. Clin. Investigation, Harvey Soc. (sec. 1984—), Soc. Study Inborn Errors of Metabolism, Am. Soc. Biol. Chemists, Am. Pediatric Soc., Am. Soc. Microbiology, Assn. Am. Physicians, Sigma Xi. Current work: Human molecular and biochemical genetics. Subspecialties: Genetics and genetic engineering (medicine); Genetics and genetic engineering (biology). Office: Mt Sinai Sch Medicine 5th Ave and 100th St New York NY 10029

DESOER, CHARLES AUGUSTE, electrical engineer; b. Ixelles, Belgium, Jan. 11, 1926; came to U.S., 1949, naturalized, 1958; s. Jean Charles and Yvonne Louise (Peltzer) D.; m. Jacqueline K. Johnson, July 21, 1966; children—Marc J., Michele M., Craig M. Ingenieur Radio-Electricien, U. Liege, Belgium, 1949, D.Sc. (hon.), 1976; Sc.D. in Elec. Engring, M.I.T., 1953. Research asst. M.I.T., 1951-53; mem. tech. staff Bell Telephone Labs., Murray Hill, N.J., 1953-58; asso. prof. elec. engring. and computer scis. U. Calif., Berkeley, 1958-62, prof., 1962—, Miller research prof., 1970-71. Author: (with L. A. Zadeh) Linear System Theory, 1963, (with E. S. Kuh) Basic Circuit Theory, 1969, (with M. Vidyasagar) Feedback Systems: Input Output Properties, 1975, Notes for a Second Course on Linear Systems, 1970, (with F. M. Collier) Multivariable Feedback Systems; contbr. numerous articles on systems and circuits to profl. jours. Served with Belgian Arty., 1944-45. Decorated Vol.'s medal; recipient Best Paper prize Joint Automatic Control Conf., 1962, Univ. medal U. Liege, 1970, Disting. Teaching award U. Calif., Berkeley, 1971, Prix Montefiore Inst. Montefiore, 1975; award for outstanding paper Control Systems Soc., 1981; award for outstanding paper IEEE, 1979; Guggenheim fellow, 1970-71. Fellow IEEE (Edison medal 1975), AAAS; mem. Nat. Acad. Engring., Am. Math. Soc., Math. Assn. Am., Soc. Indsl. and Applied Math. Current Work: Systems: controls and circuits. Office: Dept Elec Engring and Computer Sci U Calif Berkeley CA 94720

DESSER, KENNETH BARRY, cardiologist, researcher; b. N.Y.C., Mar. 24, 1940; s. George and Sarah Ruth (Kaplan) D.; m. Carmen Yvonne Fletcher, Sept. 3, 1981; children: Brett Karen, Lori Helene. B.A., NYU, 1961; M.D., N.Y. Med. Coll., 1965. Diplomate: Am. Bd. Internal Medicine. Intern Beth Israel Med. Ctr., N.Y.C., 1965-66, resident, 1968-70; cardiology fellow Inst. for Cardiovascular Diseases, Phoenix, 1970-72, now dir. cardiology fellowship program; cons. in field. Contbr. numerous articles to med. jours.; mem. editorial bds.: Am. Jour. Cardiology, 1980-82, Jour. Am. Coll. Cardiology, 1983-85. Served to capt. M.C. U.S. Army, 1966-68, Vietnam. Recipient Best Research Project award Beth Israel div. Mt. Sinai Sch. Medicine, 1966. Fellow ACP, Am. Coll. Cardiology, Am. Coll. Chest Physicians, Internat. Coll. Angiology; mem. Am. Fedn. for Clin Research, N.Y. Acad. Scis. Applied Doppler ultrasonic flowmeter for human study. Current Work: Genetics of mitral valve prolapse, Dopplar ultrasonic shifts in cardiovascular disease. Subspecialties: Cardiology; Internal medicine. Home: 77 E Missouri Ave Phoenix AZ 85012 Office: Inst for Cardiovasvular Disease Good Samaritan Med Center 1003 E McDowell Rd Phoenix AZ 85006

DESSLER, ALEX J., space physicist. Dir. Space Scis. Lab., Marshall Space Flight Ctr., Huntsville, Ala. Subspecialty: Space physics. Office: NASA Marshall Space Flight Ctr Space Scis Lab Huntsville AL 35812

DESSY, RAYMOND EDWIN, chemistry educator; b. Reynoldsville, Pa., Sept. 3, 1931; b. Raymond John and Martha Ellen (Orr) D.; m. Annabelle Lee, Sept. 8, 1959. B.A., U. Pitts., 1953, Ph.D., 1956. Postdoctoral fellow, instr. Ohio State U., Columbus, 1956-57; asst. prof. U. Cin., 1957-61, assoc. prof., 1961-66; prof. chemistry Va. Poly. Inst. and State U., Blacksburg, 1966—. Author books and numerous articles. Sloan fellow, 1961-64; recipient award Sigma Xi, 1961. Mem. Am. Chem. Soc. Current Work: Instrument design and automation including design of new detectors for use in analytical chemistry, laboratory automation using networks. Subspecialties: Analytical chemistry; Distributed systems and networks. Office: Va Poly Inst and State U 325 Davidson Hall Blacksburg VA 24061

DETORRES, CORY DELGADO, psychologist, organizational consultant; b. N.Y.C., Aug. 3, 1942; d. Frank Joseph and Mildred (Kahn) Cohen; m. Fernando Delgado de Torres, June 25, 1966 (div. 1970); m. Tibor St. John de Cholnoky, Mar. 15, 1975; 1 son, Eric. A.B., Barnard Coll, 1964; Ph.D., Temple U., 1979. Lic. clin. psychologist, Pa. Staff assoc. Eastern Inst. Transactional Analysis and Gestalt, Phila., 1973-75; staff assoc. Laurel Inst., Inc., Phila., 1975-78; founding assoc. Phila. Profl. Assocs., Phila., 1978-79; dir. tng. and consultations Access Centers, Inc., Phila., 1979-82; dir. Cory de Torres Assocs., Phila., 1982—; cons. Influence Tng. Systems, Phila., 1980—. Contbr. articles to profl. jours. Mem. Am. Psychol. Assn., Pa. Psychol Assn., Phila. Soc. Clin. Psychology, Internat. Transactional Analysis Assn., Soc. Neuro-Linguistic Programming (cert. trainer). Current Work: Interpersonal power and conflict resolution; interpersonal communications technology. Subspecialty: Neurolinguistic programming. Office: Cory de Torres Assocs 1900 Spruce St Philadelphia PA 19103

DETRA, RALPH WILLIAM, research laboratory administrator; b. Thompsontown, Pa., Mar. 23, 1925; s. Ralph Emerson and Sara Jane (Portzline) D.; m. Charlesanna Francis Eberly, June 21, 1947; children—Stephen William, David Eberly. B.S. in Mech. Engring, Cornell U., 1946, M. Aero.Engring, 1951; Dr. sc. techn. (NRC fellow 1951-52), Eidgenossische Technische Hochschule, Zurich, Switzerland, 1953. Supr. aerodynamic research, aviation gas turbine div. Westinghouse Corp., Kansas City, Mo., 1953-55; prin. research scientist Avco Everett Research Labs. Inc. (Mass.), 1955-59, v.p. fossil energy tech., 1972-81, gen. mgr., pres., 1981—, v.p., gen. mgr. systems div., Wilmington, Mass., 1966-71; pres. Tyco Labs. Inc., Waltham, Mass., 1971-72. Author papers in field. Served with USN, 1943-47. Asso. fellow AIAA; mem. Sigma Xi, Tau Beta Pi. Republican. Episcopalian. Club: Winchester Country. Subspecialties: Plasma physics; Combustion processes. Home: 15 Frost St Arlington MA 02174 Office: 2385 Revere Beach Pkwy Everett MA 02149

DETTBARN, WOLF-DIETRICH, pharmacologist, educator; b. Berlin, Ger., Jan. 30, 1928; s. Erwin B. and Maria M. (Conrady) D.; children: Donata-Andrea, Henning Christian. M.D., U Gottingen, Ger., 1953. Intern. Univ. Clinic, Gottingen, 1953-54; research assoc. biology dept. Ciba Co., Basel, Switzerland, 1954-55, Physiology Inst., U. Saarland, Hamburg, Germany, 1955-58; research assoc. dept. neurology Coll. Physicians and Surgeons, Columbia U., N.Y.C., asst. prof., 1961-67, assoc. prof., 1967-68; prof. pharmacology Med. Sch., Vanderbilt U., Nashville, 1968—; cons. U.S. Army Med. Research and Devel. Command, Nat. Acad. Sci.; corp. mem. Marine Biol. Lab., Woods Hole, Mass. Contbr. articles to profl. jours. Mem. Am. Physiol. Soc., Am. Soc. Pharmacology and Exptl. Therapeutics, Am. Soc. Neurochemistry, Soc. Gen. Physiologists, Soc. Neurosci. Current Work: Neurotrophic regulation of muscle; organophosphates. Subspecialties: Neuropharmacology; Neurochemistry.

DETTERMAN, ROBERT LINWOOD, nuclear engineer; b. Norfolk, Va., May 1, 1931; s. George William and Jenneille (Watson) D.; m. Virginia Armstrong, Apr. 19, 1958; children; Janine, Patricia, William Arthur. B.S., Va. Poly. Inst., 1953; Ph.D. in Nuclear Engring, Oak Ridge Sch. Reactor Tech., 1954. Test dir. Foster Wheeler, N.Y.C., 1955-59; sr. research engr. Atomics Internat., Canoga Park, Calif., 1959-62, chief projects engr., 1962-68; dir. bus. devel. Atomics Internat. (Energy Systems Group), 1968—; chmn. space safety com. Atomic Indsl. Forum, N.Y.C., 1968; nuclear cons. Danish Govt., Riso, 1960. Author: Livermore Pool-Type Reactor, 1961, Safe Disposal of Reactors, 1965. Trustee Morris Animal Found., Arabian Horse Trust; adv. Calif. State Poly. U.; pres. Bo-Gin, Inc., Thousand Oaks. Mem. Am. Nuclear Soc. (dir. aerospace div. 1965-70), Atomic Indsl Forum, Tau Beta Phi, Phi Kappa Phi, Eta Kappa Nu. Republican. Clubs: Magic Cast (Los Angeles), SPVA (Los Angeles). Patentee central rod activator, 1955, mechanism termination nuclear reactor, 1965. Current Work: Nuclear reactor development, liquid metal fast breeder, space systems, computer applications. Subspecialties: Nuclear fission; Microchip technology (engineering). Home: 120 Colt Ln Thousand Oaks CA 91360 Office: Rockwell International Corp 6633 Canoga Ave Canoga Park CA 91304

DETWEILER, DAVID KENNETH, veterinary physiologist, educator; b. Phila., Oct. 23, 1919; s. David Rieser and Pearl Irene (Overholt) D.; m. Inge E. A. Kludt, Feb. 2, 1965; children: Ellen, Diane, Judith, David, Inge, Kenneth. V.M.D., U. Pa., 1942, M.S., 1949; Sc.D. (hon.), Ohio State U., 1966; M.V.D. (hon.), U. Vienna (Austria), 1968; D.M.V. (hon.), U. Turin (Italy), 1969. Asst. instr. physiology and pharmacology Sch. Vet. Medicine, U. Pa., Phila., 1942-43, instr., 1943-45, assoc. in physiology, pharmacology, 1945-47, asst. prof., 1947-51, assoc. prof., 1951-62, prof. physiology, 1962—. Sch. Vet. Medicine, U. Pa. (Grad. Sch. Arts and Scis.); chmn. dept. vet. med. scis. Sch. Vet. Medicine, U. Pa. (Grad. Sch. Medicine), 1956-68, dir. comparative cardiovascular studies unit, 1960—, prof., head lab. physiology and pharmacology, 1962-68, prof., head lab. physiology, 1968—, prof. faculty arts and scis., 1968—, chmn. grad. group comparative med. scis., 1971—; mem. Inst. Medicine, Nat. Acad. Scis., 1974—; cons. cardiovascular toxicology, 1950—. Contbr. numerous articles to various publs. Guggenheim fellow, 1955-56; Recipient Gaines award and medal Am. Vet. Med. Assn., 1960; D.K. Detweiler prize in cardiology established in his honor German Group of World Vet. Med. Assn., 1982. Fellow AAAAS; mem. Am. Physiol. Soc., Am. Assn. Vet. Physiology and Pharmacology (pres.), N.Y. Acad. Scis., Am. Vet. Med. Assn., Council Basic Scis., Am. Heart Assn., Acad. Vet. Cardiology (pres.), Am. Coll. Vet. Internal Medicine (cardiology group), Phi Zeta. Subspecialties: Animal physiology; Internal medicine (veterinary medicine). Office: Sch Vet Medicine 3800 Spruce St Philadelphia PA 19104

DEUPREE, ROBERT GASTON, hydrodynamicist; b. Washington, Aug. 5, 1946; s. Robert Gaston and Mildred (Avery) D.; m. Janet Hammersley, June 22, 1968; children: Alexander, Michael. B.A., U. Wis., Madison, 1968; M.S., U. Colo., Boulder, 1970; Ph.D., U. Toronto, 1974. Postdoctoral fellow dept. astrophys. scis. Princeton U., 1974-75; postdoctoral asst. Los Alamos Sci. Lab., 1975-77; asst. prof. dept. astronomy Boston U., 1978-80; mem. staff Los Alamos Nat. Lab., 1980—. Contbr. articles to sci. jours. NSF grantee, 1978-79, 79-80. Mem. Am. Astron. Soc., Internat. Astron. Union. Current Work: Hydrodynamics of stellar interiors; shock response of different geological media to nuclear explosions; Monte Carlo modelling of big hole logging tools. Subspecialties: Nuclear shock effects; Theoretical astrophysics. Home: 1981 41st St Los Alamos NM 87544 Office: ESS-5 MS F-665 Los Alamos Nat Lab PO Box 1663 Los Alamos NM 87545

DEUSCHLE, KURT WALTER, physician, educator; b. Kongen, Germany, Mar. 14, 1923; came to U.S., 1924, naturalized, 1949; s. John and Marie (Schaefer) D.; m. Jeanne Magagna, 1975; children by previous marriage—Kurt J., Sally, James. B.S. cum laude, Kent State U., 1944; M.D., U. Mich., 1948. Intern Colo. Gen. Hosp., Denver, 1948-49; resident medicine, fellow oncology Upstate Med. Center of State U. N.Y. at Syracuse, 1950-52, instr. medicine, 1954-55; asst. prof. pub. health and preventive medicine Cornell Med. Coll., 1955-60; prof., chmn. dept. community medicine U. Ky., 1960-68; Ethel H. Wise prof., chmn. and dir. dept. community medicine Mt. Sinai Sch. of Medicine of City U. N.Y., 1968—; Merrimon lectr. U. N.C., Chapel Hill, 1975; vis. prof. U. Lagos, Nigeria, 1977; mem. tech. bd. Milbank Meml. Fund; mem. Tb control adv. com. Center Disease Control Dept. HEW; cons. manpower intelligence NIH; mem. Inst. Medicine of Nat. Acad. Scis., Washington; mem. rural health systems del. to China, 1978. Author: (with J. Adair) The People's Health: Anthropology and Medicine in a Navajo Community, 1970; Contbr. to: (ed. John Norman) Medicine in the Ghetto, 1969, Community Medicine: Teaching, Research and Health Care, (ed. Lathem and Newberry), 1970. Served with AUS, 1943-46. Commonwealth Fund sr. health fellow, 1966-67. Fellow Am. Coll. Preventive Medicine (past pres., Distinguished Service award 1975); mem. Am. Pub. Health Assn. (award for excellence in domestic health 1975), Am. Thoracic Soc., Assn. Tchrs. Preventive Medicine, Internat. Epidemiol. Assn., Alpha Omega Alpha. Subspecialty: Preventive medicine. Home: 1212 Fifth Ave New York NY 10029 Office: Fifth Ave and 100th St New York NY 10029

DEUTSCH, DALE GEORGE, toxicologist, neurobiochemist, educator; b. Liberty, N.Y., Feb. 22, 1943; s. Bernard and Sylvia (Nathanson) D.; m. Lou Charnon, July 2, 1946. B.A., SUNY-Buffalo, 1965; Ph.D., Purdue U., 1972. Postdoctoral fellow U. Colo., 1972-73; research assoc. U. Chgo., 1973-76; research asst. SUNY-Stony Brook, 1976-80, research asst. prof., 1980-81, asst. prof. pathology and biochemistry, head toxicology research on psychoactive drugs, 1981—; cons. in toxicology. Contbr. articles to profl. publs. Grantee USPHS; Grantee Nat. Inst. Drug Abuse; Pub. Sci. Citation Classic, 1983. Mem. Am. Soc. Neurochemistry, Soc. Neurosci., Electron Microscopy Soc. Am., AAAS, Suffolk County Mental Health Assn., Am. Assn. Clin. Chemistry. Current Work: Effect of psychoactive drugs upon brain and liver biochemistry. Subspecialties: Toxicology (medicine); Neurochemistry. Home: 21 Stony Brook Ave Stony Brook NY 11790 Office: University Hosp SUNY Stony Brook NY 11794

DEVANEY, JOSEPH JAMES, physicist; b. Boston, Apr. 29, 1924; s. Joseph Patrick and Madeline Elinor (Darragh) D.; m. Marjorie Ann Jones, Sept. 9, 1954; 1 dau., Kathleen. B.S., MIT, 1947, Ph.D., 1950. Research asst. MIT, Cambridge, 1942, 46, 47, 48; staff physicist Los Alamos Nat. Lab., 1950—; adj. prof. math. U. N.Mex., Los Alamos, 1956-59, adj. prof. physics, 1959-70. Contbr. articles in field to profl. jours. Adv. Gov.'s Policy Bd.-Pollution, Santa Fe, N.Mex., 1969-70; mem. County and State Central Co., Los Alamos, Santa Fe, N.Mex., 1953-71; co-founder Anti-Smog Fedn., N.Mex., 1967; nat. patrolman Nat. Ski Patrol, 1953-79; water safety/first aid instr. ARC, Los Alamos, 1952-79. Served with USCG, 1944-45; Served with AUS, 1942-44. Recipient Scholarships M.I.T., 1941, 42, 45, 46, 47; AEC fellow M.I.T., 1947-50. Mem. Am. Phys. Soc., Am. Nuclear Soc. Club: Ski (Los Alamos) (Patrol leader 1962-63). Current Work: Physics for particle transport, air pollution, solar energy, comparative hazards of energy production, laser fusion, nuclear physics, mathematical physics, defense of the U.S. and Free World. Subspecialties: Theoretical physics; Laser fusion. Home: 4792 Sandia Dr Los Alamos NM 87544 Office: Los Alamos Nat Lab MS-B226 X6 Los Alamos NM 87545

DE VAUCOULEURS, GERARD HENRI, astronomer, educator; b. Paris, Apr. 25, 1918; U.S., 1957, naturalized, 1962; m. Antoinette Pietra, Oct. 31, 1944. Ph.D., U. Paris, 1949; D.Sc., Australian Nat. U., Canberra, 1957. Research attache Nat. Center Sci. Research, Sorbonne and Astrophysics Inst., Paris, 1943-49; research fellow Australian Nat. U. Mt. Stromlo Obs., 1951-54; observer-in-charge Yale-Columbia So. Sta., 1954-57; astronomer Lowell Obs., Flagstaff, Ariz., 1957-58; research asso. Harvard U. Obs., 1958-60; asso. prof. astronomy U. Tex., Austin, 1960-63, prof., 1964-80, Ashbel Smith prof., 1981-82, Blumberg prof., 1983—; vis. prof. Coll. de France, Paris, 1976, Royal Obs., Edinburgh, Scotland, 1976; cons. in field. Author 20 books, 350 research papers in field. Grantee NSF, NASA, others. Mem. Internat. Astron. Union, Am. Astron. Soc., Royal Astron. Soc. (Herschel medal 1980), Astron. Soc. Pacific, French Phys. Soc. Current work: Extragalactic astronomy; cosmology. Subspecialties: Cosmology; Optical astronomy. Address: Astronomy Dept RLM 16 316 U Tex Austin TX 78712

DEVEREUX, WILLIAM PATRICK, aerospace co. adminstr.; b. Yonkers, N.Y., Mar. 21, 1923; s. William Thomas and Mary Catherine (McCormack) D.; m. Theodora, May 30, 1955; 1 son, Lawrence M. A.B., Woodstock Coll., 1946, Ph.L., 1947. Instr. Canisius Coll., Buffalo, 1947-50; tech. instr. Bell Aircraft Corp., Buffalo, 1952-56; physicist Farrand Optical Co., Inc., Bronx, N.Y., 1956-59; scientist, physicist Gen. Dynamics-Elec. Boat, Groton, Conn., 1960-62; prin. engr. optics Kollsman Instrument Corp., Syosset, N.Y., 1962-71; mgr. electrooptics design Ball Aerospace Systems Div., Boulder, Colo., 1971—. Contbr. articles to profl. jours. Mem. Optical Soc. Am., Soc. Photo-optical Instrumentation Engrs. Democrat. Roman Catholic. Lodge: KC. Patentee in field. Current Work: Design of instrumentation for space astronomy and navigation. Subspecialties: Aerospace engineering and technology; Optical engineering. Home: 805 Agate St Broomfield CO 80020 Office: Ball Aerospace Systems Div PO Box 1062 Boulder CO 80306

DEVINCENZI, RONALD GEORGE, dental consultant; b. San Francisco, Oct. 11, 1930; s. George Louis and Elvyra (DeLuca) DeV.; m. Donna Rita Vondra, June 27, 1953; children—Mark, Ronald George, Paul, Robert, Maria, Dianna, Andrea. B.S., Creighton U., 1952, D.D.S., 1956. Pvt. practice dentistry, Monterey, Calif., 1960-71; ptnr. Monterey Peninsula Dental Group, 1971-79; research investigator Calif. Found. Dental Health, Los Angeles, 1976-79; Western regional dir. Am. Dental Examiners, Monterey, 1980—; dir. Calif. Dental Service Corp., 1976-77; cons. socio-econ. research Calif. Found. Dental Health, Los Angeles, 1976-79. Served to capt. AUS, 1955-60. Named Dentist of Yr. Monterey Bay Dental Soc., 1974. Fellow Am. Coll. Dentists, Am. Inst. Oral Biology; mem. Calif. Dental Assn. (trustee 1976-79), ADA (del. 1974-79), Internat. Assn. Dental Research, Am. Assn. Pub. Health Dentists. Republican. Roman Catholic. Current Work: Dental health insurance administration; dental health care evaluation, health policy research. Home: 1141 Wildcat Canyon Rd Pebble Peach CA 93953

DEVINEY, MARVIN LEE, JR., industrial research scientist, research administrator; b. Kingsville, Tex., Dec. 5, 1929; s. Marvin Lee and Esther Lee (Gambrell) D.; m. Marie Carole Massey, June 7, 1975; children—Marvin Lee III, John H., Ann-Marie Karen. B.S., S.W. Tex. State U., 1949; M.A., U. Tex., Austin, 1952, Ph.D. in Phys. Chemistry, 1956. Cert. profl. chemist. Devel. chemist Celanese Corp. Bishop, Tex., 1956-58; research chemist Shell Chem. Co., Deer Park, Houston 1958-66; sr. scientist, head phys. and radiochem. group Ashland Chem. Co., Houston, 1966-68, mgr. phys. and analytical chemistry sect., 1968-71, mgr. phys. chemistry Research and Devel. Lab., Columbus, Ohio, 1971-78, research assoc., supr. applied surface chemistry Ashland Ventures Research and Devel., 1978-84, supr. elec. microscopy, advanced aerospace composites and research contracts, 1984—; mem. sci. adv. bd. Am. Petroleum Inst., 1968-74; adj. prof. chemistry U. Tex.-San Antonio, 1973-75; mem. ednl. adv. com. Columbus Tech. Inst., 1974-84, Central Ohio Tech. Coll., 1975-82. Co-editor books on catalysis-surface chemistry and carbon-graphite chemistry. Contbr. numerous articles to sci. jours. Patentee in field. Humble Oil research fellow, 1954. Fellow Am. Inst. Chemists (pres. Ohio chpt. 1978-82, chmn. nat. com. 1984—); mem. Am. Chem. Soc. (chmn. Houston area, chief exec. officer 1969), Ohio Acad. Sci., Tex. Acad. Sci., Electron Microscopy Soc. Am., Materials Research Soc., Am. Def. Preparedness Soc., Am. Carbon Soc., Engrs. Council Houston (sr. councilor 1970-71), Sigma Xi, Phi Lambda Upsilon, Sigma Pi Sigma, Alpha Chi Sigma. Republican. Methodist. Current work: Advanced polymeric composites; catalysis surface chemistry; electron microscopy, high temperature aerospace materials and chemicals; polymer test methods; analytic chemistry; fuel cell electrochemistry; elastomer reinforcement. Subspecialties: Surface chemistry; Composite materials. Home: 6810 Hayhurst St Worthington OH 43085 Office: Ashland Chem Co Ventures Research and Devel Box 2219 Columbus OH 43216

DEVITA, VINCENT THEODORE, JR., oncologist; b. Bronx, N.Y., Mar. 7, 1935; s. Vincent Theodore and Isabel DeV.; m. Mary Kay Bush, Aug. 3, 1957; children: Teddy (dec.), Elizabeth. B.S., Coll. William and Mary, 1957; M.D., George Washington U., 1961. Diplomate: Nat. Bd. Med. Examiners, Am. Bd. Internal Medicine. Intern U. Mich. Med. Center, Ann Arbor, 1961-62; resident in medicine George Washington U. Med. Service D.C. Gen. Hosp., 1962-73; sr. resident in medicine Yale New Haven Med. Center, 1965-66; clin. asso. lab. chem. pharmacology Nat. Cancer Inst. NIH, Bethesda, Md., 1963-65, mem. staff, 1966—, chief med. br., 1971-74, dir. div. cancer treatment, 1974-81, clin. dir. inst., 1975-81, dir., 1981—; mem. faculty George Washington U. Med. Sch., 1971—, prof. medicine, 1975—; mem. expert advisory panel WHO, 1976; mem. Lasker Award Jury, 1976; chmn. Com. French-Am. Agreement on Cancer Treatment Research, 1976—; vis. prof. Stanford U. Med. Sch., 1972; 1st ann. Clowes lectr. Roswell Park Meml. Inst. Buffalo, 1973. Contbr. numerous articles to med. jours. Served with USMCR, 1955-61. Tobacco Research Industry fellow, 1959; recipient Albert and Mary Lasker Med. Research award, 1972; Superior Service award HEW, 1975; Esther Langer Found. award, 1976; Alumni medallion Coll. William and Mary, 1976; Jeffrey Gottliev award, 1976; decorated Oren del Sol en el Grando Oficial Peru, 1970. Fellow A.C.P.; mem. Am. Soc. Clin. Oncology (chmn. program com. 1972, dir. 1973-76, pres. 1977-78), Am. Cancer Soc., Inst. Medicine, Am. Soc. Hematology, Am. Assn. Cancer Research (dir. 1976-79), AMA, Am. Fedn. Clin. Research, Am. Soc. Clin. Investigation, Soc. Surg. Oncology, Smith-Reed-Russel Med. Soc., Alpha Omega Alpha. Subspecialties: Cancer research (medicine); Hematology. Office: Nat Cancer Inst 900 Rockville Pike Bethesda MD 20014*

DEVONS, SAMUEL, physics educator; b. Bangor, Eng., Sept. 30, 1914; s. David I. and Edith (Edlestein) D.; m. Celia Ruth Toubkin, Sept. 7, 1938; children—Susan D., Judith R., Amanda J., Cathryn A.J. B.A., Trinity Coll., Cambridge U., Eng., 1935, M.A., Ph.D., 1939; A.R.C.S. (hon.), Imperial Coll., 1954; M.Sc. (hon.), Manchester U., 1958. Fellow, dir. studies, lectr. Trinity Coll., Cambridge U., 1946-49; prof. physics Imperial Coll. Sci., London, 1950-54; Langworthy prof. physics Manchester U., Eng., 1954-60; prof. physics Columbia U., N.Y.C., 1960-84, prof. emeritus, 1985—. dir. Barnard-Columbia History of Physics Lab., Barnard Coll., N.Y.C., 1969—. Author, editor various articles and profl. jours. Bd. govs. Weizmann Inst. Sci., Rehovot, Israel, 1972—. Recipient Rutherford medal and prize Inst. Physics, 1970. Fellow Royal Soc., Am. Phys. Soc.; mem. Am. Assn. Physics Tchrs., Phi Beta Kappa (hon.). Subspecialty: Nuclear physics. Office: Columbia U Box 33 Pupin St New York NY 10533

DEVORE, DALE PAUL, biochemist, researcher; b. Phillipsburg, N.J., Mar. 31, 1943; s. David Henry and Anna Elizabeth (Paul) DeV.; m. Sandra Bernice Grebowiec, Dec. 27, 1965; children: Mychelle, Braden. B.A., Rutgers U., 1966, M.S., 1972, Ph.D., 1973. Research asst. Rutgers U., New Brunswick, N.J., 1966-72; research scientist Battelle Meml. Inst., Columbus, Ohio, 1972-74, prin. research biochemist, 1974-79; research specialist Riker Research div. 3M Corp., St. Paul, 1979-81, sr. research specialist biochemistry, mgr. collagen products labs. McGhan Med. div., 1981—; mem. faculty U. Minn., 1981—; dir. product devel. MedChem, Woburn, Mass. Contbr. chpts. to books, articles to profl. jours. Inventor collagen reconstitution. Commr. Vadnais Heights (Minn.) Planning Commn., 1981—. Mem. Am. Rheumatism Assn., Internat. Assn. for Dental Research, Soc. for Biomaterials, Midwest Connective Tissue Assn., Sigma Xi, Alpha Zeta. Current Work: Biochemistry of connective tissue. Investigation of connective tissue degradation in rheumatoid arthritis. Development of collagen-based and hyaluronic acid-based biomedical implants. Subspecialties: Biochemistry (medicine); Artificial organs and prostheses. Home: 4334 Greenhaven Circle Vadnais Heights MN 55110 Office: Med Chem Products Woburn MA 01801

DEVORE, DUANE THOMAS, oral surgeon, lawyer, educator; b. Park Ridge, Ill., May 14, 1933; s. Jacques Joseph and Nellie (Liddil) DeV.; m. Patricia Kilgarriff; 1 dau., Katherine Margaret. D.D.S., Loyola U., Chgo., 1956; Ph.D., U. London, 1975; J.D., U. Md.-Balt., 1979. Bar: Md 1980, D.C 1980; diplomate: Am. Bd. Oral Surgery, Am. Bd. Forensic Odontology; lic. dentist, Ill., Ga., Md. Individual practice dentistry specializing in oral surgery, Savannah, Ga., 1960-67, Balt., 1971—; hon. Research fellow London Hosp., 1968-71; mem. faculty U. Md. Dental Sch., Balt., 1971—, prof. oral and maxillofacial surgery, 1976—, pvt. practice legal and med. cons., Balt., 1971—. Mem. Am. Heart Assn. (dir. Balt. chpt. 1973-78), Charles Village Civic Assn. (dir. 1982-83), ADA, ABA, Am. Assn. Dental Research (councillor 1975—). Current Work: Microvascular surgery; bone replacement materials; clinical research; forensic odontology; medico-legal. Subspecialties: Oral and maxillofacial surgery; Microsurgery. Home: 2701 N Calvert St Baltimore MD 21218 Office: U Md Dental Sch 666 W Baltimore St Baltimore MD 21201

DE VRIES, GEORGE HENRY, neurobiologist; b. Paterson, N.J., Dec. 22, 1942; s. Henry and Jeanette (Greydanus) DeV.; m. Helen T. De Vries, Aug. 21, 1965; children: Jori Elizabeth, James Thomson. B.S. in Zoology cum laude, Wheaton Coll, 1964; Ph.D. in Biochemistry, U. Ill. Med. Ctr., Chgo., 1969. Postdoctoral fellow Albert Einstein Coll. Medicine, 1969-71; asst. prof. biochemistry Med. Coll. Va., 1972-75, assoc. prof., 1975-83, prof., 1983—; Fogarty Found. fellow, Nice, France, 1980. Contbr. numerous articles to profl. jours. Bd. dirs. Multiple Sclerosis Assn., Richmond. Roche Found. fellow, 1975-76; NIH grantee, 1973; NSF grantee, 1976-78; Kroc Found. grantee, 1982-83; Javits neurosci. scholar, 1984—. Mem. Am. Soc. Neurochemistry (council), Internat. Soc. Neurochemistry, Soc. Neurosci., Am. Soc. Cell Biology. Presbyterian. Club: Highland Hills Swim. Current Work: Research in mechanisms of myelination, neuronal influences in demyelinating disease, isolation of axonal plasma membrane, neuron-glial interactions. Subspecialties: Neurobiology; Biochemistry (biology). Home: 2329 Tuscora Rd Richmond VA 23235 Office: Dept Biochemistry Med Coll Va Richmond VA 23298

DE VRIES, KENNETH LAWRENCE, mechanical engineer, educator; b. Ogden, Utah, Oct. 27, 1933; s. Sam and Fern (Slater) DeV.; m. Kay M. DeVries, Mar. 1, 1959; children—Kenneth, Susan. A.B., Weber State Coll., 1953; B.S., U. Utah, 1959, Ph.D., 1962. With Convair, Fort Worth, 1957; mem. faculty U. Utah, Salt Lake City, 1961—, prof. mech. engring., 1969-76, prof. dept. mech. and indsl. engring., 1976—, chmn. dept., 1970-81, assoc. dean Coll. Engring., 1983—; head polymer program NSF, 1975-76; mem. Utah Council Sci. and Tech., 1973-77. Author: Analysis and Testing of Adhesive Bonds, 1977; contbr. articles on polymers, dental materials, rock mechanics, adhesive design to profl. jours. Mem. ASME, Am. Phys. Soc., Internat. Soc. Dental Research, Am. Chem. Soc., ASTM, Material Soc. Mormon. Current Work: Research in material failure, polymers and composites. Subspecialties: Mechanical engineering; Materials (engineering). Home: 1466 Penrose St Salt Lake City UT 84103 Office: 3008 Mech Engring Bldg U Utah Salt Lake City UT 84112

DEVRIES, MARVIN FRANK, manufacturing engineering educator, manufacturing systems engineering director; b. Grand Rapids, Mich., Oct. 31, 1937; s. Ralph B. and Grace (Buurma) DeV.; m. Martha Lou Kannegieter, Aug. 28, 1959; children—Mark, Michael, Matthew. B.S., Calvin Coll., 1960; B.S.M.E., U. Mich., 1960, M.S.M.E., 1961, Ph.D., 1966. Registered profl. engr., Wis.; cert. manufacturing engr. Asst. prof. U. Wis.-Madison, 1966-70, assoc. prof., 1970-77, prof. mfg. engring., 1977—, dir. mfg. systems engring., 1981—. Author: Group Technology, 1976. Contbr. articles to profl. jours. Fulbright-Hays vis. prof., 1979-80. Mem. Soc. Mfg. Engrs. (pres. 1985-86), Interactional Inst. for Prodn. Engring. Research, ASME (chmn. prodn. engring. div. 1972-73). Mem. Christian Ref. Ch. Current work: Director of a graduate program in manufacturing systems engineering. Administer program of more than 50 students, yearly budget more than $1,000,000. Subspecialties: Mechanical engineering; Manufacturing engineering. Office: U Wis 1513 University Ave Madison WI 53706

DEVRIES, WILLIAM CASTLE, surgeon, educator; b. Bklyn., Dec. 19, 1943; s. Hendrik and Cathryn Lucille (Castle) DeV.; m. Ane Karen Olsen, June 12, 1965; children: Jon, Adrie, Kathryn, Andrew, Janna, William, Diana. B.S., U. Utah, 1966, M.D., 1970. Intern Duke U. Med. Center, 1970-71, resident in cardiovascular and thoracic surgery, 1971-79; formerly asst. prof. surgery U. Utah, chmn. div. cardiovascular and thoracic surgery, chief thoracic surgery Salt Lake VA Hosp.; now with Humana Hosp. Audubon, Louisville. Recipient Wintrobe award, 1970. Mem. A.C.S., Utah Med. Assn., AMA, Intermountain Thoracic Soc., Salt Lake Surg. Soc., Utah Heart Assn., Assn. VA Surgeons, Utah Lung Assn., Alpha Omega Alpha. Mormon. Subspecialties: Artificial organs and prostheses; Cardiac surgery. Office: Humana Hosp Audubon 1 Audubon Plaza Dr Louisville KY 40217

DEWAR, MICHAEL JAMES STEUART, chemistry educator; b. Ahmednagar, India, Sept. 24, 1918; came to U.S., 1959, naturalized, 1980; s. Francis and Nan (Keith) D.; m. Mary Williamson, June 3, 1944; children: Robert Berriedale Keith, Charles Edward Steuart. B.A., Oxford (Eng.) U., 1940, D.Phil., 1942, M.A., 1943. Imperial Chem. Industries fellow Oxford U., 1945; phys. chemist Courtaulds Ltd., 1945-51; prof. chemistry, head dept. Queen Mary Coll., U. London, Eng., 1941-59; prof. chemistry U. Chgo., 1959-63; Robert A. Welch prof. chemistry U. Tex., 1963—; Reilly lectr. U. Notre Dame, 1951; Tilden lectr. Chem. Soc. London, 1954; vis. prof. Yale U., 1957; Falk-Plaut lectr. Columbia U., 1963; William Pyle Phillips visitor Haverford Coll., 1964, 70; Arthur D. Little vis. prof. MIT, 1966; Marchon vis. lectr. U. Newcastle (Eng.), 1966; Glidden Co. lectr. Kent State U., 1967; Gnehm lectr. Eldg. Technische Hochschule, Zurich, Switzerland, 1968; Barton lectr. U. Okla., 1969; Disting. vis. lectr. Yeshiva U., 1970; Kahlbaum lectr. U. Basel, Switzerland, 1970; Benjamin Rush lectr. U. Pa., 1971; Kharasch vis. prof. U. Chgo., 1971; Phi Lambda Upsilon lectr. Johns Hopkins U., 1972; Firth vis. prof. U. Sheffield, 1972; Foster lectr. SUNY-Buffalo, 1973; Five Colls. lectr., Mass., 1973; Sprague lectr. U. Wis., 1974; Disting. Bicentennial prof. U. Utah, 1976; Bircher lectr. Vanderbilt U., 1976; Pahlavi lectr., Iran, 1977; Michael Faraday lectr. U. No. Ill., 1977; Priestley lectr. Pa. State U., 1980; cons. to industry. Author: Electronic Theory of Organic Chemistry, 1949, Hyperconjugation, 1962, Introduction to Modern Organic Chemistry, 1965, Computer Compilation of Molecular Weights and Percentage Compositions of Organic Compounds, 1969, The Molecular Orbital Theory of Organic Chemistry, 1969, The PMO Theory of Organic Chemistry, 1975; also articles. Recipient Harrison Howe award Am. Chem. Soc., 1961, S.W. regional award, 1978; Robert Robinson Lecture, Chem. Soc., 1974; G.W. Wheland Meml. medal U. Chgo., 1976; Evans award Ohio State U., 1977; hon. fellow Balliol Coll., 1974. Fellow Royal Soc. (Davy medal 1982), Am. Acad. Arts and Scis., Chem. Soc. London; mem. Am. Chem. Soc. (Norris award in phys. organic chemistry), Nat. Acad. Sci., Sigma Xi. Home: 6808 Mesa Dr Austin TX 78731 Office: Dept Chemistry U Tex Austin TX 78712

DEWART, DOROTHY BOARDMAN, clinical psychologist, consultant, researcher; b. Boston, Aug. 19, 1948; d. Thomas Dennie and Dorothy (Potter) Boardman. B.A. in Psychology and Sociology, Salem Coll., 1972; M.A. in Clin. Psychology, Xavier U., 1976; postgrad., U. Cin., 1975-77; Ph.D. in Clin. Psychology, Temple U., 1981. Research asst. Cin. Ctr. Devel. Disorders, 1974-75, psychology trainee, 1975, U. Cin., 1975-76, Rollman' Psychiat. Inst., Cin., 1975-76; psychologist Cen. Psychiat. Clinic, Cin., 1976-77; asst. dir. Psychol. Services, Clermont Gen. and Tech. Coll., U. Cin., 1976-77; supr. Psychol. Services Ctr., Temple U., 1978, clin. asst., 1980, psychology intern, 1980-81, staff psychologist, dept. psychiat. and chronic pain clinic, 1981-82; cons. maxillo-facial pain clinic, 1981—, clin. instr. dept. psychiatry, 1981—. Profl. com. Wissahickon Hospice, Chestnut Hill, Pa. Research Incentive Fund grantee Temple U. Hosp., 1981—; Pew Meml Trust grantee, 1981—; recipient NIMH assistantship, 1977-78. Mem. Am. Psychol. Assn., Phila. Soc. Clin. Psychologists, Am. Pain Soc. Current Work: Psychotherapy with patients who present significant physical illness; research in effects of tryptophan on chronic pain; supervise and teach psychiatry residents, psychology interns, consultant to physicians. Subspecialties: Diagnosis and control of chronic pain; Clinical psychology. Home: 748 St George's Rd Philadelphia PA 19119

DEWERD, LARRY A., med. physicist, educator; b. Milw., July 18, 1941; s. Anthony L. and Dorothy M. (Heling) DeW.; m. Vada M. Anderson, Sept. 14, 1963; children: Scott, Mark, Eric. B.S., U. Wis.-Milw., 1963, M.S., 1965; Ph.D., U. Wis.-Madison, 1970. Research assoc. U. Wash., Seattle, 1970-72, research asst. prof. mining, metall. and ceramic engring., 1972-75; vis. asst. prof. U. Wis.-Madison, 1975-76, clin. asst. prof. radiology-med. physics, 1976-79, clin. assoc. prof., 1979—; dir. U. Wis.-Madison (Midwest Ctr. for Radiol. Physics), 1981—. Contbr. articles to profl. jours. Mem. Am. Assn. Physicists in Medicine, Am. Phys. Soc., Health Physics Soc., Soc. Photographic-Instrumentation Engrs. Patentee in field. Current Work: Diagnostic and therapeutic medical physics. Subspecialties: Medical physics; Radiology. Home: 13 Pilgrim Circle Madison WI 53711 Office: UNIV-AVE Med Physics U Wis 1570 MSC/1300 Madison WI 53706

DE WIT, MICHIEL, physicist; b. Amsterdam, Netherlands, June 6, 1933; came to U.S., 1951, naturalized, 1968; s. Louis Willem and Marianne (Carels) DeW.; m. Catharine C. Courtney, Dec. 27, 1957; children: Kirsten, Deirdre, Seth, Damiane. B.S., Ohio U., 1954; Ph.D., Yale U., 1960. Mem. tech. staff Tex. Instruments Inc., Dallas, 1959-79, sr. mem. tech. staff, 1979—; occasional lectr. Contbr. articles to profl. publs. Mem. Am. Phys. Soc., Optical Soc. Am., IEEE, AAAS. Patentee in field. Current Work: Analog MOS integrated circuit design; research and development work. Subspecialties: Integrated circuits; Atomic and molecular physics. Office: MS 369 PO Box 225621 Dallas TX 75265

DE WOLF, DAVID ALTER, elec. engr., educator; b. Dordrecht, Netherlands, July 23, 1934; came to U.S., 1962, naturalized, 1979; s. Marinus and Esfira (Frigind) de W.; m. Hilfman, Aug. 22, 1958 (div. Apr. 1964); children: Naomi, Jiska; m. Peggy L. Lumpkin, May 9, 1975. B.Sc., U. Amsterdam, 1955, Doctorandus in Theoretical Physics, 1959; D.Tech., U. Eindhoven, Netherlands, 1968. Research scientist Nuclear Def. Lab., Edgewood Arsenal, Md., 1962; mem. tech. staff David Sarnoff Research Center, RCA Labs., Princeton, N.J., 1962-82; prof. elec. engring. Va. Poly. Inst. and State U., Blacksburg, 1982—. Asso. editor: Jour. Optical Soc. Am, 1969-81; author articles. Served to 1st lt. Royal Dutch Army, 1960-61. Recipient Achievement award RCA Labs., 1976. Mem. IEEE, Optical Soc. Am., Netherlands Phys. Soc., Internat. Union Radio Sci. (mem. commns. B, C and F of U.S. nat. com.), AAAS, Sigma Xi. Patentee in field. Current Work: Electromagnetic wave propagation, optics, diffraction, electron optics, scattering of waves. Subspecialties: Electrical engineering; Theoretical physics. Home: 200 Craig Dr Blacksburg VA 24060 Office: Dept Elec Engring Va Poly Inst and State U Blacksburg VA 24061

DEWYS, WILLIAM DALE, physician, cancer researcher; b. Zeeland, Mich., Sept. 14, 1939; s. Peter and Jennie (Morslnk) DeW.; m. Alice Grace Schut, June 10, 1961; children: Alisa Kay, William Dale, Pamela Jane. B.S., Calvin Coll., Grand Rapids, Mich., 1960; M.D. cum laude, U. Mich., 1964. Diplomate: Am. Bd. Internal Medicine; Am. Bd. Med. Oncology. Asst. prof. internal medicine U. Rochester, 1971-73; assoc. prof. internal medicine Northwestern U., Chgo., 1973-78, prof., 1978-79, chief sect. med. oncology, 1973-79; head nutrition sect. clin. investigations br. Nat. Cancer Inst., Bethesda, Md., 1979-82, chief clin. investigations br., 1980-82, assoc. dir. prevention program, 1982—. Contbr. articles to med. jours. Served to sr. surgeon USPHS, 1966-68. Fellow ACP; mem. Am. Assn. Cancer Research, Am. Soc. Clin. Oncology, Soc. Clin. Trials, Alpha Omega Alpha, Phi Kappa Phi. Current Work: Clinical trials in cancer prevention; physiologic studies of cancer cachexia; clinical trials of supportive care in cancer. Subspecialties: Cancer research (medicine); Nutrition (medicine). Home: 6830 Hillmead Rd Bethesda MD 20817 Office: 8300 Colesville Rd Bethesda MD 20205

DEY, ARABINDA NARAYAN, electrochemist, inventor; b. Bangladesh, Oct. 3, 1937; came to U.S., 1962, naturalized, 1969; s. Amarendra Narayan and Anima (Biswas) D.; m. Adrienne Steinacker, May 9, 1963; 1 dau., Monica. B.Sc., Calcutta U. (India), 1956, Ph.D., 1966; M.Sc., Patna U. (India), 1959. Research fellow U. Pa., Phila., 1962-64; research chemist Hooker Chem., Niagara Falls, N.Y., 1964-66; staff scientist Mallory Co., Burlington, Mass., 1966-68, research supr., 1968-70; tech. dir. Duracell Inc., Burlington, 1980—. Contbr. articles to profl. jours. Patentee in field. Fullbright scholar India, 1962. Mem. Am. Chem. Soc., Electrochem. Soc. (chmn. Boston sect. 1974-76), Indian Assn. Cultivation Sci. (life). Democrat. Hindu. Current work: Research and development on high energy density lithium batteries for advanced power sources and for energy storage. Home: 215 Fisher St Needham MA 02192 Office: Duracell Inc 37 A St Needham MA 02194

DEYOUNG, DAVID SPENCER, astrophysicist, observatory director; b. Colorado Springs, Colo., Nov. 29, 1940. B.A. magna cum laude, U. Colo., 1962; Ph.D., Cornell U., 1967. Sci. staff mem. Los Alamos Nat. Lab., 1967-69; astronomer Nat. Radio Astronomy Obs., Charlottesville, Va., 1969-80; astronomer Kitt Peak Nat. Obs., Tucson, 1980—, assoc. dir., 1982—; mem. adv. bd. Aspen Ctr. Physics; chmn. radio astronomy experiment selection panel NASA Deep Space Network. Contbr. articles in field to profl. jours. Mem. Am. Phys. Soc., Am. Astron. Soc., Internat. Astron. Union., Internat. Union Radio Sci. Current Work: Theoretical astrophysics. Subspecialty: Theoretical astrophysics. Office: PO Box 26732 Tucson AZ 85726

DHADESUGOOR, VAMAN RAO, computer science, electrical engineering educator; b. Bellary, India, Sept. 4, 1948; came to U.S., 1974; s. Sreenivasa Rao and Sethamma D.; m. Janaki V., June 16, 1976; children—Sreesha, Smitha. B.E.E., Regional Engring. Coll., Warangal, India, 1970, M.Tech. in Electronic Instrumentation, 1972; M.S. in Elec. Engring., CCNY, 1975; Ph.D. in Elec. Engring., CUNY, 1979. Systems engr. Space Applications Ctr., Ahmedabad, India, 1972-74; research assoc. CCNY, 1974-79; mem. tech. staff Network Analysis York Corp., Vienna, Va., 1979-81, Comsat Labs., Clarksburg, Md., 1981-84; assoc. prof. computer sci. and elec. engring. Stevens Inst. Tech., Hoboken, N.J., 1984—; cons. Timeplex Corp., Rochelle Park, N.J., 1984—, VMX Corp., Dallas, 1984—. Contbr. articles to engring. jours. Mem. IEEE (sr. mem.; program chmn. Info. Theory chpt. Washington 1982-84, mem. communications theory com. 1982—), Eta Kappa Nu, Tau Beta Pi. Current work: Computer networks; local area networks and distributed processing; integrated voice and data systems; signal processing and signal identification; systems applications; teleconferencing, remote control processing (process control). Subspecialty: Computer engineering. Home: 5678 Pebble Dr Frederick MD 21701 Office: Dept Computer Sci Stevens Inst Tech Castlepoint Sta Hoboken NJ 07030

DHALIWAL, RANJIT SINGH, mathematician, educator; b. Bilaspur, India, June 21, 1930; s. Bharpur Singh and Bachan Kaur (Grewal) D.; m. Gurdev Kaur, July 1, 1958; 1 son, Gurminder Singh. M.A., Punjab U., 1955; Ph.D., Indian Inst. Tech., Kharagpur, 1960. Lectr. Indian Inst. Tech., New Delhi, 1961-63, asst. prof., 1963-66; asso.prof. U. Calgary, Alta., Can., 1966-71, prof. math., 1971—; visitor Imperial Coll. Sci. and Tech., London, 1964-65; vis. prof. City U. London, 1971-72. Author book; contbr. articles to profl. jours. Mem. Am. Math. Soc., Soc. Indsl. and Applied Math., Can. Math. Congress, London Math. Soc. Current Work: Solid mechanics; elasticity,thermoelasticity, and fracture mechanics. Subspecialty: Applied mathematics. Home: 44 Patterson Dr Calgary AB Canada Office: Dept Math U Calgary Calgary AB Canada

DHAR, AMIYA KANTI, neurology educator, laboratory director; b. Calcutta, India, Jan. 12, 1939; came to U.S., 1969; s. Upendra Chandra and Chinmoyee (Ghosh) D.; m. Bani Mazumdar, June 5, 1965; children—Panchali, Aninda. B.Sc. with honors, Presidency Coll., Calcutta, 1959; M.Sc., U. Calcutta, 1961, D.Sc., 1969. Research fellow U. N.M., Albuquerque, 1969-70; research assoc. U. Tex. Med. Br., Galveston, 1970-74, Cornell Med. Coll., N.Y.C., 1974-80, assoc. lab. dir. Epilepsy Research Lab., 1981—, research asst. prof. neurology, 1980—; pres., lab. dir. Eastern Lab. Ltd., N.Y.C., 1983—. Contbr. articles to profl. jours. Mem. Am. Chem. Soc., N.Y. Acad. Sci. Current work: Toxicology, drug metabolism, therapeutic drug monitoring, pharmacology, detection and quantitation of drugs of abuse. Subspecialties: Toxicology (agriculture); Clinical chemistry. Office: Cornell Univ Med Coll 411 E 69th St New York NY 10021

DHARA, SUDHIR CHANDRA, chemist, technical administrator; b. Calcutta, India, Sept. 20, 1939; came to U.S., 1972; s. Satyeswar and Susanbala (Sahu) D.; m. Chhaya Guha, Mar. 3, 1974. B.S. with honors, Calcutta U., 1961, M.S., 1963; Ph.D., Leningrad U., USSR, 1968; postgrad. London U., 1970-73; cert. Am. Mgmt. Assn., 1976. Sci. officer Bhaba Atomic Research Ctr., Bombay, India, 1969-70; mgr. refining lab. Engelhard Corp., Newark, 1973-78, reserch assoc., Menlo Park, N.J., 1979-80; ops. dir. Noble Metals, New Orleans, 1980-81; tech. mgr. PGP Industries, Santa Fe Springs, Calif., 1981-82, tech. dir., 1982—. Contbr. articles to profl. jours. Mem. Am. Chem. Soc., AIME (Metallurgical Soc.), Internat. Precious Metal Inst. Democrat. Current work: The reclamation, extraction, refining of all noble metals, various exotic and base metals from different industrial, mining, domestic materials; manufacturing and fabricating of chemicals and catalysts. Subspecialties: Materials processing; Inorganic chemistry. Home: 2100 Dalewood Ave Fullerton CA 92633 Office: PGP Industries Inc 13429 Alondra Blvd Santa Fe Springs CA 90670

DHARAMSI, AMIN NURDIN, engineering educator; researcher; b. Jan. 2, 1951; s. Nurdin Dharamsi and Kulsum (Walji) Rawji; m. Yasmin Shamshudin Lakhani, Apr. 28, 1979; children—Aisha. B.S. in Elec. Engring., U. Nairobi, 1973; M.S. in Elec. Engring., U. Alta., 1977, Ph.D., 1981. Instr. Old Dominion U., Norfolk, Va., 1980-81, asst. prof., 1981—; dir. Quantum Electronics Research Lab. Old Dominion U. Contbr. articles to profl. jours. NSF grantee; 1983-84; summer research fellow Old Dominion U., 1981. Mem. IEEE, Am. Inst. Physics. Current work: Visible, ultraviolet laser development, pumping mechanisms, spectroscopy, kinetics of molecules and molecular complexes. Subspecialties: Excimers; Laser spectroscopy. Office: Dept Elec Engring Old Dominion U Norfolk VA 23508

DHONG, SANG HOO, electrical engineer, researcher; b. Jin-Ju, Kyung sang namdo, Rep. of Korea, Mar. 13, 1952; came to U.S. 1976; s. Zi Young and Ok Ju (Park) D.; m. Mi Kyung Bae, Dec. 30, 1983. B.S.E.E. summa cum laude, Korea U., Seoul, Republic of Korea, 1974; M.S.E.E., U. Calif.-Berkeley, 1980, Ph.D. E.E., 1983. Mem. research staff IBM Watson Research Ctr., Yorktown Heights, N.Y., 1983—. Served to 1st lt. Army, 1974-76, Dae Jon, Republic of Korea. Mem. IEEE, Electrochemical Soc. Current work: Plasma, reactive-ion etch of silicon related materials such as silicon, silicon oxide, and silicon nitride. Subspecialties: Semiconductors; Superconductors. Home: 244 West St #6B Mount Kisco NY 10549 Office: IBM Watson Research Ctr PO Box 218 Yorktown Heights NY 10598

DIADDARIO, LEONARD LAWRENCE, JR., chemist; b. Garfield Heights, Ohio, Jan. 24, 1951; s. Leonard Lawrence and Frances M. (Szeremet) D.; m. Sandra Mendolera, Jan. 5, 1974; children—Jennifer Ann, Leonard Lawrence, III. B.S., John Carroll U., 1973; M.S., Wayne State U., 1977, Ph.D., 1979. Research scientist Purdue U., West Lafayette, Ind., 1979-82; sr. research chemist Va. Chems., Inc., Portsmouth, 1982-84, project leader, 1984—. Contbr. articles to profl. jours. Mem. Am. Chem. Soc., Sigma Xi, Phi Lambda Upsilon (sec. Alpha Psi chpt. 1976-78). Roman Catholic. Current work: Solid-state reaction mechanisms; characterization of solid-state reactions by thermal analysis; thermal hazards evaluation; electrochemistry. Subspecialties: Kinetics; X-ray crystallography. Home: 5732 Brookmere Ln Portsmouth VA 23703 Office: Va Chems Inc 3340 W Norfolk Rd Portsmouth VA 23703

DIAMANDOPOULOS, GEORGE THEODORE, physician, researcher; b. Herakleion, Crete, Greece, Nov. 21, 1929; came to U.S., 1948, naturalized, 1964; s. Theodore George and Rita Theodore (Mouzenidis) D. B.A., Lawrence Coll., Appleton, Wis., 1951; M.D., U. Vt., Burlington, 1955; A.M. (hon.), Harvard U., 1975. Diplomate: Am. Bd. Pathology. Intern New Eng. Ctr. Hosp., Boston, 1955-56, resident in medicine, 1956-57; resident in pathology Peter Bent Brigham Hosp., Boston, 1957-59, Children's Hosp., Boston, 1959, Boston Lying-In Hosp., 1960; mem. faculty Harvard U. Med. Sch., 1965—, prof. pathology, 1980—. Mem. AAAS, Am. Assn. Pathologists, Soc. Exptl.

Biology and Medicine, Am. Assn. Acad. Pathologists, Am. Assn. Cancer Research, Am. Soc. Exptl. Pathology, Alpha Omeha Alpha. Current Work: etiopathology of human leukemia. Subspecialties: Pathology (medicine); Cancer research (medicine).

DIAMOND, HERBERT, research chemist, environmental researcher; b. Chgo., July 28, 1925; s. Max H. and Jeanne (Winchester) D.; m. Ruth S. Shoskey, Dec. 19, 1948; 1 child, Linda. B.S., U. Chgo., 1948. Chemist Argonne Nat. Lab., Ill., 1949—. Contbr. articles to profl. jours. Dir. Argonne Credit Union, Ill., 1970, Old-Town NW Neighborhood Assn., Western Springs, Ill., 19—. Served to s/sgt. U.S. Army, 1943-46, ETO. Mem. Am. Chem. Soc., Am. Phys. Soc. Current work: Development of separations chemistry pertinent to nuclear waste management; determination of species and structures of metal-organic solutes in organic solutions. Subspecialties: Inorganic chemistry; Nuclear chemistry. Home: 3837 Forest Ave Western Springs IL 60558 Office: Argonne Nat Lab 200 M119 Argonne IL 60439

DIAMOND, JARED MASON, biologist; b. Boston, Sept. 10, 1937; s. Louis K. and Flora K. D. B.A., Harvard U., 1958; Ph.D., Cambridge (Eng.) U., 1961. Jr. fellow Soc. Fellows, Harvard U., 1962-65; asso. in biophysics (Med. Sch.), 1965-66; asso. prof. physiology U. Calif. Med. Center, Los Angeles, 1966-68, prof., 1968—; cons. in conservation and nat. park planning govts., Papua New Guinea, Solomon Islands, Indonesia. Author: Avifauna of the Eastern Highlands of New Guinea, 1972, Ecology and Evolution of Communities, 1975. Recipient Burr medal Nat. Geog. Soc., 1979, Bowditch prize Am. Physiol. Soc., 1976, Disting. Achievement award Am. Gastroent. Assn., 1975; MacArthur Found. fellow, 1985. Fellow Am. Acad. Arts and Scis.; mem. Nat. Acad. Scis. Research in membrane physiology, ecology. Subspecialties: Ecology (environmental science); Physiology (biology). Office: Physiology Dept UCLA Med Center Los Angeles CA 90024

DIANA, JOHN NICHOLAS, physiologist, educator; b. Lake Placid, N.Y., Dec. 19, 1930; s. Alphose Walton and Dolores (Mirto) K.; m. Anita Louise Harris, May 8, 1966; children—Gina Sue, Lisa Ann, John Nicholas. B.A., Norwich U., 1952; M.A., U. Louisville, 1961, Ph.D., 1965. Asst. prof. Coll. Medicine Mich. State U., East Lansing, 1966-68; assoc. prof. Coll. Medicine U. Iowa, Iowa City, 1968-74, prof., 1974-78; prof., chmn. dept. medicine La. State U., Shreveport, 1978-85; dir. Cardiovascular Research Ctr., U. Ky. Coll. Medicine, 1985—. Patentee in field. Mem. editorial bd. profl. jours. Grantee NIH, Nat. Heart, Lung and Blood Inst., 1966-87. Mem. Microcirculatory Soc. (pres. 1977-78), Am. Physiol. Soc. (council circulation), Am. Heart Assn., Iowa Heart Assn. (com. review 1974-78), La. Heart Assn. (review com. 1978—), Am. Fedn. Clin. Research, Sigma Xi. Current work: Studies on regulation of capillary permeability; microvascular circulatory dynamics; characterization of pressures; flows and trancapillary exchange in normal and pathophysiologic states. Subspecialties: Physiology (medicine); Cardiology. Home: 3656 Eleuthera Ct Lexington KY 40509 Office: T&H Research Inst Cooper and Alumni Drives Lexington KY 40536

DIAZ, JULIO CESAR, computer science educator; b. Trujillo, Valle, Colombia, Dec. 3, 1948; came to U.S., 1970; s. Luis Eduardo and Josefina (Velasco) D.; m. Pamela Sue Jenkins, Aug. 19, 1978; children—Diana Cristina, Adriana Carolina. Licenciado Matematicas U. de Los Andes, Bogota, Colombia, 1970; M.A., Rice U., 1974, Ph.D., 1974. Prof. U. Los Andes, Bogota, 1970; postdoctoral fellow U. Ky., Lexington, 1974-75, asst. prof., 1975-81; vis. asst. prof. U. Toronto, Can., 1978-79; sr. research math. Mobil Research and Devel., Dallas, 1981-84; assoc. prof. U. Okla., Norman, 1984—. Contbr. articles to profl. jours. U. Los Andes scholar, 1966; fellow Rice U., 1970-74, U. Ky., 1976. Mem. Soc. Industl. Applied Math., Soc. Petroleum Engring., Soc. Exploration Geophysicists, Soc. Colombiana de Matematicas. Current work: Parallel processing for large scale scientific computing applications; numerical techniques for non linear partial differential equations. Subspecialties: Numerical analysis (computer science); Mathematical software. Office: U Okla EECS 202 W Boyd Room 219 Norman OK 73019

DIBIANCA, FRANK ANTHONY, physicist, research scientist; b. Atlantic City, N.J., Apr. 8, 1940; s. Vincent Joseph and Sarina Cardamone DiB.; m. Kay Carpenter, Mar. 14, 1970; 1 son, Arthur Nicholas. Ph.D. in Physics, Carnegie-Mellon U., 1970. Research assoc. dept. physics Case Western Res. U., 1970-73; research assoc. dept. physics FermiLab, Batavia, Ill., 1973-76; sr. physicist Gen. Electric Med. Systems, Milw, 1976-81; assoc. prof. radiology and biomedical engring. U. N.C., Chapel Hill, 1981—, dir. biomed. microelectronics program, 1981—. Contbr. articles in field to profl. jours. Served with USNR, 1962-64. Recipient Gen. Electric Co. award for devel. of digital radiography instrument, 1979. Mem. Am. Assn. Physicists in Medicine, Internat. Soc. Optical Engring., Internat. Soc. Hybrid Microelectronics. Current Work: Medical imaging instrumentation research, biomedical microelectronics research. Subspecialties: Biomedical engineering; Imaging technology. Office: University of North Carolina 144 Mac Nider Hall Chapel Hill NC 27514

DIBNER, MARK DOUGLAS, neurobiologist, strategic planner; b. N.Y.C., Nov. 7, 1951; s. David Robert and Dorothy Joyce (Siegel) D. B.A., U. Pa., 1973; Ph.D., Cornell U., 1977; M.B.A., Widener U., 1985. Postdoctoral fellow Med. Sch., U. Colo., Denver, 1977-79; research fellow, instr. U. Calif., San Diego, 1979-80; lectr. psychology Nat. U., San Diego, 1980; research neurobiologist E.I. DuPont Exptl. Sta., Wilmington, Del., Lab., Glenolden, Pa., 1980—. Mem. Am. Soc. Pharmacology and Exptl. Therapeutics, Soc. for Neurosci., AAAS. Current Work: Researcher in neuropharmacology and cell biology; strategic planner in biotechnology. Subspecialties: Neuropharmacology; Neurobiology. Office: E I DuPont Exptl Sta E 400 Wilmington DE 19898

DICELLO, JOHN FRANCIS, JR., physicist, educator; b. Bradford, Pa., Dec. 18, 1938; s. John Francis and Nicolina Carmille (Costello) D.; m. Shirley Ann Rodgers, Aug. 25, 1962; children—John Francis III, Paul T. B.S., St. Bonaventure U., 1960; M.S., U. Pitts., 1962; Ph.D., Tex. A&M U., 1968. Instr. St. Bonaventure U., 1962-63; AEC-Assoc. Western Univs. grad fellow Los Alamos Sci. Lab., 1965-67, staff scientist, 1973-84; research assoc. Columbia U., N.Y.C., 1967-73; prof. physics Clarkson U., Potsdam, N.Y., 1982—. Contbr. articles to profl. jours. Bd. dirs. N.Mex. div. Am. Cancer Soc., 1978-82. Recipient Young Scientist travel award Am. Assn. Physicists in Medicine, 1972. Mem. Am. Assn. Physicists in Medicine, Radiation Research Soc., Am. Phys. Soc. Roman Catholic. Current Work: Biophysics, nuclear physics, electronics. Subspecialties: Radiation biology; Cancer research (medicine). Office: Dept Physics Clarkson Coll Potsdam NY 13676

DICK, CHARLES EDWARD, physicist; b. Ft. Wayne, Ind., Apr. 24, 1937; s. Melvin L. and Virginia Viola (Laemmle) D.; m. Vivian Claire Dick, Aug. 16, 1958; children: Timothy M., Victoria M. B.S., Ill. Benedictine Coll., Lisle, Ill., 1958; Ph.D., U. Notre Dame, 1963. Physicist Nat. Bur. Standards, Washington, 1962—. Contbr. articles to profl. jours. Mem. Am. Phys. Soc., AAAS, Soc. Photo-Optical Instrumentation Engrs., Sigma Xi. Democrat. Roman Catholic. Current Work: Applications of digital techniques to diagnostic imaging, interaction of electrons and photons with matter. Subspecialties: Atomic and molecular physics; Imaging technology. Home: 14000 Manorvale Rd Rockville MD 20853 Office: Nat Bur Standards C 216 Bldg 245 Gaithersburg MD 20899

DICK, HENRY JONATHAN BIDDLE, marine geologist; b. Portland, Oreg., Aug. 30, 1946; s. Hugh Lenox Hodge and Helene (Biddle) D. B.A., U. Pa., 1969; M.Phil., Yale U., 1971, Ph.D., 1976. Postdoctoral investigator Woods Hole (Mass.) Oceanographic Instn., 1975-76, asst. scientist, 1976-80, assoc. scientist, 1980—. Editor: Magma Genesis, 1977; contbr. articles to profl. jours. Pres. Pinecrest Beach Neighborhood Assn., Falmouth, Mass., 1980—; chmn. bd. dirs. Citizens for Protection of Waquoit Bay, Falmouth, 1981—; bd. dirs. Big Bros./Big Sisters of Cape Cod. Mem. Am. Geophys. Union, Geol. Soc. Am. Republican. Episcopalian. Current Work: Igneous petrology of the abyssal upper mantle, geology of ophiolites, petrology and tectonics of the ocean crust. Subspecialties: Petrology; Sea floor spreading. Office: Woods Hole Oceanographic Instn Woods Hole MA 02543

DICK, ROBERT JAMES, electrical engineer; b. Quincy, Mass., Nov. 1, 1943; s. James Fred and Elizabeth Helen (Macy) D.; m. Barbara Gale Cornelius, May 22, 1976; 1 son, Robert James. B.S. in Elec. Engring., MIT, 1964; M.S., Cornell U., 1967, Ph.D., 1973. Teaching asst. Cornell U., Ithaca, N.Y., 1964-71, research assoc., 1973-75; sr. staff mem. P.A.R. Tech., Utica, N.Y., 1976-83; sr. mem. tech. staff RCA, Somerville, N.J., 1983—. Developer automatic single sideband tuner. Mem. IEEE. Republican. Lodges: Mega, Prometheus (membership officer 1983—). Current work: Digital signal processing; electronic communications; error control coding. Subspecialties: Electronics; Systems engineering. Home: 13 Speer St Somerville NJ 08876 Office: RCA Mail Zone 46 Route 202 Somerville NJ 08876

DICK, WILLIAM ALLEN, composite materials engr.; b. Belleville, Ill., June 7, 1956; s. William Allen and Ruth Anne (Racine) D.; m. Kim Mary Smith, Aug. 11, 1978. B.M.E., U. Del., 1979. Instnl. research and fin. planning U. Del., 1975-79, research assoc. I, 1979-80, research assoc. II, 1980-81; asst. dir. (Ctr. for Composite Materials), 1981-82, research assoc. III, asst. dir. Ctr., 1982—; cons.; guest lectr. Contbr. articles to tech. jours. Recipient K. C. Citizenship award, 1974. Mem. ASME, ASTM. Republican. Christian Scientist. Current Work: Composite materials; processing science; damage and repair mechanisms in composite structures; mechanical behavior of materials; composites testing and design. Subspecialties: Composite materials; Theoretical and applied mechanics. Home: 9 Elan Hall Newark DE 19711 Office: 201 Spencer Lab Newark DE 19711

DICKEL, HELENE RAMSEVER, astronomer, educator; b. Cambridge, Mass., Mar. 19, 1938; d. Frank Wells and Linda Chapin (Marcus) Ramseyer; m. John Rush Dickel, June 17, 1961; children—Cynthia, Rebecca. A.B. magna cum laude, Mt. Holyoke Coll., 1959; M.A. in Astronomy, U. Mich., 1961, Ph.D., 1964. Research assoc. astronomy U. Ill., Urbana, 1965-70, 71-77, research assoc. prof., 1977—, vis. assoc. prof., 1983—; vis. fellow div. radiophysics Commonwealth Sci. Indsl. Research Ogn., Epping, New South Wales, Australia, 1970-71; vis. astronomer Sterrewacht te Leiden, The Netherlands, 1977-79; cons. Aerospace Corp., Los Angeles, 1975—, Los Alamos Nat. Lab., 1983—; lectr. in field. Contbr. articles to profl. jours. Mt. Holyoke scholar, 1959-66; Rackham fellow U. Mich., Ann Arbor, 1963-64; grantee NSF, 1972-80, NATO, 1980-83, Am. Astronomical Soc., 1982-85. Mem. Am. Astronomical Soc., Astronomical Soc. Pacific, Internat. Sci. Radio Union (commn.), Assn. Women Sci., Internat. Astronomical Union (chmn. commn. 1979—), Mt. Holyoke Alumni Assn., Sierra Club, Sigma Xi, Phi Beta Kappa. Current work: Investigation of physical conditions and evolution of dense cores of molecular clouds with active star formation by high resolution; aperture synthesis molecular spectroscopy analyzed by employing results of computer computations of the radioactive transfer through such regions. Subspecialties: Radio and microwave astronomy; Optical astronomy. Office: U Ill Dept Astronomy 1011 W Springfield Ave Urbana IL 6108-3000

DICKENS, ELMER DOUGLAS, JR., research physicist; b. Charleston, W.Va., Dec. 26, 1942; s. Elmer D. and Gennevie (Duff) D.; m. Helen Marie Lively, Aug. 3, 1962; children: Tony, Mark. B.S., Morris Harvey Coll., Charleston, 1965; M.S., W.Va. U., 1967, Ph.D., 1970. Research physicist B.F.Goodrich Research and Devel. Center, Brecksville, Ohio, 1970-72, sr. research physicist, 1972-74, group leader new products, 1974-77, sect. leader new ventures, 1977-78, mgr. new ventures, 1978-81, mgr. corp. research, 1981-82, research fellow, 1983—. NASA fellow, 1967-70. Mem. Am. Phys. Soc., Combustion Inst., AIAA, Sigma Xi, Sigma Pi Sigma. Patentee in field. Current Work: Polymer combustion, fire testing, fire modeling, low temperature plasmas, applied magnetism, magnetic materials, mathematical modeling. artificial intelligence. Subspecialties: Polymer physics; Electronic materials. Home: 4160 Maple Dr Richfield OH 44286 Office: BF Goodrich Research and Devel Center 9921 Brecksville Rd Brecksville OH 44141

DICKENS, JUSTIN KIRK, physicist, nuclear engineer; b. Syracuse, N.Y., Nov. 2, 1931; s. Milton Clifford and Jennette Martin (Holmes) D.; m. Marcay Cosette Jordan, Dec. 21, 1957; children: Alan Russell, Leonard Raymond, Steven Kenneth, Michael Loren. A.B., U. So. Calif., 1955, Ph.D. in Physics, 1962; M.S., U. Chgo., 1956. Mem. research staff Oak Ridge Nat. Lab., 1962—. Treas. Oak Ridge High Sch. PTA, 1981-86; bd. dirs. Oak Ridge Community Playhouse, 1975-76, 85-86. Served with U.S. Army, 1950-52. Mem. Am. Phys. Soc., Am. Nuclear Soc., Sigma Xi. Current Work: Experimental research; nuclear interaction; safety of nuclear reactors; nuclear fission; computer control of nuclear experiments; nuclear damage in fusion energy; man-to-machine interactions. Subspecialties: Nuclear physics; Nuclear fission. Office: Oak Ridge Nat Lab PO Box X Oak Ridge TN 37831

DICKERMAN, HERBERT W, endocrinologist; b. N.Y.C., Aug. 3, 1928; s. Leopold and Bertha Lee D.; m. Mary Cole, Feb. 3, 1963; children—Leah, Samuel, Sara; 1 dau. from previous marriage, Lisa Akchin. Student U. Wis.-Madison, 1945-47; M.D., SUNY Downstate Med. Ctr., 1952; Ph.D., Johns Hopkins U., 1960. Intern Johns Hopkins Hosp., 1952-53; asst. resident Stanford U. Hosp., San Francisco, 1953-54; instr. medicine Johns Hopkins U., 1960-63, assoc. prof., 1965-75; investigator NIH, Bethesda, Md., 1963-66; asst. dir. clin. research Wadsworth Ctr. Labs. and Research, N.Y. State Dept. Health, Albany, 1975-82, dir. div. clin. sci., 1982—. Contbr. articles to profl. jours. NIH grantee. Mem. Am. Soc. Biol. Chemists, Endocrine Soc. Clubs: No. N.Y. Paddlers, Adirondack Mountain. Current work: Mechanism of action of estrogens including estrogen receptors; DNA interaction and estrogen control of specific protein synthesis. Subspecialties: Biochemistry (biology); Reproductive biology. Home: 450 Loudonville Rd Loudonville NY 12211 Office: Wadsworth Ctr Labs and Research NY State Dept Health Albany NY 12201

DICKERSON, CHARLESWORTH LEE, chemist; b. Fredericksburg, Va., Dec. 14, 1927; s. Laurence Major and Arlene Reed (Eubank) D.; m. Ruth Loraine Bittorf, Sept. 19, 1959; children—Laurence Edward, Bruce Owen Lee. B.S., Coll. William and Mary, 1949; M.S., U. Va., 1951, Ph.D., 1954. Research chemist Am. Enka Corp., N.C., 1954-55; sr. research chemist S.C. Johnson & Son, Inc., Racine, Wis., 1957-67, librarian, 1967-74, product safety coordinator, 1974-80, sr. product safety coordinator, 1980-84, group leader product safety, 1984—. Contbr. numerous articles to profl. jours. Committeeman Boy Scouts Am., Racine, 1978-79; mem. exec. bd. United Fund, Racine, 1973; vestryman St. Michaels Episcopal Ch., Racine, 1984—. Served with U.S. Army, 1955-57. Mem. Am. Chem. Soc., Am. Coll. of Toxicology, AAAS, Internat. Soc. Regulatory Toxicology and Pharmacology, Order of the White Jacket. Current work: Toxcology of pesticides, household cleaners and polishes. Subspecialties: Toxicology (agriculture); Toxicology (medicine). Office: 1525 Howe St Racine WI 53403

DICKERSON, DEAN STUART, research chemist; b. Mount Vernon, Ill., Oct. 25, 1958; s. Paul E. and Mary M. (Flamm) D.; m. Judy Kay Rodgers. B.S. in Chemistry, Eastern Ill. U., 1980. Research chemist ARDL Inc., Mount Vernon, 1980—. Mem. Civil Def. Scuba Rescue Team, Mount Vernon, 1980—; mem. planning comm. City of Mt. Vernon. Mem. Mount Vernon Jaycees (pres. 1984-85, treas. 1982-83). Subspecialty: Analytical chemistry. Home: 2500 Casey Ave Mount Vernon IL 62864Office: ARDL Inc 1801 Forest Mount Vernon IL 62864

DICKERSON, RICHARD EARL, physical biochemist. Prof. Molecular Biology Inst. UCLA. Subspecialties: Biophysical chemistry; Molecular evolution. Office: UCLA Molecular Biology Inst Los Angeles CA 90024

DICKEY, JOAN MARION, physicist, educator; b. Manchester, U.K. B.A., Cambridge U., 1959, Ph.D., 1963. Lectr. U. Ghana, 1963-66; research assoc. asst. physicist, Brookhaven Nat. Lab., Upton, N.Y., 1967-70, assoc. physicist, physicist, 1975-79, cons., 1979—, guest scientist, 1970-75; asst. prof. Queens Coll., NYU, 1970-75, prof., 1979—. Mem. Am. Phys. Soc., Sigma Xi. Current work: Condensed matter, surface physics, nuclear reactor safety and risk assessment. Office: Physics Dept Queens Coll Flushing NY 11367

DICKIE, HELEN AIRD, physician, educator; b. North Freedom, Wis., Feb. 19, 1913; s. Robert Bruce and Anna (Adams) D. B.A., U. Wis., 1935; M.D., 1937. Intern, chest resident Los Angeles County Hosp., 1937-40; resident medicine U. Wis. Med. Sch., 1940-42, staff instr. medicine, 1942-43, asst. prof., 1943-45, assoc. prof., 1945-55, prof. medicine, 1955—; cons. VA Hosp. Master A.C.P.; mem. Central Soc. Clin. Research, Am. Thoracic Soc., Am. Fedn. Clin. Research, Wis. Tb and Respiratory Diseases Assn. (pres. 1968, dir.), Alpha Omega Alpha. Research on farmer's lung, Tb, acute histoplasmosis, spontaneous mediastinal emphysema. Subspecialty: Internal medicine. Home: 501 Clifden Dr Madison WI 53711

DICKINSON, BRADLEY WILLIAM, engineering educator; b. St. Marys, Pa., Apr. 28, 1948; s. William A. and Maxine I Dickinson; m. Colette Merri Aldrich, Mar. 12, 1983; 1 child, James Aldrich. B.S.E., Case Inst. Tech., 1970; M.S.E.E., Stanford U., 1971, Ph.D., 1974. Asst. prof. Princeton U., 1974-80, assoc. prof. dept. elec. engring., 1980-85, prof., 1985—. Contbr. articles to tech. jours. Reader, Rec. for the Blind, Princeton, 1978—. Mem. IEEE (sr. mem.), Soc. for Am. Baseball Research, Sigma Xi, Tau Beta Pi. Current work: Research in signal processing, statistical system theory and info. theory. Subspecialties: Electrical engineering; Systems engineering. Office: Dept of Elec Engring Princeton U Princeton NJ 08544

DICKINSON, LEONARD CHARLES, research chemist, educator; b. Glasgow, Ky., Dec. 12, 1941; s. Joseph Rogers and Inez Marie (Schneider) D.; m. Ellen Marie Spathelf, June 18, 1966; children—Emma Marie, William Charles. A.B., Bellarmine Coll., Louisville, 1963; Ph.D., U. Wis.-Madison, 1968. Postdoctoral fellow, U. Leicester, Eng., 1969, postdoctoral, 1970-72, research assoc., 1972-76; asst. prof. chemistry U. Mass., Amherst, 1976—. Contbr. articles to profl. jours. Pres. Pioneer Valley Early Music Soc., 1983—. Mem. Am. Chem. Soc., Am. Recorder Soc., Sigma Xi. Current work: Metal sites in enzymes; paracrystalline structure of conducting polymers, nuclear magnetic resonance in solid polymers. Subspecialties: Biophysical chemistry; Electron spin resonance. Office: Univ Mass Dept Chemistry Amherst MA 01003

DICKINSON, WINIFRED BALL, biologist, educator, researcher; b. Pitts., Sept. 10, 1933; d. Breese Morse and Winifred (Brown) D. B.S., Pa. Coll. for Women (now Chatham Coll.), 1955; M.S., U. Colo., 1957; Ph.D., U. Pitts., 1971. Lab. asst. Biophysics Research Lab., Eye and Ear Hosp., Pitts., 1952-55, Pa. Coll. for Women, 1951-55; teaching asst. U. Colo., 1955-57; research asst. U. Pitts. Sch. Medicine, 1957-61; adminstrv. asst., head dept. biology St. Paul's Sch., Walla Walla, Wash., 1961-63; instr. Point Park Coll, 1964-65, 78; teaching asst. U. Pitts., 1965-66, teaching fellow, 1965-66, 67-71, adv. to undergrads., 1967-71, instr. univ. community ednl. programs, 1971-72, asst. instr., 1971-72, instr., 1972-73; asst. prof. biology Pa. State U., Beaver Campus, Monaca, 1973-79; assoc. prof. U. Steubenville, 1979—. Contbr. articles, revs. to profl. jours. Am. Cancer Soc. grantee, 1970-71; Pa. State U. grantee, 1974-75, 77-78. Mem. Pa. Acad. Sci., Western Pa. Conservancy, Nature Conservancy, AAAS, Am. Inst. Biol. Sci., Bot. Soc. Am. Republican. Current Work: Development Pteridium aquilinum gametophyte. Subspecialties: Cell and tissue culture; Developmental biology. Home: 83 Union Ave Pittsburgh PA 15205 Office: U Steubenville Franciscan Way Steubenville OH 43952

DICKMAN, ROBERT LAURENCE, astrophysicist; b. N.Y.C., May 16, 1947; s. Sidney and Eve D.; m. Albertina Catharina Otter, Sept. 18, 1975; children: Joshua, Ilana. A.B., Columbia U., 1969, M.A., 1972, Ph.D., 1976. Postdoctoral research assoc. physics dept. Rensselaer Poly. Ins., Troy, N.Y., 1975-78; mem. tech. staff Aerospace Corp., Los Angeles, 1978-80; faculty research assoc. U. Mass., Amherst, 1980-85, assoc. prof. astronomy, 1985—; mgr. U. Mass. (Five Coll. Radio Astronomy Obs.), 1980—. Contbr. articles to profl. jours. Mem. Am. Astron. Soc., Am. Phys. Soc., Sigma Xi. Current Work: Interstellar cloud dynamics, star formation, turbulence. Receiver development for radio astronomy. Subspecialty: Radio and microwave astronomy. Office: Radio Astronomy GRC Univ Mass Amherst MA 01003

DICKSON, PAUL WESLEY, JR., physicist; b. Sharon, Pa., Sept. 14, 1931; s. Paul Wesley and Elizabeth Ella (Trevethan) D.; m. Eleanor Ann Dunning, Nov. 17, 1952; children: Gretchen Ann, Heather Elizabeth, Paul Wesley III. B.S. in Metall. Engring, U. Ariz., 1954, M.S. in Metall. Engring, 1954; Ph.D. in Physics, N.C. State U., 1962. With Westinghouse Electric Corp., Large, Pa., 1963-83, mgr. advanced projects, 1969-72, mgr. reactor analysis and core design, Madison, Pa., 1975-79; tech. dir. Westinghouse Electric Corp. (Clinch River Breeder Reactor project), Oak Ridge, 1979-83; mgr. new tech. devel. EG & G Idaho, 1983—; mem. adv. com. on advanced propulsion systems NASA, Washington, 1970-72; mem. adv. com. reactor physics AEC/Dept. Energy, 1974-79; mem. rev. com. applied physics Argonne (Ill.) Nat. Lab., 1978-83, chmn., 1980, mem. rev. com. EBR-II, 1984, mem. sci. and tech. adv. com., 1985—; mem. fellow selection com. Dept. Energy, 1981-82; mem. rev. com. engring. physics Oak Ridge Nat. Lab., 1982—. Contbr. numerous sci. articles to profl. pubs. Served to capt. USAF, 1955-63. Phelps Dodge fellow, 1953-54. Mem. Am. Nuclear Soc. (mem. reactor physics div. exec. com. 1984—), Am. Phys. Soc., N.Y. Acad. Scis., AIME (pres. student chpt. 1953-54), AAAS. Republican. Methodist. Current Work: Nuclear reactor development. Subspecialties: Nuclear fission; Nuclear engineering. Home: 4850 Loma Circle Idaho Falls ID 83401 Office: EG & G Idaho Inc PO Box 1625 Idaho Falls ID 83401

DICUS, DUANE ALFRED, physics educator, researcher; b. Okanogan, Wash., Nov. 23, 1938; s. Everest Alfred and Norma May (Greenaway) D.; m. Mary Sandra Schultz, Sept. 1, 1957; children—James, Steven, Richard. B.S. in Physics, U. Wash., 1961, M.S. in Physics, 1963; Ph.D. in Physics, UCLA, 1968. Research physicist Boeing Co., Seattle, 1963-64; research assoc. MIT, Cambridge, 1969-71, U. Rochester (N.Y.), 1971-73; asst. prof. physics, assoc. prof., prof. U. Tex., Austin, 1973—. Contbr. articles to physics jours. Current work: Theoretical elementary particle physics and particle physics in astrophysics and cosmology. Subspecialties: Particle physics; Theoretical astrophysics. Home: 3305 Woodbriar Austin TX 78723 Office: Center for Particle Theory U Tex Austin TX 78712

DI DONATO, ARMIDO RICHARD, mathematician, researcher; b. Pitts., June 8, 1922; s. Aronne and Delia DiD.; m. Annie Jean Breaux, Nov. 22, 1971; children: Judy, Laurie, Thomas, Robert. B.S., Duquesne U., 1950; S.M., M.I.T., 1951; postgrad., Carnegie-Mellon U., 1964-66, Ph.D., 1972. Mathematician duPont de Nemours, Wilmington, Del., 1951-53, Melpar, Alexandria, Va., 1953-54, Naval Surface Weapons Center, Dahlgren, Va., 1954—. Subspecialties: Numerical analysis (computer science); Applied mathematics. Home: PO Box 907 Dahlgren VA 22448 Office: Naval Surface Weapons Center Dahlgren VA 22448

DIEFENDORF, RUSSELL JUDD, materials engineering educator; b. Mount Vernon, N.Y., Aug. 28, 1931; s. Warren Edwin and Catherine Martha (Mechling) D.; m. Myrle Jeanne Warn, Sept. 6, 1952; children—Richard, Catherine, Amy, Sara. B.S. in Chemistry, U. Rochester, 1953; Ph.D. in Phys. Chemistry, U. Toronto, 1958. Scientist, Research Lab. Missile and Space div. Gen. Electric Corp., Phila., 1958-59, Schenectady, 1960-65; prof. materials engring. Rensselaer Poly. Inst., Troy, N.Y., 1965—. Contbr. articles to profl. jours. Patentee in field. Tchr. Reformed Dutch Ch. Youth Group, Schenectady, 1958-68. Recipient Cordiner award Gen. Electric, 1960; Humboldt prize Humboldt Found., Fed. Republic Germany, 1974; Graffin award Am. Carbon Soc., 1978. Mem. Am. Chem. Soc., Am. Ceramic Soc., ASTM (com. chmn. 1962-70), Am. Soc. for Metals (chpt. chmn.), Am. Helicopter Soc. Subspecialties: Composite materials; High-temperature materials. Office: Rensselaer Poly Inst Troy NY 12180-3590

DIENER, EDWARD FRANCIS, psychologist; b. Glendale, Calif., July 25, 1946; s. Frank C. and Mary Alice (Ferry) D.; m. Carol I. Merk, Dec. 27, 1966; children: Marissa, Mary Beth, Robert. B.A., Calif. State U.-Fresno, 1968; Ph.D., U. Wash., 1974. Asst. prof. U. Ill., Champaign, 1974-79, assoc. prof. psychology, 1979—. Author: Ethics in Social and Behavioral Research, 1978; Contbr. articles to profl. jours. Mem. Soc. Exptl. Social Psychology, Internat. Soc. for Research on Aggression, Am. Psychol. Assn., Soc. Psychol. Study of Social Issues. Current Work: Mood; positive effect; life satisfaction. Subspecialty: Social psychology. Home: 1711 Mayfair Rd Champaign IL 61821 Office: Dept Psychology U Ill 603 E Daniel St Champaign IL 61820

DIENER, THEODOR OTTO, plant pathologist; b. Zurich, Switzerland, Feb. 28, 1921; came to U.S., 1949, naturalized, 1955; s. Theodor Emanuel and Hedwig Rosa (Baumann) D.; m. Sybil Mary Fox, May 11, 1968; children by previous marriage: Theodor W., Robert A., Michael S. Dipl. Sc. Nat. E.T.H., Swiss Fed. Inst. Tech., 1946, D. Sc. Nat., 1948. Asst. Swiss Fed. Inst. Tech., Zurich, 1946-48; plant pathologist Swiss Fed. Exptl. Sta., Waedenswil, 1949-50; asst. prof. plant pathology R.I. State U., Kingston, 1950; asst. plant pathologist Wash. State U., Prosser, 1950-55, asso. plant pathologist, 1955-59; research plant pathologist Agrl. Research Service, USDA, Beltsville, Md., 1959—; lectr. univs. and research insts.; Regents' lectr. U. Calif., Riverside, 1970; Andrew D. White prof.-at-large Cornell U., 1979-81. Author: Viroids and Viroid Diseases, 1979; asso. editor: jour. Virology, 1964-66, 74-76; editor jour., 1967-71; mem. editorial com.: jour. Ann. Rev. Phytopathology, 1970-74, Annales de Virologie, 1980—; contbr. articles to sci. publs. Recipient Campbell award Am. Inst. Biol. Scis., 1968; Alexander von Humboldt award, 1975; Superior Service award USDA, 1969; Distinguished Service award, 1977. Fellow Am. Phytopath. Soc. (Ruth Allen award 1976), N.Y. Acad. Scis., Am. Acad. Arts and Scis.; mem. AAAS, Nat. Acad. Scis., Leopoldina, German Acad. Natural Scientists. Discoverer novel class of pathogens (viroids), 1971.

Current Work: Fundamental research and research leadership on subviral pathogens of plants and animals. Subspecialties: Plant pathology; Plant virology. Home: 4530 Powder Mill Rd PO Box 272 Beltsville MD 20705 Office: Plant Virology Lab Agrl Research Center USDA Beltsville MD 20705

DIENSTAG, JULES LEONARD, physician, educator; b. N.Y.C., Dec. 10, 1946; s. Baruch and Josephine D.; m. Judy Iris Gordon, Feb. 3, 1974; children: Joshua, Jonathan. A.B., Columbia U., 1968, M.D., 1972. Diplomate: Am. Bd. Internal Medicine, Nat. Bd. Med. Examiners. Intern U. Chgo., Billings Hosp, 1972-73, resident, 1973-74; research assoc. Lab. Infectious Diseases, Nat. Inst. Allergy and Infectious Diseases, NIH, 1974-76; research fellow in medicine Harvard Med. Sch., 1976-78, asst. prof. medicine, 1978-82, assoc. prof., 1982—; clin. and research fellow in medicine Mass. Gen. Hosp., Boston, 1976-78, asst. in medicine, 1979-82, asst. physician, 1983—; vis. scientist Lab. Epidemiology, Lindsley F. Kimball Research Inst., N.Y. Blood Center, 1980—. Mem. editorial bd.: Hepatology, 1980—, Jour. Clin. Microbiology, 1977—, Gastroenterology, 1981—, Infectious Disease series, Marcel Dekker Med. Div., 1981—; contbr. articles to profl. jours. Served with USPHS, 1974-76. USPHS grantee, 1978-79, 79-82. Fellow ACP; mem. Am. Soc. Microbiology, AAAS, Am. Fedn. Clin. Research, Am. Assn. Immunologists, Internat. Assn. Study of the Liver, Am. Assn. Study of Liver Diseases, Am. Gastroent. Assn., N.Y. Acad. Sci., Phi Beta Kappa. Current Work: Viral hepatitis, liver immunology, medical research. Subspecialty: Gastroenterology. Home: 4 Lincoln Rd Wayland MA 01778 Office: Gastrointestinal Unit Mass Gen Hosp Boston MA 02114

DIESEM, CHARLES DAVID, vet. anatomist, educator; b. Galion, Ohio, July 5, 1921; s. John Elmer and Mary Florence (Burwell) D.; m. Janet Moore, Jan. 18, 1945; children: Mary Lynn Diesem Peoples, Nancy Sue, Robert C. D.V.M., Ohio State U., 1943, M.Sc., 1949, Ph.D., 1956. Gen. practice vet. medicine, Mt. Gilead, Ohio, 1943-44; instr. dept. vet. anatomy Ohio State U., Columbus, 1947-56, asst. prof., 1956-59, assoc. prof., 1959-61, prof., 1961—. Co-author: Anatomy and Histology of the Eye and Orbit and Orbit in Domestic Animals, 1960, The Rabbit in Eye Research, 1964, The Anatomy of Domestic Animals, 5th edit, 1975. Dep. health commr. City of Upper Arlington, Ohio, 1954-76. Served with Vet. Corps. U.S. Army, 1945-47. Mem. AVMA, Ohio Vet. Med. Assn., Am. Assn. Anatomists, Am. Assn. Vet. Anatomists, World Assn. Vet. Anatomists, Sigma Xi. Lodge: Masons. Current Work: Ophthalmic anatomy and peripheral nervous system. Subspecialty: Ophthalmology. Home: 1872 Berkshire Rd Columbus OH 43221 Office: Dept Vet Anatomy Ohio State U 1900 Coffee Rd Columbus OH 43210

DIETENBERGER, MARK ANTHONY, research physicist; b. Reedsburg, Wis., Aug. 10, 1952; s. William Karl and Cleo (Rockweiler) D.; m. Joleen Ann Soper, June 31, 1979; children: Nicole, Angela, Elizabeth. B.S., U. Wis.-Milw., 1974; M.S., U. Dayton, 1978. Research physicist U. Dayton, Ohio, 1977—. Contbr. articles to profl. jours. Mem. AIAA, Am. Phys. Soc. Roman Catholic. Current Work: Primary general interest is in computer modeling of physical systems; current research is in aviation safety whereby numerical analysis is applied to atmospheric (winds, rain, ice, frost, fire) impacts on aerospace systems. Subspecialties: Aerospace engineering and technology; Numerical analysis (computer science). Office: U Dayton Research Inst Applied Systems Analysis 300 College Park Ave Dayton OH 45469

DIETRICH, JOHN WILLIAM, endocrinologist; b. Syracuse, N.Y., June 28, 1946; s. Joseph F. and Elizabeth (Lawler) D.; m. Marilyn Jean Fuller, July 26, 1969; children: Tamera, Brian. B.S., LeMoyne Coll., 1968; M.S., U. Dayton, 1970; Ph.D. in Pharmacology, U. N.C., 1973. Postdoctoral fellow U. Conn. Health Center, Farmington, 1974-76; asst. prof. U. Ill. Sch. Medicine, Peoria, 1976-79; dir. endocrinology Revlon Health Care Group, Tuckahoe, N.Y., 1979—. Contbr. articles to profl. jours. Pharm. Mfrs. research grantee, 1974; NIH grantee, 1975. Mem. AAAS, Am. Soc. Bone and Mineral Research, Endocrine So., Fedn. Am. Soc. Exptl. Biology. Roman Catholic. Current Work: Endocrinology drug discover, bone and calcium metabolism. Subspecialty: Endocrinology. Office: Revlon Health Care Center 1 Scarsdale Rd Tuckahoe NY 10707

DIETRICH, RICHARD VINCENT, geology educator, researcher; b. LaFargeville, N.Y., Feb. 7, 1924; s. Roy Eugene and Mida A. (Vincent) D.; m. Frances Elizabeth Smith, Dec. 28, 1946; children—Richard Smith, Kurt Robert, Krista Gayle Brown. A.B., Colgate U., 1947; M.S., Yale U., 1950, Ph.D., 1951. Geologist, N.Y. State Educ. Service, Brier Hill Quadrangle, N.Y., 1949-50; Fulbright research prof. U. Oslo, Norway, 1958-59; from asst. prof. to assoc. prof. geology Va. Poly. Inst., Blacksburg, 1951-69, assoc. dean arts and scis., 1966-68, acting dean, 1968-69; dean arts and scis. Central Mich. U., Mt. Pleasant, 1969-75, prof., 1969—. Author: Geology and Virginia, 1970; Rocks and Rock Minerals, 1979; Mineralogy: Concepts, Descriptions, Determinations, 2d edit., 1983, others. Contbr. articles to profl. jours. Served to sgt. USAAC, 1943-46; PTO. Recipient citation Mich. Acad. Sci., Letters and Arts, 1978; Sci. Book award N.Y. Acad. Sci., 1981. Yale U. fellow. Fellow Mineral. Soc. Am., Soc. Econ. Geology; mem. Assn. Earth Sci. Editors, Norges Geologisk Forbund (life mem.), Geol. Soc. Finland (life mem.), Phi Beta Kappa, Sigma Xi, Phi Kappa Phi. Current work: Tourmaline group minerals and Migmatite petrology. Subspecialties: Petrology; Mineralogy. Home: 1323 Center Dr Mount Pleasant MI 48858 Office: Central Mich U Geology Dept Mount Pleasant MI 48859

DIETSCHY, JOHN MAURICE, internal medicine educator, researcher; b. Alton, Ill., Sept. 23, 1932; s. John C. and Clara A. (Sahner) D.; m. Beverly A. Robertson, Apr. 18, 1959; children: John, Daniel, Michael, Karen. A.B., Washington U., St. Louis, 1954, M.D., 1958. Intern St. Joseph's Hosp., Denver, 1958-59; resident in medicine VA Hosp., Denver, 1959-61; research fellow Boston U., 1961-63; research fellow U. Tex. Southwestern Med. Sch., 1963-65, asst. prof. internal medicine, 1965-69, assoc. prof., 1969-71, prof., 1971—, dir. div. gastroenterology, 1979—. Med. research publs.; editor: Gastroenterology Monographs, 1976—, Lipid Metabolism, 1978, Textbooks of Medicine, 1978-83. Markle scholar, 1966-71; NIH grantee, 1964—; recipient Heinrich-Wieland prize, 1983. Mem. Am. Physiol. Soc. (chmn. com. 1977), Am. Gastroent. Assn. (Disting. achievement award 1978), Am. Soc. Clin. Investigation, Assn. Am. Physicians, Am. Soc. Biol. Chemists, Am. Fedn. Clin. Research (pres. So. sect. 1975), So. Soc. Clin. Investigation (pres. 1983). Roman Catholic. Current Work: Regulation cholesterol metabolism, atherosclerosis; intestinal absorption; gastrointestinal infections. Subspecialties: Internal medicine; Gastroenterology. Office: Dept Internal Medicine U Tex Health Sci Ctr 5323 Harry Hines Blvd Dallas TX 75235

DIFILIPPO, FELIX CARLOS, physicist; b. Buenos Aires, Argentina, July 24, 1943; came to U.S., 1979; s. Miguel and Angela (Portuese) D.; m. Nuria Maria Hernandez, Jan. 13, 1967; children: Ernesto Antonio, Eduardo Pablo. M.Physics, Instituto Balseiro, Bariloche, Rio Negro, Argentina, 1967, Ph.D., 1978. Aux. prof. U. Buenos Aires, 1968-69; researcher AEC Argentina, Buenos Aires, 1968-79; research asst. prof. U. Tenn., Oak Ridge Nat. Lab., 1979-83; research staff mem. Oak Ridge Nat. Lab., 1983—; lectr. Nat. U. Cordoba, Argentina, 1972, Peruvian Inst. Nuclear Energy, Lima, 1978-79. Contbr. articles in field to profl. jours. IAEA fellow Vienna, 1974. Mem. Am. Phys. Soc., Am. Nuclear Soc. Current Work: Design of a high-flux reactor, noise analysis of nuclear reactors, mathematical modeling of nuclear power plants, in general applied physics. Subspecialties: Nuclear fission; Nuclear engineering. Home: 102 Westwind Dr Oak Ridge TN 37830 Office: Oak Ridge Nat Lab PO Box X Bldg 6025 Oak Ridge TN 37830

DIFOGGIO, ROCCO, physicist; b. Chgo., Aug. 12, 1952; s. Daniel Joseph and Phyllis Helen (DeSantis) DiF. B.S., Ill. Inst. Tech., 1974; M.S. in Physics, U. Chgo., 1977, Ph.D., 1980. Research assoc. U. Chgo., 1980-81; research physicist Shell Devel. Co., Houston, 1981—. Contbr. articles to sci. jours. Patentee in field. Recipient Nottingham prize in surface sci. Conf. Phys. Electronics, 1980; mem. Honors Research Participation Program, AEC, NSF, Argonne Nat. Lab., 1972, Fermi Nat. Lab., 1973. Mem. Am. Phys. Soc., Soc. Petroleum Engrs., Soc. Profl. Well Log Analysts, N.Y. Acad. Scis., AAAS. Current work: Measuring relative permeabilities and other physical properties of reservoir rock; developing new well-logging tools and other well-evaluation techniques and equipment. Subspecialties: Petrophysics; Petroleum engineering. Office: Shell Devel Co PO Box 481 Houston TX 77001

DIGBY, PETER SAKI BASSETT, biology educator, researcher; b. London, Jan. 15, 1921; came to Can., 1967, Can. citizen, 1977; s. George Bassett and Dorothy Stewart (Johnson) D.; m. Violet Valerie Wilson, Aug. 2, 1945; children—Susan Ann, Claire Margaret, Karen Venetia, Robin Peter. B.A., Cambridge U., 1942, M.A., 1944; D.Sc., London U., 1967. Mem. research staff Agrl. Adv. Service, Eng., 1944-46, Plymouth Marine Lab., Eng., 1946-48, Zool. Lab., Oxford U., 1948-52, Overwintering Expedition to Greenland, 1950-51; summer expeditions to Spitsbergen, 1948, 56; lectr., then sr. lectr. St. Thomas' Hosp. Med. Sch., London, 1951-64; prof. biology McGill U., Montreal, Que., Can., 1967—. Co-author: Beyond the Pack-Ice, 1954. Grantee Browne Fund, Royal Soc. London, 1950-51, Percy Sladen Fund, 1948, 56, Nat. Sci. and Engring. Research Council Can., 1968-80. Mem. Royal Geog. Soc., Linnean Soc. London (council 1964-67), Marine Biol. Assn. U.K., Am. Zool. Soc., Am. Phyisol., Soc., Royal Entomol. Soc., Royal Meteorol. Soc., Soc. Exptl. Biology, Inst. Biology, Can. Physiol. Soc., Am. Ecol. Soc., Ecol. Soc. Gt. Britain, Challenger Soc., Norfolk and Norwich Naturalists Soc., Zool. Soc. London. Anglican. Club: Faculty. Current work: Physiology of calcification in shell, crustaceans, coral reef organisms and bone, ecology of seas, shores and artic and alpine regions. Subspecialties: Ecology (biology); Marine biology. Home: 52 Lakeview Blvd Beaconsfield PQ H9W 4R1 Canada Office: Dept Biology McGill U 1205 Ave Docteur Penfield Montreal PQ H3A 1B1 Canada

DIGGS, CARTER LEE, immunologist, researcher, army officer; b. Deltaville, Va., Dec. 31, 1934; s. Harvey Lee and Jewel (Carter) D.; m. Virginia Mabry, June 5, 1956; children: Carter Lee, Diana, Daniel Christopher. B.S., Randolph-Macon Coll., 1956; M.D., Med. Coll. Va., 1960; Ph.D. (Univ. fellow), Johns Hopkins U., 1968. Intern, Med. Coll. Va., 1960-61, resident in pathology, 1961-62; commd. capt. M.C., U.S. Army, 1962, advanced through grades to col., 1976; research assoc. dept. med. zoology Walter Reed Army Inst. Research, Washington, 1962-64, sr. research assoc. dept. med. zoology, dept. dir. div. communicable diseases and immunology, 1970-73, chief dept. immunology, 1973-80, dir. div. communicable diseases and immunology, 1979—; chmn. dept. parasitology SEATO Med. Research Lab., Bangbok, Thailand, 1968-70; cons. in field. Contbr. numerous articles to profl. jours. Mem. Am. Assn. Immunologists, Am. Soc. Tropical Medicine and Hygiene, Phi Beta Kappa. Current Work: Parasite immunology; malaria, trypanosomiasis; vaccine development. Subspecialties: Infectious diseases; Microbiology (medicine). Home: 11202 Landy Ct Kensington MD 20895 Office: Walter Reed Army Inst Research Div Communicable Diseases and Immunology WRAMC Washington DC 20012

DIJKSTRA, EDSGER W., computer scientist. Holder Schlumberger Centennial chair dept. computer sci. U. Tex., Austin, 1984—. Office: Univ Texas Dept Computer Sci Austin TX 78712*

DILCHER, DAVID LEONARD, paleobotany researcher, educator; b. Cedar Falls, Iowa, July 10, 1936; s. Leonard George and Hannah Eliza (Short) D.; m. Katherine Rose Swanson, Sept. 10, 1961; children: Peter Corbin, Ann Katherine. B.S., U. Minn., 1958, M.A., 1960; Ph.D., Yale U., 1964. NSF postdoctoral fellow Senckenberg Mus., Frankfurt, W.Ger., 1964-65; instr. Yale U., New Haven, 1965-66; asst. prof. paleobotany Ind. U., Bloomington, 1966-69, assoc. prof., 1969-75, prof., 1975—; Mem. Utility Service Bd., 1975-77. Author books and articles. Cullman fellow, 1964; NSF fellow, 1964-65; Guggenheim fellow, 1972-73; Amax Research grantee, 1979-80; NSF grantee, 1966-84. Fellow Linnean Soc., Ind. Acad. Sci.; mem. Bot. Soc. Am., AAAS, Geol. Soc. Am., Orgn. Tropical Biology. Current Work: Evolution of flowering plants. Subspecialties: Evolutionary biology; Paleobiology. Office: Dept Biology Ind U Bloomington IN 47405

DILL, KENNETH AUSTIN, pharmaceutical chemistry educator; b. Oklahoma City, Dec. 11, 1947; s. Austin Glenn and Margaret (Blocker) D. S.B., Mass. Inst. Tech., 1971, S.M., 1971; Ph.D., U. Calif.-San Diego, 1978. Damon Runyon-Walter Winchell fellow Stanford (Calif.) U., 1978-81; asst. prof. chemistry U. Fla., Gainesville, 1981-82; asst. prof. pharm. chemistry and pharmacy U. Calif., San Francisco, 1982-85, assoc. prof., 1985—. Contbr. numerous sci. articles to profl. publs. Patentee in field. Mem. Am. Chem. Soc., Am. Phys. Soc., Biophys. Soc., AAAS. Current Work: Statistical mechanical theory of biological molecules, surfactants and proteins. Subspecialties: Biophysical chemistry; Polymer physics. Home: 665 Lancaster St Moss Beach CA 94038 Office: Pharm Chemistry Dept Univ Calif San Francisco CA 94143

DILLEY, RICHARD A., biologist, educator; b. South Haven, Mich., Jan. 12, 1936; s. Varnum M. and Marion (Dahlquist) D.; m. Janette G. Fitzsimons, Aug. 13, 1960; children: John, Thomas, David, Neil. B.S., Mich. State U., 1958, M.S., 1959; Ph.D., Purdue U., 1963. Research assoc. C.F. Kettering Lab., Yellow Springs, Ohio, 1963-64, U. Rochester, 1965; staff scientist C.F. Kettering Research Lab., Yellow Springs, Ohio, 1966-70; assoc. prof. Purdue U., West Lafayette, Ind., 1970-75, prof., 1975—; mem. peer. rev. panel NSF, U.S. Dept. Agr. Mem. editorial bd.: Jour. Biol. Chemistry. NSF, NIH, Dept. Agr. grantee; von Humboldt fellow, 1982-83. Mem. Am. Soc. Biol. Chemists, Am. Soc. Plant Physiologists, Am. Soc. Photobiology, AAAS. Roman Catholic. Current Work: Research in photosynthesis, membrane biochemistry and membrane structure. Subspecialties: Photosynthesis; Biochemistry (biology). Office: Dept Bicl Scis Purdue U West Lafayette IN 47907

DILLON, DONALD JOSEPH, psychologist; b. N.Y.C., Apr. 26, 1926; s. Will F. and Mae (Hockman) D.; m. Helene R. Cooney, Sept. 3, 1955; children: Linda M., Donald J., James J., Kathleen M., Richard P. B.S., Yale U., 1949; M.A., Fordham U., 1952, Ph.D., 1955. Lic. psychologist, N.Y. Teaching fellow Fordham U., 1953-54; Research psychologist N.Y. Psychiat. Inst., N.Y.C., 1955-57, sr. research psychologist, 1957-74; instr. psychology Columbia U., N.Y.C., 1958-67; adj. asst. prof. Manhattan Coll., Riverdale, N.Y., 1963-67; research assoc. psychology Columbia U., 1967-69; assoc. research psychologist N.Y. Psychiat. Inst., 1974—; adj. assoc. prof. Manhattan Coll., 1967—; asst. prof. Columbia U., 1969—. Chmn. religious edn. bd. St. William the Abbot Ch., Seaford, N.Y., 1973-76; committeeman Boy Scouts Am., Massapequa, 1970-71. U.S. Navy research asst. 1952-54. Mem. AAAS, Am. Psychol. Assn., Soc. Sigma Xi, Psychonomic Soc., N.Y. Acad. Sci. Republican. Roman Catholic. Current Work: Research, diagnosis and treatment anxiety disorders; research into basic psychophysical measures of pain, teaching undergrads. Subspecialties: Psychobiology; Sensory processes. Home: 77 Chicago Ave Massapqua NY 11758 Office: 722 W 168th St New York NY 10032

DIMANT, JACOB, physician, medical educator; b. Rehovot, Israel, Apr. 27, 1947; s. Symcha and Ita D.; m. Rose Bea Jearolman, Sept. 11, 1974. M.D., Hebrew U., Jerusalem, 1972. Diplomate: Am. Bd. Internal Medicine, Am. Bd. Rheumatology, Am. Bd. Quality Assurance and Utilization Rev. Physicians. Resident in medicine Maimonides Med. Ctr., Bklyn., 1972-76, asst. dir. med. edn., 1978-80, dir. rheumatology, 1978—; fellow in rheumatology SUNY-Downstate Med. Ctr., Bklyn., 1976-78, asst. prof. medicine, 1978—; med. dir. Prospect Park Nursing Home, Bklyn., 1977—, Crown Nursing Home, Bklyn., 1983—; adj. prof. clin. pharmacy Bklyn. Coll. Pharmacy, 1975-76; hon. prof. Universidad Autonoma de Guadalajara, Mex., 1979-80, hon. police surgeon, N.Y.C., 1982—. Contbr. articles to profl. jours. Research fellow Arthritis Found., 1977-78; recipient research award Maimonides Med. Ctr., 1980. Fellow ACP; mem. Am. Fedn. Clin. Research, Am. Rheumatism Assn., Am. Geriatric Soc. Current Work: Rheumatic disease in the elderly; aging research. Subspecialties: Internal medicine; Gerontology. Office: Kingsboro Med Group 3245 Nostrand Ave Brooklyn NY 11229

DIMENT, WILLIAM HORACE, research geophysicist, consultant; b. Oswego, N.Y., Oct. 15, 1927; s. James Smith and Priscilla Rose (Faatz) D.; m. Evelyn Virginia East, Nov. 12, 1958; children: Evelyn Patricia Diment Chamberlain, James Howell, William David. A.B., Williams Coll., 1949; A.M., Harvard U., 1951, Ph.D., 1954. Registered geophysicist, Calif. Geophysicist Standard Oil Co. Calif., New Orleans, 1953-56; geophysicist, br. chief U.S. Geol. Survey, Washington, Menlo Park, Calif., Denver, 1956-65, research geophysicist, 1973-83, Golden, Colo., 1973—; prof. geology U. Rochester, N.Y., 1965-73; cons. on reactor siting U.S. AEC, Washington, 1965-69; cons. on reactor siting U.S. Dept. Interior, 1965-69, cons. on radioactive waste disposal, 1965-69, 1971; mem. various panels, coms. NSF, NRC. Served with USNR, 1945-46; served to 1st lt. USAFR, 1949-58. Sr. postdoctoral fellow NSF, Yale U., 1964-65; prin. investigator NSF grants, 1966-73. Fellow AAAS (council 1961-62), Geol. Soc. Am.; mem. Soc. Exploration Geophysicists (rep. AAAS council 1961-62). Republican. Congretationalist. Current Work: Regional geophysics; exploration geophysics, seismicity eastern U.S.; geothermal systems and geothermal energy; physical limnology. Subspecialties: Geophysics; Tectonics. Home: 1822 Arapahoe St Golden CO 80401 Office: US Geol Survey 1711 Illinois St Golden CO 80401

DINARELLO, CHARLES A., medical researcher. Assoc. prof. dept. medicine Tufts U Sch. Medicine, Boston. Subspecialty: Molecular biology. Office: Tufts U Sch Medicine 136 Harrison Ave Boston MA 02111

DINERSTEIN, HARRIET, astronomer. Lectr. dept. astronomy U. Tex., Austin, 1984—. Recipient Annie Jump Cannon award in Astronomy AAUW, 1984. Subspecialty: Infrared astronomy. Office: U Tex Austin Dept Astronomy Austin TX 78712

DINGLE, RICHARD DOUGLAS HUGH, entomology educator; b. Penang, Malaysia, Nov. 4, 1936; came to U.S., 1942; s. Walter Hugh and Mildred Burns (Porter) D.; m. Geraldine Joyce Palmer, Aug. 29, 1959; children: Jennifer Leigh, Hilary Alison, Tracy Alexandra. B.A., Cornell U., 1958; M.S., U. Mich., 1959, Ph.D., 1962. Asst. prof. U. Iowa, Iowa City, 1964-67, assoc. prof., 1967-73, prof., 1973-82; vis. lectr. U. Nairobi, Kenya, 1969-70; prof. U. Calif.-Davis, 1982—. Editor: Evolution of Insect Migration and Diapause, 1978; co-editor: Insect Life History Patterns, 1981, Evolution and Genetics of Life Histories, 1982. NIH fellow, 1969-70; NSF grantee, 1964-85. Fellow AAAS; mem. Ecol. Soc. Am., Am. Soc. Naturalists, Soc. Study Evolution, Animal Behavior Soc. Democrat. Current Work: Evolution and genetics of insect migration and life histories. Subspecialties: Genome organization; Behavioral ecology. Home: 1204 Colby Dr Davis CA 95616 Office: U Calif Dept Entomology Davis CA 95616

DINNEEN, GERALD PAUL, elec. engr., corp. exec., former govt. ofcl., educator; b. Elmhurst, N.Y., Oct. 23, 1924; s. Walter James and Anna Constance (Costello) D.; m. Mary Purington, June 28, 1947; children—Patricia, Barbara (Mrs. Timothy J. Sehr), Michael. B.S., Queens Coll., 1947; M.S., U. Wis., 1948, Ph.D., 1952. Mathematician Goodyear Aircraft Corp., Akron, Ohio, 1951-53; with Mass. Inst. Tech., Lexington, Mass., 1953-77; dir. Lincoln Lab., 1970-77, prof. elec. engring., 1971-77; asst. sec. def. for communications, command, control and intelligence, 1977-81; corp. v.p. sci. and tech. Honeywell, Inc., Mpls., 1981—; Mem. sci. adv. bd. USAF, 1960-64, 70-77; vice chmn. 1971-75, chmn., 1975-77; cons. Def. Dept., NASA, USN, USAF. Served with AC AUS, 1943-46. Recipient Exceptional Civilian Service award USAF, 1966; Disting. Public Service award Dept. Def., 1981. Mem. Nat. Acad. Engring., Am. Math. Soc., Math. Assn. Am., Sigma Xi. Club: Cosmos (Washington). Subspecialty: Electrical engineering. Home: 6400 Barrie Rd Edina MN 55435 Office: Honeywell Inc Honeywell Plaza Minneapolis MN 55408

DIONNE, GERALD FRANCIS, research physicist, engineer; b. Montreal, Que., Can., Feb. 5, 1935; came to U.S., 1964; s. Louis Philip and Clare Isabel (Flood) D.; m. Claudette LeBlanc, June 29, 1963; 1 child, Stephen. B.Sc. summa cum laude, Concordia U., Montreal, 1956; B.Eng. with honors, McGill U., Montreal, 1958, Ph.D. in Physics, 1964; M.S. in Physics, Carnegie-Mellon U., 1959. Registered profl. engr., Que. Teaching asst. Carnegie-Mellon U., Pitts., 1958-59; jr. engr. IBM Corp., Poughkeepsie, N.Y., 1959-60; sr. engr. Sylvania GTE, Woburn, Mass., 1960-61; research asst., lectr. McGill U., 1963-64; sr. research assoc. United Technologies, North Haven, Conn., 1964-66; mem. tech. staff MIT Lincoln Lab., Lexington, Mass., 1966—; mem. tech. program com. Magnetism and Magnetic Materials Conf., Boston, 1973, 3d Internat, Conf. on Ferrites, Paris, 1976. Contbr. articles to profl. jours. Univ. scholar McGill U., 1958; Nat. Research Council Can. fellow, 1961-63. Mem. IEEE (sr.), Am. Phys. Soc., Corp. Profl. Engrs. Que., Sigma Xi. Roman Catholic. Current work: Magnetic and magnetoelastic properties of solids, microwave and millimeter-wave interactions with ferrimagnetic oxides, far-infrared and submillimeter-wave heterodyne radiometry, thermionic and secondary electron emission phenomena. Subspecialties: Magnetic physics; Infrared spectroscopy. Home: 182 High St Winchester MA 01890 Office: MIT Lincoln Lab 244 Wood St Lexington MA 02173

DIORIO, MARK LEWIS, mech. engr., metallurgist; b. Norwalk, Conn., Feb. 18, 1957; s. Joseph P. and Susan DiO.; m. Constance Pratt, June 27, 1981. B.S. in Mech. Engring. and Materials Engring, U. Conn., 1979; postgrad., St. Louis U. Sch. Bus., 1980-81. Market devel. engr. Olin Fineweld Tube, Olin Brass div. Olin Corp., East Alton, Ill., 1979-81; market devel. engr. Somers Thinstrip, Olin Brass, Waterbury, Conn., 1981; sales engr. Olin Brass, San Francisco, 1982—. Mem. ASME, Micro Electronic Packaging and Processing Engrs. Current Work: Marketing and developing copper alloys for semiconductor applications. Subspecialties: Metallurgy; Mechanical engineering. Home: 10194 Parwood Dr Cupertino CA 95014 Office: 20430 Town Center Ln 5-I Cupertino CA 95014

DIPAOLO, JOSEPH AMEDEO, geneticist, lavoratory director; b. Bridgeport, Conn., June 13, 1924; s. John Anthony and Nancy (Montagano) DiP.; m. Arleta Mae Schreib, June 14, 1952; children: Nancy, John. A.B., Wesleyan U., 1948; M.S., Western Res. U., 1949; Ph.D., Northwestern U., 1951. Instr. genetics and bacteriology dept. biology Loyola U., Chgo., 1951-53; instr. clin. and exptl. pathology dept. pathology Northwestern U. Sch. Med., Evanston, Ill., 1953-55; sr. cancer research scientist Roswell Park Meml. Inst., Buffalo, N.Y., 1955-63; research pharmacologist, cell biologist biology br. div. cancer etiology Nat. Cancer Inst., Bethesda, Md., 1963-76, chief lab. biology, div. cancer cause and prevention, 1976—; assoc. profl. lectr. anatomy George Washington U., Washington, 1973-76; chmn. U.S.-USSR Mammalian Somatic Cell Genetics Related to Neoplasia, 1973-76, U.S.-Germany Cancer Program Area for Environ. Carcinogenesis, 1979—. Assoc. editor: Jour. Nat. Cancer Inst, 1968-71, Cancer Research, 1970-78, Teratogenesis, Carcinogenesis and Mutagenesis, 1982—; editor: Chemical Carcinogenesis, 1974. Served with USN, 1943-46. Fellow AAAS, N.Y. Acad. Sci.; mem. Am. Assn. Cancer Research (dir. 1983-87), Am. Soc. Human Genetics, Am. Soc. Exptl. Pathology, Genetics Soc. Am., Teratology Soc., Hamster Soc., Tissue Culture Assn., Sigma Xi. Current Work: Modulation of neoplasia, DNA metabolism, cell surface changes, cytogenetics, in vitro transformation. Subspecialties: Cancer research (medicine); Cell biology. Office: Bldg 37 Room 2A-19 NIH-Nat Cancer Inst 9000 Rockville Pike Bethesda MD 20205

DI PASQUALE, GENE, pharmacologist, researcher; b. N.Y.C., July 17, 1932; s. Emidio and Maria (De Gennaro) Di P.; m. Anita Famiglietti, Sept. 7, 1962; children: Lora, Dean. B.S., Iona Coll., 1954; M.S., L.I. U., 1960; Ph.D., N.Y.U., 1970. From asst. scientist to assoc. dir. pharmacodynamics Warner Lambert Research Inst., Morris Plains, N.J., 1957-77; sect. mgr. immunopharmacology I.C.I., Wilmington, Del., 1977—. Contbr. articles to sci. jours. Served with M.C. U.S. Army, 1954-56. Recipient Founders Day award N.Y.U., 1970. Mem. Soc. Study of Reprodn., Am. Physiol. Soc., Am. Soc. Pharmacology and Exptl. Therapeutics, Endocrine Soc., N.Y. Acad. Scis., AAAS, Sigma Xi, Phi Sigma. Co-discoverer Benisone (Flurobate) and Isoxicam (Maxicam). Current Work: Anti-arthritic research. Subspecialties: Pharmacology; Biochemistry (medicine). Office: Murphy and Concord Rd Wilmington DE 19897

DIRIENZO, JOSEPH MICHAEL, microbiologist, researcher, educator; b. Derby, Conn., Sept. 20, 1950; s. Joseph and Concetta (Ricciardi) DiR.; m. Sharon Barbara Mills, Aug. 31, 1974; children—Elizabeth Anne, Brian David. B.Sc., Providence Coll., 1972; Ph.D., McGill U., Montreal, Que. Can., 1977. Postdoctoral fellow SUNY-Stony Brook, 1976-79; asst. prof. microbiology Sch. Dental Medicine, U. Pa., Phila., 1980—. Invited reviewer profl. jours. Recipient Faculty grant and award U. Pa., 1980; grantee Am. Cancer Soc., 1980, NIH, 1983. Mem. Am. Soc. Microbiology, AAAS, Internat. Assn. Dental Research. Democrat. Roman Catholic. Current work: Biochemistry and genetics of pathogenesis of oral microorganisms; molecular basis of cell-cell aggregation of oral bacteria. Subspecialties: Microbiology; Molecular biology. Office: U Pa Sch Dental Medicine Dept Microbiology 4001 Spruce St Philadelphia PA 19104

DIRKS, LESLIE CHANT, physicist; b. New Ulm, Minn., Mar. 7, 1936; s. Emereld Francis and Eva (Gay) D.; m. Eleanor G. McPeake, Feb. 10, 1959; children: Anthony, Jason, Elizabeth. B.S. in Physics, MIT, 1958, Oxford (Eng.) U., 1960. Instr. physics Phillips Acad., Andover, Mass., 1960-61; with CIA, 1961-82, dep. dir. sci. and tech., 1976-82. Recipient Disting. Intelligence medal CIA, 1977, Nat. Security medal, 1978; ann. award IEEE, 1980. Mem. Nat. Acad. Engring. Subspecialties: Microelectronics; Aerospace engineering and technology. Home: 45 Hancock St Lexington MA 02173 Office: Hughes Aircraft Co Los Angeles CA 90009

DIRKSEN, THOMAS REED, II, dental educator, biochemist, dentist; b. Pekin, Ill., Nov. 5, 1931; s. Thomas Reed and Mildred Roslyn (Neville) D.; m. Jean Kathryn Twietmeyer, Dec. 17, 1955; children: Thomas R., Peter T., John S., James C., Robert S., Kathryn A. B.S., Bradley U., 1953; D.D.S., U.

Ill.-Chgo., 1957; M.S., U. Rochester, 1960, Ph.D., 1967. Lic. tchr., Ga. lic. dental bds. Ill., N.Y. Assoc. prof. Sch. Dentistry, Med. Coll. Ga., Augusta, 1967-70, prof., 1970—; assoc. dean Sch. Dentistry, Med. Coll. Ga. (Sch. Dentistry), 1977—; mem. Nat. Adv. Dental Research Council, Nat. Inst. Dental Research, Washington, 1982-85, Biomed. Research Support Subcom., HEW, Washington, 1979-80. Co-editor: Boucher's Clinical Dental Terminology, 1982; contbr. to books. Bd. dirs. Dirksen Ctr., Pekin, 1979-85, Bd. Edn. Adv. Com., Augusta, 1978—; bd. dirs. Richmond County Library, Augusta, 1974-79, chmn., 1977-79. Served to capt. USAF, 1960-62. Research grantee Nat. Inst. Arthritis and Metabolic Diseases, 1968, 71; Research grantee Juvenile Diabetes Found., 1976; Research grantee Nat. Inst. Dental Research, 1981. Fellow Am. Coll. Dentists; mem. Internat. Assn. Dental Research, Am. Assn. Dental Research (chmn. nat. affairs com. 1982—), Am. Assn. Dental Schs. (sect. chmn. 1974-75, 82-83), ADA (dental and dental hygiene test const. com. 1978-82). Current Work: Lipids of calcified issues, cariology, lipid metabolism of oral structures. Subspecialties: Oral biology; Biochemistry (medicine).

DI SALVO, NICHOLAS ARMAND, dental educator, orthodontist; b. N.Y.C., Nov. 2, 1920; s. Frank and Mary (Ruberto) DiS; m. Pauline Rose Pluta, June 2, 1945; children: Allan, Donald. B.S., CCNY, 1942; D.D.S., Columbia U., 1945, Ph.D. in Physiology, 1952, cert. in orthodontics, 1957. Diplomate: Am. Bd. Orthodontics. Fellow Inst. Dental Research, Columbia U., 1950-52; instr. in physiology Coll. Physicians and Surgeons, Columbia U., 1948-51, asst. prof. physiology, 1952-57, assoc. prof., 1957-58, prof. dentistry, 1958—, dir. orthodontics, 1957—; attending dentist Presbyn. Hosp., N.Y.C., 1975—; cons. N.Y. State Dept. Health, 1970—, VA, N.Y.C., 1975—, Project/HOPE/Egypt, Alexandria and Cairo, 1976, Nat. Def. Med. Center, Taipei, Taiwan, 1982. Contbg. editor book chpts.; contbr. articles to profl. jours. Pres. Hartsdale-Fels Civic Assn., 1960-66. Served to lt. USNR, 1945-50. Recipient Disting. Service award Orthodontic Alumni Soc. Columbia U., 1973; fellow 8th Inst. Advanced Edn. in Dental Research. Mem. Am. Assn. Orthodontists (del. 1970-76), Northeastern Soc. Orthodontists (pres. 1974-75), Angle Soc. of Orthodontists (pres. 1977-79), Internat. Soc. Craniofacial Biology (pres. 1965-66). Republican. Roman Catholic. Current Work: Growth and development of occlusion. Subspecialty: Orthodontics. Office: Columbia U Dental Sch 630 W 168th St New York NY 10032

DISHMAN, RODNEY KING, exercise and sport psychologist, physical educator; b. Springfield, Mo., Feb. 4, 1951; s. Willard King and Virginia Lanette (Potter) D.; m. Sharon Emily Alter, Aug. 17, 1974; children: Jessica E., Amanda Corinne, Adrienne King. B.S., Southwest Mo. State U., 1973; M.S., U. Wis., 1975, Ph.D., 1978. Grad. asst. U. Wis.-Madison, 1973-77, research asst., 1976; vis. lectr. N. Tex. State U., 1977-78; assoc. prof. Southwest Mo. State U., 1978-83, U. Calif.-Davis, 1983-85; dir. behavioral fitness lab. U. Ga., 1985—. Author: Essentials of Fitness, 1980. Assoc. editor Medicine and Science in Sports and Exercise. Contbr. articles to profl. jours. Recipient A. J. McDonald award S.W. Mo. State U., 1973. Fellow Am. Coll. Sports Medicine, AAHPER and Dance (chmn. research div. Mo. chpt. 1981); mem. Am. Psychol. Assn. Methodist. Current Work: Mental health; medical compliance psychogenic aids in sports. Subspecialties: Exercise and sport psychology; Sports medicine. Office: U Ga Behavioral Fitness Lab Athens GA 30602

DITERS, RICHARD WILLIAM, veterinary pathologist, educator; b. Hartford, Conn., Nov. 27, 1952; s. Richard Henry and Wilma (Kimmerle) D. B.S., U. N.H., 1974, D.V.M., U. Pa., 1981. Grad. asst. U. Conn., Storrs, 1975-77; resident in pathology Cornell U., Ithaca, N.Y., 1981-82, sr. resident, 1982-83; sr. lectr., head necropsy service U. Pa., Phila., 1983—. Contbr. articles to profl. jours. Recipient Scholarship awards U. N.H., 1972, 73, 74; medal of Achievement in Pathology, U. Pa., 1981. Mem. AVMA, Internat. Acad. Pathology, Wildlife Disease Assn. Current work: Diagnostic veterinary pathology, comparative aspects of ocular disease, morphology and morphogenesis of animal tumors. Subspecialties: Pathology (veterinary medicine); Cancer research (veterinary medicine). Home: 1443 Conway Dr Swarthmore PA 19081 Office: Dept Pathology U Pa Sch Vet Medicine 3800 Spruce St Philadelphia PA 19104

DIVINE, THEODORE EMRY, research engineer; b. Hailey, Idaho, May 27, 1943; s. Theodore Clyde and Muriel Juanita (Kirtley) D.; m. Roberta Louise Erickson, Mar. 19, 1966; children—Timothy Shannon, Brianna Kristine, Rachel Melissa. B.S. in Elec. Engring., U. Wash., 1966, M.B.A., 1970. Engr. Gen. Telephone Co. of Northwest, Everett, Wash., 1968-69; mem. tech. staff Computer Sci. Corp., Richland, Wash., 1970-73; from research engr. to research mgr. and staff engr. Battelle Pacific Northwest Labs., Richland, 1973—. Editorial adv. bd. Internat. Jour. Computers, Electronics in Agr. Ruling elder 1st Presbyn. Ch., Prosser, Wash., 1982-84. Served to capt. U.S. Army, 1966-68, Vietnam. Decorated Bronze Star. Mem. IEEE, Am. Soc. Agrl. Engrs. (regional div. chmn. 1977, nat. com. chmn. 1977-78, 82-83, chmn. nat. conf. on electronics 1983, asst. editor jour. 1983), Assn. of U.S. Army, Am. Def. Preparedness Assn., Mid-Columbian Sci. Fair Assn. (pres. 1975-76), Beta Gamma Sigma. Current work: Microelectronics and computers; robotics in agr. Subspecialties: Microelectronics; Agricultural engineering.

DIWAN, BHALCHANDRA APPARAO, oncologist; b. Sangli, Maharashtra, India, Apr. 27, 1937; came to U.S., 1971; s. Apparao P. and Mainabai A. Diwan; m. Sanjivani B. Joshi, June 5, 1966; children—Ashutosh, Sachin. B.S., Willington Coll., Sangli, 1959; M.S., U. Poona, India, 1961, Ph.D., 1964. Prin. scientist Meloy Labs., Springfield, Va., 1976-80; spl. expert Nat. Cancer Inst., Frederick, Md., 1981—. Contbr. articles to profl. jours. Fellow NIH, 1971-74, Leukemia Soc. Am., 1974-76. Mem. Am. Assn. Cancer Research, AAAS. Subspecialties: Cancer research (medicine); Teratology. Office: Nat Cancer Inst Frederick Cancer Research Facility Frederick MD 21701

DIWAN, JOYCE JOHNSON, biology educator; b. Bklyn., Dec. 25, 1940; d. John Henry and Lillian Freida (Russ) Johnson; m. Romesh Kumar Diwan, Oct. 25, 1970. A.B., Mt. Holyoke Coll., 1962; Ph.D., U. Ill., 1967. Postdoctoral fellow U. Pa., 1966-69; asst. prof. Rensselaer Poly. Inst., 1969-75, assoc. prof., 1975—; vis. fellow U. Warwick, Eng., 1976-77. Contbr. to profl. jours. USPHS fellow, 1966-69; NSF grantee, 1970-72; USPHS grantee, 1974-76, 77-81, 83—. Mem. Am. Soc. Biol. Chemists, Am. Soc. Cell Biology, Biophys. Soc., AAAS, AAUP, Assn. Women in Sci., N.Y. Acad. Sci. Current Work: Bioenergetics, mitochondrial ion transport and metabolism. Subspecialties: Cell biology; Membrane biology. Home: 6 Bolivar Ave Troy NY 12180 Office: Dept Biology Rensselaer Polytechnic Inst Troy NY 12180

DIXEN, JEAN MARIE, psychologist; b. Owatonna, Minn., May 31, 1954; d. Jens Alfred and Mary Ann (Johnson) D. B.A., U. Minn., 1975; M.A., Mankata State U., 1977; Ph.D., U. Ga., 1971. Lic. marriage, family and child counselor, Calif.; lic. psychologist, Calif. Clin. psychology intern Palo Alto VA Med. Ctr., Calif., 1979-80; research asst. U. Ga., Athens, 1980-81, practicum supr., 1980-81, marriage and family counselor in pvt. practice, Palo Alto, Calif., 1982—; postdoctoral scholar Stanford U., 1981-83; outpatient psychiatrist Kaiser Hosp., Martinez, Calif., 1984—; research cons. Gender Dysphoria Program, Palo Alto, 1980—. Contbr. articles to profl. jours. Recipient Sci. award Bausch & Lomb, 1972; U. Ga. fellow, 1978-79, 80-81. Mem. Am. Psychol. Assn., AAAS, Calif. Assn. Marriage and Family Therapists, Assn. for Advancement Psychology, Mensa. Democrat. Lutheran. Current Work: Effects of estrogen replacement therapy on sexual function and depression in postmenopausal women; the relative effects of age and menopause on sexuality in women; evaluation of surgical sex reassignment for gender dysphoria. Subspecialties: Psychophysiology; Behavioral psychology. Home: 1312 Bel Aire Rd San Mateo CA 94402 Office: Kaiser Hosp Dept Outpatient Psychiatry Martinez CA 94402

DIXIT, SUDHIR SHARAN, electronics engineer; b. Lucknow, India, June 20, 1951; came to U.S., 1980; s. Shambhoo S. and Urmila (Dube) D.; m. Asha Shukla, Feb. 21, 1981; 1 child, Sapna. B.E., Maulana Azad Coll. Tech., India, 1972; M.E., Birla Inst. Tech. and Sci., India, 1974; Ph.D., U. Strathclyde, Glasgow, Scotland, 1979; M.B.A., Fla. Inst. Tech., 1983. Asst. lectr. Birla Inst. Tech. and Sci., Pilani, India, 1974; adj. lectr. Glasgow coll. Tech., 1976; postgrad. research engr. ITT Standard Telecommunication Labs., Harlow, Eng., 1978-80; assoc. prin. engr. Harris Corp., Melbourne, Fla., 1980-83; prin. engr. Codex Corp., Canton, Mass., 1983—. Contbr. articles to profl. publs. Patentee in field. Mem. IEEE. Current work: Artificial intelligence; image processing; pattern recognition; computer graphics; robotics; data compression; airborne navigation systems. Subspecialties: Computer engineering; Telecommunications. Home: 25 Devon Rd Norwood MA 02062 Office: Codex Corp 20 Cabot Blve Mansfield MA 02048

DIXON, FRANK JAMES, medical scientist, educator; b. St. Paul, Mar. 9, 1920; s. Frank James and Rose Augusta (Kuhfeld) D.; m. Marion Edwards, Mar. 14, 1946; children: Janet Wynne, Frank, Michael. B.S., U. Minn., 1941, M.B., 1943, M.D., 1944; D.Sc. (hon.), Med. Coll. Ohio, 1983. Diplomate Am. Bd. Pathology. Intern U.S. Naval Hosp., Great Lakes, Ill., 1943-44; research asst. dept. pathology Harvard, 1946-48; instr. dept. pathology Washington U., 1948-50, asst. prof., 1950-51; prof., chmn. dept. pathology U. Pitts. Med. Sch., 1951-60; chmn. dept. exptl. pathology Scripps Clinic and Research Found., La Jolla, Calif., 1961-74, chmn. biomed. research depts., 1970-74, dir. research inst., 1974—; research assoc. dept. biology U. Calif. at San Diego, 1961-64, prof. in residence in dept. biology, 1965-68, adj. prof. dept. pathology, 1968—; sci. adviser NIH, Nat. Found., Helen Hay Whitney Found.; mem. expert adv. panel on immunology WHO; sci. adv. bd. Nat. Kidney Found.; Pahlavi lectr. Ministry of Sci. and Higher Tech., Iran, 1976. Editor Advances in Immunology; Editorial bd. Excerpta Medica, Jour. Exptl. Medicine, Am. Jour. Pathology, Cellular Immunology, Kidney Hosp. Practice, Perspectives in Biology and Medicine; contbr. articles to profl. jours. Bd. dirs. Irvington House Med. Research; sci. adv. com. Mass. Gen. Hosp. Served with M.C. USNR, 1943-46. Recipient Theobald Smith award, 1952; Parke-Davis award in exptl. pathology, 1957; Disting. Achievement award Modern Medicine, 1961; Martin E. Rehfuss award in internal medicine, 1966; Von Pirquet medal Ann. Forum on Allergy, 1967; Bunim medal Am. Rheumatism Assn., 1968; Internat. award Gairdner Found., 1969; Mayo Soley award Western Soc. Clin. Research, 1969; Albert Lasker Basic Med. Research award, 1975; Dickson prize U. Pitts., 1975; Homer Smith award N.Y. Heart Assn., 1976; Rous-Whipple award Am. Assn. Pathologists, 1979, regents award U. Minn., 1985. Mem. Nat. Acad. Scis., N.Y. Acad. Scis. Western Assn. Physicians, Western Soc. Clin. Research, Soc. Exptl. Biology and Medicine, Transplantation Soc., AAAS, Am. Soc. Clin. Investigation, Am. Acad. Allergists, Interurban Path. Soc., Harvey Soc. (lectr. 1962), Am. Soc. Exptl. Pathology (pres. 1966), Am. Assn. Immunologists (pres. 1972), Am. Assn. for Cancer Research, Assn. Am. Physicians, Am. Acad. Arts and Scis., Sigma Xi, Nu Sigma Nu, Alpha Omega Alpha. Current Work: Genetics influencing autoimmunity. Subspecialties: Immunology (medicine); Immunogenetics. Home: 2355 Avenida de La Playa La Jolla CA 92037 Office: 10666 N Torrey Pines Rd La Jolla CA 92037

DIXON, GORDON HENRY, biochemist; b. Durban, South Africa, Mar. 25, 1930; s. Walter James and Ruth (Nightingale) D.; m. Sylvia W. Gillen, Nov. 20, 1954; children: Frances Anne, Walter Timothy, Christopher James, Robin Jonathan. M.A. with honors, U. Cambridge, Eng., 1951; Ph.D., U. Toronto, 1956. Research asso. U. Wash., 1956-58; research asso. U. Oxford, Eng., 1958-59; asst. prof. biochemistry U. Toronto, 1959-61, asso. prof., 1961-63; prof. U. B.C., 1963-72; prof., chmn. dept. biochemistry U. Sussex, Eng., 1972-74; prof. med. biochemistry U. Calgary, Alta., Can., 1974—, chmn., 1983—. Contbr. articles to profl. jours. Recipient Steacie prize, 1966. Fellow Royal Soc. London, Royal Soc. Can. (Flavelle medal 1980); mem. Am. Soc. Biol. Chemists, Can. Biochemistry Soc. (pres. 1982-83 Ayerst award), Pan Am. Biochem. Socs. (v.p. 1984—). Current Work: Mechanism of differential gene expression; organization and expression of sperm-specific genes. Subspecialties: Molecular biology; Genetics and genetic engineering (biology). Home: 3424 Underwood Pl NW Calgary AB T2N 4G7 Canada Office: Dept Med Biochemistry Health Scis Centre 3330 Hospital Dr NW Univ of Calgary Calgary AB T2N 4N1 Canada

DIXON, JACK E., biochemistry educator; b. Nashville, June 16, 1943; s. Margaret and Jesse D. D.; m. Claudia Kent, July 25, 1981. B.A., UCLA, 1966; Ph.D., U. Calif.-Santa Barbara, 1971. Teaching asst. U. Calif.-Santa Barbara, 1967-68, research asst., 1968-71; asst. prof. Purdue U., West Lafayette, Ind., 1973-78, assoc. prof., 1978-82, prof. biochemistry, 1982—; adj. assoc. prof. Ind. U., Bloomington, 1978—. NSF postdoctoral research fellow, 1971-73; recipient outstanding counselor Purdue U., 1975; travel award Am. Soc. Biol. Chemistry, 1976-81; career devel. award USPHS, 1976-81. Mem. Am. Chem. Soc., AAAS, Am. Assn. Biol. Chemists. Current Work: Molecular biology of peptide hormones. Subspecialties: Biochemistry (biology); Molecular biology. Home: 3743 Capilano Dr West Lafayette IN 47906 Office: Purdue U West Lafayette IN 47907

DIXON, RICHARD WAYNE, physicist; b. Hubbard, Oreg., Sept. 25, 1936; s. Harlow C. and Mabel (Nillson) D.; m. Rosina O. Berry, July 4, 1970; children—Erica, Douglas, Andrew. B.A., Harvard U., 1958, M.A., 1960, Ph.D., 1964. Tech. staff mem. Bell Labs., Murray Hill, N.J., 1965, supr. lightwave lasers group, 1968-79, head optoelectronics devices dept., 1979—. Editor: IEEE Electronic Device Letters, 1980-84, dir. Lightwave Devices Lab., 1984—. Contbr. articles to profl. jours. NSF fellow, 1959-63; Nat. scholar 1955-58. Fellow IEEE; mem. Am. Phys. Soc., AAAS, Ass Subspecialty: Laser research and development. Office: AT&T Bell Labs 600 Mountain Ave Murray Hill NJ 07974*

DIXON, ROBERT L., pharmacologist, toxicologist; b. Sacramento, Feb. 9, 1936; s. Wilbur Harold and Frances M. (Schafer) D.; m. Marilyn Veva Roth, June 8, 1958; children—Wendy C., Diane F., David R. B.S. in Pharmacy, Idaho State U., 1958; M.S. in Pharmacology, U. Iowa, 1961, Ph.D., 1963. Asst./assoc. prof. dept. pharmacology U. Wash., Seattle, 1965-69; sr. investigator Nat. Cancer Inst., Bethesda, Md., 1963-65, chief toxicology lab., 1969-72; chief lab. reproductive and devel. toxicology Nat. Inst. Environ. Health Scis., Research Triangle Park, N.C., 1972-84, asst. to dir. for internat. programs, 1979-80; dir. EPA Office of Health Research, Washington, 1984—; sr. policy analyst Office of Sci. and Tech. Policy, Exec. Office of Pres., Washington, 1977-78. Mem. editorial bd.: Environ. Health Perspectives, 1972—, Fundamental and Applied Toxicology, 1982—, Toxicology and Applied Pharmacology, 1973—, Jour. Toxicology and Environ. Health, 1978—, others; contbr. articles to encys. and profl. jours. Served with U.S. Army, 1959. Recipient Dir.'s award NIH, 1977. Mem. AAAS, Am. Assn. for Cancer Research, Am. Pub. Health Assn., Am. Soc. for Pharmacology and Exptl. Therapeutics, Am. Soc. Andrology, Am. Chem. Soc. (dir. chem. health and safety), Internat. Soc. Study of Xenobiotics, Internat. Union Pharmacology (sect. toxicology), Mt. Desert Island Biol. Lab. Soc., Soc. for Exptl. Biology and Medicine, Soc. for Occupational and Environ. Health, Soc. for Risk Analysis, Soc. Study of Reprodn., Soc. Ecotoxicology and Environ. Safety, Soc. Toxicology (pres. 1982-83, Achievement award 1972), Western Pharmacology Soc., Sigma Xi, Rho Chi. Lutheran. Current Work: Reproductive toxicology, developmental toxicology; extrapolation of laboratory data to man; risk analysis. Subspecialties: Toxicology (medicine); Pharmacology. Home: 6208 Winthrop Dr Raleigh NC 127612 Office: RO-683 401 M St SW Washington DC 20460

DIXON, ROBERT MORTON, scientist, land revegetation consultant; b. Leon, Kans., May 30, 1929; s. William Gill and Vivian (Marshall) D. B.S., Kans. State U., 1959, M.S., 1960; Ph.D., U. Wis., 1966. With USDA, various locations, 1960—, research soil scientist, Reno, 1967-73, Tucson, 1973—. Irrigation cons. Ford Found., Cairo, 1967; agrl. cons. AID, Haiti, 1978; irrigation del. People to People Internat., China, 1982; cons. agrl. colls., univs., land mgmt. agencies, pvt. land mgrs. Patentee land treatment method, imprinting, and land treatment machine, imprinter. Mem. Am. Soc. Agronomy, Soil Sci. Soc. Am, Internat. Soil Sci. Soc., Am. Soc. Agrl. Engrs., Soil Conservation Soc. Am., Am. Geophys. Union, Sierra Club, Nat. Wildlife Fedn., Audubon Soc., Defenders of Wildlife, Natural Resource Def. Council, Wilderness Soc., Nature Conservancy, Sigma Xi, Phi Kappa Phi, Gamma Sigma Delta. Democrat. Unitarian/Universalist. Development of land imprinting concepts and land imprinting machines for reversing global land desertification, to enhance natural resource conservation and food production. Subspecialties: Soil science; Resource conservation. Home: 1231 E Big Rock Rd Tucson AZ 85718 Office: USDA Agrl Research Service 2000 E Allen Rd Tucson AZ 85719

DIXON, WILFRID JOSEPH, statistics educator; b. Portland, Oreg.; m. Glorya Duffy, June 25, 1983; children—Janet Dixon Elashoff, Kathleen Dixon Nebert. B.A., Oreg. State Coll., 1938; M.A., U. Wis., 1939; Ph.D., Princeton, 1944. Asst. prof. math. U. Okla., 1942-44, 45-46; mem. joint Army-Navy Target Group, Washington and, Guam, 1944-45; asso. prof., then prof. math. U. Oreg., 1946-55; prof. preventive medicine UCLA, 1955-67, prof., 1967—, chmn. dept. biomath., 1967-74; pres. BMDP Statis. Software, Inc., 1981—; math. stat. VA Brentwood. Author: (with F.J. Massey) Introduction to Statistical Analysis, 4th edit., 1982; also articles.; Assoc. editor: Biometrics, 1955-65, Annals of Math. Statistics, 1955-58. Cons. NIH, 1960—; cons. NRC, 1948—, NSF, 1968—, Calif. Dept. Mental Hygiene and Public Health, 1963—. Fellow AAAS, Royal Statis. Soc.; mem. Inst. Math. Statistics, Internat. Statis. Inst., Am. Statis. Assn. (v.p. 1969-70, 78-81). Current Work: Statistical software with applications to environmental and medical research on analyzing incomplete data. Subspecialties: Mathematical software; Statistics. Home: 3821 Diamante Pl Encino CA 91436 Office: Univ Calif Los Angeles CA 90024

DIZER, JOHN THOMAS, JR., indsl. engr., educator, coll. dean, cons.; b. Norwood, Mass., Nov. 7, 1921; s. John Thomas and Eunice Haven (Homer) D.; m. Marie Leerkamp, Dec. 25, 1947; children: John Thomas III, Jane E., William D., Ann E., Mary L. B.S., Northeastern U., 1943; M.S. in Indsl. Engring, Purdue U., 1947, Ph.D. in Indsl. Engring, 1969. Registered profl. engr., N.Y. State cert. mfg. engr. Standards engr. E. I. du Pont de Nemours & Co., Inc., East Chicago, Ill., 1947-50; prodn. engr., supr. Cummins Engine Co., Columbus, Ind., 1952-59; mem. faculty Mohawk Valley Community Coll., Utica, 1959—, head mech. engring. tech. dept., 1968-82, dean tech. and bus., 1982—, NSF cons., India, 1969. Author: Tom Swift & Co, 1982; contbr. numerous articles on engring. edn. to profl. jours.; also writer juvenile lit. Bd. dirs. Oneida Hist. Soc.; dist. advancement chmn. Boy Scouts Am. Served to lt. USN, 1944-46, 50-52, PTO; Korea. Recipient Excellence in Adminstrn. award Mohawk Valley Community Coll., 1982. Mem. Am. Soc. for Engring. Edn., ASME (past chmn. Mohawk Valley chpt., Outstanding Engr. award 1971, Centennial medal 1981), Soc. Mfg. Engrs. (past chmn. Mohawk Valley chpt., Outstanding Engr. award 1973), Inst. Indsl. Engrs. (past pres. Mohawk Valley chpt.), Mohawk Valley Engrs. Exec. Council (past chmn., Outstanding Engr. award 1978), N.Y. State Engring. Tech. Assn. (pres.), Tau Beta Pi. Mem. Ch. of Christ. Lodge: Masons. Current Work: Electrochemical machining; physics of metal removal. Subspecialties: Industrial engineering; Mechanical engineering. Home: 10332 Ridgecrest Rd Utica NY 13502 Office: 1101 Sherman Dr Utica NY 13501

DJERASSI, CARL, educator, chemist; b. Vienna, Austria, Oct. 29, 1923; s. Samuel and Alice (Friedmann) D.; m. Norma Lundholm (div. 1976); children: Dale, Pamela (dec.); m. Diane W. Middlebrook, 1985. A.B. summa cum laude, Kenyon Coll., 1942, D.Sc. (hon.), 1958; Ph.D., U. Wis., 1945; D.Sc. (hon.), Nat. U. Mex., 1953, Fed. U., Rio de Janeiro, 1969, Worcester Poly. Inst., 1972, Wayne State U., 1974, Columbia, 1975, Uppsala U., 1977, Coe Coll., 1978, U. Geneva, 1978, U. Ghent, 1985, U. Man., 1985. Research chemist Ciba Pharm. Products, Inc., Summit, N.J., 1942-43, 45-49; asso. dir. research Syntex, Mexico City, 1949-52, research v.p., 1957-60; v.p. Syntex Labs., Palo Alto, Calif., 1960-62; v.p. Syntex Research, 1962-68, pres., 1968-72, Zoecon Corp., 1968-83; Prof. chemistry Wayne State U., 1952-59, Stanford, 1959—; dir. Cetus Corp., Zoecon Corp., Ridge Vineyards, Teknowledge, Inc.; Andrews lectr. U. New South Wales, Australia; Debye lectr. Cornell U.; Reynaud lectr. Mich. State U.; Venable lectr. U. N.C.; Edgar Fahs Smith Meml. lectr. U. Pa.; O.H. Smith lectr. Okla. State U.; Stieglitz lectr. U. Chgo.; Bachman lectr. U. Mich.; Mack lectr. Ohio State U.; Dreyfus lectr. Dartmouth; Fuson lectr U. Nev.; Dreyfus Disting. scholar Duke U.; Gregory Pincus Meml. lectr. Worcester Found.; Baker lectr. U. Calif. (Santa Barbara); Osborne lectr. Rockefeller U.; Purves lectr. McGill U.; Redman lectr. McMaster U.; ann. chemistry lectr. Royal Swedish Acad. Engring.; Scheele lectr. Swedish Pharm. Soc. Mem. editorial bd.: Jour. Organic Chemistry, 1955-59, Tetrahedron, 1958—, Steroids, 1963—, Proc. of Nat. Acad. Scis, 1964-70, Jour. Am. Chem. Soc, 1966-75, Organic Mass Spectrometry, 1968—; Author 7 books.; Contbr. numerous articles to profl. jours. Recipient Intrasci. Research Found. award, 1969; Freedman Patent award Am. Inst. Chemists, 1970; Chem. Pioneer award, 1973; Nat. Medal Sci., 1973; Perkin medal, 1975; Wolf prize in chemistry, 1978; John and Samuel Bard award in Sci. and Medicine, 1983; named to Nat. Inventors Hall of Fame, 1978. Mem. Nat. Acad. Scis., Am. Chem. Soc. (award pure chemistry 1958, Baekeland medal 1959, Fritzsche award 1960, award for creative invention 1973, award in chemistry of contemporary tech. problems 1983), Swiss Chem. Soc., Royal Soc. Chemistry (hon. fellow, Centenary lectr. 1964), Am. Acad. Arts and Scis., German Acad. (Leopoldina), Royal Swedish Acad. Scis. (fgn.), Royal Swedish Acad. Engring. Scis. (fgn.), Am. Acad. Pharm. Scis. (hon.), Brazilian Acad. Scis. (fgn.), Mexican Acad. Sci. Investigation, Bulgarian Acad. Scis. (fgn.), Phi Beta Kappa, Sigma Xi, Phi Lambda Upsilon (hon.). Current Work: Chemistry of natural products (antibiotics, alkaloids, steroids and terpenoids), medicinal chemistry (oral contraceptives, antiinflammatory agents), applications of physical measurements (optical rotatory dispersion, circular dichroism and mass spectrometry) to organic chemical problems. Subspecialties: Organic chemistry; Mass spectrometry. Office: Dept Chemistry Stanford U Stanford CA 94305

DJORDJEVIC, BORISLAV BORO, materials science scientist; b. Brezice, Yugoslavia, Aug. 25, 1951; came to U.S., 1968; s. Branislav Branko and Cirila (Antolovic) D.; m. Nancy Grant, June 30, 1974. B.S., Coll. William and Mary, 1973; M.S.E., Johns Hopkins U., 1978, Ph.D., 1980. Lab. asst. Coll. William and Mary, Williamsburg, Va., 1971-72; research asst. Johns Hopkins U., Balt., 1973-79; sr. scientist, group leader Martin Marietta Labs., Balt., 1980—; cons. Nat. Bur. Standards, Washington, 1979; dr. of univ. Johns Hopkins U., 1980—. Contbr. articles to sci. jours.; patentee in field. Recipient Outstanding Achievement award Martin Marietta Corp. Research and Devel., 1983, 84; Jefferson Cup award, 1984. Mem. Am. Soc. for Non-destructive Testing (vice chmn. acoustic emission com., chmn. Chesapeake Bay sect. 1984—), Am. Phys. Soc., Am. Soc. for Metals, ASTM, Metall. Soc., Md. Inst. for Metals (chmn. 1985). Club: Johns Hopkins (Balt.). Current work: Non-destructive evaluation of composites, advanced ultrasonics, optical probing of stress-waves, amtomated-robotic NDE systems, materials science. Subspecialties: Non-destructive testing; Materials. Office: Martin Marietta Labs 1450 S Rolling Rd Baltimore MD 21227

DLHOPOLSKY, JOSEPH GERALD, human factors engineer; b. Bronx, Mar. 4, 1950; s. Joseph Jaraslav and Sophie (Kist) D.; m. Patrice Sweeney, June 2, 1973; children: Heather, Gregory. B.A., St. John's U., 1972; Ph.D., SUNY-Stony Brook, 1978. Asst. prof. dept. psychology St. John's U., S.I., 1978-84; human factors engr. Grumman Aerospace Corp., Bethpage, N.Y., 1985—; cons. to sci. and industry. Contbr. articles to profl. jours., newspapers, and mags.; author: microcomputer software Grade File System, 1982, Extra-Sensory Perception, 1981, ICON: Visual Sensory Store, 1981, Hemispheric Information Processing, 1982; Software Methods for Experimental Psychology, 1984. Mem. AAAS, Eastern Psychol. Assn., Human Factors Soc., Nat. Space Inst., Current Work: Research and design of operator-machine interfaces in artificial intelligence systems; interest in space environment as perceptual distortion and human adjustment to same. Subspecialties: Artificial intelligence; Human factors engineering. Home: 27 Wilson St Port Jefferson Station NY 11776 Office: Grumman Aerospace Corp CO4-14 Bethpage NY 11714

DOANE, WILLIAM MCKEE, biomaterials research administrator, researcher; b. Covington, Ind., Sept. 26, 1930; s. Earle Edward and Mildred Rowena (McKee) D.; m. Joan Marie, June 6, 1952; children: Diane, Steven, Robert, Karen. B.S., Purdue U., 1952, M.S., 1960, Ph.D., 1962. Cert. tchr., Ind. Exec. trainee Gen. Motors, 1952; tchr. Fountain County (Ind.) Public Schs., 1954-55; grad. asst. Purdue U., 1955-62; with No. Regional Research Center, Dept. Agr., Peoria, Ill., 1962—, research leader, 1970-79; chief Biomaterials Conversion Lab., 1980—; lectr. Bradley U., 1965-80. Contbr. numerous articles, chpts. to profl. publs. Served with U.S. Army, 1952-54. Recipient Indsl. Research IR-100 award Dept. Agr., 1975, 78, Disting. Service award, 1976, Pollution Abatement award, 1978, Superior Service award, 1979; Don Wood award Am. Electroplaters Soc., 1978. Mem. Am. Chem. Soc., AAAS, Controlled Release Soc., Weed Sci. Soc. Patentee in field. Current Work: Chemistry and biochemistry of plant materials; research leadership on structure-property realtinships of biomaterials—plant polymers and composites. Subspecialties: Biomaterials; Polymers (materials science). Office: 181 Regional Research Center 1815 N University Peoria IL 61604

DOANE, WINIFRED WALSH, zoologist, geneticist, educator, researcher, cons.; b. Bronx, N.Y., Jan. 7, 1929; d. Harold Vandervoort and Helen Harper (Loucks) Walsh; m. Charles Chesley Doane, July 5, 1953; 1 child, Timothy Price. B.A. magna cum laude, Hunter Coll., CUNY, 1950; M.S., U. Wis., 1952; Ph.D. (NSF fellow), Yale U., 1960. E. Seringhaus scholar Woods Hole Marine Biol. Lab., 1950; teaching asst. U. Wis., Madison, 1950-51, research asst., 1951-53; asst. prof. Millsaps Coll., Jackson, Miss., 1954-55; lab. asst. Yale U., New Haven, 1956-58, NIH postdoctoral research trainee in genetics, 1960-62, faculty research assoc., 1962-75, lectr., 1965-75, assoc. prof. biology, 1975-77; prof. zoology Ariz. State U., Tempe, 1977—; prin. investigator research grants NSF, 1965-75; prin. investigator research grants NIH, 1973—, cons. genetics study sect. div. research grants, 1972, 74-77, 79; cons. genetic basis of disease rev. com. Nat. Inst. Gen. Med. Scis., NIH, 1980-84; cons. biomed. scis. study sect. div. research grants, 1985—. cons. Alan T. Waterman award com. NSF, 1979-81, chair com., 1981. Assoc. editor: Devel. Genetics, 1979-81; contbr. numerous articles to sci. jours. and books. Recipient Hall of Fame award Hunter Coll. Alumni Assn., 1972. Fellow AAAS; mem. Am. Inst. Biol. Scis., Am. Soc. Cell Biology, Am. Soc. Naturalists, Am. Soc. Zoologist, Genetics Soc. Am., Internat. Soc. Devel. Biology, Soc. for Devel. Biology (sec. 1976-79), Phi Beta Kappa. Current Work: Developmental, biochemical and molecular genetics of Drosophila; genetic regulatory mechanisms in cellular differentiation using A-amylase gene-enzyme system as a model; current work uses recombinant DNA technology. Subspecialties: Gene actions; Developmental biology.

DOBBS, GREGORY MELVILLE, chemist, computer scientist, educator; b. Teaneck, N.J., Aug. 19, 1947; s. Melville George and Madeline Veronica (Schlesler) D.; m. Mary Elizabeth Connor, Jan. 15, 1977; children: Katherine Michelle, John Gregory. A.B., Dartmouth Coll., 1969; M.A., Princeton U., 1972, Ph.D. in Chemistry, 1975. Systems programmer Kiewit Computation Center, Hanover, N.H., 1966-69; resident research fellow, central research dept. E.I. DuPont de Nemours & Co., Wilmington, Del., 1969; NSF trainee Princeton U., 1969-70, asst. in instrn., 1971-74; postdoctoral research assoc. dept. chemistry M.I.T., 1974-76; sr. research scientist, chem. physics United Techs. Research Center, East Hartford, Conn., 1976—; adj. lectr. dept. computer and info. sci. Hartford (Conn.) Grad. Center, 1978—. Contbr. articles to profl. jours. Recipient John G. Kemeny prize in computing Dartmouth Coll., 1969, E.B. Hartshorn medal in chemistry, 1969. Mem. Am. Chem. Soc., Am. Phys. Soc., Combustion Inst., Am. Inst. Aeros. and Astronautics, Phi Beta Kappa. Current Work: Laser diagnostic spectroscopy; laser-induced chemistry; systems programming; laboratory data acquisition. Subspecialties: Laser-induced chemistry; Laser spectroscopy. Home: 103 Farmstead Ln Glastonbury CT 06033 Office: Mail Stop 90 United Techs Research Center Silver Ln East Hartford CT 06108

DOBKIN, DAVID PAUL, computer science educator; b. Pitts., Feb. 29, 1948; s. Ben G. and Sylvia June (Swartz) D.; m. Kathy Kram, Sept. 6, 1970 (div. Dec. 1976); m. Suzanne Gespass, April 17, 1983. S.B., M.I.T., 1970; M.S., Harvard U., 1971, Ph.D., 1973. Asst. prof. Yale U., 1973-78; assoc. prof. U. Ariz., 1978-81; prof. computer sci. Princeton U., 1981—. Editor: Foundations of Secure Computation, 1978; contbr. articles profl. jours. Mem. Assn. Computing Machinery, Soc. Indsl. and Applied Math., Sigma Xi. Subspecialties: Algorithms; Graphics, image processing, and pattern recognition. Home: 463 Prospect Ave Princeton NJ 08540 Office: EECS Dept Princeton U Princeton NJ 08544

DOCHERTY, JOHN JOSEPH, microbiologist, educator; b. Youngstown, Ohio, Dec. 5, 1941; s. John Henry and Viola Jean (Sovak) D.; m. Pamela Ann, Aug. 21, 1965; children: Patricia, Susan. B.A., Youngstown U., 1964; M.S., Miami U., Oxford, Ohio, 1966; Ph.D., U. Ariz., 1970. Postdoctoral fellow Med. Sch., Pa. State U., 1970-72, asst. prof. microbiology, 1972-76, asso. prof., 1976—. Contbr. articles to profl. jours. Mem. Am. Soc. Microbiology, AAAS, Am. Soc. Virology, Sigma Xi, Phi Sigma. Current Work: Herpes simplex virus genital infections and relation to cancer induction. Subspecialties: Virology (biology); Microbiology. Home: 852 Webster Dr State College PA 16801 Office: Pa State U 310 S Frear Bldg University Park PA 16802

DOCHERTY, JOHN PATRICK, psychiatrist; b. Bklyn., Sept. 8, 1944; s. John Francis and Bernadine Julia (Szmythkowski) D.; children—Jennifer, Christine. A.B. magna cum laude, Boston Coll., 1966; M.D., U. Pa., 1970. Diplomate Am. Bd. Psychiatry and Neurology. Intern, Hosp. of U. Pa., Phila., 1970-71; resident in psychiatry Yale U., New Haven, 1971-74; dir. psychiat. research West Haven Vets. Hosp., Conn., 1976-78; dir. edn. Yale Psychiat. Inst., New Haven, 1978-81, chief schizophrenia unit, 1978-79, chief adolescent unit, 1979-81; chief spl. studies sect. NIMH, Rochville, Md., 1981, chief psychosocial treatments research br., 1983-85; med. dir. Nashua-Brookside Hosp., Nashua, N.H., 1985—; faculty grad. program NIH, Bethesda, Md., 1975-76, 84; co-dir. med. studies program Washington Sch. Psychiatry, 1982—; clin. research cons. Sheppard-Pratt Hosp., Balt., 1983—. Author abstracts, audio-visual publs., book chpts., articles. Served to comdr. USPHS, 1974-75, 81—. Recipient Hamilton Watch award, 1966; Kenneth E. Appel award, 1970; Seymour Lustman award, 1974; Outstanding Tchr. award Yale Psychiatry Residents, 1981. Mem. Am. Psychiat. Assn., AMA, Soc. Psychotherapy Research, AAAS. Current work: Psychotherapy research; psychiatric diagnosis; psychology of drug addiction. Subspecialty: Psychiatry. Office: Nashua-Brookside Hosp 11 Northwest Blvd Nashua NH 03063

DODS, RICHARD FREDERICK, clinical biochemist, consultant; b. Flushing, N.Y., Oct. 6, 1938; s. William and Elizabeth (Menson) D.; m. Linda Yuccas, June 18, 1967; 1 child, Steven. B.S., Bklyn. Coll., 1957-61; M.S., NYU, 1963; Ph.D., U. Conn., 1968. Diplomate Am. Bd. Clin. Chemistry. Research assoc. NYU Med. Ctr., N.Y.C., 1970-72; Northwestern U. Med. Ctr., Chgo., 1972-74; postdoctoral fellow Michael Reese Med. Ctr., Chgo., 1974-76; clin. asst. prof. U. Ill. Med. Sch., 1976-82; dir. biochemistry Louis A. Weiss Meml. Hosp., Chgo., 1976-82; dir. toxicology satellite lab. Smith Kline Clin. Labs., Schaumburg, Ill., 1978-81; dir. Clin. Lab. Consultants, Palatine, Ill. Author (audio cassette course) Introduction to Clinical Chemistry. Contbr. articles to profl. jours. Mem. Am. Assn. Clin. Chemistry, Nat. Acad. Clin. Biochemists, Am. Chem. Soc., AAAS. Home: 243 E Forest Ln Palatine IL Office: Clinical Lab Consultants 243 E Forest Ln Palatine IL

DODSON, CHARLES LEON, JR., chemistry educator; b. Knoxville, Tenn., Mar. 15, 1935; s. Charles Leon and Margaret Glen (Berry) D.; m. Vernell Laura Woodard, Sept. 6, 1958; children: Alyssa, Bronwyn. B.S., Emory and Henry Coll., 1957; M.S., U. Tenn., 1962, Ph.D., 1963. Postdoctoral fellow U. Birmingham, Eng., 1963-64, Nat. Research Council, Ottawa, Ont., Can., 1964-66; mem. faculty U. Ala., Huntsville, 1966-81, assoc. prof. chemistry, 1969-81; applications specialist Beckman Instruments, Inc., 1981-84, prin. applications chemist, 1985—; vis. prof. Oxford U., 1972-73. Contbr. articles to profl. jours. Mem. Am. Chem. Soc., Am. Phys. Soc., Blue Key, Sigma Pi Sigma. Subspecialties: Inorganic chemistry; Physical chemistry. Home: 1982 Keokuk St Orange CA 92665 Office: Campus Drive at Jamboree Blvd Irvine CA 92713

DOEHRMAN, STEVEN R(ALPH), research clinical psychologist, consultant; b. Ft. Wayne, Ind., July 12, 1942; s. Ralph C. and Virginia Rita (Drury) D.; m. Margery Jean Adelson, May 5, 1968 (div. Apr. 1981); children: Eric, David. A.B., U. Mich., 1965, Ph.D., 1971. Supervising clin. psychologist U. Mich., 1974-80, lectr. dept. psychology, 1974-81, research coordinator psychol. clinic, 1976-81; project dir. Inst. Social Research, Ann Arbor, Mich., 1977-81; clin. psychologist, research dir. Orchard Hills Psychiat. Center, Farmington Hilsl, Mich., 1980—; lectr. Univ. Extension Service, Grand Rapids, Mich., 1971; speaker for civic, bus. groups, Ann Arbor area, 1979—, cons. in field. Author: (with J.R. French) Stress, social support and adjustment, 1982. NIMH postdoctoral fellow, 1973-75; Center for Clin. Study Personality grantee, 1977-80. Mem. Am. Psychol. Assn., Soc. Psychotherapy Research, Assn. Advancement Psychology. Clubs: Ski (Ann Arbor), Parents Without Partners (speaker) (Ann Arbor), Ann Arbor Track (Ann Arbor). Current Work: Social support as a buffer against deleterious effects of environmental stress upon individual strain; prevention and treatment for anorexia nervosa and bulimia. Subspecialties: Social psychology; Health psychology. Office: Orchard Hills Psychiat Center 23800 Orchard Lake Rd Farmington Hills MI 48024

DOELLGAST, GEORGE JOHN, biochemist, educator; b. Bklyn., Aug. 18, 1944; s. Johann George and Marie (Brand) D.; m. Janet Menke, Aug. 26, 1972; children—Virginia Lee, Johann. B.S. in Chemistry, Fordham U., 1966; B.S. in Chem. Engring., Columbia U., 1967; Ph.D. in Biochemistry, Purdue U., 1972. Postdoctoral fellow Tufts U., Boston, 1972-75, instr., Boston, 1975-76; asst. prof. Wake Forest U., Winston-Salem, N.C., 1976-80, assoc. prof. biochemistry, 1980—. Mem. Am. Soc. Biol. Chemists. Current work: Tissue specific proteins; clotting factors. Subspecialties: Biochemistry (medicine); Immunology (medicine). Home and office: 4291 Lantern Dr Winston-Salem NC 27106

DOERING, DALE LARRY, research physicist; b. Akron, Ohio, Aug. 12, 1955; s. Larry L. and Jean Louise (Boughton) D.; m. Toyoko Tsukuda, Nov. 14, 1981. B.S. in Physics, Wash. State U., 1977, M.S. in Physics, 1978, Ph.D. in Physics, 1981. Research asst. Wash. State U., Pullman, 1976-81, postdoctoral assoc., 1981; NRC postdoctoral fellow Nat. Bur. Standards, Gaithersburg, Md., 1981-83; asst. research scientist U. Fla., Gainesville, 1983—. Contbr. articles to profl. publs. Adviser U. Fla. Internat. Folkdancers, 1984—. Mem. Am. Phys. Soc., Am. Vacuum Soc., Phi Beta Kappa. Current work: Surface structure, thin films, ultra high vacuum, surface chemistry, orientational ordering on metals and semiconductors, epitaxy. Subspecialties: Condensed matter physics; Surface chemistry. Home: 5923 NW 36th Pl Gainesville FL 32606 Office: Dept Physics Univ Fla Gainesville FL 32611

DOERNER, ROBERT CARL, reactor physicist; b. St. Cloud, Minn., Sept. 26, 1926; s. Carl A. and Marcella (Krieger) D.; m. Elizabeth Dalton, Oct. 25, 1954; children: Katherine, Mary, Joanne, David, James. B.S., St. Johns U., Collegeville, Minn., 1949; Ph.D., St. Louis U., 1955. Research assoc. Argonne Nat. Lab., Ill., 1955-56, asst. physicist, 1956-59, assoc. physicist, 1959—; vis. assoc. prof. Cornell U., 1962-64. Chmn. Gov.'s Planning Council Developmental Disabilities, 1981-83; bd. dirs. Ill. Advocacy Authority, 1977—. Served with USN, 1944-46, PTO, ETO. Mem. Am. Nuclear Soc. (vice chmn. sect. 1969-70, chmn. 1970-71, Meritorious award 1972). Current Work: Water reactor plant safety analysis, code development and implimentation. Fast-reactor physics experiments and analysis. Subspecialties: Nuclear engineering; Nuclear physics. Home: 615 Knollwood Wheaton IL 60187 Office: Argonne Nat Lab 9600 Cass Ave Argonne IL 60439

DOERR, ROBERT DOUGLAS, psychologist, educator, poet; b. Burlington, Vt., Apr. 9, 1944; s. Robert Joseph and Betty Jane (Whitney) Stubbings D.; m. Lorinda Ferland; 1 child, Eli T. B.A., Rollins Coll., 1966; M.A., San Francisco State U., 1971; Ph.D., Saybrook Inst., 1978. Cert. Biofeedback Cert. Inst. Am. Clinician behavioral medicine, dir. Alameda (Calif.) Biofeedback Center, 1978—; prof. psychology and communication arts Columbia Coll., 1978—; prof. sci. fiction Chabot Coll., Hayward, Calif., 1971—; mem. adj. faculty Sierra U., 1981. Editor: Saybrook Review and Humanistic Psychology Inst. Review, 1978—; author: Canto Libre, 1979, The Peace Corps Experience: A Dialogal Analysis, 1981; 7 books of poetry. Mem. Kensington Symphony Orch., 1979—. Fellow Am. Psychol. Assn.; mem. Biofeedback Soc. Am., Assn. Humanistic Psychology, Am. Fedn. Tchrs., Alameda C. of C. Taoist. Current Work: The use of biofeedback to aid in self-regulation of vascular and muscular disorders; the phenomenon of mind-body resistance in the above context; application of subliminal techniques in psycho-neuro-immunology. Subspecialties: Biofeedback; Physiological psychology. Home: 1517 B Saint Charles St Alameda CA 94501

DOHERTY, MARK FITZGERALD, computer systems analyst; b. Norfolk, Va., Dec. 8, 1953; s. Robert Emmett and Mary Elizabeth (Fitzgerald) D.; m. Linda Jean Noeske, Sept. 6, 1980; children: Jonathan Alexander, Anna Elise. Student, Chaminade U. Honolulu, 1972-74; B.A., Cath. U. Am., 1976; postgrad., U. Md., 1982—. Programmer Son-Chief Electrics, Winstead, Conn., 1974-75; sr. mem. tech. staff ConTel Info. Systems, Bethesda, Md., 1976-82. State chmn. Libertarian party Md., Bethesda, Md., 1979. Mem. Assn. Computing Machinery, Phi Beta Kappa. Libertarian. Current Work: Autonomous navigation, spatial representations of objects. Subspecialties: Distributed systems and networks; Graphics, image processing, and pattern recognition. Home: 7324 Willow Ave Takoma Park MD 20912

DOI, KUNIO, medical physicist; b. Tokyo, Japan, Sept. 28, 1939; s. Umekiti and Mitiko (Nakamura) D.; m. Akiko Doi, Feb. 15, 1962; children: Hitoshi, Takeshi. B.Sc., Waseda U., Tokyo, 1962, Ph.D., 1969. Dir. Kurt Rossmann Labs. for Radiologic Image Research dept. radiology U. Chgo., 1976—, prof. radiology, 1976—. Mem. Am. Assn. Physicists in Medicine. Current Work: Digital radiography, monte carlo simulation, transfer function analysis, monoenergetic x-ray source, screen film systems. Subspecialties: Diagnostic radiology; Imaging technology. Home: 6415 Lane Ct Hinsdale IL 60521 Office: 5841 S Maryland Ave Chicago IL 60637

DOI, ROY HIROSHI, biochemistry educator; b. Sacramento, Calif., Mar. 26, 1933; s. Thomas Toshiteru and Ima (Sato) D.; m. Joyce Takahashi, Aug. 30, 1958; children: Kathryn Ellen, Douglas Alan. B.A. in Physiology, U. Calif.-Berkeley, 1953, B.A. in Bacteriology, 1957; M.S. in Bacteriology, U. Wis.-Madison, 1958, Ph.D., 1960. Asst. prof. biochemistry Syracuse U., 1963-65; asst. prof. U. Calif.-Davis, 1965-66, assoc. prof., 1966-69, prof., 1969—; chmn. microbial chemistry study sect. NIH, Bethesda, 1978-79; v.p., treas. Internat. Spore Conf., Inc., Boston, 1982—. Served with U.S. Army, 1953-55. NIH fellow, 1960-63; NSF fellow, 1971-72; recipient Sr. U.S. Scientist award Alexander von Humboldt Found., 1978-79. Mem. AAAS, Am. Soc. Biol. Chemists, Am. Soc. Microbiology, Sigma Xi. Democrat. Unitarian. Current Work: Use of expression-probe plasmids to study promoter structure and function, heterologous gene expression, and gene organization in Bacillus subtilis. Subspecialties: Molecular biology; Microbiology. Home: 1520 Lemon Ln Davis CA 95616 Office: Dept Biochemistry and Biophysics U Calif Davis CA 95616

DOIRON, DAVID JOHN, astronomy educator, radio astronomer; b. Lowell, Mass., Sept. 15, 1952; s. David D. and Rita H. (Furtado) D. B.S. in Physics, MIT, 1974; M.S., U. N.H., 1976; Ph.D., U. Iowa, 1984. Teaching asst. U. N.H., Durham, 1974-76; teaching asst. U. Iowa, 1976-84, research asst., 1983; asst. prof. Clemson U., S.C., 1984—. Contbr. articles to profl. jours. Mem. rules com. Johnson County Democratic Party, Iowa, 1980-84; mem. credentials com. Iowa Dem. Party, Des Moines, 1984. Mem. Am. Astron. Soc. (assoc.), Am. Phys. Soc., Astron. Soc. Pacific, AAAS. Current work: Radio emission, binary stars, interferometry. Subspecialties: Radio and microwave astronomy; Solar physics. Office: Dept Physics and Astronomy Clemson U Clemson SC 29631

DOLAK, TERENCE MARTIN, research chemist, research administrator; b. Youngstown, Ohio, Sept. 24, 1951; s. Edward Andrew and Verona R. (Hugoboom) D.; m. Lisa Ann Pavlick, Apr. 20, 1985. B.S. in Biochemistry, Ohio State U., 1973; Ph.D. in Chemistry, U. S.C., 1977. Research assoc. Wayne State U., Detroit, 1977-78; scientist Bristol-Myers Co., Evansville, Ind., 1979:80, sr. scientist, 1981-82, mem. antihypertensive group, 1983-84; sect. head Ayerst Labs. Research, Princeton, N.J., 1984—; lectr. in field. Patentee, author in field. Mem. Am. Chem. Soc., N.Y. Acad. Scis., AAAS. Roman Catholic. Current work: Design and synthesis of new drug entities; have worked on Beta-blockers, diuretics, ACE inhibitors, vasodilators, Alpha-blockers and calcium antagonists. Subspecialties: Organic chemistry; Biochemistry (biology). Office: Ayerst Labs Research CN 8000 Princeton NJ 08540

DOLAN, JOSEPH FRANCIS, astronomer; b. Rochester, N.Y., Sept. 17, 1939; s. Edwin Joseph and Helen Virginia (McAnnally) D.; m. Susan Marie, Aug. 14, 1971; children: Lee Marie, John Henry. B.S., St. Bonaventure U., Olean, N.Y., 1961; A.M., Harvard U., 1963, Ph.D., 1966. Physicist Smithsonian Astrophys. Obs., Cambridge, Mass., 1964-66; sr. scientist Jet Propulsion Lab., Pasadena, Calif., 1966-68; asst. prof. Warner & Swasey Obs., Case Western Res. U., Cleve., 1968-75; sr. fellow Nat. Acad. Scis., NASA Goddard Space Flight Ctr., Greenbelt, Md., 1975-77, astrophysicist, 1977—; co-investigator high speed photometer experiment Space Telescope Satellite, Hipparcos satellite. Contbr. articles to profl. jours. in field. Mem. Internat. Astron. Union, Am. Astron. Soc. Current Work: Galactic X-ray sources, close binaries, astronomical polarization. Subspecialties: X-ray high energy astrophysics; Optical astronomy. Home: 16007 Jerald Rd Laurel MD 20707 Office: Code 681 NASA Goddard Space Flight Ctr Greenbelt MD 20771

DOLAN, LINDA CAPANO, nuclear fuels company executive; b. Cin., Dec. 7, 1953; d. Arnold Frank and Velma Emily (Craig) Capano; m. Jerome Francis Dolan, July 23, 1977; 1 dau.: Jacqueline Michelle. B.S., Xavier U., Cin., 1976, postgrad., 1986; M.S. in Nuclear Engring, U. Cin., 1977. Instr. Xavier U., Cin., 1976-77; engr. Gen. Electric Co., San Jose, Calif., 1977-79, Evendale, Ohio, 1979-81; chief systems and facilities safety NLO, Inc., Cin., 1981—; Chmn. Gen. Electric Task Force on Human Factors, Evendale, 1980. U. Cin. grad. fellow, 1976. Mem. Am. Nuclear Soc., Soc. Women Engrs., Sigma Pi Sigma. Republican. Current Work: Nuclear criticality safety of fuel elements, particularly in transportation applications. Subspecialties: Nuclear engineering; Nuclear fission. Home: 5750 Desertgold Dr Cincinnati OH 45239 Office: NLO Inc PO Box 39158 Cincinnati OH 45239

DOLAN, LINDA SUTLIFF, alternative energy research executive, consultant; b. Danville, Pa., Sept. 10, 1951; d. William Bruce and June (Mausteller) Sutliff; m. Roderick Norman Dolan; 1 son, Troy Norman. B.A. in Biology and Earth Sci, Clarion (Pa.) State Coll., 1974; M.S. in Forest Mgmt. (music scholar, Weyerhaeuser Found. fellow), Oreg. State U., Corvallis, 1981. Exec. asst. Clarion County Conservation Dist., 1972-74; forest researcher Oreg. State U., 1976-77; dist. mgr. Spokane County Conservation Dist., 1978; chief cons. Dolan & Assocs., Seattle, 1978-79; biomass program mgr. Seattle City Light, 1979—; cons., curriculum adv., program reviewer. Contbr. articles to profl. jours. Program adv. MetroCenter YMCA, 1981—; mem. Democratic Women's Caucus, 1982, 84. Mem. Soc. Am. Foresters, Biomass Energy Research Assn. (nat. bd. dirs.), Poplar Council Can., Biomass Invisible Coll. Brazil, Bio-Energy Council, Seattle Mgmt. Assn., Seattle Women in Govt. Methodist. Club: Seattle City. Current Work: Cultivating and marketing crops as fuel for energy production biomass, energy farms, renewable resources, wood-fired power-plants, bio-fuels, bio-energy, silviculture, gasification. Subspecialties: Combustion processes; Fuels. Office: Seattle City Light 1015 3d Ave Seattle WA 98104

DOLENZ, JOHN JOSEPH, psychologist; b. Barton, Wis., July 17, 1931; s. Joseph John and Martha Mary (Kircher) D.; m. Jetta Maxine Parmer, Dec. 27, 1962; 1 son, John Andrew. Cert., Cath. U. Am., 1957; M.A., U. Tulsa, 1962; postgrad., U. Kans., 1961-64; Ph.D., U. Ottowa, Ont., 1970. Lic. psychologist, Tex., Kans.; diplomate in neuropsychology Am. Bd. Profl. Neuropsychology. Clin. psychologist Psychol. Services, Kansas City, Mo., 1962-68; dir. services Tarrant County Hosp. Dist., Ft. Worth, Tex., 1970-73; with alcohol unit VAMC, Marion, Ind., 1973-76; dir. mental hygiene clinic VA-Outpatient, Evansville, Ind., 1976-79; coordinator alcohol treatment unit VA Med. Ctr., Big Spring, Tex., 1979—; cons. Tex. Tech Med. Sch. Alcohol Unit, Lubbock, 1983. Editor, co-author: Participant Manual, 1982; contbr. articles to profl. jours. Recipient Superior Performance award VA Med. Ctr., Big Spring, 1980, 82, 83, 85. Canadian Psychol. Assn., Tex. Psychol. Assn., Kans. Psychol. Assn., Council for Nat. Register of Health Service Providers in Psychology, Psychol. Assn. Greater West Tex. (pres. 1983, 85). Clubs: Sertoma (sec. Evansville 1978-79), Garden (pres. 1982-85). Lodge: Rotary (dir. Big Spring 1982-83). Current Work: Cognitive impairment from excessive use mind altering drugs especially alcohol. Subspecialties: Neuropsychology; Toxicology (medicine). Home: 2519 E 25th St Big Spring TX 79720 Office: 2400 S Gregg St Big Spring TX 79720

DOLL, EUGENE CARTER, soil scientist; b. Fort Benton, Mont., Feb. 15, 1921; s. Frank Bryan and Nancy Ann (Carter) D.; m. Mary Margaret Nash, July 7, 1949 (dec.); children—Carol Ann, Elizabeth Jane, William Eugene. B.S. in Soil Sci., Mont. State U., 1949, M.S. in Botany, 1951; Ph.D. in Soil Sci., U. Wis.-Madison, 1953. Agronomist, U. Ky., Lexington, 1953-60; prof. soil sci. Mich. State U., 1960-74; soil scientist Internat. Fertilizer Devel. Ctr. and TVA, Muscle Shoals, Ala., 1974-76; agriculturist TVA, Muscle Shoals, 1976-78; programming adminstr. Office Internat. Coop. and Devel., USDA, Washington, 1978-81; supt., soil scientist Land Reclamation Research Ctr., N.D. State U., Mandan, 1981—. Contbr. numerous articles to profl. jours. Served to 1st lt. U.S. Army, 1943-46. Fellow Am. Soc. Agronomy, Soil Sci. Soc. Am. Roman Catholic. Current work: Reclamation of surface-mined land, soil chemistry, soil fertility, international agricultural development Subspecialty: Soil science. Office: ND State U Reclamation PO Box 459 Mandan ND 58554

DOLLING, DAVID STANLEY, fluid dynamics researcher, aerospace engineer, educator; b. Bournemouth, Dorset, Eng., Mar. 21, 1950; came to U.S., 1976; s. Stanley Henry and Irene (Lucas) D. B.Sc. in Engring, London U., 1971, Ph.D., 1977; diploma, Von Karman Inst., Brussels, 1974. Aerodynamicist Hawker-Siddeley Dynamics, Hertfordshire, Eng., 1971-73; researcher, lectr. Princeton U., 1976—. Contbr. numerous articles to profl. publs., 1976—. Mem. Royal Aero. Soc. (London) (Undergrad. prize 1971), AIAA (chmn. Princeton sect. 1980-81, sr.), AAAS. Current Work: Supersonic flows, interactions of shock waves with boundary layers, high frequency instrumentation. Subspecialties: Aeronautical engineering; Aerospace engineering and technology. Home: 65 S Stanworth Dr Princeton NJ 08540 Office: Gas Dynamics Lab James Forrestal Campus Princeton U Princeton NJ 08544

DOLUISIO, JAMES THOMAS, educator; b. Bethlehem, Pa., Sept. 28, 1935; s. Dominic and Sue (Powell) D.; m. Phyllis M. Sabolski, June 20, 1959; children—Thomas, James, Rebecca. B.S. in Pharmacy, Temple U., 1957, M.S., 1959; Ph.D., Purdue U., 1962. From asst. prof. to asso. prof. pharmacy Phila. Coll. Pharmacy and Sci., 1961-67, also asso. dir. dept., 1965-67; prof., chmn. dept. pharmacy U. Ky., Lexington, 1967-73; prof., dean U. Tex., Austin, 1973—; Cons. Smith Kline & French Labs., Phila., 1962-67, McNeil Labs., Ft. Washington, Pa., 1967-72, Hoechst Labs., Somerville, N.J., 1973—, Nat. Inst. Drug Abuse, 1976-78, HEW, U.S. Surgeon Gen., 1975-83. Contbr. to profl. and sci. jours. NSF fellow, 1959-61; Am. Found. Pharm. Edn. fellow, 1957-59. Mem. Am. Pharm. Assn., Am. Assn. Colls. Pharmacy, Am. Soc. Hosp. Pharmacy, Rho Chi. Current work: Drug Absorption. Subspecialty: Pharmacokinetics. Office: Office of Dean Coll Pharmacy U Texas Austin TX 78712

DOMAN, ROBERT CHARLES, materials scientist; b. Lancaster, Pa., July 3, 1930; s. James Charles and Anna Sophia (Kipphorn) D.; m. Nancy Ann Barrett, Jan. 24, 1959; children—Linda E., Charles R. B.S. in Geology, Franklin and Marshall Coll., 1953; M.A., Washington U., 1955; Ph.D., U. Wis., 1961. Petroleum geologist Shell Oil Co., Abilene, Tex., 1955-57; scientist ceramics Corning Glass Works, N.Y., 1960-74, mgr. ceramic product devel., 1974-78, mgr. glass ceramics research, 1978-82, sr. research assoc., 1982-83, mgr. materials research, 1984—, mgr. engring. research, 1983-84. Contbr. articles to profl. jours. Patentee in field. Mem. Mineralogical Soc. Am., Am. Chem. Soc., Am. Ceramic Soc., Sigma Xi. Republican. Lutheran. Current work: Fiber and whisker reinforced glass and glass ceramics, glass ceramics, fine particulate ceramics. Subspecialties: Ceramics; Composite materials. Home: 3 W Chatfield Pl Painted Post NY 14870 Office: Corning Glass Works Sullivan Park Corning NY 14831

DOMBECK, THOMAS WALTER, physicist; b. Ellwood City, Pa., Feb. 7, 1945; s. Walter John and Cecelia Mary (Topolski) D.; m. Bonnie Marcia Rosen, Dec. 20, 1968; children—Heidi Jane, Daniel Andrew. B.A., Columbia U., 1967; Ph.D., Northwestern U., 1972. Research asst. Imperial Coll., London, 1972-74; postdoctoral fellow Argonne Nat. Lab., 1974-75; vis. sr. physicist Lab. High Energy, Dubna, USSR, 1975; asst. prof. U. Md., College Park, 1976-81; staff mem. Los Alamos Nat. Lab., 1981—; pres. Adminstrv. Planning and Computing Co., N.Y.C., 1967. Contbr. articles to profl. jours. Mem. Am. Phys. Soc., AAAS, Am. Hist. Soc. Democrat. Current work: Neutrino interactions with nuclei and electrons, neutron properties, neutron interferometry, gravitational interactions with neutrons. Subspecialties: Particle physics; Nuclear physics. Home: 550 Canyon Rd Los Alamos NM 87544 Office: Los Alamos Nat Lab Box 1663 Los Alamos NM 87545

DOMBRO, ROY SANDOR, biochemist, educator; b. Bklyn., Oct. 21, 1933; s. Max and Esther (Shapiro) D.; m. Marcia Ann Winters, Sept. 10, 1967; children—Rayna, Meryl. B.S., Bklyn. Coll., 1954; M.S., U. Wis.-Madison, 1956, Ph.D., 1958. Research assoc. Rockefeller U., N.Y.C., 1958-64, Inst. Muscle Disease, N.Y.C., 1964-65; asst. prof. surgery and biochemistry Albert Einstein Coll. Medicine, Bronx, N.Y., 1965-70; research asst. prof. surgery U. Miami Med. Sch., Fla., 1970—; chemist VA Hosp., Miami, 1970—. Contbr. articles to profl. jours. Mem. Am. Chem. Soc., AAAS. Current work: Amino acid and lipid metabolism related to liver disease. Subspecialties: Biochemistry (medicine); Pharmacology. Home: 9841 SW 123d St Miami FL 33176 Office: VA Med Ctr 1201 NW 16th St Miami FL 33125

DOMER, FLOYD RAY, pharmacologist, educator; b. Cedar Rapids, Iowa, July 12, 1931; s. William Ray and Caroline Anne (Zimmer) D.; m. Judith Elaine Kofroth, 1965. B.S., State U. Iowa, 1954, M.S., 1956; Ph.D., Tulane U., 1959. Life Ins. Med. Research Fund postdoctoral fellow Nat. Inst. Med. Research, London, 1959-60; with USAF Research and Devel. Command, Istituto Superiore di Sanita, Rome, 1960-61; asst. prof. pharmacology U. Cin., 1961-62; asst. prof. pharmacology Tulane U., 1963-64, asso. prof., 1965-74, prof., 1974—. Author: Animal Experiments in Pharmacological Analysis, 1971. Recipient award for teaching Owl Club, 1982, 83. Mem. Am. Soc. Pharmacology and Exptl. Therapeutics, Soc. Neurosci., Soc. Exptl. Biology and Medicine. Club: Trojan. Current Work: The effects of drugs on function of blood-brain barrier, genitourinary tract. Subspecialties: Pharmacology; Neuropharmacology. Home: 4420 Copernicus St New Orleans LA 70114 Office: 1430 Tulane Ave New Orleans LA 70112

DOMER, JUDITH ELAINE, microbiologist; b. Millersville, Pa., Apr. 9, 1939; d. Richard Harvey and Dorothy Alice (Peters) Kofroth; m. Floyd R. Domer, Apr. 15, 1965. B.A., Tusculum Coll., 1961; Ph.D., Tulane U., 1966. Diplomate: Am. Bd. Med. Microbiology. Instr. dept. biology St. Mary's Dominican Coll., New Orleans, 1966-67, asst. prof., 1967-68; research assoc. dept. microbiology and immunology Tulane U. Med. Sch., New Orleans, 1968-71; research fellow Kennedy Inst. Rheumatology, London, 1971-72; asst. prof. dept. microbiology Tulane U. Med. Sch., 1972-77, assoc. prof., 1977—;

mem. bacteriology and mycology study sect. NIH, 1975-79; guest researcher NIAID, NIH, 1984-85. Mem. editorial bd.: Exptl. Mycology, 1976-79, assoc. editor, 1979-83; mem. editorial bd.: Infection and Immunity, 1981-86. Contbr. articles to profl. jours. NIH grantee; Cancer Assn. Greater New Orleans grantee. Mem. Am. Soc. Microbiology (chmn.-elect med. mycology div. 1982-83, chmn. 1983-84), Med. Mycol. Soc. Ams., Internat. Soc. Human and Animal Mycology, Am. Assn. Immunologists, Am. Acad. Microbiology, Infectious Diseases Soc. Am., Sigma Xi. Democrat. Methodist. Current Work: Immunology of fungal diseases. Subspecialties: Microbiology; Infectious diseases. Home: 4420 Copernicus St New Orleans LA 70114 Office: 1430 Tulane Ave New Orleans LA 70112

DOMINO, GEORGE, psychologist; b. Torino, Italy, June 13, 1938; came to U.S., 1949; s. Tommaso and Maria (Oglietti) D.; m. Valerie Gerencser, Aug. 14, 1965; children: Brian, Marisa, Marla. B.S., Loyola U., Los Angeles, 1960; Ph.D., U. Calif.-Berkeley, 1967. Cert. clin. psychologist, Ariz. Instr. U. San Francisco, 1962-65; asst. prof. Fresno State Coll., 1965-66; prof., dir. counseling Fordham U., 1966-75; prof., dir. clin. tng. U. Ariz., Tucson, 1975—; cons., v.p. George W. Fotis, Greenwich, Conn., 1968—. Contbr. articles to profl. jours. USPHS predoctoral fellow, 1963-65; postdoctoral fellow Am. Coll. Testing, 1970. Mem. Am. Psychol. Assn., Western Psychol. Assn., Rocky Mountain Psychol. Assn., Sigma Xi. Roman Catholic. Current Work: Psychometrics, creativity, dream content. Subspecialty: Clinical psychology. Office: University of Arizona Tucson AZ 85721

DON, NORMAN STANLEY, psychologist; b. Port Chester, N.Y., Oct. 2, 1934; s. William and Betty (Berson) D.; m. Ruth Stevens Tolman, June 28, 1958; children: Bronson Whitmarsh, Brent Tolman. M.S., U. Chgo., 1960; Ph.D., Union Grad. Sch., 1974. Researcher U. Chgo., 1961-65; cons. in field industry, fed., state govt., 1965-74; research asso. Dept. Psychiatry, U. Chgo., 1974-75; investigator Am. Dental Assn., Chgo., 1976-80; pvt. practice psychology, cons., Chgo., 1975-81; dir., pres. Kairos Found., Chgo., 1981—; lectr. in field; cons. in field. Author: The Transpersonal Crisis, 1983; contbr. articles to profl. jours.; discoverer/prin. investigator: The Canonical Effect, 1974. Epilepsy Found. Am. fellow, 1975. Mem. Biofeedback Soc. Ill. (dir. 1976-79), Am. Psychol. Assn., Biofeedback Soc. Am., AAAS. Current Work: Psychophysiology; cognitive neuroscience; consciousness research; phenomenology of conscious experience; cybernetic modeling of perceptual control. Subspecialties: Physiological psychology; Consciousness. Address: Kairos Found 35 E Wacker Dr Chicago IL 60601

DONABEDIAN, AVEDIS, physician, public health educator; b. Beirut, Lebanon, Jan. 7, 1919; came to U.S., 1955, naturalized, 1960; s. Samuel and Maritza (Der Hagopian) D.; m. Dorothy Salibian, Sept. 15, 1945; children: Haig, Bairj, Armen. B.A., Am. U. Beirut, 1940, M.D., 1944; M.P.H., Harvard U., 1955. Intern Am. U. of Beirut Hosps., 1943-44; physician, acting supt. English Mission Hosp., Jerusalem, 1945-47; instr. physiology, clin. asst. dermatology and venereology Am. U. Med. Sch., Beirut, 1943-51, univ. physician, dir. univ. health service, 1949-54; med. assoc. United Community Services Met., Boston, 1955-57; asst. prof. to assoc. prof. preventive medicine N.Y. Med. Coll., N.Y.C., 1957-61; mem. faculty U. Mich. Sch. Pub. Health, Ann Arbor, 1961—, prof. med. care orgn., 1964—, Nathan Sinai Disting. prof. pub. health, 1979—. Author: A Guide to Medical Care Administration: Medical Care Appraisal-Quality and Utilization, 1969, Aspects of Medical Care Administration, 1973, Benefits in Medical Care Programs, 1976, The Definition of Quality and Approaches to Its Assessment, 1980, The Criteria and Standards of Quality, 1982, Medical Care Chartbook, 1980, the Methods and Findings of Quality Assessment and Monitoring, 1985. Recipient Dean Conley award Am. Coll. Hosp. Adminstrs., 1969, Norman A. Welch award Nat. Assn. Blue Shield Plans, 1976; Elizur Wright award Am. Risk and Ins. Assn., 1978, Nat. Merit award Delta Omega, 1978; Richard B. Tobias award Am. Coll. Utilization Rev. Physicians, 1984; award for outstanding contbns. in health services research Assn. Health Services Research, 1985. Fellow Am. Coll. Hosp. Adminstrs. (hon.), Am. Coll. Utilization Rev. Physicians (hon.), Am. Pub. Health Assn.; mem. Inst. Medicine, Assn. Tchrs. Preventive Medicine, Am. Coll. Utilization Rev. Physicians (hon., Richard B. Tobias award 1984). Current Work: Organization; administration; financing and evaluation of personal health care services. Subspecialties: Health services research; Health care organization and administration. Home: 1739 Ivywood Dr Ann Arbor MI 48103 Office: Univ Mich Sch Public Health 109 Observatory St Ann Arbor MI 48109

DONAHUE, MICHAEL JAMES, engineer; b. Barre, Vt., Oct. 23, 1953; s. Howard James and Beatrice Therese (Demers) D. B.S. in Engring, Northeastern U., 1982. Technician Gen. Electric Ordnance Systems, Pittsfield, Mass., 1973-76; programmer/analyst Honeywell Info. Systems, Brighton, Mass., 1976-78; research and devel. engr. communications systems div. GTE Products Corp. Systems Group, Needham Heights, Mass., 1978—. Mem. IEEE, Assn for Computing Machinery. Current Work: The integration of information processing facilities in an industrial environment, inparticular product description data defined by engineering units andutilized by manufacturing units. Subspecialties: Computer-aided design; Distributed systems and networks. Home: 148 First Parish Rd Scituate MA 02066 Office: GTE Govt Systems Corp Communication Systems Div (CSD) 77 A St Needham Heights MA 02194

DONALDSON, COLEMAN DUPONT, consulting engineer; b. Phila., Sept. 22, 1922; s. John W. and Renee (duPont) D.; m. Barbara Goldsmith, Jan. 17, 1945; children: B. Beirne, Coleman duPont, Evan F., Alexander M., William M. B.S. in Aero. Engring., Rennselaer Poly. Inst., 1943; M.A., Princeton U., 1954, Ph.D., 1957. Staff, NACA, Langley Field, Va., 1943-44, head aerophysics sect., 1946-52; gen. aerodynamics USAC, Wright Field, Ohio, 1945-46; aerodynamic evaluation Bell Aircraft, Niagara Falls, N.Y., 1946; sr. cons., pres. Aero Research Assos. of Princeton, N.J., 1954-79, chmn. bd., 1979—; cons. missile guidance and control Gen. Precision Equipment Corp., 1957-68; cons. magnetohydro-dynamics Thompson Ramo Wooldridge, Inc., 1958-61; cons. aerodynamic heating, gen. aerodynamics Martin Marietta Corp., 1955-72; gen. editor Princeton series on high speed aerodynamics and jet propulsion, 1955-64; cons. boundary layer stability, aerodynamic heating, missile and ordnance systems dept. Gen. Electric Co., 1956-72; cons. Grumman Aerospace Corp., 1959-72; Robert H. Goddard vis. lectr. with rank of prof. Princeton U., 1970-71; mem. research and tech. adv. council panel on research NASA, 1969-76; mem. indsl. profl. adv. com. Pa. State U., 1970-77; mem. Pres.'s Air Quality Adv. Bd., 1973-74; chmn. lab. adv. bd. for air warfare Naval Research Adv. Com., 1972-77; mem. Marine Corps panel Naval Res. Adv. Com., 1972-77; chmn. adv. council dept. aerospace and mech. scis. Princeton U., 1973-78. Author articles on aerodynamics. Fellow AIAA (Dryden Research lecture award 1971, gen. chmn. 13th aerospace scis. meeting 1975), Nat. Acad. Engring., Am. Phys. Soc., Sigma Xi, Delta Phi. Subspecialty: Aeronautical engineering. Home: PO Box 279 Gloucester VA 23061 Office: 1800 Old Meadow Rd Suite 114 McLean VA 22102

DONALDSON, DAVID, engineer; b. Boulder City, Nev., June 17, 1932; s. Arthur and Myrtle (Dullenty) D.; m. Alfreda E. Chambers, Dec. 18, 1955 (div.); children—Bruce, Brian, Blair; m. Lea Dora Braslasky, Nov. 26, 1982; children—Ivan, Adrian, Juan Pablo. B.C.E., Mont. State U., 1955; M.S. in San. Engring., U. N.C., 1960. Registered profl. engr., N.Y., Nicaragua. San. engr. Pan Am. Health Orgn., Washington, 1966-71; assoc. dir. Camp Dresser & McKee/Washington, Arlington, Va., 1981-85; san. engr. Pan Am. Health Orgn., 1985—. Contbr. articles to profl. jours., chpt. to books. Served to lt. USNR, 1956-59. Mem. Am. Acad. Environ. Engrs. (diplomate), Am. Water Works Assn. (mem. internat. com.), ASCE, Interam. Assn. San. Engrs. (bd. dirs. U.S. sect. 1980—, pres. 1974-78). Subspecialties: Civil engineering; Environmental engineering. Home: 1606 Waters Edge Ln Reston VA 22090 Office: Pan Am Health Orgn 525 23d St NW Washington DC 20037

DONALDSON, LLOYD ERIC, reproductive physiologist, genetics company executive; b. Brisbane, Australia, Sept. 20, 1934; came to U.S., 1962, 79; s. Eric Leslie and Breta (Furness) D.; m. Morva Beatrice Parmeter, Jan. 23, 1959; children—William Lloyd, Peter Eric, Sarah Jane. B. Vet. Medicine, U. Queensland, Brisbane, 1957, M. Vet. Medicine, 1959; Ph.D., Cornell U., 1963. Vet. officer Dept. Primary Industries, State of Queensland, Australia, Townsville, 1957-62; research assoc. Cornell U., Ithaca, N.Y., 1963-64; sr. research scientist Commonwealth Sci. and Indsl. Research Orgn., Brisbane, 1964-68; cons. vet. practice Australian Breeders Service, Brisbane, 1968-79; project leader, sr. research cons. Govt. of Burma Internat. Devel. Agy. Project, Rangoon, 1976-77; vis. prof. Coll. Vet. Medicine, Miss. State U., Starkville, 1979-81; pres. Am. Genetic Engring. Services, Starkville, 1981-82; dir., research assoc. Rio Vista Internat., San Antonio, 1982-84; pres. Matterhorn Genetics, Inc., Wilsonville, Ala., 1984—. Author, editor: Artificial Breeding and Pregnancy Diagnosis in Beef Cattle. Editor: Embryo Transfer in Cattle, 1982. Contbr. numerous articles on reprodn. in cattle to profl. jours. Overseas student Australian Meat Research Council, Canberra, 1961. Mem. AVMA, Am. Assn. Animal Sci., Australian Vet. Assn., Am. Embryo Transfer Assn., Internat. Embryo Transfer Assn., Australian Coll. Vet. Scientists, Royal Coll. Vet. Surgeons, Phi Kappa Phi. Episcopalian. Current work: Endocrinology of superovulation; seeking more reliable treatment regimens for cattle. Subspecialties: Embryo transplants (veterinary medicine); Animal breeding and embryo transplants. Home: RD 1 Box 32 Wilsonville AL 35186

DONALDSON, TERRENCE LEE, chemical engineer; b. Franklin, Pa., Apr. 20, 1946. B.S., Pa. State U., 1968; Ph.D., U. Pa., 1974. Registered profl. engr., Tenn. Asst. prof., then assoc. prof. U. Rochester, N.Y., 1974-80; staff engr., group leader, biotech. coordinator Oak Ridge Nat. Lab., 1980—. Contbr. articles to profl. jours. Patentee in field. Served with U.S. Army, 1968-70, Vietnam. Recipient Undergrad. Engring. Teaching award U. Rochester, 1980; grantee NSF, Dept. Energy. Mem. Am. Inst. Chem. Engrs., Am. Chem. Soc., Sigma Xi, Tau Beta Pi. Current work: Bioprocess engineering and modeling; anaerobic digestion and biooxidation phenomena; microbial fixed-film phenomena; bioreactors; mass transfer and reaction kinetics. Subspecialties: Chemical engineering; Biochemical Engineering. Office: Oak Ridge Nat Lab PO Box X Oak Ridge TN 37831

DONALEK, PETER JOHN, engineer, mathematician; b. Chgo., Apr. 9, 1939; s. John George and Lillian (Lazarik) D.; m. Julia Ann Gallagher, Aug. 24, 1968; children—Thomas, Katherine. B.S. in Elec. Engring., U. Ill., 1961; M.S., U. Pa., 1970; M.A. in Math., U. Toledo, 1973. Registered profl. engr., Ill. Elec. engr. Westinghouse Corp., Balt., 1961-63; vol. U.S. Peace Corps, Washington, Brazil, 1963-65; elec. engr. Sargent & Lundy, Chgo., 1965-68; asst. prof. Spring Garden Coll., Phila., 1969-71; elec. engr. Harza Engring. Co., Chgo., 1973-74, sr. elec. engr., 1974-77, sr. systems engr., 1977-79, head systems studies sect., 1979—, assoc., 1985—; lectr. Internat. Atomic Energy Agy. Argonne Nat. Labs., Chgo., 1971-81. U.S. Dept. Energy-Economic Regulatory Authority grantee, 1978. Mem. IEEE (sr.; task force chmn. 1975-77, seminar chmn. 1981-82), Math. Assn. Am., Soc. for Indsl. and Applied Math., Western Soc. Engrs. Current work: Planning, design, control, and economics of interconnected electric power transmission systems. Subspecialties: Electrical engineering; Systems engineering. Office: Harza Engineering Co 150 S Wacker Dr Chicago IL 60606-4176

DONATH, FRED ARTHUR, geoscientist, educator; b. St. Cloud, Minn., July 11, 1931; s. Arnold C. and Elizabeth H. (Crary) D.; m. Mavis E. Hagen, July 19, 1952; children—Robert W., Deborah A. B.A., U. Minn., 1954; M.S., Stanford U., 1956, Ph.D., 1958. Asst. prof. San Jose State U., Calif., 1957-58; asst. prof., then prof. Columbia U., N.Y.C., 1958-67; prof. U. Ill., Urbana, 1967-80, head dept. geology, 1967-77; pres. CGS, Inc., Urbana, Ill., 1980-83; dir., prin. geoscientist Earth Tech. Corp., Long Beach, Calif., 1983—; cons. U.S. Nuclear Regulatory Commn., Washington, 1977-80; advisor Office Sci. and Tech. Policy, Washington, 1978-79; mem. bd. U.S. Nat. Commn. Rock Mechanics, Washington, 1978-81. Contbr. articles to profl. jours. Recipient Semicentennial medallion Rice U., 1962. Fellow Geol. Soc. Am. (assoc. editor 1963-74), AAAS; mem. Am. Geophys. Union (sect. sec. 1964-68). Current work: Integration of experimental, theoretical and field studies of geologic deformation; predictive geology, using computer simulations, relative to problem of nuclear waste isolation. Subspecialties: Geology; Geophysics. Home: 6230 Riviera Circle Long Beach CA 90815 Office: Earth Tech Corp 3777 Long Beach Blvd Long Beach CA 90807

DONATI, ROBERT MARIO, physician, educator; b. St. Louis, Feb. 28, 1934; s. Leo Simon and Rose Marie (Gualdoni) D. B.S., St. Louis U., 1955, M.D., 1959. Diplomate Am. Bd. Nuclear Medicine. Chief nuclear medicine service Cochran VA Hosp., St. Louis, 1968-70, St. Louis VA Med. Ctr., 1970-79, acting chief of staff, 1976-77, chief of staff, 1979-83; from instr. to assoc. prof. medicine St. Louis U., 1963-74, prof., 1974—, dir. div. nuclear medicine, 1968—, sr. assoc. dean, 1983—; exec. assoc. v.p. St. Louis U. Med. Ctr., 1985—; cons. in field; adj. prof. medicine Washington U. Sch. Medicine, 1979-83. Contbr. articles to profl. jours. Mem. desegration monitoring adv. com. U.S. Dist. Ct., St. Louis, 1981-82; mem. Citizens Edn. Task Force on Quality Edn. in Pub. Schs., 1977-78; bd. dirs. Inst. Health Mgmt., St. Louis, 1976-78; co-chmn. Italo-Am. Bicentennial Com., St. Louis, 1975-76. Served to capt. U.S. Army, 1966-68. Recipient Exceptional Service award VA, 1983, Adminstrs. Commendation, 1980, Dir.'s Commendation, 1977-78, 79, 81, Commendation medal for Meritorious Service, Walter Reed Army Inst. Research, 1968. Mem. Soc. Nuclear Medicine, Am. Bd. Nuclear Medicine (vice chmn. 1984, chmn. 1985), Am. Bd. Med. Specialities (fin. com.). Roman Catholic. Clubs: Cosmos (Washington); Racquet (St. Louis). Current work: Humoral control of cellular proliferation; clinical investigation in nuclear medicine; assessment, adoption and diffusion of medical technology. Subspecialty: Nuclear medicine. Home: 5335 Botanical Saint Louis MO 63110 Office: Saint Louis U Sch Medicine 1402 S Grand Blvd Saint Louis MO 63104

DONAWICK, WILLIAM JOSEPH, veterinarian, educator; b. Troy, N.Y., Aug. 18, 1940; s. Joseph Charles and Gladys (Marion (Fields) D.; m. Bonnie Jean Martin, Feb. 3, 1961; children—Stephanie Eileen, Melinda Jean. Student Cornell U., 1957-59, D.V.M., 1963; postgrad. U. Pa., Phila., 1966-69, M.Sc. (hon.), 1973. Veterinarian Easton and Lein Vet. Service, Machias, N.Y., 1963-64; instr. U. Pa., Phila., 1964-66, postdoctoral fellow, 1966-69, from asst. prof. to prof. surgery, 1969-82, Mark Whittier and Lila Griswold Allam prof. surgery, 1982—; cons. Profl. Exam. Service, N.Y.C., 1981—. Advisor Aero Club Pa., Phila., 1982—. USPHS-Nat. Cancer Inst. postdoctoral fellow, 1966-67; recipient Norden Disting. Teaching award U. Pa., 1970; Research Career Devel. award USPHS, 1973-78. Mem. Am. Coll. Vet. Surgeons (diplomate, pres. 1982-83, chmn. bd. regents 1983-84), AVMA, Phi Zeta, Debonaire Flyers (pres. 1978-84). Presbyterian. Club: Bentley Bunch Camp (pres. 1976-83) (Wharton, Pa.). Current work: Metabolic care of horse; laparoscopy in animals; absorption and secretion of water and electrolytes by intestine; immunology in the horse. Subspecialties: Surgery (veterinary medicine); Transplantation. Home: 1501 Brandywine Dr West Chester PA 19382 Office: New Bolton Ctr U Pa 382 W Street Rd Kennett Square PA 19348

DONCHIN, EMANUEL, psychologist, educator; b. Tel Aviv, Apr. 3, 1935; came to U.S., 1961; s. Michael and Guta D.; m. Rina Greenfarb, June 3, 1955; children: Gill, Opher, Ayala. B.A., Hebrew U., 1961, M.A., 1963; Ph.D., UCLA, 1965. Teaching and research asst. dept. psychology Hebrew U., 1958-61; research asst. dept. psychology UCLA, 1961-63, research psychologist, 1964-65; research asso. div. neurology Stanford U. Med. Sch., 1965-66, asst. prof. in residence, 1966-68; research asso. neurobiology br. NASA, Ames Research Center, Moffett Field, Calif., 1966-68; asso. prof. dept. psychology U. Ill., Urbana-Champaign, 1968-72, prof. psychology and physiology, 1972—, head dept. psychology, 1980—. Author: (with Donald B. Lindsley) Averaged Evoked Potentials, 1969; Cognitive Psychophysiology, 1985; contbr. articles to profl. jours. Served with Israeli Army, 1952-55. Fellow AAAS, Am. Psychol. Assn.; mem. Soc. Psychophysiol. Research (pres. 1980), Fedn. Behavioral, Cognitive and Psychol. Socs. (v.p. 1981—), Am. EEG Soc., Psychonomic Soc., Soc. Neuroscis., AAAS. Current Work: Biology of cognitive function; event related brain potentials; engineering psychology; complex skills; psychophysiology. Subspecialties: Psychobiology; Neuropsychology. Office: Dept Psychology U Ill 603 E Daniel St Champaign IL 61820

DONEGAN, WILLIAM LAURENCE, surgeon, educator; b. Jacksonville, Fla., Nov. 3, 1932; s. William Elton and Mildred Louise (Bullock) D.; m. Judith Higgins, Dec. 21, 1963; children: William David, Elizabeth Kathleen. B.A., Yale U., 1955, M.D., 1959. Intern Barnes Hosp., St. Louis, 1959-60, asst. resident surgery, 1960-63, resident in surgery, 1963-64, USPHS cancer clin. fellow, 1963-64; clin. asst. prof. surgery U. Mo., Columbia, 1964-65; instr. surgery Washington U., St. Louis, 1964-67; asst. prof. surgery U. Mo., Columbia, 1965-69, assoc. prof., 1969-74; prof. surgery Med. Coll. Wis., Milw., 1974—; prof. clin. oncology Am. Cancer Soc., 1975-83; surgeon Ellis Fischel State Cancer Hosp., Columbia, 1964-74; dir. clin. research unit Cancer Research Ctr., Columbia, 1965-74, assoc. scientist, 1967-74; attending surgeon Milw. County Med. Complex, 1974—, Columbia Hosp., Milw., 1974—, Mt. Sinai Med. Ctr., 1976—, acting chief surgery, 1982-83, chief surgery, 1983—; cons. VA Med. Ctr., 1975—; sr. attending surgeon Froedtert Meml. Luth. Hosp., Milw., 1981—; cons. in field. Contbr. numerous articles to profl. jours. Sterling-Winthrop Research Inst. grantee; Am. Cancer Soc. grantee, 1975—; Nat. Cancer Inst. grantee, 1982—; others. Fellow ACS; mem. Am. Assn. Cancer Research, Soc. Surgery of Alimentary Tract, Central Surg. Assn., Am. Assn. Cancer Edn., Milw. Acad. Surgery, Soc. of Head and Neck Surgeons, Soc. Surg. Oncology, Milw. Acad. Medicine, Wis. Surg. Soc., Am. Soc. Clin. Oncology, Pan-Pacific Surg. Assn., Collegium Internationale Chirurgiae Digestivae, Am. Radium Soc., Sigma Xi, Phi Beta Kappa. Current Work: Research in cancer. Subspecialties: Surgery; Oncology. Home: 9421 N Lake Dr Bayside WI 53217 Office: 950 N 12th St Milwaukee WI 53201

DONIVAN, FRANK FORBES, JR., astronomer; b. Inglewood, Calif., Oct. 19, 1943; s. Frank Forbes and Daisy Dean (Lambert) D.; m. Margaret R. Gates; children: Laura, Erin. B.A., UCLA, 1966; Ph.D., U. Fla., Gainesville, 1970. Assoc. prof. astronomy U. Fla., 1970-79; asst. dean (Grad. Sch.), 1971-73; vis. asst. scientist Nat. Radio Obs. Astronomy, Charlottesville, VA., 1976; mem. tech. staff Jet Propulsion Lab., Pasadena, Calif., 1979-84, radio sci. and VLBI system engr., 1984—. Mem. Am. Astron. Soc., Sigma Pi Sigma. Current Work: Very Long Baseline Interferometry (VLBI) applied to interplanetary and earth orbiter navigation; development of radio science systems for planetary occultations. Subspecialties: Radio and microwave astronomy; Astronautics. Office: 4800 Oak Grove Dr Pasadena CA 91103

DONN, WILLIAM L., research scientist, consultant; b. Bklyn., Mar. 2, 1918; s. Nathan and Tina D.; m. Renee M. Brilliant, Jan 23, 1960; children: Matthew, Tara. B.A., Bklyn. Coll., 1939; M.A., Columbia U., 1946, Ph.D., 1951. Sr. research scientist Lamont-Doherty Obs., Columbia U., Palisades, N.Y., 1951—; instr. to prof. geology Bklyn. Coll., 1946-63; prof. geology CCNY, N.Y.C., 1963-77; research cons. Woods Hole (Mass.) Oceanographic Instn., 1947-49; heat meteorology sect. U.S. Merchant Marine Acad., 1942-45; aerologist Naval Air Navigation Sch., 1945; geologist N.Atlantic Dist. C.E. U.S. Army, 1941-42, Del. Aqueduct Program, 1941; cons. various indsl. and legal orgns., 1951—; White House cons. Office Sci. and Tech., Washington, 1979-81; mem. com. on long waves ASCE; commn. on microseisms Internat. Union Geodesy and Geophysics; review com. prevention and mitigation of flood losses NRC. Author: textbooks Meteorology - With Marine Applications, 1946, 2d edit., 1951, 3d edit., 1965, 4th edit., 1975, Graphic Methods in Structural Geology, 1958, The Earth, 1973; editor: textbooks Glossary of Geology, 4th edit, 1980, International Geophysics Series, 1979—; contbr. research articles to profl. publs. Trustee Village Bd. Grand View-on-Hudson, N.Y., 1968—, dep. mayor, 1975—, police commr., 1968—. Served with USCGR, 1942; served to lt. s.g. USNR, 1942-46. Disting. nat. lectr. Am. Assn. Petroleum Geologists, 1960; Disting. nat. lectr. Soc. Exploration Geophysicists, 1960; NSF sr. postdoctoral fellow, 1959-60; fellow in geology Bklyn. Coll., 1940-41; chief scientist, prin., co-prin., dir. project and grants, 1941—. Fellow AAAS, Geol. Soc. Am., Explorers Club; mem. Seismol. Soc. Am., Am. Geophys. Union, N.Y. Acad. Scis. (council 1950-52, chmn. sect. oceanography and neteorology 1950-52), Am. Meteorol. Soc. (profl., chmn. com. on paleoclimatology 1965), Phi Beta Kappa, Sigma Xi. Current Work: Prediction of monthly and seasonal climate with thermodynamic model, study of evolution of climate; application of infrasound as atmospheric probe. Subspecialties: Climatology; Atmospheric infrasound. Home: 302 River Rd Grand View-on-Hudson NY 10990 Office: Lamont-Doherty Geol Observatory Palisades NY 10960

DONNELLAN, JAMES EDWARD, JR., biophysicist; b. Cleve., May 27, 1932; s. James Edward and Edith May (Bissell) D.; m. Elizabeth Thomas Lott, June 12, 1954; children—James Edward III, Douglas Arthur. B.S. in Physics, Yale U., 1954, Ph.D. in biophysics, 1958. Physicist, instr. radiology Grace New Haven Hosp., Conn., 1957-60; research physicist U.S. Army Natick Labs., Mass., 1960-63; research biologist Oak Ridge Nat. Lab., 1963-78; second officer IAEA, Vienna, Austria, 1973-77; research affiliate Yale U., New Haven, 1979—. Contbr. articles to profl. jours. Treas. Oak Ridge Unitarian Ch., 1971-73; cubmaster Gt. Smoky Mountains council Boy Scouts Am., Oak Ridge, 1968-72. Mem. AAAS, Biophys. Soc., Radiation Research Soc., Sigma Xi. Current work: Biophysics of bacterial spores; molecular effects of radiation; repair of radiation effects; DNA repair; significance of photoproducts in bacterial spores. Subspecialties: Molecular biology; Radiation biology. Home: 15 Lookout Rd Westbrook CT 06498 Office: Yale U Dept Molecular Biophysics and Biochemistry New Haven CT 06510

DONNELLEY, JAMES ELLIS, computer scientist, consultant; b. Palo Alto, Calif., July 5, 1948; s. John Donovan and Rachael Ellis (Millard) D. B.S. in Math, U. Calif.-Davis, 1970, B.A. in Physics, 1970, M.S. in Math, 1972. Technician Hewlett Packard Co., Palo Alto, 1966; hydrologist U.S. Geol. Survey, Menlo Park, Calif., 1968-72; computer scientist Lawrence Livermore Lab., Calif., 1972—; cons. Aerospace Corp., Los Angeles, 1980—, Dietrich, Glasrud & Jones (Law Firm), Fresno, Calif., 1981—. Contbr. articles to profl. jours. Recipient cert. for outstanding achievement in undergrad. math. U. Calif.-Davis, 1970. Mem. Assn. Computing Machinery, IEEE, Planetary Soc., Nat. Space Inst., ACLU. Mem. Libertarian party. Current Work: Capability-based network operating systems; asynchronous cellular data flow computers. Subspecialties: Distributed systems and networks; Computer architecture. Home: 288 Scherman Way Livermore CA 94550 Office: PO Box 808 Livermore CA 94550

DONNELLY, RICHARD FRANK, solar terrestrial physicist, research scientist; b. Sioux Falls, S.D., Mar. 26, 1937; s. Richard James and Doris Gail (Lynum) D.; m. Elizabeth Ann Lindahl, June 18, 1966; children—Richard Scot, Lora Elizabeth. B.S., S.D. Sch. Mines and Tech., 1959; M.S., U. Ill., 1961, Ph.D., 1966. Physicist U.S. Dept. Commerce, Boulder, Colo., 1964—. Contbr. articles to profl. jours. Mem. Am. Astron. Soc., Am. Geophys. Am. Meteorol. Soc., Sigma Xi, Eta Kappa Nu, Sigma Tau. Methodist. Current work: Research of temporal variations of solar ultraviolet radiation, their stratospheric effects on ozone density and temperature, and their possible effects on climate. Subspecialties: Solar physics; Climatology. Office: Air Resources Lab NOAA ERL US Dept Commerce 325 Broadway Boulder CO 80303

DONNELLY, RUSSELL JAMES, physicist, educator; b. Hamilton, Ont., Can., Apr. 16, 1930; s. Clifford Ernest and Bessie (Harrison) D.; m. Marian Card, Jan. 21, 1956; 1 son, James. B.Sc., McMaster U., 1951, M.Sc., 1952; M.S., Yale, 1953, Ph.D., 1956. Faculty U. Chgo., 1956-66, prof. physics, 1965-66, U. Oreg., Eugene, 1966—, chmn. dept., 1966-72, 82-83; vis. prof. Niels Bohr Inst., Copenhagen, Denmark, 1972; co-founder Pine Mountain Obs., 1967; cons. Gen. Motors Co. Research Labs., 1958-68, NSF, 1968-73, 79-83, mem. adv. panel for physics, 1970-73, chmn., 1971-72, mem. adv. coms. on materials research, 1979-83; cons. Jet Propulsion Lab., Calif. Inst. Tech., Pasadena, 1973-82. Contbr. papers to profl. lit.; editor: (with Herman, Prigogine) Non-Equilibrium Thermodynamics Variational Techniques and Stability, 1966, (with Parks, Glaberson) Experimental Superfluidity, 1967; (with A.W. Francis) Cryogenic Science and Technology, 1985; assoc. editor: Physics of Fluids, 1966-68; mem. editorial bd.: Phys. Rev. A, 1978-84. Bd. dirs. U. Oreg. Devel. Fund, 1970-72; bd. dirs. Oreg. Mus. Park, 1975—, chmn., 1975-82. Alfred P. Sloan fellow, 1959-63; sr. vis. fellow Sci. Research Council, U.K., 1978. Fellow Am. Phys. Soc. (exec. com. div. fluid dynamics 1966-72, 80—, sec-treas. 1967-70, chmn. 1971-72, 82-83, Otto Laporte Meml. lectr. 1974), AAAS; mem. AAUP, Am. Assn. Physics Tchrs. Episcopalian. Clubs: (Washington); Town (Eugene). Research on physics fluids, especially hydrodynamic stability and superfluidity. Current Work: Superfluid turbulence; Couette and Benard flows. Subspecialties: Low temperature physics; Fluid mechanics. Home: 2175 Olive St Eugene OR 97405 Office: Dept Physics Univ Oreg Eugene OR 97403

DONNELLY, THOMAS EDWARD, JR., pharmacology educator; b. Chelsea, Mass., Sept. 16, 1943; s. Thomas Edward and Catherine S. (Ross) D.; m. Thorkatla Thorkelsdottir, Jan. 31, 1975; children: Karina, Erling. B.S., Mass. Coll. Pharmacy, 1966; M.A., Harvard U., 1968; Ph.D., Yale U., 1972. Postdoctoral fellow U. Copenhagen, 1972-73; biochemist Leo Pharm. Products, Ballerup, Denmark, 1973-74; research assoc. Emory U., Atlanta, 1974; asst. prof. U. Nebr. Med. Ctr., Omaha, 1974-78, assoc. prof. pharmacology, 1978—. Contbr. articles to sci. jours. NIH grantee, 1976-79, 78-81, 84—. Mem. Am. Soc. Pharmacology and Exptl. Therapeutics, N.Y. Acad. Sci., AAAS. Current Work: Role of calcium-dependent and cyclic nucleotide-dependent protein kinases in cellular proliferation; biochemical basis of Duchenne muscular dystrophy. Subspecialties: Molecular pharmacology; Biochemistry (medicine). Home: 10713 Valley St Omaha NE 68124 Office: 42nd St and Dewey Ave Omaha NE 68105

DONNELLY, THOMAS WILLIAM, physicist, educator; b. Victoria, B.C., Can., June 1, 1943; s. Thomas Howard Grant and Gertrude Florence (Hord) D.; m. Barbara Louise Nicol, Jan. 6, 1979. B.S. with honors, U. B.C., 1964, Ph.D., 1967. Research assoc. Stanford U. (Calif.), 1967-69, asst. prof. physics, 1971-79; sr. postdoctoral fellow U. Toronto (Ont., Can.), 1969-70, lectr., 1970-71; sr. research scientist MIT, Cambridge, 1979—; cons. Los Alamos Nat. Lab. (N.Mex.), 1978-81, Lawrence Livermore Nat. Lab. (Calif.), 1981—. Contbr. articles to physics jours. Recipient Alexander von Humboldt Sr. U.S. Scientist award, 1985; Nat. Research Council Can. fellow, 1967-69; A.P. Sloan Found. fellow, 1974-76. Mem. Am. Phys. Soc., Can. Assn. Physicists, Sierra Club. Current work: Intermediate-energy theoretical nuclear physics-electromagnetic and weak interactions in nuclei. Subspecialties: Nuclear physics; Theoretical physics. Home: 1 Hartford Rd Arlington MA 02174 Office: MIT 6-301 Cambridge MA 02139

DONNELLY, TIMOTHY CHRISTOPHER, chemistry educator; b. Berkeley, Calif., June 11, 1947. B.S. in Chemistry, Calif. State U.-Hayward, 1970, M.S. in Chemistry, 1975; Ph.D. in Chemistry, U. Calif.-Davis, 1979. Research chemist Clorox Corp., Pleasanton, Calif., 1978-79; vis. lectr. U. Calif.-Davis, 1979—, dir. in person enrollment, 1982—, faculty lectr., summer adv., 1981-83; pres. TiDon Research Inst., Vacaville, Calif., 1976—, cons. to industry, 1976—. Author: Raman Spectroscopic Studies of Lithium and Calcium Ions in Aqueous Environment, 1979. Contbr. articles to profl. jours. Inventor in field. Mem. Am. Chem. Soc. Club: Faculty. Current work: Applications of lasers to vascular disease; Raman spectroscopy of aqueous systems; applications of surface active agents to hydrocarbon systems. Subspecialties: Physical chemistry; Laser medicine. Office: U Calif Dept Chemistry Davis CA 95616

DONOHO, CLIVE WELLINGTON, JR., dean, horticulture and plant physiologist; b. Nashville, Tenn., Jan. 16, 1930; s. Clive Wellington and Daisy Donoho; m. Cynthia T. Debish, May 21, 1955; children—Gary, Anne, Theresa, Glen. B.S., U. Ky., 1952; M.S., N.C. State U., 1958; Ph.D., Mich. State U., 1960. From asst. prof. to prof. horticulture Ohio Agrl. Research and Devel. Ctr., Ohio State U.-Wooster, 1960-67, assoc. dir., 1973-82, dir., 1982-84; head dept. hort. sci. N.C. State U., Raleigh, 1967-73; assoc. dean, dir. Ga. Agrl. Expt. Stas., U. Ga., Athens, 1984. Contbr. articles to profl. jours. Served as staff sgt. USAF, 1952-56. Fellow Am. Soc. Hort. Sci.; mem. Council Agrl. Sci. and Tech. (bd. dirs. 1984—), Agrl. Research Inst. (bd. dirs. 1980-83), Wooster C. of C. (bd. dirs. 1981-84). Subspecialty: Agricultural administration. Office: U Ga 107 Conner Hall Athens GA 30602

DONOHUE, TERENCE, research chemist, laser physicist; b. Altadena, Calif., Oct. 15, 1946; s. Jerry and Patricia Ann (Schreier) D.; m. Ann Elizabeth O'Hara, Aug. 3, 1974. B.S., UCLA, 1968; M.S., Cornell U., 1971, Ph.D., 1973. Teaching research asst. Cornell U., Ithaca, N.Y., 1968-73, postdoctoral research assoc., 1973-75; research chemist Naval Research Lab., Washington, 1975—. Contbr. articles to profl. jours., chpts. to books. Patentee in field. Recipient Publ. awards Naval Research Lab., 1977, 78; NSF fellow, summer 1966, 67. Mem. Am. Chem. Soc., Inter-Am. Photochem. Soc., Sigma Xi. Club: BMW Car (Washington). Current work: Use of lasers in new types of photochemistry for applications in elemental and isotope separation and surface processing and modification; rare earth photochemistry. Subspecialties: Laser photochemistry; Surface chemistry. Home: 5917 Valley View Dr Alexandria VA 22310 Office: Laser Physics Br Naval Research Lab Washington DC 20375

DONOVAN, JOHN CHARLES, veterinarian, researcher, consultant; b. Canton, Ohio, Aug. 5, 1950; s. Edward Francis and Theda Bessie (Rohrer) D.; m. Marilyn Blum, Mar. 18, 1977; children—Erin, Kerry, Colleen. B.S., U.S. Mil. Acad., 1972; D.V.M., Ohio State U., 1977. Diplomate Am. Coll. Lab. Animal Medicine. Commd. 2d lt. U.S. Army, 1972; commd. officer USPHS., advanced through grades to lt. comdr., 1985; chief animal care facility U.S. Army Research Inst. Environ. Medicine, Natick, Mass., 1977-80; postdoctoral trainee U.S. Army Med. Research Inst., Infectious Diseases, Ft. Detrick, Md., 1980-83; chief dept. animal resources Walter Reed Army Inst. Research, Washington, 1983; head unit on research animal Resources, Nat. Inst. Child Health and Human Devel., Bethesda, Md., 1984—; cons., site visitor Am. Assn. Accreditation Lab. Animal Care, New Lenox, Ill., 1983—. Contbr. articles to profl. lit. Mem. Am. Soc. Lab. Animal Practitioners, AVMA, Am. Assn. Lab. Animal Sci., AAAS. Current work: Improving and defining laboratory animal health; clinical research on laboratory animal problems; nonhuman primate medicine and surgery; research animal programs management. Subspecialties: Laboratory animal medicine; Comparative physiology. Office: Bldg 10 Room 8C407 NIH Nat Inst Child Health and Human Devel 9000 Rockville Pike Bethesda MD 20205

DONZANTI, BRUCE ARMAND, pharmacologist, army officer; b. Phila., Aug. 15, 1956; s. Vincent Peter and Elda Barbara (D'Angelo) D.; m. Sandra Sue Simmons, Aug. 27, 1983. B.S. in Biology, Phila. Coll. Pharmacy and Sci., 1978, M.S. in Pharmacology, 1980; Ph.D. in Pharmacology, Ohio State U., 1983. Capt., U.S. Army, 1983; prin. investigator Med. Research Inst. Chem. Def., Edgewood, Md., 1984—; contract rep., Edgewood, 1984—. Author sci. articles. Mem. Am. Inst. Biol. Scis. (award 1978), Soc. Neurosci., AAAS, Sigma Xi. Democrat. Roman Catholic. Current work: Behavioral toxicology and pharmacology of potentially new treatment compounds for organophosphate (nerve gas)-induced poisoning. Subspecialties: Neuropharmacology; Toxicology (medicine). Home: 304 E Bel Crest Rd Bel Air MD 21014 Office: US Army Med Research Inst Chem Def Aberdeen Proving Ground Edgewood MD 21010

DOOB, JOSEPH LEO, mathematician, educator; b. Cin., Feb. 27, 1910; s. Leo and Mollie (Doerfler) D.; m. Elsie Haviland Field, June 26, 1931; children—Stephen, Peter, Deborah. B.A., Harvard U., 1930, M.A., 1931, Ph.D., 1932; D.Sc. (hon.), U. Ill., 1981. Faculty U. Ill., Urbana, 1935—, successively asso., asst. prof., asso. prof., 1935-45, prof. math., 1945—, now emeritus prof. Recipient Nat. Medal of Sci., 1979. Mem. Nat. Acad. Scis., Am. Acad. Arts and Scis., Acad. Scis. (Paris) (fgn. asso.). Subspecialty: Probability. Home: 208 W High St Urbana IL 61801

DOODLESACK, GARY ABBOTT, electrical engineer; b. Boston, July 21, 1957; s. Louis and Thelma (Abbott) D. S.B., Brown U., 1979, S.M., 1981. Engr., Stone and Webster Engring. Corp., Boston, 1982-83; mem tech. staff The Mitre Corp., Bedford, Mass., 1983—. Mem. Am. Phys. Soc., IEEE. Congregationalist. Club: Brown Rowing Assn. (Providence). Current work: Electron device physics applications to very large scale integrated circuit design, performance enhancement and down scaling. Subspecialties: Microchip technology (engineering); Semiconductors. Home: 100-4 Main St Stoneham MA 02180 Office: The Mitre Corp PO Box 208 Bedford MA 01730

DOOLITTLE, DONALD PRESTON, geneticist, educator; b. Torrington, Conn., May 14, 1933; s. Merton Elford and Louva Edna (Mack) D.; m. Maria Zergenyi, Nov. 23, 1957; children: Andrew Donald, Thomas Robert. B.S., U. Conn., 1954; M.S., Cornell U., 1956, Ph.D., 1959. Postdoctoral fellow Jackson Lab., Bar Harbor, Maine, 1958-60; asst. research prof. biometry Grad. Sch. Public Health, U. Pitts., 1960-65; asst. prof. genetics W.Va. U., Morgantown, 1966-67, assoc. prof., 1967; assoc. prof. animal scis. Purdue U., West Lafayette, Ind., 1967—; vis. assoc. prof. animal sci. Cornell U., 1985. Contbr. articles to profl. jours. Mem. West Lafayette Citizens Community Devel. Com., 1979-84. Mem. Am. Genetics Assn., Genetics Soc. Am. Lutheran. Current Work: Researcher in population genetics, quantitative genetics, genetics of the mouse. Subspecialties: Animal genetics; Evolutionary biology. Office: Dept Animal Scis Purdue Univ West Lafayette IN 47907

DOOLITTLE, ROBERT F., II, physicist, computer systems programmer; b. Chgo., Dec. 21, 1925; s. Arthur K. and Dortha B. D.; m. Mary P., Apr. 30, 1955 (dec.); children: Robert A., Nancy E.; m. Karen K., Dec. 28, 1976. A.B., Oberlin Coll., 1948; M.S., U. Mich., 1950, Ph.D., 1958. Asst. prof. physics San Diego State U., 1958-60; sr. scientist TRW Electronics and Def., Redondo Beach, Calif., 1960-83; sr. systems programmer Ashton-Tate, Culver City, 1983—. Served with USNR, 1944-46; served to lt. comdr. 1952-54. Mem. Am. Astron. Soc., Am. Phys. Soc. Current Work: Computer graphics, algorithms and operating systems. Subspecialties: Cosmic ray high energy astrophysics; Gamma ray high energy astrophysics. Home: 1290 Monument Pacific Palisades CA 90272 Office: Ashton-Tate 10150 W Jefferson Blvd Culver City CA 90230

DORA, EORS ISTVAN, medical educator, researcher; b. Budapest, Hungray, May 1, 1943; came to U.S., 1981; s. Tivadar Tibor and Ilona (Toth) D.; m. Tunde Nagy, Dec. 7, 1974; 1 dau., Melinda. M.D., Semmelweis U. Med. Sch., Budapest, 1968; Ch.D., Hungarian Acad. Scis., 1978. Diplomate: Med. diplomate. Researcher Semmelweis U. Med. Sch., 1968-78, adj., 1978—; research assoc. U. Pa., Phila., 1972-73, assoc. prof., 1981—. Contbr. numerous articles to med. jours. Mem. Hungarian Physiol. Soc., Internat. Soc. for Oxygen Transport to Tissue, Am. Physiol. Soc., Internat. Soc. Cerebral Blood Flow and Metabolism. Current Work: Regulation of cerebral blood flow and energy metabolism under hypoxia, increased brain activity and autoregulation; mechanism of brain damage during ischemia and shock; mechanism of oxidative phosphorylation of in vivo, in situ mitochondria. Subspecialties: Neurochemistry; Neurophysiology. Home: Hajanlka U 4 Budapest Hungary 1121 Office: Experimental Research Dept & 2nd Institute Physiology Semmelweis Univ Med Sch Budapest Hungary 1082

DOREMUS, ROBERT HEWARD, ceramic engineering educator; b. Denver, Sept. 16, 1928; s. Francis Heward and Elsie Marion (Segelke) D.; m. Germaine Briancon, Mar. 19, 1956; children—Marc Francis, Elaine, Carol, Natalie. B.S., U. Colo., 1950; M.S., U. Ill., 1951, Ph.D., 1953; Ph.D. (Fulbright fellow), U. Cambridge, Eng., 1956. Phys. chemist Gen. Electric Research and Devel. Center, Schenectady, 1956-71; N.Y. State prof. glass and ceramics Rensselaer Poly. Inst., Troy, N.Y., 1971—; cons. in field. Author: Glass Science, 1973; Co-editor; Growth and Perfection of Crystals, 1958; Contbr. articles to profl. jours. Bd. dirs. Phila. Luth. Sem., 1967-76. Fellow Am. Ceramic Soc.; mem. AAAS, Sigma Xi, Sigma Tau, Tau Beta Pi. Lutheran. Current work: Glass science (diffusion, fracture, crystallization, chemical properties); sintering of ceramics, biomaterials, crystal growth, optical properties. Subspecialties: Ceramics; Biomaterials. Home: 1544 Keyes Ave Schenectady NY 12309 Office: Materials Dept Rensselaer Polytechnic Inst Troy NY 12181

DORFMAN, MYRON HERBERT, petroleum engineer, educator; b. Shreveport, La., July 3, 1927; s. Samuel Yandell and Rose (Gold) D.; children: Shelley Fonda Dorfman Roberts, Cynthia Renee. B.S., U. Tex., 1950, M.S., 1972, Ph.D., 1975. Registered profl. engr., Tex. Geologist engr. Sklar Oil Co., Shreveport, 1950-56, mgr. prodn. and devel., 1957-59, partner, 1958-59; owner Dorfman Oil Properties, Shreveport, 1950-71, Austin, Tex., 1971—; prof. petroleum engring. U. Tex., Austin, 1976—, H.B. Harkins prof. petroleum engineering, 1980—, W.A. Moncrief Jr. Centennial chair in petroleum engring., 1983—, dir. Center Energy Studies, 1977—, chmn. dept. petroleum engring., 1978—; dir. Tex. Petroleum Research Commn., Tex. R.R. Commn., 1982—; disting. lectr. Soc. Petroleum Engrs. of AIME, 1978-79, disting. author, 1982—. Contbr. articles to profl. jours. Pres. Shreveport Community Council, 1966; bd. dirs. Gov.'s Com. Employment Handicapped, 1966-68, La. Youth Opportunity Center, Shreveport, 1966-71, ARC, Caddo Parish, La., 1964-71; pres. La. Mental Health Center, Shreveport, 1967. Served with USNR, 1945-46, PTO. Recipient medal State of Israel, 1963. Fellow Geol. Soc. Am.; mem. Am. Geophys. Union, Nat. Acad. Scis., Am. Assn. Petroleum Geologists, Soc. Profl. Well Log Analysts, AIME, Shreveport Geol. Soc., Petroleum Club Shreveport, Shreveport Jewish Fedn. (pres. 1967), Pi Epsilon Tau., Tau Beta Pi. Club: Shreveport Skeet (pres. 1964). Current Work: Geopressured geothermal energy. director geothermal studies, center for energy studies, university of Texas, facies characterization of gelogic environments by use of well logs, general petroleum engineering studies of enhanced oil and gas recovery. Subspecialties: Petroleum engineering; Sedimentology. Home: 6413 Five Acre Wood Austin TX 78746 Office: Dept Petroleum Engring U Tex Austin TX 78712

DORGAN, CHARLES EDWARD, engineering educator; b. Cullison, Kans., Apr. 21, 1937; s. John Henry and Mary Margaret (Probst) D.; m. Joan Marie Roth, Aug. 10, 1963; children—Marie, Jason, Chad. B.S. in Agrl. Engring., Kans. State U., 1959; M.S.M.E., U. Pitts., 1965; Ph.D. in Mech. Engring., U. Wis., 1976. Registered profl. engr., Wis., Ohio, Kans., Pa. Engr. USAF, 1960-69; course dir. Air Force Inst. Tech., Dayton, Ohio, 1969-71; energy cons. HSR Assocs., LaCrosse, Wis., 1981-83; engring. cons. Dorgan, McMahon Assocs., Madison, Wis., 1983—; prof. engring., program dir. U. Wis., Madison, 1971—, dir. Energy Tech. Ctr., 1976—. Contbr. articles to profl. jours. Recipient Energy Mgmt. Diploma, Nat. Univ. Countinuing Edn. Assn., Denver, 1981; Spl. Energy Innovation award U.S. Dept. Energy, 1984. Fellow ASHRAE (mem. energy mgmt. com., regional v.p. 1978-83; Energy Design award 1982); mem. Wis. Soc. Profl. Engrs., Nat. Soc. Profl. Engrs. (state gov. 1984, energy chmn. 1980-83; Engr. of Year award 1982). Republican. Roman Catholic. Current work: Off-peak energy storage with heat pumps and ice; energy system design with personal computers; planned economic energy management; safety design of products and systems. Subspecialty: Computer-aided design. Home: 305 Valley View St Verona WI 53593 Office: U Wis 432 N Lake St Madison WI 53706

DORKO, ERNEST A(LEXANDER), chemist, educator, cons., researcher; b. Detroit, Sept. 16, 1936; s. John and Julia Anne (Pala) D.; m. Betty Jane, June 18, 1971; 1 son, Thomas. B.Ch.E., U. Detroit, 1959; M.S., U. Chgo., 1961, Ph.D. in Chemistry, 1964. Research chemist Phys. Scis. Lab., Redstone Arsenal, Ala., 1964-67; asst. prof. chemistry, dept. physics Air Force Inst. Tech., Wright-Patterson AFB, Ohio, 1967-70, assoc. prof., 1970-77, prof., 1977—; vis. scientist Air Force Weapons Lab., 1985-86. Contbr. numerous articles to profl. publs. Trustee Dayton (Ohio) View Triangle Assn. Served to capt. U.S. Army, 1964-66. Decorated Army Commendation medal; recipient Sci. Achievement award USAF, 1972. Mem. Am. Chem. Soc., AAAS, Sigma Xi, Tau Beta Pi. Roman Catholic. Patentee in field. Current Work: Kinetics and spectroscopic analysis in flow tubes and shock tubes, kinetics and mechanism of degradation of laser dyes. Subspecialties: Kinetics; Photochemistry. Office: Air Force Inst Tech/ENP Dept Physics Wright-Patterson AFB OH 45433

DORMER, KENNETH JOHN, cardiovascular physiologist, clinical neurophysiologist; b. Ashland, Pa., Mar. 10, 1944; s. Allen Gilgore and Grace Jones; m. Karen Marie Kyne, June 12, 1966; children—Kelly Noel, Kristin Lee, Kevin James. B.S. in Marine Biology, Cornell U., 1966; M.S. in Physiology, UCLA, 1969, Ph.D. in Biology, 1974. Postdoctoral fellow U. Tex. Med. Branch, Galveston, 1974-77; adj. asst. prof. psychiatry U. Okla. Coll. Med., Oklahoma City, 1979—, assoc. prof. physiology and biophysics, 1983—, v.p. Central Ear Research Inst., Oklahoma City, 1982—; clinical neurophysiologist Cochlear Implant Clinic Baptist Med. Ctr., Oklahoma City, 1980—. Contbr. articles to profl. jours. and book. Patentee in field. Research grantee NIH, 1970—. Mem. Am. Physiolo. Soc. (pub. affairs com. 1983—), Soc. for Neuroscience, Von Bekesy Soc. (chtr.); fellow Am. Sci. Affiliation. Current work: Neural control of the cardiovascular system, mechanisms of alcohol-induced cardiac dysfunction, auditory neural prostheses for the deaf. Subspecialties: Physiology (medicine); Otorhinolaryngology. Home: 1601 Edgewood Dr Edmond OK 73034 Office: Univ Okla Health Scis Ctr Dept Physiology and Biophysics PO Box 26901 Oklahoma City OK 73190

DORN, GORDON LEE, institute administrator, educator; b. Chgo., June 8, 1937; s. Irvin Arleigh and Grace (Jahr) D.; m. Kathie Lee Dorn, Oct. 30, 1969; children: Scott Lee, Kelly Lee. B.Sc. cum laude, Purdue U., 1958, M.Sc., 1960, Ph.D., 1961. Teaching asst. Purdue U., 1958-59; research assoc. Glasgow (Scotland) U., 1961-63; asst. prof. Albert Einstein Coll. Medicine, 1964-67; assoc. prof. microbiology Baylor U., 1968-70; adj. prof. North Tex. State U., Denton, 1974—; chmn. dept. microbiology Wadley Insts. Molecular Medicine, Dallas, also; dir. clin. microbiology; pres. Dorn Microbiol. Cons., Inc. Contbr. articles to profl. jours. NSF grantee, 1964; NIH grantee, 1965-67; Blanche Mary Taxis Found. grantee, 1970-71; recipient IR 100 award, 1982. Mem. Genetics Soc. Am., AAAS, Am. Genetics Assn., N.Y. Acad. Sci., Am. Soc. Microbiology, Am. Soc. Quality Control. Christian Sci. Patentee in field; inventor DuPont isolator systems. Current Work: Major research interests include interferon prodn., diagnostics test in the areas of bacteriology and mycology; spl. interests include blood, sputum, urine, and throat cultures and antibiotic susceptibility testing. Subspecialties: Microbiology (medicine); Genetics and genetic engineering (medicine). Home: 1232 Lausanne St Dallas TX 75208 Office: 9000 Harry Hines Blvd Suite 311 Dallas TX 75235

DORNBUSH, RHEA L., psychologist, consultant; b. N.Y.C.; d. Barnett and Betty (Shore) D. B.A., Queens Coll., 1962, M.A., 1963; M.P.H., Columbia U., 1981; Ph.D., CUNY, 1967. Lic. psychologist, N.Y. Asst. prof. psychology Rutgers U., New Brunswick, N.J., 1965-68; asst., then assoc. prof. psychiatry N.Y. Med. Coll., N.Y.C., 1968-76, assoc. prof., 1978-80, prof., 1980—; lectr. in med. psychology in psychiatry Washington U. Sch. Medicine, St. Louis, 1976-78; sr. research scientist Reproductive Biology Research Found., St. Louis, 1976-78; dir. Bradford Nat. Corp., Bradford Trust Co. Contbr. articles to profl. jours. Grantee NIMH, Am. Philos. Soc., Sigma Xi, Nat. 1966-86. Mem. AAAS, AAUP, Am. Psychol. Assn. Soc., Biol. Psychiatry, N.Y. Acad. Scis., Am. Public Health Assn. Current Work: Humanism in medicine; research, consulting, teaching, administration. Office: Dept Psychiatry NY Ned Coll Valhalla NY 10595

DOROGY, WILLIAM EUGENE, JR., research chemist; b. Wilkinsburg, Pa., Aug. 11, 1953; s. William Eugene and Claire J. (Tabor) D. B.S., Lehigh U., 1975; M.S., Ohio State U., 1977, Ph.D., 1982. Grad. teaching asst. Ohio State U., Columbus, 1975-80, grad. research assoc., 1981; research chemist Badische Corp., Williamsburg, Va., 1982—. Contbr. articles to profl. jours. Mem. Am. Chem. Soc. (inorganic chemistry div., polymer chemistry div., polymeric materials sci. and engring. div.), Psi Upsilon. Republican. Greek Orthodox. Club: Peninsula Ski. Current work: Reduce flammability and alter the chemical-physical structure of polyacrylonitrile fibers. Subspecialties: Inorganic chemistry; Polymer chemistry. Home: 1008 Myrtle Ct Newport News VA 23602 Office: Badische Corp PO Drawer D Williamsburg VA 23187

DORRELL, DOUGLAS GORDON, research administrator; b. Ashcroft, B.C., Can., Oct. 24, 1940; s. Daniel Cedric and Sheila (Bonallo) D.; m. Lora Valerie Petko, Oct. 4, 1963; children—Craig Stephen, Jan Melissa. B.S.A., U. B.C., 1962; M.Sc., U. Sask., 1963; Ph.D., Mich. State U., 1968; postgrad. Nat. Def. Coll., Kingston, Ont., 1980. Research scientist Agr. Can. Research Sta., Morden, Man., 1968-74, acting dir., 1974-75, research scientist, 1975-78, spl. adviser, Ottawa, Ont., 1978-80, dir., Winnipeg, Man., 1980-83, Lethbridge, Alta., 1983—. Councillor Town of Morden, 1975-77; chmn. Morden and Dist. Hosp. Bd., 1978. Mem. Agrl. Inst. Can. Lodge: Rotary. Subspecialty: Agricultural research administration. Office: Research Sta Agr Can Lethbridge AB T1J 4B1 Canada

DORSEY, JOHN HENRY, marine biologist; b. Long Beach, Calif., Oct. 7, 1949; s. John Ward and Mildred Barbara (Henry) D.; m. Deborah Ann Colbert, Jan. 12, 1973. B.S. in Marine Biology, Calif. State U.-Long Beach, 1972, M.A. in Biology, 1975; Ph.D. in Zoology, U. Melbourne, Australia, 1982. Marine technologist Marine Biol. Cons., Inc., Costa Mesa, Calif., 1969-73, marine biologist, 1975-76, cons. polychaete taxonomy, 1984—; research asst. Calif. State U. Found., Long Beach, 1973-75; part-time lectr. dept. zoology U. Melbourne, Parkville, Australia, 1976-80; oceanographer Interstate Electronics Corp., Anaheim, Calif., 1980-82; water biologist City Los Angeles Hyperion Treatment Plant, Playa Del Rey, Calif., 1983—; cons. marine survey Caldwell-Connell Engrs., Melbourne, Australia, 1978; cons. pollution ecology Seaventures, Dana Point, Calif., 1982—; Contbr. articles to profl. jours. Mem. AAAS, Biol. Soc. Washington, Ecol. Soc. Am., So. Calif. Acad. Sci., So. Calif. Assn. Marine Invertebrate Taxonomists (charter; pres. 1985—), Western Soc. Naturalists. Democrat. Current work: Marine pollution monitoring and research, especially on benthic communities; polychaetous annelid taxonomy, policy and regulations for marine monitoring. Subspecialties: Marine biology; Taxonomy. Home: 533 Hillcrest St El Segundo CA 90245 Office: Hyperion Treatment Plant Biology Lab 12000 Vista Del Mar Playa Del Rey CA 90291

DOS, SERGE JACQUES, surgeon, physiology researcher; b. Paris, Jan. 24, 1934; came to U.S., 1957; s. Octave Pierre Marie and Fernande Lucienne (Daire) D.; m. Rasma Kupers, Aug. 19, 1966; children: Soshana, Yasmin, Maiya. M.D., U. Paris, 1964; Ph.D. in Physiology, U. Minn., 1965. Diplomate Am. Bd. Surgery. Lab. instr. physiology U. Minn., Mpls., 1962-65; instr. in surgery Cornell U., N.Y.C., 1971-73; asst. prof. surgery SUNY-Stony Brook, 1973, asst. prof. clin. physiology, 1973-76; surgeon St. John's Episcopal Hosp., Smithtown, N.Y., 1978—; research com. VA Hosp., Northport, N.Y., 1974-76. Contbr. chpt. to book. USPHS trainee., 1962-65; various research grants NIH; various research grants Am. Heart Assn.; various research grants pvt. labs.; Laureate (Silver Medal) Faculty of Medicine U. Paris, 1966. Fellow N.Y. Acad. Scis.; mem. Am. Fedn. Clin. Research, AAAS, Am. Physiol. Soc., Assn. Acad. Surgery. Current Work: Physiology, history. Subspecialties: Surgery; Cardiac surgery. Home: 16 Crooked Oak Rd Belle Terre NY 11777 Office: St John's Episcopal Hosp Route 25A Smithtown NY 11787

DOSTER, JOSEPH MICHAEL, nuclear engineering educator, consultant; b. Chapel Hill, N.C., Dec. 3, 1954; s. Joseph C. and Ann Howard D.; m. Ellen Winship Rogers, June 6, 1981. B.S., N.C. State U., Raleigh, 1977, Ph.D., 1982. Vis. instr. N.C. State U., Raleigh, 1980-81, instr., 1981-82, asst. prof. nuclear engring., 1982—; cons. Research Triangle Inst., Research Triangle Park, N.C., 1980—. Mem. Am. Nuclear Soc., Sigma Xi. Democrat. Current Work: Parallel processing, nuclear reactor shielding. Monte Carlo simulation. Subspecialties: Algorithms; Numerical analysis (computer science). Office: Box 7909 NC State U Raleigh NC 27655

DOUBEK, CLIFFORD JAMES, chem. engr.; b. Chgo., Mar. 27, 1925; s. James Frank and Sylvia (Fara) D.; m. Mary Lillian Vinduska, Nov. 5, 1949; 1 dau., Annette Mary. B.S. in Chem. Engring, Ill. Inst. Tech., 1949. Registered profl. engr., Calif. Research engr., mgr. quality assurance, asst. nat. dir. microbiology Johnson & Johnson Co., Chgo. and New Brunswick, N.J., 1949-69; mgr. quality assurance C.R. Bard Co., Murray Hill, N.J., 1970, Abbott Labs., North Chicago, Ill., 1971-74; dir. quality assurance Hancock Extracorporeal Co., Anaheim, Calif., 1974—. Served with U.S. Army, 1943-46, ETO. Fellow Am. Soc. Quality Control (cert. reliability engr., nat. chmn. biomed. div.), Soc. Advancement Mgmt./Am. Mgmt. Assn. (profl. mgr. 1979, internat. chmn. bd., internat pres.); mem. VFW. Current Work: Heart valve development; quality assurance in the manufacture of porcine and pericardial heart valves and cardiovascular devices. Subspecialties: Chemical engineering; Biomedical engineering. Office: 4633 E La Palma Ave Anaheim CA 92807

DOUGHERTY, GEORGE JOHN, computer sciences company manager; b. Lakewood, N.J., Jan. 30, 1943; s. Edward George and Jean Gilroy (McIntyre) D.; m. Karen Ann O'Hern, Aug. 30, 1969; children: Dawn Ann, Erin Jean. B.Gen. Studies, U. Nebr., 1971; grad, U.S. Army Command and Gen. Staff Coll., 1978; M.S., Boston U., Heidelberg, Ger., 1979. Commd. officer U.S. Army, advanced through grades to maj. Res.; comdr. Hdqrs. Battery 1st Bn. 5th Field Arty., Fort Riley, Kans., 1976-77, intelligence officer, 1977, emergency action officer Hdqrs. U.S Army Europe, Heidelberg, Ger., 1977-80; programmer analyst (Hdqrs. U.S Army Europe), 1980-81, (Joint Deployment Agy.), Tampa, Fla., 1981-82; sr. mem. tech. staff Computer Scis. Corp., Tampa, 1982-83, work area mgr., 1983—; adj. lectr. City Colls. Chgo., Heidelberg, 1980-81, Boston U., Heidelberg, 1980-81, U. Tampa, 1982; adj. instr. Fla. Inst. Tech., St. Petersburg, 1982—. Pres., Butterfield Homeowners Assn., Manhattan, Kans., 1974; bd. dirs. Twelve Oaks Homeowners Assn.; treas. Soc. Pen and Sword, Omaha, 1970; mem. bus. adv. council Abilities Inc. of Clearwater (Fla.). Decorated Silver Star. Mem. Assn. U.S. Army, Inst. Cert. of Computer Profls., Assn. Computing Machinery (v.p. chpt.), Data Processing Mgmt. Assn., Processing Mgmt. Assn. Roman Catholic. Current Work: Distributed database structures for decision support systems. Subspecialties: Database systems; Distributed systems and networks. Home: 7517 Mayfair Ct Tampa FL 33614 Office: Computer Scis Corp PO Box 19188 Tampa FL 33686

DOUGHERTY, JOSEPH CHARLES, nephrologist; b. Troy, N.Y., Feb. 13, 1934; s. William Joseph and Dorothy Dewar (Anker) D.; m. Katherine Irene Barron, June 6, 1959; children: William R., Suzanne V., Timothy J., Laura E. B.S., Manhattan Coll., 1956; M.D., Cornell U., 1960. Diplomate: Am. Bd. Internal Medicine, Intern Albany (N.Y.) Med. Center Hosp., 1960-61. Resident in internal medicine Bellevue Hosp. Center, N.Y.C.; fellow N.Y. Heart Assn., 1964-67; asst. prof. medicine Cornell U. Med. Coll., 1967-68, Albert Einstein Coll. Medicine, 1968-71; assoc. prof. medicine U. Tex. Health Sci. Ctr., San Antonio, 1971-76; assoc. dir. Moses Taylor Hypertension Inst., Scranton, Pa., 1976-80; ptnr. Valley Diagnostic Clinic, Harlingen, Tex., 1980—; exec. com. ESRD Network 11, Dallas, 1980-82; med. dir. Watson W. Wise Dialysis Ctr., Harlingen, 1980—. Author: Concise Textbook on Nephrology, 1977; contbr.: to Hand Book of Nutrition, 1978; contbg. editor: to Med. Times Resident and Staff Physician, 1966-78; contbr. articles sci. jours. Med. adv. bd. Kidney Found. So. Tex., 1973-76, Tex. Dept. Pub. Safety, Drivers Lic., Austin, 1973-76, Keystone Heart Assn., 1977-80; dir. Cameron County Heart Assn., 1980-83. Mead Johnson fellow, 1962-63; N.Y. Heart Assn. fellow, 1964-68; sr. investigator, 1969-71. Fellow ACP; mem. Am. Soc. Artificial Internal Organs, Transplantation Soc., Am. Soc. Nephrology. Roman Catholic. Current Work: Economics of health care especially out-patient services, assessment of nutritional needs in dialysis patients. Subspecialties: Nephrology; Internal medicine. Office: Valley Diagnostic Clinic 2200 Haine Dr Harlingen TX 78550

DOUGHERTY, ROBERT MALVIN, microbiologist, researcher; b. Long Branch, N.J., May 25, 1929; s. Robert L. and Justine (Mernone) D.; m. Barbara Geran, June 26, 1950; children: Karen, Joyce. B.S., Rutgers U., 1952, M.S., 1954, Ph.D., 1957. Instr. U. Rochester, 1957-60; USPHS Spl. Research fellow Imperial Cancer Research Fund, London, 1960-62; assoc. prof. microbiology SUNY Upstate Med. Center, Syracuse, 1962-69, prof., 1969—. Contbr. numerous articles profl. jours. Served to cpl. AUS, 1946-48. Research grantee Am. Cancer Soc., 1963-68; Research grantee USPHS, 1965-79; Research grantee NSF, 1967-72. Mem. Am. Assn. Immunology, AAAS, Am. Soc. Microbiology, Soc. Exptl. Biology and Medicine, Sigma Xi. Current Work: Biology of oncogenic viruses. Subspecialties: Microbiology; Virology (biology). Office: 766 Irving Ave Syracuse NY 13210

DOUGLAS, BRYCE, pharmaceutical company executive; b. Glasgow, Scotland, Jan. 6, 1924; came to U.S., 1958; s. Alexander and Mary (Turner) D.; m. Joyce M. Flynn, Aug. 24, 1955; children: Alan David, Neal Malcolm, Iain Graham. B.Sc. with honors, Glasgow U., 1944; Ph.D. in Organic Chemistry, Edinburgh (Scotland) U., 1948. Chemotherapy researcher, research lab. Royal Coll. Physicians, Edinburgh, 1947-49; research asst. biol. chemistry Aberdeen (Scotland) U., 1949; research fellow in alkaloid chemistry NRC Can., Ottawa, 1949-51; research fellow dept. pharmacology Harvard U., 1952-53; research asso., lectr. Ind. U., Bloomington, 1953-56; vis. research asso. U. Malaya, Singapore, 1956-58; with Smith Kline & French Labs., Phila., 1956—, v.p. research and devel., 1971-80, pres. research and devel., 1980-81, v.p. sci. and tech., 1981—. Contbr. articles to profl. jours. Bd. dirs. Royal Soc. Medicine Found.; bd. overseers U. Pa. Sch. Dental Medicine; bd. mgrs. Franklin Inst. of Phila.; bd. dirs. Southeastern Pa. chpt. ARC. Fellow Royal Soc. Chemistry (U.K.), Coll. Physicians Phila.; mem. N.Y. Acad. Scis., AAAS, Am. Chem. Soc. Patentee in field. Subspecialty: Medicinal chemistry. Home: Box 672 Kimberton PA 19442 Office: PO Box 7929 Philadelphia PA 19101

DOUGLAS, DEXTER RICHARD, plant pathologist, consultant, researcher; b. Benton, Ohio, Nov. 14, 1937; s. Richard Loren and Dortney Ann (Phillabaum) D.; m. Bernadine Bresson, May 26, 1962; children: Laura Ann, Cynthia Marie. B.S. in Biology, Kent State U., 1962; M.S. in Plant Pathology, U. Wyo., 1965; Ph.D. in Plant Pathology, U. Minn.-St. Paul, 1968. Research plant pathologist U.S. Dept. Agr., Aberdeen, Idaho, 1968-75; pvt. researcher Chem. Supply Co. Inc., Twin Falls, Idaho, 1976-77; pvt. cons., pres., gen. mgr. Hi-Alta Inc., Moore, Idaho, 1978—; area mgr. Idaho Crop Improvement Assn., Potato Seed Cert., Idaho Falls, Idaho, 1980-82; expert witness on potato diseases. Contbr. articles to profl. jours. Served with U.S. Army, 1962-64. Mem. Am. Phytopathol. Soc., Am. Potato Assn. Lodge: Lions. Current Work: Potato diseases, control of seed piece decay, seed certification; seed potato prodn. Subspecialty: Plant pathology. Home: RD 1 Box 394 Arco ID 83213 Office: Box 916 Moore ID 83255

DOUGLAS, J. FIELDING, toxicologist, biochemist; b. Delta, Utah, Jan. 25, 1927; s. Ben and Amelia (Fielding) D.; m. Rose Terrazzino, Sept. 16, 1951; children: David, Pamela, Jason. B.S. with high honors, U. Ill., 1948; M.A., Columbia U., 1950, Ph.D., 1953. Project leader Johnson & Johnson, New Brunswick, N.J., 1952-58; dir. biochemistry Carter-Wallace, Cranbury, N.J., 1958-74; dep. dir. carcinogenesis testing program Nat. Cancer Inst., Bethesda, Md., 1976-80; chief program ops. br. nat. toxicology program Nat. Inst. Environ. Health Scis., Bethesda, 1980-84; pres. Sci. Services, Inc., 1984—; cons., 1974-80. Contbr. Author: Carcinogenesis and Mutagenesis Testing, 1984. Contbr. articles to sci. jours. Served in U.S. Army, 1944-46, ATO. Recipient award Richard Neff Soc., 1966; USPHS fellow, 1950-52. Mem. Am. Chem. Soc. (dir. sect.), Soc. Toxicology, Am. Soc. Pharmacology and Exptl. Therapeutics, Soc. Exptl. Biology and Medicine, AAAS, N.Y. Acad. Scis. Patentee in field. Current Work: Chemical carcinogenesis and toxicology; evaluation of environmental and industrial chemicals for carcinogenicity and toxicology. Subspecialties: Toxicology (medicine); Cancer research (medicine). Home: Hermitage Farm PO Box 533 Front Royal VA 22630 Office: Sci Services Inc PO Box 533 Front Royal VA 22630

DOUGLAS, JAMES NATHANIEL, astronomer. Dir., Radio Astronomy Obs., U. Tex., Austin. Subspecialty: Radio and microwave astronomy. Office: U Tex-Austin Radio Astronomy Obs Austin TX 78712*

DOUGLAS, WILLIAM HUGH, dental educator; b. Belfast, No. Ireland, Aug. 18, 1937; came to U.S., 1977; s. James and Susan (Marno) D.; m. Margaret Elizabeth Cartwright, July 17, 1971; children: Emma Susan, Harriet Irene. B.S., U. Belfast, 1959, M.S., 1961, Ph.D., 1965; B.D.S., U. London, 1970. Licentiate in dental surgery Royal Coll. Surgeons (Eng.). Lectr. dental materials U. Belfast, 1961; Nuffield fellow Guys Hosp., London, 1965-70; lectr. dentistry Welsh Nat. Sch. Medicine, Cardiff, Wales, 1971-78; vis. assoc. prof. Sch. Dentistry, U. Mich., Ann Arbor, 1977; dir. biomaterials program Sch. Dentistry, U. Minn., Mpls., 1978—, assoc. prof., 1983-85, prof., 1985—; cons. Contbr. articles to dental jours. Mem. Internat. Assn. Dental Research, Omicron Kappa. Upsilon. Presbyterian. Co-patentee in field; developer artifical mouth for testing dental materials. Current Work: Composite technology and adhesives; composite, resin, filler, dentin, enamel, acid etch, adhesive, robotics, computer graphics, clinical measurement. Subspecialties: Biomaterials; Restorative dentistry. Office: University of Minnesota 16-212 HSUA Minneapolis MN 55455

DOW, DANIEL GOULD, educator; b. Ann Arbor, Mich., Apr. 26, 1930; s. William Gould and Edna Lois (Sontag) D.; m. Kathleen Mary Bond, June 19, 1954; children—Sarah, Suzanne, Jennifer, Gordon. B.S. in Engring, U. Mich., 1952, M.S., 1953; Ph.D., Stanford U., 1958. Asst. prof. elec. engring. Calif. Inst. Tech., Pasadena, 1958-61; with Varian Assos., Palo Alto, Calif., 1961-68; prof. U. Wash., Seattle, 1968—, chmn. dept. elec. engring., 1968-77; asso. dir. Applied Physics Lab., 1977-79; dir. Washington Energy Research Center, 1979-81; cons. Hughes Aircraft, Malibu, Calif., 1958-61, Varian Assos., 1968-71, Boeing Co., 1973-74, John Fluke Co., 1979—; mem. Adv. Group on Electron Devices, Microwave Working Group, 1965-76, Wash. Energy Policy Council, 1973-74; mem. subpanel on energy research Energy Research Adv. Bd., 1980; mem. panel on measurement services Nat. Acad. Scis.-Nat. Bur. Standards. Served to lt. USAF, 1953-55. Mem. IEEE. (sr. mem.). Current Work: Microwaves, semiconductor modeling. Subspecialties: Electronics; Semiconductors. Home: 9620 NE 31st St Bellevue WA 98004

DOW, LOIS WEYMAN, physician, consultant; b. Cin., Mar. 11, 1942; d. Albert Dames and Else Marion (Krug) W.; children: Elizabeth, Alan. B.A. summa cum laude, Cornell U., 1964; M.D. cum laude, Harvard U., 1968. Diplomate: Am. Bd. Internal Medicine with spltys. hematology, med. oncology. Intern Bronx Mcpl. Hosp. Center, 1968-69; resident Presbyn. Hosp., N.Y.C., 1969-70; fellow in hematology Columbia U., 1970-72; instr. U. Tenn., Memphis, 1972-73, assoc. prof., 1973-74; research assoc. St. Jude's Children's Research Hosp., Memphis, 1974-77, asst. mem., 1977-80, assoc. mem., 1980—; cons. Nat. Cancer Inst., 1978-82. Contbr. articles to profl. jours. NIH grantee. Mem. Am. Fedn. Clin. Research, ACP, Am. Soc. Hematology, Am. Assn. Cancer Research, Internat. Soc. Exptl. Hematology, Am. Soc. Clin. Oncology, Phi Beta Kappa, Phi Kappa Phi, Alpha Lambda Delta, Alpha Epsilon Delta. Current Work: Cell culture studies of normal and malignant cells; cell kinetics. Subspecialties: Cancer research (medicine); Cell and tissue culture. Office: Div Hematology/Oncolog St Jude Children's Research Hosp Memphis TN 38101

DOWD, JOHN PETER, physics educator and researcher; b. New Bedford, Mass., Feb. 1, 1938; s. John Henry and Estelle (Fournier) D.; m. Mary Beth Vancini, Feb. 12, 1960; children: Michael, Paul. B.S., MIT, 1959, Ph.D., 1966. Vis. researcher German Electron Synchrotron, Hamburg, W.Ger., 1966-67; asst. prof. physics Southeastern Mass. U., North Dartmouth, 1967-72, assoc. prof., 1972-77, prof., 1978—, chmn. dept., 1985—; guest researcher Cambridge (Mass.) Electron Accelerator, 1967-72, Brookhaven Nat. Lab., Upton, N.Y., 1972—; guest scientist U. Bonn, W.Ger., 1978-79. NSF grantee. Mem. Am. Phys. Soc., Am. Assn. Physics Tchrs., AAAS, Sigma Xi. Current Work: Experiment high energy physics; application of microcomputers to physics laboratory instruction. Subspecialty: Particle physics. Home: Box 833 Fairhaven MA 02719 Office: Dept Physics Southeastern Mass U North Dartmouth MA 02747

DOWDLE, WALTER REID, microbiologist; b. Irvington, Ala., Dec. 11, 1930; s. Ruble C. and Rebecca (Powell) D.; m. Mable Irene Graham, Apr. 2, 1953; children—Greta Denise Dowdle Rackley, Robert Reid, Jennifer Leigh. B.S., U. Ala., 1955, M.S., 1957; Ph.D., U. Md., 1960. Chief respiratory virology Ctrs. for Disease Control, Atlanta, 1964-73, dir. virology div., 1973-79, asst. dir. for sci., 1979-81, dir. Ctr. for Infectious Diseases, 1981—; hon. fellow John Curtin Sch. Med. Research, Canberra, Australia, 1972-73; chmn. Interagy. Reye Syndrome Task Force, USPHS, 1982—. Author: (with Jack La Patra) Informed Consent, 1983. Mem. editorial bd. Jour. Clin. Microbiology, 1974—. Contbr. articles to profl. jours. Served with USAF, 1948-52. Recipient Disting. Service award HHS, 1981, 82; Presdl. Rank Award, 1984; named Fed. Exec. of Yr., Sr. Exec. Assn., Washington, 1983. Mem. Am. Acad. Microbiology (bd. govs. 1984—), Am. Pub. Health Assn., Infectious Diseases Soc. Am., AAAS, Am. Soc. Virology. Subspecialty: Infectious diseases. Office: Centers for Disease Control 1600 Clifton Rd Altanta GA 30333

DOWELL, EARL HUGH, university dean, aerospace and mechanical engineering educator; b. Macomb, Ill., Nov. 16, 1937; s. Earl S. and Edna Bernice (Dean) D.; m. Lynn M. Cary, July 21, 1981; children: Marla Lorraine, Janice Lynelle, Michael Hugh. B.S., U. Ill., 1959; S.M., Mass. Inst. Tech., 1961, Sc.D., 1964. Research engr. Boeing Co., 1962-63; research asst. Mass. Inst. Tech., 1963-64, research engr., 1964, asst. prof., 1964-65; asst. prof. aerospace and mech. engring. Princeton U., 1964-68, asso. prof., 1968-72, prof., 1972-83, assoc. chmn., 1975-77, acting chmn., 1979; dean Sch. Engring. Duke U., Durham, N.C., 1983—; cons. to industry and govt. Author: Aeroelasticity of Plates and Shells, 1974, A Modern Course in Aeroelasticity, 1978; Assoc. editor: AIAA Jour, 1969-72; Contbr. articles to profl. jours. Chmn. N.J. Noise Control Council, 1972-76. Named outstanding young alumnus U. Ill. Sch. Aero. and Astronautical Engring., 1973, disting. alumnus, 1975. Fellow AIAA (Structures, Structural Dynamics and Material award 1980, v.p. publs. 1981-83), Am. Acad. Mechanics; mem. Acoustical Soc. Am., ASME. Current Work: Nonlinear dynamics, aeroelastilcity, structural dynamics, acoustics. Subspecialties: Aerospace engineering and technology; Theoretical and applied mechanics. Home: duke univ school of engineering Durham NC 27706 Office: Sch of Engring Duke U Durham NC

DOWELL, FLONNIE, theoretical physicist, researcher; b. Marietta, Ga., Feb. 7, 1947. B.A., U. S. Fla., 1969; M.S., Tex. Woman's U., 1974; Ph.D., Georgetown U., 1977. Tchr., Ocala, Fla. and Carrollton-Farmer's Branch, Tex., 1969-71; research and teaching asst. Tex. Woman's U., Denton, 1971-73; Georgetown U., Washington, 1973-77; research scientist Nat. Bur. Standards, Washington, 1977-79, Oak Ridge Nat. Lab., 1979-81, Los Alamos Nat. Lab., 1981—. Contbr. articles to profl. jours. Recipient travel award NSF, 1977, 10th Internat. Liquid Crystal Conf., 1984. Mem. Am. Phys. Soc., N.Y. Acad. Scis., AAAS, Royal Soc. Chemistry (assoc.), Sigma Xi. Current work: Statistical physics of chain molecules (including polymers) and their mixtures in the liquid, liquid-crystalline, crystal, and glass states; theoretical design of molecules. Subspecialties: Theoretical physics; Statistical physics. Office: Los Alamos Nat Lab Theoretical Div Los Alamos NM 87545

DOWLEY, MARK WILLIAM, physicist, business exec.; b. Dundalk, Ireland, Apr. 28, 1934; came to U.S., 1959, naturalized, 1964; s. Arthur Gerard and Sheila Mary (Williams) D.; m. Mary F. Donnelly, Mar. 29, 1967; children: A. David, Aoife, Patrick. B.Sc. with 1st class honours, Univ. Coll., Dublin, 1956; M.A., U. Toronto, 1957, Ph.D., 1959. Postdoctoral research fellow in physics U. Calif., Berkeley, 1959-61; with IBM Research Labs., San Jose, Calif., 1961-67, Spectra Physics, Mountain View, Calif., 1967-68; dir. researcher Coherent Radiation, Palo Alto, Calif., 1968-72; pres. chmn. bd. Liconix, Sunnyvale, Calif., 1972—; Lectr. U. Calif., Berkeley, Calif. State U., San Jose. Contbr. numerous articles to sci. jours. Numerous scholarships and fellowships, 1952-62. Mem. IEEE, Optical Soc. Am., Am. Phys. Soc. Roman Catholic. Clubs: University (Palo Alto); Richmond (Calif.) Yacht. Patentee laser tech. field. Current Work: Design and physics of helium cadmium lasers; strategic planning and finance in high technology company, laser optics. Subspecialty: Laser research. Office: 1390 Borregas Sunnyvale CA 94086

DOWNEY, JAMES MERRITT, physiology educator; b. Wabash, Ind., Nov. 1, 1944; s. Richard Merritt and Janet Mildred (Fisher) D.; m. Patty Ann Froebe, June 18, 1967 (div. 1979); children: Michael, Douglas. B.S., Manchester Coll., 1967; M.S., U. Ill., 1969, Ph.D., 1971. Research fellow Harvard Med. Sch., Boston, 1970-72; asst. prof. physiology U. South Fla., Tampa, 1972-75; assoc. prof. physiology U. South Ala., Mobile, 1975-79, prof., 1979—; cons. scientist Rayne Inst., St. Thomas Hosp., London, 1980—. Co-author: PET Interfacing, 1980, Interfacing Projects for the Sinclair Computers, 1983, Easy Interfacing Projects for the Commodore 64, 1985. Served with U.S. Army, 1962. NIH grantee, 1976—; Am. Heart Assn. grantee, 1982—. Fellow Am. Heart Assn. (Circulation Council), Am. Physiol. Soc. (circulation group); mem. Am. Fedn. Clin. Research. Democrat. Methodist. Current Work: Laboratory research concerning protection of the heart in the presence of coronary artery disease; basic biophysics and drug evaluation. Subspecialties: Physiology (medicine); Pharmacology. Home: 5453 Old Shell Rd 264 Mobile AL 36608 Office: Coll Medicine U South Ala MSB 3024 Mobile AL 36688

DOWNING, ROBERT GREGORY, research chemist; b. St. Joseph, Mo., Dec. 1, 1953; s. Robert Isaac and Beverly Ann (Lawhon) D.; m. Eva Sharon Boggs, Aug. 9, 1980; 1 dau., Holly Priscilla. B.S., Mo. Western State Coll., 1976; Ph.D., U. Mo.-Rolla, 1981. Lectr., Tex. A&M U., College Station, 1980-81; Postdoctoral fellow Nat. Bur. Standards, Gaithersburg, Md., 1981-83, research chemist, 1983—. Contbr. articles to profl. jours. Recipient Cert. Pioneer Research, Nat. Bur. Standards Dirs. Office, 1984. Mem. Am. Chem. Soc., Microbeam Analysis Soc., Materials Research Soc., Meteoritical Soc., Sigma Xi. Current work: Analytical neutron techniques, multidimensional profiling using neutron reactions, materials characterization, cold neutron instrumentation, analytical chemistry. Subspecialties: Nuclear chemistry; Analytical chemistry. Home: 77 Longmeadow Dr Gaithersburg MD 20878 Office: Nat Bur Standards Reactor B108 Gaithersburg MD 20899

DOYLE, EARL HOWARD, JR., civil engineer, researcher; b. Providence, Sept. 26, 1943; s. Earl Howard and Helen Marie (Aust) D.; m. Carol A. Mahoney, June 1, 1968 (div. 1972); 1 child, Timothy; m. Roberta Louise Platt, Mar. 29, 1974; children—Benjamin, Rachel, Daniel. Assoc. Sci. Roger Williams Coll., 1963; B.S. in Civil Engring., U. R.I., 1966, M.S. in Ocean Engring., 1968. Registered profl. engr., Tex. Research engr. Shell Devel. Co., Houston, 1968-76, sr. research engr., 1976-82, staff research engr., 1982—. Mem. Marine Programs Adv. Council, U. R.I., Narragansett, 1983—; mem. La. State U. Indsl. Assn. Program, Coastal Studies Inst., Baton Rouge, 1983—. Chmn. bd. elders Sugar Land Bible Ch., 1982-84. Mem. ASCE, Earthquake Engring. Research Inst. Republican. Current work: Geological hazards in offshore, foundations for offshore structures. Subspecialties: Civil engineering; Ocean engineering. Home: 13802 Vinehill Dr Sugar Land TX 77478 Office: Shell Devel Co 3737 Bellaire Blvd Houston TX 77025

DOYLE, FRANK LAWRENCE, hydrogeologist, research administrator; b. San Antonio, Oct. 16, 1926; s. William Michael and Elizabeth Lillian (Black) D.; m. Giovanna Maria Scorza, June 9, 1962; 1 son, Michael Joseph. B.S. in Geology, U. Tex.-Austin, 1950; M.S., La. State U., 1955; Ph.D., U. Ill., 1958. Registered geologist, Calif. Instr. St. Mary's U., San Antonio, 1950-53, asst. prof. geology, 1958-60, assoc. prof., 1960-62, chmn. dept. geology, 1961-62; petroleum geologist Seeligson Engring. Com., San Antonio, 1952-53; asst. geologist Ill. Geol. Survey, Urbana, 1956-58, assoc. geologist/research affiliate, 1959-61; geologist U.S. Geol. Survey, Mont., 1955, Colo., Ariz. 1962-63; assoc. prof. U. Conn., 1963-65; cons. hydrogeologist, Panama, Nicaragua, Algeria, 1965-71; regional geologist for North Ala. Geol. Survey Ala., 1971-77; cons. Kenneth E. Johnson Environ. and Energy Ctr., U. Ala.-Huntsville, 1971-77; adj. prof. hydrology, chmn. environ. sci. program Sch. Sci. and Engring., U. Ala.-Huntsville, 1971-77; cons. hydrogeologist, Fla., 1977-78; chief hydrogeologist Metcalf and Eddy, Inc., Boston, 1978-79; sr. hydrogeologist/program mgr. for waste mgmt. research U.S. Nuclear Regulatory Commn., Washington, 1979—. Sr. author: Environmental Geology and Hydrology, Huntsville and Madison County, Alabama, 1975; co-editor: Karst Hydrogeology, 1977. Active Huntsville/Madison County Local Govt. Study Com., Huntsville Solid Waste Mgmt. Com., 1972-75. Served with AUS, 1945-46. U. Ill. fellow, 1954-55. Fellow Geol. Soc. Am.; mem. Am. Assn. Petroleum Geologists (del. 1975-76), Internat. Assn. Hydrogeologists (gen. chmn. 12th Internat. Congress 1975, adv. council 1977-80, sec.-treas. U.S. com. 1980—), Am. Geophys. Union, Am. Inst. Profl. Geologists, Sigma Xi. Current Work: Research management: hydrogeology of high-level nuclear waste management; application of remotely-sensed data to ground water contamination; geomorphology; field geology. Subspecialties: Hydrology; Geology. Home: 4875 Wheatstone Dr Fairfax VA 22032 Office: US Nuclear Regulatory Commn Mail Stop 1130-SS Washington DC 20555

DOYLE, JOHN LAURENCE, manufacturing company executive; b. Whitestone, Devon, Eng., Sept. 7, 1931; came to U.S., 1953; s. John Edgcumbe and Grace Vera (Burd) D.; m. Judith Anne Nannizzi, Apr. 24, 1965; children—Jeffrey Michael, Peter John. B.S., Stanford U., 1956, M.S., 1959. Gen. mgr. AMD Hewlett Packard, Palo Alto, Calif., 1969-70; v.p., gen. mgr. Aerotherm, Sunnyvale, Calif., 1970-72; dir. corp. devel. Hewlett Packard, Palo Alto, 1972-76; v.p. personnel, 1976-81, v.p. research and devel., 1981-84, exec. v.p., 1984—; dir. Hexcel, San Francisco. Chmn. bd. C.I.S. Adv. Com., Stanford, 1980—; bd. dirs. Urban Coalition, Stanford, 1978—; cabinet Calif. Poly. Inst., San Louis Obispo, 1980—. RAF, 1951-53. Office: Hewlett-Packard Co 1501 Page Mill Rd Palo Alto CA 94025

DOYLE, WALTER ARNETT, pedodontist, orthodontist; b. Los Angeles, Aug. 9, 1933; s. Walter and Ruth D.; m. Betty Ann Parrot, Dec. 27, 1957 (div. June 1975); children: Shannon, Elizabeth, Sarah, Walter; m. Elizabeth Lewis, July 17, 1977. D.D.S., Emory U., 1959; M.S.D., Ind. U.-Indpls., 1961; postgrad., Boston U., 1974-76. Diplomate: Am. Bd. Pedodontics, Am. Bd. Orthodontics. Pvt. practice pedodontics, Lexington, Ky., 1962—, pvt. practice orthodontics, 1976—; instr. pedodontics Ind. U., 1961-62; instr. pedodontics U. Ky., 1964-65, guest lectr. dept. community dentistry, 1972-74, asst. field prof., 1972-74; vis. assoc. prof. pedodontics Northwestern U., 1972-74; vis. clin. prof. pedodontics Boston U. Sch. Grad. Dentistry, 1975—; mem. staff Good Samaratin, St. Joseph, Central Baptist, Humana hosps.; cons., contbr. Health Info. Systems, Inc.; dental cons. Medcom, Inc.; bd. dirs. Ky. Dental Service Corp., 1964-69; S. S. White Centennial teaching fellow. Contbr. articles to profl. jours. Trustee Hunter Found., 1972-74; mem. Bluegrass Trust for Historic Preservation, 1968—, Lexington Council for Arts, 1976—, Boston U. Alumni Area Rep. Fellow U. Ky.; Recipient award for leadership in dental progress Thomas Hinman, 1972, 76. Fellow Am. Acad. Pedodontics, Internat. Coll. Dentists, Am. Coll. Dentists.; Mem. Am. Soc. Preventive Dentistry (pres. Ky. unit 1972), Am. Soc. Dentistry for Children (mem. exec. council 1972—, pres. 1976-77), Internat. Assn. Dental Research, Am. Dental Assn., Assn. Pedodontic Diplomates (pres.-elect. 1968), Southeastern Soc. Pedodontics (pres. 1968), Ky. Soc. Dentistry for Children (pres. 1963), Psi Omega, Lexington C. of C. Clubs: Lexington Polo, Keeneland, Sierra, Ind. U. Century. Current Work: Orthodontics; pedodontics. Subspecialties: Dental growth and development; Orthodontics. Home: 3284 Paris Pike Lexington KY 40511 Office: 1628 Nicholasville Rd Lexington KY 40503

DOYLE, WILLIAM THOMAS, biologist, research center administrator; b. Coalinga, Calif., June 1, 1929; s. John Robert and Flora Mary (Hollingsworth) D.; m. Glendawyn A. Cox, Aug. 23, 1955; children—Shelley Suzanne, Carol Diane, Jean Kathryn, Mary Katherine. B.A., U. Calif.-Berkeley, 1957, Ph.D., 1960. Instr. biology Northwestern U., 1960-61, asst. prof., 1961-65; asst. prof. U. Calif., Santa Cruz, 1965-67, assoc. prof., 1967-72, prof., 1972, chmn. dept. biology 1967-68, 70-72, dean Div. Natural Sci., 1980-83, dir. Inst. Marine Scis., 1975—. Author: Nonseed Plants: Form and Function, 1970; Biology of the Higher Cryptogams, 1970. Served with USAF, 1948-53. Mem. Bot. Soc. Am., AAAS, Am. Soc. Plant Physiologists, Calif. Bot. Soc. Lodge: Rotary. Current work: The form and development of lower plants. Subspecialties: Morphology; Plant physiology (biology). Office: Univ Calif Inst Marine Sciences Santa Cruz CA 95064

DRAGO, JOSEPH ROSARIO, urologist; b. Jersey City, N.J., Oct. 28, 1947; s. Rosario P. and Betty L. (Brisgal) D.; m. Diane Mary Lavacca, June 17, 1972; children: Andrea, Daniella, Denise. B.S., U. Ill., 1965; M.D., 1972. Diplomate: Am. Bd. Urology. Intern gen. surgery Milton S. Hershey Med. Ctr., Pa. State U., Hershey, 1972-73, resident in urology, 1973-77; instr. urology Milton S. Hershey Med. Ctr., Pa. State U. (Coll. Medicine), 1976-77, asst. prof. urology, dir. urologic oncology, 1979-80, assoc. prof. surgery, dir. urologic oncology, 1980-85; prof. surgery, chmn. div. urology Ohio State U., Columbus, 1985—; asst. prof. urology, dir. urologic oncology U. Calif., Davis, 1977-79; mem. Nat. Prostatic Cancer Task Force, 1980-83; mem. cancer research coordinating com. U. Calif., 1978-79. Contbr. articles in field to profl. jours. Elsa U. Pardee Found. grantee, 1978; U. Calif. faculty research grantee, 1977. Mem. Am. Urologic Assn., Assn. Acad. Surgery, AMA, Am. Fertility Soc., Am. Soc. Andrology, Crippled Children's Services, Soc. Clin. Trials, Soc. Univ. Urologists, Pan-Pacific Surg. Assn., Western Assn. Transplant Surgeons, Pa. Med. Soc., Dauphin County Med. Soc., Phila. Urologic Soc. Roman Catholic. Current Work: Urologic oncology, tumor model systems, both bladder cancer model and prostrate cancer model, urologic-endocrinologic management carcinoma, chemotherapeutic measurements in animal model systems Subspecialties: Oncology; Urology. Home: 1512 Teeway Dr Columbus OH 43220 Office: 456 Clinic Dr Columbus OH 43210

DRAKE, AVERY ALA, JR., geologist, b. Kansas City, Mo., Jan. 17, 1927; s. Avery Ala and Mary Geneieve (Wilson) D.; m. Colette J. J. E. Buino, Aug. 10, 1963; children—Avery Ala III, Isabelle G.P. B.S., Mo. Sch. of Mines, 1950, M.S., 1952. Geologist, U.S. Geol. Survey, Denver, Washington, 1952-78, Reston, Va., 1985—, asst. chief geologist, Reston, 1979-84. Contbr. articles to profl. jours. Served with U.S. Army, 1945-46, ETO. Fellow Geol. Soc. Am.; mem. Soc. Econ. Geologists. Club: Cosmos (Washington). Current work: Geology of the Appalachian orogen, particularly the central Appalachians. Subspecialty: Tectonics. Home: 1551 44th St NW Washington DC 20007 Office: US Geol Survey 928 National Center Reston VA 22092

DRAKE, FRANK DONALD, astronomer; b. Chgo., May 28, 1930; s. Richard Carvel and Winifred Pearl (Thompson) D.; m. Amahl Z. Shakhashiri, Mar. 4, 1978; children: Nadia Meghann, Leila Marlyss; children by previous marriage: Stephen David, Richard Procter, Paul Robert. B. Engring. Physics, Cornell U., 1952; M.A., Harvard, 1956, Ph.D., 1958. Mem. Harvard Radio Astronomy Project, 1955-58; dir. Astron. Research Group, Ewen-Knight Corp., 1958; head telescope operations div. and sci. services div., radio studies Venus and Jupiter Nat. Radio Astronomy Obs., 1958-63; chief lunar and planetary scis. sect. Jet Propulsion Lab., 1963-64; assoc. prof. astronomy Cornell U., Ithaca, N.Y., 1964-66, prof., 1966-85, Goldwin Smith prof. astronomy, 1976-85, chmn. dept., 1968-71, assoc. dir. Center for Radiophysics and Space Research, 1965-74; prof. astronomy and astrophysics U. Calif.-Santa Cruz, 1984—, dean natural scis., 1984—; dir. Arecibo Ionospheric Obs., 1966-68, Nat. Astronomy and Ionosphere Center, 1971-81; mem. NRC, 1969-71; adviser govt. coms. on space research and astronomy. Author: Intelligent Life in Space, 1962, Murmurs of Earth: The Voyager Interstellar Record, 1978; Editorial adv. bd.: World Book Ency. Bd. dirs. Extrasolar Planetary Found. Mem. Am. Astron. Soc. (councillor, past chmn. div. planetary scis.), AAAS (past v.p., past chmn. astronomy sect.), Nat. Acad. Scis., Astron. Soc. Pacific (bd. dirs. 1985—), Am. Acad. Arts Scis., Internat. Astron. Union (v.p. commn. on life in universe, vice chmn. U.S. nat. com.), Internat. Sci. Radio Union, Planetary Soc. (dir.), Sigma Xi, Tau Beta Pi. Club: Explorers. Organized pioneer search for extra-terrestrial life, project OZMA, 1960. Subspecialty: Radio and microwave astronomy. Office: U Calif Santa Cruz Dept Astronomy Santa Cruz CA 95064

DRAKE, MICHAEL LEE, applied research engineer; b. Dayton, Ohio, Feb. 9, 1949; s. Ralph L. and Fannie R. (Britton) D.; m. Rebecca Ann Kerns, Oct. 16, 1971; children: Dawn Michelle, Benjamin Phillip. B.S. in Aerospace Engring, U. Cin., 1972, M.S., 1973. Research engr., group leader vibration analysis and control group U. Dayton, 1973—. Contbr. articles to profl. jours. Mem. ASME, Soc. Exptl. Stress Analysis, Inst. Environ. Scis. Subspecialties: Mechanical engineering; Aerospace engineering and technology. Office: 300 College Park Dr Dayton OH 45469

DRAPER, ERNEST LINN, JR., electric utility executive, nuclear engineer; b. Houston, Feb. 6, 1942; s. Ernest L. and Marcia Lee (Saylor) d.; m. Mary Deborah Doyle, June 9, 1962; children: Susan, Robert, Barbara, David. Student, Williams Coll., 1960-62; B.A., Rice U., 1964, B.S., 1965; Ph.D., Cornell U., 1970. Registered profl. engr., Tex. Asst. prof. U. Tex.-Austin, 1969-72, assoc. prof. mech. engring., 1972-79; tech. asst. to chmn. bd. Gulf States Utilities, Beaumont, Tex., 1979-80, v.p. nuclear tech., 1980-81, sr. v.p. engring. and tech. service, 1981-82, sr. v.p. external affairs, 1982—; cons.; mem. Commn. Radioactive Waste Mgmt., Tex. Energy and Nat. Resources Adv., Austin, 1979—; cons. Congressional Office of Tech. Assessment, Washington, 1982—. Editor: Proc. Tex. Symposium on Tech. Controlled Thermonuclear Fusion Experiments and Engring. Aspects of Fusion Reactors, 1974, Proc. Implications of Nuclear Power for Tex, 1973. NSF fellow, 1965, 66; AEC fellow, 1967, 68; recipient Faculty award U. Tex. Mem. Am. Nuclear Soc. (exec. com., dir.), Am. Phys. Soc. Current Work: Nuclear waste management, public understanding of energy issues. Subspecialties: Nuclear engineering; Nuclear fusion. Home: 1190 Dowlen Beaumont TX 77706 Office: Gulf States Utilities PO Box 2951 Beaumont TX 77704

DRAPKIN, ROBERT L., oncologist, clinical investigator; b. Albany, N.Y., Sept. 22, 1944; s. Isadore and Francis D.; m. Renee Mary Kumaraperv, Oct. 24, 1978; children: Julia, Jessica. B.S., Union Coll., 1966; M.S., Rensselaer Poly. Inst., 1967; M.D., Wayne State U., 1971. Intern U. Ill.Hosp., Chgo., 1971-72, resident in internal medicine, 1972-74, instr. in medicine, 1974-75; fellow oncology Meml. Hosp., Sloan Kettering Cancer Ctr., N.Y.C., 1975-78; physician Roswell Meml. Inst., Buffalo, 1978-79; assoc. prof. U. South Fla., Tampa, 1979—; attending physician Morton Plant Hosp., Clearwater, Fla., 1979—, Clearwater Community Hosp., 1979—, Mease Hosp., Dunedin, Fla., 1979—. Contbr. chpts. to book, articles to profl. jours. Fellow ACP; mem. Am. Soc. Clin. Oncology. Current Work: Physician and clinical investigator. Subspecialties: Chemotherapy; Oncology.

DRAWE, DALE LYNN, wildlife foundation executive, researcher; b. Mercedes, Tex., Nov. 3, 1942; s. Dale Umland and Doris Faye (Garrison) D.; m. Kathleen Kious, Aug. 24, 1964; children—Kimberly Anne, Pamela Lynn. B.S., Tex. A&I U., 1964; M.S., Tex. Tech U., 1967; Ph.D., Utah State U., 1971. Assoc. prof. Tex. A&I U., Kingsville, 1970-74; asst. dir. Welder Wildlife Found., Sinton, Tex., 1974—; cons. Winrock Internat., Morrilton, Ark., 1982. Author: (with others) Plant Communities of Welder Refuge, 1978. Editor Proc. of Welder Found. Symposium, 1978. Contbr. articles to profl. jours. Bd. dirs. Sinton Parks Adv. Bd., 1981—, Sinton Ind. Sch. Dist., 1983—, Coastal Bend Agri-Bus. Council, Robstown, Tex., 1970-74. Recipient Disting. Conservation award San Patricio Soil and Water Conservation Dist., 1977; named hon. state farmer Future Farmers Am., 1983. Mem. Soc. for Range Mgmt. (bd. dirs. Tex. sect. 1977-79), Wildlife Soc., Southwestern Assn. Naturalists, Tex. Acad. Sci., Am. Soc. Animal Sci., Sinton C. of C. (bd. dirs. 1981-83). Republican. Methodist. Lodges: Rotary, Kiwanis. Current work: Livestock grazing systems, white-tailed deer ecology, prescribed burning, wildlife-livestock-range interactions. Subspecialty: Resource management. Home: PO Drawer 1400 Sinton TX 78287

DRAYER, JAN IGNATIUS, physician; b. Amsterdam, Netherlands, Jan. 31, 1946; came to U.S., 1980; s. Roelof Pieter and Anna Betsie (DeSwart) D.; m. Thea Jacoba van Kalmthout, July 3, 1971; children: Myke, Joris. H.B.S.-B., St. Joris Coll., 1963; M.D., U. Nijmegen, 1971, Ph.D., 1975. Research asso. Cornell U., N.Y.C., 1975-77; internist U. Nijmegen, Netherlands, 1977-80; asso. chief clin. pharmacology/hypertension VA Med. Center, Long Beach, Calif., 1980—. Contbr. articles to profl. jours.; editor: Introduction to Echocardiography, 1980, Mineralocarticoids in Essential and Secondary Hypertension, 1982. Bd. dirs. Am. Heart Assn., Orange County, 1981—. Grantee Am. Heart Assn., 1982. Fellow Council for High Blood Pressure Research, Am. Coll. Clin. Pharmacology; mem. Am. Soc. Clin. Pharmacology and Therapeutics, Internat. Soc. Hypertension, Endocrine Soc. Current Work: Clin. pharmacology of cardiovascular agts.; endrocine aspects of hypertension; non-invasive monitoring and evaluation of hypertensive patients. Subspecialties: Internal medicine; Pharmacology. Home: 5401 Catowba Ln Irvine CA 92715 Office: VA Med Center 5901 E 7th St Long Beach CA 90822

DRAZNIN, BORIS, physician, researcher, educator; b. Kharkov, USSR, Oct. 1, 1945; came to U.S., 1977; s. Nahum and Rosa (Rips) D.; m. Elena Lerman, Dec. 25, 1965; children: Julie, Micky, Ann. M.D., Minsk (USSR) State Med. Inst., 1968; Ph.D., Vilnus (USSR) Inst. Exptl. Medicine, 1972. Diplomate: Am. Bd. Internal Medicine. Intern Molodechno City Hosp., 1968-69; resident in medicine Minsk Regional Hosp., 1969-71, research assoc., 1971-73, staff physician, 1973; research assoc. Tel Aviv Med. Ctr., 1974-77; fellow endocrinology U. Colo. Med. Ctr., 1977-80; asst. prof. medicine U. Colo. Health Sci. Ctr., Denver, 1980-85; assoc. prof. U. Colo. Med. Ctr., 1985—; research assoc. VA Med. Ctr., Denver, 1980-83, clin. investigator, 1983—. Mem. Am. Fedn. Clin. Research, Am. Diabetes Assn., Endocrine Soc., ACP, Am. Physiol. Soc., Am. Soc. Cell Biology. Jewish. Current Work: Insulin release and action; intracellular movement of proteins and receptors. Subspecialties: Endocrinology; Cell biology. Office: U Colo Health Sci Ctr 1055 Clermont St Denver CO 80220

DREITLEIN, RAYMOND PAUL, alcoholism counselor, consultant; b. Bklyn., Sept. 14, 1943; s. Michael George and Madelyn (Zamitka) D.; m. Carol Ann Lays, Jan. 23; children: Raymond, William, Karen, Scott, Adam, James, Kevin. B.A., St. Francis Coll., Bklyn., 1967; M.A., Seton Hall U., 1969. Cert. alcoholism counselor, N.J. Dept. head counseling and evaluation Mt. Carmel Guild, Newark, 1971-73. Clin. and project dir. A.T.U. Runnels Hosp., Berkeley Heights, N.J., 1973-76; dir., founder SSDC Detoxication Ctr., Elizabeth, N.J., 1977-79; regional counselor Employee Adv. Service, State of N.J., Newark, 1979-82; alcoholism counselor in pvt. practice, Morristown, N.J., 1982—; dir. out patient dept. alcoholism treatment unit Fair Oaks Hosp., Summit, N.J., 1983—; mem. faculty Rutgers U., 1976—; aftercare coordinator Mountainside Hosp., Montclair, N.J., 1980—; police instr. Union County Police Chief Acad., Cranford, N.J., 1974—. Recipient Alcoholism Recognition award Union County Counselors in Alcoholism, 1977. Mem. N.J. Assn. Alcoholism Counselors, N.J. Psychol. Assn. (assoc.), Am. Psychol. Assn. (assoc.), N.J. Assn. Profl. Psychologists (charter). Democrat. Roman Catholic. Current Work: Research on alcoholism treatment; professionals and dynamic of burnout and its aftermath on staffs and program, developed treatment mode for burnout dynamic. Subspecialties: Alcoholism rehabilitation counseling; Burnout alcoholism treatment personnel. Home: 726 Prospect St Maplewood NJ 07040 Office: 181 South St Morristown NJ 07960

DREIZEN, SAMUEL, oncology educator, researcher; b. N.Y.C., Sept. 12, 1918; s. Charles and Rose (Schneider) D.; m. Jo Gilley, Aug. 3, 1956; 1 dau., Pamela. B.A., Bklyn. Coll., 1941; D.D.S., Western Res. U., 1945; M.D., Northwestern U., 1958. Research asso. Nutrition Clinic, Hillman Hosp., Birmingham, 1945-47; instr. nutrition and metabolism Northwestern U. Med. Sch., Chgo., 1947-48, asst. prof., 1948-58, asso. prof., 1958-66; prof. pathology U. Tex. Dental Br., Houston, 1966-76, prof. and chmn. dental oncology, 1976—; cons. ADA, M.D. Anderson Hosp., Houston, 1966—. Author: multi media package Mouth in Medicine, 1979; book Experimental Stomatology, 1981; guest editor profl. jours., 1971, 74. Served to capt. U.S. Army, 1953-60. Recipient Propylaea award Bklyn. Coll., 1940. Fellow AAAS; mem. Internat. Assn. Dental Research, Am. Assn. Phys. Anthropologists, Soc. Research in Child Devel., Sigma Xi, Alpha Omega Alpha, Omicron Kappa Upsilon. Current Work: Oral complications of cancer therapy; effect of substandard nutrition on human growth; role of nutrition in diseases of the mouth. Subspecialties: Oncology; Nutrition (biology). Home: 5218 Dumfries Dr Houston TX 77096 Office: U Tex Dental Br PO Box 20068 Houston TX 77025

DRELL, SIDNEY DAVID, physics educator; b. Atlantic City, Sept. 13, 1926; s. Tulla and Rose (White) D.; m. Harriet Stainback, Mar. 22, 1952; children—Daniel White, Persis Sydney, Joanna Harriet. A.B., Princeton U., 1946; M.A., U. Ill., 1947, Ph.D., 1949, D.Sci. (hon.), 1981. Research assoc. U. Ill., 1949-50; instr. physics Stanford, Calif., 1950-52, assoc. prof., 1956-60, prof., 1960-63, Stanford Linear Accelerator Ctr., 1963—, Lewis M. Terman prof. and fellow, 1979-84, dep. dir., exec. head theoretical physics, 1969—, co-dir. Stanford Ctr. for Internat. Security and Arms Control, 1984—; research assoc. MIT, 1952-53, asst. prof., 1953-56; vis. scientist Guggenheim fellow CERN Lab., Switzerland, 1961, U. Rome, 1972; vis. prof., Loeb lectr. Harvard U., 1962, 70; vis. Schrodinger prof. theoretical physics U. Vienna, 1975; cons. Office Sci. and Tech., 1960-73, Office Sci. and Tech. Policy, 1977-81, ACDA, 1969-81, Office Tech. Assessment U.S. Congress, 1975—, NSC, 1978-81; mem. high energy physics adv. panel Dept. Energy, 1973—, chmn., 1974-82, mem. energy research adv. bd., 1978-80; mem. Jason, 1960—; Richtmyer lectr. to Am. Assn. Physics Tchrs., San Francisco, 1978; I.I. Rabi prof. Columbia U., 1984; MacArthur fellow, 1984—; vis. fellow All Souls Coll., Oxford, Eng., 1979; Danz lectr. U. Wash., 1983. Author 3 books; Contbr. articles to profl. jours. Trustee Inst. Advanced Study, Princeton, 1974-83; bd. govs. Weizmann Inst. Sci., Rehovoth, Israel, 1970—; bd. dirs. Ann. Revs., Inc.; mem. Pres. Sci. Adv. Com., 1966-70. Recipient Ernest Orlando Lawrence Meml. award and medal for research in theoretical physics AEC, 1972; Alumni award for disting. service in engring. U. Ill., 1973. Fellow Am. Phys. Soc. (Leo Szilard award for physics in the pub. interest 1980; pres. elect); mem. Nat. Acad. Scis., Am. Acad. Arts and Scis., Arms Control Assn. (bd. dirs. 1978—), Council on Fgn. Relations. Current work: Specialist in arms control and national security. Subspecialties: Particle physics; Theoretical physics. Home: 570 Alvarado Row Stanford CA 94305 Office: SLAC PO Box 4349 Stanford CA 94305

DRESCHHOFF, GISELA AUGUSTE MARIE, physicist, educator, researcher; b. Monchengladbach, Germany, Sept. 13, 1938; came to U.S., 1967; d. Gustav Julius and Hildegard Friederieke (Krug) D. VOR Diploma in Physics, Tech. U., Braunschweig, Germany, 1961, Diploma in Physics, 1965, Ph.D. in Physics, 1972. Staff scientist Fed. Inst. Physics and Tech., Germany, 1965-67; research assoc. Kans. Geol. Survey, Lawrence, 1971-72; vis. asst. prof. physics dept., U. Kans., Lawrence, 1972-74, adj. asst. prof., 1979—, dep. dir. radiation physics lab. Space Tech. Ctr., 1972-78, assoc. dir., 1979—; assoc. program mgr. NSF, Washington, 1978-79. Contbr. articles to profl. jours. Patentee in field. Recipient U.S. Antarctic Service medal NSF, 1979; Group Achievement award, NASA, 1983; named to Women's Hall of Fame, U. Kans., 1978. Fellow Explorer's Club; mem. U.S. Naval Inst. Am. Phys. Soc., Am. Geophys. Union, AAAS, Am. Polar Soc., Antarctican Soc., Sigma Xi. Current work: Main activity in polar geophysics doing airborne radioactivity surveys in Antarctica and studies of polar ice geochemistry in relation to solar activity; studies of naturally occurring hydrogen gas in subsurface geological formations. Subspecialties: Geophysics; Condensed matter physics. Home: 2908 W 19th St Lawrence KS 66044 Office: U Kans Space Tech Ctr Campus West Lawrence KS 66045

DRESSELHAUS, MILDRED SPIEWAK, engineering educator; b. Bklyn., Nov. 11, 1930; d. Meyer and Ethel (Teichtheil) Spiewak; m. Gene F. Dresselhaus, May 25, 1958; children: Marianne, Carl Eric, Paul David, Eliot Michael. A.B., Hunter Coll., 1951, D.Sc. (hon.), 1982; Fulbright fellow, Cambridge (Eng.) U., 1951-52; A.M., Radcliffe Coll., 1953; Ph.D. in Physics, U. Chgo., 1958; D.Engring. (hon.), Worcester Poly. Inst., 1976; D.Sc. (hon.), Smith Coll., 1980. NSF postdoctoral fellow Cornell U., 1958-60; mem. staff Lincoln Lab., MIT, 1960-67, prof. elec. engring., 1968—, asso. dept. head elec. engring., 1972-74; Abby Rockefeller Mauzé vis. prof. MIT, 1967-68, Abby Rockefeller Mauzé prof., 1973—; dir. MIT (Center for Materials Sci. and Engring.), 1977-83; vis. prof. dept. physics U. Campinas (Brazil), summer 1971, Technion, Israel Inst. Tech., Haifa, Israel, summer 1972, Nihon and Aoyama Gakuin Univs., Tokyo, summer 1973, IVIC, Caracas, Venezuela, summer 1977; mem. solid state scis. panel and com. NRC, 1973—; mem. exec. com. assembly of math. and phys. scis. Nat. Acad. Scis., 1975-78; chmn. steering com. of evaluation panels Nat. Bur. Standards, 1978-83. Contbr. articles to profl. jours. Named to Hunter Coll. Hall of Fame, 1972; recipient Alumnae medal Radcliffe Coll., 1973. Fellow Am. Phys. Soc. (chmn. nominating com. 1975, chmn. Buckley Prize com. 1977, v.p. 1982, pres.-elect 1983, pres. 1984), Am. Acad. Arts and Scis., IEEE; mem. Nat. Acad. Scis., Nat. Acad. Engring., Soc. Women Engrs. (Achievement award 1977); corr. mem. Brazilian Acad. Sci. Current Work: Condensed matter physics, especially modification of material properties by intercalation and ion implantation. Subspecialties: Condensed matter physics; Materials (engineering). Home: 147 Jason St Arlington MA 02174 Office: Mass Inst Tech Cambridge MA 02139

DRESSER, MILES JOEL, physicist, educator; b. Spokane, Wash., Dec. 19, 1935; s. Lloyd Joel and Stella Christine (Nelson) D.; m. Muriel Louise Hunt, June 7, 1959; children: Don Joel, Marilyn Louise, Laura Jill. B.A., Linfield Coll., McMinnville, Oreg., 1957; Ph.D., Iowa State U., Ames, 1964. Teaching asst. Iowa State U., 1957-60; research asst. Ames Lab., 1960-63; asst. prof. physics Wash. State U., Pullman, 1963-70, assoc. prof., 1970—; physicist Nat. Bur. Standards, 1972; sr. vis. research prof. Surface Sci. Ctr., U. Pitts., 1984-85. Contbr. articles to profl. jours. Bd. dirs. Pullman United Way, 1972-75. Mem. Am. Assn. Physics Tchrs., Am. Phys. Soc., Am. Vacuum Soc., Sigma Xi. Baptist. Current Work: Desorption of ions and mefastable neutrals by electronic transitions, vacuum surface phenomena, impact excitation processes, ionization mechanisms, electroluminescence. Subspecialties: Condensed matter physics; Surface chemistry. Office: 2814 Physics Washington State U Pullman WA 99164

DRESSLER, ALAN, astronomer; b. Cin., Mar. 23, 1948; s. Charles and Gay (Stein) D. B.A. in Physics, U. Calif., Berkeley, 1970; Ph.D. in Astronomy and Astrophysics, U. Calif., Santa Cruz, 1976. Carnegie fellow Hale Obs., Pasadena, Calif., 1976-78, Las Campanas fellow, 1978-81; mem. sci. staff Mt. Wilson and Las Campanas Obs., Carnegie Instn. Washingtin, Pasadena, 1981—; researcher. Contbr. papers to sci. jours. Mem. Am. Astron. Soc. (Pierce prize 1983). Current Work: Formation and evolution of galaxies; studies structure, morphology and stellar populations of galaxies as function of environment and cosmological age. Subspecialty: Optical astronomy. Office: 813 Santa Barbara St Pasadena CA 91101

DREVER, JAMES IRVING, geochemist, educator; b. Edinburgh, Apr. 6, 1942; came to U.S., 1964; s. James and Joan Isabel (Budge) D.; m. Irene Brigitte Cargill, Apr. 29, 1967; children—Anita Isabel, James Cargill. B.A., Cambridge U., Eng., 1964, M.A., 1968; A.M., Princeton U., 1967, Ph.D., 1968. Postdoctoral researcher Scripps Inst. Oceanography, La Jolla, Calif., 1968-71; faculty dept. geology and geophysics U. Wyo., Laramie, 1971—, prof., 1977—. Author: book; editor 2 books; mem. editorial bd. Chem. Geology, 1977—, Geology, 1984—; assoc. editor Geochimica et Cosmochimica Acta, 1982—. Contbr. articles to profl. jours. Research grantee NSF, EPA; conf. grantee NATO, Rodez, France, 1984. Mem. Geochem. Soc., Geol. Soc. Am., Mineral. Soc. Am., Internat. Assn. Geochemistry and Cosmochemistry, Internat. Humic Substances Soc. Current work: Chemistry of surface waters and groundwaters; weathering processes including effects of acid deposition; contaminant migration in groundwater; global geochemical cycles. Subspecialties: Geochemistry; Environmental chemistry. Home: 413 S 12th St Laramie WY 82070 Office: Univ Wyo Dept Geology and Geophysics Laramie WY 82071

DREW, ALLAN PIERCE, forest biologist, researcher; b. Chgo., Jan. 15, 1943; s. Freeman Pierce and Ruth Jesse (Knight) D.; m. Elizabeth Mary McTarnaghan, July 24, 1982; 1 child, Katherine Elizabeth. B.S. in Forestry, U. Ill., 1965; M.S. in Watershed Mgmt., U. Ariz., 1967; Ph.D. in Forest Mgmt., Oreg. State U., 1974. Asst. cons. forests Dept. Forestry and Game, Malawi, Central Africa, 1967-69; research assoc. Yale U., New Haven, 1973-75; research assoc. U. Ill.-Urbana, 1975-77; asst. prof. Mich. Tech. U., Houghton, 1977-80; assoc. prof. SUNY-Coll. Environ. Sci. and Forestry, Syracuse, 1980—. Contbr. articles to profl. jours. Coordinator spl. adult ch. sch. program Univ. United Meth. Ch., Syracuse, 1982—; bd. dirs. Citizen Advocacy Onondaga County, Syracuse, 1983-84. Served with U.S. Peace Corps, 1967-69. Recipient Weyerhaeuser fellow, 1970-72; Nat. Model Project award United Meth. Ch., 1984. Mem. Ecol. Soc. Am., Internat. Soc. Tropical Foresters, Poplar Council U.S. (exec. com. 1984-86), Sigma Xi. Current work: Physiological genetics, environmental physiology, specific research on gas exchange of woody plants (conifers, hybrid poplar) and growth physiology. Subspecialties: Ecology (biology); Plant physiology (biology). Office: SUNY-Coll Environ Sci and Forestry Syracuse NY 13210

DREW, BRUCE ARTHUR, statistician, mathematician; b. Detroit, Mar. 9, 1924; s. Merton Hesselton and Victoria (Kopicenski) D.; m. Margaret Ann Elliot, Mar. 25, 1948; children—Nancy Ann, Christopher Alan, Jennifer, Jonathan Elliot, Mary Josephine. B.S. in Chem. Engring., Wayne State U., 1950. Jr. chem. engr., Parke, Davis & Co., Detroit, 1949-50; paint formulator Rinshed-Mason Co., Detroit, 1950-52; devel. engr. Huron Milling Co., Harbor Beach, Mich., 1952-57; sr. chemist Hercules Powder Co., Hopewell, Va., 1957-59; statistician Pillsbury Co., Mpls., 1959-74, research fellow, 1974—. Served with U.S. Army, 1943-45. Fellow Royal Statis. Soc.; mem. Am. Statis. Assn. (pres. Twin City chpt. 1976-78), Am. Inst. Chem. Engrs., Am. Assn. Cereal Chemists, Soc. for Indsl. and Applied Math. Current work: Mathematical models. Subspecialties: Statistics; Chemical engineering. Office: Pillsbury Co 311 2d St SE Minneapolis MN 55414

DREWINKO, BENJAMIN, physician, researcher; b. Buenos Aires, Argentina, Feb. 10, 1940; came to U.S., 1963, naturalized, 1973; s. Aaron Joseph and Aida (Kadecka) D.; m. Rita M. McKinley, Jan. 15, 1985; children—William Joseph, David Shawn; children by previous marriage—Andrea P., Henry D., Marla G., Alejandra J.; stepchildren—William J., David S. B.Sc. and B.A., Nat. Coll., 1956; M.D., Buenos Aires U., 1961; Ph.D., U. Tex., 1970. Cert. Am. Bd. Pathology. Intern Mt. Sinai Hosp., Chgo., 1963-64; resident Mt. Sinai Hosp. (N.Y.), N.Y.C., 1964-65; fellow M.D. Anderson Hosp. & Tumor Inst., Houston, 1967-70, chief sect. hematology dept. lab. medicine, 1970—, assoc. pathologist, 1973; dir. Schs. Med. Tech. and Blood Banking, 1973-74, prof. pathology, 1979—. Assoc. editor: Cancer Research, 1982—; contbr. chpts. to books and articles to profl. jours. Served to capt. MC U.S. Army, 1964-65. NIH grantee, 1976—; recipient Research Career Devel. award Nat. Cancer Inst., 1969. Mem. Am. Soc. Clin. Pathologists, Internat. Acad. Pathology, Am. Soc. Hematology, Cell Kinetics Soc. (pres. 1980-81), AAAS, Am. Assn. Cancer Research, Am. Soc. Clin. Oncology. Jewish. Current Work: Cellular pharmacology, interactions of antitumor drugs and cells, in vitro cell killing mechanisms, cell cycle progression delay, models of cell killing, combination of drugs in vitro; cell kinetics, growth kinetics of tissue cultured cells, experimental tumors and human (clinical) neoplasms, methods of, model, experimental therapy. Subspecialties: Cancer research (medicine); Cellular pharmacology. Home: 2603 Rice Blvd Houston TX 77005 Office: 6723 Bertner Ave Houston TX 77030

DREXLER, HENRY, microbial geneticist, educator; b. Glendale, Pa., June 24, 1927; s. John Henry and Helena Catherine (Kieffer) D.; m. Susan Jane Schneider, June 15, 1957; children: Patricia Ann, Wesley Mark. B.Sc., Pa. State U., 1954; Ph.D., U. Rochester, 1960. Instr. U. Soc. Calif., Los Angeles, 1960-62; USPHS postdoctoral fellow Karolinska Inst., Stockholm, 1962-64; asst. prof. microbiology Med. Sch., Wake Forest U., Winston-Salem, N.C., 1964-69, assoc. prof., 1969-75, prof., 1975—. Served with U.S. Army, 1945-46. Mem. Am. Soc. Microbiology. Current Work: Packaging of DNA by bacterial viruses, basic recombination, and the genetics of bacteriophage T1. Subspecialties: Genetics and genetic engineering (biology); Microbiology. Office: Dept Microbiolog Sch Medicine Wake Forest U Winston-Salem NC 27103

DREYFUS, EDWARD A., clinical psychologist; b. N.Y.C., Mar. 27, 1937; s. Herbert and Estelle (Soussi) D.; m. Estelle Dobbs, June 15, 1958 (div. June 1972); children: David E., Ronald C., Lydia M.; m. Judith K. Jones, Aug. 3, 1980 (div. 1983); m. Barbara F. Reade, Feb. 14, 1985. B.B.A., CUNY, 1958, M.S., 1960; Ph.D., U. Kans., 1964. Diplomate Am. Bd. Psychotherapy, Internat. Acad. Psychotherapy and Counseling; lic. psychologist; lic. marriage, family and child counselor, Calif.; cert. sex therapist and educator Am. Acad. Sex Educators, Counselors and Therapist. Psychologist VA Hosp., Palo Alto, Calif., 1964-65, UCLA, 1965-73, pvt. practice clin. psychology, Santa Monica, Calif., 1965—. Author: Youth: Search for Meaning, 1972, Adolescence, 1976; contbr. articles to profl. jours. Fellow Am. Univ. Sex. Educators and Therapists; mem. Am. Psychol. Assn. Am. Assn. Marriage and Family Therapists, Calif. State Psychol. Assn., Los Angeles County Psychol. Assn., Los Angeles Soc. Clin. Psychologists. Current Work: Psychotherapy, psycho-social issues. Subspecialties: Behavioral psychology; Cognition. Office: 1421 Santa Monica Blvd Santa Monica CA 90404

DRICKAMER, HARRY GEORGE, chemistry educator; b. Cleve., Nov. 19, 1918; s. George Henry and Louise (Strempel) D.; m. Mae Elizabeth McFillen, Oct. 28, 1942; children: Lee Charles, Lynn Louise, Lowell Kurt, Margaret Ann, Priscilla. B.S., U. Mich., 1941, M.S., 1942, Ph.D., 1946. Chem. engr. Pan Am Refining Corp., 1942-46; asst. prof. U. Ill. at Urbana, 1946-49, asso. prof., 1949-53, prof. phys. chemistry and chem. engring., 1953—. Recipient Bendix award, 1968; P.W. Bridgman award Internat. Assn. High Pressure Sci. and Tech., 1977; Guggenheim fellow, 1952; Michelson-Morley award Case Western Res. U., 1978; John Scott award City of Phila., 1984. Fellow Am. Phys. Soc. (Buckley Solid State Physics award 1967), Am. Geophys. Union; mem. Nat. Acad. Engring., Am. Chem. Soc. (Ipatieff prize 1956, Langmuir award in chem. physics 1974), Am. Inst. Chemists (Chem. Pioneers award 1983), Am. Inst. Chem. Engrs. (Colburn award 1947, Alpha Chi Sigma award 1967, Walker award 1972), Faraday Soc., Nat. Acad. Scis., Am. Acad. Arts and Sci., Am. Philos. Soc., Center for Advanced Studies. Current Work: Use of high pressure to study electronic phenomena in condensed phases. Subspecialties: Physical chemistry; Condensed matter physics. Home: 304 E Pennsylvania St Urbana IL 61801

DRIESSEL, KENNETH R., applied mathematician; b. Milw., 1940; s. Richard H. and Margaret (Otto) D. B.S., U. Chgo., 1962; M.S., Oreg. State U., Corvallis, 1965, Ph.D., 1967. Research scientist Amoco Research, Tulsa, 1971—; asst. prof. U. Colo., Denver, 1967-71. Mem. Am. Math. Soc., Soc. Indsl. and Applied Math., Assn. Computer Machinery, Assn. Symbolic Logic, U.S. Cycling Fedn. (Okla. dist. rep. 1974-81). Club: Tulsa Bicycle (pres. 1974-75). Current Work: Mathematical aspects of exploration seismology. Subspecialties: Applied mathematics; Mathematical software. Home: 3734 S Madison Tulsa OK 74105 Office: Amoco Research PO Box 3385 Tulsa OK 74102

DRIGGERS, LOUIS BYNUM, agricultural engineer, educator; b. Manning, S.C., July 18, 1935; s. Louis and Hattie Alice (Mahoney) D.; m. Kay Freeman, Aug. 10, 1957; children—Louis Bynum Jr., Pamela Kay. B.S., Clemson U., 1957; M.S., Va. Tech. U., 1965. Registered profl. engr., N.C. Extension instr. Va. Tech. U., Blacksburg, 1957-62, extension asst. prof., 1962-66; extension asst. prof. N.C. State U., Raleigh, 1966-70, extension assoc. prof., 1970-77, extension prof., 1977—; cons. U.S. Feed Grains Council, Taiwan, 1984; tech. cons. Nat. Hog Farmer, St. Paul, 1976—; farm bldgs. cons., 1972—. Contbr. chpts. to books. Recipient Outstanding Extension Service award N.C. State U., 1974, Superior Leadership award, 1978; Engring. Achievement award Am. Soc. Agrl. Engrs., 1975, Metal Bldg. Mfrs. Assn. award, 1981, 9 Blue Ribbon awards, 1972-84. Sr. mem. Am. Soc. Agrl. Engrs.; mem. Nat. Soc. Profl. Engrs., Profl. Engrs. N.C., Epsilon Sigma Phi; hon. mem. Nat. Frame Builders Assn. Democrat. Methodist. Club: Raleigh Cotillion (pres. 1979-80). Current work: Housing systems and environmental control for swine and poultry structures planning and design of farm buildings. Subspecialty: Agricultural engineering. Home: 2213 Nancy Ann Dr Raleigh NC 27607 Office: NC State U Box 7625 Raleigh NC 27695

DRING, ROBERT PAUL, engineer; b. N.Y.C., Jan. 31, 1941; s. Robert Jan Paul and Madeline (Schwab) D.; m. Saundra Sue Pultz, June 15, 1963; children—Robert Jan, Thomas Paul. B.S., Clarkson Coll., Potsdam, N.Y., 1962; M.S., Cornell U., 1965, Ph.D., 1968. Project engr. Pratt & Whitney Aircraft, East Hartford, Conn., 1968-75; mgr. gas turbine tech. United Techs. Research Ctr., East Hartford, 1975—. Contbr. articles to profl. jours. Elder Glastonbury Community Ch., Conn., 1977-83. Mem. ASME, AIAA (assoc. editor Jour. Propulsion and Power 1984—, Air Breathing Propulsion award 1984). Current work: Research on gas turbine technology aerodynamics and heat transfer Subspecialties: Aeronautical engineering; Mechanical engineering. Office: United Technologies Research Ctr East Hartford CT 06108

DRISCOLL, TIMOTHY JOHN, physicist; b. Washington, Oct. 17, 1941; s. Timothy John and Rose Mary (Gallogly) D. B.A., Cath. U. Am., 1964, M.S., 1966, Ph.D., 1977. Physicist U.S. Bur. Mines, Avondale, Md., 1964-69, research physicist, 1969—. Contbr. articles to profl. pubs. Mem. Am. Phys. Soc., Am. Vacuum Soc. Current Work: Applying techniques of surface physics to study of oxidation and corrosion of metals; studying incentive behavior of light metals in mines; studying interaction of particle beams with oxides. Subspecialties: Surface physics; Metallurgy. Office: 4900 LaSalle Rd Avondale MD 20782

DRITSCHILO, ANATOLY, radiation oncologist; b. Reigersfeld, Ger., Oct. 10, 1944; s. Peter and Maria (Kardash) D.; m. Joy Ann Ickenroth, Apr. 6, 1968; children: Peter, Andrea, Lisa. B.S., U. Pa., 1967; M.S., Newark Coll. Engring., 1969; M.D., Coll. Medicine N.J., 1973. Cert. in therapeutic radiology. Intern Cin. Gen. Hosp., 1973-74; resident Joint Center Radiation Therapy, Harvard U., 1974-77; chmn. dept. radiation medicine Georgetown U., 1980—; dir. radiation oncology Vincent Lombardi Comprehensive Cancer Center, 1979—. Contbr. articles to profl. jours. NSF fellow, 1967-68; Am. Cancer Soc. clin. fellow, 1978. Mem. Am. Soc. Therapeutic Radiologists, Radiation Research Soc., Am. Assn. Cancer Research, Am. Soc. Clin. Oncologists. Republican. Russian Orthodox. Current Work: Response of human cells in tissue culture to radiation. Subspecialties: Radiology; Cell biology. Office: 3800 Reservoir Rd NW Washington DC 20007

DROLSOM, PAUL NEWELL, agronomist; b. Martell, Wis., July 15, 1925; s. Peter and Inga Marie (Qualle) D.; m. Marian Eda Zwerg, Aug. 19, 1950; children: Amy Ann, Ann Marie. B.S., U. Wis., 1949, M.S., 1950, Ph.D., 1953. Research asst. U. Wis., Madison, 1949-52, asst. prof., 1958-61, assoc. prof., 1961-66, prof., 1966—; pathologist U.S. Dept. Agr., Oxford, N.C., 1953-58. Contbr. articles in field to profl. jours. Served with U.S. Army, 1943-46. Mem. Am. Soc. Agronomy, Am. Genetic Assn., Am. Forage and Grassland Council, Am. Inst. Biol. Scis. Lutheran. Club: Kiwanis. Current Work: Researcher in corn breeding, especially for earliness with cold tolerance and disease resistance. Subspecialty: Plant genetics. Office: University of Wisconsin Dept.Agronomy Madison WI 53706

DROWN, EUGENE ARDENT, forest engineer, resource consultant; b. Ellenburg, N.Y., Apr. 25, 1915; s. Frank Arthur and Jessie (Kate) D.; m.

Marian Munroe, Mar. 5, 1938; children—Linda Harriet, Margaret Ruth. B.S., Utah State U., 1938; M.S. in Tactics, Command and Gen. Staff Coll., 1960; cert. Indsl. Coll. Armed Forces, 1957-60; Ph.D., U. Beverly Hills, 1979. Registered profl. engr., Calif. Park ranger Nat. Park Service, Yosemite, Calif., 1940-47; forester U.S. Forest Service, Quincy, Calif., 1947-56; staff forester Bureau Land Mgmt., Denver, 1956-79; forest engr. Tiger Engring. Service, Sacramento, 1979—; vegetation, forest mgmt. specialist Frederiksen, Kamine & Assocs., Sacramento, 1977—; Service Corps Ret. Execs. counselor Small Bus. Adminstrn., Sacramento, 1980—. Editor (manual) Timber Appraisal, 1966. Author: (manual) Land Management, 1970. First Aid instr. ARC Calif., 1952-82; mem. forestry adv. bd. Sierra Coll., Rocklin, Calif.; leader Golden Empire council Boy Scouts Am.; cert. lay speaker United Methodist Ch., Sacramento. Served to lt. col. U.S. Army, 1940-45, PTO. Recipient Presdl. citation U.S. Army, 1945, Nat. Service Medal ARC, 1964; noted for superior performance Bur. Land Mgmt., 1970, excellence of service, 1976. Mem. Soc. Am. Foresters (cert.), Nat. Soc. Profl. Engrs., Am. Inst. Biol. Scientists, Ecol. Soc. Am., Res. Officers Assn. Republican. Clubs: Bulldog Sentinels (pres. 1977-79); High Twelve (Sacramento) (pres. 1984—). Lodge: Masons (commander 1979, master 1981). Current work: Computer programming for resource inventory and management. Subspecialties: Resource management; Civil engineering. Home: 5624 Bonniemae Way Sacramento CA 95824 Office: Tiger Engineering Services Sacramento CA

DROZD, ANDREW LOUIS STEPHAN, electromagnetics engineer, software support consultant; b. Vucht, Belgium, Jan. 14, 1956; came to U.S., 1956, naturalized, 1978; s. Matthew Thomas and Mary (Sandak) D. B.S. in Physics-Math, Syracuse U., Utica Coll., 1978; M.S. in Elec. Engring, Syracuse U., 1982. Electromagnetics/systems engr. IIT Research Inst., Griffiss AFB, N.Y., 1978-84; engr. Kaman Scis. Corp., Utica, N.Y., 1984—. Mem. Am. Inst. Physics, Assn. for Computing Machinery, IEEE. Democrat. Roman Catholic. Club: Optimist. Lodge: KC (Rome, N.Y.). Current Work: Software applications to electromagnetics analysis; software/database support, electromagnetic theory; conducting workshops/courses in computer-aided electromagnetics analysis. Subspecialties: Systems engineering; Computer engineering. Home: 7755 Turin Rd Rome NY 13440 Office: Kaman Scis Corp 258 Genesee St Utica NY 15302

DRUCKER, DANIEL CHARLES, engineer, educator; b. N.Y.C., June 3, 1918; s. Moses Abraham and Henrietta (Weinstein) D.; m. Ann Bodin, Aug. 19, 1939; children: R. David, Mady. B.S., Columbia U., 1937, C.E., 1938, Ph.D., 1940; D.Engring. (hon.), Lehigh U., 1976; D.Sc. in Tech. (hon.), Technion, Israel Inst. Tech., 1983; D.Sc. (hon.), Brown U., 1984, Northwestern U., 1985. Instr. Cornell U., 1940-43; supr. Armour Research Found., Chgo., 1943-45; asst. prof. Ill. Tech., 1946-47; assoc. prof. Brown U., Providence, 1947-50, prof., 1950-64, L. Herbert Ballou Univ. prof., 1964-68, chmn. div. engring., 1953-59, chmn. phys. scis. council, 1960-63; dean Coll. Engring., U. Ill., Urbana, 1968-84; grad. research prof. engring. scis. U. Fla., 1984—; Marburg lectr. ASTM, 1966; Mem., past chmn. U.S. Nat. Com. on Theoretical and Applied Mechanics; treas. Internat. Union Theoretical and Applied Mechanics, 1972-80, pres., 1980-84, v.p., 1984—; past. mem. gen. com. Internat. Council Sci. Unions; past chmn. adv. com. for engring. NSF; hon. chmn. 3d SESA Internat. Congress on Exptl. Mechanics. Author: Introduction to Mechanics of Deformable Solids, 1967; Contbr. chpts. in tech. books, also tech. papers to mech. and sci. jours. Guggenheim fellow, 1960-61; NATO Sr. Sci. fellow, 1968; Fulbright travel grantee, 1968; Gustave Trasenster medal U. Liège, Belgium, 1979; Thomas Egleston medal Columbia U. Sch. Engring. and Applied Sci., 1978; John Fritz medal, 1985. Fellow ASME (hon. mem., chmn. applied mechanics div. 1963-64, v.p. policy bd. communications 1969-71, pres. 1973-74, Timoshenko medal 1983), Am. Acad. Mechanics (past pres.), Am. Acad. Arts and Scis., AAAS (past chmn. sect. engring., mem. council), Am. Inst. Aero. and Astronautical Scis. (assoc. fellow), ASCE (von Karman medal 1966, past pres. New Eng. council, past pres. Providence sect., past chmn. exec. com. engring. mechanics div.); mem. Nat., R.I., Ill. (hon.) socs. profl engrs., Soc. Exptl. Stress Analysis (hon.; past pres., W. M. Murray lectr. 1967, M.M. Frocht award 1971), Am. Technion Soc. (past pres. So. N.E. chpt.), Soc. of Rheology, Am. Soc. Engring. Edn. (charter fellow mem., past 1st v.p., past chmn. engring. coll. council, dir., pres. 1981-82, Lamme award 1967, Disting. Educator, Mechanics Div. 1985), Nat. Acad. Engring. (mem. com. on pub. engring. policy 1972-75, chmn. membership policy com. 1982-85), Soc. Engring. Sci. (Wiliam Prager medal 1982), Polish Acad. Scis. (fgn. mem.), Sigma Xi (past pres. Brown U. chpt.), Phi Kappa Phi, Tau Beta Pi, Pi Tau Sigma, Chi Epsilon, Sigma Tau. Current Work: Stress-strain relations; finite plasticity; stability; fracture and flow on macroscale and microscale. Subspecialties: Theoretical and applied mechanics; Materials (engineering). Office: 231 Aerospace Engring Bldg U Fla Gainesville FL 32611

DRUGER, STEPHEN DAVID, physicist; b. Bklyn., May 1, 1942; s. Harry and Ida (Taks) Druger. B.S., Bklyn. Coll., 1963; M.A., U. Rochester, 1966, Ph.D., 1969. Research assoc. Coll. William and Mary, Williamsburg, Va., 1969-70; assoc. research scientist NYU, N.Y.C., 1970-72; asst. prof. SUNY-Binghamton, 1972-73; research assoc. U. Rochester, N.Y., 1973-76; adj. asst. prof. Clarkson U., Potsdam, N.Y., 1976-82; research fellow Northwestern U., Evanston, Ill., 1982—. Contbr. numerous articles to sci. jours. Mem. Am. Phys. Soc., Sigma Xi. Current work: Theory of charge transport in ionic conductors and molecular crystals, theory of fluorescent and Raman light scattering. Subspecialty: Condensed matter physics. Home: 4820 Greenleaf St Skokie IL 60077 Office: Chemistry Dept Northwestern Univ Evanston IL 60201

DRUM, BRUCE ALAN, visual psychophysicist, consultant; b. Wauseon, Ohio, May 18, 1947; s. Virgil Ward and Clela Laverne (Overly) D.; m. Pamela Joy Neff, June 16, 1973; children—Rachel Lynne Neff, Kevin Michael Neff. B.S., Ohio State U., 1969, Ph.D., 1973. Vis. research assoc. Ohio State U., 1973; postdoctoral fellow Johns Hopkins U., Balt., 1973-75; asst. research prof. George Washington U., Washington, 1975-79, research scientist, 1979-83, sr. research scientist, 1983-84; co-founder, sec. Vision Research Assos., Inc., Balt., 1981— asst. prof. Johns Hopkins U., Balt., 1984—. Author book chpt., jour. articles. Postdoctoral fellow Seeing Eye, Inc., Balt., 1974; biomed. research support grantee George Washington U., 1978-79; research grantee Nat Eye Inst., NIH, 1975-78, 79-82, 81-84, 85—. Mem. AAAS, Assn. for Research in Vision and Ophthalmology, Optical Soc. Am., Psychonomic Soc., Internat. Research Group for Color Vision Deficiencies, Internat. Perimetric Soc., Fedn. Am. Scientists. Current Work: Correlations between neural processes and visual sensation; color vision; light and dark adaptation; rod-cone interactions; chromatic and achromatic brightness sensations; peripheral vision and perimetry; visual function in glaucoma. Subspecialties: Psychophysics; Sensory processes. Home: 4932 Pale Orchis Ct Columbia MD 21044 Office: Wilmer Ophthal Inst B-27 Johns Hopkins U Sch Medicine Baltimore MD 21205

DRUMMOND, ROBERT JOHN, psychologist, consultant; b. Newark, Mar. 30, 1929; s. Lester Linwood and Marie (Pester) D.; m. Gloria E. Erickson, Nov. 11, 1968; children: Robin, Heather. A.B., Waynesburg Coll., 1949; A.M., Columbia U., 1952, 56, Ed.D., 1959. Prof., chmn. dept. psychology Waynesburg (Pa.) Coll., 1957-69; vis. prof. U. Pitts., 1966-67; prof., coordinator field research U. Maine, Orono, 1969-81; acting chmn. div. ednl. services and research U. North Fla., Jacksonville, 1981—; cons. Inst. Can. Bankers, Montreal, 1977-82; evaluator dept. Edn. and Cult Services, Augusta, Maine, 1969-81. Contbr. articles to profl. jours. Recipient Impact Computer Guidance Systems award Maine Occupational Info. Coordinating Com., 1980. Fellow Am. Psychol. Assn.; mem. Am. Personnel and Guidance Assn., Am. Edn. Research Assn. Methodist. Current Work: Computer guidance systems, computer applications in education, computer anxiety, learning style and computer utilization. Subspecialties: Learning; Social psychology. Home: 3405 Compass Rose Dr Jacksonville FL 32216 Office: U N Fla PO Box 17074 Jacksonville FL 32216

DRUMMOND, ROGER OTTO, acarologist, entomologist; b. Peoria, Ill., Aug. 11, 1931; s. Jay Elmer and Edna Louise (Leben) D.; m. Ellen Peare, Sept. 6, 1953; children—Diane, Douglas Alan. A.B., Wabash Coll., 1953; Ph.D., U. Md., 1956. Diplomate Am. Registry Profl. Entomologists. Entomologist, USDA-Agrl. Research Service, U.S. Livestock Insects Lab., Kerrville, Tex., 1956-70, investigations leader, 1970-72, research leader, 1972-77, lab. dir., 1977—. Contbr. articles to profl. jours. Recipient Cert. of Merit, USDA, 1981; Rockefeller Found. grantee, 1966; U. Ark. scholar, 1984. Fellow AAAS; mem. Am. Soc. Parasitologists, Entomol. Soc. Am. (pres. S.W. br. 1972), Entomol. Soc. Washington, Council for Agrl. Sci. and Tech. Presbyterian. Current work: Biology and control of insects, ticks, and mites affecting livestock. Subspecialties: Veterinary acarology; Integrated pest management. Office: USDA-ARS U S Livestock Insects Lab PO Box 232 Kerrville TX 78029

DRZEWIECKI, GARY MICHAEL, bioengineering educator, researcher; b. Buffalo, Oct. 14, 1954; s. Norbert F. and Aurea F. (Stempin) D. B.S., SUNY-Buffalo, 1976; M.S., U. Pa., 1979, Ph.D., 1985. Research fellow U. Pa., Phila., 1978-83, asst. prof. Rutgers U., Piscataway, N.J., 1983—. Contbr. chpt. to book. Mem. IEEE Engr. in Medicine and Biology Soc. Roman Catholic. Current work: Hemodynamics; noninvasive cardiovascular measurements; collapsible vessel mechanics. Subspecialty: Biomedical engineering. Home: 3114 Quail Ridge Dr Plainsboro NJ 08536 Office: Rutgers U Coll Engring Biomed Engr Program Piscataway NJ 08854

DU, SEN-WO, mathematician, researcher, educator; b. Taipei, Taiwan, Republic of China, Mar. 3, 1953; came to U.S., 1978, naturalized, 1984; s. Chen-Ohu and Chin-Yu (Wang) D.; m. Tina Shu-Cheng Chan, Mar. 29, 1980; 1 child, Jihone. B.S., Chuang-Yuan U., Chuang-Li, Taiwan, 1976; Ph.D., U. Tex.-Arlington, 1982. Asst. prof. math. U. Southwestern La., Lafayette, 1982-83, 85—, Miami U., Oxford, Ohio, 1983-85. Named Outstanding Young Man Am., U.S. Jaycees, 1982. Mem. Assn. Computing Machinery, Am. Math. Soc., Soc. Indsl. and Applied Math. Sigma Xi. Current work: Functional differential equations; database design; stochastic systems. Subspecialties: Analysis; Numerical analysis (computer science). Office: Dept Math PO Box 41010 Lafayette LA 70504

DUA, SURESH KUMAR, microbiologist, veterinary medical officer; b. New Delhi, June 1, 1944; came to U.S., 1972, naturalized, 1978; s. Madan Lal and Ram Rakhi (Bajaj) D.; m. Nisha Ohri, Dec. 12, 1970; children—Vikas, Sumit. B.Vet.Sci., Coll. Vet. Medicine, Mhow, India, 1965, D.V.M., 1965; M.Vet.Sci. in Microbiology, Indian Vet. Research Inst., Mukteswar, India, 1967; Ph.D. in Vet. Microbiology, Coll. Vet. Medicine, St. Paul, 1978. Contbr. sci. publs. to profl. jours. Fellow Indian Council Agr. Research, 1965-67, 70. Mem. AVMA, Fed. Vet. Assn. Republican. Hindu. Club: Hindu Soc. Current work: Veterinary medical officer working under United States Department of Agriculture since 1978 in regulatory veterinary medicine; eradication disease program and public health. Subspecialties: Microbiology (veterinary medicine); Pathology (veterinary medicine). Home: 214 Drake Ave Rochelle IL 61068

DUARTE, CRISTOBAL G., physician, educator, researcher, scientist; b. Concepión, Paraguay, July 17, 1929; s. Cristobal Duarte and Emilia Miltos. B.S., Colegio de San JoséAsuncón, 1947; M.D., Nat. U. Asunción, 1953. Intern De Goesbriand Meml. Hosp., Burlington, Vt., 1956; resident in medicine Carney Hosp. and St. Elizabeth's Hosp., Boston, 1956-58; fellow in medicine Lahey Clinc, Boston, 1959; fellow hypertension and renal medicine Hahnemann Hosp., Phila., 1960; assoc. in medicine U. Vt. Coll. Medicine, 1962-65; clin. investigator VA, 1966-68, staff physician, 1968-73; dir. Renal Function Lab., Mayo Clinic and Found., Rochester, Minn., 1973-77; asst. prof. lab. medicine Mayo Med. Sch., 1973-77; commd. lt. col. U.S. Army, 1977; assoc. prof. medicine and physiology Uniformed Services U. Health Scis., Bethesda, Md., 1977-84, attending in medicine Walter Reed Army Med. Ctr., Washington, 1977-84; chief nephrology service Bay Pines VA Med. Ctr., 1984—; assoc. prof. medicine U. South Fla., Tampa, 1984—. Editor: Renal Function Tests, 1980; contbr. articles to profl. jours., chpts. to books. Recipient cert. of accomplishment VA, 1969; physician's recognition award AMA, 1981; Cordell Hull Found. fellow, 1958-59. Fellow Am. Coll. Nutrition; mem. Nat. Kidney Found., Latin Am. Soc. Nephrology, Am. Fedn. Clin. Research, Am. Physiol. Soc., Am. Soc. Pharmacology and Exptl. Therapeutics, Midwest Salt and Water Club, Am. Soc. for Clin. Research, Central Soc. for Clin. Research, Am. Soc. Nephrology, Sigma Xi. Roman Catholic. Current Work: Radio-contrast-induced renal failure. Subspecialty: Nephrology. Office: 4008 Bay Pines Sta Bay Pines FL 33504

DUBAR, JULES RAMON, geogolist; b. Canton, Ohio, June 30, 1923; s. Joseph Adolphe and Inez Ismay (Simlar) DuB.; m. Susan Stokes Davidson, July 29, 1964; children: Nicole Mae, Scott Johnson. B.S., Kent State U., 1949; M.S., Oreg. State U., 1950; Ph.D., U. Kans., 1957. Assoc. prof. geology Duke U., Durham, N.C., 1962-64; sr. research assoc. Esso Prodn. Research Co., Houston, 1964-67; chmn., prof. geosci. Morehead (Ky.) State U., 1967-81; exploration mgr. Internat. Resource Devel. Corp., Pepper Pike, Ohio, 1981-82; research scientist U. Tex. Bur. Econ. Geology, Austin, 1982—; cons. Fla. Geol. Survey, Tallahassee, 1953-58, Internat. Minerals and Chem. Corp., Lakeland, Fla., 1963-64, 76-77, William Bird Sales Co., Charleston, S.C., 1972-74; professorial research appointee U.S. Geol. Survey, 1979-81. Author: Stratigraphy Neogene Stratigraphy Southern Florida, 1958, Neogene Stratigraphy of Carolinas, 1971, Biostratigraphy of Southwestern Florida, 1962; author, editor: Post-Miocene Stratigraphy, 1974. Served with USCG, 1942-46, PTO. Grantee NSF, 1959-65, 68-70, 77-79, 79-81. Fellow Geol. Soc. Am., AAAS, Explorers Club; mem. Am. Assn. Petroleum Geologists. Democrat. Current Work: Evaluations of hydrocarbon potentials in Gulf of Pexico Province, Michigan Basin, and Appalachian Basin based on siesmic, geophysical log, and sample analyses. Subspecialties: Geology; Paleontology, paleoecology. Home: 6637 Sedro Trail Georgetown TX 78628 Office: Bur Econ Geology Univ Tex Univ Sta Box X Austin TX 78712

DUBE, ROGER RAYMOND, exptl. physicist; b. Portland, Maine, Nov. 24, 1949; s. Roger Joseph and Doris Ruth (Roy) D.; m. Marilyn Markman, Dec. 9, 1972; children: Dawn, Danielle, Laura. A.B., Cornell U., 1972; M.A., Princeton U., 1974, Ph.D., 1976. Postdoctoral Kitt Peak Nat. Obs., 1976-77; mem. sr. staff Jet Propulsion Lab., Pasadena, Calif., 1977-78; asst. prof. physics U. Mich., 1978-80, U. Ariz, 1980-82; mem. staff IBM Gen. Products div., Tucson, 1982—; cons. Grantee in field. Mem. AAAS, N.Y. Acad. Sci., Soc. Advancement of Chicanos and Native Americans in Sci., Am. Astron Soc. Current Work: Astronomy instrumentation, computer applications, research and devel., high speed instrumentation, electronic data processing performance evaluation. Subspecialties: Relativity and gravitation; Optical astronomy. Office: Department 67E/041-2 IBM Corporation Tucson AZ 85744

DUBES, GEORGE RICHARD, geneticist; b. Sioux City, Iowa, Oct. 12, 1926; s. George W. and Regina E. (Kelleher) D.; m. Margaret J. Tumberger, July 25, 1964; children: George, David, Deanna, Kenneth, Deborah, Keith. B.S., Iowa State U., 1949; Ph.D., Calif. Inst. Tech., 1953. Research assoc. Johns Hopkins U., Balt., 1953-54; successively research assoc., asst. prof., assoc. prof. U. Kans. Sch. Medicine, Kansas City, 1954-64; assoc. prof., then prof. med. microbiology U. Nebr. Coll. medicine, Omaha, 1964—. Contbr. articles and abstracts to sci. lit. Mem. citizen's adv. com. Omaha Pub. Schs., 1977-80. Served with U.S. Army, 1945-46, PTO. NIH grantee, 1966-69. Mem. Am. Assn. Cancer Research, AAAS, Am. Genetic Assn., Am. Inst. Biol. Scis., Am. Soc. Microbiology, Biometric Soc., Genetics Soc. Am., Internat. Soc. Oncodevel. Biology and Medicine, Tissue Culture Assn., Nebr. Acad. Scis., N.Y. Acad. Scis., Sigma Xi. Current Work: Methods for transfecting cells; mechanism of copper-mediated inactivation of nucleic acids; opal mutants of viruses; effects of virus transformation of mammalian cells on their requirements for hormones and other growth factors; effects of oxygen limitation on virus multiplication; role of asbestos in transformation. Subspecialties: Genetics and genetic engineering (biology); Virology (biology). Home: 7061 Starlite Dr Omaha NE 68152 Office: 42d St and Dewey Ave Omaha NE 68105

DUBIN, MARK WILLIAM, biology educator; b. N.Y.C., Aug. 30, 1942; s. Sidney Stanley and Dorothy (Cirinsky) D.; m. Alma Heller, June 27, 1964; children—Lila, Miriam. B.A., Amherst Coll., 1964; Ph.D., Johns Hopkins U., 1969. Research fellow Australian Nat. U., Canberra, 1969-71; asst. prof. biology U. Colo., Boulder, 1971-77, assoc. prof., 1977-82, prof., 1982—, chmn. dept., 1983—. Contbr. articles to profl. jours. Mem. steering council Boulder Council Chs. and Synagogues, 1979-83. NSF fellow, 1966-69. Mem. Assn. for Research in Vision and Ophthalmology, Soc. for Neurosci., Internat. Soc. for Devel. Neurosci., AAAS, Sigma Xi. Democrat. Jewish. Current work: Mechanisms of development of proper synaptic connections in the vertebrate CNS; vertebrate visual system development and structure function correlations. Subspecialty: Neurobiology. Home: 1868 Del Rosa Ct Boulder CO 80302 Office: U Colo CB 347 Dept MCD Biology Boulder CO 80309

DUBINSKY, WILLIAM PAUL, JR., physiology educator, researcher; b. Waterbury, Conn., Aug. 30, 1948; s. William Paul and Caroline (Hallock) D.; m. Stephanie Joy Gabor, Apr. 1, 1972; 1 child, Caroline Joy. B.A., Northeastern U., 1971; Ph.D., St. Louis U., 1975. Research technician Uniroyal, Naugatuck, Conn., 1967-71; postdoctoral fellow Cornell U., Ithaca, N.Y., 1975-79; asst. prof. U. Tex. Med. Sch., Houston, 1979—, U. Tex. Grad. Sch., 1980—. Recipient Claire Y. Svrcek award Am. Heart Assn., Texas, 1983-84; Mem. AAAS, N.Y. Acad. Scis., Biophys. Soc., Mt. Desert Island Biol. Lab. Congregationalist. Current work: Studies of the mechanisms and regulation of ion transport in epithelial tissues using isolated membrane vesicles reconstitution phospholipid vesicles as an experimental approach. Subspecialties: Membrane biology; Biochemistry (medicine). Home: 3635 Drummond Houston TX 77025 Office: Dept Physiology and Cell Biology U Tex Health Sci Ctr 6431 Fannin Houston TX 77225

DUBOIS, ARTHUR BROOKS, physiologist, educator; b. N.Y.C., Nov. 21, 1923; s. Eugene Floyd and Rebeckah (Rutter) DuB.; m. Roberdeau Callery, June 21, 1950; children—Anne R., Brooks, James E.F. Student, Harvard U., 1941-43; M.D., Cornell U., 1946. Intern in medicine N.Y. Hosp., N.Y.C., 1946-47; med. research fellow U. Rochester, N.Y., 1949-51; asst. resident Peter Bent Brigham Hosp., Boston, 1951-52; from asst prof. to prof. physiology and medicine U. Pa., Phila., 1952-74; prof. epidemiology and physiology Yale U., New Haven, 1974—, dir. John B. Pierce Found. Lab. Author: the Lung, 1955, 2d edit. 1962; Body Plethysmography, 1969. Contbr. articles to profl. jours. Served with USNR, 1947-49. Recipient Research Career award NIH, 1963-74. Mem. Am. Physiol. Soc. Am Soc. Clin. Investigation, Assn. Am. Physicians, Undersea Med. Soc. Democrat. Clubs: Harvard, Cosmos. Current work: Environmental health and function of the lungs. Subspecialties: Physiology (medicine); Physiology (biology). Home: 370 Livingston St New Haven CT 06511 Office: 290 Congress Ave New Haven CT 06519

DUBOIS DALCQ, MONIQUE ELIZABETH, neurobiologist, virologist; b. Brussels, Mar. 4, 1939; came to U.S., 1971; d. Albert Marie and Irene (Rousseau) Dalcq; m. Andre Dubois, Apr. 15, 1964; (div. Oct. 1977); children—Joel, Laurent. Candidature in Natural and Med. Scis. cum laude, Free U. Brussels, 1959, M.D. magna cum laude, 1963. Intern, Univ. Hosp. Brussels, 1960-63; resident dept. neurology Bunge Inst., Antwerp, Belgium, 1963-64; fellow in pediatric neurology Ctr. Neonatal Biol. Research, Paris, Dept. Pediatrics and Obstetrics Univ. Hosp., Free U., Brussels, 1964-66, researcher lab. depts. neuropathology, electron microscopy Belgian Found. Sci. Research, 1967-71; postdoctoral fellow Nat. Multiple Sclerosis Soc., Infectious Diseases br. NIH, Bethesda, 1972-73, vis. scientist, head electron microscopy unit, 1974-75, head electron microscopy sect., 1976-82, head sect. on neural and molecular ultrastructure, lab. of molecular genetics, 1982—; fgn. study assignment Univ. Coll., London, 1985; lectr. numerous univs. and research instns.; mem. adv. com. on fellowships Multiple Sclerosis Soc., N.Y.C., 1979—. Author: Assembly of Enveloped RNA Viruses, 1984. Mem. editorial bd. Jours. of Neuropathology and Exptl. Neurology, 1984. Contbr. articles to profl. jours. and chpts. to books. Mem. Amnesty Internat., N.Y.C., 1981—. Sane Nuclear Policy, Washington, 1984, Bethesda PTA. Recipient USPHS Spl. Recognition award HEW, 1980, Spl. Achievement Award NIH, 1981. Mem. Am. Soc. Microbiology, Am. Assn. Neuropathologists, Am. Soc. Neurosci., Am. Soc. Cell Biology, Chesapeake Soc. Electron Microscopy. Current work: Myelin formation, viral and demyelinating diseases of the nervous system, assembly of enveloped RNA viruses. Subspecialties: Virology (biology); Neurobiology. Office: NINDCS NIH LMG Bldg 36 Rm 4A01 Rockville Pike Bethesda MD 20205

DUBOSE, THOMAS DURWARD, JR., medicine, physiology, and biophysics educator; b. Gadsden, Ala., Oct. 7, 1944; s. T. Durward and Norma Jeanne (Hatley) D.; m. Linda Gail Baswell, Jan. 22, 1966; children—Nathan Scott, Emily Lauren. B.S., U. Ala., 1966, M.D., 1970. Diplomate Am. Bd. Internal Medicine/Nephrology. Resident in internal medicine Parkland Hosp., Dallas, 1971-73; postdoctoral fellow U. Tex. Health Sci. Ctr., Dallas, 1975-77; asst. prof. U. Tex. Southwestern, Dallas, 1978-81, assoc. prof. Med. Br., 1981-84, prof. physiology, Galveston, 1984—, prof. medicine, 1984—. Served to maj. USAF, 1973-75. Recipient Career Devel. award NIH, USPHS, 1981. Fellow Am. Coll. Physicians; mem. Am. Soc. Clin. Investigation, Am. Physiol. Soc., So. Soc. Clin. Investigation. Current work: Role of the kidney in acid-base homeostasis; renal bicarbonate transport; role of renal carbonic anhydrase; ammonia transport; renal tubular acidosis. Subspecialties: Nephrology; Physiology (medicine). Home: 22 N Dansby Galveston TX 77551 Office: U Tex Med Br Galveston TX 77550

DUCE, ROBERT ARTHUR, atmospheric chemistry educator; b. Midland, Ont., Can., Apr. 9, 1935; s. Leonard Arthur and Irma Harriet (Gynn) D.; m. Mary Elizabeth Untz, June 8, 1968; children—Patricia, David. B.A., Baylor U., 1957; postgrad. MIT, 1957-58, Ph.D., 1964. Research assoc. MIT, 1964-65; asst. prof. U. Hawaii, Honolulu, 1965-68, assoc. prof., 1968-70; assoc. prof. U. R.I., Kingston, 1970-73, prof. atmospheric chemistry, 1973—, dir. Ctr. for Atmospheric Chemistry Studies, 1981—; mem. bd. on atmospheric scis. and climate Nat. Acad. Scis., Washington, 1982—; pres. Internat. Commn. on Atmospheric Chemistry and Global Pollution, Boulder, Colo., 1983—; mem. adv. com. for atmospheric sci. NSF, Washington, 1984—. Contbr. numerous sci. articles to profl. jours. Served to capt. USAFR, 1957-61. Fellow Am. Meteorol. Soc.; mem. Am. Chem. Soc. (sect. sec., chmn. elect 1968-70), Am. Geophys. Union, Geochem. Soc., AAAS. Current work: Cycles of trace substances in global atmosphere; air/sea chemical exchange. Subspecialties: Atmospheric chemistry; Environmental chemistry. Office: Ctr for Atmospheric Chemistry Studies Grad Sch Oceanography U RI Kingston RI 02881

DUCHARME, DONALD WALTER, pharmacologist, researcher; b. Saginaw, Mich., June 14, 1937; s. WalterArnold and Marion (Law); m. Doris Barbara Rieck, Aug. 30, 1958; children: Michael, Mark, Daniel. A.B., Central Mich. U., 1959; Ph.D. (USPHS fellow), U. Mich., 1965. Scientist Upjohn Co., Kalamazoo, Mich., 1965-67, research scientist, 1967-70, sr. research scientist, 1970-73, sr. scientist, 1973-78, research head, 1978-85, assoc. dir., 1985—; adj. asso. prof. dept. pharmacology Med. Coll. of Ohio. Contbr. articles on pharmacology to profl. jours. Pres. Kalamazoo (Mich.) County Heart Unit Bd., 1971-72. Recipient W. E. Upjohn award, 1977. Fellow Council for High Blood Pressure Research; mem. Am. Heart Assn. (pres. Mich. affiliate 1981-82, chmn. north central region research adv. com. 1981-83, regional heart com., nat. regional research com.), Am. Soc. for Pharmacology and Exptl. Therapeutics, Council for Kidney in Cardiovascular Disease, Mich. Steelhead and Salmon Fisherman's Assn. Patentee in field. Current Work: Cardiovascular pharmacology, etiology of hypertension, research administration, hypertension, neurogenic and humoral control of circulatory system, prostaglandins. Subspecialties: Pharmacology; Cardiology. Home: 287 Fineview Kalamazoo MI 49007 Office: Cardiovascular Disease Research The Upjohn Co Kalamazoo MI 49001

DUCHOWNY, MICHAEL SAMUEL, neurologist, neurophysiologist, educator; b. N.Y.C., Nov. 17, 1945; s. Boris M. and Helen (Ledman) D.; m. Bonnie L. (maiden name please) Levin, May 26, 1979; 1 dau., Alexandra. A.B., Cornell U., 1966; M.D., Albert Einstein Coll. Medicine, 1970. Research assoc. NIH, Bethesda, Md., 1972-74; clin. fellow in neurology Harvard U. Med. Sch., Boston, 1974-77, instr. in neurology, 1977-80, asst. prof. neurology, 1980; dir. EEG labs. and seizure unit Miami (Fla.) Children's Hosp., 1980—; clin. asst. prof. neurology and pediatrics U. Miami, 1980-83, clin. assoc. prof., 1983—. Contbr. articles to profl. publs. Served to lt. comdr. USPHS, 1972-74. Manealoff fellow, 1969; Grass fellow, 1978-79. Mem. Am. Acad. Pediatrics, Am. Acad. Neurology, Child Neurology Soc., Soc. Neurosci., Soc. Clin. Neurologists, Am. EEG Soc., Am. Epilepsy Soc. Current Work: Clinical neurophysiology and epilepsy. Subspecialty: Neurology. Home: 5420 SW 92d St Miami FL 33156 Office: Miami Children's Hosp 6125 SW 31 St Miami FL 33155

DUCKLES, SUE PIPER, pharmacologist, educator, researcher; b. Oakland, Calif., Mar. 1, 1946; d. Carl Frank Piper and Joan (Brashares) Robert; m. Lawrence T. Duckles, Mar. 21, 1968; children: Ian Muir, Galen Vincent. B.A., U. Calif., Berkeley, 1968; Ph.D., U. Calif., San Francisco, 1973. Fellow UCLA, 1973-76, asst. prof. in residence, 1976-79; asst. prof. pharmacology U. Ariz., Tucson, 1979-83, assoc. prof., 1983-85; assoc. prof. U. Calif.-Irvine, 1985—; established investigator Am. Heart Assn., 1982—. Assoc. editor: Life Scis. Jour, 1980—; mem. editorial adv. bd.: Jour. Pharmacology and Exptl. Therapeutics, 1983—. Recipient Faculty Devel. award Pharm. Mfrs. Assn., Inc., 1976-78. Mem. Am. Soc. Pharmacology and exptl. Therapeutics, Soc. Neuroscience, Western Pharmacology Soc., Phi Beta Kappa. Current Work: Control of vascular smooth muscle, cerebral circulation, autonomic nervous system, peptide neurotransmitters, receptors. Subspecialties: Pharmacology; Neuropharmacology. Office: Department Pharmacology College Medicine U Calif-Irvine Irvine CA 95717

DUCKWORTH, DONNA HARDY, microbiologist, educator; b. Balt., Sept. 12, 1935; d. Albert Victor and Grace (Campbell) Hardy; m. Alistair Duckworth, June 13, 1964; children: Alexandra, Edward. B.A., Fla. State U., 1957; Ph.D., Johns Hopkins U., 1966. Asst. prof. U. Va., Charlottesville, 1967-73; asst. prof. U. Fla., Gainesville, 1973-77, assoc. prof., 1977-81, prof. dept. immunology and med. microbiology, 1981—. Pres.'s scholar U. Fla., 1976; Macy Faculty scholar, 1977. Mem. Am. Soc. Microbiology, AAAS, Sigma Xi. Current Work: Role of bacterial plasmids in disease; interactions between bacteriophage and plasmids, molecular genetics of plasmids. Subspecialties: Genetics and genetic engineering (biology); Genetics and genetic engineering (medicine). Home: 1720 NW 26 Way Gainesville FL 32605 Office: Box J266 JHM Health Center Gainesville FL 32610

DUCKWORTH, WINSTON HOWARD, ceramic engineer, materials scientist; b. Greenfield, Ohio, Oct. 15, 1918; s. Benton Raymond and Carrie Lois (Schrock) D.; m. Clara Elizabeth Ayres, Dec. 15, 1941; children—Winston (dec.), Christopher. B.Chem. Engring., Ohio State U., 1940, M.S. in Ceramic Engring., 1941. Registered profl. engr., Ohio. Research engr. Battelle Columbus Labs., Ohio, 1946-48, asst. chief ceramic research, 1948-52, chief ceramic research, 1952-66, fellow, 1966—, dir. metall. and ceramic info. ctr., 1967-71, mem. research council, 1979—; bd. dirs. Engrs. Council for Profl. Devel., 1969-73; mem. coms. Nat. Materials Adv. Bd.; mem. adv. com. ceramic dept. Ohio State U., U. Ill., U. Wash., 1979—. Author: Engineering Properties of Ceramics, 1966; also papers and articles. Served to col. USAF, 1941-46, MTO. Fellow Am. Ceramic Soc. (trustee 1968-74, v.p. 1976, chmn. various coms., Cramer award 1963, disting. life mem.); mem. Nat. Inst. Ceramic Engrs. (pres. 1964, trustee 1963-74, permanent sec. 1978—), Can. Ceramic Soc., AAAS, Ohio Acad. Sci., Engrs. Joint Council (trustee 1975-77), Keramos, Sigma Xi. Current work: Ceramic and glass science and engineering, brittle fracture, fracture mechanics. Subspecialties: Ceramic engineering; Fracture mechanics. Home: 63 Brevoort Rd Columbus OH 43214 Office: Battelle Columbus Labs 505 King Ave Columbus OH 43201

DUDA, RICHARD FRANK, nuclear fuel cycle planning mgr.; b. N.Y.C., Sept. 23, 1923; s. Frank Joseph and Emma (Jazek) D.; m. Wynema Jane Bond, May 3, 1945; children: Wynema J. Duda Duffy, Richard F., Jr., Lesley J. Duda Koluder, Desiree J. B.Chem. Engring., Rensselaer Polytechnic Inst., 1948; cert. meteorology, N.Y. U., 1944. Registered profl. engr., N.Y. Design engr., project mgr. Vitro Engring. Co., N.Y.C., 1948-60, chief process engr., mgr. chem. program, 1960-68; program dir., project mgr. Numec, Apollo, Pa., 1968-71; mgr. design and constrn., design engr. mgr. nuclear fuels Westinghouse Electric Corp., Pitts., 1971-78; mgr. fuel cycle activities Westinghouse Electric Corp. (Advanced Energy Systems div.), 1978—; project mgr. Unique Extractive Metallurgy, 1956-57. Cubmaster North Bergen Council Boy Scouts Am., Paramus, N.J., 1960, asst. cubmaster, 1962. Served to 1st lt. AC U.S. Army, 1943-46. Mem. Am. Nuclear Soc., Inst. Nuclear Materials Mgmt. (chmn. govt. laison subcom.), ASTM, Phi Lambda Upsilon. Current Work: Currently investigating commercialization of reprocessing, plutonium conversion and mixed oxide fuel fabrication; providing in-house consultation on nuclear fuel cycle technology. Subspecialties: Nuclear fission; Chemical engineering. Home: RD 9 Box 535 Greensburg PA 15601 Office: Westinghouse Electric Corporation Advanced Energy Systems Division PO Box 10864 Pittsburgh PA 15236

DUDLEY, JOHN WESLEY, plant genetics in agronomy educator; b. Huntsville, Ind., Sept. 29, 1931; s. Gerald Wayne and Mary Laura (Freer) D.; m. Norma Lou Kizer, Jan. 27, 1951; children—John, Jane, Jo, James. B.S., Purdue U., 1953; M.S., Iowa State U., 1955, Ph.D., 1956. Research geneticist Agrl. Research Service, U.S. Dept. Agr., Fort Collins, Colo., 1957-59, Raleigh, N.C., 1959-65; assoc. prof., then prof. agronomy U. Ill., Urbana, 1965—. Editor: Seventy Generations of Selection for Oil and Protein in Maize, 1974. Contbr. numerous articles to profl. jours. Fellow Am. Soc. Agronomy; mem. Crop Sci. Soc. Am. (editor 1971, 76), Am. Genetic Assn., Biometrics Soc. Current work: Quantitative genetics, corn breeding, teaching plant breeding. Subspecialties: Agronomy; Plant genetics. Home: 1802 Augusta Dr Champaign IL 61821 Office: Agronomy Dept Univ Illinois 1102 S Goodwin Ave Urbana IL 61801

DUDOCK, BERNARD SAMUEL, biochemistry educator; b. N.Y.C., Nov. 17, 1939; s. Julius and Betty D. B.S., CCNY, 1961; Ph.D., Pa. State U., 1966. NIH fellow in biochemistry Cornell U., Ithaca, N.Y., 1966-68; asst. prof. biochemistry SUNY, Stony Brook, 1968-73, assoc. prof., 1973-81, prof., 1981—, dept. chmn., 1978-81. Contbr. articles to profl. jours. Mem. Am. Soc. Biol. Chemists, AAAS. Current work: Engaged in basic research on structure and function of Eukaryotic genes. Subspecialties: Biochemistry (biology); Biochemistry (medicine). Office: Dept Biochemistry SUNY Stony Brook NY 11794

DUDZINSKI, DIANE MARIE, biology educator; b. Erie, Pa., July 23, 1946; d. Maxim and Sophie (Wisniewski) D. B.S., Villa Maria Coll., 1968; M.S., Fordham U., 1970, Ph.D., 1974. Teaching fellow Fordham U., 1970-73; instr. Manhattan Coll., 1973-74, asst. prof., 1974-78; assoc. prof. Coll. Santa Fe, N.Mex., 1978-83, prof. biology, 1983—, chair-person math. and sci. dept., 1982—. Contbr. articles to profl. jours. Treas., bd. dirs. N.Mex. Network for Women in Sci. and Engring., Albuquerque, 1981-82. Villa Maria Coll. Hon. scholar, 1964-68; Fordham U. fellow 1970-73; NASA/ASEE fellow, 1982—. Mem. Am. Inst. Biol. Scis., Ecol. Soc. Am., AAAS, Sigma Xi. Roman Catholic. Current work: Examining microorganisms in controlled environment life support systems using higher plants grown hydroponically at NASA Ames Research Center. Subspecialties: Ecology (biology); Ecosystems analysis. Office: Coll of Santa Fe St Michael's Dr Santa Fe NM 87501

DUECK, JOHN, research executive; b. Altona, Man., Can., Aug. 11, 1941; s. Gerhard and Elizabeth (Funk) D.; m. Mary Enns, Sept. 8, 1962; children—Harvey, Cheryl, Kenneth. B.S., U. Man., 1964; M.S., U. Minn., 1966, Ph.D., 1971. Agronomist Man. Dept. Agr., Winnipeg, 1966-68; plant pathologist Agr. Can., Harrow, Ont., 1971-73; chief tech. sect. plant quarantine, Ottawa, 1973-74, plant pathologist, Arg. Can. Research Sta., Saskatoon, Sask., 1974-81, dir., Regina, Sask., 1981—. Mem. Agrl. Inst. Can. Sask. Inst. Hydrologists, Can. Phytopthological Soc., Am. Phytopthological Soc. Mennonite. Current work: Disease of oilseed crops, biological control of weeds, bacterial diseases of fruit and vegetable crops. Subspecialty: Plant pathology. Office: BARD Project GPO1785 Islamakad Pakistan

DUERR, J. STEPHEN, materials consultant, metallurgist; b. Erie, Pa., Apr. 8, 1943; s. John S. and Jodine J. (Sparks) D.; m. Judith M. Duerr, Oct. 17, 1964; children: Karen L., Kristen M., Craig M. S.B., MIT, 1965, S.M., 1967, Ph.D., 1971. Registered profl. engr., N.J. Sr. metallurgist Westinghouse Bettis Atomic Power Lab., West Mifflin, Pa., 1971-74; dir. analytical services PhotoMetrics, Inc., Woburn, Mass., 1974-77; tech. dir. Structure Probe, Inc., Metuchen, N.J., 1977—; pres. Metuchen Analytical, Inc., 1978—; course dir. Center Profl. Advancement, East Brunswick, N.J., 1980—. Contbr. articles on electron microscopy, microanalysis and metall. failure analysis to profl. jours. Mem. Microbeam Analysis Soc., Am. Soc. Metals (past chmn. N.J. chpt.), ASTM, Internat. Soc. Hybrid Microelectronics, Alpha Tau Omega. Current Work: Primary interest is characterization of materials by electron and ion microbeam techniques applied to analytical investigations and their court presentation. Subspecialties: Metallurgy; Metallurgical engineering. Office: 230 Forrest St Metuchen NJ 08840

DUERRE, JOHN ARDEN, microbial biologist, molecular biologist, educator; b. Webster, S.D., Aug. 21, 1930; s. Dewey H. and Stella M. (Barber) D.; m. BennaBee Harris, June 16, 1957; children—Gail, Dawn, Arden. B.S., S.D. State U., 1952, M.S., 1956; Ph.D., U. Minn., 1960. Asst. prof. microbiology, U. N.D., Grand Forks, 1963-65, assoc. prof., 1965-71, prof., 1971—; vis. scientist Neuropsychiat. Research Unit, Research Council Lab., Carshalton, Surrey, Eng., 1969-70; vis. prof. Walter Reed Army Inst. Research, Washington, 1984-85. Contbr. articles to profl. jours., chpts. to books. Chmn. Grand Forks County Wildlife Fedn., 1965-68, 77-78, Ducks Unltd., Grand Forks, 1969-71, 77-79. Served with U.S. Army, 1953-55. Recipient Career Devel. award NIH, 1965, 70; AEC fellow, 1960-61; NIH grantee, 1966, 71-84. Mem. Am. Soc. Microbiologists, Am. Soc. Biochemists, N.D. Acad. Sci., Sigma Xi (Outstanding Research award 1977). Democrat. Clubs: Curling (bd. dirs. 1980-84), Gun (Grand Forks). Lodge: Elks. Current work: sulfur amino acid metabolism and methylation of macromolecules, especially chromosomal proteins. Subspecialties: Biochemistry (medicine); Cell biology (medicine). Home: 918 N 26th St Grand Forks ND 58201 Office: U ND Med Sch Grand Forks ND 58202

DUFF, JAMES THOMAS, microbiologist, virologist; b. Sandusky, Ohio, Jan. 23, 1925; s. William John and Winifred Kathryn (Breining) D. B.S., Ohio State U., 1947, M.S., 1949; Ph.D., U. Tex., 1960. Microbiologist, immunology br., med. investigations div. U.S. Army Biol. Lab., Ft. Detrick, Md., 1949-56, 59-65; with Nat. Cancer Inst., Bethesda, Md., 1965-83, chief biol. carcinogenesis br., 1978-83. Contbr. articles to profl. jours. Served with U.S. Navy, 1943-46. Mem. Am. Soc. Microbiology., Tissue Culture Assn., Internat. Assn. Comparative Research on Leukemia and Related Diseases, Sigma Xi. Republican. Current Work: Azotobacter bacteriophage, Clostridium botulinum toxins and toxoids, tissue culture, psittacosis vaccines, viral oncology. Subspecialties: Virology (biology); Cancer research (medicine). Home: 1329 Midwood Pl Silver Spring MD 20910

DUFF, RONALD GEORGE, virologist, cell biologist; b. Billings, Mont., Dec. 8, 1936; s. Ross I. and Alda Mable (Markholt) D.; m. Naomi Darlene, Aug. 12, 1962; children: Kelle Amber, Ross Alan. Mus.B., U. Mont., 1959; Ph.D. in Pathology, U. Colo. Med. Sch., 1968. Assoc. prof. microbiology Milton S. Hershey (Pa.) Med. Center, 1969-74; head viral and cell biology Abbott Labs., North Chicago, Ill., 1974-83; prof. microbiology Chgo. Med. Sch., North Chicago, 1978-83; v.p. devel. Damon Biotech, Needham Heights, 1983-84, sr. v.p. research and devel., 1984—. Contbr. numerous articles to profl. publs. Bd. dirs. Deerfield (Ill.) Park Dist. Bands, 1981-84. Mem. Am. Soc. Microbiology, AAAS, Am. Assn. Cancer Research, Sigma Xi, Phi Sigma. Current Work: Anti-cancer agents, viral diagnostics, cancer diagnostics, molecular biology of cancer; cancer immunology, monoclonal antibodies, molecular control mechanisms. Subspecialties: Virology (biology); Cell and tissue culture. Home: 11 Shawnee Rd Medfield MA 02052 Office: 119 4th Ave Needham Heights MA 02194

DUFFEY, GEORGE HENRY, physics educator, researcher; b. Manchester, Iowa, Dec. 24, 1920; s. Henry Alfred and Marion Ella (Barr) D.; m. Helen Susie Hooper, Sept. 17, 1945; children—Ann Elizabeth Gibson, James Roy, Mary Kay (dec.). B.A., Cornell Coll., 1942; cert., Brown U., 1942; A.M., Princeton U., 1944, Ph.D., 1945. Asst. prof. chemistry S.D. State Coll., Brookings, 1945-49, assoc. prof. chemistry, 1949-55, prof. chemistry, 1955-58; prof. physics, 1959—; prof. chemistry and physics U. Miss., Oxford, 1958-59; vis. lectr. U. Western Australia, Nedlands, 1977. Author: Physical Chemistry, 1962; Theoretical Physics, 1980; A Development of Quantum Mechanics, 1984. Contbr. articles to profl. jours. Recipient Excellence in Instrn. award N. Midwest Sect. Am. Soc. Engring. Edn. 1971-72. Mem. Am. Chem. Soc., Am. Phys. Soc., Societa Italiana di Fisica, AAAS, Sigma Xi. Baptist. Current work: Foundations of quantum mechanics, applications to chemical bonding, detonation waves, hierarchy of fields (gravitational, electric, quark). Subspecialties: Theoretical physics; Theoretical chemistry. Home: 628 11th Ave Brookings SD 57006 Office: SD State U Dept Physics Brookings SD 57007

DUFFEY, PAUL STEPHEN, microbiologist, researcher; b. Oakland, Calif., Nov. 24, 1939; s. David Norman and Saphrona Carol (Korkus) D.; m. Marlen Gregory, Jan. 12, 1962 (dec. July 1975). B.A., San Jose State U., 1963; postgrad. U. Calif.-Berkeley, 1967-68; Ph.D., U. Mich., 1973. Microbiologist Calif. Dept. Health, Berkeley, 1963-68, research microbiologist, 1981—; asst. prof. microbiology and immunology U. Mich., Ann Arbor, 1973-76, U. Tex. Health Sci. Ctr., San Antonio, 1976-81. Mem. N.Y. Acad. Scis., Am. Immunologists, Sigma Xi (assoc.). Current work: Monoclonal antibody technology; design and development of diagnostic assays; nucleic acid technology; use of recombinant DNA methods for diagnostic assays. Subspecialties: Immunobiology and immunology; Microbiology (medicine). Home: 166 Miramonte Dr Moraga CA 94556 Office: Calif Dept Health Services 2151 Berkeley Way Berkeley CA 94704

DUFFIE, JOHN ATWATER, chemical engineer, educator; b. White Plains, N.Y., Mar. 31, 1925; s. Archibald Duncan and Lulie Adele (Atwater) D.; m. Patricia Ellerton, Nov. 22, 1947; children: Neil A., Judith A. Duffie Schwarzmeier, Susan L. Duffie Buse. B.Ch.E., Rensselaer Poly. Inst., 1945, M.Ch.E., 1948; Ph.D., U. Wis., 1951. Registered profl. engr., Wis. Instr. chem. engring. Rensselaer Poly. Inst., 1946-49; research asst. U. Wis., 1949-1951; research engr. DuPont, 1951; sci. liaison officer Office Naval Research, 1952-53; mem. faculty dept. chem. engring. U. Wis.-Madison, 1954—, prof., 1957—, dir. solar energy lab., 1956—; Fulbright scholar U. Queensland, Australia, 1964; sr. Fulbright-Hays scholar Commonwealth Sci. and Indsl. Research Orgn., Australia, 1977; hon. sr. research fellow U. Birmingham (Eng.), 1984. Author: (with W.A. Beckman) Solar Energy Thermal Processes, 1974, (with W.A. Beckman, S.A. Klein) Solar Heating Design, 1977, (with W.A. Beckman) Solar Engineering of Thermal Processes, 1980. Served with USN, 1943-46. Recipient Charles G. Abbot award Am. sect. Internat. Solar Energy Soc., 1976. Fellow Am. Inst. Chem. Engrs.; mem. Internat. Solar Energy Soc. (past pres.), AAAS. Current Work: Research on solar energy thermal processes and teaching chemical engineering. Subspecialties: Solar energy; Chemical engineering. Home: 5710 Dorsett Dr Madison WI 53711 Office: 1500 Johnson Dr Madison WI 53706

DUFFIN, RICHARD JAMES, See *Who's Who in America,* 43rd edition.

DUFFY, LAWRENCE KEVIN, biochemist, educator; b. Bklyn., Feb. 1, 1948; s. Michael and Anne (Browne) D.; m. Geraldine Antoinette Sheridan, Nov. 10, 1972; children—Anne Marie, Kevin Michael. B.S., Fordham U., 1969; M.S., U. Alaska, 1972, Ph.D., 1977. Teaching asst. dept. chemistry U. Alaska, 1969-71, research asst. inst. arctic biology, 1974-77; postdoctoral fellow Boston U., 1977-78, Roche Inst. Molecular Biology, 1978-80; research asst. prof. U. Tex. Med. Br., 1980-82; asst. prof. neurology (biol. chemistry) Harvard Med. Sch., Cambridge, Mass., 1982—, adv. biochemistry instr., 1983—; organic chem. instr. Roxbury Community Coll., Boston, 1984—Contbr. articles to profl. jours. Disaster control coordinator Warren County CD, N.J., 1979; treas. youth Commn., Acton, Mass., 1984. Served as lt. USNR, 1971-73. NSF trainee, 1971; J.W. McLaughlin fellow, 1981; W.F. Milton scholar, 1983. Mem. Am. Soc. Biol. Chemists, N.Y. Acad. Sci., Am. Soc. Zoologists, Am. Chem. Soc. (chem. edn. com. 1984; Analytical Chemistry award 1969), Intern Soc. Toxinologists, Sigma Xi. Phi Lambda Upsilon. Roman Catholic. Current work: Use of HPLC protein isolation, monoclonal antibodies as protein structural probes; NMR of proteins, mechanism of action of proteins and toxins in human disease; biochemical and medical education. Subspecialties: Biochemistry (biology); Biochemistry (medicine). Office: Ctr for Neurol Diseases Brigham and Women's Hosp Boston MA 02115

DUFFY, ROBERT ALOYSIUS, aeronautical engineer; b. Buck Run, Pa., Sept. 9, 1921; s. Joseph Albert and Jane Veronica (Archer) D.; m. Elizabeth Reed Orr, Aug. 19, 1945; children: Michael Gordon, Barclay Robert, Marian Orr, Judith Elizabeth, Patricia Archer. B.S. in Aero. Engring, Ga. Inst. Tech., 1951. Commd. 2d lt. U.S. Army, 1942; commd. U.S. Air Force, advanced through grades to brig. gen, 1967, service in, C.Z., Morocco, Algeria, Tunisia, Sicily, Italy, Vietnam; vice comdr. USAF Space and Missile Systems Orgn., Los Angeles, 1970-71; ret., 1971; v.p., dir. Draper Lab. div. M.I.T., Cambridge, Mass., 1971-73; pres., dir., chief exec. officer Charles Stark Draper Lab., Inc., 1973—; chmn. USAF-NOAA weather satellite program rev. Dept Def.-NASA, 1972; chmn Fed. Contract Research Center Task Force, Dept. Def., 1975; mem. indsl. and profl. adv. council Pa. State U. Sch. Engring., 1979—. Contbr. articles to profl. jours. Decorated Disting. Service medal, Legion of Merit; recipient Thomas D. White award Nat. Geog. Soc., 1970. Fellow AIAA; mem. Nat. Acad. Engring., Inst. Navigation (Thurlow award 1964, pres. 1976-77), Air Force Assn., U.S. Naval Inst. Clubs: Algonquin (Boston); Concord Country. Subspecialties: Aeronautical engineering; Research administration. Home: 115 Indian Pipe Ln Concord MA 01742 Office: 555 Technology Sq Cambridge MA 02139

DUFFY, THOMAS HYATT, biomedical researcher; b. Santa Monica, Calif., May 27, 1953; s. Thomas and Patricia (Hyatt) D. B.A. in Chemistry, Whittier Coll., 1975; Ph.D. in Chemistry, U. Notre Dame, 1982. Lab. dir., chemistry instr. Peace Corps, Ghana, 1975-76, Belize, 1976-78; research asst. U. Notre Dame, Ind., 1978-82; research assoc. Scripps Clinic and Research Inst., La Jolla, Calif., 1982—. Contbr. articles to profl. jours. Scholarship organizer Peace Corps, Belize, 1976-78. Zahm fellow, 1980; Am. Cancer Soc. fellow, 1984; NIH fellow, 1985. Mem. Am. Chem. Soc., AAAS, Biophys. Soc., Soc. Fellows Scripps Clinic (dept. basic and clin. research rep. 1984). Current work: Multiple forms of dihydrofolate reductase differing in affinity for the anti-neoplastic agent methotrexate. Subspecialties: Biophysical chemistry; Nuclear magnetic resonance. Office: Scripps Clinic and Research Found Div Biochemistry 10666 N Torrey Pines Rd La Jolla CA 92037

DUFFY, WILLIAM THOMAS, JR., physics educator, researcher; b. San Francisco, June 30, 1930; s. William Thomas and Adele Leone (Fagothey) D.; m. Katherine Maria Koster, June 27, 1959; children—Judith A., Mary K., Christopher W. B.E.E., U. Santa Clara, 1953; M.S., Stanford U., 1954, Ph.D., 1959. Asst. prof. U. Santa Clara, Calif., 1959-61, assoc. prof., 1962-68, prof. physics, 1969—, chmn. physics dept., 1974—; NSF postdoctoral fellow U. Leiden, Netherlands, 1961-62; research assoc. Stanford U., Calif., 1968-69. Author: Low Temperature Physics: A KWIC Index to the Conference Literature 1958-69, 1970. Contbr. articles to profl. jours. Research grantee NSF, 1962-85, Research Corp., 1978-82. Mem. Am. Phys. Soc., Sigma Xi, Sigma Pi Sigma. Current work: Magnetism of crystalline free radicals and charge transfer complexes, internal friction in metals at ultra-low temperatures. Subspecialties: Low temperature physics; Magnetic physics. Home: 20637 Leonard Rd Saratoga CA 95070 Office: Dept Physics U Santa Clara Santa Clara CA 95053

DUGAN, CHARLES HAMMOND, physicist, educator; b. Balt., Apr. 2, 1931; s. Hammond J. and Frances L. (Smith) D.; m. Gwendolyn Finn, Nov. 4, 1954; children: Melanie, Alison, Ann, Frances, John. B.S., U. Ky., 1951; M.A., UCLA, 1954; Ph.D., Harvard U. Staff Smithsonian Astrophys. Obs., 1963-66; asst. prof. physics York U., Downsview, Ont., Can., 1967-74, prof., 1975—; assoc. dean York U. (Faculty Grad. Studies), 1978-79; vis. fellow dept. elec. engring. Cornell U., Ithaca, N.Y., 1981; vis. fellow dept. physics Imperial Coll., London, 1973-74. Contbr. articles to profl. jours. Served with U.S. Army, 1954-56. Grantee NRC Can.; Grantee Def. Research Bd. Can.; Grantee Province Ont. Mem. Am. Phys. Soc., AAAS, Can. Assn. Physicists. Current Work: Research in photodissociation of molecules. Subspecialties: Atomic and molecular physics; Laser spectroscopy. Home: 37 Johnson St Thornhill ON L3T 2N9 Canada Office: York U Petrie Bldg Downsview ON M3J 1P3 Canada

DUGGIN, MICHAEL JOHN, physics educator; b. Dorking, Surrey, Eng., July 30, 1937; came to U.S., 1979; s. Walter J. and Winnifred L. (Button) D.; m. Maggie Amelia Beveridge, July 16, 1978; children: John Bruce, Blake Michael. B.Sc., Melbourne (Austrlia) U., 1959; Ph.D., Monash U., Melbourne, 1965. Teaching fellow Monash U., Melbourne, Australia, 1962-64; postdoctoral fellow U. Pitts., 1965, asst. prof., 1966; research scientist CSIRO, Sydney, Australia, 1967-71, sr. research scientist, 1971-79; prof. physics, div. engring. Coll. Environ. Sci. and Forestry SUNY-Syracuse, 1979—; cons. in field. Contbr. numerous articles to profl. jours. Assoc. fellow AIAA; fellow Inst. Physics; fellow Royal Astron. Soc.; mem. Am. Inst. Physics, Am. Soc. Photogrammetry, Internat. Remote Sensing Assn., Soc. of Photo-Optical Instrumentation Engrs. Current Work: Physics of remote sensing processes; fundamental remote sensing research; visible and IR clutter studies; discrimination studies; spectral reflectance factor measurement; remote sensing data acquisition and analysis optimization. Subspecialties: Satellite studies; Aerospace engineering and technology. Home: 212 Robinhood Ln Camillus NY 13031 Office: 308 Bray Hall Suny Syracuse NY 13210

DUGUAY, LINDA EMMA, marine scientist; b. Providence, Feb. 20, 1947; d. J. Roland and A. Emma (Begin) D.; m. Douglas G. Capone, Feb. 17, 1979; children—Jennifer Linn, Rebecca Marie. A.B., U. R.I., 1968; M.S., U. Miami, 1973, Ph.D., 1979. Research asst. U. Miami, Fla., 1975-78; adj. asst. prof. marine sci. SUNY-Stony Brook, 1980-82, research asst. prof. marine sci., 1982—; asst. prof. Southampton Coll., N.Y., 1982-83. Contbr. articles to sci. jours. Maytag fellow U. Miami, 1969-72, Koczy fellow U. Miami, 1978-79. Mem. AAAS, Am. Soc. Limnology and Oceanography, Am. Inst. Biol. Scis., Physol. Soc. Am., Western Soc. Naturalists, Am. Women in Sci. Current work: Physiological ecology benthic foraminifera, Ctenophones, Algai-Invertebrate symbioses. Subspecialties: Ecology (biology); Deep-sea biology. Office: Marine Scis Research Ctr SUNY Stony Brook NY 11794

DUKE, SCHERER PRESTON SANDERS, immunochemist, educator; b. Wilmington, Del., Feb. 26, 1955; d. Carl William and Henrietta Sarah (Trower) Sanders; m. George Wesley Duke, June 10, 1978. B.S. in Chemistry, Coll. William and Mary, 1977; Ph.D. in Medicinal Chemistry, Va. Commonwealth U., 1981. Teaching asst., instr. Va. Commonwealth U., Richmond, 1977-81, postdoctoral research fellow, 1981-83; research chemist A.H. Robbins Co., Inc., Richmond, 1981; research instr. Vanderbilt U., Nashville, 1983—. Contbr. articles to profl. jours.; chpt. to book. Mem. Am. Chem. Soc., Sigma Xi, Sigma Zeta, Rho Chi, Phi Kappa Phi, Kappa Alpha Theta (chmn. recommendations 1982-83). Current work: Role of immune response and prostaglandins and leukotrienes in lung injury and disease. Subspecialties: Immunocytochemistry; Immunotoxicology. Home: 110 Riverwood Dr Franklin TN 37064 Office: Vanderbilt U B-1308 Med Ctr N Nashville TN 37232

DUKE, STEPHEN OSCAR, plant physiologist; b. Battle Creek, Mich., Oct. 9, 1944; s. Oscar and Azalee Rosa (Tallant) D.; m. Barbara Alice Rowe, June 2, 1967; children: Gregory Ivan, Robin Anne. B.S., Henderson State U., 1966; M.S., U. Ark., 1968; Ph.D., Duke U., 1975. Instr. Duke U., 1974-75; NSF research assoc. So. Weed Sci. Lab., Stoneville, Miss., 1975-76, staff scientist, 1976-85, research leader, 1985—. Editor: Weed Physiology, vol. I and II, 1985; assoc. editor: Weed Sci., 1980-85; contbr. numerous articles and book chpts. Served to 1st lt., M.S.C. U.S. Army, 1968-70. Decorated Bronze Star; recipient Outstanding Young Weed Scientist award Weed Sci. Soc. Am., 1984. Mem. AAAS, Am. Inst. Biol. Sci., Bot. Soc. Am., Am. Soc. Plant Physiology, Am. Soc. Photobiology, Am. Soc. Plant Physiology, Scandinavian Soc. Plant Physiology, Japan Soc. Plant Physiology, Weed Sci. Soc. Am., Sigma Xi. Club: Soccer (Greenville, Miss.). Current Work: Herbicide mechanism of action, plant photobiology, secondary metabolism. Subspecialties: Plant physiology (biology); Photosynthesis. Home: 1741 W Azalea St Greenville MS 38701 Office: US Dept Ag Agrl Research Service So Weed Sci Lab PO Box 225 Stoneville MS 38776

DUKER, NAHUM JOHANAN, experimental pathologist; b. N.Y.C., Oct. 27, 1942; s. Abraham G. and Lillian (Sandrow); m. Naomi Ruth Maisel, June 4, 1972; children: Eli, Joshua, Jonathan, Ezra. M.D., U. Ill., 1966. Diplomate: Am. Bd. Pathology, 1978. Intern Bellevue Hosp., N.Y.C., 1966-67; resident in pathology N.Y. U. Med. Ctr., 1970-76; instr. pathology N.Y. U. Med. Sch., 1976-77; asst. prof. pathology Fels Research Inst., Temple U. Med. Sch., 1977-82, assoc. prof. pathology, 1982—. Author papers on DNA damage and repair. Served to capt. M.C. USAR, 1967-69. Grantee USPHS, 1978—; USPHS research career devel. award, 1983. Mem. Internat. Acad. Pathology, Am. Assn. Pathologists, Am. Assn. Cancer Research, Am. Soc. Biol. Chemists, Am. Soc. Photobiology., Environ. Mutagen Soc. Jewish. Current Work: Physical and chemical damage to DNA and its repair. Subspecialties: Biochemistry (biology); Molecular biology. Office: 3400 N Broad St Philadelphia PA 19140

DUKLER, ABRAHAM EMANUEL, chemical engineer; b. Newark, Jan. 5, 1925; s. Louis and Netty (Charles) D.; children—Martin Alan, Ellen Leah, Malcolm Stephen. B.S., Yale U., 1945; M.S., U. Del., 1950, Ph.D., 1951. Devel. engr. Rohm & Haas Co., Phila., 1945-48; research engr. Shell Oil Co., Houston, 1950-52; mem. faculty dept. chem. engring. U. Houston, 1952—, prof., 1963—, chmn. dept., 1967-73, dean engring., 1976-83; dir. State of Tex. Energy Council, 1973-75; cons. U.S. Nuclear Regulatory Commn., Brookhaven Nat. Lab., Shell Devel. Co., Exxon, others. Contbr. chpts. to books, articles to profl. jours. Recipient Research award Alpha Chi Sigma, 1974. Fellow Am. Inst. Chem. Engrs., Nat. Acad. Engring., Am. Soc. Engring. Edn. (research lectureship award 1976); mem. Am. Inst. Chem. Engrs., ASME, AAAS, Am. Chem. Soc., AAUP, Sigma Xi, Tau Beta Pi. Current Work: Theoretical and experimental studies of two phase gas liquid flow and related energy and mass transfer questions. Subspecialty: Fluid mechanics. Office: Coll of Engring Univ of Houston Houston TX 77004

DULEY, WALTER WINSTON, physicist, educator; b. Montreal, Que., Can., Oct. 8, 1941; s. Walter Albert and Ella (Harnum) D.; m. Irmgardt Zunker, July 3, 1965; children: Nicholas, Mark. B.S., McGill U., 1963; D.I.C., Imperial Coll., 1966; Ph.D., U. London, Eng., 1966, D.Sc., 1982. Scientist Def. Research Bd., Quebec City, Que., Can., 1966-67; asst. prof. York U., Toronto, 1967-70, assoc. prof., 1970-74, prof., 1974—; assoc. research chemist U. Calif., Berkeley, 1973; vis. prof. Swiss Inst. Tech., Zurich, 1974; vis. prof. theoretical physics Oxford U., 1981; research chemist, Harwell, Eng., 1981; cons. lasers; pres. Powerlasers Ltd., King City, Ont., Can., 1976—. Contbr. numerous articles to profl. jours.; Author: CO_2 Lasers, 1976, Laser Processing, 1983, Interstellar Chemistry, 1984. Recipient U.K. SRC Sr. Vis. Research Fellowship award, 1978, 80. Fellow Royal Astron. Soc., Royal Soc. Arts; mem. Internat. Astron. Union. Current Work: Laser spectroscopy, materials processing with lasers, laboratory studies of interstellar dust, theoretical astrophysics. Subspecialties:

Laser spectroscopy; Laboratory astrophysics. Home: 136 Dew St Box 453 King City ON LOG 1KO Canada Office: 4700 Keele St Toronto ON M3J 1P3 Canada

DUMAS, HERBERT MONROE, (JR.), physicist, elec. engr., research and devel. lab. exec.; b. Eldorado, Ark., Dec. 16, 1927; s. Herbert Monroe and Emma Villa (Woodard) D.; m. Patricia Ann Johnson, May 9, 1953; 1 son, Herbert Scott. B.A. in Physics, U. Ark., 1954, B.S. in Physics, 1955, M.S. in Physics, 1956. With Sandia Nat. Labs., Albuquerque, 1956—, super. div. seismic systems, 1965-76, mgr. dept. space systems, 1976—. Served with USN, 1946-49; to 2d lt. USAR, 1952-53. Recipient Physics Achievement award U. Ark., 1955. Mem. Optical Soc. Am., Phi Beta Kappa, Sigma Xi, Kappa Sigma. Democrat. Club: U. Ark. Alumni (Albuquerque) (bd. dirs. 1971-73, v.p. 1977). Current Work: Instrumentation systems for satellite applications; mgmt. research engrng. of satellite instrumentation and sensor systems and satellite data processing stas. Subspecialties: Satellite studies; Optical engineering. Home: 1304 Florida NE Albuquerque NM 87110 Office: PO Box 5800 7240 (880/B-42) Albuquerque NM 87165

DUMLAO, ROSA, plant breeder, researcher; b. Paoay, Ilocos Norte, Philippines, July 25, 1929; came to U.S., 1964; d. Gregorio Reyno Dumlao and Francisca Castillo Cacatian. B.S. in Agr., U. Philippines, 1957, M.Sc., 1964; Ph.D., U. Conn., 1968. Agronomist, U. Philippines, Coll. Laguna, 1958-60, research instr., 1961-64; research asst. U. Conn., Storrs, 1964-66; grad. fellow, 1967-68; plant breeder Joseph Harris Seed Co. Inc., Rochester, N.Y., 1968—. Research and publs. on rice and corn seed. Active First Aid and CPR programs ARC, Rochester, 1981—. Entrance scholar U. Philippines, 1954, Univ. scholar, 1957; grad. fellow U. Conn., 1967. Mem. Tissue Culture Assn., N.Y. Acad. Scis., Am. Genetic Assn., Sigma Xi, Gamma Sigma, Phi Sigma. Current work: Evolving superior varieties of vegetables and ornamentals. Subspecialties: Plant genetics; Genetics and genetic engineering (agriculture). Home: 3641 Westside Dr Churchville NY 14428 Office: Harris Moran Seed Co 3670 Buffalo Rd Rochester NY 14624

DUMONTELLE, PAUL BERTRAND, geologist; b. Kankakee, Ill., June 22, 1933; s. Lester Vernon and Helen (McKinstry) DuM.; m. Dollie Louise Bridgewater, June 5, 1955; children: John, Jeffrey, Jo, James, Jay. B.A., DePauw U., 1955; M.S., Lehigh U., 1957. Geologist Lehigh Portland Cement Co., Allentown, Pa., 1956-57, Homestake Mining Co., Lead, S.D., 1957-63; asst. geologist Ill. State Geol. Survey, Champaign, 1963-70, assoc. geologist, 1970-78, geologist, 1979—, coordinator environ. geology, 1975-79, geologist, head engrng. geology sect., 1979—, dir. Ill. subsidence research program. Fellow Geol. Soc. Am.; mem. Assn. Engrng. Geologists (chmn. nat. awards com.), Am. Inst. Profl. Geologists, Am. Congress on Surveying and Mapping, Ill. Geol. Soc., Sigma Xi. Lodge: Kiwanis. Current Work: Engineering geology, including slope stability, soil problems, mine subsidence, and computerization of geological information. Subspecialty: Geology. Home: 2020 Burlison Dr Urbana IL 61801 Office: Ill State Geol Survey 615 E Peabody St Champaign IL 61801

DUNAYEVSKY, VICTOR ARKADY, applied mathematician, researcher; b. Ashchabad, Turkmenia, USSR, 1942; came to U.S., 1978; s. Arkady Samual and Rozalia (Shklovsky-Tictinsky) D.; m. Evelina Aisenberg, Oct. 1, 1968 (div. 1977). M.S., Civil Engrng. Inst., Kharkov, USSR, 1964; Ph.D., Siberian Div. Acadamy of Sci., Novosibirsk, USSR, 1973, Northwestern U., 1980. Assoc. prof. Elec. Engrng. Inst., Novosibirsk, USSR, 1974-78; project leader Standard Oil Co. Research Center, Warrensville, Ohio, 1982—; vis. scholar Northwestern U., 1978-82. Mem. Soc. Indsl. and Applied Math., ASME. Current Work: Crack propagation in an elastic-plastic medium; fracture mechanics; dynamic fracture; stability of elastic structures. Subspecialties: Fracture mechanics; Solid mechanics. Home: 6805 Mayfield Rd Apt 1004 Mayfield Heights OH 44124 Office: Standard Oil Co Research Center 4440 Warrensville Rd Cleveland OH 44128

DUNBAR, GEOFFREY THORNE, telecommunications corporation executive; b. Evanston, Ill., June 24, 1946; s. James Harrison and Barbara (Cook) D.; children—Kimberly Reid, Brittany Thorne, Christopher James. Premier degree, U. Grenoble, France, 1966; B.A., Lake Forest Coll., 1974; M.B.A., Stanford U., 1976. Sr. assoc. Booz, Allen & Hamilton, Chgo., 1976-81; pres., dir. Interand Corp., Chgo., 1981—. Mem. Chgo. Forum, 1978-80. Club: Chicago. Subspecialties: Information systems (Information science); Distributed systems and networks. Office: Interand Corp 3200 W Peterson Ave Chicago IL 60659

DUNBAR, JAN ROBERT, battalion fire chief, fire technology educator; b. Sacramento, Sept. 21, 1942; s. Warren Robert and Jeannette (Cippa) D. A.A., Am. River Coll., 19—; grad. in chemistry, Sacramento State Coll., 1967. Fire fighter Sacramento Fire Dept., 1965-75, engr., 1975-77, capt., 1977-83, bn. chief, 1983—; cons. Biddle & Assocs., Sacramento, 1982—, Am. Environ., Sacramento, 1979—. Mem. Pacific Burn Inst., Nat. Fire Protection Assn., Internat. Assn. Fire Chiefs, Nat. Radiol. Emergency Response Team. Republican. Roman Catholic. Current work: Develop hazardous materials response team; neutralization, cleanup, disposal of chemicals; develop new breathing apparatus with built in microphone; develop new chemical suit with embilical fed air. Subspecialties: Hazardous waste disposal; Environmental toxicology. Home: 6825 Garden Hwy Sacramento CA 95837 Office: Sacramento Fire Dept 915 I St Sacramento CA 95814

DUNCAN, CONSTANCE CATHARINE, psychologist; b. Watertown, Wis., Nov. 2, 1948; d. Howard Burton and Mary Elizabeth (Fagan) Duncan. B.A., Northwestern U., 1970; A.M., U. Ill., 1973, Ph.D., 1978. Research analyst Adolf Meyer Mental Health Ctr., Decatur, Ill., 1971-73; research and teaching asst. dept. psychology U. Ill., Champaign, 1974-78; postdoctoral scholar dept. psychiatry and behavioral scis. Stanford U. Sch. Medicine, Calif., 1978-81; research psychologist VA Med. Ctr., Palo Alto, Calif., 1978-81; sr. staff fellow psychology and psychopathology lab. NIMH, Bethesda, Md., 1981—, chief. unit on psychophysiology, 1982—. Contbr. articles to profl. jours. Recipient Nat. Research Service award NIH, 1978-81; USPHS fellow, 1970-74; AAUW Golden Anniversary scholar, 1974. Mem. Soc. Psychophysiol. Research (bd. dirs. 1982-85, various coms., Disting. Sci. award for early career contbn. 1980), Am. Psychol. Assn., Soc. Neurosci., Internat. Neuropsychol. Soc., Am. Epilepsy Soc., Mortar Board, Shi-Ai, Phi Beta Kappa, Alpha Lambda Delta, Pi Mu Epsilon, Phi Kappa Phi. Current work: Electrophysiological and neuropsychological investigations of psychiatric and neurologic disorders. Subspecialty: Neuropsychology. Office: Psychology and Psychopathology Lab NIMH Bldg 10 Room 4C110 Bethesda MD 20205

DUNCAN, DORIS GOTTSCHALK, information systems educator; b. Seattle, Nov. 19, 1944; d. Raymond Robert and Marian (Onstad) D.; m. Robert George Gottschalk, Sept. 12, 1971 (div. 1983). B.A., U. Wash., Seattle, 1967, M.B.A., 1968; Ph.D., Golden Gate U., 1978. Cert. data processor; cert. systems profl.; cert. data educator. Communications cons. Pacific NW Bell Telephone Co., Seattle, 1968-71; mktg. supr. AT&T, San Francisco, 1971-73; sr. cons., project leader Quantum Sci. Corp., Palo Alto, Calif., 1973-75; dir. analysis program Input Inc., Palo Alto, 1975-76; prof. accounting, information systems Calif. State U., Hayward, 1976—; dir. information sci. dept. Golden Gate U., San Francisco, 1982-83; cons. pvt. cos., 1975—. Author: Computers and Remote Computing Services, 1983; contbr. articles to profl. jours. Loaned exec. United Good Neighbors, Seattle, 1969; nat. committeewoman, bd. dirs. Young Republicans, Wash., 1970-71; adv. Jr. Achievement, San Francisco, 1971-72. Mem. Data Processing Mgmt. Assn. (past v.p., sec. San Francisco chpt., pres. chpt. 1986, bd. dirs. 1984—, bd. dirs. spl. interest group in edn. 1985-86, Individual Performance award 1984), Assn. Computing Machinery. Club: Junior (Seattle). Current Work: curriculum development, professionalism in data processing field, professional certification, industry standards, computer literacy and user education, design of data bases and data banks. Subspecialties: Information systems (Information science); Database systems. Office: Calif State U-Hayward Sch Bus and Econs Hayward CA 94542

DUNCAN, ROBERT LEON, JR., immunologist; b. Ayer, Mass., Nov. 1, 1951; s. Robert L. and Ardinelle (Bean) D.; m. Susan L. Horvath, May 24, 1975; 1 dau., Olivia Susan. B.A., Bloomsburg U., 1974; M.A., U. Pa., 1977, Ph.D., 1980. Assoc. in dermatology Emory U., Atlanta, 1980-82, sr. research assoc. in microbiology and immunology, 1982-84, asst. prof., 1984—. Contbr. articles to profl. jours. Mem. Am. Assn. Immunologists, Am. Soc. for Microbiology, Southeastern Immunology Conf. Democrat. Methodist. Current work: Macrophage processing of bacterial lipopolysaccharides and immunomodulatory activities of bacterial constituents. Subspecialties: Immunology (medicine); Infectious diseases. Home: 5216 Mountain Village Ct Stone Mountain GA 30083 Office: Emory U 1462 Clifton Rd NE Atlanta GA 30322

DUNCAN, STARKEY DAVIS, JR., behavioral sciences educator; b. San Antonio, Aug. 24, 1935; s. Starkey Davis and Catherine (Poulson) D.; m. Susan Morton, June 30, 1960; children: Arne, Sarah, Owen. B.A., Vanderbilt U., 1957; Ph.D., U. Chgo., 1965. Postdoctoral fellow U. Chgo., 1965-67, asst. prof. behavioral scis., 1967-74, assoc. prof., 1974-81, prof., 1981—. Author: (with others) Face-to-face Interaction, 1977, Interaction Structure and Strategy, 1985; contbr. articles profl. jours. Served to lt. (j.g.) USNR, 1957-59. Grantee NSF, 1972, 75, 80, NIMH, 1978, 1983. Fellow Am. Psychol. Assn., AAAS, Linguistic Soc. Am. Current Work: Structure and strategy of face-to-face interaction, nonverbal communication. Subspecialty: Cognition. Office: Dept of Behavioral Sciences University of Chicago 5848 S University Ave Chicago IL 60637

DUNCAN, THOMAS MICHAEL, chemical engineer; b. Charleston, S.C., Aug. 11, 1953; s. Thomas Marshall and JoAnne (Bean) D.; m. Deborah Lynne Ryerson, Dec. 22, 1979. B.S. in Chem. Engrng., U. Mich., 1975; M.S. in Chem. Engrng., Calif. Inst. Tech., 1977, Ph.D., 1980. Mem. tech. staff AT&T Bell Labs., Murray Hill, N.J., 1980—. Contbr. articles to profl. jours. Mem. Am. Chem. Soc., Am. Phys. Soc., Am. Inst. Chem. Engrs., Tau Beta Pi. Current work: Spectroscopic characterization of reactive intermediates absorbed on heterogeneous catalysts, especially nuclear magnetic resonance and infrared. Subspecialties: Catalysis chemistry; Nuclear magnetic resonance. Office: AT&T Bell Labs 600 Mountain Ave Murray Hill NJ 07974

DUNG, H.C., anatomy educator, acupuncturist, algologist; b. Pingtung, Taiwan, Mar. 7, 1936; came to U.S., 1963, naturalized, 1971; s. Sun Tu and Moon Khan (Chen) D.; m. Elizabeth Izu Dunn, July 30, 1963; children—Y. Ben Dunn, Joeming Wolfe Dunn. Cert. Nat. Taiwan Normal U., 1956; B.Sc., Nat. Taiwan U., 1960; Ph.D., U. Louisville, 1969. Lic. acupuncturist, Republic of China. Research assoc. U. Louisville, Ky., 1969-70; instr. U. Tex. Med. Sch., San Antonio, 1970-71, asst. prof., 1972-80, assoc. prof. U. Tex. Health Sci. Ctr., San Antonio, 1981—; vis. prof. Nat. Yang-Ming Med. Coll., Taipei, Taiwan, 1977; mem. acupuncture adv. com. Tex. State Bd. Med. Examiners, 1982—; mem. nat. adv. bd. Nat. Back Found., Little Rock, 1984—. Mem. editorial bd. Am. Jour. Chinese Medicine, N.Y., 1984—. Contbr. articles to profl. jours. Pres. Taiwan Benevolent Assn. of Am., Washington, 1980; mem. Overseas Chinese Affairs Commn.; Recipient Outstanding Community Service citation Sec. State Calif., 1982; named Most Outstanding Tchr. of Yr., Nat. Yang-Ming Med. Coll., 1977. Mem. Am. Assn. Anatomists, Soc. for Neurosci., Am. Soc. Cell Biology, Internat. Assn. Study of Pain, Am. Congress of Rehab. Medicine, World Affairs council (San Antonio chpt.). Current work: Immunologic deficiencies of neurological mutant mice, anatomic basis of acupuncture, clinical application of acupuncture in pain managements. Subspecialty: Anatomy and embryology. Home: 6426 Flint Rock San Antonio TX 78238 Office: Dept Cellular and Structural Biology U Tex Health Sci Ctr San Antonio TX 78284

DUNHAM, PHILIP BIGELOW, biology educator, physiology researcher; b. Columbus, Ohio, Apr. 26, 1937; s. T. Chadbourne and Margaret (Bigelow) D.; m. Joyce Enderle, Aug. 20, 1965 (div. Dec. 1969); m. Gudrun Bjarnarson, Mar. 9, 1985. B.A., Swarthmore Coll., 1958; Ph.D., U. Chgo., 1962. USPHS postdoctoral fellow Carlsberg Found., Copenhagen, 1962-63; asst. prof. zoology Suracuse U., 1963-67, assoc. prof., 1967-71, prof., 1971—; vis. assoc. prof. physiology Yale U. Sch. Medicine, 1968-70; vis. scientist Physiol. Lab., U. Cambridge, Eng., 1969; vis. honors examiner Swarthmore Coll., 1966-67, 73-74, mem. alumni council, 1971-73; mem. exec. com. of bd. trustees Marine Biol. Lab., Woods Hole, Mass., 1972-76. Assoc. editor Am. Jour. Physiology, Cell, 1984-87. Research numerous publs. in field. Mem. Soc. Gen. Physiologists (council 1967-69), Am. Physiol. Soc., Red Cell Club, Biophys. Soc. Current Work: Mechanism and cellular function of passive and active membrane transport of sodium and potassium in mammalian erythrocytes. Subspecialties: Physiology (biology); Biophysics (biology). Home: 2311 E Genesee St Syracuse NY 13210 Office: Syracuse U 130 College Pl Syracuse NY 13210

DUNIGAN, PAUL FRANCIS XAVIER, chemical engineer, consultant; b. Boston, Mar. 9, 1918; s. John Joseph and Therese Florence (Donoghue) D.; m. Eva Lucile Reckley, July 2, 1942; 1 son, Paul Francis Xavier. B.A., Boston Coll., 1939; M.Ed. in Biology/Chemistry, Mass. State Tchrs. Coll., Boston, 1940. Tchr. sci. St. Rose High Sch., Chelsea, Mass., 1940; with E.I. duPont de Nemours, 1941-46; sr. supr. Hanford (Wash.) Engr. Works, 1944-46; mgr. facilities operation Gen. Electric Co., Hanford, 1946-65; mgr. plant ops. Battelle N.W., Richland, Wash., 1965-70; mgr. facilities utilization Westinghouse Hanford Co., Richland, 1970-84; facility utilization cons., 1984—. Dist. chmn. Blue Mountain council Boy Scouts Am., Richland, 1967; mem. Lay Com. on Edn., 1957-58; res. officer Aux. Police, 1962-63; sec. CeeKay Fed. Credit Union, 1970. Mem. Am. Chem. Soc. (sec. Richland 1952), Am. Nuclear Soc. (vice chmn. remote systems tech. div. 1961), Am. Inst. Chem. Engrs. (nuclear div.), AAAS. Democrat. Roman Catholic. Current Work: Design and utilization of research and development facilities. Subspecialties: Nuclear engineering; Chemical engineering. Home: 1942 Davison Ave Richland WA 99352

DUNIWAY, JOHN M., plant pathologist; b. San Francisco, Nov. 6, 1942; s. Ben C. and Ruth M. D.; m. Catherine C. Cohrs, June 10, 1965; children: Sarah, Michael. B.A. in Biology, Carleton Coll., Northfield, Minn., 1964; Ph.D. in Plant Pathology, U. Wis., 1969. NSF postdoctoral fellow Australian Nat. U., Canberra, 1969-70; mem. faculty dept. plant pathology U. Calif., Davis, 1970—, prof., 1982—. Contbr. articles to profl. jours. Mem. Am. Phytopath. Soc. (CIBA-GEIGY award for research 1982), Am. Soc. Plant Physiologists. Current Work: Water relations of plants and soil fungi. Subspecialties: Plant pathology; Plant physiology (agriculture). Office: Dept Plant Pathology U Calif Davis CA 95616

DUNKER, ALAN MELVIN, research physical chemist; b. Detroit, May 22, 1946; s. Melvin Frederick William and Viola Edith (List) D.; m. Janet Elise Barnes, Sept. 24, 1983. B.S., U. Mich., 1968; M.S., Harvard U., 1972, Ph.D., 1974. Postdoctoral research assoc. Brown U., Providence, 1974-76; sr. research scientist Gen. Motors Research Labs., Warren, Mich., 1976-80, staff research scientist, 1980—. Contbr. articles to profl. jours. Mem. Am. Chem. Soc., Sigma Xi. Current work: Modeling kinetics of tropospheric chemistry; sensitivity analysis of complex models; development of numerical algorithms for detailed models. Subspecialties: Atmospheric chemistry; Kinetics. Office: Environ Sci Dept Gen Motors Research Labs Warren MI 48090

DUNLAP, R. BRUCE, chemist, educator; b. Elgin, Ill., Oct. 14, 1942; s. Robert J. and Carol C. D.; children: Heather Diane, Edward Joseph. B.S. with honors, Beloit (Wis.) Coll., 1964; Ph.D. in Chemistry, Ind. U., 1968. NIH postdoctoral fellow dept. biochemistry Scripps Clinic and Research Found., LaJolla, Calif., 1968-71; asst. prof. dept. chemistry U. S.C., 1971-74, assoc. prof., 1974-78, prof., 1978—. Contbr. articles to profl. jours. Am. Cancer Soc. awardee, 1976-80. Mem. AAAS, Am. Assn. Cancer Research, Am. Chem. Soc., Am. Soc. Biol. Chemists, Am. Cancer Soc. (dir. S.C. div.). Current Work: Enzymology and protein chemistry, selenium biochemistry, mechanism of action of folate enzymes, development of analytical technique of room temperature phosphorescence, application of nuclear magnetic resonance spectroscopy to biochemical problems. Subspecialty: Biochemistry (biology). Home: 1409 Brookview Columbia SC 29210 Office: Dept Chemistr U SC Columbia SC 29208

DUNLOP, ROBERT HUGH, See *Who's Who in America,* 43rd edition.

DUNLOP, TERRENCE WARD, psychologist; b. San Antonio, Nov. 29, 1943; s. Ward Carl and Laura Louise (Laue) D. B.A., Bradley U., 1972; M.A., U. Conn., 1974, Ph.D., 1976. Pvt. practice psychology, Balt., 1976—; postdoctoral fellow dept. psychiatry Johns Hopkins U., Balt., 1976-78, assoc. dir. Cortical Function Lab., 1978-80; chief psychologist Social Security Adminstrn., Office Disability Program, Balt., 1980—. Mem. profl. service com. United Cerebral Palsy, Annapolis, Md., 1981—. Served with U.S. Army, 1966-69. Recipient Acad. Excellence Citation, Bradley U., 1972; cert. of recognition Psychol. Info., 1981; Johns Hopkins U. neuropsychol. grantee, 1978. Mem. Internat. Neuropsychol. Soc., Am. Psychol. Assn., Nat. Acad. Neuropsychologists, Neurol. Soc. Md. Current Work: Neuropsychological evaluation and rehabilitation, determination of disability. Subspecialties: Neuropsychology; Behavioral psychology. Home: 1231-L Gemini Dr Annapolis MD 21403 Office: Social Security Adminstrn Dickinson Bldg Suite 2414 Woodlawn MD 21241

DUNN, ADRIAN JOHN, neuroscience educator; b. London, June 16, 1943; came to U.S., 1970; s. John Charles and Gwendolyn (Gracie) D.; m. Glenda Bradley, Oct. 6, 1973. B.A., U. Cambridge, 1965, M.A., 1968, Ph.D., 1968. Asst. prof. biochemistry U. N.C., Chapel Hill, 1973; asst. prof. neurosci. U. Fla., Gainesville, 1973-77, assoc. prof., 1977-85, prof., 1985—; mem. neuropsychology research rev. com. NIMH, 1980-84. Author: Functional Chemistry of the Brain, 1974, Peptides, Hormones and Behavior, 1984. Mem. Biochem. Soc., Internat. Soc. Neurochemistry, Am. Soc. for Neurochemistry, Soc. for Neurosci., AAAS, European Soc. for Neurochemistry. Current Work: Mechanisms of ACTH action on the brain, neurochemistry of stress. Subspecialties: Neurochemistry; Neuroendocrinology. Office: U Fla PO Box J-244 Gainesville FL 32610

DUNN, ANNE ROBERTS, optical engineer; b. Champaign, Ill., Nov. 23, 1940; d. Howard Creighton and Elizabeth (Clifford) Roberts; m. Karl Lindemann Dunn, June 24, 1967. B.S., Beloit (Wis.) Coll., 1962; M.S., Rensselaer Poly. Inst., 1965, Ph.D., 1969. Research physicist Teledyne Brown Engrng., Huntsville, Ala., 1969-76; staff engr. McDonnell Douglas Astronautics Co., Huntsville, 1976-78; sr. scientist Nichols Research Corp., Huntsville, 1978—. Contbr. articles to profl. jours. Mem. Am. Astron. Soc., AAAS. Current Work: Processing and analysis of data from large infrared detector arrays; military infrared optics; electrooptics; photoelectric mosaic arrays; sensor calibration; data reduction and analysis. Subspecialties: Optical engineering; Infrared technology. Home: 1044 Joe Quick Rd Hazel Green AL 35750 Office: 4040 S Memorial Pkwy Suite A Huntsville AL 35802

DUNN, BRUCE SIDNEY, engineering educator; b. Chgo., Apr. 22, 1948; s. George Bernard and Goldye Rosalyn (Opper) D.; m. Wendy Joan Rader, June 7, 1970; 1 child, Julianne. B.S., Rutgers U., 1970; M.S., UCLA, 1972, Ph.D., 1974. Research scientist Gen. Electric Co., Schenectady, 1976-80; assoc. prof. materials dept. UCLA, 1980—. Contbr. numerous articles to tech. jours. Patentee in field. Mem. Am. Ceramic Soc., Electrochem. Soc., AAAS. Current work: Ion transport in solids; electrochemical devices based on solid electrolytes; laser materials for integrated optics. Subspecialties: Electronic materials; Solid state chemistry. Office: UCLA 6531 Boelter Hall Los Angeles CA 90024

DUNN, DANNY LEROY, chemist; b. Wichita, Kans., July 12, 1946; s. Delmer LeRoy and LeEtta (Johnson) D.; m. Nancy Helen Nelson, Aug. 5, 1967; children—Wendy, Andrew. B.S., Wichita State U., 1968, M.S., 1970; Ph.D., North Tex. State U., 1976. Postdoctoral fellow U. Tex. Health and Sci, Ctr., Dallas, 1975-77; sr. scientist Alcon Labs, Ft. Worth, 1977—. Contbr. articles to profl. jours. Mem. Am. Chem. Soc. Current work: Analysis of pharmaceuticals using high-performance liquid chromotagraphy. Subspecialty: Analytical chemistry. Home: 1003 Yvonne Joshua TX 76058 Office: Alcon Labs 6201 South Freeway Fort Worth TX 76134

DUNN, DEAN ALAN, oceanography educator, micropaleontologist; b. Groton, Conn., Nov. 11, 1954; s. Edward Daniel Jr. and Margaret Elizabeth (Smillie) D. B.S. in Biology, U. So. Calif., 1976, B.S. in Geology, 1977; Ph.D. in Oceanography, U. R.I., 1982. Lab technician geology dept. U. So. Calif., Los Angeles, 1975-77; geophys. asst. Union Oil Co., Santa Fe Springs, Calif., summer 1976; grad. teaching asst. geology dept. Fla. State U., Tallahassee, 1977-78; grad. research asst. oceanography U. R.I., Kingston, 1978-82; staff scientist Deep Sea Drilling Project, U. Calif., San Diego, 1983—; asst. prof. geology U. So. Miss., Hattiesburg, 1983—; cruise scientist oceanography cruises U. So. Calif., 1976-77, shipboard scientist oceanography cruise U. R.I., 1979; shipboard sedimentologist Deep Sea Drilling Project, 1982; shipboard sci. rep. and sedimentologist, 1983. Author: (with others) Initial Reports of the Deep Sea Drilling Project, Vol. 85, 1985; co-author, sci. editor: Initial Reports of the Deep Sea Drilling Project, Vol. 93, 1986. Contbr. articles and abstracts to profl. jours. Faculty adviser So. Geol. Soc., U. So. Miss., 1983. Nat. Merit scholar-trustee scholar U. So. Calif., 1972-77. Mem. Am. Assn. Petroleum Geologists, Geol. Soc. Am., Am. Geophys. Union, Soc. Econ. Paleontologists and Mineralogists (N.Am. micropaleontology sect.), Sigma Xi. Presbyterian. Current work: Marine sedimentation processes, micropaleontology and biostratigraphy of Tertiary radiolaria and calcareous nannofossils, paleo-climatology and paleo-oceanography of Pacific Ocean. Subspecialties: Oceanography; Paleontology, paleoecology. Home: PO Box 8506 Hattiesburg MS 39406 Office: U So Miss Dept Geology So Station Box 5044 Hattiesburg MS 39406

DUNN, FLOYD, biophysicist, bioengineer, educator; b. Kansas City, Mo., Apr. 14, 1924; s. Louis and Ida (Leibtag) D.; m. Elsa Tanya Levine, June 11, 1950; children: Andrea Susan, Louis Brook. Student, Kansas City Jr. Coll., 1941-42, Tex. A. and M. U., 1943; B.S., U. Ill., Urbana, 1949, M.S., 1951, Ph.D., 1956. Research asso. elec. engrng. U. Ill., Urbana, 1954-57, research asst. prof. elec. engrng., 1957-61, assoc. prof. elec. engrng. and biophysics, 1961-65, prof., 1965—, prof. elec. engrng., biophysics and bioengrng., 1972—, dir. bioacoustics research lab., 1976—, chmn. bioengrng. faculty, 1978-82; vis. prof. dept. microbiology Univ. Coll., Cardiff, Wales, 1968-69; vis. sr. scientist Inst. Cancer Research, Sutton, Surrey, Eng., 1975-76, 82-83; vis. prof. Inst. Chest Diseases and Cancer, Tohoku U., Sendai, Japan, 1982, U. Nanjing, 1983; mem. radiation study sect. NIH, 1976-81; steering com. NSF workshop on interaction of ultrasound and biol. tissues, 1971-72; chmn. WHO working group on health aspects of exposure to ultrasound radiation, London, 1976; mem. tech. elec. products radiation standards com. FDA, 1974-76. Editorial bd.: Jour. Acoustical Soc. Am., Rad. Environ. Biophysics, Ultrasound Medicine and Biology; manuscript reviewer: Jour. Phys. Chemistry, Jour. Acoustical Soc. Am., IEEE Transactions, others; Contbr. articles on biophys. acoustics to profl. jours. Trustee Hensley Twp., Ill., 1980-81. Served with AUS, 1943-46. NIH spl. research fellow, 1968-69; Am. Cancer Soc.-Eleanor Roosevelt-Internat. Cancer fellow, 1975-76, 82 83; Fulbright fellow, 1982 83; Japan Soc. for Promotion of Sci. fellow, 1982. Fellow Acoustical Soc. Am. (assoc. editor Jour., pres. 1985-86), Am. Inst. Ultrasound in Medicine (William J. Fry meml. award 1984), IEEE, Inst. Acoustics (U.K.); mem. Biophys. Soc., Nat. Acad. Engrng., AAAS, Sigma Xi, Sigma Tau, Eta Kappa Nu, Tau Beta Pi, Pi Mu Epsilon, Phi Sigma. Current Work: Research in all aspects of ultrasonic propagation in, and interaction with, biological media. Subspecialties: Acoustics; Biophysics (physics). Home: Rural Route 3 Box 295 Champaign IL 61820 Office: Bioacoustics Research Lab U Ill 1406 W Green St Urbana IL 61801

DUNN, MICHAEL JAMES, engineering executive; b. Bklyn., July 13, 1947; s. Frank Nelson and Helen Macaluso (Rau) D.; m. Ann Elizabeth Lutz, Feb. 20, 1982; children: Peter James, Steven Christopher, John Andrew. B.S. in Nuclear Engrng, U. Fla., 1971, M.Engrng. in Nuclear Engrng, 1972. Registered profl. engr., Calif., Mich. Engr., group leader Bechtel Corp., San Francisco, 1972-75; project engr. Black & Veatch, Kansas City, Kans., 1975-77; supr. engrng. Bechtel Corp., Ann Arbor, Mich., 1977-82; sect. mgr. EDS Nuclear, Norcross, Ga., 1982-84; dir. Pacific Nuclear Systems, Atlanta, 1984—. Author tech. papers in field. Mem. admissions com. U. Fla., 1972. Mem. Am. Nuclear Soc. Republican. Lutheran. Current Work: Development of technology for radwaste treatment, decontamination, volume reduction and operations management software. Subspecialties: Nuclear engineering; Systems engineering. Home: 9060 Martin Rd Roswell GA 30076 Office: Pacific Nuclear Systems 2621 Sandy Plains Rd NE Suite 304 Marietta GA 30066

DUNN, WILLIAM LAWRENCE, principal scientist, consulting psychologist; b. Richmond, Va., Apr. 19, 1924; s. William Lawrence and Emily Chenault (Noble) D.; m. Elisabeth Oleknovitch, June 5, 1948; children: Olga, William Mark, Alexandra Noble, Lawrence Alexis. B.S., Lynchburg (Va.) Coll., 1947; Ph.D., Duke U., 1953. Clin. psychologist VA Hosp., Richmond, 1953-61; assoc. prin. scientist Philip Morris Research Ctr., Richmond, 1961-75, prin. scientist, 1975—; adj. prof. Va. Commonwealth U., 1956-61; cons. psychologist Va. Penitentary for Women, Goochland, 1957—; Mem. Bd. Psychologist Examiners, Richmond, 1965-75; mem. wine adv. com. Va. Alcoholic Beverage Control Bd., Richmond, 1976—. Editor: Smoking Behavior, 1973. Served to lt. USNR, 1942-46. Mem. Va. Psychol. Assn. (pres. 1965-66), Va. Acad. Clin. Psychologists (charter pres. 1976-78), Am. Psychol. Assn. Eastern Orthodox. Current Work: Investigation of the psychodynamics of smoking; methods development in consumer evaluation of products. Subspecialties: Clinical psychology; Sensory processes. Home: 4701 New Kent

Ave Richmond VA 23225 Office: Philip Morris Research Center PO Box 26583 Richmond VA 23261

DUNNING, FRANK BARRY, space physics, astronomy and physics educator; b. Tadcaster, Eng., Apr. 10, 1945; came to U.S., 1971; s. John Francis and Margaret Anne (Birbeck) D.; m. Christine Barber, Dec. 26, 1968; children—Sarah Rachel, Francis Mark. B.S. (Spl.) with 1st class honors, Univ. Coll., London, 1966, Ph.D., 1969. Postdoctoral fellow Univ. Coll., 1969-71; research assoc. Rice U., Houston, 1971-74, asst. prof. space physics, astronomy and physics, 1974-78, assoc. prof., 1978-82, prof., 1982—. Editor: Rydberg States of Atoms and Molecules, 1983. Fellow Imperial Chem. Industries, 1969, Alfred P. Sloan Found., 1976. Mem. Optical Soc. Am., Am. Phys. Soc. Current work: Study of atoms in high-lying Rydberg states; use of lasers to study atom-photon interactions; development of new spin-dependent surface spectroscopies to investigate surface electronic and magnetic properties. Subspecialties: Atomic and molecular physics; Condensed matter physics. Home: 7914 Gulfton Houston TX 77036 Office: Dept Space Physics and Astronomy Rice U Houston TX 77251

DUNNING, JAMES MORSE, dental educator; b. N.Y.C., Oct. 16, 1904; s. William Bailey and Rose (Morse) D.; m. Mae Bradford, Aug. 20, 1935; children—Cornelia Dunning Holliston, Rose; m. Nora Gladwin, Apr. 12, 1975. A.B., Harvard U., 1926, M.P.H., 1947; D.D.S., Columbia U., 1930. Diplomate Am. Bd. Dental Pub. Health. Instr. Columbia Sch. Dental and Oral Surgery, N.Y.C., 1930-35; practice dentistry, Boston, 1930—; dental dir. Met. Life Ins. Co., N.Y.C., 1935-45; dean, lectr., prof. ecol. dentistry Harvard U. Sch. Dental Medicine, Boston, 1946—; summer dentist Internat. Grenfell Assn., Labrador, Nfld., Can., 1930-32. Author: Principles of Dental Public Health, 1962, 3d edit., 1979; Dental Care for Everyone, 1976; History of Harvard School of Dental Medicine, 1981. Contbr. articles to profl. jours. Mem. adv. council Mass. Comprehensive Health Planning Council, Boston, 1965-68. Served to lt. comdr. Dental Corps, USN, 1942-46. Recipient Lemuel Shattuck award, 1962; Cert. of Recognition Div. Dental Pub. Health and Resources, USPHS, 1965; Disting. Faculty award Harvard sch. Dental Medicine, 1972. Fellow Am. Coll. Dentists, N.Y. Acad. Dentistry, Am. Acad. Dental Sci.; mem. ADA, Mass. Dental Soc. (Hon. Service awards 1972, 77), Am. Assn. Indsl. Dentists (pres. 1946-47), Fed. Dentaire Internat., Internat. Assn. for Dental Research, Am. Pub. Health Assn. (John W. Knutson Disting. Service award 1983), Am. Coll. Health Assn., (Ruth E. Boynton award 1974), Inst. Medicine, Nat. Acad. Scis. (sr. mem.), Omicron Kappa Upsilon, Delta Omega. Unitarian. Current work: Epidemiology of dental disease; preventive dentistry, fluoridation, dental auxiliary programs. Subspecialty: Preventive dentistry. Office: Harvard Sch Dental Medicine 188 Longwood Ave Boston MA 02115

DUPERON, DONALD FRANCIS, dental educator, pediatric dentist; b. Regina, Sask., Can., Dec. 18, 1937; came to U.S., 1974; s. Francis and Eugenie (Dhuez) D.; m. Donna Joy Hill, Aug. 20, 1960; children: Lori Anne, Mona Lee. Cert., Children's Hosp., Winnipeg, Man., Can., 1968; M.Sc., U. Man., 1970; D.D.S., U. Alta., 1961. Pvt. practice dentistry Weiker & Duperon, Regina, 1961-67; asst. prof. dentistry U. Man., Winnipeg, 1968-70, assoc. prof., chmn., 1970-74; assoc. prof. dentistry UCLA, 1974-83, prof., 1983—, also chmn. grad. program. Mem. Can. Dental Assn., Can. Acad. Pedodontics, Royal Coll. Dentists Can., Man. Dental Assn., Calif. Soc. Pediatric Dentistry. Current Work: Computerized cephalometric analysis, oral problems of bone marrow transplant patients, pulp therapy in pedodontics. Subspecialties: Pediatric dentistry; Dental growth and development. Home: 30169 Via Victoria Rancho Palos Verdes CA 90274 Office: UCLA 23-020 CHS Los Angeles CA 90024

DUPLESSIS, JOHN JOSEPH, metallurgical engineer; b. Winston-Salem, N.C., July 16, 1935; s. Bernard Louyis and Margaret (Browne) DuP.; m. Kitty Sue Berger, June 27, 1959; children—John Joseph, Mary Kathryn, Margaret Evelyn, Samuel Vincent, James Carme. B.S. in Nuclear Engring., B.S. in Metall. Engring., N.C. State U., 1958; M.S. in Metall. Engring., 1960. Research assoc. N.C. State U., Raleigh, 1958-60; metallurgist Allvac Metals div. Teledyne, Monroe, N.C., 1960-63; metallurgist Crucible Magnetics Div. Colt Industries, Elizabethtown, Ky., 1963-68, supt. ferrites, 1968-75, v.p. tech., 1975-80, v.p. tech. and gen. mgr. Alnico Crucible Magnetics div., 1980—. Contbr., articles to Jour. Am. Ceramic Soc., Intersci. Active Boy Scouts Am., 1968-84; pres. Let's Spruce Up, Inc., Elizabethtown, 1983-84; v.p. Acad. Boosters, Elizabethtown, 1984; mem. Elizabethtown Bd. Edn., 1985. Served as cpl. USMCR, 1955-63. Recipient award of merit Boy Scouts Am., Louisville, 1977, Silver Beaver award, Boy Scouts Am., Louisville, 1978. Mem. IEEE (v.p. 1965-66), Am. Soc. Metals, Am. Powder Metal Inst., Am. Ceramic Soc., Magnetic Materials Producers Assn. (pres.-elect), Elizabethtown Jaycees (bd. dirs. 1971-72). Lodge: Lions (bd. dirs. 1978-79). Current work: Development of permanent magnet materials and their manufacturing processes. Subspecialties: Materials; Materials processing. Home: 621 El Dorado Dr Elizabethtown KY 42701 Office: Colt Industries Crucible Magnetics Div Route 2 Leitchfield Rd Elizabethtown KY 42701

DUPREE, SAMUEL HARDY, JR., programmer/analyst; b. Phila., Feb. 25, 1953; s. Samuel H. and Louise D. B.S., Pa. State U., 1974, M.S., 1978. Programming cons. Computation Ctr., Pa. State U., 1975-78; instr. physics and computer sci. Rose-Hulman Inst. Tech., 1978-81; programmer/analyst Gen. Electric Space Systems Div., Phila., 1981—. Mem. Am. Astron. Soc., Soc. Indsl. and Applied Math., Astron. Soc. Pacific, IEEE Computer Soc., Assn. Computing Machinery, Baptist. Current Work: Computer graphics, software engineering, scientific computing, man-machine interfacing. Subspecialty: Scientific computing. Office: Gen Electric Space System Div PO Box 8555 Philadelphia PA 19101

DUPUIS, RUSSELL DEAN, materials science and electrical engineering researcher; b. Kankakee, Ill., July 9, 1947; s. Rudolph William and Evelyn Marie (Hoevet) D.; m. Dana Elizabeth Gammage, Nov. 19, 1973; 1 child, Elizabeth Anne. B.S.E.E. with highest honors, U. Ill.-Urbana, 1970, M.S.E.E., 1971, Ph.D.E.E., 1973. Mem. tech. staff Tex. Instruments, Dallas, 1973-75, Rockwell Internat., Anaheim, Calif., 1975-79, AT&T Bell Labs., Murray Hill, N.J., 1979—, Disting. mem. tech. staff, 1985—. Contbr. of articles to profl. jours. Mem. IEEE (Liebmann award 1985), Am. Phys. Soc., Electrochem. Soc., Eta Kappa Nu, Tau Beta Pi, Phi Eta Sigma. Current work: Research in metalorganic chemical vapor deposition growth of thin films of III-V compound semiconductors with applications to light-wave communications systems. Subspecialties: Semiconductors; Electronic materials. Office: AT&T Bell Labs 600 Mountain Ave Murray Hill NJ 07974-2070

DUQUE, RICHARO ERNESTO, physician, pathologist, immunopathologist; b. Bogota, Colombia, Apr. 16, 1944; came to U.S., 1949, naturalized 1985; s. Bernardo and Ines (Gonzalez) D.; m. Beatriz Turriago, Apr. 2, 1971; children—Maria F., Patricia. M.D., Univ. Nacional, Colombia, S.Am., 1973. Diplomate Am. Bd. Pathology. Intern, Hosp. San Juan de Dios, Bogota; resident in pathology Orlando Regional Med. Ctr., Fla., 1975-78; practice medicine, Orlando, 1978-81; postdoctoral research fellow, research investigator U. Mich., Ann Arbor, 1981-84, asst. prof., 1984—. Contbr. articles to profl. jours. Recipient Alfred L. Lewis, Jr., M.D., Meml. Research award Fla. Soc. pathologists, 1976. Mem. Am. Assn. Pathologists (Exptl. Pathologist In-Tng. award 1983). Subspecialties: Pathology (medicine); Immunology (medicine). Office: Dept Pathology U Mich 1315 E Catherine Rd Ann Arbor MI 48109

DURANT, JOHN RIDGEWAY, See *Who's Who in America,* 43rd edition.

DURELLI, AUGUST JOSEPH, mechanical engineer; b. Buenos Aires, Argentina, Apr. 30, 1910; came to U.S., 1939, naturalized, 1960; s. August F. and Jeannette (Natzi) D.; m. Marie-Marthe Baril, Oct. 2, 1943; children: Ana, Monica, Andrew. Civil engr., U. Buenos Aires, 1932; D. Engring., U. Paris, 1937; D. Social Scis., Cath. U. Paris, 1937. Prof. Ill. Inst. Tech., 1956-61; prof. Cath. U., Washington, 1961-75; Dodge prof. engring. Oakland U., Mich., 1975-80; Nabor Carrillo prof. U. Mexico, 1981; prof. mech. engring. U. Md., College Park, 1981—. Author: Essai sur les Mentalites Contemporaines, 1937, Nacionalismo frente al Cristianismo, 1940, Del Universo de la Universidad al Universo del Hombre, 1942, Liberation de la Liberte, 1942, (with Phillips and Tsao) Introduction to the Theoretical and Experimental Analysis of Stress and Strain, 1958, (with Riley) Introduction to Photomechanics, 1965, (with Parks) Moire Analysis of Strain, 1970, Applied Stress Analysis, 1967; also 300 articles. Recipient Sr. research award Am. Soc. Engring. Edn., 1980. Mem. AAUP (pres. Cath. U. chpt. 1973-75), ASME, N.Y. Acad. Sci., Soc. Exptl. Stress Analysis (hon.), Sigma Xi. Democrat. Roman Catholic. Current Work: Optimization of structural components, development of experimental stress analysis methods. Subspecialties: Solid mechanics; Optical engineering. Home: PO Box 6 Myersville MD 21773 Office: Mech Engring U Md College Park MD 20742

DURGUN, KANAT, mathematician; b. Istanbul, Turkey, Mar. 30, 1940; s. Resat A. and Feriha (Ulu) D.; m. Lynn K. Hogan, June 12, 1971 (div. Jan. 1979); 1 dau. Sarah K.; m. Ann Mary Moskiewicz, May 13, 1979. Ph.D., Tech. U. Istanbul, 1965; M.S., Syracuse U., 1972, Ph.D., 1976. Research collaborator Brookhaven Nat. Lab., Upton, L.I., N.Y., 1965-67; asst. prof. Tech. U. Istanbul, 1967-69, Utica (N.Y.) Coll., 1976-77, U. South Ala., Mobile, 1977-79; assoc. prof. U. Ark., Little Rock, 1981—; mem. vis. faculty NASA Johnson Space Center, Houston, 1982. Author: General Equation of Heat Conduction in Semi-Infinite and Infinite Mediums. Mem. Soc. Indsl. and Applied Math., Am. Math. Soc., Math. Assn. Am., Sigma Xi. Democrat. Roman Catholic. Current Work: Applied mathematics. Subspecialties: Applied mathematics; Civil engineering. Home: 6200 Asher St Apt 272 Little Rock AR 72204 Office: Dept Math Univ Ark Little Rock AR 72204

DUSANIC, DONALD GABRIEL, parasitologist, educator; b. Chgo., Dec. 15, 1934; s. Garbriel John and Harriet (Rojewski) D.; m. Roberta Leona Drost, June 22, 1957; children: Belinda Conrad, Donald, Karla Conrad, Allan Conrad, Robert; m. Jane Mitchell Haw, June 11, 1971. B.S., U. Chgo., 1957, M.S., 1959, Ph.D., 1963. Instr. U. Chgo., 1963-64; vis. prof. U. Philippines, 1964; asst. prof. U. Kans., 1964-68, assoc. prof., 1968-71, prof., 1971; vis. prof. Nat. Taiwan U. Sch. Medicine, 1971; prof. dept. life scis. Ind. State U., Terre Haute, 1971—; adj. prof. Ind. U. Sch. Medicine; guest faculty Rockefeller U., 1965; Universidade Catolica de Pelotas, Rio Grande do Sul, Brazil, 1980; cons. NATO, NIH, NSF, U.S. Navy. Contbr. articles to profl. jours. NSF grantee, 1982-84; NIH grantee, 1982-85. Mem. Am. Soc. Tropical Medicine and Hygiene, Am. Soc. Parasitologists, Soc. Protozoologists, Am. Assn. Immunologists, N.Y. Acad. Scis., AAAS, Sigma Xi. Current Work: Immunity in rodent and human trypanosomiases; hybridoma technology in the study of trypanosome antigens, their functions during infections and their use as vaccines and serodiagnostic reagents. Subspecialties: Immunobiology and immunology; Parasitology. Home: BOX 176A Route 24 Terre Haute IN 47802 Office: Dept Life Scis Ind State U Terre Haute IN 47809

DUSENBERY, DAVID BROCK, biophysics educator; b. Portland, Apr. 30, 1942; s. Harris and Evelyn (Shields) D. B.A., Reed Coll., 1964; Ph.D., U. Chgo., 1970. Postdoctoral fellow Calif. Inst. Tech., Pasadena, 1970-73; asst. prof. Ga. Inst. Tech., Atlanta, 1973-79, assoc. prof., 1979—. Contbr. articles to profl. jours. Mem. AAAS, Biophys. Soc., Soc. Nematologists, Assn. Chemoreception Scis. Current Work: Nematode behavior, video camera-computer tracking, laser microbeam, fluorescence. Subspecialties: Biophysics (biology); Neurobiology.

DUSKO, HAROLD GEORGE, military technology branch executive, geography educator; b. Tarentum, Pa., July 1, 1942; s. Harold Richard and Josephine Mary (Goralka) D.; m. Janet Lamonby Craig, Sept. 1, 1963; children: Steven Harold, Christopher David, Jeffrey Craig. B.S. in Edn, Slippery Rock State Coll., 1964; M.B.A., U. Dayton, 1970; postgrad., Southern Ill. U., 1965-66. Cartographer Aero. Chart and Info. Ctr., St. Louis, 1964-66; imagery analyst rgn. tech. div. Wright-Patterson AFB, Fairborn, Ohio, 1966-69, methods officer, 1970-79, br. chief, 1979—; faculty Wright State U., Fairborn, 1970—, adj. prof. geography, 1970—, cartographic cons., 1973-82; U.S. Air Force rep. Mensuration Standards Group, Washington, 1975-85, Digital Image Work Group, Washington, 1976-80; cartographic cons. Dayton (Ohio) Family Services, 1979-80. Author: Caesar Creek and Toddsfork maps, 1974, Laboratory Exercises in Cartography, 1975, Map Exercises in Remote Sensing, 1976, Digital Image Processing, 1980, Locational Cartography, 1983. Bd. dirs. New Carlisle (Ohio) Baseball Assn., 1974-78; coach Miami County (Ohio) Area Youth Soccer Assn., 1979; commr. Bethel Baseball Assn., Miami County, 1980; mem. Steering Com. for Remote Sensing, Columbus, Ohio, 1982. Recipient Outstanding Performance awards Air Force Systems Command/Fgn Tech Div, U.S. Air Force, 1975, 78, 79, Sustained Superior Performance award, 1982, 83, Outstanding Performance award, 1984. Mem. Am. Soc. Photogrammetry. Democrat. Presbyterian. Current work: Digital image processing using distributed systems and microprocessors; computer-aided design systems and software, low-cost microprocessors for education in earth sciences. Subspecialties: Graphics, image processing, and pattern recognition; Remote sensing (geoscience). Home: 5244 Eastland Dr New Carlisle OH 45344 Office: Imagery Analysis Branch Fgn Tech Div Bldg 856 Wright-Patterson AFB Fairborn OH 45433

DUTCH, STEVEN IAN, structural geology educator, researcher; b. Milford, Conn., May 10, 1947; s. Reginald Frank and Dorothy Elizabeth (Mundy) D.; m. Shawn Claire Matteson, Aug. 16, 1975; children—Christopher, Brendan. B.A., U. Calif.-Berkeley, 1969; M. Phil., Columbia U., 1974, Ph.D., 1976. Asst. prof. geology U. Wis.-Green Bay, 1976-82, assoc. prof., 1982—. Contbr. articles to profl. jours. State co-liaison Com. of Correspondence on Creation-/Evolution, 1984. Served with U.S. Army, 1970-72. U.S. Geol. Survey contract grantee, 1981. Mem. Geol. Soc. Am. Roman Catholic. Current work: Computer-assisted instruction in geology, Precambrian geology of the U.S.; numerical modelling of glacio-isostasy. Subspecialty: Tectonics. Home: 559 Peters St Green Bay WI 54302 Office: U Wis-Green Bay Dept Sci and Environ Change Green Bay WI 54301

DUTCH, SUSAN ELAINE, psychology educator; b. Providence, Nov. 5, 1950; d. Robert A. and D. Elaine (Randall) Dutch. B.A., U. Conn., 1971, M.A., 1974, Ph.D., 1980. Instr. St. Francis Coll., Ft. Wayne, Ind., 1977-80, asst. prof., 1981-82, Westfield State Coll., Mass., 1982-84, assoc. prof., 1984—. Contbr. articles to profl. jours. Grantee NSF, 1982-84, Westfield State Coll., 1982—; recipient Disting. Service award Westfield State Coll., 1983-84. Mem. Am. Psychol. Assn., New England Psychol. Assn. (steering com. 1984-86), Eastern Psychol. Assn. (co-chmn. placement service 1985). Current work: Memory, language, speech, cognition, reading processes. Subspecialty: Cognition. Office: Westfield State Coll Western Ave Westfield MA 01086

DUTCHER, JANICE PHILLIPS, oncology educator; b. Bend, Ore, Nov. 10, 1950; d. Charles Glen and May Belle (Fluit) P. B.A., U. Utah, 1971; M.D., U. Calif.-Davis, 1975. Diplomate: Am. Bd. Internal Medicine. Intern Presbyn. St. Lukes Hosp., Chgo., 1975-76, resident in medicine, 1976-78; clin. assoc. Balt. Cancer Research Ctr., Nat. Cancer Inst. NIH, 1978-81, med. investigator, 1981-82; asst. prof. med. oncology U. Md., Balt., 1982; asst. prof. medicine and oncology Albert Einstein Coll. Medicine, Bronx, 1983—; cons. in field. Bd. advisers Sunshine Found., Balt., 1982—. Served to lt. comdr. USPHS, 1978-82. Recipient Beecham award, 1983. Fellow ACP; mem. NOW, Am. Soc. Clin. Oncology, Am. Soc. Hematology, Am. Assn. Cancer Research, Am. Fedn. Clin. Research, Am. Assn. Blood Banks, Am. Med. Women's Assn., Phi Beta Kappa, Phi Kappa Phi, Alpha Omega Alpha. Democrat. Current Work: Transfusion supportive care of cancer and leukemia patients; clin. trials in acute leukemia and solid tumors, clinical and laboratory investigations in leukemia. Subspecialty: Oncology. Home: 640 W 239th St Apt 6D Riverdale NY 10463 Office: Section of Oncology Albert Einstein Coll Medicine 1300 Morris Park Ave Bronx NY 10411

DUTE, ROLAND ROY, botany educator; b. Amherst, Ohio, Nov. 9, 1947; s. Roy Casper and Donna Yvonne (Fazey) D. B.S., Ohio State U., 1969, M.S., 1972; Ph.D., U. Wis.-Madison, 1976. Research assoc. Lab. Molecular Biology U. Wis., 1976-78; research asso. dept. botany U. Ill., 1978-79; asst. prof. biology St. Ambrose Coll., 1979-82; asst. prof. botany, plant pathology and microbiology Auburn U., 1982—. Contbr. articles to profl. jours. Served with U.S. Army, 1970-72. Mem. AAAS, Bot. Soc. Am., Iowa Acad. Sci. Current Work: Ultrastructure of food-conducting systems in vascular plants; ultrastructure; sieve elements; phloem. Subspecialties: Cell biology; Developmental biology. Office: Dept Botany Auburn U Auburn AL 36849

DUTKO, FRANCIS JOSEPH, JR., molecular virologist; b. Trenton, N.J., July 5, 1951; s. Francis Joseph and Helen Antoinette (Zyla) D.; m. Angela Lynn Grossi, Apr. 19, 1975; 1 dau., Rachel. B.S. in Biology, Rensselaer Poly. Inst., 1973, M.S., 1975, Ph.D., 1977. Research fellow dept. immunology Scripps Clinic and Research Found., La Jolla, Calif., 1977-80, research assoc., 1980-83; with dept. microbiology Sterling-Winthrop Research Inst., Rensselaer, N.Y., 1983—. Contbr. articles to profl. jours. NIH fellow, 1977-79; Leukemia Soc. Am. spl. fellow, 1982-84. Mem. Am. Soc. for Microbiology, AAAS. Democrat. Roman Catholic. Current Work: Mechanism of persistent and latent viral infections. Subspecialties: Molecular biology; Virology (biology). Office: Sterling-Winthrop Research Inst Rensselaer NY 12144

DUTTA, SISIR KAMAL, educator; b. Bengal, India, Aug. 28, 1928; came to U.S., 1956, naturalized, 1974; s. Krishna K. and Satyabati (Chanda) D.; m. Minati Roy, July 1, 1955; children: Mahasweta, Basabi. M.S., Kans. State U., 1958, Ph.D., 1960. Dir., chief research officer Nat. Pineapple Research Inst., Malaysia, 1961-64; research assoc. Rice U., 1964-65; asst. prof. biology Tex. So. U., Houston, 1965-66; chmn. div. sci. and math., assoc. prof. biology Jarvis Christian Coll., 1966-67; prof. molecular genetics dept. botany Howard U., 1967—; cons. pineapple industries, Formosa, Philippines, Malaysia, various univs.; collaborator Pasteur Inst., Carnegie Instn.; lectr. Univs., U.S. and abroad. Contbr. articles to profl. jours. Vis. scientist Rockefeller U., 1968-69; vis. scientist Pasteur Inst., Paris, 1974-75, NIH, Bethesda, Md., 1974-75. Named to Hall of Fame in Molecular Genetics. Grantee NSF; grantee Dept. Energy; grantee NIH; grantee Olin Found.; grantee EPA; grantee Research Corp. N.Y.; grantee Anna Fuller Fund.; grantee USNR. Mem. AAAS, Indian Sci. Congress, Genetics Soc. Am., AAUP, Am. Mycol. Soc., Am. Soc. Environ. Mutagen, Sigma Xi, Beta Kappa Chi. Current Work: Gene isolation, gene expression, molecular genome organization. Subspecialties: Genetics and genetic engineering (biology); Genome organization. Home: 8841 Tuckerman Ln Potomac MD 20854 Office: Dept Botany Howard U Washington DC 20059

DUTTON, JOHN ALTNOW, meteorologist; b. Detroit, Sept. 11, 1936; s. Carl Evans and Velma (Altnow) D.; m. Frances Elizabeth Andrews, Jan. 13, 1962; children—Christopher Evan, John Andrews, Jan Frederik. B.S., U. Wis., 1958; M.S., 1959, Ph.D., 1962. Mem. faculty Pa. State U., University Park, 1965—, assoc. prof. meteorology, 1968-71, prof., 1971—, head dept. meteorology, 1981—; expert aero. system div. USAF, 1965-71; vis. scientist Riso Research Establishment, Roskilde, Denmark, 1971-72, summer 1975, 78-79; vis. prof. Tech. U., Denmark, 1978-79. Author: The Ceaseless Wind: An Introduction to the Theory of Atmospheric Motion, 1976; (with H.A. Panofsky) Atmospheric Turbulence Models and Methods for Engineering Applications, 1984; assoc. editor: Meteorol. Monographs, 1973-79; editor, 1979-84 contbr. articles to profl. jours. Trustee Univ. Corp. for Atmospheric Research, 1974-81, sec., 1977, treas., 1978-79, vice-chmn., 1980—; Mem. bd. atmospheric scis. and climate Nat. Acad. Scis., 1982—; mem. space and earth scis. adv. com. NASA, 1982—. Served with USAF, 1962-65. Fellow Am. Meteorol. Soc. (chmn. publs. commn. 1984—); mem. Math. Assn. Am., Soc. Indsl. and Applied Math., Sigma Xi, Phi Kappa Phi, Theta Delta Chi. Current Work: Atmospheric dynamics; spectral modeling of atmospheric and hydrodynamic flow, predictability; effects of atmospheric turbulence on structures; application of artificial intelligence methods to the atmospheric sciences. Subspecialties: Meteorology; Applied mathematics. Home: 447 Nimitz Ave State College PA 16801 Office: 503 Walker Bldg University Park PA 16802

DU WORS, ROBERT JEROME, software engineer; b. Lewisburg, Pa., June 17, 1952; s. Richard Edward and Luella Maude (Manter) DuWors; m. Leona Ion Locklin, July 17, 1982; 1 dau., Alexa Celeste. B.S. in Computer Sci. with distinction, U. Calgary, Alta., Can., 1980. Cert. computer programmer, cert. data processor. Systems programmer Technion-Israel Inst. Tech., 1971-73, Control Data France, 1973-74; systems designer Calgary Bd. Edn., 1978-79; cons. ALTEL, 1975-77; instr. U. Calgary, 1979-81; software engr. Can. Systems Group, 1981-82; sr. tech. computer analyst Petro-Can., Calgary, 1982-83; sofeware engr. radar group Intera, Environ. Cons. Ltd., Calgary, 1983—. Mem. Assn. Computing Machinery, IEEE Computer Soc., Can. Info. Processing Soc., AICCP. Club: Cu-Nim Gliding (Calgary). Current Work: System design, application languages, graphics, configuration analysis, image processing, synthetic operture radar, systems analysis. Subspecialties: Operating systems; Information systems, storage, and retrieval (computer science). Home: RR4 Calgary AB T2M 4L4 Canada Office: Intera 1200-510 5th St SW Calgary AB T2P 3S2 Canada

D'VER, ABBOTT SIMON, veterinarian, toxicologist; b. Teaneck, N.J., Mar. 24, 1939; s. Morris D'Ver and Lillian D'Ver Sirkin; m. Judith Z. Stern, Sept. 4, 1977; children—Marc, Ilana. Student Cornell U., 1957-59; V.M.D., U. Pa., 1963. Accredited veterinarian U.S. Dept. Agr. Assoc. Am. Soc. Prevention Cruelty to Animals, N.Y.C., 1965-66; dir. lab. animal services Hoffmann-La Roche, Nutley, N.J., 1966-72; pres. White Eagle Lab., Doylestown, Pa., 1972—; chmn. Biodyne Corp., 1985—; adj. prof. Union Grad. Sch., Yellow Springs, Ohio, 1970-74; cons. SUNY-Delhi, 1979—, Harcum Jr. Coll., 1981—; dir. BioDyne Corp., Doylestown. Author: Assistant Animal Technician Manual, 1972. Assoc. editor Lab. Animal Bull., 1965-66. Pres. Bd. Health, Dumont, N.J., 1971-72. Served to capt. U.S. Army, 1963-65. Mem. AVMA, Am. Assn. for Lab. Animal Sci., Am. Assn. Indsl. Veterinarians, N.J. Soc. for Med. Edn. (trustee 1968-72), Am. Assn. for Lab. Animal Practioners, Mid Atlantic Soc. Toxicology, Middle Atlantic Reproduction and Teratology Assn. Current work: Neonatal and pediatric toxicology, teratology. Subspecialties: Toxicology (medicine); Teratology. Home: 2829 Livingston St Allentown PA 18104 Office: White Eagle Labs Inc 2003 Lower State Rd Doylestown PA 18901

DVORAK, FRANK ARTHUR, business executive, scientist; b, Kerrobert, Sask., Can., Aug. 8, 1939; came to U.S., 1967; s. Frank and Evelyn May (Peterson) D.; m. E. Vivien Wallen, Dec. 20, 1963. B.Eng., Royal Mil. Coll. Can., 1962; M.Sc., U. B.C., Can., 1964; Ph.D., Cambridge U., Eng., 1967. Sr. engr. Boeing Co., Seattle, 1967-72; div. mgr. Flow Industries Inc., Kent, Wash., 1972-74; pres. Analytical Methods Inc., Redmond, Wash., 1975—. Contbr. articles to profl. jours. Tchr. U.S. Power Squadrons, Bellevue, Wash., 1974; Athlone fellow Brit. Bd. Trade, 1964, 65; Ministry of Def. grantee Brit. Govt., 1966. Assoc. fellow AIAA (applied aero tech. com.); mem. Am. Helicopter Soc., Can. Aero. and Space Inst., Federal Way C. of C. Current work: Research in viscous/potential flow interactions related to propulsion/airframe integration, separated flows. Subspecialties: Aeronautical engineering; Fluid mechanics. Home: 7681 W Mercer Way Mercer Island WA 98040Office: Analytical Methods Inc 2047 152d Ave NE Redmond WA 98052

DWIVEDI, CHANDRADHAR, biochemist; b. Jaunpur, U.P., India, July 1, 1948; s. Abhaya N. and Maharaji (Dubey) D.; m. Prabha Dwivedi, June 21, 1966; children: Sudhanshu, Neeraja, Himanshu. B.Sc., Gorakhpur U., 1964, M.Sc., 1966; Ph.D., Lucknow U., 1972. Clin. chemist Tenn. Dept. Health.; Research fellow K.G. Med. Coll., Lucknow, India, 1969-73; research assoc. Vanderbilt U., Nashville, 1973-76; asst. prof. dir. biochem. lab. Meharry Med. Coll., Nashville, 1976-82, assoc. prof., dir. biochem. lab., 1982—. Contbr. articles to profl. jours. Lady Tata Meml. scholar, 1968-69; Indian Council Med. Research scholar, 1969-73; NSF grantee, 1977-80; NIH grantee, 1981—; Bur. Maternal and Child Health Service Adminstrn. grantee, 1976-82. Mem. Soc. Explt. Biology and Medicine, Soc. Environ. Toxicology and Chemistry, Am. Assn. Clin. Chemistry, Soc. Neurosci., Am. Soc. Human Genetics, Genetics Soc. Am., Internat. Soc. Devel. Neurosci., Am. Physiol. Soc., Internat. Soc. Biochemical Pharmacology, Internat. Union Pharmacology. Hindu. Current Work: in developmental neurochemistry, environmental biochemical toxicology and oncology. Subspecialties: Cell study oncology; Neurochemistry.

DYBOWSKI, CECIL RAY, chemistry educator; b. Yorktown, Tex., Sept. 23, 1946; s. Hermin Romana and Ruth Joyce (Geffert) D.; m. Mary Agnes Kaiser, May 12, 1979. B.S. in Chemistry, U. Tex., 1969, Ph.D., 1973. Research fellow Calif. Inst. Tech., Pasadena, 1973-76; asst. prof. chemistry U. Del., Newark, 1976-82, assoc. prof., 1982—; vis. scientist E.I. Dupont de Nemours, Wilmington, Del., 1982-83. Mem. Am. Chem. Soc., Am. Phys. Soc., Am. Inst. Chem. Engrs., Materials Research Soc., Soc. Applied Spectroscopy (chmn. sect. 1982-83). Current Work: Polymer NMR; surface spectroscopy; inelastic electron tunneling spectroscopy. Subspecialties: Physical chemistry; Nuclear magnetic resonance. Home: 19 Linden St Newark DE 19711 Office: Dept Chemistry U Del Newark DE 19716

DYCK, RUDOLPH HENRY, optoelectronic engineer, electronic engineer; b. Pasadena, Calif., Apr. 17, 1931; s. Dietrich G. and Evangeline (Rempel) D.; m. Betty Chapman, June 25, 1955; children—Elizabeth, Jennifer, Margaret. A.A., Pasadena City Coll., 1950; student Bethel Coll., 1950-51; B.S. in Chemistry, U. Calif.-Berkeley, 1952, Ph.D. in Phys. Chemistry, 1955. Mem. tech. staff RCA Labs., Princeton, N.J., 1955-62; mem. tech. staff Fairchild Research and Devel. Lab., Palo Alto, Calif., 1962-67, mgr. optoelectronics, 1967-71; mgr. advance devel. Fairchild CCD Imaging, Palo Alto, 1971—. Contbr. chpts. to books, articles to profl. jours. Patentee in field. Mem. Soc. Photo-Optical Instrumentation Engrs., Am. Phys. Soc., AAAS. Democrat. Presbyterian. Current work: Solid State image sensor development: color, infrared, fiber optic types, low-noise. Subspecialties: Integrated circuits; Optical engineering. Home: 160 Ely Pl Palo Alto CA 94306 Office: Fairchild CCD Imaging 4001 Miranda Ave Palo Alto CA 94304

DYER, ROBERT STRITZINGER, neurophysiologist, toxicologist; b. White Plains, N.Y., May 26, 1944; s. Benjamin Wheeler and Deborah Ann (Stritzinger) D.; m. Lois Pratt, May 30, 1969 (div. June 1974); m. Elizabeth Lee Gurganus, May 9, 1977; children—Benjamin Wheeler, V, Rebecca Elizabeth. B.A., Grinnell Coll., 1966; Ph.D., SUNY-Buffalo, 1970. Postdoctoral fellow U. Mich., Ann Arbor, 1970-71; asst. prof. Towson State U., Balt., 1971-74; research fellow Johns Hopkins U., Balt., 1974-77; sr. research fellow Nat. Ctr. Toxicological Research, Jefferson, Ark., 1977-78; research psychologist EPA, Research Triangle Park, N.C., 1978-81, chief, neurophysiology, 1981—. Editor: Neurotoxicity of Organic Solvents and Acrylamide, 1981; Neurotoxicity of Pesticides, 1981; Neurotoxicology of the Alkyltins, 1982; Disease and Chemically- Induced Neurological Dysfunction, 1983; mem. editorial adv. bd. Neurotoxicology, 1982—; neurophysiology editor Neuro-behavioral Toxicology and Teratology, 1983—. Contbr. articles to profl. lit. Grantee Towson State U., 1972, NIMH, 1972, Grass Found., 1973, Fight-for-Sight, 1975. Mem. AAAS, Eastern Psychol. Assn., Soc. Neurosci., Internat. Brain Research Orgn., Soc. Toxicology. Democrat. Current work: Development of Neurophysiological methods for detection and characterization of neurotoxicity. Subspecialties: Toxicology (medicine); Neurophysiology. Home: 416 Elm St Raleigh NC 27604 Office: Neurotoxicology Div MD74B EPA Research Triangle Park NC 27711

DYKSTRA, CLIFFORD ELLIOT, educator, research chemist; b. Chgo., Oct. 30, 1952; s. Raymond and Vivian (Mishkutz) D. B.S. in Chemistry and Physics, U. Ill., 1973; Ph.D., U. Calif.-Berkeley, 1976. Research assoc. U. Calif., 1976-77; asst. prof. chemistry U. Ill., 1977-83, assoc. prof. chemistry, 1983—; cons. chemistry div. Argonne Nat. Lab., Ill., 1978-80. Editor: Advanced Theories and Computational Approaches to the Electronic Structure of Molecules. Contbr. articles to profl. jours. Alfred P. Sloan fellow, 1979-81. Mem. Am. Phys. Soc. Current Work: Electron correlation in molecules, hydrogen bonding, molecular structure and stability, interstellar and prebiotic chemistry. Subspecialties: Physical chemistry; Theoretical chemistry. Office: Dept Chemistry U Ill 505 S Matthews Urbana IL 61801

DYM, CLIVE LIONEL, engineering educator; b. Leeds, Eng., July 15, 1942; came to U.S., 1949, naturalized, 1954; s. Isaac and Anna (Hochmann) D.; children: Jordana, Miriam. B.C.E., Cooper Union, 1962; M.S., Poly. Inst. Bklyn., 1964; Ph.D., Stanford U., 1967. Asst. prof. SUNY, Buffalo, 1966-69; asso. professorial lectr. George Washington U., Washington, 1969; research staff Inst. Def. Analyses, Arlington, Va., 1969-70; asso. prof. Carnegie-Mellon U., Pitts., 1970-74; vis. asso. prof. TECHNION, Israel, 1971; sr. scientist Bolt Beranek and Newman, Inc., Cambridge, Mass., 1974-77; prof., head civil engring. dept. U. Mass., Amherst, 1977-85, prof., 1985—; vis. sr. research fellow Inst. Sound and Vibration Research, U. Southampton, Eng., 1973; vis. scientist Xerox PARC, 1983-84; vis. prof. civil engring. Stanford U., 1983-84; cons. Bell Aerospace Co., 1967-69, Dravo Corp., 1970-71, Salem Corp., 1972, Gen. Analytics Inc., 1972, ORI, Inc., 1979, BBN Inc., 1979, AVCO, 1981-83, 85—, TASC, 1985—. Mem. editorial bd. Jour. of Sound and Vibration. Author: (with I.H. Shames) Solid Mechanics: A Variational Approach, 1973; Introduction to the Theory of Shells, 1974; Stability Theory and Its Applications to Structural Mechanics, 1974; (with A. Kalnins) Vibration: Beams, Plates, and Shells, 1977; (With E.S. Ivey) Principles of Mathematical Modeling, 1980; (with I.H. Shames) Energy and Finite Element Methods in Structural Mechanics, 1985. Contbr. articles and tech. reports to profl. publs. NATO sr. fellow in sci., 1973. Fellow Acoustical Soc. Am., ASME, ASCE (Walter L. Huber research prize 1980); mem. AAAS, Inst. Noise Control Engring., Am. Soc. Engring. Edn. (Western Electric Fund award New Eng. Sect. 1983). Jewish. Current Work: Structural dynamics and stability; vibration and acoustics; expert systems for engineering design. Subspecialties: Theoretical and applied mechanics; Civil engineering. Office: Civil Engineering Dept U Mass Amherst MA 01003

DYMINSKI, JOHN W(LADYSLAW), immunologist, researcher; b. Lindau, Germany, Feb. 13, 1945; came to U.S., 1949, naturalized, 1955; s. Jan and Wanda (Michionek) D. A.B., U. Rochester, 1967; M.S., Syracuse U., 1970, Ph.D., 1972. Postdoctoral fellow U. Fla. Coll. Medicine, 1972-76; asst. prof. Children's Hosp., Cin., 1976-80; sect. leader Bethesda Research Labs., Gaithersburg, Md., 1980-82; research mgr. Mast Immunosystems, Mountain View, Calif., 1982-83, Paragon Diagnostics, Sunnyvale, Calif., 1983-84, Pan Ab Labs., San Jose, Calif., 1984—. Contbr. articles to profl. jours. Nat. Inst. Arthritis and Infectious Diseases fellow, 1975-76. Mem. Am. Assn. Immunologists, Transplantation Soc. Democrat. Roman Catholic. Current Work: Development of in vitro diagnostic systems in fields of immunobiology, oncology, infectious diseases and allergy. Subspecialties: Immunology (medicine); Immunobiology and immunology.

DYMSZA, HENRY ADAM, nutrition and food science educator, researcher; b. Newton, N.H., Jan. 14, 1922; s. Alexander and Malvina (Luckasiewicz) D.; m. Janina Helen Kaminski, June 3, 1956; children—Valerie, Darlene, Andrea, Cheryl. B.S., Pa. State U., 1943; Ph.D., 1954; M.S., U. Wis.-Madison, 1950. Nutritional technician Gen. Foods Corp., Tarrytown, N.Y., 1954-59; sr. research assoc. MIT, Cambridge, 1959-64; head metabolism group U.S. Army Research and Devel. Labs., Natick, Mass., 1964-66; chmn. food and nutrition U. R.I., Kingston, 1966-67, prof. food and nutrition, 1978—; chief clin. nutrition FDA Bur. Foods, Washington, 1979-80. Author abstracts; also articles. Served with USMC, 1943-46. Recipient Commendation for Research, U.S. Army, 1966; grantee NSF, Health and Human Services, FDA, U.S. Army, USPH Ctr. Disease Control. Mem. Am. Chem. Soc., Am. Diabetic Assn., Am. Inst. Nutrition, Inst. Food Technologists (exec. com. nutrition div. 1981-83, scholarship com. 1981-83), Sigma Xi (pres. U. R.I. chpt. 1975), Phi Kappa Phi (v.p. U. R.I. chpt. 1984-85, pres. 1985-86). Current work: Aquaculture nutrition, geriatric nutrition, food safety and regulation, food preservation, mega-nutrition effects, nutritional assessment and synthetic foods. Home: 15 Blueberry Dr East Greenwich RI 02818 Office: U RI Dept Food Sci and Nutrition Kingston RI 02881

DYNKIN, EUGENE B. (EVGENII BORISOVICH), mathematics educator; b. Leningrad, USSR, May 11, 1924; came to U.S., 1977, naturalized, 1983; s. Boris and Rebekka (Sheindlin) D.; m. Irene Pakshrer, June 2, 1959; 1 child, Olga. B.A., Moscow U., 1945, Ph.D., 1948, D.Physics and Math., 1951. Asst. prof. Moscow U., 1948-49, assoc. prof., 1949-54, prof., 1954-68; sr. research scholar Central Inst. for Math. and Econs., Acad. Sci. USSR, 1968-76; vis. prof. Weizmann Inst. Sci., Rehovot, Israel, 1976; prof. dept. math. Cornell U., Ithaca, N.Y., 1977—. Author books including: Theory of Markov Processes, 1960; Markov Processes, Vols. 1 and 2, 1965. Contbr. articles to profl. jours. Fellow Am. Acad. Arts and Scis., Inst. Math. Stats.; mem. Nat. Acad. Scis., Am. Math. Soc., Bernoulli Soc. for Math. Stats. and Probability. Current work: Stochastic processes, especially Markov processes; applications to economics and to physics, and to optimal control. Subspecialties: Probability; Algebra and number theory. Home: 107 Lake St Ithaca NY 14850 Office: Dept Math Cornell U Ithaca NY 14853

DYOTT, RICHARD BURNABY, electrical engineer, researcher; b. Tientsin, China, June 19, 1924; came to Eng., 1936; came to U.S., 1979; s. Hugh Felton and Winifred Okell (Weaver) D.; m. Jean Margaret Butler, Oct. 18, 1952; children—Rosemary Jane, Penelope Anne, Caroline Mary. B.Sc. in Engring., U. London, 1949, D. Sc., 1985. Research engr. Gen. Electric Co., London, 1949-67; sect. leader Brit. Telecom Research, London, 1967-75; research fellow Imperial Coll., London U., 1975-79; mgr. optical fiber research and devel. Andrew Corp., Chgo., 1979—. Contbr. numerous papers to profl. publs. Patentee in field. Fellow Instn. Elec. Engrs. (Electronics award 1979); mem. IEEE, Optical Soc. Am. Current work: Optical fiber sensors; polarization holding fiber and fiber components. Subspecialty: Fiber optics. Office: Andrew Corp 10500 W 153d St Orland Park IL 60462

DYSON, FREEMAN JOHN, physicist; b. Crowthorne, Eng., Dec. 15, 1923; s. George and Mildred Lucy (Atkey) D.; m. Verena Haefeli-Huber, Aug. 11, 1950 (div. 1958); children—Esther, George; m. Imme Jung, Nov. 21, 1958; children—Dorothy, Emily, Miriam, Rebecca. B.A., Cambridge U., 1945. Operations research R.A.F. Bomber Command, 1943-45; fellow Trinity Coll., Cambridge U., Eng., 1946-49; Commonwealth fellow Cornell U., Princeton, 1947-49; prof. physics Cornell U., 1951-53; prof. Inst. Advanced Study, Princeton, 1953—. Author: Disturbing the Universe, 1979; Weapons and Hope, 1984. Recipient Lorentz medal Royal Netherlands Acad. Scis., 1966; Hughes medal Royal Soc., 1968; Max Planck medal German Phys. Soc., 1969; Harvey prize Israel Inst. Tech., 1977; Wolf prize, 1981. Fellow Royal Soc. London; mem. Am. Phys. Soc., Nat. Acad. Scis. Current work: Quantum field theory, statistical mechanics. Subspecialty: Theoretical physics. Office: Inst Advanced Study Princeton NJ 08540

DZIEWONSKI, ADAM MARIAN, geology educator; b. Lwow, Poland, Nov. 15, 1936. M.S., U. Warsaw, 1960; Dr. Tech. Sci. in Applied Geology, Acad. Mining and Metallurgy-Krakow, 1965. Research asst. seismology Inst. Geophys., Polish Acad. Sci., 1961-65, research assoc., 1965, S.W. Center Advanced Studies, 1965-69; asst. prof. geophysics U. Tex.-Dallas, 1969-71; assoc. prof. geophysics, assoc. Ctr. Earth and Planetary Physics, Harvard U., Cambridge, Mass., 1972-76; prof. geology, mem. Center Earth and Planetary Physics, Harvard U., 1976—; chmn. dept. geol. sci. Harvard U., 1982—; Disting. Fairchild Scholar Calif. Inst. Tech., 1983-84; mem. Polish Sci. del., N. Vietnam, 1958-59. Mem. Seismology Soc. Am., Am. Geophys. Union, Soc. Exploration Geophysicists, AAAS. Subspecialty: Geophysics. Office: Dept Geol Scis Harvard U Cambridge MA 02138*

EADES, JOHN ALWYN, physicist; b. Ashbourne, Eng., Dec. 27, 1939, came to U.S., 1981; s. Rafael Alwyn and Winifred Elizabeth (Woolley) E. B.A., Trinity Coll., U. Cambridge, Eng., 1962, Ph.D., Cavendish Lab., 1967. Investigator dept. physics U. de Chile, Santiago, 1967-73; research assoc. dept. physics U. Bristol, Eng., 1974-76, lectr., 1977-81; prin. research scientist Materials Research Lab., U. Ill., Urbana, 1981—. Mem. Amnesty Internat. Fellow Royal Microscopical Soc.; mem. Inst. Physics, Soc. Latino Americano de Microscopia Electronica. Current work: Electron microscopy; electron diffraction; crystallography; instrumentation. Subspecialties: Condensed matter physics; Materials. Office: Materials Research Lab 104 S Goodwin Urbana IL 61801

EAGAR, ROBERT GOULDMAN, JR., chemist; b. Richmond, Va., Feb. 12, 1947; s. Robert Gouldman and Virginia Louise (Smith) E.; m. Miriam Joan Oberstein, Sept. 2, 1973; children—Robyn Elizabeth, Kristine Virginia. B.Sc., Va. Poly. Inst., 1969; Ph.D., Calif. Inst. Tech., 1974. Research fellow Calif. Inst. Tech., Pasadena, 1974-75; sr. chemist Union Carbide Corp., Tarrytown, N.Y., 1975-79, project chemist, 1980-82, group leader, 1982—. Patentee Mildewcidal Silane Compounds, Pentachlorophenyl Propyl Ether. Mem. Am. Chem., Soc., Am. Soc. for Microbiology, Soc. for Cosmetic Chemists, AAAS. Current work: Research programs for microbiocides and cosmetic chem. Subspecialties: Organic chemistry; Microbiology. Home: 57 Muirfield Ln Bridgewater NJ 08807 Office: Union Carbide Corp Spl Chem Div PO Box 670 Bound Brook NJ 08805

EAGLESON, PETER STURGES, educator, hydrologist; b. Phila., Feb. 27, 1928; s. William Boal and Helen (Sturges) E.; m. Marguerite Anne Partridge, May 28, 1949 (div.); children: Helen Marie, Peter Sturges, Jeffrey Partridge; m. Beverly Grossmann Rich, Dec. 27, 1974. B.S. in Civil Engring, Lehigh U., 1949, M.S., 1952; Sc.D., MIT, 1956. Jr. engr. George B. Mebus (cons. engr.), Glenside, Pa., 1950-51; teaching asst. Lehigh U., 1951-52; research asst. Mass. Inst. Tech., 1952-54; mem. faculty MIT, 1954—, prof. civil engring., 1965—, Edmund K. Turner prof., 1984—, head dept. civil engring., 1970-75; vis. assoc. Calif. Inst. Tech., 1975-76; Fulbright sr. research scholar Commonwealth Sci. and Indsl. Research Orgn., Canberra, Australia, 1966-67. Author: (with others) Estuary and Coastline Hydrodynamics, 1966, Dynamic Hydrology, 1970. Served to 2d lt. C.E. AUS, 1949-50. Recipient Desmond Fitzgerald medal, 1959, Clemens Herschel prize, 1965 (both Boston Soc. Civil Engrs.); research prize 1963. Fellow Am. Geophys. Union (Robert E. Horton award 1979); mem. Nat. Acad. Engring., ASCE. Current Work: Interrelationships of climate, soil and vegetation. Subspecialty: Hydrology. Office: Dept Civil Engring Room 48-335 Mass Inst Tech Cambridge MA 02139

EAGLETON, LEE CHANDLER, chemical engineer, educator; b. Vallejo, Calif., July 27, 1923; s. William L. and Mary Louise (Chandler) E.; m. Mary E. Stewart, Feb. 21, 1953; children: James C., William L., Elizabeth L. S.B., MIT, 1946, S.M., 1947; D.Eng., Yale U., 1950. Research asso. Columbia U., 1950-51; devel. engr. Rohm & Haas Co., Phila., 1951-56; lectr. Drexel Inst. Tech., 1954; lectr. U. Pa., Phila., 1954-55, asso. prof., 1956-65, prof., 1966-69; prof. head dept. chem. engring. Pa. State U., 1970—; cons. Rohm & Haas, 1956-74, Inst. for Def. Analyses, 1961-63, Martin Marietta Co., 1970-72, 74. Served with AUS, 1942-46. Fellow Am. Inst. Chem. Engrs. (dir. 1980-82); mem. Am. Soc. Engring. Edn. (chmn. chem. engring. div. 1970-71), Am. Chem. Soc., AAUP. Subspecialty: Chemical engineering. Home: 445 Cricklewood Dr State College PA 16801 Office: 160 Fenske Lab Pa State U University Park PA 16802

EAGON, ROBERT GARFIELD, microbiology educator; b. Salesville, Ohio, Oct. 29, 1927; m. Margretta Isabel Buchanan, Aug. 30, 1952; 1 dau., Victoria Margretta. B.Sc., Ohio State U., 1951, M.Sc., 1952, Ph.D., 1954. Fulbright scholar Pasteur Inst., Paris, 1954-55; asst. prof. microbiology U. Ga., Athens, 1955-59, assoc. prof., 1959-66, prof., 1966—. Contbr. chpts. to books, articles to profl. jours. Served to col. U.S. Army. Recipient M.G. Michael award U. Ga., 1962. Fellow Am. Acad. Microbiology; mem. Am. Soc. Microbiology (P.R. Edwards award S.E. br. 1976), Soc. Indsl. Microbiology, AAAS. Current Work: Structure and function of the bacterial cell envelope; mechanisms and bioenergetics of solute transport in the bacterial cell; mechanisms of bacterial antibiotic susceptibility and resistance. Subspecialties: Microbiology; Biochemistry (biology). Office: Dept Microbiology U Ga Athens GA 30602

EAMES, DAVID ROBSON, plasma physicist; b. Detroit, July 15, 1952; s. Robson MacDonald and Jane Bell (Brunton) E. B.S. with honors in Math., U. Mich., 1974, B.S.E. in Physics, 1974, B.S.E. in Elec. Engring, 1974; Ph.D. in Plasma Physics, Princeton U., 1981. Research asst. Princeton Plasma Physics Lab., 1975-80; sr. scientist GA Technologies, San Diego, Calif., 1981—. Recipient NSF grad. fellowship award, 1975-78. Mem. Am. Phys. Soc. Clubs: San Diego Orienteering, San Diego Table Tennis. Current Work: Plasma physics of tokamaks; laser-induced fluorescence diagnostics on the Doublet III Tokamak. Subspecialty: Plasma physics. Home: 5710 Ferber St San Diego CA 92122 Office: GA Technologies PO Box 85608 San Diego CA 92138

EANES, EDWARD DAVID, research chemist; b. Rochester, N.Y., Sept. 2, 1934; s. Edward Wilbur and Harriet Lura (Briggs) E.; m. Beverly Elaine Kinsman, Aug. 19, 1961; children—Mark David, Donna Ruth. B.S., Coll. William and Mary, 1957; M.A., Johns Hopkins U., 1959, Ph.D., 1961. Commd. officer USPHS, Bethesda, Md., 1961-63; asst. prof. phys. chemistry Cornell U. Med. Coll., N.Y.C., 1963-67; assoc. scientist Hosp. Spl. Surgery, N.Y.C., 1963-67; chief skeletal biophysics sect. Nat. Inst. Dental Research, Bethesda, 1967—. Author numerous research articles, revs., book chpts. Recipient Dir.'s award NIH, 1978. Fellow AAAS; mem. Internat. Assn. Dental Research (Biol. Mineralization award 1983), Am. Chem. Soc., Am. Crystallographic Assn., Sigma Xi, Phi Beta Kappa, Phi Lambda Upsilon. Democrat. Methodist. Current work: Chemical and physical characterization of mineral phases in skeletal tissues; dynamics of calcium phosphate formation in aqueous solutions; mechanisms of biological calcification. Subspecialties: Biophysical chemistry; Inorganic chemistry. Home: 5404 Alta Vista Rd Bethesda MD 20814 Office: Bldg 30 Room 106 Nat Inst Dental Research Bethesda MD 20892

EARHART, CHARLES FRANKLIN, JR., microbiologist, educator; b. Melrose Park, Ill., Oct. 26, 1941; s. Charles Franklin and Katherine Anne (Laho) E. B.A., Knox Coll., 1962; Ph.D., Purdue U., 1967. Assoc. prof. dept. microbiology U. Tex., Austin, 1977-83, prof. microbiology, 1983—. Editorial bd.: Jour. Bacteriology. Mem. Am. Soc. Microbiology, Genetics Soc. Am., Sigma Xi, Phi Lambda Upsilon. Current Work: Microbial iron assimilation Escherichia coli, siderophores, outer membrane. Subspecialties: Microbiology; Membrane biology.

EARL, BOYD LOREL, chemist, educator, researcher; b. Burley, Idaho, Aug. 17, 1944; s. Boyd W. and Alismae (Melton) E.; m. Judy Mathewson Nye, June 1, 1980. B.S. in Chemistry, U. Idaho, 1966; M.S. in Phys. Chemistry (NSF fellow), U. Calif., Berkeley, 1969, Ph.D. in Phys. Chemistry, 1973. Postdoctoral fellow CUNY, 1973-76; asst. prof. Bklyn. Coll., CUNY, 1973-74, adj. asst. prof., 1974-75; asst. prof. chemistry U. Nev., 1976-81, assoc. prof., 1981—. Contbr. articles to profl. jours. Mem. Am. Chem. Soc., AAAS, Sigma Xi. Current Work: Carbon dioxide laser induced chemical reactions. Subspecialties: Laser photochemistry; Laser-induced chemistry. Office: Dept Chemistry U Nev Las Vegas NV 89154

EARLE, ALVIN MATHEWS, anatomist, neuroanatomy educator, researcher; b. Topeka, Mar. 20, 1931; s. Alvin Mathews Earle and Millie Rae (Nelson) Krueger; m. Adah Marie Corson, Sept. 12, 1954; children—David Jeffrey, Lisa Marie, Daniel Steven. A.S., Wright Jr. Coll., 1950; B.S., Loyola U., Chgo., 1954; M.S., U. Colo., 1958, Ph.D., 1962. Chmn. dept. biology Regis. Coll., Denver, 1960-66; NIH postdoctoral fellow U. Kans. Med. Ctr., Kansas City, 1966-68; prof. anatomy U. Nebr. Med. Ctr., Omaha, 1968—. Author: Neuroanatomy Review, 1977; contbr. articles to profl. jours. Bd. dirs. Prairie Lane Assn., Omaha, 1976—; scoutmaster, Explorer advisor Mid-Am. Council Boy Scouts Am., Omaha, 1968—. Served to capt. USNR, 1951—. Recipient Golden Apple award, freshman med. class U. Nebr., 1980, 83, 84, Disting. Teaching award Coll. Medicine U. Nebr., 1982; NIH predoctoral research fellow, 1959-60. Mem. Am. Assn. Antomists, Soc. Neurosci., Cajal Club, Sigma Xi. Republican. Episcopalian. Current work: Experimental neuroanatomy and neurophysiology. Subspecialty: Neurobiology. Home: 3610 S 119th St Omaha NE 68144 Office: U Nebr Med Ctr 42d and Dewey Omaha NE 68105

EARLE, SYLVIA ALICE, oceanographer; b. Gibbstown, N.J., Aug. 30, 1935; d. Lewis Reade and Alice Freas (Richie) E. B.S., Fla. State U., 1955; M.A., Duke U., 1956, Ph.D., 1966. Resident dir. Cape Haze Marine Lab., Sarasota, Fla., 1966-67; research scholar Radcliffe Inst., 1967-69; research fellow Farlow Herbarium Harvard U., 1967-75, research assoc., 1975—; research assoc. botany Natural History Mus. Los Angeles County, 1970-75; research biologist, curator Calif. Acad. Scis., San Francisco, 1976—; research assoc. U. Calif., Berkeley, 1969—; v.p., sec.-treas. Deep Ocean Tech., Inc., Oakland, Calif. Author: Exploring the Deep Frontier, 1980; editor: Scientific Results of the Textite II Project, 1972-75; contbr. articles to profl. jours. V.p., sec.-treas. Deep Ocean Engring., Oakland, 19782—; trustee World Wildlife Fund U.S., World Wildlife Fund Internat., Charles A. Lindbergh Fund, Ocean Trust Found.; council mem. Internat. Union Conservation Nature; corp. mem. Woods Hole Oceanographic Inst.; mem. Nat. Adv. Com. Oceans and Atmosphere. Recipient Conservation Service award U.S. Dept. Interior, 1970; recipient Boston Sea Rovers award, 1972, 79, Nogi award Underwater Soc. Am., 1976, Conservation service award Calif. Acad. Sci., 1979, Lowell Thomas award Explorer's Club, 1980, Order of Golden Ark Prince Netherlands, 1980; named Woman of Year Los Angeles Times, 1970, Scientist of Year Calif. Mus. Sci. and Industry, 1981. Fellow Marine Tech. Soc.; mem. Internat. Phycological Soc. (sec. 1974-80), Phycological Soc. Am., Am. Soc. Ichthyologists and Herpetologists, Am. Inst. Biol. Scis., AAAS, Brit. Phycological Soc., Marine Tech. Soc., Ecol. Soc. Am., Internat. Soc. Plant Taxonomists. Current Work: Ecology and distribution of marine plants; deepwater ecology; marine mammal behavior; development and use of technology for ocean exploration andwork; conservation of natural resources, management of Rand D and operations companies for ocean technology. Subspecialties: Ecology (environmental science); Deep-sea biology. Office: Calif Acad Scis Golden Gate Park San Francisco CA 94118

EARLEY, JOSEPH EMMET, chemist, educator; b. Providence, Apr. 6, 1932; s. Daniel McGlynn and Margaret T. (Doran) E.; m. Shirley Ann Titus, June 23, 1956; children: Thomas D., David G., Joseph Emmett. B.S., Providence Coll., 1954; Ph.D., Brown U., 1957. Faculty U. Chgo., 1958; faculty Georgetown U., Washington, 1958—, prof. chemistry, 1969—, chmn. dept., 1984—; vis. faculty Calif. Inst. Tech., 1968-69, Free U. Brussels, 1976; coordinator chemistry and atmospheric scis. research evaluation U.S. Air Force Office Sci. Research. Author articles, chpts. in books, revs. Served to 1st lt. U.S. Army, 1958. Recipient Potter prize Brown U., 1958. Mem. Am. Chem. Soc., AAAS. Democrat. Roman Catholic. Lodge: KC. Current Work: Solution-phase redox reactions involving ruthenium and titanium compounds. Subspecialties: Inorganic chemistry; Kinetics. Home: 2348 Greenwich St Falls Church VA 22046 Office: Reiss Sci Ctr Georgetown U Washington DC 20057

EARLY, JAMES MICHAEL, semiconductor company executive; b. Syracuse, N.Y., July 25, 1922; s. Frank J. and Rhoda Gray E.; m. Mary Agnes Valentine, Dec. 28, 1948; children—Mary, Kathleen, Joan Early Farrell, Rhoda Early Alexander, Maureen Early Mathews, James, Margaret Mary. B.S., N.Y. Coll. Forestry, Syracuse, N.Y., 1943; M.S., Ohio State U., 1948, Ph.D., 1951. Instr., research asso. Ohio State U., Columbus, 1946-51; dir. lab. Bell Telephone Labs., Murray Hill, N.J., 1951-64, Allentown, Pa., 1964-69; research and devel. dir. Fairchild Camera and Instrument Corp., Palo Alto, Calif., 1969—. Served with U.S. Army, 1943-45. Fellow IEEE (recipient J.J. Ebers award IEEE Electron Device Soc. 1979); mem. AAAS, Am. Phys. Soc., Electrochem. Soc., Internat. Platform Assn. Roman Catholic. Club: Palo Alto (Calif.) Yacht. Current Work: Direct development of VLSI (very large scale integration)technology. Subspecialties: Microchip technology (engineering); Microelectronics. Home: 740 Center Dr Palo Alto CA 94301 Office: 4001 Miranda Ave Palo Alto CA 94304

EASTER, STEPHEN SHERMAN, JR., biology educator; b. New Orleans, Feb. 12, 1938; s. Stephen Sherman and Myrtle Olivia (Bekkedahl) E.; m. Janine Eliane Piot, June 4, 1963; children: Michele, Kim. B.S., Yale U., 1960; postgrad., Harvard U., 1961; Ph.D., Johns Hopkins U., 1966. Postdoctoral fellow Cambridge (Eng.) U., 1967, U. Calif., Berkeley, 1968-69; asst. prof. biology U. Mich., Ann Arbor, 1970-74, assoc. prof., 1974-78, prof., 1978—. Editor: Vision Research, 1978—. Mem. Soc. Neuroscience, Assn. Research in Vision and Ophthalmology. Subspecialties: Neurobiology; Regeneration. Home: 2204 Brockman Blvd Ann Arbor MI 48104 Office: Division Biological Sciences University of Michigan 2109 Natural Science Bldg Ann Arbor MI 48109

EASTMAN, MICHAEL PAUL, chemistry educator, researcher; b. Lancaster, Wis., Apr. 14, 1941; s. LeRoy Irons and Virginia Marie (Anderson) E.; m. Frances Rose Barto, Oct. 24, 1963; children: Michael E., Nathanial L.; m. Carol Oden Eastman, Aug. 23, 1980. B.A., Carleton Coll., 1963; Ph.D., Cornell U., 1968. Fellow Los Alamos Nat. Lab., 1968-70; asst. prof. U. Tex., 1970-74, assoc. prof., 1974-80, prof. chemistry, 1980—, asst. dean sci., 1981-84, asst. v.p., 1984—; vis. staff mem. U. Calif. Los Alamos Nat. Lab. Contbr. articles to profl. jours. Mem. Am. Chem. Soc. Current Work: Magnetic resonance and low temperature geochemistry. Subspecialties: Physical chemistry; Geochemistry. Home: 1308 Madeline St El Paso TX 79902

EASTOE, CHRISTOPHER JOHN, geoscience educator, researcher; b. Launceston, Australia, Aug. 13, 1952; came to U.S., 1982; s. Raymond Jack and Billie Margaret (Mills) E. B.S., U. Tasmania, 1972, B.S. with honors, 1973, Ph.D., 1979. Cons., Geol. Soc. Australia, Hobart, Tasmania, 1979; contract geologist Getty Oil Devel. Co., Queenstown, Tasmania, 1980-82; asst. prof. geosci. U. Ariz., Tucson, 1982—. Contbr. articles to profl. jours. Mem. Soc. Econ. Geologists, Geol. Soc. Am., Geol Soc. Australia, Ariz. Geol. Soc., Can. Inst. Mining and Metallurgy. Anglican. Current work: Hydrothermal deposits, especially massive sulfides and porphyrytype, application of stable isotopes and fluid inclusions. Subspecialties: Geology; Geochemistry. Office: Dept Geoscis U Ariz Tucson AZ 85721

EASTON, MYRIAM PERDICES, research scientist; b. Havana, Cuba, Nov. 29, 1949; came to U.S., 1970, naturalized, 1974; d. Rafael and Isabel (Acaba) P.; m. N. Roy Easton, Jr., Dec. 9, 1972; 1 child, Elizabeth Anne. B.A., Mt. St. Mary's Coll., 1972; M.S., UCLA, 1976. Research asst. UCLA, 1975-77; assoc. tech. staff Aerospace Corp, El Segundo, Calif., 1977-80, staff research scientist, Los Angeles, 1980—. Mem. Am. Chem. Soc. Current work: Environmental science, chemistry of industrial hazardous waste disposal. Subspecialties: Environmental chemistry; Analytical chemistry. Office: Aerospace Corps (M2-275) PO Box 92957 Los Angeles CA 90009

EATON, BARBARA RUTH, biochemist; b. Somerville, Mass., Aug. 14, 1928; d. Laurence Clifford and Josephine H. (Connell) E. A.B., Emmanuel Coll., Boston, 1950; M.S., Cath. U. Am., Washington, 1963; Ph.D., U. Calif., San Diego, 1975. Tchr. high sch. sci., sci. supr., Boston, 1953-66; instr. dept. chemistry Emmanuel Coll., Boston, 1966-76, asst. prof., 1976-80, assoc. prof. biochemistry, 1980—. Mem. Sisters of Notre Dame de Namur, Boston province, 1950—. USPHS intern, 1970-75; NSF fellow, 1960-63. Mem. Am. Chem. Soc., New Eng. Assn. Chemistry Tchrs., Hastings Center, Sigma Xi. Democrat. Roman Catholic. Current Work: Characterization and kinetics of phospholipases. Subspecialties: Biochemistry (medicine); Membrane biology. Office: Chemistry Dept Emmanuel Coll Boston MA 02115

EATON, DAVID FIELDER, chemist; b. Peterborough, N.H., Oct. 4, 1946; s. David Church and Ruth (Fielder) E.; m. Carroll Price, Oct. 5, 1974. A.B.,

Wesleyan U., 1968; Ph.D., Calif. Inst. Tech., 1972. Research fellow U. Calif.-San Diego, La Jolla, 1972-73; mem. research staff central research dept. DuPont, Wilmington, Del., 1973-79, sr. research chemist photo product dept., 19790-80, group leader central research dept., 1980-81, research supr., 1982—. Contbr. articles to profl. jours.; patentee in field. Mem. Inter-Am. Photochem. Soc., Soc. for Photog. Scientists and Engrs., Am. Chem. Soc., Internat. Union of Pure and Applied Chemistry Commn. on Photochemistry. Current work: Photoimaging chemistry; dynamics of excited state processes. Subspecialty: Photochemistry. Office: EI DuPont de Nemours Co Central Research and Devel Dept Exptl Station Wilmington DE 19898

EATON, DAVID J., environmental sciences educator; b. Detroit, Dec. 18, 1949; s. Joseph W. and Helen F. E. A.B., Oberlin Coll., 1971; M.P.W., U. Pitts., 1972, M.Sc., 1972; Ph.D., Johns Hopkins U., 1977. Asst. prof. environ. systems LBJ Sch. Pub. Affairs, U. Tex., Austin, 1976-80, assoc. prof., 1980-85, prof., 1985—. Author: A Systems Analysis of Grain Reserves, 1980; contbr. articles to profl. jours. Fulbright fellow, 1981-82; Lady Davis fellow, 1982. Current Work: Applications of systems analysis to natural resources. Subspecialties: Water supply and wastewater treatment; Operations research (engineering). Office: LBJ Sch Public Affairs U Tex Austin TX 78712

EATON, GARETH RICHARD, chemist, educator; b. Lockport, N.Y., Nov. 3, 1940; s. Mark Dutcher and Ruth Emma (Ruston) E.; m. Sandra Y. Shaw, Mar. 29, 1969. B.A., Harvard U., 1962; Ph.D., M.I.T., 1972. Asst. prof. chemistry U. Denver, 1972-76, asso. prof., 1976-80, prof., 1980—, dean natural scis., 1984—. Contbr. numerous articles on chemistry to profl. jours. Served to lt. USN, 1962-67. Mem. Am. Chem. Soc., AAAS, Chem. Soc. (London), Internat. Soc. for Magnetic Resonance, Soc. Applied Spectroscopy. Current Work: Synthetic chemistry and magnetic resonance spectroscopy. Subspecialties: Inorganic chemistry; Physical chemistry. Office: Dept Chemistry U Denver Denver CO 80208

EATON, JOHN KELLY, mechanical engineering educator, consultant; b. Camden, N.J., May 22, 1954; s. George Warren and Dorothy (Kelly) E.; m. Laura I. Jameson, June 24, 1984. B.S.M.E., Stanford U., 1976, M.S.M.E., 1977, Ph.D. in mech. Engring, 1980. Student engr. Airesearch Corp., Phoenix, 1974; mech. engr. Hewlett Packard, San Diego, 1975-76; assoc. prof. mech. engring. Stanford U., 1980—; founder, pres. GDK Engring.; dir. Bus. Computer Corp., Santa Clara, Calif.; cons. to industry. Contbr. articles to profl. jours. Recipient Silver medal Royal Soc. Arts, 1976; NSF grad. fellow, 1976-79; NSF, NASA, and Dept. Energy research grantee, 1980-85; Wheeler Found. research grantee, 1982-84; recipient Presdl. Young Investigator award, 1984. Mem. ASME, AIAA. Democrat. Current Work: Experimental studies of complex turbulent flows and convective heat transfer; particle transport in fluidized beds; computer-aided experimentation. Subspecialty: Fluid mechanics. Home: 12 Peter Coutts Circle Stanford CA 94305 Office: Dept Mechanical Engineering Stanford University Stanford CA 94305

EATON, PHILIP EUGENE, chemist. Prof. dept. chemistry, U. Chgo. Subspecialties: Organic chemistry; Synthetic chemistry. Office: U Chgo Dept Chemistry Chicago IL 60637

EAVES, REUBEN ELCO, electrical engineer; b. Balt., Jan. 20, 1944; s. Reuben Elco and Mattie Mae (Callaway) E. B.E.S., Johns Hopkins U., 1964; Sc.M., Brown U., 1966, Ph.D., 1969. Electronics engr. NASA, Cambridge, Mass., 1968-70, U.S. Dept. Transp., Cambridge, 1970-76; vis. asst. prof. Brown U., Providence, 1973-76; mem. tech. staff Lincoln Lab., MIT, Lexington, 1976-81; mgr. satellite design Communications Satellite Corp., Washington, 1981-84; dept. head advanced communications systems Mitre Corp., Bedford, Mass., 1984—. Contbr. articles to profl. jours. Inventor acoustic delay for TDMA signal storage. Fellow AIAA (assoc., tech. com. on communication systems); mem. IEEE (sr., com. on space communications), Sigma Xi, Tau Beta Pi, Eta Kappa Nu. Current work: Satellite communications, communications systems. Subspecialties: Aerospace engineering and technology; Telecommunications. Home: 987 Memorial Dr Cambridge MA 02138 Office: MITRE Corp Burlington Rd Bedford MA 01730

EBDON, DAVID WILLIAM, chemist, educator, researcher; b. Detroit, Apr. 9, 1939; s. William George and Lillian (Smith) E.; m. Priscilla Ann Ragle, June 9, 1967; children: Melanie Ann, Derek William, Deren George. B.S.Chem., U. Mich., 1961; Ph.D. in Phys. Chemistry, U. Md., 1967. Sr. research scientist Nat. Biomed. Research Found., Washington, 1967-68; lectr. U. Md., 1967-68; asst. prof. chemistry Eastern Ill. U., 1968-73, assoc. prof., 1973-80, prof., 1980—, chmn. dept. chemistry, 1977—; vis. prof. U. Okla., summers 1972, 75; research scientist U. Tex., Austin, 1978-79. Mem. Am. Chem. Soc., Royal Soc. Chemistry, Ill. State Acad. Sci. Current Work: Physical chemistry of electrolyte solutions; solution chemistry of surfactant systems; surfactant ion-selective electrodes; computer modeling of natural water systems; activity coefficients in multicomponent solutions; ion assn. equilibria; chem. oceanography. Subspecialties: Physical chemistry; Surface chemistry. Home: 2506 Salem Charleston IL 61920 Office: Dept Chemistry Eastern Ill U Charleston IL 61920

EBEL, MARVIN EMERSON, physicist, university administrator; b. Waterloo, Iowa, Sept. 23, 1930; s. Louis August and Emily (Mussett) E.; m. Barbara Ann Schuck, July 22, 1960; children—Frederick, Charles, Elizabeth, Katherine. Student Iowa State Tchrs. Coll., 1946-47; B.S., Iowa State Coll., 1950, M.S., 1952, Ph.D., 1953. NSF postdoctoral fellow Inst. Theoretical Physics, Copenhagen, 1953-54; instr., asst. prof. Yale U., New Haven, 1954-57; asst. prof. U. Wis.-Madison, 1957-59, assoc. prof., 1959-65, prof. physics, 1965—, assoc. dean grad. sch., 1976—; cons. Inst. Def. Analyses, Washington, 1962-64, Los Alamos Sci. Lab., N.Mex., 1959-73; bd. mgmt. Council Govtl. Relations, Washington, 1984—. Contbr. articles to profl. jours. Fellow Research Corp., 1952, NSF, 1953-54, Sloan Found., 1957-62. Fellow Am. Phys. Soc.; mem. AAUP, AAAS, Sigma Xi. Presbyterian. Current work: Theories of weak interactions of elementary particles; behaviour of ions traversing solids. Subspecialties: Particle physics; Theoretical physics. Home: 910 Hampshire Pl Madison WI 53711 Office: U Wis 500 Lincoln Dr Madison WI 53706

EBELING, DICK WINFIELD, consulting structural engineer; b. Portland, Oreg., July 2, 1919; s. Louis Augustus and Jessie Mae (Green) E.; m. Florence Shook, June 14, 1942; children—Ardabeth, Lois, Cheryl, Michelle. B.S. in Civil Engring., Oreg. State U., 1941, M.S. in Civil Engring., 1943. Registered profl. engr., Oreg., Wash., Idaho, Alaska, Mont., Calif., Nev., Utah, Ariz., N.Mex., Colo., Iowa, Wis., Pa., Fla., Tenn., Tex. Instr. Oreg. State U., Corvallis, 1941-43; engr. Curtis Wright Corp., 1943-44, U.S. Army Corps Engrs., 1944-46, O.C. Schoenwerk, Longview, Wash., 1946, Timber Structures, Inc., Portland, 1946-52; engr.-assoc. Cooper & Rose and Assocs., Portland, 1952-62; pres. Dick W. Ebeling, Inc., Portland, 1962—. Contbg. author: ASCE-Wood Structures, 1975, Evaluation, Maintenance and Upgrading of Wood Structures, 1982; Wood Engineering and Construction Handbook, 1986. Fellow ASCE (life); mem. Internat. Assn. Bridge and Structural Engrs., Earthquake Engring. Research Inst., Am. Concrete Inst., Am. Inst. Timber Constrn., Am. Cons. Engrs. Council, Internat. Conf. Bldg. Ofcls., Structural Engrs. Assn. Oreg. (life), Structural Engrs. Assn. No. Calif., Am. Inst. Steel Constrn., Sigma Xi. Subspecialties: Structural engineering; Civil engineering. Home: 7725 SW 82d Ave Portland OR 97223 Office: 9370 SW Greenburg Rd Portland OR 97223

EBENEZER, JOB SELVARAYAN, univ. adminstr., cons.; b. Vellore, India, Oct. 10, 1941; came to U.S., 1967; s. Titus and Kanthammal (Selvarayan) E.; m. Marjorie Rasilini Doraiswamy, July 4, 1969; children: Roshini, Suresh, Arul. M.S., U. Madras, India, 1962, Indian Inst. Sci., Bangalore, 1967; Ph.D., Stevens Inst. Tech., 1973. Asst. prof. N.Y. Inst. Tech., 1972-76; vis. asst. prof. U. N.Mex., Albuquerque, 1976-79, dir. div. energy conservation design, 1978-79; asst. dir. tech./vocat. edn. U. N.Mex. (Valencia Campus), Belen, 1981—; dir. Rural Appropriate Tech. Ctr., Madras, 1980; sr. mgr. tech. application Solar Am., Inc., Albuquerque, 1981; exec. dir. Appropriate Rural Tech. Assn., Inc., Los Lunas, N.Mex.; cons. Appropriate Tech. Internat., Washington. Contbr. articles to profl. publs. Mem. N.Mex. Solar Energy Assn., Am. Vocat. Assn., N.Mex. Vocat. Assn. Lutheran. Club: Optimists (Belen). Inventor bicycle conversion attachment for prime mover function; modifications of small-scale agrl. implements. Current Work: Third world rural technologies. Subspecialties: Solar energy; Pedal power.

EBERHARDT, ALLEN CRAIG, engineer educator; b. Cin., Aug. 30, 1950; s. Alfred John and Elfriede M. (Vollmer) E.; m. Mary Drake, June 9, 1973; children—William Craig, Laura Elizabeth. Ph.D., N.C. State U., 1977. Asst. prof. mech. engring. N.C. State U., Raleigh, 1977-81, assoc. prof., 1981—; dir. Integrated Mfg. Systems Engring. Inst., 1984—; cons. structural mechanics and acoustics. Mem. ASME, Soc. Automotive Engrs. (Teetor award 1980), Am. Soc. Engring. Educators, Acoustical Soc. Am., Sigma Xi. Current Work: Computer-aided design, robotics, signal analysis, experimental data acquisition design, acoustics, vibration, stress analysis. Subspecialties: Mechanical engineering; Solid mechanics. Office: NC State U Box 7915 Broughton Hall Raleigh NC 27695

EBERHART, ROBERT CLYDE, biomedical engineer; b. Oakland, Calif., Apr. 17, 1937; s. George Perrin and Roberta Louise (Anderson) E.; m. Carol Paulette Venel, Aug. 4, 1963; children—Charles, Robert, Annalise. B.S., Harvard U., 1959; M.S., U. Calif.-Berkeley, 1960, Ph.D., 1965. Research assoc. Inst. Med. Scis., San Francisco, 1964-70, sr. research mem., 1970-75; assoc. prof. mech. engring. U. Tex., Austin, 1975-76; assoc. prof. surgery U. Tex. Health Sci. Ctr., 1976—, chmn. biomed. engring. program U. Tex. Health Sci. Ctr., Dallas and U. Tex., Arlington, 1984—; prof. biomed. engring. U. Tex., Arlington, 1984—; cons. med. tech. industries, 1974—. Assoc. editor Jour. Biomech. Engring., 1982—, Critical Care Medicine, 1974—; editor: Heat Transfer in Medicine and Biology, 1984; contbr. articles to profl. jours.; patentee in blood compatible plastics. Grantee: NIH, Nat. Heart, Lung and Blood Inst.; Harvard Coll. scholar, 1955-59. Mem. AMSE, Am. Soc. Artificial Internal Organs, Am. Soc. Engring. Edn., IEEE, Soc. Critical Care Medicine. Republican. Club: Harvard (Dallas). Current work: Biomaterials, artifical blood vessels, biosensors, bioheat transfer; ethics in high technology medicine. Subspecialties: Biomaterials; Biomedical engineering. Office: Dept Surgery U Tex Health Sci Ctr 5323 Harry Hines Blvd Dallas TX 75235

EBERHART, ROBERT JAMES, veterinary science researcher, educator; b. Lock Haven, Pa., Sept. 9, 1930; s. Harry James Eberhart and Ruth Elinor (Moyer) Eberhart Jackson; m. Dec. 3, 1953; children—Suzanne, Andrew, Gretchen, Peter. A.B., Cornell U., 1952; V.M.D., U. Pa., 1959; M.S., Pa. State U., 1964, Ph.D., 1966. Instr. dept. vet. sci. Pa. State U., University Park, 1959-66, asst. prof., 1966-72, assoc. prof., 1972-78, prof., 1978—. Served as lt. (j.g.) USN, 1952-55. Mem. AVMA, AAAS, Am. Dairy Sci. Assn., Nat. Mastitis Council (pres. 1984-85). Republican. Current work: Epidemiology, pathogenesis and prevention of bovine mastitis. Subspecialties: Microbiology (veterinary medicine); Preventive medicine (veterinary medicine). Home: 143 Hartswick Ave State College PA 16803 Office: Pa State U Dept Vet Sci University Park PA 16802

EBERLY, WILLIAM ROBERT, biology educator; b. North Manchester, Ind., Oct. 4, 1926; s. John H. and Ollie M. (Heaston) E.; m. Eloise L. Whitehead, June 30, 1946; children—Diana Sue, Brenda Kay, Sandra Jo. B.A., Manchester Coll., 1948; M.S., Ind. U., 1955, Ph.D., 1958. Tchr. pub. schs. Wabash County, Ind., 1947-52; teaching asst. Ind. U., Bloomington, 1952-55; asst. prof. Manchester Coll., North Manchester, Ind., 1955-60, assoc. prof., 1960-67, prof., 1967—; cons. Ind. Dept. Natural Resources, Indpls., 1968, 76-82. Author: History of the Church of the Brethren in Northwest Ohio, 1982. Contbr. numerous articles to jours. Mem. Ind. Pesticide Rev. Bd., Indpls., 1971-83. Named Sagamore of Wabash, Gov. of Ind., 1983. Fellow Ind. Acad. Sci. (editor 1965-69, pres. 1982); mem. Am. Soc. Limnology and Oceanography, Internat. Soc. Limnology, Am. Inst. Biol. Scis. Republican. Mem. Ch. of Brethren. Current work: Acid precipitation; water quality; environmental education. Subspecialties: Ecology (environmental science); Limnology. Home: 304 Sunset Ct North Manchester IN 46962 Office: Manchester Coll North Manchester IN 46962

EBERSTEIN, ARTHUR, biophysicist, educator; b. Chgo., Apr. 23, 1928; s. Nathan and Sara (Estes) E.; married; children—Sharon, Laura. B.S., Ill. Inst. Tech., 1950; M.S., U. Ill., 1951; Ph.D., Ohio State U., 1957. Physicist Lundy Inc., Glen Head, N.Y., 1959-61; prof., dir. research dept. rehab. medicine NYU, 1961—. Author: (with others) Electrodiagnosis of Nerve and Muscle Disease, 1983. NSF fellow, Copenhagen, 1958. Mem. Am. Physiol. Soc., Am. Assn. Electromyography and Electrodiagnosis, Am. Biophys. Soc. Jewish. Current work: Muscle physiology; electromyography; nerve regeneration. Subspecialties: Neurophysiology; Biofeedback. Office: NYU Med Ctr 400 E 34th St New York NY 10016

EBERT, JAMES DAVID, research biologist; b. Bentleyville, Pa., Dec. 11, 1921; s. Alva Charles and Anna Frances (Brundege) E.; m. Alma Christine Goodwin, Apr. 19, 1946; children—Frances Diane, David Brian, Rebecca Susan. A.B., Washington and Jefferson Coll., 1942, Sc.D., 1969; Ph.D., Johns Hopkins, 1950; Sc.D., Yale, 1973, Ind. U., 1975; LL.D., Moravian Coll., 1979. Jr. instr. biology Johns Hopkins, 1946-49, Adam T. Bruce fellow biology, 1949-50, hon. prof. biology, 1956—, hon. prof. embryology, 1956—; instr. biology Mass. Inst. Tech., 1950-51; asst. prof. zoology Ind. U., 1951-54, asso. prof., 1954-56, Patten vis. prof., 1963; dir. dept. embryology Carnegie Instn. of Washington, 1956-76, pres., 1978—; vis. scientist med. dept. Brookhaven Nat. Lab., 1953-54; Philips vis. prof. Haverford Coll., 1961; instr. in charge embryology tng. program Marine Biol. Lab., summers 1962-66, trustee, 1964—, pres., 1970-78, dir., 1970-75, 77-78; mem. Commn. on Undergrad. Edn. in Biol. Scis., 1963-66; mem. vis. com. for biol. and phys. scis. Western Res. U., 1964-68; Mem. panels on morphogenesis and biology of neoplasia of com. on growth NRC, 1954-56; mem. adv. panel on genetic and developmental biology NSF, 1955-56, mem. divisional com. for biology and medicine, 1962-66, mem. univ. sci. devel. panel, 1965-70, adv. com. for instl. devel., 1970-72; mem. panel basic biol. research in aging Am. Inst. Biol. Sci., 1957-60; mem. panel on cell biology NIH, USPHS, 1958-62, mem. child health and human devel. tng. com., 1963-66; mem. bd. sci. counselors Nat. Cancer, Inst., 1967-71, Nat. Inst. Child Health, 1973-77; mem. Com. on Scholarly Communication with People's Republic of China, 1978-81; mem. vis. com. to dept. biology Mass. Inst. Tech., 1959-68; mem. vis. com. biology Harvard, 1969-75, Princeton, 1970-76; chmn. bd. sci. overseers Jackson Lab., 1976-80; mem. Inst. Medicine. Author: (with others) The Chick Embryo in Biological Research, 1952, Molecular Events in Differentiation Related to Specificity of Cell Type, 1955, Aspects of Synthesis and Order in Growth, 1955, Interacting Systems in Development, 2d edit, 1970, Biology, 1973, Mechanisms of Cell Change, 1979; Mem. editorial bd.: Abstracts of Human Developmental Biology; editor: Oceanus; Contbr. articles to profl. jours. Trustee Jackson Lab. Served as lt. USNR, 1942-46. Decorated Purple Heart. Fellow AAAS (v.p. med. scis. 1964), Am. Acad. Arts and Scis., Internat. Soc. Developmental Biology; mem. Nat. Acad. Scis. (chmn. assembley life scis. 1973-77, v.p. 1981—), Am Philos. Soc. Royal Soc. Medicine London (affiliate), Am. Inst. Biol. Scis. (pres. 1963, Pres.'s medal 1972), Am. Soc. Naturalists, Am. Soc. Zoologists (pres. 1970), Soc. Study Growth and Devel. (pres. 1957-58). Phi Beta Kappa, Sigma Xi, Phi Sigma. Subspecialties: Developmental biology; Immunobiology and immunology. Home: 2101 Connecticut Ave NW Washington DC 20008 Office: Carnegie Instn 1530 P St NW Washington DC 20005

EBERT, MARLIN J., business executive, nuclear engineering consultant; b. Bryn Athyn, Pa., Dec. 2, 1938; s. Stanley F. and Sarah Jane (Heilman) E.; m. Linda Brinsley, Jan. 28, 1961 (div. 1970); children: Winfrey, Nina, Benjamin; m. Norma Jean Smith, Ja. 23, 1982. B.S., Pa. State U., 1961, M.Sc., 1963. Registered profl. nuclearengr., Calif. Research engr. Nuclear Materials and Equipment Corp. Atlantic Richfield Corp., Apllo, Pa., 1968-70; sr. mktg. engr. Gen. Elec. Nuclear Corp., Pleasanton, Calif., 1970-76; pres. Life Science Systems, Inc., Livermore, Calif., 1976—; gen. mgr. Livermore Engring., Inc., 1976—; cons. U.S. Navy, 1978-81, U.S. Army, 1972—. Bd. dirs. Water Mgmt. Agy., 1978-80; mem. Livermore City Council, 1978-82. Served to capt., C.E. U.S. Army, 1961-68, Vietnam. NDEA fellow, 1961-63; decorated Bronze Star, Air medal. Mem. Soc. Nuclear Medicine, Am. Nuclear Soc. Republican. Lodge: Masons. Developer toxic material nuclear anti-contamination kit, 1978; co-developer Xenon-133 ventilation study system, 1974. Current Work: Toxic material personal anticontamination; nuclear biological chemical warfare protection; medical and industrial application of radionuclides; wastewater irradiation. Subspecialties: Nuclear medicine; Nuclear engineering. Home: 1182 Burgundy Way Livermore CA 94550 Office: 4049 1st St Livermore CA 94550

EBERT, PAUL STOUDT, biochemist; b. Palmerton, Pa., Apr. 13, 1933; s. Paul F. and Ellen S. (Stoudt) E.; m. Linda P. Romig, Nov. 26, 1964; children: Robert, Mindy. B.S., Pa. State U., 1955; Ph.D., Rutgers U., 1962. Chemist Merck & Co., Rahway, N.J., 1955-57; research asst. Rutgers U., New Brunswick, N.J., 1957-61; postdoctoral fellow U. Pa., Phila., 1961-65; research chemist Lab. Molecular Oncology, Div. Cancer Etiology, Nat. Cancer Inst., NIH, Bethesda, Md., 1965—. Contbr. numerous sci. articles to profl. publs. Deacon 4th Presbyterian Ch., Bethesda, 1978-81. Muscular Dystrophy Assn. grantee, 1964-65. Mem. Am. Assn. Cancer Research, N.Y. Acad. Scis., Sigma Xi. Current Work: Control mechanisms in erythropoiesis; pharmacology of heme pathway inhibitor, succinylacetone; mechanism of photoinactivation of tumor cells with hematoporphyrin; mechanisms of cell transformation. Subspecialties: Cancer research (medicine); Cell study oncology. Home: 10004 Sinnott Dr Bethesda MD 20817 Office: Nat Cancer Inst Frederick Cancer Research Facility Frederick MD 21701

EBERT-FLATTAU, PAMELA, study administrator; b. Chgo., Dec. 24, 1946; d. Raymond C. and Sylvia Ann (Jones) E.; m. Edward S. Flattau, Feb. 1, 1977; children—Jeremy Paul, Victoria Celeste. B.Sc. with honors, Leeds U., 1969; M.S., U. Ga., 1972, Ph.D., 1974. AAAS-Am. Psychol. Assn. Congressional Sci. fellow U.S. Senate, 1974-75; staff officer Nat. Research Council, Washington, 1975-80, sr. staff officer, 1980-81; sci. policy analyst Sci. Indicators unit NSF, Washington, 1981-85; dir. studies on policies related to vision research, 1985—. Author: A Legislative Guide, 1980. Mem. Am. Psychol. Assn., AAAS, Assn. Advancement Psychology (trustee 1976—), Sigma Xi, Psi Chi. Current Work: Vision research, policy. Subspecialty: Behavioral psychology. Office: Nat Acad Sci/NRC JH819 2101 Constitution Ave NW Washington DC 20418

EBLE, JOHN NELSON, pathologist; b. Madison, Wis., Sept. 15, 1951; s. John Nelson and Jane Mildred (Brewer) E.; children—Nicholas, Benjamin, Elizabeth. Student, City U. London, 1969-70; B.S., Ind. U., 1973, M.D., 1976. Diplomate Am. Bd. Pathology. Resident pathologist Ind. U. Sch. Medicine, Indpls., 1977-80, asst. prof. pathology, 1980-81, asst. prof. pathology and exptl. oncology, 1981-85, assoc. prof. pathology and exptl. oncology, 1985—; chief pathologist Richard L. Roudebush VA Med. Ctr., Indpls., 1982—. Contbr. articles to profl. jours. Fellow Coll. Am. Pathologists, Am. Soc. Clin. Pathologists; mem. AMA, Internat. Acad. Pathology, Am. Soc. Microbiology. Current work: Surgical and biochemical pathology of cancer; urologic pathology, surgical pathology, metabolism of cancer, urogenital cancer. Subspecialties: Pathology (medicine); Cancer research (medicine).

EBNER, KURT EWALD, biochemistry educator, researcher; b. New Westminster, B.C., Can., Mar. 30, 1931; came to U.S., 1957; s. Sebastian Alois and Martha (Gmundner) E.; m. Dorothy Colleen Reader, May 4, 1957; children—Roger, Michael Colleen, Paul. B.S.A., U. B.C., 1955, M.S.A., 1957; Ph.D., U. Ill., 1960. Asst. prof. Okla. State U., Stillwater, 1961-64, assoc. prof., 1964-67, prof., 1967-70, regent's prof., 1970-74; prof., chmn. dept. biochemistry U. Kans. Med. Ctr., Kansas City, Kans., 1974—. Author, editor: Protein Subunits, 1975. Mem. dist. com. Boy Scouts Am., Overland Park, Kans., 1975—. Mem. Am. Chem. Soc. (Borden award in chemistry of milk 1968), Am. Soc. Biol. Chemists, AAAS. Presbyterian. Current work: Enzymology, protein structure, hormone receptors gene cloning and sequencing, protein mutagenesis. Subspecialty: Biochemistry (medicine). Home: 7210 W 101 Terr Overland Park KS 66212 Office: Dept Biochemistry U Kans Med Ctr Kansas City KS 66103

EBNER, TIMOTHY JOHN, neurophysiologist; b. Mpls., July 15, 1949; s. Leo Bud and Stella Agnus (Andryski) E.; m. Rita A. Evans, Dec. 18, 1971; children—Ezra C., Stella V., Dylan T. B.S., U. Minn., 1971, M.D., 1979, Ph.D., 1979. Jr. scientist U. Minn., Mpls., 1976-78, teaching asst., 1976-77, research specialist dept. neurosurgery, 1979, asst. prof., 1979-85, lab. dir., 1984—, assoc. prof., 1985—; neurophysiologist Mpls. VA Hosp., 1978-79. Contbr. articles to profl. jours. Recipient Hans Berger award Am. Encephalographic Soc., 1979; NIH grantee, 1982—; NSF grantee, 1984—. Mem. Am. Physiol. Soc., Soc. for Neurosci., N.Y. Acad. Scis. Current work: Research on the relationship of structure and function in the cerebellar cortex, pathophysiology of movement disorders. Home: 5308 3d Ave S Minneapolis MN 55419 Office: U Minn Dept Neurosurgery B590 Mayo 420 Delaware St SE Minneapolis MN 55455

EBY, DAVID EUGENE, geologist, researcher; b. Harrisburg, Pa., Sept. 26, 1947; s. Eugene Elwood and Ruth Dunkleburger (Crozier) E.; m. I. Marie Cooper, Aug. 1968; children—Rebecca L., Matthew A. A.B., Franklin and Marshall Coll., 1969; M.S., Brown U., 1972; Ph.D., SUNY-Stony Brook, 1977. Asst. prof. geology L.I. U., Southampton, N.Y., 1973, Franklin and Marshall Coll., Lancaster, Pa., 1973-74, U. Tex.-Dallas, Richardson, 1975-79; sr. research geologist Mobil Research & Devel. Corp., Dallas, 1979-83; staff geologist Champlin Petroleum, Englewood, Colo., 1983—; adj. asst. prof. U. Tex.-Dallas and U. Tex.-Arlington, 1979-83; thesis adviser univs., 1975-83. Co-editor: Geology of the Ft. Worth Basin, 1982; co-editor workshop: Carbonate Reservoirs of the Rocky Mountain Basins, 1985. Contbr. articles on carbonate rocks to profl. jours., 1975—. Pres., bd. dirs. Lookout Community Presch., Richardson, 1977-78. Recipient Best Tchr. award Amoco, 1978, Best Tchr. award M. P. Stephens Found., 1979; Appel scholar Franklin and Marshall Coll., 1965-69; Geol. Soc. Am. grantee-in-aid Brown U., Providence, 1972. Mem. Am. Assn. Petroleum Geologists (chmn. student chpt. com. 1984, editor, assoc. editor AAPG Bull., and co-author field trip guidebooks 1983-84), Nat. Assn. Geology Tchrs., Soc. Econ. Paleontologists and Mineralogists, Dallas Geol. Soc. (first v.p. 1981-82, Disting. Service award 1980), Rocky Mountain Assn. Geologists Democrat. Current work: Sedimentary petrology; sedimentology of carbonate rocks; petroleum geology; paleoecology and paleontology of Paleozoic and Mesozoic rocks; Precambrian geology. Subspecialties: Sedimentology; Paleontology, paleoecology. Home: 1324 E Easter Circle Littleton CO 80122 Office: Champlin Petroleum Co PO Box 1257 Englewood CO 80150

EBY, RONALD K., physics educator; b. Reading, Pa., May 7, 1929; s. H. Elmer and Ruth K. (Kraft) E.; m. Barbara L. Leacock, July 19, 1952; children—Ronald, Douglas. Sc.B. in Physics, Lafayette Coll., 1952; M.S., Brown U., 1955, Ph.D. in Physics, 1957. Physicist plastics dept. E.I. DuPont de Nemours & Co., Inc., Wilmington, Del., 1957-63; physicist polymers div. Nat. Bur. Standards, Washington, 1963-67, chief polymer physics, 1967-68, chief polymers div., 1968-84; prof. materials sci. and engring. Johns Hopkins U., Balt., 1984—; cons. U. Utah, 1984, Wash. State U., 1984, 85, U. Tenn., 1985. Assoc. editor Polymer, 1976—, Rev. Sci. Instruments, 1973-79; editor: Durability of Macromolecular Materials, 1979. Trustee Nat. Plastics Mus., Leominister, Mass., 1983—. Fellow Am. Phys. Soc. (chmn. exec. com. div. high polymer phys. 1972-73, councilor 1985—), Acoustical Soc. Am., Soc. Plastics Engrs. (bd. dirs. 1975-78, 84—); mem. ASTM (chmn. coms.), Am. Chem. Soc. (vice chmn. polymer chem. div.). Clubs: Cosmos (Washington); Hopkins (Balt.). Current work: Structure, morphology and properties of polymers; composites, physical acoustics and ultrasonic propagation. Subspecialties: Polymer physics; Acoustics. Office: Materials Sci and Engring Johns Hopkins U Baltimore MD 21218

ECCLESHALL, DONALD, physicist; b. Warrington, Eng., July 8, 1927, came to U.S., 1966, naturalized, 1972; s. Donald and Jane (Houghton) E.; m. Sylvia Mary Plant, June 10, 1957; children—Julian A., Olivia C. B.Sc. with honors, U. Liverpool, Eng., 1952, Ph.D., 1955. Research fellow U. Liverpool. Eng., 1955-56; prin. sci. officer U.K. Atomic Energy Authority, Aldermaston, 1956-66, 1967-68; research fellow U. Pa., Phila., 1966-67; supr. research physicist Ball Research Lab., Aberdeen Proving Ground, Md., 1967—. Contbr. articles to profl. jours. Recipient Research and Devel. award U.S. Army, 1978, 82. Mem. Am. Phys. Soc., Sigma Xi. Current work: Research high current particle accelerators; EM guns; radar absorbing material; refractory materials. Subspecialty: Plasma physics. Home: 1513 Charter Oak Ave Bel Air MD 21014 Office: US Army Ballistics Research Lab Aberdeen Proving Ground MD 21005

ECKARDT, MICHAEL JON, psychologist; b. Glendale, Calif., Apr. 3, 1943; s. Ralph Benjamin and Betty June (Davey) Voelker; m. Johneen Pofahl, Aug. 9, 1968; children: Shea Michael, Neil Edward, Rory Lawrence. B.A., Calif. State U.-Northridge, 1966; M.S., U. So. Calif., 1967, U. Mich., 1970; Ph.D., U. Oreg. Helath Sci. Ctr., 1975. Lic. psychologist, Md. Vice pres. J & M Enterprises, Inc., Glendale, Calif., 1963-65; lectr. U. Mich., 1970; psychologist VA Hosp., Sepulveda, Calif., 1975-76; fellow U. Calif.-Irvine, 1976; psychologist Nat. Inst. Alcohol Abuse, Bethesda, Md., 1976—. Contbr. articles to profl. jours. Trustee Bridge, A Way Across, Inc., Burbank, Calif., 1976-76; co-chmn. community services com. Cinnamon Woods, Inc., Germantown, Md., 1982-84. Recipient Outstanding Biologist award Calif. State U., 1966; Superior Service award USPHS, 1982. Fellow Md. Psychol. Assn.; mem. Am. Psychol. Assn., Soc. Neurosci., AAAS. Current Work: Investigating the acute and chronic effects of alcohol and other addictive substances on various anatomic and physiological systems. Subspecialties: Neuropsychology; Medical psychology. Home: 14013 Castaway Dr Rockville MD 20853 Office: Laboratory of Clinical Studies National Institute on Alcohol Abuse and Alcoholism Bldg 10 Room 3C-218 900 Rockville Pike Bethesda MD

ECKELMANN, GEORGE WILLIAM, See *Who's Who in America,* 43rd edition.

ECKENFELDER, W. WESLEY, chemical engineering educator; b. N.Y.C., Nov. 15, 1926; s. William Wesley and Martha Ann (Richter) E.; m. Kathleen Hurley, Nov. 17, 1974; children—Lawrence William, Janice Ann. B.C.E., Manhattan Coll., 1946; M.S., Pa. State U., 1949; M.C.E., NYU, 1954. Registered profl. engr., Tex. Assoc. prof. Manhattan Coll., N.Y.C., 1952-63; vis. prof. U. Wis.-Madison, 1963-64; prof. U. Tex. Austin, 1965-70; Disting. prof. Vanderbilt U., Nashville, 1970—; ptnr. Weston Eckenfelder & Assocs., Phila., 1952-56; pres. Hydrosci., Inc., Leonia, N.J., 1958-63; chmn. bd. Aware, Inc., Nashville, 1970-84. Author: Biological Waste Treatment, 1961; Industrial Water Pollution Control, 1967; Principles of Water Quality Management, 1980. Fellow Am. Inst. Chemists; mem. Internat. Assn. Water Pollution Research (pres. 1962-64), Am. Inst. Chem. Engrs., ASCE, Am. Chem. Soc. Republican. Current work: Water pollution control, industrial waste treatment, biological waste treatment. Subspecialties: Water supply and wastewater treatment; Environmental chemistry. Office: Ctr for Indsl Water Quality Mgmt Vanderbilt U Box 6222 Nashville TN 37235

ECKENHOFF, JAMES EDWARD, physician, educator; b. Easton, Md., Apr. 2, 1915; s. George L. and Ada (Ferguson) E.; m. Bonnie Lee Youngerman, June 4, 1938 (div. Jan. 1973); children: Edward Alvin, James Benjamin, Walter Leroy, Roderic George; m. Jane M. Mackey, Sept. 22, 1973. B.S., U. Ky., 1937; M.D., U. Pa., 1941; D.Sc., Transylvania U., 1970. Diplomate: Am. Bd. Anesthesiology (bd. dirs. 1965-73, pres. 1972-73). Intern Good Samaritan Hosp., Lexington, Ky., 1941-42; Harrison fellow anesthesia U. Pa., 1945-48; mem. faculty U. Pa. (Med. Sch. and Grad. Sch.), 1948-65, prof. anesthesiology, 1955-65; physician anesthetist Hosp. U. Pa., 1948-65; prof. anesthesia Northwestern U. Med. Sch., Chgo., 1966-85, chmn. dept., 1966-70; dean Northwestern U. Med. Sch., 1970-83; pres. McGaw Med. Center, 1980-85; fellow faculty anesthesia, also Hunterian prof. Royal Coll. Surgeons.; VA Disting. physician, 1984—; chief anesthesia Passavant Meml. Hosp., Chgo., 1966-70; chmn. anesthesia Chgo. Wesley Hosp., 1966-70; cons. VA Research Hosp., Childrens Hosp., Chgo., 1966—, surgeon gen. U.S. Navy, 1964—; Mem. surgery study sect. NIH, 1962-66, anesthesia tng. com., 1966-70; vis. prof. Australian and New Zealand Soc. Anesthetists, 1968, South African Soc. Anesthetists, 1970; dir. Nat. Bd. Med. Examiners, 1975—, treas., 1979-83. Author: (with others) Introduction to Anesthesia, 6th edit, 1982, Anesthesia from Colonial Times, 1966, also numerous articles.; Editor: (with others) Science and Practice in Anesthesia, 1965, (with J. Beal) Intensive and Recovery Room Care, 1969, Jour. Anesthesiology, 1958-62, Yearbook of Anesthesia, 1970-81, Controversy in Anesthesiology, 1979. Trustee Evanston Hosp., 1972-83, Rehab. Inst. Chgo., 1972-83, Northwestern Meml. Hosp., 1973—, Children's Meml. Hosp., 1977—, Ill. Hosp. Assn., 1983—. Served to capt. M.C. AUS, 1942-45, ETO. Commonwealth Fund fellow Queen Victoria Hosp., East Grinstead, Eng., 1961-62. Fellow Inst. Medicine Chgo., A.C.P.; mem. Australian, New Zealand, South African socs. anesthesiologists, Soc. Acad. Anesthesia Chairmen (pres. 1967-68), Soc. Med. Consultants to Armed Forces, Am. Soc. Anesthesiologists (Disting. Service award 1981, Ralph Waters award 1984), AMA, Assn. Univ. Anesthetists (pres. 1962), Inst. Medicine of Chicago (George H. Coleman medal 1985), AAUP, Ill. Council Med. Deans (pres. 1973-74), Chgo., Ill. med. socs., Am. Physicians Art Assn., Am. Physiol. Soc. Home: Stokelea 8601 N State Rd 39 La Porte IN 46350 Office: VA Lakeside Med Ctr 333 E Huron St Chicago IL 60611

ECKERT, CHARLES ALAN, chemical engineering educator; b. St. Louis, Dec. 13, 1938; married, 1961; 2 children. S.B., MIT, 1960, S.M., 1961; Ph.D. in Chem. Engring, U. Calif.-Berkeley, 1965. NATO fellow high pressure physics High Pressure Lab., Nat. Ctr. Sci. Research, Bellevue, France, 1964-65; from asst. prof. to assoc. prof. U. Ill., Urbana, 1965-73, prof. chem. engring., 1973—, head dept. chem. engring., 1980—; cons. various cos.; vis. prof. Stanford U., 1971-72. Guggenheim fellow, 1971. Mem. AIME, Am. Chem. Soc. (Ipatieff prize 1977), Am. Inst. Chem. Engrs. (Allan Colburn award 1973), Am. Soc. Engring. Edn., Nat. Acad. Engring., Chem. Soc. London. Subspecialty: Chemical engineering. Office: Dept Chem Engring 113 RAL U Ill Urbana IL 61801*

ECKERT, ERNST R. G., emeritus mechanical engineering educator; b. Prague, Czechoslovakia, Sept. 13, 1904; came to U.S., 1945, naturalized, 1955; s. Georg and Margarete (Pfrogner) E.; m. Josefine Binder, Jan. 30, 1931; children: Rosemarie Christa Eckert Koehler, Elke, Karin Eckert Winter, Dieter. Diploma Ing., German Inst. Tech., Prague, 1927, Dr.Ing., 1931; Dr. habil., Inst. Technology, Danzig, 1938; Dozent, Inst. of Technol., Braunschweig, Germany, 1940; hon. doctorates, Inst. Tech., Munich, 1968, Purdue U., 1968, U. Manchester, Eng., 1968, U. Notre Dame, 1970, Poly. Inst. Romania, Jassy, 1973. Registered profl. engr., Minn. Chief engr., lectr. Inst. Technology, Danzig, 1934-38; sect. chief thermodynamics Aero. Research Inst., Braunschweig, 1938-45; prof., dir. Inst. Technology, Prague, 1943-45; cons. USAF, 1945-49, Lewis Flight Propulsion Lab., NASA, 1949-51; prof. mech. engring. dept. U. Minn., 1951-73, dir. thermodynamics and heat transfer and of heat transfer lab., 1955-73, Regents' prof. emeritus mech. engring., 1966-73; former vis. prof. Purdue U.; cons. Gen. Electric Co.; former cons. Trane Co.; U.S. rep. aerodynamics panel Internat. Com. Flame Radiation. Author: Introduction to the Transfer of Heat and Mass, 1950, 2d edit., 1959, Heat and Mass Transfer, (translated by J.F. Gross), 1963; others in German and Russian, (with Goldstein) Measurement Techniques in Heat Transfer, 1970, 2d edit., 1976, (with Drake) Analysis of Heat and Mass Transfer, 1972; Chmn. hon. editorial adv. bd.: (with Drake) Internat. Jour. Heat and Mass Transfer; Editor: (with Drake) Thermal Sciences series, Wadsworth Pub. Co., Belmont, Cal.; editor: (with Drake) Thermo and Fluid Dynamics; co-chmn. adv. editorial bd.: (with Drake) Heat Transfer-Japanese Research; co-editor: (with Drake) Energy Developments in Japan; chmn. hon. editorial adv. bd.: (with Drake) Letters in Heat and Mass Transfer; editorial adv. bd.: (with Drake) Numerical Heat Transfer; Contbr. (with Drake) articles to sci. mags. Mem. Nat. Commn. Fire Prevention and Control, 1970-73. Recipient Max Jacob Meml. award, 1961, Distinguished Teaching award U. Minn., 1965, Western Electric Fund award, 1965, Gold medal French Inst. Energy and Fuel, 1967, Vincent Bendix award, 1972; Alexander von Humboldt U.S. Sr. Scientist award, 1980; Recipient A.V. Luikov medal, 1979; research fellow Japan Soc. Promotion Sci., 1982. Fellow N.Y. Acad. Scis., AIAA; mem. Am. Soc. Engring. Edn. (hon.), Wissenschaftliche Gesellschaft für Luft and Raumfahrt, Sigma Xi, Pi Tau Sigma, Tau Beta Pi. Current work: Heat transfer in energy production and conservation, advanced gas turbines, energy storage. Subspecialty: Mechanical engineering. Home: 60 W Wentworth Ave W St Paul MN 55118 Office: U Minn Minneapolis MN 55455

ECKERT, ROGER OTTO, educator; b. N.Y.C., Dec. 12, 1934; s. Otto and Karla Henrietta (Heims) E.; children—Kevin, Glenn, Bryan, Timothy. B.A., Atlantic Union Coll., 1956; M.A., Columbia U., 1957, Ph.D., 1961. Asst. prof. Syracuse U., N.Y., 1962-65, assoc. prof., 1965-68; research fellow Harvard U., Cambridge, Mass., 1961-62; prof. neurobiology UCLA, 1968—. Author: Animal Physiology, 1978, 2d edit. 1983. Recipient Alexander von Humbolt award, 1973; Fogarty Internat. award, 1985; Javits award, 1985. Mem. Biophys. Soc., Soc. for Neurosci., Soc. Gen. Physiologists, Am. Physiol. Soc., Am. Soc. Cell Biology. Current work: Mechanisms of function of membrane channels, especially calcium and potassium channels; regulation of ion channels by intra and extra-cellular messengers and modulators. Subspecialties: Neurobiology; Biophysics (biology). Office: Dept Biology UCLA 405 Hilgard Ave Los Angeles CA 90024

ECKHARDT, CRAIG JON, chemistry educator; b. Rapid City, S.D., June 26, 1940; s. Reuben H. and Hilda W. (Craig) E. B.A., U. Colo., 1962; M.S., Yale U., 1964, Ph.D., 1967. Asst. prof. chemistry U. Nebr., Lincoln, 1967-72, assoc. prof., 1972-78, prof., 1978—; cons. NSF, Washington, 1977-81, 3M Corp., St. Paul, 1979—. Contbr. articles to profl. jours. Fellow NSF, 1962, NIH, 1964-67, Yale U., 1967, Guggenheim Found., 1979-80. Mem. Am. Phys. Soc., Optical Soc. Am., Soc. Photog. Scientists and Engrs., Royal Soc. Chemistry, Am. Assn. Physics Tchrs. Current work: Energy transfer in solids and liquids, light scattering, piezomodulation spectroscopy, lattice dynamics, liquid crystals, organic solid state chemistry. Subspecialties: Solid state chemistry; Physical chemistry. Office: 524 Hamilton Hall Univ Nebr Lincoln NE 68588-0304

ECKHARDT, HELMUT KARL, physicist, researcher; b. Homberg, Fed. Republic Germany, Oct. 5, 1946; came to U.S., 1977; s. Kurt and Katharina (Herold) E.; m. Marie DeSimone, May 27, 1984. M.S. in Physics, U. Giessen, Fed. Republic Germany, 1973, Ph.D., 1977. Research assoc. dept. chemistry, U. Nebr., Lincoln, 1977-79; research assoc., group leader research and devel. Allied Corp., Morristown, N.J., 1979—. Contbr. articles to profl. jours. Patentee in field. Served to 1st lt. German Army, 1966-68. Mem. Am. Phys. Soc., German Phys. Soc. Current work: Materials research, conducting polymers, conjugated polymers, charge-transfer compounds. Subspecialties: Condensed matter physics; Polymers (materials science). Home: 23 Laurel Way Madison NJ 07940 Office: Allied Corp PO Box 1021R Morristown NJ 07960

ECKMAN, RICHARD RAYMOND, research chemist; b. Cleve., June 10, 1952; s. Donald Preston Eckman and Jeanette (Putman) Eckman Tuve; children—Noadiah Shanti, Nathan Preston. B.S., Southeastern Mass. U., 1976; Ph.D., U. Calif.-Berkeley, 1982. Teaching asst. U. Calif.-Berkeley, 1976-78; research asst. Lawrence Berkeley Lab., Calif., 1978-82; vis. sci. DuPont Central Research, Wilmington, Del., 1982-83; research chemist Exxon Chem. Co., Baytown, Tex., 1983—. Contbr. articles to profl. jours. Mem. Am. Chem. Soc. Current work: Development novel techniques for NMR of solids and catalysts; application of NMR to surface science and heterogeneous catalysts; catalysis using zeolites. Subspecialties: Nuclear magnetic resonance; Physical chemistry. Office: Exxon Chem Co 5200 Bayway Dr Baytown TX 77520

ECKSTEIN, EUGENE CHARLES, biomechanical engineering educator, researcher; b. Bucyrus, Ohio, Oct. 31, 1946; s. Robert Frederick and Catherine Caroline (Pessefall) E.; m. Jane Bernstein, Sept. 1, 1968; children—Matthew, Sarah, Adam. S.B. in Mech. Engring., S.M. in Mech. Engring., MIT, 1970, Ph.D. in Mech. Engring., 1975. Assoc. in medicine, bioengring. Peter Bent Brigham Hosp., Harvard Sch. Medicine, Boston, 1975; asst. prof. biomed. engring. U. Miami, Coral Gables, Fla., 1975-79, assoc. prof., 1979—; cons. in field. Contbr. articles to profl. jours. NIH grantee, 1976—. Mem. Am. Soc. Artificial Internal Organs, Internat. Soc. for Artificial Organs, Soc. for Biomaterials, ASME. Current work: Development of urological prostheses, rheological studies related to thrombosis and hemostasis. Subspecialties: Biomedical engineering; Artificial organs and prostheses. Office: Dept Biomed Engring U Miami PO Box 24829 Coral Gables FL 33124

ECONOMOS, GEORGE, materials scientist; b. Haverhill, Mass., Aug. 22, 1919; s. James George and Angelina Mary (Matsuka) E.; m. Bessie Anna Kasida, July 24, 1947; children—Gayle Virginia, James William. B.S. in Chemistry, Northeastern U., 1949; S.M. in Ceramics, MIT, 1951, Sc.D. in Materials Sci., 1954. Asst. prof. metallurgy MIT, Cambridge, Mass., 1954-61, materials group leader Lab. Insulation Research, 1951-61, research asst. Lincoln Lab., 1951-54; mem. ednl. council, 1961-71; sr. sci. cons. Allen-Bradley Co., Milw., 1961-71, cons., 1954-61; vis. prof. materials sci. U. Wis.-Milw., 1971-72; chief engr. Sprague Electric Co., Grafton, Wis., 1972-77; staff scientist Nat. Acad. Sci., Washington, 1977—; magnetic materials cons. Sperry Rand UNIVAC div., Phila., 1956-61. Contbr. articles to profl. jours. and books; patentee in field. Mem. Citizens Adv. Com. Human Relations, Shorewood, Wis., 1965; mem. parish council Greek Orthodox Ch. Milw., 1967. Served with USAF, 1941-45, ETO, prisoner of war, Germany. Fellow AAAS, Am. Ceramic Soc. (treas. Boston sect., v.p. Chgo. sect.); mem. Am. Chem. Soc., Am. Soc. Metals (co. rep. Milw.), AIME, Am. Legion, Sigma Xi. Republican. Club: MIT (v.p. Milw. cptr. 1964-67). Current work: Technical aspects of critical and strategic materials for the National Defense Stockpile, studies on strength of materials, and assessment of semiconductor and electronics materials and processing. Subspecialties: Electronic materials; Ceramics. Home: 6204 Bradley Blvd Bethesda MD 20817 Office: Nat Acad Scis/Nat Materials Adv Bd 2101 Constitution Ave NW Washington DC 20418

EDAHIRO, TAKAO, electronics engineer; b. Hoten, China, Sept. 8, 1943, came to U.S., 1983; s. Isamu and Kiyoko Edahiro; m. Miyoshi Tanimoto; children—Takaaki, Toshie, Hisanao. B.E., Osaka U., Japan, 1966, M.E., 1968, D.E., 1982. Engr. Ibaraki Nippon Tel. & Tel., Japan, 1968-75; staff engr. Research and Devel. Bur., Tokyo, 1975-77; sr. staff engr. Ibaraki Lab. Nippon Tel. & Tel., 1977-83; dir. N.Y. office Nippon Tel. & Tel., N.Y.C., 1983—; lectr. Ibaraki U., Japan, 1980-82. Author: Optical Fiber Communication, 1981,84. Recipient Paper award Inst. Electronics and Communications Engrs. Japan, 1983. Current work: Fiber optics; lightwave guide; electromagnetic field; crystalline structure. Subspecialties: Fiber optics; Condensed matter physics. Home: 23 Walter Ct Harrington Park NJ 07640 Office: Nippon Tel & Tel 200 Park Ave 2905 New York NY 10166

EDELMAN, ANN LYNN, psychologist, computer programmer, systems analyst, laboratory supervisor; b. N.Y.C., Dec. 17, 1944; d. Eugene and Sarah Dorothy (Paris) E.; m. Alfred Henry Letourneau, Aug. 6, 1972. B.A., Case Western Res. U., 1967; M.A., Boston U., 1969, Ph.D., 1974. Cert and lic. psychologist, Mass. Psychologist Emmanuel Coll., Boston, 1971-76; chief psychologist Brockton (Mass.) Multi-Service Ctr., 1976-78; clin. dir. TRIAD, Watertown, Mass., 1970—; sr. lab. coordinator Cambridge Inst., Boston, 1982-84; Analyst I, John Hancock Co., 1984—; cons. Youth Community Action, Arlington, Mass., 1980-82. NIMH fellow, 1969, 70; Rehab. Services Adminstrn. fellow, 1968; VA fellow, 1967. Mem. Am. Psychol. Assn., Mass. Psychol. Assn., Nat. Register Health Services Providers in Psychology. Jewish. Current Work: Systems psychology—the integration of computer science and clinical psychology to study human factors in computer-related fields. Subspecialties: Social psychology; Information systems (Information science). Home: 80 Thorndike St Arlington MA 02174 Office: Cambridge Inst Computer Programming 480 Boylston St Boston MA 02116

EDELMAN, GERALD MAURICE, biochemist; b. N.Y.C., July 1, 1929; s. Edward and Anna (Freedman) E.; m. Maxine Morrison, June 11, 1950; children: Eric, David, Judith. B.S., Ursinus Coll., 1950, Sc.D., 1974; M.D., U. Pa., 1954, D.Sc., 1973; Ph.D., Rockefeller U., 1960; M.D. (hon.), U. Siena, Italy, 1974; D.Sc., Gustavus Adolphus Coll., 1975; Sc.D., Williams Coll., 1976. Med. house officer Mass. Gen. Hosp., 1954-55; asst. physician hosp. of Rockefeller U., 1957-60, mem. faculty, 1960—, assoc. dean grad. studies, 1963-66, prof., 1966-74, Vincent Astor Distinguished prof., 1974—; Mem. biophysics and biophys. chemistry study sect. NIH, 1964-67; mem. Sci. Council, Center for Theoretical Studies, 1970-72; assoc., sci. chmn. Neurosciences Research Program, 1980—, dir. Neurosci. Inst., 1981—; mem. adv. bd. Basel Inst. Immunology, 1970-77, chmn., 1975-77; non-resident fellow, trustee Salk Inst.; bd. overseers Faculty Arts and Scis., U. Pa., 1976-83; trustee, mem. adv. com. Carnegie Inst., Washington. Bd. govs. Weizmann Inst. Sci.; trustee Rockefeller Bros. Fund., 1972-82. Served to capt. M.C. AUS, 1955-57. Recipient Spencer Morris award U. Pa., 1954; Ann. Alumni award Ursinus Coll., 1969; Nobel prize for physiology or medicine, 1972; Albert Einstein Commemorative award Yeshiva U., 1974; Buchman Meml. award Calif. Inst. Tech., 1975; Rabbi Shai Shacknai meml. prize Hebrew U.-Hadassah Med. Sch., Jerusalem, 1977; Regents medal of Excellence, N.Y. State, 1984. Fellow N.Y. Acad. Scis., N.Y. Acad. Medicine; mem. Am. Philos. Soc., Am. Soc. Biol. Chemists, Am. Assn. Immunologists, Genetics Soc. Am., Harvey Soc. (pres. 1975-76, Am. Chem. Soc., Eli Lilly award biol. chemistry 1965), AAAS, Am. Acad. Arts and Scis., Nat. Acad. Sci., Am. Soc. Cell Biology, Acad. Scis. of Inst. France (fgn.), Japanese Biochem. Soc. (hon.), Pharm. Soc. Japan (hon.), Soc. Developmental Biology, Council Fgn. Relations, Sigma Xi, Alpha Omega Alpha. Research structure of antibodies, molecular and devel. biology. Subspecialties: Developmental biology; Molecular biology.

EDELMAN, NORMAN H., medical educator, researcher; b. N.Y.C., May 21, 1937; s. Irving H. and Pearl Ruth (Solomon) E.; m. Ida Nadel, July 15, 1959; children—David, Ruth, Deborah. A.B., Bklyn. Coll., 1957; M.D., NYU, 1961. Intern, then med. resident NYU, N.Y.C., 1961-63; research assoc. NIH, Balt., 1963-65; adv. research fellow Columbia U., N.Y.C., 1965-67; research assoc. Michael Reese Cardiovascular Inst., Chgo., 1967-69; asst. prof. medicine U. Pa., Phila., 1969-72; prof. medicine Rutgers Med. Sch., U. Medicine and Dentistry of N.J., New Brunswick, 1972—, assoc. dean research, 1977—, dir. N.J. Ctr. Advanced Biotech. and Medicine, 1983—. Contbr. articles to profl. jours. Editor sci. series. Served as surgeon USPHS, 1963-65. Mem. Assn. Am. Physicians, Am. Soc. Clin. Investigation, Am. Thoracic Soc. (officer), Am. Physiol. Soc. Jewish. Current work: Control of breathing, endogenous opioids, brain blood flow, lung matrix biology. Subspecialties: Pulmonary medicine; Physiology (medicine). Office: U Medicine and Dentistry NJ Rutgers Med Sch CN 19 New Brunswick NJ 08903

EDELSON, MARTIN CHARLES, research chemist; b. N.Y.C., Nov. 18, 1943; s. Samuel and Rebecca (Stamler) E.; m. Wendy Alice Lipton, July 9, 1967; 1 son, Steven Jonathan. B.S., CCNY, 1964, M.A., 1967; Ph.D., U. Oreg., 1973. Postdoctoral teaching fellow U. B.C., Vancouver, 1973-77; postdoctoral fellow Ames Lab., Iowa State U., 1978-79, assoc. chemist, 1979-82, chemist, 1982—. Contbr. articles to sci. jours. Pres. Prairie Ridge Homeowners Assn., 1981-83. N.Y. State Regents scholar, 1960-64. Mem. Soc. Applied Spectroscopy, Optical Soc. Am., ASTM. Current Work: Analytical spectroscopy applied to nuclear safeguards analysis; laser-basd spectroscopy; multi-photon spectroscopy. Subspecialties: Analytical chemistry; Laser spectroscopy. Home: RR4 Prairie Ridge Ames IA 50010 Office: Ames Lab Iowa State U Ames IA 50011

EDELSON, PAUL JEFFREY, physician, educator; b. Newport News, Va., Dec. 5, 1943; s. Harry and Ruth (Levine) E.; m. Ingrid Rosner, Jan. 11, 1981; 1 son, Jonathan M.R.; married; children by previous marriage: Christopher Peter, Nicholas James. A.B., U. Rochester, 1964; M.D., SUNY-Downstate Med. Ctr., 1969. Diplomate: Am. Bd. Pediatrics. Intern, asst. resident Yale-New Haven Hosp., 1969-71; fellow dept. medicine U. Calif.-San Francisco, 1971-72; postdoctoral fellow Rockefeller U., 1973-75, asst. prof., 1975-77, Harvard U., 1977-82; assoc. prof., dir. div. pediatric infectious diseases and immunology Cornell U., 1982—; tutor in field. Attending physician Camp for Displaced Persons, Thailand, 1980; adv. bd. Cambodian Community Mass., 1980-81. Co-editor: Methods for The Study of Mononuclear Phagocytes, 1982; contbr. articles to profl. jours. Kerb fellow Oxford (Eng.) U., 1974; Research Career Devel. award NIH, 1978-83. Mem. Am. Assn. Immunologists, Am. Soc. Cell Biology, Soc. Pediatric Research, Mass. Audubon Soc., Physicians for Social Responsibility. Current Work: Cell biology of macrophanges. Subspecialties: Infectious diseases; Cell biology. Home: 104 St Marks Ave Brooklyn NY 11217 Office: 1300 York Ave New York NY 10021

EDEN, WILLIAM MURPHEY, physicist; b. Macon, Ga., Sept. 26, 1928; s. John F. and Sula M. (Wommack) E.; m. Clara May Edwards, July 7, 1961; 1 son, Andrew Mark. A.B., Mercer U., 1955; M.S., U. Miami, Coral Gables, Fla., 1964. Surg. technician Macon Hosp., 1954-56; sanitarian Jones County Health Dept., Gray, Ga., 1956-59; public health sanitarian Volusia County Health Dept., Daytona Beach, Fla., 1959-63; public health physicist Fla. Dept. Health and Rehab. Services, Tallahassee, 1964-84; cons. radiation, 1985—. Contbr. articles to profl. jours. Served with USN, 1948-52. Mem. Health Physics Soc., Internat. Radiation Protection Assn., Am. Assn. Physicists in Medicine, Am. Coll. Radiation Physicists, Am. Conf. Govt. Indsl. Hygienists, Soc. Photooptical Instrumentation Engrs. Democrat. Baptist. Subspecialty: Health physics. Home: 2812 Duffton Loop Tallahassee FL 32303 Office: PO Box 13734 Tallahassee FL 32317

EDENBERG, HOWARD JOSEPH, biochemist; b. N.Y.C., Jan. 29, 1948; s. Benjamin and Frances Rose (Kasper) E.; m. Susan Ann Grow, June 4, 1978; children—Elizabeth, Ellen. B.A., CUNY, 1968; M.A., Stanford U., 1970, Ph.D., 1973. Fellow MIT, 1973-76, Harvard U., 1976-77; asst. prof. biochemistry Ind. U., 1977-82, assoc. prof., 1982—. Contbr. articles to profl. jours. Woodrow Wilson fellow, 1968; NSF fellow, 1968; Damon Runyon fellow, 1973-75; NIH fellow, 1975-77; NIH grantee, 1978-81, 84—; NSF grantee, 1984—. Mem. Am. Soc. Biol. Chemists, Am. Soc. Microbiology, AAAS, Biophys. Soc., N.Y. Acad. Sci. Current Work: DNA repair and replication in mammalian cells and simian virus 40; structure and regulation of mammalian genes. Subspecialties: Molecular biology; Genetics and genetic engineering (biology). Home: 5960 Lieber Rd Indianapolis IN 46208 Office: Department Biochemistry Indiana University School Medicine Indianapolis IN 46223

EDGERTON, HAROLD EUGENE, educator, elec. engr.; b. Fremont, Nebr., Apr. 6, 1903; s. Frank Eugene and Mary Nettie (Coe) C.; m. Esther May Garrett, Feb. 25, 1928; children—Mary Louise, William Eugene, Robert Frank. B.S., U. Nebr., 1925, Dr.Engring. (hon.), 1948; M.Sc., Mass. Inst. Tech., 1927, D.Sc., 1931; LL.D. (hon.), Doane Coll., 1969, U. S.C., 1969. Elec. engr. Nebr. Light & Power Co., 1920-25, Gen. Electric Co., 1925-26; Inst. prof. emeritus Mass. Inst. Tech. Author: (with James R. Killian, Jr.) Moments of Vision, 1979, Electronic Flash, Strobe, 1979, also numerous tech. articles. Recipient medal Royal Photog. Soc.; Gold medal Nat. Geog. Soc.; Modern Pioneer award; Potts medal Franklin Inst.; Albert A. Michelson medal, 1969. Fellow I.E.E.E., Am. Inst. Elec. Engrs., Soc. Motion Pictures and TV Engrs., Royal Soc. Gt. Britain; mem. Nat. Acad. Scis., Nat. Acad. Engring. (Founders medal 1983), Marine Tech. Soc., Sigma Xi, Eta Kappa Nu, Sigma Tau. Republican. Conglist. Club: Mason. Inventor of stroboscopic high-speed motion and still photography apparatus; designer underwater camera and high-resolution sonar equipment. Subspecialty: Electrical engineering. Home: 100 Memorial Dr Cambridge MA 02142 Office: Dept Elec Engring MIT Room 4-405 Cambridge MA 02139

EDGREN, RICHARD ARTHUR, biologist, science administrator; b. Chgo., May 28, 1925; s. Richard Arthur and Helga D. (Corydon) E.; m. Margery Edith Kelly, June 7, 1952; children: Susan Ann, Jean Elizabeth. B.S., Northwestern U., 1949, M.S., 1951, Ph.D., 1952. Sr. investigator G.D. Searle Co., Chgo., 1952-60; mgr. endocrinology Wyeth Labs., Phila., 1960-71; dir. endocrinology Warner-Lambert/Parke-Davis, Morristown, N.J., 1971-75, Ann Arbor, Mich., 1975-78; dir. sci. affairs Syntex Labs., Palo Alto, Calif., 1978—; cons. in field. Editorial bd., asso. editor: Internat. Jour. Fertility; contbr. numerous articles to profl. jours., chpts. to books. Bd. dirs., pres. U.S. Internat. Found. Studies in Reprodn. Served with U.S. Army, 1943-46, ETO. Decorated Purple Heart. Mem. Endocrine Soc., Am. Fertility Soc., Soc. Exptl. Biology and Medicine, Soc. Study of Reprodn., Am. Soc. Pharmacology and Exptl. Therapeutics, Ecol. Soc. Am., Am. Soc. Ichthyologists and Herpetologists, Royal Soc. Medicine, Sigma Xi, Internat. Soc. Reproductive Medicine (dir.). Patentee in field of contraceptives. Current Work: Safety of oral contraceptives; development of new contraceptive modalities, particularly analogues of LHRH. Subspecialties: Reproductive biology; Neuroendocrinology. Office: Syntex Labs 3401 Hillview Ave Polo Alto CA 94304

EDLUND, MILTON CARL, physicist, educator; b. Jamestown, N.Y., Dec. 13, 1924. B.S., M.S., U. Mich., 1948, Ph.D., 1966. Physicist reactor physics, gaseous diffusion plant, 1948-49, Oak Ridge Nat. Lab., 1949-50; physicist, lectr. Sch. Reactor Tech., 1950-51, sr. physicist and sect. chief, 1953-55; mgr. devel. dept. Babcock & Wilcox Co., 1955-65, asst. mgr. atomic energy div., 1965-66; prof. U. Mich., 1966-67; planning cons. AEC, 1967-68; exec. v.p. Nuclear Assurance Corp., Atlanta, 1968-70; chmn. nuclear engring. Va. Poly. Inst. and State U., Blacksburg, 1970-74; dir. Center for Energy Research, 1974-78, prof. nuclear engring., 1978—; Vis. lectr. Swedish Atomic Energy Com., 1953. Author: (with S. Glasstone) Elements of Nuclear Reactor Theory, 1952, (with J. Fried) Desalting Technology, 1971. Recipient Ernest Orlando Lawrence award, 1965. Fellow Am. Nuclear Soc.; mem. Nat. Acad. Engring. Spl. research neutron diffusion, nuclear reactor design, energy policy analysis. Current Work: Development of new breeder reactors. Subspecialty: Nuclear fission. Address: 302 Neil St Blacksburg VA 24060

EDMOND, JOHN MARMION, research geochemist, educator; b. Glasgow, Scotland, Apr. 27, 1943; s. Andrew John Sheilds and Christina (Marmion) E.; m. Mssoudeh Vafaei, Jan. 26, 1947; 1 son, Kazem Vafaei. B.Sc. with 1st class honors in Pure Chemistry, U. Glasgow, 1965; Ph.D. in Chem. Oceanograph, Scripps Instn. Oceanography, U. Calif.-San Diego, 1970. Asst. prof. to prof. marine geochemistry dept. earth and planetary scis. MIT, 1970—. Research, numerous publs. in field. Recipient Macelwane award Am. Geophys. Union, 1979. Mem. AAAS, Geochem. Soc. Current Work: Processes controlling chemical composition of natural waters; geochemical cycle; geochemical evolution of environment of surface of earth. Subspecialties: Geochemistry; Oceanography. Office: MIT 334-201 Cambridge MA 02139

EDMONDS, HARVEY LEE, JR., neuropharmacologist, educator, cons. toxicologist; b. Leavenworth, Kans., Sept. 23, 1942; s. Harvey Lee and Esther Jane E.; m. Jeanne Carolyn Ford, July 10, 1970; 1 son: Harvey Lee III. B.A., U. Kans., 1964, B.S. in Pharmacy, 1967; Ph.D., U. Calif., Davis, 1974. Registered pharmacist, Kans., 1967. Grad. asst. U. Calif., Davis, 1971-74; asst. prof. pharmacology Wash. State U., Pullman, 1974-77; asso. prof., dir. research dept. anesthesiology U. Louisville, 1977-82, prof., dir. research, 1982—, cons. toxicologist, 1977—. Mem. bus. adv. bd. U.S. Senate, 1980—. Served to capt. U.S. Army, 1968-70. Decorated Army Commendation medal.; Grantee Epilepsy Found. Am., 1973; Grantee G.D. Searle & Co., 1974; Grantee Ky. Heart Assn., 1979; Grantee Distilled Spirits Council, 1980; Upjohn Pharms., 1982. Mem. Am. Epilepsy Soc., Am. Soc. Pharmacology and Exptl. Therapeutics, Internat. Union Pharmacology, Research Soc. Alcoholism, Soc. Neurosics. Republican. Current Work: Epilepsy and cerebral trauma; direct a series of basic science and clinical studies concerning the causes and treatment of epilepsy and brain damage associated with head trauma. Subspecialty:

Neuropharmacology. Office: Dept Anesthesiology U Louisville Sch Medicine Louisville KY 40292

EDMONDS, MARY PATRICIA, biochemistry educator; b. Racine, Wis., May 7, 1922; s. Millard Samuel and Sarah (Gibbons) E. B.A., Milw. Downer Coll., 1943; M.A., Wellesley Coll., 1945; Ph.D., U. Pa., 1951. Research assoc. Montefiore Hosp. Research, Pitts., 1955-65; asst. prof. biochemistry U. Pitts., 1965-71, assoc. prof., 1971-76, prof., 1976—; mem. molecular biology study sect. NIH, 1973-77, mem. devel. therapeutics study sect., 1978-81. Contbr. articles to profl. jours. NIH grantee, 1962—. Mem. Am. Soc. Biol. Chemists, Am. Assn. Cancer Research. Current Work: Nucleic acid metabolism and structure. Subspecialties: Molecular biology; Biochemistry (biology). Office: University Pittsburgh 527 Lansley Hall Pittsburgh PA 15260

EDMONDSON, MORRIS STEPHEN, research chemist; b. San Antonio, Sept. 9, 1941; s. Morris Cody and Alice (Hausman) E.; m. Phyllis Jean Hill, Aug. 31, 1962; children—Bryan, Boyd. B.S., S.W. Tex. State U., 1963; Ph.D., U. Tex., 1970. Research chemist Petro-Tex Chem., Houston, 1970-77, research mgr., 1976-77; sr. research chemist Dow Chem. Co., Houston, 1977-80, research assoc., 1980-83, assoc. scientist, Freeport, Tex., 1983—. Patentee in field. Mem. Am. Chem. Soc., Alpha Chi, Phi Lambda Upsilon. Mem. Ch. of Christ. Current work: Product polymer property relationships; new product development; catalyst-polymer relationships; polyethylene product development; new product market introduction. Subspecialties: Polymer chemistry; Catalysis chemistry. Home: Route 7 130 Mohawk Dr Alvin TX 77511 Office: Dow Chem USA B-1607 Freeport TX 77541

EDMONDSON, W(ALLACE) THOMAS, limnologist, educator; b. Milw., Apr. 24, 1916; s. Clarence Edward and Marie (Kelley) E.; m. Yvette Hardman, Sept. 26, 1941. B.S., Yale U., 1938, Ph.D., 1942; postgrad., U. Wis., 1938-39. Research assoc. Am. Mus. Natural History, 1942-43, Woods Hole Oceanographic Instn., 1943-46; lectr. biology Harvard U., 1946-49; faculty U. Wash., Seattle, 1949—, prof., 1957—. Editor: Freshwater Biology (Ward and Whipple), 2d edit, 1959; contbr. articles to profl. jours. NSF sr. postdoctoral fellow Italy, Eng. and Sweden, 1959-60; recipient Einar Naumann-August Thienemann Medal Internat. Assn. Theoretical and Applied Limnology, 1980. Mem. Nat. Acad. Scis., Am. Micros. Soc., Nat. Acad. Scis. (Cottrell award 1973), AAAS, Am. Soc. Limnology and Oceanography, Internat. Assn. Limnology, Am. Soc. Naturalists, Phycol. Soc. Am., Ecol. Soc. Am. (Disting. Ecologist award 1983). Current Work: Mechanism of control of population productivity and abundance in lakes; eutrophication. Subspecialty: Limnology. Office: Dept Zoology U Wash Seattle WA 98195

EDSALL, JOHN TILESTON, biochemistry educator, modern science historian; b. Phila., Nov. 3, 1902; s. David Linn and Margaret Harding (Tileston) E.; m. Margaret Dunham, May 1, 1929; children—Lawrence D. (dec.), David Tileston, Nicholas Cranford. A.B. cum laude, Harvard Coll., 1923, M.D. cum laude, 1928; student Cambridge U., Eng., 1924-26; D.Sc. (hon.), U. Chgo., 1967, Case Western Res. U., 1967, U. Mich., 1968; M.D. (hon.), N.Y. Med. Coll., 1967; D.Philosophy (hon.), U. Goteborg, Sweden, 1972. From instr. to prof. biol. chemistry Harvard U., Cambridge, Mass., 1928-73, prof. emeritus, 1973—; pres. 6th Internat. Congress Biochem., N.Y.C., 1964. Author: (with E.J. Cohn) Proteins, Amino Acids and Peptides, 1943; (with J.Wyman) Biophysical Chemistry, 1958; (with H. Gutfreund) Biothermodynamics, 1983. Editor: (with D. Bearman) Archival Sources for History of Biochemistry, 1980; editor-in-chief Jour. Biol. Chemistry, 1958-68. Contbr. articles to profl. jours. Guggenheim fellow, Calif. Inst. Tech., 1940-41; Fulbright lectr. U. Cambridge, 1952, U. Tokyo, 1964; recipient Passano award in Med. Research, Williams and Wilkins Co., 1966. Fellow Am. Acad. Arts and Scis., Am. Philos. Soc.; mem. History of Sci. Soc., Nat. Acad Scis. (editor procs. 1968-72), Am. Chem. Soc. (Willard Gibbs medal 1972; sec., chmn. div. biol. chem. 1946-51), Am. Soc. Biol. Chemists (pres. 1957-58). Current work: History of biochemistry and molecular biology, including physiology and related areas. Subspecialties: Biophysical chemistry; Biochemistry (biology). Office: Harvard Univ Dept Biochemistry and Molecular Biology 7 Divinity Ave Cambridge MA 02138

EDWARDS, BRUCE HAVEN, mathematics educator; b. San Francisco, Feb. 13, 1946; s. William Donlan Edwards and Nancy (Dyer) Edwards Merryman; m. Consuelo Briceno, Oct. 3, 1970; 1 child, Lisa. B.S., Stanford U., 1968; Ph.D., Dartmouth U., 1976. Prof. U.S. Peace Corps., Colombia, S.Am., 1968-72; prof. math. U. Fla., Gainesville, 1976—. Contbr. articles to profl. jours. Fulbright scholar, 1980; NASA Research grantee, 1981-84. Mem. Am. Math. Soc., Soc. Indsl. and Applied Math., Math. Assn. Am. (editor Fla. newsletter). Democrat. Current work: Numerical solution to differential equations. Subspecialties: Numerical analysis (mathematics); Numerical analysis (computer science). Home: 3538 NW 46th Pl Gainesville FL 32605 Office: U Fla 201 Walker Hall Gainesville FL 32611

EDWARDS, CARL NORMAND, psychologist, institute administrator, educator; b. Norwood, Mass., Jan. 22, 1943; s. Wilfred Carl and Cecile Marie-Anne (Pepin) E.; m. Mary Louise Buyse, Jan. 22, 1982. Student, Bridgewater (Mass.) State Coll., 1960-63; M.Ed., Suffolk U., 1969; postgrad., Harvard U., 1964-71, MIT, 1977-80. Cert. Mass. Bd. Registration of Psychologists. Cons. Harvard U., 1966-69, research fellow, 1969-71, lectr. social relations, 1971-72; asst. clin. prof. psychiatry Tufts U. Sch. Medicine, 1971-78, assoc. clin. prof., 1978-82; dir. Four Oaks Inst., Dover, Mass., 1974—; chmn. MEDx Systems, Ltd., 1985—; cons. research analyst Cambridge Computer Assocs., 1966—; mem. field faculty Goddard Coll., Plainfield, Vt., 1972—; sr. assoc. Justice Resource Inst., Boston, 1972-74; chmn. Info. Industry Assn. Task Force on Edn. and Human Resource Devel., Washington, 1982—. Author: Drug Dependence, 1974; contbr. articles to profl. jours. Chmn. permanent bldg. com. Town of Norfolk, Mass., 1981-83. Served with N.G. U.S. Army, 1960-65. Mem. Am. Psychol. Assn., Am. Soc. Info. Sci., Info. Industry Assn., Am. Statis. Assn. Clubs: Harvard of Boston, Appalachian Mt. Current Work: Application of information science and technology to information and decision support systems in the health sciences and education; conceptual and organizational development of innovative programs incorporating applied information technology, and design and programming of university, corporate and government buildings to house and facilitate such programs. Subspecialties: Information systems (Information science); Health services research. Home: Four Oaks Off Springdale Box 2000 Dover MA 02030

EDWARDS, DONALD MERVIN, educator; b. Tracy, Minn., Apr. 16, 1938; s. Mervin B. and Helen L. (Halstenrud) E.; m. Judith Lee Wilson, Aug. 8, 1964; children: John, Joel, Jeffrey, Mary. B.S., S.D. State U., 1960, M.S., 1961; Ph.D. in Agrl. Engring, Purdue U., 1966. Registered profl. engr., Nebr. With Soil Conservation Service, U.S. Dept. Agr., Marshall, Minn., 1957-62; teaching, research asst. S.D. State U. and Purdue U., 1960-66; asso. prof. agrl. engring. U. Nebr. at Lincoln, 1966-71, prof., 1971-80; asst. dean Coll. Engring. and Architecture, 1970-73; asso. dean, dir. Engring. Research Center, 1973-80; dir. Energy Research and Devel. Center, 1976-80; prof. and chmn. dept. agrl. engring Mich. State U., East Lansing, 1980—; collaborator, cons. to numerous industries and agys., 1966—; mem. Engring Accreditation Commn. of Accreditation Bd for Engring. and Tech. Contbr. numerous articles on irrigation, water pollution, remote sensing, energy, engring. edn. to profl. jours. Active Boy Scouts Am., Am. Field Service, 4-H; bd. dirs. Nat. Safety Council; mem. adv. bd. local sch.; past chmn. bd. dirs. Lincoln Transp. System.; mem. Christian edn. com. East Lansing Trinity Ch. Mem. Profl. Engrs. Nebr. (v.p. 1976-77), Mich. Soc. Profl. Engrs. (nat. dir.), Nat. Soc. Profl. Engrs., AAAS, Am. Soc. Agrl. Engrs. (nat. dir. profl. dept. 1977-79), Nat. Assn. Coll. Tchrs. Agr., Internat. Water Resources Assn., Am. Soc. Engring. Edn. (bd. dirs. 1985—), Sigma Xi, Alpha Gamma Rho. Clubs: Farmhouse, Triangle. Current Work: Professor and chairman of programs in agricultural and food engineering, agricultural engineering technology, building construction management, power equipment technology, electrical technology. Home: 4557 Arrow Head Rd Okemos MI 48864

EDWARDS, GORDON STUART, toxicology consultant, cancer researcher; b. Greenwich, Conn., Feb. 11, 1938; s. Alfred Conway and Eleanor Angela (Turnbull) E.; married; children: Alexis, Margot. B.A., Amherst (Mass.) Coll., 1959; M.A., Harvard U., 1963; Sc.D., M.I.T., 1970. Diplomate: Am. Bd. Toxicology. Postdoctoral fellow Rockefeller U., N.Y.C., 1970-72; assoc. prof. pharmacology and genetics George Washington U., Washington, 1972-77, vice chmn. genetics program, 1974-77; chief biology sect. New Eng. Inst. Life Scis., Waltham, Mass., 1977-80; pres. ToxiCon Assocs., Natick, Mass., 1981—. Contbr. articles sci. jours. Damon Runyon fellow, 1970-72. Mem. Mutagenesis Assn. New Eng. (steering com., past pres.), Soc. Toxicology, Am. Assn. Cancer Research, Environ. Mutagen Soc., AAAS. Current Work: Chem. carcinogens, environ. and occupational toxicology, cons. toxicologist, nitroso compounds, mutagenesis, carcinogenesis, occupational toxicology. Subspecialties: Environmental toxicology; Cancer research (medicine). Office: 34 Everett St Natick MA 01760

EDWARDS, RAY CONWAY, physicist, engineering company executive; b. lb. Belleville, Ont., Can., Sept. 1, 1913; came to U.S., 1915, naturalized, 1938; s. Ernest Alfred and Augusta Ann (Fee) E.; m. Marjorie Baisch, Dec. 17, 1951; children: David, Douglas, Diane, Ruth, Robert (dec.), Helen. B.A., UCLA, 1935. Registered profl. engr., N.Y., N.J., Va., Pa. Engr. Carrier Corp., Syracuse, N.Y., 1935-42; physicist U.S. Rubber Co., Passaic, N.J., 1943-46; founder, pres., chmn. bd. Edwards Engring. Corp., Pompton Plains, N.J., 1946—. Contb. chpts. to books. Mem. ASHRAE (life), Theta Delta Chi. Republican. Club: Smoke Rise. Patentee in heat transfer field. Current Work: Heat transfer, hydrocarbon vapor condensation, noise control, air conditioning, refrigeration, automatic temperature controls, air pollution control, mechanical engineering, chemical engineering and physics shale oil. Subspecialties: Heat transfer; Environmental engineering. Home: 396 Ski Trail Kinnelon NJ 07405 Office: Edwards Engring Corp 101 Alexander Ave Pompton Plains NJ 07444

EDWARDS, WILLIAM CHARLES, educator, naturalist; b. Waukegan, Ill., May 17, 1934; s. Henry Charles and Lillian E. (Yockey) E.; m. Nancy Beal, June 10, 1961; children: Jon, Ben. B.A., Carleton Coll., 1956; M.S., U. Wyo., 1958; Ph.D., U. Nebr., 1966. Cert. tchr., Wyo. Ranger-naturalist Grand Teton Nat. Park, summers 1959, 60, 61, Rocky Mountain Nat. Park, summer 1962; biology tchr. Central High Sch., Cheyenne, Wyo., 1958-63; asso. prof. Mankato (Minn.) Sate U., 1966-70; prof. biology, ecology and geology Laramie County Community Coll., Cheyenne, 1971—; dir. Wyo. Postsecondary Energy Consortium, 1980-82; cons. Author articles and editorials. Mem. Wyo. Ho. of Reps., 1974-84. Nat. Endowment Humanities grantee, 1973—. Mem. Audubon Soc. (past pres.), Phi Delta Kappa, Sigma Xi. Democrat. Episcopalian. Lodge: Kiwanis. Current Work: Translating scientific discoveries into lay language; updating state legislation dealing with science. Subspecialty: Ecology (environmental science).

EDWARDS, WILLIAM FARRELL, physics educator; b. Logan, Utah, Oct. 5, 1931; s. Oliver Wendell and Adeline (Barber) E.; m. Ann Parrish, June 8, 1955; children—Boyd, Lynn, David, Alan, Jane, Marianne, Catherine, Farrell, Laura, John. B.S., U. Utah, 1955, M.S., 1957; Ph.D. in Physics, Calif. Inst. Tech., 1960. Prof. physics Utah State U., Logan, 1959—. Author: (with others) Fundamentals of Physics, 1973. Contbr. articles to profl. jours. Named Prof. of Yr., Utah State U., 1976. Mem. Am. Phys. Soc. Mem. Ch. of Jesus Christ of Latter-day Saints. Current work: Electromagnetic theory of charged fluids. Subspecialties: Theoretical physics; Plasma physics. Home: 565 River Heights Blvd Logan UT 84321 Office: Physics Dept Utah State U Logan UT 84322

EDWARDSON, JOHN RICHARD, agronomist; b. Kansas City, Mo., Apr. 17, 1923; s. George Edward and Louise Marie (Sundstrom) E.; m. Mickie Newbill, Dec. 26, 1969; children: George, Elizabeth, Sarah. B.S., Tex. A. and M. U., 1948, M.S., 1949; Ph.D., Harvard U., 1954. Asst. agronomist Fla. Agrl. Expt. Sta., Gainesville, 1953-60, assoc. agronomist, 1960-66, agronomist, 1966—. Served with U.S. Army, 1943-45. Mem. AAAS, Genetics Soc. Am., Am. Phytopath. Soc. Current Work: Cytoplasmic inheritance, cytology of virus induced inclusions, research on cytoplasmic male sterility in plants and on morphology, structure and location of virus inclusions. Subspecialties: Plant genetics; Plant virology. Home: 2721 SW 3d Pl Gainesville FL 32607 Office: U Fla 2559 HS and PP Bldg Gainesville FL 32611

EERNISSE, ERROL PETER, research manager; b. Rapid City, S.D., Feb. 15, 1940; s. Welles Carl and Myra Irene (Glenn) E.; m. Claudia Canady, Sept. 20, 1972; children—Adele, Shelia, Peter. B.S. in Elec. Engring., S.D. State U., 1962; M.S. in Elec. Engring., Purdue U., 1963, Ph.D., 1965; M. Indsl. Adminstrn., U. N.Mex., 1974. Mem. tech. staff Sandia Nat. Labs., Albuquerque, 1965-68; div. supr., 1969-79; dir. Quartex, Inc., Salt Lake City, 1979-80, pres. 1981—; cons. Schalumberger, Ridgefield, Conn., 1980-81, Sagem, Paris, 1980-81. Author: (with others) Design of Resonant Piezoelectric Devices, 1969. Editor: (with others) Ion Implantation, 1972. Patentee miniature force transducer. Fellow IEEE (Cady award 1983), Am. Phys. Soc.; mem. Instrument Soc. Am. (sr.), Nat. Soc. Profl. Engrs., Phi Kappa Phi. Republican. Presbyterian. Current work: Precise measurement of force related physical parameters. Subspecialties: Electronics; Condensed matter physics. Office: Quartex Inc 1020 Atherton Dr Bldg C Salt Lake City UT 84123

EFCAVITCH, J. WILLIAM, biochemist; b. Phila., Dec. 8, 1952; s. William and Beatrice (Donnelly) E.; m. Patricia Ann Books, June 6, 1981; 1 child, John Adam. B.A., LaSalle Coll., 1974; Ph.D., Ohio U., 1978. Research assoc. U. Colo., 1978-81; project dir. DNA synthesizer Applied Biosystems, Foster City, Calif., 1981—. Contbr. articles to profl. jours. Current work: Automation of synthetic chemistry, biochemistry, molecular biology processes. Subspecialties: Molecular biology; Organic chemistry. Home: 128 Arundel Rd San Carlos CA 94070 Office: Applied Biosystems 850 Lincoln Centre Foster City CA 94404

EFRON, BRADLEY, mathematician; b. St. Paul, May 24, 1938; s. Miles Jack and Esther (Kaufman) E.; m. Gael Guerin, July 1969 (div.); 1 child, Miles James. B.S. in Math., Calif. Inst. Tech., 1960; Ph.D. Stanford U., 1964. Asst. and assoc. prof. stats. Stanford U., Calif., 1965-72, chmn. dept. stats., 1976-79, chmn. math scis., 1982—, prof. stats., 1972—; statis, cons. Alza Corp., 1970—, Rand Corp., 1966—. Author: Bootstrap Methods, 1982; Biostatistics Casebook, 1980. MacArthur Found. fellow, 1983; named Outstanding Statistician of Yr. Chgo Statis. Assn., 1981; Walk and Rietz Lectr. Inst. Math. Stats., 1977, 81. Fellow Inst. Math. State., Am. Statis, Assn.; mem. Internat. Statis. Assn. Democrat. Subspecialty: Statistics. Office: Dept Statistics Sequoia Hall Stanford CA 94305*

EGAN, EDMUND A., neonatal physician, educator; b. Chgo., Apr. 24, 1941; s. William Quan and Martha (Guerin) E.; m. Mary Michael Connolly, Aug. 29, 1964; children—Edmund, Mary, William, Sarah, Elizabeth, Frances. M.D., Emory U., 1967. Diplomate Am. Bd. Pediatrics. Resident and fellow in pediatrics U. Fla., Gainesville, 1967-70; Univ. Coll. Hosp. Med. Sch., London, 1972-73; asst., then assoc. prof. pediatrics U. Fla., Gainesville, 1973-77; assoc. prof., then prof. pediatrics SUNY-Buffalo, 1977—; chief neonatology Children's Hosp., Buffalo, 1977—; ad hoc reviewer NIH, Washington, 1976—. Served to maj. U.S. Army, 1970-72. NIH grantee, 1974-85. Fellow Am. Acad. Pediatrics; mem. Soc. for Pediatric Research, Perinatal Research Soc., Am. Thoracic Soc., Am. Physiol. Soc. Current work: Exogenous surfactant therapy for neonatal lung disease; pathophysiology of lung injury; lung fluid balance. Subspecialties: Neonatology; Physiology (medicine). Office: Children's Hosp 219 Bryant St Buffalo NY 14222

EGAN, MARIANNE LOUISE, immunologist; b. Jersey City, June 9, 1942; d. Joseph Lawrence and Thecla (Roesch) E.; m. David G. Pritchard, Dec. 27, 1975; 1 dau., Barbara Lynn. A.B. with high honors, Coll. St. Elizabeth, Convent Station, N.J., 1964; Ph.D., Jefferson Med. Coll., Phila., 1969. Instr. in biochemistry Jefferson Med. Coll., Phila., 1969-70; asst. research scientist City of Hope Nat. Med. Center, Duarte, Calif., 1970-72, assoc. research scientist, 1972-76; assoc. scientist Comprehensive Cancer Center U. Ala.-Birmingham, 1977—; assoc. scientist U. Ala.-Birmingham (Multipurpose Arthritis Center), 1979—, research asst. prof. immunobiology and immunology, 1976—; mem. med. adv. bd. Nat. Multiple Sclerosis Soc., Central Ala., 1977—; co-chmn. diagnosis and therapy working group Breast Cancer Task Force Com., Nat. Cancer Inst., Bethesda, Md., 1980—. Reviewer: Cancer Research Jour. of Nat. Cancer Inst, 1977—, Arthritis and Rheumatism, 1977-81; adv. editor: Molecular Immunology, 1971-74; contbr. numerous sci. articles to profl. publs. Recipient McClung award Beta Beta Beta, 1964; Paul Pinchunk award Jefferson Med. Sch., 1969; Nat. Multiple Sclerosis Soc. grantee, 1980-83; NIH grantee, 1976—. Mem. Am. Assn. Immunologists, Am. Assn. Cancer Research, Sigma Xi. Current Work: Control of cellular interactions in autoimmune diseases; the production of murine and human hybridomas structure and function of human DR antigens. Subspecialties: Immunobiology and immunology; Cell and tissue culture. Office: Univ Ala 450 LHR Dept Microbiology Birmingham AL 35294

EGELHOFF, WILLIAM FREDERICK, JR., chemist; b. Norfolk, Va., July 8, 1949; s. William Frederick and Caroline Breckenridge (Talbot) E.; m. Natasha Gritz, Sept. 3, 1976; children—Roman, Tom, Helen. B.S., Hampden Sydney Coll., 1971; Ph.D., Cambridge U., 1975. Research fellow Calif. Inst. Tech., 1975-76; physicist Gen. Motors Research Labs., Warren, Mich., 1976-79; chemist Nat. Bur. Standards, Gaithersburg, Md., 1979—. Contbr. articles to profl. jours. Mem. Phi Beta Kappa. Current work: X-ray photoelectron spectroscopy; molecular beam epitoxy; layered materials; surface thermodynamics; reaction kinetics. Subspecialties: Surface chemistry; Condensed matter physics. Office: Nat Bur Standards Washington DC 20234

EGGER, MAURICE DAVID, neurobiologist; b. Bakersfield, Calif., June 21, 1936; d. Henry and Ida (Hoffman) E.; m. Audrey A. Egger, June 2, 1985; children: Daniel, Rachel, Gideon. B.S. in Physics, Stanford U., 1958; M.S., Yale U., 1960, Ph.D., 1962. Instr. Sch. Medicine, Yale U., 1965-66, asst. prof., 1966-69, assoc. prof., 1969-74, Rutgers U. Med. Sch., 1974-78, prof., 1978—; research scientist devel. rev. group NIMH, HEW, 1975-79; neurobiology rev. group NIH, Dept. HHS, 1982-83. Fellow Am. Psychol. Assn., AAAS; mem. Soc. Neurosci., Internat. Brain Research Orgn., Sigma Xi. Democrat. Jewish. Patentee scanning optical microscope. Current Work: Relationships between structure and function in the central nervous system. Subspecialties: Neurophysiology; Neurobiology. Office: Anatomy Rutgers Medical School Piscataway NJ 08854

EGGERS, ALFRED JOHN, JR., research corporation executive; b. Omaha, June 24, 1922; s. Alfred John and Golden May (Myers) E.; m. Elizabeth Ann Hills, Sept. 9, 1950; children—Alfred J. III, Philip Norman. B.A., U. Nebr.-Omaha, 1945; M.S., Stanford U., 1951, Ph.D., 1957. Aerospace scientist NASA Ames Research Ctr., Mountain View, Calif., 1944-64, dep. assoc. adminstr., Washington, 1964-68; Hunsaker prof. MIT, Cambridge, 1969-71; asst. dir. NSF, Washington, 1971-77; dir. Lockheed Palo Alto Research Lab., Calif., 1977-79; pres., chief exec. officer RANN, Inc., Palo Alto, 1979—, also dir.; mem. Nat. Acad. Engring. Aerospace Engring. Bd., 1973-77, U.S. Air Force Sci. Adv. Bd., Washington, 1958-72. Author: Hypersonic Flow, Handbook of Engineering Mechanics, 1962. Contbr. articles to profl. jours. Inventor in field. Vice chmn. Sch. Community Devel. Com., Los Altos Hills (Calif.), 1963-64; chmn. troop com. Washington Area council Boy Scouts Am., 1968-75; mem. ARC Safety Com., Arlington, Va., 1975-77. Served to lt. (j.g.), USN, 1943-46. Recipient Alumnus Achievement award U. Omaha, 1958; Disting. Service medal NSF, 1975; Pres. Disting. Service award U.S. Pres., 1977. Fellow AIAA (bd. dirs. 1962-66, Sylvanus Albert Reed award 1961), Am. Astronautics Soc.; AAAS; mem. Nat. Acad. Engring. (long range planning and devel. com. 1983—). Republican. Club: Washington Golf and Country (Arlington, Va.). Current work: Aerodynamics and structural dynamics of wind energy turbine blades; microgravity effects on materials processes; orbital transfer vehicle and hypersonic aircraft configurations and applications. Subspecialties: Aerospace engineering and technology; Energy research administration. Office: Rann Inc 260 Sheridan Ave Suite 414 Palo Alto CA 94306

EGGERS, DAVID FRANK, chemistry educator, researcher; b. Oak Park, Ill., July 8, 1922; s. David F. and Anne E. (Anderson) E.; m. Vera E. Dalton, Jan. 23, 1945; children—Daniel, Richard, Ann. B.S. in Chemistry, U. Ill., 1943; Ph.D. in Phys. Chemistry, U. Minn., 1951. Chemist, Tenn. Eastmen, Oak Ridge, Tenn., 1944-47; research fellow U. Minn., Mpls., 1947-50, instr., asst. prof., assoc. prof., prof. chemistry U. Wash., Seattle, 1950—. Author: Physical Chemistry, 1964. Contbr. articles to profl. jours. Grantee NSF, U.S. Air Force Office of Sci. Research. Mem. Am. Chem. Soc., Optical Soc. Am. Presbyterian. Current work: Far infrared lasers from optically-pumped gases; computer programs for analysis of complex spectra; construction of new lasers for the visible and mid-infrared. Subspecialty: Infrared spectroscopy. Office: Dept Chemistry BG-10 U Wash Seattle WA 98194

EGGERT, FRANK MICHAEL, dental educator, immunology researcher, dentist; b. Hamburg, W.Ger., Apr. 24, 1945; emigrated to Can., 1954, naturalized, 1960; s. Frank Paul and Suse (Schilling) E.; m. Susan Louise Denny, June 19, 1976; 1 son, Frank Matthew Arthur. D.D.S., U. Toronto, Ont., Can., 1969, M.Sc., 1971; Ph.D., U. Cambridge, Eng., 1978. Lectr. London Hosp. Med. Coll. Dental Sch., 1979-81; assoc. prof. stomatology Faculty Dentistry, U. Alta. (Can.), Edmonton, 1981-83, prof., 1983—. Contbr. articles on secretory immunity, histochemistry to profl. jours. Royal Coll. Surgeons Eng. research fellow, 1976; Alta. Found. Med. Research establishment grantee, 1982-85. Fellow Royal Soc. Medicine; mem. Royal Coll. Dentists Can., Biochem. Soc., Brit. Soc. Immunology, Internat. Assn. Dental Research. Club: Royal Can. Yacht (Tornto). Current Work: Immunochemistry of secretory glycoproteins that aggregate bacteria; experimental pathology and histochemistry of periodontal disease. Subspecialties: Immunology (medicine); Periodontics. Office: U Alta Faculty Dentistry Edmonton AB T6G 2N8 Canada

EGNER, JOHN DAVID, JR., electrical engineer; b. New Castle, Pa., June 30, 1957; s. John David Egner and Ann I. Nevin. B.S.E.E., U. Vt., 1979. Devel. engr. Hewlett-Packard, Sunnyvale, Calif., 1979-82, Apple Computer, Inc., Cupertino, Calif., 1982—. Vice pres. Big Redwood Park Water and Improvement Assn., Los Gatos, Calif., 1984—. Mem. IEEE (v.p. student br. 1977-78, pres. student br. 1978-79, U. Vt. student br. award for outstanding leadership 1979), Tau Beta Pi. Current work: Systems and product design for EMI suppression and FCC compliance; design and development of switching power supplies and video sweep circuits for CRTs. Subspecialties: Electrical engineering; Electronics. Home: 18492 Main Blvd Los Gatos CA 95030 Office: Apple Computer Inc 20525 Mariani Ave Cupertino CA 95014

EHLEN, JUDY, geologist; b. Portland, Oreg., June 27, 1944; d. E.A. and Mina J. (Cowgill) E. B.A., U. Oreg., 1966, 69, M.A., 1969; M.A., George Mason U., 1980. Teaching asst. U. Oreg., Eugene, 1966-68; instr. Lane Community Coll., Eugene, part-time, 1968-69; cartographic aide Army Topographic Command, Washington, 1971-72; geologist Army Engrs. Topographic Labs., Fort Belvoir, Va., 1972—. Contbr. articles to profl. jours. Treas. Dale City 10th Homeowner's Assn., Woodbridge, Va., 1980-83. Mem. Geol. Soc. Am., Geol. Soc. Washington, Assn. Women Geoscientists, Sigma Xi. Democrat. Current work: Evaluation of relations between landform, fracture type and spacing and grain size in granitic rocks to determine how these relations, if they exist, can be determined from remotely sensed imagery and used as indicators of rock type on imagery. Subspecialties: Geology; Remote sensing (geoscience). Home: 14678 Endsley Turn Woodbridge VA 22193 Office: US Army Engrs Topographic Labs Fort Belvoir VA 22060

EHLERS, ERNEST GEORGE, geology educator, petrologic researcher; b. N.Y.C., Jan. 17, 1927; s. Ernest Frederick and Elsie Frieda (Buchenroth) E.; m. Diane Wiersema, June 17, 1950; children: Karen Alice Ehlers Chipman, Ernest George. M.S., U. Chgo., 1950, Ph.D., 1952. Geologist New Jersey Zinc Co., Sweetwater, Tenn., 1952-54; asst. prof. geology Ohio State U., 1954-57, assoc. prof., 1957-65, prof., 1965—; sr. lectr. U. Utrecht, Netherlands, 1965-66, U. Athens and Greek Geol. Survey, 1970-71. Author: The Interpretation of Geological Phase Diagrams, 1972, Petrology, 1982; contbr. articles to profl. jours. Served with USN, 1945. Recipient Fulbright Hays award, 1965-66, 70-71. Fellow Geol. Soc. Am., Mineral. Soc. Am.; mem. Sigma Xi. Current Work: Igneous and metamorphic petrology; optical crystallography; mineral synthesis. Subspecialties: Petrology; Geochemistry. Office: Dept Geology and Mineralogy Ohio State U 104 W 19 Ave Columbus OH 43210

EHLERS, KENNETH WARREN, physicist, consultant; b. Dix, Nebr., Aug. 3, 1922; s. Walter Richard and Clara (Sievers) E.; m. Marion W., Mar. 4, 1947; 1 son, Gary Walter. Student, U. Colo., 1940-42; B.S., Okla. A&M U., 1944; postgrad., M.I.T., 1945; Ph.D., U. Calif., 1967. Head electronic aids dept. Landing Aids Expt. Sta., Arcata, Calif., 1946-50; staff sr. physicist Lawrence Berkeley Lab., U. Calif., 1950—; cons. Brobeck Industries, Avco Corp., Cyclotron Corp., TRW, others. Editorial bd.: Rev. Sci. Instruments; contbr. articles to profl. jours. Served with USN, 1942-46. Ford Found. grantee U. Chile, Santiago, 1970-74. Fellow Am. Phys. Soc.; mem. IEEE, Am. Vacuum Soc. (Sr., exec. bd. fusion div.), AAAS. Patentee. Current Work: Developing neutral beam injectors for heating controlled fusion reactor plasmas. Subspecialties: Plasma physics; Particle physics. Home: 3129 Via Larga Alamo CA 94507 Office: Lawrence Berkeley Lab Bldg 4 Berkeley CA 94720

EHRENFELD, ELVERA, biochemist, virologist, cons.; b. Phila., Mar. 1, 1942; s. Henry and Eughenia (Frantz) E.; m. Donald F. Summers; 1 dau., Cynthia. B.A., Brandeis U., 1962; Ph.D., U. Fla., 1967. Asst. prof. cell biology Albert Einstein Coll. Medicine, 1969-74, assoc. prof., 1974; assoc. prof. biochemistry and cell, viral, molecular biology U. Utah Coll. Medicine, 1974-79, prof., 1979—. Recipient Career Devel. award USPHS, 1971-76,

Tchr.-Scholar award Dreyfus Found., 1975-80, Faculty award Merck, 1971; NIH grantee, 1974—; NSF grantee, 1970-80. Mem. Am. Soc. Biol. Chemists, Am. Soc. Microbiology. Current Work: Replication of RNA viruses. Subspecialties: Virology (biology); Biochemistry (biology). Office: Dept Microbiology U Utah Med Center Salt Lake City UT 84132

EHRENPREIS, SEYMOUR, pharmacologist, educator; b. N.Y.C., June 20, 1927; s. William and Ethel (Balk) E.; m. Bella R. Goodman, June 30, 1954; children: Mark, Eli, Ira. B.S., CCNY, 1949; Ph.D., N.Y. U., 1953. Research assoc. U. Pitts., 1953-55; instr. chemistry Cornell U., Ithaca, N.Y., 1955-57; asst. prof. biochemistry and neurology Coll. Physicians and Surgeons, Columbia U., N.Y.C., 1957-61; assoc. prof. pharmacology Georgetown U., Washington, 1961-69; head neuropharmacy Inst. Med. Research and Studies, N.Y.C., 1969-70; head pharmacology N.Y. State Research Inst. Neurochemistry and Drug Addiction, Ward's Island, N.Y., 1971-76; adj. prof. pharmacology Columbia Coll. Pharm. Sci., N.Y.C., 1972-76; prof. chmn. dept. pharmacology Univ. Health Sci. (Chgo. Med. Sch.), North Chgo., 1976—; vis. prof. Keio and Tokyo univs., Japan, summer 1974. Contbr. numerous articles on pharmacology to profl. jours.; editor: Cholinergic Mechanisms, 1966, Neurosci. Research, 1967-71, Neurosci. Revs, 1974-76, (with A. Neidle) Methods in Narcotics Research, 1974. Served with USN, 1945-46. Recipient Meritorious Service award Coll. Pharm. Sci., Columbia U., 1976; Morris L. Parker award Univ. Health Sci./Chgo. Med. Sch., 1981; NIH grantee, 1961-82; NSF grantee, 1963-68; Hoffman-LaRoche grantee, 1976-78. Fellow AAAS, Am. Inst. Chemists; mem. Am. Soc. Biol. Chemistry, Am. Soc. Pharmacology and Exptl. Therapeutics, Soc. Neurosci., Sigma Xi. Current Work: Analgesic mechanisms, functional role of endorphins, enkephalinase inhibitors. Subspecialties: Neuropharmacology; Neurobiology. Office: 3333 Green Bay Rd North Chicago IL 60064

EHRLICH, IRA ROBERT, mechanical engineering educator; b. Washington, Sept. 1, 1926; s. Abraham Moses and Anna (Garonzik) E.; m. Sheila Lenor Kaminsky, June 11, 1950; children—Richard Mark, Heather Maureen. B.S., U.S. Mil. Acad., 1950; M.S., Purdue U., 1956; Ph.D., U. Mich., 1960; M.S. (hon.), Stevens Inst. Tech., 1982. Registered profl. engr., Mich., N.J. Supr. ITT, Paramus, N.J., 1960-62; mgr. transp. research group Stevens Inst. Tech., Hoboken, N.J., 1962-74, dean research, 1974-83, head dept. mech. engring., 1979-83, v.p. research, 1983-85, v.p. acad. affairs, 1984-85; chmn. sci. adv. com. U.S. Army Tank-Automotive Research and Devel. Command; cons. to industry; mem. N.J. Motor Vehicle Insp. Sta. Rev. Commn., chmn. safety com., 1977-81. Asso. editor: Tire Sci. and Tech, 1972-81. Served to capt. U.S. Army, 1950-60. Themis grantee, 1967-71. Mem. Internat. Soc. Terrain-Vehicle Systems (gen. sec. 1967-78, v.p. 1978-81, pres. 1981-84), Soc. Automotive Engrs. (chmn. spl. purpose vehicle com.), ASME, Am. Def. Preparedness Assn., Nat. Safety Council, Nat. Soc. Agrl. Engrs., Assn. U.S. Army, Nat. Assn. Profl. Engrs. Jewish. Club: B'nai B'rith (chpt. pres. 1967-78). Current work: Mechanical and automotive engineering. Subspecialty: Mechanical engineering. Home: 859 Columbus Dr Teaneck NJ 07666 Office: Castle Point Station Hoboken NJ 07030

EHRLICH, PAUL RALPH, biology educator; b. Phila., May 29, 1932; s. William and Ruth (Rosenberg) E.; m. Anne Fitzhugh Howland, Dec. 18, 1954; 1 dau., Lisa Marie. A.B., U. Pa., 1953; A.M., U. Kans., 1955, Ph.D., 1957. Research assoc. U. Kans., Lawrence, 1958-59; asst. prof. biol. scis. Stanford, 1959-62, asso. prof., 1962-66, prof., 1966—, Bing prof. population studies, 1976—, dir. grad. study dept. biol. scis., 1966-69, 1974-76; cons. Behavioral Research Labs., 1963-67; cons. biology, editor in population biology McGraw Hill Book Co., N.Y.C., 1964—. Author: How to Know the Butterflies, 1961, Process of Evolution, 1963, Principles of Modern Biology, 1968, Population Bomb, 1968, 2d edit., 1971, Population, Resources, Environment: Issues In Human Ecology, 1970, 2d edit., 1972, How to Be a Survivor, 1971, Global Ecology: Readings Toward a Rational Strategy for Man, 1971, Man and the Ecosphere, 1971, Introductory Biology, 1973, Human Ecology: Problems and Solutions, 1973, Ark II: Social Response to Environmental Imperatives, 1974, The End of Affluence: A Blueprint for the Future, 1974, Biology and Society, 1976, Race Bomb, 1977, Ecoscience: Population, Resources, Environment, 1977, The Golden Door: International Migration, Mexico, and the U.S, 1979, Extinction: The Causes and Consequences of the Disappearance of Species, 1981; contbr. articles to profl. jours. Fellow Calif. Acad. Scis., Am. Acad. Arts and Scis.; mem. Soc. for Study Evolution, Nat. Acad. Scis., Soc. Systematic Zoology, Am. Soc. Naturalists, Lepidopterists Soc., Am. Mus. Natural History (hon. life mem.). Current Work: Evolution and ecology of natural populations, plant-herbivore coevolution; policy research on human population/resources-/environment. Subspecialties: Population biology; Ecology (environmental science). Address: Biological Scis Stanford U Stanford CA 94305

EHRLICH, RICHARD, bacteriologist; b. Bedzin, Poland, Jan. 19, 1924; came to U.S., 1949, naturalized, 1952; s. Jacob and Gela E.; m. June Beinhorn, June 2, 1950; children—Glenn J., Jeffrey P.M.S., Tech. U. Munich, W. Ger., 1948, Ph.D., 1949, Lab. dir. Am. Butter Inst., Chgo., 1949-52; bacteriologist I.I.T. Research Inst., Chgo., 1952-57, supr. biol. research, then assoc. dir. life scis. research, 1957-63, dir. life sci. research, 1963-77, v.p. life scis. research, 1977—; mem. NOX subcom. NRC-Nat. Acad. Scis., 1975; mem. rev. com. air quality criteria EPA, 1970. Mem. editorial bd.: Advances in Modern Environ. Toxicology; Author papers in field. Mem. Air Pollution Control Assn., Am. Soc. Microbiology, AAAS, N.Y. Acad. Sci., Soc. Occupational and Environ. Health, Am. Public Health Assn., Soc. Française de la Tuberculose and Maladies Respiratoires (fgn. asso.), Sigma Xi. Subspecialties: Microbiology (medicine); Environmental toxicology. Home: 4857 Davis St Skokie IL 60077 Office: IIT Research Inst 10 W 35th St Chicago IL 60616

EHRLICH, STANLEY L(EONARD), acoustical engineer, sonar systems consultant; b. Newark, Jan. 7, 1925; s. Henry Max and Mary (Lichtenstein) E.; m. Louise Dorothy Waldfogel, June 19, 1949; children—Barbara Ellen, Stephen Mark, Michael Alan. Sc.B. in Engring., Brown U., 1944, Sc.M. in Physics, 1945; postgrad. MIT, 1945-48, U. Conn., Storrs, 1951-53. Teaching asst. Brown U., Providence, 1944-45; teaching fellow MIT, Cambridge, 1946-48; physicist U.S. Navy Underwater Sound Lab., New London, Conn., 1948-53; sr. engr. Equipment div. Raytheon Co., Boston, Newton and Wayland, Mass., 1953-59, sect. mgr. Submarine Signal div., Waltham, Mass. and Portsmouth, R.I., 1959-62, prin. engr., Portsmouth, 1962-70, cons. engr., 1970—; cons. Nat. Security Indsl. Assn., Washington, 1964—; U.S. rep. Internat. Orgn. for Standarization, Copenhagen and Washington, 1974-76; individual expert Am. Nat. Standards Inst., N.Y.C., 1983—. Translator: Fundamentals of Electroacoustics, 1955. Assoc. editor Jour. Oceanic Engring., 1975-81, editor, 1982—. Contbr. articles to profl. jours. Patentee in field. Team capt. Newport Hosp. Bldg. Fund, 1967; head class agt. ann. fund Brown U., Providence, 1970—; bd. dirs. R.I. Arts Found. at Newport, 1972-80, sec., 1977-79. Recipient Freeman award Providence Engring. Soc., 1976. Fellow Acoustical Soc. Am. (tech. council 1979-81, assoc. editor 1981—, com. on regional chpts. 1960—, chmn. 1976—, hon. life mem. Narragansett chpt.); mem. IEEE (sr. mem.; Centennial award 1984), Oceanic Engring. Soc. (adminstrv. com. 1983—), Am. Phys. Soc. Republican. Jewish. Club: Brown (pres. Newport County 1969-72). Lodge: B'nai B'rith (pres. Waltham 1957-58). Current work: Consulting on sonar systems engineering, transducers, electroacoustics, electrostriction, magnetostriction, and normal modes in solids. Subspecialties: Acoustical engineering; Ocean engineering. Home: One Acacia Dr Middletown RI 02840 Office: Raytheon Co Submarine Signal Div PO Box 360 Portsmouth RI 02871

EHRLICH, YIGAL H., neurochemist, research, educator; b. Tel Aviv, Oct. 9, 1943; came to U.S., 1972, naturalized, 1982; s. Arthur and Regina (Eisenberg) E.; m. Elizabeth H. Kornecki, Mar. 18, 1983. M.Sc. in Microbiology, Tel Aviv U., 1968; Ph.D. in Biochemistry, Weizmann Inst. Sci., Rehovot, Israel, 1972. Postdoctoral fellow Cresap Neurosci. Lab., Northwestern U., Evanston, Ill., 1972-73, vis. asst. prof. dept. psychology and dept. physiology, 1973-75; research scientist Mo. Inst. Psychiatry, St. Louis, 1975-79; assoc. prof. psychiatry and biochemistry U. Vt. Coll. Medicine, Burlington, 1980—. Sr. editor: Modulators, Mediators and Specifiers in Brain Function, 1979; contbr. articles to sci. jours. Served with Israeli Def. Army. Recipient award Epilepsy Found. Am., 1977; NSF grantee, 1975, 79, 82, 85; NIH grantee, 1979-84. Mem. Am. Soc. for Neurochemistry, Soc. for Neurosci., Internat. Soc. for Neurochemistry, N.Y. Acad. Scis., Sigma Xi. Current Work: Research on molecular mechanisms underlying neuronal adaptation and synaptic plasticity, focusing on the role of protein phosphorylation in the regulation of neural receptors and long-lasting alterations induced in their function by hormonal and pharmacological stimulations. Subspecialties: Neurochemistry; Psychobiology. Home: 16 Brookwood Dr South Burlington VT 05401 Office: Dept Psychiatry U Vt Coll Medicine Burlington VT 05405

EIBER, ROBERT JAMES, civil engineer; b. Cleve., July 7, 1933; s. Harry E. and Grace A. E.; m. Carol A. Rankin, May 28, 1960; children: Jeffrey, Jill. B.S. in Civil Engring, Case Western Res. U., 1955, M.S. in Structural Engring, 1958. Instr. Case Western Res. U., Cleve., 1955-59; researcher Battelle Columbus (Ohio) Labs., 1959-75, mgr. fracture sect., 1975-83, mgr. stress analysis and fracture sect., 1983-85, mgr. mechanics research program, 1985—. Contbr. articles to profl. jours. Mem. ASME, ASCE, ASTM, Sigma Xi, Theta Tau, Tau Beta Pi. Lutheran. Club: Columbus Yacht. Patentee in field. Current Work: Fracture initiation, propagation and arrest of fractures in piping systems. Fracture control, piping failure analyses, pipelines, railroad tank cars, nuclear piping fractures; structural integrity of transit buses. Subspecialties: Materials (engineering); Fracture mechanics. Home: 4279 Camborne Rd Columbus OH 43220 Office: 505 King Ave Columbus OH 43201

EICHER, CARL K., agricultural economics educator; b. Newberry, Mich., Apr. 3, 1930; m. 3 children. B.S., Mich. State U., 1952, M.Sc., 1956; Ph.D., Harvard U., 1961. Asst. prof. agrl. econs. Mich. State U., East Lansing, 1961-65, assoc. prof., 1965-70, prof., 1970—; econ. adviser Econ. Devel. Inst. U. Nigeria, 1963, dir., 1964-66; vis. prof. agrl. econs. U. Zimbabwe, 1983-84, also sr. agrl. adviser South Africa regional program AIS, Harare; vis. prof. Food Research Inst. Stanford U., 1968; cons. AIS mission, Tanzania, 1970, Ghana, 1971, Ethiopia, Nigeria, Kenya, Rwanda, Upper Volta, Senegal, Niger, Haiti, Bolivia, Zambia, Zimbabwe, 1972—, World Bank, 1985; mem. panel human resources and African devel. AIS, 1984. Fellow, Smithsonian Inst., 1976-77. Contbr. articles to profl. jours. Subspecialty: Agricultural economics. Office: Dept Agrl Econs Mich State U East Lansing MI 48824

EICHHOLZ, GEOFFREY G., nuclear engineering educator; b. Hamburg, W. Ger., June 29, 1920; s. Max and Adele Daisy (Elias) E. B.S. in Physics, U. Leeds, Eng., 1942, PhD., 1948, D.Sc., 1979. Exptl. officer Brit. Admiralty, Witley, Surrey, Eng., 1942-46; asst. prof. physics U. B.C. (Can.), Vancouver, 1947-51; head physics and radiotracer subdiv. Can. Bur. Mines, Ottawa, Ont., 1951-63; prof. nuclear engring. Ga. Inst. Tech., Atlanta, 1963—; nuclear cons., cons. archtl. acoustics, 1965—. Author: Environmental Aspects of Nuclear Power, 1977, Nuclear Radiation Detection, 1979; editor: Radioisotope Engineering, 1972. Recipient Outstanding Tchr. award Ga. Inst. Tech., 1973. Fellow Am. Nuclear Soc. (chmn. isotopes and radiation div. 1967-68); mem. Am. Phys. Soc., Health Physics Soc., Can. Assn. Physicists, Inst. Physics. Current Work: Migration of radioactive wastes; radiation detectors, applied radiation technology, natural radiation background, architectural acoustics. Subspecialties: Nuclear engineering; Radiation protection. Home: 1784 Noble Dr N Atlanta GA 30306 Office: Ga Inst Tech Atlanta GA 30332

EICHHORN, GUNTHER LOUIS, chemist; b. Frankfurt am Main, Germany, Feb. 8, 1927; s. Fritz David and Else Regina (Weiss) E.; m. Lotti Neuhaus, June 25, 1964; children: David Mark, Sharon Julie. A.B. in Chemistry, U. Louisville, 1947; M.S., U. Ill., 1948, Ph.D., 1950. Asst. prof., then asso. prof. chemistry La. State U., 1950-57; commd. officer USPHS, 1954-57; asso. prof. chemistry Georgetown U., 1957-58; guest scientist Naval Med. Research Inst., 1957-58; chief sect. molecular biology Gerontology Research Center, Nat. Inst. Aging, NIH, Balt., 1958-78; chief lab. cellular and molecular biology and head sect. inorganic biochemistry Gerontology Research Center, Nat. Inst. Aging, NIH (Gerontology Research Center), 1978—; pres. Nat. Inst. Child Health and Human Devel. Assembly Scientists, 1972-73; mem. panel nickel NRC, 1974; distinguished lectr. Mich. State U., 1972; Watkins vis. prof. Wichita State U., 1983; condr. seminars, lectr. in field. Editor: Inorganic Biochemistry, 1973; co-editor: Advances in Inorganic Biochemistry, 1978—; mem. editorial bds. profl. jours.; Author papers in field. Gen. Aniline and Film Co. grantee, 1949; postdoctoral fellow Ohio State U., summers 1951, 52; recipient Woodcock medal U. Louisville, 1947; Md. Chemist award, 1978; NIH Dir.'s award, 1979; Sr. Exec. Service bonus award, 1982. Fellow AAAS, Am. Inst. Chemists, Gerontol. Soc. (fin. com. 1980-82, research and edn. com. 1982-83); mem. Am. Chem. Soc., N.Y. Acad. Scis., Am. Inst. Biol. Chemists, Biophys. Soc. Subspecialty: Molecular biology. Home: 6703 97th Ave Seabrook MD 20706 Office: NIH Nat Inst on Aging Gerontology Research Ctr Baltimore MD 21224

EIDSON, ROBERT ANSEL, electronic engineering company executive; b. Topeka, May 30, 1921; s. O. Bain and Agnes (Ray) E.; m. Cecil Ruth King, June 10, 1944; children—Susan Lloyd Eidson Barclay, Robert Bain, John Rhodes. B.S., U.S. Naval Acad., 1944; M.S.E.E., U.S. Naval Postgrad. U., 1953. Commd. ensign U.S. Navy, 1944, advanced through grades to capt., 1959; mgr. engring. div. Sanders Assocs., Inc., Nashua, N.H., 1959-64; v.p., dir. engring. lab. Airtronics, Inc., Washington, 1964-67; dir. spl. systems IBM, Gaithersburg, Md., 1967-72; pres. Decisions and Designs, Inc., McLean, Va., 1972—. Trustee U.S. Naval Acad. Found., Annapolis, Md.; v.p. Tysons Transp. Assn., Tysons Corner (Va.), 1981—. Mem. IEEE, Am. Def. Preparedness Assn., Reserve Officers Assn., Sigma Chi. Republican. Presbyterian. Clubs: Navy League; Congressional Country, Burning Tree (Bethesda, Md.); Georgetown (Washington). Subspecialty: Operations research (engineering). Office: Decisions and Designs Inc 8400 Westpark Dr Suite 600 McLean VA 22101

EIGEN, DARYL JAY, psychologist, engineering administrator; b. Milw., July 29, 1947; s. David J. and Pearl (Rice) E.; m. Carol A. Kois, Mar. 30, 1972; children: Tony, Molly. B.A. in Psychology, U. Wis.-Milw., 1972, M.S. in Elec. Engring, 1973; postgrad., Rutgers U., 1974-75; Ph.D. in Indsl. Engring, Northwestern U., 1981. Teaching asst. U. Wis., Milw., 1971-72, research asst., 1972-73; mem. tech. staff Bell Labs., Piscataway, N.J., 1973-75, Naperville, Ill., 1975-81, supr. tech. staff, 1981—; reviewer Bell Labs. (Bell System Tech.), Naperville, 1980—; session chmn. Automatic Control Symposium, Milw., 1976; organizer Workplace in the Info. Age, Murray Hill, N.J., 1982. Contbr. articles in areas of pattern, recognition, human factors and methodologies exptl. to profl. jours. Adviser Explorer Scouts, Naperville, 1982; coordinator Affirmative Action. Served with USMC, 1966-68, Vietnam. Recipient outstanding personal contbns. and commitment award Bell Labs., Naperville, 1982; Chancellor's Office scholar U. Wis.-Milw., 1970; U.Wis.-Milw. grantee, 1971; NASA Grantee, 1972; Bell Labs. grantee, 1980. Mem. IEEE (sec., treas. Computer Soc. Chgo. 1982, v.p., reviewer transactions Piscataway 1973, Naperville, 1977), Am. Psychol. Assn., Human Factors Soc., AAAS, Tau Beta Pi. Designer phone service charge-a-call, 1976, calling card service, 1978, teleconferencing, 1982. Current Work: Human-machine dialogues, quasi-experimental designs, computer based tools for human factors research, controlled preservice testing of new telephone services, system analysis and performance analysis. Subspecialties: Human factors engineering; Graphics, image processing, and pattern recognition. Home: 1541 Fender Rd Naperville IL 60540 Office: Bell Labs Naperville-Wheaton Rd Naperville IL 60566

EINHELLIG, FRANK ARNOLD, plant physiologist, educator, researcher, clergyman; b. Independence, Mo., July 7, 1938; s. Robert Frank and Bernice Louise (Landsberg) E.; m. Gertrude Inez Norris, Apr. 1, 1961; children: Robert Frank, Richard Ray. A.A., Graceland Coll., 1957; B.S. in Agr. (Fribourg scholar), Kans. State U., 1960; B.S. in Edn, U. Kans., Lawrence, 1961; M.N.S., U. Okla., 1964, Ph.D. in Botany, 1969. Tchr. sci. Shawnee Mission (Kans.) High Sch. Dist., 1961-67; mem. faculty U. S.D., 1969—, asst. prof. biology, 1969-73, assoc. prof., 1973-78, prof., 1978—; dir. various grants; ordained to ministry Reorganized Ch. of Jesus Christ of Latter Day Saints, 1959, asst. pastor congregation, Sioux City, Iowa, 1979, 82-83. Contbr. articles in allelopathy to profl. jours. Served to sgt. USNG, 1956-64. NSF fellow, summers 1962-64, 65-67, 69; NDEA fellow, 1967-69; NSF grantee, 1974-80, 81-82; Dept. Energy grantee, 1979; Dept. Interior Office Water Resources grantee, 1979-82. Mem. Am. Soc. Plant Physiologists, Plant Growth Regulators Soc., Weed Sci. Soc. Am., S.D. Acad. Sci., Sigma Xi, Phi Sigma, Phi Delta Kappa. Democrat. Current Work: Research on mechanisms of action of allelochemicals, inhibitory chemicals that result in plant-plant interactions plant (allelopathy). Subspecialty: Plant physiology (biology). Home: 1111 Ridgecrest Vermillion SD 57069 Office: Dept Biology Churchill-Haines Lab U SD Vermillion SD 57069

EINHORN, DANIEL, physician; b. Tel Aviv, Israel, Mar. 1, 1951; came to U.S., 1953, naturalized, 1953; s. Marcel and Lori (Haller) E. B.A., Yale U., 1973; M.D., Tufts U., 1977. Diplomate: Am. Bd. Internal Medicine, Am. Bd. Endocrinology. Asst. chief service Douglas Hosp., Montreal, 1966-67; intern in medicine Beth Israel Hosp., Boston, 1977-78, resident in psychiatry, 1978-79, resident in medicine, 1979-81, staff, 1981—; clin. fellow Harvard Med. Sch., Boston, 1977-81, research fellow, 1981—; staff physician Jewish Meml. Hosp., Boston, 1981—, Southwood Hosp., Norfolk, Mass., 1982—; courtesy staff Malden (Mass.) Hosp., 1983. Mem. AAAS, Am. Heart Assn., Am. Fedn. Clin. Research, ACP, Phi Beta Kappa, Alpha Omega Alpha. Current Work: Metabolism, obesity, hypertension, clinical endocrinology, opiates, sympathetic nervous system, adrenal, catecholamines, steroids. Subspecialties: Neuroendocrinology; Internal medicine. Home: 7930 Frost St San Diego CA 92123 Office: Harvard Med Sch 330 Brookline Ave Boston MA 02215

EINSPRUCH, NORMAN GERALD, college dean, electrical engineering and computer educator; b. N.Y.C., June 27, 1932; s. Adolph and Mala E. (Goldblatt) E.; m. Edith Melnick, Dec. 20, 1953; children—Eric, Andrew, Franklin. B.A. in Physics, Rice U., 1953; M.S. in Physics, U. Colo., 1955; Ph.D. in Applied Math., Brown U., 1959. Tech. staff Tex. Instrn., Inc., Dallas, 1959-62, mgr. electron transp. physics br., 1962-68, dir. adv. tech. lab., 1968-69, dir. tech. chem. materials div., 1969-72, dir. ctr. research labs., 1972-75, asst. v.p., 1975-77; prof. elec. and computer engring., dean Coll. Engring., U. Miami, Coral Gables, Fla., 1977—; dir. Ogden Corp., N.Y.C., 1981—; cons. in field. Editor: VLSI Electronics-Microstructure Sciince Series, 12 vols., 1981—. Contbr. articles to profl. jours. Fellow IEEE, AAAS, Am. Phys. Soc., Acoustical Soc.; mem. Am. Inst. Indsl. Engrs., Am. Soc. Engring. Edn., Soc. Info. Display, Golden Key, Sigma Xi, Tau Beta Pi, Eta Kappa Nu, Phi Kappa Phi, Tau Sigma Delta, Alpha Pi Mu, Omicron Delta Kappa. Subspecialties: Electrical engineering; Microchip technology (engineering). Home: 1415 Trillo Ave Coral Gables FL 33146 Office: U Miami PO Box 248581 Coral Gables FL 33124

EINZIGER, ROBERT EMANUEL, research scientist, physicist; b. Asbury Park, N.J., Feb. 19, 1945. B.S. in Physics, Ga. Tech., 1967; M.S. in Physics, Rensselaer Poly. Inst., 1973, Ph.D. in Physics, 1973. Postdoctoral scientist Argonne (Ill.) Nat. Lab., 1974-76, asst. scientist, Idaho Falls, 1976-79; sr. scientist Westinghouse Hanford Co., Richland, Wash., 1979—. Mem. Am. Nuclear Soc., Am. Phys. Soc., Sigma Xi, Sigma Pi Sigma, Tau Beta Pi. Current Work: Behavior of spent nuclear fuel during dry storage or disposal. Subspecialties: Metallurgical engineering; Nuclear fission. Home: 2363 Davison Ave Richland WA 99352 Office: Westinghouse Hanford Co PO Box 1970 Mail Stop W/A-40 Richland WA 99352

EIRICH, FREDERICK ROLAND, educator, chemist; b. Vienna, Austria, May 23, 1905; came to U.S., 1947, naturalized, 1953; s. Otto George and Hermine (Perlhefter) E.; m. Maria Dorothea Dehne, Feb. 1, 1936; children—Ursula D., Richard S. Moeller, Susan H. Ph.D., U. Vienna, 1929, Dr. Phil. habil., 1938; M.A., U. Cambridge, Eng., 1939. Research asso., lectr. U. Vienna, 1934-38, U. Cambridge, 1939-47; mem. faculty Poly. Inst., Bklyn., 1948—, prof., 1952—; distinguished prof., 1969—, dean research, 1967-70; vis. prof. U. Uppsala, 1950; Unilever prof. U. Bristol, 1965; cons. Govt. Com. Chems., Plastics and Rubber Industry. Author, editor numerous books and research papers. Recipient A. Humboldt Found. award, 1980; recipient Bingham medal 1983, M. Huggins award, 1985. Fellow N.Y. Acad. Sci. (chmn. chem. sect. 1952-53), Faraday Soc., Internat. Inst. Fracture Mechanics (hon.); mem. Am. Chem. Soc. (chmn. colloid div. 1960, Distinguished Service award 1975, Merit award Rubber Div. 1978), AAAS (chmn., councillor Gordon Confs. 1959-65), Soc. Rheology (pres. 1972-73), Am. Phys. Soc. (gov. bd. 1970-74), Sigma Xi (research award 1970). Current work: Rheology, bioadhesion, chemical evolution. Subspecialties: Polymer chemistry; Surface chemistry. Home: 22 Deerfield Ave Tuckahoe NY 10707 Office: 333 Jay St Brooklyn NY 11201

EISDORFER, CARL, physician. Sr. attending physician Montefiore Med. Ctr.; prof. Albert Einstein Coll. Medicine, Bronx, N.Y. Recipient Potamkin prize, 1983. Subspecialties: Psychophysiology; Psychiatry. Office: Albert Einstein Coll Medicine 1300 Morris Park Ave Bronx NY 10461

EISENBERG, LEON, child psychiatrist; b. Phila., Aug. 8, 1922; s. Morris and and Elizabeth (Sabreen) E.; m. Ruth Harriet Bleier, June 11, 1948 (div. 1967); children: Mark Philip, Kathy Bleier; m. Carola Blitzman Guttmacher, Aug. 31, 1967; children: Laurence, Alan. A.B., U. Pa., 1944, M.D., 1946; M.A. (hon.), Harvard, 1967; D.Sc. (hon.), U. Manchester, Eng., 1973. Diplomate: in child psychiatry and psychiatry Am. Bd. Psychiatry and Neurology. Intern Mt. Sinai Hosp., N.Y.C., 1946-47; instr. physiology U. Pa., 1947-48; resident psychiatry Sheppard-Pratt Hosp., Towson, Md., 1950-52; with Johns Hopkins, 1952-67; prof. child psychiatry Med. Sch., 1961-67; psychiatrist-in-charge children's psychiat. service Harriet Lane Home, 1958-67; prof. psychiatry Harvard Med. Sch., 1967—, Maude and Lillian Presley prof. psychiatry, 1975-80, chmn. exec. com. dept. psychiatry, 1973-80, Maude and Lillian Presley prof. social medicine and chmn. dept. social medicine and health policy, 1980—; psychiatrist-in-chief Mass. Gen. Hosp., 1967-74, mem. bd. consultation, 1974—; sr. asso. in psychiatry Children's Hosp., Boston, 1974—; psychiat. cons. Crownsville (Md.) State Hosp., 1954-58, Rosewood State Tng. Sch., Owings Mills, Md., 1957-60, Balt. City Hosp., 1959-62, Children's Guild, Balt., 1954-61; cons. Sinai Hosp., Balt., 1963-67; Mapother-Lewis ann. lectr. Maudsley Hosp., London, 1977; Baan Meml. lectr. Netherlands Psychiat. Soc., Amsterdam, 1978; Royal Soc. Medicine vis. prof., London, 1983; Mem. subcom. psychiat. nomenclature, com. vital statistics USPHS; chmn. WHO Conf. Developmental Regulation, 1964-67; mem. Joint Commn. Mental Health of Children; cons. Office Mental Health, World Health Assn., 1974—; mem. adv. com. to dir. NIH, 1977-80. Editor: Am. Jour. Orthopsychiatry, 1963-73; editorial bd.: Medicine and Psychiatry. Served to capt. M.C., AUS, 1948-50. Recipient Theobald Smith award Albany Med. Coll., 1979; Orton award Orton Soc., 1980. Fellow Am. Psychiat. Assn. (trustee 1973-76), Am. Orthopsychiat. Assn., AAAS, Royal Coll. Psychiatrists (U.K.) (hon.), Soc. Research Child Devel.; mem. Inst. Medicine of Nat. Acad. Scis. (council 1975-77, program and membership coms. 1979-82), AAUP (past pres. Johns Hopkins), Am. Acad. Pediatrics (Aldrich award 1980), Am. Pediatric Soc., Assn. Research Nervous and Mental Disease, Am. Psychopath. Assn., Md. Psychiat. Soc. (past pres.), Am. Acad. Arts and Scis., Psychiat. Research Soc. (past pres.), Soc. Neurosci., Mass. Med. Soc., Greek Soc. Neurology and Psychiatry (hon.), Johns Hopkins Soc. Scholars, Phi Beta Kappa (chpt. pres.), Sigma Xi, Alpha Omega Alpha. Current Work: Effects of social class and ethnicity on illness and on care-seeking behavior. Subspecialties: Psychiatry; Epidemiology. Home: 9 Clement Circle Cambridge MA 02138 Office: Dept Social Medicine and Health Policy Harvard Med Sch Boston MA 02115

EISENBERG, M(YRON) MICHAEL, surgery educator, academic administrator; b. N.Y.C., Jan. 27, 1931; s. George H. and Dorothy E.; divorced (div.); children: Elysa Debra, Ellen Beth, Andrea Carla; m. Barbara Yetka, 1983. B.A., NYU, 1952; M.D., Harvard U., 1956. Diplomate: Am. Bd. Surgery. Intern Peter Bent Brigham Hosp., Boston; resident Yale-New Haven Med. Ctr.; instr. surgery U. Fla., 1962-63; asst. prof. surgery U. Fla. (Coll. Medicine), 1963-67, assoc. prof., 1967-68; prof. U. Minn.-Mpls., 1968-81, head gastrointestinal surgery, 1968-81; prof., vice chmn. dept. surgery SUNY Downstate Med Ctr., Bklyn., 1981—; chief surgery Mt. Sinai Hosp., Mpls., 1968-75, surgery L.I. Coll. Hosp., 1981—. Author: Ulcers, 1978; contbr. articles to profl. publs., chpts. to books. Served as capt. M.C. U.S. Army, 1958-60. Sr. investigator NIH, 1963-80. Mem. Internat. Soc. for Surgery of Digestive Tract (pres.), Phi Beta Kappa, Alpha Omega Alpha. Current Work: Physiology and surgery of gastrointestinal tract. Subspecialties: Surgery; Psychophysiology.

EISENBERG, RONALD LEE, radiology educator; b. Phila., July 11, 1945; s. Milton and Betty Ruth (Klein) E.; m. Zina Schiff, Sept. 19, 1970; children: Avlana, Cherina. A.B. in Chemistry, U. Pa., 1965, M.D., 1969. Diplomate: Am. Bd. Radiology. Intern Mt. Zion Med. Ctr., San Francisco, 1969-70; resident Mass. Gen. Hosp., Boston, 1970-71; resident U. Calif., San Francisco, 1973-75, staff radiologist, 1975-80; prof. radiology La. State U. Med. Ctr., Shreveport, 1980—, chmn. dept., 1980—. Author: Gastrointestinal Radiology, 1983; Atlas of Signs in Radiology, 1984; Diagnostic Imaging in Internal Medicine, 1985; editor: Critical Diagnostic Pathways in Radiology, 1981. Served to maj. M.C. U.S. Army, 1971-73. VA grantee, 1977; NIH grantee, 1979. Mem. Radiol. Soc. N.Am., Am. Coll. Radiology, Am. Roentgen Ray Soc., Soc. Gastrointestinal Radiology, Assn. Univ. Radiologists, Am. Physicians Fellowship for Medicine in Israel, Phi Beta Kappa, Alpha Omega Alpha. Current Work: Referral criteria, optimization of projects, cost-containment in radiology; development of imaging consultancy program in radiology residency; algorithmic approach to sequencing of radiographic imaging procedures. Subspecialty: Diagnostic radiology. Office: Dept Radiology La State U Med Center PO Box 33932 Shreveport LA 71130

EISENBUD, MERRIL, environmental scientist; b. N.Y.C., Mar. 18, 1915; s. Kalman and Leonora (Kopaloff) E.; m. Irma Onish, Jan. 22, 1939; children—Elliott, Michael, Fredrick. B.S. in Elec. Engring, N.Y. U., 1936; Sc.D. (hon.), Fairleigh Dickinson U., 1960; D.H.C., Catholic U., Rio de Janiero. Diplomate: Am. Acad. Environ. Engrs. Indsl. hygienist Liberty Mut. Ins. Co., 1936-47; assoc. prof. indsl. medicine Sch. Medicine, NYU, 1945-55, adj. prof., 1956-59, prof. environ. medicine, dir. lab. environ. studies, 1959-84, prof. emeritus, 1984—; adj. prof. U. N.C., 1984—; adminstr. N.Y.C. EPA, 1968-70; dir. health and safety lab. AEC, 1947-59; mem. Nat. Commn. on Radiation Protection and Measurements, 1965—, dir., 1971-76; mem. expert panel on radiation hazards WHO, 1956—; mem. N.Y. State Health Adv. Council, 1975-80. Author: Environmental Radioactivity, 2d edit, 1973, Environment, Technology, and Health, 1979. Bd. dirs. Blue Cross-Blue Shield Greater N.Y., 1968-75; bd. mgrs. State Community Aid Assn.; mem. adv. council Electric Power Research Inst. Recipient Gold medal AEC, 1974; Hermann Biggs medal N.Y. State Pub. Health Assn.; Arthur Holly Compton award Am. Nuclear Soc.; Power-Life award Am. Inst. Elec. and Electronic Engrs. Fellow AAAS, N.Y. Acad. Scis. (hon. life mem., gov., v.p. 1979-80), N.Y. Acad. Medicine; mem. Nat. Acad. Engring., Health Physics Soc. (pres. 1965-66), Am. Indsl. Hygiene Assn., Brazilian Acad. Sci. (corr.). Radiation Research Soc., Am. Bd. Health Physics. Clubs: Cosmos (Washington). Current Work: Environmental effects of technology development. Subspecialty: Environmental toxicology. Home: 711 Bayberry Dr Chapel Hill NC 27514

EISGRUBER, LUDWIG MARIA, educator; b. Mallersdorf, Germany, Dec. 12, 1931; came to U.S., 1955, naturalized, 1964; s. Ludwig and Maria E.; m. Eva Renate Eisgruber, Dec. 17, 1960; children—Christopher, Karen, Michelle, Ingrid. Diploma in Agr, Technische Hochschule Munchen, W. Ger., 1955; M.S., Purdue, 1957, Ph.D., 1959. Asst. prof. Purdue U., Lafayette, Ind., 1959-62, asso. prof., 1962-65, prof., 1965-73, asst. head dept. agrl. econs., 1969-73; asst. dean Purdue U. (Grad. Sch.), 1970-73; program leader applications requirements Purdue U. (Lab. Application Remote Scanning), 1970-73; prof., head dept. agrl. and resource econs Oreg. State U., Corvallis, 1973-81, asso. dean, dir. internat. agr., 1981-83, acting dean Coll. Agrl. Scis., 1984—; sr. economist Near East Bur., U.S. AID, Dept. State, Washington, 1983; cons. in field. Author: (with E.M. Babb) Management Games for Teaching and Research, 1966, (with J.L. Hesselbach) Betriebliche Entscheidungen Mittels Simulations, 1967. IBM travel grantee, 1972; Sears, Roebuck & Co. grantee, 1958. Mem. Am. Agrl. Econs. Assn., Internat. Assn. Agrl. Economists, Am. Econs. Assn., Western Agrl. Econs. Assn. (pres. 1978-79), Sigma Xi (sec.-treas. Purdue chpt. 1970-72), Gamma Sigma Delta. Current Work: Agricultural policy and analysis of Near Eastern countries. Economic feasibility analyses of agricultural development projects, administration of research and academic programs. Subspecialty: Agricultural economics. Office: Extension Hall Oreg State U Corvallis OR 97331

EISNER, THOMAS, biologist, educator; b. Berlin, June 25, 1929; s. Hans Edouard and Margarete (Heil) E.; m. Maria Lobell, June 10, 1952; children: Yvonne, Vivian, Christina. B.A., Harvard U., 1951, Ph.D., 1955; D.Sc. hon., U. Wurzburg, W. Ger., 1982, U. Zurich, Switzerland, 1983. Postdoctoral fellow Harvard U., 1955-57; asst. prof. biology Cornell U., Ithaca, N.Y., 1957-62, assoc. prof., 1962-65, prof., 1965-76, Jacob Gould Schurman prof. biology, 1976—; vis. scientist dept. entomology Sch. Agr., Wageningen, Netherlands, 1964-65; vis. scientist Smithsonian Tropical Research Lab., Barro Colorado Island, C.Z., 1968; sr. vis. scientist Max Planck Inst. für Verhaltensphysiologie, Seewisen, W. Ger., 1971, Div. Entomology, Canberra, Australia, 1972-73; Rand fellow Marine Biol. Labs., Woods Hole, Mass., 1974; vis. research prof. U. Fla., Gainesville, 1977-78; vis. prof. Stanford U., 1979-80, U. Zurich, 1980-81. Co-author: Animal Adaptation, 1964, Life on Earth, 1973, and 3 other books.; Mem. editorial bd.: Sci, 1970-71, Am. Naturalist, 1970-71, Jour. Comparative Physiology, 1974-80, Chem. Ecology, 1974—, Cornell Rev, 1976-77, Behavioral Ecology and Sociobiology, 1976—, Sci. Yr. World Books, 1979—; contbr. articles to profl. jours. Guggenheim fellow, 1964-65, 72-73; Recipient Newcomb Cleveland prize AAAS, 1967; Founder's Meml. award Entomol. Soc. Am., 1969; Recipient Archie F. Carr medal, 1983. Fellow Explorers Club, AAAS (chmn. sect. biology 1979—, mem. com. for sci. freedom and responsibility 1980—), Am. Acad. Arts and Scis., Royal Soc. Arts; mem. Nat. Acad. Sci., Zero Population Growth (dir. 1969-70), Nat. Audubon Soc. (dir. 1970-75), Nature Conservancy (nat. council 1969-74), Fedn. Am. Scientists (mem. council 1977-81). Current Work: Behavioral and chemical ecology of insects. Subspecialties: Ecology (environmental science); Ethology. Office: Dept Neurobiology and Behavior W347 Mudd Hall Cornell U Ithaca NY 14853

EISON, MICHAEL STEVEN, psychopharmacologist, researcher; b. N.Y.C., Jan. 21, 1953; s. Fred and Freda (Berg) E.; m. Arlene Stark, Aug. 19, 1979. B.A., SUNY-Buffalo, 1975; M.A., UCLA, 1976, Ph.D., 1980. Postdoctoral fellow NSF-NATO, Cambridge, Eng., 1980-81; scientist Mead Johnson Pharms, Evansville, Ind., 1981-82; sr. scientist Bristol-Myers Co., Evansville, 1982-84, assoc. dir. CNS biology, 1984—. Recipient Feldman-Cohan award SUNY-Buffalo, 1975. Mem. Soc. for Neurosci., N.Y. Acad. Sci., Am. Psychol. Assn., AAAS, Sigma Xi, Phi Beta Kappa. Current Work: Biological basis of human psychopathology. Subspecialties: Neuropharmacology; Physiological psychology. Office: Pharm and Research and Devel Div Bristol-Myers Co Evansville IN 47721

EISS, NORMAN SMITH, JR., mech. engr., educator; b. Buffalo, Mar. 13, 1931; s. Norman Smith and Elizabeth Charlotte (Hengerer) E.; m. Nancy Jean Siegrist, Mar. 27, 1975; children: Martin E., Christine C., Jennifer L. B.S. in M.E. Rensselaer Poly. Inst., 1953; M.S., Cornell U., 1959, Ph.D., 1961. With textile fibers div. duPont, Tonawanda, N.Y., 1953-54; with Cornell Aero. Lab., Cheektowaga, N.Y., 1956-58, 61-66; with Va. Poly. Inst. and State U., Blacksburg, 1966—, prof. mech. engring., 1977—; cons. tribology, stress analysis, surface topography characterization. Contbr. articles to profl. jours. Served with USAF, 1954-56. NSF Sci. Faculty fellow, 1970-71. Mem. ASME, Am. Soc. Lubrication Engrs., Am. Soc. Engring. Edn., ASTM, Sigma Xi, Pi Tau Sigma, Tau Beta Pi, Phi Kappa Phi. Current Work: Abrasive and fatigue wear of polymers. Subspecialty: Mechanical engineering. Office: Mech Engring Dep Va Poly Inst and State U Blacksburg VA 24061

EKBERG, DONALD ROY, fisheries administrator; b. Hinsdale, Ill., Dec. 23, 1928; s. Roy Harley and Evelyn Beatrice (Newman) E.; m. Anneliese G. Nattermann, May 27, 1961; children: Kenneth, Dale. B.S., U. Ill., 1950, Ph.D., 1957; M.S., U. Chgo., 1952. Physiologist Gen. Electric Co., Phila., 1958-59; postdoctoral fellow USPHS, 1959-60, physiologist and mgr. bioscis., Phila. and Bay St. Louis, Miss., 1960-76; biologist Nat. Marine Fisheries Service, St. Petersburg, Fla., 1976-77, chief environ. and tech. service div., 1977—. Served to col. USAFR, 1952—. Mem. Soc. Gen. Physiologists, Am. Soc. Zoologists, Am. Physiol. Soc., Sigma Xi. Current Work: Fish ecosystem alteration, technology transfer to fisheries. Office: Nat Marine Fisheries Service NOAA 9450 Koger Blvd Duval Bldg St Petersburg FL 33702

EKERS, RONALD DAVID, astronomer; b. Victor Harbour, South Australia, Sept. 18, 1941; came to U.S., 1967; s. Laurence and Elsie (Plaisted) E.; m. Jennifer A. Brooks, June 1, 1940; children: Brook, Daen, Erik. B.Sc., U. Adelaide, 1962, B.Sc. with honors, 1963; Ph.D., Australian Nat. U., 1967. Postdoctoral fellow Calif. Inst. Tech., Pasadena, 1967-70, Inst. Theoretical Astronomy, Cambridge, Eng., 1970-71; research worker Kapeteyn Lab., Groningen, Netherlands, 1971-80, prof., 1977—; asst. dir. Nat. Radio Astronomy Obs., Socorro, N.Mex., 1980—; bd. dirs. Netherlands Found. Radio Astronomy, 1975-80; mem. vis. com. Meudon (France) Radio Obs., 1975-77; vis. scientist Commonwealth Sci. and Indsl. Research Orgn., 1977-78; vis. fellow Australian Nat. U., 1979; mem. sci. adv. com. Inst. Millimeter Astronomy, 1979-80; adj. prof. U. N.Mex., 1981—; mem. telecommunication and data acquisition adv. council Jet. Propulsion Lab., 1982—; dir. Riotech, N.Mex. Contbr. articles to sci. jours. Mem. Internat. Astron. Union, Astron. Soc. Australia, Am. Astron. Soc., Royal Astron. Soc. Subspecialty: Radio and microwave astronomy. Office: NRAO PO Box 0 Socorro NM 87801

EKPERIGIN, HENRY EYITUOYO, veterinarian, nutritionist, epidemiologist; b. Lagos, Nigeria, Feb. 26, 1944; came to U.S., 1974; s. Harding J. and Felicia M. (Akale) E.; m. Mofoluso Modupe Daramola, Dec. 26, 1973; children—Eyituoyo, Bejutomi, Omayone, Dedejo, Tenesan. D.V.M., U. Ibadan, Nigeria, 1970; M.P.V.M., U. Calif.-Davis, 1975, Ph.D. in Nutrition, 1980. Math. and African history instr. Anglican Girls Grammar Sch., Benin-City, Nigeria, 1965; biology instr. Continuing Edn. Ctr., Benin-City, 1973-74; vet. officer to prin. vet. officer Bendel State Govt. Nigeria, 1970-74; Avian medicine resident Vet. Med. Teaching Hosp., U. Calif., Davis, 1980-82; vis. lectr., postgrad. research/epidemiologist, dept. epidemiology and preventive medicine U. Calif., Davis, 1982—; mem. nutrition com. Livestock Disease Research Lab., U. Calif., 1981. Contbr. articles to profl. jours. Pres. Orchard Park Parents' Assn., Davis, 1980. Postgrad. scholar Bendel State Govt. Nigeria, 1974. Mem. Am. Assn. Avian Pathologists, Am. Vet. Med. Assn., Am. Acad. Vet. Nutrition, Assn. Avian Vets., Poultry Sci. Assn., World Poultry Sci. Assn. (U.S. br.), Sigma Xi. Current work: Prevention and control of egg-transmitted diseases of poultry; nutrient toxicoses and their treatment/control. Subspecialty: Animal nutrition. Office: Univ California Vet Med Teaching Hosp Large Animal Clinic Davis CA 95616

EL-ACKAD, TAREK M., cardiovascular clinical research pharmacologist, human physiology educator; b. Alexandria, Egypt, Sept. 25, 1941; came to U.S., 1964; s. Mohamed Soliman and Fatma (Fahmy) El-A. B.Sc., Alexandria U., 1962; M.S., N.C. State U., 1967, Rutgers U., 1970; Ph.D., Rutgers U., 1972. Pharmacology research fellow U. Iowa Coll. Medicine, 1972-75; head cardiovascular pharmacology Pennwalt Pharms., Rochester, N.Y., 1975-77; sr. clin. research assoc. Abbott Internat., Ltd., Abbott Park, Ill., 1977-79, Abbott Hosp. Products, Abbott Park, 1979-81; sr. med. research assoc. Schering-Plough Corp., Kenilworth, N.J., 1981—; adj. assoc. prof. Fairleigh-Dickinson U. Sch. Dentistry, Hackensack, N.J., 1981—. Contbr. articles to profl. jours. Chmn. social com. Rutgers U. Grad. Student Assn., 1970-72; mem. curriculum com. Rutgers U. Physiology Program, 1970-72. Bio-Med. Telemetry scholar, 1970; NSF research asst., 1968-71; research fellow Am. and Iowa Heart Assns., 1973-74. Mem. N.Y. Acad. Scis., AAAS, Am. Heart Assn., Am. Fedn. Clin. Research, Histamine Research Soc. N.Am., Am. Soc. Parenteral and Enteral Nutrition, Schering Classical Music Lovers Club (pres.), Sigma Xi. Club: Schering Classical Music Lovers (pres.). Current Work: Clinical pharmacology research in cardiovascular antihypertensive drugs; academic teaching in gastroenterology. Subspecialties: Pharmacology; Gastroenterology. Office: Schering Plough Corp Galloping Hill Rd Kenilworth NJ 07033

ELAM, JACK GORDON, consulting geologist, oil producer; b. Glendale, Calif., Aug. 25, 1921; s. Guy Russell and Nellie Olive (Blake) E.; m. Muriel Irene Stone, Apr. 23, 1952 (div. 1972); m. Patricia Lou Malm, July 26, 1974; children—Pamela, Patricia, Peggy, Melissa. A.B., UCLA, 1943, M.A., 1948; Ph.D., Rensselaer Poly. Inst., 1960. Geologist Stanley & Stolz, Los Angeles, 1946-47, Richfield Oil Corp., Long Beach, Calif., 1947-49; dist. geologist Cameron Oil Co., Los Angeles and Midland, Tex., 1949-51; cons. geologist, Midland, 1951-56, 60—; asst. prof. petroleum geology Rensselaer Poly. Inst., Troy, N.Y., 1956-60; ind. oil producer, Midland, 1964—. Author: Creativity in Oil Exploration, 1984; also articles. Co-editor: Cyclic Sedimentation in Permian Basin, 1969. Founder, pres., chmn. bd. Permian Basin Grad. Ctr., Midland, 1967-82. Mem. West Tex. Geol. Soc. (treas. 1964-65, 1st v.p. 1965, pres. 1966, Dedicated Service award 1977), Soc. Ind. Profl. Earth Scientists (bd. dirs., editor and 1st v.p. 1967-70), Geol. Soc. Am. Republican. Subspecialties: Geology; Tectonics. Home: 2501 Princeton Midland TX 79701 Office: 219 N Main Midland TX 79701

EL-BAZ, FAROUK, corporate executive; b. Zagazig, Egypt, Jan. 2, 1938; came to U.S., 1960, naturalized, 1970; s. El-Sayed Mohammed and Zahia Abul-Ata (Hammouda) El-B.; m. Catherine Patricia O'Leary, 1963; children—Monira, Soraya, Karima, Fairouz. B.Sc., Ain Shams U., 1958; M.S., U. Mo., 1961; Ph.D., U. Mo. and Mass. Inst. Tech., 1964. Demonstrator geology dept. Assiut U., Egypt, 1958-60; lectr. Mineralogy-Petrography Inst., U. Heidelberg, Ger., 1964-65; geologist exploration dept. Pan Am.-UAR Oil Co., Egypt, 1966; supr. lunar exploration Bellcomm and Bell Telephone Labs., Washington, 1967-72; research dir. Center for Earth and Planetary Studies, Nat. Air and Space Mus., Smithsonian Instn., Washington, 1973-82; v.p. sci. and tech. Itek Optical Systems, Litton Industries, Lexington, Mass., 1982—; cons. geology; prof. geology and geophysics U. Utah, 1975-77; prof. geology Ain Shams U., Egypt, 1976-81; sci. adviser Pres. Anwar Sadat of Egypt, 1978-81. Author or co-author: Say It in Arabic, 1968, Coprolites: An Annotated Bibliography, 1968, Glossory of Mining Geology, 1970, The Moon as Viewed by Lunar Orbiter, 1970, Astronaut Observations from the Apollo-Soyuz Mission, 1977, Apollo Over the Moon: A View from Orbit, 1978, Egypt As Seen by Landsat, 1979, Apollo-Soyuz Test Project Summary Science Report: Earth Observations and Photography, 1979; Desert Landforms of Southwest Egypt: A basis for Comparison with Mars, 1982; Deserts and Arid Lands, 1984; The Geology of Egypt: An Annotated Bibliography, 1984; also articles. Decorated Order of Merit 1st class Egypt; recipient certificate merit U.S. Bur. Mines, 1961, Exceptional Sci. Achievement medal NASA, 1971, Alumni Achievement award U. Mo., 1972, Honor citation Assn. Arab-Am. U. Grads., 1973. Fellow Royal Astron. Soc., Geol. Soc. Am. (certificate commendation 1973); mem. AAAS, Sigma Xi. Clubs: Explorers, University. Current Work: Photographic systems and photointerpretation of planetary surface features and applications of space technology to high resolution photography for mapping and reconnaissance. Subspecialties: Planetary science; Satellite studies. Office: Itek Optical Systems 10 Maquire Rd Lexington MA 02173

ELBLE, RODGER JACOB, JR., neurologist, educator, neurophysiology researcher; b. Alton, Ill., Aug. 10, 1948; s. Rodger Jacob and Blanche Dee (Baughman) E.; m. Suzanne Louise Marshall, Aug. 14, 1971; children—Rodger Jacob, III, Joseph Marshall, Ann Elizabeth. B.S. in Aero. Engring., Purdue U., 1971; Ph.D. in Physiology, Ind. U., 1975, M.D., 1977. Diplomate Am. Bd. Psychiatry and Neurology. Med. intern Ind. U., Indpls., 1977-78; resident in neurology Washington U., St. Louis, 1978-81; asst. prof. So. Ill. U., Springfield, 1981—. Contbr. articles to med. jours. Mem. Soc. Neurosci., AMA, Am. Physiol. Soc., Am. Acad. Neurology, AAAS, Alpha Omega Alpha, Tau Beta Pi, Phi Kappa Phi, Sigma Gamma Tau. Current work: Neurophysiology of tremor; treatment of Parkinson disease; neurophysiology of motor control; clinical aspects and neurochemistry of Alzheimer disease. Subspecialties: Neurology; Neurophysiology. Home: 1911 Bates Ave Springfield IL 62704 Office: So Ill U Sch Medicine 800 N Rutledge Springfield IL 62708

ELDEFRAWI, AMIRA TOPPOZADA, pharmacologist, toxicologist, neurobiologist, researcher, educator; b. Giza, Egypt, Feb. 10, 1937; came to U.S., 1968, naturalized, 1974; d. Hussein K. and Fadila I. (Aref) Toppozada; m. Mohyee E. Eldefrawi, July 18, 1957; children: Mohsen, Mona, Mohab. B.Sc. in Agr, U. Alexandria, Egypt, 1957; Ph.D., U. Calif., Berkeley, 1960. Asst. prof. U. Alexandria, 1960-68; research asso., then sr. research asso. sect neurobiology and behavior Cornell U., Ithaca, N.Y., 1968-76; research prof. pharmacology U. Md. Sch. Medicine, Balt., 1976—; cons. in field. Co-editor: Myasthenia Gravis, 1983; contbr. over 150 articles to sci. jours. NIH grantee, 1975—. Mem. Am. Soc. Pharmacology and Exptl. Therapeutics, Soc. Neurosci., Entomol. Soc. Am. Republican. Moslem. Current Work: Neuropharmacology, neurotransmitter receptors and ionic channels. Subspecialties: Molecular pharmacology; Neuropharmacology. Home: 8403 Topping Rd Pikesville MD 21208 Office: Dept Pharmacology and Exptl Therapeutics U Md Sch Medicine Baltimore MD 21201

ELDRED, KENNETH MCKECHNIE, acoustical consultant; b. Springfield, Mass., Nov. 25, 1929; s. Robert Mosley and Jean McKechnie (Ashton) E.; m. Helene Barbara Koerting Fischer, May 31, 1957; 1 dau., Heidi Jean. B.S., MIT, 1950, postgrad., 1951-53; postgrad., UCLA, 1960-63. Engr. in charge vibration and sound lab. Boston Naval Shipyard, 1951-54; supervisory physicist, chief phys. acoustics sect. U.S. Air Force, Wright Field, Ohio, 1956-57; v.p., cons. acoustics Western Electro-Acoustics Labs., Los Angeles, 1957-63; v.p., tech. dir. sci. services and systems group Wyle Labs., El Segundo, Calif., 1963-73; v.p., dir. div. environ. and noise control tech. Bolt Beranek and Newman Inc., Cambridge, Mass., 1973-77, prin. cons., 1977-81; dir. Ken Eldred Engring.; mem. exec. standards council Am. Nat. Standards Inst., 1979—, vice-chmn., 1981-84, chmn. bd. dirs., 1985—; mem., past chmn. Acoustical Standards Bd.; mem. com. hearing, bioacoustics and biomedics NRC, 1963—. Served with USAF, 1954-56. Fellow Acoustical Soc. Am. (chmn. coordinating com. environ. acoustics, chmn. ASC S-12, noise), Nat. Acad. Engring., Inst. Noise Control Engring. (pres. 1976), Soc. Automotive Engrs., Soc. Naval Architects and Marine Engrs., U.S. Yacht Racing Union. Current Work: Development of better methods to control aircraft operations at airports to minimize noise impact on airport neighbors; analysis of distribution of worker noise exposure in industry and costs for its control. Subspecialties: Acoustical engineering; Acoustics. Office: PO Box 1037 Concord MA 01742

ELDRIDGE, JOHN CHARLES, medical educator; b. Chgo., June 7, 1942; s. John Godfrey and Carol Spier (Boedeker) E. B.A., N.Central Coll., Naperville, Ill., 1965; M.S., No. Ill. U., 1967; Ph.D., Med. Coll. Ga., 1971. Instr. dept. biol. and health scis. Orange County Community Coll., Middletown, N.Y., 1967-68; attaché de recherche INSERM, Bordeux, France, 1971-72; research assoc. Med. Coll. Ga., Augusta, 1973; assoc. dept. lab. medicine Med. U. S.C., Charleston, 1973-76, asst. prof., 1976-78; asst. prof. dept. physiology/pharmacology Bowman Gray Sch. Medicine, Winston-Salem, N.C., 1978—; cons. in field. Contbr. papers to profl. confs. and articles to profl. jours. Mem. Endocrine Soc., AAAS, Soc. Study Reprodn., Am. Fertility Soc., Am. Soc. Andrology. Presbyterian. Club: Twin City (Winston-Salem). Lodge: Masons. Current Work: Mechanisms controlling pituitary hormone secretion; role of adrenals in reproductive function; techniques of analyzing hormones and hormone receptor interactions. Subspecialties: Neuroendocrinology; Reproductive endocrinology. Home: 2458 Tantelon Pl Winston-Salem NC 27107 Office: Bowman Gray Sch Medicine 300 S Hawthorne Rd Winston-Salem NC 27103

ELEUTERIUS, LIONEL NUMA, botanist, laboratory administarator, researcher; b. Biloxi, Miss., Dec. 25, 1936; s. Lionel Adam and Martha Elizabeth (Tiblier) E.; m. Kathryn Sarah Poole, Dec. 25, 1969; children: Chris L., Lee L. A.S., Perkinston Jr. Coll., 1958; B.S. in Botany, U. So. Miss., 1966, M.S. in Botany, 1968; Ph.D. in Botany, Miss. State U., 1974. Biol. technician U.S. Dept. Agr. Forest Service, Plant Pathology lab., Gulfport, Miss., 1961-65; lab. instr., research asst. U. So. Miss., Hattiesburg, 1965-68; biology and botany instr. Resident Center, U. So. Miss., Keesler AFB, Biloxi, 1968-69, genetics and gen. biology instr., 1969-72; prof. botany, head botany sect. Gulf Coast Research Lab., Ocean Springs, Miss., 1968—, instr. salt marsh ecology, summers 1976—, coastal vegetation, summers 1982—; adj. assoc. prof. botany Miss. State U., 1976—; adj. asst. prof. biology U. Miss., 1977—; adj. prof. biology U. So. Miss., 1981—; mem. Deer Island Study Com. (adv.), 1978-79, Nat. Wetlands Tech. Council, Washington, Miss. Gov.'s Conf. on Coastal Zone Mgmt., 1974. Author: Tidal Marsh Plants, 1980; contbr. numerous articles on botany to profl. jours. Served to maj. Army N.G., 1959-80. Recipient grants in field. Mem. Am. Bot. Soc., Am. Soc. Plant Taxonomists, Ecol. Soc. Am., So. Appalachian Bot. Club (v.p. 1979-80), Miss. Acad. Sci. (chmn. botany sect. 1970-71), Phi Theta Kappa, Beta Beta Beta. Republican. Episcopalian. Current Work: Plant growth, plant morphology, tide-plant relations, plant genetics, plant populations, plant taxonomy. Subspecialties: Taxonomy; Ecology (environmental science). Home: 123A Red Bluff Circle Ocean Springs MS 39564 Office: E Beach Dr Ocean Springs MS 39564

EL-GEWELY, MOHAMED RAAFAT, molecular geneticist; b. Damanhour, Egypt, June 2, 1942; s. Ahmed Abdelsalam and Aziza Khatab (Makey) El-G.; m. Sara, Nov. 16, 1981. B.S., Alexandria (Egypt) U., 1963; Ph.D., U. Alta., Can., 1971. Postdoctoral fellow McGill U., Montreal, Que., Can., 1971-73; asst. prof. Cairo (Egypt) U., 1973-77; assoc. prof. Alexandria U. Sci. Ctr., 1980; research scientist U. Mich., Ann Arbor, 1977—. Contbr. articles in field to profl. publs. UNESCO fellow, 1977. Mem. Am. Soc. Microbiology, Genetics Soc. Am., Genetics Soc. Can., Egyptian Soc. Genetics, N.Y. Acad. Scis. Moslem. Current Work: Gene organization and regulation in eucaryotes and eucaryotic cell organells using recombinant DNA methodology. Expression of foreign genes in cells is also being studied. Subspecialty: Genetics and genetic engineering (biology). Office: Dept Biol Chemistry Med Sci I U Mich Ann Arbor MI 48109

EL GHATIT, ZEINAB MOHAMMED, psychologist; b. Cairo, June 11, 1936; emigrated to Can., 1974, naturalized, 1977; d. Mohammed Ali and Shahwer El G.; m. Mustafa Kamel A. Rostom, June 4, 1965; children: Alaa, Wael. M.A. in Clin. Psychology, Ohio State U., 1960. Pvt. practice psychology, Cairo, 1961-74; cons. psychologist Family Guidance, Dokki, Cairo, 1965-74, Mil. Hosp. and El Nile Hosp., Cairo, 1965-74; lectr. psychology Am. U. Cairo, 1967-74; psychometrist II Prince Edward Heights, Picton, Ont., 1974-76, unit dir., 1976-79; program supr. mental retardation services Children's Services, Ministry of Community & Social Services, Kingston Office, Ont., 1979, 1980—; prof. spl. edn. Ottawa U., 1981-83. Author: Adaptive Behavior, 1975; contbr. articles to profl. jours. Ford Found. grantee, 1973. Mem. Am. Psychol. Assn., Am. Assn. Mental Deficiency, Canadian Psychol. Assn., Que. Assn. Profl. Psychologists, Brit. Psychol. Soc., Egyptian Psychol. Assn., Am. Assn. Edn. Severely/Profoundly Handicapped, Internat. Assn. Applied Psychology, Council of Exceptional Children. Current Work: Applied deinstitutionalization. Subspecialties: Developmental psychology; Clinical psychology. Home: #227 1695 Playfair Dr Ottawa ON K1H 8J6 Canada Office: 10 Rideau St Ottawa ON K1H 7X3 Canada

EL-HAWARY, FERIAL MOHAMED, engineering educator; b. Mansoura, Egypt, Mar. 20, 1943; emigrated to Can., 1968; s. Mohamed El-Sayed and Waheba (El-Kadaah) El-Bebani; m. Mohamed El-Aref, Sept. 10, 1966; children: Bahaa el-Deen (Bobby), Rany, Elizabeth Sarah. B.Sc., Alexandria (Egypt) U., 1967; M.Sc., Alta. U., Edmonton, 1971; Ph.D., Meml. U. Nfld., St. John's, 1981. Elec. engr. Msr. Beida Dyers, Alexandria, 1967-68; grad. asst. U. Alta., 1969-71; teaching and research asst. Meml. U., Nfld., 1975-80, postdoctoral fellow, 1981; research asst. prof. Tech. U. N.S., Halifax, 1981—. Mem. IEEE, Marine Tech. Soc., Sigma Xi. Current Work: Modeling and signal processing for identifying features of the ocean subsurface layered media on the basis of acoustic reflection data. Also estimation theory and parameters identification. Subspecialties: Sea floor spreading; Ocean engineering. Home: 23 Bayview Rd Halifax 9 NS B3M 1N8 Canada Office: Tech Univ Nova Scotia PO Box 1000 Halifax NS B3J 2X4 Canada

ELIAS, HANS GEORG, research institute executive, consultant; b. Bochum Westfalia, Germany, Mar. 29, 1928; came to U.S., 1971; s. Hermann Ludwig Georg and Elisabeth Charlotte (Rowlin) E.; m. Maria Hanke, Mar. 22, 1956; children: Peter Cornelius, Rainer Martin. Diploma in Chemistry, Tech. U. Hannover, W.Ger., 1954; Dr. rer. nat., Tech. U. Munich, W.Ger., 1957; Habilitation, Swiss. Fed. Inst. Tech., Zurich, 1961. Sci. asst. Tech. Univ. Munich, 1956-59; sci. head asst. Swiss Fed. Inst. Tech., 1960-63, privatdozent, 1961-63, asst. prof., 1963-71; pres. Mich. Molecular Inst., Midland, 1971-83; cons. firms, U.S., W.Ger., Switzerland, 1956—. Author: Macromolecules, German, 4 edits., 1971-81, English, 1977, 84, others; contbr. chpts. to books, articles to profl. jours. Hon. adv. bd. Midland Symphony Orch., 1975—; mem. Midland Beautification Adv. Com., 1979-83. Served with German Armed Forces, 1944-45. Fellow Sigma Xi (paper award 1982); mem. Am. Chem. Soc. (chmn. polymer internat. membership com. 1983), Am. Phys. Soc., German Chem. Soc., Swiss Chemists Assn. Club: Torch (dir 1982-84). Patentee in field. Current Work: Polymerization reactions; association in solution; polymers from renewable resources. Subspecialties: Polymer chemistry; Polymer engineering. Home and Office: 4009 Linden Dr Midland MI 48640

ELIAS, LUIS, laser physicist. Adj. prof. dept. physics U. Calif., Santa Barbara. Subspecialty: Free-electron lasers. Office: U Calif Dept Physics Santa Barbara CA 93106*

ELIEL, ERNEST LUDWIG, educator, chemist; b. Cologne, Germany, Dec. 28, 1921; came to U.S., 1946, naturalized, 1951; s. Oskar and Luise (Tietz) E.; m. Eva Schwarz, Dec. 23, 1949; children—Ruth Louise, Carol Susan. Student, U. Edinburgh (1939-40), Scotland; D.Phys.-Chem. Sci., U. Havana, Cuba, 1946; Ph.D., U. Ill., 1948; D.Sc. (hon.), Duke U., 1983. Mem. faculty U. Notre Dame, South Bend, Ind., 1948-72, prof. chemistry, 1960-72, head dept., 1964-66; W.R. Kenan Jr. prof. chemistry U. N.C., Chapel Hill, 1972—; Le Bel Centennial lectr., Paris, 1974; Benjamin Rush lectr. U. Pa., Phila., 1978; Sir C.V. Raman vis. prof. U. Madras, India, 1981. Author: Stereochemistry of Carbon Compounds, 1962; Elements of Stereochemistry, 1969; co-author: Conformational Analysis, 1965. Co-editor: Topics in Stereochemistry, Vols. I-XVI, 1967-86. NSF sr. research fellow Harvard U., 1958, Calif. Inst. Tech., 1958-59; fellow E.T.H. Zurich, Switzerland, 1967-68; recipient Coll. Tchrs. award Mfg. Chemists Assn., 1965; Laurent Lavoisier medal French Chem.

Soc., 1968; Guggenheim fellow Stanford, Princeton U., 1975-76, Duke U., 1983-84; recipient Disting. Chemist award N.C. Inst. Chemists, 1985. Mem. Nat. Acad. Scis., Am. Acad. Arts and Scis., Am. Chem. Soc. (chmn. St. Joseph Valley sect. 1960, councillor 1965-73, 75—, dir. 1985—, chmn. com. publs. 1972, 76-78, Morley medal Cleve. sect. 1965, Harry and Carol Mogher award Santa Clara Valley sect. 1983), AAAS, Chem. Soc. London, AAUP (chpt. pres. 1971-72, 78-79), Sigma Xi (chpt. pres. 1968-69), Phi Lambda Upsilon, Phi Kappa Phi. Current Work: Stereochemistry, conformational analysis, asymmetric synthesis, carbanions, organosulfur chemistry. Subspecialties: Organic chemistry; Nuclear magnetic resonance. Office: Dept Chemistry 045A U NC Chapel Hill NC 27514

ELION, HERBERT AARON, optoelectronics company executive; b. N.Y.C., Oct. 16, 1923; s. Robert and Bertha (Kahn) E.; m. Sheila Thall, June 15, 1945; children—Gary Douglas, Glenn Richard, Jonathan Lee, Bethanne Thall. B.ME., CCNY, 1944; M.S., Poly. Inst. Bklyn., 1949, postgrad in physics, 1949-55; Ph.D. (hon.), Hamilton State U., 1973. Registered profl. engr., Mass., Pa., N.Y. Group leader RCA, Camden, N.J., 1957-59; pres. Elion Instruments, Inc., Burlington, N.J., 1959-64; assoc. dir. space sci. GCA Corp., Bedford, Mass, 1965-67; mng. dir. electro-optics Arthur D. Little Inc., Cambridge, Mass., 1967-79; pres., chief exec. officer, Internat. Communications and Energy, Inc., Farmingham, Mass., 1979—; pres. Aetna Telecommunications Cons., Centerville, Mass., 1981—, also ptnr., Hartford, Conn.; co-founder Kristallochemie M & Elion GmbH, Meudt, Fed. Republic Germany, 1961-64; cons. on data communications Exec. Office of Pres., Washington, 1978-79; cons. Ministry Internat. Trade and Industry, Tokyo, 1975-84; chmn. internat. conf. European Electro-optics Conf., Heeze, The Netherlands, 1972-78; internat. lectr. in field. Author, editor numerous books, including 9 on lightwave info. networks. Contbr. articles to profl. jours. Patentee in field. Pres. Elion Found., Princeton, N.J., 1960-67; founder Rainbow's End Camp, Ashby, Mass., 1960; elder Unitarian Ch., Princeton, 1963-64. Served with USN, 1944-46. Decorated Chevalier du Tastevin (France); recipient Presdl. awards Arthur D. Little Inc. Fellow Am. Phys. Soc.; mem. IEEE (sr.), Am. Phys. Soc., Optical Soc. Am., Soc. Photo Instrumentation Engrs., Sigma Xi, Epsilon Nu Gamma. Current work: High resolution video networks; lightwave community networks. Subspecialty: Information systems (Information science). Office: Aetna Telecommunication Cons 889 W Main St Centerville MA 02632

ELITZUR, MOSHE, astronomer, educator; b. Poland, Apr. 29, 1944; came to U.S., 1977; s. Yechieal and Sophia E.; m. Shlomit Yoskowitz; children: Ofer, Haggai, Ben. B.Sc., Hebrew U., Jerusalem, 1964; M.Sc., Weizmann Inst., Rehovot, Israel, 1966, Ph.D., 1970. Research assoc. Rockefeller U., N.Y.C., 1970-72; research fellow Calif. Inst. Tech., Pasadena, 1972-74; scientist Weizmann Inst., 1974-75, Sr. scientist, 1975-80; vis. research asst. prof. U. Ill., Urbana, 1977-80; assoc. prof. physics and astronomy U. Ky., Lexintgon, 1980—. Contbr. articles to profl. jours. Served to lt. Israel Def. Forces, 1966-69. Fulbright awardee, 1970-72; NSF grantee, 1981. Mem. Am. Astron. Soc., Internat. Astron. Union. Current Work: Research on problems in theoretical astrophysics, in particular problems related to interstellar medium and molecular emission. Subspecialties: Radio and microwave astronomy; Theoretical astrophysics. Office: Dept Physics U Ky Lexington KY 40506

ELIZAN, TERESITA S., neurologist, neuroscientist, educator; b. Naga City, Philippines, Dec. 12, 1931; d. Paulo and Nicolasa Rosales (Siguenza) E. M.D., U. Philippines, Manila, 1955. Diplomate: Am. Bd. Psychiatry and Neurology. Resident in neurology Yale U. Sch. Medicine, 1956-58, Montreal Neurol. Inst., McGill U., 1959-60; Dazian Found. fellow in neurology Mt. Sinai Hosp., N.Y.C., 1960-62, attending neurologist, head lab. neurovirology, 1977—; vis. scientist neurology and neurovirology NIH, Bethesda, Md., 1963-68; asst. prof. neurology Mt. Sinai Sch. Medicine, 1968-71, asso. prof., 1971-77, prof., 1977—. Contbr. articles to profl. jours. Fellow Am. Acad. Neurology; mem. Am. Neurol. Assn., Am. Soc. Virology, Am. Assn. Neuropathology, Am. Soc. Microbiology, Soc. Neurosci., AAAS. Current Work: Role of viruses in etiology and pathogenesis of certain degenerative brain diseases; organic dementias; the aging nervous system. Subspecialties: Neurology; Neurovirology. Home: 245 E 63d St New York NY 10021 Office: 1200 Fifth Ave New York NY 10029

ELKAYAM, URI, Cardiologist; b. Petach Tikva, Israel, Mar. 11, 1945; came to U.S., 1976, naturalized, 1978; s. Mordechai and Dvora (Shapira) E.; m. Yael Batia Nachum, Aug. 17, 1975; children by previous marriages: Ifaat, Yehonatan, Danielle. M.D., Sackler Med. Sch., Israel, 1973. Intern Ichilov Med. Ctr., Tel Aviv, Israel, 1973-74, resident, 1974-76; dir. coronary care unit U. Calif.-Irvine, Orange, 1979-81; dir. inpatient cardiology U. So. Calif., Los Angeles, 1981—. Editor: Cardiac Problems in Pregnancy, 1982; contbr. articles to med. jours. Fellow Am. Coll. Chest Physicians; mem. ACP, Am. Fedn. Clin. Research, Am. Heart Assn., Am. Coll. Cardiology. Current Work: Congestive heart failure; ischemic heart disease; cardiovascular pharmacology. Subspecialty: Cardiology. Home: 2956 Queensbury Dr Los Angeles CA 90064 Office: U So Calif Med Sch Section of Cardiology 2025 Zonal Ave Los Angeles CA 90033

ELKIN, ROBERT GLENN, nutritional biochemist, educator; b. Passaic, N.J., May 7, 1953; s. Abe and Jean Estaire (Edelman) E.; m. Emily Jill Furumoto, May 23, 1981. B.S., Pa. State U., 1975; M.S., Purdue U., 1977, Ph.D., 1981. Asst. prof. animal scis. Purdue U., West Lafayette, Ind., 1981—. Contbr. articles to profl. jours. Ralston Purina Co. research fellow, 1979-80; Monsanto Co. grantee, 1982, 84. Mem. Poultry Sci. Assn., World's Poultry Sci. Assn., AAAS, Am. Chem. Soc., Assn. Ofcl. Analytical Chemists, Sigma Xi, Gamma Sigma Delta. Jewish. Current Work: Avian amino acid nutrition and metabolism; amino acid analysis by high performance liquid chromatography. Subspecialties: Animal nutrition; Analytical chemistry. Home: 189 Blueberry Ln West Lafayette IN 47906 Office: Dept Animal Scis Purdue U West Lafayette IN 47907

ELKINS, GARY RAY, psychologist; b. Hot Springs, Ark., Oct. 5, 1952; s. Billy Ray and Jewel Dean (Edwards) E.; m. Dorothy J. Sutton, May 31, 1975. B.A., Henderson State U., 1975; M.A., East Tex. State U., 1976; Ph.D., Tex. A&M U., 1980. Sr. staff psychologist Scott and White Clinic, Temple, Tex., 1982—; program dir. Scott and White Clinic (Pain Mgmt. Ctr.), 1982—; instr. dept. psychiatry Tex. A&M Coll. Medicine, College Station, 1982—. Contbr. articles to profl. jours. Served to capt. USAF, 1979-82. Mem. Am. Psychol. Assn., Tex. Psychol. Assn., Internat. Assn. for Study of Pain, Am. Soc. for Clin. Hypnosis. Current Work: Behavioral medicine, psychology of pain, hypnosis, psychotherapy research. Home: 3409 Forest Trail Temple TX 76501 Office: Dept Psychiatry Scott and White Clinic 2401 S 31st St Temple TX 76508

EL KOUNI, MAHMOUD HAMDI, medical scientist, educator; b. Cairo, May 30, 1942; s. Mustapha Mahmoud and Zeinab A. el K.; m. Fardos Naguib Mohammed Naguib, May 30, 1966; children: Mustapha, Sarah. B.Sci. with honors, U. Alexandria, Egypt, 1964, M.Sc., 1968; Ph.D., U. Alta., 1977. Teaching asst. Cairo U., 1964-66, U. Alexandria, 1966-70; teaching, then research asst. U. Alta., 1970-77; research assoc. Syracuse U., 1977-79; research assoc. Brown U., Providence, 1979-81, asst. prof. med. scis., 1981—. Contbr. articles to profl. jours. Grantee Am. Cancer Soc., 1980-82, 85-87; grantee WHO, 1981-83, 85-88; grantee Nat. Inst. Allergy Infectious Diseases, 1985-88. Mem. AAAS, Genetics Soc., Am. Cancer Soc., Am. Soc. Tropical Medicine. Am. Moslem. Current Work: Biochemistry and regulation of nucleotide metabolism. Mechanisms of action of antimetabolites in treatment of cancer and parasites. Subspecialties: Biochemistry (medicine); Cancer research (medicine). Office: Bio-Med Scis Brown U Providence RI 02912

ELLENBOGEN, LEON, biochemist, nutritionist; b. Bklyn., May 3, 1927; s. Martin and Bella (Zalesnick) E.; m. Roslyn Barban, June 30, 1951; children: Kenneth, Richard, Cheryl. B.S., CCNY, 1949; M.S., N.Y.U., 1951; Ph.D., Ind. U., 1954. Research technician Columbia U., 1949-51; teaching asst. Ind. U., 1951-53; research biochemist Lederle Labs., Pearl River, N.Y., 1953-59, sr. research biochemist and group leader, 1959-77, chief nutritional sci., asso. dir. profl. pharm. services, 1977—; adj. prof. nutrition in medicine Cornell U., 1978—; adj. prof. nutrition N.Y. Med. Coll., 1982—. Contbr. articles to profl. jours. Served with USN, 1945-47. Fellow N.Y. Acad. Scis.; mem. Am. Heart Assn., Am. Soc. Hematology, Am. Coll. Nutrition, Am. Inst. Nutrition, Am. Soc. Clin. Nutrition, Am. Soc. Biol. Chemistry, Am. Soc. Pharmacology and Exptl. Therapeutics, Am. Chem. Soc., Soc. Exptl. Sci., Sigma Xi, Phi Lambda Upsilon. Subspecialties: Nutrition (medicine); Biochemistry (medicine). Home: 16 Morris Dr New City NY 10956 Office: Lederle Labs Pearl River NY 10965

ELLGEN, PAUL CLIFFORD, chemist; b. Osage, Iowa, Sept. 13, 1941; s. Clifford Howard and Lois Virginia (Perkins) E.; m. Katherine Urwick Bridgman, Dec. 27, 1969; children—Sarah, Clifford. B.A. in Chemistry, Carleton Coll., 1963; M.B.A., W.Va. Coll. Grad. Studies, Charleston, 1979; Ph.D. in Chemistry, Northwestern U., 1968. Asst. prof. U. Calif.-Riverside, 1968-73; research scientist Union Carbide Corp., Charleston, W.Va., 1973-80; asst. dir. research and bus. devel. Tex. Eastern Corp., Houston, 1980—. Contbr. articles to profl. publs. Patentee chem. processes. Mem. Am. Chem. Soc., S.W. Catalysis Soc. Current work: Petrochemical process development, heterogeneous and homogeneous catalysis, chemical kinetics and reaction mechanisms. Subspecialties: Catalysis chemistry; Inorganic chemistry. Office: Tex Eastern Corp 1221 McKinney Houston TX 77001

ELLINGWOOD, BRUCE RUSSELL, structural engineering researcher; b. Evanston, Ill., Oct. 11, 1944; s. Robert W. and Carolyn L. (Ehmen) E.; m. Lois J. Drager, June 7, 1969; 1 son, Geoffrey D. B.S.C.E., U. Ill., Urbana, 1968, M.S.C.E., 1969, Ph.D., 1972. Structural engr. Naval Ship Research and Devel. Ctr., Bethesda, Md., 1972-75; research structural engr. Ctr. Bldg. Tech., Nat. Bur. Standards, Washington, 1975—; lectr., cons. Contbr. articles to profl. jours. Recipient Dural Research prize U. Ill., 1968; recipient Nat. Capital award for Engring. Achievement D.C. Joint Council Engring. and Archtl. Socs., 1980, Walter L. Huber prize ASCE, 1980, Silver medal U.S. Dept. Commerce, 1980. Mem. ASCE (State of Art of Civil Engring. award 1983, Norman medal 1983), ASTM, Am. Nat. Standards Inst., Am. Inst. Steel Constrn., Sigma Xi, Chi Epsilon. Presbyterian. Current Work: Application of probability and statistics to structural engineering, specifically in developing structural loading and strength criteria for use in standards and other regulatory documents. Subspecialties: Civil engineering; Structural reliability. Office: Nat Bur Standards Gaithersburg MD 20899

ELLIOT, DAVID H., geology and mineralogy educator, administrator; b. U.K., May 22, 1936; came to U.S., 1966. B.A., Cambridge U., Eng., 1959; Ph.D., Birmingham U., Eng., 1965. Geologist Brit. Antarctic Survey, 1960-66; research assoc. Inst. Polar Studies, Ohio State U. Columbus, 1966-69, dir., 1974—, asst. prof., assoc. prof., prof. dept. geology and mineralogy, 1969—. Mem. Geol. Soc. London, Geol. Soc. Am., Am. Geophys. Union, Ohio Acad. Scis., Sigma Xi. Current work: Antarctic geology; petrology. Subspecialties: Petrology; Arctic studies. Office: Inst Polar Studies Ohio State U Columbus OH 43210

ELLIOT, JAMES LUDLOW, astronomer; b. Columbus, Ohio, June 17, 1943; s. James Ludlow and Doris Belle (Eckfeld) E.; m. Elaine Kasparian, Nov. 24, 1967; children—Lyn, Martha. S.B., M.I.T., 1965, S.M., 1965; A.M., Harvard U., 1967, Ph.D., 1972. Research assoc. Cornell U., Ithaca, N.Y., 1972-74, sr. research assoc. 1974-77, asst. prof. astronomy, 1977-78; assoc. prof. astronomy M.I.T., Cambridge, 1978-85, prof. astronomy, 1985—; dir. George R. Wallace Jr. Astrophys. Obs., 1978—. Author: (with R. Kerr) Rings: Discoveries from Galileo to Voyager, 1984. Recipient medal for exceptional sci. achievement NASA, 1977; NSF fellow, 1965-71. Mem. Am. Astron. Soc., Internat. Internat. Astron. Union. Discovered rings of Uranus, 1977. Subspecialties: Optical astronomy; Planetary science. Home: 27 Forest St Wellesley MA 02181 Office: Bldg 54-422A MIT Cambridge MA 02139

ELLIOT, JOHN MURRAY, animal science educator; b. Howick, Que., Can., Nov. 6, 1927; s. William Wallace and Christena May (Lang) E.; m. Jane Anne Preston, Aug. 4, 1951; children—John Preston, Douglas Muir. B.S. in Agr., McGill U., 1949; M.S., U. Vt., 1951; Ph.D., Cornell U., 1958. From instr. to asst. prof. U. Mass., Amherst, 1950-60; from asst. prof. to prof., animal sci. Cornell U., Ithaca, N.Y., 1960—, chmn. dept., 1983—. Contbr. numerous articles to profl. jours. Danforth Found. tchr., 1956. Mem. Am. Dairy Sci. Assn. (Ralston Purina Teaching award 1982), Am. Soc. Animal Sci., Am. Inst. Nutrition, Sigma Xi. Current work: Effects of diet on rate of absorption of nutrients and their metabolism in liver of the lactating cow. Subspecialty: Animal nutrition. Home: 2235 N Triphammer Rd Ithaca NY 14850 Office: Cornell U 149 Morrison Hall Ithaca NY 14853

ELLIOTT, CHARLES H., clinical pediatric psychologist, researcher; b. Kansas City, Mo., Dec. 30, 1948; s. Joe Bond and Suzanne (Weider) E.; m. Barbara Lynn Johnson, Apr. 24, 1971 (div.); 1 son, Brian D. B.A., U. Kans., 1971, M.A., 1974, Ph.D., 1976. Asst. prof. East Central U., Ada, Okla., 1976-79; Okla. U. Health Sci. Ctr., Oklahoma City, 1979—; clin. cons., staff psychologist Mental Health Services So. Okla., Ada, 1977-79; psychologist pediatric psychology service Okla. CHildren's Meml. Hosp., Oklahoma City, 1979-80, dir, cons.-liaison div. mental health service, 1980—; cons. Nat. Cancer Inst., Los Angeles, 1982-85, 85—; assoc. prof. U. N.Mex. Sch. Medicine, 1985—; NIH grantee, 1982-85; recipient Research and Devel. Com. award East Central U., 1977, 78; U. Okla. Health Sci. Ctr. award, 1981. Mem. Okla. Psychol. Assn., S.W. Psychol. Assn., Am. Psychol. Assn., Assn. Advancement Behavior Therapy, Soc. Behavioral Medicine, Central Okla. Pediatric Soc., AAAS, Soc. Pediatric Psychology, Assn. Advancement Psychology, Psi Chi. Current Work: Consultation-liaison psychology, pediatric psychology, and the assessment of the interaction between subject variables; also, pain management, asthma, smoking, and treatment of depression. Subspecialties: Behavioral psychology; Pediatric psychology. Office: U NMex Dept Psychiatry Programs for Children 2600 Marble St NE Albuquerque NM 87106

ELLIOTT, DAVID LEROY, engineering educator; b. Cleve., May 29, 1932; s. Reed LeRoy and Roma Cyril (Benjamin) E.; m. Kiyoko Akaeda, Mar. 24, 1956 (div. June 1980); children—Marguerite, Philip David; m. Pauline Wei-Ying Tang, Oct. 31, 1984. B.A., Pomona Coll., 1953; M.A., U. So. Calif., 1959; Ph.D., UCLA, 1969. Profl. control engr., Calif. Mathematician U.S. Naval Ocean Systems Ctr., Pasadena, Calif., 1955-69; instr., lectr. UCLA, Los Angeles, 1969-70; mem. faculty Washington U., St. Louis, 1971—, prof. engring., 1981—; adv. com. St. Louis Mus. Sci. and Natural History, 1984—. NSF grantee 1971—. Fellow IEEE; mem. Math. Assn. Am., Am. Math. Soc., Soc. Indsl. and Applied Math. Democrat. Current work: Nonlinear system theory; observability, controllability, relation between continuous and discrete time models. Subspecialties: Control system theory; Applied mathematics. Home: 6600 Washington Apt 8 University City MO 63130 Office: Washington U Dept Systems Sci and Math Box 1040 Saint Louis MO 63130

ELLIOTT, GEORGE ALGIMON, veterinary pathologist; b. Trappe, Md., June 6, 1925; s. George Algimon and Mattie Tillison (Sullivan) E.; m. Marguerite Van Zandt Hammond, Aug. 15, 1949; children—Kathleen, Elizabeth, Jennifer. D.V.M., U. Ga., 1953; M.S. in Pathology, U. Pa., 1957. Diplomate Am. Coll. Vet. Pathologist. Asst. prof. vet. pathology U. Pa., Phila., 1957-60; asst. prof. comparative pathology Vanderbilt U. Med. Sch., Nashville, 1960-62; sr. vet. pathologist-toxicologist The Upjohn Co., Kalamazoo, Mich., 1962—. Contbr. articles to profl. jours. Served with USN, 1945-46, PTO. Mem. N.Y. Acad. Scis., Internat. Acad. Pathology, AVMA. Democrat. Refomed Ch. of Am. Current work: pathology, toxicology, immunopathology. Subspecialties: Toxicology (medicine); Pathology (medicine). Home: 4430 Romence Rd Portage MI 49002 Office: The Upjohn Co Kalamazoo MI 49001

ELLIOTT, JOHN FRANK, engineering educator; b. St. Paul, July 31, 1920; s. Stowe E. and Helen (Grube) E.; m. Frances Pendleton, May 4, 1946; children: William S., Dorothy E. Sempolinski. B.S., U. Minn., 1942; Sc.D., MIT, 1949. Phys. chemist Fundamental Research Lab. U.S. Steel Corp., Kearny, N.J., 1949-51; research metallurgist Inland Steel Co., East Chicago, Ind., 1951-54, asst. supt. quality control, 1954-55; asso. prof. dept. metallurgy MIT, Cambridge, 1955-60, prof. metallurgy dept. materials sci. and engring., 1960—, now AISI Disting. prof.; dir. MIT (Mining and Mineral Resources Research Inst.), 1978—. Author: Thermochemistry for Steelmaking, vol. I, 1960, vol. II 1963, Steelmaking: The Chipman Conference, 1965; editor: The Physical Chemistry of Steelmaking, 1958; contbr. articles to profl. jours. Served to lt. comdr. USNR, 1942-46. Guggenheim fellow, 1965; Disting. mem. Iron and Steel Soc., 1976 Sir Julius Wehrner lectr. Instn. Mining and Metallurgy, 1985. Fellow Metall. Soc., AAAS, AIME (hon. mem. 1982;, Douglas Gold medal 1976, Howe Meml. lectr. 1963, extractive metallurgy lectr. 1975). Instn. Mining and Metallurgy (London) (Sir Julius Wernher Meml. lectr. 1985), Am. Soc. Metals (White disting. teaching award 1971), Am. Acad. Arts and Scis., Am. Inst. Chem. Engrs.; mem. Nat. Acad. Engring., Iron and Steel Inst. Japan (hon.), Can. Inst. Mining and Metallurgy, Venezuelan Soc. Mining and Metall. Engrs. (hon.), Société Française de Métallurgie (hon.), Sigma Xi, Tau Beta Pi. Current Work: Physical chemistry of high temperature inorganic materials process and extractive metallurgy. Subspecialties: Metallurgical engineering; High-temperature materials. Office: 77 Massachusetts Ave Cambridge MA 02139

ELLIOTT, MARTIN ANDERSON, chemical engineer, consultant, researcher; b. Balt., Feb. 21, 1909; s. Walter W. and Lillian K. (Kesnodel) E.; m. Mary Helen Elliott (dec. Sept. 1982); children—James Parker, Virginia Layfield; m. Shirley Louise Multhauf Whitlock, June 23, 1985; stepchildren—Timothy Scott Whitlock, Jean William Whitlock, Rebecca Ana Whitlock. B. Engring., Johns Hopkins U., 1930, Ph.D., 1933. Registered profl. engr., Eng. Chief synthetic liquid U.S. Bur. Mines, Pitts., 1938-52; research prof. Ill. Inst. Tech., Chgo., 1952-56; dir. Inst. Gas Tech., 1956-61, v.p., 1961-67; corp. sci. adviser Tex. Eastern Transp. Corp., 1967-74; pvt. cons., Houston, 1974—. Active LaGrange Citizens Council, 1956-61. Recipient Disting. Service award Sec. Interior, Washington, 1952; Gas Ind. Research award, 1975. Fellow AAAS; life mem. ASME. Republican. Episcopalian. Clubs: Houston; Cosmos (Washington). Current work: Energy conversion technology. Subspecialty: Chemical engineering.

ELLIOTT, WILLIAM HUECKEL, biochemistry and chemistry educator; b. St. Louis, June 4, 1918; s. William C. and Edna A. (Hueckel) E.; m. Dorothy E. Singer, Aug. 6, 1949; children—William J., Mary C. Welch, Martha A.E. Koehler, Robert J. B.S. in Chemistry, St. Louis U., 1939, M.S., 1941, Ph.D., 1944. Research asst. Ind. U., Bloomington, 1944; instr., sr. instr. in biochemistry St. Louis U. Sch. Medicine, 1944-50, from asst. prof. to assoc. prof., 1950-59, prof., 1959—, acting chmn., 1971; prof. chemistry St. Louis U., 1977—; research assoc. radioactive ctr. MIT, 1947; vis. scientist in mass spectrometry Karolinska Inst., Stockholm, Sweden, 1965; vis. prof. biochemistry U. Edinburgh Sch. Medicine, Edinburgh, Scotland, 1974; cons. USPHS, NIH, Bethesda, Md., 1962-84. Contbr. articles to profl. jours. Mem. sci. and engrng. com. Adv. to Regional Commerce and Growth Assn. of St. Louis, 1975—; choir mem. St. Joan of Arc Ch., St. Louis, 1960—. Fellow AAAS; mem. Am. Soc. Biol. Chemists, Am. Chem. Soc. (pres. St. Louis sect. 1953), Am. Soc. Mass Spectrometry, Am. Soc. Study of Liver Diseases, Soc. Exptl. Biology and Medicine (pres. Mo. chpt. 1957). Roman Catholic. Current work: Lipids (fats) particularly cholesterol and relatives and bile acid metabolism; analytical biochemistry (including mass spectrometry) of these substances. Subspecialties: Biochemistry (medicine); Organic chemistry. Home: 6300 Tholozan Ave Saint Louis MO 63109 Office: St Louis Univ Sch of Medicine 1402 South Grand Blvd Saint Louis MO 63104

ELLIS, DONALD GRIFFITH, bioengineer, design consultant; b. Colorado Springs, Colo., Aug. 10, 1940; s. William Eugene and Lucile (Mathews) E.; m. Merle Elizabeth, May 21, 1977. B.S. in Mech. Engring, U. Colo., Boulder, 1962; postgrad. in metallurgy, U. Denver, 1962-63; M.S., U. Mich., 1964, Ph.D. in Bioengring, 1970. Research engr. U. Mich. Hosp., 1964-68, research assoc., 1968-70, 72-75; postdoctoral fellow Webb-Waring Inst., 1970-72; bioengr. U. Colo. Med. Center, Denver, 1973; research assoc. U. Colo., Boulder, 1975-78, U. Colo. Health Scis. Center, Denver, 1978—; cons. design. Contbr. articles on connective tissue mechanics and lab. instrumentation and equipment to profl. jours. Mem. ACLU, Inst. Food and Devel. Policy, Town Forum., ASME, Assn. Humanistic Psychology, AAAS. Unitarian. Patentee inflatable insulating apparatus. Current Work: Biomedical research instrumentation and equipment. Subspecialties: Biomedical engineering; Bioinstrumentation. Home: Geneva Park Boulder CO 80302 Office: CVP Research B133 U Colo Health Sci Center 4200 E 9th Ave Denver CO 80262

ELLIS, HENRY CARLTON, psychology educator; b. New Bern, N.C., Oct. 23, 1927; s. Henry Alford and Frances Lee (Mays) E.; m. Florence Pettyjohn, Aug. 24, 1957; children: Joan, Diane Elizabeth, John Weldon. B.S., Coll. of William and Mary, 1951; M.A., Emory U., 1952; Ph.D., Washington U., St. Louis, 1958. Asst. prof. psychology U. N. Mex., Albuquerque, 1957-62, assoc. prof., 1962-67, prof., 1967—, chmn. dept., 1975—, ann. research lectr., 1978; disting. vis. prof. U.S. Air Force Med. Ctr., San Antonio, 1978; vis. prof. U. Calif.-Berkeley, 1971, U. Hawaii, Honolulu, 1977; cons. Am. Psychol. Assn., Washington, 1978—. Author: Human Learning and Cognition, 1972, Human Learning, Memory and Cognition, 1978, Psychology of Learning and Memory, 1979, Human Memory and Cognition, 1983. Served with USAAF, 1946-47. Van Blarcom fellow, 1956-67. Fellow Am. Psychol. Assn. (mem. and chmn. edn. and tng. bd. 1981-83, council of reps. 1983—, sec.-treas. exec. com. div. exptl. psychology 1982—), AAAS; mem. Rocky Mountain Psychol. Assn. (pres. 1967-68, disting. service award 1983), Southwestern Psychol. Assn. (pres. 1978-79), Council of Grad. Depts. Psychology (chmn. 1977-79), Psychonomic Soc., Phi Kappa Phi. Methodist. Clubs: Tennis (Albuquerque), Twenty-One (Albuquerque). Current Work: Human memory and cognitive psychology, emotional mood states and memory, organization and memory individual differences in memory and cognition, perceptual memory, eyewitness identification. Subspecialties: Cognition; Learning. Home: 1905 Amherst Dr NE Albuquerque NM 87106 Office: Dept Psychology U NMex Albuquerque NM 87131

ELLIS, HOWARD FRANKLIN, ceramic engineer; b. Pittsfield Mass., May 27, 1942; s. Delmar Burdette and Frances (Wells) E.; m. Roberta Louise Clarke, Jan. 29, 1966; children—Kim, Michael. B.S. in Ceramic Engring., Alfred U., 1964; M.S. in Indsl. Adminstrn., Union Coll., 1974. Devel. engr. ceramics Gen. Electric Co., Pittsfield, Mass., 1966-76, sr. devel. engr., 1976—. Patentee in field. Pres. Berlin Seventh Day Baptist Ch., N.Y., 1962-83, sec. bd. trustees, 1983—; pres. Berlin High Sch. Alumni Assn., 1973; pres. Eastern Assn. Ch. Meeting, Berlin, 1973. Served to 1st lt. U.S. Army, 1964-66. Recipient Outstanding Individual Contbr. award Power Systems Sector, Gen. Electric, 1979, 80, Outstanding Tech. Achievement award, 1982. Mem. Am. Ceramics Soc., Keramos. Republican. Club: Lebanon Bowling League (v.p. 1976-77). Current work: Senior development engineer responsible for the development of metal oxide varistors to meet functional and design specifications for surge arresters, including material and process developments as well as factory support of MOV ceramics. Subspecialties: Ceramics; Ceramic engineering. Home: Route 22 Stephentown NY 12168 Office: Gen Electric Co 100 Woodlawn Ave Pittsfield MA 01201

ELLIS, JACK GERALD, semiconductor technologist; b. McKinny, Tex., July 19, 1946; s. J.D. and Dorothy C. (Craft) E.; m. Patricia A. Mason, Aug. 3, 1984. B.S. in Biology, U. Tex.-Arlington, 1979. Engring. tech. Tex. Instruments, Dallas, 1968-74; design specialist Gen. Dynamics, Ft. Worth, Tex. and Pomona, Calif., 1974-81; tech. specialist Integrated Circuit Engring., Scottsdale, Ariz., 1981-82; adv. tech. specialist Anderson DeBartolo Pan, Inc., Tucson, 1982-85; exec. v.p. Systems Chemistry Inc., Hollister, Calif., 1985—. Author: VLSI Facilities Guidelines, 1982. Mem. Semiconductor Equipment and Materials Inst., IEEE, Electrochem. Soc. Current work: Planning, design and operation of advanced manufacturing facilities for semiconductor device development and production. Subspecialties: Microchip technology (engineering); Semiconductors. Home: 25 Villa Pacheco Hollister CA 95023 Office: Systems Chemistry Inc 420 San Benito St Hollister CA 95023

ELLIS, LEGRANDE CLARK, physiology educator; b. Farmington, Utah, June 20, 1932; s. Owen W. and Mary Lucile (Clark) E.; m. Marilyn P. Ellis, Sept. 18, 1952; children—Brent, LuAnn, Janet, LeGrand C. Jr., Julie, Scott, Jason. B.S., Utah State U., 1954, M.S., 1956; Ph.D., Okla. State U., 1961. Instr. Okla. State U., Stillwater, 1957-60, asst. prof., 1960-62; asst. prof. physiology, Utah State U., Logan, 1964-66, assoc. prof., 1966-71, prof., 1971—. Contbr. articles to profl. jours. Explorer leader Boy Scouts Am., Logan, 1974; dist. chmn. exploring Boy Scouts Am., 1980. Recipient Dist. award of merit Boy Scouts Am., 1983; U. Utah fellow, 1962-64. Mem. Am. Soc. Physiology, Endocrine Soc., Soc. for Exptl. Biology and Medicine, Soc. for Study Reprodn., Am. Soc. Andrology, Am. Soc. Animal Sci., Sigma Xi. Republican. Mem. Ch. of Jesus Christ of Latter-day Saints. Current work: Reproductive endocrinology; control furring cycles in mink; endocrine control of hair pigmentation. Subspecialty: Neuroendocrinology. Home: 1160 N 600 E Logan UT 84322 Office: Dept Biology UMC-53 Utah State U Logan UT 84322

ELLIS, WILLIAM R., physicist, government official; b. Greenville, S.C., Jan. 22, 1940; s. William Rufus and Mary Louise (Rogers) E.; m. Gail Maxcine Gladden, Aug. 13, 1966; children: Benjamin Brian, Jaman Nathaniel. B.S., Clemson U., 1962; M.A., Princeton U., 1965, Ph.D., 1967. Vis. scientist A.E.R.E. Culham Lab., Abingdon, Oxford, Eng., 1967-69; mem. staff Los Alamos Nat. Lab., 1970-73, assoc. group leader, 1974-75; chief open systems br. Office of Fusion Energy, ERDA, Washington, 1976-78; dir. mirror systems div. Dept. Energy, Washington, 1979-83; assoc. dir. research, dir. gen. sci. and tech. U.S. Naval Research Lab., Washington, 1983—. Author articles and newspaper columns; patentee in field. Vice chmn. Los Alamos County Council, 1975-76. NSF fellow, 1961; NASA grantee, 1962-66. Mem. Am. Phys. Soc. (div. plasma physics, exec. com. 1980-82), Am. Nuclear Soc., AAAS, Am. Geophys. Union, Sigma Xi, Sigma Tau Epsilon, Sigma Pi Sigma, Phi Eta Sigma. Patentee in field. Current Work: U.S. Fusion program technical management and oversight. Subspecialties: Fusion; Plasma physics. Home: 1613 Auburn Ave Rockville MD 20850 Office: Office of Fusion Energy US Dept Energy ER-56/MS G234 Washington DC 20545

ELLISON, ALFRED HARRIS, government research administrator, environmental scientist; b. Quincy, Mass., Dec. 23, 1923; married; 5 children. B.S., Boston Coll., 1950; M.S., Tufts U., 1951; Ph.D. in Surface Chemistry, Georgetown U., 1956. Chemist U.S. Naval Research Lab., 1951-56; research chemist Texaco Research Ctr., 1956-65, Gillette Research Inst., 1965-69; dep. dir. Environ. Sci. Research Lab., Office Research and Devel., EPA, Research Triangle Park, N.C., 1969-79, dir., 1979-84, dir. atmospheric scis. research lab., 1984—. Mem. AAAS, Air Pollution Control Assn., Am. Chem. Soc. Subspecialty: Environmental science research administration. Office: EPA MD-59 Research Triangle Park NC 27711

ELLISON, FRANK OSCAR, chemistry educator, researcher; b. Omaha, June 18, 1926; s. Frans Oscar and Hilda Josephine (Youngquist) E.; m. Joan Lowe, Sept. 9, 1959; children—James Frans, Kathe Joanne. B.S. in Chemistry, Creighton U., 1949; Ph.D. Iowa State U., 1953. Asst. prof. chemistry Carnegie Inst. Tech., Pitts., 1953-64; prof. chemistry U. Pitts., 1964—. Contbr. articles to chemistry jours.; author: Properties of Titanium Compounds and Related Substances, 1956. Councilman, Borough of Churchill, Pa., 1980—. Served with AUS, 1944-46; ETO. Mem. Am. Inst. Chemists, AAAS, Am. Phys. Soc., Am. Chem. Soc., N.Y. Acad. Scis., Sigma Xi. Republican. Lutheran. Current work: Development of theoretical methods for calculating energies and other properties of molecules in isolation and in course of reaction. Subspecialties: Theoretical chemistry; Physical chemistry. Office: Dept Chemistry U Pitts Pittsburgh PA 15260

ELLISON, MICHAEL SCOT, fiber science educator, fiber physics researcher; b. Inglewood, Calif., Nov. 7, 1944. B.S. in Physics, U. Calif.-Davis, 1971, M.A. in Physics, 1973, Ph.D. in Polymer Fiber Physics, 1982. Research assoc. Div. Textiles, U. Calif.-Davis, 1975-84; asst. prof. Sch. Textiles, Clemson U., S.C., 1984—. Mem. Am. Phys. Soc., Am. Chem. Soc. Current work: Electronic properties of fibers, physical aging and performance of fibers. Subspecialty: Polymer physics. Office: Sch Textiles Clemson U Clemson SC 29631

ELLISON, SAMUEL PORTER, JR., energy resources educator, consultant; b. Kansas City, Mo., July 1, 1914; s. Samuel Porter and Mary Frances (Edwards) E.; m. Dorothy M. Cannady, June 9, 1940; children—Samuel David, John Robert, Stephen Paul. B.A., U. Kansas City, Mo., 1936; M.A. in Geology, U. Mo.-Columbia, 1938, Ph.D., 1940. Grad. teaching asst. U.Mo.-Columbia, 1936-39; instr. geology U. Mo. Sch. Mines and Metallurgy, Rolla, 1939-43, asst. prof., 1943-44; asst. geologist U.S. Geol. Survey, Rolla, Mo., 1942-44; geologist Stanolind Oil & Gas Co., Midland, Tex., 1944-45, sr. geologist, 1945-47, dist. geologist, Wichita, Falls, Tex., 1947-48; prof. geol. sci. U. Tex.-Austin, 1948-79, cons. to Univ. Lands, 1948-52, cons. Bur. Econ. Geology, 1948-52, chmn. dept. geol. scis., 1952-62, acting dean arts and scis., 1970-71, dean Coll. Natural Scis., 1971-73, Alexander Deussen prof. energy resources in geol. scis., 1972-79, Deussen prof. emeritus, 1979—, cons., 1984; cons. William and Joe Wagner, Dallas, 1950-53, Shell Oil Co., Casper, Wyo., 1953-56, John A. Jackson, Dallas, 1957-58, Exxon USA Co., Houston, 1959-70, Republic Gypsum Co., Dallas, 1978-80, Basic Resources Internat., 1979, Alpine Resources, Houston, 1980-81, Petro-Cap Inc., Austin, 1981, Dresser Industries, Houston, 1981, Ashton Resources Ltd., Houston, 1981, A.T. Barrett, Smithville, Tex., 1981, Covington and Burling, Attys., Washington, 1984—; lectr. numerous univs., civic orgns. Contbr. numerous articles to profl. jours. Fellow Geol. Soc. Am. (councilor 1963-68); mem. Am. Assn. Petroleum Geologists (v.p. 1972-73), Paleontol. Soc. Am., Soc. Petroleum Engring., Soc. Econ. Paleontology and Mineralogy (sec.-treas. 1953-58, pres. 1959-60). Current work: Conodont research; petroleum geology. . Home: 5948 Highland Hills Dr Austin TX 78731 Office: Dept Geol Sci U Tex Austin TX 78713

ELLSTRAND, NORMAN CARL, geneticist, educator; b. Elmhurst, Ill., Jan. 1, 1952; s. Edwin A. and Beverly (Singer) E.; m. Tracy L. Kahn. B.S., U. Ill., 1974; Ph.D., U. Tex., 1978. Postdoctoral research assoc. Duke U., Durham, N.C., 1978-79; asst. prof. plant ecology, dept. botany and plant scis. U. Calif., Riverside, 1979—. Contbr. articles to sci. jours. Regents Jr. Faculty Fellow, 1981; U.S. Dept. Agr. grantee, 1980-84; NSF grantee, 1983-88. Mem. Soc. Study Evolution, Ecol. Soc. Am., Internat. Soc. Plant Population Biologists, Nat. Audubon Soc., Calif. Native Plant Soc., Riverside Art Center, Phi Beta Kappa, Sigma Xi, Phi Kappa Phi. Club: University (Riverside). Current Work: Genetic structure of populations; plant breeding systems; horticulture of subtropical fruit crops. Subspecialties: Evolutionary biology; Population biology. Office: Dept Botany and Plant Scis U Calif Riverside CA 92521

ELLSWORTH, JEFF LYNN, biochemist, cell biologist; b. Iowa City, Iowa, July 9, 1956; s. John Calvin and Melva Lea (Johnson) E.; m. Catherine Elaine Wilson, Mar. 22, 1979. B.S. in Chemistry, Ind. U., 1978; Ph.D., Coll. Medicine U. Cin., 1982. Postdoctoral fellow Sch. Medicine Stanford U., Calif., 1982—. Author jour. articles, abstracts. Participant NIH tng. grants, U. Cin., 1980-82, Stanford U., 1982-83; recipient postdoctoral nat. research service award, NIH, 1983-85. Mem. N.Y. Acad. Scis., Am. Soc. Pharmacology and Exptl. Therapeutics (student), Am. Fedn. Clin. Research. Republican. Current work: Lipoprotein synthesis and secretion in human liver, regulation of hepatic apolipoprotein gene expression. Subspecialties: Biochemistry (biology); Cell biology (medicine). Home: 330 Waverley Palo Atlo CA 94301 Office: Dept Medicine Div Gastroenterology Sch Medicine Stanford U Stanford CA 94305

ELMAGHRABY, ADEL SAID, computer science educator, researcher; b. Alexandria, Egypt, Oct. 18, 1951; s. Said Abdel-Baki and Aida Zakaria (Gazarine) E.; m. Nemat Mohamed Ekbal, 1 child, Adam Adel. Grad. Dipl. Planning, Inst. Nat. Planning, Cairo, Egypt, 1976, Grad. Dipl. Statis., U. Cairo, Egypt, 1976; B.S. in Elec. Engring., U. Alexandria, 1973; M.S.E.E., U. Wis.-Madison, 1978, Ph.D. in Elec. and Computer Engring., 1982. Analysis, programming staff Egyptian Army Stats., Cairo, 1973-75; researcher Inst. Nat. Planning, Cairo, 1975-77; research and teaching asst. U. Wis.-Madison, 1977-82; asst. prof. computer sci. U. Louisville, 1982—. Contbr. articles to sci., tech. jours. Mem. IEEE, Soc. Computer Simulation, Internat. Assn. Mathematics and Computers, Planning Execs. Inst., Sigma Xi. Moslem. Current work: Robotics and manufacturing; expert systems and simulation; voice input/output systems. Subspecialties: Computer engineering; Graphics, image processing, and pattern recognition. Office: Engring Math and Computer Sci Dept U Louisville Louisville KY 40292

EL-MANSY, YOUSSEF ALY, electronics engineer, lecturer; b. Dessouk, Egypt, Mar. 8, 1945; Aly Ibrahim and Sitt (Rizk) El-M. m. Samia I. Sultan, Sept. 10, 1969; children—Safaa, Heba, Haddy. B.S. in Electromics, Alexandria U., 1966, M.S. in Electronics, 1970; Ph.D., Carleton U., 1974. Registered profl. engr., Ont. Researcher, Carleton U., Ottawa, Ont., Can., 1970-74, adj. prof., 1976-79; mem. sci. staff Bell No. Research, Ottawa, 1974-77, project mgr., 1977-79; project mgr. Intel Corp., Aloha, Oreg., 1979-82, engring. mgr., 1982-84; dept. mgr., 1984—; adj. prof. Oreg. Grad. Ctr., Beaverton, 1980—; Author: Hardware and Software Concepts in VLSI, 1983. Contbr. articles to profl. jours. Recipient Distinction award Alexandria U., 1961-66. Mem. IEEE. Current work: Development of very large scale integrated circuits including memory and micro processor technology. Subspecialties: Integrated circuits; Computer-aided design. Office: Intel Corp 3585 SW 198th Ave Aloha OR 97007

ELMINYAWI, IMAM MOHAMED, physics educator, researcher; b. Cairo, Egypt, July 25, 1953; s. Mohamed Imam and Redha E.; m. Kawther Hassan, Jan. 7, 1983; children—Redha, Marwa. B.S., Ain Shams U., Cairo, 1975; M.S., Rensselaer Poly. Inst., 1982, Ph.D., 1984. Instr., Ain Shams U., 1975-79; teaching asst. Rensselaer Poly. Inst., Troy, N.Y., 1979-84, research asst., 1984—lectr. Siena Coll., Albany, N.Y., 1984—. Contbr. articles to physics jours. Mem. Am. Phys. Soc., Am. Assn. Physics Tchrs. Current work: Theoretical and mathematical physics-nuclear physics-light scattering, electron beam lithography. Subspecialties: Theoretical physics; Nuclear physics. Home: 1738 Highland Ave Troy NY 12180

ELMORE, DAVID, physicist, educator; b. Los Alamos, Dec. 19, 1945; s. William Cronk and Barbara Helen (Page) E.; m. Janet Louise Fox, Aug. 24, 1968; children—Andrew, Steven. B.S., Case Inst. Tech., 1968; Ph.D., U. Rochester, 1974. Research assoc. U. Rochester, N.Y., 1974—, sr. research assoc., 1980—. Contbr. articles to profl. publs. Mem. Am. Phys. Soc., Am. Geophys. Union. Republican. Current work: Tandem accelerator mass spectrometry, measurement of long lived radioactivity in nature. Subspecialty: Nuclear physics. Home: 67 Danforth Crescent Rochester NY 14618 Office: Nuclear Structure Research Lab U Rochester Rochester NY 14627

ELMORE, JAMES LEWIS, aquatic ecologist, researcher; b. Chattanooga, May 28, 1948; s. Charles Scott and Myrtle Louise (Bryant) E.; m. Barbara Victoria Bouquard, Aug. 26, 1972; 1 son, Joseph Charles. B.A., U. Tenn.-Chattanooga, 1971; M.S., U. Tenn., Knoxville, 1973; Ph.D., U. South Fla., 1980. Grad. teaching asst. U. Tenn., Knoxville, 1971-73, U. South Fla., Tampa, 1974-76; project dir. State of Fla. grant at U. South Fla., 1979-80; research assoc. Oak Ridge Nat. Lab., 1980—; cons. Biol. Research Assocs., Tampa, 1974-79. Contbr. articles and abstracts to profl. jours. Sigma Xi grantee, 1976. Mem. Am. Soc. Limnology and Oceanography, Ecol. Soc. Am., Societas Internationalis Limnologiae, N.Am. Benthological Soc., Assn. Southeastern Biologists, Am. Orchid Soc., Bromeliad Soc., Smoky Mountain Orchid Soc., Sigma Xi, Beta Beta Beta, Phi Sigma. Current work: Population biology of freshwater zooplankton; aquatic ecology of lakes; trout populations on Appalachian streams. Subspecialties: Ecology (biology); Limnology. Home: 1700 Huntwood Ln Knoxville TN 37923 Office: Oak Ridge Nat Lab PO Box X Oak Ridge TN 37831

ELMSTROM, GARY WILLIAM, horticulture educator, researcher; b. Chgo., Jan. 10, 1939; s. Rudolph Eric and Edna Katherine (Koepke) E.; m. Mary Francis Moffett, June 24, 1967; children—Michael Eric, Kristin Kathleen, Jennifer Mae. B.S., So. Ill. U., 1963, M.S., 1964; Ph.D., U. Calif.-Davis, 1969. Asst. prof. horticulture U. Fla. Agrl. Research and Edn. Ctr., Leesburg, 1969-74, assoc. prof., 1974-78, prof., 1981—; dir. Agrl. Research Ctr., 1981—. Contbr. articles to encys. and numerous articles to profl. jours. Mem. Am. Soc. Horticulture Sci., Research Ctrs. Administrs. Soc. (pres. 1984-85), Council for Agr. Sci. and Tech., Fla. State Hort. Soc., So. Assn. Agr. Scientists. Republican. Presbyterian. Lodge: Kiwanis (pres. 1977-78). Current work: Cantaloupe and squash breeding Subspecialty: Agricultural research administration. Office: Univ Fla Agrl Research and Edn Ctr PO Box 388 Leesburg FL 32749

EL-SAYED, MOSTAFA AMR, chemistry educator; b. Zifta, Egypt, May 8, 1933; came to U.S., 1953; s. Amr El-Sayed and Zakia Ahmed; m. Janice Carol Jones, Mar. 15, 1957; children—Lyla, Tarric, James, Dorea Jehan, Ivan Homer. B.S., Ein Shams U., Cairo, Egypt, 1953; Ph.D., Fla. State U., 1959. Research assoc. Calif. Inst. Tech., Pasadena, 1960-61, Yale U., New Haven, Conn., 1957, Harvard U., Cambridge, Mass., 1959-60; asst. prof. chemistry UCLA, 1961-64, assoc. prof., 1964-67, prof., 1967—; vis. prof. Am. U., Beirut, 1967-68; fgn. prof. U. So. Paris, Orsay, France, 1976; cons. Navy Electronics Labs., 1969-73, Northrop Corp., 1979-81, others. Editor: Jour. Phys. Chemistry, 1980—. Contbr. articles to profl. jours. Alfred P. Sloan fellow, 1965, 71, Guggenheim Meml. Found. fellow, 1967-68; recipient Fresenius Nat. award 1967, Alexander von Humboldt Sr. U.S. Scientist award W. German Govt., 1982; Sherman Fairchild Disting. scholar, 1980. Mem. U.S. Nat. Acad. Scis., Am. Chem. Soc. (Gold medal 1971). Current work: Laser applications to photophysics, photochemistry and photobiology; understanding the mechanism of energetic changes on a molecular level. Subspecialty: Physical chemistry. Office: Dept Chemistry UCLA Los Angeles CA 90024

EL SHAZLY, HASSAN, engineer, researcher; b. Cairo, Arab Rep. of Egypt, Aug. 20, 1953; s. El Shazly Mohamed and Constance Wilfred (Ingham) El S.; m. Mona Raouf Naaman, Oct. 27, 1975; children—Dina, Tarek. B.S., Am. U. in Cairo, 1975; M.S., U. S.C., 1982. Electronics engr. SOSSI Electronics, Cairo, 1975; computer specialist Remote Sensing Ctr., Cairo, 1975-79; research assoc. U. S.C., Columbia, 1980-83; systems programmer Policy Mgmt. Systems, Columbia, 1984—. Mem. IEEE, Assn. for Computing Machinery, Am. Soc. of Photogrammetry. Club: Yacht (Cairo). Current work: Development of a user friendly, relational database system. Development of large scale software applications. Subspecialties: Remote sensing (geoscience); Graphics, image processing, and pattern recognition. Home: 227 Vincenne Rd Columbia SC 29210

EL-TAHAN, MONA SALAH, research engineer; b. Cairo, Egypt, Aug. 27, 1950; d. Salah and Nawal (Sherif) Shahwan; m. Hussein Wabha El-Tahan, Dec. 28, 1975; children—Tahmir, Yassir. B.Sc. in Engring, Cairo U., 1975; M.Eng., Meml. U., Nfld., 1980. Lic. profl. engr., Nfld. Research asst. Meml. U., St. John's, Nfld., 1976-80; ocean engr. Fenco Nfld. Ltd., St. John's, 1980-82, project engr., 1982—. Mem. Assn. Profl. Engrs. Nfld., Women is Sci. and Engring. Marine Tech. Soc. Muslim. Developer, Iceberg Drift Prediction Model, 1980; patentee in field. Current Work: Iceberg drift precition - iceberg grounding and morphology. Subspecialties: Ocean engineering; Offshore technology. Home: 5 Hampshire P Saint John's NF A1A 4H5 Canada Office: P O Box 8246 Kenmount Rd Saint Johns NF A1B 3N4 Canada

ELTIMSAHY, ADEL H., electrical engineer, educator; b. Damanhoor, Egypt, June 10, 1936; s. Hassan H. and Hamida A. (Elzohairy) E.; m. Kathleen H. Hoag, July 1, 1967; children: Ann Mirrette, Todd Tarek. B.S.E.E., Cairo U., 1958; M.S.E.E., U. Mich., 1961, Ph.D., 1967. Instr. Cairo U., 1958-59; teaching fellow U. Mich., 1966-67; asst. prof. U. Tenn., 1967-68; asst. prof. elec. engring. U. Toledo, 1968-73, assoc. prof., 1973-78, prof., 1978—, chmn. dept. elec. engring., 1980—. Contbr. articles to profl. jours. Named Elec. Engr. of Yr. Toledo sect. IEEE, 1979-80; Dept. Energy grantee; Libbey-Owens Ford Co. grantee. Mem. IEEE, Internat. Solar Energy Soc., Am. Soc. Engring. Edn., Simulation Council. Current Work: Optimal control of solar energy systems, robotics research. Subspecialties: Electrical engineering; Solar energy. Home: 4525 Sulgrave Toledo OH 43623 Office: Dept Elec Engring U Toledo Toledo OH 43606

ELWELL, LYNN PAUL, research company microbiologist; b. Pitts., Oct. 24, 1937; s. Louis Paul and Nelle (Byrne) E.; m. Josephine Disston Terrell, Sept. 16, 1972; 1 child, Brendan Alexander. B.S., U. Pitts., 1959; M.S., U. N.H., 1964; Ph.D., U. Oreg., 1974. Researcher, Fort Detrick Labs., Frederick, Md., 1964-66; asst. prof. Linfield, Coll., McMinnville, Oreg., 1966-69; postdoctoral fellow U. Wash., Seattle, 1974-77; researcher, group leader Burroughs Wellcome Co. Research Labs., Research Triangle Park, N.C., 1977—; adj. asst. prof. Duke U., Durham, N.C., 1977—, U. N.C., Chapel Hill, 1982—. Contbr. chpts. to textbooks, articles to profl. jours. Served with AUS, 1959-61. U. Pitts. debate scholar, 1955-59; recipient Nat. Research Service award NIH, 1975-77. Mem. Am. Soc. for Microbiology, Infectious Diseases Soc. Am., Sigma Xi. Current work: Characterization of antibiotic resistance plasmids; molecular epidemiology of R plasmids; investigation of DNA topoisomerases as targets in anti-cancer chemotherapy. Subspecialties: Microbiology (medicine); Recombinant DNA technology. Office: Research Labs Burroughs Wellcome Co 3030 Cornwallis Rd Research Triangle Park NC 27709

ELY, BERTEN E., III, educator; b. Newark, Nov. 26, 1948; s. Berten E. and Ruth Dorothy (Bloy) E.; m. Tracey Allison Ward, May 30, 1970; children: Marc, Gregory. B.S., Tufts U., 1969; Ph.D., Johns Hopkins U., 1973. Asst. prof. dept. biology U. S.C., Columbia, 1973-79, assoc. prof., 1979—; asst. prof. microbiology/immunology Sch. Medicine, U. S.C., 1975-79, assoc. prof., 1979-82. Contbr. articles to profl. jours. Mem. Am. Soc. Microbiology. Mem. Christian Ch. Current Work: Constructed a genetic map for Caulobacter crescentus; cloning C. crescentus genes; analyzing gene organization and regulation. Subspecialties: Gene actions; Microbiology. Office: Dept Biology Univ SC Columbia SC 29208

EMANUEL, IRVIN, medical educator, epidemiologist; b. Balt., Oct. 9, 1926; s. David and Dora (Hollander) E.; m. Patricia Tharp, June 18, 1960 (div.); children—Gina Marie, Melissa Pauline. B.S. in Biology, Rutgers U., 1951; M.A. in Anthropology, U. Ariz., 1956; M.D., U. Rochester, 1960; M.S. in Preventive Medicine, U. Wash., 1966. Intern, Cleve. Met. Gen. Hosp., 1960-61; resident in pediatrics U. Wash., 1961-62, sr. Fellow in pediatrics and preventive medicine, 1962-66, asst. prof. epidemiology and pediatrics, 1966-70, assoc. prof., 1970-74, prof., 1974—, dir. Child Devel. and Mental Retardation Ctr., 1973-83, dir. Maternal and Child Health Program, 1983—; cons. to nat. and internat. agys. Contbr. articles to med. and epidemiol. jours. Bd. dirs. Am. Assn. U. Affiliated Programs for Persons with Devel. Disabilities, 1977-80. Served with USN, 1945-46. Nat. Inst. Child Health and Human Devel. Research career Devel. award, 1966-71. Mem. Am. Pub. Health Assn., Internat. Epidemiol. Assn., Teratology Soc., Soc. for Epidemiologic Research, Am. Epidemiol. Soc., Phi Beta Kappa. Current work: Epidemiology of maternal and child health problems; internat. health. Subspecialty: Epidemiology. Office: U Wash Dept Epidemiology SC-36 Seattle WA 98195

EMANUEL, WILLIAM ROBERT, systems ecologist; b. Denver, Sept. 16, 1949; s. Robert Frank and Francis Lee (Countryman) E.; m. Donna Mae Anderson, June 5, 1971; children—Ryan William, Brent Jason, Jennifer Lauren. B.S., Okla. State U., 1971, M.S., 1972, Ph.D., 1975. Research staff mem. Oak Ridge Nat. Lab., Tenn., 1975—; lectr. botany dept. U Tenn., Knoxville, 1978, 84—. Contbr. articles to profl. jours. and chpts. to books. Served to capt. USAR, 1971-79. Grantee Dept. Energy, NSF. Mem. Ecol. Soc. Am., Am. Geophys. Union, AAAS, Sigma Xi, Phi Kappa Phi. Current work: Global element cycling with emphasis on the role of terrestrial ecosystems. Subspecialties: Ecosystems analysis; Systems engineering. Home: 187 N LaSalle Rd Oak Ridge TN 37830 Office: Oak Ridge Nat Lab Environ Scis PO Box X Oak Ridge TN 37831

EMELE, JANE FRANCES, consumer products company executive; b. Phillipsburg, N.J., Nov. 14, 1925; d. Karl A. and Mary E. (Shafer) E. B.S., Upsala Coll., 1947; M.S., U. Ill., 1949; Ph.D., Yale U., 1954. Asst. scientist dept. pharmacology Schering Corp., 1947-48; lab. asst. U. Ill., 1948-49; chief sect. pharmacodynamics Eaton Labs., Norwich Pharmacal Co., N.Y., 1954-55; sr. scientist Warner Lambert Research Inst., Warner-Lambert Pharm. Co., Morris Plains, N.J., 1955-61, sr. research assoc., 1961-65, mgr. dept. proprietary pharmacology and toxicology, 1965-66, dir. dept. pharmacology and toxicology consumer products research div., 1966-70, assoc. dir. biol. research consumer products research div., 1970-73, dir. consumer products group, 1973-74; dir. biol. research (Am. Chicle div.), 1975-77, dir. biol. and clin. affairs, 1977-80, dir. proprietary clin. research and toxicology, 1979—; vis. scientist Rutgers U., 1964-67. Contbr. numerous articles to profl. jours. Bd. dirs. Morris County Assn. Health and Welfare Agys., 1964-66; mem. Morris County Bd. Mental Health, 1959; bd. dirs. N.J. Assn. Mental Health, 1962-64; mem. investigational rev. com. Morristown Meml. Hosp., 1978—; trustee Upsala Coll., 1978—. Mem. Am. Soc. Pharmacology and Exptl. Therapeutics, Fedn. Am. Socs. Exptl. Biology, Am. Pharm. Assn., Acad. Pharm. Scis., Am. Soc. Clin. Pharmacology and Teherapeutics, Am. Coll. Toxicology, Inst. Food Tech., Toxcology Forum, Assos. Clin, Pharmacology, AAAS, N.Y. Acad. Scis., Internat. Soc. Biochem. Pharmacology, W.T. Salter Soc., Yale U. Alumni Assn., U. Ill. Alumni Assn., Upsala Coll. Alumni Assn. (coll. Pres.s' Forum 1973—), Sigma Xi, Phi Sigma, Sigma Delta Epsilon. Subspecialties: Toxicology (medicine); Pharmacology.

EMERSON, ROBERT CHARLES, neuroscientist, research center administrator; b. Detroit, July 17, 1939; s. Kenneth Harwood and Charlotte Magdalena (Steiner) E.; m. Marie Rose Huston, Aug. 1, 1964; children: Robert Charles, David Kenneth. B.S. in Elec. Engring, Lehigh U., 1961, B.S. in Engring. Physics, 1962; M.S. in Biology, Adelphi U., 1966; Ph.D. in Physiology, U. Pa., 1973. Engr., physicist Biomed. Engring. Lab., Airborne Instruments Lab., Melville, NY., 1962-66; hardware and software cons., Phila., 1967-72; assoc. dir. Ctr. for Visual Sci., U. Rochester, N.Y., 1974—; mem. spl. study sects. NIH, 1977, 79, 80; Mem Finger Lakes Trail Conf. N.Y.; trustee Am. Diabetes Assn. (Rochester regional affiliate), 1983. Contbr. articles in field to profl. jours. USPHS trainee Inst. Neurol. Scis., U. Pa., 1966-71; Nat. Eye Inst. research grantee, 1974-81; recipient Research Career Devel. award, 1977-82, conf. grantee, 1978. Mem. Assn. Research in Vision and Ophthalmology, Soc. Neurosci, Eta Kappa Nu, Sigma Xi. Current Work: Neural coding, computers, nonlinear interactions, morphology-injected neurons. Subspecialties: Neurophysiology; Neuroanatomy. Home: 10 Squire Ln Pittsford NY 14534 Office: Ctr Visual Sci U Rochester Rochester NY 14627

EMERY, KENNETH ORRIS, marine geologist; b. Swift Current, Sask., Can., June 6, 1914; s. Clifford Almon and Agnes (Baird) E.; m. Caroline Roberta Alexander, Oct. 3, 1941 (dec. 1984); children—Barbara Kathryn Emery Alvarado, Charlet Adelia Emery Shave; m. Phyllis Helen Williams, Mar. 16, 1985. Student, North Tex. Agrl. Coll., 1933-35; B.S., U. Ill., 1937, Ph.D., 1941. Staff Ill. State Geol. Survey, Urbana, 1941-43; staff div. war research U. Calif., San Diego, 1943-45; asso. marine geologist, prof. geology U. So. Calif., Los Angeles, 1945-62; marine geologist Woods Hole (Mass.) Oceanographic Inst., 1962-75, Henry Bryant Bigelow oceanographer, 1975-79, emeritus, 1979—; mem. U.S. Geol. Survey, Los Angeles, 1945-58. Author: books including Sea Off Southern California, 1960, Oceanography in a Coastal Pond, 1967, (with E. Uchupi) Western North Atlantic, 1972; (with Uchupi) Geology of the Atlantic Ocean, 1984; contbr. (with E. Uchupi) numerous articles to profl. jours. Guggenheim fellow, 1959; recipient Shepard prize for marine geology Soc. Econ. Paleontologists and Mineralogists, 1969; Outstanding Alumnus award U. Tex. at Arlington, 1969; Prince Albert de Monaco medal U. Paris, 1971; Compass Distinguished Achievement award Marine Tech. Soc., 1974; Rosenstiel-AAAS award in oceanographic sci., 1974; Illini Achievement award U. Ill., 1977; Maurice Ewing award in geophysics, 1985. Fellow Am. Geophys. Union; mem. Am. Assn. Petroleum Geologists, Geol. Soc. Am., Soc. Econ. Paleontologists and Mineralogists, Nat. Acad. Scis., Am. Acad. Arts and Scis., China Acad. Sci., Swedish Royal Acad. Sci. Current Work: Synthesis of knowledge of ocean floor. Subspecialty: Sea floor spreading. Home: 74 Ransom Rd Falmouth MA 02540 Office: Woods Hole Oceanographic Inst Woods Hole MA 02543

EMINO, EVERETT RAYMOND, horticulture educator; b. Milford, Mass., Feb. 8, 1942; s. Gerald C. and Dorothy H. (Taft) E.; m. Sarah Jean Tripp, Dec. 16, 1967; children: James, Kathryn. A.A.S., Stockbridge Sch. Agr., 1962; B.S., U. Mass., 1965; M.S., Mich. State U., 1967, Ph.D., 1972. Instr. Mich. State U., East Lansing, 1967-72; asst. prof. U. Mass., Amherst, 1972-75; asso. prof. Tex. A&M U., College Station, 1975-82; prof. U. Conn., Storrs, 1983—. Mem. Am. Soc. Hort. Sci., Bot. Soc. Am., Internat. Plant Propagators Soc., Am. Soc. Agronomy, Crop Sci. Soc. Am. Current Work: Leaf phytotoxicity from foliar applied nutrients. Subspecialties: Morphology; Plant physiology (agriculture). Office: Dept Plant Sci U Conn Storrs CT 06268

EMMING, JAN GOOSSEM, electrical engineer; b. Enschede, The Netherlands, May 28, 1937; came to U.S., 1970; s. Jan and Eisina (Huizing) E.; m. Risje Sytske VanderHorst, Sept. 15, 1967; children—Jan, Wilmar Frederik, Ingrid Josine. B.E.E., Delft U. Tech., 1959, M.E.E., 1961. Research engr. Gen. Electric Corp., Lynchburg, Va., 1961-62; research engr. U. Utrecht, The Netherlands, 1964-69, research assoc., 1969-70; systems engr. Ball Aerospace Systems Div., Boulder, Co., 1970-76, prin. mem. tech. staff, 1976-81, sr. research engring. mgr., 1981—. Editor-in-Chief: Space Science Instrumentation, 1975-81; assoc. editor: Astrophysics and Space Science, 1981—. Editor: Electromagnetic Radiation in Space, 1967; contbr. articles to profl. jours. Patentee in field. Served with Royal Dutch Air Force, 1962-64. Mem. IEEE, Soc. Photo-Instrumentation Engrs., Sigma Xi. Clubs: Rocky Mountain VHF Soc. (v.p. 1980), Boulder Amateur Radio. Current work: System definition, design, modeling and optimization of instrumentation for the space sciences, including infrared telescopes/systems, x-and gamma ray instrumentation, optical and ultraviolet space telescope systems. Subspecialties: Aerospace engineering and technology; Electronics. Home: 8014 Sagebrush Ct Boulder CO 80301 Office: Ball Aerospace Systems Div Commerce St Boulder CO 80306

EMMONS, HOWARD WILSON, engineering educator; b. Morristown, N.J., Aug. 30, 1912; s. Peter Wilson and Margaret (Lang) E.; m. Dorothy Gertrude Allen, July 9, 1937; children—Beverly Ann, Scott Wilson, Keith Howard. M.E., Stevens Inst. tech. 1933, M.S., 1935; Sc.D. (hon.), 1963; Sc.D., Harvard U., 1937; Sc.D.,(hon.), Worcester Poly. Inst., 1983. Research engr. Westinghouse, Essington, Pa., 1937-38; asst. prof. engring. U. Pa., Phila., 1939; instr. to assoc. prof., Harvard U., Cambridge, Mass., 1940-48, prof., 1948-83, emeritus prof., 1983—; cons. in field; mem. numerous govt. coms. including Pres. Sci. Adv. Bd., 1958-70. Chmn. sch. com., Sudbury (Mass.), 1954-68. Recipient 100th Anniversary medal Stevens Inst. Tech., 1970; named Man of Yr. Soc. Fire Protection Engrs. 1982; Mem. ASME (v.p. 1967-70, Timochenko medal 1971), Internat. Combustion Inst. (bd. dirs. 1980—, Edgerton medal 1968), Am. Phys. Soc. (sec. 1946-48 Fluid Dynamics award 1982), Nat. Acad. Sci., Nat. Acad. Engring. Current work: Science of fire in buildings. Subspecialties: Combustion processes; Fluid mechanics. Office: Harvard U 308 Pierce Hall Cambridge MA 02138

EMMONS, LOUISE HICKOK, research biologist; b. Montevideo, Uruguay, Aug. 23, 1943 (parents Am. citizens); d. Arthur Brewster and Evelyn Voorhees E. B.A., Sarah Lawrence Coll., 1965; Ph.D., Cornell U., 1975. Chercheur associe Centre Nationale de la Recherche Scientifique, Brunoy, France, 1975-76; sr. project assoc. Pa. State U., State College, 1976-79; research assoc. div. mammals Smithsonian Instn., Washington, 1980—; cons. biol. survey of nat. park Ecuador Ministry Agr., Quito, 1977; cons. biol. survey of research Peruvian Ministry Agr., Lima, 1979-80; cons. Nat. Geog. Soc., Washington, 1982-83. Contbr. chpts. to books, articles to profl. jours. Grantee Cornell U., 1970, Soc. Sigma Xi, 1971, NSF, 1971-73, Nat. Geog. Soc., 1979, 80-81, Smithsonian Instn., 1984, N.Y. Zool. Soc., 1982-84, World Wildlife Fund, 1983-84. Mem. Ecol. Soc. Am., Am. Soc. Mammalogists, Internat. Soc. for Tropical Ecology, Assn. for Tropical Biology, AAAS. Current work: Tropical ecology of mammals, their natural history, community structure, evolution, plant-animal interactions and systematics particularly in tropical rain-forests. Subspecialties: Behavioral ecology; Tropical ecology. Office: Div Mammals Smithsonian Instn Washington DC 20560

EMSLIE, A. GORDON, educator; b. Hamilton, Scotland, Sept. 6, 1956; came to U.S., 1976, naturalized, 1984; s. Norman and Isabel Marion (Cowie) E.; m. Buff Day Watson, Oct. 21, 1978. B.Sc., U. Glasgow, 1976, Ph.D., 1979. Sr. research asst. Harvard Coll. Obs., 1978-79; research assoc. Inst. Plasma Research, Stanford U., 1979-81; Von Braun prof. space physics U. Ala., Huntsville, 1981—. Contbr. numerous articles to profl. jours. Named Presidential Young Investigator, 1984—; mem. Am. Astron. Soc. Current Work: Physics of energy transport in solar flares; study of early evolution of universe. Subspecialties: Solar physics; Cosmology. Office: U Ala Dept Physics SB 211 Huntsville AL 35899

ENDAL, ANDREW SAMSON, astrophysicist; b. N.Y.C., Sept. 1, 1949; s. Konrad and Gjerturd (Ramsdal) E.; m. Glenna Jeanne Mackey, Apr. 16, 1973; 1 child, Erik. B.S., U. Rochester, 1971; Ph.D., U. Fla., 1974. Research assoc. NASA/Goddard Space Flight Ctr., Greenbelt, Md., 1974-76; vis. asst. prof. Kans. State U., Manhattan, Kans., 1976-78; assoc. prof. La. State U., Baton Rouge, 1978-81; v.p. for research and devel. Applied Research Corp., Landover, Md., 1982—; cons., 1981. Contbr. articles to profl. publs. Grantee NSF, 1977—, NASA, 1982—, Def. Nuclear Agy., 1984—. Mem. Am. Astron. Soc., Am. Geophys. Union, Internat. Astron. Union. Current work: Research management/direction. Subspecialties: Theoretical astrophysics; Climatology. Home: 160 Creek Water Ln Arnold MD 21012 Office: Applied Research Corp 8201 Corporate Dr Landover MD 20785

ENDRES, JOSEPH GEORGE, food company executive, chemical engineer; b. Chgo., Aug. 15, 1932; s. Joseph animalnutrition. Johanna (Schranz) E.; m. Barbara RuthNehls, Sept. 5, 1959; children—Elizabeth, Joseph, Kurt. B.S. in Chem. Engring., U. Ill., 1955, Ph.D. in Food Sci., 1961. Asst. dir. Armour Co., Chgo., 1961-70; v.p. CFS Continental Co., Chgo., 1970-72; dir. food products Central Soya Inc., Chgo., 1972-78, dir. food research, Ft. Wayne, Ind., 1978-83, dir. corp. research, 1983—; adj. prof. U. Ill., Urbana, 1976—. Author: Careers in Food Technology, 1969. Contbr. to publs. in field. Inventor in field. Scoutmaster Boy Scouts Am., Downers Grove, Ill., 1970-78. Served to lt. USN, 1955-63. Mem. Inst. Food Technologists, Am. Oil Chemists Soc. (treas. 1971-73). Republican. Lutheran. Current work: Food science; engineering; biotechnology, animalnutrition Subspecialty: Food science and technology. Office: Central Soya Inc PO Box 1400 Fort Wayne IN 46801

ENDRIZZI, JOHN E., geneticist, educator; b. Wilberton, Okla., July 28, 1923; m. Yvonne V. Barbot, June 6, 1955; children: Colette, George, Regina, Carisa, Karena. B.S., Tex. A&M U., 1949, M.S., 1951; postgrad., U. Va., 1951-52; Ph.D., U. Md., 1955. Asst. Prof. Tex. A&M U., 1955-63; prof., head plant breeding dept. U. Ariz., Tucson, 1963-71, prof. plant gentics, 1971—. Contbr. articles to sci. jours. Served in U.S. Army, 1943-46. Nicholson fellow, 1949-50; Dupont fellow, 1951-52; Nat. Cotton Council grantee, 1958-61; recipient Cotton Genetics Research award, 1969. Mem. Genetics Soc. Am., Am. Genetics Assn., Genetics Soc. Can., Am. Inst. Biol. Scis., AAAS, Ariz.-Nev. Acad. Sci., Sigma Xi, Gamma Sigma Delta. Democrat. Roman Catholic. Current Work: Genetics and cytology. Subspecialties: Plant genetics; Genome organization. Home: 2335 E 9th St Tucson AZ 85719 Office: U Ariz Tucson AZ 85721

ENG, LAWRENCE (LARRY) PHILLIP, engineer; b. Tulsa, Okla., June 7, 1957; s. Lawrence Eng and Daisy (Gee) Geere. B. in Chemistry, So. Meth. U., 1979, postgrad. in elec. engring., 1982-84. Lab. technician Children's Med. Ctr., Dallas, 1975-79; engr. Mostek, Carrollton, Tex., 1979-82, sr. engr. research and devel., 1982-84, head sect. research and devel., 1984—. Mem. IEEE, Am. Chem. Soc. Republican. Episcopalian. Current work: Sub-micron and micron lithography; 256K and 1 megabit dynamic ram technology. Subspecialties: Microchip technology (engineering); Integrated circuits. Home: 1909 Baxley Circle Carrollton TX 75006 Office: Mostek M/S 906 1215 at Crosby St Carrollton TX 75006

ENG, NORMAN, engineering administrator, consultant; b. Chgo., Dec. 21, 1952; s. Shang Hon (Eugene) and Hop Yee (Wong) E.; m. Candice (Wei June) Chiang, June 26, 1982; 1 child, Timothy. B.S. in Civil Engring. (scholar), U. Calif., Berkeley, 1974. Prin. engr. EDS Nuclear Inc., San Francisco, 1975-78; advanced engr. Westinghouse Hanford, Richland, Wash., 1978-79; lead engr. Duke Power Co., Charlotte, N.C., 1979-80; project engr. URS/John A. Blume & Assocs., Engrs., San Francisco, 1980-81; project mgr. NUTECH Engrs., Inc., San Jose, Calif., 1981—. Dir. East Bay Asians Community Action, Oakland, Calif., 1973-74; tchr. Chinese Community Adult Sch., Oakland, 1975-77; sec. U.S. Jaycees, Berkeley, 1979-82. Mem. Am. Nuclear Soc., Am. Welding Soc., ASME, AAAS, Am. Concrete Inst., Am. Soc. Engring. Edn., N.Y. Acad. Sci., Nat. Soc. Profl. Engrs. Current Work: Nuclear power piping and pipe support technology, fast breeder reactor technology, intergranular stress corrosion cracking, induction heating stress improvement, quality assurance/quality control. Subspecialties: Civil engineering; Nuclear engineering. Home: 3285 Padilla Way San Jose CA 95148 Office: NUTECH Engrs 145 Martinvale Ln San Jose CA 95119

ENGE, HARALD ANTON, nuclear physicist; b. Fauske, Norway, Sept. 28, 1920; naturalized U.S.; m. 1947; 3 children. Eng. Diploma, Tech. U. Norway, 1947; Ph.D., U. Bergen, 1954. Lab. engr. Tech. U. Norway, 1947; research assoc. and lectr. U. Bergen, 1948-55, from instr. to assoc. prof., 1955-63; prof. physics MIT, Cambridge, 1963—; co-founder and chmn. Deltaray Corp., 1969-73, Gammaray Corp., 1981. Fellow Am. Phys. Soc. (Bonner prize 1984); mem. European Phys. Soc., Norwegian Phys. Soc. Subspecialty: Nuclear physics. Office: MIT Room 58-009 Dept Physics Cambridge MA 02139

ENGEL, ALAN JAMES, ceramic engineer; b. Jersey City, Nov. 25, 1947; s. James Anthony and Florence Elizabeth (Fields) E.; m. Grace Agnes Schmidt, Oct. 17, 1970; children—Alan, Melissa, Cynthia, Matthew, Nicholas. B.S., Rutgers U., 1970. Project engr. Gen. Refractories Co., Balt., 1971-78, sr. tech. engr., Pitts., 1978-79, assoc. mgr. prodn. devel., 1979-80, mgr. prodn. devel., 1981-82, v.p. research and devel., 1982—. Served with U.S. Army, 1970-78. Mem. Am. Ceramic Soc., Nat. Inst. Ceramic Engrs. (assoc.), Iron and Steel Soc., The Refractories Inst. (rep. tech. adv. com.), Am. Iron and Steel Soc. (mem. refractories collaborative research unit). Current work: Direction, planning and control of refractories research and development group in support of company strategies, primary emphasis on monolitics and carbon bonding. Subspecialty: Ceramic engineering. Home: 108 Brookston Dr Mars PA 16046 Office: Gen Refractories Co 600 Grant St Room 3000 Pittsburgh PA 15219

ENGEL, BERNARD THEODORE, psychologist; b. Chgo., Apr. 18, 1928; s. Marvin I. and Hannah (Hollander) E.; m. Rae Goldberg, Mar. 10, 1951; children: Sandra E., Jeffrey P., Lauren C. B.A., UCLA, 1954, Ph.D., 1956. Cert. biofeedback, 1981. Jr. research psychologist UCLA, 1956-57, research psychologist Inst. Psychosomatic and Psychiatric. Research and Tng., Michael Reese Hosp., Chgo., 1957-58; lectr. med. psychology, mem. sr. staff Cardiovascular Research Inst., U. Calif. Sch. Medicine, San Francisco, 1959-67; chief lab. behavioral scis., chief psychophysiology sect. Gerontology Research Center, Nat. Inst. Aging, NIH, Balt., 1967—; assoc. prof. behavioral biology Johns Hopkins Sch. Medicine, Balt., 1970-82, prof., 1982—. Contbr. 100 articles to sci. jours. Served in U.S. Army, 1950-52. Recipient award Pavlovian Soc., 1979. Fellow AAAS, Gerontol. Sci.; mem. Soc. Psychophysiol. Research (pres. 1970-71), Biofeedback Soc. (pres. 1981-82), Am. Psychosomatic Soc. (sec.-treas. 1981-85, pres. 1985-86), Pavlovian Soc., Soc. Behavioral Medicine, Acad. Behavioral Medicine Research, Sigma Xi. Current Work: Behavioral medicine, application of methods and principles of behavioral sciences to the assessment and treatment of patients with medical disorders; analysis of behavioral and physiological mechanisms underlying biological adaptiveness of circulation. Subspecialties: Psychophysiology; Biofeedback. Home: 106 Welford Rd Lutherville MD 21093 Office: Francis Scott Key Med Ctr Gerontology Research Ctr Baltimore MD 21224

ENGEL, LARS NORLICK, applied mathematician; b. Portland, Oreg., Nov. 2, 1934; s. Ernest Herman and Joyce (Graham) E.; m. Emily Jo Flachmeier, Dec. 28, 1957; children: Jan Kristin, Karen Gale. B.S. with honors, U. Tex., 1961, M.S.E.E, 1964. Research engr. Elec. Engring. Research Lab., U. Tex., Austin, 1961-63; microwave engr. Electro-Mechanics Co., Austin, 1963-64; engr. Westinghouse Electric., Balt., 1964-65; staff mem. Los Alamos Nat. Lab., N.Mex., 1965—. Trustee Dad's Assn. Tex. Tech. U., Lubbock, 1982—. Served to staff sgt. USAF, 1954-58. Recipient Disting. Performance award Los Alamos Nat. Lab., 1984; Recognition of Excellence award Dept. Energy, 1985. Mem. IEEE, Am. Math Soc., Ops. Research Soc. Am., Soc. Indsl. and Applied Math. Current Work: Application of non-linear optimization techniques to nuclear physics problems. Subspecialties: Operations research (engineering); Nuclear physics. Home: 1210 Myrtle Los Alamos NM 87544 Office: Los Alamos Nat Lab PO Box 1663 Los Alamos NM 87545

ENGEL, TOBY ROSS, physician, medical educator and researcher; b. N.Y.C., Mar. 6, 1942; s. Fred and Pauline (Bienstock) E.; m. Lorraine Barbara Rodney, Aug.15, 1965; children: Joshua, Jeffrey, Benjamin. B.A., N.Y.U., 1962, M.D., 1966. Diplomate: Am. Bd. Internal Medicine (subcert. in cardiovascular disease). Resident U. Pa., Phila., 1966-68; fellow, instr. Ohio State U., Columbus, 1970-73; asst. prof. Med. Coll. Pa., Phila., 1973-75, assoc. prof., 1976-79, prof. medicine, 1980-85; prof. medicine, chief div. cardiology U. Nebr. Med. Ctr., 1985—. Assoc. editor: Annals of Internal Medicine, 1977-85. Served to capt. U.S. Army, 1968-70, Korea. Recipient awards Am. Heart Assn., awards NIH, awards others. Fellow Am. Coll. Cardiology, ACP, Am. Coll. Clin. Pharmacology, Am. Heart Assn. Council on Clin. Cardiology, others. Jewish. Current Work: Electrophysiology, electrocardiography, pharmacologic and surgical and pace maker treatment of arrhythmia. Subspecialties: Cardiology; Pharmacology. Home: 2818 S 101st St Omaha NE 68124 Office: U Nebr Med Ctr 42d and Dewey Ave Omaha NE 68105

ENGELBERGER, JOSEPH FREDERICK, robotics manufacturing company executive; b. N.Y.C., July 26, 1925; s. Joseph H. and Irene E. E.; m. Margaret B. Thomas, May 24, 1954; children—Gay, Jeff. B.S., Columbia U., 1946, M.S. in Physics, 1949. With Manning Maxwell & Moore, Stanford, Conn., 1946-57, chief engr., 1953-56, div. gen. mgr., 1956-57; founder, gen. mgr. Consol. Controls Corp. (sold to Condec Corp. 1964), Old Greenwich, Conn., 1957-77, chmn. bd., 1977; also v.p., mem. exec. com. Condec Corp., 1965—; also dir.; founder, pres. Unimation Inc., Danbury, Conn., 1962—; dir. Cooper Thermometer, Anderson Labs., State Nat. Bank; founder, past chmn. Conn. Product Devel. Corp., 1973, chmn., 1973-79; mem. Pres.'s Commn. on Indsl. Innovation. Contbr. numerous articles on robotics to profl. jours. Vice pres. Fairfield County council Boy Scouts Am. Recipient Nyselius award Die Casting Inst., 1978; Progress award Soc. Mfg. Engrs., 1979. Mem. Chief Execs. Forum, World Bus. Council, Robotics Industries Assn. (founder 1973, pres. 1974, established Joseph F. Engelberger Ann. award 1977), Tau Beta Pi. Patentee in field. Current Work: Applications of robotics throughout the factory and information service area; provide robots with sensory perception. Subspecialty: Robotics. Office: Unimation Inc Shelter Rock Ln Danbury CT 06810 also Durant Ave Bethel CT 06810

ENGELBRECHT, RICHARD STEVENS, environmental engineering educator; b. Ft. Wayne, Ind., Mar. 11, 1926; s. William C. and Mary Elizabeth (Stevens) E.; m. Mary Condrey, Aug. 21, 1948; children: William, Timothy. A.B., Ind. U., 1948; M.S., M.I.T., 1952, Sc.D., 1954. Teaching asst. Ind. U. Sch. Medicine, Indpls., 1949-50; research asst. M.I.T., Cambridge, 1950-52, instr., 1952-54; asst. prof. U. Ill., Urbana-Champaign, 1954-57, assoc. prof., 1957-59, prof. environ. engring., 1959—; dir. Advanced Environ. Control Tech. Research Center, 1979—; cons. Ill. EPA, U.S. EPA, WHO; mem. Ohio River Valley Water Sanitation Commn., chmn., 1980-82. Named Ernest Victor Balsom Commemoration Lectr., 1978; recipient Eric H. Vick award Inst. Public Health Engrs., U.K., 1979, George J. Schroepfer award Central State Water Pollution Control Assn., 1985; Benjamin Garver Lamme award Am. Soc. Engring. Edn., 1985. Mem. Internat. Assn. Water Pollution Research and Control (pres. 1980—), Am. Water Works Assn. (George W. Fuller award 1974, Publ. award 1975), Water Pollution Control Fedn. (Eddy medal 1966, Arthur Sidney Bedell award 1973, pres. 1978), Nat. Acad. Engring., AAAS, Am. Soc. Microbiology, Abwasser-technische Vereini-gung (hon.). Current Work: Microbiological (bacteria, viruses) problems associated with water quality management, including water and wastewater treatment. Subspecialty: Water supply and wastewater treatment. Home: 2012 Silver Ct W Urbana IL 61801 Office: 3230 Newmark Civil Engring Lab 208 N Romine St Urbana IL 61801

ENGELDER, THEODORE CARL, physicist; b. Detroit, Aug. 31, 1927; s. Conrad John and Ruth Laura (Linsenmann) E.; m. Rita Marie Gaffney, Sept. 28, 1952; children—Laura, James. B.S., U. Mich., 1949; M.S., Yale U., 1950, Ph.D., 1953, Nuclear physicist Dow Chem. Co., Midland, Mich., 1952-56; nuclear engr. Chrysler Corp., Ann Arbor, Mich., 1956; chief exptl. physics sect. Babcock & Wilcox Co., Lynchburg, Va., 1956-67; asst. dir. Nuclear Devel. Center, 1967-71; dir. Research Center, 1971—. Contbr. tech. articles to profl. jours. Mem. Am. Nuclear Soc., Am. Phys. Soc., Atomic Indsl. Forum, Phi Beta Kappa, Sigma Xi. Patentee in field. Home: 2236 Taylor Farm Rd Lynchburg VA 24503 Office: PO Box 11165 Lynchburg VA 24506

ENGELHARD, ARTHUR WILLIAM, plant pathologist, educator; b. Dayton, Ohio, Apr. 9, 1928; s. Paul George and Louise Emma (Stroh) E.; married; children: Eric, Lisa, Arthur William. B.S., Ohio U., 1950; M.S., Yale U., 1952; Ph.D., Iowa State U., 1955. Grad. asst. Iowa State U., 1952-55; asst. plant pathologist Ill. State Natural History Survey, Urbana, 1955-56; research biologist E. I. duPont, Wilmington, Del., 1956-64, sr. research biologist, Bradenton, Fla., 1964-66; assoc. prof. plant pathology U. Fla.-Bradenton, 1966-78, prof., 1978—; cons. in field. Contbr. numerous articles to profl. jours. Recipient ann. research award for outstanding research and service to Fla. growers Fla. Ornamental Growers Assn., 1981, Medal of Merit for outstanding contbns. in plant pathology Ohio U. Nat. Alumni Bd., 1983. Mem. Am. Phytopath Soc., Fla. State Hort. Soc. (Outstanding Paper Award 1970, 74, 80, 81), Internat. Soc. Plant Pathology, Sigma Xi, Gamma Sigma Delta, Phi Kappa Phi, Theta Chi. Patentee methods to control arachnids. Current Work: Etiology and control of diseases of ornamental plants; integration of chemical-cultural-nutritional systems of disease control. Subspecialties: Integrated pest management; Plant pathology. Home: 5306 7th Ave Dr W Bradenton FL 33529 Office: 5007 60th St E Bradenton FL 33508

ENGELKING, HENRY MARK, virologist; b. Burbank, Calif., May 3, 1949; s. Henry Christian and Lorraine Katherine (Miehl) E.; m. Judy Ann Hagner, Sept. 15, 1979. B.A., U. Calif., San Diego, 1971; M.S., Oreg. State U., 1974. Research asst. dept. biochemistry-biophysics Oreg. State U., 1974-78, sr. research asst. dept. microbiology, 1978—; cons. in field. Contbr. articles to profl. jours. Mem. Am. Soc. Microbiology, Sigma Chi, Phi Kappa Phi. Current Work: Genetic engineering, sub unit vaccines, persistent viral infections, viral diseases of fish, rhabdovirus cloning, rapid diagnosis of IHN virus in salmonids. Subspecialties: Virology (biology); Molecular biology. Home: 234 NW 29th St Corvallis OR 97330 Office: Dept Microbiology Oregon State U Corvallis OR 97331

ENGEN, BYRON WAYNE, engineering executive; b. Northwood, N.D., July 19, 1933; s. E.C. and Helma A. (Herlickson) E.; m. Donna J. Fredrickson, Mar. 16, 1957; children—Todd, Mark, Lisa, Kari. B.S. in Mech. Engring., U. Minn., 1956. Registered profl. engr., Wis., Ohio, N.Y., Mich. Engr. Ellerbe Architects, St. Paul, 1956; sales supr., Worthington Corp., East Orange, N.J., 1960-68; mgr. spl. projects Modine Mfg. Co., Racine, Wis., 1968-70, mktg. mgr., Holland, Ohio, 1970-74; supr. market devel. Owens-Corning Fiberglas, Toledo, 1974-83, mgr. engring., 1983—. Tech. coordinator Planning and Designing the Office, 1981. Contbr. articles to profl. jours., chpt. to book. Scoutmaster Toledo Area council Boy Scouts Am., Sylvania, Ohio, 1972-75; pres. Olivet Lutheran Ch., Sylvania, 1979-80, Northview Athletic Boosters, Sylvania, 1982. Served to lt. USNR, 1956-60. Mem. ASHRAE, Nat. Soc. Profl. Engrs. Illuminating Engring. Soc., ASME, ASTM (vice chmn. 1979, 84), Jaycees. Republican. Current work: Design of air-supported and tension fabric structures by non-linear finite element analysis of anticlastic surfaces using anisotropic, coated, glass-reinforced fabrics. Subspecialties: Mechanical engineering; Structural engineering. Home: 5630 Bonniebrook Rd Sylvania OH 43560 Office: Owens-Corning Fiberglas Corp Fiberglas Tower Toledo OH 43659

ENGLE, MICHAEL J(EAN), biochemist, cell biologist; b. St. Louis, Mar. 22, 1947; s. John D. and Josephine A. (Colombini) E.; m. Jacquelyn A. Textor, Sept. 3, 1983. A.B. in Biology, St. Louis U., 1969, Ph.D. in Biochemistry, 1976. Postdoctoral fellow State U. Utrecht, Netherlands, 1976-77, W. Alton Jones Cell Ctr., Lake Placid, N.Y., 1977-78; affiliate scientist Wis. Regional Primate Research Ctr., Madison, 1981—; asst. scientist dept. pediatrics U. Wis., Madison, 1978-83, assoc. scientist, 1983—. Contbr. chpts. and articles to profl. publs. Served with U.S. Army, 1970-71. Recipient Research Career Devel. award NIH, 1980-85; grantee Juvenile Diabetes Assn., 1979-81, NIH, 1981-86. Mem. Am. Oil Chemists Soc., Am. Chem. Soc., AAAS, Am. Soc. Biol. Chemists (assoc.). Current work: Pulmonary carbohydrate and phospholipid metabolism in late fetal and early neonatal life. Subspecialties: Biochemistry (medicine); Cell and tissue culture. Office: Dept Pediatrics U Wis 600 Highland Ave Madison WI 53792

ENNA, SALVATORE JOSEPH, pharmacologist, cons.; b. Kansas City, Mo., Dec. 19, 1944; s. Veto Anthony and Fannie Silvia (Bonello) E.; m. Colleen Anne Nestor, July 26, 1969; children: Anne, Matthew, Katherine. B.A., Rockhurst Coll., 1965; M.S., U. Mo., Kansas City, 1967, Ph.D., 1970. Postdoctoral fellow U. Tex. Med. Sch., Dallas, 1970-72; Roche fellow F. Hoffmann-LaRoche & Co., Basel, Switzerland, 1973-74; research fellow dept. pharmacology Johns Hopkins U., 1974-76; asst. prof U. Tex. Med. Sch., Houston, 1976-77, assoc. prof., 1977-80, prof., 1980—; cons. in field. Contbr. numerous articles to profl. jours. Bd. dirs. Houston Area Parkinson Soc., 1980—. Trustee fellow U. Mo., 1967-70; NIMH fellow, 1974-76; NIH Research Career Devel. award, 1978—; Basic Sci. Teaching award U. Tex. Med. Sch., 1980-81; John Jacob Abel award, 1980. Mem. Soc. Neurosci., Am. Soc. Neurochemistry, Am. Soc. Pharmacology and Exptl. Therapy, AAAS, Am. Chem. Soc. Current Work: Neurotransmitter biochemistry and pharmacology. Subspecialties: Molecular pharmacology; Neuropharmacology. Home: 6227 Cheena Houston TX 77096 Office: Dept Pharmacology U Tex Med Sch Box 20708 Houston TX 77025

ENNIS, FRANCIS A., physician, educator; b. Boston, May 14, 1938; s. Lewis and Veronica (Pittman) E.; m. Anne M. Cavanagh, Aug. 10, 1963. A.B., Boston Coll., 1960; M.D., Tufts U., 1964. Diplomate: Am. Bd. Internal Medicine, 1971. NIH research assoc., Bethesda, Md., 1966-68; resident in medicine Cornell U., 1968-70; assoc. prof. medicine Boston U. Sch. Medicine, 1970-73; dir. div. virology Bur. Biologics, FDA, Bethesda, Md., 1973-81; prof. medicine and molecular genetics U. Mass. Med. Ctr., Worcester, 1981—. Contbr. articles to profl. jours. Served with USPHS, 1966-68, 74-81. Recipient award of Merit FDA, 1977. Mem. Am. Soc. Clin. Investigation, Am. Assn. Immunologists, Am. Soc. Virology. Current Work: Immune responses to viruses, interferons, lymphocytes. Subspecialties: Infectious diseases; Immunology (medicine). Office: 55 Lake Ave N Worcester MA 01605

ENNIS, HERBERT L., biochemist; b. Bklyn., Jan. 6, 1932; s. Rudolph and Fannie (Stringer) E.; m. Judith A. Wolper, June 5, 1960; children: Ronald D., Ethan W. B.S., Bklyn. Coll., 1953; M.S., Northwestern U., 1954, Ph.D., 1957. Postdoctoral fellow Northwestern U., 1957-58, Harvard Med. Sch., 1958-59; Am. Cancer Soc. research fellow Brandeis U., 1959-60; instr. dept. pharmacology Harvard Med. Sch., 1960-64; mem. St. Jude Children's Research Hosp.-U. Tenn. Med. Sch., 1964-69, Roche Inst. Molecular Biology, Nutley, N.J., 1969—. Contbr. articles to profl. jours.; editor: Antimicrobial Agents and Chemotherapy, 1977—. Mem. AAAS, Am. Soc. Biol. Chemistry, N.Y. Acad. Sci., Am. Soc. Microbiology, Sigma Xi. Current Work: Protein and nucleic acid synthesis; messenger RNA decay; cloning of developmentally regulated genes; mechanism of antibiotic action. Subspecialties: Molecular biology; Developmental biology. Office: Roche Inst Molecular Biology Nutley NJ 07110

ENOCH, JAY MARTIN, visual scientist, educator; b. N.Y.C., Apr. 20, 1929; s. Jerome Dee and Stella Sarah (Nathan) E.; m. Rebekah Ann Feiss, June 24, 1951; children—Harold Owen, Barbara Diane, Ann Allison. B.S. in Optics and Optometry, Columbia U., 1950; postgrad., Inst. Optics U. Rochester, 1953; Ph.D. in Physiol. Optics, Ohio State U., 1956. Asst. prof. physiol. optics Ohio State U., Columbus, 1956-58; assoc. supr. Mapping and Charting Research Lab., Ohio State U., 1956-58; fellow Nat. Phys. Lab., Teddington, Eng., 1959-60; research instr. dept. ophthalmology Washington U. Sch. Medicine, St. Louis, 1958-59, research asst. prof., 1959-64, research asso. prof., 1965-70, research prof., 1970-74; fellow Barnes Hosp., St. Louis, 1960-64, cons. ophthalmology, 1964-74; research prof. dept. psychology Washington U., St. Louis, 1970-74; grad. research prof. ophthalmology and psychology U. Fla. Coll. Medicine, Gainesville, 1974-80, grad. research prof. physics, 1979-80; dir. Center for Sensory Studies, 1976-80; dean Sch. Optometry, prof. physiol. optics and optometry U. Calif., Berkeley, 1980—, prof. physiol. optics in ophthalmology, San Francisco, 1980—, chmn. Grad. Group on Psychol. Optics, 1980—; chmn. subcom. contact lens Standards Am. Nat. Standards Inst., 1970-77; mem. nat. advisory eye council Nat. Eye Inst., NIH, 1975-77, 80-84; exec. com., com. on vision NAS-NRC, 1973-76; mem. U.S. Nat. Com. Internat. Commn. Optics, 1976-79. Author numerous book chpts. and articles on visual sci., receptor optics, perimetry, contact lenses and infant vision to sci. jours.; contbr. chpts. in field to med. books; hon. editorial bd.: Vision Research, 1974-80; editorial bd.: Internat. Ophthalmology, 1977—; asso. editor: Investigative Ophthalmology, 1965-75; 80-85, Sight-Saving Rev, 1974—, Sensory Processes, 1974-80; editorial bd. optical scis.: Springer-Verlag, Heidelberg, 1978—. Mem. nat. sci. advisory bd. Retinitis Pigmentosa Found., 1977—; U.S. rep. Internat. Perimetric Soc., 1974—; also exec. com., chmn. Research Group Standards.; Bd. dirs. Friends of Eye Research, 1977—; trustee Illuminating Engring. Research Inst., 1977-81. Served to 2d lt. U.S. Army, 1951-52. Recipient Career Devel. award NIH, 1963-73. Fellow AAAS, Am. Acad. Optometry (Glenn A. Fry award 1972, Charles F. Prentice medal award 1974), Optical Soc. Am. (chmn. vision tech. sect. 1974-76), Am. Acad. Ophthalmology Otolaryngology (assoc.; Honor award 1985); mem. Assn. for Research in Vision and Ophthalmology (trustee 1967-73, pres. 1972-73, Francis I. Proctor medal 1977), Psychonomic Soc., AAUP, Am. Psychol. Assn. (sect. 3), Sigma Xi. Home: 54 Shuey Dr Moraga CA 94556 Office: Sch Optometry U Calif Berkeley CA 94720

ENQUIST, LYNN WILLIAM, molecular biologist, biotechnology co. research administrator, educator; b. Denver, Oct. 23, 1945; s. Clarence Andrew and Doris Alice (Hajenga) E.; m. Kathleen Marie, Aug. 10, 1968; 1 son, Brian Joseph. B.S. (Woodrow Wilson fellow), S.D. State U., 1967; Ph.D., Med. Coll. Va., 1971. Postdoctoral fellow Roche Inst. Molecular Biology, Nutley, N.J., 1971-73; staff fellow NIH, Bethesda, Md., 1973-77, staff scientist, 1977-81; research dir. Molecular Genetics, Inc., Minnetonka, Minn., 1981—; instr. advanced bacterial genetics Cold Spring Harbor (N.Y.) Labs., 1981, 82, 83. Contbr. numerous articles to profl. jours.; mem. editorial bd.: Jour. Virology, 1979-81. Served to comd. USPHS, 1973-81. Mem. Am. Soc. Microbiology, AAAS, Sigma Xi, Phi Kappa Phi. Current Work: Organization and expression of genes; gene manipulation. Subspecialties: Genetics and genetic engineering (biology); Molecular biology. Office: 10320 Bren Rd E Minnetonka MN 55343

ENROTH-CUGELL, CHRISTINA A., electrical engineering, biological sciences and neurobiology educator. Med. Lic. Med. Sch. Karolinska Inst., Stockholm, 1948; Med. Dr., Karolinska Inst. Neurophysiology Lab., Sweden, 1952. Residency in ophthalmology Karolinska Inst., 1948-56; intern. Northwestern U., 1956-57; research fellow and instr., 1958-62, asst. prof., 1962-68, assoc. prof., 1968-72, prof. dep. elec. engring. and biol. scis., 1972-74, prof. dept. engring. scis. and biol. scis., 1978-84, prof., chmn. dept. neurobiology and physiology, prof. dept. engring. scis., 1984—. Gen. editor: Investigative Ophthalmology, 1979-83. Recipient Career Devel. award NIH, 1962-72, von Stallmann prize The Netherlands, 1982, Friedenwald award Assn. Research in Vision and Ophthalmology Inc.; 1983. Nat. Eye Inst. grantee, 1974-78. Fellow Am. Acad. Arts & Scis.; mem. Nat. Adv. Eye Council NIH, Soc. Neurosci. (pres. local chpt. 1984—), Am. Physiol. Soc., British Physiol. Soc., (assoc.), AAAS, Fed. Am. Scientists. Office: Northwestern U Dept Biomed Engring Evanston IL 60201

ENSMINGER, DALE, researcher, mechanical and electrical engineer; b. Mount Perry, Ohio, Sept. 26, 1923; s. Charles Henry and Mary Elfa (Koehler) E.; m. Lois Elizabeth Hamilton, Mar. 25, 1948; children—Martha Jean, Laura Lee, Charles Robert, Jonathan Dale, Mary Ann, Daniel Joseph. B.S. in Mech. Engring., Ohio State U., 1950, B.S. in Elec. Engring., 1950, M.S. in Math. and

Physics, 1953. Registered profl. engr., Ohio. From researcher to sr. researcher Battelle Columbus Labs., Ohio, 1950—. Patentee applications in ultrasonics. Author: Ultrasonics, 1973; also articles. Sec., team capt. Columbus Prison Assn., 1948—; dean Columbus Bible Inst., 1952—; bd. dirs. Baptist Mission of Trinidad and Tobago. Served with U.S. Army, 1943-46. Mem. Acoustical Soc. Am., Am. Soc. Nondestructive Testing. Republican. Current work: Research and development in the fields of ultrasonics, vibration and sound since February 1950, with nearly 900 separate projects in both low-intensity and high-intensity ultrasonics. Subspecialties: Ultrasound; Non-destructive testing. Office: Battelle Columbus Labs 505 King Ave Columbus OH 43201

EPP, MELVIN DAVID, plant geneticist, tissue culture specialist; b. Newton, Kans., June 16, 1942; s. John, Jr. and Marie (Harder) E.; m. Sylvia K. Rieger, June 26, 1964; children: David S., J. Terry. B.S., Wheaton (Ill.) Coll., 1964; M.S., U. Conn., 1967; Ph.D., Cornell U., 1971. NIH genetics trainee Cornell U., Ithaca, N.Y., 1967; Hort. trainee Pan Am. Seed Co., Paonia, Colo., 1964-65; Damon Runyon fellow Brookhaven Nat. Lab., Upton, N.Y., 1972-74; sr. research biologist Monsanto Co., St. Louis, 1974-77; research supt. Philippine Packing Corp. subs. Del Monte Corp., Manila, 1977-82, mgr. plant propagation and tissue culture research parent co., San Leandro, Calif., 1982-84; prin. scientist ARCO Plant Cell Research Inst., Dublin, Calif., 1985—. Contbr. articles to sci. jours. Mem. Genetics Soc. Am., Bot. Soc. Am., AAAS. Current Work: The application of genetic selection and genetic engineering together with plant cell and tissue culture to develop superior varieties of temperate and tropical fruits and vegetables. Subspecialties: Plant cell and tissue culture; Genetics and genetic engineering (agriculture). Office: 6560 Trinity Ct Dublin CA 94568

EPPERLY, WILLIAM ROBERT, energy company executive; b. Christiansburg, Va., Mar. 17, 1935; s. William Rangeley and Myrtle Claire (Vest) E.; m. Sarah Ann Owen, June 9, 1957; children: William Robert, Jennifer Ann, Thomas. B.S., Va. Poly. Inst., 1956, M.S., 1958. With Exxon Research & Engring. Co., and parent co., 1957—; mgr. Baytown (Tex.) research and devel. div., 1973-76, mgr. project devel. and planning, Florham Park, N.J., 1976-77, gen. mgr. liquefaction, 1977-79, gen. mgr. synthetic fuels dept., 1980-83, sr. program mgr., 1983-84, gen. mgr. Corp. research, 1984—; mem. air pollution research adv. com. Coordinating Research Council, 1969-71; mem. fossil energy program adv. com. Oak Ridge Nat. Lab., 1978-81; mem. com. synthetic fuels safety NRC, 1982, chmn. com. on coop. govt. industry research, 1983. Author. Mem. Am. Inst. Chem. Engrs. (award for chem. engring. practice 1983), Am. Petroleum Inst., AAAS. Methodist. Patentee in synthetic fuels, automotive emissions/gasoline composition, iron ore reduction, fuel cells, others. Current Work: New science and technology for petroleum, synthetic fuels and chemicals; modern management systems for complex projects; enhancement of productivity and creativity. Subspecialties: Fuels; Chemical engineering. Home: 18 Gloucester Rd Summit NJ 07901 Office: Exxon Research & Engring Co Clinton Twp Route 22E Annandale NJ 08801

EPPSTEIN, DEBORAH ANNE, biochemical researcher; b. Kalamazoo, Mich., Oct. 16, 1948; d. Samuel Hillel and Dorothy Jean (Dodd) E. A.B. with honors, Grinnell Coll., 1970; Ph.D. in Biochemistry, U. Ark., 1975. Research assoc. plant pathology U. Ark., 1974-75; research assoc. dept. biol. sci. U. Calif.-Santa Barbara, 1976-78; dept. head biochemistry Inst. Bio-Organic Chemistry Syntex, Palo Alto, Calif., 1978—. Contbr. in field. NIH fellow, 1976-78. Mem. Am. Chem. Soc., AAAS, N.Y. Acad. Sci. Current Work: Biochemical mechanism of action studies (antiviral, anticancer), polypeptide hormones, drug delivery systems. Subspecialties: Cell and tissue culture; Virology (biology). Office: 3401 Hillview Ave Palo Alto CA 94304

EPSTEIN, ALAN LEE, cancer biologist, educator, consultant; b. Bklyn., Aug. 14, 1949; s. Arthur Victor and Shirley (Blatt) E.; m. Lindsay Diane Mount, Dec. 19, 1977; children: Aaron Jacob, Seth David. B.A., Wesleyan U., Middletown, Conn., 1971; M.D., Stanford U., 1978, Ph.D., 1978. Postdoctoral fellow Eleanor Roosevelt Inst. Cancer Research, Denver, 1978-80; asst. prof. medicine Northwestern U., 1980—; cons. Techniclone Internat., Santa Ana, Calif. Hubert H. Humphrey fellow of Damon Runyon-Walter Winchell Fellowship Fund, 1979-80; Leukemia Research Found. grantee, 1980-81; Milheim Found. grantee, 1979-80; Nat. Cancer Inst. grantee, 1980—; recipient Jr. Faculty Research award Am. Cancer Soc., 1980-83; Searle scholar, 1982-83. Mem. Am. Soc. Cell Biology, Am. Soc. Hematology, Am. Assn. Cancer Research, Am. Soc. Clin. Oncology, N.Y. Acad. Sci. Democrat. Jewish. Current Work: The study of the biology of the human malignant lymphomas and leukemias; in particular, initiation of tumor cell lines and production of monoclonal antibodies to tumor-associated antigens. Subspecialties: Cancer research (medicine); Cell study oncology. Home: 812 Colfax St Evanston IL 60201 Office: Medical Oncology Section Northwestern U 303 E Chicago Ave Chicago IL 60611

EPSTEIN, BENJAMIN ROSS, engineer; b. Phila., Nov. 21, 1955; s. Donald Morris and Nancy Lea (Hyman) E. B.S.E.E., U. Rochester, 1978; M.S. in Bioengring., U. Pa., 1980, Ph.D. in Bioengring., 1982. Postdoctoral fellow Centre Nat. de la Recherche Scientifique, Paris, 1982-83; mem. tech. staff RCA Labs., Princeton, N.J., 1983—; instr. U. Pa., Phila., 1984. Contbr. articles to engring. jours. Sr. mem. Curtis Organ Restoration Soc., Phila., 1978—. Postdoctoral fellow French Govt., 1982-83; Ashton scholar, U. Pa., 1978-82; NIH assistantship, U. Pa., 1979-82. Mem. IEEE, N.Y. Acad. of Scis., AAAS, Bioelectromagnetics Soc., Automatic RF Techniques Group, Tau Beta Pi. Current work: Development of CAD and test systems used in the manufacture and design of millimeter-wave and microwave circuits and devices; dielectric properties of oil-water mixtures, tissues, and other materials. Application of microwaves in hyperthermic treatment of cancer. Subspecialties: Electrical engineering; Biomedical engineering. Home: 38B Berrien Ave Princeton Junction NJ 08550 Office: RCA Labs Washington Rd Princeton NJ 08540

EPSTEIN, EDWARD S., meteorologist; b. N.Y.C., Apr. 29, 1931; s. Herman and Julia E.; m. Alice Katzenstein, June 6, 1954; children: Debra, Harry, Nancy, William. A.B., Harvard U., 1951; M.B.A., Columbia U., 1953; M.S., Pa. State U., 1954, Ph.D., 1960. Lectr. U. Mich., 1959-61, asst. prof., 1961-63, asso. prof., 1964-68, prof., 1969-73, chmn. dept. atmospheric and oceanic sci., 1971-73; asso. adminstr. for environ. monitoring and predictions NOAA, 1973-77, acting asst. adminstr. for research and devel., 1977-78, dir. Nat Climate Program Office, Rockville, Md., 1978-81, chief Climate and Earth Scis. Lab., 1981-83, acting dir. research and applications Nat. Environ. Satellite, Data and Info. Services, 1982-83; prin. scientist Climate Analysis Ctr., 1984—; bd. dirs. Univ. Corp. for Atmospheric Research, 1969-73. Editor: Jour. Applied Meteorology, 1971-73; contbr. articles to profl. jours. Served with USAF, 1953-57. Fellow Am. Meteorol. Soc. (councillor 1974-77), AAAS (chmn. sect. hydrospheric scis. 1980); mem. Am. Geophys. Union. Jewish. Subspecialty: Meteorology. Home: 8216 Inverness Hollow Terr Potomac MD 20854 Office: World Weather Bldg Camp Springs MD 20233

EPSTEIN, EMANUEL, plant physiologist; b. Duisburg, Germany, Nov. 5, 1916; came to U.S., 1938, naturalized, 1946; s. Harry and Bertha (Lowe) E.; m. Hazel M. Leask, Nov. 26, 1943; children: Jared H. (dec.), Jonathan H. B.S., U. Calif.-Davis, 1940, M.S., 1941; Ph.D., U. Calif.-Berkeley, 1950. Plant physiologist Dept. Agr., Beltsville, Md., 1950-58; lectr., assoc. plant physiologist U. Calif., Davis, 1958-65, prof. plant nutrition, plant physiologist, 1965—, prof. botany, 1974—; cons. to govt. and pvt. agys. Author: Mineral Nutrition of Plants: Principles and Perspectives, 1972; editorial bd.: Plant Physiology, 1962-71, 76—, CRC Handbook Series in Nutrition and Food, 1975—, The Biosaline Concept: An Approach to the Utilization of Underexploited Resources, 1978, Plant Sci., 1981—, Advances in Plant Nutrition, 1981—. Served with U.S. Army, 1943-46. Recipient Gold medal Pisa (Italy) U., 1962; Guggenheim fellow, 1958; Fulbright sr. research scholar, 1965-66, 74-75. Fellow AAAS; mem. Nat. Acad. Scis., Am. Soc. Plant Physiologists, Scandinavian Soc. Plant Physiology, Australian Soc. Plant Physiologists, Am. Inst. Biol. Scis., Crop Sci. Soc. Am., Am. Soc. Agronomy, Common Cause, Save-the-Redwoods League, Sierra Club, Sigma Xi. Club: U. Calif. at Davis Faculty. Research, publs. on ion transport in plants, mineral nutrition and salt relations of plants, salt tolerant crops. Current Work: Mineral nutrition of plants, salt relations of plants, salt tolerant crops. Subspecialties: Plant physiology (agriculture); Plant genetics. Office: Land Air and Water Resources U Calif Davis CA 95616

EPSTEIN, IRVING ROBERT, chemistry educator; b. Bklyn., Aug. 9, 1945; s. Milton and Marion (Hillsberg) E.; m. Ellen Fisher, Oct. 31, 1971; children: David, Peter. A.B. (Merit scholar), Harvard U., 1966, M.A. (Woodrow Wilson fellow), 1968, Ph.D., 1971; diploma (Marshall scholar), Oxford U., 1967. NATO postdoctoral fellow Cambridge U., Eng., 1971; Asst. prof. chemistry Brandeis U., Waltham, Mass., 1971-75, assoc. prof., 1975-81, prof., 1981—, chmn. dept. chemistry, 1983—. Contbr. numerous articles on chemistry to profl. jours. NSF fellow Max Planck Inst., Gottingen, W.Ger., 1977-78; Guggenheim fellow, 1977; Humboldt fellow, 1977; recipient Dreyfus award, 1973. Mem. Am. Chem. Soc. (Liebmann award 1962), Phi Beta Kappa. Current Work: Design and analysis of oscillating chemical reactions and dynamic instabilities in chemical systems, mathematical modeling of biochemical kinetic processes. Subspecialties: Kinetics; Biophysical chemistry. Home: 28 Otis St Newton MA 02160 Office: Dept Chemistry Brandeis U Waltham MA 02254

EPSTEIN, LOIS BARTH, physician, cancer researcher, pediatric immunologist; b. Cambridge, Mass., Dec. 29, 1933; d. Benjamin and Mary Frances (Perlmutter) Barth; m. Charles Joseph Epstein, June 10, 1956; children: David Alexander, Jonathan Akiba, Paul Michael, Joanna Marguerite. A.B. cum laude, Radcliffe Coll., 1955; M.D., Harvard U., 1959. Resident in pathology Peter Bent Brigham Hosp., Boston, 1959-60; intern in medicine New Eng. Center Hosp., Boston, 1960-61; research med. officer Nat. Inst. Arthritis and Metabolic Diseases, 1962-63, Nat. Inst. Allergy, Immunology and Infectious Diseases, 1966-67; spl. NIH fellow, 1964-66; mem. faculty U. Calif. Med. Center, San Francisco, 1969—; asso. dir. Cancer Research Inst., 1972-74, prof. pediatrics, 1980—; cons. in field, mem. Study Sects. NIH, 1972-81; mem. Cancer Ctr. Support Rev. com. Nat. Cancer Inst. 1984—. Author numerous articles in field.; Mem. editorial bd.: Jour. Interferon Research, Cellular Immunology, Nat. Immunity and Cellular Growth Regulation. Bd. dirs. Marin Symphony Assn., 1979-85, Marin Dance Assn., 1980-85; fundraising chmn. Marin Youth Orch., Vienna tour, 1979; mem. Israel tour com. Bd. Jewish Edn., 1976-79. Mem. Am. Soc. Clin. Investigation, Am. Assn. Immunologists, Soc. Pediatric Research, Am. Assn. Cancer Research, Am. Soc. Hematology, Assn. Women in Sci., Tissue Culture Assn., Assn. Am. Physicians, Calif. Acad. Medicine, Western Assn. Physicians, Phi Beta Kappa. Club: Commonwealth (Calif.). Current Work: Research on prodn., structure, antitumnor, immunomodulatory and antiviral actions and genetic control in interferons and other biologic response mediators, clin. investigations primary and secondary immunodeficiency diseases, role interferon in their pathogenesis and/or correction. Subspecialties: Cancer research (medicine); Immunology (medicine). Home: 19 Noche Vista Ln Tiburon CA 94920 Office: Cancer Research Inst U Calif Med Center San Francisco CA

EPSTEIN, SAMUEL, geologist. Prof. geochemistry, William E. Leonhard Prof. Geology, Calif. Inst. Tech., Pasadena, 1984—. Subspecialties: Geology; Geochemistry. Office: Calif Inst Tech Dept Geol and Planetary Scis Pasadena CA 91125*

EPSTEIN, WILLIAM, experimental psychologist; b. N.Y.C., Nov. 23, 1931; s. Jacob and Sarah (Kaplan) E.; m. Arlene Rita Cohen, Mar. 25, 1956; children: Sara Ann, Edith Lynn. B.A., NYU, 1955; M.A., New Sch. Social Research, 1957, Ph.D., 1959. Asst. prof. psychology U. Kans., 1959-68, asso. prof., 1962-65, prof., 1965-68; prof. psychology U. Wis.-Madison, 1968—, chmn. dept., 1975-79; vis. prof. Cambridge (Eng.) U., 1972-73; Fulbright research fellow and vis. prof. Delhi (India) U., 1981-82. Author: Varieties of Perceptual Learning, 1967, (with F.C. Shontz) Psychology in Progress, 1971, Stability and Constancy in Visual Perception, 1977; Cons. editor: Perception and Psychophysics, 1971-82; editor: Jour. Exptl. Psychology: Human Perception and Performance, 1982—. NSF sr. postdoctoral fellow U. Uppsala, Sweden, 1966-67; NIMH grantee, 1959—. Fellow Am. Psychol. Assn.; mem. AAAS, Psychonomic Soc., Sigma Xi. Office: Psychology Bldg Univ of Wis Madison WI 53706

ERAN, HARUTYUN, bio-organic chemist, researcher; b. Istanbul, R.Hisar, Turkey, Apr. 16, 1953; came to U.S., 1971; s. Hirant and Lusaper (Bedrosyan) E. A.A., El Camino Coll., 1973; B.A., Calif. State U., 1975, M.S., 1978; Ph.D., U. So. Calif., 1982. Research, teaching asst. Calif. State U.-Long Beach, 1976-77; research, teaching asst. U. So. Calif., Los Angeles, 1977-82, research assoc., 1982—. Contbr. articles to profl. jours. Mem. Armenian Gen. Benevolent Union, N.J., 1971—, Orgn. Istanbul Armenians, Los Angeles, 1980—. Grantee NIH, 1983—. Mem. Am. Chem. Soc., Am. Assn. Clin. Chemistry, AAAS, N.Y. Acad. Scis., Sigma Xi. Current work: Engage in biochemical research focused on the key agricultural problems of nitrogen fixation and the enzyme nitrogenase; organic synthesis, bioanalytical chemistry, protein isolation, purification and determination techniques. Subspecialties: Biophysical chemistry; Nitrogen fixation. Home: 17135-2 Roscoe Blvd Northridge CA 91325 Office: U So Calif Sch Medicine Dept Biochemistry 2025 Zonal Ave Los Angeles CA 90033

ERDOGAN, HAYDAR, environmental engineering researcher, educator; b. Tunceli, Turkey, Mar. 18, 1951; came to U.S., 1972, naturalized, 1980; s. Hasan and Cicek E. B.S., U. Ankara, 1972; M.S., Mich. State U., 1976; Ph.D., U. Pitts., 1981. Researcher Pitts. Energy and Environ. Systems Inc., 1977; teaching, research fellow U. Pitts., 1978-81, cons. to model bioreactors for activated sludge treatment, 1981-82; asst. prof. environ. engring. Rutgers U., Piscataway, N.J., 1982-83; research Scientist N.J. Dept. Environ. Protection, Trenton, N.J., 1983—; cons. Nat. Steel Co., Pitts., 1980. Contbr. articles to profl. lit. Turkish Ministry Edn. scholar, 1964-72; State Scholarship Found. Turkey scholar, 1972-77. Mem. Am. Inst. Chem. Engring., AAUP, Assn. Environ. Engring. Profs., Turkish Inst. Chem. Engring., Can. Inst. Chem. Engring. Current Work: Modeling of mass transfer through porous media, disposal of solid liquid hazardous waste, detoxification of contaminated soils, physical-chemical and biological treatment of water and waste water, energy production from biomass. Subspecialties: Water supply and wastewater treatment; Chemical engineering. Office: Dept Engring Rutgers U PO Box 909 Piscataway NJ 08854

ERF, ROBERT K., physicist; b. Bellevue, Ohio, Oct. 29, 1931; s. Herbert A. and Frances E. (Knapp) E.; m. Mary Elva Congleton, July 3, 1954; children: Keith, Karen, Kate, Frank. B.S.E., U. Mich., 1953; M.S. in Applied Physics, Harvard U., 1954. With United Technologies Corp., East Hartford, Conn., 1954—, chief optics and acoustics, 1975-85, mgr. engring. systems, 1985—. Author: Holographic Nondestructive Testing, 1974, Speckle Metrology, 1978. Bd. mgrs. Glastonbury YMCA, 1976-82, chmn., 1980-82. Mem. Optical Soc. Am., Soc. Photo-optical Instrumentation Engrs. Republican. Mem. United Ch. of Christ. Patentee in field. Current Work: Laser applications for nondestructive testing, measurement, machining, holography, and speckle; ultrasonics, acoustic emission. Subspecialties: Holography; Acoustics. Home: 127 Carriage Dr Glastonbury CT 06033 Office: Silver Ln MS 86 East Hartford CT 06108

ERICKSEN, JERALD LAVERNE, educator, physicist; b. Portland, Oreg., Dec. 20, 1924; s. Adolph and Ethel Rebecca (Correy) E.; m. Marion Ella Pook, Feb. 24, 1946; children: Lynn Christine, Randolph Peder. B.S., U. Wash., 1947; M.A., Oreg. State Coll., 1949; Ph.D., Ind. U., 1951; D.Sc. (hon.), Nat. U. Ireland, 1984. Mathematician, solid state physicist U.S. Naval Research Lab., 1951-57; faculty Johns Hopkins U., 1957-83, prof. theoretical mechanics, 1960-83, U. Minn., Mpls., 1983—. Editorial adv. bd.: Internat. Jour. Solids and Structures; editorial bd.: Jour. Elasticity. Served with USNR, 1943-46. Recipient Bingham medal, 1968, Timoshenko medal, 1979. Mem. Soc. Rheology, Soc. Natural Philosophy, Soc. Interaction Mechanics and Math. Current Work: Transition phenomena in crystals and liquid crystals. Subspecialties: Theoretical and applied mechanics; Theories of crystals. Home: 10 Poplar Ln North Oaks MN 55110 Office: Aerospace Engring and Mechanics Dept U Minn Minneapolis MN 55455

ERICKSON, J(OHN) MARK, paleontology educator; b. Orange, N.J., Dec. 21, 1943; s. John Raymond and Eleanor Virginia (Christenson) E.; m. Cynthia Joan Munsell, July 19, 1975. B.S., Tufts U., 1965; M.S., U. N.D., 1968, Ph.D., 1971. Curatorial asst. U. N.D., Grand Forks, 1968-71; asst. prof. paleontology St. Lawrence U., Canton, N.Y., 1971-75, assoc. prof., 1975-85, prof., 1985—, chmn. geology dept., 1981—; v.p. Randolph Co., Vt., 1980-82, pres., 1982—. Author: (monograph) Revision of the Gastropoda of the Fox Hills Formation, Upper Cret. (Maastrichtian) of North Dakota, 1974. Contbr. articles to profl. jours. Bd. dirs. St. Lawrence County chpt. Am. Cancer Soc., Canton, 1977-78. Grantee NSF, 1965-68, 72-75, 81, NASA, 1975. Fellow AAAS; mem. Geol. Soc. Am., Paleontol. Soc., Palaeontol. Assn., Paleontol. Research Inst., Ducks Unltd. (treas. Grasse River Chpt. N.Y., 1983—), Sigma Xi (pres. chpt. 1985-86). Current work: Molluscan paleoecology at the Cret-Tert boundary; freshwater micropaleontology particularly ecostratigraphic applications of oribatid mites in the fossil record. Subspecialties: Paleontology, paleoecology; Limnology. Office: Dept Geology St Lawrence U Canton NY 13617

ERICKSON, ROBERT ARLEN, engineer; b. Brainerd, Minn., Jan. 12, 1932; s. Benjamin Bernhart and Ruth Amelia (Linn) E.; m. Naomi Marie Hepburn, May 18, 1956; children—Catherine, John, Benjamin. Student, Brainerd Jr. Coll.; B.A. in Physics, U. Minn., 1958. Physicist Sperry Univac Def. Systems div., St. Paul, 1958-62, sr. physicist, 1962-64, supr. engr., 1964-65, mgr., 1965-66, group mgr., 1966-70, dir. research and devel., 1970-74, dir. engring., 1974-78, v.p. product engring., 1978-80, v.p., gen. mgr. Semicondr. div., 1980-84, v.p. new product ventures, 1984—. Contbr. articles to profl. jours. Served with USAF, 1951-55. Mem. Am. Legion, various mgmt. and tech. groups, several conservation orgns. Republican. Patentee in field. Subspecialty: Semiconductors. Home: 2182 Garnet Point Saint Paul MN 55122 Office: Sperry Park PO Box 64525 Saint Paul MN 55164

ERIKSSON, LARRY JOHN, electrical engineer; b. Milw., Feb. 12, 1945; s. Henry Charles and Frances (Bartol) E.; m. Karen Ruth Kroenke, Aug. 26, 1967; children—Mark Alan, Jodi Marie. B.S. in Elec. Engring., Northwestern U., 1967; M.S. in Elec. Engring., U. Minn., 1969. Registered profl. engr., Wis. Research scientist Honeywell Corp., Hopkins, Minn., 1968-71; pres. Sonotek, New Berlin, Wis., 1971-72; acoustical engr. AMF Harley Davidson, Milw., 1972-73; v.p. research Nelson Industries Inc., Stoughton, Wis., 1973—. Contbr. articles to profl. jours., chpt. to book. Mem. IEEE (sr.), Soc. Automotive Engrs. (Outstanding Younger mem. award 1978), Acoustical Soc. Am. (Continuing Service award 1983), ASME. Lodge: Rotary. Current work: Acoustical engineering; noise control; digital signal processing; modern control theory. Subspecialties: Electrical engineering; Acoustical engineering. Home: 5301 Greenbriar Ln Madison WI 53714 Office: Nelson Industries Inc Hwy 51 Stoughton WI 53589

ERLANGER, BERNARD FERDINAND, biochemist, microbiology educator; b. N.Y.C., July 13, 1923; s. Leo and Frieda (David) E.; m. Rachel Fenichel, June 23, 1946; children—Laura, Louis, Leon. B.S., CCNY, 1943; M.A., NYU, 1948; Ph.D., Columbia U., 1951. Chemist, U.S. Indsl. Chems. Inc., Newark, 1943-44; tech. advisor Manhattan Project, Los Alamos, 1944-46; mgr. plant Hexagon Labs., 1946-48; mem. faculty Columbia U., N.Y.C., 1957—, prof. microbiology, 1966—; cons. to industry. Assoc. editor Proc. Soc. Exptl. Biology and Medicine; editor: Molecular Models of Photoresponsiveness, 1983. Contbr. numerous articles to sci. jours. Fulbright scholar U. Republic, Uruguay, 1967; Guggenheim fellow Inst. Biologie Physico-Chimique, Paris, 1969; Am. Cancer Soc. scholar Inst. Pasteur, Paris, 1979. Mem. AAAS, Am. Assn. Immunologists, Am. Chem. Soc., Am. Soc. Biol. Chemists, Am. Soc. Cell Biology, Am. Soc. Photobiology, Harvey Soc., Enzyme Club. Current work: Research on mode of action of antibiotics; investigation of mechanisms of enzyme catalysis, immunochemistry of macromolecules concerned with genetics, photoregulation, biological receptors. Subspecialties: Immunobiology and immunology; Neurobiology. Home: 163-16 15th Dr Beechhurst NY 11357 Office: Columbia Univ 701 W 168th St New York NY 10032

ERNST, DONALD MARTIN, mechanical engineer; b. Rosenburg, Tex., July 26, 1938; s. Martin Edward and Dorathea (Baur) E.; m. Diane Merle Goodwin, Dec. 27, 1961; children—David Michael, Kristin Marie, Scott Steven. B.S. in Physics, Kans. State U., 1960. Engr., RCA, Lancaster, Pa., 1962-67; program mgr. thermo Electron, Waltham, Mass., 1967-75; dir. research Isothermics, Augusta, N.J., 1975-77; v.p. Thermacore Inc., Lancaster, 1977—, also dir. Contbr. articles to profl. jours. and articles to books. Inventor in field. Mem. ASME, AIAA, Internat. Solar Energy Soc., Jaycees (dir. Lancaster 1963-65, Manheim Twp. v.p. 1965-67). Lodge: Masons. Current work: Development of high temperature and ambient temperature heat pipes for space and terrestrial applications; space station thermal management, industrial heat recovery and electronics cooling. Subspecialties: Aerospace engineering and technology; High-temperature materials. Home: 354 Sun Valley Dr Leola PA 17540 Office: Thermacore Inc 780 Eden Rd Lancaster PA 17601

ERNST, WALLACE GARY, geology educator; b. St. Louis, Dec. 14, 1931; s. Fredrick A. and Helen Grace (Mahaffey) E.; m. Charlotte Elsa Pfau, Sept. 7, 1956; children: Susan, Warren, Alan, Kevin. B.A., Carleton Coll., 1953; M.S., U. Minn., 1955; Ph.D., Johns Hopkins U., 1959. Geologist U.S. Geol. Survey, Washington, 1955-56; fellow (Geophys. Lab.), Washington, 1956-59; mem. faculty UCLA, 1960—, prof. geology and geophysics, 1968—, chmn. geology dept. (now earth and space scis. dept.), 1970-74, 78-82; chmn. NRC Bd. on Earth Scis., 1984-87. Author: Amphiboles, 1968, Earth Materials, 1969, Metamorphism and Plate Tectonic Regimes, 1975, Subduction Zone Metamorphism, 1975, Petrologic Phase Equilibria, 1976, The Geotectonic Development of California, 1981, The Environment of the Deep Sea, 1982, Energy-For Ourselves and Our Posterity, 1985. Mem. Nat. Acad. Sci. (chmn. geology sect. 1979-82), AAAS, Am. Geophys. Union, Am. Geol. Inst., Geol. Soc. Am. (pres. 1985-86), Geochem. Soc., Mineral. Soc. Am. (recipient award 1969, pres. 1979-80), Mineral. Soc. London. Subspecialties: Tectonics; Geochemistry. Home: 16939 Livorno Dr Pacific Palisades CA 90272 Office: Dept Earth and Space Scis U Calif Los Angeles CA 90024

ERSKINE, JOHN ROBERT, physicist; b. Milw., Mar. 18, 1931. B.S. in Physics, U. Rochester, 1953; Ph.D., U. Notre Dame, 1960. Postdoctoral fellow MIT, Cambridge, 1960-62; staff scientist Argonne Nat. Lab., Chgo., 1962-80; physicist U.S. Dept Energy, Washington, 1980—. Served to lt (j.g.) USN, 1953-56. Fellow Am. Phys. Soc. Current work: Program manager for facilities and instrumentation. division of nuclear physics, Office of Energy Research. Subspecialty: Nuclear physics. Office: US Dept Energy ER-23 GTN Washington DC 20545

ERTEL, NORMAN H., physician, educator; b. Bklyn., Nov. 15, 1932; s. Harry and Mamie (Zirin) E.; m. Barbara Schuster, Oct. 15, 1967; children—Wendy Anne, Emily Jane, Adam Scott. A.B., Harvard U., 1953; M.D. Columbia U., 1957. Diplomate Am. Bd. Internal Medicine, Am. Bd. Endocrinology and Metabolism. Intern, resident in medicine Albert Einstein Hosp., Bronx, N.Y., 1957-59, 62-63; research fellow Columbia U., N.Y.C., 1959-60; sr. research fellow Cornell U. Med. Ctr., N.Y.C., 1963-65; dir. steroid research lab. Jewish Hosp. and Med. Ctr., Bklyn., 1965-71; chief med. service VA Med. Ctr., East Orange, N.J., 1971—; prof. medicine U. Medicine and Dentistry of N.J.-N.J. Med. Sch., Newark, 1971—. Trustee Solomon Schechter Day Sch., Cranford, N.J., 1980—, Temple Beth-El, South Orange, 1983—. Served to capt. USAF, 1960-62. Recipient USAF Surg. Gen.'s award, 1962; Harvard Club of L.I. scholar, 1949. Mem. Am. Diabetes Assn. (bd. govs. N.J. affiliate 1975—, life dir. 1983, chmn. clin. soc. 1975-77, 81-83), N.J. Acad. Medicine (chmn. endocrinology sect. 1977-79, 82-83, sec.-treas. endocrine sect. 1977—), VA Chiefs of Medicine (governing council 1983—). Current work: Steroid metabolism, diabetes. Subspecialties: Endocrinology; Internal medicine. Home: 140 Turrell Ave South Orange NJ 07079 Office: Med Services VA Med Ctr Tremont Ave East Orange NJ 07019

ERTURK, ERDOGAN, pathologist, educator; b. Havran/Balikesir, Turkey, Sept. 25, 1930; s. Musa Kazim and Ayse E.; m. Gulten Alp Erturk, Aug. 10, 1953. D.V.M., U. Ankara, 1955, M.S., 1960, Ph.D. in Pathology, 1965. Assoc. prof. dept. pathol. anatomy U. Ankara (Turkey) Sch. Vet. Medicine, 1972-78; adj. prof. Clin. Sci. Ctr., U. Wis. Med. Sch., 1978—. Served with Turkish Army, 1955-57. Mem. Am. Assn. Cancer Research, AAAS, N.Y. Acad. Scis. Current Work: Chemical carcinogenesis and histogenesis of several malignancies including renal, liver and breast cancers. Subspecialties: Animal pathology; Oncology. Office: 600 Highland Ave Madison WI 53792

ERWIN, KEVIN LEE, systems ecologist, consultant; b. Miami Beach, Fla., Dec. 14, 1951; s. Maurice Lee Erwin and Jacqueline Shirley (Oppenheimer) Carey; m. Andrea Marjorie Horstmann, June 21, 1975; children—Kyle Lee, Chase Martin. B.A., U. South Fla., 1973. Marine biologist Nat. Marine Fisheries, St. Petersburg Beach, Fla., 1971-73; research assoc. NSF, U. South Fla., Tampa, 1971-73; area supr. Fla. Dept. Natural Resources, St. Petersburg and Ft. Myers, 1974-75; environ. specialist Fla. Dept. Environ. Regulation, Ft. Myers, 1975-80; cons. systems ecologist, Ft. Myers, 1980—; sr. advisor Fla. project INFORM, N.Y.C., 1981—. Co-author: Promised Lands Revisited, 1985. Contbr. articles to profl. publs. Chmn. adv. bd. Six Mile Cypress Basin, Lee County, Fla., 1983; mem. council S.W. Fla. Regional Planning Council, Ft. Myers, 1984—; bd. dirs. Lee County YMCA, Ft. Myers, 1984. Mem. Soc. Wetland Scientists, Ecol. Soc. Am., Am. Soc. Limnology and Oceanography, Fla. Assn. Field Biology, Fla. Audubon Soc. (bd. dirs. 1982—), S.W. Fla. Audubon Soc. (bd. dirs. 1981—), Western Soc. Naturalists, Fla. Acad. Sci.,

Nat. Acad. Sci., Am. Inst. Biol. Sci., AAAS. Democrat. Presbyterian. Club: Rotary (bd. dirs. 1983-85) (Ft. Myers). Current work: A consulting systems ecologist evaluating and researching functions, impacts and restoration of ecosystems for government and private industry. Subspecialties: Ecology (biology); Ecosystems analysis. Home: 1236 Osceola St Fort Myers FL 33901 Office: Kevin L Erwin Cons Ecologist Inc 2077 Bayside Pkwy Fort Myers FL 33901

ESAKI, LEO, physicist; b. Osaka, Japan, Mar. 12, 1925; came to U.S., 1960; s. Soichiro and Niyoko (Ito) E.; m. Masako Araki, Nov. 21, 1959; children: Nina Yvonne, Anna Eileen, Eugene Leo. B.S., U. Tokyo, 1947, Ph.D., 1959. With Sony Corp., Japan, 1956-60; with Thomas J. Watson Research Center, IBM, Yorktown Heights, N.Y., 1960—, IBM fellow, 1967—, mgr. device research, 1965—; dir. IBM-Japan. Recipient Morris N. Liebmann Meml. prize I.E.E.E., 1961; Stuart Ballantine medal Franklin Inst., 1961; Japan Acad. award, 1965; Nobel Prize in physics, 1973; decorated Order of Culture Govt. of Japan, 1974. Fellow Am. Phys. Soc. (councillor-at-large 1971-74, co-recipient Internat. Prize in new materials 1985); IEEE; Fellow Japan Phys. Soc., Am. Vacuum Soc. (dir. 1973-74); mem. Am. Acad. Arts and Scis., Nat. Acad. Scis. (fgn. asso.), Nat. Acad. Engring. (fgn. asso.), Academia Nacional de Ingenieria Mex. (corr.), Japan Acad. Inventor tunnel diode, 1957. Subspecialty: Condensed matter physics. Home: 16 Shady Ln Chappaqua NY 10514 Office: Watson Research Center IBM PO Box 218 Yorktown Heights NY 10598*

ESHELMAN, FRED NEVILLE, research pharmacologist; b. High Point, N.C., July 20, 1948; s. John Alfred and Lossie (Neville) E. B.S., U. N.C., 1972; Pharm.D., U. Cin., 1974. Registered pharmacist, Ohio, Ill., Tenn. Clin. asst. prof. U. Ill. Coll. Pharm., Chgo., 1974-76; asst. dir. Bio Basics, N.Y.C., 1976-77; dir. profl. relations and assoc. dir. clin. research Beecham Lab., Bristol, Tenn., 1977-79; assoc. dir. clin. research Glaxo, Inc., Research Triangle Park, N.C., 1979-84; dir. clin. research Boehringer Mannheim, 1984-85. Contbr. articles to profl. jours. Mem. Am. Soc. Clin. Pharmacology and Therapeutics, Am. Fedn. Clin. Research, Am. Coll. Clin. Pharmacology, Am. Coll. Clin. Pharmacy. Republican. Methodist. Current Work: Pharmaceutical product development consulting. Subspecialties: Pharmacology; Pharmacokinetics. Home and Office: 13704 Charity Ct Germantown MD 20874

ESHLEMAN, VON RUSSEL, radar astronomer; b. Darke County, Ohio, Sept. 17, 1924; s. Earl Ellsworth and Lydia Mae (Kneisly) E.; m. Patricia May Middleton, Mar. 6, 1947; children—Mary Angela, Kathleen Carol, Eric Earl, David Middleton. Student, Ohio State U., 1946-47; B.E.E., George Washington U., 1949; M.S., Stanford U., 1950, Ph.D., 1952. Research asso. electronics labs. Stanford U., 1957-57, mem. faculty, 1957—, prof. elec. engring., 1961—, co-dir. center radar astronomy, 1961—, dir. radiosci. lab., 1974—; dir. Watkins-Johnson Co.; cons. NASA, Nat. Acad. Scis., SRI Internat., N.Am. Rockwell, Inc., Nat. Oceanographic and Atmospheric Adminstrn.; dep. dir. Office of Technology Policy and Space Affairs, Dept. State Bur. Internat. Sci. and Technol. Affairs, Washington, 1973-74. Contbr. articles to profl. jours. Served with USNR, 1943-46. Fellow IEEE, AAAS, Royal Astron. Soc. (Britain); mem. Nat. Acad. Engring., Internat. Sci. Radio Union, Am. Astron. Soc., Am. Inst. Aeros. and Astronautics, Internat. Astron. Union, Internat. Aero. Congress, Am. Geophys. Union, Sigma Xi, Sigma Tau. Pioneer radar astronomy and radio links to spacecraft as techniques for studying moon, sun, planets, meteors, astron. space, man-made satellites; attained 1st radar echoes from sun, 1959. Subspecialties: Planetary science; Remote sensing (geoscience). Home: 576 Gerona Rd Stanford CA 94305

ESPOSITO, LARRY WAYNE, planetary scientist; b. Schenectady, Apr. 15, 1951; s. Albert and Beverly Jane (De La Mater) E.; m. Diane Marie McKnight, July 26, 1975; 1 dau., Rhea Marie McKnight. S.B. in Math, M.I.T., 1973; Ph.D. in Astronomy, U. Mass., 1977. Research assoc. Lab. for Atmospheric and Space Physics, U. Colo., Boulder, 1977—, univ. lectr. dept. astro-geophysics, 1979-84, assoc. prof. dept. astrophysical, planetary and atmospheric scis., 1984—. Contbr. articles to profl. jours. Mem. Am. Astron. Soc. (div. for planetary sci., H.C. Urey prize 1985), Am. Geophys. Union, Internat. Astron. Union. Methodist. Club: Boulder Go. Current Work: Studies of planetary atmospheres and planetary rings. Spacecraft studies of Venus, Jupiter, Saturn, Uranus. Subspecialty: Planetary science. Office: LASP Campus Box 392 Boulder CO 80309

ESPOSITO, VITO M., biotechnology company executive. Pres. Genex Corp., Rockville, Md., 1984—. Subspecialty: Biotechnology research and development. Office: Genex Corp 6110 Executive Blvd Suite 710 Rockville MD 20852*

ESSENBERG, MARGARET KOTTKE, biochemistry educator; b. Troy, N.Y., Apr. 21, 1943; d. Frank Joseph and Esther Crissey (Hendee) Kottke; m. Richard Charles Essenberg, July 17, 1967; children: Gavin Richard, Carla Jean. A.B., Oberlin Coll., 1965; Ph.D., Brandeis U., 1971. NSF fellow Leicester (U.K.) U., 1971, NIH fellow, 1972-73; research asso. Okla. State U., Stillwater, 1973-75, asst. prof. biochemistry, 1975-81, asso. prof., 1981-84, prof., 1984—. Contbr. articles in field to profl. jours. Herman Frasch Found. grantee, 1977-82; U.S. Dept. Agr. grantee, 1979-81; NSF grantee, 1982—. Mem. Am. Soc. Biol. Chemists, Am. Phytopath. Soc., AAAS, Sigma Xi. Democrat. Roman Catholic. Current Work: Researcher in biochemistry of interactions between plants and plant pathogenic bacteria. Subspecialties: Biochemistry (medicine); Plant pathology. Office: Oklahoma State University Dept Biochemistry Stillwater OK 74078

ESSENWANGER, OSKAR MAXIMILIAN KARL, supervisory research physicist, educator; b. Munich, Bavaria, Germany, Aug. 25, 1920; came to U.S., 1956, naturalized, 1963; s. Oskar and Anna E.; m. Katharina D. Dorfer, June 17, 1947. B.S., U. Danzig, Germany, 1941; M.S., U. Vienna, Austria, 1943; Ph.D., U. Wurzburg, Germany, 1950. Instr., meteorologist German Air Force, 1944-45; research meteorologist German Weather Service, 1946-57; project assoc. dept. meteorology U. Wis., 1956; prin. investigator Nat. Weather Records Center, Asheville, N.C., 1957-60; supervisory research physicist, research dir. U.S. Army Missile Command, Huntsville, Ala., 1961—; adj. prof. earth and environ. sci. U. Ala.-Huntsville, 1970—. Author: Applied Statistics in Atmospheric Science, 1976; contbg. author, editor: International Compendium World Survey of Climatology, vol. I, 1985; contbr. numerous articles to profl. jours. Recipient Sci. and Engring. Achievement award Missile Command, Redstone Arsenal, Ala., 1965. Fellow AIAA (assoc., Ala.-Miss. div. chmn. 1985—, Hermann Oberth award 1981); mem. Am. Soc. Quality Control (sr.), Am. Meterol. Soc. (profl.), Ala. Acad. Sci (v.p. 1973), Sigma Xi (v.p. club 1976-77, pres. chpt. 1977-82, Outstanding Researcher 1977). Current Work: Environmental design criteria for rockets, statistical analysis in climatology, solar energy. Subspecialties: Climatology; Statistics. Home: 610 Mountain Gap Dr Huntsville AL 35803

ESSEX, MYRON ELMER, microbiologist, educator; b. Coventry, R.I., Aug. 17, 1939; s. Ruth and (Knight) E.; m. Elizabeth Katherine Jordan, June 19, 1966; children: Holly Anne, Carrie Lisa. B.S., U. R.I., 1962; D.V.M., Mich. State U., 1967, M.S., 1967; Ph.D., U. Calif., 1970; M.S. (hon.), Harvard U., 1978. Vis. scientist Karolinska Inst., Stockholm, Sweden, 1970-72; asst. prof. microbiology Sch. Pub. Health, Harvard U., 1972-76, assoc. prof., 1976-78, prof., chmn. dept. microbiology, 1979—; lectr. in pathology Sch. Pub. Health, Harvard U. (Med. Sch.), 1976—; adj. prof. Cornell U., 1980—. Editor: Viruses in Naturally Occurring Cancer, 1980, Feline Leukemia Virus, 1980; Contbr. articles to profl. jours. Trustee Leukemia Soc. Am., 1979—; mem. research com. Mass. chpt. Am. Cancer Soc., 1975—. Recipient Bronze medal Am. Cancer Soc., 1980; Leukemia Soc. Am. scholar, 1972-77; research grantee Nat. Cancer Inst.; research grantee Am. Cancer Soc. Mem. Am. Assn. Cancer Research, Am. Assn. Immunologists, Am. Soc. Microbiology, Reticuloendothelial Soc., Internat. Assn. for Research on Leukemia, AVMA. Current Work: Role of viruses in naturally occurring cancers especially feline and human retroviruses and hepatitis B virus. Subspecialties: Microbiology; Cancer research (medicine). Office: 665 Huntington Ave Boston MA 02115

ESSIG, HENRY WERNER, animal nutrition scientist, educator, researcher, conultant; b. Paragould, Ark., Dec. 9, 1930; s. George and Emma Elisabeth (Rudi) E.; m. Alice H., June 7, 1953; children: Stephen W., Rebecca A. B.S.A., U. Ark., 1953, M.S., 1956; Ph.D., U. Ill., 1959. Mem. faculty dept. animal sci. Miss. State U., 1959—, asst. prof. animal sci., 1959-61, assoc. prof., 1961-66, prof., 1966—; cons. nutrition. Contbr. numerous articles to profl. jours., popular publs. Served to 1st lt. inf. U.S. Army, 1953-55. Recipient Research award Miss. State U. chpt. Gamma Sigma Delta, 1973, faculty achievement award for research Miss. State U. Alumni Assn., 1976; award of excellence for outstanding performance Miss. Agrl. and Forestry Expt. Sta., 1984. Mem. Am. Soc. Animal Sci., Am. Soc. Dairy Sci., Animal Nutrition Research Council, Am. Forage and Grassland Council (merit cert. 1978, dir. 1982—), Alpha Zeta. Lutheran. Current Work: Ruminant nutrition, forage evaluation. Subspecialty: Animal nutrition. Office: Miss State U Dept Animal Sci Box 5228 Mississippi Station MS 39762

ESTABROOK, RONALD WINFIELD, chemistry educator; b. Albany, N.Y., Jan. 3, 1926; s. George Arthur and Lillian Florence (Childs) E.; m. June Elizabeth Templeton, Aug. 23, 1947; children: Linda Estabrook Gilbert, Laura Estabrook Verinder, Jill Estabrook, David Estabrook. B.S., Rensselaer Poly. Inst., 1950; Ph.D., U. Rochester, 1954, D.Sc. (hon.), 1980; M.D. (hon.), Karolinska Inst., Stockholm, 1981. Johnson Research Found. fellow U. Pa. Sch. Medicine, 1955-58, research asso., 1958-59, asst. prof. phys. biochemistry, 1959-62, asso. prof., 1961-65, prof., 1965-68; prof. biochemistry U. Tex. Health Sci. Center, Dallas, 1968-82; dean U. Tex. Health Sci. Center (Grad. Sch. Biomed. Scis.), 1973-76; chmn. basic sci. rev. com. VA, 1972-74; cons. in field. Bd. sci. advisers St. Judes Hosp., Memphis, 1978-81; chmn. bd. toxicology and environ. health Nat. Acad. Sci., 1980-84, mem. council Inst. of Medicine; mem. Atlantic Richfield Sci. Adv. Council, 1981—. Chmn. editorial bd. Archives of Biochemistry and Biophysics, 1966-73, Cancer Research, 1980-85; editor: Jour. Pharmacology and Exptl. Therapeutics, 1969-74, Xenobiotica, 1970—, Life Scis, 1973-85; Contbr. articles to profl. jours. Served with USNR, 1943-46. Recipient Disting. Scientist award Fedn. Am. Socs. Exptl. Biologist, 1977; Claude Bernard medal U. Montreal, 1969. Mem. Inst. Medicine, Nat. Acad. Scis., Pan Am. Assn., Biochem. Socs. (sec.-gen. 1972-75), Am. Assn. Med. Schs. (adminstrv. bd. council acad. socs.; task force cost med. edn. 1971-72, liaison com. med. edn. 1975-80), Am. Soc. Biol. Chemists (treas. 1985—), Am. Soc. Pharmacology and Exptl. Therapeutics, Sigma Xi. Subspecialty: Biochemistry (medicine). Home: 5208 Preston Haven Dallas TX 75229 Office: U Tex Health Sci Center 5323 Harry Hines Blvd Dallas TX 75235

ESTEBAN, MARIANO, biochemist educator, microbiologist; b. Villalon, Spain, July 26, 1944; came to U.S., 1974, naturalized, 1981; s. Victorino and Victoria (Rodriguez) E.; m. Victoria Jimenez, Dec. 27, 1979; 1 child, Julia. M.S., U. Santiago, Spain, 1967, 1971, Ph.D., 1970. Vis. scientist Nat. Inst. Med. Research, London, 1970-74; instr. Rutgers U. Med. Sch., 1974-77; vis. prof. Molecular Biology Inst., Gent, Belgium, 1978; asst. prof. biochemistry SUNY-Bklyn., 1979-81, assoc. prof. biochemistry, 1981—. NIH grantee, 1980—; Health Research Council N.Y. prin. investigator, 1980-81. Fellow European Molecular Biology Orgn.; mem. Spanish Soc. Microbiology, Brit. Soc. Microbiology, Am. Soc. Microbiology and Virology, Harvey Soc., N.Y. Acad. Scis., Sigma Xi. Current Work: Mode of action of antiviral and antitumor drugs; interferon, prostaglandins, vaccinia virus genome organization, biomedical engineering, cancer research. Subspecialties: Animal virology; Genetics and genetic engineering (agriculture). Home: 333 E 80th St Apt 2F New York NY 10021 Office: Downstate Med Ctr SUNY 450 Clarkson Ave Brooklyn NY 11203

ESTES, WILLIAM KAYE, psychologist, educator; b. Mpls., June 17, 1919; s. George D. and Mona; m. Katherine Walker, Sept. 26, 1942; children: George E., Gregory W. Mem. faculty Ind. U., 1946-62, prof. psychology, 1955-60, research prof. psychology, 1960-62; faculty research fellow Social Sci. Research Council, 1952-55; lectr. psychology U. Wis., summer 1949; vis. prof. Northwestern U., spring 1959; fellow Center Advanced Study Behavioral Scis., 1955-56; spl. univ. lectr. U. London, Eng., 1961; prof. psychology, mem. Inst. Math. Studies Social Scis., Stanford, 1962-68; prof. Rockefeller U., 1968-79, Harvard U., 1979—; chmn. Office Sci. and Engring. Personnel, NRC, 1982-85. Author: An Experimental Study of Punishment, 1944, Learning Theory and Mental Development, 1970, Models of Learning, Memory, and Choice, 1982; co-author: Modern Learning Theory, 1954, also numerous articles. Editor: Handbook of Learning and Cognitive Processes, 1975, Jour. Comparative and Physiol. Psychology, 1962-68, Psychol. Rev., 1977-82; assoc. editor: Jour. Exptl. Psychology, 1958-62. Served with AUS, 1944-46. Fellow Am. Psychol. Assn. (pres. div. exptl. psychology 1958-59, Distinguished Sci. Contbn. award 1962), AAAS, Am. Acad. Arts and Scis.; mem. Nat. Acad. Scis., N.Y. Acad. Sci. (hon. life), Soc. Exptl. Psychologists (Warren medal 1963), Psychometric Soc., Midwestern Psychol. Assn. (pres. 1956-57), Soc. Math. Psychology (chmn. 1984). Subspecialties: Cognition; Learning. Home: 95 Irving St Cambridge MA 02138 Office: 620 W James Hall 33 Kirkland Cambridge MA 02138

ETGEN, ANNE MARIE, research scientist, biologist, educator; b. Ft. Atkinson, Wis., Oct. 1, 1953; d. William Mathias and Jesslyn Joan (Skeen) E. B.S., Coll. William and Mary, 1975; Ph.D., U. Calif., Irvine, 1979. Teaching asst. U. Calif., Irvine, 1975-79, NSF fellow, 1976-79; research scientist IV L.I. Research Inst., SUNY, Stony Brook, 1979; asst. prof. dept. biol. sci. Rutgers U., New Brunswick, N.J., 1979-85; assoc. prof. psychiatry and neuroscience Albert Einstein Coll. Med., Bronx, N.Y., 1985—; vis. scholar Columbia U., 1979-80; mem. molecular cellular neurobiology panel NSF, 1985. Contbr. articles to profl. jours. NIMH grantee, 1980-81, 82-88. Mem. Soc. Neurosci., European Soc. Comparative Physiology and Biochemistry, Phi Beta Kappa. Current Work: Cellular and molecular mechanisms of hormone action in central nervous system. Subspecialties: Neuroendocrinology; Neurobiology. Office: Dept Psychiatry Albert Einstein Coll Med 1300 Morris Park Ave Bronx NY 10461

ETTER, PAUL COURTNEY, oceanographer; b. Phila., Oct. 27, 1947; s. Richard T. and Ellen M. (Cunliffe) E.; m. Alice D. Eblighatian, June 21, 1969; children: Gregory, Andrew. B.S., Tex. A. and M. U., 1969, M.S., 1975. Technician Technitrol, Inc., Phila., 1969; research asst. Tex. A. and M. U., College Station, Tex., 1973-76; sr. engr. MAR, Inc., Rockville, Md., 1976-82; tech dir. ODSI Defense Systems, Inc., Rockville, 1982—. Served to lt. USN, 1969-73. Fellow Washington Acad. Scis.; mem. AAAS, Am. Meterol. Soc., Am. Geophys. Union, Acoustical Soc. Am., Marine Tech. Soc. Democrat. Current Work: Apply principles of physical oceanography and underwater acoustics to the development of undersea acoustic sensing technology for the U.S. Navy. Subspecialties: Oceanography; Acoustics. Home: 16609 Bethayres Rd Rockville MD 20855 Office: ODSI Defense Systems Inc 6110 Executive Blvd Rockville MD 20852

ETTINGER, ANNA MARIE, anatomist; b. Janesville, Wis., Nov. 4, 1925; d. Martin and Anna (Dawson) Conway; m. Ralph Ettinger, Apr. 26, 1969. B.S., U. Wis., 1946, M.S., 1950; Ph.D., U. Ill. Chgo. Med. Ctr., 1967. Tchr. elem. and high schs., Barrington, Ill., 1946-49; tchr. Joliet (Ill.) High Sch., Joliet Jr. Coll., 1950-55; teaching fellow in anatomy U. Wis., 1955-57; instr. dept. anatomy St. Louis U. Med. Sch., 1957-63; asst. prof., chmn. sect. anat. scis. basic sci. dept. U. Detroit Sch. Dentistry, 1967-69, assoc. prof., chmn., 1969-76, prof., chmn. dept. anatomy, 1976—. Contbr. articles to profl. jours. NSF grantee, 1965-66; NIH grantee, 1969-72. Mem. Am. Assn. Immunologists, Am. Assn. Anatomists, Assn. Anatomy (chmn.), Sigma Xi, Omicron Kappa Upsilon. Current Work: The study of cross reaction of natrual agglutinins, natural, antibody, chicks, human milk. Subspecialties: Anatomy and embryology; Immunobiology and immunology. Office: U Detroit Sch Dentistry 2985 E Jefferson Detroit MI 48207

ETTINGER, DAVID SEYMOUR, physician; b. Bklyn., Mar. 16, 1942; s. Harry and Frieda (Rose) E.; m. Phyllis Evellen Katz, June 4, 1964; children: Laura, Daniel, Kathryn. B.A., Yeshiva U., 1963; M.D., U. Louisville, 1967. Diplomate: Am. Bd Internal Medicine and Med. Oncology. Intern Albany (N.Y.) Med. Center, 1967-68; fellow in internal medicine Mayo Clinic, Rochester, Minn., 1968-71; fellow in oncology Johns Hopkins U. Sch. Medicine, Balt., 1973-75, instr. oncology and medicine, 1976-77, asst. prof., 1977-81, assoc. prof., 1981—; Mem. patient service com. Md. div. Am. Cancer Soc., 1977—. Contbr. articles to profl. jours. Served to maj. M.C. U.S. Army, 1971-73. Decorated Army Commendation medal. Fellow ACP; mem. Eastern Coop. Oncology Group, Am. Soc. Clin. Oncology, Am. Assn. Cancer Research. Democrat. Jewish. Current Work: Development and utilization of new cancer chemotherapeutic agents, drug combinations and concomitant chemotherapy with other modalities in the treatment of malignant tumor. Subspecialties: Oncology; Internal medicine. Home: 2511 Lawnside Rd Timonium MD 21093 Office: Johns Hopkins Oncology Center Baltimore MD 21205

ETTINGER, PHILIP OWEN, cardiologist, internist; b. N.Y.C., Oct. 3, 1936; s. Samuel and Charlotte (Adler) E.; m. Roxanne M. Miller, May 31, 1964; children: Alyssa Anne, Jonathan Seth. A.B., Swarthmore Coll., 1956; M.D., N.Y.U., 1960. Diplomate: Am. Bd. Internal Medicine(subspecialty cardiovascular disease). Intern Lenox Hill Hosp., N.Y.C., 1960-61; resident Bronx (N.Y.) VA Hosp., 1961-63, N.Y.U. Hosp., 1963-64; clin. assoc. prof. medicine N.J. Med. Sch., Newark, 1966—; pvt. practice cardiology, Teaneck, N.J., 1969—; attending cardiologist Englewood (N.J.) Hosp., 1969—. Served to capt. USAF, 1964-66. N.Y. State med. scholarship, 1956; NIH cardiology grantee, 1975. Fellow ACP, Am. Coll. Cardiology; mem. Am. Physiol. Soc., Phi Beta Kappa. Current Work: Cardiology practice, research involving myocardial metabolism and function, cardiac rhythm disturbances. Subspecialties: Cardiology; Internal medicine. Office: 185 Cedar Ln Teaneck NJ 07666

ETTRE, LESLIE STEPHEN, chemist; b. Szombathely, Hungary, Sept. 16, 1922; came to U.S., 1958, naturalized, 1965; s. Stephen and Mary Therese (Dunay) E.; m. Kitty Polonyi, May 16, 1953; 1 dau., Julie Suzanne. Diploma Chem. Engring, U. Tech. Scis., Hungary, 1945, D.Tech. Scis. Chemist G. Richter Pharm. Works, Budapest, Hungary, 1946-49; research chemist Research Inst. for Heavy Chem. Industries, Veszprem, Hungary, 1949-51, head tech. office, 1951-53; sr. lectr. chemistry U. Veszprem, 1951-53; head indsl. dept. Research Inst. for Plastics Industry, Budapest, 1953-56; chemist Lurgi Cos., Fankfurt, W. Ger., 1957-58; applications chemist Perkin-Elmer Corp., Norwalk, Conn., 1958-60, product specialist, 1960-62, chief applications chemist, 1962-68, sr. staff scientist, 1972—; exec. editor Ency. Indsl. Chem. Analysis John Wiley & Sons., N.Y.C., 1968-72; research asso. dept. engring. and applied scis. Yale U., New Haven, 1977-78; adj. prof. U. Houston, 1978—; chmn. Anniversary Symposium on Chromatography Am. Chem. Soc., N.Y.C., 1972, Symposium on Selective Chromatography Detectors, San Francisco, 1976, Symposium on Standard Materials in Chromatography, Atlanta, 1981, Symposium on Headspace Gas Chromatography, Chgo., 1985; co-chmn. Summer Symposium on Analytical Chemistry Miami U., Oxford, Ohio, 1973; lectr. in, U.S., Can., Europe, Asia, Africa and Australia; participant lecture tours of Chromatography Council of Acad. Scis., USSR, 1976, 78, 79, 80, 81, Estonian Acad. Scis., 1979, 81, Chinese Acad. Scis., 1980, Georgian Acad. Sci., 1981. Author: Open Tubular Columns in Gas Chromatography, 1965, (with A. Zlatkis) The Practice of Gas Chromatography, 1967, (with W.H. McFadden) Ancillary Techniques of Gas Chromatography, 1968 (transl. into Russian, 1972), Practical Gas Chromatography, 1972, Introduction to Open Tubular Columns, 1974 (transl. into German, 1976, Spanish, 1978), (with A. Zlatkis) 75 Years of Chromatography-A Historical Dialogue, 1979, Basic Relationships of Gas Chromatography, 1977, (with R.W. Yost and R.D. Conlon) Practical Liquid Chromatography, 1980; (translated into Spanish and French, 1981, Italian 1982), (with J.L. DiCesare, M.N. Dong) Introduction to High-Speed Liquid Chromatography, 1981 (translated into Spanish 1982, Italian 1983); mem. editorial bd.: Jour. Chromatographic Sci, 1963—, Jour. Liquid Chromatography, 1985—, LC Mag., 1983—; editor: Chromatographia, 1971—; contbr. numerous articles to profl. jours. Recipient Commemorative Chromatography medal Acad. Scis., USSR, 1978, Internat. Chromatography award, 1978, L.S. Palmer award Minn. Chromatography Forum, 1980, A.J.P. Martin award Brit. Chromatography Discussion Group, 1982. Fellow Am. Inst. Chemists; mem. ASTM (chmn. subcom. research of com. E-19 1966-70, subcom. on nomenclature of com. E-19 1970-73), Am. Chem Soc. (award inchromatography 1985), Chromatography Soc., N.Y. Acad. Scis., Internat. Union Pure and Applied Chemistry (nomenclature com. 1981—). Subspecialty: Analytical chemistry. Home: 157 Grumman Ave Norwalk CT 06851 Office: Perkin-Elmer Corp Main Ave Norwalk CT 06859

ETTRICK, MARCO ANTONIO, theoretical physicist, mathematician; b. Panama City, Panama, July 17, 1945; came to U.S., 1967, naturalized, 1972; s. Clemente Adolfo and Olga Rosa (Birmingham) E.; m. Adys Marie Hippolyte, Oct. 22, 1966 (div. May 1977); children—Rodolphe Antoine, Marc Edouard. B.S. in Math., Bklyn. Polytech. Inst., 1968; currently postgrad. N.Y. Poly. Inst. Lectr., Queens Coll., Flushing, N.Y., 1980-81, L.I. U., Bklyn., 1981-82, N.Y.C. Tech. Coll., Bklyn., 1982-84, Hostos Community Coll., Bronx, N.Y., 1984—. Mem. Am. Phys. Soc., Pi Mu Epsilon. Roman Catholic. Current work: Cosmology, solid state physics, nuclear physics; quantization of phasons, instantaneous space travel of energy valve. Subspecialties: Cosmology; Statistical physics. Office: Hoston Community Coll 500 Grand Concourse Bronx NY 11450

ETZLER, MARILYNN EDITH, biochemistry educator; b. Detroit, Oct. 30, 1940; d. Elmer Ellsworth and Doris (Tegge) E. B.S. and B.A., Otterbein Coll., 1962; Ph.D., Washington U., 1967. Postdoctoral fellow Coll. Physicians and Surgeons, Columbia U., N.Y.C., 1967-69; asst. prof. biochemistry U. Calif.-Davis, 1969-75, assoc. prof., 1975-79, prof. biochemistry, 1979—. Contbr. articles to profl. jours. NIH grantee, 1970—; U.S. Dept. Agr. grantee, 1979—. Mem. Am. Soc. Biol. Chemists, Am. Soc. Cell Biology, Am. Soc. Plant Physiology, Soc. Complex Carbohydrates, AAAS. Current Work: Structure and function of lectins. Subspecialties: Biochemistry (biology); Cell and tissue culture. Home: 1112 Drake Dr Davis CA 95616 Office: Dept Biochemistry and Biophysics U Calif Davis CA 95616

EULER, ARTHUR RAY, pediatric gastroenterologist; b. Hammond, Ind., Oct. 20, 1942; s. John Stanley and June Alice Biestek; m. Becky Suzanne Brashares, Feb. 6, 1966 (div. 1980); children: Elizabeth, Katherine; m. Dana Mary Pederson, May 22, 1982. B.S., Purdue U., 1965; M.D., Ind. U., 1969. Intern Ind. U. Med. Ctr., Indpls., 1969-70, resident in Pediatrics, 1970, Harbor Gen. Hosp.-UCLA Med. Ctr., Torrance, Calif., 1973-74; fellow in cystic fibrosis-gastroenterology UCLA, 1974-76, asst. prof. pediatrics, 1976-77; head div. pediatric gastroenterology Ark. Children's Hosp., Little Rock, 1977-81; research physician gastrointestinal prostaglandin program Upjohn Co., Kalamazoo, 1981—; vis. prof. Universidad Autonoma de Guadalajara, Mex., 1980, 81, 82. Contbr. numerous articles to profl. jours. Served to lt. comdr. USN, 1970-73, Vietnam. Fellow Am. Acad. Pediatrics, Am. Gastroenterology Assn., Am. Coll. Gastroenterology, Soc. Pediatric Research; mem. N.Am. Soc. Pediatric Gastroenterology, So. Calif. Soc. Gastrointestinal Endoscopy, Western Gastroenterology Assn., So. Calif. Soc. Gastroenterology, Am. Soc. Parenteral and Enteral Nutrition, Central Ark. Pediatric Soc., So. Soc. Pediatric Research, Am. Fedn. Clin. Research, AAAS, N.Y. Acad. Scis., Am. Motility Soc., Soc. Clin. Trials. Lutheran. Current Work: Gastroesophageal reflux and its complications, gastric acid secretion physiology, gastrin physiology in infants and children, therapeutic use of prostaglandins in upper and lower gastrointestinal diseases. Subspecialties: Gastroenterology; Pediatrics. Home: 2101 Bronson Blvd Kalamazoo MI 49007 Office: Upjohn Co Kalamazoo MI 49001

EURICH, ALVIN CHRISTIAN, psychologist; b. Bay City, Mich., June 14, 1902; s. Christian H. and Hulda (Steinke) E.; m. Nell Plopper, Mar. 15, 1953; children: Juliet Ann, Donald Alan. A.B., North Central Coll., 1924; M.A., U. Maine, 1926; Ph.D., U. Minn., 1929. Asst. to pres. U. Minn., Mpls., 1935-36; v.p. Stanford (Calif.) U., 1944-47, acting pres., 1948; first chancellor SUNY-Buffalo, 1949-51; exec. dir. Ford Found. Edn. Program, N.Y.C., 1951-64; pres. Aspen Inst. for Humanistic Studies, Colo., 1963-67, spl. adviser, 1972—, hon. trustee, 1982—; pres. Acad. for Ednl. Devel., Inc., N.Y.C., 1961—. Bd. dirs. Ctr. Pub. Resources; trustee Lovelace Med. Ctr. and Found. Served to comdr. USNR, 1942-44. Recipient Disting. Achievement award U. Minn., 1951; 4th Ann. award Times Sq. Club, 1953; Annual award N.Y. Acad. Pub. Edn., 19. Fellow AAAS, Am. Psychol. Assn.; mem. Am. Ednl. Research Assn. (pres. 1944), Internat. Council Ednl. Devel. (dir.), Sigma Xi. Clubs: Cosmos (Washington); University Century (N.Y.C.), Coffee House (N.Y.C.). Current Work: Learning, education and aptitude measurement. Subspecialties: Learning; Behavioral psychology. Office: Acad for Ednl Devel 680 5th Ave New York NY 10019

EVANS, BOB OVERTON, electronics executive; b. Grand Island, Nebr., Aug. 19, 1927; s. Walter Bernard and Lillian (Overton) E.; m. Maria Bowman, Nov. 19, 1949; children: Cathleen L., Robert W., David D., Douglas B. B.E.E., Iowa State U., 1949. Electric operating engr. No. Ind. Pub. Service Co., Hammond, 1949-51; with IBM, 1951-84; v.p. devel. Data Systems div., 1962-64; pres. Fed. Systems div., 1965-69, Systems Devel. div., 1970-74, Systems Communication div., 1975-77; v.p. IBM engring., programming and tech., 1977-84; ptnr. Hambrecht and Quist, 1984—; chmn. bd. Foothill Research, Inc., Am. Supercomputers, Inc.; dir. Micro MRP, Inc., Santa Barbara Labs.; mem. tech. adv. com. ComSat Corp.; mem. Stark Draper Labs., Inc.; cons. govt. agys.; area bd. mem. Md. Nat. Bank; mem. Def. Sci. Bd. Mem. exec. bd. Nat. Capital Area council Boy Scouts Am.; trustee Rensselaer Poly. Inst., N.Y. Pub. library; mem. elec. engring. vis. com. MIT. Served with USNR, 1945-46. Recipient Disting. Pub. Service award NASA; Disting. Alumni citation Iowa State U., Nat. Medal of Tech., 1985. Fellow IEEE (chmn.

computer group conf. 1970, Armstrong award 1984, Nat. Medal of Tech. 1985); mem. Nat. Acad. Engring., Profl. Group Electronic Computers, Nat. Security Indsl. Assn. (trustee), Armed Forces Communications and Electronics Assn. (trustee), Aerospace Industries Assn. (exec. bd.). Presbyterian. (elder). Designed and developed large digital electric computers. Subspecialty: Computer engineering. Home: 120 Robin Rd Hillsborough CA 94010 Office: 1 Post St 4th Floor San Francisco CA 94104

EVANS, CHARLES HAWES, medical scientist, physician; b. Orange, N.J., Apr. 16, 1940; s. Charles Hawes and Jean Marie (Robinson) E.; m. Nancy Engel, Aug. 21, 1965; 1 dau., Heather Leigh. B.S., Union Coll., 1962; M.D., U. Va., 1969, Ph.D., 1969. Diplomate: Nat. Bd. Med. Examiners. Intern pediatrics U. Va. Hosp., Charlottesville, 1969-70, resident, 1970-71; research assoc. Nat. Cancer Inst., NIH, Bethesda, Md., 1971-73, sr. scientist, 1973-76, chief tumor biology sect., 1976—. Assoc. editor: Jour. Nat. Cancer Inst, 1981—; contbr. over 70 articles in field to med. sci. jours. Served with USPHS, 1971—. Recipient USPHS Commd. Officers award, 1980; USPHS commendation, 1985; John Horsley Meml. Prize U. Va., 1982. Mem. Am. Assn. Cancer Research, Am. Assn. Immunologists, Internat. Soc. Immunopharmacology, Assn. Mil. Surgeons U.S., AAAS. Presbyterian. Lodge: Rotary. Current Work: Director biomedical research laboratory, investigating immunological and other physiological mechanisms for their potential to prevent or control cancer. Subspecialties: Cancer research (medicine); Immunopharmacology. Home: 9233 Farnsworth Dr Potomac MD 20854 Office: NIH Room 2A17 Bldg 37 Bethesda MD 20205

EVANS, DAVID ALAN, biotechnology company executive. Vice pres. corp. research DNA Plant Tech. Corp., Cinnaminson, N.J. Subspecialty: Biotechnology research and development. Office: DNA Plant Tech Corp 2611 Branch Pike Cinnaminson NJ 08077*

EVANS, DAVID HUDSON, biology educator; b. Chgo., June 9, 1940; s. Ronald George and Margaret Virginia (Ketchum) E.; m. Jean Margaret Rose, Aug. 18, 1962; children—Andrew William, Matthew Richard. B.A., DePauw U., 1962; Ph.D., Stanford U., 1967. Asst. prof. biology U. Miami, Fla., 1969-74, assoc. prof., 1974-78, prof., chmn. dept., 1978-81; prof. zoology. U. Fla., Gainesville, 1981—, chmn. dept., 1982—; cons. panel mem. White House Office Sci. Tech. Policy, Washington, 1982-83; dir. Mt. Desert Island Biology Lab., Salsbury Cove, Maine, 1983—. Mem. editorial bd. various profl. jours. Contbr. articles to profl. jours. Mem. adminstrv. bd. Trinity United Meth. Ch., Gainesville, 1983—. Grantee NIH, NSF, 1970—. Mem. Soc. Exptl. Biology, Am. Physiol. Soc., Am. Soc. Zoologists, European Soc. Physiology and Biochemistry, Sigma Xi (panel mem. 1983—). Current work: Mechanisms of solute transport across fish gill epithelium. . Home: 100 NW 28th St Gainesville FL 32607 Office: Dept Zoology Bartram Hall U Fla Gainesville FL 32611

EVANS, DAVID STANLEY, astronomer, educator; b. Cardiff, Wales, Jan. 28, 1916; came to U.S., 1968; s. Arthur Cyril and Kate (Priest) E.; m. Betty Hall Hart, Mar. 8, 1949; children: Jonathan Gareth Weston, Barnaby Huw Weston. B.A., Cambridge U., 1937, M.A., Ph.D., ScD., 1941. Research asst. Univ. Obs., Oxford, Eng., 1938-46; 2d asst. Radcliffe Obs., Pretoria, South Africa, 1946-51; chief asst., sr. prin. sci. officer Royal Obs., Cape of Good Hope, South Africa, 1951-68; prof. astronomy U. Tex., Austin, 1968—; Sr. vis. scientist NSF fellow, 1965-66. Author or editor 8 books; contbr. over 200 articles to sci. and hist. publs. Fellow Royal Astron. Soc. (London), Inst. Physics (London), Royal Soc. South Africa; mem. Astron. Soc. So. Africa (hon. mem.; past v.p., McIntyre award for astron. history 1972), Am. Astron. Soc., Internat. Astron. Union (past pres. commn.). Clubs: Owl (Cape Town, South Africa), West Province Sports (Cape Town, South Africa); Town and Gown (Austin). Current Work: Lunar occultations flare stars, multiple stars. Subspecialties: Optical astronomy; History of astronomy. Home: 6001 Mountainclimb Dr Austin TX 78731 Office: Dept Astronomy U Tex Austin TX 78712

EVANS, DENNIS HYDE, chemistry educator; b. Grinnell, Iowa, Mar. 28, 1939; s. Leonard Hyde and Clara Ethel (Parmley) E.; m. Ruth Elizabeth Turnbull, June 28, 1958; children—Susan Katherine, John Hyde, Andrew Turnbull. B.S., Ottawa U., 1960; A.M., Harvard U., 1961, Ph.D., 1964. Instr. chemistry Harvard U., Cambridge, Mass., 1964-66; asst. prof. chemistry U. Wis.-Madison, 1966-70, assoc. prof., 1970-75, prof., 1975—, Meloche-Bascom prof., 1984—, chmn. dept., 1977-80, assoc. dean Coll. Letters and Sci., 1983—. Danforth fellow, 1960-64; NIH fellow, 1961-64; NSF grantee, 1968—. Contbr. articles to profl. jours. Mem. Am. Chem. Soc., Internat. Soc. Electrochemistry. Baptist. Subspecialty: Electrochemistry. Home: 1809 Prairie Rd Madison WI 53711 Office: 1101 University Ave Madison WI 53706

EVANS, FREDERICK E., supervisory research chemist; b. Springfield, Mass., Nov. 11, 1948; s. Edward E. and Hedwig J. (Zeletzky) E.; m. Huey-Ing Tseng, Aug. 20, 1978. B.S., U. Mass., 1970; Ph.D., SUNY-Albany, 1974. Postgrad. research chemist U. Calif.-San Diego, 1975-78; chief spectroscopic techniques br., research chemist Nat. Ctr. Toxicol. Research, FDA, Jefferson, Ark., 1978—; adj. assoc. prof. U. Ark., Little Rock, 1980—. Contbr. articles to profl. jours. Mem. Am. Assn. Cancer Research, Internat. Soc. Magnetic Resonance, Am. Chem. Soc. Current Work: Responsible for the operation and supervision of a high level nuclear magnetic resonance and mass spectrometry laboratory. Application of nuclear magnetic resonance techniques to analytical chemistry and chemical carcinogenesis. Subspecialties: Nuclear magnetic resonance; Analytical chemistry. Office: Dept Chemistry Nat Center Toxicol Research FDA Jefferson AR 72079

EVANS, GARY WILLIAM, social ecology educator; b. Summit, N.J., Nov. 22, 1948. A.B. with high honors in Psychology, Colgate U., 1971; M.S., U. Mass., 1973, Ph.D. in Psychology, 1975; postgrad., U. Calif.-Irvine, 1978. Research asst. in psychology U. Mass., Amherst, 1971-73, instr. psychology and Bklyn. Career Opportunities Program, 1973-75; asst. prof. social ecology U. Calif.-Irvine, 1975-80, assoc. prof. social ecology, 1980—, assoc. dir. undergrad. affairs, 1979-81. Contbr. articles to profl. publs.; editor: Environmental Stress, (with others) Behavior, Health, & Environmental Stress, 1986; editoral rev. bd.: Rep. Research in Social Psychology, 1973-75, Man-Environ. Systems, 1975—, Environ. Psychology and Nonverbal Behavior, 1976-79, Jour. Population and Environ, 1981—, Handbook of Environmental Psychology, 1982—, Advances in Environment, Behavior and Design, 1984—; ad hoc reviewer, NSF, NIH, various jours. Grantee in field.; Univ. scholar Colgate U., 1966-71; George Cobb fellow, 1970; Phil R. Miller psychology prize, 1971; NSF dissertation yr. fellow, 1974-75; Regents' jr. faculty fellow U. Calif., 1977; Fulbright award Council Internat. Exchange of Scholars, U. Poona, India, 1981-82; Disting. Teaching award U. Calif., Irvine, 1985. Subspecialty: Environmental psychology. Office: Program in Social Ecology Univ CaliF Irvine Irvine CA 92717

EVANS, HAROLD J., plant physiologist, biochemist, educator; b. Franklin, Ky., Feb. 19, 1921; s. James H. and Allie (Uhls) E.; m. Elizabeth Dunn, Dec. 14, 1946; children: Heather Mary, Pamela. B.S., U. Ky., 1946, M.S., 1948; Ph.D. (Cook-Vorhees fellow), Rutgers U., 1950. Asst. prof. botany N.C. State U., 1952-54, asso. prof., 1954-57, prof., 1957-61; postdoctoral fellow Johns Hopkins U., Balt., 1952; prof. plant physiology Oreg. State U., Corvallis, 1961—; dir. Lab. for Nitrogen Fixation, 1978—; vis. prof. U. Sussex, Eng., 1967; George A. Miller vis. prof. U. Ill., Urbana, 1973; mem. panel for metabolic biology NSF, 1964-68; mem. U.S.-Japan Coop. Sci. Program, 1976. Contbr. articles to profl. jours. Recipient Hoblitzelle Nat. award Tex. Research Found., 1964; Basic Research award Oreg. State U., 1965; N.W. Sci. award Gov. Oreg., 1967; named Disting. Alumnus U. Ky., 1975; recipient George G. Ferguson Disting. Prof. award and Milton Harris research award Oreg. State U., 1983; Charles Reid Barnes award Am. Soc. Plant Physiologists, 1985. Mem. Am. Soc. Plant Physiologists (pres. 1971, trustee 1977—), Biochem. Soc. (U.K.), Am. Soc. Biol. Chemists, U.S. Nat. Acad. Scis., Sigma Xi (award 1968), Phi Kappa Phi. Democrat. Current Work: Cloning and transfer of hydrogenase gene in Rhizobium with goal of increasing efficiency of nitrogen fixation in legumes. Subspecialties: Nitrogen fixation; Enzyme technology. Home: 2939 Mulkey St Corvallis OR 97330 Office: Lab for Nitrogen Fixation Research Oreg State U Corvallis OR 97331

EVANS, JAMES THOMAS, surgical oncologist, researcher; b. Niagara Falls, N.Y., Apr. 12, 1942; s. James Edward and Kathleen (Walsh) E.; m. Joyce Gray, May 9, 1981. B.S., Tulane U., 1963; M.D., La. State U., 1967. Diplomate: Am. Bd. Surgery. Intern Charity Hosp., New Orleans, 1967-69; oncology fellow Roswell Park Meml. Inst., Buffalo, New Orleans, 1970-71, cancer research surgeon, Buffalo, 1973-80; resident in surgery La. State U., dept. surgery, New Orleans, 1972-73; assoc. prof. SUNY, Buffalo, 1980—. Am. Cancer Soc. fellow, 1978-81. Mem. Am. Cancer Soc. (chmn. colorectal com. 1979—, dir. N.Y. state 1980—, pres. Erie County 1981—), Am. Assn. Cancer Research, ACS (sec.-treas. 1979—), Am. Soc. Clin. Oncology, Soc. Surgery Alimentary Tract, Soc. Surgical Oncology. Mem. Christ. Ch. Current Work: Research on treatment of solid tumors with laser; research on genetic variability of chemical carcinogenesis. Subspecialties: Laser medicine; Cancer research (medicine). Home: 33 Crosby Blvd Eggertsville NY 14226 Office: SUNY Dept Surgery 1462 Grider St Buffalo NY 14215

EVANS, JAMES WARREN, physiologist, equine cons.; b. Edna, Tex., Oct. 31, 1938; s. Calvin Cecil and Thelma Waley (Williamson) E.; m. Benita M. Evans, Sept. 2, 1959; 1 son, Scott Allen. Student, Tex. A&M U., 1958-59; B.S., Colo. State U., 1964; Ph.D., U. Calif., 1968. Prof. dept. animal sci. U. Calif., 1968-85, assoc. dean, 1982-85; prof. dept. animal sci. Tex. A&M U., 1985—. Author: Horses, 1981, (with Borton, Hintz & VanVleck) The Horse, 1977; contbr. (with Borton, Hintz & VanVleck) numerous articles in field to profl. jours. Mem. Am. Physiol. Soc., Am. Soc. Animal Sci., Endocrine Soc., Equine Nutriton and Physiology Soc. Club: Cross Court (Woodland, Calif.). Current Work: Interaction of hormones at cellular level to control reproduction in mare and stallion. Subspecialties: Reproductive biology; Chronobiology.

EVANS, JOHN R., See *Who's Who in America,* 43rd edition.

EVANS, JOHN VAUGHAN, physicist; b. Manchester, Eng., July 5, 1933; s. Gyril John and Gertrude Veronica (Bayliss) E.; m. Maureen Vervain Patrick, Oct. 19, 1958; children: Carol, David, Lesley. B.Sc. in Physics with honors, Manchester U., 1954, Ph.D., 1957. Leverhulme research fellow Jodrell Bank Exptl. Sta., U. Manchester, 1957-60; mem. staff Lincoln Lab. MIT, Lexington, 1960-66, 67-70; G.A. Miller vis. prof. U. Ill.-Urbana, 1966-67; assoc. group leader surveillance techniques group Lincoln Lab. MIT, 1970-72, group leader, 1972-74, assoc. div. head aerospace div., 1974-77, asst. dir. lab., 1977-83; dir. Haystack Obs., MIT, 1980-83; also prof. meteorology; dir. research COMSAT Labs., Gaithersburg, Md., from 1983, now v.p. for research and devel., Clarksburg, Md. Editor: (with T. Hagfors) Radar Astronomy, 1968; contbr. (with T. Hagfors) numerous articles to sci. jours. Served with Royal Brit. Army, 1951-57. Recipient Appleton prize Royal Soc., London, 1954. Fellow IEEE; mem. Am. Geophys. Union, AAAS, Internat. Astron. Union, Internat. Union Radio Scis., Sigma Xi. Unitarian. Club: Cosmos (Washington). Current Work: Studies by radar of the earth's upper atmosphere, meteors, the moon and terrestrial planets. Subspecialties: Aeronomy; Remote sensing (atmospheric science). Office: COMSAT Labs 22300 Comsat Dr Gaithersburg MD 20871

EVANS, NEAL JOHN, II, astrophysicist, educator; b. San Antonio, Sept. 22, 1946; s. Neal John and Lucie D. (Barbour) E.; m. Carol Sue Kirschenbaum, Dec. 19, 1973 (div. 1984); 1 son, Daniel Spencer. B.A. in Physics, U. Calif.-Berkeley, Ph.D. in Physics, 1973. Research fellow Calif. Inst. Tech., 1973-75; asst. prof. U. Tex., Austin, 1975-80, assoc. prof. astronomy, 1980—; also writer, cons. Contbr. articles to profl. jours. Recipient 1st prize Griffith Observer essay contest, 1974. Mem. Am. Astron. Soc., Internat. Astron. Union, Internat. Union Radio Sci. Democrat. Current Work: Studies of molecular clouds and star formation using millimeter and infrared astronomy. Subspecialties: Radio and microwave astronomy; Infrared astronomy. Home: 5400 Shoalwood Ave Austin TX 78756 Office: Dept Astronom U Tex Austin TX 78712

EVANS, PATRICK JAMES, physicist; b. New Haven, Conn., July 7, 1950; s. Francis Edward and Minnie Josephine (Mizii) E.; m. Kathleen Marie King, June 17, 1972; 1 child, Gregory Francis. B.S. in Math and Physics, Boston Coll., 1972; M.S., Purdue U., 1974, Ph.D., 1978. Instr. in research Purdue U., West Lafayette, Ind., 1976-78; sr. staff physicist Applied Physics Lab., Laurel, Md., 1978-80; mem. profl. staff The Analytic Scis. Corp., Reading, Mass., 1980—. Contbr. articles to profl. jours. Tutor minorities students dept. pharmacy Purdue U., 1978. Mem. Am. Phys. Soc., Soc. Magnetic Anomaly Detection, Phi Beta Kappa, Sigma Chi, Phi Kappa Phi. Roman Catholic. Current work: Applied classical field theory to militarily important areas of hydrodynamics, acoustics and electrodynamics, secondary interest in nuclear structure and particle theory. Subspecialties: Statistical physics; Nuclear physics. Home: 159 Franklin St Stoneham MA 02180 Office: The Analytic Sciences Corp 1 Jacob Way Reading MA 01867

EVANS, WILLIAM EDWARD, pharmacokineticist, clinical pharmacist, educator; b. Clarksville, Tenn., June 27, 1950; s. Buford Joe and Wanda (Wilson) E.; m. Dianne Dewit Miller, Sept. 2, 1972; children: Leslie Rhea, Kelli Nicol. Student, Austin Peay State U., 1968-70; B.Sc., U. Tenn., 1973, Pharm.D., 1974. Diplomate: Am. Bd. Bioanalysis. Research assoc. St. Jude Children's Research Hosp., Memphis, 1976-78, asst. mem., 1978-80, dir. clin. pharmacokinetics-pharmacodynamics sect., 1981-83, dir. pharm. div., 1983—; asst. prof. pharmaceutics U. Tenn. Ctr. Health Scis., Memphis, 1974-76, assoc. prof., 1981-83, prof., 1983—, chmn. dept. clin. pharmacy, 1983—; mem. adv. com. hematologic and neoplastic diseases U.S. Pharmacopeia, 1980—. Editor: Applied Pharmacokinetics, 1980; assoc. editor: Pharmacotherapy jour; editorial adv. bd.: Jour. Investigation Anticancer Drugs, Jour. Pediatric Hematology Oncology; contbr. articles to profl. jours. Recipient Young Investigator award NIH, 1978-80; NIH grantee. Mem. AAAS (nominating com.), Am. Soc. Cancer Research, Am. Soc. Clin. Oncology, Am. Soc. Clin. Pharmacology and Therapeutics, Am. Coll. Clin. Pharmacy (pres.'s award 1982, chmn. bd. trustees Research Inst. 1982), Am. Assn. Colls. Pharmacy (research and grad. affairs com.). Methodist. Current Work: Metabolism and disposition of anticancer drugs in children. Pharmacokinetics, clinical pharmacology of antineoplastic drugs. Subspecialties: Pharmacokinetics; Cancer research (medicine). Home: 2425 Willinghurst Germantown TN 38138 Office: St Jude Children's Research Hosp 332 N Lauderdale Memphis TN 38105

EVANS, WILLIAM FREDERICK, research chemist; b. Hamilton, Ohio, Dec. 22, 1957; s. William George and Janet Lee (Jennings) E.; m. Susan Denise Heareth, Sept. 5, 1981. B.S. in chemistry, Rose-Hulman Inst. Tech., 1980. Chem. technician Monsanto/Mound, Miamisburg, Ohio, 1979, research chemist I, 1980-83, research chemist II, 1983—. Mem. Am. Chem. Soc., Tau Beta Pi. Republican. Mem. United Ch. of Christ. Current work: Isotope separation by liquid-liquid chemical exchange and chromatographic techniques; analytical methodology development; applications of electronics and computers to assist chemical investigations. Subspecialties: Analytical chemistry; Nuclear chemistry. Home: 35 Maple Hill Circle West Carrollton OH 45449 Office: Monsanto/Mound Mound Rd Miamisburg OH 45342

EVANS, WILLIS THOMAS, chemist, materials science researcher; b. Wilkensburg, Pa., Sept. 16, 1943; s. Willis T. and Louise H. (Henry) E.; m. Deloris Ann Houser, Jan. 10, 1964; 1 child, Thomas J. B.A., Indiana U. of Pa., 1966, M.S., 1969. Research assoc. Mellon Inst., Pitts., 1966-67; scientist Hercules-ABL, Cumberland, Md., 1967-68; staff scientist Alcoa Tech. Ctr., Alcoa Center, Pa., 1969—. Adviser Boy Scouts Am., North Washington, Pa., 1973-76. Mem. Am. Chem. Soc., Republican. Methodist. Current work: Using surface analysis techniques such as electron microscopy, ESCA, SAM, ISS, SIMS, FT-IR, and TPD to characterize surface chemistry of aluminum as it relates to inorganic and organic treatments. Subspecialties: Surface chemistry; Metallurgy. Home: 1055 King Arthur Dr Apollo PA 15613 Office: Alcoa Tech Ctr Alcoa Center PA 15069

EVENS, MARTHA WALTON, computer scientist; b. Boston, Jan. 1, 1935; d. C. Russell and Virgene Claribel (Dupka) Walton; m. Leonard Evens, Sept. 13, 1958; children—Sarah Evens Golab, Samuel Robert, Anne Chaia. A.B., Bryn Mawr Coll., 1955; M.A., Radcliffe Coll., 1957; Ph.D., Northwestern U., 1975. Faculty assoc. Bell Telephone Labs., Naperville, Ill., 1978; instr. math. Nat. Coll. Edn., Evanston, Ill., 1966-68; instr. computer sci. Northwestern U., Evanston, 1972-74; asst. prof. computer sci. Ill. Inst. Tech., Chgo., 1975-81, assoc. prof., 1981—. Author: (with others) Lexical-Semantic Relations, 1981. Assoc. editor Am. Math. Monthly, 1977-81, Computational Linguistics, 1982-84. Precinct capt. Democratic Orgn. of Evanston, 1972-75. Fulbright fellow, 1955-56; named Tchr. of Yr., Ill. Inst. Tech., 1984-85; NSF grantee, 1979-81, 81-83, 83-85. Mem. Assn. for Computational Linguistics (pres. 1984), IEEE Computer Soc. pres. Chgo. chpt. 1980), Assn. Computing Machinery, Am. Assn. Artificial Intelligence. Episcopalian. Current work: Man-machine communication, med. expert systems, automatic text generation of medical case reports, lexicography, lexical semantic relations. Subspecialties: Automated language processing; Artificial intelligence. Home: 2026 Orrington Ave Evanston IL 60201 Office: Computer Sci Dept IIT 10 W 31st St Chicago IL 60616

EVENS, RONALD GENE, physician, educator; b. St. Louis, Sept. 24, 1939; s. Robert and Dorothy (Lupkey) E.; m. Hanna Blunk, Sept. 3, 1960; children: Ronald Gene, Christine, Amanda. B.A. in Econs., Washington U., St. Louis, 1960, M.D., 1964, postgrad. in bus. and edn., 1970-71. Intern Barnes Hosp., St. Louis, 1964-65; resident Mallinckrodt Inst. Radiology, 1965-66, 68-70; research asso. Nat. Heart Inst., 1966-68; asst. prof. radiology, v.p. Washington U. Med. Sch., 1970-71; prof., head dept. radiology, dir. Mallinckrodt Inst. Radiology, 1971-72; Elizabeth Mallinckrodt prof., head radiology dept., dir. Mallinckrodt Inst., 1972—; radiologist in chief Barnes and Children's Hosp., St. Louis, 1971—; chmn. bd. Health Care Network, St. Louis, 1980—; mem. bd. Washington U. Med. Center, 1980-84; mem. adv. com. on splty. and geog. distbn. of physicians Inst. Medicine, Nat. Acad. Scis., 1974-76; dir. Boatmen's Bank of St. Louis.; Hickey lectr., Detroit, 1976. Carmen lectr., St. Louis, 1983, Hampton lectr., Boston, 1984. Contbr. over 120 articles to profl. jours. Lodge adviser Order Arrow, Boy Scouts Am., 1975-84; elder Glendale and Kirkwood Presbyn. Ch., 1971-74; bd. dirs. St. Louis Comprehensive Neighborhood Health Center, OEO, 1970-74. Served with USPHS, 1966-68. James Picker Found. advanced acad. fellow, 1970; recipient Disting. Service award St. Louis C. of C., 1972, Disting. Eagle Scout award Nat. Council Boy Scouts Am., 1984. Fellow Am. Coll. Radiology; mem. Mo. Radiol. Soc. (pres. 1977-78), Soc. Nuclear Medicine (trustee 1971-75), AMA, St. Louis Med. Soc., Mo. State Med. Assn., Soc. Chairmen Acad. Radiology Depts. (pres. 1979), Radiol. Soc. N.Am., Assn. Univ. Radiologists, Am. Roentgen Ray Soc. (v.p. 1982, treas. 1983—), Phi Beta Kappa, Alpha Omega Alpha (Sheard-Sanford award). Subspecialties: Radiology; Nuclear medicine. Office: 510 S Kingshighway Saint Louis MO 63110

EVENSON, WILLIAM EDWIN, ecol. physicist, cons., educator, researcher; b. Martinez, Calif., Oct. 12, 1941; s. Raymond Fox and Berta (Woolley) E.; m. Nancy Ann Woffinden, Dec. 21, 1964; children: Brian, Elizabeth, Joann, Andrew, Bengte. B.S. in Physics, Brigham Young U., 1965; Ph.D. in Theoretical Solid State Physics (Woodrow Wilson fellow, NSF fellow, Danforth fellow), Iowa State U., 1968. Research asso. U. Pa., Phila., 1968-70; NSF postdoctoral fellow, 1968-69; asst. prof. Brigham Young U., Provo, Utah, 1970-73, assoc. prof., 1973-79, prof. physics, 1979—, asso. dir. gen. edn., 1980-81, dir., 1981-82, dean, 1982—; vis. colleague in botany U. Hawaii at Manoa, Honolulu, 1977-78; cons. Eyring Research Inst., Provo, 1980-82, cons. computer programs for ecol. analysis, 1975—. Contbr. articles on ecol. physics to profl. jours. Bishop 108th ward Ch. Jesus Christ of Latter-day Saints, 1971-74, high council 1st stake, 1970-71, 1974-75, mem. Mission to France, Paris, 1961-63; chmn. Utah County Democratic Party, 1981-82, vice chmn., 1979-81; mem. Utah State Dem. Party Central Com., 1979-82. Named Brigham Young U. Prof. of Month, Feb. 1979. Mem. Am. Assn. Physics Tchrs., Am. Bot. Soc., Hawaii Bot. Soc., Hawaii Audubon Soc., Nat. Audubon Soc., Sigma Xi. Current Work: Use of computers in ecological analysis, applications of physics to solving problems in theoretical ecology, computer programming, ecological analysis, reproductive energetics. Subspecialties: Theoretical ecology; Theoretical physics. Office: Dept Physics and Astronomy Brigham Young U Provo UT 84602

EVERETT, ROBERT RIVERS, manufacturing company executive; b. Yonkers, N.Y., June 26, 1921; s. Chester McKenzie and Ruth (Melius) E.; m. Helen Burns, Oct. 21, 1944 (div. 1972); children—Robert F., Bruce M., Douglas F., Theodore J., Michael B.; m. Jean M. McGrath, Nov. 4, 1972 (dec. Nov. 1980); m. Ann T. Russell, Mar. 26, 1982. B.S., Duke, 1942; M.S., Mass. Inst. Tech., 1943. With Servomechanisms Lab. of Mass. Inst. Tech., 1942-51; asso. dir. Servomechanisms Lab. of Mass. Inst. Tech. (Digital Computer Lab.), 1951; asso. div. head Lincoln Lab., 1951-56, div. head, 1956-58; tech. dir. The Mitre Corp., Bedford, Mass., 1958-59, v.p. tech. operations, 1959-69, exec. v.p., 1969, pres., 1969—; mem. sci. adv. bd. USAF; mem. sci. adv. group Def. Communications Agy.; trustee No. Energy Corp.; cons. Def. Sci. Bd.; cons. div. adv. group Electronic Systems div. Air Force Systems Command.; Mem. sci. adv. bd. U.S. Air Force. Contbr. articles to tech. jours. Fellow IEEE; mem. Assn. Computing Machinery, AAAS, Nat. Acad. Engring., Phi Beta Kappa, Sigma Xi, Tau Beta Pi. Club: Cosmos (Washington). Patentee digital computers. Subspecialties: Information systems, storage, and retrieval (computer science); Digital computer design. Office: Mitre Corp Burlington Rd Bedford MA 01730

EVERHART, THOMAS EUGENE, electrical engineer, university official; b. Kansas City, Mo., Feb. 15, 1932; s. William Elliott and Elizabeth Ann (West) E.; m. Doris Arleen Wentz, June 21, 1953; children—Janet Sue, Nancy Jean, David William, John Thomas. A.B. in Physics magna cum laude, Harvard, 1953; M.Sc., U. Calif. at Los Angeles, 1955; Ph.D. in Engring., Cambridge (Eng.) U., 1958. Mem. tech. staff Hughes Research Labs., Culver City, Calif., 1953-55; mem. faculty U. Calif. at Berkeley, 1958-78, prof. elec. engring. and computer scis., 1967-78, Miller research prof., 1969-70, chmn. dept., 1972-77; prof. elec. engring., Joseph Silbert dean engring. Cornell U., Ithaca, N.Y., 1979-84; chancellor U. Ill., Urbana-Champaign, 1984—; fellow scientist Westinghouse Research Labs., Pitts., 1962-63; guest prof. Inst. für Angewandte Physik, U. Tuebingen, W. Germany, 1966-67, Waseda U., Tokyo, also Osaka (Japan) U., fall 1974; vis. fellow Clare Hall, Cambridge U., 1975; chmn. Electron, Ion and Photon Beam Symposium, 1977; cons. to industry; mem. sci. and ednl. adv. com. Lawrence Berkeley Lab., 1978-84, chmn, 1980-84; mem. sci. adv. com. Gen. Motors Corp., 1980—; mem. tech. adv. com. R.R. Donnelley & Sons, 1981—. NSF sr. postdoctoral fellow, 1966-67; Guggenheim fellow, 1974-75. Fellow IEEE; mem. AAAS, Nat. Acad. Engring., Electron Microscopy Soc. Am. (council 1970-72, pres. 1977), Microbeam Analysis Soc. Am., Deutsche Gesellschaft für Elektronenmikroskopie, Assn. Marshall Scholars and Alumni (pres. 1965-68), Sigma Xi, Eta Kappa Nu. Club: Faculty (Cornell U.). Office: U Ill Office of Chancellor Urbana IL 61801

EVERITT, WILLIAM LITTELL, college dean emeritus, electrical engineering educator; b. Balt., Apr. 14, 1900; s. William Littell and Margaret (Pownall) E.; m. Dorothy Wallace, 1923 (dec. 1978); children—Barbara Everitt Bryant, Bruce W., Pamela Everitt Utterback; m. Margaret Anderson Larson, June 28, 1980. B.S.E.E., Cornell U., 1922; M.S., Univ. Mich., 1926; Ph.D., Ohio State U., 1933; D.Eng. (hon.); Tri State Coll., 1964, U. of Andes, 1966, Ohio State U., 1966, Mich. Technol. U., 1967, U. Mich., 1967, U. Ill., 1969, So. Meth. U., 1972; D.Sc. (hon.), Monmouth Coll., 1964; LL.D. (hon.), U. Denver, 1968. Registered profl. engr., Ill., Ohio. Instr. elec. engring. Cornell U., Ithaca, N.Y., 1920-22; engr. N. Elec. Mfg. Co., 1922-24; instr. U. Mich., 1924-26; asst. prof. elec. engring. Ohio State U., 1926-29, assoc. prof., 1929-34, prof., 1934-44; prof., head dept. elec. engring. U. Ill., 1944-49, dean engring., 1949-68, dean emeritus, 1968—; mem. tech review bd. Univ. Patents, Inc., 1968-70; dir. Champaign Nat. Bank, 1963-71, dir. emeritus, 1979—; dir. Astronautics Corp. Am., 1968-77; mem. communication sect. Nat. Def. Research Com., 1940-42; electronics com. Joint Research and Devel. Bd., 1946-53; research and devel. tech. adv. panel electronics Dept. Def., 1954-57, tech. adv. panel gen. scis., 1957-63, adv. com. Pacific Missile Range, 1958-62; sci. adv. panel U.S. Army, 1959-70, electronics adv. group Electronics Command, 1963-65, weapons command adv. group, 1965-76, computer command adv. group, 1971-74, Ill. Sci. Adv. Council, 1967—; trustee Electronics Compatability Analysis Ctr., 1968-70; mem. Nat. Com. Devel. Scientists and Engrs., 1956-57; chmn. accreditation and edn. com. Engrs. Council Profl. Devel., 1956-58, pres., 1958-61. Author: Communication Engineering, 1932. Editor: Electrical Engrineering Series, 1945-69. Bd. dirs. U.S. Signal Sch., 1957-60; mem. nat. council YMCA, 1961-70. Served to maj. Signal Corps. Res., 1922-41. Numerous awards include: Exceptionally Meritorious Civilian award U.S. Army, 1946, Lamme medal Am. Soc. Engring. Edn., 1957, Washington award Western Soc. Engrs., 1971, Grinter medal, 1971; Disting. Profl. Achievement award U. Mich. Coll. Engring., 1968; named to Hall of Fame Engring. Educators, 1968; Number 2 Educator, 1924. Fellow AAAS, AIEE (dir. 1947-51, Elec. Engring. Edn. medal. 1957), IRE (pres. 1942-47, 1949-51, Medal of Honor 1954), IEEE (Kelly medal 1963), Nat. Acad. Engring. (charter), Engring. Coll. Adminstrv. Council (chmn. 1953-55). Ill. Soc. Profl. Engrs., Acoustical Soc. Am., Sigma Xi, Theta Chi, Tau Beta Pi, Phi Kappa Phi, Eta Kappa Nu, Pi Mu Epsilon, Gamma Alpha, Pi Tau Sigma, Etta Kappa Nu (eminent), Triangle (hon.), Omicron Delta Kappa (hon.). Presbyterian. Clubs: University, Champaign Country. Lodge: Rotary. Subspecialties: Electrical engineering; Telecommunications. Office: Univ Ill Urbana Champaign 106 Engineering Hall 1308 W Green St Urbana IL 61801

EVERLY, GEORGE STOTELMYER, JR., psychophysiologist; b. Balt., May 31, 1950; s. George Stotelmyer and Kathleen (Webster) E.; m. Gayle May Schabdach., Apr. 27, 1975; 1 dau., Marideth Rose. B.S., U. Md., 1972, M.A., 1974, Ph.D., 1978. Instr. U. Md., 1975-80, assoc. prof., 1980-82; assoc. prof. Loyola Coll. Md., Balt., 1980-85, prof., 1985—; dir. behavioral medicine lab., 1982—; dir. behavioral medicine service (Psychol. Scis. Inst.), Balt., 1982—. Author: Controlling Stress and Tension, 1979, The Nature and Treatment of the Stress Response, 1981, Occupational Health Promotion, 1985; Personality and Its Disorders, 1985. Developer: Everly Stress and Coping Inventory, 1984. Mem. Am. Psychol. Assn., Acad. Psychosomatic Medicine, Biofeedback Soc. Am., Am. Acad. Behavioral Medicine, Soc. Behavioral Medicine. Current Work: Cognitive influences in psychosomatic medicine; clinical applications for biofeedback therapy. Subspecialties: Physiological psychology; Psychobiology. Home: 204 Glenmore Ave Catonsville MD 21888 Office: Dept Psychology Loyola Coll Md Baltimore MD 21210

EVERSON, RICHARD BERNARD, physician, epidemiologist; b. Bronxville, N.Y., Dec. 20, 1946; s. George Andrew Lincoln and Helena Bernadette (Huerlander) E.; m. JoAnn Giordano; children—Benjamin Iver, Richard George. B.S., Trinity Coll., 1968; M.D., U. Rochester, 1972. Diplomate Am. Bd. Internal Medicine, Am. Bd. Medical Oncology. Intern, Stanford U., Calif., 1972-73; resident Yale U., New Haven, Conn., 1975-76; clin. assoc., staff fellow Nat. Cancer Inst., NIH, Bethesda, Md., 1973-79; med. officer Nat. Inst. Environ. Health Scis., NIH, Research Triangle Park, N.C., 1979—. Contbr. articles to profl. jours. Current work: Development and clinical evaluation of laboratory approaches to the detection of environmentally induced genetic damage in man. Subspecialties: Cancer research (medicine); Epidemiology. Home: 115 Burnwood Ct Chapel Hill NC 27514 Office: Epidemiology Branch Nat Inst Environ Health Scis PO Box 12233 Research Triangle Park NC 27709

EVIAN, CYRIL IAN, periodontics researcher, educator, periodontist; b. Johannesburg, Transvaal, South Africa, july 31, 1948; came to U.S., 1977; s. Solly and Sonia (Dembo) E.; m. Cheryl Adrienne Freedman, Dec. 12, 1971; 1 son, Allon; m. Andrea Michelle Goldin, Febv. 3, 1976; children: Samantha, Tracy, Debbie. B.D.S., U. Witwatersrand, Johannesburg, 1971, Higher Dental Diploma, 1974; cert. periodontics, U. Pa., 71979, D.M.D., 1981. Clin. instr. U. Witwatersand, 1971, 75, lectr. in preventive dentistry, 1975-76; adj. asst. prof. periodontics U. Pa., 1979-80; research assoc. in periodontics Center for Oral Health Research, 1979-80, asst. prof. periodontics, 1980—; dir. grad. periodontics center for Oral Health Research, 1983—. Contbr. articles, abstracts to profl. jours. Mem. South African Soc. Periodontology, South African Soc. Endodontics, Internat. Assn. Dental Research, ADA, Pa. Dental Soc., Am. Acad. Periodontology, Phila. Dental County Soc., South African Dental Assn. (chmn. com. preventive dentistry 1975), Brit. Dental Soc. Current Work: Periodontal research. Subspecialty: Periodontics. Home: 1124 Woodbine Ave Narberth PA 19072 Office: U Pa 4001 Spruce St Philadelphia PA 19104

EWALD, BRUCE HAROLD, veterinarian, educator; b. N.Y.C., Sept. 12, 1933; s. Harold Edwin and Dora (Hansen) E.; m. Carolyn Alford, June 22, 1984; children—David Alford, Mark Campbell. D.V.M., Iowa State U., 1957, M.S., 1965. Diplomate Am. Coll. Lab. Animal Medicine. Dir. lab. animal medicine Cornell U. Med. Coll., N.Y.C., 1965-78; dir. lab. animal resources Va. Poly. Inst. and State U., Blacksburg, Va., 1978-81; prof., chmn. div. vet. biology Va.-Md. Coll. Vet. Medicine, Blacksburg, 1978-80, asst. dean acad. affairs, 1980-81, assoc. dean research, 1981-84; dir. animal care Ciba-Geigy, 1984—; cons. Hoffman-LaRoche, Nutley, N.J., 1983-84, AAALAC, Joliet, Ill., 1978—, N.Y. Blood Ctr., N.Y.C., 1973-78. Contbr. articles to profl. pubs. Area leader United Fund No. Westchester, Westchester County, 1972; pres. Gregory and Scott Lane Assn., Millwood, N.Y., 1973; asst. cub master Westchester-Putnam council Boy Scouts Am., 1973-74; elder Mount Kisco Presbyterian Ch. (N.Y.), 1975-77. Fellow Morris Animal Found., 1962-63, Nat. Heart Assn., 1964. Fellow Am. Coll. Lab. Animal Medicine; mem. Am. Assn. Lab. Animal Sci. (pres. 1974-75), Am. Assn. Accredited Lab. Animal Care (sec. 1977-82), Phi Gamma Delta (sec. 1953-55). Republican. Current work: Laboratory animal care management and the development of animal welfare program, research program in a new college of veterinary medicine, development of renal and cardiovascular animal models. Subspecialties: Laboratory animal medicine; Comparative physiology. Home: 1 Paddock Ct Long Valley NJ 07853 Office: Va-Md Regional Coll Vet Medicine VA Poly Inst and State U Blacksburg VA 24061

EWAN, RICHARD COLIN, animal scientist; b. Cuba, Ill., Sept. 10, 1934; s. John Grafton and Zelma (Shoop) E.; m. Arlene Francis Ewan, June 23, 1956; children: William, Richard, Daniel, Christopher. B.S., U. Ill., 1956, M.S., 1957; Ph.D., U. Wis., 1966. Research asst. U. Ill., 1956-57, U. Wis., 1962-66; prof. animal sci. Iowa State U., 1966—. Contbr. in field. Active PTA, Ames, Iowa, 1967-78; active Mid-Iowa council Boy Scouts Am., 1966—. Served to 1st lt. USAF, 1957-62. Calcium Carbonate travel fellow, 1976; recipient Boy Scouts Am. Dist. award of merit, 1974, Silver Beaver award, 1980. Mem. Am. Inst. Nutrition, Am. Soc. Animal Sci. Current Work: Energy metabolism of pigs; vitamin E and selenium metabolism of pigs, nutrition, swine, energy, vitamins and minerals. Subspecialty: Animal nutrition.

EWING, BENJAMIN BAUGH, engineering educator; b. Donna, Tex., Apr. 4, 1924; s. Joshua Fulkerson and Bula Betty (Baugh) E.; m. Elizabeth Malone, Apr. 3, 1947; children: Melissa, Douglas Malone, Frederick Joshua. B.S., U. Tex., Austin, 1944, M.S., 1949; Ph.D., U. Calif. at Berkeley, 1959. Diplomate: Am. Acad. Environ. Engrs. Instr., asst. prof. U. Tex., Austin, 1947-55; asso. in civil engring., asst. research engr. U. Calif. at Berkeley, 1955-58; asso. prof., prof. U. Ill., Urbana, 1958-85, prof. emeritus, 1985—, dir. Water Resource Ctr., 1966-73, dir. Inst. for Environ. Studies, 1972-85, dir. emeritus, 1985—; cons. engr., 1959—. Trustee Urbana and Champaign San. Dist., 1974-80; public mem. Ill. Water Resources Commn., 1975-84. Served to lt. (j.g.) CEC. USNR, 1943-46. Recipient Epstein award dept. civil engring. U. Ill., 1961, Harrison Prescott Eddy award for noteworthy research, 1968. Fellow ASCE; mem. Am. Water Works Assn. (life), Am. Geophys. Union, Water Pollution Control Fedn., AAAS, Assn. Environ. Engring. Profs. Club: Rotarian. Current Work: Water quality management and pollution control, water treatment, wastewater treatment, water resources management. Subspecialties: Water supply and wastewater treatment; Civil engineering. Home: 2212 Cottage Grove Urbana IL 61801 Office: 408 S Goodwin St Urbana IL 61801

EWING, JUNE SWIFT, scientific program administrator, electron microscopist; b. Fayetteville, Ark., July 19, 1938; d. Albert Duane and Anice Gertrude (Carlisle) Swift; m. George Edward Ewing, Feb. 18, 1961; 1 dau., Alice Adair; m. Thomas Delaney Wilkerson, Jan. 1, 1978. Student, Cornell Coll., Mt. Vernon, Iowa, 1955-57; B.S. cum laude in Chemistry, U. Wis., 1959; M.S. in Phys. Chemistry, U. Calif.-Berkeley, 1961; M.P.A., U. Colo., 1976. Staff cons. CHEM study project Harvey Mudd Coll., Claremont, Calif., 1961-63; electron microscopist, dept. chemistry Ind. U., Bloomington, 1963-66; instr. dept. chemistry Rutgers U., New Brunswick, N.J., 1969-70; lab. mgr. dept. molecular, cellular and devel. biology U. Colo., Boulder, 1971-74; program mgr. Univs. Space Research Assn., Houston, 1975-77; cons. Sci. Applications, Inc., McLean, Va., 1977-79; staff officer, biomed. programs Nat. Acad. Scis., Washington, 1979—; v.p. Environ. Sci. Communications, Inc.; sec. Applied Sci. Tech., Inc. Author: (with M. A. Bonneville) Laboratory Exercises, 1973. Pres. Unitarian Ch., Boulder, 1974-76; bd. dirs. End World Hunger Benefit Com., Washington, 1981—. Mem. AAAS. Current Work: Electron microscopy of brain tissue; administration of biomedical studies; funding of neuroscience research programs; funding of international scientific travel, planning and funding of international scientific meetings. Subspecialties: Neurophysiology; Electron microscopy. Office: Nat Acad Scis 2101 Constitution Ave NW Washington DC 20416

EWING, MARTIN SIPPLE, radio astronomer, research engineer; b. Albany, N.Y., May 4, 1945; s. Galen W. and Alice C. (Sipple) E.; m. Eva R., June 11, 1966; children: Margaret, Robert, Eric. B.A., Swarthmore Coll., 1966; Ph.D., M.I.T., 1971. Research fellow Calif. Inst. Tech., Pasadena, 1971-73, mem. profl. staff, 1973—. Contbr. articles to profl. jours. Mem. Internat. Union Radio Sci., Internat. Astron. Union, Am. Astron. Soc., IEEE. Current Work: Researcher in digital systems for radio astronomy, instrumentation design and data analysis facility mgmt. Subspecialties: Radio and microwave astronomy; Computer engineering. Office: Calif Inst Tech MS 105-24 Pasadena CA 91125

EYERLY, ROBERT MICHAEL, mechanical engineer; b. Danville, Pa., Oct. 1, 1953; s. Robert Charles and June (Spalding) E.; m. Joyce Ann Kruer, Oct. 6, 1979. B.S., Lehigh U., 1975, M.S., Stanford U., 1977; M.B.A., Coll. St. Thomas, 1984. Devel. engr. Zimmer USA, Warsaw, Ind., 1977-79, sr. devel. engr., 1979-80; sr. devel. engr. orthopedic products 3M, St. Paul, 1980-83, product research specialist, 1983, tech. supr., 1983—. Mem. ASTM, ASME. Lutheran. Subspecialties: Biomedical engineering; Artificial organs and prostheses. Home: 3540 Rolling View Dr White Bear Lake MN 55110 Office: 3M Orthopedic Products Div Bldg 270 4N 09 3M Center Saint Paul MN 55144

EYLER, JOHN ROBERT, chemist, educator; b. Wilmington, Del., May 29, 1945; s. Robert Wilson and Doris Leota (Robinson) E.; m. Fonda Page Davis, June 24, 1967; children: Lisa Todd, Jason Nathaniel. B.S. in Chemistry with honors, Calif. Inst. Tech., 1967; Ph.D. in Chem. Physics, Stanford U., 1972. NRC-Nat. Bur. Standards postdoctoral assoc. Nat. Bur. Standards, Gaithersburg, Md., 1972-74; asst. prof. U. Fla., 1974-79, assoc. prof., 1979—. Contbr. articles to profl. jours. Recipient award of Merit Chem. and Engring. News, 1967, Tchr.-Scholar award Camille and Henry Dreyfus Found., 1978. Mem. Am. Chem. Soc., Inter Am. Photochem. Soc., Am. Soc. Mass Spectrometry. Current Work: Ion-molecule reactions; laser irradiation of ions, surfaces, and neutrals near surfaces; development of Fourier transform mass spectrometry. Subspecialties: Physical chemistry; Laser-induced chemistry. Office: Dept Chemistry U Fla Gainesville FL 32611

FABER, DONALD STUART, physiologist, educator; b. Buffalo, Mar. 3, 1943; s. Gilbert and Mildred (Brothman) F.; m. Jo W. Welch, Dec. 26, 1964; children: Eve S., Amy E. S.B., MIT, 1964; Ph.D., SUNY-Buffalo, 1968. Grad. asst. dept. physiology SUNY-Buffalo, 1964-68, postdoctoral research fellow in neurobiology, 1968-70, research assoc. prof. dept. physiology, 1975-78, assoc. prof., 1978-81, prof., 1981—, dir. div. neurobiology, 1978—; vis. research assoc. neurobiology div. Max Planck Inst. for Brain Research, Frankfurt, W.Ger., 1970-72; vis. research assoc. Lab. Physiology, U. Paris, 1972, 73, 76, 79, 81, 82, Pasteur Inst., 1983, 84; asst. prof. physiology U. Cin., 1972-74. Mem. editorial bd.: Neurosci; contbr. articles to sci. jours. Grass Found. fellow Marine Biol. Lab., Woods Hole, Mass., summer 1969. Mem. AAAS, Soc. for Neurosci., Am. Physiol. Soc., Internat. Brain Research Orgn., Assn. Neurosci. Depts. and Program. Current Work: Excitability and synaptic interactions in the vertebrate CNS. Subspecialties: Neurobiology; Neurophysiology. Office: SUNY Div Neurobiology 313 Cary Hall Buffalo NY 14214

FABIAN, CAROL J., oncologist; b. Kansas City, Kans., May 28, 1946; d. Bill Eugene and Margaret (Wright) Fabian; m. Stephen Roweton, Mar., 1980; 1 child, Jennifer Lyn. Student Grinnell Coll., 1964-66; B.A., U. Kans.-Kansas City, 1968, M.D., 1972. Intern, resident in internal medicine U. Kans., Wichita, 1972-75; fellow in oncology U. Kans., Kansas City, 1975-77, asst. prof. medicine/oncology, 1977-81, assoc. prof., 1981—. Contbr. articles to profl. jours. Nat. Cancer Inst. grantee, 1978. Mem. Southwest Oncology Group, Am. Assn. Cancer Research, Am. Soc. Clin. Oncology, Central Soc. Clin. Research. Republican. Current work: Pharmacology-hormonal treatment of breast cancer, monoclonal antibody treatment; lymphoma, Hodgkins disease, colon cancer. Subspecialties: Oncology; Cancer research (medicine). Home: 12701 E 63d St Kansas City MO 64133 Office: Div Clin Oncology U Kans Med Ctr 39th and Rainbow Blvd Kansas City KS 66103

FABIATO, ALEXANDRE, biophysicist, physiologist, educator; b. Paris, Nov. 7, 1937; came to U.S., 1970; s. Nicolas and Edith (Laisne) F.; m. Francoise Loulergue, Apr. 6, 1968; children: Nicolas, Francois, Denys, Helene. B.S. in Math, Lycee Saint-Louis, 1954; M.D., Université de Paris, 1969, Ph.D., 1970. Chef de Clinique Faculte de Medecine de Paris, 1969-71; instr. Harvard Med. Sch., Boston, 1971-72, asst. prof., 1972-75; prof. Med. Coll. Va., Richmond, Va., 1975—. Mem. editorial bd.: Circulation Research. Recipient Va. Commonwealth U. 1st Disting. Prof. award for research, 1982. Fellow AAAS; mem. Am. Physiol. Soc., Biophys. Soc., Soc. Gen Physiologists Assn. des Physiologistes de Langue Francaise. Roman Catholic. Current Work: Subcellular biophysics of cardiac muscle cells; skinned cardiac cells, sarcoplasmic reticulum, microscopy, micromanipulations, application of microcomputers and microprocessors to physiology. Subspecialties: Physiology (biology); Biophysics (biology). Home: 1404 Westridge Rd Richmond VA 23229 Office: Medical Coll V Dept Physiology Box 55 Richmond VA 23298

FABISH, THOMAS JOHN, physical chemist; b. Youngstown, Ohio, Feb. 27, 1938. B.A. in Aero. Engring., Ohio State U., 1960, M.S., 1966; Ph.D. in Material Sci., U. Rochester, 1975. Research engr. aero dynamics N.Am. Aviation, Ohio, 1961-63; research engr. thermal properties of material Battelle Meml. Inst., 1966-69; scientist, solid state physics Xerox Corp., 1969-80; sr. research chemist Ashland Chem. Co., 1980-83; prin. materials scientist Am. Cyanamid Co., 1983-85; tech. specialist Alcoa Tech. Ctr., 1985—. Mem. Am. Chem. Soc., Adhesion Soc., Am. Phys. Soc. Current work: Insulator physics, with emphasis on the electronics and surface properties of polymers; chemistry and physics of carbon fiber reinforced composites; absorption in microporous and chemically active materials. Subspecialties: Surface chemistry; Composite materials. Office: Alcoa Tech Ctr Alcoa Center PA 15069

FABRICANT, JILL DIANE, geneticist, biological research company executive; b. Los Angeles, Sept. 29, 1949; d. I. Robert and Lillian (Solid) Fabricant. B.A., Mills Coll., 1970; M.A., Occidental Coll., 1971; Ph.D., McGill U., Montreal, Can., 1976. Vis. scientist NIH, Bethesda, Md., 1974-76; postdoctoral fellow Pasteur Inst., Paris, 1976-78; pres. Biosyne Corp., Houston, 1983—; cons. Rockwell Internat., Los Angeles, 1982-83, NASA, 1981-83; mem. study sect. Nat. Inst. Occupational Safety and Health, NIH, 1981-83. Editor: Fabricant Report Life Science Experiments for Space Station, 1983. Rockefeller Found. scholar, 1982; INSERM fellow Govt. of France, 1976. Mem. Environ. Mutagen Soc., Am. Cell Biology, Embryo Transfer Soc., AIAA, Sigma Xi. Clubs: Sierra (Galveston, Tex.); Encore (Houston). Current work: Research and application of genetics and reproductive biology to farm animals. Subspecialties: Reproductive biology; Genetics and genetic engineering (agriculture). Home: 18210 Bal Harbor Dr Houston TX 77058Office: Biosyne Corp 2210 Maroneal Suite 302 Houston TX 77030

FABRIKANT, VALERY ISAAC, mechanics and applied mathematics researcher, consultant; b. Minsk, USSR, Jan. 28, 1940; emigrated to Can., 1979, naturalized, 1983; s. Isaac Haim and Pesya Yudel (Turetskaya) F.; m. Maya Tyker, Dec. 23, 1981; children—Isaac, Beata. B.Sc., Power Inst., Ivanovo, USSR, 1962; Ph.D., Power Inst., Moscow, 1966. Asst. prof. Aviation Technol. Inst., Rybinsk, USSR, 1967-69; prof. engring. mechanics Poly. Inst., Ulyanovsk, USSR, 1970-73; sr. researcher Automation and Control Research Inst., Ivanovo, 1973-78; research asst. Concordia U., Montreal, Que., Can., 1979-80, research assoc., 1980-82, research prof., 1982—; cons. Paper Inst., Montreal, 1981—. Contbr. articles to profl. jours. Ministry Edn. USSR spl. scholar, 1958-62. Mem. Internat. Union Theoretical and Applied Mechanics, Soc. Engring. Sci., Soc. Indsl. and Applied Math. Current Work: Elasticity theory, integral equations, potential theory, numerical methods, contact problems. Subspecialties: Solid mechanics; Applied mathematics. Home: 2170 Lincoln Ave Apt 505 Montreal PQ H3H 2N5 Canada Office: Concordia U 1455 De Maissonneuve W Montreal PQ H3G 1M8 Canada

FABRO, SERGIO EDIGIO, physician, educator, consultant, researcher; b. Trieste, Italy, Sept. 3, 1932; came to U.S., 1967, naturalized, 1979; m. Susan Sieber, July 31, 1971. M.D. summa cum laude, U. Milan, 1956; Ph.D. in Biol. Chemistry, U. Rome, 1966, Ph.D. in Pharmacology, 1968; Ph.D. in Biochemistry, U. London, 1967. Diplomate: Am. Bd. Ob-Gyn, Sub-Bd. Maternal-Fetal Medicine. Rotating intern U. Milan, 1956-57; instr. dept. internal medicine Milan U. Hosp., 1956-58; asst. prof. dept. gen. pathology U. Modena, Italy, 1958-59, asst. prof. dept. biochemistry, 1960-62; research asst. dept. biochemistry U. London, St. Mary's Hosp., 1963-67; Brit. Council fellow in biochemistry St. Mary's Hosp. Med. Sch., 1964-66; assoc. research prof. dept. pharmacology George Washington U., Washington, 1967-71, research prof. dept. pharmacology, resident in ob-gyn, 1971-74, 1971-81, prof. dept. ob-gyn, 1974-78, prof. dept. pharmacology and ob-gyn, 1981—; dir. maternal-fetal medicine div. George Washington U. Hosp., 1978-81; med. dir. ambulatory care center, dir. maternal-fetal medicine div. Columbia Hosp. for Women, Washington, 1981—; dir. Columbia Hosp. for Women (Reproductive Toxicology Ctr.), 1981—; cons. Nat. Cancer Inst., 1966-70, Nat. Found., 1977, Office Sci. and Tech. Policy, Exec. Office of Pres., 1979-80, Council Environ. Quality, Exec. Office of Pres., 1980-81; cons. Nat. Inst. Environ. Health Scis., 1969-80, 82, sr. cons. investigator devel. and reproductive toxicology br., 1975—; founder, cons. Environ. Teratology Info. Center, 1978—; mem. U.S.A.-USSR Environ. Health Coop. Program, 1977-80; mem. task force project on safety of chems. for human progeny WHO, 1981—; mem. maternal and child health research com. Nat. Inst. Child Health and Human Devel., 1980-82. Mem. editorial bd.: Teratogenesis, Carcinogenesis and Mutagenesis, Pediatric Pharmacology; ad hoc reviewer: Sci, Teratology, Ob-Gyn, Toxicology and Applied Pharmacology, Pharmacology and Exptl. Therapeutics; contbr. numerous articles to sci. jours. Recipient Biochemistry prize Accademia Nazionale dei Lincei, 1965, best tchr. award ob-gyn resident tng. program Georgetown U., 1981, 82. Mem. Am. Coll. Obstetricians and Gynecologists, Soc. Gynecol. Investigation, Perinatal Research Soc., Soc. Perinatal Obstetricians, Med. Soc. D.C., Washington Gynecol. Soc., Am. Soc. Pharmacology and Exptl. Therapeutics, Soc. Toxicology, Teratology Soc., European Teratology Soc., Biochem. Soc. (U.K.), Soc. Occupational and Environ. Health. Subspecialties: Maternal and fetal medicine; Reproductive biology (medicine). Home: 9621 Annlee Terr Bethesda MD 20817 Office: Columbia Hosp for Women 2425 L St NW Washington DC 20037

FACCI, JOHN STEPHEN, research chemist; b. Schenectady, June 8, 1955; s. Rosario and Rosaria (Ingannamorte) F.; m. Joanne Mary Thomer, Aug. 9, 1980; children—Emily Ruth, Sarah Elizabeth. B.S. in Chemistry, Union Coll., 1977; Ph.D., U. N.C.-Chapel Hill, 1982. Sr. research scientist Xerox Webster Research Ctr., N.Y., 1982—. Author articles. Mem. Am. Chem. Soc. (chmn. pub. relations Rochester sect. 1982—), Sigma Xi, Phi Beta Kappa. Current work: Chemically modified electrodes, electron hopping mechanisms in redox polymer films and in solid state redox systems, interfacial electrode reactions especially of adsorbed monolayers, surface analysis. Subspecialties: Electroanalytical chemistry; Surface chemistry. Office: Xerox Corp 0114/39D 800 Phillips Rd Webster NY 14580

FACCINI, ERNEST CARLO, mechanical engineer, consultant; b. Livo, Trento, Italy, May 28, 1949; s. Carlo Emmanuel and Elena Agnes (Pancheri) F.; m. Sharon Louise, July 23. A.A., Western Wyo. Community Coll., 1969; B.S., U. Wyo., 1972, M.S., 1976. Registered profl. engr., Wyo., 1981. Mech. engr. dept. project integration Naval Explosive Ordinance Disposal Tech. Ctr., Indian Head, Md., 1976-79; mech. engr. ops. dept. Laramie Energy Tech. Ctr., Wyo., 1979-80; sr. engr. tech. info. dept. Naval Explosive Ordinance Disposal Tech. Ctr., Indian Head, 1980-85, mech. engr. mech. engring. dept., 1985—. Contbr. articles to profl. jours. Recipient Letter of Commendation USAF, 1978; Outstanding Performance award USN, 1978; Spl. Achievement award, 1981; Letter of Commendation Project Sand Dollar, Naval Explosive Ordinance Disposal Tech. Ctr., 1982. Mem. ASME, AAAS, Am. Soc. Metals, Am. Phys. Soc. Roman Catholic. Patentee, inventor in field. Current Work: Magnetic pickup and mobile demilitarization furnace, explosive effects. Subspecialties: Mechanical engineering; Explosives phenomena. Home: PO Box 426 Marbury MD 20658 Office: Naval Explosive Ordinance Disposal Tech. Center Indian Head MD 20640

FADER, WALTER JOHN, physicist; b. Boston, Jan. 12, 1923; s. James Walter and Mary (McNamara) F.; m. Elizabeth Armstrong; 1 child, Sarah Elizabeth. A.B., Harvard U., 1949; Ph.D., MIT, 1955. Physicist, Pratt & Whitney Aircraft, East Hartford, Conn., 1955-65, United Technologies Research Ctr., East Hartford, 1965—. Served to 1st lt. U.S. Army, 1942-46, ETO. Mem. Am. Phys. Soc., Optical Soc. Am. Current work: Theory of coupled optical resonators and the behavior of phaselocked lasers. Office: United Technologies Research Ctr Silver Ln East Hartford CT 06108

FADNER, WILLARD LEE, physics educator, researcher; b. Racine, Wis., Aug. 10, 1933; s. Glenn R. and Evelyn H. (Larsen) F.; m. Alice J. Lienhard, June 27, 1959; children—Jenette M., Peter W. B.S. in Elec. Engring., Purdue U., 1955; M.S. in Physics, U. Wis.-Madison, 1962; Ph.D. in Physics, U. Colo.-Boulder, 1971. Project engr. A.C. Electronics, Milw., 1958-62; project asst. U. Wis.-Madison, 1963-64; instr. Mankato State U., Minn., 1964-68; research asst., assoc. U. Colo., Boulder, 1968-72; asst. prof., then assoc. prof. U. No. Colo., Greeley, 1972-80, prof. physics, 1980—. Contbr. articles to profl. jours. Served to lt. (j.g.) USN, 1955-58. Mem. Colo./Wyo. Acad. Sci., Am. Phys. Soc. Current work: History and philosophy of the development of physical theories, the generalized correspondence principle, nuclear physics. Subspecialty: Nuclear physics. Office: U No Colo Dept Physics Greeley CO 80639

FADULU, SUNDAY O., microbiology educator; b. Ibadan, Nigeria, Nov. 11, 1940; s. William Cornelius and Ruth (Olumade) F.; m. Jacqueline F. Counter, Oct. 26, 1968; children: Sunday, Tony, Jeannie. B.S., Okla. Bapt. U., 1964; M.S., U. Okla., 1965, Ph.D., 1969. Lectr. U. Ife, Nigeria, 1969-70; research assoc. U. Okla. Med. Ctr., Oklahoma City, 1970-72; prof. microbiology Tex. So. U., Houston, 1972—; adj. prof. U. Houston, 1981—; v.p. Adoxy Corp., Houston, 1982—. Bd. dirs. Nigerian Found., Houston, 1982—, Econ. of African Nations Aid, Inc. Mem. N.Y. Acad Scis., Am. Soc. Microbiology (planning com. Tex. br. 1983—), Beta Beta Beta. Baptist. Patentee in field. Current Work: Microbial pathogenesis; isolation of fungal toxins in immunological, hematological, cardiovascular activities; sickle cell anemia; isolation of natural products as potential antisickling agents. Subspecialties: Infectious diseases; Hematology. Home: 20115 Wickham Ct Katy TX 77450 Office: Tex So U 3200 Wheeler Ave Houston TX 77004

FADUM, RALPH EIGIL, university dean; b. Pitts., July 19, 1912; s. Torgeir Bleken and Mimi (Knudsen) F.; m. Nancy Isabelle Fields, July 19, 1939; 1 dau., Jane Fields. B.S. in Civil Engring. U. Ill., 1935; M.S., Harvard, 1937, S.D., 1941; D.Eng., Purdue U., 1963. Registered profl. engr., N.C. Parttime asst. civil engring. Harvard, 1935-37, instr., 1937-41, faculty instr., 1941- 43; asst. prof. soil mechanics Purdue U., 1943-45, asso. prof., 1945-47, prof., 1947-49; head of civil engring. dept. and prof. of civil engring. N.C. State U., Raleigh, 1949-62, dean of engring., 1962-78; cons. Dept. Def., U.S. Corps Engrs.; Mem. Army Sci. Bd. Dept. Army, 1959-81; mem. research adv. com. Fed. Hwy. Adminstrn., 1963-70; adv. bd. Ford Found., 1963-69; vice chmn. Army Sci. Adv. Panel, Dept. Army, 1966-70; chmn. adv. group to comdr. gen. Tank Automotive Command, 1967-70. Contbr. articles to profl. jours. Chmn. N.C. Water Control Adv. Council; bd. dirs. Nat. Driving Center, 1973-77; commr. Raleigh Housing Authority, 1962-72; pres. Atlantic Coast Conf., 1966-67, 71-72; v.p. Nat. Collegiate Athletic Assn., 1972-76; Chmn. bd. dirs. N.C. Water Resources Research Inst., U. N.C. Recipient Patriotic Civilian Service award Dept. Army, 1967, Meritorious Civilian Service medal, 1967, Outstanding Civilian Service medal, 1973, 77; Distinguished Civil Engring. Alumnus award U. Ill., 1969. Mem. ASCE (hon. mem., Outstanding Civil Engr. N.C. award 1971); mem. Nat. Acad. Engring., U.S. Nat. Council Soil Mechanics and Found. Engring., Nat. Soc. Profl. Engrs., N.C. Soc. Engrs. (Outstanding Engring. Achievement award 1971), Raleigh Engrs. Club (Outstanding Engr. award), Am. Soc. Engring. Edn. (hon. mem.; v.p., mem. exec. com. 1973-74, dir.), Sigma Xi, Tau Beta Pi, Chi Epsilon (nat. honor mem.), Phi Kappa Phi, Delta Upsilon. Clubs: Rotary (Raleigh); Carolina Country. Current Work: Geotechnical Engineering. Subspecialty: Civil engineering. Address: 408 Mann Hall NC State U Raleigh NC 27695

FAEHL, LARRY GENE, chemist, agricultural pesticide formulator; b. Alamogordo, N.Mex., Mar. 10, 1950; s. James Warren and Josephine Wanda (Szostek) F.; m. Pamela Ellen Vanderhide, Jan. 6, 1973; 1 son, Nicholas Warren. B.A., Miami U., Oxford, Ohio, 1972; Ph.D., N. Tex. State U., 1977. Postdoctoral fellow NSF, Lubbock, Tex., 1977-78, R.A. Welch Found., Lubbock, Tex., 1978-79; research chemist FMC Corp., Princeton, N.J., 1979—. Contbr. articles to tech. jours. Mem. Am. Chem. Soc., Alpha Chi Sigma, Alpha Phi Omega. Current work: Currently formulating in-use and experimental compounds for agriculture productivity enchancement. Subspecialties: Nuclear magnetic resonance; Agricultural chemistry. Home: 16 Rocky Brook Rd Cranbury NJ 08512 Office: FMC Corp PO Box 8 Princeton NJ 08512

FAETH, GERARD MICHAEL, aerospace engineering educator; b. N.Y.C., July 5, 1936; s. Joseph and Helen (Wagner) F.; m. Mary Ann Kordich, Dec. 27, 1959; children—Christine Louise, Lorraine Vera, Elinor Jean. B.M.E., Union Coll., 1958; M.S., Pa. State U., 1961, Ph.D., 1964. Instr. Pa. State U., University Park, 1958-59, research asst., 1959-64, asst. prof., 1964-68, assoc. prof., 1968-74, prof. mech. engring., 1974-85, prof. emeritus, 1985—; Arthur B. Modine prof. aerospace engring. U. Mich., Ann Arbor, 1985—, head Gas Dynamics Labs., 1985—. vis. prof. Air Force Office Sci. Research, Washington, 1983-84; cons. Gen. Motors Research Lab., Warren, Mich., 1977—, Applied Research Lab., Pa. State U., University Park, 1964—. Mem. editorial bd. Combustion Sci. and Tech., 1970—; contbr. numerous articles to profl. jours. Precinct chmn. Republican. Party, Centre County, 1977-84; bd. dirs. Eagles Mere Lake Assn., 1982—, Eagles Mere Park Assn., 1978—. Frank Baily scholar Union Coll., 1954-58; research awardee Pa. State U., 1979. Fellow ASME (tech. edn. com. 1981-85, sr. tech. editor 1985—, research award 1983, best paper award 1984), AIAA (assoc.; best paper award 1984); mem. Combustion Inst. (deputy edn. 1984—), Soc. Automotive Engrs., AAAS. Sigma Xi, Phi Kappa Phi, Pi Tau Sigma. Episcopalian. Current work: Fluid dynamics, heat and mass transfer and combustion. Subspecialties: Aerospace engineering and technology; Mechanical engineering. Home: 2665 Overridge Ann Arbor MI 48104 Office: Aerospace Engring Bldg U Mich Ann Arbor MI 48109

FAHIM, MOSTAFA SAFWAT, reproductive biologist, consultant; b. Cairo, Egypt., Oct. 7, 1931; came to U.S., 1966; s. Mohamed and Amna (Hussin) F.; m. Zuhal Fahim, Feb. 23, 1959; 1 child, Ayshe. B.S. in Agrl. Chemistry, U. Cairo, 1953; M.S., U. Mo., 1958, Ph.D., 1961. Research assoc. U. Mo. Health Scis. Center, Columbia, 1966-68, asst. prof., 1968-71, assoc. prof., 1971-75; prof. U. Mo. Health Scis. Center (Environ. Trace Substances Research Center), 1981—, prof., chief reproductive biology, 1975—; cons. in field. Contbr. articles to profl. jours. Mem. Am. Public Health Assn., Mo. Public Health Assn., Nutrition Today Soc., Internat. Andrology Soc., Internat. Toxicology Soc., Am. Coll. Clin. Pharmacology, Am. Soc. Pharmacology and Exptl. Therapeutics, Internat. Fertility Soc., Am. Fertility Soc., Fedn. Am. Socs. Exptl. Biology, N.Y. Acad. Scis., Soc. Environ. Geochemistry and Health, Soc. Study Reprodn., AAAS, Sigma Xi, Gamma Alpha. Patentee in field. Current Work: Contraception, electronics and reproduction, chemical sterilization. Subspecialties: Reproductive biology (medicine); Reproductive biology. Office: Dept Obstetrics and Gynecology U Mo Health Scis Center Columbia MO 65212

FAHN, STANLEY, neurologist; b. Sacramento, Nov. 6, 1933; s. Ernest and Sylvia (Schumer) F.; m. Charlotte Zmora, June 21, 1958; children: Paul N., James D. B.A., U. Calif.-, Berkeley, 1955; M.D., U. Calif.-, San Francisco, 1958. Diplomate: Am. Bd. Neurology. Resident in neurology Neurol. Inst. N.Y., 1959-62; research asso. NIH, 1962-65; faculty Columbia, 1965-68, prof., 1973-78, H. Houston Merritt prof., 1978—; dir. (Dystonia Research Center), 1981—; faculty U. Pa., 1968-73. Served with USPHS, 1962-65. NIH grantee, 1974-77, 80-82. Current Work: Clin. and basic sci. movement disorders, including pharmacology of neurotransmitters. Subspecialties: Neurology; Neuropharmacology. Home: 155 Edgars Ln Hastings NY 10706 Office: 710 W 168th St New York NY 10032

FAI, GEORGE, physics educator, researcher; b. Budapest, Hungary, May 13, 1949; came to U.S., 1984; s. Sandor and Zsuzsanna (Koppanyi) F.; m. Judith Poor, July 27, 1979; 1 child, Suzanne. Eotvos U., Hungary, Ph.D., 1974. Research assoc. Eotvos U., Budapest, Hungary, 1972-83; asst. prof. Kent State U., Ohio, 1984—; vis. scientist Niels Bohr Inst., Copenhagen, Denmark, 1977-78; staff scientist II, Lawrence Berkeley Lab., Calif., 1980-82. Contbr. articles to profl. jours. Hungarian Acad. Sci. fellow 1977. Mem. Am. Phys. Soc., Hungarian Phys. Soc. (Novobatzky award 1983). Current work: Theory of nuclear collisions (statistical models and reaction mechanisms; exclusive observables, exotic forms of hadronic matter). Subspecialties: Nuclear physics; Theoretical physics. Home: 2016 Hastings Dr Kent OH 44240 Office: Kent State U Physics Dept Kent OH 44242

FAILLA, PATRICIA MCCLEMENT, biomedical and environmental research administrator; b. N.Y.C., Dec. 22, 1925; d. Morgan Hall and Louise (Yandell) McClement; m. Gioacchino Failla, Jan. 22, 1949 (dec. 1961). A.B. cum laude, Barnard Coll., 1946; Ph.D., Columbia U., 1958; M.B.A., U. Chgo., 1976. Asst. physicist N.Y.C. Dept. Hosps., N.Y.C., 1946-48; research scientist Columbia U., N.Y.C., 1950-60; biophysicist Argonne Nat. Lab., Ill., 1960-71, asst. div. dir. to asst. lab. dir., 1971-80, program coordinator, 1980—. Contbr. articles to profl. jours. AEC fellow, 1948-50. Mem. Radiation Research Soc., AAAS, Health Physics Soc. Current work: Biological and environmental effects of radiation and other environmental pollutants. Subspecialties: Radiation biology; Environmental toxicology. Office: Argonne Nat Lab 9700 S Cass Ave Argonne IL 60439

FAIN, JOHN NICHOLAS, biochemist; b. Jefferson City, Tenn., Aug. 18, 1934; s. Samuel Clark and Virginia Manson (Hunt) F.; m. Ann Duff, June 7, 1958; children—Margaret, John N., James. B.S., Carson-Newman Coll., 1956; Ph.D. in Biochemistry, Emory U., 1960. Research assoc. and fellow NIH, 1961-65; asst. prof. Brown U., 1965-68, assoc. prof., 1968-71, prof., 1971-85, chmn. dept. biochemistry, 1975-85; chmn. prof. dept. biochemistry U. Tenn. Ctr. Health Scis., 1985—. Contbr. numerous articles to med., profl. jours., chpts. to books. Macy Faculty scholar Macy Found., Cambridge U., 1977-78, vis. fellow Clare Hall, 1977-78; sr. internat. fellow Fogarty Inst., NIH, U. Nottingham, Eng., 1984-85, vis. prof., 1984-85. Mem. Biochem. Soc., Am. Soc. Biol. Chemists, N.Y. Acad. Scis. Democrat. Presbyterian. Current work: Mode of hormone action, phospholipid turnover and receptor activation, cellular biochemistry. Subspecialties: Biochemistry (biology); Receptors. Office: Dept Biochemistry U Tenn Ctr Health Scis 800 Madison Ave Memphis TN 38163

FAINGOLD, CARL LAWRENCE, pharmacologist, educator, researcher; b. Chgo., Feb. 1, 1943; s. Charles and Ann (Glassman) F.; m. Carol Ann Baskin, June 21, 1964; children: Scott, Charles, Robert. B.S. in Pharmacy, U. Ill., Chgo., 1965; Ph.D. in Pharmacology, Northwestern U., 1970. Postdoctoral fellow Inst. Psychiatry, U. Mo., St. Louis, 1970-72; asst. prof. pharmacology Sch. Medicine, So. Ill. U., Springfield, 1972-76, asso. prof., 1976—, acting chmn. dept., 1981-83; vis. scientist Inst. Psychiatry, London, 1984. Contbr. articles to profl. jours. Nat. Inst. Neurol and Communicative Disorders grantee, 1979—. Mem. Am. Soc. Pharmacology and Exptl. Therapeutics, Soc. for Neurosci., AAAS, Am. Epilepsy Soc., N.Y. Acad. Sci., Sigma Xi. Current Work: Neurophysiology and neuropharmacology of epilepsy, hearing and neuronal correlates of behavior. Subspecialties: Neuropharmacology; Neurophysiology. Home: 60 Danbury Dr Springfield IL 62704 Office: PO Box 3926 Springfield IL 62708

FAIR, JAMES RUTHERFORD, JR., chemical engineering educator, consultant; b. Charleston, Mo., Oct. 14, 1920; s. James Rutherford and Georgia Irene (Case) F.; m. Merle Innis, Jan. 14, 1950; children: James Rutherford III, Elizabeth, Richard Innis. Student, The Citadel, 1938-40; B.S., Ga. Inst. Tech., 1942; M.S., U. Mich., 1949; Ph.D., U. Tex., 1955; D.Sc. (hon.), Wash. U., 1977. Research engr. Shell Devel. Co., Emeryville, Calif., 1954-56; with Monsanto Co., 1942-52, 56-79; engring. dir. corp. engring. dept. Monsanto Co. (World hdqrs.), St. Louis, 1969-79; Cockrell prof. chem. engring. U. Tex., Austin, 1979—; dir., v.p. Fractionation Research, Inc., Bartlesville, Okla., 1969-79. Author: North Arkansas Line, 1969, Distillation, 1971; Contbr. numerous articles to profl. publs. Bd. dirs. Nat. Mus. Transport. Recipient profl. achievement award Chemical Engineering mag., 1968. Fellow Am. Inst. Chem. Engrs. (bd. dirs. 1965-67, Walker award 1973, Practice award 1975, Founders award 1977, Inst. lectr. 1979); mem. Am. Chem. Soc., Nat. Acad. Engring., Am. Soc. Engring. Edn., Nat. Soc. Profl. Engrs., Sigma Nu. Republican. Presbyterian (elder). Clubs: Faculty (U. Tex.); Headliners (Austin). Current Work: Head separations research program at University of Texas. Subspecialty: Chemical engineering. Office: Dept Chem Engring U Tex Austin TX 78712

FAIR, RICHARD BARTON, researcher, educator; b. Los Angeles, Sept. 12, 1942; s. Paul Albertus and Emabel (McCollom) F.; m. Mary Clare Wilkinson, Sept. 12, 1964; children—Cynthia, Catherine, Peter, Denise. B.S.E.E., Duke U., 1964, Ph.D., 1969; M.S.E.E., Pa. State U., 1966. Cert. profl. engr. Mem. tech. staff Bell Labs., Reading, Pa., 1969-73, supr., 1973-81; prof. elec. engring. Duke U., Durham, N.C., 1981—; v.p. Microelectronics Ctr. of N.C., Research Triangle Park, N.C., 1981—; cons. Gen. Electric, Research Triangle Park, 1983—, Digital Equipment Corp., Hudson, Mass., 1983—, Intel Corp., Santa Clare, Calif., 1985—, MOSTEK Corp., Carrollton, Tex., 1985—; chmn. Microelectronics Adv. Com., Durham Tech. Inst., 1983—; mem. indsl. Adv. Com. Dept. Materials Engring., N.C. State U., Raleigh, 1982—. Author: Impurity Doping Processes in Semiconductors, 1980. Editor: Diffusion and Gettering Processes in Semiconductors, 1985. Loaned exec. United Way, Reading, Pa., 1973-75; bd. dirs. Women in Crisis, Reading, 1980-81. Recipient Outstanding Young Men of Am. award Eta Kappa Nu, 1973, Outstanding Young Elec. Engr. award, 1974. Mem. IEEE (sr. mem.), Electrochem. Soc. (exec. com. 1985), AIME (electronics materials com.), Materials Research Soc., Sigma Xi, Eta Kappa Nu. Democrat Episcopalian. Current work: Diffusion in silicon, process modeling, semiconductor devices and technology, and design research and technology. Subspecialties: Microchip technology (engineering); Semiconductors. Home: 3414 Cambridge Rd Durham NC 27707 Office: Microelectronics Ctr of NC PO Box 12889 Research Triangle Park NC 27709

FAIRBAIRN, DAPHNE JANICE, biology educator; b. Ottawa, Ont., Can., Jan. 28, 1949; d. Gordon and Mary (Rioux) F.; m. Derek Anthony Roff, Feb. 15, 1977; children—Graham, Robin. B.Sc. with honors, Carleton U., Ottawa, 1971; Ph.D. in Zoology, U. B.C., Vancouver, 1976. Postdoctoral fellow U. B.C., 1976-77; asst. prof. U. Alta., Edmonton, 1977-78, Concordia U., Montreal, Can., 1982—; research scientist Dept. Fisheries and Oceans, St. Johns, Nfld., 1978-80, sci. editor Can. Jour. Fisheries and Aquatic Scis., Ottawa, 1980-82. Contbr. articles to profl. jours. Nat. Research Council Can. fellow, 1976; grantee Natural Scis. and Engring. Research Council, 1983, 84-86; recipient V.A. Ewing Meml. prize in biology, 1970. Mem. Soc. for Study of Evolution, Ecol. Soc. Am., Entomol. Soc. Can. Current work: Study of gene flow, dispersal, population structure and demic adaption in populations of a semi-aquatic bug; define genetic structure and potential for demic divergence of natural populations. Subspecialties: Population biology; Ecology (biology). Office: Dept Biology Concordia U 1455 de Maisonneuve Blvd Montreal PQ H3G 1M8 Canada

FAIRBANK, WILLIAM MARTIN, JR., physicist; b. New Haven, Jan. 7, 1946; s. William Martin and Jane (Davenport) F.; m. Donna Lorraine Witter, Aug. 30, 1975; children: William Henry, Mary Helen. B. A., Pomona Coll., Claremont, Calif., 1968; M.S., Stanford U., 1969, Ph.D., 1974. Research assoc. U. Ariz., 1974-75; asst. prof. physics Colo. State U., 1975-78, assoc. prof., 1978-83, prof., 1983—; cons. in field. Contbr. articles in field to profl. jours. Alfred P. Sloan fellow, 1976-78; NSF fellow, 1968-71. Mem. Am. Phys. Soc., Optical Soc. Am., Sigma XI. Current Work: Frontier research in applications of dye laser spectroscopy and single atom detection, particularly to elementary particle physics. Subspecialties: Laser spectroscopy; Atomic and molecular physics. Home: 1712 Clearview Ct Fort Collins CO 80521 Office: Atom Science PO Box 138 Oak Ridge TN 37830

FAIRBANKS, GRANT, cell biologist, researcher; b. Iowa City, May 17, 1940; s. Grant and Helen (Cornelius) F.; m. Ellen Wolz Kelly, Dec. 30, 1962; children—Katherine, Martha. B.A. with honors in Physics, Grinnell Coll., 1961; Ph.D., MIT, 1969. Research fellow biochem. research Mass. Gen. Hosp., dept. biol. chemistry Harvard Med. Sch., Boston, 1969-70; research assoc. Worcester Found. for Exptl. Biology, Shrewsbury, Mass., 1970-71, staff scientist, 1971-77, sr. scientist, 1977—; contbr. articles to profl. jours. Grantee, fellow NIH, NSF, 1961—; recipient Alumni award Grinnell Coll., 1974; Cancer Research Scholar award Mass. div. Am. Cancer Soc., 1973-76. Mem. Am. Soc. Cell Biology, Am. Soc. Biol. Chemists, Sigma Xi, Phi Beta Kappa. Unitarian. Current work: Plasma membrane structure and function, erythrocyte and spermatozoa; membrane pathophysiology in hemolytic anemia. Subspecialty: Hematology. Office: Cell Biology Group Worcester Found for Exptl Biology Shrewsbury MA 01545

FAIRBANKS, H. LEE, biology educator; b. Grand Rapids, Mich., Jan. 25, 1940; s. Harold Lee and Anne (Blouw) F.; m. Eleanor Stetson, Aug. 7, 1976; children—Matthew Stetson, Jeremy Hamlin. B.A., U. Mont., 1972, M.A., 1975; Ph.D., U. Ariz., 1979. Grad. teaching asst. U. Mont., Missoula, 1973-74, U. Ariz., Tucson, 1975-78; research assoc. U. Ariz., 1978-79; asst. prof. zoology Pa. State U., Monaca, 1979—. Contbr. articles to profl. jours. Served with USAF, 1957-61. Pa. State U. grantee, 1981—. Mem. AAAS, Soc. for Study of Evolution, Biol. Soc. Wash., Am. Malacological Union, Sigma Xi. Current work: Study of comparative morpholoy of the species of Philomycidae a group of native slugs; goals center on taxonomy and systematics of the group. Subspecialties: Taxonomy; Systematics. Office: Pa State U Beaver Campus Brodhead Rd Monaca PA 15061

FAIRCHILD, RALPH GRANDISON, radiol. physicist; b. Trenton, N.J., Sept. 24, 1935; s. Ralph Grandison and Sara Gertrude (Edgerton) F.; m. Frances Woods, June 14, 1958; children: David, James, Stefanie, Jovi. B.S., St. Lawrence U., Canton, N.Y., 1958; M.S., Cornell U., 1961; Ph.D., Adelphi U., 1976. Physicist Lawrence Radiation Lab., Livermore, Calif., 1959, Savannah River Lab., Aiken, S.C., 1960; radiol. physicist Brookhaven Nat. Lab., Upton, N.Y., 1961—; asso. prof. SUNY, Stony Brook, 1980—; radiol. physicist VA Hosp., Northport, N.Y., 1975—. Contbr. articles to profl. jours. NIH grantee. Mem. Am. Assn. Physicists in Medicine, Soc. Nuclear Medicine, Radiation Research Soc., Sigma Xi. Quaker. Current Work: Radiological physics; development of particle beams for radiotherapy; mixed field dosimetry; neutron capture therapy. Subspecialties: Cancer research (medicine); Biophysics (physics). Home: 6 Huckleberry Ln Setauket NY 11733 Office: Med Dept Brookhaven Nat Lab Upton NY 11973

FAIRHURST, CHARLES, civil engineering educator; b. Widnes, Lancashire, Eng., Aug. 5, 1929; came to U.S., 1956, naturalized, 1967; s. Richard Lowe and Josephine (Starkey) F.; m. Margaret Ann Lloyd, Sept. 7, 1957; children: Anne Elizabeth, David Lloyd, Charles Edward, Catherine Mary, Hugh Richard, John Peter, Margaret Mary. B.Eng., U. Sheffield, Eng., 1952, Ph.D., 1955. Mining engr. trainee Nat. Coal Bd., St. Helens, Eng., 1949-56; research assoc. U. Minn., Mpls., 1956-67, prof., 1967-70, head Sch. Mineral and Metall. Engring., 1967-70, prof. dept. civil and mineral engring., 1970—, head dept., 1972—, E.P. Pfleider prof. mining engring. and rock mechanics, 1983; cons. U.S. Army C.E., Petrobras, Brazil, Itasca Cons. Group, Potasse d'Alsace, Spie Battingnolle, W.P. Cave, Sweden; Chmn. U.S. nat. commn. rock mechanics Nat. Acad. Scis., 1971-74. Mem. AIME, S. African Inst. Mining and Metallurgy, ASCE (chmn. rock mechanics com. 1978-80), Internat. Soc. Rock Mechanics (past dir.), Am. Underground Space Assn. (pres. 1976-77), Royal Swedish Acad. Engring. Scis. (fgn.), Sigma Xi. Roman Catholic. Current Work: Mining engineering; rock mechanics; underground space and construction. Subspecialties: Mining engineering; Civil engineering. Home: 417 5th Ave N South Saint Paul MN 55075 Office: Dept Civil and Mineral Engring U Minn Minneapolis MN 55455

FAJANS, STEFAN STANISLAUS, physician; b. Munich, Ger., Mar. 15, 1918; came to U.S., 1936, naturalized, 1942; s. Kasimir M. and Salomea (Kaplan) F.; m. Ruth Stine, Sept. 6, 1947; children: Peter S., John S. B.S., U. Mich., Ann Arbor, 1938, M.D., 1942. Intern Mount Sinai Hosp., N.Y.C., 1942-43; resident U. Mich., 1947-49, research fellow, 1946-47, 49-51; mem. faculty U. Mich. Med. Sch., 1950—, prof. internal medicine, 1961—, head div. endocrinology and metabolism, also dir. metabolism research unit, 1973—; dir. Mich. Diabetes Research and Tng. Center, 1977—; mem. endocrinology study sect. NIH, 1958-62, mem. diabetes and metabolism tng. grants com., 1966-70; chmn. Am. zone internat. sci. adv. com. Congresses Internat. Diabetes Fedn., 1977-79; Banting meml. lectr., 1978. Contbr. articles med. publns. Served as officer M.C. AUS, 1943-46. Research fellow in medicine A.C.P., 1949-50; fellow Life Ins. Med. Inst., 1950-51. Mem. Inst. Medicine (sr. mem.), Nat. Acad. Scis., Am. Diabetes Assn. (pres. 1971-72, Banting medal 1972, Banting Meml. award 1978), Endocrine Soc. (council 1967-71, 78-81), ACP (master), Endocrine Soc. (v.p. 1970-71), Am. Fedn. Clin. Research, Am. Soc. Clin. Investigation, Assn. Am. Physicians, Central Soc. Clin. Research, Sigma Xi, Alpha Omega Alpha. Current Work: Genetics; natural history classification and diagnosis of diabetes; diagnosis and treatment of organic hypoglycemia. Subspecialty: Endocrinology. Home: 2485 Devonshire Rd Ann Arbor MI 48104 Office: Univ Mich Hosp Ann Arbor MI 48109

FAJER, ABRAM BENCJAN, physiology educator, physician; b. Piaski, Poland, Sept. 12, 1926; came to U.S., 1963, naturalized, 1975; s. Szolma and Chaja (Birkman) F.; m. Renate Emma Fleischer, Sept. 1, 1956; children—Debora, Simone, Salo Kurt. M.D., U. Sao Paulo, Brazil, 1951, Ph.D., 1961. Asst. prof. Faculdade de Medicina, Sao Paulo, 1952-59, head exptl. endocrinology, 1959-63; scientist Worcester Found., Shrewsbury, Mass., 1963-64; faculty U. Md. Sch. Medicine, Balt., 1964—, prof. physiology, 1973—. Contbr. sects. to books, articles to profl. jours. Vis. prof. Weizmann Inst., Israel, 1973, College de France, Paris, 1981. Mem. Am. Physiol. Soc., Endocrine Soc., Soc. for Study Reprodn., Tissue Culture Assn. Current work: Ovarian development; in-vitro fertilization; gonadal metabolism. Subspecialties: Reproductive biology (medicine); Animal breeding and embryo transplants. Office: Dept Physiology U Md Sch Medicine 660 W Redwood St Baltimore MD 21201

FAKHARZADEH, ALI M., software engineer, researcher; b. Tehran, Iran, June 14, 1947; came to U.S., 1966; s. Ali-Asghar and Fatemeh (Daeian) F.; m. Marya Montazeri, Sept. 26, 1976; children: Ali-Reza, Bahman Benjamin. B.S.E.E., U. Utah, 1970, M.S., 1977. Sr. software engr. Applicon, Inc., Burlington, Mass., 1977-82; prin. software engr. Adage, Inc., Billerica, Mass., 1982-85, mgr. systems analysis group, 1985—; mgr. systems software Encore/-Resolution Systems Inc., Marlborough, Mass., 1985—. Contbr. articles to profl. jours. Mem. IEEE, Assn. for Computing Machinery, Eta Kappa Nu. Current Work: Computer graphics, solids modeling, interactive man-machine communication, robotics, developing high performance graphics firmware. Subspecialties: Graphics, image processing, and pattern recognition; Software engineering. Home: 556 Concord Ave Lexington MA 02173 Office: Adage Inc 1 Fortune Dr Billerica MA 01821

FALCO, CHARLES MAURICE, physics educator; b. Ft. Dodge, Iowa, Aug. 17, 1948; s. Joe and Mavis Margaret (Mickelson) F.; m. Dale Wendy Miller, Apr. 5, 1973; children—Lia Denise, Amelia Claire. B.A., U. Calif.-Irvine, 1970, M.S., 1971, Ph.D., 1974. Asst. physicist Argonne Nat. Lab., Ill., 1974-77, physicist, 1977-82; prof. physics and optical scis. U. Ariz., Tucson, 1982—; cons. various indsl. orgns. Patentee in field. Co-editor: Future Trends in Superconductive Electronics, 1978; contbr. articles to profl. jours. Named to Indsl. Research 100, Indsl. Research mag., 1977, Technology 100, Technology mag., 1981. Mem. Am. Phys. Soc., Am. Vacuum Soc., IEEE, Sigma Xi. Current work: Artificial metallic superlattices, low temperature metals physics, superconductivity, materials for X-UV optics. Subspecialties: Condensed matter physics; Electronic materials. Home: 6301 N Caravan Ln Tucson AZ 85704 Office: Dept Physics U Ariz Tucson AZ 85721

FALCONE, ALFONSO BENJAMIN, physician; b. Bryn Mawr, Pa., July 24; s. B. and Elvira (Galluzzo) F.; m. Patricia J. Lalim, Oct. 22; children—Christopher L., Steven B. A.B. with distinction in Chemistry, Temple U., 1944, M.D. with honors, 1947; Ph.D. in Biochemistry, U. Minn., 1954. Diplomate Am. Bd. Internal Medicine, subsplty. in endocrinology and metabolism. Intern, Phila. Gen. Hosp., 1947-48, resident in internal medicine, 1948-49; teaching fellow internal medicine U. Hosps., U. Minn., 1949-51; asst. clin. prof. medicine U. Wis.-Madison, 1956-59, assoc. clin. prof., 1959-63; asst. prof. Inst. for Enzyme Research, 1963-66, vis. prof., 1966-67; cons. practice medicine specializing in endocrine and metabolic diseases, Fresno, Calif., 1968—; mem. active staff Fresno Community Hosp., chmn. dept. medicine, 1973; mem. active staff St. Agnes Hosp., Fresno; mem. hon. staff Valley Med. Ctr., Fresno; sr. corr. Ettore Majorana Ctr. for Sci. Culture, Erice, Italy. Contbr. articles to profl. jours. Served with AUS, 1944-46; served to lt. comdr. M.C., USNR, 1954-56. NIH postdoctoral fellow, 1951-53, research grantee, 1958-68. Fellow ACP; mem. Am. Soc. Biol. Chemists, Central Soc. Clin. Research, Am. Fedn. Clin. Research, Calif. Acad. Medicine, Am. Diabetes Assn., Am. Chem. Soc., AMA, Am. Soc. Internal Medicine, Am. Assn. for Study Liver Disease, Sigma Xi, Phi Lambda Upsilon. Current work: Research in mechanisms of adenosine triphosphate synthesis, oxidative phosphorylation, biological energy transduction mechanisms, mechanisms of drug action, and membrane biochemistry. Subspecialties: Endocrinology; Biochemistry (medicine). Office: 2240 E Illinois Ave Fresno CA 93701

FALES, HENRY MARSHALL, organic chemist, mass spectrometrist; b. N.Y.C.; s. Henry Marshall and Cecile Marie (Vatet) F.; m. b. Caroline Eleanor McCullagh, Dec. 19, 1947; children: Marsha Kent Mazz, Suzanne Kent Palmer, Henry Richard. B.S., Rutgers U., 1948, Ph.D., 1953. Research asst. Rutgers U., New Brunswick, N.J., 1952, instr., 1952; chemist Nat. Heart Inst., NIH, Bethesda, Md., 1953—; chief lab. chemistry Nat. Heart, Lung and Blood Inst., 1966—; mem. adv. panel NSF; instr. Found. for Advanced Edn. in Scis. Contbr. numerous articles on organic chemistry to profl. jours.; mem. editorial bds.: Biomed. Mass Spectrometry, Analytical Chemistry, Drug Metabolism and Disposition. Served with USN, 1944-46. Mem. Am. Chem. Soc., Am. Soc. for Mass Spectroscopy. Current Work: Structural analysis of organic compounds of biological interest using mass spectrometry x-ray crystallography, nuclear magnetic resonance. Subspecialties: Organic chemistry; Analytical chemistry. Office: NIH Bldg 10 N318 Bethesda MD 20205

FALK, CHARLES DAVID, research chemist; b. chgo., July 18, 1939; s. Leo Maurice and Mildred Francine (Bloom) F.; m. Diane Sena Miller, July 16, 1965 (div. 1980); 1 child, David Andrew; m. Margaret Elizabeth Pearce, Aug. 1981, B.S. in chemistry, U. Chgo., 1961, Ph.D. in Inorganic and Phys. Chemistry, 1966. Postdoctoral fellow U. Sussex, Eng., 1966-67; research chemist E.I. DuPont, Wilmington, Del., 1967-70; mgr., tech. cons. Riverton Labs., Newark, N.H., 1970-74; sr. research chemist, mgr. Engelhard Corp., Edison, N.J., 1974-84; chem. cons., Marlboro, N.J., 1984—. Contbr. numerous articles to profl. jours. U. Chgo. scholar, 1959-61; fellow NASA, 1962-65, NIH, 1966-67. Mem. Am. Chem. Soc., Royal Soc. Chemistry, Catalysis Soc. N.Y. Current work; Homogeneous and heterogeneous catalysis, electrocatalysis, inorganic synthesis, organic synthesis, kinetics, organometallics. Subspecialties: Catalysis chemistry; Inorganic chemistry. Home and Office: 3 Jacata Rd Marlboro NJ 07746

FALK, SANDOR A., renal physiologist; b. Paterson, N.J., Dec. 20, 1949; s. Malvin Donald and Lois Helen (Slotkin) F.; m. Barbara Carol Rudenstein, June 14, 1972. Student, The Citadel, 1967-69; B.A., Franklin Pierce Coll., 1971. Research technologist U. Pa. Hosp., Phila., 1973-74; biol. researcher VA Hosp., Denver, 1974-75; researcher U. Colo. Health Sci. Center, Denver, 1975—; cons. glomerular dynamics VA Hosp., Denver, 1981—. Contbr. articles to profl. jours. Mem. Am. Fedn. for Clin. Research. Current Work: Using micropuncture techniques to study glomerular dynamics of acute renal failure. Subspecialties: Physiology (medicine); Nephrology. Home: 9591 Warhawk Rd Conifer CO 80433 Office: U Colo Health Scis Center 4200 E 9th Ave Denver CO 80262

FALVEY, HENRY THOMAS, civil engineer; b. Denver, Sept. 26, 1935. B.S.C.E. Ga. Inst. Tech., 1958; M.S.C.E., Calif. Inst. Tech., 1960; Dr.Ing., U. Karlsruhe, Germany, 1964. Engr. U.S. Bur. Reclamation, Denver, 1960-62, research engr., 1964-72, 1974—; sr. research officer Ecole Poly. Federal de Lausanne, Switzerland, 1972-74; cons. World Bank, India, UN, India, Turkey, AID, Pakistan, U.S. Bur. Reclamation, China. Author: Air-Water Flow. Contbr. articles to profl. jours. Patentee in field. Served to capt. U.S. Army, 1959-60. Mem. ASCE, Internat. Assn. Hydraulic Research, Sigma Xi, Tau Beta Pi, Chi Epsilon. Lutheran. Current work: Cavitation in hydraulics structure; air-water flows; canal automation; hydraulic transients; atmospheric flows; draft tube surging. Subspecialties: Civil engineering; Fluid mechanics. Office: US Bur Reclamation PO Box 25007 Denver CO 80225

FALZONE, ANTHONY JOSEPH, physicist, researcher; b. Rochester, N.Y., Oct. 11, 1942; s. Joseph Frank and Eva Helen (Paixao) F.; m. Rita G. Ganzini, Apr. 24, 1976; 1 child, Sonia Aurora. B.S., St. John Fisher Coll., Rochester, 1964; M.S., Kent State U., 1966; PhD., U. Queensland, Australia, 1981. Physicist, Xerox Corp., Rochester, 1966, U.S. Naval Research Lab, Washington, 1967-68, U.S. Naval Obs., Washington, 1968-77; tutor U. Queensland, 1977-81; research assoc. U. Chgo., 1982-83; research and devel. physicist Sohio Petroleum Co., Cleve., 1983—. Contbr. articles to profl. jours. Mem. Am. Phys. Soc., Am. Geophys. Union, AIME, Am. Assn. Physics Tchrs., Sigma Xi. Current work: Investigation of physical processes involved in fluid flow through porous media at elevated temperatures and pressures. Subspecialties: Geophysics; Condensed matter physics. Home: 1373 Yellowstone Rd Cleveland Heights OH 44121 Office: Sohio Research Center 4440 Warrensville Ctr Rd Cleveland OH 44128

FAMILY, FEREYDOON, physicist; b. Tehran, Iran, Sept. 18, 1945; came to U.S., 1964; s. Hassan and Aghdas (Keramaty) F.; m. Soheila Family, Apr. 20, 1966; 1 son, Afsheen. B.S., Worcester Poly. Inst., 1968; M.S., Tufts U., 1970; Ph.D., Clark U., 1974. Asst. prof. Central New Eng. Coll., Worcester, Mass., 1971-74; research assoc. MIT, 1974-75; head solid state div. Atomic Energy Orgn. of Iran, Tehran, 1975-79; research assoc. Boston U., 1979-81; vis. asst. prof. Worcester Poly. Inst., 1980-81; asst. prof. physics Emory U., 1981-83, assoc. prof., 1984—; vis. research physicist Inst. Theoretical Physics, U. Calif.-Santa Barbara, 1982; vis. assoc. prof. chemistry dept. MIT, 1985-86. Author: Kinetics of Aggregation and Gelation, 1984; mem. organizing com. Internat. Topical Conf. on Kinetics of Aggregation and Gelation, 1984. Contbr. articles, referee sci. jours. Recipient Lawton-Plimpton prize Worcester Poly. Inst., 1968, award for teaching excellence Central New Eng. Coll., 1971; NSF grantee, 1983—; Research Corp. grantee, 1982; NIH bioscis. grantee, 1982, 84; Office of Naval Research grantee, 1984, 86. Mem. Am. Phys. Soc., Am. Assn. Physics Tchrs., Sigma Xi, Sigma Pi Sigma. Current work: Condensed matter physics, theoretical polymer physics, critical phenomena, many-body problem. Subspecialties: Polymer physics; Condensed matter physics. Office: Dept Physics Emory U Atlanta GA 30322

FAN, CHANG-YUN, physics educator; b. Nantung, China, Jan. 7, 1918; came to U.S., 1947, naturalized, 1966; s. Li-Chuan and Shi-Xue (Chen) F.; m. Tsung-Ting Teng, Sept. 30, 1950; children—Paula, Anna, Michael. B.S., Central U., Nanjing, China, 1942; M.S., U. Chgo., 1950, Ph.D., 1952. Research assoc. U. Chgo., 1952-56; asst. prof. U. Ark., Fayetteville, 1956-57; research prof. Enrico Fermi Inst., Chgo., 1958-67; prof. physics U. Ariz., Tucson,

1967—. Fellow Am. Phys. Soc.; mem. Am. Geophys. Union. Current work: To study the processes of acceleration of charged particles in space plasma and in the vicinity of stellar objects; to investigate the effect of the coupling of solar energetic particles with the earth's magnetosphere. Subspecialties: High energy astrophysics; Solar physics. Home: 2 Potter Pl Tucson AZ 85719 Office: Dept Physics U Ariz Tucson AZ 85721

FAN, LIANG-TSENG, chemical engineering educator; b. Yang-Mei, Tao-Yuan, Taiwan, Aug. 7, 1929; came to U.S., 1952, naturalized, 1970; s. Chung-chan and Chien-mei (Huang) F.; m. Eva Cheung, June 2, 1958; children: Tso Yee, Judith Tso-ling. B.S. in Chem. Engring, Nat. Taiwan U., Taipei, 1951; M.S. in Chem. Engring, Kans. State U., 1954; Ph.D. in Chem. Engring, W.Va. U., 1957, M.S. in Math, 1958. Mem. faculty Kans. State U., Manhattan, 1958—, prof. chem. engring., 1963—, head chem. engring. dept., 1968—, Univ. disting. prof., 1984—. Author: The Discrete Maximum Principle, 1964, The Continuous Maximum Principle, 1966, Flow Models for Chemical Reactors, 1975, Environmental Systems Engineering, 1977; U.S. editor: Biotech. Series, 1981—; editor: Particle Sci. and Tech, 1981—; mem. editorial com.: Applied Transport Phenomena Series, 1978—. Patentee in field. Recipient Disting. Grad. Faculty award Kans. State U., Engrs., AAAS; mem. Soc. Engring. Scis. (founding mem.), Am. Chem. Soc., Am. Soc. Engring. Edn., Sigma Xi. Patentee method for wastewater treatment in fluidized bed biol. reactors, 1982. Current Work: Systems engineering; energy resources conversion; solids mixing; fluidization; transport phenomena; chemical process dynamics; chemical reactor analysis and design; environmental pollution control; biochemical engineering and biotechnology. Subspecialties: Chemical engineering; Fuels and sources. Home: 830 Lee St Manhattan KS 66502Office: Kans State Univ Chem Engring Dept Manhattan KS 66506

FANCHI, JOHN RICHARD, physicist; b. Pontiac, Ill., Nov. 17, 1952; s. John Anton and Shirley Mae (Andersen) F.; m. Katherine Frances Goedecke, Aug. 22, 1976; children—Anthony Clifford, Christopher John. B.S. in Physics, U. Denver, 1974; M.S. in Physics, U. Miss., 1975; Ph.D. in Physics, U. Houston, 1977. Research asst. Denver Research Inst., 1970-74, U. Houston, 1975-78; research engr. Getty Oil Co., Houston, 1978-79, Cities Service Co., Tulsa, 1979-81; sr. engr. Keplinger & Assocs., Tulsa, 1981-84; advanced research scientist Marathon Oil Co., Denver, 1984—; adj. prof. physics U. Tulsa, 1980-81; pres. Simulation Tech. Corp., Tulsa, 1982-83. Prin. author software systems; contbr. articles to profl. jours. Mem. central com. Colo. Republican party, Denver, 1974; facilitator Praxis Project, Tulsa, 1981-84. Grantee Colo.-Wyo. Acad. Sci., 1972. Mem. Am. Phys. Soc., Soc. Petroleum Engrs., AAAS, Sigma Xi. Republican. Lutheran. Current work: Numerical simulation of fluid flow in porous media; developing single parameter, four-space formulation of relativistic quantum theory. Subspecialties: Geophysics; Theoretical physics. Home: 1078 E Otero Ave Littleton CO 80122 Office: Marathon Research Ctr PO Box 269 Littleton CO 80160

FANG, SHU-CHERNG, research engineer; b. Nantou, Taiwan, Republic of China, June 14, 1952; s. Shaw-Han F.; m. Chi-Hsin Chao, Aug. 5, 1982. B.S., Nat. Tsing Hua U., Hsinchu, Taiwan, 1974; M.S., Johns Hopkins U., 1977; Ph.D., Northwestern U., 1979. Asst. prof. ops. research U. Md.-Balt., 1979-80; mem. research staff Western Electric Co., Princeton, N.J., 1980-82, sr. mem. research staff, 1982—. Author tech. papers and research reports. Recipient tech. achievement award AT&T, 1984; Johns Hopkins U. fellow, 1976; Murphy fellow Northwestern U., 1977; research grantee U. Md., summer 1980. Mem. Am. Soc. Indsl. Engring., Soc. Indsl. and Applied Math., Ops. Research Soc. Am., Nat. Engring. Honor Soc. Current Work: Lightwave system design, optical fiber manufacturing, operations research in computer-aided manufacturing. Subspecialties: Fiber optics; Operations research (engineering). Office: AT&T Engring Research Ctr PO Box 900 Princeton NJ 08540

FANO, UGO, physicist, educator; b. Turin, Italy, July 28, 1912; came to U.S., 1939, naturalized, 1945; s. Gino and Rosa (Cassin) F.; m. Camilla V. Lattes, Feb. 8, 1939; children: Mary, Virginia. Sc.D., U. Turin, 1934; D.Sc. (hon.), Queen's U., Belfast, No. Ireland, 1978, U. Pierre and Marie Curie, Paris, 1979. Lectr., U. Rome, 1937-38; fellow, resident investigator Carnegie Instn., Washington, 1940-46; cons. U.S. Army Ordnance, 1944-45; physicist X-ray sect. Nat. Bur. Standards, Washington, 1946-49, chief radiation theory sect., 1949-60, sr. research fellow, 1960-66; prof. physics James Franck Inst., U. Chgo., 1966-82, prof. emeritus, 1982—, chmn. dept., 1972-74; lectr. George Washington U., 1946-47; vis. prof. U. Calif., Berkeley, summer 1958, 68, Cath. U., Washington, 1963-64. Author: (with G. Racah) Irreducible Tensorial Sets, 1959, (with L. Fano) Basic Physics of Atoms and Molecules, 1959, Physics of Atoms and Molecules, 1972; also articles. Recipient Rockefeller Pub. Service award, 1956, Exceptional Service award Dept. Commerce, 1957; Stratton award Nat. Bur. Standards, 1963; Davisson-Germer prize Am. Phys. Soc., 1976. Mem. Nat. Acad. Scis., Am. Acad. Arts and Scis., Am. Phys. Soc., Radiation Research Soc. Current Work: Research describing the mechanisms of transformations of atomic and molecular structures. Subspecialties: Atomic and molecular physics; Theoretical physics. Office: Dept Physics U Chicago Chicago IL 60637

FARAGO, GEORGE, electrical engineer; b. Budapest, Hungary, Dec. 17, 1903; came to U.S., 1959; s. Joseph and Hermin (Friedmann) Klein; m. Lenke Gyongyi Leon, Apr. 4, 1947. Engr. Cand., Technikum, Germany, 1923; Elec. Engr., Polytechnikum, Oldenburg, Germany, 1926; Dipl.Elec.Engr., Tech. U. Dresden, 1927; postgrad. Tech. U. Budapest, 1952-53. Engr.-in-charge (chief engr.) research and devel. Telecommunications, Budapest, 1929-52; research fellow Acad. Scis., Budapest, 1952-53; dep. chief engr. Tungsram Works, Budapest, 1953-57; v.p. research and devel. Faracon Corp., Englewood, N.J., 1962-65; cons. in research and devel. Premier Microwave, Portchester, N.Y., 1967-72, Elec. Cons., Bklyn., 1973-82; elec. engring. cons., Albany, N.Y. Contbr. articles to profl. jours. Patentee in field. Mem. IEEE, Mfg. Tech. Soc., Biomed. Engring. Soc., Inst. Med. Climatology. Current work: Electrical cleaning systems for automobile exhaust gas. Subspecialties: Electronics; Telecommunications. Address: 175 Hollywood Ave Albany NY 12209

FARAH, BADIE NAIEM, educator, consultant; b. Nazareth, Palestine, Jan. 15, 1946; came to U.S., 1970, naturalized, 1983; s. Naim R. and Afifi (Takla) F. B.S., Damascus U., 1967, M.A., 1968; M.S., Wayne State U., 1973; M.S.I.E., Ohio State U., 1976, Ph.D., 1977. Teaching asst. Wayne State U., Detroit, 1971-73; research assoc. Ohio State U., Columbus, 1973-77; sr. systems analyst Gen. Motors Co., Detroit, 1977-78; asst. prof. Oakland U., Rochester, Mich., 1978-82; asst. prof. info. systems, ops. research Eastern Mich. U., Ypsilanti, 1982—; advisor to bd. dirs. S & G Grocer Co., Detroit, 1979-81, vis. gen. mgr., 1980-81. Contbr. articles to profl. jours. Mem. Am. Inst. Indsl. Engrs., Assn. Computing Machinery, Ops. Research Soc. Am., Inst. Mgmt. Scis., Mich. Acad. Sci., Arts and Letters, Internat. Platform Assn., Am. Inst. Decision Sci., Alpha Pi Mu. Syrian Orthodox. Current Work: Data communications and networks of computers, decision support systems for microcomputers, management information systems. Subspecialties: Distributed systems and networks; Software engineering. Home: 37 Foxboro Dr Rochester MI 48063 Office: Eastern Mich U 511 Pray-Harrold Ypsilanti MI 48197

FARAH, FUAD SALIM, dermatologist, immunologist, educator; b. Haifa, Palestine, Apr. 5, 1929; came to U.S., 1976; s. Salim and Nada (Fuleihan) F.; m. Mona Haddad, June 25, 1955; children: Richard-Salim, Ronald-Samir, Joyce-Bahia, Ramsay-Sami. B.A., Am. U., Beirut, 1950, M.D., 1954. Diplomate: Am. Bd. Dermatology. Asst. prof. medicine Am. U., Beirut, 1959-60, assoc. prof., 1960-66, prof., 1966-76; dir. WHO Immunology Research and Tng. Ctr., Beirut, 1972-76; prof. medicine, chief sect. dermatology SUNY Upstate Med. Ctr., Syracuse, 1976—. Contbr. numerous articles in immunology and dermatology to profl. jours. Decorated knight and officer Order of Cedar Lebanon). Mem. Soc. Investigative Dermatology, Am. Assn. Immunologists, Soc. Tropical Dermatology, Reticuloendothelial Soc., AAAS. Subspecialties: Immunology (agriculture); Genetics and genetic engineering (agriculture). Home: 113 Victoria Park Dr Liverpool NY 13088 Office: 750 E Adams St Syracuse NY 13210

FARBER, JOSEPH, solar energy company executive, consultant, lecturer, solar energy researcher; b. Newark, June 1, 1924; s. Samuel and Anna (Sielunchik) F.; m. Margaret A. Farber, Dec. 28, 1951; children: Jennie Lee, Steven Eric. B.S. in Chemistry and Physics, CCNY, 1945; Ph.D. in Phys. Chemistry, U. Wis.-Madison, 1951. Research engr., sr. thermal engr. Convair, Gen. Dynamics, San Diego, 1951-55; mgr. real gas engring., mgr. aero. physics Gen. Electric Co., Valley Forge, Pa., 1955-65, mgr. advanced system engring., 1965-67; chief engr. Ford Space and Re-entry Systems, Newport Beach, Calif., 1967-70; pres. KMS Tech. Center, Irvine, Calif., 1970-73; pres., cons. Solar Research Systems, Santa Ana, Calif., 1973-84; mem. Am. Diversified Tech. Div., Costa Mesa, Calif., 1984—; lectr. U. Calif.-Irvine, Orange Coast Coll., cons. to govt., nonprofit orgns., industry; bd. dirs. Solar Age Mag., 1977—. Contbr. articles to profl. jours., chpts. to books. Chmn. Solar Coalition of Orange County, 1980-81. Mem. Am. Chem. Soc., Am. Phys. Soc., AIAA, Am. Solar Energy Soc. (dir.), Internat. Solar Energy Soc. Democrat. Unitarian. Patentee in field. Current Work: Solar technology, thermal, photovoltaic, plastics systems development, solar and aerospace, energy power generation. Subspecialties: Solar energy; Systems engineering. Home: 1605 Sherington Pl Y212 Newport Beach CA 92663 Office: 3200 Park Center Costa Mesa CA 92626

FARBER, PHILLIP ANDREW, clinical cytogeneticist, educator; b. Wilkes-Barre, Pa., Sept. 19, 1934; s. Phillip Henry and Josephine Mary (Penkala) F.; m. Larice May Krebs, Oct. 11, 1974; children: Michael, Steven, Phillip. B.S., King's Coll., Wilkes-Barre, 1956; M.S., Boston Coll., 1958; postgrad., Cath. U. Am., 1963. Instr. dept. biology Georgetown U., Washington, 1962-63; research biologist Lab. Perinatal Physiology NIH, 1963-64; research instr. Inst. Phys. Medicine and Rehab., N.Y.U. Med. Center, 1964-66; prof. dept. biol. and allied health scis. U. Pa., Bloomsburg, 1966—; cons. clin. cytogenetics, dept. lab. medicine, cytogenetic lab. Geisinger Med. Center, Danville, Pa., 1967—. Contbr. articles to profl. jours. Served with USPHS, 1960. NSF grantee, 1962; NIH grantee, 1965. Mem. Am. Soc. Human Genetics, Assn. Cytogenetics Technologists, Nat. Soc. Histotech., Teratology Soc., Tissue Culture Assn., AAAS, N.Y. Acad. Scis., Pa. Acad. Scis., AAUP, Am. Fedn. Tchrs., Sigma Xi. Current Work: Human genetics, cytology and cytogenetics, histology, histological and histochemical techniques, developmental biology. Subspecialties: Cytogenetics; Cytology and histology. Home: PO Box 92 Mifflinville PA 18631 Office: Dept Biol and Allied Health Scis Hartline Sci Center U Pa Bloomsburg PA 17815

FARBER, SAUL JOSEPH, physician, educator; b. N.Y.C.; s. Isodor and Mary (Bunim) F.; m. Doris Marcia Balmuth; children—Joshua, Beth Mina Farber Loewentheil. A.B., NYU, 1938, M.D., 1942; Ph.D. (hon.), Tel Aviv U., 1983. Diplomate Am. Bd. Internal Medicine. Intern, Sinai Hosp., Balt., 1942-43; resident NYU med. research div., Goldwater Meml. Hosp., 1946-47; asst. resident NYU med. div. Bellevue Hosp., 1947-48; mem. faculty Sch. Medicine, NYU, NYC, 1953—, prof. medicine, 1962—, chmn. dept. medicine, 1966—, Frederick H. King prof. medicine, 1978—, dean for acad. affairs, 1978—; dir. med. services Bellevue Hosp., Univ. Hosp., 1966—; mem. med. adv. bd. Hadassah; trustee Sackler Sch. Medicine, Tel Aviv U., 1977—; mem. adv. com. on long term care-chronic illness Robert Wood Johnson Found., 1979—, co-chmn. clin. nurse scholars program adv. com., 1982—; adv. com. Harold C. Simmons Arthritis Research Ctr., U. Tex. Health Sci. Ctr., Dallas, 1983—. Served with M.C., USNR, 1943-46; PTO. Mem. ACP (pres. 1984-85), Federated Council for Internal Medicine (chmn. 1984-85), Am. Soc. Clin. Investigation (sec.-treas. 1951-60, councillor 1960-63), Assn. Am. Physicians, Assn. Profs. Medicine (pres. 1973), Am. Clin. and Climatological Assn., N.Y. Heart Assn. (pres. 1973-75, councillor 1978—), Inst. Medicine, Interurban Clin. Club. Current work: Teaching and training on the graduate and postgraduate level; research in renal prostaglandins; quality of health care and manpower on the local, state and national levels. Subspecialties: Internal medicine; Nephrology. Office: NYU Med Ctr 550 1st Ave New York NY 10016

FARCASIU, DAN ALEXANDRU, chemist, research scientist; b. Carei, Romania; came to U.S. 1969, naturalized 1978; s. Alexandru and Viorica (Lerman) F.; m. Malvina Furdui; 1 child, Simina Maria. Ph.D., Polytech. Inst., Timisoara, Romania, 1969. Instr. Princeton U., N.J., 1972-73; research chemist Exxon Research & Engring. Co., Linden, N.J., 1974-77, staff chemist, 1977—. Contbr. numerous articles to profl. jours. Patentee in field. Byzantine-Rite Catholic. Current work: Organic reaction mechanism and intermediates, acid catalysis. Subspecialties: Organic chemistry; Catalysis chemistry. Office: Corp Research Dept Exxon Research & Engring Co Clinton Twp Route 22 East Annandale NJ 08801

FARISS, THOMAS LEE, physicist; b. Lynchburg, Va., Oct. 28, 1953; s. Wesley James and Mildred Josephine (Rice) F.; m. Allene Teruko Shimomura, July 12, 1981. B.S., U. Va., 1976, Ph.D., 1983. Analyst ops. Ctr. Naval Analyses, Alexandria, Va., 1983—. Contbr. articles to profl. jours. Mem. Am. Phys. Soc., Sigma Xi (assoc.), Sigma Pi Sigma. Current work: Evaluation current emerging technologies on naval radar systems and electronic countermeasures. Subspecialties: Operations research (engineering); Condensed matter physics. Home: 127 Beverly Hills Circle Lynchburg VA 24502 Office: Ctr Naval Analyses 4401 Ford Ave Alexandria VA 22302

FARLEY, JOHN WILLIAM, physicist, educator; b. N.Y.C., Feb. 7, 1948; s. John and Eileen Gertrude (Gray) F. B.A., Harvard Coll., 1970; M.A., Columbia U., 1974, M. Ph., 1974, Ph.D., 1977. Postdoctoral research assoc. U. Ariz.-Tucson, 1976-80, research asst. prof. physics, 1980-81; asst. prof. physics U. Oreg., Eugene, 1981—. Contbr. articles to sci. publs. in field. NSF nat. needs postdoctoral fellow, 1978-79. Mem. Am. Phys. Soc., Optical Soc. Am. Current Work: Lasers and other quantum-electronic areas; nonlinear optics, studies of simple atomic and molecular systems; molecular ions; computers and automated instrumentation. Subspecialties: Atomic and molecular physics; Laser spectroscopy. Home: 744 E 21st Ave Eugene OR 97405 Office: Physics Dept U Oreg Eugene OR 97403

FARMER, JAMES LEE, geneticist; b. South Gate, Calif., Aug. 8, 1938; s. James Ira and Eliza Ellen (Sheeks) F.; m. Gladys Clark, Jan. 27, 1967; children: Sarah Lynn, James Clark, Rachel Lee, Jared Randall, Deborah Ann. B.S., Calif. Inst. Techn., 1960; postgrad., Brigham Young U., 1960-61; Ph.D., Brown U., 1966. Instr. biophysics U. Colo. Med. Ctr., Denver, 1966-68; asst. prof. zoology Brigham Young U., Provo, Utah, 1969-78, assoc. prof., 1978—. Contbr. articles to profl. jours. Mem. AAAS, Fedn. Am. Scientists, Genetics Soc. Am. Mem. Ch. Jesus Christ of Latter-day Saints. Current Work: Subspecialty: Genome organization. Home: 222 E 4200 N Provo UT 84604 Office: Dept Zoology Brigham Young U Provo UT 84602

FARMER, JOHN WILLIAM, solid state physics researcher, educator; b. Springfield, Mo., May 2, 1947; s. Jack Wiley and Anita Angela (Goss) F.; m. Janet Elaine Dunn, June 17, 1972; children—Christopher John, Michael Joseph. B.S., S.W. Mo. State Coll., 1969; Ph.D., Kans. State U., 1974. Postdoctoral asst. Argonne Nat. Lab., Ill., 1974-76; sr. research scientist, U. Dayton, Ohio, 1976-80; program dir. U. Mo. Research Reactor, Columbia, 1980—; cons. AT&T Techs., Kansas City, Mo., 1984—. Sec. council St. Andrews Lutheran Ch., Columbia, 1984—. Research grantee Research Corp. U. Mo., 1981. Mem. Am. Phys. Soc. Democrat. Current work: Deep levels in semiconductors, defects and impurities. Subspecialty: Condensed matter physics. Home: 1233 Ridge Rd Columbia MO 65203 Office: U Mo Research Reactor Columbia MO 65211

FARMER, JOSEPH CLARENCE, JR., physician, educator; b. Fayetteville, N.C., Oct. 14, 1937; s. Joseph Clarence and Bettie (Eatman) F.; m. Margery Jean Newton, Aug. 19, 1957; 1 son, Thomas Hackney Richardson. M.D., Duke U., 1962. Diplomate: Am. Bd. Otolaryngology. Intern, resident Duke U., Durham, N.C., 1962-65, 67-70, asst. prof. dept. surgery, 1970-75, assoc. prof., 1975—; clin. assoc. surgery br. Nat. Cancer Inst., Bethesda, Md., 1965-67; mem. core faculty F.G. Hall Environ. Research Lab., Duke U. Med. Ctr., 1970—. Contbr. articles to profl. jours. Fellow ACS, Am. Laryingological, Rhinological and Otological Soc., Am. Acad. Otolaryngology Head and Neck Surgery; mem. AMA, N.C. Med. Soc., Durham-Orange County Med. Soc., Alpha Omega Alpha. Democrat. Episcopalian. Current Work: Academic otolaryngology; effects of altered pressures on hearing and balance; otoneurology; diving medicine-otology. Subspecialties: Otorhinolaryngology; Surgery. Office: Div Otolaryngology Dept Surgery Duke U Med Ctr Durham NC 27710

FARMER, NICK A., information systems executive. Dir. research and devel. Chem. Abstracts Service. Subspecialty: Information systems (Information science). Office: Chem Abstracts Service PO Box 3012 Columbus OH 43210*

FARMER, RICHARD GILBERT, physician, foundation adminstrator; b. Kokomo, Ind., Sept. 29, 1931; s. Oscar Irvin and ElizabethJane (Gilbert) F.; m. Janice Mae Schrank, Nov. 29, 1958; children—Amy Lynn, David Richard. Student, Ind. U., 1949-52; M.D., U. Md., 1956; M.S. in Medicine, U. Minn., 1960. Diplomate: Am. Bd. Internal Medicine. Fellow in internal medicine Mayo Clinic, Rochester, Minn., 1957-60; mem. staff Cleve. Clinic Found., 1962—, chmn. dept. gastroenterology, 1977-82, chmn. div. medicine, 1975—, mem. med. ops. group, 1975—, bd. govs., 1974-79, mem. exec. com. bd. trustees, 1975-77; mem. adv. com. Cleve. Clinic Internat. Ctr. Splty. Studies, 1977—; assoc. clin. prof. medicine Case Western Res. U. Sch. Medicine, Cleve., 1980—; mem. nat. adv. bd. Nat. Commn. Digestive Diseases, 1977-79; mem. nat. sci. adv. bd. Nat. Found. Ileitis and Colitis, 1973—; chmn. grants rev. com. Nat. Found. Ileitis and Colitis, 1981-85. Editor 2 books; contbr. articles to sci. jours., chpts. to books. Served as lt. comdr. USNR, 1960-62. Fellow ACP (gov. Ohio 1980-84, health and pub. policy com. 1982—, regent 1985—), Am. Coll. Gastroenterology (pres. 1978-79), Am. Coll. Gastroenterology (trustee, exec. com. 1975-80); mem. Assn. Program Dirs. in Internal Medicine (founding pres. 1977-79, chmn. steering com. new orgn. 1977), Council Subsplty. Socs. in Internal Medicine (council 1978-85), Inst. Medicine of Nat. Acad. Scis., Am. Soc. Internal Medicine (chpt. trustee 1980-84), Am. Gastroent. Assn. (commn. on furture 1973-74, tng. and edn. com. 1975-78, chmn. subcom. grad. edn. 1975-78). Democrat. Presbyterian. Current work: Inflammatory bowel disease; clinical studies involving long-term prognosis for patients. Subspecialties: Internal medicine; Gastroenterology. Home: 150 Hunting Trail Chagrin Falls OH 44022 Office: Cleve Clinic Found 9500 Euclid Ave Cleveland OH 44106

FARQUHAR, JOHN WILLIAM, physician, educator; b. Winnipeg, Man., Can., June 13, 1927; came to U.S., 1934, naturalized, 1950; s. John Giles and Marjorie Victoria (Roberts) F.; m. Christine Louise Johnson, July 14, 1968; children: Margaret F., John C.M.; children by previous marriage: Bruce E., Douglas G. A.B., U. Calif., Berkeley, 1949; M.D., U. Calif., San Francisco, 1952. Intern U. Calif. Hosp., San Francisco, 1952-53, resident, 1953-54, 57-58, postdoctoral fellow, 1955-57; resident U. Minn., Mpls., 1954-55; research asso. Rockefeller U., N.Y.C., 1958-62; asst. prof. medicine Stanford (Calif.) U., 1962-66, asso. prof., 1966-73, prof., 1973—; dir. Stanford Ctr. for Research in Disease Prevention, 1973—; mem. staff Stanford U. Hosp.; adviser, cons. Inst. of Medicine of Nat. Acad. Scis. Author: The American Way of Life Need Not Be Hazardous to Your Health, 1978; contbr. articles to profl. jours. Served with U.S. Army, 1945-46. Recipient James D. Bruce award ACP, 1983. Mem. Am. Soc. Clin. Investigation, Acad. Behavioral Medicine, Harvey Soc., Gold Headed Cane Soc., Sigma Xi, Alpha Omega Alpha. Episcopalian. Subspecialty: Preventive medicine. Office: Sch Medicine Stanford U Stanford CA 94305

FARQUHAR, MARILYN GIST, cell biologist; b. Tulare, Calif., July 11, 1928; d. Brooks DeWitt and Alta Gertrude (Green) Gist; m. Geroge E. Palade, June 7, 1970; children—Bruce, Douglas. A.B., U. Calif., Berkeley, 1949, M.A., 1953, Ph.D., 1955. Asso. to prof. pathology U. Calif. Sch. Medicine, San Francisco, 1962-69; prof. Rockefeller U., N.Y.C., 1970-73; prof. cell biology and pathology Yale U. Sch. Medicine, New Haven, 1973—; fellow Branford Coll. Yale U., 1977—. Mem. editorial bd.: Jour. Cell Biology, 1966-70, Endocrinology, 1974-79, Kidney Internat. Jour, 1974—, Am. Jour. Pathology, 1983—, Jour. Exptl. Medicine, 1976-80, Jour. Histochemistry Cytochemistry, 1970-77; contbr. articles on cell biology, exptl. pathology and endocrinology to profl. jours. Nat. Inst. Arthritis Metabolism and Digestive Diseases research grantee, 1962—; Nat. Inst. Gen. Med. Scis. career awardee, 1965-73. Mem. Nat. Acad. Scis., Am. Soc. Cell Biology (pres. 1981-82), Am. Assn. Pathologists, Am. Assn. Anatomists, Endocrine Soc., Am. Soc. Nephrology, Internat. Soc. Nephrology, Histochemical Soc., Internat. Acad. Pathology. Current work: Routes and mechanisms of membrane traffic and protein sorting; cell biological basis of kidney diseases. Subspecialties: Cell biology (medicine); Membrane biology. Home: 22 Coachmans Ln Woodbridge CT 06525 Office: 333 Cedar St New Haven CT 06510

FARR, EDWIN H., operations research analyst, mathematician; b. Greenburg, Pa., Sept. 24, 1925; children—Carolyn, Allan; m. Joy Farr, Aug. 3, 1984. B.A., Pa. State U., 1948; M.S., NYU, 1951; Ph.D., Carnegie-Mellon U., 1956. Engr., Sperry Gyroscope Co., Great Neck, N.Y.; geophysicist Gulf Oil Corp., Pitts.; applied sci. rep. IBM, Pitts.; engring. mathematician Gen. Electric Co., Schenectady, 1958-62; sr. staff mathematician Hughes Aircraft Co., Los Angeles, 1964-68; mathematician NASA, Cambridge, Mass., 1968-70; ops. research analyst U.S. Dept. Transp., Cambridge, 1970—; lectr. Northeastern U., Boston, 1980—, U. Lowell (Mass.), 1981—. Contbr. articles to math. jours. Pres., Schenectady Ednl. Resource Council, 1961; mem. Lexington Town. Meeting, Mass., 1972. Mem. IEEE, Soc. for Indsl. and Applied Math. Ops. Research Soc. Am., Sigma Xi, Pi Mu Epsilon. Current work: Applied mathematics, including operations research, computer science, discrete mathematics, numerical analysis, coding theory. Subspecialties: Operations research (mathematics); Applied mathematics. Home: 79 Somerset Rd Brookline MA 02146 Office: US Dept Transp Kendall Sq Cambridge MA 02142

FARRIER, NOEL JOHN, epidemiologist, educator; b. Pitts., Dec. 9, 1937; s. Carroll Edwin and Ruth Mary (Diethorn) F.; m. Betty Lou Bruner Perkins, Mar. 17, 1973; 1 stepchild: Jack Lee Perkins. B.S., Carnegie Mellon U., 1960; M.S., U. Pitts., 1964; Ph.D., Ohio State U., 1969; M.P.H., U. Pitts., 1980. Asst. prof. chemistry Wittenberg U., Springfield, Ohio, 1968-69; asst. prof. U. Cin., Ohio, 1970-76; Instr. Edison State Coll., Piqua, Ohio, 1976-78; sr. research asst. U. Pitts., 1978-82; assoc. prof. phys. sci. Sinclair Coll., Dayton, Ohio, 1983—. Contbr. articles to sci. jours. Speakers bur. U. Cin., 1974-76, Edison State Coll., 1976-78, Sinclair Community Coll., 1983-84. Recipient Lubrizol award Chem. Rubber Co., Cleve., 1960, Bausch and Lomb Hon. Sci. award, Pitts., 1956, 2 Freedom Found. awards Valley Forge, Pa., 1969-70; Ohio State U. fellow, 1969-70. Mem. Am. Chem. Soc. (sec. Dayton sect.), Soc. Epidemiol. Research, Sci. and Engrs. for Secure Energy Inc., Am. Heart Assn. (council on epidemiology and arteriosclerosis), Am. Assn. Physics Tchrs. Republican. Mem. Ch. of Jesus Christ of Latter-Day Saints. Current work: Epidemiology cardiovascular diseases related to diet, hypertension, trace minerals, alcohol, smoking, exercise, vitamins and stress; Carbon monoxide in blood; sudden infant death syndrome. Subspecialties: Epidemiology; Environmental chemistry. Office: Sinclair Community Coll 444 W 3d St Dayton OH 45402

FARRINGTON, THOMAS ALEX, computer services executive; b. Chapel Hill, N.C., Nov. 12, 1943; s. Osmond Thomas and Mary F.; m. Juarez Harrel, Jan 10, 1967; children—Christopher Thomas, Trevor Alex, Tomeeka Juarez. B.S. in Elec. Engring., N.C. Agrl. and Tech. U., 1966. Engr., Aerospace Systems div. RCA, Burlington, Mass., 1966-69; pres. Input Output Computer Services, Inc., Waltham, Mass., 1969—. Mem. Black bus. support group NAACP Fair Share Program, Waltham. Named One of Ten Outstanding Young Leaders, Boston Jr. C. of C., 1975, Mem. of Yr., Nat. Assn. Black Mfrs., 1978; recipient Bus. award Mass. Black Caucus, 1979. Mem. Armed Forces Communications and Electronics Assn., Greater Boston C. of C. (bd. dirs.), Boston Pvt. Industry Council (bd. dirs.). Democrat. Baptist. Subspecialty: Computer services management. Office: Input Output Computer Services Inc 400-1 Totten Pond Rd Waltham MA 02254

FARRIS, PAUL LEONARD, agricultural economist; b. Vincennes, Ind., Nov. 10, 1919; s. James David and Fairy Julia (Kahre) F.; m. Rachel Joyce Rutherford, Aug. 16, 1953; children: Nancy, Paul, John, Carl. B.S., Purdue U., 1949; M.S., U. Ill., 1950; Ph.D., Harvard U., 1954. Asst. prof. agrl. econs. Purdue U., West Lafayette, Ind., 1952-56, asso. prof., 1956-59, prof., 1959—, head dept. agrl. econs., 1973-82; agrl. economist Dept. Agr., Washington, 1962; project leader for meat and poultry Nat. Commn. Food Mktg., Washington, 1965-66. Editor: Market Structure Research, 1964, Future Frontiers in Agricultural Marketing Research, 1983; contbr. articles to profl. jours. Served with AUS and USAAF, 1941-46. Mem. Am. Agrl. Econs. Assn., Am. Econ. Assn. Current Work: Agricultural marketing policy; agricultural futures markets. Subspecialty: Agricultural economics. Home: 1510 Woodland Ave West Lafayette IN 47906 Office: Dept Agrl Econs Purdue U West Lafayette IN 47907

FARSHIDI, ARDESHIR B., cardiologist, educator, cardiac electrophysiologist, researcher; b. Kerman, Iran, June 13, 1945; came to U.S., 1972, naturalized, 1977; s. Jamshid and Farangis F.; m. Katayoon Kavoussi, Jan. 2, 1982. M.D., Tehran U., 1969. Diplomate: Am. Bd. Internal Medicine, Am. Bd. Cardiovascular Disease. Intern, Washington, 1972-73; resident U. Pa., Phila., 1973-75, resident in cardiology, 1975-77, electrophysiologist, 1977-78; asst. prof. medicine U. Conn., Farmington, 1978-79, dir. electrophysiology, 1982-85, assoc. prof., 1982-85, attending cardiologist Hosp., 1982-85, dir. electrophysiology, 1982-85; co-dir. electrophysiology Yale U., 1979-82, asst. prof. medicine, 1979-82, attending cardiology Hosp., 1979-82, co-dir. electrophysiology, 1979-82; chief cardiology sect. VA Hosp., Newington, Conn., 1982-85; dir. electrophysiology Los Angeles Heart Inst., 1985—. Mem. editorial bd.: Jour. Am. Coll. Cardiology, 1983; contbr. articles in field to profl. jours. Served to lt. Iran Army, 1969-72. Am. Heart Assn. researcher, 1981. Fellow ACP, Am. Coll. Cardiology, Am. Heart Assn.; mem. Am. Fedn. Clin. Research, Am. Electrophysiologic Soc. Zoroastrian. Current Work: Clinical cardiac electrophysiology and arrhythmia. Subspecialties: Cardiology; Internal medicine. Office: Los Angeles Heart Inst 2131 W 3d St Los Angeles CA 90057

FARUKHI, MOHAMMAD RAHIMULLAH, materials scientist, consultant; b. Bangalore, India, Apr. 24, 1944; came to U.S., 1960, naturalized, 1976; s. Mohammad Himayathullah and Norrie Z. (Khan) F.; m. Sahibzadi Sartaj Jehan I. Khan, Sept. 25, 1967; children—Zaid H., Shermeen T., Shahzad R., Fahhad I. B.S. in Elec. Engring., Okla. State U., 1964; M.S. in Elec. Engring., U. Mo., 1965, Ph.D. in Elec. Engring., 1968. Research asst., asst. instr. U. Mo., Columbia, 1964-68; research physicist Harshaw Chem. Co., Cleve., 1968-72, mgr. nuclear products, 1974-83; mgr. crystals Teledyne Isotopes, Westwood, N.J., 1972-73; pres. Rexon Components, Inc., Cleve., 1983—; cons. NASA, 1972, law firms, 1983—. Contbr. articles to profl. jours., chpt. to book. Patentee in field. Pres., founder Islamic Ctr. Cleve., 1972, 74, 76, Pakistan-Am. League, Cleve.; Mem. IEEE, Am. Phys. Soc., Phi Eta Sigma, Phi Kappa Phi, Pi Mu Epsilon, Eta Kappa Nu, Triangle (founder Okla. State U. chpt.). Republican. Lodge: Masons. Current work: Material science aspects of luminous phosphors and scintillators as used in all nuclear radiation detection applications. Subspecialties: PET scan; Radiology in nuclear medicine. Home: 5622 Grand Pl Willoughby OH 44094 Office: Rexon Components Inc 9009 Freeway Macedonia OH 44056

FATELEY, WILLIAM GENE, scientist, inventor educator; b. Franklin, Ind., May 17, 1929; s. Nolan William and Georgia (Scott) F.; m. Wanda Lee Glover, Sept. 1, 1953; children—Leslie Kaye, W. Scott, Kevin L., Jonathan H., Robin L. A.B., Franklin Coll., 1951, D.Sc. (hon.), 1965; postgrad., Northwestern U., 1951-53, U. Minn., 1956-57; Ph.D., Kans. State U., 1956. Head phys. measurement Dow Chem. Co., Williamsburg, Va., 1958-60; fellow Mellon Inst., Pitts., 1960-62, head sci. relations, 1962-64, asst. to pres., 1964-67, sr. fellow in ind. research, 1965-72, asst. to v.p. for research, 1967-72; prof. chemistry Carnegie-Mellon U., 1970-72; prof., head dept. chemistry Kans. State U., 1972-79; vis. prof. chem. dept. U. Tokyo, 1973, 81; pres. D.O.M. Assos., Internat., 1979—; dir. Pitts. Conf. on Analytical Chemistry and Applied Spectroscopy, 1964-65, pres., 1970-71; editor Jour. Applied Spectroscopy, Raman Newsletter, also finance chmn., steering com. for interferometry. Author: Infrared and Raman Selection Rules, 1973; Characteristic Raman Frequencies, 1974; Fundamentals in Chemistry, 1985. Contbr. articles to profl. jours. Recipient Coblentz award for outstanding contbn. to molecular spectroscopy, 1965; Spectroscopy award Pitts. Conf. Analytical Chemistry and Applied Spectroscopy, 1976; named 1st outstanding grad. chemistry Kans. State U., 1964, recipient Disting. Grad. Faculty award, 1984; H.H. King award, 1979. Fellow Optical Soc. Am.; mem. Am. Chem. Soc. (pres. phys.-inorganic sect. Pitts. 1969-70), Phi Beta Kappa (hon.), Sigma Xi, Sigma Alpha Epsilon, Phi Lambda Epsilon, Pi Mu Epsilon. Current Work: Application of Fourier transform infrared spectroscopy to analytical chemistry and to time-resolved kinetic studies. Subspecialties: Analytical chemistry; Physical chemistry. Home: 1928 Leavenworth Manhattan KS 66502

FATHMAN, CHARLES GARRISON, physician, immunologist; b. Clarksville, Mo., Aug. 30, 1942; s. Alfred Stewart and Rachel Erritt (Gillum) F.; m. Ann Kohlmoos, June 16, 1968; children: Christopher Erritt, Carrie Ann, John Warner. B.A., U. Ky., 1964; M.D., Washington U., 1969. Intern, resident in medicine Dartmouth Affiliated Hosps., Hanover, N.H., 1969-71; postdoctoral fellow in immunology Stanford (Calif.) U., 1971-73; postdoctoral fellow immunology br. Nat. Cancer Inst. NIH, Bethesda, Md., 1973-75; mem. Basel Inst. Immunology, Switzerland, 1975-77; assoc. prof. Mayo Med. Sch., Mayo Clinic, Rochester, Minn., 1977-81; assoc. prof. medicine div. immunology Stanford U., 1981—; sci. advisor Cetus Corp.; acad. assoc. Nichols Inst. Assoc. editor Ann. Rev. Immunology. Contbr. articles to profl. jours. Served as lt. comdr. USPHS, 1971-73. Mem. Am. Rheumatism Assn., Am. Assn. Immunologists, Transplantation Soc., Am. Soc. Clin. Investigation. Democrat. Current Work: Isolation and characterization of immunoregulatory lymphocyte subsets as well as cell-free products involved in normal immunoregulation. Subspecialties: Immunogenetics; Internal medicine. Office: Div Immunology S155 Stanford Med Ctr Stanford CA 94305

FATIADI, ALEXANDER JOHANN, research chemist; b. Kharkov, Ukraine, Oct. 22, 1923; came to U.S., 1952, naturalized, 1957; s. Johann George and Maria Ivan (Goncharenko) F.; m. Irina Ivan Matussevich, July 20, 1952; children: Elena Fatiadi Zahirpour, Irina Fatiadi Weiss, Tamara Fatiadi Stoner, Julia Fatiadi Steimel. Dr. Nat. Sci. in Organic Chemistry, Inst. Tech. Regensburg (Germany) and U. Mainz (Germany), 1950; M.S. in Phys. Organic Chemistry, George Washington U., 1959. Research assoc. dept. chemistry George Washington U., 1954-59; research chemist in organic chemistry Nat. Bur. Standards, Washington, 1959—. Contbr. numerous articles on organic chemistry, synthetic methods, oxidation reactions, semicondrs., revs. to profl. jours.; author: Reaction of Potassium Metal with Carbon Monoxide, 1959, Reactions of Cyano Compounds, 1983. Recipient cert. commendation Nat. Bur. Standards, 1965, 68, 73, 82, Hillebrand award Chem. Soc. Washington, 1982. Mem. Am. Chem. Soc., Chem. Soc. (London), German Chem. Soc. Republican. Russian Orthodox. Patentee synthesis inositol hexasulfate; introduced periodic acid for oxidation for polycyclic aromatic hydrocarbons; proved structure of active manganese dioxide; discovered semiconducting oxocarbons. Current Work: Research on electrochemical properties of transition metal complexes of oxo-and pseudo-oxocarbons, biomedical technology (protein analysis). Subspecialties: Organic chemistry; Synthetic chemistry. Office: Nat Bur Standards Gaithersburg MD 20899

FAUCI, ANTHONY STEPHEN, government administrator; b. Bklyn., Dec. 24, 1940; s. Stephen A. and Eugenia A. F.; m. Christine Grady, May 18, 1985. A.B., Holy Cross U., 1962; M.D., Cornell U., 1966. Diplomate Am. Bd. Allergy and Immunology. Intern. dept. medicine New York Hosp., Cornell Med. Ctr., 1966-67; asst. resident, 1967-68, chief resident, dept. medicine, 1971-72, instr., 1971-72; sr. investigator Nat. Inst. Allergy and Infectious Diseases, NIH, Bethesda, Md., 1972-74, head clin. physiology sect., 1974-80, dep. clin. dir., 1977-80, chief Lab. Immunoregulation, 84—, dir. NIAID, 1984—; clin. prof. Georgetown U., Washington, 1984—; cons. Naval Med. Ctr., Bethesda, 1972—; mem. external adv. com. Multipurpose Arthritis Ctr., Duke U. Med. Ctr., 1984—; ex officio mem. Nat. Diabetes Adv. Bd., 1984—, Nat. Digestive Diseases Adv. bd., 1984—; mem. Dept. Health and Human Services Task Force on Alzheimer's Disease, dep. ethics counselor, 1985—; speaker in field. Mem. editorial bd. numerous profl. jours. Contbr. articles, abstracts to profl. publs. Served with USPHS, 1968—. Recipient Meritorious Service award USPHS, 1979, Disting. Service award, 1984; Arthur S. Flemming award, 1983, Squibb award Infectious Diseases Soc., 1983, Commr.'s Spl. citation FDA, 1984. Fellow Am. Coll. Physicians, Am. Acad. Allergy (postgrad. edn. com. 1979-82); mem. Assn. Am. Physicians, Am. Soc. Clin. Investigation, Am. Assn. Immunologists (program chmn. 1982—), Am. Physiol. Soc. (mem. subcom. on clin. scis., publs. com. 1980-84), Am. Fedn. Clin. Research, Italian-Am. Med. Assn. (mem. hon. adv. bd. 1984—). Roman Catholic. Subspecialties: Infectious diseases; Allergy. Home: 3012 43d St NW Washington 20016 Office: NIAID NIH 9000 Rockville Pike Bethesda MD 20205

FAULKNER, LARRY RAY, chemistry educator; b. Shreveport, La., Nov. 26, 1944; s. James Clifford and Doris Louise (Koch) F.; m. Mary Ann Jordan, Aug. 14, 1965; children—Brian Jordan, Susan Louise, B.S., So. Meth. U., 1966; Ph.D., U. Tex., Austin, 1969. Asst. prof. chemistry Harvard U., 1969-73; asst. prof. chemistry U. Ill., Urbana-Champaign, 1973-75, assoc. prof., 1975-79, prof., 1979-83, prof., head dept., 84—, prof. chemistry U. Tex.-Austin, 1983-84; mem. Materials Research Lab., 1978—. Author: (with A. J. Bard) Electrochemical Methods, 1980; div. editor: Jour. Electrochem. Soc, 1975-80; U.S. regional editor: Jour. Electroanalytical Chemistry, 1980-85. NSF grad. fellow, 1966-79. Mem. Electrochem. Soc. (Edward Weston fellow 1969, Young Authors prize 1976), Am. Chem. Soc., Soc. Electroanalytical Chemistry, Phi Beta Kappa (Grad. Research award Tex. Gamma chpt. 1969-70), Phi Kappa Phi. Current work: Chemical microstructures, electrochemistry, luminescence spectroscopy. Subspecialty: Analytical chemistry. Home: 602 W Pennsylvania Ave Urbana IL 61801 Office: Dept Chemistry U Ill 1209 W California St Urbana IL 61801

FAUNCE, FRANK ROLAND, pediatric dentist; b. Richmond, Ind., Sept. 5, 1938; s. Frank Harry and Leota Parilee (Elliot) F. A.B., Ind. U., 1960; D.D.S., 1964; postgrad., U. Tex., 1974. Asst. prof. Med. Coll. Ga., Augusta, 1974-75; asst. prof., grad. dir. U. Tex., Houston, 1975-79; assoc. prof., undergrad. dir. U. Miss., Jackson, 1979-82; cons. Plimark Lab., Muncie, Ind., 1982—. Author: Bonded Aesthetic Dentistry, 1982; contbr. articles in field to profl. jours. Fellow Am. Acad. Pedodontics; mem. ADA, Houston Acad. Pedodontics, Am. Assn. Dental Research, Am. Assn. Dental Schs. Presbyterian. Developer: laminate veneers, fluoridated phosphates. Current Work: Micro structured ceramic materials and fluoridated phosphate compounds and their anti-microbial activities. Subspecialties: Biomaterials; Preventive dentistry. Home: 2020 Enterprise Dr Muncie IN 47302 Office: Plimark Labs. Inc PO Box 191 Muncie IN 47305

FAURE, GUNTER, geology educator, editor; b. Tallinn, Estonia, May 11, 1934; came to U.S. 1957, naturalized 1967; s. Stella (von Harpe) F.; divorced; children—Mary Jennifer, John Eric, Pamela Anne, David Christopher. B.S. in Geology, U. Western Ont., 1957; Ph.D. in Geology, MIT, 1961. Asst. prof. Ohio State U., Columbus, 1962-65, assoc. prof., 1965-68, prof., 1968—. Author: Principles of Isotope Geology, 1977; co-author: Strontium Isotope Geology, 1972. Editor-in-chief; Isotope Geoscience, 1983—. Recipient Antarctic Service medal NSF, 1975. Fellow Geol. Soc. Am.; mem. Geochem. Soc. (councilor 1984—). Democrat. Current work: Age determinations of rocks based on radioactivity, origin of volcanic igneous rocks, formation of brines and evaporite minerals, study of glacial deposits. Subspecialties: Geochemistry; Arctic studies. Home: 1800 Lafayette Pl 8A Columbus OH 43212 Office: The Ohio State U 125 S Oval Mall Columbus OH 43201

FAUSETT, ROBERT JULIAN, engineering geologist, consultant; b. Winfield, Kans., Apr. 9, 1923; s. Carl Alva and Bessie Opal (Jones) F.; m. Patricia Mae Probst, Feb. 15, 1946; children—Rory Sean, Teresa Mae, Carl Almond. B.S., U. Wis., 1951, M.S., 1979, Ph.D., 1982. Miner Am. & Fed. Mining Cos., Coeur d' Alene, Idaho, 1948; devel. engr. mining Pickands Mather, Hibbing, Minn., 1951-52; devel. engr. taconite devel. Erie Mining Co., Aurora, Minn., 1951-52; sr. engr. U.S. Army C.E., Chgo., 1952-53; engring. geologist Constrn. & Mining, 1953-77; lectr. U. Wis.-Madison, 1955-84, 1970-82, engring. counselor, 1981-82; advisor, cons. atty. gen. Wis., Madison, 1977-81, Wis. Geol. Survey, Madison, 1974-82; lectr. beginners sci. Head Start, Madison, 1977-85. Author: An Interdisciplinary Approach to Resource Inventory, 1981; Specifications, Their Use and Derivation, 1979; Stabilization of Soils and Rock, 1977. Commr. Four Lakes council Boy Scouts Am., Explorer Scouts, Madison, 1970. Recipient Nat. Hornaday award for conservation, nat. citation for reclamation, 1970, Wis. State award for habitat establishment, 1977, also 3 restoration awards USDA. Mem. Nature Conservancy (hon. life mem.), ASTM, AIME, Geol Soc. Am., Assn. Engring. Geologists, AAAS, Soc. Mining Engrs., Soil Conservation Soc. Am., Am. Geol. Inst., Soc. Research Scientists, Sigma Xi. Roman Catholic. Current work: Resource inventory, engineering geology for evaluation, development, environmental protection, restoration, reclamation, safety, construction. Subspecialties: Environmental engineering; Materials. Office: University Hill Farms 4909 Bayfield Terr Madison WI 53705

FAUST, ROBERT JEFFREY, research chemist; b. Pitts., Oct. 23, 1949; s. Clarence and Ella (Harley) F.; m. Mercedes Jenkins, May 20, 1972. B.S. in Chemistry, Carnegie-Mellon U., 1971; Ph.D., U. Pitts., 1977. Research chemist, Calgon Corp., Pitts., 1977—. Patentee in field. Recipient Award for excellence in research and devel. Calgon Corp., 1984. Mem. Am. Chem. Soc., AAAS, Soc. Analytical Chemists of Pitts., Western Pa. Conservancy, Smithsonian Assocs., Carnegie Instn. Current work: Development, optimization and automation of analytical methods for the determination of specific analytes in aqueous solution. Subspecialties: Analytical chemistry; Physical chemistry. Office: Calgon Corp PO Box 1346 Pittsburgh PA 15230

FAWCETT, MICHAEL HAROLD, ecologist, consultant; b. Ashland, Oreg., June 14, 1945; s. Harold W. and Nancy Elaine (Ring) F. B.A. U. Calif.-Santa Barbara, 1968, M.A., 1969, Ph.D., 1979. Environ. scientist CH2M Hill, Inc., San Francisco, 1979-82; marine ecologist Ralph M. Parsons Co., Yanbu, Saudi Arabia, 1982; project scientist Woodward-Clyde Cons., Anchorage, 1983—. Contbr. articles to profl. jours. Ford Found. fellow, 1972-75; grantee NSF, 1975-77, Theodore Roosevelt Meml. Fund, 1974. Mem. Ecol. Soc. Am. Current work: Community ecology, especially predator/prey interactions in freshwater streams and marine intertidal zone; migrations and habitat requirements of Arctic anadromous fishes in the Beaufort Sea. Subspecialties: Ecology (biology); Ecology (environmental science). Home: 9617 Newhaven Loop Anchorage AK 99507 Office: Woodward-Clyde Cons 701 Sesame St Anchorage AK 99503

FAWCETT, SHERWOOD LUTHER, research laboratory executive; b. Youngstown, Ohio, Dec. 25, 1919; s. Luther T. and Clara (Sherwood) F.; m. Martha L. Simcox, Feb. 28, 1953; children—Paul, Judith, Tom. B.S., Ohio State U., 1941; M.S., Case Inst. Tech., 1948, Ph.D., 1950; hon. degrees, Ohio State U., Ohio Dominican Coll., Gonzaga U., Whitman Coll., Otterbein Coll., Detroit Inst. Tech. Registered profl. engr., Ohio. Mem. staff Columbus Labs. Battelle Meml. Inst., 1950-64, mgr. physics dept. 1959-64; dir. Pacific Northwest Labs., Richland, Wash., 1964-67; exec. v.p. Battelle Meml. Inst., Columbus, Ohio, 1967-68, pres., chief exec. officer, 1968-80, chmn., chief exec. officer, 1981-84, chmn. bd. trustees, 1985—. Served with the USNR, 1941-46. Decorated Bronze Star. Mem. Am. Phys. Soc., Am. Nuclear Soc., Nat. Soc. Profl. Engrs., Am. Inst. Metall. Engrs., Sigma Xi, Delta Chi, Sigma Pi Sigma, Tau Beta Pi. Home: 2820 Margate Rd Columbus OH 43221

FAWWAZ, RASHID ADIB, physician, educator; b. São Paulo, Brazil, May 19, 1935; came to U.S., 1961, naturalized, 1973; s. Adib Rashid and Salwa Asma (Sabra) F.; m. Marcia Mary Cosse, Jan. 30, 1966; children: Marc, Michael. M.D., Am. U. Beirut, 1961; Ph.D., U. Calif., Berkeley, 1968. Diplomate: Am. Bd. Nuclear Medicine. Intern Am. U. Beirut, 1961, resident, 1962-63; research scientist Lawrence Berkeley Lab., 1966-74; asst. prof. radiology Columbia U., N.Y.C., 1976-78, assoc. prof., 1979-85, prof., 1985—; guest scientist Brookhaven Nat. Lab., Upton, N.Y., 1981—. Contbr. articles to profl. jours. Internat. Atomic Energy fellow, 1963; Donner fellow, 1964. Mem. Am. Assn. Cancer Research, Am. Soc. Nuclear Medicine, Transplantation Soc. Democrat. Presbyterian. Current Work: Immunotherapy. Subspecialties: Nuclear medicine; Transplantation. Office: 622 W 168th St New York NY 10032

FAY, WAYNE XALPHA, refractories research engineer, ceramic consulant; b. Bement, Ill., June 25, 1914; s. Julius B. and Emma Jane (Quick) F.; m. June Balliet Fay, May 15, 1943; children—W. Richard, Robert Woods, Steven J. B.Sc., U. Ill., 1937. Registered profl. engr., Pa. Ceramic engr. Gen. Refractoris Co., Phila., 1937-41, research engr., 1945-82; cons. Cleaver Brooks Inc., Lebanon, Pa., 1984—, Gen. Refractories Co., 1984—. Patentee plastic chrome ore, refractory product. Bd. dirs. Radnor Twp. Sch. Bd., 1966-72; trustee Methodist Ch., Wayne Pa., 1980-83; bd. dirs. ARC, 1983—; mem. Radnor Town Watch, 1983—. Served to maj. AUS, 1941-46. Decorated Bronze Star. Fellow Am. Ceramic Soc. (Founders award 1981); mem. ASTM (Merit award 1980), Pa. Ceramic Assn. (chmn. nonimations 1966-82), Refractories Inst. (tech. adv. com. 1963-82). Republican. Methodist. Subspecialty: Ceramic engineering. Home: 707 Knox Rd Villanova PA 19085

FAZIO, PAUL, building engineering educator, center administrator; b. Alvito, Frosinone, Italy, Apr. 1, 1939; came to Can., 1953; s. Donato and Anna (Marini) F.; m. Lucy Lena D'Annunzio, June 4, 1966; children—Tenna, Mark, Luke. B.A.Sc., U. Windsor, 1963, M.A.Sci., 1964, Ph.D. in Civil Engring., 1968. Registered profl. engr., Que., Ont. Asst. prof. civil engring. Concordia U., Montreal, 1967-70, assoc. prof., 1970-74, prof., 1974—, chmn. dept., 1972—, dir. Ctr. for Bldg. Studies, 1977—; pres. SIRICON. Contbr. articles to profl. jours. Mem. City of Pointe Claire Planning Bd., Que. Recipient Galbraith prize Engr. Inst. Can., 1967. Fellow Can. Soc. Civil Engrs. (Gzowski medal 1979); mem. Constrn. Industry Devel. Council Govt. Can., Conseil Internat. du Batiment, Order Engrs. Que., Assn. Profl. Engrs. Ont., ASHRAE. Current work: Building envelope, computer software for construction industry, energy systems analysis, energy conservation, structures construction productivity. Subspecialty: Civil engineering. Office: 7 Ctr for Bldg Studies Concordia Univ 1455 de Maisonneuve Blvd W Montreal PQ H3G 1M8 Canada

FEDER, RALPH, physicist; b. Phila., Jan. 12, 1922; s. Abraham and Eva (Miller) F.; m. Josephine Carr, Jan. 29, 1950; children—Elizabeth Feder Greenwaldt, Jennifer G., Kerry Carr. B.A., Ind. U., 1950; M.A., U. Pa., 1955; postgrad. Temple U., 1955-57. Physicist, Frankford Arsenal, Phila., 1949-61, T.J. Watson Research Ctr. IBM, Yorktown Heights, N.Y., 1961—. Author: NATO Conference: Examining the Sub Micron World, 19. Served with U.S. Army, 1942-45, ETO. Sec. Army fellow, 1957-58. Mem. Am. Phys. Soc., N.Y. Acad. Scis., Electron Microscope Soc. Am. Current work: Development of x-ray imaging techniques for examining biological cells. Home: River Rd Hyde Park NY 12538 Office: IBM TJ Watson Research Ctr PO Box 218 Yorktown Heights NY 10538

FEDERICO, PAT-ANTHONY, research psychologist; b. Newark, Mar. 4, 1942; s. Pasquale and Vincenza (Caramanna) Federico; m. Suzanne Marie Boudreaux, Nov. 24, 1967. B.A., U. St. Thomas, Houston, 1965; M.S., Tulane U., 1967, Ph.D., 1969. Sr. research psychologist Navy Personnel Research and Devel Ctr., San Diego, 1972—; mem. hon. faculty U. Colo.-Denver, 1969-71; lectr. San Diego State U., 1972-73, 77. Sr. author: Management Information Systems and Organizational Behavior, 1980, 2d edit., 1985; co-editor: Aptitude, Learning, and Instruction: Vol. 1, Cognitive Process Analyses of Aptitude, 1980, Vol. 2, Cognitive Process Analyses of Learning and Problem Solving, 1980. Served to capt. USAF, 1969-72. NDEA fellow, 1966-69; NSF fellow, 1972-73. Mem. Human Factors Soc. (sec.-treas. San Diego chpt. 1980-81, pres. 1981-82, exec. dir. 1982-85), Cognitive Sci. Soc., Psychonomic Soc., Am. Ednl. Research Assn. Current Work: Human information processing; computer-based instruction and simulation; management information systems and organizational behavior. Subspecialties: Cognition; Learning. Office: Navy Personnel Research and Devel Center San Diego CA 92152

FEDNER, MARK LEE, psychologist, researcher; b. Phila., Dec. 10, 1947; s. Walter and Gloria (Rodin) F.; m. Sherry Lynn Weiner, Sept. 15, 1974; children: Randall Lawrance, Matthew Brant. B.S. in Psychology, Pa. State U., 1969; Ed.M. in Ednl. Psychology, Temple U., 1972, cert. in sch. psychology, 1974, Ph.D. in Sch. Psychology, 1975. Lic. psychologist, Pa. cert. sch. psychologist, Pa., N.J. Grad. asst. asst. supr. dept. sch. psychology Temple U., 1973, 74; sch. psychologist Montgomery County Intermediate Unit, Norristown, Pa., 1975-77; child and youth service dir. N.E. Mental Health Ctr., Phila., 1977-78, clin. dir., 1979-81, psychologist in pvt. practice, Phila., 1981—; presenter, trainer profl. orgns. and agencies; cons. to schs. and social service agencies; presenter, staff trainer N.E. Community Ctr., Phila., 1977-81; participating specialist Health Maintenance Orgn. of Pa.; allied health staff Montgomery Hosp., Norristown, Pa. Mem. Nat. Rifle Assn., Pa. State Alumni Assn., Sports Range, Inc.; Fellow Pa. Psychol. Assn.; mem. Am. Psychol. Assn., Phila. Soc. Clin. Psychologists, Nat. Register Health Service Providers in Psychology, Data Processing Mgmt. Assn. Phila. Current Work: Survey of univariate and multivariate statistical techniques, psychoneurological and psychobiological advances in science for psychological evaluation and assessments. Home: 639 Arbor Rd Cheltenham PA 19012

FEDOROFF, NINA VSEVOLOD, research molecular biologist; b. Cleve., Apr. 9, 1942; d. Vsevolod N Fedoroff and Olga S. (Snegireff) Stacy; children—Natasha Gaganidzo, Kyr Gaganidze. B.S., Syracuse U., 1966; Ph.D., Rockefeller U., 1972. Acting asst prof. UCLA, 1972-74, postdoctoral fellow, 1974-75; staff scientist Carnegie Inst. Washington, Balt., 1975—; cons. Congl. Office Tech. Assessment, Washington, 1980; cons., mem. NIH Recombinant DNA Adv. Com., Bethesda, 1980-85; mem. Nat. Acad. Scis. Commn. on Life Scis., Washington, 1985—; cons. United Agrigrads, Champaign, Ill., 1984—. Contbr. chpt. to book, many articles to profl. jours. NIH research grantee, 1984—. Mem. AAAS. Current work: Molecular biology of maize transportable elements. Subspecialty: Molecular biology. Office: Dept Embryology Carnegie Instn of Washington 115 W University Pkwy Baltimore MD 21212

FEENEY, DANIEL ARTHUR, veterinary radiologist; b. Butte, Mont., June 1, 1950; s. Daniel Henry and Phyllis May (Herrin) F.; m. Janet May Emrick, June 16, 1973; 1 child, Russell Dominick. Student Mont. State U., 1968-70; B.S., Colo. State U., 1972, D.V.M., 1974; M.S., U. Ga., 1978. Diplomate Am. Coll. Vet. Radiology. Intern, Purdue U., 1974-75; radiology resident U. Ga., Athens, 1975-78; asst. prof. radiology Coll. Vet. Medicine, U. Minn., St. Paul, 1978-82, assoc. prof. radiology, 1982—. Contbr. chpts. to textbook, numerous articles to sci. jours. Mem. AVMA, Radiol. Soc. N.Am., Am. Inst. Ultrasound in Medicine, Phi Zeta (sec.-treas. 1983-85), Sigma Phi Epsilon Alumni (sec. Mpls. 1980-84). Republican. Roman Catholic. Current work: Normal canine and feline excretory urograms, distension retrograde urethrocystography in male dog, effects of urethrocystography contrast media. Office: Dept Small Animal Clin Scis Coll of Vet Medicine Univ of Minn 1352 Boyd Ave Saint Paul MN 55108

FEENEY, JOSEPH JOHN, chemist, inhalation toxicologist; b. Archbald, Pa., Jan. 5, 1945; s. Joseph John and Marjorie (Kelly F.; m. Nancy Ruth Davis, Jan. 26, 1980. B.S., U. Scranton, 1967; M.S., U. Vt., 1974; Ph.D., U. Pitts., 1979. Lab. technician Eastman Kodak, Rochester, N.Y., 1966; teaching asst. U. Vt., Burlington, 1970-74; teaching fellow U. Pitts., 1974-79; tech. advisor NASA Indsl. Applications Ctr., Pitts., 1980; research chemist Chem. Research & Devel. Command Dept. Army, Aberdeen Proving Ground, Md., 1980—. Author numerous tech. and spl. reports. Served to lt. j.g. USNR, 1969-70, comdr. Res. Mem. Am. Chem. Soc., Naval Inst., Naval Res. Assn., Am. Assn. Aerosol Research, Sigma Xi (Chesapeake chpt. sec. 1982-84, pres. elect 1984). Democrat. Roman Catholic. Current work: Inhalation toxicological evaluation of various chemical compounds and mixtures; analytical methodology applicable to chemicals in either vapor or aerosol form. Subspecialty: Inorganic chemistry. Home: 616 Mauser Dr Bel Air MD 21014 Office: Dept Army Chem Research & Devl Ctr Aberdeen Proving Ground MD 21010

FEHER, LESLIE, psychologist; b. N.Y.C., Mar. 6, 1944; d. Alexander and Elizabeth (Geller) F.; m. Ralph R. Ferney, Nov. 3, 1967; 1 dau., Vanessa. B.A., Pace U., 1967; M.A., New Sch. for Social Research, 1970. Lic. therapist, N.Y. Asst. dir. Analytic Inst. for Motivational Edn., N.Y.C., 1968-74; dir., founder The E.F. Natal Therapy Inst., N.Y.C., 1974—; exec. dir., founder, pres. Assn. for Birth Psychology, N.Y.C., 1978—, pvt. practice psychology, 1974—; guest lectr. in field. Author: The Psychology of Birth: The Roots of Human Personality, 1980; editor-in-chief: Birth Psychology Bull, 1979—; contbr. articles to profl. jours. Mem. Am. Psychol. Assn., Am. Orthopsychiat. Assn., Eastern Psychol. Assn., Assn. Women in Sci., Authors League. Democrat. Unitarian. Current Work: Research into perinatal theory and effect of birth on later personality. Subspecialty: Perinatal psychology. Home: 444 E 82d St New York NY 10028 Office: New York NY 10028

FEIGELSON, ERIC DENNIS, astrophysicist, educator; b. Springfield, Ohio, Apr. 23, 1953; s. Philip and Muriel F. (Horowitz) F. B.A., Haverford (Pa.) Coll., 1975; M.A., Harvard U., 1978, Ph.D., 1980. Teaching fellow Harvard U., Cambridge, Mass., 1976-77; research assoc. Smithsonian Astrophys. Obs., Cambridge, 1977-80; staff research scientist Center for Space Research and dept. physics M.I.T., Cambridge, 1980-82; asst. prof. dept. astronomy Pa. State U., 1982-85, assoc. prof., 1985—; vis. faculty Sci. Coll., Concordia U., Montreal, 1982. Contbr. articles to profl. jours. Smithsonian predoctoral fellow, 1975-77; John Parker fellow, 1978; recipient NASA Group Achievement award, 1980; Presdl. Young Investigator award NSF, 1984—. Mem. Am. Astron. Soc., N.Y. Sci., Fedn. Am. Scientists, Union Concerned Scientists, Phi Beta Kappa, Sigma Xi. Current Work: Observational x-ray and radio astronomy; active galactic nuclei, radio galaxies, young stars. Subspecialties: X-ray high energy astrophysics; Radio and microwave astronomy. Office: PA State U Dept Astronomy State College PA 16802

FEIGEN, LARRY PHILIP, physiologist, researcher, educator; b. Everett, Mass., Mar. 27, 1942; s. Robert and Celia (Beecher) F.; m. Judy Lee Segel, Dec. 26, 1965; children: Scott, Sharon. B.A. in Physics, Northeastern U., 1964, M.S., 1966; Ph.D. in Physiology and Biophysics, U. Health Scis., Chgo. Med. Sch., 1974. Asst. prof. Tulane U., New Orleans, 1974-81, assoc. prof. physiology, 1981—. Contbr. articles, book chpts. to profl. lit. Recipient Edward G. Schlieder Found. award, 1974-78; Am. Heart Assn. grantee, 1975-77, 79-81, 83-86; NIH grantee, 1980-83. Mem. Am. Soc. Exptl. Biology (fellow circulation group), AAAS, AAUP, Am. Physiol. Soc. (fellow circulation group), Am. Soc. Pharmacology and Exptl. Therapeutics, N.Y. Acad. Scis., Am. Heart Assn. (basic sci. council, circulation council), La. Heart Assn. Jewish. Current Work: Hormonal control of the circulation and mechanisms which regulate these hormones with special emphasis on eicosanoids. Subspecialties: Physiology (medicine); Pharmacology. Home: 2157 LaSalle Ave Gretna LA 70053 Office: 1430 Tulane Ave New Orleans LA 70112

FEIGENBAUM, EDWARD ALBERT, computer scientist, educator; b. Weehawken, N.J., Jan. 20, 1936; s. Fred J. and Sara Rachman; m. H. Penny Nii, 1975; children: Janet Denise, Carol Leonora, Sheri Bryant, Karin Bryant. B.S. in Elec. Engring., Carnegie Inst. Tech., 1956, Ph.D. in Indsl. Adminstrn.,

1960. Asst., then assoc. prof. bus. adminstrn. U. Calif. at Berkeley, 1960-64; assoc. prof. computer sci., then prof. Stanford U., 1965—; prin. investigator heuristic programming project, 1965—; dir. Computation Center Stanford U., 1965-68, chmn. dept. computer sci., 1976-81; pres. Intelli Genetics Inc., 1980-81, mem. tech. adv. bd., 1983—; cons. to industry, 1957—; dir. Sperry Corp.; Mem. computer and biomath. scis. study sect. NIH, 1968-72, mem. adv. com. on artificial intelligence in medicine, from 1974; mem. adv. com. Health Care Tech. Center, U. Mo., Columbia; mem. Math. Social Sci. Bd., 1975-78; computer sci. adv. com. NSF, 1977-80; mem. Internat. Joint Council on Artificial Intelligence, from 1973. Author: (with others) Information Processing Language V Manual, 1961, (with P. McCorduck) The Fifth Generation, 1984, (with R. Lindsay, B. Buchanan, J. Lederberg) Applications of Artificial Intelligence to Organic Chemistry: the Dendral Program. Editor: (with J. Feldman) Computers and Thought, 1963, (with A. Barr and P. Cohen) Handbook of Artificial Intelligence, 1981, 82. Mem. editorial bd. Jour. Artificial Intelligence, from 1969. Fulbright scholar Gt. Britain, 1959-60. Fellow AAAS; Mem. Assn. Computing Machinery (nat. council 1966-68, chmn. spl. interest group on biol. applications 1973-76), Am. Assn. Artificial Intelligence (pres. 1980-81), Cognitive Sci. Soc. (council 1979-81), Am. Psychol. Assn., AAAS, Sigma Xi, Tau Beta Pi, Eta Kappa Nu, Pi Delta Epsilon. Current Work: Artificial intelligence, heuristic programming, expert systems, knowledge engineering, advanced computer architectures. Subspecialties: Artificial intelligence; Computer architecture. Office: Computer Sci Dept Stanford U Stanford CA 94305

FEIGENBAUM, MITCHELL JAY, theoretical physicist; b. Phila., Dec. 19, 1944; s. Abraham Joseph and Mildred (Sugar) F. B.E.E., CCNY, 1964; Ph.D. in Physics, MIT, 1970. Research assoc., instr. dept. physics Cornell U., Ithaca, N.Y., 1970-72, prof. physics, 1982—; research assoc. dept. physics Va. Poly. Inst., Blacksburg, 1972-74; mem. staff theory div. Los Alamos Nat. Lab., 1974-81, lab. fellow, 1981-82. Contbr. articles to profl. jours. Recipient Disting. Performance award Los Alamos Nat. Lab., 1980; E.O. Lawrence Meml. award Dept. Energy, 1983. Mem. Am. Phys. Soc., N.Y. Acad. Scis., Sigma Xi. Developer of universal scaling theory for the onset of chaos; prin. developer of the subdiscipline of chaotic phenomena. Current Work: Development of physical and mathematical techniques to describe the onset of turbulence (or more generally chaos) in complex dynamical systems. Subspecialties: Chaotic phenomena; Theoretical physics. Office: Cornell U 538 Clark Hall Ithaca NY 14853

FEIN, MICHAEL E., laser engineer, gas discharge device engineer; B.A., Harvard U., 1963; M.S.E.E., U. Ill., 1966, Ph.D. in Elec. E.E, 1969. Engr. Zenith Radio Corp. Research Div., Chgo., 1963-64, Owens-Illinois, Inc., Toledo, 1970-79; engring. sect. mgr. Spectra-Physics, Inc., Mountain View and San Jose, Calif., 1979-82; with KLA Instruments Corp., Santa Clara, Calif., 1982—. Contbr. papers to profl. jours. Mem. IEEE, Optical Soc. Am., Soc. Photo-optical Instrumentation Engrs. Patentee U.S. and abroad. Current Work: Designing diffraction-limited digital microscopes. Subspecialties: Optical engineering; Laser design. Home: 1909 Lime Tree Ln Mountain View CA 94040 Office: 2051 Mission College Blvd Santa Clara CA 95054

FEINBERG, GERALD, physicist, educator; b. N.Y.C., May 27, 1933; s. Leon and Florence (Weingarten) F.; m. Barbara J. Silberdick, Aug. 9, 1968; children—Jeremy Russell, Douglas Loren. B.A., Columbia U., 1953, M.A., 1954, Ph.D., 1957. Mem. Inst. Advanced Study, Princeton, N.J., 1956-57; research assoc. Brookhaven Nat. Lab., Upton, N.Y., 1957-59, cons., 1960-74; prof. physics dept. Columbia U., N.Y.C., 1959—, chmn., 1980-82. Author: The Prometheus Project, 1969, What is the World Made Of? , 1977, Consequences of Growth, 1977, Life Beyond Earth, 1980, Solid Clues, 1985; div. assoc. editor: Phys. Rev. Letter, 1983—; Contbr. articles to profl. jours. Sloan Found. fellow, 1960-64; Overseas fellow Churchill Coll., Cambridge, Eng., 1963-64; Guggenheim fellow, 1973-74. Fellow Am. Phys. Soc.; mem. Sigma Xi. Current Work: Theory of subatomic particles; quantum field theory; cosmology; conditions for, and types of, extraterrestrial life. Subspecialties: Theoretical physics; Extraterrestrial life. Home: 535 E 86th St New York NY 10028

FEINBERG, ROBERT JACOB, radiation physicist, scientific administrator; b. Chelsea, Mass., Apr. 6, 1931; s. Charles S. and Mary A. (Melamed) F.; m. Carole I. Young, May 31, 1964; children: Curt Michael, Mark William. B.S. in Physics, Boston Coll., 1953, M.S. in Physics, 1954; M.S. in Radiation Biology, U. Rochester, 1955; grad. in nuclear engring, Oak Ridge Sch. Reactor Tech., 1956. Physicist Picatinny Arsenal, Dover, N.J., 1951, Nat. Bur. Standards, Washington, 1952; astrophysicist Air Force Cambridge (Mass.) Research Center, 1953; instr. in physics Boston Coll., Chestnut Hill, Mass., 1954; health physicist Brookhaven Nat. Lab., Upton, N.Y., 1955; nuclear engr. Oak Ridge Nat. Lab., 1955-56; physicist-radiol. devel. Gen. Electric Co., Knolls Atomic Power Lab., Schenectady, 1956-58, supr. nuclear and radiol. safety, 1958-66, mgr. health physics and nuclear safety, 1966-76, project dir. radiol. controls, 1976—. AEC fellow, 1954-55. Mem. Internat. Health Physics Soc. (chmn. admissions com. 1969-72, chmn. membership com. 1972-75, dir. 1982—), Health Physics Soc. (pres. Northeastern N.Y. chpt. 1957, 69), Am. Nuclear Soc. Jewish. Inventor beta radiation dosimeter, 1958. Current Work: Radiological physics and engineering; reactor safeguards and nuclear safety; radiation dosimetry and radiation control; environmental hazards analysis; radiation effects; waste management. Subspecialties: Biophysics (physics); Nuclear fission. Home: 1223 Godfrey Ln Schenectady NY 12309 Office: Gen Electric Co Knolls Atomic Power Lab River Rd Schenectady NY 12301

FEINERMAN, BURTON, physician, cancer researcher; b. N.Y.C., July 2, 1929; s. David and Pauline (Mendelsohn) F.; m. Judith Einhorn, Oct. 23, 1960; children: Steven, Gregg. B.A., N.Y.U., 1950; M.D., N.Y. Med. Coll., 1954. Diplomate: Am. Bd. Pediatrics. Intern L.I. Coll. Hosp., 1954-55; resident in pediatrics Flower & Fifth Ave. Hosp., N.Y.C., 1955-56, Mayo Clinic, Rochester, Minn., 1956-57; chief pediatrics Cloverleaf Hosp., North Miami Beach, Fla., 1962-64, North Miami Gen. Hosp., 1972-74, Internat. Hosp., Miami, 1982—; adj. prof. microbiology also asst. clin. prof. pediatrics Southeastern Coll. Medicine, 1981—; research assoc. Papanicolaou Cancer Research Inst., 1982—; dir. research Cancer Tech., Inc., 1981—. Author articles in field. Served to capt. M.C. AUS, 1957-59. Fellow Am. Soc. Hematology; mem. Am. Soc. Clin. Oncology, Am. Acad. Pediatrics, Pediatric Soc. Hematology-Oncology, Am. Coll. Allergy, Am. Assn. Clin. Immunology and Allergy, Am. Soc. Microbiology. Current Work: Control cancer metastasis with biological response modifers, immunology of malignancy, immunodeficiencies, brain tumors and blood brain barrier. Subspecialties: Immunopharmacology; Cancer research (medicine). Office: 640 NW 18301 St Miami FL 33169

FEINSTEIN, ALVAN RICHARD, physician; b. Phila., Dec. 4, 1925; s. Joel B. and Bella (Ukasz) F.; B.S., U. Chgo., 1947, M.S. in Math, 1948, M.D., 1952; M.A. (hon.), Yale U., 1969. Intern, then resident Yale-New Haven Hosp., 1952-54; research fellow Rockefeller Inst., 1954-55; resident Columbia-Presbyn. Med. Center, N.Y.C., 1955-56; clin. dir. Irvington House, N.Y.C., 1956-62; instr., then asst. prof. N.Y. U. Sch. Medicine, 1956-62; chief clin. pharmacology VA Hosp., West Haven, Conn., 1962-64, chief clin. biostatistics, 1964-74; mem. faculty Sch. Medicine, Yale U., 1962—, prof. medicine and epidemiology, 1969—, dir. clin. scholar program, 1974—; chief Eastern Research Support Center, VA, 1967-74; Pres. New Haven area chpt. Assn. Computing Machinery, 1968-69. Author: Clinical Judgment, 1967, Clinical Biostatistics, 1977; Clinical Epidemiology, 1985; editor: Jour. Chronic Diseases; also articles. Served with AUS, 1944-46. Recipient Francis G. Blake award for outstanding teaching Yale Med. Sch., 1969. Mem. Assn. Am. Physicians, Am. Soc. Clin. Investigation, Am. Epidemiol. Soc., A.C.P., Inst. Medicine, Am. Fedn. Clin. Research, Am. Soc. Clin. Pharmacology Therapeutics, Am. Statis. Assn., Assn. Computing Machinery, Biometric Soc., Am. Heart Assn., Am. Assn. History Medicine, Alpha Omega Alpha. Current Work: Clinical epidemiology for evaluation of diagnostic, prognostic, and therapeutic strategies in medicine; clinical biostatistics. Subspecialties: Internal medicine; Epidemiology. Home: 164 Linden St New Haven CT 06511 Office: 333 Cedar St New Haven CT 06510

FEINSTEIN, JOSEPH, electronics engineer, educator; b. N.Y.C., July 8, 1925; s. David and Edith (Morgenstern) F.; m. Elaine Cantor, Mar. 2, 1952; children: Susan, David, Jonathan. B.E.E., Cooper Union, 1944; M.A. in Physics, Columbia U., 1947; Ph.D. in Physics, NYU, 1951. Mem. staff Nat. Bur. Standards, Washington, 1949-54; mem. tech. staff, dept. head Bell Telephone Labs., Murray Hill, N.J., 1954-59; dir. research S-F-D Labs., Union, N.J., 1959-64, exec. v.p., 1960-64; v.p. research Varian Assocs., Palo Alto, Calif., 1964-79; dir. electronics and phys. scis. Dept. Def., 1980-83; vis. prof., cons. in electronics Stanford U. (Calif.), 1983—. Editor, contbg. author: Crossed Field Microwave Devices, 1968, Electronics Engineers Handbook, 1975, 81. Fellow IEEE; mem. Nat. Acad. Engring. Patentee in communications, microwaves, electron tubes. Current Work: Free electron laser, E beam and x-ray lithography for microelectronics. Subspecialties: Laser power generation; Microelectronics. Home: 2398 Branner Dr Menlo Park CA 94025 Office: Stanford U Dept Elec Engring Stanford CA

FEIT, WALTER, mathematics educator, researcher; b. Vienna, Austria, Oct. 26, 1930; married, 1957; 2 children. B.A., M.S., U. Chgo., 1951; Ph.D. in Math, U. Mich., 1954. Instr. in math. Cornell U., 1953-55, from asst. prof. to assoc. prof., 1956-64; prof. math. Yale U., 1964—. NSF fellow Inst. Advanced Study, 1958-59. Mem. Nat. Acad. Sci., Am. Math. Soc. (Cole prize 1965), Math. Assn. Am. Office: Dept Math Yale U New Haven CT 06520*

FELD, MICHAEL STEPHEN, educator; b. N.Y.C., Nov. 11, 1940; s. Albert and Lillian R. Norwalk; m. Frances Aschheim, Mar. 2, 1980; children—David A., Jonathan R., Alexander A. S.B. in Humanities and Sci, M.I.T., 1963, S.M. in Physics, 1963, Ph.D. in Physics, 1967. Postdoctoral fellow M.I.T., Cambridge, 1967-68, asst. prof., 1968-73, asso. prof., 1973-79, prof. physics, 1979—, dir. spectroscopy lab., 1976—, dir. MIT Laser Research Ctr., 1979—. Editorial bd.: Laser Focus Mag; co-editor: Fundamental and Applied Laser Physics, 1973, Coherent Nonlinear Optics, 1980. Alfred P. Sloan research fellow, 1973; recipient Disting. Service award M.I.T. Minority Community, 1980, Gordon W. Billard award, 1982. Fellow Am. Optical Soc., Sigma Xi, Am. Phys. Soc. Condr. research laser saturation spectroscopy. Current Work: Lasers, coherent processes, biomedical applications. Subspecialty: Atomic and molecular physics. Home: 56 Hinckley Rd Waban MA 02168 Office: 77 Massachusetts Ave Cambridge MA 02139

FELDMAN, ALBERT WILLIAM, educator; b. Gardner, Ill., Aug. 6, 1918; s. Joseph M. and Ann (Miller) F.; m. Helen Taylor, July 21, 1944; children: Michael Ann Feldman Immerso, William Taylor. A.B., U. Ill., 1942; M.S., N.C. State U., 1944; Ph.D., U. Minn., 1947. Asst. prof. plant pathology U.R.I., Kingston, 1947-51; mgr. research and devel. Uniroyal Chem. Co., Naugatuck, Conn., 1951-58; mem. faculty U. Fla., Lake Alfred, 1958—, prof. plant pathology, 1958—. Contbr. articles to profl. jours. Mem. Internat. Orgn. Citrus Virologists, Am. Phytopath. Soc., AAAS, Am. Soc. Plant Physiologists, Soil and Crop Sci. Soc. Fla., Sigma Xi. Lodge: Elks. Patentee in field. Current Work: Researcher in disease physiology and virology. Subspecialties: Plant pathology; Plant physiology (agriculture). Office: University of Florida Lake Alfred FL 33850

FELIPPA, CARLOS ALBERTO, civil engineer, scientist; b. Cordoba, Argentina, Apr. 28, 1941; came to U.S., 1964, naturalized, 1984; s. Francisco A. and Evelina N. Felippa. Ingeniero Civil, U. Cordoba, 1963; M.S. in Civil Engring., U. Calif.-Berkeley, 1964, Ph.D. in Civil Engring., 1966. Registered profl. engr., Calif. Research asst. U. Calif.-Berkeley, 1964-66, postdoctoral fellow, 1967-68; research engr. Boeing Co., Seattle, 1968-71; research scientist Lockheed Research Lab., Palo Alto, Calif., 1971-76, staff scientist, 1976—; cons. in field; tchr. in field. Contbr. articles and tech. papers to profl. publs. Mem. Soc. Indsl. and Applied Math., ASCE. Current work: Computational mechanics, numerical analysis, computer sciences, software systems, database systems, artificial intelligence. Subspecialties: Structural engineering; Numerical analysis (computer science). Office: Applied Mechanics Lab Org 9250 B 255 Lockheed Palo Alto Research Lab 3251 Hanover St Palo Alto CA 94304

FELIX, ARTHUR MARTIN, chemist, researcher; b. N.Y., June 15, 1938; s. Barney and Beatrice (Thaler) F.; m. Maureen A. Kopelson, Oct. 28, 1967; children—Alison, Stephan. B.A., NYU, 1959; Ph.D., Poly. Inst. N.Y., 1964. Sr. research scientist Hoffmann-La Roche Inc., Nutley, N.J., 1966-75, research fellow, 1976-80, research group chief, 1980-83, asst. dir., 1983-85, dept. head, 1985—. Contbr. numerous articles to profl. jours. Patentee in field. Bd. dirs. Big Bros./Sisters of Bergen-Passaic, N.J., 1980-82; pres. Washington Sch. Home-Sch. Assn., West Caldwell, N.J., 1980-82. Mem. Am. Chem. Soc., N.J. Inst. Chemists (councilman 1983-84), Royal Soc. Chemists, Sigma Xi (pres. 1980-81), Phi Lambda Upsilon. Current work: Synthesis of biologically active peptides and proteins, preparation of novel pharmaceuticals. Subspecialties: Organic chemistry; Synthetic chemistry. Home: 257 Central Ave West Caldwell NJ 07006 Office: Hoffmann-La Roche Inc Nutley NJ 07110

FELIX, MICHAEL O(TTO), retired electronics company executive, electronic engineer; b. Birkenhead, Cheshire, Eng., Oct. 10, 1922; came to U.S., 1960, naturalized, 1965; s. Otto and Mary E. (Lindner) F.; m. Jeane Durie, Sept. 7, 1957; children—Celia E., Ian C. B.Sc. with 1st class honors, City and Guilds, London, 1942. Engr., Can. Westinghouse Co., Hamilton, Ont., 1955-60; with Ampex Advanced Tech., Redwood City, Calif., 1960-85, chief engr. various divs., 1965-81, v.p., mgr. advanced tech. div., 1981-85. Mem. IEEE (sr.), Soc. Motion Picture and TV Engrs. (Poniatoff award 1983). Subspecialties: Applied magnetics; Telecommunications. Office: Ampex Advanced Tech MS 3-08 401 Broadway Redwood City CA 94063

FELLER, DOUGLAS LEE, veterinarian researcher; b. Watseka, Ill., Dec. 27, 1951; s. Joseph Lucien and Kathleen Anne (Plotner) F.; m. Brenda Kay Lewis, Sept. 20, 1980; children—Jonathan, Sarah, Benjamin. Student Eastern Ill. U., 1970-73; B.S.V.M., U. Ill., 1975, D.V.M., 1977. Teaching assoc. Wash. State U., Pullman, 1977; anesthesiology resident U. Ill., Urbana, 1978-80; vet. cons. Ralston Purina Co., St. Louis, 1980-81; sr. scientist Eli Lilly and Co., Indpls., 1981—; chmn. animal sci. adv. council U. Minn.-St. Paul, 1984—; speaker Am. Soc. Animal Sci., Columbia, Mo., 1984. Contbr. articles to profl. jours. Jesse Sampson fellow, 1976; Sidney Marlin fellow, 1977; Ill. Vet. Med. Assn. fellow, 1977. Mem. AVMA, Am. Assn. Indsl. Veterinarians, Am. Assn. Swine Practitioners. Presbyterian. Current work: Applied animal health, physiology, and nutritional research; regulatory affairs. Subspecialty: Physiology; Veterinary pharmacology. Office: Eli Lilly and Co Lilly Corp Ctr Indianapolis IN 46285

FELLEY, DONALD LOUIS, See *Who's Who in America,* 43rd edition.

FELLOWS, W(ALTER) SCOTT, JR., nuclear engineer; b. Columbus, Ohio, Sept. 26, 1918; s. Walter Scott and Nellie Bonner (Rinesmith) F.; m. Julia Ann Grassbaugh, Feb. 14, 1948 (dec. 1979); children: Marsha, Nancy, Joanne. B.Mech.Engring., Ohio State U., 1940; M.S., Purdue U., 1950; Ph.D., Sch. Reactor Tech., Oak Ridge, 1954. Registered profl. engr., Ohio, Ala. Commd. 2d lt. U.S. Army Air Force, 1940, advanced through grades to col., 1958, ret., 1965; chief direct cycle office AEC, Washington, 1954-57; asst. mgr. for ops. AEC (Lockland Aircraft reactor ops.), Cin., 1957-60; RIFT nuclear rocket project mgr. ROVER program Marshall Space Flight Ctr., NASA, Huntsville, Ala., 1960-65, dir. ops. mgmt. office, 1965-70; sr. research engr. So. States Energy Bd., Atlanta, 1970-84. Decorated D.F.C. with one oak leaf cluster, Legion of Merit. Fellow AIAA (assoc.); mem. Am. Nuclear Soc. Current Work: Consulting engineer; nuclear engineering; astronautics. Subspecialties: Aerospace engineering and technology; Nuclear fission. Home and Office: 9450 Coleman Rd Roswell GA 30075

FELNER, ROBERT DAVID, psychology educator; b. Norwich, Conn., June 3, 1950; s. Joseph and Roslyn (Aptaker) F.; m. Tweety Jan Yates. B.A., U. Conn., 1972; M.A., U. Rochester, 1975, Ph.D., 1977. Lic. psychologist, Ala. Research asst. U. Conn., Storrs, 1971-72; clin. psychology trainee U. Rochester, N.Y., 1972-73, U. Rochester Med. Center/Convalescent Hosp., 1973-76; asst. prof. psychology Yale U., New Haven, 1976-81; assoc. prof., dir. clin. psychology program Auburn (Ala.) U., 1981—; cons. Conn. Bar Assn., 1978-81, City of New Haven Schs., 1977-82, NIMH, 1978—; mem. grant com. NIH. Author: Community and Preventive Psychology, 1984; editor: Preventive Psychology, 1983; contbr. chpts. to books, articles to profl. jours. NIMH grantee, 1976-77; Edward W. Hazen Found. grantee, 1978-81; NSF grantee, 1978—. Fellow Am. Psychol. Assn., Am. Orthopsychiat. Assn.; mem. Council Clin. Program Dirs., Council Community Psychology Program Dirs. Democrat. Jewish. Current Work: Primary prevention of emotional problems of children; life transitions; pediatric psychology; family disruption; child custody. Subspecialties: Clinical psychology; Developmental psychology. Home: 830 Moores Hill Rd Auburn AL 36830 Office: Dept Psychology Auburn U Haley Center Auburn AL 36849

FELTON, JAMES EDGAR, astrophysicist; b. Duluth, Minn., Sept. 8, 1934. B.A. cum laude, in Physics and Math., U. Minn.-Duluth, 1956; Ph.D. in Astrophysics, Cornell U., 1965. Teaching asst. dept. physics Cornell U., Ithaca, N.Y., 1957-62, du Pont teaching scholar, 1959-60, research asst. Ctr. Radiophysics and Space Research, 1962-65; physicist Ballistic Research Labs., Aberdeen Proving Ground, Md., summer 1958; asst. research engr. space physics and planetary scis. sect. Douglas Aircraft Co., Santa Monica, Calif., summers 1959-62; asst. research physicist dept. physics U. Calif.-San Diego, 1965-68, vis. research physicist, 1980; vis. fellow Inst. Theoretical Astronomy, U. Cambridge, Eng., 1968-70; IAU vis. fellow Tata Inst. Fundamental Research, Bombay, India, 1970; vis. prof. U. Padova, U. Bologna, Italy, 1970; vis. assoc. prof. and assoc. astronomer, Steward Obs., U. Ariz., Tucson, 1970-72, assoc. prof. and assoc. astronomer, 1972-75; sr. resident research assoc. Nat. Acad. Scis./NRC, NASA Goddard Space Flight Ctr., Greenbelt, Md., 1976-78; NASA sr. research assoc. dept. physics and astronomy, U. Md., College Park, 1978, vis. prof., 1978-79, NASA sr. research assoc., 1979—; vis. lectr. cosmology series U. Va., 1974-77. Contbr. writings in field to sci. publs. Fellow Am. Phys. Soc.; mem. Am. Astron. Soc., Internat. Astron. Union. Research or work interests: Theoretical high-energy astrophysics, X-ray and gamma-ray astronomy, cosmic rays, interstellar and intergalactic medium, galaxies, cosmology. Subspecialty: Theoretical astrophysics. Home: 8569 Greenbelt Rd #204 Greenbelt MD 20770 Office: NASA Code 697 Goddard Space Flight Ctr Greenbelt MD 20771

FELTS, WAYNE MOORE, geologist, consultant; b. Oakland, Calif., Aug. 5, 1912; s. Isaac Thomas and Josephine Veva (Moore) F.; m. Bettie Lou Snoddy, June 25, 1942; children—Wayne Moore Jr., Thomas Arnon. B.S., Oreg. State Coll., 1934, M.S., 1936; Ph.D., U. Cin., 1938. Geologist Phillips Petroleum Co., Amarillo Tex. and Bartlesville, Okla., 1943-47, The Tex. Co. subs. Texaco Inc., numerous locations, 1947-58; div. geologist Texaco Inc., Los Angeles, 1958-62, asst. to div. mgr., Anchorage, 1962-66, mgr. hard mineral exploration, Denver, 1966-73; ret., 1973; pvt. investigator in field, Nev., Wash., Alaska, 1973-79; prin. W.M. Felts Geol. Services, Boulder City, Nev., 1979—; vice chmn. Alaska com. Western Oil and Gas Assn., Anchorage, 1962-63; mem. ocean ops. com. Am. Petroleum Inst., Houston and Washington, 1968-71; assoc. prof. Pa. State U., 1949-50. Ohio Acad. sci. grantee, 1937. Fellow Geol. Soc. Am., AAAS; mem. Am. Assn. Petroleum Geologists (research com. 1954-57), Am. Inst. Profl. Geologists (cert. profl. geologist), SAR (pres. Las Vegas club 1975-76), Sigma Xi. Republican. Current work: Consulting petroleum geologist; petrology of cement clinker; concrete and ceramic materials. Subspecialties: Geology; Petrology. Home: PO Box 306 1438 Sorrel Boulder City NV 89005 Office: WM Felts Geol Services PO Box 306 Boulder City NV 89005

FELTS, WILLIAM ROBERT, JR., physician; b. Judsonia, Ark., Apr. 24, 1923; s. Wylie Robert and Willie Etidorpha (Lewis) F.; m. Jeanne E. Kennedy, Feb. 17, 1954 (div. 1971); children: William R. III, Thomas Wylie, Samuel Clay, Melissa Jeanne. B.S., U. Ark., 1944, M.D., 1946. Intern Garfield Meml. Hosp., Washington, 1946-47; resident in medicine Gallinger Mcpl. Hosp., Washington, 1949-51; resident in medicine George Washington U. Hosp., 1951-53, trainee in rehab. (rheumatology), 1955-57; asst. chief arthritis research unit VA Hosp., Washington, 1953-54, adj. asst. chief, 1954-58, chief, 1958-62; cons. in rheumatology U.S. Naval Hosp., Bethesda, Md., 1957-70; mem. faculty dept. medicine George Washington U., 1962—, asso. prof., 1962-80, prof., 1980—, dir. div. rheumatology, 1970-79; mem. Nat. Commn. on Arthritis and Related Musculoskeletal Diseases, 1975-76, Nat. Com. on Health and Vital Stats., 1983—, Nat. Arthritis Adv. Bd., 1977-80, 80-83; mem. nat. com. on health policy Project Hope, 1977; cons. health affairs and mem. profl. adv. bd. Control Data Corp., 1976—; mem. D.C. Health Planning Adv. Com., 1969-72; chmn. med. adv. com. D.C. chpt. Arthritis Found., 1963-86, v.p., 1983; bd. dirs. Symposium on Computer Applications in Med. Care, 1980—, pres., 1983-84; mem. WHO Task Force on Rheumatology in Developing Countries, 1982, 84. Author articles in field, especially med. socioecons.; Mem. editorial adv. bd., cons. internal medicine: Current Procedural Terminology, 3d edit, 1972-73; editorial adv. bd.: Internal Medicine News, 1976—. Bd. dirs. Nat. Capital Med. Found., 1979-84, pres., 1980-81. Served with AUS, 1943-46, 47-49. Mem. Am. Soc. Internal Medicine (dir. 1969-78, pres. 1976-77), AMA (chmn. council on legis. 1985—, chmn. editorial adv. panel CPT-4 1980—), Am. Fedn. Clin. Research, Am. Rheumatism Assn., Inst. Medicine of Nat. Acad. Scis., Nat. Acad. Practice in Medicine (founding mem. 1982), D.C. Med. Soc. (chmn. legis. com. 1972-76), D.C. Soc. Internal Medicine (exec. council 1975-78), N.Y. Acad. Scis., So. Med. Assn. (sec. sect. internal medicine 1978-79, vice-chmn. 1979-80, chmn. 1980-81, asso. councilor 1979-81), Rheumatism Soc. D.C. (pres. 1963-64), Internat. League against Rheumatism (chmn. subcom. on classification and nomenclature 1982—), Alpha Epsilon Delta, Phi Chi, Kappa Sigma. Republican. Baptist. Clubs: Masons, George Wever. Current Work: Rheumatology. Subspecialty: Internal medicine. Home: 4827 N 27th Pl Arlington VA 22207 Office: 2150 Pennsylvania Ave NW Washington DC 20037

FENNELLY, ALPHONSUS JOHN, physicist, educator; b. Bklyn., Dec. 15, 1946; s. John Wilde and Ursula Daisy (Evans) F.; m. Sara Susan Bernhardt, July 4, 1975 (div. 1977); m. Judy Ann Giles, Mar. 4, 1983; children—Martin Mandrew, John Wilde II. B.A., Manhattan Coll., 1968; M.S., Yeshiva U., 1974, Ph.D., 1975. Jours. prodn. editor Am. Elsevier, N.Y.C., 1971-72; asst. editorial dir.jours. Acad. Press, N.Y.C., 1972-74; asst. prof. physics Western Ky. U., Bowling Green, 1974-80, assoc. prof., 1980-82; sr. research assoc. Marshall Space Flight Ctr., Huntsville, Ala., 1980-82; research sci. Teledyne Brown Engring., Huntsville, Ala., 1982-84, mgr. applied physics sect., applied sci. br., 1984—; cons. Marshall Space Flight Ctr., Huntsville, 1977-80; assoc. prof. physics U. Ala., Hunstville, 1980-84; adj. assoc. prof., 1984-85. Contbr. articles to profl. jours. Active Tenn. Valley council Cub Scouts Am., 1984-85, Navy League Sea Cadets, 1985; mentor program for sci. and engring. ednl. opportunities for handicapped students FAST (Future Assets-Student Talent), 1985; provider refugee home Western Ky. Refugee Mut. Assistance Fund, Bowling Green, 1979-84. Fellow NRC, NASA; grantee Western Ky. U., NSF, NASA. Mem. IEEE, Soc. Photo-optical Instrument Engrs., Optical Soc. Am., Am. Phys. Soc., Brit. Interplanetary Soc., Am. Geophys. Union, Soc. Exploration Geophysicists, Seismological Soc. Am., Am. Soc. Photogrammetry, Soc. Indsl. and Applied Math., Am. Soc. Naval Inst., Res. Officers Assn., Air Force Assn., Am. Soc. Naval Engrs., U.S. Naval Inst., Sigma Xi, Sigma Pi Sigma, Pi Mu Epsilon. Republican. Roman Catholic. Current work: Design and analysis of sensors and sensor systems to measure all physical signatures; optical sensors; homing sensors; target discrimination; theoretical physics; general relativity. Subspecialties: Theoretical physics; General optics. Home: 1505 Sparkman Dr Apt 263 Huntsville AL 35805 Office: Teledyne Brown Engring MS-47 Cummings Research Park Huntsville AL 35807

FENSKE, PAUL RODERICK, hydrogeologist, research institute executive; b. Ellensberg, Wash., May 15, 1925; s. Reinhold August and Emma Alice (Kunnhausen) F.; m. Deloris Irene Hoff, Dec. 28, 1952; children—Gail, Cheryl, Jon, Mark. B.S., S. D. Sch. Mines & Tech., 1950; M.S., U. Mich., 1951; Ph.D., U. Colo., 1963. Registered profl. engr., Tex. Petroleum engr. Magnolia Petroleum Co., 1951-56; oil field developer Delfer Oil Co., Lubbock, Tex., 1956-59; asst. prof. geology Idaho U., Pocatello, 1963-65; mgr., hydrogeologist Teledyne Isotopes, Palo Alto, Calif., 1965-71; research prof. Desert Research Inst., Reno, 1971-81, acting dir., 1981-83, exec. dir., 1983—. Contbr. articles to profl. jours. Served to T5 U.S. Army, 1943-46, PTO. Mem. Am. Geophys. Union, Am. Water Resources Assn., AIME, Colo. River Water User's Assn. Republican. Lutheran. Current work: Groundwater hydraulics, well hydraulics, groundwater transport of contaminants. Subspecialty: Hydrology. Home: 2630 Trentham Way Reno NV 89509 Office: U Nev Desert Research Inst Water Resource Ctr 7010 Dandini Blvd Reno NV 89512

FENTON, NOEL JOHN, computer systems manufacturing company executive; b. New Haven, May 24, 1938; s. Arnold Alexander and Carla (Mathiasen) F.; m. Sarah Jane Hamilton, Aug. 14, 1965; children: Wendy, Devon, Peter, Lance. B.S., Cornell U., 1959; M.B.A., Stanford U., 1963. Research asst. Stanford (Calif.) U., 1963-64; v.p. Mail Systems Corp., Redwood City, Calif., 1964-66; v.p., gen. mgr. products div. Acurex Corp., Mountain View, Calif., 1966-72, pres., chief exec. officer, dir., 1972-83, Covalent Systems Corp., Santa Clara, Calif., 1983—; dir. Elpac Electronics, Inc., Micro Mask Inc., RPC Industries. Chmn. adv. council Resource Center for Women; mem. San Jose Econ. Devel. Task Force, 1983, Pres. Reagan's Bus. Adv. Panel. Served to lt. (j.g.) USN, 1959-61. Mem. Am. Electronics Assn. (chmn. 1978-79, dir. 1976-80), Young Pres.'s Orgn., Santa Clara County Mfrs. Group (dir.), Stanford Bus. Sch. Alumni Assn. (pres. 1976-77, dir. 1971-76). Republican. Episcopalian. Subspecialty: Electronics company management. Home: 60

Hayfields Rd Portola Valley CA 94025 Office: Coualent Systems Corp 585 Maude Court Sunnyvale CA 94086

FENWICK, BRADLEY WILLARD, research veterinary pathologist, infectious disease specialist; b. Hutchinson, Kans., Mar. 17, 1955; s. Willard Clayton Fenwick and Martha Marrie (Myers) Fenwick Bloom; m. Debbie Lynn Nuss, Jan. 1, 1977; 1 child, Benjamin Bradley. A.A., Hutchinson Jr. Coll., 1975; B.S., Kans. State U., 1977, D.V.M., 1981, M.S., 1982. Instr. pathology Kans. State U., Manhattan, 1981; grad. research assoc. U. Calif.-Davis, 1982—. Contbr. articles to profl. jours. Recipient service award Nat. Cancer Inst., U. Calif., 1981; USDA research grantee, 1983; Calif. Milk Adv. Bd. Research grantee, 1984; Excellence in Vet. Pathology award C.L. Davis Found., 1984. Mem. AVMA, AAAS, Wildlife Disease Assn., N.Y., Acad. Scis. Democrat. Presbyterian. Current work: Infectious diseases of food animals with specialization in the immunopathology of bacterial disease as related to bacterial toxins; production and testing of diagnostic reagents and subunit vaccines for use in food animals. Subspecialties: Pathology (veterinary medicine); Infectious diseases. Home: 825 Arthur Davis CA 95616 Office: Dept Vet Pathology U Calif Davis CA 95616

FERCHAU, HUGO ALFRED, plant ecologist, educator; b. Mineola, N.Y., July 22, 1929; s. Hugo and Melita (Roller) F.; m. Mary Ellen Shea, Dec. 5, 1952; children: Hugo A., Andrea Marie, Erich Marshall, Michele Suzanne. B.S., Coll. of William and Mary, 1951; postgrad., State Coll. of Wash., 1953; Ph.D., Duke U., 1959. Assoc. prof. biology Wofford Coll., Spartanburg, S.C., 1958-62; vis. assoc. prof. biology Duke U., Durham, N.C., summer 1962; asst. prof. botany Western State Coll., Gunnison, Colo., 1962-66, assoc. prof., 1966-69, prof., 1969—; vis. prof. environ. scis. Colo. Sch. Mines, Golden, 1981-82; cons. Contbr. articles on plant ecology to profl. jours. Mem. Bot. Soc. Am., Ecol. Soc. Am., AAAS, Am. Inst. Biol. Scis., S.W. Naturalist Soc., Can. Reclamation Assn., Soc. Range Mgmt., Sigma Xi. Republican. Episcopalian. Current Work: Undergraduate and graduate education development of reclamation programs for industry (mining), supervision of reclamation monitoring, soil microbiology research. Subspecialties: Ecology (environmental science); Microbiology. Home: 819 N Pine Gunnison CO 81230 Office: Biology Dept Western State Coll Gunison CO 81230

FERCHEK, GARY RANDALL, operations research manager; b. Detroit, Jan. 28, 1947; s. Matthew and Stephanie Barbara (Glowacki) F.; m. Mary Ann Pounders, Feb. 2, 1970; 1 dau., Tracie Ann. B.S., U.S. Mil. Acad., 1969; M.S. in Engring, U. Mich., 1976. Commd. 2d lt. U.S. Army, 1969, advanced through grades to maj., 1980; mem. staff and faculty U.S. Army Personnel and Adminstrn. Ctr., Ft. Benjamin Harrison, Ind., 1977-80; resigned, 1980; mgr. ops. research ISACOMM, Atlanta, 1980—. Mem. Ops. Research Soc. Am., Am. Inst. Indsl. Engrs., Mensa. Current Work: Design of an intercity satellite based network utilizing state of the art digital switching and providing voice communications, teleconferencing and digital termination service. Subspecialty: Operations research (engineering). Home: 1868 Remington Rd Atlanta GA 30341 Office: ISACOMM 1815 Century Blvd Suite 500 Atlanta GA 30345

FERER, KENNETH MICHAEL, oceanographer; b. Pitts., Dec. 12, 1937; s. Michael Kenneth and Bertha (Fonos) F.; m. Joan Byrne; children: Michael Kenneth, David Craig. Student, U. Md., 1968-70; B.S., George Washington U., 1972; student, Catholic U. Am., 1973; M.S., U. So. Miss., 1982. Nuclear reactor operator Westinghouse Testing Reactor, Waltz Mills, Pa., 1960-62; test engr. Westinghouse Astronuclear Lab., Large, Pa., 1962; reactor operator Naval Research Lab., Washington, 1963-66, test and oceanographic engr., 1966-75; project engr. naval ocean research and devel. Nat. Sci. Testing Lab. Sta., Miss., 1975-79, project mgr., 1979—; naval rep. Nuclear Power Com., Washington, 1972-75. Contbr. articles to sci. jours. Bd. dirs. 4th Ward Assn., 1981. Served with USN, 1956-58. Mem. Marine Tech. Soc. (med. edn. com.), Am. Geophys. Union. Republican. Roman Catholic. Club: Pontchartrain Yacht. Patentee cable elongation measurement; aramid fiber cable. Current Work: Development and use of new and unique oceanographic instrumentation in order to study the physical, chemical, optical, biological and magnetic properties of the ocean. Subspecialties: Nuclear fission; Ocean engineering. Home: 108 Country Club Dr Covington LA 70433 Office: Naval Research and Devel NSTL Sta MS 39529

FERGUSON, ELDON EARL, physicist; b. Rawlins, Wyo., Apr. 23, 1926; s. George Earl and Bess (Pierce) F. B.S., Okla. U., 1949, M.S., 1950, Ph.D., 1953. Physicist U.S. Naval Research Lab., Washington, 1954-57; prof. physics U. Tex., Austin, 1957-62; dir. aeronomy lab. NOAA, Dept. Commerce, Boulder, Colo., 1962—. Served with U.S. Army, 1944-45. Guggenheim Found. fellow, 1960; Humboldt fellow, 1979-80. Mem. Am. Phys. Soc., Am. Chem. Soc., Am. Geophys. Union. Subspecialty: Aeronomy. Office: 325 Broadway Boulder CO 80302

FERGUSON, JACKSON ROBERT, JR., astronautical engineer; b. Neptune, N.J., Aug. 18, 1942; s. Jackson Robert Sr. and Charlotte Carter (Rudewick) F.; m. Christina Mary Staley, Aug. 24, 1968; children—Jack Christopher, Joy Heather. B.S. in Engring. Sci., U.S. Air Force Acad., 1965; M.S. in Astronautics, Air Force Inst. Tech., 1971; Ph.D. in Aerospace Engring., U. Tex., 1983. Registered profl. engr., Tex. Commd. 2d lt. U.S. Air Force, 1965, advanced through grades to lt. col., 1981; mission dir. Air Force Satellite Control Facility, Sunnyvale, Calif., 1965-70; astronautical engr. NORAD Cheyenne Mountain Complex, Colorado Springs, Colo., 1972-75; asst. prof. astronautics U.S. Air Force Acad., Colorado Springs, 1975-80, assoc. prof., 1982-84; chief scientist European Office Aerospace Research and Devel., London, 1984—; research cons. Global Positioning System, Joint Program Office, Los Angeles, 1976-83. Contbr. articles to profl. jours. Dir. jr. high sch. religious edn. St. Catherine's Ch., Austin, Tex., 1980, dir. adult religious edn., 1982; dir. adult religious edn. Our Lady of Pines Ch., Black Forest, Colo., 1983-84. Recipient Research and Devel. award U.S. Air Force, 1980. Mem. AIAA (space systems tech. com. 1983-84), Am. Astronautical Soc. (sr.), Am. Soc. Engring. Edn. Republican. Roman Catholic. Current work: Orbit mechanics, estimation theory, spacecraft navigation, spacecraft attitude determination and control, European spacecraft subsystems. Subspecialties: Astronautics; Aerospace engineering and technology. Home: Briar House Drews Park Knotty Green Beaconsfield Buckinghamshire HP9 2TT England Office: European Office Aerospace Research and Devel Box 14 FPO New York NY 09510

FERGUSON, RONALD MAX, educator; b. South Beaver Twp., Pa., Sept. 29, 1936; s. Myrle Delbert and Nellie Madeline (Boyer) F.; m. Dorothy Smith, Mar. 15, 1964; children: Clifford Scott, Laura Gail. B.S., Clarion State Coll., 1958; M.S., Temple U., 1962, U. Conn., 1982. Techr. physics and chemistry, Crafton, Pa., 1958-61; tchr. physics Moses Brown, Providence, 1962-65; prof. chemistry Eastern Conn. State U., Willimantic, 1965—, assoc. prof. phys. scis. dept., 1982—. Mem. Am. Chem. Soc., New Eng. Chemistry Tchrs. Assn. Current Work: Atmospheric chemistry, acid rain, trace pollutants research in chem. oceanography. Subspecialties: Analytical chemistry; Atmospheric chemistry. Home: 91 Northfield Rd Coventry CT 06238 Office: Eastern Conn State U Goddard Hall Willimantic CT 06226

FERKO, ANDREW PAUL, pharmacologist; b. b, Trenton, N.J., Aug. 19, 1942; s. Andrew and Margaret (Rogaczewski) F.; m. Joan M., Apr. 24, 1971; children: Carolyn, Karen, Katharine. B.S., Phila. Coll. Pharmacy and Scis., 1965; Ph.D., Hahnemann Med. Coll. and Hosp., 1969. Jr. instr. Hahnemann Med. Coll., Phila., 1967-69, sr. instr., 1969-71, asst. prof., 1971-81, asso. prof., 1981—. Contbg. editor: Basic Pharmacology in Medicine, 1976, 81; contbr. articles to profl. jours. NIH grantee, 1965-69; recipient Lindback Found. teaching award, 1981. Mem. Am. Soc. Pharmacology and Exptl. Therapeutics, Soc. Toxicology, AAAS, N.Y. Acad. Sci., Mid-Atlantic Soc. Toxicology, Phila. Physiol. Soc., Phila. Neurosci Soc., Internat. Soc. Study Xenobiotics, Rho Chi. Current Work: Effects of ethanol on central nervous system. Subspecialties: Pharmacology; Neuropharmacology. Office: Hahnemann Univ Broad and Vine Sts Philadelphia PA 19102

FERLAND, GARY JOSEPH, astrophysicist, educator; b. Washington, May 10, 1951; s. Andrew Joseph and Ida Maria (Schneemann) F.; m. Ann Elizabeth. B.S. in Physics, U. Tex., 1973; Ph.D. in Astrophysics, 1978. Research assoc. Cambridge (Eng.) U., 1978-80; asst. prof. astrophysics U. Ky., Lexington, 1980—; cons. NASA. Contbr. chpt. to book, articles to profl. jours. Welch Found. fellow, 1977-78; NASA grantee, 1982; NSF grantee, 1980-82. Mem. Am. Astron. Soc., Astron. Soc. Pacific, Internat. Astron. Union, Royal Astron. Soc. Current Work: Active galactic nuclei, novae, emission line formation; formation of emission lines in photoionized environments, computer modeling of gaseous nebulae. Subspecialties: Ultraviolet high energy astrophysics; Theoretical astrophysics. Home: 3514 Brookview Dr Lexington KY 40503 Office: Physics Dept U Ky Lexington KY 40506

FERNANDES, DANIEL JAMES, biochemist; b. Fall River, Mass., June 22, 1948; s. Casey Louis and Gilda (Carreiro) F.; m. Kay Galliher, Mar. 13, 1982; 1 son from previous marriage, Duane. B.S., Providence Coll., 1970; Ph.D., George Washington U., 1978. Teaching fellow dept. pharmacology George Washington U., Washington, 1972-77; postdoctoral research fellow Yale U. Sch. Medicine, 1977-80; asst. prof. dept. biochemistry Bowman Gray Sch. Medicine, Wake Forest U., Winston-Salem, N.C., 1980—; pharmacology cons. Flavor and Extract Mfrs. Assn. U.S., 1976. Contbr. articles to profl. jours. USPHS fellow, 1977-80; scholar Leukemia Soc. Am., Inc., 1985-90. Mem. Am. Assn. Cancer Research, AAAS, Southeastern Cancer Research Assn. Current Work: Genetic regulation of enzymes in drug-resistant cancer cells; design and development of cancer chemotherapeutic agents. Subspecialties: Cancer research (medicine); Molecular biology. Office: 300 S Hawthorne Rd Winston-Salem NC 27103

FERNÁNDEZ, SALVADOR M., physicist; b. Guantanamo, Cuba, Mar. 14, 1943; came to U.S., 1961, naturalized, 1983; s. Salvador Fernández-Álvarez and Onelia Mola de F. B.A., Wayne State U., 1965; M.S., U. Conn., 1968, Ph.D., 1975. Asst. prof. physiology U. Conn. Health Ctr., Farmington, 1975-84; pres. Chimerix Corp., Glastonbury, Conn., 1983—; prof. dept. radiology Med. Coll. Wis., Milw., 1985—; cons. Conn. Research Found., Storrs, 1980-83. Editor: Fast Methods in Physical Biochemistry, 1983; contbr. articles to profl. jours. Mem. Am. Biophys. Soc., AAAS, Sigma Pi Sigma. Current Work: Time-resolved fluorescence spectroscopy of living cells and biomolecules employing mode-locked lasers. Subspecialties: Bioinstrumentation; Laser medicine. Office: Chimerix Corp 310 Farmington Ave Farmington CT 06032

FERNANDEZ-CRUZ, EDUARDO P., medical researcher, physician; b. Santiago de Compostela, Spain, July 16, 1946; came to U.S., 1978, naturalized, 1982; s. Arturo L. Fernandez-C. and Filis Maria S. (Perez); m. Pilar C. Sarrate, Sept. 22, 1973; children: Eduardo, Arturo, Laura. B.Scis., Loyola Coll., Spain, 1957-63; student, Sch. Medicine, U. Barcelona, Spain, 1963-66, Sch. Medicine, U. Madrid, 1966-70. Intern, resident Clinica Puerta de Hierro, Autonomous U. Madrid, 1971-76; asst. mem. dept. immunopathology, 1977-82; research fellow, research assoc. dept. immunopathaology Scripps Clinic and Research Found., La Jolla, Calif., 1978-82, sci. assoc., 1982—; research fellow dept. immunology Middlesex Hosp. Med. Sch., London, 1973-74; sci. cons. Med. Biology Inst., 1982—. Contbr. articles to profl. jours. Named Outstanding Med. Student, 1971; Juan March Found. fellow, 1974; others. Mem. Brit. Soc. Immunology, Brit. Soc. Allergy and Clin. Immunology, Spanish Soc. Immunology, Spanish Soc. Hepatology, Am. Assn. Immunologists. Roman Catholic. Current Work: Cellular mechanisms involved in the host's immune response to tumors of different origin. Experimental models of immunotherapy of cancer. Subspecialty: Immunobiology and immunology. Home: 5120 Bothe Ave San Diego CA 92122 Office: Scripps Clinic and Research Found 10666 N Torrey Pines La Jolla CA 92037

FERNANDEZ-MORAN, HUMBERTO, biophysicist; b. b, Maracaibo, Venezuela, Feb. 18, 1924; s. Luis and Elena (Villalobos) Fernandez-M.; m. Anna Browallius, Dec. 30, 1953; children—Brigida Elena, Veronica. M.D., U. Munich, Germany, 1944, U. Caracas, Venezuela, 1945; M.S., U. Stockholm, Sweden, 1951, Ph.D., 1952. Fellow neurology, neuropath. George Washington U., 1945-46; intern George Washington U. Hosp., 1945-46; resident Serafimerlasarettet, Stockholm, 1946-58; fgn. asst. Neurosurg. Clinic, Stockholm, 1946-48; research fellow Nobel Inst. Physics, Stockholm, 1947-49; research fellow Inst. Cell Research & Genetics, Karolinska Institutet, Stockholm, 1948-51, asst. prof., 1952; prof., chmn. dept. biophysics U. Caracas, 1951-58; dir. Venezuelan Inst. Neurology and Brain Research, Caracas, 1954-58; asso. biophysicist neurosurg. service Mass. Gen. Hosp., Boston, 1958-62; vis. lectr. dept. biology Mass. Inst. Tech., 1958-62; research asso. neuropath. Harvard, 1958-62; prof. biophysics U. Chgo., 1962—, now A.N.; Pritzker prof. biophysics. Sci. and cultural attaché to Venezuelan legations, Sweden, Norway, Denmark, 1947-54; head Venezuelan commn. Atomic Energy Conf., Geneva, 1955; chmn. Venezuelan commn. 1st Inter-Am.-Symposium on Nuclear Energy, Brookhaven, N.Y., 1957; minister of edn., Venezuela, 1958; mem. Orgn. Am. States adv. commn. on sci. devel. in Latin Am., Nat. Acad. Scis., 1958; mem. U.S. Nat. Com. UNESCO, 1957. Author: The Submicroscopic Organization of Vertebrate Nerve Fibres, 1952, The Submicroscopic Organization of the Internode Portion of Vertebrate Myelinated Nerve Fibers, 1953, Cryoelectronmicroscopy; Superconductivity; Diamond Knife Ultramicrotomy, 1955-76; author series publs. in fields molecular biology, nerve ultrastructure, electron and cryo-electron microscopy, electron and x-ray diffraction, cell ultrastructure, neurobiology, superconducting lenses, superconductivity, others.; Editorial bd., Jour. of Cell Biology, 1961. Decorated Knight of Polar Star Sweden; Claude Bernard medal Canada; Medalla Andres Bello Venezuela, 1973; Recipient Gold medal City Maracaibo, 1968, John Scott award for invention of diamond knife, 1967; medal Bolivarian Soc. U.S., 1973. Fellow Am. Acad. Arts and Sci.; mem. Venezuelan Acad. Medicine (hon.), Academia Ciencias Fisicas y Matematicas (Caracas), Am. Acad. Neurology (corr. mem.), Internat. Soc. Cell Biology, Buenos Aires, Santiago, Lima, socs. Neurology, Buenos Aires, Santiago, Lima, Porto Alegre societies surgery, Electron Microscopy Soc. Am. (spl. citation), Am. Nuclear Soc., Pan Am. Med. Assn., Sociedad Bolivárianade Arquitectos (Venezuela) (hon.), Pan Am. Assn. of Anatomy (hon.). Home: Apartado 362 Maracaibo Venezuela Office: Research Insts U Chgo 5640 S Ellis Ave Chicago IL 60637

FERNIE, JOHN DONALD, astronomer, educator; b. Pretoria, South Africa, Nov. 13, 1933; emigrated to Can., 1961, naturalized, 1967; s. John Fernie and Nell (Beattie) F.; m. Yvonne Anne Chaney, Dec. 23, 1955; children—Kimberly Jan, Robyn Andrea. B.Sc., U. Cape Town, 1953, 1954, M.Sc., 1955; Ph.D., Ind. U., 1958. Lectr. physics, astronomy U. Cape Town, 1958-61; asst. prof. astronomy U. Toronto, 1961-64, asso. prof., 1964-67, prof., 1967—, chmn. dept., 1978—; dir. David Dunlap Obs., 1978—. Author: Variable Stars in Globular Clusters and Related Systems, 1973, The Whisper in the Vision, 1976; Contbr. articles to profl. jours. Fellow Royal Soc. Can.; mem. Royal Astron. Soc. Can. (past pres.), Internat. Astron. Union, Am. Astron. Soc., Astron. Soc. Pacific, Can. Astron. Soc. Current work: Cepheid variable stars, photoelectric photometry. Office: Dunlap Observatory Box 360 Richmond Hill ON L4C 4Y6 Canada

FERNSTROM, JOHN DICKSON, neuroscientist, educator, consultant; b. N.Y.C., July 9, 1947; s. Karl D. and Dorothy W. (Bond) F.; m. Madelyn Hirsch, Jan. 8, 1978; children—Aaron D., Lauren A. S.B., M.I.T., 1969, Ph.D., 1972. Postdoctoral fellow Roche Inst. Molecular Biology, Hoffmann-LaRoche, Nutley, N.J., 1972-73; asst. prof. physiology M.I.T., Cambridge, Mass., 1973-77; assoc. prof. neuroendocrinology, 1977-82; assoc. prof. psychiatry and pharmacology U. Pitts., 1982—; mem. life scis. adv. com. NASA, 1980—; mem. NINCDS program project rev. com. NIH, 1978-81, chmn., 1981-82. Contbr. articles to sci. jours. Recipient NIMH research scientist devel. award, 1979—; Alfred P. Sloan fellow in neurochemistry, 1974-76. Mem. Am. Soc. Pharmacology and Exptl. Therapeutics, Am. Physiol. Soc., Soc. Neurosci., Internat. Soc. Neurochemistry, Internat. Soc. Neuroendocrinology. Current Work: Control of neurotransmitter and neuropeptide synthesis and release. Regulation of somatostatin synthesis in hypothalamus; regulation of serotonin and catecholamine synthesis and release in brain and retina. Subspecialties: Neuroendocrinology; Neuropharmacology. Office: Dept Psychiatry U Pitts Sch Medicine 3811 O'Hara St Pittsburgh PA 15213

FERRAIO, NICHOLAS LAVERNE, psychotherapist, consultant; b. Rochester, N.Y., Sept. 9, 1946; s. LaVerne Leslie and Blanche Rose (Yates) F.; m. Carroll Ann Doolittle, June 4, 1971; children: Amy Lynn, Shannon Alicia. B.S. in Psychology and Sociologywith distinction, U. Rochester, 1976, M.S. in Community Service, 1980. Research technician U. Rochester Environ. Health Sci. Center, 1968-80, cons., 1980—; psychotherapist assoc. Joseph A. Dipoala, M.D., Rochester, N.Y., 1977. Mem. Am. Psychol. Assn., Assn. Behavior Analysis (affiliate), Nat. Psychiat. Assn., Acad. Holistic Medicine, Am. Council Counselors, Educators and Therapists, Biofeedback Soc. Am., Genessee Valley Psychol. Assn., Am. Guild Hypnotherapists (registered hypnotherapist), Rochester Acad. Pain Mgmt., Acad. Sci. Hypnotherapy, Am. Assn. Profl. Hypnotherapists. Republican. Unitarian. Current Work: Holistic psychology, holistic health and medicine, psychotherapy, relaxation training, biofeedback, hypnosis. Subspecialty: Clinical psychology. Office: 2128 E Henrietta Rd Rochester NY 14623

FERRARI, DOMENICO, electrical engineering educator; b. Gragnano, Piacenza, Italy, Aug. 31, 1940; came to U.S., 1970; s. Giacomo and Erina (Fracchioni) F.; m. Alessandra Ferrari Cella-Malugani, Apr. 16, 1966; children: Giuliarachele, Ludovica. Dr.Ing., Politecnico di Milan, Italy, 1963. Asst. Politecnico di Milan, 1964-67, asst. prof., 1967-70, prof., 1976-77; asst. prof. U. Calif.-Berkeley, 1970-75, assoc. prof., 1975-79, prof., dept. elec. engring. and computer sci., 1979—, dep. vice chmn., 1977-79; cons. in field. Author: Computer Systems Performance Evaluation, 1978, (with Serazzi and Zeigner) Measurement and Tuning of Computer Systems, 1983; editor: Performance of Computer Installations, 1978, Experimental Computer Performance Evaluation, 1981, Theory and Practice of Software Technology, 1983; contbr. articles to profl. jours. Recipient Libera Docenza Italian Govt., 1969; O. Bonazzi award AEI, 1970; NSF grantee, 1974—; U. Calif. grantee, 1982—. Mem. IEEE, Computer Measurement Group, Assn. for Computing Machinery. Clubs: Berkeley City, Croara Country (Italy). Current Work: Research in performance evaluation of computer systems, especially distributed systems. Subspecialties: Operating systems; Distributed systems and networks. Office: Computer Sci Div EECS Dept Univ Calif Berkeley CA 94720

FERRARO, BERNADETTE ANGELA, cytologist; b. Newark, Apr. 19, 1952. B.A., Rutgers U.-Newark, 1974, cert. in cytology magna cum laude U. Medicine and Dentistry N.J., 1977. Clin. cytologist Martland Hosp., Coll. Hosp., Newark, 1978-80; interim cytologist program coordinator, dept. pathology Univ. Hosp., Newark, 1982; condr. tutorials in sci. writing for grad. students. Author monograph: Cilia in Normal and Pathological States, 1985. Contbr. articles to profl. publs. Mem. Am. Soc. Cytology (assoc.), Am. Soc. Clin. Pathologists (assoc., cert. in cytology), Nargis Dutt Meml. Found., N.Y. Acad. Scis., Beta Beta Beta. Current work: Cilia in normal and pathological states. Subspecialties: Cytology and histology; Cell study oncology. Home: 77 Povershon Rd Nutley NJ 07110

FERRENDELLI, JAMES ANTHONY, neurologist, educator; b. Trinidad, Colo., Dec. 5, 1936; s. Alex and Edna F.; children: Elisabeth, Cynthia, Michael. A.B. Cum laude in Chemistry, U. Colo., 1958, M.D., 1962. Diplomate: Am. Bd. Psychiatry and Neurology. Intern U. Ky. Med. Center, 1962-63; resident in neurology Cleve. Met. Gen. Hosp., 1965-68; research fellow in neurochemistry Sch. Medicine, Washington U., St. Louis, 1968-70, asst. prof. neurology and pharamacology, 1970-74, asso. prof., 1974-77, prof., 1977-, Seay prof. clin. neuropharmacology in neurology, 1977—. Contbr. numerous articles to profl. jours. Served to capt., M.C. U.S. Army, 1963-1965. Recipient Research Career Devel. award USPHS, 1971-76; Founders Day award Washington U., 1981; NIH grantee, 1971—. Mem. Am. Acad. Neurology, Am. Neurol. Assn., Am. Soc. for Pharmacology and Exptl. Therapeutics (Epilepsy award 1981), Am. Epilepsy Soc. Current Work: Molecular mechanisms of neurologic diseases and neurotropic drugs; investigations of mechanisms of action of antiepileptic drugs, of pathophysiological mechanisms of seizure disorders, and molecular mechanisms of retinal function. Subspecialties: Neurology; Neuropharmacology. Home: 4949 W Pine St 13-N Saint Louis MO 63108 Office: Dept Neurology Washington U Med Sch 660 S Euclid Ave Saint Louis MO 63110

FERRIS, BENJAMIN GREELEY, JR., environmental health educator, researcher; b. Watertown, Mass., Jan. 24, 1919; s. Benjamin Greeley and Margaret (Wright) F.; m. Sarah Brooks Upham, Dec. 20, 1942 (dec. Oct. 1979); children—Pamela, Margaret, Katharine, Patience, Sarah; m. Stefana Puleo, Dec. 7, 1980. A.B., Harvard U., 1940, M.D., 1943; D.H.C., Bourdeaux II, France, 1983. From intern to asst. resident Children's Med. Ctr., Boston, 1943-45, asst. resident, 1947-48; research fellow in physiology Sch. Pub. Health, Harvard U., Boston, 1948-50, research assoc., 1950-53, from asst. prof. to prof. environ. health and safety, 1953-71, prof., 1971—; dir. research and med. care Mary MacArthur Respirator Unit, Wellesley, Mass., 1950-58; cons. in internal medicine Mass. Gen. Hosp., Boston, 1956—; dir. environ. health and safety Univ. Health Service, Cambridge, Mass., 1958—; cons., temporary adviser, WHO, Geneva, intermittently, 1970-79. Research, numerous publs., 1944—. Served to capt. M.C., U.S. Army, 1945-47. Grantee Nat. Inst. Environ. Health, 1960—. Fellow Am. Pub. Health Assn., Am. Coll. Epidemiology, Am. Coll. Preventive Medicine; mem. Am. Physiology Soc., Am. Acad. Sci., Am. Epidemiol. Soc. (emeritus), Am. Alpine Club (chmn. safety com. 1953-73). Clubs: Harvard (Boston), St. Botolph. Current work: contaminants and their effect on health both as ambient pollution and as occupational exposures. Subspecialties: Preventive medicine; Epidemiology. Office: Harvard U Sch Pub Health 665 Huntington Ave Boston MA 02115

FERRIS, DEAM HUNTER, microbiologist, epidemiologist, parasitologist; b. Mankato, Minn., July 8, 1912; s. Joseph Alexander and Ruby (Dawson) F.; m. Merle Wildey Ferris; children: Sara Josephine Ferris Decker, Tary Jeane Ferris Tobin, Deborah, Karen. A.S., Mo. Western Coll., 1932; A.B. in Zoology, Drake U., 1934, M.A. in Parasitology, 1938; Ph.D. in Veterinary Sci, U. Wis., 1953. Prof. zoology Graceland Coll., Lamoni, Iowa, 1948-57, dir. audio-visual program, 1948-57; asso. prof. pathobiology Coll. Veterinary Medicine U. Ill., 1957-72; microbiologist Plum Island Animal Disease Center Agrl. Research Service U.S. Dept. Agr., Greenport, N.Y., 1972—; asso. team leader, dir. Arbovirus Lab. FAO-UN Near East Animal Health Inst., Cairo, Egypt, 1964-66. Contbr. articles in field to profl. jours. Served with U.S. Army, 1942-46; Served with USAR, 1946-66. NIH grantee, 1958-64. Fellow Royal Soc. Health, AAAS; mem. Am. Veterinary Med. Assn., Am. Soc. Virology, Am. Soc. Microbiology, Am. Soc. Parasitologists, Am. Soc. Tropical Medicine and Hygiene, Conf. Research Workers in Animal Disease, Conf. Public Health Veterinarian, Wildlife Disease Assn., Sigma XI, Phi Sigma Soc., Sigma Tau Delta, Phi Zeta. Current Work: Foreign animal diseases, diagnosis and control, African swine fever, malignant catarrhal fever, trypanosomiasis, devel. of diagonostic tests for these and other foreign animal disease. Subspecialties: Microbiology (veterinary medicine); Parasitology. Home: 843 Main St Greenport NY 11944 Office: PO Box 848 Greenport NY 11944

FERRY, DAVID KEANE, electrical engineering educator; b. San Antonio, Oct. 25, 1940; s. Joseph T. and Elizabeth Ferry; m. Darleen Heitkamp, Aug. 25, 1962; children—Lara, Linda. B.S., Tex. Tech. Coll., 1962; M.S., U. Tex., 1963, Ph.D., 1966. Postdoctoral fellow U. Vienna, 1966-67; from asst. to assoc. prof. elec. engring. Tex. Tech. Inst., Lubbock, 1967-73; sci. officer Office of Naval Research, Arlington, Va., 1973-77; prof., head dept. elec. engring. Colo. State U., Fort Collins, 1977-83; dir. Ctr. for Solid State Electronics Research, prof. Ariz. State Univ., Tempe, 1983—; dir. Galavis Corp., Phoenix, 1984—; cons. Materials Research Council, 1982—. Contbr. articles to profl. jours. Recipient Halliburton Research award Colo. State Univ., 1982. Fellow Am. Phys. Soc.; mem. IEEE (sr.), Sigma Xi. Republican. Methodist. Current work: Transport on sub-picosecond time scale in simiconductor devices, physics and limitations of VLSI, concurrent processing in VLSI structures. Subspecialty: Semiconductors. Office: Ariz State Univ Ctr for Solid State Electronics Coll of Engring and Applied Scis Tempe AZ 85287

FERRY, JAMES ALLEN, particle accelerator manufacturing company executive; b. Roxbury, Wis., Sept. 9, 1937; s. Darwin J. and Eleanor J. (Irwin) F.; m. Karen A. Greenwood, Feb. 8, 1964; children—Thomas E., Jennifer J. B.S. in Physics, U. Wis.-Madison, 1959, M.S. in Physics, 1962, Ph.D. in Physics, 1965. Research assoc. U. Wis.-Madison, 1965-66; with Nat. Electrostatics Corp., Middleton, Wis., 1967—, exec. v.p., chief operating officer, 1967—. Designer devices related to particle accelerators. Mem. Am. Phys. Soc. Current work: Design and construction of pelletron accelerators and MeV ion implantation systems. Subspecialty: Nuclear physics. Office: Nat Electrostatics Corp PO Box 310 Graber Rd Middleton WI 53562

FERRY, JOHN DOUGLASS, chemist; b. Dawson, Can., May 4, 1912; s. Douglass Hewitt and Eudora (Bundy) F.; m. Barbara Norton Mott, Mar. 25, 1944; children—Phyllis Leigh, John Mott. A.B., Stanford U., 1932, Ph.D., 1935; student, U. London, 1932-34. Pvt. asst. Hopkins Marine Sta., Stanford, 1935-36; instr. biochem. scis. Harvard, 1936-38; mem. Soc. Fellows, 1938-41; asso. chemist Woods Hole Oceanographic Inst., 1941-45; research asso. Harvard U., 1942-45; asst. prof. chemistry U. Wis., 1946, asso. prof., 1946-47, prof., 1947-82, prof. emeritus, 1982—, Farrington Daniels research prof., 1973-82, chmn. dept., 1959-67; chmn. Internat. Com. on Rheology, 1963-68; vis. lectr. Kyoto (Japan) U., 1968, Ecole d'Eté, U. Grenoble, France, 1973. Author: Viscoelastic Properties of Polymers, 1961, 2d edit., 1970, 3d edit., 1980; co-editor: Fortschritte der Hochpolymeren Forschung. Recipient Eli Lilly award Am. Chem. Soc., 1946, Bingham medal Soc. Rheology, 1953;

Kendall Co. award Am. Chem. Soc., 1960; Witco award, 1974; Colwyn medal Instn. Rubber Industry, U.K., 1972; Tech. award Internat. Inst. Synthetic Rubber Producers, 1977. Fellow Am. Phys. Soc. (high polymer physics prize 1966), Am. Acad. Arts and Scis.; mem. Nat. Acad. Sci., Am. Chem. Soc. (Goodyear medal Rubber div. 1981, Polymer Chemistry award polymer div. 1984), Am. Soc. Biol. Chemists, Soc. Rheology (pres. 1961-63), Internat. Soc. Hematology, d'Honneur Groupe Français Rhéologie, Soc. Rheology Japan (hon.), Phi Beta Kappa, Sigma Xi, Phi Lambda Upsilon, Alpha Chi Sigma. Club: Rotary. Current Work: Rheology of polymers; viscoelastic and other physical properties of biological macromolecules. Subspecialties: Polymer chemistry; Polymers (materials science). Home: 137 N Prospect Ave Madison WI 53705

FESHBACH, HERMAN, physicist, educator; b. N.Y.C., Feb. 2, 1917; s. David and Ida (Lapiner) F.; m. Sylvia Harris, Jan. 28, 1940; children: Carolyn Barbara, Theodore Philip, Mark Frederick. B.S., CCNY, 1937; Ph.D., MIT, 1942; D.Sci., Lowell Tech. Inst., 1975. Tutor CCNY, 1937-38; instr. MIT, 1941-45, asst. prof., 1945-47, asso. prof., 1947-55, prof., 1955—, Cecil and Ida Green prof. physics, 1976-83, Inst. prof., 1983—, dir. Center for Theoretical Physics, 1967-73, head dept. physics, 1973-83; cons. AEC; chmn. nuclear sci. adv. com. of Dept. Energy and NSF, 1979-82. Author: (with P.M. Morse) Methods of Theoretical Physics, 1953, (with A. deShalit) Theoretical Nuclear Physics, 1974; also sci. articles tech. jours.; Editor: (with A. deShalit) Annals of Physics. Recipient Harris medal Coll. City N.Y., 1977; John Simon Guggenheim Meml. Found. fellow, 1954-55; Ford fellow CERN, Geneva, Switzerland, 1962-63. Mem. Am. Phys. Soc. (chmn. div. nuclear physics 1970-71, divisional councillor 1974-78, exec. com. 1974-78, chmn. panel on pub. affairs 1976-78, v.p. 1979-80, pres. 1980-81, Bonner prize 1973), Nat. Acad. Scis., NRC, Am. Acad. Arts and Scis. (v.p. Class I 1973-76, pres. 1982-85). Current Work: Theoretical Nuclear Physics. Subspecialties: Theoretical physics; Nuclear physics. Office: MIT Dept Physics Cambridge MA 02139

FESHBACH, SEYMOUR, psychology educator; b. N.Y.C., June 21, 1925; s. Joseph and Fannie (Katzman) F.; m. Norma Deitch, Aug. 16, 1947; children: Jonathan, Laura, Andrew. B.S., Coll. City N.Y., 1947; M.A., Yale U., 1948, Ph.D., 1951. Project dir. Army Attitude Assessment Br., 1951-52; from asst. prof. to asso. prof. U. Pa., Phila., 1952-63; prof. U. Colo., Boulder, 1963-64; prof. psychology UCLA, 1964—, chmn. dept., 1977-83; dir. Fernald Sch., 1964-73; cons. CBS, Ednl. TV, 1972; vis. fellow Wolfson Coll., Oxford (Eng.) U., 1980-81. Author: Television and Aggression, 1970, Psychology, An Introduction, 1977; also others; co-author: Personality, 1982; editor: Aggression and Behavior Change: Biological and Social Processes, 1979; cons. editor: Jour. Abnormal Psychology, 1973—; Contbr. chpts. to books, articles to profl. jours. Served to 1st lt., inf. AUS, 1943-46, PTO. Recipient Ward medal Coll. City N.Y., 1947, Townsend Harris medal, Distinguished Alumnus award, 1972, Fellowship award Fund Advancement of Psychiatry, 1980-81, Disting. Scientist award Calif. Psychol. Assn., 1983; NIMH grantee; NSF grantee. Fellow Am. Psychol. Assn.; mem. Western Psychol. Assn. (pres. 1977), AAAS, Soc. for Study of Social Issues, Soc. for Research in Child Devel., Internat. Soc. for Applied Psychology, Internat. Soc. for Study of Aggression (pres. 1985—), Internat. Soc. for Study of Behavior Devel., ACLU, Phi Beta Kappa. Democrat. Jewish. Subspecialties: Developmental psychology; Personality. Home: 743 Hanley Ave Los Angeles CA 90049 Office: Dept Psychology U Calif 405 Hilgard Ave Los Angeles CA 90024

FESSLER, RICHARD GLENN, neurosurgeon, neuropharmacologist; b. Sheboygan, Wis., Oct. 21, 1952; s. Eldred Carlos and Grace Florence (Shavie) F.; m. Carol Marie Anderson, June 17, 1978; 1 child, Laura Marie. B.S., Lawrence U., Appleton, Wis., 1974; M.S., N.D. State U., 1980; Ph.D., U. Chgo., 1980, M.D. with honors, 1983. Research fellow Ill. State Psychiat. Inst., Chgo., 1976-80; postdoctoral fellow U. Chgo., 1980-81, research assoc., 1981-82, research fellow, 1982-83, resident in neurosurgery, 1983—. Contbr. numerous scientific papers to profl. jours. Recipient Outstanding Research award Chgo. Surg. Soc., 1984. Mem. AMA, Ill. Med. Soc., Chgo. Med. Soc., Soc. for Neurosci., Phi Gamma Delta. Roman Catholic. Current work: Evaluation of use and pharmacological effects of electrical brain stimulation for treatment of pain and morbid obesity, evaluation of use of transplantation of neural tissues for clinical therapeutics. Subspecialties: Neurosurgery; Neuropharmacology. Home: 1606 Talcott Rd Park Ridge IL 60068 Office: Sect Neurosurg Univ Chicago Med Ctr 5847 S Maryland Ave Chicago IL 60637

FETT, WILLIAM FREDERICK, plant pathologist; b. Hinsdale, Ill., Oct. 30, 1952; s. Walter W. and Francis H. F.; m. Maria I. DaSilva, Nov. 24, 1977; children: Andrew, Melanie. B.S., U. Ill., 1974; M.S., U. Wis.-Madison, 1977, Ph.D in Plant Pathology, 1979. NRC postdoctoral research assoc. Eastern Regional Research Ctr., U.S. Dept. Agr., Phila., 1979-80, research plant pathologist, 1980—. Contbr. articles to profl. jours. Mem. Am. Soc. Plant Physiologists, Am. Phytopathological Soc., Am. Soc. Microbiology, Sigma Xi, Phi Kappa Phi, Gamma Sigma Delta. Current Work: Determine the physiological basis for plant resistance to phytopathogenic bacteria. Subspecialties: Plant pathology; Plant physiology (agriculture). Home: 128 Reiffs Mill Rd Ambler PA 19002 Office: 600 E Mermaid Ln Philadelphia PA 19118

FETTERMAN, HAROLD RALPH, electrical engineer, educator, researcher; b. Jamaica, N.Y., Jan. 17, 1941; s. Maurice and Gloria (Jochnowitz) F.; m. Susan P. Rauchway, Aug. 15, 1965; children: David, Matthew. B.A., Brandeis U., 1962; Ph.D. in Physics, Cornell U., 1968. Asst. prof. in residence physics dept. UCLA, 1967-69, prof. elec. engring., 1982—, dir. high frequency electronics ctr., 1984—; staff physicist Lincoln Lab., MIT, Lexington, 1969-82; cons. on millimeter wave systems; dir. Millitech Corp. Patentee: Lasers, modulators, quasi-Optical systems. Recipient IR-100 award Indsl. Research Mag., 1979. Fellow Optical Soc. Am.; mem. IEEE (sr.), Sigma Xi. Current Work: Millimeter and submillimeter detectors and sources: solid state sources for millimeter and submillimeter wave generation; antenna arrays for imaging applications; field effect transitions. Subspecialties: Microelectronics; Atomic and molecular physics. Office: Elec Engring Dept UCLA Los Angeles CA 90024

FETTMAN, MARTIN JOSEPH, veterinary educator, medical researcher; b. Bklyn., Dec. 31, 1956; s. Bernard Paul and Elaine (Stazinsky) F. B.S., Cornell U., 1976, D.V.M., 1980, M.S., 1980; Ph.D., Colo. State U., 1982. Diplomate Am. Coll. Vet. Pathologists. Asst. prof. pathology Colo. State U., Ft. Collins, 1982—, also asst. prof. physiology, 1983—. Mem. AVMA, AAAS, Am. Assn. for Clin. Chemistry, Sigma Xi, Phi Zeta, Phi Kappa Phi. Current work: Pathophysiology of nutritional and metabolic diseases, with emphasis on physiological biochemistry of energy, electrolyte and fluid metabolism. Subspecialties: Pathology (veterinary medicine); Physiology (medicine). Office: Colo State U Dept of Pathology Fort Collins CO 80523

FEUERSTEIN, MICHAEL, clinical psychology educator; b. Buffalo, July 26, 1950; s. Irving Seymor and Shirley (Lapides) F.; m. Michele D. Kaplan, Dec. 26, 1971; children: Sara Elizabeth, Andrew Scott. A.B., Boston U., 1972; M.S., U. Ga., 1975, Ph.D., 1977. Lic. psychologist, N.Y., Fla. Health psychologist Stanford Research Inst., Menlo Park, Calif., 1977-78; clin. instr. Stanford U. Sch. Medicine, 1977-78; asst. prof. McGill U., Montreal, 1978-82; co-dir. behavior therapy unit Allan Meml. Inst., Montreal, 1979-82; assoc. prof. clin. psychology U. Fla., Gainesville, 1982-84; assoc. prof. dept. psychiatry U. Rochester Sch. Medicine and Dentistry, also dir. behavioral medicine program, 1984—; cons. Med. Comprehensive Health Systems Ltd., Montreal, 1982-84. Author: Mastering Pain, 1979, Health Psychology: A Psychobiological Perspective; editor: Readings in Behavioral Medicine, 1979. Recipient M.H. Erickson award of scientific excellence Am. Soc. Clin. Hypnosis, 1978, Ouroboros award, 1984; Med. Research Council Can. grantee, 1981; Health and Welfare Can. grantee, 1981; Zimmer scholar, 1977. Fellow Acad. Behavioral Medicine Research; mem. Am. Psychol. Assn., Soc. Behavioral Medicine, Soc. Psychophysiol. Research, Assn. Advancement Behavior Therapy, Sigma Xi. Jewish. Current Work: Psychophysiological mechanisms of chronic pain, pain management, health behavior, eating disorders, stress management, medical psychology. Subspecialties: Clinical psychology; Psychophysiology. Home: 18 Hunters Pointe Pittsford NY 14534 Office: Dept Psychiatry U Rochester Sch Medicine and Dentistry 300 Crittenden Blvd Rochester NY 14642

FEYNMAN, RICHARD PHILLIPS, physicist; b. N.Y.C., May 11, 1918; s. Melville Arthur and Lucille (Phillips) F. B.S., MIT, 1939; Ph.D., Princeton U., 1942. Staff atomic bomb project Princeton, 1942-43, Los Alamos, 1943-45; asso. prof. theoretical physics Cornell U., 1945-50; prof. theoretical physics Calif. Inst. Tech., 1950—. Author: Quantum Electrodynamics, 1961; Theory of Fundamental Processes, 1961; Character of Physical Law, 1965; Statistical Mechanics 1972; Photon-Hadron Interactions, 1972; Surely You're Joking, Mr. Feynman: Adventures of a Curious Character, 1985; contbr. theory of quantum electrodynamics, beta decay and liquid helium. Recipient Einstein award, 1954; Nobel prize in physics, 1965; Oersted medal, 1972; Niels Bohr Internat. Gold medal, 1973. Mem. Am. Phys. Soc., AAAS, Royal Soc. (fgn. mem.), Nat. Acad. Scis., Pi Lambda Phi. Subspecialty: Theoretical physics. Address: Physics Dept California Institute of Technology Pasadena CA 91125*

FICHTEL, CARL EDWIN, physicist; b. St. Louis, July 13, 1933; s. Edwin Blanke and Eleanora Alice (Gutsch) F. B.S., Washington U., St. Louis, 1955, Ph.D., 1960. Teaching and research asst. Washington U., 1956-59; physicist NASA Goddard Space Flight Center, Greenbelt, Md., 1959-60, sect. head, 1960-68, br. head, 1968—; sr. scientist NASA Goddard Space Flight Center (Lab. High Energy Astrophysics), 1975—; vis. lectr. U. Md., 1963-80, adj. prof., 1980—; mem. com. on space astronomy and astrophysics, mem. Astronomy Survey for the 1980's, Nat. Acad. Sci. Editor: (with others) High Energy Particles and Quanta in Astrophysics, 1974; author: (with others) Gamma Ray Astrophysics, New Insight into the Universe, 1981; contbr. (with others) numerous articles profl. jours. Recipient John C. Lindsay Meml. award NASA Goddard Space Flight Center, 1968, spl. Achievement award, 1978; Exceptional Sci. Achievement medal NASA, 1971. Fellow Am. Phys. Soc. (sec.-treas. cosmic physics div. 1974-76, vice chmn. 1982); mem. Am. Astron. Soc. (chmn. high energy div. 1979-81), Internat. Astron. Union, Sigma Xi. Current Work: High energy astrophysics, especially gamma ray astrophysics, diffuse galactic and extragalactic radiation, active galaxies, cosmic ray physics and gamma ray instruments. Subspecialties: High energy astrophysics; Gamma ray high energy astrophysics. Office: NASA Goddard Space Flight Center Code 660 Greenbelt MD 20771

FIDEL, HOWARD, biomedical engineer; b. Los Angeles, Oct. 18, 1950; s. Milton Henry and Shirley (Rubin) F.; m. Marlene Brandt, Sept. 15, 1974. B.E., Stevens Inst. Tech., 1968-72; M.S., U. Conn., Storrs, 1973; M.B.A., Pace U., 1984. Project engr. Princeton Electronic Products, North Brunswick, N.J., 1974; project engr. CBS Labs., Stamford, Conn., 1974; project engr. Searle Ultrasound, Santa Clara, Calif., 1975-77, Electronics for Medicine, Pleasantville, N.Y., 1978-80, Irex Med. Systems, Ramsey, N.J., 1980-83; sr. tech. dir. Johnson & Johnson Ultrasound, Ramsey, N.J., 1983-84, v.p. tech., 1985—. Patentee in field. Mem. Nat. Elec. Mfrs. Assn. (mem. tech. com. 1979—), IEEE, Am. Inst. Ultrasound in Medicine. Current work: Ultrasound phased array B-Mode imaging, flow mapping, tissue characterization, image processing. Subspecialties: Ultrasound; Bioinstrumentation. Home: 24 Scott Pl Hartsdale NY 10530 Office: Johnson & Johnson Ultrasound 69 Spring St Ramsey NJ 07446

FIDLER, JOHN MICHAEL, medical research scientist; b. Balt., Aug. 16, 1947; s. Glenn Leroy and Mary Kathryn (Weyandt) F. B.A. with honors in Biology, Johns Hopkins U., 1969; Ph.D. in Immunology, Purdue U., 1972. Postdoctoral research assoc. dept. biol. sci. Purdue U., 1973-74; Am. Cancer Soc. postdoctoral fellow in cellular immunology biophysics and biochemistry unit Walter and Eliza Hall Inst. Med. Research, Melbourne, Australia, 1974-76; asst. mem. dept. immunopathology Scripps Clinic and Research Found., La Jolla, Calif., 1976-82; vis. prof. dept. immunology Biomed. Research Inst., U. Mex., Mexico City, 1982; group leader, head cellular and molecular immunoregulation research unit, cellular immunology, inflammation and immunology research dept. metabolic disease research sect. Lederle Labs., Pearl River, N.Y., 1982—; adj. prof. dept. clin. immunology Johns Hopkins U. Sch. Medicine, Balt., 1982—; adj. prof. dept. microbiology N.Y. Med. Coll., Valhalla, 1983—. Recipient Md. Legis. Scholarship award Johns Hopkins U., 1965-69, David Ross predoctoral fellow Purdue U., 1971-72; Am. Cancer Soc. postdoctoral research fellow, 1974-76. Mem. Internat. Soc. Exptl. Hematology, AAAS, Am. Assn. Immunologists, Soc. Analytical Cytology. Democrat. Current Work: Immunoregulation, T lymphocyte subsets, lymphocyte differentiation and activation, immunological tolerance, immunomodulation, immunobiological research. Subspecialties: Immunobiology and immunology; Immunopharmacology. Office: Lederle Labs 60B-305 Pearl River NY 10965

FIELD, ARTHUR KIRK, virologist; b. North Adams, Mass., Jan. 6, 1938; s. Kenneth Sellers and Florence May (Kirk) F.; m. Marcia Elen Case, Sept. 4, 1960; children—Karen Lynn, Richard Kirk. B.S., Cornell U., 1960, M.S., 1961; Ph.D., U. Calif.-Berkeley, 1965. With Merck Inst. Therapeutic Research, West Point, Pa., 1965—, sr. investigator, 1980—; lectr. Gwynedd Mercy Coll. Pa., 1971—. Contbr. articles to profl. jours.; patentee in field. Mem. Twp. Planning Commn., Upper Gwynedd, Pa., 1983-84. Mem. Am. Soc. Microbiology, Am. Soc. Virology, N.Y. Acad. Sci., Soc. Explt. Biology and Medicine, Am. Assn. Immunologists, Inter Am. Soc. Chemotherapy, Internat. Soc. Interferon Research, Sigma Xi. Republican. Methodist. Current work: Antiviral chemotherapy; herpes viruses; interferon research mechanics of antiviral drug action and therapeutic utility. Subspecialties: Virology (biology); Immunobiology and immunology. Office: Dept Virus and Cell Biology Merck Research West Point PA 19486

FIELD, GEORGE BROOKS, astronomer. Sr. scientist Smithsonian Astrophys. Obs., Cambridge, Mass., 1982—, former dir. Subspecialty: Theoretical astrophysics. Office: Smithsonian Astrophys Obs 60 Garden St Cambridge MA 02138*

FIELD, MICHAEL EHRENHART, marine geologist, sedimentologist; b. Balt., June 27, 1945; s. Joseph B. and Phyllis (Hambsch) F.; m. Kathleen Ann Zoog, Oct. 28, 1967; children—Jeffrey M., Marisa K. B.S., U. Del., 1967; M.A., Duke U., 1969; Ph.D., George Washington U., 1976. Geologist Coastal Engring. Research Ctr., Ft. Belvoir, Va., 1972-75; marine geologist U.S. Geol. Survey, Menlo Park, Calif., 1975—; vis. prof. U. Calif.-,Berkeley, 1984. Contbr. articles to profl. jours. Served to capt. U.S. Army, 1969-72. Mem. Geol. Soc. Am., Soc. Econ. Paleontologists and Mineralogists, Am. Assn. Petroleum Geologists. Subspecialties: Sedimentology; Oceanography. Office: US Geol Survey Menlo Park CA 94025

FIELD, ROBERT CLIVE, research physicist; b. Belfast, No. Ireland, Feb. 11, 1943; came to U.S., 1968; s. Robert Hugh and Annie Patterson (Brown) F.; m. Eleanor Anne Selfridge, July 26, 1969; 1 child, Brent A. B.S., Queen's U., 1964; D. Phil., Oxford U., Eng., 1968. Research assoc. Lawrence Berkeley Lab., Calif., 1968-73; staff physicist Stanford Linear Accelerator Ctr., Calif., 1973—. Contbr. articles to profl. jours. Mem. Am. Phys. Soc. Current work: Production and decay properties of charmed particles; preparing equipment for study of intermediate vector bosons. Subspecialty: Particle physics. Office: SLAC PO Box 4349 Stanford CA 94305

FIELDER, LOUIS DUNN, audio engineer, physicist; b. Denver, Jan. 15, 1951; s. William Ridge and Louise (Dunn) F.; m. Marlene Marro, Aug. 11, 1984. B.S. in Engring., Calif. Inst. Tech., 1974; M.S. in Engring., UCLA, 1976. Engr., Paul Veneklasen & Assocs., Santa Monica, Calif., 1975-77; research mem. Ampex, Redwood City, Calif., 1978-83; engr. Dolby Labs., San Francisco, 1983—; electronic cons., Mem. Audio Engring. Soc., Acoustical Soc. Am., IEEE (magnetics sect.). Current work: Magnetic recording physics, magnetic data recording, audio acoustics, digital signal processing, digital-audio research and development, audio electronic design. Subspecialties: Electronics; Applied magnetics. Office: Dolby Labs 731 Sansome St San Francisco CA 94111

FIELDS, BERNARD NATHAN, microbiologist; b. Bklyn., Mar. 24, 1938; s. Julius and Martha Fields; m. Ruth Peedin; children—Edward, John, Michael, Daniel, Joshua. A.B., Brandeis U., 1958; M.D., NYU, 1962; A.M. (hon.), Harvard U., 1976. Intern, Beth Israel Hosp., Boston, 1962-63, resident in Medicine, 1963-64; asst. chief arbovirus infectious unit Nat. Communicable Disease Ctr., Atlanta, 1966-67; chief infectious disease div. Albert Einstein Coll. Medicine, Bronx, N.Y., 1971-75, Peter Bent Brigham Hosp., Boston, 1975-80; prof. microbiology and molecular genetics, Harvard Med. Sch., Boston, 1975-84, prof. medicine, 1981—, Adele Lehman prof. microbiology and molecular genetics, chmn. dept., 1984—; chief infectious disease div. Brigham and Women's Hosp., Boston, 1980—; cons. Cambridge Biosci. Corp., Hopkinton, Mass., 1982—. Editor: Virology, 1985. Contbr. articles to profl. jours. Recipient Orton Stark Lecturer award Miami U.; Thayer Lecturer award Johns Hopkins U.; Lippard Lecturer award Coll. Phys. and Surg.; Sommer Meml. Lecturer award Oreg. Health Sci. U.; Wellcome Lecturer award U. Colo.; Hattie Alexander Meml. Lecturer award Columbia U.; Carl G. Hartford Vis. Prof. award Washington U. Sch. Medicine. Mem. Nat. Acad. Sci., Am. Soc. Virology, Assn. Am. Physicians, Am. Soc. Clin. Investigation. Current work: Virology, genetics and pathogenesis, reoviruses. Subspecialty: Virology (medicine). Office: Harvard U Med Sch 25 Shattuck St Boston MA 02115

FIELDS, ELLIS KIRBY, chemical company research consultant; b. Chgo., May 10, 1917; m. Jeanette Shames, Nov. 18, 1939; children—Jennifer Fields Grunschlag, Diana Fields Carroll, Wendy Fields Abondolo. S.B., U. Chgo., 1936, Ph.D., 1938. Lilly postdoctoral grantee U. Chgo., 1938-41; research chemist Research Corp., Chgo., 1941-50; research chem. cons. Amoco Chems. Co., Naperville, Ill., 1950—; vis. lectr. King's Coll., London, 1962-63, U. Idaho, Moscow, 1979. Contbr. numerous articles to profl. jours. Patentee in field. Recipient award Chgo. Tech. Soc., 1980. Fellow Chem. Inst. Can., AAAS; mem. Am. Chem. Soc. (Petroleum Chemistry award 1978, pres. 1985—). Current work: Research in petrochemicals, polymers, catalysis. Office: Amoco Chems Co PO Box 400 Naperville IL 60566

FIELDS, PATRICK F., mus. preparator, paleobotanist, editor; b. Palo Alto, Calif., May 30, 1954; s. Earl F. and Elizabeth R. (Reay) F. B.S. in Palo-Plan Ecology, U. Calif., Davis, 1977; postrad. in paleontology, U. Calif., Berkeley, 1982—. Sr. mus. preparator paleobotany U. Calif., Berkeley, 1978—; researcher macroscopic plant fossils. Contbr. articles on paleobotany to profl. jours.; editor: Paleontologic Jour, 1981—. Mem. Internat. Assn. for Angiosperm Paleobotany, Bot. Soc. Am., Paleobot. Sect. Bot. Soc. Am., Calif. Bot. Soc., Calif. Native Plant Soc., Calif. Hort. Soc. (Golden Gate Park, San Francisco). Current Work: Tertiary megafloral paleobotany and paleoecology, paleobotany, macrofossils, tertiary, paleoecology, curation, biostratigraphy. Subspecialties: Paleontology, paleoecology; Paleobotany. Home: 2839 Ashby Ave Berkeley CA 94705 Office: Mus Paleontology U Calif Berkeley CA 94720

FIELDS, PAUL ROBERT, research chemist; b. Chgo., Feb. 4, 1919; s. Alexander and Anna (Green) F.; m. Bernice White, Jan. 3, 1943; children—Marlene Frances, Rita Norine, Donald Brian. B.S., U. Chgo., 1941. Chemist TVA, Wilson Dam, Ala., 1941-43, Metall. Lab., U. Chgo., 1943-45, Standard Oil Co., Whiting, Ind., 1945-46; sr. chemist, div. dir. Argonne Nat. Lab., Ill., 1946—, assoc. lab. dir., 1981-82, dir. sci. support div., 1982—; cons. Simon & Schuster, Cleve., 1982—. patentee in nuclear chemistry. Co-discoverer Einsteinium (element 99), Fermium (element 100) Nobelium (element 102). Author: Laboratory Experiments in Heavy Element Chemistry, 1955; Lanthanide-Actinide Chemistry, 1967; Cleaning Our Environment, 1978. Contbr. articles to sci. jours. Fellow AAAS, Am. Nuclear Soc.; mem. Am. Chem. Soc. (Nuclear Applications in Chemistry award 1970), Am. Phys. Soc., Phi Beta Kappa. Current work: Nuclear and chemical properties of transuranium elements, chemistry of rare gas compounds. Subspecialties: Nuclear chemistry; Inorganic chemistry. Home: 7308 N California Ave Chicago IL 60645 Office: Argonne Nat Lab 9700 S Cass Ave Argonne IL 60439

FIELDS, ROBERT WILLIAM, geology and paleontology educator, consultant; b. San Leandro, Calif., Sept. 17, 1920; s. William Leander and Jessie (Williams) F.; m. Charlotte Genevieve Carpenter, Apr. 14, 1945; children—Karen Judith (dec.), Mark William. B.A., U. Calif.-Berkeley, 1949, Ph.D., 1952. Geologist Shell Oil Co., Salt Lake City, 1952-55; asst. prof. dept. geology U. Mont., Missoula, 1955-58, assoc. prof., 1958-64, prof., 1964-82, prof. emeritus, 1982—, chmn. dept., 1964-70, 77-79; cons. in field; chmn. adv. council Mont. Bur. Mines and Tech., Butte, 1980—. Author sci. papers and reports. Mem. Ravalli County Planning Bd., Hamilton, Mont., 1984-86. Served with AC, U.S. Army, 1942-46. Grantee NSF, U. Mont., Elbridge and Mary Stewart Found. Fellow Geol. Soc. Am. (program chmn. 1976-77); mem. Soc. Vertebrate-Paleontology. Current work: History, paleontology and development of intermontane basins of northern basin and range province. Subspecialties: Sedimentology; Paleobiology. Office: Dept Geology U Mont Missoula MT 59812

FIENE, RICHARD JOHN, psychologist; b. Bklyn., Nov. 11, 1949; s. Richard Ludwig and Vera Ann (Garone) F.; m. Judith Theresa Gibson, July 18, 1970; children: Corinne Leah, Christopher Alan. B.A., SUNY-Stony Brook, 1971, M.A., 1973; Ph.D., Newport U., 1978. Research asst. SUNY-Stony Brook, 1970-73; instr. U. N.C., Greensboro, 1973-75; asst. prof. Guilford Tech. Inst., High Point, N.C., 1974-75; research psychologist Gov.'s Office, Harrisburg, Pa., 1975-77; adj. prof. Pa. State U., 1977-82; dir. info. systems Children and Youth, Harrisburg, 1977—; info. systems cons. Health Edn. and Welfare, 1975-77; research assoc. Millersville State U., 1977-78; panel reviewer Child Care Quar., Mpls., 1978-82. Author: Instrument Based Program Monitoring System, 1981; Editor: In the Best Interest of Children, 1977. Bd. dirs. Mulberry House Delinquents, Harrisburg, 1975-76. Nat. Child Service grantee, 1980; named Boss of the Yr. Am. Bus. Woman's Assn., 1981; N.Y. State Regents scholar, 1971; scholar incentive, 1973. Mem. Pa. Psychol. Assn. (pres. 1980-81), Am. Psychol. Assn., Evaluation Research Soc., Pa. Children's Consortium (chmn. 1977-80). Roman Catholic. Current Work: Cognitive and information processing theory in young children; compliance benefit theory in information systems science/computer science. Subspecialties: Information systems (Information science); Developmental psychology. Home: 625 Adelia St Middletown PA 17057 Office: Research Information Systems Ctr Children's Services 1514 N 2d St Harrisburg PA 17102

FIENUP, JAMES RAY, physicist, researcher; b. St. Louis, Apr. 17, 1948; s. Wilbur G. and Helen (Rozanski) F.; m. Patricia Ann, Dec. 19, 1970; children: Jonathan, Matthew, Daniel, David. A.B. in Physics and Math. magna cum laude, Holy Cross Coll., 1970; M.S. in Applied Physics (NSF fellow), Stanford, U., 1972, Ph.D in Applied Physics, 1975. Research asst. Stanford Electronics Labs., Stanford U., 1972-75; research physicist Environ. Research Inst. Mich., Ann Arbor, 1975—. Editor 1 book; Assoc. editor: Optics Letters; Contbr. articles to profl. jours. Recipient internat. prize in optics Internat. Commn. for Optics, 1983. Mem. Optical Soc. Am., Internat. Soc. Optical Engring. (Rudolf Kingslake medal and prize 1979), Soc. Photog. and Instrumentation Engrs., IEEE, Sigma Xi, Sigma Pi Sigma, Alpha Sigma Nu. Patentee in field. Current Work: Research in optical and digital information processing; holography; coherent optics. Subspecialties: Optical image processing; Algorithms. Home: 3951 Waldenwood Dr Ann Arbor MI 48105 Office: ERIM PO Box 8618 Ann Arbor MI 48107

FIGARD, JOSEPH EMERSON, research scientist; b. Leavenworth, Kans., Jan. 17, 1948; s. Emerson T. and Mary M. (Turner) F.; m. Mary Jane Eggleston, Oct. 6, 1974; children—Benjamin J., Theodore M., Daniel L. B.A. in Math. and Philosophy, Kans. U., 1971; Ph.D. in Chemistry, Kans. State U., 1979. Lectr. chemistry dept. Kans. State U., Lawrence, 1978-79; sr. research scientist Phillips Petroleum Co., Bartlesville, Okla., 1979—. Contbr. articles to tech. jours. Referee, coach Washington County Soccer Club, 1985—; active local Boy Scouts Am. Mem. Am. Chem. Soc., Am. Phys. Soc. Current work: Thin film photovoltaic cells. Subspecialties: Photochemistry; Solar energy. Home: 4006 SE Woodville Rd Bartlesville OK 74006 Office: Phillips Petroleum Co 124-AL-N Bartlesville OK 74004

FIGLEY, CHARLES RAY, psychology educator, psychotherapist; b. Chgo., Oct. 6, 1944; s. John and Geneva (Bartley) F.; m. Marilyn Gaye Reeves, 1983; 1 step dau., Jessica Reeves Burns. B.S., U. Hawaii, 1970; M.S., Pa. State U., 1971, Ph.D., 1974. Cert. marriage and family therapist cert. sex therapist lic. psychologist, Ind. Instr. Bowling Green State U., 1970-71; instr., teaching asst. Pa. State U., 1971-74; asst. prof. Purdue U., 1974-77, assoc. prof., 1977-83, prof., 1983—; dir. Child and Family Research Inst., 1978—, psychotherapist in pvt. practice, West Lafayette, Ind., 1976—, Chgo., 1983—; research cons.; founder, dir. Consortium on Vet. Studies, 1975—; pres. Groves Conf. on Marriage and the Family, 1981-84. Author, editor: Stress Disorders Among Vietnam Veterans, 1978, (with S. Leventman) Strangers at Home: Vietnam Veterans Since the War, 1980, (with H. McCubbin) Stress and the Family, Vols. I and II, 1983; contbr. (with H. McCubbin) articles to sci. jours. Bd. dirs. Lafayette ARC, 1980—; bd. dirs., pres. Planned Parenthood, 1975-79. Served with USMC, 1963-67, Vietnam. Recipient Instrnl. Innovation award Purdue Parents Assn., 1974, Sanger Founder award Planned Parenthood, 1979, Tchr. of Yr. award Sigma Delta Chi, Purdue U., 1979, Disting. Scholar award Forgotten Warriors Project, Cleve., 1970. Fellow Am. Assn. Marriage and Family Therapists, Am. Orthopsychiat. Assn., Am. Psychol. Assn. Current Work: Immediate and long-term effects of highly stressful and noxious situations on psychosocial and emotional parameters in search of effective mitigating intervention methods. Subspecialties: Social psychology; Psychiatry. Office: Purdue University 525 Russell St West Lafayette IN 47906

FIGLEY, MELVIN MORGAN, physician, educator; b. Toledo, Dec. 5, 1920; s. Karl Dean and Margaret (Morgan) F.; m. Margaret Jane Harris, Mar. 16, 1946; children: Karl Porter, Joseph Dean, Mark Thompson. Student, Dartmouth, 1938-41; M.D. magna cum laude (John Harvard fellow), Harvard, 1944. Diplomate: Am. Bd. Radiology (trustee 1967-72). Intern, resident internal medicine Western Res. U., 1944-46; resident radiology U. Mich., 1948-51, instr., asst. prof., asso. prof. radiology, 1950-58, practice medicine, specializing in radiology, Seattle, 1958—; prof. radiology, chmn. dept. U. Wash., 1958-78, prof. radiology and medicine, 1979—; mem. radiation study sect. NIH, 1963-67; mem. com. on radiology Nat. Acad. Scis.-NRC, 1964-69, chmn., 1968-69. Editor: Am. Jour. Roentgenology, 1976—; Contbr. articles profl. jours. Bd. dirs. James Picker Found., 1970—. Served to capt. M.C. AUS, 1946-48. John and Mary R. Markle scholar, 1952-57. Fellow Am. Coll. Radiology; hon. fellow Royal Coll. Radiologists (London), Royal Australian Coll. Radiologists; hon. mem. Royal Soc. Medicine; mem. Assn. Univ. Radiologists (pres. 1966, Gold medal 1983), Am. Roentgen Ray Soc. (exec. council 1970—, pres. 1983-84), N. Am. Soc. Cardiac Radiology (pres. 1974), Fleischer Soc., Radiol. Soc. N.Am., AMA, Boylston Med. Soc., Wash. Heart Assn. (past trustee), Soc. Chmn. Acad. Radiology Depts. (exec. council 1969-71), Phi Beta Kappa, Sigma Xi, Alpha Omega Alpha, Sigma Alpha Epsilon. Episcopalian. Subspecialty: Diagnostic radiology. Home: 7010 51st Ave NE Seattle WA 98115 Office: Univ Hosp Dept Radiology Seattle WA 98105

FIGUEIRA, JOSEPH F., laser physicist, researcher; b. Paris, Ill., Mar. 7, 1943; s. J. Frank and Virginia E. (Long) F.; m. Anna Marie Fahrenbacher, Aug. 7, 1965; children—E. Christine, William F. B.S., U. Ill., 1965; M.S., Ph.D., Cornell U., 1971. Mem. staff Los Alamos Nat. Lab., N.Mex., 1971-76, group leader, 1976-85. Author: (with others) High Power, Short Pulse CO2 Laser Systems for Inertial Entire Fusion, 1978. Contbr. articles to profl. jours. Chmn. Pojoaque Valley Soccer League, N.Mex.; bd. regents No. N.Mex. Community Coll. NSF fellow, 1971. Mem. Am. Phys. Soc., Material Research Soc., Sigma Tau Sigma, Tau Beta Pi. Current work: Development of high power lasers (ultraviolet to infrared), understanding of optical damage phenomenon in materials, and investigation of nonlinear optics. Office: Los Alamos Nat Lab MSJ 566 Los Alamos NM 87545

FIGUERES, MAURICE CHRISTIAN, data processing executive; b. Lyon, France, July 24, 1932; came to U.S., 1961, naturalized, 1968; s. Pierre and Antoinette Jeanne (Garde) F. Student, U. Lyon, France, 1952-53, McGill U., 1958-59; B.A., CUNY, 1971; M.B.A., NYU, 1978. Internal auditor Bankers Trust Co., N.Y.C., 1969-72; sr. EDP auditor Am. Express Co., N.Y.C., 1972-80; EDP auditor Home Life Ins. Co., N.Y.C., 1980-81; EDP audit mgr. Rockefeller Center, Inc., N.Y.C., 1981—. Reviewer: Computing Reviews, 1982. Treas. French Vets. Assn., Algerian War, N.Y.C., 1981—. Served with French Air Force, 1953-54. Decorated Commemorative medal, Combatant Cross (France). Mem. IEEE (mem. tech. coms. computer soc. 1978), Assn. Computing Machinery (mem. spl. interest groups 1976—), Am. Assn. Artificial Intelligence, IEEE Systems, Man and Cybernetics, Systems, EDP Auditors Assn., Inst. Internal Auditors, N.Y. Acad. Scis. Republican. Roman Catholic. Patentee in field. Current Work: Artificial intelligence. Subspecialties: Software engineering; Cryptography and data security. Office: Rockefeller Center Inc 1230 Ave of the Americas New York NY 10020

FIGUEROA-VIÑAS, ADOLFO, federal government astrophysicist; b. Arecibo, P.R., Nov. 11, 1949; s. Adolfo and Isabel (Vinas-Rivera) Figueroa-Ramos; m. Maria E. Rodriguez, Dec. 17, 1972; 1 child, Ricardo A. B.S., U. P.R., 1970, M.S., 1972; Ph.D., MIT, 1980. Au. physics instr. U. P.R., Mayaguez, 1969-71, instr. physics, 1971-72, Ponce, 1972-74; teaching asst. MIT, Cambridge, 1974-75, research asst., 1975-80; astrophysicist NASA-Goddard Space Flight Ctr., Greenbelt, Md., 1980—; cons. editor Revista Colombiana de Física, 1979-82. Contbr. articles to profl. jours. Mem. Am. Phys. Soc., Am. Geophys. Union, Assn. Puerto Ricans in Sci. and Engring., AAAS, Sigma Xi. Democrat. Roman Catholic. Current work: Study of plasma waves and instabilities in the solar wind and planetary magnetospheres; study of magnetohydrodymmical waves and turbulence on interplanetary shocks. Subspecialty: Plasma physics. Office: Code 692 NASA-Goddard Space Flight Center Greenbelt MD 20771

FIGULY, GARRET DANIEL, chemical manufacturing corporation executive; b. Hammond, Ind., June 6, 1954; s. Joseph Daniel and Elsie Marie (Varga) F.; m. Marianne Elizabeth Graff, July 31, 1976; children—Stephen Daniel, Susan Diane. B.S., Purdue U., 1976; Ph.D., U. Ill., 1981. Teaching asst. U. Ill., Urbana, 1976-78, research asst., 1978-81; research chemist E.I. DuPont de Nemours & Co., Inc., Wilmington, Del., 1981—. Mem. Am. Chem. Soc., Phi Beta Kappa, Sigma Xi, Alpha Chi Sigma, Phi Lambda Upsilon, Phi Kappa Phi, Phi Eta Sigma. Current work: Exploratory polymer chemistry including the synthesis and characterization of new and unusual polymer structures. Subspecialties: Polymer chemistry; Organic chemistry. Home: 18 Drummond Dr Highland West Wilmington DE 19808 Office: Expt Sta 302/322 E I DuPont de Nemours & Co Inc Wilmington DE 19898

FILBEY, ALLEN HOWARD, industrial chemical researcher; b. Fond du Lac, Wis., Jan. 14, 1927; s. Arthur Hawthorne and Wilma Kathrine (Huenink) F.; m. Mary Lee Sharpe, Aug. 20, 1949; children—Christine Elizabeth, Melissa Ann, Gwendolyn Sue, William Allen. B.S., U. Wis., 1948; M.S., U. Mich., 1949, Ph.D., 1953. Research chemist Ethyl Corp., Detroit, 1953-58, research supr., 1958-63, asst. dir., 1963-81, assoc. dir., 1981-82, dir. petroleum chem. research, 1982-83, tech. dir. research, Baton Rouge, 1983—. Served with USN, 1944-46. Mem. Am. Chem. Soc. (corp. assoc.), AAAS. Current work: Specialty chemicals; agricultural chemical and drug intermediates; bromine chemicals; alkylation and catalysis. Subspecialties: Organic chemistry; Organometallics. Home: 13443 Anne Cleves Baton Rouge LA 70816 Office: Ethyl Corp PO Box 341 Baton Rouge LA 70821

FILBY, ROYSTON HERBERT, chemistry educator; b. London, Feb. 16, 1934; married, 1965; 2 children. B.Sc., U. London, 1955; M.Sc., McMaster U., 1957; Ph.D. in Chemistry, Wash. State U., 1971. Research fellow in geochemistry U. Oslo, 1961-64; head dept. chemistry U. El Salvador, 1964-67; chemist Wash. State U., 1967-70, asst. prof. chemistry, 1970-71, assoc. prof., 1971-74, prof., 1974—; asst. dir. Nuclear Radiation Ctr., 1970-74, assoc. dir., 1974-76, dir., 1976—; Orgn. European Econ. Cooperation sr. vis. fellow European Atomic Energy Comm., Mol, Belgium, 1962; guest worker Nat. Bur. Standards, Washington, 1975-76. Fellow Am. Inst. Chemistry; mem. AAAS, Geochem. Soc., Am. Chem. Soc., Geol. Soc. Finland. Subspecialties: Geochemistry; Nuclear chemistry. Office: Nuclear Radiation Ctr Wash State U Pullman WA 99164*

FILDES, ROBERT ANTHONY, biotechnology company executive; b. London, June 5, 1938; came to U.S., 1975; s. Alfred and Olive F.; m. Mavis J. Fildes, Feb. 3, 1964; children—Nicola, Lesley. B.Sc., U. London, 1961, D.C.C., 1964, Ph.D., 1964. Research scientist Human Biochem. Genetics unit, Med. Research Council, Eng., 1964-65; dept. head Fermentation Research and Devel., Glaxo Group Ltd., Eng., 1966-74; v.p. devel. Bristol-Myers Co., Syracuse, N.Y., 1975-78, v.p. ops., 1978-80; pres. Biogen, Inc., Cambridge, Mass., 1980-82; pres., chief operating officer, dir. Cetus Corp., Emoryville, Calif., 1982—; cons. Office Tech. Assessment, Washington, 1981-83. Office: Cetus Corp 1400 Fifty Third St Emeryville CA 94608

FILER, LLOYD JACKSON, JR., medical educator, clinical investigator; b. Grove City, Pa., Sept. 30, 1919; s. Lloyd Jackson and Frances Elsie (Hosack) F.; m. Evalyn Mae Rink, May 29, 1942; children—Lloyd Jackson, Margaret Ann, Thomas Ewing. B.S. in Chemistry, U. Pitts., 1941, Ph.D. in Biochemistry, 1944; M.D., U. Rochester, 1952. Med. research fellow U. Pitts., 1944-45; instr. physiology U. Rochester, (N.Y.), 1945-47, research fellow in anatomy, 1945-52; med. dir., v.p. Ross Labs., Columbus, Ohio, 1952-65; instr., asst. clin. prof. Ohio State U., Columbus, 1952-65; prof. pediatrics U. Iowa, Iowa City, 1965—; chmn. food and nutrition bd. Nat. Acad. Sci., Washington, 1972-75; chmn. com. to evaluate generally regarded as safe substances, 1971-83; trustee, bd. dirs. Nutrition Found., Washington, 1982-84; bd. dirs. Am. Bd. Nutrition; Internat. Life Scis. Inst.-Nutrition Found., 1985—. Editor: Glutamic Acid, 1979, Parental Nutrition, 1983; Aspartame, 1984; jour. supplement Current Perspectives Hypertension, 1982. Served to capt. USAF, 1956-58. Recipient Joseph Goldberger award AMA, 1978, Outstanding Achievement award Am. Coll. Nutrition, 1979, Inst. Food Technologists, 1981. Fellow Am. Acad. Pediatrics (chmn. nutrition com. Evanston 1972-75); mem. Soc. Pediatric Research, Am. Pediatric Soc. Republican. Presbyterian. Club: Cosmos (Washington). Current work: Amino acid peptide metabolism; infant nutrition; food additives. Home: 216 Monroe St Iowa City IA 52240 Office: U Iowa Iowa City IA 52242

FILIPEK, LORRAINE HENRIETTA, research geochemist, hydrologist; b. Dearborn, Mich., Oct. 27, 1947; d. Henry Joseph and Sophie Patricia (Slaga) F.; m. Stacy Walters, Feb. 24, 1979. B.S. in Biophysics, U. Mich., 1969, Ph.D. in Chem. Oceanography, 1979; M.A. in Phys. Oceanography, Johns Hopkins U., 1974. Research asst. IAEA, Vienna, Austria, 1971-72; research geochemist U.S. Geol. Survey, Denver, 1979—. Contbr. articles and abstracts to profl. jours. Recipient scholarships Nat. Assn. Secondary Sch. Prins., 1965; William C. Doherty scholar, 1965-69; U. Mich. Regents-Alumni scholar, 1965-69; Continuing Edn. Women scholar, 1977-78; fellow Balt. Gas and Elec., 1972-73, Turner fellow, 1977, Rackham predoctoral fellow, 1978-79; NRC fellow, 1979-80. Geol. Soc. Am. (student research grantee 1977-78), Geochem. Soc., Am. Geophys. Union, Assn. Women Geoscientists (treas. Denver chpt. 1984-85), Assn. Exploration Geochemists, Sigma Xi (research grantee 1977-78). Current work: Paleo-ground water flow and transport modeling; water-rock interactions and weathering processes using sequential extraction techniques and solute transport modeling. Subspecialties: Geochemistry; Hydrology. Office: US Geol Survey Fed Ctr M S 973 Box 25046 Denver CO 80225

FILIPPENKO, ALEXEI VLADIMIR, astrophysicist; b. Berkeley, Calif., July 25, 1958; s. Vladimir Ivan and Alexandra (Karmansky) F. B.A. in Physics, U. Calif.-Santa Barbara, 1979; Ph.D. in Astronomy, Calif. Inst. Tech., 1984. Lab. asst. U. Calif.-Santa Barbara, 1976-77; instr. astronomy, 1977-79; Miller research fellow, U. Calif.-Berkeley, 1984—. Contbr. articles to profl. jours. Fannie and John Hertz Found. fellow, 1979-84, U. Calif. Regents scholar, 1975-79. Mem. Union Concerned Scientists, Am. Astron. Soc., Astron. Soc. Pacific, Soc. Physics Students, Phi Beta Kappa. Democrat. Club: Santa Barbara Astronomy. Current work: Physical properties of active galactic nuclei and quasars; relationship between normal galaxies, classical Seyferts, and starburst galaxies. Subspecialty: Optical astronomy. Office: Dept Astronomy U Calif Berkeley CA 94720

FILISKO, FRANK EDWARD, materials and metallurgical engineering educator, consultant; b. Lorain, Ohio, Jan. 29, 1942; s. Joseph John and Mary Magdelene (Cherven) F.; m. Doris Faye Call, Aug. 8, 1970; children—Theresa, Andrew, Edward. B.A., Colgate U., 1964; M.S., Purdue U., 1966; Ph.D., Case Western Res. U., 1969. Asst. prof. U. Mich., Ann Arbor, 1970-76, assoc. prof., 1972-83, prof. dept. materials and metall. engring., 1982—; cons. Indsl. Tech. Inst., Ann Arbor, 1984—, Aetna Ins. Co., Flint, Mich., 1980—, Bendix Corp., Southfield, Mich., 1980-82. Author: Introduction to Biomedical Materials, 19—; contbr. articles to sci. jours. Leader, YMCA, UWCA, Ann Arbor, 1978—. Mem. Am. Chem. Soc., Am. Phys. Soc., Soc. Rheology, Soc. Biomaterials, N.Y. Acad. Scis. Democrat. Roman Catholic. Lodge: K.C. (Ann Arbor). Current work: Characterization and processing of glassy polymers, blood-polymer interfacial interactions, rheological properties of polymers. Subspecialties: Polymers (materials science); Biomaterials. Office: Materials and Metall Engring U Mich Ann Arbor MI 48109

FILLON, RICHARD HENRY, micropaleontologist, marine geologist; b. Bklyn., Dec. 17, 1944; s. Henry Joseph and Constance (Michetti) F.; m. Jerrilyn Mary Olin, Aug. 29, 1964; children—Emily Ann, Elizabeth Aimee. B.S., Rensselaer Poly. Inst., 1966; M.S., U. Vt.-Burlington, 1970; Ph.D., U. R.I.-Kingston, 1973. Postdoctoral fellow Woods Hole Oceanographic Inst., Mass., 1973-74; research scientist Geol. Survey of Can., Bedford Inst. Oceanography, Dartmouth, N.S., 1974-81; assoc. prof. research Baruch Inst., U. S.C., Columbia, 1981-85; area micropaleontologist Texaco, Inc., New Orleans, 1985—; cons. in field. Author: Principles of Pleistocene, 1984. Contbr. articles to profl. jours. Bd. dirs., editor newsletter Columbia Audubon Soc., 1984. Mem. Geol. Soc. Am., Am. Quaternary Assn., Soc. Econ. Paleontologists and Mineralogists, Am. Assn. Petroleum Geologists. Current work: Quaternary stratigraphic studies and paleoenvironmental studies using Planktonic Foraminifera. Subspecialties: Paleontology, paleoecology; Sedimentology. Office: Texaco Inc PO Box 60252 New Orleans LA 70160

FINCH, CALEB ELLICOTT, biology educator; b. London, July 4, 1939; s. Benjamin Finch and Faith (Stratton) Campbell; m. Doris Nossamen; Stepchildren—Alec Tsongas, Michael Tsongas. B.S., Yale U., 1961; Ph.D., Rockefeller U., 1969. Prof. biology and gerontology U. So. Calif., 1978—. Editor: Handbook of Biology of Aging, 1977, 2d edit., 1985. Contbr. articles to profl. jours. Fellow Gerontol. Soc. (Kleemeier award 1984, Brookdale award 1985); mem. Endocrine Soc., Neuroscience Soc. Current work: Neuroendocrinology and neurochemistry of aging processes, role of gene activity in aging, Alzheimer's disease. Subspecialties: Neurobiology; Gerontology. Home: 2144 Crescent Dr Altadena CA 91001 Office: Univ So Calif University Park Los Angeles CA 90089

FINCH, WARREN IRVIN, geologist, researcher; b. Union County, S.D., Oct. 27, 1924; s. Julius Irvin and Dorothy (Hedden) F.; m. Mary Margaret Theisen, Sept. 1, 1951; children—Lawrence Paul, Carolanne Marie, Andrew Thomas (dec.). B.S., S.D. Sch. Mines and Tech., 1948; M.S. in Geology, U. Calif.-Berkeley, 1954; postgrad. Colo. Sch. Mines, 1958-59. Geologist, project chief U.S. Geol. Survey, Grand Junction and Denver, 1949-61, Paducah, Ky., 1962-68, Denver, 1969-71, chief br. uranium and thorium resources, 1972-77, research geologist, Golden, Colo., 1978-82, supervisory research geologist, 1983—; project leader geology working group IAEA, Vienna, Austria, 1979-84. Author: Geology of Uranium Deposits in Triassic Rocks, Colorado Plaueau, 1959; Geology of Epigenetic Uranium Deposits in Sandstone Formations, 1967; Stratigraphy, Marphology, and Paleoecology of a Fossil Peccary Herd, 1972. Editor: Sedimentary Environment of Uranium Deposits in Sandstone Formations, 1984. Scoutmaster Denver area council Boy Scouts Am., 1970-71; pres. Bicycle Racing Assn. Colo., Denver, 1977-79; bd. dirs. Mountain Bicyclists Assn. Inc., Denver, 1980—; pres. Denver Field Ornithologists, Denver, 1982. Served with U.S. Army, 1944-46. Recipient Meritorious Service award U.S. Dept. Interior, 1981, Unit award Excellence of Service, U.S. Dept. Interior, 1982. Fellow Geol. Soc. Am.; mem. Soc. Econ. Geologists, Colo. Sci. Soc., Internat. Assn. Genesis Ore Deposits, Denver Regional Exploration Geologists Soc. Lodge: K.C. Current work: Research to develop new methods to reduce subjectivity of estimating undiscovered mineral resources. Subspecialty: Geology. Home: 455 Dover St Lakewood CO 80226 Office: US Geol Survey PO Box 25046 MS 916 Denver CO 80225

FINDEISEN, HEINZ H., electronics engineer; b. Celje, Yugoslavia, Sept. 24, 1926; came to U.S., 1966; s. Heinrich Anton and Barbara (Kleindienst) F.; m. Beryl Knight, Mar. 29, 1952; children—Isabella-Barbara, Christina, Helena-Julia. B.S. in Elec. Engring., Fed. Inst. Tech., Graz, Austria, 1946, postgrad., 1946-48. Chief engr. Epsylon Research and Devel. Co. Ltd., London, 1959-66; design engr. Sangamo Electric Inc., Springfield, Ill., 1966-69; prin. engr. Honeywell Computer Inc., Framingham, Mass., 1969-83; engring. mgr. Digital Equipment Inc., Maynard, Mass., 1973-83; tech. dir. North Atlantic Industries Inc., Hopkinton, Mass., 1983—. Patentee in field. Set designer Theater Guild, Milford, Mass., 1972-76. Mem. IEEE (assoc.; exec. bd. dirs.; magnetics soc. planning bd. 1980-81 Boston chpt.). Current work: Manage research, development and design of magnetic recording disks tape systems, optical disks for computers, research and development to advance magnetic recording technology for information storage. Subspecialties: Information systems, storage, and retrieval (computer science); Laser data storage and reproduction. Home: 20 Muriel Ln Milford MA 01757

FINDL, EUGENE, bioelectrochemical engineer; b. Fredericktown, Pa., July 26, 1926; s. Max and Dora (Weinberg) F.; m. Dolores Koppelman, Apr. 14, 1954 (div. Dec. 1969); children—Marci L., Jeff D., Denise L., Kim L. B.S., U. Pitts., 1950; postgrad. U. So. Calif., 1953-54. Field engr. So. Calif. Gas Co., 1952-55; research engr. TRW Inc., 1955-59; sr. research engr. Sundstrand Corp., 1959-61; supr. chem. research Group Marquardt/CCI Corp., 1961-63; mgr. advanced tech. div. Xerox Corp., 1963-69; engring. cons., 1969-74; dir. bioelectrochemistry div. BioResearch, Inc., 1974-81; prin. investigator Brookhaven Nat. Lab., Upton, N.Y., 1982—. Contbr. articles to profl. jours. Patentee in field. Served to lt. (j.g.) USN, 1944-46, 51-52, Korea. Mem. Instrument Soc. Am. (dir. biomed. scis. div. 1984—), Am. Chem. Soc., AAAS, Electrochem. Soc., Am. Inst. Biol. Scis., BioElectroMagnetics Soc., Internat. Assn. Colloid and Interface Scientists, BioElectrochem. Soc., N.Y. Acad. Scis. Current work: Bioelectrochemistry, bioengineering, electrochemical engineering, chemical engineering. Subspeciality: Biomedical engineering.

FINDLAY, JOHN WILLIAM ADDISON, biochemist; b. Buckie, Banffshire, Scotland, Mar. 27, 1945; s. Alexander and Jessie Ross (Addison) F.; m. Jean Marjorie Hey, July 11, 1970; children: Kathleen Moira, Fiona Jean. B.Sc., U. Aberdeen, 1966, Ph.D., 1969. Research assoc. pharm. chemistry U. Va., Charlottesville, 1969-72; research biochemist dept. pathology Norfolk Gen. Hosp., Norfolk, 1972-73; research scientist Radiochem. Centre, Amersham, Eng., 1973-75; sr. research scientist Wellcome Research Labs., Research Triangle Park, N.C., 1975-81, group leader, 1981—; cons. Tobacco Research Council, 1979. Contbr. articles to profl. jours. Mem. Am. Soc. Pharmacology and Exptl. Therapeutics. Presbyterian. Current Work: Development of antisera and immunoassays: application of these to studies of drug disposition and pharmacology in animals and man. Subspecialties: Pharmacokinetics; Pharmacology. Office: Burroughs Wellcome Co 3030 Cornwallis Rd Research Triangle Park NC 27709

FINDLEY, GARY LEE, chemistry educator; b. Little Rock, Ark., Dec. 29, 1952; s. Willis Winn and Wanda Jean (Kinsinger) F.; m. Anna Marie Tringali, June 16, 1975; children—Jean-Marie, Helen Ann. B.S., U. Ark., 1974; Ph.D., La. State U., 1978. Dir. molecular spectroscopy group chemistry dept., La. State U., Baton Rouge, 1978-82; assoc. prof. chemistry dept., NYU, 1982—. Editor: Photophysics and Photochemistry in the VUV, 1985. Contbr. articles to profl. jours. NYU fellow, 1984; NATO grantee, 1982. Mem. Am. Math. Soc., Am. Phys. Soc., Am. Chem. Soc., N.Y. Acad. Scis., Phi Kappa Phi, Phi Lambda Upsilon. Democrat. Current work: Atomic and molecular spectroscopy in vacuum ultraviolet; Rydberg states; solid state spectroscopy; theoretical biology. Subspecialties: Physical chemistry; Atomic and molecular physics. Home: 2 Washington Sq Village Apt 3-L New York NY 10003 Office: Chemistry Dept NYU 4 Washington Pl New York NY 10003

FINE, ALBERT S., biochemist; b. Phila., Oct. 24, 1923; s. Max and Sylvia (Lerner) F.; m. Selma J. Skolnick, Mar. 28, 1959; 1 child, Martin Jay. B.A., CUNY-Bklyn., 1950, M.A., 1953; Ph.D., NYU, 1970. Faculty, NYU Coll. Medicine, N.Y.C., 1950-52; faculty biochemistry Columbia U., N.Y.C., 1952-56; biochemist Bklyn. VA Med. Ctr., 1956-70; chief dental research NYU VA Med. Ctr., 1970—; assoc. prof. histology-cell biology, periodontology NYU Coll. Dentistry, 1970—. Contbr. articles to profl. jours. Mem. N.Y. Acad. Sci., AAAS, Am. Chem. Soc., Internat. Assn. Dental Research, Sigma Xi. Current Wrok: Regulation of cellular proliferation during wound healing. Subspecialties: Oral biology; Biochemistry (medicine). Office: NY VA Med Ctr 1st Ave at E 24th St New York NY 10010

FINE, DONALD LEE, microbiologist, research administrator; b. Nanticoke, Pa., Jan. 14, 1943; s. Donald Harmon and Doris (Searles) F.; m. Judith Ann, June 12, 1965; children: Dawn Ann, Heather, Matthew. Ph.D. in Microbiology, Pa. State U., 1968. Chief dept. virology and cell biolgoy Frederick (Md.) Cancer Research Ctr., 1970-72, head devel. research sect., 1972-76, head immunobiology of type B retroviruses sect., 1976-78; mgr. NIH intramural research support program, 1978—; cons. in field. Author: Biological Markers of Neoplasia, 1978, Breast Cancer: New Concepts in Etiology and Control, 1980, others; contbr. articles to profl. publs. Recipient Outstanding Achievement award Dept. Army, 1969. Mem. Am. Soc. Microbiology, N.Y. Acad. Sci., AAAS, Am. Assn. Cancer Research, Soc. Exptl. Cell Biology and Medicine, Tissue Culture Assn., Internat. Leukemia Soc., Sigma Xi (chpt. program chmn. 1981), Iota Mu Pi. Subspecialties: Cancer research (medicine); Microbiology (medicine). Office: Frederick Cancer Research Facility Box B Frederick MD 21701

FINE, MICHAEL LAWRENCE, biologist, educator; b. Bklyn., Feb. 10, 1946; s. Herbert A. and Helen R. F.; m. Judith R. Slavsky, Aug. 7, 1977; 1 son, Benjamin A. B.S., U. Md., 1967; M.A., Coll. William and Mary, 1970; Ph.D., U. R.I., 1976. Oceanographer U.S. Naval Oceanographic Office, summers 1966-67; postdoctoral assoc. Cornell U., Ithaca, N.Y., 1976-79; physiologist Tunison Lab. Fish Nutrition, Fish and Wildlife Service, Cortland, N.Y., summer 1979; asst. prof. biology Va. Commonwealth U., Richmond, 1979-85, assoc. prof., 1985—. Contbr. articles to profl. jours. Mem. Soc. Neurosci., AAAS, Animal Behavior Soc., Am. Soc. Ichthyologists and Herpetologists. Jewish. Current Work: Acoustic communication in fishes, toadfish, neural substrates of behavior, sexual dimorphism of brain, hormones and behavior, auditory neurophysiology. Subspecialty: Ethology. Home: 9419 Broad Meadows Rd Glen Allen VA 23060 Office: Dept Biology Va Commonwealth U Richmond VA 23284

FINE, MORRIS EUGENE, materials engineer, educator; b. Jamestown, N.D., Apr. 12, 1918; s. Louis and Sophie (Berrington) F.; m. Mildred Eleanor Glazer, Aug. 13, 1950; children: Susan Elaine, Amy Lynn. B.Metall. Engring. with distinction, U. Minn., 1940, M.S., 1942, Ph.D., 1943. Instr. U. Minn., 1942-46; mem. tech. staff Bell Telephone Labs., Murray Hill, N.J., 1946-54; prof., chmn. dept. metallurgy Tech. Inst., Northwestern U., Evanston, Ill., 1955-57, chmn. dept. materials sci., 1958-60, prof. and chmn. materials research center, 1960-64, Walter P. Murphy prof. materials sci., 1963—; asso. dean grad. studies and research Tech. Inst., Northwestern U. (Technol. Inst.), 1973-85, Technol. Inst. prof., 1985—; vis. prof. dept. materials sci. Stanford U., 1967-68; JSPS vis. scholar, Japan, 1979; vis. disting. prof. U. Tex.-Austin, 1984-85; asso. engr. Manhattan Project, U. Chgo., also, Los Alamos, World War II; mem. materials adv. bd. Nat. Acad. Sci., 1963-68; mem. com. geol. and materials scis. NRC, 1979-82; co-chmn. Engring. Socs. Conf. on Fatigue Crack Initiation, 1980; chmn. adv. bd., program on modular methods for teaching materials Pa. State U., 1973-77; chmn. vis. com. metallurgy and materials Sci. and Materials Research Center, Lehigh U., 1965-75; vis. com. Lawrence Berkeley Lab., 1978-81, chmn., 1981, vis. com. Ames Dept. Energy Lab., 1976-80. Author numerous tech. and sci. articles on mech. properties of metals and ceramics, fatigue of metals, phase transformations and other subjects.; author: Introduction to Phase Transformation in Condensed Systems. Named Chicagoan of Year in Sci., 1961. Fellow Am. Phys. Soc., AAAS, Am. Soc. Metals (chpt. chmn. 1963, Campbell lectr. 1979, Gold medal 1986), Metall. Soc. of AIME (chmn. inst. metals div. 1966-68, dir. 1968-71, dir. inst. 1972-75, Mathewson gold medal for research 1981, James Douglas Gold medal 1983), Am. Ceramic Soc. (keynote lectr. electronic materials div. 1972); mem. Nat. Acad. Engring. (mem. astronautics space engring. bd. 1973-77, membership com. 1974-79, chmn. 1977-78), Am. Assn. Engring Edn., ASTM, AAUP, Fedn. Am. Scientists, Engring. Com. for Profl. Devel. (accreditation panel for metallurgy and materials), Sigma Xi, Tau Beta Pi, Alpha Sigma Mu, Sigma Alpha Sigma. Subspecialty: Metallurgy. Home: 1101 Manor Dr Wilmette IL 60091 Office: Northwestern U Evanston IL 60201

FINE, SAMUEL, biomedical engineering educator, researcher, consultant; b. Baranowiczach, Poland, Jan. 21, 1925; came to U.S., 1950; s. Abraham and Rose (Perlin) F. B.A. Sc., U. Toronto, Can., 1946, M.D., 1957; S.M., MIT, 1953. Registered profl. engr., Can. Staff mem. research lab. electronics MIT, Cambridge, 1951-53; biomed. engr. NIH, Bethesda, Md., 1958-59; research assoc., assoc. in medicine Brookhaven Nat. Lab., Upton, R.I., 1959-61; assoc. prof. elec. engring. Northeastern U., Boston, 1961-64, prof. biomed. engring., 1964-66, prof., chmn. biomed. engring., 1966—; clin. fellow Mass. Gen. Hosp., Boston, 1969-70; dir. Advanced Tech. Pub., Newton, Mass., 1968-81, Biometrics, Cambridge, 1968-72; mem. exptl. cardiovascular study sect. NIH, 1978-81; cons. Dept. Pub. Health, State of Mass., 1966—; mem. editorial bd. Laser Focus, Newton, 1966-81. Editor (with M. Cox and W. Bushor), Laser Industry Assn. Proceedings, 1968. Patentee in field. Mem. adv. bd. New Eng. Intercollegiate Sailing, Cambridge, 1981—. Named Klein Lectr. Northeastern U., 1969; recipient Distin. Service award Zeta Beta Tau, 1984. Mem. IEEE (chmn. E.M.B. Boston sect. 1969), Laser Inst. of Am. (mem. founding bd. of dirs. 1967-71), Am. Nat. Standards Inst. (mem. Z-136 com. 1972—), Soc. Exptl. Pathology, Sigma Xi, Tau Beta Pi, Phi Kappa Phi, Eta Kappa Nu. Jewish. Current work: Analysis of cardiac output and equivalent systems; mechanisms of interaction and effects of laser radiation with biological systems. Subspecialties: Biomedical engineering; Biophysics (biology). Home: 16 Ware St Cambridge MA 02138 Office: Northeastern U 360 Huntington Boston MA 02115

FINE, TERRENCE LEON, electrical engineering educator, applied mathematics and statistics educator; b. N.Y.C., Mar. 9, 1939; s. Abraham and Lola (Breidberg) F.; m. Susan Woodward, June 12, 1964 (div. Mar. 1981); children—David, Jennifer. B.S. in Elec. Engring., CCNY, 1958; S.M., Harvard U., 1959, Ph.D., 1963. Research assoc., lectr. Harvard U., Cambridge, Mass., 1963-64; Miller fellow U. Calif.-Berkeley, 1964-66; asst. prof. Cornell U., Ithaca, N.Y., 1966-70, assoc., prof., 1970-79, prof., 1979—; vis. prof. Stanford U., Palo Alto, Calif., 1972-73, 79-80. Author: Theories of Probability, 1973.

Patentee in field. Author numerous papers. Recipient Hon. Mention Best Paper prize IEEE Control Systems Soc., 1980. Fellow IEEE (bd. govs. info. theory group 1980—); mem. Inst. Math. Stats. Democrat. Current work: Development of new concepts of probability and their application to decision making and risk analysis; statistical problems of communication and control. Subspecialties: Probability; Telecommunications. Home: 1391 Ellis Hollow Rd Ithaca NY 14850 Office: Sch Elec Engring Cornell U Ithaca NY 14853

FINEGOLD, LEONARD X., biophysicist, educator; b. London, Feb. 15, 1935; m. Mary V.S. Krotkov, 1965; children—Alan Anthony, Geoffrey Nicholas. B.S., Queen Mary Coll., U. London, 1956, Ph.D., 1959. Research fellow Harvard U., 1959-62; research assoc. U. Calif.-Berkeley, 1962-65; research assoc., asst. prof. U. Colo., Boulder, 1965-74; prof. biophysics Drexel U., Phila., 1974—; vis. prof. Watkins Found., Wichita, Kans., 1978; Contbr. articles to profl. jours. Research scholar Am. Cancer Soc., 1971-73; spl. fellow NIH, 1971-73; Queens Quest scholar, Queen's U., Kingston, Ont., Can., 1984. Mem. Am. Phys. Soc., Biophys. Soc., Fedn., Am. Scientists, Calorimetry Conf., AAAS, Soc. Basic Irreproducible Research, ASTM, Sierra Club (coordinator Delaware County sect. 1982—). Current work: Biophysics: lipid bilayers (artificial membranes), phase transitions; polymers: effects of gamma-radiation on ultra-high molecular weight polyethylene. Subspecialties: Biophysics (physics); Polymers (materials science). Office: Dept Physics Drexel U Philadelphia PA 19104

FINK, JONATHAN HARRY,, geology educator; b. N.Y.C., May 2, 1951; s. Max and Martha (Gross) F. B.A., Colby Coll., 1973; Ph.D., Stanford U., 1978. Field geologist U.S. Geol. Survey, Menlo Park, Calif., 1975, 76, 82; postdoctoral fellow, research assoc. Weizmann Inst., Rehovot, Israel, 1979; postdoctoral fellow, research assoc. geology Ariz. State U., Tempe, 1980-82, asst. prof. geology, 1982—. Editor: Emplacement of Lava Domes, 1985. Contbr. articles to profl. jours. Research grantee NSF, 1980-85, NASA, 1980-85, Dept. Energy, 1984-86. Mem. Geol. Soc. Am., Am. Geophys. Union, AAAS, Sigma Xi, Phi Beta Kappa. Democrat. Jewish. Current work: Lava flow mechanics; magma intrusion processes; explosive volcanism; impact cratering; tectonics of icy satellites of Jupiter and Saturn; electronic surveying techniques. Subspecialties: Volcanology; Tectonics. Office: Ariz State U Geology Dept Tempe AZ 85287

FINK, LESTER HAROLD, engineer; b. Phila., May 3, 1925; s. Harold Drury and Edna Baily (Hopkins) F.; m. Ruth Naomi Veit, Dec. 10, 1955; children—Lois Hope, Carol Anne. B.S. in Elec. Engring., U. Pa., 1950, M.S. in Elec. Engring., 1961. Registered profl. engr., Pa., Va. Supervising engr. Phila. Electric Co., Phila., 1950-74; asst. dir. U.S. Dept. Energy, Washington, 1974-79; pres. Systems Engring. for Power, Inc., Annandale, Va., 1979-83; ptnr. Carlsen & Fink Assocs., Inc., Fairfax, Va., 1983—; adj. prof. Drexel U., Phila., 1961-74, U. Md., College Park, 1979-80. Patentee in field (3). Editor: Systems Engineering for Power, 1975; contbr. to books. Decorated Meritorious Service award U.S. Dept. Energy, 1979. Fellow IEEE, Inst. Soc. Am.; mem. Conf. Internat. de Grande Reseaux Electrique. Presbyterian. Current work: Control and analysis of large scale electrical energy systems. Subspecialty: Electrical engineering. Home: 11304 Full Cry Ct Oakton VA 22124 Office: Carlsen & Fink Assocs Inc 11244 Waples Mill Rd D-2 Fairfax VA 22030

FINK, RICHARD W(ALTER), chemistry educator; b. Detroit, Jan. 13, 1928; s. Bernard and Ann (Walter) F.; m. Gunilla Lena Gustafson, Oct. 4, 1960; children—Kerry Leif, Roger Gunnar. B.S. in Chemistry, U. Mich., 1948; M.S. in Chemistry, U. Calif.-Berkeley, 1949; Ph.D., U. Rochester, 1953. Asst. prof. chemistry U. Ark., Fayetteville, 1953-61, assoc. prof., 1960-61; prof. physics Marquette U., Milw., 1961-65; prof. chemistry Ga. Inst. Tech., Atlanta, 1965—; vis. research scientist Werner Inst. Nuclear Chemistry, U. Uppsala, Sweden, 1959-60; vis. prof. physics U. Hamburg, Fed. Republic Germany, 1963-64; cons. Lawrence Livermore Nat. Lab., 1961-62. Contbr. numerous articles to profl. jours. Fellow Am. Phys. Soc.; mem. Am. Chem. Soc. (div. nuclear chemistry and tech.), Univ. Isotope Separator at Oak Ridge, Sigma Xi (research awards 1971, 72, 77, 79, 83). Club: German (Atlanta). Current work: Radioactive decay and nuclear structure of nuclei far from stability; x-rays and Coster-Kronig transitions in radioactive decay; radiochemistry especially fluorine-18 for nuclear medicine. Subspecialties: Nuclear chemistry; Nuclear physics. Office: Sch Chemistry Ga Inst Tech Atlanta GA 30332

FINKELSTEIN, MICHAEL, endocrinologist; b. Sonsnowiec, Poland, Dec. 15, 1916; came to Israel, 1934; s. Eliezer and Bilha (Zmigrod) F.; m. Nehama Gilmovsky, Mar. 27, 1947; children—Elazar, Elona. M.Sc., Hebrew U., 1940, Ph.D., 1946. Sr. lectr. endocrinology, Hebrew U., Jerusalem, 1954-58, assoc. prof., 1958-67, prof., 1967—; vis. prof. U. Louisville, 1978-79; cons. WHO, New Delhi, India, 1975, prof., Bangkok, 1975. Patentee in field. Recipient Henrietta Szold award Mcpl. Council Tel-Aviv, 1961; cert. for outstanding contbns. U. Louisville, 1979. Humanitarian Trust fellow, London, 1951. Mem. Internat. Study Group for Steroid Hormones (chmn. steering com. 1963-83, vice chmn. 1983—). Current work: Endocrinology, steroid hormones in normal humans and in genetic aberrations; estimation of steroid hormones in biological fluids. Subspecialty: Endocrinology. Home: 17/8 Shai Agnon Ave Jerusalem Israel 92586 Office: Hebrew U Hadassah Med Sch Jerusalem Israel

FINKELSTEIN, RICHARD ALAN, microbiologist; b. N.Y.C., Mar. 5, 1930; s. Frank and Sylvia (Lemkin) F.; m. Helen Rosenberg, Nov. 30, 1952; children: Sheri, Mark, Laurie; m. Mary Boesman, June 20, 1976; 1 dau., Sarina Nicole. B.S., U. Okla., 1950; M.A., U. Tex., Austin, 1952, Ph.D., 1955. Teaching fellow, research scientist U. Tex., Austin, 1950-55; fellow, instr. U. Tex. Southwestern Med. Sch., Dallas, 1955-58; chief bioassay sect. Walter Reed Army Inst. Research, Washington, 1958-64; dep. chief, chief dept. bacteriology and mycology U.S. Army Med. Component, SEATO Med. Research Lab., Bangkok, Thailand, 1964-67; asso. prof. dept. microbiology U. Tex. Southwestern Med. Sch., Dallas, 1967-73, prof., 1973-79; prof., chmn. dept. microbiology Sch. Medicine U. Mo.-Columbia, 1979—; mem. Nat. Com. for Coordination of Cholera Research, Ministry of Public Health, Bangkok, 1965-67; cons. WHO, 1970—; cons. to comdg. gen. U.S. Army Med. Research and Devel. Command, 1975-79; cons. Schwarz-Mann Labs., 1974-79; vis. asso. prof. U. Med. Scis., Bangkok, 1965-67; vis. prof. U. Chgo. Med. Sch., 1977; vis. scientist Japanese Sci. Council, 1976; Ciba-Geigy lectr. Waksman Inst., Rutgers U., 1975. Contbr. articles on cholera, enterotoxins, gonorrhea, role of iron in host parasite interactions to profl. jours. Recipient numerous awards including Robert Koch prize in sci. and medicine Bonn, W. Ger., 1976; Chancellor's award for outstanding faculty research in biol. scis. U. Mo.-Columbia. Fellow Am. Acad. Microbiology, Infectious Diseases Soc. Am.; mem. Am. Soc. Microbiology (div. councilor, chmn. program com. 1979-82, pres. Tex. br. 1974-75), Am. Assn. Immunologists, Soc. Gen. Microbiology, Pathol. Soc. Gt. Britain and Ireland. Current Work: Pathogenesis and immunology of cholera and related diarrheal diseases; enterotoxins; critical role of iron in host-parasite interactions. Subspecialties: Microbiology; Immunobiology and immunology. Home: 3207 Honeysuckle Dr Columbia MO 65201 Office: Dept Microbiology Sch Medicine Univ of Mo-Columbia Columbia MO 65212

FINKL, CHARLES WILLIAM, JR., geology educator, researcher; b. Chgo., Sept. 19, 1941; s. Charles William Finkl Sr. and Marian Louella (Hamilton) Finkl Seymour; m. Charlene Bristol, May 16, 1965 (div. 1974); children—Amanda Marie, Jonathon William Frederick. B.Sc., Oreg. State U., 1964, M.Sc., 1966; Ph.D., U. Western Australia, Nedlands, 1971. Cert. profl. soil scientist, geologist. Instr. geology Oreg. State U., Corvallis, 1967; demonstrator U. Western Australia, Perth, 1968; staff geochemist Internat. Nickel Australia, Perth, Western Australia, 1970-74; dir., program prof. Inst. Coastal Studies, Nova U., Fort Lauderdale, Fla., 1980-83; prof., Fla. Atlantic U., Boca Raton, 1983—; exec. dir. Coastal Edn. and Research Found., Fort Lauderdale, 1983—. Editor/author: The Encyclopedia of Soil Science, Part I: Physics, Chemistry, Biology, Fertility, and Technology, 1979; The Encyclopedia of Applied Geology, 1983. Editor: Ency. Earth Sci., N.Y.C., 1974—; Soil Classification, 1981; editor-in-chief Jour. Coastal Research, 1983—. Contbr. articles and revs. to profl. jours. Mem. ad hoc com. Broward County Mus. Natural History and Sci. Mem. AAAS, Am. Assn. Petroleum Geologists, AAUP, Am. Geophys. Union, Am. Geog. Soc., Am. Quaternary Assn., Am. Inst. Profl. Geologists (cert. in geosci.), Am. Littoral Soc., Am. Shore and Beach Preservation Assn., Am. Soc. Photogrammetry, Am. Soc. So. Agrl. Scientists, Australian Soc. Soil Sci., Australasian Inst. Mining and Metallurgy, Brit. Geomorphological Research Group, Brit. Soc. Soil Sci., Can. Geophys. Union, Coastal Soc., Deutsche Bodenkundlishen Gesellschaft, Deutsche Geologische Vereinigung, European Assn. Sci. Editors, Estuarine and Brackish-Water Scis. Assn., Fedn. Am. Scientists, Fla. Acad. Sci., Fla. Shore and Beach Preservation Assn., Geol. Assn. Can., Geol. Soc. Am., Geol. Soc. Australia, Geol. Soc. London, Geol. Soc. Miami, Geol. Soc. S. Africa, Geoloists' Assn., Geosci. Info. Soc., Inst. Australian Geographers, Internat. Soil Sci. Soc., Internat. Union Geol. Scis., Internat. Geog. Union (comn. on river and coastal plains, comn. on geomorphological survey and mapping, subcom. on morphotectonics), Internat. Quaternary Assn. (neotectonics commn., palaeopedology working group), Mineral. Assn. Can., Mus. Sci. and Planetarium, Nat. Assn, Environ. Profls., Nature Conservancy, Nat. Parks and Conversation Assn., N.Y. Acad. Scis., Soil Sci. Soc. Am. (cert. in agronomy, crops and soil scis.), Soc. Belge de Pedologie, Soc. Econ. Paleontologists and Mineralogists, Soc. Mining Engrs. of AIME, U.S. Naval Inst., Order Orange Oar, Gamma Theta Upsilon. Republican. Presbyterian. Current work: Geomorphology and paleopedology of tropical cratons; soil stratigraphy; coastal hazard mitigation; natural resources management. Subspecialties: Geology; Coastal zones. Home: 1808 Bay View Dr Fort Lauderdale FL 33305Office: Fla Atlantic U Dept Geology Boca Raton FL 33431

FINKLE, BERNARD JOSEPH, plant biochemist, cryobiologist, tissue culturist; b. Chgo., Mar. 17, 1921; s. Nathan Ephraim and Lena F.; m. Evelyn Cohen, Dec. 9, 1944; children: Wayne Nathaniel, Claudia. B.S., U. Chgo., 1942; Ph.D., UCLA, 1950. Research assoc. U. Calif., Berkeley, 1951-53; lab. dir. Atomic Research Lab., Los Angeles, 1953-54; research instr. U. Utah, Salt Lake City, 1954-57; research biochemist Western Regional Research Center, Berkeley, 1957-83; adj. assoc. prof. food sci. U. Calif., Berkeley, 1970-72; cons. cryobiology, plant and food enzymology, tissue culture, Berkeley, 1983—; assoc. pomology U. Calif.-Davis, 1983—; lectr. Symposium Academia Sinica, Peking, China, 1982. Editor: Phenolic Compounds and Metabolic Regulation, 1967; contbr. chpts. to books. Nat. Cancer Inst. fellow UCLA, 1947-49; AEC fellow U. Cambridge, Eng., 1949-50; U.S.-Japan Coop. Sci. Found. grantee U. Kyoto, 1966-67; Japan Sci. Promotion grantee U. Hokkaido, 1974. Mem. Am. Soc. Plant Physiologists, Soc. Cryobiology, Internat. Assn. Plant Tissue Culture, Am. Soc. Biol. Chemists, Phytochem. Soc. N.Am. (v.p. 1964-65, pres. 1965-66), Orgn. Profl. Employees Dept. Agr. (chpt. pres. 1968-69, Nat. Honor Award 1970), Nat. Council Gene Resources (mem. adv. bd. 1980—), Internat. Bd. Plant Genetic Resources (mem. working group on tissue culture 1982—). Patentee treatment to prevent browning of plant tissue, 1964; prevention of freeze damage in food, 1973. Current Work: Plant tissue culture and biochemistry; cryobiology; freezing damage and the actions of cryoprotective agents; enzyme technology. Subspecialties: Plant physiology (agriculture); Resource conservation. Home: 21 Kingston Rd Berkeley CA 94707

FINKS, ROBERT MELVIN, paleontology educator; b. Portland, Maine, May 12, 1927; s. Abraham Joseph and Sarah (Bendette) F. B.S. in Biology magna cum laude, Queens Coll., 1947; M.A. in Geology, Columbia U., 1954, Ph.D., 1959. Lectr. geology Blyn. Coll., 1955-58, instr., 1959-61; lectr. geology Queens Coll., Flushing, N.Y., 1961-62, asst. prof., 1962-65, assoc. prof., 1966-70, prof. geology, 1971—, acting chmn. dept. geology and geography, 1963-64; geologist U.S. Geol. Survey, Washington, 1952-54, 63—; research assoc. Smithsonian Inst., Washington, 1968—; doctoral faculty CUNY; research assoc. Am. Mus. Natural History, N.Y.C., 1961-77. Author: Late Paleozoic Sponge Faunas of the Texas Region, 1960; editor: Guidebook to Field Excursions, 1968; contbr. articles to profl. jours. Queens Coll. scholar, 1947. Fellow AAAS, Geol. Soc. Am., Explorers Club; mem. Paleontol. Soc. (chmn. N.E. sect. 1977-78), Internat. Paleontol. Assn., Paleontol. Assn. Great Britain, Planetary Soc., Phi Beta Kappa, Sigma Xi (exec. sec. chpt. 1982-85). Current Work: Fossil sponges, taxonomy and evolution; paleoecology of reefs; life-span and growth studies of fossil populations; natural selection in fossil populations. Subspecialties: Paleobiology; Paleontology, paleoecology. Office: Dept Geology Queens Coll Flushing NY 11367

FINN, JAMES EDWARD, physicist; b. Phila., Dec. 18, 1943; s. John Hugh and Sarah Ann (Cutler) F. B.S., U. Wis.-Milw., 1975; M.S., U. Wis.-Milw., 1977; Ph.D., Purdue U., 1982. Research asst. Purdue U., 1979-82; research assoc. physics, 1984—; cons. Applied Mathematics, Gales Ferry, Conn., 1983-84. Contbr. articles to profl. jours. Recipient George Tautfest award Purdue U., 1982. Mem. Am. Phys. Soc., Sigma Xi. Current work: Critical phenomena and phase transitions in hadronic matter. Subspecialty: Particle physics. Home: 59 Point West West Lafayette IN 47906 Office: Dept Physics Purdue Univ West Lafayette IN 47907

FINN, JAMES WALTER, chemist; b. St. Paul, Oct. 3, 1946; s. Walter J. and Helen A. Finn; m. Elizabeth M. Varriano-Marston, Aug. 16, 1980; children—Julie, Stacey. B.S. in Chemistry, U. Minn., 1970; Ph.D., Kans. State U., 1981. Research profl. Pillsbury Co., Mpls., 1971-76; research chemist ICI Americas, Wilmington, Del., 1981—; lectr. U. Del., Newark, 1983—. Contbr. numerous articles to profl. jours. Mem. Am. Chem. Soc., Chromatography Forum of Del., Sigma Xi, Gamma Sigma Delta, Phi Lambda Upsilon. Current work: Liquid chromatography, super-critical fluid chromatography. Subspecialties: Analytical chemistry; Food science and technology. Home: 2011 Foulk Rd Wilmington DE 19897 Office: ICI Americas Concord Pike and New Murphy Rd Wilmington DE 19897

FINN, PATRICIA ANN, group leader, researcher; b. Oak Park, Ill.; d. LeRoy and Anne (Pavlinic) F. B.S., Mundelein Coll., 1967; Ph.D., U. Calif.-Berkeley, 1971; postdoctoral, Iowa State U., 1972-73, Argonne (Ill.) Nat. Lab., 1973-75. Asst. chemist chem. tech. div. Argonne Nat. Lab., 1975-80, chemist, 1980-82, group leader, 1982—. Contbr. numerous articles to profl. jours. Mem. Am. Ceramics Soc., Am. Chem. Soc., Am. Nuclear Soc., Assn. Women in Sci., Sigma Xi. Current Work: System design (tritium and/or blanket system for fusion). Subspecialties: Fusion; Materials (engineering). Home: 339 S Park Westmont IL 60559 Office: Argonne Nat Lab 9700 S Cass Argonne IL 60439

FINNERTY, WILLIAM ROBERT, microbiologist, educator, cons.; b. Keokuk, Iowa, May 2, 1929; s. William T. and Harriet E. (Vandervort) F.; m. Margaret V. Gallagher, Aug. 14, 1952; children: Deborah, Steven, Carrie, Beth, Todd, Stan. B.S. Gen. Sci. and Math, U. Iowa, 1955, Ph.D. in Organic Chemistry and Microbiology, 1961. Instr. U. Iowa, 1959-60; USPHS postdoctoral fellow Oak Ridge Nat. Lab., 1960-62; asst. prof. microbiology Ind. U. Med. Center, 1962-65, assoc. prof., 1965-68, U. Ga., 1968-75, prof., 1975—, head dept. microbiology, 1977—; cons. to industry; vis. prof. U. Gottingen, W.Ger., 1973. Contbr. numerous articles, chpts., revs. on microbiology or biochemistry to profl. publs. Served to sgt. USAF, 1948-52. AEC grantee, 1963-66; NSF grantee, 1965-74; NIH grantee, 1980-83; Dept. Energy grantee, 1975-83. Mem. Am. Soc. Microbiology (P.R. Edwards award S.E. sect. 1980), Am. Chem. Soc., Am. Soc. Biol. Chemists, AAAS, Sigma Xi. Current Work: Hydrocarbon and petroleum microbiology; microbial physiology, genetics and biochemistry; microbial enhanced oil recovery and production. Subspecialties: Microbiology; Genetics and genetic engineering (biology).

FINNEY, ROY PELHAM, urology surgeon; b. Gaffney, S.C., Dec. 7, 1924; s. Roy P. Finney and Mary Frances (Cannon) Woodard; m. Kay Harkness, Apr. 5, 1962; children: Wright C., James L., Joella R., Gray, Kevin. M.D., Med. Univ. S.C., 1952. Diplomate: Am. Bd. Urology. Resident in urology Johns Hopkins U., Balt., 1952-57, instr. in urology, 1957; prof. surg. urology U. South Fla., Tampa, 1972—, dir. div. urology, 1972-82. Fellow ACS; mem. Am. Urology Assn., Soc., Internationale D'Urologie, Internat. Continence Soc., Urodynamic Soc. Republican. Club: Tampa Yacht. Designer and inventor implantable prostheses, 1973—, penile, incontinence devices, ureteral stents, diving devices; developer new surg. proceedings treatment impotence, 1977. Current Work: Design implantable medical prostheses for impotence, incontinence, of the genito-urinary tract, originate new surgical procedures. Subspecialties: Urology; Biomedical engineering. Home: 4382 Aztec Ct Bayport FL 33526 Office: U South Fla PO Box 16 12901 N 30th St Tampa FL 33612

FIORE, NICHOLAS FRANCIS, chemical and metals company executive, physical metallurgy researcher, consultant; b. Pitts., Sept. 24, 1939; s. William Henry and Margaret Angeline (Scinto) F.; m. Sylvia Marie Chinque, Aug. 13, 1960; children: Maria, Nicholas Francis, Kristin, Anthony. B.S. in Metall. Engring., Carnegie-Mellon U., 1960, M.S. in Metall. Engring., 1963, Ph.D. in Metall. Engring., 1964. Asst. prof. metall. engring. and materials sci. U. Notre Dame, 1966-68, assoc. prof., 1968-70, prof., 1970-81, chmn. dept. metall. engring. and materials sci., 1969-81; v.p., corp. dir. tech. Cabot Corp., Boston, 1982—; vis. scientist Argonne Nat. Labs., 1974-75, cons., 1966-81. Contbr. numerous articles on phys. metallurgy, wear, embrittlement, internal friction to profl. jours. Chmn. bd. dirs. Primary Day Sch., Inc., South Bend, Ind. Served to 1st lt. Signal Corps U.S. Army, 1964-66. Recipient Adams Meml. award Am. Welding Soc., 1972. Fellow Am. Soc. Metals; mem. AIME, AAUP. Roman Catholic. Club: Downtown (Boston). Current Work: Degradation of materials by wear, corrosion, embrittlement; management and long-range planning of technology and research. Subspecialties: Metallurgical engineering; Materials (engineering). Home: 15 Rockport Rd Weston MA 02193 Office: 125 High St Boston MA 02110

FIORI, MARIO GIUSEPPE, clinical research manager, physician, researcher; b. Cantu', Como, Italy, June 29, 1947; came to U.S., 1978; s. Antonio and Anita (Mauri) F.; m. Mirella P. Porro Milanese, June 9, 1973; 1 child, Emiliano Bronislaw. M.D., U. Milan, Italy, 1974; Resident in neurosurgery U. Pavia Sch. Medicine and Surgery, Italy; research asst. Mario Negri Inst. Pharmacol. Research, Milan, 1974-75; research assoc. I.U. Conn., Storrs, 1978-79; postdoctoral fellow Case Western Res. U., Cleve., 1979-81; asst. prof. U. Milan Sch. Medicine, 1975-77, prof., 1981-82; vis. prof. U. Medicine and Dentistry of N.J., Newark, 1982-84; clin. research mgr. Bracco Industria Chimica S.p.A., Milan, 1984—; vis. neuropathologist Lederle Labs., Pearl River, N.Y., 1981. Contbr. chpts. to books and articles to refereed jours. Muscular Dystrophy Assn. fellow, 1980-81. Fellow Royal Micros. Soc., mem. Soc. for Neurosci., Italian Soc. Immunology and Immunopathology, N.Y. Acad. Scis., Paleopathology Assn., Roman Catholic. Current work: Animal model of peripheral neuropathies using toxic chemicals-role of axonally transported cytoskeletal proteins in regeneration of peripheral nerves. Subspecialty: Regeneration. Home: Via Accademia 5 Milano Italy I-20131 Office: Bracco Industria Chimica SpA Via Egidio Folli 50 Milano Italy I-20134

FIRESTONE, DAVID, chemist; b. N.Y.C., Sept. 15, 1923; s. Harry and Anna (Koved) F.; m. Berdie Flegenheimer, May 26, 1946; children—Richard Ira, Michael Paul, Janice Celia. B.S., CCNY, 1948; M.S. Poly. Inst. Bklyn., 1951; Ph.D., George Washington U., 1969. Chemist U.S. FDA, N.Y.C., 1948-54, Washington, 1954-63, supervisory research chemist, 1963-73, sr. research chemist, 1973—. Contbr. articles to profl. jours. Pres. Met. Lodge B'nai B'rith, 1974-75, Nat. Capital Assn. of B'nai B'rith, 1981-82. Served with U.S. Army, 1942-46, PTO. Recipient Commendable Service award FDA, 1978. Fellow Assn. Ofcl. Analytical Chemists (referee oils and fats); mem. Am. Oil Chemists' Soc. (pres. 1978-79), Am. Chem. Soc., AAAS, Internat. Union Pure and Applied Chemistry (div. com. mem. applied chemistry div., chmn. commn. on oils, fats and derivatives 1981-83), Sigma Xi. Jewish. Current work: Composition and analysis of food fats and oils; analysis and toxicology of dioxins and related environmental toxicants. Subspecialty: Analytical chemistry. Home: 906 Playford Ln Silver Spring MD 20901 Office: Div Chem Tech Ctr Food Safety and Applied Nutrition FDA 200 C St SW Washington DC 20204

FIROR, JOHN WILLIAM, physicist, science administrator; b. Athens, Ga., Oct. 18, 1927; s. John William and Mary Valentine (Moss) F.; m. Merle Jenkins, Sept. 17, 1950 (dec. 1979); children—Daniel, Katherine, James, Susan; m. Judith Eva Jacobsen, Oct. 15, 1983. B.S. Physics, Ga. Inst. Tech., 1949; Ph.D. Physics, U. Chgo., 1954. Staff mem. Carnegie Inst. of Washington, 1953-61; dir. High Altitude Obs., Boulder, Colo., 1961-68; dir. Nat. Ctr. for Atmospheric Research, Boulder, 1968-74, exec. dir., 1974-80, dir. advanced studies, 1980—; trustee Environ. Def. Fund., N.Y.C., World Resources Inst., Washington, Internat. Fed. Inst. for Advanced Studies, Stockholm, 1980. Contbr. articles to profl. jours. Pres. Colo. Music Festival, Boulder, 1982-83, Boulder County YMCA, 1972-76; active Govs. Sci. and Tech. Com., Denver, 1980-82. Served in U.S. Army, 1945-46. Barnaby lectr. Nat. Soaring Museum. Fellow Am. Meteorol. Soc., sr. fellow Hubert Humphry Inst. U. Minn., 1981; mem. Am. Astron. Soc. (chmn. solar physics div. 1970-71), Sigma Xi (nat. lectr. 1968). Current work: Climate change, interaction of climate change and society. Subspecialties: Climatology; Cosmic ray high energy astrophysics. Office: Nat Ctr for Atmospheric Research PO Box 3000 Boulder CO 80307

FISCHELL, DAVID ROSS, physicist, electrical engineer; b. Washington, Dec. 4, 1953; s. Robert Elentuch and Marian (Standard) F.; m. Sarah Thole, June 11, 1977. B.S. in Engring. Physics, Cornell U., 1975, M.S. in Applied Physics, 1978, Ph.D. in Applied Physics, 1980. Teaching asst., then research asst. Cornell U., 1975-79; mem. tech. staff Bell Labs., Holmdel, N.J., 1979-82, supr. performance objectives studies, 1982—. Mem. Optical Soc. Am., IEEE. Democrat. Jewish. Current Work: Performance evaluation of AT&T communication's new audiographic teleconferencing service. Subspecialties: Graphics, image processing, and pattern recognition; Acoustical engineering. Home: 62 Stratford Rd Tinton Falls NJ 07724 Office: 3 E 505 Bell Labs Holmdel NJ 07733

FISCHELL, ROBERT ELLENTUCH, university physicist, biomedical engineer; b. N.Y.C., Feb. 10, 1929; s. Philip and Julia (Ellentuch) F.; m. Marian Elaine Standard, Feb. 2, 1951; children—David Ross, Tim Alexander, Scott Jay Standard. B.S. in Mech. Engring., Duke U., 1951; M.S., U. Md., 1953. Physicist, Duke U., Durham, N.C., 1950-51; mech. engr., physicist Naval Ordnance Lab., White Oak, Md., 1951-56; physicist Emerson Research Lab., Silver Spring, Md., 1956-59; asst. dept. head/chief tech. transfer, applied physics lab. Johns Hopkins U., Laurel, Md., 1959—, research assoc. in medicine Sch. Medicine, Balt., 1983—; dir. Pacesetter Systems, Inc., Sylmar, Calif., Patlex Corp., Westfield, N.J.; mem. exec. panel Chief Naval Ops., Arlington, Va., 1984—. Patentee medical apparatus. Recipient Tech. Achievement award ASME, 1962, Exceptional Engring. Achievement medal NASA, Space Act award, 1984; named Inventor of Year award Intellectual Property Owner's Assn., 1983, Disting. Citizen of Yr., U. Md., College Park, 1984. Mem. Am. Heart Assn., Internat. Soc. Artificial Organs, Md. Acad. Scis. Current work: Development of implantable artificial organs; computer operated implantable medical devices. Subspecialty: Biomedical engineering. Office: Applied Physics Lab Johns Hopkins U Johns Hopkins Rd Laurel MD 20707

FISCHER, ALBERT KARL, chemist, researcher; b. Newark, N.J., Oct. 15, 1931; s. Albert Rudolf and Vilma (Czink) F.; m. Mary Elizabeth Deiwert, May 24, 1959; children—George, Charles, Steven. B.A., NYU, 1953; M.A., Harvard U., 1955, Ph.D., 1958. Research chemist, Union Carbide Metals Co., Niagara Falls, N.Y., 1957-60; research chemist Union Carbide Chem. Co., South Charleston, W.Va., 1959-62; chemist Argonne Nat. Lab., 1962—. Contbr. articles to profl. jours. Patentee in field. Mem. Am. Chem. Soc., Sigma Xi. Unitarian-Universalist. Current work: Research on the high temperature thermodynamic properties of ceramic surfaces for fusion reactor development. Subspecialties: Inorganic chemistry; Physical chemistry. Office: Argonne Nat Lab 9700 S Cass Ave Argonne IL 60439

FISCHER, HANS-PETER, chemist, researcher; b. Basle, Switzerland, Dec. 12, 1934; came to U.S., 1962-64, 84; s. Arnold and Gertrud (Baertschi) F.; m. Charlotte Margareth Belle', July 21, 1961. Ph.D., U. Basle, 1961. Research asst. U. Basle, 1961-62; postdoctoral fellow UCLA, 1962-64; lectr. Swiss Fed. Inst. Tech., Zurich, 1964-68; mgr. herbicide research J.R. Geigy A.G., Basle, 1968-74, sr. scientist Ciba-Geigy Lim., Basle, 1974-83, sr. scientist advanced techs. Ciba-Geigy Corp., Greensboro, N.C., 1984—; advisor Swiss Sci. Council, Bern, 1970-73. Author: Free Radicals, 1965. Contbr. articles to sci. jours. Patentee in field. Served with Swiss Army. Mem. Swiss Chem. Soc., Ger. Chem. Soc., Am. Chem. Soc. Current work: Biorational and computer assisted design of agrochemicals; new agro chemical technologies, chemical process development. Subspecialties: Organic chemistry; Horticultural technology assessment. Home: Burggartenstrasse 14 4103 Bottmingen Switzerland Office: Ciba-Geigy Corp Ltd CH-4002 Basel Switzerland

FISCHER, HARRY W., radiologist, educator; b. St. Louis, 1921; s. Harry William and Amy Babette (Gieselman) F.; m. Kay Fischer, 1943; 5 children. B.S., U. Chgo., 1943, M.D., 1945. Diplomate: Am. Bd. Radiology. Asst. prof., then asso. prof. radiology U. Ia. Med. Sch., 1956-63, prof., head sect. diagnostic radiology, 1963-66; prof. radiology U. Mich. Med. Sch., 1966-71; dir. dept. radiology Wayne County Gen. Hosp., 1966-71; prof. radiology, chmn. dept. U. Rochester (N.Y.) Sch. Medicine and Dentistry, 1971-85. Editorial bd.: Investigative Radiology, 1966—, Radiology, 1971—. Served to lt. (j.g.) M.C. USNR, 1946-48. Fellow Am. Coll. Radiology; mem. Radiol. Soc. N.Am., Assn. Univ. Radiologists (Gold medal), Am. Roetgen Ray Soc., Uroradiology Soc., U. Chgo. Med. Sch. Alumni Assn., Sigma Xi. Current Work: Contrast media, development and toxicity; radiology department planning and administration. Subspecialty: Diagnostic radiology. Home: 3565 Elmwood Ave Rochester NY 14610 Office: 601 Elmwood Ave Rochester NY 14642

FISCHER, TRAUGOTT ERWIN, physicist; b. Aarau, Switzerland, Jan. 21, 1932; came to U.S., 1963; s. Traugott J. and Josephine A. (Kuhn) F.; m. Marie-Claude Blanc, Sept. 7, 1958; children: Pierre F., Jacques F., Anne C. B.A., St. Michel Coll., Fribourg, Switzerland, 1952; diploma in physics, Fed. Inst. Tech., Zurich, 1956, Dr. Sc. Nat., 1963. Mem. tech. staff Bell Telephone

Labs., Murray Hill, N.J., 1963-66; assoc. prof. Yale U., New Haven, 1966-72; with Exxon Corp. Research Labs., Clinton, N.J., 1972—, sr. research assoc., 1977—; cons. CBS Labs., 1968-72. Contbr. articles to profl. jours. Served with Swiss Air Force. Recipient Kern prize Swiss Phys. Soc., 1962. Fellow Am. Phys. Soc.; mem. Am. Vacuum Soc., AIME, Am. Soc. Lubrication Engrs. Roman Catholic. Club: Metals Sci. of N.Y. Current Work: Catalysis from viewpoint of electronic structure. Surface chemistry aspects of metallurgy. Interdisciplinary approach to friction, lubrication and wear. Subspecialties: Condensed matter physics; Mechanical engineering. Home: 107 Passaic Ave Summit NJ 07901 Office: Exxon Research & Engring Co Clinton Twp Annandale NJ 08801

FISCHETTI, THOMAS LOUIS, technology consultant; aeronautical engineer; b. N.Y.C., May 30, 1930; s. Rocco and Emanuela (Greco) F.; m. Thomas M., Lawrence R., Robert F., Lisa M. B.S. in Aero. Engring., NYU, 1952. Program mgr. NASA, Washington, 1968-70, experiment mgr. Skylab, 1970-75, dep. dir. spl. projects, 1975-79, chief geodynamics div., 1979-85; pres. Tech. Mgmt. Cons., Inc., 1985—. Contbr. articles to profl. jours. Recipient NASA Exceptional Service award, 1974. Mem. Am. Geophys. Union, AIAA. Current work: Studies of the movement and deformation of the solid earth and its internal structure. Subspecialty: Geophysics.

FISH, ANDREW JOSEPH, JR., electrical engineering educator, researcher; b. New Haven, Aug. 15, 1944; s. Andrew Joseph and Katherine Pauline (Frey) F. B.S.E.E., Worcester Poly. Inst., 1966; M.S.E.E., U. Iowa, 1973; M.S. in Math, St. Mary U., San Antonio, 1974; Ph.D., U. Conn.-Storrs. Asst. prof. elec. engring. U. Hartford, West Hartford, Conn., 1979-83; asst. prof. elec. engring. Western New Eng. Coll., Springfield, Mass., 1984-85, assoc. prof., 1985—; co-chmn. nonlinear systems group Am. Control Conf., 1980. Contbr. articles to profl. publs. Gate keeper West Suffield Grange, 1982. Yale U. fellow, 1972-73. Mem. IEEE, ASME. Current Work: Modeling, analysis, control of nonlinear systems, particularly Hybrid Analog-Digital Systems. Subspecialties: Systems engineering; Applied mathematics.

FISH, FEROL FREDRIC, geophysicist, research manager; b. East Chicago, Ind., Jan. 15, 1930; s. Ferol Fredric and Edna Mae (Arms) F.; m. Joline McVicker, June 6, 1956 (div. Mar. 1983); children—Ferol, Molly, Ruth, Hannah, Matthew.; m. Lois Ann Stewart, May 21, 1983. B.S., Ind. U., 1955, A.M., 1956; Ph.D., Pa. State U., 1961. Geophys. investigator N.J. Zinc Co., Palmerton, Pa., 1960-63; staff scientist Gen. Dynamics Co., Fort Worth, 1963-64, McDonnell Douglas Co., Santa Monica, Calif., 1964-68; mgr. applied physics Borg-Warner Research Ctr., Des Plaines, Ill., 1968-79; mgr. phys. scis. Gas Research Inst., Chgo., 1979—. Contbr. articles to profl. jours. Treas. Parents Tchrs. Club, Arlington Heights, Ill., 1971-72. Served with U.S. Army, 1948-51, Korea. NSF fellow, 1958-60. Mem. Am. Geophys. Union, Soc. Petroleum Engrs., Sigma Xi. Methodist. Subspecialties: Geophysics; Geochemistry. Home: 804 N Kaspar St Arlington Heights IL 60004 Office: Gas Research Inst 8600 W Bryn Mawr Chicago IL 60631

FISHER, ANNA, physician, astronaut. Astronaut NASA Johnson Space Ctr., Houston. Subspecialty: Astronautics. Office: NASA Johnson Space Ctr Astronaut Office Houston TX 77058*

FISHER, CHARLES HAROLD, research administrator; b. Hiawatha, W.Va., Nov. 20, 1906; s. Lawrence D. and Mary (Akers) F.; m. Elizabeth Dye, Nov. 4, 1933 (dec. 1967); m. Lois Carlin, July 1968. B.S., Roanoke Coll., 1928, Sc.D.; M.S., U. Ill., 1929, Ph.D., 1932; D.Sc. (hon.), Tulane U., 1953; Sc.D. (hon.), Roanoke Coll., 1963. Teaching asst. chemistry U. Ill., 1928-32; instr. Harvard, 1932-35; asso. organic chemist U.S. Bur. Mines, Pitts., 1935-40; head carbohydrate div. E. Regional Research Lab., U.S. Dept. Agr., 1946-50; dir. So. Regional Research Lab., U.S. Dept. Agr. (So. Marketing and Nutrition Research div.), New Orleans, 1950-72; adj. research prof. Roanoke Coll., 1972—. Pres. New Orleans Sci. Fair, 1967-69. Recipient So. Chemists award, 1956, Herty medal, 1959; Chem. Pioneer award Am. Inst. Chemists, 1966. Mem. Am. Inst. Chemists (hon., pres. 1962-63, chmn. bd. dirs.), Sci. Research Soc. Am., Oil Chem. Soc., Am. Chem. Soc. (dir. region IV), Chemurgic Council (dir.), Am. Assn. Textile Chemists and Colorists, Sigma Xi, Alpha Chi Sigma, Gamma Alpha, Phi Lambda Upsilon. Club: Cosmos (Washington). Current Work: Polymer additives; relations between physical and thermodynamic properties and molecular structure. Subspecialties: Organic chemistry; Polymer chemistry. Office: Chemistry Dept Roanoke College Salem VA 24153

FISHER, DAVID GEORGE, physics educator, researcher; b. Pottsville, Pa., Aug. 1, 1955; s. Harvey Kermit and Joan Leah F. B.S. in Physics, Pa. State U., 1977; M.S. in Physics, U. Del., 1980, Ph.D. in Physics, 1983. Postgrad. fellow Bartol Research Found. of Franklin Inst., Newark, 1983-84; asst. prof. physics Lycoming Coll., Williamsport, Pa., 1984—. Mem. Am. Phys. Soc., Phi Beta Kappa, Phi Kappa Phi. Lutheran. Current work: Radiation damage effects in amorphous magnetic alloys, particularly changes in magnetic and electrical properties. Subspecialty: Condensed matter physics. Office: Dept Astronomy and Physics Lycoming Coll Williamsport PA 17701

FISHER, GENE JORDAN, chemical company executive; b. Quitman, Mass., Mar. 26, 1931; s. Ira R. and Gertrude (Jordan) F.; m. Christine Ann Hodges, May 28, 1954; children—Denise, Darrell. B.S., U. Tex., 1952. Research chemist to sr. research chemist Celanese Chem. Co., Corpus Christi, Tex., 1952-59, group leader, 1959-67, research mgr., 1967-77, dir. research, 1977-83, tech. dir., 1983—. Contbr. articles to profl. jours. Fellow Am. Inst. Chemists; mem. Am. Chem. Soc., Corpus Christi C. of C. Baptist. Club: Rotary. Patentee in Field. Office: PO Box 9077 Corpus Christi TX 78469

FISHER, GEORGE WESCOTT, university dean, geology educator; b. New Haven, May 16, 1937; s. Irving Norton and Virginia (Hays) F.; m. Frances Louisa Gilbert, Dec. 26, 1959; children: Catherine Anne, Lynn Ellen, Cynthia Lee. A.B., Dartmouth Coll., 1959; Ph.D. (Woodrow Wilson fellow, NSF fellow), Johns Hopkins U., 1963. Postdoctoral fellow Geophys. Lab., Carnegie Instn., Washington, 1964-66; asst. prof. geology Johns Hopkins U., Balt., 1966-71, asso. prof., 1971-74, prof., 1974—, chmn. dept. earth and planetary scis., 1978-83, dean Div. Arts and Scis., 1983—; geologist U.S. Geol. Survey, Beltsville, Md., 1967-72. Editor: Studies in Appalachian Geology: Central and Southern, 1970. Served with Signal Corps U.S. Army, 1962-64. NSF grantee, 1971—. Mem. Geol. Soc. Am., Mineral. Soc. Am. (treas. 1974-76), Geol. Soc. Washington, Geochem. Soc., AAAS, Phi Beta Kappa, Sigma Xi. Research in Appalachian geology and metamorphic petrology. Current Work: The dynamics of metamorphic processes; relation between metamorphism and rock deformation. Subspecialties: Petrology; Tectonics. Home: 936 Cromwell Bridge Rd Towson MD 21204 Office: Div Arts and Sciences Johns Hopkins U Baltimore MD 21218

FISHER, H. LEONARD, information scientist; b. Bronx, N.Y., Nov. 7, 1936; s. Harold Leonard and Betty (Kahn) F.; m. Yvonne Derrick, Aug. 2, 1968. B.S. in Physics, St. John's U., 1957, M.S. in Physics, 1961. Research physicist United Aircraft Research Labs., East Hartford, Conn., 1960-63; physicist Lawrence Livermore (Calif.) Nat. Lab., 1963-69, tech. info. specialist, 1969-79, head research info. group, 1981—; mem. faculty Golden Gate U., San Francisco, 1980—. Mem. Am. Soc. Info. Sci., Am. Phys. Soc., Sigma Xi, Sigma Pi Sigma. Current Work: Online retrieval, literature searching, videotex, societal effects of information technology. Subspecialties: Information systems, storage, and retrieval (computer science); Societal effects of information technology.

FISHER, HAROLD WALLACE, chemical engineer; b. Rutland, Vt., Oct. 27, 1904; s. Dean Wallace and Grace Minot (Cheney) F.; m. Hope Elisabeth Case, Sept. 29, 1930; 1 son, Dean Wallace. S.B. in Chem. Engring, Mass. Inst. Tech., 1927; D.Sc., Clarkson Coll. Tech., Potsdam, N.Y., 1960. With Exxon Corp. (and affiliates), 1927-69; joint mng. dir. Iraq Petroleum Co., 1957-59; dir. Exxon Corp., 1959-69, v.p., 1962-69; mem. adv. bd. energy lab. Mass. Inst. Tech., 1974-80, mem. corp. devel. commn., 1975—; mem. marine bd. Nat. Acad. Engring., 1969-74. Co-author: The Process of Technological Innovation, 1969; also articles. Chmn. exec. com. Community Blood Council Greater N.Y., 1969-71; trustee Sloan-Kettering Inst. Cancer Research, N.Y.C., 1964—, chmn., 1970-74. Recipient Chem. Industry medal Am. sect. Soc. Chem. Industry, 1968; Bronze Beaver award Mass. Inst. Tech. Alumni Assn., 1970. Fellow AAAS; mem. Nat. Acad. Engring., Am. Chem. Soc., Am. Inst. Chem. Engrs., Pilgrims of U.S., Kappa Sigma, Alpha Chi Sigma, Tau Beta Pi. Republican. Clubs: University (N.Y.C.); Duxbury Yacht (Mass.); Community Men's; American (London). Patentee petroleum processing, petrochem. mfr. Subspecialty: Chemical engineering. Home: 68 Goose Point Ln PO Box 1792 Duxbury MA 02331

FISHER, JAMES HAROLD, geology educator, petroleum cons.; b. Mayfield, Ky., Nov. 8, 1919; s. Clyde and Lillian (Smithson) F.; m. Anne Brown, June 6, 1943 (div.); children: James Michael, John Allan, Jeanne Ann; m. Normalee Stapler, June 12, 1982. A.B., U. Ill.-Urbana, 1943, B.S., 1947, M.S., 1949, Ph.D., 1953. Geologist McCurtain Limestone Co., Idabel, Okla., 1948-49, Pure Oil Co., Casper, Wyo., 1949-51; asst. prof. U. Ill.-Urbana, 1952-55, U. Nebr.-Lincoln, 1955-57; prof. geology Mich. State U., East Lansing, 1957-84, prof. emeritus, 1984—; cons. Tenneco Oil Co., Houston, 1960-67; exploration mgr. McClure Oil Co., Alma, Mich., 1968-69. Served to capt. U.S. Army, 1943-46, ETO. Shell Oil Co. fellow, 1951. Fellow Geol. Soc. Am.; mem. Am. Assn. Petroleum Geologists (pres. ea. sect. 1974-75), Am. Inst. Profl. Geologists, Mich. Basin Geol. Soc. (pres. 1961-62). Republican. Unitarian. Current Work: Petroleum occurrences in the Michigan basin, tectonic analysis of intercratonic basins. Subspecialties: Petroleum engineering; Sedimentology. Home: 1175-F Arbor Dr East Lansing MI 48823 Office: Dept Geology Mich State East Lansing MI 48824

FISHER, JAMES W., pharmacologist, educator; b. Startex, S.C., May 22, 1925; s. Earnest Amaziah and Mamie Viola (Turner) F.; m. Carol Brodarick, June 5, 1947; children: Candis, Patricia, Richard, William, John, Elaine. B.S., U. S.C., 1947; Ph.D. in Pharmacology, U. Louisville Med. Sch., 1958. Pharmacologist, Armour Pharm. Research Labs., Chgo., 1950-53; Pharmacologist, Lloyd Bros., Inc. Pharm. Research Labs., Cin., 1954-56; instr. dept. pharmacology U. Tenn. Med. Units, Memphis, 1958-60, asst. prof., 1960-62, assoc. prof., 1962-66, prof., 1966-68; prof., chmn. dept. pharmacology Tulane U. Sch. Medicine, New Orleans, 1968—; cons. Pharmacia Labs., Piscataway, N.J., 1973-75, Schering Corp., Bloomfield, N.J., 1976—, Upjohn Co., Kalamazoo, 1977—, Biogen, Inc., Cambridge, Mass., 1983—. Editorial bd.: Proc. Soc. Exptl. Biology and Medicine, 1971-74, 74-77; editor: Kidney Hormones, vols. I and II, 1977; mem. various editorial rev. bds.; contbr. articles to profl. jours. Served to lt. (j.g.) USNR, 1943-46, PTO. USPHS fellow, 1956-58. Mem. Am. Soc. Pharmacology and Exptl. Therapeutics, Soc. Exptl. Biology and Medicine, Am. Soc. Nephrology, Am. Soc. Hematology, Assn. Med. Sch. Pharmacology, AAAS, Internat. Soc. Nephrology, AAUP, N.Y. Acad. Scis., Am. Fedn. Clin. Research, Sigma Xi. Current Work: Hematopharmacology; endocrine pharmacology; renal pharmacology; drug effects on renal blood flow and erythropoietin; hormones and erythropoietin; anemia of chronic renal failure; prostaglandins and erythropoiesis. Subspecialties: Cellular pharmacology; Hematology. Home: 4025 Pin Oak Ave New Orleans LA 70114 Office: 1430 Tulane Ave New Orleans LA 70112

FISHER, JERID MARTIN, clinical neuropsychologist, health promotion consultant; b. Houston, July 12, 1953; s. Seymour and Rhoda (Lee) F. B.S. in Psychology, Duke U., 1975; Ph.D. in Clin. Psychology, U. Rochester, 1981. Lic. psychologist, Calif., N.Y. Dir neuropsychology service U. Rochester Med. Ctr., 1981—; ptnr. Am. Data Systems, Rochester, 1982—, pub. speaker health promotion, 1980—. Author pamphlet: Stress-Don't let it distress you, 1982. Mem. Am. Psychol. Assn., Internat. Neuropsychol. Soc., N.Y. Neuropsychol. Group, Phi Beta Kappa. Current Work: Differential diagnosis of dementing disorders; treatment and rehabilitation of the brain injured; life extension; health promotion and modification of the American lifestyle. Subspecialties: Neuropsychology; Clinical psychology. Home: 248 Crittenden Way Apt 5 Rochester NY 14623 Office: U Rochester Med Center 300 Crittenden Blvd Rochester NY 14642

FISHER, JOHN COURTNEY, surgical physicist, consultant; b. Wilkinsburg, Pa., Apr. 19, 1922; s. Edwin Henry and Elizabeth (Walden) F.; m. Patricia Kingsbury, Nov. 26, 1942; children: Carolyn Fisher Ellis, John Courtney, Stephen Kingsbury; m. Jane Clauss, July 7, 1976. B.S., Harvard U., 1942, M.S., 1947, Sc.D., 1952. Teaching fellow Harvard U., 1942-52; sonar engr. Submarine Signal Co., Boston, 1945-46; dir. electromech. engring. Calidyne Co., Winchester, Mass., 1952-55; dir. devel. privately funded research project, Maynard, Mass., 1955-60; chmn., treas. Am. Dynamics Corp., Cambridge, Mass., 1960-68; northeastern regional sales mgr. Princeton Applied Research Corp., N.J., 1968-72, cons. in sci. instrumentation, Weston, Mass., 1972—; dir. med. devel. Cavitron Lasersonics div., Stamford, Conn., 1976-81; mem. surg. staff St. Barnabas Med. Center, Livingston, N.J., 1980—. Contbr. articles to profl. jours. Mem. Weston Planning Bd., 1974-80. Fellow Am. Soc. Laser Medicine and Surgery; mem. Internat. Soc. Laser Surgery, ASME, IEEE, AAAS, Gynecologic Laser Soc., Midwest Biolaser Inst., N.Y. Acad. Scis. Patentee in field. Current Work: Applications of lasers and other light sources to medicine, biology, surgery, and therapy, development of sophisticated instrumentation for diagnosis, therapy, and surgery. Subspecialties: Laser medicine; Surgery. Home: 417 Palmtree Dr Wildewood Springs Bradenton FL 33507

FISHER, PAUL B., cell biologist, virologist, oncologist; b. Bklyn., July 5, 1945; s. George and Ray M. (Fisher) Cherkis; m. Marlene J. Weintraub, May 16, 1976; children—Danielle Leah, Damien Marc. B.A., Hunter Coll., 1968; M.A., H. Lehman Coll., CUNY, 1971; M.Phil., Rutgers U., 1973, Ph.D., 1974. Busch postdoctoral fellow Waksman Inst. Microbiology Rutgers U., 1974-75; research assoc. dept. microbiology and immunology Albert Einstein Coll. Medicine, N.Y.C., 1975-76; staff assoc. Cancer Center-Inst. Cancer Research Coll. Physicians and Surgeons, Columbia U., N.Y.C., 1976-80, research scientist prof. dept. microbiology, 1980—; assoc. prof. Bronx Community Coll. of CUNY, 1979-83, prof., 1983—; cons. EPA, Nat. Cancer Inst., NSF. Contbr. abstracts and articles to profl. jours. Mem. Am. Assn. Cancer Research, AAAS, Am. Soc. Microbiology, N.Y. Acad. Scis., Harvey Soc., Internat. Pigment Cell Soc., Tissue Culture Assn., Nat. Found. Infectious Diseases, Am. Soc. Cell Biology, Am. Inst. Biol. Sci. Current Work: Molecular basis of chemical and viral carcinogenesis; gene structure and function; mechanisms of tumor promotion and progression; cancer chemotherapy; chemical and viral transformation; membrane structure and function; cellular differentiation. Subspecialties: Cell study oncology; Virology (medicine). Home: 15 Gordon Pl Scarsdale NY 10583 Office: Dept Microbiology Cancer Ctr Inst Cancer Research Columbia U Coll Physicians and Surgeons New York NY 10032

FISHER, RICHARD KEITH, research veterinarian; b. Gallipolis, Ohio, Sept. 5, 1951; s. Richard Arlen and Doris Roberta (Fellure) F.; m. Helen Anita Walker, Aug. 4, 1974; children—Kelly Suzanne, Keith Ashley. D.V.M., Ohio State U., 1976. Gen. practitioner Athens Vet. Hosp., Ohio, 1976-78; owner Rio Grande Vet. Clinic, Ohio, 1978-83; clin. veterinarian Philips Roxane Inc., St. Joseph, Mo., 1983-84; sr. program coordinator Am. Cyanamid Co., Princeton, N.J., 1984—. Veterinarian Gallia County Jr. Fair, Gallipolis, 1980, 83. Recipient Acad. scholarship Ohio State U., 1971. Mem. AVMA, Ohio Vet. Med. Assn., Am. Assn. Indsl. Veterinarians. Republican. Baptist. Current work: Conduct clinical and non-clinical animal trials of veterinary pharmaceuticals to assure their safety and efficacy. Subspecialties: Drug delivery systems; Preventive medicine (veterinary medicine). Home: 810 Dunbury Rd Fairless Hills PA 19030Office: Am Cyanamid Co Princeton NJ 08540

FISHER, ROBERT ALAN, physicist; b. Berkeley, Calif., Apr. 19, 1943; s. Leon Harold and Phyllis (Kahn) F.; m. Andrea, Mar. 18, 1967; children: Andrew, Derek. A.B. with honors, U. Calif.-Berkeley, 1965, M.A., 1967, Ph.D., 1971. Lab. asst., programmer Lockheed Missiles & Space Co., Palo Alto, Calif., summers, 1962, 63; NSF grantee Stanford (Calif.) U. Genetics Dept., summer, 1964; programmer Stanford Linear Accelerator Center, summer 1965; with Granger Assoc., Palo Alto, 1966 (summer); teaching asst., research asst., reader U. Calif.-Berkeley, 1965-71; instr. Dept. Applied Sci., U. Calif.-Davis, 1972-74; physicist Lawrence Livermore Lab., 1971-74, Los Alamos (N.Mex.) Nat. Lab., 1974—; presider OSA Symposium on Optical Phase Conjugation, 1981; program com. Gordon Conf. on Nonlinear Optics, 1981, Internat. Quantum Electronics Conf., 1982, ann. meeting Optical Soc. Am., 1981. Editor: Optical Phase Conjugation, 1983; assoc. editor Optics Letters, Applied Optics. Contbr. articles to profl. jours.; editor spl. issue on optical phase conjugation Jour. Optical Soc. Am., 1983. Vol., cons. N.Mex. No. Schs. Chess League, 1980-82; coach N.Mex. elem. state champion chess team, 1982, 83, U.S. elem. champion chess team, 1984; mem. adv. com. to provost U. N.Mex., 1983—; mem. Air Force Red Team Study Panel, 1983—. Fellow Optical Soc. Am.; mem. Am. Phys. Soc., IEEE (sr.), Soc. Photo-Optical Instrumentation Engrs. Patentee in field. Current Work: Research in new lasers, optical phase conjugation and wavefront reversal, nonlinear laser optics, high energy lasers, molecular spectroscopy, ultraviolet laser tech. Subspecialty: Nonlinear laser optics; Optical phase conjugation. Home: Jacona Plaza Route 5 Box 23 Santa Fe NM 8750 Office: Los Alamos Nat Lab Mail Stop E535 Los Alamos NM 87545

FISHMAN, ALFRED PAUL, physician; b. N.Y.C., Sept. 24, 1918; s. Isaac and Anne (Tinter) F.; m. Florence Howitz, Aug. 23, 1948 (dec.); children: Mark, Jay; m. Linda Miltman, Oct. 7, 1984. A.B., U. Mich., 1938, M.S., 1939; M.D., U. Louisville, 1943; M.A. (hon.), U. Pa., 1971. Diplomate: Nat. Bd. Examiners, Am. Bd. Internal Medicine. Intern Jewish Hosp., Bklyn., 1943-44; Dazian Found. fellow pathology Mount Sinai Hosp., N.Y.C., 1946-47, asst. resident, resident medicine, 1947-48; Dazian Found. fellow cardiovascular physiology Michael Reese Hosp., Chgo., 1948-49; Am. Heart Assn. research fellow Bellevue Hosp., N.Y.C., 1949-50, established investigator cardiopulmonary lab., 1951-55; Am. Heart Assn. research fellow physiology Harvard U., Boston, 1950-51; instr. physiology N.Y. U., 1951-53; assoc. in medicine Columbia Coll. Physicians and Surgeons, N.Y.C., 1953-55, asst. prof., 1955-58, assoc. prof., 1958-66; prof. medicine U. Chgo., 1966-69; dir. Cardiovascular Inst., Chgo., 1966-69; dir. div. cardiovascular disease Michael Reese Hosp., Chgo., 1966-69; prof. medicine U. Pa., 1969—, William Maul Measey prof., 1972—; asso. dean U. Pa. (Sch. Medicine), 1969-75; dir. cardiovascular-pulmonary div., dir. Robinette Found., Clin. Cardiovascular Research Center, U. Pa. Med. Center, 1969-75; dir. Specialized Center of Research (Lung), 1973-81; attending physician Hosp. U. Pa., 1969—; sr. attending physician Phila. Gen. Hosp., 1970-78; physician Mass. Gen. Hosp., 1979; cons. to chancellor U. Mo., Kansas City, 1973-78; vis. prof. Harvard U., 1970, Oxford (Eng.) U., 1972, Washington U., St. Louis, 1973, Johns Hopkins U., 1974, Ben Gurion U., 1975, Emory U., Atlanta, 1976, U. Porto Alegra, Brazilia, Brazil, 1976, U. Zurich, Switzerland, 1978, Fu Wai Hosp., Peking, China, 1980; cons. Exec. Office Pres., 1961-69, U. Athens, Greece, 1980; mem. WHO Expert Panel, Geneva, 1973—; adv. council Nat. Lung Div., 1976-80, cons. to dir., 1983—; Nat. Adv. Heart and Lung chmn. Gov.'s Com. for Research on Respiratory Diseases in Coal Miners, 1974-79, Internat. Conf. on Lung, Titisee, Germany, Florence, Italy, 1976; mem. Inst. of Medicine, Nat. Acad. Sci., 1980—. Editor: (with D.W. Richards) Circulation of The Blood-Men and Ideas, 1964, 2d edit., 1984; (with H.H. Hecht) The Pulmonary Circulation and Interstitial Space, 1969; editorial bd. Handbooks of Respiratory Physiology, Am. Physiol. Soc., 1969-72; editor Physiology in Medicine, New Eng. Jour. Medicine, 1969-79, Jour. Applied Physiology, 1981—; editorial bd.: Merck Manual, 1972-82, Ann. Rev. Physiology, 1977-81, Heart Failure, 1979, (with E. M. Renkin) Pulmonary Edema, 1979, Pulmonary Diseases and Disorders, 1979; sect. editor Ency. Brit., 1984— contbr. articles to profl. jours. Bd. dirs. Polachek Found., Phila. Zool. Soc. Served to capt. M.C. U.S. Army, 1944-46. Recipient Disting. Alumni award U. Louisville, 1984. Fellow Am. Coll. Chest Physicians (hon.), Royal Coll. Physicians, A.C.P.; mem. Am. Physiol. Soc. (chmn. publs. bd. 1974-81, pres. 1983-84), Am. Soc. Clin. Investigation, AAAS, Royal Soc. Medicine (London), Assn. Am. Physicians, Am. Heart Assn. (dir. 1973-77, chmn. council on cardiopulmonary disease 1972-74, research council 1974-78, Disting. Achievement award 1980), N.Y. Heart Assn. (pres. 1965-67), Internat Union Physiol. Scis. (U.S. nat. com. 1982—), Internat. Union Physiol. Scis. (adv. com. div. health sci. policy 1982—), Am. Coll. Cardiology (hon.), Interurban Clin. Club, N.Y. County Med. Soc., Phila. Coll. Physicians, Heart Assn. Southeastern Pa. (bd. dirs.), Alpha Omega Alpha. Current Work: Cardiopulmonary physiology; integrative physiology; comparative physiology. Subspecialties: Animal physiology; Pulmonary medicine. Home: 2401 Pennsylvania Ave Apt 20-A7 Philadelphia PA 19130 Office: Hospital U Pennsylvania 3400 Spruce St Philadelphia PA 19104

FISHMAN, GERALD JAY, astrophysicist; b. St. Louis, Feb. 10, 1943; s. Irwin M. and Minnie (Kalish) F.; m. Nancy Dale Neyman, June 18, 1967; children: Lisa R., Jodi L. B.S. with honors in Physics, U. Mo., Columbia, 1965; M.S., Rice U., Houston, 1968, Ph.D., 1969. Research asst. Rice U., 1965-69, research assoc., 1969; sr. research physicist Teledyne Brown Engring. Co., Huntsville, Ala., 1969-74; part-time instr. U. Ala., Huntsville, 1972-74; with NASA (George C. Marshall Space Flight Center), Ala., 1974—; on detail NASA (Astrophysics Program Office), Washington, 1977-78; prin. investigator NASA (Gamma-Ray Obs.), 1978—, astrophysicist, 1974—. Contbr. numerous articles to sci. jours. Recipient NASA medal for exceptional sci. achievement, 1983. Mem. Am. Astron. Soc., Am. Phys. Soc., AAAS, Internat. Astron. Union. Patentee radiation detectors using multiple scintillation crystal pieces. Current Work: Gamma-ray astronomy (balloon-borne and satellites), gamma ray astrophysics, nuclear astrophysics, nuclear radiation monitors and detectors. Subspecialty: Gamma ray high energy astrophysics. Office: ES62 George C Marshall Space Flight Center NASA Space Flight Center Huntsville AL 35812

FISHMAN, ROBERT SUMNER, mathematician, systems analyst; b. Boston, May 17, 1931; s. Henry and Esther (Libman) F.; m. Judith Sheila Landau, Dec. 10, 1957; children—Joan-Ellen, Allison, Barbara, Steven. B.S., Northeastern U., 1954; M.A., U. Vermont, 1956; Ph.D., Boston U., 1961. Prof. math. Emmanuel Coll., Mass. Coll. Pharmacy, Boston, 1961-65, Salem State Coll., Mass., 1965-68; sr. sci. Raytheon, Bedford, Mass., 1968-74, RCA, Burlington, Mass., 1978-83; cons. QEI Bedford, 1975-78; systems analyst TRW, Wayland, Mass., 1983—. Fellow, scholar U. Vermont, 1954-56, Boston U., 1956-61. Mem. Soc. Indsl. and Applied Math. Jewish. Lodge: Masons. Subspecialties: Algorithms; Systems engineering. Home: 20 Ruby Ave Marblehead MA 01945

FISKE, RICHARD S., See *Who's Who in America,* 43rd edition.

FISTEDIS, STANLEY H., nuclear and mechanical engineer; married, 1953; 2 children. B.S., Robert Coll., 1947; M.S., Mont. State U., 1949; Ph.D. in Engring, Mechanics, U. Mo., 1953; M.B.A., U. Chgo., 1965. Designer Babcock & Wilcox Co., 1948-49; instr. in engring. mechanics U. Mo., 1949-52; structural engr. Western Knapp Engring. Co., 1952-53, Johnson & Johnson Co., 1953, Allen & Garcia Co., 1953-54; spl. assignments engr. Girdler Co., 1954-57; assoc. engr. Argonne Nat. Lab., 1957-63, group head engring. mechanics, 1963-66, mgr., 1966-71, program mgr., 1971—; sci. and gen. chmn. 7th Internat. Conf. Structural Mech. Reactor Tech., Chgo., 1983; chmn. Internat. Seminars Containment Nuclear Reactors, San Francisco, 1977, Berlin, 1979, Ispra, Italy, 1981, Chgo., 1983. Prin. editor: Internat. Jour. Nuclear Engring. and Design, 1980—. Fellow ASCE, ASME, Am. Nuclear Soc.; mem. Nat. Soc. Profl. Engrs., Internat. Assn. Structural Mechanics in Reactor Tech. (pres. 1981-83). Subspecialties: Nuclear engineering; Theoretical and applied mechanics. Address: 500 N Parkwood Park Ridge IL 60068

FITCH, FRANK WESLEY, pathologist, educator; b. Bushnell, Ill., May 30, 1929; s. Harold Wayne and Mary Gladys (Frank) F.; m. Shirley Dobbins, Dec. 23, 1951; children—Mary Margaret, Mark Howard. M.D., U. Chgo., 1953, S.M., 1957, Ph.D., 1960. USPHS postdoctoral research fellow, 1954-55, 57-58; faculty U. Chgo., 1957—, prof. pathology, 1967—, Albert D. Lasker prof. med. sci., 1976—; asso. dean med. and grad. edn. U. Chgo. (Div. Biol. Scis.), 1976—; vis. prof. Swiss Inst. Exptl. Cancer Research, Lausanne, Switzerland, 1974-75. Contbr. chpts. to books, articles profl. jours. Recipient Borden Undergrad. Research award, 1953, Lederle Med. Faculty award, 1958-61; Markle Found. scholar, 1961-66; Commonwealth Fund fellow U. Lausanne (Switzerland) Institut de Biochimie, 1965-66; Guggenheim fellow, 1974-75. Mem. Am. Assn. Immunologists, Am. Assn. Pathologists, Chgo. Path. Soc., Radiation Research Soc., Reticuloendothelial Soc., Sigma Xi, Alpha Omega Alpha. Current Work: Cellular immunology, T cell clones, anitibody-producing hybridomas. Subspecialties: Immunobiology and immunology; Pathology (medicine). Home: 5449 Kenwood Ave Chicago IL 60615

FITCH, VAL LOGSDON, physics educator; b. Merriman, Nebr., Mar. 10, 1923; s. Fred B. and Frances Marion (Logsdon) F.; m. Elise Cunningham, June 11, 1949 (dec. 1972); children: John Craig, Alan Peter; m. Daisy Harper Sharp, Aug. 14, 1976. B.Eng., McGill U., 1948; Ph.D., Columbia U., 1954. Instr. Columbia, 1953; instr. physics Princeton, 1954-56, asst. prof., 1956-59, 1959-60, prof., 1960—, Class 1909 prof. physics, 1968-76, Cyrus Fogg Bracket prof. physics, from 1976, now James S. McDonnell disting. univ. prof. physics. Mem. Pres.'s Sci. Adv. Com., 1970-73. Trustee Asso. Univ., Inc., 1961-67. Served with AUS, 1943-46. Recipient Research Corp. award, 1967; E.O. Lawrence award, 1968; Wetherill medal Franklin Inst., 1976; Nobel prize in physics, 1980; Sloan fellow, 1960. Fellow Am. Phys. Soc., Am. Acad. Arts and Sci., AAAS; mem. Nat. Acad. Sci. Subspecialty: Particle physics. Office: Dept Physics Princeton U Princeton NJ 08544*

FITE, KATHERINE VIRGINIA, neuroscientist; b. Tallahassee, Fla., Oct. 12, 1941; s. Van Roy and Elah Katherine (Porter) F. B.Sc., Fla. State U., 1963; M.Sc., Brown U., 1967, Ph.D. (NIH fellow), 1969. NIH postdoctoral fellow Brown U., 1968-70; asst. prof. psychology U. Mass., Amherst, 1970-74, assoc. prof., 1975-80, prof., 1980—. Editor: The Amphibian Visual System: A Multidisciplinary Approach, 1976; contbr. articles to profl. jours. Recipient

NIMH Career Devel. research awards, 1977-82; disting. vis. scholar People's Republic of China, 1985. Mem. Soc. Neurosci., Assn. Research in Vision and Ophthalmology, Internat. Brain Research Orgn., Am. Assn. Anatomists, AAAS, Sigma Xi. Current Work: Comparative anatomy and physiology of vertebrate vision, biomedical studies of inherited retinal degeneration. Subspecialties: Neurobiology; Comparative neurobiology. Office: Div Neuroscience and Behavior U Mass Amherst MA 01003

FITE, WADE LANFORD, physicist, physics educator; b. Apperson, Okla., Oct. 4, 1925; s. Luther Sherman Fite and Floe Ellen (Blue) Fite Greer; m. Ruby Rose Kauffman, Aug. 24, 1947; children—Christopher S., John C., Andrew J., Rebecca E. A.B., U.Kans., 1947; M.A., Harvard U., 1949, Ph.D., 1951; postgrad. Univ. Coll., London, 1954-55. Physicist, Philco Corp., Phila., 1951; instr., lectr. U. Pa., Phila., 1952-54; mem. staff, mgr. Gen. Atomic Co., La Jolla, Calif., 1956-63; prof. physics U. Pitts., 1963—; chmn. bd. Extranuclear Labs., Inc., Pitts., 1967—; cons. in field. Contbr. articles to profl. jours. Bd. dirs. San Dieguito Union High Sch. Dist., Encinitas, Calif., 1958-63. Served with U.S. Army, 1944-46, PTO. Fellow Am. Phys. Soc. (chmn. div. electron physics 1965-66); mem. AAAS, Am. Chem. Soc. Democrat. Current work: Atomic collisions, chemical kinetics, mass spectrometry, upper atmosphere physics, astrophysics. Subspecialties: Atomic and molecular physics; Mass spectrometry. Office: Extrel Corp PO Box 11512 Pittsburgh PA 15238

FITZGERALD, EDWIN ROGER, educator, physicist; b. Oshkosh, Wis., July 14, 1923; s. James C. and Edwina (Brown) F.; m. Carolyn H. Johnson, Aug. 30, 1946; children: Lucia Edwina, Margaret Mary, William Maurice, Alice Ann, Roger Edwin, Douglas Brendan, Thomas Michael, Jane Carolyn. B.S. in Elec. Engring, U. Wis., 1944, M.S. in Physics, 1950, Ph.D. in Physics, 1951. Registered profl. engr., Md. Physicist Phys. Research Lab., B.F. Goodrich Co., 1944-46; Project asso. chemistry U. Wis., 1951-52; mem. faculty Pa. State U., 1953-61, prof. physics, 1959-61; prof. dept. mechanics Johns Hopkins U., 1961—. Author: Particle Waves and Deformation in Crystalline Solids, 1966; Contbr. numerous tech. articles to profl. jours., sects. in books. Fellow Am. Phys. Soc. (exec. com., chmn. high polymer Physics 1958-59); mem. Acoustical Soc. Am., Materials Research Soc., Phi Beta Kappa, Sigma Xi, Eta Kappa Nu, Tau Beta Pi. Spl. research on mech. and dielectric properties solids. Current Work: Wave mechanical explanation of deformation and fracture (theoretical); dynamic mechanical measurement apparatus (experimental). Subspecialties: Polymer physics; Theoretical and applied mechanics. Home: 2445 Tracey's Store Rd Parkton MD 21120

FIVOZINSKY, SHERMAN PAUL, physicist; b. Hartford, Conn., Aug. 2, 1938; s. Irving and Betty P. (Pivnick) F.; m. Marilyn Leibowitz, June 18, 1961; children: Karen Beth, Laurie Sue. B.A., U. Conn., 1961, M.S., 1963, Ph.D., 1971. Nuclear structure researcher Nat. Bur. Standards, Washington, 1966-76; asst. to chief Office of Standard Reference Data, 1976-84, mgr. phys. data program, 1984—; adj. prof. physics Montgomery Coll., Rockville, Md., 1973—. Author: Measurements for the Safe Use of Radiation, 1976, Medical Physics Data Book, 1982; also articles. Mem. Am. Phys. Soc., Am. Assn. Physicists in Medicine, AAAS, Sigma Xi. Subspecialty: Nuclear physics. Home: 5503 Manorfield Rd Rockville MD 20853 Office: Physics Bldg A323 Gaithersburg MD 20899

FIX, GEORGE JOSEPH, mathematics educator, consultant; b. Dallas, May 10, 1939; s. George Joseph and Francis (Barlett) F.; m. Linda Mitchell, June 30, 1962; children: Paige, Blake. B.S., Tex. A&M U., 1963; M.S., Rice U., 1965; Ph.D., Harvard U., 1968. Engr. Tex. Instruments, Dallas, 1963-64; assoc. prof. U. Md., 1972-73, U. Mich., 1973-75; prof., head dept. math. Carnegie-Mellon U., Pitts., 1975—, cons. Author 2 books, numerous articles. Served in USMC, 1958-62. NASA fellow, 1981-83; grantee Office Naval Research, Army Research Office, NSF. Mem. Am. Math. Soc., Soc. Indsl. and Applied Math., AAAS, Sigma Xi, Tau Beta Pi. Current Work: Numerical analysis and scientific computing. Subspecialties: Numerical analysis (computer science); Applied mathematics. Office: Carnegie-Mellon U Pittsburgh PA 15213

FIXMAN, MARSHALL, educator, chemist; b. St. Louis, Sept. 21, 1930; s. Benjamin and Dorothy (Finkel) F.; m. Marian Ruth Beatman, July 5, 1959 (dec. Sept. 1969); children—Laura Beth, Susan Ilene, Andrew Richard; m. Branka Ladanyi, Dec. 7, 1974. A.B., Washington U., St. Louis, 1950; Ph.D., Mass. Inst. Tech., 1954. Jewett postdoctoral fellow chemistry Yale, 1953-54; instr. chemistry Harvard, 1956-59; sr. fellow Mellon Inst., Pitts., 1959-61; prof. chemistry, dir. Inst. Theoretical Sci., U. Oreg., 1961-64, prof. chemistry, research asso. inst., 1964-65; prof. chemistry Yale, New Haven, 1965-79; prof. chemistry and physics Colo. State U., Ft. Collins, 1979—. Assoc. editor: Jour. Chem. Physics, 1962-64, Jour. Phys. Chemistry, 1970-74, Macromolecules, 1970-74, Accounts Chem. Research, 1984-86. Served with AUS, 1954-56. Fellow Alfred P. Sloan Found., 1961-63; recipient Governor's award Oreg. Mus. Sci. and Industry, 1964. Mem. Nat. Acad. Scis., Am. Acad. Arts and Scis., Am. Chem. Soc. (award pure chemistry 1964), Am. Phys. Soc. (high polymer physics award 1980), Fedn. Am. Scientists. Current Work: Theory of liquids and polymers. Subspecialties: Statistical mechanics; Theoretical chemistry. Address: Dept of Chemistry Colo State U Fort Collins CO 80523

FLACK, RONALD DUMONT, JR., mechanical engineer, educator, researcher, consultant; b. South Bend, Ind., Dec. 24, 1947; s. Ronald Dumont and Alpha Jeanette F.; m. Nancy Lee Slauson, Aug. 30, 1969; children: Melissa Beth, Todd Alan. B.S.M.E., Purdue U., 1970, M.S.M.E., 1973, Ph.D. in Mech. Engring, 1975. Registered profl. engr., Va. Analytical design engr. Pratt & Whitney Aircraft Co., West Palm Beach, Fla., 1970-71; research and teaching asst. Purdue U., West Lafayette, Ind., 1971-75; asst. prof. mech. engring. U. Va., Charlottesville, 1976-81, assoc. prof., 1981—, dir. Rotating Machinery and Controls Lab., 1982—, cons. on flows on pumps, compressors and turbines, devel. lab. equipment, thermal analysis of electronic equipment. Contbr. articles on bearing lubrication, turbomachinery flows, laser velocimetry, heat transfer, rotor dynamics to profl. jours. Asst. dir. Y-Indian Guides, Charlottesville, 1982. Research grantee NIH; Research grantee ERDA/Dept. Energy; Research grantee NASA; Research grantee NSF; Research grantee Dept. Agro. Mem. ASME, Am. Soc. Lubrication Engring., Am. Soc. Engring. Edn. (Outstanding Young Faculty award 1980), Sigma Xi, Pi Tau Sigma, Tau Beta Pi, Phi Beta Phi. Current Work: Fluid mechanics on turbomachines, lubrication, laser velocimetry. Subspecialties: Mechanical engineering; Fluid mechanics. Home: 4265 Viewmont Rd Earlysville VA 22936 Office: Dept Mech and Aero Engring Thornton Hal U Va Charlottesville VA 22901

FLAGG, RAYMOND OSBOURN, biologist, scientific supply company executive; b. Martinsburg, W. Va., Jan. 31, 1933; s. Dorsey Slemons and Dorothy (Hobbs) F.; m. Ann Birmingham, May 19, 1956; children: Richard M., Elizabeth Flagg Laseau, Catherine G. B.A. with honors, Shepherd Coll., W.Va., 1957; Ph.D. in Biology, U. Va., 1961. Math. tchr. Boonsboro (Md.) High Sch., 1957; research asst. Blandy Exptl. Farm, Boyce, Va., 1957-61; research assoc. U. Va., Charlottesville, 1961-62; dir. botany Carolina Biol. Supply Co., Burlington, N.C., 1962-80, v.p., 1980—; mem. N.C. Plant Conservation Bd., 1980—. Contbr. articles to sci. jours. Patentee method and means for anesthetizing insects, 1980. Chmn. Burlington Beautification Commn., 1976-80, Burlington Hist. Commn., 1981-82; pres. Williams High Sch. PTA, 1979-80; v.p. Found. for Ednl. Devel., Research Triangle Park, N.C., 1983—. Served to cpl. U.S. Army Security Agy., 1952-55. Recipient Progressive Community Leadership award No. Piedmont Area Devel. Assn., 1977. Mem. Assn. Southeastern Biologists (pres. 1978-79), N.C. Acad. Sci. (pres. 1983-84), AAAS, Bot. Soc. Am., So. Appalachian Bot. Club, Va. Acad. Sci., Sigma Xi. Presbyterian (elder). Club: Rotary Internat. Current Work: Improved lab instruction in the sciences; administrative, endangered species, science education, lab supplies, taxonomy, genetics, plants, animals, Zephyranthes, Drosophila. Subspecialties: Systematics; Genome organization. Home: 712 W. Davis St Burlington NC 27215 Office: Carolina Biol. Supply Co Burlington NC 27215

FLANAGAN, CHARLES ALLEN, engineering administrator; b. Aultman, Pa., Oct. 14, 1931; s. Paul John and Mabel Celia (Bloomquist) F.; m. Jane Hoyt Pell, Nov. 27, 1959; children: Catherine Anne, William Patrick. B.S. in Physics, Lafayette Coll., 1953; M.B.A., U. Pitts., 1972. Jr. scientist Westinghouse-Bettis, West Mifflin, Pa., 1956-57, assoc. scientist, 1957-58, scientist, 1958-62, sr. scientist, 1962-66, supr., mgr., 1966-75, mgr., Madison, Pa., 1975-80, dep. mgr. fusion engring. design ctr., Oak Ridge, 1980—; fusion reactor studies participant IAEA, Vienna, 1980-82, 83—. Mem. editorial adv. bd. Jour. Fusion Tech. Served as 1st lt. U.S. Army, 1953-55. Recipient cert. of appreciation Dept. Energy, 1981. Mem. Am. Nuclear Soc. (chmn. fusion energy div., program com. 1977-78, vice-chmn. fusion div. 1982, chmn. div. 1983, cert. of appreciation 1983, cert. of governance 1984). Unitarian. Current Work: Design and analysis of next generation fusion devices. Subspecialties: Nuclear fusion; Nuclear fission. Home: 106 Dana Dr Oak Ridge TN 37830 Office: Fusion Engring Design Ctr Westinghouse Oak Ridge Nat Lab PO Box Y Oak Ridge TN 37830

FLANAGAN, JAMES LOTON, electrical engineer; B.S. in Elec. Engring, Miss. State U., 1948; S.M., MIT, 1950, Sc.D. 1955. Mem. elec. engring. faculty Miss. State U., 1950-52; mem. tech. staff Bell Labs., Murray Hill, N.J., 1957-61, head dept. speech and auditory research, 1961-67, head dept. acoustics research, 1967-85, dir. info. prins. research lab., 1985—. Author: Speech Analysis, Synthesis and Perception, 1972; contbr. numerous articles to profl. jours. Mem. evaluation panel Nat. Bur. Standards/NRC, 1972-77; mem. adv. panel on White House tapes U.S. Dist. Ct. for D.C., 1973-74; bd. govs. Am. Inst. Physics, 1974-77; mem. sci. adv. bd. Callier Center, U. Tex., Dallas, 1974-76; mem. sci. adv. panel on voice communications Nat. Security Agy., 1975-77; mem. sci. adv. bd. div. communications research Inst. Def. Analyses, 1975-77; commr. NRC com. engring. and tech. systems, 1984—. Recipient Disting. Service award in sci. Am. Speech and Hearing Assn., 1977; L.M. Ericson prize in telecommunications, 1985. Fellow IEEE (mem. fellow selection com. 1979-81), Acoustical Soc. Am. (assoc. editor Speech Communication 1959-62, exec. council 1970-73, v.p. 1976-77, pres. 1978-79); mem. Acoustics, Speech and Signal Processing Soc. (v.p. 1967-68, pres. 1969-70, Achievement award 1970, Soc. award 1976), Nat. Acad. Engring. of Nat. Acad. Scis. U.S. and fgn. patentee in field. Current Work: Digital communications. Subspecialty: Electrical engineering. Office: 600 Mountain Ave Murray Hill NJ 07974

FLANEGAN, JAMES BERT, microbiologist, educator, researcher; b. Tampa, Fla., Aug. 2, 1946; s. James H. and Julia L. F.; m. Dawn Elaine, July 12, 1980; children: Ryan, Jennifer, Amy. B.S., Fla. State U., 1968, M.S., 1969; Ph.D., U. Mich., 1975. Postdoctoral fellow Center for Cancer Research, M.I.T., 1975-78; assoc. prof. immunology and med. microbiology Coll. Medicine, U. Fla., 1978—. Contbr. articles to profl. jours. Served to lt. (s.g.) USNR, 1970-72. NIH postdoctoral fellow, 1975-77; NIH grantee, 1979—; NSF grantee, 1979—. Mem. Am. Soc. Microbiology, Am. Soc. Virology, Sigma Xi (Fla. chpt. Faculty Research award 1981). Current Work: Molecular biology of RNA viruses. Subspecialties: Virology (biology); Molecular biology. Office: Dept Immunology and Med Microbiology Coll Medicine Box J-266 U Fla Gainesville FL 32610

FLANZ, JACOB B., nuclear physics experimentalist, accelerator physicist; b. Queens, N.Y., Nov. 7, 1952; s. David Flanz and Miriam (Lefkowitz) Rose; m. Nancy Dale Goldman. B.S., Rensselaer Poly. Inst., 1973; M.S., U. Mass., 1975, Ph.D., 1979. Mem. research staff MIT, Cambridge and Middleton, Mass., 1979-83; assoc. group leader accelerator ops. MIT-Bates Linear Accelerator, Middleton, 1983-84, prin. research scientist, 1984—, chmn. accelerator devel. com., 1984—, asst. project leader beam recirculation project, 1979-82; accelerator design cons. U. Sask., Can., 1983. Contbr. articles to profl. jours. NSF research fellow, 1973. Mem. Am. Phys. Soc., AAAS, N.Y. Acad. Scis. Current work: Nuclear structure physics, transverse electron scattering, coincidence experiments, high momentum transfer nuclear structure; beam optics, magnetics and accelerator design. Subspecialty: Nuclear physics. Home: 99 East St Middleton MA 01949 Office: MIT Bates Accelerator Ctr PO Box 846 Middleton MA 01949-2846

FLASCHEN, STEWARD SAMUEL, corporation executive; b. Berwyn, Ill., May 28, 1926; s. Hyman Herman and Ethel (Leviton) F.; m. Joyce Davies, Apr. 21, 1949; children: John, Sheryl, David, Evan. B.S. in Chemistry, U. Ill., 1947; M.S., Miami U., Oxford, Ohio, 1948; Ph.D. in Geochemistry, Pa. State U., 1953. Supr. research dept. Bell Telephone Labs., Murray Hill, N.J., 1952-59; dir. phys. scis., research and devel., semiconductor products div. Motorola, Inc., Phoenix, 1959-64; sr. v.p., gen. tech. dir. ITT Corp., N.Y.C., 1964—; lectr. Pace U. Grad. Sch. Bus. Author: Search and Research, 1965; also articles. Mem. Phoenix Bd. Edn., 1962-64. Served with USNR, 1944-46. Fellow Am. Inst. Chemists, IEEE; mem. Electromech. Soc. Am., Am. Ceramic Soc., AAAS, Indsl. Research Inst., N.Y. Acad. Scis. Patentee in field. Subspecialty: Research and development management. Home: 592 Weed St New Canaan CT 06840 Office: 320 Park Ave New York NY 10022

FLAX, PHILIP DANIEL, geologist; b. Hackensack, N.J., May 1, 1950; s. Harold and Sylvia (Riveles) F.; m. Sonia Sofia Hernandez, Sept. 8, 1979. B.A. in Geosci., Jersey City State Coll., 1977; postgrad., Rutgers U., 1978-79; M.S. in Geology, Queens Coll. CUNY, 1985. Adj. faculty lectr. Queens Coll. CUNY, Flushing, 1982-83; research asst., 1983; exploration geologist Arco Exploration Co., Denver, 1983; research asst. Research Found. CUNY, Flushing, 1984—. Mem. Geol. Soc. Am., Am. Assn. Petroleum Geologists, Soc. Econ. Paleontologists and Mineralogists, Soc. Mining Engrs., Sigma Xi. Jewish. Current work: Carbonate-evaporite sedimentology, stratigraphy and petrology and their application to energy exploration. Subspecialties: Geology; Sedimentology. Home: 70-12 34th Ave 3B Jackson Heights NY 11372 Office: Queens Coll CUNY Geology Dept Kissena Blvd Flushing NY 11367

FLECK, DAVID CHARLES, elec. engr.; b. Findlay, Ohio, Aug. 13, 1954; s. Charles Edward and Mary Catherine (Thiry) F. B.S.E.E., U. Cin., 1978. Engr. EPA, Cin., Annapolis, Md., 1976-80; pres. Capella Cons., Laurel, Md., 1980—; sr. engr. GTCO Corp., Rockville, Md., 1982—. Mem. Assn. Computing Machinery, IEEE, AAAS. Democrat. Roman Catholic. Current Work: Computer graphics, image processing, pattern recognition; microcomputer applications, computer architectures. Subspecialties: Computer engineering; Computer architecture. Home: 16127 Kenny Rd Laurel MD 20707 Office: 1055 1st St Rockville MD 20850

FLEISCH, JEROME HERBERT, pharmacologist; b. Bronx, N.Y., June 6, 1941; s. Wolf and Miriam (Glaser) F.; m. Marlene L. Cohen, Aug. 8, 1976; children: Abby Faye, Sheryl Brynne. B.S., Columbia U., 1963; Ph.D., Georgetown U., 1967. Research fellow Harvard U. Med. Sch., Boston, 1967-68; research asso./sr. staff fellow Nat. Heart and Lung Inst., NIH, Bethesda, Md., 1968-74; research asso. Lilly Research Labs., Eli Lilly & Co., Indpls., 1974—. Contbr. articles to sci. jours. Served to lt. comdr. USPHS, 1968-70. Mem. Am. Soc. Pharmacology and Exptl. Therapeutics, Soc. Exptl. Biology and Medicine; mem. Am. Acad. Allergy and Immunology; Mem. Collegium Internationale Allergologicum. Current Work: Mechanisms involved in antigen-induced release of mediators of anaphylaxis - leukotriene receptors. Subspecialties: Pharmacology; Allergy. Office: Lilly Research Labs MC905 Indianapolis IN 46285

FLEISCHMANN, HANS HERMANN, physicist, educator; b. Munich, Germany, June 2, 1933; came to U.S., 1963, naturalized, 1978; s. Paul and Gertrud (Jaenicke) F. Dipl. Phys., Tech. U. Munich, 1959, Dr.rer.nat., 1962. Research assoc. Tech. U. Munich, 1962-63; cons. Rohde & Schwarz, Messgeraetebau, Munich, 1962-63; mem. staff Gen. Atomic, San Diego, 1963-67; prof. applied physics Sch. Applied and Engring. Physics, Cornell U., Ithaca, N.Y., 1967—; cons. to govt. and industry. Contbr. articles to profl. jours. Fellow Am. Phys. Soc. (div. plasma physics, past mem. exec. com.), IEEE, Plasma Sci. Soc. (past mem. exec. com., adminstrv.com.); mem. Am. Nuclear Soc. (past mem. exec. com.). Current Work: Plasma physics and controlled fusion in area of compact toroids and intense electron and ion beams, atomic collisions. Subspecialties: Plasma physics; Fusion. Office: Sch Applied and Engring Physics Cornell U Ithaca NY 14853

FLEMING, HUBERT LOY, research chemical engineer; b. Sutton, W.Va., Aug. 6, 1956; s. Hubert Harrison and Edra Ruth (Crawford) F.; m. Pamela Anne Monteleone, May 6, 1979; children—Jaime Lynn, Megan Ann. B.S., Alderson-Broaddus Coll., 1978; M.S., Cornell U., 1980, Ph.D., 1981. Registered profl. engr., Pa. Tech. supr., group leader Alcoa, Alcoa Center, Pa., 1981—. Contbr. articles to profl. jours. Patentee process production aluminas and adsorption processes. Vol. United Way, Pitts., 1984. NSF fellow; DuPont fellow. Mem. Am. Inst. Chem. Engrs., Am. Chem. Soc., Sigma Xi, Alpha Chi Sigma, Zeta Alpha Gamma. Republican. Club: Chess (Philippi, W.Va.) (pres. 1974-75). Current work: Gas and liquid interactions with solid surfaces; adsorption and catalysis; surface chemistry of solids; kinetics of reactions; transport phenomena in reactions. Subspecialties: Chemical engineering; Physical chemistry. Home: 2805 Camelot Dr Lower Burrell PA 15068 Office: Alcoa Tech Ctr C Alcoa Center PA 15069

FLEMING, JAMES STUART, JR., pharmacologist; b. Buffalo, Sept. 1, 1936; s. James Stuart and Pauline (McClurg) F.; m. Marilyn Joyce Bartsch, June 7, 1960; children: Lois Vernette, James Stuart III. B.A., Northwestern U., 1958; M.A., U. Buffalo, 1962; Ph.D., Ohio State U., 1965; M.B.A., Syracuse U., 1983. Teaching asst. U. Buffalo, 1961-62; research asst. Ohio State U., Columbus, 1962-65; assoc. dir. cardiovascular biology Sci. and Tech. div. Bristol-Myers Co., Syracuse, N.Y., 1965—. Contbr. articles to profl publs. NIH tng. grantee, 1958-61. Mem. Am. Soc. Pharmacology and Exptl. Therapeutics, Am. Heart Assn., Council on Thrombosis, Microcirculatory Soc., Internat. Soc. on Oxygen Transport to Tissue.; mem. Beta Gamma Sigma. Patentee pharmacologic agts in prevention of thrombosis. Current Work: Supervision and development of a comprehensive research program for identification and development of new drugs for the prevention and treatment of occlusive vascular disease, including planning of early stages of clinical testing, general cardiovascular profiling of pharmacodynamic agents. Subspecialties: Pharmacology; Hematology. Office: Dept Cardiovascular Biology Bristol-Myers Thompson Rd Syracuse NY 13201

FLEMING, KARL NEILL, nuclear scientist/engineer, consultant; b. Uniontown, Pa., July 18, 1947; s. John Nesbit and Gladys Ruth (Helmick) F.; m. Suzanne Watson, July 14, 1980. B.S. in Physics, Pa. State U., 1969; M.S. in Nuclear Sci. and Engring, Carnegie-Mellon U., 1974. Engr. Gen. Atomic Co. (name now GA Techs.), San Diego, 1974-75, sr. engr., 1975-77, staff engr., 1977-80, br. mgr., 1980-81; dir. probabilistic risk assessment methods Pickard, Lowe & Garrick, Irvine, Calif., 1981-82; project mgr. Seabrook Sta. Probabilistic Safety Assessment, 1982—; chmn. working group on probabilistic risk assessment U.S. Dept. Energy, 1982—. Author: IEEE/Am. Nuclear Soc. Probabilistic Risk Assessment Procedures Guide, 1981. Dudley Meml. scholar, 1968-69. Mem. Am. Nuclear Soc., AAAS, Sigma Pi Sigma, Pi Mu Epsilon, Phi Kappa Phi. Developer model for reliability analysis of systems called Beta Factor Method. Current Work: Made major contributions to early research and development in the new technology of probabilistic risk (safety) assessment as it is applied to assessment of nuclear reactor safety; refined the state-of-the-art in systems reliability engineering in the analysis of dependent (common cause) failures. Subspecialty: Nuclear engineering. Office: Pickard Lowe & Garrick 17840 Sky Park Irvine CA 92714

FLEMING, WENDELL HELMS, See *Who's Who in America*, 43rd edition.

FLEMINGS, MERTON CORSON, metallurgy educator, researcher; b. Syracuse, N.Y., Sept. 20, 1929; married; 4 children. S.B., MIT, 1951, S.M., 1952, SC.D. in Metallurgy, 1954. Metallurgist Am. Brake Shoe Research Lab., 1954-56; from asst. prof. to assoc. prof. metallurgy MIT, 1956-69, Abex prof., 1970-75, Ford prof., 1975-81, prof. metallurgy, 1969—, Toyota prof. materials processing, 1981—, assoc. dir. Ctr. Materials Sci. and Engring., 1973-77, dir. Materials Processing Ctr., 1979-82, head dept. materials sci. and engring., 1982—; dir. Hitchiner Mfg. Co., Inc.; cons. to govt. labs., industry, 1970—. Recipient Albert Sauveur Achievement award, 1978; overseas fellow Churchill Coll., Eng., 1970-71. Fellow Am. Soc. Metals (Henry Marion Howe medal 1973); mem. Nat. Acad. Engring., Am. Foundrymen's Soc. (Simpson Gold medal 1961), Inst. Metals London, AIME (Mathewson Gold medal 1969), Am. Acad. Arts and Scis. Subspecialty: Materials (engineering). Office: MIT Room 8-309 Cambridge MA 02139*

FLETCHER, AARON NATHANIEL, research chemist; b. Los Angeles, Dec. 24, 1925; s. Robert Eugene and Mabel Louise Fletcher; m. Edna Delora Stulce, Feb. 23, 1951; children—Clixie, Roberta, Delora, Ronald, Denise. B.S., Calif. Inst. Tech., 1949; Ph.D., UCLA, 1961. Chemist So. Pacific Co., Sacramento, 1949-54; research chemist Naval Weapons Ctr., China Lake, Calif., 1954—. Contbr. articles to profl. jours. Patentee in field. Served with USAAF, 1944-45. Fellow Naval Ordnance Test Station, 1959-60. Fellow AAAS; mem. Am. Chem. Soc., Electrochem. Soc. Current work: Dyes for laser applications, dye laser lifetime measurements, fluorescence spectroscopy, thermal battery research, safety of battery materials. Subspecialties: Physical chemistry; Analytical chemistry. Home: PO Box 1314 Ridgecrest CA 93555 Office: Naval Weapons Ctr Mail Code 3852 China Lake CA 93555-6001

FLETCHER, EDWARD ABRAHAM, educator; b. Detroit, July 30, 1924; s. Morris and Lillian (Protes) F.; m. Roslyn Silber, June 15, 1948; children—Judith Ellen, Deborah Gail, Carolyn Ruth. B.S., Wayne State U., 1948; Ph.D. (DuPont fellow, AEC fellow), Purdue U., 1952. Head propellant chemistry and flame mechanics sects. NASA, Cleve., 1952-59; asso. prof. U. Minn., Mpls., 1959-60, prof., 1960—, dir. grad. studies in mech. engring., 1965—; vis. scientist Byellorussian Acad. Scis., 1964; vis. Fulbright prof. U. Poitiers, 1968; cons. U.S. Dept. Commerce Study Waste Heat Mgmt., Minn. Energy Agy., No. States Power Co., Public Systems Research Corp.; co-chmn. com. on fire resistant hydraulic fluids NRC-Nat. Acad. Scis. Nat. Materials Adv. Bd., 1977-78; Participant adv. group for aero. research and devel. NATO Confs., 1960, 61. Editor: Isotopes, 1958-59. Bd. dirs. Minn. Com. for Technion., New Friends of Chamber Music. Served with USNR, 1943-46. Recipient NASA Spl. award, 1961; Outstanding Ski Patrolman of Western Region award Nat. Ski Patrol, 1969-70. Mem. Combustion Inst. (bd. advisers, sec. Central States sect. 1967-78, vice chmn. 1978-79, chmn. 1979-82), Am. Chem. Soc., AAAS, Sigma Xi, Tau Beta Pi, Pi Tau Sigma, Phi Lambda Upsilon. Current Work: High temperature solar thermochemistry electrolysis and applied thermodynamics and combustion. Subspecialties: Solar energy; Thermodynamics. Home: 3909 Beard Ave S Minneapolis MN 55410

FLETCHER, JAMES CHIPMAN, consulting engineer; b. Millburn, N.J., June 5, 1919; s. Harvey and Lorena (Chipman) F.; m. Fay Lee, Nov. 2, 1946; children: Virginia Lee, Mary Susan, James Stephen, Barbara Jo. A.B., Columbia U., 1940; Ph.D., Calif. Inst. Tech., 1948; D.Sc. (hon.), U. Utah, 1971, Brigham Young U., 1977; LL.D., Lehigh U., 1978. Research physicist bur. ordnance Dept. Navy, 1940-41; spl. research assoc. Cruft Lab., Harvard U., 1941-42; instr. Princeton U., 1942-45; teaching fellow Calif. Inst. Tech., 1945-48; instr. UCLA, 1948-50; dir. theory and analysis lab. Hughes Aircraft Co., 1948-54; asso. dir. guided missile lab., dir. electronics guided missile research div., later in space tech. labs. Ramo-Wooldridge Corp., 1954-58; pres., founder Space Electronics Corp., 1958; pres. Space-Gen. Corp. (merger between Space Electronics Corp. and Aerojet-Gen. Corp.), 1960; chmn. bd. Space-Gen. Corp., 1961-64; pres. U. Utah, 1964-71; adminstr. NASA, Washington, 1971-77; Whiteford prof. U. Pitts., 1977—, cons. engr., McLean, Va., 1977—; mem. subcom. on stability and control NACA, 1950-54; cons. Office Sec. Def., 1959-64; asst. sec. USAF, 1961-64, to ACDA, 1962-63, Aerojet-Gen. and Space-Gen. Corps., 1964-71; cons., then mem. Pres.'s Sci. Adv. Com., 1958-70; mem. Air Force Sci. Adv. Bd., 1962-67; chmn. tech. study team 1983; mem. strategic weapons panel, 1959-61, mil. aircraft panel, 1964-67, chmn. naval warfare panel, 1967-73; mem. Pres.'s Nat. Crime Commn., 1966; mem. tech. assessment adv. council Office of Tech. Assessment; mem. Def. Sci. Bd.; chmn. safety adv. bd. Three Mile Island No. 2; governing bd. NRC, 1978-84; v.p. Nat. Space Inst.; dir. Standard Oil Co. (Ind.), Burroughs Corp., COMARCO, Inc., Fairchild Industries, Astrotech. Internat. Author classified papers, sci. papers, chpts. in books; bd. editors, Addison-Wesley Pub. Co., 1958-64. Trustee Rockefeller Found., Theodore von Karman Meml. Found.; bd. regents Nat. Library Medicine, 1971; bd. visitors Def. Intelligence Sch., 1970-71; bd. govs. Argonne Nat. Lab., Univ. Corp. on Atmospheric Research. Recipient Disting. Service medal NASA; Exceptional Civilian Service award USAF; Dept. Energy award, 1982; John Jay award Columbia U. Fellow IEEE, Am. Acad. Arts and Sci., AIAA (hon.), Am. Astronautical Soc.; mem. Am. Phys. Soc., Nat. Acad. Engring. (council, rep. to governing bd. NRC, governing bd. 1978-81), Am. Ordnance Assn., Air Force Assn., Sigma Xi. Club: Cosmos. Subspecialties: Systems engineering; Astronautics. Home: 7721 Falstaff Rd McLean VA 22102

FLEXNER, LOUIS BARKHOUSE, scientist, educator; b. Louisville, Jan. 7, 1902; s. Washington and Ida (Barkhouse) F.; m. Josefa Barba Gosé, Aug. 23, 1937. B.S., U. Chgo., 1923; M.D., Johns Hopkins, 1927; LL.D., U. Pa. Fellow medicine Johns Hopkins Hosp., 1928-29; resident physician U. Chgo. Clinics, 1929-30; instr. and asso. anatomy Johns Hopkins Med. Sch., 1930-39; with dept. physiology Cambridge (Eng.) U., 1933-34; staff mem. dept. embryology Carnegie Instn., Washington, 1939-51, research asso., 1951—; prof. anatomy Sch. Med. U. Pa., 1951—, chmn. dept., 1951-67; dir. Inst. Neurol. Scis., 1953-66. Contbr. articles to profl. jours. Sci. adv. bds. USPHS, United Cerebral Palsy, Nat. Council to Combat Blindness, Nat. Paraplegic Soc., NRC, Nat. Found. Mem. Am. Assn. Anatomists, Nat. Acad. Scis., Am. Physiol. Soc., Am. Soc. Biol. Chemists, Am. Acad. Arts and Scis., Am. Philos. Soc. Current Work:

Memory: mechanism of cerebral spread of an engram. Subspecialty: Neurobiology. Home: 4631 Pine St Philadelphia PA 19143

FLIKKE, ARNOLD MAURICE, agricultural engineering educator; b. Viroqua, Wis., July 8, 1919; s. Arthur P. and Mabel Christine (Hermanson) F.; m. Bethel Irene Christie, June 11, 1942; children—Gary, Craig, Karen. B.S. in Agrl. Engring, U. Wis., 1941; M.S., U. Minn., 1943; Ph.D., Auburn U., 1972. Instr. agrl. engring. U. Minn., 1946-49, asst. prof., 1949-56, asso. prof., 1956-63, prof., 1963-72, prof., 1972— head dept. agrl. engring., 1972-83; cons. in field. Served with USNR, 1944-46. NSF faculty fellow, 1966. Mem. Am. Soc. Agrl. Engrs. (chmn. Minn. sect. 1962, chmn. North Central region 1972, nat. dir. 1974—), Am. Soc. for Engring. Edn., IEEE, AAAS, Sigma Xi, Phi Kappa Phi, Alpha Zeta, Gamma Sigma Delta, Alpha Gamma Rho. Lutheran. Club: Mason. Research and publs. on application of electricity for grain drying, farm power. Subspecialties: Biomass (energy science and technology); Resource conservation. Home: 3409 Downers Dr NE Minneapolis MN 55418 Office: Dept of Agrl Engring U Minn Saint Paul MN 55108

FLINN, EDWARD AMBROSE, III, geophysicist; b. Oklahoma City, Aug. 27, 1931; s. Edward Ambrose and Marion Catalina (Prater) F.; m. Jane Margaret Bott, Dec. 29, 1962; 1 dau., Susan Katherine. B.S. in Geophysics (William Barton Rogers scholar), Mass. Inst. Tech., 1953; Ph.D. in Geophysics (NSF fellow 1953-54), Calif. Inst. Tech., 1960; postgrad. (Fulbright scholar), Australian Nat. U., 1958-59; certificat, Le Cordon Bleu Ecole de Cuisine et de Patiesserie, 1971. Seismologist United ElectroDynamics Inc., Pasadena, Calif., 1960-62; chief seismologist, lab. seismic data Teledyne Geotech, Alexandria, Va., 1962-64, dir. research, 1964-68; asso. dir. Alexandria labs., 1968-74; dir. lunar programs office space sci. NASA, Washington, 1975, dep. dir., chief scientist lunar and planetary programs, 1976-77, chief scientist earth and ocean programs, 1977, chief scientist geodynamics program, 1978—; mem. joint research panel AEC-U.K. Atomic Energy Authority, 1963-74; vis. research asso. Calif. Inst. Tech., 1969, 78; vis. asso. prof. geophysics Brown U., 1970; cons. subcom. planetology steering com. space sci. and applications NASA, 1969-70, Nat. Swedish Inst. Bldg. Research, Stockholm, 1970; participant sci. exchange Nat. Acad. Sci.-Acad. Scis. USSR, 1970; mem. com. lunar and planetary exploration Nat. Acad. Scis., 1973-75, mem. com. on seismology, 1973-75, mem. com. on internat. geology, 1982—; mem. adv. com. earthquake studies U.S. Geol. Survey, 1975-80. Trans., editor 3 books; asso. editor for gen. seismology: Geophysics, 1965-67; editor sect. earth and planetary surfaces and interiors: Jour. Geophys. Research, 1973-78. Mem. adv. bd. No. Va. br. Urban League, 1970-71; mem. Alexandria Council on Human Relations, 1970—; mem. traffic bd., Alexandria, 1972-74; mem. Alexandria Democratic Com., 1970-74, exec. bd., 1971-73. Recipient NASA medal for exceptional sci. achievement, 1979. Mem. AAAS, Am. Astron. Soc., Royal Astron. Soc. (editorial bd. Geophys. Jour. 1969-74), Am. Geophys. Union (sec. sect. seismology 1970-74), Assn. Earth Sci. Editors, Internat. Union Geodesy and Geophysics (chmn. commn. planetary scis. 1976-80, sec. Commn. on Internat. Coordination of Space Techniques for Geodesy and Geodynamics 1979-85), Seismol. Soc. Am., Soc. Exploration Geophysicists, Inter-Assn. Com. Math. Geophysics (sec. 1971-75), Internat. Council Sci. Unions (sec.-gen. Inter-Union Commn. on Lithosphere 1980-86, mem. com. on publs. and communications 1981-85), 89ers Soc., Sigma Xi, Beta Theta Pi. Club: Cosmos. Research, numerous publs. on seismology, geophysics, applied maths., computer sci. Current Work: Application of space technology to geodesy, geophysics and geodynamics. Subspecialties: Tectonics; Geophysics. Home: 3605 Tupelo Pl Alexandria VA 22304 Office: NASA Hqrs Code EEG Washington DC 20546

FLINN, PAUL ANTHONY, physics educator, materials scientist; b. Mar. 25, 1926; s. Richard A. and Anna M. (Weber) F.; m. Mary Ellen Hoffman, Aug. 20, 1949; children—Juliana, Margaret, Donald, Anthony, Patrick. A.B., Columbia U., 1948, M.A., 1949; Sc.D., MIT, 1952. Asst. prof. Wayne U., Detroit, 1953-54; mem. research staff Westinghouse Research Lab., Pitts., 1954-63; prof. Carnegie-Mellon U., Pitts., 1964-78; sr. staff scientist Intel. Corp., Santa Clara, Calif., 1978—; vis. prof. Stanford U., Calif., 1984—; vis. prof. U. Nancy, France, 1967-68, U. Federal do Rio Grande du Sal, Porto Allegre, Brazil, 1975; vis. scientist Argonne Nat. Lab., Ill., 1977-78. Contbr. articles to sci. jours. Served with USN, 1944-46, PTO. Named to Disting. appointment Argonne U. Assn., 1971. Fellow Am. Phys. Soc.; mem. AIME, AAAS, Phi Beta Kappa, Tau Beta Pi. Current work: Materials problems related to VLSI devices, especially mechanical properties of thin films. Subspecialties: Condensed matter physics; Microchip technology (materials science). Home: 2162 Coronet Dr San Jose CA 95124 Office: Dept Materials Sci Engring Stanford U Stanford CA 94305

FLINN, RICHARD ALOYSIUS, metall. engr., cons., educator; b. N.Y.C.; s. Richard A. and Anna M. F.; m. Edwina R. Flinn, 1944; children: Ellen, John, Paul, Mark, Brian. B.S.Ch.E., CUNY, 1936; M.S. in Metallurgy, M.I.T., 1937, Sc.D. in Metallurgy, 1941. Research in metallurgy Internat. Nickel Co., Bayonne, N.J., 1937-39; asst. chief metallurgist ABEX, Mahwah, N.J., 1941-51; prof. metall. engring. U. Mich., Ann Arbor, 1951—, cons. legal work in failure analysis. Author: Fundamentals of Metal Casting, 1964, Engineering Materials and Their Applications, 1978, 2d edit., 1980; contbr. numerous articles profl. jours. Trustee Barton Hills Village, 1979—. Fellow Am. Soc. Metals (Howe medal 1944, 61); mem. Am. Foundrymen's Soc. (Simpson Gold medal 1947, hon. life mem.). Republican. Patentee in field. Current Work: Failure analysis, alloy devel., metal casting. Subspecialties: Materials processing; Metallurgy. Home: 140 Underdown Dr Ann Arbor MI 48105 Office: U Mich 4305 E Engineering Ann Arbor MI 48109

FLIPPEN-ANDERSON, JUDITH LEE, x-ray crystallographer; b. Winthrop, Mass., Apr. 21, 1941; d. Sidney and Mary (Levine) Dubchansky; m. Philip E. Flippen, Jr., Nov. 28, 1965 (dec. Dec. 1972); 1 child, Cheona Anne; m. Paul B. Anderson, Jan. 22, 1978. B.A., Northeastern U., 1963; M.S., Ariz. State U., 1966. X-ray crystallographer Naval Research Lab., Washington, 1966—. Contbr. articles to profl. jours. Patentee in field. Recipient Superior Service award USDA, 1984; publ. award Naval Research Lab., 1979, 84. Mem. Am. Chem. Soc., Am. Crystallographic Assn., Sigma Xi. Current work: X-ray diffraction studies on single crystals of small to medium sized organic and biological molecules. Subspecialty: X-ray crystallography. Office: Naval Research Lab Code 6030 Washington DC 20375

FLOM, TERRENCE EDSEL FLOM, electrical engineer; b. Moose Lake, Minn, Sept. 21, 1940; s. Andrew Felix and Olga (Koskey) F. B.E.E., Ga. Inst. Tech., 1964. Electronic engr. Control Data Corp., Mpls., 1964-67; electronic engr. Xerox, Pasadena, Calif., 1967-68, ITT, Van Nuys, Calif., 1968-75; supr. laser communications GTE, Mountain View, Calif., 1975-77, mgr. dept. systems engring., 1977-81, mgr. tech. devel., 1982-84; mgr. systems engring. GTE Sprint, Burlingame, Calif., 1985—. Contbr. articles to profl. jours. Mem. Optical Soc. Am., Laser Inst. Am. Current Work: Network architecture for integrated voice, data, and video telecommunications. Subspecialties: Laser communications; Telecommunications. Home: 606 Portofino Ln Foster City CA 94404 Office: 533 Airport Blvd Burlingame CA 94010

FLOOD, DOROTHY GARNETT, neurobiologist; b. Sayre, Pa., Oct. 7, 1951; d. James Murlin and Dorothy Garnett (Dietrich) F. Student, U. Ill., 1972-73; B.A. cum laude, Lawrence U., Appleton, Wis., 1973; M.S., U. Rochester, N.Y., 1980, Ph.D., 1980. Sr. instr. U. Rochester, 1980-84, asst. prof., 1984—. Contbr. articles to profl. jours. Mem. AAAS, Soc. Neurosci. Current Work: Development and aging of nervous system; plasticity. Subspecialties: Anatomy and embryology; Neurobiology. Office: Dept Neurology Box 673 U Rochester Med Center 601 Elmwood Ave Rochester NY 14642

FLORY, WALTER S., JR., botanical educator, researcher; b. Bridgewater, Va., Oct. 5, 1907; s. Walter Samuel and Ella May (Reherd) F.; m. Nellie Maude Thomas, Apr. 24, 1930 (dec. Jan. 1971); children—Kathryn Flory Maier, Walter S. III, Thomas Reherd; m. Gale Crews, June 25, 1975. B.A., Bridgewater Coll., 1928; M.A., U. Va., 1929, Ph.D., 1931. Horticulturist, Tex. A&M U., College Station, 1936-44, Va. Poly. Inst., Blacksburg, Va., 1944-47; prof. exptl. horticulture U. Va., Charlottesville, 1947-63; Babcock prof. botany Wake Forest U., Winston-Salem, N.C., 1963-80, prof. emeritus, 1980—, genetic and biosystematic researcher, 1980—; dir. Reynolds Gardens, Wake Forest U., Winston-Salem, 1964-72; curator White Research Arboretum, U. Va., Boyce, 1955-63; research cons. Fairchild Tropical Garden, Miami, Fla., 1972; botanical cons. Va. Mus. Sci., Richmond, 1973. Contbr. articles to profl. jours. Pres. Blue Ridge chpt. Va. Mus. Fine Arts, Richmond, 1962-63; trustee, exec. com., treas. Winston-Salem Nature Sci. Ctr., 1964-67; trustee Bridgewater Coll., 1958—. Recipient Pres. and Visitors Research prize U. Va., 1951, William Herbert medalist Am. Plant Life Soc., 1978. Fellow AAAS, Va. Acad. Sci. (pres. 1954-55, Horsley Research award 1949), Royal Hort. Soc. Eng.; mem. Botanical Soc. Am. (chmn. Southeast sect. 1951-52, councillor 1951-52), Assn. Southeastern Biologists (pres. 1963, Research prize 1978). Democrat. Brethren. Club: Torch (Winston-Salem) (pres. 1969-70). Current work: Biosystematics of Zephyrantheae; chromosome evolution in the cycads. Subspecialties: Evolutionary biology; Genome organization. Home: 2025 Colonial Pl Winston-Salem NC 27104Office: Dept Biology Wake Forest U Winston-Salem NC 27109

FLOWER, PHILLIP JOHN, astronomer, educator; b. Toledo, Feb. 4, 1948; s. Chester R. and Ursula (Malikowski) F. B.S. in Physics, U. Toledo, 1970; Ph.D. in Astronomy, U. Wash., Seattle, 1976. Research assoc. Inst. Astronomy, Polish Acad. Sci., Warsaw, 1974-75; postdoctoral research assoc. Joint Inst. Lab. Astrophysics, Boulder, Colo., 1976-78; asst. prof. physics and astronomy Clemson U., 1978-83, assoc. prof., 1983—. Mem. Am. Astron. Soc., AAAS, Am. Phys. Scis., Astron. Soc. Pacific, S.C. Acad. Scis. Current Work: Stellar evolution, stellar interiors, Magellanic clouds, star clusters, dwarf galaxies. Subspecialties: Theoretical astrophysics; Optical astronomy. Office: Dept Physics and Astronomy Clemson U Clemson SC 29634

FLOYD, MIDDLETON BRAWNER, JR., medicinal chemist; b. Atlanta, Aug. 8, 1938; s. M. Brawner and Fay (Hitechew) F.; m. Pamela Dineen, June 25, 1966; children—Bethany, Catherine. B.A., Emory U., 1960, M.S., 1962; Ph.D., Yale U., 1966. Postdoctoral fellow Boston U., 1965-67; sr. chemist Am. Cyanamid, Pearl River, N.Y., 1967-82, research fellow 1982—. Mem. Am. Chem. Soc., Sigma Xi. Current work: Chemical sysnthesis of prostaglandins; drugs for diabetes therapy. Subspecialties: Organic chemistry; Medicinal chemistry. Home: 5 Babbling Brook Ln Suffern NY 10901 Office: Am Cyanamid Co N Middletown Rd Pearl River NY 10965

FLOYD, ROBERT A., biochemist; b. Yosemite, Ky., Oct. 7, 1940; s. Aaron and Clarice (Williams) F.; m. Marlene Gale Rohner, Aug. 21, 1965; children: Matthew Christopher, Patrick Aaron. B.S., U. Ky., Lexington, 1963, M.S., 1965; Ph.D., Purdue U., Lafayette, Ind., 1969. Postdoctoral work U. Calif., Davis, 1968-69, U. Pa., Phila., 1969-71; research assoc. Washington U., St. Louis, 1971-74; biochemist Okla. Med. Research Found., Oklahoma City, 1974—, mem., 1983—. Editor: Free Radicals and Cancer, 1982; mem. editorial bd. Archives Gerontology and Geriatrics, Jour. Free Radicals in Biology and Medicine. Contbr. sci. articles to profl. publs. NIH grantee, 1975-85; EPA grantee, 1985-86. Mem. Am. Soc. Biol. Chemists, Biophys. Soc., Am. Chem. Soc., Am. Soc. Photobiology, N.Y. Acad. Scis., AAAS, Am. Assn. for Cancer Research, Sigma Xi. Current Work: Free radicals in biological systems, oxygen free radicals, oxidation-reduction reactions in biochemistry, bioenergetics; membrane peroxidation induced modification of dopamine synthesis in striatum synaptosomes; hydroxyl free radical adduct of deoxyguanosine: sensitive detection and mechanisms of formation. Subspecialties: Biochemistry (biology); Toxicology (agriculture). Home: 207 NW 18th St Oklahoma City OK 73103 Office: 825 NE 13th St Oklahoma City OK 73104

FLUEGGE, RONALD MARVIN, nuclear engineer; b. Cape Girardeau, Mo., Nov. 22, 1948; s. Marvin Alvin and Maxine Louise (Hamilton) F.; m. Vicki Sue Oldham, Aug. 9, 1969; children: Terasa Dawn, Jennifer Beth. B.S., U. Mo.-Rolla, 1970. Registered profl. engr., Mo., Md., Tex., Kans. Engr. Balt. Gas & Electric Co., 1970-74; reactor engr. Nuclear Regulatory Commn., Bethesda, Md., 1974-76; med. physicist Shoss Radiology Group, Cape Girardeau, Mo., 1976-78; pres. Diagnostic Services Unltd., Jackson, Mo., 1978-79; dir. Mo. Pub. Service Commn., Jefferson City, 1979-83; nuclear cons. UCCEL Corp., Dallas, 1983—; curriculum adv. U. Mo., Rolla., 1980—; econs. adv. Atomic Indsl. Forum, Washington, 1982—; tech. adv. Gov's. Office, Jefferson City, Mo., 1979-83; radiation cons. Oliver, Oliver, Waltz & Cook/Geo-Log, 1978. Vol. Mo. Nuclear Emergency Team, Jefferson City, 1979-83. Served with Md. Nat. Guard, 1970-71. Mem. Am. Nuclear Soc., ASME, Nat. Soc. Profl. Engrs., Tex. Soc. Profl. Engrs. Republican. Methodist. Current Work: Nuclear engineering, computer code development regarding nuclear fuel management physics and economics, and simulations of nuclear power plant incident emergency response. Subspecialties: Nuclear engineering; Nuclear fission. Home: 5633 N Colony Blvd The Colony TX 75056 Office: UCCEL Corp 1930 Hi Line Dr Dallas TX 75207

FLUM, ROBERT SAMUEL, SR., physicist; b. Indpls., July 3, 1925; s. Martin William and Maude (Schenck) F.; m. Rosemarie Cinkoski, July 19, 1947; chldren—Robert Samuel, William M., Catherine A., Christine M., Stephen F., Martin E., Thomas J. B.S. in Physics, Ind. U., 1949, M.S. in Physics, 1956; postgrad. U. Calif.-Berkeley, 1947-48, U. Md., 1951-55. Physicist, Naval Ordnance Lab., White Oak, Md., 1951-55; aero-hydrodynamisist Naval Ordnance Lab., 1955-61; physicist, staff U. Chgo., 1961-63; sr. analyst Naval Ordnance Lab., 1963-75; phys. scientist Space and Warfare Systems Command, Dept. Navy, Washington, 1975—; hydrodynamicist Dept. Navy, Washington, 1965—, ASW modelling staff, 1969—, arctic coordinator, 1981—. Patentee in field. Contbr. articles to profl. jours. Caretaker St. Mary's Historic Cath. Ch., Rockville, Md., 1963—. Served with U.S. Army, 1943-45. Cottrell Research Corp. fellow, 1950; recipient Superior Accomplishment award, Navy Dept., 1961, others. Mem. Ops. Research Soc. Am., Am. Phys. Soc., Mil. Ops. Research Soc., Sigma Pi Sigma. Current work: Analyze and provide solutions to anti-submarine warfare problems; computer simulation models, acoustics, databases, equipment performance and naval tactics. Subspecialties: Anti-submarine warfare; Database systems. Home: 11603 Georgetowne Ct Potomac MD 20854 Office: Naval and Space Warfare Systems Command Navy Dept Washington DC 20363

FLYNN, DANIEL LEE, medicinal chemist; b. Great Bend, Kans., Feb. 10, 1954; s. Kenneth Eugene and Willene Louise (Morrison) F.; m. Brenda Gayle Brubaker, Aug. 10, 1974; children—Emily Gayle, Mary Louise. B.S., U. Kans., 1977, M.S., 1980, Ph.D., 1981. Postdoctoral researcher Ind. U., Bloomington, 1981-83; sr. scientist Warner-Lambert Co., Ann Arbor, Mich., 1983—, chem. coordinator, 1984—. Contbr. articles to profl. jours. Putnam scholar, 1972-74; Dane G. Hansen Found. scholar, 1977; Summerfield scholar, 1975-77; fellow NIH, Sterling-Winthrop. Mem. Am. Chem. Soc. (div. medicinal chemistry, div. organic chemistry), Rho Chi, Phi Lambda Upsilon. Republican. Current work: Design and synthesis of medicinal agents; total synthesis of natural products. Subspecialties: Medicinal chemistry; Organic chemistry. Home: 2700 Lakehurst Ln Ann Arbor MI 48105 Office: Warner-Lambert Parke Davis 2800 Plymouth Rd Ann Arbor MI 48105

FLYNN, GEORGE WILLIAM, chemistry educator; b. Hartford, Conn., July 11, 1938; s. George William and Rose Margaret (Tummillo) F.; m. Jean Van Alystine Pieri, Oct. 3, 1970; children: David, Suzanne. B.S., Yale U., 1960; A.M., Harvard U., 1962, Ph.D., 1965. Postdoctoral fellow M.I.T., Cambridge, 1964-66; asst. prof. Columbia U., N.Y.C., 1967-72, assoc. prof., 1972-76, prof. chemistry, 1976—; vis. scientist M.I.T., Cambridge, 1975; dir. Columbia Radiation Lab., N.Y.C., 1979—; research collaborator Brookhaven Nat. Lab., Upton, N.Y., 1969—. Sloan Found. fellow, 1968-70; Guggenheim Found. fellow, 1974-75; NSF fellow, 1960-64, 64-65. Mem. Am. Phys. Soc., Am. Chem. Soc., N.Y. Acad. Scis., Sigma Xi. Roman Catholic. Current Work: Application of lasers to the study of vibrational relaxation, chemical reactions and photofragmentation processes. Subspecialties: Physical chemistry; Laser photochemistry. Home: 382 Summit Ave Leonia NJ 07605 Office: Columbia U 116th St New York NY 10027

FODOR, GABOR BELA, chemistry educator, foundation researcher; b. Budapest, Hungary, Dec. 5, 1915; came to U.S., 1969, naturalized, 1976; s. Domokos Victor and Paula Maria (Bayer) F. B.S., Poly. Inst. Graz, Austria, 1934; Ph.D., U. Szeged, Hungary, 1937; D.Sc., Hungarian Acad. Sci., Budapest, 1952. Univ. demonstrator Lab. Organic Chemistry, Szeged, Hungary, 1935-38; research chemist Chinoin Pharm., Ujpest, Hungary, 1938-45; assoc. prof. chemistry U. Szeged, 1945-49, prof. organic chemistry, 1949-57; head Lab. Stereochemistry Hungarian Acad. Sci., 1958-65; prof. Laval U., Que., 1965-69; Centennial prof. W.Va. U., 1969—; cons., project dir. Nat. Found. Cancer Research, Bethesda, Md., 1977—. Author: Organic Chemistry, 1960, Organische Chemie, 1966; contbr. numerous articles to profl. jours. Recipient Kossuth medal Hungary, 1950, 54, Silver medal U. Helsinki, 1958; fellow Churchill Coll., Cambridge, Eng., 1961. Mem. Am. Chem. Soc., Chem. Soc. London, Swiss Chem. Soc., Hungarian Acad. Sci., Canadian Inst. Chemistry. Republican. Calvinist. Club: Lakeview Country (Morgantown). Patentee in field. Current Work: Synthetic organic chemistry, determination of the three dimensional structure of alkaloids, sphingosine, sugars; new reactions of vitamin C, related cancer research. Subspecialties: Organic chemistry; Synthetic chemistry. Home: 829 Augusta Ave Morgantown WV 26505 Office: West Virginia University Department of Chemistry Morgantown WV 26506

FODOR, MAGDA MARIA, engineer; b. Hungary, Sept. 21, 1942; d. Jeno and Edith (Gotz) F.; 1 son, Thomas. Ed. in Europe. Civil squad leader Am. Cyanamid Co., Wayne, N.J., 1974-76; sr. engr. Merck & Co., Rahway, N.J., 1976-77; project engr. Exxon Research and Engring., Florham Park, N.J., 1977-79; mem. tech. staff TRW, Redondo Beach, Calif., 1980-81; project engr. research and devel. Todd Pacific Shipyards Corp., San Pedro, Calif., 1981-83; aerospace engr. U.S. Air Force, Los Angeles, 1983-85; supervisory gen. engr. Dept. Navy, Long Beach, Calif., 1985—. Mem. Am Soc. Naval Engrs. Current Work: Worked for DOD-STS program at Vandenberg; also MX-program; research and development of robotics for U.S. Navy; Air Force B-1 B program. Subspecialties: Robotics; Aerospace engineering and technology. Office: Long Beach Naval Shipyard C-1362 Long Beach CA 90822

FOFONOFF, NICHOLAS PAUL, oceanographer, educator; b. Queenstown, Alta., Can., Aug. 18, 1929; came to U.S., 1962; s. Paul Alexander and Anna Dimitri (Malakoff) F.; m. Mabel Beryl Hutton Deckard, June 16, 1951; children—Paul Wynn, Stephanie Anne, Timothy Wayne, Nicholas David. B.A., U. B.C., Can.), Vancouver, 1950; M.A., 1951; Ph.D., Brown U., 1955. Postdoctoral fellow Nat. Inst. Oceanography, Eng., 1955-56; scientist Fisheries Research Can., 1956-62; sr. scientist Woods Hole (Mass.) Oceanographic Instn. 1962—, chmn. dept. phys. oceanography, 1967-71, 81-85; prof. practice of phys. oceanography, Harvard U., 1968—; asso. mem. Center for Earth and Planetary Physics, 1971—. Mem. AAAS. Research in studies of ocean currents by direct measurements from moored buoys and remote measurements from satellites. Home: 6 Greengate Rd Falmouth MA 02540 Office: Woods Hole Oceanographic Instn Woods Hole MA 02543

FOGG, THOMAS ROBERT, analytical/environmental chemistry educator, consultant; b. Alton, Ill., Apr. 30, 1952; s. Perry W. and Janet (Chambers) F.; m. Beverly Ann Kennedy, June 4, 1976; children—Matthew, Thomas. B.S., Hobart Coll., 1974; M.S., U. Conn., 1976; Ph.D., U. R.I., 1983. Research asst. U. R.I., Kingston, 1977-82; postdoctoral research assoc. Ctr. for Atmospheric and Chem. Studies, Narragansett, R.I., 1982-84; asst. prof. analytical and environ. chemistry U. Lowell, Mass., 1984—; cons. Leeman Labs., Inc., Lowell, 1984, Cambridge Analytical, ERCO, Cambridge. Contbr. articles to profl. jours. Mem. Lafayette Band, North Kingston, R.I., 1972-83. NSF grantee, 1978-80; Dept. Energy grantee, 1982-83. Mem. Am. Chem. Soc., Am. Geophys. Union, Soc. Applied Spectroscopy, Delta Chi (treas. 1973-74). Clubs: Narragansett Bay Blades Hockey, Old Tymers Hockey. Current work: Atmospheric chemistry: determination of the influence of the ocean on the atmosphere; budgets and cycles of B, Hg and other trace elements in the atmosphere, chemical tracers of acid rain. Subspecialties: Atmospheric chemistry; Chemical oceanography. Office: U Lowell Dept Chemistry One University Ave Lowell MA 01854

FOGLER, HUGH SCOTT, chem. engr., educator, cons.; b. Normal, Ill., Oct. 28, 1939; s. Ralph Waldo and Ann (Scott) F.; m. Janet Meadors, July 1, 1962; children: Peter, Robert, Kirstin. B.S., U. Ill., 1962; M.S., U. Colo., 1963, Ph.D., 1965. Registered profl. engr., Calif. Vis. scientist Nat. Center Atmospheric Research, 1965; mem. faculty U. Mich., 1965—, asst. prof. chem. engring., 1968-71, assoc. prof., 1971-75, prof., 1975—; research scientist Jet Propulsion Lab., Pasadena, Calif., 1966-68, cons. chem., petroleum engring. to industry. Author: The Elements of Chemical Kinetics and Reactor Calculations, 1974; Contbr. numerous articles to profl. jours. Served as capt. U.S. Army, 1966-68. Mem. Am. Inst. Chem. Engrs. (Detroit chpt. Chem. Engr. of Yr. 1980), Am. Chem. Soc., Am. Soc. Engring. Edn. Methodist. Current Work: Emulsion stability, dissolution catalysis, petroleum engineering. Subspecialties: Chemical engineering; Surface chemistry. Office: Dept. Chem. Engring U Mich Ann Arbor MI 48109

FOLEY, CRAY LYMAN, aerospace corporation executive; b. Tulsa, Apr. 15, 1927; s. Lyndon Lyman and Margaret (Cray) F.; m. Paula Ann Vincent, Nov. 30, 1957 (div. 1980); children: Kelly Ann, Jill, Cray, Seth. Student, U. Tulsa, 1945-46, 47-48; B.S. in Mech. Engring, Okla. State U., 1951, M.S., 1953. Registered profl. engr., Okla. Jr. research engr. Lockheed Aircraft Co., Burbank, Calif., 1951-52; engr. Sperry Gyroscope Co., Great Neck, N.Y., 1953-57; sr. staff engr. Lockheed Missile & Space Co., Inc., Sunnyvale, Calif., 1957—. Pres. Homeowners Assn., San Jose, Calif., 1964-65; com. chmn. Cub Scouts of Santa Clara County, San Jose, 1971-72; mem. Republican Nat. Com., Washington, 1971—. Mem. Soc. Automotive Engrs., Nat. Soc. Profl. Engrs., Am. Def. Preparedness Assn., AIAA, Okla. Soc. Profl. Engrs., Counsteau Soc. (founding). Current Work: Studies and new business proposals in support of the company's aerospace programs, both technical aspects and cost. Subspecialties: Mechanical engineering; Aerospace engineering and technology. Home: 7090 Galli Dr San Jose CA 95129 Office: Lockheed Missile & Space Co Inc 1111 Lockheed Way Sunnyvale CA 94086

FOLEY, MICHAEL GLEN, geologist, researcher; b. Independence, Mo., July 23, 1945; s. Roy Eugene and Joyce Helen (Luken) F.; m. Katherine Elizabeth Reynolds, June 1, 1968. B.S. in Engring., Calif. Inst. Tech., 1967, M.S. in Aeros., 1968, Ph.D. in Geology, 1976. Cert. profl. geoscientist, hydrologist. Research engr. Boeing Co., Houston, 1968-69; propulsion system analyst Jet Propulsion Lab., Pasadena, Calif., 1969-70; asst. prof. geology dept. U. Mo., Columbia, 1976-80; sr. geologist Battelle-Northwest, Richland, Wash., 1980-85, staff scientist, 1985—. Contbr. articles to profl. jours. Served to capt. USAF, 1972. Alfred P. Sloan Found. scholar Calif. Inst. Tech., 1963-67; Fannie and John Hertz Found. fellow, 1968. Mem. Geol. Soc. Am., Am. Geophys. Union, Brit. Geomorphological Research Group, Can. Nuclear Soc. Current work: Safety analysis of long-term storage of radioactive wastes and mill tailings, fluvial geomorphology, sediment transport and river mechanics, expert systems. Subspecialties: Hydrology; Remote sensing (geoscience). Home: 2305 Towhee Ln West Richland WA 99352 Office: Battelle-Northwest PO Box 999 Richland WA 99352

FOLGER, DAVID WINSLOW, marine geologist; b. Woburn, Mass., Nov. 21, 1931; s. Joseph Butler and Marion (Allen) (Folger); m. Joan Carol Throckmorton, June 30, 1956 (dec. Sept. 1980); children: Susan W., Peter F., John B.; m. Carolyn Gail Merrihew, Aug. 14, 1982. B.A., Dartmouth Coll., 1953; M.A., Columbia U., 1958, Ph.D., 1968. Petroleum geologist Chevron Oil Co., Jackson, Miss., 1958-63; postdoctoral investigator Woods Hole (Mass.) Oceanographic Inst., 1968-69; prof. Middlebury (Vt.) Coll., 1969-75; coordinator environ. studies, br. chief U.S. Geol. Survey, Woods Hole, 1975-82, marine geologist, 1982—. Served to lt. (j.g.) U.S. Navy, 1953-56. Fellow Geol. Soc. Am.; mem. Am. Geophys. Union, AAAS, Soc. Exploration Paleontologists and Mineralogists, Sigma Xi. Current Work: Geologic evaluation of continental margins and ocean basins. Subspecialties: Geology; Oceanography. Home: 19 Spartina Pl West Falmouth MA 02574 Office: Br of Atlantic Geology US Geol Survey Quissett Campus Woods Hole MA 02543

FOLINSBEE, LAWRENCE JOHN, physiologist, consultant; b. Vancouver, B.C., Can., Nov. 28, 1945; came to U.S., 1974, naturalized, 19—; s. John Allan and Agnes Emily (Colpitts) F.; m. Jane Elizabeth Furchner, Aug. 24, 1969; children—John Alan, Emily Jane. B.S., U. Oreg., 1967, M.S., 1969; Ph.D., U. Calif.-Davis, 1972. Postdoctoral fellow U. Toronto, Ont. Can., 1972-73, asst. prof., 1973-74; assoc. research physiologist U. Calif.-Santa Barbara, 1974-84; research physiologist Environ. Monitoring and Services, Chapel Hill, N.C., 1984—; cons. Am. Petroleum Inst., Washington, 1983-84; mem. editorial bd. Advanced Modern Environ. Toxicology, Toxicology and Indsl. Health, 1983—; book rev. editor Sports Medicine Bull., 1985—. Editor: Environmental Stress, 1978. Contbr. articles to profl. jours., chpts. to books. Mem. Can. Nat. Diving Team, 1966-67; pres. Cannon Green Condominium Assn., Goleta, Calif., 1980-84. Grantee EPA, 1975-83, NIH, 1980-83, Am. Petroleum Inst., 1984. Fellow Am. Coll. Sports Medicine; mem. Am. Physiol. Soc. Current work: Air pollution, human inhalation toxicology, control of breathing in exercise, exercise physiology, respiratory physiology. Subspecialties: Environmental toxicology; Physiology (medicine). Home: 227 Old Forest Creek Dr Chapel Hill NC 27514 Office: Environmental Monitoring 800 Eastowne Dr #200 Chapel Hill NC 27514

FOLK, STEWART HUNTLEY, geologist, consultant, researcher; b. Urbanette, Ark., Nov. 30, 1915; s. Harry Bright and Ethel Weller (Baker) F.; m. Mary Boyd, Feb. 3, 1940; children—Harry, William, Mary, Susan. B.A. with honors, Baylor U., 1936; M.S. in Geology, U. Iowa, 1938. Cert. profl. geologist.

Geologist various petroleum and mining cos. and gov. agys., Ill., Kan., Alaska, Tex., Mex., Italy and other countries, 1938-68; exploration mgr. Jefferson Lake Sulphur Co., Houston, 1968-70; cons. geologist petroleum and mining cos., Houston, 1970—; pres. Stewart Folk & Co., Houston, 1976—; mng. dir. Universal Minerals N.Z., Wellington, 1972—. Contbr. articles to profl. jours. Patentee in field. Served to lt. (j.g.) USN, 1944-46. Fellow Geol. Soc. Am.; mem. Am. Assn. Petroleum Geologists, Am. Inst. Profl. Geologists, AIME, Soc. Independent Profl. Earth Scientists. Republican. Current work: Exploration for and evaluation of petroleum, sulphur, and other energy and mineral resources, research and development of new and improved borehole mining methods. Subspecialties: Geology; Fuels. Home: 11907 Longleaf Houston TX 77024

FOLKERS, KARL AUGUST, chemist; b. Decatur, Ill., Sept. 1, 1906; s. August William and Laura Susan (Black) F.; m. Selma Leona Johnson, July 30, 1932; children—Cynthia Carol, Richard Karl. B.S., U. Ill., 1928, D.Sc., 1973; Ph.D., U. Wis., 1931; postdoctoral research, Yale, 1931-34; D.Sc., Phila. Coll. Pharmacy and Sci., 1962, U. Wis., U. Uppsala (Sweden), 1969. With Merck & Co., Inc., Rahway, N.J., summer 1933, 34-63, asst. dir. research, 1938-45, dir. organic and biochem. research, 1945-63, asso. dir. research and devel., 1951-53, dir. organic and biol. chem. research, 1953-56, exec. dir. fundamental research, 1956-62, v.p. exploratory research, 1962-63; pres., chief exec. officer Stanford Research Inst., Menlo Park, Calif., 1963-68, mem. council bd. trustees, 1971-74; courtesy prof. chemistry Stanford, 1963-68; Ashbel Smith prof., dir. Inst. Biomed. Research, U. Tex., 1968—; Baker non-resident lectr. in chemistry Cornell U., 1953; Regents lectr. UCLA, 1960; lectr. vitamin chemistry U. Calif., Berkeley, 1963; F.F. Nord lectr. biochemistry Fordham U., 1971; mem. sci. adv. com. Inst. Microbiology, Rutgers; chmn. symposium chmn. 3d Internat. Congress Pure and Applied Chemistry, Boston, 1971; adv. council dept. chemistry Princeton, 1958-64; Walter Hartung lectr. U. N.C., Chapel Hill; chmn., lectr. sect. 1 Isolation, Chemistry and Radioimmunoassay Nobel Symposium on Substance P, Stockholm, 1976; lectr. Tohoku U. Sch. Medicine, Japan, 1981, Assn. Advancement Med. Instrumentation, Washington, 1981, U. Athens, 1981; plenary lectr., chmn. sect. on chemistry of hypothalamic hormones 2d European Colloquim on Hypothalamic Hormones U. Tübingen, Germany, 1976; chmn., lectr. Internat. Symposium on Coenzyme Q, Japan, 1976; Burger lectr. U. Va., 1977; Plenary lectr. 500th Anniversary U. Uppsala, 1977; organizer, chmn. Gordon Research Conf. on Chemotherapy of Exptl. and Clin. Cancer, 1978; lectr. Ferring Symposium, Munich, 1979, Internat. Brain Research Symposium, Zurich, 1979; co-chmn., lectr. Internat. Symposium on Coenzyme Q, Tokyo, 1979; Dreyfus Disting. scholar Reed Coll., Portland, Oreg., 1981. Mem. editorial bd.: Jour. Molecular Medicine; Contbr. sci. jours. on organic chemistry. Trustee Gordon Research Confs., 1971-77. Recipient Am. Chem. Soc. award in pure chemistry, 1941, Spencer award, 1959; Julius Sturmer Lecture award, 1957; Perkin medal Soc. Chem. Industry, 1960; Nichols medal N.Y. sect. Am. Chem. Soc., 1967; Robert A. Welch Internat. award and medal for research on life processes, 1972; award in pharm. and medicinal chemistry Am. Pharm. Assn. Found. and Acad. Pharm. Scis., 1974; award Alexander von Humboldt-Stiftung, 1977; 2d S.W. Sci. Forum award, 1979; co-recipient Van Meter prize Am. Thyroid Assn., 1969. Mem. Nat. Acad. Sci., Am. Chem. Soc. (pres. 1962, Priestley medal 1986), Am. Soc. Biol. Chemistry, Am. Inst. Nutrition, Soc. Exptl. Biology, N.Y. Acad. Sci., Am. Soc. Biol. Chemistry, Am. Inst. Nutrition, Soc. Exptl. Biology and Medicine, A.A.A.S., Am. Inst. Chemists, Royal Swedish Acad. Engring. Scis. (fgn. mem.), Societa Italiana di Scienze Farmaceutiche (hon.), Sigma Xi (Phi Lambda Upsilon, hon.), Alpha Chi Sigma, Rho Chi. Methodist. Subspecialty: Biomedical research administration. Home: 6406 Mesa Dr Austin TX 78731

FOLLINGSTAD, HENRY GEORGE, mathematics educator, scientific researcher, consultant; b. Wanamingo, Minn., Jan. 6, 1922; s. Henry A. and Lottie R. (Johnson) F.; m. Helen Jane Chrislock, May 26, 1945; children: Nancy Ellen, Daniel Mark, Karen Joy, Sharon Ruth, Carl Martin. B.E.E., U. Minn., 1947, M.S., 1971. Mem. tech. staff Bell Telephone Labs., Inc., Murray Hill, N.J., 1948-62; instr. Augsburg Coll., Mpls., 1962-66; sci. research cons. Honeywell, Mpls. and St. Paul, 1964-81; asst. prof. Augsburg Coll., 1966-78, assoc. prof., 1978—; electronics research cons. North Star Research and Devel. Inst., Mpls., 1965-66. Contbr. numerous articles to profl. jours. Trustee Luther Coll. Bible and Liberal Arts, Teaneck, N.J., 1960-63; Bible lectr. Augsburg Coll., 1983, Central Luth. Ch., Mpls., 1969-71, 81-82. Served in USAAF, 1943-46. Mem. IEEE (sr.), Math. Assn. Am., Tau Beta Pi, Sigma Pi Sigma. Lutheran. Current Work: Mathematical-logical-physical absurdities, experimental interpretation errors, and inadequacies in Einstein special and general relativity, with space-age alternatives; abuses of mathematics in scientific-academic-social-theological areas, with space-age alternatives; math-model analyses of complex physical systems. Subspecialties: Applied mathematics; Relativity and gravitation. Home: 3506 Garfield Ave S Minneapolis MN 55408 Office: 731 21st Ave S Minneapolis MN 55454

FOLSE, DEAN SYDNEY, experimental pathologist, educator; b. Kansas City, Mo., Dec. 19, 1921; s. Charles D. and Belle (Stewart) F.; m. Jean DeMaster, June 8, 1947. B.S., Tex. A&M U., 1945, D.V.M., 1945; M.S., Kans. State U., 1946; Ph.D., U. Tex. Med. Br., Galveston, 1970. Assoc. prof. Auburn U., Ala., 1948-52, Kans. State U., Manhattan, 1952-66; histopathologist AEC, Vienna, 1966-69; assoc. prof. pathology and vet. medicine U. Tex. Med. Br., 1969—, dir. pathology edn., 1983—; cons. Fla. Inst. Tech., Melbourne, 1982—. Named Tchr. of Yr., U. Tex. Med. Br., 1982; recipient Golden Apple award, 1984; McLaughlin fellow, 1961. Mem. Internat. Acad. Pathology, Am. Soc. Pathologists, AAAS, Am. Soc. Lab. Animal Sci., AVMA. Lodges: Masons, Shriners. Current work: Lymphatic filariasis, leprosy, aquatic medicine. Subspecialties: Pathology (medicine); Dermatology. Office: Pathology Dept Univ of Tex Med Br Galveston TX 77550

FOLSOME, CLAIR EDWIN, microbiology educator; b. Ann Arbor, Mich., June 26, 1935; s. Clair Edwin and Leah (Carter) F.; m. T. Grubawicz, Sept. 26, 1956 (div. Nov. 1980); children—Russell Sage, Clair Edwin, Alexander Leo, Theodore James; m. Geraldine Virginia DeBeneditti, June 20, 1982; children—Cassandra Lea, Grant Kaina. A.B., Harvard U., 1956, M.A., 1959, Ph.D., 1960. Asst. prof. genetics Boston U., 1960-62; reader in genetics Melbourne U., Australia, 1962-64; prof. microbiology U. Hawaii, Honolulu, 1964—; v.p. Bio-Foods, Inc., Honolulu, 1982—. Author: Origins of Life, 1980. Editor: Life: Origin and Evolution, 1979. Contbr. articles to profl. jours. Research grantee NASA, 1972, NSF, 1972. Fellow Brit. Interplanetary Soc. (pres. 1972), Ecoculture Assn. Honolulu (pres. 1980—), Internat. Soc. for Study of Origin of Life, N.Y. Acad. Scis., Am. Genetics Soc. (pres. 1960). Clubs: Waikiki Yacht (Honolulu), Outrigger Canoe. Current work: Chemistry of the origin of the earliest cells. Studies on bioelement fluxes in closed ecologies. Subspecialties: Chemistry of the origin of life; Closed system ecology. Home: 1761 Halekoa Dr Honolulu HI 96821 Office: U of Hawaii 2538 The Mall Honolulu HI 96822

FOLWEILER, ROBERT COOPER, materials scientist; b. Tallahassee, Aug. 2, 1933; s. Alfred David and Gertrude Lillian (Cooper) F.; m. Helen Herbert Smith, Aug. 19, 1961; children—David, Sara, Robin. B.A., Rice U., 1955, B.S., 1956, M.S., 1958. Ceramist, Gen. Electric Research Lab., Schenectady, N.Y., 1959-61; v.p., lab. dir. Lexington Labs., Cambridge, Mass., 1961-68; prin. investigator Sanders Assocs., Nashua, N.H., 1968-79; sr. program engr. Microwave Assocs., Burlington, Mass., 1979-80; mem. tech. staff GTE Labs. Inc., Waltham, Mass., 1980—; vis. scientist MIT, Cambridge, 1970-74. Contbr. articles to profl. jours. Mem. fin. com. Town of Bedford, Mass., 1968-77, selectman, 1978-84, mem. conservation com., 1984—. Served to capt. U.S. Army, 1958-59. Recipient IR-100 award Indsl. Research mag., 1977; Hughes Tool scholar, 1955-56; Alcoa fellow, 1956-58. Mem. Am. Ceramic Soc., Am. Assn. Crystal Growth (sect. chmn. 1979-80), AAAS, Tau Beta Pi. Lodge: Lions (Tail Twister 1976-77). Current work: Research in preparation of high purity fluoride compounds and glasses; preparation optical materials by novel techniques. Subspecialties: Materials processing; High temperature chemistry. Home: 45 Wildwood Dr Bedford MA 01730 Office: GTE Labs Inc 40 Sylvan Rd Waltham MA 02254

FONCK, RAYMOND JOHN, physicist; b. Joliet, Ill., Nov. 1, 1951; s. Joseph H. and Rosalie M. (Ochs) F.; m. Rosalie Ann Migas, Aug. 22, 1977. B.A. with honors, U. Wis., 1973; postgrad., Princeton U., 1973-74; Ph.D., U. Wis., 1978. Research assoc. Plasma Physics Lab, Princeton U., 1978-80, research staff II, 1980-83; research physicist Plasma Physic Lab. Princeton U., 1983—. Contbr. articles to profl. publs. NSF grad. fellow, 1974. Mem. Am. Phys. Soc., Optical Soc. Am., AAAS, Union Concerned Scientists, Fedn. Am. Scientists, ACLU, Phi Beta Kappa, Phi Kappa Phi. Current Work: Plasma spectroscopy; optical instrumentation; tokamak diagnostics; plasma confinement Development of spectroscopic diagnostics for fusion plasmas. Atomic and plasma physics research in high temperature plasmas. Subspecialties: Nuclear fusion; Atomic and molecular physics. Office: Princeton Plasma Physics Lab PO Box 451 Princeton NJ 08544

FONER, SIMON, physicist; b. Pitts., Aug. 13, 1925; B.S., Carnegie-Mellon U., 1947, M.S., 1948, D.Sc., 1952. Research physicist Carnegie-Mellon U., 1952-53; staff physicist Lincoln Lab. MIT, Cambridge, Mass., 1953-61, project leader Francis Bitter Nat. Magnet Lab., 1961-77, chief scientist, head research div., 1977—, sr. research physicist dept. physics, 1982—; dir. Advanced Study Insts., NATO, 1970, 73, 76, 80. Editor: Superconducting Machines and Devices-Large Systems Applications, 1974; Magnetism-Selected Topics, 1976; Superconductor Applications, SQUIDS and Machines, 1977; Super-Conductor Materials Science-Metallurgy, Fabrication and Applications, 1981. Contbr. numerous articles to profl. jours. Patentee in field of magnetometry and supercondrs. Named Disting. Lectr. IEEE Magnetic Soc., 1982-83. Fellow Am. Phys. Soc. (mem. exec. com. 1984, divisional councillor condensed matter physics 1982-86, chmn. exec. com. 1978-81). Current work: Condensed matter physics, superconductivity, magnetism, high magnetic fields, magnetometry. Subspecialties: Condensed matter physics; Magnetic physics. Office: Francis Bitter Nat Magnet Lab MIT 170 Albany St NW14-3117 Cambridge MA 02139

FONSECA, ANTHONY GUTIERRE, chemist, research executive; b. Chattanooga, Mar. 31, 1940; s. David and Esther (Haven) F.; m. Carolyn Hughey, Aug. 14, 1965; children—Audrey, Carlton. B.A., U. Tenn.-Chattanooga, 1962; M.S., U. Ga., 1966, Ph.D., 1968. Research scientist Conoco Inc., Ponca City, Okla., 1968-75, sr. scientist, 1975-76, group leader, 1976-82, dir., Library, Pa., 1982-83, asst. mgr., acting dir., 1983—. Patentee in field. Mem. Am. Chem. Soc., AIME. Republican. Roman Catholic. Current work: Coal utilization, ash and sulfur removal and combustion; process development research for coal company; laboratory pilot plant and field projects. Subspecialties: Coal; Inorganic chemistry. Home: 2170 Meadowmont Dr Pittsburgh PA 15241 Office: Conoco Inc Coal Research Div 4000 Brownsville Rd Library PA 15129

FONTAINE, GILLES JOSEPH, physics educator; b. Levis, Que., Can., Aug. 13, 1948; s. Emilien Joseph and Marie Louise (Roy) F.; m. Francine Fortin, July 5, 1969; children: Marc-Andre, Julie. B.Sc., U. Laval, 1969; Ph.D., U. Rochester, 1973. Postdoctoral fellow U. Montreal, Que., Can., 1973-75, research assoc., 1975-76, asst. prof. physics, 1977-80, assoc. prof., 1980—; research assoc. U. Western Ont., London, 1976-77. Contbr. articles to profl. jours. Mem. Internat. Astron. Union, Am. Astron. Soc., Canadian Assn. Physicists, Canadian Astron. Soc. Current Work: Stellar structure and evolution, white dwarf stars, pulsating white dwarfs, dense matter, diffusion theory. Subspecialties: Theoretical astrophysics; Optical astronomy.

FONTANA, MARS GUY, engr.; b. Iron Mountain, Mich., Apr. 6, 1910; s. Dominic and Rosalie (Amico) F.; m. Elizabeth Frances Carley, Aug. 21, 1937; children—Martha Jane, Mary Elizabeth, David Carley, Thomas Edward. B.S., U. Mich., 1931, M.S., 1932, Ph.D., 1935, D.Eng. (hon.), 1975. Research asst., dept. engring. research U. Mich., 1929-34; metall. engr., group supervisor engring. dept. duPont Co., Wilmington, Del., 1934-45; prof., chmn. dept. metall. engring. Ohio State U., 1945-75, prof. emeritus, 1976, Regents prof., 1967—, Duriron prof., 1970-75; dir. Corrosion Center; supr. metall. research; dir. Worthington Industries, 1973—, mem. audit com., 1975—; research NASA, USN, USAF, Nat. Sci. Found., Alloy Casting Inst.; cons. engr. several pvt. and govtl. orgns. Author: Corrosion: A Compilation, 1957, Corrosion Engineering, 1967, 2d edit., 1978; contbr.: column Indsl. and Engring. Chemistry, 1947-56; also other tech. publs. Recipient distinguished alumnus citation U. Mich., 1953, Sesquicentennial award, 1967; Frank Newman Speller award in corrosion engring. Nat. Assn. Corrosion Engrs., 1956; Native Son award Iron Mountain (Mich.) Rotary Club, 1969; Neil Armstrong award Ohio Soc. Profl. Engrs., 1973; MacQuigg Teaching award Coll. Engring., Ohio State U., 1973; Mars G. Fontana Labs. at Ohio State U. named in his honor, 1981. Fellow Am. Soc. Metals (hon.; Gold medal 1979), Am. Inst. Mining, Metall. and Petroleum Engrs., Am. Inst. Chem. Engrs.; mem. Nat. Assn. Corrosion Engrs. (pres. 1952, editor Jour. Corrosion 1962-74), Electrochem. Soc., Materials Tech. Inst. of Chem. Process Industries (exec. dir. 1977—), Nat. Acad. Engring., Nat. Soc. Profl. Engrs., Am. Soc. Engring. Edn. (award for excellence in engring. instruction 1969), Sigma Xi, Tau Beta Pi, Alpha Chi Sigma, Iota Alpha, Phi Eta Sigma, Phi Lambda Upsilon, Sphinx, Texnikoi. Clubs: Port au Villa (Naples, Fla.) (pres. 1967-70); Faculty, Univ. Golf. Patentee on corrosion testing and recording devices, also iron ore reduction and corrosion resistant alloys. Current Work: Solving corrosion problems primarily in chemical industry. Subspecialty: Materials. Home: 2086 Elgin Rd Columbus OH 43221

FONTANA, PETER ROBERT, physicist, educator, cons.; b. Bern, Switzerland, Apr. 20, 1935; came to U.S., 1956, naturalized, 1970; married. M.S., Miami U., Oxford, Ohio, 1958; Ph.D., Yale U., 1960. Research assoc. U. Chgo., 1960-62; asst. prof. U. Mich., Ann Arbor, 1962-67; assoc. prof. Oreg. State U., Corvallis, 1967-74, prof. physics, 1974—; vis. prof. physics Swiss Inst. Tech., Lausanne, 1974-77, U. Tubingen, W. Ger., 1982. Author: Atomic Radiative Processes, 1982; also articles on atomic physics. Mem. Am. Phys. Soc. Patentee multi-detector intensity interferometer. Current Work: Atomic radiative processes; quantum optics; inter-atomic forces; atomic fine and hyperfine structure. Subspecialties: Theoretical physics; Atomic and molecular physics.

FOOTE, J(OEL) LINDSLEY, biochemistry educator; b. Cleve., Jan. 11, 1928; s. Joel Lindsley and Beth Eliza (Brainard) F.; m. Alice Lydia Tanner, June 16, 1951; children—Robert Lindsley, Karen Ann. B.S., Miami U., Oxford, Ohio, 1952; postgrad. Ohio State U., summer 1955; Ph.D., Case Inst. Tech., 1960. Tchr. high sch., Wilmington, Ohio, 1952-53, Springfield, Ohio, 1953-56; teaching asst. Case Inst. Tech., Cleve., 1956-58; NSF fellow, 1958-60; postdoctoral fellow U. Mich., Ann Arbor, 1960-62, researcher biochemistry, instr., 1962-65; faculty mem. Western Mich. U., Kalamazoo, 1965—, prof. chemistry, 1979—; book manuscript reviewer, cons., intermittently 1975—. Contbr. articles to profl. jours. Project dir. booklet: Eastern Equine Encephalomyelitis in Southwestern Michigan, 1982. Chmn. City of Kalamazoo Environ. Concerns Com., 1970-72; mem. exec. com. Kalamazoo County Democrats, 1968—; pres. Peoples Ch. Unitarian-Universalist, Kalamazoo, 1981-82. Served with USN, 1946-48. NIH research grantee, 1966-69. Mem. Am. Soc. Biol. Chemists, Am. Chem. Soc., AAAS, AAUP. Current work: Teaching biochemistry and chemistry for allied health professionals; developing a chemistry course for non-science students based on ingredients in food. Subspecialties: Biochemistry (medicine); Food science and technology. Home: 3623 Lancaster Dr Kalamazoo MI 49007 Office: Dept Chemistry Western Mich U Kalamazoo MI 49008

FORAL, RALPH FRANCIS, mechanical engineer; b. Omaha, June 18, 1934; s. Ralph Adolph and Alice Marie (Hakel) F.; m. Kathryn Margaret Gaffney, May 4, 1957; children: R. David, Michael J., Mary E., Jeanne M., James E. Student, Creighton U., 1952-53; B.S.M.E., U. Nebr., 1956; M.S., U. Colo., Boulder, 1958, Ph.D., 1963. Assoc. engr. to research specialist Martin Marietta Corp., Denver, 1956-64; assoc. prof. U. Nebr., Lincoln, 1964-72, prof. engring. mechanics, 1972—; cons. Brunswick Corp., Lincoln, 1965—. Recipient Skylab Achievement award NASA, 1974, 1st Shuttle Flight Achievement award, 1981. Mem. ASTM, ASME, Am. Soc. Engring. Edn., Am. Acad. Mechanics. Roman Catholic. Patentee in field. Current Work: Mechanics of composite materials, mechanical behavior characterization of fiber/epoxy composite materials, filament wound composite pressure vessels. Subspecialties: Solid mechanics; Composite materials. Home: 1836 Morningside Dr Lincoln NE 68506 Office: U Nebr Lincoln NE 68588

FORBES, RICHARD MATHER, retired nutrition educator and researcher; b. Wooster, Ohio, Jan. 8, 1916; s. Ernest Browning and Lydia Maria (Mather) F.; m. Mary Medlicott, Feb. 26, 1944; children—Sally Allen, Anne Mather, Stephen Harding. B.S., Pa. State U., 1938, M.S., 1939; Ph.D., Cornell U., 1942. Research asst. Cornell U., Ithaca, N.Y., 1939-42; instr. Wayne State U., Detroit, 1942; research fellow Cornell U., 1942-43; asst. prof. U. Ky., Lexington, 1946-49; assoc. prof. U. nutrition U. Ill., Urbana, 1949-55, prof., 1955-85; mem. peer rev. com. NIH, Bethesda, Md., 1975-78, U.S. Dept. Agr., Washington, 1979-82; mem. Nat. Research Council-Nat. Acad. Sci. com. on animal nutrition, Washington, 1956-72. Contbr. numerous articles to sci. jours. Recipient H.H. Mitchell award dept. animal sci. U. Ill., 1981. Served to capt. AUS, 1943-46. Fellow AAAS; mem. Am. Inst. Nutrition (Borden award 1984), Am. Soc. Animal Sci. (Bohstedt award 1968), Am. Chem. Soc. Republican. Mem. United Ch. of Christ. Clubs: Exchange (pres. 1970-71), Izaak Walton (pres. 1975-76) (Urbana). Current work: Requirements, metabolism, bioavailability of mineral elements by animals. Subspecialties: Animal nutrition; Biochemistry (biology). Home: 2005 S Vine St Urbana IL 61801

FORCE, CARLTON GREGORY, pulp and paper researcher; b. Gouverneur, N.Y., Aug. 5, 1926; s. Leon Henry and Christina (Hampton) F.; m. Rosalie Marie Gotham, June 20, 1953; children—Gregory Leon, Jeffrey Harold, Stuart Dale, Ralph Jon. B.S., Clarkson U., 1952, Ph.D., 1965; M.S., U. Ill., 1957; M.B.A., The Citadel, 1985. Research chemist, Merck & Co., Rahway, N.J., 1952-56; research chemist Esso Research, Linden, N.J., 1957-59; sr. research chemist Latex Fiber Industries, Beaver Falls, N.Y., 1959-67; research assoc. Westvaco Corp., Charleston, S.C., 1967—. Author: Emulsion Polymerization, 1976, 1982; Am. Chem. Soc. Symposium series. Patentee in field. Active Jefferson-Lewis council Boys Scouts Am., Beaver Falls, N.Y., 1959-67, Coastal Carolina council, Charleston, S.C., 1967-78; deacon Presbyterian Ch., Charleston, 1968-71, Mt. Pleasant, S.C., 1974-77. Served with U.S. Army, 1945-46. Mem. Am. Chem. Soc. Republican. Clubs: Hobcaw Yacht (bd. dirs. 1976-77); Square Dance (sec. 1984). Current work: Personally developed and successfully introduced unique surfactants currently commercially utilized in latex, soap and detergent and cosmetic products. Subspecialties: Polymer chemistry; Physical chemistry. Home: 299 Hobcaw Dr Mount Pleasant SC 29464 Office: Westvaco Corp PO Box 5207 North Charleston SC 29406

FORCE, ERIC RONALD, geologist; b. Cin., Sept. 23, 1943; s. Ronald Clarence and Winifred Amelia (Schnatz) F.; m. Lucy McCartan Owens, June 24, 1965 (div. Dec. 1980); children—Jason, Chandra; m. M. Jane Brandon Dodge, Dec. 5, 1981. B.A., Occidental Coll., 1965; M.S., Lehigh U., 1967, Ph.D., 1970; postgrad. U. Otago, Dunedin, N.Z., 1967-69. Geologist, U.S. Geol. Survey, Monrovia, Liberia, 1970-72, Reston, Va., 1973—. Editor: Geology and Resources of Titanium, 1976. Contbr. articles to profl. jours. Recipient Benchmark Papers award 1982; grantee Fulbright Found., N.Z., 1967-68, 75-76, Mem. Soc. Econ. Geologists (research com. 1984—). Current work: Geology of titanium and manganese resources, paleo-oceanography, provenance and dispersal of sediments, geology of Liberia and New Zealand. Subspecialty: Geology. Home: 656 Spring St Herndon VA 22070 Office: US Geol Survey Reston VA 22092

FORCE, RONALD C(LARENCE), psychologist, researcher; b. Toledo, Apr. 10, 1917; s. Rockwell Clarence and Anna Elizabeth (Briner) F.; m. Winifred Amelia Schnatz, Dec. 15, 1941; children: Eric R., Hugh B., Bryan P., Gregory M. B.A., Heidelberg Coll., Tiffin, Ohio, 1940; M.A., Miami U., Ohio, 1941; postgrad., U.Calif.-Berkeley, 1948-50, U. Tex.-Austin, 1952. Lic. psychologist, Kans. cert. health services provider in psychology Nat. Register Health Service Providers in Psychology. Commd. 2d lt. U.S. Army AC, 1947, advanced through grades to lt. col., 1961; clin. and research psychologist (3320th Retng. Group), Amarillo AFB, Tex., 1951-56, dir. clin. services, 1961-64; psychologist (Dept. Mental Hygiene), Lackland AFB, Tex., 1957-60; ret., 1964; clin. coordinator St. Francis Boys Homes, Salina, Kans., 1966-81, cons., dir. research, 1982—; dir. Test Systems, Inc., Wichita, Kans., 1972-82; cons. U.S. Army Rehab. Ctr., Ft. Riley, Kans., 1973—, Mem. Commn. on Ministry, Presbyterian Ch., 1984-85. Author, developer: Biographical and Personal Inventory, 1971; co-author, developer: Multi-Instrument Screen, 1959; contbr. articles to profl. jours. Bd. dirs., officer Salina Symphony Orch., 1977-82. Decorated Air Force Commendation Medal, 1954, 64. Fellow AAAS; mem. Am. Psychol. Assn., Fedn. Am. Scientists, Union Concerned Scientist. Democrat. Presbyterian. Current Work: Development of factorially-derived description/predictive instruments for early intervention, differential placement and treatment of behavior-disordered youth and young adults, feed-back directed treatment modification for optimum results. Subspecialties: Behavioral psychology; Corrections psychology. Home: 2811 Melanie Ln Salina KS 67401 Office: Saint Francis Boys Homes Inc PO Box 1340 509 E Elm St Salina KS 67402

FORCHHEIMER, OTTO L., refractories technologist; b. Nurnberg, Germany, Sept. 18, 1926; came to U.S., 1951, naturalized, 1961; s. Jakob E. and Dina (Neu) F.; m. Lesesne Bell, Aug. 24, 1957; children—Margaret, Richard. B.Sc., McGill U., 1947; Ph.D., Brown U., 1951. Research chemist U. Chgo., 1951-53; sr. research chemist Gen. Abrasive Co., Niagara Falls, N.Y., 1953-59; mgr. chem. div. Trionics Corp., Madison, Wis., 1959-62; dir. research J.E. Baker Co., York, Pa., 1962-80, v.p., tech. dir., 1980—. Contbr. articles to profl. jours. Sr. warden, vestry mem. St. John's Episcopal Ch., York; Inc. trustee Diocese of Central Pa., 1982—. Soc. Advancement Mgmt. fellow, 1970. Fellow ASTM (vice chmn. com. C-8, award of merit 1982); mem. Am. Ceramic Soc., Am. Chem. Soc. Current work: Management of refractories research laboratory. Subspecialties: Ceramic engineering; High-temperature materials. Home: 330 Pine Hill Ln York PA 17403 Office: J E Baker Co PO Box 1189 York PA 17405

FORD, BYRON MILTON, computer systems consultant; b. Hayden, Colo., Feb. 24, 1939; s. William Howard and Myrtle Oretta (Christian) F.; m. Shirley Ann Edwards, Sept. 4, 1958; children: Gregory Scott, Barry Matthew. B.S., Engring., Colo. U., 1964; M.S., Johns Hopkins U., 1971. Sr. mathematician Johns Hopkins U. Applied Physics Lab., Laurel, Md., 1964-79, cons. computer systems, 1979—. Mem. Ops. Research Soc. Am., Nat. Assn. Self-Employed. Current Work: Structured programming languages; data communications. Subspecialties: Mathematical software; Operations research (mathematics). Address: 6909 Redmiles Rd Laurel MD 20707

FORD, GEORGE D, physiology and biophysics educator; b. Morgantown, W.Va., Aug. 18, 1940; s. O. Rex and Eleanor M. (Barnett) F.; m. D. Margaret Shrader, June 19, 1965; children—Laura E., Timothy R. B.S. in Physics, W.Va. U., 1961, Ph.D. in Pharmacology, 1967; M.S. in Physics, Iowa U., 1964. Phys. testing engr. Allegheny Ballistics Lab., Cumberland, Md., 1961, design engr., 1962; postdoctoral fellow U. Rochester, N.Y., 1967-69; asst. prof. Med. Coll. Va., Richmond, 1969-76, assoc. prof. phyiology and biophysics, 1976—. Contbr. articles to profl. jours. and book. Pres. Mill Quarter Golf Assn., 1980-81, 84—; basketball scorekeeper Va. Commonwealth U., Richmond, 1979—. Fulbright Found. scholar Belgium, 1982-83. Mem. Am. Physiol. Soc., Biophys. Soc., AAAS, Phi Beta Kappa, Sigma Xi, Rho Chi. Current work: Excitation-contraction coupling in vascular smooth muscle, mechanisms and regulation of membrane transport, mathematical modeling. Subspecialties: Biophysics (biology); Biophysical chemistry. Office: Med Coll Va MCV Box 551 Richmond VA 23298

FORD, RICHARD EARL, plant virologist, educator; b. Des Moines, May 25, 1933; s. Victor S. and Gertrude (Headlee) F.; m. Roberta Jean Essig, June 20, 1954; children—Nina Diane, Linda Marie, Kent Richard (dec.), Steven Earl. B.S., Iowa State U., 1956; M.S., Cornell U., 1959, Ph.D., 1961. Undergrad. research technician Iowa State U., 1952-55, undergrad. tchr. botany, 1956; grad. research asst. plant pathology Cornell U., 1956-59, grad. research asst. virology tchr., 1959-61; research plant pathologist, asst. prof. U.S. Dept. Agr. and Oreg. State U., 1961-65; prof. plant virology, virus research Iowa State U., Ames, 1965-72; prof., head dept. plant pathology U. Ill., Urbana, 1972—, cons. agrl. improvement, Europe, Asia, S.Am., others. Editor: Jour. Phytopathology; contbr. articles to profl. jours. Mem. Am. Phytopath. Soc. (sec., councilor, pres. N.C. div., nat. pres. and v.p.), Assn. Dept. Heads of Plant Pathology in U.S. (chmn.), Sigma Xi (v.p., treas. U. Ill. chpt.), Phi Kappa Phi, Phi Sigma Gamma, Gamma Sigma Delta, Gamma Gamma, FarmHouse Frat. (nat. pres., Master Builder of Men award, tres. FarmHouse Found.). Clubs: Lions, Toastmasters. Current Work: Diagnosis of plant virus diseases, identification, purification, characterization and serology of plant viruses; virus-virus/virus-host interactions; physiology and biochemistry of disease; virus, fungal and bacterial interractions in disease. Subspecialties: Plant pathology; Plant virology. Home: 11 Persimmon Circle Urbana IL 61801

FORD, STEPHEN PAUL, reproductive physiologist, educator; b. Palo Alto, Calif., Oct. 11, 1948; s. Frank George and Rosemary (Bonnot) F.; m. Marsha Ann Ford, Sept. 12, 1970; children: Tamara Lynn, Joanna Christine, Jessica Gale. B.S., Oreg. State U., 1971, Ph.D., 1977; M.S., W. Va. U., 1973. Grad. research asst. dept. animal and vet. sci. W. Va. U., 1971-73; grad. research asst. dept. animal sci. Oreg. State U., 1974-77; research physiologist Roman L. Hruska U.S. Meat Animal Research Center, Clay Center, Nebr., 1977-79; prof. animal sci. Iowa State U., Ames, 1979—. Contbr. to profl. jours. Upjohn Co. grantee, 1980-81; NIH grantee, 1982-88; Iowa High Tech. grantee, 1984-87; U.S. Dept. Agr. grantee, 1985-88. Mem. Am. Soc. Animal Sci., Soc. Study Reprodn., Sigma Xi, Gamma Sigma Delta. Current Work: Role of the uterus and ovaries in potentiating conceptus survival in domestic animals; factors controlling uterine and ovarian blood-flow during the estrous cycle and early pregnancy in the ewe, cow, and sow. Subspecialties: Reproductive biology; Animal physiology. Home: 3317 Jewel Dr Ames IA 50010 Office: 11 Kildee Hall Iowa State U Ames IA 50011

FORD, WILLIAM KENT, JR., astronomer. Astronomy staff mem. Carnegie Inst. Washington. Recipient Watson medal Nat. Acad. Scis., 1985. . Office: Carnegie Instn Washington Dept Terrestrial Magnetism 5241 Broad Branch Rd NW Washington DC 20015*

FORD, WILLIAM TIBBETS, physicist, educator; b. Los Angeles, May 7, 1941; s. William Grimshaw and Helen Elizabeth (Tibbets) F.; m. Ann Margaret Weisblat, Mar. 20, 1970; children—Stephanie Louise, Alan Michael. B.A., Carleton Coll., 1963; Ph.D., Princeton U., 1967. Research assoc. Princeton U., N.J., 1967-69; research fellow Calif. Tech. Inst., Pasadena, 1969-72; asst. prof. U. Pa., Phila., 1972-76; assoc. prof. U. Colo., Boulder, 1976-81, prof., 1981—. Contbr. articles to profl. jours. U. Colo. faculty fellow, 1981-82. Mem. Am. Phys. Soc., AAAS. Current work: Experimental particle physics, especially weak interactions: electron-position annihilation, neutrino interactions, particle decays. Subspecialty: Particle physics. Home: 901 Miami Way Boulder CO 80303 Office: U Colo Physics Dept Box 390 Boulder CO 80309

FOREMAN, FREDRICK, chemist, researcher; b. Gary, Ind., Mar. 25, 1957; s. Ulysses and Joycelyn (Brown) F.; m. Shirley Letbetter, July 16, 1983. B.S. in Chemistry, Grambling State U., 1981. Chemist, Dow Chem. Co., Midland, Mich., 1978-79, Monsanto Co., St. Louis, 1981—. Mem. New Sunny Mount Missionary Bapt. Ch., St. Louis, 1982. Named Outstanding Chemistry grad. Grambling State U., 1981. Mem. Am. Chem. Soc., Nat. Orgn. for Profl. Advancement of Black Chemists and Chem. Engrs., Kappa Alpha Psi. Democrat. Current work: Synthesis of natural products that have biological activity as herbicides and fungicides; mass spectrometer operator. Subspecialties: Organic chemistry; Analytical chemistry. Home: 1141 Donnell St Saint Louis MO 63137 Office: Monsanto Co 800 N Lindbergh St Saint Louis MO 63137

FOREMAN, JONATHAN HALE, veterinarian, veterinary educator, researcher; b. Oakland, Calif., May 11, 1956; s. Robert Peyton and Frances (Owens) F. B.S., Coll. William and Mary, 1978; D.V.M. magna cum laude, U. Ga., 1981; M.S., Wash. State U., 1984. Lic. veterinarian Wash., Idaho, Va., Ky., N.C. Intern in equine medicine and surgery Wash. State U., 1981-82, resident in equine internal medicine, 1982-84; vis. asst. prof. N.C. State U., Raleigh, N.C., 1984-85; asst. prof. U. Ill., Urbana, 1985—. Contbr. articles to profl. jours. Judge various competitive horse events, 1977—; coach Middleburg-Orange County Pony Club, Va., 1977-79, Palouse Hills Pony Club, Moscow, Idaho, 1982-84. Mem. AVMA, Am. Assn. Equine Practitioners, Ga. Vet. Med. Assn., U.S. Combined Tng. Assn., Assn. Equine Sports Medicine, N.C. State Vet. Med. Assn., Phi Beta Kappa, Phi Eta Sigma, Phi Sigma, Phi Zeta, Gamma Sigma Delta, Phi Kappa Phi. Episcopalian. Club: Nat. Beagle. Current work: Practice and teaching of equine internal medicine; research in equine exercise physiology especially in adaptations to training. Subspecialties: Internal medicine (veterinary medicine); Animal physiology. Office: U Ill CVM 1008 W Hazelwood Dr Urbana IL 61801

FOREMAN, ROBERT DALE, neurophysiologist, educator; b. Orange City, Iowa, Apr. 27, 1946; s. Wilma Nellie (Wiersma) F.; m. Charlotte Ann Poppen, June 17, 1969; children—Matthew Jin, Nathan Jon. B.S., Central Coll., 1969; Ph.D., Loyola U., 1973. Postdoctoral fellow U. Tex.-Galveston, 1973-75; asst. prof., 1975-77; asst. prof. U. Okla., Oklahoma City, 1977-81, assoc. prof., 1981—; mem. clin. scis. sect. NIH, Bethesda, Md., 1982—. Contbr. articles to profl. jours. Vice pres. Our Lord's Community Ch., Oklahoma City, 1984. Recipient Research Career Devel. award NIH, Bethesda, 1979-84; U. Okla. grantee, 1984. Mem. Am. Heart Assn. (vice chmn. 1984), Internat. Assn. Study Pain, Christian Med. Soc., Soc. Neurosci., Am. Pain Soc., Am. Physiol. Soc. (com. program adv. 1982—). Democrat. Mem. Ref. Ch. in Am. Current work: Neural control of visceral pain especially related to cardiac pain; neural mechanism for relief of visceral pain. Subspecialties: Neurophysiology; Physiology (medicine). Office: Dept Physiology and Biophysics U Okla Health Sci Ctr Coll Medicine Oklahoma City OK 73190

FORER, ARTHUR HANAN, biology educator, editor; b. Trenton, N.J., Dec. 17, 1935; came to Can., 1972; s. Bernard and Rose Ethel (Forer) F.; m. Alexandra Engberg Westengaard, Dec. 18, 1964; children—Michael, David. B.Sc. in Biology, MIT, 1957; postgrad. U. Rochester, 1957-59, U. Wash., 1959; Ph.D. in Molecular Biology, Dartmouth Coll., 1964. Research asst. Cambridge U., Eng., 1966-67; lektor Odense U., Denmark, 1970-72; assoc. prof. biology York U., Downsview, Ont., 1972-75, prof., 1975—; mem. cell biology and genetics grant selection panel Natural Scis. and Engring. Research Council Can., Ottawa, Ont., 1976-78. Editor: Mitosis/Cytokinesis, 1981. Mem. editorial bd. Jour. Cell Sci., 1972-84, Canadian Jour. Biochemistry Cell Biology, 1982—, Cell Biology Internat. Reports, 1985—. Contbr. chpts. to books and numerous articles to profl. jours. Fellow Am. Cancer Soc., 1964-66, Helen Hay Whitney Found., 1967-70. Fellow Royal Soc. Can., Acad. Scis.; mem. Am. Soc. Cell Biology, Can. Soc. Genetics, AAAS, Sci. for Peace. Current work: Mechanism of force production during cell division; mechanisms of coordination (control) during cell division. Subspecialty: Cell biology. Office: York U Dept Biology Downsview ON M3J 1P3 Canada

FOREST, HERMAN SILVA, ecology educator, researcher, consultant; b. Chattanooga, Feb. 18, 1921; s. William Hirsh and Fannie (Schutzer) S.; m. Grace Marie Wyman, Apr. 5, 1963; children—Samuel, Benjamin. A.B., U. Tenn., 1942; M.S., Mich. State U., 1948, Ph.D., 1951. Instr., U. Tenn., Knoxville, 1954-55, research assoc., 1958-60; instr. U. Okla., Norman, 1955-58, research assoc. Med. Ctr., 1960-61; research assoc. U. Rochester, N.Y., 1961-65; prof. biology SUNY Coll. at Geneseo, 1965—; exchange scientist Nat. Acad. Sci., USSR, 1964, Czechoslovakia, 1980; adviser environ. issues N.Y. State Health and Environ. Conservation, 1965-74; prin. scientist Environ. Resource Ctr., Geneseo, 1968-80; nat. lectr. Am. Inst. Biol. Sci., 1971-72; fellow, nat. lectr. Scientists Inst. for Pub. Info., 1974; mem. staff EMS Engrs., Rochester, 1980—; vis. scholar SUNY, 1974—. Author: Jessie's Children, 1959; Handbook of Algae, 1954; also numerous articles, monograph and tech. reports in profl. jours. Impact analyst Monroe County (N.Y.), Environ. Mgmt. Council, Rochester, 1971-74; sci. adviser Ctr. for Environ. Info., Rochester, 1976—, Monroe County Parks, 1982, others. Served to 1st lt. U.S. Army 1944-46, 51-53. Mem. AAAS, Ecol. Soc. Am., Bot. Soc. Am., Phycol. Soc. Am., Internat. Assn. Aquatic Vascular Plant Biologists, Internat. Assn. for Great Lakes Research, N.Am. Lake Mgmt. Soc., Rochester Acad. Sci. (Centennial fellow 1980, treas. 1982-85). Democrat. Jewish. Current work: Application of lake management knowledge to Finger Lakes; also writing in both aquatic and terrestrial ecology and systematics. Subspecialties: Ecology (biology); Ecology (environmental science). Home: 19 Genesee Park Blvd Rochester NY 14611 Office: SUNY Coll Geneseo Geneseo NY 14454

FORGHANI, BAGHER, virologist; b. Bandar Anzali, Iran, Mar. 10, 1936; came to U.S., 1969; s. Baba and Jahan (Rahimi) F.; m. Nikoo Alavi, June 12, 1969; children: Niki, Nikta. Ph.D., Justus Liebig U., Giessen, W.Ger., 1965. Postdoctoral fellow Utah State U., 1965-67; asst. prof. Nat. U. Iran, Tehran, 1967-69; postdoctoral trainee Calif. Dept. Health Services, Berkeley, 1970-72, research specialist, 1972—. Contbr. chpt., articles to profl. publs. Mem. Am. Soc. Microbiology. Moslem. Current Work: Production and characterization of monoclonal antibodies to human immunoglobulin, varicella-Zoster virus and their application to diagnosis of viral infections. Subspecialties: Virology (medicine); Infectious diseases. Home: 134 Lombardy Ln Orinda CA 94563 Office: Calif Dept Health Virus Lab 2151 Berkeley Way Berkeley CA 94704

FORKEL, CURT EMIL, mechanical engineer; b. Cameron, Tex., Oct. 26, 1922; s. Curt Emil and Mary Louise (Baade) F.; m. Chloe Tidwell, Oct. 30, 1943; children: Kaye (Mrs. Keith Lawton Bentzen), Mary Candace (Mrs. Thomas Brame Wilkinson IV), Ruth Ann. B.S., U. Tex., 1944, postgrad., 1947; postgrad., U. Denver, 1946; M.S., U. Idaho, 1969. Registered profl. engr., Okla. Draftsman N.Am. Aviation, Dallas, 1943-44; instr. U. Tex., Austin, 1944-45, U. N.Mex., 1945-46; instr. U. Denver, 1946-47, asst. prof., 1947-48; metall. engr. Phillips Petroleum Co., Bartlesville, Okla., 1948-60, design group supr., Borger, Tex., 1960-63, Idaho Falls, Idaho, 1963-69, Idaho Nuclear Corp., Idaho Falls, 1969-71, Aerojet Nuclear Co., Idaho Falls, Idaho, 1971-76; sr. project engr. EG & G Idaho Inc., Idaho Falls, 1976-77, br. mgr. design rev. and cost estimating, 1977, design sect. supr., 1977-78, br. mgr. engring. support for nuclear energy programs, 1978-80, supr. design, 1980-81, sr. program specialist, 1981—. Republican precinct committeeman, 1963-64. Mem. ASME, Nat. Rifle Assn., Pi Tau Sigma, Phi Eta Sigma. Republican. Baptist. Clubs: Idaho Nuclear Sportsmen's, Acad. Model Aeronautics, Red Baron RC Modelers Ltd. Patentee pebble heater heat transfer apparatus. Current Work: Flow induced heat exchanger tube vibration; high temperature gas cooled nuclear reactor systems and components. Subspecialties: Mechanical engineering; Nuclear engineering. Home: 2306 Koro Ave Idaho Falls ID 83401 Office: PO Box 1625 Idaho Falls ID 83415

FORMAN, DAVID SHOLEM, neurobiologist; b. Detroit, Dec. 10, 1942; s. Louis B. and Gertrude (Baroff) F. B.A. summa cum laude, Harvard U., 1964; postgrad (Knox fellow), Cambridge U., 1964-65; Ph.D., Rockefeller U., 1971. Postdoctoral fellow Lab. Neuropharmacology NIMH, Washington, 1971-75, Sloan fellow, 1974-75; research physiologist Naval Med. Research Inst., Bethesda, Md., 1975-81; assoc. prof anatomy Uniformed Services U. of Health Scis., Bethesda, Md., 1981—. Contbr. articles to profl. jours. Recipient Golden Eagle award Council Internat. Nontheatrical Events, 1976, Spl. Merit award Naval Med. Research Inst., 1978, Fed. Sustained Superior Performance award, 1980, 81. Mem. Soc. Neurosci., Am. Soc. Cell Biology, Am. Soc. Neurochemistry, Am. Assn. Anatomists, Internat. Brain Research Orgn. Jewish. Current Work: Neurobiology: axonal transport, nerve regeneration, video microscopy, cell motility. Subspecialties: Cell biology; Neurobiology. Home: 4301 Mass Ave NW #1012 Washington DC 20016 Office: Dept Anatomy Uniformed Services U Health Scis 4301 Jones Bridge Rd Bethesda MD 20814-4799

FORMAN, DONALD T., biochemist; b. N.Y.C., Feb. 27, 1932; s. Jack and Fannie (Jaffee) F.; m. Florence Sporn, Aug. 22, 1953; children—Joan Diane, Steven Lawrence, Debra Helene. B.S., Bklyn. Coll., 1953; M.S., Wayne State U., Ph.D., 1959. Clin. biochemist Mercy Hosp. Med. Center, Chgo., 1959-63; dir. clin. biochemistry, asso. prof. biochemistry and pathology Evanston Hosp./Northwestern U. Med. Sch., Chgo., 1963-78; prof. pathology and biochemistry U. N.C., Chapel Hill, 1978—, dir. clin. chemistry, 1978—; cons. clin. chemist, industry and govt., 1965—. Editor: Clinical Chemistry, 1976. Served with AUS, 1953-55. Recipient Chgo. Clin. Chemists Creativity award, 1974; Mich. Heart Assn. fellow, 1957-59. Mem. Assn. Clin. Scientists (pres. 1973-74), Am. Assn. Clin. Chemistry (dir.), Am. Bd. Clin. Chemistry, Nat. Acad. Clin. Biochemistry, AAAS, AAUP, Sigma Xi, Phi Lambda Upsilon., B'nai B'rith. Jewish. Current work: Enzymology, tumor associated antigens, atherosclerosis; developing analytical biochemical procedures to diagnose disease; research in tumor markers; research in pathobiology of alcoholism. Subspecialties: Clinical chemistry; Pathology (medicine). Home: 2559 Owens Ct Chapel Hill NC 27514 Office: Dept Pathology U NC Med Sch Chapel Hill NC 27514

FORMAN, J(OSEPH) CHARLES, professional association executive, chemical engineer; b. Chgo.; s. Joseph O. and Marie Sophie (Smith) F.; m. Ursula Diane Weston, July 22, 1953; children—Stephen Charles, Diane Brigitte, Mary Erika. B.S., MIT, 1953; M.S., Northwestern U., 1957, Ph.D., 1960. Registered profl. engr., Ill. Agrl. Vet. dir. Abbott Labs., North Chicago, Ill., 1956-77; assoc. exec. dir. Am. Inst. Chem. Engrs., N.Y.C., 1977-78, exec. dir. and sec., 1978—. Editor: Am. Inst. Chem. Engrs. history book, 75 Years of Progress, 1983; contbr. articles to profl. jours. Mem. edit. council MIT, Lake Bluff, Ill., 1961—; chmn. Lake Bluff Plan Commn., 1973-77; pres. Lake County Sch. Bd. Assn., 1969-71; pres. Lake Bluff Bd. Edn., 1967-73. Served to capt. USAF, 1953-56. Numerous fellowships and grants Northwestern U. and NSF, 1956-59. Fellow Am. Inst. Chem. Engrs. (pub. jour. 1978—); mem. Am. Chem. Soc., Am. Assn. Engring Soc. (bd. dirs. 1980—), Council of Engring. and Sci. Soc. Execs. (bd. dirs. 1980-83, sec. 1983-84, v.p. 1984-85, pres. 1985-86), Nat. Soc. Profl. Engrs., Am. Soc. Assn. Execs., Tau Beta Pi, Sigma Xi. Club: Chemists (N.Y.C.). Current work: Former research and manufacturing interests in biochemical engineering, fermentation technology, antibiotics, and project management and plant construction. Subspecialty: Chemical engineering. Office: Am Inst Chem Engrs 345 E 47th St New York NY 10017

FORMAN, RICHARD ALLAN, physicist, consultant; b. Bklyn., Mar. 5, 1939; s. George Robert and Mildred Joy (Gleberman) F.; m. Gail Iris Mozarsky, Jan. 31, 1960; 1 child, Ross Geoffrey. B.S. in Physics, Poly. Inst. Bklyn., 1959; Ph.D. in physics, U. Md., 1965. Physicist, Nat. Bur. Standards, Washington, 1959-66; vis. scientist Brown U., 1966-67; physicist Nat. Bur. Standards, 1967-77; Comsc. fellow U.S. Dept. Def., Washington, 1977-78; sr. physicist Nat. Bur. Standards, Gaithersburg, Md., 1978—; mem. chmn. Greater Washington Solid State Physics Colloquium Steering Com., 1972—. Bd. editors Rev. Sci. Inst., 1980-82. Contbr. numerous articles to profl. jours. Patentee in field. Trustee Montgomery County Library Bd., Rockville, Md., 1976—, chmn., 1980-82. Mem. Am. Phys. Soc., Japan Soc. Applied Physics, AAAS. Current work: Optical spectroscopy, x-ray topography, x-ray diffraction, raman spectroscopy, EXAFS, transport properties of solids. Subspecialties: Condensed matter physics; Electronic materials. Home: 10213 Lloyd Rd Potomac MD 20854 Office: Nat Bur Standards A331 Tech Bldg Gaithersburg MD 20899

FORNACE, ALBERT JOSEPH, JR., medical researcher, pathologist; b. Phila., Pa., Apr. 5, 1949; s. Albert Joseph Sr. and Frances Helen (Langan) F.; m. Arlene V. Ferretti, Jan. 12, 1980; 1 child, Kimberly M. B.S., Pa. State U., 1970; M.D., Jefferson Med. Coll., 1972. Diplomate Am. Bd. Anatomic Pathology. Med. intern George Washington U. Hosp, Washington, 1972-73; research assoc. NIH, Bethesda, Md., 1973-75; research scientist, 1979—; pathology resident Peter Bent Brigham Hosp., Boston, 1975-78; research assoc. Harvard U., Boston, 1976-79. Contbr. articles to profl. jours. Served with USPHS, 1973-75. Mem. Am. Assn. Cancer Research, Radiation Research Soc. Current work: DNA repair in mammalian cells; molecular biology of cellular injury. Subspecialties: Radiation biology; Pathology (medicine). Home: 8207 Moorland Ln Bethesda MD 20817 Office: NIH Radiation Oncology Br 10/B3B69 Bethesda MD 20205

FORNBERG, BENGT, applied mathematics researcher; b. Halmstad, Sweden, June 8, 1946; came to U.S., 1974, permanent resident, 1978; s. Bertil and Eva (Friese) F.; m. Jennifer Margaret Horne, Apr. 9, 1974; children—Per E., Lenalisa M., Anders J. B.A., Uppsala U., Sweden, 1969, Ph.D., 1972. Fellow, CERN, Geneva, 1972-74; instr. math. Calif. Inst. Tech., Pasadena, 1974-75, asst. prof., 1975-80, assoc. prof., 1980-84; research assoc. Exxon Research and Engring Co., Annandale, N.J., 1984—. Co-author three books. Mem. editorial bd. Jour. Computational Physics, Computers and Math. Contbr. articles to profl. jours. Guggenheim fellow Cambridge U., Eng. 1981-82. Current work: Numerical analysis, computational fluid dynamics, supercomputers. Subspecialties: Numerical analysis (mathematics); Fluid mechanics. Home: PO Box 175 Stanton NJ 08885 Office: Exxon Research and Engring Co LF-362 Annandale NJ 08801

FORNEY, GEORGE DAVID, JR., electronics company executive; b. N.Y.C., Mar. 6, 1940; s. George D. Forney and Priscilla (Brush) Forney McDonnell; m. Harriett Bascom, June 9, 1962; children—Mark H., Priscilla Jean, William McD. B.S.E., Princeton U., 1961; M.S., MIT, 1963, Sc.D., 1965. Mem. tech. staff Codex Corp., Watertown, Mass., 1965-70, v.p. research, Newton, Mass., 1970-75, v.p. research and devel., 1975-79, v.p. research, Mansfield, Mass., 1979-82; v.p., dir. tech. and planning Motorola ISG, Mansfield, 1982—. Contbr. articles to various publs. Patentee in field. Fellow IEEE; mem. Nat. Acad. Engring. Subspecialty: Electronics. Office: Motorola ISG 20 Cabot Blvd Mansfield MA 02048

FORNSHELL, RANDALL DOUGLAS, analytical chemist; b. Wichita, Kans., Jan. 28, 1956; s. Gale Edward and Betty Jane (Wheeler) F.; m. Sharon Kay Mills, June 15, 1979; 1 child, Ashley Megan. B.S. in Adminstrn. of Justice, Wichita State U., 1979, B.S. in Chemistry, 1982. Analytical chemist, owner Heuristech Labs., Wichita, Kans., 1983—, Means Labs., Inc., Wichita, 1979-83; analytical chemist Wichita Water and Wastewater Lab., 1983—. Mem. Am. Chem. Soc. Democrat. Lutheran. Current work: Trace analysis of environmental pollutants, matrix isolation to improve the quality of trace analysis results and methods developement; natural gas and liquified petroleum gas analysis. Subspecialties: Analytical chemistry; Environmental chemistry. Home: 4000 Clarendon St Wichita KS 67220 Office: Water-Wastewater Lab 1815 Pine St Wichita KS 67202

FORREST, HUGH SOMMERVILLE, zoology educator; b. Glasgow, Scotland, Apr. 28, 1924; came to U.S., 1951; s. Archibald and Margaret Watson (Peden) F.; m. Rosamond Scott Baker, June 12, 1953; children: Eleanor Scott, Anne Sommerville, Hugh Watson. B.S. with honors, U. Glasgow, 1944; Ph.D., U. London, 1947; D.Sc., 1970; Ph.D., U. Cambridge, 1951. Research scientist Med. Research Council Gt. Britain, 1947-51; research fellow Calif. Inst. Tech., Pasadena, 1951-54, sr. research fellow, 1954-55; research scientist U. Tex., Austin, 1955-56, asso. prof., 1956-63, prof. zoology, 1963—, chmn. dept., 1974-78. Editor: Biochemical Genetics, 1971—; Contbr. articles to profl. jours. Carnegie scholar, 1944-45; Gt. Britain Dept. Sci. and Indsl. Research fellow, 1948-51; USPHS research fellow, 1951-53; spl. research fellow, 1973; numerous research grants NSF; numerous research grants USPHS; numerous research grants Robert A. Welch Found. Fellow Royal Soc. Edinburgh, Royal Chem. Soc.; mem. Am. Chem. Soc., Soc. Gen. Physiologists, Soc. Biol. Chemists. Current Work: Biochemistry of new coenzyme, methoxatin, from methane-oxidizing baceteria; biochemistry of development; insect pigments. Subspecialties: Biochemistry (biology); Gene actions. Home: 3302 River Rd Austin TX 78703

FORRESTER, A(LVIN) THEODORE, physics researcher, educator; b. N.Y.C., Apr. 13, 1918; s. Joseph David and Rose Marian (Kissen) Finkelstein; m. Joy Levin, June 24, 1948 (dec. July 1954); children—Bruce Hyman, Cheri Joy; m. June Doris Berg, Oct. 5, 1956 (div. Nov. 1973); children—William Charles, Susan Joan. A.B., Cornell U., 1938, A.M., 1939, Ph.D., 1942. Research assoc. U. Calif. Radiation Lab., Berkeley, 1942-45; asst.. then assoc. prof. physics U. So. Calif., Los Angeles, 1946-55; physicist Westinghouse Research Labs., Pitts., 1955-58; dept. mgr. Electro-optical Systems, Inc., Pasadena, 1959-68; prof. physics U. Calif.-Irvine, 1965-67, UCLA, 1967—; cons. TRW, Northrop, Rockwell Atomics Internat., Meret Inc., Phrasor Sci., Los Angeles, 1965—. Contbr. articles to tech. jours. Patentee high current cathode, discharge neutralizer, laser communications. Recipient Ann. Research award AIAA, 1962. Fellow Am. Phys. Soc., IEEE; mem. AAUP, AAAS. Current work: generation and propagation of intense ion beams. Subspecialty: Plasma physics. Home: 11525 Ohio Ave Apt 4 Los Angeles CA 90025 Office: UCLA 7731 Boelter Hall Los Angeles CA 90024

FORSHEY, CHESTER GENE, pomologist, educator; b. Lower Salem, Ohio, Mar. 21, 1925; s. James Hammond and Carrie Opal (Corum) F.; m. Lorraine Clair Sweetland, Oct. 20, 1956; children—Douglas, Gregory, Patricia, Debra. B.S. in Horticulture, Ohio State U., 1950, Ph.D. in Horticulture, 1954. From asst. prof. to assoc. prof. horticulture N.Y. State Agr. Expn. Sta. Hudson Valley Labs, Highland, 1954-66, prof., 1966—, supt., 1968—; cons. Rockefeller Found., Santiago, Chile, 1963-64; spl. cons. Fundacion Chile, Santiago, 1980-83. Contbr. articles to profl. jours. Served to QM 2/C USN, 1943-46, PTO. Mem. Am. Soc. Hort. Sci., Am. Chem. Soc. Methodist. Club: University (sec. 1984—) (Poughkeepsie). Current work: Relationship between fruiting and vegetative growth in deciduous fruit trees. Subspecialties: Plant growth; Pomology. Home: 3 Circle Dr Hyde Park NY 12538 Office: Hudson Valley Lab PO Box 727 Highland NY 12528

FORSLUND, DAVID WALLACE, physicist; b. Ukiah, Calif., Feb. 18, 1944; s. Dero Bradford and Myrtle Ruth (Conner) F.; m. Jean Carolyn Monson, Aug. 17, 1968; children: Daniel, Luke. B.S., U. Santa Clara, 1964; M.A., Princeton U., 1967, Ph.D., 1969. Postdoctoral fellow Los Alamos Sci. Lab., 1969-71, mem. staff, 1971-77, assoc. group leader, 1977-78, alt. group leader, 1978-80, fellow, 1981—. Contbr. articles to profl. jours; assoc. editor: Physics of Fluids, 1982-84. Ruling elder Presbyn. Ch. in Am., 1975—. Recipient Disting. Performance award Los Alamos Nat. Lab., 1982. Fellow Am. Phys. Soc; mem. Am. Geophys. Union, Am. Astron. Soc., Astron. Soc. of Pacific. Current Work: Inertial confinement fusion, laser interaction with matter, plasma simulation methods, space plasma physics. Subspecialties: Plasma physics; Theoretical physics. Home: 309 Aragon Ave Los Alamos NM 87544 Office: Los Alamos Nat Lab MS E531 Los Alamos NM 87545

FORTIER, CLAUDE, medical scientist, physiology educator; b. Montreal, Que., Can., June 11, 1921; s. Carolus and Flore-Edith (Lanctôt) F.; m. Elise Gouin, Sept. 8, 1953; children: Anne, Michele, Nicole, Nathalie. B.A., U. Montreal, 1941, M.A. in Polit. Sci, 1941, M.D., 1948, Ph.D., 1952, D.U. (hon.), 1981; LL.D. (hon.), Dalhousie U., 1977; D.U., Ottawa U., 1981. Research asst. U. Montreal Inst. Exptl. Medicine and Surgery, 1948-51; research cons. U. Lausanne, Switzerland, 1952-53; research asso. dept. neuroendocrinology U. London, 1953-55; asso. prof. physiology, dir. neuroendocrine research lab. Baylor U. Coll. Medicine, 1955-60; dir. endocrine lab. Laval U., Quebec, Que., Can., 1960—, prof. exptl. physiology, 1961—, chmn. dept. physiology, 1964-84; mem. Med. Research Council Can., 1963-68, 70-72, vice chmn., 1965-67; chmn. study group on med. research, Govt. Que., 1968-70; vice chmn. med. research coordinating, adv. coms. Def. Research Bd. Can., 1967-70; chmn. Can. nat. com. Internat. Union Physiol. Scis., 1969-72; cons. physician Laval U. Med. Center, 1968—; mem. Killam com. Can. Council, 1967-72, Que. Med. Research Council, 1963-70; chmn. bd. Canadian Fedn. Biol. Socs., 1973-74; mem. neuroendocrinology panel IBRO, UNESCO, 1958—; advisory council Order of Can., 1974-75; chmn. Sci. Council Can., 1978-81, vice chmn., 1975-78, chmn. task force on research in Can., 1976-78; asso. Humanities and Social Scis. Research Council Can., 1981-82. Trustee Inst. Research in Pub. Policy, 1974-75, 78-81. Decorated companion Order of Can., 1970, Knight comdr. Malta, 1985; recipient Archambault Research award French Canadian Assn. Advancement Sci., 1972; Sci. award Govt. Que., 1972; Wightman award Gairdner Found., 1979; Marie-Victorin sci. award Govt. of Que., 1980; sci. achievement award French Can. Med. Assn., 1982. Fellow Royal Soc. Can. (pres. 1974-75; McLaughlin medal 1984), Royal Coll. Physicians Can.; mem. Can. Physiol. Soc. (pres. 1966-67), Am. Physiol. Soc., Endocrine Soc., Am. Thyroid Soc., AAAS, N.Y. Acad. Sci., Soc. Exptl. Biology and Medicine, Assn. Am. Physicians, Biomed. Engring. Soc., Peripatetic Club, Can. Soc. Clin. Investigation, Internat. Soc. Neuroendocrinology, Can. Soc. Endocrinology and Metabolism (Career Achievement award 1985), Assn. Sci., Engring. and Tech. Communities Can. (hon.), Can. Assn. Club of Rome. Research, publs. neurohumoral control adenohypophysial functions, pituitary-thyroid-adrenocortical interactions, biostatistics, bio-control systems, role plasma steroid-binding proteins, boundaries of knowledge, science policy. Current Work: Science policy; medical education; consultant in endocrinological research (endocrine bio-controls). Subspecialties: Endocrinology; Neuroendocrinology. Home: 1014 DeGrenoble St Quebec PQ G1V 2Z9 Canada Faculty Medicine Laval U Quebec PQ G1K 7P4 Canada

FOSTER, CHARLES STEPHEN, physician, surgeon, educator; b. Charleston, W.Va., May 19, 1942; s. Carson and Martha F.; 1 child, Marc David. B.S., Duke U., 1965, M.D., 1969. Diplomate: Am. Bd. Ophthalmology. Intern Duke U., 1969-70; resident in ophthalmology Washington U., St. Louis, 1972-75; fellow in cornea and immunology Harvard U., 1975-77, instr. ophthalmology, 1976-79, asst. prof., 1979-82, assoc. prof., 1982—; dir. immunology and uveitis unit Harvard U.-Mass. Eye and Ear Infirmary, 1981—, dir. Hilles Immunology Lab., 1984—; dir. immunopathology lab. Eye Research Inst., 1977-84. Contbr. articles to profl. jours. Served with USPHS, 1970-72. Fellow ACS; mem. AMA, Am. Acad. Ophthalmology, Mass. Med. Soc., New Eng. Ophthal. Soc., Am. Soc. Immunology, Royal Soc. Medicine, Phi Beta Kappa, Sigma Xi, Alpha Omega Alpha. Current Work: Ocular immunology; immunoregulation in the eye, corneal transplantation; diagnosis and therapy of autoimmune diseases affecting the eyes; ocular microsurgery. Subspecialties: Ophthalmology; Immunology (medicine). Home: 348 Glen Rd Weston MA 02193 Office: 243 Charles St Boston MA 02114

FOSTER, EDWIN MICHAEL, microbiologist, educator, consultant; b. Alba, Tex., Jan. 1, 1917; s. Edward Lee and Katherine (Ryan) F.; m. Winona Lively, Apr. 25, 1941; 1 son, Michael Stewart. B.A., North Tex. State Tchrs. Coll., Denton, 1936, M.A., 1937; Ph.D., U. Wis., 1940. Instr. microbiology U. Wis., Madison, 1940-41, asst. prof., 1945-46, assoc. prof., 1946-52, prof., 1952—; instr. U. Tex., Austin, 1941-42, cons. in field. Author: with others Dairy Microbiology, 1957; contbr. numerous articles to profl. jours. Served to capt. Chem. Corps U.S. Army, 1942-45. Recipient Pasteur award Ill. Soc. Microbiology, 1969; W.O. Atwater lectr. U.S. Dept. Agr., 1982. Fellow Am. Acad. Microbiology (pres. 1965-66), Inst. Food Technologists (Nicholas Appert award 1969); mem. Am. Soc. Microbiology (pres. 1969-70), Internat. Assn. Milk and Food Sanitation, Toxicology Forum (dir. 1980-87). Club: Cosmos. Current Work: I am director of a research institute that is totally involved in food safety investigations; with a faculty of nine we have major research projects in all the principal areas of food borne disease. Subspecialties: Microbiology; Food science and technology. Home: 1111 Amherst Dr Madison WI 53705 Office: University of Wisconsin 1925 Willow Dr Madison WI 53706

FOSTER, NEIL ROBERT, agricultural engineering company executive; b. N.Y.C., Nov. 15, 1934; s. Edward DeVorkin and Eleanor (Steiner) F.; m.

Sandra Rothman, Aug. 1957 (div. 1973); children—Seth Allen, Lauren Sue. A.B. in Sci., SUNY-Farmingdale, 1954; B.S., U. Ga., 1956; M.S., L.I. U., 1960. Regional sales mgr. Spot Systems, Atlanta, 1974-78; v.p. mktg. Bermad, 1978-82; pres. NRF Assocs. Co., Atlanta, 1982—. Author chpt. in ACS Jour. Yearbook, 1979; also articles in mags. Leader Greater N.Y. and Atlanta area councils Boy Scouts Am., 1957-84. Recipient Scouters award Boy Scouts Am., 1957. Mem. Am. Soc. Agrl. Engrs., Am. Water Works Assn., Irrigation Assn., Ga. Irrigation Assn., Fla. Irrigation Soc. Club: Atlanta Radio (treas. 1982-83, pres. 1984-85). Lodge: Masons. Current work: Low flow (drip) irrigation, micro irrigation. Subspecialty: Agricultural engineering. Office: NRF Assocs Ltd PO Box 29276 Atlanta GA 30359

FOTI, JOHN THOMAS, mechanical engineer; b. N.Y.C., Oct. 27, 1934; s. Michele and Rose (Luca) F.; m. Rosaline Michie, Feb. 23, 1957; children—Lauren, Thomas, John. Student Poly. Inst. N.Y., 1951-53, 58-61; B.S. in Mech. Engring., Politecnica de Buenos Aires, Argentina, 1969. With CE-TEC Internat., Stamford, Conn., 1976-79; pres. Lummus Operating Assocs., Bloomfield, N.J., 1979-81; pres. Burns & Roe-Humphreys & Glasgow Synthetic Fuels, Oradell, N.J., 1981-82, Burns & Roe Indsl. Services Corp., Oradell, 1982—; dir. Roe Engring. Inc., Oradell, Tech Systems Inc., Stamford, Conn.; mem. adv. bd. Pitts. Coal Conf., 1985—. Inventor spreader stoker improvement, 1970. Served to 1st lt. U.S. Army, 1953-55, Korea. Mem. Am. Nuclear Soc., Licensing Exec. Soc., Internat. Execs. Soc., Societya de Ingomeria de Argentina. Republican. Roman Catholic. Club: White Beeches (Haworth, N.J.). Current work: Revenue enhancement for engineering firms; solid waste management. Subspecialties: Mechanical engineering; Solid waste management. Office: Burns & Roe Indsl Services Corp 700 Kinderkamack Rd Oradell NJ 07649

FOTOPOULOS, SOPHIA STRATHOPOULOS, life science executive; b. Kansas City, Mo., Nov. 6, 1936; d. C. Marinos G. and Stauroula F. Stathopoulos. B.A., U. Kans., Lawrence, 1958, M.A., 1964, Ph.D., 1970. Research asst. U. Kans. Med. Center, Kansas City, 1958-61; NIH research fellow U. Kans., Lawrence, 1962-64; research assoc. Inst. Community Studies, Kansas City, Mo., 1965-66; lectr. U. Kans., Lawrence, 1969-70, adj. prof., 1975—; dir. Psychophysiology-Psychopharmacology Lab., Greater Kansas City Mental Health Found., 1970-73; staff assoc. neuropsychophysiology Midwest Research Inst., Kansas City, Mo., 1974-75, head psychophysiology lab., 1975-77, assoc. dir. chem. scis. div., 1977-79, dir. life scis. dept., 1979—; mem. spl. rev. com. Nat. Cancer Inst., Kansas City, Mo., 1978—; mem. nat. adv. com. Am. Cancer Soc., Kansas City, 1982—; lectr. U. Mo.-Kansas City Sch. Medicine, 1970—; NIH research fellow, 1963-64, Health and Human Services research fellow, 1965-69. Contbr. articles in field to profl. jours. Recipient Creative Scientist award Am. Inst. Research, 1971. Mem. Claude Bernard Soc., AAAS, N.Y. Acad. Scis., Sigma Xi. Club: Zonta (Kansas City, Mo) (pres. 1983—). Current Work: Medical and health research related to in vitro and in vivo metabolism studies, carcinogenesis and mutogenesis, psychophysiology; human factors and performance, effects of drugs on pharmacological and biochemical mechanisms, biochemical psychophysiological and neuroimmunologic aspects of disease onset and treatment, biodetection and toxicology of toxic substances, cell biology, microbial biochemistry and neurosciences. Subspecialty: Psychophysiology. Office: Midwest Research Inst 425 Volker Blvd Kansas City MO 64110

FOULKES, DAVID, research psychologist, educator; b. East Orange, N.J., May 29, 1935; s. Paul Bergen and Alice (Hinson) F.; m. Nancy Helen Kerr, Apr. 19, 1978; children: Alice, Anne, William, Thomas, Sarah. B.A., Swarthmore Coll., 1957; Ph.D., U. Chgo., 1960. Instr. Lawrence Coll., Appleton, Wis., 1960-63; research assoc. U. Chgo., 1963-64; from asst. prof. to prof. psychology U. Wyo., Laramie, 1964-77; prof. psychiatry Emory U., Atlanta, 1977—, adj. prof. psychology, 1977-83; dir. Cognition Research Lab., Ga. Mental Health Inst., Atlanta, 1977—. Author: The Psychology of Sleep, 1966, Grammar of Dreams, 1978, Children's Dreams, 1982; Dreaming: A Cognitive-Psychological Analysis, 1985. NSF grantee, 1965-70; NIMH grantee, 1970-74, 78-81; Nat. Inst. Child Health and Human Devel. grantee, 1970-75. Fellow Ctr. for Advanced Study in Behavioral Scis, AAAS; mem. Assn. for Psychophysiol. Study of Sleep (exec. sec. 1966-69), Midwest Psychol. Assn., Psychonomic Soc., Internat. Neuropsychol. Soc. Current Work: Information-processing models of dreaming; dream ontogeny. Subspecialty: Cognition. Home: 1420 Berkeley Ln Atlanta GA 30329 Office: 1256 Briarcliff Rd Atlanta GA 30306

FOUNDS, HENRY WILLIAM, JR., microbiologist, virologist, laboratory manager; b. Drexel Hill, Pa., Mar. 6, 1942; s. Henry W. and Elaine V. (Smargis) F.; m. Ferne A. Brunner, Nov. 6, 1971; children: Steven, Jeffrey, Jennifer, Sarah. B.S., Villanova U., 1964; M.S., U. Notre Dame, 1968; Ph.D., Rutgers U., 1981. Instr. Bayley-Ellard High Sch., Madison, N.J., 1964-68; mem. faculty County Coll. Morris, Randolph Twp., N.J., 1968-83, asst. prof., microbiology, 1971-77, assoc. prof., 1978-83; dir. Biotech. Products Group research and devel. Ventrex Labs., Inc., Portland, Maine, 1983—; cons. in field; research asso. Rutgers U. Mem. Am. Soc. Microbiology, Tissue Culture Assn., N.Y. Acad. Sci. Current Work: Study of early interactions of virus with host cells, of RNA virus-host cell interactions, cell growth research and development; infectious diseases research and development Subspecialties: Microbiology; Virology (biology). Home: 13 Hemlock Circle Scarborough ME 04074

FOUTS, GREGORY TAYLOR, psychology educator, media consultant; b. Logansport, Ind., May 22, 1943; emigrated to arrived Canada, 1974; s. Frederic Wagner and Mae (Vodicka) F.; m. Geraldine Janet Mattea, Aug. 19, 1967; children: Benjamin, Courtney. B.A., Ind. U., 1965; M.A., U. Iowa, 1968, Ph.D., 1970. Tchr. math. Paul Hadley Jr. High Sch., Mooresville, Ind., 1965-66; asst. prof. psychology U. Denver, 1969-74; assoc. prof. psychology U. Calgary (Alta., Can.), 1974-80; prof. U. Calgary, 1980—; pvt. practice psychology, Calgary, 1976—; cons. Royal Commn. on Violence in the Communications Industry, Province of Ont., 1976-77, Nat. Film Bd., Ottawa, 1978; bd. dirs. Can. Jour. Communications, Sask., 1982—. Host TV prodn.: Children and Television, 1980; contbr. numerous articles to profl. jours. Royal Commn. on Violence in the Communications Industry grantee, 1976-77; Alta. Environ. Research Trust grantee, 1977. Mem. Soc. Research in Child Devel., Am. Psychol. Assn., AAAS, Internat. Communication Assn., Internat. Assn. Applied Psychology. Current Work: Media technologies; media and education; communications science; media effects; impact of media technologies on society; socialization of children; emotional development. Subspecialties: Developmental psychology; Learning. Home: RR 1 Site 3 Box 10 Cochrane AB T0L 0W0 Canada Office: adrt Psychology U Calgary 2500 University Dr Calgary AB T2N 1N4 Canada

FOUTS, JAMES RALPH, pharmacologist, educator; b. Macomb, Ill., Aug. 8, 1929; s. Ralph Butler and Mary May (Lingenfelter) F.; m. Joan Laverne Van Dyke, June 20, 1964; children: Mary, Jeffrey, Carolyn. B.S. with highest honors (Merit Scholar), Northwestern U., 1951, Ph.D., 1954; M.Div. with highest honors, Duke U., 1984. Fellow biochemistry Northwestern U. Med. Sch., Chgo., 1952-54; postdoctoral fellow Lab. Chem. Pharmacology, Nat. Heart Inst., NIH, Bethesda, Md., 1954-56; sr. research biochemist Wellcome Research Labs., Burroughs Wellcome & Co., Tuckahoe, N.Y., 1956-57; asst. prof., assoc. prof., prof. dept. pharmacology Coll. Medicine, U. Iowa, Iowa City, 1957-70; dir. Toxicology Center, Coll. Medicine, U. Iowa, 1968-70; Claude Bernard prof. U. Montreal, (Que., Can.) Inst. of Medicine, 1970; chief pharmacology and toxicology br. Nat. Inst. Environ. Health Scis., Research Triangle Park, N.C., 1970-76, sci. dir., 1976-78, chief lab. pharmacology, 1978-81, sr. exec. service, 1981—; cons. pharmacology cos. including Smith Kline & French, Hoffman La Roche, others; adj. prof. pharmacology U. N.C. Sch. Medicine, 1970—; adj. prof. toxicology N.C. State U., 1971—; cons. coms. NIH, FDA, NIDA, EPA; chmn. Gordon Conf. on Drug Metabolism, 1977-78; vis. prof. Swiss Fed. Inst. Tech. and U. Zurich, Switzerland, 1978-79. Contbr. numerous articles on drug metabolism to profl. jours. Served to lt. USPHS, 1954-56. Recipient Marple-Schweitzer award Northwestern U., 1950; recipient Superior Achievement award NIH, 1975; Spl. award U. N.C. Sch. Nursing, 1978. Mem. Am. Soc. Pharmacology and Exptl. Therapeutics (Abel award 1964, councillor 1980-83, chmn. drug metabolism div. 1975-78), Am. Assn. for Cancer Research, Soc. of Toxicology, Mt. Desert Island Biol. Lab.; mem. Phi Beta Kappa, Sigma Xi., Phi Lambda Upsilon. Democrat. Episcopalian (deacon, chaplain). Current Work: Metabolism of chemicals/drugs; role of metabolism in effect/toxicity of chemical/drug; species differences in metabolism/toxicity; perinatal drug metabolism; metabolism of drugs by isolated organs, tissues, cells; effects of pollutants on metabolizing systems; drug/-chemical interactions at metabolizing systems. Subspecialties: Pharmacology; Environmental toxicology. Home: 212 Ridge Trail Chapel Hill NC 27514 Office: NIEHS PO Box 12233 Research Triangle Park NC 27709

FOWLER, BRUCE ANDREW, toxicologist, researcher; b. Seattle, Dec. 28, 1945; s. Andrew and Dolores (Ivey) F.; m. Mary Glenn Oler, June 9, 1968; children: Glenn Andrew, Randall Bruce. B.S. in Fisheries, U. Wash., 1968; Ph.D. in Pathology, U. Oreg., 1972. Staff fellow Nat. Inst. Environ. Health Sci., NIH, Research Triangle Park, N.C., 1972-74, sr. staff fellow, 1974-77, research biologist, 1977—; temporary adviser WHO, Geneva, 1978-79; mem. working group Internat. Agy. for Research in Cancer, Lyon, France, 1978-79. Editor: The Biological and Environmental Effects of Arsenic, 1983; Mechanisms of Cell Injury: Implications for Human Health, 1986. Mem. Am. Soc. Cell Biology, Am. Assn. Pathologists, Am. Soc. Pharmacology and Exptl. Therapeutics, Soc. Toxicology (councilor mechanisms sect. 1981-83). Current Work: Mechanisms of toxic cell injury from trace metals; role of metal-binding proteins in regulating intracellular bioavailability of metals; comparative biochemistry of metal-binding proteins in marine invertebrates. Subspecialties: Toxicology (medicine); Biochemistry (medicine). Office: PO Box 12233 Research Triangle Park NC 27709

FOWLER, CHARLES ALBERT, electronics engineer; b. Centralia, Ill., Dec. 17, 1920; s. Clarence J. and Bess (Maxwell) F.; m. Kathryn Elizabeth Grimes, Oct. 23, 1943; children: Patricia Ann, Mary Catherine. B.S. in Engring. Physics, U. Ill., 1942. Mem. staff radiation lab. MIT, 1942-45; head radar systems dept. Airborne Instruments Lab., Deer Park, N.Y., 1946-66; dep. dir. (tactical warfare) def. research and engring. Dept. Def., 1966-70; v.p., mgr. equipment devel. labs. Raytheon Co., Sudbury, Mass., 1970-76; sr. v.p. Mitre Corp., 1976—; mem. sci. adv. com. Def. Intelligence Agy., 1971—, chmn., 1976-82; mem. Air Force Sci. Adv. Bd., 1971-77, Def. Sci. Bd., 1972—, chmn., 1984—. Contbr. articles in field. Mem. East Norwich Sch. Bd., 1955-61, East Norwich Library Bd., 1956-62. Fellow IEEE, AAAS (assoc.); mem. Nat. Acad. Engring. Subspecialty: Electronics. Home: 15 Woodberry Rd Sudbury MA 01776 Office: Mitre Corp Bedford MA 01730

FOWLER, ELIZABETH, immunologist, educator; b. Schenectady, Apr. 18, 1943; d. Francis Raynor and Julia Rachel (Merchant) F. A.B., Cornell U., 1965; Ph.D., Harvard U., 1972. Postdoctoral fellow U. Wis.-Madison, 1972-76, asst. scientist, 1976-77; asst. prof. bacteriology and immunology U. N.C., Chapel Hill, 1977-83; assoc. prof. U. South Ala., Mobile, 1983-85; staff scientist Ciba Geigy Agrl. Biotech. Unit, Research Triangle Park, N.C., 1985—. Contbr. articles to profl. jours. NSF fellow, 1968-71; NIH fellow, 1972-74; Am. Cancer Soc. awardee, 1980-83. Mem. Am. Assn. Immunologists, Am. Soc. Cell Biology, AAAS, Am. Women in Sci., Phi Beta Kappa. Current Work: Control of gene expression in plants. Subspecialties: Gene actions; Molecular biology. Home: 205 N Boundary St Chapel Hill NC 27514 Office: Ciba Geigy Biotech Box 12257 Research Triangle Park NC 27709

FOWLER, HOWLAND AUCHINCLOSS, scientific administrator, researcher; b. N.Y.C., Jan. 25, 1930; s. Robert H. and Caroline (Auchincloss) F.; m. Shirley Boers, May 5, 1962; children: Joanna L., Amy A. A.B., Princeton U., 1952; M.S., Brown U., 1955, Ph.D. in Physics, 1957. With Nat. Bur. Standards, Washington, 1957—, successively physicist, project leader atomic physics div. and electricity div., 1957-71; sci. asst. to dir. Inst. Basic Standards, 1971-77, Inst. Basic Standards (Center Applied Math.), 1977—, research in computer-graphics simulation of non-linear equations. Contbr. articles to profl. publs. Mem. bd. ushers Presbyterian Ch., 1965—. Mem. Am. Phys. Soc., Soc. Indsl. and Applied Math., IEEE, Sigma Xi. Republican. Club: Princeton of N.Y. Current Work: Nonlinear systems, Josephson effect; applied mathematics, theoretical solid-state physics, general technical writing. Subspecialties: Condensed matter physics; Applied mathematics.

FOWLER, TIMOTHY JOHN, engineer. Disting. fellow Monsanto Co., St. Louis. Subspecialty: Structural engineering. Office: Monsanto Co Corp Engring Dept 800 N Lindbergh Blvd Saint Louis MO 63167*

FOWLER, WILLIAM ALFRED, physics educator; b. Pitts., Aug. 9, 1911; s. John McLeod and Jennie Summers (Watson) F.; m. Ardiane Foy Olmstead, Aug. 24, 1940; children: Mary Emily, Martha Summers Fowler Schoenemann. B.Eng. in Physics, Ohio State U., 1933, D.Sc. (hon.), 1978; Ph.D., Calif. Inst. Tech., 1936; D.Sc. (hon.), U. Chgo., 1976, Ariz. State U., 1985. Research fellow Calif. Inst. Tech., Pasadena, 1936-39, asst. prof. physics, 1939-42, assoc. prof., 1942-46, prof. physics, 1946-70, Inst. prof. physics, 1970—; asst. dir. research NDRC, 1941-45; tech. observer OSRD, South Pacific Theatre, 1944; sci. dir. project VISTA, Dept. Def., 1951-52; Fulbright lectr. Cavendish Lab., U. Cambridge, 1954-55; Guggenheim fellow dept. applied math. and theoretical physics St. John's Coll., U. Cambridge, 1961-62; vis. fellow Inst. Theoretical Astronomy, 1967-72; mem. nat. sci. bd. NSF, 1968-74; mem. space bd. Nat. Acad. Scis., 1970-73, 77-80; chmn. Nat. Acad. Scis. (Office Phys. Scis.), 1981—; mem. space program adv. council NASA, 1971-73; mem. nuclear sci. adv. com. Dept. Energy/NSF, 1977-80; cons. and lectr. in field. Contbr. articles to profl. jours. Bd. dirs. Am. Friends, Cambridge U., 1970-78. Recipient Naval Ordnance Devel. award USN, 1945, medal of merit, 1948; Lamme medal Ohio State U., 1952; U. Liège medal, 1955; Calif. Co-scientist of Yr. award, 1958; Barnard medal for sci. Columbia U., 1965; Apollo Acheivement award NASA, 1969; Vetlesen prize, 1973; Nat. Medal of Sci., 1974; Nobel Prize in Physics, 1983; Benjamin Franklin fellow Royal Soc. Arts; Bruce gold medal Astron. Soc. Pacific, 1979; Sullivant Medal Ohio State U., 1985. Fellow Am. Phys. Soc. (Bonner prize 1970, pres. 1976), Am. Acad. Arts and Scis., Royal Astron. Soc. (assoc., Eddington medal 1978); mem. Nat. Acad. Scis. (council 1974-77), AAAS, Am. Astron. Soc., Am. Inst. Physics (governing bd. 1974-80), AAUP, Am. Philos. Soc., Soc. Royal Sci. Liège (corr. mem.), Brit. Assn. Advancement Sci., Mark Twain Soc. (hon.), Phi Beta Kappa (vis. scholar 1980-81), Sigma Xi, Tau Beta Pi, Tau Kappa Epsilon. Democrat. Clubs: Athenaeum (Pasadena); Cosmos (Washington). Current Work: Research on nuclear forces and reaction rates, nuclear spectroscopy, structure of light nuclei, thermonuclear sources of stellar energy and element synthesis in stars and supernovae; study of general relativistic effects in quasar and pulsar models. Subspecialty: Nuclear physics. Office: Kellogg Radiation Lab (106-38) Calif Inst Tech Pasadena CA 91125

FOX, C. FRED, microbiologist, educator, consultant; b. Springfield, Ohio, Aug. 19, 1937; s. Charles L. and Geneva F. A. B. cum laude, Wittenberg U., 1960, D.Sc. (hon.), 1974; M.S., Ohio State U., 1961; Ph.D. (NSF predoctoral fellow), U. Chgo., 1964. Teaching asst. Ohio State U., 1959-61; research assoc. U. Chgo., 1964; postdoctoral fellow NSF, Harvard Med. Sch., 1964-66; asst. prof. biochemistry U. Chgo., 1966-70, assoc. prof., 1970-71; assoc. prof. microbiology UCLA, 1970-72, prof., 1972—, chmn. dept., 1976-81; dir., cons. INGENE, Inc., Santa Monica, Calif. Editor: more than 40 books including Membrane Research, 1972, (with A. Keith) Membrane Molecular Biology, 1972, Biochemistry of Cell Walls and Membranes, 1975, (with D. Oxender) Molecular Aspects of Membrane Transport, 1978, (with Cunningham, Watson and Goldwasser) Control of Cellular Division and Development, 1980; series editor: more than 40 books including UCLA Symposia on Molecular and Cellular Biology, 1972; editor: more than 40 books including Jour. Cell Biochemistry, 1972; contbr. numerous articles to sci. jours. Recipient Research Career Devel. award USPHS, 1969-70, 71-76. Mem. Am. Soc. Microbiology, Am. Soc. Biol. Chemists, Am. Chem. Soc. (Eli Lilly award 1973), Endocrine Soc. Current Work: Hormone action in cell culture. Subspecialties: Cell biology; Membrane biology. Office: Molecular Biology Inst UCLA Los Angeles CA 90024

FOX, EUGENE NOAH, microbiologist, cons.; b. Chgo., Dec. 9, 1927; s. Noah and Beatrice (Sender) F.; m. Eloise Block, June 14, 1964; children: Mara, Daniel. B.S., U. Ill., 1949, M.S., 1950; Ph.D., Case-Western Res. U., 1955. Successively asst. prof., assoc. prof., prof. microbiology U. Chgo., 1960-77; dir. research and devel. Cutter Labs., Berkeley, Calif., 1977-81; prin. Kensington Cons., Calif., 1981—Current Work: Consultant to biotechnology companies and venture capital institutions. Subspecialties: Infectious diseases; Microbiology. Address: 235 Willamette Ave Kensington CA 94708

FOX, GEORGE EDWARD, biochemist, educator; b. Syracuse, N.Y., Dec. 17, 1945; s. Charles Dainer and Henrietta L. (Carpentier) F.; m. Carolyne Ann Tordiglione, Sept. 1, 1973; children: Brian Trevor, Kevin William. B.S., Syracuse U., 1967, Ph.D., 1974. Research asso. dept. genetics and devel. U. Ill., Urbana-Champaign, 1973-77; asst. prof. dept. biophys. scis. U. Houston, 1977-82, assoc. prof. dept. biochem. and phys. scis., 1982—. Mem. editorial bd.: Jour. Molecular Evolution, 1980—, Molecular Biology and Evolution, 1982—; contbr. articles in field to profl. jours. NASA grantee, 1978—; NSF grantee, 1902—. Mem. AAAS, Am. Chem. Soc., Am. Inst. Chem. Engrs., Am. Soc. Microbiology, Sigma Xi, Theta Tau. Current Work: Archaebacteria, 5S rRNA structure and function, molecular evolution. Subspecialties: Molecular biology; Systematics. Office: Dept Biochem Sci U Houston Houston TX 77004

FOX, J. EUGENE, research institute director. Dir., ARCO Plant Cell Research Inst., Dublin, Calif. Subspecialty: Plant genetics. Office: ARCO Plant Cell Research Inst 6560 Trinity Court Dublin CA 94568

FOX, JACK JAY, bio-organic chemist, educator; b. N.Y.C., Dec. 21, 1916; s. Samuel and Celia (Stern) F.; m. Ruth Chiyeko Inabu, June 13, 1939; children—Dolores Merrick, John Reed. B.A., U. Colo., 1939, Ph.D., 1950. Postdoctoral fellow U. Libre Bruxelles, Belgium, 1950-52; assoc. Sloan-Kettering Inst. Cancer Research, N.Y.C., 1952-56, assoc. mem., 1956-60, mem., Rye, N.Y., 1960—, lab. head, 1956—; prof. Cornell U. Grad. Sch. Med. Scis., N.Y.C., 1958—. Contbr. numerous articles to profl. jours. and books. Served with USAAF, 1942-45, ETO. Decorated Air medal with three oak leaf clusters; recipient Sloan award in Cancer Research Sloan-Kettering Inst., N.Y.C., 1956, Pap award in cancer research Papanicoleau Cancer Inst., 1982, Norlin award U. Colo. Alumni Assn., 1984. Mem. Am. Chem. Soc. (Hudson award in carbohydrate chemistry 1977), Am. Soc. Biol. Chemists, Am. Assn. Cancer Research, Internatl. Soc. Heterocyclic Chems., Westchester Chem. Soc. (pres. 1964-65), Sigma Xi. Current work: Design and syntheses of anti-cancer and antiviral agents, carbohydrate and heterocyclic chemistry, nucleoside antibiotics. Subspecialties: Synthetic chemistry; Drug design. Home: 424 S Lexington Ave White Plains NY 10606 Office: Sloan-Kettering Inst Cancer Walker Lab 145 Boston Post Rd Rye NY 10580

FOX, KENNETH, physicist, astronomer; b. Highland Park, Mich., Aug. 16, 1935; s. Abraham and Jennie (Krakowski) F. B.S., Wayne State U., 1957; M.S., U. Mich., Ann Arbor, 1958, Ph.D., 1962. Research physicist Nuclear Physics Inst., Netherlands, 1962-63; vis. asst. prof. Vanderbilt U., 1963-64; prof. physics and astronomy U. Tenn., Knoxville, 1964—; cons. Oak Ridge Nat. Lab., Jet Propulsion Lab., Los Alamos Nat. Lab. Editor NASA Procs., 1982; Contbr. articles in field to profl. jours and books. Nat. Acad. Sci. fellow, 1967-69, 77-78; grantee in field; Fulbright scholar, 1974-75. Mem. Am. Astron. Soc., Am. Phys. Soc., N.Y. Acad. Sci., Tenn. Acad. Sci., Internat. Astron. Union, Phi Beta Kappa, Sigma Xi. Club: Explorers (N.Y.C.). Current Work: Interstellar molecules, planetary atmospheres, terrestrial environ.; laser isotope separation; theoretical physics and chem. physics; ultra high-resolution spectroscopy. Subspecialties: Atomic and molecular physics; Cosmology. Office: Department of Physics and Astronomy University of Tennessee Knoxville TN 37996

FOX, MARYE ANNE, chemistry educator; b. Canton, Ohio, Dec. 9, 1947; d. Charles Arthur and Lucille Mae (Cooper) Payne; m. R. John Fox, Jr., June 28, 1969; children—Robert, Michael, Matthew. B.S., U. Notre Dame, 1969; Ph.D., Dartmouth Coll., 1974. Asst. prof. chemistry U. Tex.-Austin, 1976-81, assoc. prof., 1981-85, prof. chemistry, 1985—; cons. in field. Contbr. articles to profl. jours. Recipient Agnes Fay Morgan Research award, Iota Sigma Pi, 1984; Best of the New Generation, Esquire, 1984; Camille and Henry Dreyfus Tchr.-Scholar, 1981; Alfred P. Sloan research fellow, 1981; Jean Holloway award, 1977. Mem. Am. Chem. Soc. (exec. com.), Army Research Office. Current work: Solar energy utilization, mechanistic organic photochemistry and electrochemistry. Subspecialties: Organic chemistry; Photochemistry. Home: 7705 Valburn Dr Austin TX 78731 Office: Dept Chemistry U Tex Austin TX 78712

FOX, MAURICE SANFORD, molecular biologist, educator; b. N.Y.C., Oct. 11, 1924; s. Albert and Ray F.; m. Sally Cherniavsky, Apr. 1, 1955; children—Jonathan, Gregory, Michael. B.S. in Meteorology, U. Chgo., 1944, M.S. in Chemistry, 1951, Ph.D., 1951. Instr. U. Chgo., 1951-53; asst. Rockefeller Inst., 1953-55, asst. prof., 1955-58, assoc. prof., 1958-62; assoc. prof. MIT, 1962-66, prof., 1966-79, Lester Wolfe prof. molecular biology, 1979—, head dept. biology, 1985—. Served with USAAF, 1943-46. USPHS fellow, 1952-53; Nuffield Research fellow, 1957. Fellow AAAS; mem. Inst. Medicine of Nat. Acad. Scis. Current work: Molecular mechanisms of genetic recombination; diagnostic and treatment criteria in medicine. Office: Massachusetts Institute Technology Cambridge MA 02139

FOX, MICHAEL HENRY, researcher, radiation biology educator; b. Great Bend, Kans., Mar. 19, 1946; s. Robert Loren and Wilma Mae (Ulrich) F.; m. Mary Ann Ryser, Oct. 8, 1946; children: Nathan Michael, Jennifer Marie. B.S., McPherson Coll., 1968; M.S., Kans. State U., 1972, Ph.D., 1977; postgrad., Colo. State U., 1979. Vol. Peace Corps, Universidad Mayor de San Andres, La Paz, Bolivia, 1968-70; asst. prof. McPherson (Kans.) Coll., 1972-73; grad. research asst. Kans. State U., Manhattan, 1973-77; postdoctoral fellow Colo. State U., Fort Collins, 1977-79, asst. prof. radiation biology, 1979—, mem. grad. faculty cellular and molecular biology, 1981—. Contbr. articles to profl. jours. Exec. com. Larimer County Democratic party, Fort Collins, Colo., 1980-85; mem. ch. bd. Foothills Unitarian Ch., Fort Collins, 1980-83; Spanish tchr. Amigos de las Americas, 1980-81; fireman Wellington Vol. Fire Dept., Wellington, Colo., 1981-83. Mem. Soc. Analytical Cytology, Radiation Research Soc. Democrat. Unitarian. Current Work: Studying the response of cells to hyperthermia utilizing multiparameter flow cytometry and cell sorting techniques to measure cell cycle, membrane fluidity, and intracellular ions. Subspecialty: Cell and tissue culture. Home: 901 Eggleston St Fort Collins CO 80524 Office: Dept Radiation Biology Colo State U Fort Collins CO 80523

FOXX, RICHARD MICHAEL, psychologist; b. Denver, Oct. 28, 1944; s. James Martin and Marie Louise (Harris) F.; m. Carolyn Lee Crofutt, Apr. 4, 1966; children: Carrie, Christopher. B.A., U. Calif., Riverside, 1967; M.A., Calif. State U., 1970; Ph.D., So. Ill. U., 1971. Research scientist IV State of Ill., Anna, 1970-74; asst. prof. pediatrics U. Md. Med. Sch., Balt., 1974-80, asso. prof. psychology, 1976-80; prof. rehab. So. Ill. U., Carbondale, 1981—; behavior modification coordinator State of Ill., Anna, 1980—; pres. HELP Services, Inc., Carbondale, Ill., 1976—; mem. AABT Peer Review Com., N.Y.C., 1982—. Bd. editors various psychol. jours.; adv. bd., Assn. for Retarded Citizens, Arlington, Tex., 1982—; Author: Increasing Behavior, 1982, Decreasing Behavior, 1982, Toilet Training in Less Than a Day, 1974, Toilet Training the Retarded, 1973. Recipient Distinguished Alumnus award Calif. State U., Fullerton, 1981; Commendation Am. Film Festival, 1981; Research award Am. Assn. Mental Deficiency, 1979; First place Internat. Rehab. Film Festival, 1980. Fellow Am. Psychol. Assn., Am. Assn. Mental Deficiency, Behavior Therapy and Research Soc.; mem. AAAS, Psi Chi. Current Work: Application of Learning based theories to clin. treatment of normal, retarded, autistic, emotionally disturbed and deaf individuals - behavioral treatments. Subspecialties: Behavioral psychology; Learning. Office: Anna Mental Health & Devel Center 1000 North Main St Anna IL 62906 X1

FRADEN, JACOB, inventor of biomedical instrumentation, researcher; b. Sverdlovsk, USSR, Apr. 12, 1945; came to U.S., 1977, nautralized, 1984; s. Vladimir and Sofia (Ugorets) F.; m. Irene Tishkoff, June 23, 1972; children—Roman, Julia. M.S., Poly. Inst., Sverdlovsk, 1967, Ph.D., Chelyabinsk, USSR, 1971. Sr. scientist Occupational Diseases Research Inst., Sverdlovsk, 1968-77; postdoctoral research fellow Case Western Res. U., Cleve., 1977-79; project mgr. WP-Instruments, Inc., New Haven, 1979-81; sr. research engr. Timex Med. Products, Waterbury, Conn., 1981-84; pres. FreMed, Inc., New Haven, 1984—; ltd. ptnr. Bio-Optical Sensors, Ltd., Oberlin, Ohio, 1979—; cons. DIMERCO Internat., Cupertino, Calif., 1982—, Diablo Research, Inc., San Jose, Calif., 1983—. Editor: Biotelemetry, 1976. Contbr. articles to profl. jours. Patentee in field. Mem. Assn. Advancement Med. Instrumentation, IEEE. Republican. Jewish. Current work: New methods of patient monitoring in hospitals and at home. Subspecialties: Biomedical engineering; Electrical engineering. Home: 72 Hampton Rd Hamden CT 06518 Office: FreMed Inc 5 Science Park New Haven CT 06511

FRADIN, FRANK YALE, materials scientist; b. Chgo., May 14, 1941; s. Harry R. and Esther (Levin) F.; m. Joan S. Blumenthel, June 10, 1963; children—Gerald, Richard, Matthew. Sc.B., MIT, 1963; Ph.D., U. Ill., 1967. Dir. materials sci. Argonne Nat. Lab., Ill.. 1967—; prof. physics No. Ill. U., DeKalb, Ill, 1970—. Contbr. articles to profl jours. Fellow Am. Phys. Soc.; mem. Materials Research Soc. Current work: Superconductivity, magnetic materials. Subspecialties: Electronic materials; Condensed matter physics. Office: Argonne Nat Lab 9700 S Cass Ave Bldg 223 Argonne IL 60439

FRADKIN, LARRY, environmental scientist; b. N.Y.C., Jan. 19, 1956. B.S., Fairleigh Dickinson U., 1977; M.S., U. Cin., 1979. Environ. scientist EPA, Cin., 1978-80, 84—; environ. engr. Argonne Nat. Lab., Ill., 1980-84. Author: Recoverable Energy and Materials, 1984; Energy from Industrial Waste Water, 1984. Recipient Disting Sci. award EPA, 1979. EPA grantee, 1977. Mem. ASTM (com. mem. 1984—), AAAS, Am. Chem. Soc., Ill. Hazardous Waste Task Force (com. mem. 1983-84), Water Pollution Control Fedn. Current work: Municipal waste water sludge reuse and disposal technologies; alternative technologies for hazardous wastes; energy technology, waste to energy, biomass, synthetic fuels. Subspecialties: Hazardous waste disposal; Resource management. Home: 572 Terrace Ave Cincinnati OH 45220 Office: EPA 26 W St Clair St Cincinnati OH 45268

FRAENKEL-CONRAT, HEINZ, research biochemist; b. Breslau, Germany, July 29, 1910; came to U.S., 1936, naturalized, 1941; s. Ludwig Fraenkel and Lili Conrat; m. Jane Opermann, July 14, 1939 (div.); children—Richard, Charles; m. Bea A. Singer, 1964. Student univs., Breslau, Munich, Vienna, Geneva; Dr. Med., U. Breslau, 1933; Ph.D. in Biochemistry, U. Edinburgh, 1936. Research in enzymatic peptide synthesis Rockefeller Inst., N.Y.C., 1936-37; crystallization of rattlesnake venom neurotoxin Inst. Butantan, Sao Paulo, Brazil, 1937-38; chemistry and biology pituitary hormones Inst. Exptl. Biology, U. Calif. at Berkeley, 1938-42; research methods protein modification Western Regional Research Lab., Dept. Agr., Albany, Calif., 1942-49; Rockefeller fellow, Eng., Denmark, 1950; staff virus lab., prof. virology U. Calif. at Berkeley, 1951—, also prof. molecular biology. Author: Design and Function at the Threshold of Life: the Viruses, 1962, the Chemistry and Biology of Viruses, 1969, Comprehensive Virology, Vol. 1, 1974, Virology, 1981. Recipient (with Schramm and Hershey) Lasker award, 1958; named Calif. Scientist of Year, 1958. Mem. Am. Soc. Biol. Chemists, Am. Chem. Soc., Nat. Acad. Scis., Am. Acad. Arts and Scis. Also research degradation and reconstitution tobacco mosaic virus, chem. research protein and nucleic acid of viruses, viral and nonviral plant enzymes, mechanism of snake venom neurotoxicity. Subspecialty: Molecular biology. Home: 870 Grizzly Peak Blvd Berkeley CA 94708

FRAHM, RICHARD RAY, geneticist, educator; b. Scottsbluff, Nebr., Nov. 17, 1939; s. Robert L. and Murial E. (Nolke) F.; m. Joyce L. Frahm, Aug. 27, 1961; children: Lorinda S., Kathy R. B.S. in Animal Sci, U. Nebr., 1961; M.S. in Genetics, N.C. State U., 1963, Ph.D. in Genetics and Stats, 1965. Cert. animal scientist. Asst. prof. dept. animal sci. Okla. State U., 1967-71, assoc. prof., 1971-76, prof., 1976—. Contbr. articles to profl. jours. Served to capt. U.S. Army, 1965-67. NSF fellow, 1961-65; grantee in field. Mem. Am. Soc. Animal Sci., Genetics Soc. Am., Okla. Cattlemen's Assn., Sigma Xi. Current Work: Breed evaluation and development of effective crossbreeding systems to improve efficiency of beef production. Subspecialties: Animal breeding and embryo transplants; Animal genetics. Home: 2106 Warren Dr Stillwater OK 74075 Office: Animal Sci Dept Okla State U Stillwater OK 74078

FRAMPTON, PAUL HOWARD, physics educator; b. Kidderminster, Eng., Oct. 31, 1943; came to U.S., 1968; s. Harold Albert and Grace Elizabeth (Howard) F. B.A., U. Oxford, Eng., 1965, M.A., 1968, D. Phil., 1968, D.Sc. (hon.), 1984. Asst. prof. physics U. N.C., Chapel Hill, 1981-83, assoc. prof., 1983-85, prof., 1985—. Author: Dual Resonance Models, 1974. Contbr. articles on elem. particle theory to profl. publs. Fellow Am. Phys. Soc. Current work: Quantum field theory and elementary particle physics. Subspecialty: Particle physics. Home: 32 Fearrington Post Pittsboro NC 27312 Office: U NC Dept Physics and Astronomy Chapel Hill NC 27514

FRANCIOSA, JOSEPH ANTHONY, cardiologist, researcher; b. Easton, Pa., Apr. 24, 1936; s. Joseph and Letizia Beatrice (Cascioli) F.; m. Antonietta Battistoni, Feb. 8, 1964 (div. 1972); m. Barbara Ann Neilan, Aug. 3, 1973; 1 son, Christopher David. B.A., U. Pa., 1958; M.D., U. Rome, Italy, 1963. Diplomate: Am. Bd. Internal Medicine. Intern USPHS Hosp., S.I., N.Y., 1964-65; resident Washington Hosp. Ctr., 1967-69; cardiology fellow VA Hosp.-Georgetown U., Washington, 1969-71; chief ICU VA Hosp., Washington, 1971-73; assoc. dir. cardiac research Georgetown U., 1973-74; dir. CCU VA Hosp., Mpls., 1974-76, cardiac research, 1976-79; chief cardiology VA Hosp., Phila., 1979-82; dir. cardiology div. U. Ark., Little Rock, 1982—; asst. prof. medicine Georgetown U., 1973-74, U. Minn., Mpls., 1974-77, assoc. prof., 1977-79; assoc. prof. U. Pa., Phila., 1979-82; prof. U. Ark., 1982—. Contbr. numerous articles to med. jours. Mem. med. research com. Am. Heart Assn., Mpls., 1976-79, Phila., 1981-82. Served to lt. comdr. USPHS, 1964-67. VA grantee, 1974-86; U. Ark. grantee, 1982-83; NHLBI grantee, 1985-91. Fellow ACP, Am. Coll. Cardiology, Am. Coll. Chest Physicians (gov. Ark. sect. 1984—, chmn. hypertension com. 1981—), Am. Heart Assn. (circulation council 1978—, council high blood pressure research 1982—); mem. Am. Soc. Clin. Pharmacology and Therapeutics (vice chmn cardiopulmonary com. 1981—), Assn. Univ. Cardiologists. Roman Catholic. Current Work: Cardiovascular physiology, hemodynamics, heart failure, exercise pathophysiology, hypertension, cardiovascular clinical pharmacology. Subspecialties: Cardiology; Internal medicine. Home: 3027 Painted Valley Dr Little Rock AR 72212 Office: Univ Ark Med Scis 4301 W Markham St Little Rock AR 72205

FRANCIS, JOHN ELBERT, aerospace, mech. and nuclear engr., educator, researcher; b. Kingfisher, Okla., Mar. 14, 1937; s. John Amos and Virginia Lorain (Mitchell) F.; m. Susan Ruth Bentley, June 2, 1962; children: John Carl, Steven Michael. B.S. in Mech. Engring, U. Okla., 1960, M.S. in Mech. Engring, 1963, Ph.D. in Engring. Sci, 1965. Registered profl. engr., Okla. Engr. Allis-Chalmers Co., Springfield, Ill., 1960; grad. asst. in mech. engring. U. Okla., Norman, 1960-61, asst. prof. aerospace and mech. engring., 1966-69, assoc. prof., 1969-74, prof. aerospace, mech. and nuclear engring., 1974—; asst. dean U. Okla. (Grad. Coll.), 1968-71; now assoc. dean U. Okla. (Coll. Engring.); asst. research scientist Continental Oil Co., Ponca City, Okla., summer 1963; asst. prof. mech. engring. U. Mo., Rolla, 1964-66; Phys. scientist Nat. Bur. Standards, summers 1978-79. Contbr. articles to profl. jours. Recipient Ralph Teetor award Soc. Automotive Engrs., 1969; Wonders of Engring. award Okla. Soc. Profl. Engrs., 1974. Mem. AIAA (chmn. thermophysics tech. com. 1978-81, gen. chmn. 15th Thermophysics Conf. 1980), ASME, Am. Soc. for Engring. Edn., Optical Soc. Am., N.Y. Acad. Scis., Sigma Xi, Pi Tau Sigma. Democrat. Roman Catholic. Lodge: Norman Rotary. Current Work: Heat transfer, thermography, solar energy; research on combined conductive and radiative heat transfer in insulating materials; administrative duties in academic programs for Engineering College. Subspecialties: Mechanical engineering; Biomedical engineering. Home: 1406 Greenbriar Dr Norman OK 73069 Office: U Okla 22 W Boyd Room 107 Norman OK 73019

FRANCIS, KENNON THOMPSON, physiologist, educator; b. Camp LeJune, N.C., July 8, 1945; s. James Ballard and Dorothy (Thompson) F.; m. Sheryl East, Dec. 29, 1966; children: Connie Jill, Wendy Kay. B.S. in Zoology, Auburn U., 1967, M.S. in Biochemistry, 1969, Ph.D., 1972. Asst. prof. dept. sci. Troy State U., Montgomery, Ala., 1973-74; prof. dept. allied health U. Ala. in Birmingham, 1974—; mem. nat. adv. com for guidance of Ph.D. Program in Phys. Therapy, U. Calif., 1977; mem. Nat. Adv. Council in Phys. Therapy Edn., 1980-83. Assoc. editor Jour. Ala. Acad. Sci.; cons. editor Clin. Mgmt. in Phys. Therapy; contbg. reviewer Phys. Therapy Jour. Contbr. articles to sci. jours. Served to capt. Signal Corps. U.S. Army, 1970-72. Faculty grantee U. Ala., 1975-77, 81-82; Linn Henley Charitable Trust grantee, 1977; also rehab. and medicine grants. Mem. Am. Physiol. Soc., Sigma Xi, Gamma Sigma Delta, Alpha Eta. Presbyterian. Current Work: Physiological basis of endurance and exercise development. Subspecialties: Physiology (medicine); Physiology (biology).

FRANCIS, MARLAN LANNING, veterinarian, animal nutritionist; b. Harper, Kans., Apr. 10, 1939; s. Harold Ray and Anna Evelyn (McClung) F.; m. Karen Sue Ioerger, Aug. 22, 1961; 1 child, Andria Marcel. B.S., Kans. State U., 1961, D.V.M., 1963. Sole practice vet. medicine, Harper, Kans., 1963-78; tech. service veterinarian Vigortone, Inc., Marion, Ohio, 1978-81; staff veterinarian Pro-Ag, Inc., Mpls., 1981-84; v.p. Agro-K Corp., Mpls., 1984—; pres. Wildcat Vet. Supply Co., Mpls., 1983—. Contbr. articles to profl. publs. Served with USNG, 1957-62. Mem. Am. Assn. Bovine Practioners, Am. Assn. Equine Practitioners, Am. Assn. Indsl. Veterinarians, AVMA, Kans. Vet. Med. Assn., Lodges: Lions, Elks. Current work: Effect of cobalt on milk production in dairy cows, increased growth rates in beef cattle; trace mineral requirements of food animals. Subspecialties: Preventive medicine (veterinary medicine); Animal nutrition. Office: Agro-K Corp 5750 Main St NE Minneapolis MN 55432

FRANCIS, ROBERT DORL, microbiologist, educator, researcher; b. West Liberty, Ohio, Sept. 28, 1920; s. Joseph C. and Nellie Viola (Wartenbe) F.; m. Lisbeth Ann Innis, Feb. 20, 1943. A.B., Franklin Coll., 1942; M.S., U. Chgo., 1945; Ph.D., U. Mich., 1955. Chemist Swift & Co., Chgo., 1942-44; research asst. U. Chgo., 1945-47; bacteriologist Emulsol Corp., Chgo., 1947-49; instr. U. Mich., 1950-52; assoc. prof. microbiology U. Ala., Birmingham, 1956—; cons. virology Ala. Health Dept., 1966-77. Served with USPHS, 1953-56. NIH grantee, 1957-74. Mem. AAAS, Am. Soc. Microbiology (E.O. King award Southeastern Br. 1976), Sigma Xi. Presbyterian. Research, publs. virology. Current Work: Comparative and molecular virology; chlamydial agents. Subspecialties: Microbiology (medicine); Virology (medicine). Office: Univ Sta CHSB 445 U Ala in Birmingham Birmingham AL 35294

FRANCKO, DAVID ALEX, biology educator, researcher; b. Cleve., Aug. 15, 1952; s. Alex Frank and Marie (Novak) F.; m. Diana Lee Whitmer, June 14, 1975; 1 child, Tyler Whitmer. B.S. in Biology, Kent State U., 1974, M.S. in Biology, 1977; Ph.D. in Botany, Mich. State U., 1980. Postdoctoral assoc. W.K. Kellog Biol. Sta., Hickory Corners, Mich., 1980-81; asst. prof. botany Okla. State U., Stillwater, 1981-85, assoc. prof., 1985—; organizer ann. meeting Great Plains Limnology Conf., Stillwater, 1984, Okla. Acad. Sci., Stillwater, 1984. Author: To Quench Our Thirst, 1983; Principles of Biology-Lab Investigations, 1984. Contbr. articles to profl. jours. Adv. various state civic groups concerned with water conservation, Mich., Okla., 1981—. Named one of Outstanding Young Mem Am., Jaycees, 1983. Research grantee NSF, 1980—, State of Okla., 1982—. Mem. Am. Soc. Limnology and Oceanography, Internat. Assn. Theoretical/Applied Limnology, Sigma Xi, Beta Beta Beta (v.p. 1973-74). Democrat. Roman Catholic. Current work: Physiological limnology, aquatic botany, nutrient dynamics, water resource policy writing. Subspecialties: Limnology; Plant physiology (biology). Office: Okla State U Dept Botany and Microbiology Stillwater OK 74078

FRANCO, JOHN VINCENT, computer science educator; b. N.Y.C., Mar. 27, 1947; s. Vincent Joseph and Concetta (Scandura) F.; m. Myra Suzanne Rowe, Feb. 16, 1975; children: Veronica, Vanessa. B.E.E., CCNY, 1969; M.S., Columbia U., 1971, Rutgers U., 1978; Ph.D., Rutgers U., 1981. Mem. tech. staff Bell Telephone Labs., Holmdel, N.J., 1969-75; asst. prof. computer sci. Case Western Res. U., Cleve., 1980-84, Ind. U., Bloomington, 1984—. Vice-pres. Ludlow Community Assn., Cleve., 1982; dir. radio broadcasting Ch. of the Saviour, Cleveland Heights, Ohio, 1982. Recipient Alumni award CCNY Engring. Alumni, 1969; Rutgers U. fellow, 1977-80. Mem. Assn. Computing Machinery, Soc. Indsl. and Applied Math., Eta Kappa Nu. Methodist. Inventor multiple digital FSK demodulator, 1975. Current Work: Probabilistic analysis of algorithms for NP hard problems, theoretical computer science, complexity classes, approximation algorithms, duality. Subspecialties: Algorithms; Theoretical computer science. Home: 2535 Spicewood Ln Bloomington IN 47401 Office: Dept Computer Sci Ind U Bloomington IN 47405

FRANCO, VICTOR, physicist, educator; b. N.Y.C., Dec. 15, 1937; s. Isaac and Regina (Ferezy) F. B.S., N.Y.U., 1958; M.A., Harvard U., 1959, Ph.D, 1963. Research asso. M.I.T., 1963-65, Lawrence Radiation Lab., Berkeley, Calif., 1965-67, Los Alamos (N. Mex.) Nat. Lab., 1967-69; asso. prof. physics Bklyn. Coll., 1969-72, prof., 1973—. Contbr. articles to profl. jours. Grantee NASA; Grantee NSF; Grantee others. Fellow Am. Phys. Soc.; mem. Sigma Xi. Current Work: Theoretical studies of nuclear and atomic scattering at medium and high energies. Subspecialties: Theoretical physics; Nuclear physics. Office: Dept Physics Brooklyn Coll Brooklyn NY 11210

FRANDSEN, WALTER JAMES, engineering consultant; b. Hammond, Ind., Jan. 1, 1936; s. Walter Neal and Edna (Smith) F.; m. Wanda Lorene Cluff, June 13, 1964; children—Debi Lynn, Walter James, Jr. B.S. in Chem. Engring., U. Utah, 1957, M.B.A., 1959; Ph.D. in Behavioral Scis., Calif. Western Coll. (now U.S. Internat. U.), 1969. Registered profl. engr., Calif. Project engr. Utah Power & Light Co., Salt Lake City, 1957; chem. process engr. U.S. Bur. Mines, Salt Lake City, 1958; engring. project coordinator Sperry Utah Engring. Lab., Salt Lake City, 1959-61; mgr. tng. and employee devel. Hercules Inc., Salt Lake City, 1961-63; cons. in engring. and mgmt. Gen. Atomic Corp., San Diego, 1963-81; human resources cons. Solar Turbines, Inc., subs. Caterpillar Tractor Co., San Diego, 1981—; prof. Sch. Bus., U. San Diego, 1980—; prof., lectr. Sch. Bus. San Diego State U., 1972—; cons., lectr. U. Calif. Extension, San Diego, 1969—, San Diego Community Colls., 1969—, Nat. U., San Diego, 1974—. Chmn. exec. com., dean's council Coll. Arts and Scis., U. San Diego, 1979—; bd. dirs. Jr. Achievement San Diego, 1981—; mem. exec. com., scout master San Diego council Boy Scouts Am., 1974—. Served with USCG, 1960. Mem. Am. Psychol. Assn., Am. Soc. for Tng. and Devel. (chpt. pres. 1967), Acad. Mgmt., U.S. Internat. Univ. Doctoral Soc. Republic. Mormon. Current work: enhancement of individual and organizational effectiveness, e.g., strategic planning and management, quality and productivity systems. Subspecialties: Human factors engineering; Behavioral psychology. Home: 500 Camino de Orchida Encinitas CA 92024

FRANK, DIETER, research company executive; b. Erfurt, Germany, May 21, 1930; came to U.S., 1975; s. Karl and Luise (Metz) F.; m. Edith Anna Laufer, July 19, 1957; children—Martin, Susanne, Beate. Dr. Ing., Tech. U. (Berlin), 1963. Tchr., Tech. U., Berlin, 1963-65; research chemist ENKA, Obernburg, W. Ger., 1965-68, sect. head, 1968-71; assoc. dir. corp. research AKZO, Obernburg, 1971-75; v.p. research AKZO Chemie Am., Chgo., 1975—. Patentee in field, (17); contbr. chpts. to books, articles to profl. jours. Mem. AAAS, Indsl. Research Inst. (bd. editors 1981-83). Current work: Applied polymer and chemical process research. Subspecialties: Polymer chemistry; Organic chemistry. Office: Akzo Chemie Am 300 S Wacker Dr Chicago IL 60606

FRANK, ELLEN RYAN, management scientist; b. N.Y.C., July 10, 1954; d. Joseph Thomas and Cleone Irene (Mekos) Ryan; m. Stephen Z. Frank, Aug. 1, 1976. B.S., C.W. Post Coll., 1976; M.A., Hofstra U., 1978, Ph.D., 1981. Research mgr. L.I. Cancer Council, Melville, N.Y., 1978-79; research asso. Inst. for Research/Eval., 1979-80; mgmt. scientist Pfizer, Inc., N.Y.C., 1980-81; mgr. ops. research Roerig/Pfizer, Inc., N.Y.C., 1981—; adj. faculty/doctoral supr. Hofstra U., Hempstead, N.Y., 1981—; lectr., cons. in field, 1980—; lectr. Micro Computer confs., Washington, 1982—. Hofstra U. grad. fellow, 1976-80. Mem. Am. Psychol. Assn., Ops. Research Soc. Am., Metro. N.Y. Assn. for Applied Psychology, Eastern Psychol. Assn., Phi Eta, Psi Chi. Current Work: Industrial psychology, decision support systems, multivariate modeling. Subspecialties: Operations research (engineering); Algorithms. Home: 235 E 42d St New York NY 10017 Office: Roerig Div Pfizer Inc 235 E 42 St New York City NY 10017

FRANK, IRWIN NORMAN, urology educator, urologist; b. Rochester, N.Y., Mar. 24, 1927; s. Harry and Bess (Smalline) F.; m. Marilyn Ellowitch, June 13, 1954; children: Gary, Steven, Lawrence. B.A., U. Rochester, 1950, M.D., 1954. Diplomate: Am. Bd. Urology. Intern Strong Meml. Hosp., Rochester, 1954-55, asst. resident, 1955-58, Nat. Cancer Inst. trainee, 1957-59, chief resident urology, 1958-59; asst. prof. urology U. Rochester, 1959-67, assoc. prof., 1967-74, prof., 1974—, acting chmn. dept. urology, 1967-69, sr. assoc. dean U. Rochester Sch. Medicine and Dentistry; med. dir. Strong Meml. Hosp.; Contbr. chpts., numerous articles to profl. publs. Med. adv. bd. Kidney Found. Upstate N.Y., Rochester. Served with USN, 1944-46, PIO. Am. Cancer Soc. fellow, 1951. Fellow ACS, Am. Acad. Pediatrics; mem. Am. Urol. Assn. (past pres. Northeastern Sect.), N.Y. State Urol. Soc. (past pres.), Sigma Xi. Club: Irondequoit Country (Rochester) (v.p. 1980-82). Current Work: Medical education, cancer research (bladder and kidney cancer), cytologic diagnosis of urologic cancer, kidney stone disease, practice of urology (patient care), ultrasonic treatment of kidney stones and urologic cancer. Subspecialties: Urology; Cancer research (medicine). Home: 221 Monteroy Rd Rochester NY 14618 Office: U Rochester Med Sch 601 Elmwood Ave Rochester NY 14642

FRANK, MICHAEL M., physician; b. Bklyn., Feb. 28, 1937; s. Robert and Helen (Prakin) F.; m. Ruth Sybil Pudolsky, Nov. 5, 1961; children—Robert E., Abigail B., Brice S.H. A.B., U. Wis., 1956; M.D., Harvard U., 1960. Intern Boston City Hosp., 1960-61; resident in pediatrics Johns Hopkins Hosp., 1961-62, 64-65; vis. scientist Nat. Inst. Med. Research, London, 1965-66; with NIH, 1967—; chief lab. of clin. investigation, clin. dir. Nat. Inst. Allergy and Infectious Diseases, Bethesda, Md., 1977—. Editor: Blood. Mem. Assn. Am. Physicians, Am. Soc. Clin. Investigation, Soc. Pediatric Research, Infectious Diseases Soc., Am. Acad. Allergy, A.C.P., Soc. Hematology. Current Work: Role of complement and immune complexes in host defense and in production of human disease. Subspecialties: Allergy; Infectious diseases. Office: Room 11N232 Clin Center NIH Bethesda MD 20205

FRANK, NEIL LAVERNE, meteorologist, meteorol. center adminstr.; b. Kans., Sept. 11, 1931; s. Clarence E. and Mary Violet F.; m. Velma L. Becker, Sept. 12, 1952; children—Pamela, Debra, Ron. B.A., Southwestern Coll., 1953; M.S., Fla. State U., 1959, Ph.D., 1967. Meteorologist Nat. Hurricane Center, Miami, Fla., 1961-73, dept. dir., 1973-74, dir., 1974—. Contbr. articles to profl. jours. Bd. dirs. Dade County Citizens Safety Council, Dade County ARC. Served with USAF, 1953-57. Mem. Am. Meteorology Soc. Methodist. Subspecialty: Meteorology. Office: Nat Hurricane Ctr 1320 S Dixie Hwy Coral Gables FL 33146

FRANKEL, VICTOR HIRSCH, orthopaedic surgeon; b. Wilmington, Del., May 14, 1925; s. Harry and Estelle (Hillersohn) F.; m. Elna Ruth Olsen, Feb. 15, 1958; children—Victor Hirsch, Dana G., Lars-Erik, Carl S., Paul A. B.A., Swarthmore Coll., 1946; M.D., U. Pa., 1951; D.Sc., U. Upsala, Sweden, 1960. Intern Grad. Hosp. U. Pa., 1951-52; resident Charlotte (N.C.) Meml. Hosp., 1954-55; resident Hosp. Joint Diseases, N.Y.C., 1955-58, attending orthopaedic surgeon, 1960-66; prof. orthopaedic surgery and bioengring. Case Western Res. U., 1966-75; prof., chmn. dept. orthopaedic surgery U. Wash. Sch. Medicine, Seattle, 1976-81; chmn. orthopaedic surgery, surgeon-in-chief Hosp. Joint Diseases, Orthopaedic Inst., N.Y.C., 1981—; prof. orthopaedic surgery Mount Sinai Med. Sch., N.Y.C., 1981-84, lectr. orthopaedic surgery, 1984—; chmn. orthopaedic panel FDA Bur. Med. Devices, 1972-75. Author: Orthopaedic Biomechanics, 1970, Basic Biomechanics of Skeletal System, 1980. Served with M.C. U.S. Army, 1952-54. Recipient Klinkicht award Am. Orthopaedic Foot Soc., 1972; award of merit U.S. Ski Assn., 1972; Citation award Am. Coll. Sports Medicine, 1974; award of Merit ASTM, 1978; citation Outstanding Performance Boeing Comml. Airplane Co., 1978; Clemson award Internat. Biomaterials Symposium, 1980; Nat. Found. fellow, 1958-60; Frauenthal fellow Hosp. Joint Diseases, 1958-60; Am. Orthopaedic Assn. exchange fellow, 1965. Mem. Internat. Soc. Orthopaedic Surgery and Traumatology, Internat. Soc. Study Lumbar Spine, AMA, Am. Acad. Orthopaedic Surgeons, Can. Orthopaedic Assn., Am. Orthopaedic Assn., Hip Soc., Am. Orthopaedic Soc. Sports Medicine. Subspecialty: Orthopedics. Office: 301 E 17th St New York NY 10003

FRANKEN, PETER ALDEN, physicist, educator; b. N.Y.C., Nov. 10, 1928; s. Sigmund Anthony and Rose Dorothy (Lewin) F.; m. Donna Marie Barbeau, Jan. 4, 1955 (div. Mar. 1979); children—Jessica, Lydia, Alicia; m. Peg Nash, Jan. 28, 1983. B.A. in Physics, Columbia U., 1948, M.A., 1950, Ph.D., 1952. Instr., then asst. prof. Stanford U., Calif., 1952-56; asst. prof. physics U. Mich., Ann Arbor, 1956-58, assoc. prof., 1959-62, prof. physics, 1962-73; prof. optical scis. and physics U. Ariz., Tucson, 1973—, dir. Optical Scis. Ctr., 1973-83, acting dir. Ariz. Research Labs., 1983-84; vis. lectr. physics Oxford U., 1959; vis. prof. physics Yale U., New Haven, 1963; dep., acting dir. Advanced Research Projects Agy., Dept. Def., 1966-68; expert Office of Emergency Preparedness, Office of Pres., 1968-73. Inventor metastable helium magnetometer; developer level cross-over spectroscopy; pioneer in modern nonlinear optics. Sloan Found. fellow, 1959-62. Fellow Optical Soc. Am. (pres. 1977, Wood prize 1979), Am. Phys. Soc. (prize 1967), AAAS; mem. Soc. Photo-Optical Instrumentation, Radiol. Soc. N.Am., Sigma Xi. Club: Cosmos (Washington). Current work: Lasers, spectroscopy, nonlinear optics, image processing. Subspecialty: Atomic and molecular physics. Home: 2105 E 4th St Tucson AZ 85719 Office: Optical Scis Ctr U Ariz Tucson AZ 85721

FRANKL, WILLIAM STEWART, physician; b. Phila., July 15, 1928; s. Louis and Vera (Simkin) F.; m. Razelle Sherr, June 17, 1951; children: Victor S. (dec.), Brian A. B.A. in Biology, Temple U., 1951, M.D., 1955, M.S. in Medicine, 1961. Diplomate: Am. Bd. Internal Medicine, Am. Bd. Cardiovascular Disease. Intern Buffalo Gen. Hosp., 1955-56; resident in medicine Temple U., Phila., 1956-57, 59-61; mem. faculty Temple U. (Sch. Medicine), 1962-68, dir. EKG sect. dept. cardiology, 1966-68, dir. cardiac care unit, 1967-68; research fellow U. Pa., Phila., 1961-62; prof. medicine, dir. div. cardiology Med. Coll. Pa., Phila., 1970-79; prof. medicine, assoc. dir. cardiology div. Thomas Jefferson U., Phila., 1979-84; prof. medicine, co-dir. William Likoff Cardiovascular Inst. Hahnemann U., Phila., 1984—; physician-in-chief Springfield (Mass.) Hosp., 1968-70, practice medicine specializing in cardiology, Phila., 1962-68, 70—; cons. cardiology Phila. Va Hosp., 1970-79; Fogarty Sr. Internat. fellow Cardiothoracic Inst., U. London, 1978-79; Pres. elect Pa. affiliate Am. Heart Assn. Contbr. articles to profl. jours. Served with M.C. U.S. Army, 1957-59. Recipient Golden Apple award Temple U. Sch. Medicine, 1967; award Med. Coll. Pa., 1972; Lindback award for distinguished teaching, 1975. Fellow A.C.P., Am. Coll. Cardiology, Phila. Coll. Physicians, Am. Coll. Clin. Pharmacology (regent), Council Clin. Cardiology, Am. Heart Assn. (council on arteriosclerosis); mem. N.Y. Acad. Scis., Am. Fedn. Clin. Research, AAUP, AAAS, Assn. Am. Med. Colls., Am. Heart Assn. (bd. govs. S.E. Pa. chpt. 1972—, pres. 1976), Am. Soc. Clin. Pharmacology and Therapeutic Therapeutics. Current Work: Cardiovascular pharmacology; electrophysiology; cardiovascular hemodynamics; myocardial metabolism; education of medical students, house staff, fellows and practicing physicians; administration; research. Subspecialties: Cardiology; Pharmacology. Home: 536 Moreno Rd Wynnewood PA 19096 Office: William Likoff Cardiovascular Inst Broad and Vine Sts Philadelphia PA 19102

FRANKLIN, PAULA ANNE, psychologist; b. Wheaton, Ill., Feb. 2, 1928; d. Paul Spangler and Ella (Daniels) Fowler; m. Richard Franklin, Aug. 13, 1950; children: Jan Patience Franklin BenDor, Timothy Vickery, Edward Lee. B.Sc., Northwestern U., 1949, postgrad., 1975; M.A., W. Va. U., 1970; Ph.D., Union of Experimenting Colls. and Univs., Cin., 1980. Lic. psychologist, Md. Group social worker Girl Scouts U.S.A., El Paso, Tex., 1949-51, Las Cruces, N.M., 1949-51; staff mem. Placement Office, Columbia U., N.Y.C., 1952-54; adult educator, writer, Kan., Ill., W.Va., 1954-69; dir. Franklin Behavioral Sci. Cons., W. Va., 1969-71, Balt., 1971—; faculty applied behavior sci. Johns Hopkins Evening Coll., Balt., 1972—; social sci. research analyst Social Security Adminstrn., Balt., 1973—. Author: (with Richard Franklin) Tomorrow's Track, 1976, Urban Decisionmaking, 1967; contbr. articles to profl. jours. Active Girl Scouts U.S.A., Boy Scouts Am. Recipient Spl. Achievement award Social Security Adminstrn., 1982; Certificate of Recognition of Psychol. Service in Pub. Interest Md. Psychol. Assn., 1981. Mem. Am. Psychol. Assn. (mem. pub. policy com. 1981—, mem. research support network 1980—), Md. Psychol. Assn., AAAS, Assn. Women in Sci., League Women Voters, Evaluation Research Soc. Democrat. Unitarian. Club: Toastmasters. Current Work: Math. modelling to estimate costs of various policy and legislative alternatives for chronically ill. Involved labor force participation, utilization of health care facilities, estimation of health care costs. Also implemented social experimentation in disability program to estimate more accurately impact of future changes from more precisely targetted data bases. Subspecialty: Social psychology. Home: 3946 Cloverhill Rd Baltimore MD 21218 Office: Div Disability Studies Office of Disability Social Security Administration Security Blvd Baltimore MD 21235

FRANKLIN, RANDALL MORROW, director regional forensic unit, clinical psychologist; b. Bloomington, Ind., May 13, 1947; s. Owen Ellsworth and Dicy Lou (Morrow) F.; m. Mary Ann La Cava, Dec. 18, 1971 (div. 1975). B.A., U. Va., 1969; M.A., Temple U., 1976, Ph.D., 1979. Lic. psychologist, Pa. Clinic asst. Temple U. Psychol. Services Center, Phila., 1974-75; ward psychologist Phila. State Hosp., 1975-78, forensic ward adminstr. and ward psychologist, 1978-80, chief psychology services and forensic ward adminstr., 1980-81, chief forensic psychologist, 1981, dir. regional forensic unit, 1981—, pvt. practice clin. psychology, Phila., 1981—; clin. asst. prof. Hahnemann Med. Center, Phila., 1980—; cons. Fairmount Inst., Phila., 1981—. Mem. Pa. Psychology Polit. Action Com., 1980—. Served with USNR, 1969-71. Temple U. fellow, 1972; Pa. Psychiatry Dept. fellow, 1973. Mem. Nat. Register Health Service Providers in Psychology, Internat. Transactional Analysis Assn., Am. Psychol. Assn., Pa. Psychol. Assn., Am. Psychology-Law Soc., Assn. Advancement Psychology, Phi Beta Kappa, Phi Sigma, Alpha Phi Omega. Current Work: Research: Competency in the trial process; treatment and research issues in forensic psychology and law. Home: 522 Hilaire Rd Saint David's PA 19087 Office: Regional Forensic Unit Phila State Hosp 14000 Roosevelt Blvd Philadelphia PA 19114

FRANSES, ELIAS I., chemical engineer educator, researcher; b. Larissa, Greece, June 19, 1951; came to U.S., 1974, naturalized, 1984; s. Iosafat S. and Linda (Roussos) F.; m. Nien-Hwa Linda Wang, Dec. 22, 1978; 1 child, Joseph. Diploma in Chem. Engring., Nat. Tech. U., Greece, 1974; Ph.D., U. Minn.,

1979. Asst. prof. chem. engring., Purdue U., West Lafayette, Ind., 1979-83, assoc. prof., 1983—. Contbr. articles to profl. jours. Recipient Dist. Paper award Am. Oil Chem. Soc., 1984, Outstanding Jr. Faculty award ARCO, 1981. Mem. Am. Inst. Chem. Engrs., Am. Chem. Soc., Soc. Petroleum Engrs. Jewish. Current work: Surfactant systems, phase behavior, microstructure, tension, dynamics, lyotropic liquid crystals, vesicles, enhanced oil recovery; light scattering, dielectric relaxation, microspheroids. Subspecialties: Chemical engineering; Surface chemistry. Home: 3732 Capilano Dr West Lafayette IN 47906 Office: Purdue U Sch Chem Engring West Lafayette IN 47907

FRANTI, CHARLES ELMER, biostatistician, consultant, researcher; b. Ewen, Mich., Apr. 29, 1933; s. John Elmer and Ida Mary (Nykanen) F.; m. Carole Joan Wisti, Aug. 25, 1956; children: Rebecca Lee, Sara Lynne, Daniel John, Michael Jacob, Matthew Benjamin. B.S., U. Mich., 1955, A.M., 1960; M.S., Mich. State U., 1960; Ph.D., U. Calif.-Berkeley, 1967. Dir. athletics, instr. Suomi Coll., Hancock, Mich., 1955-59; instr. math. Mich. Tech. U., Houghton, 1956-59, 60-62; asst. prof. U. Calif.-Davis, 1966-70, assoc. prof., 1970-76, prof. biostatistics, 1976—; cons. U. Alta., Edmonton, 1981, Royal Vet. and Agrl. Coll., Copenhagen, 1981, U.S. Dept. Agr., Sacramento, 1972-76, Calif. Dept. Mental Health, Sacramento, 1968. Author: (with others) Epidemiology in Veterinary Practice, 1977. Pres. Upper Peninsula Intercollegiate Athletic Conf., Mich., Wis., 1956-57; v.p. Little League Baseball, Davis, Calif., 1971-73; officer, coach Davis Softball League, Calif., 1971-76; bd. dirs. Davis Youth Baseball, 1978-80, 82—. Martin Luther fellow Luth. Brotherhood Ins., Mich. State U., 1959-60; named Outstanding Instr. Sch. Vet. Medicine, U. Calif.-Davis, 1967-68. Mem. Math. Assn. Am. Biometric Soc., Am. Statis. Assn., Inst. Math. Stats. Soc. Epidemiologica Research, Soc. Indsl. and Applied Math., Nat. Council Tchrs. Math., Am. Pub. Health Assn., Statis. Soc. Can., Sigma Xi, Delta Omega, Zeta Psi. Lutheran. Current Work: Applications of statistical methods in biomedical research, epidemiologic methods and applications in medicine, zoonotic diseases. Subspecialty: Epidemiology. Office: Dept Community Health U Calif Sch Medicine Davis CA 95616

FRANTZ, FREDERICK STRASSNER, JR., nuclear engineer; b. Lebanon, Pa., Jan. 21, 1922; s. Frederick Strassner and Charlotte Elizabeth (Tear) F.; m. Emma Louise Keller, June 26, 1946; children: Charlotte L., Rachel L., Marjorie E., Frederick K. B.S., Lebanon Valley Coll., 1943; M.S., U. Pa.-Phila., 1949. Physicist Nat. Bur. Standards, Washington, 1949-55; nuclear engr. Westinghouse Electric Co., Pitts., 1955—. Served to lt. (j.g.) USNR, 1943-46. Mem. Am. Nuclear Soc. Republican. Lutheran. Current Work: Project engineer for Dept. Energy supported breeder reactor technology transfer program at Advanced Energy Systems Division, responsible for cost and schedule management. Subspecialty: Nuclear fission. Home: 325 McClellan Dr Pittsburgh PA 15236

FRANZ, DONALD NORBERT, pharmacologist, researcher, author; b. Indpls., Sept. 23, 1932; s. Norbert John and Henrietta Pauline (Bluemel) F.; children: Diane V., Beth L. B.S., Butler U., 1954, M.S., 1962; Ph.D., U. Utah, 1966. Research assoc. U. Edinburgh, Scotland, 1966-68; asst. prof. U. Utah Sch. Medicine, 1968-75, assoc. prof., 1975-85, prof., 1985—. Contbg. author: The Pharmacological Basis of Therapeutics, 5th edit, 1975, 6th edit., 1980, 7th edit., 1985; contbr. research articles to profl. jours. Served with AUS, 1954-56. Grantee Utah Heart Assn., 1976-78, 83-85; Grantee Mont. Heart Assn., 1977-78; Grantee Am. Parkinson Disease Assn., 1979-81; Nat. Heart, Lung and Blood Inst. NIH grantee, 1979—; Gardner Faculty fellow U. Utah, 1981. Mem. Am. Soc. Pharmacology and Exptl. Therapeutics, Soc. Neurosci., Am. Heart Assn., AAAS. Lutheran. Current Work: Regulation of blood pressure and the autonomic nervous system by the central nervous system; essential hypertension; pharmacology of central monoaminergic systems and opiate addiction. Subspecialties: Neuropharmacology; Neurophysiology. Office: Dept Pharmacology U Utah Sch Medicine Salt Lake City UT 84132

FRANZ, HELMUT, chemist; b. Kahl Main, Bavaria, Fed. Republic Germany; Sept. 22, 1930; came to U.S., 1967; naturalized, 1973; s. Otto and Anna (Lederer) F.; m. Antonie Anna Becker, Feb. 14, 1958; children—Bettina, Jutta, Christine. B.S., U. Wurzburg, Fed. Republic Germany, 1955, M.S. in Chemistry, 1959, Ph.D. in Natural Sci., 1962. Scientist Max Planck Inst. Silicate Research, Wurzburg, 1962-67; research assoc. Rensselaer Poly. Inst., Troy, N.Y., 1967-69; sr. research assoc. PPG Industries, Pitts., 1969-71, staff scientist, 1971, sr. scientist, 1979—. Patentee in field. Contbr. articles to profl. jours. Mem. Am. Ceramic Soc., Am. Chem. Soc. Republican. Roman Catholic. Current work: Advanced materials science, surface chemistry, coatings, thin films Subspecialties: Ceramics; Surface chemistry. Home: 201 Ridge Rd Pittsburgh PA 15238 Office: PPG Industries Glass Research and Devel PO Box 11472 Pittsburgh PA 15238

FRANZBLAU, DANIEL ERIC, computer graphics software engineer; b. Chgo., Jan. 29, 1955; s. Sanford Asher and Eugenia (Wysat) F. B.S. in Art and Design, MIT, 1977, M.S., 1979. Computer graphics programmer MIT, 1980-83; computer graphics programmer Capital Children's Museum, Washington, 1980-81; programmer, cons. Graphic Devices, Brighton, Mass., 1981—; cons. Mass. Coll. Art, Boston, 1982-83, Most Media, Somerville, 1981-82. Vol. digital arts project Boston Film and Video Found., 1982; project leader Simx Inc., Boston, 1984—. Mem. IEEE, Assn. for Computing Machinery. Creator computer video art work. Current Work: Interactive computer graphics applied to page composition and makeup, video paint systems, high quality font generation, education, training. Development of computer graphic tools for artistic creation of images, computer as darkroom and postprocessor for images. Subspecialties: Graphics, image processing, and pattern recognition; Software engineering. Office: Graphic Devices 124 Sutherland Rd Apt 2 Brighton MA 02146

FRASER, CLARENCE MALCOLM, veterinarian, editor; b. Hamiota, Man., Can., June 21, 1926; s. William Kerr and Edna May (Wallace) F.; m. Dorothy Jean Black, Sept. 17, 1955; children—Stuart, Kenneth, Paul, Martha, Duncan. B.S. in Agr., U. Man. 1949; D.V.M., U. Toronto, 1954, M.V.S.C., 1963. Gen. practice vet. med., Man., 1954-57; asst. prof. Ont. Vet. Coll., Guelph, 1957-63, prof., head div. medicine, 1963-65; prof. head dept. vet. clin. studies U. Sask., Saskatoon, Can., 1965-70; assoc. editor Merck Vet. Manual, Merck & Co., Inc., Rahway, N.J., 1970-75, 76-81, editor, 1981—; mgr. clin. research Pitman-Moore, Inc., Washington Crossing, N.J., 1975-76. Mem. AVMA, Can. Vet. Med. Assn. (mem. council 1958-62, editor Can. Vet. Jour. 1963-65), Brit. Vet. Assn., Am. Assn. Indsl. Vets., Sask. Vet. Med. Assn. Current work: Handbook of veterinary diagnostics, therapy and disease control, developmental research for animal health pharmaceuticals. Subspecialties: Internal medicine (veterinary medicine); Drug delivery systems. Home: 4 Old Forge St RD 3 Flemington NJ Office: Animal Sci Research MSDRL Box 2000 Rahway NJ

FRASIER, GARY WAYNE, hydraulic engineer; b. Imperial, Nebr., July 27, 1937; s. Wilber Wayne and Edith Belle (Simms) F.; m. Alberta Jolee Rolston, Nov. 25, 1959; children—Donna J., Clay R., Wendy B. B.S., Colo. State U., 1954; M.S. in Soil Mechanics, Ariz. State U., 1966. Trainee Agrl. Research Service, USDA, Grand Junction, Colo., 1957-58, agrl. engr., Tempe Ariz., 1959-67, research hydraulic engr., Phoenix, 1967-78, Tucson, 1978—. Contbr. articles to profl. jours. Cubmaster Theodore Roosevelt Council Boy Scouts Am., Tempe, 1967-71, scoutmaster, 1971-76. Mem. Am. Soc. Agrl. Engrs., Soil Conservation Soc. Am., Soc. Range Mgmt. (assoc. editor jour. 1982—, editor 1984—). Current work: Water supply and conservation in arid and semiarid regions; revegetation of rangelands; rainfed agriculture; water use efficiency of semiarid range plants. Subspecialties: Water supply and wastewater treatment; Resource conservation. Office: SW Rangeland Watershed Research Ctr 2000 E Allen Rd Tucson AZ 85719

FRASSANITO, JOHN ROBERT, industrial designer, consultant; b. N.Y.C., July 8, 1941; B.A., Art Ctr. Coll. of Design, Pasadena, Calif., 1968. Indsl. designer Loewy Snaith Assoc., N.Y.C., 1968-69; pres. John Frassanito Assocs., San Antonio, 1969—. Mem. Indsl. Design Soc. Am. Clubs: Lake Canyon Yacht (San Antonio); Lakewood Yacht (Houston). Current work: Multi function video teleconferencing systems, space vehicle habitability design, product development. Subspecialties: Space habitat design; Industrial engineering. Office: John Frassanito and Assocs PO Box 29000 San Antonio TX 78229

FRAUENTHAL, JAMES CLAY, mathematician; b. N.Y.C., Nov. 25, 1944; s. Herman Clay and Roslyn (Lilienstern) F.; m. Margaret A. Mitchell, June 8, 1969. B.S. in Mech. Engring. summa cum laude, Tufts U., 1966; M.S. (NSF fellow), Harvard U., 1967, Ph.D., (NSF fellow), 1971. Asst. prof. mech. engring. Tufts U., Medford, Mass., 1971-73; research assoc. population studies Harvard U. Sch. Pub. Health, Cambridge, Mass., 1973-75; assoc. prof. applied math. SUNY-Stony Brook, 1975-82; mem. tech. staff AT&T Bell Labs., Holmdel, N.J., 1982—; vis. assoc. prof. math. Harvey Mudd Coll., Claremont Calif., 1981-82. Author: Introduction to Population Modeling, 1979; Mathematical Modeling in Epidemiology, 1980. Trustee Orthopaedic Inst., Hosp. for Joint Diseases, Helene Fuld Sch. Nursing. Recipient Chancellor's award for excellence in teaching SUNY, 1978; Alfred P. Sloan Found. grantee, 1975-79. Mem. Soc. Indsl. and Applied Math. (editor news 1977-84), ASME, Tau Beta Pi. Current work: Population dynamics, queueing systems, applied mechanics. Subspecialties: Applied mathematics; Mathematical software. Home: 16 Saratoga Dr Colts Neck NJ 07722 Office: AT&T Bell Labs Room 2D-612 Holmdel NJ 07733

FRAUMENI, JOSEPH FRANCIS, JR., physician, cancer research administrator; b. Boston, Apr. 1, 1933; s. Joseph Francis and Pauline Elizabeth (Malta) F.; m. Patricia Welch D'Arcy, Apr. 23, 1977. A.B., Harvard U., 1954; M.S., 1965; M.D., Duke U., 1958. Diplomate Am. Bd. Internal Medicine. Intern, resident Johns Hopkins Hosp., Balt., 1958-60; resident in medicine Meml. Sloan-Kettering Cancer Ctr., N.Y.C., 1960-62; commd. med. officer USPHS, 1962; staff assoc. epidemiology br. Nat. Cancer Inst., Bethesda, Md., 1962-65, chief ecology studies sect., 1966-75, chief environ. epidemiology br., 1976-82, dir. Epidemiology and Biostats. Program, 1981—; attending physician Clin. Ctr., NIH, Bethesda, 1966—; adj. prof. epidemiology Uniformed Services U. of Health Scis., Bethesda, 1980—. Editor: Persons at High Risk of Cancer, 1975; (with others) Genetics of Human Cancer, 1977, Cancer Epidemiology and Prevention, 1982, Radiation Carcinogenesis, 1984. Author (with others) Atlas of Cancer Mortality in the U.S., 1975. Recipient Meritorious Service medal USPHS, 1976, Disting. Service medal USPHS, 1983. Fellow ACP, Am. Coll. Epidemiology; mem. Am. Soc. Preventive Oncology (pres. 1981-83); Am. Assn. Cancer Research (bd. dirs. 1983—). Current work: Director of program of epidemiological research of the causes and means of preventing cancer. Subspecialties: Epidemiology; Cancer research (medicine). Office: Nat Cancer Inst Landow Bldg Room 4C03 7910 Woodmont Ave Bethesda MD 20205

FRAY, JOHN CORDELL SPENCER, physiologist; b. Red Hills, Jamaica, June 23, 1943; came to U.S., 1963, naturalized, 1975; d. Dudley and Enid May (Cookhorn) F.; 1 dau., Joni Michele. B.S., Howard U., 1970; M.S., MIT, 1971; Ph.D., Harvard U., 1975. Instr. physiology Harvard Med. Sch., Boston, 1975-76; asst. prof. U. Calif.-San Francisco, 1976-78; asst. prof. physiology U. Mass.-Worcester, 1978-81, assoc. prof., 1984—; assoc. prof. Hunter Coll., N.Y.C., 1981-84; mem. adv. council NSF, Washington, 1984—. Contbr. articles to profl. jours. Bd. dirs. Harvard Apparatus Found., Boston, 1982—. Mem. Am. Physiol. Soc. Current work: Blood pressure regulation and the renin-angiotensin system; cellular control of renal renin secretion. Subspecialties: Physiology (biology); Endocrinology. Home: 340 Sunderland Rd #28 Worcester MA 01604 Office: U Mass Dept Physiology 55 Lake Ave N Worcester MA 01605

FRAZIER, ALVA WILLIAM, research chemist, crystallographer; b. Johnson City, Tenn., Apr. 12, 1931; s. Alva Whittle and Stella (Weeden) F.; m. Gussie Vesta Irick, June 13, 1952; children—Gordon, Anthony, Linda. B.S. in Chemistry, U. Tenn., 1953. Analytical chemist TVA, Muscle Shoals, Ala., 1953-56, research chemist, 1956—. Author chpt. in book. Patentee in field (6). Contbr. numerous articles to profl. jours. Mem. Nat. Solution Fertilizer Assn., Am. Chem. Soc., Florence Astronomy Soc. (sec.-treas. 1963-73). Current work: Research and development for fertilizer technology and production; optical microscopy of fertilizer materials and their soil reaction products. Subspecialties: Crystallography; Inorganic chemistry. Home: 2219 Randolph St Florence AL 35630 Office: TVA Muscle Shoals AL 35660

FRAZIER, HOWARD STANLEY, physician; b. Oak Park, Ill., Jan. 16, 1926; s. Cecil Austin and Harriet DeGolyer (Greenleaf) F.; m. Lenore Callahan, June 10, 1950; children—Mark C., Reid J., Anne K., Peter B. Ph.B., U. Chgo., 1949; M.D., Harvard U., 1953. Intern, then resident in medicine Mass. Gen. Hosp., Boston, 1953-55; postdoctoral fellow Harvard U. Med. Sch., 1955-56, Cambridge U., 1956-57, Case Western Res. U. Med. Sch., 1957-58; mem. faculty Harvard U. Med. Sch., 1958—, prof. medicine, 1978—; dir. Inst. Health Research Harvard U. Med. Sch. (Sch. Public Health), 1975—; cons. NIH, Nat. Center Health Care Tech. Author papers in field. Served with USNR, 1943-46. Mem. Am. Soc. Clin. Investigation, Am. Physiol. Soc., Am. Soc. Nephrology, Inst. Medicine. Current Work: Medical technology evaluation, health practices research, research administration. Subspecialties: Health services research; Internal medicine. Office: 677 Huntington Ave Boston MA 02115

FRAZIER, OSCAR HOWARD, thoracic and cardiovascular surgeon, researcher; b. Stephenville, Tex., Apr. 16, 1940; s. Oscar H. and Adele (Jones) F.; m. Rachel Merriman, Feb. 15, 1964; children: Todd, Allison. B.A., U. Tex., 1963; M.D., Baylor U., 1967. Diplomate: Am. Bd. Surgery, 1975, Am. Bd. Thoracic Surgery, 1977. Intern Baylor Affiliated Hosps., Houston, 1967-68, resident in surgery, 1970-74; resident in thoracic and cardiovascular surgery Tex. Heart Inst. of St. Luke's Episcopal Hosp., Tex. Children's Hosp., Houston, 1974-76; assoc. surgeon Tex. Heart Inst., 1976—; staff M.D. Anderson Hsp., Hermann Hosp., both Houston, 1976—; dir. cardiovascular research St. Luke's Hosp., Houston, 1981—, also mem. courtesy staff; assoc. prof. surgery U. Tex. Med. Sch., Houston, 1976—, U. Tex.-M.D. Anderson Hosp. and Tumor Inst., 1976—; guest examiner Am. Bd. Surgery, 1982. Assoc. editor: Tex. Heart Inst. Jour, 1981—; contbr. numerous articles to sci. and med. jours. Bd. dirs. Nat. Soc. Prevention of Child Abuse, 1977—; mem. Fun Football Bd., 1978-80, team physician, 1978-80; mem. adminstrv. council St. Luke's United Methodist Ch., 1978; adv. council Nat. Heart, Lung and Blood Inst. Served as capt. U.S. Army, 1968-70, Vietnam. Recipient Outstanding Surgery Student award Baylor U., 1967. Fellow ACS, Am. Coll. Cardiology; mem. Soc. Thoracic Surgeons, AMA, Am. Coll. Chest Physicians, Am. Soc. Clin. Oncology, Tex. Med. Assn., Tex. Surg. Assn., Denton A. Cooley Cardiovascular Surg. Soc., Internat. Soc. Study of Lung Cancer, AAAS, Houston Surg. Soc., Houston Cardiology Soc., N.Y. Acad. Scis., Internat. Soc. Heart Transplantation, N.Am. Hyperthermia Group, Am. Soc. Artificial Internal Organs, N.Am. Soc. Pacing and Electrophysiology, Radiation Research Soc., Sigma Chi. Current Work: Development of an implantable left heart assist system; study of systemic hyperthermia by extracorporeal circulation; role of lasers in vascular surgery; development of a new heart valve. Subspecialties: Cardiac surgery; Transplant surgery. Home: 2241 Chilton Houston TX 77019 Office: PO Box 20345 Houston TX 77025

FRAZIER, SHERBERT HUGHES, JR., psychiatrist, institute director; b. Shreveport, La., June 12, 1921; s. Shervert Hughes and Mary (Lowman) F.; m. Gloria Barger, July 20, 1947; children—Elise, Alan, Rosalie, Stephen. Student Baylor U., 1936-39; B.S., U. Ill.-Chgo., 1941, M.D., 1943; M.S. in Psychiatry, U. Minn., 1957; cert. psychoanalytic medicine, Columbia Coll. Phys. and Surgs., 1963; M.A. (hon.), Harvard U., 1972. Diplomate Am. Bd. Psychiatry and Neurology (bd. dirs. 1965, pres. 1972), Am. Bd. Family Practice (by-laws com. 1979-80, examining com. 1979—, research and devel. com. 1979-80, chmn. patient mgmt. program panel). Intern, U. Ill. Research and Ednl. Hosp., 1943-44; fellow internal medicine Mayo Found., 1951-52, fellow psychiatry, asst. to staff, 1954-56; practice medicine Harrisburg, Ill., 1946-50, 53; adminstr. Harrisburg Med. Found., 1948-51; cons. sect. psychiatry Mayo Clinic, St. Mary's Hosp., also Meth. Hosp., Rochester, Minn., 1956-58; chief research scientist internal medicine N.Y. State Psychiat. Inst., 1958-61, dep. dir. 1968-72; asst. attending psychiatrist Presbyn. Hosp., N.Y.C., 1958-63; dir. impatient cons. service in psychiatry, 1961-62; later attending psychiatrist; dir. Houston Psychiat. Inst., 1962-65 psychiatrist in chief Ben Taub Gen. Hosp., Houston, 1962-68; cons. VA Hosp., Houston, 1962-68; sr. attending psychiatrist Meth. Hosp., Houston, 1962-68; psychiatrist-in-chief McLean Hosp., Belmont, Mass., 1972—; assoc. in psychiatry Columbia Coll. Phys. and surgery, Joske asst. prof. psychiatry, 1958-62, prof. 1968-72; profl. psychiatry, chmn. dept. Baylor U. Coll. Medicine, 1962-68; prof. psychiatry Harvard, Boston, 1972—; dir. NIMH, Dept Health and Human Services, 1984—; cons. Rice U., 1963-68; commr. Mental Health and Mental Retardation for Tex., 1965-67; pres. VI World Congress Psychiatry; mem. vis. com. Yale U., Med. Sch., 1977-81. Contbr. articles to profl. jours. Served as officer, M.C., USNR, 1944-60, PTO. Recipient Disting. Alumnus award Mayo Found., 1983. Fellow N.Y. Acad. medicine (chmn. Salmon lecture com); mem. AMA (council continuing physician edn. 1976-81), Mass. Med. Assn., Middlesex County Med. Soc., Am. Coll. Psychiatrists (regent 1972, v.p. 1977-79, pres. 1979-81), Am. Psychiat. Assn. (chmn. program com. 1965-68, chmn. joint commn. pub. affairs, sec. 1983—), World Psychiat. Assn. (v.p. 1977—), Central Neuropsychiat. Assn., Assn. Research Nervous and Mental Disease (pres. 1972, chmn. bd. 1976-78), Boston Psychoanalytic Soc. and Inst., Sigma Xi, Alpha Omega Alpha. Subspecialty: Psychiatry.

FRAZIER, WILLIAM EARL, spacecraft systems engineer; b. Walnut Creek, Calif., May 2, 1958; s. Philip Emory and Margaret (Mendenhall) F. B.S.M.E., U. Colo., 1980, M.S. in Aerospace Engring., 1982. With solar mesosphere explorer ops. Lab. for Atmospheric and Space Physics, U. Colo., Boulder, 1981, research assoc., 1981; project engr. Computer Tech. Assn., Englewood, Colo., 1982; spacecraft systems engr. Ball Aerospace Systems Div., Boulder, 1983—. Mem. Am. Astronautical Soc. (co-chmn. keystone guidance and control conf. 1984). Current work: Spacecraft systems engineering, especially attitude determination, control and mission design of CRRES spacecraft; engineering of system requirements and capabilities trade-offs of entire spacecraft. Subspecialties: Aerospace engineering and technology; Astronautics. Office: Ball Aerospace Systems Div BE-9 PO Box 1062 Boulder CO 80306

FREAR, DONALD STUART, research biochemist; b. Wakefield, R.I., Sept. 5, 1929; s. Donald E.H. and Hazel W. (Eaton) F.; m. M. Clotine Rose, Jan. 14, 1956; children—Dawnelle, Susan, Michele, Craig. B.S., Pa. State U., 1951; M.S., Ohio State U., 1953, Ph.D., 1955. Research biochemist Charles F. Kettering Found., Yellow Springs, Ohio, 1955-57; assoc. prof. biochemistry, N.D. State U., Fargo, 1957-64; research biochemist Agrl. Research Service, USDA, Fargo, 1964-68, research leader, 1968—. Editor: Xenobiotic Metabolism: In Vitro Methods, 1979. Recipient Superior Service Team award USDA, 1982. Mem. Am. Chem. Soc., Plant Growth Regulator Soc. Am., Sigma Xi. Current work: Metabolism and action of agricultural chemicals in higher plants. Subspecialties: Biochemistry (biology); Plant physiology (biology). Home: 91 19th Ave N Fargo ND 58102 Office: USDA Metabolism and Radiation Research Lab State U Sta Fargo ND 58105

FRECHETTE, VAN DERCK, ceramics engineering educator, consultant, researcher; b. Ottawa, Ont., Can., Jan. 5, 1916; came to U.S., 1936; s. Howells and Lena D. (Derick) F.; m. Sarah Wiley Houghton, Apr. 4, 1940; children—William G.H., H.V. Derck, Christopher J., Margaret Kathleen, Judith L. Student U. Toronto, 1934-36; B.S., Alfred U., 1936-38; M.S., Ph.D., U. Ill., 1942. Registered profl. engr., N.Y. Research physicist Corning Glass, N.Y., 1942-44; prof. ceramic sci. N.Y. State Coll. Ceramics, Alfred U., N.Y., 1944—; cons. to various orgns., 1944—; guest prof. U. Goettingen, Fed. Republic Germany, 1955-56, M.P.I. Silikatforschungen, Wuerzburg, Fed. Republic Germany, 1965, U. Erlangen-Nuernberg, Fed. Republic Germany, 1973. Author: Microscopy of Ceramics, 1955; editor 10 books; contbr. numerous articles to sci. jours. Chmn. Alfred Chpt. ARC, 1952. Fulbright Commn. sr. research fellow, 1955; Western Electric Fund fellow; recipient award Am. Soc. Engring. Edn., 1968. Fellow Am. Ceramic Soc (Outstanding educator award 1983); mem. Nat. Inst. Ceramic Engrs., Deutsche Keramische Gesellschaft, N.Y. Acad. Sci., Swedish Royal Acad. Sci. (hon.), Sigma Xi. Republican. Episcopalian. Current work: Failure analysis of brittle materials. Subspecialties: Ceramic engineering; Fracture mechanics. Home: 22 S Main St Alfred NY 14802 Office: NY State Coll Ceramics Alfred U Alfred NY 14802

FREDERICKSON, ARMAN FREDERICK, geologist, educator, consultant; b. Glenboro, Can., May 5, 1918, came to U.S., 1923; s. Albert and Ethel May (Wilton) F.; m. Mary Maxine Stubblefield, Sept. 18, 1943; children—Mary Christene, Clover Diane, Penny Kathlene, Kimberly Mei, Sigrid Janice. B.S. in Mining Engring., U. Wash., 1940; M.S. in Metall. Engring., Mont. Sch. Mines, 1942; Sc.D. in Geology, MIT, 1947. Registered profl. engr., Tex., Colo., Nev., Mo. Instr. Mont. Sch. Mines, 1939-42, MIT, Cambridge, 1942-43; chief geologist Cornucopia Gold Mines, Oreg., 1940-41; prof. geology and geol. engring., Washington U., St. Louis, 1947-55; Fulbright research prof., Norway, 1951-52; supr. exploration research Pan Am. Petroleum Corp., Tulsa, 1955-60; prof., chmn. dept. earth and planetary scis. U. Pitts., 1960-65, dir. Ctr. Oceanography, 1965-66; v.p., dir. research King Resources Co., Denver, 1965-69; adj. prof. environ. engring. Denver U., 1968-71; sr. v.p., dir. King Resources Co., Denver, 1969-71; pres. Sorbotec, Inc., Houston, 1971-73; owner, pres. Global Survey, Inc., 1971—; mgr., v.p. or dir. numerous cos. Middle East, Europe, Africa; Worldwide cons. in oil and mineral exploration. Editor: Geophysics, 1965. Contbr. articles to profl. jours. Patentee techniques for exploration, pollution control for chem. engring. Served to lt. USN, 1943-46. Fellow Geol. Soc. Am., AAAS; mem. AIME, Am. Assn. Petroleum Geologists, Mineral. Soc. Am., Soc. Econ. Geologists, Geochem. Soc., Soc. Econ. Paleontologists and Mineralogists. Republican. Subspecialties: Mineralogy; Petroleum engineering. Home and Office: 425 Uvalde St McAllen TX 78501

FREDERICKSON, PAUL OLIVER, computer scientist, mathematician; b. Lynd, Minn., May 30, 1936; s. Howard Milton and Dagny (Ostergaard) F.; m. Rosmarie Hohenner, Aug. 9, 1958; children—Beth, Margaret, James, Howard. B.S., U. Md., 1958, M.A., 1961; Ph.D., Nebr. U., 1964. Assoc. in math. Johns Hopkins Applied Physics Lab., Md., 1957-61; asst. prof. Case Inst. Tech., Cleve., 1964-69; assoc. prof. Lakehead U., Thunder Bay, Ont., Can., 1969-79; vis. prof. Tech. U. Munchen, Germany, 1973-74; vis. scientist NASA/Goddard, Greenbelt, Md., 1978-79; staff Los Alamos Nat. Lab., N.Mex., 1979—. NSF grantee, 1962, 63, 65-69; Nat. Research Council Can. grantee, 1971-73. Mem. Soc. Indsl. and Applied Math., Assn. for Computing Machinery, Am. Math. Soc. Club: Kiwanis. Current work: Development of high performance algorithms for parallel supercomputers. Subspecialties: Algorithms; Analysis. Address: Gimlevein 6B 5000 Bergen Norway

FREDERIKSEN, NORMAN OLIVER, geologist; b. Vienna, Austria, Aug. 11, 1932 (parents Am. citizens); s. Oliver Jul and Jane (Schwanfeldt) F.; m. Elke Elfriede-Magret Petersen, Aug. 25, 1962; 1 child, Kirsten. B.A., Hamilton Coll., 1957; M.S., Pa. State U., 1961; Ph.D., U. Wis.-Madison, 1969. Geologist Mobil Oil Corp. Dallas, 1961-63, 1965-69; assoc. prof. San Diego State U., 1969-75; geologist U.S. Geol. Survey, Reston, Va., 1975—. Contbr. articles to profl. jours. Served with U.S. Army, 1952-54. Mem. Am. Assn. Stratigraphic Palynologists (bd. dirs. 1977-78), Geol. Soc. Am., Am. Assn. Petroleum Geologists. Current work: Biostratigraphy, paleoecology, and paleobiogeography of Paleozoic to Cenozoic spores and pollen grains. Subspecialties: Paleontology; Paleobiology. Office: US Geol Survey mail stop 970 Reston VA 22092

FREDRICK, LAURENCE WILLIAM, astronomer, educator; b. Stroudsburg, Pa., Aug. 27, 1927; s. Ishmeal T. and Grace (Slider) F.; m. Frances I. Schwenk, Feb. 5, 1949; children—Laura Grace, Theodore David, Rebecca Lyn. B.A, Swarthmore Coll., 1952, M.A., 1954; Ph.D., U. Pa., 1959. Research asst. Sproul Obs., Swarthmore, Pa., 1952-56; research asso. Flower and Cook Obs., Malvern, Pa., 1957-59; astronomer Lowell Obs., Flagstaff, Ariz., 1959-63; mem. faculty U. Va., Charlottesville, 1963—, prof. astronomy, 1965—; chmn. dept., dir. Leander McCormick Obs., 1963-79, cons. in field.; Fulbright-Hays exchange lectr., Austria, 1972-73; prof. U. Vienna, 1972-73; assoc. astronomer Eur. Southern Obs., 1982-83. Co-author: An Introduction to Astronomy, 9th edit, 1980, Astronomy, 10th edit, 1976, Descriptive Astronomy, 1978. Served with USN, 1945-48. Named Alumnus of Year Milton Hershey Sch., 1961. Mem. Am. Astron. Soc. (sec. 1969-80), Internat. Astron. Union (sec. U.S. nat. com. 1970-80), Am. Inst. Physics (bd. govs. 1969-79), Univs. for Space Research Assn. (trustee), Sigma Xi. Current Work: Binary stars; stellar masses; planerary nebulae; identification of field galaxies. Subspecialty: Optical astronomy. Home: 2602 Bennington Rd Charlottesville VA 22901

FREDRICKSON, DONALD S., See *Who's Who in America*, 43rd edition.

FREDRICKSON, LEIGH HARRY, wetland ecologist, educator; b. Sioux City, Iowa, Mar. 13, 1939; s. Harry T. and Fern E. (Happel) F.; m. Judith C. Stotts, July 1965; children—Nicole L., Jill M. B.S., Iowa State U., 1961, M.S., 1963, Ph.D., 1967. Instr. Iowa State U., Ames, 1964-65; asst. prof., dir. U. Mo., Columbia, 1967-71, assoc. prof., dir., 1971-79, prof. ecology, dir., 1979—. Recipient Disting. Research award Gamma Sigma Delta, 1983. Mem. Am. Ornithologists Union, Wildlife Soc., Cooper Ornithol. Soc., Wilson Ornithol. Soc., AAAS (E. Sydney Stephens award 1985). Current work: Wetland ecology - especially lowland hardwood wetlands and glacial marshes, bioenergetics of breeding and wintering waterfowl moist-soil management, greentree reservoir management. Subspecialties: Resource conservation; Ecology (environmental science). Home: Route 1 Box 273 Puxico MO 63960 Office: Mo Gaylord Lab Puxico MO 63960

FREE, CHARLES ALFRED, biochemist, pharmacologist; b. Cleve., Apr. 19, 1936; s. Alfred H. and Dorothy (Hoffmeister) F.; m. Thora C. Meade, Oct. 21,

1961; children: Charles M., Maia E. B.S. in Chemistry, Purdue U., 1957; Ph.D. in Physiol. Chemistry, UCLA, 1962. USPHS postdoctoral research fellow Sloan-Kettering Inst. for Cancer Research, N.Y.C., 1962-65; research investigator Squibb Inst. for Med. Research, New Brunswick, N.J., 1965-69, sr. research investigator, Princeton, N.J., 1969-82, research fellow, 1982—. Contbr. articles to biochem. and pharmacologic publs. Mem. AAAS, Am. Chem. Soc., Am. Soc. for Pharmacology and Exptl. Therapeutics, Sigma Xi. Current Work: Steroid hormones, receptors and mechanisms of action; enzyme inhibitors; therapy of inflammatory and hypertensive diseases. Subspecialties: Biochemistry (medicine); Molecular pharmacology. Home: 103 Bradford Ln Pennington NJ 08534 Office: Squibb Inst for Med Research PO Box 4000 Princeton NJ 08540

FREED, KARL FREDERICK, chemist, educator; b. Bklyn., Sept. 25, 1942; s. Nathan and Pauline (Wolodarsky) F.; m. Gina P. Goldstein, June 14, 1964; children: Nicole Yvette, Michele Suzanne. B.S., Columbia U., 1963; A.M., Harvard U., 1965, Ph.D., 1967. NATO postdoctoral fellow U. Manchester, Eng., 1967-68; asst., then assoc. prof. chemistry James Franck Inst., U. Chgo., 1968-76, prof., 1976—, dir. James Franck Inst., 1983—. Adv. editor: Chem. Revs; assoc. editor: Jour Chem. Physics; Contbr. articles on chem. physics to profl. jours. Recipient Pure Chemistry award Am. Chem. Soc., 1976, Marlow medal Faraday div., 1973. Fellow Am. Phys. Soc.; mem. Royal Soc. Chemistry (London). Current Work: Radiationless processes and photochemistry; statis. mechanics of polymer systems; many-body theory; theoretical founds. of semi-empirical quantum chemistry. Subspecialties: Theoretical chemistry; Atomic and molecular physics. Office: 5640 S Ellis Ave Chicago IL 60637

FREED, NORMAN, physics educator and researcher, academic dean; b. Phila., June 11, 1936; s. Hyman David and Betty (Posner) F.; m. Marian Trygve Struble, June 12, 1960; children—Jonathan Raymond, Eric Oliver. B.S. in Physics, Antioch Coll., 1958; M.S. in Theoretical Nuclear Physics, Western Res. U., 1961, Ph.D. in Theoretical Nuclear Physics, 1964. Postdoctoral fellow U. Nebr., 1963-64; Nordic Inst. for Theoretical Atomic Physics fellow U. Lund, Sweden, 1964-65; Ford Found. fellow Niels Bohr Inst., U. Copenhagen, 1964-65; asst. prof. physics Pa. State U., University Park, 1965-68, assoc. prof., 1968-82, prof., 1982—, asst. dean Coll. Sci., 1978-79, assoc. dean for resident instrn., 1979—; inst. fellow Research Inst. Theoretical Physics, U. Helsinki, summer 1971; guest scientist Ctr. Nuclear Studies, French Atomic Energy Commn. at Saclay, 1971-72; guest prof. U. grenoble, France, summer 1973; NORDITA fellow U. Lund, summer 1975; guest prof. U. Paris at Orsay, summer 1977. Contbr. numerous articles to profl. publs. Mem. Am. Phys. Soc., AAAS, AAUP, N.Y. Acad. Scis., Sigma Xi. Current work: Theoretical nuclear physics, intermediate energy nuclear physics, pion physics, high energy electromagnetic interactions with nuclei, nuclear structure theory. Subspecialties: Theoretical physics; Nuclear physics. Home: 133 E Marylyn Ave State College PA 16801 Office: Coll of Sci and Dept of Physics 211 Whitmore Lab Pa State U University Park PA 16802

FREED, VIRGIL HAVEN, toxicology educator; b. Mendota, Ill., Nov. 18, 1919; s. Jay R. and Olive Rebecca (Edgell) F.; m. Anna May Carlson, Jan. 30, 1944; children: Kathleen, John, Linda, (dec.), David. B.S., M.S., Oreg. State U.; Ph.D., U. Oreg. Asst. prof. agrl. chemistry and farm crops Oreg. State U., Corvallis, 1944-48, assoc. prof., 1948-54, assoc. prof. chemistry, 1954-61, prof., 1960-61, head agrl. chemistry, 1961-84, dir. Environ. Health Scis. Ctr., 1967-81. Co-editor: Environ. Dynamics of Pesticides, 1975, Agromedical Practices in Pesticide Management, 1982. Active Concerned Citizens of Oreg. Recipient Gov.'s N.W. Sci. award Oreg. Mus. Sci. and Industry, 1971. Fellow AAAS, Weed Sci. Soc. (hon.); mem. Am. Weed Sci. Soc., Oreg. Acad. Scis., Jamaican Agromed. Assn., Soc. Toxicology, Phi Lambda Upsilon. Republican. Baptist. Club: Triads (Corvallis). Lodge: Kiwanis. Current Work: Biochemistry of pesticides, environmental chemodynamics, behavior of pesticides in soils and in biological systems. Subspecialties: Toxicology (agriculture); Environmental toxicology. Home: 11 NW Edgewood Way Corvallis OR 97330 Office: Dept Agrl Chemistry Oreg State U Corvallis OR 97331

FREEDBERG, IRWIN MARK, dermatology educator; b. Boston, July 4, 1931; s. Arthur Harris and Sadie (Bixby) F.; m. Irene Lisman, July 4, 1954; children—Marjorie, Kenneth, Deborah. Student Dartmouth Coll., 1952; M.D., Harvard Med. Sch., 1956. Diplomate Am. Bd. Dermatology. Intern then resident Beth Israel Hosp., Boston, 1956-59; asst. resident dermatology Mass. Gen. Hosp., Boston, 1959-61; postdoctoral fellow dept. biochemistry Brandeis U. Waltham, Mass., 1961-62; from instr. to prof. Harvard Med. Sch., Boston, 1962-77; prof., chmn. dept. dermatology Johns Hopkins Med. Ctr., Balt., 1977-81, NYU Med. Sch., N.Y.C., 1981—; adv. council Nat. Inst. Arthritis, Diabetes and Digestive and Kidney Disease, Washington, 1984—. Editor: Dermatology in General Medicine, 1985, Jour. Investigative Dermatology, 1972-77. Contbr. articles to profl. jours. Guggenheim fellow, 1969—; NIH grantee, 1962—. Fellow Am. Bd. Dermatology (bd. dirs. 1984—); mem. Soc. Investigative Dermatology (pres. 1981-82, Montagna lectr. 1980), Assn. Profs. Dermatology (pres. elect 1984—). Current work: Clinical and investigative dermatology. Subspecialty: Dermatology. Office: NYU Med Ctr Dept Dermatology 550 1st Ave New York NY 10016

FREEDLE, ROY OMER, research psychologist, editor; b. Chgo., Aug. 8, 1933; s. Edwin Lee and Goldie (Dolance) F. B.S., Roosevelt U., 1957; M.S., Columbia U., 1959, Ph.D., 1964. Research scientist Am. Insts. for Research, Washington, 1964-67; research psychologist Ednl. Testing Service, Princeton, N.J., 1967—, sr. research psychologist, 1971—. Editor-in-chief: Discourse Processes, 1978; series editor: Advances in Discourse, 1977—; author, editor: Discourse Production and Comprehension, 1977; author: Culture and Language, 1975. Mem. Am. Psychol. Assn., Am. Statis. Assn., Psychometric Soc. Republican. Current Work: Integrate and evaluate language performance as presented by specialists in the fields of psychology, computer science, linguistics and anthropology. Subspecialties: Cognition; Learning. Office: Educational Testing Service Rosedale Rd Princeton NJ 08541

FREEDMAN, DANIEL X., psychiatrist, educator; b. Lafayette, Ind., Aug. 17, 1921; s. Harry and Sophia (Feinstein) F.; m. Mary C. Neidigh, Mar. 20, 1945. B.A., Harvard U., 1947; M.D., Yale U., 1951; grad., Western New Eng. Inst. Psychoanalysis, 1966; D.Sc. (hon.), Wabash Coll., 1974, Indiana U., 1982. Intern pediatrics Yale Hosp., 1951-52, resident psychiatry, 1952-55; from instr. to prof. psychiatry Yale U., 1955-66; chmn. dept. U. Chgo., 1966-83, Louis Block prof. biol. scis., 1969-83; Judson Braun prof. psychiatry and pharmacology UCLA, 1983—; career investigator USPHS, 1957-66; dir. psychiatry and biol. sci. tng. program Yale U., 1960-66; cons. NIMH, 1960—, U.S. Army Chem. Center, Edgewood, Md., 1965-66; chmn. panel psychiat. drug efficacy study Nat. Acad. Sci.-NRC, 1966; chmn. Nat. Acad. Scis.-NRC, 1977—; mem. adv. com. FDA, 1967—; rep. to div. med. scis. NRC, 1971—, mem. com. on brain scis., 1971-73, mem. com. on problems of drug dependence, 1971—; mem. com. problems drug dependence Nat. Inst. Medicine, 1971-76, com. substance abuse, and habitual behavior, 1976—; advisor Pres.'s Biomed. Research Panel, 1975-76; mem. selection com., coordinator research task panel Pres.'s Commn. Mental Health, 1977-78; mem. Jt. Commn. Prescription Drug Use, Inc., 1977—. Author: (with N.J. Giarman) Biochemical Pharmacology of Psychotomimetic Drugs, 1965, What Is Drug Abuse? , 1970, (with F.C. Redlich) The Theory and Practice of Psychiatry, 1966, (with D. Offer) Modern Psychiatry and Clinical Research, 1972; editor: (with J. Dyrud) American Handbook of Psychiatry, Vol. V, 1975, The Biology of the Major Psychoses: A Comparative Analysis, 1975; chief editor: Archives Gen. Psychiatry, 1970—. Bd. dirs. Founds. Fund for Research in Psychiatry, 1969-72, Drug Abuse Council, 1972-80; vice chmn. Drug Abuse Council Ill., 1972—. Served with AUS, 1942-46. Recipient Distinguished Achievement award Modern Medicine, 1973; William C. Menninger award ACP, 1975; McAlpin medal for research achievment, 1979; Vestermark award for edn., 1981. Fellow Am. Acad. Arts and Scis., Am. Psychiat. Assn. (chmn. commn. on drug abuse 1971—), Am. Coll. Neuropsychopharmacology (pres. 1970—); mem. Inst. Medicine Nat. Acad. Scis., A.C.P. (William C. Menninger award 1975), Ill. Psychiat. Soc. (pres. 1971-72), Social Sci. Research Council (dir. 1968-74), Chgo. Psychoanalytic Soc., Western New Eng. Psychoanalytic Inst., Am. Soc. Pharmacology and Exptl. Therapeutics, AAAS, Am. Assn. Chairmen Depts. Psychiatry (pres. 1972-73), Am. Psychiat. Assn. (v.p. 1975-77, pres.-elect 1980-81, pres. 1981-82), Group Advancement Psychiatry, Psychiat. Research Soc., Am. Psychosomatic Soc. (councillor 1970-73), Assn. Research in Nervous and Mental Disease (pres. 1974), Soc. Biol. Psychiatry, Sigma Xi, Alpha Omega Alpha. Current Work: Biological basis of behavioral disorders pursued by use of drugs as tools to understand brain function. Subspecialties: Psychopharmacology; Neuropharmacology. Home: 806 Leonard Rd Los Angeles CA 90049 Office: 760 Westwood Plaza Los Angeles CA 90024

FREEDMAN, DANIEL Z., theoretical physicist; b. Hartford, Conn., May 3, 1939. B.A., Wesleyan U., 1960; M.S., U. Wis., 1962, Ph.D. in Physics, 1964. Research assoc. physics U. Wis., 1964; NSF fellow Imperial Coll., U. London, 1964-66; research fellow U. Calif.-Berkeley, 1965-66, instr., 1966-67; mem. Inst. Advanced Study, Princeton, N.J., 1967-68; from asst. prof. to assoc. prof. SUNY-Stony Brook, 1968-74, prof. physics, 1974-80; prof. applied math. MIT, Cambridge, 1980—, vis. scientist dept. physics, 1970-71; vis. assoc. dept. physics, Calif. Inst. Tech., 1977-78. Sloan fellow, 1969-71; Guggenheim fellow, 1973-74, 85-86. Subspecialty: Theoretical physics. Office: Dept Math MIT Cambridge MA 02139

FREEDMAN, HERBERT ALLEN, educator, research scientist; b. N.Y.C., Jan. 22, 1944; s. Abraham and Pearl (Maloff) F. B.A., N.Y. U., 1965, M.S., 1969, Ph.D., 1972. Research fellow Inst. Muscle Diseases, N.Y.C., 1967-68, Inst. Med. Research and Studies, N.Y.C., 1968-71; adj. lectr. CCNY, 1972; postdoctoral research fellow in genetics Albert Einstein Coll. Medicine, 1972-74, assoc. in genetics, 1975-76; asst. prof. pathology SUNY-Downstate Med. Center, Bklyn., 1977—. Contbr. articles in field to profl. jours. Leukemia Soc. Am. fellow, 1973-75; Spl. fellow, 1975-77; Am. Cancer Soc. grantee, 1978-82; NIH grantee, 1981-83; recipient N.Y. U. Founders Day Scholars award, 1972, Dupont-Sorvall Bios award, 1981. Mem. Am. Assn. Cancer Research, Am. Assn. Immunologists, N.Y. Acad. Sci., AAAS. Current Work: Basic research on the mechanisms of genetic control of malignancy and target cell specificity of carcinogens. Subspecialties: Cancer research (medicine); Immunogenetics. Office: 450 Clarkson Ave PO Box 25 Brooklyn NY 11203

FREEDMAN, LEON DAVID, chemistry educator; b. Balt., July 19, 1921; s. Samuel and Jennie (Greenberg) F.; m. Myrle Florence Neistadt, June 23, 1945; children—Carl Howard, Jean Rose. A.B., Johns Hopkins U., 1941, M.S., 1947, Ph.D., 1949. Chemist, USPHS, Balt., 1941-44, Chapel Hill, N.C., 1949-61; assoc. prof. N.C. State U., Raleigh, 1961-65, prof. chemistry, 1965—; dir. Organic Electronic Spectral Data, Inc., Silver Spring, Md., 1962—. Author: Organometallic Compounds of Arsenic, Antimony and Bismuth, 1970. Editor: Spectral Data, 1970; editorial bd. Phosphorus and Sulfur, 1976—. Patentee organometallic Compounds by Reaction of Dry Diazonium Compounds. Served with USNR, 1944-46. Named Outstanding Tchr., N.C. State U., 1984. Fellow AAAS; mem. Am. Chem. Soc., Phi Beta Kappa, Sigma Xi, Phi Lambda Upsilon. Democrat. Jewish. Current work: Research on synthesis, reactions and physical properties of organophosphorus and organometallic compounds. Subspecialties: Organic chemistry; Organometallics. Home: 2006 Myron Dr Raleigh NC 27607Office: Dept Chemistry N C State U Box 8204 Raleigh NC 27695-8204

FREEMAN, BRUCE L., JR., experimental physicist; b. Wharton, Tex., Apr. 2, 1949; s. Bruce L. and Audrey May (Wear) F.; m. Susan Hope Balog, Jan. 9, 1982. B.S. in Physics, Tex. A&M U., 1971; M.S. in Applied Sci., U. Calif.-Davis, 1971, Ph.D., 1974. Staff physicist Los Alamos Sci. Lab, 1974-77, Los Alamos Nat. Lab., 1977—. John and Fannie Hertz Found. fellow, 1971-74; recipient Disting. Performance award Los Alamos Nat. Lab., 1983. Mem. Am Phys. Soc., AAAS, IEEE, N.Y. Acad. Sci. Republican. Mem. United Church of Christ. Current work: Development of explosive pulsed power supplies and their application to high-energy-density plasma physical systems. Subspecialties: Plasma physics; Explosive pulsed power. Home: 1431 11th St Los Alamos NM 87544 Office: Los Alamos Nat Lab PO Box 1663 MS-J970 Los Alamos NM 87545

FREEMAN, DAVID LAURENCE, chemistry educator; b. Los Angeles, Mar. 10, 1946; s. Abe Mordicai and Edith (Cohen) F.; m. Donna Beth Meister, June 27, 1971; 1 child, Mark S. B.S., U. Calif.-Berkeley, 1967; A.M., Harvard U., 1968, Ph.D., 1973; postdoctoral fellow Battelle Inst., 1972-74. Research assoc. U. Utah, Salt Lake City, 1974-76; asst. prof. U. R.I., Kingston, 1976-80, assoc. prof. chemistry, 1980—; vis. staff mem. Los Alamos Nat. Lab., 1982-83. Co-author: The Electronic Structure of Molecules: Algebraic and Diagrammatic Methods in Many-Fermion Theory. Contbr. articles to profl. jours. Mem. Am. Phys. Soc., Am. Chem. Soc. Current work: Quantum Monte-Carlo studies of fluids, molecular clusters and alloys. Subspecialties: Theoretical chemistry; Statistical mechanics. Office: Dept Chemistry U RI Kingston RI 02881

FREEMAN, JULIA BERG, pharmacologist; b. Moline, Ill., June 7, 1940; d. Leslie Willard and Margaret Vivian Freeman; divorced; children: Margaret Louise, Brian Alexander. B.A., Radcliffe Coll., 1962; Ph.D., Ind. U., 1966. Research assoc. Harvard U., 1966-67; staff fellow NIH, 1967-69; research assoc. dept. pharmacology Ind. U., Indpls., 1970-71, asst. prof., 1971-76, assoc. prof., 1976-85, prof., 1985—, dir. grad. studies, 1977-85; dir. Ind. U. Animal Core, Diabetes Research and Tng. Ctr., Sch. Medicine, 1978-85; program dir. diabetes research Nat. Inst. Arthritis, Digestive Disease and Kidney, NIH, Bethesda, Md., 1985—. Author: (with S. F. Queener, V.B. Karb) The Pharmacological Basis of Nursing Practice, 1982. Mem. AAAS, Am. Diabetes Assn., Am. Fedn. Clin. Research, Am. Soc. Pharmacology and Exptl. Therapeutics, Endocrine Soc., Soc. Exptl. Biology and Medicine, Sigma Xi. Current Work: Hormonal regulation of metabolism research. Subspecialty: Pharmacology. Office: DDEMD NIADDK NIH Westwood Bldg 605 Bethesda MD 20205

FREEMAN, LEONARD MURRAY, radiologist, nuclear medicine physician, educator; b. N.Y.C., Apr. 20, 1937; s. Joseph and Tillie (Krutman) F.; m. Marlene Carolyn Held, Apr. 28, 1967; children: Eric Lawrence, David Robert, Joy Esther. B.A., N.Y. U., 1957; M.D., Chgo. Med. Sch., 1961. Diplomate: Am. Bd. Radiology, Am. Bd. Nuclear Medicine. Intern Beth Israel Hosp. and Med. Center, N.Y.C., 1961-62; resident in radiology Bronx Municipal Hosp. Center, 1962-65; mem. staff Bronx Municipal Hosp. Center and Hosp. of Albert Einstein Coll. Medicine, N.Y.C., 1965—, co-dir. div. nuclear medicine, 1965-83; dir. nuclear medicine Montefiore Hosp. and Med. Center, N.Y.C., 1976—, attending radiologist, 1977—; cons. nuclear medicine USPHS Hosp., S.I., N.Y., 1967—, St. Barnabas Hosp., Bronx, 1967—, Beth Israel Hosp. and Med. Center, 1974—, Maimonides Hosp. and Med. Center, 1974—; asst. instr. radiology Albert Einstein Coll. Medicine, Bronx, 1964-65, instr., 1965-67, asst. prof., 1967-72, asso. prof., 1972-77, prof., 1977—, prof. nuclear medicine, 1983—; mem. adv. com. nuclear medicine program Brookhaven Nat. Labs., Upton, N.Y., 1972—; examiner nuclear medicine Am. Bd. Radiology. Author: Clinical Scintillation Scanning, 1969, Clinical Scintillation Imaging, 1975, Freeman & Johnson's Clinical Radionuclide Imaging, 1984; co-editor: Seminars in Nuclear Medicine, 1970—, Physicians Desk Reference for Radiology and Nuclear Medicine, 1971-80; reviewer: Jour. Nuclear Medicine, 1972—; editor: Nuclear Medicine Ann, 1977—, Current Concepts in Diagnostic Nuclear Medicine, 1983—; mem. editorial bd.: European Jour. Nuclear Medicine, 1979—, Jour. Nuclear Medicine and Allied Scis., 1982—; contbr. numerous articles to jours., also book chpts. Fellow Am. Coll. Radiology; fellow Am. Coll. Nuclear Physicians; mem. Soc. Nuclear Medicine (gov. local chpt. 1973—, nat. trustee 1973-77, nat. v.p. 1977-78, nat. pres. 1979-80, chmn. pub. relations com. 1981—, chmn. correlative imaging council 1982-84, chmn. awards com. 1983—), Assn. Univ. Radiologists, Am. Roentgen Ray Soc., Radiol. Soc. N.Am., N.Y. Roentgen Soc., L.I. Radiol. Soc., Soc. Gastrointestinal Radiologists, N.Y. State Med. Soc., Nassau County Med. Soc., Pan Am. Med. Assn. (hon. life), Gissellschaft für Nuklearmedizin (hon. corr.), L.I. Soc. Nuclear Med. Technologists (hon. life). Current Work: Introduction of new and diagnostic imaging techniques using radionuclides and comparison of their usefulness with existing radiologic techniques. Subspecialties: Radiology in nuclear medicine; Nuclear medicine. Home: 65 Oak Dr East Hills NY 11576 Office: 111 E 210th St Bronx NY 10467

FREEMAN, STEPHEN MORRISON, abrasive engineer, administrator; b. N.Y.C., May 31, 1948; s. Stephen Morrison and Anne (Ciotti) F.; m. Colleen Fitzpatrick, Sept. 5, 1971; children—Jennifer, Kim. B.S., Rutgers U., 1970; M.S., Ohio State U., 1971. Researcher Ohio State U., Columbus, 1970-71; tech. dir. Sterling Abrasive Products Co., Tiffin, Ohio, 1973—; mem. com. GWI Safety Com., Cleve., 1980—. Author: High Alumina-Glass Reactions, 1971. Patentee in field. Exec. officer Tiffin PTO, Ohio, 1979-84. Served to 2d lt. U.S. Army, 1971-73. Keystone scholar, 1966, Lenox scholar, 1969; Orton fellow, 1970. Mem. Am. Ceramic Soc., Abrasive Engring. Soc., Am. Nat. Standards Inst. (B7.1 tech. com. 1980—). Democrat. Quaker. Current work: Study and development of grinding wheels and abrasives, management of quality control, research, hazardous wastes, product liability, and environmental quality. Subspecialties: Ceramic engineering; Composite materials. Office: Sterling Abrasive Products Co 2d and Wall Sts Tiffin OH 44883

FREEMAN, WADE AUSTIN, chemist, educator; b. Evanston, Ill., Nov. 20, 1940; s. Raymond Barrett and Eleanor (Knaus) F.; m. Sally Fairchild Miller, Mar. 22, 1975; children: Andrew Taylor, Neil Barrett. B.S., U. Ill., 1962; M.S., U. Mich., 1964, Ph.D., 1967. Mem. faculty U. Ill., Chgo., 1967—; asst. dean U. Ill. (Coll. Liberal Arts and Scis.), 1969-79, dir. gen. chemistry, 1979—. Mem. Am. Chem. Soc., AAAS. Current Work: Structures of transition metal complexes and relationship to their spectra. Subspecialties: X-ray crystallography; Crystallography. Office: U Ill Dept Chemistry Box 4348 Chicago IL 60680

FREI, EMIL, III, internist, institute administrator, educator, researcher; b. St. Louis, Feb. 21, 1924; m. Elizabeth Frei, 1948; 5 children. M.D., Yale U., 1948. Intern Univ. Hosp., St. Louis, 1948-49, resident in pathology, 1952-53, resident in internal medicine, 1953-55; head chemotherapy service, chief med. br. and assoc. sci. dir. Nat. Cancer Inst., 1955-65; assoc. dir. U. Tex. M.D. Anderson Hosp. and Tumor Inst., 1967-53; dir., physician-in-chief Dana-Farber Cancer Inst., Boston, 1973—; prof. medicine Harvard U., Boston, 1980—, Richard and Susan Smith prof. medicine, 1985. Recipient Lasker award, 1972, Man of Yr. award Am. Cancer Soc., 1981, Kettering prize Gen. Motors Corp., 1983; Hamao Umezawa award, 1985. Mem. Inst. Medicine of Nat. Acad. Sci., Am. Soc. Clin. Investigation, Am. Assn. Cancer Research (pres. 1971-72), Assn. Am. Physicians. Subspecialties: Chemotherapy; Internal medicine. Office: Dana-Farber Cancer Inst 44 Binney St Boston MA 02115*

FREIBERGER, WALTER FREDERICK, mathematics educator; b. Vienna, Austria, Feb. 20, 1924; came to U.S., 1955, naturalized, 1962; s. Felix and Irene (Tagany) F.; m. Christine Mildred Holmberg, Oct. 6, 1956; children: Christopher Allan, Andrew James, Nils Henry. B.A., U. Melbourne, 1947, M.A., 1949; Ph.D., U. Cambridge, Eng., 1953. Research officer Aero. Research Lab. Australian Dept. Supply, 1947-49, sr. sci. research officer, 1953-55; tutor U. Melbourne, 1947-49, 53-55; asst. prof. div. applied math. Brown U., 1956-58, assoc. prof., 1958-64, prof., 1964—, dir. Computing Center, 1963-69; dir. Center for Computer and Info. Scis., 1969-76, chmn. div. applied math., 1976—; mem. fellowship selection panel NSF. Author: (with U. Grenander) A Short Course in Computational Probability and Statistics, 1971; Editor: The International Dictionary of Applied Mathematics, 1960, (with others) Applications of Digital Computers, 1963, Advances in Computers, Volume 10, 1970, Statistical Computer Performance Evaluation, 1972; Mng. editor: Quarterly of Applied Mathematics, 1965—; Contbr. numerous articles to profl. jours. Served with Australian Army, 1943-45. Fulbright fellow, 1955-56; Guggenheim fellow, 1962-63; NSF Office Naval Research grantee in field. Mem. Am. Math. Soc. (asso. editor Math. Reviews 1957-62), Soc. for Indsl. and Applied Math., Inst. Math. Statistics, Assn. Computing Machinery. Republican. Episcopalian. Club: Univ. (Providence). Current Work: Computational probability and statistics, pattern theory and applications, computer science. Subspecialties: Applied mathematics; Statistics. Office: 182 George St Providence RI 02912

FREIS, EDWARD DAVID, physician, researcher; b. Chgo., May 13, 1912; s. Roy Joel and Rose (Goldstein) F.; m. Willa Hussey (div. 1973); children—Richard, Susan, Martha. B.S., U. Ariz., 1936; M.D., Columbia U., 1940; D.Sc. (hon.), Georgetown U., 1985. Intern Boston U. Hosp., 1940-42, resident, 1946-47, fellow hypertension, 1947-49; asst. chief, then chief medicine VA Hosp., Washington, 1949-57, sr. med. investigator, 1957—. Contbr. numerous papers on nature and treatment of hypertension to profl. jours. Recipient Lasker award in clin. research, 1971, Ciba award in hypertension research, 1982. Served as maj. M.C., U.S. Army, 1942-46. Mem. Council High Blood Pressure Research (chmn. 1962-63), Am. Soc. Clin. Investigation. Current work: Hemedynamics of antihypertensive drugs, comparative effectiveness of various drug treatments in hypertension. Subspecialties: Cardiology; Pharmacology. Home: 4515 Willard Ave Apt S-1916 Chevy Chase MD 20815 Office: VA Med Ctr 50 Irving ST NW Washington DC 20422

FREISER, BEN SHERMAN, chemistry educator; b. Pitts., Feb. 12, 1951; s. Henry and Edith (Schwartz) F.; m. Dalia Viera, Oct. 18, 1975 (div.); m. I. Helene Hagestam, May 15, 1985. B.S., UCLA, 1971; Ph.D., Calif. Inst. Tech., 1977. Asst. prof. chemistry dept. Purdue U., Lafayette, Ind., 1976-82, assoc. prof., 1982-85, prof. analytical chemistry, 1985—, head analytical div., 1984—. Contbr. articles to profl. jours. Named one of Top Ten Tchrs., Sch. of Sci., Purdue U., 1981, recipient Frank D. Martin undergrad. Teaching award Purdue U., 1983; Mem. Am. Chem. Soc. (Pure Chemistry award 1985, Fresenius award 1985, Akron sect. award 1985), Am. Soc. for Mass Spectrometry, Phi Beta Kappa, Sigma Xi. Current work: Applications of Fourier transform mass spectrometry to the study of the chemistry and photochemistry of metal ions and their clusters. Subspecialties: Analytical chemistry; Photochemistry. Office: Dept Chemistry Purdue U West Lafayette IN 47907

FREIWALD, DAVID ALLEN, engineering consulting executive; b. Cleve., June 4, 1941; s. Harry Herman and Arline (Woehrman) F.; m. Joyce Darlene Gross, Apr. 3, 1976; children—Wesley, Todd, Christopher. B.S. in Mech. Engring, Northwestern U., 1963, Ph.D., 1968. Staff mem. Sandia Nat. Labs., Albuquerque, 1967-72; staff mem., mgmt. dir. Office of Dir., Los Alamos Nat. Labs., 1972-81; sr. scientist SEA, Inc., McLean, Va., 1981-82; cons. MRJ, Inc., Oakton, Va., 1982—. Author: booklet Introduction to Laser Fusion, 1975. Mem. N.Mex. Gov.'s Land Use Legis. Com., 1971; N.Mex. rep. environ. com. Western Power Systems Coordinating Com., 1972-73; mem. Gov.'s Energy Task Force, 1973-74; adv. council State N.Mex. Energy Inst., 1978-81. Mem. Am. Am. Nuclear Soc., N.Mex. Acad. Sci. (pres. 1981), Tau Beta Pi, Pi Tau Sigma, Sigma Xi. Republican. Methodist. Current Work: Secure, survivable, sustainable energy supplies/logistics for U.S. Armed Forces, including advanced concepts and alternative fuels for present and projected force structures for deterrence and war scenarios. Subspecialty: Fluid mechanics. Home: 10401 Lloyd Rd Potomac MD 20854 Office: MRJ Inc Suite 200 10455 White Granite Dr Oakton VA 22124

FRELINGER, JEFFREY ALLEN, geneticist, educator; b. Bklyn., July 16, 1948; s. John Edgar and Alice (Andersen) F.; m. Joy Vaughan; children—Jacob Jeffrey, John Kress. B.A., U. Calif. at San Diego, 1969; Ph.D., Calif. Inst. Tech., 1973. Asst. prof. to prof. U. So. Calif., 1975-82; prof. microbiology U. N.C., 1983—; Mem. NIH Mammalian Genetics Study Sect. chmn. VA Immunology Merit Rev. Bd. Contbr. numerous articles to profl. jours. James Coffin Childs fellow; NIH grantee. Mem. AAAS, Am. Assn. Immunologists, Sigma Xi. Current Work: Use of molecular biology and hybridoma tech. to understand genetic orgn. and function of the maj. histocompatability complex. Subspecialties: Immunogenetics; Gene actions. Home: 1721 Allard Rd Chapel Hill NC 27514 Office: Dept Microbiology and Immunology U NC Chapel Hill NC 27514

FREMOUNT, HENRY NEIL, biologist, educator; b. Easton, Pa., Sept. 29, 1933; s. Henry Anthony and Lucille (DeRenzis) F.; m. Rosalyn Arlene Malone, Sept. 7, 1957. B.S., East Stroudsburg State Coll., 1956, M.Ed. in Biology, 1964; M.S. in Parasitology, Columbia U., 1966, D.P.H., 1970. Tchr. sci. jr. high sch. Delaware Valley Joint Sch. System, Milford, Pa., 1956-58; tchr. sci. Belvidere (N.J.) High Sch., 1958-65; assoc. prof. biology East Stroudsburg (Pa.) State Coll., 1966-71, prof., 1971—, chmn. dept., 1974-80; instr. parasitic diseases, lectr. histology Columbia U. Coll. Physicians and Surgeons, N.Y.C., 1965-71, NIH trainee, 1965-66, 68-70; NSF grantee Pa. State U., 1963-64; NIH trainee U. Mich. Biol. Sta., 1965; internat. fellow in tropical medicine La. State U. Faculty Medicine, 1970; vis. scientist Gorgas Meml. Lab., Panama, 1970; adj. assoc. prof. pathobiology Inst. for Pathobiology, Lehigh U., Bethlehem, Pa., 1971-78; sr. mem. Inst. for Pathobiology, Lehigh U. (Center for Health Scis.), 1973-78; assoc. sci. staff parasitic diseases Sacred Heart Hosp., Allentown, Pa., 1974—, mem. assoc. sci. staff dept. pathology, 1978—. Contbr. articles to sci. jours. Recipient cert. of excellence in teaching East Stroudsburg State Coll., 1977; NIH grantee, 1970; Commonwealth teaching fellow, 1977. Fellow Royal Soc. Tropical Medicine and Hygiene; mem. Am. Soc. Tropical Medicine and Hydiene, Am. Soc. Parasitologists, Am. Inst. Biol. Scis., AAAS, Am. Soc. Clin. Pathologist, N.Y. Soc. Tropical Medicine, N.Y. Zool. Soc., N.Y. Acad. Sci., Pa. Acad. Sci. (exec. com., editorial com.), Sigma Xi. Roman Catholic. Current Work: Ultrastructure and pathophysiology of malaria. Subspecialties: Microscopy; Immunology (medicine). Home: RD 4 Box 4441 Stroudsburg PA 18360 Office: Dept Biology East Stroudsburg Univ East Stroudsburg PA 18301

FREMOUW, EDWARD JOSEPH, ionospheric physicist, research exec.; b. Northfield, Minn., Feb. 23, 1934; s. Fred J. and Marion Elizabeth (Drozda) F.;

m. Rita Lorraine Johnson, June 26, 1960; children: Thane Edrik, Sean Fredrik. B.S.E.E., Stanford U., 1957; M.S. in Physics, U. Alaska, Fairbanks, 1963, Ph.D. in Geophysics, 1966. Engr. Boeing Co., Seattle, 1957; chief auroral obs. U.S. Antarctic Research Program, South Pole, 1958-59; grad. teaching and research asst. Geophys. Inst., U. Alaska, Fairbanks, 1960-66, asst. prof. geophysics, 1966; physicist Stanford Research Inst., Menlo Park, Calif., 1967-70, sr. physicist, 1970-76, program mgr., 1976-77; v.p., dir. Phys. Dynamics, Inc., Bellevue, Wash., 1977—; assoc. La Jolla Inst.; conf. chmn., presenter. Contbr. articles to prof. jours. Mem. student learning objectives com. Mercer Island Sch. Dist., 1981-84; trustee East Shore Unitarian Ch., 1983—. Recipient Antarctic Service Medal, 1959. Mem. AAAS, Am. Geophys. Union, IEEE, Internat. Radio Sci. Union. Unitarian. Clubs: Stanford of Western Wash. (trustee 1982—), Seattle Mountaineers. Patentee in field. Current Work: Morphology and dynamics of plasma-density irregularities in ionosphere and their effects on transionospheric communication systems. Subspecialties: Aeronomy; Satellite studies. Home: 8232 E Mercer Way Mercer Island WA 98040 Office: 300 120th Ave NE Bldg 7220 Bellevue WA 98005

FRENCH, CHARLES STACY, scientist; b. Lowell, Mass., Dec. 13, 1907; s. Charles Ephraim and Helena (Stacy) F.; m. Margaret Wendell Coolidge, Dec. 10, 1938; children—Helena Stacy, Charles Ephraim. Student, Loomis Inst., Windsor, Conn., 1921-25; B.S., Harvard, 1930, A.M., 1932, Ph.D., 1934; Ph.D. (hon.), U. Göteborg, Sweden, 1974. Asst. in gen. physiology Harvard, 1930-33; research fellow Calif. Inst. Tech., 1934-35; guest worker with Otto Warburg Kaiser Wilhelm Inst., Berlin-Dahlem, Germany, 1935-36; Austin teaching fellow in biochemistry Harvard Med. Sch., 1936-38; instr. (research) in chemistry with James Franck U. Chgo., 1938-41; asst. prof. dept. botany U. Minn., 1941-45, asso. prof., 1945-47; dir. div. plant biology Carnegie Instn. of Washington at Stanford U., 1947-73, dir. emeritus, 1973—; prof. (by courtesy) Stanford. Contbr. articles on plant physiology to sci. jours. Trustee, Trust for Hidden Villa Inc., 1979—. Mem. Am. Soc. Plant Physiologists (chmn. Western Sect. 1954, Charles Ried Barnes life mem.), Bot. Soc. Am. (award of merit 1973), Nat. Acad. Scis., Am. Acad. Arts and Scis., Am. Soc. Biol. Chemists, Soc. Gen. Physiologists (v.p. 1954, pres. 1955-56), AAAS, Biophys. Soc., Deutsche Akademie der Naturforscher Leopoldina, Friends of Hidden Villa (pres. 1977-79). Clubs: Am. Alpine, Harvard of Peninsula (pres. 1973-75), Explorers. Current Work: Spectroscopy of chlorophyll-protein complexes. Photo-oxidation by chloroplast components. Subspecialties: Photosynthesis; Plant physiology (agriculture). Home: 11970 Rhus Ridge Rd Los Altos Hills CA 94022 Office: Carnegie Institution Stanford CA 94305

FRENCH, DAVID NICHOLS, metallurgist; b. Newton, Mass., Jan. 24, 1936; s. Sydney Perkins and Donalda (Roy) F.; m. Louise Murray French, June 25, 1960; children: Katherine, Andrew, Stephen, Jonathan. B.S., MIT, 1958, M.S., 1959, Sc.D., 1962. Research scientist Linde Co., Indpls., 1962-63; mem. tech. staff Ingersoll-Rand Co., Princeton, N.J., 1963-68; phys. metallurgist Abex Corp., Mahwah, N.J., 1968-72; mem. tech. staff P.R. Mallory Co., Burlington, Mass., 1972-73; dir. corp. quality assurance Riley Stoker Corp., Worcester, Mass., 1973-82; v.p. Leighton Industries, Inc., Phoenixville, Pa., 1982-83; chief metallurgist D.G. Peterson & Assocs., Greenfield, Mass., 1983-84; pres., owner David N. French, Inc., Metallurgists, 1984—. Author: Metallurgical Failures in Fossil Fired Boilers, 1983; contbr. articles to profl. jours. Mem. ASME (mem. boiler and pressure vessel code com. SCI Power Boilers), Nat. Assn. Corrosion Engrs., Am. Soc. Metals, AIME, Sigma Xi. Current Work: Boiler corrosion, metallurgy, materials condition assessment, remaining life determination, failure analysis, metall. engring., boilers and fuel burning equipment, quality assurance. Subspecialties: Metallurgy; Corrosion. Home: 1 Lancaster Rd Northborough MA 01532 Office: David N French Inc Metallurgists One Lancaster Rd Northborough MA 01532

FRENCH, JUDSON CULL, government scientist; b. Washington, Sept. 30, 1922; s. Morrison Brady and Ethel Haviland (Cull) F.; m. Julia A. McAllister, Aug. 1, 1951; child, Judson Cull. B.S. cum laude, Am. U., 1943; M.S., Harvard U., 1949; postgrad., Bus. Sch., 1968, Johns Hopkins U., 1943-44, George Washington U., 1944-45, M.I.T., 1951. Instr. physics Johns Hopkins U., Balt., 1943-44, George Washington U., Washington, 1944-47; sec., dir. Home Title Ins. Co., Washington, 1956-71; with Nat. Bur. Standards, Commerce Dept., Washington, 1948—, asst. chief electron devices sect., 1964-68, chief electron devices sect., 1968-73, chief electronic tech. div., 1973-78; dir. Center for Electronics and Elec. Engring., 1978—. Contbr. articles to profl. jours. Recipient Silver medal for meritorious service Commerce Dept., 1964; Gold medal for exceptional service, 1978; Edward Bennett Rosa award Nat. Bur. Standards, 1971; presdl. rank of Meritorious Exec. Sr. Exec. Service, 1980, Disting. Exec., 1984. Fellow IEEE; mem. Am. Phys. Soc., ASTM, Sigma Pi Sigma, Pi Delta Epsilon, Alpha Kappa Pi. Current Work: Technical management of research and development concerning electrical, electronic, laser, fiber-optic, semi-conductor, microwave and other measurement science and services. Office: Center for Electronics and Elec Engring Nat Bur Standards Gaithersburg MD 20899

FRENCH, NORMAN ROGER, ecology educator, researcher; b. Kankakee, Ill., Mar. 7, 1927; s. Carl R. and Clara L. (Miller) F.; m. Jean H. Bachrach, June 11, 1951 (div. 1969); children—Gregory N., Dorothy M. B.A., U. Ill., 1949, M.S., U. Colo., 1951; Ph.D., U. Utah, 1954. Chief ecology br. Idaho Ops., AEC, Idaho Falls, 1955-59; research ecologist Lab. Nuclear Med. and Radiation Biology, UCLA, 1959-69; dir. field studies Grassland Biome Program, Ft. Collins, Colo., 1969-74; prof. biology Colo. State U., Ft. Collins, 1969-81; research scientist Research Inst. Colo., Ft. Collins, 1981-83; vis. prof., research assoc. Inst. Arctic and Alpine Research U. Colo., Boulder, 1983—; sec. BioScis. Info. Service, 1977-82; plenary speaker 3d Internat. Theriological Congress, 1982; trustee BioSciences Info. Service Biol. Abstracts, 1977-82. Editor: Perspectives in Grassland Ecology, 1979; Role of Animals in Biological Cycling (transl. from Russian), 1980. Treas. Amigos de las Americas, Ft. Collins, 1981; mem. religious edn. com. Foothills Unitarian Ch., Ft. Collins, 1977. Served with USN, 1945-46. Interdisciplinary Environ. Research award Colo. State U., 1977. Fellow AAAS; mem. Internat. Assn. Ecology, Cooper Ornithol. Soc. (life mem., asst. bus. mgr. 1961-67), Ecol. Soc. Am. (cert. sr. ecologist), Societe de Biogeographie. Current work: Population effects of pollution or habitat modification, evolution and biogeophraphy of Alpine birds. Subspecialties: Ecology (environmental science); Evolutionary biology. Office: Inst Arctic and Alpine Research U Colo Boulder CO 80309

FRENIERE, EDWARD RICHARD, optical engineer; b. Cambridge, Mass., Sept. 24, 1953; s. E. Richard and Gaetana G. (Celi) F.; m. Patricia E.B. O'Brien, June 18, 1977; 1 child, Ansel Edward. B.A. in Physics, Boston U., 1976; M.S. in Physics, Worcester Poly. Inst., 1978; Ph.D. in physics, U. Lowell, 1984. Sr. devel. engr. Honeywell Inc., Lexington, Mass., 1978-84; sr. optical engr. Itek Optical Systems, Lexington, 1984—. Contbr. articles to profl. jours. Mem. Optical Soc. Am., Soc. Photo-Optical Instrumentation Engrs. Democrat. Current work: Diffraction theory; electromagnetic scattering theory; Fourier optics; computer simulation optical systems. Home: 3 Maplehurst Rd Littleton MA 01460 Office: Itek Optical Systems 10 Maguire Rd Lexington MA 02173

FRENKEL, EUGENE PHILLIP, physician; b. Detroit, Aug. 27, 1929; s. David Eugene and Eva (Antin) F.; m. Rhoda Beth Smilay, Dec. 21, 1958; children: Lisa Michelle, Peter Alan. B.S., Wayne State U., 1949; M.D., U. Mich., 1953. Diplomate: Am. Bd. Internal Medicine (hematology, med. oncology; bd. govs. 1980—, chmn. subspecialty com. hematology 1980—). Intern Wayne County Gen. Hosp., Eloise, Mich., 1953-54; resident in internal medicine Boston City Hosp., 1954-55; resident in internal medicine, then instr. U. Mich. Med. Center, 1957-62; mem. faculty U. Tex. Health Sci. Center, Dallas, 1962—, prof. internal medicine and radiology, 1969—, chief div. hematology-oncology, 1962—; chief nuclear medicine, cons. hematology-oncology VA Med. Center, Dallas, 1962—; cons. com. evaluation research hematology Nat. Inst. Arthritis and Metabolic Diseases. Author numerous research papers in field. Served as officer M.C. USAF, 1955-57. Fellow A.C.P., Internat. Soc. Hematology; mem. Am. Soc. Hematology (treas. 1976-83), Am. Soc. Clin. Oncology (chmn. membership com. 1982—), Am. Cancer Soc. (pres. Dallas unit 1970-71, dir. Tex. div. 1978—, sci. adv. com. on clin. investigations II—chemotherapy and hematology 1978—, Emma Freeman prof. 1981, nat. clin. fellowship com. 1978—), Assn. Am. Physicians, Am. Assn. Cancer Research, Am. Assn. Cancer Edn., Am. Soc. Biol. Chemists, Am. Soc. Clin. Investigation, So. Soc. Clin. Investigation, Soc. Nuclear Medicine, Am. Fedn. Clin. Research, Internat. Assn. Study Lung Cancer, Alpha Omega Alpha. Subspecialties: Hematology; Oncology. Office: 5323 Harry Hines Blvd Dallas TX 75235

FRENKEL, JACOB KARL, pathologist; b. Darmstadt, Germany, Feb. 16, 1921; came to U.S., 1939, naturalized, 1944; s. Karl and Anna Maria (Kaufmann) F.; m. Rebecca L. Reese, Sept. 4, 1954; children—Lisa, Linda, Carl. A.B., U. Calif.-Berkeley, 1942, Ph.D., 1948; M.D., U. Calif.-San Francisco, 1946. Pathologist, Rocky Mountain Lab., Hamilton, Mont., 1948-50, NIH, Bethesda, Md., 1950-51; instr., resident in pathology U. Tenn., Memphis, 1951-52; asst. prof. U. Kans., Kansas City, 1952-57, assoc. prof., 1957-60, prof., 1960—; fgn. advisor Argentine Found. Study Toxoplasmosis, 1980—. Author: Toxoplasmosis, 1951; mem. editorial bd. Jour. Parasitology, 1977—, Zeitschrift fur Parasitenkunde, 1979—, Jour. Protozoology, 1982—, Exptl. Pathology, 1982—. Served to surgeon USPHS, 1948-52. Fellow Infectious Disease Soc. Am.; mem. Am. Soc. Tropical Medicine and Hygiene, Am. Assn. Pathologists, Internat. Acad. Pathologists, Deutsche Akademie der Naturforscher Leopoldina. Current work: Research in toxoplasmosis, other protozoan infections, immunity to chronic infection, vaccines for toxoplasma. Subspecialties: Pathology (medicine); Parasitology. Home: 10030 El Monte Overland Park KS 66207 Office: U Kans Sch Medicine 39th and Rainbow Blvd Kansas City KS 66103

FRESCO, JACQUES ROBERT, biochemist, educator; b. N.Y.C., May 30, 1928; s. Robert and Lucie (Asseo) F.; m. Rosalie Sarah Bernstein, Dec. 22, 1957; children—Lucille Deborah, Suzette Josie, Linda Hannah. B.A., N.Y. U., 1947, M.S., 1949, Ph.D., 1953; M.D. (hon.), U. Göteborg, Sweden, 1979. Postdoctoral fellow Sloan Kettering Inst. for Cancer Research, N.Y.C., 1952-54; instr. biochemistry N.Y. U. Coll. Medicine, 1953-54, instr. pharmacology, 1954-56; research fellow dept. chemistry Harvard, 1956-60, tutor biochem. scis., 1957-60; vis. fellow Cavendish Lab., Cambridge, Eng. and; Institut de Biologie Physico-Chimique, Paris, France, 1957; asst. prof. dept. chemistry Princeton, 1960-62, asso. prof., 1962-65, prof., 1965—, acting chmn. biochem. scis., 1965-66, prof. dept. biochem. scis., 1970—, chmn. dept., 1974-80; vis. prof. Hebrew U. of Jerusalem, 1973; dir. Nat. Cancer Inst. Basic Sci. Cancer Center, 1976—, Pfeiffer prof. life scis., 1977—; mem. adv. bd. Biopolymers, 1963-70; dir., chmn. sci. adv. com. Bio Technica Internat. Inc., 1981—; cons. sci. adv. com. Helen Hay Whitney Found.; vis. scientist MRC Lab. Molecular Biology, Cambridge, Eng., 1969-70. Mem. editorial bd.: Jour. Phys. Chemistry, 1963-70, Analytical Biochemistry, 1969-81. Recipient Am. Scientist Writing award AAAS, 1962; NIH fellow, 1952-54; Lalor Found. fellow, 1957; established investigator; Am. Heart Assn., 1958-63; Guggenheim fellow, 1969-70. Mem. Am. Chem. Soc., Am. Soc. Biol. Chemists, Sigma Xi. Current Work: Nucleic acids; base pairing; mutagenesis; carcinogenesis. Subspecialties: Biochemistry (biology); Molecular biology.

FREUND, HENRY PHILLIP, plasma physicist; b. N.Y.C., May 23, 1949; s. Andrew and Lena Katie (Levine) F.; m. Sandra Lee Cross, June 12, 1977; children—Lena Marion, Anna Jane. B.S. Rensselaer Poly. Inst., 1971; M.S., U. Md., 1975, Ph.D., 1976. Research assoc. U. Md., College Park, 1976-77, sr. research assoc., part-time 1982—; postdoctoral research fellow NRC-Naval Research Lab., Washington, 1977-79; research physicist Sci. Applications, Inc., McLean, Va., 1979—. Mem. Am. Phys. Soc., Sigma Pi Sigma. Republican. Jewish. Current work: Collective radiation processes in plasmas, strong turbulence in plasmas, free-electron lasers. Subspecialties: Plasma physics; Free-electron lasers. Office: Sci Applications Inc 1710 Goodridge Dr McLean VA 21202

FREUND, LAMBERT BEN, engineering educator, researcher, consultant; b. McHenry, Ill., Nov. 23, 1942; s. Bernard and Anita (Schaeffer) F.; m. Colleen Jean Hehl, Aug. 21, 1965; children: Jonathan Ben, Jeffrey Alan, Stephen Neil. B.S., U. Ill., 1964, M.S., 1965; Ph.D., Northwestern U., 1967. Postdoctoral fellow Brown U., Providence, 1967-69, asst. prof., 1969-73, assoc. prof., 1973-75, prof. engring., 1975—, chmn. div., 1979-83; vis. prof. Stanford (Calif.) U., 1974-75; cons. Aberdeen Proving Ground, U.S. Steel Corp.; vis. scholar Harvard U., 1983-84. Editor-in-chief: ASME Jour. Applied Mechanics, 1983—; contbr. articles to tech. jours. NSF trainee, 1964-67; grantee NSF, Office Naval Research, Army Research Office, Nat. Bur. Standards. Fellow Am. Acad. Mechanics, ASME (Henry Hess award 1974); mem. Am. Geophys. Union. Current Work: Mechanics of solids and structures; fracture mechanics; stress waves in solids; theoretical seismology. Subspecialties: Solid mechanics; Materials. Home: 3 Palisade Ln Barrington RI 02806 Office: Brown U Providence RI 02912

FREUND, ROBERT STANLEY, physicist; b. Newark, Jan. 26, 1939; s. Herman and Evelyn (Osterweil) F.; m. Joan Kesselman, June 17, 1962; children: Kevin, Wendy. B.A., Wesleyan U., 1960; M.A., Harvard U., 1962, Ph.D., 1965. Mem. tech. staff Bell Labs., Murray Hill, N.J., 1966-76, head dept. environ. chemistry, 1976-79; head dept. chem. kinetics research AT&T Bell Labs, 1979—; mem. com. atomic and molecular scis. NRC, 1976-82; mem. N.J. Gov's. Sci. Adv. Com., 1979-83. Treas., N. Jersey chpt. Juvenile Diabetes Found., 1979-81, v.p., 1982-84, pres., 1984-86. Fellow Am. Phys. Soc.; mem. Am. Chem. Soc. (alt. councillor div. phys. chemistry 1985—), Am. Vacuum Soc., Gaseous Electronics Conf. (exec. com. 1983-85). Current Work: Electron-molecule collision experiment, spectroscopy, high-Rydberg molecules. Subspecialties: Atomic and molecular physics; Physical chemistry. Office: AT&T Bell Labs Murray Hill NJ 07974

FREY, WILLIAM HOWARD II, research biochemist, research neurochemist; b. Atlanta, Nov. 19, 1947; s. William Howard and Brena (Feldman) F.; m. Barbara Katherine Hursh, Nov. 3, 1977; children: Brandl Laurie, William Howard III. B.A., Washington U., St. Louis, 1969; Ph.D., Case Western Res. U., 1974. Research specialist U. Minn., Mpls., 1974-77, asst. prof. psychiatry dept., 1977—; dir. Psychiatry Research Labs., St. Paul-Ramsey Med. Center, 1980—; research dir. Alzheimer's Treatment and Research Ctr., Dry Eye and Tear Research Ctr.; adviser Geriatric Research, Edn. and Clin. Center, VA Med. Center, Mpls., 1980—. Author: Crying: The Mystery of Tears, 1985. Grantee NIH, 1978, 82. Mem. Am. Soc. Biol. Chemists. Current Work: Research in human brain biochemistry and the neurochemistry of Alzheimer's disease, research on human emotional crying and emotional tears. Subspecialties: Neurochemistry; Behavioral psychology. Home: 1100 W Montana Ave St Paul MN 55108 Office: Psychiatry Research Labs St Paul-Ramsey Med Center 640 Jackson St St Paul MN 55101

FRIAS, JAIME LUIS, medical eduator, pediatrician; b. Concepcion, Chile, Mar. 20, 1933; s. Humberto and Olga (Fernandez) F.; m. Jacqueline M. Steel, Apr. 8, 1961; children: Jaime A., Juan Pablo, Maria Josefina, Patricio Andres. M.D., U. Concepcion, 1959. Diplomate: Am. Bd. Pediatrics, Am. Bd. Med. Genetics. Asst. prof. pediatrics U. Concepcion, 1965-69, prof., 1969-70; asst. prof. pediatrics U. Fla., Gainesville, 1970-73, assoc. prof., 1973-76, prof., 1976—. Contbr. articles to profl. jours. Fellow Am. Acad. Pediatrics; mem. Am. Soc. Human Genetics, Teratology Soc., AAAS, Sigma Xi. Roman Catholic. Current Work: Genetics and dysmorphology. Subspecialties: Pediatrics; Genetics and genetic engineering (medicine). Office: Dept Pediatrics U Fla Gainesville FL 32610

FRIBERG, EMIL EDWARDS, consulting engineer; b. Wichita Falls, Tex., Apr. 11, 1935; s. John Walter and Anne (Crumpton) F.; m. Jo Ann Rutta, Jan. 26, 1957; children: Emil Edwards, Vicki Lynn, Joe Alan. B.S. in Mech. Engring, U. Tex., 1958. Registered profl. engr., Tex., Okla., La., Miss. With Tex. Electric Service Co., Wichita Falls, 1958-64, engring. cons., Ft. Worth, 1964-69; prin. Friberg Alexander Gipson Weir, Inc., Ft. Worth, 1969—, pres., 1973—. Chmn. Energy Conservation Adv. Com., City of Ft. Worth, 1981. Served to 1st lt. C.E. U.S. Army, 1958-66. Recipient Young Engr. of Yr. award Ft. Worth chpt. Tex. Soc. Profl. Engrs., 1968; award of merit Cons. Engrs. Council Tex., 1976; award of excellence, 1977. Fellow ASHRAE (past dir., Disting. Service award 1979); mem. Cons. Engrs. Council Tex. (pres.), Nat. Soc. Profl. Engrs., Tex. Soc. Profl. Engrs., ASME, AIME. Baptist. Clubs: Ft. Worth, Sierra. Lodge: Rotary. Current Work: Energy conservation in building heating, air conditioning and lighting systems; management of counsulting engineering firm with emphasis on energy conservation. Subspecialties: Mechanical engineering; Electrical engineering. Home: 3406 Woodford Arlington TX 76013 Office: PO Box 2080 Fort Worth TX 76113

FRICKE, MARTIN PAUL, physicist, applied research administrator; b. Franklin, Pa., May 18, 1937; s. Frank Albert and Pauline Jane (Wentz) F.; m. Barbara Ann Blanton, Jan. 3, 1959. B.S., Drexel U., 1961; M.S., U. Minn., 1964, Ph.D., 1967. Various sci. positions Oak Ridge Nat. Lab., 1956-68; group leader Gulf Radiation Tech., La Jolla, Calif., 1968-73; div. and dept. mgr. Sci. Applications, Inc., La Jolla, 1974-80, v.p., 1977-80, corp. v.p., 1980-84; sr. v.p. Titan Systems, Inc., La Jolla, 1984—. Contbr. articles to physics jours. Oak Ridge Assoc. Univs. fellow, 1964-67; U. Mich. fellow, 1967. Mem. Am. Phys. Soc. (panel pub. affairs 1983—), Phi Kappa Phi. Current work: Manager of nationally recognized programs of applied research in the physical sciences and mathematics important to defense and national security. Subspecialty: Nuclear physics. Home: 8501 La Jolla Scenic Dr La Jolla CA 92037 Office: Titan Systems Inc 9191 Towne Centre Dr San Diego CA 92122

FRIDOVICH, IRWIN, biochemistry educator; b. N.Y.C., Aug. 2, 1929; s. Louis and Sylvia (Appelbaum) F.; m. Mollie Finkel; children: Sharon E., Judith L. B.S., CCNY, 1951; postgrad., Cornell U. Med. Coll., 1951-52; Ph.D., Duke U., 1955; hon. doctorate, U. Rene Descartes, Paris, 1980. Instr. biochemistry Duke U., Durham, N.C., 1956-58, assoc., 1958—; vis. research assoc. Harvard U., Cambridge, Mass., 1961-62; asst. prof. biochemistry Duke U., 1961-66, assoc. prof., 1966-71, prof., 1971-76, James B. Duke prof., 1976—; mem. study sect. Am. Cancer Soc., mem. adv. com. biochemistry and chem. carcinogenesis. Editorial bd.: Jour. Biol. Chemistry, Jour. Free Radicals in Biology and Medicine, Jour. Inorganic Biochemistry, Biochem. Jour., Analytical Biochemistry, Biochem. Pharmacology; contbr. articles to sci. jours. Recipient Founders' award Chem. Industry Inst. Toxicology, 1980; recipient Herty award Ga. sect. Am. Chem. Soc., 1980, Research Career Devel. award NIH, 1959-69. Mem. Nat. Acad. Scis., Am. Acad. Arts and Scis., Am. Soc. Biol. Chemists (pres. 1982), N.C. Acad. Scis., Phi Beta Kappa, Sigma Xi. Current Work: Enzymology, metabolism of oxygen, oxygen free radicals, superoxide dismutase. Subspecialty: Biochemistry (medicine). Home: 3517 Courtland Dr Durham NC 27707 Office: Duke U Med Center Durham NC 27710

FRIED, JERROLD, biomedical researcher; b. N.Y.C., Mar. 3, 1937; s. Max and Irene (Shapiro) F.; m. Shirley M. Rozen, Dec. 26, 1965; children: Daniel Alan, Andrew Mark. B.S., Calif. Inst. Tech., 1958; M.S., Stanford U., 1960, Ph.D., 1964. Postdoctoral fellow Hunter Coll., N.Y.C., 1965; research assoc. Sloan-Kettering Inst., N.Y.C., 1965-67, assoc., 1968-76, asso. mem., 1976—; asst. prof. biophysics Cornell U. Grad. Sch. Med. Scis., Sloan-Kettering div., 1968-78, assoc. prof., 1978—. Nat. Cancer Inst. research grantee, 1974—. Mem. Biophys. Soc., Am. Assn. Cancer Research, Cell Kinetics Soc., Soc. Analytical Cytology, Sigma Xi. Democrat. Jewish. Current Work: Antigenic modulation, complement-mediated cytotoxicity, cell kinetics, effects of cytotoxic drugs on cell survival and kinetics, application to leukemia, flow cytometry and cell sorting, computer simulation models. Subspecialties: Cell and tissue culture; Information systems, storage, and retrieval (computer science). Home: 11 Winslow Pl Larchmont NY 10538 Office: 1275 York Ave New York NY 10021

FRIED, JOHN, chemist; b. Leipzig, Germany, Oct. 7, 1929; s. Abraham and Frieda F.; m. Helene Gellen, June 29, 1955; children—David, Linda, Deborah. A.B., Cornell U., 1951, Ph.D., 1955. Steroid chemist, research asso. Merck and Co., Rahway, N.J., 1956-64; with Syntex Research, Palo Alto, Calif., 1964—, dir. inst. organic chemistry, 1967-74, exec. v.p., 1974-76, pres., 1976—; sr. v.p. Syntex Corp., 1981—, also dir. and mem. com. for sci., 1982—. Mem. Am. Chem. Soc., Chem. Soc. (London). Current work: Steroid chemistry, prosta glandin chemistry, medicinal chemistry. Office: Syntex Research 3401 Hillview Ave Palo Alto CA 94304

FRIED, JOSEF, chemist, educator; b. Przemysl, Poland, July 21, 1914; came to U.S., 1938, naturalized, 1944; s. Abraham and Frieda (Fried) F.; m. Erna Werner, Sept. 18, 1939; 1 dau., Carol Frances. Student, U. Leipzig, 1934-37, U. Zurich, 1937-38; Ph.D., Columbia U., 1941. Eli Lilly fellow Columbia U., 1941-43; research chemist Givaudan, N.Y., 1943; head dept. antibiotics and steroids Squibb Inst. Med. Research, New Brunswick, N.J., 1944-59, dir. sect. organic chemistry, 1959-63; prof. chemistry, biochemistry and Ben May Lab. Cancer Research, U. Chgo., 1963—, Louis Block prof., 1973—, chmn. dept. chemistry, 1977-79; mem. med. chem. study sect. NIH, 1963-67, 68-72, chmn., 1971; mem. com. arrangements Laurentian Hormone Conf., 1964-71; Knapp Meml. lectr. U. Wis., 1958. Mem. bd. editors: Jour. Organic Chemistry, 1964-69, Steroids, 1966—, Jour. Biol. Chemistry, 1975-81, 83—; contbr. articles to profl. jours. Recipient N.J. Patent award, 1968. Fellow AAAS, N.Y. Acad. Scis.; mem. Am. Chem. Soc. (award in medicinal chemistry 1974), Nat. Acad. Scis., Am. Acad. Arts and Scis., Am. Soc. Biol. Chemists, Swiss Chem. Socs., Brit. Chem. Socs., Sigma Xi. Patentee in field. Subspecialties: Organic chemistry; Biophysical chemistry. Home: 5715 S Kenwood Ave Chicago IL 60637

FRIED, VOJTECH, chemist, educator; b. Czechoslovakia, Aug. 27, 1921; came to U.S., 1965, naturalized, 1970; s. Maurice and Helene (Lefkovits) F.; m. Katarina Altmann, July 10, 1951; 1 son, Thomas. Student, Charles U., Prague, Czechoslovakia; M.A. in Chem. Engring. with honors, Chem. Tech. Inst., Prague, 1951, Dr.T.Sci., 1953, Dr. Chem. Sci., 1957, Dr. Phys. Chem., 1963. Inst. Chem. Tech. U., Prague, 1950-53, successively asst. prof., assoc. prof., dozent, 1953-65; prof. chemistry Bklyn. Coll. of CUNY, 1965—, Disting. prof. chemistry, 1974—; disting. vis. prof. Arya Mehr U. Tech., Tehran, Iran, 1974; M. Jorizane chair vis. prof. U. Hiroshima, Japan, 1975. Author articles and books in field. Recipient Excellence in teaching awards Chem. Tech. Inst., 1959, Excellence in teaching awards Bklyn. Coll., 1974; Czechoslovak State Prize in Sci., 1963; grantee Petroleum Research Fund, Iranian Govt.; others. Fellow Japan Soc. Promotion Sci.; mem. Am. Chem. Soc., Czechoslovak Chem. Soc. Lodge: B'nai B'rith. Patentee. Current Work: Equations of state; theories of liquid solutions; experimental and theoretical studies of PVT behavior of gases and the behavior of nonelectrolyte solutions. Subspecialties: Physical chemistry; Statistical mechanics. Home: 37 Ethan Allen Dr Community of Concordia Cranbury NJ 08512 Office: Bedford Ave and Ave H Brooklyn NY 11210

FRIEDBERG, CARL E., computer systems company executive; b. Pitts., May 2, 1942. B.A., Harvard U., 1964; M.A., Princeton U., 1969, Ph.D., 1969. Instr. Princeton (N.J.) U., 1969-71; research fellow U. Calif., Lawrence Berkeley Lab., 1971-76; asst. prof. Harvard U., Boston, 1976-79; asst. physicist Meml. Sloan Kettering Cancer Center, N.Y.C., 1979-81; pres. In House Systems, N.Y.C., 1979—; pres. Seaport Systems Inc., N.Y.C., 1983—; chmn. VAX Systems, Maynard, Mass., 1980; mem. steering com. N.Y. Met. Local Users Group, N.Y.C., 1979. Mem. Am. Assn. Physicists Medicine, Am. Inst. Physics, Assn. Computing Machinery, N.Y. Acad. Scis., Sigma Xi. Current Work: Systems studies, integration, automated software development systems. Subspecialties: Operating systems; Particle physics. Office: In House Systems 165 William St New York NY 10038

FRIEDENSON, BERNARD ALLEN, biological chemist, educator; b. Duluth, Minn., July 6, 1943; s. Fred and Sarah (Berger) F.; m. Louise Pinsky, Nov. 10, 1968; children: Rachel, Jennifer, Joel. B.A., U. Minn., 1965; Ph.D., 1970. Cancer research scientist Roswell Park Meml. Inst., Buffalo, 1971-72, sr. cancer research scientist, 1973; asst. prof. biol. chemistry U. Ill. Med. Center, Chgo., 1973-78, assoc. prof., 1978—. Contbr. articles to profl. jours. USPHS grantee; NIH research career devel. award. Mem. Am. Assn. Immunologists. Current Work: Study of mechanisms of regulation of the immune system. Subspecialties: Immunology (medicine); Biochemistry (medicine). Home: 9348 Home Circle Des Plaines IL 60016 Office: 1853 W Polk Chicago IL 60612

FRIEDHOFF, ARNOLD, medical scientist; b. Johnstown, Pa., Dec. 26, 1923; s. Abraham M. and Stella (Beerman) F.; m. Frances Wolfe, Feb. 24, 1946; children: Lawrence, Nancy, Richard. B.A., U. Pa., 1944, M.D., 1947. Diplomate: Am. Bd. Psychiatry and Neurology. Intern Western Pa. Hosp., 1947-48; resident psychiatry U.S. Army, 1952-53, Bellevue Hosp., N.Y.C., 1953-55; instr., prof. psychiatry N.Y. U. Sch. Medicine, 1956—, head psychopharmacology research unit, 1956-63; co-dir. N.Y. U. Sch. Medicine (Center for Study Psychotic Disorders), 1963-69, dir., 1970—, N.Y. U. Sch. Medicine (Millhauser Labs.), 1970—; mem. clin. projects research rev. com. NIMH, 1970-74, chmn. treatment devel. and assessment research rev. com., 1979-81; Mem. Mayors Com. on Prescription Drugs, N.Y.C. Co-editor: Yearbook of Psychiatry and Applied Mental Health, 1968-80; mem. adv. bd. Biological Psychiatry, 1969—; Contbr. numerous reports on biochem. psychiatry, psychopharmacology. Served to 1st lt. M.C. U.S. Army, 1951-53. Recipient Research Scientist award NIMH, 1967—. Fellow Am. Coll. Neuropsychopharmacology (past councillor and past pres. 1978-79), Am. Psychiat. Assn., Am. Soc. Clin. Pharmacology and Therapeutics, Royal Coll. Psychiatrists (Gt. Britain); mem. Am. Chem. Soc., Internat. Soc. Neurochemistry, Assn. for Research in Nervous and Mental Diseases (past asst. sec.-treas.), Am. Psychopath. Assn. (past pres., Samuel B. Hamilton award), Soc. Biol. Psychiatry (past pres.). Current Work: Neuropharmacology, psychobiology, biological substrate of behavior, particularly adaptive biological processes in the brain. Subspecialties: Neurobiology; Neuropharmacology. Office: 550 1st Ave New York NY 10016

FRIEDLAENDER, GARY ELLIOTT, orthopaedic surgeon, medical educator; b. Detroit, May 5, 1945; s. Alex and Eileen (Berman) F.; m. Linda Beth Krohner, Mar. 16, 1969; children—Eron, Ari. B.S., U. Mich., 1967, M.D., 1969; M.A. (hon.), Yale U., 1984. Intern, U. Mich. Med. Ctr., Ann Arbor, 1969-70, resident in surgery, 1970-71; resident in orthopaedics Yale U.-New Haven Hosp., 1971-74; dir. tissue bank Naval Med. Research Inst., Bethesda, Md., 1974-76; asst. prof. Yale U. Sch. Medicine, New Haven, 1976-79, assoc. prof., 1979-84, prof., chief dept. orthopaedics, 1984—; sr. research fellow in orthopaedics Harvard U. Med. Sch., Boston, 1983. Editor: Tissue Banking for Transplantation, 1976; Osteochondral Allografts, 1983. Contbr. numerous med. articles to profl. jours. Served to lt. comdr. M.C., USNR, 1974-76. Recipient Kappa Delta Outstanding Orthopaedic Research award Am. Acad. Orthopaedic Surgeons/Orthopaedic Research Soc., 1982. Fellow A.C.S.; mem. Am. Council on Transplantation (pres. 1983-85), Am. Assn. Tissue Banks (pres. 1983-85), Am. Acad. Orthopaedic Surgeons, Am. Soc. Transplantation Surgeons, Soc. for Surg. Oncology. Jewish. Current work: Immunology, biology, banking and clinical applications of bone and cartilage transplants. Subspecialties: Orthopedics; Transplant surgery. Office: Dept Orthopaedic Surgery Yale Univ Sch Medicine 333 Cedar St New Haven CT 06510

FRIEDLANDER, GERHART, chemist; b. Munich, Germany, July 28, 1916; came to U.S., 1936, naturalized, 1943; s. Max O. and Bella (Forchheimer) F.; m. Gertrude Maas, Feb. 6, 1941 (dec. 1966); children: Ruth Ann F. Huart, Joan Claire F. Hurley; m. Barbara Strongin, 1983. B.S., U. Calif. - Berkeley, 1939, Ph.D., 1942. Instr. U. Idaho, Moscow, 1942-43; staff Los Alamos Sci. Lab., 1943-46; research asso. Gen. Electric Co. Research Lab., Schenectady, 1946-48; vis. lectr. Washington U., St. Louis, 1948; chemist Brookhaven Nat. Lab., Upton, N.Y., 1948-52, sr. chemist, 1952-81, cons., 1981—, chmn. chemistry dept., 1968-77; Chmn. Gordon Research Conf. on Nuclear Chemistry, 1954; mem. adv. com. for chemistry Oak Ridge Nat. Lab., 1966-70; mem. program adv. com. Los Alamos Meson Physics Facility, 1971-75; chmn. vis. com. nuclear chemistry Lawrence Berkeley Lab., 1974-75; mem. tech. adv. com. electromagnetic isotope separation Oak Ridge Nat. Lab., 1983—; exec. sec. basic energy scis. lab. program panel Dept. Energy, 1976-80; mem. adv. com. for nuclear chemistry div. Lawrence Livermore Lab., 1977-83. Author: (with J.W. Kennedy) Introduction to Radiochemistry, 1949, Nuclear and Radiochemistry, 1955, (with J.M. Miller), 1964, (with E.S. Macias), 1981; also articles.; assoc. editor: Ann. Rev. Nuclear Sci., 1958-67; editor: Radiochimica Acta, 1972-73. Recipient Alexander von Humboldt award Institut für Kernchemie, Mainz, W. Ger., 1978-79. Fellow Am. Phys. Soc.; mem. Nat. Acad. Scis. (mem. assembly math. and phys. scis. 1981-82; mem. commn. phys. scis., math. and resources 1982—, chmn. ad hoc panel on future nuclear sci. 1975-76, chmn. com. on recommendations for U.S. Army basic sci. research Nat. Acad. Scis.-NRC 1977-81, mem. com. on postdoctoral and doctoral research staff NRC 1977-80), Am. Acad. Arts and Scis., Am. Chem. Soc. (chmn. div. nuclear chemistry and tech. 1967, award for nuclear applications in chemistry 1967), AAAS. Research chem. effects of nuclear transformations, properties of radioactive isotopes, mechanisms of nuclear reactions, especially those induced by protons of very high energies, solar neutrino detection. Current Work: Solar neutrino detection. Subspecialties: Physical chemistry; Nuclear chemistry. Home: 5 Lorraine Ct Smithtown NY 11787 Office: Brookhaven Nat Lab Upton NY 11973

FRIEDLANDER, SHELDON KAY, educator; b. Bronx, N.Y., Nov. 17, 1927; s. Irving and Rose (Katzewitz) F.; m. Marjorie Ellen Robbins, Aug. 17, 1958; children—Eva Kay, Amelie Elise, Antonia Zoe, Josiah. B.S., Columbia, 1949; M.S., Mass. Inst. Tech., 1951; Ph.D., U. Ill., 1954. Asst. prof. chem. engring. Columbia, 1954-57; asst. prof. then asso. prof. Johns Hopkins, 1957-62, prof. chem. engring., 1962-64; prof. chem. engring. and environ. engring. Calif. Inst. Tech., 1964-78; prof. engring. and applied sci., vice-chmn. dept. chem. engring. UCLA, 1978—; dir. Intermedia Transport Research Center, 1980—; mem. environ. sci. and engring. study sect. B USPHS, 1965-68; chmn. panel on particulate emissions NRC-Nat. Acad. Engring., 1970—; chmn. panel on photochem. oxidants and ozone NRC, 1973-76; cons. Los Angeles Air Pollution Control Dist., 1973-75; mem. environ. studies bd. NRC, 1977-80; chmn. clean air sci. adv. com. EPA, 1978—. Served with AUS, 1946-47. Fulbright scholar, 1960-61; Guggenheim fellow, 1969-70. Mem. Nat. Acad. Engring., Am. Inst. Chem. Engrs. (Colburn award 1959, Alpha Chi Sigma award 1974, Walker award 1979), Am. Chem. Soc., Sigma Xi, Tau Beta Pi. Originator theory self-preserving size distbns., aerosol dynamics, filtration theory, turbulent deposition, relation of air quality to emission sources for particulate pollution, facilitated transport. Subspecialties: Environmental engineering; Chemical engineering. Home: 1591 Oakdale St Pasadena CA 91106

FRIEDLER, GLADYS, developmental psychopharmacologist; b. Lewiston, Maine, Sept. 7, 1926; s. Max Herman and Anna Diana (Feld) F. B.A., U. Maine; M.A., U. Pa.; Ph.D., Boston U. NIH postdoctoral fellow U. Calif. San Francisco Med. Ctr.; research fellow Harvard Med. Sch., 1970-72; research fellow anesthesiology Lying-In div. Boston Hosp. for Women, 1970-72; asst. prof. psychiatry and pharmacology Boston U. Med. Sch., 1973-81, assoc. prof., 1981—. Contbr. articles to profl. jours. NIH fellow, 1964-68; NIMH trainee, 1968-70; Nat. Inst. Drug Abuse grantee, 1975-82. Mem. Behavioral Teratology Soc., Internat. Soc. Devel. Psychobiology, Am. Soc. Pharmacology and Exptl. Therapeutics, AAAS, Phi Beta Kappa, Phi Kappa Phi. Current Work: Long term and cross generational alterations in growth, behavioral and neuroendocrine development of progeny which follow parental exposure to pharmacologic agents and other environmental contaminants; exploration of comparative roles of genetic and environmental factors in etiology of the imprint. Subspecialty: Teratology. Office: 80 E Concord St Boston MA 02118

FRIEDMAN, EDWARD ALAN, college dean, educator; b. Bayonne, N.J., Sept. 29, 1935; s. Philip Arthur and Esther (Weinstein) F.; m. Arline Joan Lederman, Jan. 13, 1963; children: Millard Timur. B.S., MIT, 1957; postgrad., Stanford U., 1957-58; Ph.D., Columbia U., 1963. Philip Kerim. Asst. prof., asso. prof. physics Stevens Inst. Tech., Hoboken, N.J., 1963-69, dean of coll., 1973—, prof., 1980—, chmn. computer tng. com., 1982; v.p. Mentor Systems, Inc., 1980—; vis. prof. Kabul U., 1965-67, dir. engring. coll. devel. program, Afghanistan, 1970-73; Cons. Hudson Inst., 1962-63, Doubleday Book Co., 1969; Chmn. Civic Affairs Com., Hoboken, 1968-69; vice chmn. bd. edn. Am. Internat. Sch. of Kabul, 1971-72; chmn. bd. dirs. N.Y. Scientists Com. for Pub. Info., 1977-78; chmn. Council for Understanding of Tech. in Human Affairs, 1979-82; sr. v.p. Afghanistan Relief Com., 1980—; mem. N.J. Commn. on Grad. Tchr. Edn., 1982-83. Co-founder, co-editor: Machine-Mediated Learning Jour., 1983. Trustee Hudson Higher Edn. Consortium, 1974; bd. dirs. Assn. Ind. Colls. and Univs. N.J., 1978-82. Recipient (with R.D. Andrews) Ottens research award Stevens Inst. Tech., 1970, 1st Class Edn. medal Govt. of Afghanistan, 1973; NSF grantee to direct elementary sch. sci. program for Orange, N.J., 01969. Mem. Am. Phys. Soc., AAAS, Am. Assn. Engring. Edn., Computer Soc., Am. Soc. Tng. and Devel. Subspecialty: Technological education. Home: Colonial House Castle Point Hoboken NJ 07030

FRIEDMAN, GERALD MANFRED, geology educator, geologist; b. Berlin, July 23, 1921; came to U.S., 1946, naturalized, 1950; s. Martin and Frieda (Cohn) F.; m. Sue Tyler, June 27, 1948; children: Judith Fay Friedman Rosen, Sharon Mira Friedman Azaria, Devorah Paula Friedman Zweibach, Eva Jane Friedman Scholle, Wendy Tamar Friedman Spanier. Student, U. Cambridge, Eng., 1938-39; B.Sc., U. London, 1945, D.Sc., 1977; M.A., Columbia U., 1950, Ph.D., 1952. Lectr. Chelsea Coll., London, 1944-45; analytical chemist E. R. Squibb & Sons, New Brunswick, N.J.; also J. Lyons & Co., London, 1945-48; asst. geology Columbia U., 1950; temporary geologist N.Y. State Geol. Survey, 1950; instr., asst. prof. geology U. Cin., 1950-54; cons. geologist, Sault Ste. Marie, Ont., Can., 1954-56; mem. research dept. Amoco Prodn. Co., Tulsa, 1956-64, sr. research scientist, 1956-60, research assoc., 1960-62, supr. sedimentology research, 1962-64; Fulbright vis. prof. geology Hebrew U., Jerusalem, 1964; prof. geology Rensselaer Poly. Inst., 1964-84, prof. emeritus, 1984—; prof. geology Bklyn. Coll., Grad. Sch. and Univ. Ctr. of CUNY, 1985—; adv. Judo Club, 1964-84; research scientist Hudson Labs., Columbia U., 1965, 66-69, research assoc. dept. geology, 1968-72; vis. prof. U. Heidelberg, Germany, 1967; cons. scientist Inst. Petroleum Research and Geophysics, Israel, 1967-71; vis. scientist Geol. Survey Israel, 1970, 73, 78; lectr. Oil and Gas Cons. Internat., 1968—; pres. Gerry Exploration, Inc., 1982—. Author: (with J.E. Sanders) Principles of Sedimentology, 1978, (with A. Reekmann and ELF-Aquitaine) Exploration for Carbonate Petroleum Reservoirs, 1982, (with K. G. Johnson) Exercises in Sedimentology; editor: Jour. Sedimentary Petrology, 1964-70 (Best Paper award 1961), Northeastern Geology, 1979—, Earth Scis. History, 1982—; pub.: Northeastern Environ. Sci, 1982—; sect. editor: Chem. Abstracts, 1962-69; editorial bd.: Sedimentary Geology, 1967—, Israel Jour. Earth Scis, 1971-76, Jour. Geology, 1977—, GeoJour, 1977-84; co-editor, contbr.: Carbonate Sedimentology in Central Europe, 1968, Modern Carbonate Enviroments, 1983, Hypersaline Ecosystems: The Garish Sabkha, 1985; editor, contbr.: Depositional Environments in Carbonate Rocks, 1969; editor: Lecture Notes in Earth Sciences, 1985—; contbr. articles in field to profl. jours. Mem. phys. edn. com. Tulsa YMCA, 1958-63; bd. dirs. Troy Jewish Community Council, 1966-72, 74-77; pres. Northeastern Sci. Found., Inc., 1979—. Fellow Mineral. Soc. Am. (nominating com. for fellows 1967-69, awards com. 1976-77), Geol. Soc. Am. (mem. com. on publs. 1980-82), Geol. Assn. Can., Geol. Soc. Gt. Britain, AAAS (chmn. sect. geology and geography 1978-79, council mem. 1979-80); mem. Am. Chem. Soc. (group leader 1962-63), Am. Assn. Petroleum Geologists (disting. lectr. 1972-73, chmn. carbonate rock com. 1965-69, mem. research com. 1965-71, 75-82, marine geology com. 1974, lectr. continuing edn. program 1967—, adv. council 1974-75, disting. lectr. com. 1975-78, membership com. 1981—, ho. of dels. 1977-79, 83—, treas. eastern sect. 1980-81, v.p. eastern sect. 1981-82, pres. 1982-83, nat. v.p. 1984-85), Soc. Econ. Paleontologists and Mineralogists (hon. nat. pres. 1974-75, sect. pres. 1967-68, Best Paper award Gulf Coast sect. 1974), Assn. Geology Tchrs. (nat. treas. 1951-55, pres. Okla. 1962-63, pres. Eastern sect. 1983-84), Am. Geol. Inst. (governing bd. 1971-72, 74-75), Assn. Earth Sci. Editors (pres. 1971-72), Internat. Assn. Sedimentologists (hon., pres. 1975-78), N.Y. State Geol. Assn. (pres. 1978-79), Geol. Soc. Israel, Geol. Vereinigung, U.S. Judo Fedn., Sigma Gamma Epsilon (nat. pres. 1981—). Current Work: Research in carbonate and clastic sedimentology, especially depositional environments and diagenetic overprint. Subspecialty: Sedimentology. Home: 32 24th St Troy NY 12180 Office: Northeastern Sci Found Rensselaer Ctr Applied Geology PO Box 746 Troy NY 12181 Also: Bklyn Coll of CUNY Brooklyn NY 11210

FRIEDMAN, HAROLD IRA, surgeon; b. N.Y.C., Oct. 22, 1946; s. Joseph and Dorothy (Asnin) F.; m. Clarke Emmons, Nov. 24, 1976. B.Sc., Hobart Coll., 1967; Ph.D., U. Va., 1972, M.D., 1974. Diplomate: Nat. Bd. Med. Examiners. Intern surgery U. Va. Med. Center, Charlottesville, 1974-75; cell biologist gen. surgeon Letterman Army Inst. Research, San Francisco, 1975-78; resident gen. surgery U. Ariz. Med. Center, Tucson, 1978-82; resident in plastic surgery U. Va. Med. Center, Charlottesville, 1982—. Contbr. articles to profl. jours. Served to maj., M.C. U.S. Army, 1975-78. Recipient Van Winkle award U. Ariz., 1982; Upjohn Achievement award, 1982; decorated Army Commendation medal; recipient James Kembrough award for outstanding urologic research, 1976. Mem. Am. Inst. Nutrition, Am. Assn. Clin. Nutrition, Am. Soc. Exptl. Biology, Am. Soc. Parenteral and Enteral Nutrition, AMA, Assn. Mil. Surgeons. Current Work: Electron microscopic investigations of nutrition, prostate cancer, resuscitative fluids, obesity, blood storage products, others. Subspecialties: Cell biology (medicine); Surgery. Home: 136 Bennington Rd Charlottesville VA 22901

FRIEDMAN, HARVEY MICHAEL, physician, virologist, researcher, educator; b. Montreal, Que., Can., May 29, 1944; came to U.S., 1971; s. Sidney and Sybil (Garfinkle) F.; m. Cynthia D. Mickey, Apr. 12, 1980; children—Julie, Lisa. M.D., McGill U., Montreal, 1969. Intern Jewish Gen. Hosp., Montreal, 1969-70, resident, 1970-71; fellow in virology Wistar Inst., Phila., 1971-73; fellow in infectious disease Hosp. U. Pa., 1973-75; dir. Diagnostic Virology Lab., Children's Hosp., Phila., 1975—; assoc. prof. medicine U. Pa., 1981—; cons. infectious diseases. Contbr. numerous articles to profl. jours. NIH grantee, 1981—. Fellow Infectious Disease Soc. Am.; mem. AAAS, Am. Soc. Microbiology. Current Work: Herpes simplex virus glycoproteins. Subspecialties: Infectious diseases; Virology (medicine). Office: Children's Hospl Phila 34th and Civic Center Blvd Philadelphia PA 19146

FRIEDMAN, HOWARD STEPHEN, chemist; b. Elizabeth, N.J., Mar. 31, 1948; s. Samuel and Zelda (Gushin) F.; m. Lori Marcia Roseman, Dec. 24, 1972. A.B., N.Y.U., 1970, M.S., 1972, Ph.D., 1976. Postdoctoral scholar U. Mich., Ann Arbor, 1975-77; sr. research chemist Goodyear Tire & Rubber Co., Akron, Ohio, 1977-79; Ferro Corp., Bedford, Ohio, 1980-82; sr. chemist Velsicol Chem. Corp., Chgo., 1982—. Contbr. articles to profl. jours. Mem. Am. Chem. Soc., Royal Soc. Chemistry, N.Y. Acad. Scis., Sigma Xi. Current work: Process development of agricultural and specialty chemicals through production facility level. Subspecialty: Organic chemistry. Office: Velsicol Chem Corp 341 E Ohio St Chicago IL 60611

FRIEDMAN, MELVIN, geologist, educator; b. Orange, N.J., Nov. 14, 1930; s. Leonard and Hannah L. (Sholk) F.; m. Deborah Friedman, June 13, 1954; children: Barry D., Cheryl A. B.S., Rutgers U., 1952, M.S., 1954; Ph.D., Rice U., 1961. Geologist, research assoc., sect. leader Shell Devel. Co., 1954-67; assoc. prof. geology Tex. A&M U., College Station, 1967-69, prof., 1969—, dir. Ctr. for Tectonophysics, 1979-82, assoc. dean Coll. Geoscis., 1982-83, dean Coll. Geoscis., 1983—. Co-editor-in-chief: Jour. Tectonophysics, 1980—; contbr. articles to profl. jours. Recipient research award Internat. Soc. Commn. U.S. Rock Mechanics, 1969; Disting. Faculty Achievement award Tex. A&M U., 1975. Fellow Geol. Soc. Am., AAAS; mem. Am. Geophys. Union. Jewish. Current Work: Observational studies of deformation mechanisms in experimentally and naturally deformed rocks; application of same to problems in petroleum exploration and production, engineering rock mechanics, faulting and folding. Subspecialties: Tectonics; High-temperature materials. Office: Ctr Tectonophysics Tex A&M U College Station TX 77843

FRIEDMAN, NATHAN BARUCH, pathologist; b. N.Y.C., Jan. 30, 1911; s. Emanuel David and Rose (Borgenicht) F.; m. Helen Eugenie McFrancis; m. Isabel Williams Speers, Jan. 3, 1960; children: Sharon, Janifer, Robert, Marylou, Emily, Charles. B.S., Harvard U., 1930; M.D., Cornell U., 1934. Diplomate: Am. Bd. Pathology. Intern Montefiore Hosp., N.Y.C., 1935-36; resident U. Chgo. Clinics, 1937-38; asst. in pathology U. Chgo., 1938-39; Littauer fellow Harvard U., 1939-40; instr. in pathology Stanford U., 1941-42; dir. labs. Cedars of Lebanon Hosp., Los Angeles, 1948-70; sr. cons. in pathology Cedars Sinai Med. Ctr., Los Angeles, 1970—; clin. prof. pathology U. So. Calif. Author: Tumors of Bladder, 1959; contbr. articles on cancer, radiation, endocrines, urology to profl. jours. Served to maj. M.C. AUS, 1942-46. Mem. Am. Assn. Pathologists, Am. Soc. Clin. Pathology, Am. Assn. Cancer Research, Endocrine Soc. Current Work: Germ cell tumors, breast cancer, experimental immunology. Subspecialties: Pathology (medicine); Oncology. Home: 15150 Mulholland Dr Los Angeles CA 90077 Office: 8700 Beverly Blvd Los Angeles CA 90048

FRIEDMAN, ORRIE MAX, biotechnology company executive; b. Grenfell, Sask., Can., June 6, 1915; came to U.S., 1946, naturalized, 1962; s. Jack and Gertrude (Shulman) F.; m. Laurel E. Leeder, Jan. 2, 1959; children: Mark David, Gertrude Jane, Hugh Robert. B.Sc., U. Man., 1935; B.Sc. in Chemistry, McGill U., 1941, Ph.D., 1944. Research chemist NRCCan., Ottawa, Ont., 1944-46; research fellow chemistry Harvard U., 1946-49, research assoc., 1949-51; asst. prof. Harvard Med. Sch., 1951-53; asst. prof. Brandeis U., 1953-55, assoc. prof., 1955-58, prof. chemistry, 1958-62; pres., sci. dir. Collaborative Research, Inc., Waltham, Mass., 1962-82, chmn. bd., 1982—; cons. in field; dir. Nat. Assn. Life Sci. Industries, 1977-79; dir. Canada Fibre Can Co. Ltd., Montreal. Contbr. articles to profl. jours. Bd. dirs. Boston chpt. Am. Technion Soc., also nat. bd. dirs.; trustee Beth Israel Hosp., Boston, Worcester Found. Exptl. Biology; mem. corp. Sidney Farber Cancer Inst., Mus. Sci., Boston.; bd. govs. Technion, Israel Inst. Tech. Recipient numerous grants from various govt. agys. Fellow AAAS, Chem. Soc. London; mem. Am. Chem. Soc., Am. Assn. Cancer Research, Radiation Soc., N.Y. Acad. Sci., Sigma Xi. Current Work: Developer, manufacturer products having commercial potential in medicine, agricultural and industry and research. Subspecialties: Genetics and genetic engineering (biology); Genetics and genetic engineering (medicine). Home: 49 Warren St Brooklin MA 02146 Office: 128 Spring St Lexington MA 02173

FRIEDMAN, RAYMOND, combustion scientist; b. Portsmouth, Va., Feb. 9, 1922. B.S. in Chem. Engring., Va. Poly. Inst., 1942; Ph.D., in Chem. Engring., U. Wis.-Madison, 1948. Registered profl. engr., Mass. Research scientist Westinghouse Electric Corp., Pitts., 1943-46, 1948-55; research mgr. Atlantic Research Corp., Alexandria, Va., 1955-69; research mgr., v.p. Factory Mut. Research, Norwood, Mass., 1969—. Contbr. articles to profl. jours. Mem. Combustion Inst. (pres. 1978-82), Am. Chem. Soc. (div. chmn. 1964), Am. Inst. Chem. Engrs., AAAS, Soc. Fire Protection Engrs. Club: Cosmos (Washington). Subspecialty: Combustion processes. Home: 126 Kings Grant Rd Weston MA 02193 Office: Factory Mutual Research 1151 Boston Providence Turnpike Norwood MA 02062

FRIEDMAN, SELWYN MARVIN, microbiologist, educator; b. N.Y.C., May 17, 1929; s. Louis and Leah (Weinstein) F.; m. Rivka Teitelbaum, May 28, 1972. Student, CCNY, 1946-48; B.S., U. Mich., 1951; M.S., Purdue U., 1953, Ph.D., 1961. Postdoctoral fellow dept. biochemistry Western Res. U., 1961-62; dept. cell biology Albert Einstein Coll. Medicine, 1962-63; research fellow Columbia U. Coll. Physicians and Surgeons, 1962-66; vis. scientist dept. chemistry Columbia U., 1973; asst. prof. Hunter Coll., CUNY, 1966-69, assoc. prof. biology, 1969—; U.S. coordinator joint U.S.-Japan seminar in Biochemistry of Thermophily U.S.-Japan Coop. Sci. Program, Honolulu, 1977. Research publs. in field; editor: Biochemistry of Thermophily, 1978. Served with U.S. Army, 1954-56. USPHS grantee, 1967-70, 75-78; CUNY Faculty Research Award Program grantee, 1975-79, 81-86. Mem. N.Y. Acad. Scis., AAAS, Am. Soc. Microbiology, Harvey Soc. Democrat. Jewish. Current Work: Molecular aspects of growth at elevated temperatures; genetic exchange in thermophilic bacteria. Subspecialties: Microbiology; Genetics and genetic engineering (biology). Home: 340 E 64th St Apt 14-L New York NY 10021 Office: 695 Park Ave New York NY 10021

FRIEDRICH, OTTO MARTIN, JR., elec. engr., researcher, educator, cons.; b. Austin, Tex., Jan. 29, 1939; s. Otto Martin and Lillie Louise (Stark) F. B.S. in Elec. Engring. U. Tex., 1961, M.S. in Elec. Engring, 1962, Ph.D. in Elec. Engring, 1965. Registered profl. engr., Tex. Research engr. U. Tex., Austin, 1961-65, mem. faculty dept. elec. engring., 1965—, faculty research engr., 1969—; asst. dir. U. Tex. (Electronics Research Ctr.), 1971-75, cons. profl. engring. to industry, fed., state and local govt. Contbr. articles on electro-optics, lasers, plasma diagnostics and instrumentation to publs. of, IEEE, Instrument Soc. Am. Mem. IEEE (sr.), Instrument Soc. Am. (sr., Dr. Charles Stark Draper award 1972), Am. Phys. Soc., AAAS, AIAA, Am. Geophys. Soc., Optical Soc. Am., Nat. Soc. Profl. Engrs., Tex. Soc. Profl. Engrs. Lutheran. Current Work: Laser instrumentation and applications, including holography; electro-optics, lasers, holography, plasmas, instrumentation. Subspecialties: Electronics; Laser research. Office: U Tex Austin TX 78712

FRIES, RICHARD CYRIL, reliability engineer; b. Chgo., Dec. 8, 1942; s. Cyril C. and Sophia (Biadaszkiewicz) F.; m. Mary June Marciniak, July 6, 1968; children—Thomas Richard, Matthew Ryan. B.S. in Biology, Loyola U., Chgo., 1965; B.S.E.E., Marquette U., 1976. Research biologist Lakeside Labs., Milw., 1970-75, Milw. Blood Ctr., 1975-76; software engr. Sperry Univac, Mpls., 1976-79; reliability engr. Medtronic, Mpls., 1979-81, lead engr., 1981-83; reliability engr. Ohmeda, Madison, Wis., 1983—. Contbr. articles to profl. jours. Leader Indianhead council Boy Scouts Am., 1977-79; coach Recreation League softball and soccer, White Bear Lake, Minn., 1979, 81. Served with USN, 1965-70. Mem. Assn. for the Advancement of Med. Instrumentation (session chmn. 1985, 86), IEEE, Assn. for Computing Machinery, Am. Soc. for Quality Control, N.Y. Acad. Scis., Health Industry Mfgrs. Assn. (computer and software task force). Episcopalian. Current work: Reliability of medical devices and associated microprocessor software. Subspecialties: Biomedical engineering; Software engineering. Office: Ohmeda Ohmeda Dr Madison WI 53707

FRIESEN, LARRY JAY, software engineer; b. Salina, Kans., Sept. 7, 1946; s. Eric Jacob and Dorothy Marie (Le Clair) F. B.A., U. Kans., 1967; M.S., Rice U., 1972, Ph.D., 1974. Postdoctoral research asso. U. Ga., Athens, 1974-75; engr. guidance and control mechanics McDonnell Douglas, Houston, 1976-80, sr. engr., 1980—. Served with U.S. Army, 1969-70. Mem. AAAS, Nat. Space Inst., Am. Astron. Soc., Am. Astronautical Soc., World Space Found., L-5 Soc., Republican. Methodist. Copyrighted board game: Quadrants. Current Work: Lunar and planetary studies. Orbital operation studies, including orbital maneuvering vehicle. Subspecialty: Aerospace engineering and technology. Office: McDonnell Douglas Tech Service Mail Code G 16505 Space Center Blvd Houston TX 77062

FRIESEN, WOLFGANG OTTO, biology educator; b. Elbing, Germany, Oct. 31, 1942; came to U.S., 1950, naturalized, 1960; s. Helmuth and Trude F. B.A., Bethel Coll., Newton, Kans., 1964; M.A. in Physics, U. Calif.-Berkeley, 1966; Ph.D. in Neurosci, U. Calif.-San Diego, 1974. Research physicist Cardiovascular Research Inst., U. Calif.-San Francisco, 1969-70; research assoc., research fellow dept. molecular biology U. Calif.-Berkeley, 1974-77; asst. prof. biology U. Va., Charlottesville, 1977-82, assoc. prof., 1982—. Contbr. articles on pulmonary physiology, neurophysiology, neuroanatomy, math. modeling and instrumentation to sci. jours. NIH fellow, 1975-77; NIH research grantee, 1978-82, 84—; NSF research grantee, 1982—. Mem. AAAS, Soc. for Neurosci. Inventor infant respiratory monitor and a sonic level. Current Work: Biology, neurobiology. Subspecialties: Neurobiology; Bioinstrumentation. Home: 2821 Northfields Rd Charlottesville VA 22901 Office: Dept Biology U Va Charlottesville VA 22901

FRINK, RICHARD CLARK, electrical engineer, electromagnetics executive; b. Norwich, N.Y., May 28, 1925; s. Hoyt Peter and Mildred Elizabeth (Day) F.; m. Hazel Marie Perry, June 19, 1945; 1 dau., Barbara Jean. B.E.E., Rensselaer Poly. Inst., 1950. Engr., Gen. Lab. Assocs., Norwich, 1950-56, test lab. mgr., 1956-64, research engr., 1964-72; mgr. elec. power systems Simmonds Precision Engine Systems Div., Norwich, 1972—. Patentee in field. Membership sec. Broad St. United Meth. Ch., Norwich, 1970—. Served with AUS, 1943-46. Recipient Founders award Simmonds Precision Inc., 1983. Mem. IEEE, Am. Def. Preparedness Assn., Am. Philatelic Soc. Democrat. Lodge: Moose (Norwich). Current work: rare earth permanent magnet alternator design. Subspecialties: Aerospace engineering and technology; Applied magnetics. Home: 10 Westcott St Norwich NY 13815 Office: Engine Systems Div Simmonds Precision Group Hercules Aerospace Norwich-Oxford Rd Norwich NY 13815

FRISCH, HENRY JONATHAN, physicist, educator; b. Los Alamos, N.Mex., Aug. 21, 1944; s. David Henry and Rose Nona (Epstein) F.; m. Priscilla Diane Chapman, Nov. 29, 1971; children—Sarah Tenaya, Genevieve Alexandra. B.A. in Physics, Harvard U., 1966; Ph.D., U. Calif.-Berkeley, 1971. Instr. physics U. Chgo., 1971-73, asst. prof., 1973-77, assoc. prof., 1977-84, prof., 1984—. Mem. Am. Phys. Soc. (mem. exec. com. of particle and fields div. 1979), Fermilab Users Orgn. (mem. exec. com. 1979). Current work: Search for magnetic monopoles, detector development, ultrahigh energy p bar-p collisions. Subspecialty: Particle physics. Office: HEP 320 EFI 5640 S Ellis Ave Chicago IL 60637

FRISCH, JOSEPH, mech. engr., educator, cons.; b. Vienna, Austria, Apr. 21, 1921; came to U.S., 1940, naturalized, 1946; s. Abraham and Rachel (Lieberman) F.; m. Joan S., May 26, 1962; children: Nora Theresa, Erich Martin, Jonathan David. B.S.M.E., Duke U., 1946; M.S., U. Calif., 1950. Registered profl. engr., Calif. Mem. faculty U. Calif., Berkeley, 1947—, asst. prof. mech. engring., 1951-57, asso. prof., 1957-63, prof., 1963—; asst. dir. U. Calif. (Inst. Engring. Research), 1961-63, chmn. div. mech. design, 1966-70; asso. dean U. Calif. (Coll. Engring.), 1972-75, cons. to indsl. and govtl. labs. Contbr. numerous articles to profl. jours. Fellow ASME; mem. Phi Beta Kappa, Sigma Xi, Tau Beta Pi, Pi Tau Sigma. Clubs: U. Calif. at Berkeley Faculty, Berkeley City. Current Work: Computer-aided design and manufacturing; computer-aided systems analysis. Subspecialties: Mechanical engineering; Computer-aided design. Office: Dept Mech Engring U Calif Berkeley CA 94720

FRISELL, WILHELM RICHARD, biochemist, educator; b. Two Harbors, Minn., Apr. 27, 1920; s. Olof Wilhelm and Thyra Magnina (Falk) F.; m. Margaret Jane Fleagle, Mar. 6, 1948; children William Richard, Robert Benjamin. B.A., St. Olaf Coll., Minn., 1942; M.A., Johns Hopkins U., 1943, Ph.D., 1946, postdoctoral, 1946-49. Instr. physiol. chemistry Johns Hopkins U. and Sch. Medicine, Balt., 1950-51; asst. prof. biochemistry U. Colo. Sch. Medicine, Denver, 1951-58, asso. prof., 1958-64, prof., 1964-69; prof., chmn. dept. biochemistry N.J. Med. Sch., Newark, 1969-76; acting dean Grad. Sch. Biomed. Sci., Coll. Medicine and Dentistry N.J., Newark, 1971-73; prof., chmn. dept. biochemistry East Carolina U. Sch. Medicine, also asst. dean grad. affairs, Greenville, N.C., 1976—; mem. fellowships com. Fogarty Internat. Center, NIH, 1962-66, 67-71, 81—, chmn., 1968-71, 81, chmn. sr. fellowship com., 1981—. Author: Acid-Base Chemistry in Medicine, 1968, Human Biochemistry, 1982; also articles and revs. NDRC fellow, 1943-44; Am. Scandinavian Found. fellow Uppsala, Sweden, 1949-50. Fellow AAAS; mem. Am. Chem.

Soc., Am. Soc. Biol. Chemists, Am. Soc. Microbiology, Soc. Exptl. Biology and Medicine, N.Y. Acad. Scis., Harvey Soc., Phi Beta Kappa, Sigma Xi (pres. Colo. chpt. 1968-69). Current Work: Biosynthesis and reaction mechanisms of flavin and folate-coenzymes; metabolic pathways in prokaryotes and eukaryotic cells. Subspecialties: Biochemistry (medicine); Microbiology. Home: 209 Fairlane Rd Greenville NC 27834 Office: Sch Medicine E Carolina U Greenville NC 27834

FRITTS, HAROLD CLARK, dendrochronology educator; b. Rochester, N.Y., Dec. 17, 1928; s. Edwin Coulthard and Ava Lee (Washburn) F.; m. Barbara Smith, June 11, 1955 (dec. July 1981); children—Marcia L., Paul T.; m. Miriam Colson, July 19, 1982. B.A., Oberlin Coll., 1951; M.S., Ohio State U., 1953, Ph.D., 1956. Asst. prof. botany Eastern Ill. U., Charleston, 1956-60; faculty U Ariz., Tucson, 1960—, prof. dendrochronology, 1969—; founder, dir. Internat. Tree-Ring Data Bank, Tucson, 1974—. Author: Tree Rings and Climate, 1976. Contbr. numerous articles to sci. jours., books. Mem. local sch. bd., Tucson, 1971-72. Recipient Outstanding Achievement in Bioclimatology award Am. Meteorol. Soc., 1982; NSF grantee, 1963—; Guggenheim Found. fellow, 1968-69, NATO fellow Advanced Study Inst. on Climate Variability, Erice, Sicily, 1980. Mem. Ecol. Soc. Am., Am. Assn. Quaternary Environment, Am. Inst. Biol. Scis., AAAS, Tree-Ring Soc. Current work: Reconstruction of past climates through tree-ring studies and other proxy climate data; dendrochronology, dendroclimatology, paleoclimatic research, quaternary research. Subspecialty: Dendroclimatology. Office: Lab Tree-Ring Research Bldg 58 U Ariz Tucson AZ 85721

FRITZ, FRANK MARK, mechanical engineer; b. Milw., Jan. 10, 1954; s. Frank Rudolph and Arline May (O'Conner) F. B.S. in Mech. Engring., Milw. Sch. Engring., 1980. Project engr. Applied Power Inc., Milw., 1980—. Patentee pulse width modulated pressure regulator. Recipient 2d place Engring. Design award Am. Soc. for Engring. Edn., 1980. Mem. ASME (assoc.). Current work: Software development - electro hydraulics; computer modeling and simulation; magnetic analysis - applied magnetics. Subspecialties: Software engineering; Applied magnetics. Office: Applied Power Inc 1619 S 101st St West Allis WI 53214

FRITZ, WILLIAM JON, geology educator; b. Vancouver, Wash., Mar. 31, 1953; s. Ernest and Huldah M. (Petersen) F.; m. Terry Dale McNulty, Apr. 22, 1973; children—Tristan J. B.S., Walla Walla Coll., 1975, M.S., 1977; Ph.D., U. Mont., 1980. Grad. teaching asst. Walla Walla Coll., College Place, Wash., 1975-77; head grad. teaching asst. U. Mont., Missoula, 1978-80; petroleum geologist Amoco Prodn. Co., Denver, 1980-81; asst. prof. geology Ga. State U., Atlanta, 1981—. Author: Roadside Geology of the Yellowstone Country, 1985. Contbr. articles and abstracts to profl. jours. and meetings. Am. Philos. Soc. grantee, 1984. Mem. Soc. Econ. Paleontologists and Mineralogists (tech. program chmn.), Geol. Soc. Am., Am. Assn. Petroleum Geologists (Ho. of Dels. 1984—), Georgia Geol. Soc. (pres. 1984—), Internat. Assn. of Sedimentologists, Sigma Xi. Current work: Volcaniclastic sedimentology related to volcanic controls on sedimentation. Subspecialties: Sedimentology; Geology. Home: 1094 Chatsworth Dr Avondale Estates GA 30002 Office: Dept of Geology Ga State U Atlanta GA 30303

FROHLICH, EDWARD DAVID, physician; b. N.Y.C., Sept. 10, 1931; s. William and May (Zneimer) F.; m. Sherry Linda Fine, Nov. 1, 1959; children—Marjorie, Bruce, Lara. B.A., Washington and Jefferson Coll., 1952; M.D., U. Md., 1956; M.S., Northwestern U., 1963. Diplomate: Am. Bd. Internal Medicine. Intern, resident D.C. Gen. Hosp., 1956-58; fellow in cardiovascular research Georgetown U. Hosp., Washington, 1958-59, resident in internal medicine, 1959-60; clin. investigator VA Research Hosp., Chgo., 1962-64; asso. in medicine Northwestern U., 1963-64; staff mem. research div. Cleve. Clinic, 1964-69; faculty medicine, physiology, biophysics, dir. div. hypertensive diseases U. Okla., Oklahoma City, 1969-76, George Lynn Cross research prof., 1975-76; v.p. edn., research Alton Ochsner Med. Found., New Orleans, 1976—; div. hypertensive diseases Ochsner Clinic, 1976—; prof. medicine, physiology La. State U., 1976—; prof. medicine, adj. prof. pharmacology Tulane U., 1976—; cons. FDA, 1971-74, VA, 1972—, NIH, 1972—, WHO, 1975-82, U.S. Pharmacopeia, 1975—. Contbr. many chpts. to books, numerous articles to profl. jours.; Editor: Pathophysiology - Altered Regulatory Mechanisms in Disease, 1972, 76, 84, Rypins' Medical Licensure Examinations, 1981, 85; editor.: Jour. Lab. and Clin. Medicine, 1974-76, Am. Jour. Cardiology, 1977—, Archives of Internal Medicine, 1978—, Modern Medicine, 1980—, Hypertension, 1980—. Served to capt. M.C. AUS, 1960-62. Recipient Honors Achievement award Angiology Research Found., 1964; recipient Disting. Faculty award U. Okla., 1970, So. Med. Assn. Ann. award, 1971. Fellow A.C.P., Am. Coll. Cardiology, AAAS; mem. Am. Soc. for Clin. Investigation, Am. Soc. for Clin. Pharmacology and Therapeutics (pres. 1973-74), Internat. Soc. Hypertension (sci. council 1974-84, v.p. 1982-84), Am. Heart Assn. (dir. La. 1979-84), Am. Physiol. Soc., Am. Soc. Nephrology, Central Soc. for Clin. Research, Chi Epsilon Mu, Phi Sigma, Alpha Kappa Alpha. Jewish. Current Work: Cardiovascular, physiological and pharmacological aspects of experimental and clinical hypertension. Subspecialties: Internal medicine; Cardiology. Home: 5353 Marcia Ave New Orleans LA 70124 Office: Alton Ochsner Med Found 1516 Jefferson Hwy New Orleans LA 70121

FROHNSDORFF, GEOFFREY JAMES CARL, government official, building materials researcher; b. London, Feb. 4, 1928; came to U.S., 1960, naturalized, 1970; s. Stanley George Carl and Adeline May (Lee) F.; m. Doris Helen Keen, Aug. 10, 1956; children—Katharine Anne, Gregory James Carl, Elizabeth Susan. B.Sc. with honours, U. St. Andrews, Scotland, 1953; M.S., Lehigh U., 1956; Ph.D., Imperial Coll., London, 1959, diploma, 1959. Mgr. research and devel. Am. Cement Corp., Riverside, Calif., 1960-70; group leader Gillette Research Inst., Rockville, Md., 1970-73; sect. chief Nat. Bur. Standards, Gaithersburg, Md., 1973-81, div. chief, mem. sr. exec. service, 1981—. Pres., Jurupa Mountains Cultural Ctr., Riverside, 1969-70. Served with RAF, 1947-49. 1851 Sr. studentship Royal Commn. for the 1851 Exhbn., London, 1957-59; recipient silver medal Dept. Commerce, 1983. Fellow Am. Ceramic Soc. (v.p. 1982-83); mem. Am. Concrete Inst. (vice chmn. concrete materials research council 1985—), ASTM (P.H. Bates award 1981), Internat. Union of Materials and Structures Research and Testing Labs. (chmn. tech. adv. group 1983-84). Current work: Building materials research; cement and concrete science; service life prediction; mathematical modeling. Subspecialty: Materials. Office: Nat Bur Standards Room B368 Bldg 226 Gaithersburg MD 20899

FRÖLICHER, FRANZ, geologist, consultant, educator; b. Ridgewood, N.J., Jan. 11, 1936; s. Victor and Helene (Stehli) F.; m. Margrit Grundmann, Jan. 23, 1976; 1 dau., Britta. B.A., Don Bosco Coll., 1959, Alaska Methodist U., 1970, 1972; Ph.D., U. Edinburgh, Scotland, 1977. Researcher U. Tubingen, W.Ger., 1974-79; asst. prof. geology U. So. Miss., 1979—; dir. Swiss Field Camp, Solothurn, 1980—, Geo Kartier Kurs, Solothurn, 1979—; bd. dirs. Geo Dirs. Union, Tubingen, 1978—. Bd. dirs. West Lake Property Owners Assn., Hattiesburg, Miss., 1980—. Served to 1st lt. USAF, 1959-62. Mem. Geol. Soc. Am. Current Work: Paleoecology of estuarine system; modern coalforming environments; carboniferous paleoecology. Subspecialties: Paleontology, paleoecology; Coal. Office: U So Miss SS Box 9364 Hattiesburg MS 39406

FROMM, GERHARD HERMANN, neurologist, educator; b. Konigsberg, Germany, Sept. 7, 1931; s. Fritz Wilhelm and Ilse (Pflaum) F.; m. Antionette McKenna, May 26, 1973; children: Allison, Devin. B.S., U. P.R., Rio Piedras, 1949; M.D., Jefferson Med. Coll., Phila., 1953. Diplomate: Am. Bd. Psychiatry and Neurology. Instr. neurology Tulane U. Sch. Medicine, New Orleans, 1961-62, asst. prof., 1962-66, asso. prof., 1966-68; asso. prof. neurology U. Pitts. Sch. Medicine, 1968-81, prof., 1981—; attending physician Presbyn.-Univ. Hosp., Pitts. Contbr. articles to med. jours. Served to lt., M.C. USNR, 1956-58. NIH fellow, 1959-61; career devel. awardee, 1962-68. Mem. Am. Acad. Neurology, Am. Epilepsy Soc., Soc. Neurosci., Am. EEG Soc., Eastern Assn. EEG, Internat. Assn. for Study of Pain, Am. Pain Soc., Am. Neurol. Assn. Current Work: Neuropharmacology of anticonvulsant drugs; epilepsy; trigeminal neuralgia; pain mechanisms. Subspecialties: Neurology; Neuropharmacology. Home: 1401 N Negley Ave Pittsburgh PA 15206 Office: University of Pittsburgh 322 Scaife Hall Pittsburgh PA 15261

FROMMER, J. PEDRO, physician, medical educator; b. Santiago, Chile, Nov. 24, 1949; came to U.S., 1978; s. Guillermo and Eva (Holota) F. M.D., U. Chile, 1974. Diplomate: Am. Bd. Internal Medicine. Intern U. Toronto, Ont., Can., 1974-75, resident in internal medicine, 1975-78; fellow in nephrology Baylor U. Coll. Medicine, Houston, 1978-81; instr. medicine U. Ill. Med. Sch., Chgo., 1981-82, asst. prof., 1982-83; asst. prof. medicine Baylor Coll. Medicine, Houston, 1983—; chief renal sect. VA Med. Ctr., Houston, 1983-85. Contbr. numerous articles to med. jours. Nat. Kidney Found. fellow, 1980. Fellow ACP, Royal Coll. Physicians and Surgeons Can., Chgo. Council Fgn. Affairs. Current Work: Research interest in renal physiology, salt and water metabolism and acid base metabolism. Subspecialties: Internal medicine; Nephrology. Office: 7580 Fannin St #235 Houston TX 77054

FRONING, GLENN WESLEY, food scientist, educator; b. Gray Summit, Mo., Sept. 8, 1930; s. Gilbert Charles and Marie Juanita (Buchanan) F.; m. Lynne S., Aug. 4, 1962; children: Teri Ann, Sharon Marie. B.S. in Poultry Sci, U. Mo., 1953, M.S. in Poultry Products, 1957; Ph.D. in Food Tech, U. Minn., 1961. Asst. prof. food sci. Rutgers U., 1961-63; asst. prof. poultry sci. U. Conn., 1963-66; assoc. prof. poultry sci. U. Nebr., Lincoln, 1966-70, prof. poultry sci., 1970-72, prof. poultry and wildlife sci., chmn. dept. poultry and wildlife sci., 1972-77, prof. animal sci., 1977—. Contbr. numerous articles to profl. jours. Served to 1st lt. U.S. Army, 1953-55. Recipient Research award Nat. Turkey Fedn., 1972; named Nebr. Poultry Man of Yr. Nebr. Poultry Industries, 1982; Dept. Agr. grantee, 1967; Am. Egg Bd. grantee, 1979, 82; also various industry grants. Mem. Am. Chem. Soc., Poultry Sci. Assn. (sec.-treas.), Inst. Food Technologists, AAAS, Nat. Assn. Colls. and Tchrs. Agr., World's Poultry Sci. Assn., Sigma Xi, Phi Tau Sigma, Gamma Sigma Delta. Methodist. Lodge: Kiwanis. Current Work: Functional and chem. properties of mechanically deboned poultry meat, functional properties of eggs, color chemistry of poultry meat, study of poultry meat and egg proteins as related to functionality. Subspecialty: Food science and technology. Office: Dept Animal Sci U Nebr 122 Mussehl Hall Lincoln NE 68583

FROSCH, ROBERT ALAN, automotive company research executive; b. N.Y.C., May 22, 1928; s. Herman Louis and Rose (Bernfeld) F.; m. Jessica Rachael Denerstein, Dec. 22, 1957; children—Elizabeth Ann, Margery Ellen. A.B. in Theoretical Physics, Columbia U., 1947, M.S., 1949, Ph.D., 1952; Engr. (hon.), U. Miami, 1982, Mich. Tech. U., 1983. Research scientist assoc. Hudson Labs. Columbia U., N.Y.C., 1951-63; dir. nuclear test detection Adv. Research Projects Agy., Dept. Def., Washington, 1963-65, dep. dir., 1965-66; asst. sec. research and devel. Dept. Navy, Washington, 1966-73; asst. exec. dir. UN Environment Program, Nairobi Kenya, 1973-75; assoc. dir. applied oceanography Woods Hole Oceanographic Inst., Mass., 1975-77; adminstr. NASA, Washington, 1977-81; pres. Am. Assn. Engring. Socs., N.Y.C., 1981-82; v.p. research labs. Gen. Motors Corp., Warren, Mich., 1982—. Patentee directional filtering of summed arrays. Recipient Arthur S. Fleming award, 1966, Navy Disting. Pub. Service award, 1969; Def. Meritorious Civilian Service medal, 1973; Neptune award Am. Oceanic Orgn., 1973; Disting. Service medal NASA, 1981. Fellow AAAS, Acoustical Soc. Am., IEEE, AIAA, Am. Astron. Soc. (John F. Kennedy award 1981); mem. Nat. Acad. Engring., Am. Phys. Soc., Siesmol. Soc. Am., Marine Tech. Soc., Soc. Naval Architects and Marine Engrs., Soc. Exploration Geophysicists (Spl. Commendation award 1981), Am. Geophys. Union, Soc. Automotive Engrs., Engring. Soc. Detroit. Clubs: Columbia (N.Y.C.), Cosmos (Washington). Current work: Management of research and development. Subspecialty: Systems engineering. Office: Gen Motors Research Labs Warren MI 48090-9055

FROST, JOHN ELLIOTT, minerals company executive; b. Winchester, Mass., May 20, 1924; s. Elliott Putnam and Hazel Lavera (Carley) F.; m. Carolyn Catlin, July 12, 1945 (div. 1969); children: John Crocker, Jeffrey Putnam, Teresa Baird, Virginia Nicholl; m. Martha Hicks, June 6, 1969. B.S., Stanford U., 1949, M.S., 1950, Ph.D., 1965. Geologist Asarco, Salt Lake City, 1951-54; chief geologist, surface mines supt. Philippine Iron Mines Inc., Larap, Camarines Norte, 1954-60; chief geologist Duval Corp. (Pennzoil Corp.), Tucson, 1961-67; minerals exploration mgr. Exxon Corp., Houston, 1967-71; minerals mgr. Esso Eastern Inc. div., 1971-80; sr. v.p. Exxon Minerals Co. div., N.Y.C., 1980—; bd. dirs., mem. real estate com. United Engring. Trustees, N.Y.C., 1982—. Mem. adv. bd. Sch. Earth Scis., Stanford (Calif.) U., 1983—. Served to 1st lt. USAAF, 1943-45, PTO. Fellow Geol. Soc. Am.; mem. Soc. Econ. Geologists (councilor 1982—, program com., nominating com. chmn. 1982), AIME (chmn. edn. com. Soc. Mining Engrs. 1971), Australian Inst. Mining and Metallurgy, Sigma Xi. Republican. Congregationalist. Clubs: Mining (N.Y.C.); Mining of Southwest (Tucson). Originator porphyry copper zoning concept, 1958-60. Current Work: Management responsibilities for minerals subsidiary including overall management of minerals exploration and minerals research programs. Subspecialties: Geoscience management; Geochemistry. Home: 12 Stonehenge Dr New Canaan CT 06840 Office: Exxon Minerals Company 1251 Ave of the Americas New York NY 10020

FROST, MELVIN JESSE, geography educator; b. Salt Lake City, Aug. 14, 1920; s. Clarence Alfred and Seraphine (Smith) F.; m. Dorothy Skousan, Mar. 16, 1951; children: Susan, Luisa, Melvin S., Robert S., Rita, Paul S. B.S., Ariz. State U.-Tempe, 1959; M.S., Brigham Young U., 1961; Ph.D., U. Fla., 1964. Gen. mgr. C.A. Frost Co., Monticello, Utah, 1945-47; owner, mgr. Frost Implement Co., Monticello, 1948-52; instr. phys. sci. U. Fla., 1962-64; assoc. prof. U. So. Miss., Hattiesburg, 1964-65; dir. geography student tchrs. Ariz. State U., Tempe, 1969-74, asst. prof. geography, 1965-85; ret. Author: A Decimal System for Calculating Angles, Time & Location, 1961. Pres. Mesa Hist. and Archeol. Soc., Mesa, 1973-77; chmn. Farm Museum, 1982. Pan Am. Research Found. grantee, 1961; Caribbean Research Found. grantee, 1962; Ariz. State U. grantee, 1966, 68. Mem. Ariz. Acad. Sci. (sec. 1969-71), Latin Am. Studies Assn., Nat. Council Geographic Edn. (state coordinator 1966-68). Republican. Mormon. Patentee device for showing time and dates. Current Work: Teaching geography of Latin America and environmental studies; research in solid waste recycling and management. Subspecialties: Ecology (environmental science); Resource management. Home: 1748 N Lindsay St Mesa AZ 85203 Office: Department of Geography Arizona State University Tempe AZ 85287

FRUEH, ALFRED JOSEPH, crystallography educator; b. Passaic, N.J., Sept. 2, 1919; s. Alfred Joseph and Giuliette (Fanciulli) F.; m. Anne Torrey, Dec. 18, 1943; children: Jonathan, Carol, Timothy. B.S., MIT, 1942, M.S., 1947, Ph.D., 1949. Teaching asst. MIT, Cambridge, 1946-49; asst. prof. U. Chgo., 1949-58; assoc. prof. McGill U., Montreal, Que., Can., 1959-66, prof., 1966-69; dept. head, prof. dept. geology U. Conn., Storrs, 1969—; vis. prof. U. Oslo, 1958-59; vis. research assoc. Univ. Coll., U. London, 1976; mem. com. teaching crystallography Internat. Crystallographic Union, Chester, Eng., 1960-66; mem. com. on teaching sci. Internat. Council Sci. Unions, Paris, 1963-66. Editor: Structures Reports for 1956, 1963, Structure Reports for 1967, 1975; contbr. articles to profl. jours. Served to lt. USNR, 1942-46, PTO. Fellow Mineral. Soc. Am. (assoc. editor 1963-65); mem. Mineral. Soc. Can. (exec. com. 1962-65). Current Work: Stability of sulfide minerals, crystal structure and crystal chemistry, x-ray diffraction and non-bragg diffraction, order disorder and modulated structures, group theory in crystallography. Subspecialties: Mineralogy; X-ray crystallography. Home: 23 Bundy Ln Storrs CT 06268 Office: Dept Geology and Geophysics U Conn Storrs CT 06268

FRUMERMAN, ROBERT, chemical engineer; b. Rochester, Pa., Aug. 1924; m. Marcia; children: Bruce, Julie. B.S. in Chem. Engring, U. Pitts.; M.S. in Chemistry, Carnegie Mellon U. Registered engr., Pa., N.Y., N.J., Fla. Process engr. Elliott Co., Blaw-Knox Chem. Plants Div.; project engr. Koppers Co. E & C Div.; mgr. chem. processing NUMEC; founder, pres. Frumerman Assocs Inc., Pitts., 1962—; cons. devel. of processes and systems for chem., metall., and coal conversion, and nuclear applications. Author publs. in field. Fellow Am. Inst. Chem. Engrs. Patentee. Subspecialty: Chemical engineering. Office: Frumerman Assocs 218 S Trenton Ave Pittsburgh PA 15221

FRY, JAMES PALMER, research scientist, educator, university research group director; b. Detroit, May 2, 1939; s. Palmer Edmund and Anne Joanna (Olson) F.; m. Rosemary S. King, June 24, 1961; children: Mary Ann, James Palmer Jr., Leif Christian, Erika Diane, Benjamin Jotham, Joshua Jonathan. B.S., U. Mich., 1962, M.S. in Engring, 1963, M.S., 1974. Area engr. E.I. DuPont de Nemours & Co., Montague, Mich., 1962-63; assoc. research engr. Boeing Co., Renton, Wash., 1963-65; mem. tech. staff and project leader MITRE Corp., McLean, Va., 1965-69; mem. research staff, faculty U. Mich., Ann Arbor, 1970—; dir. info. systems research group U. Mich. (Grad. Sch. Bus. Adminstrn.), 1977—. Author: Design of Database Structure, 1981; contbr. articles to Design sci. publs. Mem. Assn. Computing Machinery (dir. 1973—), Conf. on Data Systems Lang. (chmn. stored-data definition task group 1969-74), Share Inc. (chmn. database project 1968-70). Lutheran. Subspecialties: Database systems; Distributed systems and networks. Home: 6130 Munger Rd Ypsilanti MI 48197 Office: Univ Mic Grad Sch Bus Adminstrn Ann Arbor MI 48109

FRYE, HERSCHEL GORDON, chemist, educator; b. Long Beach, Calif., Apr. 6, 1920; s. Herschel Guy and Neva Jane (Yancey) F.; m. Grace Helen Tener, Sept. 26, 1940; children: Wayne Herschel, Gordon Evans. B.A., Coll. of Pacific, 1947, M.A., 1949; Ph.D., U. Oreg., 1956. Asst. prof. chemistry U. of Pacific, Stockton, Calif., 1956-59, assoc. prof., 1959-62, prof., 1962—; partner FM Analytical Cons., Stockton, 1968—. Contbr. articles to profl. jours. Cons. to dist. atty. and pub. defender, San Joaquin County (Calif.), 1970—. Served with U.S. Army, 1944-46. Amn. Philos. Soc. grantee; Research Corp. grantee, 1958-68. Mem. Am. Chem. Soc., Am. Acad. Forensic Scis., AAAS, Cons. Chemists Assn., Calif. Assn. Toxicologists, N.Y. Acad. Scis. Current Work: Analytical chemistry of restricted drugs in biofluids; synthetic inorganic chemistry of platinum group metals. Subspecialties: Analytical chemistry; Forensic chemistry. Office: 1231 W Robinhood Dr Suite D-3 Stockton CA 95207

FRYXELL, PAUL ARNOLD, research botanist, educator; b. Moline, Ill., Feb. 2, 1927; s. Hjalmar Edward and Hulda Eunice (Peterson) F.; m. Greta A. Fryxell, Aug. 23, 1947; children: Karl J., Joan E., Glen E. B.A., Augustana Coll., Rock Island, Ill., 1949; M.S., Iowa State U., 1951, Ph.D., 1955. Asst. agronomist N.Mex State U., Las Cruces, 1952-55; asst. prof. botany U. Wichita, 1955-57; research geneticist U.S. Dept. Agr., Tempe, Ariz., 1957-65; research botanist, College Station, Tex., 1965—; mem. grad. faculty Tex. A&M U., 1965—, U. Tex., 1980—. Author: Natural History of the Cotton Tribe, 1979; contbr. over 100 articles to sci. jours. Pres. local chpt. ACLU, 1968. Served in USAAF, 1945-46. Mem. Am. Soc. Plant Taxonomists (pres. 1983-84), Bot. Soc. Am., AAAS, Internat. Assn. Plant Taxonomists, Am. Soc. Naturalists, Soc. Study of Evolution. Unitarian-Universalist. Current Work: Taxonomy of the family Malvaceae; revision of selected genera of the family; floristic studies. Subspecialties: Taxonomy; Evolutionary biology. Office: PO Drawer DN College Station TX 77841

FU, KAREN KING-WAH, radiation oncologist; b. Shanghai, China, Oct. 15, 1940; came to U.S., 1959, naturalized, 1975; d. Ping Sen and Lein Sun (Ho) F. Student, Ind. U., 1959-61; A.B., Barnard Coll., Columbia U., 1963, M.D., 1967. Cert. radiation oncologist. Intern Montreal (Que., Can.) Gen. Hosp., 1967-68; resident Princess Margaret Hosp., Toronto, Ont., Can., 1968-69, Stanford U. Hosp., 1969-71; instr. U. Utah, 1971-72; clin. instr. U. Calif.-San Francisco, 1972-73, asst. prof., 1973-76, assoc. prof., 1976-82, prof., 1982—, research assoc. Cancer Research Inst., 1973—. Contbr. articles to profl. jours. Mem. San Francisco Opera Guild, San Francisco Symphony Assn., San Francisco Ballet, Calif. Acad. Sci., De Young Mus. Am. Cancer Soc. grantee, 1982; NIH grantee, 1982. Mem. Am. Soc. Therapeutic Radiologists, Am. Med. Women's Assn., Am. Coll. Radiology, Calif. Radiation Therapy Assn., Calif. Radiol. Soc., No. Calif. Acad. Clin. Oncology, Radiation Research Soc., Am. Soc. Clin. Oncologists, Cell Kinetics Soc., Assn. Women in Sci. Current Work: Cancer research, patient care, teaching in medical school. Subspecialties: Oncology; Cancer research (medicine). Office: U Calif San Francisco Dept Radiation Oncology L-75 San Francisco CA 94143

FU, SHOU-CHENG JOSEPH, biomedicine educator; b. Peking, China, Mar. 19, 1924; came to U.S., 1946; s. W.C. Joseph and W.C. (Tsai) F.; m. Susan B. Guthrie, June 21, 1951; children: Robert W.G., Joseph H.G., James B.G. B.S., M.S., Catholic U., Peking, 1944; Ph.D., Johns Hopkins U., 1949. Gustav Bissing fellow Johns Hopkins U., at Univ. Coll., London, 1955-56; chief Enzyme and Bioorganic Chemistry Lab. Children's Cancer Research Found., 1956-67; research assoc. Harvard U. Med. Sch., Boston, 1956-67; prof., chmn. bd. chemistry Chinese U., Hong Kong, 1967-70, dean sci. faculty, 1967-69; vis. prof. Coll. Physicians and Surgeons, Columbia U., N.Y.C., 1970-71; prof. biochemistry U. Medicine & Dentistry, Newark, 1971—; asst. dean U. Medicine & Dentistry (Grad. Sch. Biomed. Scis.), 1975-77, acting dean, 1977-78. Contbr. articles to profl. jours. Served to lt. commdr. USPHS Res., 1959—. Fellow AAAS, Royal Soc. Chemistry (London); mem. Sigma Xi. Club: Royal Hong Kong Jockey: American (Hong Kong). Current Work: Amino acids, peptides and proteins; folate and anti-folate agents in cancer research; mammalian lens protein in cataractogenesis. Subspecialties: Biochemistry (medicine); Biophysical chemistry. Home: 693 Prospect St Maplewood NJ 07040 Office: 100 Bergen St Newark NJ 07103

FU, SHUMAN, research scientist; b. Canton, China, July 29, 1942; s. Tak-Yu and Lai-Sim (Tang) F.; m. Felicia Gaskin, Jan. 29, 1969; children: Kai Ming, Kai Mei. B.S., Dickinson Coll., 1965; M.D., Stanford U., 1970; Ph.D., Rockefeller U., 1975. Diplomate: Am. Bd. Internal Medicine. Intern, resident in medicine Stanford U. Med. Center, 1970-71, N.Y. Hosp., 1975-76; grad. fellow Rockefeller U., 1971-75, asst. prof., then asso. prof., 1975-82; prof. U. Okla., 1982—; mem., head immunology program Okla. Med. Research Found., 1982—. Scholar Leukemia Soc. Am., 1976-81. Mem. Am. Soc. Clin. Investigation, Am. Assn. Immunolgists, AAAS, Am. Rheumatism Assn., Phi Beta Kappa. Current Work: Human immunology with emphasis on B cell proliferation and differentiation in normal and disease states. Subspecialty: Immunology (medicine). Office: 825 NE 13th St Oklahoma City OK 73104

FUCCILLO, DAVID ANTHONY, virologist, immunologist; b. Chelsea, Mass., Aug. 20, 1930; s. Anthony and Marion (Catalano) F.; m. Norma Ellen Regis, Apr. 19, 1955; children: Joanne, David Regis. B.S. in Bacteriology, U. Mass., Amherst, 1953, M.S. in Microbiology, 1955; Ph.D. in Microbiology, Purdue U., 1960. Commd. 2d lt. U.S. Air Force, 1955, advanced through grades to capt., 1965; chief lab. services USAF Hosp., Williams AFB, 1955-57, officer charge microbiology dept. and blood bank transfusion service, Lackland AFB, 1960-62, officer in charge microbiology dept. and clin. lab., Weisbaden, W.Ger., 1962-65, ret., 1965; asst. head sect. infectious diseases Perinatal Research br. Nat. Inst. Neurol. Diseases and Stroke, NIH, 1965-71, asst. chief infectious diseases br. collaborative and field research, 1971-76; dir. advanced testing and devel. labs. Biomed. Research div. Litton Bionetics, Inc., 1976-80, mgr. biol. lab. products, Kensington, Md., 1978-80; dir. research and devel. M.A. Bioproducts, Walkersville, Md., 1980-82; dir. virology Microbiol. Assocs., Bethesda, Md., 1982—; chmn. subcom. human herpesvirus Nat. Com. Lab. Standards; advisor grad. students Hood Coll. Contbr. articles to profl. jours. Recipient USPHS commendation medal for outstanding achievement, 1976. Mem. Am. Assn. Immunologists, Am. Soc. Microbiology, Soc. Exptl. Biology and Medicine, Sigma Xi. Current Work: Development of immunological assays, development of enzyme-linked immunosorbent assays for detection of antibodies and antigens for various infections. Subspecialties: Virology (biology); Immunobiology and immunology. Home: 11801 Seven Locks Rd Rockville MD 20854 Office: 5221 River Rd Bethesda MD 20816

FUDENBERG, H. HUGH, immunologist, university administrator; b. N.Y.C., Oct. 24, 1928; married, 1955; 4 children. A.B., UCLA, 1949; M.D., U. Chgo., 1953; M.A., Boston U., 1957; Dr. h.c., U. Kuopio, Finland, 1982, Free U. Natural Sci., Padua, 1982, U. Claude Bernard, France, 1985. Intern in medicine U. Utah, 1953-54; fellow in hematology Sch. Medicine, Tufts U., 1954-56; asst. resident in medicine Mt. Sinai Hosp., N.Y.C., 1956-57, Peter Bent Brigham Hosp., Boston, 1957-58; research assoc. in immunology Rockefeller Inst., 1958-60; prof. bacteriology and immunology U. Calif.-Berkeley, 1966-75; from asst. prof. to prof. medicine U. Calif.-San Francisco, 1966-75, chief hematology unit, 1962-75; chmn. dept. basic and clin. immunology Med. U.S.C., 1975—; mem. expert com. immunology WHO, 1962-77; participant Alfred Nobel 150th Birthday Celebration, 1983; mem. sci. adv. bd. Pasteur Inst., UNESCO Research Inst. Chief editor: Jour. Clin. Immunology. Recipient Pasteur medal Inst. Pasteur Paris, 1962, Robert A. Cooke Meml. medal Am. Acad. Allergy, 1967. Fellow AAAS; mem. Am. Assn. Immunologists, Am. Soc. Human Genetics, Am. Soc. Clin. Investigation, Genetics Soc. Am. Subspecialties: Immunology (medicine); Immunogenetics. Office: Dept Basic and Clin Immunology Med U SC Charleston SC 29425*

FUERSTENAU, DOUGLAS WINSTON, materials science educator; b. Hazel, S.D., Dec. 6, 1928; s. Erwin Arnold and Hazel Pauline (Karterud) F.; m. Margaret Ann Pellett, Aug. 29, 1953; children: Lucy, Sarah, Stephen. B.S., S.D. Sch. Mines and Tech., 1949, M.S., Mont. Sch. Mines, 1950; Sc.D., MIT, 1953; Mineral Engr., Mont. Coll. Mineral Sci. and Tech., 1968. Asst. prof. mineral engring. MIT, 1953-56; sect. leader, metals research lab. Union Carbide Metals Co., Niagara Falls, N.Y., 1956-58; mgr. mineral engring. lab Kaiser Aluminum & Chem. Corp., Permanente, Calif., 1958-59; assoc. prof. metallurgy U. Calif., Berkeley, 1959-62, prof. metallurgy, 1962—, Miller research prof., 1969-70, chmn. dept. materials sci. and mineral engring., 1970-78; dir.

Homestake Mining Co.; Chmn. Engrng. Found. Research Conf. on Comminution, 1963; Mem. adv. bd. Sch. Earth Scis., Stanford, 1970-73; mem. Nat. Mineral Bd., 1975-78; Am. rep. Internat. Mineral Processing Congress Com., 1978—. Editor: Froth Flotation-50th Anniversary Vol, 1962; co-editor-in-chief: Internat. Jour. of Mineral Processing, 1974—; Mem. editorial adv. bd.: Jour. of Colloid and Interface Sci, 1968-72, Colloids and Surfaces, 1980—; Contbr. articles to profl. jours. Recipient Distinguished Teaching award U. Calif., 1974; fellow Instn. Mining and Metallurgy, London; recipient Alexander Humboldt sr. scientist award Fed. Republic Germany, 1984. Mem. Nat. Acad. Engrng., Am. Inst. Mining and Metall. Engrs. (chmn. mineral processing div. 1967, Robert Lansing Hardy Gold medal 1957, Rossiter W. Raymond award 1961, Robert H. Richards award 1975, Antoine M. Gaudin award 1978, Mineral Industry Edn. award 1983), Soc. Mining Engrs. (dir. 1968-71, Distinguished mem.), Am. Chem. Soc., Am. Inst. Chem. Engrs., Sigma Xi, Theta Tau. Congregationalist. Current Work: Extractive metallurgy, mineral processing, surface and collid chemistry, particle science and technology, marine resources, coal benefication. Subspecialties: Metallurgical engineering; Surface chemistry. Home: 1440 LeRoy Ave Berkeley CA 94708

FUHR, JEFFREY ROBERT, physicist; b. Balt., Oct. 27, 1946; s. Irvin and Ruby Lillian (Rubenstein) F.; m. Barbara Ann, Sept. 17, 1972; children: Lisa, Daniel. A.B., Earlham Coll, 1968; M.S. in Physics, Purdue U., 1970. Physicist Nat. Bur. Standards, Gaithersburg, Md., 1970—. Contbr. writings to profl. publs. in field. Mem. Am. Phys. Soc. Club: Saturday in Style Square Dance (pres.). Current Work: Compile and publish critically evaluated data on atomic transition probabilities; cons. availability and reliability atomic data. Subspecialty: Atomic and molecular physics. Home: 9 Pavilion Dr Gaithersburg MD 20878 Office: Nat Bur Standards Physics Bldg Room A267 Gaithersburg MD 20899

FUHRMAN, ROBERT ALEXANDER, See *Who's Who in America*, 43rd edition.

FUHS, ALLEN EUGENE, engineering educator, consultant; b. Laramie, Wyo., Aug. 11, 1927; s. Michael Allen and Grace Emeline (Terrill) F.; m. Emily Ann Large, Dec. 22, 1951; 1 child, Susan Elizabeth Fuhs-Huff. B.S. in Mech. Engrng., U. N.Mex., 1951; M.S. in Mech. Engrng., Calif. Inst. Tech., 1955, Ph.D., 1958. Asst. prof. Northwestern U., Evanston, Ill., 1958-59; mem. tech. staff TRW, El Segundo, Calif., 1959-60; staff scientist Aerospace Corp., El Segundo, 1960-66; prof., chmn. dept. Naval Postgrad. Sch., Monterey, Calif., 1966-68; chief scientist Air Force Aeropropulsion Lab., Wright Patterson AFB, Ohio, 1968-70, Disting. prof., 1970—, chmn. space systems, 1982—; mem. Nat. Acad. Sci./Air Force Systems Command Propulsion Panel, 1970-76; U.S. Navy rep. Adv. Group Aerospace Research and Devel., NATO, Paris, 1970-77; cons. Rand Corp., 1985, FAA, FAA Tech. Ctr., N.J., 1981, Inst. for Def. Analyses, Washington, 1974-75, 67-68. Author: Instrumentation for High Speed Plasma Flow, 1965. Editor: Energetics for Aircraft Auxiliary Power Systems, 1972; Diagnostics and Engine Condition Monitoring, 1975; Instrumentation for Air Breathing Propulsion, 1974. Editor-in-chief: Handbook of Fluid Dynamics and Fluid Machinery, 1985; Jour. Aircraft, 1975-81. Patentee in field. Served to lt. (j.g.), 1951-54; Korea. Guggenheim scholar, 1957; recipient medal of Honor Nat. Soc. DAR, 1982. Fellow AIAA (v.p. publs. 1979-81, dir.-at-large 1982-85, pres.-elect 1985), ASME; mem. Am. Phys. Soc., Am. Assn. Physics Tchrs., Optical Soc. Am., Combustion Inst., Soc. Naval Architects and Marine Engrs., Soc. Automotive Engrs. (Ralph R. Teetor award for excellence in teaching engrng. 1981), Internat. Soc. Optical Engrng., Sigma Xi. Current work: Teaching and conducting research in the areas of high energy lasers, energy, space warfare, spacecraft design, and naval weapons. Subspecialty: Aerospace engineering and technology. Office: Naval Postgrad Sch Code 67 Monterey CA 93943

FUJIMOTO, TAKEO, pediatric oncologist, educator, clinician, researcher; b. Nichinan, Miyazaki, Japan, Mar. 30, 1936; s. Usaku and Shizue F.; m. Motoko Horio, June 14, 1963; children—Ichiro, Jiro, Kazuro. B.S., Kagoshima U., 1956; M.D., Kyoto U., 1960; Ph.D., Kyushu U., 1972. Cert. Nat. Med. Bd. Japan. Asst. prof. Kyushu U. Sch. Medicine, Fukuoka, 1972, lectr., 1972-79; project investigator U. Tex. System Cancer Ctr., Houston, 1973-77; prof., chmn. Aichi Med. U., 1979—; exec. chmn. Children's Cancer and Leukemia Study Group, Aichi, 1972—. Editor: Childhood Cancer, vol. I, 1980, vol. II, 1983. Recipient Research award Japan Found. Multidisciplinary Treatment of Cancer, 1982; Spl. award Tokai Acad. Sci., 1983. Mem. Japanese Acad. Pediatrics (councilor 1982, bd. dirs. 1984), Japan Hematol. Soc. (councilor 1981), Japanese Cancer Assn., Am. Soc. Clin. Oncology, Japanese Soc. Clin. Hematology (councilor 1979), Am. Assn. Cancer Research. Current work: Pediatric hematology/oncology, chemotherapy, pharmacology. Subspecialties: Chemotherapy; Pediatrics. Home: 54-2 Shimodouchi Inokoshi Itaka Meito 465 Nagoya Japan Office: Dept Pediatrics Aichi Med U Negakute 480-11 Aichi-gun 480-11 Aichi-gun Aichi Japan

FUJIMURA, OSAMU, physicist, researcher; b. Tokyo, Aug. 29, 1927; came to U.S., 1973; s. Susumu and Sei (Tsuneyoshi) F.; m. Yoko Sugai, Dec. 15, 1957; children: Akira, Makoto. B.S. in Physics, U. Tokyo, 1952, D.Sc. in Physics, 1962. Guest researcher Royal Inst. Tech., Stockholm, 1963-65; staff research mem. M.I.T., Cambridge, 1958-61; prof. Research Inst. Logopedics and Phoniatrics, U. Tokyo, 1965-73; head dept. Bell Labs., Murray Hill, N.J., 1973—; mem. sci. adv. bed. Voice Found., N.Y.C.; mem. vis. com. for linguistics and philosophy M.I.T.; mem. vis. com. for linguistics Harvard U. Mem. editorial bd.: Sprachwissenschaft und Kommunikationsforschung, Jour. Phonetics, Phonetica; contbr. over 300 articles to sci. jours. Fellow Acoustical Soc. Am., N.Y. Acad. Scis.; mem. IEEE, Linguistic Soc. Am. (exec. com.), Soc. for Studies Japanese Lang., Phys. Soc. Japan, AAAS, Am. Assn. Physicists in Medicine, Internat. Soc. Phonetic Scis., Internat. Coll. Exptl. Phonology, Am. Speech and Hearing Assn. Clubs: Internat. House of Japan (Tokyo); Gakusikai (U. Tokyo). Patentee in U.S. and Japan. Current Work: Speech and language research. Subspecialties: Linguistics and speech science; Acoustics. Office: 600 Mountain Ave Room 2D-545 Murray Hill NJ 07974

FUJITA, TETSUYA THEODORE, educator, meteorologist; b. Kitakyushu City, Japan, Oct. 23, 1920; came to U.S., 1953, naturalized, 1968; s. Tomojiro and Yoshie (Kanesue) F.; m. Sumiko Yamamoto, June 13, 1969; 1 son, Kazuya. B.S.Eq. in Mech. Engrng, Meiji Coll. Tech., Kitakyushu City, 1943; Dr.Sci., Tokyo (Japan) U., 1953. Asst. prof. Meiji Coll. Tech., Kitakyushu, 1943-49; asst. prof. Kyushu Inst. Tech., Kitakyushu, 1949-53; sr. meteorologist U. Chgo., 1953-62, asso. prof., 1962-65, prof., 1965—. Recipient Okada award Japan Meteorol. Soc., 1959; Kamura award Kyushu Inst. Tech., 1965; Meisinger award Am. Meteorol. Soc., 1967; Aviation Week and Space Tech. Distinguished Service award Flight Safety Found., 1977; Adm. Luis de Florez Flight Safety award, 1977; Ann. award Nat. weather Assn., 1978; Disting. Public Service award NASA, 1979; Losey Atmospheric Sci. award AIAA, 1982. Mem. Am., Japan meteorol. socs., Am. Geophy. Union, Am. Optical Soc., Sigma Xi. Specialized research on servere weather phenomena and satellite meteorology. Discovered suction vortex in tornado, 1970; originated Fujita Tornado Scale, 1971; directed NASA tornado cloud overflight, 1971-77; patentee omni-directional windspeed detector. Subspecialty: Meteorology. Office: Dept Geophys Sciences U Chicago 5734 Ellis Ave Chicago IL 60637

FUKUDA, MINORU, cancer research scientist; b. Hiroshima, Japan, July 6, 1945; came to U.S., 1975, naturalized, 1980; s. Iwao and Sueko (Fujiwara) F.; m. Michiko Nishida, Apr. 8, 1970; children: Ko, Shun. B.S. in Biochemistry, U. Tokyo, 1968, M.S., 1970, Ph.D., 1973. Research assoc. U. Tokyo, 1973-75; postdoctoral assoc. Yale U., 1975-77; assoc. Hutchinson Cancer Research Ctr., Seattle, 1977-81; asst. prof. U. Wash., Seattle, 1980-81; staff scientist La Jolla (Calif.) Cancer Research Found., 1982—, dir. Carbohydrate Chemistry Lab., 1984—. Author: Biology of Glycoproteins, 1984. Nat. Cancer Inst. grantee, 1981—. Mem. Am. Soc. Cell Biology, Am. Soc. Biol. Chemists, N.Y. Acad. Scis. Current Work: Biochemistry of glycoproteins in differentiation and oncogenesis; now directing a laboratory of which the objective is to study membrane differentiation in normal and leukemic human blood cells and in gastrointestinal development. Subspecialties: Biochemistry (biology); Cancer research (medicine). Home: 2818 Passy Ave San Diego CA 92122 Office: La Jolla Cancer Research Foundation 10901 N Torrey Pines Rd La Jolla CA 92037

FUKUI, HATSUAKI, electrical engineer; b. Yokohama, Japan, Dec. 14, 1927; came to U.S., 1962, naturalized, 1973; s. Ushinosuke and Yoshi (Saito) F.; m. Atsuko Inamoto, Apr. 1, 1954 (dec. 1973); children—Mayumi, Naoki; m. Kiku Kato, Dec. 12, 1975. Diploma Miyakojima Tech. Coll., Osaka, Japan, 1949; Dr. Engrng., Osaka U., 1961. Research assoc. Osaka City U., 1949-54; sr. engr. Shimada Phys. and Chem. Indsl. Co., Tokyo, 1954-55; mgr. Sony Corp., Tokyo, 1955-62; mem. tech. staff Bell Telephone Labs., Murray Hill, N.J., 1962-69, supr., 1969-83; supr. AT&T Bell Labs., Murray Hill, N.J., 1984—. Author: Esaki Diodes, 1963; co-author Solid State FM Receivers, 1968; editor: Low-Noise Microwave Transistors and Amplifiers, 1981; contbr. articles to profl. jours., chpts. to books. Recipient Inada prize IECEJ, 1959; Fellow IEEE (Microwave prize 1980); mem. Inst. Electronics and Communication Engrs. of Japan, Japan Soc. Applied Physics, IEEE Microwave Theory and Techniques Soc. (editorial bd.), IEEE Electron Devices Soc. (Standardization com.), IEEE Quantum Electronics and Applications Soc., Inst. TV Engrs. Japan (steering com.). Current work: Semiconductor lasers for telecommunication use; microwave semiconductor devices; integrated opto-electronic devices; consumer electronics. Subspecialties: Electronics; Telecommunications. Home: 53 Drum Hill Dr Summit NJ 07901 Office: AT&T Bell Labs 600 Mountain Ave Murray Hill NJ 07974

FULDA, MICHAEL, political science educator, space policy researcher; b. Liverpool, Eng., Apr. 21, 1939; came to U.S., 1962, naturalized, 1966; s. Boris and Catherine (Von Dehn) F.; m. Rosa Bongiorno, July 19, 1970; children—Robert, George. Student Polytechnique, Grenoble, France, 1956-57, Tech. U., West Berlin, Germany, 1957-58, Karl Eberhardt Coll., Tubingen, Germany, 1963-66; M.A., Am. U., 1968, Ph.D. in Internat. Studies, 1970. Prof. polit. sci. Fairmont State Coll., W.Va., 1971—; internat. relations specialist NASA, Washington, summer 1979; fellow NASA Marshall Ctr., Huntsville, Ala., summer 1977, Langley Ctr., Hampton, Va., summer, 1976. Author: Oil and International Relations, 1979; (with others) United States Space Policy, 1985. Contbr. articles to profl. jours. Bd. dirs. Faimont Chamber Music Soc., 1983—; W.Va. state com. chmn., dir. space policy Nat. Unity Campaign for John Anderson, 1980; mem. nat. adv. com. John Glenn Presdl. Com., 1983-84. Served with U.S. Army, 1962-66. Woodrow Wilson Found. fellow, 1969-70; Humanities Found. W.Va. grantee, 1978-80. Mem. AIAA, Am. Astronautical Soc., Nat. Space Inst., World Future Soc. (pres. W.Va. chpt. 1977-80), Nat. Space Club. Mem. Nat. Unity Party. Current work: Impacts of technology, economy, and domestic and foreign politics on U.S. civilian and military space policy. Subspecialty: Space policy. Home: 166 Circle Dr Fairmont WV 26554 Office: Fairmont State Coll Fairmont WV 26554

FULKERSON, SAMUEL COLE, psychology educator, consultant; b. Cedar Rapids, Iowa, Jan. 5, 1923; s. Samuel and Ruth Amanda (DeSilva) F.; m. Katharine Alger James, May 6, 1947; children: Gregory, Heidi. B.A., U. Iowa, 1948, M.A., 1951; Ph.D., U. Tex.-Austin, 1955. Intern Worchester (Mass.) State Hosp., 1952-53; psychologist U.S. Air Force Sch. Aviation Medicine, San Antonio, 1954-58; assoc. prof. psychology U. Pitts., 1958-61; prof. U. Louisville, 1961—, cons. in field. Contbr. articles to profl. jours., 1955—. Served to cpl. USAAF, 1943-45, CBI. Recipient award for journalistic excellence Sigma Delta Chi, U. Iowa, 1948. Fellow Am. Psychol. Assn.; mem. Psychonomic Assn., U.S. Chess Fedn. (life), Am. Mycologiyal Assn., Sierra Club, Sigma Xi. Democrat. Current Work: Cognitive analysis of intelligence tasks and personality items. Subspecialty: Cognition. Home: 1021 Watterson Trail Louisville KY 40299 Office: Dept Psychology U Louisville Louisville KY 40292

FULLER, RAY WARD, pharmacologist; b. Dongola, Ill., Dec. 16, 1935; s. Lloyd M. and Wanda (Keller) F.; m. Sue Brown, Dec. 22, 1956; children: Ray W. II, Angela Lea. B.A., So. Ill. U., 1957, M.A., 1958; Ph.D., Purdue U., 1961. Dir. Biol. Research Lab., Ft. Wayne (Ind.) State Hosp., 1961-63; sr. pharmacologist Eli Lilly & Co., Indpls., 1963-67, research scientist, 1967-68, head dept. metabolic research, 1968-71, research asso., 1971-75, research advisor, 1976—; vis. lectr. MIT, 1976—; assoc. prof. biochemistry Ind. U., 1974-84, prof. neurobiology, 1985—; cons. NIMH, 1980-84, Pharm. Mfrs. Assn. Found., 1978-82, NASA, 1982—. Contbr. articles to profl. jours., chpts. in books. Mem. Am. Soc. Pharmacology and Exptl. Therapeutics, Am. Soc. Biol. Chemistry, AAAS, Am. Soc. Neurochemistry, Soc. Neurosci., Endocrine Soc. Patentee field of medicinal chemistry. Current Work: Biochem. pharmacology of brain and peripheral nervous system. Subspecialties: Pharmacology; Neuropharmacology. Office: Lilly Corp Ctr Indianapolis IN 46285

FULLER, RENEE NUNI, psychologist, publisher; b. Mannheim, Ger., Apr. 14, 1929; came to U.S., 1938; d. Eric Woldemar and Fridel Gronau (Henning) Stoetzner; m. George Ripley Fuller, Dec. 21, 1949 (dec. 1955). B.A., Swarthmore Coll., Pa., 1951; B.A. Hunter Coll, 1951; M.A., Columbia U., 1953; Ph.D., NYU, 1963. Cert. psychologist, Md. Research scientist Letchworth Village, Thiells, N.Y., 1960-66; project dir. S.I. Soc. Mental Health, S.I., N.Y., 1966-67; chief psychol. services Rosewood Hosp., Owings Mills., Md., 1967-75; pres. Ball-Stick-Bird Publs., Inc., Stony Brook, N.Y., 1975—. Author: In Search of the IQ Correlation, 1977. Mem. Am. Psychol. Assn., Am. Psychopath. Assn., Ednl. Research Assn., Behavior Genetics Assn. Developed Ball-Stick-Bird learning systems, 1974, 75. Current Work: Theretical and applied technologies for enhancing human cognition. Subspecialties: Cognition; Developmental psychology. Office: Ball-Stick-Bird Publications Inc Box 592 Stony Brook NY 11790

FULLMER, HAROLD MILTON, biomedical research administrator, researcher, educator; b. Gary, Ind., July 9, 1918; s. Howard and Rachel Eva (Tiedge) F.; m. Marjorie Lucile Engel, Dec. 31, 1942; children: Angela Sue, Pamela Rose. B.S., Ind. U., 1942, D.D.S., 1944; D. (hon.), U. Athens, Greece, 1981. Diplomate: Am. Bd. Oral Pathology. Intern Charity Hosp., New Orleans, 1946-47, resident, 1947-48, vis. dental surgeon, 1948-53; instr. Loyola U., New Orleans, 1948-49, asst. prof., 1949-50, assoc. prof. gen. and oral pathology, 1949-53; cons. pathology VA Hosps., Biloxi and Gulfport, Miss., 1950-53; asst. dental surgeon Nat. Inst. Dental Research, NIH, Bethesda, Md., 1953-54, dental surgeon, 1954-56, sr. dental surgeon, 1956-60, dental dir., 1960-70; chief sect. histochemistry Nat. Inst. Dental Research, 1967-70, chief exptl. pathology br., 1969-70, cons. to dir., 1971-72; mem. dental caries program adv. com. HEW, 1975-79, chmn., 1976-79; dir. Inst. Dental Research, prof. pathology, prof. dentistry, assoc. dean Sch. Dentistry U. Ala. Med. Center, Birmingham, 1970—; sr. scientist cancer research and tng. program, sci. adv. com. U. Ala. Med. Center (Diabetes Research and Tng. Center), 1977—; mem. med. research career devel. com. VA, 1977—. Co-editor: Histopathologic Technic and Practical Histochemistry, 1976; cons. editor: Oral Surgery, Oral Medicine, Oral Pathology, 1970; editor, founder: Jour. Oral Pathology, 1972—; assoc. editor: Jour. Cutaneous Pathology, 1973—; editorial bd.: Tissue Reactions, 1976—. Served to capt. U.S. Army, 1944-46. Recipient Isaac Schour award for outstanding research and teaching in anat. scis. Internat. Assn. Dental Research, 1973; Fulbright grantee, 1962; Disting. Alumnus of Year Ind. U. Sch. Dentistry, 1978; Disting. Alumnus award Ind. U., 1981. Fellow Am. Coll. Dentists, Am. Acad. Oral Pathology (v.p. 1984-85, pres.-elect 1985-86, pres. 1986-87), AAAS (chmn. sect. 1976-78, sec. sect. 1979—); mem. ADA (cons. Council Dental Research 1973-74), Internat. Assn. Dental Research (v.p. 1974-75, pres. 1976-77, pres. exptl. pathology group 1985-86), Am. Assn. Dental Research (pres. 1976-77), Internat. Assn. Pathologists, Internat. Assn. Oral Pathologists (co-founder, 1st pres. 1976, editor), Histochem. Soc., Nat. Soc. Med. Research (dir. 1977-79), Biol. Stain Commn. (trustee 1977—), Commd. Officers Assn. Republican. Presbyterian. Club: Exchange (pres. New Orleans 1952-53). Current Work: Biology and pathology of connective tissues; histochemical methods. Subspecialties: Pathology (medicine); Oral pathology. Home: 3514 Bethune Dr Birmingham AL 35223 Office: Univ Ala Birmingham Birmingham AL 35294

FULMER, CHARLES VIRGIL, geologic engineer, consultant; b. Council Bluffs, Iowa, Nov. 15, 1920; s. Fred Roy and Lula Belle (Cluphf) F.; m. Carol L. Fulmer; children—Charles, Steven, Clark, John. B.S., U. Wash., 1942, M.S., 1947; Ph.D., U. Calif.-Berkeley, 1950. Geologist, stratigrapher Standard Oil Calif., San Francisco, 1951-62; geologist, geophysicist Boeing Co., Seattle, 1962-72; geol. engr. King County, Seattle, 1972—; pres. Geonics Inc., Seattle, 1962—. Contbr. articles to profl. jours. Chmn. 1st dist. Republican Com., Seattle. Served to 1st lt. U.S. Army, 1942-45, PTO. Fellow Geol. Soc. Am.; mem. Assn. Engrng. Geology, N.Y. Acad. Scis., Sigma Xi. Methodist. Current work: Urban engineering geology; urban engineering geology natural determinate constraints; seismic safety analysis; landslide and geologic hazard analysis. Subspecialty: Paleontology, paleoecology. Home: 6174 NE 187th Pl Seattle WA 98155 Office: King County Bldg Dept King County Adminstrn Bldg 5th St and James St Seattle WA 98103

FULTON, CHRISTOPHER, organic chemist, researcher; b. Detroit, Nov. 10, 1955; s. Robert and Sally Arlene (Gaulin) F. B.S. in Chemistry, U. Mich., 1977; M.S. in Chemistry, U. Detroit, 1983. Research chemist Foundry Products div. Internat. Minerals and Chems. Co., Detroit, 1978-79, Energy Conversion Devices, Inc., Troy, Mich., 1979—. Chmn. Gen. Citizens Com.-Berkley/Huntington Woods Youth Asst., Mich.; co-chmn., vol. youth assistance People Listening, Understanding, Sharing Com. Mem. Am. Chem. Soc., U. Mich. Alumni Assn. Roman Catholic. Current work: Specialized materials for encapsulation of innovative solar modules. Subspecialties: Polymer chemistry; Solar energy. Home: 3669 Crooks St Apt 12 Royal Oak MI 48073

FUNG, ADRIAN KIN-CHIU, electrical engineering educator; b. Liuchow, Kwangsi, China, Dec. 25, 1936; came to U.S., 1960, naturalized, 1972; m. Jean Lee, Nov. 24, 1966; children—Lindy, Sally. B.S.E.E., Cheng Kung U., Taiwan, 1958; M.S.E.E., Brown U., 1961; Ph.D. E.E., U. Kans., 1965. Asst. prof. U. Kans., Lawrence, 1965-68, assoc. prof., 1968-72, prof., 1972-84; prof. U. Tex., Arlington, 1984—; assoc. dir. Remote Sensing Lab., Lawrence, 1970-75; dir. Wave Scattering Research Ctr., Arlington, 1984—. Author (with others): Microwave Remote Sensing, 1981. Contbg. author, editor chpt. in Manual Remote Sensing, 1983. Assoc. editor Oceanic Engineering, 1982. Recipient European Chpt. award IEEE Geosci. Remote Sensing Soc., 1984; Center for Research, Inc. award, 1984. Fellow IEEE. Current work: Radar scattering from objects and terrains, radar scattering simulation, microwave emission from land, sea, and vegetation Subspecialties: Electrical engineering; Remote sensing (geoscience). Home: 2501 Oak Manor Ct Arlington TX 76012 Office: U Texas at Arlington Box 19016 Arlington TX 76019

FUNG, KEE-YING, aeronautical engineering educator, consultant, researcher; b. Hunam, China, Dec. 20, 1948; came to U.S., 1972; s. Yuk-Kwong and Nam Hing (Tam) F.; m. EE Ho, Jan. 18, 1976 (div. Apr. 1985). B.S., Nat. Taiwan U., 1972; Ph.D., Cornell U., 1976. Research asst. Aero. dept. Cornell U., 1973-75; research assoc. aerospace and mech. engrng. dept. U. Ariz., Tucson, 1975-78, research asst. prof., 1978-79, asst. prof., 1979-85, assoc. prof., 1985—; dir. Computational Fluid Mech. Lab., 1981—; vis. scientist Inst. Theoretical Fluid Mechanics, Göttingen, W. Ger., 1981. Contbr. articles to profl. jours. Recipient Book award Nat. Taiwan U., 1970; Alexander von Humboldt fellow, 1981. Mem. AIAA. Club: Tucson Soaring. Current work: Aerodynamics; computational mechanics; applied mathematics Subspecialties: Applied mathematics; Aeronautical engineering. Home: 121 Los Pinos Vista Tucson AZ 85704 Office: Dept Aerospace and Med Engrng U Ariz Tucson AZ 85721

FUNG, YUAN-CHENG BERTRAM, bioengineering educator, author; b. Yuhong, Changchow, Kiangsu, China, Sept. 15, 1919; came to U.S., 1945, naturalized, 1957; s. Chung-Kwang and Lien (Hu) F.; m. Luna Hsien-Shih Yu, Dec. 22, 1949; children: Conrad Antung, Brenda Pingsi. B.S., Nat. Central U., Chungking, China, 1941, M.S., 1943; Ph.D., Calif. Inst. Tech., 1948. Research fellow Bur. Aero. Research China, 1943-45; research asst., then research fellow Cal. Inst. Tech., 1946-51, mem. faculty, 1951-66; prof. aeros. Calif. Inst. Tech., 1959-66; prof. bioengrng. and applied mechanics U. Calif.-San Diego, 1966—; cons. aerospace indsl. firms, 1949—. Author: The Theory of Aeroelasticity, 1956, Foundations of Solid Mechanics, 1965, A First Course in Continuum Mechanics, 1969, 77, Biomechanics, 1972, Biomechanics: Mechanical Properties of Living Tissues, 1980; also papers.; Editor: Jour. Biorheology, Jour. Biomech. Engrng. Recipient Achievement award Chinese Inst. Engrs., 1965, 68; Landis award Microcirculatory Soc., 1975; von Karman medal ASCE, 1976; Guggenheim fellow, 1958-59. Fellow AIAA, ASME (Lissner award 1978); mem. Nat. Acad. Engrng. Soc. Engrng. Sci., Microcirculatory Soc., Am. Physiol. Soc., Nat. Heart Assn., Basic Sci. Council, Sigma Xi. Current Work: Biomechanics, pulmonary circulation, international cooperation in science. Subspecialty: Biomechanics. Home: 2660 Greentree Ln La Jolla CA 92037 Office: Univ Calif-San Diego La Jolla CA 92093

FUNK, GLENN ALBERT, microbiologist/virologist, educator, consultant; b. Highland Park, Mich., Feb. 28, 1942; s. John Louis and Dorothy Emily (Fritz) F.; m. Heidi Anne Reutiman, July 16, 1966; children: Kevin Hunter, Colin Jeffrey. A.B. in Bacteriology, U. Calif.-Berkeley, 1963; M.S. in Med. Microbiol. Immunology, UCLA Med. Sch., 1965; Ph.D. in Med. Microbiology, Stanford U. Sch. Medicine, 1975. Postdoctoral fellow Baylor U. Coll. Medicine, 1974-76; asst. prof. microbiology San Jose State U., 1976-81, assoc. prof., 1981-83; mgr. research Internat. Diagnostic Tech., Santa Clara, 1981-82; expt. support scientist for spacelab GE-Mgmt. and Tech. Services Co., 1982-83, sr. scientist for Spacelab, 1983—, mgr. life scis., 1985—, cons. to industry on virus and tissue culture products and prodn. Contbr. articles to profl. publs. Served to lt. USNR, 1966-70, Vietnam. Mem. Am. Soc. Microbiology, Calif. Acad. Sci., Aerospace Med. Assn., Taiwan Internat. Med. Soc., Soc. Wine Educators. Current Work: Management and technical service to NASA's spacelab missions in the area of microbiology and science management and operations. Subspecialties: Virology (medicine); Animal virology. Home: 1664 Fairlawn Ave San Jose CA 95125 Office: Mailstop 240A-4 NASA-Ames Research Center Moffett Field CA 94035

FUNK, VICKI ANN, research scientist, herbarium curator; b. Owensboro, Ky., Nov. 26, 1947; divorced. B.S., Murray State U., 1969, M.S. in Biology, 1975; Ph.D., Ohio State U., 1980. Grad. asst. Murray State U., 1974-75; teaching assoc. Ohio State U., Columbus, 1975-76, 77-78, research assoc., 1978-79; asst. curator Herbarium, 1976-77; research fellow, 1979-80; mus. intern N.Y Bot. Garden, 1980-81; assoc. curator U.S. Nat. Herbarium, Smithsonian Instn., Washington, 1981—; curator in charge (Dynamics of Evolution Hall), Nat. Mus. Natural History. Contbr. articles to profl. jours. NSF grantee, 1977-80; Sigma Xi grantee, 1979-80; WHO grantee, 1980; Smithsonian Instn. grantee, 1981-83; NATO travel grantee, 1982. Mem. AAAS, Am. Soc. Plant Taxonomists, Bot. Soc. Am., Calif. Bot. Soc., Internat. Assn. for Plant Taxonomy, Sociedad Botanica de Mexico, Soc. Systematic Zoology, Sigma Xi, others. Current Work: Origin and evolution of Andean flora, especially the family Asteraceae; Cladistics; biogeography; computer assisted taxonomy. Subspecialties: Systematics; Evolutionary biology. Office: US Nat Herbarium Smithsonian Instn NHB 166 Washington DC 20560

FUNT, RICHARD CLAIR, horticulturist, fruit grower, educator, researcher; b. Gettysburg, Pa., Feb. 13, 1946; s. Sterling Samuel and Dorothy M. (Guise) F.; m. Shirley May Fox., Sept. 6, 1969; children—Elizabeth Anne, Caroline Claire. B.S., Del. Valley Coll., 1968; M.S., Pa. State U., 1971, Ph.D., 1974. Research assoc. Pa. State U., University Park, 1970-74; asst. prof. U. Md.-College Park, 1974-78; assoc. prof. Ohio State U., Columbus, 1978—, student adviser, 1979-83; adv. Md. Hort. Club, College Park, 1975-78. Contbr. chpts. to hort. books. Bd. dirs. Methodist Ch., Columbus, 1982-83. Served to sgt. U.S. Army, 1969-70, Vietnam. Decorated Bronze Star, Army Commendation medal Vietnam. Mem. Am. Soc. Hort. Sci., Am. Agr. Econ. Soc., N. Am. Strawberry Grower Assn. Methodist. Current Work: Apple, peach growth regulators, rootstock cultivar evaluations, strawberry, bramble-herbicides; trickle irrigation production economics. Subspecialties: Plant growth; Plant physiology (agriculture). Home: 1877 Stockwell Drive Columbus OH 43220 Office: Ohio State Univ 2001 Fyffe Ct Columbus OH 43210

FURSHPAN, EDWIN JEAN, neurobiology educator, researcher; b. Hartford, Conn., Apr. 18, 1928; married, 1957; 3 children. B.A., U. Conn., 1950; Ph.D. in Animal Physiology, Calif. Inst. Tech., 1955; A.M. (hon.), Harvard U. Med. Sch., 1967. Fellow and hon. asst. Univ. Coll., U. London, 1955-58; instr. in neurophysiology Med. Sch., Johns Hopkins U., 1958-59, assoc. in neurophysiology and neuropharmacology, 1959-62; from asst. prof. to assoc. prof. Harvard U. Med. Sch., 1962-69, prof. neurobiology, 1969—. Mem. Soc. Neurosci., Nat. Acad. Scis., Am. Acad. Arts and Sci., Harvey Soc. (hon.). Subspecialties: Neurophysiology; Neurobiology. Office: Dept Neurobiology Harvard U Med Sch Boston MA 02115*

FURTH, HAROLD PAUL, physicist, educator; b. Vienna, Austria, Jan. 1930; came to U.S., 1941, naturalized, 1947; s. Otto and Gertrude (Harteck) F.; m. Alice May Lander, June 19, 1959 (div. Dec. 1977); 1 son, John Frederick. Grad., Hill Sch., 1947; A.B., Harvard U., 1951; Ph.D., Harvard, 1960; postgrad., Cornell U., 1951-52. Physicist U., Calif. Lawrence Radiation Lab., Livermore, 1956-65, group leader, 1965-67; prof. astrophys. scis. Princeton U., 1967—; dir. Plasma Physics Lab., 1981—. Bd. editors Physics of Fluids, 1965-67, Nuclear Fusion, 1964—, Revs. Modern Physics, 1975-80, Plasma Physics and Controlled Fusion, 1984—. Contbr. articles to profl. jours. Recipient E.O. Lawrence award AEC, 1974; Joseph Priestley award Dickinson Coll., 1985. Fellow Am. Phys. Soc. (J. C. Maxwell prize 1983); mem. Nat. Acad. Scis. Patentee in field. Subspecialties: Fusion; Nuclear fusion. Home: 36 Lake Ln Princeton NJ 08540

FURTH, JOHN JACOB, molecular biologist, pathologist; b. Phila., Jan. 25, 1929; s. Jacob and Olga (Bertauer) F.; m. Mary Autry, June 24, 1959; children: Karen, Susan, Robin. B.A., Cornell U., 1950; student, Yale Law Sch., 1950-51; M.D., Duke U., 1958; M.A. (hon.), U. Pa., 1972. Intern Bellevue Hosp., N.Y.C., 1958-59; resident in pathology N.Y.U. Sch. Medicine, N.Y.C., 1959-60, postdoctoral fellow dept. microbiology, 1960-62; mem. faculty dept. pathology U. Pa. Med. Sch., Phila., 1962—, prof., 1978—. Contbr. articles to profl. jours. Pres. Assn. Preservation of Darby Creek Valley, 1972-83. Served to 2d lt. Q.M.C. U.S. Army, 1951-53. Recipient Hoffman LaRoche award, 1958; Eleanor Roosevelt fellow, 1977-78. Mem. Am. Soc. Biol. Chemists, AAAS, Am. Assn. Cancer Research, Am. Assn. Pathologists. Democrat. Quaker. Current Work: Gene regulation in normal and malignant cells. Subspecialties: Molecular biology; Pathology (medicine). Home: 43 Roselawn St Lansdowne PA 19050 Office: Dept Pathology G3 U Pa Sch Medicine Philadelphia PA 19104

FUZEK, JOHN FRANK, research chemist; b. Knoxville, Tenn., Dec. 21, 1921; s. John and Maria (Pucher) F.; m. Bettye Lynn Bean, May 31, 1943; children—Mary Ann, Mark Lynn, Martha Elizabeth. B.S. in Chem. Engring., U. Tenn., 1943, M.S. in Phys. Chemistry, 1945, Ph.D. in Phys. Chemistry, 1947. Chemist Hercules Powder Co., Wilmington, Del., 1943-44; research chemist N.Am. Rayon Corp., Elizabethton, Tenn., 1948-55; head research physics Beaunit Fibers, Elizabethton, 1955-66; sr. research chemist Tenn. Eastman Co., Kingsport, 1966-70; research assoc. Chem. div. Eastman Kodak Co., Kingsport, 1970—. Contbr. articles to sci. jours., chpt. to book. Patentee in field. Recipient Sci. Research award Oak Ridge Inst. Nuclear Studies, 1950. Fellow Am. Inst. Chemists (pres. Tenn. 1971-72), AAAS; mem. Am. Chem. Soc. (chmn. N.E. Tenn. 1957-58, nat. councilor 1964-66, nat. alt. councilor 1978-80, Speaker of Yr. award N.E. Tenn. sect. 1979), Fiber Soc. (Lectr. of Yr. award 1980-81), ASTM (cert. of appreciation 1983, 3d vice chmn. com. D13 on textiles 1984—), N.Y. Acad. Scis., Coblentz Soc., Am. Crystallographic Assn., Am. Assn. Textile Chemists and Colorists, Sigma Xi. Republican. Presbyterian. Current work: Fiber science; textile testing; fiber and polymer structure; textile products comfort; chemical kinetics. Subspecialties: Polymers (materials science); Polymer physics. Home: 4603 Mitchell Rd Kingsport TN 37664 Office: Chems Div Eastman Kodak Co PO Box 1972 Kingsport TN 37662

FYE, PAUL MCDONALD, oceanographic institution administrator, oceanographer; b. Johnstown, Pa., Aug. 6, 1912; s. Orlando Grimm and Jennie (Vesta) F.; m. Ruth Elizabeth Heym, Apr. 26, 1942; children—Kenneth, Elizabeth. B.S., Albright Coll., 1935, D.Sc., 1955; Ph.D., Columbia U., 1939; D.Sc. (hon.), Tufts U., 1970; LL.D., Northeastern U., 1974. Asst. prof. Hofstra Coll., 1939-41; research asst. Carnegie Inst. Tech., N.Y.C., 1941-42; asst. prof. chemistry U. Tenn., Knoxville, 1947-48; dep. chief, then chief Naval Ordnance Lab., Md., 1948-56, assoc. dir. research, 1956-58; dir. Woods Hole Oceanographic Inst., Mass., 1958-77, pres., 1958—; dir. Arthur D. Little, Inc., Boston, Textron, Inc., Providence, Lord Abett, Inc., N.Y.C.; mem. corp. Marine Biol. Lab., Woods Hole, 1958—; mem. Ctr. for Oceans Law and Policy, U. Va., 1975—, ocean affairs, Dept. State, 1971—, Law of the Sea, 1972—; mem. Ocean Energy Systems Council, Dept. Energy, 1979—, Internat. Atlantic Salmon Found., 1970; bd. trustees Mass. Maritime Acad., 1980—, mem., 1973—; mem. Nat. Acad. Scis. Freedom of Ocean Sci. Task Group, 1982—; chmn. Ocean Policy Com., 1979—; mem. com. New Eng. Aquarium, 1970—. Bd. dirs. Cape Cod Community Coll., 1961-81. Recipient Presdl. cert. Merit, 1948, Disting. Alumni award Albright Coll., 1951, U.S. Navy Meritorious award, 1951, cert. commendation, 1960, 66, Disting. Pub. Service award, 1977, Assn. Govt. Accts. Ann. Achievement award, 1977. Mem. Am. Acad. Arts and Scis., AAAS, Am. Chem. Soc., Am. Geophys. Union, Am. Phys. Soc., Am. Soc. Limnology and Oceanography, Council on Fgn. Relations, Inc., Marine Tech. Soc. (pres. 1968-69, pres. 1969-70, hon. mem.), U.S. Naval Inst., U.S. Navy Research and Devel. Planning Council, Sigma Xi. Pi Tau Beta, Phi Lambda Upsilon, Epsilon Chi. Clubs: Cosmos (Washington); University (N.Y.C.). Subspecialty: Oceanography. Home: 18 Widgeon Rd PO Box 309 Woods Home MA 02543 Office: Woods Home Oceanographic Inst Crowell House Woods Hole MA 02543

FYSTROM, DELL ORREN, educator, physicist, cons.; b. Mpls., Aug. 29, 1937; s. Orren Alvin and Florence (Benson) F.; m. Linda Mae Conger, Sept. 7, 1962 (div.); children: Eileen Teresa, Heather Lee, Michael Dell. B.A., St. Olaf Coll., Northfield, Minn., 1959; Ph.D. in Physics, U. Colo., Boulder, 1969. Asst. prof. U. Wis., LaCrosse, 1969-72, assoc. prof., 1972—, chmn. dept. physics, 1971-73, 82—; chmn. dept. physics Nat. U., Addis Ababa, Ethiopia, 1974-75. Chmn. Mayor's Ad Hoc Energy Commn. of LaCrosse. Mem. Am. Assn. Physics Tchrs. Lodge: Rotary. Current Work: Magnetic moment of proton in nuclear magnetons (exptl). Subspecialty: Atomic and molecular physics. Home: 2918 N Marion Rd LaCrosse WI 54601 Office: Cowley Hall University of Wisconsin 1775 Pine St LaCrosse WI 54601

GAA, PETER CHARLES, research chemist; b. Springfield, Ill., Mar. 30, 1955; s. Peter Carl and Patricia (Stewart) G.; m. Sheila Bourque, Aug. 2, 1980; children—Lillian, Peter. B.S. in Chemistry, Notre Dame U., 1977; Ph.D. in Organic Chemistry, Ga. Tech. U., 1982. Research chemist PPG Industries, Pitts., 1982-84, sr. research chemist, 1984—. Contbr. articles to profl. jours. Patentee in field of aqueous silylated polyurethane and fiberglass sizing. Mem. Am. Chem. Soc., TAPPI (bldg. products com. 1983—). Roman Catholic. Current work: Synthesize chemicals for use in coating fiber glass; investigate effects of chemicals on surface of glass and interface with matrix resin. Subspecialties: Organic chemistry; Organometallics. Home: 1248 Hazlett Rd Pittsburg PA 15237 Office: PPG Industries 201 Zeta Dr Pittsburg PA 15238

GAAFAR, SAYED M., veterinary parasitology educator; b. Tanta, Egypt, Jan. 18, 1924; came to U.S., 1947, naturalized, 1956; s. Mohammed Hegab and Bahia (Salama) G.; m. Irma Eileen Bird, Aug. 30, 1949; children—Joseph, Wayne, Daniel, Gail. B.Vet. Sci., Fouad U., 1944; M.S., Kans. State U., 1949, Ph.D., 1950; D.V.M., Tex. A&M U., 1955. Veterinarian, Vet. Service Eqypt, 1944-45; instr. dept. parasitology Cairo U., 1945-47; vet. diagnostician Vet. Path. Lab., Giza, Egypt, 1950-51; veterinarian Rutherford Vet. Hosp., Dallas, 1951-54; asst. prof. Tex. A&M U., College Station, 1954-58; asst. prof. Purdue U., Lafayette, Ind., 1958-61, assoc. prof., 1961-64; prof. parasitology, dept. vet. microbiology Purdue U., West Lafayette, Ind., 1964—; external examiner, Saudi Arabia, Nigeria, Tripoli med. schs., 1975—; cons. World Bank, Bangkok, Thailand, 1977. Editor: Pathology of Parasitic Diseases, 1970; Parasites, Pests and Predatory Diseases, 1985; Vet. Parasitology, 1972—. Egyptian Govt. scholar, 1947; NIH fellow, 1964, 68. Mem. World Assn. Vet Parasitology (pres. 1975-83), World Fedn. Parasitologists (1st v.p. 1978-82), Am. Assn. Vet. Parasitologists (pres. 1963-64). Clubs: West Lafayette, Sagamore Lions (1st v.p. 1984, pres. 1985), Optimist (pres. 1962). Lodge: Masons (worshipful master 1984). Current work: Pathogenesis of parasitic disease-immunopathology of parasitism, ectoparasitism in animals. Subspecialties: Veterinary Parasitology; Parasitology. Home: 2620 Newman Rd West Lafayette IN 47906 Office: Dept Vet Microbiology Purdue U West Lafayette IN 47906

GAARENSTROOM, STEPHEN WILLIAM, chemist; b. Mpls., Sept. 20, 1950; s. Conrad Franklin and Beverly Ann (Peterson) G.; m. Nancy Ruth Maledon, Sept. 19, 1981. B.A., Carleton Coll., 1972; Ph.D., Purdue U., 1977. Staff research chemist Gen. Motors Research Labs., Warren, Mich., 1977—. Contbr. articles to profl. jours. Mem. ASTM (chmn. subcom. 1983—), Am. Vacuum Soc., Am. Chem. Soc., Assn. Analytical Chemists, AAAS. Lutheran. Current work: Surface analysis related to corrosion wear and contamination; information content of electron spectra. Subspecialty: Analytical chemistry. Home: 11319 Ventura St Warren MI 48093 Office: Gen Motors Research Labs 30500 Mound Rd Warren MI 48090

GABELMAN, JOHN WARREN, geologist, engineer; b. Manila, Philippines, May 18, 1921; s. Charles Grover and Cyprienna (Turcotte) G.; m. Olive Alexander Thompson, Sept. 22, 1945; children: Barbara Grace, Joan Lynn. B.S., Colo. Sch. Mines, 1943, M.S. in Geol. Engring, 1948, Sc.D., 1949. Registered profl. engr., Colo. cert. profl. geologist. Jr. engr. N.J. Zinc Co., Gilman, Colo., 1943-44; geologist Colo. Fuel & Iron Corp., Pueblo, 1949-51, Am. Smelting & Refining Co., Salt Lake City, 1951-54; dist. geologist, br. chief AEC, Western U.S., S.Am., Washington, 1954-73, program mgr. geothermal, Washington, 1973-75; mgr. exploration research Utah Internat. Inc., San Francisco, 1975-83; pres. John W. Gabelman & Assocs., 1983—; v.p. Geosat Com., Inc., San Francisco, 1981-83; adv. AEC, Latin-Am. rep., 1958-61. Author: Migration of Thorium and Uranium, 1977; Contbr. numerous articles to profl. jours. Served with USNR, 1944-46. Fellow Geol. Soc. Am.; mem. Am. Assn. Petroleum Geologists, Soc. Econ. Geologists, Am. Mineralogical Soc., Am. Inst. Mining Engrs., Am. Geophys. Union. Republican. Roman Catholic. Current Work: Research in metallic ore deposits, particularly uranium, spectral remote sensing in geology; tectonics related to ore deposits; geochemistry of mineralization processes. Subspecialties: Geology; Remote sensing (geoscience). Home and Office: 23 Portland Ct Danville CA 94526

GABER, BRUCE PAUL, physical biochemist, researcher, research adminstrator; b. Chgo., Oct. 15, 1941; s. George and Ruth Sylvia (Suekoff) G.; m. Sung Suk Lee, Dec. 31, 1966 (div. 1982); children—Mi-Ai Andrea, Paula; m. Catherine Josephine Goeser, Apr. 27, 1985. B.A. in Chemistry., Hendrix Coll., 1963; Ph.D. in Biochemistry, U. So. Calif., 1968. Research assoc. IBM Watson Lab., N.Y.C., 1968-70, IBM Research Ctr., Yorktown Heights, N.Y., 1970-71; asst. prof. in chemistry U. Mich.-Dearborn, 1971-75; vis. scientist U. Oreg., Eugene, 1979-77; research chemist Naval Research Lab., Washington, 1977-84, dep. head biolmolecular engring. br., 1984—; pres. Revs. Northwest, Eugene, 1975-77, PS R and T Cons., Bethesda, Md., 1984—. cons. Fedn. Am. Socs. Exptl. Biology, Bethesda, 1984. Contbr. articles to profl. jours. Recipient Alan Berman Research Publ. award Naval Research Lab., 1984, NRC-Sigma Xi award in applied research, 1984; Nat. Cancer Inst. research fellow, 1975-77. Mem. Am. Soc. Biol. Chemists, AAAS, Biophys. Soc., Molecular Graphics Soc. (London). Jewish. Current work: Membrane structure, spectroscopy, artificial red cells, immunochemistry, molecular graphics, biosensors. Subspecialties: Biophysical chemistry; Graphics, image processing, and pattern recognition. Home: 5707 Northfield Rd Bethesda MD 20817 Office: Biolmolecular Engring Br Code 6190 Naval Research Lab Washington DC 20375-5000

GABLE, CAROL BRIGNOLI, clinical nutritionist, epidemiologist; b. N.Y.C., Dec. 28, 1945; d. Peter Joseph and Frances Veronica (Guma) Abatemarco; m. Francis Giovanni Brignoli, May 19, 1968 (div. 1981); children—Barbra Christine, James Alexander; m. Raymond Lewis Gable, Jan. 8, 1983. B.S. in Chemistry, CCNY, 1968; Ph.D., U. Md., 1973. Lectr. Montgomery Coll., Takoma Park, Md., 1972-75; nutritionist USDA, Hyattsville, Md., 1974-76; chemist FDA, Washington, 1977-82, nutritionist, biostatistician, 1982—. Contbr. articles to profl. jours. Mem. Carderock Sch. PTA, Md., N.Y. State Regents scholar; NSF fellow. Mem. Am. Chem. Soc., AAAS, N.Y. Acad. Sci., Nutrition Group of Washington. Democrat. Mem. United Ch. of Christ. Current work: Analyze NHANES II data to describe the iron status of U.S. population; review the Gras status of sugar. Subspecialties: Nutrition (medicine); Epidemiology. Home: 7715 Glenmore Spring Way Bethesda MD 20817 Office: FDA DON HFF-265 200 C St SW Washington DC 20204

GABLE, RALPH KIRKLAND, psychology educator; b. Canton, Ohio, Mar. 21, 1934; s. Harry C. and Mary (Blackburn) Schwitzgebel; m. Colleen Ryan, Dec. 28, 1963; children: Eric, Sandra. B.S., Ohio State U., 1956; Ed.D., Harvard U., 1962, J.D., 1970; Ph.D., City U. Los Angeles, 1985. Diplomate: Am. Bd. Forensic Psychology. Lectr. Harvard U., 1968-71, Northeastern U., 1969-73; Lectr. Harvard Med. Sch., 1970-74, asst. prof., 1975-78; asst. prof. psychology Calif. Luth. Coll., Thousand Oaks, 1975-77, assoc. prof., 1978-83, prof., 1983—; mem. Harvard Civil Rights-Civil Liberties Law Rev., Cambridge, 1968-70; chmn. Crime and Delinquency Rev. Com. NIMH, 1974-76; mem. Inventors Workshop Internat., Ventura, Calif., 1976—. Author: Streetcorner Research, 1964, Law and Psychological Practice, 1980, Changing Human Behavior, 1974; mem. editorial bd.: Jour. Law and Human Behavior, 1974-82; asst. editor: Internat. Jour. Psychiatry, 1963-64. Mem. Am. Psychol. Assn. (chairperson ethics com. 1974-76), Assn. Advancement Behavior Therapy (dir. 1968-80). Democrat. Patentee behavioral superivison system, 1969, antomobile camera system. Current Work: Behavioral electronics; product development law; evaluation of ethanol tolerance; interpersonal communications technology. Subspecialties: Social psychology; Distributed systems and networks. Home: 515 Fargo St Thousand Oaks CA 91360 Office: California Lutheran College 60 Olsen Rd Thousand Oaks CA 91360

GABLEHOUSE, REUBEN HAROLD, aerospace co. exec.; b. Berthoud, Colo., Aug. 31, 1923; s. Daniel Henry and Mollie Emma (Henry) G.; m. Genevieve Margaret Willburn, June 19, 1949; children: Timothy, R. Daniel, Nancy, Kelly. B.S.E.E., U. Colo., 1951; M.S.E.E., U. N.Mex., 1956. Electronics engr. instrumentation design Chance-Vought, 1951-52; staff mem. instrumentation devel. Sandia Corp., Albuquerque, 1952-60; with Ball Aerospace Systems Div., Boulder, Colo., 1960—, pres., 1980—. Bd. dirs. Fiske Planetarium, 1982—; vice chmn. United Way Campaign, Boulder, 1983. Served to 2d lt. U.S. Army, 1943-46. Mem. AIAA, Am. Astron. Soc. Methodist. Subspecialty: Electronics. Home: 1840 Forest Ave Boulder CO 80302 Office: 1600 Commerce St Boulder CO 80303

GABOR, JOHN DEWAIN, chemical engineer, researcher; b. Chgo., Aug. 8, 1932; s. John and Catherine (Hardy) G.; m. Mary Lynn Dickinson, Oct. 14, 1961; children—Cathryn Cruse, John Dickinson. B.S., U. Ill., 1954; PhD., Cornell U., 1957. Chem. engr. Argonne Nat. Lab, Ill., 1957—; vis. prof. U. Ill.-Chgo., 1974, 79, 80, 82, 84. Contbr. chpts. to books, articles to profl. jours. Patentee in field. Mem. Am. Inst. Chem. Engrs., Am. Chem. Soc. Current work: Heat transfer in particle beds; fluidization; nuclear reactor safety. Subspecialties: Chemical engineering; Nuclear fission. Home: 4135 Ellington Ave Western Springs IL 60558 Office: Argonne Nat Lab 9700 S Cass Ave D206 Argonne IL 60439

GABRIEL, MICHAEL, psychology educator; b. Phila., May 5, 1940; s. Michael and Josephine (Alesio) G.; m. Linda Prinz, June, 1967 (div.); 1 child, Joseph Michael; m. Sonda Sue Walsh, May, 1984. A.B. in Psychology, St. Joseph's Coll., 1962; M.A. in Psychology, U. Wis.-Madison, 1965, Ph.D. in Psychology, 1967. Asst. prof. Pomona Coll., Clarement, Calif., 1967-70; staff Psychologist Pacific State Hosp., Pomona, Calif., 1968-70; NIMH sr. postdoctoral fellow U. Calif., Irvine, 1970-72; asst. prof. U. Tex., Austin, 1973-77, assoc. prof., 1977-82, area chmn. Biol. Psychology Program, 1979-82; prof. psychology U. Ill., Champaign, 1982—. Author: (with Brent A. Vogt) Neural and Behavioral Biology of the Cingulate Cortex, 1984. Mem. Psychonomic Soc., Soc. for Neurosci., Sigma Xi (pres. elect Claremont Colls. 1969-70). Current work: Description of the neural substrates and mechanisms of learning and cognitive processes. Subspecialties: Neurophysiology; Learning. Home: 2103 Rodney St Champaign IL 61821 Office: U Ill Dept Psychology 603 E Daniel Champaign IL 61820

GABRIEL, OTHMAR, biochemistry educator; b. Vienna, Jan. 10, 1925; s. Othmar and Rosa (Fellner) G.; m. Rachelle Rothenberg, Aug. 5, 1965; m. Elisabeth Rehurek, May 28, 1949 (div. 1962); children—Annamaria, Harriet. Ph.D., U. Vienna, 1954. Asst. prof. U. Vienna, 1954-60; research assoc. Columbia U. Med. Sch., N.Y.C., 1958-60; research chemist NIH, Bethesda, Md., 1960-65; assoc. prof. biochemistry Georgetown U. Med. Sch., Washington, 1965-70, prof., 1970—; vis. prof. Harvard U. Med. Sch., 1973. Contbr. articles to profl. jours.; exec. editor Analytical Biochemistry, 1983—. Mem. Am. Soc. Biol. Chemists, Am. Chem. Soc., Am. Soc. Microbiology, Soc. Exptl. Biology and Medicine, Sigma Xi. Roman Catholic. Current work: Role of cell surface carbohydrates in cellular recognition. Subspecialties: Biochemistry (medicine); Microbiology (medicine). Home: 6508 Wilmett Rd Bethesda MD 20817 Office: Georgetown U Med Sch 3900 Reservoir Rd Washington DC 20007

GADDIS, M. FRANCIS, mechanical and marine engineer, environmental scientist; b. Boston, July 27, 1920; s. Michael Joseph and Catherine Agnes (Lavelle) G.; m. Marie B. Leen, Nov. 22, 1946 (dec. Feb. 1979); children—Robert L., Paul L. Student U. Ala., 1941-43; B.A., Adelphi U., 1977, M.Sc., 1979, cert. environ. mgmt., 1979; M.Phil., Columbia U., 1981, postgrad., 1981—. Chief marine engr. U.S. Army, Port of N.Y., 1944-45; service engr. Garlock Inc., Boston, 1946-47, ter. mgr., N.Y.C., 1947-61; pres., chief engr. Gaddis Engring. Co., Port Washington, N.Y., 1961—; mem. seals edn. workshop com. Dept. Energy, Office Naval Research, Am. Soc. Lubrication Engrs., ASME, 1979-80. Author: Awareness of Environmental Hazards in Risk Management, 1979. Co-developer cryogenic vapor barrier. Recipient Disting. Alumni medal Adelphi U., 1984. Mem. ASME, Am. Soc. Lubrication Engrs. (emissions com. 1980-84), Soc. Naval Architects and Marine Engrs., Assn. Environ. Profls., Marine Tech. Soc., N.Y. Acad. Scis., John Henry Newman Hon. Soc., Delta Tau Delta (MIT chpt. adviser 1946-47). Clubs: Columbia (N.Y.C.); North Shore Yacht (Port Washington). Current work: Research on hydrogeological environmental considerations in toxic waste disposal facility siting; research on materials and systems in mechanical sealing and containment. Subspecialties: Mechanical engineering; Hazardous waste disposal. Home: PO Box 411 Locust Valley NY 11560 Office: Gaddis Engring Co PO Box 689 Port Washington NY 11050

GAEKE, GOTTLIEB CHARLES, analytical research chemist; b. Goose Creek, Tex., Sept. 11, 1928; s. Gottlieb Charles and Ida Fredrica (Ludwig) G.; m. Rosemarie Theresa Gibson, Sept. 7, 1952; children—Charles Gibson, Diane Marie. B.S., U. Houston, 1950; M.S., La. State U., 1956. Research asst. U. Tex. Med. Br., Galveston, 1950-52; teaching asst. chemistry dept. La. State U., Baton Rouge, 1952-53; gen. mgr. Kem-Tech Labs., Baton Rouge, La., 1953-60; asst. prof. chemistry La. State U., Alexandria, 1960-61; sr. research assoc. Ethyl Corp., Baton Rouge, La., 1961—. Contbr. articles to tech. jours. Patentee gas sampling. Recipient Charles E. Coates award, 1983. Fellow Am. Inst. Chemists; mem. Am. Chem. Soc. (chmn. 1975-76), Baton Rouge Analytical Instrument Discussion Group (vice-chmn. 1981—), Sigma Xi. Current work: Trace analyses of gases; analysis of organic compounds via chromatographic methods; automation of analytical systems. Subspecialty: Analytical chemistry. Home: 581 College Hill Dr Baton Rouge LA 70808 Office: Ethyl Corp Research and Devel Dept PO Box 341 Baton Rouge LA 70821

GAFFAR, MARIA CORAZON SOLIS, research scientist, pharmaceutical formulator; b. Tacloban City, Leyte, Philippines, Dec. 1, 1939; d. Vincente B. and Lourdes (Mate) Solis; m. Abdul Gaffar, May 23, 1970; 1 child, Yousuf. A. B.S. in Pharmacy, U. Santo Tomas, Philippines, 1961; M.S. in Pharmacy, Mass. Coll. Pharmacy, 1964, Ph.D., 1967; M.B.A., Fairleigh Dickinson U., 1984. Instr. chemistry Emmanuel Coll., Boston, 1964-67; research scientist Colgate-Palmolive Co., Piscataway, N.J., 1967-79; sr. scientist Johnson & Johnson Products, Inc., North Brunswick, N.J., 1979—. Contbr. articles to profl. jours. Patentee in field. Mem. Am. Chem. Soc., Am. Pharm. Assn., Am. Assn. Dental Research, Internat. Assn. for Dental Research, Rho Chi. Subspecialty: Oral biology. Office: Johnson & Johnson Research Ctr Route 1 and Milltown Rd North Brunswick NJ 08902

GAFFEY, JOHN DEAN, JR., physicist; b. Washington, June 27, 1944; s. John Dean and Joan (Barrow) G.; m. Claudia Maria Correa Lima, Dec. 22, 1978. B.A., U. Calif.-Riverside, 1966; M.S., U. Calif.-San Diego, 1968, C. Phil., 1974, Ph.D., 1974. Research asst. physics U. Calif.-San Diego, 1967-74; postdoctoral fellow physics and astronomy U. Md., College Park, 1974-75, research assoc. Inst. Phys. Sci. and Tech., 1982—; assoc. prof. U. Fed. do Rio Grande do Sul, Porto Alegre, Brazil, 1975-80; research assoc. Naval Research Lab., Washington, 1980-82. Contbr. articles to profl. jours. Mem. Am. Geophys. Union, Am. Phys. Soc., Brazilian Phys. Soc., Phi Beta Kappa, Pi Mu Epsilon. Current work: Theoretical investigations of physical phenomena occuring in laboratory and space plasmas; including waves, particles, instabilities, and radiation. Subspecialties: Plasma physics; Nuclear fusion. Home: 10105 Frederick Ave Kensington MD 20895 Office: Inst Phys Sci and Tech U Md College Park MD 20742

GAFFEY, SUSAN JENKS, geologist; b. Iowa City, Jan. 9, 1946; d. John William and Edith (Cobeen) Jenks; m. Michael James Gaffey, Aug. 15, 1973. B.A., U. Iowa, 1968; M.A., Rice U., 1973; Ph.D., U. Hawaii, 1984. Teaching asst. Rice U., Houston, 1970-71; technician U. Hawaii, Honolulu, 1979-80, research asst. Planetary Geoscis., Honolulu, 1981-84; vis. research assoc. Rensselaer Poly. Inst., Troy, N.Y., 1984—. NSF fellow, 1969-72. Mem. Soc. Econ. Paleontologists and Mineralogists, Geol. Soc. Am., Internat. Assn. Sedimentologists, Phi Beta Kappa. Democrat. Episcopalian. Current work: Research on petrology of carbonate rocks; spectral properties carbonate rocks; applications in remote sensing and petrology. Subspecialties: Sedimentology; Remote sensing (geoscience). Home: 54 Pawling Ave Troy NY 12180 Office: Dept Geology Rensselaer Poly Inst West Hall Troy NY 12181

GAFFNEY, FRANCIS ANDREW, medical educator, cardiologist; b. Carlsbad, N.Mex., June 9, 1946; s. Francis Blair and Miriam Julia (Means) G.; m. Sheila Baebel, June 30, 1973; children—Andrea Elaine, Lauren Michelle. Student, U. Madrid, 1966-67; B.A., U. Calif., 1968; M.D., U. N.Mex., 1972. Diplomate Am. Bd. Internal Medicine. Intern, Cleve. Met. Gen. Hosp., 1972-73, resident in cardiology, 1973-75; fellow in cardiology U. Tex. Health Sci. Ctr., Dallas, 1975-77, asst. prof., 1979-84, assoc. prof., 1984—; payload specialist NASA, Houston, 1984—. Contbr. articles to profl. jours. Recipient Individual Research award NIH, 1978, Young Investigator award, 1981. Fellow Am. Coll. Cardiology; mem. Aerospace Med. Assn., Tex. Med. Assn., Am. Heart Assn. Current work: Study of cardiovascular regulation with emphasis on hemodynamic responses to gravitational stress; space flight and high G stress of aircraft flight; trainee crew member spacelab Life Scis. 1. Subspecialties: Cardiology; Aerospace engineering and technology. Office: Div Cardiology U Tex Health Sci Ctr 5323 Harry Hines Dallas TX 75235

GAFFNEY, JEFFREY STEVEN, chemist, researcher; b. San Bernardino, Calif., July 28, 1949; s. Jack Paul and Jeannette Theodosia (Heistand) G.; m. Linda Marie Myers, Mar. 27, 1971; children—Colleen Marie, Juliet Hope, Ryan Michael. B.S., U. Calif.-Riverside, 1971, M.S., 1973, Ph.D., 1975. Research assoc. dept. chemistry Brookhaven Nat. Lab., Upton, N.Y., 1975-77, assoc. chemist, dept. applied sci., 1977-80, chemist dept. applied sci., 1980—. Contbr. articles to tech. jours. Troop leader local Girl Scouts U.S., 1982—. Environ. scis. predoctoral trainee USPHS, 1971-72; predoctoral fellow IBM, 1973-75; prin. investigator Dept. Energy, 1980—. Mem. Am. Chem. Soc. Democrat. Roman Catholic. Current work: Air chemistry of organic pollutants, gas phase kinetics and product analysis, organic photochemistry, air pollution monitoring, chromatographic detector development, chemiluminescent reactions, natural abundance isotope ratio determination. Subspecialties: Atmospheric chemistry; Analytical chemistry. Home: 43 Wildwood Dr Sound Beach NY 11789 Office: Brookhaven Nat Lab Bldg 426 Upton NY 11973

GAFFNEY, PAUL GOLDEN, II, naval officer, oceanographer; b. Attleboro, Mass., May 30, 1946; s. Paul G. and Elfrieda L. (Piepenstock) G.; m. Linda L. Myers, Sept. 7, 1974; 1 dau., Crista Lee. B.S., U.S. Naval Acad., 1968; M.S.E., Cath. U. Am., 1969; grad. with highest distinction, Naval War Coll, 1979. Commd. ensign USN, 1968, advanced through grades to comdr., 1982; grad. research asst. Cath. U. Am., Washington, 1968-69; hydrographic advisor Vietnamese Navy, Saigon, 1971-72; oceanographic officer FleetWeather Central, Rota, Spain, 1972-75; exec. asst. Oceanographer of the Navy, Alexandria, Va., 1975-78; research fellow Naval War Coll., Newport, R.I., 1978-79; comdg. officer Ocean Unit 4, Hydrographic Survey, Indonesia, 1979-80; acting dir. arctic and earth sci. Office Naval Research, Washington, 1980-81; exec. asst. Asst. Sec. Def., Washington, 1981-83; comdg. officer Naval Oceanography Command Facility, Jacksonville, Fla., 1984—. Decorated Bronze Star medal, Def. Superior Service medal. Mem. Explorers Club, U.S. Naval Inst. Republican. Roman Catholic. Current Work: Field hydrography, research and development management in ocean environment, ocean policy, synoptic meterology. Subspecialties: Oceanography; Synoptic meteorology. Home: 2757 Pebblendge Ct Orange Park FL 32073 Office: Naval Oceanography Command Facility Jacksonville FL 32212

GAGE, DONALD SHEPARD, electrical engineering educator, consultant reliability engineering; b. Evanston, Ill., June 10, 1930; s. John Kellogg and Marion Elizabeth (Bell) G.; m. Jean Ann Veirs, Dec. 15, 1956; children—Rebecca Ann, Nancy Lynn, Catherine Sue. B.S., Northwestern U., 1953; M.S., Stanford U., 1954, Ph.D., 1958. Faculty mem. Northwestern U., Evanston, 1958-62; assoc. prof. Mich. State U., East Lansing, 1963-66; assoc. prof. U. Colo., Colorado Springs, 1966-68, prof., 1968-77; prof. elec. engring. U. Colo., Denver, 1977—; cons. IBM, Boulder, Colo., 1974, Hewlett Packard Corp., Colorado Springs, 1984—. Contbr. tech. articles to profl. jours. Sr. mem. IEEE. Presbyterian. Current work: Automated material measurements at 94 gigahertz. Subspecialties: Integrated circuits; Applied magnetics. Home: 2014 Hercules Dr Colorado Springs CO 80906 Office: Dept Engring U Colo Campus Box 104 1100 14th St Denver CO 80202

GAGE, TOMMY WILTON, dental educator, pharmacologist; b. Stamford, Tex., Oct. 6, 1935; s. Carl U. and Mildred L. (Hughes) G.; m. Loyce M. Voss, June 2, 1956; children—Sharon, Stephen, Susan, Stacey. B.S. in Pharmacy, U. Tex., 1957; D.D.S., Baylor U., 1961, Ph.D., 1969. Gen. practice dentistry, Munday, Tex., 1963-66; postdoctoral fellow Baylor Coll. Dentistry, Dallas, 1966-69, assoc. prof., chmn. dept. pharmacology, 1969-72, prof., chmn. dept. pharmacology, 1972—; cons. VA Hosp., Dallas, 1979—; mem. dental adv. panel USP/NF com. on revision, Washington, 1975—. Guest editor: Dental Clinics of North America, 1984. Served to maj. Dental Corps, USAR, 1961-63. Nat. Inst. Dental Research fellow, 1966-69. Mem. ADA, Am. Soc. Pharmacology and Exptl. Therapeutics, Internat. Assn. Dental Research, Am. Assn.

Dental Research, Tex. Dental Assn. (Cooley Trophy 1976), Am. Coll. Dentists (fellow 1981). Methodist. Current work: Local anesthetics and vasoconstrictors, jaw depressor reflex as a model for local anesthetic activity. Subspecialty: Pharmacology. Office: Baylor Coll Dentistry 3302 Gaston Ave Dallas TX 75246

GAGNEBIN, ALBERT PAUL, mining executive; b. Torrington, Conn., Jan. 23, 1909; s. Charles A. and Marguerite E. (Huguenin) G.; m. Genevieve Hope, Oct. 26, 1935; children: Anne Hope Gagnebin Coffin, Joan DeVere Gagnebin Wicks. B.S. in Mech. Engring., Yale U., 1930, M.S., 1932. With Internat. Nickel Co., Inc., 1932-74, successively staff research lab., research ferrous metallurgy, devel. ductile iron, staff devel. and research div., 1932-55, mgr. nickel sales dept., 1956-61, v.p., 1958-64, exec. v.p., 1964-67, pres., 1967-72, also dir., mem. exec. com.; v.p. Internat. Nickel Co. Can., Ltd., 1960-64, exec. v.p., 1964-67, pres., 1967-72, chmn. bd., 1972-74, ret., 1974, mem. exec. com.; former trustee Atlantic Mut. Ins. Co.; former dir. Abex Corp., Centennial Ins. Co.; dir. Am.-Swiss Assos., Inc.; dir. emeritus Ill. Central Industries; former dir. Ingersoll-Rand Co., Schering-Plough Corp., Bank of N.Y.; mem. N.Am. adv. bd. Swissair; cons. Stauffer Chem. Co. Author: The Fundamentals of Iron and Steel Castings. Decorated Ordre National du Merite France; recipient ann. award Ductile Iron Soc., 1965; Grande Medaille d'Honneur L'Association Technique de Fonderie, 1967. Mem. ASME (Charles F. Rand Meml. Gold medal 1977), AIME, Am. Soc. Metals, Am. Foundrymen's Soc. (hon. life, Peter L. Simpson gold medal award 1952), Nat. Acad. Engring., Mining and Metall. Soc. Am., Yale Engring. Assn. (dir.), Sigma Xi. Clubs: Seabright (N.J.) Beach; Down Town Assn. (N.Y.C.), Univ. (N.Y.C.), Yale (N.Y.C.); Rumson Country. Co-inventor ductile iron. Subspecialty: Metallurgy. Home: 143 Grange Ave Fair Haven NJ 07701 Office: 1 New York Plaza New York NY 10004

GAI, MOSHE, physicist; b. Bagdad, Iraq, Aug. 18, 1949; s. Shalom and Naima (Beno) Gabbay; m. Rachel Ezroni, Aug. 30, 1973 (div. 1976). B.Sc., Hebrew U., Jerusalem, 1974; M.Sc., Ph.D., SUNY-Stony Brook, 1980. Research assoc., lectr. Yale U., New Haven, 1980-84, asst. prof., 1984—. Served with Israeli Army, 1967-70. Current work: Research in experimental and theoretical nuclear physics to study fundamental modes of excitations of the nucleus and nuclear structure. Subspecialty: Nuclear physics. Home: 17 Parker Pl Branford CT 06405 Office: Dept Physics Yale U 272 Whitney Ave New Haven CT 06511

GAINER, JOSEPH HENRY, virologist, researcher; b. Atlanta, Ill., Oct. 24, 1924; s. Henry Albert and Erma Irene (Hoose) G.; m. Bridget Ginty, Jan. 2, 1954; children: Karen, Lisa, Patricia, Kelly, David, Erin. D.V.M., Ohio State U, 1946, M.S., 1947; M.S. in Virology, U. Mich., 1958. Diplomate: Am. Coll. Veterinary Microbiologists.; lic. veterinarian, Ohio, Ark., Mich. Instr. Ohio State U., 1947-49; research asst. Mayo Clinic, Rochester, Minn., 1949-50; research assoc. U. Chgo., 1950-51; asst. prof. U. Ark., 1951-53; virologist Fla. Dept. Agr., Kissimmee, 1959-66; research virologist NIH, 1967-73; veterinary med. officer FDA, Beltsville, Md., 1973—; adj. prof. N.C. State U., 1967-73. Contbr. articles in field to profl. jours. Pres. elect Kissimmee High Sch. PTA, 1965-66. Served to capt. U.S. Army, 1953-55. NIH grantee, 1962-65. Mem. Am. Veterinary Med. Assn., Am. Soc. Microbiology, Internat. Acad. Pathology, Am. Soc. Virology, Mayo Clinic Alumni Assn., AAAS, Am. Assn. Vet. Immunologists, Sigma Xi, Phi Eta Sigma, Phi Zeta. Roman Catholic. Lodge: Rotary. Current Work: Adverse/beneficial effects of chemicals on immune and interferon systems in food animals; bacterial resistance from animal feed antibiotics; medical products/drugs produced by recombinant DNA procedures. Subspecialties: Virology (veterinary medicine); Immunotoxicology. Home: 12408 Willow Green Ct Potomac MD 20854 Office: FDA Bldg 328 A Beltsville MD 20705

GAINES, ALBERT LOWERY, mechanical engineer; b. Selma, Ala., Feb. 28, 1920; s. Drummond Fletcher and Rubye Lee (Cocke) G.; m. Dorothy Lea Conley, Apr. 25, 1942; children: Albert Lowery, John Bruce, Richard Andrew, William Stuart. B.M.E., Auburn U., 1946; M.M.E., U. Mo.-Columbia, 1950. Registered profl. engr., Tenn. Mech. engr. Humble Oil & Refining, Baytown, Tex., 1948-49; asst. instr. U. Mo.-Columbia, 1949-50; engr. Union Carbide Nuclear, Oak Ridge, 1950-56; mgr. spl. products Combustion Engring., Chattanooga, 1956-65; project mgr. Combustion Engring., Windsor, Conn., 1965-84; cons. MIT, Cambridge, 1981, Gen. Atomics, San Diego, 1982, Vincent and Elkins, Houston, 1984-85; pres. A Gaines Co., 1984—. Served to 1st lt., arty. U.S. Army, 1942-46. Mem. ASME, Am. Nuclear Soc., Am. Inst. Chem. Engrs. Episcopalian. Patentee in field. Current Work: Consultation in mechanical and system engineering of advanced power technologies, project management of PWR power plant and studies in fusion and liquid metal breeder reactors. Subspecialties: Mechanical engineering; Nuclear engineering. Home and Office: 410 Leyswood Dr Greenville SC 29615

GAINES, GEORGE LOWEREE, JR., physical chemist; b. New Haven, Conn., Mar. 7, 1930; s. George Loweree and Ann Josephine (Ekman) G.; m. Margaret Earl Greene Aug. 21, 1954; children—Barbara H., George Loweree III, Elizabeth W. B.S., Yale U., 1950, M.S., 1952, Ph.D., 1954. Phys. chemist Gen. Electric Research and Devel. Ctr., Schenectady, N.Y., 1954—; adj. assoc. prof. chemistry Renssalear Poly. Inst., Troy, N.Y., 1970—. Contbr. articles to profl. jours. Patentee in field. Subspecialties: Physical chemistry; Surface chemistry. Home: RD 2 Box 94 Scotia NY 12302

GAINES, JAMES ABNER, animal science educator, researcher; b. San Antonio, Aug. 5, 1927; s. William Haney and Thelma Welch (Redmon) G.; m. Elaine Henrietta Vermeersch, July 13, 1957; children—James M., Mary E., Joseph B., Cecile M., Peter S., Alice J., John R., N. Anne, Catharine M. B.S., Tex. A&M U., 1949, M.S., 1953; Ph.D., Iowa State U., 1957. Assoc. prof. animal sci. Va. Poly. Inst., Blacksburg, 1956—; livestock adviser to Argentina, U.S. AID, Washington, 1962-64. Contbr. articles to profl. jours. Served to capt. U.S. Army, 1950-52, Korea. Recipient W.E. Wine award for teaching excellence Va. Poly. Inst. Alumni Assn., 1969. Mem. Am. Soc. Animal Sci., Am. Genetic Assn., Sigma Xi. Roman Catholic. Current work: Cattle crossbreeding, recurrent selection in sheep. Subspecialties: Animal genetics; Statistics. Home: Route 3 Box 289 Blacksburg VA 24060 Office: Animal Sci Dept Va Poly Inst Blacksburg VA 24061

GAITHER, ROBERT BARKER, mechanical engineering educator; b. North Bay, Ont., Can., Aug. 12, 1929 (parents Am. citizens); s. Edwin Hampton and Loyola Elizabeth (Barker) G.; m. Renate Konstanze Zielke, Dec. 11, 1954; children—Patricia, Vivienne, Francesca. B.M.E., Auburn U., 1951; M.S.M.E., U. Ill., 1957, Ph.D., 1962. Instr. U. Ill., Urbana, 1957-62; assoc. prof. U. Fla., Gainesville, 1962-64, prof., dept. chmn., 1964—; bd. dirs. Accreditation Bd. Engring. and Tech.; cons. U. Qatar, 1977-84. Contbr. articles to profl. jours. Chmn. Fla. Found. Future Scientists, Served to lt. USN, 1951-54, Korea. Fellow ASME (v.p. edn. 1976-80, pres. 1981-82, Centennial medallion 1980); mem. Am. Soc. Engring. Edn. Roman Catholic. Current work: High energy gas dynamics; energy conversion; administration. Subspecialty: Mechanical engineering. Home: 2100 NW 63d Terr Gainesville FL 32605 Office: Mech Engring Dept U Fla Gainesville FL 32611

GAITHER, WILLIAM SAMUEL, university president; b. Lafayette, Ind., Dec. 3, 1932; s. William Marcius and Susan Frances (Kirkpatrick) G.; m. Robin Cornwall McGraw, Aug. 1, 1959; 1 dau., Sarah Curwen. Student, Purdue U., 1950-51; B.S. in Civil Engring, Rose Poly. Inst., 1956; M. Sci. Engring., Princeton, 1962, M.A. (Arthur Le Grand Doty fellow), 1963, Ph.D. (Ford Found. fellow), 1964. Lic. profl. engr., Alaska, Calif., Del., Fla., Pa., Wis. Engr. Dravo Corp. (marine constrn.), Pitts., 1956-60; supt. Myer Corp., Neenah, Wis., 1960-61; supervising engr., chief engr. port and coastal devel., pipeline div. Bechtel Corp., San Francisco, 1965-67; asso. prof. coastal engring. dept. U. Fla. at Gainesville, 1964-65; mem. faculty U. Del. at Newark, 1967-84, assoc. prof. civil engring., 1967-70, prof. civil engring., 1970; prof., dean U. Del. at Newark (Coll. Marine Studies), 1970-84, also dir. sea grant coll. program; prof., pres. Drexel U., Phila., 1984—; dir. Roy F. Weston Inc., Mut. Assurance Co., Phila. Electric Co. mem. marine bd. NRC, 1975-81. Chmn. Gov.'s Oil Transp. Study Com., 1971-73; mem. Gov.'s Task Force Marine and Coastal Affairs, 1970-72, Gov.'s Council Sci. and Tech., Del., 1970-72; mem. ocean affairs adv. com. U.S. Dept. State; chmn. adv. council dept. civil engring. Princeton U., 1973-84; bd. dirs. Univ. City Sci. Ctr.; bd. dirs. Soc. John Gaither Descs., pres., 1985—. Served as pvt. C.E. AUS, 1953. Recipient Disting. Achievement award Rose Poly. Inst., 1975. Fellow ASCE (chmn. offshore policy com. 1979-84); mem. Del. Acad. Sci. (pres. 1971-72), Soc. Naval Architects and Marine Engrs., Marine Tech. Soc., Am. Geophys. Union, Assn. Sea Grant Program Instns. (pres. 1973-74), Sigma Xi, Phi Kappa Phi, Tau Beta Pi. Clubs: Cosmos (Washington); Union League, Downtown, Germantown Cricket (Phila.). Subspecialties: Civil engineering; Systems engineering. Home: 3705 Hamilton St Philadelphia PA 19104 Office: Drexel Univ 32d and Chestnut St Philadelphia PA 19104

GAJDUSEK, DANIEL CARLETON, pediatrician, research virologist; b. Yonkers, N.Y., Sept. 9, 1923; s. Karl A. and Ottilia D. (Dobroczki) G.; children: Ivan Mbagintao, Josede Figirliyong, Jesus Raglmar, Jesus Mororui, Mathias Maradol, Jesus Tamel, Jesus Salalu, John Paul Runman, Yavine Borima, Arthur Yolwa, Joe Yongorimah Kintoki, Thomas Youmog, Toni Wanevi, Toname Ikabala, Magame Prima, Senavayo Anua, Igitava Yoviga, Luwi Ikavara, Iram'bin'ai Undae'mai, Susanna Undapmaina, Steven Malrui, John Fasung Raglmar, Launako Wate Louise Buwana, Regina Etangthaw Raglmar, Vincent Ayan. B.S., U. Rochester, 1943; M.D., Harvard U., 1946; NRC fellow, Calif. Inst. Tech., 1948-49; D.Sc. (hon.), U. Rochester, 1977; D.Sc., Med. Coll. Ohio, 1977, Washington & Jefferson Coll., 1980, Harvard U., 1982, Hahnemann U., 1983; D.H.L., Hamilton Coll., 1977, U. Aix-Marseille, France, 1977; LL.D. (hon.), U. Aberdeen, Scotland, 1980. Diplomate: Am. Bd. Pediatrics. Intern, resident Babies Hosp., Columbia Presbyn. Med. Center, N.Y.C., 1946-47; resident pediatrics Children's Hosp., Cin., 1947-48; pediatric med. mission, Germany, 1948; resident, clin. and research fellow Childrens Hosp., Boston, 1949-51; research fellow pediatrics and infectious diseases Harvard U., 1949-52; with Walter Reed Army Inst. Research, Washington, 1952-53, Institut Pasteur, Teheran, Iran and dept. medicine U. Md., 1954-55; vis. investigator Nat. Found. Infantile Paralysis, Walter and Eliza Hall Inst. Med. Research, Melbourne, Australia, 1955-57; dir. program for study child growth and devel. and disease patterns in primitive cultures and lab. slow, latent and temperate virus infections Nat. Inst. Neurol. and Communicative Disorders and Stroke, NIH, Bethesda, Md., 1958—; chief Central Nervous System Studies Lab., 1970—; chief scientist research vessel Alpha Helix expdn. to, Banks and Torres Islands, New Hebrides, South Solomon Islands, 1972. Author: Hemorrhagic Fevers and Mycotoxicoses in the USSR, 1951, Journals, 38 vols., 1954-84, Hemorrhagic Fevers and Mycotoxicoses, 1959, Slow Latent and Temperate Virus Infections, 1965, Correspondence on the Discovery of Kuru, 1976, (with Judith Farquhar) Kuru, 1980. Recipient E. Meade Johnson award Am. Acad. Pediatrics, 1963, Superior Service award NIH, HEW, 1970, Disting. Service award HEW, 1975, Prof. Lucian Dautrebande prize in pathophysiology Belgium, 1976, Nobel prize in physiology and medicine, 1976; Gudakunst lectr. U. Mich., 1973; Dyer lectr. NIH, 1974; Heath Clark lectr. U. London, 1974; B.K. Rachford lectr. Children's Hosp. Research Found., Cin., 1975; Langmuir lectr. Center for Disease Control, Atlanta, 1975; Withering lectr. U. Birmingham, Eng., 1976; Cannon Elie lectr. Boston Children's Med. Center, 1976; Zale lectr. U. Tex., Dallas, 1976; Bayne-Jones lectr. Johns Hopkins Med. Sch., Balt., 1976; Harvey lectr. N.Y. Acad. Medicine, 1977; J.E. Smadel lectr. Infectious Disease Soc. Am., 1977; Burnet lectr. Australasian Soc. Infectious Disease, 1978; Mapother lectr. U. London, 1978; Disting. lectr. in medicine Mayo Clinic, 1978; Kaiser Meml. lectr. U. Hawaii, 1979; Eli Lilly lectr. U. Toronto, 1979; Payne lectr. Children's Hosp. D.C., 1981; Ray C. Moon lectr. Angelo State U., Tex., 1981; Silliman lectr. Yale U. Sch. Medicine, 1981; Blackfan lectr. Children's Hosp. Med. Ctr., Boston, 1981; Hitchcock Meml. lectr. U. Calif.-Berkeley, 1982; Nelson lectr. U. Calif.-Davis, 1982; Derick-MacKerres lectr. Queensland Inst. Med. Research, 1982; Bicentennial lectr. Harvard U. Sch. Medicine, 1982; Cartwright lectr. Columbia U., 1982; lectr. Chinese Acad. Med. Sci., 1983; Eastman Meml. lectr. U. Rochester, 1985. Mem. Nat. Acad. Scis., Am. Acad. Arts and Scis., Am. Philos. Soc., soc. Deutsche Akademie der Naturforscher Leopoldina, Royal Acads. Medicine, Academie de Medicina de Colombia, Pediatric Research, Am. Pediatric Soc., Am. Soc. Human Genetics, Am. Acad. Neurology (Cotzias prize 1979), Soc. Neurosci., Am. Epidemiol. Soc., Infectious Diseases Soc. Am., Société des Oceanistes, Paris, Papua and New Guinea Sci. Soc., Micronesian Acad. Sci., Slovak Acad. Scis., Academia Nacional de Medicina de Mexico, Phi Beta Kappa, Sigma Xi. Subspecialty: Virology (medicine). Home: Prospect Hill 6552 Jefferson Pike Frederick MD 21701 Office: NIH Bethesda MD 20205

GAJEWSKI, WALTER MICHAEL, nuclear reactor systems and equipment engineer; b. Hartford, Conn., Apr. 4, 1923; s. Michael Walter and Mary Ann (Boron) G.; m. Mary Christine Maglieri, Dec. 27, 1949; children: Lisa Marie, Stephen Walter, Paul Michael. B.S.E.E., U. Conn., 1949, M.S.E.E., 1951. Registered profl. engr., Calif. Engr., mgr. engring. Bettis Atomic Power Lab., Pitts., 1950-60; mgr. reactor plant Naval Reactors Facility, Arco, Idaho, 1960-68; asst. project mgr. Bettis Atomic Power Lab., 1968-70; engring. mgr. Westinghouse Hanford Co., Richland, Wash., 1970—. Served with AUS, 1943-46, ETO. Mem. IEEE (sr.), ASME (chmn. advanced reactors com./nuclear engring div. 1982—), Am. Nuclear Soc. (chmn. Pitts. chpt. 1954-56). Lodge: Elks. Inventor unique pool water reactor, various nuclear components. Current Work: Design of nuclear reactors; reactor plant equipment; fuel and waste handling; surveillance inspection—robotics. Subspecialties: Nuclear engineering; Mechanical engineering. Home: 3103 S Everett Pl Kennewick WA 99337 Office: Westinghouse Hanford Co Richland WA 99352

GAJSKI, DANIEL DANKO, computer scientist, educator; b. Zagreb, Yugoslavia, Oct. 10, 1938; came to U.S., 1969; s. Dako and Nada (Mirol) G.; m. Ana Veselic, Mar. 2, 1963. B.S.E.E., U. Zagreb, 1963, M.S., 1967; Ph.D., U. Pa., 1974. Engr. Inst. Tesla, Zagreb, Yugoslavia, 1963-69; vis. asst. prof. U. Ill, Urbana-Champaign, 1977-78, asst. prof., 1978-79, assoc. prof., 1980—; project engr. Burroughs Corp., Paoli, Pa., 1974-77, mgr. semicondr. structures, 1979-80. Contbr. articles in field to profl. jours. Mem. IEEE, Assn. Computing Machinery. Patentee in field. Current Work: Algorithms, architecture of supercomputers, hardware and silicon compilers, design methodology and expert systems. Subspecialty: Artificial intelligence. Office: 1304 W Springfield Ave Urbana IL 61801

GALABURDA, ALBERT MARK, neurologist, researcher, educator; b. Santiago, Chile, July 20, 1948; came to U.S., 1963, naturalized, 1968; s. John and Eva (Drinberg) G.; m. Margaret Okun, July 21, 1969; children: Adam, Daniel, Laura, Julia. B.A. cum laude, Boston U., 1971, M.D., 1971. Diplomate: Am. Bd. Internal Medicine, Am. Bd. Psychiatry and Neurology, Nat. Bd. Med. Examiners. Med. intern Boston City Hosp., 1971-72, asst. resident in medicine, 1972-73, resident in neurology, 1973-75, chief resident, 1975-76, asst. vis. physician, 1976-77, asso. dir. neurol. unit, 1977-82; teaching asso. Boston U. Sch. Medicine, 1972-73; clin. fellow in neurology Harvard U. Med. Sch., Boston, 1973-76, instr., 1976-80, asst. prof., 1980-84, assoc. prof., 1984—; asst. neurologist Beth Israel Hosp., Boston, 1976—; dir. Beth Israel Hosp. (Dyslexia Lab.), 1980—; dir. neurology Hebrew Rehab. Center for Aged, Roslindale, Mass., 1976-85; guest lectr., Stockholm, 1980, Frankfurt, W.Ger., 1980, Paris, 1980, Monastir, Tunisia, 1981. Contbr. articles to sci. jours. Served with U.S. Army Rev., 1971-77. Recipient Pattison prize in neurosci., 1983. Mem. Am. Acad. Neurology, Boston Soc. Psychiatry and Neurology, AAAS, N.Y. Acad. Scis., Pan Am. Med. Assn., Mass. Med. Soc., Soc. for Neurosci., Am. Assn. Anatomists, Orton Soc. (cons. 1980—), Chilean Soc. Neurology, Neurosurgery and Psychiatry. Current Work: Anatomical aspects of cerebral lateralization and language; research on neurol. basis of learning disabilities. Subspecialty: Neurology. Office: 330 Brookline Ave Room K-420 Boston MA 02215

GALAMBOS, JAMES ANDREW, cognitive scientific researcher; b. Cleve., Feb. 26, 1951; s. Henry J. and Jeannette (Turvey); m. Sylvia Joseph, Dec. 29, 1974. B.A., U. Pa.-Phila., 1974; Ph.D., U. Chgo., 1981. Research assoc. Yale U., New Haven, 1981-84; exec. v.p. Compu-Tech, Inc., New Haven, 1983-84; mgr. service design Trintex, 1985—. Co-editor: Yale Cognitive Science: New Approaches to the Study of Cognition. USPHS grantee, 1975-80; IBM grantee, 1982. Mem. Am. Psychol. Assn., Assn. for Computing Machinery, Cognitive Sci. Soc. (assoc.), Psychonomic Soc. (assoc.). Current Work: Investigating the representation and utilization of knowledge about common activities, in human and computer memory, including design of man-machine interfaces; videotex. Subspecialties: Cognition; Artificial intelligence. Office: Trintex 123 Main St White Plains NY 10601

GALANOPOULOS, KELLY, biomedical engineer; b. Athens, Greece, Jan. 4, 1952; came to U.S. 1970, naturalized, 1976; d. Panayotis and Catherine (Calas) G.; m. Dale S. Kruchten, Sept. 4, 1982; 1 child, Catherine Roberta Kruchten. B.A., CUNY, 1974; M.S., Poly. Inst. N.Y., 1978, postgrad., 1982—; postgrad. L.I. U., 1982—. Dir. bio-med. engring. Wycoff Heights Hosp., Bklyn., 1980-83, Bronx Lebanon Hosp., N.Y.C., 1983—; cons. Environ. Co., N.Y.C., 1980—, Joint Purchasing, N.Y.C., 1980—. Mem. Assn. Advancement Med. Instrumentation, IEEE, Soc. Women Engrs., N.Y. Acad. Scis. Current work: Engineering management; clinical engineering; development of medical technology. Subspecialty: Biomedical engineering. Office: Bronx Lebanon Hosp Ctr 1650 Grand Concourse Bronx NY 10457

GALAS, DAVID JOHN, biology educator; b. St. Petersburg, Fla., Feb. 25, 1944; s. David Emanuel and Catherine Elizabeth (Filan) G.; m. Linda Elaine Hubbard, July 1, 1967; children: David John, John Ryan. B.A., U. Calif.-Berkeley, 1967; M.S., U. Calif.-Davis, 1968, Ph.D., 1972. Sr. scientist U. Calif. Lawrence Livermore Lab., 1974-77; charge de recerche U. Geneva, 1977-81; asst. prof. molecular biology U. So. Calif., Los Angeles, 1981-83, assoc. prof., 1983—, dir. molecular biology, 1985—. Served to capt. USAF, 1972-74. Mem. Am. Phys. Soc., AAAS, Sigma Xi. Current Work: Molecular biology of DNA recombination transposition and DNA-protein interactions. Subspecialties: Molecular biology; Genetics and genetic engineering (biology). Office: Dept Biol Scis U So Calif University Park Los Angeles CA 90089

GALBIATI, LOUIS JOSEPH, elec. engr., educator; b. Vineland, N.J., Feb. 17, 1925; s. Louis Anthony and Mary Theresa G.; m. Jane Horan, Mar. 30, 1952; children: Louis, James, Philip, Andrew, Susan. B.E. in Elec. Engring, Johns Hopkins U., 1951; M.S., Cornell U., 1956, Ph.D., 1960; M.Ed. Adminstrn., Northeastern U., 1968. Registered profl. engr., Ohio. Instr. Cornell U., Ithaca, N.Y., 1954-60; prof. Merrimack Coll., Andover, Mass., 1960-62; engr. MITRE, Bedford, Mass., 1962-68; computer mgr. Service Tech Corp., Boston, 1968-71; engring leader RCA, Morestown, N.J., 1971-73; acad. dean, asst. pres. Hartford (N.Y.) State Coll., 1973-75; prof. U. Ark., Little Rock, 1975-77; dean SUNY Coll. Tech., Utica, 1977—; exec. dir. SUNY Coll. Tech. (Center Applied Tech.), 1982—. Mem. Mohawk Valley Engring. Exec. Council; mem. Council Engring. Tech. in N.Y. State. Served with Signal Corps U.S. Army, 1943-47. Rockefeller Found. grantee, 1976-78. Mem. IEEE, Soc. Mfg. Engrs. (grantee 1980-82, chmn. Robotics Internat. 1982—), Mohawk Valley Engring. Exec. Soc., Sigma Xi, Tau Alpha Pi. Current Work: Robotics, CAD/CAM. Subspecialties: Electronics; Software engineering. Office: SUNY 811 Court St Utica NY 13502

GALE, CHARLES, virologist, researcher; b. Wyandotte, Mich., July 7, 1926; s. John and Marcyanna (Gieraltowski) G.; m. Billie Sue Kennedy, Sept. 9, 1950; children—Charles M., Catherine C. D.V.M., Mich. State U., 1952; M.P.H., U. Minn., 1956; Ph.D., 1958. Diplomate Coll. Vet. Microbiologists (bd. dirs. 1957-61). Diagnostician, U. Minn., Mpls., 1952-56, instr., 1952-56; research veterinarian Ohio State U., Columbus, 1952-56, Ohio Agrl. Expt. Sta., Wooster, 1956-62; research assoc. Eli Lilly & Co., Greenfield, Ind., 1962—. Served with U.S. Army, 1943-45. Mem. AVMA (mem. council biols. and therapeutics 1971-81), Am. Soc. Virologists, Conf. Research Workers, AAAS, Phi Zeta, Republican. Presbyterian. Club: Rotary. Current work: Synthetic vaccines, virus vectors, anti-viral screen, also interplay with microbiology. Subspecialties: Virology (biology); Animal virology. Home: 6627 E Pleasant Run Pkwy S Dr Indianapolis IN 46219 Office: Eli Lilly and Co Box 708 Greenfield IN 46140

GALE, ROBERT PETER, physician/scientist; b. N.Y.C., Oct. 11, 1945; m. Tamar Tishler; children: Tal Britt, Shir Jessica, Elan Adam. A.B. with high honors, Hobart Coll., 1966; M.D., SUNY, Buffalo, 1970; Ph.D. in Microbiology and Immunology, UCLA, 1978. Diplomate: Am. Bd. Internal Medicine, Am. Bd. Med. Oncology. Postdoctoral scholar in immunology UCLA, 1972-76, asst. prof. medicine div. hematology-oncology, 1974-79, sr. mem. immunobiology group, 1974—; dir. UCLA (UCLA transplantation biology unit), 1977—, assoc. prof.medicine div. hematology-oncology, 1979—; chmn. Internat. Bone Marrow Transplant Registry, 1982—; Bogert fellow Leukemia Soc. Am., 1974-76; Leukemia Soc. scholar, 1976-81, SUNY Research Found. fellow, 1967, Excerpta Medica Found. traveling prof., 1979-81; Meyerhoff vis. scientist Weizmann Inst. Sci., 1982-83. Contbr. articles to sci. jours. Mem. AAAS, Am. Assn. Immunologists, ACP, Am. Fedn. Cancer Research, Am. Fedn. Clin. Research, Am. Soc. Clin. Oncology, Am. Soc. Hematology, Internat. Soc. Exptl. Hematology, N.Y. Acad. Sci., Soc. Cryobiology, Soc. Exptl. Biology and Medicine, Transplantation Soc., Western Soc. Clin. Research, Sigma Xi, Epsilon Pi Sigma. Subspecialties: Cell biology; Cancer research (medicine). Office: 14-121 UCLA Center Health Sciences Los Angeles CA 90024

GALEY, JOHN TAYLOR, natural gas operator, cons. geologist; b. Beaver, Pa., Aug. 30, 1907; s. George Banks and Vera (Taylor) G.; m. Blanche Georgene Fishback, Nov. 19, 1938; children: Margaret Elizabeth, John Taylor. B.A., princeton U., 1932; postgrad., U. Pitts., 1932-33. Certified profl. geologist. Natural gas operator John T. Galey, Pitts., 1934-66, Somerset, Pa., 1966—, cons. in field. Contbr. articles to profl. jours. Trustee Carnegie Mus. Natural History, Pitts., 1974—; trustee Mt. Lebanon Presbyn. Ch., 1947-57, pres., 1948-50, 52-54. Recipient Distinguished Service award Am. Assn. Petroleum Geologists, 1974, hon., 1980, Ben H. Parker medal Am. Inst. Profl. Geologists, 1978. Mem. Geol. Soc. Am. (fellow), Pitts. Geol. Soc. Republican. Episcopalian. Clubs: Duquesne, Harvard-Yale-Princeton, Rolling Rock, Cottage. Current Work: Investigation deeper hitherto unexplored natural gas/petroleum possibilities of Appalachians. Subspecialty: Geology. Office: Galecrest RD 4 Somerset PA 15501-8679

GALIL, KHADRY AHMED, health science educator, researcher, dentist, oral surgeon; b. Aswan, Egypt, Sept. 1, 1942; emigrated to Can., 1969; s. Ahmed and Amna G.; m. Kathleen McCully, Aug. 1974; 1 child, Ramzy. B.D.S., U. Alexandria, Egypt, 1964, D.Oral Surgery, 1967; Ph.D., U. Western Ont., 1973. Asst. prof., lectr. Alexandria (Egypt) U. Oral Surgery, 1964-69; co-dir. Mich. Alexandria X-Ray Pharoah Project, 1967-69; vis. prof. U. Mich.; fellow U. Sask., U. Western Ont., 1969-73; assoc. prof. dept. anatomy, dept. oral and maxillofacial surgery Health Scis. Centre, U. Western Ont., London, Can., 1976—; sec./treas. Midwest Anatomist Assn., U.S. and Can., 1975. Contbr. chpt. to book in field. Judge, referee Can. Amateur Boxing Assn., Ont., 1976—. Recipient awards in oral diagnosis Alexandria U., 1964, awards in pharmacology, 1962, teaching awards U. Western Ont., 1985. Fellow Acad. Gen. Dentistry; mem. Royal Coll. Dentists and Surgeons Ont., Internat. Assn. Dental Research (pres. Ont. chpt. 1973, 82-83, Am. Assn. Anatomy.). Inventor Galil, Wright & Way device (acid etch space maintainer). Current Work: Tissue adhesives, surgical glue; use of surgical glue as substitute for sutures, experimental and clinical trials, scanning electron microscopy. Dentistry; Oral biology. Office: Dept Anatomy Health Scis Centre Univ Western Ont London ON N6A 5C1 Canada

GALINSKY, RAYMOND ETHAN, pharmacy educator; b. Hartford, Conn., Jan. 27, 1948; s. Max and Cecille Marie (Smith) G. Student, San Francisco State Coll., 1966-68; B.A. in Biology, U. Calif.-Berkeley, 1970; Pharm.D., U. Calif.-San Francisco, 1975. Registered pharmacist, Calif. Resident in hops. pharmacy U. Calif.-San Francisco Hosp., 1975-76; pharmacist Summit Pharmacy, Oakland, Calif., 1976-77; instr. Phila. Coll. Pharmacy and Sci., 1977-78; postdoctoral fellow Sch. Pharmacy, SUNY-Amherst, 1978-80, research asst. prof. pharmaceutics, 1980—; guest faculty mem. Eli Lilly & Co., Indpls., 1982—; mem. speakers bur. Syva Co., Palo Alto, Calif., 1982—. Mem. Am. Fedn. Clin. Research, Am. Coll. Clin. Pharmacy, N.Y. Acad. Scis., AAAS, Federation Internationale Pharmaceutique (assoc.). Jewish. Current Work: Teaching graduate and undergraduate pharmaceutics; research in drug metabolism, drug disposition, pharmacokinetics, toxicokinetics. Subspecialty: Pharmacokinetics. Home: 273 Lisbon Ave Buffalo NY 14215 Office: Dept Pharmaceutics Sch Pharmac SUNY Amherst NY 14260

GALLAGHER, BRIAN BORU, neurologist; b. Chgo., Sept. 2, 1934; s. Thomas Francis and Beatrice (Sheehan) G.; m. Suzanne G., June 17, 1978; children: Ellen Elizabeth, Eileen Catherine, Ian Boru, Cullen Brian. B.S., U. Notre Dame, 1956; Ph.D. (NIH fellow), U. Chgo., 1960, M.D., 1963. Intern U. Chgo., 1963-64; resident in neurology Yale U., 1964-67, instr. in neurology, 1967-68, asst. prof. neurology, 1968-72, asso. prof., 1972; asso. prof. pharmacology and neurology Georgetown U., 1972-77; prof. neurology Med. Coll. Ga., 1977—; cons. to govt. agys. Contbr. numerous research articles, chpts. and revs. to profl. publs. Recipient Research Career Devel. award NIH, 1972; NIH grantee, 1967—. Mem. Am. Acad. Neurology, Am. Neurochemistry Soc., AAAS, N.Y. Acad. Sci., Am. Soc. Pharmacology and Exptl. Therapeutics, Am. Epilepsy Soc., Sigma Xi. Current Work: Research in neuropharmacology and neuroendocrinology of epilepsy. Subspecialties: Neurology; Neuropharmacology. Office: Dept Neurology Med Coll Ga Augusta GA 30912

GALLAGHER, JOHN JOSEPH, JR., energy company manager, researcher; b. Boston, Oct. 7, 1940; s. John Joseph and Margaret Theresa (Leahy) G.; m. Judy Gail Kilgore, Mar. 2, 1968; children: John Joseph, Michael Patrick, Judy

Gail, Mary Elizabeth. B.S., Boston Coll., 1962; M.A., U. Mo., Columbia, 1965; Ph.D., Tex. A&M U., 1971. Cert. petroleum geologist, Am. Assn. Petroleum Geologists cert. profl. geologist Am. Inst. Profl. Geologists. Asst. field party chief Que. Dept. Natural Resources, Que., Can., 1964; exploration geologist Am. Metal Climax of Can., Noranda, Que., 1965; research assoc. Cities Service Exploration and Prodn. Research Lab., Tulsa, 1971-78; sr. geol. assoc. Cities Service Internat. New Ventures, Houston, 1978-79, Cities Services Internat. Tech. Services, Houston, 1979-80; basin study mgr. Cities Service Co. Exploration Resources, Tulsa, 1980—; trustee, vice chmn. for confs. Basement Tectonics Com. Inc., Denver and Cairo, Egypt, 1982—; session convenor 2d World Oil and Gas Show and Conf., Dallas, 1982-83; assoc. editor tectonics Am. Geophys. Union and European Geophys. Soc., Washington and Paris, France, 1982—; session chmn. Basin Analysis Research Conf. Am. Assn. Petroleum Geology, Tucson, 1982, 83. Contbr. chpt. to book in field; convenor exploration symposium. Served to capt. C.E. U.S. Army, 1966-68. Recipient M.T. Halbouty Award Tex. A&M U., 1969. Fellow Geol. Soc. Am.; mem. Am. Assn. Petroleum Geologists, Am. Inst. Profl. Geologists, Am. Geophys. Union (supporting), Sigma Xi (ife). Republican. Roman Catholic. Current Work: Evaluation of hydrocarbonn possibilities in sedimentary basins worldwide; global tectonics; physics of basin development; rock mechanics: cataclastic flow; fractography; lithosphers mechanics. Regional Geology: China, Arctic, Africa, India, Western North America, South America, Southeast Asia-Australia; research management; remote sensing. Subspecialties: Tectonics; Geophysics. Home: 6219 E 99th St Tulsa OK 74136 Office: Cities Service Tech Center Box 3908 Tulsa OK 74102

GALLAGHER, JOSEPH PATRICK, research structural engr.; b. Phila., July 20, 1941; s. Joseph Michael and Margaret Regina (Balson) G.; m. Joan Mary Shodder, Jan. 30, 1965; children: Joseph Patrick, Timothy Adrian. B.S.C.E., Drexel U., 1964; M.S. (NSF trainee), U. Ill., Urbana, 1965, Ph.D. (NSF trainee), 1968. Grad. teaching asst. dept. theoretical and applied mechanics U. Ill., 1964-68, asst. prof. theoretical and applied mechanics, 1968-72; aerospace engr. Air Force Flight Dynamics Lab., Dayton, Ohio, 1972-77; group leader, service life mgmt. U. Dayton Research Inst., 1977—; adj. prof. materials engring., grad. program U. Dayton, 1980—; short course lectr. on fracture mechanics, 1974—; research engr. metall. div. U.S. Naval Research Lab., summer 1969; cons. Rockwell-Internat., 1982. Editor: (with T.A. Cruse) Fatigue Life Technology, 1977, (with T.W. Crooker) Structural Integrity Technology, 1979. Recipient Systems Command Tech. Achievement award USAF, 1973, 77, 2d Pl. Engring. award Air Force Assn., 1973, Gen. Foulois award Air Force Flight Dynamics Lab., 1975. Mem. ASME (exec. com. materials div. 1976-81), ASTM (Sam Tour award 1975, chmn. subcom. on subcritical crack growth), Am. Soc. Metals, Sigma Xi. Research, numerous publs. on applying fracture mechanics techniques to solution of subcritical crack growth problems; patentee crack growth gage. Current Work: Management of research and development projects that lead to improved crack damage control technologies, to enhanced structural maintenance plans or to solutions of fracture problems. Subspecialties: Fracture mechanics; Materials (engineering). Home: 3340 Ferry Rd Bellbrook OH 45305 Office: U Dayton Research Inst Dayton OH 45469

GALLAGHER, PATRICK KENT, chemist; b. Waukegan, Ill., Mar. 17, 1931; s. George Francis and Florence Kathrine (Jorgenson) G.; m. Marianne Ruth Maske, Aug. 29, 1953; children—Michael Kent, John Patrick. B.S. in Chemistry, U. Wis.-Madison, 1952, M.S. in Chemistry, 1954, Ph.D. in Inorganic Chemistry, 1959. Mem. tech. staff AT&T Bell Labs, Murray Hill, N.J., 1959—; chmn. com. E-37, ASTM, 1973-76; Editor (with others) Jour. Reactivity of Solids. Contbr. articles to profl. jours. Served to capt. USMCR, 1954-57. Fellow N.Am. Thermal Analysis Soc. (pres. 1975, Mettler award 1976, Outstanding Service award 1985) Am. Ceramic Soc.; mem. Internat. Confedn. Thermal Analysis Socs. (pres. 1982—, DuPont award 1982), Am. Chem. Soc. (councilor 1980-82), AAAS. Current work: Research in reactivity of solids-synthesis and characterization of electronic materials, primarily ceramics-thermoanalytical techniques. Subspecialties: Inorganic chemistry; Solid state chemistry. Home: 69 Harrison Brook Dr Basking Ridge NJ 07920 Office: AT&T Bell Labs Inc Room 6D-311 Murray Hill NJ 07974

GALLAGHER, RICHARD HUGO, university official and dean, engineer; b. N.Y.C., Nov. 17, 1927; s. Richard Anthony and Anna (Langer) G.; m. Therese Marylyn Doyle, May 17, 1952; children: Marylee, Richard, William, Dennis, John. B.C.E., NYU, 1950, M.C.E., 1955; Ph.D., SUNY, Buffalo, 1966. Field engr. CAA, Dept. Commerce, Jamaica, N.Y., 1950-52; structural designer Texaco, N.Y.C., 1952-55; asst. chief engr. Bell Aerospace Co., Buffalo, 1955-67; prof. civil engring. Cornell U., 1967-78, chmn. dept. structural engring., 1969-78; dean Coll. Engring., U. Ariz., 1978-84; v.p., dean faculty Worcester (Mass.) Poly. Inst., 1984—; cons. in field. Author: Finite Element Analysis, 1975, Matrix Structural Analysis, 1979; editor: Internat. Jour. Numerical Methods in Engring, 1969—. Served with USNR, 1945-47. Fulbright fellow Australia, 1973; Sci. Research Council fellow U. Wales, 1974. Fellow ASCE, ASME; mem. AIAA, Am. Soc. Engring. Edn., Nat. Acad. Engring., Soc. Exptl. Stress Analysis, Sigma Xi, Chi Epsilon, Tau Beta Pi. Roman Catholic. Current Work: Finite element analysis of plates and shells for geometrically nonlinear behavior; complementary formulations of finite element analysis. Subspecialties: Civil engineering; Solid mechanics. Home: 15 Regent St Worcester MA 01609 Office: Worcester Poly Inst Worcester MA 01609

GALLAGHER, SARAH ANN, solid state scientist, researcher; b. Lock Haven, Pa., Mar. 4, 1950; d. Charles Robert Gallagher and Katherine Dorothy (Tate) Gallagher Cox; m. Richard George Johnston, Nov. 24, 1979. B.S., Pa. State U., 1971, Ph.D., 1979. Grad. research asst. Pa. State U., University Park, 1971-77; sr. scientist Rockwell Hanford Ops., Richland, Wash., 1977—. Contbr. articles to profl. jours. NDEA fellow, 1972; recipient research assistantships AEC, ERDA, Dept. Energy, 1974-77, Young Career Woman of Yr. award Rockwell Hanford Ops., 1980. Mem. Am. Ceramic Soc., Materials Research Soc., numerous covered bridge socs., Sigma Delta Epsilon. Republican. Clubs: Antique Study (chmn. 1979-80), Rainbow Girls. Current work: Synthesis and characterization of tailored materials, inorganic ion exchange materials, solvent extraction, solid supported liquid membrane separations. Subspecialties: High-temperature materials; Solid state chemistry. Home: 1318 Sacramento Blvd Richland WA 99352 Office: Rockwell Hanford Ops PO Box 800 Richland WA 99352

GALLAGHER, THOMAS FRANCIS, physicist; b. Bronxville, N.Y., Nov. 19, 1944; s. Thomas Francis and Margaret Ann (Sheekey) G.; m. Betty Barbara Cassiman, Sept. 21, 1974; 1 son Thomas Francis. A.B., Williams Coll., 1966; M.A., Harvard U., 1968, Ph.D., 1971. Research assoc. Harvard U., 1971; research assoc. U. Utah, 1971-72; postdoctoral physicist Stanford Research Inst., Menlo Park, Calif., 1972-74, physicist, 1974-79, sr. physicist, 1979-83, program mgr., 1983-84; prof. physics U. Va., Charlottesville, 1984—. Contbr. articles in field to profl. jours. Fellow Am. Phys. Soc. Roman Catholic. Patentee in field. Current Work: Collisions and spectroscopy of highly excited atoms. Subspecialty: Atomic and molecular physics. Home: 1920 Barracks Rd Charlottesville VA 22903 Office: U Va Dept Physics Charlottesville VA 22901

GALLANT, NANETTE, medical clinic executive, consultant; b. Salt Lake City, Mar. 14, 1956; d. Richard Austin and Kathryn Amelia (Grogan) G. Student, U. Mont., 1973-74; cert., Utah Tech. Coll., 1976; B.S., U. Utah, 1980, postgrad., 1980—. Cert. surg. technologist. Cardiac surgery specialist St. Mark's Hosp., Salt Lake City, 1976-80; ops. engr. KUED-TV, Salt Lake City, 1978-80; remote ops. engr. Skaggs Telecommunications, Salt Lake City, 1981-82; chief of research Western Spinal Clinic, Salt Lake City, 1982—; cons. NGP Co., 1974—; cons. engring. to physicians, 1981-82, 82—, Zimmer-Jackson Assocs., 1982—. Mem. Assn. Surg. Technologists (pres. 1977, regional rep. 1978, Nat. Technologist of Month 1978), Soc. Photo-Optical Instrumentation Engrs., Soc. Broadcast Engrs., IEEE; assoc. mem. Soc. Motion Picture and TV Engrs., Am. Nuclear Soc. Democrat. Roman Catholic. Current Work: Application of broadcast equipment to microsurgical situation to provide accurate imaging; design and application bioinstruments to microsurgery. Subspecialties: Microsurgery; Bioinstrumentation. Home: 1408 Military Way Salt Lake City UT 84103

GALLARDO-CARPENTIER, ADRIANA, pharmacologist; b. Valparaiso, Chile, Sept. 13, 1930; d. Gustavo Rene and Lily Rebeca (Saavedra) Gallardo-C.; m. Robert Georges Carpentier, Feb. 23, 1967. D.D.S., Dental Sch. U. Chile, 1955. Lic. dentist, U.S.A. Pvt. practice dentistry, Santiago, Chile, 1955-73; instr. Coll. Dentisty U. Chile, 1964-67, asst. prof., 1966-74; asst. research pharmacologist Sch. Medicine UCLA, 1966-67; vis. fellow dept physiology SUNY Downstate Med. Center, Bklyn., 1970-72; asso. prof. exptl. medicine Med. Coll. U. Chile, 1973-76; research asso. dept. pharmacology Med. Coll. Howard U., Washington, 1977, asst. prof., 1977—. Contbr. articles to profl. jours. Mem. Am. Soc. Pharmacology and Exptl. Therapeutics, N.Y. Acad. Scis. Current Work: Alcohol and cardiac fiber, CNS. Subspecialties: Pharmacology; Neuropharmacology. Office: 520 W St NW Washington DC 20059

GALLATIN, JUDITH ESTELLE, author, research psychologist; b. Grand Rapids, Mich., Feb. 15, 1942; d. Marcus and Marilyn Gittlen Laniado; m. Charles Helppie, Jan. 2, 1975; step-children: Charles, Bruce, Kathleen. B.A., U. Mich., 1962, M.A., 1963, Ph.D., 1967. Ltd. lic. psychologist, Mich. Teaching fellow U. Mich., 1966-67; asst. prof. psychology Eastern Mich. U., 1967-72, assoc. prof., 1972-77, prof., 1977; research assoc. U. Strathclyde, 1968; cons. Ford Found., 1975; reviewer NSF, Washington, 1979-82; co-prin. Helppie & Gallatin, Portland, Oreg., 1982-84, Grand Rapids, Mich., 1984—; vis. scholar U. Mich., Ann Arbor, 1983—. Author: Adolescence and Individuality, 1975, Abnormal Psychology: Concepts, Issues, Trends, 1982; Democracy's Children: The Development of Political Thinking in Adolescents, 1985; contbg. author: Understanding Adolescence, 1976, 80, Handbook of Adolescent Psychology, 1980, Personality Theory, Moral Development and Criminal Behavior, 1983. Mem. Portland (Oreg.) Com. on Fgn. Relations, 1978-82. USPHS research fellow, 1963-66. Mem. Am. Psychol. Assn., Soc. Research in Child Devel., Am. Orthopsychiat. Assn., Phi Beta Kappa. Current Work: Author of general books and textbooks in developmental and abnormal psychology; research into virtually all areas of psychology. Subspecialties: Behavioral psychology; Cognition. Home: 2109 Glencoe Hills Dr #11 Ann Arbor MI 48104

GALLETTI, PIERRE MARIE, university executive, medical science educator; b. Monthey, Switzerland, June 11, 1927; s. Henri and Yvonne (Chamorel) G.; m. Sonia Aidan, Dec. 31, 1959; 1 son, Marc-Henri. B.A. in Classics, St. Maurice Coll., Switzerland, 1945; M.D., U. Lausanne, Switzerland, 1951, Ph.D. in Physiology and Biophysics, 1954; Sc.D. (hon.), Roger Williams Coll., U. Nancy. Asst. prof. physiology Emory U., 1958-62, assoc. prof., 1962-66, prof., 1966-67, vis. prof., 1967-68; prof. med. sci. Brown U., 1967—, chmn. div. biol. sci., 1968-72, acting dean of medicine, 1980-81, v.p. biology and medicine, 1972—; mem. acad. rev. bd. Exxon; mem. polymer adv. panel Johnson and Johnson; mem. sci. adv. com. Integrated Ionics, Princeton, N.J., 1984—; chmn. bd., chmn. sci. adv. com. Sorin Biomedica s.p.a. Torino, Italy; chmn. Consensus Devel. Conf., NIH; chmn. devices and tech. br. task force NIH; plenary lectr. World Biomaterials Conf., 1980; Hastings lectr. NIH, 1979; McNeil Pharm. Spring Sci. lectr., 1982. Author: Heart-Lung Bypass: Principles and Techniques of Extracorporeal Circulation, 1962; contbr. numerous chpts., abstracts, articles to profl. publs. Trustee Morehouse Sch. Medicine, Atlanta; mem. vis. com. Tufts U. Sch. Medicine. Recipient John H. Gibbon award Am. Soc. Extracorporeal Technology, 1980; NIH grantee, 1962—. Fellow Am. Coll. Cardiology; mem. AAAS, Biomed. Engring. Soc., Am. Physiol. Soc. Current Work: Bioresorbable vascular grafts, Implantable artificial lung; hybrid artificial pancreas; insulin delivery systems; piezoelectric polymers; hybrid articial liver. Subspecialties: Artificial organs and prostheses; Biomaterials. Office: Box G 97 Waterman St Providence RI 02912

GALLIE, THOMAS MUIR, JR., computer scientist; b. N.Y.C., Aug. 25, 1925; s. Thomas Muir and Mavis (Chubb) G.; m. Mary Frances Cordts, Nov. 22, 1945; children: Thomas Muir III, Charles Cordts, Ann Walston, Margaret Elizabeth. A.B., Harvard, 1947; M.A., U. Tex., 1949, Rice U., 1952; Ph.D., Rice U., 1954. Research engr. Humble Oil Co., Houston, 1954, 55-56; mem. faculty Duke U., Durham, N.C., 1954, 56—, prof. math, 1967-71, prof. computer sci., 1971—, chmn. dept. computer sci., 1982-84, v.p. Microelectronics Ctr. N.C.; sect. head NSF, 1968-69; vis. prof. Eidgenossische Technische Hochschule, Zurich, 1962-63, 73-74, Universidad Central de Venezuela, Caracas, 1965; chmn. bd. dirs. Triangle Univs. Computation Ctr., 1965-67, mem., 1969-73, 79—. Author: Computer Science, 1976; contbr. articles to profl. jours. Mem. Assn. Computing Machinery (nat. lectr. 1965-66)), Math. Assn. Am., Sigma Xi. Current Work: Medical applications of computers. Subspecialty: Numerical analysis (computer science). Home: 21 Glenmore Dr Durham NC 27707 Office: Dept Computer Sci Duke U Durham NC 27706

GALLIN, JOHN I., physician, researcher; b. N.Y.C., Mar. 25, 1943; s. Nathaniel M. and Helen R. (Cohen) G.; m. Elaine B. Klimerman, June 23, 1966; children: Alice, Michael. B.A. cum laude, Amherst Coll., 1965; M.D., Cornell Med. Coll., 1969. Intern, resident, then chief resident in medicine Bellevue Hosp., NYU Med. Ctr., N.Y.C., 1969-71, 74-75; clin. assoc. Nat. Inst. Allergy and Infectious Diseases, NIH, Bethesda, Md., 1971-74, sr. investigator, 1974-76, chief bacterial diseases sect. Lab. Clin. Investigation, 1976—. Editor: Advances in Host Defense Mechanisms, 1978; editor: Jour. Immunology, 1979-83, sect. editor, 1985—; mem. editorial bd.: Infection and Immunity, Blood, Jour. Leukocyte Biology, Cell Immunology, Jour. Clin. Investigations, Inflammation, Advances Inflammation Research; contbr. over 150 articles to profl. jours. Recipient Commendation medal USPHS, 1980, Outstanding Service medal, 1985. Mem. Am. Soc. Clin. Investigation, Assn. Am. Physicians, Am. Fedn. Clin. Research (Clin. Investigator award 1984), Am. Assn. Immunologists, Am. Soc. Cell Biology. Current Work: Infectious diseases, phagocyte function, inflammation; leukocyte chemotaxis and secretion. Subspecialties: Infectious diseases; Internal medicine. Office: Bldg 10 Nat Inst Allergy and Infectious Diseases NIH Bethesda MD 20205

GALLO, CHARLES FRANCIS, JR., physicist; b. Mt. Vernon, N.Y., July 22, 1935; s. Charles F. and Ann Marie (Del Vecchio) G.; m. Marilyn R. Gallo, Oct. 5, 1957; 1 child, Bonnie. B.S. in Physics (scholar), Rensselaer Poly. Inst., 1957. Engr. Gen. Electric Co.,-Rensselaer Poly. Inst. Coop. Program, Schenectady and Cleve., 1955-57; scientist Westinghouse Research, Pitts., 1957-64, Xerox Corp., Webster, N.Y., 1965-81, 3M Corp., St. Paul, 1981—; cons. sci. Rochester (N.Y.) Inner City Schs.; lectr. univs.; conf. presenter. Contbr. articles to sci. and engring. jours. Active Jobs for Inner City Students, Rochester. Recipient hon. mention for best publ. IEEE/ Indsl. Applications Soc., 1972-73, 75-76; fgn. fellow Japan Inst. Electrostatics, 1977—; recipient Bausch & Lomb hon. sci. award, 1954. Mem. Am. Phys. Soc., Electrostatics Soc. Am., Japan Inst. Electrostatics. Clubs: Carlton Racquet (St. Paul), Tartan (St. Paul). Patentee in field. Current Work: Reprographics, optical engring., gas discharge physics, electrostatics, atomic and molecular physics, data storage and reprodn., elec. engring., electronics. Home: 2440 Lisbon Ave Lake Elmo MN 55042 Office: 3M Corp 3M Center Bldg 201 PO Box 33221 Saint Paul MN 55133

GALLO, MARIO MARTIN, clinical psychologist, neuropsychologist; b. Chgo., Sept. 13, 1947; s. Mike Vito and Christina Mary (Serritella) G. B.S., Loyola U., Chgo., 1969; M.A., Roosevelt U., 1972; Ph.D., Miami U., Oxford, Ohio, 1977. Diplomate Am. Bd. Vocat. Experts. Lic. psychologist, Ill., Ohio, Ariz., Calif., Fla. Intern Greater Lawn Mental Health Ct., Chgo., 1970-71; trainee Miami U. Psychol. Clinic, Oxford, Ohio, 1972-75; psychiat. ward specialist U.S. Air Force Res., Chgo., 1972-76; intern Good Samaritan Hosp., Dayton, Ohio, 1974-75; resident Northwestern U., 1975-77; clin. dir. Kevin Coleman Mental Health Ctr., Kent, Ohio, 1978-83; pvt. practice psychology, Kent, 1978-83, Evergreen Park and Oakbrook Terrace, Ill., 1983—; vis. staff psychologist dept. neuroscis. Columbus-Cuneo-Cabrini Med. Ctr., Chgo., 1983—; profl. adv. staff Children with Learning Disabilities, Chgo., 1983—; adj. asst. prof. psychology Kent State U., 1978-83; instr. dept. behavioral scis. Northeastern Ohio U. Coll. Medicine, 1982-83. Served with USMC, 1969-70. Fellow Masters and Johnson Inst.; mem. Am. Psychol. Assn., Am. Acad. Psychotherapists, Am. Soc. Clin. Hypnosis, Internat. Neuropsychol. Soc., Nat. Acad. Neuropsychologists, Am. Assn. Marriage and Family Therapy (clin.), Am. Assn. Sex Educators, Counselors and Therapists (cert. sex therapist and counselor), Internat. Council Sex Edn. and Parenthood of Am. Univ. (approved fellow in sex therapy and counseling). Current Work: Neuropsychological assessments and rehabilitation; psychotherapy, hypnotherapy and biofeedback. Subspecialties: Neuropsychology; Clinical psychology. Office: 3830 West 95th St Suite 110 Evergreen Park IL 60642 Home: 8621 So Kostner Av Chicago IL 60652 Also: 705 Butterfield Rd Suite A Oakbrook Terrace IL 60181

GALLO, ROBERT CHARLES, research scientist; b. Waterbury, Conn., Mar. 23, 1937; s. Francis Anton and Louise Mary (Ciancuilli) G.; m. Mary Jane Hayes, July 1, 1961; children—Robert Charles, Marcus. B.A., Providence Coll., 1959, D.Sc. (hon.), 1974; M.D., Jefferson Med. Coll., 1963; hon. degrees Providence Coll., 1977, Jefferson Med. Sch., 1982, U. Rochester, 1985, U. Turino, 1985. Clin. asso. med. br. Nat. Cancer Inst., NIH, Bethesda, Md., 1965-68, sr. investigator human tumor cell biology br., 1968-69, head sect. cellular control mechanisms, 1969-72, chief lab. tumor cell biology, 1972—; adj. prof. genetics George Washington U.; adj. prof. microbiology Cornell U.; adj. prof. biology Johns Hopkins U.; U.S. rep. to world com. Internat. Comparative Leukemia and Lymphoma Assn., 1981—. Served with USPHS, 1965-68. Recipient Dameshek award Am. Hematol. Soc., 1974, CIBA-GEIGY award in biomed. sci., 1977, USPHS Superior Service award, 1979, F. Stohlman lecture award, 1979; Albert Lasker award for basic biomed. research, 1982; Gen. Motors Cancer Research award, 1983; Tel Aviv Cancer Research award, 1983; Lucy Wortham prize, 1984; Rosenstiel award, 1983; Hammer prize, 1985; Gold medal Am. Cancer Soc., 1984; Gold Plate award Am. Acad. Achievement, 1985, numerous others. Mem. Am. Soc. Clin. Investigation, Am. Soc. Biol. Chemists, Am. Microbiology Soc., Biochem. Soc., Am. Assn. Cancer Research, Alpha Omega Alpha. Research on viruses, biochemistry and leukemia. Subspecialty: Cancer research (medicine). Home: 8513 Thornden Terr Bethesda MD 20034 Office: Nat Cancer Inst 9000 Rockville Pike Bethesda MD 20014

GALLOWAY, KENNETH FRANKLIN, electrical engineer, government official, educator; b. Columbia, Tenn., Apr. 11, 1941. B.A. Vanderbilt U., 1962; Ph.D., U. S.C., 1966. Mem. faculty Ind. U., Bloomington, 1966-72, assoc. prof., 1972; research physicist Naval Weapons Support Ctr., Crane, Ind., 1972-74; mem. tech. staff Nat. Bur. Standards, Washington, 1974-81, div. chief, semicondr. devices and circuits div., 1981—; prof. elec. engring. U.Md., College Park, 1980—. Contbr. articles to archival jours. Commerce Sci. and Tech. fellow Dept. Commerce, 1979-80. Mem. Am. Phys. Soc., Electrochem. Soc., IEEE, Sigma Xi. Current work: Semiconductor devices; semiconductor measurement technology; radiation effects in semiconductor devices and circuits. Subspecialties: Semiconductors; Microelectronics. Office: Nat Bur Standards Div 726 Gaithersburg MD 20899

GALT, JOHN ALEXANDER, physicist, radio astronomer; b. Toronto, Ont., Can., Mar. 8, 1925; s. Ian and Mabel Claire (Johnston) G.; m. Rena Mabel Smith, Aug. 6, 1955; children: Sheila Jean, David Richard. B.A., U.Toronto, 1949, M.A., 1952, PH.D., 1955. Physicist DuPont of Can., Kingston, Ont., 1956-57; radio astronomer Nat. Research Council Can., Penticton, B.C., Can., 1957—; guest prof. Chalmers Tekniska Hogskola, Goteborg, Sweden, 1972-73. Serviced with Royal Can. Navy, 1944-45. Subspecialties: Radio and microwave astronomy; Atomic and molecular physics. Office: Box 248 Penticton BC V2A 6K3 Canada

GALT, JOHN KIRTLAND, physicist, laboratory administrator; b. Portland, Oreg., Sept. 1, 1920; s. Martin Happer and Elsie (Lee) G.; m. Marguerite VanNest, Dec. 30, 1949; children—James Michael (dec.), Lloyd Anthony. A.B., Reed Coll., 1941; Ph.D., MIT, 1947. Mem. tech. staff Bell Labs., Murray Hill, N.J., 1948-57, head solid state and plasma physics dept., 1957-61, dir. solid state electronics lab., 1961-74; dir. solid state scis. research orgn. Sandia Nat. Labs., Albuquerque, 1974-78, v.p., 1978-85; mem. Air Force Studies Bd., Nat. Acad. Sci., 1971-76, Air Force Sci. Adv. Bd., 1975-82. Cons. editor: McGraw-Hill Ency. Sci. and Tech., 1965—. NRC fellow, Bristol, Eng., 1947-48. Fellow Am. Phys. Soc., IEEE (Philips award 1984), AAAS. Subspecialty: Condensed matter physics. Office: Orgn 1000 Sandia Nat Lab PO Box 5800 Albuquerque NM 87185

GALTON, PETER MALCOLM, biology educator; b. London, Mar. 14, 1942; came to U.S., 1967; s. Sidney and Ena (Childs) G.; m. Natalie S. Rawls, Feb. 14, 1975. B.Sc., U. London, 1964, Ph.D., 1967, D. Sc., 1983. Curatorial assoc. Peabody Mus. Natural History, Yale U., 1967-70, research staff dept. geology, 1967-70; asst. prof. biology U. Bridgeport, Conn., 1970-74, assoc. prof., 1974-78, prof., 1978—. Contbr. articles to profl. jours. Mem. Soc. Vertebrate Paleontology, Am. Soc. Zoologists, Sigma Xi. Current Work: Vertebrate paleontology, functional morphology, systematics, relationships, evolution and zoogeography of dinosaurs. Subspecialty: Paleobiology. Office: Dept Biology U Bridgeport Bridgeport CT 06601

GALTON, VALERIE ANNE, endocrinology educator; b. Louth, Eng., May 6, 1934; came to U.S., 1959; s. Wilfrid and Eileen (Watson) Hamilton; m. Michael Galton, Aug. 26, 1956 (dec. 1968); children: Ian Andrew, Kenneth Anthony; m. Reed Detar, Dec. 28, 1976; stepchildren: James, Elizabeth, Stephen, Susan. B.Sc. with honors, U. London, 1955, Ph.D., 1958. Research assoc. Nat. Inst. for Med. Research, Mill Hill, London, 1955-58, Harvard Med. Sch., Boston, 1959-61; instr., asst. prof. Dartmouth Med. Sch., Hanover, N.H., 1961-66, assoc. prof., 1968-75, prof., 1975—; cons. NIH, Bethesda, Md., 1973—. Contbr. articles to profl. jours.; mem. editorial bd.: Endocrinology, 1982-86, Am. Jour. Physiology, 1982—. NIH grantee, 1962—. Mem. Am. Thyroid Assn., Endocrine Soc. Current Work: Mechanism of action of thyroid hormones. Subspecialties: Endocrinology; Receptors. Home: 20 Rayton Rd Hanover NH 03755 Office: Dartmouth Med. Sch Hanover NH 03756

GAMBERT, STEVEN ROSS, medical educator; b. N.Y.C., Aug. 22, 1949; s. Lawrence and Mildred G.; married; children: Christopher, Iselin. B.A. with honors, NYU, 1971; M.D., Columbia U., 1975. Intern Darmouth Med. Sch., Hanover, N.H., 1975-76, resident, 1976-77; fellow in endocrinology and geriatrics Harvard U. Med. Sch., Boston, 1977-79; asst. prof. medicine Med. Coll. Wis., Milw., 1979-81, assoc. prof. medicine, 1979-81, assoc. prof. medicine and physiology and chief geriatics and gerontology, 1981—; cons. Wis. Bur. Health, Madison, 1982—. TV host: To Better Health for the Elderly, Milw., 1982; writer health column: Sr. Citizen News, Milw., 1982; Editor: Contemporary Geriatric Medicine, 1983; contbr. numerous articles to med. jours.; mem. editorial bds.: Jour. Gerontology, 1981—, Psychit. Medicine, 1982—. Nat. Inst. Aging grantee, 1982-87; recipient Goldberger Research award AMA, 1974. Fellow ACP; mem. Endocrine Soc., Gerontol. Soc. Am. (sec.-treas. 1981-82), Soc. for Exptl. Biology and Medicine, Am. Geriatrics Soc., Am. Aging Assn., Am. Fedn. Clin. Research (councilor MW sect. 1982—), State of Wis. Med. Soc. (chmn. aging com. 1982—), Milw. County Med. Soc. (aging com.). Current Work: Aging, endocrine, thyroid and aging, neuropeptide, health service delivery to elderly, geriatrics, gerontology, health education. Subspecialties: Gerontology; Neuroendocrinology. Home: 9043 N Tennyson Dr Bayside WI 53217 Office: Med Coll Wis Care Wood VA Hosp 5000 National Ave Milwaukee WI 53193

GAMBLE, FRED RIDLEY, JR., research and engineering company executive; b. Dallas, Apr. 24, 1941; s. Fred Ridley and Leona Aileen (Crain) G.; m. Anne McCord, Sept. 12, 1964 (div. 1982); children—Katherine, John. A.B., Harvard U., 1964; Ph.D., Stanford U., 1968. Scientist Syva Corp., Palo Alto, Calif., 1964-71; group leader Exxon Corp. Research, Linden, N.J., 1971-74, lab. dir., 1974-81; div. mgr. Exxon Engring., Florham Park, N.J., 1981-83; v.p., dir. research Schlumberger-Doll Research, Ridgefield, Conn., 1983—. Contbr. articles to profl. jours. Patentee in field. Fellow Am. Phys. Soc. Subspecialties: Physical chemistry; Condensed matter physics. Home: 47 Breeds Hill Pl Wilton CT 06897 Office: Schlumberger-Doll Research Old Quarry Rd Ridgefield CT 06877-4108

GAMMON, JAMES ROBERT, zoology educator; b. Sparta, Wis., Apr. 24, 1930; s. Abner James and LeVerne Marie (Robertson) G.; m. Carolyn Patricia O'Beirne, June 16, 1952 (div. Nov. 1977); children: David M., Clifford W., Kathleen L., Robert J.; m. Sharon Ann Sanders Garner, Mar. 22, 1980; children: Shannon, Bradley. B.S., Wis. State U., Whitewater, 1956; M.S., U. Wis., 1956, Ph.D., 1961. Research asst. U. Wis., Madison, 1957-61; asst. prof. dept. zoology DePauw U., Greencastle, Ind., 1961-66, assoc. prof., 1966-73, prof., 1973—; mem. panel biol. cons. ORSANCO, Cin., 1978—; mem. Indsl. Pesticide Rev. Bd., 1983—; cons. to bus. and govt. agys. Contbr. articles to profl. jours. Served with USN, 1948-52. Danforth fellow, 1957-61. Fellow Ind. Acad. Sci. (sec. 1967-69); mem. Am. Fisheries Soc., Am. Soc. Limnology and Oceanography. Methodist. Current Work: Development of methods focusing aquatic biotic communities as an index of water and environmental quality. Subspecialties: Ecology (environmental science); Ecosystems analysis. Office: Dept Biol Sci DePauw U Greencastle IN 46135

GAMOTA, GEORGE, physicist, research and development administrator; b. Lviv, Western Ukraine, May 6, 1939; married, 1961; 3 children. B.Physics, U. Minn., 1961, M.S., 1963; Ph.D. in Physics, U. Mich., 1966. Research asst. and teaching asst. U. Minn., 1959-63; research asst. U. Mich., 1963-66, research assoc., lectr., 1966-67; prof. physics, dir. Inst. Sci. and Tech., 1981—; mem. tech. staff Bell Labs., Murray Hill, N.J., 1967-74; research specialist Office Under Sec. Def., Research and Engring., Dept. Def., 1976-78, dir. research, 1978-81; mem. adv. Council Research, 1973-75, N.J. Gov's Commn. to

Evaluate Capital Needs N.J., 1975; chmn, founder Sci. and Tech. Council for Congressman M. Rinaldo, 1974-75; exec. sec. Def. Sci. Bd. Study Fundamental Research in Univs., 1976; mem. Pres. Sci. Adv. Fed. Coordinating Council on Sci. and Engring. Tech., 1976-77; chmn Def. Com. research, 1978; mem. space system and tech. adv. com. NASA, 1979—, mem. adv. subcom. for electronics, 1983—, mem. research designee adv. com., 1983—; mem. NRC Office of Sci. and Engring. Personnel Adv. Panel to Assess the Quality of Scientists and Engrs. in Dept. of Def. Labs., 1984—. Recipient Meritorious Civilian Service award U.S. Sec. Def., 1981. Fellow AAAS; mem. Am. Phys. Soc., Ukrainian Am. Engrs. Soc., IEEE, Sigma xi. Office: Inst Sci and Tech U Mich 2200 Bonisteel Blvd Ann Arbor MI 48109*

GANDHI, SHIRISH MANILAL, consulting engineering company executive; b. Jinja, Uganda, Nov. 17, 1931; came to U.S., 1967, naturalized, 1975; s. Manilal Tricumlal and Savitri M. (Shah) G.; m. Judith Aileen Hardy, Jan. 18, 1964; children: Sunita, Rohini, Ranjana, Suschiel. B.E., Poona U., 1956, 1957; M.Sc., London U., 1961. Elec. engr. Central Electricity Generating Bd., London, 1962-67; elec. and mech. engr. Westinghouse Elec. Corp., Pitts., 1967-70; elec. engr. Bechtel Corp., San Francisco, 1970-73, Kaiser Engrs., Oakland, Calif., 1974-75; cons., dir. U. Calif.-Berkeley (Hope Cons. Group), San Francisco, 1977-81; pres. SMG Cons. Engrs., Walnut Creek, Calif., 1975—, also dir.; energy cons. U.S. Air Force; planning design and expert witness large environ. projects; mem. Chem. Engring. Product Research Panel, 1982-83. Author: Digital Computer in Power, 1962. Gen. sec., treas. Assn. Indian Engrs. in U.K., London, 1965-67; organizor ceremonies Boy Scouts Am., Walnut Creek, Calif., 1981-83. Mem. IEEE, Am. Nuclear Soc. (legislative panel 1977-78), Instrument Soc. Am., AAAS, N.Y. Acad. Scis., Fusion Power Assocs., Clubs: Royal Soc. Vis. Scientis (London) (commonwealth rep. 1959-63), Goats Internat. (London) (sr. rep. 1960-67). Current Work: Advancement of design of electrical and mechanical systems and machines with computer automation at frontiers of science and technology for processes in nuclear fission and fusion power programs, reactor development and other process facilities, including use of laser and fiber optics for power and communication purposes. Subspecialties: Electrical engineering; Mechanical engineering. Home: c/o Cons Engs 2595 Chinook Dr Walnut Creek CA 94598 Office: SMG Cons Engrs 2595 Chinook Dr Walnut Creek CA 94598

GANDLER, JOSEPH RUBIN, chemistry educator; b. Bklyn., Dec. 2, 1949; s. Benjamin and Mary (Levine) G.; m. Marlene Ryba, Mar. 24, 1974; 1 child, Rachel Karen. B.S., Bklyn. Coll., 1971; Ph.D., U. Calif.-Santa Cruz, 1978. NIH postdoctoral fellow SUNY-Buffalo, 1978-79, Brandeis U., Waltham, Mass., 1979-81; vis. scientist, summer 1983; asst. prof. chemistry Calif. State U.-Fresno, 1981-83, assoc. prof., 1984—; asst. dir. Central Valley Sci. Fair, 1982—. Contbr. articles to sci. jours. Calif. State U.-Fresno grantee, 1982. Mem. Am. Chem. Soc. (chmn. program com. San Joaquin Valley sect. 1982—, sec.-treas. 1981-82, chmn. 1984—). Current work: Multiple-structure-reactivity effects in alkene forming elimination reactions; acid-base catalysis of organic reactions. Subspecialty: Organic chemistry. Office: Dept Chemistry Calif State U Fresno CA 93740

GANDOLFI, ALLEN JAY, anesthesiology researcher; b. San Mateo, Calif., Dec. 11, 1946; s. Frank Joseph and Lorine (Wittmeier) G.; m. Judith Anne Monks, July 20, 1968; children: Christopher, Matthew, Jason. B.A., U. Calif.-Davis, 1968; Ph.D., Oreg. State U., 1972. USPHS fellow Oreg. State U., 1968-72; Mayo fellow Mayo Clinic, Rochester, Minn., 1972-75; sr. research scientist Battelle Meml. Inst., Richland, Wash., 1975-78; research asst. prof. anesthesiology and pharmacology U. Ariz., 1978—. Mem. Soc. Toxicology, Am. Soc. Pharmacology and Exptl. Therapeutics, Am. Soc. Anesthesiologists. Current Work: Toxicity and disposition of anesthetics, drugs and xenobiotics. Subspecialties: Toxicology (medicine); Anesthesiology. Home: 3231 Camino Suerte Tucson AZ 85715 Office: U Ariz Dept Anesthesiology Tucson AZ 85724

GANDOUR, RICHARD DAVID, bioorganic chemist; b. Sistersville, W.Va., Feb. 12, 1945; s. Jackson Thomas and Mary Frances (Valent) G.; m. Ruth Frances Wells, Dec. 26, 1971 (dec.); 1 child, Rochelle Marie; m. K. Jill Kiecolt, Oct. 12, 1985. B.S., Wheeling Coll., 1967; Ph.D., Rice U., 1972. Teaching assoc. Kans. U., 1971-72, research assoc., 1973-1975; asst. prof. chemistry La. State U., 1975-80, assoc. prof., 1980—. Contbr. articles to profl. jours.; author 2 undergrad. teaching supplements; editor: (with R.L. Schowen) Transition States of Biochemical Processes, 1978. Served with U.S. Army, 1969. Recipient Faculty Service award La. State U., 1979; Petroleum Research Fund grantee, 1976-79; Research Corp. grantee, 1977, 80; Am. Heart Assn.-La. grantee, 1979, 80; Dow Chem. Co. grantee, 1980, 81; Exxon Chem. Co. grantee, 1981, 83-86; Nat. Inst. Gen. Med. Scis. grantee, 1981-84. Mem. Am. Chem. Soc., AAAS. Roman Catholic. Current Work: Design and synthesis of chemical models of enzymatic catalysis; reaction rates, isotope effects and mechanisms of organic reactions; organic crystallography. Subspecialty: Organic chemistry. Home: 4659 Bennett Dr Baton Rouge LA 70808 Office: Dept Chemistry La State U Baton Rouge LA 70803

GANDT, JEROME OTTO, dentist; b. Appleton, Wis., Aug. 28, 1930; s. Otto A. and Hedwig C. (Hoppe) G.; children—Brian, Kathleen, Caroline. B.S. in Med. Sci., Marquette U., 1952, D.D.S., 1955. Pres. Valley Dental Assocs., Ltd., Green Bay, Wis., 1958—, Wilderness Watch, Inc., Green Bay, 1969—, Ultrax, Green Bay, 1980—; v.p., chief exec. officer The Dental Group, Ltd., Green Bay, 1980-83; v.p. Prepaid Profl. Services, Ltd., Green Bay, 1981—, health plan dir., 1981—, cons., 1981—; lectr. in field. Contbr. articles to profl. jours. Mem. adv. council Upper Miss. River Basin Commn., 1970-80. Recipient Environ. award Save Our Sylvania Action Com., 1970. Fellow Acad. Gen. Dentistry, Am. Endodontic Soc.; mem. ADA, Wis. Dental Assn., Chgo. Dental Soc. Club: Sturgeon Bay Yacht (Wis.). Current work: Etiology and diagnosis of periodontal disease; clinical applications of adhesive technology; health care marketing analysis. Subspecialties: Periodontics; Dental materials. Office: Valley Dental Assocs Ltd 1745 Dousman St Green Bay WI 54303

GANESAN, ADAYAPALAM TYAGARAJAN, geneticist, educator, researcher; b. Madras, India, May 15, 1932; s. Adayapalam Vasudeva Tyagarajan and Savitri; m. Ann Katherine Cook, Aug. 3, 1963. B.S., Annamalai U., Madras State, India, 1952, M.A., 1953; Ph.D. (NIH predoctoral fellow, 1959-63), Stanford U., 1963. Research fellow Indian Inst. Sci., Bangalore, 1953-55; research asst. Indian Agrl. Research Inst., New Delhi, 1955-57; research fellow Carlsberg Lab., Copenhagen, Denmark, 1957-59; successively grad. student, research assoc., asst. prof. assoc. prof. Stanford (Calif.) U., 1959-76, prof. genetics, 1977—. Contbr. writings to profl. publs. Charter mem. World Wildlife Fund, U.S.A. Fellow Indian Inst. Sci., 1953-55; Fellow Rask-Orsted Found. of Denmark, 1957-59; research career devel. awardee NIH, 1970-75; recipient Calif. Higher Med. Edn. award Am. Lung Assn., 1975-76; sabbatical yr. dept. biochemistry Oxford (Eng.) U. Mem. AAAS, Am. Soc. Microbiology, Genetics Soc. Am. Current Work: Genetic and biochemical basis of DNA replication and recombination in prokaryotes and eukaryotes. Subspecialties: Biochemistry (biology); Molecular biology. Office: Dept Genetics Stanford Univ Stanford CA 94305

GANGAROS, LOUIS PAUL, SR., dentist, pharmacologist; b. Rochester, N.Y., June 8, 1929; s. Biagio and Carmella (Bellassi) G.; m. Clara Amalfi, Sept. 4, 1950; children: Michael, Louis Paul, Maria, Alyssa. B. A. with high distinction, U. Rochester, 1952, M.S., 1961, Ph.D. in Pharmacology, 1965; D.D.S., U. Buffalo, 1955. Lic. dentist, Ga., N.Y. Pvt. practice dentistry, Rochester, 1958-61; asst. prof. U. Rochester, 1965-68; asso. prof., coordinator pharmacology Med. Coll. Ga., Augusta, 1968-71; prof. oral biology, coordinator pharmacology Med. Coll. Ga. (Sch. Dentistry), 1971—; prof. pharmacology Med. Coll. Ga. (Schs. Medicine and Grad. Studies), 1971—; cons. on iontophoresis ALZA Pharms Inc., Palo Alto, Calif., Motion Control Inc., Salt Lake City, Del Commerce Lab., Farmingdale, N.Y.; grant reviewer NIH, Nat. Inst. Dental Research. Author: (with Ciarlone and Jeske) Pharmacotherapeutics in Dentistry, 1983; also articles, monographs and abstracts.; Reviewer: (with Ciarlone and Jeske) Jour. ADA, 1965—, Jour. Acad. Gen. Dentistry, 1982; Contbg. editor: (with Ciarlone and Jeske) Methods and Findings in Exptl. and Clin. Pharmacology, 1979—. Served to capt. USAF, 1954-58. Recipient C.V. Mosby Co. award, 1955; Nat. Inst. Dental Research grantee, 1966-75, 82-84; also indsl. grantee. Mem. Am. Soc. Pharmacology and Exptl. Therapeutics, Internat. Assn. Dental Research, ADA, Soc. Exptl. Biology and Medicine, Am. Assn. Dental Schs., Am. Coll. Dentists, Am. Assn. Dental Research. Methodist. Current Work: Iontophoresis; application of drugs for treatment of caries, periodontal disease, viral ulcers and other conditions. Subspecialties: Pharmacology; Oral biology. Home: 380 Folkstone Circle Augusta GA 30907 Office: Med Coll Ga Sch Dentistry Dept Oral Biology-Pharmacology Augusta GA 30901-9990

GANGULY, ASHIT KUMAR, chemist, researcher; b. New Delhi, India, Aug. 9, 1934; came to U.S., 1967; s. Apurba Kumar and Protiva (Chatterji) G.; m. Jean Currie, Sept. 10, 1966; 1 child, Nomita. B.S. with honors, U. Delhi, 1953, M.S., 1955, Ph.D., 1958; Ph.D., D.I.C., U. London, 1961. Lectr. Delhi U., 1957-59; 1851 Exhbn. scholar Imerpial Coll., London, 1959-61; scientist Glaxo Research Labs., India, 1962-63, Ciba Research Centre, India, 1963-67; researcher Research Inst. for Medicine and Chemistry, Cambridge, Mass., 1967-68; sr. scientist Schering Corp., N.J., 1968-70, prin. scientist, 1970-71, research fellow, 1971-79, assoc. dir., 1979-82, dir. organic chem. research, 1982-83, dir. organic chem. research and sr. research fellow, v.p., 1983—, fellow, 1985—; adj. prof. chemistry Stevens presdl. Inst. Tech., Hoboken, N.J., 1974—; mem. U.S.A. delegation NSF; lectr. in field. Contbr. articles to profl. jours., chpts. to books. Patentee in field. Recipient Shshadri Meml. award Delhi U., 1982. Fellow Chem. Soc. (London), Am. Chem. Soc., N.Y. Acad. Scis., Am. Soc. Microbiology. Current work: Direct chemical research in three areas; infectious diseases, allergy, inflammation. Subspecialties: Organic chemistry; Drug design. Home: 96 Cooper Ave Upper Montclair NJ 07043 Office: Schering-Plough Corp 60 Orange St Bloomfield NJ 07003

GANGULY, SUNILENDU NARAYAN, cardiologist, educator; b. Calcutta, West Bengal, India, Dec. 27, 1936; came to U.S., 1971; s. Ramesh Chandra and Sailabasini G.; m. Kuniko Tanii, Sept. 24, 1939; children: Joya Anne, Maya Lynne. M.D., Med. Coll., Calcutta, 1960. Intern Hutzel Hosp., Detroit, 1963; resident in medicine Wayne State U., 1964-66, fellow in cardiology, 1966, asst. prof. medicine, 1972-75, assoc. prof., 1975—; fellow in cardiology Vancouver (B.C., Can.) Gen. Hosp.; chief cardiology Hutzel Hosp., 1974—. Fellow A.C.P., Am. Coll. Cardiology, Am. Coll. Angiology; mem. AMA, N.Y. Acad. Sci., Bichitra (pres. 1973), Physicians India (pres. Detroit 1979). Current Work: Cardiovascular hemodynamics; streptoinase therapy and percutaneous transluminal coronary angioplasty in acute myocardial infarction. Subspecialties: Cardiology; Internal medicine. Home: 3630 Estates Dr Troy MI 48084 Office: 4727 Saint Antoine Detroit MI 48201

GANIS, FRANK MICHAEL, biochemistry educator, college official; b. Rochester, N.Y., Nov. 26, 1924; m. Josephine Mary Ferraro, Sept. 17, 1949 (dec. Dec. 1982); children—Michael, Karen. A.B., U. Rochester, 1949, Ph.D. in Biochemistry, 1956. Research asst. U. Rochester, 1950-51, grad. research fellow, research assoc. atomic energy project, 1951-56, pub. health research fellow, 1956-58, instr. biochemistry, 1956-62, radiation biology, 1959-61, asst. prof., 1961-62, chief sect. endocrinology, 1959-62; asst. prof. lab. medicine and biochemistry U. Md. Sch. Medicine, Balt., 1962-68, biochemist, dir. labs., 1962-66, assoc. prof., 1966-71, prof., 1971-73, chmn. dept. biochemistry, 1966-73; assoc. dean scis., prof. U. Hartford, Conn., 1973-75; dean div. health scis. SUNY-Utica, Rome, 1975-76; dean Sch. Nursing and Health Scis., prof., Western Carolina U., Cullowhee, N.C., 1976-78; acad. dean, prof. Ohio Coll. Podiatric Medicine, Cleve., 1978—, v.p. acad. affairs, 1981—. Bd. editors Biochem. Medicine, Jour. Podiatric Med. Edn. Contbr. chpts. to books, articles to profl. jours. Served to col. USAF, 1943-46; col. Res. (ret.). Mem. AAAS, Am. Chem. Soc., Endocrine Soc., Am. Oil Chemists Soc., Am. Assn. Dental Schs., AAUP, Am. Inst. Chemists, N.Y. Acad. Scis., Am. Assn. Univ. Adminstrs., Am. Assn. Colls. Podiatric Medicine (council deans. v.p. 1983-84), Sigma Xi. Current work: Intermediary metabolism of steroids in cancer tissues. Subspecialties: Biochemistry (biology); Endocrinology. Home: 8696 Camelot Dr Chesterland OH 44026 Office: 10515 Carnegie Ave Cleveland OH 44106

GANLEY, MARY CONSTANCE, geologist, researcher, educator; b. Oakland, Calif., Dec. 31, 1956; d. John Joseph and Frances Flora (St. Aubin) G.; m. Stephen James Czekalski, July 14, 1983. B.S., Wright State U., 1979, M.S., 1984. Engring. aide Systems Research Lab., Dayton, Ohio, 1975-80; intelligence research specialist, imagery analyst Fgn. Tech. Div. Dept. Def., Wright Patterson AFB, Ohio, 1981-82; instr. Sinclair Community Coll., Dayton, 1982-84; adj. instr. Wright State U., 1982-84; tutor, Dayton, 1983-84. Wright State U. scholar 1982. Mem. Geol. Soc. Am., Am. Assn. Petroleum Geologists, Sigma Gamma Epsilon (sec. 1977-78). Democrat. Roman Catholic. Current work: Project development; working with environmental engineers, chemical engineers and hydrogeologists in the development of solutions and approaches to environmental remediation and investigative projects. Subspecialties: Geology; Environmental engineering. Home: 511 E Sandusky Findlay OH 45840Office: OH Materials Co State Route 224 East Findlay OH 45840

GANNATAL, JOSEPH PAUL, project engineer and administrator; b. Ventura, Calif., Sept. 9, 1955; s. Paul and Janet Gannatal; m. Sandra Jean Gannatal, Jan. 14, 1950; children—Troy, Jenny, Sarah. B.S., Calif. Poly. Inst., 1976, M.E., 1979; postgrad. U. Santa Barbara, 1984—. Registered profl. engr., Calif. Engr.-in-tng. Naval Missile Ctr., Point Mugu, Calif., 1973-79; mfg. engr. Nat. Semicondr., Santa Clara, Calif., 1979-81; project engr., mgr. Pacific Missile Test Ctr., Point Mugu, 1981—. Contbr. articles to profl. jours. Mem. bldg. com. Camarillo Baptist Ch., Calif., 1984. Mem. ASME, Am. Inst. Aeros. and Astronautics, Planetary Soc. Republican. Current work: Expert in sea shore interfaces of and analyst for in-water cabling networks, also helicopter over-water recovery systems; navy trained aircrew and diver; still and video photographer in air, land and water. Subspecialties: Ocean engineering; Mechanical engineering. Office: Underwater Systems Br Code 3144 Point Mugu CA 93042

GANNON, JOHN EDWARD, limnologist, researcher, educator; b. Detroit, Dec. 23, 1942; s. John Edward and Betty Anne (Winans) G.; m. Susan Ann Chartier, Dec. 19, 1970; children—Aron, Aura, Alene. B.S. in Biology, Wayne State U., 1965; M.S. in Fisheries, U. Mich., 1967; Ph.D. in Zoology, U. Wis.-Milw., 1972. Research scientist, lectr. Biol. Sta., U. Mich.-Pellston, 1972-78; assoc. dir. research ctr. SUNY-Oswego, 1978-83; limnologist Internat. Joint Commn., Windsor, Ont., Can., 1983—; cons. on lake mgmt. to numerous lake property owners' assns., Mich., Pa., N.Y., Fla., 1972—. Contbr. articles to profl. jours. and chpts. to textbooks. Mem. Oswego County Environ. Mmgt. Council, N.Y., 1978-83, acting chmn., 1982-83. Grantee NSF, NOAA, EPA, Nat. Park Service. Mem. Internat. Assn. Great Lakes Research (pres. 1982-83), Am. Soc. Limnology and Oceanography, Am. Fisheries Soc. (cert.), No. Am. Lake Mgmt. Soc., Sigma Xi (sec. local chpt. 1980-82). Current work: Great Lakes water pollution; curriculum development in winter ecology; water quality protection through local community involvement. Subspecialties: Limnology; Ecology (environmental science). Home: 984 Homedale Blvd Windsor ON N8S 2T2 Canada Office: Internat Joint Commn 100 Ouellette Ave 8th Fl Windsor ON N9A 6T3 Canada

GANNON, PATRICK THOMAS, meteorology educator; b. Ft. Bragg, N.C., May 4, 1930; s. Michael Vincent and Mary Lee (Ayers) G.; m. Donna Merle Neilson, Aug. 15, 1953; children: Patrick Thomas, Mary, Jane, Megan, Stephen, Elizabeth, Emily. B.S., U. Fla., 1956; postgrad., Fla. State U., 1956-57, MIT, 1965-67; M.S., U. Chgo., 1961; Ph.D., U. Miami, 1977. Weather officer USAF Air Weather Service (various locations), 1956-72; meteorology researcher NOAA/Environ. Research Labs., Coral Gables, Fla., 1975-80, Boulder, Colo., 1980-81; asst. prof. meteorology Lyndon State Coll., Lyndonville, Vt., 1981—. Served with U.S. Army, 1948-52. Decorated Bronze Star, Purple Heart; NOAA grantee, 1982-83. Mem. Am. Meteorol Soc. (chmn. Miami chpt. 1979-80), Am. Water Resources Assn., Fla. Acad. Scis., Phi Kappa Phi, Epsilon Tau Lambda. Republican. Roman Catholic. Current Work: Numerical modeling of mesoscale processes. Subspecialty: Synoptic meteorology. Office: Dept Meteorology Lyndon State Coll Vail Hill Lyndonville VT 05851

GANS, CARL, zoologist; b. Hamburg, Ger., Sept. 7, 1923; came to U.S., 1939, naturalized, 1945; s. Samuel S. and Else Hubertine (Leeser) G.; m. Kyoko Andow, Nov. 18, 1961. B.M.E., N.Y. U., 1944; M.S., Columbia U., 1950; Ph.D. in Biology, Harvard U., 1957; D.h.c., U. Antwerp, Belgium, 1985. Contract and service engr. Babcock & Wilcox Co., 1947-55; from asst. prof. to prof. biology, chmn. dept. biology State U. N.Y., Buffalo, 1958-71; prof. zoology U. Mich., Ann Arbor, 1971—, chmn. dept., 1971-75; research scientist Mus. Zoology, 1971—; research asso. Carnegie Mus., 1953—, Am. Mus. Natural History, 1958—; sec., bd. dirs. Zool. Soc. Buffalo, 1961-71; med. adv. council Detroit Zool. Park, 1973—; cons. in field, vis. prof. univs. and colls. Author: Biomechanics, 1974, Reptiles of the World, 1975; co-author: Photographic Atlas of Shark Anatomy, 1964; Gen. editor: Biology of the Reptilia, 15 vols., 1969-85; mng. editor: Jour. Morphology, 1968—. Served with AUS, 1944-47. Recipient Gold medal Soc. Royal Zoology, Antwerp, 1985; Guggenheim fellow, 1953, 77; NSF predoctoral fellow, 1956-57; postdoctoral fellow U. Fla., Gainesville, 1957-58; grantee NSF; grantee NIH; grantee others. Fellow N.Y. Zool. Soc., Zool. Soc. London, AAAS, Zool. Soc. India, Acad. Zoology India; mem. Am. Soc. Zoologists (pres. 1977), ASME, Soc. Study Evolution (v.p. 1971), Am. Soc. Ichthyology and Herpetology (gov. 1961, 70, 76, pres. 1979), Am. Inst. Biol. Scis. (gov. bd. 1975-78), Soc. Study Amphibians and Reptiles (pres. 1983), Am. Assn. Anatomists, Soc. Exptl. Biology, Am. Physiol. Soc., Senckenberg. Naturforsch. Gesellschaft (corr.). Current Work: Functional morphology, herpetology, electromyography. Subspecialties: Evolutionary biology; Morphology. Home: 2811 Park Ridge Dr Ann Arbor MI 48103 Office: 2127 Natural Scis Bldg Univ Mich Ann Arbor MI 48109

GANTT, DAVID GRAHAM, dental researcher, physical anthropologist; b. Alliance, Ohio, Sept. 18, 1943; m. Phyllis Arlene Pollard, Aug. 14, 1963; children: David Graham Jr., Tasha, Bryan. B.A., U. Wash., Seattle, 1971; M.A., Washington U., St. Louis, 1976, Ph.D., 1977. Instr., research asst. Washington U., 1974-77; asst. prof. anthropology Fla. State U., Tallahassee, 1977-81; research fellow, adj. asst. prof. U. Ala., Birmingham, 1981—; cons. U. Ala. (Lab. Molecular Biophysics), 1982—; co-dir. electron microscopy core facility U. Ala. (Inst. Dental Research), 1981—. Served with U.S. Army, 1961-64. Alexander von Humboldt-Stiftung Research fellow Frankfurt, Germany, 1979; recipient Young Investigator award Nat. Inst. Dental Research, Washington, 1978; others. Mem. Internat. Assn. for Dental Research, Am. Assn. Phys. Anthropologists, Internat. Primatology Assn. Club: Mid-State Soccer (exec. bd. St. Louis 1982—). Current Work: SEM and X-ray microanalysis of teeth, especially enamel and dentin structures. Evolutionary history of calcified dental tissues in mammals, primates, and cariology. Subspecialties: Cariology; Oral biology. Office: Inst Dental Research Sch Dentistry Univ Alabama Birmingham AL 35294

GARABEDIAN, PAUL ROESEL, mathematics educator, researcher; b. Cin., Aug. 2, 1927. A.B., Brown U., 1946; M.A., Harvard U., 1947; Ph.D. in Math, Harvard U., 1948. NRC fellow, 1948-49; asst. prof. math. U. Calif., 1949-50; from asst. prof to prof. Stanford U., 1950-59; prof. math. N.Y.U., 1959—. Recipient Birkhoff prize, 1983; Sloan fellow, 1960-62; Guggenheim fellow, 1966-67; Sherman Fairchild fellow Calif. Inst. Tech., 1975. Mem. Nat. Acad. Sci., Soc. Indsl. and Applied Math., Am. Math Soc., Am. Acad. Arts and Sci. Subspecialty: Applied mathematics. Office: Courant Inst NYU New York NY 10012

GARBARINI, EDGAR JOSEPH, civil engineer, engineering company executive; b. Jackson, Calif., Aug. 1, 1910; s. Henry Casamero and Elvira (Gardella) G.; m. Lillian Rosemarie Arata, Nov. 14, 1936; children—Paul Henry, Ann Elisabeth. B.S., U. Calif. at Berkeley, 1933. Registered profl. engr., several states. Jr. research engr. U. Cal. at Berkeley, 1933-34, research engr., 1934-38; field engr. W.A. Bechtel & Six Cos. Calif., San Francisco, 1934; civil engr. Calif. Commn., Golden Gate Internat. Expn., 1938-39, Dewell & Earl (cons. engrs.), San Francisco, 1939, Pacific Gas & Electric Co., San Francisco, 1939-40; with Bechtel Group of Cos., San Francisco, 1940—, now sr. exec. cons. Fellow ASCE; mem. Nat. Acad. Engring., Structural Engrs. Assn. No. Calif., Mining and Metall. Soc. Am., Order of Golden Bear, U. Calif. Alumni Assn., Sigma Xi, Tau Beta Pi, Chi Epsilon. Clubs: Family (San Francisco), World Trade (San Francisco), Pacific Union (San Francisco). Current Work: Improving large organizations' ability to produce government and industrial facilities. Subspecialty: Civil engineering. Office: PO Box 3221 San Francisco CA 94119

GARCIA, JULIO M., physician; b. Camaguey, Cuba, Sept. 29, 1937; s. Julio C. and Hortensia C. (Sedeno) G.; m. Marta E. Ismail, May 20, 1962; children: Marta M., Teresita M. B.S., Champagnat Sch., Cuba, 1954; M.D., Havana U., 1963. Intern Riverside Hosp., Newport News, Va., 1969-70; resident in internal medicine Mount Sinai Hosp., Miami Beach, Fla., 1970-72; med. oncology fellow U. Miami, 1972-73, practice medicine, Miami, 1973—; cons. Liga Contra el Cancer, Miami. Chmn. Ballet Concerto, Miami. Mem. Dade County Med. Assn., Fla. Med. Assn., AMA, Am. Soc. Clin. Oncology, Fla. Soc. Clin. Oncology, Am. Cancer Soc. Republican. Roman Catholic. Clubs: Big Five (Miami); Grove Isle (Coconut Grove). Current Work: Five year follow-up in cancer of breast with adjunct chemotherapy. Subspecialties: Chemotherapy; Internal medicine. Office: 3661 S Miami Ave Suite 203 Miami FL 33133

GARCIA, NICHOLAS FLORES, missiles and space company executive; b. Garden City, Kans., Dec. 6, 1931; s. Pedro Flores and Jennie (Hanson) G.; m. Alice Beth Vollenweider, Dec. 18, 1958; children—Dawn, Corinne, Nicholas, Raquel. B.S. in Mech. Engring., San Jose State Coll., 1963; M.S. in Applied Mechanics, U. Santa Clara, 1969. With Lockheed Missiles & Space Co., Sunnyvale, Calif., 1963—, sr. staff engr., to 1983, dept. mgr. advanced space structures, 1983—. Served with USAF, 1951-53. Current work: Development of large deployable space structures and antennas. Subspecialties: Large space structures; Mechanical engineering. Office: Dept 62-43 Lockheed Missiles & Space Co 1111 Lockheed Way Sunyvale CA 94088

GARD, MICHAEL FLOYD, research engineer; b. McPherson, Kans., Nov. 14, 1949; s. Floyd Milton and Dorothy Rosalee (Schulz) G.; m. Vicky Vaughn, Dec. 30, 1972; children—Amanda, Emily. B.S.E.E. magna cum laude, Kans. State U., 1971; M.S.E.E., Washington U., St. Louis, 1972. Test engr. Beech Aircraft, Wichita, Kans., 1972-75; sr. biomed. engr. VA Med. Ctr., St. Louis, 1975-80; mgr. electronics devel. Storz/Surg. Mech. Research, St. Louis, 1980-81; sr. research engr. AMOCO Prodn. Co., Tulsa, 1981-84, ARCO Oil and Gas Co., Plano, Tex., 1984—. Author: EMI Control in Medical Electronics, 1979. Contbr. articles to profl. jours. Patentee in field. Elder, Faith Lutheran Ch., Plano, 1984—. Pub. Health Service fellow, 1971-72; Nat. Elec. Contractors Assn. scholar, 1969-71; J. Seeley Mudd scholar, 1972. Mem. IEEE, Soc. Exploration Geophysists. Current work: Research and development of seismic and downhole logging instruments; digital signal processing; precision analog circuit development. Subspecialties: Electronics; Geophysics. Home: 3008 Oak Grove Plano TX 75074 Office: ARCO Oil and Gas (PAT-736) 2300 W Plano Pkwy Plano TX 75075

GARDIN, JULIUS MARKUS, cardiologist; b. Detroit, Jan. 14, 1949; s. Abram and Fania Toba (Garden) G.; m. Susan Deanne Kelemen, Dec. 19, 1982. B.S. with high distinction, U. Mich., 1968, M.D. cum laude, 1972. Diplomate: Am. Bd. Internal Medicine. Resident in medicine U. Mich., Ann Arbor, 1972-75; fellow in cardiology Georgetown U., Washington, 1975-77; dir. cardiology noninvasive lab., staff cardiologist Lakeside VA Med. Ctr., Chgo., 1977-79; staff cardiologist, asst. prof. Northwestern U. Med. Sch., Chgo., 1977-79; dir. cardiology noninvasive lab. U. Calif.-Irvine Med. Ctr., Orange, 1979-84, assoc. prof., 1984—, acting chief cardiology Long Beach (Calif.) VA Med. Ctr., 1982-84. Co-editor: Textbook of Two-Dimensional Echocardiography, 1983; editor: Update on Cardiovascular Diagnostics, 1982; corr. editor: Archives of Internal Medicine and Chest, 1978-84; contbr. articles to profl. jours. Served to maj. M.C. USAR. Am. Heart Assn. grantee, 1980-82, 83-84. Fellow ACP, Am. Coll. Cardiology, Am. Coll. Chest Physicians, Am. Heart Assn. (council clin. cardiology); mem. U. Mich. Med. Center Alumni Assn. (bd. govs. 1979-81), Internat. Cardiac Doppler Soc. (chmn. Pan-Am. sect. 1984—), Am. Soc. Echocardiography (bd. dirs.), Phi Beta Kappa, Alpha Omega Alpha, Phi Delta Epsilon. Jewish. Current Work: Doppler echocardiography. Subspecialty: Cardiology. Office: U Calif-Irvine Med Center 101 City Dr S Orange CA 92668

GARDIN, T. HERSHEL, epidemiologist, research and evaluation consultant; b. Detroit, July 21, 1947; s. Abraham and Ruth (Miedzwinski) G.; m. Joy Beth Lewis, Oct. 10, 1972; children: Naftali M., Dov E., Miriam S., Yehudis K. B.A., Wayne State U., 1969, M.A., 1971, Ph.D., 1983. Instr. Wayne State U., 1971-75; dir. psychol. services Alexandrine House, Inc., Detroit, 1975-77; planner Wayne County Substance Abuse, Detroit, 1977-79; assoc. MFA and Assocs., Bingham Farms, Mich., 1979-81; sr. research analyst Comprehensive Health Services Detroit, 1981-83, adminstr. research and reporting dept., 1984—, grant investigator, contract reviewer, research cons.; mem., contbr. Tex. Instruments, Inc., Profl. Program Exchange, 1980-83. Contbr. articles to profl. jours., chpts. to books. Mem. Am. Psychol. Assn., Am. Pub. Health Assn., Soc. Psychologists in Substance Abuse Soc., Psychol. Study of Social Issues, Psi Chi. Jewish. Current Work: Health care delivery systems and administration, experimental design and data analysis. Subspecialties: Health services research; Information systems, storage, and retrieval (computer science). Home: 1D Oak Park Oak Park MI Office: Comprehensive Health Services of Detroit 6500 John C Lodge Expressway Detroit MI 48237

GARDNER, CHARLES OLDA, agronomy educator, consultant; b. Tecumseh, Nebr., Mar. 15, 1919; s. Olda Cecil and Frances E (Stover) G.; m. Wanda Marie Steinkamp, June 9, 1947; children: Charles Olda, Lynda, Thomas, Richard. B.Sc. with highest distinction, U. Nebr., 1941, M.S., 1948; M.B.A., Harvard U., 1943; Ph.D., N.C. State U., 1951. Asst. extension agronomist U. Nebr.-Lincoln, 1946-48, assoc. prof. agronomy, 1952-57, prof., 1957-70, Found. prof. (Regents Disting. prof.) agronomy, 1970—; chmn. U. Nebr.-Lincoln Statis. Lab., 1957-68; asst. statistician N.C. State U., 1951-52; vis. prof. genetics U. Wis.-Madison, 1962-63; internat. lectr. and cons. in plant breeding, quantitative genetics and applied stats.; mem. Nat. Plant Genetics Resources Bd., 1975-81; mem. Dept. Agr. Competitive Grants Program Rev. Panel, 1978-80, Nat. Com. to Develop Title XII Internat. Maize Planning Grant Proposal, 1978-80, Nat. Corn Research Coordinating Com., 1980-82. Contbr. chpts., numerous articles to profl. publs.; assoc. editor: Crop Sci, 1964-66, Agronomy Jour, 1971-73; mem. adv. bd.: Egyptian Jour. Genetics and Cytology, from 1976, Brazilian Jour. Genetics, from 1978, Agricultural Handbook, Plant Sci. Series, from 1977. Elder, local ch. Served to capt. Q.M.C. U.S. Army, 1943-46, New Guinea, Philippines. Recipient award for outstanding research and creative activity U. Nebr., 1981. Fellow Am. Soc. Agronomy (editorial bd. 1970-73, bd. dirs. 1973-76, 81-83, chmn. bd. dirs. 1982, mem. exec. com. 1973-76, 81-83, chmn. exec. com. 1982, pres. 1982), AAAS; mem. Crop Sci. Soc. Am. (editorial bd. 1963-66, mem. exec. com. 1973-76, chmn. exec. com. 1975, bd. dirs. 1973-76, chmn. bd. dirs. 1975, pres. 1975, Crop Sci. award 1978), Biometric Soc., Genetic Soc. Am., Am. Genetic Assn., Sigma Xi, Gamma Sigma Delta (Internat. award 1977), Phi Kappa Phi. Independent Republican. Presbyterian. Current Work: Plant quantitative genetics; plant breeding systems; population improvement methods; germplasm collection, maintenance and utilization; isoenzyme studies in maize populations; corn and sorghum breeding. Subspecialties: Plant genetics; Plant breeding. Office: Dept Agronomy U Nebr Lincoln NE 68583

GARDNER, ELDON JOHN, genetics educator; b. Logan, Utah, June 5, 1909; s. John and Cynthia Evelyn (Hill) G.; m. Helen Richards, Aug. 21, 1939; children: Patricia Mahrt, Donald E., Betty Morrison, Cynthia Pulley, Alice, Mary Jane Neville. B.S., Utah State U., 1934, M.S., 1935, D.Sc. (hon.), 1980; Ph.D., U. Calif.-Berkeley, 1939. Instr., dean Salinas (Calif.) Jr. Coll., 1939-46; faculty U. Utah, Salt Lake City, 1946-49; faculty Utah State U., 1949-74, research prof. emeritus, 1974—; dean Utah State U. (Coll. Sci.), 1962-67, Utah State U. (Grad. Sch.), 1967-74; research prof. Coll. Medicine, U. Utah, Salt Lake City, 1977-80; cons. in field; dir. Utah Div. Am. Cancer Soc., 1981-82. Author: Principles of Genetics, 7th edit, 1984, History of Biology, 3rd edit, 1972, Genetics Laboratory Investigations, 8th edit, 1985; contbr. articles to profl. jours. Mem. Logan City Sch. Bd., 1962-64. Recipient Disting. Service award Utah Acad. Sci., Arts and Letters, 1957; Willard Gardner Sci. award, 1975; Sci. Achievement award Brigham Young U., 1979. Mem. Genetics Soc. Am., Am. Soc. Human Genetics, Am. Soc. Naturalists, Am. Inst. Biol. Scis., AAAS, Sigma Xi, Phi Kappa Phi. Lodge: Rotary. Current Work: Mechanism, prevention and cure of hereditary precancers; Gardner syndrome. Subspecialties: Genetics and genetic engineering (biology); Cell and tissue culture. Home: 369 N 5th E St Logan UT 84321 Office: Utah State Univ 137 NRB Bldg Logan UT 84322

GARDNER, JILL CHRISTOPHER, neuroscientist, researcher; b. Winchester, Mass., Dec. 23, 1948; d. Wallace Joseph Gardner and Lyna (Christopher) Gardner Mueller. B.Sc., Dalhousie U., 1975, M.A., 1977, Ph.D., 1981. Research assoc. Dalhousie U., Halifax, N.S., Can., 1981-82; fellow Research Lab. of Electronics, MIT, Cambridge, 1982—; pres. Kaleidoscope Project, Ltd., Cambridge, 1982—. Author sci. papers and book chpts.; composer mus. compositions. Active various presdl. campaigns; mem. staff Nat. Earth Day Com., Washington, 1969. Natural Scis. and Engring. Council Can. fellow, 1983-84. Mem. Soc. Physics Students, Soc. Neurosci., Assn. Research in Vision and Ophthalmology, Internat. Brain Research Orgn., World Fedn. Neuroscientists. Current work: Electrophysiology of neurons in visual cortex mediating sensations of stereoscopic depth; organization of perceptual systems in brain. Subspecialties: Neurophysiology; Neuropsychology. Home: 1791 Massachusetts Ave Cambridge MA 02140 Office: MIT Bldg 36-873 Cambridge MA 02139

GARDNER, JOHN WILLARD, physician, medical educator; b. Boston, May 10, 1948; s. John Hale and Olga Helen (Dotson) G.; m. Kathryn Joyce Burton, Dec. 17, 1971; children: Lisa Kathryn, Kirsten Marie, John Burton, Michael Grant, Andrea Diane. B.A., Brigham Young U., 1972, M.S., 1973; M.D., U. Utah, 1976; M.P.H., Harvard U., 1979, D.P.H., 1981. Diplomate: Nat. Bd. Med. Examiners, Am. Bd. Preventive Medicine. Intern U. Ariz. Affiliated Hosps., Tucson, 1976-77, resident in pediatrics, 1977-78; asst. prof. family and community medicine U. Utah, 1980-84, adj. asst. prof. pediatrics, 1981-84; assoc. prof. preventive medicine and biometrics Uniformed Services U. Health Scis., Bethesda, Md., 1984—, also asst. prof. pediatrics, 1984—. Served to maj. MC USAR, 1978—. Bd. dirs. Utah div. Am. Cancer Soc., 1981-84. Am. Cancer Soc. Research grantee, 1981; Nat. Cancer Inst. Research grantee, 1982. Republican. Mormon. Current Work: Research and teaching in the causes of cancer, chronic disease, and maternal and childhood diseases; methodology for epidemiologic studies in human populations. Subspecialties: Epidemiology; Preventive medicine. Home: 700 Fordham St Rockville MD 20850 Office: Dept Preventive Medicine and Biometrics Uniformed Services U Health Scis 4301 Jones Bridge Rd Bethesda MD 20814

GARDNER, MARJORIE HYER, science educator, administrator; b. Logan, Utah, Apr. 25, 1923; d. Saul Edward and Gladys (Christenson) Hyer. B.S., Utah State U., 1947, Ed.D. (hon.), 1975; M.A., Ohio State U., 1958, Ph.D., 1960; cert. ednl. mgmt., Harvard U., 1975. Asst. exec. sec. Nat. Sci. Tchrs. Assn., Washington, 1961-64; asst. prof. to prof. chemistry U. Md., after 1964; Fulbright prof. Australian Nat. Commn., Sydney, Canberra, 1973-74, Nigerian Nat. Commn., Port Harcourt, 1982-83; UNESCO cons. UNESCO, France, China, Thailand, Qatar, 1976—; dir. Lawrence Hall of Sci., U. Calif.-Berkeley, 1984—; dir. SERI div. NSF, Washington, 1979-81. Author: Chemistry in Space Age, 1965; dir.: monograph series Vistas of Science, 1963; texts and tchrs.' guides Interdisciplinary Approaches to chemistry, 1973-79. Recipient O'Haus award Nat. Sci. Tchrs. Assn., 1972, Carleton award, 1974; Catalyst award Chem Mfrs. Assn., 1982. Fellow AAAS (sect. chairperson 1975-78, mem. council 1980-83), Am. Inst. Chemists; mem. Am. Chem. Soc. (Western Conn. Vis. Scientist award 1972, div. chairperson 1982-85), Fulbright Assn. Alumni (dir. 1972-86, pres. 1980-81), Internat. Union Pure and Applied Chemistry (exec. b. com. teaching 1982—), Internat. Orgn. for Chem. Scis. in Devel. (edn., bd. 1982—), Kappa Delta (pres. 1946-47, province officer 1948-52). Current Work: Science education, a rapidly developing research area; curriculum development; learning theory; assessment. Subspecialties: Chemical education; Learning. Office: Lawrence Hall of Sci U Calif Berkeley CA 94720

GARDNER, MICHAEL PATRICK, chemist; b. Chgo., Aug. 29, 1938; s. Joseph Patrick and Dorothy Henrietta (Flory) G.; m. Lynda Lee Martin; 1 child, Thomas Michael. B.S., San Jose State U., 1965; M.S., Calif. State U.-Long Beach, 1970; Ph.D., UCLA, 1975. Analytical staff Shell Chem. Corp., Denver, 1965-66; mem. profl. staff TRW Systems Inc., Redondo Beach, Calif., 1966-75, mgr. phys. chemistry, 1976-81, asst. mgr. chemistry lab., 1982—; mem. adv. council Calif. State U.-Long Beach, 1983—. Contbr. articles to profl. jours. Served with USAF, 1956-60. TRW fellow, 1973; recipient Manned Spaceflight Awareness award NASA, 1970. Mem. Am. Chem. Soc. (chmn. fin. 1982-83, exec. com. 1984—), Planatory Soc. Club: Blizzard Youth Ski (Los Angeles) Bd. dirs. 1981—). Current work: Heterogeneous reaction kinetics; kinetics and mechanisms of gas and solid; gas liquid reaction in both catalyzed and uncatalyzed systems; emphasis on highly reactive solids and molten metallic surfaces. Subspecialties: Kinetics; Physical chemistry. Office: TRW Systems Inc 1 Space Park 01/2030 Redondo Beach CA 90278

GARFIELD, ALAN J., computer graphics and animation educator; b. Utica, N.Y., Jan. 17, 1950; s. Robert and Charlotte Hirsch G.; m. Phyllis H. Rafferty, Sept. 2, 1979; children—Eliot, Meg. B.A., U. Iowa-Iowa City, 1971; M.A., SUNY-Binghamton, 1974. Technician Univ. Art Gallery, SUNY-Binghamton, 1972-74; instr. art Converse Coll., Spartanburg, S.C., 1974-76; asst. prof. art S.W. Mo. State U., Springfield, 1976-77; asst. prof. art dept. Creighton U., Omaha, 1977-79; dir. Krasl Art Center, St. Joseph, Mich., 1979-80; chmn. art and computer graphics Marycrest Coll., Davenport, Iowa, 1980—; cons. Consortium Ind. Colls., Washington; pres. Digi Graphic Systems, Davenport, Iowa. lectr. in field. Author: Drawings by Isabel Bishop, 1976, Pastels by Pierre Prins, 1976, Alexander Beary Gavalas, 1982, The Aquarian Conspiracy: An Under-graduate Computer Graphics Curriculum, 1984. Mem. Spl. Interest Group in Graphics, Assn. Computing Machinery, Nat. Computer Graphics Assn., Spl. Interest Group in Personal Computers, Coll. Art Assn., Am. Assn. Museums. Jewish. Current Work: Interactive computer graphic software; visible line algorithms. Subspecialties: Graphics, image processing, and pattern recognition; Programming languages. Home: 34 Oak Ln Davenport IA 52804 Office: Computer Graphics Marycrest Coll 1607 W 12th St Davenport IA 52804

GARFIELD, EUGENE, information science educator; b. N.Y.C., Sept. 16, 1925; s. Ernest and Edith (Wolf) Garofano; m. Faye Byron, 1945 (div.); 1 son, Stefan; m. Winifred Koziolek, 1955 (div.); children: Laura, Joshua, Thea; m. Catheryne Stout, 1983; 1 child, Alexander Merton. B.S., Columbia U., 1949, M.S., 1954; Ph.D., U. Pa., 1961. Research chemist Evans Research & Devel. Corp., 1949-50; research chemist Columbia U., N.Y.C., 1950-51; mem. staff machine index project Johns Hopkins U., Balt., 1951-53; pres. Eugene Garfield Assocs., Phila., 1954-60; pres., founder Inst. Sci. Info., Phila., 1960—; weekly columnist Current Comments in Current Contents, 1956—; adj. prof. info. sci. U. Pa., Phila., 1974—. Author: Essays of an Information Scientist, 7 vols., 1977 (Book of Yr., Am. Soc. Info. Sci.), Citation Indexing: Its Theory and Application to Science, Technology and Humanities, 1979; editor-in-chief: Scientometrics; mem. editorial bd.: Jour. of Info. Sci.; bd. dirs. Ann. Revs.; contbr. articles to profl. jours. Served with AUS, 1943-45. Recipient John Price Wetherill medal Franklin Inst., Phila., 1984, Derek de Solla Price Meml. medal 1984. First Grolier Soc. fellow, 1953-54. Fellow AAAS (chmn. sect. T), Inst. Info. Scientists London; mem. Nat. Assn. Sci. Writers, Chem. Notation Assn. (award 1980), Soc. Scholarly Pub., IEEE (sr.), Info. Industry Assn. (corp. mem., past chmn. bd., past pres., Hall of Fame award), Spl. Libraries Assn., ACM, Authors League Am., Med. Library Assn., Am. Soc. Info. Sci. (award of merit 1975, past pres. Delaware Valley chpt.), Am. Chem. Soc. (Herman Skolnik award div. chem. info. 1977, Patterson-Crane award 1983), Drug. Info. Assn., Fedn. Am. Scientists. Developer Sci. Citation Index, 1961—, Index Chemicus, 1960—; developer sci. info. service; patentee in field. . Office: ISI 3501 Market St University City Sci Ctr Philadelphia PA 19104

GARFINKEL, DAVID, biophysicist; b. N.Y.C., May 18, 1930; s. Louis and Leah (Markosfeldt) G.; m. Lillian Magid, June 26, 1960; children: Susan Laura, Beth Diane. A.B., U. Calif.-Berkeley, 1951; Ph.D., Harvard U., 1955; M.A. (hon.), U. Pa., 1972. Postdoctoral fellow in biophysics U. Pa., Phila., 1955-58, research assoc., 1961-63, asst. prof., 1963-65, assoc. prof. biophysics, 1965-72, assoc. prof. computer sci., 1972-77, prof. computer sci., 1977—; research biochemist N.Y. State Psychiat. Inst., Columbia U., N.Y.C., 1958-60. Mem. editorial bds.: Computers and Biomed. Research, Jour. Theoretical Biology, Am. Jour. Physiology; Contbr. articles to profl. jours. NIH research grantee, 1961—. Fellow IEEE; mem. Soc. Computer Simulation (sr.), Biomed. Engring. Soc. (bd. dirs. 1982—), Am. Soc. Biol. Chemists, Am. Physio. Soc. Current Work: Computer simulation of biological systems and related biological computing. Subspecialties: Biomedical engineering; Biochemistry (medicine). Office: Moore Sch Elec Engring Univ Pennsylvania Philadelphia PA 19104

GARFINKLE, BARRY DAVID, pharmaceutical company executive; b. Newark, Oct. 3, 1946; s. Philip and Adella (Rauchwager) G.; m. Sherry Ellen Frank, Aug. 11, 1968; children: Jack, Stacey. B.S. in Bacteriology, Kans. State U., 1968; M.S. (NSF fellow), Pa. State U., 1970, Ph.D. (NSF fellow), 1972. Postdoctoral fellow Roche Inst. Molecular Biology, Nutley, N.J., 1972-74; sr. project microbiologist Merck Sharp & Dohme, West Point, Pa., 1975-77, mgr. biol. quality control tech. services, 1977-81, mgr. process validation, 1981-83, mgr. quality control pharm. prodn., 1983-85, mgr. sterile process project engring., 1985—; tchr. course on process validation. Contbr. articles to profl. jours. NIH fellow, summer 1971. Mem. Am. Soc. Microbiology, Parenteral Drug Assn. Jewish. Current Work: Sterilization validation and process development for sterile pharmaceuticals and biologicals. Subspecialties: Microbiology; Virology (biology). Home: 1274 Georgia Ln Hatfield PA 19440 Office: Merck Sharp & Dohme Sumneytown Pike Bldg 29-M West Point PA 19486

GARG, DEVENDRA PRAKASH, mech. engr., educator; b. Roorkee, India, Mar. 22, 1934; came to U.S., 1965; s. Chandra Gopal and Godawari (Devi) G.; m. Prabha Govil, Nov. 19, 1961; children—Nisha, Seema. B.Sc., Agra (India) U., 1954; B.S. in Mech. Engring, U. Roorkee, 1957; M.S. (Tech. Coop. Mission Merit scholar), U. Wis.-Madison, 1960; Ph.D., N.Y. U., 1969. Lectr. mech. engring. U. Roorkee, 1957-62, reader, 1962-65, vis. prof., 1978; instr. N.Y. U., 1965-69; asst. prof. Mass. Inst. Tech., 1969-71, asso. prof., 1971-72, chmn. engring. projects lab., 1971-72, lectr., 1972-75; prof. Duke U., 1972—, dir. undergrad. studies dept. mech. engring. and materials sci., 1977—; cons. in field. Author: An Introduction to the Theory and Use of the Analog Computer, 1963, A Textbook of Descriptive Geometry, 1964; asso. editor: Jour. Interdisciplinary Modeling and Simulation, 1978—; contbr. numerous articles to profl. jours. Recipient Founder's Day award N.Y. U., 1969. Mem. IEEE (reviewer), Instrument Soc. Am. (reviewer), ASME (reviewer, co-guest editor spl. issues on ground transp. 1974, also socioecon. and ecol. systems 1976, sec. dynamic systems and control div. 1980—), Sigma Xi (sec. chpt. 1970-72). Current Work: Technological forecasting and assessment; advanced transportation systems; analysis and design of linear and nonlinear feedback control systems. Subspecialties: Mechanical engineering; Systems engineering. Home: 2815 DeKalb St Durham NC 27705 Office: Sch Engring Duke Univ Durham NC 27706

GARG, DIWAKAR, chemical engineer, researcher; b. Kanpur, India; Sept. 11, 1952; came to U.S., 1974, naturalized, 1981; s. Amrit Lal and Pushp Mala Garg. B.S. in Chem. Engring., H.B. Tech. Inst., India, 1974; M.S., Okla. State U., 1975; Ph.D., Auburn U., 1979. Sr. research engr. Air Products, Allentown, Pa., 1979-82, prin. research engr., 1982-85, sr. prin. research engr., 1985—. Contbr. articles to profl. jours. Patentee in field. Mem. Am. Inst. Chem. Engrs., Am. Chem. Soc. Lodge: Lions. Current work: Creative work in upgrading of coal products and heavy oils hydroconversion; coal liquefaction. Subspecialty: Coal. Home: 2815 Whitemarsh Pl Macungie PA 18062 Office: Air Products & Chems PO Box 538 Allentown PA 18105

GARG, LAL CHAND, pharmacology educator; b. India, Jan. 22, 1933; s. Amar Nath and Kalawati (Jindal) G.; m. Shakuntala Goyal, Jan. 1, 1940; children: Arun, Lovey. B.S., Panjab U., 1954, M.S., 1956; Ph.D., U. Fla., 1969. Instr. Vet. Coll., Mhow, India, 1956-61, asst. prof., 1961-63; asst. prof. pharmacy Panjab U., 1963-65; grad. asst. U. Fla., Gainesville, 1965-69, instr., 1969-71, asst. prof., 1971-76, assoc. prof., 1976—. Mem. Am. Soc. Pharmacology and Exptl. Therapeutics, Am. Soc. Nephrology, Internat. Soc. Nephrology, N.Y. Acad. Scis., Sigma Xi. Current Work: Electrolyte transport, acid-base balance, hormonal regulation of transport enzymes. Subspecialties: Pharmacology; Renal pharmacology. Office: Box J-267 JHMHC Gainesville FL 32610

GARING, JOHN SEYMOUR, physicist, research executive; b. Toledo, Ohio, Nov. 6, 1930; s. Harry Raymond and Catherine Marie (Gomer) G.; m. Ione Davis, Apr. 26, 1952; children: John Davis, Susan Carolyn. B.S. summa cum laude, Ohio State U., 1951, M.S., 1954, Ph.D. in Physics, 1958. Physicist Air Force Geophysics Lab., Hanscom AFB, Mass., 1958-61, chief infared physics br., 1961-63, dir. optical physics div., 1973—. Contbr. articles to profl. jours. Served to 1st lt. USAF, 1954-57. Fellow Optical Soc. Am., AAAS; mem. AIAA, Sigma Xi, Phi Beta Kappa, Phi Eta Sigma, Pi Mu Epsilon. Current Work: Infrared physics, molecular spectroscopy, atmospheric optics and transmission, research management. Subspecialties: Atomic and molecular physics; Infrared spectroscopy. Home: 157 Cedar St Lexington MA 02173 Office: Air Force Geophysics Lab Hanscom AFB MA 01731

GARLAND, BERNARD WILLIAM, environment specialist; b. Atlanta, Aug. 6, 1950; s. Bernard O. and Martha (Klinger) G.; m. Antoinette Patricia, Keeth, Aug. 22, 1970; 1 child, Jonathan. B.S., La. Tech. U., 1972, M.S., 1974. Cert. wildlife biologist. Wildlife biologist Weyerhaeuser Co., Hot Springs, Ark., 1974-75; project biologist Dames & Moore, Cranford, N.J., 1975-81; sr. biologist Rogers, Golden & Halpern, Phila., 1981-84; environ. specialist U.S. Army, Ft. McClellan, Ala., 1984—. Contbr. articles to profl. jours. Environ. commr. Evesham Twp., N.J., 1983-84. Mem. Wildlife Soc., Soc. for Range Mgmt., Ecol. Soc. Am. Lutheran. Current work: Management responsibilities on U.S. government land involving environmental regulation, resource management and biological studies. Subspecialty: Resource management. Office: US Army ATZN-FEE Fort McClellan AL 36205

GARLAND, HOWARD, psychologist, educator; b. Bklyn., June 22, 1946; s. Murray and Norma (Luft) Garlitsky; m. Eileen Mary Cohen, Aug. 21, 1968; children: Eric Lee, Adam Marc. B.A., Bklyn. Coll., 1968; M.S., Cornell U., 1971, Ph.D., 1972. Asst. prof. psychology Upsala Coll., East Orange, N.J., 1972-74; asst. prof. psychology and mgmt. U. Tex., Arlington, 1974-75, assoc. prof. psychology and mgmt., 1976-78, prof. psychology and mgmt., 1979—. Mem. editorial bd.: Group and Orgn. Studies; contbr. articles to profl. jours. Army Research Inst. grantee, 1978-80. Mem. Am. Psychol. Assn., Soc. for Personality and Social Psychology, Soc. of Indsl. and Organizational Psychology, Soc. for Advancement of Social Psychology. Current Work: Work in the area of goals levels and task performance. In particular, research centers on looking at the facilitative effects of impossible goals on performance. Subspecialties: Organizational psychology; Social psychology. Home: 4706 Basswood Ct Arlington TX 76016 Office: Univ Texas Dept Mgmt Box 19467 Arlington TX 76010

GARLAND, JAMES C., physics educator, university research laboratory administrator; b. Columbia, Mo., Aug. 11, 1942; 2 children. A.B., Princeton U., 1964; Ph.D. in Physics, Cornell U., 1969. NSF fellow in physics Cambridge (Eng.) U., 1969-70; asst. prof. Ohio State U., 1970-75, assoc. prof. physics, 1975-80, prof. physics, 1980—, now dir. materials research lab. Mem. Am. Phys. Soc. Subspecialties: Low temperature physics; Condensed matter physics. Office: Dept Physics Smith Lab Ohio State U Columbus OH 43210*

GARLID, KERMIT LEROY, engineering educator, university administrator; b. Ellsworth, Wis., May 10, 1929; s. Emil Peter and Inga Ovidia (Knutson) G.; m. Barbara Joyce Cunningham, Sept. 18, 1954; children—Peter, Jeffrey, Jonathan, Steven. B.S., U. Wis.-River Falls, 1950. B. Chem. Engring., U. Minn., 1956, Ph.D., 1961. From asst. prof. to assoc. prof. engring. U. Wash., Seattle, 1960-71, prof. nuclear and chem. engring., 1971—, acting dean engring., 1980-81, vice provost, 1982—; cons., Battelle NW Lab., Richland, Wash., 1965-78, Nuclear Regulatory Commn., Washington, 1971-84, Math. Scis., Inc., Seattle, 1973-78. Contbr. articles, book revs. to profl. jours. Served with U.S. Army, 1951-53. NSF grantee, 1970-73. Mem. Am. Nuclear Soc., Am. Inst. Chem. Engrs., AAAS. Current work: University administration; nuclear fission fuel cycles. Subspecialties: Nuclear fission; Chemical engineering. Home: 2829 10th Ave E Seattle WA 98102 Office: U Wash AH-20 Seattle WA 98195

GARMAN, PHYLLIS METROLIS, geologist; b. Rockville, Md., Sept. 10, 1939; s. George Joseph and Mildred Evelyn (Woods) Metrolis; m. Roy Keith Garman, Sept. 2, 1961 (div. Feb. 1975); children—Keith Michael, Karen Lee, Mark Andrew. A.A., Palm Beach Jr. Coll., 1959; B.S., Fla. State U., 1962; M.S. U. Va., 1981. Registered profl. environmentalist, Tenn.; cert. profl. geologist. Geologist, Tenn. Div. Geology, Nashville, 1970-76, Tenn. Solid Waste Mgmt., 1976-84; geologist, hydrogeologist Garman Geologic Cons., Joelton, Tenn., 1984—; coordinator, chmn. Tenn. Groundwater Protection Task Force, Nashville, 1981-82. Mem. Geol. Soc. Am. (sec. treas. hydrogeology div. 1983—), Am. Inst. Profl. Geologists (pres. Tenn. sect. 1984), chmn. nat. membership com. 1985), Nat. Water Well Assn. (adv. com. for hydrogeologic settings 1984-85), Sigma Xi. Current work: Hydrogeologic investigations of waste disposal sites; ground water contamination and monitoring studies; hazardous waste reduction and management. Subspecialties: Geology; Hydrogeology. Home: 7570 Bidwell Rd Joelton TN 37080 Office: Garman Geologic Cons 7570 Bidwell Rd Joelton TN 37080

GARMIRE, GORDON PAUL, astronomer, educator; b. Portland, Oreg., Oct. 3, 1937; s. Paul W. and Ethel V. (Alsen) G.; m. Audrey B. Cook, Feb. 14, 1976; children: Geoffrey, Lisa, Marla, Chris, Rosemary, David. A.B. cum laude, Harvard U., 1959; Ph.D., M.I.T., 1962. Staff M.I.T., Cambridge, 1962-64, asst., then assoc. prof., 1964-68; sr. research fellow Calif. Inst. Tech., 1966-68, assoc. prof., 1968-72, prof. physics, 1972-81; prof. astronomy Pa. State U., State College, 1980—, Evan Pugh prof. astronomy, 1985—; cons. TRW, Los Alamos Lab., NASA. Sr Hays Fulbright fellow, 1973-74; Guggenheim fellow, 1973-74; NASA Exceptional Sci. Achievement awardee, 1978. Mem. Am. Astron. Soc. (chmn. high energy astrophysics div. 1985), Internat. Astron. Union, Sigma Xi. Co-discoverer cosmic high energy Gamma radiation; pioneer 1st diamond turned x-ray telescope; co-prin. investigator high energy astron. obs.; pioneer 1st all-sky soft x-ray survey. Current Work: Supernova remnants, hot interstellar medium, x-ray sources, radiation detectors, x-ray telescopes. Subspecialties: X-ray high energy astrophysics; High energy astrophysics. Home: Route 2 Box 256 Huntingdon PA 16652 Office: 504 Davey Lab University Park PA 16802

GARNEAU, MARC, astronaut; b. Que. Can., Feb. 23, 1949; s. Andre and Jean (Richardson) G.; m. Jacqueline Brown, Oct. 6, 1973; children—Yves, Simone. B.Eng., Royal Mil. Coll., Kingston, Ont., 1970; Ph.D., Imperial Coll.-London, Eng., 1973; Hon. Dr.Engring., Tech. U. N.S., 1985, Royal Mil. Coll., 1985; Sc.D., Laval U., 1985. Combat Systems engr. HMCS Algonquin, Halifax, N.S., 1974-76; weapons instr. Fleet Sch., Halifax, 1976-77; weapons project engr. Nat. Def. Hdqrs., Ottawa, Ont., 1977-80; maint. and trials officer Naval Engring. Unit, Halifax, 1980-82; sect. head Communications and Electronic Warfare, Ottawa, Ont., 1983-84; astronaut Nat. Research Council Can., Ottawa, 1984—. Served to comdr. Can. Navy, 1965—. Athlone scholar, 1970-72; NRC Bursary, 1973; NASA Space Flight medal, 1984; Order of Can., 1985. Current work: Canadian manned involvement in space. Subspecialties: Aerospace engineering and technology; Astronautics. Home: 720 Lonsdale Ottawa ON K1K 0K2 Canada Office: Nat Research Council Montreal Rd Ottawa ON K1A 0R6 Canada

GARNER, LAFORREST DEAN, orthodontist, educator; b. Muskogee, Okla., Aug. 20, 1933; s. Sanford and Fannie (Thompson) G.; m. Alfreida Thomas, July 18, 1964; children: Deana Yvette, Thomas LaForrest, Sanford Ernest. D.D.S., Ind. U.-Indpls., 1957, M.S., 1959. Diplomate: Am. Bd. Orthodontists. Program chmn. craniofacial biology sect. Internat. Assn. Dental Research, Washington, 1982— pres. craniofacial bilogy sect., 1984-85; chmn. dept. orthodontics Ind. U. Sch. Dentistry, Indpls., 1969—. Contbr. articles to sci. jours., chpts. to books. Bd. dirs. Ind. Boys Clubs, 1975—, Park-Tudor Sch., Indpls., 1978—, Ind. Health Careers, 1974—, Vis. Nurses Assn., 1973-76. Fellow Am. Coll. Dentists; mem. Am. Assn. Orthodontists, Edward H. Angle Soc. Orthodontists, Internat. Assn. Dental Research, Am. Cleft Palate Assn. (bd. dirs. 1974-78), Ind. Dental Assn., Ind. Soc. Orthodontists (pres. 1972-73), Omicron Kappa Upsilon. Democrat. Presbyterian. Club: Boule (Indpls.). Current Work: Cleft lip and palate rehabilitation, growth and development, mechanotherapy and instrumentation for delivery of services, student direction in growth and development. Subspecialties: Orthodontics; Dental growth and development. Home: 6245 Riverview Dr Indianapolis IN 46260 Office: Indiana University School of Dentistry 1121 W Michigan St Indianapolis IN 46202

GARNER, WENDELL RICHARD, psychology educator; b. Buffalo, Jan. 21, 1921; s. Richard Charles and Lena Belle (Cole) G.; m. Barbara Chipman Ward, Feb. 18, 1944; children: Deborah Ann, Peter Ward, Elinor. A.B., Franklin and Marshall Coll., 1942, D.Sc., 1979; A.M., Harvard U., 1943, Ph.D., 1946; M.A. (hon.), Yale U., 1967; D.H.L., Johns Hopkins U., 1983. Teaching fellow Harvard U., 1942-43, research assoc., 1943-46; instr. Johns Hopkins U., 1946; asst. prof. Johns Hopkins, 1947-51; assoc. prof. Johns Hopkins U., 1951-55, prof., 1955-67; dir. Psychol. Lab. Inst. Coop. Research, 1949-55, chmn. dept. psychology, 1954-64; James Rowland Angell prof. psychology Yale U., 1967—, dir. social scis., 1972-73, 81—, chmn. dept. psychology, 1974-77; dean Yale U. (Grad. Sch.), 1978-79; Paul M. Fitts Meml. lectr. U. Mich., 1973. Author: Uncertainty and Structure as Psychological Concepts, 1962, Processing of Information and Structure, 1974; editor: Ability Testing, 1982. Recipient alumni citation and award Franklin and Marshall Coll., 1975, Wilbur Cross medal Yale U., 1980. Fellow Am. Psychol. Assn. (Distinguished Sci. Contbn. award 1964, pres. div. exptl. psychology 1974), AAAS (v.p. psychology 1967), Acoustical Soc. Am.; mem. Soc. Exptl. Psychologists (chmn. 1959, 75, Warren medal 1976), AAUP, Md. Psychol. Assn. (pres. 1961-62), Eastern Psychol. Assn., Nat. Acad. Scis., Sigma Xi. Current Work: Visual information processing, especially perceptual structure and dimensional interactions of stimuli. Subspecialties: Cognition; Psychophysics. Home: 48 Yowago Ave Branford CT 06405 Office: Yale U New Haven CT 06520

GARNETT, ROBERT WILLIAM, physicist, electrical-optical engineer; b. Landstuhl, W.Ger., Nov. 23, 1957; s. Robert Allen and Luise G.; m. Anne Elise Blackstock, Sept. 30, 1983. B.S. in Physics, U. Calif.-Santa Barbara, 1980; M.S. in Physics, N.Mex. State U., 1983. Lab. asst. dept. physics U. Calif.-Santa Barbara, 1978-80; teaching asst. dept. physics N.Mex. State U., Las Cruces, 1981-82; research asst. Los Alamos Nat. Lab. (N.Mex.), 1982-84; software quality engr. Martin Marietta Corp., Vandenberg AFB, Calif., 1984; staff physicist aerophysics dept.-DELCO, Goleta, Calif., 1984-85; faculty N.Mex. State U., Las Cruces, 1985—. Contbr. articles to sci. jours. Mem. Am. Phys.

Soc., Sigma Pi Sigma. Current work: Infrared radiometry and spectroscopy of fast transient phenomena, numerical solution of Klein-Gordon Equation for quark confining potentials. Subspecialty: Nuclear physics. Office: Dept Physics New Mexico State U PO Box 3D Las Cruces NM 88003

GARON, CLAUDE FRANCIS, research scientist, electron microcopy researcher; b. Baton Rouge, Nov. 5, 1942; s. Ivy J. and Janith Nola (Latil) G.; m. Sally Anne Sheffield, Aug. 3, 1968; children—Michele, Anne, Julie. B.S., La. State U., 1964, M.S., 1966; Ph.D., Georgetown U., 1970. Staff fellow NIH, Bethesda, Md., 1971-74, research microbiologist, 1974-81; head electron microscopy sect. Rocky Mountain Labs, Hamilton, Mont., 1981—. Contbr. articles to profl. jours. Recipient NIH award of merit, 1979. Mem. Am. Soc. Microbiology, Am. Soc. Biol. Chemists, Am. Soc. Virology. Roman Catholic. Lodge: Lions (bd. dirs.). Current work: Using techniques of electron microscopy to relate specific regions of virus genomes to biochemical activities involved in replication and transcription. Subspecialties: Genome organization; Virology (biology). Office: Rocky Mountain Labs Hamilton MT 59840

GAROVOY, MARVIN R., physician, researcher; b. N.Y.C., June 14, 1943; s. Nathan and Ann (Braffman) G.; m. Seena Fischer, June 7, 1969; children: Natara, Jocelyn. B.A., NYU, 1964; M.D., SUNY, Downstate Med. Ctr., 1969. Diplomate: Am. Bd. Internal Medicine, 1974. Research assoc., fellow in nephrology Harvard Med. Sch., 1971-73; asst. prof. medicine, assoc. dir. tissue typing lab. Harvard Med. Sch. and Peter Bent Brigham Hosp., 1975-81; assoc. prof. surgery and medicine U. Calif.-San Francisco, 1981—, dir. immunogenetics and transplantation lab., 1981—. Contbr. articles to profl. jours. Served to maj. USAF, 1973-75. Mem. Am. Assn. Immunologists, Am. Soc. Nephrology, Am. Assn. Clin. Histocompatibility Testing, Am. Fedn. Clin. Research. Current Work: Mechanisms of kidney graft rejection; induction of graft tolerance, controlling mechanisms of antibody formation, flow cytometry. Subspecialties: Transplantation; Immunogenetics. Office: U Calif Med Ctr 3d and Parnassus Sts San Francisco CA 94143

GARRELS, ROBERT MINARD, geology educator; b. Detroit, Aug. 24, 1916; s. John C. and Margaret A. (Gibney) G.; m. Jane M. Tinen, Dec. 21, 1940 (div. 1969); children: Joan F., James C., Katherine G.; m. Cynthia A. Hunt, 1970. B.S., U. Mich., 1937, Sc.D. (hon.), 1980; M.S., Northwestern U., 1939, Ph.D., 1941; M.A. (hon.), Harvard U., 1955; Sc.D. (hon.), U. Brussels, 1969, U. Louis Pasteur, Strasbourg, France, 1976. From instr. to assoc. prof. geology Northwestern U., Evanston, Ill., 1941-52, prof. geology, 1965-69, 72-80, Scripps Instn. Oceanography, 1969-71; prof. U. South Fla., 1980—; geologist U.S. Geol. Survey, 1952-55; assoc. prof. geology Harvard U., 1955-57, prof., 1957-65, chmn. dept. geol. scis., 1963-65; Henri Speciael prof. sci. U. Brussels, Belgium, 1962-63; Capt. James Cook prof. oceanography U. Hawaii, Honolulu, 1972-74; adj. prof. Yale U., 1983—. Author: Textbook of Geology, 1951, Mineral Equilibria, 1959, (with C.L. Christ) Solutions, Minerals and Equilibria, 1965, (with F.T. Mackenzie) Evolution of Sedimentary Rocks, 1971, (with C.A. Hunt) Water, The Web of Life, 1972, (with F.T. Mackenzie, C. Hunt) Chemical Cycles and the Global Environment, 1975. Recipient Wollaston medal Geol. Soc. London, 1981. Fellow AAAS, Geol. Soc. Am. (Arthur L. Day medal 1966, Penrose medal 1978), Mineral. Soc. Am. (Roebling medal 1981); mem. Geochem. Soc. (pres. 1962, V.M. Goldschmidt award 1973), Nat. Acad. Scis., Soc. Econ. Geologists, Am. Acad. Arts and Sci., Am. Chem. Soc., Sigma Xi. Current Work: Geochemistry of low-temperature and pressure mineral-water systems; mathematical modeling of environments of geologic past. Subspecialties: Geochemistry; Geology. Office: Dept Marine Sci U South Fla Saint Petersburg FL 33701

GARRETT, EDWARD ROBERT, pharmaceutical scientist, educator; b. N.Y.C., Apr. 9, 1920; s. Murray and Stella (Abrams) G.; m. Irene Brewer, July 31, 1941; children—Jan Edward, Terry Lee, Kurt Lane. B.S., Mich. State U., 1941, M.S., 1948, Ph.D. (Hinman fellow), 1950, D.Sc. (hon.), 1974; Dr. rerum nat. honoris causa, U. Berlin, 1979. Asst. foreman Gen. Chem. Co., Claymont, Del., 1941-42; supr. TNT prodn. Keystone Ordnance Works, Meadville, Pa., 1942-43; chem. process engr. synthetic rubber Gen. Tire & Rubber Co., Baytown, Tex., 1943-45; asst. plant mgr. sulfuric acid prodn. Stauffer Chem. Co., Hammond, Ind., 1945-46; grad. asst. Mich. State U., 1946-49; sr. research scientist, group leader Upjohn Co., 1950-61; grad. research prof. U. Fla. Coll. Pharmacy, Gainesville, 1961—; chmn. grad. studies, 1968-70; vis. prof. U. Wis., 1958, U. Buenos Aires, 1965; cons. Smith Kline & French Labs., 1963-75; vis. scientist U. Calif. at San Francisco, 1964; pres. symposium indsl. pharmacy and biochemistry Latin Am. Congress Chemistry, Buenos Aires, 1962; mem. com. revision, mem. subcoms. organic and inorganic compounds, gen. tests U.S. Pharmacopeia XIX, 1970-75. Author: Drug Fate and Metabolism, Vol. I, 1977, Vol. II, 1978, Vol. III, 1980, Vol. IV, 1983, Vol. V, 1985; transl. editor: Analytical Metabolic Chemistry, 1971; contbr. numerous articles to profl. jours.; editor: Internat. Jour. Clin. Pharmacology, 1967-75; editorial bd.: Jour. Pharm. Scis. 1966-72, Chemotherapy, 1976—; cons. editor: Jour. Pharmacokinetics, 1972—; co-editor: Clinical Pharmacology and Pharmacotherapy, 2d edit., 1973, 3d edit., 1976; editor: series Drug Fate and Metabolism, Vol. 1, 1977, Vol. 2, 1978, Vol. 3, 1979, Vol. 4, 1983, Vol. 5, 1985. Recipient Lawson Essay prize Mich. State U., 1938; Upjohn award Upjohn Co., 1959; medal Italian Soc. Pharm. Scis., 1967; J.E. Purkyne medal Czechoslovakian Med. Soc., 1971; chevalier d'Armagnac, France, 1977; Volwiler Gold medal award for research excellence in pharm. scis., 1980. Fellow Acad. Pharm. Scis., Internat. Soc. Clin. Pharmacology (senator, Am. v.p. 1972-74), AAAS; hon. mem. Argentine, Chilean socs. indsl. pharmacy and biochemistry; mem. N.Y. Acad. Scis., Am. Chem. Soc., Am. Pharm. Assn. (Ebert prize 1962, Research Achievement award phys. chem. in pharm. scis. 1963, Research Achievement award in drug standards and assay 1969, Indsl. Pharm. Tech. award 1976, Stimulation of Research award 1981), Am. Soc. Microbiology, Am. Soc. Clin. Pharmacology and Therapeutics (v.p. sect.), Sigma Xi, Pi Mu Epsilon, Sigma Pi Sigma, Rho Chi, Rho Pi Phi, Alpha Chi Sigma, Rho Chi (lecture award 1985). Democrat. Unitarian. Current work: Kinetics and mechanisms of reactions of drugs; prediction of stability of pharmaceutics and antibiotics; Kinetics and mechanisms of antibiotic action on microbial growth. Home: 1826 NW 26th Way Gainesville FL 32605

GARRETT, GARY PACE, icthyologist; b. Corpus Christi, Apr. 4, 1953; s. Julian Pace and Stella Ruth (Hefte) G.; m. Linda P. Dittlinger, Aug. 17, 1974; 1 child, Nicholas Thorin. B.A., U. Tex., 1975, Ph.D., 1981. Research biologist Tex. Parks and Wildlife Dept., Ingram, 1982—. Mem. Am. Soc. Ichthyologists and Herpetologists, Am. Fisheries Soc., Soc. for Study Evolution, Southwestern Assn. Naturalists, Desert Fishes Council. Current work: Aspects of biology of fishes of Texas. Subspecialties: Reproductive biology; Species interaction. Home: Junction Star Route Box 57-d Ingram TX 78025 Office: Tex Parks and Wildlife Dept Junction Star Route Box 62 Ingram TX 78025

GARRETT, HOWARD LEROY, microscopist, analytical chemist; b. Midland, Mich., June 28, 1926; s. Clinton Hugh and Bernice Louise (Wiltse) G.; m. Kathleen Ellen Taylor, June 22, 1957; children—Sherilyn Marie, Paul Hugh, Duane Charles. B.S. in Chemistry, U. Mich., 1950; M.S. in Botany, 1957. Analytical chemist in emission spectroscopy Dow Chem. Co., Boulder, Colo., 1951-54, analytical chemist in microscopy, Midland, Mich., 1957-83, research assoc., 1983—. Contbr. articles to sci. publs. Organizer, treas., pres., bd. dirs. Chippewa Nature Ctr., Midland, 1962—. Howard L. Garrett Aboretum of Mich. trees and shrubs named in his honor Chippewa Nature Ctr., 1983. Mem. Am. Chem. Soc., Electron Microscopy Soc. Am., Microbeam Analysis Soc., Midland Camera Club (pres. 1960-62), Midland Nature Club (pres. 1962-64), Sigma Xi. Current work: Characterization of minute amounts of material using microscopical techniques; professional quality light photomicrography and photomacrography. Subspecialties: Analytical chemistry; Polymers (materials science). Home: 2107 Sylvan Ln Midland MI 48640 Office: Dow Chem Co Analytical Lab 574 Bldg Midland MI 48667

GARRICK, B. JOHN, engineering consulting firm executive; b. Eureka, Utah, Mar. 5, 1930; s. Morrison H. and Zelma (Hoffman) G.; m. Amelia Madson, Sept. 18, 1952; children: Robert Stephen, John Morrison, Ann. B.S., Brigham Young U., 1952; M.S., UCLA, 1962, Ph.D., 1968. Physicist Phillips Petroleum Co., Idaho Falls, Idaho, 1952-54, U.S. AEC, Washington, 1955-57; pres. nuclear and systems scis. group Holmes & Narver, Inc., Anaheim, Calif., 1957-75; pres. Pickard, Lowe and Garrick, Inc., Newport Beach, Calif., 1975—; adj. prof. UCLA, 1976-83; pres. Los Angeles Maintainability Assn., 1973-74; U.S. rep. Internat. Conf. on Nuclear Relia Germany, 1971. Contbr. articles to profl. jours. Fellow Inst. Advancement Engring.; mem. Am. Nuclear Soc., Atomic Indsl. Forum, Pacific Coast Elec. Assn., N.Y. Acad. Scientists. Current Work: Quantitative risk assessment of nuclear power plants and other high technology facilities plant performance analysis, management consulting, and teaching at graduate level. Subspecialties: Nuclear fission; Nuclear engineering. Office: Pickard Lowe and Garrick Inc 17840 Skypark Blvd Irvine CA 92714

GARRISON, ROBERT FREDERICK, astronomer, educator; b. Aurora, Ill., May 9, 1936; s. Robert W. and Dorothy I. (Rydquist) G.; m. Ada V. Mighell, June 7, 1957 (div. 1978); children: Forest L., Alexandra, David C. B.A. in Math, Earlham Coll., 1960; postgrad., U. Wis., 1961-62; Ph.D. in Astronomy and Astrophysics, U. Chgo., 1966. Research assoc. Mt. Wilson and Palomar Obs., Pasadena, Calif., 1966-68; asst. prof. U. Toronto, Ont., Can., 1968-74, assoc. prof., 1974-78, prof. astronomy, 1978—, also research, assoc. dir. Chile ops. Contbr. articles to profl. jours. Bd. dirs. Bruce Trail Assn., 1975-76. Served with USMC, 1954-56. Mem. Can. Astron. Soc., Am. Astron. Soc., Astron. Soc. of Pacific, Am. Assn. Variable Star Observers, Royal Astron. Soc. Can., Internat. Astron. Union. Club: U. Chgo. of Can. (v.p. schs. 1982—). Current Work: Stellar spectra, spectral classification, galactic structure, morphology of galaxies, instrumentation. Subspecialty: Optical astronomy. Office: David Dunlap Obs Box 360 Richmond Hill ON L4C 4Y6 Canada

GARTLAND, WILLIAM JOSEPH, scientific research administrator, biochemist; b. N.Y.C., Apr. 15, 1941; s. William Joseph and Mary Elizabeth (Klik) G.; m. Margaret Louise Wenstadt, June 20, 1981. B.S. in Chemistry, Holy Cross Coll., 1962; M.A., Princeton U., 1964, Ph.D. in Biochemistry, 1967. Asst. research scientist dept. biochemistry NYU Med. Ctr., 1967-69; postgrad. research biologist dept. biology U. Calif.-San Diego, La Jolla, 1969-70; grants assoc. div. research grants NIH, Bethesda, Md., 1970-71, program adminstr. genetics program Nat. Inst. Gen. Med. Scis., 1971-76, dir. Office Recombinant DNA Activities, from 1976; dir. NIH Office Recombinant DNA Activities Nat. Inst. Allergy and Infectious Diseases, 1979—; exec. sec. Recombinant DNA Adv. Com. NIH, 1975—; U.S. head U.S.-Japan Coop. Program for Recombinant DNA Research, from 1980. Contbr. articles on genetics and biochemistry to profl. jours. Recipient NIH Dir.'s award, 1978. Mem. Am. Soc. for Human Genetics, AAAS; mem. Am. Soc. Microbiology. Current Work: Oversight of recombinant DNA research, administration of NIH guidelines, risk assessment studies. Subspecialties: Genetics and genetic engineering (biology); Molecular biology. Office: NIH Bldg 31 Bethesda MD 20205

GARTNER, LAWRENCE MITCHEL, pediatrician, medical college administrator; b. Bklyn., Apr. 24, 1933; s. Samuel and Bertha (Brimberg) G.; m. Carol Sue Blicker, Aug. 12, 1956; children—Alex David, Madeline Hallie. A.B., Columbia U., 1954; M.D., Johns Hopkins U., 1958. Intern pediatrics Johns Hopkins Hosp., 1958-59; resident pediatrics Albert Einstein Coll. Medicine, 1959-60, chief resident, 1960-61, instr. pediatrics, 1962-64, asst. prof., 1964-69, asso. prof., 1969-74, prof., 1974-80, dir. div. neonatology, 1967-80, dir. div. pediatric hepatology, 1967-80; dir. clin. research unit Rose F. Kennedy Center, 1972-80; attending physician Hosp. Albert Einstein Coll. Medicine; prof., chmn. dept. pediatrics U. Chgo. Pritzker Sch. Medicine, 1980—; dir. Wyler Children's Hosp., U. Chgo. Med. Center, 1980—; mem. maternal and child health com. Nat. Inst. Child Health and Human Devel., 1984—; mem. Ill. Exptl. Organ Transplant Bd., 1985—. Contbr. articles to med. jours. and textbooks. Mem. adv. bd. Children's Liver Found.; trustee Wyler Children's Hosp. of U. Chgo., La Rabida Children's Hosp., Internat. Pediatric Research Found., 1984—. Recipient award NIH, 1967-74; Appleton Century Crofts prize, 1956; Mosby book award, 1958; NIH grantee, 1967—. Mem. Am. Pediatric Soc. (exec. council 1984—), Soc. Pediatric Research, Perinatal Research Soc., Am. Assn. Study Liver Disease, Am. Acad. Pediatrics, AAAS, N.Am. Soc. Pediatric Gastroenterology (pres. 1974- 75), LaLeche League Internat., Chgo. Pediatric Soc., Assn. Med. Sch. Pediatric Dept. Chairmen (exec. council 1984—), Phi Beta Kappa, Alpha Omega Alpha. Current Work: Jaundice in newborn infants and studies of bilirubin metabolism in fetus and newborn, including animal studies; studies of liver disease in children. Subspecialties: Pediatrics; Neonatology. Office: Pritzker Sch Medicine 5841 S Maryland Ave Chicago IL 60637

GARTRELL, CHARLES FREDERICK, space scientist, engineer, researcher; b. Balt., Nov. 4, 1951; s. Charles Collins Gartwell and Viviane Jeanne (Brown) Cole; m. Vanessa Lynn vanManen, May 19, 1975; 1 son, Charles Michael. B.A., U. Md.-Balt., 1973; postgrad., Johns Hopkins U., 1974-75, 79-80, Rutgers U., 1976-77. Task mgr./analyst Computer Scis. Corp., Silver Spring, Md., 1973-75; systems analyst RCA Am. Communications, Princeton, N.J., 1975-78; sr. engr. Gen. Research Corp., McLean, Va., 1978—. Author/editor: Military Space Systems Technology Model, 1982, 83, NASA Space Systems Technology Model, 1980-85. Mem. Optical Soc. Am., AIAA. Republican. Baptist. Clubs: Nat. Model R.R. Assn. (Indpls.); B & O R.R. Hist. Soc. Current Work: Research and planning for advanced civilian and military space systems technology, covering next 20-30 years; design/studies of advanced earth observation, radar and communication satellites, orbital transfer vehicles and spacecraft control. Subspecialties: Aerospace engineering and technology; Satellite studies. Home: 10332 Ridgeline Dr Gaithersburg MD 20879 Office: Gen Research Corp 7655 Old Springhouse Rd McLean VA 22102

GARVEY, PETER MEDFORD, irrigation consultant, agricultural engineer; b. Jacksonville, Fla., Jan. 15, 1953; s. Laverne Hugh and Mary Jo (Medford) G.; m. Katherine Grosh, Dec. 11, 1973; children—Jennifer Katherine, Allison Victoria, Jonathan Peter. A.S., Abraham Baldwin Agrl. Coll., 1973; B.S. in Agrl. Engring. with honors, U. Ga., 1975, M.S., 1977. Registered profl. engr. in tng., Ga. Grad. asst. U. Ga. Athens, 1975-77; extension engr., irrigation U. Ga. Coop Extension Service, Attapulaus, 1977-78; owner, operator peach orchard, Tifton, Ga., 1978—; owner, pres. Garvey Irrigation Co., Tifton, 1978—. Patentee liquid chem. spray apparatus. Mem. Ga. Irrigation Assn. (bd. dirs. 1980—, chmn. standards com. 1981—), Am. Soc. Agrl. Engrs. (recipient 1st place in design competition Ga. sect. 1975; named Engr. of Yr. 1983), Blue Key, Mu Alpha Theta, Alpha Zeta, Gamma Sigma Delta, Phi Kappa Phi. Baptist. Current work: Design, specs, bidding and installation supervision of all types of irrigation systems in Georgia; chemical application to row crops using new patented process. Subspecialty: Agricultural engineering. Home and office: Route 1 Box 186 Lenox GA 31637

GARY, DALE EVERETT, astrophysics researcher; b. Flint, Mich., Nov. 5, 1953; s. Ora Douglas and Bertha Emily (Wicks) G.; m. Kyle Ann Micol, Aug. 11, 1973; children—Isaac Allen, Benjamin Michael. B.S., U. Mich., 1976; Ph.D., U. Colo., 1982. Research fellow Calif. Inst. Tech., Pasadena, 1982—. Contbr. articles to sci. jours. Mem. Am. Astron. Soc., Am. Geophys. Union. Current work: Radio observations and physical processes of sun and solar-type stars. Subspecialties: Radio and microwave astronomy; Solar physics. Office: Solar Astronomy 264-33 Calif Inst Tech Pasadena CA 91125

GARZIA, MARIO RICARDO, mathematician; b. Buenos Aires, Mar. 6, 1955; came to US, 1967; s. Ricardo Francisco and Julia Elisa (Berrud) G.; m. Marjorie Ann Wilson, Oct. 3, 1975; 1 son, Daniel Ricardo. B.S. in Math, U. Akron, 1975; M.S., 1977; Ph.D. in Systems Engring, Case Western Reserve U., 1982. Grad. teaching asst. dept. math. sci. U. Akron, 1975-76; sci. programmer Babcock & Wilcox Co., Barberton, Ohio, 1976-82; mem. tech. staff Bell Labs., Holmdel, N.J., 1982—. Contbr. articles in field to profl. jours. Mem. IEEE, Soc. Indsl. & Applied Math., Am. Math. Soc., Pi Mu Epsilon. Current Work: Computer simulation, mathematical modeling and geometric systems theory. Subspecialties: Applied mathematics; Systems engineering. Home: 126-1000 Oaks Dr Atlantic Highlands NJ 07716 Office: Bell Labs WB1K207 Holmdel NJ 07733

GARZIA, RICARDO FRANCISCO, computer company executive; b. Lomas de Zamora, Argentina, Sept. 19, 1926; came to U.S., 1967; s. Mario Francisco and Zulema (Alvarez) G.; m. Julia E. Berrud, Oct. 2, 1948; children: Liliana Julia, Silvia Cristina, Mario Ricardo, Fernando Marcelo. B.S.E.E., Otto Krause Sch., Argentina, 1945; M.S.E.E., La Plata (Argentina) U., 1950. Prof. Nat. Indsl. Sch., Buenos Aires, 1950-53; prof. electricity Nat. Tech. U., Buenos Aires, 1954-67, chmn. dept., dir. computer ctr., 1954-67; leader computer applications Gen. Dynamics, Rochester, N.Y., 1967-69; sr. computer scientist Computer Sci. Corp., Huntsville, Ala., 1969-71; mgr. tech. applications Babcock & Wilcox Co., Barberton, Ohio, 1971-83, sr. engring. cons., 1983-84; mem. tech. staff AT&T Bell Labs., 1984—. Author: Transformada Z, 1966, Introduccion a la Computacion Digital, 1968; contbr. chpts. to books in field. Mem. IEEE (chmn. tech. com. 1983—), Instrument Soc. Am. (editor jour. 1975-78), Ops. Research Soc. Roman Catholic. Current Work: Mathematical modeling and simulation, continuous and discrete, control systems. Subspecialties: Algorithms; Mathematical software. Home: 220 Old Trail Dr Columbus OH 43213 Office: AT&T Bell Labs 6200 E Broad St Columbus OH 43213

GASICH, WELKO ELTON, aerospace company executive; b. Cupertino, Calif., Mar. 28, 1922; s. Elija John and Catherine Louise (Paviso) G.; m. Patricia Ann Gudgel, Dec. 28, 1973; 1 child, Mark David. A.B., Stanford U., 1943, M.S., 1947; prof. degree in Aero. Engring., Calif. Inst. Tech., 1948; postgrad. Stanford Bus. Sch., 1967. Registered profl. mech. engr., Calif. Aerodynamicist Douglas Aircraft, El Segundo, Calif., 1942-44, structures engr., 1948-51; systems analyst Rand Corp., Santa Monica, Calif., 1951-53; chief preliminary designer Northrop Corp., Los Angeles, 1953-57, v.p. engring., 1957-60, asst. gen. mgr., 1960-66, gen. mgr., group exec., sr. v.p., 1966-85, exec. v.p., 1985—. Designer T-38 and F-5 aircraft. Explorers Southwest Los Angeles execu Boy Scouts Am., 1965. Served to lt., USN, 1944-46. Fellow AIAA, Soc. Automotive Engrs.; mem. Stanford Sch. Engring. (adv. council chmn. 1981-83), Stanford Bus. Sch. Alumni Assn. (pres. 1971). Republican. Clubs: Bel Air Country (Los Angeles); Wings (N.Y.C.). Current work: Early work in aerodynamics and structures leading to design integration of fighter type aircraft. Subspecialty: Aeronautical engineering. Office: Northrop Corp 1840 Century Park East Los Angeles CA 90067

GASPARRINI, WILLIAM GERARD, clinical psychologist; b. Greenwich, Conn., Oct. 25, 1951; s. Joseph William and Rose Marie (Cianci) G.; m. Martha Sue Dodd, May 24, 1981. B.A., Lehigh U., 1972, M.A., 1973; Ph.D., U. Fla., 1977. Lic. psychologist, Miss. Psychology trainee VA Hosp., Gainesville, Fla., 1974-76; teaching asst. U. Fla., Gainesville, 1973-74; psychology intern VA Hosp., New Orleans, 1976-77, staff psychologist, Gulfport, Miss., 1978-81; adj. faculty U. So. Miss., Long Beach, 1978—; pvt. practice clin. psychology, Gulfport, 1983—. Contbr. articles to profl. jours. Mem. Am. Psychol. Assn., Southeastern Psychol. Assn., Miss. Psychol. Assn., Internat. Neuropsychol. Assn., Internat. Council Psychologists, Phi Beta Kappa. Current Work: Neuropsychology, biofeedback, behavioral medicine, personality assessment, behavior therapy children's temperament, oncology. Subspecialties: Neuropsychology; Behavioral psychology. Home: 153 Markham Dr Gulfport MS 39501

GASSMAN, PAUL GEORGE, chemistry educator; b. Alden, N.Y., June 22, 1935; s. Joseph Martin and Florence Marie (Rautenstrauch) G.; m. Gerda Ann Rozler, Aug. 17, 1957; children: Deborah, Michael, Vicki, Nancy, Amy, Kimberly, Eric. B.S., Canisius Coll., 1957; Ph.D., Cornell U., 1960. Asst. prof. Ohio State U., Columbus, 1961-66, assoc. prof., 1966-69, prof., 1969-74; prof. dept. chemistry U. Minn., Mpls., 1974—, chmn. dept., 1975-79. Editor books in field; contbr. articles to profl. jours.; editor bd.: Reviews of Chem. Intermediates, 1978—. Recipient James R. Crowdle Disting. Alumni award Canisius Coll., 1971; Alfred P. Sloan Found fellow, 1967-69; Japan Soc. for Promotion of Sci. fellow, 1981. Fellow AAAS; mem. Am. Chem. Soc. (award in petroleum chemistry 1972, award phys. organic chemistry 1985, chmn. Columbus sect. 1970, nat. councilor 1971-74, chmn. organic div. 1980), Chem. Soc. (London), Am. Inst. Chemists. Roman Catholic. Patentee. Current Work: Organic chemistry: catalysis chemistry, photochemistry, organoelectrochemistry, and synthetic chemistry. Subspecialties: Organic chemistry; Catalysis chemistry. Office: University of Minnesota 207 Pleasant St SE Minneapolis MN 55455

GAST, ROBERT G., university dean, soil chemist; b. Philadelphia, Mo., July 28, 1931; s. Fred W. and Lolabel (McPike) G.; married, June 6, 1954; children—Regina, Roger, Kimberly. B.S., U. Mo., 1953, M.S., 1956, Ph.D., 1959. Asst. prof. U. Tenn.-AEC Agrl. Research Lab., Oak Ridge, after 1959, then assoc. prof., to 1970; prof. U. Minn., St. Paul, 1970-77; head dept. agronomy U. Nebr., Lincoln, 1977-83; assoc. dean, dir. Mich. Agr. Experiment Sta., Mich. State U., East Lansing, 1983—. Contbr. articles to sci. jours. Served to 1st lt. USAF, 1953-55; Korea. Recipient Alumni award U. Mo., 1982. Fellow Am. Soc. Agronomy (exec. com. 1981-83), Soil Sci. Soc. Am. (pres. 1982); mem. Clay Minerals Soc. (bd. dirs. 1974). Current work: Soil chemistry and mineralogy with emphasis on surface chemistry and ionexchange; clay mineralogy. Subspecialty: Soil science. Office: Mich Agrl Experiment Sta 109 Ag Hall Mich State U East Lansing MI 48824

GATCHELL, SUSANNE MARIE, automobile manufacturing company executive, industrial engineer; b. Detroit, July 14, 1947; d. Gilbert M. and Dorothy K. (Hofweber) G. B.S., Oakland U., Rochester, Mich., 1969; M.S., U. Mich., 1972, Ph.D., 1977. Asst. supt. indsl. engring. Pontiac Motor div. Gen. Motors Corp., Mich., 1978-79, engr.-in-charge Fisher Body Plant, Warren, Mich., 1979-84, asst. chief engr. Chevrolet-Pontiac Can. Group, Pontiac, 1985, mgr. tech. assessment, planning, 1985—. Chmn. small bus. sect. United Found. campaign, Detroit, 1984. Gen. Motors Corp. fellow, 1971-76; recipient Best of New Generation award Esquire mag., 1984. Mem. Human Factors Soc. (sec./treas. 1980-82, exec. council 1982—), Ergonomics Soc. Current work: Technology assessment, planning and development; human factors engineering; automotive research. Subspecialties: Industrial engineering; Human factors engineering.

GATES, BRUCE CLARK, chemical engineering educator, consultant; b. Richmond, Calif., July 5, 1940; s. George Laurence and Frances G. (Wilson) G.; m. Jutta Margarete Reichert, July 17, 1967; children—Robert Clark, Andrea Margarete. B.S., U. Calif.-Berkeley, 1961; Ph.D., U. Wash., 1966. Research engr. Chevron Research Co., Richmond, Calif., 1967-69; asst. prof. chem. engring. U. Del., Newark, 1969-73, assoc. prof., 1973-77, prof., 1977—, H. Rodney Sharp prof., 1985—; dir. Ctr. for Catalytic Sci. and Tech., 1981—. Author: Chemistry of Catalytic Processes, 1979. Contbr. articles to profl. jours. Fulbright grantee, 1966-67, 75-76, 83-84. Mem. Am. Chem. Soc., Am. Inst. Chem. Engrs. Subspecialties: Catalysis chemistry; Chemical engineering. Office: Univ Del Ctr for Catalytic Sci and Tech Dept Chem Engrings Newark DE 19716

GATES, DAVID MURRAY, botany educator; b. Manhattan, Kans., May 27, 1921; s. Frank Caleb and Margaret Henry (Thompson) G.; m. Marian Francis Penley, June 4, 1944; children: Murray Penley, Julie Mary, Heather Margaret, Marilyn Joan. B.S., U. Mich., 1942, M.S., 1944, Ph.D., 1948. Faculty, U. Denver, 1947-57; sci. dir. Office Naval Research, Am. embassy, London, 1955-57; cons. to dir., asst. chief upper atmosphere and space physics div. Boulder Labs., Nat. Bur. Standards, Colo., 1957-64; prof. natural history U. Colo., 1964-65; prof. biology Washington U., dir. Mo. Bot. Garden, St. Louis, 1965-71; prof. botany U. Mich.; dir. Biol. Sta., Ann Arbor, 1971—; dir. Detroit Edison Corp.; mem. nat. sci. bd. NSF, 1970-76; chmn. environ. studies bd. Nat. Acad. Scis. and Nat. Acad. Engring., 1970-73; mem. panel sci. and tech. Com. Sci. and Astronautics, U.S. Ho. of Reps., 1970-74. Author: Energy Exchange in the Biosphere, 1962, Atlas of Energy Exchange for Plant Leaves, 1971, Man and His Environment: Climate, 1972, Perspectives of Biophysical Ecology, 1975, Biophysical Ecology, 1980; Energy and Ecology, 1985. Contbr. numerous articles to profl. jours. Bd. dirs. Conservation Found., Washington, 1970—, Nat. Audubon Soc., 1972-78, Cranbrook Inst. Sci. Recipient Gold Seal award Nat. Council State Garden Clubs, 1971; Recipient Disting. Faculty Achievement award U. Mich., 1982. Mem. Am. Inst. Biol. Scis. (dir. 1970-76, pres. 1975, Outstanding Achievement in Biolclimatology award), Am. Meteorol. Soc. Club: Cosmos (Washington). Subspecialty: Ecology (environmental science). Home: 442 Huntington Pl Ann Arbor MI 48104

GATES, MARSHALL DEMOTTE, JR., chemistry educator emeritus; b. Boyne City, Mich., Sept. 25, 1915; s. Marshall DeMotte and Virginia (Orton) G.; m. Martha Louise Meyer, Sept. 9, 1941; children—Christopher David, Catharine Louise, Marshall DeMotte III, Virginia Alice. B.S., Rice Inst., 1936, M.S., 1938; Ph.D., Harvard, 1941; D.Sc. (hon.), MacMurray Coll., 1963. Asst. prof. chemistry Bryn Mawr Coll., 1941-43; vis. prof. Harvard, 1946, asso. prof., 1947-49, Max Tishler lectr., 1953; tech. aid NDRC, 1943-46; lectr. chemistry U. Rochester, 1949-52, part-time prof., 1952-60, prof., 1960-68, Charles Frederick Houghton prof. chemistry, 1968-81, prof. emeritus, 1981—; Welch Found. lectr., 1960; adv. bd. Chem. Abstracts Services, 1974-76; vis. prof. Dartmouth Coll., 1982, 84, 85. Mem. com. on drug addiction and narcotics, div. med. scis. NRC, 1956-70, also com. on organic nomenclature div. of chemistry; mem. Pres.'s Com. on Nat. Medal of Sci., 1968-70. Recipient Edward Peck Curtis award for excellence in undergrad. teaching, 1967; Armed Services certificate Appreciation, 1946. Fellow Am. Acad. Arts and Scis., N.Y. Acad. Scis.; mem. Am. Chem. Soc. (editor Jour. 1963-69), Nat. Acad. Scis. Current Work: Synthesis of narcotics and narcotic antagonist; chemistry of opium alkaloids. Subspecialties: Organic chemistry; Synthetic chemistry. Home: 41 W Brook Rd Pittsford NY 14534 Office: U Rochester Rochester NY 14627

GATES, WILLIAM LAWRENCE, meteorologist, educator; b. South Pasadena, Calif., Sept. 14, 1928; married, 1951; 3 children. S.B., M.I.T., 1950, S.M.,

1951, Sc.D., 1955. Asst. M.I.T., 1950-53; research meteorologist Air Force Cambridge Research Ctr., 1953-57; asst. prof. meteorology UCLA, 1957-59, assoc. prof., 1959-66; research scientist Rand Corp., 1966-76; prof. atmospheric sci., chmn. dept. atmospheric sci., dir. climatology research inst. Oreg. State U., 1976—. Mem. Am. Meteorol. Soc., Am. Geophys. Union, Royal Meteorol. Soc. Subspecialties: Meteorology; Climatology. Office: Dept Atmospheric Sci Oreg State U Corvallis OR 97331

GATEWOOD, GEORGE DAVID, astronomer; b. St. Petersburg, Fla., May 10, 1940; s. George Harry and Virginia V. G.; m. Carolyn Virginia Scott, Mar. 10, 1959; children: Sara, Ann. B.A., U. South Fla., 1965, M.A., 1968; Ph.D., U. Pitts., 1972. Asst. prof. U. Pitts., 1972-77, assoc. prof., 1977—; dir. Allegheny Obs., 1977—; cons. NASA. Contbr. articles to profl. jours. NSF grantee, 1974—; NASA grantee, 1975—. Mem. Am. Astron. Soc., Internat. Astron. Union. Current Work: Determination of stellar distances and masses. Subspecialties: Astrometry; Computer interfacing. Office: Allegheny Obs Pittsburgh PA 15214

GATHERUM, GORDON ELWOOD, forestry educator; b. Salt Lake City, Oct. 22, 1923; s. James Elwood and Jessie Margaret (Robertson) G.; m. Patricia Jeanne Brandley, July 31, 1947; children: Laurie Patricia, Mark Gordon, Kristin Lee. B.S. in Forest Mgmt., U. Wash., 1949; M.S. in Range Mgmt., Utah State U., 1951; Ph.D., Iowa State U., 1959. Mem. faculty dept. forestry Iowa State U., 1953-69; chmn. dept. forestry Ohio State U., also Ohio Agrl. Research and Devel. Center, 1969-75; dir. Sch. Natural Resources, asso. dean Coll. Agr., Ohio State U. and Ohio Agrl. Research and Devel. Center, 1975-84, prof. forestry; AID cons., Brazil. Contbr. articles to profl. jours. NSF grantee. Mem. Nat. Assn. Profl. Forestry Schs. and Colls. (regional chmn.), Soc. Am. Foresters, Sigma Xi, Phi Eta Sigma, Xi Sigma Pi. Current Work: The interactions of genetic and enviromental factors on metabolic processes underlying forest tree production. Subspecialties: Plant physiology (agriculture); Resource management. Home: 5710 Strathmore Ln Dublin OH 43017

GATTOZZI, ANGELO LUCIANO, electrical engineering executive; b. Matrice, Molise, Italy, Dec. 12, 1947; came to U.S. 1970, naturalized, 1979; s. Domenico Germano and Angiolina (Appugliese) G.; m. Marianna Storto, Dec. 27, 1984. B.S., Case Western Res. U., 1971, M.S., 1975, Ph.D., 1978; cert. in acctg. John Carroll U., 1976. Grad. asst. Case Western Res. U., Cleve., 1971-74; engr. Reliance Electric Co., Cleve., 1974-77, project mgr., 1977-80; pres. Tyler Power Systems, Ins., Mentor, Ohio, 1980—. Treas. Health Hill Hosp. Aux., Cleve., 1983—. Mem. IEEE, ASTM, Am. Mgmt. Assn., Am. Math. Assn., Ohio Soc. C.P.A.s (assoc.). Roman Catholic. Current work: Electromechanics, superconductivity, electromagnetics, robotics industrial controls, automation, power generation. Subspecialties: Applied magnetics; Superconductors. Home: 2110 Apple Dr Euclid OH 44143 Office: Tyler Power Systems Inc 8648 Tyler Blvd Mentor OH 44060

GAUDINO, MARIO, physician, pharmaceutical company executive; b. Buenos Aires, Argentina, May 22, 1918; came to U.S., 1946; s. Nicolas Manlio and Maria Teresa (Ferrari) G.; m. Ann Murray, Sept. 24, 1947 (div. Jan. 1983); children—David, Brian; m. Judith Ann Jenkins, May 19, 1984. B.A., U. Buenos Aires, 1934, M.D. with honors, 1944; Ph.D., NYU, 1950. Lic. physician, N.J., N.Y. Intern, then resident and chief resident Ramos Mejia Hosp., Buenos Aires, 1939-44; 1941-44; research asst., chief of Lab. Inst. Physiology, Sch. Medicine U. Buenos Aires, 1944-46; fellow dept. physiology NYU Coll. Medicine, N.Y.C., 1946-49; asst. prof. physiology Tex. U. Med. Br., Galveston, 1949; chair dept. biol. physics Sch. Medicine, U. La Plata, Argentina, 1950; research assoc. prof. dept. surgery NYU Coll. Medicine, 1951-55, assoc. prof. surgery (biochemistry), 1955-57; lectr. dept. medicine Northwestern U. Med. Sch., Chgo., 1959, asst. prof., 1960; med. dir. Abbott Labs. Internat. Co. and Abbott Universal Ltd., Chgo., 1957-61; assoc. med. dir. Pfizer Internat. Inc., N.Y.C., 1962-67; assoc. dir. advanced clin. research, med. affairs internat. Merck Sharp & Dohme Research Labs., N.Y.C., 1967-69, dir. advanced clin. research, 1969-71, sr. dir. clin. research Commonwealth, Far East and Middle East, 1971, sr. dir. clin. research Europe, Rahway, N.J., 1971-74; dir. med. compliance, drug regulatory affairs CIBA-Geigy Corp., Summit, N.J., 1974-80, assoc. dir. med. services, pharms. div., 1980-85, dir., 1985—; clin. asst. prof. medicine Cornell U. Med. Sch., N.Y.C., 1971-77; established investigator Am. Heart Assn., 1954-57. Contbr. articles to med. and sci. jours. Millet and Roux fellow Argentine Assn. Advancement of Sci., 1943; Argentine Nat. Cultural Commn. fellow, 1945; U.S. Dept. State fellow, 1946-48; Dazian Found. Med. Research fellow, 1947-49. Fellow N.Y. Acad. Scis.; mem. Acad. Medicine N.J., Am. Acad. Clin. Toxicology, Am. Fedn. Clin. Research, AMA (Physician's Recognition award 1984), Am. Physiol. Soc., Am. Soc. Clin. Pharamcology and Therapeutics, Am. Soc. Nephrology, Drug Info. Assn., Harvey Soc., Internat. Soc. Nephrology, Microcirculatory Soc., Soc. Exptl. Biology and Medicine, Summit Med. Soc., N Current work: Experimental hypertension; kidney, body water and electrolytes membrane permeability; clinical research; psychiatry; pharmaceutical industry management. Subspecialties: Physiology (medicine); Psychiatry. Office: CIBA-Geigy 556 Morris Ave Summit NJ 07901

GAULT, N.L., JR., physician, educator; b. Austin, Tex., Aug. 22, 1920; s. N.L. and Pauline (Johnson) G.; m. Sarah Jane Dickie, June 28, 1947; children—Elizabeth Jean, John Dickie, Paul Alan. Student, U. Tex., 1938-42, Baylor U. Med. Sch., 1946-48; B.A., U. Tex., 1950; M.B., U. Minn., 1950, M.D., 1951, student Grad. Sch., 1951-54. Intern Mpls. Gen. Hosp., 1950-51; resident internal medicine Mpls. VA Hosp., 1951-52; chief resident internal medicine Ancker Hosp., St. Paul, 1952, U. Minn. Hosp., 1953-54; faculty U. Minn. Med. Sch., Mpls., 1953-67, 72—, asso. prof. internal medicine, asso. dean, 1962-67; prof. medicine, U. Minn. Med. Sch. 1972—, dean, 1972-84; prof. medicine U. Hawaii; asso. dean U. Hawaii Med. Sch., 1967-72; chief adviser Seoul Nat. U. Coll. Medicine, 1959-61; med. edn. cons. China Med. Board, N.Y.C., 1963, 71, AID, 1964-68; dir. postgrad. med. edn. program for, Ryukyu Islands, 1967-69; cons. Mpls. VA Hosp., 1956-67. Sec.-treas. Minn. Med. Found., 1956-67. Served to capt. AUS, USAAF, 1942-46. Decorated Commendation medal.; Recipient Supreme award Japan Med. Assn., 1969. Mem. AMA, Assn. Am. Med. Colls. (exec. council 1974-80, chmn. council deans MidWest-Gt. Plains region 1974-76), Minn. Med. Assn., Hennepin County Med. Soc. Subspecialties: Internal medicine; Medical education. Address: Medical Sch U Minn Minneapolis MN 55455

GAUT, NORMAN EUGENE, environmental consulting firm executive; b. Gilman, Colo., Sept. 20, 1937; s. Marvin Joseph and Margaret Elmo (Carl) G.; m. Madeleine Suzanne Dupuy, Aug. 29, 1964; children: Christopher Carl, Eric Kerwin, Jeffrey Gareth. B.S. in Physics, UCLA, 1959; S.M. in Meteorology, M.I.T., 1964, Ph.D. in Meteorology, 1967. Pres. Environ. Research and Tech., Inc., Concord, Mass., 1968—. Served with USAF, 1959-62. NASA grantee, 1963-67. Mem. Am. Meteorol. Soc., Am. Geophys. Union, AAAS. Subspecialties: Meteorology; Resource management. Home: 25 Marrett St Lexington MA 02173 Office: 696 Virginia Rd Concord MA 01742

GAUT, ZANE NOEL, physician, medical research administrator; b. Nauvoo, Ala, Aug. 29, 1929; s. Noel and Gladys (Odom) G.; m. Laura Tarence, June 25, 1955; children: Douglas, Julie, David. B.S., Birmingham-So. Coll., Ala., 1950; M.D., Tulane U., 1954; Ph.D. in Biochemistry, 1964; postgrad., Oak Ridge (Tenn.) Inst. Nuclear studies, 1966. Intern Vanderbilt U. affiliated St. Thomas Hosp., Nashville, 1955; flight surgeon and examiner Gen. Dynamics Corp., Fort Worth, 1958-60; asst. prof. depts. biochemistry and medicine Tulane U, New Orleans, 1961-66; mem. attending and teaching staff dept. medicine Martland Med. Center, Newark, 1966-71; staff physician, 1966-71; assoc. dept. clin. pharmacology Hoffmann-La Roche Inc., Nutley, N.J., 1966-71, sect. head dept. biochem. nutrition, 1971-76, asst. dir. dept. clin. pharmacology, 1976-78, dir. clin. research/endocrinology-metabolism, dept. med. research, 1978—; mem. attending staff Newark Presbyn. and Newark Beth Israel Hosps., 1966-69, Newark Beth-Israel Hosp., 1971—; asst. attending staff St. Luke's Hosp., N.Y.C., 1972—; mem. attending staff East Orange VA Hosp., N.J., 1969—; clin. asst. prof. N.J. Coll. Medicine and Dentistry, Newark, 1967-72; asst. clin. prof. Columbia U. Coll. Physicians and Surgeons, 1972—; cons. Reid-Provident Pharm. Co., Atlanta. Contbr. numerous articles on pharmacology to profl. jours. Served to lt. USN, 1955-58. Fellow Am. Coll. Clin. Pharmacology, Sci. Council of Internat. Coll. Angiology; mem. AAAS, Am. Diabetes Assn., Am. Fedn. for Clin. Research, Am. Inst. Nutrition, AMA, Am. Soc. Clin. Nutrition, Am. Soc. for Clin. Pharmacology and Therapeutics, Essex County Med. Soc., Med. Soc. of N.J., N.J. acad. Medicine, N.Y. Acad. Scis., Royal Soc. Health, Am. Med. Writers Assn., Am. Chem. Soc., Sigma Xi. Subspecialties: Endocrinology; Nutrition (medicine). Address: 800 Cranford Ave Westfield NJ 07090

GAUTIERI, RONALD FRANCIS, pharmacologist, educator; b. Providence, Oct. 10, 1933; s. Emilio and Frances (Amalfitano) G.; m. Bernadette Howell, Jan. 20, 1962; 1 dau., Anne Marie. B.S., R.I. Coll. Pharmacy, 1955; M.S., Temple U., 1957, Ph.D., 1960. Asst. prof. pharmacology Temple U. Sch. Pharmacy, Phila., 1960-66, asso. prof., 1966-70, prof., 1970—, chmn. dept., 1971—. Contrbr. articles to sci. jours. Co-chmn. Cheltenham Democratic party, 1981-82. NIH grantee. Mem. Am. Pharmac. Assn., Am. Soc. Pharmacology and Exptl. Therapeutics, Sigma Xi, Rho Chi. Roman Catholic. Current Work: Birth defects; animal models; hypertensive screening; placental perfusion. Subspecialties: Pharmacology; Teratology. Home: 418 Bolton Rd Glenside PA 19038 Office: 3307 N Broad St Philadelphia PA 19140

GAUTREAUX, MARCELIAN FRANCIS, JR., chemical company executive; b. Nashville, Jan. 17, 1930; s. Marcelian Francis and Mary Eunice (Terrebonne) G.; m. Mignon Alice Thomas, Apr. 26, 1952; children—Marcelian, Marian, Kevin, Andrée. B.S.Ch.E. magna cum laude, La. State U., 1950, M.S.Ch.E., 1951, Ph.D. in Chem. Engring, 1958. With Ethyl Corp., Baton Rouge, 1951-55, 58—, gen. mgr. dept. research and devel., 1968-69, v.p., 1969-74, sr. v.p. research and devel. toxicology, med. depts., 1974-81, advisor to exec. com., 1981—, also dir.; instr. La. State U., 1955-56, asst. prof. chem. engring., 1956-58; mem. sci. adv. com. Biotech Research Lab., Inc., 1982—. Bd. dirs. Baton Rouge Community Concerts Assn., 1974-84, pres., 1981-85; trustee La. Arts and Sci. Center, Baton Rouge, 1974-77; mem. La. State U. Found.; chmn. adv. com. dept. chem. engring. La. State U. Recipient (charter) Personal Achievement in Chem. Engring. award Chem. Engring. Mag., 1968; Charles E. Coates Meml. award Am. Chem. Soc./Am. Inst. Chem. Engrs., 1976; Ann. Meml. award Chem. Mktg. Research Assn., 1978; Best Paper award, 1980; charter mem. La. State U. Engring. Hall of Distinction, 1979; named to La. State U. Hall of Distinction, 1985. Fellow Am. Inst. Chem. Engrs. (Best Presented Paper award 1952); mem. Nat. Acad. Engring., Soc. Chem. Industry, Soc. Engring. Sci. (past dir.), Inst. Amorphous Studies (sci. adv. com. 1982—). Roman Catholic. Clubs: Baton Rouge Country, Baton Rouge City, Baton Rouge Camelot. Patentee and author in field. Current Work: Chemical processing, biotechnology, photovoltaics. Subspecialty: Chemical engineering. Home: 1662 Pollard Pkwy Baton Rouge LA 70808 Office: 451 Florida Blvd Baton Rouge LA 70801

GAUVIN, WILLIAM HENRY, chemical engineer; b. Paris, Mar. 30, 1913; emigrated to Can., 1930, naturalized, 1937; s. Hectore Gustave and Albertine Marie (VanHalle) G.; m. Dorothy Strong, Aug. 23, 1965; children—Suzanne, Robin, Christopher, Ian, Geoffrey, Stephanie. B.Eng., McGill U., Montreal, 1941, M.Eng., 1942, Ph.D. in Phys. Chemistry, 1945, D.Sc., 1983; D.Eng. (hon.), U. Waterloo, Ont., 1967; D.Sc. (hon.), Queen's U., 1984. Lectr. chem. engring. McGill U., 1942-44, asso. prof., 1947-62, research asso., 1961-72, sr. research asso., 1972—; plant supt. F.W. Horner Ltd., Montreal, 1944-46; cons., then head chem. engring. div. Pulp and Paper Research Inst. Can., Montreal, 1951-61; research mgr. Noranda Research Centre, Pointe Claire, Que., 1961-70; del. gen. policy and planning Nat. Research Council Can., 1970-71; dir. research and devel. Noranda Mines Ltd., Pointe Claire, 1970-83; mem. council Nat. Research Council Can., 1964-70; pres. adv. com. Indsl. Materials Research Inst., 1978—; mem. Sci. Council uan., 1966-70, 73-76; bd. dirs. Institut National de Productivité, Que., 1979—; hon. pres. 2d World Congress Chem. Engring., Montreal, 1981; mem. Can. council Weizman Inst. Sci., 1966—; sci. adviser HydroQue. Author. Bd. govs. McGill U., 1972—. Decorated companion Order Can.; recipient Archambault medal ACFAS, 1966; Gold medal Société d'Encouragement pour la Recherche et l'Invention, 1979; Prix Scientifique du Quebec, 1984. Fellow Royal Soc. Can., Chem. Inst. Can. (pres. 1977-78, Palladium medal 1966), Inst. Chem. Engring. U.K. (Sr. Moulton medal 1964), Am. Inst. Chem. Engring.; mem. Interam. Confedn. Chem. Engring. (pres. 1979-81), Assn. de la Recherche Industrielle du Quebec (pres. 1980—), Can. Inst. Mining and Metallurgy (Alcan award 1970, Disting. Lectr. award 1972, v.p.), Can. Soc. Chem. Engring. (pres. 1966-67, award 1968, R.S. Jane Meml. Lectr. award 1963), Can. Pulp and Paper Assn. (I.H. Weldon medal 1958), Corp. Profl. Engrs. Que., Am. Mgmt. Assn. (research and devel. planning council 1968—), Conseil de la Politique Sci. Que., Acad. Sci. Can., Engring. Inst. Can., Can. Nuclear Soc., Internat. Centre Heat and Mass Transfer, Am. Inst. Chem. Engrs., Am. Inst. Mining and Metall. Engrs., Can. Research Mgmt. Assn., Indsl. Research Inst., Instn. Chem. Engrs., Brit. Non-Ferrous Metals Research Assn., TAPPI, Dechema, Soc. de Chimie Industrielle (hon.), Soc. des Ingenieurs Civils de France, Soc. Chem. Industry, AAAS, Montreal Bd. Trade. Clubs: Royal St. Lawrence Yacht; Univeristy, Faculty (Montreal). Patentee in field. Current work: Applications of high temperature plasmas to industrial processes. Subspecialty: Chemical engineering. Home: 7 Harrow Pl Beaconsfield PQ H9W 5C7 Canada Office: Noranda Research Centre 240 Hymus Blvd Pointe Claire PQ H9R 1G5 Canada

GAVALAS, GEORGE ROUSETOS, chemical engineer; b. Athens, Greece, Oct. 7, 1936; s. Lazaros R. and Belouso A. (Matha) G. B.S., Nat. Tech. U., 1958; M.S., U. Minn., 1962, Ph.D., 1964. Asst. prof. chem. engring. Calif. Inst. Tech., 1964-67, asso. prof., 1967-75, prof., 1975—; cons. in field. Author: Nonlinear Differential Equations of Chemically Reacting Systems, 1968, Coal Pyrolysis, 1983; contbr. articles to profl. jours. Mem. Soc. Petroleum Engrs., Am. Inst. Chem. Engrs. (Tech. award 1968, Wilhelm award 1983), Am. Chem. Soc. Subspecialty: Chemical engineering. Office: Caltech 208-41 Pasadena CA 91125

GAVELIS, JONAS RIMVYDAS, dentist, educator; b. Boston, Jan. 11, 1950; s. Mykolas and Janina (Povydis) G.; m. Bonnie L. Sylvester; children—Nikolas, Gregory. B.S., U. Mass., Amherst, 1971; D.M.D., U. Conn., 1975. Resident in dentistry Cabrini Health Care Center, N.Y.C., 1975-76; fellow in prosthetic dentistry Harvard U. Sch. Dental Medicine, Boston, 1976-78, instr., 1978-79; asst. prof. U. Conn. Sch. Dental Medicine, Farmington, 1979-82; practice dentistry specializing in prosthodontics Harvard Community Health Plan, Boston, 1982—; asst. prof. Harvard Sch. Dental Medicine, 1982—. Contbr. articles on prosthetic dentistry to profl. jours. Fellow Acad. Gen. Dentistry (Vernon S. Johnson award 1981); mem. ADA, Northeast Prosthodontic Soc., Internat. Assn. Dental Research, Am. Assn. Dental Schs. Roman Catholic. Clubs: Scuba Shack Dive (Rocky Hill, Conn.) (treas. 1980-82); Southboro (Mass.); Rod and Gun; New Eng. Aquarium Dive (Boston). Current Work: Clinical application and biocompatibility of ceramics, gold-palladium based and base metal alloys. Subspecialties: Prosthodontics; Dental materials. Home: 1238 Washington St Gloucester MA Office: Harvard Community Health Plan 2 Fenway Plaza Boston MA 02215

GAWIENOWSKI, ANTHONY M(ICHAEL), biochemist, educator, endocrinologist; b. Newark, Oct. 30, 1924; s. Witold and Tekla (Mieczkiewicz) G.; m. Clotilda Brewington, July 30, 1955; children—John, Anthony, Margaret, Mary, Peter. B.S., Villanova Coll., 1948; M.S., U. Mo., 1953, Ph.D., 1956. Control chemist Merck & Co., Rahway, N.J., 1948; profl. service rep. Schering Corp., Bloomfield, N.J., 1949-52; asst. prof. biochemistry Kans. State U., Manhattan, 1957-63; prof. U. Mass., Amherst, 1963—; research scientist IV, U. Tex., Austin, 1956-57; guest worker NIH, Bethesda, Md., 1969-70; guest scientist Oak Ridge Assoc. Univs., 1978. Research and publs. in field. Served to lt. (j.g.) USNR, 1943-46; PTO, ETO. Grantee NASA, NIH, NSF, Am. Cancer Soc., Army Research Office, U. Mass., 1961-84. Fellow AAAS; mem. Am. Chem Soc. (chmn. Kans. State U. sect. 1962), Endorcine Soc., Sigma Xi (chmn. U. Mass. chpt. 1971). Republican. Roman Catholic. Current work: Ovarian terpenoid biochemistry; interphylum hormone interactions. Subspecialties: Biochemistry (biology); Neuroendocrinology. Home: 902 E Pleasant St Amherst MA 01002 Office: U Mass Dept Biochemistry Amherst MA 01003

GAY, CHARLES FRANCIS, physical chemist, solar engineer, research and development executive; b. Redlands, Calif., Oct. 2, 1946. B.S., U. Calif.-Riverside, 1968, Ph.D. in Chemistry, 1978. Engr. Spectrolab, 1975-78; dir. research Arco Solar, Chatsworth, Calif., 1978-80, v.p. research and devel., 1980—. Mem. Electrochem. Soc., Sigma Xi. Subspecialty: Solar energy. Office: Arco Solar PO Box 2105 Chatsworth CA 91313

GAY, TIMOTHY JAMES, physics educator; b. Ashtabula, Ohio, Mar. 23, 1953; s. William Coddington and Anne Elizabeth (McClelland) G.; m. Anna Christine Nothstine, Sept. 6, 1975. B.S., Calif. Inst. Tech., 1975; M.S., U. Chgo., 1976, Ph.D., 1980. Research asso., instr. Yale U., New Haven, 1980-82; asst. prof. U. Mo.-Rolla, 1983—. Mem. Am. Phys. Soc. Current Work: Electron-Atomic collisions, ion-atom collisions. Subspecialty: Atomic and molecular physics.

GAYLES, JOSEPH NATHAN WEBSTER, JR., educational administrator, chemist, consultant; b. Birmingham, Ala., Aug. 7, 1937; s. Joseph Nathan and Ernestine (Williams) G.; m. Gloria Jean Wade, Aug. 21, 1976; children—Jonathan Ifeanyi-Chukw, Monica Saleyeka. A.B. summa cum laude, Dillard U., 1958, LL.D., 1983; Ph.D., Brown U., 1962. Asst. prof. Morehouse Coll., Atlanta, 1963-66, prof. chemistry, 1969-77, v.p. Sch. Medicine, 1983—; staff scientist IBM, San Jose, Calif., 1966-69; pres. Talladega Coll., Ala., 1977-83; cons. NSF, Washington, 1971—, NIH, Bethesda, Md., 1972—; dir. Woodrow Wilson Found., Princeton, N.J., 1978—. Contbr. articles to profl. jours., chpts. to books. Bd. dirs. Metro Atlanta Council on Alcohol & Drugs, 1974-76; bd. dirs. North Central Ga. Health Systems Agy. Atlanta, 1975-77, North Central Ga. Health Systems Agy., Atlanta, 1975-77; bd. visitors MIT, 1981—. Named Alumnus of Yr. Dillard U., 1977; recipient Camille & Henry Dreyfus Found. tchr.-scholar award, 1970; Woodrow Wilson fellow, 1958. Mem. Am. Chem. Soc., Am. Phys. Soc., AAAS, Am. Assn. Polit. and Social Scientists, Phi Beta Kappa, Sigma Xi, Alpha Phi Alpha, Sigma Pi Phi. Current work: Higher education management and curriculum development; spectroscopy in the infrared and laser technology; computer science and data management; light scattering phenomena; the interaction of physical and biological sciences; the mind-body problem. Subspecialties: Physical chemistry; Laser spectroscopy. Home: 1515 Austin Rd SW Atlanta GA 30331

GAYLOR, DAVID WILLIAM, statistician, government official; b. Waterloo, Iowa, Apr. 8, 1930; s. David P. and Lena Ruth (Livingston) G.; m. Nannette Dolores Riley, June 19, 1954 (div. Jan. 1984); children—Craig, Thomas, Caroline, Julie. B.S. in Stats., Iowa State U., 1951, M.S. in Stats., 1953; Ph.D. in Stats., N.C. State U., 1960. Statistician, Gen. Dynamics Corp., Ft. Worth, 1955-57, Gen. Electric Co., Pleasanton, Calif., 1960-62, Research Triangle Inst., Research Triangle Park, N.C., 1962-68; chief biometry Nat. Inst. for Environ. Health Sci., Research Triangle Park, 1968-72; dir. biometry Nat. Ctr. for Toxicol. Research, Jefferson, Ark., 1972—; adj. prof. U. Ark. for Med. Scis., Little Rock, 1973—; mem. steering com. VA Southeast Regional Health Services Research and Devel., Little Rock, 1983—. Mem. editorial bd. Risk Analysis, 1980—. Contbr. articles to profl. jours. Recipient Shewell award Am. Soc. for Quality Control, 1968, Frank Wilcoxin prize Am. Soc. for Quality Control, 1970; award of Merit FDA, 1980. Fellow Am. Statis. Assn. (chmn. biopharm. sect. 1985); mem. Biometric Soc., Soc. for Risk Analysis, Soc. of Toxicology (South Central chpt.). Current work: Health risk assessment of environmental, food, drug, and cosmetic chemicals. Subspecialty: Statistics. Office: Nat Ctr for Toxicological Research Jefferson AR 72079

GAYLORD, NORMAN GRANT, chemist, research laboratory executive; b. Bklyn., Feb. 16, 1923; s. Irving M. and Tillie (Horowitz) G.; m. Marilyn Einhorn, June 24, 1945; children: Lori Gaylord Wright, Kathy Gaylord Fleegler, Richard, Cory Gaylord-Ross. B.S., CCNY, 1943; M.S., Poly. Inst., Bklyn., 1949, Ph.D., 1950. Chemist Elko Chem. Works, Pittstown, N.J., 1943-44, Pa. Salt Mfg. Co., Pittstown, 1945, Merck & Co., Rahway, N.J., 1946-48; research chemist E.I. duPont de Nemours & Co., Buffalo, 1950-54; group leader Interchem. Corp., N.Y.C., 1955-56, asst. dept. dir., 1957-59; v.p. Western Petrochem. Corp., Newark, 1959-61; pres., research dir. Gaylord Research Inst., Whippany, N.J., 1961—; adj. prof. polymer chemistry Canisius Coll., Buffalo, 1951-54, Poly. Inst. Bklyn., 1955-62, U. Lowell, Mass., 1981—. Author: Reduction with Complex Metal Hydrides, 1956, Linear and Stereoregular Addition Polymers, 1959, Polyalkylene Sulfides and Other Polythioethers, 1962, Polyalkylene Oxides and Other Polyethers, 1963; mem. editorial adv. bd.: Jour. Macromolecular Sci.-Chemistry, 1968—, Macromolecular Syntheses, 1963—, Jour. Polymer Sci, 1959—, Jour. Applied Polymer Sci, 1959-74, Ency. of Polymer Sci. and Tech, 1964-72, Soc. Plastics Engrs. Transactions, 1963-64, Polymer Engring. and Sci, 1965-66, Revs. in Macromolecular Chemistry, 1968-73; contbr. articles to profl. publs. Served with USAAF, 1945-46. Recipient Honor scroll N.J. Inst. Chemists, 1984. Mem. Am. Chem. Soc., Soc. Plastics Engrs., TAPPI, Chem. Soc. Japan, Polymer Soc. Japan, Sigma Xi. Patentee in field. Current Work: Charge transfer polymerization; graft copolymerization; polymer modification. Subspecialties: Polymer chemistry; Photochemistry. Home: 28 Newcomb Dr New Providence NJ 07974 Office: 156 Algonquin Pkwy Whippany NJ 07981

GAYNOR, HAROLD MARVIN, dentist, consultant; b. Phila., Apr. 25, 1930; s. David J. and Ida (Kremens) G.; m. Sandra L. Woodoff, June 25, 1955; 1 son, Eric Reid. B.S. in Pharmacy cum laude, Phila. Coll. Pharmacy and Scis., 1953; D.D.S., Temple Dental Sch., 1957; postgrad., Yale Sch. Pub. Health, 1973-75. Registered pharmacist. Dir. U. Conn. Sch. Dental Medicine, Farmington, 1975-76, asst. dean, 1976-77, assoc. dean, 1977-82, univ. dir., 1982-83, pvt. practice dentistry, Branford, Conn., 1983—; cons. Bowman Gray Med. Sch., Winston-Salem, N.C., 1982—, ADA Council on Dental Therapeutics. Dir. Bd. Health Branford, 1974-76; bd. dirs. East Shore Health Dist., Branford, 1974-76. Served to capt. U.S. Army, 1957-59. Fellow Am. Coll. Dentistry, Acad. Gen. Dentistry (mastership 1982); mem. Conn. State Dental Assn., Pierre Fauchard Acad., New Eng. Dental Soc. Club: Cosmopolitan (marshall 1960-61). Current Work: Research directed to clinical application and clinical research into pharmacology of drugs applicable to dentistry. Subspecialties: Oral biology; Periodontics. Home: 35 Oxbow Ln Woodbridge CT 06525

GEARING, ALAN EUGENE, electronics engineer; b. Pittsfield, Mass., Oct. 19, 1950; s. Franklin A. and Jennie H. (Berlt) G. B.S.E.E., SUNY-Buffalo, 1972; postgrad. Brown U., 1972-73. Registered profl. engr., D.C. Jr. engr. Jules Cohen & Assocs., P.C., Washington, 1973-75, sr. engr., 1975-83, prin., 1983—. Mem. East Chatham Vol. Fire Co., N.Y., 1969—. Mem. Soc. Motion Picture and TV Engrs., Assn. Fed. Communications Commn. Cons. Engrs. (exec. com. 1984—), IEEE (adminstrv. com. broadcast tech. soc. 1984—; Centennial Young Engr. 1984), Nat. Soc. Profl. Engrs., Tau Beta Pi., Am. Radio Relay League, Radio Amateur Satellite Corp., Amateur Radio R&D Corp. Lodge: Grange (gatekeeper and steward). Current work: Telecommunications engineering, principally broadcasting and cellular mobile radiotelephone systems. Subspecialties: Telecommunications; Electronics. Home: 2737-B S Walter Reed Dr Arlington VA 22206 Office: 1730 M St NW Suite 400 Washington DC 20036

GEARY, WILLIAM CHARLES, engineer; b. Olean, N.Y., Feb. 2, 1944; s. Raymond R. Geary and Kathryn M. Wagner; m. Marilyn Kahan, Dec. 7, 1969; children—Kimberly Michelle, Matthew Elliot. B.S.M.E., U. Detroit, 1967; M.S.M.E., Purdue U., 1976. Registered profl. engr., Ind., Okla. Devel. test engr. Teledyne, Detroit, 1967-68, Detroit Diesel Allison, Detroit and Indpls., 1968-77; sr. engr. Cummins Engine Co., Columbus, Ind., 1977-79; devel. supr. Mech. Technology, Inc., Latham, N.Y., 1979-81; chief engr. Arrow Splty. Co., Tulsa, 1981-85; founder Creative Technologies, 1985—; cons. Forness Found. scholar, 1961. Recipient Product of Yr. award Masco Industries, 1984. Mem. ASME (chpt. chmn. 1976, Meritorious Service award 1985), Soc. Autmotive Engrs., Tulsa Engring. Soc., Soc. Petroleum Engrs. Republican. Current work: Ceramic technology, engines; microprocessors; photovoltaics, automation; advanced manufacturing and processes; CAD/CAM; fuels and combustion. Subspecialties: Mechanical engineering; Software engineering. Home and Office: 22333 E 67th St Broken Arrow OK 74014

GEBALLE, THEODORE HENRY, educator; b. San Francisco, Jan. 20, 1920; s. Oscar and Alice (Glaser) G.; m. Frances C. Koshland, Oct. 19, 1941; children—Gordon, Alison, Adam, Monica Ruth, Jennifer, Ernest. B.S. in Chemistry, U. Calif. at Berkeley, 1941, Ph.D. in Chemistry, 1950. Research asso. Low Temperature Lab., U. Calif. at Berkeley, 1949-51; mem. staff Bell Telephone Lab., Murray Hill, N.J., 1952—, head low temperature physics dept., 1958-67, research cons., 1967—; prof. applied physics Stanford, 1967—. Served to capt. AUS, 1941-46. Guggenheim fellow, 1974-75. Fellow Am. Phys. Soc. (Oliver E. Buckley solid state physics prize 1970); mem. Nat. Acad. Scis., Am. Acad. Arts and Scis., Am. Chem. Soc., Phi Beta Kappa, Sigma Xi. Subspecialty: Low temperature physics. Home: 259 Kings Mountain Rd Woodside CA 94062 Office: Dept Applied Physics Stanford Univ Stanford CA 94305

GEDNEY, LARRY DANIEL, seismologist, geophysicist; b. Salt Lake City, Jan. 22, 1938; s. Roy Jay and Vinita (Manly) G.; m. Joan Marie Talarski, Mar. 28, 1957; children: Gregory Monroe, Jeffrey Jay, Douglas Kevin, Laura Anne. B.S., U. Nev.-Reno, 1960, M.S., 1966. Grad. Asst. U. Nev., Reno, 1964-66; asst. geophysicist Geophys. Inst., U. Alaska, Fairbanks, 1966-70; geophysicist U.S. Geol. Survey, San Francisco, 1970-71; assoc. prof. Geophys. Inst., U. Alaska, Fairbanks, 1971—. Weekly sci. columnist Anchorage Times, Fairbanks Daily News-Miner, 1981—. Contbr. articles in field to profl. jours. Served to capt. U.S. Army, 1960-64. Mem. Seismol. Soc. Am., Am. Geophys. Union,

AAAS, Alaska Geol. Current Work: Ongoing tectonic deformation of Alaska. Subspecialty: Geophysics. Home: Willow Ct Fairbanks AK 99725 Office: Geophys Inst U Alaska Fairbanks AK 99775

GEER, RONALD LAMAR, mechanical engineer, oil company executive; b. West Palm Beach, Fla., Sept. 2, 1926; s. Marion Wood and Bertha (Lightfoot) G.; m. Geneva Yvonne Chappell, Dec. 24, 1951; children—Ronald Lamar, Mark Randall. B.M.E., Ga. Inst. Tech., 1951. With Shell Oil Co., 1951—, sr. staff mech. engr., head office, Houston, 1969-71, cons. mech. engr., 1971—; mem. various govt., univ. adv. coms. Contbr. articles on petroleum drilling and prodn. to profl. jours. Recipient Disting. Achievement award Offshore Tech. Conf., 1984. Mem. Nat. Acad. Engring., NRC (marine bd.), Nat. Security Indsl. Assn. (petroleum panel, research and engring. adv. com.), ASME (hon.), Marine Tech. Soc., Am. Petroleum Inst., Model-A Ford Club Am., Classic T-Bird Club Internat., Thistle Class Assn., Pi Tau Sigma. Republican. Patentee petroleum drilling and prodn. equipment; mem. Shell Oil Co. team recognized in Offshore Tech. Conf. Disting. Achievement award to co., 1971. Subspecialty: Petroleum engineering. Home: 14723 Oak Bend Dr Houston TX 77079 Office: One Shell Plaza Houston TX 77001

GEERTZ, CLIFFORD JAMES, anthropology educator; b. San Francisco, Aug. 23, 1926; s. Clifford James and Lois (Brieger) G.; m. Hildred Storey, Oct. 30, 1948 (div. 1981); children—Erika, Benjamin. A.B., Antioch Coll., 1950; Ph.D., Harvard U., 1956, LL.D. (hon.), 1974, L.H.D., No. Mich. U., 1975, U. Chgo., 1979, Bates Coll., 1980, Knox Coll., 1982, Brandeis U., 1984, Swarthmore Coll., 1984. Asst. prof. to prof. dept. anthropology U. Chgo., 1960-70; prof. dept. social sci. Inst. for Advanced Study, Princeton, N.J., 1970—; Eastman prof. Oxford U., 1978-79. Author: The Religion of Java, 1960, Peddlers and Princes, 1963, Agricultural Involution, 1963, The Social History of an Indonesian Town, 1965, Islam Observed, 1968, The Interpretation of Cultures, 1973, (with H. Geertz) Kinship in Bali, 1975, (with L. Rosen and H. Geertz) Meaning and Order in Moroccan Society, 1979, Negara: The Theatre State in Nineteenth-Century Bali, 1980, Local Knowledge, 1983. Served with USNR, 1943-45. Nat. Acad. Scis. fellow, 1973—. Fellow Am. Philos. Soc., Am. Acad. Arts and Scis., AAAS; mem. Am. Anthrop. Assn., Assn. for Asian Studies, Middle East Studies Assn. Home: 5 Newlin Rd Princeton NJ 08540 Office: Institute for Advanced Study Princeton NJ 08540

GEFTER, MALCOLM LAWRENCE, biochemistry educator; b. N.Y.C., Mar. 16, 1942; s. David Harry and Elaine Pearl (Gurski) G.; m. Sharon Lee Bergen, Aug. 18, 1966 (div. 1976); 1 child, Donna Michele; m. Martha Louise Gross, July 25, 1982; 1 child, Matthew Adam. B.S., U. Md., 1963; Ph.D., Albert Einstein Coll. Medicine, 1967. Postdoctoral fellow Med. Research Council, Cambridge, Eng., 1967-69; asst. prof. Columbia U., N.Y.C., 1969-71, assoc. prof., 1971-76; assoc. prof. biology MIT, Cambridge, 1976, prof. biochemistry, 1976—, exec. officer dept. biology, 1977-82; cons. in field. Author: (with Vickie Sato) Cellular Immunology: Selected Readings and Critical Commentary, 1981. Mem. editorial bd. Jour. Biol. Chemistry, 1974-84, Archives of Biochemistry and Biophysics, 1970-81, Nucleic Acids Research, 1979-82. Recipient Pfizer award in enzyme chemistry Am. Chem. Soc., 1975. Mem. Am. Soc. Biol. Chemists, Harvey Soc., Am. Assn. Immunologists. Jewish. Current work: Molecular biological and genetic analysis of the immune response. Subspecialties: Immunobiology and immunology; Molecular biology. Office: MIT 77 Massachusetts Ave Cambridge MA 02139

GEHA, ALEXANDER SALIM, Cardiothoracic surgeon, educator; b. Beirut, Lebanon, June 18, 1936; came to U.S., 1963; s. Salim M. and Alice I. (Hayek) G.; m. Diane L. Redalen, Nov. 25, 1967; children: Samia, Rula, Nada. B.S. in Biology, Am. U. Beirut, 1955, M.D., 1959; M.S. in Surgery and Physiology, U. Minn.-Rochester, 1967; M.S. (hon.), Yale U., 1978. Asst. prof. U. Vt., Burlington, 1967-69; Asst. prof. Washington U., St. Louis, 1969-73, assoc. prof., 1973-75, Yale U., New Haven, 1975-78, prof., chief cardiothoracic surgery, 1978—; cons. VA Hosp., West Haven, Conn., 1975—, Waterbury Hosp., 1976—, Sharon Hosp., 1981—; mem. study sect. Nat. Heart, Lung and Blood Inst., 1981-85. Editor: Thoracic and Cardio-vascular Surgery, 1983, Basic Surgery, 1984. Bd. dirs. New Haven Heart Assn., 1981—. Mem. Assn. Clin. Cardiac Surgery (chmn. membership com. 1979-80, sec.-treas. 1980-83), Am. Heart Assn. (bd. dirs. 1981-85, councils on cardiovascular surgery and basic research), Am. Coll. Chest Physicians (steering com. 1980-84), Am. Assn. Thoracic Surgery, Am. Coll. Cardiology, ACS (coordinating com. on continuing edn. in thoracic surgery), AMA, Am. Physiol. Soc., Am. Surg. Assn., Am. Thoracic Soc., Assn. for Acad. Surgery, Central Surg. Assn., Internat. Soc. Cardiovascular Surgery, Lebanese Order Physicians, New Eng. Surg. Soc., Pan Am. Med. Assn., Halsted Soc., Société Internationale Chirurgie, Soc. Thoracic Surgery (govt. relations com., manpower com.), Soc. Univ. Surgeons, Soc. Vascular Surgery, Societa di Richerche in Chirugia, Thoracic Surgery Dirs. Assn., Sigma Xi, Alpha Omega Alpha. Current Work: Clinical cardiothoracic surgery and cardiovascular research into cardiac hypertrophy and its physiological effects and characteristics; cardiac electrophysiology; cardiac transplantation and cardiac preservation, short term (hours) and long term (days). Subspecialties: Cardiac surgery; Transplant surgery. Home: 345 Ridge Rd Hamden CT 06517 Office: Yale U Sch Medicine 333 Cedar St New Haven CT 06510

GEHRELS, NEIL, astrophysicist; b. Lake Geneva, Wis., Oct. 3, 1952; s. Tom and Aleida (de Stoppelaar) G.; m. Ellen D. Williams, Apr. 5, 1980. Mus.B., U. Ariz., 1976; B.S. in physics, 1976; Ph.D., Calif. Inst. Tech., 1981. Research asst. Calif. Inst. Tech., Pasadena, 1977-81; NRC research assoc. Goddard Space Flight Center, Greenbelt, Md., 1981-83, astrophysicist, 1983—. Contbr. articles to profl. jours. Mem. Am. Phys. Soc., Am. Geophys. Union, Am. Astron. Union, Phi Beta Kappa. Current Work: Researcher in gamma ray line spectroscopy. Subspecialty: Gamma ray high energy astrophysics. Office: Code 661 Goddard Space Flight Center Greenbelt MD 20771

GEHRELS, TOM, astronomer; Ph.D., U. Chgo., 1956. Research assoc. Ind. U., 1956-61; assoc. prof. U. Ariz., Tucson, 1961-67, prof., 1967—; Sarabhai prof. and fellow Phys. Research Lab, Ahmedabad, India, 1978—. Author articles on astron. polarimetry, surveying of asteroids and comets. Served with Spl. Services 1944-47. Recipient NASA medal for exceptional sci. achievement, 1974. Mem. Am. Astron. Soc., Internat. Astron. Union. Current Work: Surveying of the solar system. Subspecialty: Planetary science. Office: Lunar Lab U Ariz Tucson AZ 85721

GEHRING, FREDERICK WILLIAM, mathematician, educator; b. Ann Arbor, Mich., Aug. 7, 1925; s. Carl E. and Hester McNeal (Reed) G.; m. Lois Caroline Bigger, Aug. 29, 1953; children: Kalle Burgess, Peter Motz. B.S.E. in Math, U. Mich., 1946, M.A. in Math, 1949; Ph.D. (Fulbright fellow) in Math, Cambridge U., Eng., 1952, Sc.D., 1976; Ph.D. (hon.), U. Helsinki (Finland), 1977. Benjamin Peirce instr. Harvard U., Cambridge, Mass., 1952-55; instr. math. U. Mich., Ann Arbor, 1955-56, asst. prof., 1956-59, asso. prof., 1959-62, prof., 1962—, T.H. Hildebrandt prof. math., 1984—, chmn. dept. math., 1973-75, 77-84; vis. prof. Harvard U., 1964-65, Stanford U., 1964, U. Minn., 1971, Inst. Mittag-Leffler, Sweden, 1972. Editor: Duke Math. Jour, 1963-80, D. Van Nostrand Pub. Co., 1963-69, North Holland Pub. Co., 1970—, Springer-Verlag, 1974—, editorial bd., Procs. Am. Math. Soc., 1962-65, Ind. U. Math. Jour., 1967-75, Math. Revs., 1969-75, Bull. Am. Math. Soc., 1979-84, Complex Variables, 1981—; contbr. numerous articles on research in pure math. to sci. jours. Served with USNR, 1943-46. NSF fellow, 1959-60; Fulbright fellow, 1958-59; Guggenheim fellow, 1958-59; Sci. Research Council sr. fellow, 1981; Humboldt fellow, 1981. Mem. Assn. Women in Math., Math. Assn. Am., Am. Math Soc. (council 1980-83, trustee 1983—), Inst. for Math. and Its Applications (gov. 1981-84), Swiss Math Soc., Swedish Math. Soc., Finnish Math Soc., London Math. Soc., Finnish Acad. Sci. Subspecialty: Complex analysis. Home: 2139 Melrose Ave Ann Arbor MI 48104

GEHRZ, ROBERT DOUGLAS, physicist, astronomer, educator; b. Evanston, Ill., Dec. 28, 1944; s. Robert Gustave and Mary Gilbert (Laubscher) G.; m. Susan Lucille Laurel, May 1, 1970; children: Alexander Robert, Andre Laurel. B.A. in Physics, U. Minn., 1967, Ph.D., 1971. Research asst. U. Minn., 1968-71, research assoc., 1971-72; asst. prof. physics and astronomy U. Wyo., 1972-78, asso. prof. physics and astronomy, 1978-83, prof. physics and astronomy, 1983-85, dir. Wyo. Infrared Obs., 1985; prof. astronomy U. Minn., 1985—; dir. at large AURA, Inc., 1976-79; Chmn. NSF Optical-Infrared Subcom., 1978-80, Astronomy Adv. com., 1977-80; chmn. AURA Obs. Vis. Com., 1982—; mem. U. Calif. Ten Meter Telescope Infrared Working Group, 1981—. Contbr. numerous articles to profl. jours. Chmn. Laramie (Wyo.) Parks and Recreation Bd., 1981-85. Mem. Am. Astron. Soc. (mem. astronomy survey com. 1978—, chmn. galactic astronomy working group 1978—), AAAS (chmn. astronomy and pub. policy 1985), Royal Astron. Soc., Internat. Astron. Union, Sigma Xi. Episcopalian. Clubs: Explorers Club, Laramie Adult Hockey (sec.-treas.). Current Work: Observational astrophysics, experimental instrumentation and development; teaching, research, consulting. Subspecialties: Infrared astronomy; Low temperature physics. 2285 Folwell Ave Saint Paul MN 55108 Office: Dept Astronomy Sch Physics and Astronomy U Minn 116 Church St SE Minneapolis MN 55455

GEIDUSCHEK, E(RNEST) PETER, biophysicist, educator; b. Vienna, Austria, Apr. 11, 1928; came to U.S., 1945, naturalized, 1946; s. Sigmund and Frieda (Tauber) G.; m. Joyce Barbara Brous; 2 children. B.A., Columbia, 1948; A.M., Harvard, 1950, Ph.D., 1952. Instr. chemistry Yale, 1952-53, 55-57; asst. prof. chemistry U. Mich., 1957-59; asst. prof. biophysics U. Chgo., 1959-62, asso. prof., 1962-64, prof., 1964-70; prof. biology U. Calif. at San Diego, LaJolla, 1970—, chmn. dept., 1981-83; Cons. USPHS, 1963-69. Editorial bd.: Biophys. Jour, 1967-69, Ann. Revs. Biophysics and Bioengring, 1971-74, Virology, 1972—, Science, 1977-84. Served with AUS, 1953-55. Recipient Research award Am. Postgrad. Med. Assn., 1962, Research Career Devel. award USPHS, 1962; Guggenheim Found. fellow, 1964-65. Fellow Am. Acad. Arts and Scis.; mem. Nat. Acad. Scis., Am. Soc. Biol. Chemists, Biophys. Soc. (council 1964-66), AAAS, Am. Soc. for Microbiology, Am. Soc. Virology (council 1985—). Research in biophys. chemistry, molecular biology, virology. Current Work: Research in biophysical chemistry, molecular biology, virology, genetic regulation, enzymology of transcription. Subspecialties: Molecular biology; Virology (biology). Home: 8460 Cliffridge Ln La Jolla CA 92037

GEIER, JAMES AYLWARD DEVELIN, manufacturing executive; b. Cin., Dec. 29, 1925; s. Frederick V. and Amey (Develin) G.; children—Deborah Anne, James Develin, Aylward Whittier. Attended, Williams Coll., 1947-50. With Cin. Milacron Inc., 1951—, became v.p., 1964, dir., 1966, exec. v.p., 1969, pres., chief exec. officer, 1970, also chmn.; dir. Clark Equipment Co., Central Bancorp., U.S. Steel Corp. Pres. Cin. Museum Natural History; mem. adv. bd. Cin. Council on World Affairs; mem. Kenton County Airport Bd.; trustee Children's Home of Cin. Served with USAAF, 1944-46. Mem. NMTBA Conf. Bd., Engring. Soc. Cin. Republican. Clubs: Commercial, Commonwealth, Queen City, Camargo. Office: Cin Milacron Inc 4701 Marburg Ave Cincinnati OH 45209

GEIGER, JON ROSS, bacterial geneticist; b. Phila., Nov. 28, 1943; s. Gordon R. and Violet M. (Anderson) G.; m. Margaret Jeffrey, June 25, 1966; children: Michael Gil, Douglas Jeffrey. B.S., Pa. State U., 1965; Ph.D., U. Conn., 1976. Asst. prof. Smith Coll., Northampton, Mass., 1976-80; vis. scientist biology dept. M.I.T., Cambridge, Mass., 1980-81; sr. research biologist Olin Research Center, Cheshire, Conn., 1981-84, research assoc., 1984—. Contbr. articles to sci. lit. Served to lt. USN, 1965-70, Vietnam. NSF, Commonwealth Fund grantee. Mem. AAAS, Am. Soc. Microbioloy, Environ. Mutagen Soc., Genetics Soc. Am., Inst., Soc., Ethics and Life Scis., Sigma Xi. Unitarian. Current Work: Molecular genetics and recombinant DNA; mutagenesis in bacteria; applications of biotech. in chem. industry. Subspecialties: Genetics and genetic engineering (biology); Microbiology. Home: 9 Sunrise Hill Dr West Hartford CT 06107 Office: Olin Research Center PO Box 586 Cheshire CT 06410

GEIST, JACOB MYER, chemical engineer; b. Bridgeport, Conn., Feb. 2, 1921; s. David and Anne Rose (Steinschreiber) G.; m. Sandra Levy, Nov. 17, 1972; children by previous marriage—Eric D., Ellen A., David C. B.S. in Chem. Engring, Purdue U., 1940; M.S., Pa. State U., 1942; Ph.D., U. Mich., 1951. Instr. Pa. State U., 1943-44; teaching fellow, part-time instr. U. Mich., 1946-48; instr., then asst. prof. Mass. Inst. Tech., 1950-52; sr. lectr. Technion, 1952-55; with Air Products and Chems., Inc., Allentown, Pa., 1955-82, assoc. dir. research and devel., 1961-63, assoc. chief engr., 1963-69, chief engr., 1969-82; pres. Geist Tech., 1982—; lectr., adj. prof. Lehigh U., Bethlehem, Pa., 1960—. Author. Served to 2d lt. AUS, 1944-46. Hon. fellow Indian Cryogenic Soc., 1975; named Outstanding Engring. Alumnus, Pa. State U., 1985. Fellow Am. Inst. Chem. Engrs. (award chem. engring. practice 1976), AAAS; mem. Nat. Acad. Engring., Am. Chem. Soc., Internat. Inst. Refrigeration (v.p.; laureate 1983), Cryogenic Engring. Conf. (dir.), Sigma Xi, Tau Beta Pi, Phi Lambda Upsilon. Patentee in field. Current Work: Cryogenics, separations, process engineering. Subspecialty: Cryogenics. Home and Office: 2720 Highland St Allentown PA 18104

GELBARD, FRED, chemical engineer; b. Bklyn., Dec. 17, 1952; B.S., MIT, 1974; M.S., Calif. Inst. Tech., 1975, Ph.D., 1978. Mem. research staff Sandia Lab., Albuquerque, 1978-80; prof. chem. engring., MIT, Cambridge, 1980-81; research engr. Chevron, LaHabra, Calif., 1981—. Mem. editorial bd. Jour. Aerosol Sci. and Tech., 1982—. Current work: Computer simulation; flow through porous media; interactive computer graphics; aerosols; air pollution: Subspecialties: Chemical engineering; Fuels. Office: Chevron Oil Fields PO Box 446 LaHabra CA 90631

GELBKE, CLAUS-KONRAD, physics educator; b. Celle, W.Ger., May 31, 1947; came to U.S., 1976; s. Heinz and Gertraud (Laube) G.; m. Briggitte Zabeschek, Apr. 6, 1973; children—Susanne, Martin. Diploma Physics, U. Heidelberg, W.Ger., 1970, Dr. rer. nat., 1973. Asst. Max Planck Inst., Heidelberg, 1973-76; physicst Lawrence Berkeley Lab. Berkeley, Calif., 1976-77; assoc. prof. physics Mich. State U., East Lansing, 1977-81, prof., 1981—. Contbr. articles to physics jours.; co-editor: Classical and Quantum, 1975; Nucleus-Nucleus Collisions, 1983. Alfred P. Sloan fellow. Fellow Am. Phys. Soc. Current work: Nuclear collisions at intermediate and high energies. Subspecialty: Nuclear physics. Home: 4684 Sandstone Dr Williamston MI 48895 Office: Mich State U Cyclotron Lab East Lansing MI 48824

GELBOIN, HARRY VICTOR, biochemist; b. Chgo., Dec. 21, 1929; s. Herman and Eva (Jurkowsky) G.; m. Marlena Maisels, Apr. 1, 1962; children: Michele Ida, Lisa Rebecca, Sharon Anna, Tamara Rachel. A.B., U. Ill., 1951; M.S., U. Wis., 1956, Ph.D., 1958. Devel. chemist U.S. Rubber Co., 1952-54; research asst. McArdle Meml. Lab. Cancer Research, U. Wis., 1954-58; biochemist NIMH, 1958-61; supervisory biochemist Nat. Cancer Inst., 1962-64, head chemistry sect., 1964-66; chief Lab. Molecular Carcinogens div. cancer etiology, 1966—; adj. prof. Mt. Vernon Jr. Coll., Washington, Georgetown U., 1978; cons. Am. Cancer Soc., EPA, Nat. Acad. Sci., Fedn. Am. Soc. Exptl. Biology, NSF, others.; Predoctoral fellow Nat. Cancer Inst., 1957-58; keynote speaker Gordon Research Conf. Cancer, 1965; Franz Bielschowsky Meml. lectr., Dunedin, New Zealand, 1966, Smith, Kline and French hon. lectr., 1974, 76. Author more than 200 articles, chpts. in books.; Asso. editor: Chem.-Biol. Interactions; assoc. editor: Cancer Research, 1983-86; editor: Jour. Biochemistry-Toxicology, 1976. Recipient Claude Bernard award U. Montreal, 1970; New Horizons award lectr. Radiol. Soc. N.Am., 1970; Superior Service award NIH, 1970. Mem. AAAS, Am. Assn. Cancer Research Am., Soc. Biol. Chemists, Am. Soc. Pharmacology and Exptl. Therapeutics. Jewish religion (trustee congregation 1972—). Club: Mem. B'nai B'rith. Subspecialty: Biochemistry (biology). Home: 2806 Abilene Dr Chevy Chase MD 20015 Office: Nat Insts Health Bethesda MD 20014

GELFAND, DAVID H., biologist, genetic research administrator; b. N.Y.C., June 9, 1944; s. Sidney J. and Gigi P. (Levinson) G.; m. Ellen Daniell, Dec. 29, 1980; 1 dau., Duskie Lynn. A.B., Brandeis U., 1966; Ph.D. in Biology, U. Calif., San Diego, 1970. Research asst. biochemistry Brandeis U., Waltham, Mass., 1965; research asso. biology U. Calif.-San Diego, 1966; NIH trainee molecular genetics U. Calif., 1966-70, staff research biochemist, 1970-72; asst. research prof. U. Calif.-San Francisco, asst. research biochemist and lab. mgr., 1972-76; dir. recombinant molecular research Cetus Corp., Berkeley, Calif., 1977-81, v.p. sci. affairs, 1979—; mem. sci. adv. council NSF, 1980-84. Contbr. articles on molecular research in genetics to sci. jours. Mem. Am. Soc. Biol. Chemists, Am. Soc. for Microbiology, AAAS. Subspecialty: Molecular biology. Office: 1400 53rd st Emeryville CA 94608

GELINAS, ROBERT JOSEPH, scientist; b. Muskegon, Mich., Sept. 25, 1937; s. Robert Joseph and Vivian (Van Westen) G.; m. Mary R. Halfpap, June 18, 1960; 1 son, Robert H. Student, Muskegon (Mich.) Community Coll., 1955-57; B.S. in Chem. Engring, U. Mich., Ann Arbor, 1960, M.S. in Nuclear Engring, 1961, Ph.D., 1965. With Gen. Atomic, San Diego, 1960; student research asso. U. Mich., Ann Arbor, 1963-65; group leader, theoretical computational physics Lawrence Livermore (Calif.) Lab., 1966-75; sr. scientist, mgr. basic scis. div. Sci. Applications, Inc., Pleasanton, Calif., 1975-85; group leader computational analysis/design Lawrence Livermore (Calif.) Lab., 1985—. Contbr. articles to sci. jours. Mem. Am. Nuclear Soc. (Mark Mills award 1965), Am. Phys. Soc., AAAS, Am. Chem. Soc., Combustion Inst., Internat. Assn. Math., Sigma Xi, Phi Kappa Phi. Current Work: Non-equilibrium fluid dynamics; laser physics; thermo elasticity; optics; free electron laser modeling; shock phenomena in gases and solids; transport of radiation and matter; continuum mechanics. Subspecialties: Non-equilibrium fluid dynamics; Combustion processes. Office: Lawrence Livermore Nat Lab Mail Code L-487 Livermore CA 94550

GELLER, BERNARD DOV, electrical engineer; b. Fergana, Uzbekistan, USSR, Dec. 10, 1945; came to U.S., 1955, naturalized, 1961; s. Solomon and Rachel (Durchfort) G.; m. Joan Dianne Tacchetti, Apr. 18, 1982; 1 child, Emily Claire. B.S.E.E., Johns Hopkins U., 1967; M.S.E.E., U. Md., 1974. Engr. Advanced Tech. Lab., Westinghouse Corp., Balt., 1967-79; mem. tech. staff Comsat Labs., Clarksburg, Md., 1979-83, mgr., 1983—. Contbr. articles to profl. jours. Mem. IEEE (sr.), Microwave Theory and Techniques Soc. (chmn. Balt. chpt. 1977-78, vice chmn. tech. program com. 1986 symposium). Current work: Monolithic microwave integrated circuits, passive and active microwave circuits. Subspecialties: Integrated circuits; Microwave circuits. Office: Comsat Labs 22300 Comsat Dr Clarksburg MD 20871

GELLES, RUBIN, metrological instrumentation company executive; b. N.Y.C., Feb. 16, 1926; s. Louis and Celia (Jordan) G.; m. Dorothy Gelles, Jan. 31, 1927; 1 son, Adam. B.A., Cooper Union, 1948; B.S., CCNY, 1958; postgrad., NYU, 1958-60, Baruch Coll. Sch. Bus., 1979-81. Optical engr. Servo Corp. Am., Hicksville, N.Y., 1957-60; sr. optical engr. Kollsman Instrument Co., Syosset, N.Y., 1960-68, exec. engr., 1972-74, cons., 1974-77; v.p. engring. Spl. Optics, Little Falls, N.J., 1977-79; dir. research and devel. MKG Optical Instrument Corp., Woodside, N.Y., 1968-72; ops. mgr. Keuffel & Esser Co., Morristown, N.J., 1979—. Contbr. articles on optical engring., lens design, geometrical optics to profl. jours. Mem. Optical Soc. Am., Soc. Photo-Optical Instrumentation Engrs., Am. Mgmt. Assn. Current Work: Development of integrated metrology systems for automated factory and robotics control. Subspecialties: Optical engineering; Robotics.

GELL-MANN, MURRAY, theoretical physicist; b. N.Y.C., Sept. 15, 1929; s. Arthur and Pauline (Reichstein) Gell-M.; m. J. Margaret Dow, Apr. 19, 1955 (dec. 1981); children: Elizabeth, Nicholas. B.S., Yale, 1948; Ph.D., Mass. Inst. Tech., 1951. Mem. Inst. for Advanced Study, 1951; instr. U. Chgo., 1952-53, asst. prof., 1953-54, asso. prof., 1954, Calif. Inst. Tech., Pasadena, 1955-56, prof., 1956—, now R.A. Millikan prof. physics.; Mem. Pres.'s Sci. Adv. Com., 1969-72. Author: (with Y. Ne'eman) Eightfold Way. Regent Smithsonian Instn., 1974—; bd. dirs. J.D. and C.T. MacArthur Found., 1979—. NSF post doctoral fellow, vis. prof. Coll. de France and U. Paris, 1959-60; Recipient Dannie Heineman prize Am. Phys. Soc., 1959; E.O. Lawrence Meml. award AEC, 1966; Franklin medal, 1967; Carty medal Nat. Acad. Scis., 1968; Research Corp. award, 1969; Nobel prize in physics, 1969. Fellow Am. Phys. Soc.; mem. Nat. Acad. Scis., Royal Soc. (fgn.), Am. Acad. Arts and Scis. Clubs: Cosmos, Century. Research theory of weak interactions, research dispersion relations Research theory of weak interactions, research dispersion relations. Subspecialty: Theoretical physics. Office: Dept Physics Calif Inst Tech Pasadena CA 91125

GENEST, JACQUES, physician, research administrator, educator; b. Montreal, Que., Can., May 29, 1919; s. Rosario and Annette (Girouard) G.; m. Estelle Deschamps, Oct. 3, 1953; children: Paul, Suzanne, Jacques, Marie, Helene. B.A., Coll. Jean de Brebeuf, Montreal, 1937; M.D., U. Montreal, 1942; LL.D. (hon.), Queen's U., 1966, U. Toronto, Ont., Can., 1970, U. Ottawa, Ont., Can., 1983; D.Sc. (hon.), Laval U., Quebec, Que., 1973, Sherbrooke U., 1974, Meml. U. Nfld., 1978, St. Xavier U., 1983, SUNY-Buffalo, 1984. Postgrad. tng. Harvard U. Med. Sch., Boston, 1938, 39; resident Hôtel-Dieu Hosp., Montreal, 1942-45, Johns Hopkins Hosp., Balt., 1945-48, Harvard Sch. Chemistry, Boston, 1948, Rockefeller Hosp. Med. Research, N.Y.C., 1948-51; cons. practice medicine specializing in nephrology, endocrinology and internal medicine, dir. clin. research physician Hôtel-Dieu Hosp., Montreal, 1952—; prof. medicine U. Montreal, 1965—; prof. exptl. medicine McGill U., Montreal, 1960—; sci. dir. Clin. Research Inst. Montreal, 1965—; dir. Merck & Co., Rahway, N.J., Montreal Trust Co. Editor: (with Erich Koiw) Hypertension, 1972, (with Erich Koiw and Otto Kuchel) Hypertension: Physiopathology and Treatment, 1977, 2d edit., 1983. Bd. dirs. Robarts Research Inst. Decorated companion Order of Can.; recipient award Gairdner Found., 1963; Archambault medal Can. Assn. Advancement of Sci., 1965; Stouffer prize Am. Heart Assn., Cleve., 1969; Marie-Victorin Sci. prize Govt. Que., Que., 1977; Royal Bank award, 1980; Sims Commonwealth travelling prof., 1970. Fellow Royal Coll. Physicians and Surgeons Can., A.C.P., Royal Soc. Can. (Flavelle medal and award 1968); mem. Peripatetic Club U.S.A. (master), Assn. Am. Physicians, Am. Clin. and Climatol. Assn., Am. Heart Assn. Roman Catholic. Clubs: St.-Denis (Montreal); Century Assn. and Club (N.Y.C.). Current Work: Mechanisms and management of arterial hypertension. Subspecialties: Nephrology; Endocrinology. Home: 5955 Wilderton PH-L Montreal PQ H38 2V1 Canada Office: 110 Pine Ave W Montreal PQ H2W 1R7 Canada

GENOWAYS, HUGH HOWARD, museum curator; b. Scottsbluff, Nebr., Dec. 24, 1940; s. Theodore Thompson and Sarah Louise (Beales) G.; m. Joyce Elaine Cox, July 28, 1963; children—Margaret Louise, Theodore Howard. A.B., Hastings Coll.; postgrad. U. Western Australia, 1964; Ph.D., U. Kans., 1971. Research asst. U. Kans., Lawrence, 1970-71; research assoc., Tex. Tech U., Lubbock, 1971-72, curator of mammals, 1972-76, lectr. mus. sci. program. 1974-76, acting coordinator for research, the Mus., 1975-76; curator of mammals Carnegie Mus. Natural History, Pitts., 1976—; publs. editor, 1977—; chmn. com. Mammals of Spl. Concern in Pa., Harrisburg, 1979—. Author: Systematics and Evolutionary Relationships of Liomys, 1973. Editor-author: Mammalian Biology in South America, 1982; Natural History of the Dog, 1984; Species of Special Concern in Pennsylvania, 1985. Packmaster, Allegheny Trails council Boy Scouts Am., 1981-83, asst. scoutmaster, 1983—; mem. Shaler Area Sch. Dist. Adv. Com., Glenshaw, 1981-83. Fulbright scholar, 1964; NSF grantee, 1978-80; Alcoa Found. grantee, 1979-81. Mem. Am. Soc. Mammalogists (pres. 1984—), mng. editor Jour. Mammalogy, 1974-78, Southwestern Assn. Naturalists (pres. 1984—), Am. Assn. Museums, Council Biology Editors, Sigma Xi. Methodist. Current work: Systematics and zoogeography of small mammals occurring in the New World; museology, especially the management of biological collections. Subspecialties: Systematics; Taxonomy. Office: Carnegie Mus Natural History 4400 Forbes Ave Pittsburgh PA 15213

GENSEL, PATRICIA GABBEY, paleobotany educator; b. Buffalo, Mar. 18, 1944; d. Scott Seburn and Elinor (Dikeman) Gabbey; m. William Howard Gensel, June 7, 1968. B.A., Hope Coll., 1966; M.S., U. Conn., 1969, Ph.D., 1972. Research asst. dept. geology King's Coll., London, 1966-67; research assoc. biology sci. group U. Conn., Storrs, 1972-75; asst. prof. dept. botany U. N.C., Chapel Hill, 1975-80, assoc. prof., 1980-82, assoc. prof. dept. biology, 1982—. Author: (with H.N. Andrews) Plant Life in the Devonian, 1984. Contbr. sci. articles to profl. jours. Grantee: NSF, 1977—, U. N.C. Research Council, 1975-77, 81-85. Mem. Bot. Soc. Am. (rep. to editorial bd. 1979-82, chmn. paleontol. bot. sect. 1984-85), Am. Assn. Stratigraphic Palynologists, Am. Fern Soc., Paleontol. Assn., Internat. Fedn. Palynology, Internat. Orgn. Paleobotany, Sigma Xi. Current Work: Study fossil plants of Devonian and Carboniferous ages to better understand their nature and evolutionary significance. Subspecialties: Paleobiology; Morphology. Office: Dept Biology Coker 010 U-NC Chapel Hill NC 27514

GENSLER, HELEN LYNCH, molecular biologist; b. Stamford, Conn., Jan. 12, 1934; d. Joseph Martin and Lauretta (Murphy) Lynch; m. William George Gensler, July 8, 1961. B.A., Albertus Magnus Coll., 1955; M.S., U. Rochester, 1958; Ph.D., U. Ariz., 1979. Grad. fellow Sch. Medicine, U. Rochester, N.Y., 1955-58; research asst. Arthur D. Little Co., Cambridge, Mass. 1958-59; instr. physiology Coll. Nursing, U. Buffalo, 1961-62; cancer research scientist to sr. cancer research scientist Roswell Pk. Meml. Inst., Buffalo, 1959-63; research assoc. U. Pitts., 1967-68; research fellow dept. microbiology U. Ariz., Tucson, 1974-79, research assoc. dept. radiation oncology, 1981-84, asst. prof. dept. radiation oncology, 1985—; research assoc. Ariz. Center Occupational Safety and Health, Tucson, 1980-84. Contbr. articles to profl. jours. USPHS fellow, 1978-79; NIH grantee, 1980-81; Cancer Biology grantee, 1981-82, 84-85. Mem. Genetics Soc. Am., Am. Soc. Microbiology. Current Work: Genetic toxicology, DNA repair, oncology, gerontology. Subspecialties: Genetics and genetic engineering (biology); Oncology. Office: Dept Radiation Oncology Univ Ariz Health Sci Center Tucson AZ 85724

GENTILE, ARTHUR CHRISTOPHER, university dean; b. N.Y.C., Nov. 24, 1926; s. Leo and Grace (Leone) G.; m. Gloria Lenore Ennevor, Jan. 22, 1949; 1 dau., Flora. B.S., CCNY, 1948; M.S., Brown U., 1951; Ph.D., U. Chgo., 1953. Plant physiologist U.S. Forest Service, Lake City, Fla., 1955-56; mem. faculty U. Mass., Amherst, 1956-72, prof. botany, 1964-72; asso. dean U. Mass. (Grad. Sch.), 1965-72; dean Grad. Coll., v.p. research adminstrn. U. Okla., 1972-74; v.p. for acad. affairs U. Nev., Las Vegas, 1974-79; exec. dir. Am. Inst. Biol. Scis., 1979-83; dean acad. affairs Ind. U.-Kokomo, 1983—; Bd. dirs. Midcontinent Environ. Council Assn., 1972-74; mem. Sci. Manpower Commn., 1980-83; trustee Am. Type Culture Collection, 1980-83, Bioscis. Info. Service, 1981—. Author: Plant Growth, 1971. Served with AUS, 1945-46. USPHS research fellow Nat. Cancer Inst., 1954-55. Mem. AAUP, AAAS, Sigma Xi, Alpha Epsilon Delta. Subspecialties: Plant physiology (biology); Cell and tissue culture. Office: Ind U-Kokomo 2300 S Washington St Kokomo IN 46902

GENTLEMAN, JANE F., statistician; b. Washington, Apr. 8, 1940; d. Joseph and Florence (Roberts) Forer; children—David, Wendy. B.A. in Math., U. Chgo., M.S. in Stats., Ph.D. in Stats., U. Waterloo, Assoc. mem. tech. staff Bell Labs., Murray Hill, N.J., 1965-68; instr. U. Waterloo, Ont., Can., 1969-73, asst. prof., 1973-77, assoc. prof., stats., 1977—; sr. research officer Dept. Stats., Ottawa, Ont., 1982—; statis. cons. Ont. Ministry Labour. Contbr. articles to profl. jours. Mem. Am. Statis. Assn., Statis. Soc. Can. Current work: Research and data analysis. Subspecialties: Statistics; Graphics, image processing, and pattern recognition. Office: Research Analysis Div Dept Stats U Waterloo Waterloo ON N2L 3G1 Canada

GEORGE, AJAX ELIS, neuroradiologist; b. Athens, Greece, Jan. 16, 1941; came to U.S., 1947; s. Elis P. and Helen E. (Palaiogiannidoy) G.; m. Bia Lapiotis, Aug. 22, 1982. M.D., Nat. U., Athens, Greece, 1966. Diplomate: Am. Bd. Diagnostic Radiology. Intern St. Joseph's Hosp., Paterson, N.J., 1966-67; resident in radiology NYU Med. Ctr., 1968-69, neuroradiology fellow, 1970-71, dir. computed tomography, 1979—, prof. radiology (neuroradiology), 1981—; dir. neuroradiology Bellevue Hosp., N.Y.C., 1972-78, attending radiologist, 1972—; med. adv. bd. Gen. Electric Co., Milw., 1983. Author: Neuroradiology Case Studies, 1977; con. reviewer: Am. Journal Neuroradiology, 1980—. NIH grantee, 1982—. Mem. Am. Soc. Neuroradiology, Radiologic Soc. N.Am., N.Y. Med. Soc. Greek Orthodox. Current Work: Research activities; aging and cognitive dysfunctions of aging, computed tomography, cat scanning, positron tomography, pet scanning, nuclear magnetic resonance. Subspecialties: Diagnostic radiology; CAT scan. Home: 245 E. 40th St Apt 33E New York NY 10016 Office: Dept Radiolog NYU Sch Medicine 550 1st Ave New York NY 10016

GEORGE, JAMES, research physicist; b. Lynn, Mass., Dec. 29, 1922; s. John Jeanto and Thalia Anne (Pappas) Zorzy; m. Winifred Rose Nazzaro, Mar. 8, 1952; children: James Kevin, Carolyn Anne. B.S., Northeastern U., 1948; postgrad., Georgetown U., 1951-55. Physicist high energy radiation physics div. NIH, Nuclear Radiation Physics Lab., Bethesda, Md., 1948-53; physicist Mass Spectrometry Lab., U.S. Naval Med. Research Inst., Bethesda, 1953-55; sr. physicist dept. physics Cesium atomic beams Nat. Co., Melrose, Mass., 1955-66; dir. atomic research Frequency Electronics Inc., New Hyde Park, N.Y., 1973-78; research physicist JG Research & Tech., Salem, Mass., 1969—; dir. Electronautics Corp., Maynard, Mass., 1964-66; pres., treas. Frequency Control Corp., Topsfield, Mass., 1966-69. Contbr. articles to profl. jours. Mem. Am. Phys. Soc., N.Y. Acad. Scis., Internat. Platform Assn. Patentee in field. Current Work: Investigations in the hyperfine energy transitions of cesium, surface ionization of atoms, atomic collisions with surfaces, atomic and ionic impact phenomena on metal surfaces; secondary electron emissions. Subspecialties: Atomic and molecular physics; Statistical physics. Home: 15 Oakledge Rd Swampscott MA 01907 Office: 89 Washington St Melrose MA 02176

GEORGE, SARAH BREWSTER, mammalogist, museum curator; b. Tacoma, Nov. 16, 1956; d. H.C. and Shawn Brewster (Nims) G. B.S., U. Puget Sound, 1978; M.S., Fort Hays State U., 1980; Ph.D., U. N.Mex., 1984. Asst. curator mammals Los Angeles County Mus. Natural History, Los Angeles, 1984—. Durning fellow Delta Delta Delta, 1983-84; Theodore Roosevelt Meml. Fund grantee Am. Mus. Natural History, 1979, 83. Mem. Am. Soc. Mammalogists (com. chmn. 1984—; grantee 1983), Soc. Systematic Zoology, Soc. Study of Evolution, Southwestern Assn. Naturalists, Pacific N.W. Bird and Mammal Soc. Democrat. Current work: Mammalian systematics, taxonomy, historical biogeography. Subspecialties: Systematics; Taxonomy. Office: Div Life Scis Los Angeles County Mus Natural History 900 Exposition Blvd Los Angeles CA 90007

GEORGE, THYCODAM VARKKEY, government engineering executive, physicist; b. Pulthuppally, India, Aug. 19, 1938; came to U.S., 1956, naturalized, 1971; s. T. K. and Mariamma Varkkey; m. Achamma Mathew, June 14, 1964; children: Asha, Shobha, Sageev. B.Sc., U. Madras, India, 1956; Ph.D., U. Ill., 1964. Asst. prof. elec. engring. U. Ill.-Urbana, 1963-66; sr. engr. Westinghouse Research and Devel. Ctr., Pitts., 1966-75; with Office Fusion Energy, Dept. Energy, 1975—; program mgr. Office Fusion Energy, Dept. Energy (Mirror Confinement Program), 1975-82, program mgr. microwave (plasma) heating tech., gyrotron devel. program, Washington, 1982—. Mem. Am. Phys. Soc., Sigma Xi. Democrat. Current Work: Research in Thomson scattering, Rayleigh scattering, measurement of plasma properties with far-infrared absorption techniques. Management of research and development efforts related to fusion programs in industry and universities. Subspecialties: Electrical engineering; Fusion.

GEORGI, HOWARD MASON, III, physicist, educator; b. San Bernardino, Calif., Jan. 6, 1947; s. Howard Mason and Mary Alice (Mack) G.; m. Ann Rutledge Blake, June 14, 1969; children: Geoffrey Barnes, Justin Avery. B.A., Harvard U., 1967; Ph.D., Yale U., 1971. Mem. faculty Harvard U., Cambridge, Mass., 1976—, prof. physics, 1980—. Contbr. articles on theoretical particle physics to profl. jours.; author Lie Algebras in Particle Physics. NSF postdoctoral fellow, 1971-73; Sloan Found. fellow, 1976-80. Mem. Am. Phys. Soc., Harvard Soc. of Fellows.; fellow Am. Acad. Arts and Scis. Episcopalian. Current Work: Grand unified theories; properties of quarks and leptons. Subspecialties: Particle physics; Theoretical physics. Office: Physics Dept Harvard U Cambridge MA 02138

GEORGIADES, JERZY ALEXANDER, biological research and development company executive; b. Drohobycz, Lwow, Poland, Apr. 18, 1928; came to U.S., 1963, naturalized, 1982; s. Jerzy and Elizabeth G.; m. Izolda Schroeder, Sept. 20, 1960; 1 son, George B. Ph.D., Med. Acad. Krakow, Poland, 1963; M.D., Sch. Medicine, Gdansk, Poland, 1960; postgrad., Sch. Chemistry, Szczecin, Poland, 1943-48. Asst. prof. State Inst. Marine and Tropical Medicine, Gdansk, 1953-60; assoc. prof. dept. microbiology Krakow Coll. Medicine, 1960-63, prof., 1964-67, 69-70; vis. prof. Inst. Med. Pathology, U. Naples, Italy, 1967-69, 70-71; asst. prof. virology, virologist, dept. virology U. Tex. System, Cancer Ctr., M.D. Anderson Hosp. and Tumor Inst., Houston, 1971-75; vis. prof. K.U. Leuven, Belgium, 1976-77; research assoc., dept. microbiology U. Tex. Med. Br., Galveston, 1977-78, faculty assoc., dept. microbiology, 1978-80; v.p., sci. dir. Immuno Modulators Labs., Inc., Stafford, Tex., 1980—. Fellow WHO, London, 1958, State Inst. Microbiology, Epidemiology and Hygiene, Prague, Czechoslovakia, 1956. Current Work: Research and development of interferon and related products. Subspecialties: Virology (medicine); Microbiology (medicine). Office: Immuno Modulators Labs Inc 10511 Corporate Dr Stafford TX 77477

GERAN, RUTH I., biologist in cancer research; b. Middletown, Ohio, Nov. 27, 1922; d. Harry Clayton and Ethel Lacy (Kinney) G. B.A., Am. U., 1944; M.S., George Washington U., 1954, M.Phil., 1969, Ph.D., 1971. Biologist Nat. Cancer Inst., Bethesda, Md., 1958-83; sci. adviser VSE Corp., Alexandria, Va., 1984—. Contbr. articles to profl. jours. Mem. Am. Assn. for Cancer Research, Am. Inst. Biol. Scis., Am. Soc. Zoologists, Mortar Board, Kappa Delta, Beta Beta Beta. Methodist. Club: Potomac Appalachian Trail. Current Work: Searching for new or improved compounds for the treatment of cancer. Subspecialties: Cancer research (medicine); Chemotherapy. Office: VSE Corp 4217 Wheeler Ave Alexandria VA 22304

GERE, JAMES MONROE, civil engineering educator, writer, lecturer; b. Syracuse, N.Y., June 14, 1925; s. William Stanton and Carol Elizabeth (Hixson) G.; m. Janice Macauley Platt, June 1, 1946; children—Susan M., William P., David S. B.C.E., Rensselaer Poly. Inst., 1949, M.C.E., 1951; Ph.D., Stanford U., 1954. Registered civil engr., Calif., N.Y. Instr. civil engring. Rensselaer Poly. Inst., Troy, N.Y., 1949-52; from asst. to assoc. prof. Stanford U., Calif., 1954-62, prof., 1962—, assoc. dean Sch. Engring., 1960-70, chmn. dept. civil engring., 1967-72; cons. Author several textbooks. Served with USAF, 1943-46, ETO. Fellow ASCE; mem. Am. Soc. Engring. Edn., Earthquake Engring. Research Inst. Current work: Analysis and design of structures to withstand the effects of earthquakes. Subspecialties: Structural engineering; Civil engineering. Home: 932 Valdez Pl Stanford CA 94305 Office: Stanford U Dept Civil Engring Stanford CA 94305

GEREK, JAMES MICHAEL, chemist; b. East Stroudsburg, Pa., Apr. 11, 1953; s. Stephen and Virginia (Rutt) G.; m. Mary-Louise Robert, Sept. 20, 1975. B.S. in Chemistry, Juniata Coll., 1975. Product devel. chemist Kodak Co., Rochester, N.Y., 1975-76, process devel. chemist, 1976-80; supervising chemist Eastman Kodak Co., Rochester, 1980—. Chmn. bd. Focus on Rehab. 19, Inc., Rochester; mem. 19th Ward Community Assn., Rochester. Mem. Am. Chem. Soc., Soc. Photog. Scientists and Engrs. Democrat. Current work: Efficient synthesis of photographic developers; application of statistical quality control to batch production processes; synthesis of photosensitive compounds for microelectronic applications. Subspecialties: Organic chemistry; Synthetic chemistry. Home: 369 Ravenwood Ave Rochester NY 14619 Office: Eastman Kodak Co Kodak Park Bldg 119 Rochester NY 14650

GERETY, ROBERT JOHN, research physician; b. Jersey City, Oct. 16, 1939; s. James Leo and Helen (Beck) G.; m. Joan Imelda Grant, Feb. 3, 1967; children: Andrew Lawrence, Kathleen Suzanne, Nancy Grant. B.A., Rutgers U., 1962; M.A., Stanford U., 1966, Ph.D., 1971; M.D., George Washington U., 1970. Research assoc. Stanford U., 1970, intern, resident in pediatrics, 1971, 74-75; comdr. USPHS, 1971; advanced to med. dir.; clin. assoc. NIH, 1971-73; chief hepatitis br. Office of Biologics, FDA, Bethesda, Md., 1972-84; exec. dir., head virus and cell biology research Merck, Sharp & Dohme, West Point, Pa., 1984—; cons. NIH, WHO; prof. Found. for Advanced Edn. in the Scis., NIH, 1973-81. Editor: Non-A, Non-B Hepatitis, 1981; Hepatitis A, 1984, Hepatitis B, 1985; contbr. articles to profl. jours. USPHS fellow, 1962-66; recipient Commendation medal USPHS, 1979, Outstanding Service medal, 1982, Disting. Service medal, 1985. Mem. Am. Assn. Immunologists, Infectious Diseases Soc. Am., William Beaumont Soc., Sigma Xi. Patentee in field. Current Work: Vaccine development, development of biologics, anti-viral and anti-cancer substances, specifically those related to monoclonal antibodies and gene splicing technology. Subspecialties: Pediatrics; Infectious diseases. Home: 871 Village Circle Blue Bell PA 19422 Office Merck Sharp & Dohme: West Point PA 19486

GERGELY, PETER, structural engineering educator, researcher; b. Budapest, Feb. 12, 1936; came to U.S., 1960; s. Istvan and Maria (Csanky) G.; m. Kinga M. Mecs, Dec. 26, 1964; children—Zoltan E., Illa L. Student Tech. U., 1954-56; B.Engring., McGill U., Montreal, 1960; M.S., U. Ill., 1962, Ph.D., 1963. Registered profl. engr., N.Y. Asst. prof. dept. structural engring. Cornell U., 1963-68, assoc. prof., 1968-75, prof., 1975—, chmn. dept., 1983—, dir. Sch. Civil and Environ. Engring., 1985—; vis. prof. U. Toronto, 1976; cons. in field. Contbr. numerous articles to profl. jours. Nat. Acad. Sci. grantee, 1976. Fellow ASCE (com. chmn. 1980-84), Am. Concrete Inst. (D.L. Bloem Disting. Service award 1981, bd. dirs. 1985—); mem. Earthquake Engring. Research Inst., Internat. Assn. Bridge and Structural Engring. Current work: Earthquake engineering, structural engineering, reinforced concrete, nuclear reactor structures. Subspecialties: Structural engineering; Civil engineering. Home: 106 Juniper Dr Ithaca NY 14850 Office: Cornell U Hollister Hall Ithaca NY 14853

GERGELY, TOMAS ESTEBAN, astronomer, researcher; b. Budapest, Hungary, Oct. 14, 1943; Came to U.S., 1976; naturalized, 1982; s. Tibor and Magda (Szilasi) G.; m. Ana Lajmanovich, Mar. 6, 1970; children—Gabriela S., Esteban A., Daniel M. Licenciado in Physics, U. of Buenos Aires, Argentina, 1967; Ph.D. in Astronomy, U. Md., 1974. Asst. prof. Nat. Tech. U., Buenos Aires, 1974; researcher Instituto Argentino de Radio astronomia, Consejo Nacional de Investigaciones Cientificas y Tecnicas, Buenos Aires, 1975; research assoc. U. Md., College Park, 1976-81, sr. research assoc., 1981-82, assoc. research scientist, 1982—. Co-editor: Radio Physics of the Sun, 1980. Contbr. articles to profl. jours. Recipient Young Scientists award French Govt., Paris, 1976. Mem. Internat. Astron. Union, Am. Astron. Soc. (Solar physics div.), Internat. Radio Physics Union. Current work: Solar radio emission at meter-decameter wavelengths, particularly emission of the quiet Sun and type II-type IV bursts; long wavelength emission of comet tails. Subspecialties: Solar physics; Radio and microwave astronomy. Home: 2908 Terrace Dr Chevy Chase MD 20815 Office: Astronomy Program U Md College Park MD 20742

GERHARDT, PHILIPP, microbiologist, educator; b. Milw., Dec. 30, 1921; s. Philipp W. and Agnes (Daigh) G.; m. Vera Mary Armstrong, Feb. 24, 1945; children: Ellen Daigh, Stephen Philipp, Doris Mary. Ph.B. with honors, U. Wis., 1943, M.S., 1947, Ph.D., 1949. Diplomate: Am. Bd. Med. Microbiology. Faculty microbiology Oreg. State U., 1949-51, U. Mich. Med. Sch., 1953-65; prof., chmn. dept. microbiology and pub. health Colls. Natural Sci., Human Medicine, Osteo. Medicine, Vet. Medicine and Agr. Expt. Sta., Mich. State U., 1965-75; prof., asso. dean for research and grad. study Coll. Osteo. Medicine, Mich. State U., 1975—; adj. prof. Mich. Biotech. Inst.; cons. various univs. and corps.; mem. U.S. nat. com. Internat. Union Microbiology Socs. Editor: Manual of Methods for General Bacteriology, 1981. Served with AUS, 1943-46, 51-52. Wis. Alumni Research Found. fellow, 1946-47; NIH research fellow, 1947-49. Fellow AAAS; mem. Am. Soc. for Microbiology (sec. 1961-67, v.p. 1973-74, pres. 1974-75), Am. Acad. Microbiology (charter fellow, bd. govs. 1970-76), Brit. Soc. Gen. Microbiology, Internat. Union Microbiol. Socs. (pres. 1982-86), Phi Beta Kappa, Sigma Xi. Research and publs. on microbial endospores, permeability, fermentations. Subspecialties: Microbiology; Microbiology (medicine). Home: 529 Woodland Dr East Lansing MI 48823

GERKING, SHELBY DELOS, zoology educator; b. Elkhart, Ind., Nov. 16, 1918; s. Shelby Delos and Fezon Thankful (Churchill) G.; m. Louisa Burke Pfretzschner, Dec. 28, 1943; children—Shelby D., Timothy C., Andrew A. A.B., DePauw U., 1940; Ph.D., Ind. U., 1944. Instr. zoology Ind. U., Bloomington, 1946-49, asst. prof., 1949-54, assoc. prof., 1954-59, prof., 1959-67; prof., chmn. dept. zoology Ariz. State U., Tempe, 1967-74, prof., 1974-83, prof. emeritus 1983—; mem. adv. panel environ. biology NSF, 1965-68; mem. Internat. Congress Limnology, Warsaw, Poland, 1964-68; mem. U.S. nat. com. Internat. Biol. Programme, 1964-68; organizer Symposium on Fish Prodn., Reading, Eng., 1966; mem. external rev. com. Grad. and Research Program dept. entomology, fisheries and wildlife, U. Minn., 1976, Ecology Program, Battelle Northwest, 1976; CSIR vis. fellow U. Cape Town, South Africa, 1982; lectr., cons. in field. Assoc. editor Ecol. Monographs, Jour. Fish Biology, Environ. Biology Fishes, 1980—, Marine Ecology Progress Series. Contbr. articles to profl. publs. Fellow Conservation Dept., U. Ind., NSF, 1959; NSF grantee. Fellow AAAS, Am. Inst. Fishery Research Biologists, Ind. Acad. Sci.; mem. Am. Fisheries Soc. (2d v.p. 1983-84, 1st v.p. 1984-85, pres.-elect, 1985. Assoc. editor trans. 1954-63, 68, Silver medal, 1980), Am. Soc. Limnology and Oceanography, Am. Soc. Ichthyologists and Herpetologists, Am. Soc. Zoologists, Ecol. Soc. Am. (treas. 1969-72), Internat. Soc. Limnology, Internat. Assn. Ecology, Sigma Xi (sec. 1954-57, v.p. 1962-63, pres. 1963-64). Democrat. Episcopalian. Club: Mesa Country (Ariz.). Lodge: Rotary. Current work: fish biology; movements, growth nutrition, production, reproduction stress, thermal stress, feeding relationships. Subspecialty: Ecology (biology). Home: 418 E Alameda St Tempe AZ 85282 Office: Ariz State U Dept Zoology Tempe AZ 85287

GERMAN, RICHARD BARRY, engineering company executive; b. Halifax, N.S., Can., Nov. 19, 1950; s. Andrew Barry Crawford and Sage Janet (Ley) G.; m. Debra June Pepler, Sept. 9, 1978; 1 son, Andrew. B.S., Queen's U., Can., 1973. Registered profl. engr., Ont. Oceanological engr. Geocon Ltd., Toronto, Ont., Can., 1972-74, sr. project engr., joint venture, Lagos, Nigeria, 1974-75, mgr. field services, 1977-82; mgr. Geocon Offshore, Toronto, 1976—; mgr. bus. devel. Geocon, Inc., Toronto, 1982—; mem. task group on marine geotech. engring. NRC of Can., 1978-82. Richardson scholar Queen's U., 1969. Mem. Marine Tech. Soc., Arctic Inst. N.Am., Canadian Inst. Mining and Metallurgy, Prospectors and Developers Assn., Cons. Engrs. of Ont. Current Work: Marine geotechnical engineering, offshore drilling and sampling, ocean mining, systems development, offshore technology. Subspecialties: Ocean engineering; Mining engineering. Home: 147 Old Orchard Grove Toronto ON M5M 2E1 Canada Office: Geocon Offshore 33 Yonge St Toronto ON Canada

GERMANO, DON JOSEPH, chemist; b. Chgo., July 18, 1953; s. Joseph Michael and Eleanor Louise (Herbst) G. B.A., Benedictine Coll., 1975; Ph.D., U. Pitts., 1980. Sr. research chemist Dow Chem. U.S.A., Freeport, Tex., 1980-82, project leader, 1982-85, research leader, 1985—. Bd. dirs. Brazosport Little Theatre, 1983—, pres., 1984-85; v.p. for drama Brazosport Fine Arts Council, 1984-85; bd. govs. Benedictine Coll., 1985—. Mem. Am. Phys. Soc., Am. Chem. Soc., Am. Soc. Testing and Materials, Phi Lambda Upsilon. Roman Catholic. Current Work: Direct a research group which utilizes servo-hydraulic physical testing, thermal analysis, microscopy, x-ray and molecular techniques to study polymers, composites and metals. Subspecialties: Polymers (materials science); Thermodynamics. Home: 420 Garland Dr Apt 513 Lake Jackson TX 77566 Office: Dow Chem USA Tex Operations B-1218 Freeport TX 77541

GERMROTH, TED CALVIN, research chemist; b. Latrobe, Pa., Feb. 21, 1952; s. Calvin George and Dorothy Louise (Wheeler) G.; m. Deborah Sue Shoemaker, Aug. 29, 1975; children—Kristal April, Kara Ashley. B.S. summa cum laude, Coll. William and Mary, 1974; M.S., U. Calif.-Berkeley, 1976, Ph.D., 1979. Research chemist Eastman Kodak, Kingsport, Tenn., 1979-83, sr. research chemist, 1983—. Author articles. Regents scholar U. Calif.-Berkeley, 1974-75, 75-76. Mem. Am. chem. Soc. (treas. 1982-83, sec. 1983-84, pres. 1986-87), Phi Beta Kappa. Presbyterian. Club: Woodworking (pres. Kingsport 1984-85). Current work: Research in efficient synthesis of cellulose-based polymers including cellulose acetate and cellulose acetate butymate, etc. Subspecialties: Polymer chemistry; Synthetic chemistry. Home: 4538 Grace Dr Kingsport TN 37664 Office: Eastman Kodak Box 1972 Kingsport TN 37664

GERRITSEN, JEROEN, ecologist; b. Leiden, Netherlands, Nov. 6, 1951; came to U.S., 1956; s. Alexander Nicolaas and Jacqueline (Koolhaas) G.; m. Jine-i Kou, July 7, 1979; 1 child—Tristan Ming. B.S., Antioch Coll., 1974; M.A., Johns Hopkins U., 1976, Ph.D., 1978. Research assoc. U. Ga., Athens, 1978-81, research coordinator, 1981-82, asst. ecologist, 1982—; sci. cons. Nat. Geog. Soc., N.Y.C., 1982—; proposal reviewer NSF, Washington, 1983—. Contbr. articles to profl. jours. NSF grantee, 1983—. Mem. AAAS, Am. Soc. Limnology and Oceanography, Ecol. Soc. Am., Sigma Xi. Current work: Effect of surface chemistry on filter feeding; body size relations of animals; succession in wetlands and ecological theory. Subspecialties: Ecology (biology); Limnology. Office: U Ga Inst Ecology Athens GA 30602

GERSHBEIN, LEON LEE, biochemist, research inst. exec., clin. chemist; b. Chgo., Dec. 22, 1917; s. Meyer and Ida (Shutman) G.; m. Ruth, Sept. 30 1956; children: Joel Dan, Marcia Renee, Carla Ann. S.B. (Oscar Blumenthal Meml. Scholar), U. Chgo., 1938, S.M. in Chemistry, 1939, Ph.D. in Chemistry, Northwestern U., 1944. Research asso. in chemistry, Nat. Def. Research Council and Pitts. Plate Glass postdoctoral fellow Northwestern U., 1944-47; asst. prof. biochemistry U. Ill. Coll. Medicine, Chgo., 1947-53; asso. prof. biology Ill. Inst. Tech., 1953-57, adj. prof., 1957—; pres. and dir. Northwest Inst. for Med. Research, Chgo., 1957—; dir. labs. Northwest Hosp., Chgo., 1957—. Research numerous publs. in clin. chemistry and biochemistry, neurobiology, sebaceous lipids, liver regeneration, nutrition and endocrine metabolism. Recipient merit award in chromatography Chgo. Gas Chromatography Discussion Group, 1978, citation Ill. State Acad. Sci., 1975-79. Mem. Am. Chem. Soc., Am. Inst. Chemists, Am. Oil Chemists' Soc., AAAS, Ill. State Acad. Scis., N.Y. Acad. Sci., Soc. Exptl. Biology and Medicine, Soc. Applied Spectroscopy, Soc. Cosmetic Chemists, Am. Fedn. Clin. Research, Am. Assn. Cancer Research, Sigma Xi, Phi Lambda Upsilon. Current Work: Tumorigenesis; liver regeneration; tissue enzymes and isoenzymes, lipid metabolism with emphasis on sebaceous types. Subspecialties: Biochemistry (medicine); Clinical chemistry. Home: 2836 Birchwood Ave Wilmette IL 60091 Office: 5645 W Addison St Chicago IL 60634

GERSHON, ELLIOT SHELDON, psychiatrist; s. David and Ann (Pohorille) G.; m. Faye Deborah Saltman, Nov. 4, 1967; children: Ari Andrew, Ethan Daniel. A.B., Harvard U., 1961, M.D., 1965. Intern Mt. Sinai Hosp., N.Y.C., 1965-66; teaching fellow psychiatry Harvard U. Med. Sch.; also resident in psychiatry Mass. Mental Health Center, Boston, 1966-69; cons. Peter Bent Brigham Hosp., Boston, 1968-69, Prince George's County (Md.) Health Dept., 1969-70; with NIMH, Bethesda, Md., 1969—, unit chief, sect. psychogenetics, biol. psychiatry br., 1974—, sect. chief, 1978—, mem. faculty staff coll., 1977—; now chief clin. neurogenetics br.; dir. research Jerusalem (Israel) Mental Health Center, 1971-74; mem. faculty Washington Sch. Psychiatry, from 1976; sci. adv. bd. Israel Center Psychobiology, 1972-74; sr. surgeon USPHS, 1969-71, 75-80, med. dir., 1980—; Mem. sci. adv. bd. Am. Friends of Jerusalem Mental Health Center, 1978—. Author: Impact of Biology on Modern Psychiatry, 1977, Genetic Research Strategies for Psychobiology and Psychiatry, 1981; also articles; editorial bd.: Jour. Affective Disorders, 1978—, Psychiatry Research: An Internat. Jour. for Rapid Communications, 1978—, Psychiat. Devels., 1982—, Jour. Psychiat. Research, 1983. Recipient Anna Monika Found. prize, 1979; USPHS Commd. Officer's Commendation medal, 1979. Mem. AAAS, Am. Psychiat. Assn., Am. Psychopath. Assn., Psychiat. Research Soc., Am. Coll. Neuropsychopharmacology, Soc. for Neurosci. Jewish. Current Work: Clinical and biological inherited factors in major psychiatric disorders. Psychopharmacology and pharmacogenetics. Human population genetics, biochemical genetics, chromosomal linkage. Subspecialty: Psychopharmacology. Address: Bldg 10 Room 3N218 NIMH 9000 Rockville Pike Bethesda MD 20205

GERSHON, MICHAEL DAVID, anatomist, educator; b. N.Y.C., Mar. 3, 1938; s. Murray Huda and Juliette (Levinson) G.; m. Elda Anne Angen, June 10, 1961; children: Perry, Timothy, Dana. B.A., Cornell U., 1958, M.D., 1963. Fellow, instr. Cornell U. Med. Coll., N.Y.C., 1963-65, asst. prof., 1965-69, assoc. prof. anatomy, 1969-74, prof., 1974-75; research assoc. Oxford (Eng.) U., 1965-66; prof. anatomy and cell biology, chmn. dept. Columbia U. Coll. Phys. and Surgeons, 1975—; mem. neurol. disorders program project rev. com. NIH, 1972-75, Neurology A study sect., 1980—. Contbr. med. jours.; Editorial bd.: Neurochemistry Internat., Jour. Histochemistry, Anat. Record, Jour. Comparative Neurology and Anatomy and Embryology. Recipient Borden Undergrad. research prize, 1963; N.Y.C. Health Research Council Career Scientist award, 1971; Markle Found. scholar acad. medicine, 1968; grantee NIH. Mem. Am. Assn. Anatomists, Am. Gastroenterol. Assn., Am. Soc. Cell Biology, Am. Physiol. Soc., AAAS, Endocrine Soc., Soc. Neurosci., N.Y. Soc. Electron Microscopists (pres. 1977-78), N.Y. Acad. Sci., Internat. Soc. Devel. Neurosci., Phi Beta Kappa, Sigma Xi, Alpha Epsilon Delta, Phi Kappa Phi. Club: Cajal. Subspecialty: Neurobiology. Office: 630 W 168th St New York NY 10032

GERSTEN, JEROME WILLIAM, physician, educator; b. N.Y.C., Apr. 20, 1917; s. Louis and Bessie (Abrams) G.; m. Rhoda Rich., Nov. 8, 1941; children—Steven, Wendy, Christopher, Dennis, Madeleine. B.S., CCNY, 1935; M.D., NYU, 1939; M.S. in Physiology, U. Minn., 1949. Diplomate Am. Bd. Phys. Medicine and Rehab. Intern, Morrisania City Hosp., N.Y.C., 1939-40; intern Montefiore Hosp., N.Y.C., 1940-41, resident, 1941; resident MIT, Cambridge, 1946, Columbia U., N.Y.C., 1946-47, Mayo Clinic, Rochester, Minn., 1947-49; asst. prof. phys. medicine and rehab. U. Colo., Denver, 1949-52, assoc. prof., 1952-57, prof., 1957—, dept. chmn., 1955-81; dir. Rehab. Research and Tng. Ctr., HEW, 1965-74. Contbr. articles to profl. jours.. Served to maj. U.S. Army, 1941-46. Fellow Council Cerebrovascular Disease of Am. Heart Assn.; mem. Am. Congress Rehab. Medicine, Am. Assn. Electromyography, Am. Inst. Ultrasonics in Medicine, Phi Beta Kappa, Alpha Omega Alpha. Democrat. Current work: Major current research activity is management of chronic pain with emphasis on behavioral aspects. Subspecialty: Physical medicine and rehabilitation. Home: 1370 Forest St Denver CO 80220 Office: U Colo Sch Medicine 4200 E 9th Ave Denver CO 80262

GERSTENBERGER, DAVID CHARLES, electrical engineer; b. Thompson Falls, Mont., Nov. 11, 1952; s. Albert Frank and Violet Mae (Franck) G. B.S, Tulane U., 1974; M.S., Stanford U., 1975; Ph.D., Colo. State U., 1980. Laser engr. Spectra Physics, Mountain View, Calif., 1980—. Contbr. articles to profl. jours. Mem Am. Phys. Soc., IEEE, Palo Alto Rock Climbing Club. Current work: OEM gas lasers; laser spectroscopy; nonlinear optics; gas discharge physics. Subspecialty: Gas lasers. Home: 777 W Middlefield Rd Apt 199 Mountain View CA 94043 Office: Spectra Physics 18-45 1250 W Middlefield Rd Mountain View CA 94042

GERSTLE, FRANK P., JR., materials scientist, research adminstr.; b. Louisville, June 23, 1942; s. Frank P. and Marie E. (Marrone) G.; children: Ron, David. B.A. in Math.Physics, St. Joseph's Coll., 1965; S.B. and S.M. in Mech. Engring, M.I.T., 1966; Ph.D. in Mech. Engring. and Materials Sci, Duke U., 1972. Mem. staff Sandia Labs., Albuquerque, 1966-68, mem. tech. staff div. composite materials, 1972-73, div. mechanics of materials, 1973-74, supr. div.

composites and polymer mechanics, 1974-83, supr. div. ceramics devel., 1984—; grad. asst. Duke U., 1968-72; mem. com. on organic matrix composites Nat. Materials Adv. Bd., 1978-80, mem. com. on lightweight mil. vehicles, 1981-82; chmn. Gordon Research Conf. on Composites, 1981. Mem. Com. nonconventional materials in guns and guntubes Nat. Materials Adv. Bd., 1984-85. Albuquerque Mountain Rescue Council; mem. N.Mex. State Search and Rescue Rev. Bd. Mem. ASME, Soc. Engring. Sci., Am. Ceramics Soc. Club: N.Mex. Mountain. Current Work: Mech. behavior of materials; design of composite structures; supervision activities in composite materials, ceramics, brittle fracture and failure analysis; research in creep rupture in composites. Subspecialties: Composite materials; Theoretical and applied mechanics. Office: Sandia Nat Labs Div 1845 Albuquerque NM 87185

GERWICK, BEN CLIFFORD, JR., construction engineer, educator; b. Berkeley, Calif., Feb. 22, 1919; s. Ben Clifford and Bernice (Coultrap) G.; m. Martelle Louise Beverly, July 28, 1941; children: Beverly (Mrs. Robert A. Brian), Virginia (Mrs. Roy Wallace), Ben Clifford III, William. B.S., U. Calif., 1940. With Ben C. Gerwick, Inc., San Francisco, 1939-70, j1pres, 1952-70; exec. v.p. Santa Fe-Pomeroy, Inc., 1968-71; prof. civil engring. U. Calif., Berkeley, 1971—; sponsoring mgr. Richmond-San Rafael Bridge substructure, 1953-56, San Mateo-Hayward bridge, 1964-66; lectr. constrn. engring. Stanford U., 1962-68; cons. major bridge and marine constrn. projects; cons. constrn. engr. for ocean structures, also concrete offshore structures in, North Sea, Arctic Sea, Japan, Australia, Indonesia, Arabian Gulf; past chmn. marine bd., mem. polar research bd. NRC; mem. Commn. on Engring. and Tech. Systems, NRC; mem. Nat. Acad. Engring., Norwegian Acad. Tech. Scis., Verein Deutscher Ingenieure. Author: (with Peter V. Peters) Russian-English Dictionary of Prestressed Concrete and Concrete Construction, 1966, Construction of Prestressed Concrete Structures, 1971, (with John C. Woolery) Construction and Engineering Marketing for Major Project Services; Contbr. articles to profl. jours. Served with USNR, 1940-46; comdr. Res. ret. Recipient Lockheed award Marine Tech. Soc., 1977. Fellow ASCE (Karp award 1976, Hon. Mem. 1985), Am. Concrete Inst. (dir. 1960, hon. mem., Turner award 1974, Corbetta award 1981, R.E. Davis lectr. 1985); mem. Federation Internationale de la Precontrainte (pres. 1974-78, now hon. pres., Freyssinet medal 1982), Prestressed Concrete Inst. (pres. 1957-58, hon.), Deutscher Beton Verein (hon., Emil Mörsch medal 1979), Concrete Soc. U.K. (hon.), Association Francaise du Beton (hon.), Moles, Soc. Naval Architects and Marine Engrs. (Blakely Smith award 1981), Beavers (Engring. award 1975), Phi Beta Kappa, Tau Beta Pi, Sigma Xi, Chi Epsilon, Kappa Sigma. Conglist. Clubs: Bohemian (San Francisco); Claremont Country (Oakland). Current Work: Offshore construction with emphasis on Arctic and sub-arctic marine environment; prestressed concrete application to marine construction. Subspecialties: Offshore technology; Ocean engineering. Home: 5874 Margarido Dr Oakland CA 94618 Office: 217 McLaughlin Hall U Calif Berkeley CA 94720 also 500 Sansome St San Francisco CA 94111

GERWIN, BRENDA ISEN, biochemist, researcher; b. Boston, May 2, 1939; d. Maurice M. and Jeannette Hershon Isen; m. Robert David Gerwin, Dec. 18, 1960; children: David, Daniel, Joel. B.A. cum laude in Biochemistry, Radcliffe Coll., 1960; Ph.D. in Biochemistry, U. Chgo., 1964. Instr. biochemistry Rockefeller U., 1964-66, Case Western Res. U., 1966-69; biochemist molecular anatomy program Oak Ridge Nat. Lab., 1969-70; sr. staff fellow viral leukemia and lymphoma br. Nat. Cancer Inst., Bethesda, Md., 1971-73; chemist viral biochemistry sect. Nat. Cancer Inst. Lab. Tumor Virus Genetics, 1973-81; research chemist Nat. Cancer Inst. Lab. Molecular Oncology, 1981-83, Lab. Human Carcinogenesis, 1983—. Contbr. chpts. and articles to profl. publs. Mem. Am. Soc. Biol. Chemists, Am. Soc. Microbiology, Am. Chem. Soc., AAAS, Sigma Xi. Current Work: Sequencing DNA of mutant RNA tumor viruses to determine which sequences encode or control important functions; examining intermediates in copying of RNA to DNA by reverse transcriptase. Subspecialties: Biochemistry (biology); Genome organization. Office: Nat Cancer Inst Bldg 37 Rm 2C15 Bethesda MD 20852

GESLICKI, MARK LOUIS, engineering administrator; b. Rome, N.Y., Nov. 24, 1949; s. Paul and Elaine (Legendre) G. B.S. in Physics, Rochester Inst. Tech., 1972. Assoc. engr. optical design Xerox Corp., Rochester, N.Y., 1972-74, sr. engr. optical design, Dallas, 1974-79, engring. mgr. design laser scanning systems, El Segundo, Calif., 1980-81, imaging systems devel. mgr., 1981—. Mem. Optical Soc. Am. Republican. Current Work: Program management of raster scanning systems for digital printing, using lasers as light sources, system integration and architecture of laser scanners in host printing systems. Subspecialties: Laser scanning systems; Laser optics design. Office: 1500 S Shamrock Ave Monrovia CA 91016

GESSOW, ALFRED, aerospace engineer, educator; b. Jersey City, Oct. 1922; s. Morris Samuel and Emma (Levovsky) G.; m. Elaine E. Silverman, Nov. 23, 1947; children: Laura Gessow Goldman, Lisa Gessow Michelson, Miles Jory, Andrew Jody. B.C.E., CCNY, 1943; M.Aero. Engring., NYU, 1944. Aero. research scientist, nat. adv. com. on aeros. Langley Research Center, Va., 1944-59; chief fluid physics research NASA, Washington, 1959-66, asst. dir. research div., 1966-70, dir. for aerodynamics, 1970-79; prof., chmn. dept. aerospace engring. U. Md., College Park, 1979—; lectr. U. Va., Va. Poly. Inst.; adj. prof. NYU, Cath. U. Am.; vis. prof. Korean Inst. Advanced Sci.; cons. NATO; chmn. aerospace div. adv. council Pa. State U.; mem. Nat. Acad. Sci/NRC bd. Army Sci. and Tech., 1982—. Sr. author: Aerodynamics of the Helicopter, 3d edit, 1967; contbr. articles to encys. and profl. jours. Recipient medal for exceptional service NASA, 1974. Fellow Am. Helicopter Soc., AIAA. Jewish. Current Work: Aerospace education; research in rotorcraft aerodynamics and flight dynamics. Subspecialties: Aeronautical engineering; Aerospace engineering and technology. Home: 7308 Durbin Terr Bethesda MD 20817 Office: U Md College Park MD 20742

GETZELS, JACOB WARREN, psychologist, educator; b. Bialystok, Poland, Feb. 7, 1912; came to U.S., 1921, naturalized, 1933; es. Hirsch and Frieda (Solon) G.; m. Judith Nelson, Dec. 24, 1949; children: Katharine, Peter, Julia. B.A., Bklyn. Coll., 1936; M.A., Columbia U., 1939; Ph.D., Harvard U., 1951; L.H.D. (hon.), Hofstra U., 1984. Instr. ednl. psychology U. Chgo., 1951, asst. prof. ednl. psychology, 1952-54, assoc. prof., 1955-57, prof., 1957-84, R. Wendell Harrison Disting. Service prof. edn. and behavioral scis. emeritus; vis. prof. psychology U. P.R., summer, 1962, Stanford U., summer, 1963; mem. U.S. Office Edn. Mission to Soviet Russia, 1960, mem. research adv. council, 1964-70; mem. council of scholars Library of Congress, 1980-83. Author: (with A. Coladarci) The Use of Theory in Educational Administration, 1955, (with P.W. Jackson) Creativity and Intelligence: Explorations with Gifted Students, 1962, (with J.M. Lipham and R.F. Campbell) Educational Administration as a Social Process, 1968, (with I. Taylor) Perspectives in Creativity, 1975, (with M. Csikszentmihalyi) The Creative Vision: A Longitudinal Study of Problem Finding in Art, 1976; contbr. articles to profl. jours. Mem. bd. visitors Learning Research and Devel. Center, U. Pitts., 1973-79; bd. dirs. Spencer Found., 1971—. Recipient Research award Am. Personnel and Guidance Assn., 1959; Tchrs. Coll. medal, 1977; Nicholas Murray Butler medal for theory or philosophy of edn. Columbia U., 1980; Disting. Alumnus award Bklyn. Coll., 1984; Center for Advanced Study in Behavioral Scis. fellow, 1960-61; Center for Policy Study (U. Chgo.) fellow, 1967-75. Fellow AAAS; mem. Am. Psychol. Assn., Nat. Acad. Edn. (1st. v.p. 1972-76), Nat. Soc. for Study Edn. (dir. 1975-77), Am. Ednl. Research Assn. Current Work: Longitudinal studies of development of artists; research on creative thought processes of children and artists; the social context of creativity. Subspecialties: Cognition; Social psychology. Office: 5835 S Kimbark Ave Chicago IL 60637

GEWARTOWSKI, JAMES WALTER, electrical engineer; b. Chgo., Nov. 10, 1930; s. Joseph Walter and Irene Dorothy (Dziekanowski) G.; m. Marion Ruth Wakeman), June 23, 1956; children—Marion, Diane, Patricia, John, Karen. B.S. in Elec. Engring., Ill. Inst. Tech., 1952; S.M. in Elec. Engring., MIT, 1953; Ph.D. in Elec. Engring., Stanford U., 1958. Supr. microwave source group Bell Telephone Labs., Inc., Murray Hill, N.J., 1957-71, supr. lightwave subsystems and reliability group, Allentown, Pa., 1971—. Co-author: Principles of Electron Tubes, 1965; Fundamentals of Electron Tubes, 1969; contbr. articles to profl. jours. Fellow IEEE (Browder J. Thompson Meml. prize 1960). Republican. Roman Catholic. Current work: Transmitter and receiver optical subsystems for fiber optic communication systems. Subspecialties: Electronics; Fiber optics. Home: 2908 Edgemont Dr Allentown PA 18103 Office: AT&T Bell Labs 555 Union Blvd Allentown PA 18103

GEYER, WAYNE ALLAN, forest scientist; b. Oak Park, Ill., Nov. 24, 1933; s. Herman M. and Alice J. (Miller) G.; m. Patricia Joyce Wheeler, Aug. 20, 1960; children: Keith, Kevin. B.S., Iowa State U., 1955; M.S.F., Purdue U., 1962; Ph.D., U. Minn., 1971. Field forester Ga. Kraft Paper Co., Macon, 1957-59; research assoc. forestry U. Ill., Simpson, 1962-65; forest scientist Kans. State U., Manhattan, 1966—, prof. forestry, 1982—. Contbr. articles to profl. jours. Served with USNR, 1955-57. Mem. Soc. Am. Foresters. Current Work: Reclamation of mined areas; fuelwood forestry plantations; herbicides; soil-site studies. Subspecialty: Biomass (agriculture). Office: Call Hall Forestry Dept Kans State U Manhattan KS 66506

GEZARI, DANIEL YSA, astrophysicist; b. N.Y.C., Nov. 6, 1942; s. Zvi and Temima G.; m. Pirjo Kortelainen, July 27, 1974; 2 children. A.B., Cornell U., 1966; M.S., N.Y.U., 1969; Ph.D., Stony Brook U., 1973. Research asst. Woods Hole Oceanographic Inst., 1963, Kitt Peak Nat. Obs., 1969; research fellow Calif. Inst. Tech., Pasadena, 1973-76; resident research asso. NRC, Washington, 1976-78; astrophysicist NASA/Goddard Spare Flight Center, Greenbelt, Md., 1978—; Robert A. Millikan research fellow in astrophysics Calif. Inst. Tech., 1973. Contbr. 30 articles in field to profl. jours. Mem. Internat. Astron. Union, Am. Astron. Soc. Patentee in field. Current Work: Infrared observational astrophysics star formation regions, speckle interferometry, cryogenic instrumentation, space physics and technology; infared array detectors. Subspecialties: Infrared astronomy; Biomedical engineering. Office: NASA/-Goddard Space Flight Center Greenbelt MD 20771

GHANGAS, GURDEV S., molecular biologist; b. Ghangas, Punjab, India, Nov. 15, 1942; s. Gurbachan S. and Dalip Kaur (Virk) G.; m. Surinder P. Kaur, Aug. 1972; children: Imroz, Param, Roop. B.Sc. (Merit scholar), Punjab Agrl. U., 1963, M.S., 1966; Ph.D., Syracuse U., 1971. Lectr. Punjab Agrl. U., 1966; Carver fellow Tuskegee Inst., Ala., 1966-67; research asso. Cornell U., Ithaca, N.Y., 1971-74, vis. scientist, 1983—; postgrad. research biochemist U. Calif., Berkeley, 1974-76; asso. research scientist N.Y. U. Med. Center, N.Y.C., 1977-78; vis. asst. prof. Cornell U., 1979-80; vis. asso. prof. N.Y. Med. Coll., 1981; mgr. cell biology Biol. Energy Corp., Valley Forge, Pa., 1982-83; cons. Contbr. articles to profl. jours. NIH fellow, 1977-79. Mem. Am. Chem. Soc., Am. Assn. Immunologists, Genetics Soc. Am. Current Work: Gene structure and function in procaryotes, eucaryotes, viruses and plasmids, biotechnology. Subspecialties: Genetics and genetic engineering (agriculture); Molecular biology. Home: 700 Warren Rd Apt 13-1F Ithaca NY 14850 Office: Cornell U Wing Hall Ithaca NY 14853

GHANTA, BABU MADHUR, computer science educator; b. Guntur, Andhra Pradesh, India, Mar. 5, 1941; s. Rattaiah and Venkata Subbamma (Gogineni) G.; m. Vijaya Madhur Vemulapalli, June 24, 1970. B.S., Andhra U., 1959; B.Tech. with honors, Indian Inst. Tech., 1963; M.S., MIT, 1969; Ph.D., N.Y. U., 1980. Indsl. engr. Guest Keen Nettlefolds, Bombay, India, 1963-64; tool engr. Godrej & Boyce, Inc., Bombay, 1964-65; mfg. engr. IBM, Bombay, 1965-67; sr. systems cons. Equitable Life Assurance Co., N.Y.C., 1971-77; sr. staff analyst Arthur D. Little, Cambridge, Mass., 1979-80; prof. mgmt. sci. Manhattan Coll., 1980-84; cons. AT&T Communications, 1984—. Mem. Assn. Computing Machinery, Am. Mktg. Assn. Current Work: Human factors aspects of software engring.; automated factories. Subspecialties: Software engineering; Graphics, image processing, and pattern recognition. Home: 89 Oakview Terr Short Hills NJ 07078 Office: AT&T Communications Basking Ridge NJ 07920

GHAUSI, MOHAMMED SHUAIB, electrical engineering educator, administrator; b. Kabul, Afghanistan, Feb. 16, 1930; came to U.S., 1951; s. Omar M. and Homaira Ghausi; m. Marilyn Ghausi, June 12, 1961; children—Nadjya, Simine. B.S. in Elec. Engring., U. Calif.-Berkeley, 1956, M.S. in Elec. Engring., 1957, Ph.D. in Elec. Engring., 1960. Prof., NYU, 1960-62; head elec. and computer engring. NSF, Washington, 1972-74; chmn. dept. elec. engring. Wayne State U., Detroit, 1974-78; dean engring. Oakland U., Rochester, Mich., 1978-83, U. Calif.-Davis, 1983—; bd. dirs. Calif. Engring. Found., Sacramento, 1983—. Author 3 textbooks; co-author 2 textbooks. Contbr. numerous articles to profl. jours. Recipient A. Humboldt prize, 1984. Fellow IEEE (Centennial award 1984); mem. Cir. and Systems Soc. (pres. 1976). Subspecialties: Computer engineering; Integrated circuits. Home: 2894 N El Macero Dr El Macero CA 95618 Office: U Calif-Davis Bainer Hall Davis CA 95616

GHEBREHIWET, BERHANE, immunologist, educator; b. Asmara, Ethiopia, Sept. 28, 1946. D.V.M., Sch. Vet. Medicine, Warsaw, Poland, 1971; M.V.Sc., Ecole Nationale Veterinaire D'Alfort, France, 1973; D.Sc., U. Paris, 1974. Research assoc. dept. molecular immunology Scripps Clinic and Research Found., La Jolla, Calif., 1974-79; asst. prof. medicine SUNY, Stony Brook, 1979-85, asst. prof. pathology, 1983-85, assoc. prof. medicine and pathology, 1985—. Contbr. articles to profl. jours. Mem. Am. Assn. Immunology, Am. Fedn. Clin. Research, N.Y. Acad. Sci., Am. Chem. Soc., AAAS., Am. Assn. Vet. Immunology. Coptic Orthodox. Subspecialties: Immunology (medicine); Biochemistry (medicine). Office: SUNY at Stony Brook HSC T-16 Room 040 Stony Brook NY 11794

GHEORGHIADE, MIHAI, cardiologist, physician, educator; b. Bucarest, Rumania, Feb. 19, 1946; came to U.S., 1972, naturalized, 1978; s. Cosma and Matilda (Sneer) G.; m. Anborg Reidun Lindblom, Sept. 8, 1968. Maturita, Matei Basarab, Bucharest, 1963; M.D., U. Rome, 1972. Diplomate: Am. Bd. Internal Medicine, Am. Bd. Cardiology. Intern Miriam Hosp. Brown U., Providence, 1972-73, resident, 1973-76, chief resident, 1976-77, fellow in cardiology, 1977-79; chief cardiology sect. VA Med. Ctr., Salem, Va., 1979—; asst prof. medicine U. Va., Charlottesville, 1979-83, assoc. prof., 1983—. Contbr. articles to profl. jours. Recipient Outstanding Attending award U. Va., 1981. Fellow Am. Coll. Cardiology; mem. ACP, Roanoke Acad. Medicine, Am. Fedn. Clin. Research, Am. Heart Assn. (dir. 1979—), Porsche Club Am. Current Work: Left ventricular functions and cardiac pharmacology (inotropic agents). Subspecialties: Internal medicine; Cardiology. Home: 5260 Crossbow Circle Roanoke VA 24014 Office: VA Medical Center University of Virginia Salem VA 24011

GHER, MARLIN EUGENE, JR., periodontist, naval officer, educator; b. Harrisburg, Pa., Jan. 8, 1947; s. Marlin E. and Joan E. (Ewing) G.; m. Sharon R. Sumler, May 23, 1970; children: Steven Todd, Jaime Malia. D.D.S., U. Mo.-Kansas City, 1971; M.Ed., George Washington U., 1981. Diplomate: Am. Bd. Oral Medicine, Am. Bd. Periodontics; cert. in periodontics Nat. Naval Dental Center, Bethesda, Md., 1979. Commd. lt. U.S. Navy Dental Corps, 1971, advanced through grades to comdr., 1979; asst. dental officer USN, Twentynine Palms, Calif., 1971-73, Kaneohe, Hawaii, 1973-77, resident in periodontics, Bethesda, 1977-79; mem. staff periodontal dept. Nat. Naval Dental Ctr., Bethesda, 1979-81; head periodontal dept., regional cons. Naval Dental Center, San Diego, 1981—; assoc. prof. U. Md., 1979-81; guest lectr. U. So. Calif., 1982; cons. Uniform Services U. of Health Scis., 1979-81; Research in immunogenicity of freeze-dried skin allografts, 1977-81, inventor collapsible image viewing device. Mem. ADA, Am. Acad. Periodontology, Am. Acad. Oral Medicine, Internat. Assn. Dental Research, Am. Assn. Dental Research. Republican. Episcopalian. Current Work: Immunology and clinical application of freeze-dried skin used as a grafting material; treatment of patients with periodontal disease. Subspecialty: Periodontics. Home: 2804 Atadero Ct Carlsbad CA 92008 Office: NRDC Naval Sta Box 147 San Diego CA 92136

GHETTI, BERNARDINO, neuropathologist, neurobiology researcher; b. Pisa, Italy, Mar. 28, 1941; s. Getulio and Iris (Mugnetti) G.; m. Caterina Genovese, Oct. 8, 1966; children: Chiara, Simone. M.D. cum laude, U. Pisa, 1966, specialist in mental and nervous diseases, 1969. Diplomate: Am. Bd. Pathology.; Lic. physician, Italy cert. Edn. Council for Fgn. Med. Grads. Postdoctoral fellow U. Pisa, 1966-70; research fellow in neuropathology Albert Einstein Coll. Medicine, Bronx, N.Y., 1970-73, resident, clin. fellow in pathology, 1973-75, resident in neuropathology, 1975-76; asst. prof. pathology Ind. U., Indpls., 1976-77, asst. prof. pathology and psychiatry, 1977-78, assoc. prof. pathology and psychiatry, 1978-83, prof., 1983—. Contbr. articles and abstracts to profl. jours. Mem. Am. Assn. Neuropathologists, Soc. Neurosci., Assn. Research in Nervous and Mental Diseases, Am. Soc. Cell Biology, Italian Soc. Psychiatry, Italian Soc. Neurology, Sigma Xi. Roman Catholic. Current Work: Pathologic reactions of neuronal cytoskeleton to toxic compounds, experimental models induced by natural agents, neurobiology and neuropathology of genetically determined cerebellar degenerations in mutant mice. Subspecialties: Pathology (medicine); Neurobiology. Home: 1124 Frederick S Dr Indianapolis IN 46260 Office: 635 Barnhill Dr Room 157 Indianapolis IN 46223

GHOSHAL, NANI GOPAL, veterinary anatomist, educator; b. Dacca, India, Dec. 1, 1934; came to U.S., 1963; s. Priya Kanta and Kiron Bala (Thakurata) G.; m. Chhanda Banerjee, Jan. 24, 1971; 1 dau., Nupur. G.V.Sc., B.V.C., India, 1955; D.T.V.M., U. Edinburgh, 1961; Dr. med. vet., Tieraerztliche Hochschule Hannover, W. Ger., 1962; Ph.D., Iowa State U., 1966. Vet. asst. surgeon West Bengal (India) State Govt., 1955-56; instr. Bengal Vet. Coll., U. Calcutta, 1955-56; research asst. M.P. Govt. Coll. Vet. Sci. and Animal Husbandry, Mhow, India, 1956-59; research officer Indian Council Agrl. Research, India, 1963; instr. Iowa State U., Ames, 1963-66, asst. prof., 1967-70, assoc. prof., 1970-74, prof. vet. gross anatomy, 1974—; chmn. Internat. Vet. Medicine Com., 1967-79. Co-author, editor: Getty's Anatomy of Domestic Animals, 1975; author: (with Tankred Koch, Peter Popesko) Venous Drainage of Domestic Animals, 1981; contbr. (with Tankred Koch, Peter Popesko) chpts. to books, articles to profl. jours. Recipient various scholarships and grants. Fellow Royal Zool. Soc. Scotland (life); mem. World Assn. Vet. Anatomists, Am. Assn. Vet. Anatomists, AAAS, Am. Assn. Anatomists, Pan Am. Assn. Anatomy, N.Y. Acad. Scis., Iowa Vet. Med. Assn., Sigma Xi, Phi Zeta, Gamma Sigma Delta, Phi Kappa Phi. Current Work: Morphology of various organ systems, brain temperature regulation, audio-visual education, developmental anatomy, anatomy of laboratory animals. Subspecialties: Morphology; Biomedical engineering. Home: 1310 Glendale Ave Ames IA 50010 Office: Coll Vet Medicine Iowa State U 1070 Vet Anatomy Ames IA 50011

GIACCO, ALEXANDER FORTUNATUS, diversified chemical company executive; b. St. John, Italy, Aug. 24, 1919 (parents Am. citizens). s. Salvatore J. and Maria Concetta (de Maria) G.; m. Edith Brown, Feb. 16, 1946; children—Alexander Fortunatus, Richard John, Mary P. Giacco Walsh, Elizabeth B., Marissa A., Giacco Rath. B.S. in Chem. Engring, Va. Poly. Inst., 1942; postgrad. in mgmt., Harvard U., 1965; D.B.A. (hon.), William Carey Coll., Hattiesburg, Miss., 1980, Goldey Beacome Coll., 1984; LL.D. (hon.), Widener U., 1984. With Hercules Inc., Wilmington, Del., 1942—, gen. mgr. polymers dept., 1968-73, dir., 1970—, gen. mgr. operating dept., 1973, v.p. parent co., 1974-76, mem. exec. com., 1974—, exec. v.p., 1976-77, pres., chief exec. officer, chmn. exec. com., 1977—, chmn. bd., 1980, Himont Inc., 1983; dir. Del. Trust Co., Montedison S.p.A. and Erbamont, N.V.; mem. U.S. Com. on New Initiatives in East-West Co-op., 1976—. Hon. chmn., mem. nat. bd. dirs. Jr. Achievement Del., 1975; trustee, bd. dirs., mem. exec. com. Med. Ctr. of Del., 1975—; rector, trustee, bd. visitors Va. Poly. Inst., 1979; bd. dirs. Greater Wilmington Devel. Council, WHYY, Inc.; chmn. bd. Grand Opera House, Wilmington. Named One of Ten Outstanding Chief Exec. Officers Fin. World, 1980, Best Chief Exec. Officer in Chem. Industry Fin. World, 1981, Outstanding Chief Exec. Officer in the Chem. Industry Wall Street Transcript, 1983, 84, 85. Mem. Chem. Mfrs. Assn. (dir.), Soc. Plastics Industry, Soc. Chem. Industry, Soc. Automotive Engrs., Man-Made Fiber Producers Assn., Am. Ordnance Assn. (past dep. chmn.), Del. Roundtable (chmn. econ. devel. com.). Clubs: Wilmington, Wilmington Country (bd. dirs.), Vicmead Hunt, Hercules Country, Rehoboth Beach Country, Rodney Square (bd. dirs.), Jonathan's Landing Country (Fla.). Patentee in field. . Home: Greenville DE 19807 Office: Hercules Plaza Wilmington DE 19894

GIACCONI, RICCARDO, science institute director, educator; b. Genoa, Italy, Oct. 6, 1931; came to U.S., 1956; s. Antonio and Elsa (Canni) G.; m. Mirella Manaira, Feb. 15, 1957; children—Guia, Anna Lee, Marc Antonio. Ph.D. in Physics, U. Milan, Italy, 1954; D.Sc. (hon.), U. Chgo., 1983; Laurea honoris causa, in Astronomics, U. Padua, Italy, 1984. Asst. prof. physics U. Milan, 1954-56; research assoc., Fulbright fellow Ind. U., Bloomington, 1956-58; research assoc. Cosmic Ray Lab., Princeton U., N.J., 1958-59; sr. scientist Am. Sci. and Engring. Inc., Cambridge, Mass., 1959-62, dir., 1966-73, exec. v.p., 1969-73; assoc. dir. high energy astrophysics div. Harvard/Smithsonian Ctr. for Astrophysics, 1973-81; prof. astronomy Harvard U., Cambridge, 1973-82; prin. investigator NASA, 1960—; dir. Space Telescope Sci. Inst., Balt., 1981—; prof. astrophysics Johns Hopkins U., Balt., 1982—; cons. and lectr. in field. Contbr. articles to profl. jours. Recipient numerous awards for sci. excellence, most recent being Gold medal Royal Astron. Soc., 1982; A. Cressy Morrison award in natural scis. N.Y. Acad. Scis., 1982. Fellow AAAS; mem. Am. Astron. Soc. (councilor 1979-82), Am. Phys. Soc., Internat. Astron. Union (pres. com. 48), Nat. Acad. Scis., Md. Acad. Scis. (sci. council), Italian Phys. Soc., Fachbereit, Max-Planck Inst. for Physics and Astrophysics, Centro Internazionale di Stora dello Spazio e del Tempo (sci. com.). Current Work: X-ray astronomy. Subspecialties: X-ray high energy astrophysics; Cosmology. Home: 4205 Underwood Rd Baltimore MD 21218 Office: Space Telescope Sci Inst 3700 San Martin Dr Baltimore MD 21218

GIAEVER, IVAR, physicist; b. Bergen, Norway, Apr. 5, 1929; came to U.S., 1957, naturalized, 1963; s. John A. and Gudrun (Skaarud) G.; m. Inger Skramstad, Nov. 8, 1952; children: John, Anne Kari, Guri, Trine. Siv. Ing., Norwegian Inst. Tech., Trondheim, 1952; Ph.D., Rensselaer Poly. Inst., 1964. Patent examiner Norweigian Patent Office, Oslo, 1953-54; mech. engr. Can. Gen. Electric Co., Peterborough, Ont., 1954-56; applied mathematician Gen. Electric Co., Schenectady, 1956-58; physicist Gen. Electric Co. (Research and Devel. Center), 1958—. Served with Norwegian Army, 1952-53. Recipient Nobel Prize for Physics, 1973; Guggenheim fellow, 1970. Fellow Am. Phys. Soc. (Oliver E. Buckley prize 1965); mem. IEEE, Norwegian Profl. Engrs., Nat. Acad. Sci., Nat. Acad. Engring. (V.K. Zworykin award 1974), Am. Acad. Arts and Scis., Norwegian Acad. Sci., Norwegian Acad. Tech. Current Work: biophysics. Subspecialties: Biophysics (physics); Condensed matter physics. Office: Gen Electric Co Corp Research & Devel PO Box 8 Schenectady NY 12301*

GIAMBALVO, CECILIA TANG, psychopharmacologist, educator; b. Canton, China, Oct. 5, 1946; came to U.S., 1966, naturalized, 1974; d. Stephen W.W. and Mary P. Tang; m. Vincent W. Giambalvo, July, 1971. B.S., U. Conn., 1970, Ph.D., 1975. Postdoctoral fellow Harvard Med. Sch., Boston, 1975-77; research assoc. Children's Hosp., Boston, 1975-79; instr. Harvard Med. Sch., Boston, 1977-79; psychopharmacologist State R.I., Cranston, 1979—; asst. prof. research Brown U., Providence, 1979—; asst. adj. prof. U. R.I., Kingston, 1979—. Contbr. articles to profl. jours. NIH grantee, 1983. Mem. Am. Soc. Neurosci., Internat. Soc. Neurochemistry, AAAS. Current work: Biochemical basis of neuronal functions and how it affects physiology and behavior and relates to psychiatric illnesses. Subspecialties: Neurochemistry; Psychopharmacology. Office: RI Psychiatric Research and Training Ctr Howard Ave Cranston RI 02920

GIANNETTA, CARL LEE, nutrition scientist; b. Pueblo, Colo., Mar. 31, 1937; s. Carl Joseph and Patricia Beatrice (Carlino) G.; m. Juaniva Marion Wood, June 11, 1960; children—Patricia Corrinne Giannetta Horstkamp, Deborah Kathleen, Stephanie Elizabeth Giannetta Mijo. B.A., Western State Coll., Gunnison, Colo., 1955-59; M.S., Trinity U., San Antonio, 1963-68; Ph.D., Tex. A&M U., 1973; diploma Internat. Correspondence Sch., 1975. Research chemist Sch. Aerospace Medicine, San Antonio, 1963-77; consumer safety officer FDA, Washington, 1977-81; nutrition scientist Agrl. Research Service, Houston, 1981—; asst. dir. for program mgmt. Children's Nutrition Research Ctr., Houston, 1982—. Lectr. K.C., Houston, 1984. Recipient Cert. of Appreciation EPA, 1980, Superior Performance award FDA, 1981. Fellow AM. Coll. Nutrition, Royal Soc. Health; mem. Am. Chem. Soc., N.Y. Acad. Scis., AAAS. Roman Catholic. Current work: Scientific administration with consultation in mineral metabolism and analytical chemistry. Subspecialties: Nutrition (biology); Clinical chemistry. Home: 3643 Storm Creek Dr Houston TX 77088 Office: Children's Nutrition Research Ctr 6608 Fannin Suite 601 Houston TX 77030

GIANNINI, A. JAMES, psychiatrist, educator; b. Youngstown, Ohio, June 11, 1947; s. Matthew and Grace Carla (Nistri) G.; m. Judith Ludvik, Apr. 26, 1975; children—Juliette Nicole, Jocelyn Danielle. B.S., Youngstown State U., Ohio, 1970; M.D., U. Pitts., 1974; postgrad., Yale U., 1974-78. Diplomate: Nat. Bd. Med. Eximiners. Intern St. Elizabeth Med. Ctr., Youngstown, 1974; resident dept. psychiatry Yale U., New Haven, 1975-78, chief resident, 1977-78; assoc. psychiatrist Elmcrest Psychiat. Inst., Portland, Conn., 1976-78; acting ward chief Conn. Mental Health Center, New Haven, 1977; assoc. dir. family medicine, psychiatry St. Elizabeth Med. Ctr., Youngstown, 1978-80; assoc. prof. dept. psychiatry Northeast Ohio Med. Coll., 1978-84, prof., 1984—, program dir., 1980—; assoc. clin. prof. dept psychiatry Ohio State U., 1983—; sr. cons. Fair Oaks Hosp., Summit, N.J., 1980—, Regent Hosp., N.Y.C., 1981—, chmn. Nat. Adv. Council Prevention and Control of Rape, NIMH, Rockville, Md., 1984—; dir. depts. psychiatry and toxicology Western Res. Health Systems, 1985—. Author: (with Henry Black) Psychiatric, Psychogenic, Sumatopsychic Disorders, 1978; (with Robert Gilliland) Neurologic, Neurogenic and Neuropsychiatric Disorders, 1982; (with Andrew Slaby) Overdose and Detoxification Emergencies, 1983; Clinical Foundation of Biological Psychiatry, 1985. Contbr. numerous articles to profl. jours. Vice chmn. Mahoning County (Ohio) Mental Health Bd.; councilor Nat. Italian Am. Found. Recipient James Earley award U. Pitts., 1974, Upjohn Research prize Upjohn Co., 1974; recipient Fair Oaks Research award Fair Oaks Hosp., 1979, Bronze award Brit. Med. Assn. Fellow N.J. Acad. Medicine, Am. Coll. Clin. Pharmacology; mem. Soc. Neurosci. Brit. Brain Soc., Brit. Brain Soc., European Neurosci. Soc., N.Y. Acad. Scis., Am. Psychiat. Assn., Acad. Clin. Psychiatry, Sigma Xi. Roman Catholic. Club: Youngstown. Current Work: Central effects of phencyclidine; effect of ambient ions upon mood, mood-modulating effects of clonidine. Subspecialties: Psychopharmacology; Neurophysiology. Office: PO Box 2169 Youngstown OH 44504

GIARDINA, PAUL ANTHONY, environmental hazard administrator; b. Rockville Centre, N.Y., June 7, 1949; s. Anthony J. and Carolyn A. (Tamburello) G.; m. Jane Cranston, May 13, 1972. B.S., U. Mich., 1971; M.S., N.Y.U., 1973. Engr. Consolidated Edison, N.Y.C., 1971-74, Ebasco Services, N.Y.C., 1974-75; chief radiation EPA, N.Y.C., 1975-79; dir. N.J. DEP, Trenton, 1979—; adv. council Environ. Hazard Mgmt. Inst., Portsmouth, N.H., 1979—; dir. chem. control clean-up, 1980-81. Author: govt. report Summary Report on the Low-Level Radioactive Waste Burial Site, West Valley, 1977. Named Outstanding Young Man of Am. Jaycees, 1979; USPHS fellow, 1971; U.S. Army scholar, 1967. Mem. AAAS, Am. Nuclear Soc., Health Physics Soc., N.Y. Acad. Scis., Planetary Soc. Republican. Current Work: The control of hazardous materials and toxic substances, including radioactive materials, specializing in developing new clean-up and disposal technology. Subspecialty: Environmental engineering. Home: 152 Three Mile Harbor Rd East Hampton NY 11937

GIBBONS, HARRY LAWRENCE, JR., limnologist, consultant, researcher; b. Spokane, Wash., Sept. 21, 1950; s. Harry Lawrence and Jackie Ann (Payne) G.; m. Maribeth Vivian Hanussak, Aug. 4, 1973; 1 son, Ryan Holt. B.S., Gonzaga U., 1973; M.S., Wash. State U., 1976, Ph.D., 1981. Research asst. Wash. State U., Pullman, 1973-81, postdoctoral research assoc., 1981-85; chief limnologist KCM, Inc., Seattle, 1985—; pres. Water, Pullman, 1983-84. Contbr. articles to profl. jours. Grantee Dept. Ecology, 1981-85, U.S. Army C.E., 1981-85, Dept. Interior, 1982-83, local govts., 1982-85. Mem. N.Am. Lake Mgmt. Soc. (program chmn. 1984), Pacific N.W. Pollution Control Assn. (chmn. water resources 1984-85), Am. Soc. Limnology and Oceanography, Aquatic Plant Mgmt. Soc. Sigma Xi. Roman Catholic. Current work: Lake restoration, aquatic macrophyte control, aquaculture, pollution biology, acid rain, nutrient cycles. Subspecialties: Limnology; Resource management. Home: 9515 Wind Song Loop NE Bainbridge Island WA 98110 Office: Kramer Chin & Mayo Inc 1917 1st Ave Seattle WA 98101

GIBBONS, JAMES F., electrical engineer; b. Leavenworth, Kans., Sept. 19, 1931; married; 3 children. B.S., Northwestern U., 1953; M.S. in Elec. Engring., Stanford U., 1954, Ph.D., in Elec. Engring., 1956. Fulbright fellow Cambridge U., 1956-57; from asst. prof. to assoc. prof. Stanford U., Calif., 1957-64, prof. elec. engring., 1964—, dean Sch. of Engring., 1984—; mem. tech. staff Bell Telephone Labs., Inc., 1956; NSF sr. fellow, 1963-64; Fulbright lectr., 1963-64; mem. grad. fellow panel NSF, 1964-70, chmn. engring. fellow panel, 1968-70; cons. Fairchild Camera and Instrument Co., 1966-70. Subspecialty: Electronics. Office: Stanford U Sch Engring Stanford CA 94305*

GIBBONS, MICHAEL FRANCIS, JR., anthropology educator, anatomy researcher; b. Laconia, N.H., Mar. 20, 1941; s. Michael Francis and Mary Jo (Leso) G. B.A., Yale U., 1963, M.Phil., 1970, Ph.D., 1974. Teaching fellow anatomy Yale U., New Haven, 1970-72; instr. anthropology U. Mass., Boston, 1972-74, asst. prof., 1974-78, assoc. prof., 1979—; vis. prof. U. Alaska-S.E., Juneau, 1977-78; cons. Children's Hosp., Boston, 1974-76; vis. scientist Mass. Audubon Soc., Wenham, 1978-79. Author: Dissection Guide to Higher Primates, 1979; monograph Phyletics of Oreopithecus, 1963 (Dean's prize). Sec. The Conservation Agy., Jamestown, R.I., 1981—. Served to lt. USN, 1963-68. Yale Univ. fellow, 1968, 70; NIH fellow, 1969; NSF grantee, 1973. Fellow Am. Anthrop. Assn.; mem. Am. Assn. Anatomists, N.Y. Acad. Scis., Systematics Assn. (London), Conservation Agy. Clubs: Elizabethan; Yale (New Haven). Current Work: Mechanisms of speech sound generation; anatomy, embryology and evolution of the human head and neck; evolution of speech. Subspecialties: Anatomy and embryology; Acoustics. Home: 125 Chestnut St Wakefield MA 01880 Office: U Mass Harbor Campus Boston MA 02125

GIBBS, DAVID EUGENE, actuary; b. Spencer, Iowa, Jan. 13, 1940; s. E. Eugene and Helen Catherine (Glessner) G.; m. Inez Harmon, Mar. 25, 1972; children—David Matthew, Steven Eugene, Karen Alicia. B.A., U. Calif.-Berkeley, 1963, M.A., 1967; Ph.D., U. Va. 1971. Researcher, U. Bonn., 1971-73; asst. prof. math. La. State U., Baton Rouge, 1973-78; chmn. math. dept. Murray State U., Ky., 1978-82; actuary Met. Life Ins. Co. N.Y.C., from 1982; now with Aetna Life & Casualty Co., Hartford, Conn. NSF summer fellow, 1968, 69, 70, grantee, 1975; U. Va. Gov.'s fellow, 1970-71; La. State U. grantee, 1976. Mem. Soc. Actuaries, Soc. Indsl. and Applied Math, Sigma Xi. Republican. Episcopalian. Current work: Application of applied math and stats. to investment problems as well as insurance problems. Subspecialties: Applied mathematics; Statistics. Home: 407 Old Stage Rd Glastonbury CT 06033 Office: Aetna Life and Casualty Co 151 Farmington Ave Hartford CT 06156

GIBBS, E(DWARD) PAUL J(OHNSON), veterinary educator, virologist; b. Neath, Wales, Apr. 6, 1945; came to U.S., 1979; s. Stanley Johnson and Margaret Kathleen (James) G.; m. Christine Frances Mayo, Aug. 24, 1968; children—Katherine Anna, Samantha Elizabeth. B.V.Sc., U. Bristol (Eng.), 1967, Ph.D., 1970. Prin. vet. research officer Animal Virus Research Inst., Pirbright, Eng., 1970-79; prof. virology Coll. Vet. Medicine, U. Fla., Gainesville, 1979—; advisor Inter Am. Inst. Coop. Agr., Costa Rica, 1980—, FAO, UN, Rome, 1984—. Editor: Virus Diseases Food Animals, 1981; co-author: Veterinary Virology, 1985; also articles. Recipient Career Travelling award Agrl. Research Council, 1974. Mem. AVMA, Am. Soc. Virology, Brit. Vet. Assn., Am. Soc. Tropical Medicine and Hygiene, U.S. Animal Health Assn., Phi Zeta. Current work: Epidemiology of virus diseases of international importance. Subspecialties: Virology (veterinary medicine); Genetics and genetic engineering (veterinary medicine). Home: 3650 NW 30th Pl Gainesville FL 32605 Office: Coll Vet Medicine U Fla J-137 Gainesville FL 32610

GIBBS, GARRY WAYNE, physicist; b. Watrous, Sask., Can., July 22, 1943; came to U.S., 1952, naturalized, 1964; s. Clarence Darrel and Inga Marie (Austring) G.; 1 child, Michelle Marie. B.S., U. N.D., 1965, M.S., 1967; grad. Naval War Coll., 1975; M.S., U. So. Calif., 1977. Head high energy laser br. Naval Missile Ctr., Point Mugu, Calif., 1973-75; sr. project mgr. spl. projects Pacific Missile Test Ctr., Point Mugu, 1975-77, acting head surface weapons project, 1977; mgr. systems analysis high energy laser program U.S. Navy, Washington, 1977-80; laser physicist OIF, Dept. Energy, Washington, 1981-82, laser program mgr., 1982—, mem. sr. exec. service devel. program, 1984-85. Patent disclosure Explosive driven gas dynamic laser, 1972. Contbr. articles to profl. jours. Recipient Performance awards U.S. Navy and U.S. Dept. Energy, 1971, 77, 78, 79, 83, 85. Mem. Optical Soc. Am., Sigma Xi. Current work: Laser fusion research and development, directed energy weapons technology, high energy lasers technology, lasers and electrooptics, energy research and development. Subspecialties: Laser fusion; Nuclear fusion. Office: Office Inertial Fusion US Dept Energy DP-231 Washington DC 20545

GIBBS, HYATT MCDONALD, physicist, educator; b. Hendersonville, N.C., Aug. 6, 1938; s. Robert Shuford and Isabella Frances (Gamble) G.; m. Lethia Elizabeth Archer, June 3, 1960; children: Alexander Robert, Vanetta Lea. A.A., Mars Hill Coll., 1958; B.S.E.E., B.S.Engring. Physics, N.C. State U., Raleigh, 1960; Ph.D., U. Calif., Berkeley, 1965. Acting asst. prof. U. Calif., Berkeley, 1965-67; exchange scientist Philips Research Labs., Eindhoven, 1975-76; mem. tech. staff Bell Labs., Murray Hill, N.J., 1967-80; prof. optical scis. U. Ariz., Tucson, 1980—, dir. optical circuitry coop., 1984—; vis. lectr. Princeton U., 1978-79. Mem. editorial bd. Phys. Review A, 1982—; assoc. editor Optics Letters, 1983—. Mem. Warren Twp. Planning Bd., 1973, 74, Bd. Edn., 1978-80. Recipient Michelson medal Franklin Inst., 1984. Fellow Am. Phys. Soc., Optical Soc. Am. (bd. dirs. 1985—), AAAS; mem. IEEE (com. 1985—), N.Y. Acad. Sci., Sigma Xi, Sigma Pi Sigma, Phi Kappa Phi, Eta Kappa Nu, Tau Beta Pi. Presbyterian. Patentee in field. Current Work: Optical bistability: basic experiments and development practical all-optical logic and switching devices, nonlinear optics, coherent pulse propagation, optical chaos, fundamental tests. Subspecialties: Condensed matter physics; Optical signal processing. Home: 4900 E Calle Barril Tucson AZ 85718 Office: Optical Scis Center Tucson AZ 85721

GIBBS, MARTIN, educator, biologist; b. Phila., Nov. 11, 1922; s. Samuel and Rose (Sugarman) G.; m. Svanhild Karen Kvale, Oct. 11, 1950; children—Janet Helene, Laura Jean, Steven Joseph, Michael Seland, Robert Kvale. B.S., Phila. Coll. Pharmacy, 1943; Ph.D., U. Ill., 1947. Scientist Brookhaven Nat. Lab., 1947-56; prof. biochemistry Cornell U., 1957-64; prof. biology, chmn. dept. Brandeis U., Waltham, Mass., 1965—; Cons. NSF, 1961-64, 69-72, NIH, 1966-69; mem. corp. Marine Biol. Lab., Woods Hole, Mass., 1970—; RESA lectr., 1969; NATO cons. fellowship bd., 1968-70; mem. Council Internat. Exchange of Scholars, 1976-82; chmn. adv. com. selection Fulbright scholars for Eastern Europe; adj. prof. Bot. Inst., U. Münster, W.Ger. Author: Structure and Function of Chloroplasts; Editor-in-chief: Plant Physiology, 1963—; assoc. editor: Physiologie Vegetale, 1966-76, Ann. Rev. Plant Physiology, 1966-71. Mem. AAUP, Am., Japanese socs. plant physiologists, Am. Acad. Arts and Scis., Am. Soc. Biol. Chemists, Council Biology Editors, Nat. Acad. Scis., Sigma Xi. Current Work: Plant: carbohydrate metabolism, carbon flow in photosynthesis. Subspecialty: Plant physiology (biology). Home: 32 Slocum Rd Lexington MA 02173 Office: Brandeis Univ Waltham MA 02254

GIBBS, ROBERT HENRY, JR., ichthyologist, biological oceanographer; b. New London, Conn., July 30, 1929; s. Robert Henry and Elizabeth Carrington (Kilgore) G.; m. Sarah Preble Bowker, June 19, 1951 (div. 1962); 1 dau., Elizabeth; m. Frigga Katharina Elizabeth Bahr, Mar. 2, 1963; children—Hans-Martin, Hans-Thomas, Adrienne. B.A., Cornell U., 1951, Ph.D., 1955. Asst. prof. Plattsburgh State U., N.Y., 1955-56; research assoc. Woods Hole Oceanographic Inst., Mass., 1956-58; asst. prof. Boston U., 1958-62, assoc. prof., 1962-63; assoc. curator Smithsonian Inst., Washington, 1963-66, curator, 1967—, chmn. dept. vertebrate zoology, 1972-77. Contbr. numerous articles to profl. jours. Mem. Am. Soc. Ichthyologists and Herpetologists (treas. 1967-72), Ichthyological Soc. Japan, SociétéFrançaise d'Ichtyologie, Soc. Systematic Zoology. Current work: Systematics and biology of epipelagic and mesopelagic fishes, especially stomioid dragon fishes; ecology of mesopelagic systems. Subspecialties: Marine biology; Taxonomy. Home: 4017 Simms Dr Kensington MD 20895 Office: Div Fishes Nat Mus Natural History Washington DC 20560

GIBBS, WILLIAM EUGENE, chemical company executive; b. Akron, Ohio, Sept. 23, 1930; s. Marvin Hill and Mary Myrtle (Frame) G.; m. Carol Lois Ullrich, Oct. 13, 1958 (div. 1968); children—Sheryl, Shelley, Susan, Sharon, Scott; m. Susie Janet Cottingim, Aug. 30, 1970; stepchildren—David, Leslie, Eric Sullender. B.S in Chemistry, U. Akron, 1954, M.S in Chemistry, 1954, Ph.D. in Polymer Chemistry, 1959. Research chemist U. Akron, 1953-55; Goodyear Tire and Rubber Co., Akron, 1955-58; commd. officer U.S. Air Force, 1955, advanced through ranks to maj.; research chemist, Wright-Patterson AFB, Ohio, 1958-60, lab. chief, 1960-70; ret., 1975; v.p. research and devel. plastics div. Am. Hoechst Corp., Leominster, Mass. and Chesapeake, Va., 1970—. Contbr. chpts. to books, articles to profl. jours. Bd. dirs. Leominster C. of C., 1972-78; bd. dirs. United Way North Central Mass., Leominster, 1976-84, pres., 1980-82. Recipient Outstanding Fed. Service award U.S. Govt., 1968. Mem. Am. Chem. Soc. (councilor 1972—), Faraday Soc., Soc. Plastics Engrs. Club: Oak Hill Country. Current work: Kinetics and mechanisms of polymerization, high temperature polymers, vinyl polymerization, plastic materials, polymer degradation, thermodynamics. Subspecialty: Polymer chemistry. Office: Am Hoechst Corp 5100 Bainbridge Blvd Chesapeake VA 23320

GIBLETT, ELOISE ROSALIE, hematology educator; b. Tacoma, Wash., Jan. 17, 1921; d. William Richard and Rose (Godfrey) G. B.S., U. Wash., 1942, M.S., 1947, M.D. with honors, 1951. Mem. faculty U. Wash. Sch. Medicine, 1957—, research prof., 1967—; asso. dir., head immunogenetics Puget Sound Blood Center, 1955-79, exec. dir., 1979—; former mem. several research coms. NIH. Author: Genetic Markers in Human Blood, 1969; Editorial bd.: Transfusion; Contbr. over 180 articles to profl. jours. Recipient fellowships, grants, Emily Cooley, Karl Landsteiner, Philip Levine and Alexander Wiener immunohematology awards. Fellow AAAS; Mem. Nat. Acad. Scis., Am. Soc. Human Genetics (pres. 1973), Am. Soc. Hematology, Am. Assn. Immunologists, Brit. Soc. Immunology, Internat. Soc. Hematologists, Am. Fedn. Clin. Research, Western Assn. Physicians, Assn. Am. Physicians, Sigma Xi, Alpha Omega Alpha. Current Work: Administration, teaching, research in blood transfusion science, immunohematology, medical genetics, genetic markers in human blood, biochemistry of immunodeficiency disease, enzyme polymorphisms. Subspecialties: Immunology (medicine); Hematology. Home: 6533 53d St NE Seattle WA 98115 Office: Puget Sound Blood Center Terry and Madison Sts Seattle WA 98104

GIBSON, ELEANOR JACK, psychology educator; b. Peoria, Ill., Dec. 7, 1910; d. William A. and Isabel (Grier) Jack; m. James J. Gibson, Sept. 17, 1932; children: James J., Jean Grier. B.A., Smith Coll., 1931, M.A., 1933, D.Sc., 1972; Ph.D., Yale U., 1938; D.Sc., Rutgers U., 1973, Trinity Coll., 1982, Bates Coll., 1985; L.H.D., SUNY-Albany, 1984. Asst., instr., asst. prof. Smith Coll., 1931-49; research assoc. psychology Cornell U., Ithaca, N.Y., 1949-66, prof., 1972—, Susan Linm Sage prof. psychology, 1972—; fellow Inst. for Advanced Study, Princeton, 1959-60, Inst. for Advanced Study in Behavioral Scis., Stanford, Calif., 1963-64; vis. prof. Mass. Inst. Tech., 1973, Inst. Child Devel., U. Minn., 1980; vis. disting. prof. U. Calif., Davis, 1978; vis. scientist Salk Inst., La Jolla, Calif., 1979; vis. prof. U. Pa., 1984. Author: Principles of Perceptual Learning and Development, 1967 (Century award), (with H. Levin) The Psychology of Reading, 1975. Recipient Wilbur Cross medal Yale U., 1973; Howard Crosby Warren medal, 1977; medal for disting. service Tchrs. Coll., Columbia U., 1983; Guggenheim fellow, 1972-73. Fellow AAAS (div. chairperson 1983), Am. Psychol. Assn. (Distinguished Scientist award 1968, G. Stanley Hall award 1970, pres. div. 3 1977); mem. Eastern Psychol. Assn. (pres. 1968), Soc. Exptl. Psychologists, Nat. Acad. Edn., Psychonomic Soc., Soc. Research in Child Devel. (Disting. Sci. Contbn. award 1981), Nat. Acad. Sci., Am. Acad. Arts and Scis., Brit. Psychol. Soc. (hon.), N.Y Acad. Scis. (hon.), Italian Soc. Research in Child Devel. (hon.), Phi Beta Kappa, Sigma Xi. Current Work: Perceptual development. Subspecialties: Developmental psychology; Cognition. Home: 111 Oak Hill Rd Ithaca NY 14850

GIBSON, GEORGE WILLIAM, metallurgical engineer; b. Los Angeles, Nov. 5, 1921; s. George Imboden and Florence (Huse) G.; m. Aleene Neely, Sept. 11, 1948; children: George N., David H., Howard E., Richard B. B.S., U. Ariz., 1943; postgrad., Yale U., 1946; M.S., U. Idaho, 1966. Metall. engr. ASARCO, Los Angeles, 1946-55, Braden Copper Co., Caletones, Chile, 1955-58, Idaho Nat. Engring. Lab., Idaho Falls, 1958-71, So. Peru Copper Co., Ilo, 1971-73, Idaho Nat. Engring. Lab., Idaho Falls, 1973-83, cons., 1983—. Served to 1st lt. USAF, 1943-46. Mem. AIME. Republican. Current Work: Development of processes for disposal of nuclear waste; design and fabrication of nuclear fuels. Subspecialties: Metallurgical engineering; Nuclear engineering. Home: PO Box 923 Hailey ID 83333 Office: PO Box 923 Hailey ID 83333

GIBSON, JEAN M., radiation physicist; b. Columbia, Utah, Dec. 1, 1930; d. George J. and Mary (Pizzuto) G. B.A., Coll. St. Benedict, 1956; M.S., U. Iowa, 1966, Ph.D., 1969. Tchr. high sch., Cold Spring, Minn., 1958-63; asst. prof. physics Coll. St. Benedict, St. Joseph, Minn., 1969-75; physicist St. Benedict's Hosp., Ogden, Utah, 1975—. Contbr. articles to profl. jours. NASA trainee, 1968-69. Mem. Am. Assn. Physicists in Medicine. Roman Catholic. Current Work: Computer software evaluation for radiation therapy, calibration of linear accelerators and other x-ray machines; computer treatment planning for radiation therapy. Subspecialty: Medical physics. Home: 309 E 5450 S Ogden UT 84405 Office: 5475 S 500 E Ogden UT 84405

GIBSON, SAM THOMPSON, physician; b. Covington, Ga., Jan. 1, 1916; s. Count Dillon and Julia (Thompson) G.; m. Alice Chase Gibson, Oct. 31, 1942 (dec. Jan. 1971); children: Lena S., Stephen C., Judith Gibson Hammer, Lucy F. B.S. in Chemistry, Ga. Inst. Tech., 1936; M.D., Emory U., 1940. Diplomate: Am. Bd. Internal Medicine. Med. house officer Peter Bent Brigham Hosp., Boston, 1940-41, asst. resident in medicine, 1946-47; research fellow in medicine Harvard Med. Sch., 1941-43, Milton research fellow, 1947-49; asst. to assoc. dir. ARC Blood Program, Washington, 1949-56, nat. dir., 1956-66, sr. med. officer, 1957-67; clin. asst. prof. medicine George Washington U. Med. Sch., 1963—, Uniformed Services U. Health Scis., 1981—; asst. dir. Div. Biol. Standards, NIH, Bethesda, Md., 1967-72; asst. to dir. Bur. Biologics, FDA, Bethesda, 1972-77, dir. div. biologics evaluation, 1977-82, dir. div. biol. product compliance, 1982—; cons. Care-Medico, 1970—. Editorial bd.: Jour. Vox Sanguinis, 1956-76. Served to capt. USNR, 1941-46. Recipient service award FDA, 1977, merit award, 1978. Mem. Internat. Soc. Blood Transfusion (dir. 1962-66), Internat. Soc. Hematology, Am. Soc. Hematology, N.Y. Acad. Scis., AMA. Club: George Washington U. Current Work: Regulation of biologics production. Subspecialty: Regulatory medicine. Home: 5801 Rossmore Dr Bethesda MD 20814 Office: FDA Ctr Drugs and Biologics 5600 Fishers Ln Rockville MD 20857

GIDDA, JASWANT SINGH, physiologist, educator; b. Panjab, India, Oct. 1, 1946; s. R.S. Singh and Shakuntla (Devi) G.; m. Raj K., May 2, 1948; children: Archana R., Vipul J. B.S. with honors, Panjab U., 1967, M.S. with honors, 1968, Ph.D., 1973. Research scientist U. Tex.-Dallas, 1973-78; instr. U. Tex. Health Sci. Center-San Antonio, 1978-81; instr. physiology Harvard Med. Sch., 1981-84; sr. research scientist Bristol-Myers Co., 1984—; research asst. prof. Upstate Med. Ctr., 1984—. Jr. research fellow Council Sci. and Indsl. Research, India, 1968-72. Contbr. articles to sci. jours. Mem. AAAS, Neurosci. Soc., Am. Gastroenterology Assn. Current Work: Neuromuscular control of gut motility. Neurophysiology, motility, smooth muscle physiology, neuropharmacology. Subspecialties: Gastroenterology; Neurophysiology. Home: 4794 Hyde Rd Manlius NY 13104 Office: 330 Brookline Ave Boston MA 02215

GIDDINGS, JOHN CALVIN, educator, researcher; b. American Fork, Utah, Sept. 26, 1930; s. Luther W. and Berniece (Crandall) G.; married; children: Steven B., Michael C. B.S., Brigham Young U., 1952; Ph.D., U. Utah, 1954. Asst. prof. chemistry U. Utah, 1957-59, assoc. prof., 1959-62, research prof., 1962-66, prof., 1966—; mem. adv. bd. Negative Population Growth, Inc. Author: Dynamics of Chromatography, 1965, Chemistry, Man and Environmental Change, 1973; editor: Our Chemical Environment, 1972, Advances in Chromatography, Vols. 1-24; exec. editor: Separation & Technology, 1966—; mem. editorial bd.: Jour. Liquid Chromatography, 1978—; contbr. articles to profl. jours. Fulbright grantee, 1974; recipient Tswett medal in chromatography, 1978, Stephen Dal Nogare Chromatography award, 1979, U. Utah Disting. Research award, 1979, Russian Sci. Council Chromatography award, 1980. Mem. Am. Chem. Soc. (award in chromatography and electrophoresis 1967, award in analytical chemistry 1980). Club: Wasatch Mt. (Salt Lake City). Organizer expedition for exploration and descent of the upper canyons of the Apurimac River in Peru, 1975. Current Work: Chromatography and field flow fractionation; active in research relating chromatographic separability to the underlying molecular processes and research on general separation theory and methods; new separation methodology, macromolecular separations, devel. of techniques for diffusion coefficient measurements, theory of diffusion and chemical kinetics. Subspecialties: Analytical chemistry; Ecosystems analysis. Home: 3978 Emigration Canyon Salt Lake City UT 84108 Office: University of Utah Department of Chemistry Salt Lake City UT 84112

GIEBISCH, GERHARD HANS, physiology educator, research; b. Vienna, Austria, Jan. 17, 1927, came to U.S., 1951, naturalized 1962; s. Hans and Valery (Bruckner) G.; m. Ilse Riebeth, Dec. 10, 1952; children—Christina Maria, Robert Gerhard. M.D., U. Vienna, Austria, 1951; D. "hon.", U. Bern. Switzerland, 1979, Uppsala U., 1977. Instr. pharmacology, U. Vienna Med. Sch., Austria, 1951; intern Milw. Hosp., Wis., 1952-53; fellow physiology Cornell U. Med. Coll., Ithaca, N.Y., 1953-54, instr. physiology, 1955-56, asst. prof., 1957-60, assoc. prof., 1960-65, prof., 1965-68; prof., chmn. dept. physiology Yale U. Sch. Medicine, New Haven, Conn., 1968-73, Sterling prof., 1970—; mem. physiology study sect. NIH, 1964-69, 1982-84. Editor: Physiological Reviews, 1985; sect. editor: Am. Jour. Applied Physiology, Am. Jour. Physiology, Kidney and Electrolyte Metabolism, 1967-69; mem. editorial bd.: Quarterly Jour. Physiology, Pflugers Archives, Jour. Membrane Biology, Kidney Internat. Recipient Pub. Health Research Career award, 1962-68, Faculty Scholar award, Josiah Macy Jr. Found., 1974-75, Homer Smith award, 1971, Disting. Service award, Cornell U. Med. Coll. Alumni Soc., 1983. Mem. Nat. Acad. Scis. Am. Acad. Arts and Scis., German Physiol. Soc. (Johannes Muller medal 1980), Am. Soc. Nephrology (pres. 1971-72), Soc. Gen. Physiol. (council mem. 1980-82), N.Y. Heart Assn. (adv. com. 1978-81, established investigator 1957-62), Internat. Nephrological Soc., (exec. com. 1969-81), Austrian Acad. Sci. (hon. mem.), Austrian Physiol. and Nephrological Soc. (hon. mem.), Am. Phys. Soc., Biophysical Soc., Soc. Clin. Research. Protestant. Current work: Renal physiology, particularly cellular mechanisms of electrolyte transport and control of electrolyte homeostasis. Subspecialties: Physiology (medicine); Nephrology. Office: Yale Univ Sch Medicine Dept Physiology 333 Cedar St New Haven CT 06510

GIESSEN, BILL CORMANN, chemistry educator, cons.; b. Pitts., June 8, 1932; s. Ernst Aloys and Gustel (Cormann) G.; m. Mary Burns; 1 dau., Nora. Dr.Sci.Nat., U. Göttingen, W.Ger., 1958. Research assoc. MIT, Cambridge, 1959-68; assoc. prof. chemistry Northeastern U., Boston, 1968-72, prof., 1972—; assoc. dir. Barnett Inst. Chem. Analysis and Material Sci. Northeastern U. 1973—; dir. Marko Materials, Inc., North Billerica, Mass., Energy Materials Corp., South Lancaster, Mass., Cambridge Analytical Assocs., Inc., Boston, Cambridge Data Analysis Corp., Mass. Editor: Structural Chemistry of Alloy Phases, 1969, (with others) Rapidly Quenched Metals, 1976, Rapidly Solidified Amorphous and Crystalline Alloys, 1982, Alloy Phase Diagrams, 1983; Rapidly Solidified Metastable Materials, 1984; Synthetic Modulated Structures, 1985. Mem. AIME, Materials Research Soc. (sec. 1980-83), Am. Chem. Soc., Am. Crystallographic Assn. Current Work: Synthesis and structural, thermal, mechanical and electronic characterization of new metallic glasses and metastable alloys. Semiconductor studies. Subspecialties: Metallurgy; Solid state chemistry. Office: Northeastern U Boston MA 02115

GIESY, JOHN PAUL, toxicology educator, researcher; b. Youngston, Ohio, Aug. 9, 1948; s. John Paul and Betty Jean (Auld) G.; m. Susan Elaine Damerell, Sept. 5, 1970; 1 child, Emily Jean. B.S., Alma Coll., 1970; M.S., Mich. State U., 1971, Ph.D., 1974. Assoc. prof. U.Ga., Athens, 1974-81; assoc. prof. toxicology Mich. State U., East Lansing, 1981-85, assoc. prof., 1985—; cons. in field. Editor: Microcosms in Ecological Research, 1982; also numerous articles, chpts., 1970—. Counselor Chief Okemos council Boy Scouts Am., 1982—; coordinator United Way, East Lansing, 1984. Woodrow Wilson fellow Mich. State U., 1970; grantee EPA, NIH, Dept. Energy, 1970-84. Mem. Soc. Environ. Toxicology and Chemistry (charter, pres. regional tech. com. 1980-84), Sigma Xi, Beta Beta Beta (pres. regional chpt. 1970), also numerous others. Current work: Aquatic toxicology; trace metal chemistry; pesticide chemistry; microcosms; simulation models. Subspecialty: Environmental toxicology. Home: 2355 Bravender Rd Williamston MI 48895 Office: Mich State U 201 Pesticide Research Ctr East Lansing MI 48824

GIFFORD, ERNEST MILTON, JR., botanist, educator; b. Riverside, Calif., Jan. 17, 1920; s. Ernest and Mildred (Campbell) G.; m. Jean Duncan, July 15, 1942; 1 dau., Jeanette. A.B., U. Calif., Berkeley, 1942, Ph.D., 1950. Asst. prof. botany U. Calif., Davis, 1950-56, assoc. prof., 1957-61, prof., 1962—, chmn. dept., 1963-67, 73-78, asst. botanist agrl. expt. sta., 1950-56, assoc. botantist, 1957-61, botanist, 1962—. Editor-in-chief: Am. Jour. Botany, 1975-79; co-author: Comparative Morphology of Vascular Plants, 2d edit, 1974; co-editor: Mechanisms and Control of Cell Division, 1977; contbr. over 90 articles to sci. jours. Served with U.S. Army, 1942-46; to col. Res. 1948-73. Decorated Bronze Star; Merck sr. postdoctoral fellow Harvard U., 1956; Guggenheim fellow, 1966; Fulbright scholar France, 1966; NATO sr. sci. fellow, 1973; NSF grantee, 1958-66, 79-81. Mem. Bot. Soc. Am. (cert. of merit 1981, pres. 1982), Internat. Soc. Plant Morphologists (v.p. 1980-84), Am. Inst. Biol. Scis. Democrat. Current Work: Morphology and anatomy of vascular plants; morphogenesis and ultrastructure, especially of meristems; spermatogenesis. Subspecialties: Developmental biology; Plant anatomy. Home: 1023 Ovejas Ave Davis CA 95616 Office: U Calif Davis CA 95616

GIFFORD, GEORGE EDWIN, microbiologist, researcher; b. Mpls., Dec. 6, 1924; s. Ernest Wilbur and Hulda Victoria (Widen) G.; m. June Marie Pirila, Dec. 27, 1955 (dec.); children: Charles Stephen, Sheryl Byrne. B.S. cum laude, U. Minn., Mpls., 1949, M.S., 1953, Ph.D., 1955. Grad. asst. U. Minn., 1950-55, instr., 1955-56; asst. prof. U. Fla. Coll. Medicine, Gainesville, 1957-64, assoc. prof., 1964-68, prof., 1968—, co-prof. microbiology and cell sci., 1969—, mem. ctr. macromolecular sci., 1969—. Contbr. numerous research articles to pubs. USPHS fellow London, 1962; USPHS and Am. Cancer Soc. grantee, 1957—. Fellow Am. Acad. Microbiology, AAAS; mem. Am. Soc. Microbiology, Am. Assn. Immunologists, Am. Assn. Virologists, Union Concerned Scientists, Sigma Xi (pres. Fla. chpt. 1981). Current Work: Natural resistance to viral disease at the cellular level; nature, production and action interferon; production and action of tumor necrosis factor and oncolytic factors. Subspecialties: Immunology (medicine); Cancer research (medicine). Home:

1013 NW 91st Terr Gainesville FL 32606 Office: Dept Immunology and Med Microbiology U Fla Coll Medicine Box J-266 Gainesville FL 32610

GIFFORD, GERALD F., university administrator, forestry, wildlife and range educator; b. Chanute, Kans., Oct. 24, 1939; s. Gerald Leo and Marion Lou (Browne) G.; m. Cinda Jean Lowman, June 26, 1982. Student U. Kans., 1957-60; B.S. in Range Mgmt., Utah State U., 1962, M.S. in Watershed Mgmt., 1964, Ph.D. in Watershed Sci., 1968. Lectr., U. Nev., Reno, 1965-67, prof., head range wildlife and forestry, 1984—; asst. prof. watershed sci. Utah State U., Logan, 1967-72, assoc. prof., 1972-80, prof., 1980-84; cons. in field. co-author: Rangeland Hydrology, 1981. Assoc. editor: Jour. Range Management, 1982—, Arid Soil Research & Rehabilitation, 1985—. Contbr. articles to profl. jours. NSF grantee, 1973-74. Mem. Nat. Acad. Sci., Soc. Range Mgmt., Am. Water Resources Assn., Soil Conservation Soc. Am. Current work: Administration of natural resource programs; interested in hydrology of semiarid rangelands. Subspecialties: Range management; Soil science. Office: Univ Nev Range Wildlife & Forestry 1000 Valley Rd Reno NV 89512

GIFT, JAMES JOSEPH, environmental consultant; b. Trenton, July 25, 1942; s. Robert Ayres Jr. and Katharine M. (Weil) G.; m. Audrey Geyer, Feb. 4, 1967; children—Craig Robert, Andrea Marie. A.B., Harvard U., 1964; M.S., Rutgers U., 1968, Ph.D., 1970. Sr. research biologist Ichthyological Assocs., Middletown, Del., 1970-73, lab. research dir., Brigantine, N.J., 1973-75; dir. ops. Ecol. Analysts, Melville, N.Y., 1975-79, dir. environ. toxicology and chemistry, Towson, Md., 1979-81, v.p., Sparks, Md., 1981-83; sr. v.p. EA Engring. Sci. and Tech., Sparks, 1983—. Contbr. articles to profl. jours. Com. chmn. pack 444 Balt. Area council Cub Scouts Am., 1981-83, troop 444, Boy Scouts Am., 1983—. Mem. Soc. Environ. Toxicology and Chemistry (charter), Water Pollution Control Fedn., Am. Fisheries Soc., Ecol. Soc. Am., Soc. Limnology and Oceanography. Republican. Presbyterian. Current work: Multimedia waste assessment and management, risk management; behavioral and physiological effects of pollutants on freshwater, estuarine and marine organisms. Subspecialties: Environmental toxicology; Ecology (biology). Home: 13717 Summer Hill Dr Phoenix MD 21131 Office: EA Engring Sci and Tech 15 Loveton Ctr Sparks MD 21152

GILBERT, ROBERT PERTSCH, mathematician, educator; b. N.Y.C., Jan. 8, 1932; s. Ralph H. and Ruth (Pertsch) G.; m. E. Eileen Manton, Oct. 28, 1955 (div. Jan. 1975); m. Ursula Murach, June 27, 1975 (div. Mar. 1979); m. Elizabeth Ann Page, Aug. 12, 1979; 1 dau., Jennifer Page. B.S., Bklyn. Coll., 1952; M.S. in Physics, Carnegie-Mellon U., 1955, M.S. in Math, 1955, Ph.D. in Math, 1958. Faculty U. Pitts., 1957-60, Mich. State U., 1960-63; research asst. prof. Inst. for Fluid Dynamics and Applied Math., U. Md., 1961-64, research asso. prof., 1964-65; prof. dept. math. Georgetown U., Washington, 1965-66; prof. math. Ind. U., Bloomington, 1966-75; dir. Ind. U. (Systems Analysis Inst.), 1973-75; Unidel prof. math. U. Del., 1975—; also dir. U. Del. (Applied Math. Inst.), 1975—; Cons. spl. coal research div. U.S. Bur. Mines, 1958-60, Naval Ordnance Lab., 1961-64; vis. Unidel prof. U. Del., 1972-73; guest prof. U. Glasgow, 1972, U. Dortmund, Germany, 1972, Hahn Meitner Inst. Nuclear Physics, Berlin, 1974, Free U. Berlin, 1974-75; vis. prof. Tech. U. Denmark, 1979, U. Karlsruhe, 1980, Oxford U., 1981-82. Author: Function Theoretic Methods in Partial Differential Equations, 1969, Constructive Methods for Elliptic Equations, 1973; co-author: Foundations of Applied Mathematics, First Order Elliptic Systems, 1983; Co-editor: Analytic Methods in Mathematical Physics, 1970; editor-in-chief: an internat. jour. Applicable Analysis; Complex Variables; assoc. editor: Jour. Nonlinear Analysis; adv. editor: Math. Method in Applied Scis; cons. editor, Pitman Press, London. Recipient von Humboldt Sr. Scientist award, 1975, 85. Mem. Am. Math. Soc. (mem. council), Soc. for Indsl. and Applied Math. (asso. editor jour.), Washington Acad. Scis., Sigma Xi, Pi Mu Epsilon. Research and publs. on analysis, especially harmonic functions, boundary value problems, math. physics, partial differential equations, numerical analysis. Current Work: Moving boundary problems; porous media problems; underwater acoustics. Subspecialty: Applied mathematics. Home: 112 Briar Ln Newark DE 19711

GILBERT, WALTER, scientist, molecular biologist; b. Boston, Mar. 21, 1932; s. Richard V. and Emma (Cohen) G.; m. Celia Stone, Dec. 29, 1953; children—John Richard, Kate. B.A., Harvard U., 1953, A.M., 1954; D.Phil., Cambridge U., Eng., 1957; D.Sc. (hon.), U. Chgo., 1978, Columbia U., 1978, U. Rochester, 1979. NSF postdoctoral fellow Harvard, 1957-58, lectr. physics, 1958-59, asst. prof. physics, 1959-64, asso. prof. biophysics, 1964-68, prof. molecular biology, 1968—, Am. Cancer Soc. prof. molecular biology, 1972—. Recipient U.S. Steel Found. award Nat. Acad. Sci., 1968; Ledlie prize Harvard, 1969; Guggenheim fellow, 1968-69; V.D. Mattia lectr. Roche Inst. Molecular Biology, 1976; Warren triennial prize Mass. Gen. Hosp., 1977; Louis and Bert Freedman Found. award N.Y. Acad. Scis., 1977; Prix Charles-Leopold Mayer Academie des Scis., Inst. de France, 1977; Nobel prize in chemistry, 1980; co-winner Louisa Gross Horwitz prize Columbia U., 1979; Gairdner prize, 1979; Albert Lasker Basic Sci. award, 1979. Mem. Nat. Acad. Scis., Am. Phys. Soc., Am. Soc. Biol. Chemists, Am. Acad. Arts and Scis. Subspecialty: Molecular biology.*

GILBOE, DAVID DOUGHERTY, surgery and physiology educator; b. Richland Ctr., Wis., July 13, 1929; s. Harvey Bernard and Margaret Lucille (Dougherty) G.; m. Myrtle Marie Kroll, Aug. 18, 1951; children—Andrew J., Sarah A. B.A. in chemistry, Miami U., 1951; M.S. in Biochemistry, U. Wis.-Madison, 1955, Ph.D. in Biochemistry, 1958. Research asst. U. Wis., Madison, 1955-58, instr. physiol. chemistry and surgery, 1958-61, asst. prof., 1961-65, asst. prof. surgery and physiology, 1965-67, assoc. prof., 1967-73, prof., 1973—; neurology study sect. NIH, Bethesda, Md., 1980-84. Ad hoc referee Am. Jour. Physiology. Served with USN, 1951-54, Korea. Wis. Alumni Research Found. fellow, 1958-59; Fulbright fellow U. Chile, 1970. Mem. Am. Physiology Soc., Am. Soc. Biol. Chemists, Am. Soc. Neurochemistry, Internat. Soc. Neurochemistry, Soc. for Neurosci. Roman Catholic. Lodge: Rotary (Madison). Current work: Research in metabolism and physiology of isolated canine brain preparation. Subspecialties: Physiology (medicine); Neurochemistry. Home: 409 Blue Ridge Pkwy Madison WI 53705 Office: U Wis Med Sch Dept Surgery 4630 MSC 1300 Univ Ave Madison WI 53706

GILDENBLAT, GENNADY, physicist; b. Lenningrad, USSR, Aug. 30, 1952, came to U.S., 1979; s. Sholom and Klara (Weinfeld) G. M.S.E.E. with honors, Lenningrad Elec. Engring. Inst., USSR, 1975; Ph.D. in Physics, Rensselaer Poly. Inst., 1984. Research engr. State Inst. Resistors and Capacitors, Lenningrad, 1975-78; mem. research staff Gen. Elec. Corp. Research and Devel., Schenectady, 1979-84; prin. engr. Digital Equipment Corp. Adv. Semiconductor Devel., Hudson, Mass., 1984—. Author: Metal-Semiconductor Contacts and Devices, 1986. Contbr. articles to profl. jours. Mem. IEEE, Electron Device Soc. IEEE, Sigma Xi. Current work: Microelectronics; interfaces; device physics; quantum theory of solids; theory of magnetism; parametric testing of semiconductors. Subspecialties: Condensed matter physics; Semiconductors. Office: Digital Equipment Corp 75 Reed Rd Hudson MA 01749

GILES, NORMAN HENRY, educator, geneticist; b. Atlanta, Aug. 6, 1915; s. Norman Henry and Alice (Guerard) G.; m. Dorothy Lunsford, Aug. 26, 1939 (dec. Jan. 1967); children—Annette Guerard, David Lunsford; m. Doris Vos Weaver, Aug. 1, 1969; stepchildren—Gayle Weaver (dec.), Alix Weaver. A.B., Emory U., 1937, Sc.D. (hon.), 1980; M.A., Harvard U., 1938, Ph.D., 1940; M.A. (hon.), Yale, 1951. Instr. botany Yale, 1941-45, asst. prof., 1945-46, asso. prof., 1946-51, prof., 1951-61, Eugene Higgins prof. genetics, 1961-72; Fuller E. Callaway prof. genetics U. Ga., 1972—; prin. biologist Oak Ridge Nat. Lab., 1947-50; cons. AEC, 1954-64; mem. genetics study sect. NIH, 1960-64, mem. genetics tng. com., 1966-70; ednl. adv. bd. John Simon Guggenheim Meml. Found., 1977-85. Editorial bd.: Radiation Research, 1953-58, Am. Naturalist, 1961-64, Devel. Genetics, 1979—. Bd. dirs. U. Ga. Research Found., 1979-85. Recipient Bicentennial Silver medallion U. Ga., 1984; Parker fellow Harvard U., 1940-41; Fulbright and Guggenheim fellow U. Genetics Inst., Copenhagen, 1959-60; Guggenheim fellow Australian Nat. U., Canberra, 1966. Fellow Am. Acad. Arts and Scis., AAAS; mem. Nat. Acad. Scis. (chmn. genetics sect. 1976-79), Genetics Soc. Am. (treas. 1954-56, pres. 1970), Bot. Am., Am. Soc. Naturalists (pres. 1977), Am. Inst. Biol. Scis., Genetics Soc. Japan (hon.), Am. Ornithologists Union, Royal Danish Acad. Scis. and Letters (fgn.), Phi Beta Kappa, Sigma Xi. Current Work: Gene organization and regulation in lower eukaryotes. Subspecialties: Gene actions; Genetics and genetic engineering (biology). Home: 289 Hanover Dr Bogart GA 30622 Office: Dept Genetics U Ga Athens GA 30602

GILES, RALPH EDSON, pharmacologist; b. Rahway, N.J., Mar. 26, 1941; s. Edson Remmick and Lena Margaret (Tram) G.; m. Trudy Anne Moran, Dec. 28, 1963; children: Thomas, Deborah, Monica, Mary Ellen, Patrick. B.S. in Pharmacy, Fordham U., 1962; Ph.D. in Pharmacology, U. Minn., 1966. Asst. prof. pharmacology Fordham U., Bronx, N.Y., 1966-67; scientist Warner-Lambert, 1967-69, sr. scientist, 1969-72, sr. research assoc., 1972-75; mgr. pharmacology Stuart Pharms. div. ICI-Ams., Wilmington, Del., 1975-79, dir. pharmacology, 1979—. Contbr. articles and abstracts to sci. jours. Mem. Soc. Exptl. Biology and Medicine, Royal Soc. Medicine, Western Pharm. Soc., Am. Pharm. Assn., Acad. Pharm. Scis., N.Y. Acad. Scis., Am. Chem. Soc. (div. med. chemistry), Sigma Xi, Rho Chi., Am. Soc. Pharmacology and Exptl. Therapeutics. Roman Catholic. Current Work: Pulmonary, CNS, GI, renal, cardiovascular, anti-arthritic pharmacology administration; director of pharmacology department. Subspecialties: Pharmacology; Biochemistry (medicine). Home: 1303 Grayson Rd Wilmington DE 19803 Office: Stuart Pharms Div ICI-Americas Murphy Rd and Concord Pike Wilmington DE 19897

GILKESON, ROBERT FAIRBAIRN, utility company executive; b. Phila., June 26, 1917; s. Fairbairn and Helen (Geiger) G.; m. KMarie Whitwell, Apr. 26, 1941 (dec. May 1985); children—Katherine Gilkeson Hughes, Richard, Thomas, David, Elizabeth Gilkeson Aikens. E.E., Cornell U., 1939. Registered profl. engr., Pa. Engr. operating dept. Phila. Electric Co., 1939-60, v.p. engring. and research, 1961-62, exec. v.p., 1962-66, pres., 1965-71, chmn. bd., chief exec. officer, 1971-82, chmn. exec. com., 1973—; mem. bd. mgrs. Germantown Savs. Bank, Bala Cynwyd, Pa.; mem. Nat. Sci. Bd., 1982—. Patentee supplemental energy registers. Served to maj. AUS, 1940-45. Mem. IEEE, Soc. Am. Mil. Engrs. Republican. Episcopalian. Club: Phila. Country (Gladwyne, Pa.). Lodge: Masons. Subspecialty: Electrical engineering. Office: Phila Electric Co 2301 Market St Philadelphia PA 19101

GILL, AYESHA ELENIN, geneticist, biology educator; b. Fresno, Calif., Oct., 31, 1933; d. Suret Singh and Kartar Kaur (Dhillon) G.; children: Piara Gil Andersen, Erika Pilar Andersen. B.A. in Physics, U. Calif.-Berkeley, 1957, B.A. in Slavic Langs. and Lit, 1961, Ph.D. in Genetics, 1972. Physicist Gen. Electric Vallecitos Atomic Lab., Pleasanton, Calif., 1957-58; research linguist Mechanolinguistics Project, U. Calif.-Berkeley, 1961-64; asst. prof. biology UCLA, 1972-79; asst. prof. biology U. Nev., Reno, 1979-81, assoc. prof., 1981-84; research human med. genetics N.Y.State Dept. Health, 1984—; human/medical geneticist State of Nev., Reno, 1979-81; dir. genetics program, 1981-82. Translator: Soviet Education, 1965; contbr. articles to profl. jours. Nat. Acad. Scis. exchange scholar, 1978, 80; grantee NIH, 1967, 75; NSF, 1968, 69, 77; Ford Found., 1972. Mem. Genetics Soc. Am., Soc. Study of Evolution, Am. Soc. Human Genetics, Am. Soc. Mammalogists, AAAS, Soc. Systematic Zoology, Sigma Xi, Phi Beta Kappa. Current Work: Human genetic diseases, care and prevention; study of speciation and genetic variability in mammals using cytogenetic and biochemical analyses; human chromosome analysis and counseling. Subspecialties: Genetics and genetic engineering (biology); Evolutionary biology. Office: NY State Dept Health 789 Tower Albany NY 12237

GILL, DENNIS HOWARD, electrical engineer; b. Monticello, Akr., Jan. 5, 1939; s. William Howard and Dorothy Lauree G.; m. Opal Lee Clark, Sept. 3, 1939; children: John Howard, David Dennis. B.A., Rice U., 1961, B.S.E.E., 1962; M.S.E.E., U. Tex., 1963, Ph.D., 1966. With Los Alamos Nat. Lab., 1966—, group leader tunable laser research group, 1980-83, assoc. div. leader chemistry div., 1983-85, dep. div. leader chemistry div., 1985—. Contbr. articles to profl. jours. Mem. Los Alamos Bd. Edn., 1979—, v.p., 1981-83, pres., 1983—; pres. adv. bd. Los Alamos br. U. N.Mex., 1981—. Mem. IEEE (sr.), Optical Soc. Am. Republican. Methodist. Current Work: Technical management of laser system research and development, especially for applications related to photochemistry, spectroscopy, remote detection and laser fusion. Subspecialties: Laser-induced chemistry; Optical engineering. Home: 2403 Club Rd Los Alamos NM 87544 Office: Los Alamos Nat Lab MS J563 Los Alamo NM 87545

GILL, HARDAYAL SINGH, physicist, scientist; b. Amritsar, Punjab, India, Aug. 18, 1952, came to U.S., 1974; s. Shamer S. and Satwant K. G.; m. Inderbir K. Dhillon, Jan. 3, 1982. B.Sc. with honors, Punjabi U., Patiala, India, 1971, M.Sc., 1973; Ph.D., U. Minn., 1978. Teaching assoc. U. Minn., 1974-78; sect. head Nat. Semiconductor, Santa Clara, Calif., 1978-81; scientist Hewlett-Packard, Palo Alto, Calif., 1981-83, project leader, 1983-85, project mgr., 1985—. Author: Amorphous Materials, 1983. Contbr. articles to profl. jours. Patentee in field. IBM fellow, 1977. Mem. IEEE, Am. Phys. Soc., IEEE Magnetics Soc. of Santa Clara Valley (program chmn. 1985-86). Current work: Design of magnetic recording, head/disc systems, fabrication of head/disc, project management. Subspecialties: Information systems, storage, and retrieval (computer science); Applied magnetics. Home: 321 Cuesta Dr Los Altos CA 94022 Office: 3500 Deer Creek Rd Palo Alto CA 94304

GILL, JASBIR SINGH, research chemist; b. Dault Pur, Panjab, India, Jan. 1, 1947; came to U.S., 1976, naturalized, 1985; s. Beant S. and Pritam K. (Thandi) G.; m. Paramjit K. Sandhu, Jan. 26, 1977; children—Sonika, Inderjit. B.S., Punjab U., 1967; M.S., U. Roorkee, India, 1970, Ph.D., 1973. Vis. scholar U. Perugia, Italy, 1974-75; vis. lectr. U. Salford, Eng., 1975-76; asst. research prof. SUNY-Buffalo, 1976-79; group leader Calgon Corp., Pitts., 1979-83, sr. research assoc., 1983—; cons. Magnesium Elecktron, Swinton, Manchester, Eng., 1975-76. Patentee in field. Contbr. articles to tech. jours. Cultural sec., coordinator Tri-Sate Sikh Cultural Soc., Pitts., 1981. Fellow Univ. Grants Commn., 1971-73, Am. Chem. Soc., 1976-79. Mem. Am. Chem. Soc., Colloid and Surface Sci. Sikh. Current work: Inorganic ion-exchangers, ion exchange equilibria, solution chemistry, crystal growth from aqueous solutions, electrochemical techniques in corrosion, corrosion inhibition, scale/deposit control, phosphate equilibria in soil and soil conditioning. Subspecialties: Physical chemistry; Analytical chemistry. Home: 123 Darnley Dr Corapolis PA 15108 Office: Calgon Corp PO Box 1346 Pittsburgh PA 15230

GILL, THOMAS JAMES, III, physician, educator; b. Malden, Mass., July 2, 1932; s. Thomas James and Marguerite (Capobianco) G.; m. Faith Libbie Etoll, July 8, 1961; children: Elizabeth Ruth, Thomas James IV, Christopher Gregory. A.B. summa cum laude, Harvard U., 1953, M.A. in Chemistry, 1957, M.D., 1957. Diplomate Am. Bd. Pathology; subcert. in immunopathology. Asst. pathology Peter Bent Brigham Hosp., Boston, 1957-58; intern N.Y. Hosp.-Cornell Med. Center, 1958-59; jr. fellow Soc. Fellows Harvard U., 1959-62; mem. faculty Harvard Med. Sch., 1962-71, assoc. prof. pathology, 1970-71; prof. pathology, chmn. dept. U. Pitts. Med. Sch., 1971—; pathologist-in-chief Univ. Health Center Pitts., 1971—; cons. to govt. and industry; mem. sci. adv. bd. St. Jude Children's Research Hosp., Memphis, 1969-77, chmn., 1974-76; mem. allergy and immunology research com. Nat. Inst. Allergy and Infectious Diseases, 1973-76; mem. med. research service merit rev. bd. in immunology VA, 1976-79, chmn., 1977-79; mem. sci. adv. com. Damon Runyon-Walter Winchell Cancer Fund, 1978-81; mem. com. on animal models and genetic stocks NRC, 1978—, chmn. com., 1983—, mem. com. on rabbit genetic resources, 1979-80; mem. surgery, anesthesiology and trauma study sect. NIH, 1983—; mem. Armed Forces Epidemiol. Bd., 1966-72. Editorial bds. several sci. and med. jours.; contbr. articles to profl. jours. Bd. dirs. Easter Seal Soc., Allegheny County, 1972-77, Univs. Asso. for Research and Edn. in Pathology, 1979—; trustee Am. Bd. Pathology, 1981—. Recipient Lederle med. faculty award, 1962-65, research career devel. award NIH, 1965-71; certificate appreciation for patriotic civilian service Dept. Army, 1973. Fellow Am. Soc. Clin. Pathologists, Am. Acad. Allergy, Assn. Pathology Chairmen (pres. 1978); mem. Am. Assn. Immunologists, Am. Assn. Pathologists, Am. Soc. Biol. Chemists, Internat. Acad. Pathology, Am. Soc. Human Genetics, Transplantation Soc. (v.p. 1982-84), Internat. Soc. Immunology Reprodn. (Sec.-gen. 1983—), Am. Chem. Soc., Am. Soc. Cell Biology, Genetics Soc. Am., AMA. Clubs: Harvard (Western Pa.); Harvard (Boston); Fox Chapel Racquet (Pitts.); Pitts. Athletic Assn, Harvard Varsity. Current Work: Major interest is in basic immunogenetics of the rat and application of this knowledge to problems of transplantation and reproduction. Subspecialties: Immunogenetics; Transplantation. Home: 117 Crofton Dr Pittsburgh PA 15238

GILLELAND, JOHN ROGERS, research scientist; b. Gadsden, Ala., Jan. 12, 1941; s. Earl Rogers and Margaret (Kilpatrick) G.; m. Ruth Magnuson, Nov. 14, 1964; children: John Rogers Jr., David Reid. B.S. in Physics, Yale U., 1963; M.S. in Physics, U. Mich., Ann Arbor, 1964, Ph.D. in Physics, 1969. Research scientist U. Mich., 1964-69; assoc., sr. to staff scientist Gen. Atomic Co. (name now GA Techs. Inc.), San Diego, 1970-73; project mgr. Gen. Atomic Co. (Doublet III program), 1973-78, mgr. fusion projects, 1978-80; dir. Gen. Atomic Co. (Doublet III div.), 1980—; mem. U.S. del. to UN Internat. Tokanak Reactor design team, 1979; exec. dir. Fusion Engring. Device Tech. Mgmt. Bd., Washington, 1980-81; mem., panel chmn. Magnetic Fusion Adv. Com., Washington, 1982—; participant Nat. Research Council on Fusion, Washington; founding mem. Atomic Indsl. Forum Com. on Fusion; mem. exec. adv. bd. U.S. Internat. Tokanak Reactor Study, 1980-82. Mng. editor, author: The Fusion Engineering Device, vols. L-IV, 1981. Recipient Young Mem. Achievement award Am. Nuclear Soc., 1980; Cert. of Appreciation U.S. Dept. Energy, 1981. Mem. Am. Phys. Soc., Am. Nuclear Soc., Yale Sci. and Engring. Assn., Fusion Power Assocs., Sigma Xi. Current Work: Director of largest operating magnetic fusion experiment in the world. Member of magnetic fusion advisory committee, reports through Director of Research to Secretary of Energy. Subspecialties: Fusion; Plasma (energy science and technology). Office: GA Techs Inc 10955 John Jay Hopkins Dr San Diego CA 92121

GILLESPIE, DAVID HUTTON, biological chemistry educator, research scientist; b. Stoneham, Mass., Jan. 22, 1940; s. Edward Hutton and Ella Gracie (Blanchard) G.; m. Sally Marie Crisler, Dec. 31, 1964; children—William, Robert. B.S. in Biology, Tufts U., 1961; Ph.D. in Microbiology, U. Ill., 1966. Prof. biotech. Hahnemann U., Phila., 1979—, prof. biol. chemistry dept. biol. chemistry Sch. Medicine, 1980—, dir. basic research, 1979—; adj. prof. virology U. Pa., Phila., 1980—; v.p. Diogenes, Inc., Phila., 1984—; cons. in field. Inventor in field. Current work: DNA evolution; molecular biology of human disease processes. Subspecialty: Molecular biology. Office: Hahnemann U Broad and Vine Sts Philadelphia PA 19102

GILLESPIE, ELIZABETH, biochemical pharmacologist; b. Montreal, Que., Can., May 7, 1936; came to U.S., 1966; d. George and Madeline Maud (Deller) G. B.Sc., McGill U., 1957, Ph.D., 1966. Info. scientist Explosives and Ammunition divs. Can. Industries Ltd., Montreal, 1957-59; sr. research technician U. Mich., Ann Arbor, 1959-62; postdoctoral fellow dept. pharmacology Yale U. Sch. Medicine, New Haven, 1966-68, research asso., 1968-71; instr. clin. immunology div. dept. medicine Johns Hopkins U. Sch. Medicine, Balt., 1971-73, asst. prof. medicine, 1973-81; with Wellcome Research Labs., Beckenham, Kent, Eng., 1978-79; sect. mgr. respiratory pharm. div. Bristol-Myers Co., Evansville, Ind., 1981-82, sr. research scientist cardiovascular pharm. div., 1982—. Contbr. articles and abstracts to sci. jours., also chpts. to books. NIH grantee, 1974-81. Mem. Am. Assn. Immunology, Am. Soc. Pharmacology and Exptl. Therapeutics. Current Work: Drug development. Subspecialties: Immunopharmacology; Allergy. Home: 619 College Hwy Evansville IN 47714 Office: Mead Johnson Pharm Div Bristol Myers Co 2400 Pennsylvania Ave Evansville IN 47721

GILLESPIE, GEORGE HUBERT, physicist; b. Dallas, Sept. 9, 1945; s. Hubert W. and Frieda S. Gillespie; children—James S., Colin H., Ian G. B.A., Rice U., 1968, M.E.E., 1968, M.S. in Physics, 1969; Ph.D., U. Calif., San Diego, 1974. Engr., IBM, Lexington, Ky., summer 1967; research asst. Los Alamos Sci. Lab., summer 1968, U. Calif., San Diego, 1968-74; assoc. LaJolla (Calif.) Inst., 1976—; staff scientist Physical Dynamics, Inc., LaJolla, 1975—. Contbr. articles to profl. jours. Trustee, Sky Mountain Life Sch. Inc., 1983-86. Served to capt. USAR, 1968-76. Mem. Am. Phys. Soc., AAAS. Current Work: Theoretical applied physics; primary interests in scattering theory, quantum mechanics, atomic physics and plasma physics; with applications in magnetic confinement fusion, ion-beam fusion, and particle accelerators. Subspecialties: Theoretical physics; Atomic and molecular physics. Home: 364 Hillcrest Dr Leucadia CA 92024 Office: Physical Dynamics Inc PO Box 1883 La Jolla CA 92038

GILLESPIE, SHERRY JACQUELINE, microcircuit engineer; b. N.Y.C., June 2, 1943; d. Rubin and Anne (Sloter) Victor; divorced (div.); children: Neil Gillespie, Tristan Gillespie. A.B., Vassar Coll., 1965; M.S., U. Pa., 1966; Ph.D., Temple U., 1975. Tchr. physics Abington (Pa.) High Sch., 1967-68; engr. IBM, Burlington, Vt., 1975—. Contbr. articles to physics, engring. jours. NSF trainee, summer 1971. Mem. Am. Phys. Soc. Current Work: Manager of process development for electron beam technology. Subspecialties: Microchip technology (engineering); Semiconductors. Home: 6 Nahma Ave Essex Junction VT 05452 Office: IBM Corp Essex Junction VT 05452

GILLETTE, PAUL CRAWFORD, pediatric cardiologist, electrophysiologist; b. Winston-Salem, N.C., Dec. 1, 1942; s. Crawford Paul and Eilene (O'Rounke) G.; m. Sarah Nelle Stone, July 1, 1964; 2 children. A.B., U. N.C., 1965; M.D., Med. U.S.C., 1969. Resident in pediatrics Baylor Coll. Medicine, Houston, 1969-71, fellow, pediatric cardiology, 1971-74, asst. prof., 1974-77, assoc. prof., 1977-80, prof., 1980-84; prof., dir. pediatric cardiology Med. U. S.C., Charleston, 1984—; cons. Richland Meml. Hosp., Columbia, S.C., 1984—, Greenville Hosp. System, S.C., 1984—, St. Francis Hosp., Charleston, 1985—, Roper Hosp., Charleston, 1985—. Editor 4 books. Contbr. over 110 articles to profl. jours. Mem. clin. research ctr. adv. com. Tex. Children's Hosp., 1978-84; adminstrv. policy rev. com. Med. U. S.C., 1984—, instnl. rev. bd. com. 1984—, univ. research council, 1984—. Recipient Moseby scholarship award, 1969; Rich Scholarship award, 1969; Am. Acad. Pediatrics grantee, 1970, Young Investigators award, 1975. Fellow, Am. Coll. Cardiology (learning ctr. com. 1982-85; bd. dirs. 1985—), Am. Acad. Pediatrics; mem. Am. Heart Assn. (council cardiovascular disease young 1975—, council basic research 1975—, Houston bd. dirs. 1980-84, exec. com. 1982-84, v.p. 1982-84), AMA, Soc. Pediatric Research, Southeastern Soc. Pediatric Research, Southeastern Pediatric Cardiology Soc. (pres. 1979), N.Am. Soc. Pacing and Electrophysiology (exec. com. 1982—, v.p. 1984—, pres. elect 1985), So. Med. Assn., Tex. Med. Assn., Tex. Pediatric Soc., Harris County Med. Soc., Houston Electrophysiology Soc. (trustee 1981-84, pres. 1982), Houston Cardiology Soc., Houston Pediatric Soc., Am. Coll. Chest Physicians, S.C. Heart Assn. (bd. dirs. 1984—), Alpha Omega Alpha, Phi Chi. Republican. Roman Catholic. Current work: Developmental cardiac electrophysiology basic and clinical, cardiac pacing and pediatric cardiology. Subspecialty: Cardiology. Office: Med Univ SC 171 Ashley Ave Charleston SC 29425

GILLIAM, JAMES KARL, applied ecologist; b. Coronado, Calif., Mar. 30, 1950; s. William Morgan and Gertrude Ann (Schettler) G.; m. Mary Kim Malone, June 10, 1972; children—Jessica Margaret, Andrew David. B.S., U. Ill., Urbana, 1971; M.S., Eastern Ill. U., 1973. Cert. ecologist. ESA-Ecologist Commonwealth Assocs., Jackson, Mich., 1974-76, U.S. Army C.E., Chgo., 1976-77, U.S. Fish and Wildlife Service, Anchorage, 1977-79; insp. U.S. Office Surface Mining, Evansville, Ind., 1979-81; ecologist U.S. Bur. Land Mgmt., Anchorage, 1981—. Mem. Ecol. Soc. Am. Current work: Environmental aspects of Trans-Alaska pipeline system and mineral/petroleum development in Alaskan Arctic. Subspecialties: Ecology (biology); Resource management. Home: 7020 Altoona Dr Anchorage AK 99502 Office: Br Pipeline Monitoring US Bur Land Mgmt 701 C St Box 30 Anchorage AK 99513

GILLIGAN, JOHN GERARD, nuclear engineering educator; b. Beach Grove, Ind., Jan. 17, 1949; s. John Bernard and Mary Ann (Prieshoff) G.; m. Barbara Ann Bertolami, Dec. 8, 1979; children—Theresa Marie, Lisa C. B.S., Purdue U., 1971; M.S., U. Mich., 1973, Ph.D., 1977. Research assoc. Princeton (N.J.) Plasma Physics. Lab., 1974-77; asst. prof. dept. nuclear engring. U. Ill., Champaign, 1977-83, affiliate asst. prof. mech. engring., 1982-83; assoc. prof. dept. nuclear engring. N.C. State U., 1983—; cons. SAI, La Jolla, Calif., 1980—. Argonne Nat. Lab. summer faculty fellow, 1982, 83. Mem. Am. Nuclear Soc. (fusion exec. com. 1980-83, edn. exec. com. 1985—), IEEE, Univ. Fusion Assn., Fusion Power Assocs. Roman Catholic. Current Work: Technology of fusion reactors for electrical production, plasma physics, particle and energy transport. Subspecialties: Nuclear fusion; Nuclear fission. Home: 1028 Sturdivant Dr Cary NC 27511 Office: Box 7909 Dept Nuclear Engring NC State U Raleigh NC 27695

GILLILAND, RONALD LYNN, astrophysicist; b. Emporia, Kans., July 16, 1952; s. Rodney and Reta Frances (Jones) G. B.A., U. Kans., 1974; Ph.D., U. Calif., Santa Cruz, 1979. Postdoctoral fellow Advanced Study Program, Nat. Ctr. for Atmospheric Research, Boulder, Colo., 1979-81; staff scientist High Altitude Obs., Boulder. Mem. Am. Astron. Soc., Internat. Astron. Union, Pi Mu Epsilon, Sigma Pi Sigma. Current Work: Solar and stellar variability. Subspecialties: Theoretical astrophysics; Solar physics. Office: PO Box 3000 Boulder CO 80307

GILLIOM, RICHARD D., chemist, educator, researcher, consultant; b. Bluffton, Ind., June 25, 1934; s. Andrew and Roberta Aldine (Dowty) G.; m. Patricia Ann Hastings, Mar. 7, 1958; children: Laura Rhea, Andrea Lee, Bruce Hastings. Student, Centenary Coll., 1952-54; B.S., Southwestern at Memphis, 1956; Ph.D. (Sun Oil Co. fellow), M.I.T., 1960. Research chemist Esso

Research Labs., Baton Rouge, 1960-61; asst. prof. chemistry Southwestern at Memphis (now Rhodes Coll.), 1961-64, assoc. prof., 1964-71, prof., 1971—, cons. in field; undergrad. research participation dir. NSF, 1966-68, 71, 75, 81. Author: Introduction to Physical Organic Chemistry, 1970; contbr. articles to profl. jours. Fulbright Hays lectr., 1968-69; NSF grantee, 1970-73; Research Corp. grantee, 1962-63. Mem. Am. Chem. Soc. Patentee in field. Current Work: Mechanisms of hydrogen abstraction reactions, linear free energy relationships, drug design, computational chemistry. Subspecialties: Organic chemistry; Theoretical chemistry. Home: 3017 Dumbarton Rd Memphis TN 38128 Office: 2000 N Parkway Memphis TN 38112

GILLIS, STEVEN, immunologist; b. Phila., Apr. 25, 1953; s. Herbert and Rosalie Henrietta (Segal) G.; m. Anne Cynthia Edgar, June 26, 1976. B.A., Williams Coll., 1975; Ph.D., Dartmouth Coll., 1978. Research fellow Norris Cotton Cancer Ctr., Hanover, N.H., 1977-78; research assoc. Dartmouth Med. Sch., Hanover, 1978-79; vis. assoc. Sloan Kettering Inst., N.Y.C., 1979-80; asst. mem. Hutchinson Cancer Research Ctr., Seattle, 1980-82; also asst. prof. U. Wash.; exec. v.p. Immunex Corp., Seattle, 1982—; affiliate Hutchinson Cancer Ctr., 1982—. Contbr. articles to profl. jours. Leukemia Soc. spl. fellow, 1978-82. Mem. Am. Assn. Immunologists, N.Y. Acad. Sci., Phi Beta Kappa, Sigma Xi. Current Work: Biochemical and molecular characterization of lymphokines, hormones which control the immune response. Subspecialties: Cellular engineering; Immunopharmacology. Office: 51 University St Suite 600 Seattle WA 98101

GILLS, JAMES PITZER, ophthalmologist; b. Bluefield, W.Va., Aug. 30, 1934; s. James Pitzer and Lucille (Martin) G.; m. Margaret Rose Rogers, June 15, 1962; children—Shea, James Pitzer III. B.S. with honors, Va. Poly. Inst., 1955; M.D., Duke U., 1959. Diplomate Am. Bd. Ophthalmology. Intern Duke U., Med. Ctr., Durham, N.C., 1959-60; resident Wilmer Ophthal. Inst. of John Hopkins U., Balt., 1962-65. Asst. prof. ophthalmology Duke U. Med. Ctr., 1965-68; practice medicine specializing in ophthalmology St. Luke's Cataract and Intraocular Lens Clinic, New Port Richey, Fla., 1969—, dir. ednl. seminars for ophthalmologists, 1979-84, dir. ednl. seminars for optometrists, 1980-84. Contbr. articles to profl. jours. Served with USPHS, 1960-62. Fellow Am. Acad. Ophthalmology; mem. St. Luke's Eye Bank, Inc., Gills Cataract Teaching Found., Inc., AMA, Am. Med. Joggers Assn., Assn. Research in Ophthalmology, Am. Intra-Ocular Implant Soc., Community Hosp. Assn., Bayonet/Hudson Regional Med. Ctr., Council Med. Staff, Christian Med. Soc., Contact lens Assn. Ophthalmology, Fla. Med. Assn., Internat. Soc. Refractive Surgery, John Hopkins U. Alumni Assn., Kerato-Refractive Soc., Internat. Eye Found., Soc. of Eye Surgeons, Fla. Physician's Assn., N.C. Med. Assn., So. Med. Assn., N.Y. Acad. Scis., Nat. Assn. Prevention of Blindness, Pasco County Med. Soc., Pasco Better Bus. Assn., Ophthal. Assn., Outpatient Ophthalmic Surgery Soc., Internat. Glaucoma Congress, Research to Prevent Blindness, Tampa Bay Opthal. Soc., Am. Soc. Contemporary Ophthalmology, Tarpon Springs Hosp. Found., Vision Edn., West Pasco C. of C., Royal Soc. Medicine, Internat. Assn. Ocular Surgeons, Soc. for Office Based Surgery, Am. Running and Fitness Assn., St. Petersburg Bicycle Club, Internat. Windsurfer Class Assn., Suncoast Runners Club, Tampa Bay Triathletes, Project Orbis, Sigma Xi, others. Lodge: Lions. Subspecialty: Ophthalmology. Office: Saint Luke's Eye Clinic 118 High St New Port Richey FL 33552

GILMAN, ALFRED G., medical researcher. Chmn. dept pharmacology U. Tex. Southwestern Med. Sch. at Dallas. Recipient Gairdner Found. Internat. award, 1984. Subspecialty: Pharmacology. Office: U Tex Southwestern Med Sch at Dallas Dept Pharmacology 5323 Harry Hines Blvd Dallas TX 75235

GILMAN, SID, neurology educator, neuroscientist; b. Los Angeles, Oct. 19, 1932; s. Morris and Sarah Rose (Cooper) G. B.A., UCLA, 1954, M.D., 1957. Diplomate: Am. Bd. Psychiatry and Neurology. Research assoc. NIH, Bethesda, Md., 1958-60; resident in neurology Harvard Med. Sch., Boston, 1960-63, instr. to assoc., 1965-68; from asst. prof. to prof. neurology Columbia U., N.Y.C., 1968-76, H.H. Merritt prof., 1976-77; prof., chmn. dept. neurology U. Mich., Ann Arbor, 1977—; mem. sci. programs adv. com. Nat. Inst. Neurol. Communicative Diseases and Stroke, NIH, 1982-84; chmn. sci. adv. council Nat. ALS Found., N.Y.C., 1981-83; mem. profl. adv. bd. Epilepsy Found. Am., 1976-84; mem. research adv. council United Cerebral Palsy, 1973—; mem. peripheral and central nervous system drugs adv. com. FDA, 1983—. Author: Disorders of the Cerebellum, 1981, Essentials of Clinical Neuroanatomy and Neurophysiology, 1982; contr. numerous articles to sci. jours. Served as sr. asst. surgeon USPHS, 1958-60. Recipient Weinstein-Goldenson award United Cerebral Palsy, 1981, Lucy G. Moses prize Columbia U., 1973, NIH Career devel. award, 1966; NIH fellow, 1962. Fellow Am. Acad. Neurology; mem. Am. Neurol. Assn. (v.p. 1980-81, 85-86), Am. Soc. Clin. Investigation, Am. Physiol. Soc., Soc. Neurosci. Current Work: Cerebellar neurophysiology; mechanisms underlying spasticity and movement disorders; studies of cerebral metabolism with positron emission tomography; regenerative activity in the nervous system after injury. Subspecialties: Neurology; Neurophysiology. Home: 3411 Geddes Rd Ann Arbor MI 48105 Office: 1405 E Ann St Ann Arbor MI 48109

GILMARTIN, AMY JEAN, botanist, herbarium director, educator; b. Red Bluff, Calif., Oct. 15, 1932; d. Ruy H. and Margaret Helena (Harvey) Finch; div. 1974; children: Malvern, Dale Moana, Sheila Ann, Ian Harvey. B.A., Pomona Coll., 1954; M.S., U. Hawaii, 1956, Ph.D (AAUW fellow), 1968. Research asst. Hawaii Agrl. Exptl. Sta., 1954-56; curatorial asst. U. B.C. (Can.), Vancouver, 1956-58; prof. contratada U. Guayaquil, Ecuador, 1962-64; asso. researcher Smithsonian Instn., Washington, 1969-70; instr. biology Monterey (Calif.) Peninsula Coll., 1970-75; dir. Ownbey Herbarium, Pullman, Wash., 1975—; asst. prof. Wash. State U., Pullman, 1975-79, assoc. prof., 1979-83, prof., 1983—; cons. environ. surveys. Author: Bromeliads of Ecuador, 1972; contbr. articles on botany to numerous sci. and popular jours.; editorial bd., Calif. Bot. Soc., Internat. Assn. Plant Taxonomy. NSF grantee, 1971-86; sr. Fulbright prof. Bogota, Colombia, 1980; AAUW postdoctoral fellow, 1982-83. Mem. Bromeliad Soc. (dir.), Soc. Study of Evolution, Am. Soc. Plant Taxonomists, Soc. Systematic Zoology, Internat. Assn. Plant Taxonomy, N.W. Sci. Assn., AAAS. Democrat. Current Work: Evolution and phylogeny of flowering plants, numerical taxonomy, phylogenetic inference, speciation, bromeliads, umbellifers. Subspecialties: Evolutionary biology; Numerical analysis (computer science). Office: Ownbey Herbarium Wash State U Pullman WA 99164-4320

GILMORE, SHIRLEY ANN, anatomist, educator; b. Connellsville, Pa., Jan. 1, 1935; d. Jesse Stauffer and Alberta (Ridenour) G. A.B., Thiel Coll., 1957; Ph.D., U. Cin., 1961. Postdoctoral fellow U. Upsala, Sweden, 1961-62; instr. U. Ark. for Med. Sci., Little Rock, 1962-63, asst. prof., 1963-67, assoc. prof., 1967-75, prof. anatomy, 1975—, chmn. dept. anatomy, 1984—; assoc. Nat. Commn. Human Resources Nat. Research Council, Washington, 1981. Contbr. articles to profl. jours. Recipient Disting. Alumnus award Thiel Coll., 1975. Mem. Am. Assn. Anatomists, Am. Assn. for History of Medicine, Am. Inst. Biol. Sci., Soc. Neurosci. Internat. Soc. Devel. Neurosci. Current work: Maturation of the nervous system especially neuroglia of spinal cord; repair and regeneration of the immature spinal cord; reconstruction of the spinal cord. Subspecialties: Anatomy and embryology; Neurobiology. Office: Univ Ark for Med Sci Dept Anatomy 4301 W Markham Little Rock AR 72205

GILMOUR, WILLIAM ALEXANDER, computer based energy conservation systems co. exec.; b. Elizabeth, N.J., May 26, 1934; s. Alexander W. and Kathleen (Sullivan) G.; m. Margaret E. Gillich, Oct. 6, 1954; m. Madeleine C. Clark, Dec. 7, 1973; children: William J., Joyce M., Lynn A., Margaret E., Barbara Anne. Student, Union Coll., Cranford, N.J., 1957; A.S., U. Md., 1958. Research chemist Exxon Research & Devel., Linden, N.J., 1957-61; asst. div. mgr. Sargent Welch Sci. Co., Skokie, Ill., 1961-70; v.p. eastern ops. Environ. Data Corp., Monrovia, Calif., 1970-79; founder, pres., chmn. bd. Princeton Sensors Inc., N.J., 1979—. Mem. Presdl. Task Force; trustee Covenent Christian Sch., Cranford, N.J. Served with U.S. Army, 1952-54. Mem. Instrument Soc. Am. (sr., author tech. publs. 1979-80), TAPPI. Republican. Patentee in field; developed microprocessor-based stack gas monitor, 1979. Current Work: Development of optical sensors, computer based, for non-compliance monitoring of gases, specifically as related to improving efficiency of fossil fuel fired combustion processes. Subspecialties: Infrared spectroscopy; Combustion processes. Office: Princeton Sensors Inc Research Park 1101-B Princeton NJ 08540

GILRUTH, ROBERT ROWE, aerospace consultant; b. Nashwauk, Minn., Oct. 8, 1913; s. Henry Augustus and Frances Marion (Rowe) G.; m. E. Jean Barnhill, Apr. 24, 1937 (dec. 1972); 1 dau., Barbara Jean (Mrs. John Wyatt); m. Georgene Hubbard Evans, July 14, 1973. B.S. in Aero. Engring, U. Minn., 1935, M.S., 1936, D.Sc., 1962; D.Sc., George Washington U., 1962, Ind. Inst. Tech., 1962; D.Eng., Mich. Tech. U., 1963; LL.D., N.Mex. State U., 1970. Flight research engr. Langley Aero. Lab., NACA, Langley Field, Va., 1937-45, chief pilotless aircraft research div., 1945-50, asst. dir., 1950-58; dir. NASA Project Mercury, 1958-61; dir. NASA Manned Spacecraft Center, Houston, 1961-72, dir. key personnel devel., 1972-73, ret., 1973; cons. to adminstr. NASA, 1974—; dir. Bunker Ramo Corp. Ind. experimenter and cons. hydrofoil craft, 1938-58; advisor on guided missiles, aeros. and structures, high temperature facilities U.S. Dept. Def., 1947-58; mem. com. space systems NASA Space Adv. Council, 1972—; chmn. mgmt. devel. edn. panel NASA, 1972-73; mem. ad hoc com. fire safety aspects of polymeric materials Nat. Materials Adv. Bd., 1973-74. Recipient Outstanding Achievement award U. Minn., 1954, Great Living Am. award U.S. C. of C., 1962, Distinguished Fed. Civilian Service award Pres. U.S., 1962, Americanism award CBI Vets. Assn., 1965, Spirit of St. Louis medal, 1965, Internat. Astronautics award Daniel and Florence Guggenheim, 1966, Distinguished Service medal NASA, spring 1969, fall 1969, Pub. Service at Large award Rockefeller Found., 1969, ASME medal, 1970, James Watt Internat. medal, 1971; Achievement award Nat. Aviation Club, 1971; Robert J. Collier trophy with Nat Aero. Assn., 1972; Space Transp. award Louis W. Hill; Distinguished Service medal NASA; medal of honor N.Y.C.; Robert H. Goddard Meml. trophy Nat. Rocket Club; named to Nat. Space Hall of Fame, 1969, Internat. Space Hall of Fame, 1976. Mem. Nat. Acad. Engring. (aeros. and space bd. 1974—), Nat. Acad. Scis. Subspecialties: Aerospace engineering and technology; Astronautics. Home: Route 1 Box 1486 Kilmarnock VA 22482

GIMARC, BENJAMIN MAURICE, chemist, educator, researcher; b. Nogales, Ariz., Dec. 5, 1934; s. John and Virgie Dill (Ringo) G.; m. Jerry Dell, Nov. 4, 1936. B.A. in Chemistry, Rice U., 1956; Ph.D. in Chemistry, Northwestern U., 1963. Instr. Northwestern U., Evanston, Ill., 1961-62; USPHS fellow, lectr. Johns Hopkins U., Balt., 1962-64; asst. prof. Ga. Inst. Tech., Atlanta, 1964-66; asst. prof. chemistry U. S.C., Columbia, 1966-72, assoc. prof., 1972-78, prof., 1978—, dept. head, 1973-76, chmn. dept. chemistry, 1982—; Nat. Acad. Scis. exchange scientist, Zagreb, Yugoslavia, 1978, 82, 84. Author: Molecular Structure and Bonding, 1978; contbr. numberous articles to profl. jours. Served to lt. (j.g.) USN, 1956-58. Mem. Am. Chem. Soc., Am. Phys. Soc., AAAS. Current Work: The development and application of qualitative theories of chemical valence. Subspecialty: Theoretical chemistry. Home: 316 Wateree Ave Columbia SC 29205 Office: Dept. Chemistry U SC Columbia SC 29208

GINOS, JAMES ZISSIS, research scientist; b. Hillsboro, Ill., Feb. 1, 1923; s. Zissis and Nicoletta M. (Sakellaris) G.; m. Chrisilla Paul Katsas, June 13, 1947; children: Geoffrey, Milton. B.A., Columbia U., 1954; M.S. in Chem. Engring., Stevens Inst. Tech., 1962, Ph.D. in Organic Chemistry, 1964. Chemist, Colgate Palmolive Co., Jersey City, 1953-57; chief chemist Diamond Shamrock Corp., Newark, 1957-58; project coordinator Nopco Chem. Co., Harrison, N.J., 1959-64; asst. scientist Brookhaven Nat. Labs., Upton, N.Y., 1964-68; research asst. prof. Mt. Sinai Sch. Medicine, N.Y.C., 1968-70; assoc. scientist Brookhaven Nat. Labs., 1970-74, scientist, 1974-75; research assoc. prof. Cornell U., 1975—; assoc. lab. mem. Lab. Meml. Sloan-Kettering Cancer Ctr., N.Y.C., 1980—. Contbr. articles to profl. jours. Mem. Am. Chem. Soc., AAAS, Harvey Soc., Am. Soc. Pharmacology and Exptl. Therapeutics, N.Y. Acad. Sci. Patentee in field. Current Work: synthesis of radiopharmaceuticals labelled with short-lived positron emitting radioisotopes used in positron emission tomography. Subspecialties: Nuclear medicine; Synthetic chemistry. Home: 200 Winston Dr Cliffside Park NJ 07010 Office: 1275 York Ave New York NY 10021

GINSBERG, HAROLD SAMUEL, virologist, educator; b. Daytona Beach, Fla., May 27, 1917; s. Jacob and Anne (Kalb) G.; m. Marion Reibstein, Aug. 4, 1949; children: Benjamin Langer, Peter Robert, Ann Meredith, Jane Elizabeth. A.B., Duke, 1937; M.D., Tulane U., 1941. Resident Mallory Inst. Pathology, Boston, 1941-42; intern, asst. resident Boston City Hosp., 4th Med. Service, 1942-43; resident physician, asso. Rockefeller Inst., 1946-51; asso. prof. preventive medicine Western Res. U. Sch. Medicine, 1951-60; prof. microbiology, chmn. dept. U. Pa. Sch. Medicine, 1960-73, Coll. Phys. and Surg. Columbia, 1973—; Mem. commn. acute respiratory diseases Armed Forces Epidemiological Bd., 1959-73; cons. NIH, 1959-72, 75—, Army Chem. Corps, 1962-64, NASA, 1969—, Am. Cancer Soc., 1969-73, mem. council on research and personnel, 1976-80; v.p. Internat. Com. on Nomenclature of Viruses, 1966-75; mem. space sci. bd., chmn. panel microbiology Nat. Acad. Sci., 1973-74; chmn. microbiology exam. com. Nat. Bd. Med. Examiners, 1974-79; mem. microbiology and infectious disease com. Nat. Inst. Allergy and Infectious Disease, NIH, 1976-81, chmn., 1979-81. Contbr. textbooks.; Co-author: Microbiology, 1967, 3d edit., 1980; mem. editorial bd.: Jour. Infectious Diseases, Jour. Immunology, Jour. Exptl. Medicine, Jour. Virology and Bacteriological Revs.; editor: Jour. Virology, 1979—, Cancer Research, 1978—. Served to maj. M.C. AUS, 1943-46. Decorated Legion of Merit. Mem. Nat. Acad. Scis.; Mem. Inst. Medicine of Nat. Acad. Scis., Assn. Am. Physicians, Am. Acad. Microbiologists (chmn. bd. govs. 1971-72), Am. Soc. Clin. Investigation (councillor 1958-60), Am. Assn. Immunologists, Am. Soc. Microbiology (chmn. virology div. 1961-62, councilor div. 1977—), Soc. Exptl. Biology and Medicine, Assn. Med. Sch. Microbiology Chairmen (pres. 1972-73), Harvey Soc. (pres.-elect 1983), Central Soc. Clin. Research, Am. Soc. Biol. Chemists, Am. Soc. Virology (pres. 1983), Alpha Omega Alpha. Current Work: Study of viral gene regulation and function of viral gene products using DNA-containing animal viruses. Subspecialties: Virology (biology); Microbiology. Home: 450 Riverside Dr New York NY 10027 Office: Dept Microbiology Columbia U Coll Physicians and Surgeons 701 W 168th St New York NY 10032

GINSBURG, ARTHUR PHILLIP, biophysicist; b. Revere, Mass., Jan. 8, 1942; s. Morris Peter and Lee Esther (Gropman) G.; children—David, Richard; m. Charlotte Ann Whitmer, June 30, 1984. B.S.E.E., Widener Coll., 1969; M.S.E.E., Air Force Inst. Tech., 1971; Ph.D., Cambridge U., 1980. Producer, dir. Aviation Vision Lab., Air Force Aerospace Med. Research Labs., Wright-Patterson AFB, Ohio, 1977-85; chmn., chief exec. officer, dir. research and devel. Vistech Cons., Inc., Dayton, Ohio, 1985—. Author: Visual Information Processing Based on Spatial Filters by Biological Data, 1978. Contbr. articles to profl. jours. Patentee in field Vice pres. Inventor's Council of Dayton, 1983—. Served to maj. USAF, 1960-85. Mem. Optical Soc. Am., Advancement for Research in Vision and Ophthalmology, AAAS, Sigma Xi, Tau Beta Pi, Sigma Pi Sigma. Current work: Basic and applied vision research to model filtering characteristics of vision and develop performance related vision tests based on contrast sensitivity for earth and space environments; disease detection and display analysis. Subspecialty: Vision research. Home: 4753 Shaunee Creek Dr Dayton OH 45415 Office: Vistech Cons Inc 1372 N Fairfield Rd Dayton OH 45432

GINTER, MARSHALL LLOYD, physicist, educator; b. Oroville, Calif., Aug. 24, 1935; s. Lloyd J. and Lois (Chapman) G.; m. Dorothy Spencer, Sept. 1, 1957; children: Karl Lloyd, Gretchen E. A.B., Chico State U., 1957; Ph.D., Vanderbilt U., 1961. Research asst. Vanderbilt U., Nashville, 1961, acting dir. Spectroscopy Lab., 1961-62; research assoc. U. Chgo. Lab. Molecular Structure and Spectra, 1962-66; vis. research assoc. Physikalische Anstalt der Universitat Basel, Switzerland, 1966; asst. prof. Inst. for Phys. Sci. and Tech., U. Md., College Park, 1966-69, assoc. prof., 1969-74, prof., 1974—; cons. Naval Research Lab. Contbr. articles to profl. jours. Grantee NSF; Grantee NASA; Grantee Air Force Office of Sci. Research. Fellow Optical Soc. Am.; mem. Am. Phys. Soc., Am. Chem. Soc., Sigma Xi. Current Work: Atomic and molecular electronic structure, high resolution electronic spectroscopy, high vacuum optical systems. Subspecialty: Atomic and molecular physics. Home: 12240 Valerie Ln Laurel MD 20708 Office: Inst. Phys Sci and Tech U Md College Park MD 20742

GINWALA, KYMUS, chemical engineer; b. Durban, South Africa, Mar. 27, 1931; came to U.S. 1949; s. Kekobad and Alamai (Bodhanwala) G.; m. Genevieve Teresa Modzelewski, May 15, 1955; children—Darius, Cyrus, Jay. B.Sc., MIT, 1952, M.S., 1954. Mem. research staff, div. sponsored research MIT, Cambridge, Mass., 1954; sr. engr. S.E. Ginwala Fibros, Mozambique, South Africa, 1955, Arthur D. Little, Inc., Cambridge, 1955-59; pres. No. Research and Engring. Corp., Woburn, Mass., 1959—. Mem. AIAA, Am. Inst. Chem. Engrs., Am. Chem. Soc., Nat. Computer Graphics Assn. Club: Oakley Country (Watertown, Mass.). Subspecialty: Research and development management. Office: Northern Research and Engring Corp 39 Olympia Ave Woburn MA 01801

GINZLER, EDWARD RICHARD, chemist, researcher; b. N.Y.C., May 20, 1950; s. Robert Morton and Alice Rhoda (Tolmach) G. B.A. in Chemistry, Kalamazoo Coll., 1972; M.S., in Biochemistry, U. Ill., 1975. Researcher, NIH, Bethesda, Md., 1970-72; teaching asst. U. Ill., Urbana, 1972-75; sr. chemist Mo. Analytical Labs., Inc., St. Louis, 1976—. Contbr. articles to profl. jours. Mem. Am. Chem. Soc., N.Y. Acad. Scis., Am. Assn. Dental Research, Internat. Assn. Dental Research. Democrat. Club: Sierra. Current work: Methods for testing pharmaceuticals and dentifrice products. Subspecialties: Analytical chemistry; Biochemistry (biology). Office: Mo Analytical Labs Inc 1820 Delmar Blvd Saint Louis MO 63103

GINZTON, EDWARD LEONARD, engineering corporation executive; b. Dnepropetrovsk, Ukraine, Dec. 27, 1915; came to U.S., 1929; s. Leonard Louis and Natalie P. (Philipova) G.; m. Artemas A. McCann; children: Anne, Leonard, Nancy, David. B.S., U. Calif., 1936, M.S., 1937; E.E., Stanford U., 1938, Ph.D., 1940. Research engr. Sperry Gyroscope Co., N.Y.C., 1940-46; asst. prof. applied physics and elec. engring. Stanford U., 1946-47, assoc. prof., 1947-50, prof., 1951-68; dir. Microwave Lab., 1949-59; dir. Varian Assocs., 1948—, chmn. bd., 1959-84, chmn. exec. com., 1984—, chief exec. officer, 1959-72, pres., 1964-68; dir. Stanford Bank, 1967-71, Stanford Project M, Stanford Linear Accelerator Center, 1957-60; Mem. commn. 1 U.S. nat. com. Internat. Sci. Radio Union, 1958-68; mem. Lawrence Berkeley Lab. Sci. and Adv. Com., 1972-79; chmn. adv. bd. Sch. Engring., Stanford U., 1968-70; bd. dirs., mem. exec. com. co-chmn. Stanford Mid-Peninsula Urban Coalition, 1968-72; bd. dirs. Nat. Bur. Econ. Research, 1981—, mem. panel on sci. communication and nat. security Nat. Acad. Sci., mem. Sci. policy bd. Stanford Synchrotron Radiation Lab. Author: Microwave Measurements, 1957; Contbr. articles to tech. jours. Bd. dirs. Mid-Peninsula Housing Devel. Corp., 1970—, Stanford Hosp., 1975-80; trustee Stanford U., 1977—. Recipient Morris Liebmann Meml. prize I.R.E., 1958, Calif. Manufacturer of Yr. award, 1974. Fellow IEEE (bd. dirs. 1971-72, chmn. awards bd. 1971-72, medal of honor 1969); mem. Nat. Acad. Scis. (chmn. com. on motor vehicle emissions 1971-74, co-chmn. com. nuclear energy study 1975-80), Am. Acad. Arts and Scis., Nat. Acad. Engring. (mem. council 1974-80), Sigma Xi, Eta Kappa Nu, Tau Beta Pi. Patentee in field. Current Work: Microwave tubes; linear electron acceleration. Subspecialty: Electronics. Home: 28014 Natoma Rd Los Altos Hills CA 94022 Office: 611 Hansen Way Palo Alto CA 94303

GIORGI, ELSIE AGNES, physician, university educator; b. N.Y.C. B.A., Hunter Coll., 1931; M.D., Coll. Physicians and Surgeons, Columbia U., 1949. Diplomate Am. Bd. Internal Medicine. Resident in internal medicine Bellevue Hosp., N.Y.C., 1949-53; asst. prof. clin. medicine Cornell U. Med. Coll., Ithaca, N.Y., 1957-62; asst. prof. UCLA, 1962-66, assoc. clin. prof., 1972—; asst. prof. medicine U. So. Calif. Sch. Medicine, Los Angeles, 1966-69; assoc. clin. prof. community and family medicine U. Calif. Med. Coll.-Irvine, 1969-72; guest lectr. Sch. Social Welfare, 1964—; attending physician dept. medicine Cedars-Sinai Hosp., Los Angeles, 1962—, Los Angeles County Hosp., U. So. Calif. Med. Ctr., 1966-71, St. John's Hosp., Calif., 1970—; assoc. mem. dept. internal medicine Orange County Med. Ctr., 1969—. Mem. Inst. Medicine, Gerontology Soc., Am. Pub. Health Assn. Current work: Private practice medicine and teaching. Subspecialty: Internal medicine. Address: 153 S Lasky Dr Suite 3 Beverly Hills CA 90202

GIPSON, GARY STEVEN, civil engineering educator; b. Jackson, Miss., Jan. 4, 1952; s. James Luther and Johnnie Lavera (Ferguson) G.; m. Cheryl Martinez, Feb. 24, 1953. B.S., La. State U., 1975, M.S., 1978, Ph.D., 1982. Instr. dept. civil engring. La. State U., 1977-80; research asso. Inst. Environ. Studies, 1980-82, asst. prof. dept. civil engring, 1982—. Contbr. articles to profl. jours. Mem. Am. Acad. Mechanics, ASME, Soc. Engring. Sci., Am. Phys. Soc., Nat. Soc. Profl. Engrs., La. Engring. Soc., Mensa, Sigma Xi. Current Work: Numerical modelling, applied physics, theoretical mechanics; boundary integral equations applied to mechanics. Subspecialties: Theoretical and applied mechanics; Applied mathematics. Home: 17735 Creek Hollow Rd Baton Rouge LA 70816 Office: Dept Civil Engring La State U Baton Rouge LA 70803

GIRDEN, ELLEN ROBINSON, psychology educator; b. Bklyn., May 14, 1936; d. Robert and Sarah (Bellinoff) R.; m. Edward Girden, Sept. 8, 1977. B.A., CUNY-Bklyn., 1956; M.A., 1958; Ph.D., Northwestern U., 1962. Instr. Northwestern U., 1961-62; asst. prof. Hobart and William Smith Coll., 1961-63; assoc. prof. Yeshiva U., 1963-77, Fla. Sch. Profl. Psychology, 1978-81; assoc. prof. Nova U., 1981-84, prof., 1984—. Contbr. articles to profl. jours. NIH Research grantee, 1963; CUNY fellow, 1956-58. Mem. AAAS, Am. Psychol. Assn. Democrat. Jewish. Current Work: Amygdala and motivation; time estimation; litter size and crowding effects on learning and retention by white rats. Subspecialties: Research design; Statistics. Home: 2851 NE 183d St Apt 1204 North Miami Beach FL 33160 Office: Sch Profl Psychology Nova U 3301 College Ave Fort Lauderdale FL 33314

GIROU, MICHAEL, computer systems executive; b. St. Louis, July 2, 1947; s. Jack J. and Patricia S. (Sittner) G.; m. Lynn R. Fessler, Apr. 16, 1965 (div. 1974); 1 child, Beverly; m. Theodora L. Dygert, Dec. 13, 1974; 1 child, Jim. B.A. in Math., U. Mo., 1969; Ph.D. in Math, 1985. Tech. analyst McDonnell Aircraft Co., St. Louis, 1965-67; sr. systems programmer U. Mo., 1967-69; prin. systems analyst Honeywell, Mpls., 1969-73; pres. SSM, Inc., 1973-79, M.F.D., Inc., 1979-84; program dir. Presearch, Inc., Aiken. S.C., 1984—; dir. Omni 360, Tonka Tackle. Designer computer system. Bd. dirs. Amicus, 1978. Curators scholar U. Mo., 1964. Mem. Soc. Indsl. and Applied Math. Am. Math. Soc., IEEE, Assn. Computing Machinery, U. Mo. Alumni Arts and Scis. (trustee 1982—); Pi Mu Epsilon. Republican. Club: Houndslake Country. Current work: Research and development of novel computer architectures and the design of new algorithms and techniques that exploit those architectures. Subspecialties: Algorithms; Computer architecture. Home: 11 Inverness E Aiken SC 29801 Office: Presearch Inc 39 Varden Aiken SC 29801

GISLASON, ERIC ARNI, chemist, educator; b. Oak Park, Ill., Sept. 9, 1940; s. Raymond Spencer and Jane Ann (Clifford) G.; m. Nancy Davis Brown, Sept. 11, 1962; children: Kristina Elizabeth, John Harrison. B.A. summa cum laude in Chemistry, Oberlin Coll., 1962; Ph.D. in Chem. Physics, Harvard U., 1967. Postdoctoral fellow Nat. Center for Air Pollution Control, U. Calif., Berkeley, 1967-69; asst. prof. chemistry U. Ill. at Chgo., 1969-73, assoc. prof., 1973-77, prof., 1977—; vis. scientist FOM-Inst. for Atomic and Molecular Physics, Amsterdam, Netherlands, 1977-78. Contbr. articles on chemistry to profl. jours. Recipient Silver Circle award U. Ill. at Chgo., 1982. Mem. Am. Chem. Soc., Am. Phys. Soc., Sigma Xi, Phi Beta Kappa. Congregationalist. Current Work: Molecular beam studies of molecular interactions, theoretical studies of molecular collisions, theory of nonadiabatic processes in atom-molecule collisions. Subspecialties: Atomic and molecular physics; Theoretical chemistry. Home: 7227 Oak Ave River Forest IL 60305 Office: Chemistry Dept PO Box 4348 Chicago IL 60680

GITOMER, STEVEN JOEL, physicist; b. Camden, N.J., Nov. 6, 1942; s. Martin and Miriam (Greenetz) G.; m. Joyce Kaufman, July 3, 1966; children—Michele, Alana. B.S. in Elec. Engring., Johns Hopkins U., 1964, M.S., 1966; Ph.D., U. Wis., 1969. Asst. prof. U. Pa., Phila., 1969-73; staff mem. Los Alamos Nat. Lab., N.Mex., 1974—. Editor, IEEE Transactions on Plasma Sci. Jour., 1984—. Mem. IEEE (sr., centennial medal 1984), Am. Phys. Soc. Democrat. Jewish. Current work: Laser fusion target design and experimental modelling. Subspecialties: Plasma physics; Laser fusion. Home: 1428 Miracerros S Santa Fe NM 87501 Office: Los Alamos Nat Lab Group X-1 Mail Stop E531 Los Alamos NM 87545

GIVAN, GUY VAN, ceramic engineer, researcher; b. Independence, Mo., Dec. 15, 1946; s. Victor Howell and Alice Elizabeth (Bradica) G.; m. Doris Jean Prindable, May 17, 1975; children—Gordon Victor, Gerard John, Geoff Matthew, Geri Rose. B.S. in Ceramic Engring., U. Mo.-Rolla, 1969, M.S., 1970. Mgmt. trainee Gen. Steel Co., Granite City, Ill., 1966-67; research engr. Alcoa, East St. Louis, Ill., 1970-75; ceramic engr. Rocky Mt. Refractories, Salt Lake City, 1975-84, Gunning Refractories, South Webster, Ohio, 1984—. Mem. Am. Ceramic Soc., Nat. Inst. Ceramic Engrs., Am. Concrete Inst., Keramos. Subspecialty: Ceramic engineering. Home: 2239 Concord Dr Wheelersburg OH 45694 Office: Gunning Refractories PO Box 267 South Webster OH 45682

GLACKIN, DAVID LANGDON, astronomer; b. Jamestown, N.Y., July 28, 1952; s. Franklin Pennell and Joann Elizabeth (Langdon) G.; m. Carlotta Allen, June 21, 1975. B.S., Calif. Inst. Tech., 1974; M.S., U. Colo., 1977. Research asst. Calif. Inst. Tech. Big Bear Solar Observatory, summers 1971, 72, 73, undergrad. teaching asst. dept. physics, 1974; research astronomer Sacramento Peak Observatory, Sunspot, N. Mex., 1974; research asst. Joint Inst. for Lab. Astrophysics, U. Colo., Boulder, 1974-77; profl. research asst. Goddard Space Flight Center, Greenbelt, Md., 1978; sr. scientist Jet Propulsion Lab., Pasadena, Calif., 1978—. Contbr. articles to profl. jours. Recipient Calif. Inst. Tech. chpt. Sigma Xi award for Outstanding Research, 1974; Calif. Inst. Tech. President's Fund grantee, 1979,80. Mem. Am. Astronom. Soc., Am. Geophysical Union. Current Work: Very long baseline interferometry with application to measuring earth rotation and polar motion; atmospheric effects on earth rotation. Subspecialties: Solar physics; Graphics, image processing, and pattern recognition. Office: Jet Propulsion Lab 264-700 4800 Oak Grove Dr Pasadena CA 91109

GLADFELTER, WAYNE LEWIS, chemistry educator, researcher; b. Bryn Mawr, Pa., Feb. 16, 1953; s. Stanley Lewis and Jean Roberts (Davis) G.; m. Elizabeth Joan Jedziniak, Aug. 19, 1978. B.S. in Chemistry, Colo. Sch. Mines, 1975; Ph.D. in Chemistry, Pa. State U., 1978. NSF postdoctoral fellow Calif. Inst. Tech., Pasadena, 1978-79; asst. prof. chemistry U. Minn., Mpls., 1979—. Contbr. articles to profl. jours. Fellow Alfred P. Sloan Found., 1983-85; Harry Bright scholar, Pa. State U., 1977. Mem. Am. Chem. Soc. (Nobel Laureate Signature award 1980), Sigma Xi (research award 1978). Current work: Synthetic, structural and mechanistic studies of transition metal clusters. Subspecialties: Organometallics; Inorganic chemistry. Home: 1754 Arona Ave Saint Paul MN 55113 Office: U Minn Dept Chemistry Minneapolis MN 55455

GLADFELTER, WILBERT EUGENE, physiologist, educator; b. York, Pa., Apr. 29, 1928; s. Paul John and Marea Bernadette (Miller) G.; m. Ruth Ballantyne, Jan. 26, 1952; children: James W., Charles D., Mary A. A.B. magna cum laude, Gettysburg Coll., 1952; Ph.D. (NSF fellow), U. Pa., 1960. Asst. instr. physiology U. Pa., Phila., 1954-56, 58-59, NIH trainee fellow, 1958-59; instr. physiology W. Va. U. Med. Center, Morgantown, 1959-61, asst. prof., 1961-69, asso. prof., 1969—. Contbr. articles to profl. jours. Treas. Monongalia County Heart Assn., 1976—. Served with USN, 1946-48. Mem. Am. Physiol. Soc., Soc. for Neurosci., Am. Soc. Zoologists, N.Y. Acad. Scis., Phi Beta Kappa, Sigma Xi, Beta Beta Beta. Lutheran. Current Work: Hypothalamic control of the excitability of the motor system; teaching medical, dental and graduate students; research. Subspecialties: Neurophysiology; Physiology (medicine). Home: Route 7 Box 528 Morgantown WV 26505 Office: Dept. Physiology WVa U Med Center Morgantown WV 26506

GLADNEY, HENRY MARTIN, computer scientist, researcher; b. Prague, Czechoslovakia, Feb. 8, 1938; came to U.S., 1960; s. Kurt Paul and Eva Maria (Horwich) G.; m. Helga Hedwig Beinhoff, Oct. 2, 1968; children—Stephanie Olivia, Sebastian Henry. B.A., U. Toronto, Ont., Can., 1960; M.A., Princeton u., 1962, Ph.D., 1963. Mem. research staff IBM Research, Jan Jose, Calif., 1963-69, tech. adviser, Armonk, N.J., 1970, mgr. computing service, San Jose, 1971-74, 77-80, research staff mem., 1980—. Contbr. articles to profl. publs. Fellow Am. Phys. Soc.; mem. Assn. Computing Machinery. Current work: Distributed access to databases, linguistics and cognitive theories for specification of information processing, programming languages. Subspecialties: Distributed systems and networks; Programming languages. Home: 20044 Glen Brae Dr Saratoga CA 95070 Office: IBM Research K51/282 5600 Cottle Rd San Jose CA 95193

GLAESER, ANDREAS MICHAEL, materials science educator; researcher; b. Dresden, Fed. Republic Germany, Mar. 29, 1954; came to U.S., 1959; s. Alexander Johannes and Charlotte (Wachs) G. B.S., MIT, 1976, Sc.D., 1981. Asst. prof. materials sci. U. Calif.-Berkeley, 1981—; prin. investigator Lawrence Berkeley Lab., 1981—; cons. IBM, Austin, Tex., 1983—, ERG, Oakland, Calif., 1983—. Author, inventor in field. Hertz Found. fellow, 1976-81; Arco jr. faculty fellow, 1982-83; regents jr. faculty fellow U. Calif.-Berkeley, 1982. Mem. Am. Ceramic Soc. Current work: Ceramic/materials processing, microstructure development, powder processing, thermodynamics, phase transformations, sintering, grain growth. Subspecialties: Ceramic engineering; Materials processing. Home: 1203 Melville Sq Apt 415 Richmond CA 94804 Office: U Calif Hearst Mining Bldg Berkeley CA 94720

GLAMKOWSKI, EDWARD JOSEPH, medicinal chemist; b. Bklyn., May 20, 1936; s. S. John and Nellie (Novakowski) G.; m. Shirley Marie van Horn, Apr. 28, 1963; children—Diane, Catherine, Edward. B.S. with honors in Chemistry, Fordham U., 1958; Ph.D. in Organic Chemistry, Ohio State U., 1963. Sr. research chemist Merck Sharp & Dohme Research Labs., Rahway, N.J., 1963-71; research assoc. Hoechst-Roussel Pharms. Inc., Somerville, N.J., 1971-76, research group mgr., 1977—. Editor: Drug Development Research, 1981. Contbr. articles to profl. jours.; patentee in field. Kettering fellow, 1960-61. Mem. Am. Chem. Soc. (chmn. membership com. div. medicinal chemistry 1982-84, alt. councilor 1984-85), Phi Lambda Upsilon. Current work: Design and synthesis of new therapeutic agents having psychotropic, cardiovascular, diuretic, analgesic or antiinflammatory properties; heterocyclic chemistry; indoles and related compounds. Subspecialties: Medicinal chemistry; Organic chemistry. Home: 7 Owens Dr Warren NJ 07060 Office: Hoechst-Roussel Pharms Inc Route N202-206 Somerville NJ 08876

GLANTZ, STANTON ARNOLD, medicine educator; b. Cleve., May 3, 1946; s. Louis and Frieda (Stern) G.; m. Marsha Kramar, Mar. 26, 1972; children—Aaron, Frieda. B.S., U. Cin., 1969; M.S., Stanford U., 1970, Ph.D., 1973. Engr., Manned Space Ctr., NASA, Houston, 1965-69; research fellow Stanford U., Palo Alto, Calif., 1973-75; research fellow U. Calif.-San Francisco, 1975-77, asst. prof. medicine, 1977-81, assoc. prof., 1981—; mem. cardiovascular research inst., U. Calif.-San Francisco, 1977—, chmn. bioengring. grad. group, 1984—. Author: Mathematics for Biomedical Applications, 1979; Primer of Biostatics, 1981. Mem. editorial bd. Circulation Research, 1981—; Circulation, 1982—. Treas. Californians for Nonsmokers Rights, Berkeley, 1981-83, pres., 1983—. Recipient Research Career Devel. award NIH, 1977-81, Mem. Am. Heart Assn., IEEE (best paper award 1980), AAAS, Am. Physiol. Soc. Current work: Cardiac mechanics, computers in medicine, effects of involuntary smoking. Subspecialties: Cardiology; Biomedical engineering. Home: 1474 24th Ave San Francisco CA 94122 Office: U Calif San Francisco Div Cardiology 1186M San Francisco CA 94143

GLASCOCK, HOMER HOPSON, II, physicist, electrical engineer; b. Hannibal, Mo., Apr. 10, 1929; s. Homer Hopson and Mary Dodd (Neale) G.; m. Nancy Louise Senior, June 29, 1958; children—Homer H., Colin F., Thomas D. B.S. in Edn., U. Mo.-Columbia, 1951, M.S., 1956, Ph.D., 1960 Physicist, Gen. Electric Co., Schenectady, 1960—. Patentee in field. Contbr. articles to sci. jours. Served with U.S. Army, 1951-53. U. Mo. fellow, 1956; NSF fellow, 1959; recipient Albert Eisenstein award U. Mo., 1960. Mem. Am. Phys. Soc., IEEE, Sigma Xi, Elfun Soc. Presbyterian. Current work: Semiconductor packaging; thermalanalysis; material properties; environmental effects; thermionic and field emission. Subspecialties: Condensed matter physics; Semiconductors. Home: 43 Cypress Dr Scotia NY 12302 Office: Gen Electric Co PO Box 8 Schenectady NY 12301

GLASER, DONALD A(RTHUR), physicist; b. Cleve., Sept. 21, 1926; s. William Joseph Glaser. B.S., Case Inst. Tech., 1946, Sc.D., 1959; Ph.D., Cal. Inst. Tech., 1949. Prof. physics U. Mich., 1949-59; prof. physics U. Calif. at Berkeley, 1959—, prof. physics and molecular biology, 1964—. Recipient Henry Russel award U. Mich., 1955; Charles V. Boys prize Phys. Soc., London, 1958; Nobel prize in physics, 1960; NSF fellow, 1961; Guggenheim fellow, 1961-62. Fellow Am. Physics Soc. (prize 1959); mem. Nat. Acad. Scis., Sigma Xi, Tau Kappa Alpha, Theta Tau. Current Work: Understanding human vision through psychophysical experiments and theoretical models. Subspecialties: Psychophysics; Neurobiology. Office: Molecular Biology Dept U Calif Berkeley CA 94720*

GLASER, GILBERT HERBERT, educator, physician, neuroscientist; b. N.Y.C., Nov. 10, 1920; s. Burnard Richard and Sidelle (Rogers) G.; m. Morfydd Mai Pugh, Mar. 17, 1946; children—Gareth Evan, Sara Elizabeth. A.B., Columbia, 1940, M.D., 1943, Med. Sc.D., 1951; M.A. (hon.), Yale, 1963. Diplomate: Am. Bd. Psychiatry and Neurology. Intern Mt. Sinai Hosp., N.Y.C., 1943-44; resident neurology N.Y. Neurol. Inst., 1944-46; from research asst. to asso. neurology Columbia Coll. Physicians and Surgeons, 1948-52; research scientist N.Y. Psychiat. Inst., 1948-50; head. sect. neurology Yale Sch. Medicine, 1952-71, chmn. dept. neurology, 1971—, asst. prof. neurology, 1952-55, asso. prof., 1955-63, prof. neurology, 1963—; Commonwealth Fund vis. prof. neurology U. London, Eng., 1965-66; cons. West Haven (Conn.) VA Hosp., 1955—; vis. prof. neurology Nat. Hosp., London, 1972, Park Hosp., Oxford, 1973—; Fulbright disting. prof., 1981; mem. neurology research adv. com. USPHS, 1956-60, 68-72, spl. cons., 1973, epilepsy adv. com., 1974-77, chmn. basic sci. subcom., 1974-77; mem. neurobiology rev. com. VA, 1975-78; chmn., 1977-78. Author: EEG and Behavior, 1963; Editor: Epilepsia, 1958-76, adv. editor, 1976-84; editor: Recent Advances in Clinical Neurology, 1978, 81, 84, Antiepileptic Drugs: Mechanisms of Action, 1980; mem. editorial bd.: Jour. Nervous and Mental Diseases, Jour. Neurol. Scis. Contbr. articles to profl. jours. Served as capt. M.C. AUS, 1946-48. Recipient Janeway prize Columbia U., 1943, Bicentennial medal award, 1968, Book award Commonwealth Fund, 1975. Fellow Royal Soc. Medicine, A.C.P.; mem. Am. Neurol. Assn. (1st v.p. 1977-78), Am. Acad. Neurology (pres. 1973-75), Am. Epilepsy Soc. (pres. 1963), Am. Electroencephalographic Soc. (council 1958-61, bd. qualifications), Eastern Assn. Electroencephalographers (pres. 1958), EEG Soc. (Gt. Britain), Assn. Brit. Neurologists, Soc. for Neurosci., Epilepsy Found. Am. (med. adv. bd.), Myasthenia Gravis Foundation (med. adv. bd. chmn. 1964-65), Multiple Sclerosis Soc. (chmn. research programs com. 1973-74, med. adv. bd.). Club: Athenaeum (London). Subspecialty: Neurology. Home: 205 Millbrook Rd Hamden CT 06518 Office: 333 Cedar St New Haven CT 06510

GLASER, PETER EDWARD, mechanical engineer; b. Zatec, Czechoslovakia, Sept. 5, 1923; came to U.S., 1948; s. Hugo and Helen (Weiss) G.; m. Eva F. Graf, Oct. 16, 1955; children: David, Steven, Susan. Diploma, Coll. Tech., Leeds, Eng., 1943; state exam., Tech. U., Prague, 1948; M.S., Columbia U., 1951, Ph.D., 1955. Head design dept. Werner Mgmt., N.Y.C., 1948-53; v.p. Arthur D. Little, Inc., Cambridge, Mass., 1955—; cons. NASA, 1969-71, Office Tech. Assessment, Washington, 1980-81. Editor: Thermal Imaging, 1964, Aerodynamically Heated Structures, 1962, Solar Energy, 1973-85. Trustee Combined Jewish Philanthropies, 1976—. Served in Free Czechoslovak Army, 1943-45. Recipient Carl F. Kayan medal Columbia U., 1974. Mem. Internat. Solar Energy Soc. (pres. 1968-70, Farrington Daniels award 1983), Am. Astronautical Soc. (dir. 1976-84), Internat. Astronautical Fedn. (com. chmn. 1982—), ASME (com. chmn. 1958-60), Internat. Inst. Refrigeration (v.p. 1969-73), SUNSAT Energy Council (pres. 1978—). Club: Cosmos (Washington). Invented concept of solar power satellite, 1973. Current Work: solar energy applications, solar power satellite, space shuttle experiments, space commercialization, space station. Subspecialties: Solar energy; Aerospace engineering and technology. Home: 62 Turning Mill Rd Lexington MA 02173 Office: Arthur D Little Inc 20 Acorn Park Cambridge MA 02140

GLASER, RONALD, microbiology educator; b. N.Y.C., Feb. 27, 1939; s. Irving and Pauline G.; m. Janice Kiecolt, Jan. 17, 1980; children: Andrew, Eric. B.A., U. Bridgeport, 1962; M.S., U. R.I., 1964; Ph.D., U. Conn., 1968; postgrad., Baylor Coll. Medicine, 1968-69. Asst. prof. microbiology Pa. State U., Hershey, 1970-73, assoc. prof., 1973-77, prof., 1977-78; prof. chmn. dept. med. microbiology and immunology Ohio State U., Columbus, 1978—, prof. Medicine, 1978—; ad hoc reviewer NIH study sects. Author: (with T. Gottleib-Stematsky) Human Herpes Virus Infections: Clinical Aspects, 1982. NIH fellow, 1968-69; Franco-Am. exchange Program; Fogarty Internat. Center; NIH and INSRM fellow, 1975, 77; Leukemia Soc. Am. scholar, 1974-79. Mem. Am. Soc. Microbiology, AAAS, Am. Assn. Cancer Research, Soc. Exptl. Biology and Medicine. Current Work: Human oncogenic herpesviruses and cancer. Subspecialties: Virology (medicine); Cell study oncology. Office: 333 W 10th Ave Columbus OH 43210

GLASGOW, GLENN PATRICK, med. physicist; b. Lebanon, Ky., Feb. 8, 1944; s. Glenn Shirley and Frances (Tutt) G.; m. Lyndia Rouse Glasgow, June 2, 1968. B.S., Western Ky. U., 1965; M.S., U. Ky., 1969, Ph.D., 1974. Diplomate: Am. Bd. Radiology, Am. Bd. Health Physics. Fellow Washington U., St. Louis, 1974-75, instr. radiation physic in radiology, 1975-78, asst. prof., 1978-85; prof. Loyola U., 1985—. Contbr. numerous articles to profl. jours. Mem. Am. Phys. Soc., Health Physic Soc., Am. Soc. Therapeutic Radiologists, Am. Coll. Radiology, Am. Assn. Physicists in Medicine (Mo. River Valley chpt. sec. treas. 1977-78, pres. elect 1979, pres. 1980). Democrat. Methodist. Current Work: Medical uses of radiation. Subspecialties: Cancer research (medicine); Nuclear physics. Home: 942 Monore St River Forest IL 60305 Office: Loyola-Hines Dept Radiotherapy Hines VA Hosp 114B Hines IL 60141

GLAS-GREENWALT, PIA, physician, investigator; b. Sigmaringen, Fed. Republic Germany, Jan. 3, 1932; came to U.S., 1961; naturalized, 1975; d. Alois August and Johanna (Kirchhardt) Glas; m. Tibor J. Greenwalt, Feb. 27, 1971; 1 stepchild, Peter H. M.D., U. Tubingen, Fed. Republic Germany, 1960. Intern U. Tubingen, 1960-61, resident, 1967-70; research investigator James F. Mitchell Found. Inst. Med. Research, Washington, 1961-67, sr. investigator, 1970-75; dir. Coagulation Lab. Naval Med. Research Inst., Bethesda, Md., 1975-79; research assoc. U. Cin., 1979-81, asst. prof., 1981—, dir. Fibrinolysis Lab., 1981—, cons., 1981—. Mem. Am. Heart Assn. Internat. Soc. Thrombosis and Haemostasis, Am. Fedn. Clin. Research, Am. Soc. Hematology, Soc. Exptl. Biol. Medicine, Internat. Soc. Blood Transfusion, Internat. Soc. Hematology. Current work: Active clinical and basic research in clotting problems in a variety of diseases. Subspecialties: Biochemistry (medicine); Hematology. Home: 328 Compton Hills Dr Cincinnati OH 45215 Office: U Cin 231 Bethesda Ave Cincinnati OH 45267

GLASHAUSSER, CHARLES MICHAEL, physics educator; b. Newark, Dec. 7, 1939; s. Charles and Ruth Glashausser; m. Suellen O'Brien; children—Alexander, Allegra. B.S., Boston Coll., 1961; Ph.D., Princeton U., 1966. Physicist, Saclay, France, 1965-67, vis. physicist, 1981; physicist Lawrence Berkeley Lab. Calif., 1967-69; prof. physics Rutgers U., New Brunswick, N.J., 1969—; guest prof. U. Munich, Fed. Republic Germany, 1975-76. Contbr. articles to profl. jours. Fellow Am. Phys. Soc.; mem. Lampf Users Group, AAAS. Current work: experimental intermediate energy nuclear physics, polarization, spin excitations, delta resonance. Subspecialty: Nuclear physics. Home: 202 S 2d Ave Highland Park NJ 08904 Office: Rutgers U Physics Dept Box 849 Piscataway NJ 08854

GLASHOW, SHELDON LEE, physicist, educator; b. N.Y.C., Dec. 5, 1932; s. Lewis and Bella (Rubin) G.; m. Joan Glashow; children: Jason David, Jordan, Brian Lewis, Rebecca Lee. A.B., Cornell U., 1954; A.M., Harvard U., 1955, Ph.D., 1958; D.Sc. (hon.), Yeshiva U., 1978, U. Marseille, 1982. NSF fellow U. Copenhagen, Denmark, 1958-60; research fellow Calif. Inst. Tech., 1960-61; asst. prof. Stanford U., 1961-62; asst. prof., asso. prof. U. Calif. at Berkeley, 1962-66; faculty Harvard U., 1966—, prof. physics, 1967—, Higgins prof. physics, 1979—; cons. Brookhaven Nat. Lab., 1966-73, 75—; mem. sci. policy com. CERN, 1979—; vis. prof. U. Marseille, 1971, MIT, 1974, 80, Boston U., 1983; affiliated sr. scientist U. Houston, 1983—; univ. scholar Tex. A & M U., 1983—. Contbr. articles to profl. jours. and popular mags. Pres. Andrei Sakharov Inst., 1980—. Recipient J.R. Oppenheimer Meml. prize, 1977; George Ledlie prize, 1978; Nobel prize in physics, 1979; Castiglione di Sicilia prize, 1983; NSF fellow, 1955-60; Sloan fellow, 1962-66; CERN vis. fellow, 1968. Fellow Am. Phys. Soc., AAAS; mem. Am. Acad. Arts and Scis., Nat. Acad. Scis., Sigma Xi. Subspecialty: Theoretical physics. Office: Harvard U Dept Physics Cambridge MA 02138

GLASS, ALEXANDER JACOB, business executive; b. Pittsfield Twp., N.Y., Jan. 4, 1933; s. Lawrence Louis and Anna Constance (Kaufman) G.; m. Joanna McClelland, Dec. 18, 1959 (div. 1976); children—Jennifer, Mavis, Lawrence; m. 2d Judith Anderson, Aug. 7, 1977. B.S. in Physics, Rensselaer Poly. Inst., 1954, M.S., Yale U., 1955, Ph.D., Rensselaer Poly. Inst., 1963; D.Sc. hon., Eastern Mich. U., 1983. Prof. elec. engring. Wayne State U., Detroit, 1968-70, chmn. elec. engring., 1970-73; lectr. applied sci. U. Calif.-Davis, 1973-81; head laser design group Lawrence Livermore Nat. Lab., Calif., 1973-78, asst. assoc. dir. lasers, 1978-81; pres KMS Fusion Inc., Ann Arbor, 1981—; dir. KMS Industries, Ann Arbor, 1983—; chmn. and pres. Covalent Tech., Ann Arbor, 1983—; staff scientist Dept. Energy, Washington, 1978; cons. LaJolla Inst., Calif., 1976-80. Co-editor ann. procs. profl. conf., 1969-80; contbr. articles to profl. publs. Served as capt. U.S. Army, 1955-57. Sterling fellow Yale U., 1960; recipient Outstanding Tchr. award Wayne State U., 1969. Fellow Optical Soc. Am. (dir. 1980-82), IEEE; mem. Am. Phys. Soc. (sec. treas. Joint Council on Quantum Electronics 1972—). Democrat. Subspecialty: Laser fusion. Office: KMS Fusion Inc PO Box 1567 Ann Arbor MI 48106

GLASSER, JULIAN, metallurgist, researcher; b. Chgo., May 23, 1912; s. Jacob David and Sarah (Permut) G.; m. Mildred Lavina Demmel, June 27, 1942 (dec. 1976); children—William J., James E.; m. 2d, Dorothea Justice, Nov. 6, 1983. B.S. in Chemistry, U. Ill., 1933, M.S., 1935; Ph.D. in Phys. Chemistry, Pa. State U., 1938. Grad. asst. Pa. State U., State College, 1935-38; research chemist Gen. Electric Co., Schnectady, N.Y., 1937; research engr. Battelle Meml. Inst., Columbus, Ohio, 1938-42; chief chemist, chief metallurgist Olin Industries, Inc. aluminum div., Tacoma, 1942-45; dir. research Gen. Abrasive Co., Niagara Falls, N.Y., 1945-47; supr. Armour Research Found., Chgo., 1947-53; cons. to head metallurgy br. Navy Dept., Office Naval Research, Washington, 1952-53; staff metallurgist, cons. Materials Adv. Bd., Nat. Research Council, Washington, 1951-53; tech. dir. Cramet Inc., Chattanooga, 1953-58; prof. Vanderbilt U., Nashville, 1958-59; cons. Julian Glasser, Chattanooga, 1958-60; pres. Chem. and Metall. Research, Inc., Chattanooga, 1960—. Contbr. articles to profl. jours. Patentee in field. Mem. Am. Chem. Soc. (chmn. Chattanooga sect. 1973-74), Am. Soc. Metals (chmn. Chattanooga chpt. 1956-57), Am. Inst. Mining, Metall. and Petroleum Engrs. (chmn. publs. com. 1951-53), Electrochem. Soc. (chmn. electrothermics div. 1949-51, treas. Chgo. chpt. 1948-49), Am. Soc. Nondestructive Testing (chmn. Chattanooga sect. 1969-70), Am. Ceramic Soc., Am. Powder Metallurgy Inst. Jewish. Current work: Research in materials science and engineering. Subspecialties: Physical chemistry; Metallurgical engineering. Home: 3400 Glendon Dr Chattanooga TN 37411 Office: Chem and Metall Research Inc PO Box 80156 Chattanooga TN 37411

GLASSER, LEO G., See *Who's Who in America*, 43rd edition.

GLASSMAN, ARMAND BARRY, physician, scientist, educator; b. Paterson, N.J., Sept. 9, 1938; s. Paul Glassman and Rosa Glassman Ackerman; m. Alberta C. Macri, Aug. 30, 1958; children—Armand P., Steven B., Brian A. B.A., Rutgers U., 1960; M.D. magna cum laude, Georgetown U., 1964. Diplomate Am. Bd. Pathology, Am. Bd. Nuclear Medicine. Med intern Georgetown U. Hosp., 1964-65; resident in anat. pathology Yale-New Haven Hosp., 1965-67, spl. fellow, 1968-69; resident in clin. pathology West Haven VA Hosp., 1967-68; asst. prof. U. Fla., Gainsville, 1969-71; assoc. prof. Med. Coll. Ga., 1971-76, chmn. dept. med. tech. sch. Allied Health Scis., 1971-76, prof. dept path. and med. tech., 1974-76; prof., chmn. dept. lab. medicine Med. U. of S.C., 1976—, assoc. dean Coll. Medicine, 1979, assoc. med. dir. Med. Univ. Hosp., 1982—, asst. dean, dir. sch. Applied Lab. Sci., 1984—; dir. clin. labs. Charleston Meml. Hosp., S.C, 1976-81, 84—, acting chmn. dept. basic and clin. immunology and microbiology, 1985—; cons. lab. and nuclear medicine VA Med. Ctr., Charleston, 1976—. Contbr. articles to profl. jours. Bd. dirs. Franklin C. Fetter Family Health Ctr., Charleston unit Am. Cancer Soc., 1984—, Low Country ARC Blood Bank, Charleston, 1983—; mem. Charleston Historic Soc., 1976—; adminstrv. adv. com. Trident Tech. Coll., Charleston, 1977—; mem. dean's com. VA Hosp., Charleston, 1978—, mem. med. adv. com. ARC Regional Blood Services, 1983—. mem. adv. bd. Cobra Sickle Cell, 1980—; founder, dir. Thomas W. Holbrook Meml. Dept. Lab. Medicine Fund, 1983—. Recipient Jacobi (pediatrics) award Washington, 1964; Outstanding Tchr. award Med. Coll. Ga., 1974; scholar N.J. State, Johnson Found., Avalon Found.; grantee NIH, Abbott Co., Med. Research Found. Ga. Fellow ACP, Coll. Physicians, Coll. Am. Pathologists (bd. editors 1979-81, various coms.), Am. Soc. Clin. Pathologists (council immunohematology, 1982—), Coll. Nuclear Medicine, Soc. Nuclear Medicine (reviewer jour., S.E. chpt. Young Investigator of Yr. 1971, acad. council 1979—); mem. AMA (sect. med. schs. 1980—, Physicians Recognition award 1970-82), Acad. Clin. Lab. Physicians and Scientists (pres. 1982-83, exec. com. 1983-84), Am. Bd. Pathology, Am. Assn. Blood Banks (chmn. cryobiology com. 1974-84), AAAS, N.Y. Acad. Scis., Assn. Clin. Scis., Assn. Am. Med. Colls., Soc. Cryobiology (treas., mem. exec. com. 1980-82), Charleston Med. Soc. (editor newsletter 1980—), Sigma Xi, Alpha Omega Alpha, Alpha Eta Soc. Clubs: Charleston Tennis, Running. Current work: Host agent immunologic responses especially Leishmania donovani lymphocyte function and metabolism; role of prostaglandins in diabetic lymphocytes. Subspecialties: Pathology (medicine); Nuclear medicine. Office: Dept Lab Medicine Med U SC 171 Ashley Ave Charleston SC 29425

GLASSMAN, EDWARD, biochemistry and nutrition educator; b. N.Y.C., Mar. 18, 1929; s. J. Stanley and Riesa (Bronfman) G.; m. Ann Terrell, Feb. 16, 1956 (div. 1976); children—Lyn Judith, Susan Fiona, Ellen Ruth Glassman Volgarino, Marjorie Riesa. B.A., NYU 1949, M.S., 1951; Ph.D., Johns Hopkins U., 1955. Am. Cancer Soc. postdoctoral fellow Calif. Inst. Tech., Pasadena, 1955-57; NIH postdoctoral fellow U. Edinburgh, Scotland and Zurich, Switzerland, 1958-59; staff mem. dept. genetics City of Hope Med. Ctr., Duarte, Calif., 1959-60; from asst. prof. to assoc. prof. biochemistry, U. N.C. Sch. Medicine, Chapel Hill, 1960-67, prof. biochemistry and genetics, 1967—, dir. neurobiology program, 1965-72, dir. div. chem. neurobiology, 1971-78, head program team effectiveness, 1982—; vis. prof. Stanford U., 1968-69, U. Calif.-Irvine, 1978; vis. fellow Ctr. Creative Leadership, Greensboro, N.C., 1983; cons. in field; mem., chmn. numerous coms. Author: Molecular Approach to Psychobiology, 1967. Contbr. articles to profl. jours., also mem. editorial bds. Recipient Career Devel. award NIH, 1961-71; Guggenheim fellow, 1968-69. Fellow Royal Soc. Edinburgh, AAAS; mem. Am. Soc. Biol. Chemists, Am. Soc. Neurochemistry, European Brain Behavior Soc., AALP, Am. Soc. Tng. and Devel., Elisha Mitchell Sci. Soc. (v.p. 1965-66), Soc. Neursci. (pres. N.C. chpt. 1974), N.C. Assn. Humanistic Educators (bd. dirs. 1976). Current work: Research on alcohol metabolism in mammals; teach nutrition; consult on creativity and leadership training. Subspecialties: Genetics and genetic engineering (biology); Biochemistry (biology). Home: 112 Kenan St Chapel Hill NC 27514 Office: U N C Med Sch Biochemistry Dept Chapel Hill NC 27514

GLASSMAN, IRVIN, engineering educator, consultant; b. Balt., Sept. 19, 1923; s. Abraham and Bessie (Snyder) G.; m. Beverly Wolfe, June 17, 1951; children: Shari Powell, Diane Geinger, Barbara Ann. B.E., Johns Hopkins U., 1943, D.Eng., 1950. Research asst. Manhattan Project, Columbia U., N.Y.C., 1943-46; mem. faculty Princeton U. (N.J.), 1950—, prof. mech. and aero. engring., 1964—, cons. to industry. Author: (with R.F. Sawyer) Performance of Chemical Propellants, 1971, Combustion, 1977; editor 3 books; contbr. articles to tech. jours. Served with U.S. Army, 1944-46. NSF fellow, 1966-67. Mem. Combustion Inst. (Sir Alfred Edgerton Gold medal 1982), Am. Chem. Soc., AAUP, Tau Beta Pi. Patentee rocket propellants (2). Current Work: Combustion of multicomponent fuels, soot formation, hydrocarbon oxidation kinetics, fire safety. Subspecialties: Combustion processes; Fuels. Home: PO Box 14 Princeton NJ 08540 Office: Princeton U Princeton NJ 08544

GLASSMAN, JEROME MARTIN, clinical pharmacologist, educator; b. Phila., Mar. 2, 1919; s. Martin K. and Dorothea (Largeman) G.; m. Justine Helena Rizinsky, June 15, 1952; children: Martin J., Lorna R., Gary J. A.B., U. Pa., 1939, M.A., 1942; Ph.D., Yale U., 1950. Research asso. lab. applied physiology Yale U., New Haven, 1950-51; head dept. pharmacology Wyeth Labs., Phila., 1951-62; dir. biol. research USV/Revlon, Yonkers, N.Y., 1962-69; dir. clin. research and pharmacology Wampole Labs., Stamford, Conn., 1969-75; asso. dir. clin. investigation Wallace Labs., Cranbury, N.J., 1975—; adj. assoc. prof. pharmacology N.Y. Med. Coll., 1973-82. Contbr. articles to profl. jours. Scoutmaster Boy Scouts Am., 1957-62, chmn. troop com., 1976-81. Recipient Cert. of Merit, U.S. Office Sci. Research and Devel., Washington, 1945. Fellow AAAS, N.Y. Acad. Scis., Am. Coll. Clin. Pharmacology, Am. Coll. Clin. Pharmacology and Chemotherapy; mem. Biometric Soc., Am. Soc. Pharmacology and Exptl. Therapeutics, Soc. Exptl. Biol. Medicine, Soc. Toxicology, Sigma Xi. Patentee in field. Current Work: Pharmacology and toxicology of therapeutic agts. in clinical medicine. Subspecialties: Pharmacology; Toxicology (medicine). Home: 280 Sleepy Hollow Rd Briarcliff Manor NY 10510 Office: Wallace Labs Half Acre Rd Cranbury NJ 08512

GLATZ, ALFRED CHRISTIAN, physical chemist, researcher; b. New Rochelle, N.Y., Dec. 25, 1930; s. Albert Adolph and Elsie A. (Rapp) G.; m. Norma A. DeMarzo, Sept. 10, 1955; children—Christopher A., Lisa A. B.S., Muhlenberg Coll., 1953; Ph.D. in Chemistry, Poly. Inst. Bklyn., 1960; M.B.A., Iona Coll., New Rochelle, 1975. Sr. phys. chemist Carrier Corp., Syracuse, N.Y., 1960-66; phys. scientist NASA-Electronics Research Ctr., Cambridge, Mass., 1966-73; research scientist Gen. Foods Corp., Tarrytown, N.Y., 1973-83; group leader BOC Tech. Ctr., Murray Hill, N.J., 1983—. Asst. scoutmaster Fairfield County council Boy Scouts Am., 1980-81. Mem. Am. Chem. Soc. Club: Gideons Internat. (treas. 1984—). Current work: Research interests include studies of the physico-chemical properties of sub-and super-critical fluids with emphasis on separation processes for natural products.

Subspecialties: Physical chemistry; Food science and technology. Office: BOC Tech Ctr 100 Mountain Ave Murray Hill NJ 07974

GLATZMAIER, GARY ANDREW, physicist; b. St Cloud, Minn., Jan. 4, 1949; s. Andrew J. and Vera A. (Oehrlein) G. B.S., Marquette U., 1971; postgrad. Johns Hopkins U., 1972-73, U. N.Mex., 1976; Ph.D., U. Colo., 1980. Instr. physics Naval Nuclear Power Sch., Bainbridge, Md., 1971-75; postdoctoral researcher Nat. Ctr. Atmospheric Research, Boulder, Colo., 1980-81, U. Newcastle upon Tyne, Eng., 1981-82; postdoctoral researcher Los Alamos Nat. Lab., 1982-84, staff scientist, 1984—. Contbr. articles to profl. jours. Served to lt. USN, 1971-75. Mem. Am. Astron. Soc., Phi Beta Kappa. Current work: Three dimensional, nonlinear simulations of convection and magnetic field generation in sun's atmosphere and of global circulations in the earth's atmosphere. Subspecialties: Climatology; Solar physics. Home: 4727 Trinity Dr Los Alamos NM 87544 Office: Los Alamos Nat Lab Los Alamos NM 87545

GLAZER, HOWARD IRWIN, psychologist; b. Toronto, Ont., Can., May 8, 1946; s. Max and Leah (Osolky) G.; m. Roberta Lynn Hoff, May 8, 1969 (div. Dec. 1982). B.A. with honors, U. Toronto, 1969; Ph.D., U. Tex., 1972. Lic. psychologist, N.Y. Asst. prof. U. Tex., Austin, 1972-73, Rockefeller U., N.Y.C., 1977-80; clin. asst. prof. Cornell U. Med. Coll., N.Y.C., 1977—; pres. Corp. Psychol. Examiners, N.Y.C., 1978—, Corp. Stress Control Services Inc., N.Y.C., 1981—; asst. prof. Loyola U. of Montreal, Que., Can., 1975-77; sr. scientist Postgrad. Center for Mental Health, N.Y.C., 1980-81; asst. attending psychologist N.Y. Hosp., N.Y.C., 1977—. Editor, author: Directive and Behavioral Intervention Strategies in Depression, 1981; editor: Behavioral Psychotherapy, 1983; contbr. articles to profl. jours. Woodrow Wilson fellow, 1969-71; Foundations Fund for Research in Psychiatry fellow, 1973-75. Mem. Am. Psychol. Assn., N.Y. State Psychol. Assn., N.Y. Acad. Scis., Nat. Registers of Health Service Providers in Psychology, Sigma Xi. Current Work: The effects of psychological stressors on brain chemistry and behavioral deficits. Development of clinical service programs for major U.S. corporations. Subspecialties: Clinical/organizational psychology; Psychobiology. Home: 127 W 92d St 2A New York NY 10025 Office: Corporate Stress Control Services Inc 320 E 65th St 117 New York NY 10021

GLEASON, ANDREW MATTEI, educator; b. Fresno, Calif., Nov. 4, 1921; s. Henry Allan and Eleanor Theodalinda (Mattei) G.; m. Jean Berko, Jan. 26, 1959; children—Katherine Anne, Pamela, Cynthia. B.S., Yale, 1942; jr. fellow, Soc. Fellows, Harvard, 1946-50, M.A. (hon.), 1953. Asst. prof. math. Harvard, 1950-53, asso. prof., 1953-57, prof., 1957—, Hollis prof. math. and natural philosophy, 1969—. Author: Fundamentals of Abstract Analysis, 1966. Served from ensign to lt. (s.g.) USNR, 1942-46; lt. comdr. 1950-52. Recipient Newcomb Cleveland prize AAAS, 1952. Mem. Am. Math. Soc. (pres. 1981-82), Math. Assn. Am., Am. Philos. Soc., Societe Mathematique de France, Am. Acad. Arts and Scis., Nat. Acad. Scis. Club: Cosmos (Washington). Subspecialties: Probability; Abstract analysis. Home: 110 Larchwood Dr Cambridge MA 02138

GLEICHER, NORBERT, obstetrician-gynecologist, medical administrator and educator; b. Cracow, Poland, Aug. 20, 1948; came to U.S., 1975; s. Arnold and Eugenie (Volk) G. Student, Sch. Medicine Vienna U., 1966-70; M.D., Tel-Aviv U., 1973. Diplomate: Am. Bd. Ob-Gyn. Rotating intern Ihilov Mcpl. Hosp., Tel-Aviv, Israel, 1973-74; research fellow dept. ob-gyn Mt. Sinai Med. Ctr., N.Y.C., 1975, resident in ob-gyn, 1975-78, chief resident, 1978-79; asst. prof. dept. ob-gyn Mt. Sinai Sch. Medicine of CUNY, N.Y.C., 1979-81, dir. lab. reproductive immunology, course dir. reproduction course, dir. med. education dept. ob-gyn, 1979-81, dir. div. reproductive immunology, 1979-81, chmn. med. edn. com., 1980-81; course dir. reproduction sect. pathophysiology course CUNY, 1981—; chmn. dept. ob-gyn Mt. Sinai Med. Ctr., Chgo., 1981—; prof. ob-gyn, asst. prof. immunology and microbiology Rush Med. Coll., Chgo.; mem. Internat. Coordination Com. for Immunology of Reproduction, 1981-82; bd. dirs. profl. edn. com., chmn. physicians' subcom. Am. Cancer Soc., Chgo. Unit, 1982—; program dir., program chmn., session chmn., panelist profl. confs., seminars in field. Editor: Reproductive Immunology, vol. 70, 1981; co-editor: Cardiac Problems in Pregnancy, Diagnosis and Management of Maternal and Fetal Disease, 1982; Principles of Medical Therapy in Pregnancy, 1985; editorial bd.: Mt. Sinai Jour. Medicine, 1979—; editor-in-chief: Am. Jour. Reproductive Immunology, 1980—; contbr. articles to profl. publs., papers to profl. confs., U.S., Israel, Austria, Italy, Bulgaria. Recipient Dr. Solomon Silver award in Clin. Medicine Richard and Hilda Rosenthal Found., 1979; Lalor Found. fellow, 1979-80. Mem. AMA, Am. Coll. Ob-Gyn, ACS, Am. Assn. Gynecologic Laparoscopists, Am. Soc. for Immunology of Reproduction (v.p. 1980-82), Am. Soc. Abdominal Surgeons, Am. Med. Soc. of Vienna, Assn. Profs. of Gyn and Ob, N.Y. Acad. Scis., Am. Fedn. Clin. Research, Internat. Soc. for Study of Hypertension in Pregnancy, Central Assn. Obstetricians and Gynecologists, Israel Med. Soc., Chgo. Gynecol. Soc. Current Work: Co-dir. in vitro fertilization program; research in reproductive immunology, immunology of lipids, red cell immunology, cancer immunology, microbiology of pelvic inflammatory disease, cardiac and other medical diseases in pregnancy, cesarean section indications and rates. Subspecialties: Microbiology; Immunobiology and immunology. Office: Mt Sinai Hosp Med Center Dept Ob Gyn California Ave at 15th St Chicago IL 60608

GLENDINNING, WILLIAM BERNARD, integrated electronics technologist, physical scientist; b. West New York, N.J., Jan. 23, 1926; s. James and Angelina Frances (Callaghan) G.; m. Viola Helen Meidell, July 23, 1949; children—William Olaf, Priscilla Christine, James Edwin, Timothy Andrew, Brigette Ann, Shawn Ashley, Tor Erin. B.S.E.E., N.J. Tech. Inst., 1951; M.S.E.E., Monmouth Coll., 1973. Gas discharge devel. engr. Westinghouse Electric Co., Bloomfield, N.J., 1951-52, Bendix Aviation Corp., Eatontown, N.J., 1952-54; phys. research scientist Electronics Tech. and Devices Lab., Ft. Monmouth, N.J., 1954—. Contbr. articles to profl. jours. Patentee in field. Active Boy Scouts Am., PTA, Monmouth Arts Assn., Middletown, N.J., 1965-80. Served with USN, 1943-45, PTO. Mem. IEEE, VFW. Club: Nobleboro Hist. Lodge: Noreg. Current work: Submicron patterning lithography concerning direct-write electron: beam backscatter distortion/automated electronic device measurement metrology, overlay error metrology, simplified e-beam peripheral writing, and X-ray mask pattern distortions. Subspecialties: Microchip technology (engineering); Integrated circuits. Office: Electronics Tech & Devices Lab Fort Monmouth NJ 07703

GLENN, ROBERT EDWARD, industrial hygienist, research administrator; b. Florence, S.C., Jan. 19, 1944; s. David Douglas and Wilma (Aiken) G.; m. Sandra Leigh Holmes, Mar. 23, 1968; children—Robert Edward Jr., Marshall McMeekin, Lesley Elizabeth. B.S., Clemson U., 1967; M.P.H., U. Minn.-Mpls., 1976. Diplomate Am. Bd. Indsl. Hygiene. Commd. 2d lt. Med. Service Corps U.S. Army, 1968, advanced through grades to maj., service in Vietnam, resigned 1978; indsl. hygienist, Div. Respiratory Disease Studies, Nat. Inst. for Occupational Safety and Health, Morgantown, W.Va., 1978-79, chief environ. investigation br., 1979-81, dir. Div. Respiratory Disease Studies Morgantown, 1981—; adj. assoc. prof. indsl. engring. W.Va. U., 1978—. Contbr. chpts. to books. Mem. Am. Indsl. Hygiene Assn. (cert.), Am. Conf. Govtl. Indsl. Hygienists (mem. nominating com. 1985—, mem. editorial bd. 1985—), Am. Acad. Indsl. Hygiene, Commissioned Officers Assn. USPHS. Southern Baptist. Current work: Direction of staff whose interests include epidemiologic and clinical studies of occupational lung disease. Subspecialties: Industrial hygiene; Epidemiology. Office: Nat Inst for Occupational Safety and Health 944 Chestnut Ridge Rd Morgantown WV 26505

GLESS, RICHARD DOUGLAS, JR., chemist; b. Cocosolo, Panama, Nov. 13, 1948 (parents Am. citizens); s. Richard Douglas and Audrey Mae (Taylor) G.; m. Janet Lois Kuckein, June 17, 1972. B.S. in Chemistry, U. Calif.-Berkeley, 1971, Ph.D., 1978. Research chemist Dynapol, Palo Alto, Calif., 1972-74; assoc. research chemist Stauffer Chem. Co., Richmond, Calif., 1978-80, research chemist, 1980-82, group supr., 1982—. Contbr. articles to profl. jours. Served with USNR, 1967-69. Standard Oil scholar, 1977. Mem. Am. Chem. Soc. Current work: Agricultural chemical research and development. Subspecialties: Organic chemistry; Synthetic chemistry. Office: Stauffer Chem Co 1200 S 47th St Richmond CA 94804

GLICK, J. LESLIE, biotechnology company executive; b. N.Y.C., Mar. 2, 1940; s. Arthur Harvey and Hilda Lillian (Lichtenfeld) G.; m. Judith Sumiye Mihara; children: Geoffrey Michael, Jessica Michele. A.B., Columbia U., 1961, Ph.D., 1964. Nat. Cancer Inst. postdoctoral fellow Princeton U., 1964-65; sr., then asso. cancer research scientist Roswell Park Meml. Inst., Buffalo, 1965-69; assoc. research prof. physiology, physiology chmn. Roswell Park div. SUNY, Buffalo, 1968-70; from exec. v.p. to chmn. bd. Asso. Biomedic Systems, Inc., Buffalo, 1969-77; pres. Inst. Sci. and Social Accountability, Washington, 1975-79; from pres. to chmn. bd. Genex Corp., Rockville, Md., 1977—; chmn. HTI Corp., Buffalo, 1972-75; dir. Nat. Assn. Life Sci. Industries, 1975-77; dir. Indsl. Biotech. Assn., 1981-84; overseer Simon's Rock of Bard Coll., 1984-85; research prof. biology Niagara (N.Y.) U., Canisius Coll., Buffalo, 1968-70; exec. com. SUNY Grad. Sch., Buffalo, 1968-70; vis. lectr. NATO Advanced Study Inst., Brussels, 1970. Author: Fundamentals of Human Lymphoid Cell Culture, 1980; also articles. Mem. Am. Assn. Cancer Research, Am. Physiol. Soc., Tissue Culture Assn., N.Y. Acad. Scis., Sigma Xi. Current Work: Corporate management; technology assessment; product development. Subspecialties: Cell and tissue culture; Genetics and genetic engineering (biology). Office: Genex Corp 6110 Executive Blvd Rockville MD 20852

GLICKMAN, MYRON, mechanical engineer; b. Chgo., Sept. 21, 1936; s. Jack and Ida (Berkowitz) G.; m. Benita Rae Moline, Dec. 17, 1961; children—James, Michael, Steven. B.S.M.E., Ill. Inst. Tech., 1959, M.S.M.E., 1962. Assoc. research engr. Ill. Inst. Tech. Research Inst., Chgo., 1962-65, research engr., 1967-69; sr. engr. Martin Marietta, Balt., 1965-67, T.R.W. Corp., Cleve., 1966-67; ptnr. Dynamic Tech. Inc., Chgo., 1969-76; chief engr. Mi-Jack Products Inc., Hazel Crest, Ill., 1976—; Procs. editor Fluid System Design Conf., 1969; also articles. Patentee container retrieval system, tracked crane for large objects. Mem. ASME, Fluid Power Soc. (pres. Chgo. chpt. 1969-70). Jewish. Current work: Development of advanced concepts in heavy material handling equipment, particularly cranes for container and trailer handling and handling large, long, heavy industrial products. Subspecialties: Mechanical engineering; Systems engineering. Home: 7520 Churchill St Morton Grove IL 60053 Office: Mi-Jack Products Inc 3111 W 167th St Hazel Crest IL 60429

GLICKSMAN, ARVIN SIGMUND, radiation medicine educator, physician; b. Bklyn., Mar. 14, 1924; s. Charles and Myrtle (Fetner) G.; m. Bernice R. Grobstein, Jan. 30, 1956; children—Jonathan, Jane Ellen, Merrylee, Caroline, Jeanette. M.B., M.D., U. Chgo., 1949. Intern, Kings County Hosp., Bklyn., 1948-50; resident in medicine Meml. Hosp., N.Y.C., 1952-54; faculty Brown U., Providence, 1973—, prof., chmn. dept. radiation medicine, 1973—; chmn. dept. radiation oncology R.I. Hosp., Providence, 1973-84, chmn. dept. radiation medicine and biology research, 1984—, dir. Quality Assurance Rev. Ctr., Providence, 1980—; chmn. community cancer care evaluation adv. com. Nat. Cancer Inst., Bethesda, Md., 1983—. Author: Adaptation to Life-Threatening Illness, 1985. Editor: Computers in Radiotherapy, 1972. Recipient Research Career Devel. award NIH, Royal Marsden Hosp. and Inst. for Cancer Research, London, 1962-64, Disting. Alumnus award Chgo. Med. Sch., 1982. Current work: Radiobiology: modification of radiation response by maturational agents; effect of human tumor heterogeneity on radiation response; three-dimensional treatment planning for radiation of tumors in humans; multidisciplinary cooperative group clinical trials of cancer treatment; quality control of radiotherapy in collaborative group trials. Subspecialties: Radiation biology; Oncology. Home: Old Blackstone Rd Uxbridge MA 01569 Office: Dept Radiation Medicine R I Hosp 593 Eddy St Providence RI 02902

GLICKSMAN, MAURICE, physicist, university administrator. Prof., provost Brown U., Providence, R.I. Subspecialty: Condensed matter physics. Office: Brown U Office of the Provost Providence RI 02912

GLIMM, JAMES GILBERT, mathematician; b. Peoria, Ill., Mar. 24, 1934; s. William Frederick and Barbara Gilbert (Hooper) G.; m. Adele Strauss, June 30, 1957; 1 dau., Alison. A.B., Columbia U., 1956, A.M., 1957, Ph.D., 1959. From asst. prof. to prof. math. MIT, 1960-69; prof. Courant Inst., NYU, 1969-74; prof. math. Rockefeller U., N.Y.C., 1974-82; prof. Courant Inst., NYU, N.Y.C., 1982—. Co-author: Quantum Physics, 1981; Collected Papers, Vol. I, II, 1985; mem. editorial bds. profl. jours.; contbr. articles to sci. publs. Recipient Dannie Heineman prize in math. physics, 1980; Guggenheim fellow, 1963, 65. Mem. Internat. Assn. Math. Physicists, Am. Math. Soc., Nat. Acad. Scis., Soc. Indsl. and Applied Math., Am. Acad. Arts and Scis., Soc. Petroleum Engrs., N.Y. Acad. Scis. (award in phys. and math. scis. 1979). Subspecialties: Numerical analysis (computer science); Petroleum engineering. Office: Courant Inst 251 Mercer St New York NY 10012

GLODOWSKI, ROBERT JOHN, metallurgist, researcher; b. Williston, N.D., Jan. 4, 1946; s. Daniel Louis and Katheryne Josephine (Polley) G.; m. Amy Marie Burgess, Nov. 7, 1964; children: Camille, Ronald, Gregory, Teresa. B.S. in Metallurgy, S.D. Sch. Mines and Tech., 1967. Metallurgist Armco Inc., Middletown, Ohio, 1967-75, sr. metallurgist, 1975-81, sr. staff metallurgist carbon and alloy products, 1981—. Contbr. articles on stress relaxation testing to profl. publs.; editor: Through Thickness Tension Testing of Steel, 1982. Mem. ASME, ASTM, Am. Soc. Metals, Pressure Vessel Research Council, Internat. Standards Orgn. Invented a steel heat treatment. Current Work: Steel alloy development; steel processing improvements; rod and wire products; grinding media. Subspecialties: Metallurgical engineering; Metallurgy. Office: Research and Tech Armco Inc Middletown OH 45043

GLOSSER, ROBERT physics educator; b. Johnstown, Pa., Dec. 14, 1937; s. Frank and Beatrice (Werfel) G.; m. Joan Kathleen Thorn, Aug. 4, 1963; 1 child, Jeremy David. B.S., MIT, 1959; M.S., U. Chgo., 1962, Ph.D., 1967. Lectr. U. Calif.-Santa Barbara, 1969-71; asst. prof. physics U. Md., College Park, 1971-75; assoc. prof. physics U. Tex.-Dallas, Richardson, 1975—; cons. Naval Weapons Ctr., China Lake, Calif., summer 1974, VARO, Inc., Garland, Tex., 1984. Contbr. articles to profl. jours. Sec. Congregation Beth Torah, Richardson, 1976, v.p., 1978, treas., 1983. Served to capt. U.S. Army, 1967-69. Mem. Am. Phys. Soc., Sigma Xi. Jewish. Current work: Optical properties of solids, hydrogen in metals. Subspecialties: Condensed matter physics; Materials. Home: 2909 Deep Valley Trail Plano TX 75075 Office: PO Box 830688 Richardson TX 75083

GLOWER, DONALD DUANE, university dean, mechanical engineer; b. Shelby, Ohio, July 29, 1926; s. Raymond W.W. and Irva (Scheerer) G.; m. Betty Stahl, June 18, 1953; children: Donald, Michel, Leilani, Jacob. B.S., U.S. Mcht. Marine Acad., 1946, Antioch Coll., 1953; M.S., Iowa State U., 1958, Ph.D. (NSF fellow), 1960. Engring. officer Grace Lines, Inc., San Francisco, 1947-49; research engr. Battelle Meml. Inst., Columbus, Ohio, 1953-54; asst. prof. Coll. Engring., Iowa State U., 1954-58, 60-61; mem. research staff Sandia Corp., Albuquerque, 1961-63; head radiation effects dept. Gen. Motors Corp., Milw., 1963-64; prof., chmn. dept. mech. and nuclear engring. Ohio State U., 1964-76; dean Ohio State U. (Coll. Engring.), 1976—; also dir. Engring. Expt. Sta.; cons. to industry, 1964—; dir. AccuRay Corp., CADimensions. Author: Graphical Theory and Application, 1957, Basic Drawing and Projection, 1957, Working Drawings and Applied Graphics, 1957, Experimental Reactor Analysis and Radiation Measurements, 1965. Bd. dirs. Ohio Transp. Research Center; bd. dirs. Indsl. Tech. Enterprise Bd. Ohio; Bd. dirs. Orton Found., OSU Devel. Fund, Nat. Regulatory Research Inst. Recipient Outstanding Bus. Achievement award U.S. Mcht. Marine Acad., 1961; Outstanding Profl. Achievement award Iowa State U., 1979. Fellow Am. Nuclear Soc.; fellow ASME; mem. Am. Soc. Engring. Edn., Ohio Acad. Sci., Argonne Univs. Assn., Ohio Energy Task Force, Sigma Xi, Tau Beta Pi, Texnikoi. Subspecialties: Mechanical engineering; Nuclear engineering. Home: 2338 Kensington Dr Columbus OH 43221 Office: Hitchcock Hall 2070 Neil Ave Columbus OH 43210

GLOYNA, EARNEST FREDERICK, environmental engineer, educator, dean; b. Vernon, Tex., June 30, 1921; s. Herman Ernst and Johanna Bertha (Reithmayer) G.; m. Agnes Mary Lehman, Feb. 17, 1946; children: David Frederick, Lisa Anna (Mrs. Jack Grosskopf). B.S. in Civil Engring, Tex. Technol. U., 1946; M.S. in Civil Engring, U. Tex., 1949; Dr. Engring., Johns Hopkins U., 1952. Registered profl. engr. Engr. Tex. Hwy. Dept., 1945-46; office engr. Magnolia Petroleum Co., 1946-47; instr. civil engring. U. Tex., Austin, 1947-49, asst. prof., 1949-53, assoc. prof., 1953-59, prof., 1959—, Joe J. King prof. engring., 1970-82, Bettie Margaret Smith prof. environ. engring., 1982—, dir. Environ. Health Engring. Labs., 1953-70, dir. Center for Research in Water Resources, 1963-73, dean Coll. Engring., 1970—, dir. Bur. Engring. Research, 1970—; cons. on water and wastewater treatment and water resources, 1947—; dir. Parker Drilling Co.; cons. numerous industries, WHO, U.S. Air Force, U.S. Army, U.S. Senate, fgn. cities and govts., UN, 1952—; mem., past chmn. sci. adv. bd. EPA. Author: Waste Stabilization Ponds, 1971 (also French and Spanish edits), (with Joe O. Ledbetter) Principles of Radiological Health, 1969; Editor: (with W. Wesley Eckenfelder, Jr.) Advances in Water Quality Improvement, 1968, Water Quality Improvement by Physical and Chemical Processes, 1970, (with William S. Butcher) Conflicts in Water Resources Planning, 1972, (with Woodson and Drew) Water Management by Electric Power Industry, 1975, (with Malina and Davis) Ponds as a Wastewater Treatment Alternative, 1976; Contbr. numerous articles to profl. jours. Served with Corps Engrs. AUS, 1942-46, ETO. Recipient Harrison Prescott Eddy medal Water Pollution Control Fedn., 1959, Gordon Maskew Fair medal, 1979, Hon. Mem. award, 1980; Water Resources Div. award Am. Water Works Assn., 1959; named Distinguished Engr. Grad. Tex. Tech. U., 1971, Distinguished Alumnus, 1973, Disting. Engring. Grad. U. Tex., Austin, 1982; recipient Joe J. King award U. Tex., Austin, 1982, EPA regional environ. educator award, 1977, Nat. Environ. Devel. award, 1983, Order of Henri Pittier, Nat. Conservation medal Venezuela, 1983. Fellow ASCE (Meritorious Paper award Tex. sect. 1968, award of honor Tex. sect. 1985); mem. Nat. Acad. Engring. governing council mem.), Am. Inst. Chem. Engrs., Assn. Environ. Engring. Profs. (past pres.), Am. Soc. for Engring. Edn., Am. Water Works Assn., Am. Acad. Environ. Engrs. (diplomate, past pres. Gorden Maskew Fair award), Water Pollution Control Fedn. (past nat. dir., pres.-elect), Tex. Soc. Profl. Engrs. (Engr. of Year award Travis chpt. 1972), Southwestern Soc. Nuclear Medicine (hon.), Nat. Acad. Engring. Mex. (fgn. corr. mem.), Nat. Acad. Scis. Venezuela (fgn. corr.), Sociedad Mexicana de Aguas (Jack Hubbert award), Sigma Xi, Tau Beta Pi, Chi Epsilon, Phi Kappa Phi, Pi Epsilon Tau (hon.), Omicron Delta Kappa. Clubs: Cosmos (Washington); Headliners (Austin), Faculty Center (Austin). Lodge: Rotary (Austin). Current Work: Environmental, water supply and wastewater treatment. Subspecialty: Water supply and wastewater treatment. Home: 3317 River Rd Austin TX 78703

GLUSKER, JENNY PICKWORTH, chemist; b. Birmingham, Eng., June 28, 1931; came to U.S., 1955, naturalized, 1977; d. Frederick Alfred and Jane Wylie (Stocks) Pickworth; m. Donald Leonard Glusker, Dec. 18, 1955; children: Ann, Mark John, Katharine. B. A. in Chemistry, Oxford (Eng.) U., 1953, M. A. in Chemistry, 1957, D.Phil. in Chemistry, 1957. Postdoctoral research fellow Calif. Inst. Tech., Pasadena, 1955-56; research fellow Inst. for Cancer Research, Fox Chase Cancer Center, Phila., 1956, research assoc., 1957-67, asst. mem., 1967, assoc. mem., 1967-79, sr. mem., 1979—; mem. faculty U. Pa., Phila., 1969—, adj. prof. biochemistry and biophysics, 1980—; mem. U.S.A. Nat. Com. for Crystallography, 1974-76, 80, sec.-treas., 1977-79, chmn., 1982-84, del. to internat. meeting, Warsaw, 1978, Ottawa, Ont., Can., 1981, chmn. del. to internat. meeting, Hamburg, Fed. Author: (with K.N. Trueblood) Crystal Structure Analysis: A Primer (transl. into Russian and Polish), 1972, 2d edit., 1985. editor: Structural Crystallography in Chemistry and Biology, 1981, (with Dodson and Sayre) Structure of Molecules of Biological Interest, 1981, (with McLachlan) Crystallography in North America, 1982; mem. editorial bd.: Biophys. Jour, 1981—; mem. editorial adv. bd.: Accounts of Chem. Research, 1982—; Contbr. articles to profl. sci. jours. Mem. Am. Chem. Soc. (Phila. sect. award 1978, Garvan medal 1979), Am. Crystallographic Assn. (pres. 1979), Am. Inst. Physics (governing bd. 1980-83), AAAS, Biophys. Soc., Am. Soc. Biol. Chemists, Chem. Soc., Am. Assn. for Cancer Research, Am. Phys. Soc., N.Y. Acad. Scis., Sigma Xi. Current Work: Research on enzyme mechanisms and chemical carcinogenesis; basic research. Subspecialties: Biophysical chemistry; X-ray crystallography.

GODDARD, WILLIAM ANDREW, III, scientist, educator; b. El Centro, Calif., Mar. 29, 1937; s. William Andrew and Barbara Worth (Bright) G.; m. Yvonne Amelia Correy, Oct. 27, 1957; children—William Andrew IV, Susan Yvonne, Cecelia Monique, Lisa Sharell. B.S. in Engring., UCLA, 1960; Ph.D. in Engring. Sci., Calif. Inst. Tech., 1964. From Noyes research fellow in chemistry to prof. chemistry and applied physics Calif. Inst. Tech., Pasadena, 1964-84, Charles and Mary Ferkel prof. chemistry and applied physics, 1984—, mem. sci. adv. bd. Triton Bioscis. Inc., Alameda, Calif., 1984—; cons. in field. Mem. adv. editorial bd. Chem. Physics, 1972—, Jour. Phys. Chemistry, 1976-80, Langmuir, 1984—, Am. Chem. Soc. Jour., 1985—. Contbr. articles to sci. jours. Mem. NSF adv. com., chemistry div., Washington, 1983—. Fellow NSF, 1960-61, Shell Cos. Found., 1961-62, NSF, 1962-64, Alfred P. Sloan Found., 1967-69; recipient Buck-Whitney medal for major contbns. to theoretical chemistry in N.Am., 1978. Fellow Am. Phys. Soc.; mem. Nat. Acad. Scis., Am. Chem. Soc., Am. Vacuum Soc. Current work: Reaction mechanisms, including homogeneous and heterogeneous catalysis; biological oxidations; electronic properties of surfaces, semiconductors, metal, and metal oxides; dynamics and simulation of biological and surface processes. Subspecialties: Catalysis chemistry; Theoretical chemistry. Office: Dept Chemistry Room 127-72 Calif Inst Tech Pasadena CA 91125

GODFREY, HENRY PHILIP, immunologist; b. Poughkeepsie, N.Y., Aug. 7, 1941; s. Joseph and Mildred (Hoffman) G.; m. Ginger Schnaper, May 6, 1977; 2 sons, Thomas, David. A.B., Harvard U., 1961, M.D., 1965; Ph.D., U. Birmingham, (Eng.), 1980. Intern Barnes Hosp., St. Louis, 1965-66; Mosley travelling fellow Harvard U., 1970-72; hon. research fellow, dept. exptl. pathology U. Birmingham, Eng., 1970-78; asst. prof. Inst. Exptl. Immunology U. Copenhagen, 1972; assoc. prof., 1972-75; asst. prof. pathology SUNY-Stony Brook, 1975-82; assoc. prof. pathology N.Y. Med. Coll., Valhalla, 1982—. Contbr. articles to profl. jours. Served with USPHS, 1966-70. Mem. N.Y. Acad. Scis., Am. Assn. Immunologists, Brit. Soc. Immunology, Harvey Soc., Am. Soc. Microbiology, AAAS, Sigma Xi. Current Work: Biochemical mechanisms underlying delayed hypersensitivity and cellular immunity; isolation of lymphokines employing monoclonal antibody technology. Subspecialties: Immunopharmacology; Biochemistry (biology). Office: Dept Pathology NY Med Col Valhalla NY 10595

GODLEWSKI, HARRY HENRY, JR., electrical engineer, development engineer; b. Pitts., Nov. 27, 1950; s. Harry Henry and Florence Delores (Czarniak) G.; m. Lois Ann Meyers, June 19, 1971; children—Joseph Edward, David Allen, Stephen Andrew (dec.). Student Clarion State Coll., 1968-70; cert. Air Force Tech. Sch., 1971; B.E.E., U. Pitts., 1976; M.E.E., Northeastern U., 1981. Enlisted U.S. Air Force, 1971, advanced through grades to 1st lt., 1978; electronics devel. engr. RADC, Hanscom AFB, Bedford, Mass., 1977-80; ret., 1980; mem. tech. staff MITRE Corp., Bedford, 1980-82, GTE Sylvania, Needham Heights, Mass., 1982-84; devel. engr. CTI Cryogenics, Helix, Waltham, Mass., 1984—. Assoc. mem., contbr. Physicians Social Responsibility, Boston, 1984. Lutheran. Current work: Power conversion systems, advanced electromechanical drives (linear), electrical/electronic control systems. Subspecialties: Applied magnetics; Electronics. Office: Helix CTI Cryogenics 266 2d Ave Waltham MA 02254

GODLEY, WILLIE CECIL, animal scientist, educator; b. Miley, S.C., Oct. 3, 1922; married, 1944; 3 children. B.S., Clemson Coll., 1943; M.S., N.C. State Coll., 1949, Ph.D., 1955. From instr. to asst. prof. animal husbandry Clemson U., 1946-47, assoc. prof., 1952-57, prof. animal sci., 1957—; assoc. animal husbandman S.C. Agrl. Expt. Sta., 1954-57, animal husbandman and geneticist, 1957-64, assoc. dir., 1973-75, assoc. dean and dir., 1975—. Mem. Am. Soc. Animal Sci., Am. Genetic Assn. Subspecialty: Animal genetics. Office: 103 Lewis Rd Clemson SC 29631*

GODLOVE, TERRY F., physicist; b. Balt., June 23, 1927; s. Isaac H. and Esther A. (Hurlbut) G.; m. Dorothy C. Miller, Aug. 16, 1952; children—Terry F., Karen E. Godlove Malley. Student U.Md., 1946-47; B.S., Lafayette Coll., 1950; M.S., Yale U., 1951, Ph.D., 1955. Physicist, Naval Research Lab., Washington, 1955-77, Dept. Energy, Germantown, Md., 1977—. Contbr. articles to profl. jours. Patentee. Served with USN, 1945-46. Recipient Ann. Nat. Capital award D.C. Council Engrs. and Architects Socs. and Wash. Acad. Scis., 1959. Mem. Am. Phys. Soc., Sigma Xi. Presbyterian. Current work: Particle accelerator physics/engineering; nuclear physics; gyrotrons; free electron lasers; management of program in heavy ion fusion accelerator research. Subspecialty: Nuclear fusion. Office: Dept Energy ER-20 2/GTN Washington DC 20545

GODSON, G. NIGEL, biochemistry educator; b. London, June 20, 1936; came to U.S., 1969; s. Godfrey E. and Elsie G.; m. Barbara Cohen, Aug. 1969; children: Rebecca Charlotte, Vanessa Alexandra. B.Sc., London U., 1957, M.Sc., 1958, Ph.D., 1961, D.Sc. (hon.), 1983. Biochemist/sci. staff Chester Beatty Inst., London, 1961-64; postdoctoral fellow Calif. Inst. Tec., Pasadena, 1964-66; research assoc. Yale U., New Haven, 1966-67, asst. prof., 1969-74, assoc. prof., 1974-80; prof., chmn., dept. biochemistry NYU Md. Ctr., N.Y.C., 1980—; biochemist/sci. staff Nat. Inst. Med. Research, London, 1967-69; mem. exec. com. Sackler Inst. Grad. Biomed. Scis., NYU, 1981—; mem. com. Med. Scientist Tng. Program, NYU, 1981—; mem. biochemistry sect. Nat. Bd. Med. Examiners, 1985—; mem. NIH, NIAID, Tropical Medicine and Parasitology Study Sect., 1985—. Contbr. articles and revs. to sci. jours. Mem. Am. Soc. Exptl. Biology, N.Y. Acad. Scis., Am. Soc. Biol. Chemists, Harvey Soc. Current Work: Study of gene expression in E. coli and plasmodium;

development of an anti-malarial vaccine using recombinant DNA techniques. Subspecialties: Gene actions; Genetics and genetic engineering (agriculture). Office: 550 1st Ave New York NY 10016

GOE, DON RICHARD, chiropractor; b. Baker, Mont., Mar. 23, 1923; s. Don Alfred and Eula Gladys (Sparks) G; m. June Waskey, June 17, 1951; children—Richard Alan, Douglas Edward. B.A., Pacific Union Coll., 1945; M.A., Walla Walla Coll., 1950; Ph.D., U. So. Calif., 1958; D.C., Western States Chiropractic Coll., 1982; course in physiology Marine Biology Lab., 1955. Instr. physiology Loma Linda U., Calif., 1954-60; assoc. prof. biology Walla Walla Coll., Wash., 1960-61; dir. pulmonary research VA Hosp., Walla Walla, 1961-65; prin. Rainbow Valley Exptl. Sch., Southwest City, Mo., 1965-69; dir. profl. relations ICN-United Med. Labs., Portland, 1969-74; prof. physiology Western States Chiropractic Coll., Portland, 1974-83; dir. clin. neuro-physiology Western States Chiropractic Coll., 1983-84, clin. neurophysiologist Chiropractic Physicians and Cons. Group, 1984—. Editor Lab. News, 1969-74. Author programmed texts: Lipids, Hypertension, 1972, 73. Served with USN, 1956-58; PTO. Mem. N.Y. Acad. Sci., Am. Chiropractic Assn., Am. Physiol. Soc., Sigma Xi, Phi Sigma. Current work: Clinical significance and utility of nerve conduction velocity, electromyography and evoked potential latency in traumatic and metabolic neuropathic conditions. Subspecialties: Neurophysiology; Neuropharmacology. Home: 21020 NE Wistful Vista Troutdale OR 97060 Office: 2442 SE 101st Ave Portland OR 97216

GOE, GERALD LEE, chemical company executive; b. Kansas City, Mo., Aug. 17, 1942; s. Tom A. and Lucille (Bauer) G.; m. Mary Ellen Stapleton; 1 child, Jason A. B.S., U. Mo., 1963; Ph.D., MIT, 1967. Postdoctoral fellow Iowa State U., Ames, 1967-69; asst. prof. U. Notre Dame, Ind., 1969-73; chemist Reilly Tar & Chem. Corp., Indpls., 1973—, research dir., 1980—. Mem. Am. Chem. Soc., AAAS, Soc. of Chem. Industry. Current work: Pyridine and other heterocyclic chemistry. Subspecialty: Organic chemistry. Office: Reilly Tar & Chem Corp 1500 S Tibbs St Indianapolis IN 46241

GOEBEL, WALTHER FREDERICK, biochemist; b. Palo Alto, Calif., Dec. 24, 1899; s. Julius and Kathryn (Vreel) G.; m. Cornelia Van Rensselaer Robb, Oct. 23, 1930 (dec. Oct. 1974); children—Cornelia Van Rensselaer Bronson, Anne Kathryn Barkman; m. Alice Lawrence Behn, Nov. 12, 1976. A.B., U. Ill., 1920, A.M., 1921, Ph.D., 1923, scholar in chemistry, 1920-21, fellow, 1921-23; postgrad., U. Munich, Germany, 1923-24; D.Sc. (hon.), Middlebury (Vt.) Coll., 1959, Rockefeller U., 1978. Research asst. Rockefeller U., 1924-27, assoc., 1927-34, assoc. mem., 1934-44, mem., 1944-57, prof., 1957-70, prof. emeritus, 1970—. Contbr. monographs, reports and articles on chem. and immunological subjects sci. jours. Mem. Nat. Acad. Scis., Am. Chem. Soc., Am. Soc. Biol. Chemists, Harvey Soc., Am. Assn. Immunologists, Am. Soc. Microbiology, Conn. Acad. Sci. and Engring., Gesellschaft für Immunologie (Avery-Landsteiner award 1973), Phi Beta Kappa, Sigma Xi, Phi Lambda Upsilon, Phi Eta. Current Work: Immunologically active carbohydrates; synthetic antigens. Subspecialties: Immunochemistry; Immunology (medicine). Home: 15 Lyon Farm Dr E Greenwich CT 06830 Office: Rockefeller U New York NY 10021

GOEDDEL, DAVID VAN NORMAN, biochemist; b. Pasadena, Calif., May 3, 1951; s. Walter Van Norman and Barbara Lou (Haist) G.; m. Carol Lynn Smiley, Jan. 13, 1973. B.A. in Chemistry, U. Calif. at San Diego, 1972; Ph.D. in Biochemistry, U. Colo., 1977. Dir. Stanley Andrews Mountaineering Sch. and Guide Service, San Diego, 1970-73; teaching asst., research asst. dept. chemistry U. Colo., Boulder, 1973-77; postdoctoral fellow Stanford Research Inst., Menlo Park, Calif., 1977-78; research scientist Genentech, Inc., South San Francisco, Calif., 1978—. Mem. Am. Chem. Soc., AAAS. Co-inventor first bacterial production of human insulin, 1978, of human growth hormone, 1979, of human interferon, 1980. Subspecialty: Molecular biology. Office: 460 Point San Bruno Blvd South San Francisco CA 94080

GOEPP, ROBERT AUGUST, dental educator, researcher; b. Chgo., Nov. 3, 1930; s. Charles August and Ernestine Josephine (Mertz) G.; m. Iraida Pineiro, July 9, 1960; children: Robert C., Heidi M., Myra J. B.S., Loyola U., Chgo., 1953, D.D.S., 1957; M.S., U. Chgo., 1961, Ph.D., 1967. Diplomate: Am. Bd. Oral Pathology, Am. Bd. Oral and Maxillofacial Radiology.; Lic. dentist. Instr. Pritzker Sch. Medicine, U. Chgo., 1961-64, asst. prof., 1964-70, assoc. prof., 1970-75; prof. U. Chgo., 1975—. Contbr. to textbooks; author articles to sci. jours. USPHS career devel. awardee, 1970; grantee NIH, Am. Cancer Soc., 1962-80. Fellow Am. Coll. Dentists; mem. ADA (chmn. Council on Dental Research 1981-82), Am. Acad. Dental Radiology (pres. 1974), Soc. Oral Pathologists Ill. (pres. 1977-78), Med. Radiation Adv. Council, Nat. Council on Radiation Protection and Measurements. Roman Catholic. Club: Quadrangle (U. Chgo.). Co-inventor custom cervical cap. Current Work: Biologic effects of ionizing radiation, epithelial cell propulation kinetics in abnormal growth, cervical cap as a means of barrier fertility control. Subspecialties: Oral biology; Radiology. Home: 5928 N Kilbourn Chicago IL 60646 Office: Zoller Dental Clinic Box 418 950 E 59th St Chicago IL 60637

GOETZ, FRANK, industrial chemist; b. Hoboken, N.J., Mar. 23, 1949; s. Ludwig and Jennie (Alasio) G.; B.A. cum laude, Alfred U., 1971; M.S., Marquette U., 1974; Ph.D., U. Del., 1978. Research chemist U. Dayton Research Inst. at Air Force Rocket Propulsion Lab., Edwards AFB, Calif., 1978-80; sr. chemist Morton-Thiokol, Elkton, Md., 1980—. Contbr. articles to profl. jours. Mem. Am. Chem. Soc., Soc. Applied Spectroscopy, Royal Soc. Chemistry, Phi Kappa Phi. Republican. Current work: Development of solid propellant formulations for use in tactical rocket motors and low flame temperature formulations for gas generator applications; program chemist on a space defense initiative concept development program. Subspecialties: Propellant chemistry; Aerospace engineering and technology. Home: 34 Highland Ave Elkton MD 21921 Office: Morton Thiokol/Elkton Div PO Box 241 Elkton MD 21921

GOFFMAN, MARTIN, chemist; b. Phila., June 22, 1940; s. Benjamin and Evelyn (Pollack) G.; m. Renee Cooperstein, Nov. 28, 1965; children—Robert, Vivian, Deborah. B.A., Temple U., 1961, M.A., 1963, Ph.D., 1965. Research chemist ASARCO Inc., South Plainfield, N.J., 1965-70, sr. research chemist, 1970-78, project leader, 1978-84, sect. head chemistry, 1985—. Patentee in field. Fellow Am. Inst. Chemists; mem. Electrochem. Soc. (local sect. chmn. 1972-73), Am. Chem. Soc., Am. Soc. Metals, Sigma Xi. Jewish. Current work: Electrochemistry-development of new and improved processes; computer aided chemistry for process control and automated operations. Subspecialty: Physical chemistry. Home: 3 Dellview Dr Edison NJ 08820 Office: ASARCO Inc 901 Oak Tree Rd South Plainfield NJ 07080

GOGUE, GEORGE PAUL, electrical engineer; b. Basrah, Iraq, Oct. 3, 1949; came to U.S., 1981; s. Paul Essa and Mary (Francis) G.; m. Kathryn Sayles, Apr. 25, 1981. B.S.E.E., U. Basrah, 1969; M.S.E.E., U. Aston, Eng., 1976, Ph.D. in Elec. Engring., 1980. Registered profl. engr. Lectr. U. Basrah, Iraq, 1969-75; design engr. Walter Jones Co., London, 1980; research engr. Electro-Craft Corp., Hopkins, Minn., 1981-83; sr. design engr. Synektron Corp., Portland, Oreg., 1983—. Patentee brushless motor magnetics, single-phase winding. Mem. IEEE. Current work: Brushless direct current motors and their power-electronics drivers in computer peripheral industry, disc drives, tape drives. Subspecialties: Applied magnetics; Power electronics. Home: 9775 SW Rodeo Pl Beaverton OR 97005 Office: Synektron Corp 12000 Garden Pl Portland OR 97223

GOH, DAVID SHUH JEN, psychology educator; b. Kiangsu, China, July 9, 1941; came to U.S., 1967, naturalized, 1977; s. Ying-Hwa and Pei-Shuo (Chao) G.; m. Jane M. Chen, Sept. 1, 1973; children: Alice, Nancy. M.S, Ill. State U., 1969; Ph.D., U. Wis., 1973. Lic. psychologist, Mich., Wis., Ill. Psychologist Lincoln (Ill.) Devel. Ctr., 1969-70; asst. prof. U. Wis.-LaCrosse, 1973-75; asst. prof., then assoc. prof. Central Mich. U., Mt. Pleasant, 1975-80; assoc. prof., then prof. So. Ill. U., Carbondale, 1980—; also staff psychologist So. Ill. U. (Clin. Ctr.), 1980—. Contbr. articles to profl. jours., chpts. to books.; Editorial bd.: Psychology in the Schs. Jour, 1980—; reviewer various other jours., 1977—. Mem. Am. Psychol. Assn., Nat. Assn. Sch. Psychologists, Soc. Personality Assessment, Am. Assn. Asian Psychologists, Nat. Council for Measurement and Evaluation. Current Work: Research/teaching in areas of individual differences in cognitive processes and personality, psychological assessment and consultation; microcomputer applications in psychology. Subspecialties: Behavioral psychology; Cognition. Home: 4 View Valley Dr Heritage Hills Carbondale IL 62901 Office: So Ill Univ Carbondale IL 62901

GOH, EDWARD HUA SENG, pharmacologist, educator, researcher; b. Sarawak, Malaysia, Jan. 20, 1942; came to U.S., 1964, naturalized, 1974; s. Chee Kuan and Chai Ting (Lim) G.; m. Sharon Ratliff, June 17, 1949; children: Melisa Hua-Linn, Andrew Hua-Seng. A.A., Warren Wilson Coll., Swannonoa, N.C., 1966; B.A., Berea Coll., 1968; Ph.D., Vanderbilt U., 1974; postgrad., U. Mo., 1974-75. Instr. U. Mo., Columbia, 1975-77; asst. prof. pharmacology Ind. U., Bloomington, 1977-82, asso. prof., 1982—. Contbr. articles on metabolism of blood cholesterol to sci. jours. NSF grantee, 1979-82; Am. Heart Assn. grantee, 1978-81; Pharm. Mfrs. Assn. Found. Inc. grantee, 1977-79; Am. Diabetes Assn. grantee, 1982. Mem. Am. Soc. Pharmacology and Therapeutics, Am. Heart Assn., Internat. Soc. for Study Xenobiotics. Current Work: Current research activities involve the metabolism of lipoprotein cholesterol and the developmental testing of new drugs, in relation to their metabolism and toxicology, used to regulate blood cholesterol levels. Subspecialties: Pharmacology; Biochemistry (medicine). Office: Ind U Med Scis Program Myers Hall 306 Bloomington IN 47405

GOHAR, MOHAMED YOUSRY AHMED, nuclear engineer; b. Kom-Hamada, Behira, Egypt, Feb. 3, 1947; s. Ahmed Ahmed and Doria A. (Gharib) G.; m. Iman Esmat O, El-Dib, July 23, 1978. B.S. in Nuclear Engring, Alexandria (Egypt) U., 1967, M.S. in Nuclear Engring, 1970, Ph.D. in Nuclear Engring, 1974. Asst. prof. Atomic Energy Establishment of Egypt, Cairo, 1967-74; research assoc. nuclear engring. dept. U. Wis., Madison, 1974-77; nuclear engr. Argonne (Ill.) Nat. Lab., 1977—; researcher Fusion Engring. Design Center, Oak Ridge, 1981—. Recipient longevity service award Argonne Nat. Lab., 1982. Mem. Am. Nuclear Soc. Current Work: Nuclear fission and fusion reactor design, computational methods in nuclear engineering, nuclear data, applied numerical methods, mathematical software. Subspecialties: Nuclear engineering; Nuclear fusion. Office: Argonne National Laboratory 9700 S Cass Ave Argonne IL 60439

GOINS, WILLIAM (DORIS), III, govt. research adminstr.; b. Cleve., Apr. 6, 1943; s. William D. and Lillian L. (Palmer) G.; m. Diane Johnston, Sept. 5, 1964; children: William D. IV, Clay Paul. B.S. in Nuclear Engring, U. Tenn., 1966, M.S. in Metall. Engring, 1969. Supr. Welding lab Combustion Engring., Chattanooga, 1970-77, lab. Welding engring., 1970-77; with TVA, Chattanooga, 1977—, lab. supr., project mgr., 1977-79, program mgr. nuclear research, 1979—; mem. Edison Electric Inst. Metallurgy, Piping, Welding, and Corrosion Task Force. Mem. ASME (chmn. working group on repair welding Boiler and Pressure Vessel Code Sect. XI), Am. Welding Soc., Am. Nuclear Soc., Welding Research Council (chmn. utilities adv. com), Am. Soc. Metals, Sigma Xi. Baptist. Current Work: Research projects include light water reactor safety; materials; corrosion; radioactive waste; gamma thermometers; nuclear fuel dry storage; decontamination and advanced systems; fusion; high temperature gas-cooled reactors; liquid metal fast breeder reactors. Subspecialties: Materials (engineering); Metallurgical engineering. Home: 2506 Big Cedar Rd Soddy TN 37379 Office: TVA 1050 Chestnut St Tower II Chattanooga TN 37401

GOLAND, MARTIN, research institute executive; b. N.Y.C., July 12, 1919; s. Herman and Josephine (Bloch) G.; m. Charlotte Nelson, Oct. 16, 1948; children—Claudia, Lawrence, Nelson. M.E., Cornell U., 1940; LL.D. (hon.), St. Mary's U., San Antonio. Instr. mech. engring. Cornell U., 1940-42; sect. head structures dept. research lab., airplane div. Curtiss-Wright Corp., Buffalo, 1942-46; chmn. div. engring. Midwest Research Inst., Kansas City, Mo., 1946-50, dir. for engring. scis., 1950-55; v.p. Southwest Research Inst., San Antonio, 1955-57, dir., 1957-59, pres., 1959—; pres. Southwest Found. Research and Edn., San Antonio, 1972-82; dir. Nat. Bancshares Corp. Tex., Gulf States Utilities Corp. Chmn. subcom. vibration and flutter NACA, 1952-60; chmn. research adv. com. on aircraft structures NASA, 1960-68, chmn. materials and structures group, aeros. adv. com., 1979-82; sci. adv. com. Harry Diamond Labs., U.S. Amry Materiel Command, 1955-75; adv. panel com. sci. and astronautics Ho. of Reps., 1960-73; mem. nat. inventors council, 1966-67, mem. state tech. services evaluation com., 1967-69; mem. adv. bd. on undersea warfare Dept. Navy, 1968-70, chmn., 1970-73; mem. spl. aviation fire reduction com. FAA, 1979-80; sci. adv. panel Dept. Army, 1966-77; chmn. U.S. Army Weapons Command Adv. Group, 1966-72; mem. materiels adv. bd. NRC, 1969-74; vice-chmn. Naval Research Adv. Com., 1974-77, chmn., 1977, dir. Nat. Bank Commerce, San Antonio.; Dir. Engrs. Joint Council, 1966-69; mem. adv. group U.S. Armament Command, 1972-76; mem. sci. adv. com. Gen. Motors, 1971-81; mem. Nat. Commn. on Libraries and Info. Scis., 1971-78, Nat. Bd. on Grad. Edn., 1972-75; mem. adv. bd. on mil. personnel supplies Nat. Acad. Sci., 1973-76; chmn. NRC Bd. Army Sci. and Tech., 1982—. Editor: Applied Mechanics Review, 1952-59; editorial adviser, 1959-84. Bd. govs. St. Mary's U., San Antonio, 1970-76; pres. San Antonio Symphony, 1968-70, chmn. bd., 1970-71; bd. dirs. So. Meth. U. Found. Sci. and Engring., Dallas, 1979-84; trustee Univs. Research Assos., Inc., 1979-84. Recipient Spirit of St. Louis jr. award ASME, 1945, jr. award, 1946, Alfred E. Nobel prize ASCE, 1947. Fellow A.A.A.S., Am. Inst. Aeros. and Astronautics (pres. 1971); hon. mem. ASME (dir., mem. bd. tech., mem. tech. devel. com., v.p. communications); mem. C. of C. (dir.), Nat. Acad. Engring., Research Soc. Am., Sigma Xi, Tau Beta Pi. Current Work: President research institute. Subspecialties: Aeronautical engineering; Theoretical and applied mechanics. Home: 306 Country Ln San Antonio TX 78209 Office: 6220 Culebra Rd San Antonio TX 78284

GOLBERG, LEON, physician, educator, consultant; b. Limassol, Cyprus, Aug. 22, 1915; came to U.S., 1967, naturalized, 1974; s. Aron and Bertha (Lurie) G.; m. Bertha Klempman, July 4, 1944; children: Michael Gregory, Estelle Laura, Aron Anthony. B.Sc., U. Witwatersrand, 1934, M.Sc., 1936, D.Sc., 1946; D.Phil., Oxford U., 1939; M.A., M.B. B.Chir. (sr. scholar), Cambridge U., 1951; D.Sc. (hon.), Phila. Coll. Pharmacy and Scis., 1983. Registered Gen. Med. Council, U.K. Sr. lectr. chem. pathology U. Manchester, Eng., 1951-55; med. research dir. Fisons Pharms. Ltd., Holmes Chapel, Eng., 1955-61; dir. BIBRA, Carshalton, Surrey, Eng., 1961-67; research prof. pathology Albany (N.Y.) Med. Coll., 1967-76; pres. Chem. Industry Inst. Toxicology, Research Triangle Park, N.C., 1976-81; prof. community/occupational medicine Duke U. Med. Center, Durham, N.C., 1981—; Milroy lectr. Royal Coll. Physicians London, 1967; adj. prof. pharmacology, pathology, toxicology. Author: Toxicology: Has a New Era Dawned? , 1980, The Revolution in Toxicology: Real or Imaginary, 1981, The Hierarchy of Hazard Evaluation, 1982; contbr. articles to sci. jours. Recipient George Scott Meml. award Toxicology Forum, 1983. Fellow Royal Soc. Chemistry, Royal Coll. Pathologists (founder fellow), Soc. Toxicology (pres. 1978-79, ambassador of toxicology 1981, Disting. fellow 1981, John Barnes lectr. 1983); mem. Am. Chem. Soc., Environ. Mutagen Soc., Japanese Cosmetic Sci. Soc. (hon.). Current Work: Promoting agents in experimental neoplasia; occupational medicine; toxicology; consulting; teaching; cancer research; biotechnology. Subspecialties: Toxicology (medicine); Cancer research (medicine). Home: 2109 Nancy Ann Dr Raleigh NC 27607 Office: Duke U Med Center Div Community/Occupational Medicine Box 2914 Durham NC 27710

GOLD, MICHAEL NATHAN, research, technology and finance manager; b. Chgo., May 3, 1952; s. Julius and Sarah (Blitzblau) G.; m. Cynthia Bilicki, June 19, 1976. B.A., Kalamazoo Coll., 1976. Research fellow Sinai Hosp., Detroit, 1976; research assoc. Molecular Biological Inst., UCLA, Los Angeles, 1976-77; lab mgr., adminstr. Biomed. Engring. Ctr., U. So. Calif., Los Angeles, 1977-80; asst. dir. Crump Inst., Los Angeles, 1980-84, assoc. dir. Crump Inst. for Med. Engring., UCLA, Los Angeles, 1984—. Mem. IEEE, Assn. for Advancement of Med. Instrumentation, Clin. Ligand Assay Soc., Am. Assn. for Med. Systems and Informatics. Current work: Technology transfer, management of research and development, finance, cost effective medical technology, business development. Subspecialties: Biomedical engineering; Physiology (medicine). Home: 1933 Selby Ave Los Angeles CA 90025 Office: Crump Inst for Med Engring UCLA 405 Hilgard Ave Los Angeles CA 90024

GOLD, STEVEN HARVEY, physicist; b. Phila., Sept 3, 1946; s. Bernard and Laura (Tischler) G.; m. Sue Ellen Sloca, Jan. 1, 1974; children—David Jason, Kathryn Maureen. B.A., Haverford Coll., 1968; M.S., U. Md., 1970, Ph.D., 1978. Research assoc. Naval Research Lab., Washington, 1978-80, research physicist, 1980—. Inventor free electron laser injection oscillator (NRL invention award 1983), free electron laser with tapered axial magnetic field (NRL award 1984). Mem. Am. Phys. Soc., Optical Soc. Am., AAAS High power Microwave generation. Subspecialties: Free-electron lasers; Plasma physics. Home: 6203 Westbrook Dr New Carrollton MD 20784 Office: Naval Research Lab Code 4740 Washington DC 20375

GOLD, THOMAS, educator, astronomer; b. Vienna, Austria, May 22, 1920; s. Max and Josefine (Martin) G.; m. Merle Eleanor Tuberg, June 21, 1947; children—Linda, Lucy, Tanya; m. Carvel Lee Beyer, Dec. 27, 1972; 1 dau., Lauren. B.A., Cambridge (Eng.) U., 1942, M.A., 1945, Sc.D., 1969; fellow, Trinity Coll., Cambridge, 1947; M.A. (hon.), Harvard, 1957. Lectr. physics Cambridge (Eng.) U., 1948-52; chief asst. to Astronomer Royal, Gt. Britain, 1952-56; prof. astronomy Harvard, 1958, Robert Wheeler Willson prof., 1958-59; prof. astronomy, dir. Center Radiophysics and Space Research Cornell U., 1959-81, chmn. dept., 1959-68, asst. v.p. for research, 1970-71, John L. Wetherill prof., 1971—. Contbr. articles to profl. jours. Recipient Gold medal Royal Astronomical Soc., 1985. Fellow Royal Soc. London; mem. U.S. Nat. Acad. Sci., Am. Philos. Soc., Am. Acad. Arts and Scis., Royal Astron. Soc. (past councillor), Am. Astron. Soc., Am. Geophys. Union. Subspecialties: Geophysics; Radio and microwave astronomy. Address: Space Scis Bldg Cornell U Ithaca NY 14853

GOLDBAUM, MICHAEL HENRY, ophthalmology educator, researcher; b. Bklyn., Apr. 17, 1939; s. Samuel Zolomon and Sarah (Kramer) G.; m. Brenda Scott Leggio, July 7, 1964; children: David, Stephen, Rachel. B.A., Syracuse U., 1961; M.D., Tulane U., 1965. Diplomate: Am. Bd. Ophthalmology. Retina fellow Cornell U. Med. Sch., N.Y.C., 1973, instr., fellow ophthalmology, 1972-73; asst. prof. ophthalmology U. Ill. Eye and Ear Infirmary, Chgo., 1973-77; assoc. prof. ophthalmology U. Calif.-San Diego, 1977—. Contbr. articles to profl. jours. Served to lt. comdr. USN, 1967-72. Fellow Am. Acad. Ophthalmology, San Diego Acad. Ophthalmology; mem. AMA, Assn. for Research in Vision and Ophthalmology, Macula Soc., Retina Soc. San Diego Assn. Retarded Citizens. Current Work: Neovascularization and angiogenesis in the eye, macular degeneration. Subspecialties: Ophthalmology; Laser medicine. Home: 8435 Cliffridge Ln La Jolla CA 92037 Office: U Calif San Diego Eye Ctr Sir William Osler Ln M-018 La Jolla CA 92093

GOLDBERG, ALAN MARVIN, toxicologist, educator; b. Bklyn., Nov. 20, 1939; s. William and Celia Ida (Tudman) G.; m. Helene S. Schwenbach, Aug. 14, 1960; children: Michael David, Naomi Jill. B.S., Bklyn Coll. Pharmacy, 1961; Ph.D. in Pharmacology, U. Minn., 1962. Research asst. U. Wis., 1961-62, U. Minn., 1962-66; research assoc. Inst. Psychiat. Research Ind. U., 1966-67; asst. prof. dept. pharmacology Ind. U., 1967-69; asst. prof. environ. medicine Johns Hopkins U., 1969-71, assoc. prof., 1971-78, prof. dept. environ. health scis., 1978—, assoc. chmn. dept., 1978-80, acting dir. div. toxicology, 1979-80, dir. div. toxicology, 1980-82; dir. (Center for Alts. to Animal Testing), 1980-83, assoc. dean for research prin. research scientist Chesapeake Bay Inst., 1979—; mem. Health Hazard Evaluation Team of Chem. Wastes Dumps, State of Tenn., EPA Rev. Panel, 1980-82; cons. Wrightsville Marine Biomed. Labs., Astra Pharm. Co.; mem. sect. on neurobiology NSF; environ. health scis. NIH. Mem. editorial bd.: Jour. Am. Coll. Toxicology; Contbr. articles to profl. jours. Recipient award Ind. Neurol. Soc., 1967. Mem. AAAS, Am. Soc. Pharmacology and Exptl. Therapeutics, Soc. Neurosci. (pres. Balt. chpt. 1971-73), Am. Soc. Neurochemistry, Am. Epilepsy Soc., Internat. Soc. Neurochemistry, Soc. Toxicology, Internat. Study Group on Memory Disorders, Internat. Union Pharmacology. Current Work: Neurotoxicology, in vitro methodology development. Subspecialties: Environmental toxicology; Neurobiology. Home: 2231 Crest Rd Baltimore MD 21209 Office: 615 N Wolfe St Baltimore MD 21205

GOLDBERG, EDWARD DAVID, geochemist, educator; b. Sacramento, Aug. 2, 1921; s. Edward Davidow and Lillian (Rothholz) G.; m. Kathe Bertine, Dec. 26, 1973; children: David Wilkes, Wendy Jean, Kathi Kiri, Beck Bertine. B.S., U. Calif. at Berkeley, 1942; Ph.D., U. Chgo., 1949. Mem. faculty Scripps Instn. Oceanography, La Jolla, Calif., 1949—, prof. chemistry, 1960—; provost Revelle Coll., U. Calif. at San Diego, 1965-66. Author: (with J. Geiss) Earth Sciences and Meteorites, 1964, Guide to Marine Pollution, 1972, North Sea Science, 1973, The Sea: Marine Chemistry, Vol. V, 1974, The Health of the Oceans, 1976; Black Carbon in the Environment, 1985. Contbr. numerous articles to profl. jours. Guggenheim fellow, 1961; NATO fellow, 1970. Mem. Am. Geophys. Union, AAAS, Geochem. Soc., U.S. Acad. Scis., Sigma Xi. Research, publs. primarily on marine pollution, chem. composition sea water, sediments, marine organisms, environmental mgmt.; radioactive dating techniques in marine environment and glaciers. Subspecialty: Geochemistry. Home: 750 Val Sereno Dr Encinitas CA 92024

GOLDBERG, IVAN D., microbiologist, educator; b. Phila., May 13, 1934; s. Max and Frances G.; m. Noveta McCracken, July 27, 1979; children: Micki, Judy, Lisa; married; stepchildren: Nick, Vikki Russell. A.B., U. Pa., 1956; Ph.D., U. Ill., 1961. Postdoctoral fellow Rutgers U., 1961-62, Oreg. State U., 1962-63; NRC postdoctoral research assoc. U.S. Army Biol. Labs., Frederick, Md., 1963-65, microbial geneticist, 1965-71; assoc. prof. dept. microbiology U. Kans. Sch. Medicine, 1971-77, prof. microbiology, 1977—. Contbr. articles to sci. jours. NIH grantee, 1972-80; recipient Leroy D. Fothergill Sci. award, 1970. Mem. Am. Soc. Microbiology (pres. Mo. Valley br. 1974), Sigma Xi. Democrat. Jewish. Current Work: Genetics of Neisseria gonorrhea, Bacillus sp. and Legionella pneumophila. Utilization of recombinant DNA technology to elucidate the genetic bases of thermophily; organisms utilized are B.stearothermophilus, B. coagulans and B. subtilis. Subspecialties: Genetics and genetic engineering (biology); Microbiology. Home: 14409 W. 90th Terrace Lenexa KS 66215 Office: 39th and Rainbow Blvd Kansas City KS 66103

GOLDBERG, LEON ISADORE, clinical pharmacologist; b. Charleston, S.C., Sept. 26, 1926; s. Harry and Goldy (Cohen) G.; m. Faye Joan Girsh, Feb. 2, 1958 (div.); children—Mark, Claudia. B.S. Pharmacy, Med. U. S.C., 1946, M.S., 1951, Ph.D., 1952; D.H.L.; M.D. cum laude, Harvard U., 1956. Intern Mass. Gen. Hosp., Boston, 1956-57, intern, asst. resident in medicine, 1957-58, research fellow anesthesia, 1954-56; research asst. in pharmacology Med. Coll. S.C., 1949-52, research asso., 1952-54; clin. asso. Exptl. Therapeutics Br., NIH, 1958-61; prof. medicine, pharmacology, dir. clin. pharmacology program Emory U., Atlanta, 1961-74; prof. medicine, pharmacology, chmn. com. on clin. pharmacology U. Chgo., 1974—; cons. NIH, VA, FDA, Nat. Acad. Scis. Editor: Jour. Cardiovascular Pharmacology; mem. editorial bds. several pharmacology jours., 1961—; contbr. chpts. to books, numerous articles on clin. pharmacology, cardiovascular pharmacology to profl. jours. Served as surgeon USPHS, 1958-61. Burroughs Welcome Fund scholar in clin. pharmacology, 1961-66. Fellow Am. Coll. Cardiology; mem. Am. Soc. Clin. Investigation, Am. Soc. for Pharmacology and Exptl. Therapeutics, Soc. for Exptl. Biology and Medicine, Am. Soc. for Clin. Pharmacology and Therapeutics, Am. Heart Assn., Council for High Blood Pressure Research, Assn. Am. Physicians. Current Work: Fundamentals and clinical studies of cardiovascular drugs. Subspecialties: Pharmacology; Internal medicine. Home: 5000 S Cornell Apt 21B Chicago IL 60615 Office: Dept Pharmacology Sch Medicine U Chgo 947 E 58th St Chicago IL 60637

GOLDBERG, ROBERT NATHAN, chemist; b. Stamford, Conn., Dec. 11, 1943; s. Isaac and Claire (Richards) G. B.A., Johns Hopkins U., 1965; Ph.D., Carnegie Mellon U., 1969. Research chemist Nat. Bur. Standards, Gaithersburg, Md., 1969—. Contbr. articles to profl. jours. Mem. Am. Chem. Soc., U.S. Calorimetry Conf. Current work: Solutions, biochemical equilibria, biotechnology, electrolytes, calorimetry, thermodynamics and data evaluation. Subspecialties: Physical chemistry; Thermodynamics. Office: Nat Bur Standards Chem Thermodynamics Div Gaithersburg MD 20899

GOLDBERGER, MARVIN L., educator, physicist, institute technology president; b. Chgo., Oct. 22, 1922; s. Joseph and Mildred (Sedwitz) G.; m. Mildred Ginsburg, Nov. 25, 1945; children: Samuel M., Joel S. B.S., Carnegie Inst. Tech., 1943; Ph.D., U. Chgo., 1948. Research asso. Radiation Lab., U. Calif., 1948-49; research asso. Mass. Inst. Tech., 1949-50; asst.-asso. prof. U. Chgo., 1950-55, prof., 1955-57; Higgins prof. physics Princeton U., 1953-54, 57-78, chmn. dept., 1970-76, Joseph Henry prof. physics, 1977-78; pres. Calif. Inst. Tech., Pasadena, 1978—; Mem. President's Sci. Adv. Com., 1965-69; Chmn. Fedn. Am. Scientists, 1971-73; dir. Gen. Motors Corp., Haskel, Inc., Interactive Systems Corp. Fellow Am. Phys. Soc., Am. Acad. Arts and Scis.; mem. Nat. Acad. Scis., Am. Philos. Soc., Council on Fgn. Relations. Club: Princeton (N.Y.C.). Subspecialties: Theoretical physics; Particle physics. Home: 415 S Hill Ave Pasadena CA 91106

GOLDE, DAVID WILLIAM, educator, physician, scientist; b. N.Y.C., Oct. 23, 1940; s. Harvey and Esther (Bobrove) Goldstein; children: Daniel, Michael. B.S. in Chemistry, Fairleigh Dickinson U., 1962; M.D., McGill U., Montreal, Que., Can., 1966. Diplomate: Am. Bd. Internal Medicine, 1972, Nat. Bd. Med. Examiners. Intern U. Calif. Hosps., San Francisco, 1966-67; resident in clin. pathology Clin. Center, NIH, Bethesda, Md., 1968-69; hematology fellow and resident in clin. pathology Clin. Center, NIH (Hematology Service, Clin. Center), 1969-70; resident in medicine U. Calif. Hosps., San Francisco, 1970-71; fellow Cancer Research Inst., 1971-72, resident in medicine, 1971-72; staff cons. continuing edn. and tng. br. div. regional med. programs NIH, 1967-68; instr. medicine U. Calif., San Francisco, 1972, asst. prof., 1973, UCLA, 1974, assoc. prof., 1975-79, prof., 1979—, chief div. hematology/oncology, 1981—; co-dir. UCLA (Chem. Research Ctr.), 1974—; mem. (VA hematology study sect.), 1978-80, (NIH hematology study sect.), 1979-81; mem. cancer coordinating com. U. Calif., 1982—. Contbr. numerous articles on hematology to profl. jours.; mem. editorial bds.: Leukemia Research, 1977, Blood, 1978, Leukemia Revs, 1980, Am. Jour. Hematology, 1985. Served to lt. comdr. USPHS, 1966-70. Recipient J. Francis Williams prize McGill U. Dept. Medicine, 1966. Fellow ACP; mem. Am. Assn. for Cancer Research, AAAS, Am. Fedn. Clin. Research, Am. Soc. Clin. Investigation, Am. Soc. Hematology, Internat. Assn. Comparative Research on Leukemia and Related Diseases, Internat. Soc. Exptl. Hematology, Reticuloendothelial Soc., Soc. Exptl. Biology and Medicine, Western Soc. Clin. Research, Alpha Omega Alpha, Phi Omega Epsilon. Subspecialties: Hematology; Oncology. Office: UCLA Sch Medicine Los Angeles CA 90024

GOLDEN, DAVID EDWARD, physicist, university administrator, researcher; b. N.Y.C., May 27, 1932; s. Barnet Dade and Rose (Rosenbaum) G.; m. Paula Englander, July 18, 1962; children: Jeffrey Bertram, Leila Justine. B.A., NYU, 1954, Ph.D. in Physics, 1960. Asst. prof. physics dept. N.Y.U., 1960-61; asst. prof. Adelphi U., 1961-62; engring. specialist Gen. Telephone & Electronics Lab., Palo Alto, Calif., 1962-63; staff scientist Lockheed Research Lab., Palo Alto, 1962-67; vis. prof. in physics U. Bari, 1967-70; assoc. prof. physics U. Nebr., Lincoln, 1970-72, prof., 1972-75; prof., chmn. dept. physics and astronomy U. Okla., Norman, 1975-85, George Lynn Cross prof. physics, 1985; provost, v.p. acad. affairs North Tex. State U., 1985—; hon. lectr. Mid Am. State Univ. Assn., 1982-83; cons. Autometric Corp., 1961-62, ARIS, 1970-72, Tracor, 1972-74, Lawrence Radiation Lab., 1975-80; gen. com. Internat. Conf. on Physics of Electron and Atomic Collisions, 1979-83; com. on atomic and molecular sci NRC, 1982-85. Contbr. articles to profl. pubis. Grantee NSF, 1982—; Grantee Dept. Energy, 1982—. Fellow Am. Phys. Soc. (exec. com. div. electron and atomic physics 1981-83). Patentee. Current Work: Atomic scattering, electron spectroscopy, lasers, electron-photon angular correlation, scattering with spin polarized electrons. Subspecialty: Atomic and molecular physics. Office: Office of Provost North Tex State U Denton TX 76203

GOLDENBERG, BARBARA L., chemical physicist; b. Trenton, N.J., Feb. 22, 1952; d. David and Sylvia (Schain) G. A.B., Occidental Coll., 1973; postgrad. MIT, 1973-74; Ph.D., Brandeis U., 1982. Research specialist U. Minn., Mpls., 1981-84; prin. research scientist Honeywell, Inc., Bloomington, Minn., 1984—. Contbr. articles to profl. jours. Mem. AAAS, Am. Chem. Soc., Am. Phys. Soc., Assn. Women in Sci., Phi Beta Kappa, Pi Mu Epsilon, Alpha Mu Gamma. Current work: Growth of semiconducting materials by MOCVD; characterization of thin films. Subspecialties: Electronic materials; Condensed matter physics. Home: 9705 Pleasant Ave S Apt 3G Bloomington MN 55420 Office: Honeywell Phys Scis Ctr 10701 Lyndale Ave S Bloomington MN 55420

GOLDFARB, STANLEY, physician, physiology educator; b. N.Y.C., Dec. 18, 1943; s. Robert Melvin and Mary Ann (Siegel) G.; m. Rayna Block, Aug. 31, 1970; children: Rachael Fay, Michael Louis. A.B. cum laude, Princeton U., 1965; M.D., U. Rochester, 1969. Diplomate: Am. Bd. Internal Medicine, Am. Bd. Internal Medicine in Nephrology. Intern Hosp. U. Pa., 1969-70, resident, 1970-72; clin. instr. U. Pa. Sch. Medicine, 1974-75, asst. prof. medicine, 1975-81, assoc. prof., 1981—. N.Y. State Regents Scholar, 1961-65; NIH Clin. Investigator awardee, 1978-81; grantee, 1983—. Fellow Am. Coll. Physicians; mem. Am. Fedn. Clin. Research, Am. Soc. Nephrology, Internat. Soc. Nephrology, N.Y. Acad. Scis. Jewish. Club: Rolling Green Golf. Current Work: Renal regulation of divalent ion metabolism; nephrolithiasis; thiophosphate pharmacology. Subspecialties: Nephrology; Physiology (medicine). Home: 34 Rosedale Rd Overbrook Hills PA 19151 Office: Renal-Electrolyte Sect Hosp U Pa 860 Gates 3400 Spruce St Philadelphia PA 19104

GOLDFEDER, ANNA, cancer and radiobiol. researcher; b. Lubin, Poland, July 25, 1897; came to U.S., 1931, naturalized, 1940; d. Chaim and Tauba (Friedman) Godlfeder. D.Sc., Karl U., Prague, 1923; M.U.C., Masaryk U., Brno, Czechoslovakia, 1931. Fellow Harvard U. Med. Sch., 1931-33; dir. Cancer Research Lab. City of N.Y., 1934-77; dir. cancer and radiobiological research lab. N.Y.U., 1977—. Contbr. articles to profl. jours. Mem. Radiol. Soc. N. Am. (recipient award 1940), N.Y. Acad. Sci. (recipient Gold medal 1981). Current Work: Cell Biology, cell kinetics, cell radiosensitizers. Subspecialties: Cell and tissue culture; Membrane biology. Home: 2 Washington Square Village 91 New York NY 10012 Office: 100 Washington Square New York NY 10003

GOLDFISCHER, SIDNEY LEO, pathology educator; b. N.Y.C., Dec. 28, 1926; s. Samuel and Ida (Lerner) G.; widowed: children—Carl Samuel, Susan, Michael Jean, Madeline Louise. B.S., Columbia U., 1958; M.D., NYU, 1961. Assoc. prof. Albert Einstein Coll. Medicine, Bronx, N.Y., 1970, prof. pathology, 1974, acting chmn. dept. pathology, 1984; dir. office indsl. liason A. Einstein Coll. Medicine, Bronx, 1983—. Contbr. articles to profl. jours. Fellow N.Y. Acad. Medicine; mem. Histochem. Soc. (pres.), N.Y. Soc. Electron Microscopy, Am. Soc. Cell Biology, Société Francaise de Microscopie Electronique. Jewish. Subspecialties: Pathology (medicine); Cell biology (medicine). Office: Albert Einstein Coll Medicine Dept Pathology 1300 Morris Park Ave Bronx NY 10461

GOLDHABER, JACOB KOPEL, mathematician, educator; b. Bklyn., Apr. 12, 1924; s. Joseph and Shirley (Heller) G.; m. Ruth Last, Dec. 25, 1951; children—Doreet, David, Aviva. B.A., Bklyn. Coll., 1944; M.A., Harvard, 1945; Ph.D., U. Wis., 1950. Instr. U. Conn., Storrs, 1950-53; instr. Cornell U., Ithaca, N.Y., 1953- 54; asst. prof. Washington U., St. Louis, 1954-59, assoc. prof., 1959- 61, U. Md., College Park, 1961-62, prof., 1962—, chmn. math. dept., 1968-77; exec. sec. Office Math. Scis., NRC, 1975-83, acting dean grad. studies and research, 1984—; vis. research assoc. (NSF Sci. Faculty fellow) U. London (Eng.), 1966-67. Author: (with Gertrude Ehrlich) Algebra, 1970. Contbr. papers to profl. jours. Mem. AAAS, Am. Math. Soc., Math. Assn. Am., Sigma Xi. Subspecialty: Algebra and number theory. Home: 5517 39th St NW Washington DC 20015 Office: Dept Math U Md College Park MD 20742

GOLDHABER, MAURICE, physicist; b. Lemberg, Austria, Apr. 18, 1911; came to U.S., 1938, naturalized, 1944; s. Charles and Ethel (Frisch) G.; m. Gertrude Scharff, May 24, 1939; children: Alfred S., Michael H. Ph.D., Cambridge U., Eng., 1936; Ph.D. (hon.), Tel-Aviv U., Israel, 1974; Dr. (hon.), U. Louvain-La-Neuve, Belgium, 1982; D.Sc. (hon.), SUNY, Stony Brook, 1983. Bye fellow Magdalene Coll., Cambridge, 1936-38; asst. prof. physics U. Ill., 1938-43, assoc. prof., 1943-45, prof., 1945-50; sr. sci. Brookhaven Nat. Lab., 1950-60, chmn. dept. physics, 1960-61, dir., 1961-73, Associated Univs. Inc. disting. scientist, 1973—; cons. labs. AEC; Morris Loeb lectr Harvard U., 1955; adj. prof. physics SUNY, Stony Brook, 1965—; Mem. nuclear sci. com. NRC. Assoc. editor: Phys. Rev, 1951-53; Contbr. articles on nuclear physics to sci. jours. Mem. bd. govs. Weizmann Inst. Sci., Rehovoth, Israel, Tel Aviv U.; trustee Univs. Research Assn. Recipient citation for meritorious contbns. U.S. AEC, 1973, J. Robert Oppenheimer meml. prize, 1982. Fellow Am. Phys. Soc. (pres. 1982), Am. Acad. Arts and Scis., AAAS; mem. Nat. Acad. Sci., Am. Philos. Soc. (Tom W. Bonner prize in nuclear physics 1971). Subspecialty: Nuclear physics. Home: 91 S Gillette Ave Bayport NY 11705 Office: Brookhaven Nat Laboratory Upton NY 11973

GOLDIN, STANLEY MICHAEL, neuroscientist, educator; b. N.Y.C., 1948; B.S. in Chem. Engring, M.I.T., 1970; M.S. in Chem. Engring., MIT, 1970; Ph.D. in Biochemistry, Harvard U., 1977. Jr. fellow Harvard U., Cambridge, Mass., 1976-78, asst. prof. pharmacology Med. Sch., Boston, 1979-83, assoc. prof., 1983—. Contbr. articles to profl. jours. Recipient Alfred P. Sloan award in neurosci., 1979, McKnight Scholar's award, 1981, Searle Scholar's award, 1981, Rita Allen award, 1985. Mem. Soc. Neurosci., Sigma Xi, Phi Lambda Upsilon. Patentee biologically active membrane material. Current Work: Molecular basis of regulation of neuronal electrical activity; ion gates and pumps; nerve cell membranes; membrane reconstitution; immunocytochemical localization. Subspecialties: Membrane biology; Neurobiology. Office: 250 Longwood Ave Boston MA 02115

GOLDMAN, ALEXANDER, psychologist; b. Bklyn., Apr. 3, 1910; s. Harry and Bertha (Bloch) G.; m. Florence Halperin, Jan. 19, 1944; children: Harriet Elen, Thomas J., Henry J. B.S., L.I. U., 1931; M.A., Columbia U., 1947; Ph.D., NYU, 1959. Lic. psychologist, N.Y. Research psychologist U.S. Navy-O.N.R., Port Washington, N.Y., 1951-59; head human factors Republic Aviation, Farmingdale, N.Y., 1959-64; chief psychologist phys. medicine Meadowbrook Hosp., East Meadow, N.Y., 1964-66; sr. life scientist Grumman Aerospace, Osyter Bay, N.Y., 1968-72; psychologist U.S. VA, Bklyn., 1972-79, pvt. practice psychology, N.Y.C., 1979-85. Contbr. articles to profl. jours. Bd. dirs. for Southeast U.S., Internat. Inst. for Safety in Transp. Served to 1st lt. U.S. Army, 1942-47. Recipient Founders Day award NYU, 1960; commendation U.S. VA, 1978. Mem. Human Factors Soc., Am. Psychol. Assn., Product Safety Assn. (bd. dirs. Los Angeles 1981—), System Safety Soc. (pres. 1977-78). Current Work: Application of behavioral sciences to design and safety in use of the products of technology to protect health, life, welfare of individuals. Subspecialties: Human factors engineering; Neuropsychology. Home: 1210 Haddington Circle Sun City Center FL 33570 Office: PO Box 5358 Sun City Center FL 33571-5358

GOLDMAN, ALLEN SEYMOUR, pediatrician; b. Providence, Oct. 25, 1929; s. Louis Henry and Sonia Evelyn (Brodsky) G.; m. Mary Lemann, Aug. 7, 1957 (div. 1982); children—Jonathan, Benjamin Allen, Adam Louis; m. 2d Rachel Bok, Nov. 29, 1982; stepchildren—Jefferson Bok Kise, Charles Curtis Kise. A.B., Brown U., 1951, Sc.M., 1953; postgrad. Yale U., 1954; M.D., SUNY-Syracuse, 1958; M.A. (hon.), U. Pa., 1971. Diplomate Am. Bd. Pediatrics. Intern Yale-Grace New Haven Hosp., 1958-59; resident Children's Hosp. of Phila., 1959-60, chief resident, 1960-61; instr. dept. pediatrics U. Pa., Phila., 1961-64, assoc. in pediatrics, 1964-66, asst. prof., 1966-69, assoc. prof., 1969-78, research prof. pediatrics and pediatrics in pharmacology, 1978-86; practice medicine specializing in pediatrics, Phila., 1961-86; prof. pediatrics and genetics U. Ill. Coll. Medicine, Chgo., 1986—, dir. Ctr. for Craniofacial Anomalies, 1986—; mem. staff Children's Hosp. Contbr. articles to profl. jours. Mem. AAAS, Am. Chem. Soc., Am. Pediatric Soc., Phila. County Med. Soc., Soc. for Study of Reproduction, Endocrine Soc., Lawson Wilkins Pediatric Endocrine Soc., Teratology Soc., Soc. for Exptl. Biology and Medicine, Phila. Endocrine Soc., Soc. Endocrinology (London), Coll. Physicians Phila., Assocs. Phi Beta Kappa, Phi Beta Kappa, Sigma Xi. Democrat. Jewish. Club: Phila. Racquet. Current work: Research interests include the biochemical mechanism of the induction of a variety of birth defects by glucocorticoids, phenytoin and other teratogens, including cleft palate, neural tube defects and sexual malformations. Subspecialties: Endocrinology; Teratology. Home: 1411 N State Pkwy Chicago IL 60610 Office: Ctr for Craniofacial Anomalies U Ill Coll Medicine Box 6998 Chicago IL 60680

GOLDMAN, ARMOND SAMUEL, physician, educator, researcher; b. San Angelo, Tex., May 26, 1930; s. David and Rose (Gottesfeld) G.; m. Barbara Jean Goldman, July 31, 1950; children: Lynn, David, Daniel, Paul, Robert. M.D., U. Tex., Galveston, 1953. Diplomate: Am. Bd. Pediatrics, Am. Bd. Allergy and Immunology. Instr. dept. pediatrics U. Tex. Med. Br., Galveston, 1959-60, asst. prof., 1960-67, assoc. prof., 1967-72, prof. dept. human biol. chemistry and genetics, 1972—, dir. div. immunology, 1960—. Contbr. articles to profl. jours. Served to capt. M.C. U.S. Army, 1955-57. Mem. Am. Acad. Pediatrics, Soc. Pediatric Research, Am. Pediatric Soc., Am. Assn. Immunologists, Reticuloendothelial Soc., Sigma Xi. Current Work: Immunologic system in human milk; pathogenesis of immunodeficiency; ontogeny of immunity. Subspecialties: Pediatrics; Immunology (medicine). Home: 3801 Pine Manor Dickinson TX 77539 Office: U Tex Med Br Galveston TX 77550

GOLDMAN, JOSEPH L., scientist-technical director, consultant; b. San Francisco, Aug. 25, 1932; s. Samuel and Charlotte (Malamud) G.; m. Sylvia Shiffman, 1955 (div. 1977); children: Rachel Ann, Charles Israel, Michelle Sandra. Student, UCLA, 1955-56; B.S., Tex. A&M U., 1958, M.S., 1960; postgrad., U. Chgo., 1960-62; Ph.D., U. Okla., 1971. Cert. consulting meteorologist. Mathematician West Coast Research Lab., Los Angeles, 1955-56; research asst. to scientist Tex. A&M U., 1956-60; research meteorologist U. Chgo., 1960-65; prin. investigator Nat. Engring. Sci. Co., Houston, 1965-66; exec. v.p. Inst. Storm Research, Houston, 1966-75; tech. dir. Internat. Ctr. for the Solution of Environ. Problems, Houston, 1976—; mng. dir. Sea & Storm Service Specialists Ltd., London, 1973-79; assoc. prof. U. St. Thomas, Houston, 1967-76. Contbr. chpts. to books and numerous articles to profl. jours. Bd. dirs. ARC, Houston, 1976—; gen. chmn. Sci. & Engring. Fair, 1976—. Served with USAF, 1951-55. NSF grantee, 1971-72. Fellow Royal Meteorl. Soc.; mem. Am. Meteorol. Soc., Am. Geophysical Union, N.Y. Acad. Sci., AAAS, Engrs. Council Houston (v.p., exec. bd. 1975-82), Marine Tech. Soc., Sigma Xi (dir. Rice Med. Ctr. chpt. 1982, co-chmn. S.E. Tex. council 1984—). Lodge: B'nai B'rith. Originator Sculpture of Storm motion, 1967. Current Work: Risk analysis, projections of urban growth and related problems-health, hazards, transportation, waste utilization, structural integrity, water, socio-economics, energy, climate. Subspecialty: Meteorology. Office: International Center for the Solution of Environmental Problems 3818 Graustark St Houston TX 77006

GOLDMAN, LAWRENCE, physiologist, educator; b. Boston, May 6, 1936; s. Theodore T. and Sophye (Altshuler) G.; m. Faith Kordis, July 11, 1968 (div.); 1 dau. Ann Kordis. B.S. summa cum laude, Tufts U., 1958; Ph.D., UCLA, 1964. NIH postdoctoral trainee dept. neurology Columbia U. Coll. Physicians and Surgeons, 1964-65; asst. prof. dept. zoology U. Md., 1965-67; asst. prof. dept. physiology U. Md. (Sch. Medicine), 1967-70, assoc. prof., 1970-77, prof., 1977—, prof. biophysics, 1977—; NATO sr. fellow in sci. Queen Mary Coll., U. London, 1970; NIH spl. research fellow Cambridge (Eng.) U., 1973; cons. NIH, NSF. Contbr. numerous articles to sci. jours. Grantee NIH, NATO, NSF, 1966—. Fellow AAAS; mem. Am. Physiol. Soc., Biophys. Soc., Soc. Gen. Physiologists (rep. to Nat. Soc. Med. Research Council), Soc. Neurosci., N.Y. Acad. Sci., Am. Inst. Biol. Sci., Sigma Xi, Phi Beta Kappa. Current Work: Membrane biophysics, study of generation and conduction of nervous impulse. Subspecialty: Biophysics (biology). Home: 3502 Newland Rd Baltimore MD 21218 Office: Dept Physiology Sch Medicine U Md Baltimore MD 21201

GOLDMAN, LEE, physician, educator, researcher; b. Phila., Jan, 6, 1948; s. Marvin and Kathryn (Schwartz) G.; m. Jill Steinhardt, Mar. 21, 1971; children: Jeff, Daniel, Robyn Sue. B.A., Yale U., 1969, M.D., 1973, M.P.H., 1973. Diplomate: Am. Bd. Internal Medicine. Intern U. Calif.-San Francisco, 1973-74, resident in med., 1974-75, Mass. Gen. Hosp., Boston, 1975-76; fellow in cardiology Yale-New Haven Hosp., 1976-78; asst. prof. medicine Harvard U. Med. Sch., 1978-83, assoc. prof., 1983—; asst. physician-in-chief dept. med. Brigham and Women's Hosp., Boston, 1983. Contrbr. numerous articles to profl. jours. Bd. dirs. Temple Shir Tikva, Wayland, Mass., 1982-83, treas., 1983-84, v.p., 1985-86. ACP teaching and research scholar, 1980-83; Henry J. Kaiser Family Found. scholar, 1982—. Fellow ACP and Am. Coll. Cardiology; mem. Am. Fedn. Clin. Research, Soc. Med. Decision Making, Soc. Research and Edn. Primary Care Internal Medicine. Democrat. Jewish. Current Work: Application of multivariate analytic techniques to problems in medical decision making and medical diagnosis. Subspecialties: Internal medicine; Cardiology. Office: Dept of Medicine Brigham and Women's Hosp 75 Francis St Boston MA 02115

GOLDMAN, TERRANCE JACK, physicist; b. Winnipeg, Man., Can., Feb. 20, 1947; came to U.S., 1968, naturalized, 1984; s. Louis Meyer and Helen Grace (Levson) G.; m. Bernadine Zoe Gross, June 25, 1968; children—Oliver, Elizabeth, Leah, Matthew. B.S. with honors, U. Man., 1968; A.M., Harvard U., 1969, Ph.D., 1973. Postdoctoral fellow Stanford Linear Accelerator Ctr., Calif., 1973-75; postdoctoral fellow Los Alamos Lab., 1975-78, staff mem., 1978—; sr. research fellow Calif. Inst. Tech., Pasadena, 1978-80; vis. assoc. prof. U. Calif.-Santa Cruz, 1982-83; mem. gallium rev. Panel Dept. Energy, Brookhaven, N.Y., 1981. Editor: Intense Medium Energy Sources of Strangeness, 1983; Proc. of Santa Fe Meeting, 1985. Contbr. articles to profl. jours. Bd. dirs. Los Alamos Jewish Ctr., 1984—. Woodrow Wilson fellow, 1968; NRC fellow, 1970-75. Mem. Am. Phys. Soc. Current work: Gauge theories of weak interactions, grand unified theories and proton decay, quark structure of nuclei and hypernuclei. Subspecialties: Particle physics; Nuclear physics. Office: Los Alamos Nat Lab T-5 MS-B283 Los Alamos NM 87545

GOLDNER, LAURIE LINDA, aquatic ecologist, consultant; b. Yonkers, N.Y., Oct. 22, 1953; d. William and Elizabeth Emma (Roeder) G. B.S., U. R.I., 1975; Ph.D., U. Ga., 1984. Field lab. coordinator Lockheed Engring. and Mgmt. Services Corp., Las Vegas, Nev., 1984-85; ecol. cons. Ecosystem Research Inst., Logan, Utah, 1985—. Sigma Xi grantee, 1977, 80. Mem. Ecol. Soc. Am., Inst. Ecol. U. Ga. Current work: Aquatic population and community ecology (freshwater and marine systems); assessment of effects of acid deposition and toxic substances on lakes and streams. Subspecialties: Ecology (biology); Limnology. Office: Ecosystem Research Institute Logan UT

GOLDREICH, PETER MARTIN, educator, astrophysicist; b. N.Y.C., July 14, 1939; s. Paul and Edith (Rosenfield) G.; m. Susan Kroll, June 14, 1960; children—Eric, Daniel. B.Engring. Physics, Cornell U., 1960, Ph.D. in Physics, 1963. Instr. Cornell U., 1963; postdoctoral fellow Cambridge (Eng.) U., 1963-64; asst. prof. astronomy and geophysics UCLA, 1964-66; assoc. prof. astronomy and planetary sci. Calif. Inst. Tech., 1966-69, prof., 1969—, Lee A. Dubridge prof. astrophysics and planetary physics, 1981—. Mem. Nat. Acad. Sci., Am. Acad. Arts and Scis. Subspecialty: Planetary science. Home: 471 Catalina Ave Pasadena CA 91106 Office: 1201 E California Blvd Pasadena CA 91109

GOLDSBERRY, FRED LYNN, oil exploration executive; b. San Antonio, Jan. 3, 1947; s. William Donald and Freda Mae (Case) G.; m. Sharon Faye Williams, Dec. 20, 1969; children: Jeanette Louise, Dennis Hamilton. B.S.M.E. with honors, Tex. A&M U., 1968, M.S.M.E., 1969, Ph.D., 1971. Registered profl. engr., Tex. Research technologist Tex. Petroleum Research Co., College Station, Tex., 1970-71; research engr. ENSERCH Corp., Dallas, 1971-73; supervising engr. TUCO, Inc., Amarillo, Tex., 1973-75; spl. projects engr. J. M. Huber Corp., Borger, Tex., 1975-76; program mgr. Hanford (Wash.) site ERDA, 1976-79; dir. ERDA (Geopressure Projects Office), Houston, 1976-83; chief reservoir engr. Zapata Exploration Co., 1983—. adv. to Common Market, 1982. Contbr. articles to profl. jours. Bd. dirs. Epilepsy Found., Richland, Wash., 1977-79. Recipient award U.S. Dept. Energy, 1979. Mem. Tau Beta Pi, Pi Tau Sigma, Phi Eta Sigma, Phi Kappa Phi. Presbyterian. Patentee in field. Current Work: Reservoir and production engineering. Subspecialties: Petroleum engineering; Geothermal power.

GOLDSCHMIED, FABIO RENZO, consulting engineer; b. Trieste, Venezia Giulia, Italy, Oct. 25, 1919; came to U.S., 1939, naturalized, 1943; s. Rodolfo and Ada (Frankel) G.; m. Marie P. Perfumo, Mar. 14, 1942; 1 dau., Wanda Ada. Student, Swiss Fed. Poly., Zurich, 1937-39, M.I.T., 1943; B.Sc., Columbia U., 1947, M.Sc., 1948. Registered profl. engr., Pa., Utah, Mass. Adv. scientist Westinghouse Electric Corp., Pitts., 1968-81; research prof. U. Utah, Salt Lake City, 1965-68; research aerodynamicist Sperry Rand Corp., Blue Bell, Pa. and Salt Lake City, 1962-65; mgr. advanced devel. engring. Westinghouse Electric Corp., Boston, 1954-61; cons. engr. F. R. Goldschmied P.E., Monroeville, Pa., 1981—; cons. M.I.T., Electric Power Research Inst., David W. Taylor Naval Ship Research and Devel. Ctr. Contbr. articles to profl. jours. Served with U.S. Army, 1942-46, ETO. Assoc. fellow AIAA (assoc. editor Jour. Hydronautics 1980-82); mem. ASME, Soc. Naval Architects Marine Engrs. Democrat. Jewish. Patentee in field. Current Work: Optimum integration of hull design, boundary-layer control, propulsion and stability for submerged vehicles such as submarines, torpedoes, and airships. Subspecialties: Fluid mechanics; Systems engineering. Home: 1782 McClure Rd Monroeville PA 15146

GOLDSMITH, DOUGLAS HOWARD, oral and maxillofacial surgeon; b. Los Angeles, May 26, 1949; s. Leon R. and Edith (Fish) G.; m. Catherine L. Smerling, Aug. 19, 1973; children: Lisa, Sarah. D.D.S. cum laude, UCLA, 1974. Diplomate: Am. Bd. Oral and Maxillofacial Surgery. Resident in oral and maxillofacial surgery Montefiore Hosp. and Med. Ctr., Bronx, N.Y., 1974-76, chief resident in oral and maxillofacial surgery, 1976-77, adj. attending oral and maxillofacial surgeon, 1977—; oral and maxillofacial surgeon Montefiore Hosp. and Med. Ctr. (Ctr. for Craniofacial Deformities), 1977—, pvt. practice dentistry, specializing in oral and maxillofacial surgery, Scarsdale, N.Y., 1980—; instr. gross anatomy course Albert Einstein Coll. Medicine, 1977-78, asst. prof. surgery, 1977-80, assoc. clin. prof., 1981; assoc. clin. prof. Columbia Presbyn. Sch. Dentistry; mem. staff, adj. attending oral and maxillofacial surgeon North Central Bronx Hosp.; oral and maxillofacial surgery cons. Norwalk (Conn.) Hosp.; lectr. dept. oral and maxillofacial surgery NYU; mem. staff Beth Abraham Hosp., Bronx Coll. Hosp., Albert Einstein Coll. Medicine, White Plains (N.Y.) Hosp. and Med. Ctr., Columbia Presbyn. Hosp. and Med. Ctr., N.Y.C.; lectr., presenter in field; guest lectr. and surgeon, various hosps., 1977-80. Contbr. articles, chpts. to profl. pubis. Recipient 2d place award Am. Acad. History Dentistry Writing Contest, 1973; Am. Inst. Oral Biology fellow, 1973. Mem. Student ADA, So. Calif. Acad. Oral Pathology, Am. Dental Soc. Anesthesiology, Am. Inst. Oral Biology, Internat. Assn. Dental Research, First Dist. Dental Soc. (N.Y.), Am. Cleft Palate Soc., Am. Soc. Oral and Maxillofacial Surgery, N.Y. State Soc. Oral and Maxillofacial Surgery, Sigma Xi, Omicron Kappa Upsilon, Phi Eta Sigma, Alpha Omega. Subspecialties: Oral and maxillofacial surgery; Dental growth and development. Home: 37 Brite Ave Scarsdale NY 10583 Office: Dr. Douglas H Goldsmith DDS PC 495 Central Park Ave Scarsdale NY 10583

GOLDSMITH, MICHAEL ALLEN, oncologist, cancer researcher; b. Bronx, N.Y., Jan. 28, 1946; s. Walter and Bertha (Tannenberg) G.; m. Judith Harriet Plaut, June 6,1971; children: Sharon, Esther, Eva, Steven. B.A., Yeshiva U., 1967; M.D., Albert Einstein Coll. Medicine, 1971. Cert. Am. Bd. Internal Medicine (subcert. in med. oncology). Intern Bronx Mcpl. Hosp. Ctr., 1971-72; staff assoc. Nat. Cancer Inst., Bethesda, 1972-74; resident Mt. Sinai Hosp., N.Y.C., 1974-75, neoplastic disease fellow, 1975-77; asst. clin. prof. medicine and neoplastic diseases Mt. Sinai Hosp. (Sch. Medicine), 1977—, practice medicine specializing in oncology, N.Y.C., 1977—; cons. Bronx VA Hosp., 1977—. Vice-pres. Congregation Orach Chaim, N.Y.C., 1978—. Served with USPHS, 1972-74. Recipient Upjohn Achievement award Upjohn Co., 1971. Fellow ACP; mem. Am. Soc. Clin. Oncology, Am. Assn. Cancer Research, N.Y. Acad. Scis., AMA. Current Work: Clinical cancer chemotherapy, clinical trials of new anticancer agents. Subspecialties: Oncology; Chemotherapy. Office: Oncology Cons PC 1045 Fifth Ave New York NY 10028

GOLDSMITH, STANLEY JOSEPH, nuclear medicine physician, educator; b. Bklyn., Aug. 17, 1937; s. Jack and May (Greenzweig) G.; m. Miriam Schulman, June 6, 1969; children: Ira, Arthur, Beth, Mark. B.A., Columbia U., 1958; M.D., SUNY-Downstate Med. Ctr., 1962. Diplomate: Am. Bd. Internal Medicine, Am. Bd. Nuclear Medicine. Intern SUNY-Kings County Med. Center, Bklyn., 1962-63, resident, 1965-66, chief resident, 1966-67; fellow in endocrinology Mt. Sinai Hosp., N.Y.C, 1967-68; dir. Mt. Sinai Hosp. (Andre Meyer dept. physics-nuclear medicine), 1973—; research assoc. radioisotope service Bronx (N.Y.) VA Hosp., 1968-69; dir. nuclear medicine, asst. dir. endocrine dept. Nassau County Med. Ctr., East Meadow, N.Y., 1969-73; asst. prof. medicine radiology SUNY-Stony Brook Health Sci. Ctr., 1971-73; asst. prof. medicine Mt. Sinai Sch. Medicine, 1973-76, assoc. prof., 1976-84, prof., 1985—; research collborator Brookhaven Nat. Labs., Upton, N.Y., 1971-75; cons. nuclear medicine; cons. dept. health State of N.Y., 1973-77, Health Services Adminstrn., N.Y.C., 1976. Editor-in-chief: Newsline; assoc. editor Jour. Nuclear Medicine; mem. editorial bds.: Am. Jour. Cardiology, 1978-82, Picker Jour. Nuclear Medicine Instrumentation, 1980; reviewer: Israeli Jour. Med. Scis, 1979, Jour. AMA, 1983—. Served to capt. U.S. Army, 1963-65. Fellow Am. Coll. Cardiology, ACP, Am. Coll. Nuclear Physicians (chmn. nuclear med. tech. affairs); mem. AAAS, Am. Fedn. Clin. Research, Endocrine Soc., N.Y. Acad. Scis., Radiol. Soc. N.Am., Soc. Nuclear Medicine (trustee 1982-85, pres. 1985-86, sec. Greater N.Y. chpt. 1975-78, pres. 1979-80, mem. nuclear med. tech. cert. bd. 1979-81). Current Work: Radionuclidic and NMR quantitation of organ function; quantitative analysis of medical diagnosis and management. Subspecialties: Nuclear medicine; Internal medicine. Home: 72 Ivy Way Port Washington NY 11050 Office: Mt Sinai Med Center One Gustave L Levy Pl New York NY 10029

GOLDSMITH, WILLIAM ALEE, environmental engineer; b. Memphis, Nov. 5, 1941; s. Jack Gene and Louise Elizabeth (Alston) G.; m. LaVance Davis, June 1, 1965; children: Jack Gregory, William Vance, Lara Ellen. B.S., Miss. State U., 1964, M.S., 1966; Ph.D., U. Fla., 1968. San. engr. U.S. EPA, Dallas, 1971-73; asst. prof. U. So. Miss., Hattiesburg, 1973-74; staff mem. Los Alamos Sci. Lab., 1974-75; research staff mem. Oak Ridge Nat. Lab., 1975-81, remedial action survey and certification activities program mgr., 1981-82; engring. specialist Bechtel Nat., Inc., Oak Ridge, 1982—. Treas. Covenant Presbyn. Ch., Oak Ridge, 1978; stewardship chmn. First United Meth. Ch., 1981—. Served to capt. AUS, 1969-71. Mem. Am. Chem. Soc., Am. Nuclear Soc., AAAS, Health Physics Soc. (councilman East Tenn. chpt. 1979-82), N.Y. Acad. Scis., Sigma Xi, Tau Beta Pi, Phi Kappa Phi. Developer technique for Ac Measurement, mobile gamma-ray van technique for Ra measurement. Current Work: Development of environmental health physics monitoring programs and techniques, development of monitoring techniques and instrumentation for radon dosimetry. Subspecialties: Nuclear fission; Environmental engineering. Office: Bechtel Nat Inc 800 Oak Ridge Turnpike Oak Ridge TN 37830

GOLDSTEIN, CHARLES M., information scientist. Lead info. tech. Lister Hill Nat. Ctr. for Biomed. Communications, Nat. Library of Medicine, Bethesda, Md. Subspecialty: Information systems (Information science). Office: Lister Hill Nat Ctr for Biomed Communications 8600 Rockville Pike Bethesda MD 20209

GOLDSTEIN, DAVID ARTHUR, biophysicist, medical educator, computer systems design consultant; b. Rochester, N.Y., Nov. 8, 1934; s. Jacob David and Elizabeth (Brown) G.; m. Marie Elaine Nardone, May 25, 1969; 1 son, David James. A.B. in Physics, Harvard Coll., Cambridge, Mass., 1956; M.D., Harvard Med. Sch., Boston, 1960. Research fellow bio-physics lab. Harvard Med. Sch., 1960-62, research assoc., 1964-65; cons. mathematician NIMH, Bethesda, Md., 1963-64; asst. prof. radiation biology and biophysics U. Rochester Med. Sch., N.Y., 1965-68, assoc. prof. biomath. 1969-74, assoc. prof. radiation biology and biophysics, 1968—, dir. Med. Ctr. computing, 1975-77, assoc. chmn. dept. radiation biology and biophysics, 1980-85; chmn. bd., cons. Advanced Systems Labs., Lima, N.Y., 1982—. Contbr. articles to profl. jours. Treas. Southeast Pittsford Homeowners Assn., N.Y., 1970, Stormers Soccer Club, Pittsford, 1983—. Served as surgeon USPHS, 1963-64. Grantee AEC, ERDA, NSF, NIH, Dept. Energy, 1985-87. Mem. AAAS, Biophys. Soc., N.Y. Acad. Sci., The Harvey Soc. Current work: Theoretical analysis of protein structure/function, especially cytochromes; mathematical models of DNA sequence divergence. Subspecialties: Biophysics (biology); Molecular biology. Home: 75 Deer Creek Rd Pittsford NY 14534 Office: Dept Radiation Biology and Biophysics U Rochester Med Ctr Box RBB Rochester NY 14642

GOLDSTEIN, DAVID JOEL, medical geneticist, educator; b. N.Y.C., June 25, 1947; s. Milton S. and Thelma (Weinman) G.; children: Benjamin Avry Brimer, Philip Jon. B.A., Franklin and Marshall Coll., 1969; M.D., U. Tenn., 1973, Ph.D., 1975. Resident in pediatrics Mayo Grad. Sch. Medicine, Rochester, Minn., 1975-78; fellow in human genetics U. Pa., Phila., 1978-81; asst. prof. med. genetics Ind. U. Med. Sch., Indpls., 1981—, also research. Contbr. articles to profl. jours. Recipient Quigley award in physiology U. Tenn. Med. Sch., 1973; NIH fellow in genetics, 1978. Mem. Am. Soc. Human Genetics, Soc. for Neurosci., AAAS. Current Work: Biochemical genetics of essential hypertension, monoclonal antibodies. Subspecialties: Genetics and genetic engineering (medicine); Pediatrics. Office: Dept Med Genetics Ind U Med Sch Indianapolis IN 46223

GOLDSTEIN, HENRY, research chemist; b. N.Y.C., Aug. 16, 1939; s. Joseph and Mae (Prager) G.; m. Susan Roslyn Levy, Aug. 18, 1963; children—Eric Andrew, Meredith Elise, Amy Jo. B.A., NYU, 1961; M.S., Tulane U., 1965; Ph.D., U. Conn., 1970. Research chemist, project leader Amstar Corp., N.Y.C., 1970-76; from group leader to research mgr. Miller Brewing Co., Milw., 1976—. Contbr. articles to profl. jours. Patentee in field. Fellow Am. Inst. Chemists; mem. Am. Chem. Soc., Am. Soc. Brewing Chemists. Current work: Research in field of physical organic chemistry of hydrazines and nitrosamines; organic chemistry of hop compounds. Subspecialties: Organic chemistry; Analytical chemistry. Office: Miller Brewing Co 3939 W Highland Blvd Milwaukee WI 53208

GOLDSTEIN, JACK, biochemist, educator; b. Phila., June 24, 1930; s. Max and Sara (Granet) G.; m. Ellen Krueger, July 7, 1967; children: Marcus, Andrea, Elissa. B.S., Bklyn. Coll. Pharmacy, 1952; M.N.S., Cornell U., 1957, Ph.D., 1959. Vis. investigator USPHS research assoc., asst. prof. Rockefeller U., N.Y.C., 1959-66; investigator, head cell biochemistry lab. L.F. Kimball Research Inst., N.Y. Blood Ctr., N.Y.C., 1966—; vis. assoc. prof. Yale U., New Haven, 1966-67; assoc. prof. biochemistry Cornell U. Med. Coll., N.Y.C., 1968—. Contbr. articles to profl. jours. Served with M.C. U.S. Army, 1953-55. Nat. Cancer Inst. fellow, 1959-61; NIH grantee, 1966-77; Office Naval Research grantee, 1979—; Greater N.Y. Blood Program grantee, 1978—. Mem. Am. Soc. Biol. Chemists, Am. Soc. Cell Biology, Harvey Soc., Sigma Xi. Patentee enzymatic conversion of red cells for transfusion. Current Work: Enzymatic conversion of type A and B Erythrocytes to type O; isolation and characterizations of biological response modifiers. Subspecialties: Biochemistry (medicine); Hematology. Office: New York Blood Center 310 E 67th St New York NY 10021

GOLDSTEIN, JEFFREY MARC, psychopharmacologist; b. Bronx, N.Y., May 9, 1947; s. Joseph and Shirley (Scher) G.; m. Robin; children: Kevin Allen, Neal David. B.S., Colo. State U., 1970; M.S., Seton Hall U., 1973; Ph.D., U. Del., 1980. Assoc. scientist dept. pharmacology Schering Corp., Bloomfield, N.J., 1970-76; sr. research pharmacologist, biomed. research dept. ICI Americas, Inc., Wilmington, Del., 1976—. Contbr. articles to profl. jours. Mem. AAAS, N.Y. Acad. Sci., Am. Soc. Pharmacology and Explt. Therapeutics, Soc. Neuroscience, Brit. Brain Research Soc., European Brain and Behavior Soc., Sigma Xi. Current Work: Psychotherapeutic agents, mechanism and action. Subspecialties: Neuropharmacology; Psychopharmacology. Home: 4 Curry Ct Wilmington DE 19810 Office: Stuart Pharms Div ICI Americas Inc Wilmington DE 19897

GOLDSTEIN, JOSEPH LEONARD, physician, genetics educator; b. Sumter, S.C., Apr. 18, 1940; s. Isadore E. and Fannie A. G. B.S., Washington and Lee U., Lexington, Va., 1962; M.D., U. Tex., Dallas, 1966; D.Sc. (hon.), U. Chgo., 1982, Rensselaer Poly. Inst., 1982. Intern, then resident in medicine Mass. Gen. Hosp., Boston, 1966-68; clin. assoc. NIH, 1968-70; postdoctoral fellow U. Wash., Seattle, 1970-72; mem. faculty U. Tex. Health Scis. Center, Dallas, 1972—, Paul J. Thomas prof. medicine, chmn. dept. molecular genetics, 1977—; Harvey Soc. lectr., 1977; mem. sci. rev. bd. Howard Hughes Med. Inst., 1978-84, med. adv. bd., 1985—; non-resident fellow The Salk Inst., 1983—. Co-author: The Metabolic Basis of Inherited Disease, 5th edit., 1983; editorial bd.: Jour. Biol. Chemistry, 1981-85, Cell, 1983—, Jour. Clin. Investigation, 1977-82, Ann. Rev. Genetics, 1980-85, Arteriosclerosis, 1981—, Sci., 1985—. Recipient Heinrich-Wieland prize, 1974, Pfizer award in enzyme chemistry Am. Chem. Soc., 1976; Passano award Johns Hopkins U., 1978; Gairdner Found. award, 1981; award in biol. and med. scis. N.Y. Acad. Scis., 1981; Lita Annenberg Hazen award, 1982; Research Achievement award Am. Heart Assn., 1984; Louisa Gross Horwitz award, 1984; 3M Life Scis. award, 1984; Nobel prize, 1985. Mem. Nat. Acad. Scis. (Lounsbery award 1979), Am. Acad. Arts and Scis., Assn. Am. Physicians, Am. Soc. Clin. Investigation (pres. 1985-86), Am. Soc. Human Genetics, Am. Soc. Biol. Chemists, A.C.P., Am. Fedn. Clin. Research, Phi Beta Kappa, Alpha Omega Alpha. Subspecialty: Genetics and genetic engineering (medicine). Home: 3730 Holland Ave Apt H Dallas TX 75219 Office: 5323 Harry Hines Blvd Dallas TX 75235

GOLDSTEIN, LESTER, biology educator; b. Bklyn., June 28, 1924; s. Charles and Gussie (Silverman) G.; children: Natasha, Nina. A.B., Bklyn. Coll., 1948; Ph.D., U. Pa., 1953. Instr. biology Queens Coll., 1950; teaching asst. zoology U. Pa., Phila., 1950-51, univ. fellow, 1951-52, USPHS predoctoral fellow, 1952-53; USPHS postdoctoral fellow U. Calif.-Berkeley, 1953-55; Damon Runyon fellow U. Calif.-San Francisco, 1955-56; research assoc. U. Calif. Med. Ctr., San Francisco, 1955-59; assoc. prof. biology U. Pa., Phila., 1959-64, prof., 1964-67, Inst. Devel. Biology, U. Colo., Boulder, 1967-68, prof. cell biology, 1968-82; ACS research scholar dept. genetics U. Wash., Seattle, 1977-78; prof., dir. Thomas Hunt Morgan Sch. Biol. Scis., U. Ky., Lexington, 1982—. Cons. editor, McGraw Hill, 1970-80; editor: Acad. Press, 1975-80, Springer Verlag, 1981—; contbr. articles to profl. jours. Served with U.S. Army, 1943-46. Lalor Found. fellow Haverford Coll., summer 1959; UPSPHS spl. fellow U. Colo. Med. Ctr., Denver, 1965-66; recipient Disting. Alumnus award Bklyn. Coll., 1975; Am. Cancer Soc. scholar, 1977; U. Colo. faculty fellow, 1977. Fellow AAAS; mem. Genetics Soc. Am., Am. Soc. Cell Biology (council 1970-72), AAAS. Subspecialty: Cell biology. Office: Morgan Sch Biol Scis Univ Ky Lexington KY 40506

GOLDSTEIN, MARK KINGSTON LEVIN, high technology executive, researcher; b. Burlington, Vt., Aug. 22, 1941; s. Harold Meyer Levin and Roberta (Butterfield) G.; m. Kyoko Matsubara, Mar. 8, 1985. B.S. in Chemistry, U. Vt., 1964; Ph.D. in Chemistry, U. Miami-Coral Gables, 1971. Pres. IBR, Inc., Coral Gables, Fla., 1970-74; group leader Brookhaven Nat. Lab., Upton, N.Y., 1974-77; sr. researcher East-West Ctr., Honolulu, 1977-79; sr. tech. advisor JGC Corp., Tokyo, 1979-81; pres., chmn. bd. Quantum Group, Inc., La Jolla, Calif., 1981—; exec. dir. Magnatek, Inc., Brotas, Brazil, 1982—. Contbr. articles to profl. jours.; contbr. poetry to mag. NSF fellow, 1964, 65. Mem. Am. Nuclear Soc., Am. Chem. Soc., AAAS. Club: Hawaii Yacht (Honolulu). Patentee in field. Current Work: Gas Safety, appliance controls, carbon monoxide detectors, health effects of toxic materials, nuclear waste management, forensic science and engineering, fire protection, energy, toxic gas detection and purification. Subspecialties: Physical chemistry; Nuclear fission. Office: Quantum Group Inc 11211 Sorrento Valley Rd Suite D San Diego CA 92121

GOLDSTEIN, MURRAY, osteopathic physician, government official; b. N.Y.C., Oct. 13, 1925; s. Israel and Yetta (Zeigen) G.; m. Mary Susan Michael, June 13, 1957; children—Patricia Sue, Barbara Jean. A.B. in Biology, N.Y. U., 1947; D.O., Des Moines Still Coll. Osteo Medicine, 1950; M.P.H. in Epidemiology, U. Calif., 1959; D.Sc. (hon.), Kirksville Coll. Osteo. Medicine, 1966; D.D.L. (hon.), N.Y. Inst. Tech., 1982. Intern Des Moines Still Coll. Osteo Medicine Hosp., 1950-51, resident in internal medicine, 1951-53; commd. sr. asst. surgeon USPHS, 1953, advanced through ranks to asst. surgeon gen., 1980; asst. chief grants and tng. br. Nat. Heart Inst., NIH, Bethesda, Md., 1953-58; asst. chief research grants rev. br., dir. epidemiology and biometry tng. grant program div. research grants NIH, Bethesda, 1956-60; acting sect. chief Bur. Acute Communicable Disease, Calif. Dept. Public Health, Berkeley, 1958; chief spl. projects br. Nat. Inst. Neurol. Diseases and Blindness NIH, Bethesda, 1960-61; dir. extramural programs Nat. Inst. Neurol. and Communicative Disorders and Stroke, NIH, Bethesda, 1961-76, dir. stroke and trauma program, 1976-78; dep. dir. NINCDS-NIH, 1978-82, dir., 1982—; vis. scientist Mayo Clinic and Grad. Sch., Rochester, Minn., 1967-68; v.p. Eisenhower Inst. for Stroke Research; cons. WHO; clin. prof. medicine N.Y. Coll. Osteo Medicine, N.Y. Inst. Tech.; trustee Am. Osteo. Coll. Public Health and Preventive Medicine; mem. med. adv. bd. Am. Parkinson's Disease Assn.; bd. dirs. United Cerebral Palsy Research and Edn. Found. Editorial bd.: Osteo. Annals, 1973—, Internat. Jour. Neurology, 1980—, Jour. Neuroepidemiology. Served with U.S. Army, 1943-45. Decorated Silver Star, Purple Heart.; Recipient Meritorious Service medal USPHS, 1971, Disting. Service medal USPHS, 1983. Fellow Am. Public Health Assn., Am. Heart Assn. (liaison mem. exec. com. Council on Stroke, asso. editor Stroke, Jour. Cerebral Circulation 1976—), Am. Coll. Osteo. Internists (hon.), Am. Acad. Neurology; mem. Am. Neurol. Assn. (2d v.p., cert. merit), Am. Osteo. Assn., AAAS, Assn. Research in Nervous and Mental Disease, Soc. Neurosci., Am. Osteo. Coll. Public Health and Preventive Medicine, World Fedn. Neurology. Subspecialties: Neurology; Epidemiology. Office: 9000 Rockville Pike Bethesda MD 20205

GOLDSTEIN, NORMAN, dermatologist; b. Bklyn., July 14, 1934; s. Joseph Harry and Bertha (Doctoroff) G.; m. Ramsay Goldstein, Feb. 14, 1980; children: Richard David, Heidi Lee. B.A., Columbia U., 1955; M.D., SUNY, Bklyn., 1959. Diplomate: Am. Bd.Dermatology. Intern Maimonides Hosp., N.Y.C., 1959-60; dermatology resident skin and cancer unit N.Y.U. Med. Center, 1960-61, Bellevue Hosp., 1961-62; partner Honolulu Med. Group (pvt. practice dermatology), 1972—; assoc. clin. prof. dermatology U. Hawaii, 1973—; bd. dirs. Honolulu Med. Group Research/Edn. Found., 1970—; task force mem., adv. council Am. Acad. Dermatology Biomed. Communications Network, 1979—; tech. adv. com. Cancer Center Hawaii; exec. bd. Physicians Exchange; adv. Nat. Skin Cancer Found.; trustee Dermatology Found., 1979-82. Contbr. articles to profl. jours. Active Hawaii Council on Culture and Arts; trustee Hawaii Jewish Fedn., 1976-79, 82—, Historic Hawaii Found.; mem. Hawaii Visitors Bur., Downtown Improvement Assn.; pres. Friends of the Alexander Young Bldg., 1980. Served with U.S. Army, 1963-64. Decorated Army Commendation medal. Mem. AMA, Soc. Investigative Dermatology, Internat. Soc. Tropical Dermatology, Assn. Mil. Dermatologists, Hawaii Dermatol. Soc. (pres. 1970-72), Honolulu County Med. Soc. (bd. govs. 1978-80), Hawaii Med. Assn., Micronesian Med. Assn., Hawaii Pub. Health Assn., AAAS, Am. Soc. Photobiology, Environ. Health and Light Research Inst., Am. Assn. Clin. Oncology, Pacific Dermatol. Assn., Hawaii Assn. for Physicians for Idemnification (dir. 1977), Hawaii Planned Parenthood, Pacific Health Research Inst., Biologic Photographic Assn., Internat. Solar Energy Soc., Photographic Soc.Am., Health Scis. Communications Assn. Clubs: Outrigger Canoe, Waikiki, Plaza, Honolulu, Honolulu Club. Lodge: Rotary. Subspecialties: Dermatology; Medical photography.

GOLDSTEIN, PAUL, marine engineering company executive, consultant; b. N.Y.C., Dec. 2, 1934; s. Joseph and Gertrude (Myers) G.; m. Susan Jennings Hough (div.); 3 daus. B.S. in Marine Engring., U.S. Mcht. Marine Acad., 1956. Test engr. Gen. Electric Co., Schenectady, 1956-57; marine engr. various cos., 1959; research project engr. Foster Wheeler Corp., N.Y.C., 1959-65; research project mgr. CE Inc., Windsor, Conn., 1965-68; sr. v.p., gen. mgr., project mgr. Superfund div. NUS corp., Pitts., Arlington, Va., 1968—, cons. environ. engr. Contbr. articles to profl. jours.; editorial bd.: ASME Handbook on Water in Thermal Power Systems. Chmn. twp. planning commn., cognizant exec. minority scholarship program, Pitts. Served to lt. (j.g.) USNR, 1957-59. Recipient Am. Seamen's Friend Soc. award, 1956. Mem. ASME (Prime Movers award 1968), TAPPI, ASTM, Engring. Soc. Western Pa. (meml. scholarship com., internat. water conf. award of merit 1980), Water Pollution Control Fedn. Patentee in field. Current Work: Hazardous waste management, water pollution control, thermal power system water technology. Subspecialties: Environmental engineering; Chemical engineering. Home: RD #2 Prosperity PA 15329 Office: NUS Corp Park West 2 Cliffmine Rd Pittsburgh PA 15275

GOLDSTEIN, RICHARD JAY, engineer, educator; b. N.Y.C., Mar. 27, 1928; s. Henry and Rose (Steierman) G.; m. Anita Nancy Klein, Sept. 5, 1963; children: Arthur Sander, Jonathan Jacob, Benjamin Samuel, Naomi Sarith. B.M.E., Cornell U., 1948; M.S.M.E., U. Minn., 1950, M.S. in Physics, 1951, Ph.D., 1959. Instr. U. Minn., 1948-51, instr., research fellow, 1956-58, mem. faculty, 1961—, prof. mech. engring., 1965—, head dept., 1977—; research engr. Oak Ridge Nat. Lab., 1951-54; asst. prof. Brown U., 1959-61; cons. in field, 1956—; NSF sr. postdoctoral fellow, vis. prof. Cambridge (Eng.) U., 1971-72. Served to 1st lt. AUS, 1954-55. Honeywell fellow, 1955-57; NATO fellow Paris, 1960-61; Lady Davis fellow Technion, Israel, 1976; recipient NASA award tech. innovation, 1977. Fellow ASME (Heat Transfer Meml. award 1978, Centennial medallion 1980); mem. AAAS, Am. Phys. Soc., Nat. Acad. Engring., Minn. Acad. Sci., Am. Soc. Engring. Edn., Sigma Xi, Tau Beta Pi, Pi Tau Sigma. Research, publs. in thermodynamics, fluid mechanics, heat transfer, optical measuring techniques. Subspecialty: Mechanical engineering. Home: 520 Janalyn Circle Golden Valley MN 55416 Office: Dept Mech Engring U Minn Minneapolis MN 55455

GOLDSTEIN, SIDNEY, pharmacologist; b. Phila., Mar. 27, 1932; s. Israel and Gertrude (Stein) G.; m. Janice Levy, June 19, 1955; children: Rhonda, David, Nina. B.Sc., Phila. Coll. Pharmacy, 1954, M.Sc., 1955, D.Sc., 1958. Registered pharmacist. Head antiinflammatory unit Eaton Labs., 1958-59; head cardiovascular unit Lederle Labs., 1959-61; sect. head Nat. Drug Co., 1961-64, dir. pharmacology, 1964-67, dir. devel., 1967-70; sect. head Merrell Dow Pharms. Inc., 1970-72, assoc. group dir. clin. pharmacology, 1972-74, exec. asst. to v.p. research, 1974-76, dir. pharm. scis., 1976-82, U.S. dir. pharm. scis., 1982—; lectr. Rutgers State U., 1963-66, Phila. Coll. Pharmacy, 1967-70; adj. assoc. prof. U. Cin. Sch. Pharmacy, 1984—. Contbr. articles to profl. jours. Vice-pres., sr. adv. B'nai B'rith Youth Orgn., 1978; bd. dirs. Glen Manor Home for the Aged, 1983—. Recipient Bausch and Lomb Sci. award, 1950. Mem. Am. Soc. Pharmacology and Exptl. Therapeutics, Soc. Exptl. Biology and Medicine, Am. Pharm. Assn., Acad. Pharm. Sci., Am. Soc. Clin. Pharmacology and Therapeutics. Jewish. Club: Cresthill Country (Cin.). Lodge: B'nai B'rith. Current Work: Pharmaceutics product devel. Subspecialty: Pharmacology. Home: 259 Compton Rdge Dr Cincinnati OH 45215 Office: 2110 E Galbraith Rd Cincinnati OH 45215

GOLDSTEIN, STEVEN EDWARD, psychologist; b. N.Y.C., Nov. 25, 1948; s. Maurice and Matilda (Weiss) G. B.S., CCNY, 1970, M.S., 1971; Ed.D., U. No. Colo., 1976. Registered sch. psychologist, N.Y. Sch. psychologist Denver pub. schs., 1975; teaching asst. U. No. Colo., Greeley, 1975-76; asst. prof. psychology Northeastern Okla. State U., Tahlequah, 1976-78; psychologist-/dir. inpatient Winnemucca Mental Health Ctr., Nev., 1978-80; psychologist-/dir. tng. Desert Devel. Ctr., Las Vegas, 1980-82; sr. psychologist Las Vegas Mental Health Ctr., 1982—; sec. grad. council CCNY, 1970-71, chmn., 1970-71; tchr./counselor N.Y.C. pub. schs., 1971-74; cons. U.S. Dept. Edn., Region IX, 1981-82. NSF scholar, 1975-76; others. Mem. Am. Psychol. Assn., Biofeedback Soc. Am., Am. Soc. Tng. and Devel., Biofeedback Soc. Nev., Nat. Assn. Sch. Psychologists. Jewish. Current Work: Stress management, biofeedback, values clarification, management training, training the trainer, family/couples counseling. Subspecialties: Behavioral psychology; Stress management. Office: Las Vegas Mental Health Center 6161 W Charleston Blvd Las Vegas NV 89158

GOLDSTINE, HERMAN HEINE, mathematician; b. Chgo., Sept. 13, 1913; s. Isaac Oscar and Bessie (Lipsey) G.; m. Adele Katz, Sept. 15, 1941 (dec. 1964); children—Madlen, Jonathan; m. Ellen Watson, Jan. 8, 1966. B.S., U. Chgo., 1933, M.S., 1934, Ph.D., 1936; Ph.D. honoris causa, U. Lund, Sweden, 1974; D.Sc., Adelphi U., 1978, Amherst Coll., 1978. Engaged as research asst. U. Chgo., 1936-37, instr., 1937-39, U. Mich., 1939-42, asst. prof., 1942-45; asst. project dir., electronic computer project Inst. for Advanced Study, Princeton, 1946-55, acting project dir., 1954-57, permanent mem., 1952—; formerly dir. math. scis. dept. IBM Research, dir. sci. devel. IBM Data Processing Hdqrs., White Plains, N.Y., cons. to dir. research IBM; now IBM fellow; cons. various govt., mil. agys.; mem. report rev. com. Nat. Acad. Scis.; Mem. vis. com., phys. sci. div. U. Chgo. Author: A History of the Calculus of Variations from the 17th through the 19th Century. Served as lt. col. AUS, World War II. Recipient book award in sci. Phi Beta Kappa, 1973, U. Chgo. Alumni Achievement award, 1974, Nat. Medal of Sci., 1985. Mem. Am. Math. Soc., Am. Philos. Soc. (exec. officer), Nat. Acad. Sci. Math. Assn. Am., Phi Beta Kappa, Sigma Xi. Current Work: Mathematics of computer science and work of John and James Bernoulli in the calculus of variations. Subspecialties: Theoretical computer science; Applied mathematics. Office: Inst Advanced Study Princeton NJ 08540

GOLDWASSER, EUGENE, biochemist, educator; b. N.Y.C., Oct. 14, 1922; s. Herman and Anna (Ackerman) G.; m. Florence Cohen, Dec. 22, 1949 (dec.); children—Thomas Alan, Matthew Laurence, James Herman. B.S., U. Chgo., 1943, Ph.D., 1950. Am. Cancer Soc. fellow U. Copenhagen, Denmark, 1950-52; research asso. U. Chgo., 1952-61, mem. faculty, 1962—, prof. biochemistry, 1963—, chmn. com. on developmental biology. Served with AUS, 1944-46. Guggenheim fellow U. Oxford (Eng.), 1966-67. Mem. Am. Soc. Biol. Chemists, Biochem. Soc., AAAS, Internat. Soc. Developmental Biologists, Internat. Soc. Exptl. Hematology, Endocrine Soc., Sigma Xi. Research biochemistry red blood cell formation. Subspecialty: Developmental biology. Home: 5727 Dorchester Ave Chicago IL 60637 Office: Dept Biochemistry U Chgo Chicago IL 60637

GOLDYNE, MARC ELLIS, dermatology educator, researcher; b. San Francisco, Oct. 15, 1944; s. Alfred Josef and Helen Sandra (Newman) G.; m. Gail Anne Sokolow, Sept. 5, 1971; children: Serena, Avram. A.B., U. Calif.-Berkeley, 1966; M.D., U. Calif.-San Francisco, 1970; Ph.D., U. Minn.-Rochester, 1975. Intern, French Hosp. Med. Center, San Francisco, 1970-71; resident in dermatology Mayo Clinic, Rochester, Minn., 1971-75; fellow in dermatology Mayo Grad. Sch. Medicine, 1971-75; instr. Mayo Med. Sch., 1974-75; research fellow Karolinska Inst., Stockholm, 1975-78; assoc. prof. dermatology and medicine U. Calif.-San Francisco, 1978—; head dermatol. research San Francisco Gen. Hosp., 1978-80; asst. chief dept dermatology San Francisco VA Hosp., 1985—. Fellow Am. Acad. Dermatology; mem. Soc. Investigative Dermatology (dir. 1972-74), Western Regional Soc. Investigative Dermatology (pres. 1983-84), Am. Fedn. Clin. Research, Am. Assn. Immunologists, Soc. Exptl. Biology Medicine. Current Work: Prostaglandin and related eicosanoid metabolism by human monocytes in relation to immune response and host tumor defenses. Subspecialties: Dermatology; Biochemistry (medicine). Office: University of California 400 Parnassus Ave San Francisco CA 94143

GOLIGHTLY, DANOLD WAYNE, research chemist; b. Cape Girardeau, Mo., Apr. 12, 1941; s. Jay Cee and Dorothy Rosina (Koch) G.; m. Marilyn Victoria Brodine, May 2, 1969; 1 child, Yvonne Marie. A.B., Southeast Mo. State U., 1962; M.S., Iowa State U., 1965, Ph.D., 1967. Postdoctoral assoc. Materials Research Lab., U. Ill.-Urbana, 1967-69; stagier etranger Centre d'Etudes Nucleaires de Grenoble, France, 1969-70; postdoctoral assoc., Iowa State U., Ames, 1970-71; research chemist Nat. Bur. Standards, Gaithersburg, Md., 1971-73; U.S. Geol. Survey, Reston, Va., 1973—. Contbr. articles to profl. jours. Patentee in field. Mem. Am. Chem. Soc., Soc. Applied Spectroscopy (Balt.-Washington sect. pres. 1984-85), Am. Optical Soc. Current work: Spectroradiometry of atomic sources, laser-induced fluorescence of ions in crystalline phases, analysis methods by inductively coupled plasma spectrometry. Subspecialty: Analytical chemistry. Office: US Geol Survey 957 National Ctr Reston VA 22092

GOLL, DARREL EUGENE, biochemist, educator; b. Garner, Iowa, Apr. 19, 1936; s. Leon Oscar and Maire Eleanor (Nonnweiler) G.; m. Rosalie Elaine Bullock, Jan. 11, 1958; children: Laurene Elaine, Jeffrey Eugene, Kathleen Kay. B.S., Iowa State U., 1957, M.S., 1959; Ph.D., U. Wis., 1962. Asst. prof. depts. animal sci. and food tech. Iowa State U., Ames, 1962-65, assoc. prof. depts. animal sci., food tech., and biochemistry and biophysics, 1965-70, prof., 1970-76; prof. depts. biochemistry and nutrition and food sci. U. Ariz., Tucson, 1976—, head dept. nutrition and food sci., 1976-84; mem. com. on animal products, adv. bd. on mil. personnel supplies NRC, 1975-78; ad hoc mem. molecular cytology study sect. NIH, 1979—; mem. tech. adv. peer panel for grants in food quality and safety U.S. Dept. Agr., 1982. Contbr. chpts. to books, articles to profl. jours. NIH spl. fellow UCLA, 1966-67; NIH spl. fellow Oxford (Eng.) U., 1972; NSF scholar, 1974. Mem. AAAS, Am. Chem. Soc., Am. Meat Sci. Assn. (Disting. Meats Research award 1972), Am. Soc. for Animal Sci. (Meats Research award 1974), Am. Soc. Biol. Chemists, Biophys. Soc., Inst. Food Technologists (Samuel Cate Prescott award 1971), Nutrition Today Soc., Phi Kappa Phi. Presbyterian. Current Work: Biochemistry and metabolic turnover of contractile proteins, muscle growth, role of interactions of contractile proteins on their functions in motility and development, properties of proteolytic enzymes involved in metabolic turnover of contractile proteins. Subspecialties: Biochemistry (biology); Biophysics (biology). Office: Muscle Biology Group U Ariz Tucson AZ 85721

GOLLAHALLI, SUBRAMANYAM RAMAPPA, mechanical engineer; b. Sadali, India, Nov. 26, 1942; s. Bagepalli and Nagalakshamma (Rao) Ramappa; m. Rangamani Gollahalli, Dec. 25, 1967; children: Suma, Anil. B.E., Mysore U., 1963; M.E., Indian Inst. Sci., 1965; M.A.Sc., U. Waterloo, Ont., Can., 1970, Ph.D., 1973. Registered profl. engr., Okla. Lectr. Indian Inst. Sci., 1965-68; research and devel. engr. John Fowler's Ltd., Bangalore, India, 1968; research asst. prof., asst. prof. U. Waterloo, 1973-76; asst. prof. U. Okla., Norman, 1976-80, assoc. prof., 1980-84, prof., 1984—. Contbr. articles to profl. jours. Recipient Robert Angus medal Can. Soc. Mech. Engrs., 1978; Regents award superior teaching U. Okla., 1983, Haliburton Disting. Lectr. award, 1984. Mem. ASME, AIAA, Soc. Auto. Engrs. (Ralph Teetor award 1978), Combustion Inst., Okla. Acad. Sci., Sigma Xi, Pi Tau Sigma. Current Work: Combustion of low BTU gases, soot production in synthetic fuel flames, emulsified fuel combustion, sulfur oxide production in flames. Subspecialties: Combustion processes; Fuels. Home: 4105 Morrison Ct Norman OK 73069 Office: Sch Aerospace Mech Nuclear Engring U Okla Norman OK 73019

GOLLOBIN, LEONARD PAUL, chemical engineer, research/engineering company executive; b. N.Y.C., July 2, 1928; s. Morris and Jennie (Levine) G.; m. Charlotte Weissman, Jan. 21, 1951; children: Michael L., Susan D. B.Chem. Engring., CUNY, 1951; M.S., Kans. State U.-Manhattan, 1952; SCMP, Harvard U., 1975. Design engr. Foster Wheeler Corp., N.Y.C., 1952-55; mfg. engr. Gen. Electric Co., Waterford, N.Y., 1955-58; program dir. ORI, Inc., Silver Spring, Md., 1958-63; pres. Presearch, Inc., Fairfax, Va., 1963—; sec., dir. Petroleum Ops. Support Services Inc., Houston, 1981—. Bd. dirs. Cultural Alliance Greater Washington, 1980—. Mem. Nat. Security Indsl. Assn. (trustee 1980—, antisubmarine warfare exec. com. 1982—), Naval Undersea Warfare Found. Mus. (v.p. 1982—). Club: Kenwood (Bethesda, Md.). Current Work: Major system planning and resources allocation. Subspecialties: Systems engineering; Operations research (mathematics). Home: 6710 Bradley Blvd Bethesda MD 20817 Office: Presearch Inc 8500 Executive Park Ave Fairfax VA 22031

GOLOMB, FREDERICK MARTIN, surgeon, educator; b. N.Y.C., Dec. 18, 1924; s. Jacob Jay and Hannah (Loewy) G.; m. Joan Ellen Schneider, Nov. 28, 1954; children—James, Susan. B.S., Yale U., 1945; M.D., U. Rochester, 1949. Diplomate Am. Bd. Surgery. Intern in surgery Johns Hopkins Hosp., Balt., 1949-50; resident in surgery Bellevue Hosp., N.Y.C., 1950-56; instr. to assoc. prof. NYU Sch. Medicine, N.Y.C., 1956-67, prof. clin. surgery, 1977—; dir. chemo immuno therapy div. tumor service dept. surgery NYU Sch. Medicine, 1967—; chmn. melanoma com. Eastern Coop. Oncology Group, Madison, Wis., 1978-80, co-prin. investigator NYU, 1978—. Contbr. articles to med. lit. Served to capt. M.C., AUS, 1953-54, Korea. Fellow Am. Coll. Surgeons; mem.

Am. Soc. Clin. Oncology (founding), Am. Assn. Cancer Research, N.Y. Cancer Soc. (pres. 1974-75). Current work: Surgical oncology and immunology. Subspecialties: Cancer research (medicine); Oncology. Office: NYU Med Ctr 550 1st Ave New York City NY 10016

GOLOMBEK, MATTHEW PHILIP, geologist, research scientist; b. New Haven, Sept. 20, 1954; s. Martin I. and Sonia (Stambler) G.; m. Connie M. Morgan, Apr. 26, 1980. A.B., Rutgers U., 1976; M.S., U. Mass., 1978, Ph.D., 1981. Research/teaching asst. U. Mass., Amherst, 1976-81; vis. postdoctoral fellow Lunar and Planetary Inst., Houston, 1981-82, vis. scientist, 1982-83; lectr. U. Houston, Clear Lake City, Tex., 1983; sr. scientist Jet Propulsion Lab., Calif. Inst. Tech., Pasadena, 1983-84, mem. tech. staff, 1984—. Contbr. articles and abstracts to profl. jours. Schlumberger scholar Rutgers U., 1975-76; planetary structure and Western U.S. tectonics grantee NASA, 1983—. Mem. Am. Geophys. Union, Geol. Soc. Am. Current work: Structure and tectonics of grabens and rifts on the earth, planets and satellites, planetary geologic problems, NASA-geodynamics-global positioning system applications, Caribbean. Subspecialties: Tectonics; Planetology. Home: 4919 Crown Ave La Canada Flintridge CA 91011 Office: Jet Propulsion Lab MS 183-501 4800 Oak Grove Dr Pasadena CA 91109

GOLTZ, ROBERT WILLIAM, physician, educator; b. St. Paul, Sept. 21, 1923; s. Edward Victor and Clare (O'Neill) G.; m. Patricia Ann Sweeney, Sept. 27, 1945; children: Leni, Paul Robert. B.S., U. Minn., 1943, M.D., 1945. Diplomate: Am. Bd. Dermatology (pres. 1975-76). Intern Ancker Hosp., St. Paul, 1944-45; resident in dermatology Mpls. Gen. Hosp., 1945-46, 48-49, U. Minn. Hosp., 1949-50; practice medicine specializing in dermatology, Mpls., 1950-65; clin. instr. U. Minn. Grad. Sch., 1950-58, clin. asst. prof., 1958-60, clin. asso. prof., 1960-65, prof., head dept. dermatology, 1971-85; prof. dermatology, head div. dermatology U. Colo. Med. Sch., Denver, 1965-71; prof. div. dermatology U. Calif.-San Diego, 1985—. Editorial bd.: Archives of Dermatology; editor: Dermatology Digest. Served from 1st lt. to capt., M.C. U.S. Army, 1946-48. Mem. Am. Dermatol. Assn. (dir. 1976—; pres. 1985-86), Am. Soc. Dermatopathologists (pres. 1981), Am. Dermatology Soc. Allergy and Immunology (pres. 1981), AMA (chmn. sect. on dermatology 1973-75), Dermatology Found. (past dir.), Minn. Dermatol. Soc., Soc. Investigative Dermatology (pres. 1972-73), Histochem. Soc., Am. Acad. Dermatology (pres. 1978-79, past dir.), Brit. Assn. Dermatology (hon.), Chilean Dermatology Soc. (hon.), Colombian Dermatol. Soc. (corr. mem.), Can. Dermatol. Soc. (hon. mem.), Pacific Dermatol. Soc. (hon.-mem.), S. African Dermatol. Soc. (hon. mem.), Rocky Mountain Dermatol. Soc., Chgo. Dermatol. Soc., Assn. Profs. Dermatology (sec.-treas. 1970-72, pres. 1973-74). Current Work: Dermatopathology, immunopathology of skin disorders. Subspecialties: Dermatology; Pathology (medicine). Home: 2234 Lee Ave N Minneapolis MN 55422 Office: Div Dermatology U Calif-San Diego 225 Dickinson St San Diego CA

GOLUB, ELLIS ECKSTEIN, biochemist; b. N.Y.C., Nov. 1, 1942; s. Harry Eckstein and Nancy (Spiegel) Golub; m. Linda Bender, Oct. 15, 1964; children—Michael, Daniel, Caryn. B.A., Brandeis U., 1963; Ph.D., Tufts U., 1969. Research fellow Calif. Inst. Tech., Pasadena, 1969-72; research assoc. U. Conn. Health Ctr., Farmington, 1972-77; asst. prof. biochemistry U. Pa., Phila., 1977-84, assoc. prof., 1984—. Mem. Am. Soc. Biol. Chemists, Am. Chem. Soc., N.Y. Acad. Scis. Democrat. Jewish. Current work: Calcification of bone and cardiovascular bioprosthetic devices; calcium transport and binding; salivary protera function; application of computers to biochemistry. Subspecialties: Biochemistry (biology); Biochemical computing. Home: 202 Drakes Drum Dr Bryn Mawr PA 19010 Office: Sch Dental Medicine U Pa 4001 Spruce St Philadelphia PA 19104

GOLUB, LORNE MALCOLM, oral biology and pathology/dentistry educator, researcher; b. Winnipeg, Man., Can., Jan. 13, 1941; came to U.S., 1973; s. Sydney Alexander and Edith (Simovitch) G.; m. Bonny Louise Moss, Aug. 2, 1964; children: Marlo Frances, Michael Benjamin. D.M.D., U. Man., Winnipeg, 1963, M.Sc., 1965; cert. in periodontology, Harvard U., 1968. Postdoctoral fellow Harvard U. Sch. Dental Medicine, Boston, 1965-68; assoc. prof. oral biology U. Man., 1968-70, assoc. prof. periodontics, 1970-73; assoc. prof. oral biology and pathology SUNY-Stony Brook, 1973-77, prof. oral biology, 1977—; cons. in field; mem. sci. adv. com. Center for Oral Health Research, U. Pa., 1982—. Contbr. numerous articles to profl. jours.; editorial rev. bd. Jour. Dental Research, 1977-84, Jour. Peridontal Research, 1985—. Mem. Hebrew sch. com. Temple Beth Sholom, Smithtown, N.Y., 1982—. Med. Research Council Can. postdoctoral fellow, 1966-68; NIH grantee, 1974—; N.Y. Diabetes Assn. grantee, 1976-78; Kroc Found. grantee, 1981-84. Mem. Am. Acad. Periodontology, Internat. Assn. Dental Research, Internat. Group Periodontal Research, AAAS, Omega Kappa Upsilon. Jewish. Patentee in field. Current Work: Gingival collagen metabolism; reduction of excessive collagenolytic enzyme activity by chemo theraphy; leucocyte dysfunctions in chemotaxis and neutral protease activity during diabetes mellitus; gingival crevicular fluid; relationship of these to periodontal disease. Subspecialties: Periodontics; Oral biology. Home: 29 Whitney Gate Smithtown NY 11787 Office: Sch Dental Medicine SUNY Stony Brook NY 11794

GOMER, ROBERT, scientist; b. Vienna, Austria, Mar. 24, 1924; m. Anne Olah, 1955; children: Richard, Maria. B.A., Pomona Coll., 1944; Ph.D. in Chemistry, U. Rochester, 1949; AEC fellow chemistry, Harvard, 1949-50. Instr. dept. chemistry and James Franck Inst. U. Chgo., 1950-51, asst. prof., 1951-54, asso. prof., 1954-58, prof., 1958—, William Eisendrath disting. service prof., 1984—; dir. James Franck Inst. U. Chgo., 1977-83. Bd. dirs. Bull. Atomic Scientists, 1960-84. Served with AUS, 1944-46. Recipient Kendall award in surface chemistry Am. Chem. Soc., 1975; Davisson-Germer prize Am. Phys. Soc., 1981; Sloan fellow, 1958-62; Guggenheim fellow, 1969-70; Bourke lectr. Eng., 1959. Mem. Leopoldina Acad. Scis., Nat. Acad. Scis., Am. Acad. Arts and Sci. Current Work: Chemisorption; surface diffusion; electron stimulated desorption. Subspecialties: Surface chemistry; Condensed matter physics. Home: 4824 Kimbark Ave Chicago IL 60615 Office: 5640 Ellis Ave Chicago IL 60637

GOMOLL, ALLEN WARREN, cardiovascular pharmacologist; b. Chgo., July 10, 1933; s. Herbert F. and Sara E. (Cowan) G.; m. Elaine L. Kirkpatrick, Sept. 17, 1955; children: Gary A., Lisa E. B.S., Coll. Pharmacy, U. Ill., 1955; M.S., Coll. Medicine, 1958, Ph.D., 1961. Registered pharmacist, Ill. Asst. prof. pharmacology Coll. Medicine, U. Ill., 1961-66; group leader cardiovascular pharmacology Mead Johnson, Evansville, Ind., 1966-69, sect. leader cardiovascular pharmacology, 1969-76, prin. research assoc. biol. research, 1976-80, sect. mgr. biol. research, 1980-82; prin. research scientist cardiovascular biology Bristol-Myers Pharm. Research and Devel. Div., Evansville, 1982-84, research fellow, 1984—; lectr. U. Evansville Coll. Nursing, 1977-81. Contbr. articles to profl. jours. Fellow Councils of Circulation and Basic Sci., Am. Heart Assn., Am. Coll. Cardiology; mem. Am. Soc. Pharmacology and Exptl. Therapeutics, AAAS, Soc. Exptl. Biol. Medicine, N.Y. Acad. Scis., Internat. Soc. Heart Research (Am. sect.), Am. Chem. Soc. Presbyterian. Current Work: Antiarrhythmic/cardiac dysfunction drug devel., myocardial ischemic models, renal pharmacology. Subspecialties: Pharmacology; Cardiology. Office: 2404 Pennsylvania Ave Evansville IN 47721

GOMORY, RALPH EDWARD, mathematician, business machines manufacturing company executive; b. Brooklyn Heights, N.Y., May 7, 1929; s. Andrew L. and Marian (Schellenberg) G.; m. Laura Dumper, 1954 (div. 1968); children: Andrew C., Susan S., Stephen H. B.A., Williams Coll., 1950, Sc.D. (hon.), 1973; student, Kings Coll., Cambridge (Eng.) U., 1950-51; Ph.D., Princeton U., 1954. Research assoc. Princeton U., 1951-54, asst. prof. math., Higgins lectr., 1957-59; with IBM, Yorktown Heights, N.Y., 1959—, IBM fellow, dir. math. scis., research div., 1968-70, mem. corp. tech. com., 1970, dir. research, 1970—, v.p., 1973-84, sr. v.p., 1984—, also mem. corp. mgmt. bd.; Andrew D. White prof.-at-large Cornell U., 1970-76; dir. IBM World Trade Ams./Far East Corp., Bank of N.Y.; Mem. vis. com. Sloan Sch. Mgmt., M.I.T., 1971-77; mem. adv. council dept. math. Princeton U., 1974-83, chmn., 1983-85, mem. adv. council Sch. Engring., Stanford U., 1978-85. Univ. trustee, 1985—; Trustee Hampshire Coll., 1977—; mem. governing bd. Nat. Research Council., 1980-83. Served with USN, 1954-57. Recipient Lanchester prize Ops. Research Soc. Am., 1963; John Von Neumann theory prize Ops. Research Soc. Am., 1984; Indsl. Research Inst. Medal, 1985; Harry Goode Meml. award Am. Fedn. Info. Processing Socs., 1984. Fellow Econometric Soc., Am. Acad. Arts and Scis.; mem. Nat. Acad. Scis. (council 1977-78, 80-83), Nat. Acad. Engring. Research integer and linear programming, non-linear differential equations. Subspecialty: Applied mathematics. Home: 260 Douglas Rd Chappaqua NY 10514 Office: IBM Thomas J Watson Research Center Box 218 Yorktown Heights NY 10598

GONCZY, STEPHEN THOMAS, research scientist, manager; b. Tuebingen, Germany, Oct. 8, 1947; s. Stephen I. and Doris E. (Eberhardt) G.; m. Anne Marie Laporte, Apr. 21, 1979; 1 dau., Teresa Elizabeth. B.S.M.E., Marquette U., 1969; Ph.D., Northwestern U., 1978. Research group leader Signal Research Ctr., Des Plaines, Ill., 1978—. Served to maj. U.S. Army, 1969—. NSF grad fellow, 1969; Gen. Electric fellow, 1976. Mem. Am. Soc. for Metals, Am. Ceramic Soc., Materials Research Soc., ASME. Patentee in field. Current Work: New materials for advanced ceramics and advanced heat transfer technology. Subspecialties: Ceramic engineering; Ceramics.

GONZÁLEZ, RICARDO, surgeon, educator, researcher, consultant; b. Buenos Aires, Argentina, June 26, 1943; came to U.S., 1968; naturalized, 1981; s. Salvador María Rafael Juan and Clyde Alcira (Prevettoni) G.; m. María Graciela Estévez, Dec. 16, 1968; children—Diego Andrés, Carlos Ricardo. M.D., U. Buenos Aires, 1965. Diplomate Am. Bd. Urology. Med. fellow U. Minn., Mpls., 1968-74, instr., 1974-76; asst. prof., 1976-78; assoc. prof., 1978-84, prof., 1985—, dir. pediatric urology 1981—. Contbr. articles to profl. publs., Nat. Kidney Found. fellow, 1974-76. Fellow Am. Acad. Pediatrics; mem. Am. Urol. Assn., Argentina Urol. Assn. (corr.), Argentine Urol. Confedn. (hon.), Mex. Coll. Urology (hon.), Latin Am. Soc. Pediatric Urology, Argentine Soc. Transurethral Surgery (hon.). Home: 1752 Morgan Rd Long Lake MN 55356 Office: PO Box 45 Mayo Bldg 412 Delaware St SE Minneapolis MN 55455

GONZALEZ FLORES, AGUSTIN EDUARDO, physics educator; b. Orizaba, Veracruz, Mex., Dec. 27, 1948; s. Guillermo and Angela (Flores) G. B.S., Nat. U. Mex., 1973, M.S., 1977; Ph.D., Boston U., 1981. Assoc. prof. Met. U., Mexico City, 1977-77; adj. asst. prof. UCLA, 1981-82; vis. research physicist Inst. Theoretical Physics, U. Calif.-Santa Barbara, 1982-83; investigator Nat. U. Mex., Mexico City, 1983—. Consejo Nacional de Ciencia Y Technologia fellow, 1977. Contbr. articles to profl. jours. Mem. Am. Phys. Soc., Am. Chem. Soc. (polymer div.). Roman Catholic. Current work: General statistical physics with an emphasis on lattice magnetic models, percolation, branched polymers and polymer gelation, polymer viscoelasticity, dispersion forces. Subspecialties: Polymer physics; Statistical physics. Home: Cerro del Quetzal 289 04200 Mexico DF Mexico Office: Apdo Postal 20-364 Instituto de Fisica UNAM Delegacion Alvaro Obregon 01000 Mexico DF Mexico

GONZALEZ-LIMA, FRANCISCO MARIA, neuroanatomist, educator, researcher; b. Havana, Cuba, Dec. 7, 1955; s. Francisco and Jacinta (Lima) Gonzalez-L.; m. Erika V. Musiol, 1981. B.S. in Biology, Tulane U., 1976, B.A. in Psychology, 1977; Ph.D. in Anatomy, U. P.R., 1980; Ph.D. in Psychology, Am. Western U., 1981. Postdoctoral research fellow Lab. Neurophysiology U. P.R., San Juan, 1981; asst. prof. Ponce Sch. Medicine, 1980-83, assoc. prof., 1983-85; asst. prof. med. anatomy Tex. A&M U., 1985—; cons. in field. Contbr. articles to profl. jours. NSF grantee, 1981-83; NIH grantee, 1982-83, NIMH grantee, 1983—; research fellow Alexander von Humboldt Found., 1982-83; grantee Resource Ctr. Sci. and Engring., summers 1982, 83. Mem. Soc. Neurosci., Nat. Soc. Med. Research, Animal Behavior Soc. Current Work: Definition of neural processes underlying motivational and sensory interactions, structures responsible for normal integration of these processes, alteration of these activities in the brain. Subspecialty: Neurophysiology. Home: Cond el Mirador 19F Ponce PR 00731 Office: Tex A&M U Coll Medicine Dept Anatomy College Station TX 77843

GOOCH, JAN WOODALL, chemist; b. Danville, Ark., Jan. 15, 1946; d. Luther Woodall and Lottie May (Michiel) G.; divorced, Jan. 1975; 1 child, Sonja Dawn. B.S., Ark. Poly. Coll., 1971; Ph.D., U. So. Miss., 1979. Tech. dir. Wrape Enterprises, Little Rock, 1971-76; sr. engr. Bechtel Group, Inc., San Francisco, 1979-82; group leader Cook Paint and Varnish Co., Kansas City, Mo., 1982; sr. research scientist Ga. Inst. Tech., Atlanta, 1983—. Patentee in field. Contbr. articles to profl. jours. Served as sgt. USAFR, 1967-73. Mem. Polymer Group, Am. Chem. Soc., Nat. Assn. Corrosion Engrs., Soc. Plastics Engrs., Sigma Xi. Republican. Current work: Polymer characterization and coatings. Subspecialty: Polymer chemistry. Home: 200 26th St NW Atlanta GA 30309 Office: Georgia Inst Tech Atlanta GA 30332

GOOD, MARY LOWE, business executive, chemist; b. Grapevine, Tex., June 20, 1931; d. John W. and Winnie (Mercer) Lowe; m. Billy Jewel Good, May 17, 1952; children: Billy, James. B.S., Ark. State Tchrs. Coll., 1950; M.S., U. Ark., 1953, Ph.D., 1955, LL.D. (hon.), 1979; D.Sc. (hon.), U. Ill., Chgo., 1983. Instr. Ark. State Tchrs. Coll., Conway, summer 1949; instr. La. State U., Baton Rouge, 1954-56, asst. prof., 1956-58, asso. prof., New Orleans, 1958-63, prof., 1963-80, Boyd prof. materials sci., div. engring. research, Baton Rouge, 1979-80; v.p., dir. research UOP, Inc., Des Plaines, Ill., 1980-84; pres. Signal Research Ctr., Inc., Des Plains, 1985—; chmn. Pres.'s Com. for Nat. Medal Sci., 1979-82; mem. Nat. Sci. Bd., 1980-86. Contbr. articles to profl. jours. Bd. dirs. Oak Ridge Asso. Univs. Recipient Agnes Faye Morgan research award, 1969; Distinguished Alumni citation U. Ark., 1973; Scientist of Yr. award Indsl. R & D Mag., 1982; AEC tng. grantee, 1967; NSF internat. travel grantee, 1968; NSF research grantee, 1969-80. Fellow Am. Inst. Chemistry (Gold medal 1983), Chem. Soc. London; mem. Am. Chem. Soc. (1st woman dir. 1971-74, regional dir. 1972-80, chmn. bd. 1978, 80, Garvan medal 1973, Herty medal 1975, award Fla. sect. 1979), Phi Beta Kappa, Sigma Xi, Iota Sigma Pi (regional dir. 1967—, hon. mem. 1983). Club: Zonta (past pres. New Orleans club, chmn. dist. status of women com. and nominating com., chmn. internat. Amelia Earhart scholarship com.). Current Work: Heterogeneous catalysis, surface science, materials. Subspecialties: Catalysis chemistry; Surface chemistry. Home: 295 Park Dr Palatine IL 60067 Office: Signal Research Center Inc 50 E Algonquin Rd Box 5016 Des Plaines IL 60017

GOOD, ROBERT ALAN, physician, educator; b. Crosby, Minn., May 21, 1922; s. Roy Homer and Ethel Gay (Whitcomb) G.; children: Robert Michael, Mark Thomas, Alan Maclyn, Margaret Eugenia, Mary Elizabeth. B.A., U. Minn., 1944, M.B., 1946, Ph.D., 1947, M.D., 1947; M.D. (hon.), U. Uppsala, Sweden, 1966; D.Sc. (hon.), N.Y. Med. Coll., 1973, Med. Coll. Ohio, 1973, Coll. Medicine and Dentistry N.J., 1974, Hahnemann Med. Coll., 1974, U. Chgo., 1974, St. John's U., 1977, U. Health Scis., Chgo. Med. Sch., 1978. Teaching asst. dept. anatomy U. Minn., Mpls., 1944-45; instr. pediatrics U. Minn. (Med. Sch.), 1950-51, asst. prof., 1951-53, asso. prof., 1953-54, Am. Legion Meml. research prof. pediatrics, 1954-73, prof. microbiology, 1962-72, Regents prof. pediatrics and microbiology, 1969-73, prof., head dept. pathology, 1970-72; intern U. Minn. Hosps., 1947, asst. resident pediatrics, 1948-49; pres., dir. Sloan-Kettering Inst. for Cancer Research, 1973-80, mem., 1973-81; prof. pathology Sloan-Kettering div. Grad. Sch. Med. Scis. Cornell U., 1973-81, dir., 1973-80; adj. prof., vis. physician Rockefeller U., 1973-81; prof. medicine and pediatrics Cornell U. Med. Coll., 1973-81; dir. research Meml. Sloan-Kettering Cancer Ctr., v.p., 1980-81; dir. research Meml. Hosp. for Cancer and Allied Diseases, 1973-80, also attending physician depts. medicine and pediatrics; attending pediatrician N.Y. Hosp., 1973-81; mem., head cancer research program Okla. Med. Research Found., 1982-85; prof. pediatrics, research prof. medicine, OMRF prof. microbiology and immunology U. Okla. Health Scis. Ctr., 1982-85; attending physician, head div. immunology Okla. Children's Meml. Hosp., 1982-85; attending physician in internal medicine Okla. Meml. Hosp., 1983-85; physician-in-chief All Children's Hosp., St. Petersburg, Fla., 1985—; prof., chmn. dept. pediatrics U. South Fla., St. Petersburg, 1985—; vis. investigator Rockefeller Inst. for Med. Research, N.Y.C., 1949-50, asst. physician to Hosp., 1949-50; attending pediatrician Hennepin County Gen. Hosp., 1950-73, cons., 1960-73; Mem. Unitarian Service Commn. Med. Exchange Team to, France, Germany, Switzerland and Czechoslovakia, 1958; cons. VA Hosp., Mpls., 1959-60; cons., sci. adviser Nat. Jewish Hosp., Denver and Childrens Asthma Research Inst. and Hosp., Denver, 1964-69; mem. study sects. USPHS, 1952-69; mem. expert adv. panel on immunology WHO, 1967—; cons. Merck & Co., N.J., 1968—, Nat. Cancer Inst., 1973-74; mem. ad hoc com. President's Sci. Adv. Council on Biol. and Med. Sci., 1970, Pres.'s Cancer Panel, 1972; mem. Lyndon B. Johnson Found. awards com., 1972; mem. adv. com. Bone Marrow Transplant Registry, 1973—; fgn. adv. Acad. Med. Scis., People's Republic of China, 1980—. Author, editor numerous books.; Contbr. articles to profl. jours. Mem. adv. council Childrens Hosp. Research Found., Cin., 1954-58; bd. dirs. Allergy Found. Am., 1973; bd. sci. advisers Jane Coffin Childs Meml. Fund Med. Research, 1972-74, Merck Inst. Therapeutic Research, 1972-76; chmn. Internat. Bone Marrow Registry, 1977-79. Recipient Borden Undergrad. Research award U. Minn. Med. Sch., 1946; E. Mead Johnson First award, 1955; Theobald Smith award, 1955; Parke-Davis 6th Ann. award, 1962; Rectors medal U. Helsinki, 1963-64; Pemberton Lectureship award, 1966; Gordon Wilson Gold medal, 1967; R.E. Dyer Lectureship award, 1967; Clemens Von Pirquet Gold medal 9th Ann. Forum on Allergy, 1968; Presidents medal U. Padua, Italy, 1968; Robert A. Cooke Gold medal Am. Acad. Allergy, 1968; John Stewart Meml. award Dalhousie U., 1969; Borden award Assn. Am. Med. Colls., 1970; Howard Taylor Ricketts award U. Chgo., 1970; Gairdner Found. award, 1970; City of Hope award, 1970; Am. Acad. Achievement golden plate award, 1970; Albert Lasker award for clin. and med. research, 1970; A.C.P. award, 1972; Am. Coll. Chest Physicians award, 1974; Lila Gruber award Am. Acad. Dermatology, 1974; award in cancer immunology Cancer Research Inst. N.Y., 1975; Outstanding Achievement award U. Minn., 1978; award Am. Dermatological Soc. Allergy and Immunology, 1978; 1st Sarasota Med. award, 1979; sect. on mil. pediatrics award Am. Acad. Pediatrics, 1980; recipient Univ. medal Hacettepe U., Ankara, Turkey, 1982; numerous others.; Fellow Nat. Found. for Infantile Paralysis, 1947; Helen Hay Whitney Found. fellow, 1948-50; Markle Found. scholar, 1950-55. Fellow Acad. Multidisciplinary Research, AAAS, N.Y. Acad. Sci., Am. Acad. Arts and Scis.; mem. Am. Assn. History of Medicine, Am. Fedn. Clin. Research, Am. Assn. Anatomists, Am. Assn. Immunologists (past pres.), AAUP, Am., Mpls., Northwestern pediatric socs., Am. Rheumatism Assn., Am. Soc. Clin. Investigation (past pres.), Am. Soc. Exptl. Pathology (past pres.), Am. Soc. Microbiology, Assn. Am. Physicians, Central Soc. Clin. Research (past pres.), Harvey Soc., Infectious Disease Soc. Am. (Squibb award 1968), Internat. Soc. Nephrology, Internat. Acad. Pathology, Internat. Soc. for Transplantation Biology, Minn. State Med. Assn., Nat. Acad. Sci., Nat. Acad. Sci. Inst. Medicine (charter), Reticuloendothelial Soc. (past pres.), Soc. for Exptl. Biology and Medicine, Soc. for Pediatric Research, Am. Clin. and Climatol. Assn. (Gordon Wilson Gold medal 1967), Detroit Surg. Assn. (McGraw medal 1969), Internat. Soc. Blood, Transfusion, Practitioners' Soc., Am. Assn. Pathologists, Internat. Soc. Exptl. Hematology, Transplant Soc., Western Assn. Immunologists, Internat. Soc. Immunopharmacology (founding mem.), Phi Beta Kappa, Sigma Xi, Alpha Omega Alpha. Subspecialties: Immunopharmacology; Pediatrics. Office: All Children's Hosp 801 Sixth St Saint Petersburg FL 33701

GOOD, ROLAND HAMILTON, JR., educator, theoretical physicist; b. Toronto, Ont., Can., Oct. 22, 1923; came to U.S., 1948, naturalized, 1950; s. Roland Hamilton and Marie (Smith) G.; m. Ferol Hendrickson, May 7, 1944; children—Roland Hamilton III, Patricia Gail, Sue Marie. B.M.E., Lawrence Inst. Tech., 1944; M.A.E., Chrysler Inst. Engring., 1946; M.S., U. Mich., 1948, Ph.D., 1951. Engr. Chrysler Corp., Windsor, Ont. and Highland Park, Mich., 1942-47; instr. U. Calif., Berkeley, 1951-53; asst. prof., asso. prof. Pa. State U., 1953-56, prof., 1972—, head physics dept., 1972-81; asso. prof., prof. physics Iowa State U., Ames, 1956-72, distinguished prof. scis. and humanities, 1970—; physicist, sr. physicist Ames Lab. of U.S. AEC, 1956-72; vis. lectr. U. Colo., summer 1958; NSF sr. postdoctoral fellow Inst. Advanced Study, Princeton, 1960-61; vis. prof. Inst. Math. Sci., Madras, India, 1968, Seoul Nat. U., 1979; guest Stanford Linear Accelerator Center, 1968-69. Author: (with T.J. Nelson) Classical Theory of Electric and Magnetic Fields, 1971. Fellow Am. Phys. Soc. Research, publs. theoretical physics, especially relativistic wave equations, polarization of elementary particles, metallic binding, electron emission from metals and spectroscopy of rare earths. Current Work: High energy scattering, field emission processes. Subspecialties: Theoretical physics; Particle physics. Home: 24 S Barkway Ln State College PA 16803

GOODE, GLENN AMOS, JR., nuclear engineer; b. Yuma, Ariz., May 5, 1946; s. Glenn Amos and Virginia Lee (Altstatt Schilliger) G.; m. Sandra Rose Mackensen, June 17, 1972 (div. Apr. 1982). A.S., Ariz. Western Coll., 1974; B.S., U. Ariz., 1976; M.B.A., Kent State U., 1982. Registered profl engr., Ohio. Electronics technician U.S. Navy, 1965-67; nuclear reactor operator 1967-71; startup engr. Gen. Electric Co., San Jose, Calif., 1976-82, lead startup engr., 1982-83, ops. mgr., 1983—; cons. Hatch Nuclear Plant, Ga., 1983—. Served with USN, 1965-71. Mem. Am. Nuclear Soc., Nat. Soc. Profl. Engrs., Am. Welding Soc., Ohio Soc. Profl. Engrs. Republican. Lutheran. Current Work: Nuclear steam supply systems. Subspecialties: Nuclear engineering; Nuclear fission. Home: 112 Bloomfield Rd Vidalia GA 30474

GOODELL, HORACE GRANT, environmental sciences educator, consultant; b. Decatur, Ill., Oct. 12, 1925; s. Horace Holbrook and Frieda May (Smith) G.; m. Mona Lee Cluck, Sept. 3, 1956; children: Laurie, Katherine, Zachary. B.A., So. Methodist U., 1955; Ph.D., Northwestern U., 1957. Asst. prof. Fla. State U., 1956-60, assoc. prof., 1960-68, prof., 1968-70; prof. environ. scis. U. Va., 1970—, chmn. dept. environ. scis., 1971-78. Served to capt. USNR, 1943-49, 51-52. Decorated Air medal with 2 gold stars, Purple Heart. Fellow Geol. Soc. Am.; mem. Am. Geophys. Union, Am. Assn. Petroleum Geologists, Soc. Econ. Paleontologists and Mineralogists, Sigma Xi. Current Work: Hydrogeology, marine geology—teaching/research. Subspecialties: Hydrology; Geochemistry. Office: U Va Clark Hall Charlottesville VA 22903

GOODEN, ROBERT, chemist; b. Shreveport, La., Jan. 4, 1949; s. Arthur and Geneva (Knighten) G.; div.; children—Nakida, Michele. B.S., So. U., 1974; Ph.D., Stanford U., 1979. Mem. tech. staff Bell Labs., Murray Hill, N.J., 1978—. Contbr. articles to profl. jours. Served with USMC, 1969-72. Bell Labs Coop. Research fellow, 1974-78. Mem. Am. Chem. Soc., AAAS, Nat. Orgn. for Profl. Advancement Black Chemists and Chem. Engrs. Current work: Photochemical reactions in organic compounds and polymers, polymer degradation and stabilization. Subspecialties: Organic chemistry; Photochemistry. Home: 300 N Randolphville Rd Piscataway NJ 08854 Office: Am Tel and Tel Bell Labs 600 Mountain Ave Murray Hill NJ 07974

GOODENOUGH, SAMUEL HENRY, biomedical engineer, consultant; b. Oakland, Calif., Sept. 8, 1919; s. Samuel Henry and Katherine Mary (Amet) G.; m. Frances Carolyn, Oct. 12, 1940; m. Kathleen Eula, Sept. 15, 1962; 1 son, John Samuel. Student, U. Calif., 1943-51. Registered profl. mech. engr., Ill. Chief tool engr. Warwick Mfg. Corp., Chgo., 1959-61; sr. research engr. Cutter Biomed. Inc., San Diego and Berkeley, Calif., 1963-77; sr. engr. Shiley Labs., Irvine, Calif., 1979-82; v.p. engring. and mfg. Mitral Med. Internat. Inc., Irvine, 1979-82, cons. mech. engring., biomed. engring, Carlsbad, Calif., 1982—; cons. and expert witness in product liability litigation. Mem. Assn. Advancement Med. Instrumentation, Nat. Soc. Profl. Engrs., ASME. Patentee cardiac valve prostheses. Current Work: Cardiac valve prostheses; manufacturing processes for metal working. Subspecialties: Biomedical engineering; Mechanical engineering. Home and Office: 6472 Camino Del Parque Carlsbad CA 92008

GOODFRIEND, PAUL LOUIS, chemist, educator; b. Dallas, Aug. 10, 1930; s. Isidore and Anna (Berger) G.; m. Beverly Lebar, June 28, 1953; children: Benedict, Jason. B.S., U. Va., 1952; Ph.D., Ga. Inst. Tech., 1957. Postdoctoral fellow U. Rochester, N.Y., 1956-58; asst. prof. chemistry Coll. William and Mary, 1958-61; sr. research chemist Texaco Export Inc., Richmond, Va., 1961-63; assoc. prof. chemistry U. Maine, Orono, 1966-70, prof., 1970—. Contbr. articles to sci. jours. Mem. Am. Chem. Soc., Sigma Xi. Democrat. Jewish. Current Work: Molecular quantum mechanics, spectroscopy, kinetics. Subspecialties: Theoretical chemistry; Physical chemistry. Home: 118 Howard St Bangor ME 04401 Office: Dept Chemistry U Maine Orono ME 04469

GOODGOLD, JOSEPH, physician, educator; b. N.Y.C., Mar. 21, 1920; m. Mildred Simons; 2 children. B.A., Bklyn. Coll., 1942; M.D., Middlesex U., 1945. Diplomate Am. Bd. Phys. Medicine and Rehab. Intern, then resident in medicine Beth-El Hosp., Bklyn., 1945-47; fellow Inst. Rehab. Medicine, NYU, 1953-54, now Howard A. Rusk prof. rehab. research, chmn. dept., project dir., also dir.; attending physician, dir. electodiagnostic sect. dept. rehab. medicine Bellevue Hosp.; attending physician St. Vincent's Hosp. and Med. Ctr., N.Y.C.; cons. in field. Mem. internat. editorial bd. sect. 19 Excerpta Medica Amsterdam, Netherlands. Mem. adv. com. Vis. Fulbright-Hays Scholar Program, N.Y.C., 1970-76; mem. med. adv. bd. Mucscular Dystrophy Assn., Inc. Served to capt. M.C., U.S. Army, 1950-53. Fellow Am. Coll. Cardiology, ACP, Am. Acad. Compensations Medicine (sec. treas. 1968-71), N.Y. Acad. Medicine, mem. AMA, Am. Congress Rehab. Medicine (com. mem. 1971-72), Am. Rheumatism Assn., Am. Assn. Electromyography and Electrodiagnosis (long range com. 1980—), Am. Acad. Phys. Medicine and Rehab. (pres. 1977-78, bd. govs. 1972-82, com. mem. 1971-72, 82, Krusen award for outstanding physiatrist 1985), Am. Assn. Acad. Physiatrists (v.p. 1971-72, pres. 1973-74, bd. govs. 1971—), Med. Soc. of County of Kings, N.Y. Acad. Sci. (adv. com. biomed. engring. sect. 1973—), Am. Paraplegia Soc., Soc. Neuroscis. Home: 300 E 40th St New York NY 10016

GOODHEART, CLYDE RAYMOND, microbiologist, executive; b. Erie, Pa., June 9, 1931; s. Edmund James and Hannah Helen (Husted) G.; m. Barbara Jean Peterson, Dec. 26, 1953; children—Kenneth James, Karen Jean, Diane Louise. B.S. with honors, Northwestern U., 1953, M.S., 1957, M.D., 1957. Postdoctoral fellow Calif. Inst. Tech., Pasadena, 1958-61; asst. prof., then assoc. prof. U. So. Calif. Sch. Medicine, Los Angeles, 1961-65; assoc. mem., mem. Inst. for Biomed. Research, AMA-ERF, 1965-70; pres. BioLabs. Inc., Northbrook, Ill., 1969—. Author: An Introduction to Virology, 1969; (with others) Fundamentals of Microbiology, 1974. Contbr. numerous articles to profl. jours. Mem., Sec., pres. Bd. Edn., Dist. 103, Lake County, Ill., 1968-72. Mem. AAAS, Am. Soc. Microbiology, Ill. Soc. Microbiology (pres. 1974), Am. Assn. Cancer Research, Phi Beta Kappa. Current work: Molecular biology of cancer virology, especially herpes virology. Subspecialties: Cell and tissue culture; Virology (biology). Home: 15 Sheffield Ct Lincolnshire IL 60015 Office: BioLabs Inc 15 Sheffield Ct Lincolnshire IL 60015

GOODIN, JOE RAY, plant physiologist, biological sciences educator; b. Claude, Tex., July 28, 1934; s. Emery Lee and Leta Elizabeth (Culver) G. B.S., Tex. Tech. U., 1955; M.S., Mich. State U., 1958; Ph.D., UCLA, 1963. Asst. prof., asst. agronomist U. Calif., Riverside, 1964-70; assoc. prof., prof. biology Tex. Tech. U., Lubbock, 1970—, now chmn. dept. biol. scis.; dep. dir. Tex. Tech. U. (Internat. Ctr. Arid and Semi-Arid Land Studies); cons. Nat. Acad. Scis., AAAS, U.S. Congress. Contbr. numerous articles on plant physiology to profl. jours. Served to capt. USAF, 1955-57. Grantee Pacific Sci. Congress, Tokyo, 1967; Internat. Grasslands Congress, Sydney, Australia, 1970; Smithsonian Instn. Egypt, 1976. Mem. Am. Soc. Plant Physiologists, Bot. Soc. Am., AAAS, Soc. Developmental Biology. Methodist. Current Work: Physiology and biochemistry of water and salt stress in plants, environmental stresses and crop productivity, biomass for energy production. Subspecialties: Plant physiology (biology); Tissue culture. Office: Tex Tech U Dept Biol Sci Lubbock TX 79409

GOODING, CHARLES THOMAS, dean; b. Tampa, Fla., Nov. 18, 1931; s. Charles Thomas and Gladys Violet (Bingman) G.; m. Shirley Ann Puckett, June 7, 1953; children: Steven Thomas, Carol Ann, David Lee, Mark Charles. B.A., U. Fla., 1954; postgrad., U. Tampa, 1957-58; M.Ed., U. Fla., 1962, Ed.D., 1964. Tchr. Meml. Sch., Tampa, Fla., 1957-58, tchr., prin., St. Mary's Sch., Tampa, 1958-62; instr. U. Fla., Gainesville, 1963-64; assoc. prof. to prof. SUNY-Oswego, 1964—, dean grad. studies, 1982—, co-dir. Classroom Interaction Lab., 1985—; vis. prof. U. Liverpool, Eng., 1979-80; grad. fellow U. Fla., 1962-63; cons. Sodus (N.Y.) Pub. Schs., 1970, Norfolk (Va.) Pub. Schs., 1973, Jamesville-Dewitt (N.Y.) Pub. Schs., 1982, Liverpool (N.Y.) Pub. Schs., 1982. Author: (with Combs) Florida Studies in Helping Professions, 1969, (with Pittenger), Learning Theories in Educational Practice, 1971; contbr. articles to profl. jours. Bd. dirs. Oswego County unit Am. Cancer Soc., 1972-73, 82—. Served to 1st lt. U.S. Army, 1954-56. SUNY Research Found. grantee, 1966, 69, 70; N.Y. Dept. Edn. grantee, 1971-72; vis. scholar grantee U. Liverpool, 1979-80; NSF grantee, 1980-82, 85—. Mem. AAAS, AAUP, Am. Ednl. Research Assn., Am. Psychol. Assn., Brit. Ednl. Research Assn., Eastern Ednl. Research Assn. (v.p. 1979-81, council 1982—). Democrat. Episcopalian. Clubs: Classic Jaguar Assn. Internat, Pathfinder Antique Auto (pres. 1980-82). Current Work: Educational psychology and human learning and cognition; evaluation of human interaction and learning. Descriptors: Discussion, wait time and learning interaction. Subspecialties: Learning; Cognition. Home: 4169 W River Rd PO Box 231 Minetto NY 13115 Office: Office Grad Studies Culkin Hall SUNY Oswego NY 13126

GOODMAN, ARDEN PATRICIA, chemist, breeder Arabian horses; b. Flushing, N.Y., Aug. 16, 1949; d. Sheldon Stuart and Elizabeth Lillian (Weiss) G.; m. Joseph Theodore Gacsi, Dec. 26, 1976; children: Ted, Vickie. B.S. in Chemistry/Life Sci. (scholar), U. Ill., 1971. Quality assurance chemist Ferro Corp., Huntington Beach, Calif., 1971-72, Beckman Instruments Co., Fullerton, Calif., 1972-73; research chemist Edwards Labs. div. Am. Hosp. Supply Corp., Irvine, Calif., 1974-80; mgr. quality assurance Edwards Labs. div. Am. Hosp. Supply Corp. (Am. Med. Optics div.), 1980-81, mgr. quality assurance engring., 1981—. Contbr. articles to sci. jours. Mem. Am. Chem. Soc., Am. Soc. for Quality Control, Am. Horse Show Assn., Internat. Arabian Horse Assn.. Current Work: New product review prior to market introduction of Class II and Class III medical devices, including implants, for use by ophthalmic surgeons; ensure that all good manufacturing practice requirements for product release have been met. Subspecialties: Ophthalmology; Physical medicine and rehabilitation. Office: 1402 E Alton Ave Irvine CA 92714

GOODMAN, BARBARA EASON, physiologist; b. Hanover, N.H., Nov. 17, 1949; d. Robert Henry and Helen Esther (Mansfield) Eason; m. Douglas Robert Goodman, May 14, 1972; children—Rebekah Corey, Timothy DeForest. B.A., Duke U., 1972; Ph.D., U. Minn., 1981. Grad. asst. Jacksonville State U. (Ala.), 1973-74, Auburn U. (Ala.), 1974-75; research asst. U. Minn., Mpls., 1975-80; postdoctoral fellow UCLA, 1980-83, asst. research faculty mem., 1984—. Pres. United Meth. Women, Inglewood, Calif., 1983-84. Recipient Young Investigators award So. Calif. Pulmonary Research Conf., 1984. Mem. Am. Physiol. Soc. (assoc.), NOW (local pres. 1976-77, state coordinator Ala. 1974-75). Current work: Pulmonary alveolar epithelial transport properties in mammalian lungs. Subspecialty: Membrane transport. Home: 246 N Hillcrest Blvd Inglewood CA 90301 Office: UCLA Dept Medicine Div Pulmonary Disease Los Angeles CA 90024

GOODMAN, CHARLES DAVID, physics researcher; b. N.Y.C., May 9, 1928; s. Jacob and Libby (Freed) G.; m. Joan Louise Wright, June 11, 1952; children—Henry Nicholas, Diana Ruth. A.B., Clark U., 1949; Ph.D., U. Rochester, 1955. Physicist, Oak Ridge Nat. Lab., 1955-80; vis. scientist Weizmann Inst. Sci., Rehovot, Israel, 1966; vis. prof. U. Colo., Boulder, 1972-73; prof. physics Ind. U., Bloomington, 1980—; cons. Lawrence Livermore Nat. Lab., Calif., 1980—. Editor several conf. procs., 1965-85. Contbr. articles to profl. jours. Fellow Am. Phys. Soc. (Tom W. Bonner prize 1983); mem. IEEE, AAAS, Sigma Xi. Current work: Experimental nuclear physics concerning nuclear models; apparatus design for basic nuclear research. Subspecialty: Nuclear physics. Office: Dept Physics Indiana Univ 2401 Milo Sampson Ln Bloomington IN 47405

GOODMAN, DAVID BARRY POLIAKOFF, biochem. endocrinologist, clin. pathologist; b. Lynn, Mass., June 1, 1942; s. Nathan and Eva (Poliakoff) G.; m. Constance Cutler, Aug. 22, 1965; children: Derek, Alex. A.B., Harvard U., 1964; M.D., U. Pa., 1968, Ph.D. in Biochemistry, 1972. Lic. physician, Pa., Conn. Research asst. prof. pediatrics U. Pa. Med. Sch., Phila., 1972-76; from asst. prof. to asso. prof. medicine Yale U. Sch. Medicine, New Haven, 1976-80; asso. prof. dept. pathology and lab. medicine U. Pa. Med. Sch., 1980-82, prof., 1982—; dir. div. lab. medicine U. Pa. Med. Sch. (Univ. Hosp.), 1980-83; cons. NIH, NSF, VA. Mgn. editor: Metabolic Bone Disease and Related Research, 1978—; Contbr. over 100 articles to sci. jours. Recipient Achievement award Upjohn Co., 1968; established investigator Am. Heart Assn., 1977. Mem. N.Y. Acad. Scis. (Laport award 1981), AAAS, Am. Fedn. Clin. Research, Acad. Clin. Lab. Physicians and Scientists, Am. Assn. Pathologists, Am. Heart Assn., Am. Physiol. Soc., Am. Soc. Bone and Mineral Research, Soc. Developmental Biology, Soc. Neurosci. Current Work: Role of lipids and hormones in control of membrane permeability; diagnostic biochemistry. Subspecialties: Membrane biology; Endocrinology. Office: 3400 Spruce St Philadelphia PA 19104

GOODMAN, DEWITT STETTEN, physician, biomedical scientist, educator; b. N.Y.C., July 18, 1930; s. Max and Jennie (Katz) G.; m. Ann Bregstein, July 7, 1957; children—Daniel W., Elizabeth Goodman Reed. A.B., Harvard Coll., 1951, M.D., 1955. Intern, then asst. resident Presbyn. Hosp., N.Y.C., 1955-59; investigator Nat. Heart Inst., Bethesda, Md., 1956-58, 60-62; vis. fellow Hammersmith Hosp., London, Eng., 1959-60, Clare Hall, Cambridge U., 1972-73; from asst. prof. to assoc. prof. Columbia U., N.Y.C., 1962-69, prof. medicine, 1969—; Tilden-Weger Bieler prof., 1971—; bd. dirs. N.Y. Heart Assn., 1983—, Am. Heart Assn., 1979-81; adv. com. Nat. Heart Lung Blood Inst., Bethesda, 1979—; mem. staff Presbyn. Hosp., 1962, attending physician, 1971—; adj. prof. Rockefeller U., N.Y.C., 1974-77; vis. prof. Hebrew U., Hadassah Med. Sch., Jerusalem, 1981-82. Assoc. editor, then editor Jour. Clin. Investigation, 1967-72; editorial bd. Jour. Biol. Chemistry, 1979-85, Arteriosclerosis, 1981—; editorial bd. Jour. Lipid Research, 1965-70, adv. bd., 1974—. Contbr. articles to profl. jours. Recipient Meltzer award Soc. Exptl. Biology and Medicine, 1963. Career Scientist award Health Research Council of N.Y., 1964-74, Stevens Triennial prize Columbia U., 1971; Guggenheim fellow, 1972-73; Macy Faculty scholar, 1981-82. Fellow Council Arteriosclerosis of Am. Heart Assn. (chmn. 1979-81); mem. Assn. Am. Physicians, Am. Soc. Clin. Investigation (councillor 1973-76), Interurban Clin. Club (councillor 1982-84, pres. 1985-86), Harvey Soc. (pres. 1982-83), Am. Inst. Nutrition (Osborne-Mendel award 1974), Am. Soc. Biol. Chemists, Am. Oil Chemists Soc., AAAS, Phi Beta Kappa, Alpha Omega Alpha. Current work: Cholesterol metabolism; atherosclerosis research; vitamin A and retinoids. Subspecialties: Arteriosclerosis; Biochemistry (medicine). Home: 7 Ernst Pl Tenafly NJ 07670 Office: Columbia U Coll Physicians and Surgeons 630 W 168th St New York NY 10032

GOODMAN, DOUGLAS SEYMORE, optical physicist and engineer; b. Memphis, Feb. 17, 1947; s. E. Edwin and Lillian (Epsberg) G.; m. Carolyn Wenk. B.S. in Physics, Rhodes Coll., 1969; M.S. in Physics, U. Ill., 1971; Ph.D. in Optics, U. Ariz., 1979. Mem. research staff IBM research, Yorktown Heights, N.Y., 1979—. Office: IBM PO Box 218 Yorktown Heights NY 10598

GOODMAN, HOWARD M., biochemistry educator; b. Bklyn., Nov. 29, 1938; s. Samuel G.; children: Sylena, William. Ed., Williams Coll., Mass. Inst. Tech., Cambridge (Eng.) U. Asst. prof. biochemistry U. Geneva, 1969-70; asst. prof. U. Calif., San Francisco, 1970-71, assoc. prof., 1971-76, prof., 1976-81; investigator Howard Hughes Med. Inst., 1978-81; chief dept. molecular biology Mass. Gen. Hosp., Boston, 1981—; prof. genetics Harvard Med. Sch., 1981—. Contbr. articles to profl. jours. Helen Hay Whitney Found. fellow; Am. Cancer Soc. fellow; Josiah Macy Faculty scholar. Mem. Am. Soc. Biol. Chemists. Subspecialty: Molecular biology. Office: Dept Molecular Biology Mass Gen Hosp Boston MA 02114

GOODMAN, IRVING JACK, psychologist, educator, researcher; b. Detroit, Jan. 9, 1933; s. Dave and Marion E. (Malina) G.; m. Sharon J. Jacobs, Jan. 31, 1960; children—Eric, Rachel, Jonathan. Ph.D., U. Rochester, 1968. Prof. W.Va. U., Morgantown, 1966—; vis. prof. U. Pisa, Italy, 1973-74, Campinas State U., Brazil, 1980, Princeton U., N.J., 1983. Editor: Birds: Brain and Behavior, 1974, Contbr, articles to profl. jours. Served with USN, 1955-57, Mem. Soc. Neuroscis., Am. Psychol. Assn., Internat. Soc. Psychophysiology, AAAS. Current work: Behavioral neuroscience, physiological psychology. Subspecialties: Physiological psychology; Psychobiology. Home: 232 Wilson Ave Morgantown WV 26505Office: W Va U Oglebay Hall Morgantown WV 26506

GOODMAN, JOEL WARREN, research scientist; b. N.Y.C., Jan. 2, 1933; s. Herman Joseph and Ann (Citron) G.; m. Janet Carol Petersen, July 18, 1964; children: Mark Craig, Clifford Scott. B.A., Bklyn. Coll., 1953; Ph.D., Columbia U., 1959. Asst. prof. U. Calif., San Francisco, 1960-65, assoc. prof., 1965-70, prof. microbiology and immunology, 1970—. Research grantee NIH; Research grantee NSF; Research grantee ACS. Mem. Am. Assn. Immunologists, AAAS, Planetary Soc. Current Work: Molecular basis of lymphocyte activation in the immune response. Subspecialties: Immunobiology and immunology; Molecular biology.

GOODMAN, JOSEPH WILFRED, electrical engineering educator; b. Boston, Feb. 8, 1936; s. Joseph and Doris (Ryan) G.; m. Hon Mai Lam, Dec. 5, 1962; 1 dau., Michele Ann. B.A., Harvard, U., 1958; M.S. in E.E., Stanford U., 1960, Ph.D., 1963. Postdoctoral fellow Norwegian Def. Research Establishment, Oslo, 1962-63; research asso. Stanford U., 1963-67, asst. prof., 1967-69, asso. prof., 1969-72, prof. elec. engring., 1972—; vis. prof. Univ. Paris XI, Orsay, France, 1973-74; dir. Info. Systems lab., dept. elec. engring., Stanford U., 1981-83; v.p. Internat. Commn. Optics, 1985—; cons. to govt. and industry, 1965—. Author: Introduction to Fourier Optics, 1968; Statistical Optics, 1985; contbr. articles to profl. jours. Recipient F.E. Terman award Am. Soc. Engring. Edn., 1971; research grants NSF; Air Force Office Sci. Research Office Naval Research. Fellow Optical Soc. Am. (dir. 1977-83, Max Born award 1983), IEEE, Soc. Photo-optical Instrumentation Engrs. (bd. govs. 1979-82); mem. AAAS, Sigma Xi. Current work: Optical interconnections in computer architecture and for integrated circuits. Home: 570 University Terrace Los Altos CA 94022 Office: Dept Elec Engring Durand 127 Stanford U Stanford CA 94305

GOODMAN, JULIUS, nuclear engineer, consultant, researcher; b. Odessa, USSR, July 19, 1935; came to U.S., 1979; s. Isaac and Eugenia (Lusher) Guttman; m. Rachel Bezpalko, July 4, 1959; 1 dau., Marina. M.S. in Theoretical Physics, State U., Odessa, 1958; Ph.D. in Theoretical Physics, Inst. Nuclear Physics, Tashkent, USSR, 1962; Ph.D. hon. degree in nuclear physics, Inst. Tech. Odessa, 1965. Sr. researcher Inst. Nuclear Physics, Tashkent, Acad. Sci., USSR, 1958-63; prof. Inst. Tech., Odessa, 1963-70, Poly U., Odessa, 1970-76; sr. engr. Bechtel Power Corp., Norwalk, Calif., 1980—. Author: Professional Education, 1975, (with P.U. Arifov) Positron Diagnostic, 1978; contbr. numerous articles to profl. jours. Pres. Hatchiya (Revival), Orange County, Calif., 1982—. Mem. Am. Nuclear Soc., Internat. Soc. Reliability Engrs., Los Angeles Council Engrs. and Scientists, So. Calif. Council for Soviet Jewry, Internat. Platform Assn., U.S. Com. for Energy Awareness, U.S. Def. Com., Com. on Internat. Freedom of Scientists. Club: Toastmaster (Fullerton, Calif.). Lodge: B'nai B'rith. Patentee nuclear reactor with UF-6. Current Work: Probabilistic risk assessment; general theory, external hazards-earthquakes, tornado, transportation of toxic and explosive chemicals; general relativity, atomic and nuclear physics, physics of nuclear reactors. Subspecialties: Nuclear engineering; Theoretical physics. Home: 1630 Via Linda Fullerton CA 92633 Office: Bechtel Power Corp 12400 E Imperial Hwy Norwalk CA 90650

GOODMAN, MAJOR M., geneticist, educator; b. Des Moines, Sept. 13, 1938; s. Jarrett W. and Mabel O. (Michael) G.; m. Sheila D. Balfour, Aug. 8, 1970; stepchildren: Sean Balfour Dail, Andrew Scot Dail. B.S., Iowa State U., 1960; M.S., N.C. State U., 1963, Ph.D., 1965. NSF postdoctoral fellow Instituto de Genetica, Escola Superior de Agricultura Luiz de Quiroz, Piracicaba, Sao Paulo, Brazil, 1965-67; vis. asst. prof., then asst. prof., then assoc. N.C. State U., Raleigh, from 1967, now prof. crop sci., statistics, genetics and botany; chmn. Maize Crop Adv. Com., U.S. Dept. Agr. Author: Races of Maize in Brazil and Adjacent Areas, 1977; also articles. Recipient research awards, scholarships and fellowships. Mem. Crop Sci. Soc., Genetics Soc. Am., Soc. Econ. Botany, Systematic Zoology Soc., Soc. Am. Naturalists, Am. Bot. Soc., Internat. Soc. Plant Taxonomy, Classification Soc., Sigma Xi. Current Work: Classification and Utilization of races of maize; maize isozyme genetics. Subspecialties: Plant genetics; Evolutionary biology. Office: Crop Science Dept NC State U Box 7620 Raleigh NC 27695

GOODMAN, MURRAY, chemistry educator; b. N.Y.C., July 6, 1928; s. Louis and Frieda (Bercun) G.; m. Zelda Silverman, Aug. 26, 1951; children—Andrew, Joshua, David. B.S., Bklyn. Coll., 1949; Ph.D., U. Calif.-Berkeley, 1952. Research asst. U. Calif.-Berkeley, 1949-52; research assoc. MIT, Cambridge, 1952-55; NRC fellow Cambridge U., Eng., 1955-56; asst. prof. chemistry Poly. Inst., Bklyn., 1956-60, assoc. prof., 1960-64, prof., 1964-71, dir. Polymer Research Inst., 1967-71; prof. U. Calif.-San Diego, 1971—; Alta. vis. prof. U. Alta., 1981; Lady Davis vis. prof. Hebrew U., 1982; Goldberg chair biomed. engring. Technion-Israel Inst. Tech., 1982; William H. Rauscher lectr. Rensselaer Poly. Inst., 1982. Contbr. articles to profl. jours.; editor Biopolymers Jour., 1971—. Mem. steering com. WHO, 1974—; Recipient Disting. Alumnus medal Bklyn. Coll., 1965, Scoffone medal U. Padua, Italy, 1980. Fellow AAAS; mem. Internat. Union Pure and Applied Chemists (U.S. nat. com. 1980—), Am. Chem. Soc., Am. Soc. Biol. Chemists, Chem. Soc. of Eng., Biophys. Soc., Sigma Xi. Jewish. Current work: Peptide synthesis; conformational analysis of peptides and protein model systems; study of biologically-active peptides and their analogs and carrier-drug conjugates. Home: 9760 Blackgold Rd La Jolla CA 92037 Office: U Calif Dept Chemistry La Jolla CA 92093

GOODMAN, NANCY B., physicist; b. Palo Alto, Calif., May 8, 1952; d. Merrill and Phoebe (Blank) G.; m. Peter A. Torpey, July 2, 1983. B.A., Bryn Mawr Coll., 1974; M.S., U. Chgo., 1977, Ph.D., 1981. Post-doctoral fellow Max Planck Institut, Stuttgart, Fed. Republic Germany, 1981-82; mem. research staff Xerox Corp., Webster, N.Y., 1982—. Contbr. articles to profl. jours. Fannie and John Hertz Found. fellow, 1977-81, NATO postdoctoral fellow NSF, 1981-82. Current work: Evaluation of thin film devices and the development of automated testing capabilities for doing so; latitude studies of xerographic systems. Subspecialties: Condensed matter physics; Computer engineering. Office: Xerox Corp 0201-03L 800 Phillips Rd Webster NY 14580

GOODMAN, STEVEN RICHARD, cell biologist; b. N.Y.C., Dec. 29, 1949; s. Martin Jay and Natalie (Hochberg) G.; m. Amy Lou Bobula, Dec. 20, 1980; 1 dau., Laela Beth. B.S., SUNY-Stony Brook, 1971; Ph.D., St. Louis U., 1976. Postdoctoral fellow Harvard Med. Sch., Boston, 1976-77; NIH research fellow Harvard U., Cambridge, Mass., 1977-79; asst. prof. Pa. State U., Hershey, 1979-83, assoc. prof., 1983—; dir. Multidiscipline Labs., Milton S. Hershey Med. Ctr., Hershey, Pa., 1979—, dir. div. cell and molecular biology, 1985—; cons. program project Nat. Heart, Lung and Blood Inst., Nat. Inst. Arthritis, Metabolism and Digestive Diseases, NIH, 1981—; established investigator Am. Heart Assn., 1982—. Editorial bd. Am. Jour. Physiology: Cell Physiology, 1983—. Mem. Am. Soc. Cell Biology, Biophys. Soc., Am. Soc. Hematology, Am. Soc. Biol. Chemists, Am. Physiol. Soc., AAAS, N.Y. Acad. Sci. Current Work: Research involves structure and function of membrane-associated cytoskeletal proteins of erythrocytes as well as nonerythroid cells, determination of genetic defects in some of these proteins in pathophysiological erythrocytes. Subspecialties: Membrane biology; Cell biology (medicine). Home: 2405 Rudy Rd Harrisburg PA 17104 Office: Pa State U Milton S Hershey Med Ctr PO Box 850 Hershey PA 17033

GOODRICH, JAMES TAIT, neuroscientist, neurosurgeon; b. Portland, Ore., Apr. 16, 1946; s. Richard and Gail (Josselyn) G.; m. Judy Loudin, Dec. 27, 1970. Student, Golden West Coll., 1971-72; A.A., Orange Coast Coll., 1972; B.S. cum laude, U. Calif., Irvine, 1974; M.Phil., Columbia U. Grad. Sch. Arts and Scis., 1979, Ph.D., 1970; M.D., Coll. Physicians & Surgeons, 1980. Neuroscientist N.Y. Neurol. Inst., N.Y.C., 1981—. Contbr. articles to profl. jours. Recipient Roche Labs. award in neuroscis., 1978, Mead-Johnson award, 1978, Bronze medal Alumni Assn. Coll. Physicians and Surgeons, 1980, Sandoz award for outstanding research, 1980; Willamette Industries scholar; NIH grantee. Fellow Royal Soc. Medicine (London); mem. N.Y. Acad. Medicine (Melicow award 1980), Am. Assn. History of Medicine (Sir William Osler medal 1977-78), AMA, Brit. Brain Research Assn., European Brain Research Assn., Friends of Columbia U. Libraries, Friends of Osler Library of McGill U., N.Y. Acad. Scis., Med. History Soc. N.J., ISIS History of Sci. Soc., Soc. for Bibliography of Natural History (London), Columbia Presbyterian Med. Soc., U. Calif. Alumni Assn., Soc. Ancient Medicine, AAAS, Am. Osler Soc., Les Amis du Vin, South Coast Wine Explorers Club (past chmn.), Friends of Bacchus Wine Club (past chmn.), Dionysius Council of Presbyn. Hosp. of N.Y.C., Sigma Xi, Alpha Gamma Sigma. Current Work: Research in neuronal regeneration and brain reconstruction. Subspecialties: Anatomy and embryology; Regeneration. Home: 214 Everett Pl Englewood NJ 07631 Office: Dept Neurosurgery NY Neurol Inst New York NY 10032

GOODWIN, FREDERICK K., psychiatrist. Dir. intramural research NIMH, Rockville, Md. Subspecialty: Psychiatry. Office: NIMH 5600 Fishers Ln Rockville MD 20857

GOODWIN, RICHARD CLARKE, air force officer, physicist, educator; b. Hancock, Mich., Mar. 24, 1949; s. Robert Clement and Jean (Gibson) G.; m. Linda Wells, Oct. 30, 1971. B.S., U.S. Mil. Acad., 1971; M.S. in Systems Mgmt, U. So. Calif., 1976; M..S. in Nuclear Engring, Air Force Inst. Tech., Wright-Patterson AFB, Ohio, 1978; postgrad. Air Command and Staff Coll., 1984-85, U. Ala., 1984—. Commd. 2d lt. U.S. Air Force, 1971, advanced through grades to maj., 1983, navigator, Mather AFB, Calif., 1971-76; asst. prof. physics U.S. Mil. Acad., 1978-81, radar navigator, K.I. Sawyer AFB, Mich., 1981-84; research fellow Ctr. Aerospace Doctrine, Research and Edn., Maxwell AFB, Ala., 1985—. Mem. Soc. Am. Mil. Engrs. (pres. 1979-80), Am. Nuclear Soc., Air Force Assn., Alfa Romeo Owners Club. Current Work: Defense policy analysis. Subspecialties: Nuclear engineering; Laser physics. Home: 533A 12th St Maxwell AFB AL 36112 Office: CADRE/RIA Maxwell AFB AL 45412

GOODY, RICHARD MEAD, geophysicist; b. Welwyn-Garden-City, Eng., June 19, 1921; came to U.S., 1958, naturalized, 1966; s. Harold Earnest and Lilian (Rankine) G.; m. Elfriede Koch, Sept. 11, 1946; 1 dau., Brigid. Ph.D., Cambridge U., 1949; M.A. (hon.), Harvard U., 1958. With Brit. Civil Service, 1942-46; fellow St. John's Coll., Cambridge, 1950-53; reader London U., 1953-58; prof. div. applied scis. Harvard U., 1958—; dir. Blue Hill Obs., 1958-70, Center for Earth and Planetary Physics, 1970-71. Author: Physics of the Stratosphere, 1947, Atmospheric Radiation, 1964, Atmospheres, 1974. Mem. Royal Meteorol. Soc. (Buchan prize 1955), Am. Meteorol. Soc. (50th Anniversary medal 1970, Cleveland Abbé award 1977), Am. Acad. Arts and Scis., Nat. Acad. Scis. Club: Cosmos (Washington). Subspecialty: Geophysics. Home: Box 430 Falmouth MA 02541 Office: Pierce Hall 29 Oxford St Cambridge MA 02138

GOODYEAR, WAYNE DAVID, structural engineer, consultant; b. Passaic, N.J., May 11, 1951; s. Charles Harrold and Catherine (Young) G.; m. Jennifer Palmer, Oct. 27, 1973; children—Andrew, Michelle. B.S., Cornell U., 1973; M.C.E., 1974. Registered profl. engr., W.Va., Mass., Wash., R.I. With Stone & Webster, Boston, 1974-77; sr. civil engr. Wash. Pub. Power Supply System, Richland, 1978-80; sr. engr. Arvid Grant & Assocs., Olympia, Wash., 1980—; structural assoc. Tera Corp., Berkeley, Calif., 1982—. Designer: Toutle River Bridge (Wash. Post Tensioning Inst. award 1983), 1982; Dame Point Alt. cable stayed bridge, 1984. Mem. ASCE, Earthquake Engring. and Research Inst., Post Tensioning Inst. (ad hoc com. cable stays 1984), Am. Concrete Inst., Structural Engring. Assn. Wash., Internat. Assn. Bridge and Structural Engring. Presbyterian. Current work: Stay cable materials for bridges, stay cable damping devices, construction methods for cable stayed bridges, non-linear response of bridges, computer aided engineering for bridge design, non-linear response of structures to impact loads. Subspecialties: Dynamics; Civil engineering. Home: 2320 Dublin Dr NW Olympia WA 98502 Office: Arvid Grant & Assocs 1600 E 4th Ave Olympia WA 98506

GOONERATNE, SAROJITH RAVI, veterinary researcher; b. Colombo, Sri Lanka, Aug. 4, 1947; naturalized Australian, 1981; came to Can., 1982; s. Fredrick Warnasuriya and Margaret Ethel (Dias) G.; m. Anoma Dayani Jayasuriya, May 23, 1975; children—Ruchith Prasanna, Dinesh Priyantha. B.V.Sc., U. Sri Lanka, Peradeniya, 1972; Ph.D., Murdoch U., Australia, 1979. Asst. lectr. Vet. Sch., U. Sri-Lanka, 1973-74; govt. vet. surgeon Sri Lanka Dept. Agr., 1974-75; postdoctoral researcher Murdoch U., 1979-82; profl. research assoc. in trace mineral metabolism U. Sask., Saskatoon, 1982—, vis. lectr., 1983-85. Author: Metabolism of Copper in Animals and Man, 1986; also articles. Mem. Sri Lanka Vet. Surgeons Assn., Australian Nutrition Soc., Am. Soc. Animal Sci., AVMA (assoc.), Internat. Soc. Trace Element Research in Humans (founding). Current work: Morphological and biochemical studies in trace mineral disorders with special reference to copper deficiency and toxicity. Subspecialties: Animal nutrition; Pathology (veterinary medicine). Home: 604 Rusholme Rd Saskatoon SK S7L 0G7 Canada Office: U Sask Dept Animal and Poultry Sci Saskatoon SK S7N 0W0 Canada

GOORVITCH, DAVID, research scientist; b. San Pedro, Calif., July 16,1941; s. Philip and Helen (Isbitz) G.; m. Norma Ruth Rubenstein, June 3, 1966; children: Stephen, Laura. B.A., U. Calif.-Berkeley, 1963, Ph.D., 1967. With NASA, Ames Research Center, Moffett Field, Calif., 1967—, research scientist lab. molecular spectroscopy, 1972—. Contbr. articles to physics and astronomy jours. Mem. Am. Phys. Soc., Optical Soc. Am., Am. Astron. Assn., Sigma Xi. Current Work: Molecular spectroscopy, infrared observations of the planets. Subspecialties: Atomic and molecular physics; Infrared astronomy. Office: N245-6 Moffett Field CA 94035

GOOTMAN, PHYLLIS MYRNA, physiologist, educator; b. N.Y.C., June 8, 1938; d. Albert S. and Ida (Krieger) Adler; m. Norman Gootman, June 1, 1958; children: Sharon Hillary, Craig Seth. B.A., Barnard Coll., Columbia U., 1959; Ph.D., Albert Einstein Coll. Medicine, Yeshiva U., 1967. Assoc. prof. sch. grad. studies Downstate Med. Center SUNY, 1975-81, prof., 1981—, assoc. prof. dept. physiology, 1975-81, prof., 1981—; staff pediatrics dept. Schneider Children's Hosp., L.I. Jewish Med. Center, New Hyde Park, 1976—; lectr. in field; mem. cardiovascular and renal study sect. NIH, 1981-85. Contbr. numerous articles to profl. jours. John Miles Davidson fellow, 1973. Mem. AAAS, Soc. Neurosci., Biophys. Soc., Am. Physiol. Soc., Am. Heart Assn., Am. Inst. Biol. Scis., Microcirculatory Soc., Soc. Exptl. Biology and Medicine, Internat. Soc. Devel. Neurosci., Am. Assn. Lab. Animal Sci., Sigma Xi. Current Work: Research in development of autonomic nervous system, development of autonomic regulation of cardiovascular function; development of central respiratory function. Subspecialties: Comparative physiology; Neurophysiology. Office: Dept Physiology Box 31 Downstate Medical Center 450 Clarkson Ave Brooklyn NY 11203

GOPIKANTH, MYSORE LAXMIKANTH, electrochemical engineer, research scientist, consultant; b. Mysore, India, Aug. 9, 1954; came to U.S., 1978, naturalized, 1981; s. M.K. Lakshmikanth and M.K.S. Lakshmi. B.S., U. Mysore, 1968-72; M.S., Birla Inst. Tech. and Sci., Pilani, India, 1972-74; Ph.D., Indian Inst. Sci., Bangalore, 1974-78; M.B.A., Northeastern U., 1985. Research assoc. Indian Inst. Sci., 1978. Ill. Inst. Tech., Chgo., 1979-80; sr. research scientist Cardiac Pacemakers, Inc., St. Paul, 1980-82; sr. staff scientist Duracell, Inc., Burlington, Mass., 1982—; battery cons. to pvt. corps., 1976-80, 85—; corrosion cons. to pvt. corps., 1976—. Contbr. articles to profl. jours. Patentee in field. Mem. Am. Chem. Soc., Electrochem. Soc., AAAS, N.Y. Acad. Scis., Am. Inst. Chem. Engrs., Assn. M.B.A. Execs., Boston Computer Soc., Soc. for Advancement of Electrochem. Sci. and Tech., Sigma Xi. Current work: Advanced high energy chemical power sources, electrochemical sensors, corrosion of metals, electro-plating, photo-voltaics. Subspecialty: Physical chemistry. Home: 12 Hallmark Gardents 6 Burlington MA 01803

GORBMAN, AUBREY, biologist, educator; b. Detroit, Dec. 13, 1914; s. David and Esther (Korenblit) G.; m. Genevieve D. Tapperman, Dec. 25, 1938; children—Beryl Ann, Leila Harriet, Claudia Louise, Eric Jay. A.B., Wayne State U., 1935, M.S., 1936; Ph.D., U. Calif., 1940. Research asso. U. Calif., 1940-41; instr. zoology Wayne U., 1941-44; Jane Coffin Childs fellow in anatomy Yale, 1944-46; asst. prof. zoology Barnard Coll., Columbia, 1946-49, asso. prof., 1949-53, prof., 1953-63, exec. officer dept. zoology, 1952-55; prof. zoology U. Wash., Seattle, 1963-85, prof. emeritus, 1985—, chmn. zoology dept., 1963-66; biologist Brookhaven Nat. Lab., 1952-58; Fulbright scholar College de France, Paris, 1951-52; Guggenheim fellow U. Hawaii, 1955-56; vis. prof. biochemistry Nagoya U. Japan, 1956, Tokyo U., 1960. Editor: Comparative Endocrinology; editorial bd.: Endocrinology, 1957-61; editor-in-chief: Gen. and Comparative Endocrinology. Fellow AAAS, N.Y. Zool. Soc., N.Y. Acad. Sci., Japan Soc. Promotion Sci.; mem. Endocrine Soc., Am. Inst. Biol. Scis. (governing bd. 1969-75), Am. Soc. Zoologists (pres. 1976), Phi Beta Kappa. Current work: Comparative endocrinology; textbook writing and editing in endocrinology. Subspecialties: Animal physiology; Neuroendocrinology. Home: 4218 55th Ave NE Seattle WA 98105

GORDON, CHARLES NATHAN, chemist; b. Buffalo, Apr. 13, 1935; s. Frank E. and Alice (Halperin) G. B.A., NYU, 1964, Ph.D., 1969. Asst. prof. U. Calif.-Irvine, 1969-77; chemist Nutrilite Products, Buena Park, Calif., 1980-82, Kal Kan Foods, Vernon, Calif., 1982—. Contbr. articles to profl. jours. Mem. Am. Soc. Biol. Chemists, Am. Chem. Soc., AAAS, Inst. Food Technologists, Phi Beta Kappa. Current work: Development of new main-meal and snack foods for pets (cats and dogs). Subspecialty: Food science and technology. Office: Kal Kan Foods Inc 3386 E 44th St Vernon CA 90058

GORDON, EDWARD BARRY, systems programmer; b. Boston, Sept. 10, 1952; s. Louis and Marion (Shuman) G. B.S. with distinction in Computer Sci, Worcester Poly. Inst., 1974; postgrad., Wayne State U., 1974-77, Villanova U., 1979-81. Engring. programmer Burroughs Corp., Detroit, 1974-77; tech. adv. Fed. Res. Bank, Boston, 1977-78; engring. programmer Racal-Milgo, Inc., Miami, Fla., 1978-79, Decision Data Computer Corp., Horsham, Pa., 1979-81; prin. systems programmer Racal-Milgo, Inc., Ft. Lauderdale, Fla., 1981-82; sr. engring. programmer Autech Data Systems, Pompano Beach, Fla., 1982-85; mem. tech. staff Bell Labs., North Andover, Mass., 1985—. Mem. Assn. Computing Machinery, IEEE, Mensa. Jewish. Current Work: Specification, design and development of computers and computer peripherals for telecommunications systems. Subspecialties: Software engineering; Computer architecture. Office: Bell Labs 1600 Osgood St North Andover MA 01845

GORDON, EUGENE IRVING, telecommunications consultant; b. N.Y.C., Sept. 14, 1930; s. Sol and Gertrude (Lassen) G.; m. Barbara Young, Aug. 19, 1956; children—Laurence Mark, Peter Eliot. B.S., CCNY, 1952; Ph.D., Mass. Inst. Tech., 1957. Research asso. Mass. Inst. Tech., Cambridge, 1957; mem. tech. staff Bell Labs., Murray Hill, N.J., 1957-59, supr., 1959-63, dept. head, 1963-68, dir., 1968-83, cons., 1983—. Patentee in field.; Editor: EDS Trans, 1963-64, Jour. Quantum Electronics, 1964-76; Contbr. articles to profl. jours. Fellow IEEE (Zworykin award 1975, Edison medal 1984); mem. Nat. Acad. Engring., Am. Phys. Soc. Democrat. Jewish. Club: B'nai Brith. Current Work: Development of devices for fiber optic. Communication, display devices. Subspecialties: Electrical engineering; Electronics. Home: 14 Braidburn Way Convent NJ 07961 Office: Bell Laboratories 600 Mountain Ave Murray Hill NJ 07974

GORDON, MARK AITKEN, astronomer, observatory director; b. Springfield, Mass., Oct. 13, 1937; s. Alexander Dorward and Josephine Pease (Aitken) G.; m. Mary Abigail Anderson, Aug. 19, 1961; children: Paige Abigail, Sarah Aitken; m. Julia Brown Perry, Aug. 12, 1980. B.A., Yale U., 1959; Ph.D., U. Colo., 1966. Mem. U.S. Antarctic Research Program, 1959-62; staff mem. M.I.T. Lincoln Lab., 1966-69; asst. scientist Nat. Radio Astronomy Obs., Charlottesville, Va., 1969-72, assoc. scientist, Tucson, 1972-77, scientist, 1977—, asst. dir. for Ariz. Obs., 1973-84. Contbr. articles to sci. publs. Mem. Am. Astron. Soc., Internat. Astron. Union, U.S. Nat. Com. for Radio Sci. Current Work: Interstellar medium, galactic structure. Subspecialty: Radio and microwave astronomy. Office: Campus Bldg 65 Tucson AZ 85721-0655

GORDON, MARK GARDINER, engineer; b. Kansas City, Mo., Nov. 21, 1954; s. Gerald and Sarah Elizabeth (Gardiner) G.; m. Ellen Knight, June 17, 1978. B.S.M.E., Calif. State Poly. U., 1979. Mech. engr. Burroughs Corp., Westlake Village, Calif., 1979-81; sr. staff engr. Am. Edwards Labs., Santa Ana, Calif., 1981—; cons. engring. analysis optics Christopher Group, Irvine, Calif., 1984. Patentee continuous flow pump. Mem. ASME (assoc.), Soc. Photo-Optical Instrumentation Engrs. Current work: Computer aided engineering analysis; image scanning techniques; engineering A.I.; information systems. Subspecialties: Graphics, image processing, and pattern recognition; Systems engineering. Home: 13182 Woodland Dr Tustin CA 92680 Office: Am Edwards Labs Box 11150 Santa Ana CA 92711

GORDON, ROBERT THOMAS, surgeon, educator; b. Chgo., Feb. 13, 1950; s. David and Eunice (Wienshienk) G. B.S. in Medicine with highest distinction, Northwestern U., M.D., 1972. Diplomate: Am. Bd. Surgery, Am. Bd. Thoracic Surgery. Resident in gen. surgery Northwestern U. Hosp., Chgo., 1972-77, resident in cardiac surgery, 1977-79; clin. asst. prof. surgery U. Ill., Chgo., 1979—; mem. attending staff, chief dept. cardiac surgery Lutheran Gen. Hosp., Park Ridge, Ill., 1979—; also chief cardiac surgery resident and nurses tng. program; mem. attending staff Highland Park (Ill.) Hosp., Edgewater Hosp., Chgo., Mt. Sinai Hosp., Chgo., Holy Family Hosp., Des Plaines, Ill., Humana Hosp., Hoffman Estates, Ill., Good Shepherd Hosp.; instr. gen. and thoracic surgery Northwestern U.; staff assoc. HEW, Bethesda, Md. Contbr. articles to profl. jours. Chmn. Ill. Commn. Conservation, 1966-67. Recipient awards Hoffmann-LaRoche, awards NASA, awards Am. Chem. Soc.; G.D. Searle fellow; Macy Found. Research fellow. Fellow ACS; mem. Internat. Bio-Electro Magnetic Soc., Internat. Coll. Surgeons, Royal Soc. Medicine, Flying Physicians Assn., Internat. Platform Assn., AMA, Ill. Thoracic Soc., Am. Coll. Chest Physicians, Chgo. Med. Assn., Ill. State Med. Assn., Soc. Contemporary Medicine and Surgery, Ill. Jr. Acad. Scis. (pres., hon. life mem.), Alpha Omega Alpha, Phi Beta Pi, Phi Eta Sigma. Patentee in field. Current Work: Cardiac surgery and related research; also research and innovations in biophysics (cancer diagnosis, treatment and prevention; also heart disease and other diseases); genetic engineering and instrumentation. Subspecialties: Cancer research (medicine); Cardiac surgery. Office: 9301 Golf Rd Des Plaines IL 60016

GORDY, WALTER, emeritus physics educator; b. Miss., Apr. 20, 1909; s. Walter Kalin and Gertrude (Jones) G.; m. Vida Brown Miller, June 19, 1935; children: Eileen, Walter Terrell. A.B., Miss. Coll., 1932, LL.D., 1959; M.A., U. N.C., 1933, Ph.D., 1935; Dr. honoris causa, U. Lille, France, 1955; D.Sc. hon., Emory U., 1983. Assoc. prof. math. and physics Mary Hardin-Baylor Coll., 1935-41; NRC fellow Calif. Inst. Tech., 1941-42; staff radiation lab. Mass. Inst. Tech., 1942-46; assoc. prof. physics Duke, Durham, N.C., 1946-48, prof., 1948-79, James B. Duke prof., 1958-79, James B. Duke prof. emeritus, 1979—; Vis. prof. U. Tex., 1958; Mem. NRC, 1954-57, 68-74. Author: (with W.V. Smith, R.F. Trambarulo) Microwave Spectroscopy, 1953, (with Robert L. Cook) Microwave Molecular Spectra, 1970, 3d edit., 1984; Theory and Applications of Electron Spin Resonance, 1980; assoc. editor: Jour. Chem. Physics, 1954-58, Spectrochimia Acta, 1957-60; editorial bd.: Radiation Research, 1969-72. Recipient Sci. research award Oak Ridge Inst. Nuclear Studies, 1949, Disting. Alumnus award U. N.C., 1976, N.C. award for sci., 1979; 50th Anniversary award Miss. Acad. Scis., 1980. Fellow Am. Phys. Soc. (chmn. S.E. sect. 1953-54, mem. council 1967-71, 73-77, recipient Jesse W. Beams award Southeastern sect. 1974, Earle K. Plyler prize 1980), AAAS (council 1955); mem. Radiation Research Soc. (mem. council 1961-64), Nat. Acad. Scis., Sigma Xi. Current Work: Microwave spectroscopy and electron spin resonance spectra. Subspecialties: Atomic and molecular physics; Biophysics (physics). Home: 2521 Perkins Rd Durham NC 27706

GORENC, EDWARD JOSEPH, engineer; b. Cleve., Nov. 23, 1955; s. Edward and Stannie (Rudolph) G. B.S.M.E., Case Inst. Tech., 1978; M.B.A., Case Western Res. U., 1983. Registered profl. engr., Ohio. Mfg. engr. Parker Hannifin Corp., Cleve., 1978-79, project engr., 1979-81, project mgr. new product devel., 1981-82, mgr. product engring., 1982—; cons. to industry. Ambassador, Cleve. Jr. Achievement; sponsor Cleve. Patrolman's Assn. Benefit. Mem. Am. Soc. Profl. Engrs., ASME, Soc. Automotive Engrs., Cleve. Engring. Soc., North Coast Performance Auto Club, Case Western Res. Alumni Assn. (bd. dirs.). Republican. Roman Catholic. Current work: Integration of specialized target and channel marketing techniques into technically oriented industry for unit sales maximization. Subspecialties: Mechanical engineering; Fluid mechanics.

GORENSTEIN, PAUL, physicist; b. N.Y.C., Aug. 15, 1934; s. Isidore and Bess (Evans) G. B.Engring. Physics, Cornell U., 1957; Ph.D. in Physics, M.I.T., 1962. Fulbright postdoctoral fellow, cons. Italian Nuclear Energy Com., 1963-65; sr. scientist Am. Sci. and Engring., Cambridge, Mass., 1965-73; sr. astrophysicist Smithsonian Astrophy. Obs., Cambridge, 1973—. Contbr. articles to profl. jours. Recipient contbns. to new tech. awards NASA, medal for outstanding sci. achievement, 1973. Mem. Am. Phys. Soc., Am. Astron. Soc., AAAS. Current Work: Supernova remanants, clusters of galaxies, instrumentation for x-ray astronomy. Subspecialties: X-ray high energy astrophysics; Nuclear physics. Office: 60 Garden St B-434 Cambridge MA 02138

GORGES, HEINZ A., engineering company executive; b. Stettin, Ger., July 22, 1913; came to U.S., 1959; s. Gustav and Marga (Benda) G.; m. Sapienza T. Coco, Sept. 2, 1957. M.S. Mech. Engring, Tech. U. Dresden, Ger., 1938; Ph.D., Tech. U. Hanover, Ger., 1946. Cert. profl. engr., D.C. Group leader Aero. Research Establishment, Braunschweig, Ger., 1940-45; sci. Royal Aircraft Establishment, Farnborough, Eng., 1946-49; prin. sci. officer Weapons Research Establishment, Adelaide, Australia, 1949-59; sci. asst. Marshall Space Flight Ctr., NASA, Huntsville, Ala., 1959-61; dir. advanced projects Cook Tech. Ctr., Morton Grove, Ill., 1961-62; sci. adv. Inst. Tech. Research, Chgo., 1962-66; asst. v.p. environ. and phys. scis. Tracor Inc., Austin, Tex., 1966-72; v.p., Rockville, Md., 1972-75; pres. Vineta Inc., Falls Church, Va., 1975—; prof. U. Ala.-Redstone Extension, 1960-61. Contbr. articles to profl. jours. Fellow AIAA (assoc.); mem. ASME, Acoustical Soc. Am., N.Y. Acad. Scis. Clubs: Cosmos (Washington), Palaver (Washington), Nat. Press (Washington). Current Work: Cogeneration; waste to energy conversion; economics; optimization techniques. Subspecialties: Mechanical engineering; Thermodynamics. Office: Vineta Inc 3705 Sleepy Hollow Rd Falls Church VA 22041

GORHAM, EVILLE, scientist, educator; b. Halifax, N.S., Can., Oct. 15, 1925; s. Ralph Arthur and Shirley Agatha (Eville) G.; m. Ada Verne MacLeod, Sept. 29, 1948; children—Kerstin, Vivien, Jocelyn, James. B.S. in Biology with distinction, Dalhousie U., 1945, M.S. in Zoology, 1947; Ph.D. in Botany, U. London, 1951. Lectr. botany Univ. Coll., London, 1951-54; sr. sci. officer Freshwater Biol. Assn., Ambleside, Eng., 1954-58; lectr., asst. prof. botany U. Toronto, 1958-62; assoc. prof. botany U. Minn., Mpls., 1962-65, prof., 1966-84, head dept., 1967-71, prof. ecology, 1975-84, Regents prof. ecology and botany, 1984—; prof., head dept. biology U. Calgary, Alta., Can., 1965-66; mem. for Can., Internat. Commn. on Atmospheric Chemistry and Radioactivity, 1959-62; mem. Scientists Inst. for Pub. Info., 1971—, fellow, 1972—; mem. vis. panel to rev. toxicology programs Nat. Acad. Scis.-NRC, 1974-75, mem. coordinating com. for sci. and tech. assessment of environ. pollutants Environ. Studies Bd., 1975-78, mem. com. on med. and biologic effects of environ. pollutants Assembly Life Scis., 1976-77; mem. com. on atmosphere and biophsere Bd. Agr. and Renewable Resources, 1979-81; mem. panel on environ. impact Diesel Impact Study Com., Nat. Acad. Engring.-NRC, 1980-81; mem. U.S./Can. Joint Sci. Com. on acid precipitation Environ. Studies Bd., (now U.S./Can./Mexican joint sci Commn.), Nat. Acad. Scis.-NRC-Royal Soc. Can., 1981—; mem. steering com. on flux measurements NASA Office of Space Sci. and Applications, 1983; mem. joint U.S.-Can. com. on air pollution Royal Soc. Can., 1983; mem. panel on fed. govt. research on long-range transport of air pollutants Royal Soc. Can., 1984. Mem. editorial bd. Ecology, 1965-67, Limnology and Oceanography, 1970-72. Contbr. articles to profl. jours. Royal Soc. Can. fellow State Forest Research Inst., Stockholm, 1950-51; grantee NSF, AEC, NIH, ERDA, NRC Can.; grantee Office Water Resources Research, Dept. Interior; recipient Regents medal for acad. distinction U. Minn., 1984. Mem. Am. Soc. Limnology and Oceanography, Ecol. Soc. Am., Internat. Assn. Pure and Applied Limnology, Internat. Ecology, Internat. Peat Soc., Soc. Wetland Scientists. Current work: Ecology, limnology, biogeochemistry, acid rain, peatlands, lakes. Subspecialties: Ecology (biology); Environmental toxicology. Home: 1933 E River Terr Minneapolis MN 55414 Office: U Minn Zoology Bldg Minneapolis MN 55455

GORONKIN, HERBERT, physicist; b. Pitts., Jan. 9, 1936; s. Sander and Mae (Shulman) G.; m. Beverly Smith, June 7, 1959 (div. 1980): children—David, Jeffrey, Michael; m. Pamela Louise Cooper, Oct. 4, 1980; Rebecca L., Theresa L., James D. A.B., Temple U., 1961, A.M., 1962, Ph.D., 1973. Physicist Internat. Resistance Corp., Phila., 1963-65; sr. research physicist Honeywell Inc., Ft. Washington, Pa., 1965-66; sect. head Am. Elec. lab., Colmar, Pa., 1966-69; project engr. Gen. Elec. Co., Syracuse, N.Y., 1969-75; mgr. semiconductor Varian Assoc., Beverly, Mass., 1975-77; project leader Motorola Inc., Phoenix, 1977-79, sect. mgr., 1979-84, chief sci., 1984—; chmn. workshop on Compound Semiconductor Microwave Materials and Devices, 1984—; mem. tech. program com. Internat. Electron Devices Meeting, 1983—. Contbr. articles to profl. jours. patentee electron devices. Served with USAF, 1954-57. Mem. IEEE (sr. mem.; chpt. chmn. Waves and devices, 1982-83), Am. Phys. Soc., Sigma Xi. Republican Jewish. Current work: Management and planning of technical development for high speed microchips; relationship of materials and processes to microchip performance; dependence of noise and switching speed on deep level impurities and defects. Subspecialties: Condensed matter physics; Microchip technology (engineering). Home: 1849 A N 77th St Scottsdale AZ 85257 Office: Motorola Inc 5005 E McDowell Rd Phoenix AZ 85008

GORSKI, STANLEY FRANCIS, weed scientist, educator; b. Indpls., Feb. 26, 1949; s. Stanley F. and Ruth A. (Fulmer) G.; m. Mary Jo Dowling, Apr. 18, 1970; 1 child, Stanley Bryce. B.S., Purdue U., 1973; M.S., U. Ill., 1975, Ph.D., 1978. Grad. research asst. U. Ill., Urbana, 1974-77; asst. prof. soils and crops Rutgers U., 1978-79; asst. prof. horticulture Ohio State U., 1979-83, assoc. prof., 1983—. Contbr. numerous articles to profl. jours. Grantee in field. Mem. Am. Soc. Hort. Sci., Weed Sci. Soc. Am., Northeastern Weed Sci. Soc., North Central Weed Sci. Soc., Gamma Sigma Delta. Roman Catholic. Current Work: Conduct research and teach in the area of weed science; secondly I conduct research and teach in the area of vegetable crops and vegetable crop physiology. Subspecialties: Weed science; Plant physiology (agriculture). Home: 960 Lambeth Dr Columbus OH 43220 Office: Ohio State University Department of Horticulture 2001 Fyffe Ct Columbus OH 43210

GOSALVEZ, MARIO, cancer pharmacology biochemist, educator; b. Madrid, Sept. 11, 1940; s. Fernando and Concepcion G.; m. Maria Flor Blanco, Oct. 2, 1964; children—Mario, David, Elena. Licenciate in medicine and surgery U. Complutense, Madrid, 1963, Dr. Medicine and Surgery, 1967; postgrad. Karolinska Inst., Stockholm, 1967, U. Pa., Asst. and lecturing prof. U. Complutense, 1964-67; 1968-69. research assoc. Fels Research Inst. Sch. Medicine, Phila., 1969-70; prof. asociado Sch. Medicine, U., Autonoma, Madrid, 1971-73, prof. agregado, 1974-77; head research biochemistry sector Clinica Puerta de Hierro, Madrid, 1974—; prof. titular biochemistry and molecular biology Spanish U. System, 1985—; pres. Internat. Found. Advancement of Knowledge, 1976; v.p. Spanish Assn. for Cancer Research, Madrid, 1982—. Contbr. numerous articles to med. jours. Patentee in field. Painter. Writer poetry and fiction. Recipient Extraordinary award Univ. Complutense, 1968, Nat. prize in Biochemistry Social Security (Ministry of Health), 1977, 79; Premio Rodriguez Pascual, 1979. Mem. Am. Assn. Cancer Research (corr.), Biochem. Soc. Gt. Brit., Spanish Biochem. Soc., European Assn. Cancer Research, Internat. Soc. Oxygen Transport to Tissue, Spanish Acad. Surgery. Liberal. Roman Catholic. Current work: Biochemical Pharmacology of cancer, leading to reversal of cancer to normality, tumor-reduct-targetted cytotoxic drugs carcinogenesis, cell sociology, femtomolar biochemistry, in vivo fluorometry. Subspecialties: Cancer research (medicine); Drug design. Home: Caleruega 21 7. A Madrid 28033 SpainOffice: Clinica Puerta de Hierro San Martin de Porres 4 Madrid 28035 Spain

GOSLING, JOHN THOMAS, physicist; b. Akron, Ohio, July 10, 1938; s. Arthur Warrington and Wilhelmena (Bell) G.; m. Marie Ann Turner, Dec. 21, 1963; children: Mark Raymond, Steven Arthur. B.S. in Physics, Ohio U., 1960; Ph.D. in Physics, U. Calif., Berkeley, 1965. Mem. Sci. staff Nat. Ctr. Atmospheric Research, Boulder, Colo., 1967-75; staff mem. Los Alamos Sci. Lab., 1965-67, 75—. Asso. editor: Jour. Geophys. Research, 1980-83; contbr. articles to profl. jours. Recipient Tech. Achievement award Nat. Ctr. Atmospheric Research, 1974. Mem. Am. Geophys. Union, Am. Astron. Soc., Internat. Astron. Union, AAAS. Current Work: Solar-terrestrial physics, solar wind physics; collisionless shocks, particle acceleration mechanisms, reconnection, experimental plasma physics and magnetohydrodynamics. Subspecialties: Space plasma physics; Solar physics. Home: 1420 45th St Los Alamos NM 87544 Office: Los Alamos Nat Lab Los Alamos NM 87545

GOSSARD, ARTHUR CHARLES, communications laboratory physicist; b. Ottawa, Ill., June 18, 1935; s. Arthur Paul and Mary Catherine (Lineberger) G.; m. Marsha Jean Palmer, Jan. 8, 1965; children—Girard Christopher, Elinore Suzanne. B.A., Harvard U., 1956; Ph.D., U. Calif., 1960. NSF postdoctoral fellow Centre d'Etudes Nucleaires, Saclay, France, 1962-63; mem. tech. staff AT&T Bell Labs., Murray Hill, N.J., 1960—. Contbr. numerous tech. papers to profl. lit. Fellow Am. Phys. Soc. (Oliver Buckley prize for condensed matter physics 1964); mem. Materials Research Soc. Current work: Molecular beam epitaxial crystal growth; man-made quantum wells; semiconductor superlattices; quantum Hall effect. Subspecialty: Condensed matter physics. Office: AT&T Bell Labs 600 Mountain Ave Murray Hill NJ 07974

GOSSETT, DORSEY MCPEAKE, university administrator; b. Camden, Tenn., Dec. 10, 1931; m. Marjorie Evans, Feb. 2, 1957; 1 child, John. B.S., U. Tenn.-Martin, 1955; M.S., U. Ill., 1957; Ph.D., N.C. State U., 1961. Asst. prof. N.C. State U., Raleigh, 1961-64; asst. prof. U. Tenn.-Knoxville, 1965-67, assoc. prof., 1967-70, supt. West Tenn. exptl. sta., Jackson, 1970-72, asst. dean expt. sta., Knoxville, 1972-76, dean, 1976—. Vice chmn. Tenn. Air Pollution Control Bd., Nashville. Mem. So. Assn. Agrl. Scientists, Sigma Xi, Gamma Sigma Delta, Phi Kappa Phi, Alpha Zeta, Epsilon Sigma Phi. Lodge: Rotary. Current work: research administration. Subspecialties: Agronomy; Plant physiology (agriculture). Office: Univ Tenn Agrl Exptl Sta PO Box 1071 Knoxville TN 37901

GOTCHER, JACK EVERETT, JR., oral and maxillofacial surgeon, researcher; b. Wichita Falls, Tex., May 11, 1949; s. Jack Everett and Josephine Caroline (Kruh) G.; m. Kathyanne Mary King, Dec. 30, 1972; children: Elizabeth Gayle, Jeffrey Everett. B.S., Midwestern U., 1971; D.M.D., Harvard U., 1975; Ph.D., U. Utah, 1979. Postdoctoral fellow U. Utah, Salt Lake City, 1975-78; resident U. Tenn. Meml. Hosp., Knoxville, 1978-82; asst. prof. dept. oral and maxillofacial surgery Sch. Dentistry Emory U., Atlanta, 1982-83; assoc. prof. dept. oral and maxillofacial surgery U. Tenn., Knoxville, 1983—; cons. oral surgery VA Hosp., Atlanta, 1982-83; cons. bone research Proctor & Gamble, Cin., 1977-79. Contbr. articles to profl. jours. in field. First prize resident research award U. Tenn., 1982; Am. Cancer Soc. grantee, 1978; NIH grantee, 1975-78; Johnson & Johnson travel grantee, 1975. Fellow Am. Assn. Oral and Maxillofacial Surgery; mem. ADA, Internat. Assn. Dental Research. Democrat. Presbyterian. Current Work: Mineralized tissues; metabolic inflammatory and nutritional effects on bone, diphosphonate effects on bone; morphometry in bone research; heterotransplantation of human neoplasia. Subspecialties: Oral and maxillofacial surgery; Anatomy and embryology. Home: 7620 Hawthorne Dr Knoxville TN 37919 Office: 1928 Alcoa Hwy Suite 305 Knoxville TN 37920

GOTT, JOHN RICHARD, III, astronomer; b. Louisville, Feb. 8, 1947; s. John Richard and Marjorie (Crosby) G.; m. Lucy Pollard-Gott, June 10, 1978. A.B., Harvard U., 1969; Ph.D., Princeton U., 1972. Fellow Calif. Inst. Tech., 1973-74; vis. fellow Cambridge (Eng.) U., 1975; asst. prof. astronomy Princeton U., 1976-80, assoc. prof., 1980—, dir. grad. studies dept. astrophys. scis., 1977—. Contbr. articles to profl. jours. Sloan fellow, 1977; recipient R. J. Trumpler award Astron. Soc. Pacific, 1975. Mem. Internat. Astron. Union. Current Work: Cosmology, general relativity, galaxy formation, galaxy clustering. Subspecialties: Cosmology; General relativity. Office: Princeton University Peyton Hall Princeton NJ 08544

GOTT, VINCENT LYNN, physician; b. Wichita, Kans., Apr. 14, 1927; s. Henry Vivian and Helen (Lynn) G.; m. Iveagh Foreman, Sept. 4, 1954; children—Deborah Lynn, Kevin Douglas, Cameron Bradley. B.A., Wichita U., 1951; M.D., Yale, 1953. Intern U. Minn. Hosp., 1953-54; resident surgery U. Minn. Hosps., 1954-60; asst. prof. surgery U. Wis., 1960-65; asso. prof. surgery Johns Hopkins, 1965-68, prof., 1968—; cardiac surgeon in charge Johns Hopkins, Hosp., 1965—. Contbr. articles to profl. jours. Served with USNR, 1945-46. Recipient Hektoen gold medal A.M.A., 1957; John and Mary R. Markle scholar, 1962. Fellow A.C.S.; mem. Am. Surg. Assn., Soc. Univ. Surgeons, Am. Assn. Thoracic Surgery, Soc. Thoracic Surgeons, Soc. Vascular Surgeons, Am. Heart Assn. Co-developer Gott-Daggett artificial heart valve, 1963; developer graphite-benzalkonium-heparin coating for plastic surfaces. Subspecialty: Cardiac surgery. Home: 203 Kemble Rd Baltimore MD 21218

GOTTESMAN, STEPHEN THANCY, astronomer, educator; b. N.Y.C., Feb. 23, 1939; s. Jacob Frank and Edna Beatrice (Goldner) G.; m. Celia Frances Docherty, Feb. 24, 1947; children: Lorna Rachel, Ian Kenneth Jacob, Emily Caitlin. B.A. magna cum laude, Colgate U., 1960; Ph.D., Victoria U., Manchester, Eng., 1967. Lectr. in physics and astronomy U. Keele, Eng., 1969; research assoc. Nat. Radio Astron. Obs., Charlottesville, Va., 1969-71; research fellow Calif. Inst. Tech., Pasadena, 1971; asst., then assoc. prof. astronomy U. Fla., Gainesville, 1972-81, prof. astronomy, 1981—; project cons. Nat. Endowment Humanities; cons. astron. textbooks. Contbr. numerous articles to sci. pubs. Fulbright scholar, 1960-61; Leverhulme fellow, 1961-64; grantee Internat. Astron. Union, 1972; grantee CNRS, France, 1974; grantee NSF, 1974, 78, 79, 80, 82; grantee So. Regional Edn. Bd., 1975-77; grantee Sigma Xi, 1976; grantee NRC/Nat. Acad Scis., 1979, 82. Mem. Am. Astron. Soc., Royal Astron. Soc., Internat. Union Radio Sci. (comm. J), Internat. Astron. Union, Phi Beta Kappa. Democrat. Current Work: Structure and kinematics of Milky Way and of extra-galactic nebulae. Atomic and molecular emissions from interstellar medium from our own and other galaxier. Subspecialty: Radio and microwave astronomy. Office: Dept Astronomy U Fla Gainesville FL 32611

GOTTLIEB, LEONARD SOLOMON, pathology educator; b. Boston, May 26, 1927; s. Julius and Jeanette (Miller) G.; m. Dorothy Helen Apt, Mar. 23, 1952; children: Julie Ann Gottlieb Texeira, William Apt, Andrew Richard. A.B., Bowdoin Coll., 1946; M.D., Tufts U., 1950; M.P.H., Harvard U., 1969. Diplomate: Am. Bd. Anatomic Pathology. Intern and resident in pathology Boston City Hosp., 1950-55; asst. chief pathology U.S. Naval Hosp., Chelsea, Mass., 1955-57; assoc. pathologist Mallory Inst. Pathology, Boston, 1957-66, assoc. dir., 1966-72, dir., 1972—; prof. pathology Boston U. Sch. Medicine, 1970—, chmn. dept., 1980—; dir. Mallory Inst. Pathology Found., 1980—; lectr. Harvard U., 1963—; chmn. pathology rev. com. Nat. Polyp Study, 1981—. Contbr. over 100 articles on exptl. and human gastrointestinal and liver diseases. Served to lt. M.C. USNR, 1955-57; to lt. comdr. 1960-63. James Bowdoin scholar, 1945. Mem. Am. Soc. Exptl. Pathology, Am. Assn. Study of Liver Disease, Internat. Acad. Pathology, Am. Soc. Cell Biology, Am. Gastroent. Assn., New Eng. Soc. Pathologists, Am. Soc. Clin. Pathology, Mass. Soc. Pathology, Coll. Am. Pathologists, Am. Inst. Nutrition. Current Work: Tumor antigens in gastrointestinal malignancy; role of colonic polyps in pathogenesis of malignancy; alcoholic liver disease. Subspecialties: Pathology (medicine); Gastroenterology. Home: 120 Willard Rd Brookline MA 02146 Office: 784 Massachusetts Ave Boston MA 02118

GOTTSCHALK, CARL WILLIAM, physician, educator; b. Salem, Va., Apr. 28, 1922; s. Carl and Lula (Helbig) G.; m. Helen Marie Scott, Nov. 22, 1947; children—Carl S., Walter P., Karen E. B.S., Roanoke Coll., 1942, Sc.D., 1966; M.D., U. Va., 1945. Intern, asst. resident, resident in medicine Mass. Gen. Hosp., Boston, 1945-52; research fellow physiology Harvard, 1948-50; fellow U. N.C. Med. Sch., Chapel Hill, 1952-53, faculty, 1953—, Kenan prof. medicine and physiology, 1969—; established investigator Am. Heart Assn., 1957-61, career investigator, 1961; Bowditch lectr., 1960, Harvey lectr., 1962; Mem. physiology study sect. NIH, 1961-65; mem. research career award com. Nat. Inst. Gen. Med. Scis., 1965-69, mem. physiology tng. com., 1970-73, mem.

med. scientist tng. com., 1973; chmn. com. chronic kidney disease Bur. Budget, 1966-67; adv. com. biol. and med. scis. NSF, 1967-69, vice chmn., 1968, chmn., 1969; mem. Inst. Medicine of Nat. Acad. Scis., Nat. Adv. Gen. Med. Scis. Council, 1977-80, Nat. Arthritis, Diabetes and Digestive and Kidney Diseases Adv. Council, 1982—. Author books and papers on physiology of kidney. Mem. adv. com. Burroughs Wellcome Fund for Clin. Pharmacology, 1980—; Pres. Children's Theatre N.C., 1967-68. Served to capt., M.C. AUS, 1946-48. Recipient N.C. award, 1967, Modern Medicine Distinguished Achievement award, 1966, Horsley Meml. prize U. Va., 1956, Homer W. Smith award N.Y. Heart Assn., 1970, David Hume award Nat. Kidney Found., 1976, O. Max Gardner award U. N.C., 1978. Mem. Assn. Am. Physicians, Am. Physiol. Soc., Am. Soc. Clin. Investigation, Am. Clin. and Climatol. Assn., Soc. Exptl. Biology and Medicine, A.C.P., AAUP (council 1970-73), Nat. Acad. Scis., Am. Soc. Nephrology (council 1971-77, pres. 1975-76), Am. Acad. Arts and Scis., Phi Beta Kappa, Sigma Xi. Current Work: Micropuncture studies of mammalian renal physiology; neural control of renal function. Subspecialty: Physiology (medicine). Home: 1300 Mason Farm Rd Chapel Hill NC 27514

GOUGH, DAVID ARTHUR, bioengineering educator, researcher, consultant; b. Salt Lake City, Aug. 16, 1946; s. Samuel Leland and Amber Fern (Reynolds) G.; m. Carol M. Gillett, Mar. 17, 1970; children—Monica, Andrea, Daniel, James. B.S. in Biology, U. Utah, 1970, B.A. in Chemistry, 1971, Ph.D. in Materials Sci. and Engring., 1974. Research assoc. in medicine Harvard U., Boston, 1974-76; assoc. Peter Bent Brigham Hosp., Boston, 1974-76; asst. prof. bioengring. U. Calif.-San Deigo, 1976-82, assoc. prof., 1982—. Contbr. numerous articles to profl. jours. Recipient William F. Talbert Research Project award Juvenile Diabetes Found.; NIH fellow, 1974-76; grantee in field. Mem. AAAS, Am. Inst. Chem. Engrs., Am. Soc. Artificial Internal Organs. Current work: Development of a glucose sensor for diabetes; reaction-diffusion problems in bioengineering; biotechnology reactor design. Subspecialty: Biomedical engineering. Office: Ames Bioengring U Calif San Diego La Jolla CA 92093

GOUGH, FRANCIS JACOB, plant pathologist; b. Grafton, W.Va., Apr. 9, 1928; s. Claude Ernest and Cordie Melissa (Weaver) G.; m. Ruby G. Nestor, Sept. 10, 1950; children: Rodney K., Jennifer Lynn. B.S., W.Va. U., 1951, M.S., 1953, Ph.D., 1957. Research plant pathologist Dept. Agr., Fargo, N.D., 1957-67, College Station, Tex., 1967-74, Stillwater, Okla., 1974—, dir. Plant Sci. and Water Conservation Lab., USDA, Stillwater. Contbr. numerous articles to profl. jours., 1956—. Served as cpl. USAAF, then USAF, 1946-49. Mem. Am. Phytopathol. Soc., Internat. Soc. Plant Pathologists, N.Y. Acad. Scis., Sigma Xi. Democrat. Lodge: Masons. Current Work: Genetics of host parasite interactions; epidemiology. Subspecialties: Plant pathology; Plant genetics.

GOULD, CHARLES LAVERNE, aerospace engineer; b. Winston, Mo., Oct. 26, 1933; s. Clem and Nora (Harris) G.; divorced; children: Anita, Katherine. B.S.M.E., Iowa State U., 1956; cert. bus. mgmt., UCLA, 1966; Ph.D. in Bus. Adminstrn, Calif. Western U., 1978. Cert. profl. mgr., Calif. Aerospace engr. USAF, Dayton, Ohio, 1959-62; project engr. Rockwell Internat., Downey, Calif., 1962-66, asst. chief engr. space sta., 1968-72, mgr. tech. programs, 1972-76, program mgr. space industrialization, 1976-80, shuttle utilization, 1980-84, chief projects engr., advanced tech. and systems, 1984—. Author tech. reports; contbr. articles to profl. jours. Chmn. bd. Methodist Ch., Anaheim, Calif., 1967. Served to lt USAF, 1956-59. Recipient Sustained Superior Service award USAF, 1962; Assoc. fellow AIAA. Republican. Methodist. Current Work: Management of research and technology, computer tool development, and advanced system concepts for space transportation and systems. Subspecialties: Aerospace engineering and technology; Satellite studies. Home: 1832 Sunset Ln Fullerton CA 92633 Office: Rockwell International 12214 Lakewood Blvd Downey CA

GOULD, GORDON, physicist, optical communications executive; b. N.Y.C., July 17, 1920; s. Kenneth Miller and Helen Vaughn (Rue) G. B.S. in Physics, Union Coll., 1941, D.Sc., 1978; M.S. in Physics, Yale U., 1943, Columbia U., 1952. Physicist Western Electric Co., Kearny, N.J., 1941; instr. Yale U., 1941-43; physicist Manhattan Project, 1943-45; engr. Semon Bache Co., N.Y.C., 1945-50; instr. CCNY, 1947-54; research asst. Columbia U., 1954-57; research dir. TRG, Inc./Control Data Corp., Melville, N.Y., 1958-67; prof. electrophysics Bklyn. Poly. Inst., 1967-74; v.p. engring./mktg., dir. Optelecom, Inc., Gaithersburg, Md., 1974—. Contbr. sci. articles to profl. jours. Recipient 63 research grants and contracts, 1958—; named Inventor of Year for laser amplifier Patent Office Soc., 1978. Mem. Am. Inst. Physics, Optical Soc. Am., IEEE, AAAS, Fiber Optic Communications Soc., Laser Inst. Am. (pres. 1971-73, dir. from 1971). Patentee in field. Current Work: Development of optical communication systems, optical instrumentation; fiber optic cables. Subspecialties: Optical engineering; Fiber optics.

GOULD, PHILLIP LOUIS, civil engineer, educator; b. Chgo., May 24, 1937; s. David J. and Belle (Blair) G.; m. Deborah Paula Rothholtz, Feb. 5, 1961; children: Elizabeth, Nathan, Rebecca, Joshua. B.S., U. Ill., 1959, M.S., 1960; Ph.D., Northwestern U., 1966. Structural designer Skidmore, Owings & Merrill, Chgo., 1960-63; structural engr. Westenhoff & Novick, Chgo., 1963-64; NASA trainee Northwestern U., Evanston, Ill., 1964-66; Harold D. Jolley prof., chmn. dept. civil engring. Washington U., St. Louis, 1966—; cons. various pvt. firms, utilities U.S. Nat. Bur. Standards, 1968—. Author: Static Analysis of Shells: A Unified Development of Surface Structures, 1977, (with others) Dynamic Response of Structures, 1980, Introduction to Linear Elasticity, 1983; Finite Element Analysis of Shells of Revolution, 1985; editor: Environmental Forces on Engineering Structures, 1979, (with others) Engring. Structures; contbr. over 100 articles to profl. jours. Served to 1st lt. U.S. Army, 1959-60, 62. Recipient Sr. U.S. Scientist award Alex V. Humboldt Found., W.Ger., 1974. Fellow ASCE; mem. Internat. Assn. Shell Structures, Am. Soc. Engring. Edn., Am. Acad. Mechanics, Sigma Xi. Current Work: Analysis and design of thin-shell structures including dynamic and interaction effects. Finite element analysis of rotational shells. Subspecialties: Civil engineering; Solid mechanics. Home: 102 Lake Forest Richmond Heights MO 63117 Office: Dept Civil Engring Washington Univ Campus Box 1130 St Louis MO 63130

GOULD, ROBERT JOSEPH, physicist; b. Providence, May 31, 1935; s. Howard Jerome and Julia Lillian (Gladhill) G. B.S., Providence Coll., 1957; Ph.D., Cornell U, 1963. Postgrad. research physicist U. Calif. at San Diego, La Jolla, 1963-65, ast. prof. physics, 1965-68, assoc. prof., 1968-76, prof., 1976—; vis. sr. lectr. U. Sydney, Australia, 1968; vis. scholar Stanford U., 1976. Contbr. numerous articles to profl. jours. Mem. Am. Phys. Soc., Am. Astron. Soc. Current Work: Atomic and particle physics with applications in astrophysics; statistical mechanics; plasma physics. Subspecialties: Theoretical physics; High energy astrophysics. Home: 3938 La Jolla Village Dr La Jolla CA 92037 Office: Dept Physics B-019 U Calif at San Diego La Jolla CA 92093

GOULD, ROY WALTER, engineer, physicist, educator; b. Los Angeles, Apr. 25, 1927; s. Roy Walter and Rosamonde (Stokes) G.; m. Ethel Savage Stratton, Aug. 23, 1952; children: Diana Stratton, Robert Clarke. B.S., Calif. Inst. Tech., 1949, Ph.D., 1956; M.S., Stanford, 1950. Mem. faculty Calif. Inst. Tech., Pasadena, 1955—, exec. officer for applied physics, 1973-79, chmn. div. engring. and applied sci., 1979-84, Simon Ramo prof. engring., 1980—; dir. div. controlled thermonuclear research AEC, 1970-72. Served with USNR, 1945-46. Fellow Am. Phys. Soc., IEEE; mem. Nat. Acad. Scis., Nat. Acad. Arts and Scis., Nat. Acad. Engring. Home: 808 Linda Vista Ave Pasadena CA 91103

GOULD, STEPHEN JAY, paleontologist, educator; b. N.Y.C., Sept. 10, 1941; s. Leonard and Eleanor (Rosenberg) G.; m. Deborah Ann Lee, Oct. 3, 1965; children: Jesse, Ethan. A.B., Antioch Coll., Yellow Springs, Ohio, 1963; Ph.D., Columbia U., 1967. Mem. faculty Harvard U., 1967—, prof. geology, 1973—. Author: Ontogeny and Phylogeny, 1977, Ever Since Darwin, 1977, The Panda's Thumb, 1980, A View of Life, 1981, The Mismeasure of Man, 1981, Hen's Teeth and Horse's Toes, 1983, The Flamingo's Smile, 1985; also numerous articles, monthly column This View of Life in Natural History mag. Recipient Nat. Mag. award for essays and criticism, 1980; Nat. Book award in sci., 1981; award for gen. non-fiction Nat. Book Critics Circle, 1982; McArthur Found. prize fellow, 1981—; grantee NSF. Fellow AAAS; mem. Paleontological Soc. (Schuchert award 1975), Soc. Study Evolution, Soc. Systematic Zoology, Am. Soc. Naturalists, Sigma Xi. Subspecialties: Paleobiology; Evolutionary biology. Address: Museum Comparative Zoology Harvard Univ Cambridge MA 02138

GOULIANOS, KONSTANTIN, physics educator; b. Salonica, Greece, Nov. 9, 1935; came to U.S., 1958, naturalized, 1967; s. Achilles and Olga (Nakopoulou) G. Student, U. Salonica, 1953-58; Ph.D., Columbia U., 1963. Research assoc. Columbia U., N.Y.C., 1963-64; instr. Princeton U., 1964-67, asst. prof., 1967-71; assoc. prof. Rockefeller U., N.Y.C., 1971-81, prof. physics, 1981—. Fulbright scholar, 1958-59. Patentee electronic device for analysis of radioactively labeled gel electrophoretograms. Current Work: Research in experimental high energy physics. Subspecialty: Particle physics.

GOUSE, S. WILLIAM, JR., scientist; b. Utica, N.Y., Dec. 15, 1931; s. S. William and Charlotte Virginia (Parzych) G.; m. Jacqueline Ann McLaughlin, Aug. 6, 1955; children: Linda Ellen, S. William III. S.B., S.M., MIT, 1954, Sc.D., 1958. Instr. mech. engring. MIT, 1956-57, asst. prof., 1957-61, 62-65, asso. prof., 1965-67, lectr., 1967-68; prof. mech. engring., prin. research engr. Transportation Research Inst. of Carnegie-Mellon U., 1967-69; staff mem. Office Sci. and Tech. of Exec. Office of the Pres., Washington, 1969-70; asso. dean Carnegie Inst. Tech. and Sch. Urban and Pub. Affairs of Carnegie-Mellon U., 1971-73; dir. Office Research and Devel. and sci. adviser to sec. U.S. Dept. Interior, 1973-75; acting dir. Office Coal Research, 1974-75; dep. asst. adminstr. fossil energy ERDA, 1974-77; chief scientist Mitre Corp., 1977-79, v.p., 1979-80, v.p., gen. mgr., 1980-83, sr. v.p., gen. mgr., 1984—; cons. to industry. Contbr. articles to profl. jours. Served with ordnance AUS, 1961-62. Visking Corp. fellow, 1954-55; Gen. Electric Co. W. Rice Jr. fellow, 1955-56; recipient Ralph Teetor award Soc. Automotive Engrs., 1966. Clubs: Cosmos, Explorers. Subspecialties: Mechanical engineering; Systems engineering. Home: PO Box 9085 McLean VA 22102

GOUST, JEAN-MICHEL CHRISTIAN, immunologist, educator; b. St. Mande, France, Jan. 21, 1941; naturalized, 1984; s. Francois Joseph and Marie Odile (Mirabail) G.; m. Marie Francoise Montassut, Sept. 5, 1963; children: Olivier, Thierry. B.S., U. Paris, 1958, M.D., 1971. Intern Hopitaux de Paris, 1963-66, resident, 1968-72; instr. CHU Pitie Salpetriere, Paris, 1968-72, clin. chief, asst. physician exptl. pathology and medicine, 1972-75; asst. prof. immunology Med. U. S.C., Charleston, 1975-80, asst. prof. medicine, 1976-80, assoc. prof. medicine, 1980-81, assoc. prof. immunology and neurology, 1981-84, prof. immunology, 1984—; chmn. med. adv. com. Trident chpt. Multiple Sclerosis Soc., 1980—, mem. med. adv. task force S.C. chpt., 1984—; spl. reviewer Nat. Inst. Neurol. Diseases, NIH, 1980—. Mem. editorial bd.: Clin. Immunology and Immunopathology; contbr. articles to profl. jours. Nat. Multiple Sclerosis Soc. grantee; NIH grantee; Owen-Ceatham Found for Research in Multiple Sclerosis grantee. Mem. Am. Fedn. Clin. Research, Am. Assn. Immunologists, Am. Soc. Microbiology, Soc. Exptl., Biology and Medicine, AAAS. Roman Catholic. Patentee in field. Current Work: Research in multiple sclerosis and other neurological diseases with immunological abnormalities. Subspecialties: Immunobiology and immunology; Neurology. Home: 29 27th Ave Isle of Palms SC 29451 Office: Dept Basic and Clin Immunology and Microbiology Med U SC 171 Ashley Av Charleston SC 29425

GOUTERMAN, MARTIN PAUL, chemistry educator; b. Phila., Dec. 26, 1931; s. Bernard and Melba (Buxbaum) G. B.A., Central High Sch., Phila., 1949, U. Chgo., 1951; M.Sc., U. Chgo., 1955, Ph.D. in Physics (NSF Predoctoral fellow), 1958. Faculty Harvard U., Cambridge, Mass., 1958-66; successively postdoctoral fellow, instr., asst. prof. chemistry dept.; faculty U. Wash., Seattle, 1966—, prof. chemistry, 1968—. Fellow Am. Inst. Physics; mem. Am. Chem. Soc., Sigma Xi. Research and publs. in spectroscopy, quantum chemistry, and solid state electronic properties of porphyrins, porphyrins as optical sensors. Current Work: Electronic spectra and structure of porphyrins and related molecules; solid state electronic properties of porphyrin films. Subspecialties: Physical chemistry; Theoretical chemistry. Office: Dept Chemistry U Wash Seattle WA 98195

GOVE, HARRY EDMUND, nuclear physicist, educator; b. Niagara Falls, Can., May 22, 1922; came to U.S., 1963, naturalized, 1969; s. Harry Golden and Lucia (Olmsted) G.; m. Elizabeth Alice dePencier, Aug. 20, 1945; children: Pauline Lucia, Diana Elizabeth. B.Sc., Queen's U., Kingston, Ont., 1944; Ph.D., MIT, 1950. Research asst. Nat. Research Council, Chalk River, Can., 1945-46; Research asst. Mass. Inst. Tech., 1946-50, research asso., 1950-52; asso. research officer Atomic Energy of Can., Ltd., Chalk River, 1952-59, br. head nuclear physics, 1956-63, sr. research officer, 1959-63; on leave with Niels Bohr Inst., Copenhagen, 1961-62; prof. physics, dir. nuclear structure research lab. U. Rochester, 1963—, chmn. dept. physics and astronomy, 1977-80; on leave with Lab. de Physique Nucléaire et d'Instrumentation Nucléaire, C.R.N., Strasbourg, 1971-72; R.T. French vis. prof. Worcester Coll., Oxford U., Eng., 1983-84. Mem. vis. com. Mass. Inst. Tech. Lab. Nuclear Research, 1966-68, Argonne Nat. Lab. physics div., 1966-69, Queen's U. Coll. Engring., 1968-70; mem. adv. com. physics div. NSF, 1969-71; mem. grant selection com. nuclear physics Nat. Sci. and Engring. Research Council Can., 1979-81; mem. ad hoc panel on meson factories Office Sci. and Tech., 1963; mem. selection panel NSF Postdoctoral Fellows, 1967, 69, 70; mem. vis. com. physics and accelerator depts. Brookhaven Nat. Lab., 1979-83; mem. nat. heavy-ion lab. policy com. Oak Ridge Nat. Lab., 1975-76; chmn. panel on basic nuclear data compilations NRC-Nat. Acad. Scis., 1975-80, mem. panel on future of nuclear sci., 1975-77; chmn. vis. com. Cyclotron Lab., U. Md., 1977-79. Contbr. articles to newspapers and mags. Divisional assoc. editor Phys. Rev. Letters, 1975-79; assoc. editor Ann. Rev. Nuclear Sci. Contbr. articles to profl. jours. Pres. Metro Act of Rochester, Inc., 1970-71; trustee Associated Univs., Inc., 1978-83. Served from sublt. to lt. Royal Canadian Navy, 1944-45. Recipient Pergamon Press Jari award, 1980. Fellow Am. Phys. Soc.; mem. Canadian Assn. Physicists. Democrat. Episcopalian. Club: Cosmos (Washington). Current Work: Detection of cosmogenic radioisotopes using an accelerator based mass spectrometry technique. Subspecialty: Nuclear physics. Home: 113 Burrows Hill Dr Rochester NY 14625

GOWANS, CHARLES SHIELDS, educator; b. Salt Lake City, Sept. 17, 1923; s. George Henry and Frances Ruth (Shields) G.; m. Ann Midgley, Mar. 30, 1950; children: Kathleen Gowans DeVries, Margaret Gowans Blinn, Susan. A.B. in Zoology, U. Utah, 1949; Ph.D., Stanford U., 1957. USPHS fellow Ind. U., Bloomington, 1956-57; asst. prof. biol. scis. U. Mo., Columbia, 1957-63, assoc. prof., 1963-68, prof., 1968—. Contbr. articles to profl. jours. Served with U.S. Army, 1942-45. NSF grantee, 1961-69; NIH grantee, 1961-63; Ocean Genetics Inc. grantee, 1982—. Mem. AAAS, Am. Inst. Biol. Sci., Internat. Soc. Phycology, Genetics Soc. Am., Phycological Soc. Am., Am. Soc. Microbiology, Soc. Protozoologists. Current Work: Investigation of and engring. prodn. of organic materials by algae. Subspecialties: Genetics and genetic engineering (biology); Microbiology. Office: U Mo Div Biological Science Columbia MO 65211

GOWDA, BYRE VENKATARAMANA, research and devel. engr.; b. Bangarapet, India, Mar. 3, 1940; s. Venkataramana and Muniyamma G.; m. Usha Gowda; children: Jayanth, Jeevan, Arathi. M.S. with distinction, Inst. Sci., India, 1965; Ph.D., U. Waterloo, Can., 1968. Registered profl. engr., Pa. Asst. prof. U. Waterloo, 1969-74; analyst Babcock & Wilcox Can., Ltd., 1974; sr. engr. Westinghouse Electric Corp., Pitts., 1974-76, prin. engr., 1976—. Contbr. articles to profl. jours. Exec. com. Hindu Temple. Recipient 3 Gold medals U. Mysore, India; research grantee U.S. Air Force, 1972-74; research grantee NRC, 1969-74. Mem. ASME (chmn. Westmoreland sect.), Acad. Mechanics, Am. Soc. Metals, ASTM. Patentee in field. Current Work: Strength and stability of structural systems, materials applications in energy systems, dynamics of structures degradations mechanisms like fatigue, fracture, corrosion and wear. Subspecialties: Nuclear fission; High-temperature materials.

GOWE, ROBB SHELTON, research institute administrator, researcher; b. St. Boniface, Mont., Can., Oct. 9, 1921; s. Shelton Loran and Carrie Ethyl (Wilson) G.; m. Christa B. Olsen; children—Bernard, Thomas, Margaret, Beverly. B.S.A., U. Toronto, 1945; M.Sc., Cornell U., 1947, Ph.D., 1949. Head poultry genetics Poultry Div. Agr. Can., Ottawa, Ont., 1949-59, chief animal genetics Animal Research Inst., 1959-65, dir. Animal Research Ctr., 1965—. Contbr. numerous articles to profl. jours. Founding exec. mem. Queensway Gen. Hosp., Ottawa, 1967-79, chmn., 1978-79; exec. mem., chmn. Ottawa Regional Hosp. Planning Council, 1969-75. Recipient Tom Newman Internat Poultry award, London, 1960; Merit award Govt. Can., 1980. Fellow Poultry Sci. Assn.; mem. Can. Soc. Animal Sci. (merit award 1984), Genetics Soc. Can., Am. Genetics Assn., Genetics Soc. Am. Current work: Concerned with improving the efficiency of selection in domestic poultry species where several traits must be improved simultaneously. Subspecialties: Animal genetics; Animal research administration. Office: Can Agr Animal Research Ctr Ottawa ON K1A 0C6 Canada

GOWEN, RICHARD JOSEPH, electrical engineer, educational administrator; b. New Brunswick, N.J., July 6, 1935; s. Charles David and Esther Ann (Hughes) G.; m. Nancy A. Applegate, Dec. 28, 1955; children—Jeff, Cindy, Betsy, Susan, Kerry. B.S. in Elec. Engring., Rutgers U., 1957; M.S., Iowa State U., 1961, Ph.D., 1962. Registered profl. engr., Colo. Research engr. RCA Labs., Princeton, N.J., 1957; commd. USAF; ground electronics officer Yaak AFB, Mont., 1957-59; instr. USAF Acad., 1962-63, research assoc., 1963-64, asst. prof., 1964-65, assoc. prof., 1965-66, tenure assoc. prof. elec. engring., 1966-70, tenure prof. elec. engring, 1973-73, dir., prin. investigator NASA instrumentation group for cardiovascular studies, 1968-77; mem. NASA launch and recovery med. team Johnson Space Center, 1971-77; v.p., dean engring., profl. elec. engring. S.D. Sch. Mines and Tech., Rapid City, 1977—; dir., prin. investigator NASA Program in support space cardiovascular studies, 1977—; co-chmn. Joint Industry; Nuclear Regulatory IEEE; Am. Nuclear Soc. Probabilistic Risk Assessment Guidelines for Nuclear Power Plants Project, 1980-83; mem. Dept. Def. Software Engring. Inst. Panel, 1983. Contbr. articles to profl. jours.; patentee in field. Bd. dirs. St. Martins Acad., Rapid City, S.D. Named Outstanding Young Man of Colorado Springs Jaycees, 1967; recipient Marrs Arnold Air Soc., 1967; recipient Outstanding Achievement in Field of Engring. Rutgers U., 1977, Profl. Achievement Citation in Engring. Iowa State U., 1983. Fellow IEEE (pres.-elect 1983, pres. 1984); mem. Sigma Xi, Phi Kappa Phi, Tau Beta Phi, Eta Kappa Nu, Pi Mu Epsilon. Roman Catholic. Club: Rotary (Rapid City, S.D.). Subspecialty: Electrical engineering. Home: 1609 Palo Verde Rapid City SD 57701 Office: SD Sch Mines and Tech 500 E St Joseph St Rapid City SD 57701

GOWN, ALLEN MICHAEL, pathologist, educator; b. N.Y.C., Nov. 12, 1950; s. Daniel and Theresa Rosalie (Gottleib) G.; m. Carol Safron, Dec. 26, 1971; children—Jacob, Benjamin. B.S., SUNYStony Brook, 1971; M.D., Albert Einstein Coll. Medicine, 1975. Diplomate Am. Bd. Pathology. Resident in pathology U. Wash., Seattle, 1975-79, instr., 1979-81, asst. prof. 1981—. Contbr. articles to profl. jours. Mem. Histochem. Soc., Internat. Acad. Pathology. Current work: Monoclonal antibodies as tools in cancer diagnosis; immunocytochemistry. Subspecialty: Pathology (medicine). Office: U Wash Dept Pathology Seattle WA 98195

GOY, ROBERT WILLIAM, psychologist, research administrator; b. Detroit, Jan. 25, 1924; s. George Frederick and Charlotte Elizabeth (McDowell) G.; m. Barbara Elaine Perry, Nov. 13, 1948; children: Michael Frederick, Peter William, Elizabeth Ruth. B.S., U. Mich., 1947; Ph.D., U. Chgo., 1953. Assoc. prof. anatomy U. Kans. Med. Sch., 1954-63; prof. med. psychology U. Oreg. Med. Sch.; chmn. dept. reproductive physiology and behavior Oreg. Regional Primate Research Center, 1963-71; prof. psychology U. Wis.; dir. Wis. Regional Primate Research Center, 1971—. Author: (with B.S. McEwen) Sexual Differentiation of the Brain, 1980; assoc. editor: Archives of Sexual Behavior, 1968—; editor: Hormones and Behavior, 1976—. Served with U.S. Army, 1943-46. USPHS postdoctoral fellow, 1954-56; USPHS grantee, 1954-56; NIMH grantee, 1963—. Mem. Am. Assn. Anatomists, Am. Psychol. Assn., Soc. Study Fertility, Soc. Study Reprodn., Endocrine Soc., Internat. Acad. Sex Research. Subspecialty: Physiological psychology. Home: 1845 Summit Madison WI 53705 Office: 1220 Capitol Ct Madison WI 53706

GOYAL, GREESH CHAND, chemist, researcher; b. Narnaul, Haryana, India, Nov. 10, 1942; came to U.S., 1974, naturalized, 1983; s. Rambilas and Premlata (Garg) G.; m. Saroj Garg, July 19, 1972; children—Abhinav, Neel. B.Sc., Agra U., Meerut, India; M.Sc., Rajasthan U., Jaipur, Rajasthan, India, 1963; Ph.D., Calgary U., Alta., Can., 1974. Sci. officer Atomic Energy Establishment, Trombay, Bombay, India, 1964-68; postdoctoral fellow Brandeis U., Waltham, Mass., 1974-75; research assoc. Ill. Inst. Tech., Chgo., 1976-78, sr. research assoc., 1981-84; clin. biochemist Augustana Hosp., Chgo., 1978-81; group leader Ayerst labs., Rouses Point, N.Y., 1984—. Contbr. articles to profl. jours. Mem. Am. Chem. Soc. Current work: Analytical research and development work on pharmaceuticals; biological and biochemical effects of ionizing and non-ionizing radiations. Subspecialties: Analytical chemistry; Biophysical chemistry. Home: 2 133 Lake St Apt 2 Rouses Point NY 12979 Office: Ayerst Labs Inc 64 Maple St Rouses Point NY 12979

GOYAL, RAJ K., physician; b. Hissar, India, May 6, 1937; came to U.S. Faculty in Scis., Govt. Coll., Hissar, 1955; M.B., B.S., Panjab U., Chandigarh, India, 1960; M.D. in Internal Medicine, Gastroenterology, Maulana Azad Med. Coll., New Delhi, India, 1965; A.M. (hon.) Harvard Med. Sch., 1982. Diplomate Am. Bd. Internal Medicine; cert. E.C.F.M.G. examination, Commonwealth of Mass. Bd. Registrations and Medicine; lic. Tex. State Bd. Med. Examiners. Intern in internal medicine and surgery Irwin Hosp., M.A. Med. Coll., New Delhi, 1961-62, resident in internal medicine, 1964-67; asst. research officer in internal medicine M.A. Med. Coll., 1962-63, dir. gen. health services scholar, 1963-64; resident in gastroenterology Hosp. of St. Raphael, New Haven, Conn., 1967-68; postdoc. research fellow in gastroenterology Yale U. Sch. Medicine, New Haven, 1968-69; postdoc. fellow in medicine Baylor Coll. Medicine, Houston, 1970-71; instr. in medicine Yale U. Sch. Medicine, 1969-70; asst. prof. medicine Baylor Coll. Medicine, 1971-73; prof. medicine U. Tex. Health Ctr., Dallas, 1973-77, prof. internal medicine, 1977-78, San Antonio, 1978-81; asst. attending physician in internal medicine Ben Taub Ben. Hosp., Houston, 1971-73; sr. attending physician, dir. gastroenterology Parkland Meml. Hosp., Dallas, 1973-78; attending physician Bexar County Hosp., San Antonio, 1978-81; physician, dir. gastroenterology div. Beth Israel Hosp., Boston, 1981—; Mallinckrodt prof. medicine Harvard Med. Sch., Boston, 1981-84, Charlotte F. and Irving W. Rabb prof. medicine, 1984—; cons. VA Hosp., Houston, 1971-73, Dallas, 1973-77, Audie L. Murphy VA Hosp., San Antonio, 1978-81; mem. com. on medical knowledge self-assessment program V Am. Bd. Internal Medicine, 1978-79; ad hoc mem. NIH study sect., 1979—; mem. study sect. VA review group for Gastroenterology, 1980-83; mem. faculty assembly U. Tex. Health Sci. Ctr., Dallas, 1975-77; mem. faculty senate U. Tex. Southwestern Med. Sch., 1975-77, mem. exec. com., faculty senate, 1976-77, chmn. internship adv. com., 1978-79; mem. faculty tenure and promotions com. U. Tex. Health Sci. Ctr., San Antonio, 1980-81, participant gastrointestinal pathophysiology course, 1973-77, participant gastrointestinal module, 1977—; mem. faculty council Harvard Med. Sch., 1983-84; course developer, dir. gastrointestinal pathophysiology Baylor Coll. Medicine, 1971-73; course dir. gastrointestinal pathophysiology Harvard Med. Sch., Boston, 1985—, Update in Gastroenterology, 1982—. Mem. editorial bd. Gastroenterology, 1975-77, assoc. editor, 1977-84. Author numerous abstracts and presentations. Contbr. numerous articles to profl. jours. Recipient Mohan Lal Nayyar award Irwin Hosp., 1966-67; Outstanding Tchr. award Baylor Coll. Medicine Class of 1973, 72, 73 75; Disting. Faculty award Internal Medicine Housestaff, 1980. Mem. Am. Fedn. Clinical Research (counselor so. sect. 1974-79), Am. Gastroenterological Assn. (mem. com. on research 1978-81), So. Soc. for Clinical Investigation, Am. Physiol. Soc., Am. Soc. for Clinical Investigation, Am. Assn. for Physicians, Am. Motility Soc. (pres. 1984-85, mem. steering com., program chmn., 1980). Subspecialty: Gastroenterology. Home: 61 Winston Rd Newton MA 02159 Office: Div Gastroenterology Beth Israel Hosp 330 Brookline Ave Boston MA 02215

GOYAL, SATISH CHANDRA, engineering educator, administrator, consultant; b. Kasganj, India, Sept. 10, 1921; came to U.S., 1979; s. Bankeylal and Ram Devi (Agrawal) Karariwale; m. Kunti Kumari, Jan 16, 1941; children—Ashok Kumar, Sushma Rani, Arun Kumar, Arvind Kumar, Anand Kumar. B.S., Agra U., India, 1940; B.E., Thomason Coll. Civil Engring. (now U. Roorkee), 1943; M.S. in Civil Engring., U. Calif.-Berkeley, 1961. Engr. P.W.D. Govt., Agra, Gonda, Basti, U.P, India, 1943-47; lectr., reader Roorkee U., India, 1947-54; prof. structural engring. M.B.M. Engring. Coll., Jodhpur U., India, 1954-63, 69-72, 77-79, dean engring., 1971-74, 63-66, vice chancellor, 1974-77; dean engring. Pant Engring., Pantnagar, India, 1966-69; prof. civil engring. Tri-State U., Angola, Ind., 1979—; cons. structural design work, U.S. and India. Author: (with Dropjain) Manual of Estimating, 1954; (with S. Divakaran) Design of Structures in Structural Steel, 1961; (with B.C. Punmia) Theory of Structures and Strength of Materials, 1964; (with M.R. Sethia) Engineering Mechanics, 1977. Bd. dirs., chmn. Univ. Ctr. of Desert Studies, Jodhpur, 1976-77; dir. Rural Housing Wing, Jodhpur, 1977-79. U.S. AID exchange visitor to U.S., 1960. Fellow ASCE, Instn. Engrs. India (chmn. Rajasthan Ctr., citation 1974), Indian Soc. Desert Tech. (pres.); mem. ASME. Hindu. Lodge: Rotary (pres.). Current work: Structural engineering and applied mechanics. Subspecialties: Civil engineering; Theoretical and applied mechanics. Home: 42451 Ravina Ct Northville MI 48167 Office: Tri-State U Angola IN 46703 Also: 1 Residency Rd Jodhpur 342001 India

GOYAL, SHRI KRISHNA, telecommunications and computer technologist, researcher; b. Barrakpur, India, Oct. 29, 1939; came to U.S., 1969, naturalized, 1971; s. Pirthi Singh and Somavati G.; m. Vibha Garg, Feb. 14, 1966; children—Deepi, Moki. M.S. in Tech., Allahabad U., India, 1961; Ph.D., N.C. State U., 1974. Scientist, Electronics Research Inst., Pilani, India, 1961-69; research asst. N.C. State U., Raleigh, 1969-74; mem. tech. staff GTE Labs, Waltham, Mass., 1974-80, tech. mgr., 1980—; mem. Indian Standards Inst., New Delhi, 1965-68; chmn. task force on teletext standards Electronics Industries Assn., Washington, 1978-82. Patentee in field. Recipient Nat. Import Substitution award Invention Promotion Bd., 1979. Mem. IEEE (sr.), Assn. Computer Machinery, Am. Assn. Artificial Intelligence, Phi Kappa Phi. Current work: Information processing; AI applications to info services; expert systems research; distributed artificial intelligence. Subspecialties: Artificial intelligence; Information systems (Information science). Home: 8 Axdell Rd Sudbury MA 01776 Office: GTE Labs 40 Sylvan Rd Waltham MA 02254

GOYAN, JERE EDWIN, university dean, former government official; b. Oakland Calif., Aug. 3, 1930; s. Gerald H. and Lucille (Johnson) G.; children—Pamela, Terrence H., Andrea. B.S., U. Calif. Sch. Pharmacy, 1952, Ph.D., 1957. Asst. prof. pharmacy U. Mich., 1956-61, assoc. prof., 1961-63; assoc. prof. pharmacy and pharm. chemistry U. Calif. at San Francisco, 1963-65, prof., 1965-79, 81—; assoc. dean Sch. Pharmacy, 1966-67, dean, 1967-79, 80—; commr. FDA, 1979-81. Fellow AAAS, Acad. Pharm. Scis.; mem. Inst. Medicine, Nat. Acad. Scis., N.Y. Acad. Scis., Am. Pharm. Assn., Calif. Pharm. Assn., Am. Assn. Colls. Pharmacy (pres. 1978-79), Sigma Xi, Rho Chi, Phi Lambda Upsilon. Current work: Properties of drugs in solutions. Subspecialty: Pharmacokinetics. Office: U Calif Sch Pharmacy San Francisco CA 94143

GRACE, RICHARD EDWARD, engineering educator; b. Chgo., June 26, 1930; s. Richard Edward and Louise (Koko) G.; m. Consuela Cummings Fotos, Jan. 29, 1955; children: Virginia Louise, Richard Cummings (dec.). B.S. in Metall. Engring., Purdue U., 1951; Ph.D., Carnegie Inst. Tech., 1954. Registered profl. engr., N.J. Asst. prof. Purdue U., West Lafayette, Ind., 1954-58, asso. prof., 1958-62, prof., 1962—, head sch. materials sci. and metall. engring., 1965-72, head div. interdisciplinary engring. studies, 1969-82, head freshman engring. dept., asst. dean engring., 1981—; cons. to Midwest industries. Contbr. articles to profl. jours. Past dir. and officer engring. edn. and accreditation com. Engrs. Council for Profl. Devel. Mem. Am. Soc. Metals (tchr. award 1962, fellow award 1974), AIME, Am. Soc. Engring. Edn., AAUP, Sigma Xi, Tau Beta Pi, Omicron Delta Kappa, Phi Gamma Delta. Clubs: Rotary, Elks, Lafayette Country. Current Work: Corrsion, transport processes. Subspecialties: Materials (engineering); Metallurgical engineering. Home: 2175 Tecumseh Park Ln West Lafayette IN 47906

GRACE, THOMAS PETER, computer scientist, educator; b. Evergreen Park, Ill., Jan. 30, 1955; s. Thomas George and Norma Fay (Rawls) G. B.S., U. Ill., Chgo., 1976, M.S., 1979, Ph.D., 1982. Programmer, analyst N.E. Ill. Planning Commn., Chgo., 1974-76; resident student assoc. Argonne Nat. Lab., Ill., 1976-78; programmer, analyst Speakeasy Computing, Chgo., 1978-80; teaching and research asst. U. Ill., 1977-82; asst. prof. computer sci. Ill. Inst. Tech., Chgo., 1982—; cons. Nat. Opinion Research Ctr., U. Chgo., 1981, Chgo. Area Geog. Info. Survey, 1978. Contbr. articles to profl. jours. Mem. Assn. Computing Machinery, Math. Assn. Am., Am. Math. Soc., Computer Soc. of IEEE. Roman Catholic. Current Work: Combinatorial algorithms, graph-theoretic algorithms, computer graphics, image representation and display, general graph theory. Subspecialties: Mathematical software; Graphics, image processing, and pattern recognition. Home: 650 River Dr Calumet City IL 60409 Office: Dept Computer Sci Ill Inst Tech Chicago IL 60616

GRADIJAN, JACK ROBERTSON, software engineer; b. Worcester, Mass., May 12, 1932; s. John and Viola May (Watt) G.; m. Christine Malin, Apr. 21, 1963; children—Paul, Stephen, Mark, David. B.S. in Elec. Engring., MIT, 1955, M.S., 1955. Trainee in neurobiology U. Rochester, 1963-66; computer cons. Rockland Research, Orangeburg, N.Y., 1966-75; computer scientist Lederle Lab., Pearl River, N.Y., 1975-77; software engr. GTE-Sylvania, Needham, Mass., 1977-79; mgr. software devel. Datamedix, Sharon, Mass., 1979-82; Instrumentation Lab., Lexington, Mass., 1982—. Contbr. articles to profl. jours. Mem. IEEE. Lutheran. Current work: Development of computer systems for biomedical applications, clinical instrumentation, cardiac monitoring, electroencephalography analysis. Subspecialties: Software engineering; Biomedical engineering. Home: 52 Walnut St Needham MA 02192 Office: Instrumentation Lab 113 Hartwell Ave Lexington MA 02173

GRADY, ARTHUR LYNN, aerospace company executive; b. Obion County, Tenn., June 22, 1933; s. Coy Emerson and Eva Myrl (Ferguson) G.; m. Anna B. Petrarca, July 11, 1959 (div. 1974); children—Lisa Ann, Cary Lynn. B.S.E.E., U. Tenn.; postgrad. Northwestern U. Gen. supr life sics. Northrop Space Labs., Hampton, Va., 1967-70; dir., mgr. aerophysics Northrop Services, Inc., Huntsville, Ala., 1970-71, mgr. adv. engring. and mktg., 1971-73, mgr. environ. scis., 1973-76, Research Triangle Park, N.C., 1976-79, v.p., 1979—; speaker's bur. Research Triangle Found., 1977—; Northrop rep. to Research Triangle Park area bus. and community orgns., pres. Northrop Mgmt. Club, 1970-77. Mem. Owners and Tenants Assn., Research Triangle Park, 1977—; bd. dirs. Triangle Emergency Med. Services, Inc., 1977—; chmn. bd. dirs. North Ala. Multiple Sclerosis Soc., Huntsville, 1970-77; dir. civic affairs Huntsville Jaycees, 1970-77; mem. Civic Arts Council, Huntsville, 1970-77; mem. exec., patronage policy coms. Madison County Republicans (Ala.), 1970-77; campaign mgr. county commn. chmn. Rep. candidate, mem. reception com. for U.S. Atty. Gen., mem. reception com. for Pres. Nixon's visit, Huntsville; Recipient Outstanding Leadership award Multiple Sclerosis Soc. Mem. Triangle Area Research Dirs. Assn. (chmn.). Lodge: Rotary (pres. Research Triangle Park, mem. dist. council). Subspecialty: Aerospace engineering and technology. Office: Northrup Services Inc 2 Triangle Dr Research Triangle Park NC 27709

GRAEDON, JOE DAVID, pharmacologist, author, lecturer; b. N.Y.C., Aug. 8, 1945; s. Sid and Helen (Ars) G.; m. Teresa Lynn Frost, Aug. 29, 1970; children—David, Alena. B.S., Pa. State U., 1967; M.S., U. Mich., 1971. Research asst. N.J. Neuropsychiat. Inst., Princeton, 1967-69; clin. prof. pharmacology U. Oaxaca, Mexico, 1973-74; asst. prof. clin. pharmacy Sch. Pharmacy, U. Calif.-San Francisco, 1982-83, mem. adv. bd. to drug studies unit, 1983—; guest lectr. Duke U., Durham, N.C., 1975-80, U. N.C., Chapel Hill, 1979-83; commentator Sta. WUNC-FM, Chapel Hill, 1978—, show host, 1983—. Author: People's Pharmacy (Med. Self-Care award 1976), 1975; People's Pharmacy-2, 1980; The New People's Pharmacy-3, 1985. Syndicated columnist: The People's Pharmacy, 1978—. Mem. Soc. Neurosci., Am. Med. Writers Assn. (editorial bd. 1983—), Sleep Research Soc., AAAS. Subspecialty: Neuropharmacology.

GRAFF, WILLIAM ARTHUR, engineering executive, glass technologist; b. Highland, Ill., Dec. 25, 1923; s. Arthur Oscar and Stella Emily (Koch) G.; m. Roberta Pauline Partridge, Apr. 7, 1945; children—Arthur Steven, Trudy Ann. B.S., U. Ill., 1946, M.S., 1947, Ph.D., 1949. Registered profl. engr., Ill. Research glass technologist, Gen. Electric Co., Cleve., 1949-57, Research supr., Richmond Heights, 1957-66, mgr. glass research lab., Richmond Heights, 1966-74, mgr. materials lab., Richmond Heights, 1974-80, mgr. engring. support, Richmond Heights, 1980—. Patentee lamp and electronic glasses. Served with U.S. Army, 1943. Owens-Ill. Glass Co. fellow U. Ill., 1947-49. Mem. Am. Ceramic Soc., Am. Chem. Soc., Soc. Glass Tech., Deutsche Glastechnische Gesells, Sigma Xi. Presbyterian. Current work: Glass and vitreous silica technology and engineering administration. Subspecialties: Ceramics; Electronic materials. Office: Glass and Metall Products Dept 24400 Highland Rd Richmond Heights OH 44143

GRAGOUDAS, EVANGELOS STELIOS, ophthalmologist, educator; b. Lesbos, Greece, 1941. M.D., Athens U., 1965. Diplomate: Am. Bd. Ophthalmology. Rotating intern Waltham (Mass.) Hosp., 1969-70; resident in ophthalmology Boston U., 1970-73; research fellow Joslin Research Lab., 1970; retina fellow Mass. Eye and Ear Infirmary, Boston, 1973-75, asst. in ophthalmology, 1975—; dir. Mass. Eye and Ear Infirmary (Fluorescein Angiography Lab.), 1975—; assoc. dir. retina service, 1976-85, dir. retina service, 1985—, acting dir. Laser Ctr., 1985—; asst. prof. ophthalmology Harvard U., Boston, 1978-81, assoc. prof., 1981—. Served to 2d lt., M.C. Greek Army, 1966-68. Fellow Am. Acad. Ophthalmology; mem. Assn. Research in Vision and Ophthalmology, Retina Soc. Current Work: Proton-beam irradiation of intraocular melanomas. Subspecialty: Ophthalmology. Office: Harvard U Med Sch Boston MA*

GRAHAM, DAVID TREDWAY, medical educator, physician; b. Mason City, Iowa, June 20, 1917; s. Evarts Ambrose and Helen (Tredway) G.; m. Frances Jeanette Keesler, June 14, 1941; children: Norma VanSurdam, Andrew Tredway, Mary Brewster. B.A., Princeton U., 1938; M.A., Yale U., 1941; M.D., Washington U., St. Louis, 1943. Intern Barnes Hosp., St. Louis, 1944, asst. resident medicine, 1944-45, 47-48; research fellow medicine Cornell U. Med. Coll., 1948-51; asst. prof. medicine Washington U. Med. Sch., 1951-57, asst. prof. psychiatry, 1956-57; assoc. prof. medicine U. Wis. Med. Sch., 1957-63, prof. medicine, 1963—, assoc. chmn. dept., 1969-71, chmn., 1971-80, asst. dean and/or chmn. med. sch. admissions, 1964-69; vis. prof. psychiatry U. Va. Sch. Medicine, 1960; Ripley lectr. U. Wash., 1976. Editor: Clin. Research Proc, 1954-59. Alt. del. Democratic Nat. Conv., 1968. Served to capt., M.C. AUS, 1945-47. Fellow ACP (emeritus); mem. State Med. Soc. Wis., Am. Fedn. Clin. Research, Am. Psychosomatic Soc. (council 1952-55, 64-67, pres. 1978-79), Soc. Psychophysiol. Research (bd. dirs. 1964-67, pres. 1969-70), Central Soc. Clin. Research. Current Work: Psychosomatic medicine. Subspecialties: Internal medicine; Psychophysiology. Home: 2927 Harvard Dr Madison WI 53705

GRAHAM, DONALD LEE, chemical engineer; b. Hymera, Ind., May 1, 1931; s. Ross Raymond and Hazel Mae (McClanahan) G.; m. Phyllis Ann Seymour, Sept. 2, 1950; children: Stephen Lee, Cynthia Ann Graham Bruzewski, Diane Kay Graham McBeath, Robert Bruce. B.S. in Chem. Engring., Purdue U., 1953. With Dow Chem. Co., 1953—, plastics devel. engr., mem. staff plastics tech. service and devel., sect. head fabricated constrn. materials plastics devel. and service, Midland, Mich., 1964-68, tech. mgr. constrn. materials research and devel., 1968-73, dir. research and devel. functional products and systems, 1973-76, dir. research and devel. western div., Pittsburg, Calif., 1976-82, dir. western applied sci. and tech., 1982-83; v.p., dir. ops. and research and devel. Dow Chem. Latin Am., 1983—; dir. Cynara Co.; trustee Product Research Com., 1975-79. Mem. pres.'s council Purdue U., 1979—. Mem. AAAS, Soc. Chem. Industry, Am. Chem. Soc., Am. Inst. Chem Engrs., Walnut Creek C. of C. (v.p. 1977-78). Republican. Methodist. Patentee in field. Current Work: Directing technical service and development and nine manufacturing plants serving Mexico, Central America, Caribbean and South America for agricultural, pharmaceutical, plastics and specialty chemicals. Subspecialties: Chemical engineering; Organic chemistry. Home: 7951 SW 167 St Miami FL 33157 Office: Dow Chem Latin Am 2801 Ponce de Leon Blvd PO Box 140400 Coral Gables FL 33114

GRAHAM, FREDERICK MITCHELL, educator; b. Des Moines, Feb. 7, 1921; s. Fred and Anna Mae (Mitchell) G.; m. Lillian L. Miller, Aug. 29, 1948; children: Frederick M., Stephen, Anita. B.S., Iowa State U., 1948, M.S., 1950, Ph.D., 1966. Prof., dept. head Prairie View (Tex.) A&M U., 1950-59; prof. engring. sci. and mechanics Iowa State U., Ames, 1962—; cons. McDonnell Douglas, 1972-73, Meredith Pub. Co., 1968-70, VanGorp Corp, 1970—, Sundstrand Corp., 1979. Contbr. articles to profl. jours. Served with USAAF, 1943-46. NSF fellow, 1959-61; named Superior Engring. Tchrs. of the Yr. Iowa State U., 1978, Outstanding Engring. Sci. and Mechanics Prof., 1984. Mem. Am. Soc. Engring. Edn., Nat. Soc. Profl. Engrs. (pres. 1983-84), Tau Beta Pi. Democrat. Episcopalian. Current Work: Experimentation with innovative structural components; investigation of complex industrial failures. Subspecialties: Civil engineering; Theoretical and applied mechanics. Home: 134 S Franklin St Ames IA 50010 Office: Iowa State Univ 3009 ME/ESM Ames IA 50011

GRAHAM, HARRY MORGAN, entomologist, researcher, educator; b. Whittier, Calif., June 18, 1929; s. Harry R. and May A. (Morgan) G.; m. Dorothy D. Denson, Sept. 22, 1962; children: Nancy J., Robert M. A.A., Fullerton Jr. Coll., 1949; B.S. with highest honors, U. Calif.-Berkeley, 1951, M.S., 1953, Ph.D., 1959. Research entomologist Dept. Agr. Agrl. Research Service, Brownsville, Tex., 1958-77, Tucson, 1977—; adj. prof. entomology U. Ariz. Contbr. numerous articles to profl. publs. Served to cpl. U.S. Army, 1953-55. Mem. AAAS, Entomol. Soc. Am., S.W. Entomol. Soc., Internat. Biol. Control Orgn., Ariz.-Nev. Acad. Sci. Presbyterian. Current Work: Insect ecology, biological control of insects, biological control of insects pests of field crops. Subspecialties: Integrated pest management; Ecology (environmental science).

GRAHAM, JOHN BORDEN, medical educator; b. Goldsboro, N.C., Jan. 26, 1918; s. Ernest Heap and Mary (Borden) G.; m. Ruby Barrett, Mar. 23, 1943; children: Charles Barrett, Virginia Borden, Thomas Wentworth. B.S., Davidson Coll., 1938, D.Sc. (hon.), 1984; M.D., Cornell U., 1942. Asst. Cornell U., 1943-44; mem. faculty U. N.C., Chapel Hill, 1946—, Alumni Disting. prof. pathology, 1966—, chmn. genetics curriculum, 1963-85, assoc. dean medicine for basic scis., 1968-70, coordinator interdisciplinary grad. programs in biology, 1968—, dir. hemostasis program, 1974—; vis. prof. haematology St. Thomas's Hosp. Med. Sch., London, 1972; vis. prof. Teikyo U. Med. Sch., Tokyo, 1976; mem. selection com. NIH research career awards, 1959-62; genetics tng. com. USPHS, 1962-66, chmn., 1967-71; mem. genetic basis of disease com. Nat. Inst. Gen. Med. Scis., 1977-80; mem. pathology test com. Nat. Bd. Med. Examiners, 1963-67; mem. research adv. com. U. Colo. Inst. Behavioral Genetics, 1967-71; mem. Internat. Com. Haemostasis and Thrombosis, 1963-67; chmn. bd. U. N.C. Population Program, 1964-67; sec. policy bd. Carolina Population Center, 1972-78; cons. Environ. Health Center, USPHS, WHO, Bolt, Beranek & Newman, Inc.; mem. med. and sci. adv. council Nat. Hemophilia Found., 1972-76; hon. cons. in genetics Margaret Pyke Centre, London, 1972—. Mem. editorial bd.: N.C. Med. Jour., 1949-66, Am. Jour. Human Genetics, 1958-61, Soc. Exptl. Biology and Medicine, 1959-62, Human Genetics Abstracts, 1962-72, Haemostasis, 1975-80, Christian Scholar, 1958-60. Markle scholar in med. sci., 1949-54; Recipient O. Max Gardner award U. N.C., 1968. Mem. AMA, AAAS, Elisha Mitchell Sci. Soc. (pres. 1963), AAUP, Soc. Exptl. Biology and Medicine, Am. Soc. Exptl. Pathology, Assn. Univ. Pathologists, Am. Assn. Pathologists and Bacteriologists, Am. Soc. Human Genetics (sec. 1964-67, pres. 1972), Genetics Soc. Am., Internat. Soc. Hematology, Am. Inst. Biol. Sci., Royal Soc. Medicine (London), Med. Soc. N.C., Mayflower Soc., Sigma Xi. Democrat. Presbyterian. Club:, (). Publs. on blood clotting, inherited diseases in humans, human population dynamics; co-discoverer blood coagulant Factor X (Stuart factor). Current Work: Program director for research on thrombosis and hemostasis utilizing monoclonal antibodies and recombinant DNA. Subspecialties: Genetics and genetic engineering (biology); Genetics and genetic engineering (medicine). Home: 108 Glendale Dr Chapel Hill NC 27514

GRAHAM, KENNETH ROBERT, psychology educator; b. Phila., June 5, 1943; s. Edgar and Margit (Leafgreen) G.; m. Michele C. Monroe, Aug. 10, 1968; children: Mark A., Richard A. B.A., U. Pa.-Phila., 1964; Ph.D., Stanford U., 1969. Research psychologist Inst. Pa. Hosp., Phila., 1969-70; asst. prof. Muhlenberg Coll., Allentown, Pa., 1970-76, assoc. prof. psychology, 1976-83, prof., 1983—, head dept. psychology, 1984—. Author: Psychological Research, 1977; editorial bd.: Am. Jour. Clin. Hypnosis, 1974—. Bd. dirs. Lehigh Valley Child Care, Inc., Allentown, Pa., 1979-85, pres. bd., 1981-84. Mem. Am. Psychol. Assn. (council reps. 1982), Am. Soc. Clin. Hypnosis, Soc. Clin. and Exptl. Hypnosis, Eastern Psychol. Assn., Sigma Xi. Democrat. Lutheran. Lodge: Kiwanis. Current Work: Relation between susceptibility to hypnosis and the persuasive effects of the mass media, especially television. Subspecialties: Social psychology; Clinical psychology. Home: 2949 Tilghman St Allentown PA 18104 Office: Muhlenberg Coll Allentown PA 18104

GRAHAM, LESLIE STEPHEN, medical physicist; b. Frankfort, Ind., Jan. 3, 1933; s. Forest P. and Iva E. (Davis) G.; m. Marianne E. Graham, Jan. 25, 1959; children: Michael S., Daryl T. B.A., Pasadena Coll., 1955; B.D., Talbot Sem., La Mirada, Calif., 1959; M.A., Calif. State U., Long Beach, 1962; Ph.D., UCLA, 1971. Diplomate: Am. Bd. Radiology. Med. physicist UCLA, 1971-77; prof. UCLA (Sch. Medicine), 1971—; med. physicist VA Med. Center, Sepulveda, Calif., 1977—; cons. in field. Contbr chpts. to books and articles to profl. jours. USPHS fellow, 1968-69. Mem. Am. Assn. Physicists in Medicine, Soc. Nuclear Medicine, IEEE. Current Work: Computer applications in nuclear medicine; computer modeling, dosimetry, computer analysis of instrumentation function. Subspecialty: Diagnostic radiology. Office: 16111 Plummer St Sepulveda CA 91343

GRAHAM, RONALD L., mathematician. Dir. Math. and Stats. Research Ctr., AT&T Bell Labs., Murray Hill, N.J. . Office: AT&T Bell Labs Math and Stats Research Ctr Murray Hill NJ 07974

GRAHAM, TERRENCE LEE, biochemist; b. Corning, N.Y., Sept. 24, 1947; s. Paul N. W. and Grace (Link) G.; m. Lian-Mei Yang, June 7, 1975. B.S., Pa. State U., 1969; Ph.D., Purdue U., 1975. NIH postdoctoral trainee in pathology U. Wis., Madison, 1975-77; project leader plant pathogen project Monsanto Co., St. Louis, 1977-80, sr. group leader host-modification program, 1980-82, sci. fellow, sr. group leader plant biochemistry program, 1982-83, sci. fellow, research mgr., biol. control program, 1983-85, mgr. cellular and molecular biology research, 1985—. Contbr. articles to profl. jours. Charles Gerth scholar., 1967-68; John White fellow, 1969; Purdue U. fellow, 1969. Mem. Am. Chem. Soc., Am. Phytopathol. Soc., Am. Soc. Microbiology, Am. Soc. Plant Physiologists. Current Work: Biochemical components of the plant cell; cell membrane and cell wall as they relate to cascade regulation of gene expression in whole plants and tissue culture; plant developmental and stress metabolism and the response of plants to chemical messengers, biological control of agricultural pests through genetic engineered microbes and plants. Subspecialties: Plant physiology (agriculture); Biochemistry (biology). Home: 1559 Meadowside Dr Creve Coeur MO 63146 Office: Monsanto Chem Co 800 N Lindbergh Blvd Saint Louis MO 63166

GRAHAM, WILLIAM HARDIN, chemist, researcher; b. Birmingham, Ala., Apr. 27, 1932; s. David Franklin and Roberta Lee (Hardin) G.; m. Anna Montalbano, June 9, 1956; children—Carol Anne, Michael David, Janet Lee, Patrick Hardin, Alan Gleason. B.S., La. State U., 1953, M.S., 1955; Ph.D., Fla. State U., 1958; postgrad. Calif. Inst. Tech., 1958-59; research chemist Rohm & Haas Co., Huntsville, Ala., 1959-70, group supr., 1970, Bristol, Pa., 1970-72; sr. research chemist Morton Thiokol Co., Huntsville, 1972-83, group supr., 1983—. Contbr. articles to Jour. Am. Chem. Soc., Jour. Organic Chemistry, Jour. Phys. Chemistry, also others. Patentee in field. Pres., Internat. Little League, Huntsville, 1981; chmn. Madison County Republican Com., Huntsville, 1966-68, 1975-80; elector Ala. Rep. Com., 1968, del. Rep. Nat. Conv., 1976, 84; chmn. 5th Congl. Dist. Rep. Com., 1982—; NSF fellow, 1957-58; Arthur Ames Noyes research fellow, 1958-59. Mem. Am. Chem. Soc., Assn. U.S. Army, Huntsville Assn. Tech. Socs. (treas. 1978). Roman Catholic. Club: Rohm & Haas Employees Assn. (pres. 1967). Current work: Solid propellant chemistry; energetic materials; isocyanate cure chemistry; nitrogen-flourine compounds, diazirines; nitrate esters. Subspecialties: Organic chemistry; Polymer chemistry. Home: 3019 Barcody Rd Huntsville AL 35802 Office: Morton Thiokol Inc Redstone Arsenal Huntsville AL 35807

GRALLO, RICHARD MARTIN, educational psychologist, social science research consultant; b. Winthrop, Mass., Feb. 15, 1947; s. Frederick Michael and Jennie Antonia (Ferrario) G. A.B., Boston Coll., 1969; M.S., MIT, 1972; M.A., NYU, 1976. Research asst. NYU, 1977-79; mem. faculty New Sch. for Social Research, 1978; research assoc. Inst. Developmental Studies, N.Y.C., 1979—; research cons., 1980—; prof. Coll. Human Services, N.Y.C., 1980—. John A. Lyons fellow, 1969-72. Mem. Am. Psychol. Assn. (assoc.), Am. Philos. Assn., N.Y. Acad. Scis. (adv. com. Psychology Sect. 1980—), Eastern Edl. Research Assn., Phi Delta Kappa. Current Work: Teaching in psycho-educational measurement; research design and evaluation; conducting psychoeducational research; social science research consulting. Subspecialties: Developmental psychology; Learning. Home: 1257 E 7th St Plainfield NJ Office: Coll Human Services 345 Hudson St New York NY 10014

GRAND, DIANA LEIGH, software engineer; b. Detroit, Dec. 15, 1945; d. Salman and Evelyn (Patt) G.; m. Richard M. Karp, Aug. 12, 1979. B.A., U. Mich., 1966; M.S. in Computer Sci, U. Calif.-Berkeley, 1976. Devel. engr. Hewlett Packard, Cupertino, Calif., 1975; computer scientist Lawrence Berkeley Lab., Berkeley, Calif., 1976—; software engr. Varian Assocs., Walnut Creek, Calif., 1982-84; founder, v.p. Project Tech., Inc., 1984—. Mem. Assn. for Computing Machinery, IEEE Computer Soc., N.Y. Acad. Scis. Current Work: Automated analysis and design approaches to large scale software development projects. Subspecialties: Software engineering; Distributed systems and networks. Office: 1051 Keith Ave Berkeley CA 94708

GRANDON, GARY MICHAEL, psychologist; b. Detroit, Nov. 24, 1948; s. Samuel Francis and Sylvia (Chase) G.; m. Jane Ray Rosen, June 2, 1974; children: Jessica Rose Rosen, Benjamin Seth Rosen. B.S., U. Mich., 1970; M.Ed., Wayne State U., 1972; Ph.D., U. Conn., 1978. Asso. dir. Roper Center Inc., Storrs, Conn., 1977-81, Inst. Social Inquiry, Storrs, 1976-81; asst. prof. U. Conn., Storrs, 1978-81; asso. dir. Computer Research Center, Tampa, Fla., 1981—; asst. prof. U.S. Fla., Tampa, 1981—. Author: Kera 4.0 Radial Keratotomy Prediction System, 1985, Statistical Package A-STAT 83, 1979-83, Optimizing High School Curriculum Assignments, 1979. Mem. Am. Ednl. Research Assn., Am. Statis. Assn., Assn. Computing Machinery, Am. Psychol. Assn., Assn. Ednl. Data Systems, Sigma Xi, Phi Delta Kappa. Jewish. Current Work: Biostatistics decision support systems; development of microcomputer based statistical systems; investigations into the causation of human intelligence. Subspecialties: Statistics; Educational measurement. Home: 7807 Whittier St Tampa FL 33617 Office: SVC 409 Univ S Fla Tampa FL 33620

GRANEAU, PETER, scientist, educator; b. Lissa, Poland, Mar. 13, 1921; came to U.S., 1967; m. Brigitte Weil, Oct. 24, 1955; 1 child, Neal. B.Sc., Nottingham U., Eng., 1955, Ph.D., 1961. Dept. head BICC Research Lab., London, 1955-62; asst. mgr., 1962-67; tech. dir. Simplex Wire and Cable, Cambridge, Mass., 1967-70; pres. U.P.C. Corp., Weston, Mass., 1970—; vis. sci. MIT, Cambridge, Mass., 1972—; vis. prof. Northeastern U., Boston, 1984—. Author: Underground Power Transmission, 1979; contbr. articles to profl. jours. Chmn. Mcpl. Light Bd., Concord, Mass., 1980. Fellow Inst. Physics; mem. IEEE (sr.). Current work: Classical electromagnetism. Subspecialties: Magnetic physics; Applied magnetics. Home: 205 Holden Wood Rd Concord MA 01742 Office: Northeastern U Ctr Electromagnetics Research Huntington Ave Boston MA 02115

GRANGER, CLARK ALLEN, state entomologist; b. Burlington, Vt., Nov. 13, 1941; s. Ralph Hawthorne and Doris Arlene (Hartwell) G.; m. Rosemarie Rowell, Aug. 31, 1965; children: Kimberly, Gregory. B.S., U. N.H., 1963, M.S., 1965; Ph.D., U. Maine, 1968. Registered forester, Maine. Asst. prof. U. Maine, Augusta, Auburn, 1968-69; asst. state entomologist Maine Dept. Forestry, Augusta, 1969-78, state entomologist, 1981—; dir. div. community forestry Maine Dept. Conservation, Augusta, 1978-81; pres. Northwoods Evergreens Corp., Bath, Maine, 1979—; mem. State of Maine Arborist Examining Bd., 1981—. Contbr. articles to profl. jours. Exec. dir. Pine Tree State Arboretum, 1982. Mem. Am. Rhododendron Soc., No. Nut Growers Assn., Maine Christmas Tree Assn. (bd. dirs.), Nat. Christmas Tree Growers Assn. Lodge: Elks. Current Work: Integrated pest management, soil-plant relationships, herbicides. Subspecialty: Resource conservation. Home: RFD 3 Wiscasset ME 04578 Office: Maine Forest Service State House Sta 22 Augusta ME 04333

GRANT, DONALD ANDREW, educator; b. Cherryfield, Maine, Jan. 3, 1936; s. Morton Andrew and Eunice Violet (Harrington) G.; m. June Elaine Farren, Aug. 29, 1957; children: Judith Dawn, Jeffrey Donald. B.S. in M.E, U. Maine, 1956, M.S. in M.E, 1963; Ph.D., U. R.I., 1969. Registered profl. engr., Maine. Flight test engr. NATC, Md., 1956; instr. U. Maine, Orono, 1956-63, asst. prof. mech. engring. dept., 1963-68, assoc. prof., 1968-76, prof., 1976—; cons. Contbr. articles to profl. jours. Mem. ASME. Republican. Baptist. Lodge: Masons. Current Work: Vibrations of timoshenko beams and vibrations of time dependent boundary conditions. Subspecialties: Mechanical engineering; Theoretical and applied mechanics. Office: 246 Boardman Hall Orono ME 04469

GRANT, EDWARD ROBERT, chemistry educator; b. Tacoma, Sept. 23, 1947; s. Melven Edwin and Estelle Elizabeth (Gleuck) G.; m. Catherine Janine Carey, Aug. 10, 1980; 1 child, Alexander Edward. B.A., Occidental Coll., 1969; Ph.D., U. Calif.-Davis, 1974. Asst. prof. chemistry Cornell U., Ithaca, N.Y., 1977-83, assoc. prof. 1983—; cons. Newport Corp., Fountain Valley, Calif., 1982—, Corning Glass Works, N.Y., 1983. Contbr. numerous articles to profl. jours. Mem. Am. Chem. Soc., Am. Phys. Soc. Current work: Photochemistry and photophysics; multiphoton spectroscopy and dynamics; vibronic coupling and intramolecular dynamics of isolated Jahn-Teller molecules; laser initiated organometallic catalysis. Subspecialties: Laser-induced chemistry; Laser spectroscopy. Office: Dept Chemistry Cornell U Baker Lab Ithaca NY 14853

GRANT, JOHN WALLACE, JR., biomechanics educator, consultant, researcher; b. Weston, W.Va., May 12, 1942; s. John Wallace, Sr. and Grace

(White) G.; m. Joy Starring, June 14, 1969; children—Stephen, David, John. B.S.M.E., W.Va. Inst. Tech., 1965; M.S.M.E., Tulane U., 1971, Ph.D., 1974. Prodn. engr. Union Carbinde, Charleston, W.Va., 1965-69; sr. research engr. DuPont Co., Wilmington, Del., 1974-79; asst. prof. Va. Poly. Inst. and State U., Blackburg, 1979—. Contbr. articles to profl. jours. Mem. ASME, Am. Assn. Blood Banks, Biomed. Engrs. Soc., Am. Assn. Engring. Edn. Current work: Vestibular mechanics, blood flow, microcirculation, acceletation physiology. Subspecialties: Biomedical engineering; Theoretical and applied mechanics. Office: Engring Sci and Mechanics Dept VA Poly Inst and State U Blacksburg VA 24061

GRANT, VERNE EDWIN, biology educator; b. San Francisco, Oct. 17, 1917; S. Edwin and Bessie (Swallow) G.; m. Alva Day, June 12, 1946 (div. Aug. 1959); children: Joyce Grant Mixon, Brian, Brenda Grant Aley; m. Karen Alt, Nov. 3, 1960. A.B., U. Calif.-Berkeley, 1940, Ph.D., 1949. Teaching asst. botany U. Calif.-Berkeley, 1946-49; NRC fellow Carnegie Inst., Stanford, Calif., 1949-50; geneticist Rancho Santa Ana Bot. Garden, Claremont, Calif., 1950-67; asst. prof. Claremont Grad. Sch., 1951-53, assoc. prof., 1953-57, prof., 1957-67; prof. biology Inst. Life Sci., Tex. A&M U., College Station, 1967-68; prof., dir. Boyce Thompson Southwestern Arboretum, U. Ariz.-Superior, 1968-70; prof. botany U. Tex.-Austin, 1970—. Author: Natural History of the Phlox Family, 1959, The Origin of Adaptations, 1963, The Architecture of the Germplasm, 1964, (with Karen Grant) Flower Pollination in the Phlox Family, 1965, Hummingbirds and Their Flowers, 1968, Plant Speciation, 1971, 2d edit., 1981, Genetics of Flowering Plants, 1975, Organismic Evolution, 1977; The Evolutionary Process, 1985; editorial bd.: Ency. Americana, 1955-64, Brittonia, 1957-62, Evolution, 1960-62, Am. Naturalist, 1964-67, Biologisches Zentralblatt, 1974—; contbr. numerous articles to profl. jours. Recipient Sci. award Phi Beta Kappa, 1964. Fellow Am. Acad. Arts and Scis.; mem. Nat. Acad. Scis., Am. Soc. Naturalists, Soc. for Study of Evolution (pres. 1968), Bot. Soc. Am. (cert. of merit 1971), Internat. Soc. Plant Taxonomists, Am. Soc. Plant Taxonomists, Southwestern Assn. Naturalists, Soc. Systematic Zoology. Current Work: Population biology; teaching, writing, research. Subspecialties: Evolutionary biology; Population biology. Home: 2811 Fresco St Austin TX 78731 Office: Dept Botany U Tex Austin TX 78712

GRASDALEN, GARY LARS, astronomer; b. Albert Lea, Minn., Oct. 7, 1945; s. Lars G. and Lillie (Olsen) G. A.B., Harvard U., 1967; M.S., U. Calif., Berkeley, 1970, Ph.D., 1972. Research asst. dept. astron. U. Calif., Berkeley, 1970-72; asst. astronomer Kitt Peak Nat. Obs., Tucson, 1972-75, assoc. astronomer, 1975-77; asst. prof. dept. physics and astronomy U. Wyo., Laramie, 1977-80, assoc. prof., 1980—. Contbr. articles to profl. jours. Mem. Am. Astron. Soc., Internat. Astron. Union, AAAS, Astron. Soc. Pacific. Current Work: Star formation, H II regions, galaxies; image processing, process control, infrared detectors. Subspecialty: Infrared astronomy. Office: Dept Physics and Astronomy U Wyo Box 3905 Univ Sta Laramie WY 82071

GRATT, BARTON MICHAEL, oral radiology educator, dentist; b. Chgo., Aug. 23, 1945; m. Karren Hakanson, June 3, 1979. D.D.S., UCLA, 1971. Diplomate: Am. Bd. Oral-Maxillofacial Radiology. Asst. prof. U. Calif.-San Francisco, 1975-79; assoc. prof. UCLA, 1979—; cons. dental xeroradiography Xerox Corp., Pasadena, Calif., 1977—; cons. panoramic radiography Gen. Electric Corp., Milw., 1980—. NIH grantee, 1978; Am. Fund Dental Health grantee, 1980. Fellow Am. Acad. Dental Radiology. Inventor dental xeroradiography, 1976. Current Work: Dental xeroradiography, dental radiology quality control, image analysis. Subspecialties: Diagnostic radiology; Imaging technology. Home: 2619 Federal Ave Los Angeles CA 90064Office: UCLA Sch Dentistry Los Angeles CA 90024

GRAY, EOIN WEDDERBURN, physicist, cons.; b. Larne, No. Ireland, May 7, 1942; s. Charles and Irene (Mason) G.; married; children: Liam Charles, Michael Eoin. B.Sc. (hons.), Queens U., Belfast, No. Ireland, 1964, Ph.D., 1967. Demonstrator in physics Queens U., 1964-67; postdoctoral research U. B.C., Can., 1967-69; mem. tech. staff Bell Labs., Columbus, Ohio, 1969—. Contbr numerous articles to profl. jours. Recipient prize Holm Conf. Elec. Contacts, 1977. Fellow Inst. Physics; mem. IEEE (sr.), Can. Inst. Chemistry (sr.), European Phys. Soc., Am. Inst. Physics, Am. Phys. Soc., Can. Assn. Physicists. Anglican. Patentee in field. Current Work: plasma-surface interactions, arc physics, electrical insulation. Subspecialties: Plasma physics; Electronics. Office: Bell Labs 6200 E Broad St Columbus OH 43213

GRAY, FESTUS GAIL, electrical engineering educator, researcher; b. Moundsville, W.Va., Aug. 16, 1943; s. Festus P. and Elsie V. (Rine) G.; m. Caryl Evelyn Anderson, Aug. 24, 1968; children: David, Andrew, Daniel. B.S.E.E., W.Va. U., 1965, M.S.E.E., 1967; Ph.D., U. Mich., 1971. Instr. W.Va. U., Morgantown, 1966-67; teaching fellow U. Mich., 1967-70; asst. prof. Va. Poly. Inst. and State U., Blacksburg, 1971-77, assoc. prof., 1977-82, prof., 1983—; faculty fellow NASA, 1975; cons. Inland Motors, Radford, Va., 1980; researcher Rome Air Devel. Ctr., N.Y., 1980-81, Naval Surface Weapons Ctr., Dahlgren, Va., 1982-83, Army Research Office, Research Triangle Park, N.C., 1983-85. Contbr. articles to sci. jours. Bd. deacons Northside Presbyterian Ch., Blacksburg, 1980-83; coach S.W. Va. Soccer Assn., 1980-85. Grantee NSF; Grantee Office Naval Research; Grantee NASA. Mem. IEEE (chpt. chmn. 1979-80), Assn. Computing Machinery, Sigma Xi. Democrat. Current Work: Investigation of fault tolerance, diagnosis, testing, and reliability issues for VLSI; distributed and multiprocessor computer architectures. Subspecialties: Computer engineering; Computer architecture. Home: 304 Fincastle Dr Blacksburg VA 24060 Office: Va Poly Inst and State U Blacksburg VA 24061

GRAY, HARRY BARKUS, chemistry educator; b. Woodburn, Ky., Nov. 14, 1935; s. Barkus and Ruby (Hopper) G.; m. Shirley Barnes, June 2, 1957; children: Victoria Lynn, Andrew Thomas, Noah Harry Barkus. B.S., Western Ky. U., 1957; Ph.D., Northwestern U., 1960. Postdoctoral fellow U. Copenhagen, 1960-61; faculty Columbia U., 1961-66, prof., 1965-66; prof. chemistry Calif. Inst. Tech., Pasadena, 1966—, now Arnold O. Beckman prof. chemistry; vis. prof. Rockefeller U., Harvard U., U. Iowa, Pa. State U., Yeshiva U., U. Copenhagen, U. Witwatersrand, Johannesburg, South Africa, U. Canterbury, Christchurch, New Zealand; cons. govt., industry. Author: Electrons and Chemical Bonding, 1965, Molecular Orbital Theory, 1965, Ligand Substitution Processes, 1966, Basic Principles of Chemistry, 1967, Chemical Dynamics, 1968, Chemical Principles, 1970, Models in Chemical Science, 1971, Chemical Bonds, 1973, Chemical Structure and Bonding, 1980, Molecular Electronic Structures, 1980. Recipient Franklin Meml. award, 1967; Fresenius award, 1970; Shoemaker award, 1970; Harrison Howe award, 1972; award for excellence in teaching Mfg. Chemists Assn., 1972; Remsen Meml. award, 1979; Tolman medal, 1979; Guggenheim fellow, 1972-73; Phi Beta Kappa scholar, 1973-74. Mem. Nat. Acad. Scis., Am. Chem. Soc. (award pure chemistry 1970, award inorganic chemistry 1978, award for disting. service in advancement of inorganic chemistry 1984), Royal Danish Acad. Scis. and Letters, Alpha Chi Sigma, Phi Lambda Upsilon. Current Work: Bioinorganic chemistry; inorganic photochemistry; oxidation-reduction reactions. Subspecialties: Inorganic chemistry; Photochemistry. Home: 1415 E California Blvd Pasadena CA 91106

GRAY, JOE WILLIAM, biomed. scientist; b. Hobbs, N.Nex., Apr. 26, 1946; s. Frank Omer and Rosalin Revae (Bauman) G.; m. Jane Ellin Madison, Jan. 28, 1967; 1 son, Gerald Todd. Ph.D., Kans. State U., 1972. Mineral engr. Colo. Sch. Mines, 1968; Biomed. scientist Lawrence Livermore Nat. Lab., Calif., 1972—, sect. leader cytophysics, 1982—; asst. adj. prof. U. Calif.-Davis, 1976—; adj. prof. lab. medicine U. Calif.-San Francisco. Contbr. numerous articles to profl. jours. Served to capt. AUS, 1972. NIH grantee; recipient Radiation Research Soc. research award, 1985. Mem. Am. Assn. Cancer Research, Cell Kinetics Soc. (pres. 1983), Soc. Analytical Cytology, Am. Phys. Soc., AAAS. Rebublican. Current Work: Cell cycle analysis, quantitative cytogenetics, flow cytometry. Subspecialties: Cancer research (medicine); Genome organization. Office: Biomed Scis Div PO Box 5507 Livermore CA 94550

GRAY, LEONARD WESLEY, chemist, applied researcher; b. Waycross, Ga., June 18, 1941; s. Harvey Carlton and Annie Louise (Williams) G.; m. Jeanette Joyce, June 8, 1963; children—Leonard LeVerne, Andrea Suzzanne. B.S., N. Mex. Inst. Mining and Tech., 1964; M.S., Tex. Tech. Coll., 1967; Ph.D., U. S.C., 1972. Chemist, DuPont-Savannah River Lab., Aiken, S.C., 1966-68, research chemist, 1972-75, process chemist, 1975-79; staff chemist, 1980-85, research staff chemist, 1985—; staff chemist Kaiser Aluminum & Chem. Co., Baton Rouge, La., 1979-80. Contbr. articles to profl. jours. Bd. dirs. Augusta Reading Found., R.L. Shedd Sch. for Children with Learning Disabilities, Augusta, Ga., 1977—, pres., 1980-81. Mem. Am. Chem. Soc. (chmn. local sect. 1977-78, com. on chem. safety 1981—). Baptist. Current work: Dissolution, separation, and purification of uranium, plutonium, neptunium, americium, and curium from low-grade sources and reactor targets. Subspecialty: Inorganic chemistry. Home: 1908 Brenda Dr North Augusta SC 29841 Office: E I duPont de Nemours & Co Inc Savannah River Lab Aiken SC 29808

GRAY, PAUL EDWARD, university president; b. Newark, Feb. 7, 1932; s. Kenneth Frank and Florence (Gilleo) G.; m. Priscilla Wilson King, June 18, 1955; children: Virginia Wilson, Amy Brewer, Andrew King, Louise Meyer. S.B., Mass. Inst. Tech., 1954, S.M., 1955, Sc.D., 1960. Mem. faculty Mass. Inst. Tech., 1960-71, Class of 1922 prof. elec. engring., 1968-71; dean MIT Sch. Engring., 1970-71, chancellor, 1971-80, pres., 1980—, mem. MIT Corp., 1971—; dir. Shawmut Bank, Boston, New Eng. Mut. Life Ins. Co., Boston, A.D. Little Inc., Cambridge, Cabot Corp., Boston. Trustee, mem. corp. Mus. of Sci., Boston, Woods Hole Oceanographic Inst.; chmn. bd. trustees Wheaton Coll., Mass., 1976—; trustee Carroll Sch., also Cole Ctr. for Dyslexia, Lincoln, Mass.; ex-officio mem. WGBH Ednl. Found.; mem. Whitaker Health Scis. Fund; mem. White House Sci. Council, 1982—. Served to 1st lt. AUS, 1955-57. Recipient C.E. Tucker award teaching Mass. Inst. Tech. Fellow Am. Acad. Arts and Scis., IEEE (publs. bd. 1969-70); mem. Nat. Acad. Engring., Mex. Nat. Acad. Engring., AAAS, Sigma Xi, Eta Kappa Nu, Tau Beta Pi, Phi Sigma Kappa. Mem. United Ch. Christ (deacon 1969-72, moderator 1973-77). Current Work: Electrical engineering. Subspecialty: Electrical engineering. Home: 111 Memorial Dr Cambridge MA 02142 Office: 77 Massachusetts Ave Cambridge MA 02139

GRAY, PAUL RUSSELL, electrical engineering and computer science educator. Prof. dept. elec. engring. and computer sci. U. Calif., Berkeley. Recipient Morris N. Liebmann Meml. award IEEE, 1983. Subspecialty: Integrated circuits. Office: U Calif Dept Elec Engring and Computer Sci Berkeley CA 94720

GRAY, PETER VANCE, physicist; b. Oak Park, Ill., July 17, 1928; s. Leland Merton and Marie Louise (Didion) G.; m. Mary Elizabeth Tressel, June 23, 1956; children—Jennifer Ruth, Margaret Ellen, Elizabeth Diane. B.S. Union Coll., 1958; M.S., U. Ill., 1959, Ph.D., 1962. Physicist, Gen. Electric Co., Schenectady, 1963—. Contbr. articles to profl. jours. Patentee in field. Served with USN, 1951-54. Recipient IR-100 award Indsl. Research mag., 1982, 83. Mem. Am. Phys. Soc., IEEE, Greenhouse and Indoor Plant Assn. (pres. 1980-81), Phi Beta Kappa, Sigma Xi. Lutheran. Club: Adirondack Mountain (Schenectady). Current work: New power electronic devices; power integrated circuits; semiconductor surface phenomena; modeling; design; research; invention. Subspecialties: Condensed matter physics; Semiconductors. Home: 121 Acorn Dr Scotia NY 12302 Office: Gen Electric Co CRD PO Box 43 Schenectady NY 12345

GRAY, PHILIP HOWARD, psychologist, educator; b. Cape Rosier, Maine, July 4, 1926; s. Asa and Bernice (Lawrence) G.; m. Iris McKinney, Dec. 31, 1954; children: Cindelyn, Howard. M.A., U. Chgo., 1958; Ph.D., U. Wash., 1960. Asst. prof. dept. psychology Mont. State U., Bozeman, 1960-65, assoc. prof., 1965-75, prof., 1975—; vis. prof. U. Man., Winnipeg, Can., 1968-70; pres. Mont. Psychol. Assn., 1968-70; chmn. Mont. Bd. Psychologist Examiners, 1972-74; speaker sci. and geneal. meetings on ancestry of U.S. presidents. Organized exhbns. folk art in Mont. and Maine, 1972-79; Author: The Comparative Analysis of Behavior, 1966, (with F.L. Ruch and N. Warren) Working with Psychology, 1963, A Directory of Eskimo Artists in Sculpture and Prints, 1974; Science Citations Salaries, 1974; The Science That Lost Its Mind, 1985. Contbr. numerous articles on behavior to psychol. jours., poetry to lit. jours. Served with U.S. Army, 1944-46. Recipient Am. and Can. research grants. Fellow Am. Psychol. Assn., AAAS, Internat. Soc. Research on Aggression; mem. History of Sci. Soc., Nat. Geneal. Soc., New Eng. Hist. Geneal. Soc., Deer Isle-Stonington Hist. Soc., Psychonomic Soc., Internat. Soc. for Human Ethology, Internat. Council Psychologists; Rocky Mountain Psychol. Assn., Descs. of Illegitimate Sons and Daus. of Kings of Britain, Piscataqua Pioneers, Animal Behavior Soc., Mountain Psychol. Assn.; Flagon and Trencher, SAR, Sigma Xi. Current Work: Computer analysis of poetry and humor; quantification of hereditary genius of Ameican presidents; imprinting and murderous behavior; Darwinian evolution of mind; ethnic origins of science in conquests of Europe. Subspecialties: Behavioral psychology; Ethology. Home: 1207 S Black Ave Bozeman MT 59715 Office: Dept Psychology Montana State U Bozeman MT 59717

GRAYBEAL, JACK DANIEL, chemist, educator; b. Detroit, May 16, 1930; s. Paul Herman and Polly Dale (McClintic) G.; m. Evelyn Alice Nicolai, June 13, 1954; children: Daniel L., David E., Dale K. B.S., W.Va. U., 1951; M.S., U. Wis., 1953, Ph.D., 1955. Mem. tech. staff Bell Telephone Labs., 1955-57; asst. prof. chemistry W.Va. U., 1957-62, assoc. prof., 1962-68; assoc. prof. chemistry Va. Poly. Inst. and State U., Blacksburg, 1968-69, prof., 1969—, assoc. head dept., 1975—. Contbr. articles on microwave spectroscopy, nuclear quadrupole spectroscopy, molecular structure to sci. jours. Mem. Am. Chem. Soc., Am. Phys. Soc., Sigma Xi, Phi Lambda Upsilon (nat. editor Register). Current Work: Microwave spectroscopy, nuclear quadropole resonance, molecular structure determination. Subspecialty: Physical chemistry. Home: 312 Apperson Dr Blacksburg VA 24060 Office: Davidson Hall Va Poly Inst and State U Blacksburg VA 24061

GRAYBIEL, ASHTON, physician; b. Port Huron, Mich., July 24, 1902; s. William and Lucy Ann (Young) G.; m. Moira Barkley Martin, Mar. 23, 1934; children—Ashton L., Ann M. Moseley. A.B., U. So. Calif., 1924, A.M., 1925; M.D., Harvard U., 1930. Diplomate: Am. Bd. Preventive Medicine (aviation med.). Traveling fellow, 1932-33, Dalton fellow, 1933-34; Intern Mass. Gen. Hosp., Boston, 1930-32; (cardiac clinic), 1934-42; asso. Harvard Fatigue Lab., 1936-42; instr. medicine and grad. courses Harvard, 1940-42, research staff, 1942-45; dir. research Naval Aerospace Med. Inst., Pensacola, Fla., 1945-70; spl. asst. sci. programs, head biol. scis. dept. Naval Aerospace Med. Research Lab., Pensacola, 1970-80; chief sci. advisor, 1980—; adj. prof. psychology Brandeis U., Waltham, Mass., 1981—. Author: Clinical Electrocardiography, 1950, (with P.D. White, L. Wheeler, C. Williams) Electrocardiography in Practice, 3d edit., 1952. Recipient Theodore C. Lyster award for researches in aviation medicine, 1950; Legion of Merit, 1952, with gold star, 1967; Adm. William S. Parsons award for sci. and technical progress Navy League, 1960; The Eric J. Liljencrantz award for contbns. aviation and space medicine, 1961; John J. Jeffries Award, 1962; Melbourne W. Boynton award for space medicine, 1962; Groedel Meml. award Am. Coll. Cardiology, 1962; Hubertus Strughold award for space medicine, 1963; Arnold J. Tuttle award aviation medicine, 1965; Capt. Robert Dexter Conrad award for tech. and sci. achievement in research and devel. for Navy, 1965; Exceptional Sci. Achievement medal NASA, 1974; Disting. Service medal NASA, 1982; Ashton Graybiel Spatial Orientation Lab. at Brandeis U. named in his honor, 1982. Fellow Aerospace Med. Assn. (pres., Louis H. Bauer Founders award 1983), AAAS; mem. Am. Coll. Cardiology (past pres.), Assn. Mil. Surgeons, Am. Coll. Sports Medicine, Internat. Acad. Aviation Medicine, Space Medicine Assn., Am. Physiol. Soc., Am. Heart Assn., Am. Inst. Aeros. and Astronautics, Fla. Acad. Scis., Internat. Acad. Astronautics (trustee). Club: Cosmos (Washington). Subspecialty: Space medicine. Office: Naval Aerospace Med Research Lab Pensacola FL 32508

GRAYHACK, JOHN THOMAS, urologist, educator; b. Kankakee, Ill., Aug. 21, 1923; s. John and Marie (Keckich) G.; m. Elizabeth Houlehin, June 3, 1950; children: Elizabeth, Anne Marie, Linda Jean, John, William. B.S., U. Chgo., 1945, M.D., 1947. Diplomate Am. Bd. Urology. Intern medicine Billings Hosp., Chgo., 1947; intern gen. surgery Johns Hopkins Hosp., 1947-48, asst. resident, 1948-49, fellow urology, 1949-50, asst. resident, 1950-52, resident urology, 1952-53; dir. Kretschmer Lab., Northwestern U. Med. Sch., 1956—, prof. urology, 1963—, chmn. dept.; Cons. VA Research Hosp. Editor: Year Book of Urology, 1963-78; mem. editorial bd.: Surgery, Gynecology and Obstetrics; assoc. editor: Jour. Urology. Served to capt. USAF, 1954-56. Recipient Outstanding Achievement award USAF.; Fellow Am. Cancer Soc., 1949-50; Fellow Damon Runyon Fund, 1953-54. Mem. AMA, Ill., Chgo. med. socs., Am. Assn. Genitourinary Surgeons (Barringer medal), Am. Urology Assn. (Hugh H. Young award), Chgo. Urology Soc., Endocrine Soc., Clin. Soc. Genitourinary Surgeons, Am. Surg. Assn., Soc. Univ. Urologists, Nephrology Soc., Phi Beta Kappa, Alpha Omega Alpha. Current Work: Prostate, normal, benign hyper-plasma; clinical urology. Subspecialty: Urology. Home: 95 N Park Rd LaGrange IL 60525 Office: 303 E Chicago Ave Chicago IL 60611

GRAYSON, HENRY, psychoanalyst; b. Atmore, Ala., Oct. 25, 1935; s. Henry T. and Ethel (Sagasen) G.; m. Elizabeth Cauthen, Apr. 1, 1959; children: Regine, Douglas. A.B., Asbury Coll., 1957; S.T.M., Boston U., 1963, Ph.D., 1967; postdoctoral cert. in psychotherapy and psychoanalysis Postgrad. Ctr. for Mental Health, N.Y.C., 1971. Lic. psychologist, N.Y. Instr. dept. psychology Mt. Ida Jr. Coll., Newton, Mass., 1963-67; from asst. to assoc. prof. CUNY, Bklyn., 1967-78; sole practice psychology, N.Y.C., 1967—; founder, exec. dir. Nat. Inst. Psychotherapies, N.Y.C., 1970-82, chmn. bd., 1970—; dir. Counseling and Family Therapy Assocs., Mahopac, N.Y., 1981—; bd. dirs. Ctr. Marital and Family Therapy, N.Y.C., 1981—; pres. F.A.T. Seminars, N.Y.C., 1982—. Author: Three Psychotherapies, 1975; author, editor: Short-term Approaches to the Psychotherapies, 1979, Changing Approaches to the Psychotherapies, 1978. Fellow Am. Group Psychotherapy Assn.; mem. Eastern Group Psychotherapy Soc. (treas. 1978-79), Am. Psychol. Assn., Am. Acad. Psychotherapists, N.Y. State Psychol. Assn. Current Work: Eating disorders, mind-body relationships. Subspecialty: Psychobiology. Office: 330 W 58th St New York NY 10019

GRAYSTON, J. THOMAS, medical educator; b. Wichita, Kans., Sept. 6, 1924; s. Jesse T. and Luzia B. (Thomas) G.; children: Susan, Jesse, David; m. M. Nan Bryant, June 7, 1980. Student, Carleton Coll., 1942-43; B.S., U. Chgo., 1947, M.D., 1948, M.S., 1952. Diplomate: Am. Bd. Internal Medicine, Am. Bd. Preventive Medicine. Intern Albany (N.Y.) Med. Sch., 1948-49; Seymour Coman fellow preventive medicine U. Chgo., 1949-50, asst. resident medicine, 1950-51; epidemiologist epidemic intelligence service USPHS, U. Kans. Med. Center, 1951-53; chief resident medicine U. Chgo., 1953-54, instr. medicine, 1953-55; fellow Nat. Found. Infantile Paralysis, 1954-56; asst. prof. medicine U. Chgo., 1955-60, asso. prof., 1960; chief div. microbiology and epidemiology U.S. Naval Med. Research Unit 2, Taipei, Taiwan, 1957-60, cons., 1960-79; prof. preventive medicine, chmn. dept. Sch. Medicine, U. Wash., 1960-70, dean Sch. Pub. Health and Community Medicine, 1970-71, v.p. for health scis., 1971-83, prof. dept. epidemiology, 1970—, adj. prof. pathobiology, 1982—; mem. exec. com. Regional Primate Research Center, 1964-70, research affiliate, 1967-70; attending physician medicine Univ. Hosp., Seattle, 1960-70; asso. mem. commn. acute respiratory diseases Armed Forces Epidemiol. Bd., 1962-65, mem., 1965-73; mem. research and engring. adv. panel biology and medicine Dept. Def., 1963-67; sci. group trachoma research WHO, 1963; virology and rickettsiology study sect. NIH, 1963-67; mem. internat. centers com. Nat. Inst. Allergy and Infectious Diseases, 1967-71; mem. expert adv. panel on Trachoma, WHO, 1970—; chmn. exec. com., mem. nat. adv. council on health professions edn. NIH, 1972-75. Contbr. numerous articles to profl. jours. Fellow Am. Coll. Preventive Medicine (v.p. gen. preventive medicine 1970-71, regent 1971-74), Am. Pub. Health Assn. (governing bd. 1978-80); mem. Am. Assn. Immunologists, Am. Assn. Physicians, Am. Epidemiol. Soc. (pres. 1982-83), Am. Fedn. Clin. Research, Am. Soc. Clin. Investigation, Am. Soc. Tropical Medicine and Hygiene, Assn. Acad. Health Centers (dir. 1975-80, pres. 1978-79), Assn. Tchrs. Preventive Medicine, Infectious Diseases Soc., Internat. Epidemiol. Assn., Soc. Exptl. Biology and Medicine, Inst. Medicine of Nat. Acad. Scis., Western Assn. Physicians, Western Soc. Clin. Research, Sigma Xi. Current Work: Epidemiology and immunology of infectious diseases. Subspecialties: Epidemiology; Infectious diseases. Office: Dept Epidemiology SC-36 U Wash Seattle WA 98195

GRAZIANO, KENNETH DONALD, microbiologist; b. Dunkirk, N.Y., Apr. 10, 1942; s. Russell James and Antoinette Joan (Valvo) G. B.A., Colgate U., 1963; M.S., Syracuse U., 1965; Ph.D., Johns Hopkins U., 1970. Fellow Johns Hopkins U. Sch. Medicine, Balt., 1969-72; staff fellow Nat. Cancer Inst., Balt., 1972-74; instr. Johns Hopkins U., 1974-75; research microbiologist FDA, Bethesda, Md., 1975-78, rev. microbiologist, 1978-85; mgr. regulatory affairs Hybritech, Inc., 1985—. Contbr. articles to profl. jours. Mem. Am. Assn. Immunologists, Am. Soc. Microbiology, AAAS, N.Y. Acad. Sci., Johns Hopkins U. Med. and Surg. Assn., Regulatory Affairs Profls. Assn., Assn. Biotech. Cos., Johns Hopkins U. Immunology Council, Nat. Aquarium. Roman Catholic. Club: Vintage Japanese Motorcycle. Current Work: Represents biotechnology company in its dealings with governmental agencies. Subspecialties: Immunobiology and immunology; Cellular engineering. Office: 11095 Torreyana Rd San Diego CA 92121

GRECO, GARY, drug specialist, researcher, lecturer; b. Bklyn., May 2, 1950; s. Alfonso Joseph and Ann Adelaina (Crescenzo) G.; m. Joan Patricia Buonocore, July 21, 1979. A.A., St. John's U., 1971, B.S., 1974. Chemist Schering Plough, Union, N.J., 1974-76; drug expert FDA, Bklyn., 1976—; project leader compendial monographs evaluation and devel. program U.S. Pharmacopia through FDA, Bklyn., 1985—; lectr. 95th ann. meeting Assn. Ofcl. Analytical Chemists, 1981, 23rd Eastern Analytical Annual Symposium, 1984. Contbr. articles to profl. jours. Recipient commendation FDA, 1983. Mem. Am. Chem. Soc., Assoc. Musicians of Greater N.Y. Current work: Presentation at E.A.S. 11/84; completing journal for publication on sample preparation effects on the assay value results for enteric coated drug tablets; CMED project leader. Subspecialties: Analytical chemistry; Drug delivery systems. Office: 850 3d Ave Brooklyn NY 11232

GRECO, RICHARD JAMES, software engr.; b. Portland, Oreg., July 6, 1952; s. I. James and Clara Ann (Ferrante) G. B.T.E.E., Oreg. Inst. Tech., 1975. Systems programmer Lewis and Clark Coll., Portland, 1975-79; software engr. Tektronix, Wilsonville, Oreg., 1979—; cons. engr. Technigraph, Portland, 1979—. Active Portland Art Assn., 1981. Mem. Assn. for Computing Machinery, IEEE Computer Soc., Portland Internat. Gormet Soc. Daoist. Current Work: Human interfaces to computers utilizing pictures as a communication media. Subspecialties: Computer architecture; Graphics, image processing, and pattern recognition. Office: PO Box 1000 Wilsonville OR 97070

GREEN, DAVID WILLIAM, chemist, research laboratory executive; b. Hudson, Mich., Nov. 19, 1942; s. Francis Harger and Dorotha Louise (Onweller) G.; m. Mary Sarah McCullough, July 8, 1967; children—Laura, Brenda, Mark, Brian, William. B.A., Albion Coll., 1964; Ph.D., U. Calif., 1968. Lectr. chemistry dept. U. Calif.-Berkeley, 1968; reearch assoc. U. Chgo., 1968-71; mem. faculty Albion Coll., Mich., 1971-75; chemist Argonne Nat. Lab., Ill., 1975-82, mgr. analytical chemistry, 1982—. Contbr. chpts. to books, articles to tech. jours. Mem. Dist. 58 Bd. Edn., Downers Grove, Ill., 1977-81, pres., 1978-81; bd. dirs. Assn. on Pub. Sch. Fin., Downers Grove. Mem. Am. Chem. Soc., Analytical Lab. Mgrs. Assn. (chmn. 1984-85), Sigma Xi. Current work: Matrix-isolation spectroscopy, thermodynamic properties at high temperatures, spectroscopic analytical techniques. Subspecialties: Analytical chemistry; High temperature chemistry. Home: 5625 Carpenter St Downers Grove IL 60516 Office: Dept Analytical Chemistry Argonne Nat Lab 9700 S Cass Ave Argonne IL 60439

GREEN, DONALD EUGENE, analytical toxicologist, researcher; b. Napa, Calif., Nov. 25, 1926; s. Joseph and Helen (Rubin) G.; m. Margaret Ann Maurer, July 29, 1951; children: Dennis, Gretchen, Mark, Gary, Sheryl. B.S., U. Calif., Berkeley, 1948; M.S., U. Calif.-San Francisco, 1952, B.S. in Pharmacy, 1955; Ph.D., Wash. State U., 1962. Instr. pharm. chemistry Idaho State U., Pocatello, 1955-57, 58-60, Wash. State U., Pullamn, 1957-58; research biochemist VA Med. Center, Palo Alto, Calif., 1962-64; sr. engr. Varian Assoc., Palo Alto, 1962-70; research asso. Stanford Med. Sch., Palo Alto, 1970-74; sr. research scientist Inst. Chem. Biology, U. San Francisco, 1974-81; research biochemist VA Med. Center, Palo Alto, 1981-85; cons. Universal Monitor Corp., Pasadena, Calif., 1971-76, Environ. Devices, Inc., Sacramento, 1984-85. Contbr. articles to profl. jours. Served with USNR, 1944-46, 51-53. Mem. Am. Chem. Soc. (chmn. Santa Clara Valley sect. 1971-72, councillor 1975-81, 83—), Am. Pharm. Assn., Internat. Assn. Forensic Toxicologists, Calif. Assn. Toxicologists, Western Pharmacology Soc., Am. Soc. Pharmacology and Exptl. Therapeutics, U. Calif. Alumni Assn. Club: Santa Clara Country (pres. 1980-82). Patentee in field. Current Work: Development of analysis procedures for drug metabolites, bioinstrumentation, mass spectrometry, new drug development. Subspecialties: Medicinal chemistry; Mass spectrometry.

GREEN, ELMER ELLSWORTH, psychophysiologist; b. La Grande, Oreg., Oct. 10, 1917; s. Marble F. and Marie L. (Bolton) G.; m. Alyce M. Mattson, Feb. 25, 1941; children—Patricia, Douglas, Sandra, Judith. B.S. in Physics, U. Minn., 1942; Ph.D. in Psychology, U. Chgo., 1962. Fire-control assembly methods engr. tech rep. Honeywell Corp. to U.S. Air Force, Mpls., 1942-45; head assessments div. evaluation of research of rockets and guided missiles U.S. Naval Ordnance Test Sta., China Lake, Calif., 1948-58; research assoc. in med. psychology dept. medicine U. Chgo., 1962-64; dir. psychophysiology lab., voluntary controls program, biofeedback lab. research dept. Menninger

Found., Topeka, 1964—. Subspecialties: Psychophysiology; Biofeedback. Office: Menninger Found Box 829 Topeka KS 66601*

GREEN, GEOFFREY FRANCIS, mechanical engineer; b. Phila., Jan. 20, 1945; s. George Albert G.; m. Margaret Ann Wells, Nov. 1, 1975; children—David, Denise. A.A., Pa. State U., 1966, B.S., 1970, M.S., 1972. Draftsman design Pressure Products, Warminister, Pa., 1966-70; project leader David Taylor Naval Ship Research and Devel. Ctr., Annapolis, MD., 1972-80, sect. leader, 1980—. Patentee in field. Contbr. articles to profl. jours. Recipient Spl. Service award Dept. Navy, 1981. Mem. ASME, Cryogenic Soc. Am., Pi Tau Sigma. Republican. Baptist. Current work: Modeling magnetocaloric effect and heat transfer characteristics in liquefying gases; development of low temperature regenerative type heat exchanger near 4K and investigation of isothermal gas compression technique. Subspecialty: Fluid mechanics. Home: 607 Truxton Rd Annapolis MD 21401 Office: David Taylor Naval Ship Research Ctr Code 2712 Annapolis MD 21402

GREEN, HARRY, retired pharmaceutical company executive; b. Phila., Sept. 7, 1917; s. Samuel and Mary (Bogatin) G.; m. Harriett Borten, Oct. 6, 1945; children: Ann Frankel, Jane. A.B. in Chemistry, U. Pa., 1938; M.S., 1939, Ph.D. (Harrison fellow), 1942. Research chemist Lion Oil Refining Co., El Dorado, Ark., 1941-44; sr. research organic chemist Pennsalt Mfg. Co., Phila., 1944-47; research assoc. in physiol. chemistry U. Pa. Med. Sch., Phila., 1947-52; asst. prof. U. Pa. Med. Sch. (Grad. Sch. Medicine), 1954-68; chief biochem. research Wills Eye Hosp., Phila., 1952-58; sr. research biochemist Smith Kline & French Labs., Phila., 1958-61, group leader, 1961-64, head neurobiochemistry, 1964-67, dir. biochemistry, 1967-75, dir. sci. liaison, 1975-80; v.p. sci. liaison and tech. Smith Kline Beckman Corp., Phila., 1980-83, ret., 1983. Mem. Am. Soc. Biol. Chemists, Am. Soc. Pharmacology and Exptl. Therapeutics, Am. Chem. Soc., AAAS, Assn. Research in Nervous and Mental Diseases, Internat. Soc. Biochem. Pharmacology, N.Y. Acad. Scis., Sigma Xi. Current Work: Intermediary metabolism, ocular biochemistry and physiology, enzymology corticosteroids, neurobiochemistry, drug metabolism, molecular biology, recombinant DNA research and technology, neuropharmacology, monoclonal antibodies. Subspecialties: Neurochemistry; Molecular biology. Home: 305 Penbree Terr Bala Cynwyd PA 19004 Also: 5771 Fairway Park Ct Boynton Beach FL 33437

GREEN, HARRY WESTERN, II, geology educator; b. Orange, N.J., Mar. 13, 1940; s. Harry Beutel and Mabel (Hendrickson) G.; m. Maria Manuela Martins, May 15, 1975; children: Mark, Stephen, Carolyn, Jennifer, Alice, Miquel, Maria. B.A., UCLA, 1963, M.S., 1967, Ph.D. with distinction, 1968. Postdoctoral assoc. Case Western Res. U., Cleve., 1968-70; asst. prof. geology U. Calif.-Davis, 1970-74, assoc. prof., 1974-80, prof., 1980—, acting chmn. dept., 1983, chmn. dept., 1984—; exchange scientist U. Nantes (France), 1973, vis. prof., 1978-79; vis. prof. Monash U., Melbourne, Australia, 1984. NSF grantee, 1970—. Mem. Am. Geophys. Union, Geol. Soc. Am., Mineral. Soc. Am. Current Work: The nature and history of the earth's mantle, especially the convective flow responsible for continental drift; utilizing transmission electron microscopy, electron energy-loss, spectroscopy and infrared spectroscopy to examine the deformation of natural mantle rocks, their volatile constituents and experimental analogs. Subspecialties: Geophysics; High-temperature materials. Home: 1225 Purdue Dr Davis CA 95616 Office: Dept Geology U Calif Davis CA 95616

GREEN, HOWARD, physiologist; b. Toronto, Ont., Can., 1925. M.D., U. Toronto, 1947; M.S. in Physiology, Northwestern U., 1950. Research asst. dept. physiology Northwestern U., Evanston, Ill., 1948-50; research assoc., instr. biochemistry U. Chgo., 1951-53; instr. pharmacology NYU Sch. Medicine, 1954-55, asst. prof. chem. pathology, 1956-59, assoc. prof. pathology, 1959-65, prof., 1965-68, prof., chmn. cell biology dept., 1968-70; prof. cell biology MIT, Cambridge, 1970-80; Higgins prof. cellular physiology, chmn. dept. physiology and biophysics Harvard U. Med. Sch., Boston, 1980—; lectr. in field. Served to capt. M.C. USAR, 1955-56. Recipient Mr. And Mrs. J. N. Taub Internat. Meml. award, 1977, Selman A. Waksman award, 1978, Lewis S. Rosenstiel award, 1980, Lila Gruber Research award Am. Acad. Dermatology, 1980. Mem. Am. Acad. Arts and Scis., Nat. Acad. Scis. Subspecialty: Physiology (medicine). Office: Dept Physiology and Biophysics Harvard Med Sch 25 Shattuck St Boston MA 02115

GREEN, JEROME JOSEPH, engineer, physicist; b. Chgo., Oct. 10, 1932; s. Harry Green and Josephine (Soloske) Dorn; m. Rosemary Elenore Hines, Sept. 6, 1958; children—Paula, Kenneth, Catherine, David. B.S., Northwestern U., 1954; M.A., Harvard U., 1955, Ph.D., 1960. Research asst. IBM, Pohkipsie, N.Y., 1955; prin. research sci. Raytheon Co., Waltham and Lexington, Mass., 1956—. Contbr. articles to profl. jours.; patentee microwaves. Town meeting mem. Lexington, Mass., 1975-78. Mem. IEEE (sr.). Roman Catholic. Current work: High frequency application magnetic materials. Subspecialties: Applied magnetics; Magnetic physics. Home: 28 Winchester Dr Lexington MA 02173 Office: Raytheon Co 131 Spring St Lexington MA 02173

GREEN, JONATHAN BREGSTONE, physicist; b. Chgo., Apr. 18, 1955; s. Robert Howard and Lois (Lascoe) G. S.B., MIT, 1977; M.S., Stanford U., 1979, Ph.D., 1982. Teaching asst. MIT, Cambridge, Mass., 1977, physicist Lincoln Lab., Lexington, Mass., 1982—; research asst. Stanford U., Calif., 1977-82; cons. TRW, Inc., Redondo Beach, Calif., 1981-82. Contbr. sci. articles to profl. jours. Patentee monolithic combined charge transfer and surface acoustic wave device. Mem. Am. Phys. Soc., AAAS, IEEE, Sigma Xi. Current work: Development of signal processing devices utilizing superconductivity, surface acoustic waves and semiconductor materials. Subspecialties: Condensed matter physics; Semiconductors. Home: 244 Beacon St Boston MA 02116 Office: MIT Lincoln Lab 244 Wood St Lexington MA 02173

GREEN, KEITH, physiologist, ophthalmologist, educator; b. Nuneaton, Warwickshire, Eng., Aug. 16, 1940; came to U.S., 1964, naturalized, 1973; s. Henry and Doris Sarah (Prime) G.; m. Mary Allan Vallance, Sept. 5, 1964; children—Kathryn Anne, John Philip Ross. B.Sc., U. Leicester, Eng., 1961; Ph.D., U. Andrews, Scotland, 1964, D.Sc., 1984. Research fellow Johns Hopkins U. Sch. Medicine, 1964-66, from instr. to assoc. prof., 1966-74; assoc. prof. ophthalmology Med. Coll Ga., Augusta, 1974-76, prof. ophthalmology, 1976-78, prof. physiology, 1977-78, Regents prof. ophthalmology and physiology, 1978—; cons. in field. Contbr. numerous articles to profl. jours. and chpts. to books. Recipient Career Devel. award NIH, 1969-74, Manpower award Research to Prevent Blindness, 1980-81, Disting. Faculty award for research, Med. Coll. Ga., 1984; Fogarty sr. internat. fellow, 1982-83. Mem. Am. Phys. Soc., Assn. Research in Ophthalmology, AAAS, Biophys. Soc., N.Y. Acad. Scis. Current work: Physiology and pharmacology of the eye, glaucoma, corneal transport mechanisms; cannabis compounds and treatment of disease; drug penetration into eye. Subspecialties: Physiology (medicine); Ophthalmology. Home: 3069 Westwood Rd Augusta GA 30909 Office: Dept Ophthalmology Med Coll Georgia Augusta GA 30912

GREEN, MICHAEL I(RVING), physicist, researcher; b. Suffern, N.Y., Mar. 21, 1930; s. Herman and Sylvia Katherine (Silverman) G.; m. Susan Lea Simon, Feb. 6, 1959; children—Deborah, William Harold. B.S., U. Ala., 1953; Ph.D., Wayne State U., 1972. Engr., Westinghouse Co., Bloomfield, N.Y., 1955-57; sr. scientist Lockheed Research Labs., Palo Alto, Calif., 1958-63; sr. physicist Bendix Research Labs., Detroit, 1963-64; instr. Wayne State U., Detroit, 1972-74; cons. physics, Detroit, 1964-74; accelerator physicist Lawrence Berkeley Lab., Calif., 1974—; dir. Magnetic Measurements Workshops, 1981—. Contbr. articles to profl. jours. Active Boy Scouts Am., 1953—, Mt. Diablo council, 1985—; mem. Santa Clara County Democratic Central Com., Calif., 1961-63; Dem. precinct chmn., Mount View, Calif. Served to pfc. U.S. Army, 1953-55. Mem. Am. Phys. Soc., IEEE, AAAS, Soaring Soc. Am., Pacific Soaring Council (v.p. Calif. 1984-85), Ames Soaring Club (v.p. 1982-83). Jewish. Current work: Creation of systems to measure strength and quality of magnets and fields associated with accelerators. Subspecialties: Magnetic physics; Applied magnetics. Home: 117 Rheem Blvd Orinda CA 94563 Office: Lawrence Berkeley Lab Bldg 46-125 1 Cyclotron Rd Berkeley CA 94720

GREEN, PAUL BARNETT, biology educator; b. Phila., Feb. 15, 1931; s. Otis Howard and Mabel (Barnett) G.; m. Margaret E. Cornett, Feb. 2, 1957; children: Robert, Peter, Katherine. B.A., U. Pa., 1952; Ph.D., Princeton U., 1957. Asst. to full prof. U. Pa., Phila., 1957-70; prof. biology Stanford (Calif.) U., 1971—. Contbr. articles to profl. jours.; author: Developmental Order: Its Origin and Regulation, 1982; assoc. editor: Ann. Rev. Plant Physiology, 1972-82. Recipient Darbaker Prize, 1964; Pelton award, 1974. Mem. Soc. for Developmental Biology, Bot. Soc. Am. Democrat. Congregationalist. Current Work: Morphogenesis - the initiation of new organs in plants; control of cell division planes, control of microtubule orientation. Subspecialties: Developmental biology; Plant growth. Home: 997 Cottrell Way Stanford CA 94305 Office: Stanford U Dept Biol Sci Stanford CA 94305

GREEN, PAUL ELIOT, JR., communication scientist; b. Durham, N.C., Jan. 14, 1924; s. Paul Eliot and Elizabeth Atkinson (Lay) G.; m. Dorrit L. Gegan, Oct. 30, 1948; children: Dorrit Green Rodemeyer, Nancy E., Judy J., Paul M., Gordon M. A.B., U. N.C.-Chapel Hill, 1943; M.S., N.C. State U., 1948; Sc.D., MIT, 1953. Group leader MIT Lincoln Lab., Lexington, 1951-69; sr. mgr. IBM Research Div., Yorktown Heights, N.Y., 1969-80, mem. corp. tech. com., Armonk, N.Y., 1980-82, research staff, 1982—. Served to lt. comdr. USNR, 1943-60; ret. Named Disting. Engring. Alumnus N.C. State U., 1983. Fellow IEEE (Aerospace Pioneer award 1981); mem. Nat. Acad. Engring. Current Work: Advanced protocols for architectures for large dynamic computer networks. Subspecialty: Distributed systems and networks. Home: Roseholm Pl Mount Kisco NY 10549 Office: IBM Research Staff PO Box 218 Yorktown Heights NY 10598

GREEN, RALPH ELLIS, nuclear research establishment executive; b. St. John's, Nfld., Can., Feb. 8, 1931; s. Hayward and Linda (Rowe) G.; m. Marie Flora Skanes, Sept. 18, 1952; children—Linda, Ward, Anne, Robert. B.Sc., Dalhousie U., 1952, M.Sc., 1954; Ph.D., McGill U., 1956. Research officer Chalk River Nuclear Labs., Ont., Can., 1956-70, head reactor control, 1970-78; sr. advisor to exec. v.p. AECL-Research Co., Ottawa, Ont., 1979-81; v.p., gen. mgr. Whiteshell Nuclear Research Establishment, Pinawa, Man., Can., 1981—. Contbr. sci. reports, articles to profl. lit. Mem. Can. Assn. Physicists, Can. Nuclear Soc. Clubs: Deep River Tennis (pres.), Deep River Ski (pres.) (Ont.). Current work: Research in nuclear fuel waste management, reactor safety, nuclear fuel reprocessing; study of radiation effects on cells, plants and animals. Subspecialties: Nuclear energy research management; Nuclear engineering. Home: 26 Prescott Crescent Pinawa MB R0E 1L0 Canada Office: Whiteshell Nuclear Research Establishment Pinawa MB R0E 1L0 Canada

GREEN, RICHARD FREDERICK, astronomer; b. Omaha, Feb. 13, 1949; s. Jack Maxwell and Bernice (Bordy) G.; m. Joan Auerbach, June 16, 1974; children: Alexander Simon, Nathaniel Martin. A.B., Harvard Coll., 1971; Ph.D. in astronomy, Calif. Inst. Tech., 1977. Research fellow in astronomy Hale Obs., Calif. Inst. Tech., 1977-79; asst. astronomer Steward Obs., U. Ariz., Tucson, 1979-83; asst. astronomer Kitt Peak Nat. Obs., 1983-85, assoc. astronomer, 1985—. Author: The Palomar-Green Catalogue. Mem. Am. Astron. Soc., Astron. Soc. Pacific, Phi Beta Kappa. Jewish. Current Work: Optical and space ultraviolet spectroscopy of quasars and hot stars; studies of faint clusters of galaxies around quasars; wide-field photographic surveying for rare stellar ojects. Subspecialties: Optical astronomy; Ultraviolet high energy astrophysics. Office: Kitt Peak Nat Obs PO Box 26732 Tucson AZ 85721

GREEN, ROBERT EDWARD, JR., educator, physicist; b. Clifton Forge, Va., Jan. 17, 1932; s. Robert Edward and Hazle Hall (Smith) G.; m. Sydney Sue Truitt, Feb. 1, 1962; children: Kirsten Adair, Heather Scott. B.S., William and Mary Coll., 1953; Ph.D., Brown U., 1959; postgrad. (Fulbright grantee), Aachen (Germany) Technische Hochschule, 1959-60. Physicist underwater explosions research div. Norfolk (Va.) Naval Shipyard, 61959; asst. prof. mechanics Johns Hopkins, Balt., 1960-65, assoc. prof., 1965-70, prof., 1970—, chmn. mechanics dept., 1970-72, chmn. mechanics and materials sci. dept., 1972-73, chmn. civil engring./materials sci. and engring. dept., 1979-82, chmn. materials sci. and engring. dept., 1982-85, dir. ctr. for non-destructive evaluation, 1985—. Ford Found. resident sr. engr. RCA, Lancaster, Pa., 1966-67; cons. U.S. Army Ballistic Research Labs., Aberdeen Proving Ground, Md., 1973-74; physicist Center for Materials Sci., U.S. Nat. Bur. Standards, Washington, 1974—. Author: Ultrasonic Investigation of Mechanical Properties (Treatise on Materials Science and Technology, Vol. 3), 1973; also articles. Mem. Am. Phys. Soc., Acoustical Soc. Am., Am. Inst. Mining, Metall. and Petroleum Engrs., Am. Soc. for Metals, Am. Soc. Nondestructive Testing, AAAS, Sigma Xi, Tau Beta Pi, Alpha Sigma Mu, Sigma Nu. Methodist. Research in recovery, recrystallization, elasticity, plasticity, crystal growth and orientation, X-ray diffraction, electro-optical systems, linear and non-linear elastic wave propagation, light-sound interactions, high-power ultrasonics, ultrasonic attenuation, dislocation damping, fatigue, acoustic emission, non-destructive testing, polymers, biomaterials. Current Work: Nondestructive characterization of materials; nondestructive evaluation of surgical implants, x-ray topographic examination of materials using synchrotron radiation. Subspecialties: Materials; Materials (engineering). Home: 936 Ellendale Dr Towson MD 21204 Office: Materials Sci and Engring Dept Johns Hopkins U Baltimore MD 21218

GREEN, ROBERT G., engineer; b. Lima, Ohio, June 11, 1920; m. Edna Meyer, June 28, 1941; children—Robert W., Thomas G., Daniel J. B.S. in Mech. Engring., Detroit Inst. Tech. Vice pres., gen. mgr. Eaton Springs Can., Ltd.; dir. product engring. Monroe Auto Equipment Co., Mich.; gen. mgr. automotive div. Teleflex Inc.; dir. research and devel. and engring. ITT Thompson Industries, exec. engr. ITT Corp., 1978—. Served with USN, 1943-46. Mem. Soc. Automotive Engrs., Engring. Soc. of Detroit, Engrs. Council for Profl. Devel. Subspecialty: Robotics. Home: 5407 Brookshire Monroe MI 48161

GREEN, ROBERT LESTER, ceramist; b. Pitts., Sept. 14, 1915; s. Samuel and Esther Adler G.; m. Eva Rebecca Kravif, July 27, 1940; children—Ellen Thea, Vivien Rachel. B.S. in Chemistry, U. Pitts., 1937; Sc.D. in Ceramics, MIT, 1940. Research ceramist Gen. Electric Research Lab., Schenectady, N.Y., 1939-47; lab. dir. Lenox China Inc., Trenton, N.J., 1947-80, dir. ceramic research, Pomona, N.J., 1980—. Contbr. articles to profl. jours. Named Man of Yr. N.J. Ceramic Assn., 1979. Fellow Am. Ceramic Soc.; mem. Nat. Inst. Ceramic Engrs. Democrat. Jewish. Subspecialty: Ceramics. Home: 22 E Riding Dr Cherry Hill NJ 08003 Office: Lenox China Inc Tilton Rd Pomona NJ 08240

GREEN, SAMUEL ISAAC, electronic engineer, consultant; b. Chgo., Aug. 15, 1942; s. Joseph and Belle (Lepkovsky) G.; m. Judith Arlene Tarantur, June 19, 1966; children—Meg, Steven. B.S.E.E., Northwestern U., 1964; M.S., U. Ill., 1966, Ph.D., 1969. Registered profl. engr., Mo. Sr. tech. specialist McDonnell Douglas Astronautics Co., St. Louis, 1969—. Contbr. articles to profl. jours. Patentee gated detector synchronization, 1974, broadband EO modulator, 1976, high speed photodetector, 1978. Mem. IEEE, Soc. Photo Optical Instrumentation Engrs., St. Louis Area Computer Club (bd. dirs. 1981-84). Current work: Photodetector characterization and development. Subspecialties: Electronics; Fiber optics. Home: 13052 Ferntrails Creve Coeur MO 63141 Office: McDonnell Douglas Astronautics Co Bldg 101A/230 PO Box 516 Saint Louis MO 63166

GREEN, VICTOR EUGENE, JR., research agronomist, educator; b. De Ridder, La., Sept. 3, 1922; s. Victor Eugene and Laura Mae (Harris) G.; m. Ada Ruth Hellert, June 5, 1945; children: Judy Ellen Green Brewer, Philip Martin. B.S., La. State U., 1947, M.S., 1948; Ph.D., Purdue U., 1951. Cert. Am. Soc. Agronomy. Asst. prof. La. Agrl. Expt. Sta., Baton Rouge, 1948-49; from asst. to assoc. prof. Fla. Agrl. Expt. Sta., Everglades, 1951-65, prof., 1968-70, prof./agronomist, Gainesville, 1970—; prof./adv. AID, San Jose, Costa Rica, 1965-68; cons. World Bank, Jamaica Sch. Agr., others. Recipient diploma of honor Costa Rica Ministry of Agr., 1968, diploma of honor PCCMCA, Guatemala, 1980. Mem. Soil and Crop Sci. Soc. Fla. (pres. 1965, editor-in-chief 1984-85), Am. Soc. Agronomy, Internat. Sunflower Assn., Crop Sci. Soc. Am., Soil Sci. Soc. Am. Republican. Lutheran. Current Work: Oil production and fatty acid composition through nuclear magnetic resonance and gas-liquid chromotography techniques. Subspecialties: Plant physiology (agriculture); Sunflower crop production. Home: 3915 SW 3d Ave Gainesville FL 32607 Office: U Fla Bldg 65 Gainesville FL 32611

GREENBAUM, ELIAS, research scientist; b. Bklyn., May 12, 1944; s. Bernard and Bess (Zweifach) G.; m. Anne Rochelle Deutsch, Nov. 4, 1973; children—Michael P., Bess G., Susan N. B.S. in Physics, Bklyn. Coll., 1965; M.S., Columbia U., 1967, Ph.D., 1970. Research assoc. U. Ill., Urbana, 1970-72; asst. prof. physics Rockefeller U., N.Y.C., 1972-77; research scientist Union Carbide Corp., Tarrytown, N.Y., 1977-79; group leader Oak Ridge Nat. Lab., 1979—. Patentee in field. Dept. Energy grantee, 1979—; Gas Research Inst. grantee, 1981—; Solar Energy Research Inst. grantee, 1981—. Fellow Am. Phys. Soc.; mem. Am. Solar Energy Soc. Current work: Production of fuels and chemical feedstocks from renewable inorganic resources; fundamental studies on the physics and chemistry of photosynthesis. Subspecialties: Photosynthesis; Solar energy. Home: 972 W Outer Dr Oak Ridge TN 37830 Office: Oak Ridge Nat Lab PO Box X Oak Ridge TN 37831

GREENBAUM, LOWELL MARVIN, pharmacologist, educator; b. N.Y.C., June 13, 1928; s. Benjamin and Belle (Gordon) G.; m. Gloria R. Rubin, June 13, 1950; children—Matthew, Daniel, Jessica. B.S., CCNY, 1949; Ph.D., Tufts U., 1953. Asst. prof. Downstate Med. Ctr., Bklyn., 1956-64; prof., Columbia U., N.Y.C., 1964-79; prof. dept. Pharmacology and toxicology Med. Coll. Ga., Augusta, 1979—, chmn. dept., 1979-85, v.p. research, dean Sch. Grad. Studies, 1985. Contbr. numerous articles to sci. publs. Bd. dirs. Walton Way Temple, Augusta, 1982—. Named Career Scientist, Health Research Council, N.Y.C., 1965-75; NIH grantee, 1958—. Mem. Assn. Med. Sch. Pharmacologists (pres. 1984-86), Am. Soc. Pharmacology and Therapeutics (chmn. pub. affairs com. 1973-79), Am. Soc. Biol. Chemistry, Assn. Am. Med. Colls. (council Acad. Soc. 1980-84), Internat. Kinin Congress (pres. 1984). Current work: Research in vasoactive peptides, proteases and anti-proteases, inflammation, arthritis, cancer; discoverer leukokinins, T-Kinin and T-Kininogen. Subspecialties: Pharmacology; Molecular pharmacology. Office: Dept Pharmacology and Toxicology Med Coll Ga Augusta GA 30912

GREENBERG, CHARLES BERNARD, ceramic scientist; b. Elizabeth, N.J., Dec. 20, 1939; s. Nathan and Claire (Cohen) G.; m. Susan Irma Silverman, May 28, 1967; 3 children. B.S., Rutgers U., 1961; M.S., U. Ill., 1962, Ph.D., 1965. Sr. research ceramist Glass Research Ctr., PPG Industries, Inc. Pitts., 1965-68, research assoc., 1968-71, sr. research assoc., 1971-77, staff scientist, 1977—; reviewer Am. Chem. Soc., 1984. Contbr. articles to sci. jours. Patentee in field. Adminstr., coach Murrysville Area Soccer Assn., Pa., 1978—; baseball coach Franklin Area Athletic Assn., Murrysville, 1978-82; pres. Murrysville Midget Baseball League, 1978-80. Gen. Ceramics Corp. scholar, 1960-61; Edward Orton Jr. fellow Orton Soc., 1961-62; Internat. Lead-Zinc Research Orgn. fellow, 1962-65. Mem. Am. Ceramic Soc., Electrochem. Soc., AAAS. Current work: Thin films deposited by electroless chemistry, CVD and spray pyrolysis, optically and electrically switching film materials, film durability. Office: PPG Industries Inc Glass Research Ctr Pittsburgh PA 15238

GREENBERG, DAVID ALEXANDER, oceanographer, researcher; b. Ottawa, Ont., Can., Dec. 27, 1946; s. Louis and Nancy (Lawson) G.; m. Cheryl Ann Marie Plomske, Aug. 1, 1970; 1 child, Alexander Luke. B. Math., U. Waterloo, Ont., 1969, M. Math., 1970; Ph.D., U. Liverpool, 1975. Phys. scientist Marine Environ. Data Service, Ottawa, Ont., 1970-73, 75-77; research scientist Bedford Inst. Oceanography, Dartmouth, N.S., Can., 1977—. Contbr. articles to profl. jours. Mem. Can. Oceanographic and Meteorological Soc. Current work: Numerical modelling of coastal seas and continental shelves, tides, circulation, storm surges. Subspecialties: Numerical modelling; Oceanography. Office: Bedford Inst Oceanography PO Box 1006 Dartmouth NS B2Y 4A2 Canada

GREENBERG, HAROLD PAUL, electronics co. exec.; b. Balt., May 10, 1933; s. Harry and Pauline Henrietta (Levin) G.; m. Lois Ann Lavine, Feb. 2, 1958; 1 dau., Roberta. A.S., Northeastern U., 1961, B.S., 1964, M.B.A., 1970. Registered profl. engr., Mass. Sr. engr. GTE Sylvania, Needham, Mass., 1965-70; sr. engr., mgr. vendor quality assurance Polaroid Corp., Cambridge, Mass., 1971-74; quality assurance sect. head GTE Sylvania, Needham, Mass., 1974-79; dir. reliability and regulatory affairs Analogic Corp., Wakefield, Mass., 1979-84; cons., 1984—; cons. in field. mem. faculty North Shore Community Coll., Beverly, Mass. Served with U.S. Army, 1953-55. Fellow Am. Soc. Quality Control (cert. quality engr., cert. reliability engr.); mem. Engring. Socs. New Eng. (past pres.). Lodge: Masons. Current work: Developing and implementing quality and reliability systems. Subspecialties: Quality engineering; Electronics. Home and Office: 6 Coe Rd Framingham MA 01701

GREENBERG, NEIL, zoologist, educator; b. Newark, Oct. 30, 1941; s. Henry and Norma (Wexelman) G.; m. Alicia Carolyn Berry, June 29, 1969; 1 dau.: Haley Jessica Elise. B.A., Drew U., 1963; M.S., Rutgers U., 1968, Ph.D., 1973. Research ethologist NIMH, Bethesda, Md., 1973-78; research assoc. Mu. Comparative Zoology, Harvard U., 1977-82; asst. prof. zoology U. Tenn., Knoxville, 1978-82, assoc. prof., 1982—; cons., lectr. in field. Contbr. articles to profl. jours.; editor: Behavior and Neurology of Lizards, 1978. NIMH Grant Found. fellow, 1973-75; 1st Tenn. Bank scholar, 1981; Danforth assoc., 1981. Mem. Am. Soc. Zoologists, Animal Behavior Soc., Soc. Neurosci., Sigma Xi. Current Work: Reciprocal relationships of social behavior, stress, and repro endocrinology. Subspecialties: Ethology; Comparative neurobiology. Office: Dept Zoology U Tenn Knoxville TN 37996

GREENBERG, PHILIP JOEL, theoretical physicist, educator; b. Bronx, N.Y., Apr. 22, 1942; s. Aaron and Gertrude (Schechter) G.; m. Susan Turner Driehaus, July 22, 1973 (div. Aug. 1979). B.S., Stevens Inst. Tech., 1963; M.S., Stanford U., 1964; Ph.D., U. Chgo., 1970; M.B.A., Boston U., 1980. Asst. prof. math. MIT, 1969-73; postdoctoral fellow physics U. Alta., 1973-76; staff scientist Atmospheric and Environ. Research, Cambridge, Mass., 1980-81; mem. tech. staff Bell Labs., Holmdel, N.J., 1981-83; assoc. prof. math. Monmouth Coll., West Long Branch, N.J., 1984—; tchr. Cambridge Adult Edn. Ctr., 1976-81. Contbr. articles to profl. jours. NSF fellow, 1964; NASA trainee, 1968; fellow U. Alta., 1973. Mem. Am. Phys. Soc., N.Y. Acad. Scis., Tau Beta Pi. Democrat. Jewish. Current work: Research in special and general relativistic hydrodynamics; studies on Lorentz-transformation properties of relativistic gravitational fields; computational physics. astrophysics; Subspecialties: Theoretical astrophysics; Relativity and gravitation. Home: 17 Wedgewood Circle Eatontown NJ 07724 Office: Dept of Math and Computer Sci Monmouth Coll West Long Branch NJ 07764

GREENBERG, STAN SHIMEN, pharmacologist, educator, researcher; b. Bklyn., Sept. 14, 1945; s. Louis Meyer and Anna (Pinckosowitz) G.; m. Patricia Ann Powers, Oct. 13, 1978; 1 son, Jonathan Michael. B.S. magna cum laude, Bklyn. Coll. Pharmacy, L.I. U., 1968; M.S., U. Iowa, Ph.D., 1972. Postdoctoral fellow div. clin. pharmacology U. Iowa, Iowa City, 1972-73; NIH postdoctoral scholar dept. physiology U. Mich., Ann Arbor, 1973-74; instr. pharmacology and myocardial biology Baylor Coll. Medicine, 1974-75; asst. prof. pharmacology Ohio State U. Coll. Medicine, 1975-77; assoc. prof. pharmacology U.S. Ala. Coll. Medicine, Mobile, 1977—. Author: (with T.M. Glenn) Prostanoids in Cardiovascular and Cardiopulmonary Disease, 1981, Physiology of Smooth Muscle, 1982, Procs. Soc. Exptl. Biology and Medicine; mem. editorial bd.: Methods and Findings in Clin. and Exptl. Therapeutics; contbr. articles to profl. jours. NIH grantee, 1977—; Am. Heart Assn. grantee, 1975-78. Fellow Royal Soc. Medicine; mem. Am. Fedn. Clin. research, Internat. Study Group for Research in Cardiac Metabolism, AAAS, Western Pharmacology Soc., Am. Soc. Pharmacology and Exptl. Therapeutics, Am. Physiol. Soc., Soc. Exptl. Biology and Medicine, High Blood Pressure Council Am. Heart Assn. (fellow med. adv. bd.), Mobile Area High Blood Pressure Council (v.p.), Shock Soc., Microcirculatory Soc., Sigma Xi. Jewish. Current work: Vascular smooth muscle function in hypertension, animal research to elucidate the pathogenesis of renal hypertension and coronary artery disease. Subspecialties: Pharmacology; Cellular pharmacology. Home: 33 Lakeview Dr Morris Plains NJ 07950 Office: Dept Physiology U Medicine and Dentistry of NJ Berley Labs Cedar Knolls NJ 07927

GREENBLATT, SAMUEL HAROLD, neurosurgeon; b. Potsdam., N.Y., May 16, 1939; s. Louis and Rose Leah (Clopman) G.; m. Judith Ruth Shapiro, June 23, 1963; children: Rachel, Daniel, Miriam. B.A., Cornell U., 1961, M.D., 1966; M.A., Johns Hopkins U., 1964. Diplomate: Am. Bd. Neurol. Surgery. Intern Boston City Hosp., 1966-67; resident in neurology Boston VA Hosp., 1967-68; resident in neurol. surgery Dartmouth Affiliated Hosp., Hanover, N.H., 1970-74; hon. sr. registrar Nurosurg. unit Guy's, Maudlsey and King's Coll. Hosps., London, 1972; instr. neurol. surgery Albert Einstein Coll. Medicine, Bronx, N.Y., 1974-77; asst. attending neurol. surgeon Bronx Mcpl. Hosp. Ctr., 1974-77; asst. prof. neurol. surgery Med. Coll. Ohio, Toledo, 1977-80, assoc. prof., 1980—, staff neurosurgeon, 1977—; clin. asst. neurol. surgery St. Barnabas Hosp., Bronx, 1975, research asst. neurol. surgery, 1976-77; assoc. staff neurosurgeon Mercy Hosp., Toledo, 1977-80, courtesy staff neurosurgeon, 1980—. Contbr. articles to profl. jours. and books. Served with U.S. Army, 1968-70. USPHS fellow, 1963-64; Tiffany Blake fellow, 1972-73. Fellow A.C.S.; mem. History Sci. Soc., Am. Assn. History Medicine, Internat. Neuropsychol. Soc., Am. Epilepsy Soc., Soc. health and Human Values, Soc. Neurosci., N.Y. Acad. Scis., Acad. Medicine Toledo, Ohio State Med. Assn., Behavioral Neurology Soc., Ohio State Neurosurg. Soc., Am. Assn. Neurol. Surgeons, Congress Neurol. Surgeons, Acad. of Aphasia. Jewish.

Current Work: Primary research concerns the anatomical correlates of neurobehavioral abnormalities (especially alexia) and normal brain substratum of cognitive behavior. Subspecialty: Neuropsychology. Office: Medical College of Ohio Department of Neurol Surgery CS 10008 Toledo OH 43699

GREENE, ARTHUR EDWARD, physicist; b. Chgo., Dec. 10, 1945; s. Shirley Edward and Ellen Catherine (Tweedy) G.; m. Nancy Ellen Green, Sept. 12, 1970; 1 child, Ellen Dorothy. Student, Doane Coll., Crete, Nebr., 1963-65; B.S., Ohio State U., 1967, Ph.D. in Astronomy, 1971. Staff mem. Los Alamos Nat. Lab., 1975—, mem. theoretical chemistry and molecular physics group, 1975-81, mem. thermonuclear applications group, 1981—. Contbr. articles to profl. jours. Served with USAF, 1971-75. Mem. Am. Phys. Soc., Phi Beta Kappa. Current Work: Plasma physics and radiation transport, laser physics, stellar atmospheres of evolved stars. Subspecialties: Atomic and molecular physics; Plasma physics. Office: MS-B220 Los Alamos National Laboratory Los Alamos NM 87545

GREENE, CHRIS H., physics educator; b. Lincoln, Nebr., Aug. 1, 1954; s. William Henry and Helen (Kiesselbach) G.; m. Christy Ann, Sept. 15, 1977. B.S., U. Nebr., 1976; M.S., U. Chgo., 1977, Ph.D., 1980. Research assoc. Stanford (Calif.) U., 1980-81; asst. prof. physics and astronomy La. State U., Baton Rouge, 1981—. Contbr. articles in field to profl. jours. IBM fellow, 1979-80. Mem. Am. Phys. soc. Current Work: Research on basic properties of atoms and molecules, electron correlation, photoionization and quantum defect theory. Subspecialties: Atomic and molecular physics; Theoretical physics. Office: La State U Dept Physics and Astronomy Baton Rouge LA 70803

GREENE, DUANE WESLEY, horticulture educator; b. Troy, N.Y., May 24, 1942; s. Phillip A. Greene and Mary Elizabeth Greene Peck; m. AnnaCelia Ferrazzani, Jan. 7, 1978. B.A. in Botany, Colgate U., 1964; M.S. in Horticulture, Mich. State U., 1966, Ph.D. in Horticulture, 1969. Asst. prof. plant and soil sci. dept. U. Mass., Amherst, 1969-75, assoc. prof., 1976-82, prof., 1982—. Mem. Am. Soc. for Hort. Sci. (pres. northeast region 1984-85), Am. Soc. Plant Physiologists, Dwarf Fruit Tree Assn. Current work: Use of plant growth regulators and cultural techniques to regulate growth, flowering and fruit set in fruit trees. Subspecialty: Plant growth. Office: U Mass Plant and Soil Sci Dept Amherst MA 01003

GREENE, JOHN CLIFFORD, dentist, university dean; b. Ashland, Ky., July 19, 1926; s. G. Norman and Ella R. G.; m. Gwen Rustin, Nov. 17, 1957; children: Alan, Lisa, Laura. A.A., Ashland Jr. Coll., 1947; student, Marshall Coll., 1948; D.M.D., U. Louisville, 1952, Sc.D. (hon.), 1980; M.P.H., U. Calif., Berkeley, 1961; Sc.D. (hon.), U. Ky., 1972, Boston U., 1975. Diplomate: Am. Bd. Dental Public Health (pres.). Intern USPHS Hosp., Chgo., 1952-53, staff, San Francisco, 1953-54; asst. regional dental cons. Region IX, San Francisco, 1954-56, asst. to chief dental officer, Washington, 1958-60; chief epidemiology program Dental Health Center, 1961-66; dep. dir. Div. Dental Health, 1966-70, acting dir., 1970, dir., 1970-73; acting dir. Bur. Health Resources Devel., 1973-74, dir., 1974-75; chief dental officer USPHS, 1974-81, dep. surgeon gen., 1978-81; with Epidemic Intelligence Service, Communicable Disease Center, Altanta and Kansas City, Mo., 1956-57; epidemiology and biometry br. Nat. Inst. Dental Research, NIH, Bethesda, Md., 1957-58; dean. Sch. Dentistry,U. Calif., San Francisco, 1981—; spl. cons. WHO, India, 1957; faculty Calif., U. Mich., U. Pa.; cons. Am. Dental Assn. Council, Nat. Health Professions Placement Network. Contbr. writings to profl. publs. Served with USN, 1945-46. Recipient citation Sch. Grad. Dentistry Boston U., 1971, citation U. of the Pacific, 1977, Meritorious and Disting. Service awards HEW, 1972, 75, Outstanding Alumnus award U. Louisville, 1980, award of merit FDI, 1978. Fellow Am. Coll. Dentists; mem. ADA, Calif. Dental Assn., San Francisco Dental Soc., Internat. Assn. Dental Research (pres.-elect), Am. Assn. Public Health Dentists, Am. Acad. Periodontology, Am. Assn. Dental Schs. (v.p.), Western Conf. Dental Deans and Examiners (pres.), U.S. Preventive Services Task Force, Inst. of Medicine of Nat. Acad. Sci., Federation Dentaire Internationale (chmn. commn. on public dental health, mem. WHO panel of experts on dental health), Omicron Kappa Upsilon, Delta Omega. Current Work: Changes in disease patterns affecting dentistry; dental care delivery systems. Subspecialties: Preventive dentistry; Epidemiology. Home: 103 Peacock Dr San Rafael CA 94901 Office: U Calif Sch Dentistry: San Francisco CA 94143

GREENE, JOHN PHILIP, physicist, researcher; b. Chgo., Oct. 13, 1955; s. Robert Raymond and Kathleen Veronica (Shepherd) G. A.A., Wright Jr. Coll., 1975; B.A., U. Ill., 1978; M.S. in Physics, DePaul U., 1982. Project chemist Desoto Inc., Des Plaines, Ill., 1978-82; sci. asst. Argonne Nat. Lab., Ill., 1982—. Contbr. articles to profl. jours. Patentee in field. Mem. Am. Phys. Soc., Am. Chem. Soc. (chmn. analytical group Chgo. sect. 1984—), Sigma Xi. Republican. Roman Catholic. Current work: Photoionization and photoelectron spectroscopy; chemical health and safety. Subspecialties: Atomic and molecular physics; Laser photochemistry. Home: 7331 S Woodward Apt G-105 Woodridge IL 60517Office: Argonne Nat Lab 9700 S Cass Ave Argonne IL 60439

GREENE, MURRAY A., cardiologist.; b. Bklyn., May 20, 1927; s. Max and Beatrice (Kolomer) G.; m. Eileen Smolkin, Dec. 19, 1953; children: Barry T., Larry B. A.B., NYU, 1948; M.D., Columbia U., 1952. Diplomate: Am. Bd. Internal Medicine. Intern Maimonides Hosp., Bklyn., asst. resident in medicine, 1953-54; resident in medicine Montefiore Hosp., N.Y.C., 1955-56; research fellow Cardiopulmonary Lab., Maimonides Hosp. and SUNY-Downstate Med. Center, 1954-55, 56-57; chief div. cardiovascular diseases Bronx-Lebanon Hosp., N.Y.C., 1957-71, dir. intensive care unit and Cardiopulmonary Lab., 1957-71, attending physician dept. medicine, 1957—; asst. clin. prof. medicine Albert Einstein Coll. Medicine, N.Y.C., 1972—. Contbr. numerous articles to med. jours. Served with U.S. Army, 1945-47. Fellow ACP, Am. Coll. Chest Physicians, Am. Fedn. Clin. Research; mem. AMA, Am. Physicians Fellowship Assn., N.Y. Acad. Scis., Am. Heart Assn., N.Y. Heart Assn., Am. Soc. Internal Medicine, N.Y. Soc. Internal Medicine, Med. Soc. State N.Y., Phi Beta Kappa. Subspecialties: Cardiology; Physiology (medicine).

GREENE, RICHARD MELVYN, electrical engineer; b. Queens, N.Y., Feb. 5, 1942; s. Alexander Elias and Lillian (Greenberg) G.; divorced; children—Stacie, David, Tammy. B.E.E., Clarkson U., 1963, M.S., 1964. Elec. engr. G.T.&E. Labs, Bayside, N.Y., 1964-69, G.I., Hicksville, N.Y., 1969-70; sr. engr. MOS Tech., Valley Forge, Pa., 1970-76; sr. prin. engr. Solid State Sci., Willow Grove, Pa., 1976-85; cons., 1985—. Patentee in field. Contbr. articles to profl. jours. Mem. IEEE, Audubon Oaks Jaycees (v.p. 1975-76). Democrat. Jewish. Lodge: B'nai B'rith. Current work: Advanced development of memory products with emphasis on CMOS technology. Subspecialties: Microchip technology (engineering); Integrated circuits. Office: Stevens Ln Tabernacle NJ 08088

GREENE, STEVEN JOSEPH, nuclear physicist; b. Redwood Falls, Minn., Aug. 9, 1951; s. Joseph J. and Lorraine Theresa (Carroll) G. B.A., U. Colo., 1975; Ph.D., U. Tex., 1981. Vis. staff Los Alamos Nat. Lab., 1973-83, mem. staff, 1983—; research assoc. N.Mex. State U., Las Cruces, 1982-83, asst. prof., 1983. Contbr. articles to profl. jours. Welch Found. fellow, 1976, 77, 79. Mem. Am. Phys. Soc., Planetary Soc., Nat. Geog. Soc. Current work: Medium energy physics; nuclear structure and reactions with pi mesons; pion double charge excange reactions and nucleon-nucleon interactions. Subspecialties: Nuclear physics; Particle physics. Office: Los Alamos Nat Lab MP-10 MS H841 Los Alamos NM 87545

GREENFIELD, PATRICIA ANN MARKS, psychology educator; b. Newark, N.J., July 18, 1940; d. David and Doris Jeanette (Pollard) Marks; m. Sheldon Greenfield (div. 1983); children—Lauren, Matthew Michael. A.B. summa cum laude, Radcliffe Coll., 1962; Ph.D. in Social Psychology, Harvard U., 1966. Research fellow in psychology Ctr. for Cognitive Studies Harvard U., Cambridge, Mass., 1968-72; vis. asst. prof. psychology Stanford U., 1972-73; asst. prof. psychology U. Calif.-Santa Cruz, 1973-74; assoc. prof. psychology UCLA, 1974-78, prof. psychology, 1978—; external examiner U. Lagos, Nigeria, 1977-79; collaborating scientist Yerkes Regional Primate Research Ctr. Emory U., Atlanta, 1979—. Author: Mind and Media: The Effects of Television, Video Games, and Computers, 1984. Bd. dirs. Westside Women's Clinic, Santa Monica, Calif., 1977—; mem. Com. for Econ. Democracy, Santa Monica, 1981—, Alliance for Survival, Los Angeles, 1983—. Spencer Found. grantee, 1975-81. Fellow AAAS, Am. Psychol. Assn.; mem. Soc. for Research Child Devel. Current work: Research on cognitive effects of video games, tv, and radio; cognitive aspects of chimpanzee language. Subspecialties: Developmental psychology; Cognition. Home: 42 Park Ave Venice CA 90291 Office: Dept Psychology UCLA Los Angeles CA 90024

GREENFIELD, STANLEY MARSHALL, consulting company executive, researcher; b. N.Y.C., Apr. 16, 1927; s. Harry William and Millie (Jaller) G.; m. Rhoda Claire Barish, Sept. 1, 1951; children: Diane, David. B.S., NYU, 1950; Ph.D., UCLA, 1967. Head environ. scis. dept. Rand Corp., Santa Monica, Calif., 1950-71; asst. adminstr. for research and devel. EPA, Washington, 1971-74; sr. mem. tech. staff Flow Resources Corp., San Rafael, Calif., pres., 1974-78; sr. v.p. and tech. dir. Teknekron Research Inc., Berkeley, Calif., 1978-81; pres. Systems Applications, Inc., San Rafael, 1981—; Mem. various com. and panels Nat. Acad. Scis., 1960-83; mem. adv. bds. U.S. Air Force Sci. Adv. Bd., 1959-70, Space sci. panels NASA, 1957-70; mem. adv. sci. and tech. panel Calif. State Legislature, Sacramento, 1969-71. Contbr. over 30 sci. articles to profl. publs. Served with USN, 1943-45. Recipient award for research leading to first meteorol. satellite, NOAA, 1985. Fellow Am. Meteorol. Soc. (Spl. award 1961); mem. Pan Am. Med. Assn., AAAS, Internat. Acad. Environ. Safety. Current Work: Environmental science with particular emphasis on air pollution; acid deposition; energy impacts; risk assessment; data base management. Subspecialties: Meteorologic instrumentation; Air pollution dispersion. Home: 133 Knollwood Dr San Rafael CA 94901 Office: 101 Lucas Valley Rd San Rafael CA 94903

GREENKORN, ROBERT ALBERT, chemical engineering educator; b. Oshkosh, Wis., Oct. 12, 1928; s. Frederick John and Sophie (Phillips) G.; m. Rosemary Drexler, Aug. 16, 1952; children: David Michael, Eileen Anne, Susan Marie, Nancy Joanne. Student, Oshkosh State Coll., 1951-52; B.S., U. Wis., 1954, M.S., 1955, Ph.D., 1957. Postdoctoral fellow Norwegian Tech. Inst., 1957-58; research engr. Jersey Prodn. Research Co., Tulsa, 1958-63; lectr. U. Tulsa, 1958-63; asso. prof. theoretical and applied mechanics Marquette U., Milw., 1963-65; asso. prof. Sch. Chem. Engring., Purdue U., Lafayette, Ind., 1965-67; prof., head Sch. Chem. Engring., 1967-72, asst. dean engring., 1972-76; asso. dean engring., dir. Engring. Expt. Sta., 1976-80; v.p., asso. provost, v.p. for programs Purdue Research Found., 1980—. Author: (with D.P. Kessler) Transfer Operations, 1972, (with K.C. Chao) Thermodynamics of Fluids: An Introduction to Equilibrium Theory, 1975, (with D.P. Kessler) Modeling and Data Analysis for Engineers and Scientists, 1980, Flow Phenomena in Porous Media, 1983; Contbr. articles to profl. jours. Served with USN, 1946-51. Decorated D.F.C., Air medal with two oak leaf clusters. Fellow Am. Inst. Chem. Engrs.; Mem. Soc. Petroleum Engrs., Am. Inst. Mining, Am. Soc. Engring. Edn., Metall. and Petroleum Engrs., Am. Chem. Soc., Am. Geophys. Union, Sigma Xi, Phi Eta Sigma, Tau Beta Pi, Phi Gamma Delta. Roman Catholic. Patentee in field. Current Work: Flow phenomena in porous media; thermo dynamics of fluids; coal liquefaction; environmental modeling. Subspecialties: Chemical engineering; Petroleum engineering. Home: 151 Knox Dr West Lafayette IN 47906

GREENLICK, MERWYN RONALD, health services researcher; b. Detroit, Mar. 12, 1935; s. Emanuel and Fay (Ettinger) G.; m. Harriet Cohen, Aug. 19, 1956; children—Phyllis, Michael, Vicki. B.S., Wayne State U., 1957; M.S., U. Mich., 1961, Ph.D., 1967. Pharmacist, Detroit, 1957-60; spl. instr., instr. pharmacy adminstrn. Coll. Pharmacy Wayne State U., 1958-62; dir. of research Kaiser Permanente N.W. region, Portland, 1964—; v.p. (research) Kaiser Found. Hosps., 1981—; adj. prof. sociology Portland State U., 1965—; clin. prof. preventive medicine and pub. health Oreg. Health Sci. U., 1971—; mem. study com. on health delivery systems Gov.'s Comprehensive Health Planning Council; cons. Gov.'s Health Manpower Council. Bd. dirs. Washington County Community Action Orgn., 1966-70; pres. Jewish Edn. Assn., Portland, 1976-78; bd. dirs. Jewish Fedn., 1975-79. USPHS trainee, 1962-63, 63-64. Fellow Am. Pub. Health Assn. (governing council); mem. AAAS, Am. Sociol. Assn., Am. Statis. Assn., Group Health Assn. Am., Nat. Acad. Scis., Inst. Medicine. Jewish. Subspecialty: Health services research. Home: 712 NW Spring Portland OR 97229 Office: 4610 SE Belmont Portland OR 97215

GREENSPAN, MARTIN, physicist, consultant; b. N.Y.C., May 8, 1912; m. 1937; 3 children. B.S., Cooper Union, 1933. Physicist, Nat. Bur Standards, Washington, 1935-76, editor Jour. Research, 1962-73, chief sound sec., 1967-74; mem. governing bd. Am. Inst. Physics, 1974-79; cons. 1976—; vis. lectr. UCLA, 1958-59; mem. U.S. Nat. Com. Internat. Union Pure and Applied Physics, 1966-72; adj. prof. Catholic U. Am., 1968—; mem. NRC, 1969-72. Recipient Silver medal Phys. Acoustics, Acoustical Soc. Am., 1977; Harry Diamond award IEEE. Fellow AAAS, Acoustical Soc. Am. (v.p. 1963-64, pres. 1966-67, Gold medal), Am. Phys. Soc. Subspecialty: Acoustical engineering. *

GREENSTEIN, JESSE LEONARD, astronomer, emeritus educator; b. N.Y.C., Oct. 15, 1909; s. Maurice and Leah (Feingold) G.; m. Naomi Kitay, Jan. 7, 1934; children: George Samuel, Peter Daniel. A.B., Harvard U., 1929, A.M., 1930, Ph.D., 1937. Engaged in real estate and investments, 1930-34, Nat. Research fellow, 1937-39; assoc. prof. Yerkes Obs., U. Chgo., 1939-48; research assoc. McDonald Obs., U. Tex., 1939-48; mil. research under OSRD (optical design), Yerkes Obs.), 1942-45; prof. Calif. Inst. Tech., 1948-70, Lee A. DuBridge prof. astrophysics, 1971-81, prof. emeritus, 1981—; also staff mem. Hale Obs., 1949—, Palomar Obs., 1979—, exec. officer for astronomy, 1949-72; chmn. of faculty of inst., 1965-67; mem. obs. com. Hale Observatories; mem. staff Owens Valley Radio Obs.; cons., also com. mem. NASA and NSF on astronomy and radio astronomy; chmn. astronomy survey Nat. Acad. Scis., 1969-72; spl. cons. NASA, 1978—; vis. prof. Princeton, 1955, Inst. for Advanced Studies, 1964, 68-69, U. Hawaii, 1979, Niels Bohr Inst., 1979, NORDITA, Copenhagen, 1972, U. Del., 1981; lectr. in field; cons. Sci. Adv. Bd. USAF; past dir. Itek Corp., Hycon Corp. Chmn. bd. dirs. Associated Univs. Research in Astronomy, 1974-77; bd. overseers Harvard, 1965-71; bd. dirs. Pacific Asia Mus. Author sects. of treatises, 400 tech. papers.; Editor: Stellar Atmospheres, 1960; Contbr. sci. articles; author govt. reports. Named Calif. Scientist of Yr., 1964; recipient Apollo award, Disting. Public Service medal NASA, 1974. Mem. Royal Astron. Soc. (asso., gold medal 1975), Astron. Soc. Pacific (Bruce medalist 1971), Am. Astron. Soc. (councillor 1947-50, v.p. 1955-57, Russell lectr. 1970), Internat. Astron. Union (pres. commn. on spectroscopy 1952-58, chmn. U.S. del. 1969-72, Rennie Taylor award 1982), Nat. Acad. Scis. (councillor, sect. chmn. com. on sci. and pub. policy), Am. Philos. Soc., Am. Acad. Arts and Scis., Phi Beta Kappa. Club: Athenaeum (Pasadena) (bd. govs.). Current Work: Observation of faint stars at the end of their evolution; composition and cooling of condensed matter. Subspecialties: Optical astronomy; Theoretical astrophysics.

GREENSTOCK, CLIVE LEWIS, research scientist, consultant; b. High Wycombe, Eng., Aug. 14, 1939; s. George Henry and Clarice Irene (Lewis) G.; m. Gwen Dorothy Johns, July 17, 1965; children: Erica Jane, Andrea Gail. B.Sc. in Physics with honors, U. Leeds, Eng., 1960; M.Sc. in Radiation Physics, U. London, 1963; Ph.D. in Radiation Biochemistry, U. Toronto, Can., 1968. Hosp. physicist Cardiff (Wales) Radiotherapy Centre, 1960-61; sci. officer Nat. Phys. Lab., Teddington, Eng., 1963-64; postdoctoral fellow Cancer Research Campaign, Mt. Vernon Hosp., Eng., 1969-70; research officer, chmn. long-range research study group Atomic Energy Can., Ltd., Pinawa, Man., Can., 1970—; vis. scientist NRC, Ottawa; sabbatical fellow Christie Hosp. and Holt Radium Inst. Manchester, 1983-84; cons. Radiation Chemistry Data Center of U. Notre Dame, Nat. Cancer Program, HEW, Fed. Strategy for Research of NIH; lectr. radiation protection tng. course; grant reviewer. Assoc. editor: Radiation Research Jour, 1977-80; editor; Advances in Oxygen Radicals and Radioprotectors; contbr. articles and revs. to profl. jours., chpts. to books. Nat. coach Cross Country Ski Assn., Gymnastics Assn.; chmn. Pinawa Library Bd.; sch. tchr. Pinawa Christian Fellowship, sci. fair judge. Grantee Sci. Research Council, 1961-63; awardee Can. Cancer Research, 1964-68; Nat. Cancer Inst. fellow, 1969-70; recipient sr. scientist award Heineman Found. West Germany and Royal Soc. London, 1983-84. Mem. Am. Assn. Cancer Research, Radiation Research Soc. (chmn. membership com. 1979-80), Biophys. Soc., Antioxidant Soc., Brit. Assn. Cancer Research, Brit. Assn. Radiation Research, Brit. Inst. Radiology, Am. Radio Relay League., Mensa Soc., Sigma Xi. Anglican. Current Work: Molecular radiobiology, radiation damage in DNA, lipids and proteins, radioprotection and sensitization, free radical mechanisms in radiation and chemical carcinogenesis and its prevention, redox processes in metabolism, toxicity activated oxygen and its control by redox enzymes; pulse radiolysis and chemical kinetics, structure-function relationships in biopolymers; cancer screening proneness of early diagnosis using fluorescence. Subspecialties: Cancer research (medicine); Radiation biology. Home: 112 Burrows Rd Pinawa MB ROE 1L0 Canada Office: Medical Biophysics Br Atomic Energy of Canada Ltd Pinawa MB ROE 1L0 Canada

GREENWALD, EDWARD S., physician, medical oncologist; b. New Rochelle, N.Y., May 13, 1928; s. Irving and Belle Elizabeth (Jacobson) G.; m. Edith Deborah Greenwald, Dec. 4, 1949; children: David, Daniel, Joel, Joshua. B.A., Amherst Coll., 1948; M.D., N.Y. U., 1952. Diplomate: Am. Bd. Internal Medicine. Practice medicine specializing in med. oncology, New Rochelle, N.Y., 1958—; acting chief dept. oncology Montefiore Hosp., Bronx, N.Y., 1976-82; clin. prof. medicine Albert Einstein Coll. Medicine, Bronx, 1982—. Author: Cancer Chemotherapy, 2d edit, 1973. Served to capt. USAF, 1953-55. Fellow ACP; mem. AMA, Am. Soc. Clin. Oncology, Am. Assn. Cancer Research, Phi Beta Kappa. Democrat. Jewish. Current Work: Cancer chemotherapy, chemotherapy research, cancer epidemiology. Subspecialties: Oncology; Cancer research (medicine). Home: 39 Disbrow Circle New Rochelle NY 10804 Office: 838 Pelhamdale Ave New Rochelle NY 10801

GREENWALD, PETER, physician, government medical research administrator; b. Newburgh, N.Y., Nov. 7, 1936; s. Louis and Pearl (Reingold) G.; m. Harriet Reif, Sept. 6, 1968; children: Rebecca, Laura, Daniel. B.A., Colgate U., 1957; M.D., SUNY Coll. Medicine, 1961; M.P.H., Harvard U., 1967, Dr. P.H., 1974. Intern Los Angeles County Hosp., 1961-62; resident in internal medicine Boston City Hosp., 1964-66; asst. in medicine Peter Bent Brigham Hosp., 1967-68; mem. epidemiology and disease control study sect. NIH, 1974-78; mem. N.Y. State Gov.'s Breast Task Force, 1976-78; with N.Y. State Dept. Health, Albany, 1968-81; dir. N.Y. State Dept. Health (Cancer Control Bur.), 1968-76, dir. epidemiology, 1976-81; clin. prof. medicine Albany Med. Coll., 1976-81; attending physician Albany Med. Ctr. Hosp., 1968-81; adj. prof. biomed. engring. Rensselaer Poly. Inst., Troy, N.Y., 1976-81; assoc. scientist Sloan-Kettering Inst. for Cancer Research, N.Y.C., 1977-81; dir. Div. Resources, Ctr. and Community Activities, Nat. Cancer Inst., NIH, Bethesda, Md., 1981-83, dir. Div. Cancer Prevention and Control, 1983—; mem. VA Merit Rev. Bd. Med. Oncology, Washington, 1972-74. Editor in chief: Jour. Nat. Cancer Inst, NIH, 1981—; contbr. articles to profl. jours. Served with USPHS, 1962-64, 81—. Recipient Disting. Service award N.Y. State Dept. Health, 1975; Redway medal and award for med. writing N.Y. State Jour. Medicine, 1977; N.Y. State Gov.'s Citation for pub. health achievement, 1981. Fellow ACP, Am. Coll. Preventive Medicine, Am. Pub. Health Assn. (epidemiology sect. chmn. 1981-83); mem. Am. Assn. Cancer Research, Am. Coll. Epidemiology (bd. dirs. 1981-82), Am. Cancer Soc., Nat. Com. Cancer Prevention and Detection, Am. Soc. Preventive Oncology, Internat. Cancer Registry Assn., Internat. Epidemiology Soc., Nat. Acad. Scis. (food and nutrition bd.). Subspecialty: Preventive medicine. Office: NIH Bldg 31 Room 4A32 9000 Rockville Pike Bethesda MD 20205*

GREENWOOD, ALLAN NUNNS, electrical engineering educator; b. Leeds, Eng.; s. William Nunns and Ethel May (Burrell) G.; m. Grace Ruth Neville, July 24, 1944; children: Janet Penelope, Stephen Richard, Hilary Jane. B.A., Cambridge U., 1943, M.A., 1948; Ph.D., Leeds U., 1952. Devel. engr. Imperial Chem. Industries, Stourport, Eng., 1946-48; lectr. U. Leeds, 1948-54; vis. prof. U. Toronto, Ont., Can., 1954-55; cons. engr. sr. cons. engr. Gen. Electric Co., Phila., 1955-72; Philip Sporn prof., dir. Center Electric Power Engring., Rensselaer Poly. Inst., Troy, N.Y., 1972—; cons., industry, govt. Author: Electrical Transients in Power Systems, 1971, (with Lafferty et al) Vacuum Arcs, 1980, (with Tanaka) Advanced Power Cable Technology, Vols. I and II, 1983; contbr. articles to profl. jours. Served to lt. Royal Navy, 1943-46. Fellow IEEE; mem. Conf. Internat. des Grands Reseaux Electriques, Sigma Xi, Eta Kappa Nu. Unitarian. Patentee in power-switching technology. Subspecialty: Electrical engineering. Office: Rensselaer Poly Inst Troy NY 12181

GREENWOOD, MICHAEL SARGENT, plant physiologist; b. Winthrop, Mass., Nov. 7, 1940; s. Willard Priest and Nancy Hacker (Brown) G.; m. Susan Fowle, June 10, 1961; children: Willard, Davis. B.A. in Botany, Brown U., 1963; M.F., Yale U., 1965, M.S., 1966; Ph.D., 1969. Asst. prof. Middlebury Coll., 1968-74; vis. scientist U. Glasgow, Scotland, 1971-72; tree physiologist Weyerhaeuser Co., Hot Springs, Ark., 1974—; adj. asst. prof. N.C. State U., 1981-84; prof. U. Maine, Orono, 1984—. Mem. Union Concerned Scientists. Conbtr. articles to profl. jours. AEC fellow, 1965-67. Mem. Am. Bot. Soc., Am. Soc. Plant Physiologists, AAAS. Democrat. Patentee method of inducing flowering in pines, 1979; developed operational procedures for breeding pines more rapidly. Current Work: Forest tree breeding. Subspecialties: Plant physiology (agriculture); Plant genetics. Office: Dept Forest Biology U Maine Orono ME 04469

GREER, JAMES ALAN, physicist; b. N.Y.C., Oct. 23, 1952; s. Alan and Suzanne (Martin) G.; m. Kathleen Martha Gilligan, June 1984. B.S., Stevens Inst. Tech., 1975, M.S., 1976, Ph.D., 1983. Orthopaedic cons. Columbia U.-Presbyn. Med. Ctr., N.Y.C., 1978-83; instr. orthopedics Harvard U. Med. Sch., Boston, 1983—; sr. biomechanics engr. Mass. Gen. Hosp., Boston, 1983—. Mem. Am. Phys. Soc. Jewish. Current work: Research and design of current total hip replacements; improvement of properties of polymethyacrylate bone cement; study of mechanical properties of cancellous bone and stress related remodeling. Subspecialties: Biomedical engineering; Orthopedics. Home: 1 Temple Pl Andover MA 01810 Office: Jackson 10-03 Massachusetts General Hosp Boston MA 02114

GREGG, JAY MASON, geologist; b. Pitts., Jan. 24, 1951; s. Jay B. and Patricia L. (Mason) G.; m. Elizabeth Michelle Prudot, Sept. 3, 1977; children—Patricia Michelle, Nicholas Mason, Jay William. B.S., Bowling Green State U., 1974; M.S., Okla. State U., 1976; Ph.D., Mich. State U., 1982. Prodn. geologist Sun Oil Co., Midland, Tex., 1976-78; sr. research asst. Mich. State U., East Lansing, 1978-82; sr. research geologist St. Joe Minerals Corp., Viburnum, Mo., 1982—; adj. prof. geology U. Mo.-Rolla, 1985. Contbr. articles to profl. jours. Grantee Geol. Soc. Am., 1980, Sigma Xi, 1980. Mem. Am. Assn. Petroleum Geologists, Soc. Econ. Paleontologists and Mineralogists, Geol. Soc. Am., Internat. Assn. Sedimentologists, AAAS. Current work: Origin and occurrence of carbonate hosted Mississippi Valley type mineralization; origin of dolomite textures; distribution and origin of ancient dolomites in relation to basin evolution. Subspecialties: Sedimentology; Petrology. Home: PO Box 414 11 Maple St Viburnum MO 65566 Office: St Joe Minerals Corp PO Box 500 Viburnum MO 65566

GREGORIOU, GREGOR GEORG, aerodynamicist, researcher; b. Athens, Greece, Feb. 5, 1937; emigrated to Germany, 1956; s. Georg and Athina (Koulia) G.; m. Josephine Nievelstein, Aug. 31, 1962; children: Lauretta, Katja. Dipl.-Ing., Tech. U., Aachen, Ger., 1962; Dr.-Ing., Tech. U., Munich, Ger., 1973. Aerodynamicist Vereinigte Flugtechn Werke, Bremen, Ger., 1963-64; aerodynamicist Messerschmitt-Bolkow-Blohm, Ottobrunn, W.Ger., 1964-71, mgr. aerodynamics, 1971-84; pres. ENVIRO, Putzbrunn, W.Ger., 1985—; cons. Army Research Ctr., Athens, 1982—. Contbr. articles to profl. jours. Mem. AIAA, Gesellschaft für Angewandte Mathematik und Mechanik, Deutsche Gesellschaft für Luft und Raumfahrt. Current Work: Research in missile aerodynamics. Subspecialty: Aeronautical engineering. Office: Oedenstockacher Strasse 5 Putzbrunn 8011 Federal Republic of Germany

GREGORY, DONALD CLIFFORD, research physicist; b. Tyler, Tex., Sept. 12, 1949; s. John Clifford and Dorothy (Kingston) G.; m. Jean Wheat, Dec. 28, 1971; children: Eric William, Lauren Elizabeth. B.S., U. Tex., Austin, 1971, M.A., 1973, Ph.D., 1976. Exchange scientist Hungarian Acad. Scis., Budapest, 1974-75; Welch Found. fellow physics and chemistry depts. U. Tex., Austin, 1975-76; research assoc. Joint Inst. for Lab. Astrophysics, Boulder, Colo., 1976-78; asst. physicist Brookhaven Nat. Lab., Upton, N.Y., 1978-79, assoc. physicist, 1979-80; staff scientist Oak Ridge (Tenn.) Nat. Lab., 1980—. Contbr. articles to profl. jours. Mem. Am. Phys. Soc., Amateur Radio Club of Oak Ridge, Sigma Xi, Sigma Pi Sigma. Current Work: Experimental studies of electron impact processes on multiply charged ions. Subspecialty: Atomic and molecular physics. Office: Oak Ridge Nat Lab Bldg 6003 PO Box X Oak Ridge TN 37830

GREGORY, GAROLD FAY, plant pathologist; b. Arkansas City, Kans., Aug. 15, 1926; s. John Fay and Birdie Maude (Inman) G.; m. Flossy June Lewman, Dec. 25, 1953; children: Cherylynn Gay, Andrew Fay. B.S., Kans. State U., 1951; M.S., Iowa State U., 1956; Ph.D., Cornell U., 1962. Plant pathologist U.S. Dept. Agr. Forest Service, Delaware, Ohio, 1962—. Contbr. articles to profl. jours. Served with U.S. Army, 1951-53. Allied Chem. and Dye fellow, 1960-61. Mem. Am. Phytopathol. Soc. Mem. Ch. of God. Current Work: Application of biotechnology to tree insect and disease problems and their biological control. Subspecialties: Plant pathology; Plant physiology (biology).

GREGORY, JEAN WINFREY, ecologist; b. Richmond, Va., Feb. 13, 1947; d. Thomas Edloe and Kathryn Wilson (McFarlane) Winfrey; m. Ronald Alfred Gregory, Dec. 13, 1973. B.S. in Biology, Mary Wash. Coll., 1969; M.S. in Biology, Va. Commonwealth U., 1975; M.A. in Environ. Sci., U. Va., 1983; Pollution control specialist A, State Water Control Bd., Richmond, 1970-77, specialist B, 1977-81; adj. faculty Va. Commonwealth U., Richmond, 1978—; ecologist State Water Control Bd., 1981-85, ecology programs supr., 1985—. Bd. dirs. North Am. Lake Mgmt. Soc., Washington, 1982—. EPA fellow, VA., 1974-75; named one of Outstanding Young Women of Am., Va., 1974. Mem. Am. Soc. Limnology and Oceanography, Ecol. Soc. Am., Phycological Soc. Am., Aquatic Plant Mgmt. Soc., North Am. Benthological Soc., Am. Soc. Pub. Adminstrn., AAUW (mem.-at-large). Current work: Restoration and management of man-made lakes, job satisfaction of scientists and engineers, minimum instream flow policy, water quality standards setting. Subspecialties: Limnology; Ecology (biology). Office: State Water Control Bd PO Box 11143 Richmond VA 23230

GREGORY, JOEL PATRICK, petroleum geologist; b. Danville, Va., Aug. 19, 1956; s. Andrew Harrison and Christine (Burton) G.; m. Bernardine Zimmerman, Mar. 27, 1982 (div. Dec. 1984). B.S. in Geology, Coll. William and Mary, 1978; M.S., U. N.C., 1982. Geologist, Chapel Hill, N.C., 1980-81; petroleum geologist Gulf Oil Exploration & Prodn. Co., Oklahoma City, 1981-84, Enserch Exploration, Dallas, 1984—. Mem. Am. Assn. Petroleum Geologists, Soc. Exploration Geophysicists, Geol. Soc. Am. Current work: Exploration geology in Arkoma Basin; evolution of continents. Subspecialties: Tectonics; Mineralogy. Home: 8201 Fair Oaks Crossing Apt 1021 Dallas TX 75231 Office: Enserch Exploration Inc 4849 Greenville Ave Dallas TX 75206

GREGORY, KEITH EDWARD, animal geneticist; b. Franklin, N.C., Oct. 27, 1924; s. Parker and Leila (Woodard) G.; m. Wanda Clara Eldridge, Nov. 17, 1951; children—Mark, Greta. B.S., N.C. State U., 1947; M.S., U. Nebr., 1949; Ph.D., U. Mo., 1951. Assoc. prof. Auburn U., Ala., 1951-55; investigations leader for beef cattle breeding research, Agrl. Research Service, U.S. Dept. Agr., Lincoln, Nebr., 1955-66, dir. USMARC, Clay Center, Nebr., 1966-77, research geneticist, 1977-83, research leader, 1983—; cons. U.S. Feed Grains Council, 1981, ILCA, Addis Ababa, 1980, 83; chmn. task force on germ plasm preservation and utilization CAST, Ames, Iowa, 1983-84. Contbr. articles to sci. and profl. jours. Recipient Award for pub. service in research and edn. N.E. Agri-Bus. Club, 1967, Pioneer award Beef Improvement Fedn., 1975, Hall of Merit award, Am. Polled Hereford Assn., 1972, Beef Cattle Prodn. Research award Nat. Cattlemen's Assn., 1985. Fellow AAAS, Am. Soc. Animal Sci. (hon., Animal Breeding and Genetics award 1967); mem. Am. Genetic Assn., Sigma Xi. Current work: Beef cattle breeding, heterosis, selection, germ plasm evaluation, germ plasm utilization. Subspecialty: Animal genetics. Office: USDA ARS US Meat Animal Research Ctr PO Box 166 Clay Center NE 68933

GREGSON, VICTOR GREGORY, laser scientist; b. East St. Louis, Ill., June 10, 1935; s. Victor Gregory and Dorothy Mae (Glaze) G.; m. Lois Jean Rigden, May 30, 1964; children: Christopher Todd, Jennifer. A.B., Washington U., St. Louis, 1958; M.A., 1959; Ph.D., Stanford U., 1965. Project physicist Poulter Labs., Stanford (Calif.) Research Inst., 1961-64; sr. engr. Ill. Inst. Tech. Research Inst., Chgo., 1964-69; tech. leader Mfg. Staff Gen. Motors Tech. Ctr., 1969-71; product mgr. Western div. GTE Sylvania, Mountain View, Calif., 1977-79; product mgr./mktg. Indsl. div. Coherent, Inc., Palo Alto, Calif., 1979-83; tech. mgr. laser ctr. Marine div. Westinghouse Electric Corp., Sunnyvale, Calif., 1983—. Author: (with others) Guide for Material Processing by Lasers, 1977; contbr. (with others) articles to profl. jours. Mem. IEEE, Optical Soc. Am., Laser Inst. Am. (bd. dirs. 1973-82). Republican. Presbyterian. Current Work: Computer modelling of industrial laser processes; industrial laser processing. Subspecialties: Industrial laser processing; Materials processing. Home: 10894 Dryden Ave Cupertino CA 95014 Office: Westinghouse Electric Corp Hendy Ave Sunnyvale CA 94088

GREINER, JACK VOLKER, surgeon, ophthalmologist, scientist; b. Fountain Hill, Pa., Aug. 25, 1949; s. Harry Sandt and Vera Lilian G.; m. Cynthia Ann Mis, May 17, 1980; 1 child, Ashley Lauren. A.A., Valley Forge Mil. Acad., 1969; B.A., U. Vt., 1971; M.S. in Anatomy, Purdue U., 1974; Ph.D. in Anatomy, U. Toledo, 1975; D.O., Chgo. Coll. Osteo. Medicine, 1982. Research fellow in ophthalmology Howe Lab. of Ophthalmology, Harvard U. Med. Sch. and Mass. Eye and Ear Infirmary, Boston, 1974-76; research fellow in corneal and external diseases of eye Eye Research Inst., Retina Found., 1976-78; research fellow in ophthalmology Harvard U. Med. Sch., Boston, 1975-78; research assoc. in ophthalmology U. Ill. Eye and Ear Infirmary, Chgo., 1979-81, research asst. prof. ophthalmology, 1981-83; med. intern Cook County Hosp., Chgo., 1982-83; resident in ophthalmology Georgetown U. Med. Ctr., 1983-86; adj. asst. scientist Eye Research Inst., Retina Found., Boston, 1978; adj. asst. prof. ophthalmic pathology Chgo. Coll. Osteo. Medicine, 1979-82, asst. prof. dept. pathology, 1982-83, assoc. prof., 1983—; co-dir. Eye Research Lab., Chgo. Osteo. Hosp., 1980—. Contbr. chpts. to books, articles to profl. publs. Served to capt. C.E. USAR, 1971-78. Fight For Sight grantee, 1980-82; Nat. Soc. to Prevent Blindness grantee, 1981-82; NIH Nat. Eye Inst. grantee, 1982-85. Mem. Am. Assn. Anatomists, Assn. Research in Vision and Ophthalmology, Soc. Exptl. Biology and Medicine, N.Y. Acad. Scis., AMA, Chgo. Med. Soc., Cook County Med. Soc., Am. Acad. Ophthalmology, Sigma Xi, Phi Kappa Phi, Sigma Sigma Phi. Current Work: Phosphorus-31, sodium-23, hydrogen-1, nuclear magnetic resonance and histopathology of corneal diseases and crystalline lens cataracts; specific clinical interests include diseases of cornea and external ocular tissues. Subspecialties: Ophthalmology; Nuclear magnetic resonance. Office: Dept Ophthalmology Georgetown U 3800 Reservoir Rd NW Washington DC 20007

GREISEN, KENNETH INGVARD, physicist; b. Perth Amboy, N.J., Jan. 24, 1918; s. Ingvard C. and Signa (Nielsen) G.; m. Elizabeth C. Chase, Apr. 12, 1941 (dec.); children: Eric Winslow, Kathryn Elise; m. Helen A. Leeds, Mar. 27, 1976. Student, Wagner Coll., 1934-35; B.S., Franklin and Marshall Coll., 1938; Ph.D., Cornell U., 1942. Instr. Cornell U., 1942-43, asst. prof., 1946-48, assoc. prof., 1948-50, prof. physics, 1950-84, prof. emeritus, 1984—, chmn. dept. astronomy, 1976-79, univ. ombudsman, 1975-77, dean faculty, 1978-83; scientist Manhattan Project, Los Alamos, 1943-46. Fellow Am Phys. Soc.; mem. Am. Astron. Soc., Internat. Astron. Union, Nat. Acad. Sci., AAUP. Research cosmic rays. Subspecialties: Cosmic ray high energy astrophysics; Gamma ray high energy astrophysics. Home: 336 Forest Home Dr Ithaca NY 14850

GREMBOWSKI, DAVID EMIL, urban planner, researcher, health services researcher; b. San Diego, May 26, 1951; s. Emil Dem and Delphine (Kurowski) G.; m. Mary West, June 22, 1974; children—Megan, Leda. B.A. in Sociology, Wash. State U., 1973, M.A. in Sociology, 1975; Ph.D. in Urban Planning, U. Wash., 1982. Research analyst Stanford Research Inst., Menlo Park, Calif., 1974-76; systems designer Flexible Intergovernmental Grant Project, Tacoma, 1979-80; research asst. prof. dept. community dentistry, U. Wash., Seattle, 1981—. Contbr. articles to profl. jours. Mem. Am. Planning Assn., Am. Assn. Dental Schs., Internat. Assn. Dental Research, Phi Beta Kappa. Current work: Causal models in plan evaluation, evaluation of employment and training programs, fluoridation and insurance effects on dental care demand, health services utilization, systems analysis of organizations, information system design. Subspecialty: Statistics. Office: Community Dentistry SM35 U Wash Seattle WA 98195

GRENANDER, ULF, mathematics educator, consultant; b. Vastervik, Sweden, July 23, 1923; came to U.S., 1966; s. Sven and Maria (Persson) G.; m. Emma-Stina Hallquist, 1946; children—Sven, Angela, Charlotte. Fil. Kand., U. Stockholm, 1945, Fil. Lic., 1948, Fil. Dr., 1950. Docent U. Stockholm, 1950-57, prof. mathematics, 1959-65; prof. Brown U., Providence, R.I., 1958-59, 66—. Author books. Fellow Royal Swedish Acad. Sci. Current work: Mathematical theory of patterns. Subspecialties: Statistics; Pattern theory. Office: Dept Math Brown U Providence RI 02912

GRENFELL, RAYMOND FREDERIC, physician, researcher, educator; b. West Bridgewater, Pa., Nov. 23, 1917; s. Elisha Raymond and Pearl (Bolland) G.; m. Maude Byrnes Chisholm, Aug. 19, 1944; children: Raymond Frederic, Milton Wilfred, James Byrnes, Robert Chisholm. B.S., U. Pitts., 1939, M.D., 1941. Intern Western Pa. Hosp., Pitts., 1941-42, practice medicine specializing in internal medicine, Jackson, 1946-79, practice medicine specializing in diagnosis and treatment of hypertension, 1979—; mem. staffs Hinds Gen. Hosp., Riverside Hosp., St. Dominic-Jackson Meml. Hosp., Miss. Bapt. Hosp., Doctor's Hosp.; clin. instr. U. Miss. Med. Sch., Jackson, 1955-59, clin. asst. prof. medicine, 1959—, vis. teaching physician, 1977—, head hypertension clinic, 1956-79. Pres. Jackson Symphony Orch. Assn., 1961, Duling PTA, Jackson, 1963; deacon First Baptist Ch., 1960—. Served to maj. U.S. Army, 1942-46. Recipient bronze medal Am. Heart Assn., 1963, silver medal, 1965. Fellow Am. Coll. Angiology (gov. 1979—), Internat. Coll. Angiology, Am. Coll. Chest Physicians; mem. Am. Soc. Clin. Pharmacology and Therapeutics (dir. 1968, v.p. 1976), Am. Fedn. Clin. Research, So. Med. Assn. (councilor 1968-73), Miss. Heart Assn. (pres. 1964-65). Republican. Clubs: Country (Jackson), Univ. (Jackson) (Dir. 1974—). Current Work: Investigation of antihypertensive drugs with pioneer work in short and long term double-blind, controlled studies of antihypertensive drugs in premarketing phase. Subspecialty: Internal medicine. Home: 190 Ridge Dr Jackson MS 39216 Office: 514-H E Woodrow Wilson Jackson MS 39216

GRESS-GORDON, JEAN ANNE, toxicologist; b. Pa., Jan. 8, 1939; d. Desiderius Edmund and Irene Grace (McClintock) G.; divorced (div.); children: Scott Eugene, April Dawn. B.S. in Microbiology, Calif. State U., Long Beach, 1970; M.S. in Med. Tech, Calif. State U., Carson, 1978. Med. technologist Pediatric Cardiopulmonary Lab. UCLA, 1972-75, Clin. Labs.-Chemistry/Phlebotomy, 1975-78, Clin. Labs.-Chemistry/Toxicology, 1978-79, clin. specialist, 1979-80, sr. supervising clin. lab. technologist, 1980—. Mem. So. Calif. Med. Technologists Educators, Calif. Assn. Toxicologists (sec.-treas. 1981-83, chmn. membership com. 1983-85), Am. Soc. Clin. Pathologists (affiliate), Am. Assn. Clin. Chemistry, Soc. Applied Spectroscopy. Disciples of Christ. Current Work: Clinical and acute overdose analytical toxicology. Subspecialties: Toxicology (medicine); Clinical chemistry. Office: UCLA CHS A2-250 10833 Le Conte Ave Los Angeles CA 90024

GREULICH, RICHARD CURTICE, anatomist, gerontologist; b. Denver, Mar. 22, 1928; s. William Walter and Mildred Almena (Libby) G.; m. Betty Brent Mitchell, Dec. 19, 1948 (div. 1955); children: Christopher, Robert; m. Leonora Faye Colleasure, Dec. 27, 1958; children: Jeffrey, Hilary. A.B., Stanford U., 1949; Ph.D. (AEC fellow), McGill U. (Can.), 1953. Instr. Sch. Medicine, UCLA, 1953-55, asst. prof. anatomy, 1955-61, asso. prof. anatomy, 1961-64, prof. anatomy, 1964-66, asso. prof. oral biology Sch. Dentistry, 1961-64, prof. oral biology, 1964-66; sci. dir. Nat. Inst. Dental Research, NIH, Bethesda, Md., 1966-74; acting dir. Nat. Inst. Aging, Bethesda, 1975-76; dir. Gerontology Research Center and sci. dir. Nat. Inst. Aging, Balt., 1976—; staff dir. U.S. Pres.'s Biomed. Research Panel, 1974-75; vis. investigator Karolinska Inst., Stockholm, 1955-57, U. London, 1962-63, McGill U., 1963; vis. prof. anatomy U. Va., 1966-73. Served with F.A., U.S. Army, 1946-48. Recipient award for basic research in oral sci. Internat. Assn. Dental Research, 1963, Superior Service award HEW, 1971; Bank of Am.-Giannini Found. fellow, 1955-57; USPHS spl. fellow, 1962-63. Mem. Am. Assn. Anatomists, Gerontol. Soc., Am. Inst. Biol. Scis., AAAS, Am. Soc. Cell Biology, Sigma Xi. Club: Cosmos (Washington). Research, publs. on growth, differentiation and aging at cellular and organismic level. Subspecialties: Anatomy and embryology; Gerontology. Office: Gerontology Research Center Francis Scott Key Med Ctr Baltimore MD 21224

GREULING, JACQUELIN WREN, psychologist; b. Fort Worth, Sept. 24, 1931; d. Jack and Rose (Clymer) Wren; m. William Nash Greuling, Sr., May 29, 1954; children: William Nash, Jr., Robert Wren. B.A., U. Tex., 1953; M.A., U. Tex. El Paso, 1972; Ph.D., N. Mex. State U., 1979. Paraprofl. William Beaumont Army Med. Ctr., El Paso, 1971-73; psychometrist Child Guidance Ctr., El Paso, 1972-75; cons. psychology Crisis Line, Hobbs, N. Mex., 1972-74, William Beaumont Army Med. Ctr., El Paso, 1981-82, fellow health psychology, 1982-83; vice chmn. women and smoking Tex. div. Am. Cancer Soc., 1982—. Trainer, coordinator Am. Cancer Soc., El Paso, 1982. Mem. Am Psychol. Assn., Am. Soc. Clin. Hypnosis, El Paso Psychol. Assn. Democrat. Episcopalian. Current Work: The role of hypnotizability in the surgical procedure and in the post-operative period. Subspecialty: Health psychology. Home: 330 Olivia Circle El Paso TX 79912 Office: William Beaumont Army Med Center El Paso TX 79920

GREVE, JOHN HENRY, veterinary parasitology educator, consultant, researcher; b. Pitts., Aug. 11, 1934; s. John Welch and Edna Viola (Thuenen) G.; m. Sally Jeanette Doane, June 21, 1956; children—John Haven, Suzanne Carol, Pamela Jean. B.S., Mich. State U., 1956, D.V.M., 1958, M.S., 1959; Ph.D., Purdue U., 1963. Assoc. instr. Mich. State U., East Lansing, 1958-59; instr. Purdue U., West Lafayette, Ind., 1959-63; asst. prof. Iowa State U., Ames, 1963-64, assoc. prof., 1964-68, prof. vet. parasitology, 1968—; cons. on parasitisms to various zoos, 1966—. Author articles and book chpts. Reviewing editor several jours., 1971—. Named Disting. Tchr., Norden Labs., Lincoln, Nebr., 1965, Outstanding Tchr., Amoco, 1972; recipient faculty citation Iowa State U. Alumni Assn., 1978. Mem. AVMA (outstanding service award Iowa State U. student chpt. 1977, 79), Helminthological Soc. Wash., Iowa Vet. Medicine Assn., Midwestern Conf. Parasitologists (pres. 1975-76), Am. Assn. Vet. Parasitologists (pres. 1968-70), Am. Soc. Parasitologists. Current work: Pathology of veterinary parasitisms, especially those parasitisms caused by nematodes and arthropods, including zoo and laboratory animals. Subspecialty: Pathology (veterinary medicine). Home: 334 24th St Ames IA 50010 Office: Dept Vet Pathology Iowa State U Ames IA 50011

GREYTAK, THOMAS JOHN, physicist. Prof. dept. physics MIT, Cambridge. Subspecialty: Low temperature physics. Office: MIT Dept Physics Cambridge MA 02139

GREYWALL, MAHESH, engineer, educator; b. Patiala, India, Oct. 15, 1934; came to U.S., 1954; naturalized, 1965; m. Hermine F. Fischer, Apr. 18, 1960; children—Shaun, Paul. B.S., U. Calif., Berkeley, 1957, M.S., 1959, Ph.D., 1962. Mem. tech. staff Aerospace Corp., El Segundo, Calif., 1963-65; theoretical physicist L.L. Radiation Lab., Livermore, Calif., 1965-69; prof. Wichita State U., Kans., 1969—. Contbr. articles to profl. jours. Mem. Am. Phys. Soc., AIAA, ASME. Current work: Computational fluid dynamics. Subspecialties: Mechanical engineering; Aeronautical engineering. Home: 922 S Laurel Wichita KS 67207 Office: Wichita State U Wichita KS 67208

GRIESBACH, ROBERT JAMES, research geneticist; b. Chgo., June 21, 1955; s. Robert Anthony and Mary Lou (Stoegbauer) G.; m. Pamela Dawn Bateman, Sept. 8, 1984. B.S., DePaul U., 1977; Ph.D., Mich. State U., 1980. Research assoc. Mich. State U., East Lansing, 1980-81, U. Md., 1981; research geneticist USDA-BARC West, Florist and Nursery Crops, Beltsville, Md., 1981—; dir. Am. Orchid Soc. Fund for Research and Edn., West Palm Beach, Fla. Contbr. articles to profl. jours. Mem. AAAS, Am. Genetics Assn., Am. Soc. Hort. Sci., Plant Molecular Biology Assn. Current work: Development of techniques for microinjection of chromosomes into plant protoplasts; transfer polygenic characteristics between sexually incompatible species. Subspecialties: Genetics and genetic engineering (agriculture); Plant cell and tissue culture. Home: 3574 Conchita Dr Ellicott City MD 20143 Office: USDA Florist and Nursery Crops BARC-W Beltsville MD 20705

GRIFFIN, DONALD R(EDFIELD), zoology educator; b. Southampton, N.Y., Aug. 3, 1915; s. Henry Farrand and Mary Whitney (Redfield) G.; m. Ruth M. Castle, Sept. 6, 1941 (div. Aug. 1965); children: Nancy Griffin Jackson, Janet Griffin Abbott, Margaret, John H.; m. Jocelyn Crane, Dec. 16, 1965. B.S., Harvard U., 1938, M.A., 1940, Ph.D., 1942. Jr. fellow Harvard U., Cambridge, Mass., 1940-41, 46, research assoc., 1942-45, prof., 1953-65; asst. prof. Cornell U., Ithaca, N.Y., 1946-47, assoc. prof., 1947-52, prof., 1952-53, Rockefeller U., N.Y.C., 1965—, trustee, 1973-76; pres. Harry Frank Guggenheim Found., 1979-84. Author: Listening in the Dark, 1958 (Nat. Acad. Scis. Elliot medal 1961), Echoes of Bats and Men, 1959, Animal Structure and Function, 1962, Bird Migration, 1964 (Phi Beta Kappa prize 1966), The Question of Animal Awareness, 1976, Animal Thinking, 1984. Mem. Am. Ornithologists Union, Am. Soc. Zoologists, Am. Physiol. Soc., Ecol. Soc. Am., Am. Acad. Arts and Scis., Nat. Acad. Scis., Am. Philos. Soc., Am. Soc. Naturalists, Phi Beta Kappa, Sigma Xi. Current Work: Animal navigation, sensory physiology; cognitive ethology. Subspecialties: Ethology; Comparative neurobiology. Office: Rockefeller U 1230 York Ave New York NY 10021

GRIFFIN, GERALD DUANE, aeronautical engineer; b. Athens, Tex., Dec. 25, 1934; s. Herschel Hayden and Helen Elizabeth (Boswell) G.; m. Sandra Jo Huber, Apr. 19, 1958; children: Kirk Laurence, Gwendolyn Diane. B.S. in Aero. Engring, Tex. A. and M. U., 1956. With Douglas Aircraft Co., Long Beach, Calif., 1956, Lockheed Missiles and Space Co., Sunnyvale, Calif., 1960-62, Gen. Dynamics Co., Ft. Worth, 1962-64; with NASA, 1964-81, 82—; dir. NASA Johnson Space Center, Houston, 1982—; v.p. systems engring. and mgmt. Scott Sci. and Tech., Inc., Lancaster, Calif., 1981-82. Served as navigator USAF, 1956-60. Recipient Exceptional Service medal, Outstanding Leadership medal NASA; Presdl. rank Meritorious Sr. Exec.; Presdl. Medal of Freedom group award; named Old Master Purdue U. Asso. fellow AIAA; mem. Tau Beta Pi. Subspecialty: Aerospace engineering and technology. Office: Office of Dir Johnson Space Ctr Houston TX 77058

GRIFFIN, HENRY CLAUDE, chemist, chemistry educator; b. Greenville, S.C., Feb. 14, 1937; s. Arthur Gwynn and Christa (Wilson) G.; m. Barbara Jean Pierson, Sept. 3, 1960; children—Gwen, Lyle. B.S., Davidson Coll., 1958; Ph.D., MIT, 1962. Cert. secondary tchr., Mass. Instr. math. New Prep. Sch., Cambridge, Mass., 1962-63; asst. prof. chemistry U. Mich., Ann Arbor, 1964-71, assoc. prof., 1971—; vis. sci. Swiss Fed. Reactor Inst., Wurenlinger, 1971-72; vis. research engr. dept. nuclear engring. U. Calif.-Berkeley, 1978-79; mgr. nuclear studies Environ. Research Group, Ann Arbor, 1980-82; cons. Energy Data Systems, Ann Arbor, 1984; developer analytical procedures Contbr. articles to profl. jours. Mem. AAAS, Am. Chem. Soc., Am. Phys. Soc. Baptist. Current work: Nuclear spectroscopy, fast radiochemical separations, spectrum analysis, novel radiation detectors. Subspecialties: Nuclear chemistry; Nuclear fission. Home: 1410 Harbrooke Ann Arbor MI 48103 Office: Dept Chemistry Univ Mich Ann Arbor MI 48109

GRIFFIN, JOHN HENRY, medical researcher; b. Seattle, June 26, 1943; s. John Henry and Lillian Louise (O'Connell) G.; m. Antonia Lastreto, 1965 (div. 1984); children—John, Deanna, Paul. B.S., U. Santa Clara, 1965; Ph.D., U. Calif.-Davis, 1969. Teaching asst. U. Calif., 1967-69; research fellow Harvard U. Med. Sch., 1969-71; guest worker NIH, 1971-73; on staff Service de Biochimie Centre d'Etudes Nucleaires, Saclay, France, 1973-74; asst. dept immunopathology Scripps Clinic and Research Found., La Jolla, Calif., 1974-75, assoc. depts. immunopathology and molecular biology, 1975-80, assoc. mem. dept. immunology, 1980—; peer rev. com. NIH, 1979—. Contbr. articles to profl. jours. Treas. San Diego Assn. Gifted Children, 1978-81; active Pub. Sch. Cluster Com., University City, S.D., 1984—; mem. adv. com. High Sch. Community, University City, 1979-82. Recipient Research Career Devel. award NIH, 1976-81. RCA physics scholar 1961-64; fellow NIH, 1966-69, 72-73, Helen Hay Whitney Found. 1969-72. Mem. Am. Chem. Soc., Am. Soc. Biol. Chemists, Am. Assn. Pathologists, Am. Assn. Immunologists, Internat. Soc. Thrombosis and Hemostasis, Am. Heart Assn., Sigma Xi, Alpha Sigma Nu, Phi Kappa Phi. Current work: Basic and clinical research on regulation of hemostasis and thrombosis. Subspecialties: Biochemistry (medicine); Hematology. Office: Dept Immunology IMM8 Scripps Clinic and Research Found 10666 N Torrey Pines Rd La Jolla CA 92037

GRIFFITH, JAMES EDWARD, energy engineer, energy utilization researcher; b. Camden, N.J., Feb. 15, 1920; s. Walter Anker and Gertrude Dorothy (Mathews) G.; m. Helen Marsh Thompson, May 7, 1943; 1 child, Robert D. B.S. in Natural Sci., Upsala Coll., 1972. Plant chem. engr. Pub. Service Electric & Gas Co., Camden, 1942-60, airconditioning engr., Newark, 1960-72, sr. engr.-research, 1972-75; prin. engr.-research P.S.E.&G. Research Co., Maplewood, N.J., 1975—; research adviser Gas Research Inst., Chgo., 1977—. Mem. ASHRAE, Am. Soc. Gas Engrs. (pres. East Coast 1980), Phi Lambda Upsilon. Lodge: Masons. Current work: Gas and electric space heating and cooling research and development. Subspecialty: Space heating and cooling. Office: PSE&G Research Corp 200 Boyden Ave Maplewood NJ 07040

GRIFFITH, WILLIAM SCHULER, mathematical scientist, applied probabilist; b. Bradford, Pa., Oct. 10, 1949; s. William H. and Hazel Marjorie (Schuler) G.; m. Deborah Ann Fragale, Aug. 12, 1972; children—Mark Robert, Lisa Michelle. B.S., Grove City (Pa.) Coll., 1971; M.A., U. Pitts., 1973, Ph.D., 1979. Lectr. Carlow Coll., Pitts., 1976-77; mathematician Westinghouse Research and Devel. Ctr., Pitts., 1977-79; asst. prof. stats. U. Ky.-Lexington, 1979-85, assoc. prof., 1985—. Mem. Am. Statis. Assn., Inst. Math. Statis., Biometrics Soc., Ops. Research Soc. Am., Soc. Indsl. and Applied Math. Current Work: Mathematical theory of reliability, applied probability. Subspecialties: Probability; Statistics. Home: 3338 Snaffle Rd Lexington KY 40513 Office: Dept Stats U Ky Lexington KY 40506 0027

GRIFFITHS, JOHN DAVID, systems engineer; b. Lansing, Mich., Jan. 23, 1933; s. Percy Lewis and Onnellee Jane (McDonald) G.; m. Patricia Ann Bradley, Nov. 19, 1954 (dec. 1983); 1 child, Bruce David. B.S., MIT, 1954; M.E.E., Syracuse U., 1961, Ph.D., 1965. Assoc. prof. Air Force Acad., Colorado Springs, Colo., 1969-74; chief advanced technology Air Force Tech. Applications Ctr., Patrick AFB, Fla., 1974-77; dir. space systems Sec. of Def., Washington, 1977-78; program tech. dir. Def. Intelligence Agy., Washington, 1978-80, chief systems simulation, 1980-84; com. chmn. Intelligence Community Staff, Washington, 1984—; cons., Springfield, Va., 1980—. Author: National Imagery System Model, 1984. Inventor: SSB Carrier Generator, 1961; Sound Level Meter, 1973. Contbr. articles to profl. jours. Served to col. USAF, 1954-80. Decorated Legion of Merit, USAF, 1980. Mem. IEEE, ACM, Soc. Computer Simulation, Acoustical Soc. Am., Am. Assn. Artificial Intelligence, Sigma Xi, Alpha Tau Omega. Episcopalian. Current work: Large scale interactive systems simulation modeling; adaptive models, interaction and modeling of combinations of technical and social systems. Subspecialties: Systems engineering; Artificial intelligence. Office: Intelligence Community Staff Washington DC 20505

GRIFFITHS, ROBERT B., physics educator; b. Etah, U.P., India, Feb. 25, 1937 (parents Am. citizens); s. Walter D. and Margaret (Hamilton) G. A.B., Princeton U., 1957; M.S., Stanford U., 1958, Ph.D., 1962. Asst. prof. Carnegie-Mellon U., Pitts., 1964-67, assoc. prof., 1967-69, prof. physics, 1969—. Contbr. articles to profl. jours. Recipient U.S. Sr. Scientist award A. von Humboldt Found., 1973; NSF postdoctoral fellow, 1962, A.P. Sloan Found. research fellow, 1966. Fellow Am. Phys. Soc. (Dannie Heineman prize 1984), Am. Sci. Affiliation. Presbyterian. Current work: Thermodynamics and statistical mechanics of phase transitions, with particular reference to surfaces. Also exact mathematical results in statistical mechanics. Subspecialties: Statistical physics; Condensed matter physics. Office: Carnegie-Mellow Univ Physics Dept Schenley Park Pittsburgh PA 15213

GRIFFITHS, THOMAS ALAN, biology educator; b. Lewiston, Maine, Sept. 16, 1951; s. Arthur Morgan and Lois Marilyn (Spofford) G.; m. Cara-Sue Thurston, Feb. 3, 1973; children—Jennifer Sue, Anne Elizabeth. B.S., Bates Coll., 1973; M.S., U. Vt., 1976; Ph.D., U. Mass., 1981. Instr. SUNY-Plattsburgh, 1977-78; asst. prof. biology, Ill. Wesleyan U., Bloomington, 1981—; research assoc. Am. Mus. Natural History, N.Y.C., 1984—. Contbr. numerous articles to sci. publs. Mem. Am. Soc. Mammalogists (honorarium award 1982), Am. Soc. Zoologists, Soc. Study Evolution, Soc. Vertebrate Paleontology, Sigma Xi. Current work: Comparative anatomy and histology of bats; evolution and systematics of bats. Subspecialties: Morphology; Evolutionary biology. Home: 612 E Walnut St Bloomington IL 61701 Office: Dept Biology Ill Wesleyan U Bloomington IL 61702

GRIFFY, THOMAS ALAN, physicist, educator, researcher; b. Oklahoma City, Dec. 16, 1936; s. Judson H. and Dicie (Johnston) G.; m. Peggy Lynn Walker, June 6, 1958; children: David, Alan, Marjorie. B.A., Rice U., 1959, M.A., 1960, Ph.D., 1961. Asst. prof. physics Duke U., 1961-62; research assoc. High Energy Physics Lab., Stanford U., 1962-65; assoc. prof. physics U. Tex.-Austin, 1965-68, prof., 1968—; chmn. dept. physics, 1974-84, assoc. dean Grad. Sch., 1970-73. Contbr. articles to profl. jours. Fellow Am. Phys. Soc. Methodist. Current Work: Underwater acoustics, nuclear energy. Subspecialties: Acoustics; Nuclear physics. Office: Dept Physics U Tex Austin TX 78712

GRIGORIU, MIRCEA DAN, civil engineering educator; b. Bucharest, Romania, Mar. 2, 1943; came to U.S., 1973; s. Radu and Victoria (Dumitrescu) G.; m. Cornelia Enescu, July 19, 1969; 1 child, Bogdan. Diploma Ing., Bucharest Inst. Civil Engring., 1967; diploma Math. U. Bucharest, 1972; Ph.D. in Civil Engring., MIT, 1976. Asst., Bucharest Inst. Civil Engring., 1967-73; assoc. prof. Simon Bolivar U., Caraeas, Venezuela, 1976-77; research assoc. McGill U., Montreal, Que., Can., 1977-78; vis. assoc. prof. U. Waterloo, Can., 1979-80, 81; assoc. prof. Cornell U., Ithaca, N.Y., 1980—; vis. assoc. prof. Johns Hopkins U., Balt., 1983; cons. Electric Power Research Inst., Palo Alto, Calif., 1982—. Contbr. articles to profl. jours. Mem. ASCE, Am. Acad. Mechanics. Current work: Reliability analysis, random vibrations, applications of probability theory and statistics to engineering. Office: Coll Engring Cornell U Ithaca NY 14853

GRILLER, DAVID, chemist. Head organic chemistry NRC of Can. Recipient Merck, Sharp and Dohme Lecture award Chem. Inst. Can., 1985. Subspecialty: Organic chemistry. Office: NRC of Can Div of Chemistry Ottawa ON K1A OR6 Canada

GRIM, MICHAEL DAVID, chemist; b. York, Pa., Sept. 16, 1954; s. Palmer Warner and Mildred Jean (Wert) G. B.S., U. Ga., 1977, M.S., 1980. Assoc. scientist CIBA-Geigy Corp., Ardsley, N.Y., 1980-83, scientist I, 1983—. Mem. Am. Chem. Soc., N.Y. Acad. Scis., Sigma Xi. Republican. Current work: Synthesis, purification and characterization of novel compounds for testing as new medicinal agents; special interests include peptide chemistry and enzyme inhibition. Subspecialties: Organic chemistry; Medicinal chemistry. Office: CIBA-Geigy Corp 444 Saw Mill River Rd Ardsley NY 10502

GRIMES, DALE MILLS, electrical engineering educator; b. Marshall County, Iowa, Sept. 7, 1926; s. LeRoy and Helen (Mills) G.; m. Janet LaVonne Moore, Mar. 22, 1947; children: Prudence Rae, Craig Alan. B.S. in Physics, Math. and Chemistry, Iowa State U., 1950, M.S. in Physics and Math, 1951; Ph.D. in Elec. Engring, U. Mich., Ann Arbor, 1956. From research asso. to prof. elec. engring. U. Mich., 1951-76; chief scientist Conductron Corp., Ann Arbor, 1960-63; prof. elec. engring., chmn. dept. U. Tex., El Paso, 1976-79; prof. elec. engring. Pa. State U., 1979—, head dept., 1979-85; pres. Crale Inc., 1985—; cons. to govt. and industry. Author: Electromagnetism and Quantum Theory, 1969, Automotive Electronics, 1974; also articles on radar, biconical antennas, electromagnetic radiation. Served with USNR, 1943-46. Fellow AAAS; mem. IEEE, Am. Phys. Soc., Soc. Automotive Engrs., Am. Soc. Engring. Edn. Patentee ferrite radar absorbing material, magnetic absorbers, automotive radar. Home: 2548 Sleepy Hollow Dr State College PA 16803 Office: Elec Engring Dept Pa State Univ University Park PA 16802

GRIMLEY, LIAM KELLY, educator; b. Dublin, Ireland, Apr. 4, 1936; came to U.S., 1970; s. William and Eileen (Kelly) G.; m. Marie Sadon, Aug. 26, 1973; children: Kevin, Conor. B.A., Nat. U. Ireland, 1960; L.Ph., Faculte Libre, Paris, 1963; H.D.Ed., Clongowes Wood Coll., Ireland, 1964; Th.B., Inst. Philosophy and Theology, Dublin, 1968, S.T.L., 1970; M.Ed., Kent State U., 1971, Ph.D., 1973. Tchr. English Lycee Moderne, LePuy, France, 1961-62; asst. dir. Summer Sch. English, Observatorio del Ebro, Tortosa, Spain, 1961-62; tchr. math and modern langs. Clongowes Wood High Sch., Ireland, 1963-64; tchr. math, classical langs. St. Ignatius Elementary and Secondary Sch., Galway, Ireland, 1964-66; instr. statistics and probability theory Univ. Coll., Galway, 1965-66; prof. theology Conf. Major Religious Superiors, Dublin, 1969-70; counselor Newman Center, Syracuse U., 1970; tchr. social studies Walsh Jesuit High Sch., Cuyahoga Falls, Ohio, 1971; asst. dir. Ohio Soc. Crippled Children and Adults, Tiffin, summer 1971; intern sch. psychologist Kent State U., 1972-73, research and devel. dir. lab. schs., 1972-73; prof. spl. edn. Ind. State U., Terre Haute, 1973—, chmn. dept., 1975-81, dir. Inst. Continuing Edn. in Psychology, 1976-78; cons. Joseph P. Kennedy Found., 1973—; mem. State Adv. Com., Div. Pupil Personnel, 1975-78; Mem. Ind. State Manpower Steering Com., 1977-80; chmn. State Adv. Bd. on Pupil Personnel Services, 1980—; mem. State Council on Edn. of Handicapped, 1979—. Editor: The Sch. Psychology Digest, 1976-79; contbr. articles to profl. jours. Mem. Am. Psychol. Assn., Ind. Psychol. Assn. (pres. div. sch. psychology 1980-81), Nat. Assn. Sch. Psychologists. Roman Catholic. Current Work: Developer of Grimley Personality scale for children. Subspecialty: Developmental psychology. Home: 43 Allendale Terre Haute IN 47802 Office: Dept Ednl and Sch Psychology Ind State U Terre Haute IN 47809

GRIMM, ELIZABETH ANN, cellular immunologist; b. Charleston, W.Va., Nov. 24, 1949; d. Harper Granville and Nellie (Simmons) G.; m. Jack Alan Roth, Jan. 29, 1945. A.B. in Chemistry, Randolph-Macon Woman's Coll., 1971; Ph.D. in Microbiology and Immunology, UCLA, 1979. Research assoc. Harvard U. Med. Sch., 1971, tech. supr. research lab., 1972-73; tech. supr. tumor immunology research labs. Sepulveda (Calif.) VA Hosp., 1973-75; teaching asst. microbiology and immunology UCLA Sch. Medicine, 1975-79; postdoctoral fellow Molecular Biology Inst., UCLA Sch. Arts and Scis., 1979-80; cancer expert surgery br. Nat. Cancer Inst., NIH, Bethesda, Md., 1980-84, chief cellular immunology unit SNB, NINCDS, 1984—. Contbr. articles to profl. jours. Muscular Dystrophy Assn. fellow, 1979. Mem. Am. Assn. Immunologists, Am. Assn. Cancer Research. Current Work: Research in basic cellular immunology with direct applications to adoptive immunotherapy of human cancer; specifically immunologic memory and development of cytolic effector cells. Subspecialties: Immunology (medicine); Cancer research (medicine). Office: NINCOS NIH Bldg 10A 3E 68 Bethesda MD 20892

GRIMM, LOUIS J., mathematics educator; b. St. Louis, Nov. 30, 1933; s. Louis and Florence (Hammond) G.; m. Barbara Mitko, May 6, 1967; children: Thomas Hammond, Mary Elizabeth. B.S., St. Louis U., 1954; M.S., Ga. Inst. Tech., 1960; Ph.D., U. Minn., 1965. Asst. prof. U. Utah, Salt Lake City, 1965-69; assoc. prof. U. Mo.-Rolla, 1969-74, prof. math., 1974—, chmn. math. and stats. dept., 1981—, dir. Inst. Applied Math., 1983—; vis. prof. U. Nebr., Lincoln, 1978-79, U. Gdansk, Poland, 1985; Smurfit fellow Univ. Coll. Dublin, 1984. Contbr. articles to profl. jours. NSF research grantee, 1969-73, 76-79; Nat. Acad. Scis. exchange scholar, 1981. Mem. Am. Math. Soc., Soc. Indsl. and Applied Math., Polish Math. Soc., Gesellschaft für angewandte Mathematik und Mechanik. Current Work: Analytic theory of ordinary differential and difference equations. Numerical solution of ordinary and functional differential equations. Subspecialties: Applied mathematics; Numerical analysis (computer science). Office: Dept Math and Stats U Mo Rolla MO 65401

GRINDEL, JOSEPH MICHAEL, pharmaceutical company executive; b. Kansas City, Mo., Dec. 18, 1946; s. Edward A. and Inez (Weber) G.; m. Cecelia M. Gatson, Aug. 1, 1970; children: Charles, Mary, David. B.Sc., Benedictine Coll., Kans., 1969; Ph.D., U. Kans., 1973. Chief clin. drug metabolism lab. Walter Reed Army Inst. Research, Washington, 1973-76; with McNeil Pharm., Spring House, Pa., 1976—, dir. dept. drug metabolism, 1980-82, exec. dir. research and devel. project planning, 1982-85, exec. dir. quality improvement, 1985—. Contbr. articles to profl. jours. Cubmaster Boy Scouts Am., 1979-82; pres. St. Stanislaus Sch. Bd., 1982-84. Served to 1st lt. AUS, 1973-76. Mem. Am. Chem. Soc., Am. Soc. Pharmacology and Exptl. Therapeutics, Drug Metabolism Discussion Group, Project Mgmt. Inst., Drug Info. Assn. Roman Catholic. Current Work: Drug development program design and implementation, project management. Subspecialty: Pharmacokinetics. Home: 1787 Cindy Ln Hatfield PA 19440 Office: McNeil Pharm McKean Rd Spring House PA 19477

GRINNAN, EDWARD LEONARD, biochemist; b. Phila., Oct. 14, 1922; s. Edward J. and May F. (Daily) G.; m. Agnes C. Vollmer, Aug. 21, 1954; 1 child, Gloria. B.S., Pa. Mil. Coll., 1949; M.S., U. Del., 1950, Ph.D., 1952. Sr. biochemist Eli Lilly & Co., Indpls., 1952-58, dept. head, 1958-67, sr. scientist, 1967-77, research assoc., 1977—. Contbr. articles to profl. jours. Served with USN, 1944-46. U. Del. Fellow, 1949-52. Mem. Am. Chem. Soc., N.Y. Acad. Sci., AAAS. Republican. Roman Catholic. Current work: Recombinant DNA technology; purification and characterization of peptide hormones. Subspecialties: Biochemistry (medicine); Endocrinology. Home: 3441 Eden Hollow Pl Carmel IN 46032 Office: Eli Lilly & Co Corp Ctr Indianapolis IN 46285

GRISCHKOWSKY, DANIEL, laser scientist. With IBM T.J. Watson Research Ctr., Yorktown Heights, N.Y. Subspecialty: Ultrafast lasers. Office: T J Watson Research Ctr PO Box 218 Yorktown Heights NY 10598

GRISSOM, MICHAEL PHILLIP, radiation science specialist, naval officer; b. Warren, Ohio, Oct. 25, 1948; s. Edward Henry and Cala Beatrice (Pickens) G.; m. Linda Marie Gerou, June 25, 1974. B.S. in Biol. Scis, Colo. State U., 1970; M.S.E. in Nuclear Sci. and Engring, Catholic U. Am., 1977. Commd. ensign Med. Service Corps U.S. Navy, 1971, advanced through grades to lt. comdr., 1980, radiation health officer in support of med. div. and Navy Nuclear Power Program, 1972-74, research biophysicist Armed Forces Radiobiology Research Inst., Bethesda, Md., 1974-76, radiation specialist Armed Forces Radiobiology Research Inst., 1977-82, dir. med. records search Navy Nuclear Test Personnel Rev., Arlington, Va., 1982-84; NTPR coordinator WNY, Washington, 1984-85; dir. radiation safety and med. physics U.S. Naval Hosp., Oakland, Calif., 1985—; cons. health physicist Three Mile Island Nuclear Generating Sta. during recovery ops., 1979, 80. Contbr. articles to profl. jours. Active Mountaingate Homeowners' Assn., Frederick, Md., 1978-80, including acting treas., 1979, bd. dirs., 1980. Decorated Nat. Def. medal; decorated Def. Meritorious Service medal; Recipient Citizenship award Col. SAR, 1966, Order of World Wars award San Diego Naval Hosp., 1971; Nat. Heart, Lung and Blood Inst. grantee, 1974-75. Mem. Health Physics Soc., Soc. Nuclear Medicine, Am. Assn. Physicians in Medicine, AAAS, U.S. Naval Inst. Club: U.S. Navy Officer's (Oakland). Current Work: Development of imaging techniques in the clinical environment; application of single photon tomographic methods, planar imaging, and nuclear magnetic resonance; use of receptor bound radiopharmaceuticals in nuclear imaging; radiation risk assessment. Subspecialties: Nuclear medicine; Imaging technology. Home: 21 Merlin Ct Oakland CA 94605 Office: Nuclear Medicine Clinic US Naval Hosp Oakland CA 94627

GROB, DAVID, physician, educator, researcher; b. N.Y.C., Feb. 23, 1919; s. Hyman and Fannie (Baumwall) G.; m. Elizabeth Nussbaum, Dec. 26, 1948; children: Charles, Susan, Emily, Philip. B.S., CCNY, 1937; postgrad., Columbia U., 1937-38; M.D., Johns Hopkins U., 1942. Med. intern Johns Hopkins Hosp., Balt., 1942-43, asst. resident in medicine, 1945-46, 47-48; fellow in medicine Johns Hopkins U. Sch. Medicine, 1946-47, instr., 1948-51, asst. prof., 1951-55, instr. pharmacology and exptl. therapeutics, 1953-54; assoc. prof. medicine, 1955-58; prof. medicine SUNY Coll. Medicine, Bklyn., 1958—, asst. dean, 1962-67, clin. assoc. dean, 1979—; dir. med. services Maimonides Med. Ctr., Bklyn., 1958—, dir. research and edn., 1960-67, dir. med. edn., 1970—, med. dir. Research and Devel. Found., 1982—. Editor: Myasthenia Gravis, 1976, Myasthenia Gravis: Pathophysiology and Management, 1981; contbr. over 110 articles to sci. jours., chpts. to sci. books. Mem. med. adv. bd. Myasthenia Gravis Found., 1953—, chmn., 1961-63. Served to 1st lt. and capt. M.C., U.S. Army, 1943-45, ETO. Decorated Bronze Star; recipient Townsend D. Harris medal CCNY Alumni Assn., 1964; Honor award Fedn. Jewish Philanthropies N.Y., 1964; Humanitarian award Myasthenia Gravis Found., 1963; Kermit Osserman award, 1982. Fellow ACP; mem. Am. Soc. Clin. Investigation, Am. Physiol. Soc., Am. Soc. Pharmacology and Exptl. Therapeutics, Assn. Am. Physicians, Phi Beta Kappa, Alpha Omega Alpha, Assn. Program Dirs. in Internal Medicine (councilor 1977-81, pres.-elect 1978-79, pres. 1979-80). Current Work: Physiology, pharmacology and immunology of diseases of the neuromuscular system, Key terminology: neuromuscular transmission, muscle function, fatigue, acetylcholine receptor and antibodies, myasthenia gravis, myasthenic syndromes, weakness, immunobiology and neuroimmunology. Subspecialties: Internal medicine; Neurophysiology. Home: 20 Fern Dr Roslyn NY 11576 Office: 4802 10th Ave Brooklyn NY 11219

GROB, ROBERT LEE, chemistry educator; b. Wheeling, W.Va., Feb. 13, 1927; s. William E. and Mary Margaret (Shanley) G.; m. Marjorie D. Sage, Aug. 4, 1928; children: R. Kent, G. Duane, J. Allyson, M. Michele. B.S., Coll. of Steubenville, 1951; M.S., U. Va., 1954, Ph. D., 1955. Research analytical chemist Esso Research, Linden, N.J., 1955-57; prof. chemistry Wheeling (W.Va.) Coll., 1957-63; prof. analytical chemistry Villanova (Pa.) U., 1963—. Served with U.S. Army, 1945-47. Pratt fellow U. Va., 1954. Mem. Am. Chem. Soc., Am. Inst. Chemists, Chromatography Discussion Group London, Chromatography Forum Delaware Valley, Sigma Xi. Republican. Roman Catholic. Current Work: Gas and liquid chromatography, trace metal analysis, environmental chemistry. Subspecialties: Analytical chemistry; Ecosystems analysis. Office: Chem Dept Villanova U Villanova PA 19085

GROBSTEIN, PAUL, neurobiologist, educator; b. Long Beach, Calif., Mar. 21, 1946; s. Clifford and Rose (Gruver) G.; m. Margaret Anne Hollyday, 1983; children—Jediah Peter, Rachel Elizabeth. B.A., Harvard U., 1969; M.A., Stanford U., 1970, Ph.D., 1973. Postdoctoral fellow Johns Hopkins U., Balt., 1972-73; Stanford U., Calif., 1973-74; asst. prof. U. Chgo., 1974-81, assoc. prof. neurobiology, 1981—. Contbr. articles to profl. jours. Alfred P. Sloan Found. fellow; grantee NIH, NSF. Mem. Soc. Neurosci., Soc. Developmental Biology. Current work: Spatial information processing; organization and development of neuronal circuitry; regeneration. Subspecialties: Neurobiology; Developmental biology.

GROEBER, EDWARD OTTO, JR., electronics engineer; b. Hempstead, N.Y., June 28, 1946; s. Edward Otto and Evelyn Ruth (Laufle) G.; m. Matilda Brown Eaton, June 23, 1968; children: Jennifer Jane, Jill Ann. B.S. in Nuclear Engring, N.Y. U.-Bronx, 1968; M.E.E., Fairleigh Dickinson U., 1980. Sect. chief U.S. Air Force Weapons Lab., Kirtland AFB, N.Mex., 1970-72; with CS&TA Lab., Ft. Monmouth, N.J., 1972—, br. chief., 1981-84, div. dir., 1984—; mem. dosimeter task group Am. Nat. Standards Inst., Washington, 1982—. Contbr. numerous articles in field to profl. publs. Served to capt USAF, 1968-72. Recipient Outstanding Performance awards CS&TA Lab., 1977-79, Exceptional Performance award, 1984. Mem. Am. Nuclear Soc., Eta Kappa Nu. Democrat. Current Work: Management of the research, development and initial production of nuclear radiation detection devices and systems for the U.S. Army. Subspecialties: Electronics; Nuclear engineering. Home: 24 Woodland Ln Jackson NJ 08527 Office: CS&TA Lab DELCS-K Fort Monmouth NJ 07703

GROENIER, WILLIAM SAMUEL, chemical engineering executive, researcher; b. Chgo., Feb. 5, 1936; s. Willis Lambert and Bernice E. (Kress) G.; m. Janet Marie Goodenow, June 19, 1960; children: Laurice Ann, Katherine Elizabeth. B.S., Northwestern U., 1958, M.S., 1959. Chem. engr. Tee-Pak, Inc., Chgo., 1954-59; chem. engr. Union Carbide Corp., Oak Ridge, 1959-62; chem. engr. Oak Ridge Nat. Lab., 1962-75, program mgr., 1975-80, sect. head, 1980—. Contbr. numerous articles to govt. reports and profl. jours. Mem Am. Nuclear Soc., Am. Inst. Chem. Engrs., Sigma Xi. Republican. Current Work: Manage chemistry and chemical engineering activites of research and development nature for reprocessing nuclear breeder reactor fuels. Subspecialties: Chemical engineering; Nuclear fission. Office: Oak Ridge National Laboratory PO Box X Oak Ridge TN 37830

GROFF, DONALD WILLIAM, geology educator; b. Lancaster, Pa., Apr. 11, 1928; s. Frank Lester and Martha Elizabeth Groff; m. Anata Mae Reese, Dec. 27, 1948 (div. 1950); m. Mary Polly Elliot Graves, Dec. 28, 1957; 1 child, Dana D. B.S., U. Redlands, 1952; postgrad., Pa. State U., 1952-55; Ph.D., U. Pitts., 1965. Party chief Huntley & Huntley Cons., Inc., Pitts., 1959-61; instr. U. Pitts., 1957-61; prof. geology Lock Haven State Coll., Pa., 1961-62, Indiana U. of Pa., 1962-66; cons. D. Groff & Assoc., Brookfield Ctr., Conn., 1969—; prof., chmn. earth scis. Western Conn. State Coll., Danbury, 1966-81, prof., chmn. geology, 1981—; mem. Council Edn. in Geol. Scis., Washington, 1969-73; scientist Environ. Impact Commn., Danbury, 1973-81. Editor: Quantitative Mineral Prospecting, 1973. Carnegie-Mellon Fellow, 1966; grantee NSF, 1967-70. Mem. Geol. Soc. Am., Soc. Exploration Paleontologists and Mineralogists, Soil Sci. Soc. Am., Am. Soc. Agronomy, Internat. Assn. Sedimentologists, Danbury Mineral Soc., Appalachian Mountain Club, Sierra Club, Sigma Xi. Republican. Current work: Earth surface sedimentary processes; geohydrology; soils. Subspecialties: Sedimentology; Soil science. Home: 31 Merwin Brook Rd Brookfield Center CT 06805 Office: Western Conn State U Dept Geology 181 White St Danbury CT 06810

GROFF, GERALD CHARLES, air-conditioning company executive, mechanical engineer; b. Cedar Rapids, Iowa, Mar. 4, 1934; s. Phil and Loretta Ann (Voelkel) G.; m. Beth Ann Bursch, June 22, 1956; children—Paul Andrew, Jennifer Lynn, Lee Ann. B.S. in Mech. Engring., U. Minn., 1955, M.S. in Mech. Engring., 1960; M.S. in Engring. Adminstrn., Syracuse U., 1970. Air-conditioning research mgr. Carrier Corp., Syracuse, N.Y., 1960-72, assoc. dir. research div., 1972-78, dir. corp. research div., 1978-84, corp. dir. technology planning, 1984-85, div. research and prodn. adminstrn. Europe/Africa, 1985—. Editor: Heat Pumps and Space Conditioning Systems, 1979. Patentee fan design. Chmn. Operation Enterprise, mem. bd. govs. Citizens Found., Syracuse, 1976—. Served to lt. (j.g.) USN, 1956-59. Mem. Internat. Inst. Refrigeration (U.S. nat. com.), ASHRAE, ASME, Sigma Xi. Presbyterian. Clubs: Cazenovia (N.Y.); Willow Bank Yacht. Current work: Building energy systems; advanced building design; heat pumps; heating and air-conditioning equipment and systems. Subspecialties: Mechanical engineering; Energy systems in buildings. Office: Carrier Corp Carrier Pkwy Syracuse NY 13221

GROGAN, JAMES BIGBEE, immunologist, educator; b. Edwards, Miss., May 15, 1932; s. Kenneth Forbes and Elfie (Bigby) G.; m. Nita Pauline Young, June 17, 1956; children: Frankie L., Paula D. B.S., Miss. Coll., 1955; M.S. in Bacteriology, U. Wis., 1957; Ph.D., U. Miss., 1963. Teaching asst., research asst. U. Wis.-Madison, 1955-57; supr. surg. research bacteriology lab. U. Miss. Sch. Medicine, 1957-63, fellow dept. microbiology, 1957-63, asst. prof. surgery, 1965-68, asst. prof. microbiology, 1965-72, assoc. prof. surgery, 1968-74, assoc. prof. microbiology, 1972—, prof. surgery, 1974—. Contbr. articles to profl. jours. Served with U.S. Army, 1950-52. NIH grantee. Mem. Am. Soc. Microbiology, Miss. Acad. Scis., Transplantation Soc., Reticuloendothelial Soc., Am. Assn. Immunologists, So. Soc. Clin. Investigation, Sigma Xi. Baptist. Subspecialties: Immunology (medicine); Microbiology. Home: 5124 N Hill Dr Jackson MS 39211 Office: U Miss Med Center 2500 N State St Jackson MS 39216

GROMMESH, DONALD JOSEPH, aerospace engineer; b. Fargo, N.D., Aug. 13, 1931; s. Ralph H. and Eva N. (Rademacher) G.; m. Joanne Margaret Herman, Nov. 26, 1952; children—Michael, Mark, Melinda, Belinda, Joseph, Kristine. B.S., N.D. State U., 1953. Aerodynamics engr. Cessna Aircraft Co., Wichita, Kans., 1953-55, structures engr., structures engring. group leader, 1957-62; chief structures engring., chief engr., v.p. research and engring. Gates Learjet Corp., Wichita, 1962—. Served with USAF, 1955-57. Mem. Soc. Automotive Engrs., Am. Inst. Aeronautics Astronautics, Aerospace Industries Assn. Am., Gen. Aviation Mfrs. Assn. Roman Catholic. Home: 3101 Wilma St Wichita KS 67218 Office: 8220 W Harry St Wichita KS 67277

GROOPMAN, JOHN DAVIS, toxicologist; b. N.Y.C., Nov. 19, 1952; s. John and Rose (Alterman) G.; m. Hilary Reece, Sept. 13, 1981; 1 child, Alena. B.A., Elmira Coll., 1974; Ph.D., MIT, 1979. Postdoctoral fellow MIT, Cambridge, Mass., 1979-80; staff fellow Nat. Cancer Inst.-NIH, Bethesda, Md., 1980-81; asst. prof. toxicology Boston U. Sch. Pub. Health, 1981-84, assoc. prof., 1984—. Mem. Am. Assn. Cancer Research, Phi Beta Kappa. Current work: Chemical carcinogenesis and related toxicities. Subspecialties: Environmental toxicology; Cancer research (medicine). Office: Boston U Sch Pub Health 80 E Concord St Boston MA 02118

GROPP, WILLIAM DOUGLAS, computer science educator; b. Gainesville, Fla., Sept. 23, 1955; s. Armin Henry and Clare (Morgan) G.; m. Marla Joan Hoffman. B.S., Case Western Res. U., 1977; M.S. in Physics, U. Wash., 1977-78; M.S. in Computer Sci., Stanford U., 1982, Ph.D., 1982. Asst. prof. computer sci. Yale U., New Haven, 1982—; cons. Sci. Computing Assocs., New Haven, 1982—. Mem. Soc. Indsl. and Applied Math., Am. Math. Soc. Current work: Adaptive mesh refinement for partial differential equations; parallel computing; software environment for scientific computing. Subspecialty: Numerical analysis (computer science). Office: Dept Computer Sci Yale U PO Box 2158 New Haven CT 06520

GROSCH, DANIEL SWARTWOOD, genetics educator; b. Bethlehem, Pa., Oct. 25, 1918; s. E. Samuel and Laura F. (Hoodmaker) G.; m. Edith D. Taft, Mar. 27, 1944; children: Laura D., Barbara T., Douglas T., Robert L., Gustav. B.S., Moravian Coll., 1939; M.S., Lehigh U., 1940; Ph.D., U. Pa., 1944. Instr. zoology U. Pa., 1941-44; instr. meterology Navy Pre-Flight Sch., Phila., 1943-44; asst. prof. zoology N.C. State U., Raleigh, 1946-51, assoc. prof. genetics, 1951-57, prof. genetics, 1957—; co-investigator U.S. Biosatellite Program, 1964-71. Author: Biological Effects of Radiation, 2d edit, 1979; contbr. articles to profl. jours. Served with M.C. U.S. Army, 1944-46. Recipient Comenius Alumni award Moravian Coll., 1964; Lehigh U. scholar, 1939-40. Fellow AAAS; mem. Am. Inst. Biol. Sci., Am. Soc. Naturalists, Entomol. Soc. Am., Genetics Soc. Am., Radiation Research Soc., Soc. Devel. Biology, N.C. Acad. Scis., Sigma Xi, Phi Kappa Phi. Moravian. Current Work: Chemical and physical agents which alter fecundity and fertility; comparative sensitivity of the cell types in oogenesis and spermatogenesis to cytotoxic compounds and mutagens; effects of radiation combined with weightlessness, vibration and acceleration profiles of space flight. Subspecialties: Space biology; Toxicology (agriculture). Office: NC State U Genetics Dept Gardner Hall Raleigh NC 27650

GROSJEAN, DANIEL, researcher, consultant; b. Remoncourt, Vosges, France, Jan. 9, 1944; came to U.S., 1972; s. Paulette, (Villemin) G.; m. Francoise Y. Duret, Aug. 17, 1965; children—Fabrice, Eric. B.S., U. Nancy (France), 1964; M.S., U. Paris, 1965, 3d cycle Doctorate, 1970, Ph.D., 1972. Maitre asst. U. Picardie, St. Quentin, France, 1969-73; research fellow Calif. Inst. Tech., Pasadena, 1973-75; assoc. research chemist U. Calif.-Riverside, 1975-78; sr. sci. adviser ERT, Inc., Westlake Village, Calif., 1979-81, tech. dir., 1981-83; pres. Daniel Grosjean & Assocs., Inc., Camarillo, Calif., 1983—; vis. assoc. Calif. Inst. Tech., Pasadena, 1979—. Editor: Nitrogenous Air Pollutants, 1979; The Character and Origins of Smog Aerosols, 1980; assoc. editor Advances in Environ. Sci. and Tech., 1976-80, Advances in Photochemistry, 1977-80. Mem. com. Nat. Acad. Scis./NRC, 1976-77, 80-81, 81-83. NATO fellow, 1972. Mem. Am. Chem. Soc., Air Pollution Control Assn., French Chem. Soc., Am. Assn. Aerosol Research, N.Y. Acad. Scis., Am. Geophys. Union. Current work: Atmospheric chemistry of trace organics. Experimental studies of aerosol formation. Chemical and physical transformations of organic pollutants in urban air and in the troposphere. Subspecialties: Atmospheric chemistry; Environmental engineering. Home: 2740 Dorman St Camarillo CA 93010 Office: Daniel Grosjean and Assocs Suite 645 350 N Lantana St Camarillo CA 93010

GROSS, AL, electronics and electrical engineer; b. Toronto, Ont., Can., Feb. 22, 1918; came to U.S., 1919, naturalized, 1929; s. Nathan and Bertha (Rappaport) G.; m. Helen Mary Makse, Dec. 15, 1979 (dec. Dec. 1980); m. Ethel Marie Stanka, May 29, 1982. B.S.E.E., Case Western Res. U., 1939. Chief engr. Gilmore Industries, Cleve., 1974-76; staff engr. Hickok Elec. Instrument Co., Cleve., 1976; nat. sales mgr., chief engr. Fiberglass Communication Antennas div. True Temper Corp., Cleve., 1976-78; sr. engr. controls Parsons-Peebles Electric Products, Cleve., 1979-82; specialist product design ITT Cannon Electric Co., Phoenix, 1983—. Author: Military Standard for Printed Circuits, 1962; Results of Electric Field Measurements on Missiles and Reentry Vehicles, 1969. Patentee in field. Recipient Presdl. Commendation, 1981. Fellow IEEE (exec. bd. Phoenix chpt. 1982—), Radio Club Am.; mem. World Citizens' Band Union, European Citizens' Band Fedn. (hon. life), Federazione Italiana Ricetraamissioni CB (hon. life), Nat. Citizens' Band Council (hon. life), Netherland Citizens' Band Fedn. (hon. life), Deutscher CB Dachverband e.V. (hon. life), La Federazione CB Ticino (hon. life), Assn. Francaise des Amateuro Radio (hon.), Radio Club Austria (hon.), Citizens Band Assn. U.K. (hon.). Lodge: Fraternal Order Police. Current work: Electromagnetic compatibility of electronic equipment and systems including radio frequency interference and electromagnetic pulse suppression. Subspecialties: Telecommunications; Electronics. Office: ITT Cannon 2801 Air Ln Phoenix AZ 85034

GROSS, BOB DEAN, oral and maxillofacial surgery educator, researcher; b. Freeman, S.D., Dec. 21, 1942; s. George A. (G.); m. Nancy A. Dufton, May 5, 1979. B.S., Colo. State U., 1964; D.D.S., U. Mo., 1968; M.S., U. Tex.-Houston, 1971. Diplomate: Am. Bd. Oral and Maxillofacial Surgery (examiner). Resident in oral and maxillofacial surgery U. Tex.-Houston, 1971-74; pvt. practice and group practice oral surgery, Vallejo, Calif., 1974-75; asst. prof. U. Conn. Health Center, Farmington, 1975-78; assoc. prof. oral and maxillofacial surgery La. State U. Med. Center, Shreveport, 1978—; part-time practice Drs. Worley, Clark and Gross, Shreveport, 1979—; cons. USAF Barksdale AFB, Bossier City, La., 1980—. Contbr. articles to profl. jours. Served with USAF, 1968-70. Co-investigator NIH grant, 1983. Fellow Am. Soc. Central Anesthesiologists; mem. La. State Assn. Oral and Maxillofacial Surgeons (v.p. 1981-82), ADA, Southeastern Soc. Oral and Maxillofacial Surgeons, Am. Assn. Dental Research, Internat. Assn. Dental Research, Omicron Kappa Upsilon. Republican. Current Work: Electrical stimulation of bone healing, bone induction mechanisms, ultrasound analysis of bone healing, biomechanical stress testing of facial bones and fixation devices. Subspecialty: Oral and maxillofacial surgery. Home: 7450 S Lakeshore Dr Shreveport LA 71119 Office: Dept Surgery La State Univ Med Center 1501 Kings Highway Shreveport LA 71130

GROSS, DAN ARTHUR, physicist, researcher; b. Bucharest, Romania, Dec. 2, 1946; came to U.S., 1961, naturalized, 1967; s. Albert M. and Barbara (Blibaum) G.; m. Francette Gabrielle Josub, Nov. 3, 1973 (div. 1981); m. Mery Rosendorn, Dec. 26, 1982; 1 child, David Albert. B.S., CCNY, 1968; Ph.D., U. Rochester, 1974. Research assoc. U. Rochester, N.Y., 1974-77; applied scientist Fermi Nat. Accelerator, Batavia, Ill., 1977-82; research and devel. scientist Gen. Electric Corp., Schenectady, N.Y., 1982—. NSF fellow, 1972-73. Mem. Am. Phys. Soc., AAAS, N.Y. Acad. Sci. Current work: Development of NMR magnets; optimization techniques for NMR homogeneity; quench analysis for superconducting magnets; imaging methods for NMR magnets. Subspecialties: Particle physics; Magnetic physics. Home: 2135 Alexis Ave Niskayuna NY 12309 Office: Gen Electric Co 1 River Rd Suite 57-377 Schenectady NY 12345

GROSS, DAVID JONATHAN, physics educator; b. Washington, Feb. 19, 1941; s. Bertram and Nora (Faine) G.; m. Shulamith Toaff, Mar. 30, 1962; children—Ariela, Elisheva. B.Sc., Hebrew U., Israel, 1962; Ph.D., U. Calif.-Berkeley, 1966. Jr. fellow Harvard Soc. Fellows, Cambridge, Mass., 1966-69; asst. prof. physics, Princeton U., N.J., 1969-71, assoc. prof., 1971-73, prof., 1973—. Contbr. articles to profl. jours. A.P. Sloan fellow 1970. Fellow Am. Phys. Soc., Am. Acad. Arts and Scis. Current work: Quantum chromodynamics, quantum gravity, unified field theories, spin glasses. Subspecialties: Theoretical physics; Particle physics. Home: 264 Hartley Ave Princeton NJ 08540 Office: Princeton U Physics Dept Jadwin Hall Princeton NJ 08544

GROSS, DONALD, operations research educator; b. Pitts., Oct. 20, 1934; s. Frank and Marion (Horovitz) G.; m. Alice Gold, Sept. 20, 1959; children: Stephanie Lynne, Joanne Susan. B.S., Carnegie-Mellon U., 1956; M.S., Cornell U., 1959, Ph.D., 1961. Ops. research analyst Atlantic Refining Co., Phila., 1961-65; from asst. prof. to prof. dept. ops. research George Washington U., Washington, 1965—, chmn. dept., 1976—; cons. industry and fed. agys. Co-author: Fundamentals of Queueing Theory, 1974, 2d edit., 1985; contbr. articles to sci. jours. Treas. Williamsburg Civic Assn., Arlington, Va., 1978-79. Served to capt., Signal Corps U.S. Army, 1962-63. Grantee NASA; Grantee NSF; Grantee Office Naval Research; Grantee USAF. Mem. Ops. Research Soc. Am. (council 1982-85), Inst. Mgmt. Scis., Inst. Indsl. Engrs., Washington Ops. Research Mgmt. Council (trustee 1969-73, pres. 1974-75), Sigma Xi, Tau Beta Pi. Current Work: Queuing theory; inventory theory; model development and numerical solution techniques. Subspecialties: Operations research (engineering); Probability. Home: 3530 N Rockingham St Arlington VA 22213 Office: George Washington U Washington DC 20052

GROSS, JONATHAN LIGHT, computer science educator; b. Phila., June 11, 1941; s. Nathan K. and Henrietta E. (Light) G.; m. Susan Fay Kodner, Aug. 29, 1976; children—Aaron, Jessica, Joshua, Rena Lea, Alisa Sharon. B.S., MIT, 1964; M.A., Dartmouth Coll., 1966, Ph.D., 1968. Instr. math. Princeton U., N.J., 1968-69; assoc. prof. math. stats. Columbia U., N.Y.C., 1969-72, assoc. prof., 1973-78, prof., 1978-79, prof. computer sci., math., 1979—, vice chmn. dept. computer sci., 1982—; cons. Russell Sage Found., Inst. Def. Analyses, Bell Labs., Alfred P. Sloan Found. Author: (with others) Fundamental Programming Concepts, 1972, Fortran 77 Programming, 1978, Introduction to Computer Programming, 1979, Pascal Programming, 1982, Pascal, 1984, Measuring Culture, 1985. Adv. editor Jour. Graph Theory, Computers and Electronics, Fortran 77 Fundamentals and Style, 1985. Contbr. articles to profl. jours. IBM postdoctoral fellow, 1972-73; Sloan fellow in math., 1973-75. Mem. Am. Math. Soc., Assn. Computing Machinery, Soc. Indsl. and Applied Math. Jewish. Current work: Applications of topological and probabilistic models to computer science and organization theory. Subspecialties: Theoretical computer science; Topology and foundations. Home: 150 Hightstown Rd Princeton Junction NJ 08550 Office: 450 Computer Sci Bldg Columbia U New York NY 10027

GROSS, LEO, biophysicist, cons.; b. Bklyn., Feb. 13, 1915; s. Isador and Rose (Lichenstein) G.; married; children: Alan, Walter, Joan. B.S., Bklyn. Coll., 1934; M.A., Columbia U., 1934; Ph.D., N.Y. U., 1963. Technician inhalation therapy dept. Coll. Physicians and Surgeons, Columbia U., 1935-36; tchr. physics N.Y.C. Bd. Edn., 1936-41; physicist Bur. Ordanance, U.S. Navy, 1941-42; physicist, mem. tech. staff Los Alamos Sci. Lab., U. Calif., 1943-46; mem. tech. staff Bell Telephone Labs., 1946-49; chief systems engr. Polarad Electronics Corp., Lake Success, N.Y., 1949-54; pres. Hub Electronics Corp., White Plains, N.Y., 1954-58; adminstr., dir. biophysics, dir. ednl. programs Waldemar Med. Research Found., Bayside, N.Y., 1958—; nat. Acad. Sci. internat. exchange scholar, 1973. Contbr. articles to profl. jours. Served to 1st lt., C.E. U.S. Army, 1943-46. Mem. Am. Phys. Soc., IEEE, Optical Soc. Am., Soc. Photo-Optical Instrumentation Engrs., N. Y. Acad. Scis., Biophys. Soc., Nat. Sci. Tchrs. Assn. (Sci. Teaching Achievement award 1975), Nat. Assn. Biology Tchrs. Subspecialties: Biophysics (biology); Electronics. Home: 36-11 217th St Bayside NY 11361 Office: Waldemar Med Research Found Bayside NY 11361

GROSS, LUDWIK, physician; b. Cracow, Poland, Sept. 11, 1904; came to U.S., 1940, naturalized, 1943; s. Adolf and Augusta (Alexander) G.; m. Dorothy L. Nelson, Oct. 7, 1943; 1 dau., Augusta H. M.D., Iagellon U., Cracow, 1929; Prix Chevillon, Acad. Medicine, Paris, 1937; Dr.Sci. honoris causa, Mt. Sinai Sch. Medicine, CUNY, 1983. Diplomate: Am. Bd. Internal Medicine. Intern and resident St. Lazar Gen. Hosp., Cracow, 1929-32; part time research exptl. cancer Pasteur Inst., Paris; postgrad. clin. tng. Salpetriere, U. Paris, 1932- 39; cancer research Christ Hosp., Cin., 1941-43; chief cancer research VA Med Center, Bronx, 1946—; Distinguished physician VA Med Center, Bronx, 1977-81; research prof. dept. medicine Mt. Sinai Sch. Medicine, N.Y.C., 1971-73, emeritus prof., 1973—; cons. Sloan Kettering Inst., Meml. Center, N.Y.C., 1955-57, assoc. scientist, 1957-60; Distinguished Leukemia lectr. U. So. Ala., 1976; 17th G.H.A. Clowes Meml. lectr., 1977. Author: Oncogenic Viruses, 1961, 3d edit., 1983; author numerous papers on cancer and leukemia in profl. jours. Served from capt. to maj. M.C. AUS, 1943-46. Decorated chevalier Legion of Honor France; recipient Robert R. De Villiers award for research on leukemia Leukemia Soc. N.Y., 1953, Walker prize Royal Coll. Surgeons Eng., 1962, Pasteur Silver medal Pasteur Inst., 1962, Lucy Wortham James award James Ewing Soc., 1962, WHO UN prize, 1962, The Bertner Found. award, 1963, Albert Einstein Centennial medal, 1965, Albion O. Bernstein award Med. Soc. N.Y. State, 1971, Spl. Virus Cancer Program award Nat. Cancer Inst., 1972, William S. Middleton award VA, 1973, Albert Lasker Basic Med. Research award, 1974, Founders award Cancer Research Inst., 1975; prin. Paul Ehrlich-Ludwig Darmstaedter prize, 1978; Prix Griffuel Paris, 1978; Exceptional Service award VA, 1979. Fellow A.C.P., AAAS, Internat. Soc. of Hematology, N.Y. Acad. Scis.; mem. Am. Soc. Hematology, AMA, Nat. Acad. Scis., Am. Assn. Cancer Research (dir. 1973-76), Assn. Mil. Surgeons U.S., Soc. of Exptl. Biology and Medicine, Bronx County, N.Y. State med. socs. Current Work: Etiology of cancer and leukemia; oncogenic viruses. Subspecialties: Cancer research (medicine); Virology (medicine). Home: 29 Ramona Ct New Rochelle NY 10804

GROSS, M. GRANT, ocean science administrator, oceanographer; b. Childress, Tex., Jan. 5, 1933; s. Meredith and Mary (Stevens) G.; m. Nancy Hayward, Aug. 15, 1954 (div. May 1978); children—Alison, Jeffrey, Anne. A.B., Princeton U., 1954; M.S., Calif. Inst. Tech., 1959, Ph.D., 1961. Prof. marine sci. SUNY-Stony Brook, 1969-72, acting dir. marine sci. research ctr., 1970-72; head oceanography sect. NSF, Washington, 1972-74, head internat. decade of ocean exploration, 1978-80, dir. div. ocean sci., 1980—; bd. dirs. Chesapeake Bay Inst., Johns Hopkins U., Balt., 1974-78. Served to 1st lt. U.S. Army, 1955-57. Fellow Geol. Soc. Am.; mem. Am. Geophys. Union, Am. Soc. Limnology and Oceanography, Phi Beta Kappa, Sigma Xi. Current work: Coastal ocean processes; waste disposal in ocean. Subspecialty: Oceanography.

GROSS, NICHOLAS JABOB, physician; b. Kuala Lumpur, Malaysia, Aug. 14, 1935; came to U.S., 1964; s. Reginald David and Nora Marguerite (Gayer) G.; m. Marda Jean Phoenix, Jan. 28, 1957; children—Michael D., Simon A., Julian S. B.A., Cambridge U., 1957, M.B., B.S., 1960, M.A., 1967; Ph.D., U. Chgo., 1970, M.D., 1972. House physician Guy's Hosp., London, 1960, Royal Postgrad. Med. Sch., 1963, Nat. Heart Hosp., 1964; fellow in medicine Johns Hopkins Hosp., Balt., 1964-65; fellow in cardiology U. Chgo., 1965-69, asst. prof. internal medicine, 1970-76, assoc. prof., 1977; assoc. prof. Loyola U. Med. Sch., Maywood, Ill., 1978-84, prof., 1984—; mem. staff Hines VA Hosp. Author: Asthma, 1974. Contbr. articles to profl. jours. Fellow ACP, Royal Coll. Physicians; mem. Royal Soc. Medicine, Am. Fedn. Clin. Research, Am. Physiol. Soc., Central Soc. Clin. Research, ACLU, Common Cause. Current work: Biology of lung, cell biology of lung cells, effects of radiation on lungs, pharmacology and physiology of pulmonary airways. Subspecialties: Pulmonary medicine; Cell and tissue culture. Home: 1309 E 55th St Chicago IL 60615Office: Hines VA Hosp PO Box 505 Hines IL 60141

GROSS, PAUL RANDOLPH, biologist, laboratory administrator; b. Phila., Nov. 27, 1928; s. Nathan and Kate (Segal) G.; m. Mona Lee Feld, Mar. 27, 1949; 1 dau., Wendy Loren. B.A., U. Pa., 1950, Ph.D. (Harrison and NSF fellow), 1954; M.A., Brown U., 1963; D.Sc., Med. Coll. Ohio, 1979. Asst. prof. biology N.Y. U., 1954-58, asso. prof., 1958-61; asso. prof. biology Brown U., 1962-65; prof. biology M.I.T., 1965-71; prof., chmn. dept. biology U. Rochester, 1972-78, dean grad. studies, 1975-78; chmn. sci. adv. com. U. Rochester (Cancer Center), 1974-78; pres., dir. Marine Biol. Lab., Woods Hole, Mass., 1978—; prin. investigator research and tng. grants from NSF and NIH, 1955—; mem., advisor to doctoral council N.Y. State Edn. Dept.; mem. adv. com. cell and developmental biology Am. Cancer Soc.; mem. oversight com. Assn. Am. Colls.; mem. nat. adv. council Nat. Inst. Child Health and Human Devel.; mem. sci. adv. com. Tufts U. Sch. Vet. Medicine; mem. council U. Va. Ctr. for Advanced Studies. Contbr. sci. articles to profl. jours. Mem. Indsl. Devel. Corp., Town of Falmouth (Mass.); trustee U. Rochester. Lalor fellow, 1954-55; NSF fellow U. Edinburgh, 1961-62. Fellow Am. Acad. Arts and Scis.; mem. Internat. Soc. for Developmental Biology, Am. Physiol. Soc., Am. Soc. Zoologists (chmn. sect. on developmental biology), AAAS, Am. Soc. Cell Biology. Clubs: Woods Hole Yacht, Cosmos. Subspecialties: Developmental biology; Biochemistry (biology). Office: Marine Biological Laboratory Woods Hole MA 02543

GROSS, PETER ALAN, physician, researcher; b. Newark, Nov. 18, 1938; s. Meyer P. and Nathalie (Bass) Denburg) G.; m. Regina Teri Gittlin, May 30, 1964; children: Deborah Karen, Michael Philip, Daniel Brian. B.A. cum laude, Amherst Coll., 1960; M.D., Yale U., 1964. Diplomate: Am. Bd. Internal Medicine. NIH fellow virology dept. epidemiology Yale U., New Haven, 1969-71; intern Yale-New Haven Hosp., 1964-65, jr. resident, 1965-66; sr. resident Peter Bent Brigham Hosp., Boston, 1968-69; research and edn. assoc. VA Hosp., West Haven, Conn., 1971-73, acting chief infectious disease sect., 1972-73, chief infectious disease sect., 1973-74, Hackensack (N.J.) Med. Center, 1974—, chmn. dept. medicine, 1980—; prof. medicine N.J. Med. Sch., Newark, 1981—; assoc. clin. prof. medicine Columbia U. Coll. Phys. and Surgs., N.Y.C., 1977-81, asst. clin. prof., 1974-77; asst. prof. medicine Yale U. Sch. Medicine, New Haven, 1971-74; ad hoc reviewer NIH, Nat. Inst. Allergy and Infectious Diseases research grants, 1974—. Author: Gram Strain Recognition, 1975, 2d edit., 1980; editorial bd.: Jour. Clin. Microbiology, 1980—, Infection Control, 1980—. Served to lt. comdr. USPHS, 1966-68. NIH fellow, 1969-71. Fellow Infectious Disease Soc. Am., ACP; mem. Am. Soc. Virology, AAAS, Am. Soc. Microbiology. Republican. Jewish. Current Work: Immune response to influenza vaccine, hospital-acquired infections in the elderly. Subspecialties: Infectious diseases; Epidemiology. Home: 242 McKinley Place Ridgewood NJ 07450 Office: Hackensack Med Ctr Hackensack NJ 07601

GROSS, THOMAS ALFRED OTTO, electrical engineer, consultant; b. Brunswick, Maine, Mar. 18, 1918; s. Alfred Otto and Edna Grace (Gross) G.; m. Judith Cogswell Fiske, June 29, 1948; children—Winthrop, Anne, Thomas, Kathryn, Amanda. B.S. in Physics, Bowdoin Coll., 1940; Electronics Engr., Harvard U., 1941. Mgr. advanced devel. Raytheon Co., Waltham, Mass., 1956-58, ops. mgr., 1959-61; pres. Spectran Electronics Corp., Maynard, Mass., 1961-64, T.A.O. Gross, Inc., Lincoln, Mass., 1964—. Author tech. papers. Patentee in field. Mem. IEEE, Am. Phys. Soc. Episcopalian. Subspecialties: Applied magnetics; Electronics. Office: TAO Gross Inc 230 Concord Rd Lincoln MA 01773

GROSS, WILLIAM ALLEN, mechanical engineering educator, consultant; b. Los Angeles, Nov. 17, 1924; s. William Allen and Margaret Florence (Hill) G.; m. Shirley Mae Jackson, Aug. 10, 1948 (dec. Apr. 1968); children—Constance, Ellen, Mark, David; m. Sharon Carol Philbrick, Aug. 22, 1970. B.S., U.S. Coast Guard Acad., 1945; M.S., U. Calif.-Berkeley, 1949, Ph.D., 1951. Registered profl. engineer, N.Mex. From lectr. to asst. prof. U. Calif.-Berkeley, 1949-52; asst. prof. Iowa State U., Ames, 1952-55; mem. tech. staff Bell Telephone Labs., Murray Hill, N.J., 1955-56; mem. research staff IBM, San Jose, Calif., 1956-61; v.p. advanced tech. div., dir. research AMPEX, Redwood City, Calif., 1961-72; vis. lectr. U. Calif.-Berkeley, 1973; dean engring. U. N.Mex., Albuquerque, 1974-80, prof., 1974—; cons. on gas lubricated bearings and renewable energy, U.S. and overseas, 1968—; bd. dirs. Lovelace Inhalation Toxicology Research Inst., Albuquerque. Author: Gas Film Lubrication, 1962. Editor: Fluid Film Lubrication, 1961, 82. Patentee in field. Contbr. numerous articles to profl. jours. Served to lt. (j.g.) USCG, 1945-48. Recipient Chief Manualito award Navajo Tribe, 1982. Fellow ASME (Centennial award 1980, chmn. applied mech. div. west coast sect. 1959); mem. IEEE (sr. mem.). Mem. Soc. of Friends. Current work: Co-director technological innovation program to aid technological entrepreneurs to start up their own businesses in New Mexico. Subspecialties: Theoretical and applied mechanics; Renewable energy. Office: Dept Mech Engring U N Mex Albuquerque NM 87131

GROSSER, GEORGE SAMUEL, psychology educator, research consultant; b. Boston, Aug. 14, 1929; s. Sidney and Eva Risa (Shapiro) G. A.B. cum laude, Harvard Coll., 1951; M.A., Boston U., 1952, Ph.D., 1957. Exptl. and physiol. psychologist U.S. Army Chem. Corps, Edgewood, Md., 1957-58; asst. prof. Am. Internat. Coll., Springfield, Mass., 1958-64, assoc. prof., 1964—; researcher and pres. Consumer Behavior Research Assn., Springfield, 1980-82. Author: (with W. Zinn) Vitametrics: Human Self-Evaluation Formula, 1980; editor: (with others) General Psychology, 1967. USPHS grantee, 1959-60. Mem. AAAS, Am. Psychol. Assn., N.Y. Acad. Scis., Sigma Xi. Jewish. Clubs: Springfield Chess, Springfield Bridge. Current Work: Vision; memory trace; attitude scaling; learning. Subspecialties: Physiological psychology; Social psychology. Home: 335 Maple Rd Longmeadow MA 01106 Office: Am Internat Coll 1000 State St Springfield MA 01109

GROSSMAN, BERNARD, aerospace and ocean engineering educator; b. Bklyn., Dec. 7, 1942; s. Rubin and Marion (Shapiro) G.; m. Sharon Douglas, Mar. 29, 1980; children—Robyn, Mara. B.S., Poly. Inst. Bklyn., 1964, M.S., 1965, Ph.D., 1969. Advanced devel. engr. Grumman Aerospace Corp., Bethpage, N.Y., 1968-75, head theoretical aerodynamics lab., 1975-80, cons., 1980—; assoc. prof. aerospace and mech. engring. Poly. Inst. N.Y., Bklyn., 1980-82; prof. aerospace and ocean engring. Va. Poly. Inst. and State U., Blacksburg, 1982—; cons. U.S. Naval Surface Weapon Ctr., Dahlgren, Va., 1984—. Contbr. articles to profl. jours. Mem. AIAA, Soc. Indsl. and Applied Math., Am. Phys. Soc., Am. Soc. Engring. Edn. Club: University. Current work: computational fluid mechanics. Subspecialties: Aerospace engineering and technology; Fluid mechanics. Home: 304 Pearman Rd Blacksburg VA 24060 Office: Va Poly Inst Dept Aerospace and Ocean Engring Blacksburg VA 24061

GROSSMAN, IRVING GROSS, hydrogeologist; b. N.Y.C., Mar. 4, 1917; s. Harry and Charlotte (Gross) G.; m. Rose Opas, Aug. 28, 1943 (div. 1953); 1 child, Barbara Louise; m. Ann Safran, Aug. 12, 1956; children—Joshua Seth, Gilbert Elias. B.A., Bklyn. Coll., 1944; M.A., Columbia U., 1947. Instr. geology U. N.D., Grand Forks, 1946-49; lectr. U. Conn., Storrs, 1948; geologist U.S. Geol. Survey, Albany, N.Y., San Juan, P.R., Hartford, Conn., Reston, Va., Trenton, 1949—; assoc. lectr. Am. U., Washington, 1980-81. Author ground water reports, 1950-70. Editor water reports, 1970-84. Pres. Nat. Hist. Soc. P.R., 1960-62; mem. Open Space Com., Reston, 1980-83. Fellow Geol. Soc. Am., AAAS; mem. Soc. Econ. Geologists, Assn. Geoscientists for Internat. Devel., Audubon Soc., Sigma Xi. Jewish. Current work: Review and editing scientific reports on hydrology; automation of report reviews and processing. Subspecialties: Hydrology; Geology. Home: 224 Flint Ct Yardley PA 19067

GROSSMAN, LAWRENCE, biochemist, educator; b. Bklyn., Jan. 23, 1924; s. Isidor Harry and Anna (Lipkin) G.; m. Barbara Meta Grossman, June 24, 1949; children: Jon David, Carl Henry, Ilene Rebecca. Student, CCNY, 1946-47; B.A., Hofstra U., 1949; Ph.D., U. So. Calif., 1954. Scientist NIH, Bethesda, Md., 1957-62; asst. prof. biochemistry Brandeis U., Waltham, Mass., 1957-62, assoc. prof., 1962-67, prof., 1967-75; E.V. McCollum prof., chmn. dept., biochemistry Johns Hopkins U., Balt., 1975—; sci. adv. com. Am. Cancer Soc.; cons. Author: Methods in Nucleic Acids, 11 vols; contbr. numerous articles to sci. jours. Served to lt. USNR, 1942-45. Decorated D.F.C. (2), Air medal (3).; Commonwealth Fund fellow, 1963; Guggenheim fellow, 1973; recipient Career Devel. award NIH, 1964-74; research grantee NIH; research grantee NSF; research grantee Dept. Energy. Mem. Am. Soc. Biol. Chemists. Club: Alberg 30 (Annapolis, Md.). Current Work: Genes and enzymes that repair damaged DNA in bacteria and human cells. Subspecialties: Biochemistry (biology); Genetics and genetic engineering (biology). Home: 5723 Uffington Rd Baltimore MD 21209 Office: 615 N Wolfe St Baltimore MD 21705

GROSSMAN, LAWRENCE, geochemistry educator, consultant; b. Toronto, Ont., Can., Feb. 2, 1946; s. David Saul and Marian Lillian (Jacobs) G.; m. Karen Lee Fruitman, Aug. 11, 1968; children: Sheryl Gloria, Daniel Martin. B.Sc. with honours in Chemistry and Geology, McMaster U., 1968; M.Phil. in Geochemistry, Yale U., 1970, Ph.D. in Geochemistry, 1972. Asst. prof. geochemistry U. Chgo., 1972-76, assoc. prof., 1976-81, prof., 1981—; Caswell Silver disting. lectr. U. N.Mex., 1981; Lady Davis vis. prof. Hebrew U. of Jerusalem, 1981-82. Recipient award for advancement basic and applied sci. Yale Sci. and Engring. Assn., 1982; Alfred P. Sloan research fellow, 1976-78. Fellow Am. Geophys. Union (James B. Macelwane award 1980), Mineral. Soc. Am., Meteoritical Soc.; mem. Geochem. Soc. (F.W. Clarke medal 1974), Internat. Astron. Union. Current Work: Chemical processes in the early solar system; origin of meteorites, planets and the solar system; cosmochemistry; mineralogical, chemical and isotopic composition of meteorites. Subspecialties: Geochemistry; Planetology. Office: Dept Geophys Scis and Enrico Fermi Inst U Chgo 5734 S Ellis Ave Chicago IL 60637

GROSSMAN, LAWRENCE I., molecular biology educator, researcher; b. N.Y.C., Nov. 15, 1939; s. David Morris and Dora (Turkenich) G.; m. Esta P. Shaftel, Dec. 27, 1970; 1 child, Daniel Alan. B.S., CCNY, 1961; Ph.D., Albert Einstein Coll. Medicine, 1970. Research fellow in biology Calif. Inst. Tech., Pasadena, 1970-74; asst. prof. biochemistry Wayne State U., Detroit, 1974-78, U. Mich., Ann Arbor, 1978—. Contbr. articles to profl. jours. NIH and NSF grantee, 1974—; NIH fellow Albert Einstein Coll. Medicine, 1968-69; Jane Coffin Childs Meml. fellow Calif. Inst. Tech., 1971-72; recipient Samuel Rubin prize CCNY, 1961. Mem. Am. Soc. Biol. Chemists, Biophys. Soc., Am. Soc. Microbiology, N.Y. Acad. Scis., Sigma Xi. Current work: Structure, function, evolution of DNA, mitochondrial DNA, nuclear genes for mitochondrial proteins. Subspecialties: Molecular biology; Genome organization. Home: 206 Crest Ave Ann Arbor MI 48103 Office: Div Biol Scis U Mich Ann Arbor MI 48109

GROSSMAN, MICHAEL, geneticist; b. N.Y.C., Dec. 21, 1940; s. Benjamin Harry and Alice (Berkowitz) G.; m. Margaret Rosso, June 27, 1970; children: Aaron William, Daniel Benjamin. BS., CCNY, 1962; M.S., Va. Poly. Inst. and State U., 1965; Ph.D., Purdue U., 1969. Asst. prof. U. Ill., Champaign, 1969-74, assoc. prof., 1974-85, prof., 1985—; vis. prof. Instituto de Fitotecnia, INTA, Argentina, 1970, Gadjah Mada U., Yogyakarta, Indonesia, 1974. Contbr. articles to sci. jours. Recipient teaching awards U. Ill., 1971, 72; award AMOCO Found. Inc., 1972; Danforth faculty assoc., 1976. Mem. AAAS, Am. Dairy Sci. Assn., Am. Genetic Assn., Am. Soc. Animal Sci., Biometric Soc., Genetics Soc. Am., Gamma Sigma Delta, Phi Sigma, Sigma Xi. Current Work: Theoretical and experimental population and quantitative genetics; estimation of genetic parameters; analysis of dairy goat lactation records. Subspecialties: Animal genetics; Statistics. Home: 2206 Valley Brook Dr Champaign IL 61821 Office: Animal Scis Lab 1207 W Gregory Dr Urbana IL 60801

GROSSMAN, SEBASTIAN PETER, biopsychology educator; b. Coburg, Germany, Jan. 21, 1934; came to U.S., 1954, naturalized, 1955; s. Otto Grossman and Arnet (Peipers) Dietrich-Grossman; m. Lore Bensel, June 30, 1955. B.A., U. Md., 1958; M.S., Yale U., 1959, Ph.D., 1961. Asst. prof. U. Iowa, Iowa City, 1961-64; assoc. prof. U. Chgo., 1964-67, prof., 1967—, chmn. dept. biopsychology, 1967-73, 76—; regional editor Physiology and Behavior, 1966—, Pharmacology, Biochemistry and Behavior, 1968—, Neurosci. and Biobehavior Rev., 1976—. Author: A Textbook of Physiological Psychology, 1967; Essentials of Physiological Psychology, 1973. Contbr. articles to profl. jours., chpts. to textbooks. Served with U.S. Army, 1954-56. Fellow Ctr. for Advanced Study of Behavioral Sci., 1975-76, Netherland Inst. Advanced Study, 1982-83. Fellow Am. Psychol. Assn., AAAS; mem. Am. Physiol. Soc., Neurosci. Soc. Lutheran. Current work: Neuroanatomical and neuropharmacological bases of primary motivational states. Subspecialties: Psychobiology; Physiological psychology. Office: Dept Behavioral Science U Chicago 5848 S University Ave Chicago IL 60637

GROSSMAN, STEVEN HARRIS, biochemistry educator; b. N.Y.C., May 18, 1945; s. Saul E. and Pauline (Kahan) G.; m. Martha E. Hadley, Jan. 17, 1970; children—Daniel, Sara. B.A., NYU, 1967; Ph.D., Purdue U., 1972. Postdoctoral fellow U. Wis.-Madison, 1972-74; research scientist Union Carbide Corp., Tarrytown, N.Y., 1974-76; asst. prof. U. Southwest La., Lafayette, 1978-81; assoc. prof. biochemistry U. South Fla., Tampa, 1981—. Contbr. articles to sci. jours. Mem. Am. Chem. Soc. (chmn. subsect. 1983), Am. Soc. Biol. Chemists, Am. Assn. Clin. Chemists, N.Y. Acad. Scis. Current work: Protein folding; clinical enzymology. Subspecialties: Biophysical chemistry; Clinical chemistry. Home: 7010 Whittier St Tampa FL 33617 Office: U South Fla Tampa FL 33620

GROSSNICKLE, NEVIN EDWIN, biology educator, limnologist; b. Elgin, Ill., Mar. 3, 1950; s. Edwin Eugene and Victoria Fern (Dilling) G.; m. Jane Burton Luhman, Dec. 28, 1971; 1 child, Amy. B.S. in Natural Resources, U. Mich., 1972; M.S. in Zoology, U. Wis.-Milw., 1974; Ph.D. in Zoology, U. Wis.-Madison, 1978. Research asst. U. Wis.-Milw., 1973-74, tchg. asst., 1974-75, research asst., 1975-78; postdoctoral fellow Harbor Branch Inst., Ft. Pierce, Fla., 1978-79; asst. research sci. U. Mich., Ann Arbor, 1979-82; asst. prof. biology Grand Canyon coll., Phoenix, 1982-85, assoc. prof., 1985—; chmn. biology sect. Ariz.-Nev. Acad. Scis., Phoenix, 1984-85. Bd. editors Hydrobiologia Mysid Issue, 1981-82; bd. reviewers Freshwater Invertebrate Biology, 1982—; contbr. articles to profl. jours. Mem. AAAS, Am. Soc. Limnology and Oceanography, Ecol. Soc. Am., Internat. Assn. Great Lakes Research, Internat. Assn. Theoretical and Applied Limnology. Current work: Feeding and vertical migration of aquatic invertebrates, especially crustacean zooplankton. Subspecialty: Limnology. Office: Grand Canyon Coll PO Box 11097 Phoenix AZ 85061

GROSSWEINER, LEONARD IRWIN, physicist, educator; b. Atlantic City, Aug. 16, 1924; s. Jules H. and Rae (Goldberger) G.; m. Bess Tornheim, Sept. 9, 1951; children—Karen Ann, Jane (dec.), James Benjamin, Eric William. B.S., Coll. City N.Y., 1947; M.S., Ill. Inst. Tech., 1950, Ph.D., 1955. Asst. chemist Argonne (Ill.) Nat. Lab., 1947-50, asso. physicist, 1950-57; assoc. prof. physics Ill. Inst. Tech., Chgo., 1957-62, prof. physics, 1962—, chmn. dept. physics, 1970-81, Sang Exchange lectr., 1972-73; vis. prof. radiology Stanford U. Sch. Medicine, 1979; vis. prof. physics U. Ill. Coll. Medicine-Chgo., 1983—; cons. Donner Lab. U. Calif., Berkeley, Chgo. Med. Sch., North Chicago, Ill., Hines (Ill.) VA Hosp., Michael Reese Med. Center, Chgo.; cons. Ravenswood Hosp. Med. Ctr., Chgo. Mem. U.S. Nat. Com. Photobiology, 1977-81, chmn., 1980-81. Author: Organic Photoconductors in Electrophotography, 1970; Contbr. articles to profl. jours. Served with AUS, 1944-46. Fellow Am. Phys. Soc. (sec.-treas. div. biol. physics 1973-76, chmn. 1977-78), N.Y. Acad. Scis.; mem. Am. Chem. Soc., AAAS, Radiation Research Soc., Am. Soc. Photobiology (council 1977-80, sec.-treas. 1981—), Biophys. Soc., Inter-Am. Photochem. Soc. (exec. com. 1976-78), Midwest Bio-Laser Inst. (exec. com. 1984—), Sigma Xi (distinguished faculty lectr. 1970). Current Work: Laser flash photolysis research in photobiology relevant to clinical phototherapy, especially tumor phototherapy with porphyrins and light, radiant energy damage to the eye, and PUVA phototherapy of human skin diseases, tissue dosimetry in phototherapy. Subspecialties: Laser photochemistry; Cancer research (medicine). Home: 231 Wentworth Ave Glencoe IL 60022 Office: Ill Inst Tech IIT Center Chicago IL 60616

GROSZMANN, ROBERTO JOSE, physician; b. Buenos Aires, Argentina, Aug. 17, 1939; came to U.S., 1965, naturalized, 1979; s. Jose and Sofia (Hirsch) G.; m. Aida Zugman, May 2, 1965; children: Yvette, Daniel. Bachiller, Buenos Aires U., 1958, M.D., 1964. Intern Mt. Sinai Hosp., Chgo., 1965-66; resident internal medicine VA Hosp., Washington, 1966-68, research fellow hemodynamics program, 1968-71; asst. prof. medicine Buenos Aires, U., 1972-75; asst. prof. medicine Yale U., New Haven, 1975-79, asso. prof., 1979—; dir. hepatic hemodynamic lab. W. Haven VA Hosp., 1980—. Editor: Gastroenterologia y Hepatologia, 2 vols, 1982; author balloon catheter technique for measuring wedged hepatic venous pressure, 1979. NIH Career Devel. award, 1979—; Bonarino Udaondo award Argentina Soc. Gastroenterology, 1975. Mem. Am. Assn. Study Liver Diseases, Internat. Assn. Study Liver Diseases, Am. Soc. Clin. Investigation. Current Work: Portal hypertension, hepatic circulation. Subspecialty: Gastroenterology. Home: 33 Pine Ridge Rd Woodbridge CT 06525 Office: VA Med Center West Spring St West Haven CT 06516

GROTA, LEE JAMES, psychologist, neuroendocrinologist, educator; b. Sturgeon Bay, Wis., May 12, 1937; s. Hubert D. and Carrol C. (Bartmann) G.; m. Mary Peterson, June 20, 1959; children: Catherine, Steven, Michael, Carl. B.S., Marquette U., 1959; M.S., Purdue U., Lafayette, Ind., 1961, Ph.D., 1963. Postdoctoral fellow dept. biochemistry U. Utah, 1963-65; asst. prof. psychiatry and psychology U. Rochester, 1965-71, assoc. prof., 1971—; vis. assoc. prof. neuroscis. and psychiatry McMaster U., Hamilton, Ont., Can., 1977—. Contbr. numerous articles, chpts. to profl. publs.; author numerous profl. papers. Mem. Endocrine Soc., Soc. Neurosci., Internat. Soc. Devel. Psychobiology. Current Work: Neuroendocrinology of indolealkylamines; central nervous system modulates immune reactivity. Subspecialties: Neuroendocrinology;

Neuroimmunology. Office: Dept Psychiatry 1-9045 U Rochester Med Center Rochester NY 14642

GROTBERG, JAMES BERNARD, engineering and anesthesia educator; b. Oak Park, Ill., July, 22, 1950; married. Ph.D. in Fluid Mechanics, Johns Hopkins U., 1977; M.D., U. Chgo., 1980. Resident dept. anesthesia Northwestern U. Med. Sch., Chgo., 1980-81, asst. prof., 1981—; asst. prof. dept. engring. scis. and applied math. Tech. Inst., Northwestern U., Evanston, Ill., 1981—. Contbr. articles to profl. jours. Grantee Whitaker Found., NIH, Gen. Motors Corp., NSF; NSF fellow, Mem. Phi Beta Kappa, Tau Beta Pi. Current work: Fluid mechanics and transport processes in physiological systems, including pulmonary gas exchange, deposition of toxic inhalants, flutter instability of flexible tube flows and interfacial phenomena. Subspecialties: Biomedical engineering; Fluid mechanics. Home: 2730 Simpson St Evanston IL 60201 Office: Tech Inst Dept Engring Scis and Applied Math Northwestern U Evanston IL 60201

GROUMPOS, PETER, electrical engineering educator, researcher; b. Xylocastron, Corinthia, Greece, June 23, 1950; came to U.S., 1969; s. Periandros and Marie (Koronioti) G.; m. Alexandra Lotsaris, June 4, 1977; 1 child, Demetrios. B.S. in Elec. Engring., SUNY-Buffalo, 1974, M.S. in Elec. Engring., 1976, Ph.D. in Elec. Engring., 1979. Research engr. Calspan Corp., Buffalo, 1978-79; assoc. prof. dept. elec. engring. Cleve. State U., 1979—; dir. ELE Communications Research Lab., Cleve., 1981-84, ELE Energy Research Ctr., Cleve., 1981—; owner Sunrise Assocs., Cleve., 1983—. Contbr. chpt. to book Advances in Control and Dynamic Systems, 1983; author tech. papers and reports in photovoltaics, large scale systems, communications. Recipient Photovoltaics award NASA Lewis Research Ctr., 1981, Communications award, 1981, Large Scale Systems award Cleve. State U., 1980, Use of Computers in Edn. award NSF, 1982. Mem. IEEE, Control Soc. (assoc. editor mag. 1981—), Internat. Fedn. Automation (chmn. robotics group 1983—), Global Energy Assn., Tau Beta Pi, Eta Kappa Nu. Club: Krikos (N.Y.C.). Current work: I am involved in terrestrial photovoltaic application, space station research, satellite communications, large scale and hierarchical systems and computer use in engineering education. Subspecialties: Solar energy; Electrical engineering. Home: 1211 Oxford Rd Cleveland Heights OH 44121 Office: Cleve State U Dept Elec Engring 1983 E 24th St Cleveland OH 44115

GROUSE, LAWRENCE DOUGLAS, editor, association executive, biochemical researcher, medical educator; b. Mpls., Nov. 18, 1946; s. Tom and Helene Dorothea (Burnson) G.; m. Jan Ellen Lindtwed, Oct. 27, 1973; children: Eric Roger, Carrie Katherine. B.A., Carleton Coll., 1968; M.D., U. Wash., 1973, Ph.D., 1973. Intern in internal medicine U. Calif.-San Diego, 1973-74; research assoc. NIH, Bethesda, Md., 1974-76, med. officer, 1976-79; sr. editor Jour. AMA, 1971-84; dir. dept. sci. activities AMA, Chgo., from 1979; now sr. med. editor Cable Health Network, Los Angeles; vis. scientist U. Chgo.; vis. asst. prof. preventive medicine and family practice Rush Med. Coll. Contbr. articles to profl. publs. Served to lt. comdr. USPHS, 1976-79. Mem. Am. Fedn. Clin. Research, Soc. Neurosci., AMA, Med. Soc. Va. Current Work: Gene expression in nerve cells. Subspecialties: Medical education; Neurochemistry. Office: Cable Health Network 3575 Cahuenga Blvd W Suite 500 Los Angeles CA 90068

GROVE, ANDREW S., electrical engineer, engineering physicist, corporate executive; b. Budapest, Hungary, Sept. 2, 1936; married, 1958; 2 children. B.S., CCNY, 1960; Ph.D., U. Calif.-Berkeley, 1963. Mem. tech. staff Fairchild Semicondr. Research Lab., 1963-66, head sect. surface and device physics, 1966-67, asst. dir. research and devel., 1967-68; v.p., dir. ops. Intel Corp., Santa Clara, Calif., 1968-75, exec. v.p., 1975-79, pres., 1979—, chief operating officer, 1976—; lectr. dept. elec. engring. and computer sci. U. Calif.-Berkeley, 1966-72. Recipient Medal award Am. Inst. Chemists, 1960; cert. merit Franklin Inst., 1975; Townsend Harris medal CCNY, 1980. Fellow IEEE (Achievement award 1969, J. J. Ebers award 1974); mem. Nat. Acad. Engring. Subspecialties: Electronics; Integrated circuits. Office: Intel Corp 3065 Bowers Ave Santa Clara CA 95051*

GROVER, PUSHPINDER SINGH, periodontist, research dentist, army officer; b. Amritsar, Punjab, India, Feb. 16, 1946; came to U.S., 1971, naturalized, 1978; s. Mohan Singh and Mohinder (Kaur) G.; m. Surinder K. Moonga, Oct. 2, 1970; children: Amrita K., Ajeet K., Davinder S. B.Sc., Khalsa Coll., Amritsar, 1964; B.D.S., Punjab Govt. Dental Coll., Amritsar, 1969; D.M.D., Tufts U., 1977; postgrad. Med. Coll. Ga., 1985; grad. Command and Gen. Staff Coll., Ft. Leavenworth, Kans., 1985. Commd. capt. Dental Corps, U.S. Army, 1977, advanced through grades to maj., 1982, gen. dental officer, Ft. Leonard Wood, Mo., 1977-80; research dental officer Inst. Dental Research, Walter Reed Army Med. Center, Washington, 1980-82, Inst. Dental Research at Letterman Army Inst. Research, Presidio of San Francisco, Calif., 1982-84; periodontist, Ft. Gordon, Ga., 1985—. Contbr. numerous articles to profl. jours. Recipient Patient Care award Ft. Leonard Wood, 1979. Mem. ADA, Internat. Assn. Dental Research, Am. Assn. Forensic Dentistry, Am. Assn. Dental Research. Current Work: Predictability of dental emergencies by radiographs; rapid indentification of combat casualties and mass disaster victims using radiographs and computers; co-investigator various research projects (development of a portable field x-ray unit, design and development of a protective facial mask). Subspecialty: Preventive dentistry. Home: 835-A Ginger Ct Fort Gordon GA 30905 Office: US Army DENTAC Fort Gordon GA 30905

GRUBER, SAMUEL HARVEY, marine biologist, educator; b. Bklyn., May 13, 1938; s. Sidney and Claire (Mednick) G.; m. Mariko Hirata; children: Meegan Minori, Marisa Aya. B.S. in Zoology, U. Miami, 1960; M.S. in Marine Sci, Inst. of Marine and Atmospheric Sci., U. Miami, 1966, Ph.D. in Marine Scis, 1969. Research scientist Rosenstiel Sch. of Marine and Atmospheric Sci., U. Miami, 1969-73, research asst. prof., 1972-73; asst. prof. U. Miami, 1973-76, assoc. prof., 1976-84, prof., 1985—; vis. scientist Max Planck Inst., 1971-72, Al Ghardaqua Marine Lab., Hurghada, Egypt, 1984. Contbr. articles on marine biology to profl. jours. NSF grantee; Delfiner Found. grantee, 1974-75; Binational Sci. Found. (U.S.-Israel) grantee, 1982-85; Office of Naval Research grantee, 1970-85. Mem. Am. Fishery Soc., Am. Inst. Fishery Research Biologists, Assn. for Research in Vision and Opthalmology, Internat. Assn. for Aquatic Animal Medicine, Internat. Assn. for Marine Animal Trainers, Soc. Neurosci., Optical Soc. Am., Am. Elasmobranch Soc. (founder, pres.), Am. Soc. Ichthyologists and Herpetologists, Am. Soc. Zoologists, Sigma Xi. Democrat. Current Work: Behavioral ecology of apex marine predators; researcher in shark-human interactions. Subspecialties: Marine biology; Behavioral ecology. Office: RSMAS U Miami Rickenbacker Causeway Miami FL 33149

GRUBER, SHELDON, electrical engineering educator; b. N.Y.C., Sept. 9, 1930; s. Leon Edward and Bess (Shapiro) G.; m. Lucille Evelyn Pachter, Jan. 25, 1955; children—Alexandra, Rachel. B.S. Elec. Engring., Purdue U., 1952; Sc.D., MIT, 1958. Asst. prof. MIT, Cambridge, 1958-62; scientist French Atomic Energy Agy., Saclay, 1962-63; scientist Sperry Rand Research Center, Sudbury, Mass., 1963-67; prof. elec. engring. Case Western Res. U., Cleve., 1967—. Served to capt. USAF, 1957-58. Mem. Am. Phys. Soc., IEEE (sr.; chmn. Cleve. 1984). Current work: Sensory based robotic control; simulation of large scale systems in real time. Subspecialty: Computer-aided design. Home: 2430 Demington Dr Cleveland Heights OH Office: EEAP Dept Case Western Res U Cleveland OH 44106

GRUBMAN, MARVIN, biochemist; b. Bronx, N.Y., Nov. 4, 1945; s. Abe and Ruth (Weiner) G.; m. Annette, Nov. 21, 1970; children: David, Susan. B.S., CCNY, 1967; Ph.D., U. Pitts., 1972. Research assoc. Albert Einstein Coll. Medicine, 1972-76; research chemist Plum Island Animal Disease Center, 1976—; NIH fellow, 1973. Contbr. articles to profl. jours. Recipient U.S. Dept. Agr. Disting. Service award, 1982. Mem. Am. Soc. Microbiology, Am. Soc. Virology, AAAS (Newcomb-Cleveland award), N.Y. Acad. Sci., Picornavirus Study Group. Current Work: Molecular biology of foot and mouth disease virus, bluetongue virus, study replication of virus and viral specific RNA and proteins. Subspecialties: Virology (biology); Molecular biology. Office: PO Box 848 Greenport NY 11944

GRUHN, JOHN GEORGE, pathologist, educator; b. Bklyn., Sept. 8, 1918; s. John and Annamarie (Brecht) G.; m. Helen Mandelsberg, Apr. 22, 1943; children—George, William, Susan, Paul. B.S., Manhattan Coll., 1941; M.D., L.I. Coll. Medicine, 1944. Intern Bklyn. Hosp., 1944-45; resident in medicine L.I. Coll. Medicine, Bklyn., 1947-49; resident in pathology Montefiore Hosp., N.Y.C., 1949-54; practice medicine specializing in pathology; dir. labs. St. Joseph Hosp., Pitts., 1955-60; asst. prof. U. Pitts., 1958-60; pathologist Mount Sinai Hosp., Chgo., 1960-64; lab. dir. Skokie Valley Hosp., Ill., 1964-81; assoc. prof. Rush Med. Coll., Chgo., 1980-81, Northwestern U. Hosp., Chgo., 1981—. Contbr. articles to profl. jours. Served to capt. M.C., USAAF, 1946-47. Fellow Am. Soc. Clin. Pathologists, Am. Assn. Pathologists, Coll. Am. Pathologists, Internat. Acad. Pathology; mem. AMA. Unitarian. Current work: Current interest and publications in history of pathology. Subspecialties: Pathology (medicine); Laser medicine. Home: 9238 Normandy Ave Morton Grove IL 60053 Office: Northwestern Meml Hosp Dept Pathology 303 E Superior St Chicago IL 60611

GRUN, JACOB, physicist; b. Krakow, Poland, Oct. 21, 1951; came to U.S., 1962, naturalized, 1968; s. Benjamin and Ann (Gleitman) G.; m. Yudith Biedny, Aug. 29, 1974; children—Ayelet, Yael, Tamar. B.S. summa cum laude, Poly. Inst. Bklyn., 1974; M.S., U. Md., 1977, Ph.D., 1981. Research physicist Mission Research Corp., Alexandria, Va., 1980-83, Naval Research Lab., Washington, 1983—. Contbr. articles to profl. jours. Mem. Am. Phys. Soc. Current work: Investigation of laser driven inertial confinement fusion; hydrodynamics of imploding systems, high altitute phenomena. Subspecialties: Laser fusion; Plasma physics. Office: Naval Research Lab Washington DC 20375

GRUNDER, HERMANN AUGUST, physicist. Dept. dir. gen. sci. Lawrence Berkeley Lab., Calif.; dir. Continuous Electron Beam Accelerator Facility (CEBAF) project, Newport News, Va., 1985—. Subspecialty: Accelerator physics. Office: Lawrence Berkeley Lab 1 Cyclotron Blvd Berkeley CA 94720

GRUNES, DAVID LEON, research soil scientist, educator, editor; b. Paterson, N.J., June 29, 1921; s. Jacob and Gussie (Griggs) G.; m. Willa Freeman Grunes, June 26, 1949; children: Lee Alan, Mitchell Ray, Rima Louise. B.S., Rutgers U., 1944; Ph.D., U. Calif., 1951. With U.S. Dept. Agr., 1950—, research soil scientist, Ithaca, N.Y., 1964—; assoc. prof. agronomy dept. Cornell U., 1967-76, prof., 1976—; cons. editor soils, agr. McGraw-Hill Ency., Sci. and Tech., 1965—. Contbr. chpts. to books and articles to profl. jours. Served with U.S. Army, 1944-45. Recipient U.S. Dept. Agr. award for research, 1959. Fellow AAAS, Am. Inst. Chemists, Am. Soc. Agronomy, Soil Sci. Soc. Am.; mem. Internat. Soc. Soil Sci., Western Soc. Soil Sci., Council for Agri. Sci. and Tech., Sigma Xi. Current Work: Agronomic aspects of crop quality for humans and animals; research in plant nutrition; serve on committees of assns. Subspecialties: Soil science; Plant growth. Office: US Plant Soil and Nutrition Lab Tower Rd Ithaca NY 14853

GUARINO, ANTHONY MICHAEL, toxicologist; b. Framingham, Mass., Dec. 11, 1934; s. Alfred Vincent and Nellie Lucy G.; m. Aida Iris Guarino, Nov. 11, 1957; children. B.S., Boston Coll., 1956; M.S., U. R.I., 1963, Ph.D., 1966. Research assoc. Nat. Heart Inst., NIH, 1966-68; research pharmacologist Lab. Chem. Pharmacology, Nat. Cancer Inst., 1968-73, chief toxicology lab., 1973-80; regulatory pharmacologist/toxicologist Office New Drugs, Nat. Ctr. Drugs and Biologics, FDA, Rockville, Md., 1980—; mem. faculty, chmn. dept. pharmacology and toxicology NIH Grad. Sch., Bethesda, 1970—. Contbr. 90 articles to profl. jours. Served to lt. (j.g.) USN, 1957-60; scientist officer USPHS, 1966—; capt. USPHS, 1975—. Mem. Am. Soc. Pharmacology and Explt. Therapeutics, Soc. Toxicology, Am. Chem. Soc. Current Work: Drug (xenobiotic) transport, drug (xenobiotic) Toxicology, biliary transport, drug metabolism, marine pharmacology and toxicology, quantitative toxicology, regulatory toxicology, biochemical toxicology. Subspecialties: Toxicology (medicine); Pharmacology. Home: 5903 Melvern Dr Bethesda MD 20817 Office: FDA PO Box 158 Dauphin Island AL 36528

GUASTAFERRO, ANGELO, aerospace company executive; b. Hoboken, N.J., June 4, 1932; s. Carlo and Rafaela Nancy (Gioffi) G.; m. Eleanor Lago, Sept. 12, 1954; children: Carl, Mark, John Brian. B.S. in Mech. Engring, N.J. Inst. Tech., 1954; M.B.A., Fla. State U., 1963; Advanced Mgmt. Program, Harvard U., 1984. With NASA, 1963-85; dep. project mgr. NASA (Viking Project), 1974-76, dir. planetary programs, Washington, 1979-81; dep. dir. Ames Research Center, Moffett Field, Calif., 1981-85; program dir. Lockheed Missiles and Space, Sunnyvale, Calif., 1985—; v.p., bd. dirs. Langley Fed. Credit Union, 1977-79; cons. in field. Served with USAF, 1955-58. Recipient Langley Spl. Achievement award NASA, 1974, 77, 78, Outstanding Leadership medal, 1977, Superior Performance award, 1980, Exceptional Service medal, 1981, Presdl. Meritorious rank, 1982. Fellow AAAS, AIAA (Space Systems medal 1982); mem. Planetary Soc., Mars First Landing Soc. (pres. 1978-79). Roman Catholic. Clubs: Toastmasters (Eglin AFB, Fla.) (past pres.); K.C. (grand knight). Subspecialties: Aerospace engineering and technology; Systems engineering. Office: Lockheed Missiles & Space Space Sta Program Bldg 580 Sunnyvale CA 94086

GUBERMAN, STEVEN LAWRENCE, physicist; b. Bklyn., Dec. 11, 1945; s. Irving and Rosalind (Levine) G. B.A., SUNY, Binghamton, 1967; Ph.D., Calif. Inst. Tech., 1972. Research fellow, lectr. Harvard Coll. Obs., Cambridge, Mass., 1973-78; Nat. Acad. Scis., NRC sr. resident research assoc. Air Force Geophysics Lab., Hanscom AFB, Mass., 1978-79; prin. scientist Phys. Scis., Inc., Woburn, Mass., 1979-80; vis. fgn. scientist fellow Max-Planck Inst. für Physik und Astrophysik, Munich, W.Ger., 1980; sr. research physicist Boston Coll., Newton, Mass., 1980-83, pres., physicist Inst. Sci. Research, Stoneham, Mass.; physicist Harvard-Smithsonian Ctr. for Astrophysics, 1983—. Contbr. articles to profl. jours. NASA grantee, 1981—; Air Force Geophysics Lab. grantee, 1980—. Mem. Am. Phys. Soc., Am. Chem. Soc., Am. Geophys. Union, Sigma Xi. Current Work: The development of new techniques in quantum chemical physics with application to important processes in the upper atmosphere, interstellar space, lasers. Subspecialty: Theoretical chemistry. Home: 22 Bonad Rd Winchester MA 01890 Office: Inst Sci Research 271 Main St Suite 302 Stoneham MA 02180 Also: Harvard Smithsonian Ctr for Astrophysics 60 Garden Ct Cambridge MA 02138

GUDEHUS, DONALD HENRY, astrophysicist; b. Jersey City, Sept. 13, 1939; s. Herman Andrew and Katherine Pauline (Hirner) G.; m. Linda Hope Gudehus, Sept. 19, 1968. B.S. in Physics, MIT, 1961; A.M. in Physics, Columbia U., 1963; Ph.D. in Astronomy (NASA predoctoral trainee), UCLA, 1971. Engr., scientist McDonnell Douglas, El Segundo, Calif., 1964-67; postdoctoral scholar astronomy UCLA, 1971-75; asst. prof. physics Los Angeles City Coll., 1974-81; asst. research scientist physics U. Mich., Ann Arbor, 1981—. Contbr. articles to profl. jours. Recipient grant in aid in research Sigma Xi, 1974. Mem. Am. Astron. Soc., Lorquin Entomol. Soc. Current Work: Observational cosmology with a CCD camera, clusters of galaxies, redshift, CCD, photometry, spectroscopy, extragalactic astronomy, instrumentation. Subspecialties: Cosmology; Optical astronomy. Office: Randall Lab U Mich Ann Arbor MI 48109

GUENTHER, ARTHUR HENRY, physicist; b. Hoboken, N.J., Apr. 20, 1931; s. George G. and Florence B. (Roberts) G.; m. Joan Eileen Roth, Nov. 21, 1954; children—Tracie Katherine, Wendy Katherine. B.S., Rutgers U., 1953; Ph.D., Pa. State U., 1957; D.Sc., U. Albuquerque, 1973. Supervisory physicist Air Force Weapons Lab., Kirtland AFB, N.Mex., 1959-62, supervisory research physicist, 1962-65, sci. advisor, chief simulation group, 1965-66, chief scientist support group, 1966-69, chief tech. div., 1969-70, sci. dir., tech. div., 1970-74, chief scientist, 1974—; bd. dirs., cons. Ctr. Occupational Research and Devel., 1970—; mem. N.Mex. Sci. and Tech. Adv. Com.; adj. prof. physics Air Force Inst. Tech., Wright-Patterson AFB, Ohio, 1967—; adj. prof. elec. engring., physics Tex. Tech. U., 1971; adj. prof. chemistry U. N.Mex., 1978—. Contbr. articles to profl. jours. Served with USAF, 1957-59. Recipient Disting. Scientist of Yr. award N.Mex. Acad. Sci., 1977; Harry Diamond award IEEE, 1971; Disting. Pub. Service award State of N.Mex., 1981; Arthur L. Schawlow medal, Laser Inst. Am., 1983. Fellow Optical Soc. Am., IEEE; mem. Am. Inst. Physics, Am. Chem. Soc., N.Mex. Acad. Scis., ASTM, Sigma Xi, Phi Lambda Upsilon. Patentee in field. Home: 6304 Rogers Ave NE Albuquerque NM 87110 Office: Air Force Weapons Lab Kirtland AFB NM 87117

GUENTHER, BOB DEAN, physicist; b. St. Louis, Feb. 13, 1939; s. George S. and Elaine M. (Kelly) G.; m. Sharon L. Stauder, Aug. 6, 1961; children—Valerie Kelly, Brett Dean. B.S., Baylor U., 1960; M.S., U. Mo., 1963, Ph.D., 1968. Physicist, Army Missile Command, Huntsville, Ala., 1965-72; army sr. rep. Air Force Weapons Lab., Albuquerque, 1972-75; physicist Army Missile Command, Huntsville, 1975-79, Army Research Office, Research Triangle Park, N.C., 1979—; cons. in field. Patentee optics related inventions; guest editor Jour. Quantum Electronics, 1982; contbr. articles to profl. jours. Referee U.S. Soccer Fedn., N.C. Mem. Am. Phys. Soc., Optical Soc. Am. (com. chmn. 1983), Soc. Photo Indsl. Engrs. Current work: Optics, image processing and submillimeter wave technology. Subspecialties: Optical signal processing; Atomic and molecular physics. Home: 1002 Queensferry Rd Cary NC 27511 Office: US Army Research Office PO Box 12211 Research Triangle Park Cary NC 27511

GUERIGUIAN, JOHN LEO, government official, consultant, researcher; b. Alexandria, Egypt, Sept. 20, 1935; s. Levon Artin and Valentine (Mamigonian) G.; m. Ida Fai-Fong; children: Leo Fong, Vincent John, Florence Marie. B.S., U. Paris, 1958, M.S. in Chemistry, 1964, M.D., 1965. Research fellow Harvard U. Med. Sch., 1965-67; attendant staff Peter Bent Brigham Hosp., Boston, 1965-67; research scientist dept. biochemistry U. Paris Med. Sch., 1967-69; asst. prof. U. N.C., Chapel Hill, 1969-73; assoc. prof. U. Minn. Sch. Medicine, Duluth, 1973-78, adj. asso. prof., 1978—; supervisory med. officer Nat. Center for Drugs and Biologics, FDA, Rockville, Md., 1978—, cons. in field. Contbr. articles to profl. jours., also several editorships. Co-founder, bd. dirs. Mamigonian Found., Rockville. Mem. Endocrine Soc., Am. Soc. Clin. Pharmacology and Therapeutics, Am. Soc. Pharmacology and Exptl. Therapeutics. Mem. Armenian Apostolic Ch. Current Work: Reproductive endocrinology; modern methods in communication; heuristics of drug development and regulation. Subspecialties: Pharmacology; Endocrinology. Home: 14513 Woodcrest Dr Rockville MD 20853 Office: 5600 Fishers Ln Rockville MD 20857

GUETTER, HARRY HENDRIK, astronomer; b. Andijk, Netherlands, Feb. 1, 1935; s. John and Neeltje (Cupido) G.; m. Joan Adriana Boodt, July 5, 1963; children: Mark, Adrian, Stephanie. B.Sc. with honors in Physics and Math, Queen's U., Can., 1961; M.A. in Astronomy, U. Toronto, Ont., Can., 1963. Research asso. David Dunlop Obs., Richmond Hill., Ont., 1963-64; astronomer U.S. Naval Obs., Flagstaff (Ariz.) Sta., 1964—. Contbr. articles to profl. jours. Mem. Am. Astron. Soc., Internat. Astron. Union, Astron. Soc. Pacific, Sigma Xi. Democrat. Baptist. Current Work: Determination of trigonometric stellar parallexes; spectroscopy, polarimetry, near-infrared and optical photometry of young stars in galactic clusters. Subspecialties: Optical astronomy; Infrared astronomy. Home: 526 W Havasupai Rd Flagstaff AZ 86001 Office: PO Box 1149 Flagstaff AZ 86002

GUILBAULT, GEORGE GERALD, chemistry educator, researcher; b. New Orleans, Dec. 22, 1936; s. George Robert and Valerie (Kothe) G.; m. Susan Glorgh-Bachman, Mar. 28, 1983; children: George G., Ann Marie, Eve Michelle, Stephen C. B.S., Loyola U., New Orleans, 1958; M.S., Princeton U., 1960, Ph.D., 1961. Sr. research scientist U.S. Army, Edgewood Arsenal, Md., 1961-66; prof. chemistry U. New Orleans, 1966—; vis. prof. U. Denmark, Copenhagen, 1973-75, U. Lund, 1982-83, U. Cl. Bernard, Lyon, France, 1982-83; pres. Universal Sensors, New Orleans, 1981—. Author: Instrumental Analysis, 1969, Modern Quantitative Analysis: Experiments for Non-Majors, 1970, Practical Fluorescence, 1973, Handbook of Enzymatic Methods of Analysis, 1976, Handbook of Immobilized Enzymes, 1983; others; editor: Jour. Analytical Letters, 1967—; contbr. chpts. to books and articles to profl. jours. Served to 1st lt. U.S. Army, 1961-62. Mem. Am. Chem. Soc.; Internat. Union Pure and Applied Chemistry (chmn. nomenclature com.), Nat. Clin. Lab. Standards (chmn.), N.Y. Acad. Sci., NRC. Roman Catholic. Current Work: Research in analytical biochemistry/clinical chemistry and environmental analysis; immobilized enzymes, immunochemistry, fluoresence, piezoelectric crystals, immunoanalysis, microbiology, enzyme electrodes. Subspecialties: Analytical chemistry; Clinical chemistry. Home: 2300 Edenbron St Apt 376 Metairie LA 70001 Office: Chemistry Dept U New Orleans Lakefront Campus New Orleans LA 70148

GUILL, FREDERICK CHARLES, mechanical engineer; b. Berkeley, Calif., Mar. 13, 1938; s. Samuel Gardner and Betty Jane (Goss) G. Student U.S. Coast Guard Acad., 1955-59; B.S. in Mech. Engring., U. Wash., 1961; M.Engring. Adminstrn., George Washington U., 1966; postgrad. Cath. U. Am., 1966-68, Nat. Def. U., 1984—. Mech. engr. Bur. Naval Weapons, Washington, 1963-66, Naval Air Systems Command, Washington, 1966-74, sr. engr., 1974—. Mem. ASME, Am. Soc. Metals, Human Factors Soc., Aerospace Med. Assn. Republican. Engineering/systems acquisition program management. Current work: Established specifications for, and managed design, development, test and acquisition of U.S. Navy aircrew escape systems; investigating Navy in-service usage experience (severe injury causation) with escape and life support systems. Subspecialty: Mechanical engineering. Home: 380 Severnview Dr Crownsville MD 21032 Office: Crew Systems Div Naval Air Systems Command Washington DC 20361

GUILLAUME, GERMAINE GABRIELLE CORNELISSEN, chronobiologist, statistician, researcher; b. Schaerbeek, Belgium, Nov. 22, 1949; came to U.S., 1976; d. Alphonse and Helene A (Minne) Cornelissen; m. Francis M. Guillaume, Nov. 22, 1975. M. Physics, U. Brussels, 1971, M. Ed., 1971, Ph.D. in Physics, 1976. Tchr. sci. Lycee E. Max, Brussels, 1971-73; Irsia fellow U. Brussels, 1974-76; research fellow U. Minn.-Mpls., 1976-82, research assoc., 1982—; chairperson/co-organizer various profl. meetings, 1975—. Contbr. articles to profl. jours.; referee various profl. jours., 1978—. NIH grantee, 1981—. Mem. Groupe D'Etude Des Rythmes Biologiques, Internat. Soc. Chronobiology, Societe Belge de Physique, Am. Phys. Soc., Soc. Indsl. and Applied Math., AAAS, Biometric Soc., Am. Statis. Assn. Current Work: Implementation and application of methods of time series analysis to biologic and medical data, with emphasis on treatment and prevention of cancer and high blood pressure. Subspecialties: Chronobiology; Statistics. Home: 2008 Brewster Apt 205 Saint Paul MN 55108 Office: U Minn 420 Washington Ave SE Minneapolis MN 55455

GUILLEMIN, ROGER, physiologist; b. Dijon, France, Jan. 11, 1924; came to U.S., 1953, naturalized, 1963; s. Raymond and Blanche (Rigollot) G.; m. Lucienne Jeanne Billard, Mar. 22, 1951; children—Chantal, François, Claire, Helene, Elizabeth, Cecile. B.A., U. Dijon, 1941, B.Sc., 1942; M.D., Faculty of Medicine, Lyons, France, 1949; Ph.D., U. Montreal, 1953; Ph.D. (hon.), U. Rochester, 1976, U. Chgo., 1977, Baylor Coll. Medicine, 1978, U. Ulm, Germany, 1978, U. Dijon, France, 1978, Free U. Brussels, 1979, U. Montreal, 1979. Intern, resident univs. hosps., Dijon, 1949-51; asso. dir., asst. prof. Inst. Exptl. Medicine and Surgery, U. Montreal, 1951-53; asso. dir. dept. exptl. endocrinology Coll. de France, Paris, 1960-63; prof. physiology Baylor Coll. Medicine, 1953—; adj. prof. medicine U. Calif. at San Diego, 1970—; resident fellow Salk Inst., 1970—. Decorated Legion of Honor France, 1974; recipient Gairdner Internat. award, 1974; U.S. Nat. Medal of Sci., 1977; co-recipient Nobel prize for medicine, 1977; recipient Lasker Found. award, 1975; Dickson prize in medicine, 1976; Passano award med. sci., 1976; Schmitt medal neurosci., 1977; Barren gold medal, 1979; Dale medal Soc. for Endocrinology U.K., 1980. Fellow AAAS; Mem. Am. Physiol. Soc., Endocrine Soc. (council), Soc. Exptl. Biology and Medicine, A.A.A.S., Internat. Brain Research Orgn., Internat. Soc. Research Biology Reprodn., Soc. Neuro-scis., Nat. Acad. Scis., Am. Acad. Arts and Scis., Club of Rome. Subspecialty: Neuroendocrinology. Office: Salk Inst Box 85800 San Diego CA 92138

GUILLEMIN, VICTOR W., mathematician. Prof. dept. math. MIT, Cambridge. . Office: MIT Dept Math Cambridge MA 02139

GUIST, GUYER GORDON, JR., research chemist; b. Tarentum, Pa., Apr. 19, 1950; s. Guyer Gordon and Marjorie Kathryn (Cole) G.; m. Robin Carol Brown, Jan. 15, 1972. B.S., Bethany Coll., 1972; M.A., U. South Fla., 1974. Biologist Marine Colloids Inc., Rockland, Maine, 1974-79; chemist Marine Colloids div. FMC Corp., Rockland, 1979—. Vice pres. Camden First Aid Assn., Maine, 1983. Mem. Phycol. Soc. Am., Am. Chem. Soc. Current work: Seaweed mariculture, process and characterization of seaweed hydrocolloids. Subspecialty: Marine biology. Home: 7 Pleasant Ridge Dr Camden ME 04843 Office: Marine Colloids Div FMC Corp Crocketts Point PO Box 308 Rockland ME 04841

GUJRATI, BITTHAL DAS, mechanical engineer; b. Varanasi, India, June 15, 1942; came to U.S., 1967, naturalized, 1982; s. Baldeo and Krishna (Devi) Das.; m. Meena Bhatia, July 14, 1975; children: Manu, Kusha. B.Sc. with honors, Banaras Hindu U., India, 1960; B.Sc. in Mech. Engring, 1964; M.S., Pa. State U., 1970; Ph.D., U. Mich., 1974. Scientist Indian Inst. Petroleum, Dehradun, 1964-67; research asst. U. Mich., Ann Arbor, 1969-74; research engr. Amoco Chems. Corp., Naperville, Ill., 1974-79, staff research engr., 1979; research scientist Internat. Harvester Co. Sci. and Tech. Lab., Hinsdale, Ill., 1979-81, mgr. tech. planning, 1981-82; project mgr. Wilson Sporting Goods Co., River Grove, Ill., 1982-84; dir. engring. and tech. Trek Bicycle Corp., Waterloo, Wis., 1985—; mem. tech adv. com. Metal Properties Council, Inc. Contbr. articles to profl. jours. Recipient Prince of Wales gold medal Banaras Hindu U., 1964. Mem. ASME, Soc. for Advancement of Materials and Process Engring., Soc. Plastics Engrs., ASTM (student award 1973). Current Work: Advanced composite material including composites based bicycle frame development; composite material processing facility development; engineering and research management; material technology assessment; composite and plastic products/processes; friction/wear/lubrication including elastohydrodynamics. Subspecialties: Composite materials; Materials processing. Office: 801 W Madison St Waterloo WI 53594

GULARI, ERDOGAN, chem. engr., educator; b. Erzincan, Turkey, Nov. 6, 1946; s. Fahri Hasan and Sahsenem (Buklu) G.; m. Esin Ayse, June 29, 1969; 1 child, Bora. B.S., Roberts Coll., Istanbul, Turkey, 1969; Ph.D. in Chem. Engring, Calif. Inst. Tech., 1973. Postdoctoral assoc. SUNY, Stony Brook, 1973-74; plant mgr. Komili, Inc., Turkey, 1974-76; postdoctoral assoc. SUNY, Stony Brook, 1974-78; prof. chem. engring. U. Mich., Ann Arbor, 1985—. Contbr. articles to profl. jours. Mem. Am. Chem. Soc., Am. Inst. Chem. Engrs., Catalysis Soc. N.Am. Moslem. Current Work: Liquid state physics, catalysis, colloidal phenomena; catalysis by clusters, tertiary oil recovery, micellization and microemulsions, infrared, laser and x-ray spectroscopy. Subspecialties: Chemical engineering; Physical chemistry. Office: U Mich 3168B Dow Bldg Ann Arbor MI 48109

GULATI, SURESH THAKURDAS, glass scientist, researcher; b. Kot Adu, Punjab, West Pakistan, Nov. 13, 1936; came to U.S. 1958, naturalized 1975; s. Thakur Das and Vishan Devi (Kathuria) G.; m. Teresa Antoinette Davids, Aug. 19, 1961; children—Raj, Prem, Sonya. B.S. in Mech. Engring., U. Bombay, India, 1957; M.S. in Mech. Engring., Ill. Inst. Tech., 1959; Ph.D., U. Colo., 1966. Registered profl. engr. N.Y. Stress analyst Continental Can Co., Chgo., 1959-62; instr. U. Colo., Boulder, 1966-67; adj. prof. Cornell U., Ithaca, N.Y., 1968-70; research fellow Corning Glass Works, N.Y., 1967—. Contbr. numerous articles to tech. jours. Patentee in field. Pres. Internatl. Club Finger Lakes, Corning, N.Y., 1975, Am. Field Service, Elmira, N.Y., 1971. Mem. ASME, Am. Ceramic Soc., Sigma Xi. Democrat. Hindu. Lodge: Rotary. Current work: Fracture mechanics, brittle material behavior, fiber optics, composite materials, porous honeycomb materials, strong glasses. Subspecialties: Theoretical and applied mechanics; Ceramics. Home: 1001 West Water St Elmira NY 14905 Office: Corning Glass Works Sullivan Park RB4 Corning NY 14831

GULL, THEODORE RAYMOND, astrophysicist; b. Hot Springs, S.D., Aug. 17, 1944; s. Albert Henry and Virginia Irene (Sieger) G.; m. Hazel Joy Constantine, July 1, 1967; children: Michael, Matthew. B.S. in Physics, MIT, 1966; Ph.D., Cornell U., 1971; M.B.A., Loyola Coll., Balt., 1985. Research asst. Yerkes Obs., U. Chgo., Williams Bay, Wis., 1971-72; asst. astronomer Kitt Peak Nat. Obs., Tucson, 1972-75; engr. prin. Lockheed Elec. Corp., Houston, 1975-77; astrophysicist Goddard Space Flight Ctr., Greenbelt, Md., 1977—, assoc. chief Lab. for Astronomy and Solar Physics, 1985—; cons. in field; study scientist Space Lab Wide Angle Telescope; mission scientist Astro Shuttle Missions. Contbr. articles to profl. jours. Mem. Am. Astron. Soc., Astron. Soc. Pacific, Internat. Astron. Union, AIAA, Sigma Xi, Alpha Sigma Nu. Current Work: Interstellar medium, star formation and death, structure of interstellar medium; design/development of space/ground-based astronomical instruments. Subspecialties: Optical astronomy; Ultraviolet high energy astrophysics. Office: Goddard Space Flight Center Code 683 Greenbelt MD 20771

GUM, ERNEST KEMP, JR., biochemist; b. Weston, W.Va., Feb. 1, 1949; s. Ernest Kemp and Ethel Marie (Garrett) G.; m. Mary Lou Bishop, June 1, 1968. B.S. in Chemistry, W.Va. U., 1970; Ph.D. in Biochemistry, Va. Poly. Inst. and State U., 1974. Research assoc., dept. biochemistry Va. Poly. Inst. and State U., Blacksburg, 1974-75, asst. prof., 1975-77; research scientist Union Carbide Corp., Tarrytown, N.Y., 1977-79; project specialist Gen. Foods Corp., Tarrytown, 1979-81, group leader, 1981—. Mem. Am. Chem. Soc., AAAS, Am. Soc. Metals, Sigma Xi. Subspecialty: Enzyme technology. Office: Gen Food Tech Ctr 555 S Broadway Tarrytown NY 10591

GUMMEL, HERMANN KARL, physicist; b. Hannover, Germany, July 6, 1923; came to U.S. 1953; s. Johannes and Charlotte (Elgeti) G.; m. Erika Ilse Reich, Aug. 31, 1952; children—Monica Ruth, Margaret Grace. Diploma Phys. Philipps U., Germany, 1952; M.S., Syracuse U., 1952, Ph.D., 1957. Mem. tech. staff AT&T Bell Labs., Murray Hill, N.J., 1957-62, supr., 1962-67, dept. head, 1967-82, asst. dir., 1982-84, dir., 1984—. Contbr. articles to profl. jours. Patentee in field. Fellow IEEE (Guillemin-Cauer Prize Paper award 1977, David Sarnoff award 1983); mem. Am. Phys. Soc., Nat. Acad. Engring., Sigma Xi. Subspecialty: Computer-aided design. Office: AT&T Bell Labs 600 Mountain View Ave Murray Hill NJ 07974

GUMPORT, RICHARD I., biochemistry educator; b. Pocatello, Idaho, June 23, 1937; s. Isaac and Helen Roberta (Burkey) G.; m. Roberta Helene Kugell, Sept. 18, 1960; children: Susan Rachel, William Isaac. B.S., U. Chgo., 1960, Ph.D., 1968; postgrad., Stanford U., 1968-71. Asst. prof. biochemistry U. Ill., Urbana, 1971-77; vis. scholar biochemistry Harvard U., 1979-80; assoc. prof. biochemistry U. Ill., Urbana, 1978—; assoc. Ctr. Advanced Study, U. Ill., 1985-86. Contbr. articles to profl. jours. Recipient Career Devel. awards USPHS, 1972-77; Guggenheim fellow, 1979-80; NIH research grantee, 1972—. Mem. Am. Soc. Biol. Chemists, Am. Chem. Soc., Am. Soc. Microbiology, AAAS. Current Work: Chemical and enzymatic synthesis of defined sequences of DNA, protein-nucleic acid interactions, control of gene expression by attenuation; mechanism of site specific recombination. Subspecialties: Biochemistry (biology); Genetics and genetic engineering (biology). Home: 2009 S Anderson St Urbana IL 61801 Office: U Ill 506 S Mathews St Urbana IL 61801

GUNDERSEN, MARTIN ADOLPH, physicist, educator; b. Glenwood, Minn., May 19, 1940; s. Gilbert Theodore and Frances (Iverson) G.; m. Roberta McShirley, Dec. 20, 1963; children: Gilbert, Martin. B.A., U. Calif., Berkeley, 1965; Ph.D. in Physics, U. So. Calif., 1973. Assoc. prof. elec. engring. and physics Tex. Tech. U., 1973-77, assoc. prof., 1977-80; assoc. prof. elec. engring. and physics U. So. Calif., Los Angeles, 1980—. Contbr. numerous articles in field of quantum electronics, pulsed power and laser physics to profl. jours. Current Work: Infrared and ultraviolet lasers, semiconductor physics, spectroscopy, pulsed power physics. Subspecialties: Quantum electronics; Optical engineering. Office: Dept Elec Engring and Physics SSC 420 U So Calif Los Angeles CA 90089

GUNN, CHARLES ROWLEY, aerospace engineer; b. Washington, Apr. 23, 1934; s. Ross and Gladys Jeanette (Rowley) G.; m. Meredith Ann Miller, Jan. 26, 1957; children—Kimberly Ann, Patricia Leigh, Meredith Ellen, Barbara Jean, Charles Miller. B.S. in Aero. Engring., U. Mich., 1956, M.S. in Aero. Engring., 1957. Tech. dir. Delta launch vehicle NASA Greenbelt Space Flight Ctr., Md., 1962-75, project mgr., 1975-77, project mgr. Landsat, 1977-79, dir. shuttle ops., NASA Hdqrs., Washington, 1979—. Served to 1st lt., U.S. Army, 1957. Recipient Exceptional Service medal NASA, 1968, Disting. Service medal, NASA, 1972. Mem. AIAA, Soc. Automotive Engrs. Republican. Club: Nat. Space (Washington). Current work: Space launch vehicle operations. Subspecialty: Aerospace engineering and technology. Office: NASA Hdqrs 600 Independence Ave SE Washington DC 20546

GUNN, JAMES EDWARD, astrophysicist; b. Livingstone, Tex., Oct. 21, 1938; s. James Edward and Rhea (Mason) G. B.S., Rice U., Houston, 1961; Ph.D., Calif. Inst. Tech., 1966. Sr. space scientist Jet Propulsion Lab., 1966-69; asst. prof. Princeton (N.J.) U., 1969-70, Eugene Higgins prof. astrophysics, 1980—; asst. prof., then prof. astrophysics Calif. Inst. Tech., 1970-80; dep. prin. investigator space telescope wide field camera NASA, 1977—. Served with C.E. USAR, 1967. Sloan Found. fellow, 1972-76; MacArthur Found. grantee, 1983. Mem. Am. Astron. Soc., Astron. Survey Com., Nat. Acad. Scis. Democrat. Subspecialty: Cosmology. Office: Peyton Hall Princeton U Princeton NJ 08544

GUNNER, HAIM BERNARD, environmental biologist; b. Ottawa, Ont., Can., June 18, 1924; came to U.S., 1963; s. Louis and Rachel (Dector) G.; m. Jeannette Benet, Nov. 8, 1951; children—Naomi, Raphael. B.S.A., U. Toronto, 1946; M.Sc., U. Man., Can., 1948; Ph.D., Cornell U., 1962. Field crops supr. Sasa Coop. Farm, Israel, 1949-51, farm mgr., 1951-53, soil conservation supr., 1953-55; asst. coordinator agrl. research Research Council Israel, Jerusalem, 1955-56, coordinator, 1956-57; research asst. soil microbiology Cornell U., Ithaca, N.Y., 1957-61; research officer Microbiology Research Inst., Ont., Can., 1961-63; asst. prof., then assoc. prof. U. Mass., Amherst, 1963-71, prof. environ. microbiology, acting head dept. environ. sci., 1971-72, co-dir. Tech. Guidance Ctr. Indsl. Environ. Control, 1968; assoc. dir. research Ctr. for Internat. Agrl. Studies, 1969-72; vis. prof. U. Tel Aviv, Israel, 1971—; sec. Northeast Regional Research Com. Nitrogen Transformation Soil and Water, 1969, chmn. soil biol. sect., 1969, 72-76, 76-80. Grantee NSF, 1964-66, USPHS, 1966-69, Dept. Interior Office Water Resources Research, 1967-70, U.S. Army C.E., 1980—, Canusa, 1982—. Mem. Am. Soc. Agronomy, Am. Soc. Micro-biology, AAAS, Can. Soc. Microbiologists, Internat. Soc. Soil Sci., Internat. Orgn. for Biol. Control of Noxious Animals, Sigma Xi. Current work: Ecosystem stress induced by chemical pesticides, biological control of insect pests, plant pathogens and weed plants. Subspecialties: Integrated pest management; Enzyme technology. Office: Dept Environ Scis U Mass Marshall Hall Amherst MA 01003

GUNTER, WILLIAM DAYLE, JR., physicist; b. Mitchell, S.D., Jan. 10, 1932; s. William Dayle and Lamerta Berneice (Hockensmith) G.; m. Shirley Marie Teshera, Oct. 24, 1955; children—Maria Jo, Robert Paul. B.S. in Physics with distinction, Stanford U., 1957, M.S., 1959. Physicist Ames Research Ctr. NASA, Moffett Field, Calif., 1960-81, asst. br. chief electronic optical engring., 1981—. Patentee in field. Contbr. articles to profl. jours. Served with U.S. Army, 1953-55. Recipient Westinghouse Sci. Talent Search award, 1950; various awards NASA; Stanford U. scholar, 1950. Mem. Optical Soc. Am., IEEE (sr.), Am. Phys. Soc., Soc. Photo-Optical Instrumentation Engrs., Planetary Soc., Nat. Space Inst. Current work: Optical system design for laser velocimetry; space probe instrumentation and other purposes; laser safety; optical consulting. Office: NASA Ames Research Ctr Moffett Field CA 94035

GUPTA, AJAYA KUMAR, civil engineering educator, researcher, consultant; b. Allahabad India, Sept. 27, 1944; came to U.S., 1968, naturalized, 1977; s. Chhailbihari Lal and Taravali (Jain) G.; m. Purnima Rani Mital, Feb. 28, 1968; children—Aparna Mini, Suvarna. B.S., U. Roorkee, India, 1966, M.S., 1968; Ph.D., U. Ill., 1971. Supervising engr. Sargent & Lundy, Chgo., 1971-76; sr. research engr. ITT Research Inst., Chgo., 1976-78; assoc. prof. Ill. Inst. Tech., Chgo., 1979-80; assoc. prof. civil engring. N.C. State U., Raleigh, 1980-83, prof. civil engring., 1983—; dir. Southeastern U.S. Seismic Safety Consortium, Charleston, S.C., 1981—, Tech. Transfer and Devel. Council, 1982—; cons. industry and research orgns. Editor: Seismic Performance of Low-Rise Buildings, 1981; contbr. articles to profl. jours. NSF grantee, 1979—. Mem. ASCE (Walter L. Huber prize 1982), Am. Concrete Inst. (chmn. shell reinforcement subcom. 1972—), Earthquake Engring. Research Inst., ASME, Internat. Assoc. Structural Mechanics in Reactor Tech., U. Ill. Alumni Assoc., U. Roorkee Alumni Assoc., Hindu Soc. N.C., Phi Kappa Phi. Hindu. Current work: Reinforced concrete structures, shells, hyperbolic cooling towers; earthquake engineering, multicomponent design, modal combination, secondary systems, low-rise buildings; finite element analysis, nonlinear and dynamic analysis, nuclear power plant structural analysis and design. Subspecialties: Civil engineering; Structural engineering. Office: Dept Civil Engring NC State U Box 7908 Raleigh NC 27695 7908

GUPTA, BHUPENDER SINGH, textile physics educator, administrator, researcher; b. Delhi, India, Mar. 29, 1937; came to U.S. 1963; s. Om Parkash and Lila Vati (Arya) G.; m. Vasudha Gupta, Jan. 31, 1967; children—Sumedha, Apurve, Anoopum. B.Sc. in Textiles, Punjab U., Bhiwani, India, 1958; Ph.D., U. Manchester, Eng., 1963. Supr. Modi Textile Mills, Modinagar, India, 1959-60; vis. lectr. N.C. State U., Raleigh, 1963-66, asst. prof., 1966-73, assoc. prof., 1973-79, prof., 1979—, grad. adminstr., 1983—, assoc. head dept. textile engring. and sci., 1985—. Contbr. articles to profl. jours; numerous presentations at sci. confs. Vice pres. India Heritage Soc., Raleigh, 1981—. Fellow Textile Inst.; mem. Am. Chem. Soc., Am. Assn. Textile Tech. (chpt. adviser 1979-84), Fiber Soc., Sigma Xi, Phi Kappa Phi. Current work: Structural mechanics of nonwoven fabrics, chlorine and weathering effects on structure of hair, absorbent textiles, use of polymers in surgical sutures and vascular grafts, also formation of high performance fibers. Subspecialty: Polymer engineering. Home: 5005 Lakemont Dr Raleigh NC 27609 Office: Dept Textile Engring and Sci NC State U Box 8301 Raleigh NC 27695-8301

GUPTA, MADHU SUDAN, electrical engineering educator; b. Lucknow, India, July 13, 1945; came to U.S., 1966, naturalized, 1974; s. Manohar Lai and Premvati (Gupta) G.; m. Vijaya Lakshmi Tayal, July 9, 1970; children—Jay Mohan, Vineet Mohan. M.S., Allahabad U., India, 1963-66; M.S., Fla. State U., 1966-67; M.A., U. Mich., 1967-68, Ph.D., 1972. Registered profl. engr., Ont. Teaching fellow U. Mich., Ann Arbor, 1968-72; asst. prof. Queen's U., Kingston, Ont., 1972-73; asst. prof. MIT, Cambridge, Mass., 1973-78, assoc. prof., 1978-79; assoc. prof. U. Ill.-Chgo., 1979-84; prof., 1984—, dir. grad. studies, 1980-83; cons. MIT Lincoln Lab., Lexington, Mass., 1976-79. Editor: Electrical Noise, 1977; Engineering Education, 1985. Contbr. articles to profl. jours. Lilly fellow, 1974-75. Mem. IEEE (sr. mem.), IEEE-Microwave Soc. Chgo. (vice chmn. 1984—). Current work: Noise and fluctuation phenomenon in electronic devices; microwave electronics; semiconductor devices; electronic circuits; engineering education. Subspecialties: Electrical engineering; Microelectronics. Office: U Ill-Chgo Box 4348 Chicago IL 60680

GUPTA, PREM KAMAL, cardiologist, educator; b. Jammu, India, Sept. 22, 1941; came to U.S., 1966, naturalized, 1979; s. Bodh R. and Kaushlya (Devi) G.; m. Neelam Mahajan, Jan. 7, 1973; 1 child Sumita. I.Sc., G.G.M. Science, Jammu, 1959; M.B.B.S., Govt. Med. Coll., Srinagar, India, 1964. Diplomate: Am. Bd. Internal Medicine. Intern Bekman Downtown Hosp., N.Y.C., 1966-67; resident VA Hosp., N.Y.C., 1967-68; resident VA Hosp, Bronx, N.Y., 1968-71, practice medicine specializing in cardiology, Bklyn., 1976-; assoc. dir. cardiology Mt. Sinai-City Hosp., Elmhurst, N.Y., 1971-76; assoc. dir. cardiology Maimonides Hosp., Bklyn., 1976-79, attending cardiology, 1979—; assoc in medicine Mt. Sinai Med. Sch., N.Y.C., 1971-73; asst. prof. clin. medicine, 1973-76; assoc. prof. medicine SUNY-Bklyn., 1976—. Fellow ACP, Am. Coll. Cardiology, Am. Heart Assn., Royal Coll. Physicians and Surgeons, Can.; mem. Am. Fedn. Clin. Research. Current Work: Echo cardiography, including 2-dimentional and Doppler effect. Subspecialty: Cardiology. Office: 909 49th St Brooklyn NY 1219

GUPTA, RAJENDRA, physicist; b. Mauranipur, India, Jan. 1, 1943; came to U.S., 1962; s. Mahipal and Ramati (Devi) G.; m. Usha Chand, July 11, 1970; children: Tripti, Sangeet. B.Sc., Agra U., 1959; M.Sc., 1961; Ph.D., Boston U., 1970. Research assoc. Columbia U., N.Y.C., 1970-73, lectr., 1973-74, asst. prof., 1974-78, U. Ark., Fayetteville, 1978-81, assoc. prof., 1981-85, prof., 1985—. Contbr. articles to profl. jours. Research Corp. grantee, 1979-82; USAF grantee, 1980—; NSF grantee, 1980—. Mem. Am. Phys. Soc., Am. Assn. Physics Tchrs., Sigma Xi. Current Work: Laser spectroscopy, application of laser spectroscopy to basic and applied problems in physics. Subspecialty: Atomic and molecular physics. Office: Dept Physics Univ Ark Fayetteville AR 72701

GUPTA, SATYENDRA KUMAR, chemist, researcher; b. Lucknow, India, Dec. 15, 1935; came to U.S., 1968, naturalized, 1980; s. Jahangiri Lal and Sabudra (Devi) G.; m. Manjula Rastogi, Jan. 26, 1968; children—Seema, Neera. Grad. Agra U., India, 1960, Ph.D., 1968. Postdoctoral fellow Cleve. Clinic, 1968-71, spl. fellow, 1976-77, clin. assoc., 1977-82; research assoc. Case Western Res. U., Cleve., 1971-76; dir. research Internat. Bio-products, Cleve., 1982—. Contbr. articles to profl. jours. Fellow Nat. Acad. Clin. Chemistry; mem. Am. Chem. Soc., Am. Assn. for Clin. Chemistry. Subspecialties: Clinical chemistry; Synthetic chemistry. Home: 2108 Helmsdale Dr Euclid OH 44143 Office: Internat Bio-products Corp 2108 Helmsdale Dr Euclid OH 44143

GUPTA, VIJAY KUMAR, chemistry educator; b. Ambala Cantt, Haryana, India, Apr. 27, 1941; s. Rattan Lal and Sharda Devi (Singal) G.; m. Surjit Mohini Aggarwal, Sept. 5, 1968; children: Sonia, Angela, Ashish. B.Sc., Panjab. U., Chandigarh, India, 1961, M.Sc., 1962, Ph.D., 1969. Lectr. Punjab Engring. Coll., Chandigarh, 1962-64, asst. prof., 1967-68; postdoctoral assoc. Wright State U., Dayton, 1968-69; prof. chemistry Central State U., Wilberforce, Ohio, 1969—; research chemist Lawrence Livermore (Calif.) Nat. Lab., 1980. Contbr. articles to profl. jours. Mem. constn. com. Hindu Community Orgn., Dayton, 1982. Nat. Urban League fellow, 1973, 76; NSF fellow, 1979; summer faculty fellow Wright-Paterson AFB, Ohio, 1981, 84, 85; U.S. Air Force grantee, 1982-83, 84-85; NASA grantee, 1976-79. Mem. Electrochem. Soc., Am. Chem. Soc., Ohio Acad. Scis., Assn. Energy Engrs., AAUP. Democrat. Hindu. Club: India (Dayton). Current Work: Production of synthetic fuels, high energy density battery systems, development and characterization of hydraulic fluids; thermodynamics of solutions, energy conservation and energy conversion technologies. Subspecialties: Fuels and sources; Thermodynamics. Home: 1447 New Way Dr Xenia OH 45385 Office: Dept Chemistry Central State U Wilberforce OH 45384

GUR, DAVID, radiation physicist; b. Haifa, Israel, Apr. 7, 1947; s. Zeev and Kedma Gurfinkel; m. Zipora, Aug. 31, 1971; children: Saar, Ilan. B.S. in Physics, Technion Israel Inst. Tech., 1973; M.S. in Radiation Health, Grad. Sch. Pub. Health U. Pitts., 1976, Sc.D. in Radiation Health, 1977. Sr. pilot, flight instr. Shahaf Aviation Service, Tel-Aviv, Israel, 1971-73; asst. prof. radiation health and radiology U. Pitts., 1977-80, assoc. prof. radiology and radiation health, 1980-83, prof. radiation health, 1983—, prof. radiology, 1984—. Served with Israeli Mil. Forces, 1965-68. Mem. Health Physics Soc., Am. Assn. Physicists in Medicine, Am. Heart Assn., Pa. Acad. Sci. Current Work: Development safe noninvasive techniques for derivation of in vivo functional information with improved anatomic specificity; perform research enhancing understanding of normal and abnormal tissue function resulting from local and regional alterations of tissue function. Subspecialties: Imaging technology; Comparative physiology. Office: Univ Pitts Pittsburgh PA 15261

GUR, RUBEN C., neuropsychologist, educator; b. Zagreb, Yugoslavia, Aug. 13, 1947; came to U.S., 1970, naturalized, 1983; s. Moshe Mavro and Ella (Gluck) Cohen; m. Raquel E. Gur, Aug. 19, 1969; 1 dau., Tamar Lea. B.A., Hebrew U. Jerusalem, 1970; M.A., Mich. State U., 1971, Ph.D., 1973. Research assoc. Stanford U., Palo Alto, Calif., 1973-74; asst. prof. psychology U. Pa., Phila., 1974-80, assoc. prof. neuropsychology, 1980—; dir. neuropsychology (Grad. Hosp.), Phila., 1981—; co-dir. Brain Research Lab., dir. neuro-psychology U. Pa. Sch. Medicine, 1984—. Contbr. articles to profl. jours. Spencer Found. grantee, 1979, 82; NSF grantee, 1975; NIH grantee, 1976—; NIMH grantee, 1978—; NIA grantee, 1982—. Mem. Am. Psychol. Assn., AAAS, Internat. Neuropsychol. Soc., N.Y. Acad. Scis., Am. Speech-Lang.-Hearing Assn. Current Work: Regional brain physiology in relation to behavior and psychopathology. Subspecialties: Neuropsychology; PET scan. Home: 815 St Georges Rd Philadelphia PA 19119 Office: U Pa Dept Psychiatry 205 Piersol Philadelphia PA 19104

GUR, TURGUT MEHMET, chemicals corporation executive; b. Istanbul, Turkey, Dec. 19, 1944; came to U.S., 1970; s. Talat Hasan and Cahide (Unal) G.; m. Gulay Yerman, Aug. 17, 1970; children—Yerman, Doga. B.S., Middle East Tech. U., Ankara, Turkey, 1966, M.Sc. Chem. Engring., 1969; M.Sc. in Engring. Stanford U., 1971, M.Sci in Materials Sci. and Engring., 1973, Ph.D., 1976. Process engr. Petkim Petrochem. Industries, Ltd., Izmit, Turkey, 1969-70; asst. prof. chem. engring. Middle East Tech. U., 1976-79, EITIA Chem. Engring. Sch., Eskisehir, Turkey, 1976-78; sr. research assoc. Stanford U., Calif., 1979-80; staff scientist Energy Systems Lab., Cupertino, Calif., 1980-81; sr. staff scientist Raychem Corp., Menlo Park, Calif., 1982-85. Contbr. articles to profl. jours. Patentee in field. Mem. Turkish Edn. Found., 1975-85. AID jr. fellow, 1970-74, Petkim Petrochem. Industries scholar, 1963-66. Mem. Electrochem. Soc., Am. Chem. Soc., Am. Ceramic Soc. (No. Calif. sect.). Current work: Role of solid state electrochemistry in catalysis of heterogeneous reactions; chemical sensors for gas and humidity detection; getters and chemotronic devices; fast ion conductors; membranes for separation processes; electronic ceramics, corrosion. Subspecialties: Solid state ionics; Physical chemistry. Home: Nisbetiye Cad Feruze Sk Ceylan Apt 1/30 Etiler Istanbul Turkey Office: Tusa AS Buyukdere Cad Lale Is Hani No 62 Kat 3 Mecidiyekoy Istanbul Turkey

GUR, YIGAL, physicist, educator; b. Jitomir, Ukraine, USSR, Apr. 21, 1944; s. Vladimir Grigorevich and Faina Prikopievna (Chija) Gorbov; m. Galia Josef Geshmishener, Oct. 10, 1964; children—Zeev, Avi. Came to U.S. 1979. M.S., Inst. Phys. Engring., Dolgoprudny, USSR, 1968; D.Sc., Technion, Haifa, 1978. Asst. prof. Politech. Inst., Novocherkassk, USSR, 1969-72; sr. researcher Technion Research & Devel., Haifa, 1974-79; vis. prof. SUNY-Buffalo, 1979-80; sr. physicist Moore Research Ctr., Grand Island, N.Y., 1980-81; sr. scientist Diconix, A Kodak Co., Dayton, Ohio, 1981—; adj. prof. systems analysis Miami U., Oxford, Ohio, 1983—. Contbr. articles to profl. jours. Mem. Soc. Indsl. and Applied Math., Am. Phys. Soc., Soc. Photo-Optical Instrumentation Engrs., N.Y. Acad.. Scis. Current work: Image processing by ink-jet printers; numerical modeling of ink-jet process; numerical simulations in electrostatics; visual perception of print quality. Subspecialties: Applied mathematics; Graphics, image processing, and pattern recognition. Office: Diconix A Kodak Co 3100 Research Blvd PO Box 3100 Dayton OH 45420

GURD, RUTH SIGHTS, physician, biochemist, researcher, educator; b. Chgo., Sept. 17, 1927; d. Warren Preston and Helen (Coleman) Sights; m. Frank Ross Newman Gurd, June 12, 1956; children: Martha Helen, Charles Baillie. B.S., U. Mich., 1949; M.D., Washington U., St. Louis, 1957. Life Ins. Med. Research Fund postdoctoral fellow in physiology Cornell U. Coll. Medicine, 1957; med. cons. Aerospace Research Application Ctr., Ind. U., Bloomington, 1963-66, sr. research assoc. dept chemistry, 1966-71, asst. prof. biochemistry med. sci. program, 1973-77, assoc. prof., 1978-85, prof., 1985—. Contbr. articles to sci. jours. NSF fellow, 1954-55. Mem. Am. Inst. Nutrition, Biophys. Soc.; mem. Am. Soc. Biol. Chemistry; Mem. N.Y. Acad. Scis., Nat. Soc. Arts and Letters, Kappa Kappa Gamma. Current Work: Structure function relationships of proteins and peptides; peptide structure, function, hormones, glucagon, receptors, diabetes mellitus, physical methods, synthesis, semisynthesis. Subspecialties: Biochemistry (medicine); Receptors. Home: 2600 Fairoaks Ln Bloomington IN 47401 Office: Dept Chemistry Ind U Bloomington IN 47405

GURFINKEL, GERMAN RUBEN, civil engineering educator, structural engineering consultant; b. Havana, Cuba, Sept. 14, 1932; came to U.S., 1962, naturalized, 1969; s. Oscar and Rebecca (Greenstein) G.; m. Ana Fainstein, Sept. 2, 1956; children—Brunhilda, Gustavo, Daniel, Paul. Civil Engr., U. Havana, 1955; M.S.C.E., U. Ill., 1957, Ph.D. in Civil Engring., 1966. Registered structural engr., Ill. Asst. prof. U. Havana, 1959-61; asst. prof. U. Ill., Urbana, 1962-68, assoc. prof., 1968-74, prof. civil engring., 1974—; pvt. practice structural engring., Champaign, Ill., 1962-78; pres. German Gurfinkel, P.C., Champaign, 1978—; designer New Campus of U. Havana, major bridges, tanks, bldgs., stadiums, others. Author: Wood Engineering, 1981; (with others) Prestressed Concrete, 1969. Recipient Design prizes Lincoln Arc Welding Found., 1973, 1977-83; Fellow ASCE; mem. Am. Soc. Agrl. Engrs., ASTM, Am. Concrete Inst., Structural Engrs. Ill. (Most Innovative Structural Design award 1981, 84). Current work: Wood structures, storage structures including grain silos, steel and concrete tall buildings. Subspecialty: Structural engineering. Home: 2510 S Prospect Ave Champaign IL 61820 Office: U Ill Civil Engring Dept 208 N Romine St Urbana IL 61801

GURNEY, ELIZABETH TUCKER GUICE, biologist; b. Berkeley, Calif., Apr. 4, 1941; d. Clarence Norman and Elizabeth Lillian (Eichbauer) Guice; m. Theodore Gurney, Jr., June 18, 1966. B.A., U. Chgo., 1962; M.S., U. Calif.-Berkeley, 1970, Ph.D., 1975. Tech. asst. dept. biology M.I.T., 1963-67; postgrad. research biochemist U. Calif., 1970-73; postdoctoral fellow U. Utah, 1975-77, research asst. prof. biology, 1976—. Contbr. articles in field to profl. jours. NIH grantee, 1977—. Mem. AAAS, Am. Soc. Cell Biology, Am. Soc. Microbiology. Current Work: Control of cellular growth, tumor virus transformation, moncional antibodies. Subspecialties: Genetics and genetic engineering (biology); Cell and tissue culture. Home: 203 4th Ave Salt Lake City UT 84103 Office: Dept Biology U Utah Salt Lake City UT 84112

GURTIN, MORTON EDWARD, educator; b. Jersey City, Mar. 7, 1934; s. Saul Gurtin and Irene (Hoffman) Burns: children—Amy Lynn, William Robert. B.M.E., Rensselaer Poly. Inst., 1955; Ph.D., Brown U., 1961. Structures engr. Douglas Aircraft Co., 1955-56, Gen. Electric Co., 1956-59; research asso. Brown U., 1961-62, asst. prof., 1962-64, assoc. prof., 1964-66; prof. math. Carnegie Mellon U., 1966—; Sr. Fulbright-Hays fellow, Guggenheim fellow U. Pisa, Italy, 1974; lectr., Europe, South Am., Can., cons. to industry. Author: (with B.D. Coleman, I Herrera, and C. Truesdell) Wave Propagation in Dissipative Media, 1965, An Introduction to Continuum Mechanics, 1981; Assoc. editor. Archive for Rational Mechanics and Analysis, Jour. Elasticity; Contbr. articles to profl. jours., including Handbuch der Physik. Mem. Soc. Natural Philosophy, Am. Math. Soc., Sigma Xi. Current work: Population dynamics; developing mathematical description of dispersal and solidification.. Office: Dept Math Carnegie-Mellon U Pittsburgh PA 15213

GURTOO, HIRA L., research biochemical pharmacologist, geneticist; b. Kashmir, India, Apr. 13, 1938; came to U.S., 1965; s. Rugh Nath and Kamala

(Kamala) G.; m. Lalita Durani, Apr. 13, 1937; children: Lalit, Rajeev. B.V.Sc., Madras Vet. Coll., 1959, M.V.Sc., 1962; Ph.D. in Biochemistry, Va. Poly. Inst., 1968. Vet. surgeon, Kashmir, 1959-60; asst. prof. Sch. Agr., Kashmir, 1963-65; postdoctoral tng. Yale U. Med. Sch., New Haven, 1968-70; research pharmacologist Miles Labs., Elkhart, Ind., 1970-78; cancer research scientist III, IV & V Roswell Park Meml. Inst., Buffalo, 1978-80, assoc. chief cancer research sci., 1980—. Contbr. numerous articles and abstracts to sci. jours., also chpts. to books. Grantee NIH; Grantee Nat. Cancer Inst.; Grantee Nat. Inst. Environ. Health Sci.; Grantee Am. Cancer Soc.; Grantee U.S. Council for Tobacco Research. Mem. Am. Assn. for Cancer Research, AVMA. Hindu. Current Work: Chemical carcinogenesis and chemotherapy; cytochrome P-450 cloning, benzo(a)pyrene metabolism, aflatoxin metabolism and carcinogenesis, cyclophosphamide metabolism and chemotherapy. Subspecialties: Environmental toxicology; Molecular pharmacology.

GUSDON, JOHN PAUL, JR., gynecologist/obstetrician, educator; b. Cleve., Feb. 13, 1931; s. John and Pauline (Malencek) G.; m. Marcelle Simone Deiber, June 16, 1956 (dec.); children: Marguerite, John, Veronique. B.A., U. Va., 1952, M.D., 1959. Diplomate: Am. Bd. Ob-Gyn. Intern, resident Univ. Hosps., Cleve., 1959-64; asst. prof. Western Res. U. Sch. Medicine, 1964-67; asst. prof. ob-gyn Bowman Gray Sch. Medicine, Wake Forest U., Winston-Salem, N.C., 1967-71, asso. prof., 1971-74, prof., 1974—. Contbr. numerous papers to sci. jours. Served with USN, 1952-55. Mem. Am. Coll. Obstetricians and Gynecologists (Pres.'s award 1977, Found. prize 1971), Am. Assn. Immunologists, Am. Gynecol. and Obstet. Soc., Soc. Gynecol. Investigation, S. Atlantic Assn. Obstetricians and Gynecologists, So. Med. Assn. Roman Catholic. Current Work: Immunology of reprodn., immunology of cancer and immunotherapy. Subspecialties: Obstetrics and gynecology; Immunology (medicine). Office: Bowman Gray Sch Medicine Winston-Salem NC 27103

GUSSIN, ROBERT ZALMON, pharmaceutical company executive; b. Pitts., Jan. 5, 1938; s. Carl and Yetta G. B.S. in Pharmacy, Duquesne U., 1959, M.S. in Pharmacology, 1961, Ph.D., U. Mich., 1965. Research fellow dept. pharmacology SUNY, 1965-67; research pharmacologist Lederle Labs., N.Y.C., 1967-69, group leader dept. cardiovascular renal pharmacology, 1969-73, dir. cardiovascular renal disease therapy sect., 1973-74; exec. dir. research McNeil Labs., Ft. Washington, Pa., 1974-78, v.p. research div., 1978, v.p. research and devel., 1978-79; v.p. sci. affairs Spring House, Pa., 1979—. Author: Introduction to Cardiovascular Pharmacology, 1976; mem. editorial bd.: New Drug Evaluations, Drug Devel; contbr. in field. Mem. Am. Soc. Pharmacology and Exptl. Therapeutics, Am. Soc. Clin. Pharmacology and Therapeutics, Am. Soc. Nephrology, Am. Fedn. Clin. Research, AAAS, N.Y. Acad. Scis., Am. Heart Assn. Research, Pharmaco Therapy. Office: McNeil Pharmaceutical Spring House PA 19477

GUSTAFSON, JOHN PERRY, geneticist; b. Greeley, Colo., Aug. 1, 1944; s. Elmer R. and Barbara N. (Wilson) G.; m. Christine S. McKinstry, Mar. 13, 1977; 1 dau., Kathryn. B.S., Colo. State U., 1967, M.S., 1968; Ph.D., U. Calif., Davis, 1972. Research asst. U. Calif., Davis, 1968-72; research prof. U. Man., Can., 1972-76, research asso., 1976-77, assoc. prof., 1977-82; research geneticist U.S. Dept. Agr., U. Mo., Columbia, 1982—. Contbr. articles to profl. jours. Union Pacific R.R. scholar, 1962; Nat. Sci. and Engring. Research Council Can. grantee, 1973-81. Mem. AAAS, Am. Soc. Agronomy, Am. Genetic Assn., Genetics Soc. Am., Sigma Xi, Gamma Sigma Delta, Phi Kappa Phi. Current Work: Researcher in plant genetics, plant breeding, cytogenetics and evolution. Subspecialties: Plant genetics; Genome organization. Home: 3103 Crawford St Columbia MO 65201 Office: U Mo 208 Curtis Hall Columbia MO 65211

GUSTAFSSON, BORJE KARL, veterinarian, educator; b. Varnamo, Sweden, Feb. 26, 1930; s. Albin Karl and Svea Gertrud (Andersson) G.; m. Gunilla A. Granzelius, July 11, 1958; children: Katarina, Charlotte, Lars. B.Vet. Sci., Royal Vet. Coll., Stockholm, 1953, D.V.M., 1960, Ph.D., 1966. Research assoc., instr., asst. prof. Royal Vet. Coll. Stockholm, 1960-67, tchr., researcher animal reproduction, head clinics dept. Ob-Gyn, 1967-75, acting prof., chmn. dept. Ob-Gyn, 1970-73; vis. prof. U. Minn. Coll. Agr., St. Paul, 1974; prof. theriogenology Coll. Vet. Medicine, 1976-78; dir. grad. edn. in theriogenology U. Minn., 1976-78; prof., head dept. vet. clin. medicine Coll. Vet. Medicine, U. Ill., Urbana-Champaign, 1978—. Contbr. numerous articles in field of animal reproduction to profl. jours. Served with Swedish Vet Corps, 1952-54. Lagerlof's fellow, 1974. Mem. Swedish Vet. Med. Assn., AVMA, Assn. Am. Vet. Med. Colls., Am. Assn. Vet. Clinicians, Soc. Study Reproduction, World Assn. Vet. Physiologists, Pharmacologists and Biochemists. Current Work: Testicular and epididymal function; female genital infections; prostaglandins and reproduction; bovine mastitis; pathophysiology of inflammation. Subspecialties: Theriogenology; Reproductive biology (medicine). Home: 2102 S Race St Urbana IL 61801 Office: 1008 W Hazelwood St Urbana IL 61801

GUTH, ALAN HARVEY, physicist; b. New Brunswick, N.J., Feb. 27, 1947; s. Hyman and Elaine (Cheiten) G.; m. Susan Tisch, Mar. 28, 1971; 1 son, Lawrence David. S.B. and S.M., MIT, 1969, Ph.D. in Physics, 1972. Instr. Princeton (N.J.) U., 1971-74; research assoc. Columbia U., N.Y.C., 1974-77, Cornell U., Ithaca, N.Y., 1977-79, Stanford Linear Accelerator Ctr., Calif., 1979-80; assoc. prof. Physics MIT, Cambridge, 1980—. Alfred P. Sloan fellow, 1981. Mem. Am. Phys. Soc. Current Work: Applications of particle physics (particularly grand unified theories) to the very early universe; consequences of the inflationary universe scenario. Subspecialties: Particle physics; Cosmology. Office: Center Theoretical Physics MIT Cambridge MA 02139

GUTHERMANN, HOWARD EDGAR, chemical engineer, chemist; b. N.Y.C., Dec. 5, 1949; s. Justin and Rita Regina (Speyer) G.; m. Deborah Natalie Mass, Aug. 8, 1976; children—Joshua, Rachel. B.S. in Chem. Engring., Cooper Union, 1969; M.S. in Chem. Engring., Northwestern U., 1972, Ph.D. in Chem. Engring., 1977. Sr. Chem.E. BioResearch, Inc., Farmingdale, N.Y., 1978-81; sr. research scientist Corning Med. Ctr., Medfield, Mass., 1981-84; sr. chemist Analytix, Inc., Cambridge, Mass., 1984—. Contbr. articles to profl. jours. Served with USAR, 1970-1976. NIH traineeship, 1969. Mem. Am. Inst. Chem. Engrs., Am. Chem. Soc., AAAS, Internat. Soc. Oxygen Transport to Tissue, Sigma Xi. Jewish. Current work: Electrochemical devices and instrumentation applied to clinical, biomedical, industrial, or environmental needs. Subspecialties: Clinical chemistry; Biomedical engineering. Home: 31 Rochester Rd Newton MA 02158 Office: Analytix Inc 155 2d St Cambridge MA 02142

GUTHRIE, FRANK EDWIN, entomologist, educator; b. Louisville, Jan. 14, 1923; s. Blaine and Lera May (Waller) G.; m. Bernice Button, Dec. 26, 1947; children—Janet, Caroline. B.S., U. Ky., 1947; M.S., U. Ill., 1949, Ph.D., 1952. Asst. prof. entomology U. Fla., Quincy, 1952-54; asst. prof. entomology N.C. State U., Raleigh, 1954-59, asso. prof., 1959-62, prof., 1962—; asst. dean Grad. Sch., 1962-64, dir. research and tng. programs in pesticide toxicology, 1964—. Co-author: Concepts of Pest Management, 1970, Biochemical Toxicology, 1980, Environmental Toxicology, 1980; contbr. articles to profl. jours. Served with USMCR, 1943-46, 51-52. Mem. Entomol. Soc. Am., Am. Chem. Soc., Soc. Toxicology. Current Work: Absorption and distribution by blood macromolecules of pesticides. Subspecialties: Toxicology (agriculture); Entomology. Home: 823 Beaver Dam Rd Raleigh NC 27607 Office: Dept Entomology NC State U Raleigh NC 27695

GUTHRIE, WILBUR DEAN, entomologist, researcher; b. Woodward, Okla., Mar. 3, 1924; s. Ivens and Frances (Moser) G.; m. Mary Edna Peters, Sept. 9, 1946; children—Justina, Yvonne, Larry, Gary, Scott. B.S., Okla. State U., 1950, M.S., 1951; Ph.D., Ohio State U., 1958. Research entomologist U.S. Dept. Agr., Agrl. Research Service, Ankeny, Iowa, 1951-52, Wooster, Ohio, 1952-64, 1964-73, research leader, Ankeny, 1973—; cons. agrl. services world-wide, 1966—. Contbr. articles to profl. jours. Served with USN, 1944-46. Mem. Entomol. Soc. Am., North Central Branch Entomol. Soc. Am., Crop. Sci. Soc. Am., Kans. Entomol. Soc., S.C. Entomol. Soc. Current work: Resistance of crop plants to insects. Office: Agrl Research Services US Dept Agr Ankeny IA 50021

GUTIERREZ, FERNANDO JOSE, psychologist; b. Matanzas, Cuba, Mar. 1, 1951; s. Alberto Rodolfo and Mariana Elena (Cartaya) G. B.A., Mich. State U., 1973; M.S. in Edn, Purdue U., 1974; Ed. D., Boston U., 1981. Staff counselor U. Wis.-Stevens Point, 1975-77; counseling psychologist San Francisco State U., 1980-81, U. Santa Clara, 1981—; Western region coordinator profl. workshops Nat. Assn. Minority Students and Educators in Higher Edn., 1982-84. Mem. adv. com. to Commr. Mental Health-Children's Com., 1980; pres. Hispanic Orientation, Recreation and the Arts Assn., 1980; co-chmn. Nat. Caucus Gay and Lesbian Counselors, 1985—. Title VII fellow HEW, 1978; recipient Operation Kindness service award Mass. Dept. Edn. and United Community Services, 1968. Mem. Am. Psychol. Assn., Am. Assn. Counseling and devel. (rep. to human rights com. 1985—), Bicultural Assn. Spanish-speaking Therapists and Advs., Kappa Delta Pi, Pi Lambda Theta. Democrat. Roman Catholic. Current Work: Bilcultural personality development; cross-cultural clinical applications, biofeedback training and stress related disorders. Subspecialties: Developmental psychology; Social psychology. Home: 500 King Dr 1008 Daly City CA 94015 Office: University of Santa Clara 208 Benson Center Santa Clara CA 95053

GUTIERREZ, PETER LUIS, biophysicist cancer research, educator; b. Monteria, Colombia, S.A., June 9, 1939; came to U.S., 1957; s. Pedro Antonio and Fanny Edith G.; m. Sarah Ann Hanchett, Sept. 2, 1966; children—Fanny Elizabeth, Ann Carolyn. B.S. in Physics, Wheaton Coll., 1962; M.S. in Physics, Calif. State U., 1970; Ph.D. in Biophysics So. Ill. U., 1973. Instr. biochemistry Tulane U., 1973-74; staff biophysicist Nat. Biomed. E.P.R. Ctr., Med. Coll. Wis., 1974-78; sr. investigator Balt. Cancer Research Ctr., Balt., 1978-82; asst. prof. biochemistry and oncology U. Md. Cancer Ctr., Balt., 1982—. Contbr. articles to sci. jours.; chpt. to Biochemical Mechanisms of Liver Injury, 1978. Nat. Cancer Inst. Research grantee, 1983; Lederle Labs. Research grantee, 1983; Bressler Research Found., U. Md. Research grantee, 1982—. Mem. Biophys. Soc., Am. Assn. Cancer Research, Internat. Soc. Magnetic Resonance, Radiation Research Soc., Sigma Pi Sigma. Current work: Free radical intermediates in the activation of anti-tumoragents; effects of oxygen free radicals on cell membrane lipids. Subspecialties: Electron spin resonance; Molecular pharmacology. Office: Developmental Therapeutics Univ Md Cancer Ctr 655 W Baltimore St Baltimore MD 21201

GUTMANN, RONALD JAY, electrical engineering educator, electrophysicist, researcher; b. Bklyn., Nov. 16, 1940; s. Ludwig G. and Dorothy (Levy) G.; m. Suzanne Frech, Aug. 27, 1967; children—David A., Jennifer L. B.E.E., Rensselaer Poly Inst., 1962, Ph.D., 1970; M.E.E., NYU, 1964. Mem. tech. staff Bell Telephone Labs., Whippany, N.J., 1962-66; sr. engr. Lockheed Electronics Co., Plainfield, N.J., 1966-67; research engr. Rensselaer Research Corp., Troy, N.Y., 1967-70; asst. prof. elec. engring. Rensselaer Poly. Inst., Troy, 1970-76, assoc. prof., 1976-80, prof., 1980; program dir. NSF, Washington, 1981-83; cons. to numerous indsl. and govt. labs., 1972—; speaker at numerous univs., indsl. labs. Author/editor continuing edn. series in electronics, 1976, 79; also numerous articles, conf. papers. Recipient Outstanding Performance award NSF, 1983. Mem. IEEE (sr., chmn. awards planning and policy com. 1984—), AAUP, AAAS, Sigma Xi, Tau Beta Pi, Eta Kappa Nu. Current work: Semiconductor devices; microwave techniques; submicron devices; microwave monolithic integrated circuits; radiation effects. Subspecialties: Semiconductors; Microelectronics. Home: 64 23d St Troy NY 12180 Office: Rensselaer Poly Inst ECSE/JEC6050 Troy NY 12181

GUTOWSKY, HERBERT SANDER, chemistry educator; b. Bridgman, Mich., Nov. 8, 1919; s. Otto and Hattie (Meyers) G.; m. Barbara Stuart, June 1949 (div. Sept. 1981); children: Daniel Kurt (dec.), Robb Edward, Christopher Carl.; m. Virginia Warner, Aug. 1982. A.B., Ind. U., 1940, D.Sc. (hon.), 1983; M.S., U. Calif.-Berkeley, 1946; Ph.D., Harvard U., 1949. Mem. faculty U. Ill. at Urbana, 1948—, prof. chemistry, 1956—, mem. Ctr. for Advanced Study, 1983—, head div. phys. chemistry, 1956-63, head dept. chemistry and chem. engring., 1967-70; dir. Sch. Chem. Scis., head dept. chemistry, 1970-83; mem. chemistry panel NSF, 1963-66, chmn. panel, 1965-66, mem. adv. com. on planning, 1971-74; mem. Ill. Bd. Natural Resources and Conservation, 1973—; G.N. Lewis Meml. lectr., 1976, G.B. Kistiakowsky lectr., 1980; King lectr., 1984. Mem. adv. bd. Petroleum Research Fund, 1959-61; mem. selection and scheduling com. Gordon Research Conf., 1959-64, 68-72, trustee, 1969-72, chmn. bd. trustees, 1971-72. Served to capt., chem. warfare service AUS, 1941-45. Recipient 1966 $5000 Irving Langmuir award Am. Chem. Soc.; Midwest award St. Louis sect., 1973; 1974 $1000 prize Internat. Soc. Magnetic Research; Peter Debye award in phys. chemistry Am. Chem. Soc., 1975; Nat. medal of Sci., 1977; Wolf prize in chemistry, 1983; Guggenheim fellow, 1954-55. Fellow Am. Phys. Soc. (chmn. div. chem. physics 1973-74), AAAS, Am. Philos. Soc., Am. Acad. Arts and Scis., mem., Nat. Acad. Scis. (mem. com. sci. and pub. policy 1972-75, chmn. panel on atmospheric chemistry 1975-77, mem. com. impacts of stratospheric change 1975-77), Am. Chem. Soc. (chmn. div. phys. chemistry 1966-67, com. on profl. tng. 1969-77, chmn. 1974-77), AAUP, Phi Beta Kappa, Sigma Xi. Current Work: Magnetic resonance; dynamic structure of membranes; the mechanism of photosynthetic oxygen evolution; rotational spectra and structure of small molecular clusters and of other transient species. Subspecialty: Nuclear magnetic resonance. Home: 202 W Delaware Ave Urbana IL 61801 Office: Noyes Lab 505 S Mathews St Urbana IL 61801

GUTTAG, KARL MARION, electrical engineer; b. Washington, May 29, 1954; s. Alvin and Norma (Samons) G. B.S. in Elec. Engring, Bradley U., Peoria, Ill., 1976; M.S. in Elec.Engring, U. Mich., 1977. Design engr. Tex. Instruments, Houston, 1977-79, project engr., 1980-81, graphics strategy mgr., 1982—. Recipient Sr. Mem. Tech. Staff award Tex. Instruments, 1982. Mem. IEEE, Assn. Computing Machinery. Patentee in field of video-display processors. Current Work: VLSI logic and system design and definition; computer graphics. Subspecialty: Integrated circuits. Home: 11602 Ensbrook St Houston TX 77099 Office: Tex Instruments PO Box 1443 Houston TX 77001

GUTTMAN, CHARLES MARTIN, physical chemist, educator; b. Cin. Apr. 11, 1939; s. Ervan Edward and Eva (Bloom) G.; m. Judith Atwood, Sept. 5, 1960 (div. 1972); children—Hannah, Harry; m. Evelyne Lee Barry, Feb. 15, 1975; 1 child, Damiana. B.A., Earlham Coll., 1961; Ph.D., Brandeis U., 1967. Postdoctoral fellow Bell Labs., Murray Hill, N.J., 1967; research chemist Nat. Bur. Standards, Washington, 1967—; adj. prof. U. Md., College Pk., 1983—. Contbr. articles to profl. jours. Mem. maintenance com. Mont Village Found., Gaithersburg, Md., 1979; group leader Cub Scout Pack 1933, Gaithersburg, Md., 1973. Mem. Am. Chem. Soc., Am. Phys. Soc., ASTM (task force leader). Jewish. Current work: Computer simulation of polymer conformations in solution and crystals; small molecule diffusion in polymer. Subspecialties: Polymer physics; Polymers (materials science). Office: Nat Bur Standards Polymer Div Gaithersburg MD 20899

GUTTMAN, HELENE NATHAN, research center administrator, consultant; b. N.Y.C., July 21, 1930; d. Arthur and Mollie (Bergovoy) Nathan. B.A., Bklyn. Coll., 1951; A.M., Harvard U., 1956; M.A., Columbia U., 1958; Ph.D., Rutgers U., 1960. Prof. cell and molecular biology and microbiology U. Ill.-Chgo., and Med. Sch., 1967-75, assoc. dir. research Urban Systems Lab., 1974-75; expert, research resources coordinator Nat. Heart, Lung and Blood Inst., NIH, Bethesda, Md., 1975-79; dep. dir. sci. adv. bd. EPA, Washington, 1979-80; program coordinator U.S. Dept. Agr., Beltsville, Md., 1982-83; assoc. dir. policy and research Beltsville Human Nutrition Research Ctr., 1983—; pres. HNG Assocs., Bethesda, 1983—; dir. Multisystems Group, Silver Spring, Md.; cons. to various fed. agys. Author; (with others) Experiments in Cellular Biodynamics, 1972. Co-editor Proc. 1st Joint USA-USSR Symposium on Blood Transfusion, 1975. Contbr. articles to profl. jours. Co-discoverer vitamin biopterin. Bd. dirs. DuPage County Comprehensive Health Care Planning Agy., Ill., 1974-75, Montgomery Area Sci. Fair Assn., Md., 1980—, McLean Ballet Co., Va., 1981-83. Recipient Thomas Jefferson Murray award Theobald Smith Soc., 1959, spl. award for research in Germany, Deutscher Forschungs Gemeinschaft, 1960; Andelot fellow Harvard Med. Sch., 1954-55; Dazian Found. fellow for med. research, 1956; Rutgers scholar, 1958-60. Fellow AAAS, Am. Inst. Chemists (chmn. profl. opportunities for women com. 1974-78), N.Y. Acad. Scis., Am. Acad. Microbiology (civil service affairs com. 1979—, nominating com. 1979-82), Sigma Delta Epsilon; mem. Am. Soc. Microbiology (status women microbiology com. 1980—, pub. service and adult edn. com. bd. edn. and tng. 1981—, Pres.'s fellow 1957), Am. Soc. Neurochemistry, Am. Soc. Biol. Chemists, Am. Soc. Cell Biology (chmn. ednl. policy com. 1966-69), Am. Soc. Clin. Nutrition (tellers/auditing com. 1980-82), Am. Chem. Soc., Am. Soc. Tropical Medicine and Hygiene, Neuroscis. Soc., Soc. Gen. Microbiology (Eng.), Soc. Protozoology (exec. com. 1970-75, editorial bd. jour. 1972-75), Soc. Exptl. Biol. Medicine, Royal Soc. Chemists (chartered chemist), Tissue Culture Assn. (nominating com. 1975-76), Reticuloendothelial Soc., Sigma Xi. Current work: Biochemistry of human micronutrients and their effects on human physical and mental productivity; translation of biomedical research findings to lay and/or governmental audiences; technology transfer. Subspecialties: Biochemistry (medicine); Microbiology (medicine).

GUVENIS, ALBERT, medical educator; b. Istanbul, Turkey, Apr. 4, 1955; s. Jacqes and Alicia (Edery) G. B.Sc., Bogazici U., Istanbul, Turkey, 1978; M.Sc., Drexel U., 1980, Ph.D., 1983. Instr. Drexel U., Phila., 1979-82; research specialist IV Hosp. of U. Pa., radiology, Phila., 1982-83, asst. prof., 1983-84; asst. prof. Bogazici U., 1984—. Editor BME Bull., Bogazici U., 1985; mem. editorial bd. Medica Jour., Istanbul, 1984—; researcher new software for new pet system, 1982-84. Mem. Soc. Nuclear Medicine, Engring. in Medicine Soc. and Biology Soc. of IEEE, Computer Soc. of IEEE, Circuits and Systems Soc. of IEEE. Current work: Imaging technology, nuclear medicine instrumentation, scintigraphic data processing, positron emission tomography, reconstruction algorithms. Subspecialties: PET scan; Bioinstrumentation. Home: Sisli Periahn Sok No 118/12 Istanbul Turkey Office: Bogazici U Bebek Istanbul Turkey

GUZE, SAMUEL BARRY, psychiatrist, educator, univ. ofcl.; b. N.Y.C., Oct. 18, 1923; s. Jacob and Jenny (Berry) G.; m. Joy Lawrence Campbell, June 7, 1946; children—Jonathan, Ann. Student, Coll. City N.Y., 1939-41; M.D., Washington U., 1945. Diplomate: Am. Bd. Internal Medicine, Am. Bd. Psychiatry and Neurology. Faculty Washington U. Sch. Medicine, St. Louis, 1951—, prof. psychiatry, asso. prof. medicine, 1964—, asst. to dean, 1965-71, vice chancellor for med. affairs, 1971—, co-head dept. psychiatry, 1974-75, head dept., 1975—, Spencer T. Olin prof., 1974—; pres. Washington U. Med. Center, 1971—; staff Barnes Hosp., St. Louis, 1951—, psychiatrist-in-chief, 1975—; staff Renard Hosp., 1953—, psychiatrist-in-chief, 1975—; asst. dir. Psychiatry Clinic, Washington U. Sch. Medicine, 1951-55, dir., 1955-75. Contbr. articles to profl. jours. Fellow A.C.P., Am. Psychiat. Assn., Royal Coll. Psychiatry, Am. Coll. Psychiatry; mem. Am. Fedn. for Clin. Research, Psychiat. Research Soc., AMA, Am. Psychosomatic Soc., Assn. for Research in Nervous and Mental Diseases, Am. Psychopathol. Soc., Soc. Biol. Psychiatry, Soc. Neurosci., Inst. of Medicine of Nat. Acad. Scis., Sigma Xi, Alpha Omega Alpha. Current Work: Psychiatric diagnosis and classification; alcoholism; criminality; psychiatric genetics; predicting course and outcome of illness. Subspecialty: Psychiatry. Home: 17 Ridgemoor Dr St Louis MO 63105 Office: 4940 Audubon Ave Saint Louis MO 63110

GWAZDAUSKAS, FRANCIS CHARLES, endocrinologist, educator; b. Waterbury, Conn., July 25, 1943; s. Francis Julius and Agnes Eva (Lizauskas) G.; m. Judy Keller, Mar. 20, 1971; children: Jennifer, James, John, Peter. B.S. in Animal Husbandry, U. Conn., 1966; M.S. in Dairy Sci, U. Fla., 1972, Ph.D. in Animal Sci, 1974. Assoc. prof. dept. dairy sci. Va. Poly. Inst. & State U., Blacksburg, 1980—, asst. prof., 1974-80. Contbr. to profl. jours. Served with U.S. Army, 1967-68. Mem. Am. Dairy Sci. Assn., Am. Soc. Animal Sci., Soc. Study Reprodn., Soc. Exptl. Medicine and Biology. Roman Catholic. Current Work: Uterine protein contribution to early embryo development; timing of artifical insemination; environmental effects on fertility. Subspecialties: Animal physiology; Animal breeding and embryo transplants. Office: Va Inst and State U 2070 Animal Sci Bldg Blacksburg VA 24061

GWO, TAI-CHUAN, electronic engineer; b. Tainan, Taiwan, Republic of China, June 21, 1953; came to U.S., 1977; s. Pei-Yi and Pi-Yung (Chu) G.; m. Julie Cheih-Ju Yuan, Apr. 12, 1981; children—Wendy, Joanne. B.S. in Elec. Engring., Nat. Taiwan U., Taipei, 1975; M.S. in Elec. Engring., U. Kans., 1980. Registered engr.-in-tng., Calif. Process engr. Fairchild Co., Mountain View, Calif., 1980-83; sr. product engr. Advanced Micro Devices, Sunnyvale, Calif., 1983-85, Gould, Santa Clara, Calif., 1985—. Mem. IEEE, Electro-chem. Soc. Current work: Integrated circuits. Subspecialties: Semiconductors; Integrated circuits. Home: 3001-E Kaiser Dr Santa Clara CA 95051

GWYN, CHARLES WILLIAM, electrical engineer; researcher; b. Sterling, Colo., Sept. 3, 1936; s. William Newton and Gertrude Marie (Morgan) G.; m. Carol Jean Carlton, July 4, 1957; children—Kevin, Karen, Bryan. B.S.E.E. with highest distinction, Kans., 1961; M.S.E.E., U. N.Mex., 1963, Ph.D., 1968. Registered profl. engr., N.Mex. Mem. tech. staff Sandia Labs., Albuquerque, 1961-73, div. supr., 1973-78, dept mgr., 1978-82; asst. gen. mgr. United Techs. Microelectronics Ctr., Colorado Springs, Colo., 1983—; assoc. mem. Adv. Group on Electron Devices, Washington, 1981-82; panel mem. Commn., on Phys. Sci., NRC, 1983-85. Contbr. articles to profl. jours. Fellow IEEE (assoc. editor Trans. on CAD of Integrated Circuits 1980-83), Phi Kappa Phi, Tau Beta Pi, Eta Kappa Nu. Republican. Baptist. Current work: Manager of computer aided design, integrated circuit design, device and reliability physics, quality assurance and research and development programs. Subspecialties: Integrated circuits; Computer-aided design. Home: 16 Red Wing Terr Colorado Springs CO 80906

GYFTOPOULOS, ELIAS PANAYIOTIS, mechanical and nuclear engineering educator, consultant, researcher; b. Athens, Greece, July 4, 1927; came to U.S., 1953, naturalized, 1963; s. Panayiotis Elias and Despina (Louvaris) G.; m. Artemis E. Scalleri, Sept. 3, 1962; children: Vasso, Maro, Rena. Diploma in Mech. and Elec. Engring, Tech. U., Athens, 1953; Sc.D. in Elec. Engring, M.I.T., 1958. Registered profl. engr., Mass. Research asst. in elec. engring. M.I.T., 1953-55, instr., 1955-58, asst. prof. elec. engring, 1958-60, asst. prof. elec. and nuclear engring, 1960-61, assoc. prof. nuclear engring., 1961-64, prof., 1964-70, Ford prof. engrin., 1970—; cons. in field; dir. Thermo Electron Corp. Author: Thermionic Engery Conversion, vol. 1, 1973, vol. 2, 1979, Potential Fuel Effectiveness in Industry, 1974; editor: Manuals on Energy Conservation, vols. 1-17, 1982. Served with Greek Navy, 1948-51. Fellow Am. Acad. Arts and Scis., Am. Nuclear Soc., Acad. Athens, Nat. Acad. Engring.; mem. Am. Nuclear Soc., ASME, Am. Phys. Soc., AAAS. Current Work: Foundations of quantum mechanics and thermodynamics; energy conservation; nuclear reactor safety. Subspecialties: Thermodynamics; Energy conservation. Office: MIT Room 24-109 Cambridge MA 02139

HAACKE, EWART MARK, research scientist, consultant; b. Toronto, Ont., Can., Jan. 24, 1951; came to U.S., 1978, naturalized, 1980; s. Ewart Mortimer and Helena Doris (Davies) H.; m. Linda Theresa Clarke, July 19, 1975; 1 son, Bryon Clarke. B.Sc., U. Toronto, 1973, M.Sc., 1975, Ph.D., 1978. Postdoctoral fellow Toronto (Ont., Can.) U., 1978; research assoc. Case Western Res. U., Cleve., 1978-80, instr., 1980-81, sr. research assoc., 1981-83, instr., 1984-85; research scientist Gulf Research & Devel. Co., Pitts., 1981-83; sr. research scientist Picker Internat., Cleve., 1983-85; asst. prof. dept. physics and radiology Case Western Res. U., 1985—; cons. dept. medicine Case Western Res. U., Cleve., 1981-83. Contbr. articles to profl. jours. Mem. geneal. com. Western Res. Hist. Soc., Cleve., 1981—. Burton fellow U. Toronto, 1977; Ont. grad. fellow, 1975-76; Stevens fellow, 1974; Victoria Coll. fellow, 1970; recipient Ont. scholar award Ont. Govt., 1969. Mem. Am. Phys. Soc., Soc. Exploration Geophysicists, Soc. Indsl. and Applied Math., Ont. Geneal. Soc. Current Work: Tomographic and wave equation inversion techniques, NMR and CT medical imaging, gauge field theories and parton properties, imaging physics Subspecialties: Magnetic resonance imaging; Particle physics. Home: 2312 Glendon Rd University Heights OH 44118 Office: Dept Physics Case Western Res U Cleveland OH 44106

HAACKE, GOTTFRIED, physicist; b. Bad Lausick, Germany, Nov. 27, 1930; came to U.S., 1962, naturalized, 1978; s. Erich and Dora (Grahl) H.; m. Consuelo Velarde, Dec. 14, 1964; children—Frances, Annette. Diploma in Physics, U. Cologne, Fed. Republic Germany, 1954, Ph.D. in Physics, 1957. Research physicist AEG-Telefunken, Frankfurt, Fed. Republic Germany, 1958-61; research physicist Am. Cyanamid Co., Stamford, Conn., 1962-68, group leader, 1968-77, mgr., 1977-84, research fellow, 1984—. Contbr. articles to profl. jours. Patentee in field. Mem. IEEE (sr.), Am. Phys. Soc., Internat. Solar Energy Soc. Current work: growth and characterization of thin film semiconductors; metalorganic chemical vapor deposition; solar energy conversion. Subspecialties: Condensed matter physics; Electronic materials. Office: Am Cyanamid Co 1937 W Main St Stamford CT 06904

HAALAND, DAVID MICHAEL, chemist; b. Chgo., Mar. 16, 1946; s. John Emil and Christine (Rasmussen) H.; m. Kathleen Mary York, June 6, 1968; 1 child, Ryan York. B.S., U. N.Mex., 1968; Ph.D., U. Rochester, 1972. Chemist, Sandia Nat. Labs., Albuquerque, 1972—. Contbr. articles to profl. jours. Patentee internal reference oxygen sensor. Mem. Sandia Search and Rescue Team, Albuquerque, 1974-82. Kodak fellow, 1970, U Uniroyal fellow, 1971. Mem. Fedn. Am. Scientists, Am. Phys. Soc., Am. Chem. Soc., Soc. Applied Spectroscopy, AAAS, N.Mex. Acad. Scis. Current work: Fourier transform infrared spectroscopy, catalyst studies, silicon solar cells, glass formation and structure, quantitative spectroscopy. Subspecialties: Physical chemistry; Analytical chemistry. Home: 716 Cagua St SE Albuquerque NM 87185 Office: Sandia Nat Labs Div 1923 Albuquerque NM 87185

HAAN, CHARLES THOMAS, agricultural engineering educator; b. Randolph County, Ind., July 10, 1941; s. Charles Leo and Dorothy Mae (Smith) H.; m. Janice Kay Johnson, June 3, 1967; children: Patricia Kay, Christopher Thomas, Pamela Lynn. B.S. in Agrl. Engring, Purdue U., 1963, M.S., 1965; Ph.D. in Agrl. Engring, Iowa State U., 1967. Grad. asst. Purdue U., W. Lafayette, Ind., 1963-64; research asso. Iowa State U., Ames, 1964-67; asst. prof., asso. prof., prof. U. Ky., Lexington, 1967-78; prof., head agrl. engring. dept. Okla. State U., Stillwater, 1978-85, prof. agrl. engring., 1985—; cons. in area of hydrology various firms and govtl. orgns. Author: Statistical Methods in Hydrology, 1977, Hydrology and Sedimentology of Surface Mined Lands, 1978; editor: Hydrologic Modeling of Small Watersheds, 1981; contbr. tech. papers and reports to publs. and confs. Recipient and/or adminstr. various research grants. Mem. Am. Soc. Agrl. Engrs. (Young Researcher of 1975, research paper award 1969), Nat. Soc. Profl. Engrs., Okla. Soc. Profl. Engrs., Am. Soc. for Engring. Edn., Am. Inst. Hydrologists, Sigma Xi, Tau Beta Pi, Alpha Epsilon, Gamma Sigma Delta, Phi Kappa Phi. Roman Catholic. Current Work: Hydrologic modeling. Subspecialties: Agricultural engineering; Hydrology. Home: 720 Lakeshore Dr Stillwater OK 74075 Office: Oklahoma State Univ Stillwater OK 74078

HAAS, ERWIN, researcher; b. Budapest Hungary, Sept. 11, 1906; m. Elisabeth Haas; children—Wolfgang, Robert. Ph.D., U. Chgo., 1942. Asst. prof. exptl. pathology Western Res. U., Cleve., 1945-46; asst. dir. Inst. Med. Research, Cedars of Lebanon Hosp., Los Angeles, 1946-53; dir. L.D. Beaumont Meml. Research Labs., Mt. Sinai Med. Ctr., Univ. Circle, Cleve., 1953—. Contbr. articles to profl. jours. Discoverer antibacterial enzymes. Recipient Goodman award, Mt. Sinai Hosp., 1965; NIH grantee, 1954-81. Mem. Am. Heart Assn. Council for High Blood Pressure Research, Internat. Soc. Cardiology, Sci. Council on Hypertension, Am. Soc. Biol. Chemists, Nat. Soc. Med. Research, Am. Chem. Soc. Current work: Medical research on hypertension. Subspecialty: Biochemistry (medicine). Home: 1081 Carver Rd Cleveland Heights OH 44112 Office: L D Beaumont Meml Research Mount Sinai Med Ctr University Circle Cleveland OH 44106

HAAS, THOMAS STEWART, pharmacist; b. Salina, Kans., Oct. 29, 1957; s. Thomas Elwin and Frances Irene (Shepard) H.; m. Tammie Louise Proffitt, Aug. 15, 1979 (div. 1983); m. Sally Ann Scanlan, Dec. 28, 1985. B.S. in Chemistry and Biology magna cum laude, Friends U., 1979; B.S. in Pharmacy, U. Kans., 1984. Lab. asst. U. Kans. Sch. Pharmacy, Lawrence, 1979-83; pharmacist St. Francis Hosp., Topeka, 1982-83, St. John's Hosp., Salina, 1983-84, Walgreen's, Des Moines, 1984—. Contbr. sci. papers, U. Kans., 1979-81. Kans. Bd. Regents scholar, 1984; recipient Am. Inst. Chemists award, 1979. Mem. Am. Soc. Hosp. Pharmacists, Kans. State Pharmacists Assn., Student Osteo. Med. Assn., Am. Chem. Soc., AAAS, Phi Kappa Phi, Kappa Psi, Rho Chi. Republican. Methodist. Current work: Oncology and medical management of oncology patient. Subspecialties: Pathology (medicine); Oncology. Home: 2533 Forest Dr Des Moines IA 50312

HABER, HOWARD ELI, physicist, educator; b. Bklyn., Feb. 3, 1952; s. Leo Max and Sylvia (Bittkower) H.; m. Marjorie Anne Gorker, Aug. 21, 1980. S.B. in Math., Mass. Inst. Tech., 1973, S.B. in Physics, 1973, S.M. in Physics, 1973; Ph.D. in Physics, U. Mich., 1978. Postdoctoral researcher Lawrence Berkeley Lab., Berkeley, Calif., 1978-80, U. Pa., Phila., 1980-82, U. Calif.-Santa Cruz, 1982-84; adj. asst. prof. physics, U. Calif.-Santa Cruz, 1984—. Co-editor Procs. of Theoretical Symposium on Intense Medium Energy Sources of Strangeness, 1983. Mem. Am. Phys. Soc., Am. Assn. Physics Tchrs., Sigma Xi. Democrat. Jewish. Current work: Phenomenological implications of supersymmetry as an explanation for new physics beyond the standard model, how to search for effects of Higgs bosons. Subspecialties: Particle physics; Theoretical physics. Home: 1300 Karmen Ct Santa Clara CA 95051 Office: U Calif Dept Physics Santa Cruz CA 95064

HABERMAN, CHARLES MORRIS, engineering educator; b. Bakersfield, Calif., Dec. 10, 1927; s. Carl Morris and Rose Marie (Braun) H. B.S., UCLA, 1951; M.S. in Mech. Engring., U. So. Calif., 1954, Engr. in Mech. Engring., 1957, M.S. in Aero. Engring., 1961. Lead, sr., group engr. Northrop Aircraft Corp., Hawthorne, Calif., 1951-59; mem. faculty Calif. State U.-Los Angeles, 1959—, prof. mech. engring., 1967. Author: Engineering Systems Analysis, 1965, Use of Computers for Engineering Applications, 1966, Vibration Analysis, 1968, Basic Aerodynamics, 1971. Served with AUS, 1946-47. Mem. Am. Acad. Mechanics, AAUP, AIAA, Am. Soc. Engring. Edn. Democrat. Roman Catholic. Current Work: Heat transfer, fluid mechanics, aerodynamics, vibrations and systems analysis. Subspecialties: Mechanical engineering; Aeronautical engineering.

HABERMAN, JOHN PHILLIP, industrial research chemist; b. Techumseh, Nebr., June 2, 1938; s. John George and Doris Marie (Erickson) H.; m. Kathryn Louise Wollangk, Aug. 18, 1962; children—Jillian Carol, Gwen Kathryn. B.Sc., U. Nebr., 1960; Ph.D., U. Wis., 1966. Tech. staff Proctor and Gamble, Cin., 1966-79; chief chemist ORSANCO, Cin., 1979-80; research chemist Texaco, Houston, 1980—. Author: (with others) Fresh Water Pollution I, 1973. Patentee in field. Pres. Pub. Sch. Planning Commn., Mt. Healthy, Ohio, 1977. Mem. Am. Chem. Soc., AAAS, Soc. Petroleum Engrs. Republican. Methodist. Lodge: Masons. Current work: Fluid loss and formation damage from drilling and completion fluids under simulated well conditions; stabilization of shales; acidizing; test equipment design. Subspecialties: Chemistry of oil and gas production; Analytical chemistry. Home: 3018 Triway Ln Houston TX 77043 Office: Texaco Inc Bellaire Research Labs 5901 S Rice Ave Bellaire TX 77401

HABERMANN, CLARENCE EDWARD, chemist; b. Cutler, Ill., Nov. 16, 1931; s. Albert W. and Lily (Liefer) H.; m. Marlene Ann Messerli, Dec. 27, 1952; children—David, Steven, Dale Eric. B.Sc., So. Ill. U., 1953; M.A., Iowa State U., 1961, Ph.D., 1963. Chemist, AEC, Ames, Iowa, 1956-63; research chemist Dow Chem. Co., Midland, Mich., 1963—. Contbr. articles to profl. jours. Patentee in field. Served with U.S. Army, 1953-56. Recipient Engring. Achievement award Soc. Chem. Engrs., 1974. Mem. Am. Chem. Soc., Am. Soc. Metals (treas. 1973, sec. 1974, vice chmn. 1975, chmn. 1976). Republican. Lutheran. Current work: Analytical chemistry; catalysis; high temperature chemistry; inorganic chemistry; organic chemistry; physical chemistry; solid state and surface chemistry. Subspecialties: Catalysis chemistry; Metallurgical engineering. Home: 3615 Blarney Dr Midland MI 48640 Office: Dow Chem Co 1776 Bldg Midland MI 48640

HABIB, MOHAMMAD MUNIR, research chemist; s. Munir and Suad (Kair-Allah) H.; m. Maria Elina Santiago, Aug. 19, 1977; children—Manny Munir, Omar Pablo. B.Sc. with honors, Ain Shams U., Cairo, 1967; M.Sc., Ball State U., 1975; Ph.D., U. S.C., 1978. Sci. tchr. ARAMCO, Suadi Arabia, 1967-72; postdoctoral research Ala. U., Tuscaloosa, 1978-79; research chemist Gulf Oil Co., Pitts., 1979—. Contbr. articles on catalysis and synthesis gas area to profl. jours. U.S. and fgn. patentee in field. Recipient Joseph Bouknight Teaching award U. S.C., 1976, 77, 78. Mem. Am. Chem. Soc., Catalysis Soc., Pitts. Catalysis Soc., Organic Reactions Catalysis Soc., Alpha-Gamma Grad. Sci. Soc. (pres. 1973-75). Current work: Organometallic chemistry; catalysis, especially in synthesis gas area and synthetic fuels. Subspecialties: Organometallics; Catalysis chemistry. Home: 3426 Huntertown Rd Allison Park PA 15101 Office: Gulf R&D Co PO Drawer 2038 Pittsburgh PA 15230

HACKLEMAN, DAVID EUGENE, chemist; b. Coos Bay, Oreg., Oct. 15, 1951; s. Willis N. and Fanny (LaPollo) H.; m. Debbie Bond, July 25, 1981. B.S.E.E. with honors, Oreg. State U., 1973; Ph.D. in Chemistry, U. N.C., 1978. Mem. tech. staff Hewlett-Packard, Corvallis, Oreg., 1978—. Contbr. articles to profl. jours. Patentee in field. Staff mem. Nat. Youth Sci. Camp, Charleston, W.Va., 1977-78, hon. lectr., 1979—; net control sta. Amateur Radio Emergency Services, 1978—. Mem. IEEE, Am. Chem. Soc., Electrochem. Soc. (past chmn. Oreg. sect.) Amateur Radio Relay League. Current work: Ink jet ink development. Subspecialties: Analytical chemistry; Physical chemistry. Home: 39125 Military Rd Monmouth OR 97261 Office: Hewlett-Packard 1000 NE Circle Blvd Corvallis OR 97330

HACKMAN, E(LMER) ELLSWORTH, III, chemical engineer; b. Phila., Mar. 22, 1928; s. Elmer Ellsworth, Jr. and Leone (Hershberger) H.; m. Edna Oaks, Apr. 4, 1953; children—Matthew, Christian. B.S., Juniata Coll., 1949; M.S., U. Pa., 1957; Ph.D., U. Del., 1967. Mgr. research projects Thiokol Corp., 1958-73; asst. mgr. spl. projects ARCO, 1955-57; pres. NST Engrs. Inc., Wilmington, Del., 1973—; seminar leader McGraw-Hill Chem. Engring. Mag., 1979-82. Author: Toxic Organic Chemicals, Destruction and Waste Treatment, 1978. Contbr. articles to profl. jours. Patentee in field. Air Force Office Sci. Research grantee. Mem. Am. Inst. Chem. Engrs., Am. Chem. Soc. Current work: Providing engineering services, research and development and consulting; preparation of chemical plant operating manuals. Subspecialties: Chemical engineering; Hazardous waste disposal. Home: Millcreek Rd Box 303 RD1 Hockessin DE 19707 Office: NST Engrs Inc Box 2857 Wilmington DE 19805

HACKMAN, JOHN CLEMENT, neurophysiologist, educator; b. Dayton, Ohio, May 16, 1947; s. Clem Frank and Martha Virginia (Schneble) H.; m. Susan Joan Pollard, June 3, 1968; children: Dawn, Jeff, Mark. Ph.D. in Biology, U. Miami, 1979. Adj. prof. neurology U. Miami (Fla.) Sch. Medicine, 1979-80, research asst. prof. neurology, 1980-82, asst. prof., 1982—, asst. prof. pharmacology, 1983—; research physiologist VA Med. Ctr., Miami, 1979—. Contbr. articles to sci. jours. Mem. attendance boundary com. Dade County Sch. Bd., 1981-82; v.p. Devonaire Elem. Sch. PTA, 1981-82. United Way grantee, 1980—; Nat. Parkinson Found. grantee, 1981—; recipient VA Merit Rev. award, 1985—. Mem. AAAS, Soc. for Neursci., Am. Physiol. Soc., Am. Soc. Pharmacology and Exptl. Therapeutics. Republican. Roman Catholic. Current Work: Currently studying the modulation of sensory input into the spinal cord through the use of neurophysiological, neuropharmacological technique. Subspecialties: Neuropharmacology; Neurophysiology. Home: 12244 SW 105 Ln Miami FL 33186 Office: Dept Neurology U Miami Sch Medicine PO Box 16189 Miami FL 33101

HACYAN, SHAHEN, physicist; b. Istambul, Turkey, Oct. 24, 1947; s. Migirdic and Adrine (Saleryan) H.; m. Deborah Dultzin; children: Arturo, Esther. B.Sc., U. Mex., 1968; Ph.D., U. Sussex (Eng.), 1972. Assoc. researcher Universidad Nacional Autonoma de Mexico, 1973-76, researcher, 1976—, physics tchr., 1973—. Contbr. articles to sci. jours. Mem. Internat. Astron. Union, Am. Astron. Soc., Internat. Soc. Gen. Relativity and Gravitation, Academia de la Investigacion Cientifica. Current Work: Relativistic astrophysics and general relativity. Subspecialty: General relativity. Home: Monserrat 157-6 Mexico DF 04330 Mexico Office: Instituto de Astronomia A P 70-264 Mexico DF 04510 Mexico

HADDAD, GEORGE ILYAS, educator, research scientist; b. Aindara, Lebanon, Apr. 7, 1935; came to U.S., 1952, naturalized, 1961; s. Elias Ferris and Fahima H.; m. Mary Louella Nixon, June 23, 1958; children: Theodore N., Susan Anne. B.S.E.E., U. Mich., 1956; M.S.E.E., 1958, Ph.D., 1963. Asst. prof. elec. and computer engring. U. Mich., Ann Arbor, 1963-65, assoc. prof., 1965-69, prof., 1969—, chmn. dept., 1975—; cons. Contbr. articles to profl. jours., chpt. in book. Ford Found. fellow, 1967-68. Fellow IEEE; mem. Am. Phys. Soc., Am. Soc. Engring. Edn. (Curtis W. McGraw research award 1970). Current Work: Microwave solid-state devices and circuits, millimeter-wave devices, transit-time devices, MESFETS. Subspecialties: Semiconductors; Microelectronics. Home: 1340 Morehead St Ann Arbor MI 48103 Office: U Mich 2501 East Engineering Bldg Ann Arbor MI 48109

HADEEN, KENNETH DOYLE, meteorologist; b. Haxton, Colo., Mar. 8, 1931; s. Caleb Samuel and Susie Geneva (Bane) H.; m. Barbara Alieve Foster, Dec. 20, 1953; children—Mark D., Denise. B.S., Colo. State U., 1953; M.S., Tex. A&M U., 1959, Ph.D., 1966. Commd. 2d lt. U.S. Air Force, 1953, advanced through grades to col., 1977, chief spl. analysis team 1st Weather Wing, Saigon, Vietnam, 1971-72, chief tech. services div., Hdqrs. Air Weather Service, Belleville, Ill., 1972-73, wing vice comdr. Global Weather Ctr., Omaha, 1973-76, assoc. dir. global weather expt. Dept. Def., Rockville, Md., 1976-77; dep. dir. Assessment and Info. Services Ctr., Washington, 1977-84; dir. Nat. Climatic Data Ctr., Asheville, N.C., 1984—. Developer Numerical Boundary Layer Model, 1970 (Merewether award 1971). Bd. dirs. Asheville-Buncombe county United Way, (N.C.), 1984. Decorated numerous mil. awards. Mem. AAAS, Am. Meteorol. Soc. (local offices). Lodge: Rotary. Current work: Applied environmental support, both meteorology, climatology. Subspecialties: Meteorology; Climatology.

HADIDI, MOHAMED TAHER, electrical engineer; b. Domyat, Egypt, Feb. 15, 1951; came to U.S. 1974; s. Taher Abdel Razzak and Mawahib (Minawi) H. B.Sc. in Elec. Engring., Cairo U., 1972, B.Sc. in Math., 1974; M.S. in Elec. Engring., Stanford U., 1975, Ph.D. in Elec. Engring., 1983. Teaching demonstrator Cairo U., 1972-74; research asst. Stanford U., Calif., 1978-83; sr. staff elec. engr. Mobil Research & Devel. Corp., Dallas, 1983—. Mem. IEEE, Soc. Exploration Geophysicists, Am. Assn. Petroleum Geologists, Sigma Xi. Current work: Application of signal processing techniques to seismic data; design of fast algorithms; two-dimensional signal processing. Subspecialties: Information systems (Information science); Geophysics. Home: 5330 Bent Tree Forest Dr Apt 727 Dallas TX 75248 Office: Mobil Research & Devel Corp 13777 Midway Rd Dallas TX 75234

HADLER, HERBERT ISAAC, biochemist, educator; b. Toronto, Ont., Aug. 22, 1920; s. Moses and Annie (Rosenberg) H.; m. Miriam Celia Perenson, Feb. 23, 1947; children: Laurie, Mitchell Reuben, Kenneth. B.A.Sc., U. Toronto, 1942; Ph.D., U. Wis., 1952. Postdoctoral fellow McArdle Lab., U. Wis.-Madison, 1951-53; asst. prof. Enzyme Inst., 1960-66; assoc. prof. div. oncology Chgo. Med. Sch., 1953-60; prof. So. Ill. U., Carbondale, 1966—. Contbr. articles to profl. jours. Mem. Am. Soc. Biol. Chemists, Am. Assn. Cancer Research., Am. Chem. Soc., Sigma Xi. Current Work: Oxidative phosphorylation, mitochondrial genes. Subspecialties: Biochemistry (biology); Cosmic ray high energy astrophysics. Home: 302 Wedgewood Ln Carbondale IL 62901 Office: Dept Chemistry and Biochemistry So Ill U Carbondale IL 62901

HADLER, NORTIN M., physician; b. N.Y.C., Nov. 13, 1942; s. Morris H. and Lucille (Hochberg) H.; m. Carol S. Spiegel, June 20, 1965; children: Jeffrey, Elana. A.B., Yale U., 1964; M.D., Harvard U., 1969. Diplomate Am. Bd. Internal Medicine with subspltys. in rheumatology, allergy and immunology. Med. resident Mass. Gen. Hosp., Boston, 1968-70; clin. assoc. ARB-NIAMDD, NIH, Bethesda, Md., 1970-72; resident, rheumatology fellow Mass. Gen. Hosp.-Harvard U., 1972-73; guest scientist Clin. Research Ctr., Harrow, Eng., 1973-74, 79-80; asst. prof. medicine and bacteriology U. N.C., 1974-78, assoc. prof., 1978-85, prof., 1985—. Contbr. articles to profl. jours. Served with USPHS, 1970-72. Investigator Am. Heart Assn., 1976-81. Fellow ACP; mem. Am. Rheumatism Assn., Am. Assn. Immunologists, Am. Soc. Clin. Investigation. Current Work: Biology of joints; industrial rheumatology. Subspecialty: Internal medicine. Office: U NC 932 Floor 231H Dept Medicine Chapel Hill NC 27514

HADLOCK, DANIEL C., oncologist, medical administrator, educator; b. Wilmington, Del., June 5, 1941; s. Canfield and Josephine (Cook) H.; children: Timothy, Amy, Joel, Karen. B.A. in English, Dartmouth Coll., 1962, B.M.S., 1964; M.D., U. Pa., 1966; M.S., U. Minn., 1975. Diplomate: Am. Bd. Internal Medicine (medical oncology). Intern Johns Hopkins Hosp., Balt., 1966-67, resident in internal medicine, 1967-70, practice medicine specializing in oncology, Orlando, Fla., 1975-80; med. dir. Hospice Orlando, Fla., 1976-80, Riverside Hospice, Boonton, N.J., 1980-81; med. dir./prof. edn. Hospice Inc., Miami/Ft. Lauderdale, Fla., 1981, med. dir., 1981-83; asst. clin. prof. oncology U. Miami, Fla., 1982—. Contr. chpt. to book, articles to profl. jours. Served as maj. U.S. Army, 1970-72. Am. Cancer Soc. fellow, 1974-75; recipient cert. merit Madigan Gen. Hosp., 1972; Hospice Pioneer plaque Fla. State Hospice Orgn., 1980. Fellow ACP; mem. Am. Soc. Clin. Oncology, AMA, Am. Geriatric Soc., N.Y. Acad. Sci., Nat. Hospice Orgn. (v.p. 1979-80, pres. 1980-81). Republican. Current Work: Palliative care. Subspecialties: Internal medicine; Oncology. Office: Hospice Inc 111 NW 10th Ave Miami FL 33128

HAEBERLE, FREDERICK ROLAND, oil company scientist; b. Phila., Oct. 6, 1919; s. Frederick Edward and Faye Vivian (Davis) H.; m. Cynthia Lee Davis, Feb. 22, 1946; children: Cynthia Faye, Frederick Edward. B.S., Yale U., 1947, M.S, 1948; M.B.A., Columbia U., 1962. Geologist Standard Oil Calif., Houston, 1948-52; chief geologist J. J. Lynn Oil Div., Abilene, Tex., 1952-53; div. mgr. Mayfair Minerals, Abilene, 1953-54; cons. geologist, Abilene, 1954-57; chief subsurface geologist Atlantic Refining Co., Caracas, Venezuela, 1957-60; geol. specialist Mobil Oil Corp., Dallas, 1962-83, cons. geologist, 1983—; asst. prof. U. Houston, 1948-50; prof. McMurray Coll., Abilene, Tex., 1954-57. Contbr. articles to profl. jours. Served to 1st lt U.S. Army, 1941-46 PTO. Fellow Geol. Soc. Am.; mem. Am. Assn. Petroleum Geologists, Soc. Profl. Well Log Analysts, Assn. Profl. Geol. Scientists, Tex. Acad. Sci. Republican. Presbyterian. Club: Brook Haven Country (Dallas). Current Work: Statistical studies of exploration drilling activity and reserves recovered, applications of computers to geological work. Subspecialties: Geology; Information systems (Information science). Office: 4036 Northview Ln Dallas TX 75229

HAERING, RUDOLPH ROLAND, physics educator, researcher; b. Basle, Switzlerland, Feb. 27, 1934; emigrated to Can., 1947; s. Rudolph and Selma (Tschudin) H.; m. Mary P. Peatfield, Aug. 6, 1954; children—Susan J., Linda J. B.A., U. B.C., 1954, M.A., 1955; Ph.D., McGill U., 1957. Head dept. physics Simon Fraser U., Burnaby, B.C., 1964-68, v.p. acad., 1968-69, prof. physics, 1964-72; head dept. physics U. B.C., 1973-77, prof. physics, 1973—; pres. CTF systems, Post Coquitlam, B.C., 1970-73; chmn. bd. CTF Systems, Port Coquitlam, B.C., 1973-77; dir. Moli Energy Ltd., Burnaby, 1977—, cons., 1977—. Editor: Can. Jour. Physics, 1968-72. Decorated Order of Can. Fellow Royal Soc. Can.; mem. Can. Assn. Physicists (pres. 1978-79, Herzberg medal 1970, pres. 1978-79, CAP medal 1982), Am. Phys. Soc. Current work: Energy storage, intercalation, phase transitions. Office: Dept Physics U British Columbia Vancouver BC V6T 1W5 Canada

HAFLER, DAVID ALLEN, neurologist; b. N.Y.C., Oct. 13, 1952; s. Manny and Ann (Greenwood) H.; m. Janet Jean Palmer; children—Brian Palmer, Jason Palmer. B.S., Emory U., 1974, M.S. magna cum laude, 1974; M.D., U. Miami, 1978. Intern, Johns Hopkins Hosp., Balt., 1978-79; resident Cornell-N.Y. Hosp., N.Y.C., 1979-81, chief resident, 1981-82, Meml. Sloan Kettering Hosp., N.Y.C., 1981; fellow neurosci. Harvard U., Boston, 1982-84, instr., 1984-85, asst. prof., 1985—. Contbr. articles to profl. jours. Recipient Upjohn award U. Miami, 1978, Nat. Research Service award NIH, 1983-85, Clin. Investigator Devel. award, NIH, 1985; Harry Weaver Neurosci. scholar Nat. Multiple Sclerosis Soc., 1985. Mem. Am. Acad. Neurology, Am. Assn. Immunologists, Sigma Xi, Pi Alpha, Alpha Omega Alpha. Current work: Neuroimmunology; cellular immunology in particular as related to multiple sclerosis; immunosuppresion in multiple sclerosis. Subspecialties: Neuroimmunology; Neurology. Home: 34 Morton Rd Newton Center MA 02159 Office: Brigham and Woman's Hosp 75 Francis St Boston MA 02115

HAFNER, JOHN CHRISTOPHER, biology educator, curator, researcher; b. Vallejo, Calif., Dec. 7, 1950; s. George Fredrick and Naomi Fern (Lanman) H.; m. Patti Marion Storrs, Sept. 12, 1970; children—James Martin, Rheanna Chrystine. A.B. in Zoology, U. Calif.-Berkeley, 1973, Ph.D. in Zoology, 1981; M.A. in Zoology, Tex. Tech U., 1976. Research asst. U. Calif., Sagenen Creek Field Sta., Calif., 1970; curatorial asst. Mus. Vertebrate Zoology, U. Calif., Berkeley, 1971-73, research and teaching asst., 1976-80; research and teaching asst. Tex. Tech U., Lubbock, 1973-76; postdoctoral fellow Nat. Mus. Natural History, Smithsonian Instn., Washington, 1980-82; asst. prof. biology, curator birds and mammals Moore Lab. Zoology, Occidental Coll., Los Angeles, 1982—, MacArthur research prof., 1985—. Contbr. articles to profl. jours. Mus. tour guide for various minority programs and local pub. and pvt. grade schs., Los Angeles, 1982—. Grad. research grantee Tex. Tech. U., 1975; Louise M. Kellogg grantee Mus. Vertebrate Zoology, U. Calif., 1978-79; NSF grantee, 1979-80. Mem. AAAS, Am. Ornithologists' Union, Am. Soc. Mammalogists (systematics collections com.), Soc. Study Evolution, Soc. Systematic Zoology. Republican. Current work: Evolutionary biology of geomyoid rodents; geographic variation, hybridization and cline theory; developmental underpinnings of macroevolution; heteromyid systematics. Subspecialties: Evolutionary biology; Systematics. Home: 1140 Palm Terr Pasadena CA 91104 Office: Occidental Coll Moore Lab Zoology Los Angeles CA 90041

HAGEDORN, DONALD JAMES, phytopathologist, educator, agrl. cons.; b. Moscow, Idaho, May 18, 1919; s. Frederick William and Elizabeth Viola (Scheyer) H.; m. Eloise Tierney, July 18, 1943; 1 son, James William. B.S., U. Idaho, 1941, D.Sc. (hon.), 1979; M.S., U. Wis., 1943, Ph.D., 1948. Prof. agronomy and plant pathology U. Wis.-Madison, 1948-64, prof. plant pathology, 1964—; courtesy prof. plant pathology Oreg. State U., Corvallis, 1972-73; vis. scientist DSIR Lincoln Research Center, Christchurch, N.Z., 1980-81. Contbr. chpts. to books, articles to profl. jours. Served with USAAF, 1943-46. Recipient Campbell award AAAS, 1961; CIBA-Geigy award, 1974; Meritorious Service award Nat. Pea Improvement Assn., 1979; Meritorious Service award Bean Improvement Coop., 1979; Forty-Niners award, 1983; NSF sr. postdoctoral fellow, 1957. Fellow Am. Phytopath. Soc.; mem. Sigma Xi, Gamma Sigma Delta, Alpha Zeta. Methodist. Lodge: Kiwanis. Current Work: Diseases of peas and beans; breeding peas and beans for multiple disease resistance. Subspecialties: Plant pathology; Plant genetics. Home: 927 University Bay Dr Madison WI 53705 Office: U Wis 1630 Linden Dr 583 Russell Labs Madison WI 53706

HAGEDORN, SCOTT RICHARD, microbial biochemist, researcher; b. Fond du Lac, Wisc., Nov. 15, 1951; s. Clarence Richard and Anola (Tews) H. B.S. in Molecular Biology, U. Wis.-Madison, 1975; Ph.D. in Biochemistry, U. Minn.-St. Paul, 1980. Biochemist Celanese Research Co., Summit, N.J., 1980—. Contbr. articles to profl. jours. NIH grantee, 1976-79. Mem. Am. Soc. Microbiology, Soc. Gen. Microbiology, Soc. Indsl. Microbiology, Am. Chem. Soc. Current work: Application of microbial aromatic biochemistry to industrial processes. Subspecialty: Biochemistry (biology). Home: Old Coach Rd Summit NJ 07901 Office: Celanese Research Co 86 Morris Ave Summit NJ 07901

HAGEL, ANDREW RICHARD, computer scientist; b. N.Y.C., Sept. 14, 1949; s. Morris and Florence Lyla (Brodsky) H. M.S. in Computer Sci, SUNY-Albany, 1979. Systems analyst Sperry Univac, Albany, 1979-81; telecommunications analyst NBC, N.Y.C., 1981; sr. software engr. Wang Labs., Inc., Lowell, Mass., 1981—. Served with U.S. Army, 1972-75. Mem. Assn. for Computing Machinery, Soc. Indsl. and Applied Math., IEEE. Current Work: Office automation. Subspecialties: Information systems, storage, and retrieval (computer science); Software engineering. Home: 27 Boylston Ln Lowell MA 01852 Office: 1 Industrial M/S 1393 Lowell MA 01861

HAGEN, ARNULF PEDER, chemist, educator; b. Tacoma, Wash., June 6, 1942; s. Carl A. and Marjorie W. (Black) H. B.S., U. Wash., 1964; Ph.D., U. Pa., 1968. Assoc. prof. U. Okla., 1967-83, prof., 1983—. Contbr. articles to profl. jours. Mem. Am. Chem. Soc., Assn. Asphalt Paving Technologists. Current Work: Chemical interactions which will lead to an in-situ mining of coal, reactions at high pressures, asphalt technology. Subspecialty: Inorganic chemistry. Office: Dept Chemistry U Okla Norman OK 73019

HAGEN, CHARLES ALFRED, microbiologist; b. East Rutherford, N.J., Feb. 1, 1925; s. Charles Alfred and Lina Dorothea (Scharch) H.; m. Alice Diana Wiltse, Dec. 14, 1951; children: Erich Christoph, Kristine Ann, Susan Lynn. A.B., U. Chgo., 1952, M.S., 1956. Microbiologist U. Chgo., 1954-55; sr. med. technologist Inst. Tb Research, Chgo., 1955-56; research microbiologist Kraftco, Glenview, Ill., 1956-62; microbiologist Ill. Inst. Tech., Chgo., 1962-69; lab. mgr. Avco Jet Propulsion Lab., Pasadena, Calif., 1967-72, Bionetics Corp. Jet Propulsion Lab., Pasadena, 1972-76; chief bacteriologist Becton Dickinson Lab., Oxnard, Calif., 1976-79, regulatory affairs officer, 1979—. Contbr. articles to profl. jours. Served with USN, 1943-46. Mem. AAAS, Am. Assn. Lab. Animal Sci., Am. Soc. Microbiology, Soc. Indsl. Microbiology, Am. Soc. Quality Control. Republican. Lutheran. Current Work: Assure compliance with state, federal and corporate medical device manufacturing regulations; sterilization procedures-ethylene oxide and radiation; clean room techniques and contamination control procedures. Subspecialty: Microbiology. Home: 2085 Lyndhurst Ave Camarillo CA 93010 Office: 1950 Williams Dr Oxnard CA 93010

HAGEN, LAWRENCE JACOB, agricultural engineer; b. Rugby, N.D., Mar. 6, 1940; s. Lars and Alice O. (Hannem) H.; m. Betty A. Gault. B.S., N.D. State U., 1962, M.S., 1967; Ph.D., Kans. State U., 1980. Research agrl. engr. Agrl. Research Service U.S. Dept Agr., Manhattan, Kans., 1967—. Contbr. articles to prof. jours. Mem. Am. Soc. Agrl. Engrs., Soil Conservation Soc. Am. Current work: Research on wind erosion. Subspecialty: Agricultural engineering. Office: Rm 105 Waters Hall KSU Manhattan KS 66506

HAGER, CHESTER BRADLEY, medical diagnosis company executive; b. Madison, W.Va., Oct. 15, 1938; s. Chester Robertson and Reba Mae (Bradley) H.; m. Nancy Jeanine Beane, Apr. 19, 1962; children—Jennifer Lynn, Valerie Anne. A.B., W.Va. U., 1961, M.S., 1964, Ph.D., 1966. Research scientist Oak Ridge Nat. Lab., 1966-68; research scientist Ames Co., div. of Miles Labs., Elkhart, Ind., 1968-72, dir. tech. service, 1972-75, dir. research and devel., planning Miles Research Products, 1975-81; dir. research and devel. Micromedic Systems, Inc., Horsham, Pa., 1981—; adj. prof. Goshen Coll., Ind., 1980-81. Contbr. articles to profl. jours. Inventor in field. Bd. dirs. Diabetic Childrens'

Camp, Elkhart, 1972-77. Nat. Cancer Inst. fellow, 1964-66, NIH, Am. Cancer Inst. fellow, 1966-68; named Outstanding Young Men of Am. U.S. Jaycees, 1974. Mem. Assn. Clin. Scientists, Am. Assn. Clin. Chemists, N.Y. Acad. Scis., Am. Chem. Soc., Sigma Xi, Sigma Nu. Lodges: Elks, Jaycees. Current work: Diagnostic medicine, endocrinology, molecular biology. Subspecialties: Biochemistry (medicine); Immunology (medicine). Office: Micromedic Systems Inc 102 Witmer Rd Horsham PA 19044

HAGER-RICH, JEAN CAROL, cancer research scientist; b. Avalon, Calif., Aug. 11, 1943; d. Herbert Frank and Marion Arlene (Hammer) H.; m. Marvin A. Rich, 1981. B.S., Bates Coll., Lewiston, Maine, 1965; M.S., U. Ill., Urbana, 1969, Ph.D., 1974. Research assoc. U. Ill., 1974-75; instr. Brown U., Providence, 1975-78, asst. prof., 1978-79; research assoc. Roger Williams Gen. Hosp., Providence, 1975-79; scientist Mich. Cancer Found., Detroit, 1979-80, asst. mem., 1981; asst. prof. pathology Wayne State U., 1979-81; scientist AMC Cancer Research Center, Denver 1981-85; sr. scientist, dir extramural programs AMC Cancer Research Ctr., Denver, 1985—. Contbr. chpts. to books and articles in field to profl. jours. Mem. Internat. Assn. Breast Cancer Research (asst. sec. gen. 1980—), Am. Assn. Cancer Research, Tissue Culture Assn., Internat. Assn. Comparative Research on Leukemia and Related Diseases, Electron Microscopy Soc. Am. Current Work: Cancer cell biology, metastatic process in breast cancer, role of immunological mechanisms in breast cancer and leukemia. Subspecialties: Cancer research (medicine); Immunology (medicine). Home: 1733 S Sand Lily Dr Golden CO 80401 Office: 1600 Pierce St Denver CO 80214

HAGFORS, TOR, astronomy center administrator, electrical engineering and astronomy educator; b. Oslo, Dec. 18, 1930; U.S., 1963; s. Vidar Johan and Hanna Viktoria (Edmundson) H.; m. Gillian Patricia Hart, Jan. 3, 1953; children—John, Toril, Martin, Vivien. M.Engring., U. Trondheim, Norway, 1955; Ph.D., U. Oslo, 1959. Scientist Norwegian Def. Research Labs., Kjeller, 1955-59, 61-63; research asst. Stanford U., Calif., 1961-63; staff mem. Lincoln Labs. MIT, Lexington, Mass., 1963-69, 71-73; dir. Jicamarca Obs., Lima, Peru, 1969-71; prof. elec. engring. and astronomy U. Trondheim, 1973-82; dir. Nat. Astronomy and Ionosphere Ctr. Cornell U., Ithaca, N.Y., 1982—; mem. Fachbeirat Max-Planck Inst. für Astronomie, Lindau-Hanz, Ger., 1977-82, Swedish Space Research Bd., Stockholm, 1978-82. Author, editor: Radar Astronomy, 1967, High Latitude Space Plasma Physics, 1983. Mem. IEEE, Am. Astron. Soc., Am. Geophys. Union, Internat. Union Radio Sci. . Office: Nat Astronomy and Ionosphere Ctr Space Scis Bldg Cornell Univ Ithaca NY 14853

HAGGAG, FAHMY MAHMOUD, nuclear engineer, researcher; b. Alexandria, Egypt, Jan. 1, 1948; came to U.S., 1979; s. Mahmoud Mohamed Haggag and Farida (Abd El-Aziz) El-Basyouni; m. Hassnaa Abd El-Kader, Aug. 4, 1981; children—Mohamad-Nazim, Mona Fahmy. B.S. in Nuclear Engring, U. Alexandria, 1970, M.S. in Nuclear Engring, 1976; M.S. in Nuclear Engring, U. Calif.-Santa Barbara, 1980. Mil. engr. Egyptian Air Force, 1970-72; research engr. AEC, Cairo, 1972-76; instr. U. Algiers, Algeria, 1976-79; research asst. U. Calif.-Santa Barbara, 1979-80; sr. engr. Idaho Nat. Engring. Lab., Idaho Falls, 1980—; cons. Centre Des Sciences Et La Technologie Nucleaires, Algiers, 1977-79. Mem. Egyptian Gymnastics Olympic Team, Egyptian Gymnastics Fedn., 1965-72; coach YMCA, Idaho Falls, 1981-82. Mem. Am. Nuclear Soc. (Best Contributed Paper in Materials Sci. for 1981), Am. Soc. Metals. Inventor semi-pilot prodn. of uranium metal, 1972-76. Current Work: Fracture mechanics; nuclear fuel behavior and manufacturing, materials engineering, and nuclear safety analysis, including severe reactor core accidents. Subspecialties: Materials (engineering); Nuclear engineering. Home: 724 Saturn Ave Apt 8 Idaho Falls ID 83042 Office: Idaho Nat Engring Lab PO Box 1625 Idaho Falls ID 83415

HAGMANN, DEAN BERRY, engineer; b. Cleve., Sept., 24, 1934; s. Vern and Elizabeth (Berry) H.; married; children: DeAnn, Lynda, Teresa. B.S.M.E., U. Wyo., 1959; postgrad., U. Idaho, 1959-70. Engr. Phillips Petroleum Co., Idaho Falls, Idaho, 1959-63; supr. Idaho Nuclear Corp., Idaho Falls, 1963-69; project engr. Argonne Nat. Lab., Idaho Falls, 1969-75, assoc. dir., 1976-82; v.p. Remotec, Oak Ridge, Tenn., 1982-83; staff engr. GA Technologies, San Diego, 1983—. Mem. Am. Nuclear Soc. (bd. dirs. 1978—). Club: Ski. Current Work: Application of remote technology-radioactive materials handling and remote maintenance applied to both fission and fusion plants. Subspecialties: Mechanical engineering; Nuclear fission. Home: 2714 Caminito Verdugo San Diego CA 92014 Office: GA Technologies Inc PO Box 85608 San Diego CA 92138

HAGMANN, MARK JOSEPH, biomedical engineer, researcher; b. Phila., Feb. 14, 1939; s. Mark Herman and Ruth Elizabeth (Walters) H.; m. Sharon Lynne Fritz, Dec. 18, 1959; children—children—Scott, Cathy Lynne, Wendy Kim., Angela Lynn, Mark Anand, Stephen Anand. B.S. in Physics. Brigham Young U., 1960; M.Sc. in Edn., U. Utah, 1966, Ph.D. in Elec. Engring., 1978. Research scientist IRECO Chems., West Jordan, Utah, 1968-76; research assoc. U. Utah, Salt Lake City, 1978-80, research asst. prof., 1980-81; vis. prof. U. Hawaii, Honolulu, 1981-82; biomed. engr. NIH, Bethesda, Md., 1982—; mem. subcom. Am. Nat. Standards Inst., 1978-79, 84—. Contbr. numerous articles to profl. jours.; presenter of 44 symposiums. Patentee in field. Mem. Antennas and Propagation Soc. of IEEE, Engring. Med. and Biology Soc. of IEEE, Microwave Theory and Techniques Soc. of IEEE, Radiation Research Soc., Bioelectromagnetics Soc., Sigma Xi. Current work: Hyperthermia for cancer treatment, electromagnetic imaging, computational electromagnetics. Subspecialties: Biomedical engineering; Electrical engineering. Office: Bldg 13 Room 3 W-13 NIH Bethesda MD 20205

HAGOOD, MELVIN ARDENE, irrigation specialist, educator, consultant; b. Norman, Okla., Apr. 15, 1922; s. Alvus Andrew and Edith Marie (Kessler) H.; m. Helen Patricia Glenn, Dec. 18, 1944; children—Diane C., Nancy G., Cathy L., Michael C. B.S. in Soils, Oreg. State U., 1948; M.S. in Irrigation, U. of Calif.-Davis, 1960. Irrigation specialist Oreg. State U., Corvallis, 1948-51, Wash. State U., Prosser, 1960-77; irrigation cons., Grandview, Wa., 1977—; irrigation leader Wash. State U., Ephrata, 1951-60; irrigation cons. FAO, of United Nations, Rome, 1966-67, other firms 1967—. Contbr. articles to prof. jours. Served to sgt., U.S. Army, 1942-45. Mem. Am. Soc. Agrl. Engrs. Democrat. Presbyterian. Current work: Irrigation feasability, water requirements, system selection, design of on farm systems, water management on farms, control of salinity, water-holding capacities of soils, in developing countries and as expert witness in U.S. Subspecialties: Agricultural engineering; Soil science. Home: 1007 Stassen Way Grandview WA 98930

HAHN, ERWIN LOUIS, physicist, educator; b. Sharon, Pa., June 9, 1921; s. Israel and Mary (Weiss) H.; m. Marian Ethel Failing, Apr. 8, 1944 (dec. Sept. 1978); children: David L., Deborah A., Katherine L.; m. Natalie Woodford Hodgson, Apr. 12, 1980. B.S., Juniata Coll., 1943, D.Sc., 1966; M.S., U. Ill., 1947, Ph.D., 1949; D.Sc., Purdue U., 1975. Asst. Purdue U., 1943-44; research assoc. U. Ill., 1950; NRC fellow Stanford, 1950-51, instr., 1951-52; research physicist Watson IBM Lab., N.Y.C., 1952-55; assoc. Columbia U., 1952-55; faculty U. Calif. at Berkeley, 1955—, prof. physics, 1961—; assoc. prof. Miller Inst. for Basic Research, Berkeley, 1958-59, prof., 1966-67; vis. fellow Brasenose Coll., Oxford (Eng.) U., 1981-82; cons. Office Naval Research, Stanford, 1950-52, AEC, 1955—; spl. cons. USN, 1959; adv. panel mem. Nat. Bur. Standards, Radio Standards div., 1961-64; mem. Nat. Acad. Sci./NRC com. on basic research; adv. to U.S. Army Research Office, 1967-69. Author: (with T.P. Das) Nuclear Quadrupole Resonance Spectroscopy, 1958. Served with USNR, 1944-46. Recipient Oliver E. Buckley prize Am. Phys. Soc., 1971; prize Internat. Soc. Magnetic Resonance, 1971; award Humboldt Found., Germany, 1976-77; co-winner Wolf Found. prize in physics, 1983-84; named to Calif. Inventor Hall of Fame, 1984; Guggenheim fellow, 1961-62, 69-70; NSF fellow, 1961-62; vis. fellow Brasenose Coll., Oxford, 1969-70; lifetime hon. fellow Brasenose Coll., Oxford, 1984. Fellow Am. Phys. Soc. (past mem. exec. com. div. solid state physics); mem. Am. Acad. Arts and Scis., Nat. Acad. Scis., N.Y. Acad. Scis., Slovenian Acad. Scis. and Arts (fgn.). Office: Dept Physics U Calif Berkeley CA 94720

HAHN, GEORGE LEROY, agricultural engineer, biometeorologist; b. Muncie, Kans., Nov. 12, 1934; s. Vernon Leslie and Marguerite Alberta (Breeden) H.; m. Clovice Elaine Christensen, Dec. 3, 1955; children—Valerie, Cecile, Steven, Melanie. B.S., U. Mo., Columbia, 1957, Ph.D., 1971; M.S., U. Calif., Davis, 1961. Agrl. engr., project leader and tech. advisor Agrl. Research Service, U.S. Dept. Agr., Columbia, Mo., 1957, Davis, Calif., 1958-61, Columbia, 1961-78, Clay Center, Nebr., 1978—. Contbr. articles to tech. jours. and books on impact of climatic and other environ. factors on livestock stress and resultant performance, and evaluation of methods of reducing impact. Recipient award Am. Soc. Agrl. Engrs.-Metal Bldgs. Mfrs. Assn., 1976. Mem. Am. Meteorol. Soc. (award for outstanding achievement in bioclimatology 1976), Am. Soc. Agrl. Engrs., Internat. Soc. Biometeorology, AAAS, Am. Soc. Animal Sci. Current Work: Evalution of livestock responses(production; reproduction; efficiency; behavior, health) to environmental factors, primarily thermal factors; and methods of reducing their impact. Subspecialty: Agricultural engineering. Office: US Meat Animal Research Center PO Box 166 Clay Center NE 68933

HAHN, HONG THOMAS, engineering educator; b. Seoul, Korea, Feb. 5, 1942; came to U.S., 1966, naturalized, 1975; s. Baek-Hyo and Sang-Soon (Lee) H.; m. Hoon Pat Paik, Sept. 16, 1967; children—Heryun, Hejin, Jeanie. B.S., Seoul Nat. U., 1964; M.S., Pa. State U., 1968, Ph.D., 1971. Research assoc. Air Force Materials Lab., Dayton, Ohio, 1972-74, materials research engr., 1977-78; research engr. U. Dayton Research Inst., 1974-77; mech. engr. Lawrence Livermore lab. (Calif.), 1978-79; assoc. prof. engring. Washington U., St. Louis, 1979-81, prof., 1981—; cons. in field. Co-author: Introduction to Composite Materials, 1980. Editor Jour. Composite Materials, 1980—. Mem. editorial adv. bd. Composites Tech. Rev., 1979—. Contbr. articles to profl. publs. Served to lt. Korean Army, 1964-66. Grantee NSF, 1982, NASA, 1982. Mem. Korean Assn. St. Louis (pres. 1984), Korean Scientists and Engrs. in Am. (pres. St. Louis chpt. 1980), ASME, AIAA, ASTM, Soc. Exptl. Mechanics, Sigma Xi. Current work: Composite materials and polymers, mechanics, non-destructive testing, processing, fatigue and fracture, reliability. Subspecialties: Composite materials; Theoretical and applied mechanics. Home: 1562 Mason Knoll Rd St Louis MO 63131 Office: Washington U Campus Box 1087 St Louis MO 63130

HAIDLE, RUDY HENRY, chemist, consultant; b. Rochester, N.Y., Sept. 4, 1945; s. Rudolph Emil and Julianne (Bowman) H. Assoc. in Applied Sci. Rochester Inst. Tech., 1966, B.S., 1969; M.S., Cornell U., 1971. Co-op employment Xerox Corp., Webster, N.Y., 1965-69; v.p. research and devel. Creative Plastics, Rochester, 1971-72; mgr. electronics and machine shop Northwestern U., Chgo., 1972-75, analytical instrument specialist, Evanston, Ill., 1975—; cons. Columbia Coll., Chgo., 1979—; mem. bd. cons. Fine Arts Research and Holographic Ctr., Chgo., 1979—. Contbr. articles to profl. jours. Patentee in field. Recipient DuPont Teaching award, 1970. Mem. Analytical lab. Mgrs. Assn. (co-founder, Treas. 1979—, bd. dirs. 1979—), Am. Chem. Soc. (Chgo. chpt. bd. dirs. 1978—), AAAS, Soc. Applied Spectroscopy (bd. dirs. 1981-83). Current work: Medical application of lasers, optics monitor on space shuttle, analysis of trace components, instrument design. Subspecialties: Analytical chemistry; Laser medicine. Home: 1514 South Blvd Evanston IL 60602 Office: Northwestern Univ Dept Chemistry 2145 Sheridan Rd B107 Evanston IL 60201

HAIGLER, HENRY JAMES, neuropharmacologist; b. Columbia, S.C., July 23, 1941; s. Harry Delk and Evelyn (Talton) H.; m. Jean Smith, July 25, 1964; children: Henry James, Elizabeth Ashley. B.S., Wake Forest U., 1963; Ph.D., Bowman Gray Sch. Medicine, 1969. Postdoctoral fellow Mental Health Research Inst., U. Mich., 1969-71; research asso. dept. psychiatry Yale U. Sch. Medicine, New Haven, 1971-74; asst., then assoc. prof. dept. pharmacology Emory U., Atlanta, 1974-82, dir. grad. studies dept. pharmacology, 1980-82; sect. head CNS pharmacology Searle Research & Devel., Skokie, Ill., 1982—; Magistral lectr. Neurol. Congress, 1980. Contbr. articles to profl. jours., chpts. in books. Deacon Clairmont Presbyn. Ch., 1981-82. Nat. Inst. Drug Abuse grantee, 1975-82. Mem. Soc. for Neurosci. (pres. Atlanta chpt. 1981-82), Am. Soc. Pharmacology and Exptl. Therapeutics, AAAS. Current Work: Neuropharmacological studies of the mechanism of action of neurotropic drugs such as narcotic analgesics and psychotomimetics. Subspecialties: Cellular pharmacology; Neurobiology. Office: 4901 Searle Pkwy Skokie IL 60077

HAINSWORTH, F. REED, biologist; researcher; b. Norfolk, Va., June 25, 1941; s. Waldo Reed and Willie Frances (Hodges) H.; m. Diane Smith, June 25, 1970; children—Charlotte Anna, Emily Amanda. A.B., Clark U., 1963; Ph.D., U. Pa., 1968; postdoctoral, Duke U., 1968-69. Asst. prof. Syracuse U., N.Y., 1969-71, assoc. prof., 1971-74, prof., 1974—. Author: Animal Physiology, 1981. Contbr. articles to profl. jours. Mem. Am. Soc. Naturalists, Am. Soc. Zoologists, Soc. for Study of Evolution, Am. Inst. Biol. Scis. Current work: Experimental tests of optimal design theory; study of model systems for evolution of separate sexes; adaptations in energy and resource use by organisms. Subspecialties: Evolutionary biology; Comparative physiology. Home: 110 Harrington Rd Syracuse NY 13224 Office: Dept Biology Lyman Hall Syracuse U Syracuse NY 13210

HAIRE, MARVIN JONATHAN, nuclear engineer, research scientist; b. Jackson, Ala., Sept. 18, 1943; s. Marvin Reynolds and Abalene (Creson) H.; m. Janet Gewn Newsom, June 20, 1965; children: Sarah Elizabeth, Rebecca Anne. B.S., N.C. State U., 1965, M.S., 1967, Ph.D., 1970. Registered profl. engr., Calif. Staff engr., section leader Gen. Atomic Co., La Jolla, Calif., 1970-76; asst. prof. nuclear engring. Ga. Inst. Tech., Atlanta, 1976-78; staff mem. Oak Ridge Lab., Tenn., 1978—; cons. Contbr. articles to profl. jours. Mem. Am. Nuclear Soc., Soc. for Risk Analysis, Personal Computers Club, Sigma Xi, Tau Beta Pi, Sigma Pi Sigma. Current Work: Risk analysis, systems analysis economic evaluations, radioactivity source terms, heat transfer, ventillation systems. Subspecialties: Nuclear fission; Nuclear engineering. Office: Oak Ridge Nat Lab PO Box X Oak Ridge TN 37830

HAIRE, MICHAEL JOSEPH, research chemist; b. Kansas City, Mo., Jan. 18, 1947; s. Joseph Miller and Agnes Lois (Gatton) H.; m. Theresa Marie Asher, Oct. 25, 1968; children—Michael John, Christopher Alan, Matthew James. Student St. Benedict's Coll., 1965-67; B.S. in Chemistry, U. Kans., 1969; Ph.D. in Chemistry, U. Wis.-Madison, 1974. Research chemist, central research E.I. duPont de Nemours & Co., Inc., Wilmington, Del., 1974-79, Ortho Div. Chevron Chem. Co., Richmond, Calif., 1979—; invited lectr. U. Ky., U. Kans., U. Wash., San Francisco State U., 1977—. Contbr. articles to profl. jours.; referee Jour. Organic Chemistry, 1975—. Patentee pharms. and agrichems. Mem. Del. Med. Malpractice Rev. Bd., 1977-78; scholarship adminstr. Casa Grande Music Assn., Petaluma, Calif., 1984. Mem. Am. Chem. Soc., Alpha Chi Sigma. Current work: Synthesis of novel structures to elicit useful biological effects in pharmaceutical and agricultural chemical fields; relationship of computers to chemistry, research management. Subspecialties: Organic chemistry; Synthetic chemistry. Office: Chevron Chem Ortho 940 Hensley St Richmond CA 94802

HAISCH, BERNHARD MICHAEL, astrophysicist; b. Stuttgart-Bad Canstatt, W.Ger., Aug. 23, 1949; came to U.S., 1952, naturalized, 1961; s. Friedrich Wilhelm and Gertrud Paula (Dammbacher) H.; m. Pamela S. Eakins, July 29, 1977; children: Katherine Stuart, Christopher Taylor. Student, St. Meinrad Coll., 1967-68; B.S. in Astrophysics magna cum laude, Ind. U., Bloomington, 1971; M.S. (Wis. Alumni Research Found. fellow), U. Wis., Madison, 1973, Ph.D. in Astrophysics, 1975. Research assoc. Joint Inst. for Lab. Astrophysics, U. Colo., Boulder, 1975-77, 78-79; vis. scientist Rijksuniversiteit Utrecht (Netherlands), Astron. Inst., 1977-78; research scientist Space Scis. Lab., Lockheed Palo Alto Research Lab., Palo Alto, 1979-83, staff scientist, 1983—. Research, publs. in field. Fellow Royal Astron. Soc.; Mem. Internat. Astron. Union, Am. Astron. Soc., Astron. Soc. Pacific, Phi Beta Kappa, Sigma Xi, Phi Kappa Phi. Club: Lockheed Tae Kwon Do (Karate, rank of blackbelt, 1st deg.) (Sunnyvale, Calif.). Current Work: Development of concepts and technologies for future space research; studies of solar and stellar atmospheres, coronae and flares. Subspecialties: Theoretical astrophysics; X-ray high energy astrophysics. Home: 847 San Ramon Muss Beach CA 94038 Office: Div 91-20 Bldg 255 Lockheed Palo Alto Research Lab 3251 Hanover St Palo Alto CA 94304

HAKALA, REINO WILLIAM, mathematics, computer science and chemistry educator; b. Albany, N.Y., Aug. 25, 1923; s. Toivo Wiljami and Emma Liisa (Kujanpaa) H.; m. Eunice Irma Kazanowski, June 17, 1950; children: Jonathan, Lisamaria, Christina. A.B., Columbia Coll., 1946; M.A., Columbia U., 1947; Ph.D., Syracuse U., 1965. Assoc. prof. chemistry and math. Mich. Tech. U., Houghton, 1964-67; chmn. math. and physics Oklahoma City U., 1967-70, prof. math., 1967-72; dean Sch. Sci. and Tech., Lake Superior State Coll., Sault Ste Marie, Mich., 1973-77, prof. chemistry, math, and physics, 1973-80, asst. to v.p. acad. affairs, 1977; dean Coll. Arts and Scis. Govs. State U., Park Forest South, Ill., 1980-81, spl. asst. to provost, 1982, prof. math., phys. scis. and environ. scis., 1982—; cons. Nat. Bur. Standards, Washington, 1962-63. Contbr. articles in field to profl. jours. Co-chmn. Adv. Com. to Dir. of Bd. Health on PBB Problem, Chippewa County, Mich., 1975; chmn. Air Quality Control Variance Bd. City of Oklahoma City, 1970-72. Served with U.S. Army, 1943-44. Danforth assoc. Danforth Found., St. Louis, 1979-85; Washington Acad. Scis. fellow, 1960; NSF faculty fellow, 1963-64. Mem. Soc. Indsl. and Applied Math., Assn. Computing Machinery, Chemometrics Soc., Sigma Xi, Phi Lambda Upsilon, Sigma Pi Sigma. Mem. Soc. of Friends. Current Work: Mathematical modeling, iteration acceleration techniques, equations of state, critical region of fluids, teaching computer programming, numerical analysis, operations research, calculus, advanced inorganic chemistry; treatment of experimental data. Subspecialties: Numerical analysis (computer science); Condensed matter physics. Home: 2945 Chayes Park Dr Homewood IL 60430 Office: Govs State U University Park IL 60466

HALARIS, ANGELOS, psychiatrist, educator; b. Athens, Greece, Nov. 30, 1942; came to U. S., 1971, naturalized, 1979; s. Eleftherios and Elli (Georgiadou) H.; m. Ann L. Lyons, June 15, 1980. M.D., Ph.D., U. Munich, 1967. Diplomate: Am. Bd. Psychiatry and Neurology. Resident, fellow U. Chgo., 1971-77, asst. prof. psychiatry, 1975-77, assoc. prof., 1978-80, UCLA Sch. Medicine, 1980-82, prof., 1982-84; prof. Case Western Res. U., 1984—; dir. dept. psychiatry Cleve. Met. Gen. Hosp., 1984—; vice chmn. dept. psychiatry Univ. Hosps. Cleve.; chief Biol. Psychiatry Lab.; cons. Cedars-Sinai Med. Ctr., Los Angeles. Contbr. numerouus articles on psychiatry to profl. jours. Served with Greek Army, 1970-71. Fulbright Scholar, 1955-60; Founds. Fund for Research in Psychiatry fellow, 1971-73. Mem. Am. Hellenic Inst., N.Y. Acad. Scis., AMA, Am. Psychiat. Assn., Am. Coll. Neuropsychopharmacology, Internat. Coll. Neuropsychopharmacology. Current Work: Research in biological psychiatry and psychopharmacology. Subspecialties: Psychiatry; Psychopharmacology. Office: 3395 Scranton Rd Cleveland OH 44109

HALASI-KUN, GEORGE JOSEPH, hydrologist, educator, topographer; b. Zagreb, Austria-Hungary, July 28, 1916; came to U.S., 1958, naturalized, 1963; s. Tibor and Priscilla (Tholt) H.; m. Elisabeth Christina Szorad, Mar. 10, 1945; children—Beatrice, Georgie. B.A. summa cum laude, Coll. Budapest, Hungary, 1934; M.S. in Civil Engring. summa cum laude, Inst. Tech., Budapest, 1938; C.E., Slovak Tech. U., Bratislava, Czechoslovakia, 1949; D. Engring. Sci. cum laude, Tech. U., Brunswick, W.Ger. Registered profl. engr., Conn., N.J.; cert. profl. hydrologist. Sect. engr. State Hwy. Dept., L. Mikulas, Czechoslovakia, 1946-48; prof. hydrology Tech. U., Kosice, Czechoslovakia, 1948-53; mgr., chief engr. PS Constrn. Co., Kosice, 1954-57; project mgr. Columbia U., N.Y.C., 1958-71; topog. engr. State of N.J., Trenton, 1971—; chmn. water resources Columbia U., N.Y.C., 1967—; adj. prof. hydrology N.Y. Inst. Tech., N.Y.C., 1971-76, Rutgers U., 1976-79, Fairleigh Dickinson U., Rutherford, N.J., 1979—. Contbr. articles to profl. jours. Nat. Acad. Sci. fellow 1977, 82, 84. Fellow ASCE, Geol. Soc. Am.; mem. Internat. Water Resources Assn., Am. Water Resources Assn., Société des Ingenieurs Civil de France etc. Current work: Interdisciplinary program on pollution and water resources; methodology of water resource data collection for data bank; remote sensing in toxic waste; XVI-XIX century map evaluation. Subspecialties: Civil engineering; Hydrology.

HALBERSTAM, HEINI, mathematician; b. Most, Czechoslovakia, Sept. 11, 1926; came to Eng., 1939, naturalized, 1947; s. Michael and Judith (Honig) H.; m. Heather M. Peacock, Mar. 11, 1950 (dec. 1971); children: Naomi Deborah, Judith Marion, Lucy Rebecca, Michael Welsford; m. Doreen Bramley, Sept. 28, 1972. B.S. with honours, Univ. Coll., London U., 1946; M.S., London U., 1948, Ph.D., 1952. Lectr. math. U. Exeter, 1949-57; reader Royal Holloway Coll., London U., 1957-62; Erasmus Smith prof. Trinity Coll., Dublin, Ireland, 1962-64; prof. Nottingham U., England, 1964-80; prof. math., head dept. U. Ill., Urbana-Champaign, 1980—; vis. lectr. Brown U., 1955-56; vis. prof. U. Mich., 1966, U. Tel Aviv, 1973, U. Paris-South, 1972. Co-author: Sequences, 1966, 2d edit., 1983, Sieve Methods, 1975; co-editor math. papers of, W.R. Hamilton, H. Davenport; contbr. articles to profl. jours. Mem. London Math. Soc. (v.p. 1962-63, 74-77), Math. Assn. Am., Edinburgh Math. Soc., Am. Math Soc. Subspecialty: Number theory. *

HALBERT, MELVYN LEONARD, physicist; b. Phila., Aug. 12, 1929; s. Herman and Florence Mildred (Nachman) H.; m. Edith Helen Conrad, Mar. 25, 1951; children—Daniel C., Joel M., Alan L. A.B., Cornell U., 1950; Ph.D., U. Rochester, 1955. Physicist, Oak Ridge Nat. Lab., Tenn., 1955—. Pres., Oak Ridge Symphony Orch., 1965-68, treas., 1982—. Fellow Am. Phys. Soc. Jewish. Lodge: B'nai B'rith (treas. 1980—). Current work: Heavy-ion induced reactions, nuclear reaction mechanisms, nuclear spectroscopy. Subspecialty: Nuclear physics. Home: 104 Morgan Rd Oak Ridge TN 37830 Office: Oak Ridge Nat Lab Physics Div PO Box X Oak Ridge TN 37830

HALBOUTY, MICHEL THOMAS, geologist, petroleum engineer, petroleum operator; b. Beaumont, Tex., June 21, 1909; s. Tom Christian and Sodia (Manolley) H.; 1 dau., Linda Fay. B.S., Tex. A. and M. U., 1930, M.S., 1931, Profl. Degree in Geol. Engring, 1956; D.Eng. (hon.), Mont. Coll. Mineral Sci. and Tech., 1966. Geologist, petroleum engr. Yount-Lee Oil Co., Beaumont, 1931-33, chief geologist, petroleum engr., 1933-35; v.p., gen. mgr., chief geologist and petroleum engr. Glenn H. McCarthy, Inc., Houston, 1935-37, owner firm cons. geologists and petroleum engrs., 1937-81; chmn., chief exec. officer Michel T. Halbouty Energy Co., 1981—; discoverer numerous oil and gas fields, La. and Tex.; adj. prof. Tex. Tech U.; vis. prof. Tex. A. and M. U. Author several books.; Contbr. numerous papers on geology and petroleum engring. to profl. jours. Served as lt. col. AUS, 1942-45. Recipient Tex. Mid-Continent Oil and Gas Assn. distinguished service award for an ind., 1965; named engr. of year Tex. Soc. Profl. Engrs. and Engrs. Council, 1968; Distinguished Alumni award Tex. A. and M. U., 1968; Michel T. Halbouty Geoscis. Bldg. named for him, 1977; DeGolyer Distinguished Service medal Soc. Petroleum Engrs. of Am. Inst. Mining, Metall. and Petroleum Engrs., 1971; hon. mem. Spindletop sect., 1972; hon. mem. inst., 1973; Anthony F. Lucas Gold medal, 1975; Pecora award NASA, 1977; Horatio Alger award Am. Schs. and Colls. Assn., 1978; Spirit of Life award Industry Council of City of Hope, 1978; Breath of Life award Cystic Fibrosis Found., 1981; Medal of Merit, Circum-Pacific Council for Energy and Mineral Resources, 1982; Hoover medal Am. Assn. Engring. Socs., 1982; Disting. Service award Paul Carrington chpt. SAR, 1983; Tex. Heritage award Angleton C. of C., Tex., 1983. Mem. Am. Assn. Petroleum Geologists (hon., pres. 1966-67, Human Needs award 1975, Sidney Powers Meml. medal 1977), Am. Soc. Oceanography, Internat. Assn. Sedimentology, Inst. Petroleum, London, Am. Petroleum Inst., Am. Inst. Mining and Metall. Engrs. (1st disting. lectr. emeritus 1982), Soc. Paleontologists and Mineralogists, Soc. Econ. Geologists, Mineral. Soc. Am., Geol. Soc. Am., Soc. Exploration Geophysicists (hon.), Nat. Acad. Engring., Houston Geol. Soc. (hon.), N.Y. Acad. Scis., Tex. Acad. Sci. (Disting. Tex. Scientist of Yr. award 1983), AAAS, Am. Inst. Profl. Geologists, Am. Geol. Inst., Tex., Nat. socs. profl. engrs., Gulf Coast Assn. Geol. Socs. (hon. 1982). Episcopalian. Clubs: Ramada (Houston), Houston (Houston), Petroleum (Houston), River Oaks Country (Houston); Dallas Petroleum; Eldorado Country (Palm Desert, Calif.), Vintage (Palm Desert, Calif.); New Orleans Petroleum; Cosmos (Washington); Broadmoor (Colorado Springs, Colo.), Kissing Camels (Colorado Springs, Colo.). Subspecialties: Geology; Petroleum engineering. Home: 49 Briar Hollow Houston TX 77027 Office: Halbouty Center 5100 Westheimer Rd Houston TX 77056

HALBREICH, URIEL, psychiatrist; b. Jerusalem, Israel, Nov. 23, 1943; came to U.S., 1978, naturalized, 1982; s. Mordechai and Zipora (Tennenbaum) H.; m. Tatiana Or, Feb. 1, 1966; 1 child, Jasmine. M.D., Hebrew U., 1969. Diplomate: Tel Aviv U. Psychiatry and Psychotherapy. Vice chief med. officer Israel Navy, 1970-72; second, then first asst. Hadassah U. Hosp., Jerusalem, 1972-78, temp. chief physician, 1978; chief psychiatrist Israel Navy, 1977-78; asst. prof., research psychiatrist Columbia U., N.Y.C., 1978-80; asso. prof. dir. Div. Biol. Psychiatry, Albert Einstein Coll. Medicine, N.Y.C., 1982-85; prof. psychiatry, dir. biobehavioral research SUNY-Buffalo, 1985—. Contbr. over 100 articles to profl. jours.; editor: Transient Psychosis, 1983; Harmones and Depression, 1986; Resistance to Antidepressants, 1986. Served to comdr. Israeli Navy, 1970-78. Recipient Ben Gurion award Gen. Fedn. Labor, 1976; Yair Gon award Hebrew U. Hadassah Med. Sch., 1978; Nat. Research Service award NIH, 1978; NIMH grantee, 1982. Mem. Am. Coll. Neuropsychopharmacology, Am. Psychopathology Assn., Soc. Biol. Psychiatry, Endocrine Soc., others. Jewish. Current Work: Research is in biol. psychiatry especially behavioral endocrinology and psychopharmacology of affective disorders and hormone related mood and behavior in women. Subspecialties: Psychopharmacology; Neuroendocrinology. Home: 497 Delaware Ave Buffalo NY 14202 Office: SUNY Dept Psychiatry 462 Grider St K-Annex Buffalo NY 14215

HALE, JACK K., mathematics educator, researcher; b. Dudley, Ky., Oct. 3, 1928; s. James M. and Cora Lee (Kelly) H.; m. Hazel I. Reynolds, June 6, 1949. A.B. in Math., Berea Coll., 1949; M.Sc., Purdue U., 1951, Ph.D., 1953; D.Sc. (hon.), U. Ghent, 1983. Instr. math. Purdue U., West Lafayette, Ind., 1949-54; staff mem. Sandia Corp., Albuquerque, 1954-57, Remington-Rand-Univac, St. Paul, 1957-58, RIAS, Balt., 1958-64; prof. math. Brown U., 1964—; vis. prof. UCLA-U. So. Calif., 1968-69, U. Florence, Italy, 1971-72, Heriot-Watt U., Edinburg, Scotland, 1976. Author: Nonlinear Oscillations, 1963, Ordinary Differential Equations, 1969, Functional Differential Equations, 1977, Bifurcation Theory, 1982. Editor: Differential Equations, 1980—. Recipient Chauvenent prize Math. Assn. Am., 1964; Fulbright scholar, 1971; Guggenheim fellow, 1979. Fellow Am. Acad. Mechanics; mem. Am. Math. Soc., Brazilian Acad. Sci., Sigma Xi. Current work: Asymptotic behavior and qualitative theory or ordinary, partial and functional differential equations. Subspecialty: Differential equations. Office: Div Applied Math Brown U Providence RI 02912

HALE, WILLIAM KENT, operations research analyst; b. Charleston, W. Va., Aug. 24, 1941; s. Joseph William and Eloise (Keely) H.; m. Callie Jones, Aug. 22, 1964; children: Clifford Wade, Christine Calore. B.S., W. Va. U., 1966, M.S., 1967. Prof. math. Radford (Va.) U., 1968-73; mathematician Def. Communications Agy., Reston, Va., 1973-1979, ops. research analyst, 1982—, electronics engr. Inst. for Telecommunications Scis., Boulder, Colo., 1979-81; ops. research analyst Dept. Army, Washington, 1981-82. Author: Bibliography-Frequency Assignment Methodology, 1981; contbr. research articles to publs. Organizer Nat. Soc. Profs., Radford, Va., 1970-72; faculty sponsor ACLU, Radford, 1970-72; coach Little League Baseball, Summit Point, W.Va., 1975-79. Recipient Meritorious Service Award Def. Communications Agy., Reston, 1979; research grantee NSF, Chgo., 1971; research fellow, 1968. Mem. IEEE, Ops. Research Soc. Am., Math. Assn. Am. Baptist. Current Work: Application of recent developments in discrete mathematics, computational complexity and artificial intelligence to problems in communication systems engineering. Subspecialties: Algorithms; Distributed systems and networks. Home: Box 208 Summit Point WV 25446 Office: Def Communications Agy 1860 Wiehle Ave Reston VA 22090

HALEMANE, THIRUMALA RAYA, physics educator; b. Ednad Village, India, May 27, 1953; s. H. Shama Bhat and Thirumaleshwari; m. Usha Kumari Kailar, Aug. 30, 1976; 1 child, Kaviraj. B.Sc., Bangalore U., 1972; M.Sc., Indian Inst. Tech., Madras, 1974; M.A. in Math., U. Rochester, 1980, M.A. Physics, 1976; Ph.D., 1980. Research assoc. Rutgers U., Piscataway, N.J., 1979-81; asst. prof. SUNY Fredonia, N.Y., 1981—; vis. asst. prof. Pa. State U., University Park, 1984 summer; vis. scientist Phys. Research Lab., Ahmedabad, India, 1983 summer. Rush Rhees fellow, 1974; SUNY Found grantee, 1982. Mem. Am. Phys. Soc., Materials Research Soc., AAUP. Hindu. Lodge: Rotary. Contbr. articles to profl. jours. Current work: Phase transitions in ferroelectrics; phenomenology; dielectric properties; statistical nuclear physics; electromagnetic properties; moment of inertia. Subspecialty: Theoretical physics. Home: 90 Brigham Rd #C-14 Fredonia NY 14063 Office: Dept Physics SUNY Fredonia NY 14063

HALER, LAWRENCE EUGENE, nuclear reactor company analyst; b. Iowa City, Jan. 24, 1951; s. Eugene Hilbert and Mary Elizabeth (Hans) H.; m. Jenifer Lea Leitz, June 1, 1974. B.A. in Liberal Arts, Pacific Lutheran U., 1974. Pacific Luth. U. intern Wash. State Ho. of Reps., Olympia, 1972; in public adminstrn. City of Tacoma, 1974; with UNC-United Nuclear Corp., Richland, Wash., 1974—, mgr. tng. devel. and adminstrn., 1982, investigative analyst, 1982—. Chmn. Benton County (Wash.) Republican Party, 1976-78. Mem. Am. Nuclear Soc. Lutheran. Current Work: Analyze unusual events and occurrences at nuclear reactor; also analyze operational trends as they occur at nuclear reactor. Subspecialty: Nuclear fission. Home: 4265 Ironton Dr West Richland WA 99352Office: UNC-United Nuclear Corp PO Box 490 Richland WA 99352

HALES, CHARLES ALBERT, internist, educator; b. Greeley, Colo., Apr. 27, 1941; s. Charles A. and Dorothy G. (Henkle) H.; m. Mary Ann Little, June 12, 1965; children—Sam E., Chris A., John S. B.A., Emory U., 1962, M.D., 1966. Diplomate Am. Bd. Internal Medicine, Am. Bd. Pulmonary Disease. Assoc. dir. Pulmonary Unit, Mass. Gen. Hosp., Boston, 1976—; assoc. prof. medicine Harvard U., Boston, 1979—. Contbr. articles to profl. jours. Served to lt. comdr. USNR, 1968-70, Vietnam. Recipient Pulmonary Embolism award NIH, 1983; Lung Injury in Fires award, NIH, 1982. Mem. Am. Soc. Clin. Investigation, Am. Thoracic Soc., Am. Physiol. Soc., Mass. Thoracic Soc. Presbyterian. Current work: Research on phusiology of the lung and in particular the lung vasculature. Subspecialties: Pulmonary medicine; Physiology (medicine). Office: Mass Gen Hosp Pulmonary Unit Fruit St Boston MA 02114

HALEVY, SIMON, physician, educator; b. Bucharest, Romania, June 5, 1929; came to U.S., 1963, naturalized, 1970; s. Meyer Abraham H. and Rebecca (Landau) H.; m. Hilda M. Valdes, 1968; 1 son, Daniel Abraham. M.D., U. Bucharest, 1953. Diplomate: Am. Bd. Anesthesiology. Intern Univ. Hosp., Coltzea, Romania, 1952-53, resident, 1953-54, practice medicine specializing in anesthesiology, 1955—; instr. anesthesia Postgrad. Inst. Medicine, Bucharest, 1955-57, chief lab. in anesthesia, 1957-60; preparator, instr. anatomy U. Bucharest Med. Sch., 1950; attending anesthesiologist Univ. Hosp., Fundeni, Bucharest, 1960-63; intern Community Hosp., Glen Cove, N.Y., 1964-65; resident Mt. Sinai Hosp., N.Y.C., 1965-67; asst. prof. anesthesiology Mt. Sinai Sch. Medicine, 1967-68; asst. prof. Albert Einstein Coll. Medicine, 1969-74; assoc. prof. Coll. Physicians and Surgeons, Columbia U., 1974-75; prof. SUNY, 1976—; asst. attending anesthesiologist Mt. Sinai Hosp. Services and Bronx Mcpl. Hosp. Center, 1967-71, attending anesthesiologist, 1973-74; attending anesthesiologist, assoc.-anesthesiologist-in-chief, dir. obstet. anesthesiology Nassau County Med. Center, 1976—; Chmn. com. on sci. exhibits Postgrad. Assembly in Anesthesiology, N.Y.C., 1971-80. Mem. editorial bd.: Microcirculation, Convergences Médicales; Contbr. articles to sci. jours. Fellow Am. Coll. Anesthesiologists; mem. AMA, Am. Soc. Anesthesiologists, Assn. des Anesthésiologistes Français, Deutche Gesellschaft für Anaesthesiologie und Intensivmedizin; Fellow Société Française d'Anesthésie et de Réanimation mem. Association Internationale des Anesthésiologistes d'Expression Française (v.p., mem. adminstrv. council), N.Y. Acad. Scis., AAAS, Am. Soc. Pharmacology and Exptl. Therapeutics. Current Work: Pathophysiology of shock syndrome, pharmacology of thyroid hormones, histamine and antihistamines, perinatology. Office: Nassau County Med Center 2201 Hempstead Turnpike East Meadow NY 11554

HALL, BARRY GORDON, molecular biologist, researcher, educator; b. N.Y.C., July 17, 1942; s. S. Henry and Helen (Norton) H.; m. Susan Marie Hall, May 2, 1964; children: Steven John, Scott Owen, Rebecca Anne. B.S. in Genetics, U. Wis., Madison, 1968; Ph.D., U. Wash., 1971. Research assoc. Inst. Molecular Biology, U. Oreg., Euegene, 1971-72, postdoctoral fellow, 1972-73, U. Minn., 1973-74; asst. prof. molecular biology Faculty of Medicine, Meml. U. Nfld. (Can.), St. John's, 1974-77; asst. prof. biology U. Conn., Storrs, 1977-80, assoc. prof., 1980—; vis. professorial fellow applied biology dept. U. Wales Inst. Sci. and Tech., 1984-85; Contbr. articles to sci. jours. NIH fellow, 1968-73; Fulbright sr. fellow, 1984-85; Career Devel. awardee, 1980—; Med. Research Council Can. grantee, 1974-77; NIH, NSF grantee, 1978—. Mem. Genetics Soc. Am., Am. Soc. Naturalists, Am. Soc. Biol. Chemists, Am. Soc. Microbiology, Sigma Xi, Gamma Sigma Delta. Current Work: Evolution of new enzymes in the laboratory; experimental evolution. Subspecialties: Evolutionary biology; Genetics and genetic engineering (biology). Office: Biol Scis U Conn Storrs CT 06268

HALL, CARL WILLIAM, research foundation administrator; b. Tiffin, Ohio, Nov. 16, 1924; s. Lester C. and Irene E. (Routzahn) H.; m. Mildred Evelyn Wagner, Sept. 4, 1949; 1 child, Claudia Hall Genuardi. B.S., B.A.E. summa cum laude, Ohio State U., 1948; M.M.E., U. Del., 1950; Ph.D., Mich. State U., 1952. Registered profl. engr. Ohio, Mich., Wash. Instr. then asst. prof. U. Del., Newark, 1948-51; from asst. prof. to dept. chmn., Mich. State U., East Lansing, 1951-70; dean engring., prof. mech. engring. Wash. State U., Pullman, 1970-82, now dean emeritus; dep. asst. dir. acctg., asst. dir. engring. NSF, D.C., 1982-83; pres. ACA Cons. Engr., Reynoldsburg, Ohio, 1960-70, Wash. State U. Research Found., Pullman, 1974-82. Author or co-author 20 books on drying, energy, processing, and food engineering; contbr. 250 articles to profl. jours. Editor internat. jour. Drying Tech. Served to sgt. U.S. Army, 1943-46, ETO. Decorated Bronze Star; recipient Disting. Faculty award Mich. State U., 1963; Centennial Achievement award Ohio State U., 1970; Massey-Ferguson Gold medal Am. Soc. Agrl. Engrs., 1976; Cyrus Hall McCormick medal, 1984, Max Eyth medal Max Eyth Gesellschaft, 1979. Fellow AAAS, Am. Soc. Agrl. Engrs. (pres. 1974-75), ASME (life); mem. Engrs. Council Profl. Devel. (sec. 1973-74), Nat. Soc. Profl. Engrs. (bd. dirs. 1974-78), Internat. Commn. Agrl. Engrs. (v.p. 1967-74). Subspecialties: Agricultural engineering; Mechanical engineering. Home: 3017 N Nottingham St Arlington VA 22207 Office: Directorate Engring NSF 1800 G St NW Washington DC 20550

HALL, CHARLES DENIS, telecommunications equipment executive; b. Lennoxville, Que., Can., July 1, 1938; s. Charles Wayne and Grace Elizabeth H.; m. Florence May Falkingham, Nov. 23, 1963; 1 son, Jeffrey. B.Engring., McGill U., Montreal, 1960; M.Sc., U. Sask., 1961, Ph.D., 1964. Registered profl. engr., Ont. With No. Electric Co. Ltd., Montreal, 1964-71, exec. v.p. devel., 1974-76; v.p. switching devel. Bell-No. Research Ltd., Ottawa, 1972-74, exec. v.p. devel., 1974-76, pres., 1976-81; exec. v.p. mktg. and tech. No. Telecom Can. Ltd., Islington, Ont., 1981-82, sr. v.p. tech., Mississauga, Ont., 1982—. Author articles in field. Mem. Engring. Inst. Can., IEEE, Assn. Profl. Engrs. Ont. Christian Scientist. Current work: Management of technology in communications, electronics and software. Address: 33 City Centre Dr Mississauga ON L5B 2N5 Canada

HALL, CHARLES FREDERICK, space scientist, govt. adminstr.; b. San Francisco, Apr. 7, 1920; s. Charles Rogers and Edna Mary (Gibson) H.; m. Constance Vivienne Andrews, Sept. 18, 1942; children—Steven R., Charles Frederick, Frank A. B.S., U. Calif., Berkeley, 1942. Aero. research scientist NACA (later NASA), Moffett Field, Calif., 1942-60, mem. staff space projects, 1960-63; mgr. NACA (Pioneer Project), 1963-80. Recipient Disting. Service medal NASA, 1974, Achievement award Am. Astronautical Soc., 1974, Spl. Achievement award Nat. Civil Service League, 1976, Astronautics Engr. award Nat. Space Club, 1979. Research, reports on performance of wings and inlets at transonic and supersonic speeds, on conical-cambered wings at transonic and supersonic speeds, 1942-60; Pioneer Project launched 4 solar orbiting, 2 Jupiter and 2 Venus spacecraft. Subspecialties: Aerospace engineering and technology; Aeronautical engineering. Home: 817 Berry St Los Altos CA 94022

HALL, C(HARLES) WILLIAM, surgical researcher; b. Gage, Okla., Feb. 8, 1922; s. Cecil Asbury and Helen Maude (Greene) H.; m. Sheila Fowler, Dec. 3, 1979; m. Shirley Thomson, Oct. 20, 1962 (dec.); m. Betty Woodring, June 6, 1943 (div. 1962); children—Daniel C., Kendall W. (dec.), Gregory A., Patrick C., Connan L; 1 stepchild, M'Lis Watkins Brewer. B.A., Kans. U., 1951, M.A., 1952, M.D., 1956; D.Eng. (hon.), Rose-Hulman Inst. Tech., 1985. Diplomate Am. Bd. Surgery. Intern, Kans. U., Kansas City, 1956-57, resident in surgery, 1957-62, fellow in medicine 1959-60; fellow in cardiovascular surgery Baylor Coll. Medicine, Houston, 1962-64, asst. prof. surgery and physiology, 1964-69; project dir. Nat. Heart Inst., 1964; dir. dept. bioengring. SW Research Inst., San Antonio, 1969-74, inst. med. scientist, 1975—; clin. prof. surgery U. Tex. Med. Sch., San Antonio, 1969—. Editorial bd. Jour. Biomed. Materials Research, 1967-85. Contbr. articles to profl jours. Developed and performed 1st implanted blood pump. Patentee 2 artificial hearts and permanently attached artificial limb. Served as cpl. USAAF, 1942-46. Recipient Medalla de Oro, Argentina, 1974; named prof. hon. causa U. Catolica Cordoba, 1965. Fellow Acad. Surg. Research (cofounder 1984, pres. 1985), Am. Coll. Cardiology, Am. Coll. Chest Physicians; mem. AMA, Am. Heart Assn. (pres. San Antonio chpt. 1972-73), Am. Soc. Artificial Internal Organs, Soc. Biomaterials (founding pres., Clemson award 1977), Am. Burn Assn., Internat. Cardiovascular Soc., Sigma Xi, Delta Upsilon. Republican. Unitarian. Lodges: Masons (32 deg.); Shriners. Current work: Artificial organs, surgical research, biomaterial application. Subspecialties: Artificial organs and prostheses; Biomaterials. Office: 6220 Culebra Rd PO Drawer 28510 San Antonio TX 78284

HALL, DAVID LEE, computer scientist, researcher; b. Blockton, Iowa, June 15, 1946; s. Clarence Beryl and Dorothy (Keenan) H.; m. Mary Jane Moyer, Aug. 23, 1969; children—Sonya Anne, Cristin Marie. B.A., U. Iowa, 1967; M.S., Pa. State U., 1968, Ph.D., 1976. Staff scientist MIT Lincoln Lab., Lexington, 1976-77; prin. engr. Computer Scis. Corp., Silver Spring, Md., 1977-79; engring. mgr. HRB-Singer, Inc., State Coll., Pa., 1969—; physics instr. U. Colo., Colorado Springs, 1970-72. Author: A Programmed Basic Physics Laboratory Manual, 1971. Contbr. articles to profl. jours. Served with USAF, 1969-72. Mem. Am. Astron. Soc., Am. Astronautical Soc., Sigma Xi. Republican. Lutheran. Current work: Artificial intelligence; software engineering; numerical analysis; computer architecture. Subspecialties: Software engineering; Satellite studies. Office: HRB-Singer Inc PO Box 60 State College PA 16804

HALL, DONALD NORMAN BLAKE, astronomer; b. Sydney, Australia, June 26, 1944; m. 1967; 2 children. B.Sc., U. Sydney, 1966; Ph.D. in Astronomy, Harvard U., 1970. Exptl. officer physics, div physics Commonwealth Sci and Indsl. Research Orgn., Sydney, 1966-67, 1967-70; research assoc astronomy, 1970-72, assoc., 1972-76; astronomer Kitt Peak Nat. Obs., Tucson, 1976-84; dep. dir. Space Telescope Sci. Inst., Balt., 1977-84; dir. U. Hawaii Inst. Astronomy, 1984—. Recipient Slade prize U. Sydney, 1964; Newton Lacey Pierce prize, Am. Astron. Soc., 1978. Mem. Am. Astron Soc., Internat. Astron. Union. Subspecialty: Astronomical research administration. Office: U Hawaii Inst for Astronomy 2680 Woodlawn Dr Honolulu HI 96822

HALL, EDWARD DALLAS, pharmacologist, biological scientist, med. educator; b. Bedford, Ohio, June 16, 1950; s. Edward Ellis and Martha Elaine (Johnston) H.; m. Marilynn Frances Gay, Sept. 12, 1970; children: Edward William, Christian David. B.S., Mt. Union Coll., Alliance, Ohio, 1972; Ph.D. (Nat. Inst. Gen. Med. Sci. fellow), Cornell U., 1976. Postdoctoral fellow dept. pharmacology Cornell U. Med. Coll., N.Y.C., 1976-77; asst. prof. pharmacology Northeastern Ohio Univs. Coll. Medicine, Rootstown, 1978-82, assoc. prof., 1982; asst. prof. Kent State U., 1978-82; research scientist The Upjohn Co., Kalamazoo, 1982-85, sr. research scientist, 1985—; adj. assoc. prof. Western Mich. U., 1983—; adj. assoc. prof. Med. Coll. Ohio, Toledo, 1984—; cons. on drug-related issues. Contbr. articles and abstracts to sci. and med. jours., chpt. to book. Elder Randolph (Ohio) Christian Ch., 1981-82; v.p. Portage County Combined Gen. Health Dist. Bd.; deacon Oakland Dr. Ch. of Christ, 1983—. NIMH grantee, 1978-79, 80-82; Amyotrophic Lateral Sclerosis Soc. Am. grantee, 1978-81, 81-82. Mem. Am. Soc. for Pharmacology and Exptl. Therapeutics, Soc. for Neurosci., Soc. for Exptl. Biology and Medicine, AAAS, Am. Paralysis Assn. (sci. adv. council), N.Y. Acad. Scis., Sigma Xi, Phi Sigma. Lodge: Randolph Lions. Current Work: Pathophysiology and pharmacol. treatment of acute brain and spinal cord injury and stroke; pharmacol. inhibition of nerve cell degeneration. Subspecialties: Pharmacology; Neuropharmacology. Home: 1432 Woodland Ave Portage MI 49002 Office: CNS Research Unit The Upjohn Co Kalamazoo MI 49001

HALL, FREEMAN FRANKLIN, JR., meteorologist, remote sensing researcher; b. Kansas City, Mo., Sept. 29, 1928; s. Freeman Franklin and Ruth Agatha (Morton) H.; m. Worth Butler Chapman, Dec. 19, 1952; children—Rebecca L., Russell F., Bernice R., Bradley A. A.B. in Physics, Occidental Coll., 1950; M.S. in Applied Physics UCLA, 1957, Ph.D. in Meteorology, 1967. Research scientist Lockheed Missiles Div., Van Nuys, Calif., 1954-57; assoc. dir. electro-opt. ITT Fed. Labs., San Fernando, Calif., 1957-66; dir. environ. sci. Douglas Adv. Research Labs., Huntington Beach, Calif., 1966-70; chief atmosphere acoustics NOAA Wave Propagation Lab., Boulder, Colo., 1970-77, chief atmosphere lidar, 1977—; chmn. publs. Optical Soc. Am., Washington, 1982—. Editor: Laser Applications Geosci., 1970. Contbr. articles to profl. jours., NOAA Outstanding author, 1978. Served to sgt. USMC, 1951-53. Recipient Edn., Industry award South Coast Coll. Dist., Santa Ana, Calif., 1968, Unit Commendation award NOAA Environ. Research Labs., Boulder, Colo., 1971. Fellow Optical Soc. Am. (dir. 1975-77, 1982—), Soc. Photo-Optical Instrumentation Engrs.; mem. Am. Meteorol. Soc., Phi Beta Kappa, Sigma Xi. Club: Boulder Audubon Soc. (dir. 1974-80). Current work: Develop and apply laser radar (lidar) techniques for atmospheric remote sensing, especially infrared, Doppler (heterodyne) lidars. Analyse lidar results - winds, aerosol and clouds. Subspecialties: Remote sensing (atmospheric science); Optical engineering. Office: NOAA Wave Propagation Lab 325 Broadway Boulder CO 80303

HALL, HERBERT JOSEPH, physicist, consultant; b. Springfield, Mass., Sept. 30, 1916; s. Herbert C. and Jospheine A. (Whalan) H.; m. Georgine Fleming, Sept. 21, 1949; children: Molly J., John L., Stephen W.; m. Jean Cummings, Nov. 4, 1962. B.S., Trinity Coll., Conn., 1939; M.S., U. Mich., 1940, doctoral candidate, 1939-41. Mem. staff radiation lab. MIT, Cambridge, 1941-45; mem. staff for Bikinitests Los Alamos Lab., 1946; physicist, sr. physicist, then asst. dir. research Research Cottrell, Inc., Bound Brook, N.J., 1946-58; sci. cons., N.J., 1959-61; dir. research and devel. Research Cottrell, Inc., 1962-68; v.p. Recon Systems, Inc., Princeton, N.J., 1969-72; pres. H.J. Hall Assocs., Inc. (Sci. Cons.), Princeton, 1973—; dir. corps. Contbr. articles to sci. jours. Served with OSRD, U.K. and Europe; liaison Brit. Air Ministry and USAF, 1943-45. H.E. Russell fellow, 1939; recipient Internat. Fellow award for outstanding contbns. to sci. and application of electrostatic precipitation. Mem. Am. Phys. Soc., AAAS, NY. Acad. Scis., Air Pollution Control Assn. Republican. Patentee in field. Current Work: Electrostatic precipitation; air pollution control systems and equipment; frontier technology; aerosol and gaseous discharge physics; litigation problems. Subspecialties: Gas cleaning systems; Condensed matter physics. Office: Mass Gen Hosp Boston MA 02114

HALL, HOWARD RALPH, psychology educator, researcher, clinician; b. Yokohama, Japan, Sept. 14, 1950; s. Howard Ralph and Dorothy Lillian (Johns) H.; m. Clara Jean Mosley, Aug. 12, 1978; Ilea Elizabeth Mosley. B.S., Del. State Coll., 1973; M.A., Princeton U., 1975, Ph.D., 1978; Psy.D., Rutgers U., Piscataway, N.J., 1982. Postdoctoral fellow Center Alcohol Studies, Rutgers U.-Piscataway, 1978-80; intern in psychology Coll. Medicine and Dentistry N.J./Rutgers U. Med Sch., Piscataway, 1979-80; asst. prof. psychology Pa. State U., 1980—; mem. adv. bd. Claremont Sch. Theology Inst. for Religion and Wholeness, 1982. Vice pres. Pa. State U. Forum on Black Affairs, 1981-82. Nat. Inst. Alcohol Abuse and Alcoholism grantee, 1979. Mem. Am. Psychol. Assn., Soc. Clin. and Exptl. Hypnosis, Kappa Alpha Psi. Current Work: Effects of hypnosis and imagery on lymphocyte functioning. Subspecialty: Behavioral psychology. Home: 510 Galen Dr State College PA 16803 Office: Pa State U 311 More Bldg University Park PA 16802

HALL, JEROME WILLIAM, engineering educator, researcher; b. Brunswick, Ga., Dec. 1, 1943; s. William L. and Frances (Wickie) H.; m. Loretta E. Hood, Aug. 28, 1965; children—Jennifer, Bridget, Bernadette. B.S. in Physics, Harvey Mudd Coll., 1965; M.S. in Engring., U. Wash., 1968, Ph.D. in Civil Engring., 1969. Registered profl. engr., N.Mex., Va., D.C. Assoc. prof. civil engring. U. Md., College Pk., 1970-77, prof. U. N. Mex. 1977—, dir. bur. engring. research, 1981—, asst. dean engring., 1985—; traffic safety cons., 1971—. Contbr. articles to profl. jours. Recipient Teetor award Soc. Automotive Engrs., 1975. Fellow Inst. Transportation Engrs. (pres. N. Mex. sect. 1984—); mem. Transp. Research Bd., Am. Road Transportation Builders Assn., Am. Soc. Engring. Edn. Republican. Roman Catholic. Current work: Safety research related to highway design and operation, evaluation of highway safety improvements, cost- effectiveness analyses. .

HALL, JOHN LEWIS, physicist, educator; b. Denver, Aug. 21, 1934; s. John Earnest and Elizabeth Rae (Long) H.; m. Marilyn Charlene Robinson, Mar. 1, 1958; children—Thomas Charles, Carolyn Gay, Jonathan Lawrence. B.S., Carnegie Mellon U., 1956, M.S., 1958, Ph.D., 1961. Nat. Acad. Sci. research assoc. Nat. Bur. Standards, Washington, 1961-62, physicist Joint Inst. Lab. Astrophysics, Boulder, Colo., 1962-76, sr. scientist, 1976—; lectr. dept. physics U. Colo., Boulder, 1963—. Editor: Laser Spectroscopy 3, 1977. Contbr. numerous articles to profl. jours. Patentee in field. Recipient Gold medal U.S. Dept. Commerce, 1969; S.W. Stratton award Nat. Bur. Standards, 1971; E.U. Condon award Nat. Bur. Standards, 1979; Meritorious Alumnus award Carnegie Mellon U., 1985. Fellow Am. Phys. Soc., Optical Soc. Am. (C. H. Thownes award 1984); mem. Acad. Sci. Current work: Stabilized lasers; precision measurement, fundamental constants, application of lasers to fundamental measurements. Subspecialties: Atomic and molecular physics; Laser spectroscopy. Office: Nat Bur Standards Joint Inst Lab Astrophysics 325 Broadway Boulder CO 80303

HALL, KENNETH RICHARD, chemical engineering educator, consultant; b. Tulsa, Nov. 5, 1939; s. Snipes Webster and Selina Rose (Scarpin) H.; m. Janet Beulah Blood, June 1964 (div. Jan. 1975); children—Tara Marie, Deirdre Rene; m. 2d, Frieda Maria Karner, Mar. 12, 1976; 1 child, Kent Max. B.S. in Chem. Engring., U. Tulsa, 1962; M.S., U. Calif.-Berkeley, 1964; Ph.D., U. Okla., 1967. Registered profl. engr., Tex. Asst. prof. chem. engring. U. Va., Charlottesville, 1967-70, 71-74; asst. to pres. Chem Share, Norman, Okla., 1970; sr. research engr. AMOCO, Tulsa, 1970-71; assoc. prof. chem. engring. Tex. A&M U., College Station, 1974-78, prof., 1978-79, prof., dir., 1979—; cons. PMI, Duncanville, Tex., OPC, Houston. Contbr. numerous articles to profl. jours. Mem. Am. Inst. Chem. Engrs., Am. Chem. Soc., ASME, Am. Soc. Engring. Edn., ASHRAE. Current work: Thermodynamics Subspecialties: Thermodynamics; Chemical engineering. Office: Tex A & M Univ Chem Engring College Station TX 77843

HALL, LEROY BROOKS, JR., veterinary pathologist, educator; b. Pensacola, Fla., Oct. 7, 1950; m. Earnestine Cotton, May 19, 1972. B.S., Tuskegee Inst., 1975, D.V.M., 1976; M.S., Iowa State U., 1980, Ph.D., 1982. Intern Tuskegee Inst., 1977; instr. vet. pathology Iowa State U., 1977—. Mem. AVMA, Fla. Vet. Med. Assn. Current Work: Pathogenesis of pseudorabies (Aujeszky's disease), virus infection of the reproductive tract of boars and gilts. Subspecialty: Pathology (veterinary medicine). Office: Dept Vet Pathology Iowa State U Ames IA 50011

HALL, NANCY ROSE, software engineer; b. Englewood, N.J., Jan. 16, 1942; d. Stephen R. and Lucy A. (Pastor) Gardiner; m. John L. Hall, Apr. 23, 1966 (div. 1971). B.A., N.Y. U., 1963, M.S., 1967; Ph.D., Poly. Inst. N.Y., 1983. Programmer IBM, N.Y.C., 1966-70, project programmer, mgr., Morristown, N.J., 1972-76, mgr., devel. programmer, Wayland, Mass., 1976-80, adv. programmer fed. systems div., Bethesda, Md., 1980-84, sr. programmer, 1984—; adj. faculty U. Md., College Park, 1984-85; teaching cons. Poly. Inst. N.Y., N.Y.C., 1979-80; mem. adj. faculty Fairleigh Dickinson U., Madison, N.J., 1975-76. N.Y. U. Alumni scholar, 1959-63. Mem. Assn. Computing Machinery, Soc. Indsl. and Applied Math. Current Work: Software engineering education for IBM and specialty distributed systems and networks. software complexity measurement for networks and architecture. Subspecialties: Software engineering; Distributed systems and networks. Office: IBM 6600 Rockledge Dr Bethesda MD 20817

HALL, RICHARD LELAND, food processing company executive; b. Roseland, Nebr., June 14, 1923; s. Leland R. and Hazel Ann (Parks) H.; m. Barbara Ann Abbott, Sept. 11, 1948; children—Ann Whitney Hall Dorr, Nancy Abbott Hall Cooper, Elizabeth Woodward. S.B., Harvard U., 1943, A.M., 1946, Ph.D. in Chemistry, 1951. Research chemist McCormick & Co., Inc., Balt., 1950-51, research dir., 1951-57, dir. research and devel., 1957-68, v.p. research and devel., Hunt Valley, Md., 1968-75, v.p. sci. and tech., 1975—, dir., 1955—. Editor: (with Jurg Solms) Criteria of Food Acceptance, How Man Chooses What He Eats, 1981. Served to 1st lt. USAAF, 1943-45; ETO. Named Chemist of Yr., Md. sect. Am. Chem. Soc., 1976. Fellow Inst. Food Technologists (pres. 1971-72, Nicholas Appert award 1977, Phila. Sect. award 1978, Disting. Food Scientist award N.Y. sect. 1980), AAAS; mem. Soc. of Toxicology, N.Y. Acad. Scis. Clubs: Chemists (N.Y.C.); Cosmos (Washington). Current work: Flavor and odor constituents of spices and other natural products; food toxicology and safety evaluation. Subspecialty: Food science and technology. Office: McCormick & Co Inc 11350 McCormick Rd Hunt Valley MD 21031

HALL, STAN S., chemistry educator; b. Platteville, Wis., July 4, 1938; s. Stanley LaVern and Carrie R. (Hoffland) H.; m. Barbara Lindsay, June 26, 1982; children—Jacqueline, Travis. B.S., U. Wis.-Madison, 1963; Ph.D., MIT, 1967. Postdoctoral research fellow Stanford U., Calif., 1967-68; faculty Rutgers U., Newark, 1968—, now prof. chemistry. Contbr. articles to profl. jours. CIBA-Geigy grantee, 1980. Mem. Am. Chem. Soc. (councilor 1980—, chmn. N.J. sect. 1983-84). Current work: Development of new synthetic methods; synthesis of complex molecules. Subspecialties: Organic chemistry; Organometallics. Office: Dept Chemistry Rutgers U Newark NJ 07102

HALL, STEPHEN A., geography educator; b. Ponca City, Okla., Aug. 11, 1942; s. Richard Frank and Maurine (McKnight) H.; m. Ann Dibrell Alley, Sept. 16, 1968; children—John Dibrell, James Austin. B.S., U. Okla., 1967; M.S., U. Iowa, 1971; Ph.D., U. Mich., 1975. Petrographic asst. Field Mus. Natural History, Chgo., 1967-68; research asst. U. Mich., Ann Arbor, 1971-75; research assoc. No. Ill. U., De-Kalb, 1975; asst. prof. North Tex. State U., Denton, 1977-83, assoc. prof. geography, 1983-85, assoc. prof. geography U. Tex., Austin, 1985—; cons. paleoecology of archeologic sites to many univs., govt. agys., 1972—. Contbr. articles to profl. jours. NSF grantee 1973, 79—. Mem. AAAS, Assn. Am. Geographers, Geol. Soc. Am., Internat. Assn. for Aerobiology (sec. gen. 1982—), Am. Assn. Stratigraphic Palynologists. Current work: Quaternary geomorphology and paleoecology of the American

Southwest and plains. Subspecialties: Geology; Paleontology, paleoecology. Home: 11512 Juniper Ridge Austin TX 78759 Office: Dept Geography U Tex Austin TX 78712

HALL, THOMAS CHRISTOPHER, pharmacologist, educator, medical program administrator; b. N.Y.C., Nov. 26, 1921; s. John Clarence and Theresa (McDonald) H.; m. Lorina A. Friesen, July 30, 1978; children: Christopher, Thomas, Seth, Amity, Bronwen, Nathan, Jinny, Nicholas. M.D., Harvard U., 1949. Diplomate Am. Bd. Internal Medicine, Am. Bd. Med. Oncology. Intern Peter Bent Brigham Hosp., Boston, 1949-50, assoc. in medicine, 1964; research fellow Harvard Med. Sch., 1950-53, teaching fellow, 1954, asst. in medicine, 1955; clin. and research fellow Mass. Gen. Hosp., Boston, 1951-53, resident, 1954, asst. in medicine, 1955; sr. research assoc. in biochemistry Brandeis U., Waltham, Mass., 1959, adj. assoc. prof., 1961; asst. physician Children's Hosp. Med. Ctr., Boston, 1961, research assoc. in pathology, 1961, sr. assoc. in medicine, 1963; sr. assoc. Children's Cancer Research Found., 1961, chief clin. and biochem., pharmacology, 1964; dir. div. oncology U. Rochester (N.Y.), 1968-72, prof. medicine and pharmacology, 1968-72; physician Strong Meml. Hosp., 1968-72; prof. medicine and biochemistry Los Angeles County/U. So. Calif. Cancer Hosp. and Research Center, 1972-75; dir. Cancer Control Agy. of B.C., 1975-76; prof. medicine U. B.C. Faculty of Medicine, 1975-77; scientist Pasadena (Calif.) Found for Med. Research, 1977; clin. prof. U. Calif., Irvine, 1978—; dir. cancer control Cancer Ctr. of Hawaii, U. Hawaii, 1978—; cons. in internal medicine and oncology to various hosps. Contbr. articles to profl. jours. Recipient grants in field, various lectureships. Mem. AAAS, Am. Assn. for Cancer Edn., Am. Assn. for Cancer Research (dir. 1971-74), Am. Soc. Clin. Pharmacology and Chemotherapy, A.C.P., Internat. Soc. for Biochem. Pharmacology, Am. Fedn. for Clin. Research, Am. Soc. Clin. Oncology, Am. Soc. Hematology, Am. Soc. for Pharmacology and Exptl. Therapeutics, AAUP, Endocrine Soc., James Ewing Soc., Histochem. Soc., Internat. Soc. Chemotherapy, Radiation Research Soc., Internat. Lung Cancer Working Party, Soc. for Cryobiology, Soc. for Devel. Biology, Western Assn. Physicians, Soc. for Exptl. Biology and Medicine, Western Soc. for Clin. Research, Can. Oncologic Soc., Sigma Xi, Alpha Omega Alpha. Current Work: Pharmacology and cancer control. Subspecialties: Cancer research (medicine); Chemotherapy. Home: 263 Kakahiaka St Kailua HI 96734 Office: Cancer Control Edn and Outreach Program Cancer Center Hawaii U Hawaii 1236 Lauhala St Honolulu HI 96813

HALL, TIMOTHY C., biology educator, administrator, consultant; b. Darlington, Eng., Aug. 29, 1937; came to U.S. 1965; s. Gilbert Leslie and Dorothea Olive (Lindemann) H.; m. Sandra Severn, Sept. 20, 1960; children—Anna, Liza, Peter. B.Sc. in botany with honors, U. Nottingham, Eng., 1962, Ph.D. in Plant Physiology, 1965. Prof. horticulture U. Wis.-Madison, 1966-82, adj. prof. biophysics and genetics, 1982-84; dir. advanced research Agrigenetics Corp., Madison, 1980-84; head biology dept. Tex. A&M U., College Station, 1984—; dir. Agrigenetics Research Corp., Boulder, Colo., 1981-84. Co-editor, author: Nucleic Acids in Plants, 1979; Organization and Expression of the Plant Genome, 1985. Served to flying officer RAF, 1958-62. NIH grantee Tex. A&M U., 1984—; grantee U. Wis.-Madison, 1973-84; Herman Frasch Found. grantee, 1977-82. Mem. Biochem. Soc. U.K., Am. Soc. Biol. Chemists, Am. Soc. Microbiology, Am. Soc. Virology, Am. Soc. Plant Physiologists. Current work: Transfer and expression of genes, especially seed proteins, from one plant to another, use of site-directed mutagenesis to understand viral infections. Subspecialties: Genetics and genetic engineering (biology); Plant virology. Home: 1044 Rose Circle College Station TX 77840 Office: Dept Biology Tex A & M U College Station TX 77843

HALL, WILLIAM JACKSON, statistician, educator; b. Beltsville, Md., Nov. 13, 1929; s. Reginald Foster and Lily (Hambleton) H.; m. Helen Bloxom Cox, Mar. 27, 1954 (div. 1981); children: Jacqueline Arden, Rebecca Clayton, Bryan Hambleton, Kay Randall.; m. Nancy T. Hufsmith, Jan. 1, 1982. A.B., Johns Hopkins U., 1950; M.A., U. Mich., 1951; Ph.D., U. N.C., 1955; postgrad., Manchester (Eng.) U., 1953, Cambridge (Eng.) U., 1954. Statistician Bell Telephone Labs., N.Y.C., 1954-55; asst. chief Polio Surveillance Unit, Communicable Disease Center, USPHS, Atlanta, 1955-57; lectr. U. Calif. at Berkeley, 1957, vis. prof., 1969; asst. prof. U. N.C., 1957-61, assoc. prof., 1961-66, prof. statistics, 1966-69; vis. prof. Stanford, 1967-69; prof. dept. stats. and div. biostats. U. Rochester, N.Y., 1969—, chmn. dept. stats., 1969-81; vis. prof. stats. and biostats. U. Washington, 1982. Asso. editor: Annals of Mathematical Statistics, 1968-73, Jour. Am. Statis. Assn, 1976-78. Fellow AAAS, Am. Statis. Assn., Inst. Math. Stats. (council 1973-76); mem. Royal Statis. Soc. Current Work: Statistical theory; biostatistics. Subspecialty: Statistics. Home: 75 Chelmsford Rd Rochester NY 14618

HALL, WILLIAM JOEL, educator, consulting civil engineer; b. Berkeley, Calif., Apr. 13, 1926; s. Eugene Raymond and Mary (Harkey) H.; m. Elaine Frances Thalman, Dec. 18, 1948; children—Martha Jane, James Frederick, Carolyn Marie. Student, U. Calif. at Berkeley, 1943-44, U.S. Mcht. Marine Acad., 1944-45; B.S. in Civil Engring, U. Kans., 1948; M.S., U. Ill., Urbana, 1951, Ph.D., 1954. Teaching asst. U. Kans., 1947-48; engr. Sohio Pipe Line Co., 1948-49; mem. faculty U. Ill., Urbana, 1949—, prof. civil engring., 1959—, head dept. civil engring., 1984—; cons. structural dynamics seismic, materials to govt. orgns. and industry. Author books, articles, chpts. in books, revs. Recipient A. Epstein Meml. award U. Ill., 1958; Halliburton Engring. Edn. Leadership award, 1980. Fellow ASCE (pres. Central Ill. sect. 1967-68, chmn. structural div. exec. com. 1973—, chmn. tech. council on lifeline earthquake engring. exec. com. 1982—, Kan. sect. award 1948, Walter L. Huber award 1963, Nathan M. Newmark medal 1984, Ernest E. Howard award 1984), AAAS; mem. Nat. Acad. Engring., Am. Concrete Inst., ASME, Am. Welding Soc. (Adams Meml. membership award 1967), Internat. Assn. Bridge and Structural Engrs., Earthquake Engring. Research Inst., Seismol. Soc. Am., ASTM, Soc. Exptl. Stress Analysis, Am. Soc. Engring Edn., Ill., Nat. socs. profl. engrs., Sigma Xi, Tau Beta Pi, Sigma Tau, Chi Epsilon, Phi Kappa Phi. Current Work: Earthquake engineering, structural dynamics, and research-/design activity on military systems hardness development. Subspecialties: Civil engineering; Theoretical and applied mechanics. Home: 3105 Valley Brook Dr Champaign IL 61821 Office: 1114 Newmark Civil Engring Lab 208 N Romine St Urbana IL 61801

HALL, WILLIAM STERLING, psychology educator; b. Lonoke County, Ark., July 6, 1934; s. Joseph William and Mattie (Brock) H. A.B., Roosevelt U., 1957; Ph.D., U. Chgo., 1968. Instr., asst. prof. ednl. psychology N.Y. U., 1966-68; assoc. research psychologist Ednl. Testing Service, Princeton, N.J., 1968-70; asst. prof. psychology Princeton (N.J.) U., 1970-73; assoc. prof. psychology Vassar Coll., Poughkeepsie, N.Y., 1973-74, Rockefeller U., N.Y.C., 1974-78; prof. psychology and ednl. psychology U. Ill., Urbana-Champaign, 1978-81, U. Md., College Park, 1981—; mem. study sect. NIMH, 1977-81; mem. grad. evaluation panel NRC. Mem. Lazurus Awards Com., N.Y.C., 1975-82; bd. dirs. Nat. Coll. Adv. Service, 1982—. Carnegie Corp. grantee, 1975, 77; Ford Found. grantee, 1975. Fellow Am. Psychol. Assn. N.Y. Acad. Scis.; mem. AAAS (sci. fellows selection com. 1983), Soc. Research Child Devel., Sigma Xi, Alpha Phi Alpha. Republican. Current Work: Cultural context of language development; developmental psycholinguistics. Subspecialty: Developmental psychology. Home: 1140 23d St NW Washington DC 20037 Office: Dept Psychology U Md College Park MD 20742

HALLER, IVAN, research chemist; b. Budapest, Hungary, June 8, 1934; came to U.S., 1957; s. Tibor and Magdolna (Neubauer) H.; m. Flora E. Woolf, Oct. 16, 1965; children—Paul J., Drew A. B.S. in Chem. Engring., U. Tech. Scis., Budapest, 1956; Ph.D. in Chemistry, U. Calif.-Berkeley, 1960. Mem. research staff IBM Watson Research Ctr., Yorktown Heights, N.Y., 1960—. Contbr. articles to profl. jours. Patentee in field. Coach Am. Youth Soccer Orgn. region 75, Chappaqua, N.Y., 1975-82; chmn. troop 57 Boy Scouts Am., Chappaqua, 1985—. Recipient Outstanding Contbr. award IBM Corp., 1973, Outstanding Innovation award, 1976. Mem. Am. Chem. Soc., Am. Phys. Soc. Democrat. Roman Catholic. Current work: plasma chemistry, amorphous semiconductors, thin film materials. Subspecialties: Physical chemistry; Electronic materials. Home: 901 Hardscrabble Rd Chappaqua NY 10514 Office: IBM Watson Research Ctr PO Box 218 Yorktown Heights NY 10598

HALLETT, MARK, physician, researcher, educator; b. Phila., Oct. 22, 1943; s. Joseph W. and Estelle (Barg) H.; m. Judith Peller, June 26, 1966; children: Nicholas, Victoria. A.B magna cum laude, Harvard U., 1965, M.D. cum laude, 1969. Diplomate: Am. Bd. Psychiatry and Neurology, Am. Bd. EEG. Medicine intern Peter Bent Brigham Hosp., Boston, 1969-70; research fellow NIH, 1970-72, Inst. Psychiatry, London, 1975-76; resident in neurology Mass. Gen. Hosp., Boston, 1972-75; dir. clin. neurophysiology Brigham and Women's Hosp., Boston, 1976-84; asst. prof. neurology Harvard U. Med. Sch., Boston, 1977-83, assoc. prof., 1983-84; clin. dir. Nat. Inst. Neurol. and Communicative Disorders and Stroke, 1984—. Contbr. numerous articles to sci. jours. Served with USPHS, 1970-72, 84—. Mem. Am. Acad. Neurology, Am. Assn. Electromyography and Electrodiagnosis, Am. EEG Soc., Soc. for Neurosci., Am. Neurol. Assn., Phi Beta Kappa, Alpha Omega Alpha. Current Work: Neurophysiology of control of movement in man, neurology, neurophysiology, electromyography, electroencephalography. Subspecialties: Neurology; Neurophysiology. Home: 5147 Westbard Ave Bethesda MD 20816 Office: NIH Bldg 10 Room 5N226 Bethesda MD 20205

HALLGREN, RICHARD EDWIN, meteorologist; b. Kersey, Pa., Mar. 15, 1932; s. Edwin Leonard and Edith Marie H.; m. Maxine Hope Anderson, Apr. 17, 1954; children—Scott, Douglas, Lynette. B.S., Pa. State U., 1953, Ph.D., 1960. Systems engr. IBM Corp., 1960-64; sci. adv. to asst. sec. of commerce, 1964-66; dir. world weather systems ESSA, Rockville, Md. 1966-69, asst. adminstrn., 1969-71. assoc. adminstr. environ. monitoring and prediction, NOAA, 1971-73, asst. adminstr. for ocean and atmospheric services, 1977-79; dep. dir. Nat. Weather Service, Silver Spring, Md., 1973-77, dir., 1979—; permanent U.S. rep. World Meteorol. Orgn. Contbr. articles to sci. jours. Served with USAF, 1954-56. Recipient Arthur S. Flemming award U.S. C. of C., 1968; Gold medal Dept. Commerce, 1969; named Meritorious Sr. Exec., 1980. Fellow Am. Meteorol. Soc. (pres.); mem. Am. Oceanic Orgn., Sigma Xi. Lutheran. Home: 6121 Wayside Dr Rockville MD 20852 Office: Nat Weather Service 8060 13th St Silver Spring MD 20910

HALLIDAY, JAKE, research institute director. Dir. Charles F. Kettering Research Lab., Yellow Springs, Ohio, 1984—. . Office: Charles F Kettering Research Lab 150 E South College St Yellow Springs OH 45387

HALLIGAN, JAMES EDMUND, university president, chemical engineer; b. Moorland, Iowa, June 23, 1936; s. Raymond Anthony and Margaret Ann (Crawford) H.; m. Ann Elizabeth Sorenson, June 29, 1957; children: Michael, Patrick, Christopher. M.S. in Chem. Engring, Iowa State U., 1962, M.S., 1965, Ph.D., 1968. Process engr. Humble Oil Co., 1962-64; mem. faculty Tex. Tech U., 1968-77; dean engring. U. Mo., Rolla, 1977-79; dean engring. U. Ark., Fayetteville, 1979-82, vice chancellor for acad. affairs, 1982-83, interim chancellor, 1983; now pres. N.Mex. State U., Las Cruces; v.p. engring. Kandahar Cons. Ltd.; mem. Gov. Tex. Energy Adv. Council, 1972-74. Served with USAF, 1954-58. Recipient Disting. Teaching award Tex. Tech U., 1972, Disting. Research award, 1975, 76; Disting. Teaching award U. Mo., Rolla, 1978. Mem. Am. Inst. Chem. Engrs., Am. Soc. Engring. Edn., Tau Beta Pi, Phi Kappa Phi, Pi Mu Epsilon. Roman Catholic. Club: Rotary. Subspecialty: Chemical engineering. Office: Hadley Hall N Mex State U Las Cruces NM 88003

HALLOCK, ROBERT BRUCE, physicist, educator; b. Washington, Dec. 9, 1943; s. Robert F. and Dorothy (Mengel) H.; m. Norma E., June 19, 1965; children—Robert W., Kevin F. B.S., U. Mass., 1965; M.S., Stanford U., 1967, Ph.D., 1969. Asst. prof. physics U. Mass. Amherst, 1970-74, assoc. prof., 1974-78, prof., 1978—. Contbr. articles to physics jours. Fellow AFOSR-NRC, 1969, A. P. Sloan Found., 1972. Fellow Am. Phys. Soc. Current work: Superfluidity, cryogenics; condensed matter. Subspecialties: Low temperature physics; Condensed matter physics. Office: Dept Physics Hasbrouck Lab U Mass Amherst MA 01003

HALME, JOUKO KALERVO, endocrinologist; b. Helsinki, Finland, Oct. 23, 1942; came to U.S., 1977; s. Kalervo A.A. and Helmi E.A. (Tuominen) H.; m. Anja-Pirkko Larkio, Oct. 29, 1976; children: Anna, Orvokki; married; 1 dau. by previous marriage: Kati. M.B., U. Helsinki, 1964, M.D., 1968, Ph.D., 1970, docent, 1977. Lic. physician, Finland, Mo., N.C. Postdoctoral fellow in biochemistry U. Miami, Fla., 1970-71; resident in obstetrics/gynecology U. Helsinki, 1972-75, acting asso. prof., 1976; instr. medicine Washington U., St. Louis, 1977-80; fellow reproductive endocrinology U. N.C., Dept. Obstetrics and Gynecology, Chapel Hill, 1980-82, asst. prof., 1982—. Contbr. articles to profl. jours. NIH grantee, 1983—. Fellow Am. Coll. Obstetricians and Gynecologists; mem. Am. Fedn. Clin. Research, N.C. Med. Soc., Finnish Med. Assn., Finnish Gynecol. Assn. (sec. 1973-74). Current Work: Endometriosis and cell-mediated immunology; mechanism of infertility in endometriosis. Subspecialties: Reproductive biology (medicine); Immunology (medicine). Home: 149 Dixie Dr Chapel Hill NC 27514 Office: Univ NC 214 Macnider Bldg 202H Chapel Hill NC 27514

HALONEN, MARILYN JEAN, immunologist, educator; b. Duluth, Minn.; d. George and Helmi E. (Aalto) Wainio; m. Michael A. Cusanovich, 1 son, Darren Anthony. B.S., U. Minn., 1963; M.S., Iowa State U., 1968; Ph.D., U. Ariz., 1974. Research asso. dept. microbiology U. Ariz. Coll. Medicine, Tucson, 1974-77, adj. asst. prof. medicine, div. respiratory scis., 1977-83, research assoc. prof. medicine, 1983—, mem. faculty grad. program molecular biology, 1977—; guest worker Nat. Inst. Allergy and Infectious Disease, NIH, Bethesda, Md., 1981-82. Contbr. articles to sci. jours. NIH grantee, 1975, 77—. Mem. Am. Assn. Immunologists, Internat. Soc. Immunopharmacology. Current Work: Research in animal models of acute allergic reactions. Subspecialties: Immunobiology and immunology; Immunopharmacology. Office: Div Respiratory Scis Coll Medicine U Ariz Tucson AZ 85724

HALPERIN, BERTRAND ISRAEL, physics educator; b. Bklyn., Dec. 6, 1941; s. Morris and Eva (Teplitsky) H.; m. Helena Stacy French, Sept. 23, 1962; children: Jeffery Arnold, Julia Stacy. A.B., Harvard U., 1961; A.M., U. Calif., 1963, Ph.D., 1965; vis. grad. student, Princeton U., 1964-65. NSF postdoctoral fellow U. Paris, 1965-66; mem. tech. staff Bell Labs., Murray Hill, N.J., 1966-76; lectr. Harvard U., 1969-70, prof. physics, 1976—; cons. AT&T Bell Labs., Schlumberger-Doll Research Labs. Assoc. editor: Revs. Modern Physics, 1973-80. Fellow Am. Phys. Soc. (Oliver Buckley prize 1982), Am. Acad. Arts and Scis.; mem. Nat. Acad. Scis. Research in solid state theory, statistical physics. Subspecialty: Condensed matter physics. Office: Dept Physics Harvard U Cambridge MA 02138

HALPERIN, ROBERT MILTON, electrical machinery company executive; b. Chgo., June 1, 1928; s. Herman and Edna Pearl (Rosenberg) H.; m. Ruth Levison, June 19, 1955; children—Mark, Margaret, Philip. Ph.B., U. Chgo., 1949; B.Mech. Engring., Cornell U., 1949; M.B.A., Harvard U., 1952. Engr. Electro-Motive div. Gen. Motors Corp., La Grange, Ill., 1949-50; trust rep. Bank of Am., San Francisco, 1954-56; adminstr. Dumont Corp., San Rafael, Calif., 1956-57; pres. Raychem Corp., Menlo Park, Calif., 1957—, dir., 1961—. Served to lt. USAF, 1952-53. Club: Harvard of New York City. Home: 80 Reservoir Rd Atherton CA 94025 Office: 300 Constitution Dr Menlo Park CA 94025

HALPERN, ARTHUR M(ERRILL), chemist, educator; b. Bayonne, N.J., Aug. 4, 1943; s. Maurice and Edna (Green) H.; m. Janis M. Kaye; children: Sharon, Alison, David, Maura. B.A., Rutgers U., 1964; Ph.D., Northeastern U., 1968. Research assoc. U. Minn., 1968-70; mem. tech. staff Bell Labs., 1970-71; asst. prof. chemistry N.Y.U., 1970-73; asst. prof. chemistry Northeastern U., Boston, 1973-77, assoc. prof., 1977-81, prof., 1981—; indsl. cons. Author books, articles and revs. Alfred P. Sloan fellow, 1974-76; NATO sr. scientist fellow, 1981; grantee NSF; grantee NIH; grantee Research Corp.; grantee Petroleum Research Fund Am Chemistry; grantee Air Force Office Sci. Research. Mem. Am. Chem. Soc., Am. Phys. Soc., AAAS, European Photochem. Assn. Current Work: Photochemistry and photophysics of organic molecules; photoassociation, photokinetics; thermodynamics and kinetics of excited dimers and complexes. Subspecialties: Laser photochemistry; Photochemistry. Office: 360 Huntington Ave Boston MA 02115

HALPERN, JACK, chemistry educator; b. Poland, Jan. 19, 1925; came to U.S., 1962; s. Philip and Anna (Sass) H.; m. Helen Peritz, June 30, 1949; children: Janice Deborah, Nina Phyllis. B.Sc., McGill U., 1946, Ph.D., 1949. Postdoctorate overseas fellow NRC, U. Manchester (Eng.), 1949-50; instr. chemistry U. B.C., 1950, prof., 1961-62; Nuffield Found. traveling fellow Cambridge (Eng.) U., 1959-60; prof. chemistry U. Chgo., 1962-71, Louis Block prof. chemistry, 1971-84, Louis Block Disting. Service prof., 1984—; vis. prof. U. Minn., 1962, Harvard, 1966-67, Calif. Inst. Tech., 1968-69, Princeton U., 1970-71, Max. Planck Institut, Mulheim, W. Ger; external sci. mem. Max Planck Inst., Mulheim, W. Ger., 1983—; vis. prof. U. Copenhagen, 1978; Sherman Fairchild Disting. scholar Calif. Inst. Tech., 1979; guest scholar Kyoto U., 1981; Firth vis. prof. U. Sheffield, 1982; numerous guest lectureships; cons. editor Macmillan Co., 1963-65, Oxford U. Press; cons. Am. Oil Co., Monsanto Co., Argonne Nat. Lab., IBM, Air Products Co.; mem. adv. panel on chemistry NSF, 1967-70; mem. adv. bd. Am. Chem. Soc. Petroleum Research Fund, 1972-74; mem. medicinal chemistry sect. NIH, 1975-78, chmn., 1976-78; mem. chemistry adv. council Princeton U., 1982—; Mem. Art Inst. Chgo., 1964—; mem. adv. com. Ency. Britannica, 1985—. Asso. editor: Inorganica Chimica Acta, Jour. Am. Chem. Soc; co-editor: Collected Accounts of Transition Metal Chemistry, vol. 1, 1973, vol. 2, 1977; editorial bd.: Jour. Organometallic Chemistry; Contbr. articles to research jours., Ency. Britannica. Mem. editorial bd. Accounts of Chem. Research, Catalysis Revs., Jour. of Catalysis, Jour. Molecular Catalysis, Jour. Coordination Chemistry, Gazzetta Chimica Italiana, Organometallics. Trustee Gordon Research Confs., 1968-70. Recipient Young Author's prize Electrochem. Soc., 1953; award in inorganic chemistry Am. Chem. Soc., 1968; award in catalysis Noble Metals Chem. Soc., London, 1976; Humboldt award, 1977; Richard Kokes award Johns Hopkins U., 1978; Alfred P. Sloan research fellow, 1959-63. Fellow Royal Soc. (London), AAAS, Am. Acad. Arts and Scis., Chem. Inst. Can., Royal Soc. Chemistry (London), N.Y. Acad. Scis.; mem. Am. Chem. Soc. (editorial bd. Advances in Chemistry series 1963-65, 78-81, chmn. inorganic chemistry div. 1971, Disting. Service in advancement of inorganic chemistry award 1985), Nat. Acad. Scis. (fgn. assoc.), Max Planck Soc., Renaissance Soc. (bd. dirs. 1984—), Sigma Xi. Current Work: Inorganic, organometallic and bioinorganic chemistry; kinetics and mechanisms of inorganic and organometallic reactions; catalysis. Subspecialties: Inorganic chemistry; Catalysis chemistry. Home: 5630 Dorchester Ave Chicago IL 60637 Office: U Chgo Dept Chemistry Chicago IL 60637

HALPIN, DANIEL WILLIAM, civil engineering educator, consultant; b. Covington, Ky., Sept. 29, 1938; s. Jordan W. and Gladys E. (Moore) H.; m. Maria Kirchner, Feb. 8, 1963; 1 son, Rainer. B.S., U.S. Mil. Acad., 1961; M.S.C.E., U. Ill., 1969, Ph.D., 1973. Research analyst Constrn. Engring. Research Lab., Champaign, Ill., 1970-72; faculty U. Ill.-Urbana, 1972-73; mem. faculty Ga. Inst. Tech., Atlanta, 1973-85, prof., 1981-85; Clark prof. Constrn mgmt. U. Md., College Park, 1985—; cons. constrn. mgmt.; vis. assoc. prof. U. Sydney, Australia, 1981; vis. prof. Swiss Tech. Inst., Zurich, 1985—. Author: Design of Construction and Process Operations, 1976, Construction Management, 1980, Planung und Kontrolle von Bauproduktionsprozessen, 1979, Constructo - A Heuristic Game for Construction Management, 1973; Financial and Cost Concepts for Construction Management, 1985. Served with C.E., U.S. Army, 1961-67. Decorated Bronze Star; recipient Walter L.Huber prize ASCE, 1979; grantee NSF, Dept. Energy. Mem. ASCE (past sect. pres. 1981-82), Am. Soc. Engring. Edn., Sigma Xi. Methodist. Current Work: Simulation of construction operations using computers; applications of microcomputers in construction management. Subspecialties: Civil engineering; Systems engineering. Office: Dept Civil Engring U Md College Park MD 20742

HALSEY, WILLIAM GUY, nuclear engineer, researcher; b. Battle Creek, Mich., Sept. 23, 1953; s. Leroy W. and Margaret E. (Wood) H. Student, Mich. Technol. U., Houghton, 1971-73; B.S. in Nuclear Engring, U. Mich., Ann Arbor, 1975, M.S. in Nuclear Engring, 1976, M.S. in Metall. Engring, 1978, Ph.D. in Nuclear Engring, 1980. Physicist Lawrence Livermore (Calif.) Lab., 1980-81, measurements group leader, 1981—. Mem. Am. Nuclear Soc., Am. Soc. for Metals. Current Work: Material science in support of fusion energy research. Subspecialty: Nuclear engineering. Home: 99 Mozden Ln Pleasant Hill CA 94523 Office: Lawrence Livermore Lab L-482 PO Box 5508 Livermore CA 94550

HALSTEAD, BRUCE WALTER, biotoxicologist; b. San Francisco, Mar. 28, 1920; s. Walter and Ethel Muriel (Shanks) H.; m. Joy Arloa Mallory, Aug. 3, 1941; children: Linda, Sandra, David, Larry, Claudia, Shari. A.A., San Francisco City Coll., 1941; B.A., U. Calif.-Berkeley, 1943; M.D., Loma Linda U., 1948. Research asst. in ichthyology Calif. Acad. Scis., 1935-43; instr. Pacific Union Coll., 1943-44; mem. faculty Loma Linda U., 1948- 58; research asso. Lab. Neurol. Research, Sch. Medicine, 1964—; dir. World Life Research Inst., Colton, Calif., 1959—, Internat. Biotoxicol. Center; research asso. in ichthyology Los Angeles County Mus., 1964—; instr. Walla Walla Coll., summers 1964—; Cons. to govt. agys., pvt. corps; mem. editorial staff Exerpta Medica, 1959—, Toxicon, 1962—; mem. joint group experts on sci. aspects marine pollution UN; Dir. Nat. Assn. Underwater Instrs., Internat. Underwater Enterprises, Internat. Bots., Inc. Author: Poisonous and Venomous Marine Animals of the World, 4 vols., 1966; others.; contbr. numerous articles to profl. jours. Fellow AAAS, Internat. Soc. Toxicology (a founder), N.Y. Acad. Scis., Royal Soc. Tropical Medicine and Hygiene; mem. Am. Inst. Biol. Scis., Am. Micros. Soc., Am. Soc. Ichthyologists and Herpetologists, Am. Soc. Limnology and Oceanography, numerous others. Current Work: Natural products research, immunology and degenerative diseases. Subspecialties: Preventive medicine; Biotoxicology. Address: 23000 Grand Terrace Rd Colton CA 92324

HALVERSON, THOMAS GEORGE, nuclear facility safety exec.; b. Madison, Wis., Apr. 14, 1948; s. Arthur John and Mary Jane (Hoffman) H.; m. Linda Sue Vandine, Feb. 17, 1977; children: Aaron, Brian, Wendy, Margot. B.S. in Nuclear Engring, U. Wis., 1971. Tech. engr. Commonwealth Edison Co., Zion, Ill., 1971-74; design engr. Westinghouse Hanford Co., Richland, Wash., 1974-76, engring. sect. mgr., 1976-80; mgr. safety Fast Flux Test Facility, 1980-81, mgr. nuclear facility safety, 1981—. Pres. Lower Columbia Basin Search and Rescue, Kennewick, Wash., 1982; reservist Benton County Sheriff's Office, Kennewick, 1982. Mem. Am. Nuclear Soc. (progrma chmn. 1980-82). Lutheran. Club: Atomic Ducks Dive (Kennewick) (pres. 1981-82). Current Work: Liquid metal fast reactor nuclear safety. Application of nuclear safety principles to operation of the Fast Flux Test Facility and advanced fuel research laboratories. Subspecialties: Nuclear engineering; Nuclear fission. Office: Westinghouse Hanford Co PO Box 1970 W/C 75 Richland WA 99352

HAMBER, HERBERT WALTER, physicist, researcher; b. Milan, Italy, Feb. 1, 1953; came to U.S., 1977; s. Heinz Arthur and Vittoria (Emiliani) H.; m. Franca Filippucci, July 28, 1977; 1 child, Jane. Lurea cum laude, U. Milan, 1976; Ph.D., U. Calif.-Santa Barbara, 1980. Research assoc. U. Calif.-Santa Barbara, 1980; Brookhaven Nat. Lab., N.Y., 1980-82; mem. Inst. Advanced Studies, Princeton, N.J., 1982—. Fullbright fellow 1977-81. Mem. Am. Phys. Soc. Current work: Study of gauge theories of elementary particle interactions, non perturbative phenomena in quantum field theory quantization of gravity and the statistical mechanics of random systems. Subspecialties: Theoretical physics; Particle physics. Office: Inst Advanced Studies Princeton NJ 08560

HAMBLEN, JOHN WESLEY, computer scientist; b. Story, Ind., Sept. 25, 1924; s. James William and Mary Etta (Morrison) H.; m. Brenda F. Harrod, Mar. 1, 1947 (div. 1979); 1 son, James. A.B., Ind. U., 1947; M.S., Purdue U., 1952; Ph.D., 1955. Tchr. math and sci. Kingsbury (Ind.) High Sch., 1946-48, Bluffton (Ind.) High Sch., 1948-51; asst. prof. math. Okla. State U., Stillwater, 1955-57; cons. in statis. methods for research staff Agrl. Expt. Sta., 1955-56, asso. prof. math., 1957-58; dir. Computing Center, 1957-58; asso. prof. stats., dir. Computing Center, U. Ky., Lexington, 1958-61; prof. math and technology Southern Ill. U., Carbondale, 1961-65; dir. Data Processing and Computing Center, 1961-65; project dir. computer scis. So. Regional Edn. Bd., Atlanta, 1965-72; prof. U. Mo., Rolla, 1972—, chmn. dept. computer sci., 1972-81; mem. tech. adv. com. Creative Application of Tech. to Edn., Tex. A. and M. U., 1966-68; mem. tech. adv. panel Western Interstate Commn. for Higher Edn., 1969-70; vis. scientist Ctr. for Applied Math. Nat. Bur. Standards, 1981-83; program chmn. World Conf. Computers in Edn., 1985; assoc. program dir. NSF, 1985—; cons. FTC, 1978-80, NSF, 1975-76. Editor: Ednl. Data Processing Newsletter, 1964-65; asso. editor: Jour. Ednl. Data Processing, 1965-67; editor: Jour. Assn. Ednl. Data Systems, 1967-68; asso. editor, 1968—; contbr. articles to profl. jours. Purdue Research Found. fellow, 1954-55; NSF grantee, 1966-81. Fellow AAAS; mem. Assn. Computing Machinery (sec. 1972-76, chmn. curriculum com. computer sci. 1976-80, gen. chmn. 1981 Computer Scis. Conf. 1979-81, chmn. Disting. Ser. Award com. 1980-81, rep. Sci. Manpower Commn. 1983—, vice chmn. computer scis. conf. com. 1985—), IEEE Computer Soc., Assn. Ednl. Data Systems (chmn. conv. adv. com. 1977-80, pres. 1968-69, sec. 1976-77, dir. 1965-70, 76-79, Aid award 1971), Am. Fedn. Info. Processing Socs. (dir. 1981—, chmn. edn. com. 1971-72, 79-84, Edn. award 1985), Soc. Indsl. and Applied Math, Am. Statis. Assn., Sigma Xi, Pi Mu Epsilon, Theta Chi, Upsilon Pi Epsilon, Alpha Chi Sigma. Club: Rotary. Subspecialty: Information systems, storage, and retrieval (computer science). Home: 9224 Sandy Lake Circle Gaithersburg MD 20879 Office: NSF Washington DC 20550

HAMBLIN, RALPH HUGH, petroleum geologist; b. Easton, N.Y., Apr. 25, 1913; s. Benjamin Reuben and Harriet (Wheldon) H.; m. Gertrude M. Drost,

Oct. 19, 1939; children—Erika Erna, Ursula Helga. A.B., Colgate U., 1936; M.S., U. Mont., 1939. With geology dept. Anaconda Copper Mining Co., 1940-43; dist. geologist Cities Service Oil Co., 1943-51; indsl. cons. Denver and Dallas, 1951—; pres. Ralph Hamblin, Inc., Marion, Ohio, 1951—; petroleum tech. del. to People's Republic of China, People to People Internat.; dir. Transcontinental Oil Corp., Whitney Oil Corp. Mem. Am. Assn. Petroleum Geologists, Ind. Petroleum Assn., Ohio Oil and Gas Assn., Geol. Soc. Am., Am. Inst. Profl. Geologists, Soc. Econ. Paleontologists and Mineralogists, Ohio Geol. Soc. Mem. Nat. Republican Senatorial Com., Washington. Clubs: Marion Country (Ohio); Petroleum. Lodge: Elks. Home and Office: 846 Richland Terr Marion OH 43302

HAMBURGER, MAX I., physician, educator; b. Long Branch., N.J., June 20, 1947; s. Aaron and Dorothy (Friedl) H.; m. Frances Marsha, Nov. 21, 1971; children: Jordan, Micole, Brian. B.A., Rutgers U., 1969; M.D., Albert Einstein Coll. Medicine, 1973. Intern Bellevue Hosp. Ctr., N.Y.C., 1973-74, resident in medicine, 1974-76; clin. assoc. clin. immunology sect. Lab. Clin. Investigation, Nat. Inst. Allergy and Infectious Diseases, NIH, Bethesda, Md., 1976-79; asst. prof. dept. medicine div. allergy and rheumatology, dir. therapeutic pheresis SUNY, Stony Brook, 1979—. Sr. editor: Plasma Therapy and Transfusion Tech, 1982—; editor: Jour. Clin. Apheresis, 1982—; Contbr. articles to profl. jours. Pres., chmn. profl. adv. com. L.I. Arthritis Found.; mem. exec. council N.Y. Arthritis Found. Served to lt. comdr. USPHS, 1976-79. Mem. Am. Fedn. Clin. Research, Am. Assn. Immunologists, Am. Rheumatism Assn., Suffolk County Med. Soc., N.Y. Rheumatism Assn., Am. Soc. Apheresis (dir.), Phi Beta Kappa, Delta Phi Alpha. Current Work: Immune complex diseases, complement proteins, immunoadsorption. Subspecialties: Immunology (medicine); Infectious diseases. Office: 222 E Main St Suite 115 Smithtown NY 11787 Also: 7 Medical Dr Port Jefferson NY 11776

HAMELINK, JERRY LEE, environmental toxicology researcher, aquatic environment, fisheries consultant; b. Grand Rapids, Mich., May 23, 1941; s. John William and Jane (Jelsma) H.; m. Mary Jill Bolich, Dec. 28, 1964; children—John Richard, Jason Clark. B.S., Mich. State U., 1963, Ph.D., 1969. Park ranger Mich. Dept. Conservation, Lansing, 1960-62, predoctoral fellow, Ann Arbor, 1963-69; asst. prof. Purdue U., West Lafayette, Ind., 1969-74; sr. toxicologist Eli Lilly & Co., Greenfield, Ind., 1974-78, research scientist, 1978—; co-author ASTM Standard Bioconcentration Test Method, 1974-84. Editor: Aquatic Toxicology and Hazard Evaluation, 1977. Mem. Am. Fisheries Soc. (Best Student Paper award 1969), Soc. Environ. Toxicology and Chemistry (chmn. awards com. 1984—), AAAS, Am. Chem. Soc. Unitarian. Current work: Fate and effects of agricultural chemicals and chemical manufacturing wastes in and on the environment. Subspecialties: Limnology; Environmental toxicology. Home: 1406 Sherwood Dr Greenfield IN Office: Eli Lilly and Co PO Box 708 B418/G993 Greenfield IN 46140

HAMID, MOHAMED AHMED-ABDEL, neurophysiologist, biomedical engineering consultant; b. Cairo, Mar. 6, 1947; m. Fadia M. El-Tobgy; children—Seif, Youssef. B.Sc. in Electronic and Communication Engring., Ain Shams U., Cairo, 1968; DIC in Biol. Signal Analysis, U. London, 1979, Ph.D. in Applied Neurophysiology, 1979. Research asst. Imperial Coll., London, 1975-78; vestibular scientist Royal Nat. Ear, Nose and Throat Hosp., London, 1978-80; spl. fellow Cleve. Clinic, 1980-81, dir. vestibular lab., 1981—; adj. prof. Kent State U., Ohio, 1983—. Mem. Barany Soc., N.Y. Acad. Scis., Northeastern Ohio Otolaryngology and Maxillofacial Surg. Soc., Am. Neurotology Soc., Am. Neuroscis. Current work: Vestibular physiology; oculomotor physiology; biological signal analysis; computer applications in medicine. Subspecialty: Neurophysiology. Home: 18133 Lamond Blvd Shaker Heights OH 44122 Office: Cleve Clin Found 9500 Euclid Ave Cleveland OH 44106

HAMILL, ROBERT WALLACE, neurologist, research neurobiologist; b. Hartford, July 30, 1942; s. Robert Francis and Sarah (Wallace) H.; m. Donna Gail Kole, June 26, 1966; children: Kara, Heidi, Meghan. B.S. in Biology, Springfield (Mass.) Coll., 1964; M.D., Bowman Gray Sch. Medicine, 1968. Diplomate: Am. Bd. Neurology and Psychiatry. Intern U. Rochester Med. Center-Strong Meml. Hosp., 1968-69, resident, 1969-70; resident in neurology N.Y. Hosp.-Cornell Med. Ctr., 1973-76; assoc. prof. neurology and brain research U. Rochester, N.Y.; dir. neurology unit Monroe Community Hosp., Rochester, 1980—. Contbr. articles to profl. jours. Served to lt. comdr. U.S. Navy, 1970-73. Nat. Inst. Neurol., Communicative Disorders and Stroke fellow, 1978-80; Sloan Found. fellow, 1975-76; Jordan fellow, 1977. Mem. Am. Acad. Neurology, Soc. Neurosci., AAAS. Current Work: Autonomic nervous system; degenerative neurological diseases, Alzheimer's disease; paraplegia; hormonal regulation of sympathetic neurons; development of sympathetic neurons. Subspecialties: Neurology; Neurobiology. Office: Dept Neurology U Rochester Sch. Medicine and Dentistry 601 Elmwood Ave Rochester NY 14642

HAMILTON, CARLOS ROBERT, JR., endocrinologist, consultant; b. Houston, June 12, 1939; s. Carlos Robert and Berta (Denman) H.; m. Carolyn Frances Burton, Aug. 12, 1961; children: Carlos Robert, Patricia Frances. B.A., U. Tex., 1961; M.Sc., Baylor U. Coll. Medicine, 1966, M.D., 1966. Cert. Am. Bd. Internal Medicine cert. endocrinology, metabolism. Intern Johns Hopkins Hosp., Balt., 1966-67, resident in endocrinology, 1966-69, fellow, 1966-69; postdoctoral research fellow Mass. Gen. Hosp., Boston, 1969-70; chief resident, instr. Johns Hopkins Hosp., 1970-71; asst. prof. Johns Hopkins U., 1971-72; dir. endocrine research Wilford Hall, USAF Med. Ctr., San Antonio, 1972-74; clin. asst. prof., cons. Baylor Coll. and Med. Clinic, Houston, 1974—. Served as lt. col. USAF, 1972-74. Fellow ACP; mem. Endocrine Soc., Am. Thyroid Assn., AMA, Am. Soc. Internal Medicine, Explorers Club. Baptist. Current Work: Metabolic bone disease. Subspecialties: Endocrinology; Internal medicine. Home: 3713 Chevy Chase Houston TX 77019 Office: Med Clinic Houston 1707 Sunset Blvd Houston TX 77005

HAMILTON, EUGENE PHILLIP, research mathematician; b. Wilmington, Del., Dec. 22, 1947; s. Eugene Cook and Phyllis (Brinkman) H. B.S., U. Del., 1968; M.S., Cornell U., 1970, Ph.D., 1973. Asst. prof. math. Vanderbilt U., 1973-77; ops. analyst Ctr. Naval Analyses, Arlington, Va., 1977-78; asst. prof. math. Washington Coll., Chestertown, Md., 1978-84, assoc. prof. math., 1984—. Mem. Math. Assn. Am., Soc. Indsl and Applied Math., Am. Math. Soc., N.Y. Acad. Scis., Sigma Xi. Democrat. Current Work: Construction of variational principles for differential equations, quantum field theory. Subspecialty: Applied mathematics. Home: 121A Washington Ave Apt 2 Chestertown MD 21620 Office: Washington College Chestertown MD 21620

HAMILTON, JOSEPH HANTS, JR., physicist, educator; b. Ferriday, La., Aug. 14, 1932; s. Joseph Hants and Letha (Gibson) H.; m. Jannelle Jauree Landrum, Aug. 5, 1960; children: Melissa Claire, Christopher Landrum. B.S., Miss. Coll., 1954, D.Sc. (hon.), 1982; M.S., Ind. U., 1956, Ph.D., 1958. Mem. faculty Vanderbilt U., 1958—, prof. physics, 1966—, Landon C. Garland prof. physics, 1981—; NSF postdoctoral fellow U. Uppsala, Sweden, 1958-59; research fellow Inst. Nuclear Studies, Amsterdam, 1963; vis. prof. U. Frankfort, 1979-80; mem. adv. panel Nat. Heavy Ion Labs., 1971-73; mem. nat. policy bd. Holifield Heavy Ion Facility, from 1974; organizer, chmn. exec. com., prin. investigator Univ. Isotope Separator, Oak Ridge, from 1970; cons. Oak Ridge Nat. Lab, from 1972; cons.; mem. council Oak Ridge Asso. Univs., 1974-80; organizer, dir. Joint Inst. for Heavy Ion Research, Oak Ridge, from 1980; chmn. Internat. Conf. Internal Conversion Processes, 1965, Internat. Conf. Radioactivity in Nuclear Spectroscopy, 1969; Internat. Conf. Future Directions in Studies Nuclei far from Stability, 1979, Internat. Symposium on Directions in Nuclear Structure Research, 1984. Co-author: Science: Faith and Learning, 1972; ORAU from the Beginning, 1980; Graphs of Conversion Coefficients, 1984; co-author, editor: Internal Conversion Processes, 1966, Radioactivity in Nuclear Spectroscopy, 1972, Reactions Between Complex Nuclei, 1974, Future Directions in Studies of Nuclei Far from Stability, 1980; contbr. articles to profl. jours., chpts. to books. Mem. Mayor Nashville Citizens Adv. Com. Housing, 1970-74; bd. dirs. Vineyard Conf. Center, Louisville, 1972-77, Danforth asso., 1965—, So. Bapt. Conv. Hist. Commn., 1983—. Harvie Branscomb Disting. Prof. award Vanderbilt U., 1983-84; NSF grantee, 1959-76; ERDA-Dept. Energy grantee, 1975—; Humbolt prize W. Ger., 1979. Fellow Am. Phys. Soc. (vice chmn. Southeastern sect. 1972-73, chmn. Southeastern sect. 1973-74, Jesse Beams gold medal for research 1975), AAAS; mem. Sigma Xi (chpt. pres. 1970). Current Work: Experimental studies of nuclear structures via heavy ion Coulomb excitation, in-beam gamma-ray spectroscopy, on-line mass separator studies of nuclei far from stability ; nuclear reaction mechanisms; standardization of radioactivity measurements; measurements of absolute alpha and beta radioactivites of drinking water as required by Tennessee law. Subspecialties: Nuclear physics; Water supply and wastewater treatment. Address: 305 Hildreth Ct Nashville TN 37215

HAMILTON, LEONARD DERWENT, physician, molecular biologist; b. Manchester, Eng., May 7, 1921; came to U.S., 1949, naturalized, 1964; s. Jacob and Sara (Sandelson) H.; m. Ann Twynam Blake, July 20, 1945; children: Jane Derwent, Stephen David, Robin Michael. B.A., Balliol Coll., Oxford (Eng.) U., 1943, B.M., 1945, M.A., 1946, D.M., 1951; M.A., Trinity Coll., Cambridge (Eng.) U., 1948, Ph.D., 1952. Diplomate: Am. Bd. Pathology. USPHS research fellow U. Utah, 1949-50; mem. staff Sloan-Kettering Inst., N.Y.C., 1950—, head isotope studies sect., 1957-64, asso. scientist, 1965—; mem. staff Meml. Hosp., N.Y.C., 1950-65, asst. attending physician dept. medicine, 1958-65; mem. faculty Sloan-Kettering div. Grad. Sch. Med. Scis., Cornell U. Med. Coll., 1956-64; sr. scientist, head div. microbiology Med. Research Center, Brookhaven Nat. Lab., Upton, N.Y., 1964-76; head Office Environ. Policy Analysis, 1976—; also attending physician Hosp. Med. Research Center, 1964—; prof. medicine Health Sci. Center, SUNY-Stony Brook, 1968—cons. HEW Center for Disease Control, Nat. Inst. Occupational Safety and Health Epidemiologic Study of Portsmouth Naval Shipyard, 1978—; vis. fellow St. Catherine's Coll., Oxford U., 1972-73; mem. internat. panel of experts on fossil fuel UN Environment Programme, 1978, panel on nuclear energy, 1978-79, panel on renewable sources, 1980, panel on comparative assessment of different sources, 1980; mem. WHO Focal Point on Health and Environ. Effects of Energy Systems, 1983—; mem. various coms. Nat. Acad. Sci.-NRC, Washington, 1975-80; mem. N.Y.C. Mayor's Tech. Adv. Com. on Radiation, 1963-77, N.Y.C. Commr. of Health Tech. Adv. Com. on Radiation, 1978—. Editor: Gerrard Winstanley, Selections From His Works, 1944, Physical Factors and Modification of Radiation Injury, 1964, The Health and Environmental Effects of Electricity Generation—a Preliminary Report, 1974. Am. Cancer Soc. scholar, 1953-58; Commonwealth Fund grantee, 1955-62. Mem. Am. Assn. Cancer Research, Am. Soc. Clin. Investigation, Am. Assn. Pathologists, Brit. Med. Assn., Harvey Soc. Current Work: Research on life-span of lymphocytes and their function in immunity; collaborator on proof of three-dimensional structure of DNA; effects of various chemicals and ionizing radiation on cells and man; the health and environmental effects of different energy technologies. Subspecialties: Molecular biology; Environmental effects of energy technologies. Home: Childs Ln Old Field Setauket NY 11733 Office: Brookhaven Nat Lab Upton NY 11973

HAMILTON, ROBERT MORRISON, geophysicist; b. Houston, June 20, 1936; s. Robert Gilbert and Marieta Josephine (Heisser) H.; m. Mary Edith Hudson, Mar. 12, 1977; 1 child by previous marriage, Margaret Emily. Geophys. Engr., Colo. Sch. Mines, 1958; M.A., U. Calif., Berkeley, 1963, Ph.D., 1965. Research seismologist N.Z. Dept. Sci. and Indsl. Research, Wellington, 1965-68; geophysicist U.S. Geol. Survey, Menlo Park, Calif., 1968-72, dep. for earthquake geophysics then chief Office Earthquake Studies, Reston, Va., 1972-78, research geophysicist Office Earthquake Studies, 1978-82, chief geologist Geologic Div., 1982—, chmn. sci. adv. com. 1980-81. Served with AUS, 1959. Nat. scholar, 1954-58; Socony-Mobil Oil Co. scholar, 1958; Pan Am. Petroleum Found. scholar, 1963-64; recipient Cecil Green medal for outstanding geophysics grad., 1958, Dept. Interior Meritorious Service award, 1978. Fellow Geol. Soc. Am.; mem. Am. Geophys. Union, Seismological Soc. Am. (pres., bd. dirs.), Soc. Exploration Geophysics, Earthquake Engring. Research Inst., AAAS. Current work: Research Management. Subspecialties: Seismology; Geophysics. Home: 2020 Mock Orange Ct Reston VA 22091 Office: US Geol Survey National Center Stop 911 Reston VA 22092

HAMMER, CARL, computer scientist, former computer co. exec.; b. Chgo., May 10, 1914; s. Karl Heinrich and Kaethe (Patzig) H.; m. T. Jeannette George, Sept. 23, 1944. Dipl. Math. Statistics, U. Munich, 1936, Ph.D. magna cum laude, 1938. Mathematician, statistician Tex. Co. Research Labs., Beacon, N.Y., 1938-43; statistician Pillsbury Mills Inc., N.Y.C., 1944-47; chmn. div. tech. edn. Walter Hervey Jr. Coll., 1947-51; sr. staff engr. Franklin Inst., Phila., 1951-55; dir. UNIVAC European Computing Center Sperry Rand Corp., Frankfurt/Main, Germany, 1955-57; staff cons., acting mgr. programming and analysis dept. Sylvania Electronic Products, Inc., Needham, Mass., 1957-59; sr. engring. scientist surface communications div. RCA, N.Y.C., 1959-61, mgr. sci. computer applications, Washington, 1961-63; dir. computer sci. UNIVAC, Washington, 1963-81; instr. German for staff officers U.S. Mil. Acad., summer 1942; instr. math. Pratt Inst., 1945-46; instr. math. and statistics Sch. Gen. Studies, Hunter Coll., 1947-52; adj. prof. Am. U., 1962-80; vis. prof. Indsl. Coll. Armed Forces, Washington, 1967—. Author: Viscosity Index Tables, 1941, Rank Correlation of Cities, 1951, Univac Programming with Compilers, 1956, Computers and Simulation, Vol. IV, Number 4, 1961, High-Speed Digital Communication Networks, 1963, Statistical Validation of Mathematical Computer Routines, 1967, Signature Simulation and Certain Cryptographic Codes, 1971, Space Communications Procs., Panel Sci. and Tech, 1972, Computers in Research, Procs. Internat. Symposium, 1974; contbr. articles in field of computer tech. to profl. jours. Mem. Nat. Def. Exec. Res., 1970—. Recipient Computer Sci. Man of Year award Data Processing Mgmt. Assn., 1973; Disting. Service award Am. Fedn. Info. Processing Socs., 1985. Fellow AAAS, N.Y. Acad. Scis., Assn. Computer Programmers and Analysts; mem. IEEE (sr.), AAUP, Am. Math. Soc., Am. Soc. for Cybernetics (sec. 1967, v.p. 1968, pres. 1969-72), Am. Statis. Assn., Assn. for Computing Machinery (chpt. chmn. Washington 1966-68, rep. Capital region 1968-77, chmn. accreditation com. 1968-70, nat. lectr. 1969-70, chmn. nominating com. 1971-73, Disting. Service award 1979), N.Y. Acad. Scis., Assn. Systems Mgmt. (dir. Washington chpt. 1969-71), Inst. Math. Statistics, Math. Assn. Am., Soc. Indsl. and Applied Math. (treas. 1953-55), Research Soc. Am. Subspecialties: Computer architecture; Cryptography and data security.

HAMMER, DAVID ANDREW, plasma physics educator, researcher, consultant; b. N.Y.C., Apr. 5, 1943; s. Benjamin and Helen (Gross) H.; m. Tove Helland, Aug. 31, 1968; 1 child, Cailin B. B.S., Calif. Inst. Tech., 1964; Ph.D., Cornell U., 1969. Research physicist Naval Research Lab., Washington, 1969-70, supr., research physicist, 1970-76; assoc. prof. UCLA, 1976-77; assoc. prof. nuclear sci. and engring. Cornell U., Ithaca, N.Y., 1977-84, prof., 1984—, assoc. dir. Lab. Plasma Studies, 1984-85, dir., 1985—; Sci. and Engring. Research Council vis. sr. fellow Imperial Coll., London, 1983-84; cons. SRI Internat., Menlo Park, Calif., 1979-82, Mitre Corp. (Jason), McLean, Va., 1983-85. Contbr. articles to profl. jours. Fulbright fellow, 1964-65; Ford Engring. fellow Cornell U., 1968-69; NSF fellow, 1983-84. Fellow Am. Phys. Soc. (program com. 1981, publ. com. 1982, 85); mem. IEEE (sr.), AAAS. Current work: Plasma physics and controlled fusion. Subspecialties: Plasma physics; Fusion. Office: Lab Plasma Studies Upson Hall Cornell Univ Ithaca NY 14853

HAMMER, JACOB MEYER, physicist; b. N.Y.C., Sept. 14, 1927; s. Joseph Israel and Miriam (Silverman) H.; married; children: Daniel, Jonathan, Miriam. B.S., N.Y. U., 1950, Ph.D., 1956; M.S., U. Ill., 1951. Mem. tech. staff Bell Telephone Labs., Murray Hill, N.J., 1956-59, RCA Labs., Princeton, N.J., 1959-68, 69—; sr. visitor Cavendish Lab., Cambridge, Eng., 1968-69; adj. prof. elec. engring. Poly. Inst. N.Y., 1981. Contbr. sect. to book, articles to profl. jours. in field. Served with AUS, 1946-47. Recipient Founders Day award N.Y. U., 1956; outstanding achievement award RCA Labs., 1962, 64, 73. Mem. Am. Phys. Soc., IEEE (sr.), AAAS. Patentee. Current Work: Application of optical waveguides to communication and technology. Subspecialty: Fiber optics. Office: RCA Labs Princeton NJ 086540

HAMMER, PAUL ALLEN, horticulturist, consultant; b. Raleigh, N.C., Sept. 2, 1945; s. Paul Otto and Eula Mae (Whitley) H.; m. Sarah Doris Wilson, June 10, 1967; children—Christie Lynn, Paul David. B.S., N.C. State U., 1967; M.S., Cornell U., 1970, Ph.D., 1973. Research asst. Cornell U., 1967-73; asst. prof. dept. horticulture Purdue U., West Lafayette, Ind., 1973-77, assoc. prof., 1977—. Contbr. chpts. to books and articles to profl. jours. Capt., Wabash Twp. Vol. Fire Dept., West Lafayette, 1980—. Served with USAR, 1969-75. Recipient Silver medal Chgo. Flower and Garden Show, 1976; Purdue Research Found. Internat. Travel grantee, 1978. Mem. Am. Soc. Horticulture Sci. (chmn. growth chamber and controlled environments working group 1978-80), Biometric Soc., Internat. Soc. Horticulture Sci., Bedding Plant, Inc., Ind. Flower frowers Assn. (sec. treas. 1982—), Produce Mktg. Assn., State Florists Assn. Ind. (bd. dirs. 1974—), Soc. Am. Florists. Republican. Lutheran. Current work: Controlled environment research, greenhouse management computer application, plant growth models. Subspecialty: Horticulture. Office: Dept Horticulture Purdue U West Lafayette IN 47907

HAMMES, GORDON G., chemistry educator; b. Fond du Lac, Wis., Aug. 10, 1934; s. Jacob and Betty (Sadoff) H.; m. Judith Ellen Frank, June 14, 1959; children: Laura Anne, Stephen R., Sharon Lyn. A.B., Princeton, 1956; Ph.D., U. Wis., 1959. NSF postdoctoral fellow Max Planck Inst. fur physikalische Chemie, Göttingen, Germany, 1959-60; from instr. to asso. prof. Mass. Inst. Tech., Cambridge, 1960-65; prof. Cornell U., Ithaca, N.Y., 1965—, chmn. dept. chemistry, 1970-75, Horace White prof. chemistry and biochemistry, 1975—, dir. biotech. program, 1983—; mem. physiol. chemistry study sect., tng. grant com. NIH; bd. counselors Nat. Cancer Inst., 1976-80; mem. adv. council chemistry dept. Princeton, 1970-75, Poly. Inst. N.Y., 1977-78, Boston U., 1977—. Author: Principles of Chemical Kinetics, Enzyme Catalysis and Regulation, Chemical Kinetics: Principles and Selected Topics; also articles. NSF sr. postdoctoral fellow, 1968-69; NIH Fogarty scholar, 1975-76. Mem. Am. Chem. Soc. (award biol. chemistry 1967, editorial bd. jours., exec. com. div. phys. chemistry 1976-79, exec. com. div. biol. chemistry 1977—), Am. Soc. Biol. Chemists (editorial bd. jour., councilor), Nat. Acad. Scis., Am. Acad. Arts and Scis., Phi Beta Kappa, Sigma Xi, Phi Lambda Upsilon. Current Work: Enzyme catalysis and regulation; membrane bound enzymes; multienzyme complexes; ion transport across membranes. Subspecialties: Biophysical chemistry; Biochemistry (biology). Home: 107 Warwick Pl Ithaca NY 14850

HAMMILL, TERRENCE MICHAEL, biologist, educator; b. Potsdam, N.Y., Dec. 28, 1940; s. Jeremiah James and Margaret Mae (Blanchard) H.; m. Martha Lois Trembley, Aug. 24, 1963; children: Michael Sean, Jeffery Terrence. B.S., SUNY, Potsdam, 1963; M.Ed., U. Ga., 1968; Ph.D., SUNY Coll. Forestry, Syracuse, 1971, Syracuse U., 1971. Tchr. sci. Indian River Central High Sch., Phila., 1963-67; asst. prof. biology SUNY, Oswego, 1971-74, assoc. prof., 1974-85, prof., 1985, dir. Lab. for Ultrastructural Studies, 1984—. Contbr. articles to research jours. Active Oswego Little League Baseball, Oswego Maritime Found. NSF grantee, 1974-76, 80-82; Research Corp. grantee, 1974; SUNY Awards Council grantee, 1974. Mem. AAAS, Am. Inst. Biol. Sci., Bot. Soc. Am., Brit. Mycol. Soc., Electron Microscopy Soc. Am., Mycol. Soc. Am. Democrat. Current Work: Developmental biology of fungi; research on devel. biology and ultrastructural cytology. Subspecialties: Microbiology; Developmental biology. Home: 69 W 5th St Oswego NY 13126 Office: SUNY B-18 Piez Hall Oswego NY 13126

HAMMOND, BENJAMIN FRANKLIN, microbiologist, educator; b. Austin, Tex., Feb. 28, 1934; s. Virgil Thomas and Helen Marguerite (Smith) H. B.A., U. Kans., 1954; D.D.S., Meharry Med. Coll., 1958; Ph.D., U. Pa., 1962. Mem. faculty U. Pa. Sch. Dental Medicine, Phila., 1958—, prof. microbiology, 1970—, chmn. dept., 1972-85; Pres.'s lectr. U. Pa., 1981, assoc. dean acad. affairs, 1984; Mem. oral medicine study sect. NIH, 1972-75; mem. Nat. Adv. Dental Research Council, 1975—; Turpin Meml. lectr. Meharry Med. Coll., 1985; cons. in field. Recipient USPHS Research Career Devel. award, 1965, Lindback award U. Pa., 1969; Médaille d'Argent City of Paris, 1978; NIH grantee, 1981—. Mem. Am. Soc. Microbiology, Internat. Assn. Dental Research (E.H. Hatton award 1959), Am. Assn. Dental Research (pres. 1978-79), Coll. Physicians of Phila. Current Work: Oral microbial ecology; bacterial physiology, periodontal microbiology. Subspecialty: Microbiology. Home: 560 N 23d St Philadelphia PA 19130

HAMMOND, CHARLES BESSELLIEU, obstetrician, gynecologist, educator; b. Ft. Leavenworth, Kans., July 24, 1936; s. Claude G. and Alice (Sims) H.; m. Peggy R. Hammond, June 21, 1958; children—Sharon L., Charles B. Student, The Citadel, 1957; B.S., M.D., Duke U., 1961. Intern Duke U., 1961-62, resident, 1962-63, 66-69, fellow in reproductive endocrinology, 1963-64, asst. prof. dept. ob-gyn, 1969-73, asso. prof., 1973-78, prof., 1978-81, E.C. Hamblen prof., 1981—, chmn., 1980—. Contbr. in field. Served with USPHS, 1964-66. Mem. Am. Bd. Ob-Gyn, Am. Fertility Soc. (dir. 1979—, pres. 1985), Am. Coll. Obstetricians and Gynecologists, Assn. Profs. Obstetrics and Gynecology, Am. Gynecologic Soc., Am. Assn. Obstetricians and Gynecologists, Soc. Gynecologic Investigation, N.C. Med. Soc., N.C. Soc. Obstetricians and Gynecologists. Presbyterian. Current work: Reproductive endocrinology; trophoblastic neoplasia. . Home: 2827 McDowell Rd Durham NC 27705 Office: PO Box 3853 Duke Med Center Durham NC 27710

HAMMOND, DONALD L., physical science research administrator; b. Kansas City, Mo., Aug. 7, 1927; s. Clark E. and Laila G. (Morris) H.; m. Phyllis E. Whitmore, Aug. 21, 1949; children: Deborah Ruth, Katherine Ilene, Carol Linda, Nancy Linda, Paul David. B.S. in Physics, Colo. State U., 1950, M.S., 1952, D.Sc. (hon.), 1974. Chief crystal research U.S. Army Electronics Command, Fort Monmouth, N.J., 1952-56; dir. research Scientific Electronic Products, Fort Collins, Colo., 1956-59; former mgr. precision quartz crystal devel. Hewlett-Packard, Palo Alto, Calif., dir. phys. electronics lab., dir. phys. research ctr.; now dir. Hewlett-Packard Labs., Bristol, Eng., lectr. CB Sawyer Frequency Control Symposium, 1970. Mem. bd. edn. Palo Alto Unified Sch. Dist., 1971-81, also pres. Served as ensign USN, 1945. Fellow IEEE; mem. Am. Inst. Physics. Current Work: Physical acoustics; electron optics; chemical instrumentation; medical electronics; submicron lithography; research and development management. Subspecialties: Electronics; Research administration. Office: Hewlett-Packard Labs Bristol Filton Rd Stoke Gifford Bristol BS12 6QZ England

HAMMOND, MARY ELIZABETH HALE, pathologist, electron microscopist; b. Salt Lake City, Jan. 5, 1942; d. Edward Girard and Ruth (Hansen) Hale; m. John Morgan Hammond, Dec. 30, 1964; children—Jonathan Hale, Thomas Hale, Kathleen Hale. B.S., U. Utah, 1963, M.D., 1967. Diplomate Am. Bd. Pathology. Intern, U. Utah. Coll. Medicine, Salt Lake City, 1967-68; postdoctoral fellow USPHS, NIH, Stockholm, 1968-69; resident, fellow Mass. Gen. Hosp., Boston, 1970-73, staff pathologist, 1974-77; staff pathologist LDS Hosp., Salt Lake City, 1977—, dir. Electron Microscopy Lab., 1978—; instr. Harvard U. Med. Sch., Boston, 1974-76, asst. prof., 1977; assoc. prof. U. Utah Coll. Medicine, 1977—; lectr. nat. pathology meetings. Contbr. articles to profl. jours. Bd. dirs. Deseret Found., 1977—, Thrasher Found., Salt Lake City, 1984—. Am.; Cancer research scholar, 1974. Mem. Am. Soc. Clin. Pathologists, Utah Soc. Pathologists (pres. 1982-85), Am. Assn. Immunologists, Phi Beta Kappa, Alpha Omega Alpha. Mem. Ch. of Jesus Christ of Latter-day Saints. Current work: Ultrastructure and immunocytochemistry of human tumors; ultrastructure of cardiomyopathies, application of computers to ultrastructural classification of tumors. Subspecialty: Pathology (medicine). Office: Electron Microscopy Lab LDS Hosp 8th Ave and C Salt Lake City UT 84103

HAMMOND, THOMAS JOSEPH, optical engineer; b. Warren, Ohio, Dec. 21, 1940; s. Francis Raymond and Anne (Birskovich) H.; m. Nancy Ann Kines, Apr. 14, 1962; children: Scott Alan, Brian Marshall, Jonathan Kendall. A.E.E., DeVry Tech. Inst., 1964; B.S. in Math. and Physics, U. Rochester, 1969, postgrad. in Mech. Engring., 1969-70. Research aide, physics lab. Xerox Corp., Rochester, N.Y., 1965-67, sr. physicist, 1969-80, tech. specialist, project mgr. optical tech., 1980—. Contbr. articles to profl. jours. Mem. Penfield (N.Y.) Zoning Com., 1971-72. Served with USN, 1958-62. Mem. Optical Soc. Am., Am. Wine Soc. (pres. chpt. 1980). Republican. Lutheran. Patentee in field. Current Work: Develop and carry from concept to product issue, light sources for use in electrophotography. Subspecialties: Plasma physics; Optical engineering. Home: 108 Henderson Dr Penfield NY 14526 Office: Xerox Sq 147 Rochester NY 14644

HAMMOND, WELDON WOOLF, JR., geology educator; b. San Antonio, May 17, 1937; s. Weldon Woolf and Thelma (Vandever) H.; m. Linda Lou Cowden; children—Weldon Woolf, Rory Cowden. B.A., U. Tex.-Austin, 1960, M.A., 1969, Ph.D., 1984. Cert. profl. geologist. Geologist, Tex. Water Devel. Bd., Austin, 1965-69; program mgr. Alamo Area Council of Govts., San Antonio, 1969-78; lectr. U. Tex.-San Antonio, 1978-83, asst. prof. geology, 1983—. Contbr. articles to profl. jours. Bd. dirs. Big Bros./Big Sisters, San Antonio, 1983—, San Antonio Parks Council, 1980-83, Tex. Transp. Mus., 1979-82. Served as lt. USN, 1960-63. USPHS fellow, 1965. Mem. Geol. Soc. Am., Internat. Assn. Hydrologists, South Tex. Geol. Soc., Sigma Xi, Phi Kappa Phi, Sigma Gamma Epsilon. Methodist. Current work: Hydrogeology of carbonate aquifers, isotopic dating of groundwater. Subspecialty: Hydrology. Home: 106 Tyrol Pl San Antonio TX 78209 Office: U Tex Earth and Phys Scis San Antonio TX 78285

HAMNING, RICHARD RUDOLPH, clinical psychologist, consultant researcher; b. Harvey, Ill., July 2, 1953; s. Rudolph and E. and Virginia (Phelps) H. B.S., Iowa State U., 1975; M.S., George Peabody Coll., 1978; Ph.D., Peabody Coll., Vanderbilt U., 1981. Lic. psychologist, Tenn. Psychol. examiner

Middle Tenn. Mental Health Inst., Nashville, 1978-80; clin. psychologist children and youth programs, 1981-82; dir., clin. psychologist Brentwood (Tenn.) Counseling Ctr., 1982—; adj. prof. psychology George Peabody Coll., Vanderbilt U., 1982—; cons. Giles County Schs., Pulaski, Tenn., 1982—, Giles County Schs. (Regional Intervention Program), Nashville, 1982—; dir. spl. needs unit Spencer Youth Ctr., 1983—. Mem. Am. Psychol. Assn. Methodist. Current Work: Social adaptation in psychopathology; role attribution in deviant family systems; neuroanatomical repair and psychological functioning; epistemology. Subspecialty: Neuropsychology. Office: Brentwood Counseling Ctr 783 Old Hickory Blvd Brentwood TN 37027

HAMON, DANNY JOE, entomologist, botanical consultant; b. Bakersfield, Calif., Mar. 9, 1947; s. Daniel Boone and Josemae (Glover) H.; m. Veronica Lynn Hamon, Dec. 6, 1969; children: Jennifer Lynn, Deborah Jo. A.A., Porterville (Calif.) City Coll., 1973; B.A., Calif. State U., Fresno, 1977, M.A. candidate. Cert. U.S. Dept. Agr. Profl. Devel. Sch., 1981. Botanist, Sierra Nat. Forest, Calif., 1978-80; plant protection biologist U.S. Dept. Agr., Stockton, Calif., 1980—; speaker. Contbr. articles to profl. jours. Served with U.S. Army, 1966-69, Vietnam. Recipient Lillian Wells award in Botany Calif. State U., 1979. Mem. Calif. Bot. Soc., No. Calif. Entomology Soc., Nature Conservancy, Calif. Native Plant Soc. Democrat. Current Work: Rare plant populations and plant community interactions; plant quarantine and pest control. Subspecialties: Resource management; Species interaction.

HAMPAR, BERGE, research facility exec.; b. Rockaway, N.Y., Aug. 20, 1932; s. Yervant and Dikranouhi H.; m. Nancy C. Landes, June 7, 1976; children: Adrienne, Natalie. B.A., Columbia U., 1954, D.D.S., 1960; J.D., Balt. U., 1984. Bar: Md. 1984. Postdoctoral fellow dept. microbiology Columbia U., 1960-62; sr. scientist Nat. Inst. Dental Research, 1962-67; asst. chief. head microbiology sect. Lab. Molecular Oncology NIH, 1967-81; gen. mgr. Frederick (Md.) Cancer Research Facility, Nat. Cancer Inst., 1981—. Contbr. articles to profl. jours. Served with USN, 1954-56; Served with USPHS, 1962—. Mem. Am. Assn. Immunologists, Am. Assn. Cancer Research, Am. Soc. Virology, Omicron Kappa Upsilon. Current Work: Studies on human herpes viruses and their association with cancer. Subspecialties: Virology (medicine); Cancer research (medicine). Office: Nat Cancer Inst NCI-FCRF Bldg 427 Frederick MD 21701

HAMPTON, JAMES WILBURN, physician; b. Durant, Okla., Sept. 15, 1931; s. Hollis Eugene and Ouida (Mackey) H.; m. Carol McDonald, Feb. 22, 1958; children: Jaime, Clay, Diana, Neal. B.A., U. Okla., 1952, M.D., 1956. Intern U. Okla. Hosps., 1956-57; also resident; instr. to prof. U. Okla., Oklahoma City, 1959-77, head hematology/oncology, 1972-77; head hematology research Okla. Med. Research Found., Oklahoma City, 1972-77; dir. cancer program and med. oncology Baptist Med. Center, 1977-85, med. dir. Cancer Ctr. of Southwest, 1985—; chmn. med. adv. com. Hospice of Central Okla., 1981. Contbr. over 100 articles to profl. jours. Bd. dirs. Heritage Hills, Oklahoma City, 1972, Am. Cancer Soc., 1982; co-chmn. Save St. Paul's Episcopal Cathedral com., 1983, others. NIH Career Devel. Award., 1966-67. Mem. Am. Fedn. Clin. Research (pres. 1970-71), Central Soc. Clin. Research (asso. editor jour. 1975-76), Okla. County Med. Soc. (editor bull.), ACP (fellow), Internat. Soc. Thrombosis and Hematosis. Clubs: Oklahoma City Golf and Country, Blue Cord, Chaine des Rotisseurs. Current Work: Hyperviscosity syndrome; preleukemia syndrome, hospice and palliative care. Subspecialties: Cancer research (medicine); Hematology. Home: 1414 N Hudson St Oklahoma City OK 73112 Office: Bapt Med Center 3300 NW Expressway Oklahoma City OK 73112

HAMRICK, JOSEPH THOMAS, mechanical engineer, corporate executive; b. Carrollton, Ga., Mar. 20, 1921; s. James Mayfield and Mattie Almon (Gaston) H.; m. Dorothy Elizabeth Jones, June 19, 1948; children: Jane Elizabeth Hamrick Kneisley, Nancy Ann Hamrick Owen, Thomas Mayfield. B.M.E., Ga. Inst. Tech., 1946, M.S.M.E., 1948. With NACA, Cleve., 1948-55, Thompson Ramo Wooldridge, Euclid, Ohio, 1955-61; pres. Aerospace Research Corp., Roanoke, Va., 1961—; dir. Cogeneration of Tenn., Inc., Roanoke, ptnr. RBS Electric, Knoxville, Tenn. Contbr. articles to profl. jours. Pres. North Franklin County Pub. Park, Inc. Served to 1st lt. USAAF, 1943-46, PTO. Dept. of Energy grantee, 1978-85; NSF grantee, 1980. Mem. ASME. Republican. Unitarian. Patentee in field. Current Work: Research on fueling gas turbines with wood, operation of 4000-hp gas turbine with wood fuel. Subspecialties: Biomass (energy science and technology); Combustion processes. Home: 6364 JAE Valley Rd SE Roanoke VA 24014 Office: 5454 JAE Valley Rd SE Roanoke VA 24014

HAN, JAOK, medical educator, cardiologist, researcher; b. Chinnampo, Korea, July 16, 1930; came to U.S. 1955, naturalized 1970; s. Choon H. and Chung R. (Kim) H.; m. Yangsook Chun, Jan. 21, 1961; children—Sylvia, Julia, Andrew. M.D., Kyong-Puk Nat. U., Taegu, Korea, 1951; Ph.D., SUNY-Syracuse, 1962. Intern Jersey City Med. Ctr., N.J., 1955-56, resident in medicine Mercy Hosp., Pitts., 1956-57; research assoc. Masonic Med. Research Lab., Utica, N.Y., 1961-66; fellow in cardiology U. Rochester, N.Y., 1966-67; assoc. prof. med., Albany Med. Coll., N.Y., 1968-73, dir. electrocardiography, 1968—, prof., 1973—. Mem. research com. N.Y. State Heart Assn., 1968-73, mem. rev. com. for Ischemic Heart Disease Research Ctr. Nat. Heart and Lung Inst., Bethesda, Md., 1975, rev. com. on beta blocker heart attack trial, 1979, review com. Cardiac Arrhythmia study, 1982, cardiology adv. com., 1981—. Author: Cardiac Arrhythmias, 1972. Mem. editorial bd. Jour. Electrocardiology, 1984—. Contbr. numerous articles to profl. jours. Postdoctoral fellow Internat. Soc. Cardiology Found., 1960-61, Masonic Found. Med. Research, 1961-63; NIH grantee, 1969—. Fellow Am. Heart Assn. (council on circulation, pres. Northeastern N.Y. chpt. 1980-82); mem. N.Y. Acad. Sci., Am. Fed. Clin. Research, Am. Physiol. Soc., Am. Coll. Cardiology, Sigma Xi. Current work: Clinical and research cardiology, electrophysiology of cardiac arrhythmias. Subspecialties: Cardiology; Physiology (medicine). Home: 29 Cobble Hill Rd Loudonville NY 12211 Office: Dept Medicine Albany Med Coll Albany NY 12208

HAN, KI SUP, physicist; b. Seoul, Korea, Apr. 7, 1929; came to Sweden, 1961; s. Pyo Hyung Han and Ta Suen Lee; m. Nock Soun Sohn, Nov. 15, 1956; children—Jae Kyung, Phillip Jaeho. B.S., Seoul Nat. U., 1957; diploma U. Uppsala (Sweden), 1962; M.S., Mich. State U., 1964; Ph.D., U. Mich., 1970. Instr., Korea U./Po Sung High Sch., Seoul, 1957-62; research asst. Mich. State U., East Lansing, 1962-64; asst. prof. Aquinas Coll., Grand Rapids, Mich., 1964-67; research assoc. U. Mich., Ann Arbor, 1967-72; asst. group leader Los Alamos Nat. Lab. (N.Mex.), 1972-79; mem. tech. staff Rockwell Internat., Anaheim, Calif., 1979—; cons. Los Alamos Nat. Lab., 1979-81. Author: Physics for High School Student, 1959. Patentee in field. Pres., Po Sung High Sch. Alumni Assn., Los Angeles, 1983; bd. dirs. Korean Scientist and Engrs. Assn., Irvine, Calif., 1982. Served to capt. Korean Army, 1950-55. Internat. Atomic Energy Agy. fellow, 1961. Mem. Am. Phys. Soc., AAUP, Korean Phys. Soc. Buddhist. Current work: Real time electro-optical imaging systems engineering including optical image processing and infrared detector modelling; nuclear and particle physics spectroscopy; coded apertare imaging applicable to nuclear reactions. Subspecialties: Particle physics; Infrared spectroscopy. Home: 990 S Jay Circle Anaheim CA 92808 Office: Rockwell Internat 3370 Miraloma Anaheim CA 92803

HAN, MOO-YOUNG, physicist; b. Seoul, Korea, Nov. 30, 1934; came to U.S., 1954; s. Sunghoon and Kiejer (Kim) H.; m. Changki Hong, Aug. 29, 1959; children: Grace, Chris, Tony. B.S., Carroll Coll., Waukesha, Wis., 1957; Ph.D., U. Rochester, 1964. Research assoc. Syracuse U., 1964-65; asst. prof. U. Pitts., 1965-67; asst. prof. physics Duke U., Durham, N.C., 1967-71, assoc. prof., 1971-77, prof., 1977—; vis. prof. Kyoto U., 1974. Recipient Outstanding Prof. award Duke U., 1971; recipient Disting. Teaching award, 1972, Disting. Fgn. Scholar award Kyoto U., 1974. Mem. Am. Phys. Soc. Current Work: nature and symmetry of fundamental building blocks of matter, leptons and quarks. Subspecialties: Particle physics; Theoretical physics. Home: 615 Duluth St Durham NC 27705 Office: Dept Physics Duke U Durham NC 27706

HAN, STELLA C., biochemist; b. Canton, China, May 29, 1937; came to U.S., 1961, naturalized, 1973; d. Huai-Kao and Yuan-chin (HO) Wang; m. George Shu-Ping Han, Feb. 26, 1966; children—Gregory, Eric, David. B.S., Nat. Taiwan U., 1961; M.S., U. Iowa, 1964. Research asst. Abbott Labs., North Chicago, Ill., 1964; sr. research chemist L.I. Jewish Med. Ctr., New Hyde Park, N.Y., 1966-70; research asst. Cornell U., Ithaca, N.Y., 1970-71; research biochemist Roche Inst. Molecular Biology, Nutley, N.J., 1971; research asst. II, Princeton U., N.J., 1977—. Contbr. articles to profl. jours. Mem. Am. Chem. Soc. Current work: By using the tissue culture of Drosophila cell, we are studying the relationship between DNA sequence organization and chromatin structure; we are also using the molecular cloning technique to study various genes expression. Subspecialties: Genome organization; Cell and tissue culture. Office: Princeton U Dept Biology Washington Rd Princeton NJ 08540

HAN, YOUN WOO, microbiologist, researcher; b. Taegu, Korea, Apr. 28, 1933; came to U.S., 1961, naturalized, 1971; s. Hyo Dong and Ok (Lee) H.; m. Sung Ja Kim, Mar. 31, 1965; children—Michael K., John K., Jenny S. B.S., Kyung Pook Nat. U. (Korea), 1960; M.S., Va. Poly., 1964; Ph.D., La. State U., 1969. Asst. prof. La. State U., Baton Rouge, 1969-71; assoc. prof. (courtesy) Oreg. State U., Corvallis, 1973-78; AID invited prof. Seoul Nat. U., Korea, 1978-79; fulbright profl U. Abidjan, Ivory Coast, 1983-84; research microbiologist Agrl. Research Service, Dept. Agr., New Orleans, 1971—. Contbr. over 100 articles to profl. jours. Patentee in field. Fellow Am. Inst. Chemists; mem. Am. Soc. Microbiology, Soc. Indsl. Microbiology, Am. Chem. Soc., Inst. Food Tech., Sigma Xi. Current work: Agricultural waste utilization; genetic engineering for over production of industrial enzymes. Subspecialties: Genetics and genetic engineering (agriculture); Enzyme technology. Home: 1359 Mendez St New Orleans LA 70122 Office: USDA Agrl Research Service So Regional Research Ctr 1100 Robert E Lee Blvd New Orleans LA 70179

HANAFUSA, HIDESABURO, virologist; b. Nishinomiya, Japan, Dec. 1, 1929; came to U.S., 1961; s. Kamehachi and Tomi H.; m. Teruko Inoue, May 11, 1958; 1 dau., Kei. B.S., Osaka (Japan) U., 1953, Ph.D., 1960. Research asso. Research Inst. for Microbial Diseases, Osaka U., 1958-61; postdoctoral fellow virus lab. U. Calif., Berkeley, 1961-64; vis. scientist College de France, Paris, 1964-66; asso. mem., chief dept. viral oncology Public Health Research Inst. of City N.Y. Inc., 1966-68, mem., 1968-73; prof. Rockefeller U., 1973—. Mem. editorial bd.: Internat. Jour. Cancer, from 1974, Jour. Virology, from 1975, BBA Rev. Cancer, from 1973, Intervirology, from 1972, Jour. Exptl. Medicine, from 1976, Cell, from 1979; contbr. articles to profl. jours. Recipient Howard Taylor Ricketts award, 1981, Albert Lasker Basic Med. Research award, 1982; Nat. Cancer Inst. grantee, 1966—; Am. Cancer Soc. grantee, 1976—. Mem. Am. Soc. Microbiology, AAAS, Nat. Acad. Scis., N.Y. Acad. Sci. Research on RNA tumor viruses. Subspecialties: Molecular biology; Cancer research (medicine). Home: 500 E 63d St New York NY 10021 Office: Rockefeller U 1230 York Ave New York NY 10021

HANCOCK, JOHN CHARLES, pharmacologist; b. Lockwood, Mo., Aug. 20, 1938; s. Daniel L. and Cordelia (Oats) H. B.S., U. Mo.-Kansas City, 1962; M.S., U. Tex., 1965, Ph.D., 1967. Postdoctoral fellow U. Conn., Hartford, 1967-68, instr., 1968-69, asst. prof., 1969-71, La. State U., New Orleans, 1971-73, assoc. prof., 1973-77; prof., dep. chmn. pharmacology, chmn. curriculum com. Coll. Medicine, dir. neurosci. tng. program East Tenn. State U., Johnson City, 1977—. Contbr. articles nat. and internat. jours. Grantee U. Conn. Research Found., 1971-72; Grantee La. State U. Research Found., 1972-73; Grantee AMA, 1971-73; Grantee NIMH, 1974-75; Grantee Nat. Inst. Neurol. Diseases and Stroke, 1974-77; Grantee E. Tenn. Research Found., 1979-80; Tenn affiliate Am. Heart Assn., 1979-81, 83-84; Tenn affiliate Biomed. Research Devel., 1979-80, 81-82. Mem. Am. Soc. Pharmacology and Exptl. Therapeutics, Soc. Neurosci. (pres. Appalachian chpt.), AAAS, Sigma Xi. Current Work: Central nervous system regulation of the heart and blood pressure, electrophysiology, baroreceptor function, cardiovascular regulation, neuropeptides. Subspecialties: Pharmacology; Neuropharmacology. Home: 1306 Althea St Johnson City TN 37601 Office: Dept of Pharmacology Quillen Dishner Coll of Medicine East Tenn State U Johnson City TN 37614

HAND, CADET HAMMOND, JR., marine biologist, educator; b. Patchogue, N.Y., Apr. 23, 1920; s. Cadet Hammond and Myra (Wells) H.; m. Winifred Werdelin, June 6, 1942; children—Cadet Hammond III.; Gary Alan. B.S., U. Conn., 1946; M.A., U. Calif. at Berkeley, 1948, Ph.D., 1951 Instr. Mills Coll., 1948-50, asst. prof., 1950-51; research biologist Scripps Inst. Oceanography, 1951-53; mem. faculty U. Calif. at Berkeley, 1953—, prof. zoology, 1963—; dir. Bodega Marine Lab., 1961—; Cons. NIH, 1964-66, NSF, 1964-69; mem. atomic safety and licensing bd. panel Nuclear Regulatory Commn., 1971—, adminstrv. judge atomic safety and licensing bd. panel, 1980—; NSF sr. postdoctoral fellow, 1959-60; Guggenheim fellow, 1967-68. Contbr. articles to profl. jours. Fellow Calif. Acad. Scis., Wash. acads. scis.; mem. No. Calif. Malacozool. Soc. (pres. 1963—), Soc. Systemic Zoology, Ecol. Soc. Am., Ray Soc. (Gt. Britain), Am. Soc. Zoologists (chmn. div. invertebrate zoology 1977-78), Soc. Limnology and Oceanography. Current work: Life history and taxonomy of coelenterates; symbiotic partnerships between marine metazoans; behavior of marine animals. Home: Star Route Bogeda Bay CA 94923 Office: Bodega Marine Lab Bodega Bay CA 94923

HANDE, KENNETH ROBERT, physician; b. Mpls., Jan. 20, 1946; s. Edwin Kenneth and Evelyn Dorothy (Ogrosky) H.; m. Mary Saunders, Aug. 22, 1970; 3 children. A.B., Princeton U., 1968; M.D., Johns Hopkins U., 1972. Intern, resident Barnes Hosp., St. Louis, 1972-74; clin. assoc., career expert Nat. Cancer Inst., Bethesda, Md., 1974-78; asst. prof. medicine and pharmacology Vanderbilt U., Nashville, 1978-82, assoc. prof., 1982—Current Work: Antineoplastic drug pharmacology. Subspecialties: Chemotherapy; Pharmacology. Home: 502 W Hillwood Nashville TN 37205 Office: Dept Medicine Div Oncology Vanderbilt U Sch Medicine Nashville TN 37232

HANDLER, ROBERT ALPHONSE, mechanical engineer, researcher; b. Newark, Aug. 17, 1951; s. Herbert and Bernice (Zoppi) H. B.E., Stevens Inst. Tech., 1973; M.S.E., U. Mich., 1974; S.M., M.I.T., 1976; Ph.D., U. Minn., 1980. Research asst. M.I.T., Cambridge, 1974-76; teaching assoc. U. Minn., Mpls., 1976-79; mech. engr. Naval Ship Research and Devel. Ctr., Bethesda, Md., 1980-81, Naval Research Lab., Washington, 1981—. Mem. Acoustical Soc. Am. Current Work: Computational and theoretical work in turbulence; hydrodynamic noise; fluid-structure interactions. Subspecialties: Fluid mechanics; Theoretical and applied mechanics. Home: 11978 Home Guard Dr Woodbridge VA 22192 Office: Naval Research Lab 4555 Overlook Ave SW Washington DC 22303

HANDORF, CHARLES RUSSELL, pathologist, medicinal chemist; b. Memphis, Jan. 9, 1951; s. Everett Charles and Lucille (Preston) H.; m. Miriam Howard Fulmer, Dec. 28, 1976; children: Charles Russell II, Jennifer Anne. B.A., Rice U., 1973; M.D., U. Tenn., 1977, Ph.D., 1981. Diplomate: Am. Bd. Pathology. Teaching asst. Rice U., Houston, 1972-73; research asst. VA Hosp., Memphis, 1977-78; resident in pathology U. Tenn.-Memphis, 1978-80, Meth. Hosp., Memphis, 1980-82; assoc. pathologist Duckworth Pathology Group, Memphis, 1982—; adj. instr. U. Tenn., 1978-80; jr. med. staff Meth. Hosp., 1982—; jr. med. staff Eastwood Hosp., Memphis, 1982—, dir. labs., 1985—. Marion Labs. fellow, 1973-74; recipient Lange award U. Tenn., 1977. Mem. So. Med. Assn., Coll. Am. Pathologists, Am. Soc. Clin. Pathologists, AMA, Sigma Xi, Phi Chi, Rho Chi. Methodist. Current Work: Development and implementation of novel approaches to problems in clinical toxicology and psychotherapeutic drug monitoring. Subspecialties: Pathology (medicine); Medicinal chemistry. Home: 470 Greenfield Rd Memphis TN 38117 Office: Duckworth Pathology Group 1331 Union St Suite 1005 Memphis TN 38104

HANDY, LYMAN LEE, chemist, educator; b. Payette, Idaho, Aug. 4, 1919; s. Clarence Lee and Lillie (Hall) H.; m. Lenore E. Ross, Aug. 28, 1948; children—Mark Ross, Gail Eileen. Student, Western Wash. Coll., 1938-40; B.S., U. Wash., 1942, Ph.D., 1951. With Chevron Oil Field Research Co., 1951-66; mem. faculty U. So. Calif., 1966—, prof. chem. and petroleum engring., chmn. petroleum engring., 1966—, chmn. chem. engring., 1969-76, Omar B. Milligan prof. petroleum engring., 1976—; cons. in field. Mem. editorial bd., Trans. Am. Inst. Mining Engrs., 1960, 68, 69; Contbr. articles to profl. jours. Served to lt. USNR, 1942-46. Mem. Am. Chem. Soc. (chmn. Orange County sect. 1969), Soc. Petroleum Engrs. (dir. Los Angeles basin sect. 1971-75, chmn. 1974, nat. dir.-at-large 1978—), Am. Inst. Chem. Engrs., A.A.A.S., Phi Beta Kappa, Sigma Xi, Phi Lambda Upsilon, Tau Beta Pi. Current Work: Fluid flow through porous materials and new methods for enhanced recovery of oil. Subspecialties: Petroleum engineering; Surface chemistry. Home: 1401 Dana Pl Fullerton CA 92631 Office: University Park Los Angeles CA 90007

HANIFIN, LEO EUGENE, manufacturing and research administrator, mechanical engineer; b. Binghamton, N.Y., Aug. 2, 1946; s. Leo Francis and Mary Hanna (McDonald) H.; m. Angela Papa, Aug. 2, 1980; children: Jacqueline, Sonia, Leo Daniel. Student, St. Bonaventure U., 1964-66; B.M.E., U. Detroit, 1969, M. in M.E., 1972, Dr. Engring. and Mfg. Systems, 1976; postgrad., UCLA, 1969-71. Hughes fellow Hughes Aircraft Co., 1969-70, mem. staff, 1971; engr. Aerojet Gen. Corp., Culver City, Calif., 1970-71; systems coordinator gen. mfg. div. Chrysler Corp., Detroit, 1971-78, project mgr., Syracuse, N.Y., 1972-80; dir. Center for Mfg. Productivity and Tech. Transfer, Rensselaer Poly. Inst., Troy, N.Y., 1980—; adj. assoc. prof. U. Mich., 1978; cons. for mfg. productivity improvements. Mem. Soc. Mfg. Engrs. (vice chmn. mfg. mgmt. council, outstanding young mfg. engr. of yr. 1981, lectr.), Am. Inst. Indsl. Engrs. Democrat. Roman Catholic. Current Work: Improving productivity and application of advanced technologies, education for manufacturing engineers, robotics-inspection, manufacturing systems design and analysis, control systems, quality systems. Subspecialties: Manufacturing productivity; Robotics.

HANIN, ISRAEL, pharmacologist, educator, researcher; b. Shanghai, China, Mar. 29, 1937; s. Leo and Rebecca (Lubarsky) H.; m. Leda Toni, June 12, 1960; children: Adam, Dahlia. B.S., UCLA, 1962, M.S., 1965, Ph.D. in Pharmacology, 1968. Vis. scientist dept. toxicology Karolinska Inst., Stockholm, 1968; pharmacologist Lab. Preclin. Pharmacology NIMH, Bethesda, Md., 1969-73; from asst. prof. to assoc. prof. psychiatry and pharmacology U. Pitts. Sch. Medicine, 1973-81, prof., 1981—; also dir. psychopharmacology program Western Psychiat. Inst. and Clinic; mem. research grant rev. com. NIMH, 1979-82. Editor 10 books; contbr. over 200 articles to sci. jours. Served to 2d lt. Armored Corps Israeli Army, 1955-58. NIMH grantee, 1965—. Mem. Pitts. Neurosci. Soc. (pres. 1982-83), Am. Chem. Soc., Am. Soc. Pharmacology and Exptl. Therapeutics, Am. Soc. Neurochemistry, Am. Coll. Neuropsychopharmacology. Current Work: Elucidation of factors controlling neurotransmitter synthesis with particular emphasis on cholinergic system; clin. correlates; animal models. Subspecialties: Neuropharmacology; Neurochemistry. Office: 3811 O'Hara St Pittsburgh PA 15213

HANISKO, JOHN-CYRIL PATRICK, engineer, physicist; b. Detroit, Mar. 17, 1937; s. John Joseph and Pauline Victoria (Vrabel) H. B.E.E., U. Detroit, 1963, M.S.E., 1965; M.A. in Physics, Wayne State U., 1972, postgrad., 1977-85. Engr. Burroughs Corp., Detroit, 1962-65; research engr. Boeing Co., Seattle, 1965-67; sr. engr. Eastman Kodak, Rochester, N.Y., 1967-68, Udylite Co., Warren, Mich., 1973-75; staff engr. Kent-Moore Corp., Warren, 1971-73, TRW, Farmington Hills, Mich., 1980—; cons. engring., 1975-76; project engr. Bendix, Troy, Mich., 1976-80. Contbr. articles to profl. jours. Patentee in field. Mem. AAAS, IEEE (sr. mem.), Inst. Theol. Encounter with Sci. and Tech. (pres. 1976), Fellowship Cath. Scholars. Current work: Miniaturized magnetic-based sensors, application of chaos theory to classical and quantum dynamics. Subspecialties: Electronics; Theoretical physics. Home: 21888 Murray Crescent Southfield MI 48076 Office: TRW 24175 Research Dr Farmington Hills MI 48024

HANKES, LAWRENCE VALENTINE, clinical biochemical researcher; b. Chgo., Nov. 24, 1919; s. Michael John and Matilda Ann (Bachman) H.; m. Mary Catherine Hamm, Sept. 16, 1951; children: Lawrence Michael, Catherine Ann, Matthew William. A.B., DePauw U., 1942; M.S., Mich. State U., 1943; Ph.D., U. Wis., 1949, Ph.D. (hon.), 1950. Registered clin. lab. dir., N.Y. Instr. biochemistry Mich. State U., East Lansing, 1942-43; instr. biochemistry Northwestern U. Dental Sch., Chgo., 1943-44; indsl. research fellow U. Wis., Madison, 1947-49; head allergy group VA Hosp., Aspinwall, Pa., 1950; head clin. chemistry med. ctr. Brookhaven Nat. Lab., Upton, N.Y., 1951—, sr. scientist, 1968—; cons. and researcher in field. Contbr. articles in field to profl. jours. Fellow Brit. Chem. Soc., Nat. Acad. Clin. Biochemists; mem. Am. Chem. Soc., Am. Soc. Biol. Chemists, Soc. Exptl. Biology & Medicine, Am. Assn. Clin. Chemists, Alpha Chi Sigma, Sigma Xi, Phi Sigma. Club: Explorer's. Current Work: Research on tryptophan metabolism in cancer, scleroderma, scurvy and pellagra synthesis of labeled metabolites; clinical chemistry methods. Subspecialties: Clinical chemistry; Nutrition (medicine). Home: 11 Maple Rd Setauket NY 11733 Office: Med Research Ctr Brookhaven Nat Lab Upton NY 11973

HANKINS, TIMOTHY HAMILTON, educator, radioastronomer; b. Miami, Fla., Mar. 13, 1941; s. Frank Hamilton, Jr. and Anne Chapin (Hudson) H.; m. Mary E. Nutt, Oct. 1, 1977; 1 son, Samuel Clark. B.A., Dartmouth Coll., 1962, M.S., 1967; Ph.D., U. Calif., San Diego, 1971. Research physicist, instr. U. Calif., San Diego, 1971-74; research assoc. Arecibo (P.R.) Obs., 1974-81; Alexander von Humboldt fellow Max Planck Inst. for Radioastronomy, Bonn, W.Ger., 1978-79; assoc. prof. Thayer Sch. Engring., Dartmouth Coll., Hanover, N.H., 1981—. Contbr. tech. papers to sci. publs. Served to lt. USN, 1962-64. Various research grants NSF. Mem. Am. Astron. Soc., Internat. Astron. Union, Internat. Sci. Radio Union. Current Work: Radio pulsar studies, signal processing, microprocessors. Subspecialties: Radio and microwave astronomy; Computer engineering. Office: Dartmouth Coll HB 8000 Hanover NH 03755

HANLEY, KEVIN JOSEPH, orthodontist, researcher, dental educator; b. Utica, N.Y., Oct. 25, 1952; s. Richard Joseph and Mary Teresa (Cain) H.; m. Carmella Marie Rosetti, June 24, 1978. B.A., SUNY, Buffalo, 1974, D.D.S., 1978. Cert. orthodonics U Conn., 1980. Clin. asst. prof. in residence orthodontics U. Conn. Sch. Dental Medicine, Farmington, 1980—. Author: (C.J. Burstone) Syllabus-Modern Edgewise Mechanics Segmented Arch Technique, 1982. Mem. Am. Assn. Orthodontists, ADA, Northeastern Soc. Orthodontists, Conn. State Dental Assn., Hartford Dental Soc. Republican. Roman Catholic. Clubs: Energy Independent (Simsbury, Conn.); Am. Mus. Natural History (N.Y.C.). Current Work: Effects of pulsating electromagnetic fields on osteoblasts in culture, clinical application of biomechanics in orthodontics. Subspecialties: Orthodontics; Cell and tissue culture. Home: 7 Cornfield Rd Simsbury CT 06070 Office: 345 N Main St West Hartford CT 06117

HANLEY, STEPHEN THURE, research scientist; b. Washington, Sept. 10, 1945; s. Thure Emil and John Lee (Smith) H. B.S. in Physics, U. Wash., 1967, M.S. in Physics, 1970, Ph.D. in Physics, 1973. Electronic technician Naval Hydrographic Office, Suitland, Md., 1963-67; predoctoral assoc. U. Wash., Seattle, 1967-70; physicist Naval Research Lab., Washington, 1970-79; sr. scientist OptiMetrics, Inc., Las Cruces, N.Mex., 1979—. Inventor Radiation Focus Meter, 1977, Cassegrain Laser Power Amplifier System, 1976. Mem. Am. Phys. Soc., Optical Soc. Am., Phi Beta Kappa. Current work: Research on electro-optical propagation through natural and obscurred atmospheres. Subspecialties: Infrared spectroscopy; Laser spectroscopy. Home: 6661 Vista Hermosa Las Cruces NM 88005 Office: OptiMetrics Inc 106 E Idaho Suite G Las Cruces NM 88001

HANNA, MICHAEL GEORGE, JR., biotechnology reseach scientist, administrator; b. Cleve., July 7, 1936; s. Michael George and Camella (Karem) H.; m. Barbara Ann Pearson, Sept. 6, 1958; children—Michael George III, Christine, Suzanne. B.S., Baldwin-Wallace Coll., 1958; M.S., Notre Dame U., 1960; Ph.D., U. Tenn., 1964. Research biologist biology div., Oak Ridge Nat. Lab., 1964-68, dir. immunology of carcinogenesis group, 1968-75; dir. cancer biology program Nat. Cancer Inst.-Frederick Cancer Research Facility, Md., 1975-79, dir. of Facility, 1979-82; dir. Litton Inst. Applied Biotech., Rockville, Md., 1982—; cons. med. research and ops. div. NASA, Houston, 1967-69. Editor: Lymphatic Tissue and Germinal Centers in Immune Response, 1969; gen. editor: (book series) Contemporary Topics in Immunology, 1971—; assoc. editor Jour. Cancer Research, 1980—, Jour. Biol. Response Modifiers, 1982—, Immunopharmacology, 1982—, Jour. Metastasis, 1983—. Chmn. tech. adv. com. on biotech. U.S. Dept. Commerce, 1985—. Contbr. articles to profl. jours. Recipient Charles B. Thornton Advanced Tech. award Litton Industries, 1984. Mem. Soc. Exptl. Pathology, Am. Assn. Cancer Research, Am. Assn. Immunologists, AAAS, Reticuloendothelial Soc., Sigma Xi. Republican. Eastern Orthodox. Current work: Host-tumor interaction, immunomodulation in the therapy of malignant diseases, immunodiagnostics of cancer and immunotherapy in multimodality settings. Subspecialties: Cancer research (medicine); Immunology (medicine). Home: 113 Fairview Ave Frederick MD 21701 Office: Litton Inst Applied Biotech 1330 Piccard Dr Rockville MD 20850

HANNAH, DAVID, JR., space launch service company executive; b. Houston, Apr. 9, 1922; s. David and Ethel May (Bloomfield) H.; m. Catherine Coburn, June 26, 1943; children: David III, Douglas, Glen Hannah Cole. B.A., Rice U., 1944. Pres. Ayrshire Corp., Houston, 1946-75, Castlewood Corp., Denver, 1975-80; pres. Space Services of Am., Houston, from 1981, chmn. bd., 1982—. Trustee Hermann Hosp. Estate, from 1980, chmn. Houston Com. Fgn. Relations, 1982-83. Presbyterian. Club: Houston Country. Lodge: Kiwanis. Current Work: Chairman of the board of company engaged in developing private commercialization of space launch services. Subspecialty: Space launch service. Office: Space Services Inc of Am 7015 Gulf Freeway Houston TX 77087

HANNAN, EDWARD LEES, state health services agency administrator, researcher; b. Troy, N.Y., Aug. 21, 1943; s. Edward J. and Marian (Cooper) H.; m. Maryanne Casey, Mar. 25, 1983; children—Elizabeth, Kathleen. B.S., Union Coll., 1964; M.S., 1970; M.S., Syracuse U., 1966; Ph.D., U. Mass., 1973. Instr. math. SUNY-Albany, 1966-68; sr. statistician N.Y. State Dept. Transp., Albany, 1968-70; asst. prof. Inst. Adminstrn. & Mgmt., Union Coll., Schenectady, 1973-78; asst. prof. Sch. Bus., Fla. Internat. U., Miami, 1978-80; dir. Bur. Health Care Research and Info. Services, N.Y. State Dept. Health, Albany, 1980—; cons. U.S. Coast Guard, 1978-80, N.Y. State Health Dept., 1973-78, Am. Lung Assn., 1972-73. Mem. planning com. Albany area chpt. ARC, 1982-83. Mem. Ops. Research Soc. Am., Am. Pub. Health Assn., Am. Statis. Assn., Inst. Mgmt. Scis., Am. Inst. for Decision Scis., Sigma Xi, Kappa Mu Epsilon, Alpha Pi Mu. Current work: Design and evaluation of health care programs; application of operations research techniques to public sector problems. Subspecialties: Health services research; Operations research (mathematics). Home: 7 Locust Ave Troy NY 12180 Office: Bur Health Care Research and Info Services 2084 Tower Bldg Empire State Plaza Albany NY 12237

HANNAY, N(ORMAN) BRUCE, chemist, educator; b. Mt. Vernon, Wash., Feb. 9, 1921; s. Norman Bond and Winnie (Evans) H.; m. Joan Anderson, May 27, 1943; children: Robin, Brooke. B.A., Swarthmore Coll., 1942, D.Sc. (hon.), 1979; M.S., Princeton U., 1943, Ph.D., 1944; Ph.D. (hon.), Tel Aviv U., 1978; D.Sc. (hon.), Poly. Inst. N.Y., 1981. With Bell Telephone Labs., Murray Hill, N.J., 1944-82, exec. dir. materials research div., 1967-73, v.p. research and patents, 1973-82, ret., 1982; dir. Plenum Pub. Co., Gen. Signal Corp., Flag Investors Fund, Rohm and Haas Co., Alex Brown Cash Res. Fund; Chmn. sci. adv. council Atlantic Richfield Corp., Gulf Applied Techs.; Regents' prof. UCLA, 1976, U. Calif., San Diego, 1979; cons. Alexander von Humboldt Found. Author: Solid State Chemistry, 1967, also articles.; Mem. numerous editorial bds.; editor: Semiconductors, 1959, Treatise on Solid State Chemistry, 1974. Recipient Acheson medal, 1976, Perkin medal, 1983. Fellow Am. Phys. Soc.; mem. Nat. Acad. Engring. (past fgn. sec.), Nat. Acad. Scis., Am. Acad. Arts and Scis., Mexican Nat. Acad. Engring., Am. Chem. Soc., Electrochem. Soc. (past pres.), Indsl. Research Inst. (past pres., medal 1982), Dirs. of Indsl. Research (past chmn.). Research on dipole moments and molecular structure, thermionic emission, mass spectroscopy, analysis of solids, solid state chemistry, semiconductors, superconductors. Current Work: Business and research consultant in high technology fields: electronics, materials, communications, specialty chemicals, and energy resources. Subspecialties: Materials; Electronics. Home: Friday Harbor WA Office: Nat Acad Engring 2101 Constitution Ave Washington DC 20418

HANOVER, JAMES WILLIAM, forestry educator, consultant; b. Dec. 10, 1930; married; 5 children. B.S., U. Wash., 1953; Ph.D., Wash. State U., 1963. Tree physiologist U.S. Forest Service, Moscow, Idaho, 1956-65; assoc. prof. Yale U., New Haven, 1965-66; prof. forestry Mich. State U., East Lansing, 1966—; cons. wood quality, forest tree improvement, tree seedling prodn., 1970—. Editor assoc. Forest Sci. jour., 1974-80; contbr. articles to profl. jours. Grantee state, fed. and pvt. agys.; recipient Disting. Service award Mich. Christmas Tree Assn., 1984. Mem. Soc. Am. Foresters (sec. tree physiology working group; chmn. tree improvement working group 1980-82). Developer American Spruce, tri-hybrid planted on U.S. Capitol grounds, 1976. Current work: Systems for accelerated growth of trees. Subspecialty: Plant genetics. Office: Dept Forestry Mich State U East Lansing MI 48824

HANRATTY, THOMAS JOSEPH, chemical engineer, educator; b. Phila., Nov. 9, 1926; s. John Joseph and Elizabeth Marie (O'Connor) H.; m. Joan L. Hertel, Aug. 25, 1956; children: John, Vincent, Maria, Michael, Peter. B.S. Chem. Engring., Villanova U., 1947; B.S. Chem. Engring. hon. doctorate, 1979; M.S., Ohio State U., 1950; Ph.D., Princeton U., 1953. Engr. Fischer & Porter, 1947-48; research engr. Battelle Meml. Inst., 1948-50; engr. Rohm & Haas, Phila., summer 1951; research engr. Shell Devel. Co., Emeryville, Calif., 1954; faculty U. Ill., Urbana, 1953—, assoc. prof., 1958-63, prof. chem. engring., 1963—, Shell disting. prof., 1981; cons. in field; vis. assoc. prof. Brown U., 1962-63. Contbr. articles to profl. jours. Mem. U.S. Nat. Com. on Theoretical and Applied Mechanics. NSF sr. postdoctoral fellow, 1962; recipient Curtis W. McGraw award Am. Soc. Engring. Edn., 1963, Sr. Research award, 1979; Disting. Engring. Alumnus award Ohio State U., 1984. Fellow Am. Phys. Soc., Am. Acad. Scis.; mem. Nat. Acad. Engrs., Am. Inst. Chem. Engrs. (Colburn award 1957, Walker award 1964, Profl. Progress award 1967), Am. Chem. Soc. Roman Catholic. Club: Serra Internat. Subspecialties: Chemical engineering; Fluid mechanics. Home: 1019 W Charles St Champaign IL 61820 Office: 205 Roger Adams Lab U Ill Urbana IL 61801

HANSCH, CORWIN HERMAN, educator; b. Kenmare, N.D., Oct. 6, 1918; s. Herman William and Rachel (Corwine) H.; m. Gloria J. Tomasulo, Jan. 8, 1944; children—Clifford, Carol. B.S., U. Ill., 1940; Ph.D., N.Y.U., 1944. Research chemist Manhattan project E.I. du Pont de Nemours & Co., Inc., 1944-45, research chemist, 1945-46; prof. chemistry Pomona Coll., 1946—; spl. research relationship chem. structure and drug action. Guggenheim fellow Fed. Inst. Tech., Zurich, Switzerland, 1952-53; Guggenheim fellow Pomona Coll., 1966-67; Petroleum Research Fund fellow U. Munich, Germany, 1959-60; Recipient medal Italian Soc. Pharm. Sci., 1967; Coll. Chemistry Teaching award Mfg. Chemists Assn., 1969; Research Achievement award Am. Pharm. Assn., 1969; E.A. Smissman award Medicinal Chemistry Am. Chem. Soc., 1975; Tolman award Los Angeles sect., 1976. Subspecialty: Organic chemistry. Home: 4070 Olive Knoll Pl Claremont CA 91711

HANSCH, THEODOR WOLFGANG, physicist; b. Heidelberg, W. Germany, Oct. 30, 1941; came to U.S., 1970; s. Karl E. and Martha (Kiefer) H. Abitur, Helmholtz Gymnasium, Heldelberg, 1961; M.S., U. Heidelberg, 1966, Ph.D., 1969. Asst. prof. physics U. Heidelberg, 1969-70; NATO fellow Stanford U., 1970-72, assoc. prof. physics, 1972-75, prof., 1975—. Co-editor: Metrologia, 1975—; adv. editor: Optics Communications, 1975—; assoc. editor: Applied Physics B, 1983. Contbr. articles to profl. jours. Named Calif. Scientist of Yr., 1973; recipient Alexander von Humboldt Sr. U.S. Scientist award, 1978-79; Otto Klung award, 1980, Cyrus B. Comstock prize Nast. acad. scis., 1983; Alfred P. Sloan fellow, 1973-75. Fellow Am. Phys. soc. (Herbert Broida prize 1983), Optical Soc. Am. (assoc. editor jour. 1982—); mem. Am. Acad. Arts and Scis., Deutsche Physikalische Gesellschaft, Sigma Xi. Roman Catholic. Current work: Researcher spectroscopy and quantumelelectronics, developer powerful monochromatic pulsed dye lasers, high resolution nonlinear spectroscopy of atoms and molecules. Subspecialties: Dye lasers; Spectroscopy. Office: Dept Physics Stanford U Stanford CA 94305*

HANSCHE, BRUCE DAVID, electrical engineer; b. Albuquerque, Dec. 8, 1947; s. George Everett and Helen Barbara (Johnson) H.; m. Christina Cripps Husted, Dec. 21, 1968; children: Heather, Jena. B.S.E.E., Mich. State U., 1969; M.S.E.E., Stanford U., 1970; Ph.D. in Elec. Engring., U. Mich., 1976. Mem. staff nondestructive testing tech. Sandia Labs., Albuquerque, 1969—. Contbr. articles to profl. jours. Mem. Optical Soc. Am., Eta Kappa Nu, Tau Beta Pi. Current Work: Advanced non-destructive testing technology, image processing for radiography, holographic interferometry, computed tomography. Subspecialties: Optical engineering; Graphics, image processing, and pattern recognition. Home: Box 962 Tijeras NM 87059 Office: Sandia Labs Div 7551 Albuquerque NM 87185

HANSEL, WILLIAM, physiology educator; b. Vale Summit, Md., Sept. 16, 1918; s. John William and Helen M. (Sperlein) H.; m. Milbrey Downey, Aug. 16, 1942; children—Barbara Ann, Kay Elizabeth. B.S., U. Md., 1940; M.S., Cornell U., 1947, Ph.D., 1949. Grad. asst. Cornell U., Ithaca, N.Y., 1946-49; mem. faculty N.Y. State Coll. Agr., Life Scis. and Vet. Medicine, 1949—, prof. physiology, 1961—, chmn. dept., 1973-83; cons. Schering Corp., N.J., Am. Cyanamid Corp., N.Y., Merck Sharpe & Dhome, N.J., 1981-85. Contbr. numerous chpts. to books, sci. papers to profl. lit. Served to maj. AUS, 1942-46. Liberty Hyde Bailey prof. Cornell U., 1978. Mem. Soc. for Study Reprodn. (pres. 1975-76, Carl G. Hartman award 1980), Am. Soc. Animal Sci. (Morrison award 1979), Am. Dairy Sci. Assn. (N.A.A.B. award 1973, Borden award 1972), Endocrine Soc., Am. Physiol. Soc., Soc. for Study Fertility (Hammond lectr. 1985), Soc. for Exptl. Biology and Medicine (treas. 1980-81). Republican. Current work: Reproductive physiology and endocrinology. Subspecialty: Animal physiology. Office: Dept Physiology 816 Veterinary Research Tower Vet Medicine NY State Coll Cornell U Ithaca NY 14853

HANSEN, CARL TAMS, geneticist; b. Greeley, Colo., July 22, 1929; s. Jens and Marie (Andersen) H.; m. Janet Coyle, June 8, 1962; children: Alan, Carol. B.S. in Agr, Colo. State U., 1951; M.S., S.D. State U., 1959; Ph.D. in Genetics, U. Wis., 1967. Geneticist Vet. Resources br. Div. Research Services, NIH, Bethesda, Md., 1964—. Contbr. articles on genetic models for biomedresearch to profl. publs. Served to capt. USMC, 1951-53. Recipient Superior Service award HEW, 1975. Mem. Genetics Soc. Am., Am. Genetics Assn., AAAS. Current Work: The use of genetics, genetic engineering and animal breeding techniques to develop mammalian model systems of human diseases. Subspecialties: Genetics and genetic engineering (medicine); Animal breeding and embryo transplants. Office: NIH Bldg 14A Room 102 Bethesda MD 20892

HANSEN, GRANT LEWIS, aerospace and information systems executive; b. Bancroft, Idaho, Nov. 5, 1921; s. Paul Ezra and Leona Sarah (Lewis) H.; m. Iris Rose Heyden, Apr. 21, 1945; children: Alan Lee, Brian Craig, Carol Margaret, David James, Ellen Diane. B.S. in Elec. Engring., Ill. Inst. Tech., 1948; postgrad. engring. and mgmt., UCLA, Calif. Inst. Tech.; D.Sc., Nat. U., 1978. With Douglas Aircraft Co., 1948-60; v.p., program dir. for Centaur (Convair div.), 1960-65; v.p. launch vehicle programs Convair div. Gen. Dynamics Corp., 1965-69; asst. sec. air force for research and devel., 1969-73; v.p. Gen. Dynamics Corp., San Diego, 1974-78; v.p., gen. mgr. Gen. Dynamics Corp. (Convair div.), 1973-78; exec. v.p. System Devel. Corp., Santa Monica, Calif., 1978—; also pres. SDC Systems Group, 1978—; U.S. del. NATO (Adv. Group for Aerospace Research and Devel.), 1969-73; U.S. mem. sci. com. for nat. reps. SHAPE Tech. Center, The Hague, Netherlands, 1969-73; mem. research and tech. adv. council NASA, 1971-73; mem. sci. adv. bd. Dept. Air Force, 1976—. Served with USNR, World War II. Decorated Purple Heart; recipient Pub. Service award NASA, 1966, Disting. Pub. Service award, 1975; Alumni Recognition award Ill. Inst. Tech., 1967; USAF Exceptional Civilian Service medal, 1973, 83. Fellow AIAA (nat. pres. 1975), Am. Astronautical Soc., AAAS, Internat. Acad. Astronautics; mem. IEEE (sr.), German Soc. Air and Space Travel (corr.), Nat. Alliance Businessmen (nat. bd. dirs., dir. region IX), Nat. Acad. Engring. (aeros. and space engring. bd.), NRC, Eta Kappa Nu, Tau Beta Pi. Current Work: Aeronautical and space vehicles and technology; computer based information, command and control and intelligence systems. Subspecialties: Aerospace engineering and technology; Information systems (Information science). Home: 10737 Fuerte Dr LaMesa CA 92041 Office: System Devel Corp 4065 Hancock St San Diego CA 92110

HANSEN, JAMES VERNON, computer science and information systems educator, researcher; b. Idaho Falls, May 31, 1936; s. Heber Lorenzo and Myrtle Jane (Simmons) H.; m. Diane Lynne Bradbury, Sept. 18, 1963; children: Tamsin, Jeffrey, Dale, Peter. B.S., Brigham Young U., 1963, M.S., 1966; Ph.D., U. Wash., 1973. Systems analyst TRW, Redondo Beach, Calif., 1966-69; sr. research scientist Battelle Meml. Inst., Richland, Wash., 1972-74; asst. prof. Ind. U., Bloomington, 1974-77, assoc. prof., 1978-81; prof. Brigham Young U., Provo, Utah, 1982—; prin. Phil Johnson & Assocs., Phoenix, 1980—; cons. Battelle Meml. Inst. Author: Controls in Microcomputer Systems, 1984; Primer on Telecommunications, 1985; Auditing Telecommunications Systems, 1985; also monographs. Advanced Systems Analysis. Mem. dist. scout council Boy Scouts Am., Ind., 1978. Served with U.S. Army, 1959-62. Grantee Peat, Marwick, Mitchell Found., 1982-85, Inst. Internal. Auditors, 1983, 85, Kellogg Found., 1972. Mem. Assn. Computing Machinery, Inst. Mgmt. Sci., Ops. Research Soc. Am., Am. Assn. Artificial Intelligence, Sierra Club. Independent. Mem. Ch. Jesus Christ of Latter-day Saints. Current Work: Design and testing of expert systems, application of relational database Concepts to decision support systems, applications of operations research methods to analysis and design of computer networks. Subspecialties: Information systems (Information science); Artificial intelligence. Office: Brigham Young U Provo UT 84602

HANSEN, KENT FORREST, nuclear engineering educator; b. Chgo., Aug. 10, 1931; s. Kay Frost and Mary (Cummins) H.; m. Katherine Elizabeth Kavanagh, June 13, 1959 (dec. Dec. 1975); children—Thomas Kay, Katherine Mary; m. Deborah Lea Hill, June 26, 1977; 1 child, Gordon Benedict. S.B., MIT, 1953, Sc.D., 1959. Mem. faculty Mass. Inst. Tech., 1960—, prof. nuclear engring., 1969—, exec. officer nuclear engring. dept., 1972-76, acting head dept., 1975—, assoc. dean engring., 1979-81, assoc. dir. energy lab., 1984; dir. EG&G, Inc.; cons. to industry. Co-author: Numerical Methods of Reactor Analysis, 1964, Advances in Nuclear Science and Technology, Vol. 8, 1975. Ford postdoctoral fellow, 1960-61. Fellow Am. Nuclear Soc. (dir., Arthur Holly Compton award 1978); mem. Soc. Indsl. and Applied Math., Assn. Computing Machines, Am. Soc. Engring. Edn., Nat. Acad. Engring., Sigma Xi, Sigma Chi. Current Work: Nuclear reactor analysis and safety; nuclear fuel management; energy systems. Subspecialty: Nuclear engineering. Home: Baker Bridge Rd Lincoln MA 01773 Office: Mass Inst Tech Massachusetts Ave Cambridge MA 02139

HANSEN, MORRIS HOWARD, statistician, former govt. ofcl.; b. Thermopolis, Wyo., Dec. 15, 1910; s. Hans C. and Maud Ellen (Omstead) H.; m. Mildred R. Latham, Aug. 31, 1930 (dec. 1983); children—Evelyn Maxine, Morris Howard, James Hans, Kristine Ellen. B.S., U. Wyo., 1934; M.A., Am. U., 1940; LL.D., U. Wyo., 1959. Statistician Wyo. Relief Adminstrn., 1934; statistician U.S. Bur. of Census, Washington, 1935-43, statis. asst. dir., 1944-49, asst. dir. statis. standards, 1949-61, asso. dir. research and devel., 1961-68; sr. v.p. Westat, Inc., 1968—; instr. statistics grad. sch. Dept. Agr., 1945-50; formerly statis. cons. Nat. Analysts, Inc. Co-author: Sample Survey Methods and Theory, 2 vols, 1953; Contbr. articles to statis. jours. Recipient Rockefeller Pub. Service award, 1962. Fellow Am. Statis. Assn. (pres. 1960), Royal Statis. Soc. (hon.), A.A.A.S., Inst. Math. Statistics (pres. 1953); mem. Internat. Statis. Inst. (hon. mem.), Inter-Am. Statis. Inst., Population Assn. Am., Nat. Acad. Sci. (com. nat. statistics 1972-76), Internat. Assn. Survey Statisticians (pres. 1973-77), Sigma Xi, Alpha Tau Omega, Phi Kappa Phi. Current Work: Design of systems for obtaining and utilizing information. Subspecialties: Statistics; Operations research (mathematics). Home: 5212 Goddard Rd Bethesda MD 20014

HANSEN, ROBERT SUTTLE, chemistry educator; b. Salt Lake City, June 17, 1918; s. Charles Andrew and Bessie (Suttle) H.; m. Gilda Cappannari, Apr. 8, 1939; 1 child, Edward Charles. B.S. in Chemistry, U. Mich., 1940, M.S. in Chemistry, 1941, Ph.D. in Chemistry, 1948; D.S., Lehigh U., 1978 (hon.). From asst. prof. to prof. chemistry Iowa State U., Ames, 1948—, chmn. chemistry dept. 1965-68; from assoc. chemist to sr. chemist Ames Lab., U.S. Dept. Energy, 1948—, chief chemistry div., 1965-68, dir., 1968—; cons. Union Carbide Corp., Bound Brook, N.J., 1951—, Interchem. Corp., N.Y.C., 1956-68, Proctor & Gamble, Cin., 1961—; mem. adv. panel for chemistry NSF, Washington, 1970-75, mem. adv. panel for materials research, 1975-77. Contbr. articles to profl. publs. Mem. Gov.'s Sci. Adv. Council, Des Moines, 1977—; vice chmn. Iowa State Energy Policy Council, Des Moines, 1978—. Named Disting. Prof. Sci. and Humanities, Iowa State U., 1967. Fellow Iowa Acad. Scis.; mem. Am. Chem. Soc. (Kendall award in surface chemistry 1966, Midwest award St. Louis sect. 1980, sec.-treas. div. colloid and surface chemistry 1951-55, chmn. 1972), AAAS, Am. Phys. Soc. Current work: Catalytic reactions on clean metal surfaces, adsorption thermodynamics and kinetics, viscoelastic properties of monolayers, corrosion mechanisms. Subspecialties: Surface chemistry; Catalysis chemistry. Home: 2030 McCarthy Rd Ames IA 50010 Office: Ames Lab US Dept Energy Iowa State U Ames IA 50011

HANSEN, STANLEY SEVERIN, II, aerospace engineer, astrophysicist, computer scientist; b. St. Joseph, Mo., Sept. 16, 1945; s. Stanley Severin and Gertrude (Campbell) H. B.S. in Physics, U. Mo.-Rolla, 1967; M.S. in Astrophysics, U. Mass.-Amherst, 1972, Ph.D., 1980. Research asst. Oak Ridge Associated Univs., 1966; systems devel. staff IBM, Poughkeepsie, N.Y., 1967-70; faculty Mount Holyoke Coll., South Hadley, Mass., 1971-73, U. Mass., Amherst, 1974; astronomer Onsala Space Obs., Rao, Onsala, Sweden, 1974, Nat. Radio Astronomy Obs., Charlottesville, Va., 1974-81; mem. tech. staff Aerospace Corp., El Segundo, Calif., 1982—. Contbr. articles to profl. jours. Mem. Am. Astron. Soc., Tau Beta Pi. Current Work: Aerospace technology, space sciences, cosmic rays, avionics, systems analysis, systems integration, onboard flight software, operating systems, computer simulation, trajectory analysis, signal processing, image formation, molecular masers, very long baseline interferometry, astrophysics. Subspecialties: Aerospace engineering and technology; Radio and microwave astronomy. Home: 420 S Catalina Ave Apt 208 Redondo Beach CA 90277 Office: The Aerospace Corp 2350 E El Segundo Blvd El Segundo CA 90245

HANSL, NIKOLAUS RUDOLF, pharmacologist, executive; b. Wiener Neustadt, Austria, Oct. 24, 1923; came to U.S., 1948; s. Rudolf and Luise (Fulop) H.; m. Adele Y. Bertagnolli, Jan. 23, 1971; 1 dau., Liesl Marie. Ph.D., Vienna U., 1946. Asst. dir. research Sahyun Labs., Santa Barbara, Calif., 1957-64; pres. Pacific Research Labs., Santa Barbara, and Omaha, 1964—; prof. Creighton U., Omaha, 1967—; cons. Hoffmann-LaRoche, Nutley, N.J., 1971-75. Mem. Am. Chem. Soc., AAAS, Santa Barbara Research Council, N.Y. Acad. Scis., Nebr. Acad. Scis. (co-chmn. biology and medicine sect.). Republican. Roman Catholic. Patentee in field. Current Work: Inception and development of novel compounds facilitating cognition in man, the normal adult and the geriatric with impaired cognitive function, biochemistry of cognition. Subspecialties: Neuropharmacology; Cognition. Home: 7815 Pine St Omaha NE 68124 Office: Creighton U 2500 California St Omaha NE 68178

HANSLER, RICHARD LOWELL, research physicist; b. Mpls., Aug. 21, 1924; s. George C. and Dorothy (Schultheiss) H.; m. Wanda Hansler, Aug. 20, 1949; children: James, Mark, Stephen, Susan. Student, Capital U., 1945-47; B.S., U. Chgo., 1948; Ph. D., Ohio State U., 1952. With Lighting Research Lab., Gen. Electric Co., Cleve., 1952—, sr. research adviser physics and optics, 1981—. Pres. Lutheran Housing Corp., 1974-81. Served with USAAF, 1942-45. Mem. Optical Soc. Am. Democrat. Lutheran. Current Work: Devel. of new light sources and methods of mfr. Subspecialties: Laser processing; Plasma physics. Home: 28120 Belcourt Rd Cleveland OH 44124 Office: Nela Park Department 8431 Cleveland OH 44112

HANSON, DOUGLAS M., biochemist, consultant; b. Clinton, Mass., July 1, 1942; s. Joseph Perry and Noel Neal (Picket) H.; m. Lorraine Nancy Haigh, July 20, 1968; children: Michael, Jeff, Brian, Laura. B.A., Nasson Coll., Springvale, Maine, 1964; Ph.D., Mich. State U., 1968. Nat. Inst. Aging postdoctoral research fellow Boston U. Sch. Medicine, 1968-70; research scientist VA Hosp., Bedford, Mass., 1970-77, acting asso. chief of staff, 1975-76; exec. v.p. Bioassay Systems Corp., Wobrun, Mass., 1977—; pres. JMBL Corp., 1984—; mem. faculty Boston U. Sch. Medicine; tchr. continuing edn. in biochemistry, immunology, microbiology VA Hosp., Bedford. Contbr. articles to profl. jours; author numerous govt. contract project reports. Mem. Am. Soc. Microbiology, AAAS, Genetic Toxicology Assn., Alpha Chi. Democrat. Current Work: Developement short-term vitro toxicology assay methods; corporate developement and project management in biotechnology, toxicology and in-vitro research and developement. Subspecialties: Toxicology (medicine); Biochemistry (medicine). Office: 7 Alfred St Suite 150 Woburn MA 01801

HANSON, GAIL GULLEDGE, physicist; b. Dayton, Ohio, Feb. 22, 1947; d. Karl Nelson and Alice Mildred (Hand) Gulledge; m. Andrew Jorgen Hanson, Dec. 28, 1968; 1 child, Russell Whitney. B.S., MIT, 1968, Ph.D., 1973. Research assoc. Stanford Linear Accelerator Ctr., Calif., 1973-76, continuing staff physicist, 1976-84, permanent staff physicist, 1984—. Contbr. articles to profl. publs. Fellow AAAS, mem. Am. Phys. Soc. Current work: Experimental high energy physics, specifically studying the annihilation final states. Subspecialty: Particle physics. Home: 640 Kendall Ave Palo Alto CA 94306 Office: Stanford Linear Accelerator Ctr Bin 61 PO Box 4349 Stanford CA 94305

HANSON, GEORGE PETER, botanist; b. Conde, S.D., July 20, 1933; s. George Henry and Rosa Wilhelmina (Peterson) H.; m. Gloria Ann Gaunt, June 1, 1969; children: Heather, Peter; m. Barbara Jean Graves, Aug. 20, 1958; children: David, Carol. B.S., S.D. State U., 1956; M.S., 1958; Ph.D., Ind. U., 1962. Asst. prof. biology Thiel Coll., Greenville, Pa., 1962-65, Butler U., Indpl., 1965-68; biologist Los Angeles Arboretum, Arcadia, Calif., 1968-82; botanist J.W.D. Agritech Co., Los Angeles, 1982; ret. Contbr. articles to profl. jours. EPA grantee, 1969-73; NSF grantee, 1976-80; USDA grantee, 1980-82. Mem. Genetics Soc. Am., Bot. Soc. Am., Am. Inst. Biol. Scis., AAAS. Republican. Methodist. Current Work: Research in Guayule breeding to domesticate this rubber crop to U.S. semiarid climate. Subspecialty: Plant genetics. Home: 1345 W Haven Rd San Marino CA 91108

HANSON, HAROLD PALMER, physicist, administrator; b. Virginia, Minn., Dec. 27, 1921; s. Martin Bernard and Elvida Ella (Paulsen) H.; m. Mary Jean Stevenson, June 20, 1944; children—Steven Bernard, Barbara Jean, Hanson Herbert. B.S., Superior State Coll., 1942; M.S., U. Wis.-Madison, 1944, Ph.D., 1948. From instr. to prof. U. Fla., Gainesville, 1948-54, dean Grad. Sch., 1969-71, v.p. acad. affairs, 1971-74, exec v.p., 1974-78 from assoc. prof. to prof. U. Tex., Austin, 1954-59, chmn. dept. physics, 1962-69, dir. Ctr. for Structural Studies, 1967-69; provost Boston U., 1978-79; sr. v.p., provost Wayne State U., Detroit, 1982-84; exec. dir. Com. on Sci. and Tech., U.S. Ho. of Reps., Washington, 1980-82, 84—; vis. lectr. U. Wis.-Madison, 1957; research physicist MIT Lincoln Lab., Cambridge, summer 1953; fellow U. Oslo, spring 1966, Fulbright fellow, 1961-62; trustee, treas. N. Central Fla. Health Planning Council; mem. steering com. Fla. Edn. Computer Network; chmn. symposiums. Contbr. articles and revs. to profl. jours. Served with USN, 1944-45. Decorated knight Order of North Star (Sweden); recipient St. Olav's medal King of Norway, 1976; named U. Fla. Presdl. scholar, 1976; Robert A. Welch Found. grantee. Fellow Am. Phys. Soc.; mem. Am. Assn. Physics Tchrs., AAAS, Fla. Acad. Sci., Sigma Xi, Sigma Pi Sigma, Omicron Delta Kappa. Democrat. Subspecialty: Atomic and molecular physics. Office: Com on Sci and Tech US Ho of Reps 2321 Rayburn Bldg Washington DC 20515

HANSON, JOHN EDWARD, nuclear power engineer, consultant; b. Thomaston, Maine, Nov. 5, 1929; s. John Olaf and Anna Lydia (Johnson) H.; m. Darlene June White, July 26, 1950; children: Laura Jean, Rick Edward. B.S. in Mech. Engring, U. Idaho, 1956, M.S. in Mech. Engring, 1960. Registered profl. mech. engr., Wash., Calif. Profl. nuclear engr. Calif. Engr. Gen. Electric Co., Richland, Wash., 1956-61, San Jose, Calif., 1962-66; mgr. Westinghouse Hanford Co., Richland, 1966-79; mgr./prin. engr. EG&G Idaho, Inc., Idaho Falls, 1979-82; program mgr. Los Alamos Nat. Lab., 1983—. Served with USAF, 1947-52. Mem. Am. Nuclear Soc. Republican. Lodges: Elks; Masons. Current Work: Program manager space and military reactor program. Subspecialties: Nuclear engineering; High-temperature materials. Home: 15 Loma Vista Dr Los Alamos NM 87544 Office: Los Alamos Nat Lab Box 1633 Los Alamos NM 87545

HANSON, JOHN ELBERT, educator; b. Toledo, Ohio, Mar. 5, 1935; s. John E. and Ruth (Sylvia) (Fike) H.; m. Esther Ruth Johnson, June 13, 1959; children: Heidi, Heather. B.A., Olivet Nazarene Coll., 1957; postgrad., Washington U., 1957-58; Ph.D., Purdue U., 1964. Mem. faculty Olivet Nazarene Coll., Kankakee, Ill., 1961—, prof. chemistry, 1970—; research assoc. U. Chgo., 1974; vis. prof. U. Wis.-Madison, 1984-85. Precinct committeeman, 1972-74; mem. Village Task Force for Impact of Hazardous Waste Incinerator, 1981. Named Tchr. of Year Olivet Nazarene Coll., 1966, Outstanding Alumnus, 1970. Mem. Am. Chem. Soc., Ill. Acad. Sci. Mem. Ch. of the Nazarene. Current Work: Organosilicon chemistry, cobalt complexes, synthetic inorganic and organometaloid chemistry, environmental science. Subspecialty: Inorganic chemistry. Office: Chemistry Dep Olivet Nazarene Coll Kankakee IL 60901

HANSON, KENNETH WARREN, horticulturist; b. Graceville, Minn., July 15, 1922; s. Edwin William and Esther Dorothy (Lundquist) H.; m. Margaret Lucile Stokes, Apr. 28, 1946; children: Kenneth Warren, Linda L., Robert G., Edwin William II. B.S., U. Minn., 1948, M.S., 1951, Ph.D., 1952. With USDA, various locations, 1942-43, 46-51; assoc. prof. U. Ga., 1952-54; asst. prof. Cornell U., 1954-60; asso. prof. Am. U. Beirut, 1960-63; dir. sta., horticulturist Mo. Fruit Expt. Sta., S.W. Mo. State U., Mountain Grove, 1963-84, dir. emeritus, 1984—. Served to lt. USNR, 1943-46. Fellow AAAS; mem. Am. Soc. Hort. Sci., Internat. Soc. Hort. Sci., Am. Pomol. Soc. (pres. 1984-86), Mo. Hort. Soc., Ark. Hort. Soc., Am. Inst. Biol. Scis., Minn. Hort. Soc., Mountain Grove C. of C. (pres. 1967), Sigma Xi, Gamma Alpha. Republican. Methodist. Club: Rotary (pres. 1967-68, dir. 1965-67). Subspecialties: Plant genetics; Plant physiology (agriculture). Home: 104 Royal St Gulfport MS 39503 Office: Mo Fruit Expt Sta Rt 3 Box 63 Mountain Grove MO 65711

HANSON, RAY LORAIN, research chemist; b. St. Paul, Aug. 21, 1948; s. Kermit Lorain and Deloris Katheryn (Peterson) H.; m. Sue Anne Louise Thorne, Mar. 17, 1973; children—Rebecca Anne, Katherine Louise. B.A. in Chemistry, Augsburg Coll., 1970; M.S. in Chemistry, U. N.Mex., 1973, Ph.D. in Chemistry, 1975. Instr. chemistry Augsburg Coll., Mpls., 1975-76; research chemist Lovelace ITRI, Albuquerque, 1976—. Author: Analytical Methods for Coal and Coal Products, 1979; Coal and Coal Products: Analytical Characterization Techniques, 1982; Identification and Analysis of Organic Pollutants in

Air, 1984; Polynuclear Aromatic Hydrocarbons, 1979, 80. Vol. Youth Detention Ctr., Albuquerque, 1984. Mem. Am. Chem. Soc. (treas. central N.Mex. sect. 1980, chmn.-elect 1982-83; chmn. Rocky Mountain regional meeting 1983-84). Current work: Measuring phthalate ester migration from polyvinyl chloride consumer products, analysis of lung burdens of inhaled particle exposures of rodents; atomic absorption spectroscopy. Subspecialties: Analytical chemistry; Environmental chemistry. Home: 708 Landman Pl NE Albuquerque NM 87123 Office: Lovelace ITRI PO Box 5890 Albuquerque NM 87185

HANSON, RICHARD STEVEN, microbiology educator, research administrator; b. Platte, S.D., Nov. 14, 1935; s. James Walter and Mary Ann H.; m. Doreothe Ann Glynn; children—Michael Orin, Stephen Francis, Thomas Edward. B.S., S.D. State U., 1959; Ph.D., U. Ill., 1962. Asst. prof. microbiology U. Wis., Madison, 1966-69, assoc. prof., 1969-72, prof., 1979-81, chmn. dept. bacteriology, 1972-76, chmn. molecular biology undergrad. program, 1977-79; dir. Gray Freshwater Biol. Inst., Navarre, Minn., 1981—; cons. Upjohn Co., Kalamazoo, 1980-85, various Minn. municipalities and agys., 1981—; chmn. sci. adv. bd. Biotrol, Mpls., 1984—. Editor: Spores V, 1972; Microbial Growth on One-Carbon Compounds, 1984. Contbr. articles to tech. jours. Mem. Wellspring Com. on Univ./Industry Relations, Minn., 1984; mem. oversight com. Minn. Mosquito Control, 1984. USPHS fellow, 1960-62, 64, 73; Lindberg Found. grantee, 1984. Mem. Am. Soc. for Microbiology, Fedn. Am. Socs. of Biol. Chemists. Current work: Microorganisms that grow on reduced one-carbon compounds, primarily methane and methanol (Methylotrophs), including studies of ecology and role of methylotrophic bacteria in nature, biotransformations carried out by methylotrophs, isolation and characterization of enqymes, development of genetic systems. Subspecialties: Enzyme technology; Microbiology. Home: 4162 Hillcrest Rd Wayzata MN 55391 Office: Gray Freshwater Biol Inst PO Box 100 Navarre MN 55392

HANSON, TREVOR RUSSELL, computer scientist; b. Cambridge, Eng., Sept. 24, 1955; s. Norwood Russell and Frances Fay (Kenney) H. Student, U. Chgo., 1973-75. Systems programmer Sears, Roebuck & Co., Chgo., 1975-77; systems programmer Nat. CSS, Inc., Wilton, Conn., 1977-79; founder, prin. Hanson-Smith, Ltd., Shelton, Conn., 1979—. Mem. Assn. Computing Machinery, IEEE. Current Work: Non-programmer application development systems, dataflow, actor systems, compiler design, fifth generation systems, extensible systems, distributed databases, delivering technology as products. Subspecialties: Database systems; Operating systems. Office: 58 Martinka Dr Shelton CT 06484

HANSON, WAYNE CARLYLE, ecologist, consultant; b. Kennewick, Wash., Sept. 5, 1923; s. Oscar Martinius and Gladys Leone (Duffy) H.; m. Delma Ruth Duffy, Apr. 6, 1947 (div. 1970); children—Christian Martin, Eric Everett; m. Mary Ann Moser, Sept. 4, 1970. B.S., Wash. State U., 1949; M.S., Colo. State U., 1971, Ph.D., 1973. Cert. sr. ecologist, Wildlife biologist. Group leader Los Alamos Nat. Lab., N.Mex., 1973-78; sr. biologist Battelle Pacific NW, Richland, Wash., 1978-81; mgr. ecol. services Ertec Northwest, Anchorage, Alaska, 1981-82; assoc. Dames and Moore, Anchorage, 1982-84; sr. ecologist, v.p. Hanson Environ. Research, Bellingham, Wash., 1984—. Editor: Transuranic Elements in Environment, 1981. Served with USAF, 1943-45. Decorated D.F.C., Air medal; recipient Arthur S. Einarsen award Northwest Wildlife Soc., 1979. Mem. Wildlife Soc., Ecol. Soc. Am., AAAS, Arctic Inst. N. Am., Sigma Xi. Current work: Arctic ecosystems, resource development impacts, radiation ecology. Subspecialty: Ecology (biology). Home: 1902 Yew Street Rd Bellingham WA 98226

HAPKE, BRUCE WILLIAM, astronomer, educator; b. Racine, Wis., Feb. 17, 1931; s. William E. and Blanche V. H.; m. Joyce Zellinger, June 18, 1954; children: Kevin, Jeffrey, Cheryl. B.S., U. Wis., 1953; Ph.D., Cornell U., 1962. Research assoc., then sr. research assoc. Ctr. for Radiophysics and Space Research, Cornell U., Ithaca, N.Y., 1960-67; assoc. prof. dept. geology and planetary sci. U. Pitts., 1967-79, prof. planetary scis., 1979—; research assoc. Carnegie Mus. Natural History, 1980—. Contbr. articles to profl. jours. Served to lt. USNR, 1953-55. NASA grantee. Mem. AAAS, Am. Astron. Soc., Am. Geophys. Union, Planetary Soc. Current Work: Scattering of electromagnetic radiation from surfaces; nature and genesis of planetary surfaces and interiors. Subspecialty: Planetary science. Office: U Pitts 321 Old Engring Hall Pittsburgh PA 15260

HAPP, STAFFORD COLEMAN, research geologist; b. Sparrowbush, N.Y., Sept. 16, 1905; s. Conrad and Hattie Adella (Coleman) H.; m. Inez Ellen Hale, Dec. 26, 1935; 1 dau., Ellen Coleman Happ Hill. Student, Wesleyan U., 1926-27; A.B. cum laude, Marietta Coll., 1931; Ph.D. in Geology, Columbia U., 1939. Cert. geologist and engring. geologist, Calif. Head stream and valley sediment research U.S. Soil Conservation Service, Washington, 1935-43; dist. geologist U.S. Army Engrs., Ocala, Fla. and Kansas City, Mo., 1943-55; chief prodn. services br. U.S. AEC, Grand Junction, Colo., 1955-64; research geologist U.S. Geol. Survey, Denver, 1964-65, U.S. Dept. Agr. Sediment Lab., Oxford, Miss., 1965—. Author in field. Recipient Disting. Service award Trempealeau County (Wis.) Land Conservation Dept., 1982; Outstanding Service award Wis. Assn. Conservation Dists., 1982. Fellow Geol. Soc. Am. (chmn. engring. div. 1959-60); mem. ASCE, AIMME, AAAS. Republican. Methodist. Current Work: Fluvial sedimentation related to agricultural soil erosion, including recovery of sampling cross sections established 1936-41, in some 50 valleys representing severe soil erosion effects, but abandoned during World War II and records largely lost. Measurements and interpretations evaluate changing erosion rates, and sediment effects. Subspecialties: Sedimentology; Environmental engineering. Home: 503 N 14th St Oxford MS 38655 Office: IS Dept Agr Sediment Lab PO Box 1157 Oxford MS 38655

HAQUE, PROMOD, electrical engineer; b. Simla, India, Apr. 20, 1948; came to U.S., 1972, naturalized, 1984; s. Alexander and Phulwanti (Gangaram) H.; m. Dorcas A. Daniels, July 15, 1978. B.S.E.E., U. Delhi, 1969; M.S.E.E., Northwestern U., 1974, Ph.D., 1976, M.B.A., 1983. Sales engr. Siemens, New Delhi, 1969-72; research asst. Bio-Med. Center, Northwestern U., Evanston, Ill., 1972-76; lab. dir. EMI Med. Inc., Northbrook, Ill., 1976-81; v.p., chief operating officer Emergent Corp., Anaheim, Calif., 1981-82; v.p. R&D engring and mktg. Omnimed. Corp., Anaheim, 1982-83; pres., chief exec. officer Dimensional Medicine Inc., Minnetonka, Minn., 1983—. Contbr. articles to profl. jours. Mem. IEEE, Am. Assn. Physicists in Medicine. Republican. Evangelical Christian. Current Work: CAT scanners, digital fluoroscopy, radiography, ultrasound, nuclear magnetic resonance, computer based graphics, array processors and signal processing, analog and digital instrumentation. Subspecialties: Electronics; Biomedical engineering. Home: 370 Brockton Ln Plymouth MN 55447 Office: 10999 E Bren Rd Minnetonka MN 55343

HARAKAL, CONCETTA, pharmacologist; b. Chieti, Italy, Nov. 25, 1923; d. Francesco and Maria (Gagliardi) De Leo; m. Michael P. Harakal, Oct. 16, 1948. Ph.D. in Pharmacology, Temple U., 1962. Instr. Temple U. Sch. Medicine, Phila., 1962-64, asst. prof., 1964-68, asso. prof., 1968-76, prof. pharmacology, 1976—. Contbr. articles to profl. jours. Recipient Golden Apple Teaching award Temple U. Sch. Medicine, 1975, 77, 80, 83, 85; Sowell Meml. award for excellence in basic sci. teaching, 1979; Chapel of Four Chaplains Legion of Honor award, 1977; Lindback Found. award, 1980. Mem. Am. Soc. Pharmacology and Exptl. Therapeutics, AAAS, N.Y. Acad. Scis., Sigma Xi. Roman Catholic. Club: 25-Year Faculty Temple U. Current Work: Cardiovascular pharmacology. Subspecialty: Pharmacology.

HARARI, AZRIEL, research engineer; b. Tel-Aviv, Oct. 27, 1926; came to U.S. 1960, naturalized 1969; s. Shalom and Sarah (Mokah) H. m. Sheila Bette Barth, Sept. 16, 1962. B.Sc. cum laude, Technion, Haifa, Israel, 1955, M.Sc., 1959; D.Eng. Sc., Columbia U., 1967. Research engr. Weidlinger Assocs., N.Y.C., 1962-74; mech. engr. Naval Underwater Systems Ctr., Newport, R.I., 1974—; adj. prof. CUNY, 1973-74, U. R.I., Kingston, 1979-81. Contbr. articles to profl. jours. Mem. ASME. Current work: Structural acoustics and fluid-structure interaction problems. Subspecialties: Theoretical and applied mechanics; Acoustical engineering. Home: 36 Kane Ave Middletown RI 02840 Office: Naval Underwater Systems Ctr Newport RI 02840

HARBAUGH, JOHN WARVELLE, geological educator, researcher; b. Madison, Wis., Aug. 6, 1926; s. Marion Daight and Marjorie (Warvelle) H.; m. Josephine Taylor, Nov. 24, 1951; children: Robert, Dwight, Richard. B.S., U. Kans.-Lawrence, 1948, M.S., 1949; Ph.D., U. Wis.-Madison, 1955. Asst. prof. to prof geology Stanford U., 1955—; chmn. bd. Terrascis., Inc., San Francisco, 1977—. Co-author: Computer Simulation in Geology, 1970, Probability Methods in Oil Exploration, 1977. Recipient Haworth Disting. Alumni award U. Kans., 1968. Fellow Geol. Soc. Am.; mem. Am. Assn. Petroleum Geologists (A. I. Levorsen award 1970). Republican. Club: Cosmos (Washington). Current Work: Development of statistical petroleum resource forecasting procedures; computer simulation of geological processes. Subspecialties: Mathematical geology; Mathematical software. Home: 683 Salvatierra Stanford CA 94305 Office: Stanford U Geology Bldg Stanford CA 94305

HARBAY, EDWARD WILLIAM, nuclear engineer; b. Johnstown, Pa., May 16, 1937; s. Edward F. and Helen V. H.; m. Marian M. Belavic, Sept. 4, 1971; children—Katherine Mary, Julie Ann, Marla Jean. B.S., U. Pitts., 1961, postgrad., 1963-64. Rocket devel. engr. Hercules Allegany Ballistics Lab., Cumberland, Md., 1961-66; reactor core engr. Westinghouse Electric Corp. Bettis Atomic Power Lab., West Mifflin, Pa., 1966-74; nuclear engr. Detroit Edison Co., 1974—, now assigned to nuclear procurement. Mem. Nat. Soc. Profl. Engrs., Am. Nuclear Soc. Democrat. Roman Catholic. Current Work: Boiling Water Reactor nuclear fuel cycle engineering. Subspecialties: Nuclear engineering; Fuels. Home: 22271 Derby Rd Woodhaven MI 48183 Office: Detroit Edison Co Fermi 2 Nuclear Power Plant 6400 N Dixie Hwy Newport MI 48166

HARBERT, CHARLES ARMON, chemical company executive, organic chemist; b. Indpls., Apr. 7, 1940; s. Charles Homer and Ruth Laura (Griffey) H.; m. Kay Louise Strode, Sept. 9, 1961; children—Kelle Kay, Jennifer Ruth. B.S., U. Colo., 1962; Ph.D., U. Mo., 1967. Postdoctoral research Stanford U., Calif., 1967-69; research scientist Pfizer Inc., Groton, Conn., 1969-72, project leader, 1972-76, mgr., 1976-81, dir. medicinal chemistry, 1981-84, exec. dir., 1984—. Contbr. articles to profl. jours. Patentee in field. Mem. Bd. Tax Rev., Waterford, Conn., 1975-77, Bd. Fin., 1977, Bd. Edn., 1979-81; co-chmn. Town Hall Expansion Com., 1977-79. Gates Rubber & Tire scholar, 1958-62; NIH fellow, 1967-69. Mem. Am. Chem. Soc., AAAS, Sigma Xi, Phi Lambda Upsilon. Republican. Congregationalist. Current work: Head of department responsible for the discovery of drugs for the treatment of chronic diseases; selection and planning for areas of research in medicinal chemistry. Subspecialties: Medicinal chemistry; Synthetic chemistry. Home: 25 Quinley Way Waterford CT 06385 Office: Central Research Div Pfizer Inc Groton CT 06340

HARBOTTLE, GARMAN, research scientist; b. Dayton, Ohio, Sept. 25, 1923; s. William Edwin and Susan (Garman) P., June 10, 1949; 1 child, Laura. B.S., Caltech., 1944; Ph.D., Columbia U. Postdoctoral fellow AEC, Cambridge, Eng., 1951-52, Guggenheim fellow, 1957-58; dir. div. research Internat. AEA, Vienna, 1965-67; adj. prof. SUNY-Stony Brook, 1983—; sr. sci. Brookhaven Nat. Lab., Upton, N.Y., 1949—; v.p. Miami Jacobs Coll., Dayton, 1954—. Editor: Chemical Effects of Nuclear Transformations, 1979. Trustee Incorp. Village of Old Field, N.Y., 1978—, Vanderbilt Mus. and Planetarium, Centerport, N.Y., 1978—. Grantee NSF, 1980, 84; recipient George Hevesy medal J. Radioanalytical Chemistry, 1983. Mem. Soc. Am. Archeology, Soc. Mexican Archeology, Am. Chem. Soc. Current work: Radiochemistry, half-lives, application nuclear techniques to archaeology and fine arts, numerical taxonomy, carbon-14. Subspecialties: Archaeological chemistry; Nuclear chemistry. Office: Chemistry Dept Bldg 555 Brookhaven Nat Lab Upton NY 11973

HARDEKOPF, ROBERT A(LLEN), physicist; b. St. Louis, Oct. 14, 1940; s. Charles F. and Hazel W. (Wood) H.; m. Priscilla Grovenstein, Aug. 4, 1962; children—Catherine, David, Kenneth. B.S. in Physics, Auburn U., 1962; Ph.D. in Physics, Duke U., 1972. Grad. research asst. Duke U., Durham, N.C., 1968-71; postdoctoral fellow Los Alamos Lab., 1972; staff mem. Los Alamos Nat. Lab., 1972-82, dep. group leader, 1983-84, group leader, 1984—. Contbr. numerous articles, papers on polarization in nuclear reactions, accelerator technology and related subjects to profl. pubs. Served to lt. USN, 1962-67. Woodrow Wilson fellow Duke U., 1967. Mem. Am. Phys. Soc., Phi Beta Kappa. Current work: Polarization in nuclear reactions and scattering; accelerator physics and technology. Subspecialties: Nuclear physics; Accelerator physics. Home: 119 La Vista Dr Los Alamos NM 87544 Office: Los Alamos Nat Lab MS H808 Los Alamos NM 87545

HARDIN, BRYAN DAVID, biologist; b. Clinton, Okla., July 4, 1944; s. Everett Tirey and Alma Jewel (Carmichael) H.; m. Sharon Louise Davis, Sept. 9, 1964; children—Bryan David, Erin Elizabeth. B.S., U. Okla., 1966, 70, M.S., 1972; Ph.D., U. Cin., 1983. Commd. lt. (j.g.) USPHS, 1972, advanced through grades to comdr., 1984; criteria document mgr. Nat. Inst. for Occupational Safety and Health, Rockville, Md., 1972-75, research biologist exptl. toxicology br., Cin., 1977—; trainee U. Cin., 1975-77. Served as 2d lt. U.S. Army, 1966. Decorated Commendation medal; named Profl./Sci. Fed. Employee of Yr., Greater Cin. Fed. Exec. Bd. and Fed. Bus. Assn., 1983. Mem. AAAS, Teratology Soc., Sigma Xi, Phi Sigma. Current work: Reproductive and developmental toxicology of industrial chemicals; occupational reproductive health hazards; teratology; andrology. Subspecialties: Toxicology (medicine); Teratology. Home: 8060 Debonair Ct Cincinnati OH 45237 Office: Exptl Toxicology Br Nat Inst for Occupational Safety and Health 4676 Columbia Pkwy Cincinnati OH 45226

HARDIN, IAN RUSSELL, textile chemistry educator; b. Glasgow, Scotland, Aug. 3, 1944 (father U.S. citizen); s. William Russell and Jeanette Mason (Donaghy) H.; m. Ferris Hendley, June 10, 1967; children—Wendy, Andrew. B.S. in Textile Sci., Auburn U., 1965; M.S. in Textile Engring., Inst. Textile Tech., 1967; Ph.D. in Chemistry, Clemson U., 1970. Asst. prof. Auburn U., Ala., 1971-76, assoc. prof., 1976—, head textile sci., 1977-82, chmn.-elect gen. faculty, 1984-86. Editor: A Change of Perspective, 1976. Contbr. articles to sci. jours. Scoutmaster Chattahoochee council Boy Scouts Am., 1973-77; gen. drive chmn., v.p., pres. Auburn United Fund, 1975-78; scoutmaster Concharty council Girl Scouts U.S.A., 1980-81. Mem. Am. Chem. Soc. (exec. bd. cellulose div. 1975-78), Am. Assn. Textile Chemists (chmn. S.E. sect. research com. 1983—), Fiber Soc., Sigma Xi (pres. Auburn chpt. 1980-81). Democrat. Methodist. Current work: Cellulose pyrolysis, flame retardant chemistry, analysis of historic textiles, interaction of textiles and pesticides. Subspecialties: Polymer chemistry; Polymer engineering. Home: 735 McKinley Ave Auburn AL 36830 Office: Dept Consumer Affairs Auburn U Auburn AL 36849

HARDING, ALICE KUST, astrophysicist, researcher; b. N.Y.C., Aug. 12, 1951; d. Leonard Eugene and Henrietta Bryan (Logan) Kust; m. David Scott Harding, Aug. 13, 1977. B.A., Bryn Mawr Coll., 1973; M.S., U. Mass. 1977, Ph.D., 1979. Teaching asst. U. Mass., Amherst, 1974-78; summer research asst. Nat. Radio Astronomy Obs., Charlottesville, Va., 1975; research asst. U. Mass., Amherst, 1979; NAS research assoc. NASA/Goddard Space Flight Ctr., Greenbelt, Md., 1979-80, astrophysicist, 1980—. Editor: Positron-Electron Pairs in Astrophysics, 1983. Contbr. articles to tech. jours. Fellow AAUW; mem. Am. Astronomical Soc. (high energy astrophysics div.), Am. Physical Soc. (astrophysics div.). Current work: Theory of X-ray and gamma-ray sources, physics of neutron stars, galactic structure. Subspecialties: High energy astrophysics; Theoretical astrophysics. Home: 1527 Eton Way Crofton MD 21114 Office: Code 665 NASA Goddard Space Flight Ctr Greenbelt MD 20771

HARDORP, JOHANNES C., astronomer; b. Bremen, Germany, 1929; came to U.S., 1965; s. Gerhard D. and Clara (Karstensen) H.; m. Ingeborg M. S. Arndt, 1954; children: Detlef, Agnes. Ph.D. in Astronomy, U. Hamburg, W.Ger., 1960. Tchr., researcher Hamburg U., 1958-68; research physicist U. Calif., San Diego, 1965-66; research assoc. U. Mich., Ann Arbor, 1966-67; mem. staff Inst. Theoretical Astronomy, Cambridge (Eng.) U., 1968-69; assoc. prof. astronomy SUNY-Stony Brook, 1969—; professeur associéu College de France, Paris, 1976-. Contbr. numerous articles to sci. jours. Mem. Deutsche Astronomische Gesellschaft, Internat. Astron. Union. Current Work: Stellar atmospheres, stellar rotation, peculiar stars, solar twins. Subspecialty: Optical astronomy. Office: Dept Earth and Space Sci SUNY Stony Brook NY 11794

HARDS, KATHRYN ELISA, industrial psychologist; b. Chgo.; d. Arthur Oliver and Della Caroline (Redcliffe) Olsen; m. William Clarence Hards; 1 child, Eric Arthur. B.A., San Jose State U., 1972, M.S., 1976. Indsl. psychologist Four-Phase Systems, Cupertino, Calif., 1976-79; dir. K and H Assocs., Cupertino, 1980—; instr. indsl. psychologist San Jose State U., Calif., 1979—; expert witness Tech. Adv. Service for Attys., 1980—. Contbr. articles to profl. jours., mags. and newspapers. Mem. Am. Psychol. Assn., Western Psychol. Assn., Profl. and Tech. Cons. Assn., Nat. Assn. Indsl. and Orgnl. Psychologists, Can. Soc. Psychology. Current work: Personnel selection and testing; training and program design and evaluation; productivity improvement; market research; including survey design and analysis. Office: K and H Assocs PO Box 1078 Cupertino CA 95015

HARDY, JOHN CHRISTOPHER, physicist; b. Montreal, Que., Can., July 10, 1941; s. Noel Woodburn and Ethel May (Collins) H.; m. Lynn Helen Frederick, June 3, 1964; children—Ericka, Kirsten, Bruce, Alana. B.Sc., McGill U., Montreal, 1961, M.Sc., 1963, Ph.D. (D.W. Ambridge prize 1965), 1965. NRC Can. post-doctoral fellow Oxford (Eng.) Nuclear Physics Lab., 1965-67; Miller research fellow Lawrence Radiation Lab., Berkeley, Calif., 1967-70; asso. research officer Atomic Energy Can. Ltd., Chalk River, Ont., 1970-74, sr. research officer, 1975—, head nuclear physics br., 1983—; sci. asso. CERN, Geneva, 1976-77. Contbr. articles to profl. jours. Fellow Royal Soc. Can. (Rutherford medal in physics 1981), Am. Phys. Soc. mem. Can. Assn. Physicists (Herzberg medal 1976). Current work: Exotic nuclei, Weak interactions, delayed particle decay, heavy-ion physics. . Office: Chalk River Nuclear Labs Chalk River ON K0J 1J0 Canada

HARDY, MARK ADAM, surgeon, immunologist; b. Lwow, Poland, Jan. 5, 1938; s. Paul and Rose (Pomeranz) H.; m. Ruth C. Komisarow, Jan. 14, 1967; children: Peter, Arthur, Karen. A.B., Columbia U., 1958; M.D., Albert Einstein Coll. Medicine, 1962. Diplomate: Am. Bd. Surgery. Asst. instr. surgery U. Rochester, 1962-64; asst. prof. Albert Einstein Coll. Medicine, 1971-75; assoc. prof. Columbia Coll. Physicians and Surgeons, 1975-80, prof., 1980—, dir. transplantation. Served to lt. comdr. USNR, 1964-70. NIH scholar. Mem. Soc. Univ. Surgeons, Transplantation Soc., ACS, Am. Assn. Immunology. Current Work: Immunosuppression and Immunostimulation radiobiology. Subspecialties: Transplant surgery; Vascular surgery.

HARDY, RALPH W.F., biochemist; b. Lindsay, Ont., Can., July 27, 1934; s. Wilbur and Elsie H.; m. Jacqueline M. Thayer, Dec. 26, 1954; children: Steven, Chris, Barbara, Ralph, Jon. B.S.A., U. Toronto, 1956; M.S., U. Wis.-Madison, 1958, Ph.D., 1959. Asst. prof. U. Guelph, Ont., Can., 1960-63; research biochemist DuPont deNemours & Co., Wilmington, Del., 1963-67, research supr., 1967-74, assoc. dir., 1974-79, dir. life scis., 1979-84; ret., 1984; vis. prof. life scis. Cornell U.; pres. BioTechnica Internat. Inc., Cambridge, Mass.; chmn. BioTechnica Diagnostics, Cambridge; mem. exec. com. bd. agr., mem. Commn. on Life Scis., bd. on basic biology Nat. Acad. Sci.; editorial bd. sci. jours. Author: Nitrogen Fixation, 1975, A Treatise on Dinitrogen Fixation, 3 vols, 1977-79; contbr. over 100 articles to sci. jours. Recipient Gov. Gen.'s Silver medal, 1956; WARF fellow, 1956-58; DuPont fellow, 1958-59. Mem. Am. Chem. Soc. (exec. com. biol. chemistry div., Del. award 1969), Am. Soc. Biol. Chemists, Am. Soc. Plant Physiology (exec. com.), Am. Soc. Agronomy, Am. Soc. Microbiology. Episcopalian. Patentee (2). Current Work: Biochemistry of key plant processes -N_2 fixation, photosynthesis. Subspecialties: Plant physiology (agriculture); Nitrogen fixation. Home: Box 364 Unionville PA 19375 Office: BioTechnica Internat Inc 85 Bolton St Cambridge MA 02140

HARE, BEN DEAN, geologist; b. Tampa, Fla., Aug. 11, 1945; s. Aubrey Dean and Betty Marie (Crooks) H.; m. Linda Ann Bandsma, June 17, 1966 (div. 1970); 1 child, Patrick Dean; m. Carol Rae Gardner, June 19, 1971; 1 child, Christopher. B.S. in Geology, Lamar U., 1967; M.S. in Geology, Okla. U., 1969, Ph.D., 1973. Sr. geologist Amerada Hess Corp., Tulsa, 1971-73; project dir. Atlantic Richfield Internat., Los Angeles, 1973-77; area geologist, Denver, 1977-78, sr. staff geologist, Dallas, 1978-81; geol. mgr. Edwin L. and Berry R. Cox Oil Producers, Dallas, 1981—. NSF trainee, 1968. Mem. Am. Assn. Petroleum Geologists (pub. info. commn., edn. commn.), Geol. Soc. Am., Soc. Econ. Paleontologists and Mineralogists, Dallas Geol. Soc., Ind. Petroleum Assn. Am., Sigma Xi. Club; Dallas Petroleum. Current work: Petroleum exploration, depositional and diagenetic environments of carbonate and siliciclastic rocks, organic geochemistry. Subspecialties: Petrology; Geochemistry. Office: Edwin L and Berry R Cox Oil Producers 3800 Interfirst One Dallas TX 75202

HARFORD, CARL GAYLER, retired microbiologist, educator; b. St. Louis, June 27, 1906; s. Edwin Marvin and Agnes (Gayler) H.; m. Mary Cowan (dec. Aug. 5, 1933); children: John, Gayler, Carolyn; m. Viola Graves, May 23, 1982. A.B., Amherst Coll., 1928; M.D., Washington U., St. Louis, 1933; postgrad., Rockefeller Inst. for Med. Research, 1936-38. Diplomate: Am. Bd. Internal Medicine, Nat. Bd. Med. Examiners. Instr. bacteriology and clin. medicine Washington U., 1938-43, asst. prof. medicine and preventive medicine, 1943-49, assoc. prof. medicine, 1949-63, acting head dept. microbiology, 1952,59, prof. medicine, 1964-74, prof. emeritus, 1974—, ret., 1985; assoc. mem. Commn. on Acute Respiratory Diseases, Armed Forces, 1950-71. Mem. editorial bd.: Procs. Soc. Exptl. Biology and Medicine, 1974—; author articles. Recipient Founders Day award Washington U., 1973, Alumni/Faculty award, 1982. Mem. Am. Soc. Microbiologists, Central Soc. for Clin. Research (sec.-treas. 1944-45), Am. Soc. for Clin. Investigation, Assn. Am. Physicians, St. Louis Med. Soc., St. Louis Soc. Internal Medicine, Common Cause, Sigma Xi, Alpha Omega Alpha. Current Work: Aim to make cultured cells susceptible to viruses. Subspecialties: Infectious diseases; Virology (medicine).

HARFORD, JAMES JOSEPH, association executive; b. Jersey City, Aug. 19, 1924; s. Thomas William and Jane Hume (Henderson) H.; m. Mildred Rita Waters, Apr. 19, 1952; children—Susan Gately, James Joseph, Peter Benedict (dec.), Jennifer, Christoher. B.S. in Mech. Engring., Yale U., 1945. Sales engr. Worthington Corp., 1946-49; assoc. editor Modern Industry, 1950-52; free-lance writer, Europe, 1952-53; exec. sec. Am. Rocket Soc., 1953-63; exec. dir. Am. Inst. Aeros. and Astronautics, 1963—; mem. U.S. del. Internat. Astronautical Congresses, 1959—. Author: (with others) China Space Report, 1979. Served as ensign USNR, 1945-46. Fellow AIAA Brit. Interplanetary Soc., AAAS, Royal Aero. Soc. (assoc.); mem. Internat. Acad. Astronautics. Subspecialties: Aerospace engineering and technology; Astronautics. Home: 601 Lake Dr Princeton NJ 08540 Office: Am Inst of Aeros & Astronautics 1633 Broadway New York NY 10019

HARGENS, ALAN ROBERT, surgery educator; b. Great Falls, Mont., Feb. 6, 1944; s. Lowell Luverne and Ada (Ruth) H.; m. Gunvor Margrethe Sorenson, May 30, 1973; children—Tor, Lars. B.A. summa cum laude, U. Minn., 1966; Ph.D., U. Calif.-San Diego, 1971. NSF-NATO postdoctoral fellow U. Copenhagen, 1971-72; asst prof. U. Aarhus, Denmark, 1972; adv. postdoctoral fellow U. Calif.-San Diego, 1973-76, asst. research bioengr., 1975-76, asst. research physiologist, 1976-78, assoc. research physiologist, 1978-79, assoc. prof. surgery, 1979-84, prof. surgery, 1984—, dir. Orthopaedic Physiology, 1976—; cons. Howmedica, Inc., Rutherford, N.J., Intermedics Orthopedics, Austin, Tex. Author: Compartment Syndromes, 1981. Editor: Tissue Fluid Pressure, 1981; Tissue Nutrition and Viability, 1986. Patentee wick catheter and process, 1979. Recipient Career Devel. award NIH, 1979. Mem. Am. Chem. Soc., Am. Physiol. Soc., U.S. Microcirculatory Soc. (co-chmn. 1982-84), European Soc. for Microcirculation (award 1982), Aerospace Med. Assn., U. Calif.-San Diego Alumni Assn. (chms. alumni relations com. 1984-85), A. Baird Hastings Soc., Phi Beta Kappa. Current work: Skeletal muscle physiology; trauma; tissue fluid balance; weightlessness physiology; microcirculation; tissue nutrition; polar biology; intervertebral disc. Subspecialties: Orthopedics; Space medicine. Home: 1103 Sea Village Dr Cardiff By The Sea CA 92007 Office: U Calif and VA Med Ctr Div Orthopedics and Rehab San Diego CA 92161

HARIHARAN, SUBRAMANIYA IYER, mathematics educator; b. Jaffna, Sri-Lanka, Oct. 27, 1951; came to U.S., 1977, naturalized, 1981; s. Aiyathurai Iyer and Seethalakshmi Subramaniya; m. Jeanette Bryan, Jan. 8, 1983. B.Sc., U. Sri-Lanka, 1974; M.Sc., U. Salford, Eng., 1977; M.S., Carnegie-Mellon U., 1979; Ph.D., 1980. Asst. lectr. U. Sri-Lanka, 1974-76; teaching asst. U. Salford, 1976-77; teaching fellow Carnegie-Mellon U., Pitts., 1978-80; staff scientist ICASE, NASA Langley Research Ctr., Hampton, Va., 1980-83; cons., 1983—; assoc. prof. math. U. Tenn., Space Inst., Tullahoma, after 1983; now with dept. math. U. Akron, Ohio. Editor: (with T. H. Moulden) Numerical Methods for Partial Differential Equations, 1986. Contbr. articles to profl. jours. Mem. Soc. Indsl. and Applied Math., Am. Math. Soc., Soc. Engring. Sci., AIAA, sigma Xi. Current work: Study of linear and nonlinear wave propagation phenomena; fluid mechanics; inverse problems in electromagnetics and acoustics. Subspecialties: Applied mathematics; Numerical analysis (mathematics). Office: Dept Math U Akron Akron OH 44325

HARKER, ALAN BUTLER, research chemist; b. Exeter, N.H., May 7, 1946; s. George Stanley and Janet (Collins) H.; m. Judith Elise Olsen, June 19, 1968. B.A., Oberlin Coll., 1968; Ph.D., U. Calif.-Berkeley, 1972. Research staff Lawrence Berkeley Lab., 1972-73; mem. tech. staff, group mgr. Rockwell

Internat. Sci. Ctr., Thousand Oaks Calif., 1973—, mgr. applied spectroscopy, 1976—. Contbr. articles to profl. jours. Patentee in field. Mem. Am. Chem. Soc., Am. Ceramic Soc., Materials Research Soc., Sigma Xi. Current work: Optical thin film deposition, ceramic nuclear waste form development, surface spectroscopy, surface chemistry. Subspecialties: Surface chemistry; Physical chemistry. Office: Rockwell Internat Sci Ctr PO Box 1085 1049 Camino Dos Rios Thousand Oaks CA 91360

HARKINS, STEPHEN WAYNE, gerontology, psychiatry and psychology educator, researcher; b. Pitts., Aug. 20, 1942; s. Ralph Watson and Elizabeth (Barrington) H.; 1 dau., Emily. Ph.D., U. N.C.-Chapel Hill, 1974. Research asst. Ctr. Study of Aging & Human Devel. Duke U., Durham, 1969-74; fellow dept. psychiatry and behavioral scis. U. Wash., Seattle, 1974-76, asst. prof. anesthesiology and psychiatry, 1976-79; assoc. prof. gerontology, psychiatry, psychology Med. Coll. Va., Va. Commonwealth U., Richmond, 1979—. Editor: (with L. Poon) Aging in the 1980's: Psychological Issues, 1980; mem. editorial bd.: Jour. Gerontology, 1981; contbr. chpts. to books, articles in field to profl. jours. Founder Alzheimer's Disease Support Group, Richmond, 1981. NIA fellow, 1974-76. Mem. Am. Psychol. Assn., Internat. Assn. Study Pain, Soc. Psychophysiol. Research, Gerontol. Soc. Am. Current Work: Gerontology, psychophysiology. Subspecialties: Psychobiology; Cognition. Home: 3455 Northview Pl Richmond VA 23225 Office: Medical College Virginia Box 228 MCV Station Richmond VA 23298

HARKNESS, JOHN BARRETT LONG, chemical engineer, environmental engineer; b. St. Louis, Nov. 27, 1941; s. John Barrett and Elizabeth Ann (Hayes) H.; m. Carol Jean Peplinski, Sept. 30, 1972. B.A., Pomona Coll., 1963; B.S., Calif. Inst. Tech., 1965; Ph.D., MIT, 1971. Research engr. Amoco Chems., Naperville, Ill., 1970-77; chem. engr. Argonne Nat. Lab., Ill., 1977—; lectr. on environ. topics. Contbr. articles on environ. subjects to profl. jours. Patentee in field. Mem. Am. Inst. Chem. Engrs., AAAS. Club: Chgo. Mountaineering (pres. 1982-84). Current work: Evaluation and development of flue gas environmental control technologies for coal combustion, especially high-sulfur coal. Subspecialties: Chemical engineering; Gas cleaning systems. Office: EES Div Argonne Nat Lab Bldg 362 Argonne IL 60439

HARLAN, JACK RODNEY, geneticist, educator; b. Washington, June 7, 1917; s. Harry Vaughn and Augusta (Griffing) H.; m. Jean Yocum, Aug. 4, 1939; children—Sue (Mrs. Robert Hughes), Harry, Sherry (Mrs. Mark Wilson), Richard Edwin. B.S. in Botany with distinction, George Washington U., 1938; Ph.D. in Genetics, U. Calif. at Berkeley, 1942. Research asst. Tela R.R. Co., Honduras, 1942; geneticist Dept. Agr., Woodward, Okla., 1942-51, Stillwater, Okla., 1951-61; prof. agronomy Okla. State U., 1951-66; prof. gentics U. Ill. at Urbana, 1966—; botanist Dept. of Agr. (plant exploration and introduction), Turkey, Syria and Iraq, 1948, Iran, Afghanistan, Pakistan, India and Ethiopia, 1960; sr. staff mem. Iranian prehistoric project Oriental Inst. U. Chgo., 1960, sr. staff mem. Turkish prehistoric project, 1964; mem. Dead Sea Archaeol. Project, 1977, 79, 83; plant exploration, Africa, Asia, Latin Am.; Cons. FAO, 1970-71. Mem. internat. bd.: Plant Genetic Resources, 1974-79; contbr. profl. jours. Fellow AAAS, Am. Soc. Agronomy, Am. Acad. Arts and Sci.: mem. Nat. Acad. Scis., Crop Sci. Soc. Am. (pres. 1966), Am. Inst. Biol. Scientists, Bot. Soc. Am., Am. Soc. Agronomy, Soc. for Econ. Botany, Phi Beta Kappa, Sigma Xi, Phi Kappa Phi. Presbyn. (elder). Current work: Crop evolution, genetic conservation. Home: 1822 Crescent Dr Champaign IL 61820 Office: care Dept Agronomy U Ill Turner Hall Urbana IL 61801

HARLOW, ROBERT DEAN, biochemist, researcher; b. Denver, Apr. 17, 1926; s. Floyd DeWitt and Rose (Haller) H.; m. Elizabeth Vail, July 1, 1967; children—Margaret, Mary, Christina. B.S. in Chem. Engring., U. Colo., 1948; postgrad. Tex. A&M U., 1963-66. Engr., Baroid, Houston, 1958-62; biochemist Tex. A&M U., 1962-67, Oak Ridge Assoc. Univs., 1967-71, Warren Med. Inst., Tulsa, 1971—. Mem. Am. Chem. Soc., Am. Oil Chemists Soc., AAAS. Republican. Presbyterian. Lodge: Lions. Current work: Developing and using analytical methods used in cancer research and other types of research. Subspecialties: Biochemistry (medicine); Cancer research (medicine). Home: 1519 S 124th E Ave Tulsa OK 71128 Office: Warren Med Inst 6465 S Yale St Suite 1010 Tulsa OK 74177

HARMAN, GARY ELVAN, seed microbiologist, educator; b. La Junta, Colo., Nov. 13, 1944; s. Ivan D. and Ruth A. (Bloyd) H.; m. B. Jean Wilkinson, Sept. 22, 1965; children: Douglas, Jeffrey, Trieu. B.S., Colo. State U., 1966; Ph.D., Oreg. State U., 1970. Postdoctoral assoc. N.C. State U., 1969-70; asst. prof. seed microbiology N.Y. State Agr. Expt. Sta., Cornell U., Geneva, 1970-76, assoc. prof., 1976-83, prof., 1983—. Contbr. articles to sci. jours. Grantee Snap Bean Research Assn., 1978-79; Grantee Rockefeller Found., 1978-81; Grantee Am. Seed Research Found., 1979-82; Grantee N.Y. Seed Assn., 1980-81; Grantee U.S.-Israel Binat. Agr. Research Devel. Orgn., 1981-84; Grantee U.S. Dept. Agr., 1982-84. Mem. Am. Phytopathol. Soc., AAAS, Sigma Xi. Presbyterian. Current Work: Biological control of seed and root-rotting fungi; detection and control of seed-borne plant pathogens, including fungi, bacteria, and viruses; mechanisms of aging in seeds. Subspecialties: Plant pathology; Microbiology. Office: Dept Horticultural Sciences NY State Agr Expt Station Cornell U Geneva NY 14456

HARMAN, GEORGE GIBSON, physicist, consultant; b. Norfolk, Va., Dec. 7, 1924; s. George G. Harman and Annie Wall Baldwin Harman; m. Ann W. Worischek, Jan. 31, 1953 (separated); children—Joyce Catherine, Arthur Lawrence, Stewart Thomas. B.S. in Physics, Va. Poly. Inst., 1949; M.S. in Physics, U. Md., 1959; research fellow U. Reading, Eng., 1962-63. With Nat. Bur. Standards, Washington, 1950—, sr. research scientist, 1976—; cons. Harman Assocs., Gaithersburg, Md., 1980—. Contbr. articles to profl. jours. Patentee in field. Served as staff sgt. U.S. Army, 1943-46, PTO. Recipient Silver medal U.S. Dept. Commerce, 1973, Gold Medal, 1979. Fellow IEEE (chmn. nominating com. 1980—; Centennial medal 1984), Internat. Soc. Hybrid Microelectronics (chpt. pres. 1980-82; Technical Achievement award 1981, Lewis F. Miller award 1984); mem. ASTM, Am. Phys. Soc., Sigma Xi, Sigma Pi Sigma. Club: Cosmos (Washington). Current work: Hybrid microcircuit and VLSI packaging, interconnections, device long term reliability. Subspecialties: Microelectronics; Microchip technology (materials science). Home: 20226 Maple Leaf Ct Gaithersburg MD 20879 Office: Nat Bur Standards Devices and Circuits Div Washington DC 20234

HARMAN, WILLARD NELSON, malacologist educator, benthic researcher; b. Geneva, N.Y., Apr. 20, 1937; s. Samuel Willard and Mary Nelson (Covert) H.; m. Susan Beth Mead, June 12, 1968 (div. 1979); children—Rebecca Mary, Willard Wade; m. Barbara Ann Stong, July 16, 1980; 1 child, Jessica Mary. Student Hobart Coll., 1954-55; B.S., SUNY-Syracuse, 1965; Ph.D., Cornell U., 1968; postdoctoral Marine Biology Lab., 1968. Research asst. Cornell U., Ithaca, N.Y., 1965-66, teaching asst., 1966-68; asst. prof. biology SUNY-Oneonta, 1968-69, assoc. prof., 1979-76, prof., 1976—, chmn. biology dept., 1981—. Contbr. articles to profl. jours. Served with USN, 1956-61. Pres. Otsego County Conservation Assn., Cooperstown, N.Y., 1978-78, 80-81, chmn. lake com., 1981—. Recipient Excellence in Teaching award SUNY Chancellor, 1974, 75. Mem. Soc. Limnology and Oceanography, Calif. Malacological Union, N.Am. Benthological Soc., Soc. Exptl. and Descriptive Malacology, Sigma Xi, Phi Kappa Phi. Republican. Episcopalian. Current work: Fresh water behthic malacology. Subspecialties: Limnology; Marine biology. Home: RD 2 Box 829 Cooperstown NY 13326 Office: Biology Dept SUNY Oneonta NY 13820

HARMON, BRUCE N., physics educator; b. Grand Rapids, Mich., Mar. 30, 1947; m. Bonnnie J. Harmon; children—Dion Kane, Alyssa Dawn. B.S., Ill. Inst. Tech., 1968; M.S., Northwestern U., 1969, Ph.D., 1973. Postdoctoral fellow Ames Lab., Iowa, 1973-75; asst. prof. physics Iowa State U., Ames, 1975-78, assoc. prof., 1978-82, prof., 1982—; guest scientist Kernforschungszentrum, Karlsruhe, Fed. Republic Germany, 1980-81; program dir. solid state physics div. Ames Lab.-U.S. Dept. Energy, 1983—. Contbr. articles to sci. jours. Mem. Am. Phys. Soc., Am. Assn. Physics Tchrs. Current work: Lattice dynamics, electronic structure, magnetism, superconductivity, computer modeling, superlattices. Subspecialties: Condensed matter physics; Magnetic physics. Home: 1804 Wilson Ames IA 50010 Office: Physics Dept Iowa State U Ames IA 50011

HARMON, DAVID E., JR., oil company executive, consultant; b. Kittanning, Pa., Aug. 12, 1932; s. David E. and Martha E. (Cochran) H.; m. Paula Ann Younker, Oct. 8, 1960; children: David Michael, Sabrina Marie, John Matthew Wills, Patrick Kevin, Paul Charles, Robert Jude. A.B. in Geology, Marietta Coll., 1954. Cert. profl. engr., Ky., Ind. profl. land surveyor, Ind. profl. geologist, Ga. Geologist B.H. Putnam, Marietta, Ohio, 1954-58, F.E. Moran Oil Co., Owensboro, Ky., 1958-64; chief engr. Dept. Pub. Works Jefferson County, Louisville, 1967-69; chief geologist Guernsey Petroleum Corp. Atlanta, 1969-72, cons., 1972-73; v.p. Johnston Petroleum Corp., Cambridge, Ohio, 1973-75; v.p., dir. O'Neal Petroleum, Inc., New Concord, Ohio, 1975-83, Belleville, Ill., 1976-83; pres. Concord Energy, Inc., New Concord, Ohio, 1983—; cons. Ind. Glass Sand Corp., Elizabeth, Ind., 1964-66, Duchsherer and Assoc., Louisville, 1966-67, Ballard and Cordell, Atlanta, 1972-73. Pres. and dir. East Muskingum Swimming Pool Assn., 1976; dir. S.E. Ohio Symphony Orch., 1978; nat. research assoc. Smithsonian Instn., 1980. Served with U.S. Army, 1955-57. Fellow Geol. Soc. Am.; mem. Am. Assn. Petroleum Geologists, Soc. Petroleum Engrs., Am. Inst. Profl. Geologists. Roman Catholic. Lodge: KC (4th degree). Subspecialties: Geology; Fuels. Home: Morgan House Route #2 New Concord OH 43762 Office: Concord Energy Inc PO Box 111 New Concord OH 43762

HARMON, FREDERICK ROBERT, research biochemist, immunochemist; b. Kittanning, Pa., Mar. 27, 1948; s. Roy Leonard and Elizabeth Louise (Miller) H. B.A. in Chemistry, Thiel Coll., Greenville, Pa., 1970; Ph.D., U. Del., 1976. Research assoc. Case-Western Res. U., Cleve., 1975-80; asst. prof. pharmacology Baylor Coll. Medicine, 1980-84, research asst. prof. virology, 1984—. Contbr. articles to profl. jours. Recipient Sr. award Pitts. Soc. Analytic Chemists, 1970. Mem. Biophys. Soc., Am. Soc. Cell Biology, N.Y. Acad. Scis. Current work: Use of synthetic peptides for 2d generation vaccines; immunochemistry of proteins and antigen-antibody interactions; chemical modification of proteins; RNA protein complexes and subcellular particles. Subspecialties: Infectious diseases; Biochemistry (medicine). Home: 5500 N Braeswood #214 Houston TX 77096 Office: Dept Virology Baylor Coll Medicine 1 Baylor Plaza Houston TX 77030

HARMON, GARY R., engineer; b. Ravenna, Ohio, Jan. 7, 1950; s. Raymond A. and Betty J. (Hassler) H.; m. Jacquelyn Mitchell, Sept. 6, 1981. B.Sc. in Physics, Ohio State U., 1972, M.Sc., 1974. Commd. 2d lt. USAF, 1974, advanced through grades to maj., 1984; space program mgr. Hdqrs. Aerospace Def. Command, Colorado Springs, Colo., 1977-79; policy and issue analyst Office ofSec. of Air Force, Washington, 1979-81; devel. engr. Sec. of Air Force Office of Spl. Projects, Los Angeles, 1981-84, Office of Sec. of Air Force, Washington, D.C., 1984—. Decorated Air Force Commendation medal with oak leaf cluster, Meritorious Service medal with oak leaf cluster. Def. Meritorious Service medal. Mem. IEEE, Air Force Assn. Republican. Baptist. Club: Colo. Mountain (Colorado Springs). Current Work: Aerospace technology. Subspecialties: Plasma physics; Laser-induced chemistry. Home: 13909 Cristo Ct Centreville VA 22020

HARMON, JOHN WATSON, surgeon; b. White Plains, N.Y., Aug. 22, 1943; s. Frederick W. and Anne (Page) H.; m. Gail McGreevy, June 11, 1969; children: James, Eve. B.A., Harvard U., 1965; M.D., Columbia U., 1969. Intern Harvard U. Service, Boston City Hosp., 1969-70; surg. resident Harvard U. Med. Sch., 1969-75; commd. 1st lt. U.S. Army, 1969, advanced through grades to lt. col., 1983; investigator Walter Reed Army Inst. Research, Washington, 1975-85; assoc. prof. surgery Uniformed Services U., Bethesda, Md., 1985—; U.S. Army rep. surg. study group NIH, Bethesda, 1982. Editor: Mechanisms of Mucosal Injury, 1982. Recipient William Beaumont award Fed. Gastroenterologists, 1982. Fellow ACS; mem. Am. Physiol. Soc., Soc. Univ. Surgeons, Am. A Gastroent. Soc., Assn. Acad. Surgery, Alpha Omega Alpha. Episcopalian. Clubs: Cosmos; St. Marys River Yacht (St. Marys City, Md.). Current Work: Surgical gastroenterology and endocrinology. Subspecialties: Surgery; Comparative physiology. Office: Dept Surgery Washington VA Med Ctr Washington DC 20422

HARMS, ARCHIE ARKADIUS, engineering physics educator, researcher; b. Nova-Dwor, Poland, Apr. 18, 1934; emigrated to Can., 1948; s. Paul and Wilhelmina (Kliewer) H.; m. Ursula Margareta Claassen, Aug. 17, 1957; children: Trudy, Dolores, Theodore. B.Sc., U. B.C., Can.), Vancouver, 1963; M.Sc.Eng., U. Wash., 1965, Ph.D., 1969. Engr. Internat. Power Engring. Cons., Vancouver, 1963-65; asst. prof. engring. physics McMaster U., Hamilton, Ont., 1969-72, assoc. prof., 1972-79, prof., 1979—; cons. in field; vis. scholar Internat. Inst. Applied Systems Analysts, Laxenburg, Austria, 1980. Author: Nuclear Energy Synergetics, 1982. Mem. Am. Phys. Soc., Am. Nuclear Soc., Can. Assn. Physicists. Subspecialties: Nuclear fission; Nuclear fusion. Home: 245 Taylor Rd Ancaster ON L9G 1P6 Canada Office: McMaster U Hamilton ON L8S 4M1 Canada

HARMS, WELDON MENNO, oilfield research chemist; b. Gotebo, Okla., Mar. 26, 1944; s. Menno and Mildred Elizabeth (Neubert) H.; children—Peter W., Samuel Frederick. B.S. in Chem. Physics, Northwestern Okla. State U., 1967; Ph.D. in Organic Chemistry, Okla. State U., 1972. Postdoctoral fellow U. Tex., Austin, 1971-74; asst. prof. U. Tex., 1972-74; research chemist Halliburton Services, Duncan, Okla., 1974—; v.p. HWH Aviation, Inc., 1976—. Contbr. articles to profl. jours. Inventor in field. Mem. Am. Chem. Soc., Blue Key Honor Soc., Sigma Xi, Phi Lambda Upsilon. Republican. Baptist. Current work: Oil field service chemicals, low density additives, viscosity control polymers and crosslinkers, surfactants, foam cement, water-oil-ratio modifiers, clay stabilization additives, water soluble polymers. Subspecialty: Biomaterials. Home: Rt 2 Box 76 Duncan OK 73533

HARPER, CAROL LYNN MOUNT, ecologist; b. Camden, N.J., Sept. 28, 1942; d. Edward Hunt and Carolyn Reid (Johnes) Mount; m. Charles Alan Harper, June 27, 1964. B.S., Bowling Green State U., 1964; M.S., U. So. Calif., 1967; Ph.D., U. Fla., 1971. Interim instr. U. Fla., Gainesville, 1972; sr. scientist Bechtel Group Inc., San Francisco, 1972-85. Contbr. articles to profl. jours. Mem. Am. Ornithologists Union, Am. Soc. Limnologists and Oceanographers, Ecol. Soc. Am. Current work: Environmental impact assessment. Subspecialties: Ecology (environmental science); Limnology.

HARPER, DOYAL ALEXANDER, JR., astronomer, educator; b. Atlanta, Oct. 9, 1944; s. Doyal Alexander and Emily (Brown) H.; m. Carolyn James, Mar. 11, 1967; children: Scott Alexander, Nathan Todd, Amy Claire, Evan James. B.A. in Elec. Engring, Rice U., Houston, 1966, Ph.D. in Space Sci, 1971. Asst. prof. astronomy and astrophysics U. Chgo., 1971, assoc. prof., 1976-80, prof., 1980—; dir. Yerkes Obs., 1982—. Mem. Am. Astron. Soc. (Newton Lacy Pierce prize o61979), Astron. Soc. Pacific. Current Work: Infrared observations of galaxies, stars, planets, star formation regions, far infrared detectors, cryogenics, optical systems. Subspecialty: Infrared astronomy. Home: Yerkes Observatory Williams Bay WI 53191

HARPER, JEFFREY FREDERICK, pharmacologist, educator; b. Muncie, Ind., Jan. 3, 1952; s. Henry Miller and Marjorie (Petty) H.; m. Mary Pieroni, June 23, 1973; children—Katherine Anne, Andrew Mario. A.B., Brown U., 1973; Ph.D., U. Va., 1978. Asst. prof. U. Tex. Med. Sch., Houston, 1980—. Contbr. articles to profl. jours. Grantee NIH, 1983—, Cystic Fibrosis Found., 1984—. Current work: Regulation of secretion by cyclic nucleotides; regulation of adenosine 3, 5-cyclic monophosphate synthesis by desensitization and mechanisms of desensitization. Subspecialties: Molecular pharmacology; Cell biology. Home: 2343 McClendon St Houston TX 77030 Office: Div Endocrinology U Tex Med Sch Box 20708 Houston TX 77225

HARPER, MICHAEL JOHN KENNEDY, medical educator, cons.; b. London, Feb. 25, 1935; came to U.S., 1964; s. John Kennedy and Helen Malvina (Koeller) H.; m. Marian Kennedy Wedd, July 23, 1960 (div. Feb. 1982); children: Charlotte G.K., Tristram J. K., Felicity W. K.; m. Ann Carlene Vandeventer, Feb. 16, 1985. B.A. in Agr. U. Cambridge, Eng., 1957, Ph.D., 1962, Sc.D., 1979; diploma agr., U. Reading, Eng., 1958. Tech. officer Imperial Chem. Industries, Alderley Edge, Cheshire, Eng., 1961-64, 1965-66; vis. scientist Worcester Found. for Exptl. Biology, Shrewsbury, Mass., 1964-65, staff scientist, 1966-68, sr. scientist, 1968-72; scientist WHO, Geneva, 1972-75; assoc. prof. ob-gyn U. Tex. Health Sci. Ctr., San Antonio, 1975-81, prof., 1981—; mem. task force com. WHO, 1972—, chmn., 1984—, mem. adv. group human reproduction, 1982-84; cons. Am. Pub. Health Assn., 1982—, NSF, 1983—; mem. ad hoc adv. com. contraceptive devel. br. Nat. Inst. Child Health and Human Devel., 1975—. Author: Birth Control Technologies, 1983; contbr. numerous articles on reprodn.to profl. jours. Recipient Woodman prize U. Cambridge, 1957; Agrl. Food Products prize U. Reading, 1958; NIH grantee, 1969-83; others. Fellow Inst. Biology (Eng.); mem. Endocrine Soc. U.S.A., Soc. Endocrinology (U.K.), Soc. Study of Reproduction, Soc. Study of Fertility (U.K.), Am. Fertility Soc., Am. Assn. Anatomists, Soc. Gynecol. Investigation, Am. Physiol. Soc. Republican. Inventor tamoxifen, 1963; patentee in field. Current Work: Pre-implantation stages of pregnancy, prostaglandins, contraceptive research and development. Subspecialties: Reproductive biology; Reproductive biology (medicine). Home: 13282 Hunters Lark San Antonio TX 78230 Office: U Tex Health Sci Center Dept Ob-Gyn 7703 Floyd Curl Dr San Antonio TX 78284

HARRELL, RUTH FLINN, mental-nutritional research educator; b. Americus, Ga., Apr. 19, 1900; d. Daniel and Neva (Poley) Flinn; m. William Lee Harrell, Nov. 24, 1928 (dec. Apr. 1972); children: Ruth Harrell Capp-Bell. B.S., Wesleyan Coll., Macon, Ga., 1920; M.A., Columbia U., 1924, Ph.D., 1942. Diplomate: Am. Psychol. Assn. Bd. Pub. sch. psychologist, Norfolk, Va., 1926-39; rehab. psychologist neuro-surgery Johns Hopkins Hosp., Balt., 1936-47; faculty mem. Old Dominion U., Norfolk, 1955-70, prof. psychology, to 1970; research prof. Old Dominion U. (Research Found.), 1976—. Author: Effect of Added Thiamin on Learning, 1943, Further Effects of Added Thiamin on Learning, 1947, Effect of Mothers' Diets on Intelligence of Offspring, 1955, Can Nutritional Supplements Help Mentally Retarded Children? , 1981. Recipient Ann. award for advancing research on mental retardation-nutrition Atlanta Med. Research Found., 1982. Mem. Am. Psychol. Assn., N.Y. Acad. Scis., Delta Kappa Gamma. Presbyterian. Current Work: Study of Epilepsy as related to nutrition - i.e. seizures may be a manifestation of nutritional deficiencies. Subspecialties: Nutrition (biology); Learning. Home: 3100 Shore Dr #928 Virginia Beach VA 23451 Office: Research Found Old Dominion U Norfolk VA 23508

HARRIMAN, PHILIP DARLING, geneticist, government official; b. San Rafael, Calif., Nov. 24, 1937; s. Theodore Darling and Luciel Harriet (Muller) H.; m. Jenny Elizabeth Flack, June 12, 1959; 1 son, Marc Stuart. B.S. in Physics, Calif. Inst. Tech., 1959; Ph.D. in Biophysics, U. Calif., Berkeley, 1964. Postdoctoral fellow U. Cologne, W.Ger., 1964-65, Pasteur Inst., Paris, 1965-66, Cold Spring Harbor Lab., N.Y., 1966-68; asst. prof. biochemistry Duke U. Med. Center, Durham, N.C., 1968-75; assoc. prof. biology U. Mo., Kansas City, 1975-77; program dir. for genetic biology NSF, Washington, 1977—, sr. scientist office of Asst. Dir. Biology, Behavioral and Social Scis., 1981-82. Contbr. articles to profl. jours. Legis. asst. Congressman Dave McCurdy of Okla., 1980-81. Served to 1st lt. USAFR, 1962—. Congressional fellow U.S. Office Personnel Mgmt., 1980-81. Mem. AAAS, Genetics Soc. Am., Am. Soc. Microbiology. Unitarian. Current Work: I evaluate and fund research proposals in area of genetics and genetic engineering. Subspecialties: Genetics and genetic engineering (biology); Molecular biology. Home: 2606 Arcola Ave Wheaton MD 20902 Office: Nat Sci Found Room 326 Washington DC 20550

HARRINGTON, DEAN BUTLER, retired electrical engineer; b. Schenectady; s. Elliott D. Harrington and Catherine (Butler) Harrington Johnson; m. Barbara J. Stibbe, Apr. 17, 1949; children—Kim. M., Kevin D., Jeffrey L. B.S.E.E., MIT, 1944. Engr., Gen. Electric Co., Schenectady, 1944-67, mgr. generator advance engring., 1967-82. Recipient Charles P. Steinmetz award Gen. Electric Co., 1977. Fellow IEEE (chmn. synchronous machinery subcom. 1964-66, chmn. rotating machinery com. 1969-70, Nikola Tesla award 1981); mem. Nat. Acad. Engring., Internat. Electrotech. Commn. (chmn. subcom. 2J classification of elec. insulation). Methodist. Current work: Electric machine theory, electromagnetic phenomena, management of development work, electric power engineering, rotating electric machinery engineering. Subspecialty: Electrical engineering.

HARRINGTON, JOHN VINCENT, consultant, retired communications company executive, engineer, educator; b. N.Y.C., May, 9, 1919; s. John Joseph and Dorothy (Neisel) H.; m. Frances Cullinane, Jan. 23, 1943; children—John F., Nancy Harrington Higgins, Jeffrey, Richard, Brian. B.E.E., Cooper Union, 1940; M.E.E., Poly. Inst. Bklyn., 1948; Sc.D., Mass. Inst. Tech., 1957. Research engr. U.S. Air Force Cambridge Research Lab., Mass., 1946-51; leader data transmission group Lincoln Lab., M.I.T., Cambridge, 1951-56, asso. div. head aircraft control and warning, 1956-58, head radio physics div., 1958-63; prof. aeros., astronautics and elec. engring., 1st dir. Center Space Research, M.I.T., 1963-73; v.p. research and engring. Communications Satellite Corp., Washington, 1973-79; sr. v.p. research and devel., dir. COMSAT Labs., Clarksburg, Md., 1979-83; dir. Epsco, Inc., 1964-72, Shawmut County Bank, Cambridge, 1964-73, COMSAT Gen. Telesystems, Inc., Washington, 1973-81, Environ. Research and Tech., Inc., Concord, Mass., 1981-82; mem. Space Applications Bd., NRC, 1975-81. Contbr. articles to profl. jours. Served to lt. USN, 1942-46. Recipient Exceptional Civilian Service medal U.S. Air Force, 1952; Exceptional Profl. Achievement citation Cooper Union, 1965; Gano Dunn award Cooper Union, 1983. Fellow IEEE (dir. New Eng. regional meeting 1964-66), AAAS, AIAA. Office: care Communication Satellite Corp 950 L'Enfant Plaza SW Washington DC 20024

HARRINGTON, ROBERT SUTTON, astronomer; b. Newport News, Va., Oct. 21, 1942; s. Jean Carl and Virginia Hall (Sutton) H.; m. Betty Jean, July 23, 1976; children: Amy Lucille, Ann Charon. B.A. in Physics, Swarthmore Coll., 1964; Ph.D. in Astronomy, U. Tex., 1968. Astronomer U.S. Naval Obs., Washington, 1967—. Contbr. tech. articles to profl. publs. Mem. Internat. Astron. Union, Am. Astron. Soc., AAAS, Sigma Xi. Current Work: Stellar distances and motions, solar system dynamics. Subspecialties: Astrometry; Celestial mechanics. Office: Naval Obs Washington DC 20390

HARRINGTON, RODNEY ELBERT, biochemist; b. Mayville, N.D., Jan. 9, 1932; s. Elbert Wellington and Marjorie H.; married; children: Tiffany Anne, Jennifer Ellen; m. Ilga Butelis, Jan. 26, 1979. B.A., U. S.D., 1953; Ph.D., U. Wash., 1960. Research chemist Ames Lab., Iowa State U., 1953; research asst. U. Wash., 1957; research assoc. U. Calif.-San Diego, 1960; asst. prof. U. Ariz., 1962; assoc. prof. U. Calif.-Davis, 1964; prof. chemistry U. Nev., Reno, 1972-82, chmn. dept. chemistry, 1972-76, prof. biochemistry, 1982—. Bd. dirs. Nev. Opera Co., 1973-78; mem. Community Relations Bd., U. Nev., 1977-79. NIH and NSF research grantee, 1961—. Mem. Am. Chem. Soc., Am. Phys. Soc., Biophys. Soc., AAAS, Sigma Xi. Lutheran. Current Work: Chromatin structure and gene regulation, fundamental research. Subspecialties: Biochemistry (biology); Molecular biology. Office: Dept Biochemistry U Nev Reno NV 89557

HARRINGTON, ROY VICTOR, chemist; b. Bklyn., Sept. 28, 1928; s. Victor Earl and Karen (Hanson) H.; m. Catherine Elisabeth Wiese, June 14, 1952; children—Bruce Allan, Karen Jane, Thomas Andrew. B.S. in Chemistry, Poly. Inst. Bklyn., 1952; Ph.D., U. Colo., 1955. Chemist Gen. Foods Corp., Hoboken, N.J., 1949-52, Corning Glass Works, N.Y., 1955-68; with Ferro Corp., Independence, Ohio, 1968—, asso. dir., then dir. research and devel., now v.p. research and devel.; pres. Cleve. Assn. Research Dirs., 1975; mem. panel radioactive waste disposal Nat. Acad. Scis., 1979-80. Author. Founder, pres. Corning Sci. Seminars Gifted High Sch. Students, 1960-67; Mem. steering com. Case Assos., Case Western Res. U. Mem. Am. Chem. Soc. (sect. chmn. 1978), Am. Ceramic Soc. Club: Lakeside Yacht (Cleve.). Patentee in field. Current Work: Broad materials interests, glass, ceramics, composites, electronic materials, plastics, high temperature chemistry radiochemistry. Subspecialties: Inorganic chemistry; Materials. Office: 7500 E Pleasant Valley Rd Independence OH 44131

HARRIS, ALAN WILLIAM, scientist, researcher; b. Portland, Oreg., Aug. 3, 1944; s. James Stewart and Jane Ann (Gordon) H.; m. Rose Marie Spitt, Aug. 22, 1970; children: W. Donald, David S., Catherine R. B.S., Calif. Inst. Tech., 1966; M.S., UCLA, 1967, Ph.D., 1974. Geophysicist space div. Rockwell Internat., Downey, Calif., 1967-70; physics tchr. Immaculate Heart High Sch., Hollywood, Calif., 1970-74; instr. physics Santa Monica (Calif.) Coll., 1970-71; research scientist, earth and space scis. div. JPL, Pasadena, Calif., 1974—; prin. investigator, lunar and planetary program NASA, 1976—. Contbr. articles to profl. jours. Mem. Internat. Astron. Union, Am. Astron. Soc., Am. Geophys. Union. Current Work: Dynamical theory of plant formation, observation and theoretical research on asteroid rotation and collisional processes. Subspecialties: Planetary science; Optical astronomy. Home: 4603 Orange Knoll La Canada CA 91011 Office: JPL 4800 Oak Knoll Dr 183-501 Pasadena CA 91109

HARRIS, CYRIL MANTON, electrical engineering and architecture educator, consulting acoustical engineer; b. Detroit, June 20, 1917; s. Bernard O. and Ida (Moss) H.; m. Ann Schakne, July 12, 1949; children: Nicholas Bennett, Katherine Anne. B.A., UCLA, 1938, M.A., 1940; Ph.D., MIT, 1945; Sc.D. (hon.), N.J. Inst. Tech., 1981. Teaching asst. UCLA, 1939-40; research fellow MIT, 1940; war research OSRD, 1941-44, teaching fellow, 1943-45; war research Carnegie Instn. Washington, 1941; mem. staff Bell Telephone Labs.,

1945-51; cons. Office Naval Research, London, Eng., 1951; Fulbright lectr. Tech. U., Delft, Holland, 1951-52; now Charles Batchelor prof. elec. engring., prof. architecture and chmn. div. archtl. tech. Columbia U.; vis. Fulbright prof. U. Tokyo, 1960; acoustical cons. Met. Opera House, N.Y.C., John F. Kennedy Center for Performing Arts, Washington, Krannert Center for Performing Arts, U. Ill., Powell Symphony Hall, St. Louis, Nat. Acad. Scis. Auditorium, Washington, Minn. Orch. Hall, Mpls., Nat. Centre for Performing Arts, Bombay, India, new Avery Fisher Hall, State Theater reconstruction Lincoln Center, N.Y.C., Symphony Hall, Salt Lake City; past dir. U.S. Inst. Theatre Tech.; mem. noise control group, com. undersea warfare NRC, 1955-57; mem. council hearing and bio-acoustics Armed Forces-NRC, 1953-55; mem. NRC adv. panel 213 to Nat. Bur. Standards, 1966-69, chmn., 1969-71; mem. bldg. research adv. bd. NRC, 1977-79. Author: (with V.O. Knudsen) Acoustical Designing in Architecture, 1950, rev., 1980, Handbook of Noise Control, 1957, 2d edit., 1979, (with C.E. Crede) Shock and Vibration Handbook, 1961, 2d edit., 1976, Dictionary of Architecture and Construction, 1975; author: Historic Architecture Sourcebook, 1977, Illustrated Dictionary of Historic Architecture, 1983; Contbr. articles to profl. jours.; Editorial adv. bd.: Physics Today, 1955-66. Bd. dirs. Armstrong Meml. Research Found., 1976—; hon. v.p. St. Louis Symphony Soc., 1977—; mem. nat. adv. bd. Utah Symphony Orch., 1976—. Recipient Franklin medal, 1977, Emile Berliner award, 1977, Hon. award U.S. ITT, 1977, Wallace Clement Sabine medal, 1979, AIA medal, 1980, Gold Medal Audio Engring. Soc., 1984. Fellow Acoustical Soc. Am. (pres. 1964-65, asso. editor jour. 1959-70), IEEE (chmn. profl. group ultrasonic engring. 1957-58), I.E.E.E. (profl. group audio 1961-62), Audio Engring. Soc. (hon. mem.); mem. Am. Inst. Physics (governing bd. 1965-66), Nat. Acad. Scis., Nat. Acad. Engring., Sigma Xi, Tau Beta Pi. Current Work: Architectural acoustics, noise control. Subspecialties: Acoustics; Acoustical engineering. Office: Mudd Bldg Columbia U New York NY 10027

HARRIS, DANIEL EVERETT, astronomer; b. Summit, N.J., Aug. 5, 1934; s. Pierson P. and Ella M. (Freas) H.; m. Barbara A. Jeffrey, June 24, 1967; children—Justine, Seth, Leila. B.A., Haverford Coll., 1956; M.S., Calif. Inst. Tech., 1957, Ph.D., 1961. Research assoc. Istituto di Fisica, Bologna, Italy, 1962-64; research assoc. Arecibo Obs., P.R., 1965-69, Instituto Argentino de Radio astronomia, Buenos Aires, Argentina, 1969-70, Harvard Coll. Obs., Cambridge, Mass., 1970-74, Netherlands Found. for Radio Astronomy, Dwingeloo, Netherlands, 1974-77, Dominion Radio Astrophys. Obs., Penticton, B.C., Can., 1977-80; astronomer Smithsonian Astrophy. Obs., Cambridge, 1980—. Mem. Am. Astron. Soc., Internat. Astron. Union, Union Radio Sci. Engrs. Current work: non-thermal emission processes in extra-galactic sources, clusters of galaxies, radio sources, quasars. Subspecialties: X-ray high energy astrophysics; Radio and microwave astronomy. Office: HEA CFA 60 Garden St Cambridge MA 02138

HARRIS, DEVERLE PORTER, mineral economics educator; b. Lovell, Wyo., Jan. 21, 1931; s. David Lel and Winiferd (Porter) H.; m. Jean Marie Partridge, Nov. 23, 1949 (div. Oct. 1966); children: Randall Scott, David Vernon, Richard Partridge; m. Sandra Ellen Hall, Jan. 21, 1967; children: Kirstan Ellen, Brett DeVerle, Todd William. B.S., Brigham Young U., 1956, M.S., 1958; Ph.D., Pa. State U.-University Park, 1965. Grad. asst. Pa. State U., University Park, 1960-62; geologist Geophoto Services, Denver, Calgary, Alta., 1957-60; research asst. Pa. State U., University Park, 1962-65; geostatistician Union Oil Co., Brea, Calif., 1965-66; prof. mineral econs. Pa. State U., University Park, 1966-74; prof. mineral econs., prof. geol. engring. U. Ariz., Tucson, 1974—; cons. Inter-Am. Devel. Bank, Washington, 1982—, U.S. Dept. Energy, Grand Junction, Colo., 1972-81. Author: Mineral Resources Appraisal, 1983. Mem. AIME (chmn. sessions of nat. meeting 1977-83), Am. Econ. Assn., Soc. Econ. Geologists (program chmn. nat. meeting 1980). Republican. Mem. Ch. of Jesus Christ of Latter-day Saints. Current Work: Formalization of geoscience for the probabilistic estimation of mineral and energy endowments, and the design and use of engineering-economic systems for the estimation of potential supply of minerals and energy. Subspecialty: Mineral and energy resources. Home: 3330 N Jackson St Tucson AZ 85719 Office: U Ariz Dept Mining and Geol Engring Coll Mines Tucson AZ 85721

HARRIS, DEWEY LYNN, animal research geneticist; b. Red Rock, Tex., June 23, 1933; s. Leland P. and Ethel Mae (Ingram) H.; m. Eugenia Scott, Aug. 22, 1955; children—Scott, Jeff, Todd. B.S., Tex. A&M U., 1954, M.S., 1958; Ph.D., Iowa State U., 1961. Asst. prof. Iowa State U., 1960-64; geneticist DeKalb AgResearch, Inc., Ill., 1964-71, dir. poultry research, 1971-74; chief animal and poultry research A.R.I. Agriculture Can., Ottawa, Ont., 1974-76; research leader animal genetics Dept of Animal Scis. Agrl. Research Service, Dept. Agr., West Lafayette, Ind., 1976—. Contbr. articles to profl. jours. Served to 1st lt. U.S. Army, 1955-57, Korea. Mem. Am. Soc. Animal Sci., Poultry Sci. Assn., Am. Dairy Sci. Assn., Biometric Soc., Am. Genetic Assn. Current work: Quantitative genetic and statistical aspects of livestock improvement through selection and cross breeding. Subspecialties: Animal genetics; Statistics. Home: 2025 Old Oak Dr West Lafayette IN 47906 Office: Agrl Research Service Dept Agr Dept of Animal Scis Purdue Univ West Lafayette IN 47907

HARRIS, DON NAVARRO, biochemist, biochem. pharmacologist, cons.; b. N.Y.C., June 17, 1929; s. John Henry and Margaret Vivian (Berkeley) H.; m. Regina G. Brooks, July 29, 1954; children: Donna Michele, John Craig, Scott Anthony. A.B., Lincoln U., 1951; M.S., Rutgers U., 1959, Ph.D., 1963. Research fellow dept. pharmacology Squibb Inst. for Med. Research, Princeton, N.J., 1965—; coadj. assoc. prof. biochemistry Univ. Coll. of Rutger U., New Brunswick, N.J., 1975-77; mem. U.S. Army Sci. Bd. Contbr. articles on biochemistry and pharmacology to profl. jours. Mem. adv. coms. Frank Twp.Sch. Bd. and Library Bd. Served with U.S. Army, 1951-53. Mem. AAAS, Am. Chem. Soc., N.Y. Acad. Scis., Physiol. Soc. of Phila., Am. Heart Assn., Am. Soc. Pharmacology and Exptl. Therapeutics, Sigma Xi, Alpha Phi Alpha. Democrat. Baptist. Patentee in field. Current Work: Biochemistry of Arachidonic acid metabolites, blood platelet function, cyclic nucleotide function. Subspecialties: Biochemistry (biology); Molecular pharmacology. Home: 26 Summerall Rd Somerset NJ 08873 Office: Dept Pharmacolog Squibb Inst Med Research Princeton NJ 08540

HARRIS, FREDERICK ALLAN, physicist, educator; b. Bay City, Mich., Dec. 27, 1941; s. John and Margaret Wilhelmina (Large) H.; m. Joan Page Williamson, May 1, 1965; children—Frederick Allan, Robert Daniel. B.S.E., U. Mich., 1963, M.S., 1965, Ph.D., 1970. Asst. physicist U. Hawaii, 1970-76, assoc. physicist, 1976-78, assoc. prof., 1978—. Mem. Am Phys. Soc., Sigma Xi. Club: Pacific Bonsai. Current work: Neutrino physics using a hybrid bubble chamber detector; colliding beam physics. Subspecialty: Particle physics. Home: 675 Iana St Kailua HI 96734 Office: Dept Physics and Astronomy U Hawaii 2505 Correa Rd Honolulu HI 96822

HARRIS, GALE ION, radiology and physics educator; b. Arlington, Calif., Aug. 7, 1935; s. Albert I. and Carmine A. (Waters) H.; m. Bonnie J. Hazlett, Mar. 31, 1956; children: Gayla Jean, Nathan Ward. B.S., U. Kans., 1957, M.S., 1959, Ph.D., 1962; S.M., M.I.T., 1973, J.D., Cooley Law Sch., 1985—. Project leader nuclear physics Aerospace Research Lab. GS-15, Wright-Paterson AFB, Ohio, 1965-72; dep. dir., sr. scientist Aerospace Research Lab. GS-15 (Solid State Physics Lab.), 1973-74; asst. prof. adminstrn. dept. radiology, dir. Office Mgmt. Research, Johns Hopkins Med. Sch., Balt., 1974-75; assoc. prof. radiology and physics Mich. State U., East Lansing, 1975—; pres., trustee Mich. Research Ctr., Inc., East Lansing, 1975—; dir. Am. Technetronic Corp., 1982—. Contbr. articles to profl. jours. Served from 1st lt. to capt. USAF, 1962-65. Named Outstanding Profl. Employee Dayton Met. Area Soc. Personnel Adminstrn., Dayton C. of C., 1970; Sloan fellow Mass. Inst. Tech., 1972-73. Mem. Am. Phys. Soc., Soc. Nuclear Medicine, AAAS, Am. Assn. Physicists in Medicine, Assn. Univ. Radiologists. Current Work: Diagnostic imaging systems, nuclear spectroscopy. Subspecialties: Nuclear physics; Radiology in nuclear medicine. Home: 1312 Basswood Circle East Lansing MI 48864 Office: Mich State U B-220 Clin Center East Lansing MI 48824-1315

HARRIS, HAROLD HART, chemist, educator; b. Council Bluffs, Iowa, Mar. 12, 1940; s. Arthur A. and Opal E. (Hart) H.; m. Mary E. Cline, June 25, 1966; children: Matthew M., Jill E. B.S. in Chemistry, Harvey Mudd Coll., 1962; Ph.D. in Phys. Chemistry, Mich. State U., 1967. Postdoctoral fellow U. Calif., Irvine, 1966-67, instr. in chemistry, 1967-70; asst. prof. U. Mo., St. Louis, 1970-75, assoc. prof. chemistry, 1975—. Contbr. articles to profl. jours. Mem. Am. Phys. Soc., Am. Chem. Soc., AAAS, Am. Soc. Mass Spectrometry, Fedn. Am. Scientists, Sigma Xi. Current Work: Teaching chemistry and spectroscopy; polarization spectroscopy and quasielastic laser light scattering. Subspecialties: Laser spectroscopy; Physical chemistry.

HARRIS, JAMES RIDOUT, retired electrical engineer; b. Lockhart, Tex., Apr. 14, 1920; s. Walter Karl and Hortense (Ridout) H.; m. Frances Elizabeth Wiley, June 23, 1943; children—Richard Wells, Betty Anne, Beverly Jean. B.S., U. Richmond, 1941; M.E.E., Poly. Inst. N.Y., 1948; postgrad Williams Coll., summer 1959. Engr., Chesapeake & Potomac Tel. Co., Richmond, Va., 1941-42; with Bell Labs., N.Y. and N.J., 1942-82, dir. customer equipment studies ctr., Holmdel, N.J., 1971-81, dir. data network spl. studies ctr., 1981-82; dir. spl. studies ctr. AT&T Info. Systems Labs., Lincroft, N.J., 1982-83. Pioneer in solid state computing equipment; patentee in computing, communications, and solid state circuits. Elder, trustee, pres. corp. Presbyterian Ch., 1949-82. Mem. Am. Phys. Soc., IEEE (sr.), Phi Beta Kappa, Sigma Xi, Subspecialties: Systems engineering; Information systems (Information science). Home: 8 Dogwood Ln Rumson NJ 07760

HARRIS, JAMES STEWART, JR., electronics engineer, educator, researcher; b. Portland, Oreg., Aug. 22, 1942; s. James Stewart and Jane Ann (Gordon) H.; m. Joyce Emelyn Christensen, June 12, 1965; children—Geoffrey Stewart, Gregory Alan. B.S., Stanford U., 1964, M.S., 1965, Ph.D., 1969. Instr. Stanford U., Calif., 1968-69, prof. elec. engring., 1982—, dir. solid state lab., 1984—; mem. tech. staff Rockwell Internat., Thousand Oaks, Calif., 1969-73, mgr.-infrared devices, 1973-79, prin. scientist, 1979-81, dir. optoelectronics, 1981-82; cons. NRC, Washington, 1980, Varian Assocs., Palo Alto, Calif., 1982—. Author: International Conference on GaAs, 1976, 78, 80, 82; also articles. Editor Jour. Electrochem. Soc., 1978-84. Inventor GaAs charge coupled device, 1977. Coach Am. Youth Soccer Orgn., Palo Alto, Calif., 1980-84; scoutmaster Boy Scouts Am., 1982-84. Tektronix fellow Stanford U., 1965-66. Mem. IEEE (sr., exec. com. 1980-84), Electrochem. Soc., Am. Phys. Soc., Unio Concerned Scientists, Fedn. Am. Scientists, Physicians for Social Responsibility, Sigma Xi, Tau Beta Pi. Mem. United Ch. of Christ. Current work: Microelectronics; molecular beam epitaxial crystal growth of III-V compound semiconductors with structures of ultra-small dimensions for application to new, very high speed electronics and 3-dimensional integrated circuits. Subspecialties: Semiconductors; Microelectronics. Home: 763 Esplanada Way Stanford CA 94305 Office: Stanford Electronics Labs McCullough 208 Stanford CA 94305

HARRIS, LEE ERROL, engineering consultant, educator; b. Ft. Pierce, Fla., Oct. 29, 1953; s. Kenneth Albert and Betty Patricia (Patterson) H.; m. Jo Ann King, June 16, 1975; children—Jeffrey Lee, Sarah Jo. Student, Fla. Inst. Tech., Melbourne, 1971-72, postgrad., 1981—; B.S. in Ocean Engring, Fla. Atlantic U., Boca Raton, 1972-74; M.E. in Coastal Engring, U. Fla., Gainesville, 1975. Registered profl. engr., Fla. Research asst. U. Fla. Coastal and Oceanographic Engring. Lab., Gainesville, 1974-75; coastal engr. U.S. Army C.E., Jacksonville, Fla., 1975-77; cons. engr. Coastal Data and Engring., Inc., Jensen Beach, Fla., 1977—; assoc. prof., head dept. engring. scis. and oceanographic tech. Fla. Inst. Tech., Jensen Beach, 1980—; cons. engr. Harris Engring. and Surveying, Jensen Beach, 1977—. Contbr. articles and reports to profl. jours. Mem. Fla. Oceanographic Soc. (dir. 1979—, pres. 1980-82), Internat. Oceanographic Found., Marine Tech. Soc., Fla. Shore and Beach Preservation Assn., Oceanic Soc., Am. Geophys. Union, Am. Congress on Surveying and Mapping, Nat. Soc. Profl. Surveyors. Current Work: Hydrodynamics of coastal tidal inlets; beach erosion and coastal processes; education in fields of engineering studies, especially oceanographic technology. Subspecialties: Ocean engineering; Civil engineering. Office: Fla Inst Tech 1707 NE Indian River Dr Jensen Beach FL 33457

HARRIS, LOUIS SELIG, pharmacologist, consultant; b. Boston, Mar. 27, 1927; s. Max and Pearl (Oppochinsky) H.; m. Ruth I. Schaufus, Aug. 25, 1952; 1 son, Charles Allan. B.A. in Chemistry, Harvard U., 1954, M.S. in Med. Scis, 1956, Ph.D. in Pharmacology, 1958. Research asst. in anesthesiology Mass. Gen. Hosp., Boston, 1951-52; research biologist Sterling-Winthrop Research Inst., 1960-61, assoc. mem., 1961-62, sect. head, sr. research biologist, 1962-66; assoc. prof. U. N.C., Chapel Hill, 1966-70, prof., 1970-73; cons. in field; Harvey Haag prof., chmn. dept. pharmacology Med. Coll. Va./Va. Commonwealth U., Richmond, 1972—; dir. Quintox, Inc. Contbr. numerous articles to profl. jours. Bd. dirs. Human Services, Inc., Com. of 1000. Fellow Am. Coll. Neuropsychopharmacology; mem. Am. Pharm. Found., Acad. Pharmacol. Scis., Am. Soc. Pharmacology and Exptl. Therapeutics, Am. Chem. Soc., Am. Assn. Med. Sch. Pharmacology, AAAS, Assn. Harvard Chemists, Internat. Anesthesia Research Soc., Internat. Narcotic Enforcement Officers Assn., AAUP, Assn. Neurosci., Internat. Soc. Biochem. Pharmacology, Internat. Soc. Study Pain, Va. Acad. Sci., Am. Pain Soc. Club: Harvard. Current Work: Pharmacology of substances which effect the central nervous system and drug development. Subspecialties: Pharmacology; Neuropharmacology. Home: 7830 Rockfalls Dr Richmond VA 23225 Work: Dept Pharmacology Va Commonwealth U Richmond VA 23298

HARRIS, MILTON, chemist; b. Los Angeles, Mar. 21, 1906; s. Louis and Naomi (Granish) H.; m. Carolyn Wolf, Mar. 30, 1934; children: Barney Dreyfuss (adopted), John. B.Sc., Oreg. State Coll., 1926; Ph.D., Yale, 1929; Dr. Textile Sci., Phila. Textile Inst., 1955. Research asso. Am. Assn. Textile Chemists and Colorists, Nat. Bur. Standards, 1931-39; dir. research Textile Found., 1939-45; pres. and founder Harris Research Labs., 1945-61; dir. research Gillette Co. (its subsidiaries), 1956-66, v.p. corp., 1957-66; dir., chmn. exec. com. Sealectro Corp.; dir. Warner Lambert Co.; adv. bd. Jour. Polymer Sci.; asso. editor Textile Research Jour.; cons. Exec. Office of Pres., Office Sci. and Technology, 1962-65; Adv. bd., cons. O.Q.M.G., World War II; chmn. com. on textiles and cordage, tropical deterioration project Nat. Def. Research Com.; sec. com. on clothing NRC, World War II; chmn. Wool Conservation Bd., World War II; mem. panel on clothing Research and Devel. Bd., World War II; mem. Yale Council, 1964-69, Yale Devel. Bd., 1964-67; exec. bd. Yale Grad. Sch. Assn., 1965—; mem. adv. com. Nat. Bur. Standards, 1971—, chmn. vis. com., 1973—; mem. sub-com. Food and Agrl. Orgn. UN; mem. Utilization research and devel. adv. com. U.S. Dept. Agr., 1966—; mem. adv. com. planning NSF, 1968—; mem. Pres.'s Sci. Adv. Com. Panel on Environment, 1968—; observer-cons. Task Group Nat. Systems Sci. and Tech. Information, Fed. Council Sci. and Tech., 1968—. Contbr. articles to tech. jours.; Editor: Chemistry in the U.S. Economy. Trustee Phila. Textile Inst., 1956-60; dir. Dermatology Found., Textile Research Inst.; bd. dirs. Sci. Service, Acorn Fund, Chgo. Recipient award Wash. Acad. Sci., 1943, Olney medal for textile chemistry research, 1945; honor award Am. Inst. Chemists, 1957; Harold DeWitt Smith Meml. medal, 1966; Distinguished Service award Oreg. State U., 1967; Perkin Medal award Soc. Chem. Industry, 1970; Wilbur Lucius Cross medal Yale, 1974; award for meritorious service Yale Sci. and Engring. Assn., 1983. Fellow Textile Inst., N.Y. Acad. Sci.; mem. Am. Assn. Textile Tech., Yale Chemists Assn. (past pres.), Am. Soc. Biol. Chemists, Nat. Acad. Engring., Am. Inst. Chemists (pres. 1960-61 Gold medal), N.A.M., Textile Research Inst., Am. Assn. Textile Colorists and Chemists, Am. Oil Chemists Soc., Soc. Cosmetic Chemists, Fiber Soc. (hon.), Am. Chem. Soc. (chmn. bd. dirs. 1966-70, dir.-at-large, treas. 1973—Priestley medal), AAAS (editorial bd. publ. Sci. 1968-70), Soc. Chem. Industry, Wash. Acad. Sci., Sigma Xi, Tau Beta Pi, Phi Lambda Upsilon, Phi Kappa Phi, Gamma Alpha. Clubs: Cosmos (Washington); Chemists (N.Y.C.). Subspecialties: Polymer chemistry; Natural and synthetic fibers. Home: 4101 Linnean Ave Washington DC 20008 Office: 3300 Whitehaven St NW Washington DC 20007

HARRIS, RONALD DAVID, chemical engineer, food company research executive; b. Norman, Okla., Apr. 9, 1938; s. Loyd Ervin and Maurine Cora (Dill) H.; m. Judith Anne Wright, July 28, 1962; children—Todd David, Scott Howard, Susanna Katherine. B.Chem. Engring., Ohio State U., 1961, M.Sc., 1961; M.B.A., U. Cin., 1971, postgrad. in law, 1970-71. Chem. engr.-foods Procter & Gamble Co., Cin., 1961-64, group leader-foods, 1964-71; mgr. food product devel. Clorox Co., Oakland, Calif., 1971-73, dir. research and devel., 1973-77; v.p. research and devel. Anderson Clayton Foods, Dallas, 1977-81, v.p. tech. and productivity, 1981—; mem. com. for tomorrow Ohio State U., 1980—, chem. adv. com. U. Tex.-Dallas, 1981—, food and nutrition adv. com. U. Minn., St. Paul, 1981—. Patentee absorbent bleaching process, fluffy frosting mixes. Mem. Richardson City Council (Tex.), 1983—; trustee San Ramon Valley Unified Sch. Dist., Danville, Calif., 1977; bd. dirs. Richardson Symphony Orch., 1982-85, Richardson YMCA, 1984—, Heard Natural Sci. Mus., 1985—. Mem. Inst. Food Technologists, Am. Chem. Soc., Am. Oil Chemists Soc., Richardson C. of C. (pres. 1982), Tau Beta Pi, Phi Eta Sigma, Phi Lambda Upsilon, Delta Mu Delta, Kappa Sigma. Republican. Methodist. Club: Lions (pres. 1982) (Richardson). Current work: Research and development of new and improved food and household chemical products. Subspecialties: Food science and technology; Chemical engineering. Home: 2503 Springwood Ln Richardson TX 75081 Office: WL Clayton Research Ctr 3333 N Central Expressway Richardson TX 75080

HARRIS, RONALD LEE, chemical company executive; b. Lincoln, Nebr., Aug. 1, 1942; s. Lewis Eldon and Antonia (Synovec) H.; m. Christine Marie Olson, June 19, 1965; children—Jennifer, Brett. B.S. in Bus. and Chemistry, U. Nebr., 1965, M.B.A., 1968. Cert. Adminstrv. mgr. Vice pres. Harris Labs., Inc., Lincoln, 1969-74, pres., 1974-84, vice-chmn., chief exec. officer, 1984—; pres. Fin. Systems, Inc., Kearney, Nebr., 1982—; pres. Harris Tech. Group, Inc., Lincoln, 1984—; pres. Assoc. Industries of Lincoln, 1975; pres. Am. Council of Independent Labs., Washington, 1982-84. Mem. adv. bd. Lincoln Parks and Recreation Dept., 1975-80; bd. dirs. Lower Platte South Natural Resources, Lincoln, 1978-82; commr. Nebr. Commn. on Drugs, Lincoln, 1982; mem. council Greater Lincoln Pvt. Industry Council, 1983. Recipient Disting. Service award Am. Council Independent Labs., 1970, Giesenbier award Nebr. Jaycees; named Outstanding Young Men Nebr. Jaycees, 1974, 74. Mem. Young Pres.' Orgn., Assn. Official Racing Chemists, Nebr. Assn. Commerce and Industry, Am. Pharm. Assn., Inst. Food Technologists, Lincoln C. of C. (bd. dirs. 1979-81). . Office: Harris Tech Group Inc 624 Peach St Box 80837 Lincoln NE 68501

HARRIS, ROY M(ARTIN), animal geneticist and physiologist, educator, researcher, cons.; b. Ogden, Utah, July 7, 1927; s. LeRoy and Cornelia (Sanders) H.; m. Mary E.; children: Mark (adopted), Chad. B.S., Utah State Agrl. Coll., 1952; M.S., Utah State U., 1954, Ph.D., 1970. Researcher Utah State U., 1952-54; asst. prof. animal genetics and reproductive physiology Calif. Poly. State U., 1954-62, asso. prof., 1962-68, prof., 1968—; cons. research div Eli Lilly, 1979-81, Govt. Mexico, 1980—. Author: The Occurrence of Estrus in the Domestic Ewe, 1974; Contbr. articles to profl. jours. Served with U.S. Army, 1944-46. Eli Lilly grantee, 1979-81; Syntex grantee, 1978-79; CARE grantee, 1977-78. Mem. Am. Soc. Animal Sci., Am. Registry Cert. Animal Scientists. Current Work: Chemotherapy of bio-rhythms in cattle, sheep and horses; genetic studies of horse motion as it relates to speed, development coring mechanism for muscle tissue. Subspecialties: Genetics and genetic engineering (agriculture); Animal physiology. Home: 934 Longhorn Ln Arroyo Grande CA 93420 Office: Dept Animal/Vet Sci Calif Poly State U San Luis Obispo CA 93407

HARRIS, THOMAS R., biomedical engineering educator; b. San Angelo, Tex., Feb. 19, 1937; s. Loyd Franklin and Rubye (Mitchell) H.; m. Carol Ann Cox, June 1, 1963; children—Calvin Thomas, Andrew Mitchell. B.S., Tex. A&M U., 1958, M.S., 1962; Ph.D., Tulane U., 1964; M.D., Vanderbilt U., 1974. Asst. prof. chem. engring. Vanderbilt U., Nashville, 1964-67, assoc. prof. chem. engring. and biomed. engring., 1967-76, prof., 1976—, assoc. prof. medicine, 1980—; cons. NIH, Bethesda, Md., 1980—. Contbr. articles to profl. jours. Served to 2d lt. U.S. Army, 1958-59. NIH and Am. Heart Assn. grantee, 1974—. Mem. Am. Physiol. Soc., Am. Inst. Chem. Engrs., Am. Soc. Engring. Edn., IEEE, Biomed. Engring. Soc. (pres. 1985—). Baptist. Current work: Physiol. transport phenomena, lung fluid balance, med. computing, math. modeling of physiol. exchange processes, cardiopulmonary physiology. Subspecialties: Biomedical engineering; Physiology (biology). Home: 415 Fairfax Ave Nashville TN 37212 Office: Vanderbilt U Room B-1318 Med Ctr N Nashville TN 37235

HARRIS, THOMAS VAN, research chemist; b. Cambridge, Md., Oct. 19, 1951; s. Van Thomas and Claire Semmes (Laskowski) H.; m. Diane Barbara Van Arsdale, July 24, 1982. B.S. in Chemistry, Coll. William and Mary, 1973; M.S. in Chemistry, Cornell U., 1976, Ph.D. in Chemistry, 1978. Postdoctoral research asst. Princeton U., N.J., 1978-79; research chemist Gulf Oil Corp., Pitts., 1979-85, Chevron Research Co., 1985—. Contbr. articles to profl. jours. Mem. Am. Chem. Soc. Roman Catholic. Club: Western Pa. Woodworkers (Pitts.) Current works: Inorganic and organometallic chemistry, catlysis, petrochemicals, enhanced oil recovery, physical chemistry at high pressure. Subspecialties: Organometallics; Catalysis chemistry. Home: 183 Seaview Dr Benicia CA 94510 Office: Chevron Research Co PO Box 1627 Richmond CA 94802

HARRIS, WESLEY LEROY, aeronautics educator, consultant; b. Richmond, Va., Oct. 29, 1941; s. William M. and Rosa P. (Minor) H.; m. Myrtle A. Satterwhite, June 14, 1960; children: Wesley, Zelda, Kamau, Kalomo. B.Aero.Engring., U. Va., 1964; M.A., Princeton U., 1965, Ph.D., 1968. Asst. prof. U. Va., Charlottesville, 1968-70; assoc. prof. So. U., Baton Rouge, 1970-71, U. Va., 1971-72; prof. aeronautics and astronautics MIT, Cambridge, Mass., 1972—; mem. U.S. Army Sci. Bd., Washington, 1979—; bd. dirs. Nat. Tech. Assocs., Inc., Washington, 1978-82. Editor: Jour. Nat. Tech. Assocs, 1978—. Recipient M.L. King Jr. achievement award, 1978; Black Achiever award YMCA, 1979; Sizer award MIT, 1979. Mem. Am. Helicopter Soc., AIAA, Nat. Tech. Assn., N.Y. Acad. Scis., Sigma Xi, Tau Beta Pi, Phi Beta Sigma. Current Work: Theoretical transonics: analytical and exptl. aeroacoustics. Subspecialties: Aeronautical engineering; Acoustical engineering. Home: 19 Rangeley Rd Newton MA 02165 Office: MIT Room 37-435 77 Massachusetts Ave Cambridge MA 02139

HARRISON, ANNA JANE, chemist, educator; b. Benton City, Mo., Dec. 23, 1912; d. Albert S.J. and Mary (Jones) H. Student, Lindenwood Coll., 1929-31, L.H.D. (hon.), 1977; A.B., U. Mo., 1933, B.S., 1935, M.A., 1937, Ph.D., 1940, D.Sc. (hon.), 1983, Tulane U., 1975, Smith Coll., 1975, Williams Coll., 1978, Am. Internat. Coll., 1978, Vincennes U., 1978, Lehigh U., 1979, Hood Coll., 1979, Hartford U., 1979, Worcester Poly. Inst., 1979, Suffolk U., 1979, Eastern Mich. U., 1983, L.H.D., Emmanuel Coll., 1983. Instr. chemistry Newcomb Coll., 1940-42, asst. prof., 1942-45; asst. prof. chemistry Mt. Holyoke Coll., 1945-47, asso. prof., 1947-50, prof., 1950-79, prof. emeritus, 1979—, chmn. dept., 1960-66, William R. Kenan, Jr. prof., 1976-79; Mem. Nat. Sci. Bd., 1972-78. Contbr. articles to profl. jours. Recipient Frank Forrest award Am. Ceramic Soc., 1949; James Flack Norris award in chem. edn. Northeastern sect. Am. Chem. Soc., 1977; AAUW Sarah Berliner fellow Cambridge U., Eng., 1952-53; Am. Chem. Soc. Petroleum Research Fund Internat. fellow NRC Can., 1959-60; recipient Coll. Chemistry Tchr. award Mfg. Chemists Assn., 1969. Mem. AAAS (dir. 1979—, pres. 1983), Am. Chem. Soc. (chmn. div. chem. edn. 1971, pres. 1978, dir. 1976-79, award in chem. edn. 1982), Internat. Union Pure and Applied Chemistry (U.S. nat. com. 1978-81), Sigma Xi. Subspecialty: Physical chemistry. Address: Dept Chemistry Mount Holyoke Coll South Hadley MA 01075

HARRISON, DONALD CAREY, cardiologist; b. Blount County, Ala., Feb. 24, 1934; s. Walter Carey and Sovola (Thompson) H.; m. Laura Jane McAnnally, July 24, 1955; children—Douglas, Elizabeth, Donna Marie. B.S. in Chemistry, Birmingham So. Coll., 1954; M.D., U. Ala., 1958. Diplomate: Am. Bd. Internal Medicine (cardiovascular disease). Intern, asst. resident Peter Bent Brigham Hosp., 1958-60; fellow in cardiology Harvard U., 1961, NIH, 1961-63; mem. faculty Stanford U. Med. Sch., 1963—, chief div. cardiology, 1967—, prof. medicine, 1971—; chief cardiology Stanford U. Hosp., 1967—, William G. Irwin prof. cardiology, 1972—; cons. to local hosps., industry, govt. Editorial bd.: Am. Jour. Cardiology, 1970-78, Chest, Heart and Lung Jour, 1973-78, Drugs; Practical Cardiology, Clin. Cardiology; Contbr. articles to med. jours., chpts. to books. Served with USPHS, 1961-63. Fellow Interam. Soc. Cardiology (v.p. 1980—), Am. Coll. Cardiology (membership chmn., v.p. 1972-73, sec. 1969-70, trustee 1972-78), Am. Heart Assn. (fellow council circulation, clin. cardiology and basic sci., chmn. program com. 1972-76, chmn. publs. com. 1976-80, pres.-elect 1980-81, pres. 1981—); mem. Am. Soc. Clin. Investigation, Am. Fedn. Clin. Research, Am. Soc. Pharmacology and Exptl. Therapeutics, Am. Assn. Physicians, Am. Physiol. Soc., Calif. Acad. Medicine, A.C.P., Assn. U. Cardiologists. Current Work: Design of computer based arrhyghmia program; pharmacology of antiarrhythmic drugs. Subspecialty: Cardiology. Home: 151 Mountain View Ave Los Altos CA 94022 Office: Room C-248 Stanford Univ Med Sch Stanford CA 94305

HARRISON, J(AMES) M(ERRITT), geologist; b. Regina, Sask., Can., Sept. 20, 1915; s. Roland O. and Vera F. (Merritt) H.; m. Herta von Boehmer Sliter, May 1944; 1 child, Norman. M.A., Queen's U., Kingston, Ont., 1941, Ph.D., 1943; hon. doctorate U. Man., Queen's U., McMaster U., Calgary U., U. N.B., Carleton U. Geologist Geol. Survey Can., Ottawa, 1943-64, div. chief, 1955-56, dir., 1956-64; sr. asst. dep. minister Dept. Mines and Resources, Ottawa, 1964-72; asst. dir. gen. (sci.) UNESCO, Paris, 1973-76; chmn. Sci. Inst., Northwest Terrs., 1983—; cons. to various orgns. and agys.; chmn. Can. com.

UNESCO, 1984—. Decorated Companion of Can.; recipient Achievement award Pub. Service of Can., 1970. Fellow Royal Soc. Can. (pres. 1967-68), Geol. Assn. Can. (pres. 1960-61, Logan medal 1969); mem. Can. Inst. Mining and Metallurgy (Blaylock medal 1966) pres. 1969-70), Internat. Council Sci. Unions (pres. 1966-68); fgn. assoc. Nat. Acad. Scis. Current work: Science policy and organization; natural resource policy and management. Subspecialty: Economic geology. Home and Office: 4 Kippewa Dr Ottawa ON K1S 3G4 Canada

HARRISON, JEAN BURCH, neurophysiologist, naturalist; b. Paris, Feb. 15, 1936; came to U.S., 1936; d. George and Betty (Brand) Burch; m. Theodore Harrison (div.); 1 child, Eleanor; m. Richard Siegler; children—Elisabeth, Catherine. B.A., Radcliffe Coll., 1958, M.A., 1959, Ph.D., 1962. Instr. Harvard U., Cambridge, Mass., 1962-65; asst. prof. Wellesley Coll., Mass., 1965-71, assoc. prof., 1971-74; lectr. UCLA, 1974-80, research physiologist, 1980—. Contbr. articles to profl. jours. NSF grantee. Mem. Soc. for Neurosci., AAAS, Animal Behavior Soc. Mem. Soc. of Friends. Current work: Auditory physiology, cognitive electrophysiology. Subspecialties: Animal physiology; Neurophysiology. Home: 1712 N Beverly Glen Blvd Los Angeles CA 90077Office: Physiology Dept UCLA Los Angeles CA 90024

HARRISON, JOHN HENRY, IV, chemistry and biology educator, research scientist; b. Pitts., Aug. 8, 1936; s. John Henry, III and Jeanne (Leach) H.; m. Judith Henrietta Cline, Dec. 27, 1962; children: John Henry, Robert Nathaniel. B.S., U. Tex.-Austin, 1958, Ph.D., 1964. Postdoctoral research fellow Harvard Med. Sch., Boston, 1964-67; asst. prof. chemistry U. N.C., Chapel Hill, 1967-72, assoc. prof. chemistry, 1972-76, prof. chemistry and biology, 1976—, assoc. provost, 1985—; vis. scientist dept. biochemistry Oxford (Eng.) U., 1978-79; vis. prof. chemistry U. P.R., Mayaguez, 1982. Contbr. writings in field to sci. publs. Served to capt. USMC, 1958-60. Recipient Career Devel. Award U.S. NIH, 1974-79; Jane Coffin Childs fellow Jane Coffin Childs Meml. Fund for Med. Research, 1965-67. Mem. Am. Soc. Biol. Chemists, N.Y. Acad. Scis., Am. Chem. Soc., Sigma Xi, Alpha Chi Sigma. Republican. Current Work: Physicochemical investigation of mechanism of action of pyridine nucleotide dependent dehydrogenase enzymes. Subspecialties: Biochemistry (medicine); Biophysical chemistry. Home: 806 Kenmore Rd Chapel Hill NC 27514 Office: Univ NC Dept Chemistry Venable Hall Chapel Hill NC 27514

HARRISON, KEITH GRAHAM, ecologist; b. Dowagiac, Mich., Jan. 10, 1950; s. John Barnard Harrison and Maxine Pearl (Lewis) McCormick; m. Linda Diane Dodson, Apr. 3, 1976; 1 child, Nathan Lewis. B.S., Mich. State U., 1972; M.A., Western Mich. U., 1974. Chief environ. planner Michiana Area Council of Govts., South Bend, Ind., 1975-78; environ. program coordinator Tri-County Regional Planning Commn., Lansing, Mich., 1978-79; project ecologist Snell Environ. Group, Inc., Lansing, 1979-80; project cons. Mich. Dept. Pub. Health, Lansing, 1980-84; sr. environ. specialist Mich. Toxic Substance Control Commn., Lansing, 1984—. Author: Cass County, Michigan: A Natural History, 1979. Contbr. articles to profl. jours. Upjohn Co. fellow, 1973, 74; grantee Western Mich. U., 1974. Mem. Ecol. Soc. Am. (cert ecologist), Mich. Assn. Environ. Profls., Mich. Audubon Soc. (bd. dirs. 1976—), 7th Mich. Vol. Inf. Co. B., Inc. (treas. 1983—), Sons of Union Vets. of Civil War (camp comdr. 1983—, Mich. dept. comdr. 1985—), Sons of Revolution in Mich. (state sec. 1985—), Soc. Mayflower Descs. in Mich. Republican. Presbyterian. Current work: Toxicological impacts of solid and hazardous waste disposal alternatives on terrestrial and aquatic ecosystems, and biological alternatives to pest control. Subspecialties: Ecosystems analysis; Environmental toxicology. Home: 1837 Shadywood Lane Okemos MI 48864 Office: Mich Toxic Substance Control Commn PO Box 30026 Lansing MI

HARRISON, MARTIN BERNARD, plant pathology educator; b. N.Y.C., Dec. 8, 1924; s. Harold and Belle (Drucker) H.; children: Amy R., Juliet R. B.S., Cornell U., 1950; Ph.D., 1955; M.S., Kans. State U., 1951. Mem. faculty Cornell U., 1955—, assoc. prof. plant pathology, 1960—. Contbr. articles to profl. jours. Served with AUS, 1943-46. Mem. Am. Phytopathol. Soc., Soc. Nematologists, European Soc. Nematologists. Current Work: Plant parasitc nematode biology and control. Subspecialty: Plant pathology. Home: 516 Warren Rd Ithaca NY 14850 Office: Plant Pathology Cornell U Ithaca NY 14852

HARRISON, STEADMAN DARNELL, JR., toxicologist, cons.; b. New Albany, Miss., Apr. 13, 1947; s. Steadman Darnell and Peggy Anne (Caldwell) H.; m. Anita Hardy, June 6, 1969; 1 child, Steadman Darnell III. B.S., Miss. State U., 1969; M.S., Ind. U., 1972, Ph.D. (NIH predoctoral fellow), 1973. Diplomate: Am. Bd. Toxicology. Research pharmacologist to head pharmacology sect. So. Research Inst., Birmingham, Ala., 1973-80; assoc. prof. toxicology U. Ky., 1980-84; adj. assoc. prof. U. Ala.-Birmingham, 1984—; head tumor biology and treatment sect. So. Research Inst., Birmingham, 1984-85, head chemotherapy div., 1985—; researcher, cons. Contbr. articles and abstracts to profl. jours. Mem. Soc. Toxicology, Am. Assn. Cancer Research, Royal Soc. Chemistry, Nat. Acad. Clin. Biochemistry, Soc. Risk Analysis, Sigma Xi. Baptist. Patentee in field. Current Work: Mechanisms of toxicity, vitamin A analogs, arachidonate metabolism, metals and alkylating agts., calcium; experimental therapeutics. Subspecialties: Toxicology (medicine); Pharmacology. Office: So Research Inst PO Box 55305 Birmingham AL 35255

HARRISON, YVONNE ELOIS, pharmacologist; b. Norfolk, Va., Apr. 29, 1939; d. Herman H. and Georgia M. (Hall) H.; m. Melvin C. Johnson, Sept. 27, 1975. B.S., Howard U., 1959, M.S., 1970, Ph.D., 1972. Research asst. Burroughs Wellcome & Co., 1964-69; research assoc. dept. pharmacology Howard U., 1970-72; biol. research coordinator Hoffmann-La Roche, Inc., 1972-73, asst. dir. dept. exptl. therapeutics, 1974-79, asst. dir. pharm. research and devel., 1980-82, dir. pharm. research and development coordination, 1983-84, dir. research and devel. coordination, 1984-85, asst. to v.p. research and devel., 1985—. Bd. dirs. Consumer Health Info. and Resource Center, 1981-84. Named Black Achiever in Industry YMCA, 1974; recipient Twin Tribute to Women in Industry YWCA, 1975; recipient Disting. Corporate Alumni award Nat. Assn. Equal Opportunity in Higher Edn., 1982. Mem. AAAS, Soc. Research Adminstrn., Ind. Research Inst., Am. Pharm. Assn. Acad. Pharm. Scis., Am. Physiol. Soc., Am. Soc. Pharmacology and Exptl. Therapeutics, Assn. Women in Sci., Fedn. Am. Scientists, Fedn. Am. Socs. Exptl. Biology, Internat. Soc. Ecotoxicity and Environ. Safety, N.Y. Acad. Scis., Sigma Xi. Current Work: Evaluation of research programs and priorities for the research division, comprising 1100 people in the major therapeutic areas of preclinical and clinical development. Subspecialties: Pharmacology; Biochemistry (medicine). Office: 340 Kingsland St Nutley NJ 07110

HARRIS-WARRICK, RONALD MORGAN, neurobiologist, educator; b. Berkeley, Calif., July 28, 1949; s. Morgan and Marjorie Ruth (Mason) Harris-W.; m. Rebecca Lamar, Apr. 5, 1975; children: Sheridan, Thomas. B.A., Stanford U., 1970, Ph.D. in Genetics, 1976. NIH fellow dept. neurobiology Stanford U., 1976-78; Muscular Dystrophy Assn. fellow dept. neurobiology Harvard U., 1978-80; asst. prof. sect. neurobiology and behavior Cornell U., 1980—; mem. faculty Marine Biol. Lab., Woods Hole, Mass., 1978-85. Contbr. articles to profl. jours. NIH grantee, 1981—; Muscular Dystrophy Assn. grantee, 1981—. Mem. Soc. Neurosci., AAAS, Sierra Club, Audubon Soc., Phi Beta Kappa. Current Work: Mechanism of action of neuromodulators; modulation of motor activity by biogenic amines. Subspecialties: Neurophysiology; Neurochemistry. Office: Section of Neurobiology and Behavior Cornell University Ithaca NY 14850

HARROFF, H(OMER) HUGH, JR., veterinarian, researcher; b. Youngstown, Ohio, Apr. 23, 1941; s. Homer Hugh and Lois Agnes (Miller) H.; m. Judith Ann Pfau, Aug. 22, 1964; children—Brian Hugh, Bradley Richard, Allyson Lynn. D.V.M., Ohio State U., 1965. Vet. practitioner Canfield Vet. Clinic (Ohio), 1967-69; chief div. meat inspection Ohio Dept. Agr., Columbus, 1969-74; assoc. prof. Southwestern Med. Sch., Dallas, 1974-77; chief veterinarian Columbus labs. Battelle Meml. Inst., 1977—. Chmn. Citizens Com. for Sch. Bond Issue, Gahanna, Ohio, 1976, 82; pres. Gahanna High Sch. Athletic Boosters, 1984. Served to capt. U.S. Army, 1965-67. Mem. Am. Assn. for Lab. Animal Sci. (chmn. 5th dist. arrangements com. 1984), AVMA, Am. Soc. Lab. Animal Practitioners, Ohio Vet. Med. Assn., Am. Coll. Toxicology. Current work: Laboratory animal medicine, toxicology, pharmacology. Subspecialties: Laboratory animal medicine; Toxicology (agriculture). Home: 606 Fawndale Pl Gahanna OH 43230 Office: Battelle Meml Inst 505 King Ave Columbus OH 43201

HARSHBARGER, JOHN CARL, JR., pathobiologist; b. Weyers Cave, Va., May 9, 1936; s. John Carl and Myn Alma (Baker) H. B.A., Bridgewater Coll., 1957; M.S., Va. Poly. Inst., 1959; Ph.D., Rutgers U., 1962. NSF postdoctoral research assoc. Insect Pathology Lab., U.S. Dept. Agr., Beltsville, Md., 1962-64; asst. research pathobiologist U. Calif., Irvine, 1964-67; dir. registry of tumors in lower animals Nat. Mus. Natural History, Smithsonian Instn., Washington, 1967—. Editor: (with others) Neoplasms and Related Disorders of Invertebrate and Lower Vertebrate Animals, 1969, Aquatic Pollutants and Biologic Effects with Emphasis on Neoplasia, 1977, Phyletic Approaches to Cancer, 1981; contbr. (with others) articles to profl. jours. Mem. AAAS, Am. Assn. for Cancer Research, Southeastern Cancer Research Assn., Interagy. Collaborative Group on Environ. Carcinogenesis, Internat. Assn. for Comparative Research on Leukemia and Related Diseases (world com. 1979—), N.Y. Acad. Scis., Soc. for Invertebrate Pathology (sec. 1974-76, v.p. 1984-86), Sigma Xi (sec. D.C. chpt. 1976-78, v.p. 1978-80, pres. 1980-82). Club: Cosmos (Washington). Current Work: Pathology of neoplasms in ectothermic vertebrate and invertebrate animals. Subspecialties: Pathobiology; Oncology. Home: 2038 Columbia Pike Apt 3 Arlington VA 22204 Office: Nat Mus Natural History Smithsonian Inst Room W216A Washington DC 20560

HART, FRED CLINTON, environmental consultant; b. Sharon, Pa., July 5, 1940; s. Fred Clinton and Elizabeth (Innis) H.; m. Elizabeth H. Semple, Mar. 13, 1982; 1 dau., Meredith. B.C.E., Cornell U., 1963; M.S., Stanford U., 1964; M.B.A., U. Conn., 1970. Registered profl. engr., N.Y. With Dorr-Oliver, Inc., Stamford, Conn., 1966-68, Internat. Paper Co., N.Y.C., 1969-70; commr. Dept. Air Resources, City of N.Y., 1970-74; pres. Fred C. Hart Assocs., Inc., N.Y.C., 1975—, dir., 1975—; chmn. bd. Alternate Gas Inc., 1983—; lectr. toxicology Sch. Journalism, NYU. Contbr. articles to profl. jours. Served with U.S. Army, 1964-66. Decorated Bronze Star medal; named Outstanding Grad. U. Conn. Bus. Sch., 1972. Mem. Air Pollution Control Assn., ASCE, ASME. Subspecialty: Environmental engineering. Office: Fred C Hart Associates Inc 530 Fifth Ave New York NY 10036

HART, JOHN BIRDSALL, physics educator; b. Hamilton, Ohio, Aug. 24, 1924; s. John Wilson and Elizabeth (Birdsall) H.; m. Agnes Marie Roegner, June 17, 1948 (dec. Oct. 1960); 1 dau., Mary Agnes. B.S., Xavier U., Cin., 1948, M.S., 1950. Instr. physics Xavier U., 1950-56, asst. prof., 1956-62, assoc. prof., 1962-68, prof., 1968—, chmn. physics, 1958-71, 82-83; vis. prof., cons. Fla. State U., 1967-68; cons. prof. Ohio U., 1970-71, Miami U., summer 1974. Author: (with Richard Gadske) The National Curriculum in Navigation for U.S. Naval Reserve, 1957, Lectures in Atomic Physics; contbr. articles to profl. jours. Chmn. exhibits com. Cin. Ctr. Sci. and Industry, 1966-67. Served with USNR, 1943-46. Mem. Am. Assn. Physics Tchrs., Ohio Acad. Sci., Am. Phys. Soc., Space Studies Inst., Sigma Pi Sigma. Patentee. Current Work: Foundations of operational general physics. Subspecialties: Operational general physics; Psychophysics. Home: 3836 Ledgewood Dr Cincinnati OH 45207 Office: Xavier University 3800 Victory Pkwy Cincinnati OH 45207

HART, LAWRENCE AUSTIN, chemist, consultant; b. Hollywood, Calif., Feb. 16, 1960; s. Robert Ray and Faye Irene (Wohlers) H. B.S. in Chem., Calif. State U.-Fullerton, 1982. Quality control and research and devel. supr. Hitco Materials, Santa Ana, Calif., 1979-82; chemist Hart's Labs., Brea, Calif., 1981—; research and devel. supr. in chem. tech. Xenotech Labs., Irvine, Calif., 1982—; cons. U.S. State Dept., Washington, 1980. Mem. Soc. Plastics Engrs., AAAS, Am. Chem. Soc. Delta Sigma Phi. Republican. Episcopalian. Current work: Tendon and ligament bioprosthesis; long distance prototype electric vehicle; research in chemical crystalizations. Subspecialties: Biochemistry (medicine); Aerospace engineering and technology. Home: PO Box 393 Brea CA 92621-0393

HART, RAYMOND KENNETH, materials consultant; b. Newcastle, N.S.W., Australia, Feb. 15, 1928; s. William Kenneth and Olive (Palmer) H.; m. Betty Joyce Bingemann, Sept. 5, 1952; children: Timothy Kenneth, Rowena Jane. A.S.T.C., Sydney Tech. Coll., 1949; D.I.C., Imperial Coll., London, 1952; Ph.D., U. Cambridge, Eng., 1955. Research officer Aeronautical Research Labs., Melbourne, Australia, 1955-58; research scientist Argonne Nat. Lab., Ill., 1958-66, sr. research scientist, 1967-69; prin. research scientist Ga. Inst. Tech., 1970-75; pres., dir. research Pasat Research Assocs., Inc., Atlanta, 1976—, materials cons., expert witness. Contbr. articles to profl. jours. Com. chmn. Boy Scouts Am., 1965-67, com. mem., 1971-72. Recipient NASA cert. of recognition, 1976. Fellow Inst. Physics (London), Royal Australian Chem. Inst.; mem. Am. Acad. Forensic Scis., Electron Microscopy Soc. Am., Am. Phys. Soc., Sigma Xi. Republican. Episcopalian. Current Work: High resolution analytical electron microscopy, material defect and failure analysis, environ. metal toxins, forensic sci. Subspecialties: Metallurgy; Microscopy. Home and Office: 585 Royervista Dr Atlanta GA 30342

HART, ROBERT JOSEPH, hydrologist, biologist; b. Omaha, Oct. 3, 1953; s. Joseph Montraville Jr. and Wilma Harriet (Stutt) H.; m. Kimberly Ann McKenzie, Sept. 2, 1978; B.S., U. Nebr.-Omaha 1976; postgrad. U. Nebr., Lincoln, 1979, U. Kans., 1980—. Biol. aide U.S. Fish and Wildlife Service, Marquette, Mich., 1977; hydrologic technologist U.S. Bur. Land Mgmt., Rawlins, Wyo., 1978; hydrologist U.S. Geol. Survey, Lawrence, Kans., 1979—. Author tech. papers. Mem. Wildlife Mgmt. Inst., Am. Geophys. Union. Current work: Water quality of lakes, streams and groundwater; investigation of pesticide concentrations in lakes and streams; investigation of hazardous waste sites. Subspecialties: Hydrology; Limnology. Office: US Geol Survey WRD 1950 Constant Ave Lawrence KS 66045

HART, ROGER DOUGLAS, construction company executive, energy physicist; b. Pontiac, Mich., Sept. 21, 1946; s. Earl Joseph and Fleurdelis Lola (Taffer) H.; m. Anna Santa-croce; children—Sherri Ann, Melissa Nicole, Elizabeth Danielle. B.S., Eastern Mich. U., 1969, M.S., 1971; cert. Am. Soc. Nondestructive Testing, 1983, Tech. Seminar, 1984. Cert. reliability engr., quality engr., inspection engr. Instr. physics Southwestern Mich. Coll., Dowagiac, 1970-72; supr. engring. lab. Textron Corp., Meadville, Pa., 1972-74; sr. engr. Bechtel Power Corp., San Francisco, 1974-76; corp. supr. reliability and adminstrn. N.Y. State Electricity and Gas, Binghamton, 1976-81; corp. officer for quality Perini Corp., Framingham, Mass., 1981—; proctor engring. SUNY-Binghamton and Am. Soc. Quality Control, 1978-79, edn. chmn., 1979-80; part time instr. engring. SUNY-Binghamton, 1979; standard reviewer Internat. Atomic Energy Agy., 1984—. Author, editor teach. writings in field. Active New Eng. Area, Boy Scouts Am., 1984. Grad. teaching fellow Eastern Mich. U., Ypsilanti, 1969; instn. grantee NSF, 1973; 1983. Mem. Am. Soc. Quality Control (nat. moderator 1983, mem. constrn. tech. com.), Am. Phys. Soc. (alt. energy div.), Am. Nuclear Soc., Am. Concrete Inst., ASME (Code Stamp award nat. bd.), Am. Mgmt. Assn. Current work: Further development of energy/power generation science and technology. Subspecialty: Fusion. Office: Perini Corp 73 Mt Wayte Ave Framingham MA 01701

HARTER, DONALD HARRY, medical educator; b. Breslau, Germany, May 16, 1933; came to U.S., 1940, naturalized, 1945; s. Harry Morton and Leonor Evelyn (Goldmann) H.; m. Lee Grossman, Dec. 18, 1960 (div. 1976); children: Kathryne, Jennifer, Amy, David; m. Rikki Horne, May 18, 1985. A.B., U. Pa., 1953; M.D., Columbia U., 1957. Diplomate: Am. Bd. Psychiatry and Neurology. Intern in medicine Yale-New Haven Med. Center, 1957-58; asst. resident, then resident neurology N.Y. Neurol. Inst., 1958-61; guest investigator Rockefeller U., 1963-66; mem. faculty Columbia Coll. Physicians and Surgeons, 1960-75, prof. neurology and microbiology, 1973-75; vis. fellow Clare Hall, Cambridge, Eng., 1973-74; attending neurologist N.Y. Neurol. Inst., Presbyn. Hosp., 1973-75; Charles L. Mix prof., chmn. dept. neurology Northwestern U., 1975-85, Benjamin and Virginia T. Boshes prof., 1985—; chmn. dept. neurology Northwestern Meml. Hosp., Chgo., 1975—; mem. adv. com. on fellowships Nat. Multiple Sclerosis Soc., 1976-79, chmn., 1977-79; mem. Nat. Commn. on Venereal Disease, HEW, 1970-72; mem. med. adv. bd. Am. Parkinsons' Disease Assn., 1976—, Myasthenia Gravis Found., 1980—; mem. sci. adv. council Nat. ALS Found., 1978-85; mem. neurol. disorders program project rev. A com. Nat. Inst. Neurol. and Communicative Disorders and Stroke, NIH, HHS, 1981-85. Editorial bd.: Neurology, 1976-82, Anns. of Neurology, 1983—; adv. bd.: Archives of Virology, 1975-81. USPHS spl. fellow, 1963-66; Am. Cancer Soc. scholar, 1973-74; Guggenheim fellow, 1973; recipient Joseph Mather Smith prize Columbia U., 1970, Lucy G. Moses award, 1970, 72. Mem. Am. Soc. Clin. Investigation, Am. Neurol. Assn. (membership adv. com. 1980-82), Am. Assn. Neuropathologists, Soc. Exptl. Biology and Medicine, Assn. Univ. Profs. Neurology, Infectious Disease Soc. Am., Soc. Neurosci., Am. Acad. Neurology (alt. rep. to Council of Med. Splty. Socs. 1979-82), Am. Assn. Immunologists, Am. Soc. Microbiology, Soc. Gen. Microbiology, Am. Epilepsy Soc., Am. Assn. for Study Headache, Am. Assn. for History Medicine, Pan Am Med. Assn., Phi Beta Kappa, Sigma Xi. Current Work: Virus-nerve cell interactions; neurobiology of viral infections; slow viral diseases of the nervous system. Subspecialties: Neurology; Virology (medicine). Home: 330 W Diversey Pkwy Chicago IL 60657 Office: Dept Neurology Northwestern U Med Sch 303 E Chicago Ave Chicago IL 60611

HARTH, ERICH, physicist; b. Vienna, Austria, Nov. 16, 1919; s. Martin Nassau and Sofie H.; m. Dorothy E. Feldmann, Feb. 4, 1951; children: Peter, Rick. Ph.D., Syracuse U., 1951. Scientist U.S. Naval Research Lab., Washington, 1951-54; research assoc. dept. physics Duke U., Durham, N.C., 1954-57; asst. prof. dept. physics Syracuse (N.Y.) U., 1957-60, assoc. prof., 1960-65, prof., 1965—. Author: Windows on the Mind: Reflections on the Physical Basis of Consciousness, 1982; contbr. articles to profl. jours. Served with U.S. Army, 1944-46. Mem. Am. Phys. Soc., Soc. Neuroscience, AAAS, AAUP, N.Y. Acad. Scis. Current Work: Visual Information Processing and Sensory Motor Interactions; higher information processing; dynamic properties of neural systems. Subspecialties: Biophysics (physics); Sensory processes. Home: 4451 Lafayette Rd Jamesville NY 13078 Office: Dept Physics Syracuse U Syracuse NY 13210

HARTIG, ELMER OTTO, aerospace company executive; b. Evansville, Ind., Jan. 23, 1923; s. Otto E. and Frieda K. (Sunderman) H.; m. Evelyn Ann Cameron, Aug. 21, 1949; children—Pamela Ann, Jeffery C., Gregory W., Bradley A. B.S.E.E., U. N.H., 1946, M.S. in Physics, 1947; Ph.D., Harvard U., 1950. With Goodyear Aerospace Corp., Akron, Ohio, 1950—, dir. research and engring., Litchfield Park, Ariz., 1976, v.p. research and engring., Akron, 1976-81, v.p. ops., def. and energy, 1981-85, v.p. engring. and research, 1985—; mem. U.S. Army Sci. Bd., 1979-83. Fellow IEEE; mem. AIAA. Subspecialties: Aerospace engineering and technology; Electronics. Office: 1210 Massillon Rd Akron OH 44315

HARTMAN, PATRICK JAMES, mechanical engineer, researcher; b. Ann Arbor, Mich., Dec. 5, 1944; s. Norman James and Mary Jane (Cottrill) H.; m. Lee Ann Walraff, Oct. 5, 1968; children: Elizabeth Marie, Suzanne Caroline. B.M.E., Marquette U., 1968; M.S., U. R.I., 1974, Ph.D., 1976. Researcher U. R.I., Kingston, 1972-76; research engr. E. I. duPont de Nemours Co., Wilmington, Del., 1976-79; sr. ocean engr. Gould, Inc., Glen Burnie, Md., 1979-80; sr. mech. engr. USN, Washington, 1980—. Organizer, Community Assn. Tasks, Columbia, Md., 1982. Served to lt. (j.g.) USCG, 1969-72. Recipient Sci. award Bausch and Lomb, 1963, Vigil Honor award Boy Scouts Am., 1963; M. Kollinski Found. scholar, 1967; U. R.I. fellow, 1972-74. Mem. ASME (chmn. Ocean engring. div. 1982-84), Soc. Reliability Engrs., Nat. Soc. Profl. Engrs., Tau Beta Pi, Pi Tau Sigma. Current Work: Mechanical, ocean and reliability engineering using analyses on vector supercomputers to improve shipboard equipment design. Subspecialties: Mechanical engineering; Ocean engineering. Home: PO Box 922 Columbia MD 21044 Office: Naval Sea Systems Command Code 05MR Washington DC 20362

HARTMAN, ROBERT DALE, plant pathologist; b. Miami, Mar. 31, 1948; s. John Robert and Audrey Deloris (McGrady) H.; m. Linda Diane Rockwell, Oct. 25, 1969; children: Sandee, Dawn, Kristy, Robert. B.S., U. Fla., 1970, Ph.D., 1974. Research dir. Pan Am. Plant Co., West Chicago, Ill., 1974-77; partner, mgr. Hartman's, Palmdale, Fla., 1977-84; pres. Hartman's Plants, Inc., 1985—. Contbr. articles to profl. jours. Served with Army NG, 1970-76. NDEA fellow, 1971-72; U. Fla., 1971-72. Mem. Tissue Culture Assn., Am. Phytopathol. Soc., Am. Soc. Hort. Sci., Internat. Assn. Plant Tissue Culture. Current Work: In vitro propagation of certified plants; in vitro maintenance of genetic lines for breeding; disease elimination. Subspecialties: Plant cell and tissue culture; Plant virology. Home: 164 Blue Moon Ave Lake Placid FL 33852 Office: PO Box 90 County Rd 733 Palmdale FL 33944

HARTMAN, ROBERT JOHN, research chemist; b. Fort Wayne, Ind., July 20, 1926; s. George A. and Mary E. (Ditlinger) H.; m. Betty R. Brinker, May 22, 1984; children—Carolyn, Mark, Ann, James, Anita. B.S., DePaul U., 1952, M.S., Wayne State U., 1954. Research chemist BASF Wyandotte Corp., Mich., 1954. Contbr. articles to profl. jours. Patentee in field. Served with USN, 1944-46. Mem. Am. Chem. Soc. Roman Catholic. Current work: Currently involved in synthesis and evaluation of polyether polyols for use in polyurethane applications. Subspecialties: Organic chemistry; Polymer chemistry. Home: 14676 Yorkshire Southgate MI 48195 Office: BASF Wyandotte Corp Wyandotte MI 48192

HARTMANIS, JURIS, computer scientist, educator; b. Riga, Latvia, July 5, 1928; came to U.S., 1950, naturalized, 1956; s. Martins and Irma (Liepins) H.; m. Ellymaria Rehwald, May 16, 1959; children—Reneta, Martin, Audrey. Student, U. Marburg, 1947-49; M.A., U. Kansas City, 1951; Ph.D., Calif. Inst. Tech., 1955. Instr. Cornell U., Ithaca, N.Y., 1955-57, prof., 1965—, Walter R. Read prof. engring., 1980—, chmn. dept. computer sci., 1965-71, 77-82; asst. prof. Ohio State U., 1957-58; research mathematician Gen. Electric Research & Devel. Center, Schenectady, 1957-65. Author: (with R.E. Stearns) Algebraic Structure Theory For Sequential Machines, 1966, Feasible Computations and Provable Complexity Properties, 1978; Editor: SIAM Jour. Computing; assoc. editor: Jour. Computer and Systems Scis, 1966—, Jour. Math. Systems Theory, 1966—; co-editor: Springer-Verlag Lecture Notes in Computer Sci, 1973—. Mem. Am. Math. Soc., Math. Assn. Am., Assn. Computing Machinery, Sigma Xi. Current Work: Theory of computation, computatonal complexity. Subspecialties: Theoretical computer science; Foundations of computer science. Home: 324 Brookfield Rd Ithaca NY 14850

HARTMANN, DAN JOHN, petrophysical geologist; b. Fredericksburg, Tex., Apr. 16, 1940; s. Karl A. and Esther (Kneese) H.; m. Nancy LaNell Jones, Aug. 3, 1962; children—Laurie, Holly. B.S. in Geology, N.Mex. Inst. Mining and Tech., 1963. Exploration geologist Pan Am. Oil Co., Tyler, Tex., 1963-65; project geologist Pan Am./Amoco Oil Co., Houston, 1965-72; research scientist and supr. Amoco Research Co., Tulsa, 1972-77; supr. and mgr. Amoco Prdon. Co., Denver, 1977-81; vp., gen. mgr. Mitchell Energy Co., Denver, 1981-84; owner DJH Energy Cons., Fredericksburg, 1984—; lectr. Bd. devel. Okla. Christian Coll., 1980-82; mem. Bear Creek Water and Sanitation Dist., 1977-82. Mem. Am. Assn. Petroleum Geologists, Soc. Petroleum Engrs., Soc. Profl. Well Log Analysts, S. Tex. Geol. Soc., Gillespie County Hist. Soc. (life). Republican. Mem. Ch. of Christ. Current work: Petrophysical principles and applications to extraction of hydro-carbon from the reservoir. Subspecialties: Geology; Petroleum engineering. Home: Kerr Rt Box 631 Fredericksburg TX 78624 Office: DJH Energy Cons PO Box 271 Fredericksburg TX 78624

HARTMANN, ERNEST LOUIS, psychiatrist, educator; b. Vienna, Austria, Feb. 25, 1934; s. Heinz and Dora (Karplus) H.; m. Barbara Hengst, Dec. 26, 1961; m. Eva Neumann, Aug. 20, 1975; children: Jonathan, Katherine. A.B., U. Chgo., 1952; M.D., Yale U., 1958. Diplomate: Am. Bd. Psychiatry and Neurology. Clin. assoc. NIMH, Bethesda, Md., 1962-64; mem. faculty dept. psychiatry Tufts U. Sch. Medicine, Boston, 1964—; prof., 1975—; sr. psychiatrist, dir. Sleep Lab. Boston State Hosp., 1964-80; sr. psychiatrist, dir. Sleep Lab. and Sleep Disorders Center West-Ros Park Mental Health Center, Lemuel Shattuck Hosp., 1980—; dir. Sleep Disorders Ctr., Newton-Wellesley Hosp., 1984—; practice medicine specializing in psychiatry and sleep disorders, Boston, 1964—. Author: The Biology of Dreaming, 1967, Adolescents in a Mental Hospital, 1968, The Functions of Sleep, 1973, The Sleeping Pill, 1978, The Nightmare, 1984; contbr. numerous articles to profl. jours. Served to lt. comdr. USPHS, 1962-64. Recipient Holt prize Yale U., 1956; Psychopharmacology prize Am. Psychol. Assn., 1970. Mem. Am. Psychiat. Assn., Boston Psychoanalytic Soc. and Inst., AAAS, Am. Coll. Neuropsychopharmacology, Assn. Psycholphysiol. Study of Sleep. Current Work: Sleep, schizophrenia. Subspecialties: Psychopharmacology; Neuropharmacology. Office: 170 Morton St Jamaica Plain (Boston) MA 02130

HARTMANN, WILLIAM HERMAN, pathologist; b. N.Y.C., Mar. 13, 1931; m. Loreen Moyer; children—Daniel M., William Geoffrey, Lindsey M. B.A., Syracuse U., 1951; M.D., SUNY-Syracuse, 1955. Diplomate Am. Bd. Pathology. Intern Detroit Receiving Hosp., 1955-56; resident Henry Ford Hosp., Detroit, 1956-58, Meml. Hosp. Cancer and Allied Disease, N.Y.C., 1958-60; fellow Nat. Cancer Inst., 1958-60; asst. then assoc. prof. Johns Hopkins U. Sch. Medicine, Balt., 1962-67; prof. U. Tenn., Memphis, 1968; assoc. pathologist El Camino Hosp., Mountain View, Calif., 1968-71; prof., dir. surg. pathology Vanderbilt U., Nashville, 1971-73, prof., chmn. dept., 1973—, dir. hosp. lab. system, 1973-79, chief pathologist Vanderbilt U. Hosp., 1973—; vis. pathologist Ludwig Inst. Cancer Research, Bern, Switzerland, 1981-82; dir. Am.

Cancer Soc.; dir.-at-large Univs. Assoc. for Research and Edn. Pathology; exchange prof. Cayetano-Heredia Sch. Medicine, Lima, Peru, 1965; exchange scientist Japan, 1976, U.S.S.R., 1978. Bd. dirs. Am. Jour. Surg. Pathology, 1976—, Surg. Rounds jour., 1977—, Oncology jour., 1979—, Jour. Soviet Oncology, 1980—. Contbr. articles to profl. jours. Active ARC, 1979—, Leadership, Nashville, 1979—. Fellow Am. Soc. Clin. Pathologists (cancer task force 1975-76), Coll. Am. Pathologists (mem. task force, 1976); mem. Am. Bd. Pathologists (trustee 1983), Sociedad Latino Americana de Patologia, Nashville Acad. Medicine, Assn. Pathology Chmn., AMA, Arthur Purdy Stout Soc. Surg. Pathologists, Soc. Med. Cons. to Armed Forces, Am. Assn. History Medicine. Current work: Breast disease. Office: Vanderbilt U Sch Medicine Dept Pathology Nashville TN 37232

HARTMANN, WILLIAM LAWRENCE, veterinary pathologist, veterinarian; b. St. Cloud, Minn., Jan. 2, 1951; s. Elwin Lauren and Marian Elizabeth (Aleckson) H.; m. Annette Margaret Aldrich, Aug. 17, 1974; A.A., St. Cloud State U. 1974; B.S., U. Minn., 1976, D.V.M., 1978, M.S., 1984. Veterinarian Saugus Animal Hosp., Mass., 1978-79, Fresh Pond Animal Hosp., Cambridge, Mass., 1979-81; vet. pathologist U. Minn.-St. Paul, 1981—. Mem. AVMA. Current work: Veterinary and comparative dermatohistopathology; diagnostic veterinary pathology. Subspecialty: Pathology (veterinary medicine). Home: 1693 W Minnehaha Ave Saint Paul MN 55104Office: Vet Diagnostic Labs Coll Vet Medicine U Minn 1943 Carter Ave E-220 Saint Paul MN 55108

HARTTER, DARYL EDWARD, physiologist; b. Sabetha, Kans., Nov. 8, 1952; s. Eli Edward and Margaret Ellen (Cramer) H. B.S., U. Kans., 1974; M.S., Iowa State U., 1976; M.S., U. Ill., 1979, Ph.D., 1983. Teaching asst. U. Ill., Urbana, 1976-77, reprodn. biology trainee, 1978-81, research asst., 1981-82, research assoc., 1982-84; research assoc. U. Kans., Lawrence, 1984—. Contbr. articles to profl. jours. Mem. Am. Soc. Cell Biology, AAAS, N.Y. Acad. Sci., Soc. for Neurosci. Current work: Research with cell biology, biochemistry of olfactory neuron microtubules. Subspecialties: Physiology (biology); Cell biology. Home: 2449 W 24th Terr Apt 4 Lawrence KS 66046 Office: U Kans Dept Physiology and Cell Biology Lawrence KS 66045

HARVEY, BRYAN, crop science educator, researcher, administrator; b. Newport, Gwent, Wales, Nov. 1, 1937; came to Can., 1948; s. William James Laurence and Ethel Irene Doris (Stoneman) H.; m. Eileen Bernice Pfeifer, Sept. 24, 1960; children—Donald James, James Morgan. B.S.A., U. Sask., 1960, M.Sc., 1961; Ph.D., U. Calif.-Davis, 1964. Asst. prof. U. Guelph, Ont., 1964-66; asst. prof. crop sci. U. Sask., Saskatoon, 1966-69, assoc. prof., 1969-75, prof., 1975—, chmn. genetics group, 1977-81, asst. dean agr., 1980-83, dir. Crop Devel. Ctr., 1983—, head crop sci. and plant ecology, 1983—. Contbr. articles to profl. jours. Mem. Agrl. Inst. Can. (v.p. 1979-80), Assn. Faculties of Agr. (pres. 1982-83), Expert Com. Grain Breeding (chmn. 1983—), Am. Barley Workers (pres. 1974-78), Can. Soc. Genetics (dir. 1969-72). Club: Saskatoon Nutana (dir. 1982-83). Lodge: Rotary. Current work: breeding and genetics of malting barley. Subspecialty: Plant genetics. Office: Crop Sci and Plant Ecology Univ Sask Saskatoon SK S7N 0W0 Canada

HARVEY, LEONARD A., chem. co. exec.; b. St. Catharines, Ont., Can., Aug. 20, 1925; came to U.S., 1952, naturalized, 1960; m. Shirley Williams, Oct. 7, 1950; children—Brian, Bruce, Christopher. B.Sc. with honors, Queens U., 1950. With Borg Warner Chems. Inc., 1952—, pres., Parkersburg, W.Va., 1976—, exec. v.p. Borg Warner Corp.; dir. McGean Chem. Co., Parkersburg Nat. Bank. Served with RCAF, World War II. Mem. Soc. Plastics Industry, Chem. Mfrs. Assn., NAM (bd. dirs.), Parkersburg C. of C. (pres. 1981-82). Subspecialty: Polymer chemistry. Home: 402 Country Club Dr Vienna WV 26105 Address: Box 1868 Parkersburg WV 26101

HARVEY, TERENCE, veterinarian, pharmacologist; b. Grass Valley, Calif., July 13, 1944; s. Theodore Richard and Doreen (Beckerleg) H.; m. Rosemary Wilson, June 17, 1966; children—Michele Marie, Scott Terence. A.S. in Chemistry, Belleville Jr. Coll., 1964; B.S., U. Ill., 1966, D.V.M., 1968. Lic. veterinarian, Ill., Mo. Veterinarian, Golf Rose Animal Clinic, Palatine, Ill., 1968; chief food animal br. FDA, Rockville, Md., 1968-78, dep. dir. bur. vet. medicine, 1978-83; dir. regulatory affair nutrition chem. div. Monsanto Co., St. Louis, 1984—; dir. internat. visitors program FDA, Rockville, Md., 1980-82; Author: Current Therapy V, 1974. Contbr. articles to profl. jours. Chmn., Citizens for Real Estate Tax Reform, Bowie, Md., 1973, Churchill South Village Homeowners Assn., Germantown, Md., 1976-79; coach Montgomery County Basketball, Olney, Md., 1981-84, Parkway Basketball Assn., Manchester, Mo., 1984-85. Recipient Exec. Performance award FDA, 1972, 81. Fellow Am. Acad. Vet. Pharmacology and Therapeutics (program chmn. 1982-84, chmn. symposium on dose determination 1983), Acad. Vet. and Comparative Toxicology; mem. AVMA. Comparative biological effects of recombinantly derived polypeptides in animals and man. Subspecialties: Internal medicine (veterinary medicine); Pharmacology. Office: Monsanto Co NCD 800 N Lindbergh Blvd A3SB Saint Louis MO 63167

HASCALL, VINCENT CHARLES, JR., biochemist, researcher; b. Burwell, Nebr., May 26, 1940; s. Vincent Charles and Kathryn Ellen (Signer) H.; m. Gretchen Katharine Knecht, Oct. 29, 1969 (div. 1984); children—Alan Jay, Shanda Renee. B.S., Calif. Inst. Tech., 1962; Ph.D., Rockefeller U., 1969. Asst. prof., assoc. prof. depts. oral biology and biol. chemistry U. Mich., Ann Arbor, 1969-75; sr. staff fellow Nat. Inst. Dental Research, Bethesda, Md., 1975-1976, research chemist, 1976—; mem. pathobiol. chemistry study sect. NIH, Bethesda, 1976-80; mem. Juvenile Diabetes Research Council, J.D. Found., N.Y.C., 1984—. Mem. editorial bd. various research jours., 1977—. Contbr. articles to profl. jours. Recipient Merit award NIH, 1979; Superior Service award Pub. Health Service, 1984; Dreyfus Found. scholar, 1962-66. Mem. Am. Soc. Biol. Chemists, Orthopaedic Research Soc., Soc. for Complex Carbohydrates (exec. com. 1979-82), Am. Soc. Cell Biologists, Sigma Xi. Democrat. Current work: Research on the biosynthesis, structure and function of proteoglycan macromolecules isolated from normal and diseased connective tissues such as cartliage, cornea, vascular. Subspecialty: Biochemistry (biology). Home: 10667 Montrose Ave Apt 4 Bethesda MD 20814 Office: Nat Inst Dental Research/NIH Bldg 30 Room 106 Bethesda MD 20205

HASCHEK-HOCK, WANDA MARIA, veterinary pathologist, toxicologist, educator; b. London, Sept. 7, 1949; came to U.S., 1974; d. Karol A. and Maria U. (Adamska) Haschek; m. Vincent F. Hock, Jr., Aug. 7, 1976. B.V.Sc., Sydney U., Australia, 1972; Ph.D., Cornell U., 1977. Diplomate Am. Bd. Toxicology, Am. Coll. Vet. Pathologists (editorial bd. 1983-86). Grad. research asst. Cornell U., Ithaca, N.Y., 1974-77, postdoctoral fellow, 1977; research assoc. Oak Ridge Nat. Lab., 1978-80, research staff mem. I, 1981-82; assoc. prof. vet. pathobiology Coll. Vet. Medicine, U. Ill., Urbana, 1982—, affiliate Inst. Environ. Studies, 1983—; cons. vet. pathology Toxigenics, Inc., Decatur, Ill., 1982-83. Contbr. articles to profl. jours., 1976—. Fellow Am. Acad. Vet. and Comparative Toxicologists; mem. Soc. Toxicology (editorial bd. 1984—), AVMA, AAAS, Comparative Respiratory Soc. (bd. dirs.), Phi Kappa Phi. Current work: Response of respiratory tract to chemical injury and modulation by exogenous and endogenous factors; pathophysiology of T-2 mycotoxicosis and blue-green algae toxicity. Subspecialty: Pathology (veterinary medicine). Office: U Ill Dept Vet Pathobiology 2001 S Lincoln Ave Urbana IL 61801

HASEGAWA, AKIRA, physicist, educator; b. Tokyo, June 17, 1934, came to U.S., 1968; s. Kuichi Hasegawa and Kaoru (Takata) Takata; m. Miyoko Okada, Mar. 25, 1961; children—Tomohiro, Atsushi, Akiko. B.Eng., Osaka U., Japan, 1957, M. Eng., 1959; D. Sci., Nagoya U., Japan, 1966; Ph.D., U. Calif.-Berkeley, 1964. Assoc. prof. Osaka U., 1964-68; disting. mem. tech. staff AT&T Bell Labs., Murray Hill, N.J., 1968—; adj. prof. Columbia U., N.Y.C., 1971—. Author: Plasma Instabilites and Nonlinear Effects, 1975; The Alfven Wave, 1981. Patentee optical Soliton. Fulbright fellow, 1961. Fellow Am. Phys. Soc. (exec. com., 1978-80, 85—), IEEE; mem. Phys. Soc. Japan, Am. Geophys. Union, Sigma Xi. Current work: Theoretical plasma physics; nonlinear optics; hydrodynamics. Subspecialties: Plasma physics; Fiber optics. Home: 82 Stoneridge Rd Summit NJ 07901 Office: AT&T Bell Labs 600 Mountain Ave Murray Hill NJ 07974

HASEGAWA, TONY SEISUKE, computer graphics consultant; b. Tokyo, Dec. 21, 1941; came to U.S., 1973, naturalized, 1982; s. Sukesaburo and Chiyo (Sano) H. B.S., U. Electro-Communications, Tokyo, 1965; M.S., U. Santa Clara, 1979. Systems analyst, project mgr. Control Data Far East, Inc., Tokyo, 1967-74; computer graphics cons. Control Data Corp., 1974-82; advance project cons. NASA Ames Research Center, Moffett Field, Calif., 1975-82; pres. Fine Tech. Corp., 1983—. Recipient Spl. Scholarship Japanese Govt., 1961-65. Mem. Assn. Computing Machinery., AIAA. Republican. Roman Catholic. Club: Ski (Moffett Field, Calif.). Current Work: Bible to Sartre, math. to Chopin, computer graphics to Renoir, super-computers to computational fluid dynamics. Subspecialties: Graphics, image processing, and pattern recognition; Aerospace engineering and technology. Office: Fine Tech Corp 2083 Landings Dr Mountain View CA 94043

HASELKORN, ROBERT, biophysicist; b. Bklyn., Nov. 7, 1934; s. Barney and Mildred (Seplowin) H.; m. Margot Block, June 23, 1957; children—Deborah, David. A.B., Princeton U., 1956; Ph.D., Harvard U., 1959. Asst. prof. biophysics U. Chgo., 1961-64, asso. prof., 1964-69, prof., chmn. dept., 1969—, F.L. Pritzker prof. biol. scis., 1973—; Cons. virology and rickettsiology study sect. USPHS, 1969-73; mem. sci. adv. bd. Sloan-Kettering Inst., 1972—; chmn. virology study sect. NIH, 1978-80; chmn. sci. adv. bd. Sloan Kettering Inst., 1978-79; mem. nitrogen fixation panel U.S. Dept. Agr., 1978-79. Editor: Virology, 1973—; contbr. to sci. jours. Am. Cancer Soc. postdoctoral research fellow ARC Virus Research Unit, Cambridge, Eng., 1959-61; Guggenheim fellow Institut Pasteur, Paris, 1975; recipient USPHS Research Career Devel. award, 1963-69, Interstate Postgrad. Med. Assn. Research award, 1967. Mem. Am. Soc. Virology (founding; council), Internat. Soc. Plant Molecular Biology (founding; council), Bot. Soc. Am. (Darbaker prize 1982). Subspecialties: Virology (biology); Biophysics (biology). Office: U Chgo Dept Biophysics and Theoretical Biology Chicago IL 60637

HASIMOTO, HIDENORI, physicist, educator; b. Ueki-Machi, Komamoto, Japan, Feb. 10, 1926; s. Hideo and Hatsune (Ohashi) H.; m. Setsuko Hasimoto, Nov. 11, 1955; children—Hidemi, Hironori, Junko. B.Sc., U. Tokyo, 1947; D.Sc. Ministry of Edn., Tokyo, 1955. Vice asst. Faculty of Sci., U. Tokyo, 1947-49, asst., 1949-56, assoc. prof. Inst. Aero. Sci., 1961-64, prof. Inst. Space and Aeros., 1964-74, prof. Faculty of Sci., 1973—; asst. prof. Faculty of Engring., U. Kyoto, Japan, 1956-61; vis. research scientist Johns Hopkins U., Balt., 1958-60, vis. assoc. prof., 1964, vis. prof., 1964-65. Fellow AIAA (assoc.); mem. Phys. Soc. Japan (chief of editors 1970-72), Japan Soc. Fluid Mechanics (pres. 1982-83). Current work: Fluid mechanics (vortex, waves, microfluid mechanics). Subspecialties: Theoretical physics; Applied mathematics. Home: Tamagawa-Gakuen 4-12-2 Machida-Shi 194 113 Tokyo Japan Office: Dept Physics U Tokyo Hongo Bunkyo-ku 113 Tokyo Japan

HASKINS, FRANCIS ARTHUR, geneticist; b. Omaha, Aug. 20, 1922; s. William Forrest and Lona Abbie (Davis) H.; m. Dorothy Genevieve Masters, Dec. 3, 1951; children: John, Ann Olney, Katherine, William. B.Sc., U. Nebr., 1943; M.Sc., 1948; Ph.D., Calif. Inst. Tech., 1951. Research fellow Calif. Inst. Tech., 1951-52; research scientist U. Tex., 1952-53; asst. prof. U. Nebr., Lincoln, 1953-55, assoc. prof., 1955-58, prof., 1958—, Regents prof., 1967—. Contbr. articles to profl. jours. Served with AUS, 1943-45. NSF grantee; AEC grantee; U.S. Dept. Agr. grantee. Fellow AAAS, Am. Soc. Agronomy; mem. Genetics Soc. Am., Am. Soc. Plant Physiologists, Am. Inst. Biol. Scis., Phytochem. Soc. N.Am. Republican. Presbyterian. Current Work: Researcher in genetics, breeding and biochemistry of Melilotus and Sorghum. Subspecialty: Plant genetics. Home: 820 Robert Rd Lincoln NE 68510 Office: Dept Agronomy U Nebr Lincoln NE 68583

HASKINS, ROGER ALLEN, geologist; b. South Haven, Mich., May 3, 1951; s. Ward Alfred and Meradene Irene (Cameron) H.; m. Susan Miller Marcus, Aug. 25, 1973. B.S., Grand Valley State, 1973; postgrad., U. Man., 1974. Registered geologist Oreg., Va. Exploration geologist Dept. Mines, Winnipeg, Man., Can., 1974-78; geothermal and mining law geologist U.S. Dept. Interior Bur. Land Mgmt., Riverside, Calif., 1978-80, geothermal specialist, Sacramento, 1980-82, mining law specialist, 1982—. Contbr. articles to profl. jours. Recipient spl. achievement award Bur. Land Mgmt., U.S. Dept. Interior, 1982. Mem. Geol. Soc. Am., Soc. Mining Engrs., Am. Inst. Profl. Geologists. Current work: Valuation of federal mining claims under 1872 mining law, geothermal energy, mineral property valuation. Subspecialty: Geothermal power. Home: 13205 Moss Ranch Ln Fairfax VA 22033 Office: Bur Land Mgmt US Dept Interior (680) 1800 C St NW Washington DC 20240

HASLAM, JOHN LEE, chemist; b. Salt Lake City, Jan. 4, 1939; s. LeGrand and Mary Agneline (Berg) H.; m. Gale Anne Christiansen, Aug. 26, 1966; children—Jeffrey John, Kirk Steven. B.A., U. Utah, 1963, Ph.D., 1966. Postdoctoral fellow Cornell U., 1966-68; asst. prof. chemistry U. Kans., Lawrence, 1968-73; sr. research fellow INTERX Research Corp., Lawrence, 1973—. Contbr. articles to profl. jours. Patentee in field. Mem. Am. Chem. Soc., Am. Pharm. Assn., Sigma Xi. Mem. Ch. of Jesus Christ of Latter-day Saints. Current work: Chemical kinetics; drug delivery; drug delivery system. Subspecialties: Physical chemistry; Drug delivery systems. Home: Rural Route 2 Box 259B Lawrence KS 66046 Office: INTERX Research Corp 2201 W 21st St Lawrence KS 66044

HASLER, ARTHUR DAVIS, educator; b. Lehi, Utah, Jan. 5, 1908; s. Walter Thalmann and Ada (Broomhead) H.; m. Hanna Prusse, Sept. 6, 1932 (dec.); children: Sylvia (Mrs. Gilbert Thatcher), A. Frederick, Mark, Bruce, Galen, Karl; m. Hatheway Minton, July 24, 1971. B.A., Brigham Young U., 1932; Ph.D., U. Wis., 1937; D.Sc., U. Nfld., 1967. Aquatic biologist U.S. Fish and Wildlife Service, 1935-37; instr., prof. U. Wis., Madison, 1937-78, prof. emeritus, 1979—, chmn. dept. zoology, 1953, 55-57, dir. Lab. Limnology, 1963-79; chmn. com. freshwater productivity internat. biol. program, 1964-74, Nat. Acad. Sci.-NRC, 1963-70; chmn. nat. com. Internat. Union Biol. Scis., 1965-69, chmn. com. ecology, 1966-69; pres. Internat. Congress Limnology, 1962, Internat. Assn. Ecology, 1962-74; dir. The Inst. Ecology, 1971-74; Disting. prof. U. Va., 1981, Tex. A & M U., 1979. Author: Underwater Guideposts, 1966; Contbr. articles to profl. jours. French horn player, mem. exec. com. Madison Civic Music Assn., 1937-65; chmn. Lake Mendota Problems Com., 1965-72. Fulbright research scholar Germany, 1955; Fulbright research scholar Finland, 1963; recipient Disting. Service award Am. Inst. Biol. Scis., 1980, Disting. Service award Soil Sci. Soc. Am., 1980, Disting. Service award Nat. Sea Grant Assn., 1980. Fellow Societas Zoologica Botanica Fennica Finland, Phila. Acad. Sci., Am. Acad. Arts and Sci., Royal Netherlands Acad. Sci.; mem. Am. Behavioral Soc., A.A.A.S. (past v.p. div. F), Am. Soc. Limnology and Oceanography (past pres.), Ecol. Soc. Am. (past pres.), Am. Fisheries Soc. (award of excellence 1977), Am. Soc. Naturalists (past v.p.), Am. Soc. Zoologists (pres. 1971), Nat. Acad. Scis. U.S., Internat. Assn. Limnology, Phi Kappa Phi (hon.). Mem. Ch. of Jesus Christ of Latter-day Saints. Subspecialty: Ecology (environmental science). Home: 1233 Sweet Briar Rd Madison WI 53705

HASS, ALAN JOSEPH, chemist; b. Grand Haven, Mich., Sept. 27, 1951; s. Andrew Thomas and Arlene Iona (Van Hall) H.; m. Robert L., Jan. 15, 1977 (div. Jan. 1982); 1 child, Melanie Joy. B.S. in Chemistry, Mich. State U., 1976; B.S. in Math., Central Mich. U., 1973. Rubber chemist ITT Blackburn, Spring Lake, Mich., 1976-77, engr., 1977-78; product chemist Sealed Power Corp., Muskegon, Mich., 1979-81; product engr. chem. services, 1981—. Adviser, Explorer Scouts, Muskegon, 1984. Mem. Am. Chem. Soc. (sec. 1983). Subspecialty: Analytical chemistry. Office: 2001 Sanford Muskegon MI 49443

HASS, JAMES RONALD, chemical company executive, chemistry educator; b. Statesville, N.C., Sept. 17, 1945; s. Lee Brooks and Martha Louise (Stewart) H.; m. Lina Carolyn Teague, Aug. 21, 1965; 1 child, Jennifer Caroline. B.A., Appalachian State U., 1967; Ph.D., U. N.C., 1972. Research fellow, U. Warwick, Coventry, Eng., 1972-73; vis. asst. prof. N.C. State U., Raleigh, 1973-74; fellow Nat. Inst. Environ. Health Scis., Research Triangle Park, N.C., 1974-78, group leader, 1978-84; pres. Triangle Labs., Inc., Research Triangle Park, 1984—; adj. assoc. prof., U.N.C., Chapel Hill, 1976—; dir. Asilomar Conf. on Mass Spectrometry, Calif., 1981—. Author numerous research papers. Recipient cert. of merit NIH, 1977. Mem. Am. Soc. Mass Spectrometry, Am. Chem. Soc., Research Trianle Park Mass Spectrometry Discussion Group (chmn. 1976—). Methodist. Current work: Analytical applications of mass spectrometry, mass spectrometry of biologic molecules, application of mass spectrometry to problems in environmental and health sciences, characterization of organics on surfaces. Subspecialties: Analytical chemistry; Environmental chemistry. Office: Triangle Laboratories Inc PO Box 13484 Research Triangle Park NC 27709

HASSETT, CAROL ALICE, psychologist; b. Bklyn., Apr. 19, 1947; d. Joseph and Anna (Portanova) Lusardi; m. John J. Hassett, June 29, 1968; 1 son, John J. B.S., St. John's U., 1968; M.A. in Edn, Hofstra U., 1974, M.A. in Psychology, 1978, Ph.D., 1981. Tchr. N.Y.C. Bd. Edn., Bklyn, 1968-69; grad. teaching asst. Hofstra U., Hempstead, N.Y., 1978-79, adj. asst. prof., 1980—; asst. psychologist South Nassau Community Hosp., Oceanside, N.Y., 1982, Nassau County Dept. Drug and Alcohol, East Meadow, N.Y., 1981-84; supervising psychologist Queens Outreach Project, 1985—. Contbr. articles to profl. jours. Bd. dirs. Malverne Vol. Ambulance Corps, N.Y., 1972—. Mem. Am. Psychol. Assn., Nassau County Psychol. Assn., N.Y. Psychol. Assn., Adj. Assn. of Hofstra U. Republican. Roman Catholic. Subspecialty: Physiological psychology. Home: 105 Franklin Ave Malverne NY 11565 Office: 230 Hilton Ave Hempstead NY 11550

HASSON, DENNIS FRANCIS, engineering educator; b. Balt., June 1, 1934; s. Leonard Vincent and Edith Mary (Rufe) H.; m. Eugenia Frances Eyring, May 20, 1961; children—Dennis, Leonard. B.E.S. in Mech. Engring., Johns Hopkins U., 1955; M.S., Va. Poly Inst., 1958; Ph.D., U. Md., 1970. Registered profl. engr. Md. Aerro research engr. NACA, Langley Field, Va., 1955-60; aerodynamicist Johns Hopkins Applied Physics Lab., Silver Springs, Md., 1960-61; aerospace technologist NASA-Goddard, Greenbelt, Md., 1961-67; instr. U. Md., Coll. Park, 1969-71; assoc. prof. U. D.C., 1971-73; prof. U.S. Naval Acad., Annapolis, Md., 1973—; cons. Comsat Corp., Clarksburg, Md., 1970-71, David Taylor Naval Ship Research Devel. Ctr., Annapolis, 1973, Naval Surface Weapons Ctr., White Oak, Md., 1977—; lctr. Catholic U. Am., 1978-84, U. So. Calif. Eastern Region, 1977—. Editor: Advanced Processing Methods for Titanium, 1982. Tech. editor jour. Exptl. Mechanics, 1975-78. Editorial adv. Jour. Metals, 1984—. Contbr. articles to profl. jours., also chpts. to books in field. Coach Coll. Park Boys Club, Md., 1971-74. Goddard Research Study fellow NASA. Mem. AIME, Am. Soc. Metals, ASME, Phi Kappa Phi (pres. local chpt. 1977-80), Sigma Xi (pres. local chpt. 1979), Alpha Sigma Mu, Pi Tau Sigma. Current work: Elastic plastic dynamic fracture behavior in steels; welding of ferrous and nonferrous alloys; fatigue and corrosion fatigue and fracture behavior in metal and ceramic matrix composites. Subspecialties: Materials (engineering); Materials. Office: US Naval Acad Dept Mech Engring Annapolis MD 21402

HAST, MALCOLM HOWARD, medical educator; b. N.Y.C., May 28, 1931; s. Irving William and Rose Lillian (Berlin) H.; m. Adele Krongelb, Feb. 1, 1953; children—David Jay, Howard Arthur. B.A., Bklyn. Coll., 1953; postgrad., U. So. Calif., 1955-57; M.A., Ohio State U., 1958, Ph.D. (NIH fellow), 1961. Instr. U. Iowa, 1961-63, NIH spl. fellow in otolaryngology Coll. of Medicine, 1963-65, asst. prof., 1965-69; assoc. prof. otolaryngology Med. Sch., Northwestern U., 1969-74, prof., 1974—, dir. research otolaryngology, 1969—; prof. anatomy med. and dental schs. Northwestern U., 1977—; asso. staff Northwestern Meml. Hosp., 1969—; guest scientist Max Planck Inst. für Psychiatrie, 1976; vis. prof. Royal Coll. Surgeons Eng., 1980—; mem. task force on new materials Am. Bd. Otolaryngology, 1969-72; dir. Ill. Soc. Med. Research, 1973-77. Contbr. articles to profl. jours.; chpts. to books. Mem. adv. bd. Center on Deafness, 1977-80; bd. dirs. Cliff Dwellers Arts Found., 1979-82; trustee Wilmette Library Bd., 1982-83. Served with AUS, 1953-55. Recipient Gould Internat. award, 1971; Alumnus award of honor Bklyn. Coll., 1977, Alumnus of year, 1984; Arnott Demonstrator, Royal Coll. Surgeons, Eng., 1985; NIH research grantee, 1964-84; NSF research grantee, 1975-77; NATO sr. fellow in Sci. Oxford (Eng.) U., 1978. Fellow Linnean Soc. (London), Am. Speech and Hearing Assn., Royal Soc. Medicine, AAAS, Am. Acad. Otolaryngology—Head and Neck Surgery; mem. Am. Physiol. Soc. (animal care and experimentation com. 1976-82), N.Y. Acad. Scis., Am. Soc. Mammalogists, Am. Assn. Clin. Anatomists, Chgo. Laryngd. and Otol. Soc., AAUP (chpt. pres. 1977-82), Anat. Soc. Gt. Britain and Ireland, Am. Assn. Anatomists, Am. Assn. History of Medicine, Sigma Xi (pres. chpt. 1971-72), Sigma Alpha Eta. Club: Cliff Dwellers. Current work: Comparative anatomy of the larynx-evolution and function; taxonomy of mammals; human anatomy-morphology and function. Subspecialties: Otorhinolaryngology; Evolutionary biology. Office: Northwestern Med Sch 303 E Chicago Ave Chicago IL 60611

HASTINGS, DAVID ALAN, research geoscientist, consultant, educator; b. Newton, Mass., Dec. 26, 1946; s. Carlton Herbert and Frances J. (McMahon) H.; m. Vasanta Devi Suppiah, June 6, 1979. Cert. in Italian, U. degli Studi, Bologna, Italy, 1968; B.A. in Physics, Tufts U., 1969; postgrad. in geophysics, Brown U., 1969-70; M.S. in Geol. Engring., U. Ariz., 1972; postgrad. in geophysics/geology U. Alaska, 1976—. Lectr., U. Sci. and Tech., U.S. Peace Corps, Kumasi, Ghana, 1972-74; cons., researcher EnerDesign Assocs., Weston, Mass., 1974-75; sr. geophysicist, asst. dir. Ghana Geol. Survey, Takoradi, 1976-78; vis. instr. Mich. Tech. U., Houghton, 1978-80; sr. applications scientist geophysics/geology Technicolor Govt. Services Inc., EROS Data Ctr., Sioux Falls, S.D., 1980—; mem. non renewable resources program adv. panel NASA, Washington, 1979-81; adj. prin. geophysicist Ghana Geol. Survey, Accra, 1983—; cons./advisor various orgns., U.S. and overseas. Co-author: Geology and Mineral Resources of West Africa, 1985. Editor: Geophysics, Tectonics and Mineral Deposits in Africa, 1980-82; mem. editorial com. Geodynamique Jour., 1984—. Contbr. articles to profl. jours. Recipient Magsat Research award NASA, 1983, hon. mention paper award U.S. Geol. Survey, 1984. Mem. Soc. Exploration Geophysicists (geophys. activity com. 1977-84), Geol. Soc. Am., Am. Geophys. Union, Am. Inst. Profl. Geologists (cert. profl. geol. scientist), Assn. Geoscientists for Internat. Devel. Current work: Combining geophysical, geological, remotely sensed, and other data for resource exploration, and for investigations of regional geology; design and implementation of new techniques of data integration in the geosciences. Subspecialties: Geophysics; Remote sensing (geoscience). Office: Technicolor Govt Services Inc EROS Data Ctr Sioux Falls SD 57198

HASTINGS, ROBERT CLYDE, physician, educator; b. Tipton County, Tenn., Apr. 23, 1938; s. Robert Simpson and Margaret Marie (Peterson) H.; m. Virginia Ruth Thomas, Jan. 3, 1981; children: Cynthia Margaret, Robert Clyde, Jeffrey Scott. Ph.D., Tulane U., 1971; M.D., U. Tenn., 1962. Lic. physician, La., Tenn. Intern City of Memphis hosps., 1963-64; staff physician USPHS Hosp., Carville, La., 1964-68; chief pharmacology research dept. Nat. Hansen's Disease Center, 1971—; adj. clin. prof. Tulane U., 1974—, assoc. staff, 1977—. Editor: Internat. Jour. Leprosy, 1979—; Contbr. articles to profl. jours. Served with USPHS, 1964—. Mem. Southeastern Pharmacology Soc., Am. Soc. Clin. Pharmacology and Therapeutics, N.Y. Acad. Scis., Soc. Exptl. Biology and Medicine, Am. Soc. Pharmacol. and Exptl. Therapeutics, Am. Fedn. Clin. Research, Am. Chem. Soc., Reticuloendothelial Soc., Am. Soc. Tropical Medicine and Hygiene, Internat. Leprosy Assn., USPHS Commd. Officers Assn., Council Biology Editors, Sigma Xi, Alpha Omega Alpha. Democrat. Methodist. Current Work: Immunology and pharmacology of leprosy. Subspecialties: Pharmacology; Immunopharmacology. Office: Nat Hansen's Disease Center Carville LA 70721

HATCH, ROGER CONANT, pharmacologist, toxicologist, veterinarian; b. St. Joseph, Mich., Jan. 23, 1935; s. Conant Hopkins and Helen Ann (First) H.; m. Judith Earleen Hatch, Nov. 23, 1956; children: Roger Stephen, Timothy Paul. B.S., Mich. State U., 1957, D.V.M., 1959; M.S., Purdue U., 1964, Ph.D., 1966. Gen practice vet. medicine, Berwyn, Ill., 1959-60; instr. pharmacology and toxicology Purdue U., West Lafayette, Ind., 1962-66; assoc. prof. U. Guelph, Ont., Can., 1966-73; prof. U. Ga., Athens, 1973—. Contbr. to Veterinary Pharmacology and Therapeutics, 1977, 5th edit., 1982. Mem. editorial bd. Toxicology and Applied Pharmacology. Contbr. articles to profl. jours. Served to capt. U.S. Army, 1960-62. Fellow Am. Acad. Vet. Pharmacology and Therapeutics, Soc. Toxicology, Am. Acad. Vet. and Comparative Toxicology; mem. N.Y. Acad. Sci., Internat. Soc. Chem. Ecology, Phi Zeta. Republican. Current Work: Beneficial and harmful interactions between drugs and chemicals; research in pharmacology and toxicology; teach these 2 subjects to veterinary students; diagnostic toxicology service for veterinarians; consultations. Subspecialties: Toxicology (medicine); Pharmacology. Home: 1170 Hickory Hill Dr Watkinsville GA 30677 Office: College Vet Medicine Athens GA 30602

HATCHELL, WILLIAM O'DONALD, geologist; b. Florence, S.C., Nov. 9, 1938; s. John Lee and Mildren Colleen (Hicks) H. B.S., U. S.C., 1964; M.S., U. N.Mex., 1967. Geologist, AEC, Grand Junction, Colo., 1967-68; exploration geologist Kerr-McGee Corp., Salt Lake City, 1968-70; hwy. geologist State of N.Mex., Santa Fe, 1970-72, chief uranium geologist energy and minerals dept. Resource Assessment Bur., 1979—; uranium geologist Phillips Petroleum Co., Albuquerque, 1972-74; research geologist Goethermal Services, Inc., San Diego, 1974-79; mem. State Mapping Adv. Com., Albuquerque, 1984—. Author N.Mex. State Geol. Hwy Marker Program, 1984. Contbr. articles to geol. jours. NSF grantee, 1964; geol. research grantee Mus. of No. Ariz., 1966. Mem. Geol. Soc. Am., Am. Inst. Profl. Geologists (cert.), Am. Assn. Petroleum Geologists, N.Mex. Geol. Soc., AIME, Sigma Gamma Epsilon. Current work:

Stratigraphy and sedimentation, eolian processes, uranium geology and economics; research on sedimentary structures indicative of the eolian dune-interdune contact zone; preparing paper on bottomset adhesion lamination structure in the Navajo Sandstone, Navajo Mountain, Utah. Subspecialties: Sedimentology; Fuels and sources. Home: 2855 Plaza Roja Santa Fe NM 87505 Office: Energy and Minerals Dept State of NMex 525 Camino de los Marquez Santa Fe NM 87501

HATCHER, JOHN CHRISTOPHER, psychology educator; b. Atlanta, Sept. 18, 1946; s. John William and Kay (Carney) H. B.A., U. Ga., 1968, M.S., 1970, Ph.D., 1972. Psychologist Clayton Mental Health Ctr., Atlanta, 1971-72; dir. intern tng. psychology service Beaumony Med. Ctr., El Paso, 1972-74; assoc. clin. prof. psychology U. Calif.-San Francisco, 1974—; faculty U.S. Fire Acad., U.S. Fire Adminstrn., 1981—; cons. Fed. Emergency Mgmt. Agy., Calif. Office of Emergency Services, others; spl. asst. to mayor San Francisco, 1975—. Author: (with Brooks) Handbook of Gestalt Therapy, 1976, (with Himmelstein) Innovation in Psychology, 1977; (with Gaynor) Child Firestarters; editor: Am. Jour. Family Therapy, 1980. Chmn. Mayor's Commn. on Family Violence, San Francisco, 1978-80; adv. Arson Task Force, San Francisco Fire Dept., 1977—, Calif. Gov.'s Task Force on Earthquake Preparedness, 1981-82; advisor Kevin Collins Found. for Missing Children, 1984-85. U.S. Army Med. Research and Devel. grantee, 1971; Western Army Inst. Grantee, 1972; Maxicare Health Found. grantee, 1977; Nat. Inst. Corrections grantee, 1983; Calif. Dept. Corrections grantee, 1984, 85; others. Mem. Am. Psychol. Assn., Western Psychol. Assn., Calif. Psychol. Assn., Phi Kappa Phi. Current Work: Psychology of crisis and emergency, assistance of state, federal and foreign government in management of disasters both natural and man-made. Subspecialty: Social psychology. Office: U Calif Psychiatry Dept Langley Porter Inst PO Box 33C 401 Parnassus Ave San Francisco CA 94143

HATFIELD, JERRY LEE, plant physiologist; b. Wamego, Kans., May 1, 1949; s. Virgil Hiram and Elsie Louise (Fischer) H.; m. Patricia JoAnn Reigle, Sept. 1, 1968; children: Mark Edward, Andrew James. B.S., Kans. State U., 1971; M.S., U. Ky., 1972; Ph.D., Iowa State U., 1975. Research asst. U. Ky., Lexington, 1971-72; teaching asst. Iowa State U., Ames, 1973-75; biometeorologist U. Calif.-Davis, 1975-83; plant physiologist Cropping Systems Research Lab., Agrl. Research Service, USDA, 1983—. Editor: (with I.J. Thomason) Biometeorology and Integrated Pest Management, 1982; assoc. editor: Agronomy Jour, 1981-84, tech. editor, 1985—. Research grantee U.S. Dept. Agr., NASA, Dept. Energy, USGS, State of Calif., 1975—. Mem. Am. Soc. Agronomy (div. chmn. 1980-82), Am. Meteorol. Soc. (chmn. com. on agr. and forest meteorology 1982-84). Republican. Mem. Christian Ch. Current Work: Evaluation of energy exchanges in soil-plant-atmosphere systems with emphasis on plant adaptation and genetic diversity to water use through measurements with remote sensing and ground based technologies. Subspecialties: Micrometeorology; Remote sensing (atmospheric science). Home: 3707 97th St Lubbock TX 79413 Office: USDA Agrl Research Service Route 3 Lubbock TX 79401

HATHAWAY, GARY MICHAEL, biochemist, educator; b. Los Angeles, Mar. 6, 1937; s. Clint Adrian and Edith Helen (Irving) H.; m. Wilhelmina E. York, Aug. 6, 1966 (div. 1982); children—John, Sean. B.S. in Chemistry, Calif. State U.-Long Beach, 1964; Ph.D. U. Calif.-Davis, 1967. Asst. research biochemist Scripps Clinic, La Jolla, Calif., 1967-71; asst. research biochemist U. Calif.-Riverside, 1971-76, research assoc., 1976-85, acad. coordinator biotech. instrumentation facility, 1985—; instr. Calif. State Coll., 1974-76. Co-author: Methods in Enzymology, 1979; Current Topics Cell Regulation, 1982; Methods in Enzymology, 1983. Mem. AAAS, Am. Soc. Biol. Chemists. Current work: Protein chemistry of protein kinases. Subspecialties: Biochemistry (biology); Cell and tissue culture. Home: 11854 Graham St Sunnymead CA 92388 Office: Biochemistry Dept U Calif Riverside CA 92521

HATTON, GLENN IRWIN, neurobiology educator, academic administrator; b. Chgo., Dec. 12, 1934; s. Irwin Alfred and Anita Claussen (Richter) H.; m. Patricia J. Dougherty, Oct. 16, 1954; children: James D., William G., Christopher J., Jennifer K., Trent D., Tracey E. B.A., North Central Coll., Naperville, Ill., 1960; M.A., U. Ill., 1962, Ph.D., 1964. NIMH postdoctoral fellow U. Ill., Urbana, 1964; asst. prof. neurobiology Mich. State U., East Lansing, 1965-68, assoc. prof., 1968-73, prof., 1973—, dir. neurosci. program, 1979—; vis. prof. U. Calif.-Irvine, 1976; sr. research scholar Corpus Christi Coll., U. Cambridge, Eng., 1982-83; vis. scientist Agrl. Research Council Inst. Animal Physiology, Babraham, Cambridge, 1982-83, 85. Contbr. chpts. to books, articles to profl. publs. Recipient Career Devel. award NIH, 1970-75; NIH Fogarty Sr. Internat. fellow, 1982-83; NIH grantee, 1967—. Mem. Soc. Neurosci., Physiological Soc. (London), Am. Assn. Anatomists, N.Y. Acad. Scis., AAAS. Current Work: Neural control of hypothalamic neuroendocrine cells; electrophysiology; electron microscopy; immunocytochemistry; brain slices. Subspecialties: Neurophysiology; Neuroendocrinology. Office: Neurosci Program Mich State U East Lansing MI 48824

HATTON, KAY SMITH, geologist; b. Henryetta, Okla., Dec. 22, 1937; d. Hayward Bennett and Mary Kathryn (Ford) Smith; m. Donal Clay Hatton, Mar. 21, 1964; 1 child, Karen Markley. B.S., U. Tulsa, 1960; postgrad., U. Colo., U. San Carlos, Lab. technician Scripps Inst. Oceanography, La Jolla, Calif., summer 1959; geol. librarian Exxon, Tulsa, 1960-62; lab. technician Amoco, Tulsa and Oklahoma City, 1962-66; field environmentalist N.Mex. Environ. Improvement Agy., Santa Fe, 1974-76; staff geologist IV, N.Mex. Energy and Minerals Dept., Santa Fe., 1976—; v.p. N.Mex. Geol. Soc., Socorro, mem. exec. com. 1983—. Author: (with others) New Mexico's Energy Resources, 1976-85; Oil and Gas Fields of the Four Corners Area, 1978; Geothermal Exploration and Research in New Mexico, 1980; Keystone Coal Industry Manual, 1983, 84, 85; Geothermal Resources Council Trans., Vol. 8, 1984; Interstate Oil Compact Commn., Vol. XXIII, No. 2, 1981. U. Tulsa scholar, 1955-60; U. San Carlos scholar 1960. Mem. Geol. Soc. Am., Am. Assn. Petroleum Geologists (cert.), Am. Inst. Profl. Geologists (cert.), AIME. Current work: Determination of New Mexico's coal and geothermal reserves; remote sensing as related to mineral discovery and non-energy minerals research. Subspecialties: Geology; Remote sensing (geoscience). Home: Route 4 Box 35 Santa Fe NM 87501 Office: NMex Energy and Minerals Dept 525 Camino de los Marquez Santa Fe NM 87501

HATZIOS, KRITON KLEANTHIS, plant physiology educator, weed scientist; b. Florina, Greece, Aug. 6, 1949; came to U.S., 1976; s. Kleanthis Matthews and Adamantia Vasil (Tsougos) H.; m. Maria Kriton Grammatikakis, Sept. 8, 1979; children: Adamantia Kriton, Artemis Kriton. B.S. in Agr, Aristotelian U., Thessaloniki, Greece, 1972; M.S. in Crop Sci, Mich. State U., 1977, Ph.D. in Plant Physiology, 1979. Research asst. Mich. State U., East Lansing, 1976-79; asst. prof. plant physiology Va. Poly. Inst. and State U., Blacksburg, 1979-84, assoc. prof., 1984—; cons. Breton Pubs., 1981, 82. Author: Metabolism of Herbicides, in Higher Plants, 1982; mem. editorial bd.: Weed Sci, 1982—. Advisor Hellenic Assn. Va. Poly. Inst. and State U., 1980-82. Served to 1st lt. Greek Air Force, 1973-75. Named Outstanding Scientist dept. plant physiology Va. Poly. Inst. and State U., 1982; recipient Gamma Sigma Delta research award, 1985. Mem. Am. Soc. Plant Physiologists, AAAS, Am. Soc. Photobiology, Weed Sci. Soc. Am., Am. Chem. Soc. (pesticide chemistry div.). Greek Orthodox. Subspecialties: Plant physiology (agriculture); Photosynthesis. Office: Dept Plant Pathology and Physiolog VA Poly Inst and State U Blacksburg VA 24061

HAUBRICH, ROBERT RICE, biology educator; b. Claremont, N.H., May 4, 1923; s. Frederick William and Marian Norma (Rice) H. B.S. in Forestry, Mich. State U., 1949, M.S. in Zoology, 1952; Ph.D. in Biology, U. Fla., 1957. Asst. prof. biology E. Carolina U., Greenville, N.C., 1947-61; asst. prof. biology Oberlin (Ohio) Coll., 1961-62; asst. to assoc. prof. biology Denison U., Granville, Ohio, 1962-68, prof., 1968—; assoc. dir. Earlham Biology Sta., Richmond, Ind., 1967-72; Sci. Coordinating rep. Great Lakes Coll. Assn., Ann Arbor, Mich., 1966-67; Faculty rep. Denison U. Jour. Biol. Sci., 1963—. Served as sgt. USAF, 1943-46. Fellow Ohio Acad. Sci. (v.p. zoology sect. 1972), AAAS; mem. Animal Behavior Soc., Nat. Wildlife Fedn., Sigma Xi. Current Work: Behavior and ecology of the starhead topminnow; conceptual structure of biology. Subspecialties: Sociobiology; Evolutionary biology. Office: Dept Biology Denison U Granville OH 43023

HAUCK, JAMES PIERRE, research engineer; b. St. Cloud, Minn., Jan. 23, 1946; s. Harold and Marie Teresa (Pollard) H.; m. Gail Elaine Norfolk, June 16, 1968; m. Linda Lehman, Jan. 28, 1973; children: Thomas, Tiffany, Barbara, Beverly. B.S. in Physics; B.S. in Math, Calif. State Poly. U., 1968; M.A. in Physics (NDEA Title IV fellow), U. Calif., Irvine, 1970, Ph.D. in Physics (NDEA TITLE IV fellow), 1976. NOAA fellow U. Colo., 1971; research asst. U. Calif., Irvine, 1971-76, instr. physics, 1971-73, vis. lectr. elec. engring., 1982—; mem. tech. staff Rockwell Internat., Anaheim, Calif., 1976-79, staff scientist, 1980-82; research engr. Northrop Corp., Hawthorne, Calif., 1983—; dir. engring. Illumination Industries Inc., Sunnyvale, Calif., 1979-80; adj. prof. physics Calif. State U., Fullerton, 1982—, instr. physics and astronomy, Long Beach, 1977—. Contbr. articles to profl. jours. Active Boy Scouts Am. Mem. Am. Phys. Soc. (div. plasma physics), IEEE (div. nuclear and plasma sci.), Optical Soc. Am. Patentee apparatus for generating temporally shaped laser pulses. Current Work: Free-electron lasers, plasmas and lasers, especially excimer lasers, laser gyroscopes and laser radars, laser physics, electrophoresis, cataphoresis, laser resonators, spectroscopy, laser systems. Subspecialties: Plasma physics; Laser gyroscopes and radars. Home: 1391 Longmont Pl Santa Ana CA 92705 Office: 2301 W 120th Street Hawthorne CA 90250

HAUDENSCHILD, CHRISTIAN C., pathologist, educator; b. St. Gallen, Switzerland, May 5, 1939; came to U.S., 1973. M.D., U. Basel, Switzerland, 1968. Diplomate Am. Bd. Pathology. Research assoc. F. Hoffman-LaRoche, Basel, 1968-72; research assoc. in surgery pathology Children's Hosp., Boston, 1973-76; resident Boston City Hosp., 1975-76; instr. pathology Harvard U. Med. Sch., 1976-80; assoc. pathologist Mallory Inst. Pathology, Boston, 1977—; prof. pathology Boston U. Med. Sch., 1982—; cons. pathologist VA Hosp., Boston, 1978—; cons. NIH, Washington, 1977—. Contbr. numerous articles to sci. jours. NIH grantee, 1979—. Mem. AMA, Mass. Med. Soc., Am. Heart Assn. (council of arteriosclerosis), Am. Assn. Pathologists, Am. Soc. Cell Biology, Internat. Acad. Pathology. Current work: Cardiovascular disease: structure and function of vascular cells in diabetes, hypertension and vascularization of tumors. Subspecialties: Pathology (medicine); Cell biology (medicine). Office: Mallory Inst Pathology 784 Massachusetts Ave Boston MA 02118

HAUER, JEROME MAURICE, physiologist; b. N.Y.C., Oct. 31, 1951; s. Milton and Rose (Muscatine) H.; m. Glenda Reed, Sept. 27, 1980. B.A., NYU, 1976; M.H.S., Johns Hopkins U., 1978; doctoral candidate, Tufts U. Sch. Medicine. Assoc. adminstr. ARC Blood Services, Boston, 1970-80; research assoc. Johns Hopkins Sch. Medicine, Balt., 1976-78; asst. dir. transfusion services U. Md. Sch. Medicine, Balt., 1978-79; research assoc. Beth Israel Hosp. Harvard Med. Sch., Boston, 1980—. Contbr. articles to profl. jours. Served to lt. USAR, 1981—. Mem. Am. Heart Assn., Assn. Advancement Med. Instrumentation, Am. Pub. Health Assn., Am. Fedn. Clin. Research, Am. Assn. Blood Banks, Internat. Soc. Blood Transfusion, N.Y. Acad. Scis. Democrat. Jewish. Current Work: Investigations in the nature of coagulation defects in massive transfusion and trauma and alternates to homolgous blood transfusions. Subspecialties: Hematology; Physiology (medicine). Home: PO Box 1267 Hightstown NJ 08520 Office: Beth Israel Hosp Harvard Med Sch 330 Brookline Ave Boston MA 02166

HAUG, PETER TIFFANY, systems ecologist, environmental analyst, consultant; b. Mineola, N.Y., Jan. 22, 1936; s. Waldemar Henry and Florence Helen (Tiffany) H.; m. Jolie Victoria Smithem, Aug. 12, 1961; children—Linda Marie, Daniel Brian, Tom Davis. A.B., Hamilton Coll., 1960; M.S., Colo. State U., 1970, Ph.D., 1975. Profl. writer, editor newspapers and pub. relations firms, 1960-65; instr. Colo. State U., Ft. Collins, 1968-69; asst. prof. Concord Coll., Athens, W.Va., 1974-76; sr. scientist, mgr. Environ. Research & Tech., Ft. Collins., 1977-78; systems ecologist Bur. Land Mgmt., Washington, 1978-84; self-employed systems ecologist and environ. analyst, Tumwater, Wash., 1983—; cons. various govtl. agys., univs. and pvt. corps., 1974—, Internat. Joint Commn., Washington, 1984—. Contbr. articles to profl. jours. Served with U.S. Army, 1954-56. Mem. Soc. Computer Simulation, Internat. Soc. Ecol. Modelling, AAAS, Am. Inst. Biol. Scis., Ecol. Soc. Am., Internat. Assn. Ecology, Sigma Xi, Xi Sigma Pi, Beta Beta Beta. Bahài. Current work: Application of systems ecology techniques to natural resource decision making; systems approaches to environmental planning; training and technical assistance in environmental impact analysis, and monitoring, scientific writing, interdisciplinary team building. Subspecialties: Ecosystems analysis; Resource management. Home and Office: 1005 Lake Park Dr Tumwater WA 98502

HAUGHEE, SHARON MARIE, public health veterinarian; b. Agana, Guam, June 26, 1957; d. David Allen and Mary Allene (Boykin) H. D.V.M., La. State U., 1981; M.S. in Vet. Pub. Health, Tex. A&M U., 1984. Environ. edn. coordinator Youth Conservation Corps., Mt. Ida, Ark., 1979; vet. student trainee USDA, Jacksonville, Fla., 1980; vol. Peace Corps, Bukavu, Zaire, 1981; lectr. dept. vet. pub. health Tex. A&M U., College Station, 1982-85; vet. med. officer USDA, Hollister, Calif., 1985—. Contbr. articles to profl. jours. Recipient Lorio Student Meml. scholarship La. State U., 1980. Mem. Am. Vet. Med. Assn., Am. Pub. Health Assn., Conf. Pub. Health Veterinarians. Democrat. Current work: Microcomputer applications in public health; potential applications of computer technologies in international health strategies. Subspecialties: Preventive medicine (veterinary medicine); Epidemiology. Home: 1219 Caroline Dr Bossier City LA 71112

HAUN, ROBERT DEE, JR., electric products manufacturing company research exec.; b. Lexington, Ky., Apr. 3, 1930; s. Robert Dee and Edna May (Minor) H.; m. Shirley Anne Porter, June 20, 1954 (div.); m. Karen Blash, June 4, 1977; children: Barbara L., Lynn Ellen Haun Betts, Janet D. B.S. in Physics, U. Ky., 1952; Ph.D. in Physics, MIT, 1957. With Westinghouse Electric, 1957—, dir. applied physics and math. Westinghouse Research and Devel. Ctr., Pitts., 1969-74, mgr. applied scis. research and devel., 1974-81, dir. industry products research and devel., Pitts., 1981-83, dir. energy and advanced tech. research and devel., 1983-85, dir. bus. unit tech., 1985—. Fellow AAAS; mem. Am. Phys. Soc., Optical Soc. Am., IEEE, Phi Beta Kappa, Sigma Xi. Designer cesium atomic beam frequency standard thesis apparatus on exhibit in Smithsonian Nat. Mus. History and Tech., Washington. Current Work: Research managment. Subspecialties: Atomic and molecular physics; Laser research. Office: Westinghouse Research and Devel Center 1310 Beulah Rd Pittsburgh PA 15235

HAUPIN, WARREN EMERSON, researcher, engineer, educator; b. Youngsville, Pa., Apr. 4, 1920; s. Orie Bert and Edna Earl (Donaldson) H.; m. Edna Hazel Oyler, Sept. 3, 1949; children—Barbara, Laura, Carol. B.S., Pa. State U., 1942. Registered profl. engr., Pa. Research engr. Aluminum Co. Am., New Kensington, Pa., 1943-59, electrochem. sect. head, 1959-61, sr. sci. 1961-65, sci. assoc., 1965-81; fellow Aluminum Co. Am., Alcoa Center, Pa., 1981-83, sr. fellow, 1983—; adj. instr. Pa. State U., New Kensington, 1962-65; adj. instr. Carnegie-Mellon U., Pitts., 1976-77; adj. instr. Chatham Coll., Pitts., 1979-80; vis. sci. Norwegian Inst. Tech., Trondheim, 1981. Contbr. articles to profl. jours., chpts. to books; patentee in field. Recipient Wasserman award Am. Welding Soc., 1970, Frary award Aluminum Co. Am., 1984. Mem. Am. Chem. Soc., Instrument Soc. Am., Metall. Soc. of AIME (vice chmn. Pitts. sect., 1984-85; Light Metals award 1985), Electrochem. Soc. (pres. Pitts. sect. 1961-62), Internat. Soc. Electrochemistry, Am. Inst. Chem. Engring. Republican. Methodist. Club: Toastmasters (chpt. pres. 1977-79). Current work: Physical chemistry molten salts; electrochemical engineering process modeling; environmental engineering. Subspecialties: Chemical engineering; High temperature chemistry. Home: 2820 7th St Rd Lower Burrell PA 15068 Office: Alcoa Labs PO Box 772 New Kensington PA 15068

HAUPTMAN, JOHN MICHAEL, physics educator, researcher; b. Seattle, Sept. 25, 1946; s. Carl Ashford Sylvester Hauptman and Ila Byrdine (Peck) Nehre; m. Ruth Kuznets, Aug. 29, 1980; 1 child, Miriam Anna. B.A. in Physics, U. Calif.-Berkeley, 1968, Ph.D. in High Energy Physics, 1974. Adj. asst. prof., research assoc. UCLA, 1974-80; staff scientist Lawrence Berkeley Lab., Berkeley, Calif., 1980-82; asst. prof., research assoc. physics Ames Lab., Iowa State U., 1982—. Mem. Am. Phys. Soc., AAAS, European Phys. Soc., Iowa Acad. Scis. Current work: The interactions of quarks and leptons, primarily in electron-positron annihilation experiments; design of detectors and accelerators in high energy physics experiments; pattern recognition, numerical analysis, and artificial intelligence. Subspecialties: Particle physics; Numerical analysis (computer science). Office: Physics Dept Iowa State Univ Ames IA 50011

HAUROWITZ, FELIX, biochemist, educator; b. Prague, Czechoslovakia, Mar. 1, 1896; came to U.S., 1948, naturalized, 1952; s. Rudolf and Emilie (Russ) H.; m. Gina Perutz, June 23, 1925 (dec. June 1938). M.D., German U., Prague, 1922, Sc.D., 1923; M.D. (hon.), U. Istanbul, Turkey, 1973; Ph.D. (hon.), Ind. U., 1974. Asst. prof. physiol. chemistry Med. Sch. German U., Prague, 1925-30, asso. prof., 1930-39; head dept. biol. chemistry, also prof. Med. Sch. U. Istanbul, Turkey, 1939-48; prof. chemistry Ind. U., 1948—, Distinguished prof., 1958—. Author: Biochemistry, 1955, Progress in Biochemistry, since 1949, 1959, Chemistry and Function of Proteins, 1963; Immunochemistry and the Biosynthesis of Antibodies, 1968. Recipient Paul Ehrlich prize and gold plaquette Paul Ehrlich Fund, Frankfurt, Germany, 1960. Fellow Am. Acad. Arts and Sci.; mem. Am. Chem. Soc. (chmn. div. biol. chemistry 1962-63), Leopoldina Acad. Scis., Am. Soc. Biol. Chemists, Am. Assn. Immunologists, Nat. Acad. Scis., Am. Soc. Microbiology (hon.), Societe de Chimie Biologique (hon.), Societe Immunologique (hon.). Spl. research protein chemistry and immunochemistry. Current Work: Mechanism of antibody production. Subspecialty: Biophysical chemistry. Home: 901 Juniper Pl Bloomington IN 47401

HAURWITZ, BERNHARD, educator; b. Glogau, Germany, Aug. 14, 1905; came to the U.S., 1941, naturalized, 1946; s. Paul and Betty (Cohn) H.; m. Eva Schick, May 11, 1934 (div. Nov. 1946); 1 son, Frank David; m. Marion B. Wood, Jan. 16, 1961. Ph.D., U. of Leipzig, 1927. Privatdozent U. of Leipzig; 1931-32; research asso. Harvard, 1932-35; lectr. U. Toronto, 1935-37; meteorologist, Dominion, Can., 1937-41; asso. prof. meteorology Mass. Inst. Tech., 1941-47; asso. Woods Hole Oceanographic Inst., 1947- 59; prof., chmn. dept. meteorology and oceanography N.Y.U., 1947-59; prof. astrogeophysics U. Colo., 1959-64, prof. geophysics, 1960; with Nat. Center Atmospheric Research, Boulder, Colo., 1964—, dir. advanced study program, 1968-69; prof. atmospheric scis. U. Tex., 1966-68, also Colo. State U.; prof. U. Alaska, 1970—. Contbr. tech. articles to numerous publs. Decorated Cross of Merit 1st class Fed. Republic of Germany; recipient Recipient Rossby award Am. Meteorol. Soc., 1962. Mem. Nat. Acad. Sci., Deutsche Akademie der Naturforscher Leopoldina, Royal Meteorol. Soc., Am. Meteorol. Soc. (hon. mem.), Am. Geophys. Union (Bowie award 1970), ACLU, Sigma Xi. Subspecialty: Dynamic meteorology. Home: 2523 Constitution Ave Fort Collins CO 80526 Office: Dept Atmospheric Sci Colo State Univ Fort Collins CO 80523

HAUS, HERMANN ANTON, electrical engineering educator; b. Ljubljana, Yugoslavia, Aug. 8, 1925; came to U.S., 1948, naturalized, 1956; s. Otto Maxmilian and Helene (Hynek) H.; m. Eleanor Laggis, Jan. 24, 1953; children: William Peter, Stephen Christopher, Cristina Ann, Mary Ellen. Student, Technische Hochschule, Graz, 1946-48, Technische Hochschule, Vienna, 1948; B.S., Union Coll., 1949; M.S., Rensselaer Poly. Inst., 1951; Sc.D., Mass. Inst. Tech., 1954. Asst. prof. Mass. Inst. Tech., Cambridge, 1954-58, asso. prof., 1958-62, prof. elec. engring., 1962-73, Elihu Thomson prof. elec. engring., 1973—; vis. prof. Technische Hochschule, Vienna, 1959-60, Tokyo Inst. Tech., 1980; vis. MacKay prof. U. Calif., Berkeley, summer 1968; cons. Raytheon Co., 1956—, Lincoln Labs., 1963—; mem. Nat. Acad. Scis. adv. panel, Radio Propagation Lab. Nat. Bur. Standards, 1965-67; Bell communications research, summer, 1984; researcher AT&T Bell Labs, fall 1984, Nippon Telegraph and Telephone, Tokyo, winter, 1984-85. Author: (with R.B. Adler) Circuit Theory of Linear Noisy Networks, 1959, (with L.D. Smullin) Noise in Electron Devices, 1959, (with P. Penfield, Jr.) Electrodynamics of Moving Media, 1967; Waves and Fields in Optoelectronics, 1984. Mem. editorial bd.: Jour. Applied Physics, 1960-63, (with P. Penfield, Jr.) Electronics Letters, 1965-73, Internat. Jour. Electronics, 1975-80. Guggenheim fellow, 1959-60; Fulbright scholar, 1985. Fellow IEEE, Am. Acad. Arts and Scis.; mem. Nat. Acad. Engring., Am. Phys. Soc., Sigma Xi, Eta Kappa Nu., Tau Beta Pi, Phi Delta Theta. Current Work: Waveguide optics, picosecond optics; electrodynamics. Subspecialties: Electronics; Optical signal processing. Home: 3 Jeffrey Terr Lexington MA 02173 Office: 77 Massachusetts Ave Cambridge MA 02139

HAUSER, RAY LOUIS, materials engr.; b. Litchfield, Ill., Apr. 16, 1927; s. A. Vernon and Grace Baker (Gregg) H.; m. Consuelo W. Minnich, Sept. 2, 1951; children: Beth, Cynthia, Dewi, Chris. B.S. in Chem. Enging, U. Ill., 1950; M. Enging., Yale U., 1952; Ph.D., U. Colo., 1957. Registered profl. engr., Colo., Calif. Project engr. Conn. Hard Rubber Co., New Haven, 1950-52; mem. research staff U. Colo., Boulder, 1954-57; head materials enging. Martin Co., Denver, 1957-61; dir. research Hauser Labs., Boulder, 1961—; mem. faculty U. Colo., 1954-70. Contbr. articles to profl. jours. Pres. Boulder Civic Opera, 1969-71. Served with U.S. Navy, 1945-46; Served with U.S. Army, 1952-54. Mem. AAAS, Am. Inst. Chem. Engrs., Soc. Plastics Engrs., ASTM, Soc. Advancement Materials and Process Engrs. Presbyterian. Patentee in field. Current Work: Adhesives and bonding processes; expert testimony. Subspecialties: Polymers (materials science); Chemical engineering. Office: PO Box G Boulder CO 80306

HAUSMAN, HERSHEL JUDAH, physics educator; b. Pitts., Aug. 19, 1923; s. David and Sophie H.; m. Korene Brenner, May 18, 1944; children: Herbert A., Sally Z., William B. B.S., Carnegie-Mellon U., 1948, M.S., 1949; Ph.D., U. Pitts., 1952. Asst. prof. physics Ohio State U., Columbus, 1952-57, assoc. prof., 1957-63, prof., 1963—, supr. cyclotron lab., 1952-63; supr. Van de Graaff Accelerator Lab., 1963—. Contbr. articles to profl. jours. Served to 1st lt. USAAF, 1943-45. Decorated Air medal with 3 oak leaf clusters. Fellow Am. Phys. Soc.; mem. AAAS, AAUP. Current Work: Research in medium-energy particle-capture reactions; nuclear astrophysics. Subspecialties: Nuclear physics; Nuclear astrophysics. Office: Ohio State University Van de Graaff Accelerator Laboratory 1302 Kinnear Rd Columbus OH 43212

HAUSMANN, WERNER KARL, consultant; b. Edigheim, Germany, Mar. 9, 1921; came to U.S., 1948, naturalized, 1954; s. Carl and Johanna (Sprenger) H.; m. Helen Margaret Vas, Sept. 29, 1949; 1 son, Gregory. M.S. in Chem. Engring, Swiss Fed. Inst. Tech., 1945; D.Sc., 1947. Cert. quality engr. Research fellow U. London, 1947-48; research asso. Rockefeller Inst. for Med. Research, N.Y.C., 1949-57; research group leader Lederle Labs., Pearl River, N.Y., 1957-66; ass. dir. quality control Ayerst Labs., Rouses Point, N.Y., 1966-71; dir. quality control Stuart Pharms., Pasadena, Calif., 1971-74; dir. quality assurance, analytical research and devel. Adria Labs. Inc., Columbus, Ohio, 1974-84; cons., Columbus, 1985—. Contbr. articles to profl. jours. Pres. Ednl. TV Assn., 1970-71; radiation officer CD, 1962-66. Served to 1st lt. Swiss Army, 1939-46. Fellow N.Y. Acad. Scis., AAAS, Am. Soc. Quality Control (chmn. Columbus sect.), Am. Inst. Chemists, Chem. Soc. London, Royal Soc. Chemistry; mem. Acad. Pharm. Scis., Am. Soc. Biol. Chemists, Am. Chem. Soc., Am. Inst. Chemists, Royal Soc. Chemistry, Chem. Soc. London, Am. Soc. Microbiology, Parenteral Drug Assn., Federation Internationale Pharmaceutique. Presbyterian. Club: Sawmill Athletic (Columbus). Patentee antibiotics. Current Work: research and development of analytical methods of drug substances and dosage forms as such and in biological fluids, with emphasis on high performance liquid chromatography and gas chromatography; quality control and assurance. Subspecialties: Analytical chemistry; Organic chemistry. Office: 4610 Sandringham Dr Columbus OH 43220

HAUSRATH, ALAN RICHARD, mathematics educator; b. East Cleveland, Ohio, Sept. 12, 1945; s. Albert and Esther (Reker) H.; m. Anne Stites, Aug. 17, 1971; children—Elisabeth McIntyre, Katherine Merida MacMartin. Sc.B., MIT, 1967; Ph.D., Brown U., 1972; M.Ed., Wash. State U., 1975. Asst. prof. math. U. Pitts., 1971-76; assoc. prof. Boise State U., Idaho, 1976—; vis. prof. U. de los Andes, Merida, Venezuela, 1978-79. Contbr. articles to profl. jours. Pres. Idaho Environ. Council, 1982—. Mem. Am. Math. Soc., Soc. Indsl. and Applied Math., Math. Assn. Am., Nat. Council Tchrs. Math., Idaho Council Tchrs. Math. Current work: Existence and stability properties of periodic solutions of periodically forced differential equations. Subspecialties: Applied mathematics; Analysis. Office: Dept Math Boise State Univ Boise ID 83725

HAUSWIRTH, WILLIAM WALTER, molecular biology educator, researcher; b. San Francisco, Jan. 1, 1945; s. Armin Otto and Louise Loretta (Inserra) H.; m. Judith Wittkop, Oct. 30, 1970 (div. Mar. 1978); m. Erin Kathleen Lyles, Jan. 1, 1980; children—Casey Jay, Cory Elizabeth, Matthew Aaron, Megan Kathleen. B.S., Stanford U., 1966; Ph.D., Oregon State U., 1971. NIH postdoctoral fellow Johns Hopkins U. Sch. Hygiene, Balt., 1971-73, asst. prof., 1973-74; research assoc. Johns Hopkins U. Sch. Med., Balt., 1974-75; asst. prof. U. Fla. Coll. Med., Gainesville, 1976-80, assoc. prof., 1980-85, prof., 1985—; vis. scholar Stanford U. Sch. Med., Calif., 1983-84; cons. Nat. Commn. Biomed. and Behavioral Research, 1975-78, Nat. Acad. Sci. Bd. Agr., 1984; ad hoc mem. NIH Genetics Study Sect., 1983-84. Contbr. articles to profl. jours. and book. Grantee NIH, 1985—, NSF, 1979—; recipient J.W. Graham award Johns Hopkins U., 1974. Mem. Am. Chem. Soc., Am. Soc. Microbiology, Am. Soc. Biol. Chemists. Sigma Xi. Current work: Mammalian and plant mitochondrial DNA gene organization, sequence evolution, and molecular mechanisms of inheritance. Subspecialty: Genetics and genetic engineering (medicine). Office: Dept Immunology and Med Microbiology Box J 266 JHMHC Gainesville FL 32610

HAVILAND, JAMES WEST, physician; b. Glens Falls, N.Y., July 18, 1911; s. Morrison LeRoy and Mabel Eva (West) H.; m. Marion Cranston Bertram, Oct. 23, 1943; children—James Marshall, Elizabeth Bullard, Donald Sherman, Martha Adams. A.B., Union Coll., Schenectady, 1932; M.D., Johns Hopkins, 1936. Intern medicine Johns Hopkins Hosp., 1936-37, intern, asst. resident, chief outpatient dept. pediatrics, 1937-38, asst. resident medicine, 1939-40, New Haven Hosp., 1938-39; instr. medicine Yale Med. Sch., 1938-39, Johns Hopkins Sch. Medicine, 1939-40; chief services crippled children Wash. Dept. Social Security, also Dept. Health, 1940- 42; lectr. medicine U. Wash. Sch. Nursing, 1946-60; practice medicine, Seattle, 1946—; clin. asst. prof., to clin. prof. U. Wash. Sch. Medicine, 1947—, asst. dean, 1949-53, 1954-59, acting dean, 1953-54, asso. dean, 1972-76. Trustee Seattle Artificial Kidney Center, Seattle Symphony Orch. Served as lt. comdr., M.C. USNR, 1942-46. Fellow Am. Geog. Soc. N.Y., Am. Heart Assn.; mem. Wash. State Med. Assn. (sec.-treas. 1948-51), Seattle Acad. Internal Medicine (pres. 1952-53), King County Med. Soc. (pres. 1962), AMA (council med. edn. 1966-76, chmn. 1974-76), Pacific Interurban Clin. Club, AAAS, Am. Fed. Med. Research, Western Soc. Clin. Research, North Pacific Soc. Internal Medicine, A.C.P. (pres. 1970), Am. Clin. and Climatol. Assn. (pres. 1981), Am. Assn. History Medicine, Nat. Acad. Scis. (Inst. Medicine), Phi Beta Kappa, Sigma Xi, Alpha Omega Alpha, Kappa Alpha. Subspecialty: Internal medicine. Home: 8208 SE 30th St Mercer Island WA 98040 Office: 721 Minor Ave Seattle WA 98104

HAVLEN, ROBERT JAMES, astronomer; b. Utica, N.Y., Sept. 16, 1943; s. Frank James and Marian (Briggs) H.; m. Carolyn Wolf, Sept. 2, 1967. B.S. in Astrophysics, U. Rochester, 1965; Ph.D. in Astronomy, U. Ariz., 1969. Staff astronomer European So. Obs., Santiago, Chile, 1970-77; vis. lectr. U. Va., 1977-79; asst. to dir./assoc. scientist Nat. Radio Astronomy Obs., Charlottesville, Va., 1979— head obs. services, 1985—. Contbr. articles on astronomy, astrophysics to profl. jours., 1972-78. Mem. Am. Astron. Soc., Internat. Astron. Union. Methodist. Current Work: Stellar assns., galactic structure, clusters of galaxies. Subspecialties: Optical astronomy; Radio and microwave astronomy. Office: Nat Radio Astronomy Obs Edgemont Rd Charlottesville VA 22901

HAWK, HAROLD WILLIAM, physiologist, researcher, government research leader; b. Meadville, Pa., Dec. 29, 1927; s. Stewart Dean and Anna Belle (Smith) H.; m. Donna Gail Haney, July 31, 1953; children: Sharon, Susan, Kevin. B.S., Pa. State U., 1951; M.S., U. Wis., 1953, Ph.D., 1956. Research physiologist Dept. Agr., 1956-64; leader physiology investigations unit Beltsville (Md.) Agrl. Research Ctr., 1964-72; chief Animal Reprodn. Lab., 1972—; Upjohn lectr. Am. Fertility Soc., 1969. Recipient Superior Service award Dept. Agr., 1966, Physiology and Endocrinology award Am. Soc. Animal Sci., 1972. Current Work: Reproductive physiology of domestic animals. Subspecialties: Animal physiology; Reproductive biology. Office: Agrl Research Center Beltsville MD 20705

HAWKES, GRAHAM SIDNEY, ocean engineer; b. London, Dec. 23, 1947; came to U.S., 1981; s. Sidney Charles and Winifred Florence (Brooks) H. H.N.D. Mech. Engring. with honors, Borough Poly., London, 1969. Engr. Plessy Underwater Weapons Unit, U.K., 1971-75; engr. D. H. B. Constrn., Ltd., U.K., 1975-76; co-founder, mng. dir. Offshore Submersible, Ltd., Great Yarmouth, 1977, Osel Mantis, Ltd., Great Yarmouth, 1978, Osel Group, Great Yarmouth, 1979-81; co-founder, pres., chmn. Deep Ocean Tech., Inc., Oakland, Calif., 1981—, Deep Ocean Engring., Inc., Oakland, 1982—; adv. Oceanic Soc., Stamford, Conn., 1982; mem. adv. bd. Ocean Trust Found., San Francisco, 1980—; indsl. adv. Sci. Research Council U.K., 1979—. Recipient Canadian Forces cert. mil. achievement, 1978, Charles A. Lindbergh award Charles A. Lindbergh Found., 1981. Mem. ASME, Soc. Underwater Tech., Marine Tech. Soc., Oceanic Soc. Clubs: Yacht (San Francisco), Single-handed Sailing Soc. (San Francisco). Patentee in field. Current Work: Management of research and development and offshore operations companies, design and development of subsea technology including sensory manipulator systems, robotic and manned submersible systems for ocean exploration and industrial uses. Subspecialties: Robotics; Systems engineering. Office: Deep Ocean Tech Inc 12812 Skyline Blvd Oakland CA 94619

HAWKINS, EDWARD FREDERICK, endocrinologist, researcher; b. Woodford, Essex, Eng., Feb. 12, 1946; came to U.S., Jan. 1977; s. Edward Charles and Eileen May (Cotton) H.; m. Ghislaine Marie-Therese Gallez, Aug. 14, 1976; 1 child, Edward Gregory. B.Sc., Sheffield U., Eng., 1967, Ph.D., 1970. Research endocrinologist Inst. Bordet, U. Brussels, 1973-77; research assoc. Johns Hopkins U., Balt., 1977-78; sr. research assoc. U. So. Calif. Comprehensive Cancer Center, Los Angeles, 1978-80, asst. prof. research physiology, 1980-83; asst. prof. neurology U. So. Calif. Neuromuscular Ctr., Los Angeles, 1983—. Contbr. articles to profl. jours., also chpts. to books. NATO fellow; Harkness fellow; Mem. Endocrine Soc., grantee Muscular Dystrophy Assn., Nat. ALS Found. Soc. For Neurosci., AAAS, Internat. Brain Research Orgn., N.Y. Acad. Scis., Sigma Xi. Current work: Role of neuropeptide hormones and neurotransmitters in motor neuron function and neuromuscular diseases. Subspecialties: Biochemistry (medicine); Neuroendocrinology. Office: Neuromuscular Ctr U So Calif 637 S Lucas Ave Los Angeles CA 90017

HAWKINS, GILBERT A., physicist, electrical engineer; b. Wichita, Kans., Dec. 10, 1946; s. Theodore William and Lola (McGinnis) H.; m. Judith Ann White, Mar. 29, 1969; 1 child, Eleanor S. B.S., Stanford U., 1969; Ph.D., MIT, 1973. Miller research fellow U. Calif.-Berkeley, 1973-75; research physicist Eastman Kodak Co., Rochester, N.Y., 1976—. Author numerous tech. publs. Patentee in field. Woodrow Wilson fellow, 1969—. Mem. Am. Phys. Soc., IEEE, Electron Device Soc. (pres. Rochester chpt. 1984-85). Current work: Silicon/silicon dioxide interface states, electronic imaging, VLSI fabrication technology. Subspecialties: Semiconductors; Condensed matter physics. Home: 50 Drumlin View Mendon NY 14506 Office: Research Labs Eastman Kodak Co Rochester NY 14650

HAWKINS, NEIL MIDDLETON, educator, civil engineer; b. Sydney, Australia, Jan. 31, 1935; s. Cecil Alfred and Sybil Mabel (Ralph) H.; m. Saundra Ann Youmans, Sept. 15, 1961; children: Susan Elizabeth, David Clark. B.Sc., U. Sydney, 1955, B.E., 1957; M.S., U. Ill., 1959, Ph.D., 1961. Cons. engr., Sydney, 1958; lectr. U. Sydney, 1962-65, sr. lectr., 1966-68; devel. engr. Portland Cement Assn., Chgo., 1965-66; asso. prof. U. Wash., Seattle, 1968-72, prof., 1972—, chmn. dept. civil engring., 1978—, prin. investigator NSF projects on seismic resistance of structures, 1973—. Contbr. articles to profl. jours. Served to 2d lt. Australian Citizen Mil. Forces, 1953-62. Fellow Am. Concrete Inst. (dir. 1982—, Wason medal 1970, Raymond C. Reese award 1978); mem. Australian Instn. Engrs. (Edward Noyes prize 1967), ASCE (State of the Art award 1974, Raymond C. Reese award 1976), Earthquake Engring. Research Inst. (dir. 1984—), Post-Tensioning Inst. Current Work: Reinforced and prestressed concrete structures,mixed steel and concret structures subject to dynamic and repeated loads. Subspecialty: Civil engineering. Home: 18204 NE 28th St Redmond WA 98502 Office: U Wash Seattle WA 98195

HAWKINS, WALTER LINCOLN, engineer; b. Washington, Mar. 21, 1911; s. William Langston and Catherine Elizabeth (Johnson) H.; m. Lilyan Varina Bobo, Aug. 19, 1939; children: W. Gordon, Philip L. Chem.E., Rensselaer Poly. Inst., Troy, N.Y., 1932; M.S., Howard U., Washington, 1934; Ph.D., McGill U., Montreal, Que., 1938; LL.D., Montclair State Coll., 1974, Kean State Coll., 1983; D.Eng., Stevens Inst. Tech., 1979; D.Sci., Howard U., 1984. Sessional lectr. McGill U., 1938-41; NRC fellow Columbia U., 1941-42; with Bell Telephone Labs., Inc., Murray Hill, N.J., 1942-76. Editor: Polymer Stabilization; Contbr. articles to profl. jours., chpts. to books. Trustee Montclair State Coll. Recipient Honor scroll Am. Inst. Chemists, 1970; Internat. award Soc. Plastics Engrs., 1984. Mem. Nat. Acad. Engring. Patentee in field. Current Work: Stabilization of synthetic polymers against environmental degradation; recycling of plastic scrap. Subspecialties: Polymer chemistry; Polymers (materials science). Home: 26 High St Montclair NJ 07042 Office: Bell Telephone Labs Murray Hill NJ 07971

HAWKINS, WILLIS MOORE, aircraft company executive; b. Kansas City, Mo., Dec. 1, 1913; s. Willis Moore and Elizabeth (Daniels) H.; m. Anita E. Stanfil, June 22, 1940 (dec. Nov. 5, 192); children—Nancy Gay, Willis Moore, James Walter; m. Fredericka B. Cleveland, Jan. 21, 1984. Student, Ill. Coll., 1932-34, D.Sc., 1966; B.S. in Aero. Engring, U. Mich., 1937, D.Eng., 1964. Engr. trainee Grumman Aircraft Co., 1936-37; with Lockheed Aircraft Co., 1937-54, dir. advanced design, 1942-54; with Lockheed Missiles and Space Div., Sunnyvale, Calif., 1954-63, asst. gen. mgr., 1957-61, v.p., gen. mgr. space systems, 1961-62, corporate v.p. engring., 1962-63; lectr. aerospace scis. and mgmt. U. Calif. at, Los Angeles, 1954-55; asst. sec. army for research and devel., 1963-66; v.p. sci. and engring. Lockheed Aircraft Corp., Burbank, Calif., 1966-70, sr. v.p., 1970-74, sr. adviser, 1974-76, dir, 1972-80; pres. Lockheed Calif. Co., 1976-79, sr. v.p. (aircraft), 1979-80, sr. advisor, 1980—; dir. Wackenhut Corp., AVEMCO; mem. Army Sci. Adv. Panel, 1957-74; adviser NACA, 1952-54; mem. adv. council NASA, 1978-83, chmn. safety adv. panel, 1981-83. Recipient Disting. Pub. Service medal for contbns. to Polaris fleet ballistic missile system Navy Dept., 1961; Disting. Civilian Service medal Dept. Army, 1965; with laurel, 1966; Disting. Civilian Service medal NASA, 1975; Wright Bros. Meml. Trophy, 1982. Hon. fellow AIAA, Royal Aero. Soc.; mem. Nat. Acad. Engring., Tau Beta Pi. Subspecialty: Aeronautical engineering. Home: 5239 Bubbling Well Rd LaCañada CA 91011 Office: Lockheed Corp Burbank CA 91520

HAWKINSON, THOMAS EDWIN, industrial hygienist; b. Worthington, Minn., Oct. 15, 1952; s. Robert Edwin and Vivian Julia (Foss) H.; m. Ann Elizabeth Koepsell, Aug. 14, 1977; 1 child, Timothy. B.A. in Chemistry, St. Olaf Coll., 1974; M.S. in Environ. Health U. Minn., 1978. Cert. indsl. hygienist. Research assoc. Indsl. Health Engring., Mpls., 1976-77; tchg. asst. U. Minn., 1977-78; indsl. hygienist Medtronic, Inc., Mpls., 1978—. Mem. Am. Indsl. Hygiene Assn., Am. Chem. Soc. Current work: Ethylene oxide evolution and control, air ionization. Subspecialty: Industrial hygiene. Home: 4349 McLeod St NE Columbia Heights MN 55421

HAWLEY, ROBERT JOHN, microbiologist, program researcher and developer; b. Astoria, N.Y., July 13, 1940; s. John Robert and Margaret Veronica (Miksch) H.; m. Evelyn Marie Downs, June 26, 1976; children—Pamela Ann, Karen Deanna, Eileen Denise. B.S., Pa. Military Coll., 1962; M.S., Cath. U. Am., 1966; Ph.D., Coll. Medicine and Dentistry of N.J., 1974. Postdoctoral fellow Georgetown U., Washington, 1974-75, instr., 1975-77, asst. prof., 1979-81; research microbiology 1st Nat. Inst. Dental Research, NIH, Bethesda, Md., 1977-79; clin. microbiologist Holy Cross Hosp., Silver Spring, Md., 1981-82; lectr. U. Md., College Park, 1982-85; microbiologist Dept. Army, Ft. Detrick, Frederick, Md., 1985—; cons. Precision Media, Inc., Silver Spring, 1977-79. Author: Diagnostic Atlas Off Bact, 1978. Contbr. articles to profl. jours. Block coordinator Shady Grove Station West Civic Assn., Gaithersburg, Md., 1980—. Served to capt. U.S. Army, 1967-70, USAR, 1983—. Research grantee Georgetown U., Noxell, NIH, 1979-84. Mem. Am. Soc. Microbiology, N.Y. Acad. Scis., Electron Microscopic Soc. Am., Sigma Xi (pres. 1981-82). Democrat. Roman Catholic. Current work: Product research and development. Subspecialties: Microbiology (medicine); Molecular biology. Home: 8240 Cambourne Ct Gaithersburg MD 20877 Office: SGRD-UMB-T USAMMDA Fort Detrick Frederick MD 21701

HAWLEY, SANDRA SUE, electrical engineer; b. Spirit Lake, Iowa, May 7, 1948; d. Byrnard Leroy and Dorothy Virginia (Fischbeck) Smith; m. Michael John Hawley, June 7, 1970; children—Alexander Tristin. B.S. in Math. and Stats., Iowa State U., 1970; M.S. in Stats., U. Del., 1975; B.S. in Elec. Engring., U. Dayton, 1981. Research analyst State of Wis., Madison, 1970-71; research asst. Del. State Coll., Dover, 1972-73; asst. prof. math. and stats. Wesley Coll., Dover, 1974-81, chmn. dept. math and computer sci., 1978-81; asst. prof. stats. U. Del., part-time 1980; elec. engr. Control Data Corp., Bloomington, Minn., 1982-85; sr. devel. engr. Custom Integrated Circuits, Mpls., 1985—. Mem. IEEE, Assn. Women in Sci., Am. Statis. Assn., Delta Sigma Epsilon. Current work: design and development of custom chips for digital and linear applications. Subspecialty: Microchip technology (engineering). Home: 7724 W 85th Street Circle Bloomington MN 55438 Office: Custom Integrated Circuits 5353 Wayzata Blvd Minneapolis MN 55416

HAWRYLO, FRANK ZYGMUNT, research scientist; b. Trenton, N.J., Feb. 16, 1936; s. Frank John and Laura Josephine (Mackiewicz) H.; m. Elizabeth Margaret Ovat, Feb. 8, 1958; children—Kathleen, Judy, Karen, Joanne, Frank T., Richard. B.S. in Material Scis., Thomas A. Edison State Coll., 1979. Assoc. mem. tech. staff RCA David Sarnoff Research Ctr., Princeton, N.J., 1960-81, mem. tech. staff, 1981—. Contbr. articles to profl. jours. Patentee in field. Recipient IR-100 award Indsl. Research mag., 1969, NASA tech. brief awards, 1976, 77, 80, 82. Mem. Am. Phys. Soc., IEEE (sr.), Am. Assn. Crystal Growth, ASCAP, Thomas A. Edison State Coll. Alumni Assn. (pres., 1984-85). Current work: Liquid phase epitaxy of semiconductor lasers; device fabrication and flux-free diode machine bonding technologies. Subspecialties: Semiconductors; Metallurgy. Home: 6 Verona Ave Trenton NJ 08619 Office: RCA David Sarnoff Research Ctr PO 432 Princeton NJ 08540

HAY, ELIZABETH DEXTER, physician, educator; b. St. Augustine, Fla., Apr. 2, 1927; d. Isaac Morris and Lucille (Lynn) H.; A.B., Smith Coll., 1948, D.Sc. (hon.), 1973; M.D., Johns Hopkins, 1952; M.S. (hon.), Harvard U., 1964. Intern, Johns Hopkins U. Hosp., 1952-53; instr. Johns Hopkins U. Med. Sch., 1953-56. asst. prof. 1956-57; asst. prof. Cornell Med. Coll., 1957-60; asst. prof. Harvard U. Med. Sch., 1960-64, Louise Foote Pfeiffer assoc. prof. embryology, 1964-70, Louise Foote Pfeiffer prof. embryology, 1970—, chmn. dept. anatomy, 1975—; cons. NIH. Editor-in-chief Devel. Biology, 1971-75, adv. editor, 1975—. Contbr. articles to profl. jours. Mem. Am. Assn. Anatomists, Am. Assn. Zoologists, Internat. Inst. Embryology, Soc. Devel. Biology, Soc. Cell Biology, Phi Beta Kappa, Sigma Xi, Alpha Omega Alpha. Subspecialty: Developmental biology. Office: Dept Anatomy and Cellular Biology Harvard Med Sch 25 Shattuck St Boston MA 02115

HAY, MARK EDWARD, marine ecology educator; b. Georgetown, Ky., May 3, 1952; s. Meddis Reed and Elinor (Chaney) H.; m. Patricia Jean Fuller, July 10, 1982. B.A. in Zoology and Philosophy, U. Ky., 1974; M.S. in Ecology and Evolution, U. Calif.-Irvine, 1977, Ph.D. in Ecology and Evolution, 1980. Predoctoral fellow Smithsonian Tropical Research Inst., Balboa, Republic of Panama, 1977-79; postdoctoral fellow Smithsonian Instn., Washington, 1980-81, research assoc., 1981—; vis. asst. prof. Coll. of Virgin Islands, St. Thomas, 1982; asst. prof. marine scis. U. N.C., Chapel Hill, 1982—; vis. asst. prof. Duke U. Marine Lab., Beaufort, summers 1983—. Contbr. articles to sci. jours. Mem. Ecol. Soc. Am., Am. Soc. Naturalists, Assn. for Tropical Biology, Brit. Ecol. Soc., Soc. Study of Evolution. Current work: Plant-herbivore interactions and their effects on the organization of benthic marine communities, also the functional morphology of seaweeds. Subspecialties: Ecology (biology); Marine biology. Home: 112 Ann St Beaufort NC 28516 Office: U NC-Chapel Hill Inst Marine Scis 3407 Arendell St Morehead City NC 28557

HAY, WILLIAM WINN, educator; b. Dallas, Oct. 12, 1934; s. Stephen John and Avella (Winn) H. Student, Universitaet Muenchen, Germany, 1953-54; B.S., So. Methodist U., 1955; postgrad., Universitaet Zuerich, Switzerland, 1955-56; M.S., U. Ill., 1958; Ph.D., Leland Stanford Jr. U., 1960; NSF postdoctoral fellow, Universitaet Basel, Switzerland, 1959-60. Asst. prof. U. Ill., Urbana, 1960-63, asso. prof., 1963-68, prof., 1968-73; adj. prof. Inst. Marine Scis., U. Miami, Fla., 1966-68; prof. Rosenstiel Sch. Marine and Atmospheric Sci., 1968—, chmn. div. marine geology and geophysics, 1974-76, interim dean, 1976-77, dean, 1977-80; pres. Joint Oceanographic Instns. Inc., Washington, 1980—; mem. Joides Planning Com., 1969-76, chmn., 1972-74; mem. Joides Exec. Com., 1976-80; chmn. SEPM Research Symposium, 1970; hon. research fellow U. Coll., U. London, Eng.; mem. ocean sci. bd. NRC, 1977-80; mem. Am. Commn. Strategic Nomenclature, 1975-78; mem. code com. Am. Stratigraphic Commn., 1978—. Contbr. articles to profl. jours. Trustee Internat. Oceanographic Found. Fellow AAAS, Geol. Soc. Am., Geol. Soc. (London); mem. Am. Assn. Petroleum Geologists (ad hoc com. on revision and updating stratigraphic corr. charts N.Am. 1974, Internat. Stratigraphic Commn. working group for establishing biostratigraphic zonation of Cretaceous-Tertiary deep-sea beds 1975—), Am. Geophys. Union, Am. Micros. Soc., European Geophys. Soc., Deutsche Geol. Gesellschaft (Leopold von Buch medal 1976), Nat. Assn. Geology Tchrs., Geol. Vereinigung, Paleontol. Research Instn., Internat. Assn. Sedimentologists, Internat. Assn. Math. Geologists, Soc. Econ. Paleontologists and Mineralogists (pres. Gulf Coast sect. 1971-72), Marine Council, Paleontol. Soc., Paleontol. Assn., Schweiz. Geol. Ges., Schweiz. Paleontol. Ges., Soc. Geol. France, Phi Beta Kappa, Sigma Xi, Phi Eta Sigma, Delta Phi Alpha, Omicron Delta Kappa (gold key). Clubs: Whitehall (Chgo.); Cosmos (Washington); Dial (Urbana); Ocean Reef (Key Largo, Fla.). Current Work: Interaction of tectonics, paleoclimatology, sedimentology and distbn. of organisms in time and space. Subspecialties: Sedimentology; Paleontology. Office: Joint Oceanographic Instns Inc 2600 Virginia Ave NW Suite 512 Washington DC 20037

HAYASHI, KATSUMI, organic chemist; b. Tokyo, Feb. 23, 1932; came to U.S., 1966; s. Shigezo and Fumi (Murata) H.; m. Eiko Liu, Jan. 14, 1956; children—Naoki D., Akiko K. M.S., Tokyo Inst. Tech., 1956, Ph.D., 1959. Faculty, Tokyo Inst. Tech., 1959-63, U. Tokyo, 1963-66; sr. chemist Lubrizol Corp., Wickliffe, Ohio, 1966—. Mem. Am. Chem. Soc. Current work: Research and development in the fields of lubricant oil additives, plastics and synthetic fibers. Home: 8290 Mentorwood Dr Mentor OH 44060 Office: Lubrizol Corp 29400 Lakeland Blvd Wickliffe OH 44092

HAYDEN, HOWARD CORWIN, JR., physicist, educator; b. Pueblo, Colo., June 20, 1940; s. Howard Corwin and Virginia Dayle (Burr) H.; m. Jill Moring; children: Alexis, Vanessa. B.S. in Physics, U. Denver, 1962, M.S., 1964, Ph.D., 1967. Research asst. U. Conn., 1967; vis. asst. prof. U. Tenn., 1974, 75; asst. prof. physics U. Conn., 1968-75, asso. prof., 1975—; cons. ion implantation. Mem. Am. Phys. Soc., Am. Assn. Physicists Tech., Sigma Xi. Current Work: Atomic and ionic collisions, ion implantation, energy, atomic collision spectroscopy, surface modification through ion implantation, textbook writing. Subspecialties: Atomic and molecular physics; Ion implantation. Office: Dept Physics U Conn Storrs CT 06868

HAYEK, THEODORE CRAIG, human resources development manager, organizational and industrial psychologist; b. N.Y.C., July 15, 1953; s. Henry and Ann (Spadaro) H. B.A. in Psychology, Bard Coll., 1975; M.A. in Psychology, New Sch. Social Research, 1977; M.A. in Human Resources Mgmt. and Devel. candidate, 1982—. Supr. rehab. services Community Mental Health Program, Trenton, N.J., 1977; orgnl. devel. specialist Ins. Services Office, N.Y.C., 1978-79; mgmt. devel. specialist SCM Corp., N.Y.C., 1979-81, mgr. human resources devel., 1981—; cons., N.Y.C., 1979—. N.Y. State Regents scholar, 1971-75; Bard Coll. scholar, 1971-75; New Sch. scholar, 1975-77; N.Y. State scholar, 1971-75; N.Y. State Tuition scholar, 1975-77. Mem. Am. Psychol. Assn., Soc. Orgnl. and Indsl. Psychology, Am. Human Resources Planning Soc., N.Y. Human Resource Planners Assn. Current Work: Succession and manpower planning; organizational planning and development; climate and attitude survey research; training and development; internal staffing; performance appraisal systems; selection and assessment. Subspecialty: Human resources management and development; Organizational and industrial psychology. Home: 14 W 88th St Apt 2A New York NY 10024 Office: Human Resources Devel SCM Corp 299 Park Ave New York NY 10171

HAYES, ARTHUR HULL, JR., physician, clinical pharmacology educator, medical school dean; b. Highland Park, Mich., July 18, 1933; s. Arthur Hull Sr. and Florence Margaret (Gruber) H.; m. Barbara Anne Carey, July 16, 1960; children—Arthur Hull III, Elizabeth, Katherine. A.B. magna cum laude, U. Santa Clara, 1955, D.Pub. Service (hon.), 1980; M.A., Oxford U., 1957; postgrad., Georgetown U., 1957-60; M.D., Cornell U., 1964; LL.D. (hon.), St. John's U., 1983, D.Sc., N.Y. Med. Coll., 1983. Intern in medicine N.Y. Hosp., N.Y.C., 1964-65, resident in cardiology, 1967-68; assoc. prof. pharmacology, asst. prof. medicine, assoc. dean Cornell U. Med. Coll., N.Y.C., 1968-72; prof. pharmacology and medicine, chief div. clin. pharmacology Pa. State Coll. Medicine, Hershey Med. Ctr., 1972-81; U.S. commr. food and drugs, asst. surgeon gen. USPHS, Rockville, Md., 1981-83; provost, dean, prof. medicine, pharmacology and community and preventive medicine N.Y. Med. Coll., 1983—; dir. Cadbury-Schweppes, Stamford Conn. Contbr. articles to profl. jours. Pres., U.S. Pharmacopeial Conv., 1985—; bd. dirs. Peace Found., N.Y.C., Food and Drug Law Inst., Washington, Westchester Artificial Kidney Ctr., Valhalla, N.Y. Served as capt. M.C., U.S. Army, 1965-67. Recipient Foch medal Govt. of France, 1953; Nobili medal U. Santa Clara, 1955; Good Physician award Cornell Med. Coll., 1964; Faculty Devel. award Pharm. Mfrs. Assn. Found., 1968; Bronze Medallion Seal award HHS, 1982, Disting. Pub. Service award, 1983, Cert. of Meritorious Service, Am. Acad. Family Physicians; Rhodes scholar, 1955; Danforth fellow, 1955; NIH fellow, 1960-62. Fellow N.Y. Acad. Medicine, Am. Coll. Clin. Pharmacology, Acad. Pharm. Scis.; mem. Am. Soc. Clin. Pharmacology and Therapeutics (pres. 1980-81), Am. Soc. Pharmacology and Exptl. Therapeutics, Am. Fedn. Clin. Research, N.Y. Acad. Scis., Harvey Soc., AMA, Assn. Am. Med. Colls. (council of deans, council acad. socs.), Phi Beta Kappa, Sigma Xi, Alpha Sigma Nu, Alpha Omega Alpha. Roman Catholic (permanent deacon). Lodge: Knights of Holy Sepulchre. Subspecialties: Cardiology; Pharmacology. Office: NY Med Coll Elmwood Hall Valhalla NY 10595

HAYES, DORA KRUSE, research chemist, chronobiologist; b. Kindred, N.D., June 16, 1931; d. Martin George and Dorothy (Strehlow) Kruse; m. John Clifford Hayes, Nov. 22, 1953 (dec. 1979); children: Robert Martin, John Wallace. B.S., Hamline U., 1952; M.S., U. Wis., 1953; Ph.D., U. Minn., 1961. Chemist Gen. Mills, Mpls., 1953-54; jr. scientist U. Minn., Mpls., 1955-57, teaching asst., 1957-61; research chemist U.S. Dept. Army, Dugway Proving Ground, Utah, 1961-65; research leader Livestock Insects Lab., U.S. Dept. Agr. (Agrl. Research Service, Agrl. Environ. Quality Inst., Livestock Insects Lab.), Beltsville, Md., 1965—; cons. UN Indsl. Devel. Orgn., N.Y.C., 1981—; Chmn. Gordon Research Conf., Andover, N.H., 1981. Contbr. over 90 sci. articles to profl. publs. Wis. Alumni Research Assn. fellow, 1952; USPHS fellow, 1959, 60. Mem. Internat. Soc. Chronobiology (bd. dirs. 1982-83, sec.-treas. 1983—, life. mem.), AAAS, Am. Chem. Soc., Am. Soc. Photobiology, Entomol. Soc. Am., Am. Soc. Biol. Chemistry, Federally Employed Women (nat. exec. v.p. 1982-83). Lutheran. Club: Bus. and Profl. Women's (Falls Church). Current Work: Insect hibernation-diapause; chronobiology; insect hormones and neurotransmitters. Subspecialties: Chronobiology; Biochemistry (biology). Home: 9105 Shasta Ct Fairfax VA 22031 Office: US Dept Agr Agrl Research Service Agrl Environ Quality Inst LivestockInsects Lab Room 120 Bldg 307 BARC-East Beltsville MD 20705

HAYES, JOHN GEORGE, oceanographer; b. Montclair, N.J., Jan. 17, 1948; s. John Joseph and Jane F. (Waskewicz) H.; m. Linda Louise Perry, Aug. 23, 1975; children—Ashley, Laura. B.S., NYU, 1970, M.S., 1973, Ph.D., 1977. Sr. lectr. in oceanography Rutgers U., New Brunswick, N.J., 1974-75; sr. oceanographer Fleet Numerical Oceanographic Ctr., U.S. Navy, Monterey, Calif., 1975-77; program mgr., tech. dir. Environ. Research & Tech., Inc., Concord, Mass., 1977-81; pres., chief exec. officer Global Sci., Inc., Concord, 1981-83; dir. office oceanography NOAA, Washington, 1983—. Contbr. articles to tech. publs. Mem. Republican Task Force. Mem. Nat. Ocean Industries Assn. (chmn. ocean sensing com. 1982-83), Am. Meteorol. Soc., Am. Geophys. Union, Marine Tech. Soc., Chi Epsilon Pi. Republican. Roman Catholic. Current work: Systems concept development of real-time oceanographic products and services, satellite oceanography, international scientific business development. Subspecialties: Oceanography; Remote sensing (geoscience). Office: NOAA/NOS 6001 Executive Blvd Rockville MD 20852

HAYES, JOHNNIE RAY, toxicologist, educator; b. Winston-Salem, N.C., June 18, 1942; s. John Roy and Virginia Elizabeth (McMillian) H.; m. Hilda Lynn Clodfelter; children—Jason, Daniel. B.S., Pfeiffer Coll., 1966; M.S., Appalachian State U., 1968; Ph.D., Va. Poly. Inst. and State U., 1973. Research assoc. Cornell U., Ithaca, N.Y., 1975-79; asst. prof. Med. Coll. Va., Richmond, 1979—; cons. Toxicology and Applied Pharmacology, Inc., Richmond, 1984—; sci. cons. Am. Inst. Cancer Research, Washington, 1983—. Contbr. articles, reviews to profl. jours. Bd. dirs. Salem Woods Homeowners Assn., Richmond, 1983—. Grantee, NIH, EPA, Am. Cancer Soc. Mem. Am. Inst. Nutrition, Am. Soc. Pharmacology and Exptl. Therapeutics, Soc. Toxicology, Am. Coll. Toxicology, Sigma Xi. Methodist. Current work: Role of nutrition in altering cancer sustibility, xerobiotic metabolism, environmental toxicology, carcinogenic mycototoxins. Office: Med Coll Va Box 613 MCV Sta Richmond VA 23298

HAYES, MONSON HENRY, III, electrical engineering educator; b. Washington, Oct. 27, 1949; s. Monson Henry Jr. and Anna Lois (Tufts) H.; m. Sandra Gayle Song, Dec. 18, 1971; children—Michael Young, Kimberly Song. B.A., U. Calif., Berkeley, 1971; S.M. in Elec. Engring., MIT, 1978, Sc.D., 1981. Systems engr. Aerojet Electrosystems, Azusa, Calif., 1971-74; tchr., research asst. MIT, Cambridge, Mass., 1974-81; asst. prof. Ga. Inst. tech., Atlanta, 1981—; cons. Hayes Microcomputers, Norcross, Ga., 1983-84, Lockheed-Ga., Marietta, 1985—. Contbr. articles to profl. jours. Recipient NSF Presdl. Young Investigator award, 1984. Mem. IEEE (chmn. digital signal processing tech. com. 1985—, assoc. editor 1984—, sr. award 1983). Current work: Digital signal processing, multidimensional signal processing, image processing, algorithm development, spectrum estimation, and artificial intelligence. Subspecialties: Electrical engineering; Graphics, image processing, and pattern recognition. Office: Ga Inst Tech Sch Elec Engring Atlanta GA 30332

HAYES, WAYLAND JACKSON, JR., toxicologist, educator; b. Charlottesville, Va., Apr. 29, 1917; s. Wayland Jackson and Mary Lula (Turner) H.; m. Barnita Donkle, Feb. 1, 1942; children: Marie Hayes Sarneski, Maryetta Hayes Hacskaylo, Lula Hayes McCoy, Wayland, Roche del Hayes Moser. B.S., U. Va., 1938, M.D., 1946; M.A., U. Wis., 1940, Ph.D., 1942. Chief vector-transmission investigations USPHS, Savannah, Ga., 1947-48, chief toxicology sect., 1949-60, Atlanta, 1960-67, chief toxicologist, 1967-68; prof. biochemistry Vanderbilt U. Sch. Medicine, Nashville, 1968—; Vol. asso. prof. pharmacology Emory U., Atlanta, 1962-68; cons. WHO, 1950—, Nat. Acad. Scis.-NRC, 1964—. Author: Clinical Handbook on Economic Poisons, 1963, Toxicology of Pesticides, 1975, Pesticides Studied in Man, 1982; Mem. editorial bds.: Jour. Pharmacology and Exptl. Therapeutics, 1962-64, Archives Environmental Health, 1965-72, 76—, Food and Cosmetics Toxicology, 1967-78, Essays in Toxicology, 1972-76; Contbr. sci. papers to profl. lit. Served with AUS, 1943-46. Recipient Meritorious Service medal USPHS, 1964. Mem. Soc. Toxicology (charter, pres. 1971-72), Am. Soc. Pharmacology and Exptl. Therapeutics, Am. Soc. Tropical Medicine and Hygiene, Am. Conf. Govtl. Indsl. Hygienists. Current Work: Toxicology of pesticides. Subspecialty: Toxicology (medicine). Home: 2317 Golf Club Ln Nashville TN 37215

HAYES-ROTH, FREDERICK, artificial intelligence company executive; b. Los Angeles, Nov. 12, 1947; s. Irving B. and Shirley (Wilder) R.; m. Barbara Ann Hayes, June 6, 1970; children—Aaron, Nora. A.B. in Applied Math., Harvard U., 1969; M.S. in Computer and Communication Sci., U. Mich., 1972, Ph.D., in Math. Psychology, 1974. Research assoc. MIT, Cambridge, 1970-71; vis. assoc. prof. Stanford U., Calif. 1979-80; research computer scientist Carnegie-Mellon U., Pitts., 1974-76; research program dir. Rand, Santa Monica, Calif., 1976-81; chief scientist Teknowledge, Inc., Palo Alto, Calif., 1981—. Mng. editor Addison-Wesley Teknowledge Series in Knowledge Engring., 1983—; editor: Building Expert Systems, 1983; Pattern-Directed Inference systems, 1984. Contbr. articles to profl. jours. NSF grantee 1978—. Mem. IEEE (editorial bd. Spectrum, 1985—), Assn. for Computing Machinery. Current work: Artificial intelligence; knowledge engineering; expert systems. Subspecialty: Artificial intelligence. Office: Teknowldege Inc 525 University Ave Palo Alto CA 94301

HAYFLICK, LEONARD, cell biologist, educator, researcher; b. Phila., May 20, 1928; s. Nathan Albert and Edna (Silbert) H.; m. Ruth Louise Hayflick, Apr. 11, 1926; children: Joel, Deborah, Susan, Rachel, Anne. B.A., U. Pa., 1951, M.S., 1953, Ph.D., 1956. Research asst. Merck, Sharp and Dohme, Inc., 1951-52; assoc. mem. Wistar Inst., Phila., 1958-68; asst. prof. research medicine U. Pa., 1966-68; prof. med. microbiology Stanford U., 1968-76; research cell biologist Children's Hosp. Med. Ctr., Oakland, Calif., 1976-81; prof. zoology, microbiology and immunology U. Fla., Gainesville, 1981—, dir. Ctr. Gerontol. Studies, 1981—. Contbr. articles to profl. jours. Served with U.S. Army, 1946-48. James W. McLaughlin fellow, 1956-58; recipient Career Devel. award Nat. Cancer Inst., 1962-70, Biomed. Sci. and Aging award U. So. Calif., 1974, Kesten award, 1974. Fellow Gerontol. Soc. Am. (pres. 1982—, Robert W. Kleemeier award 1972, Brookdale award 1980); mem. Am. Soc. Microbiology, AAAS, Tissue Culture Assn., Soc. Exptl. Biology and Medicine, Am. Cancer Soc., Am. Gerontol Assn., Am. Fedn. Aging Research (dir.), Soc. Exptl. Biology and Medicine (council 1984—), Am. Assn. Cancer Research, Am. Assn. Cell Biology, Am. Assn. Pathologists, Am. Longevity Assn. Current Work: Cell biology of aging, transformation of normal human cells, cell biology, transformation, aging, gerontology, cell fusion, mycoplasmology, virus vaccines, cancer biology. Subspecialties: Cell and tissue culture; Gerontology. Office: U Fla Center for Gerontological Studies 3357 GPA Gainesville FL 32611

HAYNER, GEORGE OLIVER, metallurgist supervisor, researcher; b. Port Huron, Mich. Apr. 6, 1945; s. George Ernest and Ruby Mae (Brahmer) H.; m. Lorraine Ella Grabbitt, June 12, 1965; children—Constance Jean, Stephanie Ann, George Raymond. A.S., Port Huron Jr. Coll., 1965; B.S., Mich. State U., 1967; M. in Nuclear Sci., U. of Idaho, 1973. Metallurgist, Aerojet Nuclear Co., Idaho Falls, 1967-73; lead metall. engr. Argonne Nat. Lab., Idaho Falls, 1973-79; research specialist Babcock & Wilcox, Lynchburg, Va., 1979-82, supr., 1982—; cons. EG&G Idaho, Idaho Falls, 1981—. Contbr. articles to prof. jours. Scholar, Mueller Brass Co., 1963-65. Mem. Am. Soc. of Metals, ASTM. Republican. Baptist. Current work: Physical metallurgy of high strength alloys, forensic metallurgy, metallurgical examination techniques, contract management, line supervision; Three Island - 2 (TMI-2) core examination activities. Subspecialties: Metallurgy; Materials. Home: 123 Londonberry Rd Forest VA 24551 Office: Babcock & Wilcox Lynchburg Research Ctr PO Box 1165 Lynchburg VA 24506

HAYNES, DUNCAN HAROLD, pharmacology educator, biomedical research scientist; b. Owosso, Mich., June 27, 1945; s. Alfred Cleveland and Mary Frances (MacDonald) H.; m. Celeste Ann Howard, Oct. 10, 1965 (div. 1969); 1 child, Norman Douglas; m. Gisela Busche, June 28, 1974; children—Karl Harold, Ellen Ursula. B.S., Butler U., 1966; Ph.D., U. Pa., 1970. Postdoctoral fellow Max Planck Inst. für biophysikalische Chemie, Göttingen, Fed. Republic Germany, 1970-73; asst. prof. pharmacology U. Miami Med. Sch., Fla., 1973-77, assoc. prof., 1977-82, prof., 1982—. Mem. editorial bd. Membrane Biochemistry, 1979—. Contbr. numerous articles to sci. jours. Judge South Fla. Regional Sci. Fair, Miami, 1981—; coach S.W. YMCA Youth Soccer League, Miami, 1982—. Served as lt. Med. Service Corps, USNR, 1980—. Research grantee USPHS, 1973—, Fla. affiliate Am. Heart Assn., 1978, 84. Mem. Biophys. Soc., Am. Soc. Pharmacology and Exptl. Therapeutics, Soc. Clin. Investigation, Soc. Gen. Physiologists, Soc. Armed Forces Med. Scientists, Assn. Mil. Surgeons of U.S., U.S. Naval Inst., Naval Res. Assn., Res. Officers Assn. Current work: Cellular calcium regulation in muscle contraction and blood clotting; development of fluorescent probe methods for continuous and non-destructive readout of cellular activation events in health and disease. Subspecialties: Pharmacology; Hematology. Home: 4051 Barbarossa Ave Miami FL 33133 Office: Dept Pharmacology U Miami Med Sch PO Box 016-189 Miami FL 33101

HAYNES, LYNN O., biochemist, educator; b. Louisville, Sept. 18, 1955; s. Robert L. and Nan C. (Cox) H. B.S., Va. Poly. Inst. and State U., 1977; M.S., N.C. Agrl. and Tech. State U., Greensboro, 1979. Instr., researcher SUNY-Syracuse, 1979-80; research chemist The Upjohn Co., Kalamazoo, Mich., 1980—. Reader, Western Mich. Rehab. for the Blind, Kalamazoo, 1982-84; set designer Civic Theater, Kalamazoo, 1984. Mem. Am. Chem. Soc., Am. Pharm. Assn., Phi Lambda Upsilon. Republican. Episcopalian. Current work: Design and delivery of drugs to specific tissues; cellular differentiation and function. Subspecialties: Drug delivery systems; Cell and tissue culture. Home: 1200 Banbury Rd Apt 12 Kalamazoo MI 49001 Office: The Upjohn Co Portage Rd Kalamazoo MI 49001

HAYNES, ROBERT HALL, biophysicist; b. London, Ont., Can., Aug. 27, 1931; s. James Wilson and Lillian May (Hall) H.; m. Nancy Joanne May, Sept 23, 1954; children—Mark Douglas, Geoffrey Alexander, Paul Robert; m. Charlotte Jane Banfield, June 2, 1966. B.Sc., U. Western Ont., 1953, Ph.D., 1957. British Empire Cancer Campaign fellow dept physics St. Bartholomew's Hosp., Med. Coll., U. London, 1957-58; asst. prof. biophysics U. Chgo., 1958-64; asso. prof. biophysics U. Calif., Berkeley, 1964-68; prof. biology York U., Toronto, Ont., 1968—; mem. Nat. Research Council Can., 1975-82; chmn. ministerial com. on mutagenesis Can. Dept. Nat. Health & Welfare, 1978—; mem. tech. adv. com. on nuclear fuel waste mgmt. program Atomic Energy of Can. Ltd., 1979—. Contbr. articles to profl. jours.; editor: The Molecular Basis of Life, 1968, The Chemical Basis of Life, 1973, Man and the Biological Revolution, 1976. 0ecorated Queen Elizabeth II Silver Jubilee medal; Research award Environ. Mutagen Soc., 1984; Gold medal Biol Council Can., 1984; USSR Acad. Scis. exchange visitor, 1972, 78; Brit. Council exchange visitor, 1973; Japan Soc. for Promotion of Sci. exchange visitor, 1979; Academia Sinica exchange visitor, 1980. Fellow Royal Soc. Can.; mem. Genetics Soc. Can. (pres. 1983-85), Environ. Mutagen Soc. (councillor), Sigma Xi, Beta Theta Pi. Club: Univ. Toronto. Current Work: DNA repair, mutation and recombination in yeast; environ. mutagenesis; radiation microbiology. Subspecialties: Genetics and genetic engineering (biology); Biophysics (biology). Home: 15 Queen Mary's Dr Toronto ON M8X 1S1 Canada Office: 4700 Keele St 306 Farquharson Bldg Toronto ON M3J 1P3 Canada

HAYWOOD, ANNE MOWBRAY, biochemist, virologist, pediatrician, educator; b. Balt., Feb. 5, 1935; d. Richard Mansfield and Margaret (Mowbray) H. B.A. in Chemistry, Bryn Mawr Coll., 1955; M.D., Harvard U., 1959. Diplomate: Am. Bd. Pediatrics. Intern in pediatrics U. Calif. Med. Center, San Francisco, 1959-60; postdoctoral fellow div. biology Calif. Inst. Tech., 1960-61, 62-64; postdoctoral fellow in biochemistry Columbia U., 1961-62; asst. prof. microbiology Northwestern U. Med. Sch., Chgo., 1964-66, Yale U. Med. Sch., 1966-73; vis. scientist biophys. unit Agrl. Research Council, Cambridge, Eng., 1972-74; resident in pediatrics U. Wash., 1974-75, fellow in pediatric infectious diseases, 1975-76, Vanderbilt U., 1976-77; asso. prof. pediatrics, medicine, and microbiology U. Rochester Med. Center, 1977—; vis. asst. prof. Rockefeller U., 1971-72; cons. in field. Contbr. articles to prfl. publs. Am. Cancer Soc. postdoctoral fellow, 1960-62; NIH spl. fellow, 1971-73; European Molecular Biology Orgn. fellow, 1973-74. Mem. Am. Soc. Biol. Chemists, Infectious Diseases Soc. Am., Am. Soc. Microbiology. Democrat. Quaker. Current Work: Virus replication with emphasis on membrane-related aspects; persistent viral infections; interactions between membranes. Subspecialties: Cell biology; Virology (medicine). Office: Dept Pediatric U Rochester Rochester NY 14642

HAYWOOD, L. JULIAN, educator, physician; b. Reidsville, N.C., Apr. 13, 1927; s. Thomas Woodly and Louise Viola (Hayley) H.; m. Virginia Elizabeth Paige, Dec. 3, 1953; 1 son, Julian Anthony. B.S., Hampton Inst., 1948; M.D., Howard U., 1952. Intern St. Mary's Hosp., Rochester, N.Y., 1952-53; resident Los Angeles County Hosp., 1956-58; fellow cardiology White Meml. Hosp., 1959-61; traveling fellow U. Oxford, Eng., 1963; instr. medicine Loma Linda (Calif.) U., 1960-61, asst. prof., 1961-72, asso. clin. prof., 1973—; asst. prof. medicine U. So. Calif., 1963-68, asso. prof., 1968-76, prof., 1976—; dir. comprehensive sickle cell ctr. Los Angeles County-U. So. Calif. Med. Center, dir. coronary care unit; past dir. physicians tng. program (Regional Med. Programs), 1970-75; cons. Los Angeles County Coroner, Indsl. Accident Bd. Calif., Health Care Tech. Div., USPHS, Nat. Heart and Lung Inst.; past mem. cardiology adv. com. div. heart and vascular diseases. Bd. dirs., pres. Sickle Cell Disease Research Found. Contbr. articles profl. jours.; Mem. editorial bds.: Jour. Nat. Med. Assn., Med. Instrumentation, Served with M.C. USNR, 1954-56. Recipient award of merit Los Angeles County Heart Assn., 1968, 69, 73, 75, 85. Fellow Los Angeles Acad. Medicine, A.C.P., Am. Coll. Cardiology, Am. Heart Assn. (fellow council on clin. cardiology; mem. council on athero sclerosis; mem. exec. com. council on epidemiology; mem. long-range planning com., dir., past sec., v.p., pres. Greater Los Angeles affiliate, mem. Am. Fedn. Clin. Research, AAAS, Western Soc. Clin. Investigation, Assn. Advancement Med. Instrumentation, AMA, Nat. Med. Assn. (Charles Drew Med. Soc.), N.Y. Acad. Scis., Hampton Inst. Alumni Assn. (past pres. Los Angeles chpt.), Med. Faculty Assn. U. So. Calif. Sch. Medicine (past pres.), Los Angeles Soc. Internal Medicine (past pres.), Western Assn. Physicians, AAUP, Fedn. Am. Scientists, Alpha Omega Alpha. Subspecialty: Cardiology. Home: 3551 Lowry Rd Los Angeles CA 90027 Office: 1200 N State St Los Angeles CA 90033

HAZEN, MARTHA L(OCKE), astronomer; b. Cambridge, Mass., July, 1931; d. Harold L. and Katherine P. (Salisbury) Hazen; m. William Liller (div.); children: John Avery, Hilary Webb. A.B., Mt. Holyoke Coll., 1953; M.A., U. Mich., 1955, Ph.D., 1958. Instr. U. Mich., summer 1957, research assoc., lectr., 1959-60; instr. Mt. Holyoke Coll., 1957-59; lectr. Wellesley Coll., 1961-63, 66-67; research fellow Harvard U., 1957-59, 60-69; adj. assoc. prof. Boston U., 1979; curator astron. photographs Harvard Coll. Obs., Harvard U., Cambridge, Mass., 1969—; lectr. Harvard U., 1983—. Contbr. numerous articles to profl. jours. Mem. Am. Astron. Soc., Internat. Astron. Union, Phi Beta Kappa, Sigma Xi. Current Work: Research in globular star clusters, variable stars, stellar evolution. Subspecialty: Optical astronomy. Office: Harvard Coll Observatory 60 Garden S Cambridge MA 02138

HEAD, JAMES W., educator; b. Richmond, Va., Aug. 4, 1941. B.S., Washington and Lee U., 1964; Ph.D., Brown U., 1969. With Bellcomm, Inc., Washington, 1968-72; interim dir. Lunar Sci. Inst., Houston, 1973-74; ednl. vis. scientist Space Shuttle Astronaut Tng. Program, Lunar and Planetary Inst., Houston, 1978; asst. prof. research Brown U., 1973-74, asso. prof., research, 1974-75, asso. prof., 1975-80, prof., 1980—; Mem. Office of President-Elect Transition Team, 1980; mem. space and terrestrial applications adv. com. subcom. on geodynamics and geology NASA, NRC; mem. NASA Solar System Exploration Com.-Sci. Working Group on Inner Plant Missions, 1981—. Contbr. articles to sci. jours. Mem. Geol. Soc. Am. (spl. commendation for participation in Apollo program 1973). Current Work: Study of the processes operating to form and modify planetary surfaces and lithospheres - volcanism, tectonism and impact cratering. Subspecialty: Planetology. Office: Dept Geol Scis Brown U Providence RI 02912

HEALEY, FRANK HENRY, research company executive; b. Worcester, Mass., Oct. 5, 1924; s. Frank Henry and Elizabeth M. (McGillivray) H.; m. Loretta Marguerite Finnigan, June 5, 1948; children—Steven, Elaine, Frank. A.B., Clark U., 1947, Ph.D., 1949. Asst. prof chemistry Lehigh U., Bethlehem, Pa., 1949-56; sect. chief physics Lever Bros. Co., Edgewater, N.J., 1956-58, detergents processing chief, 1958-60; mgr. processing, 1960; dir. research and devel., 1960-64, v.p. research and devel., 1964-73, research v.p., 1973-78, v.p. research and engring., 1978-80, research v.p., 1980-82, pres. Lever Research, Inc., 1982—. Served to lt. (j.g.) USN, 1943-46, PTO. Mem. Industrial Research Inst. (pres. 1976-77), Am. Chem. Soc. (div. pres. 1964), Assn. Research Dirs., Dirs. Indsl. Research, Soap and Detergent Assn. Club: Ridgewood Country (sec. 1980-83). Current work: Research and development in consumer products. Subspecialties: Physical chemistry; Surface chemistry. Office: Lever Research Inc 45 River Rd Edgewater NJ 07020

HEALEY, MARK CALVIN, immunoparasitologist, veterinarian, educator; b. Salt Lake City, Mar. 7, 1947; s. Calvin Everette and Frances Mildred (White) H.; m. JoAnn Wade, June 20, 1969; children—Rachelle, Jeffrey, Christopher. B.S., U. Utah, 1971, M.S., 1973; Ph.D., Purdue U., 1976; D.V.M., Miss. State U., 1981. Teaching fellow U. Utah, Salt Lake City, 1971-73; grad. instr. Purdue U., West Lafayette, Ind., 1973-76; instr. Tex. A&M U., College Station, 1976-78; resident Miss. State U., Starkville, 1978-81; research asst. prof. Utah State U., Logan, 1982-83, asst. prof., 1983—; cons. Penwalt Pharm. div. Penwalt Corp., Rochester, N.Y., 1983—; sec. Western Regional Coordinating Com. on Ram Epididymitis, 1984—. Contbr. articles to profl. jours. Served with USMC, 1970-76. Dept. Agr. grantee, 1983, 84. Mem. AVMA, Utah Vet. Med. Assn., No. Utah Vet. Med. Assn., Am. Soc. Parasitologists, AAAS, Soc. Exptl. Biology and Medicine, Intermountain Vet. Med. Assn., Conf. Research Workers in Animal Disease, Rocky Mountain Conf. Parasitologists, Am. Assn. Vet. Parasitologists, Sigma Xi, Phi Kappa Phi, Gamma Sigma Delta, Phi Sigma. Current work: Effect of xanthene dyes on infective larvae of sheep nematodes; application of monoclonal antibodies to animal disease agents. Subspecialties: Parasitology; Genetics and genetic engineering (veterinary medicine). Home: 578 East 1200 North Logan UT 84321 Office: Utah State U UMC 56 Logan UT 84322

HEARD, HARRY GORDON, computer scientist, executive; b. Reines, Tenn., Sept. 23, 1922; s. Pascal Harrison and Cliffie Muse (Page) H.; m. Allison Louise Norcross, Aug. 27, 1947; children: Pamela Suzanne, Todd Addison Crandall. B.S., U. Calif.-Berkeley, 1949, M.S., 1951. Research engr. Lawrence Berkeley Labs., 1951-59; chief engr. Levinthal Electronic Products, 1959-60; v.p. Radiation, Inc., 1959-60, Energy Systems, Inc., 1960-64, HNU Systems, div. Ohio Steel, 1964-68; pres. Resalab, Inc., Menlo Park, Calif., 1968-70; v.p. Info. Systems, MBA, Menlo Park, 1970-74; scientist Inst. Advanced Computation, ZS1, Santa Clara, Calif., 1975—; dir. Intronex, Inc., Menlo Park, 1975—. Author: Laser Parameter Measurements Handbook, 1966; contbr. articles in field to profl. jours. Served with USAF, 1943-46. Mem. Am. Phys. Soc., Research Soc. Am. (chpt. pres. 1961), Optical Soc. Am., IEEE, Assn. Computing Machinery, Sigma Xi, Tau Beta Pi, Eta Kappa Nu. Current Work: Super computer system architecture, optical data storage and retrieval, software engineering. Subspecialties: Computer architecture; Information systems, storage, and retrieval (computer science). Home: 1032 Wood Mill Dr Cranbury NJ 08512

HEATH, BARBARA ANITA, engineer; b. Freeport, Tex., Dec. 11, 1951; d. John Al and Helen Mae (Richter) H. B.A. in Chemistry, U. Tex., 1973; Ph.D. in Phys. Chemistry, Brandeis U., 1979. Postdoctoral fellow Bell Labs., Murray Hill, N.J., 1978-79; staff mem. Gen. Electric CR & D, Schenectady, N.Y., 1979-82; sr. process engr. Inmos Corp., Colorado Springs, Colo., 1982-83, mgr. dram tech., 1983—. Contbr. articles to sci. jours. Vice pres. YWCA, Schenectady, 1982; mem. United Way Allocations Panel, Youth Services, Schenectady, 1982. Mem. IEEE, Am. Phys. Soc., Electrochem. Soc., Phi Beta Kappa. Current work: Microelectronic circuit processing techniques, microelectronic circuit technology. Subspecialties: Microchip technology (engineering); Integrated circuits. Office: Inmos Corp PO Box 16000 Colorado Springs CO 80935

HEATH, LARRY FRANCIS, mathematics educator; b. Independence, Kans., Apr. 18, 1938; s. Floyd Francis and Ruth E. (Brown) H.; m. Carolyn Marie Paul, June 7, 1964; children—Susan, Christine, Brenda, Gregory. B.S., Washburn U., 1960; M.A., U. Kans., 1962, Ph.D., 1965. Asst. prof. U. Tex., Arlington, 1965-68, assoc. prof., 1968—; vis. assoc. prof. U. Ky., Lexington, 1976-77. Contbr. articles to profl. jours. Mem. Math. Assn. Am., Assn. Computing Machinery, Soc. Indsl. and Applied Math., Sigma XI (v.p. 1983—). Mem. Disciples of Christ. Lodge: Kiwanis (pres. Arlington chpt. 1984). Current work: Research using computer graphics with computer software; work interest is making TV tapes of calculus. Subspecialties: Analysis; Mathematical software. Home: 1804 Park Hill Dr Arlington TX 76012 Office: U Tex Arlington TX 76019

HEATH, MICHAEL THOMAS, computer scientist, researcher; b. Atlanta, Dec. 11, 1946; s. Lawrence Hasten Heath and Calistine (Cox) Heath Duncan; m. Mona Lynn Brewer, Dec. 20, 1975. B.A., U. Ky., 1968; M.S., U. Tenn., 1974; Ph.D., Stanford U., 1978. Computer analyst Oak Ridge Nat. Lab., Tenn., 1968-74, computer scientist, 1978—; cons. Environ. Systems Corp., Knoxville, 1973-74. Editor: Sparse Matrix Software Catalog, 1982; contbr. articles to profl. jours. Woodrow Wilson fellow, 1968; Fannie and John Hertz Found. fellow, 1975-78; Eugene P. Wigner Postdoctoral fellow Oak Ridge Nat. Lab., 1978-80. Mem. Soc. Indsl. and Applied Math., ACM, IEEE, Am. Math. Soc., Math. Assn. Am., Math. Programming Soc. Current work: Sparse matrix computations, parallel computing, numerical optimization. Subspecialties: Numerical analysis (computer science); Mathematical software. Home: 108 Newport Dr Oak Ridge TN 37830 Office: Oak Ridge Nat Lab PO Box Y Bldg 9207 Oak Ridge TN 37831

HEBB, DONALD OLDING, neurophychology educator; b. Chester, N.S., Can.; s. Arthur M. and Mary Clara (Olding) H.; widowed. B.A., Dalhousie U., 1925; M.A., McGill U., Montreal, 1932; Ph.D., Harvard U., 1936. Prof. neurophychology McGill U., Montreal, 1947-72; hon. prof. Dalhousie U., Halifax, N.S., 1978—. Author: Organization of Behavior, 1949; Essay on Mind, 1980. Fellow Can. Psychol. Assn. (pres. 1953), Am. Psychol. Assn. (pres. 1960), Royal Soc. London; mem. Nat. Acad. Scis. (fgn. assoc.). Subspecialty: Neuropsychology.

HECHT, LEE MARTIN, artificial intelligence company executive; b. Phila., May 11, 1942; s. Hymen Nathan and Anne Rosalee (Brodsky) H.; 1 child, Kimberley Kenney. M.S. in Physics, U. Chgo., 1965, M.B.A. (NDEA fellow), 1969. Teaching asst. physics, research asst. U. Chgo., lectr. physics, 1966-67; applied maths. U. Chgo. (Sch. Bus.), 1967-69, policy studies, 1973-80; pres., chief exec. officer Phoenix-Hecht Inc. (computer services co.), Chgo., 1968-75, dir., 1968-76; chmn., chief exec. officer Phoenix-Hecht Cash Mgmt. Services Inc., Chgo., 1973-75, dir., 1973-76; pres., chief exec. officer Kenwood-Pacific Corp., San Francisco, 1973-84; dir. Holloway Mgmt. Group, Ltd., Chgo., 1973-82, chmn., 1976-82; chmn., chief exec. officer Electron Storage Ring Corp., San Francisco, 1977-84; chmn., chief exec. officer Teknowledge, Inc., Palo Alto, Calif., 1981—; pres. Middlefield Group Inc., 1981—, Middlefield Capital Corp., 1981-84; dir. U.S. Home Corp., Houston, Digital Pathways, Inc., electronics co., Palo Alto, 1976-82; chmn. Kenwood Group Inc., 1978-82; lectr. bus. adminstrn. U. Calif.-Berkeley, 1975-77; vis. lectr. mgmt. Stanford U., 1976; v.p. Nat. Vidiograph Inc. (motion picture prodn.), Berkeley, 1975-77. Mem. Am. Assn. Artificial Intelligence, Am. Phys. Soc. Clubs: Economic (Chgo.), Tavern (Chgo.). Subspecialty: Artificial intelligence. Address: 532 Channing Ave Palo Alto CA 94301

HECKMAN, RICHARD AINSWORTH, nuclear engineer; b. Phoenix, July 15, 1929; s. Harris and Ann (Sells) H.; m. Olive Anne Biddle, Dec. 17, 1950; children: Mark, Bruce. B.S. in Chem. Engring, U. Calif.-Berkeley, 1950. Chem. engr U. Calif. Radiation Lab., 1950-51; Calif. Research and Devel. Co., Livermore, 1951-53; program leader Lawrence Livermore Nat. Lab., 1953-81, project leader, 1981—. Co-author: Nuclear Waste Management, 1982. Bd. dirs. Calif. Industries for the Blind, Inc., Los Angeles, 1977, sec. corp., 1978; bd. dirs. Hands of Tri-Valley, Inc., Livermore, 1980. Mem. AAAS, Am. Nuclear Soc., N.Y. Acad. Sci. Democrat. Clubs: Island Yacht (Alameda, Calif.) (commodore 1971); Midget Ocean Racing (San Francisco) (commodore 1972). Patentee nuclear engring. (6). Current Work: Research and development, next generation nuclear reactor fuel cycle, utilizing laser isotope separation in front andback of the fuel cycle. Subspecialties: Nuclear fission; Chemical engineering. Home: 5683 Greenridge Rd Castro Valley CA 94546 Office: Lawrence Livermore Nat Lab PO Box 808 Livermore CA 94552

HECKMAN, THOMAS PAUL, mechanical engineer; b. Kokomo, Ind., July 28, 1917; s. Thomas S. and Mary (Grosswege) H.; m. Jane C.Stewart, Mar. 27, 1955; children: Eric, Jan, Mark. B.S.M.E., Purdue U., 1940. Registered profl. engr., Wash. Project engr., classification officer, tech. info. officer AEC, 1956-70; pres. T.P. Heckman Assocs., Lombard, Ill., 1970—; cons. Argonne Nat. Lab. Bd. dirs. Schizophrenia Assn. West Suburban Chgo., 1985—. Served with USN, 1943-46. Mem. ASME, Am. Nuclear Soc. Unitarian. Patentee in field. Current Work: Research and development of permanent magnet connectors and levitation; home and yard devices and procedures for handicapped persons. Subspecialty: Mechanical engineering. Home and Office: 20 W 533 Edgewood Rd Lombard IL 60148

HEDGCOTH, CHARLES, biochemist, educator; b. Graham, Tex., Jan. 29, 1936; s. Charlie and Edna Mae Pearl (Pirkle) H.; m. Barbara Anne Graham, June 20, 1956; children: Kelli, Kimberly, Charles Michael. B.S. in Chemistry, U. Tex., Austin, 1961, Ph.D. in Chemistry (Rosalie B. Hite fellow, NIH fellow), 1965. Asst. prof. biochemistry Kans. State U., Manhattan, 1965-68, assoc. prof., 1968-76, prof., 1976—, ancillary prof. div. biology, 1979—; vis. assoc. prof. U. B.C. (Can.), Vancouver, 1975. Served with USCG, 1954-58. NATO/NSF sr. fellow, 1975; NSF, NIH, U.S. Dept. Agr., Nat. Cancer Inst. grantee. Mem. Am. Soc. Biol. Chemists, Am. Chem. Soc., AAAS, Sigma Xi. Current Work: Characterization of wheat storage protein genes; wheat mitochondrial DNA; perturbations of lysine transfer ribonucleic acids in transformed cells. Subspecialties: Cancer research (medicine); Genetics and genetic engineering (agriculture). Home: 1305 Waters St Manhattan KS 66502 Office: Dept Biochemistry Kans State U Manhattan KS 66506

HEDGES, HARRY GEORGE, educator; b. Lansing, Mich., Oct. 7, 1923; s. Charles William and Elsie (Frost) H.; m. Mary J. Corbishley, June 14, 1944 (dec.); children—Susan, Martha. B.S., Mich. State U., 1949, Ph.D., 1960; M.S., U. Mich., 1954. Electronics engr. USAF Wright Air Devel. Center, Dayton, Ohio, 1949-51; research asso. U. Mich., 1951-54; instr. Mich. State U., East Lansing, 1954-60, asst. prof., 1960-63, asso. prof., 1963-69, prof., chmn. dept. computer sci., 1969—; Dir. Nat. Electronics Conf., Inc., 1968—. Tech. editor: Analysis of Discrete Physical Systems, 1967; mem.: Computer Sci. Bd, 1973—; chmn., 1974-75. Chmn. Selective Service Bd. 264, Lansing, 1970-76. Served with AUS, 1943-46, PTO. NSF sci. faculty fellow, 1960. Mem. Am. Soc. Engring. Edn. (chmn. N.Central sect. 1968-69), IEEE (dir. 1967-69, treas. 1969, vice chmn. 1973, chmn. 1974, Southeastern Mich. sect.). Subspecialty: Computer engineering. Home: 1623 Woodside Dr East Lansing MI 48823

HEDSTROM, JOSEPH CHARLES, operations research analyst; b. Dothan, Ala., Sept. 21, 1952; s. Robert Allan and Elizabeth (Menchion) H. B.S. in Indsl. Engring, U. Ala-Tuscaloosa, 1975; M.S. in Indsl. Engring, Ga. Tech. U., 1976, now postgrad. Indsl. engr. Ford Motor Co., Sterling Heights, Mich., 1977-78; ops. research analyst Lockheed-Ga. Co., Marietta, Ga., 1978-80, sr. ops. research analyst, 1980—. Recipient Indsl. Engring. award U. Ala., 1975. Mem. Ops. Research Soc. Am., Am. Inst. Indsl. Engrs. (chpt. v.p. 1974-75), AIAA, Tau Beta Pi. Roman Catholic. Current Work: Operations research. Subspecialties: Operations research (engineering); Industrial engineering. Home: 4001 Oak Forest Circle Marietta GA 30062 Office: Lockheed-Georgia Company Marietta GA 30063

HEEGER, ALAN JAY, physicist; b. Sioux City, Iowa, Jan. 22, 1936; s. Peter J. and Alice (Minkin) H.; m. Ruthann Chudacoff, Aug. 11, 1957; children—Peter S., David J. B.A., U. Nebr., 1957; Ph.D., U. Calif., Berkeley, 1961. Asst. prof. U. Pa., Phila., 1962-64, asso. prof., 1964-66, prof. physics, 1966-82, U. Calif.-Santa Barbara, 1982—; dir. Lab. for Research on Structure of Matter, 1974-81, acting vice provost for research, 1981-82; Morris Loeb lectr. Harvard U., 1973; cons. various sci. labs. Contbr. sci. articles to profl. jours. Recipient Oliver E. Backley prize in solid state physics, 1983; Alfred P. Sloan fellow; Guggenheim fellow; Govt. grantee; Internat. Exchange scholar, USSR, 1976, Japan, 1978. Mem. Am. Phys. Soc. Patentee in field. Office: Dept Physics U Calif Santa Barbara CA 93103

HEER, CLIFFORD V., physicist, educator; b. Fulton County, Ohio, May 31, 1920; s. Nelson Veer and Minnie May (Leu) H.; m. Esther Jean Leonard, Dec. 17, 1949; children: Barbara Jean, Deborah Ann, Daniel Nelson. B.Sc. in physics, Ohio State U., 1942, Ph.D., 1949. Faculty dept. physics Ohio State U., 1949—, prof. physics, 1961—; cons. Ramo-Wooldridge Corp., 1956-58, Space Tech. Lab., 1958-65; Honeywell, Inc., 1964-65, TRW, 1965-70, Litton Corp., 1981-82. Author, 1972, also articles.; Inventor laser gyroscope. Served to lt. Signal Corps U.S. Army, 1942-46. Fellow Am. Phys. Soc. Republican. Methodist. Current Work: Current research is related to laser physics. Subspecialties: Atomic and molecular physics; Statistical physics.

HEESCHEN, DAVID SUTPHIN, astronomer, educator; b. Davenport, Iowa, Mar. 12, 1926; s. Richard George and Emily (Sutphin) H.; m. Eloise St. Clair, June 11, 1950; children: Lisa Clair, David William, Richard Mark. B.S., U. Ill., 1949, M.S., 1951; Ph.D., Harvard U., 1954; Sc.D. (hon.), W.Va. Inst. Tech., 1974. Instr. Wesleyan U., Middletown, Conn., 1954-55; lectr., research assoc. Harvard U., 1955-56; scientist Nat. Radio Astronomy Obs., 1956-77, sr. scientist, 1977—, dir., 1962-78; research prof. astronomy U. Va., 1980—; Cons. NASA, 1960-61, 68-72. Contbr. sci. jours. G.R. Agassiz fellow Harvard Obs., 1953-54; recipient Disting. Pub. Service award NSF, 1980, Alexander von Humboldt Sr. Scientist award, 1985. Fellow AAAS; mem. Am. Astron. Soc. (v.p. 1969-71, pres. 1980-82), Internat. Astron. Union (v.p. 1976-82), Internat Sci. Radio Union, Nat. Acad. Sci., Am. Acad. Arts and Sci., Am. Philos. Soc. Current Work: Variability of extra galactic sources; star formation in galaxies; nature of quasars.

HEESCHEN, JERRY PARKER, chemist; b. Marshall, Minn., Apr. 14, 1932; s. George Matern and Lucille Marie (Luetje) H.; m. Barbara Ann Stuhlmacher, Sept. 30, 1956; children—William Andrew, Paul Richard, James Matern. B.S., Western Res. U., 1953; Ph.D., U. Ill., Urbana, 1959. Research chemist The Dow Chem. Co., Midland, Mich., 1958—, research assoc., 1976—. Contbr. articles to tech. jours. Mem. Am. Chem. Soc., AAAS. Presbyterian. Current work: Structure determination, composition, molecular dynamics, solid state, liquid state, chemical reactions, data storage and retrieval. Subspecialties: Nuclear magnetic resonance; Analytical chemistry. Home: 4426 Gladding Ct Midland MI 48640 Office: Mich Div Analyt Labs 574 Dow Chem USA Midland MI 48667

HEFFNER, REID RUSSELL, JR., pathologist, neuropathologist, educator; b. Phila., Apr. 16, 1938; s. Reid Russell and Katherine (Dewey) H.; m. Elenora Markunas, July 24, 1965; children: Honora, Reid. B.A., Yale U, 1960, M.D., 1965. Diplomate: Am. Bd. Pathology. Chief neuromuscular disease div. Armed Forces Inst. Pathology, Washington, 1972-76; prof. pathology and neurology SUNY, Buffalo, 1976—; chief div. neuropathology SUNY (Sch. Medicine), 1976—, assoc. chmn. dept. pathology, 1985; dir. dept. pathology Erie County Med. Center, Buffalo, 1979—; med. adv. Buffalo Assn. Neurologic Disease; mem. med. adv. bd. Western N.Y. Alzheimer's Disease Assn.; cons. Buffalo Gen. Hosp., VA Med. Center, Millard Fillmore Hosp., all Buffalo. Contbr. articles to profl. jours. Served to maj. M.C. U.S. Army, 1970-72. Mem. Am. Assn. Neuropathologists, Am. Acad. Neurology, Am. Soc. Clin. Pathologists, Internat. Acad. Pathology, N.Y. Acad. Scis. Republician. Episcopalian. Club: Wanakah (N.Y.) Country. Current Work: Neuromuscular disease; inflammatory myopathy. Subspecialty: Pathology (medicine). Office: 462 Grider St Buffalo NY 14215

HEFFNER, THOMAS GARY, psychopharmacologist, researcher; b. Salem, Ohio, Sept. 20, 1949; s. Fred Curtis and Irma Virginia (Buchanan) H. B.S., U. Pitts., 1971, Ph.D., 1976. Teaching asst. U. Pitts., 1971-74, teaching fellow, 1974-76; postdoctoral fellow U. Chgo., 1976-79, research asst. prof. pharmacology and physiol. scis., 1979-83; research assoc. (group leader) antipsychotic drug research Warner Lambert/Parke-Davis Pharm. Research, Ann Arbor, Mich., 1983—. Contbr. articles to profl. jours. Brain Research Found. grantee, 1982. Mem. Soc. Neurosci., Am. Soc. Pharmacology and Exptl. Therapeutics, Am. Psychol. Assn., Sigma Xi. Current Work: Psychopharmacology, antipsychotic drugs, use of animal models to understand psychoactive drug action in humans with mental disorders. Subspecialties: Pharmacology; Neuropharmacology. Home: 636 Duane Ct Ann Arbor MI 48103 Office: Dept Pharmacology Warner Lambert/Parke-Davis 2800 Plymouth Rd Ann Arbor MI 48105

HEFZY, MOHAMED SAMIR W. M., engineering educator; b. Cairo, Feb. 26, 1951; came to U.S., 1976; s. Wahba Mohamed and Samya Mohamed (El-Mahdi) H.; m. Nabila A. H. Gomaa, July 28, 1976; children—Hebah, Muhammad Sheriff, B.Sc. in Civil Engring, Cairo U., 1972; B.Sc. in Math, Ain Shams U., 1974; M.S. in Applied Mechanics, U. Cin., 1977, Ph.D. in Applied Mechanics, 1981. Instr. dept. math. and phys. engring. Cairo U., 1972-76; teaching and research asst. aero. engring. dept. U. Cin., 1976-81, asst. prof. evening coll., 1981-83, research assoc. biomechanics lab., dept. orthopedic surgery, 1981-83, research asst. prof. dept. orthopaedic surgery, 1985—; asst. prof. engring. scis., dept. physics and engring. Grand Valley State Coll., Allendale, Mich., 1983-84. Recipient NASA award, 1981. Mem. Am. Soc. Engring. Edn., ASME, Am. Acad. Mechanics, Soc. Engring. Sci. Current Work: Modeling the knee joint using structural mechanics and finite elements; kinematics of the clinical laxity examinations; biomechanics of the cruciate substitutes; continuum modeling of the mechanical behavior of discrete repetitive large structures. Subspecialties: Theoretical and applied mechanics; Biomedical engineering. Office: Giannestras Biomechanics Lab Dept Orthopaedic Surgery U Cin Cincinnati OH 45267

HEGSTED, DAVID MARK, biochemistry educator, research administrator; b. Rexburg, Idaho, Mar. 25, 1914; s. John and Edna Margaret (Porter) H.; m. Maxine Scow, May 26, 1941; children: Christina, Eric John. B.S., U. Idaho, 1936; M.S., U. Wis., 1938, Ph.D., 1940; A.M. (hon.), Harvard U., 1962. Research asst. U. Wis., 1936-41; research chemist Abbott Labs., 1941-42; assoc. nutrition Harvard Schs. of Medicine and Pub. Health, 1942-43, asst. prof., 1943-48, assoc. prof., 1948-62, prof., 1962-80, prof. nutritron emeritus, 1980—; assoc. dir. research New Eng. Regional Primate Research Ctr. Harvard Sch. Medicine, 1982—; adminstr. Human Nutrition Center, U.S. Dept. Agr., Washington, 1978-82; Cons. nutrition to Colombian Govt., 1946; nutritionist Inst. Inter-Am. Affairs, Peru, 1950-51; cons. UN FAO, Chile, 1956, Rome, 1961, 69; cons. WHO, 1962, 70, NIH, 1958—; mem. food and nutrition bd. NRC, 1955-72, chmn. food and nutrition bd., 1968-72. Editor: Nutrition Revs, 1968-78; contbr. articles, chpts. profl. jours. and books. Named to U. Idaho Hall of Fame, 1976. Mem. Am. Inst. Nutrition (Osborne Mendel award 1965, Conrad A. Elvehjem award 1979, pres. 1972-73), Am. Chem. Soc., Am. Pub. Health Assn., N.Y. Acad. Scis., Peruvian Pub. Health Soc., A.M.A. (council foods and nutrition 1960-68), Nat. Acad. Scis., Am. Dietetic Assn. (hon.), Sigma Xi, Alpha Chi Sigma, Sigma Alpha Epsilon. Clubs: Harvard, Cosmos. Subspecialties: Nutrition (medicine); Nutrition (biology). Home: 58 Boulder Rd Wellesley Hills MA 02115

HEIBERG, ELVIN RAGNVALD, III, civil engineer, army officer; b. Schofield Barracks, Hawaii, Mar. 2, 1932; s. Elvin R. and Evelyn (Lytle) H.; m. Kathryn Louise Schrimpf, June 16, 1953; children—Kathryn Anna Heiberg Young, Walter Dodge, Elvin Ragnvald IV, Kay Louise. B.S., U.S. Mil. Acad., 1953; M.S.C.E., MIT, 1958; M.A. in Govt. George Washington U., 1961; M.S. in Adminstrn, George Washington U., 1971. Registered profl. engr., La. Commd. 2d lt. U.S. Army, 1953, advanced through grades to lt. gen., 1984; service in Korea, 1954-55, co. comdr., Germany, 1961-62; faculty U.S. Mil. Acad., 1965-68; bn. comdr., Vietnam, 1968-69, detailed to Exec. Office of Pres., 1969-70, staff positions in Pentagon, 1971-74, dist. engr. C.E., New Orleans, 1974-75, div. engr. C.E., Ohio River, 1975-78; engr. U.S. Army-Europe, 1978-79; dir. civil works, Washington, 1979-82, dep. chief of engrs., 1982-83; program mgr. Army Ballistic Missile Dep. Orgn., Washington, 1983-84; chief of engrs. U.S. Army, 1984—; v.p. Permanent Internat. Assn. Nav. Congresses, 1983—. Pres. Stratford-on-the-Potomac Citizens Assn., 1972-73; mem. Mississippi River Commn., 1975-78, Ohio River Commn., 1975-78. Decorated D.S.M., Silver Star, Legion of Merit (3), D.F.C.; recipient Meritorious Service award Office Emergency Preparedness, 1970. Mem. ASCE, Soc. Am. Mil. Engrs., Assn. U.S. Army, Assn. Grads. U.S. Mil. Acad., Res. Officers Assn., Ret. Officers Assn. Methodist. Subspecialty: Civil engineering. Office: Chief of Engrs US Army DAEN-ZA Washington DC 20314

HEICKLEN, JULIAN PHILLIP, chemist, educator; b. Rochester, N.Y., Mar. 9, 1932; s. Arnold and Eva (Muchnick) H.; m. Susan Alice Hook, May 2, 1959; children—Judith, Alice, Deborah. B.Chem. Engring., Cornell U., 1954; Ph.D., U. Rochester, 1958. Postdoctoral fellow U. Minn., Mpls., 1958-60, U. Calif.-Berkeley, 1960-62; mem. tech. staff Aerospace Corp., El Segundo, Calif., 1962-67, sect. mgr., 1965-67; assoc. prof. chemistry Pa. State U., 1967-71, prof., 1971—; vis. prof. Hebrew U., 1973-74. Author: Colloid Formation & Growth: A Chemical Kinetics Approach, 1976, Atmospheric Chemistry, 1976. Action chmn. Los Angeles Congress of Racial Equality, 1963; bd. dirs. Citizens for Edn., State College, Pa., 1977-79; treas. Jewish Community Ctr., State College, 1969-71, v.p., 1971-72. Fellow N.Y. Acad. Scis. (Boris Pregel award 1984), Am. Phys. Soc., AAAS; mem. Am. Chem. Soc. (Creative Advances Environ Sci. award 1984), Air Pollution Control Assn. (Frank Chambers award 1985). Current work: atmospheric chemistry, reaction kinetics, carcinogenesis, mutagenesis, gerontology Subspecialties: Atmospheric chemistry; Environmental toxicology. Office: Pa State U 152 Davey Lab University Park PA 16802

HEIDRICK, LEE EDWARD, plant pathologist, agricultural researcher; b. Little Valley, N.Y., June 23, 1921; s. Otto Paul and Martha (Frenz) H.; m. Esther Marie Lisdell, Sept. 6, 1952. B.S., Cornell U., 1943, M.S., 1950; Ph.D. W.Va. U, 1955. Research specialist Rockefeller Found., Mexico City, 1950-53, Bogota, Colombia, 1953-63; agrl. research specialist Chevron Chem. Co., Mt. Laurel, N.J., 1963-84. Research publs. in phytopathology. Served to lt. USN, 1943-46. Mem. AAAS, Am. Phytophatol. Soc., Sigma Xi. Congregationalist. Lodge: Elks. Patentee pesticide synergists. Current Work: Pesticide research on fungicides, insecticides, herbicides, plant growth regulators, activity, efficacy, toxicology, mode of action. Subspecialties: Plant pathology; Plant physiology (agriculture). Home: 100 Winthrop Dr Ithaca NY 14850 Office: Box 118 Moorestown NJ 08057

HEIL, MATTHEW FRANCIS, immunologist; b. Charleston, W. Va., June 15, 1954; s. Eugene Jacob and Marion Virginia (Burke) H. B.A. in Philosophy, Biology with honors, Loyola U.-Chgo., 1976; M.A. in Philosophy, U. Toronto, Can., 1978; Ph.D. in Immunology, Syracuse U., 1983. Asst. instr. Syracuse U., N.Y., 1978-83; fellow N.Y. Med. Coll., Valhalla, 1983-84, instr., 1984—; cons. N.Y.C., 1984—. Assoc. editor The Med. Bus. Jour., 1985—. Contbr. articles to profl. jours. Mem. N.Y. Acad. Sci., AAAS, Am. Microbiol. Soc., Am. Assn. Immunologists, Am. Fedn. Clin. Research, Alpha Sigma Nu. Current work: Lymphokine biology and growth regulation in cancer cells; development new pharmaceutical agents; lymphokines and monoclonal antibodies in current biotechnology industry. Subspecialties: Cellular engineering; Cell study oncology. Home: 117 S Highland Ave #2C Ossining NY 10562 Office: N Y Med Coll Basic Sci Bldg 622 Valhalla NY 10595

HEILMEIER, GEORGE HARRY, research electrical engineer; b. Phila., May 22, 1936; s. George C. and Anna I. (Heineman) H.; m. Janet S. Faunce, June 24, 1961; 1 child, Elizabeth. B.S. in Elec. Engring., U. Pa., 1958; M.S. in Engring., Princeton U., 1960, A.M., 1961, Ph.D., 1962. With RCA Labs., Princeton, N.J., 1958-70, dir. solid state device research, 1965-68, dir. device concepts, 1968-70, White House fellow, spl. asst. to sec. def., Washington, 1970-71; asst. dir. def. research and engring. Office Sec. Def., 1971-75; dir. Def. Advanced Projects Agy., 1975-77; v.p. research, devel. and engring. Tex. Instruments Inc., 1978-83, sr. v.p., chief tech. officer, 1983—; chmn. tech. adv. bd. So. Meth. U.; mem. Def. Sci. Bd., Air Force Sci. Adv. Bd.; mem. adv. group on electron devices Dept. Def. Author. Recipient IEEE David Sarnoff award RCA, 1969; IR-100 New Product award Indsl. Research Assn., 1968, 69; Sec. Def. Disting. Civilian Service award, 1975, 77; Arthur Flemming award U.S. Jaycees, 1974; Air Force Meritorious Civilian Service award. Fellow IEEE (Sarnoff Field award 1976, Outstanding Achievement award Dallas chpt. 1984, Philips award 1985); mem. U. Pa., Princeton U. Grad. alumni assns., Nat. Acad. Engring., Sigma Xi, Tau Beta Pi, Eta Kappa Nu (Outstanding Young Engr. in U.S. award 1969). Methodist. Patentee in field. Subspecialties: Artificial intelligence; Semiconductors. Office: Tex Instruments 13500 North Central Expy Box 225474 MS 400 Dallas TX 75265

HEIMER, MALCOLM LEE, electrical engineering educator, consultant; b. Beech Creek, Pa., May 6, 1940; s. Carl Hake and Ethel Violet (Phillips) H.; m. Nancy Lea Barner, June 6, 1961 (div. 1969); 1 child, Carl Douglas. B.S. in Elec. Engring., Bucknell U., 1962; M.S. in Elec. Engring., Calif. Inst. Tech., 1963; Ph.D. in Elec. Engring., Pa. State U., 1976. Mem. tech. staff Bell Labs., Holmdel, N.J., 1963-65, Hughes Aircraft, Culver City, Calif., 1965-71; asst. prof. elec. engring. Vanderbilt U., Nashville, 1976-79; dir. biomed. div. Fidelity Electronics, Miami, Fla., 1979-81; prin. engr. Cordis Corp., Miami, 1981-83, cons., 1983—; assoc. prof. elec. engring. Fla. Internat. U., Miami, 1983—. Patentee ultra-linear sweep generator, voltage controlled ramp generator, 1968. Pres. Friendship Community Ctr., Beech Creek, Pa., 1973. Nat. Merit scholar, 1958; Fortesque fellow AIEE, 1962; Masters fellow Hughes Aircraft Co., 1962. Mem. IEEE, Assn. Advancement Med. Instrumentation, Am. Soc. Engring. Edn. Current work: Design of switched-capacitor and analog CMOS integrated circuits with applications to cardiac pacers and myo-electric prostheses. Subspecialties: Biomedical engineering; Integrated circuits. Home: 11010 SW 139th Ave Miami FL 33186 Office: Fla Internat U Tamiami Campus Miami FL 33199

HEIN, JOHN WILLIAM, dentist, educator; b. Chester, Mass., Sept. 29, 1920; s. Rudolf Jacob and Mercedes Viola H.; m. Jeanette Marie BeVier, Dec. 16, 1944. B.S., Am. Internat. Coll., 1941; D.M.D., Tufts U., 1944; Ph.D., U. Rochester, 1952; A.M. (hon.), Harvard, 1962; D.Sc. (hon.), Am. Internat. Coll., 1979. Student instr. oral pathology Tufts Coll. Dental Sch., 1943-44; head div. dental research U. Rochester, 1948-52, sr. fellow dental research, 1949-52, instr. pharmacology, 1951-53, asst. prof. dental research, 1952-55, asst. prof. pharmacology, 1954-55, chmn. dept. dentistry and dental research, 1952-55; instr. anatomy and physiology Eastman Sch. Dental Hygiene, 1950-55, lectr. dental research, 1953-55; research specialist Bur. Biol. Research, Rutgers U., 1955-59; dental dir. Colgate Palmolive Co., 1955-59; prof. preventive dentistry, dean Sch. Dental Medicine, Tufts U., 1959-62; dir. Forsyth Dental Center, 1962—; prof. dentistry Harvard Dental Sch., 1962-67. Trustee Am. Internat. Coll., 1960-76. Served to capt. AUS, 1942-47. Fellow AAAS, Internat. Coll. Dentists (regent 1967-72, pres. U.S. 1975-76, internat. pres. 1983-84); mem. ADA, Mass. Dental Soc. (pres. 1964-65), Internat. Assn. Dental Research (treas. 1978-82), Am. Acad. Dental Sci., New Eng. Dental Soc. (hon. pres. 1978), Am. Soc. Dentistry for Children, Assn. Ind. Research Insts. (1st v.p. 1980, pres. 1981-83), Royal Med. Soc. (hon.), Sigma Xi, Omicron Kappa Upsilon, Delta Sigma Delta. Club: Harvard (Boston). Subspecialty: Cariology. Home: Bridge St Medfield MA 02052 Office: 140 The Fenway Boston MA 02115

HEINEMANN, HEINZ, chemical engineer; b. Berlin, Aug. 21, 1913; married, 1948; 2 children. B.S., Technische Hochschule, Berlin, 1935; Ph.D. in Chemistry, U. Basel, Switzerland, 1937. Chief research chemist Rodessa Oil & Refining Corp., 1938-39; research chemist Danciger Oil & Refining, 1939-41; research fellow Carnegie Inst. Tech., 1941; lab. supr. Attapulgus Clay Co., 1941-48; sect. chief process research Houdry Process Corp., 1948-57; asst. to v.p. R&D, assoc. dir. research M.W. Kellogg Co., 1957-61, mgr., 1961-67, dir. chem. and engring. research, 1967-9; sr. research assoc. central research lab. Mobil R&D Corp., 1969-70, mgr. catalysis research, 1970-76, mgr. research contracts, 1976-78; staff sr. scientist Lawrence Berkeley Lab., U. Calif.-Berkeley, 1978—, lectr. chem. engring., 1979—; pres. Internat. Congress Catalysis, 1956-60; mem. Council Sci. Research, Spain, 1964—. Exec. editor Catalysis Revs. in Sci.-Engring., 1968-85. Recipient award Catalysis Club of Phila., 1968-85. Fellow Am. Inst. Chemists, Royal Soc.; mem. Nat. Acad. Engring., Am. Chem. Soc. (E.V. Murphree medal 1971), Catalysis Soc. N.Am. (E.J. Houdry award 1975). Subspecialties: Catalysis chemistry; Petroleum engineering. Address: 1588 Campus Dr Berkeley CA 94708*

HEINICKE, PETER HART, software engineer, consultant; b. Madison, Wis., Mar. 26, 1956; s. Herbert Raymond and Janet Louise (Hart) H. B.A. in Physics and Math., Washington U., St. Louis, 1977, M.A. in Math., 1977; M.A. in Physics, Princeton U., 1979; postgrad. Ill. Inst. Tech., Chgo., 1982—. Engineer Internat. Harvester, Melrose Park, Ill., 1980; systems analyst II Fermi Nat. Accelerator Lab., Batavia, Ill., 1980—; pres. Precision Computer Methods, Inc., Warrenville, Ill., 1979—; cons. businesses and univs. Author computer software. Nat. Merit scholar, 1974; Compton fellow, 1974, NSF fellow, 1977. Mem. Am. Phys. Soc. Republican. Lutheran. Club: Sigma Nu (St. Louis) (treas. 1976-77). Current work: High speed local area networks for real time data acquisition; software code mgmt. systems and project completion time estimation. Subspecialties: Distributed systems and networks; Software engineering. Home: Unit 3 2S779 Winchester Circle Warrenville IL 60555 Office: Fermi Nat Accelerator Lab MS120 PO Box 500 Batavia IL 60510

HEINRICH, MILTON ROLLIN, space life scientist, research biochemist; b. Linton, N.D., Nov. 25, 1919; s. Fred and Emma (Becker) H.; m. Ramona G. Cavanagh, May 31, 1966. A.B., U. S.D., 1941; M.S., U. Iowa, 1942, Ph.D., 1944. Postdoctoral fellow in biochemistry U. Pa., Phila., 1947-49; research assoc. Amherst (Mass.) Coll., 1949-58; spl. postdoctoral fellow U. Calif.-Berkeley, 1958-60; asst. prof. biochemistry U. So. Calif., Los Angeles, 1960-63; research scientist NASA Ames Research Ctr., Moffett Field, Calif., 1963-85, space sta. study scientist, 1982-85; pres. Zerog Corp., 1985—; lectr. space life scis. Editor: Extreme Environments, 1976; Contbr. articles to sci. jours. Served to lt. (j.g.) USN, 1944-47, PTO. USPHS fellow, 1947, 58; grantee, 1960-63; recipient Cosmos Group award NASA, 1981. Mem. Am. Soc. Biol. Chemists, Am. Chem. Soc., AAAS, Explorers Club, Phi Beta Kappa, Phi Eta Sigma, Sigma Xi, Phi Lambda Upsilon. Current Work: Consultant for planning life sciences on future space station, biochemical research on enzymes, enzyme technology, immobilized enzymes. Subspecialties: Gravitational biology; Biochemistry (medicine). Home and Office: 27200 Deer Springs Way Los Altos Hills CA 94022

HEINRICHS, WALTER EMIL, JR., mining company and exploration company executive, cons.; b. Superior, Ariz., Jan, 16, 1919; s. Walter Emil and Mary Gertrude (Smith) H.; m. Marcella Jean Heath, Aug. 1, 1941; children: Heath Douglas, Frederick Walter. Registered profl. engr., Colo., Ariz. registered geophysicist, Calif. Geol. Engr. Colo. Sch. Mines, 1940; Asst. chief geophysicist U.S. Bur. Reclamation, Denver, 1946-47, Newmont Mining Corp., N.Y.C., 1947-49; sr. ptnr. United Geophys. Corp. Mining div., Tucson, 1949-53; exploration mgr. Pima Mining Co., Tucson, 1953-55; mgr. Minerals Exploration Co., Los Angeles, 1955-58; pres., dir. Adit Resources Corp., Tucson, 1980—, Heinrichs GeoExploration Co., Tucson, 1958—; mem. and chmn. bd. govs. Ariz. Dept. Mineral Resources. Contbr. geophys. articles to profl. jours. Adviser to trustee Colo. Sch. Mines, 1962-68; precinct committeeman and alt. del. Republican Nat. Conv. Served to lt. (j.g.) USNR, 1944-46. Recipient Van Diest award Colo. Sch. Mines, 1955. Mem. AIME (Peele award 1955), Am. Inst. Profl. Geologists (cert.), Soc. Econ. Geologists. Presbyterian (deacon). Subspecialties: Geology; Geophysics. Home: 2943 E Chula Vista Dr Tucson AZ 85716 Office: Heinrichs Geo Exploration Co Box 5964 Tucson AZ 85703

HEISEY, S. RICHARD, physiologist, educator; b. Elizabethtown, Pa., Oct. 16, 1928; s. Samuel Witmer and Grace Mildred (Fink) H.; m. Sarah Ann Leftridge, June 7, 1958; children—David Richard, Janet Marie. B.S., Elizabethtown Coll., 1951; Sc.D., Johns Hopkins U., 1959. Pharmacologist, U.S. Army Med. Labs., Army Chemical Center, Md., 1953-56; NIH fellow Johns Hopkins U., Balt., 1956-59; instr. physiology Harvard Med. Sch., Boston, 1960-62, assoc., 1962-67; assoc. prof. Mich. State U., East Lansing, 1967-71, prof., 1971—. Contbr. articles to profl. jours. Served with U.S. Army, 1951-53. Fellow AAAS; mem. Am. Physiol. Soc., Soc. for Exptl. Biology and Medicine, Soc. for Neurosci., Sigma Xi. Current work: Cerebrospinal fluid physiology, respiratory physiology, regional cerebral blood flow. Subspecialties: Physiology (medicine); Comparative neurobiology. Office: Mich State U Dept Physiology Giltner Hall East Lansing MI 48824

HEISTAD, DONALD DEAN, medical educator; b. Chgo., Apr. 2, 1940; s. Wallace Ole and Sylvia Lillian (Feldman) H.; m. Sandra Jayne Jensen, Jan. 25, 1964; children—Dean, Wendy. Student U. Ill., 1959; M.D., U. Chgo., 1963. Diplomate Am. Bd. Internal Medicine. Intern U. Chgo., 1963-64, resident in internal medicine, 1964-66; cardiovascular trainee U. Iowa, Iowa City, 1966-67; research internist U.S. Army Research Inst. Environ. Medicine, Natick, Mass., 1967-70; asst. prof. medicine U. Iowa Coll. Medicine, Iowa City, 1970-73, assoc. prof. medicine, 1973-76, prof. medicine, 1976—; med. investigator VA Med. Ctr., 1978-83; 85—; mem. staff U. Iowa Hosp.; mem. sci. adv. com. Tobacco and Health Research Inst., U. Ky., 1982—. Mem. editorial bd. Jour. Cerebral Blood Flow and Metabolism, 1981-83; assoc. editor Circulation Research, 1981—. Reviewer Am. Jour. Physiology, Jour. Lab. and Clin. Medicine, Jour. Clin. Investigation, Circulation, Sci., Prostaglandins, Jour. Applied Physiology, Diabetes, Blood Vessels, Pflüger's Archives, New Eng. Jour. Medicine, Archives Neurology, Procs. of Soc. Exptl. Biology and Medicine, Trends in Neurosci., European Jour. Pharmacology. Recipient awards including Traveling fellowship Royal Soc. Medicine Found., 1973; Cecile Lehman Mayer Research award Am. Coll. Chest Physicians, 1973; Irving S. Wright award Am. Heart Assn., 1976; Harry Goldblatt award Council High Blood Pressure Research, Am. Heart Assn., 1980. Fellow Am. Heart Assn. (mem. council circulation), ACP, Am. Coll. Cardiology; mem. Am. Physiol. Soc., Council High Blood Pressure Research, Central Soc. Clin. Research, Am. Soc. Pharmacology and Exptl. Therapeutics, Am. Fedn. Clin. Research (sect., sec., treas., chmn. 1976-81), Am. Soc. Clin. Investigation, Assn. Am. Physicians. Subspecialties: Cardiology; Physiology (biology). Home: 435 Lexington St Iowa City IA 52242 Office: U Iowa Iowa City IA 52242

HEJTMANCIK, MILTON RUDOLPH, medical educator, physician; b. Caldwell, Tex., Sept. 27, 1919; s. Rudolph Joseph and Millie (Jurcak) H.; m. Myrtle Lou Erwin, Aug. 21, 1943; children—Kelly Erwin, Milton Rudolph, Peggy Lou; m. Myrtle Frances McCormick, Nov. 27, 1976. B.A., U. Tex., 1939, M.D., 1943. Diplomate: in cardiovascular diseases Am. Bd. Internal Medicine. Intern Phila. Gen. Hosp., 1943; resident internal medicine U. Tex., 1946-49, instr. internal medicine, 1949-51, asst. prof., 1951-54, assoc. prof., 1954-65, prof. internal medicine, 1965-80, dir. heart clinic, 1949-80, dir. heart sta., 1965-80; chief of staff John Sealy Hosp., 1957-58; chief staff U. Tex. Hosps., 1977-79. Contbr. articles profl. jours. Served from 1st lt. to capt., M.C. AUS, 1944-46, ETO. Fellow ACP, Am. Coll. Chest Physicians, Am. Coll. Cardiology; mem. Am. Heart Assn. (fellow council clin. cardiology), Tex. Heart Assn. (pres. 1979-80), Galveston Dist. Heart Assn. (pres. 1956), AMA (Billing's Gold medal 1973), Am. Fedn. Clin. Research, AAAS, Tex. Acad. Internal Medicine (gov. 1971-73, v.p. 1973-74, pres. 1976-77), N.Y. Acad. Scis., Tex. Club Cardiology (pres. 1972), Galveston County Med. Assn. (pres. 1971), Tex. Med. Assn. (del. 1972-80), Am. Heart Assn. (pres. Tex. affiliate 1979-80), Phi Beta Kappa, Sigma Xi, Alpha Omega Alpha, Phi Eta Sigma, Mu Delta, Phi Rho Sigma. Current Work: Electrophysiology and ultrasound. Subspecialty: Cardiology. Home: 6198 Alfton Ln Beaumont TX 77706 Office: VA Med Ctr 3385 Fannin Beaumont TX 77707

HEKMATPANAH, JAVAD, neurosurgery educator; b. Isfahan, Iran, Mar. 25, 1934; came to U.S., 1957, naturalized, 1973; m. Lyra Van Wien, Aug. 15, 1959; children: Daria, Kevin, Cameron. M.D., U. Tehran, 1956. Diplomate: Am. Bd. Neurosurgery, Am. Bd. Psychiatry and Neurology. Resident in neurology U. Wis. Gen. Hosp., Madison, 1958-61; resident in neurosurgery U. Chgo., 1961-64, asst. prof. neurosurgery, 1964-70, assoc. prof., 1970-75, prof., 1975—. Editor: Gliomas: Current Concepts in Biology, Diagnosis and Theory, 1975. Fellow A.C.S., Am. Acad. Neurology; mem. Am. Assn. Neurol. Surgeons, Chgo. Neurol. Soc., Chgo. Surg. Soc. Current Work: Cerebral circulation, cerebral compression (cardiac arrest) and brain tumors (clinical and laboratory). Subspecialties: Neurosurgery; Neurology. Office: U Chgo Hosp 950 E 59th St Box 405 Chicago IL 60637

HELD, RONALD DENNIS, systems analyst; b. Bklyn., Oct. 29, 1951; s. Arthur G. and Rosalind (Ribak) H. B.S., Rensselaer Poly. Inst., 1973, M.S., 1976, Ph.D., 1978. Systems analyst Space Systems div. Gen. Electric Co., King of Prussia, Pa., 1980—. Mem. Am. Astron. Assn., AAAS, Sigma Pi Sigma. Current Work: Math modelling, algorithm devel., stellar structure, gen. relativity and gravitation, cosmology. Subspecialties: Mathematical software; Theoretical astrophysics. Home: 959 Penn Circle C210 King of Prussia PA 19406

HELGERSON, SAM LELAND, biophysicist, research scientist; b. Centralia, Wash., May 7, 1949; s. Stanford Donald and Blanche Irene (Dean) H.; m. Elizabeth Ann Wells, Jan. 2, 1971; children—Margaret Kathryn, Christopher Wells. B.S., U. Puget Sound, 1971; Ph.D., Purdue U., 1976. NRC assoc. NASA Ames Research Ctr., Moffet Field, Calif., 1976-77; research biophysicist Cardiovascular Research Inst., U. Calif.-San Francisco, 1977—. Contbr. articles to profl. jours. Nat. Heart, Lung and Blood Inst. fellow, NIH, 1977. Mem. Biophys. Soc., Am. Chem. Soc., Internat. Cell Research Orgn. Unitarian Universalist. Current work: Mechanisms of biological energy conversion and coupling, computer modeling of bioenergetic regulatory mechanisms, time resolved absorption and fluorescence spectroscopy. Subspecialties: Biophysics (biology); Cell biology (medicine). Office: U Calif Med Sch MS 1327-M San Francisco CA 94143

HELLER, ADAM, chemist, researcher; b. Cluj, Romania, June 25, 1933; s. Ephraim and Blanche (Nissel) H.; m. Ilana Grossbard, July 26, 1956; children—Ephraim, Jonathan. M.Sc., Hebrew U., 1957, Ph.D., 1961. Postdoctoral research assoc. U. Calif.-Berkeley, 1962-63; mem. tech. staff Bell Labs., Murray Hill, N.J., 1963-64, 1975-77; mem. tech. staff GTE Labs., Bayside, N.Y., 1964-70, mgr. exploratory research, Waltham, Mass., 1970-75; head electronic materials research dept., AT&T Bell Labs., Murray Hill, 1977—; research prof. Brandeis U., Waltham, 1972-75; adj. prof. chemistry CUNY, 1968—; vis. prof. Coll. de France, Paris, 1982; regents lectr. UCLA, 1984; disting. prof. U. Guelph, Ont., Can., 1984. Editor: Semiconductor Liquid Junction Solar Cells, 1977; Inorganic Resists, 1982. Contbr. articles to profl. jours. Patentee in field. Case Western U. Centennial scholar 1981. Mem. Electrochem. Soc. (Battery Div. award 1978), Am. Chem. Soc., Am. Phys. Soc., Internat. Soc. Electrochemistry, Internat. Union Pure and Applied Chemistry (assoc.; com. photochemistry). Jewish. Current work: Transparent metals; hydrogen-evolving solar cells; photoelectrochemistry; chemistry and materials science of microelectronic devices; batteries (lithium-thionyl chloride); inorganic liquid lasers. Subspecialties: Physical chemistry; Electronic materials. Home: 7 Timberline Dr Bridgewater NJ 08807 Office: AT&T Bell Labs 600 Mountain Ave Murray Hill NJ 07974

HELLER, ALFRED, pharmacology, physiology sciences educator; b. Chgo., July 23, 1930; s. Selig and Lena (Rochelle) H.; m. Barbara R. Steigman, July 22, 1956; 1 child, Daniel Jacob. B.S. with honors, U. Ill.-Chgo., 1952; Ph.D. in Pharmacology, U. Chgo., 1956, M.D. with honors, 1960. Asst. prof. pharmacology, physiology U. Chgo., 1960-75, assoc. prof., 1965-72, prof., 1972—, acting dept. chmn., 1973, chmn., 1973—. Office: U Chgo Dept Pharmacology and Physiol Scis Abbott Hall 947 E 58th St Chicago IL 60637

HELLER, BARBARA RUTH, statistician, educator; b. Milw., May 15, 1931; d. Mitchell and Sophie Lerner (Goldberg) Steigman; m. Alfred Heller, July 22, 1956; 1 son, Daniel. Ph.B., U. Chgo., 1950; B.S., Roosevelt U., 1953; M.S., U. Chgo., 1965, Ph.D., 1979. Asst. prof. math. Ill. Inst. Tech., Chgo., 1980—. Contbr. papers to profl. jours. Mem. Inst. Math. Stats., Am. Statis. Assn., Am. Math. Soc., Soc. Indsl. and Applied Math. Current Work: Characterization of probability distributions, application of statistics in stereological problems; size distributions. Subspecialties: Statistics; Probability. Office: Dept Mat Ill Inst Tech Chicago IL 60616

HELLER, DONALD FRANKLIN, laser researcher, chemical physicist; b. Bklyn., Mar. 29, 1947; s. George M. and Florence (Gelb) H.; m. Mary R. Noberini, May 28, 1972; 1 child, Katherine Ann. B.S. with honors, U. Calif.-Berkeley, 1969; Ph.D., U. Chgo., 1972. Research assoc. James Franck Inst., Chgo., 1972-73; postdoctoral fellow U. Calif.-Berkeley, 1973-75; project assoc. U. Wis.-Madison, 1975-76; vis. prof. chemistry McGill U., Montreal, Que., Can., 1976-77; staff physicist Allied Corp., Morristown, N.J., 1977-80, sr. research physicist, 1980-83, sr. research assoc., group leader, 1983—; reviewer numerous profl. jours., 1972—, NSF, 1977—; founder Disklok, Inc., San Francisco, 1984. Contbr. articles to profl. jours. Patentee in optics, laser applications and molecular processes. Swift fellow U. Chgo., 1971; recipient Inventors award Allied Corp., 1981. Mem. Am. Chem. Soc., N.Y. Acad. Scis. Current work: Fundamental and applied research on lasers, laser applications, nonlinear processes, molecular energy transfer. Subspecialties: Laser physics; Laser-induced chemistry. Home: 740 Watchung Rd Bound Brook NJ 08805 Office: Allied Corp 7 Powderhorn Dr Mount Bethel NJ 07060

HELLER, DOUGLAS MAX, electronics and aerospace consultant; b. Dover, Kent, Eng., Feb. 23, 1918; came to U.S., 1947, naturalized, 1955; s. William Max and Dorothy (Watt) H.; m. Patricia Short, Apr. 23, 1941; children—Susan Patricia, Wendy Anne, Jennifer Jane. B.Sc. in Physics, Royal Coll. Sci., London, 1939. Mem. sci. staff research labs. Brit. Gen. Electric Co., North Wembley, Middlesex, Eng., 1939-47; from research engr. to dir. engring. and gen. mgr. Bendix Corp., Balt. and South Bend, Ind., 1947-66; research dir. Martin Marietta Aerospace, Bethesda, Md., 1966-84; pres. Max Heller Assocs., Chevy Chase, Md., 1984—. Fellow IEEE, Inst. Physics (U.K.), AIAA (assoc.); assoc. Royal Coll. Sci. Republican. Episcopalian. Subspecialties: Electronics; Aerospace engineering and technology. Home and office: 4849 Langdrum Ln Chevy Chase MD 20815

HELLER, LEON, physicist; b. N.Y.C., Dec. 16, 1929; s. Eleazer Lawrence and Henrietta (Geller) H.; m. Rosalie D. Liebschutz, June 17, 1952; children—Peter, Anthony, Jean. B.A., Bklyn. Coll., 1951; Ph.D., Cornell U., 1956. Staff mem. Los Alamos Nat. Lab., 1956—, group leader Medium Energy Physics Theory Group, 1971-73; vis. asst. prof. Case Inst., Cleve., 1962-63; AEC/U.K. Atomic Energy Authority exchange scientist Harwell, Eng., 1969-70; vis. staff mem. MIT, Cambridge, 1976-77. Contbr. articles to profl. jours. Fulbright scholar Australian-Am. Edn. Found. Univs. Adelaide and Melbourne, 1985-86. Fellow Am. Phys. Soc. Office: T5 MS B283 Los Alamos Nat Lab Los Alamos NM 87545

HELLER, LOIS JANE, physiologist, educator; b. Detroit, Jan. 4, 1942; d. John and Lona Elizabeth (Stockmeyer) Skagerberg; m. Robert Eugene Heller, May 21, 1966; children—John Robert, Suzanne Elizabeth. B.A., Albion Coll., 1964; M.S., U. Mich., 1966; Ph.D., U. Ill. Med. Ctr.-Chgo., 1970. Instr. to asst. prof. U. Ill. Med. Ctr., Chgo., 1969-71; asst. prof. to assoc. prof. physiology U. Minn. Sch. Medicine, Duluth, 1972—, asst. dean student affairs, 1973-76. Author: (with others) Cardiovascular Physiology, 1981. Contbr. articles to profl. jours. Mem. Am. Physiol. Soc., Am. Heart Assn. (Minn. chmn. bd. 1983-84, pres. 1980-81), Sigma Xi. Current work: research cardiac function under conditions stress, hypertension, tachyarrhythmias; cardiac hypertrophy; cardiac anaphylaxis. Subspecialties: Physiology (biology); Physiology (medicine). Home: 311 Halsey Duluth MN 55803 Office: U Minn Sch Medicine Basic Med Sci Bldg Duluth MN 55812

HELLIWELL, ROBERT ARTHUR, electrical engineering educator; b. Red Wing, Minn., Sept. 2, 1920; s. Harold Harlowe and Grace (Robson) H.; m. Jean Perham, Apr. 5, 1942; children: Bradley Athearn, David Robson, Richard Perham, Donna Marie. B.E.E., Stanford U., 1942, M.A., 1943, E.E., 1944, Ph.D. in Elec. Engring, 1948. Mem. faculty Stanford U., 1946—, prof. elec. engring., 1958—, dir. Ctr. for Space Sci. and Astrophysics, 1983—. Author: Whistlers and Related Ionospheric Phenomena, 1965, also articles. Recipient Antarctica Service medal Royal Soc., London, Appleton prize, 1972. Fellow IEEE, Internat. Sci. Radio Union; mem. Am. Geophys. Union, AAAS, AAUP, Nat. Acad. Scis., Phi Beta Kappa, Sigma Xi, Tau Beta Pi. Subspecialties: Radioscience; Electrical engineering. Home: 2240 Page Mill Rd Palo Alto CA 94304 Office: Star Lab Stanford CA 94305

HELLMAN, RHONA PHYLLIS, hearing science researcher, educator; b. N.Y.C., May 22, 1935; d. David and Florence (Schlesinger) Rosenberg; m. William S. Hellman, Nov. 4, 1954; children: Ronald Bruce, Adrian David. B.A. cum laude, Bklyn. Coll., 1955; M.S., Syracuse U., 1960. Research audiologist VA, 1963-64; research asst. Auditory Perception Lab., Northeastern U., Boston, 1965-66; sr. research asst. Lab. Psychophysics, Harvard U., 1967-76; adj. asst. prof. communication disorders Boston U., 1975-81, adj. assoc. prof., 1981—, establisher Communcation Scis. Lab, 1982. Reviewer: Jour. Acoustical Soc. Am; Contbr. articles to sci. jours., chpts. to books. Sponsor Arlington (Mass.) Philharm. Soc.; mem. Arlington Civil Rights Com. NASA grantee, 1979—. Mem. Acoustical Soc. Am. (psychol. and physiol. acoustics com. 1979-82, chmn. com. on auditory magnitudes), Soc. for Neurosci., AAAS, Mass. Speech and Hearing Assn. Current Work: Psychoacoustics: psychophysiology of normal and impaired hearing; sensory processes. Subspecialties: Acoustical engineering; Psychobiology. Office: 40 Cummington St Boston MA 02215

HELLSTROM, H. RICHARD, pathologist, educator; b. Marianna, Pa., Mar. 22, 1928; s. Everett Arthur and Rhoda Elizabeth (Kempfer) H.; m. Martha Clara Montag, May 25, 1975. B.S., Waynesburg Coll., 1949; M.D., U. Pitts., 1952. Diplomate Am. Bd. Pathology. Staff pathologist VA Hosp., Pitts., 1957-68, chief lab. pathologist, 1968-79; chief lab. pathologist, VA Hosp., Syracuse, N.Y., 1979—; asst. prof. U. Pitts. Sch. Medicine, Pa., 1957-68, assoc. prof., 1968-79; prof. pathology SUNY Upstate Med. Ctr.-Syracuse, 1979—. Contbr. articles to profl. jours. Fellow Am. Soc. Cli. Pathology, Coll. Am. Pathology, Am. Heart Assn. Basic Research, Internat. Acad. Pathology; mem. AAAS, Fedn. Am. Soc. Exptl. Biology. Current work: Research in anatomic pathology and cardiology. Subspecialty: Pathology (medicine). Home: 5035 Bridlepath Rd Fayetteville NY 13066

HELLWARTH, ROBERT WILLIS, physicist, educator; b. Ann Arbor, Mich., Dec. 10, 1930; s. Arlen Roosevelt and Sarah Matilda (Townsend) H.; m. Abigail Gurfein, Sept. 20, 1957 (div. 1979); children: Benjamin John, Margaret Eve, Thomas Abraham. B.S., Princeton U., 1952; D.Phil. (Rhodes scholar), St. John's Coll., Oxford (Eng.) U., 1955. Sr. scientist, mgr. Hughes Research Labs., Malibu, Calif., 1956-70; vis. asso. prof. elec. engring. and physics U. Ill., Urbana, 1964-65; research asso., sr. research fellow Calif. Inst. Tech., Pasadena, 1966-70; NSF sr. postdoctoral fellow Clarendon Lab.-St. Peter's Coll., Oxford (Eng.) U., 1970-71; George Pfleger prof. physics and elec. engring. U. So. Calif., 1970—. Author monograph, articles in field; asso. editor: IEEE Jour. Quantum Electronics, 1964-76. Grantee NSF; Grantee Dept. Energy; Grantee Air Force Office Sci. Research; Grantee U.S. Army Research Office. Fellow IEEE, Am. Phys. Soc., AAAS; mem. Nat. Acad. Engring., AAUP, Phi Beta Kappa, Sigma Xi, Eta Kappa Nu. Patentee Q-switched laser, nonlinear optical microscope, phase conjugate mirror. Subspecialty: Optical physics. Home: 711 16th St Santa Monica CA 90402 Office: SSC 303 Physics Dept U So Calif Los Angeles CA 90089

HELSDON, JOHN HEBARD, JR., atmospheric scientist, meteorology educator; b. Buffalo, Oct. 29, 1948; s. John Hebard and Elisabeth (Ball) H.; m. Dolores Ann Matszak, Aug. 19, 1977; children—Julie Ann, Kimberly, Lara, Karen Elisabeth, Kristin Michelle. Student, U.S. Air Force Acad., 1966-67; B.S. in Physics, Trinity Coll., 1970; M.S. Atmospheric Sci., SUNY-Albany, 1973, Ph.D. in Atmospheric Sci., 1979. Research asst. Research Found. SUNY-Albany, 1977-79; assoc. prof. meteorology S.D. Sch. Mines and Tech., Rapid City, 1981—, research scientist Inst. Atmospheric Scis., 1979—, acting head numerical modeling group, 1982-83; affil. faculty appt. Colo. State U., Fort Collins, Colo., 1982-83. Contbr. articles to profl. jours. Coach, Rapid City Youth Soccer League, 1980-84; mem. Black Hills Festival Chamber Singers, Rapid City, 1985. Named to Register of Outstanding Americans Under Age 40, Esquire Mag. Mem. Am. Meteorol. Soc. (com. on atmospheric electricity), Am. Geophys. Union, Sigma Xi, Sigma Pi Sigma. Episcopalian. Club: Black Hills Runners (Rapid City). Current work: use of multidimensional numerical cloud models to investigate processes leading to the electrification of thunderstorms. Subspecialty: Atmospheric electricity; Cloud physics. Home: 3216 Meadowbrook Dr Rapid City SD 57702 Office: Inst Atmospheric Scis SD Sch Mines and Tech 501 E St Joseph Rapid City SD 57701

HELSLEY, GROVER CLEVELAND, pharm. co. exec.; b. Strasburg, Va., Sept. 26, 1926; s. Grover Cleveland and Vallie Mae (Putnam) H.; m. Betty Jean Midkiff, Oct. 30, 1949; children—Grover Cleveland, Linda Suzanne, Robert Christopher. B.S. with honors, Shepherd Coll., 1954; M.S., U. Va., 1956, Ph.D. (Philip Francis duPont fellow), 1958. Research chemist E.I. duPont de Nemours & Co., Inc., Richmond, Va., 1958-62; research chemist A.H. Robins Co., Richmond, 1962-64, group leader, 1964-68, asso. dir. chem. research, 1968-70; dir. research Hoechst-Roussel Pharms. Inc., Somerville, N.J., 1970-72, v.p. pharm. research, 1972—. Contbr. sci. articles to profl. jours. Served with USAAF, 1945-47. Mem. Am. Chem. Soc., Pharm. Mfrs. Assn. (editorial adv. bd. drug devel. research 1980), Indsl. Research Inst. Mem. Disciples of Christ Ch. Patentee in field. Current Work: Chemistry of heterocyclic compounds; fluoride displacement on aromatic rings. Subspecialties: Organic chemistry; Medicinal chemistry. Home: PO Box 117 Pottersville NJ 07979 Office: Hoechst-Roussel Pharms Inc Route 202-206 N Somerville NJ 08876

HELSTROM, CARL WILHELM, electrical engineering educator, researcher; b. Easton, Pa., Feb. 22, 1925; m. Barbro Elisabeth Dahlbom, Oct. 13, 1956; children—Lars, Stefan. B.S. in Engring. Physics, Lehigh U., 1947; M.S. in Physics, Calif. Inst. Tech., 1949, Ph.D. in Physics, 1951. Adv. mathematician Westinghouse Research Labs., Pitts., 1951-66; prof. elec. engring. U. Calif.-San Diego, La Jolla, 1966—. Author: Statistical Theory of Signal Detection, 1960, 2d edit., 1968; Quantum Detection and Estimation Theory, 1976; Probability and Stochastic Processes for Engineers, 1984. Served with USNR, 1944-46; Guam. Fellow IEEE (Centennial medal 1984, editor IEEE Transactions on Info. Theory, 1967-71), Optical Soc. Am. Current work: Computation of detection probabilities in communications, radar, and optics and of cumulative distributions arising in statistics. Subspecialties: Telecommunications; Optical signal processing. Office: Dept Elec Engring and Computer Sci C-014 U Calif-San Diego La Jolla CA 92093

HELTNE, PAUL GREGORY, museum administrator, environmental biology consultant; b. Lake Mills, Iowa, July 4, 1941; s. Palmer Tilford and Grace Catherine (Hanson) H.; children—Lisa, Christian. B.A., Luther Coll., 1962; Ph.D., U. Chgo., 1970. Asst. prof. Johns Hopkins U., Balt., 1970-82; dir. Chgo. Acad. Scis., 1982—; cons. WHO, Pan Am. Health Orgn., Washington, 1976-82, Am. Petroleum Inst., Washington, 1982—. Editor, author: The Lion-Tailed Macaque, 1985; Neotropical Primates Status and Conservation, 1976. Creator mus. exhibits Weavers of Water, Weavers of Light, 1984. Mem. Assn. Sci. Mus. Dirs., AAAS, Assn. Sci. and Tech. Ctrs., Am. Assn. Mus., Assn. Tropical Biology. Lutheran. Current work: Broad approaches to conservation and development in the tropics with emphasis on productivity of natural communities. Subspecialties: Ecosystems analysis; Evolutionary biology. Office: The Chgo Acad Scis 2001 N Clark St Chicago IL 60612

HELTON, AUDUS WINZLE, plant pathologist; b. Bethel, Okla., Oct. 5, 1922; s. Leonard Huston and Berniece Gladys (Wright) H.; m. Christina Raza, July 29, 1978; children—Rebecca, John, Kathy, Thomas, Carolyn. B.A., Ohio Wesleyan U., 1947, M.S., 1948; Ph.D., Oreg. State U., 1951. Plant pathologist U. Idaho, Moscow, 1951—, prof. plant pathology, 1956—. Served with USN, World War II. Chem. Co. research grantee, 1960—. Mem. Am. Phytopath. Soc., Am. Inst. Biol. Scis., AAUP, AAAS, Idaho Acad. Scis., Wildlife Fedn., Sigma Xi. Lodges: Lions; Masons. Current Work: Fungal stem and root diseases of orchard trees. Subspecialties: Plant pathology; Plant physiology (agriculture). Office: Dept Plant Soil and Entomol Scis U Idaho Moscow ID 83843

HELZ, GEORGE RUDOLPH, chemistry educator; b. Silver Spring, Md., Mar. 4, 1942; s. Armin Werner and Adah Hubbard (Porter) H.; m. Rosalind Lenore Tuthill, Aug. 22, 1970; 1 child, Catherine. Research asst. Princeton U., 1964, Pa. State U., 1964-68; from asst. prof. to prof. chemistry U. Md., College Park, 1970—. Author: Power Plant Chlorination, 1972. Editor: Environmental Series Cambridge U. Press, 1982—. Contbr. articles to profl. jours. Mem. Am. Chem. Soc. (chmn. geochem. div. 1985), Geochem Soc. (treas. 1975-78), Geol. Soc. Washington (v.p. 1983), Geol. Soc. Am., Am. Geophys. Union. Current work: Fate of toxic substances in environment; estuarine geo-chemistry; sulfide geochemistry. Subspecialties: Environmental chemistry; Geochemistry. Home: 4120 Everett St Kensington MD 20895 Office: Dept Chemistry U Md College Park MD 20742

HEM, JOHN DAVID, geochemist; b. Starkweather, N.D., May 14, 1916; s. Hans Neilius and Josephine Augusta (Larsen) H.; m. Ruth Evans, Mar. 11, 1945; children—John David, Michael Edward. Student Minot State Coll., 1933-36, N.D. State U., 1937-38, Iowa State U., 1938; B.S., George Washington U., 1940. Lab. technician U.S. Geol. Survey, Washington, 1939-40, analytical chemist and dist. chemist, Safford, Ariz. and Roswell, N.M., 1940-44, Albuquerque, 1945-53, research chemist, Denver, 1953-63, research geochemist, Menlo Park, Calif., 1964—. Author: Study and Interpretation Chemistry of Natural Water, 1959, rev. edits., 1970, 85. Contbr. articles to profl. jours. Mem. Am. Chem. Soc., Am. Geophys. Union, Am. Water Works Assn., Geochem. Soc., Soc. Geochemistry and Health. Democrat. Lutheran. Lodge: Toastmasters. Current work: Geochemistry of natural water, thermodynamics of non equilibrium systems, aqueous chemistry of transition metals. Subspecialties: Geochemistry; Hydrology. Home: 3349 St Michael Ct Palo Alto CA 94306 Office: US Geol Survey MS427 345 Middlefield Rd Menlo Park CA 94025

HEMBREE, GEORGE HUNT, chemical company executive; b. Richmond, Ky., Sept. 2, 1930; s. George Nelson and Miriam Grace (Tuttle) H.; m. Betty Jo Williams, June 7, 1952; children—George Hunt, Elizabeth Ann, Susan Grace. B.S., Eastern Ky. U., 1952; Ph.D., Ohio State U., 1958. With E.I. du Pont de Nemours & Co., 1958—, research mgr., Rochester, N.Y., 1969-71, Parlin, N.J., 1971-73, mktg. mgr., Wilmington, Del., 1973-74, lab. dir., Wilmington, 1974-75, Brevard, N.C., 1975—. Served with AUS, 1953-55. Mem. Am. Chem. Soc., Soc. Photg. Scientists and Engrs., Ky. Acad. Scis., Sigma Xi, Phi Lambda Upsilon. Baptist. Current work: Development of materials and systems for radiological imaging. Office: PO Box 267 Brevard NC 28712

HEMENWAY, MARY KAY, astronomer, consultant; b. Akron, Ohio, Nov. 20, 1943; d. Ralph Elwood and Mary Esther (Keegan) Meacham; m. Paul Derek Hemenway, June 1, 1968; children: Anne, Sara. B.S., Notre Dame Coll., Cleve., 1965; M.A. (NDEA fellow), U. Va., 1967, Ph.D., 1971. Asst. prof. Mary Baldwin Coll., Staunton, Va., 1970-71; asst. prof., instr. U. Tex., Austin, 1975-80; dir. U. Tex. Astronomy Ednl. Services Offices, 1980—, ednl. cons. dept. sci. edn. and extension, corr. studies. Author: (with R. Robert Robbins) Modern Astronomy-An Activities Approach, 1982. Vice pres., trustee Discovery Hall (non-profit mus.); active Girl Scouts U.S.A. U. Va. fellow Sterrewacht, Leiden, Netherlands, 1968-69. Mem. Am. Astron. Soc., Sigma Xi. Roman Catholic. Current Work: Galactic structure. Subspecialty: Optical astronomy. Home: 3205 Skylark Dr Austin TX 78757 Office: Univ Tex RLM 15-308 Austin TX 78712

HEMMINGSEN, BARBARA BRUFF, microbiologist, educator; b. Whittier, Calif., Mar. 25, 1941; d. Stephen Cartl and Susanna Jane (Alexander) Bruff; m. Edvard Alfred Hemmingsen, Aug. 5, 1967; 1 dau., Grete Anne. B.A., U. Calif.-Berkeley, 1962, M.A., 1964; Ph.D., U. Calif.-San Diego, 1971. Microbiologist Ames Research Ctr., NASA, Moffitt Field, Calif., 1964-65, summer 1966; vis. asst. prof. Ecology Lab., Zoology Inst., Aarhus (Denmark) U., 1971-72; lectr. in microbiology San Diego State U., 1973-77, asst. prof. microbiology, 1977-81, assoc. prof., 1981—. Author: (with T. Fenchel) Manual of Microbial Ecology, 1974, Japanese transl., 1975; contbr. chpts., articles to profl. publs. Mem. Planned Parenthood Assn. San Diego, 1973—; mem. La Jolla (Calif.) Elem. Sch. PTA, 1980—. Mem. AAAS, Am. Soc. Microbiology, Soc. Gen. Microbiology, Soc. Protozoologists, Fedn. Am. Scientists. Democrat. Current Work: Effects of extreme gas supersaturations on microorganisms and animal cells; conditions that promote gas bubble nucleation intracellularly; taxonomy and physiology of marine bacteria. Subspecialty: Microbiology. Office: Dept Biology San Diego State San Diego CA 92182-0067

HEMP, GENE W(ILLARD), engineering mechanics educator, university executive; b. Mpls., Dec. 6, 1938; s. Willard H. and Ann (Thompson) H.; m. Evelyn H. Ploetz, Mar. 19, 1960; children: Barbara Jean, Suzanne Marie. B.S. in Aero. Engring, U. Minn., 1961, B.S.B. in Bus. Adminstrn, 1962, M.S. in Mechanics and Materials, 1963, Ph.D. in Mechanics and Materials, 1967. Asst. prof. engring. scis. U. Fla., 1967-70, assoc. prof., 1970-76, prof., 1976—, asst. dean engring., 1972-74, asst. v.p. acad. affairs, 1974-76, assoc. v.p., 1976—; cons. Harry Diamond Labs., 1970-72. Mem. ASME, AIAA, Am. Soc. Engring. Edn., Soc. Engring. Scis. Current Work: Nonlinear oscillation, dynamic material properties, vibrations of discrete and continuous media, rigid body mechanics. Subspecialties: Theoretical and applied mechanics; Applied mathematics. Home: 9909 NW 59th Pl Gainesville FL 32606 Office: U Fla 233 Tigert Hall Gainesville FL 32611

HEMSTOCK, GLEN ALTON, corporation research and development executive; b. Owen Sound, Ont., Can., Oct. 5, 1925; s. Herman Edwin and Ada May (Tyler) H.; m. Evelyn Christina Beaton, Oct. 6, 1951; children: Carol Marie, Bruce Edward. B.S., U. Toronto, 1948; Ph.D., Purdue U., 1951. Asst. prof. agronomy Purdue U., 1951-52; research assoc. Inst. Paper Chemistry, 1952-56; research supr. minerals and chemicals Philipp Corp., 1956-62, mgr. fundamental research minerals and chemicals, 1967, from asst. dir. research to dir. research, 1967-74; v.p. research and devel. Engelhard Corp., Edison, N.J., 1974-84, dir. research, 1984—; group leader Union-Bag Camp Corp., 1962-67. Sect. editor: Phys. Chemistry of Pigments and Paper Coatings, 1974-77. Mem. TAPPI, Indsl. Research Inst., Assn. Research Dirs., Am. Chem. Soc., Clay Minerals Soc., Research and Devel. Council N.J. Republican. Presbyterian. Patentee in field. Current Work: Chemistry and surface properties of clay minerals. Subspecialties: Surface chemistry; Catalysis chemistry. Home: 24 James Ct Princeton NJ 08540 Office: Engelhard Corp Menlo Park CN 28 Edison NJ 08818

HENDERSON, ANN SHIRLEY, geneticist, researcher; b. Honea Path, S.C., Aug. 29, 1938; s. William Campbell and Annie Sue (Anderson) H. B.A., Winthrop Coll., 1960; M.A., U. N.C., 1963, Ph.D., 1967. Staff researcher Internat. Lab. Genetics and Biophysics, Naples, Italy, 1968-70; research assoc. Columbia U., N.Y.C., 1971-74, asst. prof., 1975-82; prof. biol. scis. Hunter Coll., CUNY, N.Y.C., 1983—; cons. Clin. Testing-Research, Hohokus, N.J., 1981—. Contbr. articles to profl. jours. Leukemia scholar Leukemia Soc. Am., 1981—. Current Work: Studies of molecular organization of the human chromosome. Subspecialties: Genome organization; Molecular biology. Office: Hunter Coll CUNY 695 Park Ave New York NY 10021

HENDERSON, CARROL LAVERNE, state government wildlife biologist; b. Ames, Iowa, July 14, 1946; s. Curtis Delmar and Leona Joyce (Thorsnes) H.; m. Ethelle Maria Gonzalez, Dec. 13, 1969; 1 child, Craig. B.S., Iowa State U., 1968; M.Forest Resources, U. Ga., 1970; postgrad. U. Costa Rica, 1969. Instr., U. So. Miss., Biloxi, 1971, Altus Jr. Coll., Okla., 1972-73; ecology cons. DeLeuw, Cather & Co., Atlanta, 1974; asst. mgr. Lac qui Parle Wildlife Refuge, Dept. Natural Resources, Watson, Minn., 1974-77, state nongame wildlife supr., St. Paul, 1977—. Author: Woodworking for Wildlife, 1984. contbr. articles to profl. jours. Bd. dirs. N.Am. Loon Fund, Meredith, N.H.; wildlife leader 4-H Shooting Sports Program, Anoka County, Minn., 1984; bd. dirs. Deep Portage Conservation Res., Hackensack, Minn., Minn. 4-H Shooting Sports Program, Mpls. Served to capt. USAF, 1970-73. Recipient Stewardship award The Nature Conservancy, Mpls., 1976; Tropical Agr. fellow, Tropical Ecology fellow Orgn. for Tropical Studies, San Jose, Costa Rica, 1969. Mem. Nongame Wildlife Assn. N.Am. (pres. 1984-86) Wildlife Soc. (pres. Minn. chpt. 1981-82), Minn. Ornithologists Union, Minn. Fish and Wildlife Employees Assn. (pres. 1978-79), Trumpeter Swan Soc. (membership chmn. Minn. 1980-81), Minn. Prairie Chicken Soc., Phi Kappa Phi, Gamma Sigma Delta. Lutheran. Current work: Nongame wildlife ecology, endangered species, management and conservation; supervision statewide program for conservation of nongame and endangered wildlife; publicize nongame wildlife check-off on state tax forms. Subspecialties: Resource management; Ecology (environmental science). Home: 640 119th Ln NE Blaine MN 55434 Office: Box 7 Minn Dept Natural Resources 500 Lafayette Rd Saint Paul MN 55146

HENDERSON, CHARLES R., animal geneticist. Prof. emeritus dept. animal sci., Cornell U., Ithaca, N.Y. Subspecialty: Animal genetics. Office: Cornell U Dept Animal Sci Ithaca NY 14853

HENDERSON, DONALD AINSLIE, university dean; b. Cleve., Sept. 7, 1928; s. David Alexander and Grace Eleanor (McMillan) H.; m. Nana Irene Bragg, Sept. 1, 1951; children: Leigh Ainslie, David Alexander, Douglas Bruce. B.A., Oberlin (Ohio) Coll., 1950, D.Sc. (hon.), 1979; M.D., U. Rochester (N.Y.), 1954, D.Sc. (hon.), 1977; M.P.H., Johns Hopkins U., 1960; LL.D. (hon.), Marietta (Ohio) Coll., 1978; D.Sc. (hon.), U. Ill., 1979, U. Md., 1980; M.D. (hon.), U. Geneva, 1980; L.H.D. (hon.), SUNY, 1981. Diplomate: Am. Bd. Preventive Medicine. Intern, then resident Mary Imogene Bassett Hosp., Cooperstown, N.Y., 1954-55, 57-59; chief epidemic intelligence service Center Disease Control, USPHS, Atlanta, 1955-57, chief surveillance sect., 1960-66; chief med. officer smallpox edn. WHO, Geneva, 1966-77; dean Johns Hopkins U. Sch. Hygiene and Pub. Health, 1977—. Contbr. articles to med. jours. Recipient Commendation medal USPHS, 1962, Disting. Service medal, 1976; Ernst Jung prize, 1976; award Govt. India-Indian Soc. Malaria and Other Communicable Diseases, 1975; Rosenthal internat. award for excellence, 1975; George MacDonald medal London Sch. Hygiene and Tropical Medicine, Royal Soc. Tropical Medicine and Hygiene, 1976; Health medal Govt. Afghanistan, 1976; Spl. Albert Lasker Pub. Health Service award for WHO, 1976; Public Welfare medal Nat. Acad. Scis., 1978; Joseph C. Wilson award in internat. affairs, 1978; James D. Bruce Meml. award, 1978; 50th Anniversary Disting. Service award Blue Cross-Blue Shield, 1979; medal for contbns. to health Govt. of Ethiopia, 1979; Outstanding Alumnus award Delta Omega, 1980; Disting. Alumnus award Johns Hopkins U., 1982; Internat. Merit award Gairdner Found., 1983; Albert Schweitzer internat. prize for medicine, 1985. Hon. fellow Am. Acad. Pediatrics, Royal Coll. Physicians (U.K.); mem. Inst. Medicine (Nat. Acad. Scis.), Am. Public Health Assn., Internat. Epidemiol. Assn., Royal Soc. Tropical Medicine and Hygiene, Indian Soc. Malaria and Other Communicable Diseases. Current Work: Public health education; international health and development. Subspecialty: Public health education administration. Home: 3802 Greenway Baltimore MD Office: 615 N Wolfe St Baltimore MD 21205

HENDERSON, DOUGLAS JAMES, theoretical physicist; b. Calgary, Alta., Can., July 28, 1934; s. Donald Ross and Evelyn Louise (Scott) H.; m. Rose-Marie Steen-Nielssen, Jan. 21, 1960; children—Barbara, Dianne, Sharon. B.A. with honors, U. B.C., Can., 1956; Ph.D., U. Utah, 1961. Lectr. U. Utah,

Salt Lake City, 1960-61; asst. prof. U. Idaho, Moscow, 1961-62; assoc. prof. Ariz. State U., Tempe, 1962-64; prof. U. Waterloo, Ont., Can., 1964-69, research scientist research div. IBM, San Jose, Calif., 1969—; Assoc. editor Jour. Chem. Physics USA, 1976-78; mem. editorial bd Utilitas Mathematica, 1971—, Jour. Phys. Chemistry, 1984—. Vol. fireman Loma Prieta Vol. Fire Dept., Los Gatos, Calif., 1983—; missionary to Africa, 1957-59. Corning Glass fellow, 1959; Alfred P. Sloan Found. fellow, 1964,66, Ian Potter Found. fellow, 1966; recipient Johnathan Rogers award U. B.C., 1954. Fellow Am. Phys. Soc., Inst. Physics, Am. Inst. Chemists; mem. Am. Chem. Soc. (sci. adv. bd. Chem. Abstracts 1981-83), Math. Assn. Am. Democrat. Subspecialties: Polymer chemistry; Statistical physics. Office: IBM Research Lab Dept K33 Bldg 281 San Jose CA 95193

HENDERSON, FLOYD MERL, remote sensing/geography educator, researcher; b. Denison, Iowa, Feb. 23, 1946; s. Glenn Merle and Helen Mary (Flick) H.; m. Gayle June Petersen, Aug. 24, 1968. B.A., Nebr. Wesleyan U., 1968; M.A., U. Kans., 1970, Ph.D., 1973. Cert. photogrammetrist. Asst. prof. San Diego State U., 1972-73; asst. prof. SUNY-Albany, 1973-77, 77-78, assoc. remote sensing/geography, 1978—, dir. Cartographic Remote Sensing Lab., 1978—; vis. prof. La. State U., Baton Rouge, 1977. Contbr. articles to profl. jours., chpt. to books. NASA summer fellow, 1978, fellow, 1979; NSF grantee, 1981-83. Mem. Am. Soc. Photogrammetry, Assn. Am. Geographers, IEEE (sr. mem.), Internat. Soc. Photogrammetry and Remote Sensing, Sigma Xi. Club: German Am. (Albany). Current work: Effects of radar system parameters and environmental modulation on terrain feature identification; development of micro-computer based digital image analysis applications. Subspecialties: Remote sensing (geoscience); Graphics, image processing, and pattern recognition. Home: 2 Winding Rd Delmar NY 12054 Office: Dept Geography SUNY at Albany 1400 Washington Ave Albany NY 12222

HENDERSON, ISAAC CRAIG, medical oncologist, researcher; b. Paullina, Iowa, Aug. 10, 1941; s. Isaac C. and Ora E. (Tjossem) H.; m. Mary Turner Henderson, June 11, 1966; children: Isaac Craig III, Amy Hudson. A.B., Grinnell (Iowa) Coll., 1963; M.D., Columbia U., 1970. Cert. internal medicine, 1977, med. oncology, 1979. Intern Presbyterian Hosp., N.Y.C., 1970-71, resident, 1971-72; research assoc. NIH, 1972-74; instr. medicine Harvard U. Med. Sch., Boston, 1975-76, asst. prof., 1976-84, assoc. prof., 1984—; dir. Breast Evaluation Center, Dana Farber Cancer Inst., 1980—. Contbr. articles to profl. jours. Trustees, Cambridge Friends Sch. Served with USPHS, 1972-74. Fulbright Research scholar, 1964-65; Merck, Sharpe and Dohme Internat. fellow, 1966; recipient Columbia Presbyterian Med. Soc. Research prize, 1970. Mem. Am. Soc. Clin. Oncology, Am. Assn. Cancer Research. Mem. Soc. of Friends. Current Work: Clinical protocols evaluating new treatment modalities for the treatment of breast cancer; short term tissue culture assay systems for human breast cancer; clinical studies on adriamycin cardiotoxicity. Subspecialties: Oncology; Cancer research (medicine). Home: 8 Glengarry Rd Winchester MA 01890 Office: 44 Binney St Dana 1510 Boston MA 02115

HENDERSON, ROBERT EDWARD, state research agency administrator; b. Kokomo, Ind., Feb. 28, 1925; s. Chester Ellsworth and Nellie B. (Ackerson) H.; m. Shirley S. Shroyer, Dec. 30, 1967; children: Ann, Elizabeth , Carol, Katherine, Craig, James. B. A., Carleton Coll., 1949; M.A., U. Mo., 1951, Ph.D. in Physics, 1953. With Allison div. Gen. Motors Corp., 1953-73, dir. research., 1968-73; pres., chief exec. officer Indpls. Ctr. Advanced Research, 1973-83; dir. S.C. Research Authority, Columbia, 1983—. Served with U.S. Army, 1943-45. Decorated Purple Heart. Mem. IEEE, ASHRAE, Am. Phys. Soc., AIAA (assoc. fellow), Am. Solar Energy Soc., Soc. Mfg. Engrs. Episcopalian. Subspecialties: Solar energy; Photosynthesis. Office: SC Research Authority PO Box 12025 Columbia SC 29211

HENDERSON, ROSETA MCKINLEY, research chemist; b. Fairhope, Ala., Dec. 8, 1935; d. William and Arnie (Strickland) McKinley; m. James L. Henderson; children—Wayne M., Byron M. B.S., Ala. State U., 1956; M.A., Fisk U., 1958. Instr. chemistry Tex. So. U., Houston, 1958-62; research chemist DuPont Co., Wilmington, Del., 1965—. Patentee in field. Mem. Am. Chem. Soc., Sigma Xi, Delta Theta. Roman Catholic. Clubs: Jack and Jill of Am. (treas. 1982-84), Toastmasters. Current work: Medicinal chemistry. Subspecialty: Organic chemistry. Office: DuPont Exptl Sta Bldg 336/230 Wilmington DE 19898

HENDERSON, VICTOR WARREN, neurologist, educator; b. Little Rock, Aug. 20, 1951; s. Philip S. and N. Jean (Edsel) H.; m. Barbara Ann Curtiss, May 24, 1975; children—Gregory Philip, Geoffrey Victor, Stephanie Ann. B.S., U. Ga., 1972; M.D., Johns Hopkins U., 1976; Diplomate Am. Bd. Psychiatry and Neurology. Intern in internal medicine Duke U., Durham, N.C., 1976-77; resident in neurology Washington U., St. Louis, 1977-80; fellow in behavioral neurology Boston U., 1980-81, instr. Sch. Medicine, 1980-81; asst. prof. neurology U. So. Calif., Los Angeles, 1981—; co-dir. U. So. Calif. Neurobehavioral Clinic, Los Angeles, 1981—. Author: (with others) Principles of Neurologic Diagnosis, 1985. Contbr. articles to profl. jours. Nat. Merit scholar, 1968; Hurd Found. grantee, 1984. Mem. Am. Acad. Neurology, Soc. for Neurosci., Acad. of Aphasia, Behavioral Neurology Soc., Internat. Neuropsycol. Soc., Am. Soc. for Neurol. Investigation. Current work: Behavioral neurology; neural substrate of speech and language; Alzheimer's disease. Subspecialty: Neurology. Office: Dept Neurology Univ So Calif Sch Medicine 1200 N State St Los Angeles CA 90033

HENDERSON, WILLIAM DAVID, oilfield products company executive; b. El Paso, Tex., May 1, 1950; s. Weldon Oliver and Betty Joyce (Woodson) H.; m. Karen Sue George, July 22, 1972; children—Carrie Ann, Heather Marie. Student Angelo State U., 1968-70; B.S.M.E., U. Tex.-El Paso, 1974. Registered profl. engr., Tex. Design engr. Otis Engring. Corp., Dallas, 1974-81, design mgr., 1981—. Patentee in field. Mem. ASME. Baptist. Current work: Design manager for packer design in oilfield products. Subspecialty: Petroleum engineering. Home: 8524 Preston N Dr Frisco TX 75034

HENDLER, EDWIN, aerospace physiologist, consultant; b. Phila., Aug. 29, 1922; s. David and Elene (Kalman) H.; m. May Snyder, May 13, 1945; children—Lynn Karen Slotkin, Sandra Dee. B.S., Pa. State U., 1943; M.S., U. Pa., 1956, Ph.D., 1959. Physiologist, Naval Air Material Ctr., Phila., 1946-52; head, acceleration br., 1952-55; mgr. life scis. research group Naval Air Engring. Ctr., 1956-74; head, life scis. div., Naval Air Devel. Ctr., Warminster, Pa., 1975-81; cons. Essex Corp., Warminster, 1981-83; cons. Human Factors Applications, Warminster, 1983—. Co-author (with others) Unusual Environments, 1963; patentee protective helmet, 1952. Recipient Merit award for Group Achievement, Naval Air Devel. Ctr., Warminster, Pa., 1976. Fellow Aerospace Med. Assn.; mem. Am. Physiol. Soc., Biophys. Soc., Survival and Flight Equipment Assn., Sigma Xi. Current work: Research studies on human responses to acceleration and other aerospace stressors. Physiological evaluation of aerospace life support, safety and survival equipment and techniques. Subspecialties: Physiology (medicine); Space medicine. Home: 8 Sandringham Pl Cherry Hill NJ 08003

HENDLEY, JOSEPH OWEN, pediatrician; b. Chattanooga, Aug. 18, 1937; s. Flavius Josephus and Cornelia Adelaide (Smartt) H.; m. Sarah P., May 26, 1978; children. B.A., Vanderbilt U., 1959; M.D., U. Pa., 1963. Diplomate: Am. Bd. Pediatrics. Intern Duke U., 1963-64, resident, 1964-67; research fellow dept. pediatrics U. Va., 1965-67, asst. prof. pediatrics, 1970-76, assoc. prof., 1976-82, prof., 1982—; research fellow Harvard U. Sch. Public Health, Boston, 1968-70. Mem. Am. Acad. Pediatrics, Am. Epidemiol. Soc., Am. Pediatrics Soc., Am. Soc. Microbiology, Infectious Disease Soc. Am., Soc. Pediatrics Research, So. Soc. Pediatrics Research, Va. State Med. Soc., Alpha Omega Alpha. Current Work: Characterization of the capsule on N. gonorrhoeae; transmission of rhinovirus colds; study of mechanisms of human infection by and immunity to B. pertussis. Subspecialties: Pediatrics; Infectious diseases. Office: U Va PO Box 386 Charlottesville VA 22908

HENDRICKX, ANDREW GEORGE, research physiologist, human antomy educator, administrator; b. Butler, Minn., July 14, 1933; s. Louis H. and Juliana D. Hendrickx. B.S., Concordia Coll., Moorhead, Minn., 1959; M.S., Kans. State U., 1961, Ph.D., 1963. Instr. zoology Kans. State U., Manhattan, 1959-63; asst. prof. zoology So. Ill. U., Carbondale, 1963-64; head sect. embryology, dept. anatomy SW Found. for Research and Edn., San Antonio, 1964-68, assoc. found. scientist, 1969; assoc. research physiologist Calif. Primate Research Ctr., lectr. dept. clin. scis. Sch. Vet. Medicine, U. Calif.-Davis, 1969-71, assoc. research physiologist, assoc. prof. physiology, 1971-73, research physiologist, prof. reprodn. Sch. Vet. Medicine, prof. human anatomy Sch. Medicine, 1973-78, research physiologist, assoc. dir. Calif. Primate Research Ctr., prof. human anatomy Sch. Medicine 1978—; advisor spl. program research in human reprodn. WHO, 1977—. Author book; also numerous articles. Recipient Disting. Alumni award Concordia Coll., 1977; named Acad. Staff Orgn. Lectr. of Yr., U. Calif., 1973; Nat. Def. scholar, 1959-62; grantee NIH, Nat. Found.-March of Dimes, Am. Fund for Dental Edn., WHO. Mem. Am. Assn. Anatomists, AAUP, Am. Soc. Primatologists (pres. 1982-84), Internat. Soc. Primatologists, N.Y. Acad. Scis., Perinatal Research Soc., Soc. for Study Reprodn., Teratology Soc. (sec. 1979-83), Sigma Xi. Subspecialties: Teratology; Anatomy and embryology. Office: U Calif Calif Primate Research Ctr Davis CA 95615

HENDRIE, JOSEPH MALLAM, physicist, nuclear engineer, government official; b. Janesville, Wis., Mar. 18, 1925; s. Joseph Munier and Margaret Prudence (Hocking) H.; m. Elaine Kostell, July 9, 1949; children: Susan Debra, Barbara Ellen. B.S., Case Inst. Tech., 1950; Ph.D., Columbia U., 1957. Registered profl. engr., N.Y., Calif. Asst. physicist Brookhaven Nat. Lab., Upton, N.Y., 1955-57, asso. physicist, 1957-60, physicist, 1960-71, sr. physicist, 1971—, chmn. steering com., project chief engr. high flux beam reactor design and constrn., 1958-65, acting head exptl. reactor physics div., 1965-66, project mgr. pulsed fast reactor project, 1967-70, asso. head engring. div., dept. applied sci., 1967-71, head, 1971-72, chmn. dept. applied sci., 1975-77, spl. asst. to dir., 1981—; dep. dir. licensing for tech. rev. U.S. AEC, 1972-74; chmn. U.S. Nuclear Regulatory Commn., Washington, 1977-79, 81, commr., 1980; lectr. nuclear power plant safety MIT, Ga. Inst. Tech., Northwestern U., summers 1970-77; cons. radiation safety com. Columbia U., 1964-72; mem. adv. com. reactor safeguards AEC, 1966-72, chmn., 1970; U.S. mem. sr. adv. group on reactor safety standards IAEA, 1974-78. Mem. editorial adv. bd.: Nuclear Tech, 1967-77. Served with AUS, 1943-45. Recipient E.O. Lawrence award, 1970; decorated comdr. Order of Leopold II (Belgium), 1982. Fellow Am. Nuclear Soc. (dir. 1976-77, v.p. 1983-84, pres. 1984-85), ASME; mem. Nat. Acad. Engring., Am. Phys. Soc., Am. Concrete Inst., IEEE, Nat. Soc. Profl. Engrs., Sigma Xi, Tau Beta Pi. Research, publs. on physics nuclear reactors, nuclear power plant safety, engring. design reactors, elec. power transmission, chem. physics nitrogen dissociation process, structure oxygen molecule. Subspecialties: Nuclear physics; Nuclear engineering. Office: Brookhaven Nat Lab Upton NY 11973

HENDRON, JOHN ALDEN, quality assurance engineer, consultant, nondestructive testing engineer; b. Granite Falls, Wash., Mar. 23, 1920; s. John Alden and Grace Athena (Muirhead) H.; m. Mary Ann Wick, Oct. 6, 1953; children—Susan, Gail, Heather, John. Student, U. Wash., 1940-41, 46-52. Registered profl. engr., Calif. Research and devel. engr., motion picture x-ray systems for physiology research U. Wash., 1948-52; design engr., early field x-ray equipment Indsl. X-ray Engrs., Seattle, 1952-55; supr. inspection team Esso Research & Devel. Co., Fawley, Eng., 1956-59; head nondestructive test engring. group for devel. tests and equipment Polaris missile motors Aerojet Strategic Propulsion Co., Sacramento, 1959-70, cons. nondestructive testing engring., 1970-73, 77—; quality assurance mgr. Alaskan Copper Co., Seattle, 1973-77, cons. nondestructive test engring., 1977—. Contbr. articles on motion pictures x-ray research in physiology and indsl. inspection techniques to profl. jours.; nondestructive test devels. Occasional speaker in support of nuclear power to Republican groups. Served to sgt. U.S. Army, 1941-45, ETO. Recipient Tech. Utilization award AEC/NASA Nuclear Rocket Program, 1967, 1969, 1971. Mem. ASME, Am. Welding Soc., Am. Soc. Nondestructive Testing. Club: U. Wash. Alumni. Lodges: Shriners (Seattle); Masons (Eng.). Current Work: Nondestructive test development, quality assurance programs management. Subspecialties: Aerospace engineering and technology; Nuclear engineering. Office: Aerojet Strategic Propulsion Co Dept 2021 Bldg 20019 Sacramento CA 95813

HENKEL, CRAIG KENNETH, neuroscientist, educator; b. Canton, Ohio, Mar. 8, 1949; s. George E. and Dorothy Mae (Barto) H.; m. Janice Ellen Heffer, July 12, 1975; 1 son, Brian Robert. B.S., Wheaton (Ill.) Coll., 1971; Ph.D., Ohio State U., 1975. Post-docotoral research fellow dept. anatomy U. Va. Sch. Medicine, 1975-78; assoc. prof. anatomy Wake Forest U. Bowman Gray Sch. Medicine., Winston-Salem, N.C., 1978—. NSF grantee, 1980-82; Nat. Inst. Neurol. Communicable Disease and Stroke, 1982-85. Mem. Soc. Neurosci., Am. Assn. Anatomists, Cajal Club. Mem. Christian and Missionary Alliance Ch. Current Work: Orgnization of brain pathways related to acoustico-and-visual-motor behaviors. Subspecialty: Neuroanatomy.

HENLE, GERTRUDE, virologist; b. Mannheim, Germany, Apr. 3, 1912; Came to U.S., 1937, naturalized, 1943; d. Theophil and Eleneore (Baumgart) Szpingler; m. Werner Henle, Mar. 13, 1937. M.D., U. Heidelberg, Germany, 1936; D.M.S. (hon.), Med. Coll. Pa., 1975. Intern Inst. Hygiene, U. Heidelberg, 1936-37; mem. faculty U. Pa., 1937—, instr. to prof. bacteriology, 1940—, asst. to prof. virology in pediatrics, 1940—; mem. research staff Children's Hosp. of Phila., 1940—. Contbr. numerous articles on influenza, mumps, hepatitis, infectious mononucleosis and tumor viruses to sci. jour. Recipient Mead-Johnson award Am. Acad. Pediatrics, 1950, Variety of Heart award City of Phila., 1970, Smith, Kline and French award for excellence in research, 1971, Robert-Koch medaille and Robert-Koch preis Robert-Koch- Stiftung, 1971; Robert de Villiers award Leukemia Soc. Am., Inc., 1975; Virus Cancer Program award Nat. Cancer Inst., 1975; Sci. award Phila. chpt. Am. Cancer Soc., 1977; Disting. Achievement in Cancer Research award Bristol Myers Co., 1979. Mem. Am. Acad. Microbiology, Nat. Acad. Scis., Tissue Culture Assn. Current work: Epstein-Barr virus and its involvement in various diseases. Home: 533 Ott Rd Bala-Cynwyd PA 19004 Office: 34th St and Civic Center Blvd Philadelphia PA 19104

HENLEY, ERNEST MARK, physics educator; b. Frankfurt, Germany, June 10, 1924; came to U.S., 1939, naturalized, 1944; s. Fred S. and Josy (Dreyfuss) H.; m. Elaine Dimitman, Aug. 21, 1948; children: M. Bradford, Karen M. B.E.E., Coll. City N.Y., 1944; Ph.D., U. Calif. at Berkeley, 1952. Physicist Lawrence Radiation Lab., U. Calif. at Berkeley, 1950-51; research asso. physics dept. Stanford, 1951-52; lectr. physics Columbia, 1952-54; mem. faculty U. Wash., Seattle, 1954—, prof. physics, 1961—, chmn. dept., 1973-76; dean U. Wash. (Coll. Arts and Scis.), 1979—. Author: (with W. Thirring) Elementary Quantum Field Theory, 1962, (with H. Frauenfelder) Subatomic Physics, 1974, Nuclear and Particle Physics, 1975. F.B. Jewett fellow, 1952-53; NSF sr. fellow, 1958-59; Guggenheim fellow, 1967-68; NATO sr. fellow, 1976-77; sr. A. von Humboldt awardee, 1984. Mem. Am. Phys. Soc. (chmn. div. nuclear physics 1979-80), Nat. Acad. Scis., Sigma Xi. Research and numerous publs. on symmetries, nuclear reactions and high energy particle interactions. Subspecialties: Theoretical physics; Nuclear physics. Office: Physics Dept FM 15 U Wash Seattle WA 98195

HENRICKSON, JAMES SOLBERG, botany educator; b. Eau Claire, Wis., Oct. 15, 1940; s. Henry Marvel and Grace Isabel (Solberg) H.; married; children: Jonathan James. M.S., Claremont Grad. Sch., 1964, Ph.D., 1968. Asst. prof. dept. biology Calif. State U.-Los Angeles, 1966-71, assoc. prof., 1971-77, prof., 1979—; dir. Ind. Environ. Cons., Los Angeles, 1970—. Mem. AAAS, Am. Assn. Plant Taxonomists, Bot. Soc. Am., Calif. Bot. Soc., Internat. Assn. Plant Taxonomists. Current Work: Flora of Chihuahuan Desert (Mexico), flora of Mojave Desert. Subspecialty: Systematics. Home: 1409 Oneonta Knoll South Pasadena CA 91030 Office: Dept Biology Calif State U Los Angeles CA 90032

HENRY, NORMAN WHITFIELD, III, chemist; b. Phila., May 8, 1943; s. Norman W. and Ethel (Black) H.; m. Joy Lois Lessner, Apr. 15, 1967; 1 child, Heather. B.A. in Chemistry, Lafayette Coll., 1966; M.S., U. Del., 1977. Registered clin. chemist. Research chemist Haskell Lab., E.I. du Pont de Nemours & Co., Wilmington, Del., 1967—; instr. Del. Tech. Community Coll., Wilmington, 1984—, Wesley Coll., Dover, Del., 1981—. Contbr. articles to profl. jours. Mem. Del. Radiation Authority, 1980—. Mem. Am. Chem. Soc. (treas.-sec.), Am. Indsl. Hygiene Assn., ASTM (sec. com. F-23, Disting. Service award 1984). Republican. Episcopalian. Current work: Analytical health services research. Subspecialties: Analytical chemistry; Environmental chemistry. Home: 129 Ballantrae Dr Elkton MD 21921 Office: Haskell Lab EI du Pont de Nemours & Co PO Box 50 Elkton Rd Newark DE 19714

HENRY, PATRICK M., chemistry educator; b. Joliet, Ill., Sept. 29, 1928; married, 1956; 3 children. B.S., DePaul U., 1951, M.S., 1953; Ph.D. in Chemistry, Northwestern U., 1956. Research chemist Hercules Inc., 1956-71; from assoc. prof. to prof. chemistry U. Guelph, Ont., Can., 1971-81; prof., chmn., dept. chemistry Loyola U., Chgo., 1981—. Mem. Am. Chem. Soc. Subspecialties: Catalysis chemistry; Biomass (energy science and technology). Office: Loyola U 6525 N Sheridan Rd Chicago IL 60626*

HENSEL, DALE ROBERT, soil science educator; b. Camel, Ind., Sept. 8, 1931; s. Hiram A. and Neva M. (Zimmerman) H.; m. Mary Lou McClintock, Oct. 6, 1954; children—Kathleen A., Cheryl A., Marsha L., Robert A. B.S., Purdue U., 1953, M.S., 1958; Ph.D., Rutgers U., 1960. From asst. prof. to assoc. prof. soil U. Fla. Agrl. Research Ctr., Hastings, 1960-70, prof., dir. 1970—. Contbr. articles to profl. jours. Mem. Planning and Zoning Agy. St John's County, St. Augustine, Fla., 1978—. Served to 1st lt. U.S. Army, 1953-56. Fellow Am. Inst. Chemists; mem. Am. So. Agronomy, Soil and Crop Sci. Soc. Fla. (bd. dirs. 1984—), Fla. Hort. Soc. (bd. dirs. 1960—), Potato Assn. Am. (bd. dirs. 1984—). Methodist. Club: Methodist Men (pres. St. Augustine 1970-71). Lodge: Rotary (pres. 1964-65). Current work: Experiments in potato production systems, nutrition, irrigation, drainage and cultural management. Subspecialties: Soil science; Plant growth. Home: 29 Montrano Ave Saint Augustine FL 32084 Office: Agrl Research and Edn Ctr PO Box 728 Hastings FL 32045

HENSHAW, EDGAR CUMMINGS, biochemical researcher, educator; b. Cin., Dec. 14, 1929; s. Lewis Johnson and Dorothy (Cummings) H.; m. Betty Ann Barnes, Jan. 11, 1936; 1 son: Daniel. A.B., Harvard U., 1952, M.D., 1956. Lic. physician, N.Y. Intern Harvard Med. Service-Boston City Hosp., 1956-57, resident, 1959-60, fellow dept. bacteriology, 1960-62; instr. Harvard U., 1962-64, assoc., 1964-69, asst. prof., 1969-71, assoc. prof., 1971-76; prof. oncology in medicine and biochemistry U. Rochester, N.Y., 1976—; asst. dir. basic sci. U. Rochester (Cancer Ctr.), 1978—; chmn. research adv. com. United Cancer Council, Rochester. Contbr. articles to profl. jours. Served with M.C. U.S. Navy, 1957-59. Nat. Cancer Inst. grantee, 1971—. Mem. Am. Assn. Cancer Research, Am. Soc. Biol. Chemists, Am. Assn. Cancer Edn., Biochem. Soc., N.Y. Acad. Sci, Rochester Acad. Medicine, Monroe County Med. Soc. Episcopalian. Current Work: Biochemistry of cancer; regulation of cell growth; regulation of protein synthesis; effects upon cell metabolism of alteratiopns in cellular nutrition. Subspecialties: Biochemistry (medicine); Cancer research (medicine). Home: 542 Allens Creek Rd Rochester NY 14618 Office: U Rochester Cancer Center PO Box 704 Rochester NY 14642

HERB, RAYMOND GEORGE, physicist, business executive; b. Navarino, Wis., Jan. 22, 1908; s. Joseph and Annie (Stadler); m. Anne Williamson, Dec. 26, 1945; children: Stephen, Rebecca, Sara, Emily, William. Ph.D., U. Wis., 1935; hon. degrees, U. Basel, 1960, U. Sao Paulo, 1959. Research assoc. physics U. Wis., 1935-39, research assoc., asst. prof., Madison, 1939-40, assoc. prof., 1941-45, prof., 1945-61, Charles Mendenhall prof. physics, 1961-72; founder, pres., chmn. bd. Nat. Electrostatics Corp., Middleton, Wis., 1972—. Contbr. articles to profl. jours.; patentee high voltage electrostatic and ultra high vacuum equipment. Recipient Tom W. Bonner award, 1968, Disting. Service citation Coll. Engrs. U. Wis., 1976. Fellow Am. Phys. Soc.; mem. Nat. Acad. Scis. Current Work: Developer electrostatic accelerator insulated by high pressure gas. Subspecialty: Nuclear physics. Office: 7240 Graber Rd Middleton WI 53562

HERBERT, GEORGE RICHARD, research executive; b. Grand Rapids, Mich., Oct. 3, 1922; s. George Richard and Violet (Wilton) H.; m. Lois Anne Watkins, Aug. 11, 1945; children: Gordon, Patricia, Alison, Douglas, Margaret. Student, Mich. State U., 1940-42; B.S., U.S. Naval Acad., 1945; D.Sc. (hon.), N.C. State U., 1967; LL.D. (hon.), Duke U., 1978, U. N.C.-Chapel Hill, 1984. Line officer USN, 1945-47; instr. elec. engring. Mich. State U., 1947-48; asst. to dir. Stanford Research Inst., 1948-50, mgr. bus. ops., 1950-55, exec. asso. dir., 1955-56, asst. sec., 1950-56; treas. Am. & Fgn. Power Co., Inc., N.Y.C., 1956-59; pres. Research Triangle Inst., 1959—; chmn., dir. Microelectronics Center N.C.; dir. Central Carolina Bank & Trust Co., Duke Power Co.; mem. N.C. Sci. and Tech., 1963-79; mem. tech. adv. bd. U.S. Dept. Commerce, 1964-69, N.C. Atomic Energy Adv. Com., 1964-71; mem. Korea-U.S. joint com. for sci. cooperation Nat. Acad. Scis., 1973-78; mem. bd. sci. and tech. for internat. devel. Nat. Acad. Sci., 1978-83. Bd. dirs. Oak Ridge Assoc. Univs., 1971-74, 78—. Mem. Sigma Alpha Epsilon. Clubs: Cosmos (Washington); Hope Valley Country. Office: Box 12194 Research Triangle Park NC 27709

HERBERT, VICTOR, medical educator, nutrition scientist, hematologist, oncologist; b. N.Y.C., Feb. 22, 1927; s. Charles Allan and Rosaline (Margolis) H.; m. Jacqueline Lubin, June 19, 1954 (div. 1965); children—Robert, Steven, Kathy; m. Marilynne Gruber, June 23, 1968; children—Alissa, Laura. B.S., Columbia U., 1948, M.A., 1952, J.D., 1974. Prof. medicine, vice chmn. hematology Mt. Sinai Sch. Medicine, N.Y.C., 1964-70; prof. pathology and medicine Columbia U., N.Y.C., 1970—; prof. medicine SUNY-Downstate, Bklyn., 1976—; chief, hematology and nutrition VA Med. Ctr., Bronx, N.Y., 1970—; chmn. medicine Hahnemann U., Phila., 1984-85; mem. food and nutrition bd. Nat. Acad. Scis., Washington, 1979—; mem. joint subcom. human nutrition research, Office of Pres., Washington, 1979-83. Author: Nutrition Cultism, 1980; (with others) Vitamins and —Health— Foods, 1981 (FDA award 1984). Recipient Middleton award VA, 1978, Commr's Spl. Citation FDA, 1984. Mem. Am. Soc. Clin. Nutrition (pres. 1974-80, McCollum award 1972), Am. Soc. Hematology (parliamentarian 1976—), Assn. Am. Physicians, Am. soc. Clin. Investigators, Fedn. Am. Soc. Exptl. Biologists (chmn. pub. info. 1984—). Democrat. Current work: Internal medicine, hematology, nutritian, nutritional anemias, oncology, clinical pathology, development of diagnostic tests. Subspecialties: Internal medicine; Nutrition (medicine). Office: VA Med Ctr 130 W Kingsbridge Rd Bronx NY 10468

HERBICH, JOHN BRONISLAW, engineering educator; b. Warsaw, Poland, Sept. 1, 1922; came to U.S., 1953, naturalized, 1962; s. Henry Pawel and Jadwiga Eleonora (Lopienski) H.; m. Margaret Pauline Boylan, Jan. 27, 1951; children: Ann (dec.), Barbara K., Gregory J., Patricia J. B.Sc., U. Edinburgh, Scotland, 1949; M.S. in C.E, U. Minn., 1957; Ph.D., Pa. State U., 1973; postgrad., U. Calif., Berkeley, 1964, Utah State U., 1966. Registered profl. engr., Tex. Field engr. John Laing & Son, London, Eng., 1948; research engr. U. Delft, Netherlands, 1949-50; research fellow, intermediate engr. Aluminum Co. Can., Ltd., 1950-53; research fellow U. Minn., 1953-57; asst. prof. Lehigh U., 1957-60, asso. prof., 1960-65, prof., 1965-67; prof. civil engring., head ocean and hydraulic engring. group, head ocean engring. program, 1967-83, dir. Center for Dredging Studies, Tex. A&M U., College Station, 1967—; on leave as UN project mgr. Central Water and Power Research Sta., Govt. of India, Khadakwasla, Poona, 1972-73; lectr. in, Venezuela, India, China, other countries; dir. Ocean Pollution Control, Inc., Dallas; v.p. Cons. and Research Services, Inc., Bryan, Tex. Author: Coastal and Deep Ocean Dredging, 1975, Offshore Pipelines: Design Elements, 1981, Scour Around Offshore Structures, 1983; also numerous articles and reports; contbr. chpts. to Studies in Marine Environmental Pollution, 1980, articles to Ency. of Beaches and Coastal Environments, 1981. Pres. PTA Hamilton Sch., Bethlehem, Pa., 1965-66. Served with Brit. Army, 1940-45. Recipient Karl Emil Hilgard Hydraulic Prize Am. Soc. C.E., 1965-66; NSF Faculty-Sci. fellow, 1963-64. Mem. Internat. Assn. Hydraulic Research, World Dredging Assn., Am. Soc. Engring. Edn., ASCE, Marine Tech. Soc., Permanent Internat. Assn. Nav. Congresses, Sigma Xi, Phi Kappa Phi, Chi Epsilon. Patentee in field. Current Work: Coastal engineering and dredging technology, ship channel design, interaction between ships and channels, wave forces on structures. Subspecialties: Coastal engineering; Ocean engineering. Home: 764 S Rosemary Dr Bryan TX 77802 Office: Ocean Engring Program Civil Engring Dept Tex A&M U College Station TX 77843-3136

HERGET, WILLIAM FREDERICK, infrared spectroscopist, consultant; b. Wheeling, W.Va., Sept. 29, 1931; s. Frederick Welton and Katherine Ernestine (Scharf) H.; children: Frederick J., Catherine E., Allen N., Nancy L. B.S., U. Richmond, 1952; M.S., Vanderbilt U., 1955; Ph.D. in Physics, U. Tenn., 1962. Research specialist Rocketdyne div. Rockwell Internat., Canoga Park, Calif., 1962-70; chief spl. techniques group EPA, Research Triangle Park, N.C., 1970-81; sr. scientist Nicolet Instrument Corp., Madison, Wis., 1981—; cons. on infrared spectroscopy. Contbr. articles to profl. jours. Recipient Bronze medal for meritorious service EPA, 1978, Nicolet Fellow award for tech. expertise, 1984. Mem. Optical Soc. Am., Air Pollution Control Assn., Soc. Automotive Engrs., Soc. Applied Spectroscopy. Current Work: Analysis of gaseous chemical systems using infrared spectroscopy; research on the applicatiopn of Fourier transform infrared spectroscopy to the species quantification of a variety of chemical systems. Subspecialties: Infrared spectroscopy; Remote sensing (atmospheric science). Home: 5146 Anton Dr Apt 208 Madison WI 53719 Office: 5225-1 Verona Rd Madison WI 53711

HERLYN, MEENHARD FOLKEUS, immunologist, researcher; b. Upleward, Lower Saxony, Germany, Aug. 8, 1944; came to U.S., 1976; S. Meenhard and Gretchen (Ockinga) H.; m. Dorothee Schmidt-Ruppin, Apr. 25, 1970; 1 dau., Anjye. D.V.M., U. Munich, 1972. Research asst. Inst. Med. Microbiology, Munich, Germany, 1971-76; assoc. scientist Wistar Inst., Phila., 1976-79, research assoc., 1979-81, asst. prof., 1981—; cons. M.D. Anderson Cancer Inst., Houston, 1982—. Contbr. articles in field to profl. jours. Mem. Am. Assn. Cancer Research, Am. Assn. Pathologists, Am. Assn. Microbiology, Tissue Culture Assn., Soc. Immunology. Current Work: Cancer research, monoclonal antibodies, cancer diagnosis, tumor markers, tumor progression. Subspecialties: Cancer research (medicine); Cell biology. Home: 1223 Knox Rd Wynnewood PA 19096 Office: The Wistar Inst 36th at Spruce St Philadelphia PA 19104

HERMAN, HERBERT, materials science educator, consultant; b. N.Y.C., June 15, 1934; s. Samuel and Frances (Friedman) H.; m. Barbara Budin, July 1, 1963; 1 son, Daniel. B.S., DePaul U., 1956; M.S., Northwestern U., 1958, Ph.D., 1961. Research assoc. Argonne Nat. Lab., Ill., 1962-63; asst. prof. U. Pa., Phila., 1963-67; Ford prof. AT&T, Princeton, N.J., 1967-68; prof. materials sci. SUNY, Stony Brook, 1968—; liaison scientist Office Naval Research, London, 1975-76. Editor series Treatise on Materials Science and Technology, 1967. Editor-in-chief Materials Sci. and Engring. Jour., 1983—. Fulbright scholar 1961. Mem. Am. Soc. Metals, Am. Ceramic Soc., Am. Soc. Engring. Edn., Am. Welding Soc., Marine Tech. Soc. Current work: Plasma sprayed protective coatings; ion beam surface modification; surface engineering. Subspecialties: Materials; Ceramics. Office: SUNY Dept Materials Sci Stony Brook NY 11794-2275

HERMAN, WILLIAM SPARKES, zoology educator; b. Seattle, Oct. 12, 1931; s. William Sparkes and Jane Ione (Ardery) Weidel; m. Charlotte Katherine Meyer, Oct. 5, 1962; children: Alexandria, Max, Carter. B.S., Portland State Coll., 1958; M.S., Northwestern U., 1960, Ph.D., 1964. NIH postdoctoral fellow U. Calif., Berkeley, 1964-66; asst. prof. U. Minn., Mpls., 1966-70, asso. prof., 1970-75, prof. zoology, 1976—, head genetics and cell biology dept., 1981—; cons. in field. Contbr. articles to profl. jours. Served with USAF, 1954-58. Mem. AAAS, Am. Soc. Zoologists. Current Work: Anthropod neuroendocrinology. Subspecialties: Neuroendocrinology; Cell biology. Home: 79 Clarence Ave SE Minneapolis MN 55414 Office: Genetics and Cell Biology Dept Univ of Minn Saint Paul MN 55455

HERMANN, ALLEN MAX, physicist; b. New Orleans, La., July 17, 1938; s. Edward Frederick and Miriam (Davidson) H.; m. Leonora Neil Christopher, May 19, 1979; children—Miriam, Mary, Neil, Scott. B.S., Loyola U., New Orleans, 1960; M.S., Notre Dame U., 1962; Ph.D., Tex. A&M U., 1965. Research sr. scientist, Jet Propulsion Lab., Pasadena, Calif., 1965-67; prof. physics Tulane U., 1967-81; sr. scientist task leader Solar Energy Research Inst., Golden, Colo., 1980—. Founding co-editor: Applied Physics Communications, 1981. Bd. dirs. Colo. Assn. Retarded Citizens, Denver, 1982-84, Ridge Assn. Retarded Citizens, Wheat Ridge, Colo., 1984—. Recipient Outstanding Achievement award NASA, 1970-72. Fellow Am. Phys. Soc.; mem. IEEE (Sr.), Electrochem. Soc., Internat. Soc. Optical Engring., Sigma Pi Sigma. Republican. Current work: Deposition, characterization and modeling of thin-film photovoltaic devices; charge transport in solids including amorphous and molecular semiconductors; solid state batteries and electrode reactions in liquid electrolyte batteries. Subspecialties: Condensed matter physics; Solar engineering. Home: 2704 Lookout View Dr Golden CO 80401 Office: Solar Energy Research Inst 1617 Cole Blvd Golden CO 80401

HERNANDEZ, DANIEL E., neurobiology educator; b. Valdivia, Chile, Apr. 27, 1952; came to U.S., 1980; s. Daniel Hernandez and Gabriela (Hertell) H.; 1 child, Juan Hernandez Malig. B.S., Austral U., Valdivia, 1973, D.V.M., 1977. Asst. prof. Austral U., 1977-80; research fellow U. N.C., Chapel Hill, 1980-83; assoc. prof. N.C. State U., Raleigh, 1983—. Contbr. articles to profl. jours. Mem. Am. Fedn. Clin. Research, Internat. Soc. Psychoneuroendocrinology, Soc. for Neurosci., N.Y. Acad. Sci., Brit. Brain Research Assn., AAAS, Sigma Xi. Current work: Research into biology of peptides, brain research. Subspecialties: Neurobiology; Neuroendocrinology. Home: 1250 Ephesus Church Rd Chapel Hill NC 27514

HERNANDEZ, SAMUEL P., chemistry educator; b. Aguadilla, P.R., July 10, 1951; s. Samuel A. and Maria J. (Rivera) H.; m. Maria del Carmen Reinat, Aug. 31, 1974; children: Samuel E., Ricardo J. B.S., U. P.R., 1981, M.A., 1982; Ph.D., Johns Hopkins U., 1983. Asst. prof. chemistry U. P.R. Contbr. articles to profl. jours. Ford Found. fellow, 1977-81; Nat. Hispanic scholar, 1981-82. Mem. Am. Chem. Soc., Am. Inst. Chemists, Am. Phys. Soc., AAAS, N.Y. Acad. Sci. Roman Catholic. Current Work: Electron impact and laser spectroscopy of supersonic beams. Subspecialties: Physical chemistry; Satellite studies. Office: Dept Chemistry U PR Mayaguez PR 00708*

HERNDON, JAMES HENRY, orthopedic educator; b. Los Angeles, Oct. 31, 1938; s. James Greene and Kathleen Theresa (Murphy) H.; m. Geraldine Grace Armiger, Feb. 26, 1971; children: Jennifer, Jonathan. B.S., Loyola U., Los Angeles, 1961; M.D., UCLA, 1965; M.A. ad eundum, Brown U., 1979. Diplomate: Am. Bd. Orthopedic Surgery. From asst. clin. prof. to assoc. clin. prof. surgery Mich. State U., Grand Rapids, 1974-78; prof., chmn. dept. orthopedics Brown U., Providence, 1979—; orthopedic surgeon in chief R.I. Hosp., Providence, 1979—; cons. Crippled Children's Service of R.I., 1980—. Co-author: Scoliosis and other Deformities of the Axial Skeleton, 1975; editor: New Developments in Orthopedic Surgical Clinics of North America, 1983. Bd. govs. Arthritis Found. R.I., Providence, 1980; mem. joint adv. com. Palestine Temple and R.I. Hosp., 1978. Served to maj. U.S. Army, 1971-73. Recipient Edith and Carl Lasky Meml. award UCLA Med. Sch., 1965; Bronze award Am. Congress Rehab. Medicine, 1972; 1st award for clin. research N.Y. Med. Soc., 1974; OAS traveling fellow, 1978. Fellow Am. Orthopedic Assn., Am. Acad. Orthopedic Surgeons, A.C.S., Scoliosis Research Soc.; mem. Orthopedic Research Soc. Republican. Roman Catholic. Clubs: Agawam Hunt (Providence), Hope (Providence). Current Work: Fat Embolism syndrome; artificial joints; implants in the hand; child amputee; orthopedic education. Subspecialty: Orthopedics. Home: 86 Taber Ave Providence RI 02906 Office: Dept Orthopedic Surgery RI Hosp 233 Eddy St Providence RI 02902

HERON, S(TEPHEN) DUNCAN, JR., geologist, educator; b. Jackson, Miss., Sept. 18, 1926; s. Stephen Duncan and Laura Belle (Wilson) H.; m. Rebecca Ann Melton, Apr. 3, 1948; children—Stephani Ann, Stephen Duncan III. B.S., U.S.C., 1948, M.S., 1950; Ph.D., U. N.C., 1958. Prof. geology Duke U., Durham, N.C., 1950—; sec. Stagville Corp., Durham, 1984—. Editor-in-chief Jour. Southeastern Geology, 1958—. Contbr. articles to profl. jours. Bd. dirs. Eno River Assn., Durham, 1972—; pres. N.C. Mus. Life and Sci. Durham, 1985. Grantee, NSF, Nat. Park Service, others. Fellow Geol. Soc. Am. (chmn. SE Sect. 1980—); mem. Am. Assn. Petroleum Geologists, Soc. Exploration Petrologists and Paleontologists, Carolina Geol. Soc. (sec.-treas. 1968—), Sigma Xi. Democrat. Current work: Coastal plain sedementology. Subspecialties: Coastal zones; Sedimentology. Home: 4425 Kerley Rd Durham NC 27705 Office: Duke U Geology Dept Durham NC 27708

HERR, EARL BINKLEY, JR., pharm. research co. exec.; b. Lancaster, Pa., Apr. 14, 1928; s. Earl B. and Irene (Zeamer) H.; m. Elizabeth Sydney Hook, June 17, 1950; children—Audrey, Linda. B.S., Franklin and Marshall Coll., 1948; M.S. in Chemistry, U. Del., 1950, Ph.D. in Biochemistry, 1953; postgrad., Cornell U., 1953-55, Brookhaven Nat. Labs., 1955-57. With Lilly Research Labs., Indpls., 1957—, mgr. antibiotic purification devel., 1963-64, head pharm. research, 1964-65, asst. dir. prodn. devel., 1965, dir. antibiotic ops., 1965-68, exec. dir. biochem. and biol. ops., 1968-69, v.p. biochem. ops., 1969-70, v.p. indsl. relations, 1970, v.p. research, devel. and control, 1970-73, pres., 1973—; dir. Eli Lilly and Co. Bd. dirs. Ind. Sci. Edn. Fund. Mem. AAAS, Am. Chem. Soc., Sigma Xi. Subspecialty: Biochemistry (biology). Home: 12011 Eden Glen Dr Carmel IN 46032 Office: Lilly Research Labs 307 E McCarty St Indianapolis IN 46285

HERR, JOHN MERVIN, JR., biology educator, cons., researcher; b. Charlottesville, Va., July 26, 1930; s. John Mervin and Belva (Byrd) H.; m. Sue Highfield, Aug. 30, 1952; children: Susan Rebecca Herr Reich, Rachel Lynn; m. Lucrecia Linder, Dec. 30, 1974; 1 stepson, F. Brent Wahl. B.A., U. Va., 1951; M.A., 1952; Ph.D. (Coker Fellow), U. N.C., 1957. Instr. Washington and Lee U., Lexington, Va., 1952-54; Fulbright postdoctoral fellow U. Delhi, India, 1957-1958; asst. prof. Pfeiffer Coll., Misenheimer, N.C., 1958-59; asst. prof. U. S.C., Columbia, 1959-63, assoc., prof., 1963-69, prof., 1969—. Contbr. articles to profl. jours. Mem. Bot. Soc. Am., Internat. Soc. Plant Morphologists, Assn. Southeastern Biologists, Sigma Xi. Baptist. Current Work: Development of the ovule and female gametophyte in flowering plants for use in solution of taxonomic problems, development of clearing techniques to replace paraffin section techniques primarily for the above mentioned studies. Subspecialties: Reproductive biology; Systematics.

HERR, LEONARD JAY, plant pathologist; b. Orrville, Ohio, Dec. 21, 1928; s. Roy Albert and Orpha (Shoup) H.; m. Lucille Alice Adelsberger, Sept. 18, 1954; children: Lynn Allen, Karen Marie, Melissa Ann. Student, Antioch Coll., 1946-49; B.S., Ohio State U., 1952, M.S., 1953, Ph.D., 1956. Instr. Ohio Agrl. Expt. Sta., Ohio State U.-Ohio Agrl. Research and Devel. Center, Wooster, 1956-57, asst. prof., 1957-63, asso. prof., 1963-77, prof. plant pathology, 1977—. Contbr. articles to profl. jours. Mem. Am. Phytopath. Soc., AAAS, Am. Inst. Biol. Sci., Ohio Acad. Sci., N.Y. Acad. Sci., AAUP, Assn. Applied Biologists, Sigma Xi. Roman Catholic. Current Work: Soil-borne pathogens; sunflower diseases; ecology of soil-borne pathogens. Subspecialty: Plant pathology. Office: Dept Plant Pathology Ohio Agrl Research and Devel Center Wooster OH 44691

HERR, RICHARD BAESSLER, astronomer, educator; b. Phila., Mar. 3, 1936; s. Daniel Irwin and Edna Elizabeth (Baessler) H.; m. Mary Dilling, Sept. 6, 1958; 1 son, Daniel Dilling. B.S. in Physics, Franklin and Marshall Coll., 1957; M.S., U. Del., 1960; Ph.D. in Astronomy, Case Inst. Tech., 1965. Asst. prof. physics and astronomy U. Del., Newark, 1964-70, assoc. prof., 1970—; research astronomer Mt. Cuba Astron. Obs.; cons. in computer assisted instrn. Mem. Am. Astron. Soc., Internat. Astron. Union, Astron. Soc. Pacific, Royal Astron. Soc. Can. Current Work: Photoelectric photometry, computer assisted education. Subspecialty: Optical astronomy. Home: 913 Pickett Ln Newark DE 19711 Office: Dept Physics U Del Newark DE 19716

HERRICKS, EDWIN EUGENE, environmental biology educator, researcher, consultant; b. Axtell, Kans., Dec. 24, 1946; s. Robert Nicolas and Frances Mary (Loob) H.; m. Susan Leigh Varland, Aug. 31, 1968; children—Nicole Analyese, Thurston Edwin. B.S. in Zoology and English, U. Kans., 1968; M.S. in Engring., Johns Hopkins U., 1970; Ph.D. in Biology, Va. Poly. Inst. and State U., 1974. Research assoc. dept. civil engring. Va. Poly. Inst. and State U., Blacksburg, 1973, instr. agrl. engring., 1973; aquatic research biologist, field ecologist Union Carbide Corp., Tarrytown, N.Y., 1973-75; asst. prof. environ. biology U. Ill., Urbana, 1975-80, assoc. prof., 1980—; mem. Western energy and land use team rev. research program U.S. Fish and Wildlife Service, 1976-80; mem. regulatory flow work group Ill. Dept. Transp., 1977—; research scientist Rocky Mountain Biol. Lab., Crested Butte, Colo., 1977; Ill. Water Research Ctr. rep. to Ohio River Basin Commn., 1978-82; chmn. states water research Ctr. com. on instream flows Ohio River Basin Commn., 1978-82; mem. environ. subcom. of com. on surface mining and reclamation Nat. Acad. Scis./NRC, 1978-79, mem. com. on disposal of excess spoils, 1980-82; vis. asst. prof. evolution and environ. biology U. Pitts., 1979, vis. assoc. prof., 1980-82; vis. fellow Johns Hopkins U., Balt., 1983; cons. Peabody Coal Co., St. Louis, 1977-78, Ky. Bur. Environ. Protection, 1977, Resources for Future, 1979, Woodhaven Lakes Assn., Sublette, Ill., 1979—, Clark Dietz Engrs., Chgo., 1980, Homestake Mining Co., Lead, S.D., 1981-83, Schaeffer and Roland Co., Chgo., 1982, Village of Bourbonnais, Ill., 1983, Beling Cons., Moline, Ill., 1984. Editor: Recovery and Restoration, 1977. Contbr. articles and book chpts. to profl. publs. Mem. AAAS, Am. Fisheries Soc., Am. Soc. Limnology and Oceanography, Am. Water Research Assn., Assn. Southeastern Biologists, Ecology Soc. Am., Freshwater Biol. Assn., Internat. Assn. Theoretical and Applied Limnology, Internat. Assn. Water Pollution Research and Control, N.Am. Benthological Soc. (program chmn. 1980), Soc. Environ. Toxicology and Chemistry, Water Pollution Control Fedn. (chmn. ecology com. 1978—, officer other coms.). Current work: Environmental surveillance and biomonitoring restoration and recovery of damaged ecosystems, ecosystem response to stress, ecological system risk assessment, aquatic habit management, Subspecialties: Ecology (environmental science); Resource management. Home: 507 S Chicago St Champaign IL 61821 Office: Dept Civil Engring Univ Ill 208 N Romine Urbana IL 61801

HERRING, WILLIAM CONYERS, physicist; b. Scotia, N.Y., Nov. 15, 1914; s. William Conyers and Mary (Joy) H.; m. Louise C. Preusch, Nov. 30, 1946; children—Lois Mary, Alan John, Brian Charles, Gordon Robert. A.B., U. Kans., 1933; Ph.D., Princeton, 1937. NRC fellow Mass. Inst. Tech., 1937-39; instr. Princeton, 1939-40, U. Mo., 1940-41; mem. sci. staff Div. War Research, Columbia, 1941-45; prof. applied math. U. Tex., 1946; research physicist Bell Telephone Labs., Murray Hill, N.J., 1946-78; prof. applied physics Stanford (Calif.) U., 1978—; mem. Inst. Advanced Study, 1952-53. Recipient Army-Navy Cert. of Appreciation, 1947; Distinguished Service citation U. Kans., 1973; J. Murray Luck award for excellence in sci. reviewing Nat. Acad. Scis., 1980; von Hippel award Materials Research Soc., 1980; Wolf prize in physics, 1985. Fellow Am. Phys. Soc. (Oliver E. Buckley solid state physics prize 1959), Am. Acad. Arts and Scis.; mem. AAAS, Nat. Acad. Scis. Current Work: Theory of electronic and atomic structures of solids, and their magnetic and transport properties. Subspecialties: Condensed matter physics; Theoretical physics. Home: 3945 Nelson Dr Palo Alto CA 94306 Office: Dept Applied Physics Stanford U Stanford CA 94305

HERRIOTT, DONALD RICHARD, physicist; b. Rochester, N.Y., Feb. 4, 1928. Student Duke U., 1945-49, U. Rochester, 1950-51; Poly Inst. Bklyn., 1961-63. Mem. sci. bur. Bausch and Lomb Co., Rochester, N.Y., 1949-56; mem. staff Bell Telephone Lab., Murray Hill, N.J., 1956-68, head dept., 1968-81; sr. sci. adviser Perkin-Elmer Corp., Norwalk, Conn., 1981—. Inventor helium-neon laser, 1960, electron beam mask exposure system, 1970, phase measuring interferometry, 1972. Recipient Patent of Yr. award N.J. Research Council, 1978. Fellow Optical Soc. Am. (Fraunhofer award 1983, pres. 1984); mem. IEEE (sr. mem.; Cledo Brunetti award 1980), Nat. Acad. Engring. Current work: Optical and electron beam patterrings of integrated circuits. Subspecialty: Optical instrumentation. Office: 1237 Isabel Dr Sanibel FL 33957

HERRMANN, DOUGLAS J., psychology, educator; b. Wilmington, Del., Aug. 1, 1941; s. Carl Victor and Ruth Naomi (Ice) H.; m. Donna Lynn Shellenberger, Mar. 21, 1969; 1 dau., Amanda. B.S., U.S. Naval Acad., 1964; M.S., U. Del., 1972, Ph.D., 1974. Research assoc. Stanford U., 1972-73; assoc. prof. Hamilton Coll., Clinton, N.Y., 1973—; research scholar applied psychology unit Med. Research Council, Eng., 1972-73; cons. in field. Author: Inventory of Memory Experience, 1978; Contbr. articles to profl. jours. Head Refugee Sponsorship Group, Utica, N.Y., 1975—. Served to capt. USMC, 1964-67. Recipient Excellence in teaching award U. Del., 1972; Social Sci. Research Council fellow, 1972. Mem. Psychonomic Soc., Sigma Xi. Unitarian. Current Work: Research problems in psychology of language, memory and thought. Subspecialty: Cognition. Home: RD 1 Harding Rd Apt 519 Clinton NY 13323 Office: Dept Psychology College Hill Rd Clinton NY 13323

HERRMANN, KLAUS MANFRED, biochemist, educator; b. Lingen-Ems, W. Germany, June 27, 1937; came to U.S., 1967; s. Bruno and Auguste Victoria (Milse) H.; m. Elke Susanne Kuhne, Dec. 18, 1970; children—Miriam A., Till H. B.S., U. Muenster, W. Ger., 1960; M.S., U. Freiburg, W. Ger., 1964; Ph.D., 1966, Inst. Pasteur, Paris, 1966. Research assoc. U. Freiburg, 1966-67, Stanford U., Calif., 1967-69; asst. then assoc. prof. Purdue U., Lafayette, Ind., 1969-83, prof., 1983—. Editor: Amino Acids: Biosynthesis and Genetic Regulation, 1983. Contbr. articles to profl. jours. Mem. Am. Soc. Biol. Chemists, Gesellschaft Deutscher Chemiker. Current work: Elucidation of regulatory mechanisms in bacterial and plant metabolism; purification and characterization of enzymes; nuclear magnetic resonance spectroscopy of whole cells. Subspecialties: Biochemistry (biology); Molecular biology. Home: 40 Brook Hollow West Lafayette IN 47906 Office: Purdue U Dept Biochemistry West Lafayette IN 47907

HERRMANN, ROBERT ARTHUR, mathematics educator; b. Balt., Apr. 29, 1934; s. Ernest Carl and Catherine (Brostrum) H.; m. Sandi A. Baldi, Feb. 1, 1969; children: Kimberley, Laura, Diana. B.A. with honors, Johns Hopkins U., 1963; M.A. with honors, Am. U., 1968, Ph.D., 1973. Prof. math. U.S. Naval Acad., Annapolis, Md., 1968—; dir. Inst. for Math. Philosophy, Annapolis, 1980—; adviser U.S. Congress, Washington, 1980—. Author: Nonstandard Analysis, 1977, the G-Model, 1980, The Miraculous Model, 1982; Oneness, the Trinity and Logic, 1984; Nature: the Supreme Logician, 1985. Contbr. articles to profl. jours. Served with U.S. Army, 1955-57. Mem. Am. Math. Soc., Math. Assn. Am., Am. Sci. Affiliation, Phi Beta Kappa, Sigma Xi, Phi Kappa Phi. Current Work: Mathematical philosophy, nonstandard logic and modelling of natural systems, convergence space theory. Subspecialty: Applied mathematics. Office: Dept Math US Naval Acad Annapolis MD 21402

HERRON, NORMAN, inorganic coordination chemist; b. Newcastle, Eng., July 14, 1954; came to U.S., 1979; s. Robert and Rosemary (Barker) H.; m. Margaret Rowe, July 16, 1977; children—Louisa, Matthew. B.Sc. with 1st class honors, U. Warwick (Eng.), 1975, Ph.D. in Chemistry, 1978. Postdoctoral fellow Ohio State U., Columbus, 1979-81, research coordinator, 1981-83; research chemist E.I. DuPont de Nemours, Wilmington, Del., 1983—. Contbr. articles to profl. jours. Current work: Inorganic coordination chemistry, subspecialty-intrazeolite coordination chemistry, selective oxidation chemistry, photochemistry, ziolite catalysis. Subspecialty: Inorganic chemistry. Office: EI DuPont E262/419 Exptl Sta Wilmington DE 19898

HERRUP, KARL, developmental neurogeneticist, educator; b. Pitts., July 16, 1948; s. J. Lester and Florence Bernice (Hersh) H.; m. Claire Leslie Morse, Aug. 20, 1972; children—Rachael Herrup-Morse, Adam Herrup-Morse, Alexander Herrup-Morse. B.A., Brandeis U., 1970; Ph.D., Stanford U., 1974. Postdoctoral fellow Harvard U. Med. Sch., Boston, 1974-77, Biozentrum, Basel, Switzerland, 1978; asst. prof. Yale U. Med. Sch., New Haven, 1978-84, assoc. prof. dept. human genetics, 1984—. Mem. Soc. Neurosci. (sec. Conn. chpt. 1982-84). Current work: Use of mouse neurological mutants and mutant-wild type chimeras to study sites of gene action and roles of cell lineage in central nervous system. Subspecialties: Developmental biology; Neurobiology. Office: Dept Human Genetics Yale Med Sch 333 Cedar St New Haven CT 06510

HERSCOWITZ, HERBERT BERNARD, immunologist, educator; b. N.Y.C., June 19, 1939; s. Michael and Sarah (Sussman) H.; m. Ellen Carol Levine, Aug. 26, 1961; children—Robert, Stefanie, Andrew. B.S., Bklyn. Coll., 1961; M.S. cum laude, L.I. U., 1963; Ph.D., Hahnemann Med. Coll., 1968. Asst. instr. U. Pa. Sch. Dental Medicine, Phila., 1963-65; predoctoral fellow Hahnemann Med. Coll., Phila., 1965-68; postdoctoral fellow Case-Western Res. U., Cleve., 1968-70; asst. prof. microbiology Georgetown U. Schs. Medicine and Dentistry, Washington, 1970-76, asso. prof., 1976-81, prof., 1981—. Contbr. articles to profl. jours. NIH fellow, 1967-68, 68-70; named Alumnus of Year. Hahnemann Med. Coll., 1979. Mem. Am. Assn. Immunologists, Am. Soc. Microbiology, AAAS, Reticuloendothelial Soc., Sigma Xi. Current Work: Cellular interactions, alveolar macrophage function. Subspecialties: Immunopharmacology; Microbiology. Office: 3900 Reservoir Rd Washington DC 20007

HERSHBERGER, CHARLES LEE, research scientist; b. Louisville, Ill., May 1, 1942; s. Merrill George and Betty Hormel (Walsh) H.; m. Marla K., June 30, 1962; children: Mardi, C. Douglas, Jamie. B.S. in Chemistry, Eureka Coll., 1964; Ph.D. in Biochemistry, U. Ill. Coll. Medicine, 1968. Research assoc. Molecular Biology Inst. U. Wis., Madison, 1967-70; faculty dept. microbiology U. Ill., Urbana, 1970-76; sr. scientist Eli Lilly and Co., Indpls., 1976-80, research scientist, 1981—. Contbr. articles to profl. publs. Active Crossroads of Am. council Boy Scouts Am., 1967-70, 76—, scoutmaster, 1979-85, dist. chmn., 1985—; mem. Social Ministry Commn. Ind.-Ky. Synod Lutheran Ch. Am., 1981-84. Mem. Am. Soc. Biol. Chemists, Am. Soc. Microbiologists., AAAS, Sigma Xi. Current Work: Expression of mammalian proteins in bacteria, cloning genes for biosynthesis of antibiotics. Subspecialties: Genetics and genetic engineering (biology); Biochemistry (biology). Office: Eli Lilly Corporate Ctr Indianapolis IN 46285

HERSHER, LEONARD, medical educator, researcher; b. Lancaster, Pa., Mar. 30, 1925; s. Morris Jack and Mollie (Edelson) H.; m. Hilda Turoff, Sept. 6, 1948; children—Michael E., Jay K., Lisa A. B.A., NYU, 1949; Ph.D., U. Chgo., 1955. Lic. psychologist, N.Y. State. Research asst. U. Chgo., 1952-54; faculty SUNY-Syracuse Coll. Medicine, 1954—, assoc. prof. pediatrics, 1965—. Editor: Four Psychotherapies, 1970. Contbr. articles to profl. jours. Bd. dirs. N.Y. Civil Liberties Union, Syracuse. Served with inf. U.S. Army, 1943-46, ETO. Fellow Inst. for Rational Emotive Therapy; mem. Soc. for Study Evolution, N.Y. Psychol. Assn., Sigma Xi. Democrat. Current work: Behavioral pediatrics and theories of evolution. Subspecialties: Pediatrics; Psychobiology. Home: 510 Greenwood Pl Syracuse NY 13210 Office: Dept of Pediatrics Coll of Medicine SUNY-Syracuse 750 E Adams St Syracuse NY 13210

HERSHKOVITZ, PHILIP, mammalogist; b. Pitts., Oct. 12, 1909; s. Aba and Bertha (Halpern) H.; m. Anne Marie Pierrette Dodettershkovitz, Feb. 19, 1946 (dec. 1971); children—Francine, Michael, Mark. B.S., U. Mich., 1938, M.S., 1940, postgrad., 1940-41. Fellow Smithsonian Instn., Washington, 1941-43, 46-47; asst. curator, mammals Field Mus. Nat. History, Chgo., 1947-54, assoc. curator mammals, 1954-56, curator mammals, 1956-74, curator emeritus mammals, 1974—; mem. zool. expeditions, Ecuador, Peru, 1933-37, Colombia, 1941-43, 1948-52, Suiname, 1961, 62, Peru-Brazil, 1976, 80-81, Brazil, 1984; cons. Pan Am. Health Orgn., Peru, 1980-81. Author 4 books, latest being Living New World Monkeys, 1977. Contbr. articles to profl. pubs. Served to sgt. U.S. Army, 1943-46, ETO. Walteer Bacon Travelling fellow, 1941-43, 46-47; grantee NSF, 1957-60, 60-63, 60-61, 64-66, 84, NIH, 1965-68, 68-70, 71-75. Mem. Am. Soc. Mammalogists (life mem.), Explorers Club, Soc. Study Evolution, Internat. Soc. Primatology, AAAS, others. Current work: South American mammals, systematics, origin, evolution, distribution, conservation. Subspecialties: Systematics; Evolutionary biology. Office: Field Mus Nat History Roosevelt Rd and Lake Shore Dr Chicago IL 60605

HERTZ, ROY, pharmacology educator, physician; b. Cleve., June 19, 1909; married, 1934; 2 children. A.B., U. Wis., 1930, Ph.D., 1933, M.D., 1939; M.P.H., Johns Hopkins U., 1941. Asst. zoology U. Wis., 1930-34; instr. pharmacology Med. Sch., Howard U., Washington, 1934-35; intern Wis. Gen. Hosp., 1939-40; res. officer USPHS, 1941-47; endocrinologist, chmn. sect. and mem. study sect. endocrinology and metabolism Nat. Cancer Inst., NIH, 1947-65; sci. dir. Nat. Inst. Child Health and Devel., NIH, 1965-66; prof. ob-gyn Sch. Medicine, George Washington U., 1966-67; dir. reprodn. br. Nat. Inst. Child Health and Devel., 1967-69; sr. physician, assoc. dir. biomed. div. Population Council Rockefeller U., N.Y.C., 1969-72; prof. ob-gyn and medicine N.Y. Med. Coll., 1972-73; prof. pharmacology and ob-gyn Med. Sch. George Washington U., 1974—; Mem. adv. council Am. Cancer Soc. Fellow ACP, Am. Assn. Obstetricians and Gynecologists (hon.); mem. Nat. Acad. Sci., Am. Physiol. Soc., Soc. Exptl. Biology and Medicine. Subspecialties: Physiology (medicine); Endocrinology. Office: Route 3 Box 582 Hollywood MD 20636

HERTZBERG, ABRAHAM, aerospace and energy research scientist, educator; b. N.Y.C., July 8, 1922; s. Rubin and Paulien (Kalif) H.; m. Ruth Cohen, Sept. 3, 1950; children—Eleanor Ruth, Paul Elliot, Jean R. B.S. in Aero. Engring, Va. Poly Inst., 1943, M.S., Cornell U., 1949; postgrad., U. Buffalo, 1949-53. Engr. Cornell Aero. Lab., 1949-57, asst. head aerodynamics research, 1957-59, head aerodynamics research, 1959-65; prof. aeros. and astronautics, dir. aerospace research lab. U. Wash., 1966—; Cons. Aerospace Corp.; cons., mem. bd. Math. Scis. N.W. Inc., Lockheed Missiles & Space Co.; past mem. sci. adv. bd. USAF; past mem. electro-optics panel SAB, mem. various ad hoc coms.; past mem. research and tech. adv. council NASA; mem. plasma dynamics rev. panel NSF, U.S. Army; honored speaker Laser Inst. Am., 1975; mem. theory adv. com. Los Alamos Nat. Lab.; vis. lectr. Chinese Acad. Scis., Beijing, 1983. Editor: Physics of Fluids, 1968-70; Contbr. numerous articles on modern high energy engring., high powered lasers, controlled thermonuclear fusions processes, space laser and solar energy concepts to profl. jours. Served with AUS, 1944-46. Prin. investigator on numerous fed. research grants. Fellow AIAA (Dryden lectr. 1977, Agard lectr. 1978); mem. Am. Phys. Soc., Nat. Acad. Engrs., Sigma Xi. Patentee in field. Subspecialties: Aerospace engineering and technology; Laser research and development. Home: 10317 SE 28th Pl Bellevue WA 98004 Office: Aerospace & Engring Research Bldg Fl-10 U Wash Seattle WA 98195*

HERZBERG, GERHARD, physicist; b. Hamburg, Ger., Dec. 25, 1904; emigrated to Can., 1935, naturalized, 1945; s. Albin and Ella (Biber) H.; m. Luise H. Oettinger, Dec. 29, 1929 (dec.); children: Paul Albin, Agnes Margaret; m. Monika Tenthoff, Mar. 21, 1972. Dr. Ing., Darmstadt Inst. Tech., 1928; postgrad., U. Goettingen, U. Bristol, 1928-30; D.Sc. hon causa, Oxford U., 1960; D.Sc., U. Chgo., 1967, Drexel U., 1972, U. Montreal, 1972, U. Sherbrooke, 1972, McGill U., 1972, Cambridge U., 1972, U. Man., 1973, Andhra U., 1975, Osmania U., 1976, U. Delhi, 1976, U. Bristol, 1975, U. Western Ont., 1976; Fil. Hed. Dr., U. Stockholm, 1966; Ph.D., Weizmann Inst. Sci., 1976; LL.D., St. Francis Xavier U., 1972, Simon Fraser U., 1972, others. Lectr., chief asst. physics Darmstadt Inst. Tech., 1930-35; research prof.

physics U. Sask., Saskatoon, 1935-45; prof. spectroscopy Yerkes Obs., U. Chgo., 1945-48; prin. research officer NRC Can., Ottawa, 1948, dir. div. pure physics, 1949-69, disting. research scientist, 1969—Bakerian lectr. Royal Soc. London, 1960; holder Francqui chair U. Liege, 1960. Author books including: Spectra of Diatomic Molecules, 1950; Electronic Spectra and Electronic Structure of Polyatomic Molecules, 1966, The Spectra and Structures of Simple Free Radicals, 1971, (with K.P. Huber) Constants of Diatomic Molecules, 1979. Recipient Faraday medal Chem. Soc. London, 1970, Nobel prize in Chemistry, 1971; named companion Order of Can., 1968, academician Pontifical Acad. Scis., 1964. Fellow Royal Soc. London (Royal medal 1971), Royal Soc. Can. (pres. 1966, Henry Marshall Tory medal 1953), Hungarian Acad. Sci. (hon.), Indian Acad. Scis. (hon.), Am. Phys. Soc. (Plyler prize 1985), Chem. Inst. Can.; mem. Internat. Union Pure and Applied Physics (past v.p.), Am. Acad. Arts and Scis. (hon. fgn. mem.), Am. Chem. Soc. (Willard Gibbs medal 1969, Centennial fgn. fellow 1976), Nat. Acad. Sci. India, Indian Phys. Soc. (hon.), Japan Acad. (hon.), Chem. Soc. Japan (hon.), Royal Swedish Acad. Scis. (fgn., physics sect.), Nat. Acad. Sci. (fgn. asso.), Faraday Soc., Am. Astron. Soc., Can. Assn. Physicists (past pres., Achievement award 1957), Optical Soc. Am. (hon., Frederic Ives medal 1964). Current Work: Molecular spectroscopy: study of molecular structure, especially of simple free radicals. Recent studies: triatomic hydrogen (H_3)and ammonium(NH_4). Subspecialties: Atomic and molecular physics; Infrared spectroscopy. Home: 190 Lakeway Dr Rockcliffe Park Ottawa ON Canada Office: Nat Research Council Ottawa ON K1A 0R6 Canada

HESS, EARL HOLLINGER, chemical laboratory executive; b. Lancaster County, Pa., June 16, 1928; s. Abram Myer and Ruth (Stoner) H.; m. Anita F. Swords, Sept. 2, 1951; children: Kenneth Earl, Bonita Sue, Carol Denise. B.S. cum laude, Franklin and Marshall Coll., 1952; Ph.D. in Organic Biochemistry, U. Ill., 1955. Teaching asst. U. Ill., Urbana, 1952-54; Socony-Mobil research fellow, 1954-55; asst. prof. chemistry Franklin and Marshall Coll., Lancaster, Pa., 1955-57; group leader chem. research Gen. Cigar Co., Lancaster, 1957-61; pres., chief exec. officer Lancaster Labs., Inc., 1961—; dir. Standard Labs., Inc., 1983—. Contbr. chpt. to book. Mem. Conestoga Ch. of the Brethren; bd. dirs. Bethany Theol. Sem., 1981—. Recipient Spl. award Am. Council Ind. Labs., 1979; Roger W. Truesdail award, 1983; Disting. Pennsylvanian award William Penn Com. Mem. Am. Assn. Small Research Cos., Am. Assn. for Lab Accreditation (dir.), Am. Council Ind. Labs. (pres. 1985-86), ASTM, Am. Chem. Soc., Am. Pub. Health Assn., AAAS, N.Y. Acad. Scis., Nat. Fedn. Ind. Businesses, Am. Water Works Assn., Nat. Profl. Services Firm, U.S. C. of C. (small bus. council 1980—, chmn. legis. policy com.), Pa. C. of C. (vice chmn.), Lancaster C. of C. (chmn. 1985), Bus. Execs. for Nat. Security, Phi Beta Kappa, Sigma Xi. Patentee tobacco processing. Current Work: Agricultural products utilization research; new food processes and techniques; basic biochemistry studies in agriculture, food products, and environmental issues. . Home: 2435 New Holland Pike Lancaster PA 17601 Office: 2425 New Holland Pike Lancaster PA 17601

HESS, GEORGE BURNS, physics educator; b. Princeton, N.J., Sept. 17, 1936; s. Harry Hammond and Annette (Burns) H.; m. Blanche Mieko Isobe, Dec. 19, 1965; children—Harry F., Frank M. A.B., Princeton U., 1958; Ph.D., Stanford U., 1967. Research assoc. Stanford U., Calif., 1967-68; asst. prof. physics U. Va. Charlottesville, 1968-73, assoc. prof., 1973—. Contbr. articles to physics jours. Mem. Am. Phys. Soc., AAAS, Sigma Xi. Current work: Physisorption, phase transitions, superfluidity, fluid dynamics. Subspecialties: Condensed matter physics; Low temperature physics. Home: 2505 Smithfield Rd Charlottesville VA 22901 Office: U Va Dept Physics Charlottesville VA 22901

HESS, GEORGE P., biochemistry educator; b. Vienna, Austria, Nov. 18, 1926; came to U.S., 1938; s. Henry Stephen Hess and Edith (Muller) Hess Perry; m. Betsey S. Williams, Oct. 1953 (div. 1979); children—Peter, Richard, Paul, David; m. Susan E. Coombs, July 5, 1980. A.B., U. Calif.-Berkeley, 1949, Ph.D., 1953. Postdoctoral fellow MIT, Cambridge, 1953-55; instr. biochemistry Cornell U. Med. Sch., N.Y.C., 1955; asst. prof. Cornell U., Ithaca, N.Y., 1956-60, assoc. prof., 1960-65, prof. chemistry, 1965, prof. biochemistry, 1966—; vis. fellow Yale U., New Haven, Conn., 1960; U.S. State Dept. cultural exchange prof., Europe, 1963, 70; vis. prof. biophysics U. Pa., Phila., 1964-65; vis. prof. biochemistry U. Hawaii, Honolulu, 1966; vis. prof. chemistry U. Ariz., Tucson, 1968; mem. various NIH and NSF coms. Served with U.S. Army, 1944-47. Recipient Alexander von Humboldt Sr. scientist award U. Konstanz, Germany, 1982; NIH Spl. fellow, 1968-70; Guggenheim fellow, 1962-63; Sr. Fulbright grantee, 1962-63. Mem. Am. Chem. Soc., Am. Soc. Neurochemistry, AAAS, Biophys. Soc., Brit. Biophys. Soc., Fedn. Am. Socs. Exptl. Biologists, N.Y. Acad. Scis., Soc. for Neurosci. Current work: Fast reaction techniques used to study structural and functional interrelationships in membrane-bound proteins of nerve and muscle cells. Subspecialties: Biochemistry (biology); Biophysical chemistry. Office: Biochemistry Dept Cornell U 270 Clark Hall Ithaca NY 14853

HESS, ORVAN WALTER, obstetrician, gynecologist, educator; b. Bayoba, Pa., June 18, 1906; s. Philip O. and Effie F. (Shoemaker) H.; m. Carol Woodruff Maurer, Aug. 31, 1928; children: Katherine Hess Halloran, Carolyn Hess Westerfield. B.S., Lafayette Coll., 1927; M.D., SUNY-Buffalo, 1931. Diplomate Am. Bd. Ob-Gyn. Intern Children's Hosp., Buffalo, 1931-32; intern Yale-New Haven Hosp., 1932-33, asst. resident, 1934-36, resident in ob-gyn, 1936-37, now co-dir. Fetal Cardiovascular Ctr.; research fellow in surgery and gynecology Yale U. Sch. Medicine, New Haven, 1933-35, instr., 1936-37, clin. prof., 1975—, dir. regional perinatal monitoring program, div. perinatology, dept. ob-gyn, 1971—; med. dir. Conn. Welfare Dept., 1967-70, dir. bur. health services, 1970-71; pres., Conn. Med. Inst; chmn. Conn. Com. on Maternal Mortality and Morbidity; pres. Conn. Health Assn., Inc.; mem. exec. com., mem. adv. com. Conn. Regional Med. Program; dir. Corometrics Electronics, Inc.; mem. staff Yale-New Haven Med. Ctr., Hosp. of St. Raphael, Middlesex Hosp., Middletown, Conn. Contbr. articles to med. jours. Served with U.S. Army, 1942-45; col. (ret). Decorated Bronze star (5); recipient Kidd award Lafayette Coll., 1980; fellow Morse Coll. Yale. Fellow ; ACS ; Am. Coll. ob-Gyn. ; mem. AMA (sci. achievement award 1979, del. 1970-84), Assn. Mil. Surgeons U.S., IEEE, Conn. Med. Soc. (pres. 1966-67), Sigma Xi, Nu Sigma Nu. Presbyterian. Clubs: Lawn (New Haven), Yale (New Haven), Graduate (New Haven). Current Work: Fetal monitoring, telemetry, ultrasound. Subspecialties: Neonatology; Maternal and fetal medicine. Office: Yale University School of Medicine 333 Cedar St New Haven CT 06510

HESS, WILMOT NORTON, scientific administrator; b. Oberlin, Ohio, Oct. 16, 1926; s. Walter Norton and Rachel Victoria (Metcalf) H.; m. Winifred Esther Lowdermilk, June 16, 1950; children—Walter Craig, Alison Lee, Carl Ernest. B.S. in Elec. Engring, Columbia, 1946; M.A. in Physics, Oberlin Coll, 1949, D.Sc., 1970; Ph.D., U. Calif., Berkeley, 1954. Staff Lawrence Radiation Lab., U. Calif., Berkeley and Livermore, 1954-59, head Plowshare div., Livermore, 1959-61; dir. theoretical div. Goddard Spaceflight Center (NASA), Greenbelt, Md., 1961-67; dir. sci. and applications Manned Spacecraft Center, Houston, 1967-69; dir. NOAA Research Labs. (Commerce Dept.), Boulder, Colo., 1969-80, Nat. Center for Atmospheric Research, 1980—; adj. prof. U. Colo., 1970-78. Contbr. articles to profl. jours.; editor: Introduction to Space Science, 1965; author: Radiation Belt and Magnetosphere, 1968, (with others) Weather and Climate Modification, 1974; asso. editor: (with others) Jour. Geophys. Research, 1961-67, Jour. Atmospheric Sci, 1961-67, Jour. Am. Inst. Aeros. and Astronautics, 1967-69. Served with USN, 1944-46. Fellow Am. Geophys. Union, Am. Phys. Soc.; mem. Nat. Acad. Engring. Club: Cosmos (Washington). Current Work: Oil spills, acid rain. Subspecialty: Meteorology. Home: 4927 Idylwild Trail Boulder CO 80301 Office: Nat Center Atmospheric Research 1850 Table Mesa Dr Boulder CO 80303

HESSELBERTH, JOHN FREDERIC, research and development management executive; b. Lafayette, Ind., Jan. 30, 1941; s. Wilfred M. and Merno M. (King) H.; m. Judith Ellen Kemmer, June 9, 1962; children—Janet, Joyce. B.S. in Chem. Engring., Purdue U., 1962, M.S. in Chem. Engring., 1964; Ph.D. in Chem. Engring., U. Cin., 1968. Supr. research and devel. E.I. DuPont de Nemours, Wilmington, Del., 1972-73, Kinston, N.C., 1973-75; sr. supr. research and devel., 1976-79, tech. supt., Martinsville, Va., 1979-82, lab. dir., Wilmington, 1982-84, tech. dir., carpet fiber and fiberfill div. textile fibers dept., 1985—. Served to 1st lt. U.S. Army, 1963-64. Subspecialty: Chemistry and engineering research administration. Office: EI DuPont Textile Fibers Dept Nemours Bldg Wilmington DE 19898

HESSER, JAMES E(DWARD), astronomer; b. Wichita, Kans., June 23, 1941; s. J(ames) Edward and Ina (Lowe) H.; m. Betty Louise Hinsdale, Aug. 24, 1963; children: Nadja Lynn, Rebecca Ximena, Diana Gillian. B.A. in Astronomy, U. Kans., 1963; Ph.D. in Astrophys, Scis, Princeton U., 1966. Research assoc. Princeton U. Obs., 1966-68; jr. asst., assoc. astronomer Observatorio Interamericano de Cerro Tololo, La Serena, Chile, 1968-77, asst. dir., 1972-74; assoc. research officer Dominian Astrophys. Observatory, Victoria, B.C., Canada, 1977-81, sr. research officer, 1981—; vis. prof. U. Chile, 1973-74; chairperson Can. Starlab Working Group, 1979—. Contbr. articles to profl. jours. Mem. Internat. Astron. Union, Am. Astron. Soc., Astron. Soc. Pacific (dir. 1981—, bd. editors publs. 1982—), Can. Astron. Soc. Current Work: Chemical evolution of galaxies, star clusters, interstellar lines, variable stars; research. Subspecialties: Optical astronomy; Space astronomy. Home: 1874 Ventura Way Victoria BC V8N 1R3 Canada Office: 5077 W. Saanich Rd Victoria BC V8X 4M6 Canada

HESTER, JARRETT CHARLES, mechanical engineer, educator, research and development official; b. Mt. Vernon, Tex., Dec. 14, 1938; s. Jarrett B. and Edith L. (Hutson) H.; m. Marjorie M. Hester, Sept. 10, 1980; children: James, Michael, Laura. B.S.M.E., Arlington State Coll., 1962; M.S.M.E., Okla. State U., 1964, Ph.D.M.E., 1966. Registered profl. engr., Tex. Engr. LTV Aerospace Corp. Research Center, 1962-66; sr. engring. specialist LTV Aerospace Corp. Research Center (Missiles and Space div.), 1967-70; asst. prof. mech. engring. U. Tex., Austin, 1966-67; assoc. prof. mech. engring. Clemson U., 1970-71, dept. head dept. mech. engring., 1971-74; assoc. dean Clemson U. (Coll. Engring.), 1974-77, prof. mech. engring., 1977—; dir. S.C. Energy Research and Devel. Center, 1982—; cons. J.E. Sirrine Co.; mgr. advanced tech. projects, 1979-80. Served with USAFR, 1956-64. Mem. ASME, ASHRAE, Am. Soc. Engring. Educators, Sigma Xi, Tau Beta Pi, Pi Tau Sigma. Presbyterian. Patentee in field. Current Work: Energy systems. Subspecialties: Mechanical engineering; Energy systems. Home: 206 Mountain View Ln Clemson SC 29631 Office: Mechanical Engineering Clemson U Clemson SC 29631

HESTER, LAWRENCE RAY, II, mechanical engineer, researcher and developer; b. Austin, Tex., June 29, 1956; s. Lawrence Ray and Nellene (Kuempel) H.; m. Melinda Gleason, May 18, 1979. B.S.M.E., U. Tex., Austin, 1978; M.B.A. with honors, Oklahoma City U., 1983. Registered profl. engr., Okla. Research and devl. engr. Halliburton Services Co., Duncan, Okla., 1978-83, sr. research and devel. engr., 1983-85; spl. projects engr. Teledyne Merla, Garland, Tex., 1985—. Mem. ASME (assoc., exec. com. 1981), Instrument Soc. Am. (sr. mem.). Current work: Applying new technologies in development of instrumentation, controls and other electromechanical systems. Subspecialties: Mechanical engineering; Systems engineering. Home: 1828 Archery Ln Garland TX 75042 Office: Teledyne Merla PO Box 469010 Garland TX 75046

HESTER, RICHARD KELLY, pharmacologist, med. educator; b. Austin, Tex., July 30, 1947; s. Glenn Richard and Doris Pernell (Clanahan) H.; m. Joan Christine Rydman, Mar. 25, 1979; children—Edward Zachary, Kasey Clanahan. B.A. in Biology (Ford Found. grantee), Austin Coll., 1969; Ph.D. in Pharmacology (NIH fellow), U. Tex. Health Sci. Ctr., San Antonio, 1975. NIH postdoctoral fellow dept. pharmacology U. Miami (Fla.) Sch. Medicine, 1975-76; research fellow depts. pharmacology and surgery U. Tex. Health Sci. Ctr., Dallas, 1976-77, instr., 1977-78, asst. prof., 1978-79; asst. prof. med. pharmacology Coll. Medicine, Tex. A&M U., College Station, 1979-85, assoc. prof., 1985—; cons. Contbr. numerous articles to profl. jours. Am. Heart Assn. grantee, 1977-80; Nat. Heart, Lung and Blood Inst. grantee, 1980—. Fellow Am. Heart Assn.; mem. AAAS, Western Pharmacol. Soc., Microcirculatory Soc., Am. Soc. Pharmacology and Exptl. Therapeutics, Sigma Xi. Episcopalian. Current Work: Ca and excitation/contraction (relaxation) in vascular smooth muscle, vascular smooth muscle in vitro and microcirculation in vivo. Subspecialties: Cellular pharmacology; Membrane biology. Home: 3106 Hummingbird Circle Bryan TX 77801 Office: Dept Med Pharmacology Coll Medicine Tex A&M U College Station TX 77843

HETTINGER, WILLIAM PETER, JR., petroleum company executive; b. Aurora, Ill., Sept. 13, 1922; s. William Peter and Gertrude Kathryn (Schomer) H.; m. Alice May Mietz, Apr. 20, 1944; children: Diana Lee, William Peter, Scott Edward, Sally Ann (dec.). B.S. in Chemistry, Purdue U., 1947; Ph.D., Northwestern U., 1951. Dir. corp. devel. Ga. Kaolin Co., 1972-74; v.p. research and devel., N.L. Industries, 1974-76; mem. spl. staff Arthur D. Little, Inc., 1976-77; dir. research and devel. Ashland Petroleum Co., Ky., 1977-79, v.p. research and devel. automotive and product application labs., 1979-84, v.p. and pres. Ashland Carbon Fibers div., 1985—; mem. exptl. program for stimulating competitive research NSF Com. for Ky. Contbr. articles to profl. jours. Rep. Greater Severna Park council, 1966-71, v.p., 1969-70; bd. dirs. St. Paul's Lutheran Day Sch., Glen Burnie, Md., 1967-72, chmn., 1969-71; bd. mgrs. Luth. Home for Aged, Jersey City. Served with USAAF, 1943-45, ETO. Decorated Air Medal with oak leaf cluster, 4 battle stars; advanced tng. fellow in aging research NIH, 1968-71. Fellow Am. Inst. Chemists; mem. N.Y. Acad. Scis. (hon. life), Am. Chem. Soc., AAAS, Indsl. Research Inst., Catalyst Club Chgo., Catalyst Club Phila., Catalyst Club N.Y., Catalyst Club Tri-State (pres., founder 1978-80), Catalysis Soc. (rep.), Am. Inst. Chem. Engrs. (awards com.), Ky. Acad. Sci. (bd. dirs.), Research Dirs. Assn. N.Y. (pres. 1976-77), Sigma Xi, Phi Lambda Upsilon. Lutheran. Clubs: Chartwell Country of Severna Park (dir. 1970-72), Echo Lake Country (Westfield, N.J.); Nashawtuc Country (Concord, Mass.); Bellefonte (Ky.) Country. Patentee in field. Subspecialties: Catalysis chemistry; Petroleum engineering. Home: 203 Meadowlark Rd Russell KY 41169 Office: Dept Genetics NC State U PO Box 7614 Raleigh NC 27695

HEUER, MICHAEL ALEXANDER, dentist, educator; b. Grand Rapids, Mich., Apr. 27, 1932; s. Harold Maynard and Gwendolyn Ruth (Kremer) H.; m. Barbara Margaret Naines, Nov. 23, 1955; children—Kristan M., Karin E., Katrina A. D.D.S., Northwestern U., 1956; M.S., U. Mich., 1959. Practice dentistry specializing in endodontics, Chgo., 1959—; asst. prof. Northwestern U., 1960-66; asso. prof. Loyola U., Chgo., 1968-73; prof., chmn. dept. endodontics Northwestern U., 1974-83, assoc. dean acad affairs, 1983—; dir. Am. Bd. Endodontics, 1971-77, sec.-treas., 1973-76, pres., 1976-77; chmn. subcom. Am. Nat. Standards Inst.; mem. com. on advanced edn. Commn. on Accreditation of Dental Edn., 1974-77. Contbr. articles in field to profl. jours. Served with USNR, 1956-58. Fellow Am. Coll. Dentistry, Internat. Coll. Dentistry, Am. Assn. Endodontists (exec. council 1967-71, sec. 1979-84, v.p. 1984-85, pres.-elect 1984-86); mem. ADA (mem. council dental materials and devices 1972-78, chmn. 1977-78), AAAS, Internat. Assn. Dental Research, Am. Assn. Dental Schs., Chgo. Odontographic Soc. (pres. 1982-84), Edgar D. Coolidge Endodontic Soc. (trustee), Phi Eta Sigma, Omicron Kappa Upsilon, Chi Psi, Delta Sigma Delta. Current Work: Endodontic instruments, instrumentation and materials. Subspecialties: Endodontics; Biomaterials. Home: 156 Timber Ridge Lake Barrington Shores Barrington IL 60010 Office: Dental Sch Northwestern U Chicago IL 60611

HEVEZI, JAMES MICHAEL, radiological physicist; b. Gary, Ind., June 21, 1940; s. James Emery and Margaret (Olah) H.; m. Suzanne Landig, Feb. 5, 1978; children: Julie, Lloyd, Matthew, Lisa, Martin, Jane. B.S., St. Procopius Coll., 1962; Ph.D., U. Notre Dame, 1969. Cert. radiol. physicist, Am. Bd. Radiology, 1975. Asst. prof. radiology U. Wis., Madison, 1969-71, U. Tex., Houston, 1971-79; staff physicist U. Ariz., Tucson, 1979—; v.p. Tex. Radiol. Equip. Corp., Houston, 1973-77; pres. Landig-Hevezi Assoc., Rapid City, S.D., 1978-79; cons. Radiol. Phys. Service, Inc., Phoenix, 1982—. Nat. Cancer Inst. grantee, 1974, 76. Mem. Am. Assn. Physicist in Medicine (asso. editor 1976-82), Am. Coll. Radiology, Am. Soc. Therapeutic Radiologists, Radiol. Soc. N. Am. Inventor patentee "The Inverse Pinhole Camera, 1974, Light Beam Readout, 1976. Current Work: Radiol, physics, diagnostic and therapeutic radiology, hyperthermia, implant radiation oncology. Subspecialty: Radiology. Home: 2223 E Camino Rio Tucson AZ 85718 Office: Radiation Oncology Health Sci Center Univ Ariz Tucson AZ 85724

HEWLETT, WILLIAM (REDINGTON), electronics company executive, electrical engineer; b. Ann Arbor, Mich., May 20, 1913; s. Albion Walter and Louise (Redington) H.; m. Flora Lamson, Aug. 10, 1939 (dec. 1977); children—Eleanor Hewlett Gimon, Walter B., James S., William A., Mary Hewlett Jaffe; m. Rosemary Bradford, 1978. A.B., Stanford U., 1934, E.E., 1939; M.S., MIT, 1936; LL.D., U. Calif., 1966. Yale U., 1976, Mills Coll., 1983; D.Sc. (hon.), Kenyon Coll., 1978, Poly Inst. N.Y., 1978; other hon. degrees. Electromed. researcher, 1936-39; co-founder Hewlett-Packard Co., Palo Alto, Calif., 1939, ptnr., 1939-46, exec. v.p., dir., 1947-64, pres., 1964-77, chief exec. officer, 1969-78; chmn. exec. com., 1977-83, vice chmn. bd. dirs., 1983—, dir.; trustee Carnegie Inst., Washington, 1971, chmn. bd. trustees, 1980—; dir. Utah Internat. Trustee Standord U., 1963-74; mem. Pres.'s Gen. Adv. Com. on Fgn. Assistance, 1965-68, Pres.'s Sci. Adv. Com., 1966-69, San Francisco panel Commn. on White House Fellows, 1969-70; chmn. San Francisco panel Commn. on White House Fellows, 1970; bd. dirs. San Francisco Bay Area Council. Served to lt. col. AUS, 1942-45. Recipient Nat. Medal of Sci., 1985. Fellow IEEE (pres. 1954), Franklin Inst. (life), Am. Acad. Arts and Scis.; mem. Nat. Acad. Scis., Nat. Acad. Engring., Instrument Soc. Am. (hon. life), Am. Philos. Soc., Calif. Acad. Sci. (Hon. trustee). Subspecialty: Electronics. Office: Hewlett-Packard Co 3000 Hanover St Palo Alto CA 94304*

HEYDE, JOHN BRADLEY, dental researcher, dentist; b. Marion, Ill., Dec. 27, 1926. B.S. in Chemistry, U. Mich., 1950, M.S. in Biol. Chemistry, 1952, D.D.S., 1957. Cert. Dental Bds., Pa., Mich., Del. Dir. profl. research L. D. Caulk Co. div. Dentsply Internat., Inc., Milford, Del.; lectr. on dental materials and restorative dentistry. Contbr. articles on dentistry to profl. jours. Fellow Royal Soc. Health (Eng.), Acad. Dentistry Internat.; mem. Fedn. Dentaire Internationale, Internat. Assn. for Dental Research (dental materials and pulp groups), Am. Prosthodontic Soc., Pierre Fauchard Acad., ADA, Del. State Dental Soc., Kent-Sussex Dental Soc. (hon. life mem., past pres. and sec.), Acad. Operative Dentistry, Acad. Gen. Dentistry, Am. Acad. Plastics Research (past pres., meritorious service award 1972-73), Am. Soc. Dentistry for Children, Fedn. Prosthodontic Orgns. (del. 1970, 71, 72), Sigma Alpha Epsilon, Psi Omega. Current Work: New systems and techniques for use in orthodontics, periodontics, endodontics and operative dentistry. Subspecialty: Dental materials. Home: 508 Kings Hwy Milford DE 19963 Office: L D Caulk Co Div Dentsply Internat Inc Lakeview and Clarke Aves Milford DE 19963

HEYDEGGER, H(ELMUT) ROLAND, physical chemist, educator, researcher, cons.; b. Phila., Dec. 3, 1935; s. Helmut and Allyse (Paulich) H. B.S., Queens Coll., CUNY, 1956; M.S., U. Ark., Fayetteville, 1958; Ph.D. (Gen. Electric Found. fellow), U. Chgo., 1968. Phys. chemist U.S. Bur. Mines, Bartlesville, Okla., 1958; instr. Prairie State Coll., 1961-62; asst. prof. chemistry Purdue U. Calumet, Hammond, Ind., 1970-75, assoc. prof., 1975-81, prof., 1981—, head dept. chemistry and physics, 1979—, dir. Inst. Environ. Edn., 1982-84, acting dean Sch. Sci. and Nursing, 1983-84, acting dean Sch. Sci. and Nursing, 1983-84; research assoc. Enrico Fermi Inst., U. Chgo., 1968-78, sr. research assoc., 1978—; NRC resident assoc. NASA John Space Ctr., 1985—; cons. Argonne Nat. Lab., 1973-74; vis. fellow Australian Nat. U., 1976-77, 84; vis. staff mem. Los Alamos Nat. Lab., 1978—, NRC resident assoc. NASA Johnson Space Ctr., 1985—. Contbr. articles to profl. jours. Mem. Am. Chem. Soc., Am. Phys. Soc., Am. Geophys. Uion, Geochem. Soc., Internat. Assn. Geochemistry and Cosmochemistry, Meteoritical Soc. Current Work: Application of nuclear sci. to geo- and cosmochem. problems. Subspecialties: Analytical chemistry; Geochemistry. Office: Dept Chemistry and Physics Purdue U Calumet Hammond IN 46323

HEYER, ERIC JOHN, neurologist, educator; b. N.Y.C., Feb. 10, 1946; s. John W. and Dora (Kaplan) H.; m. Diana A. Steele, June 8, 1980. B.S., U. Chgo., 1968; postgrad., Rockefeller U., 1968-69; Ph.D., Albert Einstein Coll. Medicine, 1974, M.D., 1975. Instr. neurology U. Mich., 1979-80; asst. prof. neurology Mt. Sinai Med. Sch., N.Y.C., 1981—. Contbr. articles to profl. jours. R.S. Morison fellow Grass Found., 1979-80. Mem. Am. Acad. Neurology, Am. Epilepsy Soc., AAAS, N.Y. Acad. Scis., Soc. Neurosci. Current Work: Mechanism of action of dopamine on cultured basal ganglia neurons. Subspecialties: Neurophysiology; Neurology. Home: 275 W 96th St Apt 22E New York NY 10025 Office: Dept Neurology Mt Sinai Sch Medicine One Gustave L Levy Pl New York NY 10029

HEYING, THEODORE LOUIS, chemical company executive; b. Balt., Oct. 19, 1927; s. Louis Joseph and Marie Elizabeth (Scherder) H.; m. Patricia E. Worthington, Nov. 22, 1952; children—Theodore Louis, Maria T. B.S., Loyola Coll., Balt., 1948; M.S., Holy Cross Coll., Worcester, Mass., 1949; Ph.D. in Chemistry, U. Md., 1953. With Olin Corp., New Haven, 1953—, bus. mgr., 1970-72, dir. research, 1972-82, dir. internat. tech., 1982—; mng. dir. Olin Chems. Ltd., Ireland, 1971-74. Author. Mem. bd. finance, North Haven, Conn., 1966-71, chmn., 1970-71. Served with AUS, 1954-56. Mem. Am. Chem. Soc., Republican. Roman Catholic. Patentee in field. Home: 735-B Quinnipiac Ln Stratford CT 06497

HIBBS, CLAIR MAURICE, veterinary diagnostic service administrator; b. Lucerne, Mo., Oct. 10, 1923; s. Grover Clarence and Bertha E. (Cassady) H.; m. Ann Elizabeth Robinson, Dec. 26, 1946; children—Drew R., Gerald W. B.S., U. Mo., 1949, D.V.M., 1953; M.S., Kans. State U., 1962, Ph.D., 1965. Gen. practice veterinarian, David City, Nebr., 1953-60; Mark Morris fellow, Kans. State U., Manhattan, 1960-62; instr. 1962-65, asst. prof., 1965-68, assoc. prof., 1969-73; assoc. prof. U. Nebr., North Platte, 1969-70, grad. faculty, 1971-73, prof. 1973, pathologist in charge Vet. Diagnostic lab., 1969-79; research prof. U. N.Mex., Albuquerque, 1979—; dir. Vet. Diagnostic Services, Albuquerque, 1979—. Contbr. articles to profl. jours. Mem. Meml. Hosp. Bd., North Platte, 1972-74, Great Plains Med. Ctr. Hosp. Bd., North Plains, 1975-79. Recipient Meritorious Service award Neb. Vet. Med. Assn., 1979. Fellow Am. Acad. Vet. Comparative Toxicology; mem. AVMA, N.Y. Acad. Sci. Am. Assn. Vet. Lab. Diagnostics, Am. Legion, Gamma Sigma Delta. Republican. Presbyterian. Lodge: Rotary (pres. 1975-76) (North Platte). Home: 14200 Nambe NE Albuquerque NM 87123 Office: N Mex Vet Diag Services 700 Camino de Salud NE Albuquerque NM 87106

HIBBS, DAVID EDGEMON, forest ecology educator; b. Chgo., Jan. 1, 1950; s. George G. and Elizabeth Ann (Edgemon) H.; m. Sally K. Karr, Aug. 10, 1974; children—Ryan, Robin. B.A., Carleton Coll., 1972; M.S., U. Mass., 1976, Ph.D., 1978. Silvicultural fellow Harvard U. Forest, Petersham, Mass., 1978-81; asst. prof. in residence U. Conn., Storrs, 1981-83; asst. prof. forest ecology Oreg. State U., Corvallis, 1983—. Contbr. articles to profl. jours. USDA grantee, 1984. Mem. Ecol. Soc. Am., Torrey Bot. Club, Am. Forestry Assn., Soc. Am. Foresters, N.W. Sci. Soc. Current work: Research in plant community structure and dynamics, species interactions, antecology of forest tree species. Subspecialties: Ecology (biology); Species interaction. Office: Dept Forest Sci Oreg State U Corvallis OR 97331

HICKERNELL, FRED SLOCUM, physicist, electronic engineer; b. Phoenix, Jan. 16, 1932; s. Frederick Azeriah and Alice Vernece (Slocum) H.; m. Thresa Elizabeth Kerr, June 25, 1954; children—Frederick John, Diana Elizabeth, Robert Kerr, Thomas Slocum. B.A. in Edn., Ariz. State U., 1953, M.S. in Physics, 1959, Ph.D., 1966. Instr., Ariz. State U., Tempe, 1957-58, faculty assoc., 1981-83; engr. Goodyear Aerospace, Litchfield Park, Ariz., 1958-60; physicist Motorola, Inc., Phoenix, 1960—; liaison officer USAF, Phoenix, 1972-75. Patentee in field. Leader Roosevelt council Boy Scouts Am., 1971-77; chmn. Valley Christian Ctr. Bd., 1973-74. Recipient Engring. award NASA, 1974. Mem. IEEE (sr.), Am. Phys. Soc., Am. Meteorol. Soc., Am. Vacuum Soc., Ariz. State U. Alumni Assn. (adv. council 1977-82), Sigma Xi. Baptist. Current work: Microwave acoustics and integrated optics; thin-film technology; surface acoustic wave materials and devices. Subspecialties: Condensed matter physics; Integrated circuits. Office: Motorola Inc 8201 E McDowell Scottsdale AZ 85252

HICKEY, DONAL ALOYSIUS, biologist, educator; b. County Kerry, Ireland, July 13, 1948; s. William and Margaret Mary (Daly) H. B.Sc., Nat. U. Ireland, 1970; Ph.D., Harvard U., 1977. Asst. prof. biol. scis. Brock U., St. Catharines, Ont., Can., 1978-81; assoc. prof. biology U. Ottawa, Ont., 1981—. Mem. Genetics Soc. Am., AAAS, Soc. Study Evolution, Am. Soc. Naturalists. Current Work: Eucaryotic genetics; population genetics and evolutionary theory; evolutionary dynamics of transposable genetic elements; control of amylase gene expression in drosophila melanogaster. Subspecialties: Gene actions; Genome organization. Home: 36 Burnham Rd Ottawa ON K1S 0J8 Canada Office: Dept Biology U Ottawa Ottawa ON K1N 6N5 Canada

HICKEY, JOSEPH JAMES, ornithologist, educator; b. N.Y.C., Apr. 16, 1907; s. James Bernard and Sarah Theresa (Mooney) H.; m. Margaret Brooks, June 20, 1942 (dec. Dec. 1977); 1 child, Susan; m. Lola Gray Gordon, Dec. 26, 1979. B.S., NYU, 1930; M.S., U. Wis., 1943; Ph.D., U. Mich., 1949. Research asst. Wis. State Conservation Commn., Madison, 1941-43, U. Chgo., 1943-44; asst. curator mus. zoology U. Mich., Ann Arbor, 1944-46; Guggenheim Meml. fellow 1946-47; asst. then assoc. prof. U. Wis., Madison, 1948-58, prof., 1958-79; prof. Zoology U. Minn. Summer Biology Station, Lake Itasca, 1952-62; vis. scientist Vogelschutzwarte für Hessen, Rheinl-Phalz und Saarland, Frankfurt, Fed. Republic Germany, 1964. Author: A Guide to Bird Watching, 1943, Survival Studies of Banded Birds, 1952, 72. Editor: Peregrine Falcon Populations, 1969, (with others) Procs. 13th Internat. Ornithol. Congress, 1963. Treas., Nature Conservancy, Arlington, Va., 1950-56, bd. govs., 1963-70. Recipient Aldo Leopold medal Wildlife Soc., 1972, Arthur A. Allen medal Cornell U., 1976. Fellow Am. Ornithologists Union (pres. 1972-73, Coues award 1979), Linnaean Soc. N.Y. (pres. 1937-39, Eugene Eisenmann medal 1984), AAAS; mem. Wildlife Soc. (hon., editor jour. 1956-59), Wis. Soc. Ornithology (pres. 1954-55), Nat. Audubon Soc. (bd. dirs. 1974-83, Audubon medal 1984), Western Found. Vertebrate Zoology (bd. dirs.), Bodega Bay Inst. Pollution Ecology (bd. dirs.). Subspecialty: Ecology (biology). Home: 1520 Wood Lane Madison WI 53705 Office: Dept Wildlife Ecology U Wis 1630 Linden Dr Madison WI 53706

HICKEY, LEO JOSEPH, paleontologist; b. Phila., Apr. 26, 1940; s. James Joseph and Helen Marie (Schwarz) H.; m. Judith McKendry, June 29, 1968; children: Geoffrey Alan, Damian Michael, Jason Alexander. B.S., Villanova U., 1962; M.A., Princeton U., 1964, Ph.D., 1967. Postdoctoral research assoc. NRC-Smithsonian Instn., Washington, 1966-69; assoc. curator Mus. Natural History, 1969-80, curator, 1980-82; chmn. Mus. Natural History Exhibits Com., 1973-75; dir. Peabody Mus. Natural History, Yale U., New Haven, 1982—; adj. prof. U. Md., from 1979, U. Pa., from 1982; prof. biology Yale U., 1982—, geology and geophysics, 1982—. Contbr. articles on botany and paleontology to profl. jours. Smithsonian Research Found. grantee, 1972-76; Nat. Geog. Soc. grantee, 1979; recipient Best Paper award Geol. Soc. Washington, 1981; Henry Alan Gleason award N.Y. Bot. Garden, 1977. Mem. Geol. Soc. Am., Bot. Soc. Am., Torrey Bot. Club, AAAS, Paleontol. Soc., Yellowstone Bighorn Research Assn. (pres. 1981-83). Current Work: Leaf architecture of the flowering plants, dinosaurian extinction, Cretaceous and early Cenozoic paleoecology of Arctic and Rocky Mountains, early angiosperm evolution. Subspecialties: Paleobiology; Morphology.

HICKEY, RICHARD JAMES, human epidemiology and ecology scientist; b. Rock Island, Ill., Sept. 18, 1913; s. James Leonidas and Evelyn Mary (Eckhardt) H.; m. Mary Harriet Hays, June 2, 1941; children—Douglas Lee, Stephen Bruce, Marcia Ann, Jeffrey Scott. B.S. in Chemistry, U. Ill., 1935; postgrad. U. Buffalo, 1935-36; Ph.D., Iowa State U., 1941. Research scientist Comml. Solvents Corp., Terre Haute, Ind., 1941-53, 58-63; research investigator U. Pa., Phila., 1953-58, sr. research investigator, 1963—. Contbr. articles to profl. jours. Mem. Am. Chem. Soc., N.Y. Acad. Scis., AAAS, Sigma Xi, Pi Mu Epsilon, Phi Kappa Phi, Phi Lambda Upsilon. Club: Faculty (U. Pa.). Current work: Public health and policy; human ecology, epidemiology; radiation and chemical hormesis; biochemical ethology; biostatistics; fallacies and fraud; exposing scientific malpractice. Subspecialties: Ecology (biology); Radiation biology. Home: 43 E Clearfield Rd Havertown PA 19083 Office: Dept Stats The Wharton Sch U Pa Philadelphia PA 19104

HICKEY, ROGER LEE, standards engineer; b. San Diego, Sept. 26, 1949; s. Chester Oliver and Atlantis Rose (Monro) H.; m. Debra Joan Tunnell, Aug. 4, 1973; children —Rebecca, Randy, Rachael. B.S. in Physics, Calif. Baptist Coll., 1983, B.A. in Theology, 1983; M.S.E.E., U. So. Calif., 1985. Commd. E-1 U.S. Navy, 1969, advanced through grades to E-5, 1979; maintenance supr. Alin Paper Co., Riverside, Calif., 1980-82; standards engr. Bear Med. Systems, 1982-85, Hughes Aircraft Co., Long Beach, Calif., 1985—; prof. physics Calif. Bapt. Coll., Riverside, 1983—; cons. metrology, Long Beach, 1984—. Author: Calibration and Metrology, 1984. Instr., ARC, El Cajon, Calif., 1975—, mem. disaster response team, 1976. Recipient Outstanding Achievement in Sci. award Calif. Bapt. Coll., 1982. Mem. IEEE, Am. Soc. Quality Control, Precision Measurements Assn., Nat. Conf. Standards Labs (del. 1982—). Republican. Baptist. Current work: Metrology, standards and calibration, biomedical measurements. Subspecialty: Electrical engineering. Home: 2825 Chestnut Ave Long Beach CA 90806 Office: Hughes Aircraft Co M/S LB-A1-3C914 PO Box 9399 Long Beach CA 90810-0399

HICKIS, CHARLES FRANCIS, psychologist; b. Bronx, Aug. 13, 1947; s. Charles Joseph and Marion (Streng) H.; m. Judy C. Johnson, Sept. 8, 1979; children: Gregory, Rebecca, Matthew. B.A., Hofstra U., 1970, M.A., 1974; Ph.D., U. Colo., 1978. Teaching asst. psychology Hofstra U., Hempstead, N.Y., 1970-72; research asst. U. Colo., Boulder, 1972-76; asst. prof. psychology Weber State Coll., Ogden, Utah, 1977-79; postdoctoral fellow UCLA, 1979-80; clin. dir. Chem. Dependency Center, Cody, Wyo., 1980—, pvt. practice psychology, 1981—. Contbr. articles to profl. jours. NIMH fellow, 1975; NSF grantee, 1978; NIMH research service award UCLA, 1979; State of Wyo. grantee, 1981. Mem. Am. Psychol. Assn., AAAS, Rocky Mt. Psychol. Assn. Democrat. Reorganized Ch. of Jesus Christ of Latter Day Saints. Clubs: Absaroka Flycasters, N.Am. Hunting. Current Work: Application of behavioral and physiol. principles to treatment of substance abuse problems. Subspecialties: Behavioral psychology; Psychobiology. Home: 2001 29th St Cody WY 82414 Office: West Park Hosp Chemical Dependency Center Cody WY 82414

HICKMAN, JACK WILLIAM, engineering executive; b. Ponca City, Okla., Oct. 4, 1936; s. Clyde A. and Hazel L. Hutson (Gilchrist) H.; children: Kirt Clyde, Lin Anne. B.S. in Elec. Engring., Okla. State U., Stillwater, 1962; M.S. in Elec. Engring., U. N.Mex., 1964. Mem. staff Sandia Nat. Labs., Albuquerque, 1962-74, supr., 1974-83, mgr., 1983—; lectr. George Washington U., 1972-82. Mem. Am. Nuclear Soc. Current Work: Probabilistic risk assessment, nuclear power, nuclear safety. Subspecialty: Nuclear fission. Home: 9508 Avenida de la Luna NE Albuquerque NM 87111 Office: Sandia Nat Labs Albuquerque NM 87185

HICKMOTT, THOMAS WARD, physicist; b. Kalamazoo, Mich., May 1, 1929; s. DeGarmo and Evelyn (Lay) H.; m. Joan McTerney, Jan. 31, 1959; children—Donald, Andrew, Nancy, Peter. B.S., Yale U., 1950; Ph.D., Northwestern U., 1954. Mem. research staff Gen. Electric Co., Schenectady, N.Y., 1954-66; engr. IBM Corp., East Fishkill, N.Y., 1966-70, mem. research staff, Yorktown Heights, N.Y., 1970—. Mem. Electro-chem. Soc. (divisional editor 1976-83; T.D. Callinan award 1976), Am. Phys. Soc. Current work: Semiconductor interface physics, conduction in insulators. Subspecialties: Condensed matter physics; Semiconductors. Office: TJ Watson Research Ctr PO Box 281 Yorktown Heights NY 10598

HICKOK, ROBERT LYMAN, JR., electrophysics educator, researcher; b. Feb. 25, 1929; s. Robert Lyman and Nellie (Williams) H.; m. Rose Marie Kapusta, June 12, 1949; children—Robert, Susan, Sandra. B.S., Rensselaer Poly. Inst., 1951; M.A., Dartmouth Coll., 1953; Ph.D., Rensselaer Poly. Inst., 1956. Postdoctoral fellow Yale U., 1956-58; research physicist Mobil Research and Devel. Corp., Princeton, N.J., 1958-60, sr. research physicist, 1960-65, research assoc., 1965-71; assoc. prof. electrophysics Rensselaer Poly. Inst., Troy, N.Y., 1971-74, prof., 1974—. Fellow IEEE, Am. Phys. Soc.; mem. Univ. Fusion Assn. Subspecialty: Plasma physics. Office: Rensselaer Poly Inst 110 S 8th St Troy NY 12180

HICKS, DONALD ALDEN, aerospace executive; b. Ely, Nev., Feb. 20, 1925; s. William John and Mary Josephine (Williams) H.; m. Mary Lou Hansen, Aug. 26, 1972; children—Pamela, Janine. A.B., U. Calif.-Berkeley, 1950, M.A., 1954, Ph.D., 1956. Physicist, Lawrence Radiation Lab., Berkeley, 1954-56; chief sect. applied physics aerospace group Boeing-Seattle, 1956-61; v.p. tech. Ventura Div., Northrop Corp., Los Angeles, 1961-65, v.p., mgr. dept. applied research neutronics div., 1965-67, v.p., corp., research mgr. corp. labs., 1967-70, corp. v.p., mgr. Northrop Research & Tech. Ctr., 1970-74, sr. v.p. mktg. and tech. Northrop Corp., Los Angeles, 1974—; dir. Mercantile Nat. Bank; mem. Def. Sci. Bd.; mem. Coll. Engring. adv. bd. U. Calif.-Berkeley; bd. councillors Sch. Engring. U. So. Calif.; dir. Sci. Applications Internat. Corp. Bd. dirs. John Tracy Clinic. Served with AUS, 1943-46. Mem. Phi Beta Kappa. Clubs: Calif., Regency (Los Angeles). . Office: Northrop Corp 1840 Century Park East Los Angeles CA 90067

HICKS, HARRY RICHARD, plasma and computational physicist; b. Balt., May 29, 1943; s. Harry Heston and Mary Amelia (Mayer) H.; m. Karen Fay McLeod, June 10, 1967. B.S., Fla. State U., 1965; Ph.D., U. Ill., 1971. Programmer Harvard U., Cambridge, Mass., 1964; research asst. U. Ill., Urbana, 1965-70; research assoc. Carnegie-Mellon U., Pitts., 1970-72; computational physicist Union Carbide, Oak Ridge, 1972-78, group leader, 1978-84; group leader Martin Marietta, Oak Ridge, 1984—. Contbr. numerous articles to profl. jours. Mem. Am. Phys. Soc. Current work: Solution of problems in fusion energy, using computational techniques; magnetohydrodynamics. Subspecialties: Fusion; Plasma physics. Home: 1128 W Outer Dr Oak Ridge TN 37830 Office: Martin Marietta Energy Systems PO Box Y Bldg 9104-2 Oak Ridge TN 37831

HICKS, HERALINE ELAINE, developmental biologist, researcher; b. Beaufort, S.C., Sept. 27, 1951; s. Heral and Ophelia Lillie (Albergottie) H. B.A., Ohio Wesleyan U., 1973; M.S., Atlanta U., 1978, Ph.D., 1980. Cert. secondary tchr., Ohio. Sci. tchr. Dayton Pub. Schs., Ohio, 1973-76; instr. Morris Brown Coll., Atlanta, 1978-80; research assoc. Dental Research Ctr., Chapel Hill, N.C., 1980-81, NIH postdoctoral fellow, 1981-84; asst. prof. Sch. Dentistry, U. N.C., Chapel Hill, 1985—; vis. cons. prof. Naval Med. Research Inst., Bethesda, Md., 1985—. Ohio Wesleyan U. scholar, 1969, Josiah Macy Jr. scholar Marine Biol. Lab., 1979; Univ. Minority Access to Research Careers NIH fellow Atlanta U., 1977. Mem. Am. Soc. Cell Biology, N.Y. Acad. Sci., Toxicology Assn. (N.C. chpt.), Teratology Soc., Sigma Xi, Beta Kappa Chi. Presbyterian. Current work: The study of abnormal development induced by maternal or external factors, such as the induction of birth defects like cleft lip/cleft palate by maternal use of anticonvulsant drugs. Subspecialties: Developmental biology; Teratology. Home: 5539 Burnside Dr Rockville MD 20853 Office: Naval Med Research Inst Mail Stop 18 Bethesda MD 20814

HICKS, JOHN TRIMMER, rheumatologist, consultant; b. Bethesda, Md., Mar. 11, 1946; s. Samuel Pendleton and Mary Louise (Trimmer) H.; m. Deborah Rehberg, July 30, 1977; 1 child, Julie Pendleton. B.S., U. Mich., 1968; M.D., Columbia U., 1972; hon. F.A.C.P., Am. Coll. Physicians, 1982. Diplomate Am. Bd. Med. Examiners, Am. Bd. Internal Medicine. Intern St. Luke's Hosp. Ctr., Columbia U. Coll. Physicians and Surgeons, N.Y.C., 1972-73; research assoc. div. virology Bur. Biologics-FDA, Bethesda, 1973-75; resident in internal medicine Georgetown U. Hosp., Washington, 1975-76; sr. investigator div. virology Bur. Biologics, 1976-78, instr. medicine Georgetown U., 1976-78, fellow rheumatology, 1976-78; from instr. to asst. prof. medicine, fellow rheumatology W.Va. U., Morgantown, 1978-79; pvt. cons. practice rheumatology, Phila., 1979-82; clin. asst. prof. medicine and rheumatology Temple U., Phila., 1979-82; group dir. med. affairs div. rheumatology/immunology Smith Kline Beckman Corp., Phila., 1982-84; pvt. cons. rheumatology, Phila., 1982-84; med. dir. Arthritis Inst. Nat. Hosp., Arlington, Va., 1984—, pvt. cons. rheumatology, Arlington, 1984—; staff Chestnut Hill Hosp., Phila., 1979-84, Roxborough Hosp., Phila., 1979-84, Nat. Hosp. Orthopaedics and Rehab., Arlington, 1984—. Contbr. articles to profl. jours. Active Arthritis Found. (chmn. patient clubs and pub. edn. subcoms. Eastern Pa. chpt.); adv. com. Pa. Lupus Found., Inc. Served with USPHS, 1976-78. Recipient Disting. Service award Arthritis Found., 1979; Active Tchr. in Family Practice award Am. Acad. Family Practice, 1981, 82. Mem. AAAS, Am. Soc. Microbiology, ACP, Am. Fedn. Clin. Research, Am. Rheumatology Assn., Am. Assn. Immunologists, N.Y. Acad. Scis., Phila. Rheumatism Soc., Phila. Med. Club, AMA (Physician's Recog. award 1982-85), Am. Soc. Clin. Pharmacology and Therapeutics. Current work: Clinical trials of various pharmaceutical agents in rheumatic diseases; microbial etiology of rheumatic diseases. Subspecialties: Rheumatology; Virology (medicine). Office: Arthritis Inst Nat Hosp 2455 Army-Navy Dr Arlington VA 22206

HICKS, M. JOHN, pediatric dentist; microanatomist; b. Knoxville, Iowa, Jan. 1, 1951; s. Earl Huff Hicks and June Lucinda (Doty) Terry; m. Catherine Mary Flaitz, July 17, 1983. B.S., U. Iowa, 1973, D.D.S., 1976, M.S. in Pediatric Dentistry, 1978, Ph.D. in Anatomy, 1982. Fellow Am. Acad. Pediatric Dentistry. Assoc. investigator, VA Med. Ctr., Iowa City, Iowa, 1978-80; research fellow U. Iowa, Iowa City, 1980-83; asst. prof. U. Colo., Denver, 1983—, dir. basic scis in dentistry; pvt. practice pediatric dentistry; cons. U.S. Army Dental Service, Ft. Carson, Colo., 1984—; councilor Colo. Dental Research Assn., Denver, 1984—. Contbr. articles to profl. jours. Recipient Assoc. Investigator award VA, 1978, Nat. Research Service award NIH, 1980, New Investigator award NIH, 1983. Fellow Am. Acad. Pediatric Dentistry, Sigma Xi; mem. Internat. Assn. Dental Research, Electron Microscopy Soc. Am., Am. Soc. Dentistry for Children. Current work: Cariology, etiology, histology, histopathology of enamel, dentinal and root caries, enamel formation and ultrastructure. Subspecialties: Dental growth and development; Cariology. Office: Dental Research Unit 4200 E 9th Ave Denver CO 80262

HIEBERT, RONALD DEAN, science administrator, research plant ecologist; b. Clinton, Okla., Apr. 16, 1946; s. Albert F. and Frieda E. (Schlichting) H.; m. Rosalie Goertz, Aug. 19, 1966 (div. 1979); children—Lisa, Renee; m. Diane J. Gordon, Oct. 13, 1979; children—Lindsey, Cassie. B.S. in Biology, Southwestern State U., 1968; M.S. in Botany, U. Kans., 1975, Ph.D. in Botany, 1977. Research asst. U. Kans., Lawrence, 1974-77; asst. prof. U. No. Colo., Greeley, 1977-78; ecologist Heritage Conservation and Recreation Ser., U.S. Dept. Interior, Denver, 1979-81; plant ecologist Nat. Park Service Indiana Dunes Nat. Lakeshore, Porter, Ind., 1981-82, chief scientist, 1982—. Contbr. articles to prof. jours. Served with USN, 1969-72. Polson awardee and fellow U. Kans., 1975, 77; recipient unit citation U.S. Dept. Interior, 1980; Spl. Achievement award Nat. Park Service, 1984. Mem. Ecol. Soc. Am. Democrat. Current work: Restoration ecology, effects of ecosystem fragmentation, science administration. Subspecialties: Ecology (biology); Theoretical ecology. Home: 3863N 600 W LaPorte IN 46350 Office: Ind Dunes Nat Lakeshore 1100 N Mineral Springs Rd Porter IN 46304

HIERHOLZER, JOHN CHARLES, microbiologist, cons., researcher; b. Gravenhurst, Ont., Can., July 1, 1938; s. Leo Newman and Cathrine Ann (Picker) H.; m. Connie Louise McArthur, Oct. 21, 1967; children: Jack, Karl, Mike. B.S., Spring Hill Coll., 1960; M.S., U. Fla., 1962; Ph.D., U. Md., 1966. Lab asst. dept. bacteriology U. Fla., 1961-62; research microbiologist U.S. Dept. Agr., Beltsville, Md., 1962-67; supervisory research microbiologist Ctr. Disease Control, Dept. Health and Human Resources, Atlanta, 1967—; cons. Fernbank Sci. Ctr., Atlanta, 1974—; vis. fellow Faculty of Medicine, U. Newcastle, New South Wales, Australia, 1983-84. Contbr. numerous articles on med. virology and epidemiology, viral biochemistry to profl. jours. Served to lt. comdr. USN, 1967-69. Mem. Am. Soc. Microbiology, Am. Chem. Soc., N.Y. Acad. Scis., AAAS, Am. Soc. Virology, Sigma Xi. Current Work: Viral biochemistry and immunology; human respiratory virus infections. Subspecialties: Virology (medicine); Biochemistry (biology). Office: 1600 Clifton Rd NE Atlanta GA 30333

HIGASHI, GENE ISAO, immunoparasitologist; b. Gardena, Calif., Nov. 6, 1938; s. Kay Kasutaro and Takeko (Ogo) H.; m. Elizabeth Lee, Aug. 20, 1966; 1 dau., Misao Elizabeth. B.A., Swarthmore Coll., 1960; M.D., Yale U., 1964; Sc.D., Johns Hopkins U., 1973. Intern Grace-New Haven Community Hosp., Yale U. Sch. Medicine, 1964-65; asst. resident anatomic pathology Yale-New Haven Hosp. and Med. Ctr., Yale U. Sch. Medicine, 1972-73, research fellow in parasite immunology dept. pathology, 1972-73, asst. prof. dept. pathology, 1973-75, clin. asst. prof., 1975-78; head immuno-parasitology div. U.S. Naval Med. Research Unit, Cairo, 1969-72, head parasite immunology div., 1974-76, head immunology dept., 1977-79; assoc. prof. dept. epidemiology U. Mich. Sch. Pub. Health, Ann Arbor, 1979-84, prof., 1984—. Contbr. articles to profl. jours. Served to lt. comdr. USNR, 1969-72. Mem. AAAS, Am. Soc. Parasitologists, Am. Soc. Tropical Medicine and Hygiene, Royal Soc. Tropical Medicine and Hygiene, Am. Assn. Immunologists, Indian Soc. Malariology and Communicable Diseases, Alpha Omega Alpha. Subspecialties: Parasitology; Infectious diseases. Office: 109 Observatory St Ann Arbor MI 48109

HIGGINS, PATRICK JOHN, JR., government official, electrical and nuclear engineering consultant; b. El Paso, Tex., Dec. 12, 1951; s. Patrick John and Loretta Eileen (Tuggle) H.; m. Dawana Lee Mordecai, June 12, 1971; children—Karen Elizabeth, Christopher Michael, Shawn Thomas. B.S. in Elec. Engring., U. Tex.-El Paso, 1976; M.S. in Nuclear Engring., U. N.Mex., 1980, M.B.A., 1983. Electronic technician U.S. Dept. Army, White Sands Missile Range, N.Mex., 1971-76; program engr. Energy Research and Devel. Adminstrn., Albuquerque, 1976-79; asst. program engr. U.S. Dept. Energy, Albuquerque, 1979-80, assoc. program engr., 1980-81, sr. program engr., 1981-83, nuclear program mgr., 1983—; cons. Southwest Engring. Cons., Lubbock, Tex. and Albuquerque. Recipient Spl. Engring. Achievement award U.S. Dept. Energy, 1982; Superior Performance award U.S. Dept. Energy, 1983, Spl. Project Service award U.S. Dept. Energy, 1983. Mem. IEEE, Am. Nuclear Soc., Am. Mgmt. Assn. Republican. Roman Catholic. Current work: Directed nuclear energy applications. Subspecialties: Electrical engineering; Nuclear fission. Home: 5215 Cimarron St NW Albuquerque NM 87120 Office: US Dept Energy Albuquerque Ops Office Weapon Program Div PO Box 5400 Kirtland AFB NM 87115

HIGGINS, PAUL JOSEPH, molecular biologist, cancer researcher; b. Bklyn., July 30,1946; s. Vincent John and Lucille Theresa (Gendus) H.; m. Denise Laura Cote, Feb. 24, 1973; children: Jennifer Ann, Stephen Paul, Craig Evan, Erik James, Sean Patrick. B.S., Iona Coll., New Rochelle, N.Y., 1969; M.S., L.I. U., 1973; Ph.D., NYU, 1976. Research asso. Meml. Sloan-Kettering Cancer Center, 1976-79, assoc., head hepatic carcinogensis program, 1979-85; asst. prof. genetics and molecular biology Cornell U., 1980-85; assoc. prof. pathology Albany Med. Coll., 1985—; research chemist Albany VA Med. Ctr., 1985—. Author numerous sci. papers. Recipient Young Investigators award Nat. Cancer Inst., 1980-83. Mem. Harvey Soc., Am. Assn. Cancer Research, Am. Soc. Cell Biology, N.Y. Acad. Scis., Am. Soc. Microbiology. Current Work: Molecular biology of cell differentiation and transformation; cancer research; gene cloning. Subspecialties: Cancer research (medicine); Cell biology. Office: VA Med Ctr 113 Holland Ave Albany NY 12208

HIGHET, ROBERT JOHN, chemist; b. Springfield, Ill., Oct. 6, 1925; s. David Archie and Ethel (Brown) H.; m. Patricia Morse Federico, July 30, 1955; children—Joan, Catherine, Suzanne. B.S., U. Ill., 1950; Ph.D., U. Wis., 1953. Chemist E.I. duPont de Nemours, Wilmington, Del., 1952; research chemist Nat. Heart Inst., Bethesda, Md., 1953-57, research chemist, 1958-68; research fellow Am. Cancer Soc., Zurich, Switzerland, 1957-58; chief nuclear magnetic resonance sect. Nat. Heart, Lung & Blood Inst., Bethesda, Md., 1968—; evaluator Sci. Service, Washington, 1962—. Contbr. articles to profl. jours. Served to sgt. U.S. Army, 1944-46. Mem. Am. Chem. Soc., Am. Soc. Pharmacognosy. Current work: Structural investigations on natural products and metabolites. Subspecialty: Nuclear magnetic resonance. Office: Nat Heart Lung & Blood Inst Bldg 10 Room 7N320 Bethesda MD 20205

HIGHTON, RICHARD TAYLOR, zoologist; b. Chgo., Dec. 24, 1927; s. Albert Henry and Helen Irene (Taylor) H.; m. Kathryn Ann Adams, June 23, 1950; children: Barbara, Kim, Scott, Caitlin Ann. A.B., N.Y. U., 1950; M.S., U.Fla., 1953, Ph.D., 1956. Asst. prof. zoology U. Md., College Park, 1956-62, assoc. prof., 1962-73, prof., 1973—. Contbr. articles to profl. jours. Served with AUS, 1946-48. Fellow AAAS; mem. Am. Soc. Ichthyologists and Herpetologists (sec. 1967-73, pres. 1976), Am. Soc. Naturalists, Genetics Soc. Am., Soc. Systematic Zoology, Ecol. Soc. Am., Animal Behavior Soc., Soc. Study of Evolution, Herpetologists League, Soc. Study Amphibians and Reptiles, Sigma Xi. Current Work: research in evolutionary biology, population genetics, ecology and systematics of amphibians and reptiles, especially salamanders of the genus Plethodon. Subspecialties: Evolutionary biology; Systematics. Home: 3613 Van Ness St NW Washington DC 20008 Office: Dept Zoology U Md College Park MD 20742

HIGUCHI, RUSSELL GENE, molecular biologist; b. Los Angeles, Nov. 4, 1952; s. Francis Masayuki and Hideko (Sugihara) H. B.S., UCLA, 1974, Ph.D., 1980. NIH postdoctoral fellow U. Calif.-Berkeley, 1980-83, research assoc., 1983—. Contbr. articles to profl. jours. Current work: Interested in obtaining traces of hereditary material, DNA, from fossil remains in order to give information as to evolutionary relationship to modern relatives. Subspecialties: Molecular biology; Paleobiology. Office: Dept Biochemistry U Calif Berkeley CA 94720

HIGUCHI, TAKERU, chemistry educator; b. Los Altos, Calif., Jan. 1, 1918; s. Iekichi and Chiye (Shiki) H.; m. Aya Toki, Jan. 1, 1944; children: Kenji W., Junji H., Chie S., Peter T. A.B., U. Calif. at Berkeley, 1939, Ph.D., U. Wis., 1943; D.Sc. (hon.), U. Mich., 1967; D.Sc., Eidgenössische Technische Hochschule, Zurich, 1978, U. Ill., 1980, Phila. Coll. Pharmacy and Sci., 1982. Research asso. U. Wis., 1943-44; research chemist Office Rubber Research, U. Akron, 1944-47; mem. faculty U. Wis., 1947-67, prof. pharm. chemistry, 1954-64, Edward Kremers prof., 1964-67; Regents distinguished prof. chemistry and pharmacy U. Kans., Lawrence, 1967—; pres. INTERx Research Corp., 1972—; dir., chmn. bd. Oread Labs., Inc., 1984—; v.p. Merck Sharp & Dohme Research Labs.; revision com. U.S. Pharmacopoeia, 1960-70; David E. Guttman Meml. lectr. U. Ky., 1978; Rachelle lectr. Calif. State U., Long Beach, 1979; Allen I. White lectr. Wash. State U., 1982. Author numerous papers in field. Co-recipient Ebert prize Am. Pharm. Assn., 1951, 52, winner, 1954; recipient Sturmer Lectr. award PCPS chpt. Rho Chi, 1956; Research Achievement award phys. pharmacy Am. Pharm. Assn. Found., 1962; Justin Power award pharm. analysis, 1964; research achievement award in stimulation of research, 1967; hon. citation U. Wis., 1969; award for advancement indsl. pharmacy, 1974; Internat. Surfactant Chemistry prize Italian Oil Chemists' Soc., 1974; Scheele lectr. award Pharm. Soc. Sweden, 1970; Rho Chi lectr., 1971; Recipient Kolthoff Gold medal award Am. Pharm. Assn. Acad. Pharm. Scis., 1977; Volwiler award Am. Assn. Colls. Pharmacy, 1978; Citation for Disting. Service U. Kans., 1982; Recipient Roland T. Lakey award Wayne State U., 1982; Takeru Higuchi Biomed. Research Area named in honor by U. Kans., 1984. Fellow Acad. Pharm. Scis., Pharm. Soc. Gt. Britain (hon.); mem. Am. Chem. Soc. (Midwest award 1975), Am. Pharm. Assn. (life mem.; past chmn. sci. sect. Remington Honor medal), Am. Oil Chemists Soc., Chem. Soc. (London, Eng.), Acad. Pharm. Scis. (pres. 1965-67), Japanese Pharm. Soc. (hon.), Victorian Pharm. Soc. Australia (hon.), Mexican Assn. Students Pharmacy (hon.), Phi Beta Kappa (hon.), Sigma Xi, Rho Chi. Current Work: Physical chemistry of dosage forms and drug administration; analytical chemistry of pharmaceutical and organic species. Subspecialties: Physical chemistry; Thermodynamics.

HIKIDA, ROBERT SEIICHI, biology educator; b. Long Beach, Calif., June 3, 1941; s. Frederick Toshio and Shizuye (Tanabe) H.; m. Geraldine Karen Oki, June 14, 1964; 1 child, Stephen Michael. B.S., U. Ill., 1963, M.S., 1965, Ph.D., 1967. Postdoctoral fellow Columbia U., N.Y.C., 1967-69; asst. prof. Ohio U., Athens, 1969-73; prof. Columbia U., N.Y.C., 1971; assoc. prof. Ohio U., Athens, 1973-77, prof. biology, 1977—. Assoc. editor: Anatomical Record, 1980—. Contbr. articles to profl. jours. Recipient Outstanding Grad. Faculty mem. award Ohio U., 1976; grantee NIH, NSF. Mem. Am. Soc. for Cell Biology, Am. Assn. Anatomists, Soc. for Neurosci., N.Y. Acad. Sci., Am. Soc. Zoologists. Current work: Skeletal muscle regeneration; muscle fiber type maintenance and dev.; skeletal muscle adaptation in human athletes. Subspecialties: Cell biology; Developmental biology. Home: 15 Longview Heights Athens OH 45701 Office: Ohio Univ Irvine Hall Athens OH 45701

HILBERTZ, WOLF HARTMUT, marine resources company executive; b. Gutersloh, Westfalia, Germany, Apr. 16, 1938; came to U.S., 1965; s. Rudolf Robert and Erna Charlotte (Uslat) H.; children—Kai Hannes, Derrick Max August, Halona Cordula. Werkarchitekt HBK Berlin, Staatliche Hochschule Fuer Bildende Kuenste, Berlin, 1965; M.Arch., U. Mich.-Ann Arbor, 1966. Designer Max Urbahn Architects, N.Y.C., 1965-66; sr. designer Smith, Hinchman, Grylls, Detroit, 1966-67; asst. prof. dept. arch. So. U., Baton Rouge, 1967-68, assoc. prof., 1968-70, Sch. Arch., U. Tex.-Austin, 1970-81, research scientist marine sci., 1978-80; pres. Marine Resources Co., Galveston, Tex., 1979—, Sea-Crete Resources La., Lake Charles, 1982—; cons. Bekaert, Zvewegem, Belgium, 1982, Dresser Industries, Houston, 1972, Maxwell A.G., Zurich, Switzerland, 1981—, Dome Petroleum, Calgary, Alta., Can., 1981; dir. Sea-Crete Resources of Japan, Oklahoma City, 1982—, The Symbiotic Processes Lab., Austin, Tex., 1970-81. Contbr. articles in field to profl. jours. Served with German Air Force, 1959-60. So. Consumers Coop. grantee, 1969; Sea Grant Office grantee, 1976; U. Tex.-Port Aransas grantee, 1965-79; Nat. Endowment for Arts mineral accretion workshop grantee, 1979. Mem. AAAS, Am. Inst. Ocean Architecture (pres. 1981—), Assn. Study of Man-Environment Relations, Oceanic Soc., Marine Tech. Soc., Coastal Soc. Patentee in field. Current Work: Evolutionary morphological systems, ocean architecture, OTEC cold water pipes, aquaculture facilities, energy harnessing systems, shore reclamation and protection; protection of wooden structures in marine environments. Subspecialty: Marine architecture. Home: 819 Ball Ave Galveston TX 77550 Office: Marine Resources Co 819 Ball Ave Galveston TX 77550

HILBORN, ROBERT CLARENCE, physicist, educator; b. Norristown, Pa., June 24, 1943; s. Clarence L. and Dorothy (Ditzler) H.; m. Shirley A. Antosiewicz, June 27, 1970; children: Stephen, Kurt. B.A., Lehigh U., 1966; M.A., Harvard U., 1967; Ph.D., 1971. Research assoc., lectr. SUNY-Stony Brook, 1971-73; vis. researcher U. Calif.-Santa Barbara, 1979-80; prof. Oberlin (Ohio) Coll., 1973—; cons. on optics and spectroscopy. Contbr. articles to profl jours. Research Corp. grantee, 1974-82; NSF grantee, 1981—. Mem. Am. Phys. Soc., Am. Assn. Physics Tchrs., Optical Soc. Am., Phi Beta Kappa, Sigma Xi. Current Work: Atomic and molecular laser spectroscopy; nonlinear dynamics. Subspecialties: Atomic and molecular physics; Laser spectroscopy. Home: 56 Spring St Oberlin OH 44074 Office: Dept Physics Oberlin Coll Oberlin OH 44074

HILDEBRANDT, ALVIN FRANK, physicist, educator; b. Spring, Tex., Dec. 31; s. Ludwig Otto, and Anna Arina (Weindorff) H.; m. Cornelia Nelle Margaret Mohle, Dec. 23, 1950; children—George Flavius, William John Edward. B.S., Univ. Houston, 1949; Ph.D., Tex. A & M Univ., 1956. Research group supr. Jet Propulsion Lab., Pasadena, Calif., 1956-65; sr. research fellow chemistry Caif. Tech. Inst., Pasadena, 1960-63, sr. research fellow physics, 1963-65; assoc. prof. physics Univ. Houston, 1965-69, prof. chmn. dept., 1969-75, prof., dir. Solar Lab and Energy Lab., 1975—. Mem. Com. Energy and Environment, Washington. Served as AEM3C USNR, 1946. Recipient Outstanding Contbn. award DOE Solar Thermal Dev., 1982, Outstanding Contribution award Am. Solar Energy Soc., 1982. Mem. AAAS, Am. Phys. Soc., Internat. Solar Energy Soc., Phi Kappa Phi, Sigma Xi. Clubs: Cosmos, Explorers, (Washington DC). Current work: Energy research. Subspecialty: Solar energy. Office: Univ Houston Energy Lab 4800 Calhoun Houston 77004

HILDEBRANDT, THOMAS OWEN, health physicist; b. Detroit, Apr. 27, 1954; s. Nestor Owen and Elaine Theresa (Najewski) H.; m. Donna Lynn Bennet, Oct. 21, 1972; 1 dau., Kelly Suzanne. A.S., SUNY-Albany, 1979. Dosimetry specialist Miss. Power & Light Co., Port Gibson, 1980-82, supr. health physics, 1982-85, radiation control supr., 1985—. Served with USN, 1972-80. Mem. Am. Nuclear Soc., Health Physics Soc. Republican. Roman Catholic. Current Work: Health physics, radiation protection, dosimetry, radioactive waste. Subspecialty: Nuclear fission. Office: Mississippi Power & Light Co PO Box 756 Port Gibson MS 39150

HILDRETH, EUGENE A., physician, educator; b. St. Paul, Mar. 11, 1924; s. Eugene A. IV and Lila K. (Clator) H.; m. Dorothy Anne Myers, Mar. 23, 1946; children: Jeffrey Reed, William Myers, Anne Sarver, Katherine Clator. B.S., Washington Jefferson Coll., 1943; M.D., U. Va., 1947. Diplomate: Am. Bd. Internal Medicine (mem. 1969-72, 75—, cons., com. mem. 1972-75), Am Bd. Allergy and Immunology (founding com. 1970, mem. 1970-72, 1st co-chmn.). internal medicine 1970-71, cons. 1972—). Intern Johns Hopkins, 1947-48; resident in medicine Hosp. U. Pa., 1948-49, USPHS Postdoctoral Research fellow in cardio-vascular disease, 1949-51, chief resident in medicine, 1953-54, fellow in allergy and immunology, 1954-58, faculty, 1954-69, 71—; instr. medicine U. Pa., Phila., 1953-54, asso. medicine, 1954-55, asst. prof. medicine, 1955-60, asso. prof., 1960-69; asso. dean U. Pa. (Sch. Medicine), 1964-69, prof. clin. medicine, 1971—, acting chmn. dept. research medicine, 1960-64; chmn. dept. medicine Reading (Pa.) Hosp. and Med. Center.; Cons. project site visits USPHS, 1965-70, rev. devel. new methods research in chronic pulmonary disease, 1967-69; cons. VA Hosp. Phila., 1955—; nat. adv. com. Medic Alert Found. Internat., 1964-83; cons. Citizens' Com. to Study Grad. Med. Edn., 1966; Am. Bd. Med. Spltys. rep. of subsplty. Bd. Allergy and Immunology of Am. Bd. Internal Medicine, 1969-72; chmn. certifying exam. com. Am. Bd. Internal Medicine, 1978-81, mem. exec. com., 1978-82; chmn., 1981-82; mem. rep. Am. Bd. Med. Spltys., 1976—, chmn. nominating com., 1979-80, mem. evaluation procedures study com., 1979—; mem. med. adv. bd. Lupus Found. Del. Valley, 1979—; chmn. Federated Council Internal Medicine; appeals bd. liaison Council of Grad. Med. Edn., 1980—. Co-author: Low Fat Diet, 1953, also research articles, chpts. in textbooks.; Editorial bd.: Annals Internal Medicine, 1960-68, Postgrad. Medicine, 1969-75, Jour. Berks County Med. Soc, 1969-73, Internal Medicine Digest, 1971-75. Served with USNR, 1943-45, 51-53. John and Mary R. Markle scholar in acad. medicine, 1958-63; USPHS Research grantee. Fellow Am. Clin and Climatologic Assn., A.C.P.; mem. Peripatetic Soc., AAAS, Fedn. Am. Socs. for Exptl. Biology, N.Y. Acad. Scis., Am. Heart Assn., Inst. Medicine of Nat. Acad. Scis. (nominating com. 1982—), Pa. Thoracic Soc., Phila. Art Mus., AMA, Am. Acad. Allergy, Nat. Kidney Found. Current Work: Research in evaluation of medical education. Subspecialties: Internal medicine; Immunology (medicine). Home: RD 3785 Mohnton PA 19540 Office: Reading Hosp and Medical Center Reading PA 19603

HILER, EDWARD ALLAN, agricultural engineer; b. Hamilton, Ohio, May 14, 1939; s. Earl and Thelma H.; m. Patricia Ann Burke, Jan. 30, 1960; children—Karen, Richard, Scott. B.S., Ohio State U., 1963, M.S., 1966, Ph.D. (USPHS fellow 1964-65), 1966. Registered profl. engr., Tex. Instr. Ohio State U., 1962-64, Ohio Agrl. Research and Devel. Center, 1965-66; Mem. faculty Tex. A. and M. U., 1966—, prof. agrl. engring., 1973—, chmn. dept., 1974—. Contbr. articles profl. jours. Recipient Disting. Service award Tex. A&M U., 1974, Faculty Disting. Achievement award, 1973; named Disting. Alumnus Ohio State U. Coll. Engring., 1978. Fellow AAAS, Am. Soc. Agrl. Engrs. (Paper award 1972, 74, 82, Young Researcher award 1977, Disting. Young Agrl. Engr. award 1975); mem. Am. Soc. Engring. Edn., Am. Geophys. Union, Council Agrl. Sci. and Tech., Tex. Soc. Profl. Engrs., Sigma Xi (chpt. Disting. Mem. award 1975), Gamma Sigma Delta (chpt. Disting. Service award 1983). Presbyterian. Current Work: Irrigation and drainage crop requirements, irrigation and drainage system design, biomass energy. Subspecialties: Agricultural engineering; Biomass (energy science and technology). Office: Dept Agrl Engring Tex A&M U College Station TX 77843

HILGARD, ERNEST ROPIEQUET, psychologist; b. Belleville, Ill., July 25, 1904; s. George Engelmann and Laura (Ropiequet) H.; m. Josephine Rohrs, Sept. 19, 1931; children—Henry Rohrs, Elizabeth Ann. B.S., U. Ill., 1924; Ph.D., Yale, 1930; D.Sc., Kenyon Coll., 1964; LL.D., Centre Coll., 1974. Asst. instr. in psychology Yale U., 1928-29, instr., 1929-33; successively asst. prof., asso. prof., prof. psychology Stanford, 1933-69, emeritus prof., 1969—, exec. head dept., 1942-50, dean grad. div., 1951-55; Bd. dirs., pres. Ann. Reviews, Inc., 1948-73; With USDA, Washington, 1942, OWI, 1942-43, Office Civilian Requirements, WPB, 1943-44; Collaborator, div. child devel. and tchr. personnel Am. Council Edn., 1940-41; nat. adv. mental health council USPHS, 1952-56; fellow (Center Advanced Study Behavioral Scis.), 1956-57; Mem. U.S. Edn. Mission to Japan, 1946. Author: several books, latest Theories of Learning, 1948, rev. edit., 1981, Introduction to Psychology, 1953, revised edit., 1983, Hypnotic Susceptibility, 1965, Hypnosis in the Relief of Pain, 1975, Divided Consciousness, 1977, American Psychology in Historical Perspective, 1978. Bd. curators Stephens Coll., Mo., 1953-68. Recipient Warren medal in exptl. psychology, 1940; Wilbur Cross medal Yale U., 1971; Gold medal Am. Psychol. Found., 1978. Hon. fellow Brit. Psychol. Assn.; mem. Am. Psychol. Assn. (pres. 1948-49), Am. Acad. Arts and Scis., Nat. Acad. Edn., Soc. Psychol. Study Social Issues (chmn. 1944-45), AAAS, Nat. Acad. Scis., Am. Philos. Soc., Internat. Soc. Hypnosis (pres. 1973-76, Benjamin Franklin gold medal 1979), Sigma Xi. Current Work: History of American psychology. Subspecialty: Cognition. Home: 850 Webster Palo Alto CA 94301

HILGEMAN, THEODORE WILLIAM, Laboratory administrator in optical physics; b. Amityville, N.Y., Dec. 21, 1942; s. Roy John and Erma Louise (Fabian) H.; m. Susan Elenor Goldsmith, Sept. 6, 1963; children: Leslie Ann, Erica Lynn. B.S. in Physics, M.I.T., 1964; Ph.D. in Physics, Calif. Inst. Tech., Pasadena, 1970. Research scientist Grumman Aerospace Corp., Bethpage, N.Y., 1970-76, head optical physics br., 1976-79, head optical physics lab., 1979—; ednl. counselor M.I.T., 1972-80. Editor: Episcopal Expression of Marriage Encounter, 1974; author: (with Walter Egan) Optical Properties of Inhomogeneous Materials, 1979; contbr. articles in field to profl. jours. Recipient M.I.T. Presidential citation, 1972. Mem. Am Astron. Soc., Optical Soc. Am., Sigma Xi. Current Work: Airborne and spaceborne electro-optical and photonic systems remote sensing, optical properties, electro-optical systems, photonics, infrared, atmospheric properties, background radiation, detectors. Subspecialties: Remote sensing (atmospheric science); Optical engineering. Office: Grumman Aerospace Corporation M/S A01-26 Bethpage NY 11714

HILL, A. LEWIS, psychologist, researcher; b. Glen Cove, N.Y., Nov. 5, 1940; s. James C. and Ruth M. (Lewis) H.; m. Patricia Munday, June 24, 1964 (div. 1976); children: Melissa, James; m. Florence Duguid Bramley, Jan. 10, 1980; children: Gareth Bramley, Lymond Bramley. B.A., Rollins Coll., 1963; Ph.D., Yeshiva U., 1968; profl. diploma in clin. psychology, Adelphi U., 1982. Lic. psychologist, N.Y. Sr. research scientist N.Y. Inst. Basic Research, S.I., 1967-79, research scientist IV, 1980, chief div. clin. psychology, 1981—; cons. editor profl. jours.; research cons. U. Md., 1972-75; asst. prof. CUNY, 1969-72. Contbr. articles to sci. jours. Chmn. neighborhood adv. bd. Page Ave. Group Home for Retarded, S.I., 1980—. Mem. Am. Psychol. Assn., Psychonomic Soc., Eastern Psychol. Assn. Current Work: Idiot savants, developmental perception, aging, psychotherapy, biofeedback, psychometrics, mental retardation. Subspecialty: Neuropsychology. Home: 824 Page Ave Staten Island NY 10309 Office: 1050 Forest Hill Rd Staten Island NY 10314

HILL, ALAN EUGENE, physicist; b. Durango, Colo., Sept. 4, 1939; s. Glenn Worland and Minnie Willard (Hermsmeier) H.; m. Carol Ann Havens, Mar. 26, 1960; children: Larry Glenn, Roy Leon. B.S.E.E., U. Mich., 1964, M.S., 1965. Leader laser research br. Lear Siegler Corp., Ann Arbor, Mich., 1965-67; sr. scientist, tech. dir. elec. laser div. USAF Weapons Lab., Kirtland AFB, Albuquerque, 1967-77; pres., chief scientist Plasmatronics, Albuquerque, 1977—; adj. prof. U. Ariz., Tucson, 1975—; chmn. bd. Indsl. Lasers, Inc., Albuquerque, 1985—. Contbr. articles to prof. jours. Active Cave Research Found., 1963—, Nat. Speleological Soc., 1963—. Recipient sci. achievement award Air Force Systems Command, 1971; citation of honor Air Force Assn., 1972; outstanding peformance awards U.S. Air Force, 1968-72. Patentee, inventor in field. Current Work: Generation and control of large volume, high pressure plasmas; application of pulsed power technology and gas dynamic principles to high energy lasers and accelerators; control and application of plasma-acoustic interactions. Subspecialty: Laser research and development. Office: 2460 Alamo SE Suite 101 Albuquerque NM 87106

HILL, DAVID LAWRENCE, patent licensing company executive; b. Boonville, Miss., Nov. 11, 1919; s. David Alexander and Mabel Clair (Brown) H.; m. Mary M. Shadow, Dec. 31, 1950; children—David Albert, Mary Claire, Robert Lawrence, John Frederick, Cynthia Ann, Sandra Ellen, James Alexander. B.S., Calif. Inst. Tech., 1942; Ph.D., Princeton U., 1951. With U. Chgo. Metall. Lab. and Argonne Nat. Lab., 1942-46, assoc. physicist, group leader, 1944-46; asst. prof. physics Vanderbilt U., Nashville, 1949-52, assoc. prof., 1952-54; guest scholar Inst. Theoretical Physics, Copenhagen, summer 1950; cons. theoretical physics U. Calif., Los Alamos, 1950-52, Los Alamos Nat. Lab., N.Mex., 1952-54, staff mem., 1954-58, group leader theoretical nuclear physics, 1955-58; mgmt. cons., 1958-60; pres. Phys. Sci. Corp., Fairfield, Conn., 1960-62, Nanosecond Systems, Inc., Fairfield, 1963-72, Particle Measurements, Inc., Southport, Conn., 1965-81, Harbor Research Corp., 1978—; chmn. bd. Integrated Total Systems, Inc., Hingham, Mass., 1968-81; pres. Southport Computers, Inc., 1973-81, Valutron N.V., Netherlands Antilles, 1980—; lectr. in field; sci. adviser to vice presdl. nominee Sen. Estes Kefauver, 1956; incorporator, exec. v.p., dir. Los Alamos Investment Corp., 1956-58; cons. physicist. Contbr. articles to profl. jours. Mem. adv. com. on sci. and tech. Democratic Nat. Com., 1959-61. Fellow Am. Phys. Soc., AAAS; mem. IEEE, Fedn. Am. Scientists (nat. chmn. 1953-54), Sigma Xi. Current Work: Distribution of mass and charge in atomic nuclei; dynamics of collective nuclear phenomena. Subspecialties: Nuclear physics; Theoretical physics. Office: Valutron NV PO Box L Southport CT 06490

HILL, DAVID PAUL, geophysicist; b. Livingston, Mont., June 18, 1935; s. Sanford and Gerda H.; m. Ann Rivers, June 17, 1961; 1 child, Peter. B.S. in Geology, San Jose State U., 1958; M.S. in Geophysics, Colo. Sch. of Mines, 1961; Ph.D. in Geophysics, Calif. Inst. Tech., 1971. Geophysicist U.S. Geol. Survey, Denver, 1961-64, Hawaiian Volcano Obs., 1964-66, Pasadena, Calif., 1966-71, Menlo Park, Calif., 1971—, chief seismology br., 1977-82, chief scientist Long Valley Caldera studies, 1983—. Contbr. articles to profl. jours. Mem. Am. Geophys. Union (assoc. editor 1985—, editor spl. issue Jour. Geophys. Research on Long valley Caldera, 1985, editor (with others) spl. issue Bulletin Volcanologigue on Phlegraean Fields Caldera, 1985), Seismol. Soc. Am., AAAS. Current work: Structure of the earth's crust, earthquake seismology, and volcanology. Subspecialties: Seismology; Volcanology. Office: US Geol Survey MS 977 345 Middlefield Rd Menlo Park CA 94025

HILL, HENRY ALLEN, educator, physicist; b. Port Arthur, Tex., Nov. 25, 1933; s. Douglas and Florence (Kilgore) H.; m. Ethel Louise Eplin, Aug. 23, 1954; children—Henry Allen, Pamela Lynne, Kimberly Renee. B.S., U. Houston, 1953; M.S., U. Minn., 1956, Ph.D., 1957; M.A. (hon.), Wesleyan U., 1966. Research asst. U. Houston, 1952-53; teaching asst. U. Minn., 1953-54, research asst., 1954-57; research assoc. Princeton, 1957-58, instr., then asst. prof., 1958-64; assoc. prof. Wesleyan U., Middletown, Conn., 1964-66, prof. physics, 1966-74, chmn. dept., 1969-71; prof. physics U. Ariz., 1966—. Contbr. articles to profl. jours. Sloan fellow, 1966-68. Mem. Am. Phys. Soc., Am. Astron. Soc., Royal Astron. Soc., Optical Soc. Am. Research on nuclear physics, relativity and astrophysics. Current Work: Solar oscillations; their utility in studies of internal structure of sun; tests of gravitation, and determination of solar terrestrial climate relationship. Subspecialties: General relativity; Solar physics.

HILL, MARION ELZA, chemist; b. Pawnee, Okla., Jan. 18, 1920; s. Leonard Clarence and Maude May (Short) H.; m. Susan Rand Jones, May 19, 1945; children—Stephen, Thomas. Diane. B.A., U. Oreg., 1948, M.A., 1950; postgrad., Pa. State U., 1955-56. Research chemist Nat. Bur. Standards, Washington, 1949-51; research assoc. U.S. Naval Ordnance Lab., Silver Spring, Md., 1951-60; sr. research chemist, dept. chmn. SRI Internat., Menlo Park, Calif., 1960-67, dir. chemistry lab., 1967-84, sr. sci. adv., 1984—; vol. cons. Internat. Exec. Service Corp., Stamford, Conn., 1984—; indsl. cons. Asian Devel. Bank, Manila, 1979—. Contbr. articles to profl. jours. Patentee process for acetal formation and others. Served with USAF, 1943-45, Mem. Am. Chem. Soc., AAAS, Sigma Xi. Republican. Presbyterian. Current work: Organic synthesis of specialty compounds; research and development management. Subspecialties: Organic chemistry; Synthetic chemistry. Home: 4270 Pomona Ave Palo Alto CA 94306 Office: SRI Internat 333 Ravenswood Ave Menlo Park CA 94025

HILL, RAY ALLEN, botanist, cell biologist, educator; b. Houston, Sept. 16, 1942; s. Cal and Ann Mae (Stewart) H. B.S., Howard U., 1964, M.S., 1965; Ph.D., U. Calif., Berkeley, 1977. Cert. coll. chief adminstrv. officer, Calif. Instr. So. U., Baton Rouge, 1965-66, Howard U., Washington, 1966-73; asst. prof. Fisk U., Nashville, 1977-80; assoc. prof. biology Community Coll. Balt., 1980-82, Morgan State U., Balt., 1982—; staff scientist NASA Hdqrs., summer 1979, Lawrence Berkeley Lab., summer 1980; vis. research prof. U. Calif.-San Francisco, 1985. NSF fellow, 1974; Ford Found. dissertation fellow, 1975-77, other awards and fellowships. Member. AAAS, Bot. Soc. Am., Am. Soc. Cell Biology, N.Y. Acad. Sci., Tenn. Acad. Sci., Sigma Xi, Beta Kappa Chi. Roman Catholic. Current Work: Mammalian cell culture, carcinogenic and mutagenic effects of chemicals on chromosomes. Subspecialties: Plant physiology (biology); Cell and tissue culture. Home: PO Box 462 Baltimore MD 21203

HILL, ROBERT LEE, biochemistry educator; b. Kansas City, Mo., June 8, 1928; s. William Alfred and Geneva Eunice (Scurlock) H.; m. Helen Amarette Root, Oct. 24, 1948 (div.); children—Sterrette L., Amarette L., Geneva L., Rebecca M.; m. Deborah Anderson, Apr. 10, 1982. A.B., U. Kans., 1949, M.A., 1951, Ph.D., 1954. Research instr. U. Utah, Salt Lake City, 1956-57, asst. research prof., 1957-60, assoc. research prof., 1960-61; assoc. prof. Duke U., Durham, N.C., 1961-65, prof., 1965-74, chmn. dept. biochemistry, 1969—, James B. Duke prof. and chmn., 1974—; cons. NRC, 1970—; mem. vis. com. for basic scis. Harvard Bd. Overseers. Author: Principles of Biochemistry, 6th edit., 1978; Principles of Biochemistry, 7th edit., 1983. Editor: The Proteins, 3d edit., Vol. I, 1974, Vol. II, 1976, Vol. III, 1977, Vol. IV, 1979, Vol. V, 1982. NIH fellow, 1953-54, 54-56. Fellow Am. Acad. Arts and Scis.; mem. Nat. Acad. Scis., Inst. Medicine, Am. Soc. Biol. Chemists (pres. 1976-77), Internat. Union of Biochemistry (mem. U.S. nat. com. 1982—, acting gen. sec. 1983—), Assn. Med. Depts. of Biochemistry (pres. 1982-83), Am. Chem. Soc., AAAS, Assn. Am. Med. Colls. (mem. adminstrv. bd., council of acad. socs. 1979—, chmn. 1983-84), Sigma Xi, Alpha Omega Alpha. Current work: Biochemistry, enzymology, protein structure/function; structure and function of mammalian lectis and glycosyltransferases. Subspecialty: Biochemistry (medicine). Office: Dept Biochemistry Duke U Med Ctr Durham NC 27710

HILL, THOMAS WESTFALL, research scientist; b. Olean, N.Y., July 28, 1945; s. C. Cecil and Ruth Helen (Westfall) H.; m. Patricia Hofer Reiff, July 4, 1976. B.A. in Physics, Rice U., 1967, M.S. in Space Sci., 1971, Ph.D., 1973. Research assoc. Rice U., Houston, 1972-74, sr. research assoc., 1974-75, asst. prof. space physics, 1976-80, assoc. research scientist, 1980—; Nat. Acad. Sci., NRC research assoc. NOAA Environ. Research Lab., Boulder, Colo., 1975-76; mem. associateship panel NRC, Washington, 1983—. Assoc. editor Jour. Geophys. Research, 1978-80, Geophys. Research Letters, 1983—. Contbr. articles to profl. jours. Fellow Am. Geophys. Union (James B. Macelwane award 1980); mem. AAAS, Internat. Assn. Geomagnetism and Aeronomy. Current work: Theoretical study of terrestrial and planetary magnetospheres and magnetosphere-ionosphere interactions. Subspecialty: Space plasma physics. Office: Dept Space Physics and Astronomy Rice U Houston TX 77251

HILL, WALTER EDWARD, JR., geochemist; b. Moberly, Mo., June 4, 1931; s. Walter Edward and Louise Katherine (Sours) H.; m. Beverly Kinkade, Sept. 8, 1951; children—Walter Edward III, Michele, Janet, Sean, Christopher. B.S. in Chemistry, U. Kans.-Lawrence, 1955, M.S. in Geology, 1964. Chemist III, Kans. Geol. Survey, Lawrence, 1954-66; asst. dir. research CF & I Steel, Pueblo, Colo., 1967-69; chief chemist Amax Exploration, Lakewood, Colo., 1970-74; mgr. labs. Hazen Research, Golden, Colo., 1974-79; earth scis. lab. mgr., 1980-81; tech. services mgr. Marathon Gold, Craig, Colo., 1984-85; cons. in field. Contbr. articles to profl. jours. Served as sgt. U.S. Army, 1950-52. Fellow Am. Inst. Chemists; mem. Geol. Soc. Am., Assn. Exploration Geochemists, Kans. Geol. Soc. Roman Catholic. Club: Colorado Carving (Denver). Lodge: Elks. Current work: Base and precious metals mining and metallurgy and analysis. Subspecialties: Analytical chemistry; Geochemistry. Home: 1486 S Wright St Lakewood CO 80228 Office: 1486 S Wright St Lakewood CO 80228

HILLEL, DANIEL, soil physics and hydrology educator, researcher, author, consultant; b. Los Angeles, Sept. 13, 1930; s. Morris and Sarah (Fromberg) Bugeslov. B.S., U. Ga.-Athens, 1950; M.S., Rutgers U., 1951; Ph.D., Hebrew U., 1958. Research fellow U. Calif.-Davis and Berkeley, 1959-61; head soil tech. div. Agrl. Research Orgn., Rehovot-Bet Dagan, Israel, 1952-66; prof., head soil and water dept. Hebrew U., Jerusalem-Rehovot, 1966-74; vis. prof. soil physics Tex. A&M U., College Station, 1974-75; vis. prof. environ. scis. U. Va., Charlottesville, 1975-77; research fellow Internat. Food Policy Research Inst., Washington, 1977; prof. soil physics and hydrology U. Mass., Amherst, 1977—; Chmn. Israel Nat. Com. on Soil Pollution Research, Israel, 1971; mem. Group on Water Mgmt. Research-Internat. Devel. Research Ctr., Can., 1978, Adv. Panel on Water Conservation, Dept. Water Resources Calif., 1979, Joint U.S. Dept. Agr.-Land Grant Univs. New Eng. Regional Research Priorities, Mass., 1981—; irrigation cons. World Bank, 1982-83; mem. U.S. Soil Sci. del. to People's Republic of China, 1983. Author: Soil and Water: Physical Principles and Processes, 1971, Computer Simulation of Soil Water Dynamics, 1977, Fundamentals of Soil Physics, 1980, Applications of Soil Physics, 1980, Negev: Land, Water and Civilization, 1982, Introduction to Soil Physics, 1982; editor: Optimizing the Soil Physical Environment, 1972, Advances in Irrigation, vol. 1, 1982, vol. 2, 1983, vol. 3, 1985. NSF research grantee, 1978, 82. Fellow Am. Soc. Agronomy, Soil Sci. Soc. Am.; mem. Internat. Soil Sci. Soc. (vice-chmn. soil physics 1964-68, 82-86), AAAS, Am. Geophys. Union. Patentee in field. Current Work: Soil-water-solute-energy dynamics in agriculture and in the environment. Subspecialties: Integrated systems modelling and engineering; Hydrology. Home: 58 High Point Dr Amherst MA 01002 Office: U Mass Stockbridge Hall Amherst MA 01003

HILLEMAN, MAURICE RALPH, virus research scientist; b. Miles City, Mont., Aug. 30, 1919; s. Robert A. and Edith (Matson) H.; m. Lorraine Witmer, Aug. 3, 1963; children—Jeryl Lynn, Kirsten Jeanne. B.S., Mont. State U., 1941, D.Sc., 1966; Ph.D., U. Chgo., 1944; D.Sc., U. Md., 1968. Asst. bacteriologist U. Chgo., 1942-44; research asso. virus labs. E.R. Squibb & Sons, 1944-47, chief virus dept., 1947-48; chief research and diagnostic sects. virus and rickettsial diseases Army Med. Service Grad. Sch., Walter Reed Army Med. Center, 1948-56, asst. chief lab. affairs, 1953-56; chief respiratory diseases Walter Reed Army Inst. Research, Washington, 1956-57; dir. virus and cell biol. research Merck Inst. Therapeutic Research, Merck & Co. Inc., 1957-66, exec. dir., 1966-71, v.p., 1971-78, sr. v.p., 1978—; dir. virus and cell biology research, v.p. Merck, Sharp & Dohme Research Labs., 1970-78, sr. v.p., 1978—; vis. investigator Hosp. of Rockefeller Inst. for Med. Research, 1951; vis. prof. bacteriology U. Md., 1953-57; adj. prof. viology pediatrics Sch. Medicine U. Pa., 1968—; cons. Children's Hosp. of Phila., 1968—; mem. council div. biol. scis. Pritzker Sch. Medicine, 1977—; John Herr Musser lectr. Musser-Burch Soc., Tulane U. Sch. Medicine, 1969, 19th Graugnard lectr., 1978; Mem., spl. cons. panel respiratory and related viruses USPHS, 1960-64; mem. Nat. Cancer Inst. primate study group, 1964-70; mem. council analysis and projection Am. Cancer Soc., 1971-76; mem. expert adv. panel on virus diseases WHO, 1952—; bd. dirs. W. Alton Jones Cell Sci. Center, Lake Placid, N.Y., 1980-82; mem. overseas med. research labs. com. Dept. Def., 1980; mem. virology dept. rev. com. Am. Type Culture Collection, 1980. Editorial bd.: Internat. Jour. Cancer, 1964-71, Inst. Sci. Information, 1968-70, Am. Jour. Epidemiology, 1969-75, Infection and Immunity, 1970-76, Excerpta Medica, 1971—, Proc. Soc. Exptl. Biology and Medicine, 1976—, Jour. Antiviral Research, 1980—; Contbr. 400 articles to sci., profl., med. jours. Phi Kappa Phi fellow, 1941-42; Koessler fellow, 1943-44; Recipient Howard Taylor Ricketts prize, 1945; Distinguished Civilian Service award sec. def., 1957; Walter Reed Army Med. Incentive award, 1960; Dean M. McCann award, 1970; Procter award, 1971; Achievement award Indsl. Research Inst., 1975. Fellow Am. Acad. Microbiology, Am. Acad. Arts and Scis.; mem. Am. Soc. Microbiology, Soc. Exptl. Biology and Medicine (mem. editorial and publs. com. 1977—), Tissue Culture Assn. (mem. council 1977—), Am. Assn. Immunologists, Am. Assn. Cancer Research, Infectious Diseases Soc., Permanent sect. Microbiol. Standardization Internat. Assn. Microbiol. Socs. . Office: Merck Sharp & Dohme Research Labs West Point PA 19486

HILLER, JOHN RICHARD, physicist, educator; b. Scranton, Pa., July 3, 1953; s. John Robert and Lillian Mae (Hummer) H.; m. Sharon Gay Pollock, June 27, 1981. B.S., Drexel U., 1976; M.S., U. Md., 1978, Ph.D., 1980. Physicist, Harry Diamond Labs., Woodbirdge, Va., 1975-76; mem. staff Inst. for Advanced Study, Princeton, N.J., 1980-82; research assoc. Purdue U., West Lafayette, Ind., 1982-84; asst. prof. physics U. Minn-Duluth, 1984—; research collaborator Brookhaven Nat. Lab., Upton, N.Y., Aug. 1981. Contbr. articles to physics jours. Recipient Sustained Superior Performance award Harry Diamond Labs., 1975; grad. fellow NSF, 1976; Albert Einstein fellow Inst. for Advanced Study, 1981. Mem. Am. Phys. Soc. Current work: Quark models for hadrons; in particular, a consistent relativistic formulation to resolve questions of principle and improve phenomenology. Subspecialty: Particle physics. Home: 2520 N Tischer Rd Duluth MN 55804 Office: Dept Physics U Minn-Duluth Duluth MN 55812

HILLIARD, ASA GRANT, III, psychology educator, researcher; b. Galveston, Tex., Aug. 22, 1933; s. Asa Grant and (Lois) Lowe; m. Patsy Jo Morrison, Nov. 16, 1957; children: Asa Grant IV, Robi Nsenga, Nefertari Patricia, M. Hakim. B.A., U. Denver, 1955, M.A., 1961, Ed.D., 1963. Teaching fellow U. Denver, 1961-63; asst. prof. San Francisco State U., 1963-67, assoc. prof., 1967-70, prof., 1970-83; dean San Francisco State U. (Coll. Edn.), 1972-80; Fuller E. Calloway prof. Ga. State U., 1980—; dir. Nguzo Saba Film Co., San Francisco; chief desegregation cons. Portland Pub. Schs., 1979—; nat. adv. Panel Head Start Measures Project, Westport, Conn., 1980—; research in field. Bd. dirs. Mental Health Assn. Met. Atlanta, 1982, Nat. Ctr. Clin. Infant Study, 1984—; mem. research adv. com. Southern Regional Council Ednl. Improvement, 1984-85. Served to 1st lt. U.S. Army, 1955-57. Knighted Govt. Liberia, 1974; recipient Alice Miel award Columbia U., 1978; cert. honor San Francisco Mayor, 1980; Disting. Ednl. Leadership award Assn. Tchr. Educators, 1982. Mem. Am. Psychol. Assn. (bd. scientific affairs com. on psychol. tests and assessment), Nat. Assn. Black Psychologists (Outstanding Scholarship award 1984) Nat. Assn. Edn. Young Children, Omega Psi Phi, Phi Delta Kappa. Democrat. African Methodist Episcopalian. Current Work: Cultural bias and testing; research and teaching in culture, testing, cognition and learning. Subspecialties: Cognition; Cultural bias and testing. Home: 3350 Sr Henry St East Point GA 30344 Office: Georgia State University Plaza PO Box 243 Atlanta GA 30303

HILLIER, JAMES, technical management consultant, former research executive; b. Brantford, Can., Aug. 22, 1915; came to U.S., 1940, naturalized, 1945; s. James and Ethel Anne (Cooke) H.; m. Florence Marjory Bell, Oct. 24, 1936; children—James Robert, William Wynship. B.A., U. Toronto, 1937, M.A., 1938, Ph.D., 1941, D.Sc. (hon.), 1978; D.Sc. (hon.), N.J. Inst. Tech. Staff labs. RCA, also research physicist for fundamental electron microscope research, 1940-53; adminstrv. engr., 1954-55, chief engr. comml. electronics products, 1955-57, gen. mgr. RCA Labs., 1957-58, v.p., 1958-68, v.p. research and engring. RCA Corp., 1968-69, exec. v.p. research and engring., 1969-76, exec. v.p., sr. scientist, 1976-77; dir. research dept. Melpar, Inc. subs. Westinghouse Air Brake Co., 1953-54; pres. Indsl. Reactor Labs., 1964-65; vis. lectr. dept. biology Princeton U., 1950-53, chmn. adv. council, dept. elec. engring., 1965-69. Chmn. clean air and water scholarship selection com. N.J. Dept. Health, 1968-75; mem. N.J. Higher Edn. Study Com., 1963-64; mem. tech. adv. bd. Dept. Commerce, 1964-70; mem. adv. com. Coll. Engring., Cornell U., 1966—; mem. governing bd. Am. Inst. Physics, 1962-65. Recipient Lasker award for design, constrn. and perfection of electron microscope, 1960; named to Nat. Inventors Hall of Fame, 1980. Fellow AAAS, Am. Phys. Soc., IEEE (Founders medal 1981); mem. Indsl. Research Inst. (past pres., medal 1975), Electron Microscope Soc., Am. (past pres., Disting. Achievement award 1977), Nat. Acad. Engrs. (council 1971), Sigma Xi, Eta Kappa Nu. Author:

(with others) Electron Optics and the Electron Microscope, 1945. Author approximately 150 tech. articles. Patentee in fields of electron microscopy, electron microanalysis, ultra-thin sectioning and video-disc.; designer, builder (with Albert Prebus) 1st successful high resolution electron microscope in western hemisphere, 1938. Current work: Utilization of world technology for the improvement of the economies of third-world countries. Subspecialty: Technology transfer. Home and Office: 22 Arreton Rd Princeton NJ 08540

HILLIS, WILLIAM DANIEL, SR., university administrator, biology educator, physician; b. Paris, Ark., June 12, 1933; s. Charles Raymond and Carra Elizabeth Daniel (Coffee) H.; m. Argye Idell Briggs, Dec. 23, 1952; children: William Daniel Jr., David Mark, Argye Elizabeth Hillis Trupe. B.S., Baylor U., 1953; M.D., Johns Hopkins U., Balt., 1957. Intern Johns Hopkins Hosp., 1957-58; research fellow Johns Hopkins U., 1958-60, asst. prof. to assoc. prof. pathobiology, 1965-82, asst. to assoc. prof. medicine, 1972-83; prof., chmn. dept. biology Baylor U., Waco, Tex., 1981-85, exec. v.p. univ., 1985—; chmn. med. adv. bd. Endstage Renal Disease, Network 31, Balt., 1978-82; mem. Md. Kidney Disease Commn., 1977-82; dir. med. research tng. program Johns Hopkins Sch. Medicine, 1978-82. Pres. Bapt. Conv. Md., 1976-78; Md. rep. exec. com. So. Baptist Conv., Nashville, 1977-82. Served to col. USAFR, 1960—. Recipient Seaman prize Assn. Mil. Surgeons U.S., 1979; Christian Citizen of Year award United Christian Citizens Md., 1978. Mem. Am. Soc. Microbiology, Am. Assn. Immunologists, N.Y. Acad. Sci., Soc. for Exptl. Biology and Medicine, Sigma Xi, Phi Beta Kappa, Alpha Omega Alpha. Club: Johns Hopkins (Balt.). Current Work: Virology, immunology, and epidemiology of human viral hepatitis; immunopathology of mouse hepatitis virus; viral etiology of human renal disease; primate viruses and their interrelationship; respiratory viruses of children; nutritional effects in infection. Subspecialties: Immunobiology and immunology; Virology (biology). Office: Dept Biology Baylor U Waco TX 76798 3640 Alta Vista Waco TX 76706

HILLMAN, ELIZABETH ANN, biologist, researcher; b. Ft. Edward, N.Y., Oct. 23, 1938; d. Albert R. and Martha A. (Hoag) H.; m. Edwin J. Matthews, Jan. 29, 1972; 1 dau., Susan Elizabeth. B.A. with honors, Russel Sage Coll., 1960; Ph.D in Microbiology/Pathology, Duke U., 1972. Research asso. dept. pathology Med. Coll. Va., 1963-67; research asst. dept. surgery Duke U. Med. Center, 1967-71; dept. pathology U. Va., 1972; scientist II Viral Resources Lab., Frederick Cancer Research Center, Frederick, Md., 1972-76; asso. prof. pathology U. Md., 1976—, head electron microscopy, dept. pathology, 1976-82; cons. in electron microscopy. Contbr. articles, abstracts to profl. jours. Mem. Am. Soc. Cell Biology, Am. Assn. Cancer Research, Electron Microscopy Soc. Am., Chesapeake Soc. Electron Microscopy, Assn. Women in Sci. Current Work: Research in breast cancer—in vitro systems, pathology, esophageal carcinogenesis—two stage model, x-ray microanalysis. Subspecialties: Cancer research (medicine); Microscopy. Office: U Md Sch Medicine 660 W Redwood St Baltimore MD 21201

HILLS, JACK GILBERT, theoretical astrophysicist; b. Keflavik, Iceland, May 15, 1943; came to U.S., 1949, naturalized, 1965; s. Cleon Ralph and Kristin Laura H. A.B., U. Kans., 1966, M.A., 1966; Ph.D., U. Mich., 1969. Instr. astronomy dept. U. Mich., Ann Arbor, 1967-70, asst. prof. dept. astronomy, 1970-76, U. Ill., Urbana, 1976-77; assoc. dept. physics Mich. State U., East Lansing, 1977-82, prof. dept. physics, 1982-84; mem. staff theoretical astrophysics group theoretical div. Los Alamos (N.Mex.) Nat. Lab., 1981—, dep. group leader, 1983—. Contbr. articles to profl. jours. Nat. winner Westinghouse Sci. Talent Search, 1962. Fellow Am. Phys. Soc.; mem. Am. Astron. Soc., Royal Astron. Soc., Internat. Astron. Union, AAAS. Republican. Current Work: Dynamics of stellar systems; quasars; supernovae. Subspecialty: Theoretical astrophysics. Home: 11 Loma Vista Dr Los Alamos NM 87544 Office: Theoretical Div Los Alamos Nat Lab T-6 MS B288 Los Alamos NM 87545

HILLYER, GEORGE VAN ZANDT, biology educator, researcher, cons.; b. San Juan, P.R., Dec. 8, 1943; s. William V. and Ruth L. H.; m. Josefina Gomez, June 15, 1968; children: George V., Julian F. B.S. in Biology, U. P.R., Rio Piedras Campus, 1968; Ph.D. in Microbiology, U. Chgo., 1972. Asst. prof. Lab. Parasite Immunology dept. biology U. P.R. (Rio Piedras Campus), 1972-75, asso. prof., 1975-80, prof., 1980, chmn., 1981—; adj. prof. pathology U. P.R. Med. Scis. Campus; adj. prof. tropical medicine Tulane U. Sch. Public Health and Tropical Medicine; James W. McLaughlin vis. prof. U. Tex. Med. Br., Galveston, 1985; vis. prof. dept. pathology U. Cambridge; Rockefeller Found. fellow, 1985; cons. NIH Tropical Medicine and Parasitology Study Sect. Contbr. numerous articles to profl jours. Mem. Am. Assn. Immunologists, Am. Soc. Tropical Medicine and Hygiene (councilor 1983—), Am. Soc. Parasitologists (Henry Baldwin Ward medal 1982), Royal Soc. Tropical Medicine and Hygiene, Am. Soc. Microbiology, Soc. Exptl. Biology and Medicine, Sociedad de MicrobiÓlogos de Puerto Rico (pres. 1979-80), Sociedad de Alergía e Inmunologéa de Puerto Rico (pres.-elect 1984-85), Sigma Xi (pres. U. P.R. San Juan Club 1979-85). Current Work: Immunology of parasitic infections. Subspecialties: Immunology (medicine); Parasitology. Home: 254 Himalaya Urbanization Monterrey Rio Piedras PR 00926 Office: Dept Biology U PR Rio Piedras PR 00931

HILTNER, WILLIAM ALBERT, astronomy educator; b. Continental, Ohio, Aug. 27, 1914; s. John Nicholas and Ida Lavina (Schafer) H.; m. Ruth Moyer Kreider, Aug. 12, 1939; children—Phyllis Anne, Kathryn Jo, William Albert, Stephen Kreider. B.S., U. Toledo, 1937; M.S., U. Mich., 1938, Ph.D., 1942. Mem. faculty U. Chgo., 1943-70, prof. astronomy, 1955-70; dir. Yerkes Obs., 1963-66; acting dir. Cerro Tololo Inter-Am. Obs., 1966-67; prof. U. Mich. at Ann Arbor, 1970-85, prof. emeritus, 1985—, chmn. dept. astronomy, 1970-82; Bd. dirs. Assn. Univs. for Research Astronomy, 1959-71, 74-85, pres. bd., 1968-71. Co-author: Photometric Atlas of Stellar Spectra, 1946; Editor: Astronomical Techniques, 1962. NRC fellow, 1942-43. Mem. Astron. Soc. Pacific, Am. Astron. Soc. (councilor 1962-65), A.A.A.S. Current Work: Optical counterpart of x-ray sources; development of a 2.4 meter telescope and other astronomical research instruments. Subspecialty: Optical astronomy. Home: 801 Berkshire Ann Arbor MI 48104

HILTON, JAMES LEE, plant physiologist; b. Bristol, Va., Apr. 14, 1930; s. William Rhea and Hattie Lee (Moore) H.; m. Mary Katherine Reasor, Dec. 27, 1958; children—Jul Elizabeth, Ann Katherine, Mary Martha. A.B., Duke U., 1952; M.S., Iowa State U., 1954, Ph.D., 1955. Research scientist Agrl. Research Service, Dept. Agr., Raleigh, N.C., 1956, research scientist, Beltsville, Md., 1956-72, lab. chief, 1972-76, inst. chmn., 1976—. Editor: Herbicide Handbook, 1974; Agricultural Chemicals of the Future, 1985. Contbr. articles to profl. jours. Recipient Superior Service award Dept. Agr., 1982. Fellow Weed Sci. Soc. Am. (editor-in-chief 1978—); mem. Am. Soc. Plant Physiologists, AAAS, Pesticide Sci. Soc. Washington (bd. advisers 1981—), Orgn. Profl. Employees Dept. Agr. (chpt. pres. 1983-84). Democrat. Methodist. Current work: Herbicide mode of action; pest control; environmental chemistry Subspecialties: Environmental chemistry; Herbicides. Office: Agrl Research Service Dept Agr Room 233 Bldg 001 Beltsville MD 20705

HILTON, THOMAS FREDERICK, research psychologist, naval officer; b. Cin., Apr. 12, 1947; s. Frederick and Julia (Burns) H. B.A., Elmhurst Coll., 1970; M.A., Fla. Atlantic U., 1976; Ph.D., Tex. Christian U., 1980. Commd. ensign U.S. Navy, 1968, advanced through grades to lt. MSC, 1980; grad. research fellow Inst. Behavioral Research, Ft. Worth, 1977-80; research coordinator psychiatry Tarrant County Hosp. Dist., Ft. Worth, 1980-82; instr. psychiatry and psychology Southwestern Med. Sch., Dallas, 1980-82; head health psychology projects Naval Health Research Ctr., San Diego, Calif., 1982—; research cons. Ctr. Orgn. Research and Evaluation Studies, 1981-82, Inst. Behavioral Research, 1980-82; dept. phys. medicine St. Joseph's Hosp., Ft. Worth, 1982; Research fellow Inst. Behavioral Research, 1977; research asst. Fla. Atlantic U., 1976. Mem. Am. Psychol. Assn., Internat. Assn. Applied Psychology, Soc. Advancement Social Psychology (steering com. feature editor newsletter), AAAS, Psi Chi, Sigma Xi. Current Work: Occupational health, healthful lifestyles, health service delivery, client-practitioner fit, health information systems, organizational climate and performance and health. Subspecialties: Health psychology; Social psychology. Office: Naval Health Research Center PO Box 85122 San Diego CA 92138

HIMELICK, EUGENE BRYSON, plant pathologist, educator; b. Summitville, Ind., Feb. 11, 1926; s. Virgil B. and Madalene M. (Bryson) H.; m. Elizabeth Ann Oyler, June 17, 1951; children: David E., Kirk J., Douglas N. B.S., Ball State U., 1949; M.S., Purdue U., 1952; Ph.D., U. Ill., 1959. Asst. plant pathologist Ill. Natural History Survey, Urbana, 1952-58, assoc. plant pathologist, 1959-64, plant pathologist, 1965—; prof. plant pathology U. Ill., Urbana, 1973—. Contbr. articles to profl. jours., chpts. to books. Scoutmaster Boy Scouts Am., 1960-75, dist. chmn. Arrowhead council, 1975-76; chmn. Urbana Tree Commn., 1972—. Served with USN, 1945-46. Recipient Ken Frederick's award Boy Scouts Am., 1971, also; Scouters Key; Silver Beaver award. Mem. Internat. Soc. Arboriculture (hon. life; exec. dir. 1969-79, authors citation 1979, award for research 1983), Am. Phytopath. Soc., Met. Tree Improvement Alliance, Arboriculture Research and Edn. Acad., Ill. Arborists Assn. (pres. 1984, award of merit 1984), Sigma Xi, Gamma Sigma Delta. Methodist. Lodge: Masons. Current Work: Research on the causes and control of forest and urban tree diseases. Subspecialty: Plant pathology. Home: 601 Burkwood Ct E Urbana IL 61801 Office: Ill Natural History Survey 384 Natural Resources Bldg Champaign IL 61820

HIMPSEL, FRANZ JOSEF, research physicist; b. Rosenheim, Bavaria, Fed. Republic Germany, Oct. 30, 1949; came to U.S., 1977; s. Josef and Thea (Weiss) H.; m. Elizabeth L. Hoffman, June 1, 1980; children—Carl A., Peter M. Ph.D., Munich U., 1976. Vis. investigator U. Wis.-Madison, 1979; mgr. photoemission and surface physics IBM T.J. Watson Research Ctr., Yorktown Heights, N.Y., 1982—; vis. prof. U. Munich, 1984-85. Contbr. sects. to books, numerous sci. articles to profl. jours. Mem. German Phys. Soc., Am. Phys. Soc., Am. Vacuum Soc. (Peter Mark award 1985). Current work: Semiconductor surfaces and interfaces; spectroscopy of electronic states; using synchrotron radiation and inverse photoemission. Subspecialty: Condensed matter physics. Office: IBM TJ Watson Research Ctr PO Box 218 Yorktown Heights NY 10598

HINATA, SATOSHI, astrophysicist, plasma physicist; b. Tokyo, Japan., Aug. 6, 1944; s. Takao and Kikuyo (Nagano) H.; m. Yoshiko, Oct. 30, 1968; children: Kaoru, Kaede, Taroh. B.E. in Nuclear Engring, U. Tokyo, 1967; Ph.D. in Physics, U. Ill., 1973. Research assoc. in physics U. Ill., Urbana, 1973-74; postdoctoral fellow Harvard Coll. Obs., Cambridge, Mass., 1974-76; instr. Yale Obs., New Haven, 1976-78; scientist Sacramento (N.Mex.) Peak Obs., 1978-80; assoc. prof. physics Auburn (Ala.) U., 1980—. Mem. Am. Astron. Soc. Current Work: Magnetic field generation, plasma, radiation, coronal heating, pulsar; theoretical plasma physics; dynamics of small particles. Subspecialties: Theoretical astrophysics; Solar physics.

HINCKLEY, ALDEN DEXTER, ecologist, author; b. N.Y.C., Nov. 2, 1931; s. Alfred Dexter and Annette Elizabeth (Brennan) H.; m. Nora Kimiko Matsumura, Aug. 8, 1959; children—Monica, Damien, Catherine, Teresa, Frances. A.B. cum laude, Harvard U., 1953; M.S., U. Hawaii, 1956, Ph.D., 1960; postgrad. U. Calif.-Berkeley, 1956-57. Assoc. prof. environ. sci. U. Va., Charlottesville, 1970-74; assoc. dir. research Inst. Ecology, Washington, 1974-77; mem. tech. staff MITRE, McLean, Va., 1978; sr. ecologist Flow Gen., McLean, 1979-82; environ. protection specialist Office Solid Waste, EPA, Washington, 1982—. Author: Applied Ecology, 1976; Renewable Resources in Our Future, 1980. NSF fellow U. Calif.-Berkeley, 1956-57. Mem. AAAS, Am. Inst. Biol. Scis., Ecol. Soc. Am. Current work: Directing studies on wastes from mining, beneficiation and processing or ores and minerals and other large volume wastes. Subspecialties: Hazardous waste disposal; Ecology (environmental science). Office: EPA Econ Analysis Br Office Solid Waste WH565B 401 M St SW Washington DC 20460

HINMAN, EDWARD JOHN, health care administrator; b. New Orleans, Nov. 10, 1931; s. E. Harold and Katharine (Fradenburgh) H.; m. Emma Jean Richmond, June 15, 1954; children: Cynthia, Alan, David. B.A., U. Okla., 1951; M.D., Tulane U., 1955; M.P.H., Johns Hopkins U., 1971. Diplomate: Am. Bd. Preventive Medicine. Intern USPHS Hosp., New Orleans, 1955-56, resident, Balt., 1958-61; dir. spl. research and devel. project Nat. Center Health Service Research, Rockville, Md., 1973-74; asst. surgeon gen., dir. div. hosps. and clinics USPHS, 1974-78; exec. dir. Group Health Assn., Washington, 1978-83; pres. CIMA Risk Control Services, Inc., 1984—. Contbr. articles in field to profl. jours. Bd. dirs. Greater Southeast Community Hosp., Washington. Served with USPHS, 1955-78. Recipient Bronze Letzeiser medal U. Okla., 1951; Meritorious Service award USPHS, 1976; Outstanding Achievement award Md. chpt. Federally Employed Women, 1976. Fellow ACP, Am. Coll. Preventive Medicine (v.p. 1976-77), Am. Pub. Health Assn., Soc. Advanced Med. Systems (dir. 1968-82, pres. 1976-77), Am. Assn. Med. Systems and Informatics (bd. dirs. 1980—, pres. 1985—), Am. Fedn. Clin. Research, Phi Beta Kappa. Subspecialty: Preventive medicine. Home: Box 48D Cape Leonard Dr St Leonard MD 20685 Office: CIMA Risk Control Services Inc 4200 Wisconsin Ave NW Suite 201 Washington DC 20016

HINNERS, NOEL W., space flight center executive; b. Bklyn., Dec. 25, 1935; m. 1962; 2 children. B.Sc., Rutgers U., 1958; M.Sc., Calif. Inst. Tech., 1960; M.A., Princeton U., 1961; Ph.D. in Geochem. Geology, 1963. Mem. tech. staff lunar sci. Bellcomm, Inc., Washington, 1963-65, supr. 1965-70, dept. head, 1970-72, chief scientist 1972-79; dir. Nat. Air and Space Mus., Washington, 1979-82; dir. Goddard Space Flight Ctr., Greenbelt, Md., 1982—. Subspecialty: Space flight center adminstration. Home: Goddard Space Flight Ctr Greenbelt Rd Greenbelt MD 20771

HINZE, WILLIE LEE, chemist, educator, consultant; b. Burton, Tex., Jan. 17,1949; s. Willie L. H. and Alma (Tresseler) H.; m. Wen-wen Chu, Dec. 14, 1980. A.A., Blinn Coll., Brenham, Tex., 1969; B.S., Sam Houston State U., 1970, M.A., 1972; Ph.D., Tex. A&M U., 1974. Lectr. in chemistry, NIH postdoctoral fellow Tex. A&M U., 1974-75; instr. in chemistry Blinn Coll., 1974-75; asst. prof. chemistry Wake Forest U., 1975-80, assoc. prof., 1980-84, prof., 1984—; cons analytical chemistry. Contbr. articles to profl. jours. Wake Forest Research and Publ. Fund grantee, 1976-86; Am. Chem. Soc. Petroleum Research Fund grantee, 1976-80, 80-82, 82; Research Corp. Cottrell Coll. Sci. grantee, 1977-78; Sigma Xi grantee, 1980; Research Corp. Susan Greenwall Found. grantee, 1980-81; NSF grantee, 1980-86. Mem. Am. Chem. Soc., Assn. Ofcl. Analytical Chemists, Am. Inst. Chemists (cert. profl. chemist), N.C. Acad. Sci., Royal Soc. Chemistry (assoc.), Sigma Xi. Current Work: Use of micellar and cyclodextrin systems in chemical analysis (in ultraviolet-vis, fluorescence, phosphorescence and chemiluminescence determinations, and chromatographic separations). Subspecialties: Analytical chemistry; Clinical chemistry. Home: 2200 Faculty Dr Apt 1-H Winston-Salem NC 27106 Office: Dept Chemistry Wake Forest U PO Box 7486 Winston-Salem NC 27109

HIRASUNA, THOMAS JYUN, biochemical engineer, researcher; b. Honolulu, Feb. 11, 1955; s. Masao and Pauline Tsuruko (Nakachi) H.; m. Jean Bartlett Hunter, Aug. 13, 1977. S.B. in Chem. Engring., S.B. in Biology, MIT, 1976; M.S. in Chem. Engring., Columbia U., 1983. Summer engr. Proctor and Gamble, Cin., 1975; process engr. E.I. duPont de Nemours, Seaford, Del., 1976-77; asst. chem. engr. Gen. Foods Corp., Tarrytown, N.Y., 1977-78, assoc. chem. engr. 1978-80, sr. chem. engr., 1980-84, project specialist, 1984—. Patentee (with others) in field. Mem. Am. Inst. Chem. Engrs. (various local sect. positions), Am. Chem. Soc., Soc. Indsl. Microbiology, AAAS, N.Y. Acad. Scis. Current work: Biotechnology process research and development involving enzyme, fermentation, genetic, and tissue culture technology. Subspecialties: Enzyme technology; Food science and technology. Home: 150 Glenwood Ave L-3 Yonkers NY 10703 Office: Gen Foods Corp 555 S Broadway T32-1 Tarrytown NY 10591

HIRLEMAN, EDWIN DANIEL, JR., mechanical and aerospace engineer, educator, researcher, inventor; b. Wichita, Kans., Dec. 1, 1951; s. Edwin Daniel and Marcille Parker (Wohlgemuth) H.; m. Laura Kay Kennedy, Sept. 13, 1975; children: Daniel Garth, Emily Diane, Mark David. B.S.M.E., Purdue U., 1972, M.S.M.E. (NSF fellow, Howard Hughes fellow), 1974, Ph.D. in Mech. Engring; Ph.D. (NSF fellow), 1977. Mem. engring. staff Hughes Aircraft Co., 1974-77; vis. researcher Tech. U. Denmark, Copenhagen, 1974-75; asst. prof. mech. and aerospace engring. Ariz. State U., Tempe, 1977-81, assoc. prof., 1981—; cons. Argonne Nat. Lab., Phelps Dodge Corp., Digital Equipment Corp., Garrett Turbine Engine Co., EPA, NSF, Spectron Devel. Labs. Contbr. articles to profl. jours. Recipient award for significant accomplishment in research Engring. Coll., Ariz. State U., 1980, Prof. of Yr. award mech. engring. dept., 1982. Mem. Optical Soc. Am., Combustion Inst., ASME, AIAA, ASTM, IEEE, Tau Beta Pi, Pi Tau Sigma. Patentee in field. Current Work: Laser/optical instrumentation for combustion, fluid mechanics, manufacturing; intelligent, microprocessor-based instrumentation. Subspecialties: Laser instrumentation; Optical instrumentation. Office: Mech Engring Dept Ariz State U Tempe AZ 85287

HIROSE, TERUO TERRY, surgeon; b. Tokyo, Jan. 20, 1926; s. Yohei and Seiko (Ogushi) H.; m. Tomiko Kodama, June 1, 1976; 1 son, George Philamore. B.S., Tokyo Coll., 1944; M.D., Chiba U., Japan, 1948, Ph.D., 1958. Diplomate: Am. Bd. Surgery, Am. Bd. Thoracic Surgery. Intern Chiba U. Hosp., 1948-49, resident in surgery, 1949-52, Am. Hosp., Chgo., 1954; resident in thoracic surgery Hahnemann Med. Coll., Phila., 1955-56, N.Y. Med. Coll., N.Y.C., 1961-62; practice medicine specializing in surgery, Chiba, Japan, 1952-53; chief of surgery Tsushimi Hosp., Hagi, Japan, 1958-59; asst. prof. surgery Chiba U., 1959; research fellow advanced cardiovascular surgery Hahnemann Hosp., Phila., 1959; teaching fellow surgery N.Y. Med. Coll., 1959-60, instr., 1961-62, practice medicine specializing in surgery, N.Y.C., 1965—, N.J. 1975—; dir. cardiovascular lab. St. Barnabas Hosp., N.Y.C., 1965—, sr. attending surgeon, 1965—; chief vascular surgery Union Hosp., Bronx, N.Y., 1966-67; attending surgeon Flower and Fifth Ave Hosp., N.Y.C., 1973—, Jewish Hosp. Med. Center, Bklyn., 1976—, St. Vincent Hosp., N.Y.C., 1976—, Mamonides Hosp., Bklyn., 1976-78, Passaic Gen. Hosp., 1977—, Westchester (N.Y.) County Hosp., 1977-78, Yonkers (N.Y.) Profl. Hosp., 1978-79, Westchester Sq. Hosp., 1978—, Yonkers Gen. Hosp., 1980—, St. Joseph Hosp., Yonkers, 1980—; clin. prof. surgery N.Y. Med. Coll., 1974—. Contbr. articles in field of cardiovascular surgery to Am. and Japanese med. jours. Recipient Hektoen Bronze medal AMA, 1965, Gold medal, 1971. Fellow Am. Coll. Angiology, Am. Coll. Chest Physicians, A.C.S., Am. Coll. Cardiology, Internat. Coll. Surgeons, N.Y. Acad. Medicine; mem. Am. Assn. Thoracic Surgery, N.Y. Soc. Thoracic Surgery, Pan-Pacific Surg. Assn., Internat. Cardiovascular Soc., Am. Geriatric Soc., Am. Fedn. Clin. Research. Inventor single pass low prime oxygenator; pioneer aortocoronary direct bypass surgery, open heart surgery without blood transfusion. Subspecialties: Cardiac surgery; Surgery. Office: 5830 Tyndall Ave Bronx NY 10471

HIRSCH, ANN MARY, biologist, educator; b. Milw., June 2, 1947; d. Clifford and Irene (Janes) H.; m. Stefan J. Kirchanski, Sept. 26, 1970. B.S. (scholar), Marquette U., 1969; Ph.D., U. Calif.-Berkeley, 1974. Asst. prof. U. Minn., St. Paul, 1974-76; Cabot fellow Harvard U., Cambridge, Mass., 1976-78; asst. prof. Wellesley (Mass.) Coll., 1978-83, assoc. prof., 1983—; vis. scholar Harvard U., 1981-82. Contbr. articles to sci. jours. Brachman-Hoffman fellow, 1982-84; NSF trainee, 1972-73; other grants. Mem. Am. Soc. Plant Physiologists, Plant Molecular Biology Assn., Assn. for Women in Sci., Bot. Soc. Am., Am. Soc. Cell Biology, Sigma Xi. Current Work: Analysis of symbiotically defective nodules of alfalfa infected with transposon-generated mutants of Rhizobium; analysis of Rhizobium host range and nodulation genes and determination of gene products. Subspecialties: Plant physiology (biology); Nitrogen fixation. Office: Wellesley College Wellesley MA 02181

HIRSCH, JERRY, educator, biologist, psychologist; b. N.Y.C., Sept. 20, 1922; s. Samuel M. and Mollie (Barnett) H.; m. Marjorie J. Barrie, July 29, 1950; 1 son, Wesley M. Student, Johns Hopkins, 1938-40, U. Paris, Sorbonne, France, 1949-50; B.A., U. Calif.-Berkeley, 1952, Ph.D., 1955. With Cavendish Trading Corp., 1940, Cohn, Hall, Marx Co., 1940-41; pres. Jostex Corp., 1941-49; NSF fellow U. Calif. at Berkeley, 1955-57; asst. prof. psychology Columbia, 1956-60; NIH fellow Center For Advanced Study in Behavioral Scis., Stanford, Calif., 1960-61; asso. prof. U. Ill., Urbana, 1960-63, prof. psychology, 1963—, prof. zoology, 1966—, prof. ecology, ethology and evolution, 1976—; zoology research asso. U. Edinburgh, Scotland, 1968; NSF-A.A.A.S. Chautauqua course lectr., 1973-74, 74-75; mem. com. genetics and behavior Social Sci. Research Council, 1962-65; mem. behavioral scis. tng. com. Nat. Inst. Gen. Med. Scis., NIH, 1966-70; mem. U.S. nat. com. Internat. Union Biol. Scis., Assembly Life Scis. NRC-NAS, 1975-82; mem. U.S. com. XIV, XV, XVI and XVII Internat. Ethological Conf., 1975, 77, 79, 81; dir. biopsychology research tng. program NIMH, 1966-77; dir. tng. program for research on instnl. racism NIMH, 1977-86. Author, editor: Behavior-Genetic Analysis, 1967, 82; Am. editor: Animal Behaviour, 1968-72; editor Jour. Comparative Psychology, 1982—. Contbr. articles to profl. jours. Served with USAAF, 1942-43. Recipient Aux. Research award Social Sci. Research Council, 1962. Mem. AAAS, AAUP, Animal Behavior Soc. (exec. com. 1967—, pres. 1975), Am. Eugenics Soc., Am. Genetic Assn., Am. Psychol. Assn. (rep. at large exec. com. Div. 6, mem. council of editors), Behavior Genetics Assn. (charter), Am. Soc. Human Genetics, Sigma Xi. Club: Cosmos. Subspecialty: Behavioral psychology.

HIRSCH, JORGE EDUARDO, physics educator; b. Buenos Aires, Argentina, Aug. 5, 1951; came to U.S., 1976; married; 2 children. Licenciado en fisica, U. Buenos Aires, 1974; Ph.D., U. Chgo., 1980. Research asst. U. Chgo., 1976-80; research assoc. Inst. for Theoretical Physics, U. Calif.-Santa Barbara, 1980-82; asst. prof. U. Calif.-San Diego, La Jolla, 1983—. Contbr. articles to phys. jours. Fellow Sloan Found., 1984, Andrew Found., 1978, Fulbright Commn., 1976. Mem. Am. Phys. Soc. Current work: Many-body physics in condensed matters systems; magnetism, charge-density waves, superconductivity; numerical simulation (Monte Carlo) techniques, low-dimensional systems, organic charge-transfer compounds, conducting polymers. Subspecialties: Condensed matter physics; Statistical physics. Office: Dept Physics B-019 U Calif-San Diego La Jolla CA 92093

HIRSCH, MARTIN STANLEY, virologist; b. Cortland, N.Y., Apr. 16, 1939; s. Hans and Grete (Lipper) H.; m. Corinne Becker, Oct. 18, 1964; children—T-era Gretchen, Michael Edward. A.B., Hamilton Coll., 1960; M.D., Johns Hopkins U., 1964. Diplomate Am. Bd. Internal Medicine, Am. Bd. Infectious Diseases. Intern then resident U. Chgo., 1964-66; surgeon, virologist Ctrs. Disease Control, Atlanta, 1966-68; fellow Nat. Inst. Med. Research, London, 1968-69, Mass. Gen. Hosp., Boston, 1969-71; asst. then assoc. prof. Mass. Gen. Hosp. Harvard Med. Sch., Boston, 1971—. Contbr. articles to profl. jours. Served with USPHS, 1966-68. Mem. Am. Soc. Clin. Investigation, Am. Assn. Immunology, Am. Soc. Virology. Current work: Oncogenic virology; viral immunology; viral therapy. Subspecialties: Virology (medicine); Infectious diseases. Office: Mass Gen Hosp Fruit St Boston MA 02114

HIRSCHFELD, TOMAS BENO, scientist, consultant; b. Montevideo, Uruguay, Dec. 20, 1939; came to U.S., 1966, naturalized, 1972; s. Rudolf Herman and Ruth (Nordon) H.; m. Judith Berggrun, Nov. 3, 1963; children—Noemi, Dina, Susan. B.S., Nat. U. Uruguay, Montevideo, 1961, M.S., 1963, Ph.D., 1965, Ph.D., 1975. Vis. scientist N.Am. Aviation, Thousand Oaks, Calif., 1966-67; asst. prof. Nat. U. Uruguay, Montevideo, 1965-66, 67-69; staff/chief scientist Block Engring., Cambridge, Mass., 1969-79; adj. prof. Ind. U., Bloomington, 1977-83, U. Wash., Seattle, 1983—; sr. scientist Lawrence Livermore Nat. Lab., Livermore, Calif., 1973—; cons. Technicon, Tarrytown, N.Y., 1979—, Optical, Nahant, Mass., 1982—, Hewlett Packard, Palo Alto, Calif., 1983—. Contbr. articles to profl. jours. Patentee in field. Chmn. sch. com. Temple Beth Sholom, Framingham, Mass., 1975-79; activities chmn. Temple Beth Emek, Livermore, 1979-81. Recipient IR-100 award Indsl. Research and Devel. Mag., 1975, 77, 81, 83, 85. Fellow Optical Soc. Am.; mem. Gov. Brd. Coblentz Soc., Am. Chem. Soc., Am. Inst. Physics, Soc. Applied Spectroscopy (William Meggers award 1978, Louis Strait award 1984). Jewish. Lodge: B'nai B'rith. Current work: Chemical analysis, spectroscopy, remote sensing, microminiature devices. Subspecialties: Analytical chemistry; Laser spectroscopy. Home: 1262 Vancouver Way Livermore CA 94550 Office: Lawrence Livermore Nat Lab PO Box 808(L-322) Livermore CA 94550

HIRSH, IRA JEAN, scientist, educator; b. N.Y.C., Feb. 22, 1922; s. Ellis Victor and Ida (Bernstein) H.; m. Shirley Helene Kyle, Mar. 21, 1943; children—Eloise, Richard, Elizabeth, Donald. A.B., N.Y. Coll. for Tchrs., 1942; A.M., Northwestern U., 1943; M.A., Harvard, 1947, Ph.D., 1948. Research asst. psycho-acoustic lab. Harvard, Cambridge, Mass., 1946-47, research fellow, 1947-51; with Central Inst. for Deaf, St. Louis, 1951—, asst dir. research, 1958-65, dir., 1965-83; dir. emeritus Central Inst. Deaf, 1983—; mem. faculty or adminstrn. Washington U., St. Louis, 1951—, prof. psychology, 1961-84, Edward Mallinekrodt Disting. prof., 1984—, dean faculty arts and scis., 1969-73; vis. prof. U. Paris, France, 1962-63; U.S. del Internat. Standards Orgn., 1962-76; mem. Internat. Acoustics Commn., 1969-75; chmn. behavioral scis. and edn. NRC, 1982—. Author: The Measurement of Hearing, 1952; Contbr. articles to profl. jours. Served with USAAF, 1943-45; Served with AUS, 1945-46. Recipient Biennial award Acoustical Soc. Am., 1956, Assn. Honors Am. Speech and Hearing Assn., 1968. Fellow Acoustical Soc. Am. (pres. 1967-68), Am. Psychol. Assn., Am. Speech and Hearing Assn. (exec. council 1958-61, 65-68); mem. Nat. Acad. Sci. Current Work: Hearing; auditory perception; speech. Subspecialties: Sensory processes; Psychophysics. Home: 6629 Waterman Ave Saint Louis MO 63130

HIRSH, KENNETH ROY, pharmacologist, pharmacist; b. Bronx, N.Y., Nov. 7, 1944; s. Lester and Sara H.; m. Phyllis Pomerantz, Nov. 24,1965; children: Jeffrey, Jennifer. Ph.D. in Pharmacology, Columbia U., 1972. Prin. scientist

Gen. Foods Corp., Cranbury, N.J., 1972—. Mem. Am. Soc. Pharmacology and Exptl. Therapeutics. Jewish. Current Work: Central nervous system stimulants-mechanisms. Subspecialties: Neuropharmacology; Pharmacology. Home: 33 Scott Dr Morganville NJ 07751 Office: Prospect Plains Rd 025/C Cranbury NJ 08512

HITCHCOCK, CLAUDE R., surgeon, medical researcher. Pres., Mpls. Med. Research Found. Office: Minneapolis Med Research Found 501 Park Ave S Minneapolis MN 55415

HITCHINGS, GEORGE HERBERT, pharmaceutical company executive, biochemist; b. Hoquiam, Wash., Apr. 18, 1905; s. George Herbert and Lillian Bell (Matthews) H.; m. Beverly Reimer, June 24, 1933; children: Laramie Hitchings Brown, Thomas E. B.S., U. Wash., 1927, M.S., 1928; Ph.D., Harvard U., 1933; D.Sc. (hon.), U. Mich., 1971, U. Strathclyde, 1977, N.Y. Med. Coll., 1981, Emory U., 1981, Duke U., 1982, U. N.C., 1982, Mt. Sinai Sch. Medicine, CUNY, 1983. Teaching fellow U. Wash., 1926-28, Harvard U., 1928-39, sr. instr. Western Res. U., 1939-42; biochemist Burroughs Wellcome Co., Tuckahoe, N.Y., 1942-46, chief biochemist, 1946-55, asso. research dir., 1955-63, research dir., 1963-67, v.p. in charge research, 1967-75, scientist emeritus, cons., 1975—; also dir.; dir. Burroughs Wellcome Fund, 1968—, pres., 1971—; adj. prof. Duke U., 1970—, U. N.C., Chapel Hill, 1972—; vis. prof. Chuang-Ang U., Seoul, Korea, 1974-77; vis. lectr., Pakistan and Iran, 1976, Japan and India, 1980; staff dept. medicine Roger Williams Gen. Hosp., Brown U., 1980; mem. vis. com. drug research bd. Nat. Acad. Scis.-NRC, 1974-75; mem. research and evaluation adv. com. N.C. State Dept. Corrections, 1974-76; mem. Nat. Acad. Sci., 1977; vis. lectr., Republic of South Africa, 1981. Contbr. articles to profl. jours. Pres. Greater Durham Community Found. Recipient Gregor Mendel medal, 1968, Gardner award, 1968, Passano award, 1969, Robert de Villier award, 1969, Cameron prize, 1972, Bertner Found. award, 1974, Mullard award Royal Soc., 1976, NC. award in sci., 1980, C. Chester Stock award, 1981, Disting. Service award U. N.C., 1982, Oscar B. Hunter award, 1984, Alfred Burger award, 1984, Cain award, 1984. Fellow Royal Soc. Medicine (hon.), Royal Soc. Chemistry (hon.); Am. Chem. Soc., Chem. Soc. (London), Am. Assn. Cancer Research, Internat. Transplantation Soc., Royal Soc. (fgn.), Westchester Chem. Soc. (chmn. 1959-60), Phi Beta Kappa, Sigma Xi, Phi Lambda Upsilon. Subspecialty: Biochemistry (biology). Home: 4022 Bristol Rd Durham NC 27707 Office: 303 Cornwallis Rd Research Triangle Park NC 27709

HITTINGER, WILLIAM CHARLES, electronics co. exec.; b. Bethlehem, Pa., Nov. 10, 1922; s. John Tilghman and Pearl (Heimbach) H.; m. Elizabeth Herman, July 9, 1944; children—Patricia, William, David, Nancy. B.S. with honors in Metall. Engring, Lehigh U., 1944, D.Engring. (hon.), 1973. Engr. Western Electric Co., 1946-52; prodn. mgr. Semiconductor div. Nat. Union Radio Corp., 1952-54; exec. dir. Bell Telephone Labs., 1954-66; pres. Bellcomm Inc., Washington, 1966-68, Gen. Instrument Corp., N.Y.C., 1968-70; v.p., gen. mgr. RCA Corp., Somerville, NJ., 1970-72, exec. v.p., N.Y.C., 1972—, also dir.; dir. Thomas & Betts Corp., Recognition Equipment Inc. Indpls. Bd. dirs. Bethlehem (Pa.) Fgn. Policy Assn., 1960-62, Nat. Action Council for Minorities in Engring., Inc.; trustee Lehigh U.; mem. Nat. Security Telecommunications Adv. Com.; mem. Thomas A. Edison Papers Project, 1979—. Served to capt. AUS, 1943-46. Named hon. citizen Bethlehem, 1966. Fellow IEEE; mem. Nat. Acad. Engring., Dirs. Indsl. Research (bd. dirs.), Omicron Delta Kappa, Phi Gamma Delta. Home: 149 Bellevue Ave Summit NJ 07901 Office: David Sarnoff Research Center Princeton NJ 08540

HITZIG, BERNARD MICHAEL, physiology and biophysics educator; b. N.Y.C., Apr. 17, 1935; s. Joseph B. and Martha (Steiger) H.; m. Jacqueline Freeman, Feb. 8, 1960 (div. 1967); 1 child, Jennifer Beth; m. Harlyn Anne Behrmann, Aug. 5, 1972; 1 child, Kathryn Anne. B.S., Wagner Coll., 1958; postgrad. Columbia U., 1958-61; Ph.D., Brown U., 1977. Parker Francis Found. fellow Dartmouth Med. Sch., Hanover, N.H., 1978-79; asst. prof. Howard U., Washington, 1979-81; asst. prof. physiology and biophysics Harvard U. Med. Sch., Boston, 1981—; asst. biologist Mass. Gen. Hosp., Boston, 1981—; vis. scientist MIT, Cambridge, 1983—. Contbr. articles to profl. jours. Hinds Found. fellow, 1977-78; NIH grantee, 1978, 80. Mem. Am. Soc. Zoologists, Biophys. Soc., Nuclear Magnetic Resonance Soc., Sigma Xi. Current work: Nuclear magnetic resonance spectroscopy of the brain in unanesthetized animals, brain cell acid-base and high energy phosphate regulation, passive physicochemical methods of cellular ph regulation as well as active regulation. Subspecialties: Physiology (medicine); Biophysics (physics). Office: Pulmonary Unit Harvard U Med Sch Mass Gen Hosp Fruit St Boston MA 02114

HIXON, SUMNER BEST (DAVE), geologist, computer programmer, consultant; b. LaJunta, Colo., Sept. 7, 1930; s. Edward Henry and Isabelle (Palmer) H.; m. Helen Bicknell, Aug. 26, 1961; children—Nancy Jeanne, Edward Bruce, Richard James. B.A., U. Colo., 1952, postgrad., 1953; M.A., U. Tex.-Austin, 1959; Ph.D., U. Mich., 1964. Asst. prof. dept. geology and geol. engring. U. Miss., University, 1964-67; sr. scientist Lockheed Electronics Co., Houston, 1967-81; sr. geologist, geophysicist Aero Service Corp., Houston, 1981-83; pvt. cons., Houston, 1984—. Author papers and computer programs. Active Friendswood Republican Com., Tex., 1980; trustee United Meth. Ch., 1980-84. Served to lt. (j.g.) USN, 1953-56. NASA faculty fellow U. Miss., 1967. Mem. Am. Assn. Petroleum Geologists, Geol. Soc. Am., Soc. Econ. Paleontologists and Mineralogists, Am. Soc. Photogrammetry, Geochem. Soc. Methodist. Lodges: Masons, Gideons. Current work: Imagery remote sensing; computer-related work; sedimentation, seismic and air magnetic interpretation. Subspecialties: Remote sensing (geoscience); Sedimentology. Home and Office: 504 Misty Ln Friendswood TX 77546

HJELLMING, ROBERT MICHAEL, astrophysicist, educator; b. Gary, Ind., Dec. 21, 1938; s. Lester Alpheus and Valera Amelia (Guruskaus) H.; m. Carol Ann Johnson, June 13, 1959; children: Michael, Marya, Thomas, Peter, Teresa. B.Sc., U. Chgo., 1960, M.S., 1961, Ph.D., 1965. Asst. prof. astronomy Case Western Res. U., Cleve., 1965-68; assoc. scientist Nat. Radio Astronomy Obs., Charlottesville, Va., 1968-71, scientist, 1971-76, Socorro, N.Mex, 1976—; adj. prof. astrophysics N.Mex. Inst. Mining and Tech., 1976—. Contbr. articles to profl. jours. Served with USMCR, 1956-62. Mem. Am. Astron. Soc., Internat. Astron. Union, Astron. Soc. Pacific, N.Mex. Acad. Sci. Roman Catholic. Current Work: Radio emission from stars, x-ray sources, interstellar gas, radio behavior of stars and other active objects. Subspecialties: Radio and microwave astronomy; Theoretical astrophysics.

HJERTAGER, BJORN HELGE, research scientist; b. Bergen, Norway, Feb. 26, 1947; s. Harald A. and Annie E. (Hovdenes) H.; m. Inger-Lill Storhaug, Dec. 31, 1969; children: Hilde B., Lene K., Nina. Ing., Bergen Engring. Coll., 1968; M.Sc., U. Trondheim, Norway, 1972, Ph.D., 1979. Sci. asst. U. Trondheim, 1973, asst. prof., 1976-78; head dept. Norwegian Underwater Inst., Bergen, 1979; sr. scientist Christian Michelsen Inst., Bergen, 1980-83, head of research, 1984—. Author: Flow Heat Transfer and Combustion in Three-Dimensional Enclosures, 1979; contbg. author: Handbook for Heat and Mass Transfer Operations, 1985; contbr. articles to profl. jours. Served with Norwegian Navy, 1968-69. Mem. Combustion inst., AIAA, Internat. Assn. Math. and Computers in Simulation, Internat. Centre Heat and Mass Transfer, Polyteknisk Forening. Current Work: Gas explosion, turbulent flow, computer simulation, two-phase flows. Subspecialties: Combustion processes; Fluid mechanics. Home: Vakleiva 101 Bergen N-5062 Norway Office: Chr Michelsen Inst Fantoftvegen 38 Bergen N-5036 Norway

HLASS, I. JERRY, government official; m. Helen Mae Diller, Dec. 21, 1963; 1 son, George O. B. Mech. Engring., N.C. State U., 1949; M. Engring. Adminstrn., George Washington U., 1971. Dir. space shuttle facilities NASA, Washington, 1971-76, mgr. Nat. Space Tech. Labs., Bay St. Louis, Miss., 1976—. Mem. Nat., Miss. socs. profl. engrs. Methodist. Subspecialty: Space technology management. Office: Nat Space Tech Labs NSTL Station MS 39529*

HNATIUK, BOHDAN TARAS, engineering educator, researcher, consultant; b. Zaliszczyki, Tarnopil, Ukraine, July 25, 1915; came to U.S., 1949; s. Wasyl T. and Anastazja R. (Schuch) H.; m. Irene M. Tomkiw, Jan. 30, 1944; children: Bohdanna W., Irene R., Oleh W. B.S., State Seminary, Zaliszczyki, Ukraine, 1935; Diploma, Tech. U., Danzig Free City, 1943, D. Ing., 1945. Sci., research asst. Tech. U., Danzig and Vienna, 1942-45; research scientist Dornier Werke, Friedrichshafen, Germany, after 1945; asst., then assoc. prof. U. Notre Dame, South Bend, Ind., 1951-57; prof. W. Va. U., Morgantown, W. Va., 1957-60, Drexel U., Phila., 1960—; cons. analysis Bendix Aviation Corp., Mishawaka, Ind., 1955-57; cons. propulsion Allegany Ballistics Lab., Pinto, W. Va., 1959-72, Pneumo Dynamics Corp., Bethesda, Md., 1961-63; cons. aero. NASA (MSFC), Huntsville, Ala., 1967-69. Mem. Bala Cynwyd (Pa.) PTA, Merion Park (Pa.) Civic Assn. Recipient Alexander von Humboldt award Edn. Ministerium, Berlin, 1939-43; Faculty fellow awards, 1967,68. Assoc. fellow AIAA (Outstanding Faculty Advisor award 1972, past mem. council; past chmn. edn., student affairs); mem. Am. Soc. Engring. Edn., Am. Assn. Univ. Profs., AAAS, Sigma Gamma Tau, Pi Tau Sigma, Tau Beta Phi. Republican. Ukrainian Catholic. Club: Engring. (Phila.). Current Work: analytical and numerical study on reducing missile drag; wind energy potential for electrical power generation; propulsion noise reduction. Subspecialties: Aerospace engineering and technology; Astronautics. Office: Drexel U 32d & Chestnut Sts Philadelphia PA 19104

HO, CHO-YEN, physical science researcher, scientific research administrator; b. Guiping, Guangxi, China, Aug. 11, 1928; s. Yu-Chih Ho and Tsui-Chen Huang; m. Nancy Yang Wang, 1963; children—Chris Meichung Wang, Chester Meihua Wang. B.S., Nat. Taiwan U., 1955; M.S.M.E., U. Ky., 1960; Ph.D. in Thermodynamics and Heat Transfer, Purdue U., 1964. Asst. sr. researcher Purdue U. Centre Info. and Numerical Data Analysis and Synthesis, West Lafayette, Ind., 1964-69, assoc. sr. researcher, 1969-74, asst. dir. research, 1973-82, sr. researcher, 1974—, head of reference date div., 1967—, also dir.; dir. U.S. Dept. Def. Thermophysical and Electronic Properties Info. Analysis Centre; indexer Applied Mechanics Reviews, 1967-72; co-chmn. 8th Internat. Thermal Conductivity Conf., 1968; mem. standing com. Thermophysical Properties, ASME, 1968—; session chmn. ASME Symposiums Thermophysical Properties, 1970, 77, 81; lectr. Gordon Research Con., Tilton Sch., N.H., 1972; instr. NSF Course on Treatment and Critical Evaluation of Exptl. Data Pa. State U., 1973, Purdue U., 1973-74; lectr. U. Ill., 1975. Mem. editorial bd. Internat. Jour. Thermophysics, 1983-85; technical editor Thermophysical Properties of Matter the TRPC Data Series, 1970-79. Editor: (with others) McGraw Hill/Cindas Data Series on Material Properties, 1980—. Contbr. articles to profl. jours. and reports. Subspecialty: Thermophysics. Office: Purdue U Ctr Info and Numerical Data Analysis and Synthesis 2595 Yeager Rd West Lafayette IN 47906

HO, RAYMOND HOW-CHEE, neuroscientist, anatomist, educator; b. Hong Kong, Sept. 21, 1947; came to U.S., 1969; s. Cho Um Ho and Wan Sou Chan. B.S. cum laude, St. John's U., Minn., 1971; Ph.D. in Anatomy, U. Minn., 1978. Asst. prof. anatomy Ohio State U., Columbus, 1977-83, assoc. prof., 1983—; assoc. prof. dept. oral biology, 1984—; project dir. Spinal Cord Injury Research Ctr., Columbus, 1978—. Contbr. articles to profl. jours.; Recipient Teaching awards Ohio State U., 1981, 83; NIH grantee, 1978—; Ohio State U. grantee, 1977-78; Upjohn Co. grantee, 1978-79. Mem. Soc. Neurosci. (councilor Columbus chpt. 1984—), Midwest Assn. Anatomists, Am. Assn. Anatomists, Ohio Acad. Sci. Roman Catholic. Current Work: Chemically identified neuronal elements in the spinal cord; immunocytochemistry; development and plasticity; peptides, neurotransmitters, nociception, morphology. Subspecialties: Neurobiology; Immunocytochemistry.

HO, THOMAS INN MIN, computer scientist, educator; b. Honolulu, Oct. 17, 1948; s. Herbert Low Seu and Rose (Lee) H.; m. Jean Joan Kwan, Aug. 26, 1971; 1 son, Brian Koon Leong. B.S., Purdue U., 1970, M.S., 1971, Ph.D., 1974. Asst. prof. computer sci. and mgmt. Purdue U., West Lafayette, Ind., 1975-78, asso. prof., 1978-84, prof., 1984—, head computer tech., 1978—; cons. in field. Contbr. articles to profl. jours. NSF fellow, 1970-72. Mem. Assn. Computing Machinery, Data Processing Mgmt. Assn., Soc. for Info. Mgmt., Phi Kappa Phi. Subspecialties: Information systems, storage, and retrieval (computer science); Information systems (Information science). Office: Computer Tech Dept Purdue U West Lafayette IN 47907

HOAG, DAVID GARRATT, elec. engr.; b. Boston, Oct. 11, 1925; s. Alden Bomer and Helen Lucy (Garratt) H.; m. Grace Edward Griffith, May 10, 1952; children—Rebecca Wilder, Peter Griffith, Jeffrey Taber, Nicholas Alden, Lucy Seymour. B.S., MIT, 1946, M.S., 1950. Staff engr. Mass. Inst. Tech. Instrumentation Lab., Cambridge, 1946-57; tech. dir. Polaris Missile Guidance, 1957-61; tech. dir., program mgr. Apollo Spacecraft Guidance, 1961-74; advanced system dept. head C.S. Draper Lab., Inc., 1974—; Reviewer children's sci. book com. Harvard U., 1965—. Incorporator, bd. dirs. Medway Community Nursery Sch. Served with USN, 1943-46. Recipient Pub. Service award NASA, 1969, Spl. award Royal Inst. Navigation, Britain, 1970. Fellow Am. Inst. Aeros. and Astronautics (Louis W. Hill Space Transp. award 1972, chmn. New Eng. sect. 1979-80); mem. Nat. Acad. Engring., Inst. Navigation (Thurlow award 1969, pres. 1978-79), Internat. Acad. Astronautics (asso. editor ACTA Astronautica 1973—). Current Work: Guidance, navigation, control and pointing in aeronautics and astronautics. Subspecialties: Systems engineering; Aerospace engineering and technology. Home: 116 Winthrop St Medway MA 02053 Office: CS Draper Lab Inc 555 Technology Sq Cambridge MA 02139

HOAGLAND, GORDON WOOD, mathematics educator; b. Nampa, Idaho, Oct. 22, 1936; s. Clyde Mackay and Clara (Wood) H.; m. Byrnina Louise Burningham, Aug. 1, 1962; children: David, Daniel, Deborah. B.S., Brigham Young U., 1966, M.S., 1968; postgrad., Oreg. State U., 1969. Prof. math. Ricks Coll., Rexburg, Idaho, 1969—, chmn. dept., 1979—. Contbr. article to profl. jour. Bishop Ch. Jesus Christ of Latter-day Saints. Mem. Am. Math. Soc., Soc. Indsl. and Applied Math. Republican. Club: Upper Valley Square Dance. Current Work: Sampling techniques in forestry; gamma ray spectroscopy; algorithms for super computing, digital filters. Subspecialties: Applied mathematics; Numerical analysis (computer science). Home: 206 E 2d St S Rexburg ID 83440 Office: Dept Math Ricks Coll Rexburg ID 83440

HOAGLAND, MAHLON BUSH, educator, biochemist; b. Boston, Oct. 5, 1921; s. Hudson and Anna (Plummer) H.; m. Olley Virginia Jones, Jan. 10, 1961; children by previous marriage—Judith, Mahlon Bush, Robin. Student, Williams Coll., 1940-41, Harvard U., 1941-43; M.D., Harvard U., 1948; Sc.D. (hon.), Worcester Poly. Inst., 1973, U. Mass., 1984. From research fellow to asst. prof. medicine Harvard Med. Sch. at Mass. Gen. Hosp., 1948-60; asso. prof. bacteriology and immunology (Med. Sch.), 1960-67; prof. biochemistry, chmn. dept. Dartmouth Med. Sch., 1967-70; research prof. U. Mass. Med. Sch., 1970—; dir. Worcester Found. for Exptl. Biology, Shrewsbury, Mass., 1970-85; research asso. Carlsberg Labs., Copenhagen, Denmark, 1951-52, Cavendish Labs., Cambridge, Eng., 1957-58; Exec. sec. com. research Mass. Gen. Hosp., 1954-57; cons. NIH, 1961-64, Am. Cancer Soc., 1965-68; bd. sci. counselors Nat. Heart and Lung Inst., 1972-74. Bd. dirs. Mass. div. Am. Cancer Soc. Cancer research scholar Am. Cancer Soc., 1953-58; winner book award Am. Sci. Writers Assn., 1982. Contbr. articles to profl. books and jours. Fellow Am. Acad. Arts and Scis.; mem. Am. Soc. Biol. Chemists (Franklin medal 1976); mem. Nat. Acad. Scis. Research on mechanism of carcinogenic action of beryllium, mechanism of synthesis of coenzyme A; discovery mechanism of amino acid activation and role of transfer ribonucleic acid in protein synthesis. Current work: Science writing for public; advisory liaison with goverment to strengthen medical science. Subspecialty: Biochemistry (biology). Home: Box 153 Thelford VT 05074

HOAR, RICHARD MORGAN, pharmacologist, consultant, educator; b. Boston, Nov. 22, 1927; s. Carl Sherman and Ruth Dennis (Cole) H.; m. Rita Cecilia George, Aug. 27, 1949; 1 child, Andrew. A.B., Dartmouth Coll., 1950; Ph.D., U. Kans., 1956. Instr. anatomy Coll. Medicine, U. Cin., 1956-58, asst. prof. anatomy, 1958-64, assoc. prof., 1964-69; head teratology Hoffmann-La Roche Inc., Nutley, N.J., 1969-77, asst. dir. dept. toxicology and pathology, 1977-82, assoc. dir. dept. toxicology and pathology, 1982—; cons. in field; chmn. male and female reprodn. groups Conf. on Assessment of Risks to Human Reprodn. and to devel. of Human Conceptus from Exposure to Environ. Substances, EPA, 1980; co-chmn. reproductive effects subcom. of sci. com. Am. Indsl. Health Council, 1980-82; mem. adv. panel for assessment alternatives to animal use in testing and experimentation Office Tech. Assessment, 1984—; lectr. embryology and teratology Ctr. for Profl. Advancement, East Brunswick, N.J., 1973-78; lectr. biology No. Highlands Regional High Sch., Allendale, N.J., 1973—; adj. assoc. prof. anatomy Coll. Physicians and Surgeons, Columbia U., N.Y.C., 1973—; lectr. anatomy Mt. Sinai Sch. Medicine, N.Y.C., 1976—. Assoc. editor Lab. Animal Sci., 1977—, mem. editorial bd., 1982—; assoc. sect. editor Jour. Environ. Pathology and Toxicology, 1979—; chmn. databook editorial bd. of publs. com. Fedn. Am. Socs. Exptl. Biology 1983—; mem. editorial bd. Toxicology and Indsl. Health Jour., 1984—; mem. editorial adv. bd. Neurobehavioral Toxicology, 1980-83. Contbr. chpts., numerous articles to profl. publs. Chmn. bd. Raymond E. Banta Valley Ctr., Ridgewood, N.J., 1973—; pres. Allendale Bd. Health, N.J., 1980—. Served with U.S. Army, 1946-47. Fellow N.Y. Acad. Medicine; mem. Teratology Soc. (treas. 1974-78, pres. 1980), Behavioral Teratology Soc. (pres. 1981), Soc. Toxicology (councilor reprodutive and devel. toxicology specialty sect. 1983—), Am. Assn. Lab. Animal Sci. (pres. So. Ohio br. 1963-65), Congenital Anomalies Research Assn. Japan, Soc. Study Reprodn., Am. Assn. Anatomists, Am. Soc. Exptl. Pathology, AAAS, N.Y. Acad. Scis., Sigma Xi, Phi Sigma. Current work: Development of ferret as a model in studies of teratology reproduction and toxicology. Subspecialties: Teratology; Reproductive biology.

HOARE, JAMES PATRICK, research electrochemist; b. Denver, Colo., Jan. 9, 1921; s. Patrick Joseph and Mary Josephine (Breen) H.; m. Therese Clare Tressel, Aug. 29, 1953; children—Karen Marie, Patrick James, John Paul. B.Sc., Regis Coll., 1943; M.Sc., Cath. U. Am., 1948, Ph.D., 1949. Asst. prof. physics and chemistry Trinity Coll., 1949-54; phys. chemist U.S. Naval Research Labs., Washington, 1954-57; prin. research engr. Ford Motor Co., Dearborn, Mich., 1957-60; sr. research chemist Gen. Motors Research Labs., Warren, Mich., 1960-79, research fellow, 1979—. Author: The Electrochemistry of Oxygen, 1968. Contbr. articles to profl. jours. and chpts. to books. Judge local and internat. sci. fairs, Detroit, 1962-82. Served with USN, 1944-46, PTO. Recipient John Campbell award Gen. Motors Research Labs., 1980, Alumni Achievement award Cath. U. Am., 1984; Helen Bonfils scholar, 1939-43; Mullen fellow, 1943-44. Mem. Electrochem. Soc. (bd. dirs. 1971-73), Am. Chem. Soc., Internat. Soc. Electrochem., Am. Electroplater's Soc. (Silver medal 1981, 83, Gold medal 1985), N.Y. Acad. Scis., Sigma Xi. Republican. Roman Catholic. Clubs: St. Robert's Choir, St. Agatha Chorale. Current work: Hydrogen overvoltage; oxygen electrode mechanisms; electrochemical machining; mechanism of chromium deposition; high speed plating; fuel cell air electrodes; electro catalysis. Subspecialties: Electrochemistry; Catalysis chemistry. Home: 26065 Dover St Redford MI 48239 Office: Gen Motors Research Labs Dept 37 12 Mile and Mound Rds Warren MI 48090

HOBBIE, RUSSELL KLYVER, physicist; b. Albany, N.Y., Nov. 3, 1934; s. John Remington and Eulin Pomeroy (Klyver) H.; m. Cynthia Ann Borcherding, Dec. 28, 1957; children: Lynn Katherine, Erik Klyver, Sarah Elizabeth, Ann Stacey. B.S. in Physics, Mass. Inst. Tech., 1956; A.M., Harvard U., Ph.D., 1960. Research asso. U. Minn., 1960-62, mem. faculty, 1962—, prof. physics, 1972—, assoc. dean, 1984—, dir. Space Sci. Center, 1979—84. Author: Intermediate Physics for Medicine and Biology, 1978. Mem. Am. Assn. Physics Tchrs. (exec. bd. 1980-83), Am. Phys. Soc., Am. Assn. Physicists in Medicine, AAAS., Biophys. Soc. Current Work: Research in medical computing and biophysics. Subspecialty: Biophysics (physics). Home: 2151 Folwell St St Paul MN 55108 Office: 106 Lind Hall 207 Church St SE Minneapolis MN 55455

HOBBS, JOHN ROBERT, chemist; b. Plainfield, Ind., Aug. 22, 1941; s. Robert Morris and Jessie Ree (Sims) H.; m. Vivian J. Shevlin, Oct. 4, 1969. B.S., Rose Poly., Terre Haute, Ind., 1963; Ph.D., U. N.H.-Durham, 1968. Postdoctoral fellow U.S. Army Materials and Mechanics Research Ctr., Watertown, Mass., 1968-69; postdoctoral fellow Cornell U., 1969-70; program mgr. U.S. Dept. Transp., Cambridge, Mass., 1970—. Contbr. articles to profl. jours. NRC Nat. Acad. Scis. fellow, 1968. Mem. Am. Chem. Soc., N.Y. Acad. Scis., Am. Soc. Mass Spectrometry, ASTM. Current work: Trace gas detection, explosives detection/analysis, gas chromatography, mass spectrometry, liquid chromatography, hot-atom chemistry. Subspecialties: Physical chemistry; Analytical chemistry. Office: US Dept Transp Kendall Sq Cambridge MA 02142

HOBBS, LEWIS MANKIN, astronomer; b. Upper Darby, Pa., May 16, 1937; s. Lewis Samuel and Evangeline Elizabeth (Goss) H.; m. Jo Ann Faith Hagele, June 16, 1962; children: John, Michael, Dara. B.Engring. Physics, Cornell U., 1960; M.S., U. Wis., 1962, Ph.D. in Physics, 1966. Jr. astronomer Lick Obs., U. Calif., Santa Cruz, 1965-66; mem. faculty U. Chgo., 1966—, prof. astronomy and astrophysics, 1976—; also dir. Yerkes Obs., Williams Bay, Wis., 1974-82; bd. dirs. Assn. Univs. Research in Astronomy, Washington, 1974-85; mem. astronomy com. of bd. trustees Univs. Research Assn., Inc., Washington, 1979-83, chmn., 1979-81; bd. govs. Astrophys. Research Consortium, Inc., Seattle, 1984—; mem. Space Telescope Inst. Council, 1982—. Contbr. to profl. jours. Bd. dirs. Mil. Symphony Assn. of Walworth County, 1972—. Alfred P. Sloan scholar, 1955-60. Mem. Am. Astron. Soc., Am. Phys. Soc., Internat. Astron. Union, Wis. Acad. Scis. Arts and Letters. Current Work: Interstellar matter; galactic structure; interferometric spectroscopy. Subspecialties: Optical astronomy; Ultraviolet high energy astrophysics. Office: Yerkes Obs U Chgo Box 258 Williams Bay WI 53191

HOBBS, WILLARD EARL, JR., plasma physicist, administrator; b. Key West, Fla., Oct. 20, 1943; s. Willard Earl and Hazel Jane (Choate) H.; m. Ronda Kay Kaufman, June 16, 1973; children—Christopher Kaufman, Carrie Ann. B.S. in Math., U.S. Air Force Acad., 1965; M.S. in Nuclear Engring., U. Calif.-Davis, 1968, Ph.D. in Plasma Physics, 1975. Cert. life jr. coll. teaching credential, Calif. Research asst. Dept. Applied Sci., U. Calif.-Davis, 1971-75; research assoc. Naval Research Lab., Washington, 1975-77; scientist JAYCOR, Santa Barbara, Calif., 1977-83; sr. scientist Kaman Sci. Corp., Colorado Springs, Colo., 1983—; instr. Solano Coll., Fairfield, Calif., 1970-74. Contbr. articles to sci. jours. Served to capt. USAF, 1965-70. Fellow AEC, 1966, NRC, 1975. Mem. Am. Phys. Soc., AAAS, IEEE (affiliate). Current work: Analysis of nuclear radiation effects, electromagnetic pulse, plasma physics, numerical simulation, computational physics. Subspecialties: Plasma physics; Numerical analysis (mathematics). Home: 515 Foxen Dr Santa Barbara CA 93105 Office: Kaman Scis Corp PO Drawer QQ Santa Barbara CA 93102

HOBSON, J. ALLAN, psychiatrist, neurophysiologist, educator; b. Hartford, Conn., June 3, 1933. A.B., Wesleyan U., 1955; M.D., Harvard U., 1959. Intern in medicine Bellevue Hosp., N.Y.C., 1959-60; resident in psychaitry Mass. Mental Health Center, Boston, 1960-61, 64-66; spl. fellow NIMH dept. physiology U. Lyon, France, 1963-64; research assoc. dept. physiology Harvard Med. Sch., Boston, 1964-67, asst. in psychiatry, 1965-66, instr., 1966-67, asso. in psychiatry, 1967-69, asst. prof. psychiatry, 1969-74, assoc. prof., 1974-78, prof., 1978—; dir. lab. neurophysiology Mass. Mental Health Center, Boston, 1967, prin. psychiatrist, 1967—, dir. group psychotherapy tng. program, 1972; vis. scientist, lectr. U. Bordeaux, France, 1973; Sandoz lectr. dept. psychiatry U. Edinburgh, Scotland, 1975; vis. prof. Japan Soc. for Promotion of Sci., 1980; lectr. Italian NIH, 1980; vis. prof. Instituto di Psicologia U. Degli Studi, 1983; mem. sci. adv. bd. Max Planck Inst., Munich, Ger., 1985—; bd. sci. counselors NIH, 1979; dir. Dream stage, and Exptl. Portrait of the Sleeping Brain, 1977-81; cons. in electroencephalography Peter Bent Brigham Hosp., Boston, 1974-80, Sleep Disorders Clinic, Beth Israel Hosp., Boston, 1980; in electroencephalography Brigham and Women's Hosp., Boston, 1981; chmn. sci. adv. com. Boston Mus. Sci. Brain Exhibit. Author, editor books in field; contbr. chpts. to books, articles to profl. jours.; mem. editorial bd.: Jour. Cellular and Molecular Neurobiology, 1980; contbg. editor: Sleep Revs, 1970-72; assoc. editor, 1972-73, editor-in-chief, 1973-74, book rev. editor, 1975-76; cons. editor: Dreamworks, 1980—; creator: Dreamscreen, 1982. Recipient Benjamin Rush Gold medal for best sci. exhibit Am. Psychiat. Assn., 1978. Mem. Assn. Psychophysiol. Study of Sleep (program chmn. 1968-69, program co-chmn. 2d internat. sleep congress and 14 an. meeting 1975), Soc. Neurosci. (program com. 1974-76), Internat. Brain Research Orgn. (co-organizer and sci. chmn. Joint IBRO/Soc. Neurosci. internat. symposium on reticular formation revisited 1979), Sigma Xi. Current Work: Neurophysiol. basis of mind and behavior; sleep and dreaming. Subspecialties: Psychiatry; Neurophysiology. Office: Dept Psychiatry Harvard Med School 74 Fenwood Rd Boston MA 02115

HOCH, MICHAEL, engineering educator, researcher; b. Budapest, Hungary, Feb. 9, 1923; came to U.S., 1950; s. Joseph and Yollanda (Herzfeld) H.; m. Claire Szabo. M.S., Eidgenössische Technische Hochschule, Zurich, Switzerland, 1945, D.Sc., 1947. Researcher U. Zurich, 1947-50; research assoc. Ohio State U., Columbus, 1951-56; prof. engring. U. Cin., 1956—; cons. Gen. Electric Co., Cin., 1962-69, Corning Glass Works, N.Y., 1971—, EEC, Karlsrule, Fed. Republic Germany, 1979—. Fellow Am. Ceramic Soc., Am. Inst. Chemists; mem. German Ceramic Soc., AIME. Republican. Current work: Thermodynamics of alloys and ceramics, measurement of thermophysical properties at 1000-8000 deg. K, ultra fine particle technology. Subspecialties: High-temperature materials; Materials processing. Home: 2920 Scioto Apt 1402 Cincinnati OH 45219 Office: U Cin ML 12 Cincinnati OH 45221

HOCH, PAUL EDWARD, chemist, biologist; b. Phila., Nov. 6, 1920; m. Elizabeth Simon; children—Daniel, Thomas, Susan. B.A., Ohio Wesleyan U., 1942; M.S., Syracuse U., 1944; Ph.D., U. Ill., 1948. Research chemist Gen. Aniline and Film Corp., Easton, Pa., 1948-53; with Carwin Corp., New Haven, 1953-54; supr., sect. mgr. Hooker Chem. Corp., Niagara Falls, N.Y., 1954-66; dept. mgr., dir. lab., chief scientist Stauffer Chem. Corp., Richmond, Calif., 1966—; mem. Office Technology Assessment, U.S. Congress, 1979; chmn. Instl. Biosafety Com. for Recombinant DNA Research, 1981-83. Contbr. articles to profl. jours. Patentee in field. Mem. Am. Chem. Soc., Nat. Agrl. Chems. Assn. (dirs. com. 1974-78, pest mgmt. com. 1978-80), Entomology Soc. Am., Alpha Chi Sigma. Subspecialties: Integrated pest management; Organic chemistry.

HOCHMANN, PETR TOMÁS, chemistry educator, researcher; b. Pardubice, Czechoslovakia, Oct. 13, 1934; came to U.S., 1968, naturalized, 1977; s. Pavel and Marie (Neumann) H.; m. Jana Vit, May 15, 1966; children: David, Barbara. Student, Leningrad State U., 1954-58; M.S., Charles U., Prague, 1961; Ph.D., Czechoslovak Acad. Sci., Prague, 1967. Resercher Czechoslovak Acad. Sci., 1967-68; research assoc. Mich. State U., 1968-70; asst. prof. chemistry La. State U., 1970-75; assoc. prof. U. Tex., San Antonio, 1975—; adj. prof. U. Houston, 1980—. Current Work: High energy molecular excitations, interactions of molecular beams with solid surfaces. Subspecialties: Theoretical chemistry; Solid state chemistry. Office: Dept Earth Sciences U Texas San Antonio TX 78285

HOCHSTADT, JOY, biochemist, microbiologist; b. N.Y.C., May 6, 1939; d. Julius Louis and Edith (Tabatchnick) H.; m. Harvey L. Ozer, Feb. 3, 1960; 1 child, Juliane Natasha Hochstadt-Ozer. A.B., Barnard Coll., 1960; A.M. in Biol. Scis., Stanford U., 1963; Ph.D. in Microbiology, Georgetown U., 1969. Research fellow in devel. biochemistry Stanford U., 1961-62; instr. biology Coll. San Mateo, Calif., 1963; vis. fellow Karolinska Inst., Stockholm, Sweden, 1964-65; research fellow in biol. chemistry Harvard U., 1965-66; teaching asst. in microbiology Georgetown Med. Sch., 1967-68; NIH-USPHS postdoctoral fellow Nat. Heart and Lung Inst., Bethesda, Md., 1968-70; Am. Heart Assn. established investigator, 1970-75; sr. scientist Worcester Found. Exptl. Biology, Shrewsbury, Mass., 1972-76; research prof. N.Y. Med. Coll., Valhalla, 1977-81; dir. div. clin. biochemistry, dir. cell genetics research lab. Cath. Med. Ctr., Woodhaven, N.Y., 1981—; USPHS spl. trainee Cold Spring Harbor Lab., 1973; adj. prof. biochemistry Central New Eng. Colls., 1974-75; vis. prof. Weizmann Inst. Sci., Israel, 1976, U. R.I., 1976-77; vis. scholar Columbia U., 1984—; dir. N.Y. Eldorado, 300 CPW Apts. Corp.; lectr., convener nat. sci. symposia, workshops, confs.; vis. scholar dept. biol. scis. Columbia U., 1984-85; prin. investigator several research grants NIH, NSF; mem. postdoctoral fellowship evaluation panel NSF; mem. cell biology study sect., biomed. scis. rev. com. NIH; chmn. com. to distribute and administer instl. award Am. Cancer Soc., 1973-74. Contbr. research articles to profl. lit.; mem. editorial bd. Jour. Bacteriology, 1975-80; discovered that penicillinase is involved in bacterial cell wall metabolism (differentiation to spore-wall in bacillus); elucidated mechanisms of utilization of several purines and pyrimidines in bacteria and animal cells; developer first cell-free vesicle system permitting study of nutrient transport across membranes isolated from mammalian cells in culture; identified that transport changes with growth, quiescence and reactivation involve membrane alterations. Mem. alumnae council Barnard Coll. Fellow Am. Acad. Microbiology, Am. Inst. Chemists (profl. opportunities com., legis. com.); mem. Am. Heart Assn. (basic sci. council 1970—), Am. Soc. Microbiology (com. on status of women 1970-73, sec. physiology div. 1972-74, nominating com. metabolism and physiology div. 1973—, internat. travel award), Genetics Soc. Am., Am. Soc. Biology Chemists, AAAS, Fedn. Am. Scientists, Am. Assn. Cancer Researchers, Assn. Women in Sci. (affirmative action rep. 1973-75), Profl. Women's Caucus (nat. policy com. 1970-73), N.Y. Acad. Scis., Harvey Soc., Am. Assn. Clin. Scientists, Am. Assn. Clin. Chemists. Subspecialty: Microbiology. Home: 300 Central Park W New York NY 10024 Office: Cell Genetics Research Lab CMC St Anthonys Hosp Woodhaven NY 11421

HOCHULI, URS ERWIN, electrical engineering educator, researcher; b. Biel, Switzerland, Feb. 9, 1927; came to U.S., 1952; s. Erwin and Elsa (Walti) H.; m. Helen Gebhard, July 3, 1954; children—Christian, Stephan, Juerg. B.S., Technikum, Biel, 1950; M.S., U. Md., 1955; Ph.D., Cath. U. Am., 1961. Elec. engr. Brown-Boveri, Baden, Switzerland, 1950-52; research asst. Inst. Fluid Dynamics and Applied Math., U. Md., College Park, 1952-55, asst. prof. elec. engring. dept., 1955-63, assoc. prof., 1963-71, prof., 1971—; cons. Hughes Aircraft Co., various corps. in field. Inventions include gas laser, improved seal, long life gas laser. Recipient cert. of recognition NASA, 1978. Mem. Am. Phys. Soc., IEEE, Sigma Xi, Eta Kappa Nu, Tau Beta Pi. Republican. Presbyterian. Club: Cosmos (Washington). Current work: Laser life problems, cold cathodes, sealing techniques, RF excitation, materials. Home: 7011 Southwark Terr Hyattsville MD 20782 Office: Elec Engring Dept U Md College Park MD 20742

HOCHWALT, CARROLL ALONZO, JR., chemist; b. Dayton, Sept. 29, 1923; s. Carroll Alonzo and Pauline (Burkhardt) H.; m. Rita Ann Dineen, Nov. 13, 1948; children: Deberah Ann, Pauline Dineen, Carolyn Rose, Carroll Alonzo, Anne Elizabeth. B.S., Princeton U., 1944; Ph.D. in Organic Chemistry, Ohio State U., 1949. Staff chem. engr. Manhattan Dist. Project, Los Alamos, 1944-46; sales mgr. DuPont, Wilmington, Del., 1949-58; research lab. asst. dir. Inco Ltd., Sterling Forest, N.Y., 1958-67; gen. mgr. CORD Group, Inc., CPC Internat., Englewood Cliffs, N.J., 1967-73; v.p. Martin-Marietta Chems., N.Y.C., 1973-74; dir. corp. planning-bus. devel. Allied Chem. Corp., Morristown, N.J., 1974-77; gen. mgr. COGAS Devel. Co., Princeton, N.J., 1977—. Contbr. articles to profl. jours. Mem. Am. Chem. Soc., Comml. Devel. Assn., Chem. Market Research Assn., Am. Inst. Chemists, Soc. Chem. Industry. Clubs: Nassau (Princeton), Dial (Princeton). Patentee in field. Current Work: Energy and the need for synthetic fuels. Subspecialties: Combustion processes; Coal. Home: 136 Inwood Ave Upper Montclair NJ 07043 Office: PO Box 8 Princeton NJ 08540

HOCKEL, GREGORY MARTIN, drug regulator specialist, research physiologist; b. Phila., Nov. 10, 1950; s. Louis John and Joan Patricia (Kelly) H.; m. Catherine Marie Berg, Sept. 11, 1976; children—Megan Kelly, Aaron Baker. B.A. in Biology, Calif. State U.-Long Beach, 1972; Ph.D. in Physiology, Ind. U., 1977. Instr. physiology U. Miss., Jackson, 1977-79; asst. prof. 1979-80; research scientist Pfizer Central Research, Groton, Conn., 1980-83, sr. research scientist, 1983-85, liaison drug regulatory affairs. Mem. Am. Physiol. Soc., Regulatory Affairs Profl. Soc., N.Y. Acad. Sci. Current work: Submissions to U.S. and Can. regulatory authorities. Subspecialties: Physiology (medicine); Drug design. Office: Pfizer Central Research Eastern Point Rd Groton CT 06340

HODGE, IAN MOIR, industrial chemist; b. Auckland, New Zealand, Jan. 28, 1946; came to U.S., 1969; s. Gordon James and Agnes Mary (Edlington) H. B.Sc., U. Auckland, 1966, M.Sc., 1967; Ph.D., Purdue U., 1974. Postdoctoral fellow U. Aberdeen, Scotland, 1974-75, McGill U., Montreal, Que., Can., 1975-76, Purdue U., West Lafayette, Ind., 1977-78; research and devel. chemist B. F. Goodrich Co., Brecksville, Ohio, 1978—. Contbr. articles to profl. jours. Mem. Am. Chem. Soc., Am. Phys. Soc.; mem. N.Y. Acad. Sci.; Mem. N.Am. Thermal Analysis Soc. Current Work: Relaxation effects in glassy polymers; the glass transition; conducting polymers. Subspecialties: Physical chemistry; Polymer physics. Office: BF Goodrich Research and Devel Center 9921 Brecksville St Brecksville OH 44141

HODGE, PHILIP GIBSON, JR., mechanical engineering educator; b. New Haven, Nov. 9, 1920; s. Philip Gibson and Muriel (Miller) H.; m. Thea Drell, Jan. 3, 1943; children: Susan E., Philip T., Elizabeth M. A.B., Antioch Coll., 1943; Ph.D., Brown U., 1949. Research asst. Brown U., 1947-49, asso., 1949; asst. prof. math. UCLA, 1949-53; asso. prof. applied mechs. Poly. Inst. Bkly., 1953-56, prof., 1956-57; prof. mechanics Ill. Inst. Tech., 1953-71, U. Minn., Mpls., 1971—; Russell Severance Springer vis. prof. U. Calif., 1976; sec. U.S. Nat. Com./Theoretical and Applied Mechanics, 1982—. Author: 5 books, the most recent being Limit Analysis of Rotationally Symmetric Plates and Shells, 1963, Continuum Mechanics, 1971; research numerous publs. in field, 1949—; tech. editor: Jour. Applied Mechanics, 1971-76. Recipient award for disting. service Am. Acad. Mechanics, 1984. NSF sr. postdoctoral fellow, 1963. Mem. ASME (hon.; Worcester Warner Reed medal 1975), Nat. Soc. Profl. Engrs., ASCE (Theodore von Karman medal 1985), Nat. Acad. Engring. Mem. Democratic Farm Labor Party. Current Work: Theory of plasticity; numerical methods in plastic analysis. Subspecialties: Solid mechanics; Theoretical and applied mechanics. Home: 2962 W River Pkwy Minneapolis MN 55406 Office: 107 Akerman Hall U Minn Minneapolis MN 55455

HODGES, DAVID ALBERT, electrical engineering educator; b. Hackensack, N.J., Aug. 25, 1937; s. Albert R. and Katherine (Rogers) H.; m. Susan Spongberg, June 5, 1965; children—Jennifer, Alan. B.E.E., Cornell U., 1960; M.S., U. Calif., Berkeley, 1961, Ph.D. in Elec. Engring, 1966. Mem. tech. staff Bell Telephone Labs., Murray Hill, N.J., 1966-69, head system elements research dept., Holmdel, N.J., 1969-70; asso. prof. dept. elec. engring. and computer scis U. Calif., Berkeley, 1970-74, prof., 1974—. Contbr. articles to profl. jours. Trustee Deep Springs (Calif.) Coll., 1973-76; trustee Telluride Assn., Ithaca, N.Y., 1957-74, pres., 1967-69. Fellow IEEE; mem. Nat. Acad. Engring. Patentee in field. Office: Dept Elec Engring and Computer Scis Univ of Calif Berkeley CA 94720

HODGES, ROBERT EDGAR, physician, educator; b. Marshalltown, Iowa, July 30, 1922; s. Wayne Harold and Blanche Emma (McDowell) H.; m. Norma Lee Stempel, June 8, 1946; children: Jeannette Louise, Robert William, Karl Wayne, James Wolter. B.A., State U. Iowa, 1944, M.D., 1947, M.S. in Physiology, 1949. Diplomate: Nat. Bd. Med. Examiners, Am. Bd. Internal Medicine. Intern Meml. Hosp., Johnstown, Pa., 1947-48; fellow physiology, also obstetrics and gynecology, then resident in internal medicine State U. Iowa Hosp., 1948-52, dir. metabolic ward, 1952-71; mem. faculty State U. Iowa Med. Sch., 1952-71, prof. internal medicine, 1964-71, chmn. com. nutritional edn., adminstrn. grad. ednl. program nutrition, 1968-71; mem. liaison com. Maximum Security Hosp., Iowa City, 1966-71; prof. internal medicine, chief sect. nutrition U. Calif. Med. Sch., Davis, 1971-80, U. Nebr. Coll. Medicine, Omaha, 1980-82; prof. and dir. nutrition program, dept. family medicine, prof. dept. internal medicine U. Calif. Irvine Sch. Medicine, 1982—mem. nutrition study sect. NIH, 1964-68; chmn. subcom. ascorbic acid and pantothenic acid ARC, 1966-68; mem. com. nutrition overview and adjustment of food on demand Nat. Acad. Scis.-NRC, 1976; cons. to hosps., other govt. agencies. Author: Nutrition in Medical Practice, 1980, also articles.; Editor: Human Nutrition, A Comprehensive Treatise, 1980; Mem. editorial bds. med. jours. Served to capt. M.C. AUS, 1943-46, 54-56. Fellow ACP; mem. AMA, Am. Heart Assn. (fellow councils atherosclerosis, epidemiology; chmn. com. nutrition 1966-68), Am. Bd. Nutrition (pres. 1973-74), Internat. Soc. Parenteral Nutrition, Am. Soc. Parenteral and Enteral Nutrition, Soc. Exptl. Biology and Medicine, Am. Fedn. Clin. Research, Am. Inst. Nutrition, Am. Soc. Clin. Nutrition (pres. 1966-67), Nutrition Soc. (London). Subspecialty: Nutrition (medicine). Office: Dept Family Medicine U Calif Irvine Sch Medicine 101 City Dr S Orange CA 92668

HODGES, ROBERT MANLEY, pharmaceutical company executive; b. Llandrindod, Wales, July 13, 1924; came to U.S., 1955, naturalized, 1964; s. Joseph Henry and Lalla Jane (Mostyn) H.; m. Nan Powell Jones, Dec. 21, 1957; children—Robert, Jonathan, Daniel, Edward. B.Sc., U. Wales, 1950, M.B., B.Chir., 1953. Diplomate: Royal Coll. Obstetrics and Gynecology. Instr. U. Wash. Med. Sch., 1958-63; dir. Office New Drugs, med. officer U.S. FDA, Washington, 1963-68; dir. clin. research Parke, Davis & Co., Detroit, 1968-70, v.p. research and devel., 1970—, also dir.; Mem. Drug Rev. Bd. Nat. Acad. Scis., 1972-76. Author numerous sci. publs. Served with Brit. Army, 1942-47. Fellow Am. Coll. Obstetrics and Gynecology. Office: 2800 Plymouth Rd Ann Arbor MI 48106

HODGES, RONALD VERNON, research chemist; b. Kansas City, Mo., June 25, 1951; s. Floyd Vernon and Alice Fern (Walden) H. B.S. in Chemistry, Bethany Nazarene Coll., 1973; Ph.D. in Chemistry, Calif. Inst. Tech., 1978. Nat. Acad. Sci.-NRC postdoctoral research assoc. Ballistic Research Lab., Aberdeen Proving Ground, Md., 1978; vis. scientist SRI Internat., Menlo Park, Calif., 1979-80; research scientist Lockheed Missiles and Space Co., Palo Alto, Calif., 1981—. Contbr. articles to profl. jours. NSF grad. fellow Calif. Inst. Tech., 1973-77. Mem. Am. Chem. Soc., Am. Phys. Soc., Am. Sci. Affiliation. Nazarene. Current work: Gaseous electronics; electrical discharges. Subspecialty: Atomic and molecular physics. Office: Lockheed Research Lab 0/93-50 B/204 3251 Hanover St Palo Alto CA 94304

HODGES, THOMAS KENT, plant physiologist; b. Bedford, Ind., Oct. 18, 1936; s. Ollie Russell and Frances M. (Foster) H.; m. Sharon Ann Fultz, June 9, 1957; children: Christine Ann, Cynthia Lynne, Scott Russell. B.S., Purdue U., 1958; M.S., U. Calif., Davis, 1960, Ph.D., 1962. Postdoctoral fellow U. Ill., Urbana, 1962-63, asst. prof., then asso. prof. plant physiology, 1963-71; vis. prof. botany U. Calif., Davis, 1968-69; mem. faculty Purdue U., 1971—, prof. plant physiology, 1973—, head dept. botany and plant pathology, 1977-82; program mgr. plant biology grants Dept. Agr., 1981. Author papers in field. Recipient Daryl Snyder award Farm House Frat., 1976. Mem. Am. Soc. Plant Physiologists (Charles Albert Shull award 1975), Sigma Xi, Pi Alpha Xi, Phi Sigma, Alpha Zeta. Current Work: Regeneration of agronomic crops (i.e.corn)-from protoplasts; developmental physiology of plants. Subspecialties: Plant physiology (agriculture); Plant cell and tissue culture. Office: Lilly Hall Purdue U West Lafayette IN 47907

HODGMAN, JOAN ELIZABETH, neonatologist; b. Portland, Oreg., Sept. 7, 1923; d. Kenneth E. and Ann (Vannet) H.; m. Amos N. Schwartz, Jan. 30, 1949; children—Ann Vannet, Susan Lynn. B.A., Stanford U., 1943; M.D., U. Calif., San Francisco, 1946. Intern in pediatrics U. Calif. Hosp., San Francisco, 1946-47; resident in pediatrics Harbor Gen. Hosp., Torrance, Calif., 1947-48, Los Angeles County-U. So. Calif. Med. Center, 1948-50; practice medicine specializing in pediatrics, S. Pasadena, Calif., 1950-52; mem. faculty U. So. Calif. Med. Sch., 1952—, prof. pediatrics, 1969—; dir. newborn div. Los Angeles County-U. So. Calif. Med. Center, 1955—; chmn. med. adv. com. Nat. Found.-March of Dimes, 1972-75; adv. com. Western sect. UNICEF, 1975; med. adv. com. Calif. Legislature, 1970; cons. Calif. Health Dept. Author articles in field, chpts. in books. Recipient cert. appreciation Am. Cancer Soc., 1964, Cameo of Committent award B'nai B'rith, 1969, Meritorious award Nat. Found.-March of Dimes, 1969; named Woman of Year Calif. Museum Sci. and Industry, 1974, Woman of Year Los Angeles Times, 1976. Mem. Am. Pediatric Soc., Am. Acad. Pediatrics, Am. Thoracic Soc., Western Soc. Pediatric Research, Southwestern Pediatric Soc., Calif. Perinatal Assn., Calif. Med. Assn., Los Angeles County Med. Assn., Los Angeles Pediatric Soc. Subspecialty: Neonatology. Home: 494 Stanford Dr Arcadia CA 91006 Office: 1240 Mission Rd Los Angeles CA 90033

HOEG, DONALD FRANCIS, chemist; b. Bklyn., Aug. 2, 1931; s. Harry Herman and Charlotte (Bourke) H.; m. Patricia Catherine Fogarty, Aug. 30, 1952; children—Thomas Edward, Robert Francis, Donald John, Mary Beth, Susan Catherine. B.S. in Chemistry summa cum laude, St. John's U., N.Y., 1953; Ph.D. in Chemistry, Ill. Inst. Tech., 1957. Fellow in chemistry and chem. engring. Armour Research Found., 1953-54; grad. research asst. Ill. Inst. Tech., 1954-56; research chemist W.R. Grace & Co., 1956-58, sr. research chemist, 1958-61; group leader addition polymer chemistry Roy C. Ingersoll Research Center, Borg-Warner Corp., Des Plaines, Ill., 1961-64, mgr. polymer chemistry, 1964-66, asso. dir., head chem. research dept., 1966-75, dir., 1975—; mem. solid state scis. adv. bd. Nat. Acad. Scis.; Bd. overseers Lewis Coll. Scis. and Letters of Ill. Inst. Tech., 1980—; bd. dirs. Ill. Inst. Tech. Alumni, 1979-82, Mt. Prospect Combined Appeal, 1963-65. Bd. editors: Research Mgmt. Mag, 1979-82; contbr. numerous articles tech. publs., chpts. in books. TaPing Lin scholar, 1955-56; AEC asst., 1954; Armour Research Found. fellow, 1953-54; Ill. Inst. Tech. Achievement award, 1983. Mem. Am. Chem. Soc., AAAS, N.Y. Acad. Scis., Dirs. Indsl. Research, Am. Mgmt. Assn. (v.p. research and devel. council), Research Dirs. Assn. Chgo. (pres. 1977-78), Sigma Xi. Patentee in field. Current Work: Advanced materials, power transmission, fluid mechanics, manufacturing technology. Subspecialties: Polymer chemistry; Organometallics. Office: Roy C Ingersoll Research Center Wolf and Algonquin Rds Des Plaines IL 60018

HOEGERMAN, STANTON FRED, cytogeneticist, educator; b. Bklyn., May 13, 1944; s. Fred and Edith (Rost) H.; m. Georgeanne Stengele, Mar. 5, 1966; children: Elizabeth, David. B.S., Cornell U., 1965; M.S., N.C. State U., 1968, Ph.D., 1972. Instr. dept. biology Lincoln U., 1970-72; asst. biologist RER div. Argonne Nat. Lab., ILL., 1972-76; assoc. prof. biology Coll. William and Mary, Williamsburg, Va., 1976—. Contbr. numerous articles on human cytogenetics and radiation to cytogenetics to profl. pubs. Mem. Am. Soc. Human Genetics, Genetics Soc. Am., Bot. Soc. Am., AAAS. Unitarian. Current Work: Cytogenetics of fragile sites and human cytogenetics, fragile sites, Fragile X syndrome. Subspecialties: Cell and tissue culture; Genetics and genetic engineering (biology). Home: 367 Hiden Blvd Newport News VA 23606 Office: Biology Dept Coll William and Mary Williamsburg VA 23185

HOEL, LESTER A., civil engineering educator; b. Bklyn., Feb. 26, 1935; s. Johannes and Julia (Michelsen) H.; m. Unni Sonja Blegen, Jan. 24, 1959; children: Julie Britt, Sonja Leslie, Lisa Maureen. B.C.E., City Coll., N.Y., 1957; M.S. in Civil Engring, Bklyn. Poly. Inst., 1960; D.Eng., U. Calif. at Berkeley, 1963. Registered profl. engrs. Calif., Pa., Va. Asst. prof. engring. San Diego State Coll., 1962-64; Fulbright research scholar Inst. Transport Economy, Oslo, Norway, 1964-65; prin. engr. Wilbur Smith & Assos., San Francisco, 1965-66; faculty Carnegie-Mellon U., Pitts., 1966-74, prof. civil engring., 1970-74; asso. dir. Transp. Research Inst., 1966-74; Hamilton prof., chmn. dept. civil engring. U. Va., 1974—; staff cons. Gen. Analytics, Inc., 1971-78; Cons. P.R. Planning Bd., 1969-70. Editor: Public Transportation: Planning, Operations and Management, 1979; Mem. editorial bd.: Transp. Research; Author tech. papers, books and articles. Chmn. bd. mgmt. YMCA, 1968-69; mem. Churchill Boro Planning Commn., 1972-74. Recipient Alumni award in Civil Engring. Coll. City N.Y., 1957; Pyke Johnson award Transp. Research Bd., 1977; Fulbright travel grantee, 1964-65. Mem. ASCE (Huber research prize 1976), Am. Scandinavian Found., Inst. Transp. Engrs., Transp. Research Bd. (exec. com.), Am. Soc. Engring. Edn., Sigma Xi, Chi Epsilon, Tau Beta Pi. Subspecialty: Civil engineering. Home: 1703 Old Forge Rd Charlottesville VA 22901

HOELLER, LOUISE, nurse educator, nun, consultant; b. Fond du Lac, Wis., Dec. 5, 1928; d. Francis R. and Grace A. (Gilkey) H. R.N., St. Joseph Sch. Nursing, Chgo., 1953; B.S., DePaul U., 1954; M.Nursing, La. State U., 1977. Mem. Daus. of Charity of St. Vincent dePaul; supr. operating room-recovery room DePaul Hosp., St. Louis, 1956-62; Supr. operating room-recovery room Charity Hosp., New Orleans, 1962-65; clin. instr. U. Wis., St. Mary's Hosp., Milw., 1967-69; program dir. surg. tech. Forest Park Coll., St. Louis, 1970-75, Charity Hosp., New Orleans, 1975-80; asst. prof. perioperative nursing La. State U. Med. Center, Shreveport, 1981—; cons. Mo. Profl. Liability Ins. Assn., Columbia, 1980; site visitor, com. mem. Assn. Surg. Technologists, Denver, 1981-82. Author: Operating Room Technician, 1965, 2d edit., 1968, Surgical Technology: Basis for Clinical Practice, 1974. Mem. Am. Nurses Assn. (sect. chmn. 1962-65), Nat. League Nursing (nat. com. 1961-65), Assn. Operating Room Nurses, La. State U. Nursing Alumni, Sigma Theta Tau. Current Work: Competency-based learning-modular programmed instruction in surgical instruments. Subspecialties: Health services research; Human factors engineering. Home: PO Box 21976 Shreveport LA 71120 Office: La State U Med Center 1541 Kings Hwy Shreveport LA 71130

HOFER, LAWRENCE JOHN EDWARD, chemist; b. Salt Lake City, June 26, 1915; s. William Mathias and Friederike (Lodger) H.; m. Marguerite Ione Tears; 1 child, Richard Lawrence. B.A., U. Utah, 1937, M.A., 1938; Ph.D., U. Rochester, 1941. Research assoc. Carnegie Mellon U., Pitts., 1941-43; head calalytic chemistry Bur. Mines, Pitts., 1943-65; fellowship head Mellon Inst., Pitts., 1965-70; chief toxic materials div. Health Tech. Ctr., Pitts., 1970—; cons. Koppers Co., Pitts., 1970. Patentee in field. U. Rochester fellow 1940. Fellow AAAS, Am. Inst. Chemists (nat. councillor); mem. Am. Chem. Soc. Republican. Presbyterian. Current work: Toxicity of materials, composition of mine atmospheres, adsorption, surface chemistry. Subspecialties: Catalysis chemistry; Surface chemistry. Home: 236 Hays Rd Pittsburgh PA 15241 Office: Pitts Health Tech Ctr Mine Safety and Health Adminstrn 4800 Forbes Ave Pittsburgh PA 15213

HOFF, MARCIAN EDWARD, JR., electronics engineer; b. Rochester, N.Y., Oct. 28, 1937; s. Marcian Edward and Mary Elizabeth (Fitzpatrick) H.; m. Judith Schless Rytand, May 19, 1977; children: Carolyn, Lisa, Jill. B.E.E., Rensselaer Poly. Inst., Troy, N.Y., 1958; M.S., Stanford U., 1959, Ph.D., 1962. Research asso. Stanford U., 1962-68; mgr. applications research Intel Corp., Santa Clara, Calif., 1968-83; v.p. research and devel. Atari Inc., Sunnyvale, Calif., 1983-84; cons., 1984—. Author articles on adaptive systems, microcomputers. NSF fellow, 1958—; recipient Stuart Ballantine medal Franklin Inst., 1979. Mem. IEEE (Cledo Brunetti award 1980), Sigma Xi, Eta Kappa Nu, Tau Beta Pi. Patentee track circuits, electrochem. memory, digital filters, integrated circuits. Subspecialty: Electronics industry research and development management. Home: 1075 Astoria Dr Sunnyvale CA 94087

HOFF, NICHOLAS JOHN, mechanical and aerospace engineer; b. Magyarovar, Hungary, Jan. 3, 1906; came to U.S., 1939, naturalized, 1944; s. Miklos and Lenke H.; m. Vivian Church, July 20, 1940 (dec. Apr. 1969); m. Ruth Kleczewski, Nov. 17, 1972; 1 dau., Karen Brandt. M.E., Fed. Poly. Inst. Zurich, Switzerland, 1928, Dipl.-Ing., 1928; Ph.D. in Engring. Mechs, Stanford U., 1942; D.Sc. (hon.), Technion, Haifa, Israel, 1981. Airplane designer, Hungary, 1928-38; research asst. Stanford U., 1939-40, head dept. aeros., 1957-71, prof. aeros., 1957-71, prof. emeritus, 1971—; instr. aeros. Poly. Inst. Bklyn., 1940-41, asst. prof., 1941-43, asso. prof., 1943-46, prof., 1946-57, head dept. aeros., 1950-57; vis. prof. Monash (Australia) U., 1971, Ga. Inst. Tech., 1973, Cranfield (Eng.) Inst. Tech., 1974-75, Poly. Inst. Zurich, 1975; Clark/Crossan prof. engring. Rensselaer Poly. Inst., 1976-79, vis. Disting. prof., 1979-81; cons. to govt. and industry. Author: The Analysis of Structures, 1956; editor: books, including High Temperature Effects in Aircraft Structures, 1958, Creep in Structures, 1962; contbr. numerous articles on structural and stress analysis, aeros. to profl. jours. Recipient Monie A. Ferst award Soc. Sigma Xi, 1982; Daniel Guggenheim medal, 1983; I.B. Laskowitz award N.Y. Acad. Scis., 1983. Fellow AIAA (hon., Pendray award 1971, Structures, Structural Dynamics, and Materials award 1971), ASME (hon., Worcester Reed Warner medal 1967, ASME medal 1974), Royal Aero. Soc. (Gt. Britain); mem. ASCE (life, von Karman medal 1972), Aero. Soc. India (hon.), U.S. Nat. Acad. Engring., Internat. Acad. Astronautics (corr.). Current Work: Research on composite structures and history of aeronautics. Subspecialties: Aeronautical engineering; Aerospace engineering and technology. Office: Dept Aeros and Astronautics Stanford U Stanford CA 94305

HOFFLEIT, ELLEN DORRIT, astronomer; b. Florence, Ala., Mar. 12, 1907; d. Fred and Kate (Sanio) H. A.B., Radcliffe Coll., 1928, M.A., 1932, Ph.D., 1938; D.Sc. (hon.), Smith Coll., 1984. From research asst. to astronomer Harvard Coll. Obs., 1929-56; mathematician Ballistic Research Labs., Aberdeen Proving Ground, Md., 1943-48; tech. expert, 1948-62; lectr. Wellesley Coll., 1955-56; mem. faculty Yale U., 1956—, sr. research astronomer, 1974—; dir. Maria Mitchell Obs., Nantucket, Mass., 1957-78; mem. Hayden Planetarium Com., N.Y.C., 1975—; editor Meteoritical Soc., 1958-68. Author: Some Firsts in Astronomical Photography, 1950, Yale Bright Star Catalogue, 4th edit, 1982; also research papers. Recipient Caroline Wilby prize Radcliffe Coll., 1938, Grad. Soc. medal, 1964; certificate appreciation War Dept., 1946; alumnae recognition award Radcliffe Coll., 1983. Mem. Internat. Astron. Union, Am. Astron. Soc., AAAS, Am. Geophys. Union, Meteoritical Soc., Am. Assn. Variable Stars Observers, Am. Def. Preparedness Assn., Nantucket Maria Mitchell Assn. (hon.), Nantucket Hist. Soc., Phi Beta Kappa, Sigma Xi. Current Work: Variable stars, astrometry, star catalogues, history of astronomy. Subspecialty: Optical astronomy. Home: 255 Whitney Ave New Haven CT 06511 Office: Yale U Obs Box 6666 New Haven CT 06511

HOFFMAN, CYRUS MILLER, physicist; b. N.Y.C., Feb. 20, 1942; s. Cyrus Carson and Adele (Miller) H.; m. Jane Granich, Aug. 25, 1963; children—Benjamin, Lucas, Julie, Carrie. B.S., Brown U., 1962; M.A., Harvard U., 1964, Ph.D., 1969. Instr. Princeton U., N.J., 1969-70, asst. prof., 1970-74; mem. staff Los Alamos Nat. Lab., 1974-84, assoc. group leader, 1984—. Fellow Am. Phys. Soc. Current works: Study of rare particle decays. Subspecialties: Particle physics; Nuclear physics. Home: 660 Totavi Los Alamos NM 87544 Office: MP-4 Los Alamos Nat Lab MS H846 Los Alamos NM 87545

HOFFMAN, DARLEANE CHRISTIAN, nuclear chemist; b. Terril, Iowa, Nov. 8, 1926; d. Carl Benjamin and Elverna E. (Kuhlman) Christian; m. Marvin Morrison Hoffman, Dec. 26, 1951; children: Maureane R., Daryl K. B.S. in Chemistry, Iowa State U., 1948, Ph.D. in Nuclear Chemistry, 1951. NSF sr. postdoctoral fellow Institute for Atomenergi, Kjeller, Norway, 1964; staff mem. radiochemistry group Los Alamos Sci. Lab., 1953-71, assoc. group leader, 1971-79, div. leader chemistry and nuclear chemistry, 1979-82, div. leader isotope and nuclear chemistry, 1982-84; prof. U.Calif.-Berkeley, 1984—; Guggenheim fellow Lawrence Berkeley Lab., 1978-79, faculty sr. scientist, 1984—. Contbr. articles to profl. jours. Recipient Citation of Merit Coll. Scis. and Humanities, Iowa State U., 1978. Fellow Am. Inst. Chemists; mem. Am. Chem. Soc. (award for nuclear chemistry 1983, John Dustin Clark award

Central N.Mex. chpt. 1976), Am. Phys. Soc., AAAS. Current Work: Mechanisms of nuclear fission; transuranium elements; science administration; nuclear chemistry; isotope chemistry. Subspecialty: Nuclear chemistry. Home: 2277 Manzanita Dr Oakland CA 94611 Office: 70A-3307 Nuclear Sci Div Lawrence Berkeley Lab Berkeley CA 94720

HOFFMAN, DONALD RICHARD, immunologist, educator, consultant; b. Boston, Aug. 25, 1943; s. William Maurice and Laura (Rodman) H.; m. Valeria Anne Mossey, Sept. 21, 1971; children—Avram Joseph, Anthony Horatio, Maria Lauren. A.B., Harvard U., 1965; Ph.D., Calif. Inst. Tech., 1970. Cancer research scientist Roswell Park Meml. Inst., Buffalo, 1970-71; asst. prof. pediatrics U. So. Calif. Sch. Medicine, Los Angeles, 1971-75; assoc. prof. pathology Creighton U. Sch. Medicine, Omaha, 1975-77; assoc prof pathology and lab. medicine East Carolina U. Sch. Medicine, Greenville, N.C., 1977-82, prof., 1982—; cons. Pharmacia Diagnostics, T and M Immunodiagnostics. Contbr. articles to profl. jours. Mem. Am. Assn. Immunologists, AAAS, N.Y. acad. Scis., AAUP; fellow Am. Acad. Allergy and Immunology. Current Work: In vitro diagnosis of allergy; allergens; radioimmunoassay. Subspecialties: Allergy; Immunology (medicine). Home: 213 N Jarvis St Greenville NC 27834 Office: E Carolina U Sch Medcine Greenville NC 27834

HOFFMAN, EDWARD JACK, energy consultant; b. Marion, Kans., June 10, 1925; s. Chiles Edward and Mary (Lynch) H.; m. Suzanne Pierson, Mar. 7, 1953; children: Kathy Sue, Cal Edward, Paul Brian. B.S. in Chem. Engring, Okla. State U., 1944; M.S., U. Mich., 1950; postgrad., U. Colo., 1954-57. Refinery chemist Continental Oil Co., Ponca City, Okla., 1946-47; research chemist Carter Oil Co., Tulsa, 1947-48; engr. Black, Sivalls & Bryson, Oklahoma City, 1951-52; instr. Okla. State U., Stillwater, 1952-54; asst. prof. U. Colo., 1954-57; assoc. prof. U. Tulsa, 1957-62; research engr. Heat Transfer Research Inc., Alhambra, Calif., 1963-65; assoc. prof. U. Wyo., Laramie, 1965-72, energy cons., 1972—. Author: Azeotropic and Extractive Distillation, 1964, 77, The Concept of Energy: An Inquiry into Origins and Applications, 1977, Coal Conversion, 1978, Heat Transfer Rate Analysis, 1980, Coal Gasifiers, 1981, Phase and Flow Behavior in Petroleum Production, 1981, Synfuels: The Problems and the Promise, 1982. Served to lt. USN, 1944-46. Mem. Am. Inst. Chem. Engrs., Am. Chem. Soc., ASME, Inst. Briquetting and Agglomeration, Sigma Xi. Democrat. Methodist. Patentee in field. Current Work: Development and commercialization of the Hoffman process for the direct catalytic conversion of coal or other carbonaceous materials with steam to coproduce synthetic fuels and carbon dioxide for enhanced oil recovery. Subspecialties: Fuels; Chemical engineering. Address: PO Box 1352 Laramie WY 82070

HOFFMAN, ERIC ALFRED, cardiopulmonary physiologist; b. Rochester, Minn., Sept. 5, 1951; s. Murray Stanley Hoffman and Doris (Creamer) Kal. B.A., Antioch Coll, Yellow Springs, Ohio, 1974; Ph.D., U. Minn.-Mayo Grad. Sch. Medicine, 1981. Research cons. Royal Berkshire Hosp., Reading, Eng., 1972; research asst. Fels Research Inst., Yellow Springs, Ohio, 1973-74, U. Colo. Med. Ctr., Denver, 1974-75; pre-doctoral fellow Mayo Clinic Found., 1975-81, postdoctoral fellow, 1981-83, instr. physiology, 1982-83, assoc. cons., 1983—, asst. prof., 1983—; mem. research com. Colo. Heart Assn., 1974-75; new investigator Nat. Heart, Lung and Blood Inst., Washington, 1983—. Mem. Am. Thoracic Soc., Am. Heart Assn. Council Cardiopulmonary Disease, Am. Physiol. Soc. (long range planning com.), AAAS, Union Concerned Scientists. Current Work: Developing and validating new imaging techniques associated with synchronous volumetric x-ray scanning computed tomography, and utilizing these techniques to study the intrathoracic determinants of cardiac and pulmonary geometry to function relationships. Subspecialties: Physiology (biology); Imaging technology. Office: Biodynamics Research Unit Mayo Clinic 200 1st St SW Rochester MN 55905

HOFFMAN, GRAHAM WALTER, electrical engineering educator; b. Detroit, Jan. 10, 1928; s. Walter Robert and Erna Frieda (Schmidt) H.; m. Clyde M. McLeod, July 30, 1955; children—Graham Walter, Margaret Evelyn, Charles Fredrick, Paul Albert. B.S., Lafayette Coll., 1950; M.S., Harvard U., 1951, Ph.D., 1955. Scientist, Westinghouse Co., Pitts., 1955-58; assoc. prof. elec. engring. U. Tenn., Knoxville, 1959-64, prof., 1965—; vis. prof. U. Nottingham, Eng., 1970-71. Ford Found. fellow, 1966-67. Mem. IEEE (sr.), Am. Phys. Soc., Am. Soc. Engring. Edn., AAAS, AAUP, Phi Beta Kappa, Sigma Xi, Tau Beta Pi, Eta Kappa Nu. Epicopalian. Current work: Lasers; fiber optics; detectors; electro-optical systems. Subspecialty: Electrical engineering. Home: 4420 Plymouth Rd Knoxville TN 37914 Office: Ferris Hall 2100 Univ Tenn Knoxville TN 37996

HOFFMAN, JOHN DRAKE, materials science educator, researcher, consultant; b. Washington, Nov. 26, 1922; s. James Irvin and Mabel Irene (Hemminger) H.; m. Barbara Frances Smith, Sept 10, 1949 (dec. Feb. 1980); children—James P., John M., Robert C.; m. Dolores Filomena Garcia, Sept. 26, 1981; stepchildren—Carol F., Valerie R. B.S. with honors, Franklin & Marshall Coll., 1942; M.S., Princeton U., 1948, Ph.D., 1949. Research assoc. G.E. Research and Devel. Ctr., Schenectady, N.Y., 1949-54; mem. staff Nat. Bur. Standards, Gaithersburg, Md., 1954-62, dir. polymers div., 1952-67, dir. Inst. Materials Research, 1967-78, dir. Nat. Measurement Lab., 1978-82; prof., dir. engring. materials program U. Md., College Park, 1982—; trustee Gordon Research Conf., 1974-77, chmn. bd. trustees, 1976-77. Contbr. chpt. Treatise on Solid State Chemistry, 1976. Mem. editorial bd. Macromolecules, 1979-82, Jour. Polymer Science. Contbr. articles to profl. jours. Served as sgt. U.S. Army, 1944-46. Recipient Stratton award Nat. Bur. Standards, 1967, Presdl. Meritorious Exec. award Dept. Commerce, 1981. Fellow Am. Phys. Soc. (High Polymer Physics prize 1971); mem. Nat. Acad. Engring., N.Y. Acad. Scis., Am. Chem. Soc., Am. Soc. Metals, Am. Dental Assn. (hon. mem.), Sigma Xi. Republican. Presbyterian. Club: Cosmos (Washington). Lodge: Masons. Current work: polymer physics, polymer crystallization, dielectric and mechanical relaxation in polymers and molecular crystals, liquid thermal diffusion. Subspecialties: Polymers (materials science); Polymer physics. Home: 6121 Maiden Ln Bethesda MD 20817 Office: Dept Chemical and Nuclear Engring U Md College Park MD 20742

HOFFMAN, JOHN ROBERT, JR., engineering consulting company executive; b. Tuscaloosa, Ala., Nov. 3, 1945; s. John R. and Dorothy M. H.; m. Patricia J. Meyer, Aug. 5, 1967; children: Sheryl Ann, Michael Andrew, Megan Alicia. B.S.M.E., Cooper Union for Advancement Sci. and Art, 1967; M.S.N.E., U. Lowell, 1977; M.S. in Mgmt., Lesley Coll., 1985. Registered profl. engr., Mass., N.H., Vt. Primary coolant system engr. Westinghouse Electric Corp., West Mifflin, Pa., 1967-69; test engr. Pratt & Whitney Aircraft, East Hartford, Conn., 1969-71; asst. to v.p. Yankee Atomic Electric Co., Framingham, Mass., 1971—. Mem. ASME. Subspecialties: Mechanical engineering; Nuclear engineering. Home: 33 Woodlawn Dr Sturbridge MA 01566 Office: 1671 Worcester Rd Framingham MA 01701

HOFFMAN, KENNETH CHARLES, information systems company executive; b. N.Y.C., Nov. 29, 1933; s. Arthur A. and Helen M. (McElearney) H.; m. Ann Theresa Hynes, Aug. 20, 1955; children: Kenneth M., Theresa A., Charles M. B.M.E., NYU, 1954; M.S., Adelphi U., 1968; Ph.D. in Systems Engring, Poly. Inst. Bklyn., 1972. Registered profl. engr., N.Y. Mem. sci. staff Brookhaven Nat. Lab., 1956-75, chmn. dept. energy and environ., 1975-78; dir. Nat. Ctr. for Analysis of Energy Systems, 1975; sr. v.p. Mathtech Inc., Arlington, Va., 1979-83, pres., 1984; v.p., gen. mgr. Martin Marietta Data Systems, 1984—. Served with USAF, 1954-56. Fellow AAAS; mem. ASME, N.Am. Soc. Corp. Planners, Internat. Assn. Energy Economists. Roman Catholic. Current Work: Information systems. Subspecialties: Systems engineering; Resource policy. Office: Martin Marietta Data Systems 6801 Rockledge Dr Bethesda MD 20817

HOFFMAN, MARK PETER, animal scientist, livestock producer, educator; b. West Reading, Pa., Feb. 4, 1941; s. Mark Webber and Pearl Matilda (Troutman) H.; m. Lorraine Johnson, Aug. 24, 1969; children: Kourtney Katherine, Royelle Marka. B.S., Delaware Valley Coll., 1963; M.S., Iowa State U., 1967, Ph.D., 1969. Asst. prof. animal sci. Iowa State U., 1969-75, assoc. prof., 1976-80, prof., 1981—. Author: manual Introduction to Animal Science, 1976, Basic Principles of Animal Nutrition, 1972, Reproductive Physiology of Livestock, 1978; Beef Cattle Production, 1984; contbr. numerous articles on environ. factors affecting beef cattle performance to profl. jours. Mem. Am. Soc. Animal Sci. (cert. animal scientist), Am. Dairy Sci. Assn., Am. Inst. Biol. Scis., AAAS. Republican. Lutheran. Current Work: Research and teaching beef cattle production. Subspecialties: Animal nutrition; Animal physiology. Home: Rural Route 2 Ames IA 50010 Office: Iowa State U 119 Kildee Ames IA 50011

HOFFMAN, RONALD BRUCE, science manager, neuroscientist b. Balt., Mar. 29, 1939; s. Marvin Lionel and Edna Mildred (Fillman) H.; m. Carolyn Jean Phillips, July 6, 1969; children—Christine Beth, David Alexander, Matthew Todd. B.S. in Physics, U. Md., 1962; M.A. in Psychology, U. Houston, 1971, Ph.D. in Biophys. Sci., 1974. Aerospace engr. NASA Johnson Space Ctr., Houston, 1964-67; postdoctoral student NRC, 1975-77; mgr. Gen. Electric Mgmt. and Tech. Services Co., Moffett Field, Calif., 1979-80, sr. scientist, Houston, 1977-79; regional mgr. Tech. Inc., Washington, 1980-82; sr. project mgr. Gen. Electric Co., Washington, 1982-85; biotech. mgr. Advanced Tech. Inc., Reston, Va., 1985—; mgr., math. modeler Apollo re-entry simulation, 1964. Contbr. articles to sci. publs. Recipient group achievement award NASA, 1975. Mem. Soc. for Neurosci., Southwestern Psychol. Assn., Aerospace Med. Assn., Sigma Xi (research fellow 1972), Phi Kappa Phi. Current work: Memory research, research on efficacy and mechanisms of drugs in alleviation of stresses imposed by parabolic aircraft flight, management of interdisciplinary groups for technical support services. Subspecialties: Gravitational biology; Space medicine. Office: Advanced Tech Inc 12001 Sunrise Valley Dr Reston VA 22091

HOFFMAN, WILLIAM FLOYD, animal scientist, educator; b. Alvo, Nebr., Jan. 16, 1929; s. William George and Julia Ann (Paul) H.; m. Mailyn Cecile Elliott, June 10, 1968; 1 child, Linda Ann. B.S., Iowa State U., 1960; M.S., U. Mo., 1962, Ph.D. in Dairy Sci, 1965. Farmer, Akron, Iowa, 1946-52; processed foods insp. U.S. Dept. Agr., San Jose, Calif., 1960-61; research asst. U. Mo., Columbia, 1961-64; prof. dept. agrl. sci. U. Wis., Platteville, 1964—. Served with USAF, 1952-56. Gund scholar, 1959. Mem. Am. Soc. Animal Sci., Am. Dairy Sci. Assn. Methodist. Lodges: Masons; Lions. Current Work: Applied in reproductive physiology; nutrition in calves and stress on calves. Subspecialties: Animal breeding and embryo transplants; Animal physiology. Home: 1100 Hollman St Platteville WI 53818 Office: 221 Ullrich Hall U Wis Platteville WI 53818

HOFFMANN, ROALD, chemist, educator; b. Zloczow, Poland, July 18, 1937; came to U.S., 1949, naturalized, 1955; s. Hillel and Clara (Rosen) Safron (stepson Paul Hoffmann); m. Eva Börjesson, Apr. 30, 1960; children: Hillel Jan, Ingrid Helena. B.A., Columbia U., 1958; M.A., Harvard U., 1960, Ph.D., 1962; D.Tech. (hon.), Royal Inst. Tech., Stockholm, 1977; D.Sc. (hon.), Yale U., 1980, Columbia U., 1982, Hartford U., 1982, CUNY, 1983, U. P.R., 1983. Jr. fellow Soc. Fellows Harvard, 1962-65; asso. prof. Cornell U., Ithaca, N.Y., 1965-68, prof., 1968-74, John A. Newman prof. phys. sci., 1974—. Author: (with R.B. Woodward) Conservation of Orbital Symmetry, 1970. Recipient award in pure chemistry Am. Chem. Soc., 1969, Arthur C. Cope award, 1973; Fresenius award Phi Lambda Upsilon, 1969; Harrison Howe award Rochester sect. Am. Chem. Soc., 1970; ann. award Internat. Acad. Quantum Molecular Scis., 1970; Pauling award, 1974; Nobel prize in chemistry, 1981; inorganic chemistry award Am. Chem. Soc., 1982. Mem. Nat. Acad. Scis., Am. Acad. Arts and Scis., Internat. Acad. Quantum Molecular Scis. Current Work: Electronic structure of organic, inorganic, and organometallic molecules and of extended solid state structures. Subspecialty: Theoretical chemistry. Office: Cornell U Dept Chemistry Ithaca NY 14853

HOFMANN, LORENZ MARTIN, clinical pharmacologist, pharmacist; b. Chgo., Jan. 10, 1937; s. John C. and Margaret E. (Moews) H.; m. Victoria T. Knefel, May 3, 1968; children: Lorenz Martin II, Paul. B.S. in Pharmacy, U. Ill.-Chgo., 1959, M.S. in Pharmacology, 1961, Ph.D. in Pharmacology, 1964. Registered pharmacist, Ill., Ohio. Research scientist Searle Labs., 1964-76, mgr. regulatory affairs, 1976-77; asso. dir. clin. pharmaology research Ross Labs., 1977-81; asso. dir. clin. devel. Adria Labs., Columbus, Ohio, 1982-85; assoc. dir. clin. sci. Warner-Lambert/Parke-Davis, Ann Arbor, Mich., 1985—; adj. asst. prof. depts. pharmacology Sch. Medicine and Sch. Pharmacy, Ohio State U., Columbus; lectr. in field. Contbr. articles to sci. jours. Mem. Am. Soc. Clin. Pharmacology and Therapeutics, Am. Soc. Pharmacology and Exptl. Therapeutics. Current Work: Research on safety and effectiveness of antihypertensives, diuretics, analgesics and dermatologics. Subspecialties: Pharmacology; Pharmacokinetics. Home: 2341 Placid Way Ann Arbor MI 48105 Office: 2800 Plymouth Rd Ann Arbor MI 48105

HOFMANN, PETER LUDWIG, nuclear engineer, systems analyst; b. Vienna, Jan. 25, 1925; came to U.S., 1939; s. Arthur Oliver and Luise (Kamhuber) H.; m. Garda S. Steiner, May 27, 1950; children: Mark Eric, Monica Louise. B.E.E., Cooper Union, 1950; M.S., Union Coll., 1954; D. Eng. Sci., R.P.I., 1960. Mgr. nuclear design Gen. Electric Co., Schenectady, 1950-61, mgr. engring. physics, Richland, Wash., 1961-65; mgr. nuclear analysis Battelle Meml. Inst., Richland, 1965-70; mgr. systems analysis Westinghouse Co., Richland, 1970-74; assoc. dir. planning and analysis Battelle Meml. Inst., Columbus, Ohio, 1974-79, mgr. nuclear waste tech., 1979—. Contbr.: The Physics of Intermediate Spectrum Reactors, 1955, Advances in Nuclear Science and Technology, 1969, Solar Energy Technology Handbook, 1980; editor: The Technology of High-Level Nuclear Waste Management, 1981, 82. Contbr. numerous articles to profl. jours. Served with U.S. Army, 1943-46. Mem. Am. Nuclear Soc., Am. Phys. Soc., Sigma Xi, Tau Beta Pi. Current Work: Nuclear fuel cycle, reactor physics, disposal of radioactive waste, cost and systems analysis. Subspecialties: Nuclear fission; Nuclear engineering. Home: 5080 Dublin Rd Columbus OH 43220 Office: Battelle Meml Inst 505 King Ave Columbus OH 43201

HOFSTADTER, DOUGLAS RICHARD, computer scientist, educator; b. N.Y.C., Feb. 15, 1945; s. Robert and Nancy (Givan) H. B.S. in Math. with distinction, Stanford U., 1965; M.S., U. Oreg., 1972, Ph.D. in Physics, 1975. Asst. prof. computer sci. Ind. U., Bloomington, 1977-80, assoc. prof., 1980-84; Walgreen prof. Cognitive Sci. U. Mich., Ann Arbor, 1984—. Author: Gödel, Escher, Bach: an Eternal Golden Braid, 1979, Metamagical Themas, 1985. Editor: (with Daniel C. Dennett) The Mind's I, 1981. Columnist: Metamagical Themas in Sci. Am., 1981-83. Recipient Pultizer prize for gen. nonfiction, 1980; Am. Book award, 1980; Guggenheim fellow, 1980-81. Mem. Assn. for Computing Machinery, Cognitive Sci. Soc., Am. Assn. Artificial Intelligence. Subspecialty: Artificial intelligence. Office: Dept Psychology U Mich Ann Arbor MI 48109

HOFSTADTER, ROBERT, physicist, educator; b. N.Y.C., Feb. 5, 1915; s. Louis and Henrietta (Koenigsberg) H.; m. Nancy Givan, May 9, 1942; children—Douglas Richard, Laura James, Mary Hinda. B.S. magna cum laude (Kenyon prize), Coll. City N.Y., 1935; M.A. (Procter fellow), Princeton U., 1938; Ph.D., Princeton U., 1938; LL.D., City U. N.Y., 1961; D.Sc., Gustavus Adolphus Coll., 1963; Laureate Honoris Causa, U. Padua, 1965; D.Sc., Carleton U., Ottawa, Can., 1967, Seoul Nat. U., 1967; Honoris Causa, U. Clermont-Ferrnad, 1967; D.Rerum Naturalium honoris causa, Julius Maximilians U., Würzburg, W. Ger., 1982, Johannes Gutenberg U. Mainz (W. Ger.), 1983. Coffin fellow Gen. Electric Co., 1935-36; Harrison fellow U. Pa., 1939; instr. physics Princeton U., 1940-41, CCNY, 1941-42; physicist Norden Lab. Corp., 1943-46; asst. prof. physics Princeton U., 1946-50; assoc. prof. physics Stanford U., 1950-54, prof., 1954—, Max H. Stein prof. physics, 1971—, dir. high energy physics lab., 1967-74; dir. John Fluke Mfg. Co. Author: (with Robert Herman) High-Energy Electron Scattering Tables, 1960; Editor: Investigations in Physics, 1958-65, Electron Scattering and Nucleon Structure, 1963; Co-editor: Nucleon Structure, 1964; Asso. editor: Phys. Review, 1951-53; mem. editorial bd.: Review Sci. Instruments, 1953-55, Reviews of Modern Physics, 1958-61. Calif. Scientist of Year, 1959; co-recipient of Nobel prize in physics, 1961; Townsend Harris medal Coll. City N.Y., 1961; Guggenheim fellow, Geneva, Switzerland, 1958-59; Ford Found. fellow. Fellow Am. Phys. Soc., Phys. Soc. London; mem. Nat. Acad. Scis., Am. Acad. Arts and Scis., AAUP, Phi Beta Kappa, Sigma Xi. Subspecialty: High energy physics. Office: Stanford U Stanford CA 94305

HOGAN, EDWARD LEO, neurologist, neurochemist; b. Arlington, Mass., July 26, 1932; s. Patrick Francis and Margaret Mary (McSweeney) H.; m. Gail Manning, July 1, 1961; children—Patrick, Maryellen, Maura, Timothy, Michael. B.S. summa cum laude, Tufts U., 1953, M.D. magna cum laude, 1957. Diplomate Am. Bd. Psychiatry and Neurology. Intern Barnes Hosp., St. Louis, 1957-58; resident in medicine Peter Bent Brigham Hosp., Boston, 1958-59; resident in neurology Boston City Hosp., 1959-61, fellow in neurology, 1963-64; fellow in biochemistry Tufts U. Sch. Medicine, Boston, 1964-66; from asst. to assoc. prof. neurology Sch. Medicine, U. N.C., Chapel Hill, 1966-73; prof. neurology Med. U. S.C. Charleston, 1973—, chmn. dept., 1973—, dir. Muscular Dystrophy Assn. Clinic, 1978—; chmn. neurology B study sect. NIH, Washington, 1983—. Contbr. articles to profl. jours. Served to capt. U.S. Army, 1961-63. Research grantee. Fellow Am. Acad. Neurology; mem. Am. Soc. Biol. Chemists, Am. Neurol. Assn., Am. Soc. Neurochemistry, Internat. Soc. Neurochemistry. Current work: Composition and metabolism of cellular membranes of the nervous system and muscle with reference to the pathophysiology of demyelinating disease and muscular dystrophy. Subspecialties: Neurology; Neurochemistry. Home: 10 Legare St Charleston SC 29401 Office: Med Univ SC 171 Ashley Ave Charleston SC 29425

HOGAN, NEVILLE, mechanical engineer, roboticist. Assoc. prof. mech. engring. MIT, Cambridge. Subspecialty: Robotics. Office: MIT Dept Mech Engring Cambridge MA 02139

HOGAN, YVONNE HOLLAND, immunoparasitologist, biology educator; b. Bay City, Tex., Oct. 24, 1937; d. Andrew and Daisy (Revis) (McCoy)) Holl; m. John E. Perry II, May 3, 1962 (div. Sept. 1967); 1 son, John E. III; m. Booker T. Hogan, Jr., July 5, 1968 (div. 1974). B.S., Howard U., 1958, M.S., 1960, Ph.D., 1981. Grad. asst. Howard U., Washington, 1958-60; research biologist NIH, Bethesda, Md., 1961-62; bacteriologist Howard U. Med. Sch., Washington, 1962; biology tchr. Houston Ind. Sch. Dist., 1964-65; biology instr. Tex. So. U., Houston, 1965-69, asst. prof. biology, 1970-83, assoc. prof., 1983—; coordinator Tex. So. U. (MARC undergrad. honors program), 1981-83. MARC predoctoral fellow Nat. Inst. Gen. Med. Scis., NIH, 1977-81; Smith-Noirs scholar Howard U., 1959-60. Mem. Am. Inst. Biol. Sci., Tex. Acad. Scis., Sigma Xi, Beta Beta Beta, Beta Kappa Chi. Democrat. Roman Catholic. Current Work: Effect of trace metal contaminants on immune responses in rats infected with trypanosomes. Subspecialties: Parasitology; Immunobiology and immunology. Home: 5407 Burkett St Houston TX 77004 Office: Tex So U Dept Biology 3201 Wheeler Ave Houston TX 77004

HOGE, ARTHUR FRANKLIN, JR., oncologist, educator; b. Ft. Smith, Ark., Jan. 25, 1923; s. Arthur F. and Lilly Arabella (Boyd) H.; m. Barbara Standingbear, July 27, 1977; children by previous marriage: Rickert F., Libe, Arthur, Maurie, Elizabeth. B.S., Tulane U., 1945, M.D., 1949. Research fellow U. Okla. and Okla. Med. Research Found., 1971-73; intern, resident U. Md. and Bon Secours Host., Balt., 1949-51, 54-56; pvt. practice med. oncology, Ft. Smith, 1956-71; clin. and pathol. research U. Ark., Ft. Smith, 1961-71; chmn. dept. Ob-Gyn St. Edwards Hosp., Ft. Smith, 1970-71; prin. investigator, dir. Ark.-Okla. Cancer Program, 1969-71, Ark.-Okla. Cancer Program (Okla. Breast Cancer Demonstration Project), 1974-78; mem. cancer control intervention programs review com. NCI, 1977-80; prin. investigator Cancer Coop. Group N.W. Ark., 1979-81, Washington Regional Med. Center, 1980-81; staff St. Edwards Hosp., Ft. Smith, 1956-71, Sparks Regional Med. Center, Ft. Smith, 1956-71; cons. staff Crawford County Hosp., Van Buren, Ark., 1956-71; staff VA Hosp., Oklahoma City, 1971-78, Univ. Hosp., Oklahoma City, 1971-78; cons., lectr. Bapt. Med. Center, Oklahoma City, 1972-77; attending physician, assoc. mem. Okla. Med. Research Found., 1973-77; staff Children's Meml. Hosp., 1973-77, Presbyn. Hosp., Oklahoma City, 1974-77, Wash. Regional Med. Center., Fayetteville, Ark., 1977-81, Springdale Meml. Hosp., 1977-81, Rogers (Ark) Meml. Hosp., 1977-81, City of Faith Med. and Research Center, Tulsa, 1981—; assoc. prof. medicine Oral Roberts U., Tulsa, 1981—. Contbr. articles to profl. jours. Pres. Community Concers of Ark., 1965-69; pres. Noon Civics Club, 1965-66; pres. Ark. div. Am. Cancer Soc., 1969-70; mem. Arts Council Ft. Smith, 1965-71, others. Served to capt. U.S. Army, 1952-54. Fellow S.W. Surg. Congress, Am. Coll. Ob-Gyn.; mem. Am. Assn. Cancer Research, S.W. Oncology Group, Am. Soc. Clin Oncology, AMA, Okla. County Med. Soc., Okla. State Med. Soc., Stewart Wolf Soc., Okla. Gynecol. Soc., Gynecol. Soc. for Study of Breast Disease, others, Sigma Xi. Roman Catholic. Current Work: Clinical oncology and cancer immunology/endocrinology research. Subspecialties: Cancer research (medicine); Oncology. Office: 8181 S Lewis St Tulsa OK 74136

HOGG, DAVID CLARENCE, physicist; b. Vanguard, Sask., Can., Sept. 5, 1921; came to U.S., 1953, naturalized, 1964; s. Francis Sandison and Frances Katherine (Gadsby) H.; m. Jean E. MacMillan, Feb. 15, 1947; children—David Randal, Rebecca Jean. B.Sc., U. Western Ont. (Can.), London, 1949; M.Sc., McGill U., Montreal, Que., Can., 1951, Ph.D., 1953. With Bell Telephone Labs., 1953-77, head atmospheric physics research, 1966-72, head antenna and propagation research, Holmdel, N.J., 1972-77; chief environ. radiometry wave propagation lab. Environ. Research Lab., NOAA, Boulder, Colo., 1977-83, chief radio meteorology, 1983—. Research, numerous publs. on microwaves, optics, satellite communications and remote sensing; patentee microwave antennas. Served with Can. Army, 1940-45. Recipient Silver Medal award U.S. Dept. Commerce, 1983. Fellow IEEE (Disting. Achievement award Geosci. and Remote Sensing Soc. 1984); mem. AAAS, Nat. Acad. Engring., Union Radio Scientifique Internationale. Episcopalian. Subspecialty: Radiophysics. Office: NOAA WAve Propagation Lab Environ Research Lab Boulder CO 80302

HOGG, HOWARD CARL, economist; b. Union, Oreg., Aug. 24, 1935; s. Rhubein Clarance and Thelma Irene (Jenkins) H.; m. Akiko Takano, Apr. 16, 1962; children—Christopher Taro, Jeannine Hanako. B.S., Oreg. State U., 1958, M.S., 1959; Ph.D., U. Hawaii, 1965. Chief resource systems Dept. Agr., Washington, 1975-80; chief earth resources NASA, Washington, 1980-83, discipline scientist agristars, 1983-84; vis. fellow World Resources Inst., Washington, 1984—. Guest editor Geosci. and Remote Sensing, 1985. Contbr. articles to profl. jours. Served with U.S. Army, 1953-55, Korea. Mem. IEEE, Am. Agrl. Econs. Assn., Internat. Agrl. Econs. Assn. Republican. Current work: Role of remote sensing in monitoring globue resources. Subspecialty: Remote sensing (geoscience). Office: World Resources Inst 1735 New York St NW Washington DC 20006

HOGG, ROBERT VINCENT, JR., educator, mathematical statistician; b. Hannibal, Mo., Nov. 8, 1924; s. Robert Vincent and Isabelle Frances (Storrs) H.; m. Carolyn Joan Ladd, June 23, 1956; children—Mary Carolyn, Barbara Jean, Allen Ladd, Robert Mason. B.A., U. Ill., 1947; M.S., U. Iowa, 1948, Ph.D., 1950. Asst. prof. math. U. Iowa, Iowa City, 1950-56, asso. prof., 1956-62, prof. math., 1962-65, chmn. dept. statistics, prof. statistics, 1965—. Co-author: Introduction to Mathematical Statistics, 1959, 4th edit., 1978, Finite Mathematics and Calculus, 1974, Probability and Statistical Inference, 1977, 2d edit., 1983. Asso. editor: Am. Statistics, 1971-74, Jour. Am. Statis. Assn, 1978-80; Contbr. articles to profl. jours. Served with USNR, 1943-46. NIH research grantee, 1966-68, 75-78; NSF research grantee, 1969-74. Fellow Inst. Math. Statistics (program sec., exec. bd. 1968-74), Am. Statis. Assn. (pres. Iowa sect. 1962-63, council 1965-66, 73-74, vis. lectr. 1965-68, 77-84, chmn. tng. sect. 1973); mem. Math. Assn. Am. (pres. Iowa sect. 1964-65, gov. Iowa dist. 1971-74, vis. lectr. 1976-81), Internat. Statis. Inst., Sigma Xi (pres. Iowa chpt. 1970-71), Pi Kappa Alpha. Episcopalian (vestryman 1958-60, 66-68). Club: Rotarian. Subspecialty: Statistics. Home: Rural Route 6 Box 219A Iowa City IA 52240

HOGNESS, DAVID SWENSON, biochemistry educator; b. Oakland, Calif., Nov. 17, 1925; s. Thorfin Rusten and Phoebe (Swenson) H.; m. Judith Gore, Sept. 18, 1948; children: Peter Swenson, Christopher Gore. B.S., Calif. Inst. Tech., 1949, Ph.D., 1952. Prof. dept. biochemistry Stanford (Calif.) U. Sch. Medicine, 1966—. Served in USNR, 1944-46. Mem. Nat. Acad. Scis., Am. Acad. Arts and Scis. Subspecialties: Developmental biology; Genetics and genetic engineering (biology). Office: Stanford U Sch Medicine Stanford CA 94305

HOGNESS, JOHN RUSTEN, physician, association executive; b. Oakland, Calif., June 27, 1922; s. Thorfin R. and Phoebe (Swenson) H. Student, Haverford Coll., 1939-42, D.Sc. (hon.), 1973; B.S., U. Chgo., 1943, M.D., 1946; D.Sc. (hon.), Med. Coll. Ohio at Toledo, 1972; LL.D., George Washington U., 1973; D.Litt., Thomas Jefferson U., 1980. Diplomate: Am. Bd. Internal Medicine. Intern medicine Presbyn. Hosp., N.Y.C., 1946-47, asst. resident, 1949-50; chief resident King County Hosp., Seattle, 1950-51; asst. U. Wash. Sch. Medicine, 1950-52, Am. Heart Assn. research fellow, 1951-52, mem. faculty, 1954-71, prof. medicine, 1964-71, med. dir. univ. hosp., 1958-63; dean U. Wash. Sch. Medicine (Med. Sch.), chmn. bd. health scis., 1964-69, exec. v.p. univ., 1969-70; dir. Health Scis. Center, 1970-71; pres. Inst. Medicine, Nat. Acad. Scis., 1971-74, mem., 1971—; prof. medicine George Washington U., 1972-74, disting. professional lectr. dept. medicine; pres. U. Wash., Seattle, 1974-79, prof. medicine, 1974-79; pres. Assn. Acad. Health Centers, 1979—; mem. commr.'s adv. com. on exempt orgns. IRS, 1969-71; mem. adv. com. for environ. scis. NSF, 1970-71; adv. com. to dir. NIH, 1970-71; mem. Nat. Cancer

Adv. Bd., 1972-76, Nat. Sci. Bd., 1976-82; trustee China Med. Bd.; mem. selection com. for Rockefeller pub. service awards Princeton U., 1976-82; chmn. med. injury compensation study steering com. Inst. Medicine, Nat. Acad. Scis.; mem. council for biol. scis. Pritzker Sch. Medicine, U. Chgo., 1977—; chmn. adv. panel on cost-effectiveness of med. techs. Office Tech. Assessment, U.S. Congress, 1978-80; mem. Council Health Care Tech., HEW; adv. panel for study fin. grad. med. edn. Dept. Health and Human Services, 1980—; chmn. study sect. health care tech. assessment Nat. Ctr. Health Services Research and Health Care Tech. Assessment, 1985—. Contbr. articles to profl. jours. Served with AUS, 1947-49. Recipient Disting. Service award Med. Alumni Assn. U. Chgo., 1966, Profl. Achievement award Alumni Assn. U. Chgo., 1973; Convocation medal Am. Coll. Cardiology, 1973; Cartwright medal Columbia U. Coll. Physicians and Surgeons, 1978. Fellow ACP, Am. Acad. Arts and Scis.; mem. Assn. Am. Physicians, Assn. Am. Med. Colls. (exec. council, chmn.-elect council of deans 1968-69), Inst. of Medicine, Nat. Acad. Scis.; Alpha Omega Alpha. Current Work: Full-time administration. Subspecialties: Endocrinology; Internal medicine. Office: 11 DuPont Circle Washington DC 20036

HOGNESTAD, EIVIND, civil engineer; b. Time, Norway, July 17, 1921; came to U.S., 1947, naturalized, 1954; s. Hans E. and Dorthea (Norheim) H.; m. Andree S. Hognestad, Apr. 4, 1964; children: Hans E., Marta Marie, Kirsten Andree. M.Sc., Norwegian Tech. U., 1947, D.Sc., 1952; M.Sc., U. Ill., 1949. Research asst. to asso. prof. U. Ill., 1947-53; mgr. structural devel. sect. Portland Cement Assn., Skokie, Ill., 1953-66, dir. engring. devel. dept., 1966-74, dir. tech. and sci. devel., 1974—; cons. offshore devel. petroleum fields various oil cos. and contractors., condr. field and lab. investigations of concrete structures. Contbr. to: Ency. Brit, 1966, also over 100 articles on structural engring. and concrete tech. to tech. jours. Served with Royal Norwegian Navy, 1944-46. Fellow Am. Concrete Inst. (chmn. com. 357 offshore concrete structures, Wason medal 1956, Henry L. Kennedy award 1971, hon. mem. 1976, Alfred E. Lindau award 1977, Delmar L. Bloem award 1980), ASCE (past chmn. adminstrv. com. on masonry and reinforced concrete, Research prize 1956, Chgo. Civil Engr. of Yr. award 1977, Arthur J. Boase award 1981); mem. Nat. Acad. Engring., Prestressed Concrete Inst. o3(past chmn. tech. activities com.), European Concrete Com., Internat. Prestressing Fedn., Structural Engring. Soc. P.R. (hon.), Norwegian Acad. Engring., Royal Norwegian Acad. Sci. Subspecialty: Civil engineering. Home: 2222 Prairie St Glenview IL 60025 Office: 5420 Old Orchard Rd Skokie IL 60077

HOKAMA, YOSHITSUGI, immunopathologist, immunologist; b. Niulii, Kohala, Hawaii, Oct. 25, 1926; s. Royei and Kamada (Matsudo) H.; m. Haruko Yoshimoto, Feb. 3, 1951; children: Jon Keith Yoshimoto, Julie Lynn R. Yoshimoto. A.B., UCLA, 1951, M.A. in Microbiology, 1953, Ph.D., 1957. Jr. research, asst. research microbiologist UCLA, 1952-66; assoc. prof. Calif. State U., 1964-66; assoc. prof. pathology U. Hawaii, 1966-68, prof., 1968—; cons. Courtland Labs., Los Angeles, 1964-66; cons. immunologist, assoc. dir. SKCL-Accupath Labs., Honolulu, 1974—. Author: Immunology, Immunopathology, Basic Concepts, 1982; Contbr. articles to profl. jours. Served with AUS, 1945-48. Nat. Cancer Inst. Grantee, 1968-75—; FDA grantee, 1979-82; NOAA grantee, 1979-81; USAMRDC grantee, 1985—. Mem. Am. Soc. Microbiologists, Am. Assn. Immunologists, Am. Soc. Pathologists, Reticuloendothelial Soc., N.Y. Acad. Scis., Internat. Soc. Toxicology, Hawaii Soc. Pathologists, Sigma Xi. Episcopalian. Current Work: Acute phase protein (C-Reactive Protein); immunology and physiology of low Molecular Weight Marine toxins. Subspecialties: Immunobiology and immunology; Cancer research (medicine).

HOLADAY, JOHN WALDRON, neuropharmacologist; b. N.Y.C., June 9, 1945; s. Beverley Eli and Alta (Waldron) H.; m. Camilla Canty, June 1, 1968. B.S., U. Ala-Tuscaloosa, 1966, M.S., 1969; Ph.D., U. Calif.-San Francisco, 1977. Research chemist Walter Reed Army Inst. Research, Washington, 1969-74, research pharmacologist, 1976-81, chief neuropharmacology br., 1981—; assoc. prof. Uniformed Services U. Health Scis., Bethesda, Md., 1979—. Contbr. 200 articles to profl. jours. Served to capt. U.S. Army, 1969-72. Recipient U.S. Army Sci. Conf. award Dept. Def., 1980, U.S. Army Research and Devel. Achievement award, 1980, 84. Mem. Am. Soc. Pharmacology and Exptl. Therapeutics (Dean N. Calvert award 1977), Shock Soc. (treas.), Am. Coll. Neuropsychopharmacology, N.Y. Acad. Scis., Internat. Narcotics Research Conf., Sigma Xi. Patentee in narcotic antagonists in therapy of shock and spinal injury, thyrotropin releasing hormone as CNS stimulant and therapy of shock. Current Work: Role of endogenous opiates and other neuro-modulators in the etiology of circulatory shock, spinal trauma, stress reactions, seizure disorders, depression, temperature dysregulation, neuroimmunomodulation. Subspecialties: Neuropharmacology; Neuroendocrinology. Home: 4 Vallingby Circle Rockville MD 20850 Office: Neuropharmacology Br Dept Med Neuroscience Div Neuropsychiatry Walter Reed Army Inst Research Washington DC 20012

HOLCOMB, DAVID NELSON, chemist; b. Sioux City, Iowa, Sept. 12, 1936; s. Hollis N. and Kathryn J. H.; m. Doris M. Keener, May 1, 1966; children—Timothy, Mark, Samuel, Kathryn. B.S., U. Nebr., 1958; Ph.D., U. Ill., 1962; M.B.A., Roosevelt U., Chgo., 1977. Research scientist U.S. Dept. Agr., Phila., 1964-66; research scientist Kraft Inc., Glenview, Ill., 1966-70, group leader phys. chemistry, 1970-80, mgr. basic food sci., 1980—; adj. prof. Roosevelt U., 1978—, Ill. Inst. Tech., Chgo., 1984. Editor: Food Microstructure, 1982-84. Mem. adv. bd. Truman Coll., Chgo., 1980-84; mem. adv. bd. Ill. J.E.T.S., Champaign, 1982-84; precinct chmn. Niles Twp. Republican Party, Morton Grove, Ill., 1979-84. NSF fellow, 1962-64. Mem. AAAS, Am. Chem. Soc., Inst. Food Technologists, Soc. Rheology, Am. Soc. Quality Control, Sigma Xi, Beta Gamma Sigma. Lutheran. Current work: Food microstructure and rheology; flavor; protein-science management. Subspecialties: Biophysical chemistry; Food science and technology. Home: 8615 Callie St Morton Grove IL 60053 Office: Kraft Inc Research and Devel 801 Waukegan Rd Glenview IL 60025

HOLCOMB, GORDON ERNEST, plant pathologist; b. Monroe, Wis., July 6, 1932; s. Ernest and Florence (Henneman) H.; m. Alice Harriet Duff, Jan. 25, 1964; children: Janette Lynn, Amy Florence. B.S., U. Wis.-Platteville, 1959; Ph.D., U. Wis.-Madison, 1965. Research asst. U. Wis., 1959-65; asst. prof. plant pathology La. State U., 1965-70, asso. prof., 1970-78, prof., 1978—. Contbr. articles to profl. jours. Served with USAF, 1951-55. Recipient Dave Feathers award Am. Camellia Soc., 1982, 83, 84. Mem. AAAS, Am. Phytopath. Soc., Am. Inst. Biol. Scis., La. Acad. Scis., Sigma Xi. Current Work: Diseases of ornamental plants and turf, mycology, plant cell culture and turfgrass viruses. Subspecialties: Plant pathology; Plant cell and tissue culture. Home: 779 Rodney Dr Baton Rouge LA 70808 Office: Dept Plant Pathology and Crop Physiology La State U Baton Rouge LA 70803

HOLCOMBE, CRESSIE EARL, JR., ceramic engineer, researcher; b. Anderson, S.C., Dec. 18, 1945; s. Cressie Earl Sr. and Blanche Elizabeth (Keaton) H.; m. Catherine Joselyn Brockman, Dec. 27, 1966; children—Justin Kent, Eric Benjamin. B.S., Clemson U., 1966, M.S., 1967; postgrad. U. Mo.-Rolla, 1973. Assoc. devel. engr. Union Carbide Corp., Oak Ridge, 1967-72, devel. engr., 1972-76, mem. devel. staff, 1977-80, mem. advanced devel. staff, 1980-84; advanced devel. staff Martin Marietta Energy Systems, Inc., Oak Ridge, 1984—; founder ZYP Coatings Inc., Oak Ridge, 1982—. Author: (with others) Metallurgical Coatings, Vol. 1, 1976. Contbr. articles to profl. jours., unclassified spl. tech. reports for AEC/Dept. Energy. Patentee on refractory materials, metals and ceramics. Recipient Top Twenty award Materials Engring. mag., 1984; scholar Vol. Cement Co., 1964, 3-M Co., 1965; indsl. fellow Cabot Corp., 1966. Mem. Am. Ceramic Soc., Nat. Inst. Ceramic Engrs. (cert.), Keramos, Sigma Xi, Tau Beta Pi. Republican. Methodist. Current work: Refractory ceramics and metals; synthesis, fabrication, and properties; crystallography; physical and surface chemistry; high-temperature coatings. Subspecialties: Ceramic engineering; Ceramics. Home: 440 Sugarwood Dr Farragut TN 37922 Office: Martin Marietta Energy Systems Inc PO Box Y Bldg 9202 Oak Ridge TN 37830

HOLDER, DAVID GORDON, geneticist; b. Louisville, Miss., Oct. 18, 1943; s. Earl Jackson and Annie Belle (Williamson) H.; m. Sandra Frances Eayes, June 10, 1967; 1 child, Amy Kaylynnda. B.S., Miss. State U., 1965, M.S., 1967; Ph.D., Purdue U., 1971. Post-doctorate research assoc. Miss. State U., 1971-73; geneticist U.S. Sugar Corp., Clewiston, Fla., 1973—. Contbr. articles to profl. jours. Mem. Am. Soc. Agronomy, Crop Sci. Soc. Am., Am. Soc. Sugar Cane Technologists, Internat. Soc. Sugar Cane Technologists. Baptist. Lodge: Rotary. Current work: Sugar cane breeding and genetics. Subspecialties: Plant genetics; Agronomy. Office: US Sugar Corp Research Dept PO Drawer 1207 Clewiston FL 33440

HOLDER, WALTER DALTON, JR., general surgeon, oncology researcher; b. Glendive, Mont., May 3, 1945; s. Walter Dalton and Valeria Marie (Meyer) H.; m. Frances Lou Smith, June 7, 1969; children: Jane Elizabeth, Emily Blair. B.A. in Chemistry and Zoology, U. N.C., Chapel Hill, 1967, M.D., 1971. Diplomate: Am. Bd. Surgery.; Lic. physician, N.C., Calif. Intern in surgery Barnes Hosp., Washington U., St. Louis, 1971-72; research assoc. Viral Biology Br., Nat. Cancer Inst., Bethesda, Md., 1972-74; NIH postdoctoral fellow in surgery Duke U. Med. Center, Durham, N.C., 1974-76, resident in surgery, 1976-81, Am. Cancer Soc. clin. fellow, 1976-78; asst. prof. surgery Stanford U., 1981—; cons.; researcher surg. oncology. Contbr. articles to profl. jours. Served with USPHS, 1972-74. Recipient Deborah C. Leary Research award, 1971. Fellow ACS; mem. Am. Soc. Microbiology, Am. Assn. Cancer Research, Electromicroscopy Soc. Am., Soc. Surg. Oncology, Am. Soc. Clin. Oncology, Santa Clara County Med. Soc., Sigma Xi, Alpha Epsilon Delta. Current Work: Oncology, cell study, cancer research, immunology. Subspecialties: Surgery; Oncology. Home: 863 Highland Circle Los Altos CA 94022 Office: Stanford University Medical Center S067 Stanford CA 94305

HOLDREN, GEORGE R., JR., geochemistry researcher, educator; b. Philipsburg, Pa., Nov. 18, 1949; s. George R. and Joan Hallam (Clarke) H.; m. Nancy Susan McLean, Jan. 27, 1978; children—George Owen, Richard Stuart. B.S., Carnegie Mellon U., 1971; Ph.D., Johns Hopkins U., 1977. Postdoctoral fellow Yale U., New Haven, 1976-78; asst. prof. geochemistry U. Rochester, N.Y., 1978—. Contbr. articles to profl. jours. Mem. Geochem. Soc., Am. Soc. Limnology and Oceanography, AAAS, Am. Geophys. Union. Subspecialties: Geochemistry; Environmental chemistry. Home: 405 Rockingham St Rochester NY 14620 Office: Dept Geological Scis Univ Rochester NY 14627

HOLECEK, DALE ROBERT, technical administrator, physical chemist; b. Rapid City, S.D., Sept. 10, 1949; s. Charles Harry and Nora Borghild (Siverson) H.; m. Faye Louise Susag, June 19, 1971; children—Preston Reid, Nicole Dawn, Ian Charles. B.A., U. Minn.-Morris, 1971; Ph.D., U. Colo., 1975; postdoctoral fellow UCLA, 1975-77. Chemist, sr. chemist Shell Devel. Co., Houston, 1977-80, sr. supr. analysis dept., 1981-83, sr. supr. resins dept., 1983-85, mgr. devel. products, 1985—; instr. Quality Edn., Houston, 1983-84. Contbr. articles to profl. publs. Funds chmn. West Harris County Ambulance Squad, Katy, Tex., 1979, pres., 1980-81; pres. Lutheran Br. Assn., Harris County, 1981—. Mem. Am. Chem. Soc., Sigma Xi. Republican. Current work: Nuclear magnetic resonance spectroscopy and imaging, active first industrial applications nuclear magnetic resonance imaging, polymer chemistry, epoxy resins, new materials for printed circuit boards, adhesives, pipe, construction applications. Subspecialties: Nuclear magnetic resonance; Polymer chemistry. Office: One Shell Plaza Houston TX 77082

HOLLAAR, LEE ALLEN, university computer science educator; b. Litchfield, Minn., Mar. 9, 1947; s. Garritt A. and Lyma Marie (Geiger) H.; m. Audrey Mack, Nov. 26, 1968; B.S.E.E., Ill. Inst. Tech., 1969; M.S. in Computer Sci., U. Ill.-Urbana-Champaign, 1974, Ph.D. in Computer Sci., 1975. Registered profl. engr., Calif. Coordinator engring. Datalogics Inc., Chgo., 1969-71, 72-74; design engr. Automation Tech. Inc., Champaign, Ill., 1971-72; grad. research asst. U. Ill.-Champaign, 1970-75, asst. prof. aviation and computer sci., 1975-77, asst. prof. computer sci., sr. research engr., 1977-80; assoc. prof. computer sci. U. Utah, Salt Lake City, 1980—, assoc. chmn. dept., 1983—; cons. in field. Contbr. articles to profl. jours. NASA grantee 1979, 80, 82; IBM Corp. grantee, 1979, 83. Sr. mem. IEEE; mem. Assn. Computing Machinery. AIAA, Inst. Nav., Aircraft Owners and Pilots Assn., Balloon Fedn. Am., Sigma Xi, Phi Kappa Phi, Eta Kappa Nu. Current work: Information retrieval; specialized VLSI systems. Subspecialty: Information systems, storage, and retrieval (computer science). Office: U Utah Dept Computer Sci 3160 Merrill Engring Bldg Salt Lake City UT 84112

HOLLAND, MAJORIE MIRIAM, biology educator, researcher; b. Boston, Aug. 18, 1947; d. Bertram Holbrook and Margaret Florence (Hill) H.; m. Russell F. Sackett, May 27, 1972 (div. 1983). A.B. in Botany, Conn. Coll., 1969; M.A. in Ecology, Smith Coll., 1974; Ph.D. in Botany, U. Mass., 1977. Tchr. biology Mountain Sch., Vershire, Vt., 1969-70; Dover-Sherborn Regional High Sch., Mass., 1970-72; teaching fellow Smith Coll., Northampton, Mass., 1972-76; vis. asst. prof. Amherst Coll., Mass., 1976-78; exec. dir. Water Supply Citizens Adv. Com., Hadley, Mass., 1978-80; asst. prof. Coll. of New Rochelle, N.Y., 1980—. Co-author: Stone Walls and Sugar Maples, 1979; also articles. Assoc. mem. Conservation Commn., Northampton, 1975-80; active Northampton Planning Bd., 1977-80; bd. dirs. Appalachian Mountain Club, 1982-84; bd. advisors Mountain Sch. program Milton Acad., Vershire, 1983—. Recipient Stewardship award Mass. Steering Com. on Connecticut River, 1980; grantee Connecticut River Watershed Council, 1981, 82, 84, Nature Conservancy, 1983, 84. Current work: Wetlands ecology, especially plant ecology in tidal brackish marshes and old riverine oxbows. Subspecialties: Ecology (biology); Resource management. Office: Dept of Biology Coll of New Rochelle Castle Pl New Rochelle NY 10801

HOLLAND, ROBERT LOUIS, aerospace engineer; b. Athens, Ala., June 6, 1931; s. Aubrey Eli and Ruth Marie (Daniel) H.; m. Nancy Hill Hagood, Aug. 30, 1955; children: Neysa Sue, James Brandon. B.S., Athens Coll., 1957; M.A., U. Ala., 1967. Asst. prof. math. Athens (Ala.) State Coll., 1953-55; indsl. engr. Wolverine Tube, Decatur, Ala., 1956-61; aerospace engr. NASA, Huntsville, Ala., 1961—, mathematician, 1961-63, br. chief, 1965-75, space scientist, 1975—. Contbr. articles to profl. jours.; editor: Athenian newspaper, 1951-52. Chmn. Tenn. Valley Old Time Fiddlers, 1967. Served with U.S. Army, 1951-53. Mem. Jr. C. of C. (Athens chmn. 1964), Soc. Indsl. and Applied Math. Democrat. Developer gravity gradiometer, 1969. Current Work: Numerical analysis for weather prediction, solar activity prediction and its affect on weather. Subspecialties: Applied mathematics; Astronautics. Home: 609 Sudie Athens AL 35611 Office: Marshall Space Flight Ctr Huntsville AL 35812

HOLLANDER, LEWIS E., JR., physicist, consultant; b. Woodmere, N.Y., June 6, 1930; s. Lewis E. and Alice (Clark) H.; m. Hanne Weisse Olesen, Oct. 8, 1967; children—James W., Lewis S., Heather A., Alexandra, Ellen H., Lewis E. III. B.S., Adelphi U., 1951; Ph.D., Case Western Res. U., 1965. Sr. scientist Victoreen Instruments Co., 1955-57; research scientist Lockheed Missiles Corp., 1957-61; dir. solid state lab. Endevco Corp., Los Altos, Calif., 1961-65; dir. research, sec., treas. Integrated Transducers, Guynabo, P.R., 1965-68; cons. on solid state physics, Powell Butte, Oreg., 1968-83, Terrebonne, Oreg., 1983—; pres., chmn. bd. dirs. Green Mansions, Inc., 1964—; pres. LL, Inc., 1975. Author: Successful Endurance Riding. Contbr. articles to profl. jours. Patentee in field. Served to lt. (j.g.) USN, 1951-55. Fellow Am. Psychical Soc.; mem. Am. Phys. Soc., Am. Aging Assn. (nat. bd. dirs.), Am. Endurance Riding Conf. (nat. reserve champion endurance horse rider, 1973, v.p.). Subspecialties: Condensed matter physics; Biophysics (biology). Home and Office: 10225 NW 27th St Terrebonne OR 97753

HOLLANDER, MILTON BERNARD, corp. exec.; b. Bayonne, N.J., Nov. 29, 1928; s. Harry and Lena (Hutner) H.; m. Betty Ruth Grodberg, June 6, 1952; children—Eva Lynn, J. Steven, Aaron Phillip, Joel Daniel. B.S., Purdue U., 1951; M.S., Mass. Inst. Tech., 1953; Ph.D., Columbia, 1959. Dir. engring. center Am. Machine & Foundry Co., Springdale, Conn., 1956-67; v.p. tech. Am.-Standard, Inc., N.Y.C., 1967-72; chmn. bd. Gulf & Western Invention Devel. Corp., N.Y.C., 1975—; v.p. tech. Gulf & Western Industries, Inc., N.Y.C., 1972—; dir. PolyGulf Corp., Bklyn., 1973—; cons. electronics lab. Columbia U., 1955-57. Author tech. papers temperature measurement, metal cutting, instrumentation. Com. chmn. local Boy Scouts Am. Served with C.E. AUS, 1946-48, Korea. Research fellow Mass. Inst. Tech., 1952-53; duPont research fellow Columbia U., 1955-57; research fellow Am. Soc. Tool and Mfg. Engrs., 1954-55; recipient Outstanding Alumnus award Purdue U., 1972. Mem. ASME, Am. Welding Soc., Indsl. Research Inst., Sigma Xi. Patentee in field. Current Work: Research management, automated equipment; energy storage; energy conversion. Office: 1 Gulf & Western Plaza New York NY 10023

HÖLLDOBLER, BETHOLD KARL, zoology educator; b. Erling-Andechs, Fed. Republic Germany, June 25, 1936; came to U.S., 1973; s. Karl and Maria (Russmann) H.; m. Friederike Maria Probst, Feb. 9, 1980; children—Jakob, Stefan, Sebastian. Dr. rer. nat., U. Wurzburg, 1965; Dr. habil., U. Frankfurt, 1969; M.A.S. (hon.), Harvard U., 1973. Prof. zoology U. Frankfurt, 1970-72; prof. biology Harvard U., Cambridge, Mass., 1973—, Alexander Agassiz prof., 1982—; mem. psychobiology panel NSF, 1984—. Co-editor Jour. Behavioral Ecology and Sociobiology, 1976—. Fellow Deutsche Akademie der Naturforscher (Leopoldina), Am. Acad. Sci., AAAS. Current work: Animal communication and orientation; behavioral organization of territoriality and aggression; ecology and organization of insect societies; sociobiology. Subspecialties: Behavioral ecology; Ethology. Office: MCZ Labs Harvard U Cambridge MA 02138

HOLLEMAN, WILLIAM H., biochemist; b. Jamestown, Mich., Aug. 18, 1940; s. Hilbert D. and Norma Beatrice (Freeman) H.; m. Mary Elizabeth Roters, June 15, 1963; children—William Keith, Thomas Edward. B.A., Hope Coll., 1962; Ph.D., Mich. State U., 1966. Sr. biochemist Abbott Labs., North Chicago, Ill., 1966-72, group leader protein isolation, 1972-76, head sect. antithrombosis, 1977-79, chmn. dept. biochemistry, 1979-81, chmn. cardiovascular dept., 1981—; lectr. Harvard U. Med. Sch., Boston, 1983-84. Contbr. articles to profl. publs. Patentee in field. Chmn., Gurnee Ch. Bd., Ill., 1977-80; mem. Libertyville Sch. Bd. Dist. 68, Ill., 1977-83; chmn. Ill. Project for Sch. Reform, Libertyville, 1984. Mem. Am. Soc. Biol. Chemists, Sigma Xi. Current work: Design of agents to treat cardiovascular disease processes; enzymology of renin and angiotensin converting enzyme. Subspecialties: Biochemistry (medicine); Drug design. Home: 800 Timber Ln Libertyville IL 60048 Office: Abbott Labs Abbott Park IL 60064

HOLLENBERG, PAUL FREDERICK, biochemist, educator; b. Phila., Sept. 18, 1942; s. Frederick Henry and Catherine (Dentzer) H.; m. Emily Elizabeth Vanootighem, May 6, 1967; children: Kathryn Mary, David Paul. B.S. in Chemistry, Wittenberg U., Springfield, Ohio, 1964; M.S., U. Mich., 1966, Ph.D. in Biol. Chemistry, 1969. Teaching asst. in biochemistry U. Mich., Ann Arbor, 1964-69, postdoctoral fellow in biochemistry, 1969, U. Ill., Urbana, 1969-72; asst. prof. biochemistry Northwestern U. Med. Sch., Chgo., 1972-80, assoc. prof. pathology and pharmacology, 1980-81, assoc. prof. pathology and molecular biology, 1981-84, prof., 1984—. Contbr. articles to profl. jours. Schweppe Found. fellow, 1974-77; USPHS grantee, 1974—. Mem. AAAS, Am. Assn. Cancer Research, Am. Chem. Soc., Am. Soc. Biol. Chemists, Am. Soc. Pharmacology and Exptl. Therapeutics, Biophys. Soc., N.Y. Acad. Scis., Sigma Xi, Phi Kappa Phi, Phi Lambda Upsilon. Current Work: Mechanisms of enzyme action, chemical carcinogenesis and xenobiotic toxicity. Subspecialties: Biochemistry (medicine); Toxicology (medicine). Home: 3811 Louise St Skokie IL 60076 Office: Dept Pathology Northwestern U Med Sch 303 E Chicago Ave Chicago IL 60611

HOLLEY, CHARLES DEWAYEN, medical educator, researcher, psychologist; b. Borger, Tex., Dec. 26, 1945; s. James Wesley HOlley and Thelma Pearl (Crenshaw) Sparkman; m. b. Penny Lynn Barnes, Apr. 20, 1966; children: Shane Lee, Shawn DeWayne. B.S., Am. Tech. U., 1975; M.Ed., West Tex. State U., 1976; Ph.D., Tex. Christian U., 1979. Cert. psychologist, Tex. Research asst. West Tex. State U., 1975-76; research assoc. Tex. Christian U., 1976-79; sr. analyst Data Design Labs., Arlington, Va., 1979-80; asst. prof. med. edn., dir. evaluation services, acting dir. acad. info. systems Tex. Coll. Osteo. Medicine, 1980—; adj. asst. prof. basic health scis. North Tex. sTate U.; adj. asst. prof. math. Tex. Christian U.; cons. in field. Author: Performance Appraisal in Medical Schools, 1983; editor: Spatial Learning Strategies, 1983. Coach basketball team, Ft. Worth, 1981-83. Served to maj. U.S. Army, 1966-74; Served to maj. USAR, 1974—. Recipient 1st place award for article Soc. Motivational Exptl. Psychology, 1978; Nat. Inst. Edn. grantee, 1979; Dallas Ind. Sch. Dist. grantee, 1981; Am. Osteo. Assn. grantee, 1982. Mem. Am. Psychol. Assn., Southwestern Soc. Multivariate Psychology (v.p. 1979-80), Am. Ednl. Research Assn., Res. Officers Assn., Southwestern Ednl. Research Assn. Subspecialties: Cognition; Statistics. Home: 4832 Lubbock Fort Worth TX 76115 Office: Tex Coll Osteo Medicine Camp Bowie at Montgomery Fort worth TX 76107

HOLLEY, ROBERT WILLIAM, educator, scientist; b. Urbana, Ill., Jan. 28, 1922; s. Charles E. and Viola (Wolfe) H.; m. Ann Dworkin, Mar. 3, 1945; 1 son, Frederick. A.B., U. Ill., 1942; Ph.D., Cornell U., 1947. Am. Chem. Soc. fellow State Coll. Wash., 1947-48; asst. prof., then asso. prof. organic chemistry N.Y. State Agr. Expt. Sta., Cornell U., 1948-57; research chemist plant, soil and nutrition lab. U.S. Dept. Agr., Cornell U., 1957-64; prof. biochemistry Cornell U., 1964-69, chmn. dept. biochemistry, 1965-66; resident fellow Salk Inst. Biol. Studies, La Jolla, Calif., 1968—; mem. biochemistry study sect. NIH, 1962-66; vis. fellow Salk Inst. Biol. Studies; vis. prof. Scripps Clinic and Research Found., La Jolla, 1966-67. Recipient Distinguished Service award U.S. Dept. Agr., 1965, Albert Lasker award basic med. research, 1965; U.S. Steel Found. award in molecular biology Nat. Acad. Scis., 1967; Nobel prize for medicine and physiology, 1968; Guggenheim fellow Calif. Inst. Tech., 1955-56. Fellow AAAS; mem. Am. Acad. Arts and Scis., Am. Soc. Biol. Chemists, Am. Chem. Soc., Nat. Acad. Scis., Phi Beta Kappa, Sigma Xi. Current Work: Control of growth of normal and malignant cells. Subspecialty: Cell and tissue culture. Home: 7381 Rue Michael La Jolla CA 92037 Office: PO Box 85800 San Diego CA 92138

HOLLIS, BRUCE WARREN, nutrition educator; b. Elyria, Ohio, May 29, 1951; s. Warren Eugene and Evelyn Katherine (JaBusch) H.; m. Betsy Eberle, Aug. 16, 1980. B.Sc., Ohio State U., 1973, M.Sc., 1976; Ph.D. U. Guelph, Ont., 1979. Postdoctoral fellow Case Western Res. U., Cleve., 1979-82, asst. prof. nutrition, 1982—; acad. cons. Immuno Nuclear Corp., Stillwater, Minn., 1982—. Contbr. articles to profl. jours. Recipient NIH Nat. Research Service award, 1980, NIH Career Devel. award, 1982. Mem. Am. Soc. Bone and Mineral Research, Endocrine Soc., Am. Inst. Nutrition, N.Y. Acad. Sci., Sigma Xi. Current work: Investigation of nutritional requirements of newborn infant, especially the preterm infant, with emphasis on calcium metabolism. Subspecialties: Biochemistry (medicine); Obstetrics and gynecology. Home: 4931 N Barton Rd North Ridgeville OH 44039 Office: Case Western Res U Dept Nutrition Cleveland OH 44106

HOLLIS, JOHN PERCY, JR., microbiologist, plant pathologist, pest control co. exec.; b. Jennings, Okla., Nov. 1, 1981; s. John Percy and Eva Francis (Ham) H.; m. Mary Catharine Lee Billings, Sept. 14, 1943; children: Teresa Sue, Jan Claire, Barbara Ann, Megan Elizabeth, John Wesley. Ph.D., U. Nebr., 1949. Asst. plant pathologist Conn. Agr. Experiment Sta., New Haven, 1948-49; asst. prof. U. Mo., Columbia, 1949-53; plant pathologist U. Fruit Co., La Lima, Honduras, 1953-54; prof. plant pathology La. State U., Baton Rouge, 1954—; pres. Gulfpestco., Biotron; dir. research Biotron Tropical Agrl. Experiment Sta., Belize. Contbr. articles to profl. jours. Served to 2d lt. USAAF, 1943-45. Decorated Air medal; Sr. Fulbright research scholar Kenya, 1961-62; NATO sr. fellow, 1973. Mem. Am. Phytopath. Soc., Helminthological Soc., Sigma Xi. Current Work: Nematode swarming rice nematode damage, nematicide, herbicide, fungicide research by contract; crawfish research, crawfish farming. Subspecialty: Plant pathology.

HOLLISTER, LEO EDWARD, physician; b. Cin., Dec. 3, 1920; s. William B. and Ruth V. (Appling) H.; m. Louise Agnes Palmieri, Feb. 1, 1950; children—Stephen, David, Cynthia, Matthew. B.S., U. Cin., 1941, M.D., 1943. Diplomate: Am. Bd. Internal Medicine. Intern Boston City Hosp., 1944, VA Hosp., San Francisco, 1947-49; chief med. service Palo Alta (Calif.) VA Hosp., 1952-60, asso. chief of staff, 1960-70, med. investigator, 1970-76, dir. psychopharmacology research, 1976-82, sr. med. investigator, 1982—; prof. medicine, psychiatry, and pharmacology Stanford U. Sch. Medicine, 1970—. Contbr. over 300 articles to sci. jours., chpts. to books; author 3 books in field. Served to comdr. USNR, 1945-46, 50-51. Recipient Meritorious Service award VA, 1960; William S. Middleton award, 1966; Taylor Manor award, 1974; Menninger award, 1985. Mem. Am. Soc. Clin. Pharmacology and Therapeutics (pres. 1972), Am. Coll. Neuropsychopharmacology (pres. 1974), Collegium Internationale Neuropsychopharmacologicum (pres. 1978). Presbyterian. Current Work: Drug treatment of mental disorders; biol. aspects of mental disorders. Subspecialty: Neuropharmacology. Home: 1800 University Ave Palo Alto CA 94301 Office: 3801 Miranda Ave Palo Alto CA 94304

HOLLOWAY, CAROLINE TOBIA, biochemistry educator; b. N.Y.C., July 29, 1937; d. Martin Bartholomew and Margaret (Giolito) Tobia; m. Peter William Holloway, Oct. 25, 1963 (div. 1981); children: Philippa Elizabeth, Kenneth William. B.S., CCNY, 1959; Ph.D., Duke U., 1964. Research assoc. Shell Agrl. Chems., Sittingbourne, Kent, Eng., 1964-67, Duke U., Durham, N.C., 1967-69; Research assoc. U. Va., Charlottesville, 1975-76, research asst. prof., 1976—; ad hoc reviewer Lipids, 1980—. Pres., founder. Jackson Via Community Edn. Program, Charlottesville, Va., 1977; mem. Charlottesville (Va.) Sch. Bd., 1978-81, Spl. Edn. Adv. Com., Charlottesville, 1979-81. First

Milstead research fellow, 1964-67. Mem. Am. Soc. Biol. Chemists, Phi Beta Kappa. Roman Catholic. Current Work: Regulation of membrane properties in animals: in particular the way lipid components of membranes can influence membrane function, nutritional aspects of dietary lipid and their role in cardiovascular disease. Subspecialties: Biochemistry (medicine); Nutrition (medicine). Office: U Va Sch Medicine Dept Biochemistry Charlottesville VA 22908

HOLLOWAY, DENNIS ROBERT, architect, urban designer, solar architecture researcher; b. Owosso, Mich., Mar. 26, 1943; s. Robert Edwin and Antonia Louise H.; children: Adam David, Daniel Robert, Lauren Denise. B. Arch., U. Mich., 1966; M. Arch. in Urban Design, Harvard U., 1967; postgrad. (Fulbright scholar), U. Liverpool, Eng., 1968. Registered architect, Mich., Colo., Nat. Council Archtl. Registration Bds. Designer Robert Metcalf (Architect), Ann Arbor, Mich., 1962-66, Tufts-New Eng. Med. Center Planning Office, Boston, 1967; architect Conklin & Rossant (Architects), N.Y.C., 1968-70; assoc. prof. architecture U. Minn., Mpls., 1970-77; dir. Energy Self-sufficient House, 1973-77; assoc. prof. environ. design U. Colo., Boulder, 1977-80; prin. Dennis Holloway Architects and Solar Designers, Boulder, 1980—; Am. Collegiate Schs. Architecture exchange grantee, London, summer 1965; designer Farmer & Dark (Chartered Architects), London, 1965; cons., lectr. in field. Bd. dirs. Colo. Coalition for Full Employment, Denver, 1980-82. Recipient Environ. Quality award Region V EPA, 1976. Mem. Nat. Center Appropriate Tech. (founding dir. 1976-78), Colo. Solar Energy Assn. (dir. Denver chpt. 1980-81), Phi Kappa Phi, Tau Sigma Delta. Current Work: Appropriate tech. design; passive solar architecture; passive solar energy application to all scales of architecture and community design. Subspecialty: Solar energy. Home and office: 3697 Roundtree Ct Boulder CO 80302

HOLLOWAY, HARRY LEE, JR., biological, polar and water diversion parasitologist; b. York County, Va., May 22, 1926; s. Harry L. and Beatrice (Insley) H.; m. N. Juanita Yow, July 31, 1948; children: Harry Lee III, M. Ellen Holloway Betting, Ralph J., D. Bryan. B.S., Randolph Macon Coll., Ashland, Va., 1948; M.A., U. Richmond, 1951; Ph.D., U. Va., Charlottesville, 1956. Grad. teaching asst. U. Va., 1951-53; prof., chmn. dept. Roanoke Coll., Salem, Va., 1953-69; dean faculty Western Md. Coll., Westminster, 1969-71; chmn. dept. biology U. N.D., Grand Forks, 1971-74, prof. biology, 1971—; biology com. Internat. Garrison Diversion Study Bd., 1975-77; Wagner Coll. evaluation team assoc. Middle States Commn. Higher Edn., 1970; program assoc. div. polar programs NSF, Washington, 1984-85. Contbr. articles profl. jours. Served with USNR, 1944-46. Recipient Antarctic medal U.S. Congress, 1968; Mt. Holloway named in his honor, 1967; research grantee NSF; research grantee Bur. Reclamation; research grantee Nat. Marine Fisheries Service. Fellow AAAS; mem. Am. Microscopical Soc., Washington Helminthological Soc., Am. Inst. Biol. Scis., Am. Soc. Parasitologists, Sigma Xi, Kappa Alpha Order, Beta Beta Beta. Methodist. Club: Kiwanis (pres. 1980-81). Current Work: Ecology of fish parasites in North America and Antarctica, animal parasites. Subspecialties: Parasitology; Ecology (environmental science). Home: 1305 Chestnut St Grand Forks ND 58201 Office: 111 Starcher Hall U of ND Grand Forks ND 58202

HOLLOWAY, JOHN THOMAS, physicist; b. Cape Girardeau, Mo., June 19, 1922; s. Herbert Henry and Addie Mae (Cahill) H.; m. Kay Vickers, Nov. 11, 1965; children—Linda, Kim. A.B., Millikin U., Decatur, Ill., 1943; Ph.D., Iowa State U., 1957. With nuclear physics br. Office Naval Research, Washington, 1946-53, head br., 1951-52; research asst. Ames (Iowa) Lab., AEC, 1954-57; with Office Dir. Def. Research and Engring., Washington, 1958-61; dep. dir. Office Dir. Def. Research and Engring. (Office Sci.), 1959-61; with NASA, 1961-68, dep. dir. grants and research contracts, 1961-67, chief advanced programs and tech., space applications div., 1967-68; dir. Nat. Hwy. Safety Research Center, Dept. Transp., 1968-69; v.p. research Ins. Inst. Hwy. Safety, 1969-72; asso. dir. ops. Interdisciplinary Communications Program, Smithsonian Instn., 1972-77, program mgr. internat. program population analysis, 1972-77, research and devel. cons. in hwy. safety, biomed. electronics, energy conservation, 1977-78; sr. staff officer bd. on radioactive waste mgmt. Nat. Acad. Scis.-NRC, 1978—; dir. Interdisciplinary Communications Assos., Inc.; mem. conf. com. Nat. Conf. Advancement Research, 1971-75. Author papers in field; adviser documentary films. Served with USNR, 1944-46. Mem. Am. Phys. Soc., Philos. Soc. Washington, Sigma Xi. Clubs: Cosmos (Washington); Army-Navy Country (Arlington, Va.). Current Work: Management (including disposal) of high-level radioactive waste. Subspecialty: Nuclear physics. Home: 2220 Cathedral Ave NW Washington DC 20008

HOLLWEG, JOSEPH VINCENT, research physicist, educator, space science center executive; b. N.Y.C., Mar. 20, 1944; s. Joseph Julius and Rose Marie (Novak) H.; m. Leslie Francine, Dec. 23, 1976. Ph.D. in Plasma Physics and Space Sci., MIT, 1968. Research fellow Max Planck Inst., 1968-70, Calif. Inst. Tech., Pasadena, 1970-72; scientist Nat. Ctr. for Atmospheric Research, Boulder, Colo., 1972-80; research prof. U. N.H., Durham, 1980—; dir. Space Sci. Ctr., 1982-83. Contbr. chpts. to books, articles to publs. in field. Recipient publ. prize Nat. Ctr. for Atmospheric Research, 1974; Henry Webb Salisbury award MIT, 1964; Wayne B. Nottingham prize Am. Physics Soc., 1967. Mem. Am. Geophys. Union, Am. Astron. Soc. Current Work: Theoretical studies of energy and momentum balance of solar atmosphere. Subspecialties: Solar physics; Plasma physics. Office: Demeritt Hall Univ NH Durham NH 03824

HOLLY, FRANK JOSEPH, medical educator, consultant; b. Budapest, Hungary, Dec. 3, 1934; came to U.S., 1956, naturalized, 1962; s. Sandor and Maria (Acsay) H.; m. Katalin Maria Szalay, May 1, 1969; children: Thomas Ferenc, Kathleen Maria, Gloria Anna, Paul Gyorgy. Student, Tech. U., Budapest, 1953-56; Ph.D., Cornell U., 1962. Research phys. chemist Procter & Gamble Co., Cin., 1962-65; prof. chemistry U. El Salvador, San Salvador, 1965-66; research scientist Thermo Electron Corp., Waltham, Mass., 1966-68; assoc., sr. scientist Eye Research Inst., Boston, 1968-78; assoc. prof. Tex. Tech. U. Health Sci. Center, Lubbock, 1978-80, prof. ophthalmology and biochemistry, 1980—; v.p. Holles Labs., Inc., Cohasset, Mass., 1978—; cons. Burton, Parsons Co., Washington, 1972-76, Allergan Pharms., Irvine, Calif., 1978-79, Dow Corning Co., Midland, Mich., Ciba Vision Care, Atlanta, 1977-80, Bausch and Lomb, 1983—. Editor, Internat. Ophthalmol. Clinic, 1973, 80-83. Scoutmaster Hungarian Scout Assn. in Exile, Garfield, N.J., 1958-62. Nat. Eye Inst. spl. research fellow, 1972-74; Nat Eye Inst. grantee, 1975-77, 78-81, 81-84. Mem. Internat. Soc. Contact Lens Research (council mem. 1978—), Internat. Soc. Colloids and Interface Scientists, Am. Chem. Soc., Assn. Research in Vision and Ophthalmology, Brit. Soc. Cell Biology, Sigma Xi. Roman Catholic. Club: Mensa. Patentee in field. Current Work: Application of interface science and physical chemistry to medicine, ocular physiology, lacrimal physiology, basic dental research, cancer research, biomaterials such as hydrogels, contact lenses, and their biocompatibility, collyria, life sciences in general. Subspecialties: Physical chemistry; Surface chemistry. Office: Dept Ophthalmology Tex Tech U Health Scis Center Lubbock TX 79430

HOLMAN, B. LEONARD, nuclear medicine physician, educator; b. Sheboygan, Wis., June 26, 1941; s. Max and Sophia (Penn) H.; m. Dale Elyse Barkin, Jan. 22, 1971; children: Amy Lynn, Allison Stacy. B.S., U. Wis., 1963; M.D., Washington U., St. Louis, 1966. Diplomate: Am. Bd. Nuclear Medicine, Am. Bd. Radiology. Intern Mt. Zion Hosp., San Francisco, 1966-67; resident Mallinckrodt Inst. Radiology, St. Louis, 1967-70; nuclear radiologist Peter Bent Brigham Hosp., Boston, 1970-75; from instr. to assoc. prof. Harvard U. Med. Sch., Boston, 1970-82, prof. radiology, 1982—; nuclear radiologist Children's Hosp., Boston, 1970—, Dana-Farber Cancer Ctr., Boston, 1976—; attending nuclear radiologist West Roxbury (Mass.) VA Hosp., 1973—; cons. radiology New Eng. Deaconess Hosp., Boston, 1981—, Beth Israel Hosp., Boston, 1982—; dir. clin. nuclear medicine services Brigham and Women's Hosp., Boston, 1975—; Mem. med. adv. com. U.S. NRC, Bethesda, Md., 1980—; bd. dirs. Am. Bd. Nuclear Medicine, Los Angeles, 1980—. Author: (with J.A. Parker) Computer Assisted Cardiac Nuclear Medicine, 1981; editor: (with P.J. Ell) Emission Computed Tomography, 1982; others; contbr. articles to profl. jours., chpts. to books. Nat. Inst. Gen. Med. Sci. fellow, 1968-70. Fellow Am. Coll. Chest Physicians, Am. Heart Assn. (council cardiovascular radiology, council circulation), Am. Coll. Cardiology (trustee 1980-83); mem. Soc. Nuclear Medicine (trustee 1976, 80-83, sec. 1983—), Am. Coll. Radiology, Sigma Xi. Current Work: Cardiac nuclear medicine, single photon emission computed tomography, regional cerebral blood flow. Subspecialties: Nuclear medicine; Imaging technology. Home: 25 Nancy Rd Chestnut Hill MA 02167 Office: Brigham and Women's Hosp 75 Francis St Boston MA 02115

HOLMAN, RALPH THEODORE, educator, biochemist; b. Mpls., Mar. 4, 1918; s. Alfred Theodore and May (Nilson) H.; m. Karla Calais, Mar. 26, 1943; 1 son, Nils Teodor Calais. A.A., Bethel Jr. Coll., 1937; B.S., U. Minn., 1939, Ph.D., 1944; M.S., Rutgers U., 1941. Instr. U. Minn., 1944-46, asso. prof. physiol. chemistry, 1951-56; prof. Hormel Inst., 1956—, dir. inst., 1975—; prof. biochemistry Mayo Med. Sch., 1977—; asso. prof. Tex. A. and M. U., 1948-51; Mem. adv. bd. Deuel Conf. Lipids, 1958—, chmn., 1972; mem. nutrition study sect. NIH, 1960-63; mem. com. fats Food and Nutrition Bd., Nat. Acad. Scis.-NRC, 1956-62; pres. Golden Jubilee Congress on Essential Fatty Acids and Prostoglandins, 1980. Editor: (with W.O. Lundberg and T. Malkin) Progress in the Chemistry of Fats and Other Lipids, vols. 1-6, 1951-63; sole editor, vols. 7-16 (with W.O. Lundberg and T. Malkin), 1963—; assoc. editor: Lipids, 1966-74; editor, 1974—; editorial bd.: Jour. Lipid Research, 1959-61, Jour. Nutrition, 1962-66, Jour. Parenteral and Enteral Nutrition, 1977-82, Jour. Lab. and Clin. Medicine, 1979—. Pres. Mower County Council Chs., 1954-58. Recipient Fachini medal Italian Oil Chemistry Soc., 1974; NRC fellow Med. Nobel Inst., Stockholm, Sweden, 1946-47; Am. Scandinavian Found. fellow U. Uppsala, Sweden, 1947; spl. fellow NIH, U. Gothenburg, Sweden, 1962. Mem. Am. Soc. Biol. Chemists, Am. Inst. Nutrition (Borden award 1966), Am. Oil Chemists Soc. (gov. bd. 1968-70, sec. 1972, v.p. 1973, pres. 1974, Bailey award 1972, award in lipid chemistry 1978), Soc. Exptl. Biology and Medicine, Nat. Acad. Scis., Hormel Found., Am. Orchid Soc., Sigma Xi. Democrat. Conglist. Research, over 300 publs. on spectrophotometric studies fat oxidation, isolation and characterization lipoxidase, displacement chromatography lipids, biochem. characterization essential fatty acid deficiency; established nutritional requirements essential fatty acids; research on metabolism polyunsaturated fatty acids, relationship of essential fatty acid abnormalities to diseases in humans, near-infrared spectra lipids, mass spectrometry lipids; analysis of odors; fragrance and taxonomy; developed methods for lipid analysis, quantitative chem. taxonomy magnolia and orchids based on floral odor, effect of double bond structure upon metabolism of unsaturated acids, effect of partially hydrogenated fats upon nutrition and metabolism of essential fatty acids. Current Work: Lipids, oxidative deterioration of fats, lipoxidase, essential fatty acid metabolism, polyunsaturated fatty acids, methods of lipids analysis, mass spectrometry, in virto metabolism of fatty acids, quantitative chemical taxonomy. Subspecialties: Biochemistry (medicine); Nutrition (medicine). Home: 1403 2d Ave SW Austin MN 55912 Office: Hormel Inst U Minn Austin MN 55912

HOLMBERG, SCOTT A., epidemiologist. Mem. staff enteric diseases div., Ctrs. for Disease Control, Atlanta. Subspecialty: Epidemiology. Office: Ctrs for Disease Control 1600 Clifton Rd NE Atlanta GA 30333

HOLMES, DALE ARTHUR, optical scientist; b. Biwabik, Minn., Dec. 31, 1937; s. Arthur Emil and Saimie Amanda (Luoma) H.; m. Joan Christine Holmes, May 4, 1962; children: Kevin, Camille. B.S. in E.E, Purdue U., 1960; M.S. in E.E, Carnegie Inst. Tech., 1961, Ph.D. in E.E, 1965; M.S. in optics, U. Rochester, 1969. Asst. prof. Carnegie Inst. Tech., 1965-66; dir. research and tech. Rocketdyne/Rockwell Internat., Canoga Park, Calif., 1974-76, sr. staff scientist optics, 1977-83, mgr., chief scientist Advanced Optical Systems Group, 1984—. Contbr. articles to profl. jours. Served to capt. USAF, 1966-74. Recipient USAF Research and Devel. award, 1970. Mem. Optical Soc. Am., Nat. Rifle Assn. Am. Republican. Clubs: Rocketdyne Rifle & Pistol, Internat. Handgun Metallic Silhouette Assn. Current Work: Design analysis test of optical subsystems for high energy laser systems. Subspecialties: Laser optics; High energy laser systems. Home: 2307 E Knollhaven St Simi Valley CA 93065 Office: 6633 Canoga Ave FA44 Canoga Park CA 91304

HOLMES, DYER BRAINERD, corporation executive; b. N.Y.C., May 24, 1921; s. Marcellus B. and Theodora (Pomeroy) H.; m. Roberta M. Donohue. B.S. in Elec. Engring. (McMullen scholar), Cornell U., 1943; postgrad., Bowdoin Coll., M.I.T., 1943-44; hon. degrees, U. N.Mex., 1963, Worcester Poly. Inst., 1978. Registered profl. engr., N.J. Design engr. Western Electric Co.; also mem. tech. staff Bell Labs., 1945-53; gen. mgr. maj. def. systems div., 1961; project mgr. Navy Talos land based missile system devel., 1954-57, Air Force Atlas launch control and checkout equipment devel., 1957, USAF ballistic missile early warning system, 1958-61; dep. asso. adminstr. manned space flight NASA, 1961-63; sr. v.p., dir. Raytheon Co., Lexington, Mass., 1963-69, exec. v.p., 1969-75, pres., 1975—, dir., 1969—; dir. Wyman-Gordon Co., Worcester, Mass., Bank of Boston Corp. (and subsidiary), Kaman Corp., Bloomfield, Conn.; chmn. bd. Beech Aircraft Corp. (subs. Raytheon Co.). Author articles, papers in field. Mem. corp. Northeastern U. Served with USNR, 1942-45. Recipient Outstanding Leadership medal NASA; Paul T. Johns award Arnold Air Soc. Fellow IEEE, AIAA; mem. Nat. Acad. Engring., Aerospace Industries Assn. U.S. (exec. com.), Am. Def. Preparedness Assn. (dir.), Nat. Security Indsl. Assn. (trustee), Navy League, Tau Beta Pi, Eta Kappa Nu. Clubs: Nat. Space (Washington), Metropolitan (Washington); Algonquin (Boston). Initiated, developed first precision rec. transmission measuring set, other test equipment; participated devel. long distance coaxial telephone and TV systems, RCA, 1953-61. Subspecialties: Electrical engineering; Aerospace engineering and technology. Office: Raytheon Co 141 Spring St Lexington MA 02173

HOLMES, JERRY DELL, organic chemist; b. Mt. Vernon, Tex., Nov. 30, 1935; s. W.L. and Amie E. (Marshall) H.; m. Margaret L. King, June 22, 1957; children—Lisa, Melinda, Jerry, James. B.S., E. Tex. State U., 1956; Ph.D., U. Tex.-Austin, 1964. Chemist, Am. Oil Co., Texas City, 1956-60; chemist/sr. chemist Tex. Eastman Co., Longview, 1963-74, div. dir., 1974-80; staff asst. research and devel. Eastman Chem. div., Kingsport, Tenn., 1980-82; dir. research/devel. Tex. Eastman Co., Longview, 1982-84; dir. devel. Eastman Chem. Div., Kingsport, Tenn., 1984—; bd. trustees Textile Research Inst., Princeton, N.J., 1985—. Patentee in field. Contbr. articles to profl. jours. Mem. Am. Chem. Soc., Am. Inst. Textile Tech. Presbyterian. Current work: Chemicals, plastics and fibers. Subspecialty: Organic chemistry. Office: Eastman Chem div Eastman Kodak Co PO Box 1972 Kingsport TN 37662

HOLMES, PHILIP JOHN, applied mechanics educator, researcher; b. Scunthorpe, Eng., May 24, 1945; came to U.S. 1977; s. Robert Montague and Catherine Ann (Hall) H.; m. Ruth Helen Lazarus, Nov. 6, 1970; children—Maya, Avram, Benjamin, Ilana. B.A. with honors, Oxford U., Eng., 1967; Ph.D., Southampton U., Eng., 1974. Research fellow Southampton, Eng., 1973-77; asst. prof. Cornell U., Ithaca, N.Y., 1977-80, assoc. prof., 1980-84, prof., 1984—; dir. Applied Math. Ctr., Cornell U., 1981—. Author: (with John Guckenheimer) Nonlinear Oscillations, Dynamical Systems and Bifurations of Vector Fields, 1983, numerous research articles. Research grantee NSF, DOD, Washington, 1977-84; recipient Eric Gregory award, London, 1973. Mem. Am. Math. Soc., Soc. Ind. & Applied Math., Soc. for Natural Philosophy. Current work: Nonlinear phenomena, dynamical systems, chaotic motions. Subspecialties: Theoretical and applied mechanics; Applied mathematics. Office: Dept Theoretical and Applied Mechanics Cornell U Ithaca NY 14853

HOLMES, ROBERT ANTELL, veterinary and veterinary radiology educator; b. Vincennes, Ind., Feb. 25, 1947; s. Robert Samuel and Naomi Katherine (Kixmiller) H.; m. Linda Trudy Lamb, Aug. 25, 1968; children—Jason Alan, Rachel Anne. D.V.M., Purdue U., 1971; postgrad. radiology, U. Ga., 1977-80, M.S., 1983. Veterinarian, Webster Animal Hosp., Roswell, N.Mex., 1974-77; radiology resident U. Ga., 1977-80; asst. prof. La. State U., Baton Rouge, 1983—; cons. TRS Labs., Athens, Ga., 1982-83; judge Regional Sci. Fair, Baton Rouge, 1984, State Sci. Fair, Baton Rouge, 1984. Contbr. articles to profl. jours. Sunday Sch. tchr. Prince Ave. Baptist Ch., Athens, Ga., 1980-83. Served to capt. USAF, 1971-73. Mem. AVMA, Am. Assn. Vet. Parasitologists, Am. Vet. Computer Soc., Sigma Xi, Phi Zeta. Republican. Lodge: Sertoma Internat. (bd. dirs. 1974). Current work: Computer assisted morphometrics in veterinary radiology; computer algorithms for pharmacokinetics; effects of organ function on pharmacokinetics of anthelmintics. . Home: 4423 Lake Larto Circle Baton Rouge LA 70816 Office: Dept Vet Clin Scis La State Univ Baton Rouge LA 70803

HOLMGREN, HARRY D., physics and astronomy educator, researcher; b. Mpls., Apr. 21, 1928; s. Harry W. and M.A. (Dahl) H.; m. Monika Konig. B.S. in Physics, U. Minn., 1949, M.A., 1950, Ph.D., 1954. Physicist, U.S. Naval Research Lab., Washington, 1954-61; prof. physics U. Md., College Park, 1961—; pres. S.E. Univ. Research Assn., 1980—. Contbr. articles to profl. publs. Fellow Am. Phys. Soc.; mem. Phi Beta Kappa. Club: Cosmos (Washington). Current work: Nuclear structure, reaction mechanisms, accelerators, experimental facilities. Subspecialty: Nuclear physics. Home: 3044 R St NW Washington DC 20007 Office: U Md Dept Physics and Astronomy College Park MD 20742Also: SE Univ Research Assn 3401 N Fairfax Dr Suite 321 Arlington VA 22201

HOLMQUIST, GERALD PETER, geneticist, researcher; b. Chgo., Feb. 22, 1942; s. Gunnar A. and Elaine (Roehr) H.; m. Dorothy Jane, Dec. 29, 1969; 1 son, Peter Crittenden. B.S. in Physics, U. Chgo., 1964, M.S., 1967; Ph.D., U. Ill., 1971. Postdoctoral fellow Karolinska Inst., Stockholm, 1972, Harvard Med. Sch., 1973-74, City of Hope, Duarte, Calif., 1974, 76; asst. prof. medicine Baylor U. Coll. Medicine, Houston, 1976—, dir. cytogenetics lab., 1980—; assoc. prof. developmental biology City of Hope Med. Ctr., Duarte, Calif., 1985—. Active Republican politics. NIH Career devel. awardee, 1979—. Mem. Am. Soc. Cell Biology, Genetics Soc. Am., Sigma Xi. Club: Briar (Houston). Office: Beckman Research Inst City of Hope 1450 E Duarte Rd Duarte CA 91010

HOLMSTROM, VALERIE LOUISE, clinical psychologist, educator; b. Seattle, June 13, 1948; d. Frank Gottfried and Laura (Lofthus) H. A.B., Boston U., 1968; Ph.D., U. Wash., 1972. Lic. clin. psychologist, S.C. Staff psychologist VA Med. Ctr., Brockton, Mass., 1972-75, asst. chief psychology service, Charleston, S.C., 1975-81, chief psychology service, 1981—; asst. prof. dept. psychiatry and behavioral scis. Med. U. S.C., Charleston, 1975—; cons. Mass. Rehab. Commn., Boston, 1974-75, S.C. Div. Vocat. Rehab., Charleston, 1979—; lectr. Boston U., 1974, Grad. Sch. Edn., The Citadel, Charleston, 1979-80. USPHS fellow, 1968-69; recipient Outstanding Performance award VA Med. Ctr., Brockton, 1975, Outstanding Performance award VA Med. Ctr., Charleston, 1982. Mem. Am. Psychol. Assn., Am. Epilepsy Soc., VA Chiefs Assn. Democrat. Current Work: Neuropsychological and personality characteristics of epilepsy patients; post-traumatic stress disorder in former American prisoners of war. Subspecialties: Behavioral psychology; Neuropsychology. Home: 1115 Sea Oats Ct Mount Pleasant SC 29464 Office: VA Med Ctr 109 Bee St Charleston SC 29464

HOLONYAK, NICK, JR., electrical engineering educator; b. Ziegler, Ill., Nov. 3, 1928; s. Nick and Anna (Rosoha) H.; m. Katherine R.A. Jerger, Oct. 8, 1955. B.S., U. Ill., 1950, M.S., 1951, Ph.D. (Tex. Instruments fellow), 1954. Mem. tech. staff Bell Telephone Labs., Murray Hill, N.J., 1954-55; physicist, unit mgr., mgr. advanced semiconductor lab. Gen. Electric Co., Syracuse, N.Y., 1957-63; prof. elec. engring. and materials research lab. U. Ill.-Urbana, 1963—; mem. Center Advanced Study, 1977—; series editor Prentice-Hall, Inc., 1962—; cons. Monsanto Co., 1964—, Nat. Electronics Co., 1963-70, Skil Corp., 1967, GTE Labs. Tech. Adv. Council, 1973, Xerox, 1983—, Ameritech, 1985—. Author: (with others) Semiconductor Controlled Rectifiers, 1964. Served with U.S. Army, 1955-57. Recipient Cordiner award Gen. Electric Co., 1962, John Scott medal City of Phila., 1975, GaAs Conf. award with Welker medal, 1976. Fellow Am. Phys. Soc., IEEE (Morris Liebmann prize 1973, Jack A. Morton award 1981); mem. Electrochem. Soc. (Solid State Sci. and Tech. award 1983), Math. Assn. Am., AAAS, Nat. Acad. Engring., Nat. Acad. Sci., Am. Acad. Arts and Sci. Current Work: Semiconductor materials and devices (thyristors, transistors.LEDs, lasers, ICs). Subspecialties: Semiconductors; Microelectronics. Home: 2212 Fletcher St Urbana IL 61801 Office: Dept Elec and Computer Engring U Ill 1406 W Green St Urbana IL 61801

HOLT, ALAN CRAIG, government space agency administrator; b. Camp Lejeune, N.C., Mar. 16, 1945; s. Floyd Marshall and Bernice Ann (Schmidt) H.; m. Susan Carol Darnall, Aug. 8, 1970; 1 son, Christopher Scott. B.S., Iowa State U.-Ames, 1967; M.S., U. Houston, Clear Lake, 1979. Expt. procedures specialist NASA, Manned Spacecraft Ctr., Houston, 1967-70, Skylab crew proceedings and tng. specialist, 1970-74; Spacelab crew ops. specialist Johnson Space Ctr., 1974-78, Spacelab systems tng. supr., 1978-80, payload group leader, 1980—; pres. Holt Research & Devel. Co., 1983—; bd. dirs. Vehicle Internal Systems Investigative Team, Inc., Friendswood, Tex., 1978—. Recipient Sustained Superior Performance award NASA, Johnson Space Center, 1973, 82. Mem. Am. Astron. Soc. (assoc.), AIAA, Soc. Photo-Optical Instrumentation Engrs., N.Y. Acad. Scis. Lutheran. Club: AMORC (regional monitor 1979-81). Inventor field resonance propulsion system. Current Work: Hyperspatial theoretical models and advanced propulsion systems, crystal physics, anomalous aerial phenomena, parapsychology. Subspecialties: Theoretical astrophysics; Magnetic physics. Office: NASA Johnson Space Center Code CG 6 Houston TX 77058Office: Holt Research and Devel Co PO Box 5892 Houston TX 77258

HOLT, STEPHEN S., astrophysicist; b. N.Y.C., May 17, 1940; s. Aaron J. and Faye E. (Schwartz) Holtz; m. Carol Ann Weissman, June 3, 1961; children: Peter David, Eric Lawrence, Laura Kimberly. B.S., NYU, 1961, Ph.D. in Physics, 1966. Instr. physics NYU, 1964-66; astrophysicist Goddard Space Flight Center, Greenbelt, Md., 1966—; chief high energy astrophysics NASA Hdqrs., 1980-81; dir. Lab. for High Energy Astrophysics Goddard Space Flight Ctr., Greenbelt, Md., 1983—; lectr. physics U. Md., 1967—. Contbr. articles to profl. jours. Recipient medal for exceptional sci. achievement NASA, 1977, 80. Mem. Am. Phys. Soc., Am. Astron. Soc., Sigma Xi, Tau Beta Pi, Sigma Pi Sigma. Current Work: Investigator; project scientist space-borne scientific investigations including Einstein Observatory (the first X-ray astronomy telescope). Subspecialties: High energy astrophysics; X-ray high energy astrophysics. Home: 1207 Mimosa Ln Silver Spring MD 20904 Office: Code 660 Goddard Space Flight Center Greenbelt MD 20771

HOLT, WILLIAM R., mathematical statistician, entomologist; b. Phila., Feb. 17, 1930; s. William and Mabel (Price) H.; m. Betty Boal, June 7, 1952. B.S. in Forestry, Pa. State U., 1952, M.F., 1956; B.A. in Math, Ohio Wesleyan U., 1981. Forester U.S. Forest Service, Gainesville, Ga., 1952-56, research entomologist, Delaware, Ohio, 1960-69; statistician Merck Sharpe & Dohme Research Lab., Rahway, N.J., 1969-72, Boehringer Ingelheim Ltd., Elmsford, N.Y., 1972-77; math. statistician U.S. Army, Ft. Rucker, Ala., 1978—. Mem. Am. Statis. Assn., Math. Assn. Am., Math. Soc. Am., Biometric Soc. Current Work: General linear regression model theory and practice. Consultation and data analysis. Subspecialties: Statistics; Applied mathematics. Office: D-8 care Commander PO Box 577 USAARL Fort Rucker AL 36362

HOLTBY, KENNETH FRASER, aircraft manufacturing company executive; b. Escanaba, Mich., May 18, 1922; s. David William and Nina Kate (Hemenway) H.; m. Bettie Roberts, June 11, 1943; children—Michael Earle, Tracy Linda Holtby Buren, Jeffrey Thomas, Kristen Ann Holtby Buren, Matt Fraser. B.S. in M.E., Calif. Inst. Tech., 1947; M.S. in Indsl. Mgmt., MIT, 1961. With The Boeing Co., Seattle, 1947—, sr. vp., 1982—; mem. tech. adv. council Chrysler Corp., Detroit, 1985—. Mem. found. Pacific Sci. Ctr., Seattle, 1974—; mem. vis. com. U. Wash., Seattle, 1984—. Served to 1st lt. USAF, 1943-46. Fellow AIAA (Aircraft Design award 1984), Brit. Royal Aero. Soc.; mem. U.S. Nat. Acad. Engring., Nat. Research Council. Subspecialty: Aeronautical engineering. Office: The Boeing Co PO Box 3707 Seattle WA 98124

HOLTER, MARVIN ROSENKRANTZ, physicist; b. Fairport, N.Y., July 4, 1922; married, 1956; 2 children. B.S., U. Mich., 1949, M.S., 1951, 58. Research engr. Aero. Research Ctr. U. Mich., Ann Arbor, 1947-53, asst. supr. Project Wizard, missile def. systems, 1953, supr. Project Wizard, missile def. systems, 1954; research engr. Willow Run Labs., 1954-56; assoc. prof. engring. mechanics U. Toledo, 1956-57; mem. tech. ops. and long range planning staffs, lab. ops. and planning Willow Run Labs., U. Mich., 1957-58, head sensory devices group infrared lab., 1958-64; head infrared and optical sensor lab. Inst. Sci. and Tech., Willow Run Ctr., 1964-70; prof. Sch. Natural Resources, U. Mich., 1968-70; chief earth observations div. NASA Manned Spacecraft Ctr., 1970-72; dep. dir. Willow Run Labs., U. Mich., 1972-73; exec. v.p. Environ. Research Inst. Mich., Ann Arbor, 1973—; Mem. com. remote sensing for agrl. purposes Nat. Acad. Sci.-NRC, 1961-70; mem. div. adv. group aero. systems div. USAF, 1964; mem. USAF Sci. Adv. Bd., 1963-79, Joint U.S.-USSR Working Group for Sensing of Environ., 1971-77; mem. space applications com. NASA, 1971-77; mem. adv. com. Def. Intelligence Agy., 1978-81. Recipient Exceptional Sci. Achievement award NASA, 1973, Exceptional Service award Air Force Sci. Adv. Bd., 1979. Mem. Explorers Club. Subspecialty: Remote sensing (geoscience). Office: PO Box 8618 Ann Arbor MI 48107*

HOLTKAMP, DORSEY E(MIL), medical research scientist; b. New Knoxville, Ohio, May 28, 1919; s. Emil and Caroline (Meckstroth) H.; m. Marianne Church Johnson, Mar. 20, 1942 (dec. May 1956); m. Marie P. Bahm Roberts, Dec. 20, 1957 (dec. Apr. 1982); 1 son, Kurt Lee; stepchildren: Charles Timothy Roberts, Michael John Roberts. Student, Ohio State U., 1937-39; A.B., U. Colo., 1945, M.S., 1949, Ph.D., 1951; Student, Sch. Medicine, U. Colo., 2-1/2 yrs. Sr. research scientist biochemistry Smith, Kline & French Labs., Phila., 1951-57, endocrine-metabolic group leader, 1957-58; head endocrinology dept. Merrell Nat. Labs. div. Richardson-Merrell, Inc., Cin., 1958-70, group dir. endocrine clin. research, 1970-81; group dir. med. research dept. Merrell Dow Pharms. (subs. Dow Chem. Co.), Cin., 1981—; cons. Contbr. articles to profl. jours. Fellow AAAS, Am. Inst. Chemists; mem. Am. Chem. Soc., Am. Soc. Pharmacology and Exptl. Therapeutics, Soc. Exptl. Biology and Medicine, Endocrine Soc., Reticuloendothelial Soc., Pacific Coast Fertility Soc., Acad. Medicine Cin. (asso.), Am. Inst. Biol. Sci., Am. Soc. Zoologists, N.Y. Acad. Sci., Ohio Acad. Scis., Am. Assn. Lab. Animal Sci., AMA (affiliate), Soc. Study of Reprodn., Am. Soc. Clin. Pharmacology and Therapeutics, Am. Fertility Soc., Internat. Family Planning Research Assn., Sigma Xi. Republican. Presbyterian. Patentee in field. Current Work: Research and development of prescription drugs for humans in field of endocrinology. Subspecialties: Endocrinology; Pharmacology. Home: 9464 Bluewing Terr Cincinnati OH 45241 Office: 2110 E Galbraith Rd Cincinnati OH 45215

HOLTON, GREGORY ALLAN, environmental scientist; b. Jackson, Mich., Nov. 15, 1948; s. Alvin Leroy and Shirley Irene (Coy) H.; m. Doris Diane Dalton, June 13, 1970 (div. 1979); m. Victoria Ann Martin, Nov. 29, 1980. B.S., U.S. Mil. Acad., 1970; M.S. in Environ. Engring., U. N.C., 1977, Ph.D., 1981. Environ. engr. EPA, Research Triangle Park, N.C., 1976-77; cons. Research Triangle Inst., Research Triangle Park, 1977-80; cons. Environ. Resources Group Inc., Danville, Va., 1978-80; research assoc. Oak Ridge Nat. Lab., 1980-83; sr. scientist Maxima Corp., Oak Ridge, 1983-85; research scientist JBF Assocs., Inc., Knoxville, Tenn., 1985—; dep. dir. mgmt. info. systems directorate Chem. Systems Lab., USAR, Edgewood, Md., 1975-83; dep. dir. test br. Elec. Proving Ground, USAR, Fort Huachuca, Ariz., 1984—; mem. peer rev. com. health and environ. effects program U.S. Dept. Energy, Germantown, Md., 1982-83. Contbr. articles to profl. jours., chpt. to book. Cons., vol. Environ. Quality Adv. Bd., Oak Ridge, 1982—; fund raiser pub. TV, Knoxville, 1984; troop sponsor rep. Trans-Atlantic council Boy Scouts Am., Mannheim, Fed. Republic Germany, 1972-74. Served to capt. U.S. Army, 1970-75. ERDA grantee, 1975. Mem. Air Pollution Control Assn. (vice chmn. mar. emissions com. 1985—), Am. Chem. Soc., Assn. Grads. U.S. Mil. Acad., West Point Soc. N.Y. (career adv. bd. 1983—), West Point Soc. East Tenn., Phi Kappa Phi. Republican. Lutheran. Clubs: Ridge Ventures, Bowling (West Point, N.Y.) (v.p. 1969-70). Current work: Study design and implement innovative technologies to process recyclable or hazardous waste materials; analyze and assess advanced technology systems using human exposure modeling methodologies. Subspecialties: Atmospheric chemistry; Hazardous waste disposal. Home: 882 W Outer Dr Oak Ridge TN 37830 Office: JBF Assocs Inc Technology Dr Technology Park Ctr Knoxville TN 37932

HOLTON, WILLIAM COFFEEN, physicist; b. Washington, July 24, 1930; s. William Bultman and Esther M. (Coffeen) H.; m. Mary Schaeffer, Aug. 5, 1953; children: Elizabeth Ashe, William Andrew, Sarah Anne. B.S. in Physics, U. N.C., 1952; M.S., U. Ill., 1958, Ph.D., 1960. Mem. tech. staff Central Research Labs., Tex. Instruments, Dallas, 1960-66, mgr. quantum electronics br. Central Research Labs., 1966-71, dir. advanced devel. lab., 1971-78, research and devel. dir. Semicondr. Group, 1978-84; dir. microstructure scis. Semicondr. Research Corp., 1984—. Contbr. articles to profl. jours. Served to lt. (j.g.) USN, 1952-54. Recipient Josephus Daniels award U. N.C., 1952. Fellow Am. Phys. Soc., IEEE; mem. Phi Beta Kappa, Phi Eta Sigma. Patentee in field. Current Work: Solid state physics/semiconductors. Subspecialties: Semiconductors; Condensed matter physics. Home: 601 Brookview Dr Chapel Hill NC 27514 Office: 4501 Alexander Dr PO Box 12053 Suite 301 Research Triangle Park NC 27709

HOLTZMAN, SAMUEL, human-machine decision systems researcher, consultant; b. Mexico City, Feb. 9, 1955; came to U.S., 1973; s. Aaron Holtzman and Flora Dantus. S.B., M.I.T., 1977, S.M., 1980, E.E., 1980; postgrad, Stanford U., 1980—. Research and teaching asst. MIT, 1977-80; research and teaching asst. Stanford U., 1980-83, instr. engring.-econ. systems, 1983-84; assoc. Strategic Decisions Group, Menlo Park, Calif., 1981-82, cons. artificial intelligence and decision analysis; pres. Engring.-Econ. Systems, Student Assn., Stanford U., 1981. Inventor non-uniform time-scale modification system for speech and music, 1980. Mem. IEEE, Assn. Computing Machinery, AAAS, Mensa, Sigma Xi, Eta Kappa Nu. Current Work: Human-machine decision systems; application of decision analysis and artificial intelligence to design and implementation of intelligent decision aids. Subspecialties: Artificial intelligence; Operations research (engineering). Home: PO Box 5405 Stanford CA 94305 Office: Stanford U 301 Terman Engring Center Stanford CA 94305

HOLTZMAN, WAYNE HAROLD, psychologist, educator; b. Chgo., Jan. 16, 1923; s. Harold Hoover and Lillian (Manny) H.; m. Joan King, Aug. 23, 1947; children: Wayne Harold, James K., Scott E., Karl H. B.S., Northwestern U., 1944, M.S., 1947; Ph.D., Stanford, 1950; L.H.D. (hon.), Southwestern U., 1980. Asst. prof. psychology U. Tex., Austin, 1949-53, assoc. prof., 1953-59, prof., 1959—, dean Coll. Edn., 1964-70, prof. psychology and edn., 1965—; assoc. dir. Hogg Found. Mental Health, 1955-64, pres., 1970—; Dir. Social Sci. Research Council, 1957-63, Centro de Investigationes Sociales, Mex., 1960—; cons. USAF, also mem. sci. adv. bd., 1969-71; mem. com. basic research com. NRC, 1968-71; mem. behavioral sci. study sect. USPHS, 1957-59, mental health study sect., 1960, chmn. personality and cognition research rev. com., 1968-72; research adv. panel Social Security Adminstrn., 1961-62. Author: (with B. M. Moore) Tomorrow's Parents, 1964, Computer Assisted Instruction Testing and Guidance, 1971, (with R. Diaz-Guerrero and J. Swartz) Personality Development in Two Cultures, 1975, Introduction to Psychology, 1978; Editor: Jour. Ednl. Psychology, 1966-72. Trustee Ednl. Testing Service, Princeton, 1972-74; dir. Sci. Research Assos., 1975—; bd. dirs. Southwest Ednl. Devel. Lab., pres., 1974-75; mem. adv. com. computing activities NSF, 1970-73; mem. computer sci. and engring. bd. Nat. Acad. Scis., 1971-73, chmn. panel on selection and placement of mentally retarded students, 1979-82; chmn. interdisciplinary cluster on social and behavioral devel. Pres.'s Biomed. Research Panel, 1975-76; bd. dirs. Found.'s Fund for Research in Psychiatry, 1973-77, chmn., 1976-77; dir. Conf. of S.W. Found., 1976—, pres., 1978-79; trustee Ednl. Testing Service, 1977-80, 83—, J.W. and Cornelia Scarborough Found., 1977-82, Center for Applied Linguistics, 1978-80, Salado Inst. Humanities, 1980—, Population Inst., 1979-85, Menninger Found., 1982—, Population Resource Center, 1980—; mem. nat. adv. mental health council Alcohol, Drug Abuse, and Mental Health Adminstrn., 1978-81; mem. acad. info. systems adv. council IBM, 1982—, mem. Latin Am. adv. bd., 1985—. Served from ensign to lt. (j.g.) USNR, 1944-46. Faculty Research fellow Social Sci. Research Council, 1953-54; Faculty Research fellow Center Advanced Study Behavioral Scis., 1962-63. Fellow Am. Psychol. Assn.; mem. Tex. Psychol. Assn. (pres. 1957), S.W. Psychol. Assn. (pres. 1958), Am. Statis. Assn., AAAS, Interam. Soc. Psychology (pres. 1966-67), Am. Ednl. Research Assn., Internat. Union Psychol. Scis. (sec.-gen. 1972-84, pres. 1984—), Philos. Soc. Tex. (pres. 1982-83), Sigma Xi. Methodist. Current Work: Cross-cultural studies of personality, cognitive and perceptual development in children; techniques of personality assessment; mental health and educational technology. Subspecialties: Social psychology; Developmental psychology. Home: 3300 Foothill Dr Austin TX 78731

HOLUB, ROBERT F(RANTISEK), nuclear chemist, physicist; b. Prague, Czechoslovakia, Sept. 19, 1937; came to U.S., 1966; s. Stanislav and Marie (Prochazka) H.; m. Johnna S. Thames, Dec. 27, 1977; children—Robert M., John F., Elisabeth J. B.S., Charles U., Prague, 1958, M.S., 1960; Ph.D., McGill U., 1970. Research assoc. Fla. State U., Tallahassee, 1970-73; teaching intern U. Ky., Lexington, 1973-74; research physicist Bur. Mines, U.S. Dept. Interior, Denver, 1974—; cons. Internat. Atomic Energy Agy., Vienna, 1984—; faculty affiliate Colo. State U., Ft. Collins, 1982—; key participant radon intercalibration OECD, Paris, 1983—. Patentee continuous working level exposure apparatus. Contbr. articles to sci. jours. NRC Can. scholar, 1967-70. Mem. Am. Phys. Soc., Health Physics Soc. Current work: Radon measurements, gas transport in soils and rocks, aerosol physics, nuclear instrumentation. Subspecialties: Nuclear physics; Nuclear chemistry. Office: Bur of Mines Bldg 20 DFC Denver CO 80225

HOLZER, JOSEPH MANO, engineer, consultant; b. Somers Point, N.J., Jan. 18, 1952; s. Juda and Esther (Ziegler) H. B.S., Rensselaer Poly. Inst., 1974, M.Eng., 1975. Physicist Combustion Engring., Inc., Windsor, Conn., 1975-78; engr. Yankee Atomic Electric Co., Framingham, Mass., 1978-82; dir. nuclear fuel Cin. Gas & Electric Co., 1982-84, mgr. applications devel., 1984—. Contbr. articles to profl. jours. Mem. Am. Nuclear Soc. Jewish. Current Work: Nuclear engineering consulting; expert system development. Subspecialties: Nuclear engineering; Nuclear fission. Home: 108 Ferne Ave Palo Alto CA 94306 Office: Expert-Ease Systems 932 Santa Cruz Ave Menlo Park CA 94025

HOLZMAN, THOMAS FREDRIC, biochemist; b. Oakland, Calif., Dec. 31, 1950; s. George and Sara (Carlisle) H.; m. Rita Brewer, June 2, 1979; 1 child, Emily Louise Carlisle. B.S. in Biology, Western Wash. U., 1974, postgrad. in Chemistry, 1974-76; Ph.D. in Biochemistry, U. Ill., 1982. Teaching and research asst. Western Wash. U., Bellingham, 1974-76, U. Ill., Urbana, 1976-79; research asst. U. Ill., 1979-81; Upjohn fellow Tex. A&M U., College Station, 1981-83; research scientist Upjohn Co., Kalamazoo, Mich., 1983—. Contbr. articles to sci. publs. Patentee in field. Mem. Am. Chem. Soc., Biophys. Soc., Clin. Ligand Assay Soc., AAAS, Phi Lambda Upsilon. Current work: Protein and enzyme biochemistry of native and recombinant macromolecules, enzymology and physical biochemistry of bacterial luciferase, chemical modification of proteins. Subspecialties: Biophysical chemistry; Biochemistry (biology). Office: Upjohn Co 7000 Portage Rd Kalamazoo MI 49001

HOMANN, PETER HINRICH FRITZ, plant physiology educator; b. Wittenberge, Germany, Apr. 3, 1933; s. Wilhelm Hinrich and Lotte Paula (Luethke) H.; m. Ursel Hofmann, Feb. 7, 1964; children: Philip Peter, Oliver Robin. Diploma in Chemistry, Tech. U. Karlsruhe, W.Ger., 1959, Dr. rer. nat. in Chemistry, 1962. Asst. prof. dept. biol. sci. Fla. State U., Tallahassee, 1966-70, assoc. prof., 1970-78—, prof., 1978—. Contbr. articles to prof. jours. Mem. AAAS, Am. Soc. Plant Physiologists, Am. Soc. Photobiology, Biophys. Soc., Deutsche Ornithologen Gesellschaft, Sigma Xi. Current Work: Structure-function relationships of chloroplast thylakoids; variations of properties of chloroplast as related to functional adaptations. Subspecialties: Plant physiology (agriculture); Photosynthesis. Home: 117 Ridgeland Rd Tallahassee FL 32312 Office: 202 Inst Molecular Biophysics Fla State U Tallahassee FL 32306

HOMBURGER, FREDDY, physician, scientist, artist; b. St. Gall, Switzerland, Feb. 8, 1916; came to U.S., 1941, naturalized, 1952; s. Ludwig and Cécile (Gaille) H.; m. Regina Thûrlimann, Nov. 8, 1939. Student, U. Vienna, Austria, 1936-37; M.D., U. Geneva, Switzerland, 1941. Diplomate: Nat. Bd. Med. Examiners., Am. Bd. Toxicology. Research fellow, intern pathology Yale Med. Sch. and New Haven Hosps., 1941-43; intern, research fellow in medicine Harvard Med. Sch., Thorndike Meml. Lab., Boston City Hosp., 1943-45; fellow in medicine Meml. Hosp., N.Y.C., 1946-48; chief clin. investigation Sloan-Kettering Inst. Cancer Research, N.Y.C., 1945-48; instr. medicine Cornell U. Med. Coll., 1946-57, research prof. medicine, 1948-57; dir. cancer research and control unit Tufts U. Sch. Medicine, Boston, 1948-57; mem. courtesy staff Mt. Desert Island Hosp., Bar Harbor, Maine, 1955-73, Eastern Meml. Hosp., Ellsworth, Maine, 1957-60; sci. asso. Jackson Lab., Bar Harbor, 1951-60; research prof. oncology, div. basic scis. Sch. Grad. Dentistry, Boston U., 1973—; research prof. pathology Sch. Medicine, 1974—; mem. sci. staff Mallory Inst. Pathology, Boston City Hosp., 1979—; mem. Grad. Sch. Faculty Boston U., 1981—; Mem. corp. Gesell Inst. Child Devel., 1960-78; chmn. adv. com. Am. Students U. Geneva; pres., dir. Bio-Research Inst., Inc., 1957—, Bio-Research Cons., Inc., 1957—; pres. Trenton Exptl. Lab. Animal Co., Bar Harbor, 1969-81; bd. overseers Mt. Desert Island Biol. Lab., 1985—; treas., dir. Cambridge Coordinating Com. Drugs, 1972-74; hon. consul of Switzerland in, Boston, 1964-86; neutral mem. mixed med. commn. War Dept., 1944-46. Author: The Medical Care of the Aged and Chronically Ill, 3d edit, 1973, The Biological Basis of Cancer Management, 1957; also numerous sci. papers.; Editor: The Physiopathology of Cancer, 3d edit, 1974-76, Progress in Experimental Tumor Research, vols. I-XXVIII, 1960—; sr. editor: Symposia on Research Advances Applied to Medical Practice, Current Concepts in Toxicology; Exhibited paintings one-man shows, N.Y.C., Paris, Zurich, Geneva, Boston. Mem. overseers com. to visit Harvard, 1965-71, 76—; bd. dirs. Cambridge Soc. Early Music, 1970; trustee Opera Co., Boston, 1967-84; chmn. Friends Busch-Reisinger Mus., 1974—; visitor paintings Boston Mus. Fine Arts, 1974—; mem. adv. bd. Lachaise Found. Fellow AAAS, N.Y. Acad. Scis. (ednl. adv. com. 1967); mem. Nat. Hypertension Assn. (nat. adv. council 1978—), AMA, Endocrine Soc., Am. Assn. Cancer Research, Am. Fedn. Clin. Research, N.Y. Acad. Medicine, Soc. Exptl. Biology and Medicine, Am. Assn. Pathologists, Soc. Toxicology, Am. Soc. Pharmacology and Exptl. Therapeutics, Royal Soc. Health, Brit. Soc. Toxicology, Soc. Toxicologic Pathologists, Soc. Study Reproduction, Endocrine Soc., Am. Assn. Lab. Animal Scis., New Eng. Soc. Pathologists, Acad. Toxicological Scis., Cambridge C. of C. (dir. 1969-73), Sigma Xi. Clubs: Harvard (Boston); Yale (N.Y.C.); Cosmos (Washington). Current Work: Method improvement for in vivo chronic toxicity and carcinogenesis bioassays; development of animal models of human disease through inbreeding of Syrian hemsters. Subspecialties: Otorhinolaryngology; Toxicology (agriculture). Home: 759 High St Dedham MA 02026 also Trenton ME 04605 Office: 380 Green St Cambridge MA 02139

HOMMES, FRITZ AUKUSTINUS, biochemistry educator, researcher; b. Bellingwolde, Groningen, Netherlands, May 28, 1934; came to U.S., 1979; s. Aukustinus and Anje (Wester) H.; m. Grietje Renes, June 14, 1958; children: Peter, Anneliekt. M.S., U. Groningen, 1958; Ph.D., U. Nijmegen, 1961. Research asst. dept. biochemistry U. Nijmegen, Netherlands, 1959-61; Fulbright postdoctoral fellow dept. biochemistry U. Pa., Phila., 1961-63; head lab. dept. pediatrics U. Groningen, Netherlands, 1963-72, assoc. prof. dept. pediatrics, 1972-79; prof. dept. cell molecular biology Med. Coll. Ga., Augusta, 1979—, dir. biochem. genetics lab., 1980—; cons. genetic diseases Dutch Health Council, 1974-79, chmn. bioenergetics study group, 1975-77; co-chmn. comprehensive genetics systems State of Ga., 1982—. Editor: Inborn Errors of Metabolism, 1973, Normal and Pathological Development of Energy Metabolism, 1975, Models for the Study of Inborn Errors of Metabolism, 1979; contbr. articles to research publs. Bd. dirs. Parents Assn., Huize Maartenswouden, Drachten, Netherlands, 1975-79, Fountainhead Condominium Assn., Augusta, 1982-83. Genetics lectr. Japanese Govt., 1981. Mem. European Soc. Pediatric Research, Soc. Study Inherited Metabolic Diseases, N.Y. Acad. Scis., Am. Soc. Human Genetics, Soc. Study Inborn Errors of Metabolism, AAAS, Am. Soc. Biol. Chemists (lectr. 1965). Roman Catholic. Club: Round Table (Groningen) (chmn. 1970-71, chmn. No. Dist. 1973-75, nat. bd. 1974-75). Lodge: Rotary (Augusta). Patentee detection of lactaciduria. Current Work: Biochemistry of inborn errors in metabolism. Subspecialties: Biochemistry (medicine); Genetics and genetic engineering (medicine). Home: 793 Brookfield Pkwy Augusta GA 30907 Office: Dept Cell Molecular Biology Med Coll Georgia Augusta GA 30912

HONG, JEN-SHIANG, biochemist; b. Kaohsiung, Republic of China, Mar. 3, 1939; came to U.S., 1962, naturalized, 1974; s. Kim-chi and Kim-yeh (Chen) H.; m. Su-chen Lee, Dec. 20, 1969; children—Michael Lee, Audrey Margaret. B.S., Nat. Taiwan U., Taipei, 1961; M.S., Purdue U., 1965; Ph.D., U. Calif.-Berkeley, 1969. Postdoctoral fellow U. Calif.-Berkeley, 1969-71; guest worker Roche Inst. Molecular Biology, Nutley, N.J., 1971-72; asst. prof. Brandeis U., Waltham, Mass., 1972-80; staff scientist Boston Biomed. Research Inst., 1981-83, sr. staff scientist, 1983—; mem. microbial physiology and genetics study sect. NIH, 1982—. Recipient research career devel. award NIH, 1975-80; postdoctoral fellow NIH; fellow Am. Cancer Soc., Med. Found. Boston Inc. Mem. Am. Soc. Biol. Chemistry, Am. Soc. for Microbiology, AAAS, Greater Boston Chinese Cultural Assn. (treas. 1983-85). Democrat. Current work: Microbial gene regulation; molecular biology membrane transport. Subspecialties: Membrane biology; Molecular biology. Office: Boston Biomedical Research Inst 20 Staniford St Boston MA 02114

HONG, SU-DON, material scientist, research director; b. Chang-Hua, Taiwan, Republic of China, June 23, 1941; came to U.S., 1970; s. Ten-Sheng and Lee-Tze (Lee) H.; m. Grace C. Wang, Jan. 30, 1971; children: Emily W., Jennifer J. B.S., Nat. Taiwan U., 1966; M.S., U. Waterloo, Ont., Can., 1970; Ph.D., U. Mass., 1975. Teaching asst. Nat. Taiwan U., Taipei, Repulic of China, 1967-68; research assoc. U. Calif.-Berkeley, 1976-77; sr. scientist Jet Propulsion Lab., Pasadena, Calif., 1977-78, tech. group leader, 1978—; cons. Three Bond Corp., Gardena, Calif., 1980. Mem. Am. Chem. Soc., Am. Phys. Soc., Soc. Rheology, Soc. Plastic Engrs., Sigma Xi. Patentee double-beam optical method and apparatus for measuring thermal diffusibility. Current Work: Relationship between molecular relaxation mechanism and mechanical properties of polymers, physical aging and long-term performance of polymers, advanced composite materials of improved toughness. Subspecialties: Polymer physics; Composite materials. Home: 10551 E Danbury St Temple City GA 91780 Office: Calif Inst Tech Jet Propulsion Lab 4800 Oak Grove Dr Pasaden CA 91109

HONIGBERG, BRONISLAW MARK, zoology educator; b. Warsaw, Poland, May 14, 1920; came to U.S., 1941, naturalized, 1948; s. Zachary Z. and Mary (Laks) H.; m. Rhoda Springer, Feb. 7, 1948; children: Paul Mark, Martin Philip. A.B., U. Calif., Berkeley, 1943, M.A., 1946, Ph.D. (A. Rosenberg research fellow 1949-50), 1950. Instr. to prof. zoology U. Mass., Amherst, 1950—, chancellor's medalist, lectr., 1975, faculty fellow, 1981-82; asst. prof. Columbia U., summer 1954; research asso. in pathobiology Sch. Hygiene, Johns Hopkins U., 1958-59; asst. prof. Harvard U., summer 1959; guest investigator lab. parasitic diseases Nat. Inst. Allergy and Infectious Diseases, NIH, 1965-66; guest investigator, hon. fellow Centre for Tropical Veterinary Medicine, U. Edinburgh, 1973-74; dir. tng. grants NIH, 1973—; mem. Internat. Commn. Protozoology, 1965—, tropical medicine parasitology study sect. NIH, 1973-77; v.p., chmn. sci. program V, Internat. Congress Protozoology, 1977; v.p. Internat. Symposiumon Trichomoniasis, Bialystok, Poland, 1981. Editor: Jour. Protozoology, 1971-80; asso. editor: Trans. Am. Micros. Soc, 1966-71; editor N.Am.,: Zeitschrift für Parasitenkunde, 1974—; bd. reviewers: Acta Tropica, 1977-82; contbr. articles to profl. jours. Trustee Am. Type Culture Collection, 1966-72, mem. exec. com., 1971-72. Recipient Gold medal for human trichomoniasis studies Med. Faculty Comenius U., Bratislava, Czechoslovakia, 1977; Alexander von Humboldt Found. sr. scientist award, 1982; NIH research grantee, 1955—; USPHS spl. research fellow, 1965-66, 73-74. Fellow AAAS, N.Y. Acad. Sci., Royal Soc. Tropical Medicine and Hygiene; mem. Soc. belge de Médicine Tropicale (corr.), Deutsche Gesellschaft für Parasitologie (corr.), Am. Soc. Zoologists, Am. Soc. Parasitologists, Soc. Protozoologists (pres. 1965-66, hon.), Am. Micros. Soc. (pres. 1964-65), Am. Soc. Tropical Medicine and Hygiene, Biol. Stain Commn., Soc. Systematic Zoology, Phi Beta Kappa, Sigma Xi, Phi Kappa Phi. Current Work: Immunology and pathogenicity mechanisms of parasitic protozoa, especially flagellates (trichomonads and trypanosomes.). Subspecialty: Parasitology. Home: 95 Red Gate Ln Amherst MA 01002 Office: Zoology Dept Morrill Sci Center Univ Mass Amherst MA 01003

HOOD, LEROY EDWARD, biologist; b. Missoula, Mont., Oct. 10, 1938; s. Thomas Edward and Myrtle Evylan (Wadsworth) H.; m. Valerie Anne Logan, Dec. 14, 1963; children: Eran William, Marqui Leigh Jennifer. B.S., Calif. Inst. Tech., 1960, Ph.D. in Biochemistry, 1968; M.D., Johns Hopkins U., 1964. Med. officer USPHS, 1967-70; sr. investigator Nat. Cancer Inst., 1967-70; asst. prof. biology Calif. Inst. Tech., Pasadena, 1970-73, asso. prof., 1973-75, prof., 1975—, Bowles prof. biology, 1977—, chmn. div. biology, 1980—. Author: (with others) Biochemistry, a Problems Approach, 1974, Molecular Biology of Eukaryotic Cells, 1975, Immunology, 1978, Essential Concepts of Immunology, 1978. Mem. Am. Assn. Immunologists, Am. Assn. Sci., Nat. Acad. Scis., Am. Acad. Arts and Scis., Sigma Xi. Current Work: Molecular biology of antibody genes, T-all receptor genes and genes of the major histocompatability complex; microchemical instrumentation. Subspecialties: Immunobiology and immunology; Genetics and genetic engineering (biology). Home: 1453 E California Blvd Pasadena CA 91106 Office: Div Biology Calif Inst Tech Pasadena CA 91125

HOOKER, ARTHUR LEE, geneticist, plant pathologist, biotechnologist; b. Lodi, Wis., Oct. 12, 1924; s. Robert Lee and Dora Magdalena (Leuth) H.; m. Ellen Margaret Zimmerman, July 5, 1950; children: David Lee, Margaret Ann. B.S., U. Wis.-Madison, 1948, M.S., 1949, Ph.D., 1952. Project assoc. U. Wis., Madison, 1951-52, asst. prof. plant pathology, 1954-58; asst. prof. botany and plant pathology Iowa State U., Ames, 1952-54; plant pathologist U.S. Dept. Agr., 1954-58; mem. faculty U. Ill., Urbana, 1958-80, prof. plant pathology and genetics, 1963-80; biosci. dir. Pfizer Genetics, Inc., St. Louis, 1980-82; biosci. dir DeKalb-Pfizer Genetics, DeKalb, Ill., 1982—; adj. prof. biology No. Ill. U., DeKalb; cons. in field. Contbr. articles to profl. jours. Served with U.S. Army, 1944-46. Recipient Funk award U. Ill., 1974; Guggenheim Found. fellow, 1964. Fellow AAAS, Am. Phytopath. Soc., Am. Soc. Agronomy, Crop Sci. Soc. Am. Republican. Current Work: Genetics and physiology of plant parasite interactions, plant breeding, plant genetic resources and utilization, world food and agriculture, biotechnology. Subspecialties: Plant genetics; Plant pathology. Home: 39W749 Deerhaven Trail Saint Charles IL 60174 Office: 1300 Sycamore Rd DeKalb IL 60115

HOOP, BERNARD, physicist, educator; b. San Francisco, Feb. 17, 1939; s. Bernard and Annette (Barbata) H.; m. Nancy Clark Hulbert, June 15, 1965; children—Heidi Ann, Katrina Clark. B.S., Stanford U., 1960; M.S., U. Wis., 1962, Ph.D., 1965. Research asst., fellow Physikalisches Inst., U. Basel, 1965-67; mem. faculty Harvard U. Med. Sch., Boston, 1967—, research assoc., 1969—, asst. prof. medicine (physics), 1969—; mem. staff IAEA, Vienna, 1976-78. Contbr. articles to sci. jours. NIH grantee, 1969—. Mem. Am. Phys. Soc., Am. Physiol. Soc. Current work: Central nervous system control of respiration; biophysical mechanisms of neurotransmision. Home: 266 Main St Wakefield MA 01880 Office: Pulmonary Unit Mass Gen Hosp 32 Fruit St Boston MA 02114

HOOPER, GARY RAY, plant pathologist; b. Belvedere, Calif., Aug. 28, 1937; s. Claude Gerald and Rachael Ann (Palmer) H.; m. Karen Anne Nicol, Aug. 23, 1960; children: Laurie Ann, Michael C. and Boyd C. (twins). B.S., Brigham Young U., 1963; Ph.D., U. Calif.-Riverside, 1968. Plant pathologist, asst. prof. Mich. State U., East Lansing, 1968-71; dir. (Central Electron Microscope Lab.), 1972-80; asst. prof. Calif. Poly. State U., San Luis Obispo, 1971-72; head dept. plant pathology and physiology Va. Poly. Inst. and State U., Blacksburg, 1980-84, vice provost research and grad. studies, 1984—. Contbr. articles to profl. jours. Mem. sports bd. YMCA, East Lansing, 1972-80; bishop Ch. Jesus Christ of Latter-day Saints, 1976-80. Served with USAFR, 1956-64. Mem. Am. Phytopath. Soc., Weed Sci. Soc. Am., Electron Microscopy Soc. Am., Sigma Xi. Current Work: Ultrastructure of diseased plants, fungal electron microscopy, plant pathology. Subspecialties: Plant pathology; Plant virology. Office: Office Vice Provost Research and Grad Studies 304 Burruss Hall Va Poly Inst and State U Blacksburg VA 24061

HOOPER, ROBERT GEORGE, physician, medical administrator; b. New Brunswick, N.J., Dec. 15, 1943; s. John H. and Katheryn A. (Behrens) H.; m. Dana Dean Glasgow, July 24, 1965. B.S., U. Okla., 1965, M.D., 1968. Diplomate: Am. Bd. Internal Medicine, Am. Bd. Pulmonary Disease. Intern Maricopa County Hosp., Phoenix, 1968-69; resident U. Okla. Med. Center, 1969-71, Tripler Army Med. Center, 1971-72, Walter Reed Army Med. Center, 1972-74; practice medicine, specializing in pulmonary disease, Phoenix, 1979—; dir. pulmonary function lab. Walter Reed Army Med. Ctr., Washington, 1974-79, asst. chief pulmonary disease service, 1975-79; dir. dept. respiratory care services St. Luke's Hosp. Med. Ctr., Phoenix, 1979—. Contbr. articles to sci. jours. Served to lt. col. U.S. Army, 1971-79. Fellow Am. Coll. Chest Physicians, ACP; mem. Am. Thoracic Soc., Am. Heart Assn., Am. Fedn. Clin. Research, Ariz. Thoracic Soc. Current Work: Clinical evaluation of bronchogenic carcinoma; clinical physiology; respiratory care. Subspecialty: Pulmonary medicine. Office: 525 N 18th St Phoenix AZ 85006

HOOPES, PAUL JACK, veterinarian, pathologist; b. Muskogee, Okla., Aug. 13, 1951; s. Paul Jack Hoopes and Virginia (Bixby) Tarpley. Student Okla. U., 1971; D.V.M., Okla. State U., 1976; Ph.D., Colo. State U., 1984. Veterinarian, resident zoo medicine Nat. Zool. Park, Washington, 1977-79; resident pathology Colo. State U. Vet. Sch., Fort Collins, 1979-81, postdoctoral fellow in pathology and comparative oncology Comparative Oncology Unit, 1984-85. Contbg. author: Comparative Pathology of Zoo Animals, 1979. Contbr. articles to med. jours. Colo. State U., grantee, 1984. Mem. Am. Vet. Med. Assn., Am. Coll. Sports Medicine, Radiation Research Soc., Sigma Xi. Episcopalian. Current work: Comparative radiation pathology and pathogenesis, oncology, surgical oncology. Subspecialties: Pathology (veterinary medicine); Oncology. Office: Dept Anatomy Physiol Scis and Radiology Sch Veterinary Med NC State U 4700 Hillsborough St Raleigh NC 27606

HOORY, SHLOMO, Med. radiation physicist; b. Baghdad, Iraq, June 1, 1935; came to U.S., 1973, naturalized, 1980; s. Ezra and Salha (Dabby) H.; m. Hadassah Gelbgarb, Feb. 8, 1968 (div.); children: Itai, Eyal. Ph.D., The Hebrew U. Jerusalem, Israel, 1970. Chief physicist Hadassah U. Med. Center, 1962-63; chief physicist, researcher Tel-Hashomer Tel-Aviv U. Hosp., 1964; in-charge bldg. sci. and med. equipment Div. X-Rays and Highly Ionized Spectra, Hebrew U. Jerusalem, 1964-70; chief solar observatory Tel-Aviv U., Israel, 1972-73; chief physicist div. nuclear medicine L.I. Jewish Hillside Med. Center, 1974—; asst. prof. radiation physics and radiobiology L.I. Jewish Hillside Med. Center, Stony Brook U. Served with Israeli Def. Forces. Mem. Soc. Nuclear Medicine, Am. Assn. Physicists in Medicine, Health Physics Soc., AAAS., Am. Phys. Soc. Jewish. Current Work: Reconstruction of images from projections; computerization of radionuclide inventory and radioactive waste disposal; spectra of highly ionized atoms and soft x-rays, computerized nuclear medicine dosimetry; computerized quality assurance of pharmaceutical and generator eluates; new approach in bone mineral content evaluations in human. Home: 4E Mill Dr 1F Great Neck NY 11021 Office: Dept Nuclear Medicine L I Jewish Hosp New Hyde Park NY 11042

HOOSER, STEPHEN BLAIR, veterinarian; b. Champaign, Ill., Oct. 2, 1957; s. Richard Lee and Janice Louise (Cole) H.; m. Laura Conrad Nichols, Aug. 16, 1979. B.S., Eastern Ill. U., 1978; B.S., U. Ill., 1980, D.V.M., 1982. Pvt. practice vet. medicine, Charleston, Ill., 1982-83; research assoc in toxicology U. Ill., Urbana, 1983—. Mem. AVMA. Republican. Methodist. Current work: Veterinary toxicology; effects of various insecticides on domestic species; effects of methylxanthines on canines and equines. Subspecialty: Veterinary toxicology. Office: 1220 VMBSB Univ Ill 2001 S Lincoln Ave Urbana IL 61801

HOOTMAN, HARRY EDWARD, nuclear engineer, consultant; b. Oak Park, Ill., June 5, 1933; s. Merle Albert and Rachel Edith (Atkinson) H.; m. Linda Pearl Smith, Nov. 23, 1963; children: David, Holly, John. B.S. in Chemistry, Mich. Technol. U., 1959, M.S. in Nuclear Engring, 1962. Registered profl. engr., S.C. Research assoc. Argonne (Ill.) Nat. Lab., 1959-62; process engr. Savannah River Plant, Aiken, S.C., 1962-65; research staff engr. Savannah River Lab., Aiken, 1965—, cons. transuranic waste disposal and incineration. Bd. dirs. Central Savannah River Area Sci. and Engring. Fair, Inc., Augusta, Ga., 1972—. Served to sgt. USAF, 1953-57. Mem. Am. Acad. Environ. Engrs., Nat. Soc. Profl. Engrs. (local chmn. 1978-79), Am. Nuclear Soc. (local chmn. 1979-80), Am. Phys. Soc., Sigma Xi. Baptist. Inventor alpha waste incinerator. Current Work: Process and production plant design for production, separation, shielding and disposal of radioisotopic sources and products. Subspecialty: Nuclear engineering. Home: 820 Brandy Rd Aiken SC 29801 Office: Savannah River Lab Aiken SC 29808

HOOVER, WILLIAM LEICHLITER, forestry educator, researcher; b. Brownsville, Pa., July 29, 1944; s. Aaron Jones and Edith (Leichliter) H.; m. Peggy Jo Spangler, Aug. 30, 1976; children: Jennifer Mary, Monica Susan, Samuel Spangler. B.S., Pa. State U., 1966, M.S., 1971; Ph.D., Iowa State U., 1977. Research asst. Pa. State U., Iowa State U., 1970-74; asst. prof. Purdue U., West Lafayette, Ind., 1974-79, assoc. prof. dept. forestry and natural resources, 1980-84, prof., dir. indsl. forestry, 1985—; sec./treas., dir. econ. and fin. analysis Tim Tech., Inc., West Lafayette, 1978—. Asst. editor: Timber Tax Jour, 1979—; author: A Guide to Federal Income Tax for Timber Owners, 1982, Timber Tax Management, 1978, Timber Taxation and Investment Management, 1983. Served to 1st lt., C.E. U.S. Army, 1967-69. Decorated Bronze Star medal. Mem. Forest Products Research Soc., Am. Econ. Assn., Nat. Assn. Pub. Accts., Soc. Am. Foresters. Republican. Presbyterian. Current Work: Design and development of new wood based composite materials for structural applications, including marketing and strategic considerations. Subspecialties: Composite materials; Materials processing. Home: 206 Connolly St PO Box 2257 West Lafayette IN 47906 Office: Dept Forestry Purdue U West Lafayette IN 47907

HOOVIS, MARVIN LORIN, physician; b. N.Y.C., Apr. 22, 1929; s. Philip E. and Pansy Sarah (Kripser) H.; m. Beverly Ann Vigneault, Jan 6, 1959; children: Michelle, Keith, Dana, Hilary, Blaine. B.S., Bklyn. Coll., 1950; postgrad., U. Fribourg, Switzerland, 1950-52; M.D., U. Lausanne, Switzerland, 1956. Intern Coney Island Hosp., Bklyn., 1956-57, resident in internal medicine, 1957-59; chief resident in internal medicine St. Mary's Hosp., Waterbury, Conn., 1959-60, mem. staff, 1961-68, Roger Williams Gen. Hosp., Providence, 1968-74; dir. oncology Wesson Meml. Hosp., Springfield, Mass., 1974-80; mem. attending staff Union Hosp., Terre Haute, Ind., 1980—, Terre Haute Regional Hosp., 1980—, Lakeview Med. Ctr., Danville, Ill., 1982—, St. Elizabeth Hosp., Danville, 1982—; cons. med. oncology Lakeview Med. Center, Danville, Ill., 1980—, Clay County Hosp., Brazil, Ind., 1981—, Vermillion County Hosp., Clinton, Ind., 1981—, St. Elizabeth Hosp., Danville, 1981—; asst. prof. medicine Brown U., Providence, 1970-75; asst. clin. prof. medicine Yale U. Sch. Medicine, 1975-80; asst. prof. medicine U. Mass., Worcester, 1976-80. Contbr. articles to profl jours. Mem. Am. Cancer Soc. (v.p. Vigo County unit 1981-82), Am. Soc. Clin. Oncology, Am. Assn. Cancer Edn., Am. Assn. Cancer Research, Mass. Med. Soc., Am. Soc. Preventive Oncology, Vermilion County Med. Soc., Ill. State Med. Assn., AMA. Current Work: Biochemical pharmacology, and drug mechanisms of action. Clinical research and cancer education for community physicians and nurses. Subspecialties: Oncology; Hematology. Office: 806 N Logan Ave Danville IL 61832

HOPE, GEORGE MARION, research scientist; b. Waycross, Ga., Jan. 24, 1938; s. George Marion and Jessie (Norman) H.; m. Dorothy Marie Hendrix, Aug. 4, 1956; 1 son, Stephen Richard. Student, Armstrong Coll., 1957-58, Ga. Inst. Tech., 1958-60; A.B., Mercer U., 1965; M.A., U. Fla., 1967, Ph.D., 1971. Research asst. dept. ophthalmology Washington U., St. Louis, 1970-71; instr. dept. ophthalmology U. Louisville, 1972-73, asst. prof., 1974-79; assoc. research scientist dept. ophthalmology U. Fla., 1980—; dir. low vision service dept. ophthalmology U. Fla. (Coll. Medicine), 1980—; dir. U. Fla. (Center for Low Vision Study, Care and Rehab.), 1981—; cons. def. div. Brunswick Corp., Deland, Fla., 1980; dir. Low Vision Clinic, dept. ophthalmology U. Louisville Sch. Medicine, 1973-79. Contbr. articles in field to profl. jours. Active Old Louisville Neighborhood Council, 1400 Block 4th St. Orgn., Chakala Neighborhood Orgn. Recipient Med. Faculty Research award U. Louisville, 1973-74; USPHS postdoctoral fellow, 1972; grantee So. Med. Assn., 1973-74; grantee-in-aid Fight for Sight, Inc., 1973-74; grantee Eye Inst., NIH, 1975-78, Brunswick Corp., 1980-81, Multi Optics Corp., 1982-83, U.S. Army Med. Research Devel. Command, 1983-84, Brunswick Corp., 1985—. Mem. Assn. Research in Vision and Ophthalmology (dir. placement service 1972-83), Soc. Neurosci., AAAS, So. Soc. Philosophy and Psychology, N.Y. Acad. Scis., Sigma Xi. Democrat. Methodist. Current Work: Visual system structure and function, low vision, vision research low vision. Subspecialties: Visual neuroscience; Sensory processes. Home: 1930 SW 19th Way Gainesville FL 32608 Office: Dept Ophthalmology Box J-284 JHMHC U Fla Coll Medicine Gainesville FL 32610

HOPE, LAWRENCE LATIMER, physicist; b. N.Y.C., Dec. 28, 1939; s. William J. and Virginia (Latimer) H.; m. Dorett Amie Merk. Mar. 22, 1964 (div. 1984); 1 child, Timothy Lawrence. B.S. in Physics, CUNY, 1961; M.S., Stevens Inst. Tech., 1963, Ph.D., 1966; S.M. in Mgmt., MIT, 1976. Mem. tech. staff GTE Labs., Bayside, N.Y., 1966-72, Waltham, Mass., 1972-75, cons. Stow, Mass., 1975-76; program mgr. GTE Products Corp., Salem, Mass., 1976—; adj. prof. Hofstra U., Hempstead, N.Y., 1969-71. Contbr. articles to profl. jours. Patentee thin film tech. NSF grad. fellow, 1964. Mem. Soc. for Info. Display (chpt. vice chmn. 1980-81), Am. Phys. Soc., IEEE, AAAS. Current work: Electroluminescence; nonlinear optics; lasers; high field phenomena; technology management. Subspecialties: Condensed matter physics; Theoretical physics. Home: 7-5 Apple Ridge Rd Maynard MA 01754 Office: GTE Products Corp 60 Boston St Salem MA 01970

HOPFIELD, JOHN JOSEPH, biophysicist, educator; b. Chgo., July 15, 1933; s. John Joseph and Helen (Staff) H.; m. Cornelia Fuller, June 30, 1954; children—Alison, Jessica, Natalie. A.B., Swarthmore Coll., 1954; Ph.D., Cornell U., 1958. Mem. tech. staff Bell Telephone Labs., 1958-60, 73—; vis. research physicist Ecole Normale Superieure, Paris, France, 1960-61; asst. prof., then asso. prof. physics U. Calif. at Berkeley, 1961-64; prof. physics Princeton U., 1964-80, Eugene Higgins prof. physics, 1978-80; Dickinson prof. chemistry and biology Calif. Inst. Tech., Pasadena, 1980—. Guggenheim fellow, 1969; MacArthur Found. grantee, 1983. Fellow Am. Phys. Soc. (Oliver E. Buckley prize 1968, Biol. Physics prize 1985); mem. Nat. Acad. Scis., Am. Acad. Arts and Scis., Neurosci. Research Program, Phi Beta Kappa, Sigma Xi. Current Work: The relation between structure and function in biology; electron and transfer processes and solar energy; collective properties of neural networks. Subspecialties: Theoretical chemistry; Neural modelling. Office: Calif Inst Tech Pasadena CA 91106

HOPGOOD, DAVID, chemist, petroleum engineer; b. Kilkhampton, Cornwall, Eng., Mar. 8, 1942; came to U.S., 1966, naturalized, 1975; s. Lewis William Richard and Lilian May (Putt) H.; m. Diane Lynn Case, Mar. 15, 1969; children—Vanessa, Alexander. B.Sc. (spl.), Imperial Coll., London U., 1963, Ph.D., 1966. Asst. prof. chemistry U. Wis., Madison, 1969-73; head applications lab. Pfizer, Inc., Groton, Conn., 1973-76; mgr. research Kelco div. Merck, San Diego, 1976-80, Western Co. N.Am., Fort Worth, 1980-81; supr. research UNOCAL, Brea, Calif., 1981—. Contbr. articles to profl. jours. Mem. Am. Chem. Soc., Soc. Petroleum Engrs. (treas. production research 1984—), Soc. Rheology. Club: Toastmasters (sec.-treas. 1985—). Current work: Research and development in chemical and engineering aspects of oilfield operations in drilling, completions, stimulation, production and enhanced oil recovery. Subspecialty: Petroleum engineering. Office: Sci and Tech Div UNOCAL 376 S Valencia Ave Brea CA 92621

HOPKE, PHILIP KARL, environmental chemistry educator; b. Sherman, Tex., Mar. 22, 1944; s. George Karl and Dorothy Virginia (Dawson) H.; m. Eleanor Lois Frits, June 1, 1968; children—Jane Catherine, Frederick Karl. B.S., Trinity Coll., 1965; M.S., Princeton U., 1967. Ph.D., 1969. Research assoc. MIT, 1969-70; asst. prof. SUNY-Fredonia, 1970-74; from vis. asst. prof. to prof. environ. chemistry U. Ill., Urbana, 1974—; cons. Lawrence Livermore Lab,, Calif., 1976-82, Reed, Smith, Shaw & McClay, Pitts., 1982—, Constrn. Engring. Research Lab., Champaign, Ill., 1984—. Author: Receptor Modeling in Environmental Chemistry, 1985. Co-editor: Analytical Aspects of Environmental Chemistry, 1983; Atmosphere Aerosol; Source/Air Quality Relationship, 1981. Contbr. articles to profl. jours. Mem. Champaign Pub. Schs. Bd. Edn., 1978-81, pres., 1980-81. Grantee EPA, U.S. Bur. Mines, U.S. Dept. Energy. Mem. Am. Chem. Soc. (Subscription award 1965), Am. Phys. Soc., Am. Assn. Aerosol Research, Chemometrics Soc., AAAS. Current work: Statistical analysis of air quality data; radon and radon decay product chemistry; aerosol chemistry. Subspecialty: Nuclear chemistry. Home: 706 S Lynn St Champaign IL 61820 Office: U Ill 1005 W Western Ave Urbana IL 61801

HOPKINS, M. E., coal geologist, geology educator; b. Grove, Okla., Feb. 4, 1928; s. Maecenace E. and Betty Mae (Crook) H.; m. Patricia June Clardy, May 26, 1957; 1 child, Lisa. B.S., U. Ark., 1950, M.S., 1951; Ph.D., U. Ill., 1957. Geologist Ill. State Geol. Survey, Urbana, 1951-55, 1963-68, geologist, head coal sect., 1968-75; asst. prof. U. Tulsa, 1955-63; ptnr. H. Williamson Inc., Benton, Ill., 1975-81; dir. geology Peabody Devel. Co., St. Louis, 1981—; cons. various coal and oil cos. Editor: (with others) Environments of Coal Accumulation, 1968. Contbr. articles to profl. jours. Served with U.S. Army, 1945-46. Fellow Geol. Soc. Am. (chmn. coal div. 1976-77); mem. Soc. Mining Engrs. (program chmn. coal div. 1969), Soc. Econ. Paleontologists and Mineralogists, Ill. Mining Inst. (sec., treas. 1968-76), Rocky Mountain Coal Mining Inst., Sigma Xi, Phi Beta Kappa, Phi Kappa Phi. Republican. Current work: Coal reserve evaluation, coal mining geology, sedimentology, stratigraphy, economic geology. Subspecialties: Geology; Coal. Office: Peabody Devel Co 200 N Broadway Saint Louis MO 63102

HOPKINS, STEPHEN WILLIAM, mechanical engineer; b. Brockton, Mass., July 23, 1943; s. Royal Carlton and Bertha Irene (Crowell) H.; m. Sandra Grippen, June 23, 1963; children: Stephen R., Susan M., Scott C., Spencer M. A.S. in Mech. Engring, Wentworth Inst., 1963; B.S. in Mech. Engring, U. New Haven, 1971; M.S. in Applied Mechanics, Rensselaer Poly. Inst., 1974. Registered profl. engr., Calif. Exptl. research asst. Pratt & Whitney Aircraft Co., North Haven, Conn., 1963-69, sr. materials engr., Middletown, Conn., 1969-76; mng. engr. Failure Analysis Assocs., Palo Alto, Calif., 1976-82; dir. Exptl. and Materials Lab., 1982—; invited lectr. on material behavior and structural life predictions. Contbr. articles to profl. jours. Mem. Am. Acad. Mechanics, ASME, Soc. Exptl. Stress Analysis (chmn. No. Calif. sect. 1978-79), ASTM, Alpha Sigma Lambda. Current Work: Experimental stress analysis, instrumentation, data acquisition and mechanical lifetime predictions analysis as they related to structures and component behavior to real service loads. Subspecialties: Mechanical engineering; Fracture mechanics. Office: 2225 E Bayshore Rd Palo Alto CA 94303

HOPLIN, HERMAN PETER, information science educator, technical management consultant; b. Brandon, Minn., June 23, 1920; s. Peter Nelson and Edna Viola (Larson) H.; m. Eleanor Irene Johnson, Dec. 20, 1943; 1 dau., Barbara Lee. B.S., St. Cloud (Minn.) State U., 1942; M.B.A., Syracuse U., 1955; M.A. in Internat. Affairs, George Washington U., 1963, D.B.A., 1975. Commd. 2d lt. U.S. Army, 1942, advanced through grades to col., 1965, ret., 1972; mem. staff Joint Chiefs of Staff, Washington, 1967-72; research assoc. George Washington U., 1972-75; sr. mgmt. cons. Howard Finley Corp., Houston, 1973-75; professional lectr. Am. U., Washington, 1976-78, asst. prof. computers and mgmt. info. systems, 1978-79; assoc. prof. mgmt. info. systems Syracuse U., 1979—; lectr. Soc. for Mgmt. Info. Systems, 1975—; dir. Univ. Scis. Forum, Falls Church, Va., 1977-81; mem. exec. bd. Internat. Cons. Found., Washington, 1982—; mem. info. systems program and curriculum com. Data Processing Mgmt. Assn. Edn. Found., Park Ridge, Ill., 1982-84. Author, contbr. papers and articles to profl. jours., symposia and confs.; referee: Systems Research Jour., Computer Measurement Group; mem. reviewing Staff Computing Reviews. Mem. adv. bd. University Coll., Syracuse, 1982—. Decorated Legion of Merit, D.S.M.; recipient Eagle scout award Boy Scouts Am., 1938; named Indian Chief Confederated Tribes of Umatilla Reservation, Oreg., 1967. Mem. Syracuse Systems Execs. Group (acad. mem.), Assn. for Computing Machinery (chmn. Syracuse chpt. 1982—), Soc. for Gen. Systems Research, Inst. Mgmt. Scis., IEEE Computer Soc. Lodge: Rotary. Current Work: User-oriented and designed information systems, organization and management of information centers, high technology performance evaluation, and data base research in eight significant areas included distributed data base. Subspecialties: Information systems (Information science); Database systems. Home: 8188 Pembroke Dr Manlius NY 13104 Office: Syracuse U Sch Mgmt Syracuse NY 13244

HOPPENSTEADT, FRANK CHARLES, mathematician; b. Oak Park, Ill., Apr. 29, 1938; s. Frank Carl and Margaret C. H.; children—Charles, Matthew, Sarah. B.A., Butler U., 1960; M.S., U. Wis.-Madison, 1962, Ph.D., 1965. Assoc. prof. Mich. State U., East Lansing, Mich., 1965-68; prof. Courant Inst., NYU, N.Y.C., 1968-79; prof., chmn. math. dept. U. Utah, Salt Lake City, 1977—; sr. vis. fellow Oxford U., 1974, Author: Math Methods of Population biology, 1982, Introduction to Mathematics of Neurons, 1985. Mem. Am. Math. Soc. (chmn. applied math. 1976-79), Soc. for Indsl. and Applied Math., Am. Soc. Microbiology, Sigma Xi. Current work: Perturbation theory, nonlinear oscillations, integrated circuits, neuro-biology, ppopulation biology. Subspecialties: Applied mathematics; Genetics and genetic engineering (biology). Office: Math Dept U Utah Salt Lake City UT 84112

HOPPER, DARREL GENE, chemical physics and electronics engineering educator; b. Stillwater, Okla., June 10, 1944; s. Doyle Houston and Dorthea Eleen (Randolph) H.; m. Chahira Metwally, Aus. 31, 1969; children: Dalia Lee Elizabeth, Paul Darrel Alexander. B.S. with honors, Okla. State U., 1966, Ph.D., 1971. Fellow NRC, Washington, 1972-74; faculty level appointee Argonne Nat. Lab., 1974-77; sr. scientist and div. mgr. Sci. Applications, Inc., La Jolla, Calif., 1977-79; research prof. Wright State U., Dayton, Ohio, 1977-81; theoretical chemist JAYCOR, La Jolla, 1979-80; dir. Mattergy Research Inst., Dayton, 1982—; physicist USAF, Wright-Patterson AFB, Ohio, 1982—, prof. electronics engring. Air Force Inst. Tech., 1985—. Chmn. Zoning Bd. Appeals, City of Beavercreek, Ohio, 1982—. Contbr. articles to profl. jours. Mem. Am. Phys. Soc., Am. Chem. Soc., Laser Inst. Am., Internat. Assn. Optical Engring., Assn. Old Crows. Republican. Presbyterian. Club: Officers (Dayton). Current Work: Optical information processing, molecular structure; molecular structure, atmospheric chemistry, light-matter interactions. Quantum mechanical theory, ab initio methods, reaction mechanisms, molecular dynamics, photochemistry, ozone layer. Subspecialties: Atomic and molecular physics; Theoretical chemistry. Office: Air Force Inst Tech Wright-Patterson AFB OH 45433

HOPPER, GRACE BREWSTER MURRAY, mathematician; b. N.Y.C., Dec. 9, 1906; d. Walter Fletcher; m. Vincent Foster Hopper, June 15, 1930 (div. 1945). B.A., Vassar Coll., 1928; M.A. (Vassar fellow, Sterling scholar), Yale, 1930, Ph.D., 1934; postgrad. (Vassar Faculty fellow), N.Y. U., 1941-42; D.Eng. (hon.), Newark Coll. Engring., 1972; D.Sc. (hon.), C.W. Post Coll. L.I. U., 1973, Pratt Inst., 1976, Linkoping U., Sweden, 1980, Bucknell U., 1980, Acadia U., Can., 1980, So. Ill. U., 1981, Loyola U. Chgo., 1981; LL.D., U. Pa., 1974; D.Public Service, George Washington U., 1981. From instr. to assoc. prof. math. Vassar Coll., 1931-44; asst. prof. math. Barnard Coll., summer 1943; research fellow engring. scis., applied physics Computation Lab., Harvard, 1946-49; sr. mathematician Eckert-Mauchly Computer Corp., Phila., 1949-50; sr. programmer Eckert-Mauchly div. Remington Rand, 1950-59; systems engr., dir. automatic programming devel. UNIVAC div. Sperry Rand Corp., Phila., 1959-64, staff scientist systems programming, 1964-71, ret., 1971; vis. lectr. Moore Sch. Elec. Engring., U. Pa., 1959-63, vis. assoc. prof. elec. engring., 1963-74, adj. prof., 1974; professorial lectr. George Washington U., 1971—. Contbr. numerous articles to profl. jours. Served to comdr. WAVES, 1944-46, 67—; capt. USNR, 1973; presently serving active duty NAVDAC, achieved rank of commodore, 1984. Decorated Legion of Merit, Meritorious Service award; recipient Naval Ordnance Devel. award, 1946; Connelly Meml. award, 1968; Wilbur L. Cross medal Yale U., 1972; Sci. Achievement award Am. Mother's Com., 1970; Lovelace award Assn. Women in Computing, 1983; others. Distinguished fellow Brit. Computer Soc.; fellow Assn. Computer Programmers and Analysts, IEEE (McDowell award 1979), AAAS; mem. Nat. Acad. Engring., Assn. Computing Machinery, Data Processing Mgmt. Assn. (Man of Yr. award 1969), Am. Fedn. Information Processing Socs. (Harry Goode Meml. award 1970), Soc. Women Engrs. (Achievement award 1964), Franklin Inst., U.S. Naval Inst., Internat. Oceanographic Found., DAR, Dames Loyal Legion, Hist. Soc. Pa., Geneal. Soc. Pa., N.H. Hist. Soc., New Eng. Hist.-Geneal. Soc., Valley Forge Hist. Assn., Ret. Officers Assn., Huguenot Soc. Pa., Nat., N.Y. geneal. socs., Pechin Soc., Phi Beta Kappa, Sigma Xi. Office: Dept Navy NAVDAC Washington DC 20374

HOPWOOD, LARRY EUGENE, radiation biologist, researcher; b. Frederick, Md., Dec. 11, 1945; s. Guy Emmitt and Ruth (Shankle) H.; m. Victoria Piaskowski, Oct. 23, 1983; children—Kelley Piaskowski, Ian. B.S., Johns Hopkins U., 1967; Ph.D., Washington U., St. Louis, 1971. Research instr. Washington U., St. Louis, 1971-72; asst. prof. Colo. State U., Ft. Collins, 1972-77; assoc. prof. Med. Coll. Wis., Milw. 1977—; mem. Wis. State Radiation Protection Fetal Effects Com., Madison, 1984. Co-author: Biological Effects of Radiations, 1979. Contbr. articles to profl. jours. Grantee Am. Cancer Soc., 1979-84, Nat. Cancer Inst., 1978-82, 84-87; recipient Nat. Cancer Inst. Career Devel. award, 1977-82. Mem. Radiation Research Soc., Am. Soc. Therapeutic Radiologists. Home: 2436 N 88th St Wauwatosa WI 53226 Office: Med Coll of Wis 8700 W Wisconsin Box 165 Milwaukee WI 53226

HORAKOVA, ZDENKA ZAHUTOVA, toxicologist, researcher; b. Jindrichuv Hradec, Czechoslovakia, Apr. 6, 1925; d. Josef and Aloisie (Sohajova) Zahut; m. Vaclav Horak, Sept. 26, 1949; 1 son: David. Magister of Pharmacy, Charles U., Prague, 1949, Dr. of Natural Scis., 1952; Ph.D. in Pharmacology, Czechoslovakian Acad. Sci., 1961. Teaching asst. dept. pharmacology Med. Faculty, Charles U., Prague, 1949-50; research pharmacologist Research Inst. for Pharmacy and Biochemistry, Prague, 1950-58, head pharmacol. dept., 1958-68; vis. guest Zambon Pharm. Research Inst., Bresso-Milano, Italy, 1968; research pharmacologist exptl. therapeutics br. Nat. Heart and Lung Inst., NIH, Bethesda, Md., 1969-74, Lab. of Cellular Metabolism and Pulmonary Br., 1974-78; toxicologist, researcher Food Safety and Inspection Service, Residue Evaluation, Sci. div. Dept. Agr., Washington, 1978—; mem. Nat. Toxicology Program Working Group. Contbr. numerous articles on toxicology and pharmacology to profl. jours. Recipient diploma for Sci. Discovery on Inhibin Ministry of Health Prague, 1960. Mem. Am. Soc. of Pharmacology and Exptl. Therapeutics, Soc. Toxicology, Internat. Union of Pharmacology (organizing com. 2d Internat. Congress on Pharmacology 1963), Internat. Soc. for Study of Xenobiotics, Soc. for Exptl. Biology and Medicine (D.C. sect.), Cell and Molecular Biology in Space (NASA), Inflammation Research Assn., Internat. Soc. for Biochem Pharmacology, Internat. Inflammation Club, European Biol. Research Assn., Sigma Delta Epsilon. Roman Catholic. Current Work: Pharmacological testing, methodology, inflammation, toxicology-residue evaluation. Subspecialties: Pharmacology; Toxicology (medicine). Home: 5508 Oakmont Ave Bethesda MD 20817 Office: 300 12th St SW Washington DC 20250

HORANYI, MIHALY, physicist; b. Budapest, Hungary, Sept. 16, 1955; s. Mihaly and Julianna (Csepella) H.; m. Anna Hasenfratz, Dec. 28, 1980; 1 child, Eszter. M.S., Lorand Eotvos U., Budapest, 1975-80, Ph.D., 1982. Sci. assoc. Ctr. Research Inst. Physics, Budapest, 1980—; vis. scientist Space Physics Research Lab., U. Mich., Ann Arbor, 1984-85, Supercomputer Computational Research Inst., Fla. State U., Tallahassee, 1985—. Contbr. articles to profl. jours. Mem. Am. Astron. Soc., Lorand Eotvos Phys. Soc. Current work: Interstellar and interplanetary matter, atmospheres of planets, comets. Subspecialties: Planetary science; Theoretical astrophysics. Home: Zolyomi-42/B Budapest Hungary 1112 Office: Supercomputer Computational Research Inst Fla State U Tallahassee FL 32306

HORECKER, BERNARD LEONARD, biochemist; b. Chgo., Oct. 31, 1914; s. Paul and Bessie (Bornstein) H.; m. Frances Goldstein, July 12, 1936; children: Doris Colgate, Marilyn Diamond, Linda Lally. B.S., U. Chgo., 1936, Ph.D., 1939; Laureate honoris causa in Biol. Scis., U. Urbino (Italy), 1982. Research asso. chemistry U. Chgo., 1939-40; examiner U.S. Civil Service Commn., 1940-41; biochemist USPHS, NIH, Bethesda, Md., 1941-59; chief lab. of biochemistry and metabolism Nat. Inst. Arthritis and Metabolic Disease, 1956-59; professorial lectr. enzyme chemistry George Washington U., 1950-57; guest research-worker Pasteur Inst., Paris, France, 1957-58; prof. microbiology, chmn. dept. N.Y. U. Coll. Medicine, 1959-63; prof. molecular biology, chmn. dept. Albert Einstein Coll. Medicine, 1963-72, assoc. dean for sci. affairs, 1971-72; mem. Roche Inst. Molecular Biology, Nutley, N.J., 1972-84, head Lab. Molecular Enzymology, 1977-84; adj. prof. Cornell U. Med. Coll., 1972-84, prof. bio chemistry, dean Grad. Sch. Med. Scis., 1984—; vis. prof. Albert Einstein Coll. Medicine, 1972-84; vis. prof. biochemistry U. Calif., 1954, U. Parana, Brazil, 1960, 63; vis. lectr. U. Ill., 1956; Ciba lectr. Rutgers U., 1962; Phillips lectr. Haverford Coll., 1965; vis. prof. Kyoto (Japan) U., 1967; vis. prof. biochemistry and molecular biology Cornell U., 1965; vis. prof. U. Ferrara, Italy; Reilly lectr. Notre Dame U., 1969; vis. lectr. U. Rotterdam, 1970; prof. honoris causa Fed. U. Parana, Curitiba, Brazil, 1981—; mem. sci. adv. bd. Roche Inst. Molecular Biology, Nutley, N.J., 1967-72, chmn., 1971-72; dir. Academic Press, Inc., 1968-73; mem. Research Career Award com. Nat. Inst. Gen. Med. Scis., 1966-70; mem. personnel com. Am. Cancer Soc., 1968-72, mem. sci. adv. com. for biochemistry and chem. carcinogenesis, 1974-78; mem. biology div. adv. com. Oak Ridge Nat. Lab., 1976-80; mem. Med. Scientist Tng. Program Sect. NIH, 1970—. Editor: Biochem. and Biophys. Research Communications, 1959—, Current Topics in Cellular Regulation, 1969—, Archives Biochemistry and Biophysics, 1960-68; chmn. editorial bd.: Archives of Biochemistry and Biophysics, 1968-84; contbr. articles to sci. publs. Recipient Paul Lewis Labs. award in enzyme chemistry, 1952; Superior Accomplishment award Fed. Security Agy., 1952; Rockefeller Pub. Service award, 1957; Hillebrand prize Am. Chem. Soc., 1954; award in biol. scis. Washington Acad. Sci., 1954; Fulbright Travel award, 1963; Commonwealth Fund fellow, 1967. Fellow AAAS, Am. Acad. Arts and Scis.; mem. Am. Chem. Soc. (vice chmn. div. biol. chemistry 1975-76, chmn. 1976—), Biochem. Soc. (Eng.), Swiss Biochem. Soc. (hon. mem.), Spanish Biochem. Soc., hon. mem.), Japanese Biochem. Soc. (hon. mem.), Hellenic Biochem. and Biophys. Soc. (hon. mem.), Am. Soc. Biol. Chemists (pres. 1967-68, chmn. editorial com. 1962-63, Merck award 1981, Neuberg medal 1981), Nat. Acad. Scis., Harvey Soc. (v.p. 1969-70, pres. 1970-71), Brazilian Acad. Sci. (hon.), PanAm. Assn. Biochem. Socs. (vice chmn. 1971, chmn. 1972, mem. exec. com. 1971-78), Instituto de Investigaciones Citologicas (corr.), Phi Beta Kappa, Sigma Xi. Current Work: Intracellular proteinosis: their role in regulation of metabolism. Peptides and peptide hormones: structure, function and biosynthesis. Subspecialties: Biochemistry (biology); Molecular biology. Office: Cornell U Graduate School of Medical Sciences 1300 York Ave New York NY 10021

HOREN, DANIEL JOSEPH, physicist; b. New London, Conn., May 17, 1928; s. Morris Oscar and Gertrude (Tarnapol) H.; m. Margareta Friedman, May 15, 1959; children—Sharon Danielle, Risa Gertruda. S.B., MIT, 1952; Ph.D., Stanford U., 1959. AEC fellow Lawrence Radiation Lab., Berkeley, Calif., 1959-63, cons., 1963-69; physicist Navy Radiol. Def. Lab., San Francisco, 1963-67, head acceleration br., 1967-69; dir. nuclear data project Oak Ridge Nat. Lab., 1969-75, sr. staff scientist, 1975—; vis. prof. nuclear physics U. La Plata, Argentina, 1961, Inst. Nuclear Sci., U. Grenoble, France, 1973-74. Editor nuclear data sheets, 1969-75. Contbr. articles to profl. jours. Served with USN, 1946-48. Sloan Found. fellow, 1958-59. Fellow Am. Phys. Soc.; mem. AAAS, Sigma Xi. Current work: Experimental intermediate energy nuclear physics, nuclear structure. Subspecialty: Nuclear physics. Home: 16 Windhaven Ln Oak Ridge TN 37830 Office: Oak Ridge Nat Lab PO Box X Oak Ridge TN 37830

HORMAN, MELVIN HERBERT, engineer; b. Renton, Wash., Sept. 14, 1923; s. Herbert Vowels and Alvena Marie (Bloechlinger) H.; m. Joyce Pauline Malde, June 26, 1943; children—Colin Drew, Richard Neil, Melde Ross, Kimberly Joyce. B.S. in Math., U. Wash., 1950, B.S. in Physics, 1950; M.A. in Math., UCLA, 1960. Tchr. Lincoln High Sch., Tacoma; physicist Naval Ordinance Lab., Nat. Bur. Standards, Corona, Calif., 1952-54, Motorola Inc., Riverside, Calif., 1954-61; research specialist Boeing, Seattle, 1961-78; engr. specialist Northrop Corp., Anaheim, Calif., 1978—. Contbr. articles to profl. jours. Served with U.S. Army, 1942-45, PTO. Mem. Optical Soc. Am. Current work: Computer-aided analysis of electro-optical systems. Subspecialties: Aerospace engineering and technology; Computer-aided design. Home: 26492 Via Juanita Mission Viejo CA 92691 Office: Electro-Mechdn Northrop Corp 500 E Orangethorpe Anaheim CA 92801

HORN, BERTHOLD KLAUS PAUL, computer educator, consultant; b. Teplice, Czechoslovakia, Dec. 8, 1943; came to U.S., 1972, naturalized, 1974; s. Alfred J.L. and Paula F.A. (Glockner) H; m. Blenda Voslov, Feb. 4, 1966. B.Sc. in Engring., U. Witwatersrand, 1965; S.M., MIT, 1968, Ph.D., 1970. Cons. in machine vision and robotics, 1965—; jr. lectr. U. Witwatersrand, Johannesburg, S.Africa, 1966-67; lectr., 1971-72; software mgr. Perseus Computing Co., Pretoria, S.Africa, 1972-73; research assoc. Artificial Intelligence Lab., MIT, Cambridge, 1974-75, asst. prof., 1975-78, assoc. prof., 1978-82, prof. elec. engring. and computer sci., 1982—. Author: (with Patrick H. Winston) LISP, 1981; Robot Vision, 1986. Editor: Computer Vision, Graphics and Image Processing, 1983—. Patentee in field. Chamber of Mines scholar, gold medalist, Johannesburg, 1965. Mem. African Wildlife Protection Assn., S.W. Africa Sci. Assn., Swiss Alpine Club, Boston Mycol. Club. Current Work: Machine vision, robotics, visual perception, advanced automation. Subspecialty: Robotics. Office: Room 765 Artificial Intelligence Lab Mass Inst Tech 545 Technology Sq Cambridge MA 02139

HORN, DAVID JACOBS, entomology educator; b. Phila., Feb. 12, 1943; s. Henry Eyster and Catherine (Stainken) H.; m. Rosalind Ball Steimle, Sept. 10, 1966; children—Catherine Ann, Rosalind Ball. B.A., Harvard U., 1965; M.S., Cornell U., 1967, Ph.D., 1969. Research asst. Cornell U., 1965-69; asst. prof. entomology Calif. State U.-Hayward, 1969-72; assoc. prof. entomology Ohio State U., 1972-78, prof., 1978—. Editor: Biology of Insects, 1976; Analysis of Ecological Systems, 1979. Contbr. articles to profl. jours. Fellow Ohio Acad Sci.; mem. AAAS, Entomol. Soc. Am. Ecol. Soc. Am., Am. Inst. Biol. Sci. Lutheran. Current work: Role of predators and parasitoids in insect population dynamics; ecology of colonization and extinction. Subspecialties: Integrated pest management; Ecology (biology). Home: 37 Arden Rd Columbus OH 43214 Office: Ohio State U 1735 Neil Ave Columbus OH 43210

HORN, DENNIS LEE, environmental specialist; b. Appleton, Wis., Mar. 8, 1938; s. Irwin Walter and Mildred Marie (Endter) H.; m. Carmen Joan Loken, June 29, 1963; children—Rebecca, Barbara. Mill worker Fox River Paper Co., Appleton, 1961-69, lab. technician, 1969-72, environ. specialist, 1972—. Served with USAF, 1957-61. Mem. TAPPI, Water and Pollution Control Fedn., Fla. Water and Pollution Control Authority. Lodge: Eagles. Current work: Water and waste water treatment and pulp and paper microbiology. Subspecialties: Water supply and wastewater treatment; Microbiology. Home: 915 N Rankin St Appleton WI 54911 Office: 200 E Washington St Appleton WI 54913

HORN, ROGER ALAN, mathematician, educator, consultant; b. Macon, Ga., Jan. 19, 1942; s. Woodrow A. and Betty (McClure) H.; m. Susan Dadakis, July 24, 1965; children—Ceres, Corinne, Howard. B.A., Cornell U., 1963; M.S., Stanford U., 1964, Ph.D., 1967. Asst. prof. U. Santa Clara, Calif., 1967-68; asst. prof. math. Johns Hopkins U., Balt., 1968-71, assoc. prof., 1972-75, prof., 1975—; assoc. prof. U. Md.-Baltimore County, 1971-72; pres., dir. QC Inc., Balt., 1975—. Author: Matrix Analysis, 1985; Topics in Matrix Analysis, 1985; also articles. Alfred P. Sloan Found. fellow, 1975-78. Mem. Am. Math. Soc., Math. Assn. Am., Soc. Indsl. and Applied Math., Phi Beta Kappa, Sigma Xi. Current work: Matrix analysis and complex analysis as both pure disciplines and a source of important applications. Subspecialty: Analysis. Office: Dept Math Scis Johns Hopkins U Baltimore MD 21218

HORN, STANISLAV VÁCLAV, fluid dynamicist, researcher; b. Prague, Czechoslovakia, Dec. 22, 1943; came to U.S., 1978, naturalized, 1983; s. Stanislav Horn and Zdena (Borovicková) Hornová; m. Karen Marie Sherwood, June 3, 1978 (div. 1983); 1 child, Victoria. M.E., Fed. Inst. of Tech., Liberec, Czechoslovakia, 1966; Ph.D., Czechoslovakia Acad. of Scis., Prague, 19—. Research asst. Czechoslovak Metrological Inst., Prague, 1966-69; research scientist Nat. Research Inst., Prague, 1969-78; research engr. Transamerica Delaval, Trenton, N.J., 1979-81; engr. specialist RCIRC Borg Warner, Des Plaines, Ill., 1981—. Mem. ASME. Clubs: Am. Alpine (N.Y.), Mountaineer (Chgo.). Current work: Internal fluid dynamics of turbomachinery (pump hydrodynamics, compressor aerodynamics), valve fluid dynamics. Subspecialty: Fluid mechanics. Office: RCIRC Borg Warner Wolf & Algonquin Rds Des Plaines IL 60018

HORNBEIN, THOMAS F., physician; b. St. Louis, 1930. M.D., Washington U., St. Louis, 1956. Diplomate: Am. Bd. Anesthesiology. Intern King County Hosp., Seattle, 1956-57; resident in anesthesiology Washington U. Hosp., 1957-59, research fellow in respiratory physiology, 1959-61; asst. in anesthesiology Barnes Hosp., St. Louis, 1960-61; asst. prof. anesthesiology U. Wash., 1963-67, asso. prof., 1967-70, prof. anesthesiology, 1970—, prof. physiology and biophysics, 1970—, vice chmn. dept. anesthesiology, 1972-74, chmn. dept., 1978—. Served to lt. comdr. USNR, 1961-63. Current Work: Respiratory physiology, control of breathing, brain acid-base regulation, brain hypoxia-limits. Subspecialty: Anesthesiology. Office: U Wash Sch of Medicine RN-10 Seattle WA 98195

HORNE, FREDERICK HERBERT, chemistry educator; b. Kansas City, Mo., Mar. 11, 1934; s. Corwin Denzel and Ella Mae (Player) H.; m. Clara Ann Johnson, Jan. 31, 1959; children—Frederick John, James Herbert, Nancy Carolyn. A.B., Harvard U., 1956; Ph.D., U. Kans., 1962. Instr. chemistry Stanford U., 1963-64; asst. prof. chemistry Mich. State U., East Lansing, 1964-69, assoc. prof. chemistry, 1969-73, prof. chemistry, 1973—, assoc. chairperson chemistry dept., 1975-82, assoc. dean research and grad. programs Coll. Natural Sci., 1982—; vis. prof. Arya Mehr U., Tehran, Iran, 1975; vis. scientist Lawrence Livermore Lab., Calif., 1970, Odense U., Denmark, 1979; cons. various industries and govt. labs. Sci. editor Ann. Obituary, 1984—. Contbr. articles to sci. jours. Danforth assoc., 1971; NSF postdoctoral fellow, 1962-63, coop. grad. fellow, 1959-61; Harvard U. Nat. scholar, 1952-55. Mem. Am. Chem. Soc., Am. Phys. Soc., Materials Research Soc., Sigma Xi. Current work: Thermal diffusion in solid, liquid and gaseous mixtures; fast ion transport in solids; membrane transport; applied mathematics; chemical kinetics; diffusion of electrolytes in charged systems. Subspecialties: Theoretical chemistry; Thermodynamics. Home: 1428 Sylvan Glen Okemos MI 48864 Office: Coll Natural Sci Mich State U 154 Natural Sci Bldg East Lansing MI 48824

HORNER, HARRY THEODORE, botany educator; b. Chgo., Jan. 28, 1936; s. Harry Theodore and Eloise Gertrude (Blum) H.; m. Cecilia Astrid Midthun, Mar. 27, 1937; children: Kevin Scott, Amy Lynn, Allison Lee. B.A., Northwestern U., 1959, M.S., 1961, Ph.D., 1964. Pub. health postdoctoral fellow Iowa State U., Ames, 1964-66, asst. prof., 1966-69, assoc. prof., 1969-73, prof. dept. botany, 1973—; guest prof. U. Konstanz, W.Ger., 1979-80; dir. Bessey Microscopy Facility, 1970—. Contbr. articles in field to profl. jours. Recipient Centennial award Iowa Acad. Sci., 1975, Disting. Service award, 1985; Adviser award Iowa State U., 1982. Mem. Bot. Soc. Am., Am. Soc. Cell Biology, Am. Inst. Biol. Sci., Am. Micros. Soc., Am Soc. Electron Microscopy, Sigma Xi. Republican. Presbyterian. Current Work: Plant calcification/mineralization, male and female sterility. Subspecialties: Cell and tissue culture; Developmental biology. Office: Dept Botany Iowa State U Ames IA 50011

HOROVITZ, ZOLA PHILIP, pharm. co. exec.; b. Pitts., Oct. 12, 1934; s. Reuben and Jean (Liff) H.; m. Marlene Davis, Aug. 24, 1958; children: Bonna Lynn, Reid Alan. B.S. in Pharmacy, U. Pitts., 1955, M.S. in Pharmacology, 1958, Ph.D. in Pharmacology, 1960. Registered pharmacist, Pa. Vis. investigator VA Research Lab. Neuropsychiatry, Pitts., 1958-59; sr. research scientist Squibb Inst. Med. Research, E.R. Squibb & Sons Inc., Princeton, N.J., 1959-65, clin. assoc., 1965-66, dir. dept. pharmacology, 1967-72, assoc. dir. research, 1972-79, v.p. drug devel., 1979-85, v.p. research planning and sci. liaison, 1985—; vis. prof. psychiatry Rutgers Sch. Medicine, 1974-76; vis. prof. pharmacology Rutgers Coll. Pharmacy, 1979—, trustee, mem. adv. bd., 1980—; mem. sci. adv. council Princeton U., 1978—. Mem. East Brunswick (N.J.) Bd. Edn., 1967-70; pres. Jewish Center at Princeton, 1980-82. Served with U.S. N.G., 1953-62. Recipient A.E. Bennett prize in neuropsychopharmacology, 1965; Am. Found. Pharm. Edn. fellow, 1958-60. Fellow Acad. Pharm. Scis.; mem. Am. Pharmacology Soc., Brit. Pharmacology Soc. Patentee in field. Current Work: Administrator of pharmaceutical research and development. Subspecialty: Pharmacology. Home: 30 Philip Dr Princeton NJ 08540 Office: Box 4000 Princeton NJ 08540

HOROWITZ, CARL, chemist, chem. co. exec.; b. Lvov, Poland, Aug. 10, 1923; s. Nathan and Amalie (Roth) H.; m. Irene Mandel, Dec. 9, 1946; children: Alice, Terry. B.S., Columbia U., 1950; M.S. in Chemistry, Bklyn. Poly. Inst., 1961. Vice-pres. Yardney Electric Co., N.Y.C., 1951-63; pres. Polymer Research Corp., Bklyn., 1963—. Mem. Am. Chem. Soc., Electrochem. Soc., Am. Inst. Chem. Engrs., Am. Assn. Textile Chemists and Colorists. Democrat. Jewish. Patentee in field. Current Work: Chemical grafting of polymers; silver-zinc highpower batteries. Subspecialty: Polymer chemistry. Office: 2186 Mill Ave Brooklyn NY 11234

HOROWITZ, EMANUEL, materials science educator, center administrator; b. N.Y.C., Mar. 29, 1923; s. Barney and Florence (Stein) H.; m. Diane Silverman, Aug. 6, 1950; children—Amy, Andrew, Alice, Alan. B.S., CCNY, 1948; M.S. in Chemistry, George Washington U., 1956, Ph.D., 1963. Research chemist, Smithsonian Instn., Washington, 1949-51; supervisory chemist Nat. Bur. Standards, Washington, 1951-68, dep. dir. Inst. Materials Research, 1968-78, dep. dir. Nat. Measurement Lab., 1978-80, prof. materials sci. Johns Hopkins U., Balt., 1980—, dir. Ctr. for Materials Research, 1980—; chmn. interagency council for materials Nat. Acad. Scis., 1973-75. Cubmaster Boy Scouts Am., Silver Spring, Md., 1966-68; mem. Montgomery County Planning Bd., Silver Spring, 1974. Served to 1st lt. AC U.S. Army, 1943-46; PTO. Recipient Rosa award Nat. Bur. Standards, 1972, Republic of China Standards award, 1974; Gold medal Nat. Bur. Standards, 1975. Fellow Washington Acad. Sci.; mem. Am. Chem. Soc. (trustee 1980—), N.Y. Acad. Sci. ASTM (chmn. subcom.; hon. mem.), Fedn. Materials Scis. (pres. 1983). Club: Cosmos. Jewish. Current work: Characterization of materials properties, correlation of chemical composition, microstructure with properties and performance of materials. Subspecialties: Materials; Biomaterials. Office: Johns Hopkins U Ctr for Materials Research 34th St and N Charles St Baltimore MD 21218

HORST, RALPH KENNETH, educator; b. Massillon, Ohio, June 22, 1935; s. Ralph Emerson and Florence Ellen (Huff) H.; m. Nancy J. Vernon, June 11, 1960 (div.); children: Jeffrey Todd, Bradley Craig, Timothy; m. Hope T. Thorn, July 11, 1969; 1 stepdau, Anne Elizabeth. B.S., Ohio U., 1957; M.S., Ohio State U., 1959, Ph.D., 1961. Dir. plant pathology lab. Yoder Bros., Inc., Barberton, Ohio, 1962-68; asst. prof. plant pathology Cornell U., Ithaca, N.Y., 1968-74, asso. prof., 1974-80, prof., 1980—. Mem. Internat. Soc. Plant Pathology, Internat. Soc. Hort. Sci., Am. Phytopath. Soc., AAAS, Soc. Am. Florists, Tissue Culture Assn., Sigma Xi, Gamma Sigma Delta. Methodist. Club: Rotary. Current Work: Teacher and researcher in detection and therapeutic procedures for viroid diseases and diseases caused by mycoplasmalike organisms. Subspecialties: Plant virology; Plant cell and tissue culture. Home: 107 Birchwood Dr Ithaca NY 14850 Office: Cornell University Dept Plant Pathology 323 Plant Science Bldg Ithaca NY 14853

HORSTMANN, PAUL WILLIAM, electrical engineer, educator; b. St. Louis, Apr. 6, 1951; s. Alfred Christian and Irma Augusta (Krummrich) H.; m. Susan Margaret Braun. B.S. in Computer Sci. and Elec. Engring., U. Mo.-Rolla, 1973, M.S. in Computer Sci., 1974; Ph.D. in Elec. Engring., Syracuse U., 1983. Registered profl. engr., N.Y. Design engr. IBM, Hopewell Junction, N.Y., 1974-81, project mgr., Poughkeepsie, N.Y., 1983—; adj. prof. Syracuse U., N.Y., 1984—. Contbr. articles to profl. jours. IBM grad. fellow Syracuse U., 1981-83. Mem. IEEE (sr. mem.; sect. treas, 1984-85; Outstanding Contbr. award 1983), Sigma Xi, Tau Beta Pi, Phi Kappa Phi. Current work: Project manager for automatic synthesis and transformation of behavioral level digital design descriptions to physical layout using silicon compilers and expert systems. Subspecialties: Computer-aided design; Computer engineering. Home: 84 Alda Dr Poughkeepsie NY 12603 Office: IBM E34/901 PO Box 390 Poughkeepsie NY 12602

HORTON, ROBERT ANDREW, engineer; b. Oradell, N.J., Feb. 22, 1929; s. George Francis and May (Acker) H.; m. Lillian Marie Brandow, Sept. 23, 1950; children—Robert, William T., Thomas J., Nancy K. B.Ch.E., Cooper Union U., 1955. Chemist Austenal, Inc., Dover, N.J., 1955-59; pilot plant mgr. Precision Metalsmiths, Inc., Cleve., 1959-72, dir. research and devel., 1972-80; mgr. research and devel. Duradyne Techs., Mentor, Ohio, 1980-81; sect. mgr. TRW, Inc., Cleve., 1981-83, project leader, 1983—; mem. research com. Ductile Iron Soc., Mountainside, N.J., 1976-80. Contbr. articles to profl. jours. Patentee in field. Recipient Henry T. Bidwell Best Paper award Investment Casting Inst., 1983. Mem. Am. Ceramic Soc., Am. Soc. Metals. Current work: Investment casting, single crystal casting, ceramics. Subspecialties: Ceramic engineering; Metallurgy. Home: 12781 Caves Rd Chesterland OH 44026 Office: TRW Inc 23555 Euclid Ave Cleveland OH 44117

HORVATH, WILLIAM JOHN, health systems educator, research scientist; b. N.Y.C., Sept. 13, 1917; s. John and Anna (Horvath) H.; m. Rebecca Sue Badger, Feb. 23, 1963; children: Susan, John. B.S., CCNY, 1936; M.S., NYU, 1938, Ph.D., 1940. Physicist U.S. Navy-Bur. Ordnance, Washington, 1940-43; ops. analyst Chief of Naval Ops., Washington, 1943-49; sci. advisor Weapons Systems Evaluation Group, Sec. of Def., Washington, 1949-52; staff cons. Sylvania Electric Co., Bayside, N.Y., 1952-55; sect. head. Airborne Instrument Lab., Mineola, N.Y., 1955-58; prof. health systems, research scientist U. Mich., Ann Arbor, 1958—; cons. Nat. Acad. Sci., 1952-55, NIH, 1962-70, NIMH, 1967-72. Author numerous chpts. and articles in nuclear physics, ops. research, math. sociology, med. physics, health care delivery, health behavior. Bd. dirs. Washtenaw Community Services, Ann Arbor, 1978-80, Community Systems Found., 1978-81. Recipient Naval Ordnance Devel. award U.S. Dept. Navy, 1945; Presdl. Cert. of Merit, 1947. Fellow AAAS, Am. Pub. Health Assn.; mem. Am. Phys. Soc., Ops. Research Soc. Am. (Kimball medal 1977), Royal Soc. Health. Club: Cosmos (Washington). Current Work: Currently studying population health behavior, using survey methods to develop preventive measures for the promotion of better health. Subspecialties: Operations research (engineering); Health services research. Home: 2451 Trenton Ct Ann Arbor MI Office: Mental Health Research Inst U Mich Ann Arbor MI 48109

HORVITZ, DANIEL GOODMAN, statistician, educator; b. New Bedford, Mass., Mar. 4, 1921; s. Jacob A. and Lillian J. (Cohen) H.; m. Shirley Gordon, Sept. 30, 1945; children—Gary Alan, Paul Fisher, Barbara Ann. B.S., Mass. State Coll., 1943; Ph.D., Iowa State U., 1953. Asst. prof. biostats. Sch. Public Health, U. Pitts., 1951-53; asso. prof. exptl. stats. N.C. State U., Raleigh, 1953-56; statis. dir. A.J. Wood Research Corp., Phila., 1956-60; vis. prof. stats. U. Rangoon, Burma, 1960-62; sampling sect. head Research Triangle Inst., Research Triangle Park, N.C., 1962-66, dep. dir. stats. research div., 1966-71; dir. Center for Population Research and Services, 1971-73, v.p. statis. scis. group, 1974—; prof. biostats. Sch. Public Health, U. N.C., Chapel Hill, 1973-74, adj. prof., 1974—; chmn. panel on stats. for family assistance and related programs, com. on nat. stats. NRC, 1980—. Contbr. articles to profl. jours. Served with U.S. Army, 1943-46. Fellow AAAS, Am. Statis. Assn. (adv. com. to Bur. Census 1970-71, 80—, chmn. social stats sect. 1975, chmn. survey research methods sect. 1981); mem. Am. Public Health Assn., Internat. Assn. Survey Statisticians (council 1983-86), Internat. Statis. Inst. (program chmn. 1983), Population Assn. Am., Sigma Xi, Phi Kappa Phi. Jewish. Subspecialty: Statistics. Office: PO Box 12194 Research Triangle Park NC 27709

HORVITZ, HOWARD ROBERT, cell biologist. Assoc. prof. dept. biology MIT, Cambridge. Subspecialty: Cell biology. Office: MIT Dept Biology Cambridge MA 02139

HORWITT, MAX KENNETH, biochemist, educator; b. N.Y.C., Mar. 21, 1908; s. Harry and Bessie (Kenitz) H.; m. Frances Levine, 1933 (dec.); children: Ruth Ann Horwitt Singer, Mary Louise Horwitt Goldman; m. Mildred Gad Weitzman, Jan. 1, 1974. B.A., Dartmouth Coll., 1930; Ph.D., Yale U., 1935. Diplomate: Am. Bd. Nutrition, Am. Bd. Clin. Chemistry. Research fellow physiol. chemistry Yale U., 1935-37, lab. asst., 1932-34, asst., 1934-35; dir. biochem. research lab. Elgin (Ill.) State Hosp., 1937-59; dir. biochem. research lab. L.B. Mendel Research Lab., 1960-68, dir. research, 1966-68; asso. dept. biol. chemistry U. Ill. Coll. Medicine, Chgo., 1940-43, asst. prof., 1943-51, assoc. prof., 1951-62, prof., from 1962; prof. dept. biochemistry St. Louis U. Sch. Medicine, 1968-76, prof. emeritus, 1976—, cons. in nutrition div. endocrinology dept. internal medicine, 1976—, chmn. univ. instl. rev. bd., 1981-82; acting dir. div. research services Ill. Dept. Mental Health, Chgo., 1967-68; cons. human nutrition Rush Med. Sch., Chgo., 1967-83, vis. prof. dept. internal medicine, 1979-82; mem. expert group on Vitamin E WHO, 1981-82; field dir. Anemia and Malnutrition Research Center, Chiang Mai Med. Sch., Thailand, 1968-69; cons., 1976—. Contbr. numerous articles on clin. nutrition, biochemistry and psychopharmacology to profl. publs.; editorial bd.: Jour. Nutrition, 1967-71; co-editor: Am. Jour. Clin. Nutrition, 1974. Pres. Kneseth Israel Congregation, Elgin, 1965. Recipient Osborne and Mendal award Am. Inst. Nutrition, 1961. Fellow AAAS, N.Y. Acad. Scis., Am. Inst. Chemists, Gerontol. Soc.; mem. Am. Soc. Biol. Chemists, Am. Soc. Clin. Nutrition, NRC (food and nutrition bd. 1980—, com. dietary allowances), Soc. Exptl. Biology and Medicine, Soc. Biol. Psychiatry, Assn. Vitamin Chemists, Am. Chem. Soc. Current Work: Recommended dietary allowances of National Research Council, with specific assignments on Vitamin E, Thiamine, Riboflavin and Niacin-tryptophan. Subspecialty: Biochemistry (biology). Office: St Louis Univ Sch Medicine 1402 S Grand Blvd Saint Louis MO 63104

HORWITZ, ALAN F., biochemistry and biophisics educator, researcher; b. Mpls., Oct. 26, 1944; s. Burt and Helen (Bolnick) H.; m. Carole Joanne Rosen, Nov. 26, 1972; children—Jereny Joseph, Rachel Tamara. B.A. with honors, U. Wis., 1966; Ph.D., Stanford U., 1969; M.A. (hon.), U. Pa., 1978. Chemist Lawrence Berkeley Labs., Calif., 1970-73; wissenschaftlichen Mitarbeiten-Bioctr., Basel, Switzerland, 1973-74; asst. prof. U. Pa. Med. Sch., Phila., 1974-78, assoc. prof., 1978-84, prof., 1984—, chmn. biophysics program, 1978—; mem. cell and molecule basis of disease review com. NIH, 1984—. Contbr. articles to profl. jours. Author various books and book chpt. Mem. adv. com. Biochem. and Chem. Carcinogenesis, Am. Cancer Soc., 1977-81. W.D. Strouck Established Investigatorship Am. Heart Assn., 1975-79; postdoctoral fellow NIH, 1970-72. Mem. Am. Soc. Cell Biology, Am. Soc. Biological Chemists, Internat. Biophysics Soc. Subspecialties: Cell biology (medicine); Neurobiology. Office: Dept Biochemistry & Biophysics 420 Anat-Chem Bldg Sch Med U Pa Philadelphia PA 19333

HORWITZ, DAVID LARRY, health care medical executive, biomedical researcher; b. Chgo., July 13, 1942; s. Milton and Dorothy (Glass) H.; m. Gloria Jean Madian. B.A., Harvard U., 1963; M.D., U. Chgo., 1967, Ph.D., 1968. Diplomate: Am. Bd. Internal Medicine. Med. resident U. Chgo., 1971-74, asst. prof., 1974-79; assoc. prof. medicine U. Ill., Chgo., 1979—; med. dir. Travenol Labs., Deerfield, Ill., 1982—; dir. Am. Diabetes Assn. (no. Ill. affiliate), Chgo., 1977—. Contbr. articles in field to profl. jours. Served to lt. comdr. USNR, 1969-71. Recipient Research and Devel. award Am. Diabetes Assn., 1973-75; Research Career Devel. award NIH, 1975-81; named Outstanding Young Citizen Ill. Jr. C. of C., 1977. Fellow ACP; mem. Am. Diabetes Assn. (vice-chmn. research com. 1981-83), Endocrine Soc., Central Soc. Clin. Research. Current Work: Insulin secretion, insulin infusion systems, nutritional aspects of metabolic diseases, exercise physiology. Subspecialties: Endocrinology; Nutrition (medicine). Office: Travenol Labs Inc 1425 Lake Cook Rd Deerfield IL 60015

HOSENEY, RUSSELL CARL, chemistry educator; b. Coffeyville, Kans., Dec. 3, 1934; s. Russell C. and Velma H. (Riggs) H.; m. Joanna Leap, June 3, 1956; children—Cheryl, Douglas, Terri. B.S., Kans. State U., 1957, M.S., 1960, Ph.D., 1968. Research chemist U.S. Dept. Agri., Manhattan, Kans., 1956-70; prof. chemistry Kans. State U., Manhattan, 1971—; pres. C.H. Cons. Inc., Manhattan, 1982—. Contbr. articles to profl. jours.; patentee in field. Mem. Am. Assn. Cereal Chemists, Inst. Food Technologists, Am. Chem. Soc. Current work: Interaction of protiens lipids and carbohydrates in baked foods. Subspecialty: Food science and technology. Home: 852 Church St Manhattan KS 66502 Office: Dept Grain Sci Kans State U Manhattan KS 66506

HOSLER, CHARLES LUTHER, JR., meteorologist, educator, university administrator; b. Honey Brook, Pa., June 3, 1924; s. Charles Luther and Miriam Deichley (Stauffer) H.; m. Gladys Cheesbrough, 1947 (div.); children:- Sharon Elizabeth, David Charles, Lynn Rebecca, Peter William; m. Anna R. Stahel, 1971. Student, Bucknell U., 1943-44, Mass. Inst. Tech., 1944-45; B.S., Pa. State U., 1947, M.S., 1948, Ph.D., 1951. Faculty Pa. State U., University Park, 1948—, prof. meteorology, 1960—, head dept., 1961-65; dean Coll. Earth and Mineral Scis., Pa. State U., 1965-85, v.p. for research, dean Grad. Sch., 1985—; hydrographer Pa. Dept. Forests and Waters, 1949-59; meteorol. cons., 1950—, vis. prof. colls., lectr. civic and profl. groups; condr. daily TV weather program, 1957-67; spl. research microphysics of clouds; adv. com. on meteorology EPA; chmn. bd. on atmospheric scis. and climate Nat. Acad. Scis., 1984—; mem. nat. adv. com. on oceans and atmosphere; mem., chmn. bd. trustees Univ. Corp. for Atmospheric Research, Boulder, Colo., 1981-85; mem. Nat. Sci. Bd., 1985—. Contbr. articles to profl. jours. Served to lt. (j.g.) USNR, 1943-46; lt. comdr. Res. Fellow Am. Meteorol. Soc. (councilor, pres. 1976); mem. Nat. Acad. Engring., Am. Geophys. Union (award outstanding paper hydrology 1955), Am. Chem. Soc. (regional lectr. 1971-72), AAAS, Sigma Xi (nat. lectr. 1972), Tau Beta Pi, Sigma Gamma Epsilon. Subspecialty: Meteorology. Home: 1229 Smithfield Circle State College PA 16801 Office: Vice Pres for Research 114 Kern Pa State U University Park PA 16802

HOSS, WAYNE P., biochemist, educator; b. Paso Robles, Calif., Dec. 11, 1943; s. Donald D. and Rosalie M. (Gauthier) H.; m. Dorothy M. Hart, Sept. 3, 1967. B.S. in Chemistry, U. Idaho, 1966; Ph.D. in Chemistry, U. Nebr., 1971. NSF postdoctoral fellow dept. chemistry U. Rochester, 1970-72; NIH postdoctoral fellow Center for Brain Research, 1970-72, asst. prof., 1975-80, assoc. prof., 1980—, dir. undergrad. neurosci. program, 1980—; vis. assoc. prof. biochemistry Nagoya City (Japan) U., 1977. Contbr. articles to profl. jours. NIMH research career devel. awardee, 1976-81. Mem. Am. Chem. Soc., Am. Soc. Neurochemistry, Biophys. Soc., N.Y. Acad. Scis., Soc. Neurosci. Current Work: Interaction of drugs, neurotransmitters and neuroregulators with cellular membranes and their components including receptors, enzymes, lipids and ion channels. Subspecialties: Neurochemistry; Neuropharmacology. Home: 1748 Blossom Rd Rochester NY 14610 Office: Center for Brain Research Rochester Med Center Rochester NY 14642

HOSTETLER, KARL YODER, physician, educator, biochemist; b. Goshen, Ind., Nov. 17, 1939; s. Carl Milton and LaVerne (Yoder) H.; m. Margaretha Steur, Dec. 17, 1971; children: Saskia Emma, Kirsten Cornelia, Carl Martijn. B.A., DePauw U., 1961; M.D., Western Res. U., 1965. Diplomate: Am. Bd. Internal Medicine, Sub-Bd. Endocrinology and Metabolism. Intern Univ. Hosp., Cleve., 1965-66, resident, 1968-69; fellow in endocrinology metabolism Cleve. Clinc Found., 1969-70; postdoctoral fellow in biochemistry and medicine Case Western Res. U., Cleve., 1966-68, U. Utrecht, Netherlands, 1970-72; dir. Metabolism Clinic, VA Med. Ctr., San Diego, 1973—; asst. prof. medicine U. Calif.-San Diego, La Jolla, 1973-79, assoc. prof., 1979-84, prof., 1984—; exchange scientist USSR Acad. Sci., Moscow, 1974. Contbr. articles to profl. jours. Guggenheim Found. fellow, 1980. Mem. Am. Fedn. Clin. Research; mem. Western Soc. Clin. Investigation; Mem. Am. Soc. Biol. Chemists, AAAS, Am. Soc. for Clin. Investigation, Am. Diabetes Assn. (dir. So. Calif. affiliate 1976-83, pres. San Diego chpt. 1982-83, service award 1976). Current Work: Physician, scientist, diseases of endocrinology and metabolism, regulation of intracellular lipid metabolism. Subspecialties: Endocrinology; Biochemistry (medicine). Office: VA Med Ctr (111G) 3350 La Jolla Village Dr San Diego CA 92161

HOU, KENNETH CHIANG, physical chemist, chemical engineer; b. Kiang-Sui, China, Apr. 22, 1929; came to U.S., 1956, naturalized, 1972; s. Nai-Chou and Jean K. Hou; m. Catherine Feng, Sept. 4, 1965; children—Howard, Sellna. B.S., Taiwan U., 1952; M.S., U. Idaho, 1957; Ph.D., U. Tex., 1962; postdoctorate Pa. State U., 1962-64, Cornell U., 1964-66. Research chemist Celanese Corp., Summit, N.J., 1966-73; research engr. AMF Specialty Materials Group, Meriden, Conn., 1973-78, dir. research, 1978-84, v.p., 1984—. Contbr. articles to profl. publs. Patentee in field. Recipient Achievement award AMF Inc., 1976. Mem. Am. Chem. Soc., Sigma Chi, Phi Lambda Epsilon. Current work: Bio-physical chemistry on solid phase separation and purification of biomolecules as well as bio-engineering processes. Subspecialty: Biophysical chemistry. Home: 14 Huntingridge Rd Glastonbury CT 06073 Office: AMF Specialty Materials Group 400 Research Pkwy Meriden CT 06450

HOUCK, JAMES RICHARD, astronomer, educator; b. Mobile, Ala., Oct. 5, 1940; s. James Miller and Elsa (Echardt) H.; m. Elaine Vezzani, July 25, 1964; children—Christopher, Robert. B.S. in Physics, Carnegie Tech. U., 1962; Ph.D., Cornell U., 1967. Asst. prof. astronomy Cornell U., 1969-74, assoc. prof., 1974-79, prof., 1979—. Recipient Clark award Disting. Teaching Cornell U., 1977; Sloan fellow, 1971, Guggenheim fellow, 1975. Mem. AAAS, Am. Astron. Soc., Internat. Astron. Union. Current work: Infrared astronomy-studies of ionized hydrogen regions and star burst galaxies Subspecialty: Infrared astronomy. Office: Cornell U 220 Space Science Bldg Ithaca NY 14853

HOUDESHELL, JESSE WILLIAM, veterinary medicine administrator, pharmaceuticals researcher; b. Findlay, Ohio, Sept. 17, 1933; s. Elmer Henry and Ruth Idella (Neff) H.; m. Donna June Graham, Jan. 27, 1979; m. Mildred

Rheumillia Warner, Sept. 11, 1954; (div. Jan. 1979); children—Craig, David, Brian. D.V.M., Ohio State U., 1958. Practice vet. medicine, Bluffton, Ohio, 1958-67; dir. clin. research Schering Corp., Kenilworth, N.J., 1967-77, dir. pharm. research, 1977-84, v.p. research, 1984—. Contbr. articles to profl. jours. Fellow Am. Acad. Vet. Pharmacology and Therapeutics; mem. AVMA. Subspecialty: Veterinary pharmacology; Clinical veterinary medicine. Home: 1 Lake View Ct Lawrenceville NJ 08648 Office: Schering Plough Corp 2000 Galloping Hill Rd Kenilworth NJ 07033

HOUGHTON, DAVID DREW, meteorologist; b. Phila., Apr. 26, 1938; s. Willard Fairchild and Sara Nancy (Holmes) H.; m. Barbara Flora Coan, June 22, 1963; children: Eric Brian, Karen Jeanette, Steven Andrew. B.S., Pa. State U., 1959; M.S., U. Wash., 1961, Ph.D., 1963. Research scientist Nat. Center Atmospheric Research, Boulder, Colo., 1963-68; exchange scientist USSR Acad. Scis., Moscow, 1966; vis. scientist Courant Inst. Math. Scis., N.Y.C., 1966; asst. prof. dept. meteorology U. Wis., Madison, 1968-69, asso. prof., 1969-72, prof., 1972—, chmn. dept., 1976-79; scientist Internat. Sci. and Mgmt. Group for Global Atmospheric Research Program, Bracknell, Eng., 1972-73; lectr. Nanjing U., People's Republic of China, 1980. Contbr. articles to profl. jours.; editor-in-chief: Handbook of Applied Meteorology. Vice chmn. Planning Commn., Town of Dunn, Wis., 1977-81. NSF fellow, 1960-63. Fellow Am. Meteorol. Soc.; mem. AAAS, Phi Beta Kappa, Sigma Xi, Phi Kappa Phi. Quaker. Subspecialty: Meteorology. Office: Dept Meteorology U Wis Madison WI 53706

HOUGHTON, JANET ANNE, cancer research scientist; b. Grantham, Lincolnshire, Eng., May 21, 1952; came to U.S., 1977; d. George Edward and Viola Mary (Grant) Geeson; m. Peter James Houghton, July 21, 1973. B.Pharmacy, U. Bradford, Eng., 1973; Ph.D., Inst. Cancer Research, 1977. Postdoctoral fellow St. Jude Children's Research Hosp., Memphis, 1977-80, research assoc., 1980-82, asst. mem., 1982-85, assoc. mem., 1985—; cons. VA. Contbr. articles to profl. jours. Am. Cancer Soc. grantee, 1980—; Nat. Cancer Inst. grantee, 1982—. Mem. Pharm. Soc. Gt. Britain, Am. Assn. Cancer Research. Current Work: Study of characteristics of human solid tumors maintained in immune-deprived mice, relating to cell biology, biochemical pharmacology, cancer chemotherapy, drug resistance. Subspecialties: Cancer research (medicine); Chemotherapy. Home: PO Box 381 Route 1 Somerville TN 38068 Office: St Jude Children's Research Hosp 332 N Lauderdale St Memphis TN 38101

HOUGHTON, PETER JAMES, cancer research scientist; b. London, Feb. 1, 1949; came to U.S., 1977; s. George Douglas Stanley and Ruby (Power) H.; m. Janet Anne Geeson, July 21, 1973. B.Pharmacy with first class honors, U. Bradford, Eng., 1972; Ph.D., Inst. Cancer Research, 1976. Postdoctoral fellow Inst. Cancer Research, Surrey, Eng., 1976-77; postdoctoral fellow St. Jude Children's Hosp., Memphis, 1977-79, research assoc., 1979-81, asst. mem., 1981-84, assoc. mem., 1984—. Contbr articles to profl. jours. Am. Cancer Soc. grantee, 1980—; Nat. Cancer Inst. grantee, 1982—. Mem. Am. Assn. Cancer Research, Pharm. Soc. Gt. Britain. Current Work: Study of the characteristics of human solid tumors maintained in immune-deprived mice, relating to cell biology, biochemical pharmacology, cancer chemotherapy, drug resistance. Subspecialties: Cancer research (medicine); Chemotherapy. Home: Route 1 PO Box 381 Somerville TN 38068 Office: St Jude Children's Research Hosp 332 N Lauderdale St Memphis TN 38101

HOUGLAND, ARTHUR ELDON, microbiologist, educator; b. Omaha, Jan. 5, 1935; s. Arthur J. and Marie B. (Perkins) H.; m. Margaret Webb, June 4, 1961; children: Amy, Jon, Kriss. B.A., State U. Iowa, 1958; M.S., Brigham Young U., 1961; Ph.D., U. S.D., 1975. Research microbiologist Dept. Army, Ft. Detrick, Md., 1963-69; assoc. prof. biol. scis. East Tenn. State U., 1973—; asst. prof. microbiology Quillen Dishner Sch. Medicine, 1978—. Served with Med. Service Corps U.S. Army, 1961-63. Recipient S.D. br. Am. Cancer Soc. Research award, 1969-71, Oak Ridge Associated Univs. Research Contract and Faculty Participation award, 1977. Mem. Am. Soc. Microbiology, Tissue Culture Assn., Mil. Surgeons, AAAS, Res. Officers Assn. Current Work: Lipids of cells and plasma membranes; enzymes. Subspecialties: Virology (medicine); Biochemistry (medicine). Home: Route 19 Box 267 Johnson City TN 37601 Office: East Tenn State U PO Box 22690A Johnson City TN 37614

HOULBERG, WAYNE ARTHUR, plasma physicist, nuclear engineer; b. Chgo., Sept. 1, 1947; s. Arthur and June DeMares (Karnuth) H.; m. Linda Marie Mitchell, June 25, 1970; children—Brett Christian, Michele Anne, Kara Linda. B.S. in Nuclear Engring., U. Wis., 1970, M.S., 1972, Ph.D., 1977. Mem. research staff fusion energy div. Oak Ridge Nat. Lab., 1977—; adj. prof. U. Tenn., Knoxville, 1983-84; vis. scientist Jet Joint Undertaking, Abingdon, Eng., 1986. Pres. Oak Ridge Community Playhouse, 1984. Mem. Am. Phys. Soc., Am. Nuclear Soc., Sigma Xi. Current work: Theoretical plasma physics for magnetic confinement; computer model development and simulation of heating, fueling and dynamics of toroidally confined plasmas. Subspecialties: Plasma physics; Plasma engineering. Home: 105 Claremont Rd Oak Ridge TN 37830 Office: Fusion Energy Div Oak Ridge Nat Lab Oak Ridge TN 37831

HOUSE, CHARLES H., engineering administrator; b. Huntington Park, Calif., July 20, 1940; s. Everett S. and Ruth E. (Coates) H.; m. Gayle A. Baldwin, Mar. 5, 1960 (div. 1982); children—Sharon, Cynthia, Liesl, Warren; m. Nancy A. Young, June 24, 1982; stepchildren—Christopher, Shaun. B.S. in Engring. Physics, Calif. Inst. Tech., 1962; M.S. in Enlec. Engring., Stanford U., 1964; M.A. in History, U. Colo., 1970; M.B.A. in Mgmt. and Strategic Studies, Western Behavioral Scis. Inst., 1985. Designer Hewlett-Packard Co., Colorado Springs, Colo., 1962-71, research and devel. mgr., 1972-76, ops. mgr., 1976-82; corp. dir., Palo Alto, Calif., 1982—; instr. Stanford U., Calif., 1985—. Co-author: Logic Circuits and Microcomputer Systems, 1980; editor: Logic Analyzers for Microprocessors. Pres., Horticultural Arts Soc., Colorado Springs, 1970-82. Recipient award of Achievement Electronic Mag., 1977; named Computer Hall of Fame, Computer Design Mag., 1982. Mem. IEEE (bd. dirs. Psectrum mag. 1982-84), Assn. Computing Machinery. Methodist. Current work: Information systems and their impact on society; lifelong learning; office automation; measurement and control systems; computer graphics. Subspecialties: Information systems (Information science); Electronics. Office: Hewlett-Packard Co 1501 Page Mill Rd Palo Alto CA 94304

HOUSEPIAN, EDGAR MINAS, neurosurgeon; b. N.Y.C., Mar. 18, 1928; s. Moses Minas and Makrouhie (Ashjian) H.; m. Marion Lyon, Sept. 8, 1954; children: David Minas, Stephen Lyon, Jean Carleton. A.B., Columbia Coll., 1949; M.D., Columbia U., 1953. Diplomate: Am. Bd. Neurosurgery, 1961. Intern, gen surg. resident Lakeside Hosp., Cleve., 1953-55; resident Columbia Presbyn. Med. Center, N.Y.C., 1955-59; faculty Columbia U., N.Y.C., 1961—, prof. neurol. surgery, 1978—. Served to lt. comdr. M.C. USNR. Fellow A.C.S.; mem. AMA, AAAS, N.Y. Med. Soc., Am. Assn. Neurol. Surgeons, Am. Neurol. Surgery Congress U.S., Neurol. Surgery Research Soc., N.Y. Neurosurg. Soc., Phi Beta Kappa. Current Work: Researcher in tumors of the nervous system and vascular surgery, stereotaxic surgery. Subspecialties: Surgery; Neurology. Office: Columbia Dept Neurosurgery 710 W 168th St New York NY 10032

HOUSTON, WALTER SCOTT, science writer; b. Milw., May 30, 1912; s. Walter Charles and Edith Marie (Jones) H.; m. Miriam Althea Hill, Dec. 25, 1938; children—Ann Althea, Margaret Snow, Kay Pemberton. Ph.B., U. Wis.-Madison, 1935; A.M., U. Ala., 1949. Instr. Washington U., St. Louis, 1950-54, Kans. State Coll., Manhattan, 1954-60; sci. writer Wesleyan U., Middletown, Conn., 1960-69; sr. editor Xerox Ednl. Publs., Middletown, 1969-74; free-lance sci. writer, Middletown, 1974—. Author: Know About Drugs, 1968 (EdPress award 1969); contbr. monthly column to Sky and Telescope, Deep Sky, 1946—; nat. acid-rain survey, 1974. Mcpl. agent for elderly Town of Haddam, Conn., 1974-79, mem. com. for elderly, 1979—. Recipient Bruce Blair medal Western Astronomers, 1964, Astron. League award, 1966, Amateur Astronomers medal, 1976, Leslie C. Peltier award, 1983. Fellow Meteoritical Soc., AAAS; mem. Am. Assn. Variable Star Observers (council 1981—), Am. Meteor Soc. (New Eng. bd. dirs. 1960—), Nat. Assn. Sci. Writers. Democrat. Congregationalist. Current work: Increasing popular interest in astronomy which, in turn, means more grants in the future for the science; observation of SS Cyg type stars. Subspecialty: Optical astronomy.

HOVINGH, JACK, nuclear engineer; b. Grand Rapids, Mich., May 5, 1935; s. Peter and Hermina (Kraker) H.; m. Patsy VanderKam, June 22, 1956 (div. 1978); children: Mary, Mark. B.S. in Mech. Engring, U. Mich., 1958, B.S. in Math, 1958; M.S. in Engring. Sci, U. Calif.-Berkeley, 1973. Nuclear engr. Lawrence Livermore (Calif.) Nat. Lab., 1958—; Mem. rev. panels Electric Power Research Inst., Palo Alto, Calif., 1980—. Contbr. sci. articles to profl. publs. Mem. gen. plan rev. com. City of Pleasanton, Calif., 1983. Mem. Am. Nuclear Soc. Current Work: Pioneering work on the design and analyses of both magnetically and inertially confined fusion reactors for energy applications. Subspecialties: Nuclear fusion; Mechanical engineering. Home: 4250 Muirwood Dr Pleasanton CA 94566 Office: Lawrence Livermore Nat Lab PO Box 5508 L-480 Livermore CA 94550

HOVNANIAN, H. PHILIP, medical science research company executive, biomedical engineer; b. Aleppo, Syria, Dec. 17, 1920; s. Philip and Rosa (Jebejian) H.; m. Siran Norian, June 10, 1948; children—Rosemary Janice, Joan Anita, John Philip. B.S., Am. U., Beirut, 1942; postgrad. Brown U., 1947-49; M.S., State Coll., Boston, 1951; Ph.D., U. Beverly Hills. Registered profl. engr., N.Y., Mass. Prin. investigator, research grant Nat. Heart Inst., NIH; faculty dept. physics Am. U., Beirut, 1942-47, Brown U., 1947-49; sr. engr. Western Electric Co., Haverhill, Mass., 1951-52; asst. chief engr., Calidyne Co., Winchester, Mass., 1952-53; sr. physicist, project head, asst. research dir. Boston Electronics div. Norden-Ketay Corp., 1953-56; ptnr., research and devel. dir. physics Neutronics Research Co., Waltham, Mass., 1956-58; sr. staff scientist Avco Corp., 1958, mgr. med. sci. dept., 1959-66; mgr. lunar bio-sci. NASA, Washington, 1966-67; mgr. biomed. engring. and biophysics Kollsman Instrument Corp., Syosset, N.Y., 1967-68; v.p., dir. biomed. products Cavitron Corp. and Cooper Med. Corp., 1969—; dir. Donti Instruments Inc., Milab, Inc.; guest lectr. biomed. engring. Northeastern U., MIT-Harvard Study Group on Biomed. Engring.; research assoc. in surg. research Lahey Clin. Found.; mem. workshop interaction between industry and biomed. engring. Nat. Acad. Engring.; mem. ob-gyn. devices panel, former mem. panel on ear, nose and throat devices and dental devices FDA. Contbr. tech. papers to profl. jours.; patentee in field. Fellow Inst. Physics, Phys. Soc., Am. Soc. Laser Medicine and Surgery; mem. Optical Soc. Am., Am. Inst. Physics, IEEE (sr. mem. profl. group biomed. electronics), Internat. Fedn. Med. Microscopy Assn., Am. Inst. Ultrasound in Medicine, Am. Soc. Microbiology, N.Y. Acad. Scis., AAAS, Assn. Advancement Med. Instrumentation, Am. Dental Trade Assn. (com. on dental materials and devices), Am. Inst. Biol. Scis., Sigma Xi. Congregationalist (chmn. bd. trustees, moderator). Lodge: Masons. Current work: Oncology; phototherapy, lasers, hematoporphyrin derivatives; medical instrumentation: fiber optics, fluorescence, microscopy, lasers. Subspecialties: Laser medicine; Biomedical engineering. Home: 3902 Manhattan College Pkwy Riverdale NY 10471 Office: Cooper Lasertronics PO Box 10133 Stamford CT 06904Also: Am Standards Testing Bur 40 Water St New York NY 10004

HOWARD, JAMES LAWRENCE, pharmacologist; b. Glen Ellyn, Ill., Nov. 30, 1941; s. Ralph Orson and June Virginia (Underwood) H.; m. Judith Bennett Howard, Aug. 25, 1963; children: David Lawrence, Erin Kendra. B.A., U. N.C., 1963; M.S., Tulane U., 1966, Ph.D., 1968. Asst. prof. dept. psychiatry U. N.C., Chapel Hill, 1968-74; dir. behavioral pharmacology Burroughs Wellcome Co., Research Triangle Park, N.C., 1974—; adj. prof. U. N.C.-Chapel Hill, and Raleigh, 1974—; cons. N.C. Alcohol. Research Authority, NSF. Contbr. articles to profl. jours. NDEA fellow, 1964-68. Fellow Am. Psychol. Assn.; mem. Soc. Neurosci., AAAS, Behavorial Pharmacology Soc., Soc. Stimulus Properties of Drugs. Republican. Presbyterian. Current Work: Behavioral pharmacology, aging and senility. Subspecialties: Neuropsychology; Physiological psychology. Home: Route 1 Old Morrow Mill Rd Chapel Hill NC 27514 Office: Burroughs Wellcome Co Research Triangle Park NC 27709

HOWARD, JAY LLOYD, appliance manufacturing company executive; b. Olivia, Minn., June 24, 1952; s. Joe Earl and Jacquiline May (Gilmore) H., Jr.; m. Pamela Sue Dougan, Sept. 15, 1979; children: Melissa Ann, Joe Earl III, Heather Lea. B.A. in Psychology, U. Mo., Kansas City, 1972. Cert. mfg. technologist Soc. Mfg. Engrs. Chief pre-grind insp. Coors Porcelain Co., Golden, Colo., 1973-74; quality assurance dir. Dazey Products Co., Kansas City, Kans., 1974—, mgr. info. systems, 1974—, mfg./acctg. product info. control systems v.p., 1980—; instr. data based systems. Served with U.S. Army, 1970-71, Vietnam. Decorated Air medal, Purple Heart, Army Commendation medal. Mem. Am. Soc. for Quality Control, Am. Soc. for Prodn. and Inventory Control, Nat. Rifle Assn. Current Work: Establish and modify manufacturing computer database and manage its use. Subspecialties: Database systems; Information systems (Information science). Office: Industrial Airport 1 Dazey Circle Kansas City KS 66031

HOWARD, LAUREN DAVIS, biology and botany educator, phytosociologist and plant taxonomist; b. Nashua, N.H., Mar. 12, 1950; s. Lauren Alvin and Eleanor (Davis) H.; m. Judith Saunders, June 24, 1972; children: Lauren Fredrick, Scott Davis, Eric Robert. B.A. magna cum laude in Biology, Hartwick Coll., 1971; Ph.D. with distinction in Botany, U. Vt., 1979. Lectr. biology St. Michael's Coll., Winooski, Vt., 1976; asst. prof. biology Norwich U., Northfield, Vt., 1976-83, assoc. prof., 1983—; curator Norwich U. Herbarium; lectr. Vt. Council Humanities and Pub. Issues. Contbr. articles on botany to profl. jours.; author texts. Recipient Homer L. Dodge award Norwich U., 1979; Outstanding Young Alumnus award Hartwick Coll, 1981. Mem. Bot. Soc. Am., Ecol. Soc. Am., Am. Forestry Assn., New Eng. Bot. Club, Nature Conservancy, Nat. Wildlife Fedn. Republican. Current Work: Plant community structure and succession in New England, documentation of floras and development of floristic keys for the Northeast. Subspecialties: Sociobiology; Taxonomy. Office: Cabot Sci Bldg Norwich U Northfield VT 05663

HOWARD, MICHAEL E., neuropsychologist; b. Paola, Kans., Aug. 25, 1944. B.S., Emporia State U., 1974, M.S., 1978; Ph.D., U. Mo., 1981. Diplomate Am. Bd. Neuropsychology. Cert. psychologist, Kans; lic. psychologist, Mo.; registered psychologist, Ill. Psychometrist and grant writer Mental Health Ctr. East Central Kans., Emporia, 1975-76; teaching asst. Emporia State U., 1976; clin. psychology intern Newman Meml. Hosp., Emporia, 1976-77; adj. asst. prof., Emporia state U., 1976-77; project dir. Alcoholism Cons. and Treatment Services Drug Abuse Unit Community Mental Health Ctr., Emporia, 1976-77; cons. Mark Twain Mental Health Ctr., Hannibal, Mo., 1977-79, program coordinator dept. ednl. and counseling psychology U. Mo., Columbia, 1977-79, clin. psychology intern VA Med. Ctr., Topeka, 1979-80; brain trauma treatment team coordinator Rehab. Inst. Chgo., 1980-82; staff psychologist, neuropsychologist Rehab. Med. Ctr., Northwestern U., Chgo., 1980-82; coordinator neuropsychology Western Mo. Mental Health Ctr., Kansas city, 1982; cons., 1982—; dir. Neuropsychology Cons. Group, Kansas City, Mo., 1983—; asst. prof. psychology U. Mo. Sch. Medicine, Kansas City, 1982—, clin. asst. prof., 1982—; clin. neuropsychologist, dir. neuropsychology clinic VA Med. Ctr., Kansas City, 1982—; cons. Rehab. Inst., Kansas City, Columbia Ctr. for Psychiatry, U. Kans. Med. Ctr., 1982—; lectr. in field. Contbr. articles to profl. jours. Served to sgt. U.S. Army, 1962-67. Knights Templar scholar, 1972, Am. Psychol. Assn. scholar, 1974. Mem. Am. Psychol. Assn. (div. clin. neuropsychology, rehab. psychology, psychologists in pub. service), Mo. Psychol. Assn., Greater Kansas City Psychol. Assn., Nat. Acad. Neuropsychologists, Internat. Neuropsychol. Soc., Nat. Head Injury Found. (bd. dirs.), Am. Congress Rehab. Medicine, Assn. for Advancement of Behavior Therapy (behavioral neuropsychology spl. interest group), Assn. Med. Sch. Profs. Psychology, Assn. for Advancement of Psychology, Greater Kansas City Mental Health Assn. Office: Neuropsychology Clinic 116B VA Med Ctr 4801 Linwood Blvd Kansas City MO 64128

HOWARD, ROBERT FRANKLIN, astronomer; b. Delaware, Ohio, Dec. 30, 1932; s. David Dale and Clarine Edna (Morehouse) H.; m. Margaret Teresa Farnon, Oct. 4, 1958; children—Thomas Colin, Moira Catherine. B.A., Ohio Wesleyan U., 1954; Ph.D., Princeton U., 1957. Asst. prof. physics U. Mass., Amherst, 1959-61; scientist Mt. Wilson and Las Campanas Obs., Pasadena, 1961-84, asst. dir., 1982-84; assoc. dir. Nat. Optical Astron. Obs., Tucson, 1984—; dir. Nat. Solar Obs., Tucson, 1984—. Editor Solar Magnetic Fields, 1971. Mem. Am. Astron. Soc., (Solar Physics div. sec. 1969-71); Internat. Astron. Union. Current work: Solar physics, large scale magnetic and velocity fields of the sun; solar activity; sunspots. Subspecialties: Optical astronomy; Solar physics. Home: National Solar Obs 950 N Cherry Ave Tucson AZ 85726

HOWARD-PEEBLES, PATRICIA NELL, clinical cytogeneticist, educator; b. Lawton, Okla., Nov. 24, 1941; d. John Marion and Reba Leona (Prestidge) H.; m. Thomas Marvin Peebles, Aug. 16, 1975. B.S.Ed., Central Okla. State U., 1963; Ph.D. in Genetics, U. Tex., Austin, 1969. Diplomate: Am. Bd. Med. Genetics, 1982. Tchr. Piedmont (Okla.) Pub. Schs., 1963-64; biochem. technician Oak Ridge Nat. Lab., 1964-66; instr. depts. pediatrics and cytotech. Okla. U. Med. Ctr., Oklahoma City, 1971-72; asst. prof. dept. microbiology Inst. Genetics, U. So. Miss., Hattiesburg, 1973-77, assoc prof., 1977-80; assoc. prof. and clin. cytogeneticist dept. pub. health and Lab. Med. Genetics U. Ala., Birmingham, 1980-81; assoc. prof. dept. pathology, dir. cytogenetics lab. U. Tex. Health Scis. Ctr., Dallas, 1981-85, prof. dept. pathology, dir. cytogenetics lab., 1985—; genetic cons. Ellisville (Miss.) State Sch., 1973-80; attending staff dept. pathology Parkland Meml. Hosp., Dallas, 1981—; cytogenetic cons. El Paso Rehabl. Center. Contbr. articles and abstracts to profl. lit. Fellow Am. Cancer Soc., NIH, NSF, NIMH, Nat. Inst. Child Health and Human Devel.; Mem. Am Soc. Human Genetics, Genetics Soc. Am., AAAS, So. Soc. Pediatric Research, Am. Assn. Mental Deficiency, Acad. Clin. Lab. Physicians and Scientists, Tex. Genetics Soc., Sigma Xi, Alpha Omicron Pi. Baptist. Current Work: Cytogenetics of fragile sites, fragile X chromosomes and causes of mental retardation. Cytogenetics research, director of clinical cytogenetics laboratory. Subspecialties: Genetics and genetic engineering (medicine); Cell biology (medicine). Office: Dept Pathology U Tex Health Scis Center 5323 Harry Hines Blvd Dallas TX 75235

HOWE, ARTHUR TREVOR, solid state chemistry researcher; b. Melbourne, Australia, Apr. 6, 1943; came to U.S., 1981; s. Trevor Asquith and Stella Mary (Stacey) H.; m. Katherine Louise Hansell, Dec. 23, 1970; children—Celesta Anne, Keaton Neville. B.Sc., Melbourne U., 1964, M.Sc., 1967; Ph.D., U. Newcastle upon Tyne (Eng.), 1970. Royal Commn. of 1851 sr. research fellow U. Oxford (Eng.), 1971-72; lectr. chemistry U. Leeds (Eng.), 1972-81; group leader Amoco Research Ctr., Naperville, Ill., 1981—. Contbr. articles to tech. jours. Patentee proton conduction in hydrogen uranyl phosphate, multilayer photoelectrodes. Mem. Am. Chem. Soc., Am. Phys. Soc., Electrochem. Soc., Royal Soc. Chemistry, Am. Vacuum Soc., Sigma Xi. Current work: Amorphous semiconductors, photoelectrochemistry. Subspecialties: Electronic materials; Solar energy. Office: Amoco Research Ctr PO Box 400 Naperville IL 60566

HOWE, ROBERT HSI LIN, biological and environmental engineering educator; b. Swatow, China; Jan., 1922; came to U.S., 1948, naturalized 1962; s. Julin and Afia (Lin) H.; m. Jean Ma, Dec. 23, 1953; children—David J., Robert C., Albert G. B.S., Methodist U., 1943; B.S. in Engring., St. Johns U., Shanghai, 1945; M.S. in Physics, Cornell U., 1949, M. Engring., 1950; Ph.D., Purdue U., 1955; D.Sc., World Open U., 1977. With Eli Lilly & Co., Lafayette, Ind., 1952-82, research scientist, 1966-82, environ. tech. service cons., 1966-82; v.p. Advent Tech. Corp., Lafayette, 1983—; adviser water project Dept. State/Pan Am. Inst., Washington, 1958-59; prof. Istanbul Tech. U., 1965-66; professorial lectr. Milan Poly. U., Italy, 1966; spl. chair prof. Nat. Taiwan U., Taipei, 1980, Nat. Cheng Kung U., Republic of China, 1984-85. Author: Applied Chemistry for Water Purification and Wastes Treatment, vol. 1, 1967, vol. 2, 1971; contbr. articles to profl. jours. Fulbright Hays grantee, 1965-66. Felow Royal Soc. Health, Am. Pub. Health Assn., Inst. Advanced Sanitation Research; mem. Am. Chem. Soc. (sr.) Lafayette Profl. Engrs. (v.p. 1959, 84), Water Pollution Control Fedn. (William Hatfield award 1972). Club: Nat. Soc. Profl. Engrs., Sigma Xi. Toastmasters (pres., gov., Disting. Toastmaster). Lodge: Kiwanis (bd. dirs. 1984-85). Current work: Environmental pollution control; high temperature technology; minute particles separation; toxic chemicals destruction; energy recovery. Home: 307 Yoakum Pkwy #1607 Alexandria VA 22304 Home: 106 Drury Ln West Lafayette IN 47906 Office: Advent Tech Corp 1516 Main St Lafayette IN 47905

HOWELL, ROBERT WAYNE, agronomy educator; b. Houlka, Miss., Nov. 26, 1916; s. Raleigh Wayne and Frances Ethel (Stacy) H.; m. Elizabeth Virginia Blair, Sept. 25, 1940; children: Jacqueline Howell Choate, Richard James, Wayne Davis. Student, George Washington U., 1934-37; B.S., Miss. Coll., 1949; M.S., U. Wis., 1951, Ph.D., 1952. Clk., adminstrv. asst. U.S. Dept. Agr., Washington, Cheyenne, Wyo., Ithaca, N.Y., 1934-43; bus. mgr. Pineapple Research Inst., Hawaii, 1947; plant physiologist U.S. Regional Lab., Urbana, Ill., 1952-65; leader soybean investigations U.S. Dept. Agr., Beltsville, Md., 1965, chief oilseed and indsl. crops research br., 1966-71; prof. agronomy U. Ill., Urbana, 1971—, chmn. dept., 1971-82. Editor: Crop Science, 1969-71. Served to capt. AUS, 1943-46. Recipient award of merit Am. Soybean Assn., 1972. Fellow Am. Soc. Agronomy, AAAS; mem. Crop Sci. Soc. Am., Am. Soc. Plant Physiologists, Am. Soybean Assn. (hon. life), Sigma Chi. Subspecialty: Agronomy. Home: 2012 S Cottage Grove Urbana IL 61801

HOWELL, STEPHEN BARNARD, medical educator, administr., researcher; b. Shirley, Mass, Sept. 29, 1944; s. Wallace E. and Christine G. H.; m. Julianne R. Howell, 1968; children: Justin, Brett. A.B. in Biology with honors, U. Chgo., 1966; M.D. in Immunology magna cum laude, Harvard U., 1970. Diplomate: Am. Bd. Internal Medicine. Intern Mass. Gen. Hosp., Boston, 1970-71, resident, 1971-72; research assoc. Lab. Cell Biology, Nat. Cancer Inst., Bethesda, Md., 1972-74; resident U. Calif. Hosps., San Francisco, 1974-75; fellow in oncology Sidney Farber Cancer Inst., Boston, 1975-77; asst. prof. medicine U. Calif.-San Diego, 1977-80, assoc. prof., 1981—; dir. Lab. Pharmacology and Cytokinetics, 1978—; mem. biochem. modulation adv. group div. cancer treatment Nat. Cancer Inst., 1979—. Contbr. numerous articles to profl. jours. Mem. Am Assn. Cancer Research, Am. Soc. Clin. Oncology, Am. Fedn. Clin. Research, Cell Kinetics Soc., N.Y. Acad. Sci., Phi Beta Kappa, Alpha Omega Alpha. Current Work: Clinical pharmacology and molecular pharmacology of antineoplastic agents. Subspecialties: Chemotherapy; Cancer research (medicine). Office: Department of Medicine University of California San Diego La Jolla CA 92093

HOWELLS, WILLIAM WHITE, retired anthropology educator; b. N.Y.C., Nov. 27, 1908. B.S., Harvard U., 1930, Ph.D. in Anthropology, 1934; Sc.D. (hon.), Beloit Coll., 1975; D.Sc. (hon.), U. Witwatersrand, 1985. Research assoc. phys. anthropology Am. Mus. Natural History, 1932-43; asst. prof. to prof. anthropology U. Wis.-Madison, 1939-54; prof. Harvard U., 1954-74, prof. emeritus, 1974—; curator somatology Peabody Mus., Harvard U., 1955-74, emeritus curator, 1974—; dir. Am. Sch. Prehistoric Research, Cambridge, Mass., 1955—. Editor: Jour. Am. Assn. Phys. Anthropology, 194-54. Served to lt. USNR, 1943-46. Recipient Viking Fund medal Wenner-Gren Found., 1955; Broca prix du Centenaire, Soc. Anthropologie de Paris, 1980. Fellow AAAS, Am. Anthrop Assn. (pres. 1951), Am. Acad. Arts and Scis.; mem. Nat. Acad. Sci., Am. Assn. Phys. Anthropology, Royal Soc. South Africa (fgn. assoc.). Subspecialty: Paleontology. Office: Peabody Mus Harvard U Cambridge MA 02138

HOWLAND, ROBERT ALDEN, JR., engineer, educator; b. Bridgeport, Conn., May 7, 1943; s. Robert Alden and Winifred Leona (Goodell) H. B.A., Yale U., 1965, M.S., 1967; Ph.D., N.C. State U., 1974. Vis. instr. N.C. State U., Raleigh, 1974-78; asst. prof. Rose-Hulman Inst. Tech., Terre Haute, Ind., 1978-81, U. Notre Dame, South Bend, Ind., 1981—. Percussionist, South Bend Symphony Orch.; Contbr. articles to profl. publs. grantee NSF, 1980-82. Mem. Am. Acad. Mechanics, Soc. Engring. Sci., Am. Astron. Soc. (div. dynamical astronomy), Sigma Xi. Republican. Presbyterian. Current Work: accelerated asymptotic analysis of nonlinear systems; celestial mechanics. Subspecialties: Theoretical and applied mechanics; Applied mathematics. Home: 1523 Turtle Creek Dr South Bend IN 46637 Office: Aerospace/Mech Engring U Notre Dame Notre Dame IN 46556

HOWSE, HAROLD DARROW, research laboratory director, biology educator; b. Poplarville, Miss., Nov. 8, 1928; s. William Jefferson and Artie Mittie (Smith) H.; m. Mittie Hazel Gibson, Dec. 18, 1960; children: Trijetta Lynn Gibson Cropp, Claude Demitris Gibson. A.A., Pearl River Jr. Coll., Poplarville, 1947; B.S., U. So. Miss., 1959, M.S., 1960; Ph.D., Tulane U., 1967. Instr. zoology Miss. Coll., Jackson, 1960; instr. biology U. So. Miss., Hattiesburg, 1960-63; NIH trainee Tulane U., New Orleans, 1963-67; head sect. microscopy Gulf Coast Research Lab., Ocean Springs, Miss., 1967-79, asst. dir., 1971, acting dir., 1971-72, dir., 1972—; prof. biology U. Miss., 1972—; prof. zoology Miss. State U.; prof. biology U. So. Miss., 1972—. Contbr. articles to profl. jours. Chmn. Miss. Coastal Zone Mgmt. Adv. Com., 1981-84, Miss. Coastal Energy Impact Com., 1981-84. Served with U.S. Navy, 1950-54. NIH trainee, 1963-67. Mem. Am. Assn. Anatomists, AAAS, Am. Microscopical Soc., Am. Soc. for Cell Biology, Am. Soc. Zoologists, Assn. Southeastern Biologists, Electron Microscopy Soc. Am., Miss. Acad. Sci., N.Y. Acad. Scis., others. Baptist. Current Work: Comparative histology, histochemistry and ultrastructure of the several organ systems of marine invertebrates and vertebrates. Subspecialties: Cell biology; Cytology and histology. Home: PO Box AG Ocean Springs MS 39564 Office: Gulf Coast Research Lab Ocean Springs MS 39564

HOYE, ROBERT EARL, systems science educator; b. Warwick, R.I., Jan. 12, 1931; s. S. Earl and Alice M. (Landry) H.; m. Patricia Buswell, Aug. 20, 1955; children: Robert Earl, Jr., Joanne D., Peter M., Kathleen B. A.B., Providence Coll., 1953; M.S., St. John's U., 1955; Ph.D., U. Wis.-Madison, 1973. Dean Champlain Coll., Burlington, Vt., 1957-58; supt. Frontier Regional Sch., Deerfield, Mass., 1958-60; northeast dist. dir. IBM Sci. Research, Chgo., 1960-66; dir. learning systems Xerox Corp., N.Y.C., 1965; dir. instructional media U. Wis., 1966-73; prof. systems sci. U. Louisville, 1974—, mem. commn. on excellence, 1977; mem. adv. panel U.S. Congress OTA, Wshington, 1981-82. Author: Index To Computer Based Learning, 1973; editor: Education Jour, 1969-73, College Student Jour, 1969-73; contbr. numerous articles to profl. jours. Mem. Econ. Opportunity Program, Taunton, Mass., 1963-65; mem. Dighton (Mass.) Sch. Bd., 1965. Mem. Am. Psychol. Assn., Hosp. Mgmt. Systems Soc. Roman Catholic. Current Work: Systems science, health systems, information systems, instructional technology. Subspecialties: Information systems (Information science); Information systems, storage, and retrieval (computer science). Home: 2238 Wynnewood Circle Louisville KY 40222 Office: University of Louisville Louisville KY 40292

HOYUMPA, ANASTACIO MANINGO, physician, medical educator; b. Baybay, Leyte, Philippines, July 4, 1937; came to U.S., 1962; s. Anastacio Bandalan and Lamberta (Maningo) H.; m. Joan Maureen Howland, June 22, 1963; children: Rebecca, Danilo, Amelia, Benjamin. M.D., U. Santo Tomas, Manila, 1961. Rotating intern USAF Hosp., Clark AFB, Philippines, 1960-61, med. resident, 1961-62; med. intern Sinai Hosp., Balt., 1962-63, med. resident, 1963-65; gastroenterology fellow U. Cin., 1965-67; prof. medicine U. Tex. Health Sci. Center, San Antonio, 1982—; asst. prof. medicine U. Cin., 1968-72; asst. prof. medicine Vanderbilt U., Nashville, 1972-76, assoc. prof., 1976-82; chief gastroenterology VA Hosp., San Antonio, 1982—. Contbr. articles in field to profl. jours. Served to lt. col. M.C. USAR. Grantee VA, 1973-75, 76-78, 79-81. Mem. Internat. Assn. Study Liver Diseases, Internat. Soc. Biomed. Research on Alcoholism, Am. Assn. Study Liver Disease, Am. Gastroenterol. Assn., Am. Soc. Gastrointestinal Endoscopy, Am. Fedn. Clin. Research, Central Soc. Clin. Research. Roman Catholic. Current Work: Thiamin, intestinal transport, drug metabolism, fetal/alcohol syndrome. Subspecialties: Internal medicine; Gastroenterology. Home: 203 Fawn Dr San Antonio TX 78231 Office: U Tex Health Sci Center 7703 Floyd Curl Dr San Antonio TX 78284

HRADILEK, PETER JAROSLAV, civil engineer; b. Trebic, Moravia, Czechoslovakia, July 23, 1942; came to U.S., 1956, naturalized, 1965; s. Bohumil and Hedwig (Hanke) H.; m. Carmen Gloria Opazo-Larrain, Mar. 11, 1972; children—Linda Renata, Peter James. B.S.C.E., UCLA, 1968, M.S. in Structural Engrng., 1970, Ph.D. in Earthquake Engrng., 1978. Registered profl. engr., Calif. Various engrng. positions U.S. Army C.E., Los Angeles, 1968-79, Bur. Reclamation, Denver, 1979—; advisor Ministry of Agr., Lima, Peru, 1979-81, AID, Guayaquil, Ecuador, 1983—; liaison rep. com. on earthquake engrng, NRC, 1984—. Contbr. articles to profl. jours. Served with USN, 1961-63. Recipient various awards and commendations U.S. Govt.; Ford Found. fellow, 1970-71. Mem. ASCE, Earthquake Engrng. Research Inst., U.S. Com. Large Dams, Seismol. Soc. Am., U.S. Com. Irrigation and Drainage, Internat. Water Resources Assn. Republican. Current work: Earthquake safety; dam safety; foundation liquefaction determination. Subspecialties: Civil engineering; Earthquake engineering. Home: 2070 Tabor Dr Lakewood CO 80215 Office: AID Guayaquil APO Miami FL 34039

HRAZDINA, GEZA, biochemistry educator; b. Letenye, Zala, Hungary, Mar. 16, 1939; came to U.S., 1966; s. Geza and Maria (Volgyi) H.; m. Helga M. Stritzke, Apr. 29, 1964; 1 son, Geza Karoly. Dipl.ing.agr., Swiss Fed. Inst. Tech., Zurich, 1963, Dr.sc.tech., 1966. Asst. prof. biochemistry Cornell U., Geneva, N.Y., 1968-73, assoc. prof., 1973-80, prof., 1981—; vis. prof. U. Freiburg, Germany, 1974-75, Tech. U. Budapest, Hungary, 1979, U. Cologne, Germany, 1981. Editor: (with others) Cellular and Sub Cellular Localizations in Plant Metabolism, 1982. A. von Humboldt fellow, 1974; 81; Nat. Acad. Scis. fellow, 1979. Mem. Phytochem. Soc. N.Am. (pres. 1982-83), Am. Soc. Plant Physiologists, Am. Chem. Soc., Phytochem. Soc. Europe. Current Work: Enzymology of secondary plant metabolites; flavonoids, anthocyanins; subcellular localizations in plant metabolism. Subspecialties: Plant physiology (agriculture); Food science and technology. Home: 992 E Lake Rd Romulus NY 14541 Office: Cornell University Agricultural Experiment Station Geneva NY 14456

HRONES, JOHN ANTHONY, engineering educator; b. Boston, Sept 28, 1912; s. Emil and Olga Victoria (Cech) H.; m. Margaret Baylis, June 17, 1938; children: Janet H. Roach, Stephen Baylis, Mary H. Parsons, John Anthony. S.B., MIT, 1934, S.M., 1936, Sc.D., 1942. Asst. factory mgr. Coldwell Lawnmower Co., Newburgh, N.Y., 1937-39; asst. mech. engrng. dept. MIT, 1934-36, instr., 1936-37, 39-41, asst. prof., 1941-45, asso. prof., 1945-48, prof. mech. engrng., 1948, head machine design div., 1946, dir. Dynamic Analysis and Control Lab., 1950; v.p. acad. affairs Case Inst. Tech., Cleve., 1957-67, provost, 1964-67; provost sci. and tech. Case-Western Res. U., 1967-76, provost emeritus, prof. engrng., 1976—; James Clayton lectr. Inst. Mech. Engrs., 1960; cons. automatic control and machine design, 1939—; chmn. Univ. Circle Research Center Corp., 1967-73; pres. ChiCorp., 1967-68, chmn., 1967-77; research adv. com. AID, 1978-82. Author: (with Nelson) Analysis of the Four Bar Linkage, 1951; contbr. articles to engrng. publs. Trustee Cleve. Mus. Nat. History; trustee Asian Inst. Tech.; pres. A.I.T. Found. Mem. Newcomen Soc., ASME, Am. Soc. Engrng. Edn., Am. Acad. Arts and Scis., Inst. for Def. Analyses (trustee 1958-85), Nat. Acad. Engrng., Sigma Xi, Tau Beta Pi, Pi Tau Sigma. Club: Cleveland Skating (trustee 1970-73). Subspecialty: Mechanical engineering. Home: 9397 Midnight Pass Rd Apt 306 Sarasota FL 33581 Office: Case Western Res U Cleveland OH 44106

HRUBY, VICTOR JOSEPH, chemistry educator, consultant; b. Valley City, N.D., Dec. 24, 1938; s. Victor John and Helen (Berube) H.; m. Patricia A. McGovern, Aug. 1, 1966; children—Timothy J., Stephen M., Patrick A. Student Valley City State Coll., 1956-58; B.S., U. N.D., 1960, M.S., 1962; Ph.D., Cornell U., 1965. Instr. chemistry Cornell U. Med. Coll., 1965-67; asst. prof. chemistry U. Ariz., Tucson, 1968-72, assoc. prof., 1972-77, prof., 1977—; guest worker NIH, Bethesda, Md., 1975-76; rector's lectr. Free U. Brussels, 1979; cons. Gibson-Stephens Neuropharmaceuticals, Tucson, 1983—, Dow Chem. Co., Indpls., 1973—, USPHS, Bethesda, Md., 1977—. Editor: Peptides: Structure and Function, 1983. Contbr. numerous articles to sci. jours., also monographs. NSF fellow, 1963-65; USPHS research fellow, NIH, 1975-76; Fulbright-Hays fellow U. Brussels, 1979; Guggenheim Found. fellow 1984-85. Fellow AAAS, N.Y. Acad. Scis., Am. Inst. Chemists; mem. Am. Chem. Soc., Am. Soc. Biol. Chemists. Roman Catholic. Current work: Relation of conformation to biological activity of peptide hormones and neurotransmitters; physical-chemical basis for information transfer by hormones; peptide synthesis. Subspecialties: Organic chemistry; Biophysics (biology). Office: Dept Chemistry Univ Ariz Tucson AZ 85721

HRUSHESKY, WILLIAM JOHN MICHAEL, scientist, physician; b. Poughkeepsie, N.Y., Nov, 9, 1947; s. William Michael and Mary Margaret (Burns) H.; m. Patricia Ann Wood, July 17, 1953. A.B., Syracuse U., 1969; M.D., SUNY-Buffalo, 1973. Diplomate: Am. Bd. Internal Medicine, in med. oncology, 1979. Cancer researcher Roswell Park Meml. Inst., Buffalo, 1970; intern Balt. City Hosps. and Johns Hopkins, 1973-74; clin. assoc. NIH, 1974-76; resident, fellow in ocnology U. Minn., 1976-79, asst. prof. medicine and lab. medicine, 1979—. Contbr. articles to profl. jours.; patentee diagnostic med. devices, drug delivery systems, lab. instrumentation. Served to lt. comdr. USPHS, 1974-76. Grantee in field. Mem. AAAS, Am. Fed. Clin. Research, N.Y. Acad. Scis., Am. Soc. Clin. Oncology, Am. Assn. Cancer Research, Internat. Soc. Chronobiology. Club: Provocateurs (pres.). Current Work: Application of principals of biologic time structure to study of etiology and treatment of malignant disease. Subspecialties: Cancer research (medicine); Chronobiology. Home: 3123 James Ave S Minneapolis MN 55408 Office: U Minn Hosp Box 414 May Meml Bldg Minneapolis MN 55455

HRYCAK, PETER, mechanical engineer, educator; b. Przemysl, Poland, July 8, 1923; came to U.S., 1949, naturalized, 1956; s. Eugene and Ludmyla (Dobrzanska) H.; m. Rea Meta Limberg, June 13, 1949; children: Michael Paul, Orest W.T., Alexandra Martha. Student, U. Tubingen, Germany, 1946-48; B.S. with high distinction, U. Minn., 1954, M.S., 1955, Ph.D., 1960. Registered profl. engr., N.J. Instr. U. Minn., Mpls., 1955-60; mem. tech. staff Bell Telephone Labs., Murray Hill, N.J., 1960-65; sr. project engr. Curtiss-Wright Corp., Woodridge, N.J., 1965; assoc. prof. mech. engrng. N.J. Inst. Tech., 1965-68, prof., 1968—. Contbr. articles to profl. jours. NASA grantee, 1967-68; NSF grantee, 1982-84. Sr. mem. Inst. Environ. Scis.; mem. ASME, AIAA, Am. Soc. Engrng. Edn., Ukrainian Engrs. Soc. Am. (pres. 1966-67), N.Y. Acad. Scis., Am. Geophys. Union, AAUP, Shevchenko Sci. Soc., Ukrainian Acad. Arts and Scis. in U.S.A., Pi Tau Sigma, Tau Beta Pi, Sigma Xi. Current Work: Experimental investigation and analytical studies of fluid flow and heat transfer characteristics of impinging jets; world wide regulation mechanism of carbon dioxide; man-made climate changes. Subspecialties: Mechanical engineering; Fluid mechanics. Home: 19 Roselle Ave Cranford NJ 07016 Office: 323 Martin Luther King Blvd Newark NJ 07102

HSIA, HENRY TAO-SZE, consulting firm executive, consultant; b. Peking, Hepei, China, June 16, 1923; came to U.S., 1947, naturalized, 1955; s. Ching and Wen Ling (Chen) H.; m. Alice C. Chung, Dec. 21, 1947; children: Victor Kai, Jean Mei, Alexander Hao. B.S., Chiao Tung U., Shanghai, China, 1944; M.S., Harvard U., 1948; Engr., Stanford U., 1964, Ph.D., 1966. Research specialist Lockheed Missile & Space Co., Sunnyvale, Calif., 1957-62; sr. staff scientist United Technologies, Sunnyvale, 1962-73; sr. engr. EDS Nuclear, San Francisco, 1973-74; sr. staff engr., cons. MB Assocs., San Ramon, Calif., 1974-76; program mgr. Gen. Electric Co., San Jose, Calif., 1976-82; pres. Tecon Services, Palo Alto, Calif., 1982—; cons., lectr. Chungshan Inst. Sci. and Tech., Taiwan, China, 1968—; lectr. Profl. Engrs. Tech. Inst., Menlo Park, Calif., 1982—; chmn. energy group Chinese Inst. Engrs., San Francisco, 1982-83. Author: Fundamentals of Rocket Propulsion, 1968; contbr. articles to profl. jours. Bd. dirs. Chinese Culture Assn., Palo Alto, Calif., 1966-76, Soc. Chinese Performing Arts, San Francisco, 1976—, Chinese Am. Assn. Sci. and Culture, Palo Alto, 1982—. Served to maj. Chinese Army, 1944-45. Recipient Quality Performance award Gen. Electric Co., 1979. Mem. ASME, AIAA, Am. Nuclear Soc. Republican. Patentee in field. Current Work: Nuclear power plant safety related analysis and design, alternate energy sources, rocket propulsion, technology transfer to developing nations. Subspecialties: Nuclear engineering; Aeronautical engineering. Home: 865 Robb Rd Palo Alto CA 94306 Office: Tecon Services 865 Robb Rd Palo Alto CA 94306

HSIA, YU-PING, chemist, educator; b. China, May 16, 1936; came to U.S., 1961, naturalized, 1972; s. Hsiang-ming and Shu-chen (Wu) H.; m. Ting-mei Chen, Dec. 23, 1961; children: Irene, Richard. B.S., Tunghai U., 1959; M.S., U. Santa Barbara, 1963; Ph.D., Ill. Inst. Tech., 1967. Asst. prof. U. Bridgeport, Conn., 1967-68; asst., then assoc. prof. Calif. State Poly. U., Pomona, 1968-76, prof. chemistry, 1976—, also dir. grad. program. Contbr. articles to profl. jours. Petroleum research fellow, 1963-67; NSF grantee, 1971. Mem. Am. Chem. Soc., Chinese Am. Profl. Soc. in So. Calif. Current Work: Energy science; research in energy field; teaching in graduate and undergraduate level courses. Subspecialties: Physical chemistry; Coal. Office: Calif Poly U 3801 W Temple Ave Pomona CA 91768

HSIAO, TING HUAN, insect physiologist; b. Hangchow, Chekiang, China, Feb. 6, 1936; came to U.S., 1958, naturalized, 1972; s. Tze Yuan and Mou C. (Yang) H.; m. Catherine Tang, Mar. 21, 1961. M.S. in Entomology, U. Minn., St. Paul, 1961; Ph.D. in Insect Physiology, U. Ill., Urbana, 1966. Research assoc. dept. entomology U. Ill., 1966-67; asst. prof. zoology Utah State U., 1967-72, assoc. prof. biology, 1972-79, prof. biology, 1979—; vis. prof. entomology Agrl. U., Wageningen, Netherlands, 1975, 77, 78, 81. Contbr. numerous articles to profl. publs. Mem. Entomol. Soc. Am., Am. Soc. Zoologists, Am. Inst. Biol. Sci., AAAS, Sigma Xi. Current Work: Insect/host plant relationships as related to feeding behavior, chemical interactions, nutrition and host plant resistance; biotypes of insect pests; physiology; feeding behavior; nutrition; ecological genetics. Subspecialties: Animal physiology; Evolutionary biology. Office: Utah State U Dept Biology UMC 53 Logan UT 84322

HSIEH, JEN-SHU, radiation physicist; b. Taipei, Taiwan, Apr. 6, 1936; s. Yung-Ho and Shin-Fu (Li) H. B.S., Nat. Taiwan U., 1960; M.S., N.Mex. Highlands U., 1964; Ph.D. in Physics, Ohio U., 1968. Postdoctoral research assoc. Ohio U., 1968-70; NIH fellow, med. physicist UCLA, 1971-76; research physicist, cons. Internat. Sensor Tech., Santa Ana, Calif., 1973-76; health physicist radiation health div. Radiol. Control Office, Norfolk Naval Shipyard, 1976-78; physicist Armed Forced Radiobiology Research Inst., Bethesda, Md., 1978—. Contbr. articles to profl. jours. Mem. Am. Phys. Soc., AAAS, Am. Assn. Physicists in Medicine, Health Physics Soc., Radiation Research Soc., Sigma Xi, Sigma Pi Sigma, Phi Kappa Phi. Current Work: Effects of ionizing radiation; radiation transport codes for man and animal models; radiobiological dosimetry; thermoluminescense response from irradiated human teeth; Monte Carlo simulation of neutron spectra and dose distribution in phantom. Subspecialty: Medical physics. Home: 10620 Weymouth St Apt 201 Bethesda MD 20814 Office: Armed Forces Radiobiology Research Inst Bethesda MD 20814

HSIEH, KUAN HSIUNG, electrical engineer; b. Taipei, Taiwan, Republic of China, Feb. 2, 1952; came to U.S., 1978, naturalized, 1985; s. Fu-shan Hsieh and Pao-Yun (Huang) Wang; m. Betty an-Ye Wu, Aug. 17, 1980; children—Bryant Philip, Christine Lois. B.S., Nat. Taiwan U., 1974; M.S., U. Calif.-Santa Barbara, 1979; postgrad. Calif. Inst. Tech., 1980; Ph.D., Cornell U., 1983. Mem. tech. staff Jet Propulsion Lab., Pasadena, Calif., 1980-81; AT&T Bell Lab., Murray Hill, N.J., 1983; mem. tech. staff, project leader Hughes Research Lab., Malibu, Calif., 1984—; mem. tech. program com. Internat. Electron Device Meeting, Piscataway, N.J., 1984—. Contbr. articles to profl. jours. Patentee in field. Bd. dirs. Walnut garden Homeowners Assn., Van Nuys, Calif., 1985. Recipient Div. Invention award Hughes Research Lab., 1984. Mem. IEEE, Am. Phys. Soc., Sigma Xi. Mem. Evangelical Ch. Current work: High speed electronic devices especially using GaAs semiconductor and heterojunctions for microwave and minimeter wave transistors and integrated circuits. Subspecialties: Microchip technology (engineering); Microelectronics. Home: 7300 Lennox Ave J-1 Van Nuys CA 91405 Office: Hughes Research Lab RL61 3011 Malibu Canyon Rd Malibu CA 90265

HSIEH, TSUYING CARL, aerospace engineer; b. Fukien, China, May 20, 1936; came to U.S., 1960; s. Kong-Young and Sui-Ching W. Hsieh; m. Lydia C., Sept. 19, 1964; children: Mae, Stephen. B.S., Cheng-Kung U., 1956; M.S., U. Iowa, 1962; Ph.D., U. Md., 1970. Research scientist Hydronautics, Inc., Laurel, Md., 1962-68; research asst. prof. U. Md., College Park, 1968-73; aerospace engr. ARO, Inc., Arnold AFS, Tenn., 1973-79, Naval Surface Weapons Ctr., Silver Spring, Md., 1979—; dir. The Polygon, Inc., Knoxville, Tenn., 1978—. Contbr. articles to profl. jours. Served to 2d lt. Chinese Air Force, 1956-58. Mem. AIAA, Sigma Xi. Democrat. Current Work: Fluid dynamics with applications to aerospace engineering; special areas of research include computational fluid dynamics for transonic, supersonic and hypersonic flows over vehicles, bodies of revolution at high angle of attack, three-dimensional flow separation, and internal flow for ramjet inlets and diffusers. Subspecialties: Aerospace engineering and technology; Aeronautical engineering. Home: 13 Stonegate Dr Silver Spring MD 20904 Office: Naval Surface Weapons Ctr Silver Spring MD 20903

HSIUNG, GUEH-DJEN, microbiologist, educator; b. Hupeh, China, Sept. 16, 1918; d. Chu-yun and Bao-yu (Wu) H. B.S., Ginling Coll., Nanking, China, 1942; M.S., Mich. State U., 1948, Ph.D., 1951. Instr. Yale U. Sch. Medicine, 1954-57, research assoc., 1957-62, asst. prof., 1962-65; assoc. prof. N.Y. U. Sch. Medicine, 1965-67; chief virology lab. VA Med. Ctr., West Haven, Conn., 1967—; assoc. prof. dept. lab. medicine Yale U. Sch. Medicine, 1969-74, prof., 1974—. Author: Recent Advances in Clinical Virology, 1981, Diagnostic Virology, 1982; contbr. articles to profl. jours. Recipient Woman of Yr. award Fed. Exec. Assn. Greater New Haven, 1978; Career Scientist award VA, 1978. Mem. Am. Assn. Immunologists, Am. Soc. Microbiology (Becton-Dickson award in clin. microbiology 1983), Am. Acad. Microbiology (fellow), Infectious Diseases Soc. Am. (fellow). Methodist. Current Work: Medical virology; diagnostic virology; virus recognition and characterization; pathogenesis and epidemiology of virus infection; animal models for genital herpes and cytomegalovirus; endogenous virus infection and viral latency. Subspecialties: Virology (medicine); Virology (biology). Home: 30 W Haycock Point Branford CT 06405 Office: Virology Lab VA Med Center West Haven CT 06516

HSU, CHUNG Y., neurologist, neuropharmacologist, educator; b. Taipei, Republic of China, Oct. 14, 1944; came to U.S. 1971, naturalized, 1979; s. Jean Wu and Amy Yang, Dec. 27, 1974; children—Alice, Virginia, Charles. M.D., Nat. Taiwan U., 1970; Ph.D., U. Va., 1975. Chief resident Med. Univ. Hosp., Charleston, S.C., 1980-81; fellow dept. pharmacology Med. U. S.C., Charleston, 1980-81 , asst. prof., 1981-84, research coordinator dept. neurology, 1981—, attending neurologist, 1981—, assoc. prof., 1984—; dir. anticonvulsant lab. dept. neurology, 1982—; mem. stroke task force S.C. Heart Assn., 1983—; cons. VA Med. Ctr., Charleston, 1981—. Contbr. articles to profl. jours. Vice pres. Greater Charleston Chinese Soc., 1983—, pres., 1984—. Served to lt. Taiwan Navy. Recipient Tchr.-Investigator award NIH-Nat. Inst. Neurol. and Communicative Disorders and Stroke, 1983—; Nat. Research Service award USPHS, 1977, 80; grad. fellow U. Va. Sch. Med., 1971-75, NIH postdoctoral fellow, 1975-77. Fellow Am. Heart Assn. (stroke council 1983—); Mem. Am. Acad. Neurology, Am. Soc. Neurol. Investigation, Soc. for Neurosci., N.Y. Acad. Scis. Current work: Basic and clinical research in therapeutic modalities for stroke and spinal cord injuries. Subspecialties: Neurology; Neuropharmacology. Home: 934 Shetland Ct Mount Pleasant SC 29464 Office: Dept Neurology Med Univ SC 171 Ashley Ave Charleston SC 29425

HSU, CLEMENT C.S., research physician, clinical immunologist; b. Taiwan, Oct. 9, 1937; came to U.S., 1965, naturalized, 1976; s. Ma-Wong and Yui-Ju (Chen) H.; m. Yui-Li Wu, Nov. 20, 1965; children: Felix S.W., Ben S.L. M.D., Nat. Taiwan U., 1963. Diplomate: Am. Bd. Internal Medicine. Intern Jersey City Med. Center, 1965-66; resident Montefiore Hosp., N.Y.C., 1966-67, Boston City Hosp., 1967-68; fellow in liver disease N.J. Coll. Medicine and Dentistry, East Orange, 1968-69; tng. in immunology research Inst. Cancer Research, Columbia Presbyn. Med. Center and Mt. Sinai Hosp., N.Y.C., 1969-72; mem. faculty Northwestern U. Med. Sch., Chgo., 1972—, asso. prof. medicine, 1978—; chief infectious disease sect. Columbus-Cuneo-Cabrini Med. Center, Chgo., 1977—. Contbr. articles to profl. jours. Named Outstanding New Citizen Citizenship Council Met. Chgo., 1976; Leukemia Research Found. grantee, 1974, 75, 77; NIH grantee, 1974-77; Nat. Cancer Inst. grantee, 1977-80. Mem. Am. Assn. Immunologists, Am. Assn. for Cancer Research, Infectious Disease Soc. Am., Central Soc. for Clin. Research, AAAS, N.Am. Taiwanses Profs. Assn. Current Work: Membrane immunoglobulin isotypes on normal and neoplastic human lymphocytes; circulating inhibitor of lymphocyte responses in vitro; rabbit antibody inhibitor in human serum; hospital management of nursing home patients. Subspecialties: Immunobiology and immunology; Infectious diseases. Office: 2520 N Lakeview Ave Chicago IL 60614

HSU, HEI-TI, plant virologist, educator; b. Taipei, Taiwan, Sept. 3, 1939; came to U.S., 1968, naturalized, 1980; s. Chung-kuang and Cheng-Mei (Kuo) H.; m. Hsing Wu, Dec. 23, 1966; children: Elvin, Marvin. Ph.D., U. Ill., Champaign-Urbana, 1971. Research asso. U. Ill., Urbana, 1971-75; plant virologist Am. Type Culture Collection, Rockville, Md., 1975—; adj. prof. U. Md., 1981—; mem. plant virus subcom. Internat. Com. on Taxonomy of Viruses and chmn. study group Internat. Collection Plant Virus Type Cultures, 1978-84. Contbr. numerous articles to profl. publs.; asso. editor: Plant Diseases of Am. Phytopathol. Soc, 1978-82. Am. Soc. Microbiology travel awardee 3d Internat. Congress for Virology, 1975. Mem. Am. Phytopathol. Soc., Soc. Gen. Microbiology. Current Work: Plant virus characterization; monoclonal antibodies; virus systematics. Subspecialties: Plant virology; Immunobiology and immunology.

HSU, IH-CHANG, biochemist; b. Taiwan, China, Aug. 3, 1938; s. Sae and Tsu-Ying (Wong) H.; m. Chang-Mei Tung, Aug. 16, 1968; children Alexander, Daniel. B.Pharmacy, Kaohsiung Med. Coll., 1964; Ph.D. (Peterson fellow), U. Wis.-Madison, 1972. Research assoc. dept. pathology U. Wis.-Madison, 1972-75; research fellow in cancer program Oak Ridge Nat. Lab., 1975-77; expert investigator Cancer Cause and Prevention div. Nat. Cancer Inst., Bethesda, Md., 1977-82; assoc. prof. toxicology U. Md., Balt., 1982—. Contbr. sci. articles to profl. publs. Mem. Am. Assn. Cancer Research, Environ. Mutagen Soc., Sigma Xi. Presbyterian. Patentee in field; co-inventor ultra-sensitive enzymatic radioimmunoassay. Current Work: To establish systems for identification of environmental carcinogens. Research in the molecular basis of carcinogenesis and mutagenesis. Evaluation of gentoxic hazards of environmental carcinogens. Subspecialties: Cancer research (medicine); Biochemistry (medicine). Home: 3863 Spencer Ct Ellicott City MD 21403 Office: 10 S Pine St Baltimore MD 21201

HSU, MING-TEH, nuclear engineer; b. Kaoshung, Taiwan, China, June 10, 1946; came to U.S., 1969, naturalized, 1981; s. Kuai-teng and Chin-ju (Tong) H.; m. Chun-mei Lin, Jan. 27, 1979; 1 son, Johnny Meng. B.S. in Nuclear Engrng, Nat. Tsing-Hua U., Taiwan, 1968; M.S., U. Md., 1974, Ph.D., 1974. Engr. Singer Co., Silver Spring, Md, 1975; sr. application engr. Control Data Corp., Rockville, Md., 1975-78; sr. engr. Idaho Nat. Engrng. Lab., Idaho Falls, 1978-81, Bechtel, Norwalk, Calif., 1981—. Mem. Am. Nuclear Soc., Sigma Xi, Phi Kappa Phi. Current Work: The safety analysis of nuclear power plant, such as loss of coolant analysis or pipe break analysis. Subspecialties: Nuclear engineering; Fluid mechanics. Home: 513 Lyons Way Placentia CA 92670 Office: Bechtel 12400 E Imperial Hwy Norwalk CA 90650

HSU, YARSUN, electronics research scientist; b. Yengchung, Republic of China, Apr. 28, 1949; came to U.S. 1976; s. Peelin and Tsuan Hsu; m. Catherine Yang, Nov. 16, 1980. B.S., Chiaotung U., Republic of China, 1971, M.S., 1973; Ph.D., Rensselaer Polytech. Inst., 1979. Research asst. Chiaotung U., 1971-73, instr., 1975-76; instr. Navy Electronics Inst., Republic of China, 1973-75; Chiaotung U., 1975-76; research fellow, research asst. Rensselaer Poly. Inst., Troy, N.Y., 1976-79; mem. tech. staff Gen. Electric Co., Syracuse, N.Y., 1979-82; mem. research staff IBM Research Ctr., Yorktown, N.Y., 1982—; cons. Pres. Semicondr. Enterprise, Tainan, Republic of China. Contbr. articles to profl. jours. Mem. IEEE, Electrochem. Soc. Current work: Research and development of 1VLSI microelectronics chip including chip technology, device design and noval process development, power integrated circuits. Subspecialties: Microelectronics; Superconductors. Office: IBM TJ Watson Research Ctr PO Box 218 Yorktown Heights NY 10598

HU, BEI-LOK BERNARD, theoretical physicist, educator; b. Chungking, China, Oct. 4, 1947; came to U.S., 1964; s. I-Ping and Pie (Wang) H.; m. Chun-Chu A. Yee, June 24, 1972; children—Tung-Hui V., Tung-Fei A. A.B., U. Calif.-Berkeley, 1967; Ph.D., Princeton U., 1972. Mem. Inst. Advanced Study, Princeton, N.J., 1972-73; research assoc. Stanford U., Calif., 1973-74; research mathematician U. Calif.-Berkeley, 1974-76; research physicist U. Calif.-Santa Barbara, 1977-79; hon. research fellow Harvard U., Cambridge, Mass., 1979-80; asst. prof. physics U. Md., College Park, 1980-84, assoc. prof., 1984—. Contbr. articles to profl. jours., 1967—. Princeton nat. fellow Princeton U., 1967; individual investigator NSF, 1979. Mem. Am. Phys. Soc., Internat. Soc. for Gen. Relativity and Gravitation, 1971—, Chinese Soc. of Gravitation Physics and Relativistic Astrophysics (council), Assn. Mems. Inst. Advanced Study (trustee). Current work: Quantum processes in the early universe; quantum field theory in curved spacetime; finite temperature quantum field theory; symmetry breaking and critical dynamics; Bianchi and Kaluza-Klein cosmology. Subspecialties: Relativity and gravitation; Cosmology. Office: U Md Dept Physics and Astronomy College Park MD 20742

HU, CHUNG-HONG, dermatology educator; b. Taipei, Taiwan, Jan. 1, 1942; came to U.S., 1968; s. Sway-Wang and Yoh-Nee (Lin) H.; m. Mimi Wang; children: Michael, Mario. M.D., Taipei Med. Coll., 1966; postgrad., Mayo Grad. Sch. Medicine, 1970-74. Diplomate: Am. Bd. Dermatology, Am. Bd. Dermatopathology. Fellow Mayo Clinic-Mayo Found., Rochester, Minn., 1970-74; instr. U. Minn. Mayo Med. Sch., Rochester, 1974-75; asst. prof. Case Western Res. U., Cleve., 1975-79; asst. prof. Stanford (Calif.) U., 1979-82, assoc. prof., 1982—; asst. dermatologist Univ. Hosp., Cleve., 1975-79, dir. dermatopathology lab., 1977-79; chief dermatology Palo Alto (Calif.) VA Hosp., 1979—; sr. research assoc. Internat. Psoriasis Research Found., 1981—. Author: Diagnostic Electron Microscopy, 1980, Vasculitis, 1980. Chmn. bd. Chinese Acad. Cleve., 1979-79; v.p. Friends of Chinese Acad. Cleve., 1976-78; mem. med. council Ohio Lupus Found., 1978-79. Served as ensign Taiwan Navy, 1967-68. NIH grantee, 1976-79. Fellow ACP, Am. Acad. Dermatology, Am. Soc. Dermatopathology; mem. Soc. Investigative Dermatology, Internat. Soc. Tropical Dermatology. Current Work: Diagnosis and treatment of blistering diseases of the skin and skin tumors; pathogenesis and new therapeutic approaches for psoriasis. Subspecialties: Dermatology; Pathology (medicine). Office: 300 Pasteur Dr Stanford CA 94305

HUA, HSICHUN MIKE, aeronautical industry executive; b. China, Dec. 6, 1925; m. Margaret Chow, Jan. 1, 1954. M.S., Purdue U., 1965, Ph.D., 1968; postdoctoral, Harvard U., 1979. Enlisted Republic of China Air Force, 1949, advanced through ranks to lt. gen., 1983, fighter pilot, 1949-64; aerodynamicist Cessna Aircraft Co., Wichita, Kans., 1968-69; aerodynamics engr. Lockheed Aircraft Co., Burbank, Calif., 1969-70; chief aircraft design Aero Industry

Devel. Ctr., Taichung, Taiwan, Republic of China, 1970-74, dep. dir. engring. and research, 1974-82, dir., 1982—; assoc. prof. Cheng-Kung U., Taiwan, 1970-72; prof. Tunghai U., Taiwan, 1972-74; v.p. Internat. Turbine Engine Corp., Phoenix, 1982—. Contbr. numerous articles to profl. jours. Decorated D.F.C. Assoc. fellow AIAA; mem. Aero. and Astronautical Soc. (dir. 1972—), Soc. Theory and Applied Mechanics (dir. 1978—), Sigma Xi. Clubs: Am. Univ, Taipei, Taiwan, Harvard U. Current Work: Supervising development and fabrication of aircrafts and related products. Subspecialty: Aeronautical engineering.

HUANG, CHENG SCHEN, chemist, editor; b. Taipei, Taiwan, Sept. 1, 1937; came to U.S. 1966, naturalized 1983; s. Chi-hsiu and Jui-Pi (Chang) H.; m. Cheryl Ann Commons, June 20, 1980. Postgrad. Free U., Berlin, 1965-66, U. Toledo, 1967-70; Ph.D., Wayne State U., 1975. Research assoc. Med. Sch., Wayne State U., Detroit, 1975-78; chemist City of Detroit, 1978-79; assoc. editor Chem. Abstracts Service, Columbus, Ohio, 1979—; instr. Columbus Tech. Inst., 1981-82. Contbr. articles on spectroscopy/biophysics to sci. jours. Mem. Am. Chem. Soc., Biophys. Soc., N.Y. Acad. Scis. Current work: Scientific and technical information processing of published literature in environmental chemistry (air, water) and environmental engineering (waste/-water treatment). Subspecialties: Biophysics (physics); Environmental chemistry. Home: 6014 Chesterton Sq E Columbus OH 43229 Office: Chem Abstracts Service 2540 Olentangy River Rd Columbus OH 43210

HUANG, CHIA MING, physician; b. Taiwan, July 2, 1941; came to U.S., 1968, naturalized, 1979; s. Zong Ho and Kin (Lin) H.; m. Duen Mei Wung, Mar. 21, 1970; 4 children. M.D., Taipei Med. Coll., 1966. Diplomate: Am. Bd. Internal Medicine. Intern Grant Hosp., Chgo.; resident Northwestern U. Med. Sch.; practice medicine, specializing in internal medicine; assoc. prof. medicine Northwestern U., Chgo., 1975—. Mem. Am. Fedn. Clin. Research, Am. Soc. Nephrology, Internat. Soc. Nephrology, Am. Soc. Clin. Pharmacology and Therapeutics, ACP. Subspecialty: Nephrology. Office: VA Lakeside Med Center 333 E Huron St Chicago IL 60646

HUANG, CHUONG CHUN, psychiatrist, educator, neuroscientist; b. Taipei, Taiwan, China, July 1, 1936; came to U.S., 1963, naturalized, 1975; s. Tseng-Chien and Wang-Shih (Yu) H.; m. Mei-Fun WU (Frances), Dec. 28, 1968; children—Elbert Shiuh, Frederick Yuh. M.D., Nat. Taiwan U., 1962; Ph.D., UCLA, 1968. Asst. Research Physiologist, Brain Research Inst., UCLA, Los Angeles, 1960-70; asst. prof. psychiatry, U. Mo., St. Louis, 1970-73; asst. prof. Med. Coll., U. Wis., Milw., 1977—, staff psychiatrist, 1978—. Contbr. articles to profl. jours. Mem. Milw. Formosan Club, 1977—. Served to 2d lt. Taiwan Air Force, 1962-63. Recipient Physicians Recognition, AMA, 1971, 77, 81, 84; Spl. award Taipei Jen-Ai Hosp., Taiwan, 1982; Resistant Schizophrenia study Pfizer Pharms., 1982. Mem. AAAS, AMA, Am. Psychiatry Assn., N.Y. Acad. Scis., Soc. Neuroscis. Buddhist. Current work: Drug therapy and management of Schizophrenic patients, chronic pain, drug action on neuronal membrane of mammalian brain, basic mammalian brain mechanism. Subspecialties: Psychopharmacology; Neurophysiology. Home: 3304 S 123 St Milwaukee WI 53227

HUANG, ENG-SHANG, microbiology educator; b. Chia-Yi, Taiwan, Mar. 17, 1940; came to U.S., 1968; s. Jong-Sun and King-Fa (Ong) H.; m. Shu-Mei Huong, Dec. 26, 1965; children: David, Benjamin. B.S., Nat. Taiwan U., 1962, M.S. in Pub. Health, 1964; Ph.D. in Bacteriology and Immunology, U. N.C., 1971. Vis. asst. prof. U. N.C.-Chapel Hill, 1973-74, asst. prof., 1974-78, assoc. prof., 1978—; mem. virology study sect. research and grant div. NIH, Bethesda, Md., 1979-83. Contbr. articles on microbiology and virology to profl. jours. NIH Research Career Devel. awardee, 1978-83; USPHS fellow, 1972-73. Mem. Am. Soc. Microbiology, Am. Soc. Virology, N.Y. Acad. Scis., Am. Acad. Microbiology. Democrat. Current Work: Research and teaching in the molecular biology of human tumor viruses, research in molecular epidemiology of virus infection, viral oncology, antiviral and genetic engineering. Subspecialties: Virology (medicine); Genetics and genetic engineering (medicine). Office: Cancer Research Ctr U NC Sch Medicine Chapel Hill NC 27514

HUANG, HAI CHOW, nuclear engineer; b. Hankow, China, Dec. 10, 1927; came to U.S., 1963; s. Yung Ting and Chih Chuen (Shieh) H.; m. Leejen Hsueh, Dec. 21, 1961; children: Lucie, James. B.S., Nat. Taiwan U., 1955; M.S., U. Colo., 1964; Ph.D. in Nuclear Sci. and Engring., Carnegie Inst. Tech., Pitts., 1973. Registered profl. engr., Pa., Colo. Sr. engr. Rust Engring. Co., Pitts., 1964-66; chief engr. Salvucci Engrs., Inc., Pitts., 1966-69; sr. engr. Westinghouse Nuclear Energy Systems, Pitts., 1970-73; prin. engr. Advanced Reactors div. Westinghouse Electric Corp., Pitts., 1974-75, mgr. licensing standards, 1975-76, mgr. Clinch River breeder reactor plant licensing, 1976-80, mgr. Clinch River breeder reactor plant licensing and in-vessel safety analysis, 1980-81, mgr. licensing advanced reactors div., Madison, Pa., 1981—, mem. seismic criteria com., 1976—. Author tech. papers. Mem. Nat. Soc. Profl. Engrs., Am. Nuclear Soc., ASME, N.Y. Acad. Sci., AAAS, Sigma Xi. Current Work: Development of nuclear safety positions and safety and design evaluations of various concepts of liquid-metal fast breeder reactor nuclear power plants. Reactor system and in-core accident analyses. Radiological analyses for protection of public safety. Subspecialties: Nuclear engineering; Nuclear fission. Home: 594 Trotwood Ridge Dr Pittsburgh PA 15241 Office: Westinghouse Electric Corp PO Box 158 Madison PA 15663

HUANG, HSING T., science administrator, biochemist, microbiologist; b. Malacca, Malaysia, Sept. 9, 1921; came to U.S., 1947, naturalized, 1957; m. Rita L. Quan, Dec. 17, 1949; children—Pamela Clare, Terence Mark. B.S., Hong Kong U., 1941; Ph.D., Oxford U., 1947. Research biochemist Rohm & Haas Co., Phila., 1951-55; research supr. Pfizer Inc., Groton, Conn., 1955-64; dir. biol. sci. Internat. Minerals & Chemicals, Libertyville, Ill., 1964-73; tech. dir. Wallerstein Co., Morton Grove, Ill., 1973-75; program dir. NSF, Washington. 1975—. Contbr. articles to profl. jours. Patentee in field. Mem. Am. Soc. Biol. Chemists, Am. Chem. Soc. Subspecialties: Enzyme technology; Integrated pest management. Office: Nat Sci Found Washington DC 20550

HUANG, JIIN-LONG, structural engineer, consultant; b. Miao-Li, Taiwan, Republic of China, Dec. 11, 1939; came to U.S., 1967, naturalized, 1976; s. Wuh-Sheng and Tian-Mei (Cheng) H.; m. Ling-Jen Lin, Sept. 8, 1967; children—Wayne Huang, John Huang. B.S.C.E., Nat. Chung-Hsing U., Taichung, Taiwan, 1965; M.S.C.E., U. Ky., 1969. Registered civil and structural engr., Calif.; registered civil, structural and san. engr., Ky. Assoc. H. K. Bell Cons. Engrs., Lexington, Ky., 1974-78, chief structural engr., 1973—, ptnr., 1978—; adviser Ky. Gov.'s Task Force, Owensboro, 1983; mem. Ky. Gov.'s Earthquake Hazard and Safety Tech. Adv. Panel, Frankfort, 1984-85; instr. Lexington Tech. Inst., U.K., 1979. Vice pres. YMCA Judo Club, Lexington, 1967, 68. Served to 2d lt. Taiwan Army, 1965-66. Mem. Earthquake Engring. Research Inst. (reconnaissance team 1980), Nat. Soc. Profl. Engrs., ASCE. Republican. Current work: Earthquake hazards and safety; building and facility safety. Subspecialties: Structural engineering; Seismology. Home: 3329 Gondola Ct Lexington KY 40513 Office: HK Bell Cons Engrs PO Box 546 354 Waller Ave Lexington KY 40585

HUANG, KEH-NING, physicist; b. Nanking, China, Dec. 6, 1947; came to U.S., 1969; s. Han-Liang Huang and Chu-Chiu (Hu); m. Ying Kao Huang, June 18, 1972; children: Wei-Hwa, Wei-Chung. B.S., Nat. Cheng-Kung U. Tainan, Taiwan, 1968; Ph.D., Yale U., 1974. Postdoctoral fellow U. Oreg., Eugene, 1974-76; research assoc. U. Nebr., Lincoln, 1976-78; vis. asst. prof. U. Notre Dame, 1978-81; physicist Argonne (Ill.) Nat. Lab., 1981—; cons. in field. Author: Infinity and Set Theory, 1968; contbr. articles in field to profl. jours. NSF grantee, 1979-81; Cottrell grantee, 1980-82. Mem. Am. Phys. Soc., Sigma Xi. Current Work: Relativistic many-body theory and its applications; relativistic collision theory; plasma fusion related atomic processes. Subspecialties: Theoretical physics; Atomic and molecular physics. Office: Argonne National Laboratory Argonne IL 60439

HUANG, RICHARD SHIH-CHIU, mechanical engineer; b. Peking, Feb. 28, 1932; came to U.S., 1946, naturalized, 1955; s. Fang-Kang and Viola Johnson (Misner) H.; m. Adele Marrie Farren, June 4, 1960; children: William Farren, Michael Edward. B.S.M.E., Duke U., 1955; postgrad., George Washington U., 1974. Propulsion engr. Vought Corp., Dallas, 1955-60, aeroballistics engr., 1960-66, engring. mgr., 1966—. Fellow AIAA (assoc.). Republican. Clubs: Acad. Model Aeronautics (Washington) (dir. 1964); Soc. Antique Modelers (San Jose, Calif.) (rules com. 1982). Current Work: Orbital flight mechanics, cryogenics, electro-optics, and systems engineering. Subspecialties: Systems engineering; Aerospace engineering and technology. Home: 4032 Deep Valley Dr Dallas TX 75234 Office: Vought Corp PO Box 225907 Dallas TX 75265

HUANG, SHIEZEN, physicist; b. Lukang, Republic of China, Apr. 19, 1949; s. Hung-chi and Joan-En (Young) H.; m. Shee-ching Shaw, Oct. 18, 1974; children—Fanyi (Sandy), Marie. B.S., FuJen Cath. U., 1972; M.S., U. Idaho, 1976; Ph.D., U. Houston, 1981. M.S., U. Idaho, 1976; Ph.D., U. Houston, 1981. Postdoctoral fellow IBM, San Jose, Calif., 1981-83; sr. device scientist Memorex, Santa Clara, Calif., 1983—. Contbr. articles to profl. jours. Patentee combed MR head. Mem. Am. Phys. Soc., IEEE. Current work: Thin film magnetic transducer, especially in high recording density. Subspecialties: Information systems, storage, and retrieval (computer science); Condensed matter physics. Home: 6946 Randol Creek Dr San Jose CA 95120 Office: Memorex San Tomas at Central Expy Santa Clara CA 95052

HUANG, SHYHCHANG STRONG, research chemist; b. Republic of China, July 28, 1949; came to U.S., 1974; m. B.S. in Chemistry, Cheng-Kung U., Tainan, Taiwan, 1971; Ph.D. in Chemistry, U. Fla., 1981. Research assoc. Va. Poly. Inst. and State U., Blacksburg, 1981-83; research chemist Hercules Inc., Wilmington, Del., 1983—. Mem. Am. Chem. Soc. Current work: Polymer characterizations; size exclusion chromatography; light scattering; viscometry; high performance liquid chromatography, nuclear magnetic resonance and infrared spectroscopy. polymer syntheses; anionic polymerization; block copolymerization. Subspecialties: Analytical chemistry; Polymer chemistry. Office: Hercules Inc Research Ctr Wilmington DE 19894

HUANG, SUN-YI, polymer chemist, researcher; b. Su-Ao, Ilan, Taiwan, Sept. 14, 1940; came to U.S., 1966; s. Su Sen and Shaw Lin H.; m. Misa Lin, June 9, 1968; 1 son, Herman Lin. B.S., Nat. Cheng Keng U.; M.S., N.Mex. Highlands U., 1968; Ph.D., U. Mo.-Kansas City, 1973. Research assoc. U. Mo.-Kansas City, 1973-74; postdoctoral U. Akron, 1974-76; research chemist Am. Cyanamid Co., Stamford, Conn., 1976-78, sr. research chemist, 1978—. Contbr. articles to profl. jours. Served to 2d lt. Chinese Army, 1963-64. Recipient Sci. Achievement award Am. Cyanamid Co., 1981; research grantee. Mem. Am. Chem. Soc., Am. Phys. Soc., Chinese-Am. Chem. Soc., Chinese-Am. Polymer Soc. Patentee in field U.S. and fgn. countries; co-inventor long-last electrochromic device watch. Current Work: Elastomers, engineering plastics, block and Graft copolymers, water soluble polymers, novel polyelectrolytes for enhanced oil recovery, paper wet strength agts. and water treating chemicals. Subspecialties: Polymer chemistry; Synthetic chemistry. Home: 17 Loughran Ave Stamford CT 06902 Office: American Cyanamid Co 1937 W Main St Stamford CT 06904

HUANG, TSOU-CHIANG, electrical engineer; b. Taiwan, China, Oct. 9, 1936; came to U.S., 1962; naturalized, 1972; s. Chin Chuan and Hsien (Young) H.; m. Jane Chia-Tzu Lu, June 18, 1965; children—Linda, Irene, Arthur. Ph.D., Purdue U., 1969. Asst. prof. U. Detroit, 1969-72; mem. tech. staff TRW Corp., Redondo Beach, Calif., 1973-76; system engr. Lincom Corp., Los Angeles, 1976-80; mem. tech. staff Aerospace Corp., El Segundo, Calif., 1980-81, mgr., 1981—. Contbr. articles to profl. jours. Mem. IEEE (sr.) Current work: Satellite communication systems design. Subspecialties: Electrical engineering; Aerospace engineering and technology. Home: 5501 Carmelynn St Torrance CA 90503 Office: Aerospace Corp 2350 El Segundo El Segundo CA 90245

HUARD, THOMAS KING, immunologist; b. Wauseon, Ohio, Jan. 20, 1947; s. C. Paul and Donna S. H.; m. Rebecca S. Spangler, Aug. 28, 1971; 1 son, Thomas C. Student, DePauw U., 1965-69; B.S., U. Ill.-Chgo., 1970; M.S., 1976, Ph.D., 1979. Research asst. Am. Dental Assn., Chgo., 1970-72; clin. lab. technician Rush-Presbyn.-St. Luke's Med. Ctr., Chgo., 1974-78; instr. Ill. Coll. Podiatric Medicine, Chgo., 1974-78; postdoctoral scholar U. Mich., Ann Arbor, 1978-80, asst. research scientist, 1980—; cons. Internat. Biotech. Found., Denton, Tex., 1982—. Recipient Young Research award Internat. Assn. for Dental Research, 1974; NIH grantee, 1980. Mem. Am. Fedn. Clin. Research, Reticuloendothelial Soc., Sigma Xi. Repbulican. Methodist. Current Work: Cell-mediated immunity and cancer, monocyte macrophage-immunobiology, biological response modifiers (interferon) effects on immune function. Subspecialties: Immunopharmacology; Immunobiology and immunology. Home: 319 S Revena Ann Arbor MI 48103 Office: U Mich Simpson Meml Research Inst 102 Observatory Ann Arbor MI 48109

HUBBARD, G(REGORY) SCOTT, physicist, consultant; b. Lexington, Ky., Dec. 27, 1948; s. Robert Nicholas and Nancy Clay (Brown) H.; m. Susan Artimissa Ruggeri, Aug. 2, 1982. B.A., Vanderbilt U., 1970; postgrad. U. Calif.-Berkeley, 1975-77. Engr. Vanderbilt U., Nashville, 1970-73; staff scientist Lawrence Berkeley Lab., Berkeley, Calif., 1974-80; dir. research and devel. Detector Products div. Canberra Industries, Novato, Calif., 1981-82; v.p., gen. mgr. Canberra Semicondr., Novato, 1982-85; owner Hubbard Cons. Services, 1985—; cons. SRI Internat., Menlo Park, Calif., 1979—. Contbr. chpts. to books, articles to profl. jours. Recipient Founder's scholar Vanderbilt U., 1966. Mem. IEEE, Materials Research Soc., Am. Soc. Physical Research, Ky. Cols. Democrat. Current work: Electronic materials; crystal growth and purification radiation detector fabrication/ultra pure semiconductors; psychophysics: experimentation to ascertain the existence of paranormal phenomena, e.g. remote viewing and psychokinesis. Subspecialties: Electronic materials; Psychophysics. Office: SRI Internat Bldg G-220 333 Ravenswood Ave Menlo Park CA 94025

HUBBARD, HAROLD MEAD, research company executive; b. Beloit, Kans., Apr. 16, 1924; s. Clarence Richard and Elizabeth (Mead) H.; m. Doreen J. Wallace, Aug. 13, 1948 (div. 1975); children—Stuart W., David D.; m. Barbara Bell Czarnecki, 9, 1976. B.S., U. Kans., 1948, Ph.D., 1951. Instr. chemistry U. Kans., Lawrence, 1949-51; research chemist, research mgr., lab. mgr. E. I. dUpont de Nemours & Co., Inc., Wilmington, Del., 1951-69; dir. phys. sci. Midwest Research Inst., Kansas City, Mo., 1970-75, v.p. research, 1976-78, sr. v.p. ops., 1979-82; exec. v.p., dir. Solar Energy Research Inst., 1982—; dir. Guaranty State Bank. Mem. adv. com. U. Kans. Sch. Engring.; trustee U. Kansas City. Served with U.S. Army, 1942-45. Mem. Mo. Acad. Sci. (councillor at large 1977-80), Tech. Transfer Soc. (v.p. 1978-80), Am. Chem. Soc., AAAS, Am. Solar Energy Soc., Sigma Xi, Delta Upsilon. Unitarian. Club: Rockhill Tennis. Current Work: Exploratory research and advanced development in all principal solar-related technologies; biomass, combustion, wind power, materials, photo voltaics, ocean thermal energy, photosynthesis. Subspecialties: Analytical chemistry; Solar energy. Home: 2605 Vivian St Lakewood CO 80215 Office: 1617 Cole Blvd Golden CO 80401

HUBBARD, LINCOLN BEALS, radiological physicist; b. Hawkesbury, Ont., Can., Sept. 8, 1940; s. Carroll Chauncey and Mary Lunn (Beals) H.; m. Nancy Ann Krieger, Apr. 3, 1961; children: Jill, Katrina. B.S., U. N.H., 1961; Ph.D., M.I.T., 1967; postgrad. (fellow), Argonne Nat. Lab., 1966-68. Diplomate: Am. Bd. Health Physics, Am. Bd. Radiology. Asst. prof. math., physics Knoxville (Tenn.) Coll., 1968-70; asst. prof. physics Furman U., Greenville, S.C., 1970-74; chief physicist Mt. Sinai Hosp., Chgo., 1974-75, 81—; ptnr. Fields, Griffith, Hubbard & Assocs., Inc., Glencoe, Ill., 1975—; chief physicist Cook County Hosp., Chgo., 1979—; cons. in field; assoc. prof. med. physics Rush U., 1983—. Author: Mathematics for Technologists in Radiology, 1979; Computers in Radiology, 1984. NSF fellow, 1962-65; Research Corp. grantee, 1972-74. Mem. Am. Assn. Physicists in Medicine, Am. Phys. Soc., Am. Coll. Radiology, Health Physics Soc. Current Work: Application of radiation physics to all aspects of radiology imaging, nuclear medicine and radiation therapy including related safety and instructional aspects. Subspecialty: Radiology. Home: 4113 W End Rd Downers Grove IL 60515 Office: PO Box 367 Hines IL 60141

HUBBARD, WILLIAM NEILL, JR., retired pharmaceutical company executive; b. Fairmont, N.C., Oct. 15, 1919; s. William Neill and Mary Emma (Fenegan) H.; m. Elizabeth Terleski, Dec. 28, 1945; children—William Neill III, Michael J., Mary E., Elizabeth A., Susan E. A.B., Columbia, 1942; postgrad., U. N.C. Sch. Medicine; M.D., N.Y. U., 1944. Mem. house staff 3d med. div. Bellevue Hosp., N.Y.C., 1944-50; instr. medicine N.Y. U., 1950-53, asst. prof., 1953-59; asst. dean, then assoc. dean N.Y. U. Coll. Medicine, 1951-59; dean U. Mich. Med. Sch., 1959-70, asso. prof. internal medicine, 1959-64, prof., 1964-70; dir. U. Mich. Med. Center, 1969-70; gen. mgr. pharm. div., v.p. Upjohn Co., 1970-72, exec. v.p., 1972-74, pres., 1974-84, dir., 1968-84; dir. 1st Am. Bank Corp., Hoover Universal Inc., Consumers Power; bd. dirs. Pharm. Mfrs. Assn., 1978-80, 81—, chmn. bd., 1980-81; cons. USPHS. Mem. Nat. Adv. Commn. on Libraries, 1966-68; med. adv. com. W.K. Kellogg Found., 1959-67, trustee, 1979—; mem. Gov.'s Adv. Com. on Edn. Health Care, 1965-69; trustee Bronson Meth. Hosp., 1970—; chmn. Gov.'s Action Com. on Corrections, 1972-73; mem. panel ednl. consultants Commn. on Edn. for Health Adminstrn., 1973-75; mem. com. on med. edn. Brown U., 1974-77; mem. nat. sci. bd. NSF, 1974-80, cons. to bd., 1980—; bd. dirs. Internat. Fertility Research Program, 1981—; mem. bd. sci. and tech. for internat. devel. Nat. Acad. Scis., 1978-80, Council on Sci. and Tech. for Devel., 1978—; bd. visitors in East Asian studies U. Mich., 1976—, bd. dirs. devel. council, 1979—; bd. overseers Morehouse Coll., 1976-81; bd. dirs. Nat. Med. Fellowships, Inc., 1973-75, Nat. Fund. Med. Edn., 1962-75; trustee Kalamazoo Coll., 1973-78, Columbia U., N.Y.C., 1981—; mem. bd. regents Nat. Library of Medicine, 1963-67, 72-76, chmn., 1965-67, 74-76, cons., 1976—; bd. dirs. Am. Near East Refugee Aid, 1977—; dir. devel. council U. Mich., 1979—; mem. population adv. panel Office of Technology Assessment, U.S. Congress, 1979-81. Fellow A.C.P.; mem. Inst. Medicine of Nat. Acad. Scis., Harvey Soc., N.Y. Acad. Medicine, Soc. Alumni Bellevue Hosp., Mich. Med. Soc. (council 1960-62), AMA, Kalamazoo Acad. Medicine, Am. Soc. Clin. Pharmacology and Therapeutics, Assn. Am. Med. Colls. (pres. 1966-67), Sigma Xi, Alpha Omega Alpha. Home: 4630 Hickory Point Hickory Corners MI 49050

HUBBERT, MARION KING, geologist, geophysicist; b. San Saba, Tex., Oct. 5, 1903; s. William Bee and Cora Virginia (Lee) H.; m. Miriam Graddy Berry, Nov. 11, 1938. Student, Weatherford Coll., 1921-23; B.S., U. Chgo., 1926, M.S., 1928, Ph.D., 1937; D.Sc. (hon.), Syracuse U., 1972, Ind. State U., 1980. Asst. geologist Amerada Petroleum Corp., Tulsa, summer 1926, 27-28; teaching asst. geology U. Chgo., 1928-30; instr. geophysics Columbia, 1930-40; geophysicist Ill. Geol. Survey, summers 1931-32, 35-37; assoc. geologist U.S. Geol. Survey, summer 1934; pvt. research, writing, 1940-41; sr. analyst Bd. Econ. Warfare, Washington, 1942-43; research geophysicist Shell Oil Co., Houston, 1943-45, assoc. dir. research, 1945-51, chief cons. gen. geology, 1951-55; cons. gen. geology Shell Devel. Co., 1956-64; vis. prof. geology and geophysics Stanford U., 1962-63, prof., 1963-68, prof. emeritus, 1968—; vis. prof. geography Johns Hopkins U., spring 1968; regents prof. U. Calif. at Berkeley, spring 1973; mem. adv. bd. U. Calif. at Berkeley (Coll. Engring.), 1974-77; research geophysicist U.S. Geol. Survey, 1964-76, cons., 1976—; mem. U.S. delegation UN Sci. Conf. Conservation and Utilization Resources, Lake Success, N.Y., 1949; mem. com. geophysics Nat. Research Council; adviser Office Naval Research, 1949-51; mem. com. Disposal Radioactive Waste Products, 1955-63; mem. Adv. Selection Com. for Allowing Grants under Fulbright Act, 1950-51; mem. vis. com. earth scis. Mass. Inst. Tech., 1958-60; mem. earth scis. adv. panel NSF, 1953-57, chmn., 1954-57; vis. lectr. M.I.T., 1959; regents' lectr. UCLA, 1960; mem. com. natural resources Nat. Acad. Scis., 1961-62; chmn. div. earth scis. Nat. Acad. Scis.-NRC, 1963-65; nat. adv. bd. U. Nev. Desert Research Inst., 1967-73; mem. com. resources and man NRC, 1966-70. Author: The Theory of Groundwater Motion and Related Papers, U.S. Energy Resources, A Review as of 1972; co-author: Resources and Man, Structural Geology; Editor: Geophysics, 1947-49; assoc. editor: Jour. Geology, 1958-82, Bull. Am. Assn. Petroleum Geologists, 1955-74; Contbr. articles to profl. jours. Trustee, sec. Population Reference Bur., 1966-72; lectr. exec. seminars U.S. Civil Service, Office of Personnel Mgmt., 1971-84; USIA lectr., Europe, 1975, 77. Recipient Lucas medal Am. Inst. Mining, Metall. and Petroleum Engrs., 1971; Rockefeller Pub. Service award, 1977; William Smith medal Geol. Soc. London, 1978; Elliott Cresson medal for outstanding work in field of geology Franklin Inst., Phila., 1981; Vetlesen gold medal and cash award Columbia U., 1981. Fellow Am. Acad. Arts and Scis., AAAS (life), Geol. Soc. Am. (Day medal 1954, Penrose medal 1973, council 1947-49, pres. 1962), Internat. Union Geol. Scis. (U.S. nat. com. 1961-64, com. on geosci. and man 1972-76); mem. Am. Inst. Mining, Metall. and Petroleum Engrs. (hon.), Am. Assn. Petroleum Geologists (hon., Distinguished lectr. U.S. and Can. 1945, 52, 73-74), Am. Geophys. Union, Soc. Petroleum Engrs. (Distinguished lectr. 1963-64), Soc. Exploration Geophysicists (hon.), Canadian Soc. Petroleum Geologists (hon.), Nat. Acad. Scis., Sigma Xi, Gamma Alpha. Club: Cosmos (Washington). Current Work: World energy and mineral resources and their implications for human society. Subspecialties: Geology; Geophysics. Home: 5208 Westwood Dr Bethesda MD 20816

HUBE, DOUGLAS PETER, astronomer, physicist, educator; b. St. Catharines, Ont., Can., May 19, 1941; s. Clarence C. and Dorothy H. (Jago) H.; m. Joan O. Rieck, Oct. 16, 1965; children: Sharon, Susanne. B.Sc., U. Toronto, 1964, M.A., 1965, Ph.D., 1968. Vis. astronomer Radcliffe Obs., S. Africa, 1966-67; lectr. U. Toronto, 1967-68; Nat. Research Council Can. Postdoctoral fellow Kitt Peak Nat. Obs., Tucson, 1968-69; asst. prof., then assoc. prof. U. Alta., Edmonton, 1969-82, prof. physics, 1982—; founding mem. Edmonton Space Scis. Found. Contbr. articles to profl. jours., mags., newsletters and newspapers. Mem. Internat. Astron. Union, Can. Astron. Soc., Am. Astron. Soc., Royal Astron. Soc. Can. (service award 1982), Brit. Interplanetary Soc., Current Work: Spectroscopic and photometric observations and analysis of close binary stars, and peculiar A-type stars. Subspecialty: Optical astronomy. Office: Dept Physics U Alt Edmonton AB T6G 2J1 Canada

HUBER, DON MORGAN, plant pathologist; b. Mesa, Ariz., Mar. 19, 1935; s. Albert Elmo and Emma Lapreel (Davis) H.; m. Paula Elese Towery, Feb. 19, 1959; children: Brenda, Joyce, Aaron, Louise, Lynette, Sharon, Sarah, Elese, Natalie, Kevin, Derek. B.S., U. Ida., 1957, M.S., 1959; Ph.D., Mich. State U., 1963. Asst. prof. U. Ida., Moscow, 1963-68, asso. prof., 1968-71; asso. prof. plant pathology Purdue U., West Lafayette, 1971-81, prof., 1981—; research cons., 1965—; dir. Decah Mfg. Co., 1979—. Contbr. numerous articles to profl. jours. Served with AUS, 1959. Recipient Dow Chem. Research award, 1980. Mem. Am. Phytopathol. Soc., Western Soil Sci. Soc., Internat. Plant Pathology Soc., Sigma Xi, Alpha Zeta. Mormon. Patentee in field. Current Work: Basic and applied research on ecology of soil organisms, biological and cultural disease control, biology of the nitrogen cycle and physiology of pathogenesis. Subspecialties: Plant pathology; Microbiology.

HUBER, IVAN, entomologist, educator, consultant; b. Zagreb, Yugoslavia, Oct. 15, 1931; came to U.S., 1940, naturalized, 1945; s. Francis and Irene (Deutsch) H.; m. Vivienne Hirchinson, Sept. 12, 1961; children—Jonathan, Mirella. A.B., Cornell U., 1954; postgrad. U. Md., 1954-60; Ph.D., U. Kans., 1968. Microbiologist FDA, Washington, 1960-61; instr. Muhlenberg Coll., Allentown, Pa., 1966-68; asst. prof. dept. biology Fairleigh Dickinson U., Madison, N.J., 1968-74, assoc. prof., 1975-83, prof., 1984—; pres. Blatt-assocs., Inc., entomology cons., Boonton, N.J., 1979—. Contbr. articles to profl. jours. Mem. N.Y. Entomol. Soc. (treas. 1975-79), Soc. for Study Evolution, Entomol. Soc. Am., Soc. Systematic Zoology, Sigma Xi (pres. local chpt. 1971-76). Current work: Cockroaches as models in biomedical research; engaged in production of behavioral mutants for neurological research and nutritional mutants for biochemical research. Subspecialty: Gene actions. Home: 520 Lincoln St Boonton NJ 07005 Office: Dept Biology Fairleigh Dickinson U Madison NJ 07940

HUBERMAN, BENJAMIN, electrical engineer, consultant; b. Havana, Cuba, Jan. 25, 1938; came to U.S., 1947; s. Henry and Marcella (Waisman) H.; m. Gisela Bialik, Oct. 13, 1963; children—Jonathan, Martin. A.B., Columbia U., 1959, B.S. in Elec. Engring., 1960; diploma Imperial Coll. of Sci. and Industry, U. London, 1962. Nuclear engr. AEC, Washington, 1960-66; spl. asst. to dep. dir. ACDA, Washington, 1966-73; dep. dir. program analysis NSC, Washington, 1973-75; dir. policy evaluation Nuclear Regulatory Commn., Washington, 1975-77; dep. dir. White House Office Sci. and Tech. Policy, Washington, 1977-81; v.p. Cons. Internat. Group, Inc., Washington, 1981—. Served to lt. USN, 1960-66. Fulbright scholar Imperial Coll. Sci. and Industry, U. London, 1960-61. Fellow AAAS. Club: Cosmos (Washington). Current work: Consulting on nuclear, space and technology transfer issues. Subspecialties: Nuclear fission; Aerospace engineering and technology. Home: 9808 Conestoga Way Potomac MD 20854 Office: Cons Internat Group Inc 1616 H St NW Washington DC 20006

HUBERMAN, ELIEZER, microbiologist, researcher, educator; b. Lukow, Poland, Feb. 8, 1939; came to U.S., 1976, naturalized, 1982; s. Samuel and Mina (Slushni) H.; m. Lily Ginsburg, May 11, 1967; children: Ilan, Ron. M.Sc., Tel Aviv U., 1964; Ph.D., Weizmann Inst. Sci., 1969. Postdoctoral fellow McArdle Lab., U. Wis, 1969-71; scientist dept. genetics Weizmann Inst. Sci., 1971-73, sr. scientist, assoc. prof., 1973-77; sr. scientist, group leader biology div. Oak Ridge (Tenn.) Nat. Lab., 1976-81; dir. biology and med. research div. Argonne (Ill.) Nat. Lab., 1981—; prof. dept. molecular genetics and cell biology U. Chgo., 1982, dept. therapeutic radiology, 1984—. Mem. Am. Assn. for Cancer Research. Current Work: Cell differentiation and mutagenesis. Subspecialties: Cancer research (medicine); Cell and tissue culture. Home: 424 Sunset Ave LaGrange IL 60525 Office: 9700 S Cass Ave Argonne IL 60439

HUDAK, WILLIAM JOHN, pharmacologist; b. Duquesne, Pa., Jan. 3, 1929; s. Stephen and Anna (Dvorznak) H.; m. Cecelia A. Byers, Sept. 11, 1954; children: Theresa, William, Cindy, Kathy, Steve, Ralph, Agnes, Paul, Brian. B.S., U. Pitts., 1954, M.S., 1956, Ph.D. in Pharmacology (George A. Kelly fellow), 1959. Registered pharmacist, Pa. Cardiovascular sect. head Merrell Nat. Labs., Cin., 1959-70, asst. group dir., 1970-71, asso. group dir. cardiovascular clin. research, 1971-80; asst. to v.p. research ops. Merrell Nat. Labs. (Merrell Research Center), 1980-82; mgr. research ops. Merrell Dow Pharms., Inc., Cin., 1982—. Contbr. articles to sci. jours. Sec. Sharonville (Ohio) Recreation Commn., 1972-75, chmn., 1972-75, 1975-77; pres. Merrell Dow Employees Fed. Credit Union, 1973—. Nat. Heart Inst. grantee, 1958-59. Fellow AAAS; mem. Am. Soc. Clin. Pharmacology and Therapeutics, N.Y. Acad. Scis., Am. Heart Assn., Am. Soc. Pharmacology and Exptl. Therapeutics, Am. Chem. Soc., Sigma Xi, Phi Sigma, Phi Delta Chi, Rho Chi. Roman Catholic. Patentee in field (2). Current Work: Devel. of drugs for treatment of cardiovascular disease. Subspecialty: Pharmacology. Home: 10476 Wintergreen Ct Sharonville OH 45241 Office: 2110 E Galbraith Rd Cincinnati OH 45215

HUDECKI, MICHAEL STEPHEN, biologist, researcher; b. Ft. Bragg, N.C., Nov. 7, 1943; s. Stephen Edward and Veronica Aileen (Kwolek) H.; m. Rajmohini Sebastian, June 9, 1973. B.S., Niagara U., 1965, M.S., 1967, D.Sc. (hon.), 1981; M.A., SUNY, Buffalo, 1970, Ph.D., 1973. Lectr., research assoc. SUNY, Buffalo, 1979-80, research asst. prof., 1980—; cons. AAAS project on handicapped in sci., U.S. Ho. of Reps. com. on opportunities in sci. program, NSF handicapped in sci. project; adv. Office Services to Handicapped, SUNY, Buffalo. Contbr. articles in field to profl. jours. Muscular Dystrophy Assn. fellow, 1972-76; grantee, 1977—; NIH grantee, 1980-83; recipient USPHS Research Career Devel. award NIH, 1980-85. Mem. AAAS, Soc. Neuroscience, N.Y. Acad. Sci., Am. Soc. Cell Biology, Fedn. Sci. and the Handicapped, Delta Epsilon Sigma. Roman Catholic. Current Work: Drug therapy trials using chickens with inherited muscular dystrophy; high frequency stimulation of muscle. Subspecialties: Muscular dystrophy; Muscle pathology. Office: State University of New York at Buffalo 670 Cooke Department of Biological Sciences Amherst NY 14260

HUDELSON, GEORGE DAVID, air conditioning manufacturing company executive; b. Bedford, Ind., Nov. 16, 1920; s. William E. and Mabel C. (Bair) H.; m. Patricia Louise Night, June 6, 1958; children—David, Peter, Patricia. B.S.M.E., Purdue U., 1943; M.S., Ohio State U., 1951. Registered profl. engr., Ohio. Devel. engr. Wright Aero. Corp., Paterson, N.J., 1943-44; research engr. Nat. Adv. Com. for Aeronautics, Cleve., 1944-47; asst. prof. engring. Ohio State U., Columbus, 1947-57; v.p. engring. and research Carrier Corp., Syracuse, N.Y., 1957-84, v.p. corp. tech., 1984—; air conditioning design cons., Columbus, 1950-57. Recipient Disting. Engring. Alumnus award Purdue U., 1977, Disting. Engring. Alumnus award Ohio State U., 1979. Fellow ASHRAE; mem. Ohio Registered Profl. Engrs. Republican. Current work: Air conditioning research. Subspecialty: Mechanical engineering. Office: Carrier Corp Carrier Pkwy PO Box 4808 Syracuse NY 13221

HUDGIN, DONALD EDWARD, chemical research and development executive; b. Greenville, S.C., Aug. 11, 1917; s. Thomas and Virginia H.; m. Charlotte Hass, Jan. 14, 1943; children: Richard Henry, Frederick William, Charlotte Dott. B.S., Clemson U., 1938; M.S., Purdue U., 1940, Ph.D., 1947. Research chemist Procter & Gamble, Cin., 1947-52; research project leader Mallinckrodt Chem., St. Louis, 1952-55; research sect. head Celanese Corp., Summit, N.J., 1955-60; dir. research and devel. Gary Chems., East Brunswick, N.J., 1960-61; research dir. Diamond Alkali Co., Cleve., 1961-66; tech. advisor to v.p. research Exxon Research & Engring. Co., Linden, N.J., 1966-67; dir. research Princeton Chem. Research, Princeton, N.J., 1967-70; v.p. Princeton Polymer Labs., Plainsboro, N.J., 1970-80, pres., 1980—; lectr. chemistry U. Mass., 1965, Princeton U., 1972; speaker in field. Editor: Polymer Engineering Book Series, 1980; assoc. editor: Internat. Jour. Polymer Process Engring, 1980; contbr. articles to profl. jours. Exec. dir. Northeast Ohio council Boy Scouts Am., 1962-66; bd. dirs. Civil Def. Council, Summit, N.J., 1957-61. Served to maj. AUS, 1942-46, ETO; Served to maj. USAR, 1946-66. Fellow Am. Inst. Chemists; mem. Am. Chem. Soc., AAAS, N.Y. Acad. Sci., Chemists Club, Soc. Plastics Engrs., Am. Council Ind. Labs., Assn. Small Research Companies, Assn. Research Dirs. (pres. 1974-75), Plastics Edn. Found. (bd. trustee 1974-75), Sigma Xi. Republican. Unitarian. Clubs: West Windsor Tennis Assn, Ret. Officers Assn. Patentee in field. Current Work: Polymer science, technical market studies. Subspecialties: Polymer chemistry; Organic chemistry. Office: 501 Plainsboro Rd Plainsboro NJ 08536

HUDGINS, ARCHIBALD PERRIN, II, computer programmer; b. Charleston, W.Va., Sept. 15, 1943; s. Archibald Perrin and Marie (Linville) H. B.S., Presbyn. Coll., Clinton, S.C., 1965; M.P.A., Brigham Young U., 1978. Flight/ground instr. Burnside-Ott Aviation Tng. Ctr., Ft. Lauderdale, Fla., 1970-75; computer programmer Tooele Army Depot, Tooele, Utah, 1975-79; computer programmer, analyst Naval Aviation Logistics Ctr., Patuxent Naval Air Sta., Md., 1979—. Squadron comdr. CAP, 1983-85. Served to capt. AUS, 1965-69; Vietnam. Mem. Assn. Computing Machinery, Soc. Indsl. and Applied Math., Am. Mgmt. Assn., Aircraft Owners and Pilots Assn., Nat. Assn. Flight Instrs. Republican. Presbyterian. Club: Flying. Current work: Development of information storage and retrieval systems using relational database technology. Subspecialties: Information systems, storage, and retrieval (computer science); Database systems. Home: PO Box 292 Lexington Park MD 20653 Office: Naval Aviation Logistics Ctr NALC 1324B Patuxent NAS MD 20670

HUDSON, WILLIAM DONALD, JR., natural sciences educator; b. St. Johnsbury, Vt., June 28, 1950; s. William Donald and Marguerite (McConnell) H.; m. Josephine Wilcox Ewing, June 16, 1979. A.B. in French, Dartmouth Coll., 1972; M.S. in Botany, U. Vt., 1979; Ph.D. in Biology, Ind. U., 1983. Instr. Chewonki Found., Wiscasset, Maine, 1972-76, biologist, coordinator natural scis. edn., 1982—. Ind. Acad. Scis. grantee, 1980-81; Sigma Xi grantee, 1980-81. Mem. Bot. Soc. Am., Am. Soc. Plant Taxonomists, Soc. for Study of Evolution, Soc. Econ. Botany, Ecol. Soc. Am., Brit. Ecol. Soc., Inst. Biology, Am. Ornithol. Union, AAAS, New Eng. Bot. Soc., Northeastern Bird-Banding Assn., Sigma Xi. Current Work: Investigations of the origin and evolution of domesticated plants, notably members of the potato family. Solanaceae Physalis. Subspecialties: Evolutionary biology; Taxonomy. Office: Chewonki Found Wiscasset ME 04578

HUEBNER, ROBERT JOSEPH, med. research scientist; b. Cin., Feb. 23, 1914; s. Joseph Frederick and Philomena (Brickner) H.; m. Harriet Lee, Feb. 5, 1975; children by previous marriage—Elizabeth, Frances, Geraldine, James, Virginia, Roberta, Edward, Louise, Daniel. Student, Xavier U., 1932-35, U. Cin., 1937-38; M.D., St. Louis U., 1942; LL.D., U. Cin., 1965; D.Sc. (hon.), Edgecliff Coll., 1970, U. Parma, Italy, 1970; D.Sc. hon. degree, U. Leuven, 1973. Commd. jr. asst. surgeon USPHS, 1942, advanced through grades to med. dir., 1953; mil. duty Alaskan area USCG, 1943- 44; virus and rickettsial disease research NIH, 1944-56, chief virus sect., 1949-56; chief lab. infectious disease Nat. Inst. Allergy and Infectious Diseases, 1956-68; chief viral carcinogenesis br. Nat. Cancer Inst., Bethesda, Md., 1968—; Gehrman lectr. U. Ill., 1955, Eli Lilly lectr., 1957; Gudakunst lectr. U. Mich., 1958, Harvey lectr., 1960, Puckett lectr., 1960. Contbr. numerous articles to profl. jours. Recipient Bailey K. Ashford award, 1949; certificate merit St. Louis U., 1949; James D. Bruce Meml. award, 1964; Pasteur medal, 1965; Distinguished Service medal USPHS, 1966; Howard Taylor Ricketts award, 1968; Nat. medal Sci., 1969; Kimble award, 1970; Rockefeller award, 1970; Guido Lenghi award, 1971. Fellow Am. Pub. Health Assn., N.Y. Acad. Scis.; mem. Nat. Acad. Scis., A.A.A.S., Am. Assn. Immunologists, Am. Epidemiol. Soc., Fedn. Am. Socs. Exptl. Biology and Medicine, Wash. Acad. Sci. (award biol. scis. 1949), Internat. Union Against Cancer, Am. Acad. Microbiology, Am. Assn. Cancer Research, A.M.A., Md. Angus Assn. (pres. 1959-60), Sigma Xi, Alpha Omega Alpha. Current Work: Role of oncogenes(transforming celluar genes)in human cancer. Subspecialties: Cancer research (medicine); Epidemiology. Home: 12100 Whippoorwill Ln Rockville MD 20852 Office: Lab Cellular and Molecular Biology Nat Cancer Inst Bethesda MD 20205

HUESER, JAMES NICHOLAS, physician, medical oncologist; b. Clinton, Mo., Dec. 6, 1938; s. Edward John and Geneva Catherine (Putthoff) H.; m. Lorraine A. Buchanan, Oct. 23, 1965; children: Michael, Michelle, Christopher, Mark. B.S., Rockhurst Coll., 1959; M.D., U. Mo.-Columbia, 1963. Diplomate: Am. Bd. Internal Medicine and Med. Oncology. Intern San Francisco Gen. Hosp., 1963-64; resident U. Mo., Columbia, 1964-67; internist Ellis Fischel State Cancer Hosp., Columbia, 1967-69, cons. med. oncology, 1969-83; attending physician Boone Hosp. Center, Columbia, 1969—; internist, med. oncologist Columbia Clinic, 1972—; attending physician Columbia Regional Hosp., 1974—; dir. Cancer Detection Clinic Cancer Research Center, Columbia, 1971-75; cons. med. oncology Bothwell Meml. Hosp., Sedalia, Mo, 1978—, Audrain Med. Center, Mexico, Mo., 1980—, Fitzgibbon Hosp., Marshall, Mo., 1981—. Contbr. articles to profl. jours. Bd. dirs. Mo. Div. Am. Cancer Soc., Jefferson City, 1975—, pres., 1979-81, bd. Ronald McDonald House, Columbia, 1982-84; del. mem. Assn. Community Cancer Centers, 1982—. Investigator Western Cancer Study Group, Los Angeles, 1969-75; Investigator Cancer and Acute Leukemia Group B, N.Y.C., 1981-84; Investigator Nat. Surg. Adjuvant Breast Project, Pitts., 1981-83. Fellow Am. Soc. Clin. Oncology, Am. Assn. Cancer Research, ACP; mem. N.Y. Acad. Scis., AAAS. Republican. Roman Catholic. Current Work: Clinical research in cancer chemotherapy. Subspecialty: Cancer research (medicine). Home: 604 W Broadway Columbia MO 65201 Office: Columbia Clinic 401 Keene St Columbia MO 65201

HUEY, RAYMOND BRUNSON, zoology educator, author; b. Bakersfield, Calif., Sept. 14, 1944; s. Arthur S. and LaVerne (Brunson) H. A.B., U. Calif.-Berkeley, 1966; M.A., U. Tex., 1969; Ph.D., Harvard U., 1975. Miller fellow U. Calif., Berkeley, 1975-77; asst. prof. zoology U. Wash., Seattle, 1977-80, assoc. prof., 1980-84, prof., 1984—. Co-editor: Lizard Ecology, 1983; assoc. editor Oecologia, Berlin, 1983—; contbr. numerous articles to profl. jours. Research grantee Nat. Geog. Soc., 1975, NSF, 1976—. Mem. Soc. for Study Evolution, Am. Soc. Naturalists, Am. Soc. Ichthyologists and Herpetologists, Herpetologists League, Ecol. Soc. Am. Current work: Evolution of physiology. Subspecialties: Behavioral ecology; Comparative physiology. Office: Dept Zoology NJ-15 Univ Wash Seattle WA 98195

HUFF, KENNETH O., consulting geologist; b. Daleville, Ind., Dec. 17, 1926; s. George Byron and Mary Ethel (Smith) H.; m. Donna M. Huff, Mar. 25, 1957; children: John, Robert, Donald, Patricia. B.S., Ind. U., 1956; postgrad., Ball State U., 1947-48, Purdue U., 1944-45. Cert. Am. Inst. Profl. Geologists. Well logging engr., lab. mgr. Core Labs., Inc., Williston, N.D. and Farmington, N.Mex., 1956-64, lab. mgr., sales engr., Casper, Wyo. and Farmington, 1964-67, Rocky Mountain dist. supr., Casper, 1967-69, cons. geologist, 1969—; pres. Adventures, Inc., Casper, 1972—. Mem. dist. export council U.S. Dept. Commerce, 1977—. Served with U.S. Army, 1944-46, 50-51, Korea. Mem. Soc. Petroleum Engrs., Am. Assn. Petroleum Geologists, Wyo. Geol. Assn., Rocky Mountain Assn. Petroleum Geologists, Casper Petroleum Club. Patentee automated sample recovery equipment for rotary drill rigs (3). Current Work: Corporate management; sample recovery equipment for drill rigs. Subspecialties: Geology; Petroleum engineering. Office: 535 N Lenox St Casper WY 82601

HUGG, JAMES WILLIAM, physicist, researcher; b. Raceland, La., Nov. 10, 1952; s. James William and Emily Jo (Boyd) H.; m. Olivia Brooks, June 30, 1973. B.S. in Physics and Econs., Calif. Inst. Tech., 1974, M.S. in Physics, 1974; M.S. in Physics, Stanford U., 1976, Ph.D. in Physics, 1978. Research asst. Stanford U., Calif., 1974-78; research physicist Shell Devel. Co., Houston, 1978-82; staff research geophysicist Sohio Petroleum Co., Dallas, 1983-84, mgr. applied geophys. research, 1984—. Contbr. articles to profl. jours. Inventor well logging techniques. Vice chmn. bd. trustees Lamb and Lion Ministries, McKinney, Tex., 1980—; mem. steering com. Palmer Drug Abuse Program, Houston, 1979-82. Mem. Fedn. Am. Scientists, Union Concerned Scientists, Soc. Exploration Geophysicists (research com.), Am. Phys. Soc., Am. Geophys. Union, IEEE, AAAS, Mensa, Stanford Alumni Assn., Calif. Inst. Tech. Alumni Assn., Shotokan Karate of Am., Sigma Xi. Current work: Geophysical petroleum exploration and production research, especially inversion, vector computing, expert systems; geochronology; particle physics, especially unified field theories and cosmology. Subspecialties: Geophysics; Particle physics. Office: Sohio Petroleum Co 5400 LBJ Freeway Suite 1200 Dallas TX 75240

HUGGINS, WILLIAM HERBERT, electrical engineering educator; b. Rupert, Idaho, Jan. 11, 1919; s. William John and Alafretta Evelyn (Roraback) H. B.S., Oreg. State Coll., 1941, M.S., 1942; Sc.D., Mass. Inst. Tech., 1953. Instr. elec. engring. Oreg. State Coll., 1942-44; spl. research asso. radio research lab. Harvard, 1944-46; supervising scientist Air Force Research Center, Cambridge, Mass., 1946-54; research asso. Mass. Inst. Tech., 1949-54; prof. elec. engring. Johns Hopkins, 1954-84, part-time, 1985—, chmn. dept., 1970-74; Cons. editor Addison-Wesley Pub. Co., 1957-60, Blaisdell Pub. Co., 1961-65; cons. Rand Corp., 1955-73. Recipient decoration for exceptional civilian service USAF, 1954; Browder J. Thomson Meml. prize Am. I.R.E., 1948; Lindback Found. award for distinguished teaching, 1961; Western Electric Fund award Am. Soc. Engring. Edn., 1965. Fellow IEEE (Edn. medal 1966), Acoustical Soc. Am., AAAS; mem. Nat. Acad. Engring., Phi Beta Kappa, Sigma Xi. Subspecialty: Electrical engineering. Home: One E University Pkwy Unit 1005 Baltimore MD 21218

HUGHES, ERIC HILL, federal government wetlands ecologist; b. Landstahl, W.Ger., Oct. 19, 1953; came to U.S., 1956, naturalized 1960; s. George B. and Margaret C. (Hazard) H. B.S., Emory U., 1975; M.S., U. Ga., 1980. Ecol. research asst. Chesapeake Biol. Lab., Solomons, Md., 1973, Oak Ridge Nat. Lab., 1974; water quality chemist U.S. Geol. Survey, Atlanta, 1974-76; research asst. U. Ga., Athens, 1976-78; wetlands ecologist EPA, Atlanta, 1979—. Contbr. articles to profl. jours. Mem. Soc. Wetland Scientists, Estuarine Research Fedn., Southeastern Estuarine Research Soc., Nat. Resource Def. Council, Audubon Soc. Democrat. Methodist. Club: Atlanta Lacrosse (exec. com. 1982-84). Current work: Expert in wetlands ecology, ecosystems functioning, marsh carbon flow. Subspecialties: Ecology (environmental science); Resource management. Office: EPA Environ Assessment Br 345 Courtland St NE Atlanta GA 30365

HUGHES, JOHN HENRY, medical virologist, educator; b. Cleve., Jan. 7, 1942; s. James W. and Mary E. (Kostelia) H.; m. Laura Jo Hughes, July 10, 1965; children: Paula Jo, Jennifer, Darrell, Eric. M.A., Bowling Green State U., 1967; Ph.D., Ohio State U., 1972—. Clin. microbiologist Children's Hosp., Columbus, Ohio, 1971; virologist dept. med. microbiology Ohio State U., 1972—, assoc. dir. diagnostic virology, 1981—. Contbr. articles to profl. jours. Mem. AAAS, Am. Soc. Microbiology. Current Work: Diagnostic virology, antivirals, viral genetics and molecular biology of RNA viruses. Subspecialties: Animal virology; Microbiology (medicine). Home: 4326 Oak View Dr Columbus OH 43204 Office: 700 Children's Dr Ross Hall Columbus OH 43205

HUGHES, JOHN RUSSELL, physician, researcher; b. DuBois, Pa., Dec. 19, 1928; s. John Henry and Alice Fay (Cooper) H.; m. Mary Ann Dick, June 14, 1958; children—Christopher Alan, Thomas Gregory, Cheryl Ann. A.B. summa cum laude, Franklin and Marshall Coll., 1950; B.A. with honors, Oxford U., 1952, M.A. with honors, 1955, D.M. (hon.) 1976; Ph.D., Harvard U., 1954; M.D., Northwestern U., 1975. Intern Northwestern Meml. Hosp., Chgo., 1975-76; neurophysiologist NIH, Bethesda, Md., 1954-56, cons. 1970—; dir. EEG SUNY-Buffalo, 1957-62; prof. neurophysiology, dir. EEG Northwestern Med. Ctr., Chgo., 1962-77, U. Ill. Med. Ctr., Chgo., 1977—; cons. VA Hosp., Chgo., 1962—. Author 5 books on EEG. Contbr. articles to profl. jours. Col. M.C. U.S. Army Res. Mem. Eastern EEG Assn. (sec., treas. 1959-63), Am. EEG Soc. (treas. 1968-71), Am. Acad. Neurology, Am. Epilepsy Soc., Am. Med. EEG Assn. (bd. dirs. 1976). Republican. Presbyterian. Current work: Electro-clinical correlations in EEG and epilepsy. Subspecialties: Neurophysiology; Neurology. Home: 720 Roslyn Terr Evanston IL 60201

HUGHES, PHILIP ALFRED, researcher, astronomy educator; b. London, June 27, 1951; s. Derek Alfred and Irene (Seymour) H. B.Sc., Queen Mary Coll., London, 1973; M.Sc., U. Sussex, Eng., 1974, D.Phil., 1980. Research fellow U. Sussex, Brighton, 1978-81; Sci. and Engring. Research Council fellow Cavendish Lab., Cambridge, Eng., 1981-83; lectr. dept. astronomy U. Mich., Ann Arbor, 1983—. Contbr. articles to profl. jours. Fellow Royal Astron. Soc.; mem. Am. Astron. Soc. Current work: Extended and compact features of radio galaxies and quasars, with particular interest in physics of collisionless shocks, magnetic field generation and particle acceleration. Subspecialty: Theoretical astrophysics. Office: Dept of Astronomy Univ of Mich Ann Arbor MI 48109

HUGHES, THOMAS JOSEPH, mechanical engineering educator, consultant; b. Bklyn., N.Y., Aug. 3, 1943; s. Joseph Anthony and Mae (Bl) H.; m. Susan Elizabeth Weh, July 1, 1972; children: Emily, Ian, Elizabeth. B.S., Pratt Inst., 1965, M.S., 1967; M.S., U. Calif.-Berkeley, 1974, Ph.D., 1974. Mech. design engr. Grumman Aerospace, Bethpage, N.Y., 1965-66; research engr. Gen. Dynamics, Groton, Conn., 1967-69; research engr., lectr. U. Calif., Berkekely, 1974-76; assoc. prof. Calif. Inst. Tech., 1976-80; prof. Stanford U., 1980—. Author: Mathematical Foundation of Elasticity, 1983, A Short Course in Fluid Mechanics, 1976; editor: Computational Methods in Transient Analysis, 1983, Computer Methods in Applied Mechanics and Engineering, 1980. Recipient Bernard Friedman prize U. Calif., Berkeley, 1975. Fellow Am. Acad. Mechanics; mem. ASME (Melville medal 1979), Am. Soc. Civil Engrs. (Huber Research prize 1978), Soc. Engring. Sci., AIAA. Current Work: Computational methods in solid, fluid, structural and soil mechanics. Subspecialties: Mechanical engineering; Civil engineering. Office: Division of Applied Mechanics Durand Bldg Stanford University Stanford CA 94305

HUGHETT, PAUL WILLIAM, computer image generation consultant; b. San Rafael, Calif., May 19, 1950; s. Earl Howard and Shirley Helen (Hoitela) H. Student, MIT, 1966-73. Mem. tech. staff Hewlett-Packard, Palo Alto, Calif., 1973-77; system engr. Singer-Link, Sunnyvale, Calif., 1977-81; cons. Dragoncraft, Palo Alto, 1981—. Mem. Spl. Interest Group on Computer Graphics, IEEE, Profl. & Tech. Cons. Assn. (program chmn. 1983-85, Exceptional Service award 1984). Current Work: Real-time computer image generation for flight simulation; pilot visual cues and training value; visual data base design. Subspecialties: Graphics, image processing, and pattern recognition; Aeronautical engineering. Home: PO Box 60 Palo Alto CA 94302

HUGLI, TONY EDWARD, immunologist; b. Logan, Ohio, June 26, 1941; s. John and Clara (Farmer) H.; m. Judith Ann Furay, Aug. 26, 1963; children—Kevin T., Heidi E. B.S., Otterbein Coll., 1963; Ph.D., Ind. U., 1968. Mem. Scripps Clinic, La Jolla, Calif., 1972—; research assoc. Rockefeller U., 1968-72; vis. com. U. Tex. Health Ctr., Tyler, 1984; cons. Upjohn Diagnostics, Kalamazoo, Mich., 1980—. Contbr. articles to profl. jours. Recipient James W. McLaughlin Professorship Series award, Galveston, Tex., 1977. Mem. Am. Soc. Biol. Chemists, Am. Soc. Exptl. Pathology, Am. Assn. Immunologists, Am. Heart Assn. (established investigator 1974-78). Subspecialty: Biochemistry (medicine). Home: 6026 Charae St San Diego CA 92112 Office: Scripps Clinic and Research Found 10666 N Torrey Pines Rd IMM18 La Jolla CA 92037

HUI, KOON-SEA, biochemist; b. Hong Kong, Sept. 21, 1948; came to U.S., 1976; s. Yuk-Tat and Lau Kiu Hui; m. Sept. 13, 1974; 1 child, Jacqueline. B.Sc., Chinese U., Hong Kong, 1971; M.Phil., Hong Kong U., 1974; Ph.D., U. Sask., Can., 1976. Research scientist Dept. Mental Hygiene, N.Y.C., 1976-83; chief peptide research lab. N.S. Kline Inst., Orangeburg, N.Y., 1983—; asst. research prof. dept. psychiatry NYU, N.Y.C., 1981—. Author: Trace Metals, 1976; Neuropeptide, 1983; Neurochemistry, 1983; Neuromethods, 1985. Grantee NIH, 1979-81, NSF, 1979-81; sr. fellow NIH, 1981; recipient hon. mention 6th Psychiat. Forum, 1976. Mem. N.Y. Acad. Scis., Am. Soc. Neurochemistry, Internat. Soc. Neurochemistry, Am. Soc. Biol. Chemists, Internat. Brain Research Orgn. Current work: Neuropeptide metabolism, neurochemistry, enzyme manipulation. Subspecialties: Neurochemistry; Psychopharmacology. Office: Nathan S Kline Inst Orangeburg NY 10962

HUIZENGA, JOHN ROBERT, nuclear chemist, educator; b. Fulton, Ill., Apr. 21, 1921; s. Harry M. and Josie B. (Brands) H.; m. Dorothy J. Koeze, Feb. 1, 1946; children—Linda J., Jann H., Robert J., Joel T. A.B., Calvin Coll., 1944; Ph.D., U. Ill., 1949. Lab. supr. Manhattan Wartime Project, Oak Ridge, 1944-46; instr. Calvin Coll., Grand Rapids, Mich., 1946-47; asso. scientist Argonne Nat. Lab., Chgo., 1949-57, sr. scientist, 1958-67; professorial lectr. chemistry U. Chgo., 1963-67; prof. chemistry and physics U. Rochester, 1967-78, Tracy H. Harris prof. chemistry and physics, 1978—, chmn. dept. chemistry, 1983—; vis. prof. Joliot-Curie Lab., U. Paris, 1964-65, Japan Soc. for Promotion of Sci., 1968; chmn. Nat. Acad. Sci.-NRC Com. on Nuclear Sci., 1974-77. Author: (with R. Vandenbosch) Nuclear Fission, 1973; Contbr. articles to profl. jours. Fulbright fellow Netherlands, 1954-55; Guggenheim fellow Paris, 1964-65; Guggenheim fellow Berkeley, Calif., 1973; Guggenheim fellow Munich, W.Ger., 1974; Guggenheim fellow Copenhagen, 1974; recipient E.O. Lawrence award AEC, 1966; named Disting. Alumnus Calvin Coll., 1975. Fellow Am. Phys. Soc., AAAS; mem. Nat. Acad. Sci., Am. Chem. Soc. (award for nuclear applications in chemistry 1975), Phi Beta Kappa, Phi Kappa Phi, Sigma Xi. Current Work: Nuclear chemistry; nuclear reactions and structure, including nuclear fission and heavy-ion reaction mechanisms. Home: 51 Huntington Meadow Rochester NY 14625 Office: Dept Chemistry U Rochester Rochester NY 14627

HULBERT, LLOYD CLAIR, plant ecology educator; b. Lapeer, Mich., June 27, 1918; s. L. Claire and Mary (Hungerford) H.; m. Jean Elizabeth Smaltz, June 28, 1952; children: Steven L., Mark J., Thomas A., John R. B.S., Mich. State Coll., 1940, student, 1940-41; student, Cornell U., 1941-42; Ph.D., Wash. State U., 1953. Instr. math U. Minn., 1946-47; instr. botany Mont. State U., 1947-49, U. Minn., 1951-55; asst. prof. div. biology Kans. State U.-Manhattan, 1955-64, assoc. prof., 1964-72, prof., 1972—, dir. Konza Prairie Research Natural Area, 1972—. Contbr. articles to sci. jours.; Co-author: (with F. W. Oehme) Plants Poisonous to Livestock, 3d edit, 1968. NSF Research grantee, 1980—; Biol. Field Facility grantee, 1981; recipient The Nature Conservancy's Oak Leaf award, 1976, Pres.'s Stewardship award, 1978. Current Work: Productivity and composition of prairie under various treatments and effects of fire on vegetation. Subspecialty: Ecology (environmental science). Home: 2323 Bailey Dr Manhattan KS 66502 Office: Div Biology Kans State U Manhattan KS 66506

HULBURT, HUGH MCKINNEY, chemical engineering educator; b. Nashua, N.H., Oct. 27, 1917; s. Clarence Hellings and Alice Hannah (McKinney) H.; m. Ann Podlucky, June 30, 1940 (dec. 1956); children—Susan Mary Hulburt Wadelton, Margery Ann; m. Pauline Podlucky, Dec. 1, 1956; 1 child, William Hugh. B.A., Carroll Coll., Waukesha, Wis., 1938; M.S., U. Wis., 1940, Ph.D., 1942. Sr. research chemist Shell Oil Co., N.Y.C., 1943-44; temp. instr. Hunter Coll., N.Y.C., 1944-46; asst. prof., then assoc. prof. Cath. U. Am., Washington, 1946-51; sr. engr. to dir. research and devel. Chem. Constrn. Corp., N.Y.C., 1951-56; asst. to dir. chem. engring., dir. phys. research Am. Cyanamid Co., Stamford, Conn., 1956-63; prof. chem. engring. Northwestern U., Evanston, Ill., 1963—, assoc. dean Grad. Sch., 1975-80, assoc. dean Technol. Inst., 1980-83; cons. chem. and engring. cos.; vis. prof. Swiss Fed. Tech. Inst., Zurich, 1971; cons. div. engring. NSF, Washington, 1975-77. Patentee manufacture of cyanogen. Editor research jour., chem. reaction engring. books. Contbr. research papers to profl. publs. Mem. adv. panel Ill. Energy Resource Commn., Springfield, 1975-76; chmn. adv. panel Chgo. Citizens Task Force on Tunnel and Reservoir Project, 1979-81. NRC fellow, Princeton U., 1942-43. Fellow Am. Inst. Chem. Engrs. (inst. lectr. 1962), AAAS; mem. Am. Chem. Soc., Am. Phys. Soc. Club: Economic (Chgo.). Current work: Chemical reaction engineering; theory of particulate processes; computer aids to engineering education. Subspecialty: Chemical engineering. Home: 2028 Highland Ave Wilmette IL 60091 Office: Dept Chem Engring Northwestern U Evanston IL 60201

HULBURT, MARGERY ANN, geohydrology consulting company executive; b. N.Y.C., Apr. 2, 1954; d. Hugh M. and Ann (Podlucky) Hulburt; m. Arthur Held, June 11, 1976; 1 child, Kristin Pauline. B.A. in Geology and Biology, Carleton Coll., 1976; M.S. in Hydrology, U. Ariz.-Tucson, 1979. Field mgr. U. Ariz., Gillette, Wyo., 1977-78; hydrologist Gen. Electric-Tempo, Santa Barbara, Calif., 1978-79; hydrologist Land Quality div. Wyo. Dept. Environ. Quality, Cheyenne, 1979-80, chief hydrologist, 1980-81; ind. geohydrology cons., Cheyenne, Wyo., 1981-83; pres. Profl. Solutions, Inc., Cheyenne, Wyo., 1983—. Contbr. articles to tech. jours. Treas. Cheyenne chpt. NOW, 1980-81, co-pres., 1982-83. Mem. Nat. Water Well Assn., Am. Water Resources Assn., Geol. Soc. Am., Colo. Ground Water Assn., Cheyenne Women's Network. Club: Zonta Internat. (bd. dirs. Cheyenne chpt.). Current work: Ground water; mining hydrology; in-situ mining; ground water contamination monitoring, control and restoration; geologic controls on hydrologic systems; computer applications to hydrology; regulation of water use and impacts. Subspecialties: Hydrology; Geology. Office: Profl Solutions Inc 1603 Capitol Ave Cheyenne WY 82001

HULET, E. KENNETH, nuclear scientist; researcher; b. Baker, Oreg., May 7, 1926; s. Frank Ervin and Marjorie I. (Suiter) H.; m. Betty Jo Gardner, Sept. 10, 1949; children—Carri, Randall Gardner, Hulet. B.S., Stanford U., 1949; Ph.D., U. Calif.-Berkeley, 1953. AEC doctorate fellow Lawrence Berkeley Lab., Calif., 1950-53; staff scientist Lawrence Livermore Lab., Calif., 1953-66, group leader, 1966—. Author book chpts. Co-discoverer of element 106. Contbr. articles to profl. jours. Served to lt. (j.g.) USN, 1944-48. Fulbright Research scholar, 1962-63. Fellow AAAS, Am. Inst. Chemists (vice chmn. 1979-82); mem. Am. Phys. Soc., Am. Chem. Soc. (chmn.-elect div. nuclear sci. and tech. 1986). Current work: Nuclear and chemical properties of the transplutonium elements, new elements, physics of fission. Subspecialties:

Nuclear physics; Nuclear chemistry. Home: Box 411 Diablo CA 94528 Office: L-232 Lawrence Livermore Nat Lab Box 808 Livermore CA 94550

HULKE, STEVEN DELBERT, geologist; b. Elgin, Ill., Jan. 4, 1948; s. Delbert William and Elizabeth Jane (Kaufman) H.; m. Anne Muir Schultz, Apr. 5, 1977; 1 child, Sarah Caitlin. B.A., Carleton Coll., 1970; M.A., U. Tex., 1978. Geologist, Turk, Kehle & Assocs., Austin, 1974-80; sr. exploration geologist Anadarko Prodn. Co., Midland, Tex., 1980-81; sr. exploration geologist Heritage Resources, Midland, 1981-83; dist. geologist Mid Am. Petroleum Corp., Midland, 1983; sr. exploration geologist Woods Petroleum Corp., Midland, Tex., 1983-84, exploration mgr., 1984—. Mem. Am. Assn. Petroleum Geologists, Geol. Soc. Am., Am. Inst. Profl. Geologists, Soc. Econ. Paleontologists and Mineralogists, W. Tex. Geol. Soc., Roswell Geol. Soc., N.Mex., Geol. Soc. Club: W. Tex. Flyfishers. Current work: Geological and geophysical interpretation for petroleum prospect generation, West Tex and Southeast New Mexico. Subspecialty: Petroleum exploration; Petroleum geology. Office: Woods Petroleum Corp 310 W Illinois St Suite 300 Midland TX 79701

HULL, DIANA, psychologist; b. Lawrence, N.Y., Dec. 27, 1969; d. Louis Albert and Roslyn (Diamont) Jaffree; m. David Pershing Hull, Dec. 27, 1969; children: Marcy Burton, Allison Langdon Boomer. B.A., CUNY, 1946; M.S.W., U. Mich., 1954; Ph.D., U. Tex.-Houston, 1975. Asst. prof. psychology dept. psychiatry Baylor Coll. Medicine, Houston, 1976-80, clin. instr., 1966-76, cons. group psychotherapy program Child Psychiatry Clinic, 1975-80, pvt. practice psychology, Santa Barbara, Calif.; group therapist milieu treatment program and substance abuse program VA Hosp., Houston, 1962-67; cons. Child Guidance Clinic of Houston, 1967-69; editorial cons. Issue on Migration and Health Internat. Migration Rev., 1981. Contbr. articles to profl. jours. Bd. dirs. Phoenix House of Santa Barbara. Recipient sustained superior performance award VA, 1963. Fellow Am. Group Psychotherapy Assn. (Master Instr. award 1976); mem. Am. Psychol. Assn., AAAS, N.Y. Acad. Scis., Tex. Psychol. Assn., Calif. Psychol. Assn., Santa Barbara Area Psychol. Assn., Assn. Media Psychology (sec.), Southwestern Group Psychotherapy Soc., Houston Group Psychotherapy Soc. (mem. faculty and adv. bd. group psychotherapy and family therapy tng. program 1976-80, pres. 1967-69), So. Calif. Demographic Forum, Sierra Club (nat. population com.). Clubs: Birnam Wood Golf, Coral Casino. Current Work: Migration, population and environment; health psychology, media psychology, group process. Subspecialties: Social psychology; Population and environment, media psychology. Address: 815 Cima Linda Ln Santa Barbara CA 93108

HULL, HARVARD LESLIE, corporate official; b. Holstein, Neb., Oct. 23, 1906; s. Joel Leslie and Caroline Evangeline (Larsen) H.; m. Alta Zera Jones, June 9, 1928; children: Gwen Alta Hull Quackenbush, Janet Barbara Hull Clark. A.B. with distinction, Nebr. Wesleyan U., 1927, D.Sc. (hon.), 1984; Ph.D. in Physics, Columbia U., 1933. Project engr. Sperry Gyroscope Co., Bklyn, 1933-35, research engr., 1935-40, dir. remote control devel., 1940-43; introduced new equipment Sperry Gyroscope Co., Ltd., Eng., 1934, 35-36; dir. process improvement electromagnetic process of separation Uranium 235 Tenn. Eastman Corp., Oak Ridge, 1943-46; asso. dir. Argonne Nat. Lab., Chgo., 1946-49, dir. remote control engring. devel., 1949-53; v.p. research and devel. div. Capehart-Farnsworth Co., Ft. Wayne, 1953-54; pres. Farnsworth Electronics Co., Co. (div. ITT), Ft. Wayne, 1954-56; v.p. Litton Industries, Beverly Hills, Calif., 1956-57; pres. Hull Assos., Chgo., 1957—; dir., pres. Chgo. Aerial Industries, Inc., Barrington, Ill., 1962-64, Internat. Tech. Corp., Western Springs, Ill.; dir. Central Research Labs., Inc.; chmn. bd., dir. research Aero-Space Inst., Chgo., 1973—; dir. Spantel Corp., Lincoln, 1984—. Fellow AIAA (assoc.); mem. IEEE (life), Am. Nuclear Soc. (cert. of appreciation 1978), AAAS, Am. Phys. Soc., Nat. Telemetering Conf. (chmn. 1956), Sigma Xi, Phi Kappa Phi, Theta Chi. Conglist. Club: Executives. Current Work: Application of electronics, hydraulics and stereo TV to control of automated machinery and other systems. Subspecialties: Electronics; Robotics. Address: 2400 S Finley Rd Apt 350 Lombard IL 60148

HULSIZER, ROBERT INSLEE, physicist; b. E. Orange, N.J., Nov. 25, 1919; s. Robert Inslee and Dorothy Joy (Price) H.; m. Bernice Lord, June 21, 1941 (div.); children—Stephen, Ann, Morgan, Cynthia; m. Carol Enid Kasen, May 27, 1967. B.S., Bates Coll., Lewiston, Maine, 1940; M.A., Wesleyan U., Middletown, Conn., 1942; Ph.D., MIT, 1948. Research assoc. MIT, Cambridge, 1942-49, prof. physics, 1964—; asst. prof. U. Ill., Urbana, 1949-52, assoc. prof., 1952-57, prof., 1957-64; cons. Office Naval Research, Washington, 1957-60, Edn. Devel. Ctr., Watertown, Mass., 1959-65, Xerox Corp., Rochester, N.Y., 1966-69. Author: Electronic Time Measurement, 1946; The World of Physics, 1969. Sec. Chilmark Town Affairs Council, Mass., 1981-84. Fellow Am. Phys. Soc.; mem. Am. Assn. Physics Tchrs. (Outstanding Tchr. award 1960), AAUP, Phi Beta Kappa (pres. Xi chpt. 1982-84). Current work: Experimental work on high-energy hadron-hadron and neutrino-hadron interactions. Subspecialty: Particle physics. Home: 15A Madison St #2 Cambridge MA 02138 Office: Physics Dept MIT 575 Tech Sq Cambridge MA 02139

HULSMAN, ROBERT BRUCE, engineer, educator, researcher; b. Lynn, Mass., Aug. 28, 1930; s. Robert Frederick and Lottie H.; m. Lotte Hochschild, June 5, 1951; 1 child, Gene Michael. B.G.E., U. Nebr., 1965; B.S., Utah State U., 1969, M.B.A., 1971, Ph.D., 1979. Enlisted in U.S. Air force, 1948; ret., 1968; pres., mgr. Cessna ACFT Dealer, Logan, Utah, 1970-75; asst. prof. N.Mex. State U., Las Cruces, 1979—; cons. Contbr. articles to profl. jours. Mem. Am. Soc. Agrl. Engrs., ASCE, Irrigation Assn., Am. Soc. Agronomy. Democrat. Current work: Surge flow irrigation of graded, closed borders; low pressure spray devices as applied to moving laterals and center pivots; irrigation systems simulation. Subspecialties: Agricultural engineering; Civil engineering. Home: 1135 Marilissa Ln Las Cruces NM 88005 Office: N Mex State U Dept Agrl Engring Box 3268 Las Cruces NM 88003

HUMANIC, THOMAS JOHN, physicist; b. Pitts., Jan. 21, 1951; s. John Gregory and Jean Patricia (Loether) H.; m. Karyn Gale Carpenter, Mar. 24, 1979; 1 child, Paul Thomas. B.S., Calif. State U.-Northridge, 1972, M.S., 1975; Ph.D., U. Pitts., 1979. Sr. devel. physicist Monsanto Research Corp., Miamisburg, Ohio, 1979-80; postdoctoral researcher Argonne Nat. Lab., Ill., 1980-82; asst. prof. U.S. Naval Acad., Annapolis, Md., 1982-83; staff sci. Lawrence Berkeley Lab., Calif., 1983-85., guest scientist GSI, Darmstadt, resident at CERN, Geneva, 1985—. Contbr. articles to profl. jours. Mem. Am. Phys. Soc., Sigma Pi Sigma. Current work: Research in relativistic heavy-ion physics; experimental and theoretical studies using pion interferometry. Subspecialty: Nuclear physics.

HUMAYDAN, HASIB SHAHEEN, plant pathologist; b. Ain-Anoub, Lebanon, Mar. 6, 1945; came to U.S., 1971, naturalized, 1982; s. Shaheen Hamad and Amria (Magid) H.; m. Anna Maria DiLiegro, Mar. 8, 1980; 1 son: Michael James. Ph.D. in Plant Pathology and Plant Genetics, U. Wis., 1974. Dir. plant pathology and tissue culture Joseph Harris Co., Inc., Rochester, N.Y., 1974—, now v.p. for research and devel. Recipient Edgecombe award Am. U. Beirut, 1969. Mem. Am. Phytopathol. Soc., Internat. Soc. Plant Pathologists, N.Y. Acad. Scis., AAAS. Current Work: Long term disease control through breeding for multiple disease resistances in the major vegetable crops by utilizing traditional techniques as well as tissue culture, eletrophoresis and induced mutations. Subspecialties: Plant pathology; Plant genetics. Home: 34 Regina Dr Rochester NY 14606 Office: 3670 Buffalo Rd Rochester NY 14624

HUME, JAMES NAIRN PATTERSON, computer science educator; b. Bklyn., Mar. 17, 1923; s. James Smith and Jean Frances (Nairn) H.; m. Patricia Anne Molyneux, Aug. 8, 1953; children—Stephen, Philip, Harriet, Mark. B.A., U. Toronto, 1945, M.A., 1946, Ph.D., 1949. Instr. physics Rutgers U., 1950; asst. prof. physics U. Toronto, 1950-57, assoc. prof., 1957-63, prof. physics and computer sci., 1963—, assoc. dean Grad. Sch., 1968-72, chmn. computer sci. dept., 1975-80, master Massey Coll., 1981—. Author: High-Speed Data Processing, 1958. Physics in Two Volumes, 1974, Structured Programming Using PL-1, 1975; other programming books on Fortran, 1977; Fortran77, 1979, Pascal, 1980, UCSD Pascal, 1982, Pascal Under Unix, 1983, Apple Basic, 1983, IBM PC Basic, 1984, Turing, 1984, Fortran 77, 1985; ednl. TV programs State of Ohio, 1962, citation for best sci. edn. film Edison Found., 1962, Silver medal Sci. Inst. Rome, 1962, Silver Core award Internat. Fedn. for Info. Processing, 1974, Disting. Service Citation Am. Assn. Physics Tchrs., 1979, Can. Centennial medal, 1967. Fellow Royal Soc. Can.; mem. Am. Phys. Soc., Assn. for Computing Machinery, Can. Info. Processing Soc., Sigma Xi. Club: Arts and Letters (Toronto). Current work: Analysis of computer systems (user-hardware-software) by experiment, simulation, analytic modelling; performance improvement. Subspecialties: Programming languages; Operating systems. Home: 4 Devonshire Pl Toronto ON M5S 2E1 Canada Office: Dept Computer Sci U Toronto Toronto ON M5S 1A7 Canada

HUMPHREY, ARTHUR EARL, university administrator; b. Moscow, Idaho, Nov. 9, 1927; s. Samuel Earl and Iris May (Rowe) H.; m. Sheila Claire Darwin, June 13, 1951; children: Andrea Lynn, Allyson Dawn. B.S. in Chem. Engring, U. Idaho, 1948, M.S., 1950, D.Sc. (hon.), 1974; Ph.D., Columbia U., 1953; M.S. in Food Tech, Mass. Inst. Tech., 1959. Mem. faculty U. Pa., Phila., 1953-80, prof. chem. engring., 1961-80; dir. U. Pa. (Sch. Chem. Engring.), 1962-72; dean U. Pa. (Coll. Engring. and Applied Sci.), 1972-80; provost, v.p., prof. biochem. engring. Lehigh U., Bethlehem, Pa., 1980—; also co-dir. Center for Biotechnology Research; NSF sci. tchr. fellow Mass. Inst. Tech., 1957-58; Fulbright lectr. U. Tokyo, Japan, 1963, U. New South Wales, Australia, 1970; guest lectr. Inst. Biology, Czechoslovakian Acad. Sci., 1964, Tech. Inst., Budapest, 1966; I.I.T. Delhi, New Delhi, India, 1970, Tungai U., Taichung, Taiwan, 1968; cons. Merck Sharp & Dohme, 1957-63, Merck Chem. Co., 1963-64, 80-85, Sun Oil Co., 1961-68, Bioferm, 1964-67, Cryotherm, 1966-67, Fermentation Design, 1967-74, E.R. Squibb, 1967-73, Air Products, 1971—. Author: ann. Fermentation Rev., 1960-64; author textbooks on biochem. engring.; Contbr. articles to profl. jours. Pres. Phila. Trail Club, 1960-61; councilor Appalachian Trail Conf., 1961-67; chmn. space sci. panel Nat. Acad. Sci.; co-chmn. 3d Internat. Fermentation Symposium; mem. engring. adv. bd. NSF; mem. single cell protein working group, protein adv. group WHO-FAO-UN; chmn. group on prodn. substances by microbial means U.S.-USSR Cooperation in Sci. and Tech. Recipient Outstanding Tchr. award U. Pa., 1959. Mem. Nat. Acad. Engring., Internat. Assn. Microbiol. Socs. (sec.-gen. econ. and applied microbiology), Nat. Acad. Engring., Am. Chem. Soc. (chmn. div. microbial. chem. and tech. 1967, Div. Disting. Service award 1979, named Eminent Living Chem. Eng. 1983), Am. Inst. Chem. Engrs. (chmn. food and bioengring. div. 1972, Profl. Progress award 1972, Food and Bio-Engring award 1973, Inst. lectr. 1975), Franklin Inst., Japanese Soc. Fermentation Tech., Am. Soc. Microbiology, Soc. Indsl. Microbiology, Sigma Xi, Sigma Tau. Clubs: Trail (Phila.), Horse-Shoe Trail (Phila.); Appalachian Mountain (Boston). Subspecialty: Biomedical engineering. Office: Alumni Hall Lehigh U Bethlehem PA 18015

HUMPHREY, RONALD DE VERE, microbiology educator; b. Denver, Mar. 31, 1938; s. Walter D. and Edna (Carroll) H.; m. Julia Frances Hamlett, Feb. 6, 1960; children: Sean, Lara. B.S. in Biol. Sci, Colo. State U., Ft. Collins, 1960, M.S. in Bacteriology, 1963; Ph.D. in Microbiology, U. Tex.-Austin, 1970. Teaching assoc. U. Tex.-Austin, 1970; assoc. prof. biology Prairie View (Tex.) A&M U., 1970—; summer research appointee Argonne (Ill.) Nat. Lab., 1978. Referee Washington County Youth Soccer Assn. Served to lt. USNR, 1963-66. Grantee Sci. and Edn. Adminstrn. of U.S. Dept. Agr., 1978-83. Mem. Am. Soc. Microbiology, AAAS, N.Y. Acad. Scis., Nat. Inst. Sci., Sigma Xi. Lodge: Brenhem (Tex.) Evening Lions. Current Work: Physiology of nitrogen fixing legume root nodule bacteria, nitrogen fixation, legume, root nodules, pesticide. Subspecialties: Microbiology; Nitrogen fixation. Office: Dept of Biology Prairie View A&M University Prairie View TX 77445

HUMPHREYS, TOM (DANIEL), II, biologist, educator; b. Arlington, Tenn., June 22, 1936; s. Tom D. and Libbie (Kesl) H.; 1 child, Tom D. B.S., U. Chgo., 1958, Ph.D., 1962. Asst. prof. MIT, Cambridge, 1962-66; asst. prof. U. Calif.-San Diego, 1966-71; pres. Hawaii Biotech. Group, Inc., Aiea, 1982—; prof. biochemistry U. Hawaii, Honolulu, 1971—, dir. basic scis. Cancer Research Ctr., 1982—. NIH grantee, 1967—. Mem. Soc. for Devel. Biology, Am. Soc. Cell Biology, Biophys. Soc., Am. Zool. Soc., ACLU. Current work: Gene expression during development; molecular specificity of cell-cell interaction. Subspecialties: Developmental biology; Genetics and genetic engineering (agriculture). Office: Pacific Biomedical Research Center 41 Ahui St Honolulu HI 96813

HUMPHRIES, JOAN ROPES, psychology educator; b. Bklyn., Oct. 17, 1928; d. Lawrence Gardner and Adele Lydia (Zimmermann) Ropes; m. Charles C. Humphries, Apr. 6, 1957; children: Peggy Ann, Charlene Adele. B.A., U. Miami, 1950; M.S., Fla. State U., 1955; Ph.D., La. State U., 1963. Psychol. cons. East La. State Hosp., Jackson, 1961-62; part-time instr. U. Miami, Coral Gables, 1964-65; assoc. prof. Miami-Dade Community Coll., 1966. Prin. author: The Application of Scientific Behaviorism to Humanistic Phenomena, 1975, rev. edit., 1979; contbr. articles to profl. jours. Recipient award of appreciation for continuous, dedicated service to women in community AAUW, 1977. Mem. Internat. Platform Assn. (bd. govs.), Am. Psychol. Assn., AAUP (chpt. v.p. 1980, sec. 1981, pres. 1983-85, bd. dirs. 1983—), Dade County Psychol. Assn., N.Y. Acad. Scis., Phi Lambda. Current Work: Use of biofeedback techniques to help students learn. Subspecialties: Learning; Behavioral psychology. Home: 1311 Alhambra Circle Coral Gables FL 33134 Office: 11380 NW 27th Ave Miami FL 33167

HUNT, EARLE RAYMOND, JR., botanist; b. Elmer, N.J., Aug. 19, 1956; s. Earle Raymond and Anne Hunt; m. Marie Quinto, June 20, 1981. B.S., Ohio U., 1978; M.S., U. Mich., 1981; Ph.D., 1984. Postdoctoral scientist UCLA, 1984—. Contbr. articles to profl. jours. Camp nature ecology dir. Boy Scouts Am., Chillicothe, Ohio, 1977. Newcombe fellow, 1984. Mem. AAAS, Am. Inst. Biol. Scis., Am. Soc. Plant Physiologists, Ecol. Soc. Am., Alpha Phi Omega (chpt. v.p. 1976). Current work: Photosynthesis and stomatal conductance mechanisms; root growth and water relations; mineral nutrition of plants; remote sensing applications to plant ecology. Subspecialties: Ecology (biology); Plant physiology (biology). Office: LBES Warren Hall UCLA 900 Veteran Ave Los Angeles CA 90024

HUNT, ELIZABETH HOPE, psychologist, author, researcher, educator; b. Hattiesburg, Miss., Oct. 14, 1943; d. Emory Spear and Ida Elizabeth (Burkette) H.; m. John Volney Allcott III, Sept. 9, 1978; 1 son, Hunt. A.B., Sweet Briar Coll., 1965; M.S.W., U. Pa., 1971; Ph.D., U. Oreg., 1980. Vol. Peace Corps, Santiago, Chile, 1967-69; civil rights specialist HEW, Phila., 1971-74; research asst. U. Oreg., Eugene, 1978-79, lectr., 1980, pvt. practice psychology, Eugene, 1980—; workshop presented Oreg. Mental Health Assn., Eugene, 1980. Contbr. articles to profl. jours. Bd. dirs. Lane County Relief Nursery for Abused and Neglected Children, Eugene, 1982—; co-chmn. Speakers Bur., Physicians for Social Responsibility, 1982. Fellow U. Oreg., 1974-77; Nat. Inst. Handicapped Research grantee, 1977-79. Mem. Am. Psychol. Assn., Oreg. Psychol. Assn., Lane County Psychologists Assn. (pub. affairs com. 1981—), Profl. Women's Network. Current Work: Past writing chiefly behavioral; current research and writing on theory of human development, life cycle problems, diversity possible within normal range of development. Subspecialty: Developmental psychology. Home: 2650 Cresta De Ruta Eugene OR 97403 Office: Oreg Family Center 3225 Willamette St Suite 3 Eugene OR 97405

HUNT, RONALD DUNCAN, veterinary pathologist, educator; b. Los Angeles, Oct. 9, 1935; s. Charles H. and Margaret H. (Duncan) H.; B.S., U. Calif, Davis, 1957, D.V.M. with honors, 1959. Resident fellow pathology, Harvard U. Med. Sch., Boston, 1964-68, prin. assoc. pathology, 1969-72, assoc. prof. comparative pathology, 1972-77, prof. comparative pathology, 1977—; dir. various research ctrs. Harvard U. Med. Sch.; lectr. nutritional pathology MIT, 1964—; affiliate pathologist Angell Meml. Animal Hosp., Boston. Co-author: Veterinary Pathology, 4th edit., 1972, 5th edit., 1984: Co-editor: Endocrine System, 1983, Respiratory System, 1985; Urinary System, 1985; contbr. articles to profl. jours. Served to capt. U.S. Army, 1959-63. Recipient Disting. Service award Charles Louis Davis D.V.M. Found.; Charles River prize, AVMA; Bernard F. Trum award Am. Assoc. for Lab. Animal Sci.; Disting. Alumni award U. Calif.-Davis Sch. Vet. Medicine, 1985. Mem. Am. Coll. Vet. Pathology, N.Y. Acad. Sci., Internat. Acad. Pathology, Am. Soc. Clin. Pathologists, Am. Soc. Primatologists, Am. Jour. Vet. Research (bd. dirs. 1978-80), Internat. Life Scis. Inst. (bd. dirs. 1981—). Current work: Diseases of laboratory animals, especially nonhuman primates; herpesviruses; nutritional disease; animal models for human disease. Subspecialties: Laboratory animal medicine; Pathology (veterinary medicine). Office: New Eng Regional Primate Research Ctr Harvard Med Sch 1 Pine Hill Dr Southborough MA 01772

HUNTER, HARRY LAYMOND, physician, pharmaceutical company executive; b. Girard, Kans., Mar. 7, 1923; s. Adolphus Osborne and Mary Elizabeth (White) H.; m. Louise R. Leone, Aug. 19, 1949 (dec. July 21, 1982); children: John Patrick, Mary Anne; m. Emily Fisher Esau, Oct. 19, 1985. A.B., U. Ill., Urbana, 1944; B.S., U. Ill.-Chgo., 1944, M.D., 1946. Diplomate: Am. Bd. Internal Medicine. Intern Gorgas Hosp., C.Z., 1946-47, resident in internal medicine, 1947-48; resident Ill. Central Hosp., Chgo., 1949-50, U. Mich., Ann Arbor, 1950-51; assoc. chief medicine Blanchard Valley Hosp., Findlay, Ohio, 1951-52; dir. exec. health Ill. Central Hosp., Chgo., 1953-57, assoc. chief medicine, 1957-64, chief med. officer, 1968-74; clin. assoc. prof. medicine U. Ill. Coll. Medicine, Chgo., 1953-76; assoc. dir. clin. pharmacology Abbott Labs., North Chicago, Ill., 1965-67, med. dir., 1975-76; dir. clin. studies and sr. dir. med. dept. Mead Johnson & Co., Evansville, Ind., 1976—. Contbr. numerous articles to profl. jours. Bd. dirs. Ill. Council on Alcoholism, Chgo., 1970-74, Am. Cancer Soc., Evansville, 1978-80. Served to capt. U.S. Army, 1943-49, Panama. Fellow ACP, Am. Soc. Clin. Oncology, Chgo. Soc. Internal Medicine, Chgo. Inst. Medicine; mem. AMA. Current Work: involves clinical development of new drugs and new therapeutic indications. Subspecialties: Internal medicine; Oncology. Home: 4141 Orchard Rd Evansville IN 47721 Office: Mead Johnson & Co 2404 Pennsylvania Evansville IN 47721

HUNTER, JOHN STUART, statistician, consultant; b. Holyoke, Mass., June 3, 1923; s. John and Irene (Robinson) H.; m. Edna Taylor Martz, Sept. 19, 1952; 1 child, Jean Bartlett; m. T.J. Hirasuna, Aug. 13, 1977; 1 child, William Mark; m. V. Halford, Aug. 28, 1982; 1 child, Anne Robinson. Ph.D. in Exptl. Stats., N.C. State U., 1954, M.S. in Engring. Math, 1949, B.S. in Elec. Engring, 1947. Staff statistician Am. Cyanamid Co., 1954-59; with Statis. Techniques Research Group, Princeton U., 1957-59, Math. Research Center, U. Wis., 1959-61; assoc. prof. Princeton, 1962-67; prof. engring. Princeton U., 1968-82, prof. emeritus, 1982—; statistician in residence U. Wis., 1967-68; lectr. Korean Standards Research Inst., 1979, Nat. Center: Indsl. Sci. and Tech. Mgmt. Devel., Dalian, People's Republic of China, 1981, 82; Mem. staff com. nat. statistics Nat. Acad. Scis., 1975-76, mem. com., 1976-82, chmn. com. pres.'s of statis. socs., 1976-79; chmn. panel Nat. Bur. Standards, 1977-80. Author, cons., lectr. in field.; Founding editor: Technometrics, 1959-63. Served with AUS, 1942-46. Fellow Am. Statis. Assn., Am. Soc. Quality Control (Shewhart medal, 1971, Youden award 1977, Ott award 1979), AAAS (council mem. 1974-77, chmn. com. on fellows 1977); mem. Biometrics Soc., Inst. Math. Statistics, Am. Inst. Chem. Engrs., ASTM, Am. Soc. Indsl. Engrs., ASCE, Royal Statis. Soc., Internat. Statistics Inst. Episcopalian. Club: Cosmos. Current Work: Statistical design and analysis of experiments industrial process and quality enhancement. Subspecialties: Statistics; Operations research (mathematics). Home: 179 Longview Dr Princeton NJ 08540

HUNTER, RICHARD EDMUND, research plant pathologist; b. Jersey City, Jan. 26, 1923; s. Frederick William and Margaret (Dahlgren) H.; m. Earline Clark; children: Catherine Jeane, Margaret Ann, Richard Clark. B.S., Rutgers U., 1949; M.S., Okla. State U., 1951, Ph.D., 1968. Asst. in biology N.Mex. State U., 1951-55; instr. Okla State U., Stillwater, 1958-68, asst. prof., 1968-71, assoc. prof., 1971-72; research plant pathologist U. S. Dept. Agr., Stillwater, 1968-72, Nat. Cotton Pathology Lab., U.S. Dept. Agr., College Station, Tex., 1972-75; research plant pathologist, nut prodn. unit Southeastern Fruit and Nut Tree Lab., U.S. Dept Agr., Byron, Ga., 1975-79, research leader, 1976-79; research leader, location leader W.R. Poage Pecan Field Sta., U.S. Dept. Agr., Brownwood, Tex., 1979—. Contbr. articles to profl jours. Active Presbyn. Ch., Stillwater, 1958-72; ch. sch. tchr., mem. adminstrv. bd. First United Meth. Ch., Brownwood, 1979—. Served to capt. USAAF, 1943-46. Mem. Am. Phytopathol. Soc., Am. Soc. Hort. Scientists, Sigma Xi, Alpha Zeta, Phi Sigma. Current Work: Host resistance and genetic vulnerability to pecan diseases; in charge Department of Agriculture pecan genetics and improvement program. Subspecialties: Plant pathology; Plant genetics. Home: 3903 Glenwood Dr Brownwood TX 76801 Office: WR Poage Pecan Field Sta 701 Woodson Rd Brownwood TX 76801

HUNTER, THOMAS ALEXANDER, III, forensic engineer, consultant; b. La Grange, Ill., Nov. 9, 1918; s. Thomas Alexander, Jr. and Virginia Catherine (O'Neill) H.; m. Gloria Eleanore Hunter, Aug. 26, 1950; children—Thomas IV, William, Eleanore. B.S., Ill. Inst. Tech., 1940, M.S., 1944; Ph.D., U. Mich., 1952. Registered profl. engr., Ill., Conn. Fire protection engr. Indsl. Risk Insurers, Chgo., 1940-42; mem. tech. staff Bell Telephone Labs., Murray Hill, N.J., 1955-56; chief engr. ARO Corp., Cleve., 1956-59; mgr. new products Homelite Div. Textron, Inc., Port Chester, N.Y., 1965-75; tech. dir. Seal, Inc., Naugatuck, Conn., 1979-81; sr. forensic engr. Am. Standards Testing Bur., Inc., N.Y.C., 1981—; cons. Town of Westport, Conn., 1976-77, Marion Power Shovel Co., Ohio, 1964; reservist Fed. Disaster Assistance Adminstrn., N.Y.C., 1976-78. Author: Engineering Mechanics, 1959. Patentee in field. Trustee Westport Pub. Library, 1981-85; active mem. Bd. Edn., Rocky River, Ohio, 1962-65, Charter Commn., Rocky River, 1963, Planning and Zoning Commn., Westport, 1971-73. Served with USNR, 1944-46. Ill. Inst. Tech. scholar, 1936, 39. Mem. ASME, AM. Soc. Agrl. Engrs., ASTM, Am. Soc. Engring. Edn. Republican. Unitarian. Current work: Application of principles of mechanics to accident causation, products liability and legal aspects of engineering. Subspecialty: Theoretical and applied mechanics. Home: 33 High Point Rd Westport CT 06880 Office: Am Standards Testing Bur Inc 40 Water St New York NY 10004

HUNTER, TONY, molecular biologist, virologist; b. Ashford, Kent., Eng., Aug. 23, 1943; came to U.S., 1971; s. Ranulph Rex and Nellie Ruby Elsie (Hitchcock) H.; m. Philippa C. Marrack, July 19, 1969 (div. 1974). B.A., U. Cambridge, Eng., 1965, M.A., 1966, Ph.D., 1969. Research fellow U. Cambridge, 1968-71, 73-75; research assoc. Salk Inst., San Diego, 1971-73, asst. prof. molecular biology and tumor virology, 1975-78, assoc. prof., 1978-82, prof., 1982—. Contbr. numerous articles to profl. jours.

HUNTSMAN, JOHN ROBERT, geology educator, researcher; b. Johnstown, Pa., Mar. 20, 1951; s. Ralph Waldo and Mildred Belle (MacRill) H.; m. Rebecca Muriel Gallagher, Dec. 28, 1973; children—Sarah Elizabeth, Lori Rebecca. B.S., Mount Union Coll., 1973; M.A., Bryn Mawr Coll., 1975, Ph.D., 1978. Instr. Widener Coll., Chester, Pa., 1977, U. N.C., Wilmington, 1978-79, asst. prof., 1979—; cons. Dupont, Inc.-Savannah River, Aikon, S.C., 1979-80. Author geological abstracts. Contbr. articles to profl. jours. Recipient Development awards U. N.C. Research and Devel., 1979, 1980, faculty research grantee, 1981-83, 85-86; geology fellow Bryn Mawr Coll., 1974-75. Mem. Geol. Soc. Am., Carolina Geol. Soc., Sigma Xi (grant-in-aid). Methodist. Subspecialty: Geology. Office: Dept Earth Science University North Carolina 601 S College Rd Wilmington NC 28403

HUNTSMAN, LEE L., bioengineering educator, administrator, consultant, researcher; b. Tacoma, June 11, 1941; s. Walter L. and R. Elizabeth Huntsman; m. Virginia Ann Koolen, June 15, 1963; children—Scott L., Jennifer A., Mark W. B.E.E., Stanford U., 1963; Ph.D. in Biomed. Engring., U. Pa., 1968. Research asst. prof. bioengring., U. Wash., Seattle, 1968-73, research assoc. prof., 1973-81, acting dir. bioengring., 1980, dir., 1980—, prof., 1981—; cons. Coopervision, Seattle, 1981—; cardiovascular cons. NIH, 1983—; cons. Lawrence Med. Systems, Redmond, Wash., 1980—. Recipient Research Career Devel. award U. Wash., 1977-82; Stanford scholar, 1959-63; NIH fellow U. Pa., 1963-68; NIH grantee, 1968—. Mem. Biomed. Engring. Soc. (bd. dirs. 1984—), Am. Heart Assn., Cardiovascular System Dynamics Soc., Am. Inst. Ultrasound Med., AAAS. Club: Port Madison Yacht (Bainbridge Island, Wash.). Current work: Bioengineering, heart, mycardial mechanics, muscle mechanics, non-invasive measurements, ventricular performance, ultrasound, doppler, engineering, medicine. Subspecialties: Biomedical engineering; Ultrasound. Home: 6866 NE Bergman Bainbridge Island WA 98110 Office: Bioengring WD-12 U Wash Seattle WA 98195

HUPPE, FRANCIS FROWIN, chemical company executive; b. Kansas City, Mo., Dec. 11, 1934; s. Francis Frowin and Juanita Helene (Holton) H.; m. Dorothy Jean Sweeney, Aug. 12, 1961; children—John F., Susan M., Michael J. B.S. in Physics, Rockhurst Coll., 1956; M.S. in Physics, MIT, 1959; Ph.D. in Physics, U. Wis.-Madison, 1967. Research physicist E.I. DuPont de Nemours and Co., Inc., Wilmington, Del., 1966-68, research supr., 1968-71, staff asst., 1971-72, sr. supr., 1972-74, research mgr., 1974-80, lab. dir., 1981—; mem. vis. com. dept. physics U. Tex.-Austin, 1983—. Mem. Am. Phys. Soc., Sigma Xi. Roman Catholic. Home: 1401 Olive Circle Wilmington DE 19803 Office: E I Du Pont de Nemours and Co Inc Engring Physics Lab Exptl Sta Wilmington DE 19898

HURD, EDWARD NELSON, III, management consultant, nuclear engineer; b. Sewickley, Pa., Apr. 14, 1926; s. Austin Avery and Hannah (Shaffer) H.; m. Marjorie L. Harrison, Sept. 5, 1949; children: Marion H. Leonard, Edward N. B.S., U. Pitts., 1950. Testing mgr. Naval Reactor Facility, Idaho Falls, Idaho, 1961-72; U.S. rep. to Japan's Liquid Metal Fast Breeder Reactor program

Westinghouse Co., Dept. of Energy, Mito, Japan, 1978-79; prin. engr. Fast Flux Test Facility, Richland, Wash., 1972-77, 79-81, Nuclear Quality Assurance Program Ofice, Westinghouse Hanford Co., Richland, 1981-84; cons. Dept. Energy, Nuclear Quality Assurance Program Office, Richland, 1981-84. Chmn. Local Homeowners Assn., Richland, 1980-85. Served with U.S. Army, 1944-46, ETO. Mem. Am. Nuclear Soc. Republican. Episcopalian. Club: Meadow Springs Country (Richland). Current Work: Nuclear consultant assigned to Hanford N-reactor programs management. Subspecialties: Nuclear fission; Nuclear engineering. Home: 517 Greenbrook Pl Richland WA 99352 Office: Westinghouse Hanford Co PO Box 1970 Richland WA 99352

HURLEY, FRANCIS XAVIER, federal government aeronautical agency executive; b. Jersey City, July 24, 1940; s. Francis X. and Martha M. (Stetson) H.; m. Brigitte R. Breckner, Dec. 18, 1976; children—Elisabeth M., Rita I. B.A., Elizabethtown Coll., 1963; B.S., Pa. State U., 1963; M.S. Engring., Princeton U., 1965; Ph.D., Rice U., 1968. Scientist, McDonnell Douglas Research Labs., St. Louis, 1968-76; Congl. fellow AIAA, Washington, 1976-77; mgr. research and tech. Fort Worth div. Gen. Dynamics Corp., 1977-83; dep. chief scientist NASA, Washington, 1983-85; dir. tech. planning mobility exptl. devices U.S. Army Research Office, Research Triangle Park, N.C., 1985—; conf. lectr. Contbr. articles to profl. jours. Chmn., Tex. Aerospace Profls. for Reagan-Bush, 1980; chmn. indsl. and profl. adv. council, aerospace engring. dept. Pa. State U., 1983. Assoc. fellow AIAA (Appreciation certificate 1974); mem. German Air and Space Travel Assn., Am. Def. Preparedness Assn., Assn. Unmanned Vehicle Systems. Republican. Lutheran. Current work: Research and development management. Subspecialty: Aerospace engineering and technology. Office: US Army Research Office PO Box 12211 Research Triangle Park NC 27709

HURSH, STEVEN RAWLINGS, neuroscientist, research psychologist; b. N.Y.C., June 27, 1946; s. Paul David and Lenore Irene (Daniels) H.; m. Ellen Brittingham, Aug. 3, 1968; 1 child, Annemarie Elizabeth. B.A., Wake Forest U., 1968; Ph.D., U. Calif.-San Diego, 1972. Research psychologist Walter Reed Army Inst. Research, Washington, 1972-77, chief physiology and behavior branch, 1977-81, chief dept. medical neuroscience, 1981—. Mem. editorial bd. Jour. Exptl. Analysis of Behavior, 1975—. Contbr. chpts. to books and articles to profl. jours. clk. of session St. Matthew United Presbyterian Ch., Silver Spring, Md., 1983—. NIMH fell 1970-72. Served to maj. U.S. Army Res., 1972—. Mem. Assn. for Behavior Analysis, Psychonomic Soc. Eastern Psychol. Assn., AAAS. Current work: Animal behavior, behavioral economics, choice, reinforcement, aversive control, rhythmic aspects of behavior, stress, human performance, behavioral pharmacology. Subspecialties: Behavioral psychology; Neuropsychology. Office: Dept Med Neuroscis Walter Reed Army Inst Research Washington DC 20307

HURT, VALINA KAY, science educator, researcher; b. Bowling Green, Ky., Jan. 3, 1953; d. Ottis C. and Geraldine (Andrew) H. B.S. (Regents' scholar), Western Ky. U., 1975, M.S., 1979; postgrad., U. Okla., 1979—. Dental asst., Bowling Green, 1974, 75; grad. teaching asst. Western Ky. U., Bowling Green, 1978, 79, U. Okla., Norman, 1979-83; instr. sci. Hazard Community Coll., (Ky.), 1983—. Contbr. articles on botany to profl. jours. Okla. Mining and Mineral Resources Research Inst. scholar, 1980-83. Mem. AAUP, Ecology Soc. Am., Ky. Acad. Sci., Am. Genetic Assn., AAAS, Assn. for Women in Sci., Bot. Soc. Am., Southeastern Assn. Biologists, Okla. Acad. Sci., Southwestern Assn. Naturalists, Sigma Xi, Alpha Epsilon Delta, Beta Beta Beta, Beta Sigma Phi. Republican. Current Work: Strip mine revegetation and reclamation, allelopathy, old field succession, ecotypes, family size and sex preference, heterogeneity of variances. Subspecialties: Ecology (environmental science); Resource management. Home: PO Box 250 Combs KY 41729 Office: Hazard Community Coll Hazard KY 73069

HUSE, DAVID ALAN, physicist; b. Sudbury, Mass., 1958; s. Mason W. and Marjorie (Carroll) H.; m. Julia Ann Smith, 1982; 1 child, Alan. B.S., U. Mass., 1979; M.S., Cornell U., 1982, Ph.D., 1983. Mem. tech. staff AT&T Bell Labs., Murray Hill, N.J., 1982—. Contbr. articles to profl. jours. Mem. Am. Phys. Soc. Current work: Research on theory of phase transitions, random systems. Subspecialties: Condensed matter physics; Statistical physics. Office: AT&T Bell Labs Murray Hill NJ 07974

HUSTON, NORMAN EARL, nuclear engineering educator; b. Jefferson, Iowa, Jan. 24, 1919; s. Sherburn Sherwood and Helen Isadore (Briggs) H.; m. Mary Belle Felton, June 27, 1943; children—Norman Earl, Anne Marie (Mrs. Thomas Daniel Sigerstad), Susan Deane (Mrs. Alan Braddock). Student, Los Angeles City Coll., 1938-40; A.B., U. Calif. at Berkeley, 1943; Ph.D., U. So. Calif., 1952. Registered profl. engr., Wis., Calif. Physicist U. Calif. Radiation Lab., Berkeley, 1943-44; research engr., dir. dept. Atomics Internat. div. N.Am. Aviation Co., Los Angeles, 1950-65; sr. sci. adviser, asst. to v.p. Autonetics div., Anaheim, Calif., 1966; prof. nuclear engring., dir. Instrumentation Systems Center, U. Wis., Madison, 1966-84, prof. emeritus and cons., 1984—; dir. Adv. Center for Med. Tech. and Systems, 1972-78; also dir. Ocean Engring. Labs., 1967-70, U. Wis.-NASA Biomed. Application Team, 1974-77; mem. subcom. of com. on interaction of engring. in biology and medicine Nat. Acad. Engring.; reviewer, cons. NSF, AID, project leader mission to Cairo, Mgmt. Lab. Instrn., 1976; project leader Egypt Sci. and Tech. Project, Nat. Research Center for AID and NSF, Cairo, 1977; UN expert on mission Singapore Inst. Standards and Indsl. Research, 1972; mem. NSF task force on instrumentation requirements to Nat. Research Centre, Egypt, 1974, NSF team mission to Cairo, Rome, workshops sci. intruments, 1975; cons. to Indonesian Ministry Edn. and Culture, World Bank program, 1983. Contbg. author: Summary of Reactor Design, 1955, Progress in Nuclear Energy, Series VI, Vol. 3, 1959; editor: Management Systems for Lab. Instrument Services, 1980; mem. editorial bd.: Jour. Internat. Measurement Confedn., 1982—; contbr. articles to profl. jours. Served to lt. (j.g.) USNR, 1944-47. Levi Strauss scholar, 1941-43. Fellow AAAS (council mem.), Instrument Soc. Am. (v.p. edn. and research 1971-72, v.p. publs. 1974-76, sec. 1977-78, pres. 1978-79), Inst. Measurement and Control; mem. Am. Nuclear Soc., Am. Soc. Engring. Edn., Am. Phys. Soc., Nat. Mgmt. Assn. (v.p. NAA Valley chpt., treas. 1958-59), Western Boys Baseball Assn. (pres. Woodland Hills 1959), Sigma Xi, Alpha Delta Sigma, Alpha Tau Omega. Club: Rotary (Madison). Patentee in field. Current Work: Scientific instruments-management systems and research and development. Subspecialties: Instrumentation; Nuclear engineering. Home: 4556 Winnequah Rd Monona WI 53716 Office: 1500 Johnson Dr Madison WI 53706

HUTCHINGS, JOHN BARRIE, astronomer; b. Johannesburg, South Africa, July 18, 1941. B.Sc., Witwatersrand U., 1962, B.Sc. with honors, 1963, M.Sc., 1964; Ph.D., Cambridge U., 1967. NRC fellow Dominion Astrophys. Obs., Victoria, B.C., Can., 1967-69, research scientist, 1969—; sr. research officer NCR Can., 1979—. Contbr. articles to profl. jours. Mem. Am. Astron. Soc., Internat. Astron. Union, Royal Acad. Scis. Current Work: Optical, UV, X-Ray, radio investigation of stellar X-ray sources, massive stars, quasars and active galaxies. Subspecialties: Optical astronomy; Ultraviolet high energy astrophysics.

HUTCHINS, CHARLES WILLIAM, organic chemist; b. Albuquerque, Mar. 19, 1953; s. Jack Randolph and Ruth Marie (Newman) H. A.B., Cornell U., 1975; Ph.D., U. Ill., 1980. Postdoctoral asst. U. Calif., Berkeley, 1980-82; sr. research chemist Sterling-Winthrop Research Inst., Rensselaer, N.Y., 1982—. Contbr. articles to profl. jours. Mem. Am. Chem. Soc., Smithsonian Inst., AAAS, N.Y. Acad. Sci. Methodist. Current work: Drug design; synthesis of medically usefull compounds. Subspecialties: Organic chemistry; Medicinal chemistry. Office: Sterling-Winthrop Research Inst Columbia Turnpike Rensselaer NY 12144

HUTCHINSON, LAWRENCE JAY, veterinarian; b. Bryn Mawr, Pa., July 1, 1937; s. Hamilton and Eva (Cohee) H.; m. Barbara Bryson, Aug. 16, 1958; children—Steven M., Ben A., Laura L., Lee J., Nathan J. B.S., Pa. State U., 1959; D.V.M., Cornell U., 1962. Pvt. practice vet. medicine Vergennes, Vt., 1962-63, Amsterdam, N.Y., 1963-64, Honey Brook, Pa., 1964-76; extension veterinarian Pa. State U., University Park, Pa., 1976—. Contbr. numerous articles to vet. jours. Mem. Pa. Vet. Medicine Assn. (pres. 1985), Am. Assn. Extension Veterinarians (pres. 1984-85), AVMA (continuing edn. com. 1984—), Am. Assn. Bovine Practitioners (continuing edn. com. 1976—). Republican. Mem. United Ch. of Christ. Current work: Johne's disease; reproduction management; herd health programs; residue avoidance programs. Subspecialty: Preventive medicine (veterinary medicine). Home: 501 Hubler Rd State College PA 16801 Office: Pa State U 115 Henning Bldg University Park PA 16802

HUTCHINSON, THOMAS CUTHBERT, botany educator; b. Sunderland, Durham, Eng., Feb. 18, 1939; came to Can., 1967; s. Walter and Margaret A. (Bell) H.; m. Vivien Bessie Coyne, Aug. 9, 1961 (div. 1980); 1 child, Sally Louise. B.Sc. with honors, Manchester U., Eng., 1960; Ph.D., Sheffield U., Eng., 1964. Postdoctoral fellow Newcastle U., Eng., 1964-67; asst. prof. botany U. Toronto, Ont., Can., 1967-71, assoc. prof., 1971-74, prof., 1974—, prof. forestry, 1978—, chair dept. botany, 1976-82, acting dir. Inst. Environ. Studies, 1973-74. Editor: Heavy Metals in Environment, 1975; Effect of Acid Precipitation on Terrestrial Ecosystems, 1980. Recipient Faculty Alumni award U. Toronto, 1984. Fellow Royal Soc. Can., Explorers Club; mem. Can. Bot. Assn. (George Lawson medal 1983), Am. Agron. Soc., Ecol. Soc. Am., Brit. Ecol. Soc., Arctic Inst. N.Am. Current Work: Effects of stresses on natural ecosystems caused by acidification, heavy metals, oil spills; adaptations of plants to polluted environments. Subspecialties: Environmental toxicology; Ecology (biology). Home: 37 Bulwer St Toronto ON M5T 1A1 Canada Office: Dept Botany U Toronto Toronto ON M5S 1A1 Canada

HUTCHINSON, WILLIAM BURKE, surgeon, research foundation executive; b. Seattle, Sept. 6, 1909; s. Joseph Lambert and Nona Bernice (Burke) H.; m. Charlotte Martha Rigdon, Mar. 25, 1939; children: Charlotte Hutchinson Reed, William Burke, John L., Stuart, Mary Hutchinson Wiese. B.S., U. Wash., 1931; M.D., McGill U., 1936; H.H.D. (hon.), Seattle U., 1982. Diplomate: Am. Bd. Surgery. Active staff surgery Swedish Hosp., Seattle, from 1941; pres., founding dir. Pacific N.W. Research Found., 1956—; pres., founding dir. Fred Hutchinson Cancer Research Ctr., Seattle, 1972-81, pres., chmn. bd., 1981-85, pres. emeritus, 1985—; clin. prof. surgery U. Wash. Med. Sch., 1974-83; now prof. emeritus; mem. Yarborough Com., 1970; pres. 13th Internat. Cancer Congress, 1978-82. Contbr. articles to med. jours. Recipient First Citizen of Seattle award, 1976; Outstanding Alumnus award U. Wash., 1983. Mem. ACS, Pacific Coast Surg. Assn., King County Med. Soc., Western Surg. Assn., N. Pacific Surg. Assn., Soc. Surg. Oncology, AMA, Seattle Surg. Soc. Clubs: Men's Univ, Seattle Golf. Current Work: Cancer research. Subspecialty: Surgery. Home: 7126 55th Ave S Seattle WA 98118 Office: 1102 Columbia St Seattle WA 98104 Also: 1309 Summitt Seattle WA 98104

HUTCHISON, CLYDE ALLEN, JR., chemistry educator; b. Alliance, Ohio, May 5, 1913; s. Clyde Allen and Bessie Gertrude (Bicksler) H.; m. Sarah Jane West, Dec. 29, 1937; children—Clyde Allen III, Sarah Jane Dunn, Robert West. A.B., Cedarville Coll., Ohio, 1933, D.Sc. (hon.), 1953; Ph.D., Ohio State U., 1937. Postdoctoral fellow NRC, Columbia U., N.Y.C., 1937-38, research assoc., 1938-39; asst. prof. U. Buffalo, 1939-45; research assoc. SAM Labs., N.Y.C., 1943-45; research assoc. U. Va., Manhattan Project, Charlottesville, 1942-43; mem. staff metall. lab. U. Chgo., 1945-46; asst. prof. Enrico Fermi Inst., U. Chgo., 1945-48, asst. prof. dept. chemistry and Enrico Fermi Inst., 1948-50, assoc. prof., 1950-54, prof., 1954-63, chmn. dept. chemistry, 1959-62, Carl William Eisendrath prof., 1963-69, Carl William Eisendrath disting. service prof., 1969-83, Carl William Eisendrath disting. service prof. emeritus, 1983—; Eastman prof. U. Oxford, 1981-82; cons., lectr., mem. numerous adv. panels in chemistry. Contbr. articles to profl. jours. Mem. editorial bd. Jour. Chem. Physics, 1953-59; Ann. Rev. Phys. Chemistry, 1962-66; Procs. Internat. Symposium on the Triplet State, 1967. Guggenheim fellow, Oxford U., 1955-56, 1972-73; recipient Ohio State U. Centennial Achievement award, 1970. Fellow Am. Acad. Arts and Scis., Am. Phys. Soc.; mem. Nat. Acad. Scis., Am. Chem. Soc. (Peter Debye award 1972), AAAS, Sigma Xi. Subspecialties: Physical chemistry; Crystallography. Office: U Chgo 5735 S Ellis Ave Chicago IL 60637

HUTCHISON, DORRIS JEANNETTE, microbiologist, educator; b. Carrsville, Ky., Oct. 31, 1918; d. John W. and Maud Lela (Short) H.; B.S., Western Ky. State Coll., 1940, M.S., U. Ky., 1943; Ph.D., Rutgers U., 1949. Teaching asst. Western Ky. State Coll., 1939-40; research asst. U. Ky., 1940-42; instr. Russell Sage Coll., 1942-44; instr. Vassar Coll., 1944-46; research asst. Rutgers U., 1946-48, research assoc., 1948-49; instr. Wellesley Coll., 1949-51; asst. Sloan-Kettering Inst. Cancer Research, N.Y.C., 1951-56, assoc., 1956-60, assoc. mem., 1960-69, mem., 1969—, sect. head, 1956-72, acting chief div. exptl. chemotherapy, 1965-66, div. chief drug resistance, 1967-72, head lab. of drug resistance and cyto-regulation, 1973-83, co-head lab. exptl. tumor therapy, 1973-74, coordinator field of edn., 1975-81, mem. Meml. Sloan-Kettering Cancer Ctr., 1984—, instr. biology Sloan- Kettering div. Grad Sch. Med. Scis., Cornell U., 1952-53, research assoc., 1953-54, asst. prof. microbiology, 1954-58, assoc. prof., 1958-70, unit chmn. biology 1968-74, prof., 1970—, assoc. dir., 1974—, assoc. dean Grad. Sch. Med. Scis., 1978—, asst. dean Grad. Sch., 1978—. Bd. dirs. Southgate Apts., Inc., Bronxville, N.Y., 1966-83, sec., 1967-80, v.p., 1980-83; dist. capt. Republican Club, Bronxville, 1978—; charter mem., pres. So. Westchester unit Am. Cancer Soc., 1984—. USPHS fellow, 1951-53, Philippe Found. fellow, 1959; recipient Bronze Medal, award Westchester div. Am. Cancer Soc., 1984. Fellow Am. Acad. Microbiology, N.Y. Acad. Medicine; mem. AAAS, Am. Assn. Cancer Research, Am. Genetics Assn., Am. Inst. Nutrition, Am. Soc. Microbiology, Genetics Soc. Am., Harvey Soc., Internat. Soc. Biochem. Pharmacology, N.Y. Acad. Scis., Soc. Cryobiology, Am. Cancer Soc. (bd. dirs. Westchester div. 1976—, mem. exec. com. 1976—, v.p. 1979-81, pres. 1981-83, sec. 1983—). Clubs: Bronxville Field, Griffis Faculty. Contbr. numerous articles in field to profl. jours. Subspecialties: Cancer research (medicine); Microbiology (medicine). Office: Sloan-Kettering Inst for Cancer Research 1275 York Ave New York NY 10021

HUTCHISON, JAY BRYSON, JR., utilities executive; b. Ames, Iowa, July 2, 1948; s. Jay Bryson and Bernice (Farni) H.; m. Janis Johnson, Nov. 9, 1975; children—Joey-Michelle, Jayna Sheryl. B.S., Iowa State U., 1970; M.S., Fla. Inst. Tech., 1973. Aquatic biologist Orange and Rockland Utilities, Inc., Pearl River, N.Y., 1974-80, mgr. environ. services, 1980—. Contbr. articles to profl. jours. Emergency med. technician, officer Cornwall Vol. Ambulance Corp., N.Y., 1983—. Mem. AAAS, Am. Fisheries Soc. Cornwall Jaycees (officer 1978-79). Lutheran. Current work: Techniques to mitigate aquatic biological effects of major power generating facilities. Subspecialties: Ecology (environmental science); Fishery biology. Home: Angola Rd Cornwall NY 12518 Office: Orange and Rockland Utilities Inc One Blue Hill Plaza Pearl River NY 10965

HUTCHISON, ROBERT VERN, engineering executive; b. Boston, Dec. 24, 1943; s. Robert William and Janet Elaine (Hurst) H. B.S., Mich. State U., 1967. Aerospace engr. McDonnell-Douglas Corp., Huntington Beach, Calif., 1967-69; engr., engring. mgr. Burroughs Corp., San Diego, 1969-78; engring. mgr. Honeywell Corp., Phoenix, 1978-82; engring. dir. Amdahl Corp., Sunnyvale, Calif., 1982—. Patentee in field. Sr. mem. IEEE (speaker Computer Soc., Electron Devices Soc., computer elements workshops); mem. Internat. Soc. for Hybrid Microelectronics, Components, Hybrids and Mfg. Tech. Soc., Aircraft Owners and Pilots Assn., Amateur Radio Relay League. Current work: High-performance computer hardware design and development, microelectronic packaging. Subspecialties: Microelectronics; Microchip technology (engineering). Home: 779 Wichitaw Dr Fremont CA 94539 Office: Amdahl Corp MS-197 1250 E Arques Ave Sunnyvale CA 94088

HUTZLER, ERICH KURT, mathematical physicist, consultant; b.Boston, May 12, 1944; s. Albert Joseph and Ruth Marion (Harpel) H.; m. Judith Ann Stake, Dec. 28, 1974; 1 child, Megan Wayles. B.A., Sonoma State U., 1975. Cons. Gen. Electric Co., Santa Barbara, Calif., 1964-81; mem. tech. staff Gen. Research Corp., Santa Barbara, 1976-77; dir. research programs Isis Research Corp., Nevada City, Calif., 1981—; cons. Dept. Def., Washington, 1983—; dir. Isis Research Corp. Patentee optical frequency modulator. Vice pres., bd. dirs. Santa Barbara Democratic League, 1970, Santa Barbara Ballet Theatre, 1982. Mem. Am. Math. Soc., Am. Phys. Soc. Current work: Analysis of nuclear warhead design and nuclear weapons effects. Subspecialties: Analysis; Theoretical physics. Home: 311 Verano Dr Santa Barbara CA 93110 Office: Isis Research Corp 23939 Rooster Hill Rd Nevada City CA 95959

HWANG, CHING-LAI, industrial engineering educator; b. Tainan, Taiwan, Jan. 22, 1929; came to U.S., 1958, naturalized, 1972; s. Kuang-Min and Ueng (Chiu) H.; m. Meilang Liu, Jan. 22, 1954; children—Grace, Frank, Jean. B.S. Nat. Taiwan U., 1953; M.S., Kans. State U., 1960, Ph.D., 1962. Instr., research engr. Tatung Inst. Tech., Taipei, Taiwan, 1953-58; asst. prof. Washburn U., Topeka, 1962-65; asst. prof. indsl. engring. Kans. State U., Manhattan, 1964-65, assoc. prof., 1966-73, prof., 1973—. Author: Multiple Objective Decision Making, 1979; Optimization of System Reliability, 1980; Multiple Attribute Decision Making, 1981. Contbr. numerous articles to profl. jours. Research grantee Air Force Office Sci. Research, 1963, NASA, 1968, NSF, 1974, 1981, 1983, Office Naval Research, 1976. Mem. ASME, Inst. Indsl. Engring., Japan Assn. Automatic Control Engrs. Current work: Operations research, decision theory, systems engring. Subspecialties: Industrial engineering; Operations research (engineering). Home: 1604 Virginia Dr Manhattan KS 66502 Office: Dept Indsl Engring Kansas State U Manhattan KS 66506

HWANG, JENNIE SHILAN, business and technology researcher; b. China; d. Hua and Min Yu (Chen) Sang; m. Leo Shengnien Hwang, Jan. 6, 1973; children—Raymond, Rosalind. B.S., Cheng Kung U., 1969; M.S., Kent State U., 1971; M.A., Columbia U., 1973; Ph.D., Case Western Res. U., 1976. Scientist, Martin Marietta Corp., Cleve., 1976-78, mgr. research, 1978-80, dir. research, 1980-82; head adhesives research and devel. Sherwin Williams Co., Cleve., 1980-82; mgr. tech. SCM Corp., Cleve., 1982—. Patentee solder paste and vehicle. Mem. Am. Ceramic Soc., Am. Chem. Soc., Internat. Soc. Hybrid Microelectronics, Am. Soc. Metals, Am. Welding Soc., ASTM. Current work: Advancement of electronic materials especially as related to joining processes for microelectronic surface mounted components and devices. Subspecialties: Electronic materials; Materials. Home: 3439 Brainard Rd Pepper Pike OH 44122 Office: SCM Corp 11000 Cedar Ave Cleveland OH 44106

HWANG, SAN-BAO, biophysicist, researcher; b. Taiwan, Republic of China, Sept. 8, 1946; s. Dunn Tsai and Jean Hwang; m. Shu-Chen Tsai, Aug. 30, 1970; children—Sandy, Michael. B.S., Nat. Taiwan U., 1969; Ph.D., U. Calif.-Berkeley, 1976. Research assoc. U. Calif.-San Francisco, 1978-79; sr. research biophysicist Merck Sharp & Dohme, Rahway, N.J., 1979-83, research fellow, 1984—. Co-inventor PAF receptor antagonists. Mem. Biophys. Soc. Current work: Characterization of membrane receptor of platelet activating factor and search for PAF receptor antagonist for therapeutic applications. Subspecialties: Biochemistry (biology); Biophysics (biology). Home: 67 Canterbury Dr Scotch Plains NJ 07076 Office: Merck Sharp & Dohme Research Lab Scott and Lincoln Ave Rahway NJ 07065

HYMAN, ALBERT LEWIS, physician; b. New Orleans, Nov. 10, 1923; s. David and Mary (Newstadt) H.; m. Neil Steiner, Mar. 27, 1964; 1 son, Albert Arthur. B.S., La. State U., 1943; M.D., 1945; postgrad., U. Cin., U. Paris, U. London, Eng. Diplomate: Am. Bd. Internal Medicine. Intern Charity Hosp., 1945-46, resident, 1947-49, sr. vis. physician, 1959-63; resident Cin. Gen. Hosp., 1946-47; instr. medicine La. State U., 1950-56, asst. prof. medicine, 1956-57, asst. prof., Tulane U, 1957-59, asso. prof., 1959-63; asso. prof. surgery Med. Sch., 1963-70, prof. research surgery in cardiology, 1970—, adj. prof. pharmacology, 1974—; dir. Cardiac Catheterization Lab., 1957—; sr. vis. physician Touro Hosp., Touro Infirmary, Hotel Dieu; chief cardiology Sara Mayo Hosp.; cons. in cardiology USPHS, New Orleans Crippled Children's Hosp., St. Tammany Parish Hosp., Covington La. area VA, Hotel Dieu Hosp., Mercy Hosp., East Jefferson Gen. Hosp., St. Charles Gen. Hosp.; electrocardiographer Metairie Hosp., 1959-64, Sara Mayo Hosp., Touro Infirmary, St. Tammany Hosp.; cons. cardiovascular disease New Orleans VA Hosp.; cons. cardiology Baton Rouge Gen. Hosp.; Barlow lectr. in medicine U. So. Calif., 1977; mem. internat. sci. com. IV Internat. Symposium on Pulmonary Circulation, Charles U., Prague. Mem. editorial bd. Circulation Research, 1985. Contbr. articles to profl. jours. Recipient award for research of the Hadassah, 1980. Fellow ACP, Am. Coll. Chest Physicians, Am. Coll. Cardiology, Am. Fedn. Clin. Research; mem. Am. Heart Assn. (fellow council on circulation, mem. council on cardiopulmonary medicine, regional rep. council clin. cardiology, chmn. sci. com. of cardiopulmonary council 1981, chmn. cardiopulmonary council, bd. dirs., mem. research com. 1985), La. Heart Assn. (v.p. 1974, Albert L. Hyman Ann. Research award), Am. Soc. Pharmacology and Exptl. Therapeutics, So. Soc. Clin. Investigation (chmn. membership com.), So. Med. Soc., Am. Physiol. Soc., N.Am. Soc. Pacing and Electrophysiology, N.Y. Acad. Scis., AAUP, Alpha Omega Alpha. Research in cardiopulmonary circulation. Current Work: Director of surgical cardiopulmonary research laboratory at Tulane Medical School engaged in research in pulmonary circulation; interest is diverted toward pharmacology; physiology, and biochemistry of pulmonary blood flow. Subspecialties: Cardiology; Pharmacology. Home: 5550 Jacquelyn Ct New Orleans LA 70124 Office: 3601 Prytania St New Orleans LA 70115

HYMAN, CAROL BRACH, pediatric hematologist-oncologist; b. South Orange, N.J., Jan. 21, 1923; d. Leon S. and Madeline E. (Rosenthal) Brach; m. Maurice M. Hyman, Apr. 14, 1951; children: Gayle, J. Madeline, Celia. B.A., Cornell U., 1943, M.D., 1947. Diplomate: Am. Bd. Pediatrics with subsplty in pediatric hematology-oncology. Intern Newark City Hosp., 1947-49; resident Cornell-N.Y. Hosp., 1949-50, Mt. Sinai Hosp., N.Y.C., 1950-51; resident Children's Hosp. of Los Angeles, 1952-54, staff, 1954-80; faculty U. So. Calif., 1954—, assoc. prof. clin. pediatrics, 1980—; pediatric hematologist/oncologist Cedars-Sinai Med. Center, Los Angeles, 1980—; also dir. Thalassemia-Chronic Ironload Overload Program. Author articles, book chpts. in pediatric hematology-oncology. Recipient 25 Yr. Service award Children's Hosp. of Los Angeles, 1980. Mem. AMA, Am. Assn. Cancer Research, Am. Soc. Hematology, Calif. Med. Assn., Internat. Soc. Hematology, Los Angeles County Med. Soc., Los Angeles Pediatric Soc., Western Soc. Pediatric Research, Women in Bus., Sierra Club, Nat. Audubon Soc., Cornell U. Alumni Assn., Cornell U. Med. Sch. Alumni Assn. Jweish. Current Work: Pediatric hematology-oncology. Present research in Thalassemia (Cooley's Anemia) and chronic iron overload. Subspecialties: Hematology; Oncology. Office: 8700 Beverly Blvd Room 4310 Los Angeles CA 90048

HYMAN, EDWARD SIDNEY, internist, consultant, researcher; b. New Orleans, Jan. 22, 1925; s. David and Mary (Newstadt) H.; m. Jean Simons, Sept. 29, 1956; children: Judith, Sydney, Edward David, Anne. B.S., La. State U., 1944; M.D., Johns Hopkins U., 1946. Diplomate: Am. Bd. Internal Medicine. Intern Barnes Hosp., Washington U., St. Louis, 1946-47; fellow in medicine Stanford U., San Francisco, 1949-51, asst. resident in medicine, 1950-51, Peter Bent Brigham Hosp., Boston, 1951-53; teaching fellow in medicine Harvard U., Boston, 1952-53; practice medicine specializing in internal medicine, New Orleans, 1953—; dir. kidney unit Charity Hosp., New Orleans, 1953-55; investigator Touro Research Inst., New Orleans, 1959—; mem. staff Sara Mayo Hosp., 1954-79, chief of staff, 1968-70, trustee, 1970-78; mem. staff Touro Infirmary, New Orleans, St. Charles Hosp., New Orleans; panelist Pres.'s Commn on Health Needs of Nation, 1952; cons. water quality New Orleans Sewerage and Water Bd., 1978; mem. research adv. com. Cancer Assn. New Orleans, 1976—, La. Bd. Regents, 1983. Contbr. articles to profl. jours. NIH grantee, 1960-81; Am. Heart Assn. grantee, 1962-65. Fellow ACP; mem. Am. Fedn. Clin. Research, Am. Soc. Artificial Internal Organs, Am. Physiol. Soc. Biophys. Soc. (chmn. local arrangements 1971, 77, 81), Am. Soc. Microbiology, AAAS, Pvt. Doctors Am. (co-founder 1968, v.p. 1968—, Dist. Service award 1981), Orleans Parish Med. Soc. (gov. 1972-80), La. State Med. Soc. (ho. of dels. 1970-81). Jewish. Isolated aldosterone, 1949; patentee sheet plastic oxygenator (artificial heart), oil detection device; inventor telephone tranmission of electrocardiogram, early data transmission; inventor hydrogen-platinum detection of heart shunts. Current Work: Clinical internal medicine, biochemistry, biophysics, nephrology, artificial organs, water quality, government in medicine, cause of death in renal failure, significance of bacteria in urine. Subspecialties: Internal medicine; Biophysics (physics). Office: 3525 Prytania St Suite 200 New Orleans LA 70115

HYMAN, HOWARD ALLAN, physicist; b. Montreal, Que., Can., Dec. 5, 1943; s. Harold and Marcia (Rohr) H.; m. Judith Lynn Seltzer, Oct. 19, 1969; 1 son: David. B.S.E.E., U. So. Calif., 1965; Ph.D., Yale U., 1970. Research fellow Queen's U., Belfast, No. Ireland, 1970-72; prin. research scientist Avco Everett Research Lab., Inc., Mass., 1972—. Contbr. articles to profl. jours. Mem. Am. Phys. Soc. Patentee in field. Current Work: Theory of atomic collisions; spectroscopy; physics of visible uv/x-ray lasers. Subspecialties: Atomic and molecular physics; Laser physics. Office: Avco Everett Research Lab Inc Everett MA 02149

HYSON, MICHAEL TERRY, biologist, consultant; b. Rockford, Ill., July 5, 1948; s. Harvey Eugene and Norma Audry (Allison) H.; m. Emillia Ann Smith, June 15, 1970 (div. Sept. 1971). B.S. in Biology, U. Miami, Fla., 1970, M.S. in Biology, 1973, Ph.D. in Biology, 1976. Research assoc. Calif. Inst. Tech., 1977-80, vis. assoc., 1982—; NASA fellow NASA Robotics Study, Santa Clara, Calif., 1980; cons. G. C. H. Astronautics, Sunnyvale, Calif., 1980—; pres. Hy Tech Glendale, Calif., 1980—. Editor, pub.: The Caltech Space Settlement Conference, 1981; software programmer. Mem. citizens adv. com. nat. space policy L-5 Soc., Los Angeles, 1981-82. Served with USNR, 1970. Recipient Nat. Res. Service award NIH, 1977-80; NSF trainee, 1971-72; Maytag Grad.

fellow, 1973-75. Mem. L-5 Soc. (speaker 1st nat. conf. 1982), Lighter-than-air Soc. (life), Assn. Computing Machinery, Am. Soc. Photogrammetry, Soc. Photo-Optical and Illumination Engrs. Libertarian. Performed experiments in weightlessness aboard NASA KC-135. Current Work: Eye movements in binocular vision; neural models of vision; robot vision; application of robotics and teleoperation and biology to colonization of space; consulting on space-related topics; would like to see space colonized and moon and asteroids mined; interested in dolphins and interspecies communication. Subspecialties: Neurobiology; Satellite studies. Home and Office: Hy Tech 1155 N Verdugo Rd Apt C Glendale CA 91206

IACONO, JAMES M., government research center administrator. Dir. Dept. of Agr., Western Human Nutrition Research Ctr., San Francisco. Subspecialty: Nutrition (biology). Office: Western Human Nutrition Research Ctr PO Box 29997 Presidio San Francisco CA 94129

IANNA, PHILIP A., astronomer, educator; b. Phila., May 27, 1938; s. Michael and Jeanette E. (Russell) I.; m. Susan Osborne, Dec. 28, 1968 (div. 1983), B.A., Swarthmore Coll., 1960, M.A., 1962; Ph.D., Ohio State U., 1968. Research assoc. Center for Advanced Studies, U. Va., Charlottesville, 1968-70; research assoc. Leander McCormick Obs., U. Va., 1970-73; asst. prof. dept. astronomy U. Va., 1973-79, assoc. prof., 1979—. Author: (with Roger B. Culver) The Gemini Syndrome, 1979; also articles. Recipient Group Achievement award NASA, 1981. Mem. Am. Assn. Variable Star Observers, Am. Astron. Soc., Internat. Astron. Union, Sigma Xi. Current Work: Establishment of fundamental properties of nearby stars, studies of stellar open clusters. Astrometry, trigonometric parallaxes, proper motions, stellar luminosities, stellar masses. Subspecialties: Optical astronomy; Astrometry. Home: PO Box 3818 Charlottesville VA 22903 Office: Dept Astronomy Cabell Dr Charlottesville VA 22903

IANNACCONE, PHILIP MONROE, biologist, pathologist, educator; b. Syracuse, N.Y., May 3, 1948. B.Sc. in Biochemistry, Syracuse U., 1968; B.Sc. in Forestry, SUNY, Syracuse, 1968; M.D., SUNY Upstate Med. Center, 1972; Ph.D., U. Oxford (Eng.), 1977. Diplomate Am. Bd. Pathology. Intern SUNY Upstate Med. Center, 1972-73, resident in pathology, 1973-74; asst. prof. U. Calif.-San Diego, 1978-79; assoc. prof. pathology Northwestern U. Med. Sch. and Cancer Center, Chgo., 1979—. Contbr. sci. articles to profl. publs. Mem. AAAS, Internat. Acad. Pathologists, Am. Assn. Cancer Research, Am. Assn. Pathologists. Current Work: Biology of cancer, reproductive toxicology. Subspecialties: Cell and tissue culture; Cancer research (medicine). Office: 303 E Chicago Ave Chicago IL 60611

IANNUZZELLI, RAYMOND JOSEPH, mechanical engineer; b. Hoboken, N.J., Feb. 6, 1946; s. Raymond Joseph and Marie Silvestri I.; m. Nancy Newsome, July 23, 1972; children—Damon Brian, Darren Raymond. B.S. in Mech. Engring., Widner U., 1972; M.S., U. Pa., 1975. Registered profl. engr., Pa., 1984. Engring. technician Westinghouse Electric Co., Lester, Pa., 1965-71, jr. engr., 1971-75, assoc. engr., 1975-78; cons. engr. Turbo Research Inc., Lionville, Pa., 1978-79; sr. research and devel. engr. Air Products, Inc., Allentown, Pa., 1979-84; prin. mech. engr. Sperry Corp., Blue Bell, Pa., 1984—. Solar energy cons. RJI Solar Services, Media, Pa., 1972-78; rotordynamic cons. Turbo Research Inc., 1978-79. Contbr. articles to profl. jours. Served with U.S. Army, 1968-71. Mem. ASME (outstanding service award 1978). Subspecialties: Solid mechanics; Applied mathematics. Office: Sperry Corp PO Box 500 Blue Bell PA 19424

IATRIDIS, PANAYOTIS GEORGE, physician, physiology and medicine educator, university administrator; b. Alexandira, Egypt, Dec. 10, 1926; came to U.S., 1962, naturalized, 1975; s. George E. and Ioanna (Nicholaides) I.; m. Catherine P. Mouzouris, Apr. 27, 1957; children: Ioanna P., Mary P. Grad., Greek Gymnasium Ambetios Sch., Cairo, 1944; M.D., U. Athens, 1951, D.Sc. with honors in Physiology, 1968. Med. lic. Greece, Egypt, N.C., Ind., Ill. Resident Univ. Med. Clinic, Athens, 1951-53; resident Greek Hosp., Alexandria, 1953-55, asst. dir. dept. medicine, 1959-62; research assoc. dept. physiology U. N.C., Chapel Hill, 1963-66, asst. prof. physiology, 1969-72; assoc. prof. physiology Ind. U., Gary, 1972-76, prof., 1976—, prof. medicine, 1981—; dir. Ind. U. (Northwest Ctr. for Med. Edn.), 1975—; asst. dean Ind. U. (Sch. Medicine), 1979—; vis. research scientist Protein Found. and Harvard Sch. Pub. Health, 1966; research scientist dept. physiology U. Athens, 1967-69; cons. St. Mary Med. Ctr., Meth. Hosp., St. Catherine Hosp., Porter Meml. Hosp., St. Anthony Hosp. Contbr. numerous articles in field to profl. jours. Bd. dirs. Porter County (Ind.) Mental Health Assn., 1973-77; bd. dirs. Am. Heart Assn., Ind. affailiate, 1975—, Am. Lung Assn., Northwest Ind. chpt., 1977—, Am. Cancer Soc., Northwest Ind. chpt., 1978—; mem. council SS Constantine and Helen Greek Orthodox Cathedral, Merrillville, Ind., 1979-81; vice chmn. Community Health Assn., Lake County, Ind., 1979—, chmn. med. adv. com., 1979—; founder, pres. Greek Orthodox Ch. of Porter County, 1980-81. Grantee in field. Mem. Internat. Soc. Hematology, Internat. Soc. Thrombosis and Hemostasis, N.C. Acad. Sci., N.Y. Acad. Sci., Am. Physiol. Soc., AAAS, Med. Soc. Athens, Greek Hematological Soc., World Fedn. Hemophilia, Am. Thoracic Soc., Ind. Thoracic Soc., Assn. Am. Med. Colls., Assn. Ind. Dirs. Med. Edn., Sigma Xi. Current Work: Effects of 2,3-DPG on platelet aggegation and prostaglandin synthesis, blood coagulation, fibrinolysis, thrombosis, and related topics. Subspecialties: Internal medicine; Hematology. Home: 603 Hastings Terr Valpariso IN 46383 Office: Indiana U Sch Medicine 3400 Broadway St Gary IN 46408

IBEN, ICKO, JR., astrophysicist, educator; b. Champaign, Ill., June 27, 1931; s. Icko and Kathryn (Tomlin) I.; m. Miriam Genevieve Fett, Jan. 28, 1956; children: Christine, Timothy, Benjamin, Thomas. B.A., Harvard U., 1953; M.S., U. Ill., 1954, Ph.D., 1958. Asst. prof. physics Williams Coll., 1958-61; sr. research fellow in physics Calif. Inst. Tech., 1961-64; asso. prof. physics Mass. Inst. Tech., 1964-68, prof., 1968-72; vis. prof. astronomy Harvard, 1966, 68, 70; vis. fellow Joint Inst. for Lab. Astrophysics, U. Colo., 1971-72; vis. prof. astronomy and astrophysics U. Calif. at Santa Cruz, 1972; prof. astronomy and physics U. Ill., Urbana-Champaign, 1972—, head dept. astronomy, 1972-84; vis. prof. physics and astronomy Inst. for Astronomy, U. Hawaii, 1977; mem. adv. panel, astronomy sect. NSF, 1972-75; mem. vis. com. Aura Observatories, 1979-82. Contbr. articles to profl. jours. Guggenheim fellow, 1985-86. Mem. Am. Astron. Soc. (councilor 1974-77), Nat. Acad. Scis. Current Work: Evolution of asymptotic giant branch stars (dredge up and nucleosynthesis); evolution of central stars of planetary nebulae and cooling white dwarfs; evolution of binary stars and Type I supernovae. Subspecialty: Theoretical astrophysics. Home: 3910 Clubhouse Dr Champaign IL 61820 Office: Astronomy Bldg 1011 W Springfield Urbana IL 61801

IBERALL, ARTHUR SAUL, physicist, educator; b. N.Y.C., June 12, 1918; s. Benjamin and Anna (Katz) I.; m. Helene Rubenstein, Jan. 28, 1940; children—Eleanora Iberall Robbins, Pamela Iberall Rubin, Althea Valerie Iberall Slate. B.S., CCNY, 1940, postgrad. 1940-41; postgrad. George Washington U., 1942-45; D.Sci., (hon.) Ohio State U., 1976. Gen. physicist Nat. Bur. Standards, Washington, 1941-53; research dir. ARO Equipment Corp., Cleve., 1953-54; chief physicist Rand Devel. Corp., Cleve., 1954-65; chief scientist, pres. Gen. Tech. Services, Inc., Upper Darby, Pa., 1965-81; vis. scholar UCLA, 1981—. Author: Toward a General Science of Viable Systems, 1972; On Pulsatile and Steady Arterial Flow, 1973; Physics of Membrane Transport, 1973; Bridges in Science from Physics to Social Science, 1974; On Nature, Life, Mind and Society, 1976. Editor: (with others) Technical and Biological Problems of Control; A Cybernetic View, 1970; Regulation and Control in Physiological Systems, 1973. Contbr. articles to profl. jours. Fellow ASME; mem. Am. Phys. Soc., N.Y. Acad. Scis. Biomed. Engring. Soc. (Alza Disting. lectr. 1975), Am. Cybernetic Soc., Microcirculation Soc., Instrument Soc. Am., Biophysics Soc., Sigma Xi. Democrat. Jewish. Club: Cosmos. Current work: Physical foundations for complex systems, nature, life, man, mind, society. Subspecialties: Theoretical physics; Integrated systems modelling and engineering. Home: 4675 Willis Ave Sherman Oaks CA 91403 Office: UCLA Los Angeles CA 90024

IBERS, JAMES ARTHUR, chemist; b. Los Angeles, June 9, 1930; s. Max Charles and Esther (Imerman) I.; m. Joyce Audrey Henderson, June 10, 1951; children—Jill Tina, Arthur Alan. B.S., Calif. Inst. Tech., 1951, Ph.D., 1954. NSF post-doctoral fellow, Melbourne, Australia, 1954-55; chemist Shell Devel. Co., 1955-61, Brookhaven Nat. Lab., 1961-64; mem. faculty Northwestern U., 1964—, prof. chemistry, 1964. Mem. Am. Chem. Soc. (inorganic chemistry award 1979), Am. Crystallographic Assn., U.S. Nat. Acad. Scis. Current Work: Synthesis, characterization and properties of new inorganic, organometallic and solid state materials; correlation of properties with structure. Subspecialties: Inorganic chemistry; Solid state chemistry. Home: 2657 Orrington Ave Evanston IL 60201 Office: Dept Chemistry Northwestern Univ Evanston IL 60201

IBRAHIM, ALI ABD-EL-FATTAH, systems company executive, quality specialist; b. Shibrakhit, Behara, Egypt; came to U.S. 1979; s. Ali M. Ibrahim and Nagia Farahat; m. Leslie A. Lake, May 21, 1977 (div.). B.Sc. in Electronics, Spl. Physics, Alexandria U., Egypt, 1962; M.Sc. in Solid State Electronics, Birmingham U., Eng., 1965, Ph.D. in Electronic and Elec. Engring., 1969. Group leader Bell No. Research Co., Ottawa, Can., 1970-73, mgr. silicon imaging, 1973-75, mgr. silicon tech., 1975-79; mgr. spl. products devel. Microelectronic Ctr., El Segundo, Calif., 1979-81, mgr. very large scale integration design engring. dept., 1981-84; mgr. strategy devel. Xerox System Group, El-Segundo, 1984-85; mgr. electronic div. Electro-Optical Ctr., Monrovia, 1985—; mem. No. Telecom Tech. Mission to Peoples Republic China, 1978. Author and lectr. on custom design VLSI, 1982; editor for Research Studies Press, Ltd., contbr. articles to profl. jours.; patentee (12) in field. Adv. Jr. Achievement program, Torrance, Calif., 1979. Egyptian Govt. grantee, 1959-62, 64-69. Mem. IEEE (sr.). Internat. Com. Current work: Electronics applications for electronic systems development with focus on manufacturing of printheads required for current and future Xerox printing and electronic reprographics. Subspecialties: Microchip technology (engineering); Integrated circuits. Office: Xerox Corp 1500 S Shamrock Ave Monrovia CA 91016

IBRAHIM, SHAWKI AMIN, radiology educator; b. Cairo, Egypt, Mar. 27, 1942; came to U.S., 1970, naturalized, 1975; s. Amin and Venice (Michael) I.; m. Janette Yousef, Mar. 21, 1967; children: Maria, Daniel. B.S., Alexandria (Egypt) U., 1962; M.S., L.I. U., 1972; Ph.D., N.Y. U., 1980. Lab. instr. Alexandria (Egypt) U., 1962-70; chief technologist Coney Island Hosp., N.Y.C., 1972-75; research scientist N.Y. U., 1975-80; asst. prof. Colo. State U., 1980—. Contbr. articles to profl. jours. Mem. Health Physics Soc. (student award 1978). Current Work: Radiochemistry and environmental aspects of nuclear waste management. Subspecialties: Nuclear fission; Ecology (environmental science). Home: 3349 Pepperwood Ln Fort Collins CO 80525 Office: Colo State U Dept Radiation Biology Fort Collins CO 80523

ICERMAN, LARRY, university research administrator; b. Muncie, Ind., Sept. 22, 1945; s. Charles and Janelyn (Mock) I. B.S., M.I.T., 1967; M.S., U. Calif., San Diego, 1968, Ph.D., 1976; M.B.A., San Diego State U., 1976. Research engr. U. Calif., San Diego, 1976; asst. prof. tech. and human affairs Washington U., St. Louis, 1976-79, assoc. prof., 1979-80; dir. N.Mex. Energy Inst., Las Cruces, 1980-81; dir. N.Mex. State U. Energy Inst., Las Cruces, 1982-84, N.Mex. Energy Research and Devel. Inst., Santa Fe, 1984—. Author: (with S. S. Penner) Energy: Demands, Resources, Impact, Techonolgy, and Policy, 1974, 81; Energy: Non-Nuclear Energy Technologies, 1976, 84; (with R. P. Morgan) Renewable Resource Utilization for Development, 1981. Current Work: Energy tech. and policy, including research, engring., and commercialization. Subspecialties: Geothermal power; Solar energy. Home: 2999 Calle Cerrada Santa Fe NM 87505 Office: 1220 S St Francis Dr Rm 358 Santa Fe NM 87501

IDLER, DAVID RICHARD, biochemist, marine scientist, educator; b. Winnipeg, Man., Can., Mar. 13, 1923; s. Ernest and Alice (Lydon) I.; m. Myrtle Mary Betteridge, Dec. 12, 1956; children: Louise, Mark. B.A., U. B.C., Vancouver, 1949, M.A., 1950; Ph.D., U. Wis., 1954. With Fisheries Research Bd. of Can., 1953-71; dir., investigator in charge of steroid biochemistry Halifax (N.S.) Lab., 1961-69, Atlantic regional dir. research, Halifax, 1969-71; dir. Marine Sci. Research Lab.; prof. biochemistry Meml. U. Nfld., Can., St. John's, 1971—. Editor: Steroids in Nonmammalian Vertebrates, 1972; editorial bd.: Steroids, 1963—, Gen. and Comparative Endocrinology, 1966-82, Endocrine Research Communications, 1974—, Can. Jour. Zoology, 1979-82; mem. bd. corr. editors: Jour. Steroid Biochemistry, 1981—. Served with RCAF, 1942-45. Decorated D.F.C. Fellow Royal Soc. Can.; mem. European Soc. Comparative Endocrinologists (founding), Can. Biochem. Soc., Can. Zool. Soc. (v.p. 1985), Am. Chem. Soc., AAAS, Am. Zool. Soc., Endocrine Soc., N.Y. Acad. Scis. Subspecialty: Biochemistry (biology). Home: 44 Slattery Rd St John's NF A1A 1Z8 Canada Office: Marine Scis Research Lab Meml U Nfld St Johns NF A1C 5S7 Canada

IDOL, JAMES DANIEL, JR., chemical company executive, inventor; b. Harrisonville, Mo., Aug. 7, 1928; s. James Daniel and Gladys Rosita (Lile) I. A.B., William Jewell Coll., 1949; M.S., Purdue U., 1952, Ph.D., 1955, D.Sc. (hon.), 1980. With Standard Oil Co., Ohio, 1955-77, research supr., 1965-68, research mgr., 1968-77; mgr. venture research Ashland Chem. Co., Columbus, Ohio, 1977-79, v.p., dir. corp. research and devel., 1979—; mem. adv. bd. NSF Presdl. Young Investigators Awards; cons. in field. Contbr. articles to profl. jours; mem. editorial bd. profl. jours. Recipient Modern Pioneer award Nat. Assn. Mfrs., 1965, Disting. Alumnus citation William Jewell Coll., 1971. Life fellow Am. Inst. Chemists (dir. 1981, Chem. Pioneer award 1968, Mems. and Fellows lectr. 1980); mem. Soc. Plastics Industry, Am. Chem. Soc. (chmn. indsl. engring. div. 1971, Joseph P. Stewart Disting. Service award 1975, Creative Invention award 1975), Am. Inst. Chem. Engrs., Soc. Plastics Engrs., Indsl. Research Inst. (rep.), Plastics Pioneers Assn., Soc. Chem. Industry (Perkin medal 1979), Council Chem. Research (bd. govs. 1985-87; indsl. del.), Ind. Acad. Sci., AAAS, Sigma Xi, Alpha Chi Sigma, Theta Chi Delta, Kappa Mu Epsilon, Alpha Phi Omega, Phi Gamma Delta. Mem. Disciples of Christ Ch. Clubs: Cleve. Athletic, Worthington Hills Country; Cosmos (Washington). Lodges: Masons, Shriners. Patentee in field. Home: 8008 Park Ridge Ct Worthington OH 43085 Office: PO Box 2219 Columbus OH 43216

IGLEWSKI, WALLACE JOSEPH, microbiologist, researcher; b. Cleve., Aug. 17, 1938; s. Wallace Frank and Marie Ann (Sech) I.; m. Barbara Hotham Iglewski, Apr. 23, 1965; children: Eric, William. B.S., Western Res.U., 1961; M.S., Pa. State U., 1963, Ph.D., 1965. Postdoctoral fellow U. Colo. Med. Center, 1965-66, Pub. Health Research Inst., N.Y.C., 1966-68; asst. prof. microbiology U. Oreg., 1968-72; assoc. prof. Oreg. Health Sci. U., 1972-84, prof., 1984—. Contbr. articles to profl. jours. NIH grantee, 1968—; NSF grantee, 1979-82. Mem. Am. Soc. Microbiology, Am. Soc. Virology. Current Work: Biochemistry of replilation of RNA viruses; structure and function of elongation factor-2; ADP-ribosylation of proteins. Subspecialties: Virology (medicine); Molecular biology. Office: Department Microbiology and Immunology 3181 SW Sam Jackson Park Rd Portland OR 97201

IGNATIEV, ALEX, physics educator; b. Wehingen, Germany, Feb. 14, 1945; s. Nicholaj and Helene (Pesudova) Ignatjevs; m. Laura Tatarchuk, Aug. 6, 1967; children—Nicholas, Victor. B.S., U. Wis.-Milw., 1966; Ph.D., Cornell U., 1972. Asst. prof. physics U. Houston, 1974-77, assoc. prof., 1977-82, prof., 1982-83, prof. physics and chemistry, 1983—, mem. staff Energy Lab., 1975—, assoc. dir. Magnetic Info. Lab., 1984—; lektor. physics Aarhus U., Denmark, 1977-78. Contbr. articles to profl. publs. Fulbright scholar, 1983. Mem. Am. Phys. Soc., Am. Vacuum Soc., Am. Chem. Soc., Sigma Xi. Current work: Investigation of surface properties of materials with interest in catalysis, 2-D phase transitions, ion damage and photo effects in solar energy materials. Subspecialties: Condensed matter physics; Surface chemistry. Home: 4131 Grennoch Ln Houston TX 77025 Office: U Houston Dept Physics University Park Houston TX 77004

ILG, RONALD JON, marine biology researcher, educator; b. Cleve., Dec. 10, 1945; s. John and Helen May (Eschuk) I.; m. Susanne Audrey Warren/Bye, Apr. 12, 1970 (div. Dec. 1978); m. Patricia Ellen McCoy, May 19, 1982. B.Sc., Ohio State U., 1966; Ph.D., U. Tex., Austin, 1980. Shipboard biologist Lamont Geol. Obs., Columbia U., Palisades, N.Y., 1966-67; communications cons. Ohio Bell Telephone Co., Cleve., 1967-74; research asst. U. Tex., Port Aransas, 1977-80; asst. prof. biology, prin. investigator McNeese State U., Lake Charles, La., 1980—; cons. Port of Corpus Christi, Tex., 1980, Weyerhaeuser Co., Tacoma, Wash., 1981, PPG Industries, Lake Charles, La., 1981-82, S.W. La. Shrimping and Fishing Assn., Vinton, La., 1982—. Mem. Calcasieu Commn. on Arts and Humanities, Lake Charles, La., 1982. Ohio State U. stadium scholar, 1963-64. Mem. AAAS, Union Concerned Scientists, Gulf Estuarine Research Fedn., Estuarine Research Fedn., Am. Fisheries Soc., Am. Soc. Zoologists. Current Work: Physiological ecology of fish particularly regarding salinity and pollution, coastal zone management, innovative fisheries management and economical repercussions. Subspecialties: Ecology (environmental science); Resource management. Home: 625 W LaGrange St Lake Charles LA 70605 Office: McNeese State U PO Box 1468 Lake Charles LA 70609

ILLINGWORTH, GARTH D., astronomer; b. Perth, Western Australia, Mar. 14, 1947; s. Norman and Yvonne (Manning) I.; m. Wendy L. Illingworth, Apr. 19, 1969. B.Sc. with 1st class honors, U. Western Australia, 1968; Ph.D., Australia Nat. U., 1973. Postdoctoral fellow Kitts Peak Nat. Obs., Tucson, 1974-74, U. Calif.-Berkeley, 1975-77; astronomer Kitts Peak Obs., 1977-84; dep. dir. Space Telescope Sci. Inst., Balt., 1984—. Contbr. articles to profl. jours. Miller Found. fellow, 1976. Mem. Am. Astron. Soc., Internat. Astron. Union. Current work: Observational studies of structure and dynamics of galaxies, formation, composition and evolution of normal and radio galaxies, structure of globular clusters; distance scale. Subspecialty: Optical astronomy. Office: Space Telescope Sci Inst Johns Hopkins U Homewood Campus Baltimore MD 21218

IMBEMBO, ANTHONY LOUIS, surgeon, educator, educational administrator; b. N.Y.C., Nov. 8, 1942; s. Emil Anthony and Theresa (Rippert) I. A.B., Columbia U., 1963, M.D., 1967. Diplomate: Am. Bd. Surgery Am. Bd. Thoracic Surgery, Nat. Bd. Med. Examiners. Intern Mass. Gen. Hosp., 1967-68, resident, 1968-73; asst. prof. surgery Johns Hopkins U., 1973-77, assoc. prof., 1977-83; surgeon Johns Hopkins U. (Hosp.), 1973-83; prof. surgery, vice chmn. dept. Case Western Res. U., 1983—; dir. dept. surgery Cleve. Met. Gen. Hosp., 1983—; cons. Walter Reed Army Med. Ctr., 1982—. Johns Hopkins Hosp. grantee, 1976; recipient George J. Stuart award Johns Hopkins U. Sch. Medicine, 1977-82. Fellow A.C.S.; mem. Soc. Univ. Surgeons, Assn. Surg. Edn. (pres. 1982-83), Soc. Surgery of the Alimentary Tract, Internat. Cardiovascular Soc. Current Work: Surgeon (general, vascular and thoracic surgery); educator; president of Association for Surgical Education and numerous educational teaching awards; researcher implantable programmable infusion pump for delivery of insulin (human trials beginning); research role of amino acid analogues in nutrition. Subspecialties: Surgery; Artificial organs and prostheses. Home: 20901 Claythorne Rd Shaker Heights OH 44122 Office: Cleve Met Gen Hosp 3395 Scranton Rd Cleveland OH 44109

IMBRIE, JOHN Z(ELLER), physics educator; b. Englewood, N.J., May 16, 1956; s. John and Barbara (Zeller) I. A.B., Harvard, U., 1978, A.M., 1979, Ph.D., 1980. Jr. fellow Harvard U., Cambridge, Mass., 1981-84, asst. prof. physics, 1984—. Contbr. articles to profl. jours. Mem. Am. Math. Soc., Am. Phys. Soc., Internat. Assn. Math. Physics. Club: Am. Alpine. Current work: Disordered systems; properties of spin systems in random magnetic fields; quantum field theory; spectral properties of gauge theories; continuum limits. Subspecialties: Mathematical physics; Statistical physics. Home: 251 Pearl St Apt 5 Cambridge MA 02139 Office: Lyman Lab Physics Harvard U Cambridge MA 02138

IMONDI, ANTHONY ROCCO, pharmacologist; b. Providence, Aug. 21, 1940; s. Anthony and Phyllis (Cacchiotti) I.; m. Lucy Ann Corsini, July 6, 1963; children: Lisa, Michael, Gina, Gail. B.S., U. R.I., 1962; M.S., U. Maine, 1964, Ph.D., 1966. USPHS postdoctoral fellow Cornell Med. Coll., N.Y.C., 1966-69; postdoctoral fellow Sloan-Kettering Inst. for Cancer Research, N.Y.C., 1967-69; sr. pharmacologist Warren-Teed Pharms., Columbus, Ohio, 1969-74; project leader Rohm & Haas Co., Phila., 1974-77; mgr. pharmacology Adria Labs., Columbus, 1977-84, dir. research, 1984—. Contbr. articles to profl. jours. Pres. Adria Labs. Credit Union, 1981—; v.p. Rolling Ridge Co., residents assn. Mem. Am. Soc. Pharmacology and Exptl. Therapeutics, Soc. Exptl. Biology and Medicine, AAAS. Current Work: Development of new drugs for human use, research in pharmacology including drug metabolism, cancer chemotherapy, cardiovascular, central nervous system drugs and gastrointestinal pharmacology. Subspecialties: Pharmacology; Pharmacokinetics. Office: PO Box 16529 Columbus OH 43216

IMSANDE, JOHN D., genetics educator; b. Grass Range, Mont., June 14, 1931; s. Louis H. and Freda M. (Dengel) I.; m. Marcia F. Rohrbach, Aug. 13, 1976; children: Carol Lynn, Louis Daniel. B.A., U. Mont., 1953; M.S., Mont. State U., 1956; Ph.D., Duke U., 1960. Lectr., research scientist Princeton U., 1961-62; asst. prof. biology Case Western Res. U., Cleve., 1962-64, assoc. prof., 1964-68; vis. scientist U. Edinburgh, Scotland, 1968-69; prof. genetics and biochemistry Iowa State U., Ames, 1969-75, prof. genetics, 1975—; lectr. numerous univs. Contbr. chpts. to books, articles to profl. jours. Served with U.S. Army, 1953-55. NIH grantee. Mem. Am. Soc. Plant Physiologists. Current Work: Identification of plant (soybean) genotype that promotes a high level of nitrogen fixation; enhanced dinitrogen fixation. Subspecialties: Nitrogen fixation; Plant genetics. Home: 1121 N Hyland Ave Ames IA 50010 Office: Dept Genetics Iowa State U Ames IA 50011

INADA, HITOSHI, research engineer; b. Ueno, Japan, Mar. 10, 1937; came to U.S., 1964; s. Osamu and Humi (Inada) I.; m. Misako Mochida, Aug. 18, 1970; children—Maki, Tetsu. B.S.E.E., Tokyo Denki U., 1960; M.S.E.E., Northwestern U., 1966, Ph.D. in Elec. Engring., 1969. Research engr. TOA Electronics Ltd., Tokyo, 1960-64; research asst. Northwestern U., Evanston, Ill., 1964-69; asst. prof. U. Ill.-Chgo., 1969-74; staff mem. MIT Lincoln Lab., Lexington, Mass., 1975—. Contbr. articles to jours. NSF research grantee, 1971. Mem. IEEE (Recognition award antenna and propagation 1971), Inst. Electronics and Communications Engrs. of Japan, Optical Soc. Am., Internat. Sci. Radio Union. Current work: Imaging techniques, radar systems, electromagnetic wave scattering and propagation. Subspecialties: Computer engineering; Satellite studies. Office: MIT Lincoln Lab 244 Wood St Lexington MA 02173

INAGAMI, TADASHI, biochemistry, educator; b. Kobe, Japan, Feb. 20, 1931; came to U.S., 1954; s. Yoshio and Yoshi (Hoshi) I.; m. Masako Araki, Nov. 12, 1961; children: Sanae, Mary. B.S., Kyoto (Japan) U., 1953; M.S., Yale U., 1955, Ph.D., 1958. Research assoc. Kyoto U., 1959-62; instr. biochemistry Nagoya City U., 1962; research assoc. Yale U., 1962-66; asst. prof. biochemistry Vanderbilt U., Nashville, 1966-69, asso. prof., 1969-75, prof., 1975—; dir. Vanderbilt U. (Hypertension Center), 1979—; mem. cardiovascular and renal disease study sect. NIH, 1976-80, cardiovascular rev. com., 1984-87. Contbr. over 200 articles and revs. to sci. jours., chpts. to books. Recipient Ciba award Am. Heart Assn., 1985. Mem. Am. Soc. Biol. Chemists, Endocrine Soc., Am. Heart Assn., Am. Chem. Soc., Soc. for Neurosci., Internat. Soc. Hypertension, Am. Soc. Cell Biology. Current Work: Biochemistry of high blood pressure; renin, angiotensin, cell biology. Subspecialties: Biochemistry (medicine); Cell biology (medicine). Home: 2029 Kingsbury Dr Nashville TN 37215 Office: Dept Biochemistry Vanderbilt U Nashville TN 37232

INCE, LAURENCE PETER, psychologist; b. N.Y.C., June 29, 1937; s. Eugene and Ernestine (Goldstein) I.; m. Mariene Sandra Rosenberg, Aug. 3, 1963; children: Valerie, Elizabeth. B.A., Hobart Coll., 1959; M.S., L.I.U., 1961; Ph.D., Fla. State U., 1965. Cert. psychologist, N.Y. State. Sr. psychologist N.Y.U. Med. Center, Goldwater Meml. Hosp., 1966-79, now supr. psychology, dir. psychophysiology and biofeedback lab.; dir. Center for Learning Disabilities, N.Y.C.; adj. prof. psychology Queens Coll., CUNY, N.Y.C., 1968-75. Contbr. articles to profl. publs. Fellow Am. Psychol. Assn.; mem. Am. Congress Rehab. Medicine, Biofeedback Soc. Am. Current Work: Biofeedback, spinal cord functioning. Subspecialties: Behavioral psychology; Physiological psychology. Home: 295 Winthrop Rd Teaneck NJ 07666 Office: Psychology Service Goldwater Meml Hosp Roosevelt Island NY 10044

INCROPERA, FRANK PAUL, engineering educator; researcher; b. Lawrence, Mass., May 12, 1939; s. James Frank and Anna Laura (Leone) I.; m. Andrea Jeanne Eastman, Sept. 2, 1960; children—Terri Ann, Donna Renee, Shaunna Jeanne. B.S., MIT, 1961; M.S., Stanford U., 1962, Ph.D., 1966. Heat transfer engr. Lockheed Missiles and Space, Sunnyvale, Calif., 1962-64; prof. Purdue U., West Lafayette, Ind., 1966—; cons. in field. Author: Molecular Structure and Thermodynamics, 1974; Fundamentals of Heat Transfer, 1981; Fundamentals of Heat and Mass Transfer, 1985; Introduction to Heat Transfer, 1985. Recipient Andrei Potter award Purdue U., 1973, Solberg award, 1973, 77. Fellow ASME; mem. Am. Soc. Engring. Edn. (Ralph Coats Roe award 1982, George Westinghouse award 1983). Current work: Mixed convection and radiation transfer; double diffusive convection; microelectronic cooling; applications of heat transfer to materials processing and behavior. Subspecialty: Mechanical engineering. Home: 5422 Hillside Ln West Lafayette IN 47906 Office: Sch Mech Engring Purdue U West Lafayette IN 47907

INFANGER, ANN, geneticist, biologist, educator; b. Newark, Dec. 20, 1933; d. Adolph Omega and Louise Elizabeth Catherine (Stuerm) I. B.A., Seton Hill Coll., 1955; Ph.D., Cornell U., 1963. Joined Sisters of Charity of Seton Hill, Roman Catholic Ch., 1956; mem. faculty Seton Hill Coll., Greensburg, Pa., 1958—, prof. biology, 1972—. NIH grantee, 1963-69; NSF grantee, 1969-73.

Mem. Genetics Soc. Am., AAAS, Sigma Xi. Current Work: Mitochondrial genetics of Neurospora; analysis of DNA of mitochondria of mutant Neurospora. Subspecialty: Genetics and genetic engineering (biology). Home and Office: Seton Hill Coll Greensburg PA 15601

INGHAM, ROBERT KELLY, organic chemistry educator; b. Bristol, Va., Sept. 26, 1926; s. James D. and Curtis B. (Bonham) I.; m. Ruth S. Torbett, Dec. 26, 1952. B.A., King Coll., 1947; Ph.D., Iowa State U., 1952. Asst. prof. Ohio U., Athens, 1953-57, assoc. prof., 1957-63, prof. organic chemistry, 1963—. Author: Organotin Compounds, 1962. Sect. editor Chem. Abstracts, 1968—. Served with USAAF, 1945. Grantee NSF, Dept. Army, Research Corp., Fellow Royal Soc. Chemistry; mem. Am. Chem. Soc. (local sect. officer). Current work: Organometallic compounds, hetarynes. Subspecialties: Organic chemistry; Organometallics. Home: 22 Northwood Dr Athens OH 45701 Office: Dept Chemistry Ohio U Athens OH 45701

INGLE, WILLIAM MARTELL, chemist; b. Bondurant, Iowa, July 12, 1941; s. Robert Thomas and Marie (Hayden) I.; divorced. B.S. in Chemistry, San Diego State U., 1964, M.S. in Silicon Chemistry, 1966; Ph.D., U. Pa., 1973. Prin. investigator solar energy project Motorola, Inc., Phoenix, 1975-78, prin. staff scientist, 1983—; chmn. Motorola Sci. Adv. Bd. Assocs., 1983—. Contbr. articles to profl. jours. Patentee in field. Dan Noble fellow, 1984. Mem. Am. Chem. Soc. Club: Elite Bonzo Party (pres. 1983—) (Phoenix). Current work: Investigating chemical vapor deposition of advanced metallic films for developing VLSI devices with higher speed and greater reliability. Subspecialties: Inorganic chemistry; Electronic materials. Home: 8161 N 1st Ave Phoenix AZ 85021

INGLETT, GEORGE EVERETT, biochemist, researcher; b. Waltonville, Ill., Aug. 3, 1928; s. Harry Everett and Bertha Pearl (Eater) I.; m. Marilyn Jean Fawley, June 12, 1954; children—George Dale, Carolyn Janeen. B.S., U. Ill.-Urbana, 1949; Ph.D., U. Iowa, Iowa City, 1952. Postdoctoral assoc. U. Ill.; 1952-54; officer USPHS, Bethesda, Md., 1954-56; research chemist CPC Internat., Argo, Ill., 1956-60; sr. food chemist Griffith Labs., Chgo., 1960-63; mgr. natural products Internat. Minerals & Chem., Northbrook, Ill., 1963-67; chief cereal scis. No. Regional Research Ctr., Peoria, Ill., 1967—. Editor books. Contbr. numerous articles to research publs. Patentee in field. Mem. Am. Chem. Soc. (award in agr. and food chemistry 1983, councilor 1981—), Inst. Food Technologists (award Phila. sect. 1981), Plant Growth Regulator Soc. Current work: Influence of bioregulators on composition and quality of cereal grains. Subspecialties: Food science and technology; Plant physiology (agriculture). Office: No Regional Research Ctr 1815 N University St Peoria IL 61604

INGOLD, KEITH USHERWOOD, educator, chemist; b. Leeds, Eng., May 31, 1929; s. Christopher Kelk and Edith (Usherwood) I.; m. Carmen Cairine Hodgkin, Apr. 7, 1956; children—Christopher Frank, John Hilary, Diana Hilda. B.Sc. with honors in Chemistry, Univ. Coll., London, 1949; D.Phil., Oxford (Eng.) U., 1951; D.Sci., U. Gualt, Ont., 1985. Postdoctoral fellow Nat. Research Council Can., 1951-53, research officer, 1955-77, asso. dir. chemistry, 1977—; postdoctoral fellow U. B.C., 1953-55; vis. scientist Chevron Research Co., Richmond, Calif., 1966, Univ. Coll., London, 1969, 72, Ford Motor Co., 1971, Esso Research and Engring. Co., Linden, N.J., 1973, U. Western Ont., 1975, Iowa State U., 1975, U. Bologna, Italy, 1975, U. Adelaide, Australia, 1979, U. Grenoble, France, 1983. Recipient Can. Silver Jubilee medal, 1977; Carnegie fellow U. St. Andrews, Scotland, 1977; vis. fellow Japan Soc. for Promotion Sci., 1982. Fellow Royal Soc. Can. (treas. 1979-82, Centennial medal 1982, Henry Marshall Tory medal 1985), Royal Soc. (London), Chem. Inst. Can. (medal 1981, Syntex award for phys. organic chemistry 1983); mem. Am. Chem. Soc. (award petroleum chemistry 1968), Chem. Soc. (award kinetics and mechanism 1978) (London). Research papers in free radical chemistry. Subspecialty: Physical chemistry. Home: Box 712 Rural Route 5 Ottawa ON Canada Office: Nat Research Council Can Ottawa ON Canada

INGRAHAM, JOHN LYMAN, bacteriology educator; b. Berkeley, Calif., Sept. 22, 1924; s. Dean Clement and Velma Etta (Lewis) I.; m. Marjorie Frances Mitchell, June 30, 1950; children: Catherine Ann, Thomas Mitchell. B.S., U. Calif.-Berkeley, 1947, Ph.D., 1951. With DuPont Co., Newark, Del., 1951-56, Western Regional Research Lab., U.S. Dept. Agr., Albany, Calif., 1956-58; prof. bacteriology U. Calif.-Davis, 1958—; cons. in field. Author: Microbial World, 1976, Introduction to the Microbial World, 1979; author: Growth of the Bacterial Cell, 1983; contbr. articles to profl. jours. Served with USNR, 1944-46. Guggenheim fellow, 1965-66; NIH grantee, 1962-81; NSF grantee, 1977-83; U.S. Dept. Agr. grantee, 1981-83. Mem Soc. Gen. Microbiology, Am. Soc. Microbiology, Genetics Soc. Am., AAAS, Spanish Microbiol. Soc. (hon.). Democrat. Current Work: Genetic study of bacteria. Subspecialties: Microbiology; Genetics and genetic engineering (biology). Office: Dept Bacteriology Univ Calif Davis CA 95616

INGRAM, ALVIN JOHN, surgeon; b. Jackson, Tenn., Mar. 31, 1914; s. Alvin Hill and Margaret (Gallagher) I.; m. Catherine Davis, Feb. 7, 1943; children: Mildred Ingram Dyer, Catherine Ingram Doyle, Peggy Ingram Tagg. B.S., U. Tenn., 1939, M.D., 1939, M.S. in Orthopaedic Surgery, 1947. Diplomate: Am. Bd. Orthopaedic Surgery (dir. 1972-78, v.p. 1976, pres. 1976-78; mem. residency rev. commn. orthopedic surgery 1972-76, chmn. 1975-76). Intern Univ. Hosp., Ann Arbor, Mich., 1939-40, asst. resident surgery, 1940-41; fellow orthopaedic surgery Campbell Clinic, Memphis, 1941-42, 46-47, mem. staff, 1947—, dep. chief of staff, 1967-69, chief of staff, 1970-78, chief of staff emeritus, 1979—, pvt. practice orthopaedic surgery, Memphis, 1947—; med. dir. Crippled Children's Hosp., 1948-61, chief staff, 1961-70; med. dir. Les Passes Cerebral Palsy Treatment Center, 1953-56; med. adv. com. Memphis and W. Tenn. chpt. Nat. Found. Infantile Paralysis, 1947-57, chmn., 1947-55; med. adv. com. Shrine Sch. Crippled Children, 1947-56; med. adv. bd. Variety Club Convalescent Hosp., 1952-56; asso. prof. orthopaedic surgery U. Tenn. Coll. Medicine, 1960-71, prof., chmn. dept., 1971-79, prof. emeritus, 1979—; mem. staff Bapt. Meml. Hosp., exec. com. med. staff, 1969-70, chmn. orthopaedic dept., 1970-74, pres. med. staff, 1973; mem. staff St. Joseph Hosp.; cons. orthopedics Richards Med. Co., 1983—; mem. staff LeBonheur Children's Hosp. (trustee 1968-71); cons. staff Meth. Hosp. Program; chmn. 2d Tenn. Conf. Handicapped Children, 1958; chmn. med. div. United Fund Shelby County, 1961, mem. budget com., 1963-65; dir. at large Nat. Assn. Blue Shield Plans, 1965-70; mem. Gov. Tenn. Adv. Bd. Crippled Children's Service, 1961-77, chmn., 1967-77; mem. exec. com. Am. Bd. Med. Specialties, 1980-83; mem. Tenn. Bd. Med. Examiners, 1981—. Contbr. to books. Bd. dirs. Front St. Theatre, Memphis, 1963-64. Served to maj. M.C., AUS, 1942-46. Mem. Am. Acad. Orthopaedic Surgeons (chmn. program com. 1954, 71, mem. manpower com. 1974-81), Am. Orthopaedic Assn. (chmn. program com., pres. 1973), Central Orthopaedic Club (charter), Tenn. Orthopaedic Soc. (pres. 1963-64), Willis C. Campbell Club (pres. 1967), Internat. Soc. Orthopaedics and Traumatology, Am. Acad. Cerebral Palsy (chmn. program com. 1955, publs. com. 1957, exec. com. 1958, pres. 1958-59), ACS (mem. grad. edn. com. 1974-76), AMA (ho. of dels. 1961-64, trustee 1964-70, sec. treas. 1968-70, sec. bd. trustees 1968-70), So. Med. Assn., Tenn. Med. Assn., Memphis and Shelby County Med. Soc. (pres. 1962, bd. censors 1963-65, ho. of dels. 1965), Nat. Acad. Sci. Inst. Medicine (council 1972-75), Memphis Ind. Practice Assn. (med. dir. 1983—), U.S. C. of C. Methodist (ofcl. bd. 1952— , vice chmn. ofcl. bd. 1965, 66, 69, 70, chmn. 1971-72, gen. chmn. every mem. canvass 1955-57, 63, pres. men's club 1958, sec. stewardship 1964-65). Current Work: Orthopedic surgery; health care delivery—medical administration. Subspecialties: Orthopedics; Health care delivery. Home: 190 Belle Meade Ln Memphis TN 38117 Office: Campbell Clinic 869 Madison Ave Memphis TN 38173

INGRAM, ALVIN RICHARD, polymer research consultant; b. Enfield, N.H., May 16, 1918; s. Irving Ira and Wilma Amalia (Sacher) I., m. Virginia Elizabeth Long, Oct. 31, 1942; 1 child, Carl Mason. B.S. in Chemistry, U. N.H., 1940; M.S. in Phys. Chemistry, Northeastern U., 1942; Ph.D. in Organic Chemistry, U. Pitts., 1955. Control chemist Gen. Chem. Def. Corp., Point Pleasant, W.Va., 1942-43; research group leader Johnson & Johnson Co., New Brunswick, N.J., 1943-48; Koppers Co. indsl. fellow Mellon Inst., 1948-53; various research and devel. mgmt. positions Koppers Co., Pitts., 1953-74; research group mgr. ARCO Chem. Co., Monroeville and Newtown Square, Pa., 1974-84, cons. 1984—; lectr. in field. Contbr. articles to profl. jours. and chpts. to books. Patentee in field. Troop com. chmn. Beaver council Boy Scouts Am., 1957-58, scoutmaster, 1959-60. Mem. Am. Chem. Soc., U. N.H. Alumni Assn. Western Pa. (pres. 1952-60), Sigma Xi, Phi Kappa Phi, Phi Lambda Upsilon, Alpha Chi Sigma. Republican. Presbyterian. Lodge: Rotary. Current work: Expandable polystyrene beads, synthesis and applications; suspension polymerization; styrene copolymers; flame retardants; blowing agents; plaster of Paris; orthopedic bandages. Subspecialties: Polymer chemistry; Organic chemistry. Home: 439 Cardinal Ln West Chester PA 19382 Office: ARCO Chem Co 3801 West Chester Pike Newton Square PA 19073

INGRAM, LONNIE O'NEAL, microbiologist, educator; b. S.C., Dec. 30, 1947; s. Thomas Belk and Jean (Weeks) I.; m. Vickie Webb, Oct. 18, 1968; children: Thomas O'Neal, Kenneth Paul, Erin Elizabeth. B.S. in Biology, U. S.C., Columbia, 1969; Ph.D. in Biol. Scis, U. Tex., Austin, 1971. NSF summer fellow U. Tex., 1969; postdoctoral researcher Oak Ridge Nat. Lab., 1971-72; asst. prof. microbiology and cell sci., immunology and med. microbiology U. Fla., 1972-76, assoc. prof., 1976-82, prof., 1982—; speaker in field; cons. to industry. Contbr. numerous articles to profl. publs. Recipient undergrad. research award NSF, 1969; Career Devel. award Nat. Inst. Alcohol Abuse and Alcoholism, 1979-83; grantee U. Fla., 1972, 76; grantee Am. Cancer Soc., 1973-75; grantee NSF, 1975-77, 82-84; grantee Distilled Spirits Council Am., 1975-76; grantee NIH, 1975, 78-82. Mem. AAAS, Am. Soc. Microbiology (O. B. Williams award Tex. br. 1970), Sigma Xi. Current Work: Biochemical determinents of alcohol tolerance in bacteria, yeast and mammalian cells; cloning of alcohol resistance genes. Subspecialties: Biomass (energy science and technology); Genetics and genetic engineering (biology).

INGRAM, ROY LEE, geology educator; b. Mamers, N.C., Mar. 12, 1921; s. Byron Perry and Berlena (McLean) I.; Jacqueline LaVon Sparks, June 5, 1944; children—Keith Sparks, Karen Ann. B.S., U. N.C., 1941; M.S., U. Okla., 1943; Ph.D., U. Wis.-Madison, 1948. Asst. prof. U. N.C., Chapel Hill, 1947-51, assoc. prof., 1951-57, prof. geology, 1957—, chmn. dept. geology, 1957-64, 74-79; numerous cons. projects; mem. N.C. Earth Resources Council, 1974-83. Contbr. articles to profl. jours. Served to capt. U.S. Army, 1943-46, ETO. Recipient Gov's. award Excellence in Research, 1981; grantee Nat. Research Found. Fellow Geol. Soc. Am. (chmn. S.E. sect. 1959); mem. Nat. Assn. Geology Tchrs. (treas. 1965-68), Elisha Mitchell Sci. Soc. (pres. 1956), Carolina Geol. Soc. (pres. 1959), Internat. Assn. Sedimentologists, Clay Minerals Soc., Am. Assn. Petroleum Geologists. Democrat. Methodist. Current work: Environments of deposition of sedimentary rocks and clay minerals; modern sediments of N.C. coast; coastal plain formations; peat deposits. Subspecialties: Sedimentology; Coastal zones. Home: 601 Oteys Rd Chapel Hill NC 27514 Office: U NC Dept Geology 029A Chapel Hill NC 27514

INHORN, STANLEY LEE, medical educator; b. Phila., Aug. 1, 1928; s. Charles and Nan (Ostrow) Einhorn; m. Shirley Gertrude Sherburne, Aug. 22, 1954; children—Lowell Frank, Marcia Claire, Roger Charles. B.S., Western Res. U., 1949; M.D., Columbia, 1953. Diplomate: Am. Bd. Pathology, Nat. Bd. Med. Examiners. Intern U. Wis. Hosp., Madison, 1953-54, resident, 1956-60; mem. faculty Med. Sch. U. Wis., Madison, 1959—, prof. pathology and preventive medicine, 1969—, chmn. dept. pathology, 1978-81; asst. dir. Wis. Lab. Hygiene, Madison, 1960-66, dir., 1966-79, med. dir., 1979—; cons. medicare div. HEW, 1968-69, 73-74, Center Disease Control, 1968-79. Violinist, Madison Symphony Orch., 1967-74. Bd. dirs. Wis. div. Am. Cancer Soc., Wis. Youth Symphony Orch., 1974—. Served with M.C. USNR, 1954-56. Mem. Am. Soc. Clin. Pathologists, Am. Pub. Health Assn., Am. Soc. Cytology. Research in cytogenetics of congenital anomalies, diagnostic lab. practice. Current Work: Laboratory method in clinical cytology and clinical and environmental cytogenetics. Subspecialties: Pathology (medicine); Cytology and histology. Home: 210 Ozark Trail Madison WI 53705

INMAN, BOBBY RAY, advanced computer technology company executive; b. Rhonesboro, Tex., Apr. 4, 1931; s. Herman H. and Mertie F. (Hinson) I.; m. Nancy Carolyn Russo, June 14, 1958; children: Thomas, William. B.A., U. Tex., 1950; grad., Nat. War Coll., 1972. Commd. ensign U.S. Navy, 1952, advanced through grades to adm., 1981, asst. naval attache, Stockholm, 1965-67, exec. asst., sr. aide to vice chief naval ops., Washington, 1972-73, asst. chief staff intelligence on staff comdr. in chief U.S. Pacific Fleet, 1973-74; dir. Naval intelligence Dept. Navy, Washington, 1974-76; vice dir. Def. Intelligence Agy., 1976-77; dir. Nat. Security Agy., Ft. Meade, Md., 1977-81; dep. dir. CIA, 1981-82; chmn., pres., chief exec. officer Microelectronics and Computer Tech. Corp., Austin, Tex., 1983—; mem. Nat. Acad. Scis. panel on impact of nat. security controls on internat. tech. transfer, 1985—. Decorated Def. D.S.M., Navy D.S.M., Legion of Merit, Def. Superior Service medal, Meritorious Service medal, Nat. Security medal, Joint Services Commendation medal. Subspecialty: Computer technology research and development management. Office: 9430 Research Blvd Austin TX 78759 Also: 1501 Wilson Blvd Arlington VA 22209

INMAN, FRANKLIN POPE, biochemistry educator, immunologist; b. Hamlet, N.C., Aug. 2, 1937; s. Franklin Pope and Aieleen (Shelton) I.; m. Barbara J. Bullock, Aug. 30, 1959; children—Jody Lin, James Walter. A.B., U. N.C., 1959, Ph.D., 1964. Asst. prof. microbiology and biochemistry U. Ga., Athens, 1966-70, assoc. prof. microbiology and biochemistry, 1970-75, prof. microbiology and biochemistry, 1975-77; prof., chmn. dept. biochemistry Quillen-Dishner Coll. Medicine, East Tenn. State U., Johnson City, 1977—; vis. lectr. immunology Harvard U., Boston, 1975-76; presenter seminars, symposia. Contbr. numerous articles to sci. publs. Pres. Athens PTA, 1968; bd. dirs. Forest Heights Pool, Athens, 1973-75. John M. Morehead scholar U. N.C., 1955-59; recipient M.G. Michael award for research, U. Ga., 1969; Am. Cancer Soc. scholar, 1976. Mem. Am. Assn. Immunologists (faculty immunology course 1975, 76, chmn. publicity and info., mem. com. on travel awards 1977), Southeastern Immunology Workshop (founder, chmn. 1969-70), Southeastern Immunology Conf. (bd. dirs. 1979—, chmn. 1985—), Am. Soc. Biol. Chemists, Am. Soc. Microbiology, Am. Chem. Soc., Assn. Med. Sch. Depts. Biochemistry, N.Y. Acad. Scis., Jaycees. Current work: Biochemical characterization of a suppressor of lymphocyte proliferation made by human tonsil cells; response to suppressor by mouse thymoma cells; control of lymphocyte proliferation. Subspecialties: Immunobiology and immunology; Biochemistry (biology). Office: Dept Biochemistry Quillen-Dishner Coll Medicine East Tenn State U PO Box 19930A Johnson City TN 37614

INNES, DAVID LYN, physiology educator; b. Cleve., Dec. 19, 1941; s. Harry Donald and Mildred Marie (Svozil) I.; m. Janet Lynne Koons, Sept. 5, 1964; children—Debra Lynn, Jonathan Lyn. B.A., Ohio Wesleyan U., 1964; M.S., U. Cin., 1966; Ph.D., Ohio State U., 1969. Instr. Ohio State U., Columbus, 1969-70; asst. prof. physiology Temple U., Phila., 1970-76, assoc. prof., 1976-80; prof. physiology Mercer U., Macon, Ga., 1980—. Contbr. articles to profl. jours. NIH grantee, 1978. Mem. Am. Physiol. Soc., Am. Gastroent. Soc., Am. Pharma. Assn., Fedn. Am. Socs. for Exptl. Biology, Soc. Tchrs. Family Medicine. Republican. Methodist. Current work: Gastric ulcer research; methods of induction and prevention, cure. Subspecialties: Physiology (medicine); Gastroenterology. Home: 1239 Craddock Way Macon GA 31210 Office: Mercer U Sch Medicine 1550 College St Macon GA 31207

INSEL, PAUL ANTHONY, internist; b. N.Y.C., Nov. 22, 1945; s. Herman Herbert and Ruth Leona (Friedman) I.; m. Louise Rausa, Dec. 29, 1977; children: Rachel Lauren, Sarah Rebecca Jo. Student, George Washington U., 1962-64; M.D., U. Mich., 1968. Diplomate: Am. Bd. Internal Medicine. Intern, resident in medicine Harvard Med. unit Boston City Hosp., 1968-70; clin. fellow in medicine Harvard Med. Sch., 1969-70; clin. assoc., med. officer Gerontology Research Ctr., NIH, Balt., 1970-74; research fellow U. Calif.-San Francisco, 1974-77, asst. prof. in residence, 1977-78; asst. prof. medicine U. Calif.-San Diego, 1978-81, assoc. prof., 1981—; cons. NIH, NSF, Am. Cancer Soc., VA; mem. pharmacology study sect. NIH, 1982-86; Investigator Am. Heart Assn., 1977-82. Contbr. articles to profl. jours. Served with USPHS, 1970-74. U.S. France Coop. Program in Cancer Research awardee, 1981; NSF grantee, 1977—; NIH grantee, 1980—; Am. Heart Assn. grantee, 1977-82; Am. Cancer Soc. grantee, 1982-84. Mem. AAAS, Am. Fedn. Clin. Research, Western Soc. Clin. Research, Am. Soc. Pharmacology and Exptl. Therapeutics, Am. Soc. Cell Biology, Endocrine Soc., Am. Soc. Clin. Investigation, Am. Soc. Biol. Chemists, Am. Heart Assn. (basic sci. and hypertension councils). Current Work: Mechanisms of catecholamine action and regulation of catecholamine receptors, alpha adrenergic receptors, beta-adrenergic receptors, cyclic AMP, Adenylate cyclase, cultured cells, human platelets. Subspecialties: Molecular pharmacology; Cell biology (medicine). Office: Dept Medicine M-013-H U Calif San Diego LaJolla CA 92093

INSLEY, ROBERT HITESHEW, engineer; b. Washington, June 20, 1923; s. Herbert and Margarette (Hiteshew) I.; m. Betty Hughes, May 15, 1947; children—Susan, Patricia, Donald. B.A., Hamilton Coll., 1945; postgrad. U. Colo., 1947-49; M.S., Pa. State U., 1952. Research asst. Pa. State U., University Park, 1949-52; petrographer Champion Spark Plug Co., Detroit, 1952-58, sr. research engr., 1958-68, mgr. ceramic research, 1968-73, asst. dir. research and engring., 1973-74, dir. research and devel., 1975—. Served to lt. (j.g.), USNR, 1942-45. Fellow Am. Ceramic Soc. (v.p. 1978-79, Purdy award 1966), ASTM (Award of Merit 1983); mem. Deutsche Keramische Gesellschaft, Mineralogical Soc. Am. Republican. Episcopalian. Current work: Petrography of ceramic raw materials and finished products; high temperature studies of oxides; semiconductors; glass to metal seals. Subspecialties: Ceramic engineering; Ceramics. Home: 855 Pine Hill Dr Bloomfield MI 48013 Office: Champion Spark Plug Co 20000 Conner Ave Detroit MI 48234

INTAGLIETTA, MARCOS, bioengineering educator; b. Buenos Aires, Argentina, Aug. 10, 1935; came to U.S., 1953, naturalized, 1969; s. Michele and Maria (Girola) I.; children—Monica, Michelle. B.S. in Mech. Engring., U. Calif.-Berkeley, 1957; M.S., Calif. Inst. Tech., 1958, Ph.D., 1963; Prof. (hon.), Chinese Acad. Med. Scis., Beijing, 1984. Postdoctoral research fellow Calif. Inst. Tech., Pasadena, 1963-66; asst. prof. U. Calif.-San Diego, La Jolla, 1966-71, assoc. prof., 1971-76, prof. bioengring., 1976—; sr. scientist Humboldt Found., Bonn, Fed. Republic Germany, 1982-83; Disting. lectr. Abbott Internat., Caracas, Venezuela, 1984. Fellow Swedish Med. Research Council, Stockholm, 1973-74, Hoffman La Roche Found., Basel, Switzerland, 1974. Mem. Internat. Inst. for Microcirculation (bd. dirs.), Microcirculation Soc. (pres. 1985-86). Current work: Microscopic blood vessel research, applications to clinical studies. Subspecialties: Biomedical engineering; Physiology (biology). Home: 5888 Ravenswood Rd La Jolla CA 92037 Office: U Calif-San Diego Dept Bioengring M-005 La Jolla CA 92093

INTERRANTE, LEONARD VINCENT, chemistry educator; b. Bklyn., Apr. 6, 1939; s. Leonard and Mildred (Esposito) I.; m. Vita Louise McFarland, Aug. 29, 1959; children—Victoria Lynn, John Alan. A.B. in Chemistry, U. Calif.-Riverside, 1960; Ph.D. in Inorganic Chemistry, U. Ill., 1964. Postdoctoral fellow U. Coll. London, Eng., 1963-64; asst. prof. dept. chemistry U. Calif., Berkeley, 1964-67; inorganic chemist dept. research and devel. Gen. Electric Corp., Schenectady, 1968-84; prof. chemistry Rensselaer Poly. Inst., Troy, N.Y., 1985—; chmn. 1st Gordon Research Conf. on Chemistry of Electronic Materials, 1985; lectr. in field. Editorial adv. bd. Inorganic Chemistry Jour., 1985—; mem. adv. bd. Inorganic Synthesis Inc., 1980—; Contbr. articles to profl. jours. Patentee in field. Fellow AAAS; mem. Am. Chem. Soc. (inorganic div. chmn. 1982), Chem. Soc. Gt. Britain. Democrat. Unitarian Universalist. Current work: Inorganic and coordination chemistry applied to generation of novel solid state materials; design and synthesis of organometallic precursors to solid state inorganic materials; electronic materials. Subspecialties: Inorganic chemistry; Solid state chemistry. Office: Rensselaer Poly Inst Troy NY 12180

INYANG, HILARY, soil engineer; b. Uyo, Nigeria, Nov. 8, 1959, came to U.S., 1982, naturalized; d. Inyang Amos and Abigail Inyang. B.Sc. in Geology, U. Calabar, Nigeria, 1981; B.S.C.E., N.D. State U., 1985. Youth corper Ondo State Govt., Nigeria, 1981-82; soil engr. Midwest Testing Lab., Fargo, N.D., 1984—. Author: Geology of NKO and Environs. Recipient Shell Brit. Petroleum award, Nigeria, 1978, Essay award North Central chpt. ASCE, 1984. Fellow Geol. Soc. London; mem. Geol. Soc. Am., Am. Soc. Engring. Edn., Am. Soc. Profl. Engrs., Assn. Engring. Geologists, Am. Am. Concrete Inst., Geol. Soc. Calabar (dir. socials 1979). Club: Soccer (Fargo). Current work: Design of transportation facilities; asphalts; highway geology; petrology. Subspecialties: Civil engineering; Petrology. Home: PO Box 661 Moorehead MN 56560

IONSON, JAMES, astrophysicist, government program executive. B.S. in Math., Physics, and Astronomy, U. Mich., 1972, M.S. in Physics, 1973, M.S. in Aerospace Engring., 1975; Ph.D. in Physics, U. Md., 1977. Physicist, NASA/Goddard Space Flight Ctr., 1978-84; dir. Strategic Def. Initiative, Innovative Sci. and Tech. Office, U.S. Dept. Def., Washington, 1984—; adj. prof. physics U. Md. Fellow, Smithsonian Astrophys. Obs.; recipient Sci. Distinction award Dutch Orgn. Pure Sci. Research; named Outstanding Young Scientist of 1983, Md. Acad. Sci. Subspecialty: Theoretical astrophysics. Office: Dept Defense Strategic Def Initiative Innovative Sci and Tech Office The Pentagon Washington DC 20301*

IPPEN, ERICH PETER, electrical engineering educator; b. Fountain Hill, Pa., Mar. 29, 1940; s. Arthur Thomas and Elisabeth Anne (Wagenplatz) I.; m. Dorothea Ellen Swansen, Sept. 24, 1966; children—Erich Peter, Jason Timothy. S.B., MIT, 1962; M.S., U. Calif.-Berkeley, 1965, Ph.D., 1968. Mem. tech. staff Bell Labs., Holmdel, N.J., 1968-80, cons., 1981—; vis. prof. MIT, Cambridge, 1977-78, prof. elec. engring., 1980—; cons. Allied Corp., Mount Bethel, N.J., 1982—. Contbr. articles to profl. jours. Patentee in field. Recipient Edward Longstreth medal Franklin Inst., 1982. Fellow Am. Acad. Arts and Scis., Optical Soc. Am. (R.W. Wood prize 1981), IEEE (Morris E. Leeds award 1983); mem. Am. Phys. Soc., Nat. Acad. Engring., Nat. Acad. Scis. Sigma Xi. Subspecialties: Ultrashort pulse lasers; Condensed matter physics. Office: MIT 77 Massachusetts Ave Cambridge MA 02139

IPPEN-IHLER, KARIN ANN, microbiologist, educator; b. Fountain Hill, Pa., Mar. 13, 1942; d. Arthur Thomas and Elisabeth Anne (Wagenplatz) I.; m. Garret Martin Ihler, May 2, 1970; children: Elisabeth Emma, Alexander Thomas. B.A., Wellesley Coll., 1963; Ph.D., U. Calif.-Berkeley, 1967. Postdoctoral fellow in microbiology and immunology Harvard Med. Sch., Boston, 1967-69; MRC molecular genetics unit U. Edinburgh, Scotland, 1969-70; asst. prof. biophysics and microbiology U. Pitts., 1970-76; assoc. prof. med. microbiology and immunology Tex. A&M U., College Station, 1977-84, prof., 1984—. Contbr. articles to profl. jours. Nat. Inst. Allergy and Infectious Disease grantee. Mem. AAAS, Am. Soc. Microbiology. Democrat. Current Work: Genetic and biochemical basis of transfer by conjugal plasmids, F factor, conjugation, F-pili, transfer operon, pili assembly. Subspecialties: Genetics and genetic engineering (biology); Microbiology. Home: 1115 Langford St College Station TX 77840 Office: Dept Med Microbiology and Immunolog Tex A&M U College Station TX 77843

IPRI, ALFRED CHARLES, engineer; b. Phila., Oct. 29, 1942; s. Alfred James and Mary (Biello) I.; m. Averil Crossley Vickers, July 30, 1977. B.S., Drexel Inst. Tech., 1965; M.S., U. Pa., 1966, Ph.D., 1972. Sr. mem. tech. staff RCA Corp., Princeton, N.J., 1967—; engring. asst. coop. assignments Phila. Electric Co., Phila., 1962-64; lab. instr. Drexel Inst. Tech., Phila., 1964-65, research asst., 1964-65; research asst. U. Pa., Phila., 1966-67. Contbr. articles to engring. jours. Patentee in field. NSF research grantee, 1965; Ford Found. fellow, 1966. Mem. IEEE, Nat. Soc. Profl. Engrs., Pa. Soc. of Profl. Engrs., Materials Research Soc., Soc. for Info. Display, Eta Kappa Nu. Current work: Electrical characterization of silicon on sapphire films, integrated circuit fabrication processes, device characterization, circuit design, digital systems. Subspecialties: Integrated circuits; Microelectronics. Office: RCA Labs David Sarnoff Research Ctr Princeton NJ 08540

IQBAL, ZAFAR, biochemist, researcher; b. Lucknow, India, July 12, 1946; came to U.S., 1972, naturalized, 1979; s. Shujaat Ali and Saleha (Begum) Siddiqi; m. Bernida Lucile Iqbal, Nov. 27, 1974; children: Jameel, Shareen. Ph.D., All-India Inst. Med. Scis., New Delhi, 1971. Asst. research officer All India Inst. Med. Scis., New Delhi, 1968-71; research assoc. physiology Ind. U., Indpls., 1972-77, asst. prof. biochemistry, med. biophysics, 1977-82; asst. prof. neurology Northwestern U. Sch. Medicine, Chgo., 1982—. Contbr. numerous articles to profl. jours. Council Sci. and Indsl. Research fellow, 1963-66; Juvenile Diabetes Found. fellow, 1981; Am. Cancer Soc. grantee, 1979; NSF grantee, 1980; Ind. Acad. Sci. research grantee, 1979; Ind. U. research grantee, 1978; Am. Diabetes Assn. grantee, 1980. Mem. Am. Physiol. Soc., Soc. Neurosci., Internat. Brain Research Orgn., Internat. Soc. Neurochemistry, Am. Soc. Neurochemistry, Biophys. Soc., Soc. Exptl. Biology and Medicine, N.Y. Acad. Sci., Ind. Acad. Sci. (chmn. cell biology 1982-83), Soc. Biol. Chemists, Indian Acad. Neurosci., Sigma Xi. Current Work: Neurochemistry, analysis of axoplasmic transport, role of calcium-binding protein in neuronal function, role of calcium and polyamines in signal transduction. Subspecialties: Biochemistry (medicine); Neurochemistry. Office: Medical Science Bldg VALMC 333 E Huron St Chicago IL 60611

IQBAL, ZAFAR MOHD, biochemist, pharmacologist, toxicologist, cancer researcher, consultant; b. Hyderabad, India, Dec. 12, 1938; came to U.S., 1965, naturalized, 1973; s. M.A. and Haleemunissa (Begum) Rahim. B.Sc., Osmania U., 1958, M.Sc., 1962; Ph.D., U. Md., 1970. Fogarty Internat. fellow Nat. Cancer Inst., Bethesda, Md., 1970-71, staff fellow, 1971-74; asst. prof. pharmacology Case Western Res. U., Cleve., 1974-76; assoc. dir. ERC programs in occupational toxicology U. Ill. Med. Center, Chgo., 1980-81, assoc. prof. microbiology, 1977-80, assoc. prof. occupational and environ. health, 1976—, assoc. prof. preventive medicine, 1982—, cons.; grant reviewer; lectr. continuing edn. Contbr. articles profl. jours. Council Sci. and Indsl. Research of India research fellow, 1963-65; Fogarty Internat. fellow NIH, 1970-71; NSF exchange scientist, 1981. Mem. Am. Assn. Cancer Research, Am. Pancreatic Assn., N.Y. Acad. Scis., Am. Chem. Soc., Ill. Cancer Council, AAUP, AAAS, Soc. Toxicology, Sigma Xi. Current Work: Cancer research, chemical and environmental/occupational carcinogenesis, drug metabolism, DNA damage/repair in cell culture and organs, toxicology (environmental and occupational), molecular and biochemical pharmacology, science reviewer federal, state and other public interest agencies, science consultant private and governmental agencies. Subspecialties: Biochemistry (medicine); Cancer research (medicine).

IRELAND, CHRIS MICHAEL, chemistry educator; b. San Diego, Nov. 22, 1951; s. George Richard and Thelma Esther (White) I.; m. Rhonda Jean Keaton Mallory, Dec. 17, 1971 (div. 1976); 1 child, Sean Michael; m. Robyn Lynn Kennedy, Jan. 7, 1978; children—David Michael, Kristen Michelle, Leilani Ann. B.A., U. Calif.-San Diego, La Jolla, 1973; Ph.D., Scripps Inst. Oceanography, 1977. Postdoctoral fellow U. Hawaii, Honolulu, 1978-80; asst. prof. U. Conn., Storrs, 1980-83, U. Utah, Salt Lake City, 1983—. Contbr. chpt. to book, articles to profl. jours. Grantee NIH, Petroleum Research Fund. Mem. Am. Chem. Soc., Am. Soc. Pharmacognsy. Democrat. Current work: Marine natural products chemistry. Subspecialty: Organic chemistry. Home: 2282 E Claybourne Ave Salt Lake City UT 84109 Office: U Utah Dept Medicinal Chemistry Salt Lake City UT 84112

IRELAND, JOHN RICHARD, mechanical and nuclear engineer; b. Hereford, Tex., June. 25, 1951; s. Richard and Patsy Ann (Slagle) I.; m. Judith Ann Shipman, Dec. 23, 1969; children: Travis Ryle, Shannon Marie, Jamie Lee. B.S. in Mech. Engring, N.Mex. State U., 1974; M.S. in Engring, U. Calif.-Berkeley, 1977. Program engr. Gen. Electric Co., San Jose, Calif., 1974-77; sect. leader Los Alamos Nat. Lab., 1977-80, project leader, 1980-82, assoc. group leader, 1982-83, project mgr. for nuclear saftey programs, 1983—; cons. Presdl. Commn. Accident Three Mile Island. Mem. Am. Nuclear Soc., ASME. Democrat. Methodist. Current Work: Briefly, I manage a large number of programs associated with nuclear reactor safety. Subspecialties: Nuclear engineering; Nuclear fission. Home: 329 Rover Blvd Los Alamos NM 87544 Office: Los Alamos Nat Lab PO Box 1663 MSK552 Los Alamos NM 87545

IRGOLIC, KURT JOHANN, chemist, educator; b. Hartberg, Austria, Sept. 28, 1938; s. Johann and Aloisia (Staude) I.; m. Gerlinde Zillich, Feb. 1, 1964; 1 dau., Birgit Petra. Cert. elem. edn., Tchrs. Tng. Coll., Graz, Austria, 1957; postgrad., Karl Franzens U., Graz, 1957-63, Ph.D. in Inorganic and Analytical Chemistry, 1964. Postdoctoral fellow Tex. A&M U., College Station, 1964-66, asst. prof., 1966-72, assoc. prof., 1972-77, prof. chemistry, 1977—, research coordinator, 1972-75; assoc. dir. Tex. A&M U. (Center Energy and Mineral Resources), 1975—; cons. to industry. Author: (with F. L. Kolar) Chemistry for Liberal Arts Majors, 1973, The Organic Chemistry of Tellurium, 1974, (with R. O. O'Connor) Fundamentals of Chemistry in the Laboratory, 1974, 2d edit., 1981, (with F. L. Kolar) Chemistry 106 Laboratory, 1975; (with L. Peck) Fundamentals of Chemistry in the Laboratory, 1984; (with L. Peck) Environmental Inorganic Chemistry, 1985; contbr. (with A.E. Martell) chpts. to books, articles to profl. jours. R.A. Welch Found. grantee, 1969—; NIH grantee, 1974-78; NSF grantee, 1985, 86; EPA grantee, 1978; NATO grantee, 1979, 80, 82; numerous others. Mem. Am. Chem. Soc., Sigma Xi, Phi Lambda Upsilon, Brazos Valley Gem and Mineral Soc. (pres. 1971). Roman Catholic. Current Work: Synthesis of organic compounds of arsenic, selenium, tellurium; biological transformation of arsenic, selenium compounds; trace element analysis; inductively coupled plasma emission spectrometry; element-specific detectors for liquid chromatography. Subspecialties: Inorganic chemistry; Analytical chemistry. Home: 1819 Hondo College Station TX 77840 Office: Tex A&M U College Station TX 77843

IRGON, JOSEPH, researcher, energy cons., research and devel. exec.; b. Polonnoe, Ukraine, Russia, Dec. 30, 1919; came to U.S., 1922, naturalized, 1942; s. Joseph and Ida (Galperin) I.; m. Thelma Pugach, Apr. 11, 1948; children: Deborah L., Judith M., Adam E. B.S. in Chem. Engring, Northeastern U., Boston, 1943; Ph.D. in Phys. Chemistry, M.I.T., 1948. Industry project dir. or dept. head Gen. Foods Corp., 1948-52, Reaction Motors, Inc., 1952-56; founder, tech. head Fulton-Irgon Corp., 1956-60; Fulton-Irgon div. and Hydro-Space div. Lithium Corp. Am., 1960-63, Proteus, Inc., 1963-69, Ocean Recovery Systems, Inc., 1969-73; dir. Joseph Irgon Assocs., Fairfield, N.J., 1973—; cons. dir. research Energy Tech., Inc. (div. Gen. Machine & Instrument Corp.), 1979—; energy and materials researcher; cons. Author: The Most Far-reaching: Supersonic Aircraft Escape Principle, 1954, First Handbook of Rocket Propellants, 1956, First Handbook of Ocean Materials, 1964, An Emergency Buoyancy System for Deep-diving Submarines, 1966. Mem. Am. Chem. Soc., ASME. Patentee in field. Current Work: New light-focusing principle and large-scale conversion of biomass, invention and preliminary research followed by cooperative programs with industry or govts. Subspecialties: Solar energy; Biomass (energy science and technology). Home and Office: 144 Emmans Rd Flanders NJ 07836

IRIGOYEN, OSCAR HORACIO, physician, researcher; b. Buenos Aires, Argentina, May 19, 1948; s. Juan Francisco and Celia Elda (Juarez) I.; m. Matilde Margarita Irigoyen, Jan. 8, 1972; children—Ernesto Tomas, Patricia Ines. B.S., Mil. Lyceum, Buenos Aires, 1965; M.D., U. Buenos Aires, 1972. Resident Med. Research Inst., Buenos Aires, 1972-76; rheumatology fellow Columbia U., N.Y.C., 1977-80, asst. prof. medicine, 1981-83; asst. prof. medicine Albert Einstein Coll. Medicine, Bronx, N.Y., 1983—. Contbr. articles to sci. jours. Mem. Am. Rheumatism Assn., N.Y. Rheumatism Assn., Am. Fedn. Clin. Research, Am. Assn. Immunologists. Current work: Mechanisms involved in the regulation of immune responses by T lymphocytes; lymphocyte function in patients with autoimmune diseases. Subspecialties: Immunobiology and immunology; Rheumatology. Office: Dept Medicine Albert Einstein Coll Medicine 1300 Morris Park Ave Bronx NY 10461

IRIMURA, TATSURO, tumor biology educator; b. Fujisawa, Japan, Feb. 2, 1949; came to U.S., 1980; s. Tatsuo and Mie (Matsui) I.; m. Kazuko Imbe, Sept. 28, 1974; children—Sanae, Natsumi, Mineyo. B.S., U. Tokyo, Japan, 1971, M.S., 1973, Ph.D., 1977. Research asst. U. Tokyo, Japan, 1974-80; postgrad. researcher III U. Calif.-Irvine, 1980; asst. prof. U. Tex. Cancer Ctr., Houston, Tex., 1980—. Contbr. articles to profl. jours. Recipient Cancer Inst. research grantee. Mem. Am. Assn. Cancer Research, N.Y. Acad. Sci., Tissue Culture Assn., Japanese Biochem. Soc., AAAS. Current work: Cell surface biochemistry of tumor metastasis. Structures and functions of glycocinjrgates involved in tumor cell host interaction. Subspecialties: Biochemistry (medicine); Cancer research (medicine). Home: 5205 Evergreen Bellaire TX 77401 Office: U Tex MD Anderson Hosp Dept Tumor Biology 6723 Bertner Houston TX 77030

IRVINE, CYNTHIA EMBERSON, astronomer; b. Washington, Aug. 14, 1948; d. Richard Maury and Virginia Burke Nicol Emberson; m. Nelson James Irvine, June 5, 1971; 2 daus., Alice Kathleen, Laura Elizabeth. B.A., Rice U., 1970; Ph.D. in Astronomy, Case Western Res. U., 1975. Research assoc. U.S. Naval Postgrad. Sch., Monterey, Calif., 1975-81; founding mem. Monterey Inst. Research in Astronomy, 1972, exec. dir., 1981-82, pres., 1982—; instr. Lyceum of Monterey. Contbr. articles to profl. jours. Mem. Astron. Soc. Pacific, Am. Astron. Soc., Optical Soc. Am. Subspecialty: Optical astronomy. Office: 900 Major Sherman Ln Monterey CA 93940

IRVINE, EILEEN M., research scientist, consultant; b. Albuquerque, Nov. 22, 1948; d. James and Mildred Patricia (Jones) I.; m. Gene Winkler, Oct. 10, 1982. B.A. with honors, U. Calif.-Santa Barbara, 1970, M.A. in Environ. Biology, 1972. Jr. math. analyst Dynalectron Corp., Point Mugu, Calif., 1972; assoc. engr. Raytheon Co., Santa Barbara, 1972-74; research scientist ERT, Inc., Westlake Village, Calif., 1977-81, cons., 1981—. Contbr. articles to profl. jours. Mem. Ecol. Soc. Am., Bot. Soc. Am., Mortar Board. Current Work: Computer simulations—environmental impact research with emphasis on mathematical modeling. Studies on toxics in food chain model, accidental spill of hazardous chemical models, air quality dispersion models. Subspecialties: Ecosystems analysis; Integrated systems modelling and engineering. Home and office: 3040 Gibralter Rd Santa Barbara CA 93105

IRVINE, WILLIAM MICHAEL, astronomy educator; b. Los Angeles, Aug. 31, 1936; s. S. Rodman and Mary E. (Dailey) I.; m. Susan W. Ross, June 10, 1959 (div. 1975); children—Douglas R., Kenneth D., Peter R.; m. Susan R. Leschine, Feb. 4, 1984; 1 son, Jeffrey M. B.A. summa cum laude, Pomona Coll., 1957; M.A. in Physics, Harvard U., 1959, Ph.D. in Physics, 1961. Assoc. prof. U. Mass., Amherst, 1966-68, chmn. Five Coll. astronomy dept., 1966-78, chmn. astronomy program, 1966-79, prof. astronomy, 1969—; vis. prof. Kanazawa Inst. Tech., Japan, summer 1977. Chalmers U. Tech.: acting scientific dir. Onsala Space Obs., Sweden, 1979-81; trustee NEROC, Cambridge, Mass., 1981—; dir. Five Coll. Radio Astronomy Obs., U. Mass., Amherst, 1985—. Contbr. articles to profl. jours. Assoc. editor Icarus, 1974—. Fellow AAAS, Am. Chem. Soc.; mem. Am. Astron. Soc., Am. Phys. Soc., Am. Geophys. Union, Internat. Astron. Union, Internat. Sci. Radio Union, Internat. Soc. Study Origins Life, Sigma Xi, Phi Beta Kappa. Current work: Physics and chemistry of interstellar matter; planetary science. Subspecialties: Radio and microwave astronomy; Planetary science. Office: GRC Tower B U Mass Amherst MA 01003

IRVING, DONALD J., university dean; b. Arlington, Mass., May 3, 1933; m. Jewel P. Irving; children: Kevin William, Todd Lawrence. B.A., Mass. Coll. Art, 1955; M.A., Columbia U. Tchrs. Coll., 1956, Ed.D., 1963. Tchr. art White Plains (N.Y.) High Sch., 1958-60; instr. art SUNY-Oneonta, 1960-62; prof. art, dean Moore Coll. Art, Phila., 1963-67; chmn. art dept., dir. Peabody Mus. Art, George Peabody Coll. Tchrs., Nashville, 1967-69; dir. Sch. Art Inst., Chgo., 1969-82; dean Faculty Fine Arts U. Ariz., Tucson, 1982—; mem. U.S. del. Conf. Nat. Soc. Edn. Through Art, Prague, Czechoslovakia, 1966; cons. ednl. TV series Art Now, WRCV-TV, Phila. Author: Sculpture Material and Process, 1970; contbr. articles in field to profl. jours. Mem. Nat. Assn. Schs. Art (treas., dir. 1975-77), Nat. Assn. Land Grant Colls. and Univs. Arts Commn., Union Ind. Colls. Art (dir. 1972-82, chmn. 1980-82), Nat. Council Art Adminstrs. (dir.), Fedn. Ind. Ill. Colls. and Univs. (dir.), Nat. Art Edn. Assn. (officer Eastern region 1966-68), Eastern Arts Assn. (council 1964-66, mgr. conv. 1959-64), Nat. Council Arts in Edn., Internat. Soc. Edn. Through Art, Coll. Art Assn., Phi Delta Kappa. Subspecialties: Planetary science; Radio and microwave astronomy. Home: 5810 E Paseo San Valentine Tucson AZ 85715 Office: Univ of Arizona Coll of Fine Arts Tucson AZ 85721

IRVING, EDWARD, geophysicist; b. Colne, Eng., May 27, 1927; s. George Edward and Nellie (Petty) I.; m. Sheila Ann Irwin, Sept. 23, 1957; children: Kathryn Jean, Susan Patricia, Martin Edward, George Andrew. B.A., Cambridge (Eng.) U., 1950, M.A., 1957, Sc.D., 1965; D.Sc. (hon.), Carleton U., 1979. Research fellow Australian Nat. U., Canberra, 1954-57, fellow, 1957-59, sr. fellow, 1959-64; sci. officer Can. Dept. Mines and Tech. Surveys, Ottawa, Ont., 1964-66; prof. geophysics U. Leeds, Eng., 1966-67; research scientist Can. Dept. Energy Mines and Resources, Ottawa, 1967-81, Sidney, B.C., 1981—; adj. prof. geology Carleton U., Ottawa. Author: Paleomagnetism, 1964; asso. editor: Tectonphysics, Physics of Earth and Planetary Interiors; contbr. articles on paleomagnetism and related geol. topics to profl. publs. Served with Brit. Army, 1945-48. Recipient Chestien Mica Gondwana medal Mining, Geol. and Metall. Inst. India, 1965. Fellow Royal Soc. Can., Royal Soc. (London), Am. Geophys. Union (Walter H. Bucher medal 1979), Royal Astron. Soc. (U.K.), Geol. Soc. Am., Geol. Assn. Can. (Logan medal 1975). Mem. United Ch. Can. Current Work: Paleomagnetic studies in Canadian Cordillera, the Canadian shield and in Arctic Islands to determine their tectonic history. Subspecialties: Geophysics; Tectonics. Office: Pacific Geosci Ctr PO Box 6000 Sidney BC V8L 4B2 Canada

IRWIN, GEORGE RANKIN, physicist, mechanical engineering educator; b. El Paso, Tex., Feb. 26, 1907; s. William Rankin and Mary (Ross) I.; m. Georgia Shearer, June 10, 1933; children: Joseph Ross, Mary Susan Irwin Gillett, Sarah Belle Irwin Lofgren, John Shearer. A.B., Knox Coll., 1930; M.S., U. Ill., 1933, Ph.D., 1937; D.Eng. (hon.), Lehigh U., 1977. Asso. prof. physics Knox Coll., 1935-36; fellow physics U. Ill., 1936-37; physicist U.S. Naval Research Lab., 1937-67; prof. mechanics Lehigh U., 1967-72; prof. mech. engring. U. Md., 1972—; vis. prof. U. Ill., 1961, 70; hon. lectr. Internat. Congress on Fracture, 1981. Contbr. articles to profl. jours. Recipient Navy Disting. Civilian Service award, 1947; Knox Coll. Alumni Assn. Achievement award, 1949; Navy Conrad award, 1969; Grand medal French Metall. Soc., 1976; Clamer award Franklin Inst., 1978; Md. Gov.'s citation, 1982. Fellow ASTM (Dudley medal 1960, hon. mem. 1974), Washington Acad. Sci.; mem. Washington Philos. Soc., Soc. Exptl. Stress Analysis (Murray lectr. 1973, Lazan award 1977), ASME (Thurston lectr. 1966, Nadai award 1977), Am. Soc. Metals (Sauveur award 1974), Nat. Acad. Engring. Pioneer devel. fracture mechanics. Current Work: Fracture mechanics applications to structural safety, materials research and engineering education. Subspecialties: Fracture mechanics; Materials (engineering). Home: 7306 Edmonston Ave College Park MD 20740

IRWIN, JOHN DAVID, electrical engineering educator, consultant; b. Mpls., Aug. 9, 1939; s. Arthur Fowle and Virginia (Farnham) I.; m. Patricia Edith Watson, Aug. 26, 1961; children—Geri Marie, John David Jr., Laura Lynne. B.E.E., Auburn U., 1961; M.S., U. Tenn., 1962, Ph.D., 1967. Registered profl. engr., Ala., Ga., Fla. Mem. tech. staff Bell Labs., Holmdel, N.J., 1967-68, supr., 1968-69; asst. prof. elec. engring. Auburn U., Ala., 1969-72, assoc. prof., 1972-76, prof., 1976—, head elec. engring. dept., 1973—; co-founder, dir. Insouth Microsystems, Auburn, 1978-83; pres. Southeastern Ctr. for Elec. Engring. Edn., St. Cloud, Fla., 1983-84. Author: Basic Engineering Circuit Analysis, 1984; (with others) An Introduction to Computer Logic, 1976; Industrial Noise and Vibration Control, 1979. Fellow IEEE (Centennial medal 1984); mem. Indsl. Electronics Soc. IEEE (pres. 1980-81, jour. editor 1982, certs. appreciation 1982, 83). Republican. Roman Catholic. Current work: Electrical engineering, computers, electronics. Subspecialties: Electrical engineering; Electronics. Home: 127 Eastwood St Auburn AL 36830 Office: Auburn U Auburn AL 36830

IRWIN, PETER LLOYD, plant physiologist; b. Dallas, July 13, 1952; s. Aubrey Donovan and Frances (Chaney) I.; m. Christine Mary Cayer, Aug. 20, 1979. B.A., U. Tex., 1974; M.S., Tex. A&M U., 1977; Ph.D., Mich. State U., 1981. Research plant physiologist U.S. Dept. Agr. Eastern Lab., Phila., 1981—. Contbr. articles to profl. jours. Mem. Am. Chem. Soc., Am. Biophys. Soc., N.Am. Phytochem. Soc., Phi Sigma, Gamma Sigma Delta. Episcopalian. Current work: Nuclear magnetic resonance and electron paramagnetic resonance, spectroscopic studies of plant polymer systems (cell wall, cutin, suberin). Subspecialties: Nuclear magnetic resonance; Electron spin resonance. Home: 508 E Glenside Ave Wyncote PA 19095 Office: Eastern Regional Research Ctr US Dept Agr 600 E Mermaid Ln Philadelphia PA 19118

IRWINSKY, LARRY DON, mathematician; b. Anadarko, Okla., Oct. 15, 1954; s. Jerry Martin and Leta Faye (Ross) I. B.A. in Math., U. Okla., 1976, M.S. in Computer Sci., 1978. Supr. math. lab. South Oklahoma City Jr. Coll., 1976-77; tech. programmer Kerr-McGee Corp., Oklahoma City, 1977-78, mgmt. sci. analyst I, 1978-80, mgmt. sci. analyst II, 1980-84, mgmt. sci. specialist, 1984—. U. Okla. scholar, 1972; Reeves scholar, 1976. Mem. Soc. for Indsl. and Applied Math., Phi Beta Kappa, Pi Mu Epsilon. Current work: Application of simulation, linear and integer programming to surface and underground coal mines for facilities planning, product blending and loading, mine plan optimization, math modelling of offshore drilling rigs to examine stability and analyze mooring systems. Subspecialties: Applied mathematics; Operations research (mathematics). Home: 2129 SW 78th St Oklahoma City OK 73159 Office: Kerr-McGee Corp PO Box 25861 Oklahoma City OK 73125

ISAACSON, ROBERT LEE, psychologist, research scientist, center administrator, educator; b. Mich., Sept. 26, 1928; s. Emil Alfred and Evelyn Edna (Johnson) I.; m. Susan Doherty, Aug. 1, 1956; m. Ann W. Braden, Dec. 31, 1974; children: Gunnar, Lars, Mary Ingrid, Mary Christina. A.B., U. Mich., 1950, M.S., 1954, Ph.D., 1958. Asst. prof. psychology U. Mich., 1958-63, assoc. prof., 1963-67, prof., 1967-68, U. Fla., 1968-76, grad. research prof., 1976-78; Disting. prof. psychology SUNY, Binghamton, 1978—; dir. SUNY (Center for Neurobehavioral Scis.), 1978—. Author: books, the most recent being The Limbic System, 1974, 2d edit., 1982; (with N. E. Spear) The Expression of Knowledge, 1982; The Hippocampus, Vols. III and IV, 1986; contbr. numerous articles to profl. publs. Pres. Alachua County (Fla.) Assn. Retarded Children, 1970-72; mem. Fla. Gov.'s Blue Ribbon Com. for Mental Retardation, 1974. Served to lt. USN, 1950-53. NSF and NIH awardee. Fellow Am. Psychol. Assn., AAAS, Am. Physiol. Soc., Soc. Neurosci., Internat. Brain Research Orgn., Sigma Xi. Current work: Limbic system of brain; recovery from brain damage; neuropeptides and behavior. Subspecialty: Psychobiology. Office: Dept Psychology SUNY Binghamton NY 13901

ISACHSEN, YNGVAR WILLIAM, research geologist, geology educator; b. Oslo, Mar. 16, 1920; came to U.S. 1925; naturalized, 1944; s. Nils and Katrine Elizabeth (Jensen) I.; m. Anastasia Mary Keefe, Apr. 24, 1944; children—Eric John, Paul Nils, Clark Edward. B.A., Syracuse U., 1942; M.A., Washington U., St. Louis, 1949; Ph.D., Cornell U., 1953. Instr. Lafayette Coll. Easton, Pa., 1949-51; dist. geologist AEC, Grand Junction, Colo., 1953-57; assoc. prof. SUNY-Plattsburgh, 1957-58; adj. prof. geology Rensselaer Poly. Inst., Troy, N.Y., 1963—; prin. scientist N.Y. State Geol. Survey, Albany, 1958—. Author (with others:) Stratigraphy and Structural Geology of the Adirondack Mountains, New York, 1984; Geologic Map of New York, 1971. Editor/author: Origin of Anorthosite and Related Rocks, 1968. Contbr. articles to profl. jours. Campaign worker Citizens United Reform Effort, Albany, 1962; elections insp. Albany County, 1965. Recipient photog. interpretation award Am. Assn. Photogrammetry, 1974. Fellow Geol. Soc. Am. (chmn. N.E. sect. 1979-80), AAAS; mem. Am. Geophys. Union, Internat. Basement Tectonics Assn. (chmn. 1976-78, chief trustee 1983-85). Current work: Tectonic analysis of Adirondack mylonite zones; Paleostress history of Adirondacks using dike orientations and K/Ar ages; Adirondack stromatolites. Subspecialties: Tectonics; Petrology. Home: 13 Maywood Rd Delmar NY 12054 Office: NY State Geol Survey Cultural Education Ctr Albany NY 12230

ISAKOFF, SHELDON ERWIN, chemical engineer; b. Bklyn., May 25, 1925; s. Harry and Rebecca I.; m. Anita Ginsburg, Aug. 18, 1946; 1 son, Peter D. B.S., Columbia U., 1945, M.S., 1947, Ph.D., 1952. Guest fellow Brookhaven Nat. Lab., Upton, N.Y., 1949-50; with E.I. duPont de Nemours & Co., Inc., Wilmington, Del., 1951—, dir. engring. research and devel., 1975—; mem. Nat. Materials Adv. Bd., 1980-82. Served with USNR, 1943-46. Fellow Am. Inst. Chem. Engrs. (past dir., Founders award 1980, Inst. lectr. 1984), AAAS; mem. Am. Chem. Soc., Nat. Acad. Engring., Sigma Xi, Tau Beta Pi, Phi Lambda Upsilon. Subspecialty: Chemical engineering. Address: RD 1 Box 361 Chadds Ford PA 19317

ISHII, THOMAS KORYU, electrical engineering educator; b. Tokyo, Mar. 18, 1927; came to U.S., 1956, naturalized, 1963; s. Yoshitada and Taka (Furukawa) I.; m. Eiko Bernadette Ishida, Nov. 29, 1958; children—Mutsumi Michael, Naomi Bernadette, Meguni Margaret, Mayumi Mary. B.S., Nihon U., 1950; M.S., U. Wis., 1957, Ph.D., 1959; D.Eng., 1961. Registered profl. engr., Wis. Instr. Nihon U., Tokyo, 1950-56; research asst. U. Wis.-Madison, 1956-59; faculty Marquette U., Milw., 1959—, prof. elec. engring., 1964—, dir. Microwave Research Lab., 1959—. Author: Microwave Engineering, 1966; (with E.C. Okress) Microwave Power Engineering, 1968; Maser and Laser Engineering, 1980; contbr. articles to profl. jours. Mem. Nat. Soc. Profl. Engrs., IEEE, Am. Soc. Engring. Edn., Sigma Xi, Tau Beta Pi, Eta Kappa Nu. Roman Catholic. Current work: Microwaves, microwave communications, microwave navigations, microwave applications, radio frequency applications. Subspecialties: Electronics; Electrical engineering. Home: 6601 W Carolann Dr Brown Deer WI 53223 Office: Marquette U Dept Elec Engring and Computer Sci 1515 W Wisconsin Ave Milwaukee WI 53233

ISLAM, MUHAMMAD AZADUL, physicist, educator; b. Bogra, Bangladesh, Dec. 23, 1951; s. Muhammad Mohsin and Amena (Khatun) Ali; m. Forhana Begum, July 23, 1978; 1 child, Muhammad Fahd Islam. Came to U.S., 1975. B.Sc., Dhaka U., 1974; M.S., U. Ala., 1977; M.Phil., Columbia U., 1979, Ph.D., 1981. Research assoc. Joint Inst. Lab. Astrophysics, Boulder, Colo., 1981-83; asst. prof. physics San Diego State U., 1983—. Columbia U. faculty fellow, 1977-79; Nat. merit and talent scholar Bd. Edn. Bangladesh, 1969-74. Current work: Atomic and molecular physics; gaseous electronics; lasers, optics, solid state physics. Subspecialty: Atomic and molecular physics. Office: Dept Physics San Diego State U San Diego CA 92182

ISOM, GARY EUGENE, toxicology educator; b. Twin Falls, Idaho, June 21, 1946; s. Junior H. and Louise V. (Garey) I.; m. Sharon J. Hanselman, July 6, 1968; children—Randy E., Jeff A., Christia M. B.S. in Pharmacy, Idaho State U., 1969; Ph.D. in Pharmacology, Wash. State U., 1973. Assoc. prof. toxicology Purdue U., West Lafayette, Ind., 1980—, also asst. dir. div. sponsored programs. Contbr. articles to sci. jours. NIH grantee, 1982—. Mem. Soc. Toxicology, Am. Soc. Pharmacology and Exptl. Therapeutics, Am. Assn. Colls. Pharmacy. Current work: Neurotoxicology, toxicodynamics of cyanide, receptor pharmacology, opiate receptor mechanisms. Subspecialties: Toxicology (medicine); Pharmacology. Home: 1406 Meadowbrook Ct Lafayette IN 47905 Office: Dept Pharmacology-Toxicology Purdue U West Lafayette IN 47907

ISRAEL, HERBERT WILLIAM, botanist, educator; s. Elmer William and Mildred Elsa (Koepp) I.; m. Ruth Mary Goetz., June 20, 1953; children: Lynn M. Israel Walter, Carla A., Willaim J. B.S. in Elem. Edn, Concordia Tchrs. Coll., 1953; postgrad., Northwestern U., 1951-53, U. Chgo., 1954-57; M.S. in Botany-Zoology, U. Wis., 1960; Ph.D. in Botany, U. Fla., 1962. Registered referee Am. Jour. Botany, Nature, Protoplasma, Sci., Virology. Chmn. dept. sci. Luther High Sch. South Chicago, 1953-60; NSF fellow U. Wis.-Madison, 1959-60; NDEA fellow, Turtox scholar, grad. teaching research asst. dept. botany U. Fla., Gainesville, 1960-62, research assoc., 1963; NIH vis. postdoctoral fellow dept. botany Cornell U., Ithaca, N.Y., 1963-64, research assoc. lab. cell physiology, growth and devel., 1964-69, sr. research assoc., 1969-72, sr. research assoc. dept. plant pathology, 1972—; mem. SEM policy com., 1977—; lectr. in field. Contbr. numerous articles on botany to profl. jours.; assoc. editor: Phytopathology; editorial adv. bd.: Protoplasma, 1973-81. Baseball coach Kiwanis, 1975-80. Mem. AAAS, Am. Inst. Biol. Scis., Am. Phytopath. Soc. (disease and pathogen physiology com. 1974-77, editorial bd. 1981—). Republican. Lutheran. Club: Finger Lakes Cycling (Ithaca) (treas.). Current Work: Plant cell biology, plant pathology. Subspecialties: Plant cell and tissue culture; Plant pathology. Home: 954 Snyder Hill Rd Ithaca NY 14850 Office: 303 Plant Sci Bldg Cornell U Ithaca NY 14853

ISRAEL, WERNER, physics educator; b. Berlin, Oct. 4, 1931; s. Arthur and Marie (Kappauf) I.; m. Inge Margulies, Jan. 26, 1958; 1 son, Mark Abraham. B.Sc., U. Cape Town, 1951, M.Sc., 1954; Ph.D., Trinity Coll., Dublin, 1960. Asst. prof. physics U. Alta., 1958-68, prof., 1968—; Sherman Fairchild Disting. scholar Calif. Inst. Tech., 1974-75; mem. Commn. Math. Physics, Internat. Union Pure and Applied Physics. vis. prof. Dublin Inst. Advanced Studies, 1966-68, U. Cambridge, 1975-76, Institut Henri Poincare, 1976-77, U. Berne, 1980. Editor: Relativity, Astrophysics and Cosmology, 1973; co-editor: General Relativity, An Einstein Centenary Survey, 1979. Recipient Izaak Walton Killam Meml. Prize, 1984. Fellow Royal Soc. Can.; mem. Internat. Aston. Union, Can. Assn. Physicists (medal of Achievement in Physics 1981), Internat. Soc. Gen. Relativity and Gravitation. Jewish. Current work: Relativistic statistics physics; cosmology; cosmic Censorship. Subspecialties: Relativity and gravitation; Theoretical physics. Office: Physics Dept U Alberta Edmonton AB T6G 2J1 Canada

ISSELBACHER, KURT JULIUS, educator, physician; b. Wirges, Germany, Sept. 12, 1925; came to U.S., 1936, naturalized, 1945; s. Albert and Flori (Strauss) I.; m. Rhoda Solin, June 22, 1955; children: Lisa, Karen, Jody, Eric. A.B., Harvard U., 1946, M.D. cum laude, 1950. Intern, then resident Mass. Gen. Hosp., Boston, 1950-53; investigator NIH, 1953-56; chief gastrointestinal unit Mass. Gen. Hosp., 1957, chmn. com. research, 1967; prof. medicine Harvard Med. Sch., 1966—, chmn. exec. com. depts. medicine, 1968—, Mallinckrodt prof. medicine, 1972—, chmn. univ. cancer com., 1972—. Editor-in-chief: (Harrison) Principles of Internal Medicine, 1976. Fellow Am. Acad. Arts and Scis., ACP; mem. Nat. Acad. Scis., Assn. Am. Physicians (pres. 1977-78). Research in structure and function of intestinal cells, membrane changes in malignant cells and serologic tests for malignancy Research in structure and function of intestinal cells, membrane changes in malignant cells and serologic tests for malignancy. Current Work: Studies of membrane transport of sugars and amino acids in normal and malignant cells; intestinal cell structure and function, biosynthesis of membrane glycoproteins; viral hepatitis diagnosis and treatment. Monoclonal antibodies in the diagnosis and treatment of cancer. Subspecialties: Gastroenterology; Cell biology (medicine). Home: 20 Nobscot Rd Newton Center MA 02159 Office: Mass Gen Hosp Boston MA 02114

ITO, YOICHIRO, government research scientist, physician; b. Osaka, Japan, Dec. 22, 1928; came to U.S., 1968, naturalized, 1978; s. Taichi and Ai (Kubota) I.; m. Ryoko Tanioka, Dec. 23, 1963; children: Koichi, Shin. M.D., Osaka City U., 1958. Rotating intern U.S. Yokosuka (Japan) Naval Hosp., 1958-59; resident in pathology Cleve. Met. Gen. Hosp., 1959-61, Michael Reese Hosp., Chgo., 1961-63; instr. physiology Osaka City U. Med. Sch., 1963-68; vis.

scientist Nat. Heart, Lung and Blood Inst., NIH, Bethesda, Md., 1968-78, med. officer, 1978—. Mem. Japanese Am. Citizens League, Kenshinkai. Recipient 1st place award ann. sci. research presentation at Cleve. Met. Gen. Hosp., 1960, Tech. Excellence award for devel. blood cell separator, 1979; Fulbright exchange scholar, 1959-63; WHO Research Tavel Fund grantee Nat. Inst. Med. Research, London, 1968. Initiated and developed countercurrent chromatography; patentee coil planet centrifuge, rotating-seal-free flow-through centrifuge. Current Work: Innovation in separation science, including continuous development of countercurrent chromatography, cell separation methods. Subspecialties: Analytical chemistry; Chemical engineering. Office: 9000 Rockville Pike NIH Bldg 10 Room 5D-12 Bethesda MD 20205

IVERSON, GILBERT MICHAEL, immunobiologist, educator; b. San Diego, May 1, 1938; s. Gilbert and Julia Ann (Persons) I.; m. Nora Antonette Keolker, Apr. 20, 1968; children—Peter, Robert, Sven. B.A., San Jose State U., 1964; Ph.D., Nat. Inst. Med. Research, London, 1972. Fellow tumor immunology unit Imperial Cancer Research Fund, Univ. Coll., London, 1971-73; staff fellow cellular immunology sect. lab. microbiology and immunology Nat. Inst. Dental Research, Bethesda, Md., 1973-74; mem. acad. staff-research dept. genetics Stanford (Calif.) U. Sch. Medicine, 1974-78; research assoc. in pathology, lectr. biology Yale U., New Haven, 1978-80, sr. assoc. lab. cellular immunology Howard Hughes Med. Inst., Sch. Medicine, 1980—. Contbr. articles to profl. jours. Bd. dirs. Madison (Conn.) ABC Program; bd. dirs. Youth Soccer, Madison. Served with USMC, 1956-58. Recipient Disting. Alumni award San Jose State U., 1982; NIH grantee. Mem. Am. Assn. Immunologists, Brit. Soc. Immunology, Brit. Transplantation Soc. Current Work: Understanding the molecular basis of immunoregulation. Subspecialties: Immunobiology and immunology; Immunocytochemistry. Home: 501 Opening Hill Rd Madison CT 06443 Office: 310 Cedar St New Haven CT 06510

IVERSON, MARK VERNON, physicist; b. Wisconsin Rapids, Wis., Aug. 17, 1953; s. Vernon C. and Mary Ellen (Grue) I.; m. Rachel Lynn Elson, May 26, 1975; 2 children. B.A., Luther Coll., 1975; Ph.D. with honors, Okla. State U., 1979. Research assoc. U. Kans., Lawrence, 1979-80; mem. tech. staff Sandia Nat. Labs., Albuquerque, 1980-84; tech. staff mem. Rockwell Internat., Cedar Rapids, Iowa, 1984—. Contbr. articles to profl. jours. Mem. ch. council St. Luke's Luth. Ch., Albuquerque, 1983, 84. Tech. Assn. Graphic Arts fellow 1977, 78. Mem. Am. Vacuum Soc., Optical Soc. Am., Am. Phys. Soc., Soc. Photometric and Illumination Engrs. Lutheran. Current work: Optical fiber sensors, quartz resonators, manganese phosphors, vacuum technology, radiation effects. Subspecialties: Condensed matter physics; Optical engineering. Home: 7213 Parkwood Ln NE Cedar Rapids IA 52404

IVIE, GLEN WAYNE, chemist; b. Corsicana, Tex., Oct. 24, 1944; s. Wilburn David and Vera Louise (Ward) I.; m. Sue Ann Sawyer, Sept. 10, 1966; children—Amy Elizabeth, Betsy Ann. B.Sc., Tex. A&M U., 1966, M.Sc., 1968; Ph.D., U. Calif-Berkeley, 1971. Research specialist U. Ky., Lexington, 1971-72; research chemist Agrl. Research Service, USDA, College Station, Tex., 1972-75, research leader, 1975—. Editor: Fate of Pesticides in Large Animals, 1977. Contbr. chpts. to books and articles to profl. jours. Fellow Am. Chem. Soc. (chmn. pesticide chemistry div. 1983, assoc. editor Jour. of Agrl. and Food Chemistry 1982—); mem. Assn. Ofcl. Analytical Chemists, Southwestern Assn. Toxicologists. Current work: Chemistry and metabolism of pesticides in food animals; chemistry of livestock plant poisons. Subspecialties: Toxicology (agriculture); Environmental chemistry. Home: 2007 Rockwood Dr Bryan TX 77801 Office: Agrl Research Service USDA PO Drawer GE College Station TX 77841

IVOSEVIC, STANLEY WAYNE, geologic consultant; b. Stowe Twp., Pa., Aug. 9, 1939; s. George Stanley and Jewell Diak (Czopko) I. B.A. in Biology, Lafayette Coll., 1961; M.S. in Geology, U. Nev., Reno, 1976. Lab. technician Nev. Bur. Mines, Reno, 1968-71; geologic field asst. U.S. Geol. Survey, Alaska, 1969; geologist Behre Dolbear & Co., Costa Rica, 1974-75, Freeport Exploration Co., Reno, 1975-76, Houston Oil & Minerals Corp., Denver, 1976-79; cons., geologist, Denver, 1979—. Author: Gold and Silver Handbook: On Geology, Exporation, Production, Economics of Large Tonnage, Low Grade Deposits, 1984. Served with U.S. Army, 1961-65; Vietnam. Decorated Bronze Star. Mem. AIME, Colo. Mining Assn. (dir. 1983—), Geol. Soc. Am., Soc. Econ. Geologists (assoc.), VFW. Current work: Discovery of commercial mineral deposits. Subspecialty: Geology. Address: 449 Wright St Suite 2 Denver CO 80228

IYENGAR, BHASHYAM SRINIVASA, chemist, educator; b. Tumkur, Mysore, India, May 3, 1939, came to U.S., 1971, naturalized, 1981; s. Srinivasa S. and Jayamma (Jayamma) I.; m. Leela Bhashyam. B. Sc., U. Mysore, 1958, M.Sc., 1966; Ph.D., U. Lowell, 1976. Sci. tchr. Vijaya High Sch., Mysore, 1959-64; lectr. chemistry JSS Coll., U. Mysore, 1966-71; teaching asst. in chemistry, U. Lowell, Mass., 1971-75; research assoc. U. Ariz., Tucson, 1976-81; asst. research prof., 1982-84, acad. prof., 1984—. Contbr. articles to profl. jours.; patentee cancer research. Mem. Am. Chem. Soc. (organic chemistry div.), Internat. Soc. Hetrocyclic Chemistry. Current work: Designing and synthesizing potential antitumor compounds and metal complexes of antitumor drugs and their biological activities. Subspecialties: Organic chemistry; Medicinal chemistry. Home: 3653 E 2nd St Apt 210 Tucson AZ 85716 Office: Dept Pharm Scis Coll Pharmacy U Ariz Tucson AZ 85721

IYENGAR, DORESWAMY RAGHAVACHAR, scientist, consultant, educator; b. Nanjangud, Mysore, India, July 3, 1930; came to U.S., 1959, naturalized, 1974; s. Raghavachar and Shallammal (Venkataswami) I.; m. Kowsalya Garudachar, May 27, 1966; children—Veena, Pramod. B.S. with honors, U. Mysore, 1951; M.S., U. Madras, 1954; Ph.D., U. Miami, 1962. Chartered chemist, London. Instr., univ. fellow U. Miami, Coral Gables, Fla., 1959-62; Dupont fellow, research prof. chemistry Lehigh U., Bethlehem, Pa., 1962-64, 1966-70; phys. scientist U.S. Army, Pittman Dunn Lab., Phila., 1964-66; staff scientist Sherwin Williams Co., Chgo., 1970-75; sr. staff scientist BASF Wyandotte Corp., Holland, Mich., 1975—; cons. Alexandria Research Corp., Va., 1965; internal cons., educator Chemetron Corp., Holland, Mich., 1975-80. Patentee in field. Contbr. articles to book and sci. jours. Recipient U.S. Army Commendation for research work, 1967; Fulbright grantee, 1959. Fellow Royal Soc. Chemistry, Tech. Surface Coatings, Oil and Color Chemists Assn., The Am. Inst. Chemists; mem. Am. Chem. Soc., Sigma Xi. Current work: Surface chemistry and technology of catalysts, semiconductors and pigments. Dispersions, emulsions and encapsulation techniques. Subspecialties: Surface chemistry; Catalysis chemistry. Home: 369 W 35th St Holland MI 49423 Office: BASF Wyandotte Corp 491 Columbia Ave Holland MI 49423

IZANT, ROBERT JAMES, JR., pediatric surgeon, medical educator; b. Cleve., Feb. 4, 1921; s. Robert James and Grace (Goulder) I.; m. Virginia Lincoln Root, Sept. 27, 1947; children—Jonathan G. II, Mary R., Timothy H. A.B., Amherst Coll., 1943; M.D., Western Res. U., 1946. Diplomate Am. Bd. Surgery; cert. in pediatric surgery. Intern, U. Hosps. Cleve., 1946-47, resident in gen. surgery, 1949-52; resident in pediatric surgery Children's Hosp. Med. Ctr., Boston, 1952-55; clin. instr. pediatric surgery Harvard U. Med. Sch., 1954-55; asst. prof. pediatric surgery Ohio State U. Coll. Medicine, Columbus, 1955-58; asst. surgeon U. Hosp., Children's Hosp., 1955-58; asst. prof. Western Res. U. Sch. Medicine, Cleve., 1958-65, assoc. prof. Case Western Res. U., 1965-71, prof. pediatric surgery and pediatrics, 1971—; dir. div. pediatric surgery Rainbow Babies and Children's Hosp.; assoc. surgeon U. Hosps., 1958—; asst. surgeon Cleve. Met. Gen. Hosp., 1958—. Author: The Surgical Neonate - Evaluation and Care, 1978; also numerous articles. Editorial, adv. bds. Jour. Pediatric Surgery, 1970-77. Mem. med. adv. bd., exec. com. Ohio State Services for Crippled Children's Program, 1957—, chmn. legis. com., 1965-68; trustee Children's Aid Soc., 1962-72, Cuyahoga County chpt. Am. Cancer Soc., 1972-80; mem. med. adv. bd. Nat. Found., 1965-74, Cystic Fibrosis Found., 1970-76; chmn. child care task force com. Welfare Fedn. Cleve., 1968. Served to lt. (j.g.) M.C., USNR, 1947-49. Recipient Fred Waring award Western Res. Acad., Hudson, Ohio, 1983. Mem. Am. Pediatric Surg. Assn. (a founder, bd. govs.), ACS, Am. Acad. Pediatrics (surg. fellow), Am. Assn. for Surgery of Trauma, Am. Trauma Soc., Am. Burn Soc., AMA, AAAS, Brit. Assn. Pediatric Surgeons, Central Surg. Assn., Cleve. Surg. Soc. (pres. 1971-72), Lilliputian Surg. Soc., Mid-West Pediatric Surgery Soc., Ohio Med. Assn., No. Ohio Pediatric Soc., Cleve. Acad. Medicine (bd. dirs., vice chmn. edn. com. 1971—, chmn. child safety com. 1965, mem. med.-legal com. 1972-74, chmn. profl. liability com. 1974-75), Cleve. Surg. Soc. (pres. 1971-72), Columbus Surg. Soc., Cleve. Med. Library Assn. (trustee Allen Meml. Library 1965-71), Soc. Sigma Xi, Alpha Omega Alpha, Nu Sigma Nu, Delta Kappa Epsilon. Democrat. Mem. Religious Soc. Friends. Current work: Member surgical steering committee of Children's Cancer Study Group; nat. Wilms' tumor study. Subspecialties: Surgery; Pediatrics. Office: Rainbow Babies and Children's Hosp 2101 Adelbert Rd Cleveland OH 44106

IZAWA, SEIKICHI, biology educator, plant physiologist; b. Yokohama, Japan, Sept. 28, 1926; came to U.S., 1963; s. Hiroshi and Shika (Oshige) I.; m. Toyoko Tsukada, Nov. 27, 1968; 1 dau., Eri. B.S., U. Tokyo, Japan, 1950, D.Sc., 1961. Asst. prof. Tokyo Inst. Tech., 1961-63; research assoc. Mich. State U., 1963-66; assoc. prof. Queen's U., Kingston, Ont., Can., 1966-68; assoc. prof. biology Mich. State U., 1970-74; prof. biology Wayne State U., Detroit, 1974—. Contbr. numerous articles to profl. jours.; mem. editorial bd.: Plant Physiology, 1981—, Plant and Cell Physiology, 1983—. C. F. Kettering Found. Internat. fellow, 1963-64; NSF Research grantee, 1968—; Japan Soc. Promotion of Disting. Visitor fellow, 1981. Mem. Am. Soc. Biol. Chemists, Am. Soc. Plant Physiologists, Am. Soc. Photobiologists. Current Work: Research activity centered on the biochemistry and physiology of plant chloroplasts related to the mechanisms of energy transduction and oxygen evolution. Subspecialty: Photosynthesis. Home: 16974 Lauderdale Dr Birmingham MI 48009 Office: Wayne State U Detroit MI 48202

IZZO, RALPH, physicist; b. N.Y.C., Oct. 20, 1957; s. Luigi and Angelina (Barone) I.; m. Karen Ann Danowski, July 14, 1984. B.S., Columbia U., 1978, M.S., 1979, Ph.D., 1981. Research physicist Princeton U. Plasma Physics Lab., N.J., 1981—; adj. prof. physics Trenton State Coll., 1982; research cons. Exxon Research & Engring., Linden, N.J., 1978; lectr. in field; mem. Princeton Plasma Lab. Adv. Com. Contbr. articles to profl. jours. Participant Scientists-Sci. Tchr. Interaction Project, N.J., 1981—. Am. Phys. Soc.-Congl. Sci. fellow, 1985; IEEE fellow, 1982; NSF fellow, 1979-81; Illig medal, Columbia U. Sch. Engring., 1978. Mem. Am. Phys. Soc., AAAS, Scientists Inst. for Pub. Info., Tau Beta Pi. Democrat. Roman Catholic. Current work: Theoretically model and analyze the behavior of fusion plasmas. Both ideal and resistive, nonlinear, 3D models are used. Subspecialties: Fusion; Plasma physics. Office: Princeton U Plasma Physics Lab PO Box 451 Princeton NJ 08544

JAANUS, SIRET DESIREE, pharmacologist, educator; b. Tallinn, Estonia, May 17, 1937; came to U.S., 1950; s. Richard and Hedda (Klaser) J.; m. Jaak Jurison. B.S., CCNY, 1960; M.A., Hunter Coll., 1966; Ph.D., SUNY-Bklyn., 1970. Asst. prof. SUNY-N.Y.C., 1971-73; assoc. prof. So. Calif. Coll. Optometry, Fullerton, 1973-83, prof. pharmacology, 1984—; clin. investigator Allergan Pharm., Irvine, Calif., 1974-75. Author, editor: Clinical Ocular Pharmacology, 1984. Recipient Paul Yarwood Meml. award Calif. Optometric Assn., 1979. Fellow Am. Acad. Optometry; mem. Am. Soc. Pharmacology and Exptl. Therapeutics, AAUW. Current work: Side effects of drugs; ocular pharmacology. Address: So Calif Coll Optometry 2001 Associated Rd Fullerton CA 92631

JABLONSKI, DANIEL GARY, physicist, researcher; b. Washington, Nov. 15, 1954; s. Frank Edward and Dorothy Elaine (Condor) J.; m. Elizabeth Jan Trimble, Oct. 2, 1982. B.S., MIT, 1976, M.S., 1977; Ph.D., Cambridge U., Eng., 1982. Coop. student Naval Surface Weapons Ctr., Silver Spring, Md., 1974-77; cons. Gen. Electric Co., Ltd., Wembly, Eng., 1978-80; research physicist Naval Surface Weapons Ctr., Silver Spring, 1981—. Patentee in field. Contbr. articles to profl. jours. Mem. IEEE (sr.), Am. Phys. Soc. Current work: Microwave applications of superconductivity; special purpose electronic and microwave systems. Subspecialties: Superconductors; Electronics. Home: 12220 Somersworth Dr Silver Spring MD 20902 Office: Naval Surface Weapons Ctr Code R43 Bldg 24-2 Silver Spring MD 20910

JABLONSKI, DAVID, paleontologist. Asst. prof. dept. ecology and evolutionary biology U. Ariz., Tucson. Subspecialty: Paleontology. Office: U Ariz Dept Ecology and Evolutionary Biology Tucson AZ 85721

JACKEL, LAWRENCE DAVID, physicist; b. N.Y.C., June 16, 1948; s. Melvin Ely and Gloria (Itzler) J.; m. Janet Lehr, June 29, 1969; children—David Aaron, Robert Abraham. B.A., Brandeis U., 1969; M.A., Cornell U., 1971, Ph.D., 1976. Mem. tech. staff AT&T Bell Labs., Holmdel, N.J., 1975-84, dept. head device structures research dept., 1984—. Contbr. articles on microsci. to profl. jours. Patentee in field. Mem. Am. Phys. Soc., IEEE. Current work: Fabrication and measurement of ultra-small electronic devices including silicon and III-IV transistors. Subspecialties: Condensed matter physics; Microelectronics. Office: 4D 433 AT&T Bell Labs Holmdel NJ 07733

JACKSON, BENJAMIN TAYLOR, physician, investigator; b. Jacksonville, Fla., Apr. 28, 1929; s. Julian Harold and Helen (Blasingame) J.; m. Jean Davis, June 18, 1953; children—Benjamin Taylor Jr., Jean Leigh, Kimberley Louise, Jillian Davis. M.D., Duke U., 1954; M.A. (hon.), Brown U., 1982. Diplomate Am. Bd. Surgery. Intern Duke Hosp., Durham, N.C., 1954-55; asst. resident in surgery U. Minn. Hosp., Mpls., 1957-58; resident, fellow in surgery Med. Coll. Va., Richmond, 1958-62, instr. in surgery, 1963-64; prof. surgery Boston U., 1975-80, Brown U., Providence, 1980—; asst. chief surg. service Boston VA Med. Ctr., 1974-80; vis. surgeon Univ. Hosp., Boston, 1975-80; chief surg. service Providence VA Med. Ctr., 1980—. Contbr. articles to profl. jours. Served to capt. USMC, 1955-57. Research fellow USPHS, 1958-61; advanced research fellow Am. Heart Assn., 1961-63; established investigator Am. Heart Assn., 1963-68; research grantee NIH, 1960-84. Fellow ACS; mem. Soc. Univ. Surgeons, Soc. Gynecologic Investigation, Am. Assn. Pathologists, New Eng. Surg. Soc. Methodist. Current work: Fetal cardiovascular and endocrine physiology, specific investigation of ontogeny of sympathoadrenal function; clinical surgery. Subspecialties: Developmental biology; Surgery. Home: 11 October Ln Weston MA 02193 Office: Providence VA Med Ctr Davis Park Providence RI 20908

JACKSON, DAVID STANLEY, healthcare company executive, biochemist; b. Manchester, Eng., Jan. 9, 1921; s. George and Alice Catherine (Fazackerley) J.; m. Hilda Mather, Dec. 20, 1947; children—David Nicholas, Cherry Ann; m. Dorothy Betty Fitch, June 24, 1978. B.Sc., U. Manchester, 1949, Ph.D., 1954. Research assoc. Harvard U. Med. Sch., Boston, 1957-59; assoc. prof. Oreg. U. Med. Sch. Portland, 1959-62, prof., 1962-65; chmn. dept., prof. biochemistry U. Manchester, 1965-82, prof. emeritus, 1982—; sr. research fellow Johnson & Johnson Products, New Brunswick, N.J., 1981—, cons., 1960-82; cons. India Govt. Fgn. Office, Madras, 1966, 72, Ethicon Inc., Somerville, N.J., 1958-65. Editor: Internat. Rev. of Connective Tissue Research, Vol. 5, 1972, Vol. 6, 1974, Vol. 7, 1976, Vol. 8, 1979, Vol. 9, 1981, Vol. 10, 1983. Contbr. numerous sci. articles to profl. jours. Served to flight lt. RAF, 1940-46. Grantee U.K. Sci. and Engring. Research Council, Manchester, 1965-82, NIH, Portland, 1959-65; B.M. Das Meml. lectr., Madras, 1972. Mem. Biochem. Soc. Gt. Britain, Am. Soc. Biol. Chemists, Heberden Soc. (U.K.). Current work: Use of growth and other factors to enhance would healing; inhibition of excessive fibrosis; use of biodegradable materials as delivery system for biological factors purposes. Subspecialties: Biochemistry (biology); Biomaterials. Office: Johnson & Johnson Products Inc (Research) U S 1 North Brunswick NJ 08902

JACKSON, DOUGLAS WEBSTER, ecologist, consultant; b. Houston, Sept. 5, 1949; s. James Lee and Ruby Mae (Dowell) J.; m. Catherine Ann Wagner, Mar. 6, 1976; 1 child, William Douglas. B.S. in Forestry, Stephen F. Austin U., 1975, M.S. in Biology, 1977. Grad. research asst. Stephen F. Austin U., Nacogdoches, Tex., 1975-77; research scientist S.W. Research Inst., Houston, 1977-79; biologist Falcon Research and Devel. Co., Albuquerque, 1979-80; ecologist Concepts Devel., Inc., Albuquerque, 1980-82; sr. ecologist, pres. Sci. Info. Mgmt., Albuquerque, 1982—. Contbr. articles to profl. jours. Advisor for election of Eli Chavez, Dist. 21, N.Mex., 1984. Mem. Health Physics Soc., Am. Ecol. Soc., Am. Soc. Limnology and Oceanography, Sigma Xi. Current work: Prediction of hazard to man and the environment posed by release of radioactivity into the marine environment. Subspecialties: Hazardous waste disposal; Information systems, storage, and retrieval (computer science). Home: 208 Madison NE Albuquerque NM 87108 Office: Sci Info Mgmt 428 Louisiana SE Suite A-3 Albuquerque NM 87108

JACKSON, GLEN LEON, electronic engineer, computer scientist; b. Ottumwa, Iowa, Oct. 3, 1946; s. James Leon and Evelyn Melosina (Hartwig) J.; m. Crisina Manlapaz Buan, Nov. 26, 1983; 1 child, Carrie Ann. B.S. in Physics, Iowa State U., 1966, M.S. in Physics, 1968; M.S. in Elec. Engring., U. Iowa, 1975. Elec. engr. Mare Island Naval Shipyard, Vallejo, Calif., 1980-84; electronic engr. McClellan AFB, Sacramento, 1984—. Republican candidate for Iowa Senate, 1974. Served to 1st lt. U.S. Army, 1977-80. Mem. IEEE, Sigma Xi (assoc.). Baptist. Current work: Process control firmware design; microprocessor assembly language programming. Subspecialties: Electronics; Software engineering. Home: 637 Wilson Ave Sacramento CA 95833 Office: Sacramento Air Logistics Ctr McClellan AFB CA 95652

JACKSON, HAROLD EDWARD, JR., nuclear physicist; b. Pitts., Jan. 5, 1933; s. Harold Edward and Theodora Dagmar (Johnson) J.; m. Sally Moseley, June 7, 1958; children—Mark Edward, Matthew Owen, Kimberly Lynn. A.B., Princeton U., 1954; Ph.D., Cornell U., 1959. Asst. physicist Argonne Nat. Lab; Ill., 1959-62, physicist, 1962-73, sr. physicist, 1973—, research project mgr., 1981-83, acting assoc. div. dir. physics div., 1973; vis. scientist Centre d'Etudes Nucleaires de Saclay, France, 1965-67, Accelerateur Lineaire de Saclay, 1975-76; mem. U.S. Nuclear Data Com., 1967-77, sec., 1972-73, chmn., 1973-74; U.S. rep. nuclear data com., Nuclear Energy Agy., 1972-77; chmn. LEP working group Los Alamos Meson Physics Facility, 1967-77; bd. dirs. LAMPF Users Group, 1979-83, chmn., 1982; mem. nat. adv. bd. U.S. Nat. Electron Accelerator Lab., 1983—; collaborateur etranger Institut de Recherche Fondamentale, Saclay, 1984—. Contbr. articles to profl. jours. Mem. Am. Phys. Soc. Current work: Experimental studies of nuclear structure with elementary particles, particle accelerator design, instrumentation and experimental technique in nuclear physics. Subspecialty: Nuclear physics. Home: 58 Harris Ave Clarendon Hills IL 60514 Office: Argonne Nat Lab Argonne IL 60439

JACKSON, IVOR, physician, researcher; b. Glasgow, Scotland, Apr. 17, 1936; came to U.S., 1971, naturalized, 1974; s. Louis and Gertrude (Levy) J.; m. Barbara Weiss, Apr. 26, 1972; children—Heather Rochelle, Amanda Ruth. M.B., Ch.B., Glasgow, U. (Scotland), 1960. Diplomate Am. Bd. Internal Medicine, Am. Bd. Endocrinology and Metabolism. Intern Royal Infirmary, Glasgow, Scotland, 1960-61; resident in pathology Royal No. Hosp., London, 1961-62; registrar in internal medicine, endocrinology Royal Infirmary, Glasgow, 1962-69; sr. registrar Royal Victoria Infirmary, Newcastle-Upon-Tyne, Eng., 1969-71; research fellow in neuroendocrinology U. Conn., Hartford, 1971-72, Tufts New Eng. Med. Ctr., Boston, 1972-73, asst. prof. medicine, 1973-77, assoc. prof. medicine, 1977-80, prof. medicine, physician, 1980-84; chief endocrinology Brown U., Providence, 1984—; physician-in-charge div. endocrinology R.I. Hosp. Editor: (with others) Pituitary Adenoma, 1980. Contbr. articles to profl. jours. Fellow USPHS, 1971-73; grantee NIH, 1978—, NSF 1982—. Fellow ACP, Royal Coll. Physicians Edinburgh; mem. Endocrine Soc., Am. Thyroid Assn., Am. Soc. Clin. Investigation. Current work: Study of neuroendocrine regulation of hypothalamic-pituitary function: isolation, characterization of neural peptides. Subspecialties: Neuroendocrinology; Endocrinology. Home: 14 Terrace Dr Barrington RI 02806 Office: Brown U/RI Hosp 593 Eddy St Providence RI 02902

JACKSON, JAMES OSWALD, industrial hygiene manager, consultant; b. Detroit, Mar. 19, 1940; s. James Elwyn and Edna Grace (Tompkins) J.; m. Madelene Keller, June 8, 1968; children—Jeannette Madelene, Rebecca Barbara. B.S., Detroit Inst. Tech., 1968; M.S., Wayne State U., 1970; Ph.D., U. Mich., 1974. Cert. indsl. hygienist, profl. chemist. Field engr., chemist Wayne County Health Dept., Detroit, 1968-74; dir. indsl. hygiene lab. Gulf Oil Corp., Pitts., 1974-76, dir. indsl. hygiene, 1976-79; assoc. prof. U. Ariz., Tucson, 1979-80, bd. advs., 1981—; indsl. hygiene group leader Los Alamos Nat. Lab., 1980—; cons. industry and govt. orgns., 1968—; adj. prof. Colo. State U., Ft. Collins, 1981—. Contbr. articles to profl. jours. Served with U.S. Army, 1963-65. Mich. Dept. Health fellow, 1973; recipient Environ. Quality award, 1974. Fellow Am. Inst. Chemists; mem. Am. Indsl. Hygienist Assn., Am. Conf. Govt. Indsl. Hygiene, Am. Chem. Soc., Am. Acad. Indsl. Hygiene. Roman Catholic. Current work: Management and auditing of industrial hygiene programs; occupational health of alternate energy technologies; sampling and analysis of polynuclear aromatic hydrocarbons. Subspecialty: Industrial hygiene engineering. Home: 2267 Calle Cacique Santa Fe NM 87505 Office: Los Alamos Nat Lab PO Box 1663 MS K486 Los Alamos NM 87545

JACKSON, (JOHN) DAVID, physics educator; b. London, Ont., Can., Jan. 19, 1925; came to U.S., 1957; s. Walter David and Lillian Margaret (Ferguson) J.; m. Barbara Cook, June 26, 1949; children: Ian, Nan, Maureen, Mark. B.Sc., U. Western Ont., 1946; Ph.D., M.I.T., 1949. From asst. prof. to assoc. prof. math. McGill U., Montreal, Que., Can., 1950-56; from assoc. prof. to prof. physics U. Ill.-Urbana, 1957-67; prof. physics U. Calif.-Berkeley, 1967—, chmn. dept., 1978-81; assoc. dir., head physics div. U. Calif. (Lawrence Berkeley Lab.), 1982-84; mem. high energy physics adv. panel Dept. Energy, Washington, 1982-85; dep. dir. ops. Superconducting Super Collider Central Design Group, 1985—; chmn. vis. com. for Fermilab, Batavia, Ill., 1979-83; mem. sci. policy com. Stanford Linear Accelerator Ctr., 1980-83. Author: Physics of Elementary Particles, 1957, Classical Electrodynamics, 2d edit, 1975; editor: Ann. Rev. Nuclear and Particle Sci, 1977—; contbr. articles to profl. jours. Guggenheim fellow, 1956-57; vis. fellow Clare Hall, Cambridge, Eng., 1970. Fellow Am. Phys. Soc.; mem. AAUP, Berkeley Faculty Assn., ACLU. Current Work: Theoretical research in particle physics. Subspecialties: Particle physics; Theoretical physics. Office: Dept Physics U Calif Berkeley CA 94720

JACKSON, KENNETH ARTHUR, materials scientist; b. Connaught, Ont., Can., Oct. 23, 1930; s. Arthur and Suzanne May (Vatcher) J.; m. Jacqueline Jackson (div.); children—Stacy Margaret, Meredith Suzanne, Stuart Keith; m. Camilla Marie Maruszewski, June 21, 1980. B.A.Sc., U. Toronto, Ont., 1952, M.A.Sc., 1953; Ph.D., Harvard U., 1956. Postdoctoral fellow Harvard U., Cambridge, Mass., 1956-58, asst. prof., 1958-62; mem. tech. staff Bell Labs, Murray Hill, N.J., 1962-67, dept. head, 1967—; research adv. panel Air Force OSRD, 1975-78; mem. Nat. Acad. study of space application NASA, 1975, 1982. Editor: Procs. of 4th Internat. Conf. on Crystal Growth, 1975. Contbr. articles to profl. jours. Patentee in field. Mem. AIME (rep. to Council Profl. Devel. 1975-79, (Mathewson Gold medal, 1966), Am. Phys. Soc., Materials Research Soc. (councillor 1972-82, pres. 1977-78), Am. Assn. Crystal Growth (councillor 1976—, pres. 1970-76), Internat. Orgn. Crystal Growth (councillor, treas. 1979—), AAAS. Current work: Crystal growth and crystal growth processes; optical materials and novel optical phenomena for optical communications. Subspecialties: Electronic materials; Condensed matter physics. Home: 33 Bethune St New York NY 10014 Office: AT&T Bell Labs Murray Hill NJ 07974

JACKSON, MICHAEL DEAN, engineer; b. San Francisco, May 31, 1947; s. Norman William and Hazel (Shelstad) J.; m. Linda Rae Cohen, July 27, 1967; children—Jeffrey Dennis, Marc Andrew. B.S.M.E., U. Calif.-Berkeley, 1969, M.S. in Mech. Engring., 1971. Staff engr. Acurex Corp., Mountain View, Calif., 1972-75, sect. leader, 1975-77, dept. mgr., 1977-79, project mgr., 1979—. Contbr. articles to profl. publs. Mem. AAAS, ASME, Soc. Automotive Engrs. Current work: Technical viability and environmental benefits of methanol as an alternate transportation fuel for heavy-duty engines. Subspecialties: Fuels and sources; Environmental engineering. Office: Energy and Environ Div Acurex Corp 555 Clyde Ave Mountain View CA 94039

JACKSON, RAYMOND CARL, cytogeneticist, biosystematist, educator, cons; b. Medora, Ind., May 7, 1928; s. Thornton Comadore and Flossie Oliva (Booker) J.; m. T. June Jackson, Oct. 24, 1947; children: Jeffrey, Rebecca. A..B., Ind. U., 1952, A.M., 1953; Ph.D., Purdue U., 1955. Instr. biology U. N.Mex., Albuquerque, 1955-57, asst. prof., 1957-58; asst. prof. botany U. Kans., 1958-60, assoc. prof., 1961-64, prof., 1964-71, chmn. dept. botany, 1969-71; prof. biol. scis. Tex. Tech U., Lubbock, 1971—, chmn. biol. scis., 1971-78; vis. assoc. prof. U. Iowa, summer 1962, Ind. U., summer 1963. Contbr. articles to sci. jours. Served in USAF, 1946-49. Mem. Am. Soc. Naturalists, Soc. Study of Evolution, Bot. Soc. Am., AAAS, Internat. Assn. Plant Taxonomy, Am. Soc. Plant Taxonomists, Internat. Orgn. Plant Biosystematists. Current Work: Genome relationships; mathematical models to predict meiotic configurations and their frequencies in diploids and polyploids. Subspecialties: Genome organization; Systematics. Home: 3726 64th Dr Lubbock TX 79413 Office: Tex Tech U Lubbock TX 79409

JACKSON, RICHARD LEE, biochemist; b. Springfield, Ill., Dec. 30, 1939; s. Lester O. and Betty (Black) J. B.S. in Chemistry, U. Ill., 1963, Ph.D. in Microbiology, 1967. Research assoc. Brookhaven Nat. Lab., Upton, N.Y., 1967-69; staff fellow NIH, Bethesda, Md., 1969-71; asst. prof. Baylor Coll. Medicine, Houston, 1971-73, assoc. prof., 1973-77; prof. U. Cin. Coll. Medicine, 1978-84; dir. macromolecular biochemistry Merrell Dow Research Inst., Cin., 1985—; vis. prof. Hadassah U. Hosp., Jerusalem, 1974, State U., Utrecht, The Netherlands, 1978, 80-84, Chiba U., Japan, 1980, 82, Instituto Venezolano de Investigaciones Cientificas, Caracas, Venezuela, 1982, Nat.

Cardiovascular Ctr. Research Inst., Osaka, Japan, 1984, Rockefeller U., N.Y.C., 1985. Mem. editorial bd. Jour. Lipid Research, 1982—, Critical Revs. of Chemistry, 1982. Contbr. chpts. to books, articles to profl. jours. USPHS fellow, 1963-67; NIH grantee, 1971—; Am. Heart Assn. established investigator, 1972-77; recipient Louis Katz award, Am. Heart Assn., 1974; Naito Found. award Nat. Cardiovascular Ctr. Research Inst., Osaka, Japan, 1984. Mem. AAAS, Am. Soc. Pharmacology and Exptl. Therapeutics, Am. Soc. Biol. Chemists, Am. Heart Assn. (council on arteriosclerosis). Current work: Structure, function and metabolism of human plasma lipoproteins. Subspecialties: Biochemistry (biology); Biochemistry (medicine). Address: Merrell Dow Research Inst 2110 E Galbraith Rd Cincinnati OH 45215

JACKSON, SHIRLEY ANN, theoretical physicist; b. Washington; d. George Hiter and Beatrice Lewis (Cosby) J.; m. Morris Allen Washington, 1981; 1 child, Alan Jamil. B.S., MIT, 1968, Ph.D., 1973. Vis. scientist CERN, Geneva, Switzerland, 1974-75; research assoc. Fermi Nat. Accelerator Lab., Batavia, Ill., 1973-74, 75-76; vis. scientist Stanford Lineau Accelerator Ctr., Calif., 1976; mem. tech. staff AT&T Bell Labs., Murray Hill, N.J., 1976—; dir. N.J. Resources Corp. Contbr. articles to profl. jours. Vol., Boston City Hosp., 1964-65, Roxbury YMCA, Boston, 1965-68; trustee Lincoln U., Pa., 1980—. Recipient Candace award Nat. Coalition of 100 Black Women, 1982; Martin Marietta Corp. fellow, 1964-68, 72-73; Ford Found. grantee, 1971-73, 74-75. Mem. Am. Phys. Soc., AAAS, N.Y. Acad. Sci., Nat. Soc. Black Physicists, Sigma Xi, Delta Sigma Theta. Club: MIT of Princeton. Current work: Study of the electronic and bosonic properties of two demensional systems, especially the interaction of electrons with surface excitation and phase transitions in two dimensions; melting. Subspecialties: Condensed matter physics; Theoretical physics. Office: AT&T Bell Labs 1D-337 600 Mountain Ave Murray Hill NJ 07974

JACKSON, THOMAS LARRY, psychologist, educator; b. Antioch, Calif., Aug. 9, 1951; s. Thomas Larry and Mary Kathryn (Donlon) J.; m. Patricia Ann Petretic, July 28, 1978. B.A., U. Pacific, 1973; M.A., Bowling Green State U., 1975, Ph.D., 1978. Lic. psychologist, S.D. Asst. prof. psychology U. S.D., Vermillion, 1978-82, coordinator psychol. services, 1981—; cons. Neurol. Inst. and Pain Center, Sioux City, Iowa, 1978—. Contbr. articles to profl. jours. Mem. Am. Psychol. Assn., S.D. Psychol. Assn. (pres. 1982-83), Sigma Xi. Current Work: Attribution of incest blame; psychotherapy; neuropsychology; expert witness testimony; professional ethics. Subspecialties: Behavioral psychology; Neuropsychology. Home: 14 Willow St Vermillion SD 57069 Office: Dept Psychology U SD Vermillion SD 57069

JACKSON, WARREN BRUCE, physicist, researcher; b. Boulder, Colo., Jan. 19, 1954; s. Ernest Gilson Jackson and Elena (Benioff) Slusser; m. Michele Chickerella, Aug. 14, 1976. B.S. in Physics, 1976, M.A. in Physics, 1979, Ph.D. in Physics, 1981. Research asst. Stanford U. Accelerator Lab., Calif., 1973-76; teaching asst. U. Calif.-Berkeley, 1976-77; research asst. Lawrence Berkeley Nat. Lab., 1977-81; researcher Xerox-PARC, Palo Alto, Calif., 1981—. Co-developer photothermal deflection spectroscopy technique. Mem. Am. Phys. Soc., (invited speaker 1982). Optical Soc. Am., Phi Beta Kappa. Current work: Optical spectroscopy, amorphous semiconductors, electron spectroscopy, ultra fast phenomena. Subspecialties: Condensed matter physics; Laser spectroscopy. Office: Xerox + PARC 3333 Coyote Hill Rd Palo Alto CA 94304

JACKSON, WILLIAM BRUCE, biology educator, consultant; b. Milw., Sept. 10, 1926; s. Walter Raleigh and Dorothy (Greene) J.; m. Shirley Jean Slentz, Sept. 6, 1952; children—Beth, Mark, Craig. B.A., U. Wis.-Madison, 1948, M.A., 1949; D.Sc., Johns Hopkins U., 1952. Registered profl. sanitarian, Ohio; cert. pub. operator, Ohio. Biologist Am. Mus. Natural History, C.Z., 1952; sr. asst. scientist U.S. Pub. Health Services, Atlanta, 1952-55; biologist NRC, U.S. Trust Ter., 1955-57; successively asst., assoc., then prof. biol. scis. Bowling Green State U., Ohio, 1957-85, prof. emeritus, 1985—, dir. Environ. Studies Ctr., Ctr. Environ. Research, 1970-85; pres. Rodent Mgmt. Inst., Biocenotics, Inc.; sec. Internat. Pest Mgmt. Cons. Recipient Ann. Educator award Ohio Alliance for Environ. Edn., 1983, Disting. Service award Health Planning Assn., 1980, S.S. Casper Disting. Faculty award Bowling Green State U., 1968. Fellow Ohio Acad. Sci. (v.p.), AAAS; mem. ASTM (com. chmn.), Sigma Xi, Omicron Delta Kappa (faculty), Phi Kappa Phi, Pi Chi Omega (exec. dir.). Current work: Basic and applied ecology, especially in areas of pest bird and rodent population management, U.S. and developing countries. Subspecialties: Ecology (biology); Integrated pest management. Home: 315 Donbar Dr Bowling Green OH 43402Office: Dept Biol Scis Bowling Green State U Bowling Green OH 43403

JACKSON, WILLIAM DAVID, research executive; b. Edinburgh, Scotland, May 20, 1927; came to U.S., 1955, naturalized, 1968; s. Joseph and Margaret (Johnston) J.; children—Margaret Eleanor, David Foster. B.Sc., U. Glasgow, Scotland, 1947, Ph.D., 1960; postgrad., U. Strathclyde, Glasgow, 1948. Apprentice English Electric Co., Stafford, 1945-47; research asst. elec. engring. dept. U. Strathclyde, Glasgow, 1948-51; lectr. elec. engring. U. Manchester, Eng., 1951-55, 57-58; vis. lectr. dept. elec. engring. Mass. Inst. Tech., 1955-57, asst. prof., 1958-62, asso. prof., 1962-66, lectr. elec. engring., 1968-73; vis. prof. Tech. U., Berlin, Germany, 1966; prof. elec. engring., dept. energy engring. U. Ill., Chgo., 1966-67; prin. research scientist, dir. tech. edn. Avco-Everett Research Lab., Everett, Mass., 1967-72; prof. elec. engring. U. Tenn. Space Inst., Tullahoma, 1972-73; mgr. Electric Power Research Inst., Palo Alto, Calif., 1973-74; mgr. office coal research Interior Dept., Washington, 1974-75; dir. magnetohydrodynamic div. ERDA, Washington, 1975-77; dir. tech. analysis div. Office Energy Research, Dept. Energy, Washington, 1977-79; pres. Energy Cons., Inc., 1979-84, HMJ Corp., 1982—; professorial lectr. George Washington U., 1979—; cons. numerous indsl. firms and govt. agys., 1948—; mem. internat. magnetohydrodynamic liaison group Internat. Atomic Energy Agy./UNESCO, 1966—, chmn., 1969-74; coordinator coop. program magnetohydrodynamic power generation, U.S.-USSR, 1974-79, mem. numerous govt. and internat. coms. and panels. Editor: Electricity From MHD, 1968; editorial bd.: Internat. Jour. Elec. Engring. Edn, 1962-70. U.K. Fulbright scholar, 1955-57. Fellow Instn. Elec. Engrs. (U.K.) (past com. sec., chmn.), IEEE (sec.-treas. profl. group biomed. electronics Boston sect. 1962-63, energy devel. subcom. 1973—); mem. AIAA, AAUP, Am. Phys. Soc., AAAS, ASME (past chmn. energetics div.), Am. Soc. Engring. Edn., Sigma Xi. Subspecialty: Electrical engineering. Home and office: 3509 McKinley St NW Washington DC 20015

JACOB, ADIR, chemical physicist; b. Ramat-Gan, Israel, Nov. 11, 1938; came to U.S., 1968, naturalized, 1975; s. Martin and Heia (Jamszon) J.; m. Rochelle Zelmanovitch, June 27, 1965; children—Andria Leigh, Daniel Bram. B.Sc., Hebrew U., Jerusalem, 1963; Ph.D., McGill U., Montreal, Que., Can., 1967. Research assoc. chem. physics MIT, Cambridge, Mass., 1968, 69; sr. staff chemist LFE Corp., Waltham, Mass., 1969-72, sr. staff scientist, 1972-81, dir. research and devel., Clinton, Mass., 1981-84, v.p. research and devel. semicondr. equipment div., 1984—. Mem. editorial bd. Solid State Tech. Jour., 1976; tech. referee Jour. Electrochem. Soc., 1976, Solid State Tech. Jour. Contbr. articles to profl. jours. Patentee in field. Grantee Can. Def. Research Bd., 1964, Can. Nat. Research Council, 1965, AEC, 1968. Mem. Am. Inst. Physics, Am. Electrochem. Soc. Subspecialties: Kinetics; Physical chemistry. Home: 23 Juniper Ln Framingham MA 01701 Office: LFE Corp 55 Green St Clinton MA 01510

JACOB, GARY STEVEN, biochemist, researcher; b. St. Louis, Mar. 18, 1947; s. Bert and Ruth (Schrenzel) J.; m. Kathy Ann Stephenson, Aug. 3, 1975; children—Sarah Beth, Jason Aaron. B.S., U. Mo.-St. Louis, 1969; Ph.D., U. Wis.-Madison, 1976. IBM postdoctoral fellow T.J. Watson Research Ctr., Yorktown Heights, N.Y., 1976-79; sr. research biochemist Monsanto, St. Louis, 1979-82, research specialist, 1982—. Mem. Am. Chem. Soc., AAAS, Sigma Xi. Jewish. Current work: Application of solid-state 15N and 13C NMR to metabolism of microorganisms; studies of herbicide-degrading bacteria. Subspecialties: Biochemistry (biology); Nuclear magnetic resonance. Home: 11111 Bonjour Ct Creve Coeur MO 63146Office: Monsanto Co 800 N Lindbergh Blvd Saint Louis MO 63167

JACOBS, BARBARA BEAMAN, immunologist, consultant; b. Cambridge, Mass., July 23, 1929; d. Isador Richard Beaman and Rae Edna (Rodman) Beaman Edson; children—Kenneth Allen, Michael Lawrence. B.S., Mich. State U., 1950, M.S., 1952; Ph.D., Ind. U., 1956. Sr. research scientist Roswell Park Meml. Inst., Buffalo, 1959-63; assoc. research scientist Am. Med. Ctr., Lakewood, Colo., 1963-69, dir. immunology, 1969-77; prof. Nova U., Fort Lauderdale, Fla., 1978-80; U.S. Peace Corps vol., Chiang Mai, Thailand, 1980-83; cons. malaria div. Ministry Pub. Health, Chiang Mai, 1983-84; pvt. cons. in research devel., Denver, 1984—; vol. vis. prof. faculty of medicine Chiang Mai U., 1981—. Contbr. articles to profl. jours. Former mem. Colo. Democratic Women's Caucus; former Dem. com. woman, Arapahoe County, Colo. Fellow Am. Cancer Soc., 1956-58, USPHS, 1958-59; grantee USPHS, Ruth Estrin Goldberg Meml. for Cancer Research. Mem. Am. Assn. Immunologists, Am. Soc. Tropical Medicine and Hygiene, Returned Peace Corps Vol. Current work: Consulting in research implementation in developing countries-malaria immunology, development of laboratory facilities and field research. Subspecialties: Transplantation; Infectious diseases. Home and Office: 2433 S Dahlia Ln Denver CO 80222

JACOBS, DIANE MARGARET, microbiologist; b. Port of Spain, Trinidad and Tobago, Mar. 24, 1940; d. Saul and Eleanor (Rosenberger) J. A.B., Radcliffe Coll., 1961; Ph.D., Harvard U., 1967. Instr., lectr. Hadassah Med. Sch., Jerusalem, 1967-71; research fellow U. Calif.-San Diego, 1971-74; research assoc. Salk Inst. Biol. Studies, LaJolla, Calif., 1974-76; assoc. prof. SUNY-Buffalo, 1976-80, prof. microbiology, 1980—. Contbr. articles to profl. jours. NIH grantee, 1974—; Am. Cancer Soc. grantee, 1977-80. Mem. Am. Assn. Immunologists, Retic. Endoth. Soc., Am. Soc. Microbiologists, AAAS, Assn. Women in Sci. Current Work: Immunomodulatory agents of bacterial origin particularly lipopoly saccharide; lymphocyte membrane receptors, lymphocyte triggering. Subspecialty: Immunobiology and immunology. Office: 321 Sherman Hall Dept Microbiology SUNY Buffalo NY 14214

JACOBS, HOWARD LARKIN, chemical engineer; b. Cleve., July 19, 1924; s. Henry Russell and Grace Leona (Morse) J.; m. Lois Eleanore Metz, May 14, 1949; children—Leila, Daryl, Lorelei. B.S. in Chem. Engring., Cleve. State U., 1951; M.S. in Polymer Sci., Akron U., 1964. Jr. tech. man B.F. Goodrich Co., Brecksville, Ohio, 1951-57, product engr., Akron, Ohio, 1957-59, tech. man, Brecksville, 1959-60, research engr., 1960-68, sr. research engr., 1968-79, research assoc., 1979—. Contbr. articles to profl. publs., also presentations. Patentee in field. Chmn. citizen's sch. com. Brecksville-Broadview Heights Sch. Dist., 1968-69; chmn. bond issue campaign Seven Dist. Cuyahoga Valley Joint Vocat. Sch., 1969-70. Served with U.S. Army, 1943-46. Mem. Am. Chem Soc., Am. Chem. Soc. (rubber div.). Current work: Rheology of rubbers and rubber compounds, compounding, curing and testing of rubber compounds, product performance versus physical properties. Subspecialties: Polymers (materials science); Polymer chemistry. Home: 8042 Broadview Rd Broadview Heights OH 44147 Office: BF Goodrich Co 9921 Brecksville Rd Brecksville OH 44141

JACOBS, JEROME BARRY, experimental pathologist, electron microscopist, researcher; b. Worcester, Mass., Dec. 15, 1942; s. Maxwell Sol and Ruth (Jacobson) J.; m. Lois Ann Halfen, Aug. 30, 1964; children: Harry, Douglas, Rachel. B.S., U. Vt., 1965, M.S. (research fellow), 1967; teaching fellow, Clark U., 1967-68, Ph.D. (research fellow), 1971. Research fellow U. Mass., 1968-69, instr. pathology, 1973—; affiliate prof. Worcester Poly. Inst., 1975—; dir. electron microscopy St. Vincent Hosp., Worcester, 1971—. Contbr. articles to profl. jours. Gov.'s appointee Mass. Rehab. Commn., 1978-85, Mass. Devel. Disability Council, 1978-84. Mem. Am. Assn. Pathologists, Am. Soc. Clin. Pathology, Am. Assn. Cancer Research, AAAS, Am. Soc. Cell Biology, European Assn. Cancer Research, Sigma Xi. Current Work: Diagnostic electron microscopy, cancer research, pathology services. Subspecialties: Cancer research (medicine); Cell biology (medicine).

JACOBS, JOHN EDWARD, educator; b. Kansas City, June 15, 1920; s. Charles Hawley and Lucille Hartman (Boetjer) J.; m. Elizabeth Anne Brazell, Feb. 23, 1945; children—Patricia, Robert, William, Thomas, Marie, Stephen. B.S. in Elec. Engring, Northwestern Tech. Inst., 1947, M.S., 1948, Ph.D., 1950; Sc.D. (hon.), U. Strathclyde, 1972. Mgr. advance devel. X-ray dept. Gen. Electric Co., Milw., 1950-58, engring. scientist research labs., Schenectady, 1958-60; prof. elec. engring. Northwestern U., Evanston, Ill., 1960—, Walter P. Murphy prof. elec. engring. and engring. scis., 1969—; Exec. dir. Bio-med. Engring. Center, 1962-69, dir., 1969—; pres. Biomed. Engrs. Resource Corp., 1968—; cons. to industry and govt., 1961—; Spl. adviser Nat. Inst. Gen. Med. Scis., HEW, 1966-72; health manpower cons. Pres.'s adv. council mgmt. improvement, 1971-72. Mem. Com. Study Nat. Needs for Biomed. and Behavioral Research Personnel, NRC, 1975—; mem. surgery and biomed. study sect. NIH, 1982—; mem. research com. Chgo. Heart Assn., 1962-65. Served to lt. (j.g.) USNR, 1942-46. Mem. IRE (chmn. Milw. sect. 1957-58, asso. editor bio-med. trans. 1960-65), Bio-Med. Engring. Soc. (founder 1968, treas. 1968-72), Nat. Acad. Engring. Patentee in field. Subspecialties: Biomedical engineering; Electrical engineering. Home: 631 Milburn St Evanston IL 60201

JACOBS, JOSEPH DONOVAN, engineering firm executive; b. Motley, Minn., Dec. 24, 1908; s. Sherman William and Edith Mary (Donovan) J.; m. Virginia Mary O'Meara, Feb. 8, 1937; 1 son, John Michael. B.S. in Civil Engring, U. Minn., 1934. Civil engr., constrn. supr. Walsh Constrn. Co., N.Y.C. and San Francisco, 1934-54; chief engr. Kaiser-Walsh-Perini-Raymond, Australia, 1954-55; founder, sr. officer Jacobs Assocs., San Francisco, 1955—; Chmn., U.S. nat. com. on tunnelling tech. Nat. Acad. Scis., 1977. Recipient Golden Beaver award for engring., 1980; Non-Mem. award Moles, 1981. Fellow ASCE, Instn. Engrs. Australia; mem. Nat. Acad. Engring., Am. Inst. Mining and Metall. Engrs., Nat. Soc. Profl. Engrs., World Trade Club San Francisco, Engrs. Club San Francisco, Delta Chi. Club: Corinthian Yacht (San Francisco). Inventor in field of mining and tunnel excavation. Subspecialty: Construction engineering. Home: 84 Almenar Dr Greenbrae CA 94904 Office: 500 Sansome St San Francisco CA 94111

JACOBS, KEITH WILLIAM, psychologist, educator; b. Ames, Iowa, Feb. 24, 1944; s. Cyril William and Sylvia (Woodrum) J. B.A., U. No. Iowa, 1968; M.A., Eastern Ill. U., 1972; Ph.D., U. So. Miss., 1975. Lic. psychologist, La. Adj. instr. U. So. Miss., Natchez, 1974-75; asst. prof. psychology Loyola U. New Orleans, 1975-79, assoc. prof. psychology, 1979-85, prof., 1985—; lectr. Holy Cross Coll., New Orleans, 1976-78; aux. faculty William Carey Sch. Nursing, New Orleans, 1979-80; cons. in field. Contbr. articles to profl. jours. Bd. dir. Oak Harbor Homeowners Assn., Pearlington, Miss., 1979-80. Recipient Teaching award Am. Psychol. Assn., 1980. Fellow Am. Psychol. Assn.; mem. Am. Psychol. Assn., Counselors and Therapists, La. Acad. Sci., Southeastern Psychol. Assn., Southwestern Psychol. Assn., Midwestern Psychol. Assn., Nat. Rifle Assn., ACLU, Childbirth Edn. Assn., Sigma Xi. Current Work: Applications of computers to edn., psychol. effects of color, psychophysiology, personality variables in prediction of sexual behavior. Subspecialties: Behavioral psychology; Information systems, storage, and retrieval (computer science). Home: P O Box 102 Pearlington MS 39572 Office: Loyola U New Orleans LA 70118

JACOBS, ROLAND WILLIAM, psychologist; b. N.Y.C., Nov. 1, 1952; s. Stanley and Rita (Kasishka) J. B.A., Rutgers U., 1975, M.D., 1979. Resident in psychiatry UCLA, Sepulveda, 1979-83, NIMH fellow, Los Angeles, 1983-85, now Staff Brain Research Inst. Contbr. articles to profl. jours. Mem. AMA, Am. Psychiat. Assn., So. Calif. Psychia. Assn., Soc. for Neurosci., Phi Beta Kappa. Current work: Study of pathological changes in Alzheimers and related disorders causing dementia via histochemical, immunocytochemical and metabolic indices and electron microscopy. Subspecialties: Neurophysiology; Psychiatry. Home: 1127 Rosario Dr Topanga CA 90290 Office: UCLA Brain Research Inst Dept Psychology 405 Hilgard Ave Los Angeles CA 90025

JACOBS, STEVEN JAY, biochemist, physician, researcher; b. N.Y.C., Apr. 28, 1946; s. Benjamin and Sally (Blond) J.; m. Pamela Goode, Mar. 25, 1974; 1 son, James Bigby. B.A., Boston U., 1968, M.D., 1968. Diplomate: Am. Bd. Internal Medicine. Intern Mt. Sinai Hosp., N.Y.C., 1968-69, resident, 1969-72; fellow dept. pharmacology Johns Hopkins U. Sch. Medicine, Balt., 1974-75; research scientist Wellcome Research Labs., Research Triangle Park, N.C., 1975-81, group leader, 1981—; assoc. prof. dept. medicine U. N.C. Sch. Medicine, Chapel Hill, 1975—. Contbr. articles to profl. jours. Served to maj., M.C. U.S. Army, 1972-74. Mem. Endocrine Soc., Am. Soc. Biol. Chemists, Am. Soc. for Pharmacology and Exptl. Therapeutics. Current Work: Insulin receptors—structure, function and regulation. Subspecialty: Receptors. Home: 611 Kensington Dr Chapel Hill NC 27514 Office: 3030 Cornwalis Rd Research Triangle Park NC 27709

JACOBSEN, EDWARD HASTINGS, physics educator, consultant, researcher; b. Elizabeth, N.J., Jan. 2, 1926; s. Edward H. and Marie (Thomas) J.; m. Victoria Thomas, June 27, 1952. B.S., MIT, 1950, PhD., 1954. Research physicist Gen. Electric Co., Schenectady, N.Y., 1955-62; prof. physics U. Rochester, 1962—; cons. Lincoln Labs MIT, Lexington, 1978—. Contbr. articles to profl. jours. Served with USN, 1944-46. Mem. Am. Phys. Soc. Current work: Low temperature physics, condensed matter, acoustics, biophysics, electron optics, x-ray and neutron diffraction. Subspecialties: Condensed matter physics; Electron optics. Office: U Rochester Dept Physics and Astronomy Rochester NY 14627

JACOBSEN, STEPHEN CHARLES, engineering educator, researcher; b. Salt Lake City; s. Charles Jacob and Evelyn (Madsen) J.; m. Beth Vanderworth; m. Linda Diane Madiera, 1980; children—Peter Stephen, Genevieve. B.S., U. Utah, M.S.; Ph.D., MIT, 1973. Teaching asst. thermodynamics U. Utah, Salt Lake City, 1966-67, research asst. div. artificial organs, 1967-68, asst. coordinator artificial kidney, heart contracts, 1968-69, dir. Ctr. Biomed. Design, 1973—, from asst. to full prof. engineering, 1973—, dir. research; cons. in field. Served with U.S. Army, 1961-67. Contbr. articles to profl. jours. Patentee in field. Recipient Outstanding Prof. award Coll. Engring. U. Utah., 1979, Lawrence Poole prize U. Edinburgh. Mem. Soc. Mech. Engrs., Rehab. Engring. Soc. N.Am. Current work: Research in robotics, prosthetics, drug delivery systems. Subspecialties: Artificial organs and prostheses; Mechanical engineering. Office: MEB 3168 U Utah Salt Lake City UT 84112

JACOBSON, GARY R(ONALD), biochemist, microbiologist, researcher, educator; b. Ames, Iowa, Nov. 9, 1947; s. Norman Leonard and Gertrude Adelle (Neff) J.; m. Paula L. Grisafi, Sept. 29, 1984. B.S. in Biochemistry, Iowa State U., 1969; Ph.D. in Biochemistry, Stanford U., 1974. European Molecular Biology Orgn. postdoctoral fellow U. Basel, Switzerland, 1974-77; postdoctoral trainee U. Calif.-San Diego, La Jolla, 1978-79; asst. prof. biology Boston U., 1979—. Author: The Molecular Basis of Sex and Differentiation, A Comparative Study of Evolution, Mechanism and Control in Microorganisms, 1984; also articles. NSF fellow Stanford U., Calif., 1969; NIH grantee, 1980. Mem. AAAS, N.Y. Acad. Scis., Am. Soc. Microbiology, Am. Assn. Dental Research, Internat. Assn. Dental Research. Current work: Nutrient transport mechanisms in bacteria; the mannitol transport system of Escherichia coli and the sucrose transport system of Streptococcus mutans. Subspecialties: Biochemistry (biology); Membrane biology. Office: Dept Biology Boston U 2 Cummington St Boston MA 02215

JACOBSON, HAROLD GORDON, physician, educator; b. Cin., Oct. 12, 1912; s. Samuel and Regina (Dittman) J.; m. Ruth Enenstein, Aug. 10, 1941; children: Richard, Arthur. B.S., U. Cin., 1934, M.B., 1936, M.D., 1937. Diplomate: Am. Bd. Radiology (trustee 1971-82, chmn. written exams. com. in diagnostic radiology 1973-81, co-chmn. 1981—, treas. 1976-78, v.p. 1978-80, pres. 1980-82, mem. residency rev. com. 1976-82, vice-chmn. 1979-80, chmn. 1980—, exec. com. 1976—). Intern Los Angeles County Gen. Hosp., 1936-38; fellow in pathology Longview Hosp., Cin., 1938; resident Mt. Sinai Hosp., N.Y.C., 1939-41, Associated Hosps. U. Tex., 1941-42; asst. in radiology U. Tex., 1941-42; assoc. radiologist New Haven (Conn.) Hosp.; also instr. Yale U., 1952; asst. chief, asso. radiologist VA Hosp., Bronx, N.Y., 1946-50, chief radiology service, 1950-53, cons., 1958—; asst. clin. prof. N.Y. U., 1952-53, clin. prof., 1953-59, prof. clin. radiology, 1959-64; prof. radiology Albert Einstein Coll. Medicine, 1964-71; prof., chmn. Albert Einstein Coll. Medicine of Montefiore Hosp. and Med. Center, N.Y.C., 1972—; dir. dept. roentgenology Hosp. for Spl. Surgery, N.Y.C., 1953-55; radiologist-in-chief Montefiore Hosp. and Med. Center, N.Y.C., 1955—; sr. cons. in radiology Nat. Bd. Med. Examiners, 1975—, mem. bd., 1979-83; vis. prof. radiology Inst. Orthopaedics, U. London, 1975—; vis. prof., lectr., U.S.A., Israel, Brazil, Finland.; named lectures include Felson Lecture, Carman Lecture, Baylin Lecture, Beeler Lecture; named lectures include Freedman Lecture, Pfahler Lecture, Chamberlain Lecture, Evans Lecture, Sampson Lecture, Wolf Meml. Lecture, Caffey Lecture, Grubbe Lecture, Myron Melamed Lecture. Author: (with Clarence Schein, William Z. Stern) The Common Bile Duct, 1967, Neuroradiology Workshop, Vol. III, 1968, (with Ronald O. Murray) Radiology of Skeletal Disorders: Exercises in Diagnosis, 1971, 2d edit., 1977; co-author: Bone Disease Syllabus, 1972, 2d series, 1976, 3d series, 1980, Index for Roentgen Diagnosis, 3d edit, 1975; co-editor in chief: Jour. Internat. Skeletal Radiology, 1976—; editorial bd.: Excerpta Medica, 1974—, Jour. AMA, 1979—; coordinator topics in radiology, 1977-79; editor topics in radiology, 1979—; mem. editorial bd. for radiology, 1979—; contbr. articles to profl. jours. Served as maj. M.C AUS, 1942-46. Recipient Gold medal Assn. Univ. Radiologists, 1982; recipient Gold medal Phi Lambda Kappa, 1983. Fellow Am. Coll. Radiology (councilor 1960—, bd. chancellors, chmn. com. on radiol. coding 1967—, mem. commn. on credentials 1968—, chmn. commn. on affairs Am. Inst. Radiology 1971—, co-chmn. com. on diagnostic coding index and thesaurus 1973—, Gold medal 1978), Royal Coll. Radiologists (London) (hon.); mem. N.Y. Roentgen Soc. (pres. 1959-60, historian 1967—), AMA, N.Y. State, N.Y. med. socs., Soc. of Chairmen Acad. Radiology Depts. (mem. exec. council 1972—, pres. 1973-74), Radiol. Soc. N.Am. (pres. 1966-67, mem. bd. Assn. Univ. Radiologists (Gold Medal 1982), censors 1968—, gold medal 1972), Am. Roentgen Ray Soc. (Cert. of Appreciation 1983), Royal Soc. Medicine (hon.), Internat. Skeletal Soc. (co-founder, pres. 1974-75, chmn., mem. exec. com. 1976—), Alpha Omega Alpha (Rigler lectr. 1964, 70, Crookshank lectr. London 1974, Holmes lectr. Boston 1974). Current work: Radiology of Skeletal Disorders. Subspecialties: Radiology; Diagnostic radiology. Home: 3240 Henry Hudson Pkwy New York NY 10463

JACOBSON, LARRY DEAN, agricultural engineering educator; b. Perham, Minn., Sept. 8, 1950; s. Alvar Ferdinand and Lois Ann (Carlson) J.; m. Jane Louise Hesse, June 21, 1975; children—Karl Hesse, Kurt Hesse. B.Ag. Engring., U. Minn., 1972, M.S. in Ag. Engring., 1974, Ph.D. in Ag. Engring., 1983. Registered profl. engr., Minn. Research asst. U. Minn.-St. Paul, 1972-74, instr. agrl. engring., 1974-83, asst. prof., 1983—. Contbr. articles to profl. jours. Ralston Purina scholar, 1972. Mem. Am. Soc. Agrl. Engrs. Current work: Interelationships between environment and health, growth, and behavior of confinement reared livestock and poultry. Subspecialty: Agricultural engineering. Office: U Minn Room 228A 1390 Eckles Ave Saint Paul MN 55108

JACOBSON, LEON ORRIS, physician; b. Sims, N.D., Dec. 16, 1911; s. John and R. Patrine (Johnson) J.; m. Elizabeth Benton, Mar. 18, 1938; children: Eric Paul, Judith Ann. B.S., N.D. State Coll., 1935, D.Sc. (hon.), 1966; M.D., U. Chgo., 1939; D.Sc., Acadia U., N.S., 1972. Intern U. Chgo., 1939-40, asst. resident medicine, 1940-41, asst. in medicine, 1941-42, instr., 1942-45, asst. prof., 1945-48, asso. dean, div. biol. scis., 1945-51, asso. prof., 1948-51, prof. medicine, 1951—, Joseph Regenstein prof. biol. and med. scis., 1965—, chmn. dept. medicine, 1961-65, dean div. biol. scis., 1966-75; head hematology sect. U. Chgo. Clinics, 1951-61; mem. Inst. Radiobiology and Biophysics, 1949-54; dir. Franklin McLean Meml. Research Inst., 1974-77; asso. dir. health Plutonium project Manhattan Dist., 1943-45, dir. health, 1945-46; dir. Argonne Cancer Research Hosp., U. Chgo., 1951-67; U.S. rep. 1st and 2d UN Conf. on Peaceful Uses Atomic Energy, Geneva, 1955, 58, WHO conf. Research Radiation Injury, Geneva, 1959; cons. biology div. Argonne Nat. Lab.; mem. adv. com. on isotope distbn. AEC, 1952-56; mem. nat. adv. com. radiation USPHS, 1961, mem. com. radiation studies, cons. hematology study sect.; mem. com. cancer diagnosis and therapy NRC, 1949-55; mem. bd. sci. counselor Nat. Cancer Inst., 1963-67; mem. nat. adv. cancer council, nat. cancer adv. bd. NIH, 1968-72; chmn. sci. adv. bd. Council for Tobacco Research; lectr. Internat. Soc. Hematology and Internat. Congress Radiology, Eng., France, Norway, Sweden, 1950, 5th Internat. Cancer Congress, Paris, 1950, Internat. Soc. Hematology, Argentina, 1952, Paris, 1954, others. Author book on erythropoietin; contbr. chpts. on specialized items to various med. books, articles to med. jours.; Book editor: Perspectives in Biology and Medicine, 1979—. Recipient Janeway medal, 1953; Robert Roesler de Villiers award Leukemia Soc.; Borden award med. scis. Assn. Am. Med. Colls., 1962; Modern Med. and Am. Nuclear Soc. awards, 1963; John Phillips Meml. award, 1975; Theodore Roosevelt Rough Riders award State of N.D., 1977; Lincoln Laureate State of Ill., 1979; Kennecott lectr., 1963. Mem. A.C.P. (master), Am. Soc. Clin. Investigation, Assn. Am. Physicians, Soc. Exptl. Biology and Medicine, Central Soc. Clin. Research, Am. Assn. Cancer Research, Internat. Soc. Hematology, AMA, Nat. Acad. Sci., Central Clin. Research Club, AAAS, Radiation Research Soc., Am. Soc. Exptl. Pathology, Sigma Xi, Theta Chi, Nu Sigma Nu, Blue Key, Alpha Omega Alpha. Current Work: Mechanisms of red cell production and steady state maintenance; transplantation of blood-forming tissue to radiation induced or aplasia from other known mechanisms. Subspecialties: Hematology; Transplantation. Home: 5801 Dorchester Ave Apt 2B Chicago IL 60637 Office: 5841 S Maryland Chicago IL 60637

JACOBSON, ROBERT ANDREW, chemistry educator; b. Waterbury, Conn., Feb. 16, 1932; s. Carl A. and Mary Catherine (O'Donnell) J.; m.

Margaret A. McMahon, May 26, 1962; children—Robert Edward, Cheryl Ann. B.A., U. Conn., 1954; Ph.D., U. Minn., 1959. Grad. asst. U. Minn., Mpls., 1954-59; instr., asst. prof. Princeton U., N.J., 1959-64; assoc. prof., chemist Iowa State U. and Ames Lab., 1964-69, prof., sr. chemist, 1969—, asst. dean, 1982—. Contbr. over 170 articles to profl. jours. Recipient Wilkinson Teaching award chemistry dept. Iowa State U., 1974. Mem. Am. Crystallographic Assn., Am. Chem. Soc. Current work: Methods in x-ray and neutron crystallography; scientific computing; molecular structure of organometallic complexes. Subspecialties: Crystallography; Physical chemistry. Office: Chemistry Dept Iowa State U Ames IA 50011

JACOBY, HENRY DONNAN, economist, educator; b. Dallas, June 25, 1935; s. Henry Harris and Margaret Cameron (Miller) J.; m. Martha Hughes Jacoby, Apr. 4, 1959; children—Daniel Donnan, Caroline Hughes. B.S. in Mech. Engring, U. Tex., Austin, 1957; Ph.D. in Econ, Harvard U., 1967. Systems analyst Tudor Engring. Co., San Francisco, 1959-61; economist Harvard Devel. Adv. Service, Argentina Project, 1963-65; asst. prof. dept. econs. Harvard U., Cambridge, Mass., 1965-69; assoc. prof. polit. economy John F. Kennedy Sch. Govt., 1969-73; prof. mgmt. MIT, Cambridge, 1973—; dir. Center for Energy Policy Research, 1978-83; vis. scholar London Bus. Sch., 1983-84; chmn. Mass. Gov.'s Emergency Energy Tech. Adv. Com., 1973-74; mem. Nat. Petroleum Council, 1975-83. Author: (with F.S. Brooman) Macroeconomics, 1970, (with R. Dorfman and H.A. Thomas, Jr.) Models for Managing Regional Water Quality, 1973, (with J.D. Steinbruner) Clearing The Air, 1973, Analysis of Investment in Electric Power, 1979, (with R. deLucia) Energy Planning for Developing Countries, 1982. Served with USN, 1957-59. Mem. Am. Econ. Assn., Tau Beta Pi. Democrat. Episcopalian. Subspecialty: Resource management. Office: MIT Sloan Sch of Mgmt 50 Memorial Dr Cambridge MA 02139

JACOVITCH, JOHN, physicist, nuclear engineer; b. Hemphill, W.Va., Feb. 8, 1930; s. Nicolai and Domnica (Nikitoi) J.; children: John David, Michael Alan, Daniel Nicolas. B.S., Roanoke Coll., 1958; postgrad., Vanderbilt U., 1958-59; M.S., Lynchburg Coll., 1968. AEC fellow Vanderbilt U., Oak Ridge Nat. Labs., 1958-59; scientist Edgerton Germeshausen & Grier, Inc., Las Vegas, Nev., Goleta, Calif., 1959-62; nuclear research physicist Naval Civil Engring. Lab., Port Hueneme, Calif., 1962-63; radiol. engr. Atomic Internat., Canoga Park, Calif., 1963-65; health physicist, project engr. Babcock & Wilcox Co., Lynchburg, Va., 1965-70; health physicist United Nuclear Corp., Wood River Junction, R.I., 1970-71; mgr. health physics U. Mo. Research Reactor Facility, Columbia, Mo., 1971-76; cons., Columbia, 1976-78; asst. prof. med. radiology U. Ill. Med. Center, Chgo., 1978-80; project engr. Wis. Electric Power Co., Milw., 1980-84; radiation safety officer Tulane Med. Ctr., New Orleans, 1985—, clin. asst. prof., 1985—. Contbr. articles to profl. jours. Served with USN, 1947-51. Mem. Internat. Radiation Protection Assn., Health Physics Soc., Am. Assn. Physicists in Medicine, Sigma Pi Sigma. Current Work: Radiation safety; Radiological physics. Subspecialties: Nuclear physics; Nuclear engineering. Office: Tulane Med Center 1430 Tulane Ave New Orleans LA 70112

JADUSZLIWER, BERNARDO, physicist; b. Buenos Aires, Argentina, Oct. 17, 1943; came to U.S., 1974; s. Jacobo Aria and Fejga (Szichman) J.; 1 child, Ariel David. Licenciado en Ciencias, U. Buenos Aires, 1968; M.SC., U. Toronto, 1970, Ph.D., 1973. Postdoctoral fellow U. Toronto, 1973-74; research scientist, assoc. research prof. physics NYU, 1974-84; mem. tech. staff Aerospace Corp., El Segundo, Calif., 1985—; tech. advisor Physics Today buying guide Am. Inst. Physics, N.Y.C., 1983, 84. Contbr. articles to physics jours. Mem. Am. Phys. Soc. Current work: Electron scattering by atoms and molecules, atomic and molecular dipole polarizatsilities, atomic frequency standards. Subspecialty: Atomic and molecular physics.

JAEGER, KLAUS BRUNO, physicist; b. Luebeck, Germany, May 8, 1938; came to U.S., 1958, naturalized, 1964; s. Erich and Minna Wilhelmine (Evers) Jager; m. Maria Horvath, July 26, 1969; 1 child, Erik. B.S., Syracuse U., 1965, M.S., 1968, Ph.D., 1970. Postdoctoral fellow Argonne Nat. Lab., Ill., 1970-71, asst. physicist, 1971-75, assoc. physicist, 1975-80; assoc. physicist Brookhaven Nat. Lab., Upton, N.Y., 1980-81; staff specialist Lockheed Missiles and Space Co., Sunnyvale, Calif., 1982-83, supr., 1983—. Contbr. articles to profl. publs. Served with U.S. Army, 1959-61. Mem. Am. Phys. Soc., Phi Kappa Phi. Lutheran. Current work: Primary standards measurements in the electrical, physical and dimensional fields. Subspecialties: Applied magnetics; Particle physics. Home: 13685 Calle Tacuba Saratoga CA 95070 Office: Lockheed Missiles and Space Co Primary Standards 1111 Lockheed Way 0148-71 B151 Sunnyvale CA 94086

JAFFE, ARTHUR MICHAEL, physicist, mathematician, educator; b. N.Y.C., Dec. 22, 1937; s. Henry and Clarisse J.; m. Nora Frances Crow, July 24, 1971. A.B., Princeton U., 1959, Ph.D., 1965; B.A., Cambridge U., 1961. Acting asst. prof. math. Stanford U., 1966-67; asst. prof. physics Harvard U., Cambridge, Mass., 1967-69, asso. prof., 1969-70, prof. physics, 1970-77, prof. math. physics, 1977-85, Landon T. Clay prof. of math. and theoretical sci., 1985—; research fellow Princeton U., 1965-66, Stanford Linear Accelerator Center, 1966-67; mem. Inst. for Advanced Study, 1967; vis. prof. Eidgenössische Technische Hochschule, Zurich, 1968; vis. prof. math. physics Princeton U., 1971; vis. prof. Rockefeller U., 1977. Author: Vortices and Monopoles, 1980, Quantum Physics, 1981, Quantum Field Theory and Statistical Mechanics, Expositions, 1985, Selected Papers on Quantum Field Theory, 1985; Asso. editor: Jour. Math. Physics, 1970-72; editorial council: Annals of Physics, 1975-77; asst. editor, 1977—; editor: Communications Math. Physics, 1976—; chief editor, 1979—; mem. adv. bd.: Letters in Math. Physics, 1975—; editor: Progress in Physics, 1979—, Selecta Mathematica Sovetica, 1980—; contbr. articles to profl. jours. Alfred P. Sloan Found. fellow, 1968-70; Guggenheim Found. fellow, 1977-78; award Math. and Phys. Scis., N.Y. Acad. Sci., 1979; Dannie Heineman prize for Math. Physics, 1980. Fellow Am. Phys. Soc., Am. Acad. Arts and Scis.; mem. Am. Math. Soc., AAAS, Internat. Assn. Math. Physics. Subspecialty: Mathematical physics. Home: 27 Lancaster St Cambridge MA 02140

JAFFE, ERIC ALLEN, physician, educator, researcher; b. N.Y.C., Apr. 7, 1942; s. Robert Irving and Ruth (Stern) J.; m. Barbara Ruth Little, Feb. 25, 1971; children—Matthew, Alison; M.D., SUNY—Bklyn., 1966. Diplomate Am. Bd. Internal Medicine, Am. Bd. Hematology and Oncology. Intern, resident Kings County Hosp., Bklyn., 1966-68; resident, fellow N.Y. Hosp., N.Y.C., 1968-73; asst. prof. medicine Cornell U. Med. Ctr., N.Y.C., 1973-77, assoc. prof., 1977-82, prof., 1982—. Assoc. editor Microvascular Research, Boston, 1981—; editor: The Biology of Endothelial Cells, 1983. Contbr. articles to profl. jours. Recipient Career Scientist award Health Research Council, 1974-75, Irma T. Hirshal, 1976-81; Career Devel. award NIH, 1976-81; Young Scientist award Passano Found., 1977. Mem. AAP, Am. Soc. Clin. Investigation, Am. Assn. Pathologists, Am. Soc. Cell Biology, Am. Physiol. Soc. N.Y. Personal Computer Club (treas. 1982-83, pres. 1983-84). Jewish. Current work: Research on basic cell biology of endothelial cells. Subspecialties: Cell and tissue culture; Hematology. Office: Cornell U Med Ctr 1300 York Ave New York NY 10021

JAFFE, JOHN EDWARD, physicist; b. Cleve., Feb. 3, 1954; s. Hans and Mary Schuster J. B.A., Cornell U., 1974; M.S., U. Ill., 1976; Ph.D., Cornell U., 1982. Research assoc. Solar Energy Research Inst., Golden, Colo., 1981-83; research assoc. SUNY-Stony Brook, 1983—. Contbr. articles to profl. jours. Mem. Am. Phys. Soc. Current work: Transport theory for solids and quantum liquids; electronic structure of semiconductors; metal-insulator transition and high pressure superconductivity. Subspecialties: Condensed matter physics; Theoretical physics. Office: Dept Physics SUNY Stony Brook NY 11794-3800

JAFFE, NORMAN J., systems programmer; b. Vancouver, C., Can., Jan. 1, 1954; s. Jack and Marsha (Lewis) J. B.Sc. in Computing Sci. and Math, Simon Fraser U., Burnaby, B.C., 1977. Computer systems programmer Canadian Forest Products, 1973-77, systems programmer, 1977-79, Macmillan Bloedel Ltd., 1979-81; ops. mgr. Canadian Car (Pacific), Vancouver, 1981—. Recipient B.C. Profl. Engrs. award, 1971; TAPPI Found. scholar, 1971. Mem. Assn. for Computing Machinery, Pascal Users Group, HP 1000 Internat. Users Group. Current Work: Multilevel mesh-structured database systems, Actor systems, recursive systems, extensible languages, message based information systems, non-hierarchic databases, threaded languages. Subspecialties: Information systems, storage, and retrieval (computer science); Programming languages. Home: 1848 Venables St Vancouver BC V5L 2H7 Canada Office: PO Box 4200 Vancouver BC V6B 4K6 Canada

JAFFE, RANDAL CRAIG, molecular endocrinologist, educator, researcher; b. St. Louis, Dec. 18, 1947; s. Herbert Hyman and Idelle Joanne (Kolman) J.; m. Rose Lynn Pfefferman, Jan. 2, 1970; children—Tod, Aron, Tracy. B.S., U. So. Calif., 1968; Ph.D., U. Calif.-Davis, 1972. Postdoctoral fellow Vanderbilt U. Med. Sch., Nashville, 1972, Baylor Coll. Medicine, Houston, 1972-75; asst. prof. dept. physiology U. Ill. Health Sci. Ctr., Chgo., 1975-83, assoc. prof. 1983—. Mem. AAAS, Fed. Am. Socs. Exptl. Biology, Endocrine Soc. Current work: Hormone mechanism of action, comparative endocrinology, hormone receptors and their regulation. Subspecialties: Receptors; Physiology (medicine). Office: Dept Physiology U Ill Health Sci Ctr PO Box 6998 Chgo IL 60680

JAFFEE, ROBERT ISAAC, research metallurgist; b. Chgo., July 11, 1917; s. Louis Robert and Sadie (Braidman) J.; m. Edna Elspeth Winram, June 2, 1945; children: William Louis, Michael David. B.S., Ill. Inst. Tech., 1939; S.M., Harvard U., 1940; Ph.D., U. Md., 1943. Lectr. U. Md., 1942; metallurgist Leeds & Northrup, Phila., 1943, U. Calif., 1944; with Battelle Meml. Inst., Columbus, Ohio, 1944-75, asso. mgr., 1960-64, sr. fellow, 1964-73, chief materials scientist, 1973-75; sr. tech. advisor Electric Power Research Inst., Palo Alto, Calif., 1975—; cons. prof. Stanford, 1975—; Mem. Nat. Material Adv. Bd., 1970-74; mem. Acta Metall. Bd. Govs., 1969-74, chmn., 1974—; cons. PSAC, 1966; chmn. NASA Adv. Com. Materials, 1966-71; mem. NATO-AGARD Structure and Materials Panel, 1961-63, 69—; Gillett lectr. ASTM, 1976. Author: The Science, Technology and Application of Titanium, 1970, Refractory Metals and Alloys III, Applied Aspects, 1966, Refractory Metals and Alloys IV, Research and Development, 1967, Phase Stability in Metals and Alloys, 1967, Dislocation Dynamics, 1968, Inelastic Behavior of Solids, 1969, Molecular Processes on Solid Surfaces, 1970, Critical Phenomena in Alloys, Magnets and Superconductors, 1971, Interatomic Potentials and Simulation of Lattice Defects, 1972, Defects and Transport in Oxides, 1973, Titanium Science and Technology, 1973, Physical Basis of Heterogeneous Catalysis, 1974, Fundamental Aspects of Structural Alloy Design, 1975; Rotor Forgings for Turbines and Generators, 1982; Corrosion Fatigues of Steam Turbine Blade Materials, 1983; also articles. Fellow Inst. Metallurgists (London), Metall. Soc., Am. Inst. Metall. Engrs. (hon. mem.; pres. 1978), Am. Soc. Metals (Campbell lectr. 1977, James Douglas gold medal 1983; Disting. lectr. materials and soc. 1985); mem. Nat. Acad. Engring., Am. Phys. Soc., AAAS, Harvard Soc. Sci. and Engring., Sigma Xi, Tau Beta Pi, Phi Lambda Upsilon. Club: Stanford Golf. Research non-ferrous phys. metallurgy, particularly titanium and refractory metals Research non-ferrous phys. metallurgy, particularly titanium and refractory metals. Current Work: Materials for steam power plants; design of steels for rotors; application of titanium in turbine blading. Subspecialty: Metallurgy. Home: 3851 May Ct Palo Alto CA 94303 Office: 3412 Hillview Ave Palo Alto CA 94304

JAHIEL, RENÉ I., health services researcher, physician; b. Boulogne sur Seine, France, Mar. 29, 1928; s. Richard and Cécile (Lvosky) J.; m. Deborah Berg, May 8, 1955; children—Abigail, Richard, Beth. B.A., NYU, 1946; M.D., SUNY-Bklyn., 1950; Ph.D., Columbia U., 1957. Lic. physician, N.Y.; diplomate Am. Bd. Pathology. Intern, Montefiore Hosp., Bronx, N.Y., 1950-51; resident Mt. Sinai Hosp., N.Y.C., 1951-52, fellow, 1952-55, asst. attending pathologist, 1959-61; exptl. immunologist Nat. Jewish Hosp., Denver, 1957-59; asst. prof. pub. health Cornell U. Med. Coll., N.Y.C., 1961-66; research assoc. prof., then research prof. preventive medicine NYU Med. Ctr., 1967-76, research prof. dept. medicine, 1976—; cons. Nat. Ctr. for Health Services Research, Rockville, Md., 1982—; mem. grant rev. sections for adminstrn. on aging and health resources adminstrn. U.S. Dept. Health and Human Services, 1979-80; acting med. dir. NENA Health Services Ctr., N.Y.C., 1982-83; tchr. community medicine and health planning NYU. Contbr. articles to profl. jours. Elector, Shearith Israel Synagogue, 1978—; bd. dirs. N.Y. Scientists Com. for Pub. Info., 1974-79, Physicians Forum, 1975—. Named Career Scientist, N.Y.C. Health Research Council, 1961-67; grantee NIH, Nat. Center Health Services, Rockefeller Found., Miestein Found., Bruner Found. Mem. Am. Pub. Health Assn., Soc. for Social Study of Sci., N.Y. County Med. Soc., Assn. for Health Services Research. Current work: Health services research with emphasis on preventive medicine; mental retardation; research on structure and evolution of scientific fields; interferon. Office: 550 First Ave New York NY 10016

JAHN, ROBERT GEORGE, aerospace science educator; b. Kearny, N.J., Apr. 1, 1930; s. George E. and Minnie (Holroyd) J.; m. Catherine Seibert, June 20, 1953; children—Eric George, Jill Ellen, Nina Marie, Dawn Anne. B.Sc. in Mech. Engring. with highest honors, Princeton U., 1951, M.A. in Physics, 1953, Ph.D., 1955. Teaching asst. Princeton U., 1953-55; instr. Lehigh U., Bethlehem, Pa., 1955-56, asst. prof., 1956-58; asst. prof. jet propulsion Calif. Inst. Tech., Pasadena, 1958-62; asst. prof. aero. engring. Princeton U., 1962-64, assoc. prof., 1964-67, prof. aerospace scis., 1967—, dir. grad. studies aerospace and mech. scis. dept., 1968-71, dean. sch. engring. and applied sci., 1971—, exec. com. council univ. community, 1969-71, research bd., 1971—, chmn. council on energy and environ. studies; dir. Hercules Inc., 1985—; cons. editor Am. Scientist, 1966-70; mem. research adv. com. on fluid mechs. NASA, 1965-68, mem. research and tech. adv. subcom. on electrophysics, 1968-71, mem. research and tech. adv. com. on space propulsion and power, 1971-72; mem. com. on space propulsion and power NASA Research and Tech. Adv. Council, 1976-77, mem. space systems and tech. adv. com. nat. adv. council, 1978—; mem. ad hoc adv. com. minority engring. edn. Alfred P. Sloan Found., 1974-79; mem. com. edn. and employment women in sci. and engring. of commn. on human resources NRC, 1975-79; trustee Associated Univs., Inc., 1971-83, chmn. bd., 1977-79. Author: Physics of Electric Propulsion, 1968; also contbr. articles in field. Trustee Asso. Univs., Inc., 1971-83 , chmn. bd., 1977-79; chmn. council on energy and environ. studies Princeton U., 1973—. Recipient Shuichi Kusaka Meml. prize in physics, 1951, Curtis W. McGraw Research award Am. Soc. for Engring. Edn., 1969. Fellow Am. Phys. Soc., Am. Inst. Aeros. and Astronautics (lectr. electric propulsion edn. programs 1969, electric propulsion tech. com. 1963-67, 71-74); mem. AAUP (assoc.), Am. Soc. Engring. Edn., Phi Beta Kappa, Sigma Xi. Subspecialties: Aerospace engineering and technology; Plasma physics.

JAIN, NARESH KUMAR, microbiologist; b. Sunam, India, Feb. 28, 1948; came to U.S., 1981; s. Sohan L. and Swarn J.; m. Santosh Goyal, Sept. 29, 1976; children: Anshika, Vishal. B.Sc. with honors, Panjab U., Chandigarh, India, 1971, M.Sc. with honors, 1973; Ph.D., S.N. Med. Coll., Agra, India, 1981. Asst. prof. Sch. Pharmacy, Delhi U., 1973-75, Med. Sch., Agra (India) U., 1975-80; assoc. prof. Med. Sch., Meerut (India) U., 1980—; research assoc. SUNY-Buffalo, 1981—. Mem. Indian Assn. Med. Microbiology. Current Work: Purification and characterization of antigen structure of infectious mononucleosis. Subspecialties: Immunology (medicine); Infectious diseases. Home: 450-A Allenhurst Rd Amherst NY 14226 Office: Oral Biology SUNY-Buffalo Main St Campus Buffalo NY 14214

JAIN, RAKESH KUMAR, chemical engineering and biomedical engineering educator, cancer researcher; b. Lalitpur, India, Dec. 18, 1950; came to U.S., 1972; s. Sanat K. and Kailash W. Jain; m. Janet C. Taylor, Jan. 3, 1983. B.Tech. in Chem. Engring., Indian Inst. Tech., Kanpur, 1972; M. Chem. Engring., U. Del., 1974, Ph.D. in Chem. Engring., 1975. Asst. prof. chem. and biomed. engring. Columbia U., 1976-78; asst. prof. Carnegie-Mellon U., Pitts., 1978-79, assoc. prof., 1979-83, prof., 1983—; cons. Nat. Cancer Inst. Pathophysiology, Bethesda, Md., 1976—; adj. asst. prof. neurosurgery U. Pitts., 1978-80; vis. prof. chem. engring. MIT, 1983-84; vis. prof. biomed. engring. U. Calif.-La Jolla, 1984; vis. prof. radiology Stanford U., 1984. Contbr. articles to profl. jours. Recipient George Tallmann Ladd award Carnegie Mellon U., 1979, Research Career Devel. award Nat. Cancer Inst., 1980-85, Research award Internat. Inst. Microcirculation, 1984; Guggenheim fellow, 1983-84. Mem. AAAS, Am. Assn. Cancer Research, Am. Microcirculation Soc., Biomed. Engring. Soc., Radiation Research Soc., Am. Inst. Chem. Engrs., Sigma Xi. Democrat. Subspecialties: Biomedical engineering; Cancer research (medicine). Office: Carnegie Mellon U Dept Chem Engring Pittsburgh PA 15213

JAIN, S(URENDER) K(UMAR), mathematician, educator; b. Amritsar, Panjab, India, Nov. 16, 1938; came to U.S., 1969, naturalized, 1976; s. Roshan Lal and Parkash J.; m. Parvesh Jain, Dec. 8, 1965; children—Nisha, Steve. B.A. with honors, Panjab U., 1957, M.A., 1959; Ph.D., U. Delhi, India, 1963. Lectr. in math. Deshbandhu Coll., Delhi, 1959-63; vis. lectr., research mathematician U. Calif., Riverside, 1963-65; reader in math. U. Delhi, 1965-69; vis. assoc. prof. math. Ohio U., Athens, 1969-71, prof., 1971—. Co-author: First Course in Group Theory, 1974; First Course in Rings, Fields and Vector Spaces, 1977; First course in Linear Algebra, 1983. Contbr. numerous research articles on abstract algebra, applied linear algebra to profl. jours., 1963—. Mem. Am. Math. Soc., Soc. Indsl. and Applied Math., Indian Math. Soc. Current work: Noncommutative ring theory; applied algebra. Subspecialties: Algebra and number theory. Home: 3 Ransom Rd Athens OH 45701 Office: Ohio U Dept Math Athens OH 45701

JAIN, SUSHIL KUMAR, biochemistry educator, researcher; b. Nabha, Punjab, India, Mar. 31, 1950; came to U.S., 1977; s. Gian Chand and Parkash (Devi) J.; m. Shubh Laxmi, Apr. 2, 1980. B.Sc. with honors, Punjab U., 1970; M.Sc., Postgrad., Inst. Med. Edn. and Research, Chandigarh, India, 1972, PH.D., 1976. Cert. clin. chemist. Tutor in biochemistry Postgrad. Inst., Chandigarh, 1976-77; postdoctoral fellow U. So. Calif., 1977-79, U. Calif.-San Francisco, 1979-81; instr. biochemistry La. State U. Med. Ctr., Shreveport, 1981-82, asst. prof., 1983—. Contbr. articles to profl. jours. Vice pres. Indian Assn., Shreveport, 1983—. Recipient Beecham award So. Blood Group, Houston, 1982, Ross award So. Soc. Pediatric Research, 1982, Biomed. research award Nat. Inst. Health, 1982, Stiles award La. State U., 1983, Founder's award So. Soc. Pediatric Research, 1985; recipient grants from pvt. drug cos. Mem. Am. Soc. Biol. Chemistry, Am. Soc. Hematology, N.Y. Acad. Scis., Am. Fedn. Clin. Research, AAAS. Current Work: Red blood cell structure and functions, lipid metabolism, lecithin-cholesterol acyl transferase and hyperlipidemias, iron-deficiency anemia, lipid peroxidation role in cellular injury, membrane lipid peroxidation, sickle cell pathology. Subspecialties: Hematology; Nutrition (medicine). Home: 1509 Westbury Dr Shreveport LA 71105 Office: Louisiana State University Medical Center 1501 Kings Hwy Shreveport LA 71130

JAKAS, MARIO MATEO, physics researcher, educator; b. Corrientes, Argentina, Sept. 5, 1952; s. Vincent and Celia (Iglesia) J.; m. Rosa Alejandra Albisu, Jan. 19, 1974; children—Vincente, Mario, Veronica, Anthony. Lic. Fisica, Inst. Balseiro, Bariloche, Argentina, 1975, Dr. Fisica, 1983. Researcher, Comision Nacional de Energia Atomica, Bariloche, 1978-83; adj. research prof. Naval Postgrad. Sch., Monterey, Calif., 1983—. Mem. Asociacion Fisica Argentina, Am. Phys. Soc., Sigma Xi. Current work: Interaction of ions with solids; stopping power; sputtering; transport equation and computer simulation applications. Subspecialties: Atomic and molecular physics; Low temperature physics. Home: 1535 Mira Mar Ave Seaside CA 93955 Office: Naval Postgrad Sch Monterey CA 93943

JAKO, GEZA JULIUS, otolaryngologist. Assoc. surgeon in otolaryngology Mass. Eye and Ear Infirmary, Boston. Subspecialties: Otorhinolaryngology; Laser medicine. Office: Mass Eye and Ear Infirmary 243 Charles St Boston MA 02114

JAKOBSSON, ERIC GUNNAR, physiology, biophysics and bioengineering educator; b. N.Y.C., Nov. 18, 1938; s. Ejler Gunnar and Edith Nanette (Kane) G.; m. Naomi Fay Dick, Oct. 5, 1963; children—Beverly, Susan, Eric Gunnar, Garret, Jonathan, Sarah, Brenda, Linda. B.A., Columbia U., 1959, B.S. in Chem. Engring., 1960; Ph.D. in Physics, Dartmouth Coll., 1969. Cryogenic engr. Malaker Corp., High Bridge, N.J., 1962-65; postdoctoral fellow Case Western Res. U., Cleve., 1969-71; asst. prof. U. Ill., Urbana, 1971-78, assoc. prof., 1978—. Contbr. articles to profl. jours. Polit. chmn. Ill. Alliance to Prevent Nuclear War, Urbana, 1982-83, pres., 1985—; 1st vice chmn. Champaign County Democratic Orgn., 1984—. Mem. AAAS, Biophys. Soc. Unitarian. Current work: Mechanisms of ion permeation in membranes; osmoregulation and water movement across cell membranes; theoretical biology. Subspecialties: Membrane biology; Biophysics (biology). Home: 803 W Main St Urbana IL 61801 Office: Dept Physiology and Biophysics U Ill 407 S Goodwin St Urbana IL 61801

JALAL, SYED MUSTAFA, biology educator, consultant human cytogenetics; b. Ranchi, Bihar, India, Dec. 2, 1938; came to U.S., 1960, naturalized, 1973; s. Syed A. and Safia (Bano) Zafar; m. Nikhat Hoda, July 17, 1966; 1 child, Shadeen R. B.S., U. Bihar, 1959; M.S., U. Wis., 1962, Ph.D., 1965. Cert. clin. cytogeneticist Am. Bd. Med. Genetics. Asst. prof. U. N.D., Grand Forks, 1964-69, assoc. prof., 1969-77, prof. biology, 1977—, clin. cytogenetics cons. Sch. Medicine, 1980—. Contbr. articles, abstracts to profl. jours. Grad. Research prof. U. N.D. and Hill Found., summers 1972, 79, 84; vis. prof. biology U. Tex. System-M.D. Anderson Hosp. and Tumor Inst., Houston, 1974, summer 1979. Mem. Am. Soc. Human Genetics, Am. Genetic Assn., Am. Environ. Mutagen Soc., N.D. Acad. Scis., Sigma Xi. Current work: Neonatal human cytogenetics, high resolution banded chromosome analysis, environmental mutagenesis particularly herbicide induced. Subspecialty: Animal genetics. Home: 154 Columbia Ct Grand Forks ND 58201 Office: Dept Biology U ND Grand Forks ND 58201

JALURIA, RAJIV, communications engineering manager, planner; b. Lucknow, India, Nov. 23, 1952; s. Jagdishwar and Maya (Verma) J.; m. Anjali Bajaj, Jan. 1, 1979; 1 son, Samir. M.Sc., U. Delhi, India, 1974; Ph.D. candidate, Purdue U., 1976; M.B.A., Pepperdine U., 1982. Engr. ITT, Galion, Ohio, 1976-78; mem. tech. staff Bell Labs., Naperville, Ill., 1978-79; mgr. advanced network planning SP Communications, Burlingame, Calif., 1979—. Contbr. articles to profl. jours. Mem. IEEE, Assn. Computing Machinery. Current Work: Voice switching, networking and optimization; data communications; digital networks and enhancements. Subspecialties: Computer engineering; Systems engineering. Home: 983 Lurline Dr Foster City CA 94404 Office: SP Communications 1 Adrian Ct Burlingame CA 94010

JAMES, FRANCES CREWS, ecologist, educator; b. Phila., Sept. 29, 1930; m. Douglas A. James, Dec. 19, 1953; (div. 1974); 3 children. A.B., Mount Holyoke Coll., 1952; M.S. in Zoology, La. State Univ., 1956; Ph.D. in Zoology, 1970. Grad. teaching asst. La. State Univ., 1952-54; instr. botany zoology U. Ark., 1960-70, research assoc., 1971-73; research assoc. Smithsonian Inst., 1975—; from asst. to assoc. program dir. ecology NSF, Washington DC, 1973-76, assoc. program dir. population biology, physiol. ecology, 1976-77; assoc. prof., curator of birds and mamals Fla. State Univ., Tallahassee, 1977-84, prof., curator, 1984—; summer faculty Univ. Minn., 1978-81; pres. Am. Ornithologists' Union, 1984—; invited lectr. Lammi Biol. Sta., Finland, 1982; dir. World Wildlife Fund, 1984—; Cornell Lab. Ornithology, 1985—. Mem. editorial bd. Jour. Am. Birds, 1978—. Assoc. editor Jour. Am. Midland Naturalist, 1978-84. Contbr. articles to profl. jours. NSF grantee, 1979-83, Nat. Geog. Soc. grantee, 1983-84. Fellow AAAS; mem. Ecol. Soc. Am., Soc. Systematic Zoology, Am. Ornithologists' Union, Wilson Ornithol. Soc., Northeastern Bird-Banding Assn., Ark. Audubon Soc., Copper Ornithol. Soc., Fla. Ornithol. Soc., Assn., Southeastern Biologists, Am. Inst. Biol. Scis., Sigma Xi. Current work: Subspecialty: Ornithology. Office: Dept Biol Scis Fla State U Tallahassee FL 32306

JAMES, HAROLD LLOYD, geologist; b. Nanaimo, B.C., Can., June 11, 1912; s. Evan and Blodwen (Davies) J.; m. Ruth Graybeal, Feb. 13, 1936; children—David, Robert, Hugh, Herbert. Student Western Wash. U., 1933-34, U. Wash., 1938-39; B.S., Wash. State U., 1938; Ph.D., Princeton U., 1945. Geologist U.S. Geol. Survey, 1938—; instr. Princeton U., N.J., 1941-42; vis. lectr. Northwestern U., Evanston, Ill., 1953, 54; prof. U. Minn., Mpls., 1961-65. Contbr. numerous articles to profl. jours. Recipient Disting. Service award Dept. Interior, 1966. Fellow Geol. Soc. Am., Mineral. Soc. Am.; mem. Nat. Acad. Scis (chmn. sect. geology 1969-72), Soc. Econ. Geologists (Penrose medal 1976, pres. 1971-72), Geol. Assn. Can., Geochem. Soc., AAAS Current work: Precambrian iron-formations; early Earth history; Precambrian geology of southwest Montana. Subspecialties: Geology; Petrology. Home: 1617 Washington St Port Townsend WA 98368

JAMES, LARRY GEORGE, agricultural engineering educator, consultant; b. Bellingham, Wash., May 1, 1947; s. Percy L. and Alice (VanderWelle) J.; m. Elaine R. Jolly, Apr. 6, 1968; children—Gregory, Jeffrey, Elizabeth, Carolyn. B.S. in Agrl. Engring., Wash. State U., 1970; Ph.D. in Agrl. Engring., U. Minn., 1975. Asst. prof. agrl. engring. Cornell U., Ithaca, N.Y., 1975-77; asst. prof. agrl. engring. Wash. State U., Pullman, 1977-82, assoc. prof., 1982—; cons. Bonneville Power Authority, Portland, Oreg., 1982-84, N.W. Econs. Assn., Vancouver, Wash., 1983—. Contbr. articles to profl. jours. Equipment mgr. Pullman Youth Baseball Assn., 1984—. Recipient R.M. Wade award Wash. State U., 1983-84. Mem. Am. Soc. Agrl. Engring. (Engr. of Yr. award Inland Empire sect. 1983), Am. Soc. Engring. Edn. (Dow Outstanding Young Faculty award Pacific N.W. sect. 1984). Current work: Irrigation engineering; sprinkler and trickle irrigation; crop water requirements; irrigation scheduling; energy, water, and soil conservation. Subspecialty: Agricultural engineering. Office: Dept Agrl Engring Wash State U Pullman WA 99164

JAMES, PHILIP BENJAMIN, physicist, astronomer, educator; b. Kansas City, Mo., Mar. 18, 1940; s. Benjamin and Catharine (Bagley) J.; m. Sharon Lynn James, Aug. 28, 1965; children: Eric, Kevin, Kirsten. B.S., Carnegie-Mellon U., 1961; Ph.D., U. Wis., 1966. Research assoc. physics U. Ill., Urbana, 1966-68; asst. prof. physics and astronomy U. Mo., St. Louis, 1968-72, assoc. prof., 1972-78, prof., 1978—; NRC sr. assoc. Jet Propulsion Lab., 1977-78. Contbr. articles to sci. jours.; editor: Am. Jour. Physics. NASA grantee, 1978—. Mem. Am. Phys. Soc., Am. Geophys. Union, Am. Astron. Soc., AAAS. Lutheran. Current Work: Climate variability on Mars and its implications for terrestrial climate, modeling, data analysis. Subspecialties: Planetary science; Climatology. Office: 530 Benton Hall U MO Saint Louis MO 63121

JAMES, RALPH BOYD, physicist; b. Nashville, Nov. 1, 1953; s. John Edward and Gladys J. (Hurt) J.; m. Patricia G. Berry, June 7, 1975 (div. 1982); 1 child, Dale B. B.S., U. Tenn., 1976; M.S., Ga. Inst. Tech., 1977; M.S., Calif. Inst. Tech., 1978, Ph.D., 1980. Research fellow Calif. Inst. Tech., Pasadena, 1980-81; E.P. Wigner fellow Oak Ridge Nat. Lab., 1981-84; mem. tech. staff Sandia Nat. Labs., Livermore, Calif., 1984—; cons. Kavlico Corp., Chatsworth, Calif., 1980, 81. Contbr. articles to profl. jours. Presdl. fellow Ga. Inst. Tech., 1977. Mem. Am. Phys. Soc., IEEE, Optical Soc. Am., Sigma Xi, Phi Kappa Phi, Tau Beta Pi. Current work: Theoretical and experimental investigations of the optical, electrical and structural properties of semiconductors due to high intensity directed energy radiation. Subspecialties: Condensed matter physics; Theoretical physics. Home: 5420 Lenore Ave Livermore CA 94550 Office: Theoretical Div Sandia Nat Labs Box 969 Livermore CA 94550

JAMES, STEPHANIE LYNN, immunoparasitologist; b. Little Rock, Feb. 20, 1950; d. Vernal and Gene J. B.A., Hendrix Coll., Conway, Ark., 1972; Ph.D., Vanderbilt U., 1976. Research fellow in medicine Harvard Med. Sch., Boston, 1977-80; research assoc. Lab. Parasitic Diseases, NIH, Bethesda, Md., 1980-83; asst. research prof. medicine and microbiology George Washington U. Med. Ctr., 1983-85, assoc. prof. medicine and microbiology, 1985—. Contbr. articles to profl. jours. Nat. Research Service fellow, 1979-81. Mem. Am. Assn. Immunologists, Am. Soc. Tropical Medicine and Hygiene. Current Work: Immunology of parasitic diseases, particularly schistosomiasis. Subspecialties: Infectious diseases; Parasitology. Office: Room 740C Ross Hall George Washington U Med Ctr 2300 Eye St NW Washington DC 20037

JAMES, THOMAS NAUM, cardiologist, educator; b. Amory, Miss., Oct. 24, 1925; s. Naum and Kata J.; m. Gleaves Elizabeth Tynes, June 22, 1948; children—Thomas Mark, Terrence Fenner, Peter Naum. B.S., Tulane U., 1946, M.D., 1949. Diplomate: Am. Bd. Internal Medicine (mem. subsplty. bd. cardiovascular diseases 1972-78, bd. govs. 1982—). Intern Henry Ford Hosp., Detroit, 1949-50, resident in internal medicine and cardiology, 1950-53, practice medicine specializing in cardiology, Birmingham, Ala., 1968—; mem. staff Henry Ford Hosp., 1959-68, U. Ala. Hosps., 1968—; instr. medicine Tulane U., New Orleans, 1955-58, asst. prof., 1959; prof. medicine U. Ala. Med. Center, Birmingham, 1968—, prof. pathology, 1968-73, assoc. prof. physiology and biophysics, 1969-73; dir. Cardiovascular Research and Tng. Center U. Ala. Med. Center, 1970-77, chmn. dept. medicine, 1973-81, Mary Gertrude Waters prof. cardiology, 1976—; Disting. prof. of univ. U. Ala., 1981—; mem. adv. council Nat. Heart Lung and Blood Inst., 1975-79; mem. cardiology del. invited by Chinese Med. Assn. to, People's Republic of China, 1978; pres. 10th World Congress Cardiology, Washington, 1986. Author: Anatomy of the Coronary Arteries, 1961, The Etiology of Myocardial Infarction, 1963; Mem. editorial bd. Circulation, 1966-83; mem. editorial bd. Am. Jour. Cardiology, 1968-76, assoc. editor, 1976-82; mem. editorial bd. Am. Heart Jour, 1976-79; Jour. Am. Coll. Cardiology, 1983—. Contbr. articles on cardiovascular diseases to med. jours. Served as capt. M.C. U.S. Army, 1953-55. Mem. ACP (gov. Ala. 1975-79, master 1983), AMA, Am. Clin. and Climatological Assn., Assn. Am. Physicians, Am. Soc. Clin. Investigation, Assn. Univ. Cardiologists (pres. 1978-79), Am. Heart Assn. (pres. 1979-80), Am. Coll. Cardiology (v.p. 1970-71, trustee 1970-71, 76-81, First Disting. Scientist award 1982), Internat. Soc. and Fedn. Cardiology (pres. 1984-85), Am. Soc. Pharmacology and Exptl. Therapeutics, Soc. Exptl. Biology of Medicine, Am. Coll. Chest Physicians, Central Soc. Clin. Research, So. Soc. Clin. Investigation, Am. Fedn. Clin. Research, Phi Beta Kappa, Sigma Xi, Omicron Delta Kappa, Ala. Acad. Honor, Alpha Omega Alpha, Alpha Tau Omega, Phi Chi. Presbyterian. Clubs: Cosmos, Mountain Brook. Current Work: Research in internal medicine and cardiology. Subspecialties: Internal medicine; Cardiology. Office: Dept Medicine U Ala Med Center Birmingham AL 35294

JAMESON, DOROTHEA, sensory psychologist; b. Newton, Mass., Nov. 16, 1920; d. Robert and Josephine (Murray) J.; m. Leo M. Hurvich, Oct. 23, 1948. B.A., Wellesley Coll., 1942; M.A. (hon.), U. Pa., 1973. Research asst. Harvard, 1941-47; research psychologist Eastman Kodak Co., Rochester, N.Y., 1947-57; research scientist, N.Y. U., 1957-62; vis. scientist Venezuelan Inst. Sci. Research, 1965; research asso. to prof. Psychol. and Inst. Neurol. Scis., U. Pa., 1962-74; Univ. prof. U. Pa., 1975—; vis. prof. Center Visual Sci., U. Rochester, 1974, Columbia U., 1974-76; cons. in field. Mem. Nat. Acad. Sci.-NRC Commn. on Human Resources, 1977-80, chmn. com. on vision, 1980-81; mem. nat. adv. eye council NIH, 1985—; Co-author: The Perception of Brightness and Darkness, 1966; co-author: (E. Hering) introduction and English translation Outlines of a Theory of the Light Sense, 1964; Co-editor, author: Visual Psychophysics: Handbook of Sensory Physiology, vol. VII/4, 1972; Contbr. articles to profl. jours. Recipient I.H. Godlove award Inter-Soc. Color Council, 1973; Judd AIC award, 1985; Alumnae Achievement award Wellesley Coll., 1974; fellow Center for Advanced Study in the Behavioral Scis., 1981-82. Mem. Soc. Exptl. Psychologists (Howard Crosby Warren medal 1971), Internat. Brain Research Orgn., Am. Psychol. Assn. (Distinguished Sci. Contbn. award 1972), Nat. Acad. Scis., Am. Acad. Arts and Scis., AAAS, Assn. Research in Vision and Ophthalmology, Biophys. Soc., Internat. Research Group Color Vision Deficiencies, Optical Soc. Am. (Tillyer medal 1982), Psychonomic Soc., Soc. Neurosci., Sigma Xi. Current Work: Vision and perception; color and spatial vision; sensory mechanisms; brain mechanisms and art. Subspecialties: Sensory processes; Psychophysics. Home: 286 St James Pl Philadelphia PA 19106 Office: 3815 Walnut St Philadelphia PA 19104

JAMISON, HARRISON CLYDE, oil company executive; b. St. Louis, Jan. 15, 1925; s. William Clyde and Katherine Maurice (Fitzgerald) J.; m. Beverly Joy Johnson, June 26, 1946; children: Susan, David, Leslie, Daniel, Dale, Nancy, Sara. B.A. cum laude, UCLA, 1949, postgrad., 1949-50. Geologist Richfield Oil Corp., Bakersfield, Calif., 1950-52, Olympia, Wash., 1952-55, Los Angeles, 1955-60, regional exploration supr., 1961-65; Alaska dist. mgr. Atlantic Richfield Co., Anchorage, 1966-69, Alaska coordinator, Dallas, 1969-70; Alyeska pipeline mgr. ARCO Pipeline, Bellevue, Wash., 1970-72; v.p., chief geologist Atlantic Richfield Co., Dallas, 1972-80, western dist. mgr., Denver, 1980-81; pres. ARCO Exploration Co. (div. Atlantic Richfield Co.), Dallas, 1981—; sr. v.p. Atlantic Richfield Co., Los Angeles, 1981—; vice-chmn. ARCO Alaska, Inc., Anchorage, 1982—; chmn. bd. Resolution Seismic Services, Inc., Wilmington, Del., 1981—. Nat. chmn. Amigos de Ser of Ser, Jobs for Progress, Inc., Dallas, 1983-84; bd. dirs. Tex. Research League, Austin, 1981-84. Served with USN, 1943-46. Fellow Geol. Soc. Am.; mem. Am. Assn. Petroleum Geologists, Am. Inst. Petroleum Geologists, Am. Petroleum Inst., Geol. Soc. Am. Found. (trustee 1982). Republican. Club: Petroleum (Dallas); Petroleum (Anchorage) (pres. 1969). Current Work: Multi-billion dollar petroleum exploration program in North America over the next five years, utilizing a staff of 1800 people, of whom about 60% are professional explorationists. Subspecialty: Geology. Home: 6415 Forest Creek Dr Dallas TX 75230 Office: Arco Exploration Co PO Box 2819 Dallas TX 75221

JAMPLIS, ROBERT WARREN, surgeon, medical foundation executive; b. Chgo., Apr. 1, 1920; s. Mark and Janet (McKenna) J.; m. Roberta Cecelia Prior, Sept. 5, 1947; children: Mark Prior, Elizabeth Ann Jamplis Bluestone. B.S., U. Chgo., 1941, M.D., 1944; M.S., U. Minn., 1951. Diplomate: Am. Bd. Surgery, 1952, Am. Bd. Thoracic Surgery, 1953; Lic. physician, Calif., Minn., Ill. Asst. resident in surgery U. Chgo., 1946-47; fellow in thoracic surgery Mayo Clinic, Rochester, Minn., 1947-52; chief thoracic surgery Palo Alto (Calif.) Med. Clinic, 1954—, exec. dir., 1965-81; clin. prof. surgery Stanford U. Sch. Medicine, 1958—; dir. Coopers Labs., Inc.; mem. council SRI Internat.; vice-chmn. bd. TakeCare Corp.; charter mem., bd. regents Am. Coll. Physician Execs.; mem. staff Stanford Univ. Hosp., Santa Clara Valley Med. Center, San Jose, VA Hosp., Palo Alto, Sequoia Hosp., Redwood City, Calif., El Camino Hosp., Mountain View, Calif., Harold D. Chope Community Hosp., San Mateo, Calif.; pres., chief exec. officer Palo Alto Med. Found.; pres. Fedn. Am. Clinics; bd. dirs. Blue Cross Calif.; varsity football team physician Stanford U. Contbr. numerous articles to profl. jours.; author: (with G.A. Lillington) A Diagnostic Approach to Chest Diseases, 1965, 3d edit., 1984. Trustee Santa Barbara Med. Found. Clinic; pres. Calif. div. Am. Cancer Soc.; chmn. bd. Group Practice Polit. Area Com.; mem. athletic bd. Stanford U.; mem. cabinet U. Chgo.; bd. dirs. Herbert Hoover Boys' Club; past trustee No. Calif. Cancer Program; past bd. dirs. Core Communications in Health, Community Blood Res., others. Served to lt. USNR, 1944-46, 52-54. Recipient Alumni citation U. Chgo., 1968; recipient Nat. Div. award Am. Cancer Soc., 1979, Med. Exec. award Am. Coll. Med. Group Adminstrs., 1981, Russel V. Lee award lectr. Am. Group Pratice Assn., 1982. Mem. Inst. Medicine of Nat. Acad. Scis., ACS, Am. Assn. Thoracic Surgery, Western Thoracic Surg. Assn. (pres.), Western Surg. Assn., Pacific Coast Surg. Assn., San Francisco Surg. Soc. (past pres.), Portland Surg. Soc. (hon.), Doctors Mayo Soc., Am. Coll. Chest Physicians, Calif. Acad. Medicine, Am. Fedn. Clin. Research, Am. Group Practice Assn. (pres.), AMA, Calif. Med. Assn., Santa Clara County Med. Assn., Sigma Xi. Republican. Roman Catholic. Clubs: Bohemian, Pacific Union, Commonwealth of California (San Francisco); Menlo Country (Woodside, (Calif.); Menlo Circus (Atherton, Calif.); Stanford (Calif.) Golf; Rancheros Visitadores (Santa Barbara, Calif.). Current Work: Innovative and progressive administration of health care delivery, medical research and health education. Subspecialty: Surgery. Office: 400 Channing St Palo Alto CA 94301

JANDHYALA, BHAGAVAN SRIKRISHNA, pharmacology educator, researcher; b. India, Aug. 3, 1938; came to U.S., 1961, naturalized, 1976; s. Dakshina Murty and Kanaka Durgamba (Chavali) J.; m. Marie Louis Steenberg, Nov. 16, 1967; 1 son, Murty Dakshina. B. Pharmacy, Andhra U., India, 1961; M.S., U. Pitts., 1963, Ph.D., 1966. Sr. research group leader U.S.V. Pharm. Corp., N.Y.C., 1966-67; asst. prof. U. Pitts., 1967-72, assoc. prof., 1972-73, U. Houston, 1973-84, prof., 1984—; cons. in field. Contbr. numerous articles on pharmacology to profl. jours. Recipient facultl devel. award U. Houston, 1979; NIH grantee, 1974-77. Mem. Am. Soc. Pharmacology and Exptl. Therapeutics, Soc. Exptl. Biology, Internat. Soc. Hypertension, Indian Assn. of Physiologists and Pharmacologists, Sigma Chi, Rho Chi. Current Work: Cardiovascular research, pathogenesis of hypertension, salt and hypertension, central mechanisms, anti hypertensive drug research and mechanisms. Subspecialties: Pharmacology; Psychiatry. Home: 14011 Britoak Houston TX 77079 Office: 460 SR2 4800 Calhoun Houston TX 77004

JANEWAY, RICHARD, university administrator; b. Los Angeles, Feb. 12, 1933; s. VanZandt and Grace Eleanor (Bell) J.; m. Katherine Esmond Pillsbury, Dec. 23, 1955; children—Susan Kent, David VanZandt, Elizabeth Anne. A.B., Colgate U., 1954; M.D., U. Pa., 1958. Diplomate: Am. Bd. Psychiatry and Neurology. Intern Hosp. U. Pa., 1958-59; resident N.C. Baptist Hosp., Winston-Salem, 1963-66; practice medicine specializing in neurology, Winston-Salem, 1966—; mem. faculty Bowman Gray Sch. Medicine, Wake Forest U., Winston-Salem, 1966—, prof. neurology, 1971—, dir., 1969-71, dean Sch., 1971—; v.p. health affairs Wake Forest U., 1983—; dir. Forsyth Bank and Trust, 1973-82, mem. loan and investment com., 1973-82, chmn. personnel and compensation com., 1973-82, mem. exec. com., 1978-82; dir., chmn., mem. exec. com. So. Nat. Bank, Winston-Salem, 1982—; Mem. spl. task force on arteriosclerosis Nat. Heart and Lung Inst., 1971, joint com. for stroke facilities, 1969-72; mem. nat. adv. council regional med. programs HEW, 1974—; mem. N.C. Bd. Human Resources, 1975-77; Mem. adv. com. undergrad. med. evaluation Nat. Bd. Med. Examiners, 1974, chmn., 1979—, mem. at large, 1979—, mem. com. on coms., 1981—, mem. fin. com., 1981—; mem. N.C. Joint Conf. Com. on Med. Care, Inc., 1983—. Mem. personnel com. Winston-Salem/Forsyth County Bd. Edn., 1970-73, mem. policy com., 1970-73, chmn. policy com., 1972-73. Served to capt. USAF, 1959-63. USPHS fellow, 1956; Markle scholar, 1968-73. Fellow ACP, Am. Acad. Neurology; mem. Am. Neurol. Assn., Am. Heart Assn. (fellow council on stroke), AAAS, AMA, Assn. Am. Med. Colls. (council of deans adminstrv. bd. 1977—, exec. council 1977—, mem. liaison com. on grad. med. edn. 1978-80, accreditation council on grad. med. edn. 1981-83, chmn. council of deans 1982-83, exec. com. 1982—, chmn. 1984-85), Am. Clin. and Climatol. Assn., Acad. Mgmt., Soc. Neurosci., Inst. Medicine of Nat. Acad. Scis., Phi Beta Kappa, Sigma Xi, Alpha Omega Alpha. Clubs: Rotary (dir. 1977-80, v.p. 1981-82, pres. 1982-83, chmn. nominating com. 1983-84), Cosmos. Current work: Cerebrovascular diseases, stroke; health care policy, funding, cost containment. Home: 2815 Country Club Rd Winston-Salem NC 27104

JANGHORBANI, MORTEZA, biochemistry educator, researcher; b. Isfahan, Iran, Sept. 29, 1943; came to U.S., 1966; s. Mostafa and Amin (Atyar) J.; m. Kristin Karel Woods, Mar. 25, 1969; 1 child, Alexander Javad. B.S., Am. U., Beirut, 1966; M.S., Oreg. State U., 1968, Ph.D., 1972. Group leader Environ. Trace Substances Research Ctr., U. Mo., Columbia, 1975-77; prin. research scientist MIT, Cambridge, 1977-84; assoc. prof. pathology Boston U. Med. Sch., 1984—. Contbr. articles to sci. jours., chpts. to books. Mem. Am. Inst. Nutrition, Am. Soc. Clin. Nutrition, Am. Chem. Soc., N.Y. Acad. Scis. Current work: Analytical chemistry of stable isotopes, mineral metabolism, trace elements in medicine, human nutrition. Subspecialties: Analytical chemistry; Nutrition (medicine). Home: 42 Golden Ball Rd Weston MA 02193 Office: Boston U Med Ctr M1008 85 E Newton St Boston MA 02118

JANIS, RONALD ALLEN, pharmacologist, physiologist, educator; b. Mossbank, Sask., Can., Oct. 11, 1943; came to U.S., 1968; m. Adriana Beukers, Jan. 23, 1968; children: Mary Alice, Joseph Walter. B.S.P., U. B.C., 1966, M.S.P. (univ. grad. fellow), 1968; Ph.D., SUNY, Buffalo, 1972. Asst. prof. physiology Northwestern U., Chgo., 1974-80, asso. prof., 1980; prin. research scientist Miles Labs., New Haven, 1980-84; head Biochem. Pharmacology Lab., prin. staff scientist Miles Inst. for Preclin. Pharmacology, New Haven, 1980—; asso. prof. in residence dept. medicine U. Conn. Health Center, Farmington, 1981—; cons. in field. Contbr. articles to pharmacology, biochemistry and physiology jours., chpts. to books. Med. Research Council of Can. fellow, 1973; Can. Heart Found. fellow, 1973, 74; NIH grantee, 1978-82. Mem. Am. Physiol. Soc., Am. Soc. for Pharmacology and Exptl. Therapeutics, Biophys. Soc., Brit. Pharm. Soc., Pharmacology Soc. Can. Am. Soc. Neurochemistry, Soc. Gen. Physiologists. Current Work: Pharmacology of calcium antagonists and activators; new drug development; regulation of muscle contraction; calcium transport; ligand binding; isolation and characterization of neuropeptides. Subspecialties: Molecular pharmacology; Membrane biology. Home: 656 High Ridge Rd Orange CT 06477 Office: Box 1956 New Haven CT 06509

JANKELSON, BERNARD, dentist, research director; b. Bloemfontein, Orange Free State, Republic of South Africa, Sept. 8, 1902; came to U.S., 1920; s. Maurice and Sophia (Asher) J.; m. Agnes Jane Neighbors, Sept. 24, 1938; children: Robert Reed, Roland Clark. D.N.D., U. Oreg., 1924. Diplomate: Am. Bd. Prosthodontics. Pvt. practice dentistry, Seattle, 1924—; clin./research assoc. U. Wash., Seattle, 1950-60; cons. UPSHS, 1955-60, U.S. Dept. Army, 1956-58, U.S. VA, 1955-75; dir. research and devel. Myo-tronics Research, Inc., Seattle, 1967-83. Author: numerous publs. including Biophysics and Physiology of the Mandible, 1983. Recipient Diploma de Honor Colegio Chirujanos Dentistas, P.R., 1953; Cercle Paradontie Paris, 1971. Fellow Internat. Coll. Dentists, Am. Coll. Prosthodontics; mem. Internat. Coll. Craniomandibular Orthopedics, Am. Acad. Gen. Dentistry (hon.), Accademia Italiana di Paradontologia (hon.), Am. Assn. Dental Research, Am. Dental Assn., Omicron Kappa Upsilon. Patentee in field of biomed. instrumentation and chemical formulae. Current Work: Basic science research in biophysics and physiology of musculoskeletal system of head and neck; applied clinical research for diagnosis and treatment of musculoskeletal dysfunction of head and neck. Subspecialties: Biophysics (biology); Physiology (biology). Home: 1100 University St Apt 16E Seattle WA 98101 Office: Myotronics Research Inc 720 Olive Way Suite 800 Seattle WA 98101

JANSEN, GEORGE JAMES, consulting mineralogist; b. Canton, Ohio, Apr. 22, 1925; s. George Bernard and Caroline Agnes (Wilkinson) J.; m. Patricia Jean Wood, Feb. 14, 1953; children: George James, Kenneth V.; m. Marjorie Ann Molloy, June 12, 1971. B.S. in Geology, U. Notre Dame, 1951; M.A. in Geology, Bryn Mawr Coll., 1952. Geologist U.S. Geol. Survey, 1952-57; prin. geologist Battelle Meml. Inst., 1957; supr. Republic Steel Co., 1958-69; sr. scientist Amax, 1969-75; coal petrographer CT & E., 1976-77; v.p., prin. investigator Rocky Mountain Coal Petrography, Inc., Golden, Colo., 1978—. Contbr. articles to profl. jours. Mem. Colo. Right to Life, Internat. Host Family Program of Colo. Sch Mines. Served with AUS, 1943-46. Fellow Geol. Soc. Am.; mem. Mineral. Soc. Am., Mineral Assn. Can., Denver Coal Club, Colo. Mining Assn., Soc. Ind. Profl. Earth Scientists. Republican. Roman Catholic. Current Work: Microscopic and x-ray characterization of raw materials. Subspecialties: Mineralogy; Coal. Office: Box 88 Golden CO 80402

JANSSON, ROBERT EDWARD, chemical company executive; b. Westminster, London, Sept. 24, 1936; came to U.S., 1981; s. Carl Ernest and Alice Irene (Davies) J.; m. Dorothy Elizabeth Mossop, Sept. 29, 1962; children—Carl, Niall, Zoe. B.S. in Chemistry with honors, Queen Mary Coll., London, 1959, Ph.D., 1962. Postdoctoral scholar UCLA, 1962-64; research fellow Central Electricity Generating Bd., Marchwood, Eng., 1964-66; lectr. aero. and astronautics Southampton U., Eng., 1966-72, sr. lectr. electrochem. engring., 1972-81, dir. Worfson Ctr. for Electrochem. Sci., 1978-81; sr. fellow and research mgr. Monsanto Co., St. Louis, 1981—; affiliate prof. chem. engring. Washington U., St. Louis, 1984—. Author: Meet You In Munich, 1975; News Caper, 1978. Mem. editorial bd. Jour. Applied Electrochemistry, London, 1980—, Internat. Soc. Electrochemistry, 1984—. Contbr. articles to profl. jours. Patentee in field. Mem. Soc. of Chem. Industry. Current work: All aspects of applied electrochemistry and interfacial science, surface science, and solid state physics, bio materials. Subspecialties: Chemical engineering; Materials (engineering). Office: Monsanto Co Mail Zone R1C 800 N Lindbergh Blvd Saint Louis MO 63167

JANZEN, DANIEL HUNT, biologist; b. Milw., Jan 18, 1939; 2 children. Ph.D. in Entomology, U. Calif.-Berkeley, 1965. Asst. prof. biology U. Kans., 1965-68; from asst. prof. to assoc. prof. U. Chgo., 1968-72; from assoc. prof. to prof. U. Mich., 1972-76; prof. biology U. Pa., Phila., 1976—. Recipient Gleason award Am. Bot. Soc., 1975, Crafoord prize Swedish Acad. Scis., 1984. Subspecialty: Ecology (biology). Office: U Pa Dept Biology Philadelphia PA 19104*

JAPAR, STEVEN MARTIN, physical chemist, researcher; b. N.Y.C., Nov. 11, 1944; s. Romeo and Susan (Kuklish) J.; m. Teresa Martusiewicz, Feb. 11, 1984; 1 child, Mark Andrew. B.S. in Chemistry, CCNY, 1965; Ph.D. in phys. Chemistry, Case Inst. Tech., 1969. Postdoctoral fellow Nat. Research Council of Can., Ottawa, Ont., 1969-71, U. Calif.-Riverside, 1971-72; instr. Drexel U., Phila., 1972-73; sr. research scientist research staff Ford Motor Co., Dearborn, Mich., 1973-81, prin. research scientist, assoc., 1981—; lectr. in chemistry U. Mich.-Dearborn, 1975. Contbr. articles to profl. jours. Recipient Ward medal for outstanding achievement CCNY, 1965, Arch T. Colwell Merit award Soc. Automotive Engrs., 1982. Mem. Am. Chem. Soc., Optical Soc. Am., Air Pollution Control Assn., Sigma Xi. Current work: Chemistry and physics of atmospheric aerosols, including the dynamics of deposition processes; techniques for the in-situ determination of aerosols. Subspecialties: Atmospheric chemistry; Photochemistry. Office: Research Staff Ford Motor Co PO Box 2053 Dearborn MI 48121

JAQUESS, JAMES FLETCHER, nuclear power generation, quality engineering and management consultant; b. Evansville, Ind., Mar. 25, 1948; s. John Roberts Jaquess and Sybil L. (Rye) Kaho; m. Karen Louise Byrd, July 29, 1972; children—Karen Renee, Regina Kathryn. Student, Ind. U.-Bloomington, 1966-67; B.S., Ind. State U.-Evansville, 1971; M.B.A., Ind. State U.-Terre Haute, 1975; postgrad. Ga. State U. Law Sch. Cert. quality engr. Navy nuclear quality assurance engr. Babcock & Wilcox, Mt. Vernon, Ind., 1971-73, resident quality engr., 1973-76, lead quality assurance engr., Lynchburg, Va., 1976-79, internat. project mgr., 1979-82; lead sr. engr. EDS Nuclear Inc., Atlanta, 1982-84; mgr. quality assurance Impell Corp., Atlanta, 1984—. Mem. Am. Soc. for Quality Control (sr.), Am. Nuclear Soc., Soc. Mfg. Engrs., ASME, ABA, Ga. Trial Lawyers Assn., Am. Trial Lawyers Assn., Am. Soc. Internat. Law, Ind. State U. Alumni Assn. Current Work: International quality assurance consultant to electric utilities. Subspecialties: Nuclear fission; Nuclear power generation-quality engineering. Home: 3647 Frederica Rd Duluth GA 30136 Office: Impell Corp 333 Technology Park Norcross GA 30092

JARBOE, CHARLES HARRY, pharmacologist, educator, conultant; b. Louisville, Oct. 3, 1928; s. Charles Harry and Mary Elizabeth (O'Daniel) J.; m. Carla A., June 29, 1982; children: Jamisene, Charles H., Richard J., Herman H., Nancy H., Elizabeth. B.S., U. Louisville, 1951, Ph.D., 1956. Research asst. prof. chemistry U. Louisville, 1957-58; chief scientist Brown and Williamson Tobacco Corp., 1958-61; assoc. prof. pharmacology and toxicology U. Louisville, 1962-72, prof. pharmacology and toxicology, 1972—, dir.Therapeutics and Toxicology Lab., 1972—; prof. pharmacology King Faisal U., Dammam, Saudi Arabia, 1982-84, also cons. Contbr. numerous articles to profl. publs. Mem. formulary com. Ky. Med. Assistance Program; mem. Ky. Environ. Quality Commn., Jefferson County Air Pollution Control Bd. Served with USMC, 1945-58; Served with USAR, 1951-53. Research grantee public agys., also pvt. industry. Mem. N.Y. Acad. Sci., Am. Soc. Pharmacology and Exptl. Therapeutics, Am. Acad. Clin. Toxicology, Am. Soc. Clin. Pharmacology, Sigma Xi. Democrat. Patentee in field. Current Work: Human toxicology and human pharmacokinetics. I am a teaching medical school professor, director of my university Institutional Review Board and investigator in human toxico- and pharmacokinetics. Subspecialties: Molecular pharmacology; Toxicology (medicine). Home: PO Box 4053 Louisville KY 40204 Office: Dept Pharmacology and Toxicology U Louisville Louisville KY 40292

JARISCH, WOLFRAM RUDOLF, biomedical engineer, consultant; b. Vienna, Oct. 23, 1947; came to U.S., 1973; s. Rudolf and Edith (Kittler) J. B.S., U. Tech., Vienna, 1969, diploma in Engring., 1972; M.S., U. Conn., 1975, Ph.D., Carnegie-Mellon U., 1979. Sr. research analyst Sci. Systems, Cambridge, Mass., 1979-82; assoc. in medicine Harvard U. Med. Sch., Boston, 1982—; research assoc. Beth Israel Hosp., Boston, 1982—; research affiliate Harvard-MIT Health Sci. and Tech., Cambridge, 1983—; cons. Cyber Tech., Cambridge, 1982—. Contbr. articles to profl. publs. Pres. Austro-Am. Assn. Boston, Cambridge, 1982—. Fulbright scholar, 1973-74. Mem. Inst. Math. Stats., IEEE, Am. Statis. Assn. Current work: Stochastic modeling of dynamic processes in physiological systems, human arrhythmia, brain activity, intestinal motility, cybernetics in medicine, artificial intelligence like image analysis and processing. Subspecialties: Biomedical engineering; Artificial intelligence. Home: 295 Harvard St Apt 702 Cambridge MA 02139 Office: MIT Room 20A-116 77 Massachusetts Ave Cambridge MA 02139

JARMOLOW, KENNETH, corporate research executive. Pres., Martin Marietta Energy Systems, Oak Ridge. Office: Martin Marietta Energy Systems PO Box Y Oak Ridge TN 37831*

JARON, DOV, biomedical engineer, educator; b. Tel Aviv, Oct. 29, 1935; came to U.S., 1958, naturalized, 1972; s. Meir and Sara (Levit) Yarovsky; m. Brooke E. Boberg, Sept. 16, 1978; children: Shulamit, Tamara. B.S. magna cum laude, U. Denver, 1961; Ph.D., U. Pa., 1967. Sr. research asso. Maimonides Med. Center, Bklyn., 1967-70; dir. surg. research Sinai Hosp. of Detroit, 1970-73; asso. prof. elec. engring. U. R.I., Kingston, 1973-77, prof., 1977-79, coordinator biomed. engring., 1973-79; dir. Biomed. Engring. and Sci. Inst., Drexel U., Phila., 1979—, prof. elec. and computer engring., 1979—; vis. prof. elec. engring. Rutgers U., New Brunswick, N.J., 1968-73; adj. prof. biomed. engring. Wayne State U., 1971-73; adj. prof. physiology Temple U. Sch. Medicine, 1980—; adj. prof. radiology Jefferson Med. Coll., 1983—. Contbr. articles to sci. jours. NSF, NIH, Office Naval Research, pvt. founds. research grantee. Mem. Biomed. Engring. Soc., Am. Soc. Engring. Edn., Assn. Advancement Med. Instrumentation, Internat. Soc. Artificial Organs, Am. Soc. Artificial Internal Organs, Biophys. Soc., N.Y. Acad. Scis., IEEE, Am. Soc. for Engring. Edn., AAAS, AAUP, Sigma Xi, Tau Beta Pi, Eta Kappa Nu. Researcher in cardiac assist devices, cardiovascular modeling, biomed. instrumentation. Current Work: Development, control and optimization of cardiac assist devices; computer technologies applied to cardiovascular dynamics and diagnosis; bio-medical instrumentation. Subspecialties: Biomedical engineering; Artificial organs and prostheses. Home: 122 Bethlehem Pike Philadelphia PA 19118 Office: Drexel U Philadelphia PA 19104

JARRETT, ALBERT RUSSELL, agricultural engineer, soil and water consultant; b. Lewisburg, Pa., Feb. 8, 1946; s. Glen Elwood and Edith Elinore (Ocker) J.; m. Ellen Kreiser, Sept. 2, 1967; children—Aimee, Valerie, Adam. B.S. in Agrl. Engring., Pa. State U., 1968, M.S., 1970, Ph.D., 1975. Instr. Pa. State U., Mont Alto, 1969-72, agrl. engr., University Park, 1974—; engr. Arrowood Engrs., Chambersburg, Pa., 1972; grad. asst. Pa. State U., University Park, 1972-73; student trainee U.S. Dept. Agr., Agrl. Research Service, University Park, 1973-74. Author: Golf Course and Grounds Irrigation and Drainage, 1985. Contbr. articles to profl. jours. Mem. Am. Soc. Agrl. Engrs., Soil Conservation Soc. Baptist. Current work: Soil air entrapment and its effect on infiltration and soil erosion. Onlot sewage disposal. Evaluating potential hazardous waste disposal sites using tracers. Subspecialties: Agricultural engineering; Resource management. Office: The Pennsylvania State University 209 Agrl Engring Bldg University Park PA 16802

JARRETT, MARK PAUL, physician; b. Bklyn., Dec. 29, 1949; s. Irving J. and Claire (Rockower) J.; m. Michele Jonas, Aug. 15, 1974; children—Matthew, Nicole, Tyler. B.S., Muhlenberg Coll., 1971; M.D., N.Y.U., 1975. Diplomate: Am. Bd. Internal Medicine, Am. Bd. Rheumatology. Resident in medicine Montefiore Hosp., Bronx, N.Y., 1975-78, fellow in rheumatology, 1978-80; assoc. in medicine Northwestern U. Med. Sch., Chgo., 1980-81, asst. prof. medicine, 1981-82; clin. asst. prof. medicine Downstate Med. Sch., Bklyn., 1982—. Contbr. articles to profl. jours. Fellow A.C.P.; Mem. Am. Fedn. for Clin. Research, Am. Rheumatism Assn., AMA, AAAS, Phi Beta Kappa. Current Work: Immunology, cellular and humoral and its effect on collagen vascular diseases. Subspecialty: Immunology (medicine). Office: 1460 Victory Blvd Staten Island NY 10301

JARVIK, ROBERT K., artificial organs researcher, physician, educator; b. Midland, Mich., May 11, 1946; s. Norman and Edythe Jarvik; m. Elaine Levin, 1968 (div.); children—Tyler, Kate. B.A. in Zoology, Syracuse U., 1968, D.Sc. (hon.), 1983; postgrad., U. Bologna Sch. Medicine; M.A. in Occupational Biomechanics, NYU, 1971; M.D., U. Utah, 1976. Research asst. div. artificial organs U. Utah., 1971-77, acting dir. exptl. labs., div. artificial organs, 1977-78, asst. dir. exptl. labs., 1978—; also research asst. prof. surgery U. Utah. Coll. Medicine and research asst. prof. bioengring. Coll. Engring. Contbr. articles, abstracts, chpts. to profl. publs.; editorial reviewer for profl. jours. USPHS grantee. Mem. Am. Soc. Artificial Internal Organs, Internat. Soc. Artificial Organs. Patentee in field; designer Jarvik artificial hearts, 1971—; research on artificial ear. Subspecialties: Biomedical engineering; Artificial organs and prostheses. Office: Dept Surgery U Utah Coll Medicine 50 N Medical Dr Salt Lake City UT 84132*

JASIULEK, JOACHIM NORBERT, mathematics educator; b. Kassel, West Germany, Apr. 7, 1952; came to U.S., 1973; s. Heinz and Marga (Engels) J. M.A., U. Calif.-Davis, 1974, M.S.E.E., 1975, Ph.D., 1980. Lectr. research engring. U. Calif.-Davis, 1980-81; vis. asst. prof. Simon Fraser U., B.C., Can., 1981-82; vis. asst. prof. math. Case Western Res. U., Cleve., 1982—; cons. Prentice Hall, Englewood, N.J., 1982. Contbr. articles in field to profl. jours. Fulbright scholar, 1973-75. Mem. Soc. Indsl. and Applied Math., IEEE. Current Work: Development of fast algorithms for applications in signal and image processing, implementation as software packages. Subspecialties: Algorithms; Numerical analysis (computer science). Home: 1700 E 13th St Apt 16W Cleveland OH 44114 Office: Case Western Res U Math Dept Cleveland OH 44106

JASKE, ROBERT THEODORE, engineer; b. Chgo., Apr. 13, 1923; s. Anthony B. and Rose Agnes (Porzdol) Jaszkowski; m. Mary Ann Hilt, Apr. 12, 1947; children—Michael R., Margaret Ann., Jeanne Marie, Thomas R. B.S. in Chem. Engring., Northwestern U., 1944. Registered profl. engr., Wash., Oreg., Va. Prin. engr. Gen. Electric Co., Richland, Wash., 1947-64; research assoc. Battelle N.W. Lab., Richland, 1964-75; dep. dir. office state programs U.S. Nuclear Regulatory Commn., Washington, 1975-80; tech. advisor Fed. Emergency Mgmt. Agy., Washington, 1980—. Contbr. articles to profl. jours. Chmn. City Planning Commn., Richland, 1970-73; active Benton County, Republican Central Com., 1950-73; v.p. East Bethesda Citizen's Assn., 1980-83. Served with AUS, 1945-47. Named Engr. of Yr. Wash. Soc. Profl. Engrs., 1972. Fellow Am. Inst. Chem. Engrs. (bd. dirs. environ. div., Pub. Service award, 1975); mem. ASCE (chmn. energy and policy com. 1975-78), Am. Acad. Environ. Engrs. (trustee 1978-83), Wash. Soc. Engrs. Roman Catholic. Lodge: K.C. (grand knight 1953-55, state treas. 1966-68). Current work: Development and implementation of integrated emergency management information system; a national distributed data base system for plans review and evaluation; exercises and simulation and operational support. Subspecialties: Water supply and wastewater treatment; Nuclear engineering. Home: 7908 Chelton Rd Bethesda MD 20814 Office: Fed Emergency Mgmt Agy 500 C St SW Washington DC 20472

JASNY, GEORGE ROMAN, energy company executive, chemical engineer; b. Katowice, Poland, June 6, 1924; came to U.S., 1941, naturalized, 1943; s. Maurice and Irene (Heiman) J.; m. Gloria Jane Jones, June 13, 1951; children—Elizabeth Pruitt, Thomas Paul. B.S. in Chem. Engring., U. Wash., 1949; M.S. in Chem. Engring., MIT, 1952. Registered profl. engr., Tenn. Mem. tech. staff, nuclear div. Union Carbide Corp., Oak Ridge, 1950-73, dir. engring., nuclear div., 1973-80, v.p. engring. and computing, nuclear div., 1980-84; v.p. engring. and computing Martin Marietta Energy Systems, Inc., Oak Ridge, 1984—. Chmn. bd. Oak Ridge Utility Dist., 1985, Meth. Med. Ctr. Oak Ridge, 1985. Served with Constrn. Bn., USN, 1943-46; PTO. Fellow Am. Inst. Chem. Engrs.; mem. Nat. Acad. Engring., Nat. Soc. Profl. Engrs., Am. Soc. Engring. Mgmt. (pres. 1983-84), Sigma Xi, Tau Beta Pi. Democrat. Lodge: Rotary (pres.) (Oak Ridge). Current work: Management of a large engineering and computing organization. Subspecialties: Nuclear engineering; Engineering and computing organization management. Office: Martin Marietta Energy Systems Inc PO Box Y Oak Ridge TN 37831

JASTROW, ROBERT, physicist; b. N.Y.C., Sept. 7, 1925; s. Abraham and Marie (Greenfield) J. A.B., Columbia, 1944, M.A., 1945, Ph.D., 1948; post-doctoral fellow, Leiden U., 1948-49, Princeton Inst. Advanced Study, 1949-50, 53, U. Calif. at Berkeley, 1950-53; D.Sc. (hon.), Manhattan Coll., 1980. Asst. prof. Yale, 1953-54; cons. nuclear physics U.S. Naval Research Lab., Washington, 1958-62; head theoretical div. Goddard Space Flight Center NASA, 1958-61, chmn. lunar exploration com., 1959-60, mem. com., 1960-62; dir. Goddard Inst. Space Studies, N.Y.C., 1961-81; adj. prof. geology Columbia, 1961-81, dir. Summer Inst. Space Physics, 1962-70; adj. prof. astronomy Columbia (Summer Inst. Space Physics), 1977-82; adj. prof. earth sci. Dartmouth, 1973—. Author: The Evolution of Stars, Planets and Life, 1967, Astronomy: Fundamentals and Frontiers, 1972, Until the Sun Dies, 1977, God and the Astronomers, 1978, Red Giants-White Dwarfs, 1979, The Enchanted Loom, 1981. Editor: Exploration of Space, 1960; co-editor: Jour. Atmospheric Scis, 1962-74, The Origin of the Solar System, 1963, The Venus Atmosphere, 1969. Recipient Medal of Excellence Columbia, 1962, Grad. Faculties Alumni award, 1967; Arthur S. Flemming award, 1965; medal for exceptional sci. achievement NASA, 1968. Fellow Am. Geophys. Union, A.A.A.S., Am. Phys. Soc.; mem. Internat. Acad. Astronautics, Council Fgn. Relations, Leakey Found. Clubs: Cosmos, Explorers, Century. Subspecialties: Astronautics; Planetary atmospheres. Office: Dartmouth Coll Dept Earth Scis Hanover NH 03755

JASZCZAK, RONALD JACK, physicist; b. Chicago Heights, Ill., Aug. 23, 1942; s. Jacob and Julia (Gudowicz) J.; m. Nancy Jane Bober, Apr. 15, 1967; children: John, Monica. B.S. with highest honors, U. Fla., Gainesville, 1964, Ph.D., 1968. AEC postdoctoral fellow Oak Ridge (Tenn.) Nat. Lab., 1968-69, staff physicist, 1969-71; prin. research scientist Searle Diagnostics, Inc., Des Plaines, Ill., 1971-73, sr. prin. research scientist, 1973, research group leader, 1973-77, chief scientist, 1977-79; asso. prof. radiology Duke U. Med. Center, Durham, N.C., 1979—; v.p., chmn. bd. dirs. Data Spectrum Corp., Chapel Hill, N.C.; cons. Technicare Corp., 1980—, Siemens Gammasonics, Inc., 1981—. Contbr. articles in field to profl. jours. NIH sr. research fellow, 1980-82; NASA predoctoral fellow, 1964-67. Mem. Am. Phy. Soc., AAAS, Soc. Nuclear Medicine, IEEE, Am. Assn. Physicists in Medicine, Soc. Photo-Optical Instrumentation Engring., Phi Beta Kappa, Phi Kappa Phi, Sigma Tau Sigma, Sigma Pi Sigma. Patentee in field. Current Work: Medical imaging, research in design and application Single Photon Emission Computed Tomography. Research interests include physical aspects of imaging and display technologies; positron emission tomography, nuclear magnetic resonance and ultrasound. Subspecialties: Bioinstrumentation; Imaging technology. Home: 2307 Honeysuckle Rd Chapel Hill NC 27514 Office: Duke U Med Center PO Box 3949 Durham NC 27710

JAUHAR, PREM PRAKASH, cytogeneticist, researcher, consultant; b. W. Punjab, India, Sept. 15, 1939; came to the U.S., 1976, naturalized, 1984. s. Ram Lal and Maya Devi (Bhatla) J.; m. Raj Trehan, May 15, 1965; children: Rajiv, Sandeep, Suneeta. M.Sc., Agra U., India, 1959; Ph.D., New Delhi U., 1965. Assoc. prof. Indian Agr. Research Inst., New Delhi, 1963-72, postgrad. faculty, 1965-72; sr. sci. officer Welsh Plant Breeding Sta., U. Wales, Aberystwyth, 1972-75; research assoc. U. Ky., Lexington, 1976-78; research cytogeneticist U. Calif.-Riverside, 1978-81; cytogeneticist City of Hope Nat. Med. Ctr., Duarte, Calif., 1981; research dir. U.S. Agri. Labs. Research and Devel. Corp., Riverside, 1982-84; research geneticist Agrl. Research Service USDA, Western Regional Ctr., Berkeley, Calif., 1985—; Cons. genetics, cytogenetics and plant breeding; lectr. European labs. Area capt Am. Heart Assn., Riverside. Author: Cytogenetics and Breeding of Pearl Millet and Related Species, 1981; contbr. articles to profl. jours., chpts. to books. Mem. Genetics Soc. Am., Crop Sci. Soc. Am., Am. Genetic Assn., Am. Soc. Agronomy; fellow Linnean Soc. (London), Indian Soc. Genetics and Plant Breeding, Tissue culture Assn. Am. Discovered regulatory mechanism controlling chromosome pairing in polyploid species of Festuca. Current Work: Cytogenetics and plant breeding to genetically reprogram plants; plant cells and tissue culture for improving and cloning genetically superior plants; genetic control of chromosome pairing; genetic toxicology. Subspecialties: Plant genetics; Plant cell and tissue culture. Home: 230 W Campus View Drive Riverside CA 92507 Office: Western Regional Research Ctr USDA 800 Buchanan St Berkeley CA 94710

JAVEL, ERIC, neurophysiologist, educator; b. Elizabeth, N.J., Mar. 2, 1947; s. Francis Julius and Charlotte (Murray) J.; m. Mary Ellen Schuster, Dec. 28, 1968; children—Eric Daniel, Colin Christopher, Lindsay Kathryn. B.A., Johns Hopkins U., 1968; Ph.D., U. Pitts., 1972. Postdoctoral fellow U. Wis., 1975; acting dir. research Boys Town Nat. Inst., Omaha, 1976-77, staff scientist, 1976—; asst., then prof. otolaryngology Creighton U., Omaha, 1977—, From asst. prof. to prof. physiology, 1978—; assoc. prof. U. Nebr., Omaha, 1981—; vis. research fellow U. Melbourne, Australia, 1984-85. Contbr. articles to profl. jours. NIH fellow, 1973-75, grantee, 1978, 81, 84. Mem. Acoustical Soc. Am., Soc. Neurosci., Assn. Research in Otolaryngology. Current work: Sensory physiology; physiology of hearing; hearing maturation and development; computer applications in physiology. Subspecialty: Neurophysiology. Home: 676 N 58th St Omaha NE 68132 Office: Boys Town Nat Inst 555 N 30th St Omaha NE 68131

JAVID, MANUCHER J., neurosurgeon; b. Tehran, Iran, Jan. 11, 1922; came to U.S., 1944, naturalized, 1957; s. Asdolah and Touba (Ahdiyeh) J.; m. Lida Emma Fabbri, Oct. 19, 1951; children—Roxane, Daria, Jeffrey, Claudia. M.D., U. Ill., 1946. Diplomate: Am. Bd. Neurol. Surgery. Intern Augustana Hosp., Chgo., 1946-47, resident gen. surgery, 1947-48, resident neurosurgery, 1948-49; asst. in neuropathology Ill. Neuropsychiat. Inst., Chgo., 1948-49; fellow in neurosurgery Lahey Clinic, Boston, 1949; resident neurosurgery New Eng. Med. Center, Boston, 1950; clin. research fellow neurosurgery Mass. Gen. Hosp., Boston, 1950, asst. resident, 1951, sr. resident neurosurgery, 1952; teaching fellow in surgery Harvard, 1952; instr. Med. Sch. U. Wis., Madison, 1953-54, asst. prof., 1954-57, asso. prof., 1957-62, prof. neurosurgery, 1962, chmn. div. neurosurgery, 1963—; Cons. neurosurg VA Hosp., Madison. Contbr. articles profl. jours. Mem. AMA, ACS, Soc. Neurol. Surgeons, Am. Assn. Neurol. Surgeons, AAAS, Am. Assn. Med. Colls., AAUP, Am. Trauma Soc., Pan Am. Med. Assn., Soc. for Neurosci., Central Neurosurg. Soc. (pres. 1964), N.Y. Acad. Scis., Xeiron, Sigma Xi, Phi Beta Pi. Mem. Baha'i Faith. Club: Rotarian. Introduced clin. use of urea for reduction intracranial and intraocular pressure. Subspecialty: Neurosurgery. Home: 4750 Lafayette Dr Madison WI 53705 Office: Univ Wis Hosp and Clinics 600 Highland Ave Madison WI 53792

JAVID, NIKZAD SABET, prosthodontics educator, dentist; b. Kashan, Iran, May 24, 1934; came to U.S., 1969; s. Salam and Pika (Farhang) Javid-Sabet; m. Mahnaz Zolfaghari, Oct. 22, 1942; children: Nikrooz, Behrooz, Farnaz. D.M.D., U. Tehran, Iran, 1958; cert., U. Chgo., 1970; M.Sc., Ohio State U., 1971; M.Ed., U. Fla., 1981. Assoc. prof. U. Tehran, 1959-69, prof., dean, 1975-79; asst. prof. Ohio State U., 1971-73, assoc. prof., 1973-74; assoc. prof. removable prosthodontics U. Fla., 1974-75, prof., 1980—, pvt. practice dentistry specializing in prosthodontics, Gainesville, Fla., 1980—; cons. in field. Author books, including: Stress Breaker in Partial Denture, 1966, Cleft Palate Prosthetics, 1968, Complete Denture Construction, 1974, (with Sara Nawab) Essentials of Complete Denture Prosthodontics, 1979; contbr. numerous articles to profl. jours. Named Outstanding Clin. Instr. of Yr. Student Dental Council, Columbus, Ohio, 1973. Fellow Internat. Coll. Dentists, Royal Soc. Health (Eng.); mem. Iranian Dental Assn. (dir. 1975-78), ADA, Internat. Assn. Dental Research (sec.-treas. Iran div. 1978). Lodge: Lions. Current Work: Teaching and research in clinical dentistry. Subspecialty: Prosthodontics. Home: 3865 NW 38th Pl Gainesville FL 32605 Office: U Fla JHMHC Box J-435 Gainesville FL 32610

JAWAD, SARIM NAJIM, fluid mechanics educator, researcher; b. Baghdad, Iraq, July 1, 1953; s. Naji Mohammad and Radiea Ali (al-Alawiee) J. B.S., Baghdad U., 1976; M.S., Liverpool Poly. Inst., Eng., 1977; Ph.D., Hatfield Poly. Inst., Eng., 1982. Registered profl. engr. Asst. engr. Nat. Co. Vegetable Oil Products, Iraq, 1975; research assoc. Hatfield Poly. Inst., 1978-82, vis. research fellow, 1982—; cons. devl., cons. engr. Emirates Cons. Co., Abu Dhabi, United Arab Emirates, 1982-83; lectr. fluid mechanics and thermodynamics United Arab Emirates U., Al Ain, 1983—; cons. engr. Accadema Ltd., Eng., 1981-83. United Arab Emirates Ministry Edn. grantee, 1980-82. Fellow Inst. Diagnostic Engring. (fgn.); mem. ASME, AIAA, Am. Nuclear Soc., Instn. Mech. Engrs., Soc. Automotive Engrs., Royal Aero. Soc. Moslim. Current Work: Research in the aero-thermodynamic and structural design of high pressure ratio, radial flow, centrifugal compressors. Subspecialties: Fluid mechanics; Robotics. Home: PO Box 4349 Abu Dhabi United Arab Emirates Office: Engring Coll United Arab Emirates University PO Box 15551 Al Ain United Arab Emirates

JAWETZ, PINCAS, energy policy consultant; b. Czernowitz, Rumania, Dec. 20, 1935; s. Herman and Pepi (Frankel) J.; m. Irith Brenner, May 30, 1972; children: Gil-Shalom, Tom-Tsvi. M.Sc. in Chemistry, Hebrew U., Jerusalem, 1961; M.I.M., Am. Grad. Sch. Internat. Mgmt., 1975; postgrad., Rutgers U., 1968-74. Conducted studies on energy policy for Hudson Inst., GAO, Conducted studies on energy policy for countries of Colombia, Costa Rica, New Zealand, Israel, others, ind. cons. on energy policy, N.Y.C., congl. witness on energy policy. Contbr. articles profl. jours. Mem. Am. Chem. Soc., Am. Inst. Chem. Engrs., AAAS, N.Y. Acad. Scis., Internat. Assn. Energy Economists, Am. Econs. Assn. Current Work: Biofuels, integration of farm policy with energy policy, octane levels and petroleum refineries, alcohol fuels in U.S. and overseas. Subspecialties: Fuels; Agricultural economics. Home: 425 E 72d St New York NY 10021 Office: 235 E 54th St New York NY 10022

JAWOROWSKI, ANDRZEJ EDWARD, physics educator, researcher; b. Lublin, Poland, Dec. 28, 1942; came to U.S. 1978; s. Edward and Anna Bogumila (Grudzien) J.; m. Bozena Helena Nalecz, Aug. 15, 1965; 1 child, Peter Andrew. M.S. in Physics, U. Warsaw, 1966, Ph.D., 1974. Instr. physics, U. Warsaw, 1966-68, lectr., 1968-74, sr. lectr., 1974-78; sr. research assoc. SUNY-Albany, 1978-83; assoc. prof. physics Wright State U., Dayton, Ohio, 1983—; research assoc. Inst. Nuclear Research, Swierk, Poland, 1967-74; head of program Polish Acad. Scis., Warsaw, 1976-77; cons. Mobil Solar Energy Co., Waltham, Mass., 1980-83. Contbr. articles to tech. jours. Recipient Ministry of Sci. Sch. Acad. Rank and Tech. prize, Warsaw, 1975, Award of Pres. of U. Warsaw, 1975,77. Mem. European Phys. Soc., Am. Phys. Soc., Polish Phys. Soc. (sec. Warsaw dept. 1975-77), Electrochem. Soc., Materials Research Soc. Current works: Physics of electronic materials, defects in semiconductors, radiation effects and damage, ion implantation, hydrogen passivation, deep levels spectroscopy. Subspecialties: Condensed matter physics; Electronic materials. Office: Dept Physics Wright State University Dayton OH 45435

JAWORSKI, ERNEST GEORGE, biochemist; b. Mpls., Jan. 10, 1926; s. Leon and Miecieslawa (Tchorzewska) J.; m. Pauline B. Robinson, July 8, 1950; children: Diane, David, Christopher. B.S. in Chemistry, U. Minn., 1948; M.S. in Biochemistry, Oreg. State U., 1950, Ph.D. in Biochemistry, 1952. Research biochemist Monsanto Co., St. Louis, 1952-60, dir. molecular biology program, corp. research labs., 1980, Disting. Sci. fellow, dir. molecular biology program, corp. research labs., 1980-83; sci. fellow Monsanto Agrl. Products Co., St. Louis, 1960-62, sr. sci. fellow, 1962-70, disting. sci. fellow, 1970—; chmn. bd. trustees Gordon Research Confs., Inc. Contbr. chpts. to books; mem. editorial bd., Ann. Revs., Inc., 1976-81, Jour. Am. Soc. Plant Physiologists, 1973-78; editor: Trends in Biotechnology, 1983—; contbr. articles to profl. jours. Mem. Florissant (Mo.) Sch. Bd., 1957-61. Served with USN, 1944-46. Mem. Am. Chem. Soc., AAAS, N.Y. Acad. Scis., Am. Soc. Plant Physiologists, Internat. Assn. Plant Tissue Culture, Tissue Culture Assn. Patentee. Current Work: Plant and microbial genetic transformation; direction of research, plant molecular biology and cellular transformation, animal growth hormone, cellular mediators. Subspecialties: Genetics and genetic engineering (agriculture); Molecular biology.

JAY, RICHARD MARTIN, pediatric surgeon administrator, educator; b. N.Y.C., Dec. 23, 1946; s. Don F. and Blanche J.; m. Roslyn Kricheff, Mar. 15, 1980; 1 child, Kate Jenny. B.S., Bethany Coll., 1969; postgrad. in Biochemistry, California (Pa.) State U., 1969-70; D.Podiatric Medicine, Pa. Coll. Podiatric Medicine, 1976. Diplomate: Am. Bd. Podiatric Surgery. Intern J.F. Kennedy Meml. Hosp. Med. Center, Phila., 1976-77, resident, 1977-78; dir. pediatric orthopedics Pa. Coll. Podiatric Medicine, Phila., 1978—, assoc. prof. pediatric foot orthopedics, 1978—, dir. pediatric orthopedics, 1978—; dir. foot surgery residency J.F. Kennedy Hosp., Phila., 1978—; surg. cons. Inter County Hosp. Plan, Foxcroft, Pa., 1982—. Pediatrics editor: Jour. Current Podiatry, 1982; editor: Jour. Am. Podiatry Assn, 1983, 1985 Yearbook of Podiatric Medicine and Surgery. 1985 Yearbook Podiatric Medicine and Surgery; contbr. chpt. to book, article to jour. in field. Recipient Annual Foot Surgery award Am. Coll. Foot Surgeons, 1976, award Am. Coll. Foot Radiologists, 1976, Radiologists in Podiatry award Pa. Coll. Podiatric Medicine, 1976. Fellow Am. Coll. Foot Orthopedics, Am. Coll. Podopediatrics; mem. Am. Coll. Podiatric Sports Medicine, Am. Podiatry Assn. Current Work: Research in pediatric foot orthopedics for internal tibial torsion - implant designs and production for flatfeet via sinus tarsi plugs. Subspecialties: Pediatrics; Orthopedics. Office: 7915 Frankford Ave Philadelphia PA 19136 Pa Coll Podiatric Medicine 8th and Race St Philadelphia PA 19106

JAYADEV, TUMKUR SHIVA, electrical engineer, researcher; b. Bangalore, India, May 1, 1936; came to U.S. 1965; m. Leela Gundanna, July 12, 1963; children—Sumie, Raj. B. Engring., U. Mysore, India, 1958; M.S., Ill. Inst. Tech., 1965; Ph.D., U. Notre Dame, 1968. Prof., mem. Lab for Surface Studies, U. Wis., Milw., 1968-77; prin. scientist Solar Energy Research Inst., Golden, Colo., 1977-80; v.p., mgr. Energy Conversion Devices, Troy, Mich., 1980-82; sr. staff scientist Lockheed Palo Alto Research Lab., Calif., 1982—. Patentee in solid state energy conversion and solid state electronics. Burns fellow. Mem. IEEE, Electro-Chem. Soc. Current work: Conducting research on silicon-on-insulator technology and GaAs devices. Subspecialties: Semiconductors; Solar engineering. Home: 1132 Littleoak Circle San Jose CA 95129 Office: Lockheed Palo Alto Research Lab 3251 Hanover St Palo Alto CA 94304

JAYASEKARA, UPALI MATHESKANKANANGE, research pathologist, toxicologist; b. Ahungalla, Sri Lanka, Feb. 5, 1939; came to U.S., 1976; s. Robert and Mapinona (Vitharana) J.; m. Chitrangani Abeysekara, Oct. 1, 1973; children—Laleen, Sanjeewi. B.V.Sc. and A.H., E.P., Agrl. U., Mymensingh East Pakistan, 1965; M.S., U. Sask., Can., 1972; Ph.D., Kans. State U., 1978. Vet. surgeon Govt. of Sri Lanke, 1965-66; vet. research officer Vet. Research Inst., Peradeniya, Sri Lanka, 1966-76; instr. in pathology Kans. State U., Manhattan, 1976-78; research pathologist, study dir. Parke Davis Research, Ann Arbor, Mich., 1979—; vis. lectr. U. Ceylon, Peradeniya, 1974-76, Sch. Agr., Kundasale, Sri Lanka, 1973-76; cons. Ministry of Rural Devel., Sri Lanka, 1975-76. Editor, Animal Production and Health Bull., 1976. Contbr. articles to profl. jours. Served to lt. Sri Lanka Army, 1974-76. Recipient Habib Gold medal East Pakistan Agrl. U., 1965; Commonwealth scholar Can. Commonwealth Found., 1969. Mem. Ceylon Vet. Assn. (sec. 1974-76), AVMA, Soc. Toxicology, Sigma Phi Zeta, Gamma Sigma Delta. Buddhist. Club: Sri Lanka Sinha Regiment Officers (Kandy) (mess sec. 1974-76). Current work: Toxicologic pathology; congenital pathology; mechanism of action and toxicology of anti-hypertensive and anti-cancer drugs. Subspecialties: Pathology (veterinary medicine); Toxicology (medicine). Home: 2959 Burlington Ann Arbor MI 48105 Office: Parke Davis Pharm Research 2800 Plymouth Rd Ann Arbor MI 48105

JAYAWEERA, ANANDA RANJITH, biophysicist; b. Colombo, Sri Lanka, July 19, 1943; came to U.S., 1974; s. Solomon and Agnes (Fernando) J.; m. Amitha Wickramaratne, Apr. 1, 1972; 1 child, Ruwan Hasitha. B.S., U. Sri Lanka, Peradeniya, 1968, in Physics with honors, 1970; Ph.D., Portland State U., 1981. Research assoc. U. Md. Med. Sch., Balt., 1981-83, Johns Hopkins U. Sch. Hygiene, Balt., 1983—. Contbr. articles to profl. jours. Postdoctoral fellow Muscular Dystrophy Assn., 1983. Mem. AAAS, Biophys. Soc. Buddhist. Current work: Respiratory pulmonary and cardiovascular function at exercise and under drugs effecting the autonomic nervous system. Subspecialties: Biophysics (physics); Physiology (medicine). Home: 1363 Vida Dr Baltimore MD 21207 Office: Johns Hopkins U Sch Hygiene 615 N Wolfe St Baltimore MD 21205

JAYNE, BENJAMIN ANDERSON, educator; b. Enid, Okla., Oct. 10, 1928; s. Albert and Bertha Elizabeth (Anderson) J.; m. Betty Lu Bailey, Aug. 10, 1950; children—David N., Kristie A., Summer L. A.A., Boise Jr. Coll., 1949; B.S., U. Ida., 1952; M.F., Yale, 1953, Ph.D., 1955. Asst. prof. Yale, 1955-58; asso. prof. Wash. State U., 1959-62; sr. postdoctoral fellow U. Cal. at San Diego, 1963; prof. forestry N.C. State U., 1963-66, U. Wash., Seattle, 1966—; asso. dean U. Wash. (Coll. Forest Resources), 1966-71; dir. U. Wash. (Center Quantitative Sci. in Forestry, Fisheries and Wildlife), 1971-76; dean Sch. Foresty and Environmental Studies Duke U., 1976—. Editor: Wood and Fiber, Jour. Soc. Wood Sci. and Tech, 1969-72. Mem. A.A.A.S., Soc. Wood Sci. and Tech. (pres. 1968), Soc. Am. Forestry, Sigma Xi, Xi Sigma Pi. Current Work: Systems analysis applied to natural resource management. Subspecialties: Resource management; Composite materials. Home: 2610 Sevier St Durham NC 27705 Office: Sch Forestry and Environmental Studies Duke U Durham NC 27706

JAYNE, THEODORE DOUGLAS, interdisciplinary researcher; b. Painesville, Ohio, Dec. 3, 1929; s. Earl douglas and Mary Griffin (Erskine) J.; m. Penelope Sanders, Mar. 7, 1959 (div. 1980); children—Douglas T., Virginia Michelle Jayne Jones, Jillanne Mary. B.A., U. Chgo., 1950; postgrad. Case Inst. Tech., 1951-54. Head materials research lab. Rand Devel. corp., Cleve., 1950-64; dir. labs. Gen. Tech. Services, Inc., Upper Darby, Pa., 1964-69; dir. research T. Jayne Co., Painesville, Ohio, 1969—. Contbr. articles to profl. jours. Patentee in field. Current work: Interdisciplinary research, instrument research and development (process control and metrology) properties of processes and materials. Subspecialty: Research and development management.

JAYNES, EDGAR NORRIS, product researcher, surface scientist; b. Springfield, Mass., May 10, 1946; s. Edgar Norris and Mary (Bennett) J.; m. Louise Adele Hasinski, Aug. 29, 1979; children—Allison Norris, Heather Victoria. B.S. in Chemistry, W.Va. U., 1968; Ph.D., U. Wis., 1973. Postdoctoral assoc. U. Pa., Phila., 1973-76; sr. research assoc. Case Western Res. U., Cleve., 1976-79; project specialist Gen. Foods Corp., Tarrytown, N.Y., 1979-81, research specialist, 1981-84; sr. scientist S.C. Johnson & Son, Inc., Racine, Wis., 1984—; research and devel. coordinator Chem. Research and Devel. Ctr., Aberdeen Proving Ground, Md., 1977—. Contbr. articles to profl. jours. Bd. dirs. Jaycees, Yorktown Heights, N.Y., 1983. Served to lst lt. U.S. Army, 1973, to maj. USAR, 1973—. Republican. Lutheran. Current work: Researcher on skin and hair behavior and on emulsion structure and function, also gelation mechanisms and systems. Subspecialties: Organic chemistry; Surface chemistry. Home: 405 Lombard Ave Racine WI 53402 Office: S C Johnson & Son Inc 1525 Howe St Racine WI 53403

JEANLOZ, RAYMOND, geophysicist, educator; b. Winchester, Mass., Aug. 18, 1952; s. Roger and Dorothy Jeanloz. B.A. in Geology, Amherst Coll., 1975; Ph.D. in Geology and Geophysics, Calif. Inst. Tech., 1979. From asst. to assoc. prof. Harvard U., 1979-82; assoc. prof. dept. geology and geophysics Univ. Calif.-Berkeley, 1983—, mem. assoc. faculty Lawrence Berkeley Lab., 1984—; mem. lunar and planetary rev. panel NASA, 1982—. Assoc. editor Jour. Geophys. Research, 1984—. Contbr. articles to profl. jours. Recipient Presdl. Young Investigator award NSF, 1984; A.P. Sloan Found. fellow, 1981. Fellow Am. Geophys. Union (J.B. Macelwane award 1984); mem. Geol. Soc. Am., AAAS. Current work: Experimental geophysics; mineral physics; properties and evolution of planetary interiors; high pressure physics and chemistry. Subspecialties: Geophysics; Condensed matter physics. Office: Dept Geology and Geophysics Univ Calif Berkeley CA 94720

JEANLOZ, ROGER WILLIAM, biochemistry educator, consultant, editor; b. Berne, Switzerland, Nov. 3, 1917; s. Paul William Marc and Rose (Poisat) J.; m. Dorothea A.H. de Passavant, Dec. 20, 1945; children—Patrick Marc, Claude-Andre, Raymond Francois, Danielle Renee, Sylvie Anne. Baccalaureate, Coll. Calvin, Geneva, Switzerland, 1936; M.Sc., U. Geneva, 1941, D.Sc., 1943; D.Sc., (hon.), U. Paris, 1980. Sr. mem. Worcester Found. for Exptl. Biology, Mass., 1948-51; assoc. biochemistry Mass. Gen. Hosp., Boston, 1951-61, biochemist, 1961; asst. prof. Harvard Med. Sch., Boston, 1960-61, assoc. prof., 1961-69, prof. biochemistry, 1969—. Editor books on amino sugars and glycoconjugate research. Contbr. articles to profl. jours. Patentee in field. Recipient Hudson prize Am. Chem. Soc., 1973, Sr. Scientist award Alexander von Humboldt Found., 1983. Fellow Royal Soc. Chemistry, Am. Chem. Soc., AAAS; mem. Am. Soc. Biol. Chemists, Soc. for Complex Carbohydrates, Swiss Chemists Soc. Societe de Chimie Biologique, Biochem.

Soc., Commn. Congregationalist. Club: Longwood Cricket (Boston). Current work: Synthetic carbohydrate chemistry. Structure and biosynthesis of complex carbohydrates at the surface of bacterial and animal cells. Subspecialties: Biochemistry (biology); Biochemistry (medicine). Home: 42 Ruthven Rd Newton MA 02158 Office: Mass Gen Hosp Fruit St Boston MA 02114

JEDLINSKI, HENRYK, research plant pathologist; b. Bialystok, Poland, Feb. 15, 1924; s. Tomasz and Jadwiga (Weglewska) J.; m. Helena Malinowska, Dec. 31, 1958; children: Michael T., Janine V. B.S., U. Nebr., 1950, M.A., 1954, Ph.D., 1959. Research asst. U. Nebr., Lincoln, 1951; research plant pathologist Agrl. Research Service U.S. Dept. Agr., Urbana, Ill., 1959—; assoc. prof. dept. plant pathology U. Ill., Urbana, 1979—. Mem. Am. Phytopathological Soc., Internat. Soc. Plant Pathology, Am. Soc. Virology, Sigma Xi, Gamma Sigma Delta. Republican. Roman Catholic. Current Work: Diseases of cereals-oats-wheat; resistance, insect transmission of viruses; virus interactions with other pathogens. Subspecialties: Plant pathology; Plant virology. Office: 1102 S Goodwin Ave Urbana IL 61801

JEDRUCH, JACEK, nuclear engineer, computer scientist, writer; b. Warsaw, Poland, Feb. 22, 1927; came to U.S., 1951, naturalized, 1957; s. Alexander and Ann (Borsuk) J.; m. Eva Christina Hoffman, Apr. 15, 1972. B.S. in Mech. Engring, Northeastern U., 1956; M.S. in Nuclear Engring, MIT, 1958; Ph.D. in Nuclear Engring, Pa. State U., 1966. Metall. analyst Acme Type Metals Co., Everett, Mass., 1952-53; engring. trainee H.B. Smith Co., Inc., Westfield, Mass., 1953-56; ind. cons. Columbia Nat. Co., Cambridge, Mass., 1957; scientist Westinghouse Electric Co., Pitts, 1957-65, fellow scientist, 1966-82; cons., 1983—. Author: Constitutions, Elections and Legislatures of Poland, 1493-1977, 1982; Nuclear Engineering Data Bases, Standards and Numerical Analysis, 1985. Devel. chmn. Am. Youth Hostels, 1958-64; mem. Internat. Commn. for History of Rep. and Parliamentary Instns. Served with Polish Army, 1944-46; Served with Brit. Army, 1946-48. Mem. Am. Soc. Mech. Engrs., Am. Nuclear Soc. Republican. Roman Catholic. Club: MIT of Western Pa. (treas. 1978—). Current Work: Development of conceptual computational methods for neutronics, photonics of nuclear reactors; development and access to data bases; nuclear fuel cycle for power reactors. Subspecialties: Nuclear engineering; Numerical analysis (computer science). Home: 377 Maize Dr Pittsburgh PA 15236

JEFFERIES, JOHN TREVOR, astrophysicist; b. Kellerberrin, Western Australia, Apr. 2, 1925; s. John and Vera (Healy) J.; m. Charmian Candy, Sept. 10, 1949; children: Stephen R., Helen C., Trevor R. B.Sc., U. Western Australia, 1947, D.Sc., 1961; M.A., Cambridge U., 1949. Research officer Commonwealth Sci. and Indsl. Research Orgn., Sydney, Australia, 1949-60; cons. to dir. Nat. Bur. Standards, Boulder, Colo., 1960-62; fellow Joint Inst. Lab. Astrophysics, Boulder, 1962-64; prof. physics and astronomy, dir. Inst. Astronomy, U. Hawaii, 1964-83; dir. Nat. Optical Astronomy Obs., 1983—; prof. Coll. de France, 1970, 77; bd. dirs. Associated Univs. for Research in Astronomy, 1976—. Author: Spectral Line Formation, 1967; Contbr. articles profl. jours. Guggenheim fellow, 1970. Fellow Royal Astron. Soc., AAAS; mem. Internat. Astron. Union (pres. commn. X 1970-73), Am. Astron. Soc. (chmn. solar phys. div. 1971-72). Subspecialty: Solar physics. Home: 6760 Placita Manzanita Tucson AZ 85718

JEFFERY, DUANE ELDRO, evolutionary geneticist, biology educator; b. Delta, Utah, Sept. 28, 1937; s. Eldro Ether and Leona I. (Skeem) J.; m. Jacquita Kaye Westover, Sept. 15, 1961; children—Tammi, Kodi, Doni. B.S., Utah State U., 1962, M.S., 1963; M.A., U. Calif.-Berkeley, 1966, Ph.D., 1972. Asst. prof. zoology Brigham Young U., Provo, Utah, 1969-74, assoc. prof., 1976—; vis. researcher U. Hawaii, Honolulu, 1974-75; sec. Nat. Ctr. for Sci. Edn., Syosset, N.Y., 1982—. Contbr. articles to profl. jours. Served as 1st lt., inf. U.S. Army, 1962-68. Recipient various teaching excellence awards Brigham Young U. Mem. Genetics Soc. Am., Soc. for Study Evolution, AAAS. Current work: Ecological genetics of Drosophila, significance of chromosome structural aberrations, in situ hybridization mapping of comparative nucleotide sequences in Drosophila species. Subspecialties: Evolutionary biology; Genome organization. Home: 549 E 2825 N Provo UT 84604 Office: Dept Zoology Brigham Young U Provo UT 84602

JELINSKI, LYNN W., polymer scientist. Head polymer chemistry research group AT&T Bell Labs., Murray Hill, N.J. Subspecialty: Polymer chemistry. Office: AT&T Bell Labs Polymer Chemistry Research Group Murray Hill NJ 07974*

JELLISON, GERALD EARLE, JR., physicist; b. Bangor, Maine, Mar. 27, 1946; s. Gerald Earle and Gertrude (Allen) J.; m. Mary Milkovich, Mar. 14, 1970; children—Lisa, Katherine Lynn. B.A., Bowdoin Coll., 1968; M. Sc., Brown U., 1971, Ph.D., 1977. Post-doctoral fellow Naval Research Lab., Washington, 1976-78; staff scientist Oak Ridge Nat. Lab., 1978—. Contbr. articles to sci. jours. Author: (with others) Pulsed Laser Processing of Semiconductors, 1984. Served to lt. USNR, 1969-71. Fulbright-Hayes fellow, 1968. Mem. Am. Phys. Soc., Am. Optical Soc., Materials Research Soc. Current work: Laser interaction with semiconductors; time-resolved spectroscopy. Subspecialties: Condensed matter physics; Materials processing. Home: 122 Carnegie Dr Oak Ridge TN 37830 Office: Oak Ridge Nat Lab Oak Ridge TN 37830

JEN, PHILIP HUNG SUN, biology educator; b. Hung, Hunan, China, Jan. 11, 1944; s. Shou-shon and Yun In (Kuo) J.; m. Betty Yu Lee, Feb. 20, 1971. B.Sc., Tunghai U., 1967; M.A., Washington U., 1971, Ph.D., 1974. Instr. biology Chinese Air Preparatory Sch., Tung Kung, Taiwan, 1967-68; tchr. biology St. Dominics High Sch., Kaohsiung, 1968-69; teaching asst. Washington U., St. Louis, 1969-74, research assoc., 1974-75; asst. prof. U. Mo., Columbia, 1975-80, assoc. prof. dept. biol. sci., 1981-83, prof., 1984—. Contbr. articles to profl. jours. Served to 2nd lt. Chinese Army, 1967-68. Tunghai U. scholar, 1963-67; NSF research grantee, 1978, 80; NIH Research Career Devel. awardee, 1980—. Mem. Am. Soc. Zoologists, AAAS, N.Y. Acad. Sci., Soc. for Neurosci., Acoustic Soc. Am. Current Work: Behavior, neurophysiology and neuroanatomy of bat's biosonar system. Subspecialties: Neurophysiology; Neurobiology. Office: Div Biol Sci U Mo Columbia MO 65211

JENCKS, WILLIAM PLATT, educator, biochemist; b. Bar Harbor, Maine, Aug. 15, 1927; s. Gardner and Elinor (Melcher) J.; m. Miriam Ehrlich, June 3, 1950; children—Helen Esther, David Alan. Grad., St. Paul's Sch., Balt., 1944; student, Harvard, 1944-47, M.D., 1951. Intern Peter Bent Brigham Hosp., Boston, 1951-52; postdoctoral fellow Mass. Gen. Hosp., Boston, 1952-53, 55-56; postdoctoral fellow chemistry Harvard, 1956-57; mem. faculty Brandeis U., 1957—, prof. biochemistry, 1963—. Served as 1st lt., M.C. AUS, 1953-55. Mem. Am. Chem. Soc. (award biol. chemistry 1962), Am. Soc. Biol. Chemists, Am. Acad. Arts and Scis., AAAS, Nat. Acad. Scis., Alpha Omega Alpha. Current Work: Reaction mechanics and catalysis in chemistry and enzymology. Subspecialties: Biochemistry (medicine); Organic chemistry. Home: 11 Revere St Lexington MA 02173 Office: Grad Dept Biochemistry Brandeis Univ Waltham MA 02254

JENDEN, DONALD JAMES, pharmacology educator; b. Horsham, Eng., Sept. 1, 1926; came to U.S., 1950, naturalized, 1958; s. William Herbert and Kathleen Mary (Harris) J.; m. Jean Ickeringill, Nov. 18, 1950; children—Patricia Mary, Peter D., Beverly J. B.Sc. with 1st class honors, Kings Coll.-London, 1947; M.B., B.S. with honors, U. London, 1950; Ph.D. Pharm. Chem., Honoris Causa (hon.), U. Uppsala, 1980. Demonstrator in pharmacology St. Bartholomew Hosp. Med. Sch., Kings Coll., 1948-49; lectr. pharmacology U. Calif. Med. Ctr., San Francisco, 1948-49, USPHS fellow, 1951-53, asst. prof., San Francisco, Los Angeles, 1952-56, assoc. prof., Los Angeles, 1956-60, prof. pharmacology, 1960—, acting chmn. dept., 1956-57, mem. Brain Research Inst., 1961—, prof. biomath., 1967—, chmn. dept. pharmacology, 1968—; NSF sr. postdoctoral fellow dept. biophysics Univ. Coll., London, 1961-62, hon. research assoc. 1961-62; Wellcome vis. prof. U. Ala., Birmingham, 1984; cons. pharm. devel., govt. agys., instns. Mem. editorial bd. various jours. including Life Scis., Neurobiology of Aging, others. Contbr. numerous tech. articles to profl. jours. Served as lt. M.C., USNR, 1954-56. Recipient Fulbright Short-Term Sr. Scholar award, Australia. Fellow Am. Coll. Neuropsychopharmacology; mem. AAAS, Am. Chem. Soc. (div. medicinal chemistry), Am. Physiol. Soc., Am. Soc. for Mass Spectrometry, Am. Soc. for Med. Sch. Pharmacology, Am. Soc. Neurochemistry, Am. Soc. for Pharmacology and Exptl. Therapeutics, Assn. for Med. Sch. Pharmacology, Internat. Union Pharmacology (sect. toxicology), Physiol. Soc. (London), Soc. for Neurosci., W. Coast Coll. Biol. Psychology, Western Pharmacology Soc., N.Y. Acad. Scis. Current work: Cholinergic mechanisms, biomedical applications of gas chromatography/mass spectrometry and stable isotopes, neurochemistry of aging. Subspecialties: Neuropharmacology; Medicinal chemistry. Office: U Calif Sch Medicine Ctr Health Scis Dept Pharmacology Los Angeles CA 90024

JENKINS, ALEXANDER, III, analytical instrument company executive; b. Weymouth, Mass., Feb. 17, 1934; s. Alexander and Edith Gladys (Price) J.; m. Judith H. Switzer, Jan. 4, 1975; children—Alexander Tuxbury, Edith Garland, Charles Jordan. B.A., Yale U., 1956; M.B.A., Harvard U., 1961. Treas. Ocean Research Equipment Co., Falmouth, Mass., 1961-62; treas. Orion Research, Inc., Cambridge, Mass., 1962-65, 77-78, exec. v.p., 1970-71, pres., chief exec. officer, 1981—, dir., 1972—; cons., 1971-73; v.p., dir. Adcole Corp., Waltham, Mass., 1973-79; pres. Jenkins Assocs., Arlington, Mass., 1973—; treas., dir. Pintek, Inc., Newton, Mass., 1979-81; div. mgr. Spectra Physics, Bedford, Mass., 1980-81; dir. Flash Technology, Nashua, N.H., Intermetrics, Cambridge, GPM Fund, Inc., Ferranti O.R.E., Inc., Falmouth. Served with USN, 1956-59. Episcopalian. Subspecialty: Research and development management. Office: Orion Research Inc 840 Memorial Dr Cambridge MA 02139

JENKINS, ARNOLD MILTON, management information systems educator, consultant, researcher; b. Milford, Mass., June 12, 1938; s. Arnold Milton and Evelyn Estalla (Williams) J.; m. Jane Monica Biedugnis, July 20, 1964; children: Arnold Milton, Michelle Evelyn. A.Mech. Engring., Worcester Coll., 1961; B.S. in Econs., U. Albuquerque, 1969; M.B.A., U. N.Mex., 1971; Ph.D. in Mgmt. Info. Sci, U. Minn., 1977. Design engr. Whitin Machine Works, Whitinsville, Mass., 1957-62; engr., mgr. Sandia Labs., Albuquerque, 1962-72; assoc. mem. grad. faculty U. Minn., Mpls., 1972-76; prof. mgmt. info. systems Ind. U., Bloomington, 1976—; L.J. Buchan disting. prof. Oakland U., 1984—; tchr./cons. AID, U.S. Dept. State, Washington, 1978—; cons. Owens Corning Fiberglass, Toledo, 1982—, Procter & Gamble Co., Cin., 1980—, Gen. Mills, Inc., Mpls., 1980—. Author: Program of Research for Investigating MIS, 1982; editor for theory and research: Mgmt. Info. Systems Quar, 1977—. Mem. Soc. Mgmt. Info. Systems, Am. Inst. Decision Scis. (thesis competition award 1977), Assn. Systems Mgmt., Assn. Computing Machinery. Current Work: Methodologies and procedures for design, development and implementation of computerized information systems. Development of theory for user-system interface/ergonomics. Techniques for increasing productivity of knowledge workers through effective information utilization. Subspecialties: Information systems (Information science); Graphics, image processing, and pattern recognition. Home: 414 Meadowbrook Ave Bloomington IN 47401 Office: Operations and Systems Mgmt Dep Grad Sch Busines Ind U 650 Business Bldg Bloomington IN 47405

JENKINS, DONALD RALPH, mechanical engineering educator; b. New Brunswick, N.J., May 1, 1923; s. Ralph Audley and Rachel O. (Osborne) J.; m. Lavina Jane Burns, June 14, 1947; children—Winnie, Ralph, Rachel. B.S.M.E., Rutgers U., 1946; M.S.M.E., Lehigh U., 1951. Foundry engr. Ingersoll-Rand Co., Phillipsburg, N.J., 1946-47; asst. prof. mech. engring. Lafayette Coll., Easton, Pa., 1947-53, assoc. prof., 1959—; asst. prof. U. Maine, Orono, 1953-56; sr. specialist Gen. Motors Inst., Flint, Mich., 1956-59; automotive cons. Consumers Research, Washington, N.J., 1964-74; research assoc. U.S. Air Force, Dayton, Ohio, 1978; research fellow NASA, Cleve., 1980, 81. Author: I-C Engine Testing, 1969, 79; I-C Engine Fuels and Combustion, 1969. Served to 1st lt. USAF, 1943-45, ETO. Decorated Air medal with four oak leaf clusters, D.F.C. Mem. ASME (service award 1978), Am. Soc. Engring. Edn. Republican. Presbyterian. Lodge: Masons. Current work: Microprocessor based signal interfacing, data handling and control programming for computer aided testing of internal combustion engines. Subspecialties: Systems engineering; Combustion processes. Home: 142 Bullman St Phillipsburg NJ 08865 Office: Mech Engring Dept Lafayette Coll Easton PA 08865

JENKINS, EDMUND CHARLES, research scientist, clinical cytogeneticist; b. Wilkes-Barre, Pa., Sept. 15, 1942; s. Edmund and Mary Ann (Gallagher) J.; m. Valerie Ann Burhorst, July 20, 1983; 1 child, Edmund Charles. B.S., King's Coll., 1964; Ph.D., Fordham U., 1968. Diplomate Am. Bd. Med. Genetics; cert. cytogeneticist, N.Y.C., N.Y. State. Research scientist I, N.Y. State Inst. for Basic Research in Devel. Disabilities, S.I., N.Y., 1968-69, research scientist III in cytogenetics, 1969-73, research scientist V, 1973-82, research scientist VI, 1982—, chmn. cytogenetics, 1984—; adj. assoc. prof., Fordham U., Bronx, N.Y., 1983—; chmn. cytogenetics adv. com. Prenatal Diagnosis Lab. N.Y.C., 1981—; dir. cytogenetics North Shore U. Hosp. Cornell, Manhasset, N.Y., 1975-78, acting dir. cytogenetics, 1984. Contbr. articles to profl. jours.; presentor at numerous sci. mtgs. Mem. Philharmonic Soc. Lincoln Ctr., N.Y.C., 1971—. NIH trainee in devel. cytology Fordham U., 1964-68; N.Y. State/Office Mental Retardation and Devel. Disabilities, Dept. Health grantee, 1983-85; recipient Humanitarian award N.Y.C. Assn. Help Retarded Children, 1979. Mem. Council Research Scientists (exec. com., sec. 1979—), Research Found. Mental Hygiene Inc. N.Y. State (bd. dirs. 1980—), Am. Soc. Human Genetics. Democrat. Roman Catholic. Current work: Cytogenetics - the study of the Fragile X Syndrome, Down Syndrome and the identification of new chromosomal syndromes of mental retardation and developmental disability. Subspecialties: Genome organization; Developmental biology. Home: 11 Starlight Rd Staten Island NY 10301 Office: N Y State Inst Basic Research in Devel Disabilities 1050 Forest Hill Rd Staten Island NY 10314

JENKINS, JAMES THOMAS, theoretical mechanics educator; b. Chgo., June 30, 1942; s. Marvin Nicholas and Esther Alice (Nelson) J.; m. Katharine Kelly, Oct. 8, 1983; children—Thomas Nelson, Peter Kelly. B.S. in Mech. Engring., Northwestern U., 1964; Ph.D., Johns Hopkins U., 1969. Research assoc. U. Paris, Orsay, 1969-70; vis. lectr. Strathclyde U., Glasgow, 1970-71; asst. prof. theoretical mechanics Cornell U., Ithaca, N.Y., 1971-77, assoc. prof., 1977-84, prof., 1984—. Contbr. articles to profl. jours. Mem. ASME, ASCE, Soc. Indsl. and Applied Math, Soc. Rheology, Soc. Natural Philosophy. Current work: Mechanics of granular materials; biomechanics of soft tissues and membranes. Subspecialties: Theoretical and applied mechanics; Biomedical engineering. Home: 116 W Yates St Ithaca NY 14850 Office: Cornell U Dept Mechanics Ithaca NY 14853

JENKINSON, HOWARD ACIS, physicist; b. Phila., Dec. 11, 1946; s. Acis and Margaret (Abbott) J.; m. Grace Stricker, Nov. 20, 1965; children—Stephanie, Jennifer, Rebecca. B.S., Ursinus Coll., 1969; M.S., Drexel U., 1971, Ph.D., 1982. Physicist, Frankford Arsenal, Phila., 1973-77, U.S. Army - Army Research and Devel. Ctr., Dover, N.J., 1977—. Contbr. articles to profl. jours. Recipient Dept. Army Research and Devel. Achievement award, 1976. Mem. Optical Soc. Am., Materials Research Soc. Republican. Episcopalian. Current work: Infrared optical waveguiding in gallium arsenide - materials effects, fabrication, devices, applications. Subspecialties: Integrated optics; Semiconductors. Office: US Army Research and Development Ctr SMCAR-SCF-RO(D) B95 Dover NJ 07801-5001

JENNE, FREDERICK BENJAMIN, electronics engineering executive; b. Hollywood, Calif., Jan. 19, 1935; s. Harold Benjamin and Margurite Zoe (Peterson) J.; m. Shirley May Baldwin, June 30, 1956 (div.); 1 child, Michele Mae. A.A., Palomar Coll., 1959; B.S.E.E., U. Calif.-Berkeley, 1962; M.S.E.E., Long Beach State Coll., 1971. Registered profl. engr., Calif. Mgr. phys. scis. lab. McDonnell-Douglas, Long Beach, Calif., 1962-66; mgr. process devel. N.Am. Rockwell, Anaheim, Calif., 1966-71; dir. research and devel. Am. Microsystems, Santa Clara, 1971-80; mgr. tech. devel. Advanced Microdevices, Sunnyvale, Calif., 1980-83; v.p. research and devel. Cypress Semiconductor Corp., San Jose, Calif., 1983—. Co-author: Memory Design, 1978; patentee Substrate bias generator, 1971; Photon Flux integration, 1971, Buried Source memory cell, 1978. Served with USN, 1954-58. Mem. IEEE (chmn. electron devices). Republican. Current work: Expert in the management and coordination of research and development of mos technology developement and product design. Subspecialties: Integrated circuits; Microelectronics. Office: Cypress Semiconductor Corp 3901 N 1st St San Jose CA 95134

JENNETTE, JOHN CHARLES, pathologist, educator; b. New Bern, N.C., Apr. 28, 1947; s. John Benjamin and Margaret Pointer (McKinney) J.; m. Yvonne Christine Cahoon, Nov. 1, 1969; children—Jennifer Christine, Caroline Elizabeth. B.S., U. N.C., 1969, M.D., 1973. Diplomate Am. Bd. Pathology. Resident in pathology U. N.C. Sch. Medicine, 1973-75; fellow, 1977, instr., 1978, asst. prof., 1978—; research fellow Scripps Clinic, San Diego, 1975-77; dir. immunopathology lab. N.C. Meml. Hosp., Chapel Hill, 1979—. Contbr. articles to profl. jours. Am. Cancer Soc. Jr. Faculty fellow, 1978, Jefferson Pilot fellow, 1981. Mem. Am. Assn. Pathologists, Internat. Acad. Pathology, Internat. Soc. Nephrology, Am. Soc. Nephrology, N.C. Med. Soc. Current work: Diagnostic immunopathology and renal pathology; research into immune pathogenesis of renal glomerular diseases. Subspecialties: Pathology (medicine); Immunology (medicine). Home: 2516 Millwood Ct Chapel Hill NC 27514 Office: Univ NC Sch Medicine Pathology Dept Chapel Hill NC 27514

JENNINGS, FEENAN DEE, oceanographer, research administrator; b. Los Angeles, Aug. 11, 1923; s. John Thomas and Rhesa Lorraine (Owens) J.; m. Mary Lou Forman, Dec. 26, 1964; children—David Owen, Lorraine Ann. B.S. in Chem. Engring., N.Mex. A&M U., 1950; postgrad. in chem. oceanography Scripps Instn. Oceanography, 1950-54, in chemistry UCLA, 1951-52. Sr. engr. Scripps Instn. Oceanography, LaJolla, Calif., 1954-58; head oceanographer Office Naval Research, Washington, 1958-66, dep. dir. oceanography sci. and tech., 1966-70; head Office for Internat. Decade Ocean Exploration, NSF, Washington, 1970-78; dir. Sea Grant, Tex. A&M U., College Station, 1978—, exec. dir. univ. research, 1982—. Contbr. to Oceanography Ency. Yearbook, 1974-84. Served with USN, 1942-46, PTO. Recipient Navy Outstanding award USN, 1961, 63, Mil. Oceanography award Office Oceanographer of Navy, 1970; Disting. Service award NSF, 1978, Oceanography award Am. Geophys. Union, 1983. Mem. Sea Grant Assn. (pres. 1981-82), Marine Tech. Soc. (mem. editorial bd. 1980-84), Am. Geophys. Union, AAAS. Methodist. Current work: Administration of oceanographic research specifically, and of broad academic research generally. Subspecialties: Oceanography; Ocean engineering. Home: Route 5 Box 1240 College Station TX 77840 Office: Texas A&M Univ College Station TX 77843

JENNINGS, KENT RICHARD, neurobiology researcher; b. White Rock, B.C., Can., May 17, 1956; s. David Walter and Dorothy (Ross) J.; m. Linda Kable, Aug. 12, 1978; 1 child, Anne Michelle. B.Sc. in Biology, Carleton U., 1973-77; Ph.D. in Neurobiology, Calif. Tech. Inst., 1977-81. Ross research fellow Calif. Tech. Inst., Pasadena, 1977-81; vis. scientist Agr. Can., London, Ont., 1981-83; research biologist Am. Cyanamid Co., Princeton, N.J., 1983-85, group leader insecticide discovery, 1985—; sci. reviewer Pesticide Biochemistry and Physiology, 1982—. Contbr. chpt. to Peptides, 1980. Contbr. articles to profl. jours. NRC sci. scholar, 1977; L.B. Pearson scholar, Carleton U., 1973-77. Mem. Soc. for Neurosci., Am. Chem. Soc. (pesticide div.), Entomol. Soc. Canada. Presbyterian. Current work: Insecticide discovery effort targeted at insect nervous system; pharmacology; screening; SAR; computer modelling; university liaison. Subspecialties: Comparative neurobiology; Neurochemistry. Office: Insecticide Discovery American Cyanamid PO 400 Princeton NJ 08540

JENNINGS, LARRY EUGENE, computer scientist; b. Oklahoma City, Aug. 3, 1947; s. Eugene Edgar and Helen Mary (Maune) J.; m. Linda Sue Dries, Dec. 22, 1970; children: Amy, Libby, Meggin. A.S., Okla. State U., 1968; B.S. in Math, U. Albuquerque, 1978; M.S., U. N.M., 1982. Materials technician Standard Testing & Engring., Oklahoma City, 1966-68; draftsman Sandia Nat. Lab., Albuquerque, 1968-72, electro-mech. designer, 1972-76, software engr., 1976-81, database designer, 1981-82, computer scientist CAD/CAM, 1982—. Mem. Inst. Interconnecting and Packaging Electronic Circuits, Assn. Computing Machinery. Current Work: Research concerning the communication of computer based product definition and engring. data among the various agencies within the nuclear weapons complex. Subspecialty: Database systems. Home: 6104 Case de Vida NE Albuquerque NM 87111

JENNINGS, LAURENCE DUANE, materials scientist, researcher; b. New Haven, Nov. 14, 1929; s. Laurence Duane and Elizabeth Noel (Adams) J.; m. Genevieve Asch, Sept. 14, 1951; children—Noel, Mark, Lauren. S.B., MIT, 1950, Ph.D., 1955. Asst. prof. Iowa State U., Ames, 1955-57; physicist Army Research Ctr., Watertown, Mass., 1959—. Mem. Am. Phys. Soc., Am. Crystallographic Assn. Current work: Materials degradation under extreme conditions; physics of X-ray diffraction. Subspecialties: Condensed matter physics; Materials. Home: 80 Clifton St Belmont MA 02178 Office: Army Materials and Mechanics Research Ctr AMXMR-OM Watertown MA 02172

JENSEN, ARTHUR ROBERT, educator; b. San Diego, Aug. 24, 1923; s. Arthur Alfred and Linda (Schachtmayer) J.; m. Barbara Jane DeLarme, May 6, 1960; 1 dau., Roberta Ann. B.A., U. Calif. at Berkeley, 1945; Ph.D., Columbia, 1956. Asst. med. psychology U. Md., 1955-56; research fellow Inst. Psychiatry, U. London, 1956-58; prof. ednl. psychology U. Calif. at Berkeley, 1958—. Author: Genetics and Education, 1972, Educability and Group Differences, 1973, Educational Differences, 1973, Bias in Mental Testing, 1979, Straight Talk about Mental Tests, 1981; Contbr. to profl. jours., books. Guggenheim fellow, 1964-65; fellow Center Advanced Study Behavioral Scis., 1966-67. Fellow Am. Psychol. Assn., Eugenics Soc., AAAS; mem. Am. Ednl. Research Assn. (v.p. 1968-70), Psychonomic Soc., Am. Soc. Human Genetics, Soc. for Social Biology, Behavior Genetics Assn., Psychometric Soc., Sigma Xi. Current Work: Research on measurement and causes of individual and group differences in human mental abilities, particulary intelligence, using psychometric, experimental, and behavior-genetic approaches. Subspecialties: Cognition; Learning. Home: 30 Canyon View Dr Orinda CA 94563

JENSEN, BARBARA LYNNE, physicist; b. Salt Lake City, July 12, 1939; d. Howard D. and Lucile (Miner) J.; m. William D. Jensen, Sept. 18, 1965. B.S. in Physics, U. Utah, 1964, postgrad., 1964-66; M.A. in Physics, Columbia U., 1972, Ph.D. in Physics, 1973. Research asst. IBM Thomas J. Watson Research Center, Yorktown Heights, N.Y., 1970-73; instr. in physics U. Lowell, Mass., 1974-77; asst. prof. physics Boston U., 1978—. Contbr. articles to profl. jours. Mem. Am. Phys. Soc., IEEE, Am. Vacuum Soc., AAAS. Current Work: Semiconductors, solid state physics, optical communications, submillimeter waves, microelectronics. Subspecialties: Condensed matter physics; Materials. Office: Dept Physics Boston U 111 Cummington St Boston MA 02215

JENSEN, ELWOOD VERNON, biochemist; b. Fargo, N.D., Jan. 13, 1920; s. Eli A. and Vera (Morris) J.; m. Mary Welmoth Collette, June 17, 1941 (dec. Nov. 1982); children: Karen Collette, Thomas Eli; m. Hiltrud Herborg, Dec. 21, 1983. A.B., Wittenberg U., 1940, D.Sc. (hon.), 1963; Ph.D., U. Chgo., 1944; D.Sc. (hon.), Acadia U., 1976. Faculty U. Chgo., 1947—; assoc. prof. biochemistry Ben May Lab. Cancer Research, 1954-60, prof., 1960-63, Am. Cancer Soc. research prof. physiology, 1963-69; dir. Ben May Lab., 1969-82; research dir. Ludwig Inst. Cancer Research, 1983—; prof. physiology Ben May Lab., 1969-73, 77—, prof. biophysics, 1973—, prof. biochemistry, 1980—; med. dir. Ludwig Inst. for Cancer Research, 1983—; dir. Biomed. Center for Population Research, 1972-75; vis. prof. Max-Planck-Inst. für Biochemie, Munich, Germany, 1958; chmn. endocrinology panel Cancer Chemotherapy Nat. Service Center, 1960-62; mem. chemotherapy rev. bd. Nat. Cancer Inst., 1960-62, bd. sci. counselors, 1969-72; mem. Nat. Adv. Council Child Health and Human Devel., 1976-80; mem. adv. com. biochemistry and chem. carcinogenesis Am. Cancer Soc., 1968-72, council for research and clin. investigation, 1974-77; mem. assembly life scis. NRC, 1975-78; mem. com. on sci., engring. and public policy Nat. Acad. Scis., 1981-82. Editorial bd.: Perspectives in Biology and Medicine, 1966—, Archives of Biochemistry and Biophysics, 1979-85; editorial adv. bd.: Biochemistry, 1969-72, Life Scis, 1973-78, Breast Cancer Research and Treatment, 1980—; assoc. editor.: Jour. Steroid Biochemistry, 1974—; Contbr. articles to profl. jours. Guggenheim fellow, 1946-47; recipient D.R. Edwards medal, 1970; La Madonnina prize, 1973; G.H.A. Clowes award, 1975; Papanicolaou award, 1975; prix Roussel, 1976; Nat. award Am. Cancer Soc., 1976; Amory prize, 1977; Gregory Pincus Meml. award, 1978; Gairdner Found. award, 1979; Lucy Wortham James award, 1980; Charles F. Kettering prize, 1980; Nat. Acad. Clin. Biochemistry award, 1981; Pharmacia award, 1982; Hubert H. Humphrey award, 1983; Rolf Luft medal, 1983; Renzo Grattarola medal, 1984; Fred Conrad Koch award, 1984; Axel Munthe award, 1985. Mem. Nat. Acad. Scis. (council 1981-84), Am. Acad. Arts and Scis., Am. Soc. Biol. Chemists, Am. Chem. Soc., Am. Assn. Cancer Research, Endocrine Soc. (pres. 1980-81), AAAS, Soc. Study Reprodn. Clubs: Chicago Literary, Cosmos. Current Work: Responsibility for supervision and development of cancer research programs at the ten research branches of the Ludwig Institute in six countries. Subspecialties: Cancer research (medicine); Receptors. Home: Seestrasse 260 CH 8706 Feldmeilen Switzerland Office: Stadelhoferstrasse 22 Zürich CH-8001 Switzerland

JENSEN, JAMES BURT, pasasitology educator, researcher; b. Los Angeles, Mar. 8, 1943; s. Marvin James and Ottilla (McKnight) J.; m. Jane Gunderson, Feb. 26, 1965; children: Christian, Stephanie, Davidson, Levi, Leah, Joshua. B.Sc., Brigham Young U., 1970, M.Sc., 1972; postgrad., Utah State U., 1972-74; Ph.D., Auburn U., 1976; postdoctoral student, Rockefeller U., 1976-77. Asst. Prof. Rockefeller U., 1977-79; asst. prof. parasitology Mich. State U., East Lansing, 1979-82, assoc. prof., 1982—; cons. on malaria WHO,

1978—; mem. internat. bd. Kuvin Ctr. for Study Infectious and Tropical Diseases, Hadassah Med. Sch, Hebrew U., Jerusalem, 1983. Editor: Cultivation of Protozoan Parasites, 1983. Research grantee AID; Research grantee WHO; Research grantee NIH. Mem. Am. Soc. Tropical Medicine and Hygiene, Soc. Protozoologists, Am. Soc. Parasitologists, N.Y. Soc. Tropical Medicine. Republican. Mormon. Current Work: Immunologic reactions to malarial parasites in human infections of Plasmodium spp; biochemical-pharmacology of human malarial parasites; epidemiology of human malaria in Africa. Subspecialties: Parasitology; Infectious diseases. Home: 636 Charles St East Lansing MI 48823 Office: Dept of Microbiology and Public Healt Giltner Hall Michigan State University East Lansing MI 48824

JENSEN, KEITH EDWIN, scientific researcher, consultant; b. Council Grove, Kans., Sept. 6, 1924; s. Adolph George and Irma Mae (Alexander) J.; m. Betty Mae Gardner, Dec. 2, 1943; children: Dennis, Diana Jensen Marsh, Karen Jensen Manix, Michael. A.B., U. Kans., 1948, M.A., 1949; Ph.D., Jefferson Med. Coll. Phila., 1951. Diplomate: Am. Bd. Med. Microbiology. Asst. prof. Sch. Pub. Health, U. Mich., 1951-56; mgr. respiratory disease unit Ctr. Disease Control, USPHS; also dir. WHO Influenza Ctr., 1956-58; dir. biols. research and devel. Pfizer, Inc., Terre Haute, Ind., 1958-65, exec. dir. virology and cancer research, 1965-80, sr. sci. adviser, 1980—. Contbr. numerous articles to profl. jours. Chmn. Bd. Edn., Old Lyme, Conn., 1967-70; chmn. civic action program Pfizer/Groton Employees, 1981—. Served with AUS, 1943-45. Fellow Am. Acad. Microbiology; mem. Am. Assn. Immunologists, Am. Soc. Microbiology, N.Y. Acad. Sci., Sigma Xi. Republican. Methodist. Current Work: Human medicinals, animal health products. Subspecialties: Immunopharmacology; Cancer research (medicine). Home: Trumbull Rd Waterford CT 06385 Office: Pfizer Central Research Groton CT 06340

JENSEN, NORMAN PETER, chemist; b. Pontiac, Mich., Dec. 12, 1938; s. Ernest Peter and Elizabeth Marie (Thurston) J.; m. Sara Lee Mueller, Feb. 20, 1964; children—Marshall, Mitchell, Christine. B.S., U. Mich., 1967; Ph.D., MIT, 1965; postgrad. Stanford U., 1965-66. Sr. chemist Merck & Co., Rahway, N.J., 1966-73, research fellow, 1973-78, sr. research fellow, 1978-79, asst. dir., 1979-83, dir., 1984; dir. chemistry Ayerst Research Labs., Princeton, N.J., 1984—. Current work: Administrator of basic research department of medicinal chemistry. Subspecialties: Organic chemistry; Drug design. Home: 119 Linwood Circle Princeton NJ 08540 Office: Ayerst Research Labs CN 8000 Princeton NJ 08540

JENSEN, RICHARD ALAN, mechanical engineer; b. Hagerstown, Md., May 1, 1944; s. Jens and Pearl Betty (Weismann) J.; m. Betty Klainmioc, Dec. 19, 1971; children—David, Andrew, Penelope. B.Engring., Cooper Union, 1966; M.S., Columbia U., 1967, D. Engring. Sci., 1975; M.B.A., St. Johns U., S.I., N.Y., 1981. Registered profl. engr. N.Y., N.J. Prin. engr. Burns & Roe, Inc., Woodbury, N.Y., 1973—. Contbr. articles to profl. publs. Mem. S.I. Children's Mus., 1982, Jewish Community Ctr., S.I., 1983, Great Kills Community Ctr., S.I., 1984. Mem. Am. Vacuum Soc., ASME, AAAS, N.Y. Acad. Scis., Sigma Xi. Current work: Nuclear safety, fusion engineering, robotics. Subspecialties: Mechanical engineering; Fusion. Home: 630 Armstrong Ave Staten Island NY 10308 Office: Burns & Roe Inc 20 Crossways Park N Woodbury NY 11797

JENSEN, RICHARD GRANT, biochemist, educator; b. Los Angeles, Apr. 16, 1936; s. Frank Richard and Ruth (Grant) J.; m. Annette Anderson, Sept. 1, 1961; children: Karl Glenn, Jennifer Ruth, Bruce Duane, Byron Davis. B.A., Brigham Young U., 1961, Ph.D. in Biochemistry, 1965. USPHS postdoctoral fellow chem. biodynamics lab. U. Calif.-Berkeley, 1965-67; asst. prof. chemistry U. Ariz., 1967-72, assoc. prof. biochemistry, 1972-79, prof. biochemistry and plant scis., 1979—; vis. prof. Chem. Inst., Tech. U. Munich, W.Ger., 1974-75, Bot. Inst., U. Berne, Switzerland, 1975. Contbr. articles to profl. jours. Nat. Cancer Inst. fellow, 1965-67; Fulbright-Hays scholar, 1974-75. Fellow AAAS; mem. Am. Soc. Biol. Chemists, Am. Soc. Plant Physiology, Am. Chem. Soc. Mormon. Current Work: Regulation of photosynthesis and carbon metabolism in plants; biochemistry of the chloroplast, properties of the ribulose bisphosphate carboxylase and its role in CO2 fixation in plants. Subspecialties: Photosynthesis; Plant physiology (agriculture). Office: Dept Biochemistry U Ariz Tucson AZ 85721

JENSEN, ROBERT ALAN, neuroscientist, researcher; b. Bainbridge, N.Y., Sept. 25, 1940; s. Otto G. and Dorothy L. (Pierce) J. B.A., Coll. Wooster, 1965; M.A., Kent State U., 1970; Ph.D., No. Ill. U., 1976. Asst. research psychobiologist U. Calif.-Irvine, 1976-81, assoc. research psychobiologist, 1981; asst. prof. So. Ill. U., Carbondale, 1981-83, assoc. prof. neurosci., 1983—; cons. G.D. Searle, Skokie, Ill., 1984—; mem. editorial adv. bd. Behavioral Neural Biology, San Diego, Calif., 1981—, mng. editor, Irvine, Calif., 1978-81. Author: Introductory Psychology, 1986. Author/editor: Endogenous Peptides and Learning and Memory Processes, 1981. USPHS postdoctural fellow, 1976-79; grantee NIMH, 1980, Nat. Inst. Aging, 1979. Mem. AAAS, Soc. for Neurosci., Internat. Soc. for Develop. Psychobiology, Medwestern Psychol. Assn., Sigma Xi, Democrat. Presbyterian. Current work: Neurobiology of learning and memory; memory deficits in aged animals; opioid systems and the modulation of memory; psychoneuroimmunology; behavioral teratology. Subspecialties: Neuropharmacology; Psychobiology. Home: 1211 W College Carbondale IL 62901 Office: Dept Psychology So Ill U Carbondale IL 62901

JENSEN, WILLIAM AUGUST, botanist, educator; b. Chgo., Aug. 22, 1927; s. William McKinley and Gertrude (Hild) J.; m. Joan Nancy Sell, June 20, 1948; children—Scott William, Christina Cathrine. Ph.B., U. Chgo., 1948, M.S., 1950, Ph.D., 1953. NIH fellow Carlsberg Lab., Copenhagen, Denmark, 1952-53, Calif. Inst. Tech., Pasadena, 1953-55; NSF fellow U. Brussels, Belgium, 1955-56; asst. prof. dept. biology U. Va., Charlottesville, 1956-57; faculty dept. botany U. Calif. at Berkeley, 1957—, prof., 1963—, chmn. dept. botany, 1971-73, chmn. dept. biology, 1974—; asso. dean Coll. Letters and Sci., 1963-66; program dir. developmental biology NSF, Washington, 1973-74; pres. Biology Media, Berkeley, 1974—. Author: Botanical Histochemistry, 1962, The Plant Cell, 1964, 71, (with R. Park) Cell Utrastructure, 1967, (with F. Salisbury) Botany, 1972, (with B. Heinrick, D. Wake, H. Wake) Biology, 1979; Contbr. (with B. Heinrick, D. Wake, H. Wake) articles to profl. jours.; Author, producer teaching modules and multi-image lectures. Recipient Disting. Teaching award U. Calif. at Berkeley, 1960, N.Y. Bot. Garden award for bot. research, 1964, Ohaus award Nat. Sci. Tchr. Assn., 1976. Mem. Soc. for Study Devel. and Growth (past sec.), Bot. Soc. Am. (program dir. 1963-67, v.p. 1976, pres. 1978), AAAS, Am. Inst. Biol. Scis., Soc. Developmental Biology, Am. Soc. Cell Biology, Histochem. Soc. Devel. bot. histochem. procedures and application of these procedures to problems of early cell devel. in plants especially root tips and embryos; research on fertilization and early embryo devel. in flowering plants. Subspecialty: Plant physiology (biology). Home: 280 Los Altos Dr Kensington CA 94708

JENSH, RONALD PAUL, anatomy educator; b. N.Y.C., June 14, 1938; s. Werner Gunther and Dorothy (Hensle) J.; m. Ruth-Eleanor Dobson, Aug. 18, 1962; children: Victoria Lynn, Elizabeth Whitney. B.A., Bucknell U., 1960, M.A., 1962; Ph.D., Jefferson Med. Coll., Phila., 1966. Instr. dept. anatomy Jefferson Med. Coll., Phila., 1966-68, asst. prof., 1968-74, assoc. prof., 1974-82, prof., 1982—, vice chmn., 1984—; cons. in field. Contbr. articles in field to profl. jours. Mem. Teratology Soc., Behavioral Tertology Soc. (pres. 1985-86), Am. Coll. Toxicology, Am. Assn. Anatomists, Sigma Xi. Republican. Methodist. Current Work: Experimental embryology; teratology; radiation developmental biology, experimental psychology. Subspecialties: Teratology; Developmental biology. Home: 230 E Park Ave Haddonfield NJ 08033 Office: Dept Anatomy Jefferson Med Coll Thomas Jefferson U 1020 Locust St Phila PA 19107

JENSON, ALFRED BENNETT, pathologist; b. Houston, June 20, 1939; s. Alfred J. and Ann (Bennett) J.; m. Susan Hathorn, Aug. 23, 1963; children—Stephanie, Michelle, Jennifer. B.A., Tex. Christian U., 1961; M.S., Baylor U., 1966, M.D., 1966. Diplomate Am. Bd. Anatomic Pathology. Intern, Baylor Coll. Hosp., 1967; resident in pathology, 1970 Ben Taub Gen. Hosp., Houston, 1969-70; comparative pathologist U.S. Army, Edgewood Arsenal, Md., 1971-73; research assoc. immunopathology Scripps Clinic and Research Found., LaJolla, Calif., 1973-75; assoc. prof. pathology Georgetown U. Med. Sch., Washington, 1980—, vice chmn. dept., 1983—; ad hoc pathologist Am. Tupe Cultur Collection, Rockville, 1980—; chmn. animal care co. Nat. Inst. Dental Research, NIH, 1978-80. Editor: Survey Synthesis of Immunologic Research-Immunopathology, 1981—. Editorial bd. Survey and Synthesis of Pathology Research, 1982—. Contbr. articles to profl. jours. Grantee Ctrs. Disease Control, Council Toxicology Research; recipient Sheard Sanford award Am. Soc. Clin. Pathology, 1966, Service award Salvation Army Boys Club, 1967, Teaching award Phi Chi, 1970-71. Mem. Fedn. Am. Soc. Exptl. Biology, Internat. Acad. Pathologists, Am. Assn. Pathologists, Sigma Xi. Democrat. Presbyterian. Current work: Role of papillomavirus in dysplasias and neoplasias of uterine cervix; virus induces diabetes mellitus; sexually transmitted diseases. Subspecialties: Pathology (veterinary medicine); Virology (veterinary medicine). Home: 14220 Briarwood Dr Rockville MD 20853 Office: Dept Pathology Georgetown U Washington DC 20007

JEONG, TUNG HON, physicist, consultant; b. Hoyping, China, Dec. 19, 1935; came to U.S., 1948, naturalized, 1973; s. John Fong and Chung Yee Kwan; m. Anna Chimay Wong, May 19, 1962; children—Allan Chiman, Alec Chiming, Alicia Chimay. B.S., Yale U., 1957; Ph.D., U. Minn., 1963. Research assoc. U. Minn., Mpls., 1958-63; asst. prof. Lake Forest Coll., Ill., 1963-68, assoc. prof., 1968-73, A.B. Dick prof. physics, 1973—; pres. Integraf Co., Lake Forest, 1973—; dir. Internat. Symposium on Display Holography, 1985; cons. Gaertner Sci. Corp., Chgo., 1967-70, Abbott Lab., Zenith Electronics Corp., Caterpillar Tractor, McDonald's Corp., also others. Editor: Proc. of Internat. Symposium on Display Holography, 1982, 85; author motion picture: Introduction to Holography, 1972; Holography, New Window to the Future, 1971. Recipient best paper award Soc. Info. Display, 1973; Sonntag Found. grantee, 1968—; McDonald's Corp. grantee, 1985. Fellow Optical Soc. Am.; mem. Chinese Scholastic Honor Soc. (pres. 1983-84), Soc. Photo-Optical Instrument Engrs., Am. Phys. Soc., Am. Assn. Physics Tchrs. (pres. Midwest chpt. 1972-73, Robert Millikan medal 1976). Lodge: Rotary. Current work: Research and consultation in applications of optical fibers, holography, non-destructive testing, coherent optics, and liberal arts education. Office: Lake Forest Coll Sheridan and College Rds Lake Forest IL 60045

JEREB, MARJAN JOSIP, physician; b. Ljubljana, Slovenia, Oct. 5, 1930; came to U.S., 1973; s. Peter and Olga (Vodisek) J.; m. Berta Verzun, Sept. 21, 1961. M.D., U. Ljubljana, 1954. Radiologist Karolinska Hosp., Stockholm, 1963-73; asst. prof. radiology SUNY Downstate Med. Ctr., Bklyn., 1973-75, assoc. prof., 1978—; radiologist Clin. Ctr., Ljubljana, Yugoslavia, 1975-77; head chest radiology Kings County Hosp., Bklyn., 1977—. Mem. Am. Assn. Univ. Radiologists, Swedish Radiol. Soc. Current Work: Application of new technologies in the diagnosis of chest, especially mediastinal, disease. Subspecialty: Diagnostic radiology. Home: 504 E 81st St Apt 3 J New York NY 10028 Office: Downstate Med Ctr 450 Clarkson Ave Brooklyn NY 11203

JERGINS, COLVIN EDWARD, mechanical engineer; b. Hobbs, N.Mex., Mar. 26, 1943; s. George Walter and Martha Louise (Naanes) J.; m. L. Nadine Garner, May 27, 1965; children—Cynthia Kay, Stephanie Lynn. B.S. in Mech. Engring., N.Mex. State U., 1973. Registered profl. engr., Idaho. Engr., Westinghouse Electric Corp., Idaho Falls, 1973-75, supr., 1975-78, mgr., 1978-80; pres. Dynamics Inc., Idaho Falls, 1980—. Served with USN, 1961-69. Mem. ASME (chmn. 1978-79). Republican. Current work: construction of nuclear power plants and research/development facilities. Subspecialties: Nuclear fission; Mechanical engineering. Home: 775 S Fanning Ave Idaho Falls ID 83401 Office: Dynamics Inc 966 E Lincoln St PO Box 2074 Idaho Falls ID 83403

JERINA, DONALD MICHAEL, chemist, pharmacologist; b. Chgo., Jan. 17, 1940; s. Anthony and Mary J.; m. Colleen B. Burgess, Aug. 8, 1964; children: Julianne, Derek. B.A., Knox Coll., 1962; Ph.D., Northwestern U., 1966. With NIH, 1966—, chief sect. oxidation mechanisms, 1975—. Contbr. numerous articles to profl. jours. Recipient USPHS award, 1975; Hildebrant prize, 1980; B. B. Brodie award, 1982. Mem. Am. Chem. Soc., Am. Soc. Biol. Chemists, Federated Am. Soc. Exptl. Medicine and Biology, Am. Soc. Pharmacology and Exptl. Therapeutics. Current Work: Oxidative drug metabolism, chemical carcinogenesis, bay-region theory. Subspecialties: Synthetic chemistry; Cancer research (medicine). Home: 9717 Brixton Ln Bethesda MD 20817 Office: NIH Bldg 4 Room 216 Bethesda MD 20205

JERNIGAN, HOWARD MAXWELL, JR., biochemistry educator, researcher; b. Winston-Salem, N.C., Apr. 13, 1943; s. Howard Maxwell and Ruth Roland (Ray) J.; m. Diane Dee Moore, Mar. 1, 1967; 1 child, Paula. B.S. in Chemistry, W.Va. U., 1965; Ph.D. in Biochemistry, U. N.C., 1970. Postdoctoral assoc. U. Fla., Gainesville, 1970-73; asst. prof. U. Tenn., Memphis, 1973-80, assoc. prof., 1980—. Contbr. articles to profl. jours. Mem. Am. Soc. Biol. Chemists, Am. Chem. Soc., Assn. Research in Vision and Ophthalmology, AAUP, Sigma Xi. Methodist. Current work: Biochemistry of ocular lens and cataracts; amino acid and choline metabolism. Subspecialties: Biochemistry (biology); Ophthalmology. Office: U Tenn D-222 Coleman Bldg Memphis TN 38163

JERNIGAN, ROBERT LEE, research scientist; b. Portales, N.Mex., May 4, 1941; s. Frank H. and Jimmie M. (Loyd) J.; m. Marydee A. Becker, June 15, 1968; 1 son, Alexander L. B.S., Calif. Inst. Tech., 1963; Ph.D., Stanford U., 1967. Postdoctoral fellow Stanford (Calif.) U., 1967-68; NIH postdoctoral fellow U. Calif., San Diego, 1968-70; sr. staff fellow NIH, Bethesda, Md., 1970-75, theoretical phys. chemist, 1975—. Contbr. articles to profl. jours. Recipient Spl. Achievement award NIH, 1982. Mem. Biophys. Soc., Am. Chem. Soc., Am. Phys. Soc., AAAS. Current Work: Elucidation of molecular details of biochemical and biophysical processes by computer studies of macromolecular conformations. Subspecialties: Molecular biology; Polymer chemistry. Home: 3700 Dunlop St Chevy Chase MD 20815 Office: NIH Nat Cancer Inst Bldg 10 Rm 4B-56 Bethesda MD 20205

JEROME, JOSEPH WALTER, mathematics educator, research mathematician; b. Phila., June 7, 1939; s. Joseph Walter and Hermene Josephine (Ostertag) J.; m. Doreen Jean Funk, Apr. 8, 1967; children—Jon, Peter. B.S., St. Joseph's Coll., 1961; M.S., Purdue U., 1963, Ph.D., 1966. Asst. prof. Math. Research Ctr., U. Wis.-Madison, 1966-68, Case Western Res. U., Cleve., 1968-70; asst. prof. Northwestern U., Evanston, Ill., 1970-72, assoc. prof., 1972-76, prof. math., 1976—; vis. scientist Bell Labs., Murray Hill, N.J., 1982-83; vis. prof. U. Tex., Austin, 1978-79; vis. scholar U. Chgo., 1985; vis. fellow Oxford U., 1974-75. Book: Approximation Nonlinear Evolution Systems, 1983; Minimum Norm Extremals, 1975. Contbr. articles to profl. jours. Fellow NSF, 1961-65, Brit. Sci. Council, 1974-75; NSF grantee, 1970—. Mem. Am. Math. Soc., Soc. Indsl. and Applied Math. Roman Catholic. Current work: Nonlinear analysis of VLSI models/numerical simulation of transistors and algorithms for differential equations and computational complexity. Subspecialties: Applied mathematics; Numerical analysis (mathematics). Home: 2080 Drury Ln Northfield IL 60093 Office: Northwestern U 2033 Sheridan Rd Evanston IL 60201

JERVIS, HERBERT HUNTER, geneticist, educator; b. Wilmington, Del., June 25, 1942; s. Herbert Willard and Dorothy Grotz J.; m. Mary Gregory, June 9, 1974. B.S., Springfield Coll., 1964, M.Ed., 1966; M.S., Fla. State U., 1971, Ph.D., 1974. Postdoctoral fellow dept. biochemistry Va. Inst. Tech., 1974-75; asst. prof. genetics Adelphi U., 1975-80, asso. prof., 1980-83; patent agt. biotech. patents Scully, Scott, Murphy & Presser, 1982—; cons. investment group Arthur Merrill Assos., 1982—. Contbr. articles to profl. jours. Trustee Springfield Coll. Served with U.S. Army, 1966-69. Mem. AAAS, Genetics Soc. Am., Am. Soc. Microbiology, N.Y. Acad. Sci., Springfield Coll. Alumni Assn., Sigma Xi. Current Work: Fungal, genetics, developmental genetics, biotech. patents. Subspecialties: Genetics and genetic engineering (biology); Biotechnology patents. Home: 124 Brixton Rd S West Hempstead NY 11552 Office: 200 Garden City Plaza Garden City NY 11530

JESPERSEN, NIELS VESTERGAARD, research engineer; b. Graasten, Denmark, Sept. 5, 1948; came to U.S., 1977. M.S. Civil and Structural, Tech. U. Denmark, Copenhagen, 1976. Analytical engr. Gulf & Western Ind., Warwick, R.I., 1977-79; research engr. Babcock & Wilcox, Alliance, Ohio, 1979—. Inventor theoretical and numerical methods in fracture mechanics modeling. Mem. ASME (reviewer 1982-84, dir. 1983-84), Soc. Indsl. and Applied Maths., Am. Soc. Danish Engrs., Am. Ceramic Soc. (reviewer 1984). Current work: Numerical modeling of structures including finite element method, integral equations, stochastic processes, properties of composites, ceramics; theoretical modeling of cracks. Subspecialties: Structural engineering; Fracture mechanics. Home: 554 Cobblestone Ave Alliance OH 44601 Office: Babcock & Wilcox Research & Devel Div Beeson St Alliance OH 44601

JESSER, WILLIAM AUGUSTUS, materials scientist, educator; b. Waynesboro, Va., Dec. 20, 1939; s. Richard Alexander and Margaret Leonora (Fry) J.; m. Barbara Lee Schwab, Aug. 18, 1962; children: William Augustus, Nicole E. B.A., U. Va., 1962, M.A., 1964, Ph.D., 1966. Lectr. dept. physics U. Witwatersrand, Johannesburg, South Africa, 1966-67; prof. dept. materials sci. U. Va., Charlottesville, 1968—; dir. High Voltage Electron Microscopy Facility, 1976—; vis. prof. dept. metallurgy Nagoya U., Japan, 1978; dept. physics U. Pretoria, South Africa, 1982. Contbr. articles to profl. jours. Chmn. bd. dirs. Hearthstone Children's House, 1980-82; comdr. Monticello Squadron, CAP, 1980-85. Recipient Alan T. Gwathmey Prize for research U. Va., 1966. Mem. Am. Soc. Metals, Electron Microscope Soc. Am., Va. Acad. Sci., Sigma Xi. Current Work: Electron microscopy, radiation damage, phase transformations; electronic materials. Subspecialties: Metallurgy; Fusion. Home: Montvue Charlottesville VA 22901 Office: Thornton Hall U Va Charlottesville VA 22901

JESSON, JOSEPH EDWARD, electrical engineer; b. Trenton, N.J., Apr. 24, 1952; s. Joseph Ephraim and Irene (Horvath) J. B.E.E., DeVry Inst., 1973; M.S., DePaul U., 1985. Registered profl. engr., Ill. Engr. U. Chgo., 1972-74; systems engr. Motorola, Schaumberg, Ill., 1974-76; sr. engr. Oak Switch Systems, Crystal Lake, Ill., 1976-77, product mgr., 1978-80; product mgr. Switchcraft, Chgo., 1980—; cons. Exxon, Lionsville, Pa., 1978. Contbr. articles to profl. jours. Contbg. editor: Popular Communications. Mem. Assn. Computing Machinery, IEEE. Republican. Baptist. Clubs: Amsat (Washington), Antique Radio (Chgo.). Current work: Digital modulation applications; human factors regarding keyboards, graphic tablets, touch switches and advanced input units. Subspecialties: Human factors engineering; Telecommunications. Home: 21414 W Honey Ln Lake Villa IL 60046 Office: Switchcraft 5555 N Elston Chicago IL 60630

JESSUP, JOHN MILBURN, surgeon, educator; b. New Haven, Aug. 4, 1946; s. John Baker and Dorothy Milburn J.; m. Kathleen Foxen, May 7, 1977; children: Katherine Elizabeth, John Milburn. B.A., Yale U., 1968; M.D., N.Y. Med. Coll., 1972. Diplomate: Am. Bd. Surgery. Resident N.Y. Hosp., 1972-74; clin. assoc. surg. br. Nat. Cancer Inst., 1974-76; vis. scientist Basic Research Program, Frederick Cancer Research Ctr., 1976-77; resident in surgery U. Tex. Med. Sch., Houston, 1977-80; faculty assoc. dept. gen. surgery M.D. Anderson Hosp., Houston, 1980-81, asst. prof., asst. surgeon depts. gen. surgery and clin. immunology and biol. therapy, 1981—. Contbr. articles to profl. jours. Served to lt. comdr. USPHS, 1974-76. Fellow ACS, Soc. Surg. Oncology, Am. Soc. Clin. Oncology; mem. AAAS, Am. Assn. Cancer Research, Assn. Acad. Surgery, Alpha Omega Alpha. Current Work: Tumor-medicated immunosuppression, metastatic potential of human cancer cells, cloning t-cells, oncologic surgery. Subspecialties: Cancer research (medicine); Cell biology. Office: 6723 Bertner Ave Houston TX 77030

JESTER, WILLIAM ANDREW, nuclear engineering educator, consultant; b. Phila., June 16, 1934; s. William Andrew and Maud Ella (Deribelbis) J.; m. Janet Fay Tucker, Aug. 21, 1967; children—Mary Ella, William Andrew III. B.S. in Chem. Engring., Drexel Inst. Tech., 1957; M.S. in Nuclear Engring., Pa. State U., 1961, Ph.D. in Chem. Engring., 1965. Nuclear engr. Westinghouse APB, Pitts., 1961; chem. engr. Nat. Bur. Standards, Washington, 1965; asst. prof. nuclear engring. Pa. State U., University Park, 1965-72, assoc. prof., 1972—; cons. govt. agys., cos. Author: (with others) Planning Atomic Shelters, 1961, Environmental Impact of Electrical Power Generation, 1973, 75, Energy, Pennsylvania's Energy Curriculum, 1978, 80, The Ceramics of Kaminasljuyu, 1978. Patentee in field. Served to 1st lt. U.S. Army, 1957-59. Recipient Joan Hodes Queneau Palladium medal for outstanding engineering achievements in environmental conservation research Nat. Audubon Soc.-Am. Assn. Engring. Socs., 1985. Recipient numerous grants for energy and engring. research. Fellow Am. Inst. Chemists; mem. Am. Chem. Soc., Am. Soc. Engring. Edn., AAAS, Am. Nuclear Soc. (editor proc. ednl. div. tutorial publ. 1977-80, exec. com. nuclear engring. edn. for disadvantaged 1976—, scholarship awards com. 1979—, chmn., mem. various coms. 1960—), Sigma Xi, Phi Lambda Upsilon. Republican. Baptist. Current work: Utilizing nuclear techniques in solving problems in fields such as biomedicine, law enforcement, hydrology, anthropology, and environmental monitoring. Subspecialties: Nuclear engineering; Environmental engineering. Home: 135 W Mitchell Ave State College PA 16803 Office: Pa State U Breazeale Nuclear Rector University Park PA 16802

JEWELEWICZ, RAPHAEL, educator, physician; b. Nowogrodek, Poland, Dec. 26, 1932; came to U.S., 1963; s. Chaim and Chaia (Tawticky) J.; m. Ronnie Oved, July 23, 1955; children: Rachel, Dov, Daniel, Dory. M.D., Hebrew U., Israel, 1961. Intern Hadassah Hebrew U. Hosp., Jerusalem, Israel, 1960-61; resident Bellevue Hosp.-NYU Med. Ctr., N.Y.C., 1964-68; practice medicine specializing in ob.-gyn.; asst. prof. Columbia U., N.Y.C., 1969-75, assoc. prof., 1975—; dir. div. reproductive endocrinology Columbia Presbyn. Med. Center, 1975—. Contbr. articles to profl. jours. Fellow Am. Coll. Ob.-Gyn., A.C.S.; mem. Soc. for Gynecol. Investigation, Endocrine Soc., Am. Fertility Soc. Current Work: Control of menstrual cycle, induction of ovulation, infertility, in vitro fertilization and embryo transfer. Subspecialties: Obstetrics and gynecology; Endocrinology. Home: Church St Alpine NJ 07620 Office: Columbia U Dept Obstetrics and Gynecology 630 W 168 St New York NY 10032

JEWELL, WILLIAM SYLVESTER, engineering educator; b. Detroit, July 2, 1932; s. Loyd Vernon and Marion (Sylvester) J.; m. Elizabeth Gordon Wilson, July 7, 1956; children—Sarah, Thomas, Miriam, William Timothy. B.Engring. Physics, Cornell U., 1954; M.S. in Elec. Engring, MIT, 1955, Sc.D., 1958. Assoc. dir. mgmt. scis. div. Broadview Research Corp., Burlingame, Calif., 1958-60; asst. prof. dept. indsl. engring. and ops. research U. Calif.-Berkeley, 1960-63, assoc. prof., 1963-67, prof., 1967—, chmn. dept., 1967-69, 76-80; dir. Teknekron Industries, Inc., Berkeley, 1968—; cons. operations research problems, 1960—; guest prof. Eidgenössiches Technische Hochschule, Zurich, 1980-81. Contbr. articles to profl. jours. Fulbright research scholar France, 1965; research scholar Internat. Inst. Applied Systems Analysis, Austria, 1974-75. Mem. Ops. Research Soc. Am., Inst. Mgmt. Scis., Am. Risk and Ins. Assn., Actuarial Assn. Netherlands, Assn. Swiss Actuaries, Internat. Actuarial Assn., Mensa, Triangle., Sigma Xi. Current Work: Hardware and software reliability; Bayesian statistical models; risk analysis; actuarial science. Subspecialties: Operations research (engineering); Statistics. Home: 67 Loma Vista Orinda CA 94563 Office: U Cal Dept Indsl Engring and Operations Research Berkeley CA 94720

JEZL, JAMES LOUIS, research chemist; b. Tobias, Nebr., Dec. 12, 1918; s. John F. and Anna M. (Laun) J.; m. Elizabeth A. Bannister, Aug. 10, 1943 (dec. Dec. 1962); children—Barbara Ann, Patricia Jean; m. 2d, Rita M. McCartan, May 9, 1964; children—James Louis, Mary Louise, Anne Marie, John Francis. A.B. with distinction, U. Nebr., 1941; M.S., Pa. State U., 1942; Ph.D., U. Del., 1949. Supervisory chemist U.S. Rubber Co., Marion, Ohio, 1942-43; chemist, sect. chief Sun Oil Co., Toledo and Marcus Hook, Pa., 1943-60; mgr. basic research Avisun Corp., Marcus Hook, 1960-68; div. dir. Amoco Chem. Corp., Naperville, Ill., 1968-76, mgr. exploratory research, 1976-82, research cons., 1982—. Contbr. articles to profl. jours., chpts. to books; patentee in field. Mem. sch. bd. St. Charles Sch. Dist., Ill., 1982—. Mem. Am. Chem. Soc. (sec. Phila. sect. 1957-59, chmn. Phila. sect. 1961, nat. councillor 1962-66), Phi Beta Kappa, Phi Lambda Upsilon, Theta Nu, Sigma Xi. Republican. Roman Catholic. Current work: Research management; polymer research; petrochemical research; methane conversion. Subspecialties: Catalysis chemistry; Organic chemistry. Home: 35 W 094 Army Trail Rd Saint Charles IL 60174 Office: Amoco Chems Corp Amoco Research Ctr Naperville IL 60174

JIANG, JACK BAU-CHIEN, organic/medicinal chemist; b. Chengtu, Republic of China, Nov. 15, 1947; m. Lily Yang-Bai Chen, June 17, 1973; 1 child, Melody. B.S. in Chemistry, Cheng Kung U., 1970; Ph.D., in Organic Chemistry, Mich. State U., 1975. Postdoctoral researcher U. Minn., Mpls., 1975-77; research chemist Am. Cyanamid Co., Princeton, N.J., 1977-79; scientist Ortho Pharm. Corp., Raritan, N.J., 1979-80; sr. scientist, 1980-84; sr. research chemist E.I. duPont Co., Wilmington, Del., 1984—. Patentee in field. Mem. Am. Chem. Soc. Current work: Design and syntheses of medicinal agents. Subspecialties: Organic chemistry; Synthetic chemistry. Office: DuPont Co E353/338 Exptl Sta Wilmington DE 19898

JIN, SUNGHO, materials scientist; b. Daejon, Korea, Nov. 6, 1945; came to U.S., 1970, naturalized, 1982; s. Hyungha and Sookwon (Park) J.; m. Hyunju Yoo, Aug. 24, 1972; children—Lina Jin, Emily Jin. B.S., Seoul Nat. U., 1969; M.S., U. Calif.-Berkeley, 1971, Ph.D., 1974. Mem. research staff Lawrence Berkeley Lab., Calif., 1974-76; mem. tech. staff AT&T Bell Labs., Murray Hill, N.J., 1976-81, supr., 1981—. Contbr. articles to profl. jours. Patentee in field.

Mem. Metall. Soc. of AIME, IEEE. Current work: Research and development of magnetic and electronic materials and devices. Subspecialties: Composite materials; Electronic materials. Office: AT&T Bell Labs Room 1A-123 600 Mountain Ave Murray Hill NJ 07974

JIROUSEK, LUDEK, biochemist; b. Olomouc, Czechoslovakia, Aug. 18, 1925; came to U.S., 1965; s. Arnost and Zdenka (Noskova) J.; children—Zuzana, Denisa. Ph.D., Charles U., 1948. Staff mem. Research Inst. Endocrinology, Prague, Czechoslovakia, 1949-59; biochemist nuclear medicine dept. Motol Hosp., Prague, 1959-65; research assoc. dept. biochemistry Vanderbilt U., Nashville, 1965-68; research assoc. oral biology dept. U. Man., Winnipeg, 1969-71; research assoc. biochemistry dept. Brandeis U., Waltham, Mass., 1971-74; head radioiodination dept. New Eng. Nuclear Corp., Billerica, Mass., 1974-85. Contbr. articles to profl. jours. Mem. Soc. Biol. Chemists, AAAS, Am. Thyroid Assn., Czechoslovak Soc. Arts and Scis., Sigma Xi. Current work: Iodine biochemistry, goiter, Heart attack, atherosclerosis prevention by thyroid supplementation, goitrogenic compounds. Subspecialty: Medicinal chemistry. Home: 20 Redgate Rd Tewksbury MA 01876

JÖCHLE, WOLFGANG JOHANNES, veterinarian, theriogenologist; b. Munich, Germany, Oct. 5, 1927; came to U.S., 1968; s. Hans and Martha (Pupke) J.; m. Maria Frank, Jan. 3, 1964. Dr. med. vet., U. Munich, 1953. Diplomate Am. Coll. Theriogenology. Dir. Fecunda AG, Zurich, Switzerland, 1964-66; dir. vet. research and devel. Syntex Internatl., Mexico City, Mex., 1966-68, v.p., dir. Inst. Vet. Sci., Syntex Research, Palo Alto, Calif., 1968-73, v.p. internatl. vet. sect., 1973-75; pres. Wolfgang Jöchle Assocs. Inc., Denville, N.J., 1976—; lectr. Vet. Coll., Hannover, Fed. Republic Germany, 1980—; contract prof. U. Milan, Italy, 1984-85. Author: Control of Reproductive Functions in Domestic Animals, 1980. Founder, assoc. editor: Theriogenology, 1974—; editor Proc. 10th Ann. Conf. Internat. Embryo Transfer Soc., 1984. Contbr. numerous articles to profl. jours. Mem. AVMA, AAAS, Royal Soc. Med., Soc. Endocrinology, Am. Soc. Animal Sci., Soc. Lab. Animal Sci. (expert), Mexican Assn. Reproductive Animals (hon.). Current work: Planning, organizing and monitoring research and development of new animal health drugs, biologicals, feed additives and growth promotors. Subspecialties: Endocrinology; Pharmacology.

JOCIC, DUSAN, electrical engineer, consultant; b. Belgrade, Yugoslavia, Sept. 7, 1935; came to U.S., 1963; s. Zivojin Petar and Vukosava (Stojkovic) J.; m. Coral Shirley Walker, July 2, 1966. A.S., Pierce Coll., 1985. Design engring. mgr. quality control Belfuse Inc., Jersey City, 1968-74; dir. quality assurance Vanguard Electric Co., Inglewood, Calif., 1974-75; mgr. prodn. Ferrodyne Corp., Venice, Calif., 1975-76; research and devel. assoc. Litton Guidance/Control Systems, Woodland Hills, Calif., 1976-85; mem. tech. staff def. electronics ops. Autonetics Marine Systems div. Rockwell Internat., Anaheim, Calif., 1985—; cons. Encore, San Jose, Calif., 1983—. Patentee in field. Sustaining mem. Republican Nat. Com., Washington, 1980—; mem. Rep. Senatorial Club, 1980, Rep. Congl. Com., 1980. Mem. IEEE (sr. mem., adviser to exec. bd. dirs. 1984—), Internat. Power Conversion Soc. Serbian Orthodox. Current work: Development of new inductive devices for 21st century. Subspecialty: Applied magnetics. Home: 342 Maui E Dr Placentia CA 92670 Office: Rockwell Internat Tech Staff D/379-060 031-GE 22 3370 Miraloma Ave PO Box 3105 Anaheim CA 92803

JOEL, AMOS EDWARD, JR., electrical engineer; b. Phila., Mar. 12, 1918; married; 3 children. B.S., MIT, 1940, M.S., 1942. Switching systems devel. engr. Bell Telephone Labs., Holmdel, N.J., 1954-60, head electronic switching planning dept., 1960-61, dir. switching systems devel. lab., 1961-62, local switching lab., 1962-67, switching cons., 1967—. Recipient Outstanding Patent award N.J. Council R&D, 1972, Stuart Ballantine medal Franklin Inst., 1981, 2d Centenary prize Internat. Telecommunication Union, 1983; Columbian medal City of Genoa, Italy, 1984. Life fellow IEEE. (Alexander Graham Bell medal 1976); fellow Nat. Acad. Engring.; Mem. ACM, AAAS. Subspecialty: Electrical engineering. Home: 131 N Wyoming Ave South Orange NJ 07079 Office: Bell Telephone Labs Holmdel NJ 07733

JOFFE, STEPHEN NEAL, surgical educator; b. Springs, Transvaal, South Africa, Jan. 1943; s. Hirschy N. and Pearl (Cohen) J.; m. Sandra Frances Noche, Dec. 18, 1972; children—Heidi, Craig. B.S., U. Stellenbosch, Cape Province, South Africa, 1963; M.B., U. Witwatersrand, Johannesburg, South Africa, 1967. Intern surgeon Johannesburg Gen. Hosp., 1968, intern physician, 1968; med. officer South African Def. Force, Mil. Med. Inst., Voortrekkerhoote, Pretoria, 1969; resident in gen. surgery Groote Schuur Hosp., U. Cape Town, 1970, chief resident in surgery, 1972; sr. registrar and sr. tutor surgery Hammersmith Hosp. and Royal Postgrad. Med. Sch., London, U.K., 1973; resident surg. officer Hammersmith Hosp., London, 1974-75; hon. cons. surgeon, sr. lectr. surgery U. Glasgow, Univ. Dept. Surgery, Glasgow Royal Infirmary, Scotland, 1975-80; prof. surgery U. Cin. Coll. Medicine, 1980—; prof. medicine, attending physician Inst. Digestive Diseases, Cin., 1980—; attending surgeon Univ. Hosp., Cin., cons. surgeon VA Hosp., Children's Hosp. Med. Ctr., Bethesda Hosp.; mem. courtesy staff Jewish Hosp., Deaconess Hosp., Our Lady of Mercy Hosp., Good Samaritan Hosp., Christ Hosp. Author: Lasers in Medicine, 1985. Council Sci. and Indsl. Research scholar, 1964; Harwood Nash Meml. Prize U. Witwatersrand, 1966, Barnes Agranat Scholarship, 1967. Fellow Coll. Surgeons South Africa, Royal Coll. Physicians and Surgeons of Glasgow and Edinburgh, ACS; mem. Am. Fedn. Clin. Research, Am. Gastroenterol. Assn., Am. Physiol. Soc., Am. Soc. Digestive Endoscopy, Am. Assn. Endocrine Surgeons, Am. Soc. Laser Medicine and Surgery, Assn. Acad. Surgery, Assn. Surgeons Great Britain and Ireland, Assn. Gntobiotics, AMA, Acad. Medicine Cin., Brit. Soc. Gastroenterology, Caledonian Soc. Gastroenterology, Collegium Internationale Chirugiae Digestivae, Central Surg. Assn., Cin. Surg. Soc., Endocrine Soc., European Soc. Surg. Research, Internat. Assn. Endocrine Surgeons, Ohio State Med. Assn., Pancreatic Soc. Great Britain, Royal Soc. Medicine, Scottish Soc. Exptl. Medicine, Soc. Univ. Surgeons, Societe Internationale de Chirugie, Soc. Surgery of Alimentary Tract, So. Ohio GI Endoscopy Soc., Southwest Ohio Digestive Disease Soc., Surg. Research Soc. West of Scotland Surgeons, AAAS, Assn. for Advancement Med. Instrumentation. Republican. Jewish. Current work: Medical lasers, gastrointestinal hormones, gastrointestinal surgery, endocrine surgery. Subspecialties: Surgery; Laser medicine. Home: 8750 Red Fox Ln Cincinnati OH 45243 Office: Dept Surgery Bethesda Ave U Cin Med Ctr Cincinnati OH 45267

JOHANNSEN, DAVID CHARLES, physicist; b. Pasadena, Calif., Oct. 3, 1957; s. Charles Edward and Mary Jane (Boies) J. B.S. with honors, Calif. Inst. Tech., 1979; M.S., U. Calif.-Riverside, 1981, Ph.D., 1983. Mem. tech. staff Hughes Aircraft, El Segundo, Calif., 1982-83; research physicist Allied MLP, Westlake, Calif., 1983-84; engring. specialist Northrop Electronics, Hawthorne, Calif., 1984—. Contbr. articles to profl. jours. Mem. Am. Phys. Soc., Optical Soc. Am. Republican. Current work: Performance analysis and projections of new solid state laser materials, bound state spectra of relativistic particles. Subspecialty: Particle physics. Office: Northrop Electronics 2301 W 120th St N6300 Hawthorne CA 90250

JOHANNSEN, ULMER JAMES, researcher, medical technologist; b. Clinton, Iowa, Apr. 22, 1945; s. Ulmer William and Evelyn Mary (Wight) J. B.A., Coe Coll., Cedar Rapids, Iowa, 1976. Cert. med. technologist. Med. technologist Victory Hosp., Waukegan, Ill., 1976; mem. research staff U. Iowa, Iowa City, 1976—, sr. research asst., 1981—. Contbr. chpts. to books. Mem. N.Y. Acad. Scis., Am. Physiol. Soc. (assoc. mem.), Am. Soc. Clin. Pathologists (assoc.). Current Work: Neural regulation of the coronary circulation. Subspecialties: Cardiology; Physiology (medicine). Office: Univ Iowa 200A Med Lab Iowa City IA 52240

JOHANSON, CONRAD EARL, pharmacologist, educator, developmental physiologist; b. Brockton, Mass., Aug. 6, 1942; s. Axel Leonard and Edna Elizabeth (Burnell) J.; m. Nancy Lorene Williams, June 1, 1968; children—Traci, Brent, Julie, Lance. B.A., Ea. Nazarene Coll., 1965; Ph.D., U. Kans., 1970. Asst. prof. pharmacology Sch. Medicine, U. Utah, Salt Lake City, 1974-79, research asst. prof. anesthesiology, 1978—, assoc. prof. pharmacology, 1979—; mem. neurol. scis. study sect. NIH, Bethesda, Md., 1983—. Field editor Jour. Pharmacology and Exptl. Therapeutics, 1984—. Contbr. articles to profl. jours. Recipient Research Career Devel. award NIH, 1977-82; research grantee USPHS, 1977-86. Mem. Soc. Neurosci., N.Y. Acad. Scis., AAUP, Internat. Soc. Devel. Neurosci., Internat. Soc. Cerebral Blood Flow and Metabolism. Methodist. Current work: Ontogeny of ion transport in the choroid plexus-cerebrospinal fluid system and pharmacology of epithelial transport systems. Subspecialties: Cellular pharmacology; Neurochemistry. Home: 4063 Lisa Dr Salt Lake City UT 84124 Office: Dept Pharmacology Univ Utah Sch Medicine Salt Lake City UT 84132

JOHANSON, DONALD CARL, physical anthropologist; b. Chgo., June 28, 1943; s. Carl Torsten and Sally Eugenia (Johnson) J.; divorced. B.A., U. Ill., 1966; M.A., U. Chgo., 1970, Ph.D., 1974; D.Sc. (hon.), John Carroll U., 1979, Coll. of Wooster, 1985. Mem. dept. phys. anthropology Cleve. Mus. Natural History, 1972-81, curator, 1974-81; With Inst. Human Origins, Berkeley, Calif., 1981—, dir., 1981-82; adj. prof. Case Western Res. U., Kent State U.; host, narrator series Pub. Broadcasting Service, 1982. Film producer: The First Family, 1981, Lucy in Disguise, 1982; Contbr. chpts. to books, articles to profl. jours. Recipient Jared Potter Kirtland award for outstanding sci. achievement Cleve. Mus. Natural History, 1979, Am. Book award, 1982; NSF, Nat. Geog. Soc., L.S.B. Leakey Found., Cleve. Found., George Gund Found. grantee, Fellow AAAS; mem. Am. Assn. Phys. Anthropologists, Internat. Assn. Dental Research, Current Anthropology, Internat. Assn. Human Biologists, Assn. Africanist Archaeologists, Soc. Vertebrate Paleontology, Soc. Study of Human Biology, Explorers Club, Societe de l'Anthropologie de Paris. Current work: Human paleontology; evolution of human kind. Subspecialty: Paleontology. Office: Inst Human Origins 2453 Ridge Rd Berkeley CA 94709

JOHANSON, WILLIAM RICHARD, physicist, educator; b. Oakland, Calif., s. Raymond Richard and B. Louise (Youells) J. B.S., U. Hawaii, 1972; M.S., U. Calif.-Riverside, 1974, Ph.D., 1978. Postdoctoral research Argonne Nat. Lab., Ill., 1978-81, research assoc., summer, 1984; postdoctoral research fellow Los Alamos Nat. Lab., 1982-83; asst. prof. Pomona Coll., Claremont, Calif., 1983—; research assoc. U. Calif.-Riverside, 1983—. Contbr. articles to profl. jours. Served with USAF, 1968-72. Mem. Am. Phys. Soc., Am. Assn. Physics Tchrs., Sigma Xi. Current work: Low temperature solid state, specific heat, Fermi surfaces, magnetic materials, mixed valence. Subspecialties: Condensed matter physics; Low temperature physics. Office: Dept Physics and Astronomy Pomona Coll Claremont CA 91711

JOHANSSON, SONNY LENNART, pathologist, researcher; b. Falkoping, Sweden, Oct. 27, 1942; came to U.S., 1985; s. Lennart Sigfrid and Sonja Margareta (Davidsson) J.; m. Fannie Jean Gaston, Dec. 23, 1967; children—Patrik, Christian, Nicholas, Andrea. B.S. U. Goteborg, Sweden, 1965, M.D., 1972, Ph.D., 1976. Asst. prof. U. Goteborg, Sweden, 1976-81, assoc. prof., 1981-85; prof., dir. anatomy pathology U. Nebr. Med. Ctr., 1985—; lab. chief Pathology Lab. Carlanderska sjh Goteborg, Sweden, 1976—; pathology expert Swedish-Norwegian Testicular Cancer Group Study, 1981—, European Orgn. Research and Treatment Cancer, 1985—. Grantee Swedish Cancer Soc., 1979-84. Mem. Swedish Med. Assn., Internat. Acad. Pathology (sec. Swedish div. 1981-84), Am. Assn. Cancer Research. Lutheran. Current work: Urological diseases, especially urinary tract cancer and its relation to abuse of phenacetin containing analgesics, clinical and experimental studies. Home: 1318 N 127 Ave Omaha NE 68154 Office: Univ Nebr Med Ctr Dept Pathology and Microbiology 42d St and Dewey Ave Omaha NE 68105

JOHN, CHACKO JOSEPH, geologist, researcher; b. Trichur, India, Aug. 8, 1941; came to U.S., 1971; s. Chirakekaran Joseph and Jessie (Paramel) J.; m. Rosemary Holly Speck, Oct. 7, 1978; children—Joseph, Jacob. B.Sc., U. Nagpur (India), 1966, M.Sc., 1968; M.S., U. Del., 1973, Ph.D., 1977. Instr. geology U. Kerala, Trivandrum, India, 1969; geologist in charge English India Clays Ltd., Trivandrum, 1970; postdoctoral research fellow U. Del., Newark, 1977-79; sr. exploration geologist Geo-Cons. Internat., Kenner, La., 1979-80; geologist Marathon Oil Co., Lafayette, La., 1980-82, advanced geologist, Houston, 1982—; cons. Del. State Planning Office, Dover, summer 1975. Contbr. articles to profl. jours. Unidel fellow, 1971-76; M.M. Coll. Sci. scholar, India, 1966-67. Mem. Houston Geol. Soc. (continuing edn. com. 1984—), Am. Assn. Petroleum Geologists, Geol. Soc. Am., Soc. Econ. Paleontologists and Mineralogists, Soc. Profl. Well Logging Analysts, Sigma Xi (research grant 1975). Current work: Clastic depositional systems and subsurface reservoir geometry; coastal geology and processes; exploration for hydrocarbons in the Gulf of Mexico area; development of discovered oil and gas fields; prospect generation and evaluation. Subspecialties: Sedimentology; Oceanography. Home: 3830 Westmeadow Dr Houston TX 77082 Office: Marathon Oil Co PO Box 3128 Houston TX 77253

JOHN, FRITZ, educator, mathematician; b. Berlin, Germany, June 14, 1910; came to U.S., 1935, naturalized, 1941; s. Hermann and Hedwig (Buergel) Jacobsohn; m. Charlotte Woellmer; children—Thomas Franklin, Charles Frederic. Ph.D., Goettingen (Germany) U., 1933; postgrad. Cambridge (Eng.) U., 1934-35; Dr.L.c., Rome U., Bath U. Asst. then assoc. prof. U. Ky., 1935-42; mathematician Aberdeen Proving Grounds, 1942-45; prof. math. N.Y. U., 1946—; Courant prof. Courant Inst., 1976—; dir. Research Inst. Numerical Analysis, Nat. Bur. Standards, 1950-51; spl. research applied math., math. analysis; Sherman Fairchild disting. scholar Calif. Inst. Tech., 1979-80; Josioh Willard Gibbs lectr. Am. Math. Soc., 1975. Author: Plane Waves and Spherical Means, 1955, (with L. Bers and M.S. Schechter) Partial Differential Equations, 1964, (with R. Courant) Introduction to Calculus and Analysis, 1965, Partial Differential Equations, 1978. Recipient G.D. Birkhoff prize in Applied Math., 1973; Rockefeller fellow, 1935, 42; Fulbright lectr. Goettingen U., 1955; Guggenheim travel grantee, 1963; Sr. U.S. Scientist Humboldt award, W. Ger., 1980-81; Benjamin Franklin fellow Royal Soc. Arts; MacArthur fellow, 1984. Mem. Nat. Acad. Scis., Am. Math. Soc., AAAS, Math Assn. Am., Deutsche Akademie der Naturforscher Leopoldina, Sigma Xi. Current work: Nonlinear wave propagation; elasticity theory. Subspecialties: Analysis; Applied mathematics. Office: Courant Inst New York Univ 251 Mercer St New York NY 10012

JOHN-GREENE, JACQUELINE ANN, toxicologist; b. Marlboro, Mass., May 29, 1949; d. Earl G. and Lorraine K. (Cadieux) Neill; m. Tom T. John, June 3, 1972 (div. July 1979); m. Donald K. Greene, Sept. 22, 1984. B.S., U. Mass., 1971; M.A., Clark U., 1974. Project leader Dow Chem. Co., Midland, Mich., 1975-84; assoc. scientist Chem. Industry Inst. of Toxicology, Research Triangle Park, N.C., 1984—. Contbr. chpt. in book and articles to profl. jours. Pres. Bus. and Profl. Women, Midland, 1982. Mem. Teratology Soc. (council 1983-86), Behavioral Teratology Soc., Midwest Teratology Assn., Soc. Toxicology. Current work: Embryotoxicity in mammalian species from chem. exposure, teratology, fetal malformation, embryofetal metabolism, mechanisms of teratogenesis, behavioral teratology, testing methodology. Subspecialties: Teratology; Toxicology (medicine). Home: 1603 Laughridge Dr Cary NC 27511 Office: Chem Industry Inst Toxicology PO Box 12137 Research Triangle Park NC 27709

JOHNS, DEARING WARD, internist, researcher; b. Springfield, Mo., Aug. 8, 1941; d. Peter Otey and Annie (Boyd) Ward; m. Thomas Richards Johns, July 1, 1978; 1 dau., Sarah Dearing. A.B. in Physics, Sweet Briar Coll., 1963; M.D., U. Va., 1977. Asst. prof. internal medicine U. Va., 1983—. Mem. ACP, Am. Fedn. Clin. Research, Am. Coll. Cardiology. Current Work: Electrophysiology and pharmacology of vascular smooth muscle with special emphasis on its relationship to hypertension. Subspecialties: Cardiology; Internal medicine. Home: 19 Old Farm Rd Charlottesville VA 22901 Office: University of Virginia Medical Center Box 257 Charlottesville VA 22908

JOHNS, WILLIAM FRANCIS, chemist; b. Chgo., Aug. 31, 1930; s. Frank D. and Agnes (Mitrick) J.; m. Patricia J. Minehan, Nov. 11, 1950; children—Mitrick A., Daniel E., Susan L. Ph.B., U. Chgo., 1948, M.S., 1951; Ph.D., U. Wis., 1955. Chemist Merck & Co., Rahway, N.J., 1951-53; sr. chemist Searle Co., Skokie, Ill., 1955-63, research fellow, 1963-73, dir. medicinal chemistry, 1973-82; dir. medicinal chemistry Sterling-Winthrop Co., Rennsalaer, N.Y., 1982—. Editor Rev. of Steroids, 1974-75. Contbr. articles to profl. jours.; patentee in field. AAAS, Am. Chem. Soc. Current work: Director medicinal chemistry research. Subspecialties: Medicinal chemistry; Organic chemistry. Home: 9 Dennin Dr Menands NY 12204 Office: Sterling-Winthrop Research Inst Columbia Turnpike Rennselaer NY

JOHNSEN, EUGENE CARLYLE, mathematics educator, researcher; b. Mpls., Jan. 27, 1932; s. Bernhardt Thorwald and Esther Elvira (Eklund) J.; m. Marjorie Marie Wacklin, Aug. 31, 1957. B.Chem., U. Minn., 1954; Ph.D., Ohio State U., 1961. Nat. Acad. Scis.-NRC research assoc. Nat. Bur. Standards, Washington, 1962-63; lectr. in math. U. Calif.-Santa Barbara, 1963-64, asst. prof. math., 1964-68, assoc. prof. math., 1968-74, prof. math., 1974—; vis. lectr. in math. U. Mich.-Ann Arbor, 1968-69; mathematician Sperry Rand, St. Paul, summers 1956, 57; instr. chemistry and math. U. Minn., 1956-57; instr. math. Ohio State U., Columbus, 1962; vis. scholar Harvard U., 1984-85. Contbr. numerous articles to profl. jours. Recipient numerous research awards and grants. Mem. Am. Math. Soc., Math. Assn. Am., Soc. for Indsl. and Applied Math., AAAS, Internat. Network for Social Network Analysis, Phi Beta Kappa, Sigma Xi, Phi Lambda Upsilon, Pi Mu Epsilon. Clubs: Faculty, Sons of Norway. Current Work: Combinatorial designs, matrices, and algebraic structures and their applications in the biological and social sciences. Subspecialty: Applied mathematics. Office: Dept Math U Calif Santa Barbara CA 93106

JOHNSON, ANNE BRADSTREET, neuropathologist, researcher; b. Boston, Mar. 5, 1927; d. Stafford Fisher and Catherine (Tyler) J.; m. Jack Minkoff, June 19, 1948; children—Ellen Louise, Paul Andrew. B.A., Cornell U., 1948, M.D., 1951. Diplomate Am. Bd. Internal Medicine, Am. Bd. Pathology. Intern, resident Mt. Sinai Hosp., Cleve. City Hosp., Univ. Hosps., Cleve., 1951-55; practice medicine specializing in internal medicine, Cleve., 1955-57; fellow in medicine Columbia U., 1957-59; fellow in biochemistry Albert Einstein Coll. Medicine, Bronx, N.Y., 1959-61, instr., assoc. in anatomy and pathology, 1962-70, asst. prof. pathology, 1970-77, assoc. prof. pathology and neurosci., 1977—. Contbr. articles to profl. jours. Research grantee Nat. Multiple Sclerosis Soc., NIH. Mem. Am. Assn. Neuropathologists, Soc. Neurosci., Histochem. Soc., Am. Soc. Cell Biology, Internat. Acad. Pathology, N.Y. Acad. Scis., AAAS. Current work: Alzheimer's disease, studies utilizing monoclonal antibodies. Subspecialties: Pathology (medicine); Neurobiology. Office: Albert Einstein Coll Medicine Dept Pathology 1300 Morris Park Ave Bronx NY 10461

JOHNSON, ARTHUR H., soil scientist, educator; b. Phila., July 21, 1948; s. Arthur H. and Elizabeth (Deluca) J.; m. Janet Elizabeth Buttolph, June 14, 1971; children—Christopher Ross, Edward Arthur. A.B., Middlebury Coll., 1970; M.A., Dartmouth Coll., 1972; Ph.D., Cornell U., 1975; M.A. (hon.), U. Pa., 1980. Asst. prof. U. Pa., Phila., 1975-80, assoc. prof., 1980—. Contbr. articles to profl. jours. Mem. Am. Soc. Agronomy, Soil Sci. Soc. Am., AAAS. Current work: Effects of atmospheric deposition on forest elosystems. Subspecialties: Soil science; Ecosystems analysis. Office: U Pa Dept Geology Philadelphia PA 19320

JOHNSON, ARTHUR THOMAS, engineering educator, researcher; b. East Meadow, N.Y., Feb. 21, 1941; s. Arthur T. and Margaret C. (Law) J.; m. Cathleen May Throop, Sept. 7, 1963; children—Joy E., Jodi L., Paul H., Eric H. Ph.D., Cornell U., 1969. Registered profl. engr., Md. Engr. U.S. Army, Edgewood, Md., 1971-75; asst. prof. U. Md., College Park, 1975-81, assoc. prof., 1981—; cons. NBS-Office Energy Related Inventions, Gaithersberg, Md., 1978—; pres. Alliance Engring. in Medicine and Biology, Silver Spring, Md., 1984. Patentee Airflow Perturbation Device, 1975; contbr. articles to profl. jours. Balt. E. Dist. youth coordinator United Methodist Ch., 1978—. Served to capt. U.S. Army, 1969-71. Mem. Am. Soc. Agrl. Engrs. (Paper award 1970), IEEE, Am. Indsl. Hygiene Assn., Am. Soc. Engring. Edn., Internat. Soc. Respiratory Protection (chmn. bioengring. and physiol. com. 1983-84). Republican. Methodist. Current work: Instrumentation, transport processes, respiratory stress, exercise physiology, computer modelling of biological systems. Subspecialties: Agricultural engineering; Biomedical engineering. Home: 2324 Castleton Rd Darlington MD 21034 Office: U Md Agrl Engring Dept College Park MD 20742

JOHNSON, BRUCE PAUL, engineering educator, consultant; b. Lewiston, Maine, Aug. 8, 1938; s. Albert Samuel and Francis (Powers) J.; m. Marcia Ann Duarte, Feb. 1, 1961; children—Michael, Robyn, Samuel, Rebecca. B.S. in Physics, Bates Coll., 1960; M.S. in Physics, U. N.H., 1963; Ph.D. in Physics, U. Mo., 1967. Instr., physics Hobart William Smith Colls., Geneva, N.Y., 1962-64; advanced physicist Gen. Electric Med. Systems, Milw., 1967-69; group leader lamp div. Gen. Electric Cleve., 1969-74; assoc. prof., then prof. dept. elec. engring. and computer sci. U. Nev., Reno, 1974—, chmn. dept., 1978-83; mem. Acad. Adv. Council GTE Research Labs, Waltham, Mass., 1979-83; cons. Xebec Corp., Sunnyvale, Calif., 1984—. Contbr. articles to profl. jours. Mem. U.S. Metric Bd., 1978-82; mem. Nev. Metric Adv. Council, 1982—. NSF fellow. Mem. IEEE (sr. mem.; pres. No. Nev. sect. 1983-84), Sigma Xi (pres. No. Nev. chpt. 1984-85). Republican. Lodge: Masons. Current work: electronic computer aided design, manufacturing, and test from an integrated system perspective. Subspecialties: Microelectronics; Computer-aided design. Home: 3190 W 7th Reno NV 89503 Office: Dept Elec Engring U Nev Reno NV 89557

JOHNSON, CHARLES SIDNEY, JR., physical chemistry educator; b. Albany, Ga., Mar. 7, 1936; s. Charles Sidney and Mary Virginia (Reid) J.; m. Ellen McFarland, Sept. 3, 1958; children—David Mason, Daniel Cook. B.S. in Chemistry, Ga. Inst. Tech., 1958; Ph.D., in Phys. Chemistry, MIT, 1961. Nat. Acad. Scis.-NRC fellow U. Ill., Urbana, 1961-62; asst. prof. Yale U., New Haven, 1962-66, assoc. prof., 1967; prof. U. N.C., Chapel Hill, 1967—; Guggenheim fellow U. Cambridge, 1972-73. Author: Problems and Solutions in Quantum Chemistry, 1974. Contbr. articles to profl. jours. Fellow A.P. Sloan Found., 1966, J.S. Guggenheim Found., 1972. Fellow Am. Phys. Soc.; mem. Am. Chem. Soc., Sigma Xi. Current work: Laser light scattering, transient laser induced gratings, pulsed field gradient NMR, real-time electrophoresis. Subspecialties: Physical chemistry; Biophysical chemistry. Home: 1833 N Lake Shore Dr Chapel Hill NC 27514 Office: Dept Chemistry U NC 045A Chapel Hill NC 27514

JOHNSON, CHRISTOPHER PETER, III, organic/medicinal chemist; b. Richmond, Va., Oct. 5, 1943; s. Christopher Peter and Lillian Irene (Widener) J. B.S., U. Richmond, 1965, M.S., 1969; M.B.A., Va. Commonwealth U., 1984. Indsl. hygienist Va. State Dept. Health, Richmond, 1965-69; chemist Edgewood Arsenal, Md., 1969-71; chemist drug metabolism A. H. Robins Co., Inc., Richmond, Va., 1971-73, research chemist chem. research, 1973—; instr. chemistry J. Sargent Reynolds Community Coll., Richmond, Va., 1976. Patentee in field. Mem. Nat. Taxpayers Assn., Washington, 1972—; bd. dirs. Richmond Taxpayers Assn., Va., 1978—. Served with U.S. Army, 1969-71. Mem. AAAS, Am. Chem. Soc. (organic chemistry div., medicinal chemistry div.), Inst. Exec. M.B.A.s, Beta Gamma Sigma, Alpha Iota Delta. Republican. Methodist. Club: Va. Ski (Richmond). Current work: Design and synthesis of target compounds for pharmacological testing as antiarrhythmics, anti-hypertensives and calcium channel blockers in treating cardiovascular disorders. Subspecialties: Organic chemistry; Synthetic chemistry. Office: A H Robins Co Research Labs 1211 Sherwood Ave Richmond VA 23220

JOHNSON, CLARK EUGENE, JR., magnetics physicist; b. Mpls., Aug. 3, 1930; s. Clark Eugene and Elizabeth (Wiggenhorn) J.; m. Nancy Louise DeMan, Apr. 30, 1951 (div.); children—Wendy, Taylor, Brett, Clark III, Timothy, Carrie; m. Irma Shirley Rubin, Dec. 29, 1965. B.S. in Physics, U. Minn., 1950; M.S.E.E., 1961. Vice pres. Minnetech Labs., Mpls., 1963-65, Vibrac Corp., Chelmsford, Mass., 1965-72; pres. Micro communications, Waltham, Mass., 1977; dir. research and devel. Buckeye Internat. Inc., Columbus, Ohio, 1977-81; chmn., chief tech. officer Vertimag. Systems Corp., Mpls., 1981-84, chmn., 1984—; dir. Britt Corp., Mpls., High Iron Travel Corp., Milw. Railcar Corp., KRS Magnetics, Los Altos, Calif., Info. Storage and Retrieval Corp., Boulder, Calif. Mem. exec. com. Minn. Hightech. Council, Mpls., 1984—, chmn. govt. relations com., 1984—; mem. adv. com. World Trade Ctr., St. Paul, 1984—. Contbr. articles to profl. jours. Patentee in field. Mem. IEEE (sr. mem.; fin. com. 1977-81); Magnetics Soc. (sec., treas. 1979-80, v.p. 1981-82, pres. 1983-84). Democrat. Current work: Advancing high density magnetic recording by the commercialization of perpendicular magnetic recording. Subspecialties: Magnetic physics; Information systems, storage, and retrieval (computer science). Home: #803-6400 Barrie Rd Minneapolis MN 55435

JOHNSON, D. LYNN, engineering educator; b. Provo, Utah, Apr. 2, 1934; married; 5 children. B.S. in Mining Engring., U. Utah, 1956, Ph.D. in Ceramic Engring., 1962. Asst. prof. Northwestern U., Evanston, Ill., 1962-66, assoc. prof., 1966-71, prof. materials sci. and engring., 1971—, chmn. dept., 1982—. Contbr. articles to profl. jours. NSF fellow, 1960-61, fellow Am. Ceramic Soc. 1973, (trustee basic sci. div.); mem. AIME, Ceramic Edn. Council, Phi Eta Sigma, Phi Kappa Phi, Tau Beta Pi. Current work: Sintering, plasma and microwave; sintering and creep inhibition of fuel cell anodes. Office: Northwestern U Dept Materials Sci & Engring 2145 Sheridan Rd Evanston IL 60201

JOHNSON, DARYL CLYDE, veterinary epidemiologist; b. Junction City, Oreg., Feb. 6, 1933; s. H. Floyd and Selma Alfreda (Moomaw) J.; m. Elaine

Ellen Losey, May 29, 1954; children—Mark C., Deanne Kay, Bruce L. Student Manchester Coll., 1951-53, Va. Poly. Inst., 1956; D.V.M., U. Ga., 1960. Field veterinarian Ind. Livestock San. Bd., Milford, Ind., 1960-61, USDA, 1961-68; vis. rep. Plum Island Animal Disease Ctr. (N.Y.), 1968-69; poultry epidemiologist Animal and Plant Health Inspection Service, Vet. Services, USDA, Orono, Maine, 1969-72, regional epidemiologist, Athens, Ga., 1972—. Mem. AVMA, Am. Assn. Avian Pathologist (com. chmn.), Nat. Assn. of Fed. Veterinarians, U.S. Animal Health Assn. (com. mem.), Assn. of Avian Veterinarians. Baptist. Subspecialties: Preventive medicine (veterinary medicine); Veterinary Epidemiology. Home: 185 Broomsedge Trail Athens GA 30605 Office: USDA APHIS VS 934 College Station Rd Athens GA 30605

JOHNSON, DAVID EDWIN, physicist, high energy physics; b. Newark, Sept. 3, 1944; s. Lester Leonard and Alice Maude (Batchelder) J. A.B. in Physics, U. Calif.-Berkeley, 1966; Ph.D. in High Energy Physics, Iowa State U., 1972. Research and teaching asst. Ames Lab. and Iowa State U., Ames, 1966-72; postdoctoral fellow Ames Lab., 1972-73; physicist Tevatron I Project, Fermilab, Batavia, Ill., 1973—. Contbr. writings in field to profl. publs. Mem. Am. Phys. Soc., AAAS, Sigma Xi. Designer electron cooling ring and neutron cancer therapy beam, Fermilab. Current Work: Particle physics at very high energies. Design and construction of Tevatron I - intense proton-antiproton collisions at 1000 GeV x 1000GeV. Subspecialties: Particle physics; Accelerator physics. Office: Fermilab Tevatron I PO Box 500 Batavia IL 60510

JOHNSON, DAVID GREGORY, endocrinologist, internal medicine educator; b. Belvidere, Ill., July 11, 1940; s. Owen Maynard and Helen Marjorie (Carroll) J.; m. Inger Soderlund, Apr. 25, 1965; children—Elisabeth, Lars, Leif. B.A., Yale U., 1962; B.S. in Med. Sci., Dartmouth Coll., 1964; M.D., Harvard U., 1967. Diplomate Am. Bd. Internal Medicine. Asst. prof. U. Wash.-Seattle, 1973-76, assoc. prof., 1976-78; chief endocrine sect. U. Ariz.-Tucson, 1978—. Co-author (with R. Bressler): Management of Diabetes Mellitus, 1982. Bd. dirs. Tucson chpt. Am. Diabetes Assn., 1978-84. Served with USPHS, 1969-71. Recipient NIH Research Career Devel. award, 1974. Mem. Am. Diabetes Assn., Endocrine Soc., Am. Soc. Pharmacology and Exptl. Therapeutics. Lutheran. Current work: Diabetes research, metabolism, neurochemistry. Subspecialties: Neuroendocrinology; Internal medicine. Home: 1100 E Placita Linternilla Tucson AZ 85718 Office: U Ariz 1501 N Campbell Ave Tucson AZ 85724

JOHNSON, DAVID LINTON, theoretical physicist; b. Chgo., July 9, 1945; s. Marvin F.L. and Jane (Brown) J.; m. Dava Naomi Lowenthal, Feb. 26, 1972 (div. 1984); children—Kelsey Michael, Sean Philip. B.S., U. Notre Dame, 1967; M.S., U. Chgo., 1969, Ph.D., 1974. Research assoc. Michaelson Lab., China Lake, Calif., 1972-74; research assoc. Ames Lab., Iowa, 1974-76; asst. prof. Northeastern U., Boston, 1976-79; research physicist Schlumberger-Doll Research, Ridgefield, Conn., 1979—; cons. GTE Labs., Waltham, Mass., 1979. Editor: Physics and Chemistry of Porous Media, 1984. Contbr. articles to profl. jours., also Yearbook of Science and Technology. Mem. Am. Phys. Soc., Soc. Exploration Geophysicists, Acoustical Soc. Am., Am. Geophys. Union. Current work: Properties of heterogeneous media especially porous, fluid saturated solids. Subspecialties: Condensed matter physics; Acoustics. Office: Schlumberger-Doll Research Old Quarry Rd Ridgefield CT 06877

JOHNSON, DAVID NORSEEN, neuropharmacologist; b. Bronx, N.Y., Sept. 28, 1938; s. Einar Victor and Eunice Marie (Norseen) J.; m. Carolyn, Oct. 8, 1960; children: Lauren Dale, Brian David. B.S. in Biology, North Park Coll., Chgo., 1960; M.S. in Psychopharmacology, U. Louisville, 1967; Ph.D. in Neuropharmacology, Med. Coll. Va., 1975. Research pharmacologist A.H. Robins Co. Inc., Richmond, Va., 1966-69, sr. research pharmacologist, 1970-75, mgr. neuropharmacology, 1976—. Contbr. articles on treatment of mental disease, sleep research, animal models for mental disease to sci. jours., also chpts. in books. Mem. Am. Soc. Pharmacology and Exptl. Therapeutics, Soc. for Neurosci., Am. Chem. Soc. (div. medicinal chemistry). Presbyterian. Current Work: Development of new agents for treatment of mental disease; development of animal models of mental illness; effects of drugs on sleep/waking patterns in laboratory animals. Subspecialties: Neuropharmacology; Psychopharmacology. Home: 11406 Blendon Ln Richmond VA 23233 Office: 1211 Sherwood Ave Richmond VA 23261

JOHNSON, DEADRE JEANNE, research chemist; b. Newport News, Va., July 5, 1949; d. Eugene Walden and Rosa Ileana (Lee) J. B.A., Hampton Inst., 1970; postgrad. Howard U., 1970, U. Md., 1976. Clin. chemist Washington Reference Lab., Washington, 1970-72; med. technician D.C. Govt., 1972-73; chemist hematology, oncology service Walter Reed Gen. Hosp., Washington, 1973-78; research chemist hematology Walter Reed Army Inst. Research, Washington, 1978—. Contbr. articles to profl. jours. Typesetter, newsletter commn. Northeastern Presbyn. Ch., Washington, 1981-82. Recipient Commendation Outstanding Performance award Dept. Army 1976-78, 81-84, Letters Appreciation Dept. Army, D.C. Pub. Schs., 1975-84. Named one of Outstanding Young Women Am. 1982. Mem. Am. Chem. Soc., D.C. Met. Orgn. Black Scientists (scholarship chairperson 1977—), Nat. Orgn. Profl. Advancement Black Chemist and Chem. Engrs., Nat. Hampton Alumni Assn. (regional v.p. 1981—, sec. D.C. chapt. 1976-82, nat. alumni bull. com. 1981-83). Democrat. Current work: Research concerning the use of Hydroxocobalamin (Vitamin B12a) as a prophylactic agent in cyanide intoxication, also effect of environmental toxins on heme synthesis. Subspecialties: Biochemistry (medicine); Analytical chemistry. Home: 11235 Oak Leaf Dr Silver Spring MD 20901 Office: Walter Reed Army Inst Research Dept Hematology 14th & Dahlia St NW Washington DC 20307

JOHNSON, DEE LYNN, scientist, inventor, poet, photographer, futurist; b. LaJunta, Colo., Apr. 22, 1932; s. Robert Leo and Mildred Viola (Jordan) J.; m. Dorothy Ann Parmley, Sept. 1, 1956; children—Suzanne, Cynthia, Rebecca. B., U. No. Colo., 1954, M., 1958. Sr. scientist Eastman Kodak Co., Rochester, N.Y., 1958-67; sr. research specialist med. products and adhesives div. 3M, St. Paul, 1967—; lectr. in field. Contbr. articles to profl. jours., chpts. to books. Patentee in field. Precinct chmn. Woodbury Republican Com., Minn., 1974; moderator Woodbury Bapt. Ch., 1968-70. Served to capt. USAF, 1955-58. NSF fellow Princeton U., 1966-67. Mem. Am. Chem. Soc. Lodge: Lions (chmn. 1972-75). Current work: synergism of ideas and business opportunities, consultant, inventor. Subspecialties: Drug delivery systems; Polymers (materials science). Office: 3M Ctr 209-IN-20 Saint Paul MN 55144

JOHNSON, DONALD REX, scientific laboratory manager; b. Tacoma, July 19, 1938; s. Richard Carl and Freida Maria (Dahlstrom) J.; m. Karen Yvonne Neswoog, July 24, 1959; children: Eric R., Brad A. B.S. in Physics, U. Puget Sound, 1960; M.S. in Physics, U. Idaho, 1962; Ph.D. in Exptl. Physics, U. Okla., 1967. Physicist Nat. Bur. Standards, Washington, 1967—, sr. mgmt. trainee, 1976-78; dep. dir. Nat. Measurement Lab., 1978-82, dir. Nat. Measurement Lab., 1982—. Contbr. articles to tech. publs. Bd. dirs. West Riding Citizens Assn., 1971-74, pres., 1972-73; bd. dirs. Gaithersburg Area Civic Coalition, 1972-74; mem. Shady Grove Sector Plan Adv. Com., 1974-75; vice chmn. Gaithersburg Bicentennial Coordinating Com., 1975-76; sec. Gaithersburg City Planning Commn., 1977, chmn., 1978—. NSF grad. trainee in physics, 1965-67; recipient Silver medal U.S. Dept. Commerce, 1973, Gold medal, 1977; Arthur S. Flemming Award, 1976; Sr. Exec. Service meritorious exec., 1981. Fellow Am. Phys. Soc. (council 1985-83); mem. ASTM (bd. dirs. 1983-85), Am. Astron. Soc., AAAS, Internat. Astronomers Union, Sigma Xi. Student stellar atmospheres; co-discoverer various new interstellar molecules. Subspecialties: Physical chemistry; Radio and microwave astronomy.

JOHNSON, DOUGLAS BLAIKIE, engineer, lawyer; b. Chgo., Sept. 13, 1952; s. Marvin Melrose and Anne Stuart (Campbell) J.; m. Pamela Jane Tomlinson, Aug. 1, 1975; children—Richard Aaron, Lauren Stuart, Diana Blaikie, Scott Nathaniel. B.S.M.E., U. Nebr., 1974; J.D., Seton Hall U., 1980. Bar: Nebr. 1980; registered profl. engr., Nebr. Project engr. DuPont Co., Cleve., 1974-75; project engr. Exxon Chems., Linden, N.J., 1975-78, cost engr., 1978-80; sr. engr. InterNorth, Inc., Omaha, 1980-82, market planner, 1982-84, corp. planner, 1984-85, bus. mgr., 1985—. Loaned exec. Cleve. Jr. Achievement, 1974, United Way of Midlands, Omaha, 1982, Midland council Boy Scouts Am., Omaha, 1984. Mem. ASME, ASHRAE, Fed. Energy Bar Assn., ABA, Nebr. State Bar Assn, Sigma Tau, Pi Tau Sigma. Republican. Presbyterian. Current work: Energy consumption in residential and industrial applications; industrial cogeneration and gas combustion turbines; modeling of space conditioning and process technologies. Subspecialties: Mechanical engineering; Solar energy. Home: 14705 U Plaza Omaha NE 68137 Office: InterNorth Inc 2223 Dodge St Omaha NE 68102

JOHNSON, EDWARD MICHAEL, molecular biologist; b. Kenosha, Wis., Apr. 9, 1945; s. Edward and Mary Margaret (Pratch) J.; m. Elizabeth Buckingham Childs, June 14, 1969; 1 son, Nathaniel Livingston. B.A., Pomona Coll., 1967; Ph.D., Yale U., 1971. Postdoctoral fellow Rockefeller U., N.Y.C., 1971-73, asst. prof., 1975-81, assoc. prof., 1981-84; prof. dept. pathology Mt. Sinai Sch. Medicine, 1985—; research assoc. Meml. Sloan-Kettering Cancer Ctr., 1973-75, assoc. scientist, 1975-81; mem. genetics field Cornell U. Grad. Sch. Med. Scis., 1979—. Contbr. numerous articles to profl. jours. Jane Coffin Childs fellow, 1971-73; Leukemia Soc. Am. spl. fellow, 1974-76; Faculty Research award Am. Cancer Soc., 1982—. Mem. Am. Soc. Cell Biology; mem. Am. Soc. Biol. Chemists; Mem. N.Y. Acad. Scis., Am. Soc. Pharmacology and Exptl. Therapeutics. Current Work: Regulation of gene activity by chromosomal proteins; chromosomal organization of oncogenes; structure activity and chromosomal packaging of ribosomal genes, chromosome construction. Subspecialties: Gene actions; Genome organization. Home: 531 E 88th St Apt 4B New York NY 10128 Office: Dept Pathology Mt Sinai Sch Medicine 1 Gustave Levy Pl New York NY 10029

JOHNSON, ELIJAH, chemist; b. Eutawville, S.C., Dec. 30, 1947; s. Francis and Mariah (Prioleau) J. Student S.C. State Coll., 1965-67; B.S. in Chemistry, Pa. State U., 1969; Ph.D. in Chem. Physics, U. Ill., 1976. Research staff mem. Oak Ridge Nat. Lab., 1976—. Served with U.S. Army, 1969-71. Eugene P. Wigner fellow, 1977. Mem. Am. Chem. Soc. Current work: Statistical mechanical studies of fluids; analysis of x-ray and neutron scattering data on fluids. Subspecialty: Statistical mechanics. Home: PO Box 1098 Oak Ridge TN 37831 Office: Chemistry Div Oak Ridge Nat Lab PO Box X Oak Ridge TN 37831

JOHNSON, ELMER MARSHALL, reproductive toxicologist and teratologist; b. Midlothian, Ill., June 16, 1930; s. Burt and Gertrude Esther (Miller) J.; m. Sharon Ann Coyle, May 9, 1976; children—Mark Dee, Kim Lea, Erik Marshall, Lora Marlys. Student, U. Mex., 1948; diploma, Thornton Jr. Coll., 1950; B.S. (teaching asst.), Tex. A. and M. U., 1954, M.S., 1955; Ph.D. (teaching asst.), U. Calif., Berkeley, 1959. Research asst. U.S. Army Surgeon Gen./Tex. A. and M. U. Research Found., College Station, 1955; instr. anatomy and physiology Contra Costa Coll., San Pablo, Calif., 1958-59; instr. U. Fla. Coll. Medicine, Gainesville, 1960-61, asst. prof., 1961-65, asso. prof., 1965-68, prof., 1968-70, acting chmn. dept. anatomy, 1969-70; prof., chmn. dept. anatomy, prof. dept. developmental and cellular biology U. Calif., Irvine, 1970-72; prof., chmn. dept. anatomy, dir. Daniel Baugh Inst., Jefferson Med. Coll., Thomas Jefferson U., Phila., 1972—; founding pres., chmn. bd. Argus Research Labs., Inc., Perkasie, Pa.; cons. Allied Chem. Co., Dow Chem. Co., Johnson & Johnson, Argus Research Labs., Public Utilities, EPA, U.S. Naval Hosp., Phila., Shell Devel. Co., Kirkland & Ellis, Esq., Hoffman-LaRoche, Merck, Inc., McGraw-Hill, Inc., Sterling-Winthrop Research Inst., Interagy. Regulatory Liaison Group, Nat. Acad. Scis., NRC, Columbia Nitrogen Co., 3M, Xerox, PPG. Assoc. Editor: Teratology, 1974-81, Jour. Environ. Pathology and Toxicology, 1979—, Fundamental and Applied Toxicology, 1981-84. Served to 2d lt. U.S. Army, 1959. USPHS predoctoral fellow, 1953-55; March of Dimes Nat. Found. research grantee, 1962-63, 80-83, 84—; NIH research grantee, 1963—; Growth Soc. research grantee, 1972-74; NIH teratology predoctoral tng. grantee, 1955-59. Mem. AAAS, Teratology Soc., Am. Assn. Anatomists, Assn. Anatomy Chairmen, Genetic Toxicology Assn., Soc. Toxicology, Am. Coll. Toxicology, So. Soc. Anatomists, Mid Atlantic Reproduction and Teratology Assn., European Teratology Soc., Chem. Mfrs. Assn. (bd. dirs.), Am. Petroleum Inst. (bd. dirs.), Elec. Power Research Inst. (bd. dirs.), Sigma Xi. Unitarian. Subspecialties: Teratology; Toxicology (medicine). Office: 1020 Locust St Philadelphia PA 19107

JOHNSON, F. BRENT, microbiologist; b. Monroe, Utah, Mar. 31, 1942; s. Horace Jay and Ida (Christiansen) J.; m. Paula Dawn Forbush, June 18, 1965; children: Brian Kay, Matthew Glen, Christopher Jay, Wesley Terin, Stephanie Dawn. Student, Coll. So. Utah, 1960-61; B.S., Brigham Young U., 1966, M.S., 1967, Ph.D., 1970. NIH predoctoral fellow Brigham Young U., 1966-70, asst. prof. microbiology, 1972-75, assoc. prof., 1975-80, prof., 1980—; NIH postdoctoral fellow, Bethesda, Md., 1970-72, research assoc., 1977-78; dir. Adkins Research Fund. Contbr. numerous articles on parvoviruses and herpesviruses to sci. jours. NIH grantee, 1973-76; USAF summer faculty fellow, 1977; grantee, 1978-79, 79-82. Mem. Am. Soc. Microbiology, N.Y. Acad. Scis., AAAS, Sigma Xi, Phi Kappa Phi. Mormon. Current Work: The structure and biology of parvoviruses, diagnostic virology, and herpes virus oncogenicity. Subspecialties: Microbiology; Virology (biology). Office: Brigham Young U 887 WIDB Provo UT 84602

JOHNSON, FRANCIS SEVERIN, physicist; b. Omak, Wash., July 20, 1918; s. Ralston Severin and Elizabeth (Gruenes) J.; m. Maurine Marie Green, Sept. 12, 1943; 1 dau., Sharan Kaye. B.Sc. with honors in Physics, U. Alta., Can., 1940; M.A. in Physics and Meteorology, UCLA, 1942, Ph.D. in Meteorology, 1958. Head, high atmosphere research sect. U.S. Naval Research Lab., Washington, 1946-55; mgr. space physics research Lockheed Missiles & Space Co., 1955-62; head, atmospheric and space scis. div. S.W. Center Advanced Studies, Dallas, 1962-64, dir. earth and planetary scis. lab., 1964-69; acting pres. U. Tex. at Dallas, 1969-71; dir. Center for Advanced Studies, 1971-74, Cecil H. and Ida M. Green honors prof. natural sci., 1974—, exec. dean grad. studies and research, 1976-79; asst. dir. astron., atmosphere, earth and ocean scis. NSF, Washington, 1979-83; cons. ionospheric physics subcom., space scis. steering com. NASA, 1960-62, mem. planetary atmospheres subcom., space scis. steering com., 1962-67, chmn. lunar atmospheric measurements team. Apollo sci. planning teams, 1964-67; mem. adv. bd. Mars space missions, 1964-67, mem. lunar and planetary missions bd., 1967-71; mem. adv. panel atmospheric scis. NSF, 1962-67; mem. working group IV COSPAR, 1965-80, v.p., 1975-80; mem. Nat. Acad. Scis. panel adv. to central radio propagation lab. Nat. Bur. Standards, 1962-65; mem. panel weather and climate modification Nat. Acad. Scis., 1964-70; mem. adv. com. research to coordinating bd. Tex. Coll. and Univ. System, 1966-67; mem. space sci. bd. Nat. Acad. Scis., 1969-81, mem. geophysics research bd., 1971-77; mem. Nat. Acad. Scis. com. advisory to NOAA, 1966-71; mem. sci. advisory bd. USAF, 1968-79; mem. nat. adv. com. Oceans and Atmosphere, 1971-73; mem. Climate Research Bd., Nat. Acad. Scis., 1977-79; pres. Spl. Com. on Solar Terrestrial Physics, 1974-77; mem. Nat. Acad. Sci. Bd. on Atmospheric Scis. and Climate, 1983—; mem. vis. com. and Aerocibo adv. bd. Nat. Astronomy and Ionosphere Ctr., 1985—. Author: Satellite Environment Handbook, 1965; also numerous articles. Served with USAAF, 1942-46. Decorated Bronze Star medal; recipient Henryk Arctowski award Nat. Acad. Scis., 1972; Exceptional Sci. Achievement medal NASA, 1973; Meritorious Civilian Service award USAF, 1979; Outstanding Scientist award Tex. Acad. Scis., 1984. Fellow Am. Geophys. Union (vice chmn. sect. geomagnetism and aeronomy 1964-68, pres. sect. solar planetary relationships 1970-72, John Adam Fleming award 1977), AAAS (council mem. 1968-72), Am. Meteorol. Soc. (councilor 1976-78), IEEE; asso. fellow AIAA (chmn. tech. com. space and atmospheric physics 1961-64, Space Sci. award 1966); mem. Am. Phys. Soc., Am. Astron. Soc., Internat. Assn. Geomagnetism and Aeronomy (exec. com. 1967-71), Internat. Union Radio Sci. (chmn. U.S. Commn. IV 1964-67, sec. U.S. nat. com. 1967-70, vice chmn. 1970-73, chmn. 1973-76), Internat. Union Geodesy and Geophysics (U.S. nat. com. 1973-76), Sigma Xi. Current Work: Upper atmosphere structure, magneto-spheric physics. Subspecialties: Aeronomy; Satellite studies. Office: U Tex at Dallas PO Box 688 Richardson TX 75080

JOHNSON, FRANK EDWARD, surgeon, medical educator; b. Evanston, Ill., Oct. 28, 1943; s. Frank E. and Beryl Madeline (Johnson) J.; m. Tamiko Asato, Jan. 24, 1976; children—Mariko, Michael, Eric, David. B.A., U. Minn., 1964, M.D., 1967. Diplomate Am. Bd. Surgery. Clin. instr. surgery Cornell U., N.Y.C., 1977-79; asst. prof. surgery St. Louis U. Med. Ctr., 1979-84, assoc. prof. surgery, 1984—. Contbr. articles to profl. jours. Co-founder Children's Heart Fund, Mpls., 1969. Served to lt. comdr., USN, 1969-71. Decorated Bronze Star; NIH grantee, 1982-85; Am. Cancer Soc. grantee, 1978-79. Mem. Soc. Surg. Oncology, Am. Gastroenterol. Assn., AMA, Am. Assn. Clin. Research, Am. Soc. Clin. Oncology, Phi Beta Kappa. Current work: Effect of hormones on growth of normal organs and tumors; cancer surgery. Subspecialties: Cancer research (medicine); Surgery. Office: Saint Louis U Med Ctr 1325 S Grand Blvd Saint Louis MO 63104

JOHNSON, GEORGE ROBERT, educator; b. Caledonia, N.Y., Aug. 2, 1917; s. Arthur E. and Mary J. (Sinclair) J.; m. Beatrice E. Caton, Nov. 7, 1942; children: Diane K., Jane A. Eiden, Rosemary E. Johnson Kurek, Martha L. Brinkman. B.S., Cornell U., 1939; M.S., Mich. State U., 1947, Ph.D., 1954. Tchr. Corfu-East Pembroke Central Sch., Corfu, N.Y., 1939-42; asst. agrl. country agt., St. Lawrence (N.Y.) County, 1942-43; instr. animal husbandry Cornell U., 1943-47, asst. prof., 1947-48, assoc. prof., 1948-55, Ohio State U., 1955-58, prof., chmn. dept. animal sci., 1958—. Mem. Am. Soc. Animal Sci., Sigma Xi, Alpha Zeta, Gamma Sigma Delta. Subspecialty: Animal science administration. Home: 251 Fairlawn Dr Columbus OH 43214

JOHNSON, GLEN ERIC, mech. engr., educator, cons., researcher; b. Rochester, N.Y., May 29, 1951; s. Ray Clifford and Helen Francis (Lindgren) J.; m. Kathryne Ann DeLoach, May 3, 1975; children: Edward Lindgren, Eric Anders. B.S.M.E., Worcester Poly. Inst., 1973; M.S.M.E. (Pres.'s fellow), Ga. Inst. Tech., 1974; Ph.D. (Harold Stirling Vanderbilt scholar), Vanderbilt U., 1978. Registered profl. engr., Va., Tenn. Mech. engr. Tenn. Eastman Co., Kingsport, 1974-76; asst. prof. mech. engring. Vanderbilt U., 1978-79, assoc. prof., 1981—; asst. prof. U. Va., 1979-81; cons. mech. design, noise control, optimization. Contbr. articles on optimization, mech. design, noise control to profl. jours. Mem. ASME (assoc. editor Jour. Mech. Design 1981-82, Jour. Mechanisms, Transmissions, and Automation in Design, 1982-83, vice chmn. design automation com. 1984-86), Soc. Automotive Engrs. (Ralph R. Teetor award 1984), Am. Gear Mfrs. Assn., Acoustic Soc.), Math. Programming Soc., Acoustical Soc. Am. Current Work: Development and application of optimization techniques; mech. design synthesis, computer aided design, optimization, noise control. Subspecialties: Mechanical engineering; Acoustical engineering. Home: 235 Gloucester St Frankin TN 37064 Office: Vanderbilt U Box 8-B Nashville TN 37235

JOHNSON, GLENN RICHARD, plant breeder; b. Geneseo, Ill., Feb. 19, 1938; s. Glenn Carl and Josehine Maude (Miller) J. B.S., Iowa State U., 1960, Ph.D., 1965. Plant breeder DeKalb-Pfizer, Inc., Thomasboro, 1965—. Contbr. articles to profl. jours. Mem. Crop. Sci., Soc., AAAS, Am. Genetic Assn., N.Y. Acad. Sci., Sigma Xi. Current work: Corn breeding; quantitative genetic research. Subspecialties: Plant genetics; Agronomy. Office: DeKalb Pfizer Genetics Inc Rt 1 Box 162 Thomasboro IL 61878

JOHNSON, GREG WILLARD, atomic emission spectroscopist, analytical chemist; b. Hampton, Iowa, Oct. 21, 1949; s. Willard C. and Rachael Esther (Lundvall) J.; m. Mary Rose Spahn, Aug. 21, 1976; children—Geoffrey Eric, David Scott. B.S., Colo. State U., 1972, Ph.D., 1979. Applications chemist Spectrametrics, Inc., Andover, Mass., 1979-80; analytical chemist Union 76 Molycorp, Louviers, Colo., 1980—. Contbr. articles to profl. jours. Mem. Am. Chem. Soc., Rocky Mountain Soc. Applied Spectroscopy (treas. 1981-82, program chmn. 1982-83, chmn. 1983-84), Phi Kappa Phi. Roman Catholic. Current work: Analysis of various materials, especially for lanthanide elements, using atomic emission spectroscopy. Subspecialties: Atomic spectroscopy; Analytical chemistry. Home: 4851 W Oxford Ave Denver CO 80236 Office: Union 76 Molycorp PO Box 37 Louviers CO 80131

JOHNSON, HAROLD ARTHUR, manufacturing companies executive; b. Warren, Pa., May 17, 1924; s. Oscar William and Alvina Victoria (Nelson) J.; m. Alice Meredith Jones, June 15, 1955; children: Mark, Thomas. B.S. in Indsl. Engring, Pa. State U., 1950. With Pa. Furnace & Iron Co., Warren, 1941-72, sales and engring. mgr., 1961-63, sec.-treas., 1963-68, v.p., 1968-72; also dir.; exec. v.p. Allegheny Valve Co., Allegheny Coupling Co., Warren, 1972-82, pres., treas., 1982—; also dir.; exec. v.p. Rand Machine Products, Inc., Jamestown, N.Y., 1972—; also dir.; pres., treas., dir. DeFrees Family Found.; instr. short courses Ill. Inst. Tech., 1955, Mich. State U., 1956; past cons. in field; mem. U.S. del. Conferences Conseil International Pour l'Organization Scientifique, Munich, W.Ger., 1972, Caracas, Venezuela, 1975. Contbr. articles to profl. jours. Active Warren County (Pa.) Sch. Bldg. Authorities, 1961—, chmn., 1980—; chmn. Warren County Hosp. Authority, 1971—; mem. exec. bd., chief cornplanter Boy Scouts Am., 1972—, v.p., 1983—; sr. warden Trinity Meml. Ch., Warren, 1963-64, vestryman, 1962-64, treas., 1972—; trustee Erie Diocese, Episcopal Ch., 1975-81. Served with U.S. Army, 1943-46. Decorated Bronze Star. Mem. ASME, Truck Trailer Mfrs. Assn. (chmn. tank conf. engring. com. 1961-62), Tau Beta Pi, Phi Kappa Phi, Phi Eta Sigma, Phi Sigma Kappa. Republican. Clubs: Conewango Valley Country, Conewango, Grotto, Am. Legion (past officer). Lodges: Rotary; Masons; Shriners. Patentee in field; designed fueling trailers for Project Van Guard, 1st U.S. Space Satellite; early work in transp. of liquified gases at low temperatures. Current Work: Valves and equipment for liquid transportation tanks. Subspecialties: Industrial engineering; Mechanical engineering. Home: 103 Memorial Pl Rd Warren PA 16365 Office: 419 3d Ave Warren PA 16365

JOHNSON, HERBERT GARDNER, immunologist; b. Wessington, S.D., Mar. 22, 1933; s. John P. and Helen V. (Vincent) J.; m. Nita M. Hansen, Aug. 25, 1953; children—Darrell, Marilyn, Brian. B.S., U. Ill., 1958, M.S., 1959; Ph.D., U. Mich., 1969. Research asst. Upjohn Co., Kalamazoo, 1959-67, research assoc., 1969-75, sr. research sci., 1975-83, sr. sci., 1983—. Author: Allergy: Principles and Practice, 1983. Contbr. articles to profl. jours. Patentee in field. Treas. Kalamazoo Youth Ministry, Mich., 1978-80; deacon, elder 2nd Reformed Ch., Kalamazoo, 1964-84. Served with U.S. Army, 1953-55. Mem. Federated Soc. Experimental Biology. Republican. Current work: Allergy; mucus hyper-productive modulation cronic airways diseases. Subspecialties: Immunopharmacology; Pharmacology. Home: 829 Berkshire Kalamazoo MI 49007 Office: Upjohn Co 301 Henrietta St Kalamazoo MI 49001

JOHNSON, HOLLIS RALPH, astronomer, educator; b. Tremonton, Utah, Dec. 2, 1928; s. Ellwood Lewis and Ida Martha (Hansen) J.; m. Grete Margit Leed, June 3, 1954; children: Carol Ann Johnson Watson, Wayne L., Lyle David, Charlotte Johnson Willian, Lise Marie, Richard L. B.A. in Physics, Brigham Young U., 1955, M.A. in Physics, 1957; Ph.D. in Astrophysics, U. Colo., 1960. NSF postdoctoral fellow Paris Obs., 1960-61; research asso. Yale U., 1961-63; asso. prof. astronomy Ind. U., 1963-67, prof., 1967—, chmn. dept. astronomy, 1978-82. Contbr. articles to profl. jours. Served with U.S. Army, 1951-53. Recipient Vis. Scientist award High Altitude Obs., Boulder, Colo., 1971-72; Nat. Acad. Scis./NRC sr. fellow NASA Ames Research Ctr., 1982-83. Mem. Internat. Astron. Union, Am. Astron. Soc., AAAS, AAUP, Sigma Xi. Mormon. Current Work: Ultraviolet spectra of red giant stars; calculation of model atmospheres for cool stars; calculation of line opacities. Subspecialties: Ultraviolet high energy astrophysics; Theoretical astrophysics. Office: Astronomy Dept Swain W 319 Ind U Bloomington IN 47405

JOHNSON, HORACE RICHARD, electronics company executive; b. Jersey City, Apr. 26, 1926; s. Horace Adam and Grace T. (Lower) J.; m. Mary Louise Kleckner, July 29, 1950; children—Lucinda Louise, Karen Ann, Richard Adam, Russell Kleckner, David Thorp. B.E.E. with distinction, Cornell U., 1946, postgrad., 1947; Ph.D. in Physics (Research Lab. for Electronics fellow 1947-51), MIT, 1952. Mem. tech. staff Hughes Aircraft Co., Culver City, Calif., 1952-57; co-founder Watkins-Johnson Co., Palo Alto, Calif., 1958, pres., 1967—; lectr. elec. engring. UCLA, 1956-57, Stanford U., 1958-68. Contbr. articles to profl. jours. Campaign chmn. Palo Alto-Stanford chpt. United Fund, 1967; pres. Stanford area council Boy Scouts Am., 1968-70, mem. bd., 1967-77. Served with USNR, 1943-46. Fellow IEEE; mem. Nat. Acad. Engring., Am. Phys. Soc., Research Soc. Am., Newcomen Soc. N.Am., Western Electronic Mfrs. Assn. (dir. 1971-72), NAM (bd. dirs. 1983—), Sigma Xi, Eta Kappa Nu, Tau Beta Pi, Phi Kappa Phi, Gamma Alpha. Club: Commonwealth (San Francisco). Patentee in field. Office: 3333 Hillview Ave Palo Alto CA 94304

JOHNSON, HOWARD A(RTHUR), Sr., research executive, operations research consultant; b. Shelby County, Ind., Dec. 16, 1923; s. Arthur and Inez Elizabeth (Smiley) J.; m. Joy Ann Nelson, July 19, 1947; children: Howard Arthur, Kraig N. Student engring., Rose Poly. Inst., 1942; A.B. in Math, Franklin Coll. of Ind., 1949; M.A. in Physics, Wesleyan U., 1950. Chief ops. analysis 3d Air Force, Eng., 1958; dep. chief ops. analysis U.S. Air Force Europe, Germany, 1958-61; dir. operation model evaluation air force sub group for Project OMEGA, Washington, 1961-63; mgr. comparative effect research dept. Spindletop Research, Inc., Lexington, Ky., 1963-68; sci. asst. Armament Devel. and Test Ctr., Electronic Test, Eglin AFB, Fla., 1968-73; ops. research consl. Tactical Air Warfare Ctr., U.S. Air Force, Eglin AFB, Fla., 1973-84; chief exec. officer Assoc. Consultants, Ft. Walton Beach, Fla., 1984—; cons. Gulf South Research Inst., Baton Rouge, 1968—, U. Ky. Med. Ctr., 1966-67, Ministry of Def., W.Ger., 1960-61, Weapon Systems Phasing Group, Supreme Allied Powers Europe Hdqrs., 1959-61. Served to capt. USAAF, 1943-45, PTO. Alt. scholar Rose Poly. Inst., 1942; fellow Wesleyan U., 1948-50; recipient numerous govt. incentive awards, 1954-73. Mem. Ops. Research Soc. Am., Mil. Ops. Research Soc., Internat. Test and Evaluation Assn., Washington Ops. Research Council, Armed Forces Communications and Electronics Assn., Sigma Xi, Phi Delta Theta Presbyterian. Lodges: Masons; Shriners.

Current Work: C^3I (command control communications intelligence) training effectiveness and C^3I effectiveness evaluations to include weapon systems effectiveness trade-offs with C^3I. Subspecialties: Operations research (mathematics); Resource management. Home: 309 Yacht Club Dr Fort Walton Beach FL 32548 Office: PO Box 1682 Fort Walton Beach FL 32549

JOHNSON, HOWARD PAUL, agricultural engineer, educator, researcher; b. Odebolt, Iowa, Jan. 27, 1923; s. Gustaf Johan and Ruth Helen (Hanson) J.; m. Patricia Jean Larson, June 15, 1952; children—Cynthia, Lynette, Malcolm. B.S. in Agrl. Engring., Iowa State U., 1949, M.S. in Agrl. Engring., 1950, Ph.D. in Agrl. Engring. and Civil Engring., 1959; M.S. in Mechanics and Hydraulics, U. Iowa, 1954. Engring. trainee Soil Conservation Service, U.S. Dept. Agr., Sioux City, 1948-49; instr. agrl. engring. Iowa State U., Ames, 1950-59, asst. prof., 1959-60, assoc. prof., 1960-62, prof., 1962-80, head dept., 1980—. Author research papers (3 awards); editor: Hydrologic Modeling, 1982. Patentee flow meter, 1964. Served with U.S. Army, 1943-46. EPA grantee, 1975-80. Fellow Am. Soc. Agrl. Engrs. (Hancor award 1978, chmn. div. steering com. 1969-70, Engr. of Yr. award Mid-Central sect. 1982, Engr. of Yr. award Iowa sect. 1981, nat. bd. dirs. 1974-76). Republican. Lodge: Rotary. Current work: Agricultural hydrology and chemicals in environment; broad scope societal problems. Subspecialties: Agricultural engineering; Integrated systems modelling and engineering. Office: 100 Davidson Hall Iowa State U Ames IA 50012

JOHNSON, INGOLF BIRGER, electrical engineer; b. Bklyn. Sept. 29, 1913; s. Johan Ingevald and Antonie (Hansen) J.; m. Johanna Charlotte Mortensen, Sept. 6, 1942; children—Bruce Edward, Richard Birger. B.E.E., Poly. Inst. Bklyn., 1937, M.E.E., 1939. Registered profl. engr., N.Y. Grad. fellow Poly. Inst. Bklyn., 1937-39; mem. tech., teaching, managerial staff Gen. Electric Co., Pittsfield, Mass., Schenectady, 1939-78; pvt. practice elec. engring. cons., Schenectady, 1978—. Contbr. articles to profl. jours. Inventor in field. Recipient Steinmetz award Gen. Electric Co., 1975. Fellow IEEE (Habirshaw medal 1966, Centennial award 1984), AAAS; mem. Nat. Acad. Engrs., Internat. Conf. High Voltage Systems, Profl. Engring. Soc., Elvin Soc., Scandinavian Forum of Tri-Cities (v.p. 1980-81, pres. 1984—). Lutheran. Current work: Surge phenomena and protection in electric utility systems. Subspecialty: Electrical engineering. Home and Office: 1508 Barclay Pl Schenectady NY 12309

JOHNSON, IRVING STANLEY, pharmaceutical company executive, scientist; b. Grand Junction, Colo., June 30, 1925; s. Walter Glen and Frances Lucetta (Tuttle) J.; m. Alwyn Neville Ginther, Jan. 29, 1949; children—Rebecca Lyn, Bryan Glenn, Kirsten Shawn, Kevin Bruce. A.B., Washburn U., Topeka, 1948; Ph.D., U. Kans., 1953. With Lilly Research Labs., Indpls., 1953—, v.p. research, 1973—; mem. profl. edn. com. Am. Cancer Soc., 1972—; active in several areas of biol. research including cancer, virus, genetic engring.; cons. in field. Author articles in field; asso. editor: Cancer Research, 1974—; editorial bd.; Chemico-Biol. Interactions, 1968-73. Mem. edn. com. Indpls. Urban League, 1968-70; pres. Indpls. chpt. Am. Field Service Exchange Program, 1969-70; bd. dirs. Indpls. Ctr. Advanced Research. Served with USNR, 1943-46. Mem. AAAS, Am. Assn. Cancer Research, Am. Soc. Cell Biology (pub. policy com.), Environ. Mutagen Soc., Internat. Soc. Chemotherapy, Kans. Acad. Sci., N.Y. Acad. Scis., Soc. Exptl. Biology and Medicine, Sigma Xi, Phi Sigma. Episcopalian. Patentee in field. Subspecialties: Cancer research (medicine); Pharmaceutical research and development. Office: Eli Lilly and Co 307 E McCarty St Indianapolis IN 46285

JOHNSON, JACK WAYNE, research chemist; b. Red Wing, Minn., July 8, 1950; s. Merle Herbert and JoAnne (Gustafson) J.; m. Carol Cathcart, June 8, 1973; children—Luke Cathcart, Erik Boyd, Mark Edward. B.A., Carleton Coll., 1972; M.S., U. Wis., 1974, Ph.D., 1976. NSF postdoctoral fellow Cornell U., Ithaca, N.Y., 1976-77; research chemist Exxon Research & Engring., Annandale, N.J., 1977-79, sr. chemist, 1979-81, staff chemist, 1981-83, sr. staff chemist, 1983—. Contbr. articles to chemistry Jours. Patentee in field. Mem. Am. Chem. Soc., Sigma Xi. Current work: Synthesis, structure and reactivity of layered solids. Subspecialties: Inorganic chemistry; Solid state chemistry. Office: Exxon Research & Engring Annandale NJ 08801

JOHNSON, JAMES ALLEN, architectural and engineering company executive; b. Stoughton, Wis., June 2, 1924; s. Martin Helberg and Sophia Amunda (Christensen) J.; m. Kathleen Clare Smith, Nov. 26, 1949; children—Pamela Marie, James Allen, Mark Thomas, Stephen Victor. Student, U. Wis., 1942-43; B.S., U.S. Mil. Acad., 1944-47; M.S., Stanford U., 1957. Registered profl. engr., Vt. Commd. 2d lt. U.S. Army, 1947, advanced through grades to maj. gen., 1973; comdg. gen. U.S. Army Engr. Center, Ft. Belvoir, Va., 1974-77; div. engr. N. Atlantic (U.S. Army C.E.), N.Y.C., 1977-79, dep. chief engrs., Washington, 1979-80, ret., 1980; sr. v.p. Washington ops. Kuljian Corp., 1980—; dir. Eastern Indemnity Corp., Rockville, Md.; Chmn. Engring. Bd. for Rivers and Harbors, Washington, 1979-80; chmn. research devel. and rev. bd. C.E., 1979-80; assoc. mem. Def. Sci. Bd., 1985. Bd. dirs. Fairfax (Va.) chpt. Salvation Army, 1977. Decorated D.S.M. (2), Silver Star, Legion of Merit (2), Bronze Star (2), Purple Heart (2). Fellow Soc. Am. Mil. Engrs. (pres. Phila. post 1968-70, pres. N.Y.C. post 1977-78); mem. Am. Assn. Cost Engrs., Washington Soc. Profl. Engrs. Republican. Methodist. Clubs: Univ. (Washington); Army-Navy Country (Arlington, Va.); Sons of Norway. Current Work: Water supply to include rehabilitation of present systems; port development; flood control and ocean science. Subspecialties: Civil engineering; Water supply and wastewater treatment. Home: 11000 Henderson Rd Fairfax Station VA 22039 Office: Kuljian Corp 1435 G St NW Suite 1010 Washington DC 20005

JOHNSON, JAMES ROBERT, ceramic engineer, educator; b. Cin., Jan. 2, 1923; s. Charles William and Della Ramona (Schubert) J.; m. Virginia M. Bowen, Apr. 3, 1945; children—Cathy (Mrs. John Whitman), Barbara (Mrs. Charles Kallusky), Randy, John, Jamie (Mrs. J.R. Myers), Brian. B.S., Ohio State U., 1947, M.S., 1948, Ph.D., 1950. Asst. prof. U. Tex., 1950-51; tech. adviser ceramics Oak Ridge Nat. Lab., 1951-56; lab. mgr., dir., exec. scientist Minn. Mining & Mfg. Co., St. Paul, 1956-79, cons., 1979—; adj. prof. U. Wis.-Stout; U. Minn., 1979—. Contbr. articles to profl. jours. Served with C.E. AUS, 1943-46. Recipient Distinguished Alumnus award Ohio State U., 1970, 3M Carlton award, 1970. Fellow Am. Ceramic Soc. (pres. 1973-74, disting. life mem.), Wis. Acad. Arts, Letters and Sci., mem. Nat. Acad. Engring., Nat. Inst. Ceramics Engrs. (Pace award 1959, Greaves-Walker award 1985), Research Engring. Soc. Am. Patentee in field. Current Work: Consultant in materials; physical sciences. Subspecialties: Ceramic engineering; Materials (engineering). Home: Route 1 Box 231B River Falls WI 54022

JOHNSON, JEFFREY PAUL, physicist; b. Columbus, Ohio, Jan. 10, 1945; s. Samuel and Joyce Eileen (Lockary) J., Jr.; m. Rita Rae Rapino, Dec. 1, 1973; children—Jeffrey Paul, Margaret Joyce. B.S. in Physics, Ohio U., 1967; postgrad. Air Force Inst. Tech., 1969-71; M.S. in Systems Engring., Wright State U., Fairborn, Ohio, 1978. Research physicist Systems Research Labs., Dayton, Ohio, 1974-79; mem. tech. staff Rockwell Internat., Anaheim, Calif., 1979-84; staff scientist Photon Research Assocs., La Jolla, Calif., 1984—. Served to capt. USAF, 1967-74. Mem. Am. Inst. Physics, Optical Soc. Am., Soc. Photo-optical Instrumentation Engrs. Current work: Conceptual design, analysis and system engineering of electro-optical sensors (UV, visible, infrared), optical/infrared phenomenology. Subspecialties: Systems engineering; Aerospace engineering and technology. Office: Photon Research Assocs 3301 N Torrey Pines Ct La Jolla CA 92037

JOHNSON, JOHN EDLIN, JR., cell biologist, neurology educator; b. Ft. Worth, Aug. 21, 1945; s. John Edlin and Mary (Thompson) J.; m. Susan Edwards, June 15, 1968; 1 child, Cynthia Brooke. B.S. in Zoology, U. Wash., 1968; M.S. in Psychology, Tulane U., 1970, Ph.D. in Neurosci., 1973. NRC assoc. NASA Ames Research Ctr., Moffett Field, Calif., 1973-75; lectr. dept. anatomy U. Calif.-Berkeley, 1975, 78; staff electron microscopist dept. physics U. San Francisco, 1975-77; staff fellow NIH, Balt., 1977-80; asst. prof. neurology Johns Hopkins U., Balt., 1979—; pres. Joshro Inc., Balt., 1984—; dir. Sci. Design and Info., Balt., 1982—. Editor: Current Trends in Morphological Techniques, 1981; Aging and Cell Structure, 1984; Aging and Cell Function, 1984; Jour. Electron Microscopy Technique, 1983—; Contbr. articles to profl. jours. Patentee surg. device. Mem. Electron Microscopy Soc. Am., Am. Aging Assn., Soc. for Neurosci. Current work: Gerontology; drug abuse; neuroendocrine system. Subspecialties: Cell biology; Morphology. Home: 117 Woodlawn Rd Baltimore MD 21210 Office: Dept Neurology Johns Hopkins Sch Medicine 600 N Wolfe St Baltimore MD 21205

JOHNSON, JOHN MARSHALL, physiologist, educator, researcher; b. McCamey, Tex., Aug. 10, 1944; s. Marshall Theodore and Mary Imogene (Keffer) J.; m. Cheryl Rae Coffin, July 25, 1970; children—Julia, Sarah. B.A., Rice U., 1966; Ph.D., Southwestern Med. Sch., U. Tex., Dallas, 1972. Sr. fellow U. Wash., Seattle, 1972-74, research assoc., 1974-75; asst. prof. physiology U. Tex. Health Sci. Ctr., San Antonio, 1975-80, assoc. prof., 1980—; mem. central research rev. com. Tex. affiliate Am. Heart Assn., 1977-82, bd. dirs. San Antonio affiliate, 1984—; mem. external research rev. com. S.W. Found. for Research Edn., San Antonio, 1982-83; mem. research and devel. com. Audie Murphy VA Hosp., San Antonio, 1981-83. Mem. editorial bd. Jour. Applied Physiology, 1982-85. Contbr. articles to profl. publs. Grantee NIH, 1977—, Tex. Heart Assn., 1976-77. Mem. Am. Physiol. Assn., Am. Heart Assn., N.Y. Acad. Scis. Democrat. Episcopalian. Current work: Reflex regulation of skin blood flow in humans in normotension and hypertension. Subspecialty: Physiology (medicine). Home: 103 Elm Spring San Antonio TX 78231 Office: Dept Physiology U Tex Health Sci Ctr San Antonio TX 78284

JOHNSON, JOHN MORRIS, biologist, educator; b. Boise, Idaho, Mar. 16, 1937; s. Carl T. and Fannie Margaret (King) J.; m. Margaret May Horton, June 13, 1959; children: Mori Kay, Stephen Wade. B.S., Coll. Idaho, 1959; M.S., Oreg. State U., 1961, Ph.D., 1964. Postdoctoral fellow U. Chgo., 1965-66; asst. prof. biology Central Coll., Pella, Iowa, 1964-65, assoc. prof., 1966-69; prof. biology Oreg. Coll. Edn. (named changed to Western Oreg. State Coll.), Monmouth, 1969—, chmn. div. natural scis. and math., 1985—. Author: Handbook of Uncommon Plants on the Salem BLM District, 1980; contbr. articles to profl. jours. Recipient Faculty Honors award Western Oreg. State Coll., 1979; Silver Beaver award Boy Scouts Am., 1981. Mem. AAAS, Am. Soc. Cell Biology, Bot. Soc. Am., Sigma Xi, Phi Kappa Phi. Democrat. Methodist. Current Work: Plant tissue culture, somatic cell genetics, nucleolus and nucleolar vacuoles. Subspecialties: Plant cell and tissue culture; Cell and tissue culture.

JOHNSON, LAVELL R., medical equipment company executive; b. Salt Lake City, Jan. 16, 1935; s. George A. and Ethel (Rolfson) J.; m. Carol Clegg, June 6, 1958; children—Mark, Michael, Terri, Wendell, Derek, Laura. B.S., U. Utah, 1959; Ph.D., Brigham Young U., 1965. Research scientist Ames Co., Elkhart, Ind., 1965-68; assoc. dir. endocrine labs. Latter Day Saints Hosp., Salt Lake City, 1968-71; v.p., pres. Auto-Assay, Inc., Salt Lake City, 1971-76; v.p. research BDI, Salt Lake City, 1976-82; v.p. sci. affairs Advanced Diagnostic Systems, Salt Lake City, 1982—. Patentee in field. Bishop's councilor Ch. of Jesus Christ of Latter-day Saints, Salt Lake City, 1980-83, bishop, Elkhart, 1968. Mem. Am. Chem. Soc., AAAS, Am. Assn. Clin. Chemistry. Republican. Current work: immunochemistry. Subspecialty: Clinical chemistry. Office: Becton Dickinson Advanced Diagnostic Systems 810 N 2200 West Salt Lake City UT 84116

JOHNSON, LEE F(REDERICK), biochemist, educator; b. Phila., Jan. 10, 1946; s. Robert W. and Jeannette F. (Mollenkof) J.; m. Ann Marie Lester, June 10, 1967; children—Adam, Karl. B.S., Muhlenberg Coll., 1967; Ph.D., Yale U., 1972. Postdoctoral fellow MIT, Cambridge, 1972-75; asst. prof. biochemistry, Ohio State U., Columbus, 1975-80, assoc. prof. biochemistry, 1980-85, prof. biochemistry, 1985—; panel mem. NSF, Washington, 1980-84. Contbr. chpts. to books, research articles to publs. Recipient Faculty Research award Am. Cancer Soc., 1980-85. Mem. Am. Soc. Cell Biology, Am. Soc. Biol. Chemists, Am. Soc. Microbiology. Current work: Regulation of gene expression in mammalian cells. Subspecialties: Biochemistry (biology); Molecular biology. Office: Dept Biochemistry Ohio State U Columbus OH 43210

JOHNSON, PATRICK WOODRUFF, electronics engineer, bio-electronics engineer; b. Dixon, Ill., Dec. 31, 1940; s. Linton Curtis and Rowena (Woodruff) J.; m. Dorothy Anne Martin, June 8, 1963 (div. Mar. 1978); children—Amy Von Eichols, Patrick Woodruff; m. Virginia Gray, Aug. 28, 1978. B.Sc., U.S. Naval Acad., 1963; M.S.E.E., Naval Postgrad. Sch., 1971; Ph.D., Queens U., Kingston, Ont., Can., 1976. Commd. ensign U.S. Navy, 1963, advanced through grades to comdr., 1978; sea-going line officer, 1963-78; head radar/identification br. Office Chief Naval Ops., 1978-82; ret., 1982; pres. Am. Electronics, Inc., Lanham, Md., 1982—; ptnr. Technotronics Inst., Alexandria, Va., 1982—. Mem. IEEE, Electronics in Medicine and Biology. Current work: Weapons/electronic systems; bioelectronics—design and development of new devices and systems which electronically mimic physiological actions. Subspecialties: Biomedical engineering; Microelectronics. Home: 6705 Rhode Island Ave College Park MD 20740 Office: Am Electronics Inc 9332 Annapolis Rd Lanham MD 20706

JOHNSON, PETER DEXTER, phys. chemist, patent agt.; b. Norwich, Conn., July 1, 1921; s. Philip Adams and Edith Todd (Dexter) J.; m. Jessie Lois Jones, Oct. 3, 1943 (div. 1978); children: Peter Dexter, Carol, William Todd; m. Mary Grace Wood, Jan. 2, 1982. S.B., Harvard U., 1942; M.A., U. N.C., 1948, Ph.D., 1949. Registered patent agt. U.S. Patent and Trademark Office, 1981. Supr. ballistic testing Hercules Powder Co., Radford, Va., 1942-43; phys. chemist Gen. Electric Research and Devel. Center, Schenectady, 1949-84; cons. Optical Radiation, 1984—; vis. assoc. prof. physics Cornell U., 1958-59. Contbr. articles to profl. jours. Mem. Niskayuna (N.Y.) Planning and Zoning Commn., 1958-67; mem. Niskayuna Bd. Assessment Rev., 1970-75, chmn., 1972-75. Served with USAAF, 1943-46. Fellow Am. Phys. Soc.; mem. Am. Chem. Soc., Optical Soc. Am., Am. Inst. Chemists, AAAS, Eastern N.Y. Patent Law Assn., Sigma Xi. Current Work: Optical properties of solids, gases, plasmas; innovations in light and ultraviolet radiation sources. Subspecialties: Atomic and molecular physics; Optical engineering. Home: 1100 Merlin Dr Schenectady NY 12309 Office: 1100 Merlin Dr Schenectady NY 12309

JOHNSON, PHILIP LEWIS, research and educational association executive; b. Oneonta, N.Y., May 26, 1931; s. Robert A. and Hazel S. (Shaffer) J.; m. Judy Rodgers, Nov. 17, 1973. B.S. in Agr, Purdue U., 1953, M.S. in Natural Resources, 1955; Ph.D. in Ecology, Duke U., 1961. Agrl. economist fruit and vegetable div., sect. program analysis Dept. Agr., 1955; instr. botany U. Wyo., Laramie, 1959-61; botanist U.S. Forest Service, Laramie, 1961-62; ecologist U.S. Cold Regions Research and Engring. Lab., Hanover, N.H., 1962-67; asst. prof. biology Dartmouth Coll., 1963-67; asso. prof. botany and forestry U. Ga., 1967-70; program dir. ecosystem analysis program NSF, 1968-69; dep. head Office Interdisciplinary Research, 1970-71, dir. div. environ. systems and resources, 1971-74; exec. dir. Oak Ridge Asso. Univs., 1974-81, John Gray Inst., Lamar U., Beaumont, Tex., 1981—; also pres. John E. Gray Found.; research collaborator Brookhaven Nat. Lab., 1963-65; mem. N.H. Pesticide Control Bd., 1965-67; mem. primary productivity com. Internat. Biol. Program, 1967-68, adv. com. tundra biome, 1968-70, deciduous forest biome coordinating com., 1968, 70; mem. environ. panel fgn. currency program Smithsonian Instn., 1969-70; vice chmn. interagy. com. ecol. research Fed. Council Sci. and Tech./Council Environ. Quality, 1972; mem. U.S. com. Man and Biosphere Program, 1973-74; exec. com. E. Tenn. Cancer Research Center, Knoxville, 1975-77; regional com. Southeastern Plant Environ. Lab., 1975-80; fellowship adv. panel environ. affairs Rockefeller Found., 1974-78; chmn. com. on environ. research and devel. Nat. Acad. Scis., 1978-79, mem. polar research bd., 1981-85. Editorial bd.: Ecol. Monographs, 1968-70, Jour. Remote Sensing of Environ, 1971-75. Trustee Inst. of Ecology, 1976-79, chmn. bd., 1980-81; bd. dirs. Center for Natural Areas, 1979-81; mem. U.S. Commn. for UNESCO, 1978-80; chmn. Tex. Gov.'s Task Force on Advancement Labor and Mgmt. Relations, 1984—; mem. Houston Dist. Export Council, 1985—. Served with AUS, 1955-57. Recipient Commendation award Cold Regions Research and Engring. Lab., 1964, 66, Meritorious Sch. Achievement award, 1966; Meritorious Service award NSF, 1973; James B. Duke fellow 1957-59. Fellow Arctic Inst. N. Am.; mem. Ecol. Soc. Am., Brit. Ecol. Soc., N.Y. Acad. Scis., AAAS, Sigma Xi, Phi Eta Sigma, Alpha Zeta, Kappa Delta Pi, Xi Sigma Pi. Club: Cosmos (Washington). Subspecialty: Ecology (environmental science). Home: 5815 Honeysuckle St Beaumont TX 77706 Office: John E Gray Inst Lamar U Beaumont TX 77710

JOHNSON, PRATT DEEN, chemist, consultant, educator; b. Mineola, N.Y., Jan. 16, 1951; s. Pratt Herbert and Elizabeth Myrtle (Hammond) J.; m. Terri Lynn McDonald, Dec. 1, 1979; 1 child, Katie Marie. B.S., Stephen F. Austin State U., 1974, M.S., 1976. Analytical chemist, Milchem, Inc., Houston, 1977-78; chemistry supr. Northrop Services, Inc., Houston, 1978-80; trainer, cons. Varian Assocs., Sugar Land, Tex., 1980—. Co-author: (tng. course manual) Flame Atomic Absorption, 1983. Mem. Am. Chem. Soc., Soc. Applied Spectroscopy, ASTM. Current work: Analysis of metals at trace levels by graphite furnace atomic absorption spectroscopy in acid rain samples and petroleum and petroleum product samples. Subspecialties: Environmental chemistry; Analytical chemistry. Home: 7011 Tara Richmond TX 77469 Office: Varian Assocs 505 Julie Rivers Rd Suite 150 Sugar Land TX 77478

JOHNSON, RICHARD FREDERICK, research psychologist, consultant; b. Boston, July 11, 1943; s. Frederick and Alice (Kullen) J.; m. Sharyn Lois Doyle, Sept. 11, 1965; children: Wendy, Adam. B.A. with honors, Northeastern U., 1966; M.A., Brandeis U., 1968, Ph.D., 1970. Diplomate: Lic. psychologist, Mass. Commd. 2d lt. U.S. Army Res., 1966, advanced through grades to capt., 1970, active duty, 1970-72, resigned, 1974; sr. research psychologist Medfield (Mass.) Found., 1972-76; research psychologist U.S. Army Natick Research and Devel. Labs., Mass., 1976-83, research psychologist U.S. Army Research Inst. Environ. Medicine, Natick, 1983—; hypnosis cons. Blaisdell Psychol. Services, Medway, Mass., 1978-81; psychophysiology cons. Medfield Found., 1976-78; lectr. Northeastern U., Boston, 1972—. Editorial cons.: Jour. Cons. and Clin. Psychology, 1973—; corr. assoc. commentator: The Behavioral and Brain Scis, 1978—; contbr. articles to profl. jours. Chmn. human rights com. Mass. Dept. Mental Health Region V, 1974-76. Woodrow Wilson fellow, 1969-70; NASA trainee, 1966-69; NIMH grantee, 1972-76. Mem. Am. Psychol. Assn., Human Factors Soc., Am. Soc. Clin. Hypnosis, AAAS, Eastern Psychol. Assn., Soc. Personality and Social Psychology, Southeastern Psychol. Assn., Sigma Xi. Current Work: Study interaction of natural environment (cold, heat, humidity) and protective systems (e.g., cold weather clothing) on man's ability to function (mental abilities, manual dexterity, sensory performance, etc.); study bias in experimentation with humans. Subspecialties: Behavioral psychology; Human factors psychology. Home: 15 Sahlin Circle Franklin MA 02038 Office: US Army Research Inst Environ Medicine Natick MA 01760

JOHNSON, RICHARD JAMES, agricultural research administrator, animal science educator; b. Tonasket, Wash., Sept. 29; s. James Arthur and Sarah Valena (Cole) J.; m. Glea Harriet Freeby, Aug. 6, 1949; children—Judith, John, James, Richard. B.S. in Agr., Wash State U., 1960, M.S. in Animal Sci., 1963, Ph.D. in Animal Sci., 1967. From instr. to prof. animal sci. Wash. State U., Pullman, 1963-77; prof., head Southeast Kans. Expt. Sta., Kans. State U., Parsons, 1977-85; with horse, nutrition, breeding and mgmt. dept. animal scis. Wash. State U., Pullman, 1985—. Contbr. articles to profl. jours. Served to with USN, 1942-45, PTO. Mem. Am. Soc. Animal Sci. Lodge: Kiwanis (pres. 1976-77, 82-83). Current work: Cattle and horse nutrition breeding and management. Subspecialty: Agricultural research administration. Home: Route 1 Box 134 A Palouse WA 99161 Office: Dept Animal Scis Wash State U Pullman WA 99164

JOHNSON, ROBERT E., physicist, educator; b. Chgo., July 3, 1939; s. Theodore J. and Elsie M. (Johnson) J.; m. Barbara F. MacCallum; children: Amanda F. L. MacCallum, Sarah M. B.A. in Math, Colo. Coll., 1961; M.A. in Physics, Wesleyan U., 1963; Ph.D., U. Wis., 1968. With Sandia Corp., 1965; fellow Queen's U., Belfast, No. Ireland, 1968-69; asst. prof. physics So. Ill. U., Carbondale, 1969-71; asst. prof. engring. physics U. Va., Charlottesville, 1971-76, assoc. prof., 1976-84, prof., 1984—; asst. dean U. Va. (Sch. Engring. and Applied Sci.), 1982-85; vis. researcher Center for Planetary Physics, Harvard, 1977-78, Enrico Fermi Inst., U. Chgo., 1981-82; cons. Bell Telephone Labs., Murray Hill, N.J., 1979-81, 85—. Author: An Introduction to Atomic and Molecular Collisions, 1982; contbr. chpt. to book, articles to profl. jours. NATO fellow U. Copenhagen, 1976; summer fellow Argonne Nat. Lab., 1982. Mem. Am. Inst. Physics, Am. Astron. Soc., Am. Geophys. Union. Current Work: Interaction of charged particlesradiations with matter: atomic and molecular collisions; interaction of magnetospheric plasmas with satellites of Jupiter and Saturn. Subspecialties: Atomic and molecular physics; Electronic materials. Home: 135 Bollingwood Rd Charlottesville VA 22903 Office: Thornton Hall U Va Charlottesville VA 22901

JOHNSON, ROY RAGNAR, electrical engineer; b. Chgo., Jan. 23, 1932; s. Ragnar Anders and Ann Viktoria (Lundquist) J.; m. Martha Ann Mattson, June 21, 1963; children—Linnea Marit, Kaisa Ann. B.S. in Elec. Engring. U. Minn., 1954, M.S., 1956, Ph.D., 1959. Research fellow U. Minn., 1957-59; research scientist Boeing Sci. Research Labs., Seattle, 1959-72; prin. scientist KMS Fusion, Inc., Ann Arbor, Mich., 1972-74, dir. fusion expts., 1974-78, tech. dir., 1978-85, dept. head fusion and plasmas, 1985—; vis. lectr. U. Wash., Seattle, 1959-60; vis. scientist Royal Inst. Tech., Stockholm, 1963-64. Author: Nonlinear Effects in Plasmas, 1969, Plasma Physics, 1977; editorial bd. Procs. on Plasma Sci., 1972-76 contbr. to profl. publs. Bd. advisors Rose-Hulman Inst. Tech., 1982—. Decorated chevalier Order of St. George, comdr. Order of Holy Cross of Jerusalem. Fellow Am. Phys. Soc.; Mem. N.Y. Acad. Scis., IEEE (exec. com. Nuclear and Plasma Scis. Soc. 1972-75), Seattle Jr. C. of C. (treas. 1960-62), AAAS, Vasa Order Am., Am. Swedish Inst., Torpar Riddar Orden, Swedish Pioneer Hist. Soc., Swedish Council Am., Eta Kappa Nu, Gamma Alpha. Lutheran. Patentee in field. Current work: Laser fusion technology, x-ray lasers, holographic interferometry. Home: 671 Adrienne Ln Ann Arbor MI 48103 Office: 3621 S State Rd Ann Arbor MI 48104

JOHNSON, STEPHEN THOMAS, tool engineer; b. Washington, May 31, 1954; s. Glenn Elmer and Marie Veronica (Rando) J.; m. Joand Marie Wagner, Apr. 16, 1983. B.M.E.T. with honors, Northeastern U., 1978. Draftsman Hollingsworth & Vose, East Walpole, Mass., 1973-74; tech. aide U.S. Army Natick Research and Devel. Command, Natick, Mass., 1975-78; tool designer Boeing Aircraft Co., Renton, Wash., 1978-81, propulsion engr., 1981; sr. tool designer Sikorsky Aircraft, Stratford, Conn., 1981—. Mem. Am. Soc. Metals, ASME. Patentee direct ohmnic heating device. Subspecialty: Mechanical engineering. Home: 1004 Stratford RD Stratford CT 06497

JOHNSON, THOMAS EUGENE, geneticist, educator; b. Denver, June 19, 1948; s. Albert L. and Barbara J. (Bickle) J.; m. Victoria J. Simpson, Apr. 24, 1982. S.B. in Life Scis, M.I.T., 1970; Ph.D. in Genetics, U. Wash., 1975. Research assoc. in genetics and devel. Cornell U., Ithaca, N.Y., 1975-77; research assoc. in molecular biology U. Colo., 1977-82; faculty fellow Inst. Behavoral Genetics, 1981-82; asst. prof. molecular biology and biochemistry U. Calif, Irvine, 1982—; also. cons. Contbr. articles and chpts. to profl. lit. Mem. Genetics Soc. Am., Soc. Developmental Biology, AAAS, Am. Gerontol. Soc. Sufist. Current Work: Genetics and molecular biology of senescence in C. elegans. Genetics, quantitative genetics, aging, senescence, C. elegans; behavior, development and aging; biochemistry and molecular biology of aging. Subspecialties: Gene actions; Gerontology. Office: Molecular Biology and Biochemistry U Calif Irvine CA 92717

JOHNSON, VIRGIL ALLEN, agronomist; b. Newman Grove, Nebr., June 28, 1921; s. Oscar Johannas and Fairy Bell (Johnson) J.; m. Betty Ann Tisthammer, July 29, 1943; children—Karen (Mrs. Ronald Eakes), Leslie (dec.), Reed, Scott. B.S. with distinction, U. Nebr., 1948, Ph.D. (Regents Grad. fellow, Ak-Sar-Ben grad. fellow, Sears, Roebuck Grad. fellow), 1952. Agt. Agrl. Research Service, U.S. Dept. Agr., Lincoln, Nebr., 1951-52, research agronomist, 1954-75, supervisory research agronomist, 1975-78, leader wheat research, 1978—; leader wheat research, asst. agronomist U. Nebr., Lincoln, 1952-54, asso. prof., 1954-63, prof. agronomy dept., 1963—; cons. Gt. Plains Wheat, Inc.; mem. Nat. Wheat Improvement Com.; mem. tech. com. Wheat Quality Council. Contbr. articles to profl. pubs. Served in inf. U.S. Army, 1940-43, in USAAC, 1943-45. AC; Served AC. Decorated D.F.C., Air medal with 3 oak leaf clusters; recipient Agrl. Achievement award Ak-Sar-Ben, 1970, Disting. Service award Dept. Agr., 1981; AID grantee, 1966-79. Fellow Am. Soc. Agronomy, AAAS (Internat. Agronomy award 1984); mem. Crop Sci. Soc. Am. (Crop Sci. award 1975, pres. 1978, disting. career award 1985), Am. Genetics Assn., Sigma Xi, Gamma Sigma Delta (Internat. award 1969), Alpha Zeta. Lutheran. Co-developer 26 varieties of hard red winter wheat. Current Work: Genetic and physiological bases of grain protein variation in Triticum aestivum L. Subspecialties: Plant genetics; Plant physiology (agriculture). Home: 3849 Dudley St Lincoln NE 68503 Office: 324 Keim Hall East Campus U Nebr Lincoln NE 68583

JOHNSON, WAYNE ALLAN, nutrition educator, consultant; b. Graceton, Minn., June 22, 1941; s. Russell Gilbert and Grace (Williams) J.; m. Helen Oberle, Aug. 8, 1964; children—Joel, Mari. B.S., Bemidji State U., 1964; M.S., U. N.D., 1968, Ph.D., 1971. Tchr. high sch., Motley, Minn., 1964-67; faculty, head dept. S.D. State U., Brookings, 1971-83, assoc. prof., 1983; assoc. prof., chmn. dept. human nutrition Ohio State U., Columbus, 1983—; nutrition cons., S.D., Ohio, 1974—. Contbr. chpts. to books, sci. articles, abstracts to profl. lit. Mem. Soc. for Nutrition Edn., Inst. for Food Technologists, AAAS, Sigma Xi (pres. 1981), Phi Kappa Phi (sec.-treas. 1978-79). Clubs: Brookings Country. Lodge: Elks. Current work: Research on interactions of dietary components on risk factors of cardiovascular disease and cancer. Subspecialty: Nutrition (medicine). Office: Dept Human Nutrition Ohio State U 1787 Neil Ave Columbus OH 43210

JOHNSTON, BRUCE GILBERT, civil engineer; b. Detroit, Oct. 13, 1905; s. Sterling and Ida (Peake) J.; m. Ruth Elizabeth Barker, Aug. 5, 1939; children—Sterling, Carol Anne. Snow, David. B.S. in Civil Engring, U. Ill., 1930; M.S., Lehigh U., Bethlehem, Pa., 1934; Ph.D. in Sci, Columbia U., 1938. Engaged in engring. constrn. Coolidge Dam, Ariz., 1927-29; with design office Roberts & Schaefer Co., Chgo., 1930; instr. civil engring. Columbia U., 1934-38; charge structural research Fritz Engring. Lab., Lehigh U., 1938-50, asst. dir. lab., 1938-47, dir., 1947-50, mem. univ. faculty, 1938-50, prof. civil engring., 1945-50; prof. structural engring. U. Mich., 1950-68, emeritus, 1968—; prof. civil engring. U. Ariz., Tucson, 1968-70; engr. Johns Hopkins Applied Physics Lab., Silver Spring, Md., 1942-45; chmn. Column Research Council, 1956-62. Author: Basic Steel Design, 3d edit, 1986, also tech. papers.; Editor: Column Research Council Design Guide, 3 edits, 1960-76. Recipient Alumni Honor award for disting. service in engring. U. Ill., 1981. Hon. mem. ASCE (chmn. structural div. 1965-66, chmn. engring. mechanics div. 1961-62, J.J.R. Croes medal 1937, 54, Ernest E. Howard medal 1974); mem. Nat. Acad. Engring., Sigma Xi, Phi Kappa Phi, Tau Beta Pi, Chi Epsilon. Methodist. Current Work: Stability of steel columns and steel structures. Torsion of structural members. History of development of column buckling theory. Subspecialties: Civil engineering; Structural engineering. Address: 5025 E Calle Barril Tucson AZ 85718

JOHNSTON, CRAIG ALAN, neurochemist; b. Butte, Mont., May 25, 1955; s. Clayton Alan and Elisabeth Jean (Nutting) J.; m. Sharon Rae Estabrook, Aug. 7, 1976; 1 child, Hope Alicia. B.S. in Chemistry, MIT, 1977; Ph.D. in Pharmacology and Toxicology, Mich. State U., 1982, Ph.D. in Neurosciences, 1982. Postdoctoral fellow U. Tex. Health Sci. Ctr., Dallas, 1982-83; staff fellow Nat. Inst. Environ. Health Scis., N.C., 1983—; teaching asst. chemistry MIT, Cambridge, 1975-77; teaching asst. pharmacology Mich. State U., East Lansing, 1978-80; teaching asst. physiology U. Tex. Health Sci. Ctr., Dallas, 1982. Ad hoc referee for numerous jours.; contbr. articles to profl. jours. Jr. high coordinator, teacher East Lansing Community Ch., Mich., 1981. T.L. Davis scholar; T.D. Cavitt scholar; fellow MIT, Nat. Pub. Health Research Service, Nat. Inst. Environ. Health. Mem. Soc. for Neuroscience, Endocrine Soc., N.Y. Acad. Sci., AAAS, World Fed. Neuroscientists, Internat. Brain Research Orgn., Sigma Alpha Epsilon (v.p. 1976). Republican. Current work: Determining neurochemical mechanisms underlying the role of the central nervous system in the neuroendocrine regulation of prolactin. Subspecialties: Neuroendocrinology; Neurochemistry. Home: 1440 Clermont Dr Durham NC 27713 Office: Nat Inst Environ Health Sci LRDT PO Box 12233 Bldg 101 C4-07 Research Triangle Park NC 27709

JOHNSTON, DOROTHY MAE, psychologist; b. Mutual, Okla., Feb. 22, 1924; d. Harry Homer and Lena (Barnes) J. B.S. in B.A, U. Ark., 1949; M.A., U. Denver, 1952; Ph.D., N.C. State U., 1971. Engring. psychologist Douglas Aircraft Co., Tulsa, 1956-57, N.Am. Rockwell, Columbus, Ohio, 1957-60, 66-67, Boeing Co., Wichita, Kans. and; Seattle, 1960-61, 62-66, Martin Marietta, Orlando, Fla., 1961-62, Melpar, Inc., Falls Church, Va., 1968, scientist doing ind. research, Prairie Grove and Lincoln, Ark., 1971—. Contbr. articles to profl. jours.; author: Beyond the Limelight, 1983. Mem. Am. Psychol. Assn., AAAS, Soc. Women Engrs., IEEE, Assn. for Women in Sci., Optical Soc. Am., Human Factors Soc. Democrat. Methodist. Current Work: Research in visual perception. Subspecialties: Human factors engineering; Sensory processes. Address: Route 2 P O Box 79A Lincoln AR 72744

JOHNSTON, LAURANCE SCOTT, health science institute administrator; b. St. Paul, Aug. 4, 1950; s. Scott D. and Laura (Wallace) J.; m. Pauline K. Gogola, Aug. 30, 1975. B.S., Hamline U., 1972; M.S., Northwestern U., 1973, Ph.D., 1976; M.B.A., George Mason U., 1985. Fellow Runyon/Winchell Cancer Fund, Chgo. Med. Sch., 1977-78; consumer safety officer FDA, Washington, 1978-81; exec. sec. Nat. Inst. Child Health and Human Devel., Bethesda, Md., 1981—. Contbr. articles to profl. jours. Northwestern U. fellow, 1976. Mem. Am. Chem. Soc., AAAS, Found. for Advanced Edn. in Scis. Current work: Peer-review of grant applications and contract proposals for research and development research. Subspecialties: Biochemistry (biology); Biochemistry (medicine). Home: 729 Gentle Breeze Ct Herndon VA 22070 Office: Nat Inst Child Health and Human Development NIH 7910 Woodmont Ave Bethesda MD 20205

JOISHY, SURESH K., oncologist and hematologist; b. Udipi, India, Mar. 12, 1944; came to U.S., 1970, naturalized, 1978; s. Keshav K. and Sushila J.; m. Muktha S. Pau, June 28, 1972; children: Mahima, Mahanth. M.B., B.S., Jawaharlal Inst. Post Grad. Med. Edn. and Research, India, 1970. Diplomate: Am. Bd. Internal Medicine. Clin. instr. U. Rochester, N.Y., 1976-78; cons. staff VA Med. Ctr., Batavia, N.Y., 1976-78; research asst. U. Calif., San Francisco, 1978-80; clin. asst. prof. Ind. U., Bloomington, 1981—; cons. Bloomington Hosp., 1980—, Dunn Meml. Hosp., Bedford, Ind., 1981—, Bedford Med. Ctr., 1981—. Author: Tissue Healing and Regeneration Folia tramatologica Geicy, 1979. Active Am. Cancer Soc. U. Calif. grantee, 1978-80; Asian Pacific Congress Gastroenterology travel grantee, 1980. Mem. Am. Fedn. for Clin. Research, Am. Soc. Hematology, Am. Soc. Clin. Oncology, AMA, Malaysian Med. Assn. Current Work: Cancer chemotherapy, cancer in twins, hemoglobinopathies, cancer prevention studies, cancer care through patient education, medical arts-graphic and painting. Subspecialties: Hematology; Oncology. Office: Oncology and Hematology 822 W 1st St Bloomington IN 47401

JOISON, JULIO, surgeon; b. Cordoba City, Cordoba, Argentina, Oct. 2, 1932; came to U.S., 1960, naturalized, 1971; s. Moises and Sofia (Moses) J. B.S. summa cum laude, Dean Funes Coll., Cordoba, 1949; M.D., Nat. U. Cordoba, 1959; Ph.D., U. Buenos Aires, 1970. Diplomate: Am. Bd. Surgery. Intern and research asst. in surgery Sinai Hosp., Balt., 1960-61; resident in surgery Met. Hosp., N.Y.C., 1961-62; assoc. fellow in surgery Lahey Clinic, Boston, 1962; resident and chief resident in surgery Boston City Hosp., 1962-65; sr. teaching fellow in surgery Boston U., 1964-65; research fellow in surgery Harvard U. Med. Sch., Boston, 1965-66, 68-70; practice medicine specializing in surgery, Boston, 1970—; assoc. staff St. Elizabeth's Hosp., Boston, 1976—; mem. staffs Brookline (Mass.) Hosp., 1971—, Hosp. at Parker Hill, Boston, 1970—, Hahnemann Hosp., Boston, 1976—. Mem. Mass. Med. Soc., Am. Coll. Gastroenterologist, N.Y. Acad. Scis., Am. Coll. Angiology, Am. Soc. Contemporary Medicine and Surgery. Discoverer metabolic factor produced by the pancreas; developer surg. technique for transplantation of pancreas. Current Work: Surgery and transplantation. Subspecialties: Surgery; Transplantation. Home: 216 St Paul St Brookline MA 02146 Office: 1180 Beacon St Suite 3A Brookline MA 02146

JOIST, JOHANN HEINRICH, hematologist, educator; b. Bergisch Gladbach, W. Germany, Jan. 9, 1935; came to U.S., 1972; s. Heinrich and Katharina (Hasbach) J.; m. Nancy Lee Mexeiner, July 25, 1966; children: Bettina Lynn, Catherine Anne, Heidi Elaine. M.D., U. Cologne, W. Ger., 1962; Ph.D., McMaster U., Hamilton, Ont. Can., 1977. Lic. physician and surgeon Mo., 1973. Sr. Research fellow McMaster U., Hamilton, Ont., Can., 1970-72; asst. prof. medicine Washington U., St. Louis, 1972-78, assoc. prof. medicine/pathology, 1978-82, prof. medicine/pathology, 1982—; dir. Hemostasis Lab., Barnes Hosp., St. Louis, 1972-78, Div. Hematology St. Louis U. Med. Ctr., 1978-83, Div. Hematology St. Louis U. Med. Ctr. (Div. Hematology/Oncology), 1983—. Editor: Venous and Arterial Thrombosis, 1979. Mem. adv. com. Mo. Div. Health; chmn. med. adv. com. Mo./Ill. region ARC; assembly del. Am. Heart Assn. Council Thrombosis, Dallas, 1982. NIH research fellow, 1964-65; Ont. Heart Found. research fellow, 1970-72; recipient NIH individual research grant, 1982, 85. Fellow ACP; mem. Am. Heart Assn., Am. Soc. Hematology, Central Soc. Clin. Research, Am. Assn. Pathologists, St. Louis Soc. Internal Medicine. Current Work: normal and abnormal hemostasis; thrombosis; mechanisms of platelet activation in flowing blood; interaction of platelets with red cells and endothelial cells in flowing blood; thrombogenicity of abnormal vascular and artificial surfaces; hemorheology; isotopic labeling of platelets. Subspecialties: Hematology; Pathology (medicine). Home: 716 S Central Ave Clayton MO 63105 Office: St Louis U Med Center Div Hematology-Oncology 1325 S Grand Blvd St Louis MO 63104

JOKLIK, WOLFGANG KARL, biochemist, virologist, educator; b. Vienna, Austria, Nov. 16, 1926; s. Karl F. and Helene (Giessl) J.; m. Judith Vivien Nicholas, Apr. 9, 1955 (dec. Apr. 1975); children: Richard G., Vivien H.; m. Patricia Hunter Downey, Apr. 23, 1977. B.Sc. with 1st class honors, U. Sydney, Australia, 1948, M.Sc., 1949; D.Phil. (Australian Nat. U. scholar), U. Oxford, Eng., 1952. Australian Nat. U. research fellow, Copenhagen, Denmark, 1953, Canberra, Australia, 1954-56, fellow, 1957-62; assoc. prof. cell biology Albert Einstein Coll. Medicine, Bronx, N.Y., 1962-65, prof. cell biology, 1965-68, Siegfried Ullmann prof. biochem. virology, 1966-68; prof., chmn. dept. microbiology and immunology Duke U. Med. Center, Durham, N.C., 1968—, James B. Duke Distinguished prof. microbiology and immunology, 1972—. Sr. author: Zinsser Microbiology, 15th, 16th, 17th and 18th edits; Contbr. articles profl. jours. Mem. Am. Soc. Virology, Am. Soc. Microbiology, Am. Soc. Biol. Chemists, Nat. Acad. Scis., Inst. Medicine of Nat. Acad. Scis. Current Work: Properties of viruses; virus multiplication in molecular terms; arrangement of genetic material; expression of genetic information and how it is controlled. Subspecialties: Virology (medicine); Genetics and genetic engineering (medicine). Address: Dept Microbiology and Immunology Duke U Med Center Durham NC 27710

JOKSIMOVICH, VOJIN, nuclear company executive, consultant; b. Belgrade, Serbia, Yugoslavia, Apr. 17, 1936; came to U.S., 1970, naturalized, 1976; s. Bozidar Joksimovic and Sylvia Turner; m. Nada Ajh, Nov. 26, 1961 (div. Apr. 1969); m. remarried, Oct. 1969; 1 dau., Natasha. Dipl.Ing., Electrotech. Faculty, Belgrade, 1961; Ph.D, Imperial Coll. Sci. and Tech., London, 1970. Registered profl. engr. in nuclear engring., Calif. Cons. engr. Energoprojekt, Belgrade, 1961-65; group leader Atomic Power Constrns., London, 1965-70; lead engr. Westinghouse Electric Corp., Pitts., 1970-72; br. mgr. Gen. Atomic, San Diego, 1973-80, dept. mgr., 1980-81; mgr. San Diego office NUS Corp., 1981—; exec. dir. Risk Assessment Services, 1985—; chmn. various profl. conf. sessions. Contbr. articles to profl. jours. Chmn. Serbians for Reagon, San Diego, 1980; mem. Presdl. Task Force, Washington, 1982. Served with Yugoslavian Army, 1962-63. Mem. Am. Nuclear Soc. Republican. Serbian Orthodox. Club: Tennis Escondido (Calif.). Current Work: Risk assessment, nuclear safety, nuclear waste management, nuclear and non-nuclear risks. Subspecialties: Nuclear engineering; Nuclear fission. Home: 406 Hidden Hills Ln Escondido CA 92025

JOLLY, EDWARD MARTIN, consulting engineer; b. Plain Dealing, La., Dec. 24, 1924; s. Herbert Martin and Myrtice Lillian (Hamiter) J.; m. Juanita Marie Biggs, Nov. 28, 1947; children—Donna Marie, Kaye Lillian, Susan Celeste, Lisa Louise, Jennifer Ann. B.S. in Mech. Engring., La. Tech. U., 1949. Registered profl. engr., La. Rodman in survey crew E.M. Freeman & Assocs., Shreveport, La., 1949-51, survey party chief, 1951-52, designer, 1952-54, project engr., 1954-60; pres. ptnr. Aillet, Fenner, Jolly & McClelland, Inc., Shreveport, 1960—. Mem. La. Engring. Soc. (pres. 1960), Engring. and Sci. Council (pres. 1962), Cons. Engrs. Council (pres. 1968), Soc. Mil. Engrs. (pres. 1970), Constrn. Specifications Inst. (pres. 1966-67). Democrat. Methodist. Club: South Lakeside Community (pres. 1960-61) Lodge: Masons. Am. Legion (comdr. Post 14, 1976). Current work: Airports, military facilities, parks, swimming pools; design and supervision of construction. Subspecialty: Civil engineering. Office: Aillet Fenner Jolly McClelland Inc 1055 Louisiana St Shreveport LA 71101

JONA, FRANCO PAUL, physicist, educator; b. Pistoia, Italy, Oct. 10, 1922; s. Frederico S. and Gabriella (Fenoglio) J.; married; children: Frederico A., Franco S. Diplom, E.T.H., Zurich, 1946, Ph.D., 1949. Asst. prof. Pa. State U., 1952-57; research scientist Westinghouse Research Lab., Pitts., 1957-59, IBM Research Center, Yorktown Heights, N.Y., 1959-69; prof. materials sci. SUNY-Stony Brook, 1969—. Fellow Am. Phys. Soc.; mem. Italian Phys. Soc., Swiss Phys. Soc., Japanese Phys. Soc. Current Work: Surface crystallography, surface physics and chemistry, computer applications. Subspecialty: Condensed matter physics. Office: Dept Materials Sci and Engring SUNY Stony Brook NY 11794

JONAS, JIRI, chemistry educator, researcher; b. Prague, Czechoslovakia, Apr. 1, 1932; married, 1968. B.S., Tech. U. Prague, 1956; Ph.D. in Chemistry, Czechslovak Acad. Sci., 1960. Research assoc. in chemistry Czech Acad. Sci., 1960-63; vis. scientist U. Ill.-Urbana, 1963-65, asst. prof. to assoc. prof., 1966-72, prof. chemistry, 1972—, sr. staff mem. materials research, 1970—, dir. Sch. Chem. Scis., 1982—; Alfred P. Sloan found. fellow, 1967-69, Guggenheim fellow, 1972-73; assoc. mem. Ctr. Advanced Study, U. Ill., 1976-77. Fellow Am. Phys. Soc., AAAS; mem. Am. Chem. Soc. (J.H. Hildebrand award 1983), Nat. Acad. Scis. Subspecialties: Nuclear magnetic resonance; High pressure techniques. Office: Dept Chemistry U Ill Urbana IL 61801

JONES, ALFRED WELWOOD, mathematician, computer scientist; b. N.Y.C., July 6, 1915; s. Adam Leroy and Lily (Murray) J.; m. Pierette Jeanine Petas, Feb. 22, 1962; children: K. Darcy Jones Fuguet, Laurie Jones Bergamini, Alison Murray, Leroy Welwood, Bruce McKinley. B.A., Columbia U., 1937, M.A., 1939, Ph.D., 1944. Instr. U. Maine, Orono, 1939-42, Yale U., New Haven, 1942-44; asst. prof. Mich. State U., East Lansing, 1944-47; assoc. prof. Rensselaer Poly. Inst., Troy, N.Y., 1947-57; systems engr. Bell Telephone Labs., Holmdel, N.J., 1957-64; researcher Inst. Def. Analysis, Arlington, Va., 1964-69; prof. engring. Wayne State U., Detroit, 1969-83; prof. computer systems Fla. Atlantic U., Boca Raton, 1983—; vis. prof. Inst. Advanced Study, Princeton, N.J., 1950-51; cons. Inst. Def. Analysis, 1969-72, Urban Inst., Washington, 1976—, U.S. Army Corps Engrs., 1977-79. Arthor: (with C. Eringen) Continuum Physics, 1971; author: Research Simulation, 1981, 83. Flutist various symphony orchs., 1945-69; Scoutmaster Boy Scouts Am., 1973-81. Recipient Disting. Service citation USAAF, 1945. Fellow AAAS; mem. Engring. Soc. Detroit (chmn. affiliate council 1982-83), Ops. Research Soc. Am. (chmn. edn. 1980-81), Soc. Computer Simulation, Human Factors Soc., IEEE (chmn. 1973-74), Phi Beta Kappa, Sigma Xi, Psi Upsilon, Phi Mu Alpha. Episcopalian. Current Work: Design and analysis of stochastic systems using systems models which are simluatedon a high speed computer. Subspecialty: Operations research (mathematics). Home: 2616 NW 37th St Boca Raton FL 33434 Office: Dept Computer and Info Systems Fla Atlantic U Boca Raton FL 33431

JONES, BEN MORGAN, research psychologist, adminstr.; b. Lawton, Okla., Aug. 1, 1943; s. Ben Greenleaf and Cynthia (Morgan) J.; m. Marilyn Kaye Miller, May 16, 1975. B.S., Okla. State U., 1965; Ph.D., U. Okla., 1972. Asst. prof. psychiatry and behavioral scis. U. Okla Health Scis. Ctr., Oklahoma City, 1972-77, assoc. prof., 1977-78; research psychologist Okla. Ctr. Alcohol and Drug-Related Studies, Oklahoma City, 1972-78, assoc. dir., 1973-78; mem. contbg. faculty Sch. Applied and Profl. Psychology Rutgers State U. of N.J., New Brunswick, 1978-80; research psychologist, cons. in clin. psychology Carrier Clinic Found., Belle Mead, N.J., 1978-80; research assoc. prof. psychiatry SUNY-Buffalo, 1981—, adj. prof. psychology, 1983—; cons. Alcohol Rev. Bd., 1981—; exec. dir. Research Inst. on Alcoholism, Buffalo, 1980—; cons. clin. psychology VA, Buffalo, 1980—; bd. dirs. Research Found. for Mental Hygiene, Albany, N.Y., 1980—. Editor: Jour. Biol. Psychology Bull, 1971-72, Alcohol Tech. Reports, 1973-78. Mem. Erie County Com. of Alcoholism Profls., Buffalo, 1980—; mem. alcoholism/substance abuse subcom. of Erie County Mental Hygiene Community Services Bd., 1981—. NSF grantee, 1969-71. Mem. Am. Psychol. Assn., Internat. Neuropsychology Soc., N.Y. Acad. Scis., Research Soc. on Alcoholism, Sigma Xi (sec. chpt. 1981-82). Current Work: Neuropsychological functioning of male and female alcoholics as a function of age, sex differences in social drinkers, acute effects of alcohol on cognitive abilities as a function of sex hormone status and resultant ethanol and acetaldehyde levels. Subspecialties: Neuropsychology; Cognition. Home: 6862 Old Lakeshore Rd Derby NY 14047 Office: Research Inst on Alcoholism 1021 Main St Buffalo NY 14203

JONES, CLARIS EUGENE, JR., botany educator, writer; b. Columbus, Ohio, Dec. 15, 1942; s. Claris Eugene and Clara Elizabeth (Elliott) J.; m. Teresa Diane Wagner, June 26, 1966; children: Douglas Eugene, Philip Charles, Elizabeth Lynne. B.S., Ohio U., 1964; Ph.D., Ind. U., 1969. Asst. prof. botany Calif. State U., Fullerton, 1969-73, assoc. prof., 1973-77, prof., 1977—, dir. Fullerton Arboretum, 1970-80, dir. Arboretum Project, 1970-76; dir. Faye McFadden Herbarium, 1969—; vis. asst. prof. U. Mich., summer, 1972; part-time faculty Orgn. for Tropical Studies, 1970, 72; pres. Arboretum Bd. dirs. Arboretum Soc., Inc., Calif. State U., Fullerton, 1972-78. Co-author: A Dictionary of Botany, 1980; sr. editor: Handbook of Experimental Pollination Biology, 1983; Contbr. articles on botany to profl. jours. NSF grantee, 1973. Mem. Am. Inst. Biol. Sci., AAAS, Bot. Soc. Am., Am. Soc. Plant Taxonomists, Internat. Assn. for Plant Taxonomy, Soc. for the Study of Evolution, So. Calif. Botanists, Soc. Calif. Acad. Sci., Systematics Assn., Soc. for Econ. Botany, Ecol. Soc. Am., Calif. Bot. Soc., Sigma Xi (grantee 1970). Democrat. Methodist. Current Work: Pollination ecology and plant biosystematics. Subspecialties: Evolutionary biology; Systematics. Office: Dept Biol Sci Calif State U Fullerton CA 92634

JONES, DANIEL TODD, human factors project leader, human factors/systems researcher; b. San Antonio, May 18, 1950; s. Daniel Burr and Bettie Marsh (Garrison) J.; m. Susanne Elaine Miller, July 19, 1975; 1 dau., Sarah Susanne. B.S. in Engring., U. Central Fla., 1972. Registered profl. engr., Md. Indsl. engr. Naval Air Rework Facility, Jacksonville, Md., 1973, Naval Ordnance Sta., Indian Head, Md., 1973-77; human factors engr. U.S. Coast Guard, Washington, 1977—; cons. in field., 1981—. Served with USN, 1968-69. Mem. Human Factors Soc., Inst. Indsl. Engrs., AIAA, AAAS, Nat. Soc. Profl. Engrs., Phi Kappa Alpha. Republican. Methodist. Club: Methodist Men (pres. 1984-85) (Friendly, Md.). Current Work: Human factors and systems engineering research in commercial vessel and coast guard systems; problems include noise, vibration, human performance, systems design and operation, simulators. Subspecialties: Human factors engineering; Systems engineering. Home: 120 Indian Ct Waldorf MD 20601 Office: USCG 2100 2d St SW Washington DC 20593

JONES, DAVID HUNTER, reactor designer, engineer, government official; b. Youngstown, Ohio, Jan. 7, 1931; m. Helen Austin, Sept. 17, 1954; children—Laura L. Jones Hubele, David A. B.A., Oberlin Coll., 1952; M.S., U. Wash., 1956. Reactor designer, mgr. Westinghouse-Bettis Co., West Mifflin, Pa., 1956-76; ops. planning mgr. Westinghouse Hanford Co., Richland, Wash., 1976-81; rep. U.S. Dept. Energy to Power Reactor and Nuclear Fuel Devel. Corp. of Japan, Tokyo, 1981—; mem. fuel handling safeguards com. Bettis Atomic Power Lab., West Mifflin, 1966-76, Fast Flux Test Facility safeguards com. Westinghouse Hanford Co., Richland, 1976-81; U.S. rep. to JOYO Criticality, U.S. Dept. Energy, Mito, Japan, 1977. Contbr. articles to profl. jours. Patentee in field. Elder, trustee Pleasant Hills Community United Presbyterian Ch., Pitts., 1958-76; del. Republican party County Caucus, Richland, 1980. Mem. Am. Nuclear Soc., Sigma Xi. Subspecialties: Nuclear fission; Nuclear engineering. Home: Azabu Tower 1-3 Azabudai 2-Chome Minato-Ku Tokyo 106 Japan Office: Dohnen Sankaido Bldg 9-13 Akasaka 1-Chome Minato-Ku Tokyo 107 Japan

JONES, DONALD LEROY, economic research firm executive, physicist; b. St. Joseph, Mo., Feb. 5, 1932; s. Clifton Youree and Veda Belle (Goodnight) J.; m. Christine A. Kircher, Aug. 28, 1965 (div. Oct. 1982); children—Stephanie, Eric, Kit, Ashley. B.S. in Engring., B.S. in Bus., U. Colo., 1957, M.S. in Physics, 1967. Physicist Nat. Bur. Standards, Boulder, Colo., 1955-67, Gen. Electric Co., King of Prussia, Pa., 1967-71; pres. Commodity Info. Service, Phila. and Chgo., 1971—; dir. Commodity Mgmt. Service Corp., Collegeville, Pa. Contbr. articles to profl. jours., 1960—. Served with USNR, 1951-53. Mem. Math. Assn. Am, Am. Phys. Soc., Am. Geophys. Soc., Nat. Assn. Commodity Futures Advisors (founder mem.), Sigma Xi, Sigma Alpha Epsilon. Current work: Micro-economic analysis of financial markets. Subspecialties: Numerical analysis (mathematics); Database systems. Home: 109 R 2d Ave Collegeville PA 19426 Office: Comodity Info Services 327 S LaSalle St Chicag IL 60604

JONES, DOUGLAS LINWOOD, mechanical engineer educator, cons.; b. Limeton, Va., Dec. 26, 1937; s. Charlie Baxley and Irma Kathelle (Murphy) J.; m. Mary Kay O'Brien, Jan. 2, 1975. B.M.E., George Washington U., 1963, M.S. in Engring. (NASA fellow 1963-66), 1965, D.Sc., 1970. Registered profl. engr., Va. Aerospace technologist Goddard Space Flight Center, NASA, Greenbelt, Md., 1963; teaching fellow George Washington U., Washington, 1966-67, instr. engring. and applied sci., 1967-68, asst. prof., 1968-71, asst. research prof. engring., 1971-74, assoc. research prof., 1974-77, assoc. prof. engring., 1977-82, prof., 1982—, curriculum chmn. mech. engring., 1981-85, cons. in fracture mechanics, failure analysis, structural analysis and design Comsat Labs., ENSCO Corp., Battelle Meml. Inst., Systems Tech. Labs., duPont Corp. Mem. editorial adv. bd. Engring. Fracture Mechanics, 1978—. Contbr. articles to profl. jours. Bd. dirs. Wesley Found., George Washington U., 1966-77, vice-chmn., 1969-73, chmn., 1973-76; vice chmn. Commn. on Higher Edn. and Campus Ministry, Balt. Conf. of United Meth. Ch., 1977. Dept. Def. grantee, 1976—; NASA grantee, 1977-80; recipient George Washington award George Washington U., 1985. Mem. Am. Acad. Mechanics, ASME, Am. Soc. for Engring. Edn., Soc. for Exptl. Mechanics, Brit. Soc. Strain Measurement, ASTM, George Washington U. Engr. Alumni Assn. (dir. 1963—, treas. 1964-66,/69-70, pres. 1970-72, Engr. Alumni Service award 1976), Gen. Alumni Assn. George Washington U. (governing bd. 1970-72, 73-82, Alumni Service award 1974), Sigma Xi, Tau Beta Pi, Pi Tau Sigma. Current Work: Research in fracture, fatigue and mechanical behavior of engineering materials; practical development of the edge-sliding mode of fracture; studies into the fatigue behavior of composite materials. Subspecialties: Fracture mechanics; Composite materials. Home: 1818 N Cleveland St Arlington VA 22201 Office: George Washington U Washington DC 20052

JONES, HOWARD WILBUR, JR., gynecologist; b. Balt., Dec. 30, 1910; s. Howard Wilbur and Ethel Ruth (Marling) J.; m. Georgeanna Emory Seegar, June 22, 1940; children—Howard Wilbur III, Georgeanna S., Lawrence M. A.B., Amherst Coll., 1931; M.D., Johns Hopkins, 1935; Dr. Honoris Causa, Cordoba, 1968. Intern, asst. resident, resident gynecology Johns Hopkins Hosp., 1935-37, 46-48; asst. resident, resident surgery Ch. Home and Hosp., Balt., 1937-40, practice medicine, specializing in obstetrics and gynecology, 1948—; instr., asst. prof., asso. prof., prof. gynecology and obstetrics Sch. Medicine Johns Hopkins, 1948-79, prof. emeritus, 1979—; prof. obstetrics and gynecology Eastern Va. U. Med. Sch., 1978—; nat. cons. USAF, 1968-78; Dir. William & Wilkins Co. Author: (with W.W. Scott) Genital Anomalies and Related Endocrine Disorders, 1958, rev. edit., 1971, (with G.S. Jones) Textbook of Gynecology, 1965, 10th edit., 1981, (with R. Heller) Pediatric and Adolescent Gynecology, 1968, (with J.A. Rock) Reparative and Constructive Surgery of the Female Generative Tract, 1983; Editor in chief: (with G.E.S. Jones) Obstetrical and Gynecological Survey, 1957—; Contbr. (with G.E.S. Jones) articles to profl. jours. Served to maj. M.C. AUS, 1943-46. Decorated Bronze Star medal. Mem. AMA, Am. Assn. Cancer Research, Am. Cancer Soc. (dir. Md. div.), Am. Coll. Obstetrics and Gynecology, Soc. Pelvic Surgeons, Sociedad de Obstetricia Y Gynecologia die Buenos Aires, Sociedad Peruana de Obstetricia Y Ginecologia. Current Work: Reproductive biology. Subspecialty: Obstetrics and gynecology. Home: 7506 Shirland Norfolk VA 23505 Office: 825 Fairfax Norfolk VA 23507

JONES, JAMES THOMAS, JR., air force officer; b. LaGrange, Ga., Feb. 5, 1943; s. James Thomas and Louise (Priddy) J.; m. Jeanne Louise Jones, June 20, 1981; children: Andrea P., James Thomas. B.S., U. Ga., 1965; M.S., So. Meth. U., 1970. Commd. U.S. Air Force, 1965, advanced through grades to lt. col., 1981—; ops. research analyst Tactical Fighter Weapons Ctr., Nellis AFB, Nev., 1970-72; ops. research analyst (F-15 Joint Test Force), Edwards AFB, Calif., 1972-75, Eglin AFB, Fla., 1975-78, Def. Intelligence Agy., Washington, 1978-82; assoc. prof. ops. research Def. Intelligence Sch., Washington, 1982, vice dean, 1982-85, exec. officer, 1983-85; dir. govt. mktg. Liso Machines Inc., Vienna, Va., 1985—; mem. Washington Ops. Research & Mgmt. Sci. Council, 1983—. Contbr. articles to profl. jours. Leader Boy Scouts Am., Niceville, Fla., 1977-78; coach Boy's Little League, Edwards, Calif., 1972-76. Mem. Ops. Research Soc. Am., Mil. Ops. Research Soc., Am. Assn. for Artificial Intelligence. Current Work: Applications for quantitative methods in intelligence business; application for artificial intelligence to intelligence problems. Subspecialties: Operations research (engineering); Probability. Home: 6149 N Morgan St Alexandria VA 22312 Office: LMI 2020 Chain Bridge Rd Vienna VA 22180

JONES, JOHN PAUL, educator, plant pathologist; b. Warren, Ohio, Dec. 10, 1924; s. Robert Paul and Sueanna Florence (Atchison) J.; m. Joyce Shoemaker, May 7, 1950; children: Karen, Stephen, Lynn. B.S., Ohio U., 1950, M.S., 1953; Ph.D., U. Nebr., 1956. Research technician Ohio Agrl. Expt. Sta., 1949-50; research asst. U. Nebr., 1950-55; research plant pathologist U.S. Dept. Agr., Stoneville, Miss., 1955-60; prof. plant pathology U. Ark., 1960—; project leader plant protection Rice Research and Tng. Project, AID, Giza, Cairo, 1981-85. Contbr. numerous articles to profl. jours. Served with AUS, 1943-46. NSF research grantee, 1963-65; teaching grantee, 1966, 69; U. Ark. Endowment Fund grantee, 1976. Mem. Am. Phytopathol. Soc., Assn. So. Agrl. Workers, Ark. Acad. Sci., Internat. Soc. Plant Pathology, Sigma Xi, Alpha Zeta, Gamma Sigma Delta. Presbyterian. Lodge: Masons. Current Work: Etiology and control of cereal diseases, primarily wheat, oats and rice. Subspecialties: Plant pathology; Integrated pest management. Home: 4 E Sycamore St Fayetteville AR 72701

JONES, LAWRENCE WILLIAM, physics educator, administrator, researcher; b. Evanston, Ill., Nov. 16, 1925; s. Charles Herbert and Fern (Storm) J.; m. Ruth R. Drummond, June 24, 1950; children—Douglas W., Carol J. Dwyer, Ellen J. Dillman. B.S., Northwestern U., 1948, M.S., 1949; Ph.D., U. Calif.-Berkeley, 1952. Research asst. Radiation Lab., Berkeley, Calif., 1950-52, physicist Midwestern U. Research Assocs., Madison, Wis., 1956-57; prof. dept. physics U. Mich., Ann Arbor, 1952-82, prof., chmn. dept. 1982—; trustee U. Research Assoc., Washington, 1981—; vis. prof. Tata Inst., Bombay, India, 1979; vis. scientist Brookhaven Nat. Lab., Upton, N.Y., 1962-70; Fermi Nat. Accelerations Lab., Batavia, Ill., 1972. Contbr. articles on physics research to profl. jours. Bd. dirs., chmn. Ecology Ctr., Ann Arbor, 1978-76; chmn. orgn. com. First Congregational Ch., Ann Arbor, 1981-84. Served with U.S. Army, 1944-46. CERN fellow 1961-62; Guggenheim fellow, 1965; Sci. Research Council fellow, 1977; Fellow Am. Phys. Soc.; mem. AAAS. Democrat. Current work: Experiments on heavy quark production by protons at Fermilab and on 100GeV e-e annihilation at CERN; aspects of the superconducting super collider, cosmic ray physics, and hydrogen energy systems. Subspecialties: Particle physics; Cancer research (medicine). Home: 2666 Park Ridge Dr Ann Arbor MI 48103 Office: Dept Physics Univ Mich Ann Arbor MI 48109

JONES, LYLE VINCENT, psychology educator; b. Grandview, Wash., Mar. 11, 1924; s. Vincent F. and Matilda M. (Abraham) J.; m. Patricia Edison Powers, Dec. 17, 1949 (div. 1979); children: Christopher V., Susan E., Tad W. Student, Reed Coll., 1942-43; B.S., U. Wash., 1947, M.S., 1948; Ph.D., Stanford, 1950. Nat. Research fellow, 1950-51; asst. prof. psychology U. Chgo., 1951-57; vis. asso. prof. U. Tex., 1956-57; asso. prof. U. N.C., 1957-60, prof., 1960-69, Alumni disting. prof., 1969—; dir. U. N.C. (L.L. Thurstone Psychometric Lab.), 1957-74, 79—; vice chancellor, dean U. N.C. (Grad. Sch.), 1969-79; pres. Assn. Grad. Schs., 1976-77; cons. in field. Author: (with others) Studies in Aphasia: An Approach to Testing, 1961, The Measurement and Prediction of Judgment and Choice, 1968, (with others) An Assessment of Research-Doctorate Programs in the United States, 5 vols., 1982; Mng. editor: Psychometrika, 1956-61; Editorial com. for psychology, Mc-Graw-Hill, 1965-77; Contbr. articles to profl. jours. Served with USAF, 1943-46. Recipient Thomas Jefferson award U. N.C., 1979; Fellow Center Advanced Study in Behavioral Scis., 1964-65, 81-82; grantee NIH, 1957-63, NSF, 1960-63, 71-74, 83—, NIMH, 1963-74, 79—. Fellow AAAS, Am. Psychol. Assn. (pres. div. 1963-64), Am. Acad. Arts and Scis.; mem. Psychometric Soc. (pres. 1962-63), Medicine Am., Am. Statis. Assn., Inst. Medicine, Am. Ednl. Research Assn. Current Work: Assessing scholastic achievement of nation's youth. Subspecialty: Psychometrics. Home: Route 1 Pittsboro NC 27312 Office: Davie Hall U NC Chapel Hill NC 27514

JONES, MARY ELLEN, biochemistry educator; b. La Grange, Ill., Dec. 25, 1922; d. Elmer Enold and Laura Anna (Klein) J.; children from former marriage—Ethan Vincent Munson, Catherine Laura Munson. B.S., U. Chgo., 1944; Ph.D., Yale U., 1951. Mem. staff in chemistry Armour and Co., Springfield, Mo., Chgo., 1942-48; predoctoral fellow dept. physiol. chemistry USPHS, New Haven, 1950-51; postdoctoral fellow AEC, Biochem. Research Lab., Mass. Gen. Hosp., Boston, 1951-53, Am. Cancer Soc. fellow, 1953-55, assoc. biochemist Biochem. Research Lab., Mass. Gen. Hosp., 1955-57; asst. prof. dept. biochemistry Brandeis U., Waltham, Mass., 1957-60, assoc. prof., 1960-66, dir. dental tng., 1962-66; assoc. prof. dept. biochemistry Sch. Medicine, U. N.C., Chapel Hill, 1966-68, assoc. prof. dept. zoology, 1967-69, prof. dept. biochemistry Sch. Medicine, 1968-71, prof. dept. zoology, 1969-71, chmn., prof. dept. biochemistry and nutrition Sch. Medicine, 1978—, Kenan prof., 1980; prof. dept. biochemistry Sch. Medicine, U. So. Calif., Los Angeles, 1971-78; cons. and lectr. in field. Contbr. articles to profl. jours. Mem. editorial bd. Jour. Biol. Chemistry, 1975-80, 82-87, Cancer Research, 1981—. Fellow AAAS; mem. Am. Chem. Soc. (councillor 1975-79), Am. Soc. Biol. Chemists (councillor 1975-78, 1981-84, Rose award selection com. 1984—, pres.-elect 1985), Fedn. Am. Socs. for Exptl. Biology, Inst. of Medicine of Nat. Acad. Scis., Assn. Med. Sch. Depts. of Biochemistry (pres. 1985), N.Y. Acad. Scis., Sigma Xi. Current work: Enzymology; biosynthetic and transfer reactions; metabolic regulation of enzymes; multifunctional proteins; pyrimidine and amino acid biosynthesis; carbamyl phosphate; acetyloenzyme A. Subspecialties: Biochemistry (medicine); Enzyme technology. Office: U NC Dept Biochemistry and Nutrition 405 FLOB 231H Chapel Hill NC 27514

JONES, MAURICE (MO), JR., energy service co. research and development executive, consultant; b. Pasadena, Tex., Nov. 29, 1951; s. Maurice and Yvonne (Ferguson) J. B.S. in Biology, U. Houston, 1974; M.S. in Environ. Sci, U. Tex.-Houston, 1977. Biologist, technician S.W. Research Inst., Houston, 1974-76; supr. Environ. Lab., Dames & Moore, Houston, 1978-79; supr. environ. affairs IMCO Services, Houston, 1979-82, mgr. environ. services, 1982-83, mgr. research and devel., 1983—; cons. Marine Bd., NRC, Washington, 1980, 83; chmn. drilling fluids task force Petroleum Equipment Suppliers Assn., Houston, 1980-81; chmn. bioassay protocol Am. Petroleum Inst., Dallas, 1982—; co-chmn. environ. sect. Soc. Petroleum Engr./Internat. Assn. Drilling Contractors Symposium, New Orleans, 1983. Contbr. numerous articles to profl. jours.; editor: Perspective on Drilling Fluids and their Environmental Impact, 1984. USPHS trainee, 1974; Marine Biol. Lab. scholar, 1978. Mem. Ecol. Soc. Am. (cert.), Nat. Assn. Environ. Profls., Soc. Ecotoxicology and Environ. Safety, Soc. Petroleum Industry Biologists, Marine Tech. Soc. Democrat. Current Work: Drilling fluids science and technology; estuarine biology; environmental law and regulations; bioassay procedures; biometry. Subspecialties: Environmental toxicology; Offshore technology. Home: 1717 Hazard Houston TX 77019 Office: IMCO Services 2400 W Loop S Houston TX 77227

JONES, MOLLY MODRALL, clin. psychologist; b. Albuquerque, Apr. 20, 1940; d. James Ritchie and Constance (Connor) M.; m. Lawrence L. Burckmyer, Feb. 22, 1963 (div. 1968); children: Elizabeth Loring, Mary Constance. B.A., U. Colo., 1961; M.A., Harvard U., 1964, C.A.S., 1965; Ph.D., Union Grad. Sch., Cin., 1978. Licensed psychologist, N.M., D.C., Md. Sch. diagnostician Santa Fe (N.Mex.) pub. schs., 1969-72; clin. psychologist USPHS, Santa Fe, 1974-79; asso. prof. Coll. of Santa Fe, 1972-79; health sci. adminstrs. NIH, Bethesda, Md., 1979-81, clin. psychologist in pvt. practice, Chevy Chase, Md., 1981—; cons. Nat. Presbyn. Counseling Center, 1980—, N.Mex. Dept. Health & Social Services, 1974-79, Indian Health Service, Santa Fe, 1974-79. Contbr. articles to profl. jours. Cons. Rape Crisis Center, Santa Fe, 1972-79; trustee Santa Fe Prep. Sch., 1975-79; precinct capt. Democratic Party, Santa Fe, 1972-74, del., 1972-74; del. others. Am. Council on Edn. fellow, 1979-81; U. N.M. fellow, 1978-79; Indian Health Service predoctoral fellow, 1976-78; research fellow, 1973-78; Shell Oil Co. fellow, 1972. Mem. Am. Psychol. Assn., AAUP, Md. Soc. Clin. Hypnosis (treas.), Washington Psychologists for Psychoanalysis (program chmn.), Md. Psychol. Assn., D.C. Psychol. Assn. Democrat. Presbyterian. Clubs: Kenwood Golf and Tennis, Sangre de Cristo Racquet, Harvard. Current Work: Pain control, psychosomatic-psychophysiologic conditions psychodynamic psychotherapy, clin. hypnosis, pain control, relaxation tng. Subspecialties: Developmental psychology; Physiological psychology. Home: 4964 Allan Rd Bethesda MD 20816 Office: 5454 Wisconsin Ave Suite 600 Chevy Chase MD 20815

JONES, ROBERT THOMAS, aero. scientist; b. Macon, Mo., May 28, 1910; s. Edward Seward and Harriet Ellen (Johnson) J.; m. Barbara Jeanne Spagnoli, Nov. 23, 1964; children—Edward, Patricia, Harriet, David, Gregory, John. Student, U. Mo., 1928; Sc.D. (hon.), U. Colo., 1971. Aero. research scientist NACA, Langley Field, Va., 1934-46; research scientist Ames Research Center NACA-NASA, Moffet Field, Calif., 1946-62; sr. staff scientist Ames Research Center, NASA, 1970-81, research asso., 1981—; scientist Avco-Everett Research Lab., Everett, Mass., 1962-70; cons. prof. Stanford U., 1981. Author: (with Doris Cohen) High Speed Wing Theory, 1960, Collected Works of Robert T. Jones, 1976; contbr. (with Doris Cohen) articles to profl. jours. Recipient Reed award Inst. Aero. Scis., 1946; Inventions and Contbns. award NASA, 1975; Prandtl Ring award Deutsche Gesellschaft für Luft and Raumfahrt, 1978; Pres.'s medal for disting. fed. service, 1980; Langley medal Smithsonian Instn., 1981. Fellow Am. Inst. Aeros. and Astronautics (hon.); mem. Am. Acad. Arts and Scis., Nat. Acad. Scis., Nat. Acad. Engring. Subspecialties: Aerospace engineering and technology; Aeronautical engineering. Home: 25005 La Loma Dr Los Altos Hills CA 94022

JONES, ROGER CLYDE, educator; b. Lake Andes, S.D., Aug. 17, 1919; s. Robert Clyde and Martha (Albertson) J.; m. Katherine Maxine Tucker, June 7, 1952; childrn—Linda Lee, Vonnie Lynette. B.S., U. Nebr.-Lincoln, 1949; M.S., U. Md., 1953, Ph.D., 1963. Electronic scientist U.S. Naval Research Lab., Washington, 1949-57; sr. engr., project engr. Melpar, Inc., Falls Church, Va., 1957-59, sect. head physics, 1959-64, chief scientist for physics, 1964—; prof. U. Ariz., Tucson, 1964—; research assoc. U. Tex., El Paso, summer 1969; electronic scientist Ft. Huachuca, Ariz., summer 1976; guest prof. Kräftforskings instituttet, Aarhus, Denmark, 1982-83. Patentee in field. Author: (with G.A. Dawson) Planetary Electrodynamics, 1969. Served with U.S. Army, 1942-45. Fellow AAAS; mem. IEEE (sr. mem.), Optical Soc. Am., Bioelectromagnetics Soc., Am. Phys. Soc. Republican. Lutheran. Current work: Electrobiology, especially thermal and athermal effects in-vitro; photon plasma interactions; experimental quantum electronics. Home: 5809 E 3d St Tucson AZ 85711 Office: ECE Dept Coll Engring Univ Ariz Tucson AZ 85721

JONES, RUFUS SIDNEY, JR., research chemist; b. Warrenton, N.C., May 9, 1940; s. Rufus Sidney and Fannie House (Scoggin) J.; m. Martha Elizabeth Ownbey, May 25, 1968; 1 child, Laura Ruth. B.S., Duke U., 1962; Ph.D., Purdue U., 1968. Research chemist Celanese Research Co., Summit, N.J., 1968-72, sr. research chemist, 1972-81, research assoc., 1981—. Contbr. articles to profl. jours. Patentee in field. Mem. Am. Chem. Soc., Materials Research Soc., Soc. Photo-Optical Instrumentation Engrs. Current work: Project leader in development of optical data storage media based on polymeric materials; emphasis on new materials. Subspecialties: Polymer chemistry; Laser data storage and reproduction. Office: Celanese Research Co 86 Morris Ave Summit NJ 07901

JONES, RUSSELL ALLEN, oncologist; b. Waycross, Ga., Nov. 20, 1940; s. Russell Allen and Margaret (Blount) J.; m. Kate Mattison, July 3, 1967; children: Jennifer, Jason. M.D., Emory U., 1965. Diplomate: Am. Bd. Internal Medicine. Intern Grady Meml. Hosp., Atlanta, 1965-66, resident, 1966-67, U. Wash., Seattle, 1969-70; fellow in cancer and blood disease Emory U., 1970-71, practice medicine specializing in med. oncology, Clifton Forge, Va., 1971-77, Chattanooga, 1978—. Served to lt. comdr. U.S. Navy, 1967-69. Fellow A.C.P.; mem. Am. Soc. Clin. Oncology, AMA, Alpha Omega Alpha, Alpha Epsilon Upsilon. Presbyterian. Club: Signal Mountain (Tenn.) Golf and Country. Current Work: Cancer chemotherapy. Subspecialties: Chemotherapy; Cancer research (medicine). Office: Medical Oncology Associates 975 E 3d St Box 144 Chattanooga TN 37403

JONES, WALTER WILLIAM, physicist; b. Roanoke, Va., Feb. 3, 1945; s. William B. and Ruth R. Jones; m. Perlita Aliga, June 19, 1976; 1 child, Walter J. B.A., Oberlin Coll., 1967; Ph.D., U. Md., 1972. Research assoc. U. Md., Coll. Park, 1972-74; vis. asst. prof. Johns Hopkins U., Balt., 1972-73; research physicist Naval Research Lab., Washington, 1974-80, Nat. Bur. Standards, Gaithersburg, Md., 1980—. Contbr. articles to profl. jours. Recipient Sustained Superior Performance award Dept. Commerce, 1984; NSF fellow. Mem. IEEE, Assn. for Computing Machinery, Am. Phys. Soc. Club: FAA Flying (v.p. 1976-80). Current work: Numerical modeling of toxic hazard phenomenology from fires. Subspecialties: Numerical fluid dynamics; Graphics, image processing, and pattern recognition. Home: 10704 Game Preserve Rd Gaithersburg MD 20879 Office: Nat Bur Standards 224/B356 Gaithersburg MD 20899

JORDAN, ARTHUR KENT, research physicist; b. Phila., Dec. 28, 1932; s. Arthur H. and Mary (Schoff) J.; m. Mary Frances Baily, July 10, 1965; children: Thomas B., Edward M., Elizabeth A. B.Sc. in Physics, Pa. State. U., 1957; M.Sc., U. Pa., 1971, Ph.D. in Electronics Engring, 1972. Research engr. Philco Corp., Blue Bell, Pa., 1957-62; electronics engr. Radio Corp. Am., Princeton, N.J., 1962-64; aerospace physicist Gen. Electric Co., Valley Forge, Pa., 1964-69; research assoc., fellow U. Pa., Phila., 1969-73; electronics engr. Naval Research Lab., Washington, 1973-84, research physicist, 1984—; cons. Contbr. articles to sci. jours.; contbr. to books; asso. guest editor: IEEE Spl. Issue on Inverse Methods for Electromagnetics, 1981; co-editor Inverse Methods for Electromagnetic Imaging, 1985. Pres. Washington Mill Sch. PTA, 1979-80. Mem. Am. Phys. Soc., Optical Soc. Am., Union Radioscientifique Internationale, IEEE, Antennas and Propagation Soc. (chmn. Washington chpt. 1978-79). Episcopalian (vestryman 1981-84). Current Work: Inversion methods for electromagnetic wave propagation and scattering, imaging, remote sensing, applied mathematics. Subspecialties: Electronics; Inversion methods. Office: Code 4110J Space Sci Div Naval Research Lab Washington DC 20375

JORDAN, CARL FREDERICK, ecologist; b. New Brunswick, N.J., Dec. 10, 1935; s. Emil Leopold and Ethel Anabel (Augustine) J.; m. Carmen S. Vega Rivera, Jan. 14, 1967; children—Anabel, Christopher. B.S., U. Mich., 1958; M.S., Rutgers U., 1964, Ph.D., 1966. Asst. scientist, asso. scientist P.R. Nuclear Center, San Juan, 1966-69; ecologist Argonne (Ill.) Nat. Lab., 1969-74; adj. prof. Inst. Ecology U. Ga., Athens, 1974—, sr. ecologist, 1979—; vis. scientist Centro de Ecologia Insituto Venezelano de Investigaciones Cientificas, Caracas, 1974—; coordinator Internat. Study of Ecosystems., Amazon Basin, 1974—. Contbr. articles to profl. jours. Served with USNR, 1958-62. NSF grantee, 1974—; Man and Biosphere grantee, 1979—. Mem. AAAS, Ecol. Soc. Am., Sigma Xi. Current Work: Structure and function of tropical forests, tropical forestry and land mgmt. nutrient cycling and productivity. Subspecialties: Ecosystems analysis; Biomass (agriculture). Address: Inst of Ecology U Ga Athens GA 30602

JORDAN, CARL HARVEY, mechanical engineer, consultant; b. Los Angeles, June 29, 1933; s. Carlos Webster and Elizabeth Leile (Sanderson) J.; m. Wilma Fay Dupuy, Aug. 21, 1954; children—Daniel Scott, Kurt Michael. B.S. in Mech. Engring., Calif. State U.-Fresno, 1955; postgrad. U. Calif.-Berkeley. Registered profl. engr. Calif., Colo., Oreg., Wash., Nev., Hawaii, N.C. Asst. chief mech. engr. Buonaccorsi and Assocs., San Francisco, 1957-66; v.p. mech. design G.L. Gendler and Assocs., Berkeley, Calif., 1966-73; dir. mech. and elec. engring. Skidmore, Owings and Merrill, San Francisco, 1973—. Contbr. articles to profl. jours. in field. Mem. Berkeley Energy Commn., 1979-82. Served with U.S. Army, 1955-57, W. Ger. Fellow ASHRAE (pres. Golden Gate Chpt. 1976-77); mem. ASME, Nat. Soc. Profl. Engrs., Bldg. Owners and Mgrs. Assn. (affiliate). Club: Berkeley Yacht (commodores 1980). Current work: Energy consumption studies and designs related to architecture and mechanical and electrical systems in buildings. Subspecialties: Mechanical engineering; Energy systems in buildings. Home: 646 Colusa Ave Berkeley CA 94707 Office: Skidmore Owings & Merrill One Maritime Plaza San Francisco CA 94111

JORDAN, CHARLES RALPH, shipbuilder, civil engineer; b. Kinston, N.C., Dec. 21, 1927; s. George Lyman and Sallie Ballou (Herndon) J.; m. Shirley Jean Wynne, Jan. 14, 1951; children: Cynthia Karen, Charles Ralph, Pamela Jean. B.C.E., N.C. State U., Raleigh, 1951. Designer Newport News Shipbldg. & Dry Dock C., Va., 1951-56, sr. designer, 1956-64, design supr., 1964-66, sr. design supr., 1966-69, assoc. chief, 1969-72, tech. mgr., 1972-74, engring. project mgr., 1974-79, mgr. engring. research dept., 1979—. Contbr. articles profl. jours. Adminstrv. bd. 1st Methodist Ch., 1958-62, 63-74, chmn. commn. on edn., 1964-65; deacon 1st Presbyterian Ch., 1979, chmn. fin. com., 1982—. Recipient A.F. Davis Silver medal award for structural design Am. Welding Soc., 1985. Mem. Robotics Internat., Soc. Mfg. Engrs., Soc. Naval Architects and Marine Engrs. Current Work: Advancements in state of the art in marine techonolgy, new product development, design of structural welds, Artic marine transportation. Subspecialties: Naval engineering; Materials (engineering). Home: 34 N Greenfield Ave Hampton VA 23666 Office: 4101 Washington Ave Bldg 600 Newport News VA 23607

JORDAN, EDWARD CONRAD, electrical engineer, educator; b. Edmonton, Alta., Can.; Dec. 31, 1910; came to U.S., 1937; s. Conrad Edward and Erna Elizabeth (Penk) J.; m. Mary Helen Walker, Sept. 3, 1941; children—Robert E., David W., Thomas C. B.S.E.E., U. Alta., 1934, M.Sc., 1936; Ph.D., Ohio State U., 1940. Control operator Sta. CKUA, Edmonton, Alta., 1928-35; elec. engr. Internat. Nickel Co., Sudbury, Ont., Can., 1935-37; instr. elec. engring. Worcester Poly Inst., Mass., 1940-41; instr. to asst. prof. Ohio State U., Columbus, 1941-45; assoc. prof., prof., head dept. U. Ill., Urbana, 1945-79, prof., head emeritus dept. elec. engring., 1979—. Author: Electromagnetic Waves and Radiating Systems, 1950, 1968; co-author: Fundamentals of Radio, 1942, Fundamentals of Radio and Electronics, 1958. Editor: Electromagnetic Theory and Antennas, 1963; editor-in-chief: Reference Data for Engineers: Radio, Electronics, Computers & Communications, 1985. Contbr. chpts. to books, articles on antennas, wave propagation, radio direction finding. Recipient Centennial medal Ohio State U., 1970; Stanley H. Pierce award U. Ill., 1974. Fellow IEEE (edn. medal 1968, centennial award 1984); mem. Nat. Acad. Engring., Antennas and Propagation Soc. (chmn. 1960-61, hon. life mem. adminstrv. com. 1975), Internat. Union of Radio Sci. (chmn. U.S. Nat. Com., 1967-70). Lodge: Rotary (Champaign, Ill.). Subspecialty: Electronics. Office: Dept of Elec and Computer Engring Univ of Illinois 1406 W Green St Urbana IL 61801

JORDAN, RICHARD CHARLES, engineering educator; b. Mpls., Apr. 16, 1909; s. C. and Estelle R. (Martin) J.; m. Freda M. Laudon, Aug. 10, 1935; children: Mary Ann, Carol Lynn, Linda Lee. B. Aero. Engring., U. Minn., 1931, M.S., 1933, Ph.D., 1940. In charge air conditioning div. Mpls. br. Am. Radiator & Standard San. Corp., 1933-36; instr. petroleum engring. U. Tulsa, 1936-37; instr. engring. expt. sta. U. Minn., 1937-41, asst. dir., 1941-44, asso. prof., 1944-45, prof., asst. head mech. engring. dept., 1946-49, prof., head dept. mech. engring., 1950-77, prof., head Sch. Mech. and Aero. Engring., 1966-77, acting asso. dean Inst. Tech., 1977-78, asso. dean, 1978-84; dir. Onan Corp. of McGraw-Edison; cons. various refrigeration and air conditioning cos., 1937—; cons. NSF, U.S. Dept. State, Control Data Corp., others.; Mem. engring. sci. adv. panel NSF, 1954-57, chmn., 1957; mem. div. engring. and indsl. research NRC, mem. exec. com., 1957-69, chmn., 1962-65; del. OAS Conf. on Strategy for Tech. Devel. Latin Am., Chile, 1969; chmn. U.S.-Brazil Sci. Coop. Program Com. on Indsl. Research, Rio de Janeiro, 1967, Washington, 1967, Belo Horizonte, 1968, Houston, 1968; del. World Power Conf., Melbourne, 1962; v.p. sci. council Internat. Institut du Froid, 1967-71; cons. to World Bank on alternative energy for Northeastern Brazil, 1976. Author: (with Priester) Refrigeration and Air Conditioning, 1948, rev. edit., 1956, also numerous publs. on mech. engring., environ. control, solar energy, energy resources, engring. edn., tech. transfer. Contbr. to Mech. Engring. Recipient F. Paul Anderson medal ASHRAE, 1966, E.K. Campbell award, 1966, Outstanding Publs. Golden Key award, 1949; Outstanding Achievement award U. Minn., 1979; elected to Solar Energy Hall of Fame, 1980. Fellow ASME, AAAS, ASHRAE (presdl. mem.); mem. Nat. Acad. Engring., Assn. Applied Solar Energy (adv. council 1958-61), Am. Soc. Refrigerating Engrs. (1st v.p. 1952, pres. 1953, dir., council mem. 1946-53), Am. Soc. Engring. Edn., AAAS, Nat., Minn. (Engr. of Yr. award 1972), socs. profl. engrs., Internat. Inst. Refrigeration (hon. mem., del. NRC to exec. com. 1957-76, v.p. exec. com. 1959-63, v.p. sci. council 1963-71), Engr. Council Profl. Devel. (chmn. regional edn. and accreditation com.), Sigma Xi, Tau Beta Pi, Pi Tau Sigma, Sigma Chi. Club: Campus. Current Work: Alternative energy research and development and energy conservation research as related to the built environment. Subspecialties: Mechanical engineering; Solar energy. Home: 1269 N Cleveland Saint Paul MN 55108 Office: Dept Mech Engring U Minn Minneapolis MN 55455

JORDAN, STUART DAVIS, astrophysicist; b. St. Louis, July 25, 1936; s. Davis Irwin and Lillian (Maenner) J.; m. Elizabeth Susan Roemer, June 24, 1961; children: John Stuart, James William. B.S., Washington U., 1958; Ph.D., U. Colo., 1968. Research asst. JILA (NBS), Boulder, Colo., 1963-68; research astrophysicist Goddard Space Flight Center, Greenbelt, Md., 1968—; chief of solar physics NASA Hdqrs., 1973-74; project scientist Solar Optical Telescope, Goddard Space Flight Ctr., 1976-84, head solar physics br. Lab. for Astronomy and Solar Physics, 1985—. Contbr. articles to profl. jours.; Author: The Sun as a Star, 1981. Served with USAF, 1959-63. Rhodes Scholar, 1958-59. Mem. Internat. Astron. Union, Am. Phys. Soc., Am. Astronon. Soc., AAAS, Fedn. Am. Scientists, Sigma Xi, Tau Beta Pi. Clubs: Washington Area Sierra (speaker), Woods. Current Work: Structure and dynamics of solar and stellar atmospheres. Subspecialties: Solar physics; Solar, stellar astrophysics. Home: 17 Lakeside Dr Greenbelt MD 20770 Office: Goddard Space Flight Center Greenbelt MD 20771

JORDAN, THERESA JOAN, psychologist, educator; b. Irvington, N.J., Sept. 17, 1949; d. Ernest Anthony and Helen Joan (Debski) Balazs; m. Edward Todd Jordan, Sept. 12, 1970. B.A., Washington Square Coll., 1971; M.A., NYU, 1972, Ph.D., 1979. Diplomate: Lic. psychologist, N.Y. Adj. asst. prof. ednl. psychology NYU, 1975—, assoc. dir. research Inst. Devel. Studies, 1979-82; asst. prof. medicine N.J. Med. Sch., Newark, 1982—; cons. Bd. Edn., N.Y.C., 1979; mem. adv. bd. evaluation sect. N.Y. State Dept. Social Services, Albany, 1979-81. N.J. State scholar, 1967-71; NYU scholar, 1969-71; Nat. Inst. Occupational Safety and Health fellow, 1971-72, 74; Inst. Rational-Emotive Therapy fellow, 1983—. Mem. Am. Psychol. Assn., Eastern Ednl. Research Assn. (chmn. self concept spl. interest group 1979—, dir. spl. interest groups 1983—), N.Y. Acad. Scis. (adv. bd. psychology sect. 1981—), Phi Delta Kappa. Current Work: Effects of early childhood intervention programs on life-span development; role of instrumental enrichment (including computer-assisted instruction) on the growth of competence; cognitive model of self-concept development and change; losses to self-esteem incurred in medical illness. Subspecialties: Developmental psychology; Cognition. Home: 2 Washington Sq Village Apt 16-J New York NY 10012 Office: Office Primary Health Care Edn NJ Med Sch Univ Medicine and Dentistry NJ 100 Bergen St Newark NJ 07103

JORDAN, V. CRAIG, endocrine pharmacologist, educator; b. New Braunfels, Tex., July 25, 1947; s. Geoffrey Webster and Sybil Cynthia (Mottram) J.; m. Marion Yvonne Williams, July 29, 1969; children: Helen Melissa Yvonne, Alexandra Katherine Louise. B.Sc. with honors, U. Leeds, Eng., 1969, Ph.D. in Pharmacology, 1972, D.Sc. in Pharmacology, 1985. Research assoc. Worcester Found. for Exptl. Biology, Shrewsbury, Mass., 1972-73, vis. scientist, 1973-74; lectr. pharmacology U. Leeds, 1973-79; head endocrinology unit Ludwig Inst. for Cancer Research, U. Berne, Switzerland, 1979-80; asst. prof. human oncology and pharmacology U. Wis., Madison, 1978-81, assoc. prof., 1981-85, prof., 1985—, also leader pharmacology group dept. human oncology. Contbr. numerous articles to profl. jours. Served to capt. Intelligence Corps Brit. Army, 1971-76; Served to capt. Spl. Air Service, 1976-78. Med. Research Council scholar, 1969-72; co-recipient Boston Obstet. Soc. prize, 1974; UICC Internat. Cancer Research Tech. Transfer grantee, 1981; Romnes faculty fellow, 1984. Fellow Am. Inst. Chemists; mem. Am. Assn. for Cancer Research, Am. Soc. for Pharmacology and Exptl. Therapeutics, Endocrine Soc., Biochem. Soc., Brit. Pharm. Soc., Soc. for Endocrinology, Royal Soc. for Chemistry. Conservative. Mem. Ch. of England. Current Work: Mechanism of action of antiestrogens as anticancer agents. Antiestrogen structure-activity relationships, molecular pharmacology of antiestrogens, metabolism of antiestrogens in animals and man. Subspecialties: Cancer research (medicine); Endocrinology. Office: 600 Highland Ave Madison WI 53792

JORDAN, WILLIAM STONE, JR., physician, research administrator; b. Fayetteville, N.C., Sept. 28, 1917; s. William Stone and Louise Manning (Huske) J.; m. Marion Elizabeth Anderson, May 17, 1947; children—William S. III, Marion A. A.B., U. N.C., 1938; M.D., Harvard U., 1942. Diplomate Nat. Bd. Med. Examiners. Intern City Hosp., Boston, 1942-43, resident in medicine, 1946-47; from fellow to assoc. prof. Western Res. U., Cleve., 1947-58; prof., chmn. dept. preventive medicine U. Va., Charlottesville, 1958-67; dean coll. medicine U. Ky., Lexington, 1967-74; program dir. NIAID/NIH, Bethesda, Md., 1976—; cons. Dept. Army; chmn. panel respiratory and related viruses NIH, 1960-64; vis. scholar Centre Extension Tng. Community Medicine, London Sch. Hygiene and Tropical Medicine, 1974-75. Author: (with Dingle and Badger) Illness in the Home, 1964, Community Medicine in United Kingdom, 1978. Served to lt. USN, 1943-46. Recipient Outstanding Civilian Service medal Dept. Army, 1973; Bronze Laurel Leaf Cluster medal, 1981; Thomas Francis Jr. Lecture award U. Mich., 1984. Mem. Am. Acad. Microbiology, AAAS, Am. Assn. Immunologists, Am. Epidemiol. Soc. (pres. 1972-73), Am. Fedn. Clin. Research, AMA, Am. Pub. Health Assn., Am. Soc. Clin. Investigation, Am. Soc. Microbiology, Am. Soc. Tropical Medicine and Hygiene, Am. Thoracic Soc., Assn. Am. Physicians, Assn. Study Med. Edn., Assn. Tchrs. Preventive Medicine (sec. 1965-67), Central Soc. Clin. Research (sec./treas. 1956-57), Fayette County Med. Soc., Infectious Diseases Soc. Am., Internat. Epidemiol. Assn., Ky. Med. Assn., Ky. Thoracic Soc., Royal Soc. Medicine, Soc. Exptl. Biology and Medicine, Soc. Med. Cons. Armed Forces (pres. 1983). So. Soc. Clin. Research, Sigma Xi, Alpha Epsilon Delta, Alpha Tau Omega, Phi Beta Kappa, Alpha Omega Alpha. Democrat. Subspecialties: Preventive medicine; Epidemiology. Office: NIH Bldg 31 Room 7A52 Bethesda MD 20205

JORGENSEN, PALLE ERIK TIKOB, mathematics educator, researcher; b. Copenhagen, Denmark, Oct. 8, 1947; came to U.S. 1973, naturalized, 1979; s. Soren A.W. and Gyrit D. (Baden) J.; m. Soon-Min Park, Jan. 4, 1975; children—Anton Y., Greta S., Tina S. A.B., U. Aarhus, Denmark, 1968, M.S., 1970, Ph.D., 1973. Postdoctoral research fellow U. Wash., Seattle, 1973-74; postdoctoral research fellow U. Pa., Phila., 1974-77, vis. assoc. prof., 1982-84; asst. prof. Stanford U., Calif., 1977-79; assoc. prof. U. Aarhus, 1979-83; prof. U. Iowa, Iowa City, 1983—. Author: Operator Commutation Relations, 1984. Editor: Positive Semigroups of Operators, 1984; jour. Acta Applicandae Mathematicae, 1983—. Contbr. articles to profl. jours. NSF grantee; Danish Research Council grantee, 1976-77. Mem. Am. Math. Soc., Danish Math. Soc.,

Soc. Indsl. and Applied Math., Math. Assn. Am., Danish Acad. Sci. Current work: Operator algebras, non-commutative dynamical systems, unbounded operators in Hilbert space, C* -algebras, mathematical physics. Subspecialties: Analysis; Applied mathematics. Home: 708 W Park Rd Iowa City IA 52240 Office: Dept Math MLH U Iowa Iowa City IA 52242

JORSTAD, THOMAS FLOYD, geoarchaeologist, consultant; b. Chgo., May 18, 1952; s. Floyd Stan and Wanda Sophie (Szatowski) J.; B.S., No. Ill. U., 1975, B.A., 1975, M.S., U. Pitts., 1984. Advt. photographer, Chgo., Houston, Pitts., 1975—; geol. engr. NL Baroid Petroleum Services, Houston, 1976-80; geol. cons. Gulf Research & Devel. Co., Hamarville, Pa., 1981-83; archeol. geologist and photographer U. Pitts., 1980-85, cons. cultural resource mgmt. program, 1981-85. Contbr. articles to mags. and profl. jours. Mem. Geol. Soc. Am., Soc. Archeol. Scis., Archeol. Inst. Am., Am. Anthrop. Assn., AIME (jr.). Current work: Geological interpretation of sites and raw materials using sedimentological, petrographic and geochemical analyses; site geomorphology and soil processes; photographic documentation of sites and artifacts. Subspecialty: Sedimentology. Home: 5N405 Nonsu Ln Saint Charles IL 60174

JORY, VIRGINIA VICKERY, mathematician, research scientist; b. Union City, Ga., Jan. 4, 1934; d. Earl Lee and Mildred (Nolan) Cimerro Vickery; m. Philip Douglas Jory, July 11, 1953; children: Victoria Jory Dennard, Philip Douglas. B.S., Ga. Inst. Tech., 1971, M.S., 1974, Ph.D., 1979. Engring. technician Northwestern U. Aerial Measurements Lab., Patuxent River, Md., 1954-55; programmer Lockheed, Marietta, Ga., 1956-58; grad. teaching asst., instr. Ga. Inst. Tech., Atlanta, 1971-80, research scientist, 1980—; dir. Jory Concrete, Atlanta, 1970—. Named Outstanding Woman Grad. Am. Soc. Women Engrs., 1971; recipient Outstanding Math. Grad. Book award Pi Mu Epsilon, 1971. Mem. IEEE, Am. Math. Soc., Soc. Indsl. and Applied Math., Math. Assn. Am., Sigma Xi. Current Work: Antenna design and analysis, inverse problems in electromagnetic theory, regularization of ill-posed problems. Subspecialties: Applied mathematics; Remote sensing (atmospheric science). Office: Ga Inst Tech Engring Expt Sta Atlanta GA 30332

JOSHI, CHANDRASHEKHAR JANARDAN, physicist, educator; b. Wai, Maharashtra State, India, July 22, 1953; s. Janardan Digambar and Ramabai Janardan (Kirpekar) J.; m. Asha Bhatt, Jan. 18, 1982. B.S., London U., 1974; Ph.D., Hull U., England, 1977. Research assoc. NRC, Ottawa, Can., 1979-80; research engr. UCLA, 1980-83, adj. assoc. prof., 1983—; cons. Lawrence Livermore Nat. Lab., Livermore, Calif., 1984—. Contbr. articles on laser fusion, collective accelerators, to profl. jours. Recipient Queen Mary prize Inst. of Nuclear Engring., 1974; NRCC Research assoc. NRC, Can., 1979-80. Mem. IEEE, Am. Phys. Soc. Current work: Laser physics, laser-plasma interaction, accelerator physics. Subspecialty: Electrical engineering. Office: UCLA 7620-L Boelter Hall Elec Engring Dept Los Angeles CA 90024

JOSHI, JAI H.,, oncologist, hematologist, educator; b. Tavoy, Burma, June 8, 1947; s. Bhavani S. and Ratna J.; m. Paramjit K. Toor, Mar. 31, 1974; children: Amit, Arif. M.D., Christian Med. Coll., Ludhiana, India, 1971. Postdoctoral fellow in hematology and oncology U. Colo. Med. Ctr., Denver, 1976-78; postdoctoral fellow in oncology Nat. Cancer Inst., NIH, Balt. Cancer Research Ctr., 1980-81; asst. prof. medicine and oncology sect. infectious diseases and microbiology U. Md. Sch. Medicine and Cancer Ctr., Balt., 1982-85; asst. prof. medicine sect. infectious diseases U. Tex. System Cancer Ctr.-M.D. Anderson Hosp. and Tumor Inst., Houston, 1985—. Author numerous book chpts., articles and research papers. Nat. Cancer Inst.-NIH. grantee. Mem. Am. Soc. Clin. Oncology, Am. Soc. Microbiology, Am. Fedn. Clin. Research, Internat. Assn. Germ-Free Research, AAAS, Internat. Platform Assn., N.Y. Acad. Scis., Assn. Gnotobiotics. Current Work: Research in various areas of epedimiology diagnosis, prevention and treatment of infections in cancer patients. Subspecialties: Oncology; Infectious diseases. Home: 2123 Fountain Hill Dr Timonium MD 21093 Office: Sect Infectious Diseases U Tex System Cancer Ctr-MD Anderson Hosp and Tumor Inst Tex Med Ctr 6723 Bertner Ave Houston TX 77030

JOSHI, MADAN MOHAN, microbiologist; b. Almora, India, July 13, 1947; came to U.S., 1969, naturalized, 1978; s. Krishna Kant and Durga Devi (Pandey) J.; m. Lynne Diane, Aug. 9, 1974; children: Kamini Lynne. B.Sc., Agra U., 1964; M.Sc., Banaras Hindu U., 1966; M.S., Auburn U., 1972; Ph.D., La. State U., 1974. NSF research asso. La. State U., Baton Rouge, 1974-75; microbiologist, plant pathologist Kalo Labs., Inc., Quincy, Ill., 1975-76, mgr. product devel. and biol. research, 1976-79, tech. dir., 1979-80; sr. research biologist DuPont Exptl. Sta., Wilmington, Del., 1980-82, group leader plant disease control, 1982-84; research supr. plant disease control group, E.I. Du Pont de Nemours & Co., Newark, Del., 1984—. Contbr. articles in field to profl. jours. Mem. Am. Phytopath. Soc., Sigma Xi, Gamma Sigma Delta. Current Work: Researcher in development of fungicides to control plant diseases; pesticide biodegradation. Subspecialties: Plant pathology; Microbiology. Home: 204 Jackson Blvd Wilmington DE 19803 Office: Agrl Products Dept Bldg 200 Stine-Haskell Lab EI DuPont de Nemours & Co Newark DE 19711

JOVANOVIC, DRASKO D., physicist. Head physics sect. Fermi Nat. Accelerator Lab., Batavia, Ill. . Office: Fermi Nat Accelerator Lab PO Box 500 Batavia IL 60510

JOY, RICHARD CARLETON, semiconductor company executive; b. Barnstable, Mass., Mar. 30, 1938; s. Robert Edmund and Edith Francis (Small) J.; m. Connie Josephine Petak, Aug. 27, 1983; children by previous marriage—Richard Alan, Michael Scott, Kenneth Christian. A.E.E., Worcester Jr. Coll., 1958; B.S. in Elec. Engring., U. Colo., 1964; M.S. in Elec. Engring., Stanford U., 1965, Ph.D., 1968. Tech. aide Bell Telephone Labs., Murray Hill, N.J., 1958-61, mem. tech. staff, 1964-65; research asst. Stanford U., 1965-68; sr. engring. mgr. IBM, Hopewell Junction, N.Y., 1968-82; v.p. research and devel. Gould AMI Semicondrs., Santa Clara, Calif., 1982—; com. mem. Internat. Solid State Circuits Conf., 1976-82. Contbr. articles to profl. jours. Patentee in field. Com. chmn. Cub Scouts Am., Dutchess County, 1970-75, Boy Scout troop, Dutchess County, 1975-78; soccer coach East Fishkill Soccer League, 1978-79; pres. John Jay High Sch. Hockey Team, 1978-82. Mem. IEEE (sr. mem.), Gould Electronics Soc. (pres. 1983-84). Republican. Current work: Responsible for development of advanced semiconductor technology, device modeling and characterization, advanced product design, advanced packaging techniques, wafer pilot production, and mask production and engineering. Subspecialties: Microchip technology (engineering); Integrated circuits. Office: Gould AMI Semiconductors 3800 Homestead Rd Santa Clara CA 95051

JOY, ROBERT MCKERNON, educator, research scientist; b. Troy, N.Y., May 9, 1941; s. Edward M. and Rita Hannah (Sedgwick) J. Ph.D., Stanford U., 1970. Diplomate Am. Bd. Toxicology. Asst. U. Calif.-Davis, prof., 1970-77, assoc. prof., 1977-84, prof., 1984—, co-dir. health scis. neurotoxicology unit, 1981—; vis. assoc. prof. Harvard U. Med. Sch., 1977-78; vis. research assoc. Children's Hosp., Boston, 1977-78; vis. prof. pharmacology Northwestern U. Sch. Med., 1985. Assoc. editor Neurotoxicology, 1984—; mem. rev. bd. Neurobehavioral Toxicology and Teratology, 1982—. Mem. Am. Soc. Pharmacology and Exptl. Therapeutics, Soc. Toxicology, Soc. Neuroscis., AAAS, Western Pharmacology Soc. Current Work: Neurotoxicology, insecticides, neuropharmacology, kindled seizures, epilepsy. Subspecialties: Neuropharmacology; Toxicology (medicine). Home: 3104 N El Macero Dr El Macero CA 95618 Office: Sch Vet Medicine U Calif Davis CA 95616

JUDD, BRIAN RAYMOND, educator, physicist; b. Chelmsford, Eng., Feb. 13, 1931; s. Harry and Edith (Saltmarsh) J. B.A., Brasenose Coll., Oxford U., 1952, M.A., 1955, D.Phil., 1955. Fellow Magdalen Coll., Oxford U., 1955-62; instr. U. Chgo., 1957-58; asso. prof. U. Paris, 1962-64; staff mem. Lawrence Radiation Lab., Berkeley, Cal., 1964-66; prof. physics Johns Hopkins, Balt., 1966—, chmn. dept., 1979-84; Vis. Erskine fellow U. Canterbury, Christchurch, New Zealand, 1968; vis. fellow Australian Nat. U., Canberra, 1975. Author: Operator Techniques in Atomic Spectroscopy, 1963, Second Quantization and Atomic Spectroscopy, 1967, (with J.P. Elliott) Topics in Atomic and Nuclear Theory, 1970, Angular Momentum Theory For Diatomic Molecules, 1975. Hon. fellow Brasenose Coll., Oxford, 1983—. Fellow Am. Phys. Soc. Subspecialties: Atomic and molecular physics; Theoretical physics. Office: Physics and Astronomy Dept Johns Hopkins Baltimore MD 21218

JUDSON, SHELDON, geology educator; b. Utica, N.Y., Oct. 18, 1918; s. Salmon Sheldon and Dorothy (Eurich) J.; m. Anne Perrin Galpin, Feb. 13, 1943; children: Stephanie Dean, Anne Perrin, Lucy Sheldon. A.B., Princeton U., 1940; M.A., Harvard U., 1946, Ph.D., 1948. Faculty U. Wis., 1948-55, asso. prof. geology, 1955-64, Knox Taylor prof. geology, Princeton U., 1964—, chmn. dept., 1970-82; dir. Princeton Coop. Sch. Program, 1964-66; pres. Princeton Jr. Mus., 1964-67; trustee Daily Princetonian; chmn. Univ. Research Bd., Princeton U., 1972-77. Author articles in field; asso. editor: Am. Scientist, 1956-69. Served to lt. USNR, 1942-46. Faculty fellow Fund Advancement Edn., 1954-55; Guggenheim fellow, 1960-61, 66-67; Fulbright fellow, 1960-61. Fellow AAAS, Geol. Soc. Am.; mem. Arctic Inst., Sigma Xi. Clubs: Nassau (Princeton); Princeton of N.Y. Current Work: Geology of Pleistocene and Holocene with special reference to human activity. Subspecialties: Geology; Geomorphology. Home: 18 Aiken Ave Princeton NJ 08540

JULESZ, BELA, physiological psychologist, engineer; b. Budapest, Hungary, Feb. 19, 1928; came to U.S., 1956; s. Jeno and Klementin (Fleiner) J.; m. Margit Fasy, Aug. 7, 1953. Diploma in Elec. Engring., Tech. U., Budapest, 1950; D.Engring., Hungarian Acad. Sci., 1956. Asst. prof. dept. communications Tech. U. Budapest, 1950-51; mem. tech. staff Telecommunication Research Inst., Budapest, 1951-56; mem. tech. staff Bell Labs., Murray Hill, N.J., 1956-64, head sensory and perceptual processes, 1964-83; head visual perception research AT&T Bell Labs., Murray Hill, 1984—; vis. prof. dept. biology Calif. Inst. Tech., 1985—. Author: Foundations of Cyclopean Perception, 1971. Contbr. numerous articles to profl. jours. Discoverer computer generated random-dot stereogram technique. Recipient Dr. H.P. Heineken prize Royal Netherlands Acad. Scis., 1985; MacArthur Found. fellow, 1983—. Fellow Am. Acad. Arts & Scis., Optical Soc. Am. (chmn. vision 1981-82), AAAS; mem. Goettingen Acad. Sci. (corr.), Hungarian Acad. Scis. (hon.) Subspecialty: Physiological psychology. Office: AT&T Bell Labs Murray Hill NJ 07974

JURAND, ARTHUR, cell and developmental biology educator; b. Cracow, Poland, Mar. 30, 1914; came to Great Britain, 1957; s. Mark Wolf and Emily (Kaufler) Bieberstein; m. Jadwiga Reiner, Jan. 15, 1946; 1 child, Maria Kazimiera. B.Sc., Jagiellonian U., Poland, 1937, M.Sc., 1946, Ph.D., 1949; Sc.D., U. Edinburgh, Scotland, 1969; Asst. prof., docent biology Jagiellonian U., Cracow, Poland, 1944-57; sr. lectr. U. Edinburgh, 1957—; vis. scholar Ind. U., Bloomington, 1969-70, 74, 76, 78, 80, 82; vis. scholar Flinders' U., Adelaide, Australis, 1984-85. Author: The Anatomy of Paramecium Aurelia, 1969; Properties of Living Matter, 1954. Contbr. articles to profl. jours. Named hon. prof. Ind. U., 1982. Fellow Royal Soc. of Edinburgh. Current work: General, cell and developmental biology, teratology. Subspecialty: Cell biology. Office: Dept Genetics U Edinburgh W Mains Rd Edinburgh EH9 3JN Scotland

JUSTER, NORMAN JOEL, chemistry educator; b. N.Y.C., Feb. 19, 1924; s. Herman Edward and Shirley Claire (Schoenfeld) J.; m. Marian Rose Friedman, May 15, 1960; children—Jeannette, Deborah, Cindy, Robyn, Rebecca. A.A., UCLA, 1942, B.A., 1943, M.S., 1947, Ph.D., 1956. Asst. prof., assoc. chmn. John Muir Coll., Pasadena, Calif., 1947-55; sr. sci., head organic polymer lab. Motorola Semicondr. Products Inc., Phoenix, 1960-61; cons., 1961-69; vis. prof. U. Ky., Lexington, 1965-66; vis. prof. U. Hawaii, Honolulu, 1973-74, summer 1980; vis. prof. UCLA, 1963, summers 1957-84; prof. chemistry, chmn. phys. sci. depts. Pasadena City Coll., Calif., 1956-84; vis. prof. chemistry and biochemistry UCLA, 1984—; cons. Wiancko Engring., Pasadena, Calif., 1950—, Xerox Corp., Pasadena, 1960—. Author: New Concepts in Organic Chemistry, 1959. Contbr. articles to profl. jours. Patentee materials and processes. Bd. dirs. Am. Youth Hostels Assn., Los Angeles, 1968-70; cons. Honolulu Dept. Transp., 1973-74. Served to comdr. USNR, 1943-46, ETO, PTO. Recipient Catalysts of Profession award Mfg. Chemists Assn., 1974, J. Ray Risser award J. Ray Risser Found., 1978. Fellow N.Y. Acad. Scis.; mem. Am. Chem. Soc. (bd. dirs., exec. com., 1982—), Am. Assn. Cons. Chemists (pres. 1972-74 Sprenger medal and award 1976), Assn. Calif. Coll. Cons. and Adminstrs., AAAS, Ret. Officers Assn., Phi Beta Kappa, Sigma Xi, Alpha Chi Sigma, Phi Delta Kappa. Current work: Mechanisms of semiconduction in ordered and amorphous organic solids; cancer chemotherapy using certain organic semiconductors. Subspecialties: Organic chemistry; Solid state chemistry. Home: 513 N Rexford Dr Beverly Hills CA 90210 Office: Dept Chemistry and Biochemistry UCLA Los Angeles CA 90024

JUSTESEN, DON ROBERT, biomedical investigator, experimental psychology educator; b. Salt Lake City, Mar. 8, 1930; s. Richard Carvel and Elizabeth Agnes (Gustafson) J.; m. Patricia Ann Larson, Feb. 14, 1958; children: Lyle Richard, Jonille Jacelin, Tracy Ann, Anthony Raymond. B.A. in Psychology and Philosophy, U. Utah, 1955, M.A. in Psychology and Philosophy, 1957, Ph.D. in Psychology and Philosophy with distinction, 1960. Field service engr. Rocky Mountain Region Zenith Radio Corp., 1955-56; asst. prof. psychology, chmn. dept. psychology Westminster Coll., 1959-62; dir. Behavioral Radiology Labs., VA Med. Center, Kansas City, Mo., 1962—; asst. prof. psychiatry U. Kans.-Kansas City, 1963-66, assoc. prof., 1966-71, prof., 1971—; lectr. U. Mo.-Kansas City, 1963-66, assoc. prof., 1966-68, prof. psychology, 1968-75; vis. prof. psychology U. Colo., 1965; mem. commn. on metrology Internat. Union Radio Sci., Washington, 1976—; mem. subcom. Am. Nat. Standards Inst., 1976; mem. sci. com. 53 Nat. Council on Radiation Protection and Measurements, Washington, 1977—; keynote speaker for U.S. and Nat. Acad. Scis.'del. to XIXth Gen. Assembly of Internat. Union Radio Sci., Helsinki, Finland, 1978; career research scientist VA, 1980. Contbr. numerous articles, revs., abstracts to profl. publs.; co-editor or editor (biology): Special Supplements on Biological Effects of Electromagnetic Waves, Radio Science, 1977—; assoc. editor: Jour. Microwave Power, 1975—; editorial bd.: Bioelectromagnetics, 1979-83. Served to petty officer 1st class USN, 1948-52, Atlantic. Named Prof. of Yr. Students and Faculty of Westminster Coll., 1962; USPHS predoctoral research fellow, 1958; FDA grantee, 1973-80; Nat. Inst. Environ. Health Sci. grantee, 1980-85. Fellow Am. Psychol. Assn. (First Cash prize 1968), AAAS; mem. IEEE (sr.; chmn. com. on man and radiation 1979-80, mem. exec. com. 1980-83), Bioelectromagnetics Soc. (pres. 1984-85), Sigma Xi, Psi Chi. Introduced dosimetry to biol. study microwaves, 1969; research on dose-determinate conditioning of animals in microwave field, 1970; demonstration of body temperature as an evoked response to discrete stimulation, 1974; inventor behavioral experimentation involving microwaves, 1970. Current Work: Behavioral, developmental and physiological response to radio-frequency electromagnetic fields, principally microwaves and low-frequency magnetic fields. Subspecialties: Physiological psychology; Biophysics (biology). Home: 12416 Ewing Circle Grandview MO 64030 Office: Behavioral Radiology Labs VA Med Center 4801 Linwood Blvd Kansas City MO 64128

JUVET, RICHARD SPALDING, JR., scientist, chemistry educator; b. Los Angeles, Aug. 8, 1930; s. Richard Spalding and Marion Elizabeth (Dalton) J.; m. Martha Joy Myers, Jan. 29, 1955 (div. Nov. 1978); children: Victoria, David, Stephen, Richard P.; m. Evelyn Raeburn Elthon, July 1, 1984. B.S., UCLA, 1952, Ph.D., 1955. Research chemist Dupont, 1955; instr. U. Ill., 1955-57, asst. prof., 1957-61, asso. prof., 1961-70; prof. analytical chemistry Ariz. State U., Tempe, 1970—; vis. prof. UCLA, 1960, U. Cambridge, Eng., 1964-65, Nat. Taiwan U., 1968, Ecole Polytechnique, France, 1976-77; Mem. air pollution chemistry and physics adv. com. EPA, HEW, 1969-72; cons. R.J. Reynolds Industries, 1966-72; mem. adv. panel on advanced chem. alarm tech., devel. and engring. directorate Def. Systems div. Edgewood Arsenal, 1975. Author: Gas-Liquid Chromatography, Theory and Practice, 1962, Russian edit., 1966. Editorial advisor to: Jour. Chromatographic Sci, 1969—, Jour. Gas Chromatography, 1963-68, Analytica Chimica Acta, 1972-74, Analytical Chemistry, 1974-77, biennial reviewer in, 1962-76. NSF sr. postdoctoral fellow, 1964-65; Sci. Exchange Agreement awardee Czechoslovakia, Hungary, Romania and Yugoslavia, 1977. Fellow Am. Inst. Chemists; mem. Am. Chem. Soc. (nat. chmn. div. analytical chemistry 1972-73, nat. sec.-treas. div. analytical chemistry 1969-71, councilor 1978—, chmn. U. Ill. sect. 1968-69, sec. 1962-63), AAAS, Internat. Platform Assn., Am. Radio Relay League, Sigma Xi, Phi Lambda Upsilon, Alpha Chi Sigma. Presbyn. (deacon 1960— , ruling elder 1972— , commr. Grand Canyon Presbytery 1974-76). Research on gas and liquid chromatography, instrumental analysis, computer interfacing. Current Work: Development of ultra-sensitive detectors and high-accuracy, flow mointors for liquid chromatography and improved liquid chromatography/-mass spectrometry interface; computer interfacing to chemical instrumentation; chromatographic peak deconvolution; polymer identification. Subspecialties: Analytical chemistry; Photochemistry. Home: 4821 E Calle Tuberia Phoenix AZ 85018 Office: Dept Chemistry Arizona State Univ Tempe AZ 85287

KABADI, UDAYA MANOHAR, physician, endocrinologist; b. Bombay, Maharashtra, India, Jan. 6, 1942; came to U.S., 1971; s. Manohar Bapu and Suniti Manohar (Sumati) K.; m. Mary Udaya Cheruvillil, Aug. 9, 1970; children: Sajit, Rajit. M.B.B.S., Seth G.S. Med. Coll., U. Bombay, India, 1965, M.D., 1970. Diplomate: Am. Bd. Internal Medicine. Intern Jewish Meml. Hosp., N.Y.C., 1971, resident, 1971-72, Beth Israel Med. Center, N.Y.C., 1972-73; asst. physician dept. medicine, 1975-76; fellow VA Med. Center, Bronx, N.Y., 1973-74; attending physician dept. medicine Gouverneur Hosp., N.Y.C., 1975-78, chief walk-in clinic, 1976-78; staff physician VA Med. Ctr., Bklyn., 1978-80; asst. prof. medicine SUNY Downstate Med. Ctr., Bklyn., 1978-80; chief endocrinology sect. VA Med. Ctr., Des Moines, 1980—, research and devel. coordinator, 1981—; cons. endocrinology Broadlawns Med. Center, Des Moines, 1982—, Luth. Hosp. and Med. Ctr., Des Moines, 1983—; clin. asst. prof. medicine U. Iowa Sch. Medicine, Iowa City, 1981-84, clin. assoc. prof., 1985—; mem. adv. bd. Central Iowa Diabetes Edn. Center, Des Moines, 1981—. Recipient Research Grants VA Research Service, 1981—, Research Grants Am. Legion, 1981-82. Fellow Royal Coll. Physicians, ACP; mem. Endocrine Soc., Am. Fedn. Clin. Research, Am. Diabetes Assn., European Assn. Study Diabetes, Am. Assn. Lab. Animal Sci., AAAS. Current Work: Thyroid physiology and disease, carbohydrate metabolism, physiology of glucose metabolism, physiology of insulin and glucagon secretion. Subspecialties: Endocrinology; Internal medicine. Office: VA Med Center 30th and Euclid Sts Des Moines IA 50310

KABAT, ELVIN ABRAHAM, immunochemist, biochemist, educator; b. N.Y.C., Sept. 1, 1914; s. Harris and Doreen (Otis) K.; m. Sally Lennick, Nov. 28, 1942; children: Jonathan, Geoffrey, David. B.S., CCNY, 1932, M.A., Columbia U., 1934, Ph.D., 1937; LL.D. (hon.), U. Glasgow, 1976; Doctoral degree (hon.), U. Orleans (France); Ph.D. (hon.), Weizmann Inst. Sci., Rehovot, Israel. Lab. asst. immunochemistry Presbyn. Hosp., 1933-37; Rockefeller Found. fellow Inst. Phys. Chem., Upsala, Sweden, 1937-38; instr. pathology Cornell U., 1938-41; mem. faculty Columbia U., N.Y.C., 1941—, asst. prof. bacteriology, 1946-48, assoc. prof., 1948-52, prof. microbiology, 1952-85, prof. human genetics and devel., 1969-85, Higgins prof. Microbiology, 1984-85, emeritus, 1985—; mem. adv. panel on immunology WHO, 1965—; expert cons. Nat. Cancer Inst., 1975-82, Nat. Inst. Allergy and Infectious Disease, 1983—; Alexander S. Wiener lectr. N.Y. Blood Center, 1979. Author: (with M.M. Mayer) Experimental Immunochemistry, 1948, 2d edition, 1961, Blood Group Substances, Their Chemistry and Immunochemistry, 1956, Structural Concepts in Immunology and Immunochemistry, 1968, 2d edit., 1976, (with T.T. Wu and H. Bilofsky) Variable Regions of Immunoglobulin Chains, 1976, Sequences of Immunoglobulin Chains, (with others) Sequences of Proteins of Immunological Interest, 1983; Mem. editorial bd.: Jour. Immunology, 1961-76, Transplantation Bull, 1957-60. Recipient numerous awards including; Ann. Research award City of Hope, 1974; award Center for Immunology, State U. N.Y., Buffalo, 1976; Louisa Gross Horwitz award Columbia U., 1977; R.E. Dyer lectr. award NIH, 1979; Townsend Harris medal CCNY, 1980; Recipient Philip Levine award Am. Soc. Clin. Pathology, 1982, award for excellence Grad. Faculties Alumni Columbia U., 1982; Fogarty scholar NIH, 1974-75. Fellow AAAS, Am. Acad. Allergy (hon.); mem. Nat. Acad. Scis., Am. Acad. Arts and Scis., Am. Assn. Immunologists (past pres.), Am. Soc. Biol. Chemists, Am. Chem. Soc., Harvey Soc. (pres. 1976-77), Am. Soc. Microbiology, Internat. Assn. Allergists, Societe Franciaise d'Allergie (hon.), Biochem. Soc. (Eng.), Assn. for Research in Nervous and Mental Diseases, AAUP, Assn. de Microbiologists de Langue Francaise, Société de Biologie, Société de Immunologie (hon.), Phi Beta Kappa, Sigma Xi. Current Work: Size and structure of antibody and lectin combining sites, blood group substances, dextrans, monoclonal antibodies, myeloma and hybridoma antibodies. Subspecialty: Immunology (medicine). Home: 70 Haven Ave New York NY 10032 Office: Dept Microbiology Coll Physicians and Surgeons Columbia U 701 W 168th St New York NY 10032

KABELL, JACK, electronics consultant; b. Evanston, Wyo., Jan. 29, 1924; s. Louis and Ernestine Katherine (Faus) K.; m. Kathryn May Hutton, Apr. 22, 1944 (div. 1969); m. Ruth Klein, Mar. 1, 1970. B.S. in Elec. Engring. with honors, U. Colo., 1944. Sr. research engr. Stanford Research Inst., Menlo Park, Calif., 1953-60; mgr. device devel. Fairchild Semicondr., Palo Alto, Calif., 1960-68, dir. research and devel., 1968-70; dir. research and devel. Harris Semicondr., Melbourne, Fla., 1971-74; electronics cons., San Diego, 1974—. Patentee electronics systems and semicondr. components, 1948-74. Contbr. articles to profl. jours. Vice pres. Bernardo Homeowners Corp., San Diego, 1982-83. Served to lt. USNR, 1942-53. Mem. IEEE (life), Sigma Xi, Tau Beta Pi, Eta Kappa Nu. Current work: Consulting in solid state process technology and technology management. Subspecialties: Electronics; Microelectronics. Home and office: 12552 Utopia Way San Diego CA 92128

KABLER, MILTON NORRIS, research administrator, physicist; b. Roanoke, Va., Apr. 30, 1932; s. John Nelson and Alma Estelle (Norris) K.; m. Angelita Faye Suiter, June 29, 1957; children—Stephen L., Cynthia L. Student Roanoke Coll., 1950-52; B.S., Va. Poly. Inst., 1955; Ph.D., U. N.C., 1959. Research assoc. U. Ill., Urbana, 1959-62; physicist Naval Research Lab., Washington, 1962-69, br. head, 1969—; vis. scientist Oxford U., Eng., 1973-74. Contbr. articles to profl. jours. Treas. Wessynton Homes Assn., Mt. Vernon, Va., 1979, bd. dirs., 1980-82, pres., 1982. Recipient Pure Sci. award Sigma Xi/RESA Naval Research Lab., 1973. Fellow Am. Phys. Soc.; mem. Am. Optical Soc., AAAS, Sigma Xi. Current work: Research on optical properties of materials; materials research using synchrotron radiation; laser spectroscopy; research administration. Subspecialties: Condensed matter physics; Laser spectroscopy.

KABRA, POKAR MAL, clinical chemist; b. Kuchaman, Rajasthan, India, Nov. 17, 1942; came to U.S., 1967; s. Kirorimal and Ghisi (Ladha) K.; m. Usha Rani Kabra, May 16, 1966; children—Anurag, Vikas. B.Sc., U. Bombay, 1964, B.Sc.Tech., 1966; Ph.D., U. Kans., 1971. Faculty, U. Wis.-Madison, 1972-73; postdoctoral fellow U. Calif.-San Francisco, 1973-75, clin. chemist, 1975-77, asst. prof., 1977-81, assoc. prof. chemistry, 1981—; cons. Ctr. Disease Control, Atlanta, 1980-81, Bombay Hosp. Trust, India, 1983. Editor: Liquid Chromatography in Clinical Analysis, 1981; Clinical Liquid Chromatography Vol. I, II, 1984. Contbr. articles to profl. jours. U. Bombay Merit scholar, 1966. Mem. Am. Chem. Soc., Am. Assn. Clin. Chemistry, Calif. Assn. Toxicology. Current work: Clinical liquid chromatography, pharmacokinetics, therapeutic drug monitoring. Subspecialties: Clinical chemistry; Analytical chemistry. Office: U Calif M523 San Francisco CA 94143

KACHMAR, JOHN FREDERICK, clinical biochemist, educator, retired; b. Akron, Jan. 10, 1916; s. Michael and Katherine (Waytowich) K.; m. Jessie Kallman, Dec. 23, 1946; 1 dau., Carlajean Ginnis. B.S., U. Akron, 1936; M.S., U. Minn., 1947, Ph.D., 1951. Registered clin. chemist. Jr. chemist Victor Gasket Co., Chgo., 1936-37, USPHS, 1937-39; asst. chemist, 1939-42, 46; research asst. dept agrl. biochemistry U. Minn., 1947-51, research asst. dept. ob gyn, 1951-53; clin. chemist Einstein Med. Center So. div., Phila., 1953-58; clin. biochemist Rush Presbyn. St. Luke's Med. Center of Chgo., 1958—; assoc. prof. biochemistry Rush Presbyn. St. Luke's Med. Center Chgo., 1972-83, emeritus, 1983—; retired, also sr. attending biochemist; cons. in field. Contbg. author, assoc. editor: Fundamentals of Clinical Chemistry, 1970, 76. Served with U.S. Army, 1942-46. Mem. Nat. Acad. Clin. Biochemistry, Am. Chem. Soc., Am. Assn. Clin. Chemists (recipient Natelson award 1980). Current Work: Clinical enzymology, bilirubin chemistry. Subspecialties: Biochemistry (medicine); Clinical chemistry.

KACZMAREK, LEONARD KONRAD, neurobiologist; b. Edinburgh, Scotland, Aug. 2, 1947; s. Mieczyslaw and Irena (Garlinska) K.; m. Sheila Frances Hayman, Dec. 11, 1971; children: Zoe Tara, Konrad Eric. B.Sc., U. London, 1968; M.Sc., Imperial Coll., U. London, 1969; Ph.D., Charing Cross Hosp. Med. Sch., U. London, 1971. Research asst. dept. neurochemistry Inst. Neurology, U. London, 1971-72; asst. research anatomist Brain Research Inst., UCLA, 1972-74; European Sci. Exchange Program fellow U. Brussels, 1974-76; sr. research fellow div. biology Calif. Inst. Tech., Pasadena, 1976-81; asst. prof. pharmacology and physiology Yale U., New Haven, 1981-85, assoc. prof., 1985—. Contbr. articles to profl. jours. Spencer Found. fellow, 1976-79. Mem. Soc. Neurosci., Soc. Math. Biology, AAAS, N.Y. Acad. Scis. Current Work: Research into biochemical basis of long lasting changes that occur in the electrical properties of neurons; research using theoretical models in neurobiology. Subspecialties: Neurobiology; Neuropharmacology. Home: 139 Laurel Brook Dr Guilford CT 06437 Office: Department Pharmacology Yale University School Medicine 333 Cedar St New Haven CT 06510

KACZOROWSKI, GREGORY JOHN, biochemist, researcher; b. South Bend, Ind., Nov. 20, 1949; s. John Walter and Genevive (Bankowski) K.; m. Maria Luisa Garcia, June 21, 1982. B.S., U. Notre Dame, 1972; Ph.D., MIT, 1977. Postdoctoral fellow Roche Inst. Molecular Biology, Nutley, N.J., 1977-80; sr. research biochemist Merck Inst. for Therapeutic Research,

Rahway, N.J., 1980-84, research fellow, 1984—. Contbr. articles to profl. jours. Helen Hay Whitney Found. fellow, 1977-80. Mem. Am. Chem. Soc., Phi Beta Kappa. Roman Catholic. Current work: Mechanisms involved in regulation $Ca2+$ homeostasis in cardiac and neuroendocrine tissue; study of membrane receptors, channels and carriers. Subspecialties: Biochemistry (biology); Membrane biology. Home: 38 Westgate Dr Edison NJ 08820 Office: Merck Sharp & Dohme Research Labs PO Box 2000 Rahway NJ 07065

KACZYNSKI, VICTOR WALTER, environmental science executive, consultant; b. Niagara Falls, N.Y., Dec. 7, 1938; s. Walter Victor and Adolpha (Jacks) K.; m. Marianne Donnelly, June 27, 1964; children—Peter, Elizabeth, Greg. B.S., SUNY-Buffalo, 1964; M.S., Cornell U., 1967, Ph.D., 1970. Asst. prof. oceanography U. Wash., Seattle, 1969-72; environ. tech. dir. Tex. Instruments, Dallas, 1972-74; pres. Beak Cons., Inc., Portland, Oreg., 1974-77; dir. environ. scis. CH2M-Hill, Portland, 1977—; guest lectr. Oreg. State U., Corvallis, 1980-84; expert witness testimony related to effluent effects and land use practices for various indsl. cos., Ala., Wash., Oreg., Calif., N.Y., Washington, 1972—. Contbr. articles to profl. jours. Coach Little League Baseball, Beaverton, Oreg., 1982-83; trustee Portland Community Coll. Found.; mem. bicentennial adv. com. Oreg. State U. dept. fish and wildlife. Served with USAF, 1956-60, Japan. Mem. Am. Fisheries Soc. (cert. sec. treas. 1984—), Am. Soc. Limnology and Oceanography, Ecol. Soc. Am., N.Y. Acad. Sci., Sigma Xi, Kappa Delta Pi. Republican. Roman Catholic. Current work: Applied research on effects of treated effluent disposal on aquatic systems and wetlands, hazardous waste disposal, fish hatchery design, wetlands design. Subspecialties: Limnology; Hazardous waste disposal. Home: 12985 SW 135th Ave Tigard OR 97223 Office: CH2M-Hill 2020 SW 4th Ave Portland OR 97201

KADABA, PRASANNA VENKATARAMA, mechanical engineering educator; b. Gundlupet, Karnataka, India, July 4, 1931; came to U.S. 1954, naturalized 1972; s. Kadaba Venkatarama Iyengar and Kadaba Sharadamma; m. Usha Prasanna Kadaba, Nov. 14, 1966; 1 child, Vaibhav. B.S. in Mech. Engring., U. Mysore, Bangalore, India, 1952, B.E.E., 1954; M.S. in Mech. Engring., U. Ky., 1956; Ph.D. in Mech. Engring., Ill. Inst. Tech., 1964. Sr. research engr. Borg Warner Research and Devel. Corp., Des Plaines, Ill., 1963-67; sr. research scientist Westinghouse Research and Devel. Corp., Pitts., 1967-69; assoc. prof. Ga. Inst. Tech., Atlanta, 1969—; vis. prof. U. Carabobo, Valencia, Venezuela; guest worker Nat. Bur. Standards, Gaithersburg, Md., 1978; cons. Lawrence Berkeley Lab., Calif., 1979-80. Adv. Vols. for Internat. Tech. Assts., Arlington, Va., 1977—; active India Am. Cultural Assn., Atlanta, 1971—. Faculty fellow NASA, 1982, faculty research fellow NASA Lewis Research Ctr., 1984. Named Engr. of Yr. in Edn. Atlanta chpt. ASHRAE; recipient Outstanding Service award energy action com. Ga. Soc. Profl. Engrs., 1981. Mem. ASME, ASHRAE (faculty adv. 1977—), Am. Soc. Engring. Edn., Soc. Am. Mil. Engrs., Sigma Xi, Tau Beta Pi, Pi Tau Sigma. Hindu. Current work: Heat pumps, photovoltaic, heat exchangers, thermal systems. Subspecialties: Mechanical engineering; Solar energy. Home: 2756 Carolyn Dr SE Smyrna GA 30080 Office: Ga Inst Tech Sch Mech Engring Atlanta GA 30332

KADANOFF, LEO PHILIP, physicist; b. N.Y.C., Jan. 14, 1937; s. Abraham and Celia (Kibrick) K.; children: Marcia, Felice, Betsy. A.B., Harvard U., 1957, M.A., 1958, Ph.D., 1960. Fellow Neils Bohr Inst., Copenhagen, 1960-61; from asst. prof. to prof. physics U. Ill., Urbana, 1961-69; prof. physics and engring., univ. prof. Brown U., Providence, 1969-78; prof. physics U. Chgo., 1978-82, John D. MacArthur Disting. Service prof., 1982—; Mem. tech. com. R.I. Planning Program, 1972-78, mem. human services rev. com., 1977-78; pres. Urban Obs. R.I., 1972-78. Author: Electricity Magnetism and Heat, 1967; co-author: Quantum Statistical Mechanics, 1963; Adv. bd.: Sci. Year, 1975-79; editorial bd.: Statis. Physics, 1972-79, Nuclear Physics, 1980—, Annals of Physics, 1982—; contbr. articles to profl. jours. NSF fellow, 1957-61; Sloan Found. fellow, 1963-67; recipient Wolf Found. prize, 1980. Fellow Am. Phys. Soc. (Buckley prize 1977), Am. Acad. Arts and Scis.; mem. Nat. Acad. Scis. Current Work: Transitions to chaos, phase transitions, many body theory. Subspecialties: Theoretical physics; Condensed matter physics. Home: 5424 S Eastview Park Chicago IL 60615 Office: James Franck Inst U Chgo Chicago IL 60637

KADI, KAMAL SIF-EL, petroleum engineering consultant; b. Batna, Aures, Algeria, June 23, 1941; came to U.S., 1963; s. Said and Fatma (Agoune) K. B.S., Stanford U., 1966; M.S., U. Tulsa, 1974, Ph.D., 1977. Field supt. Sinclair Oil Co., Algiers, Algeria, 1966-69; asst. dir. project engring. Alcore Co., Dallas, 1969-72; simulation engr. Chevron Oil Co., Houston, 1977-79; sr staff specialist Schlumberger, Houston, 1979-81; sr. staff cons. Intercomp, resource devel. and engring., Houston, 1981-82; cons. KSK Enterprises, Houston, 1982—. Mem. Soc. Petroleum Engrs., Soc. Profl. Well Log Analysts, Soc. Indsl. and Applied Math. Current Work: Petroleum reservoir behavior prediction through use of reservoir simulation, including enhanced hydrocarbon recovery. Subspecialties: Numerical analysis (computer science); Petroleum engineering.

KADIN, ALAN MITCHELL, physicist; b. N.Y.C., Dec. 7, 1952. A.B. in Physics, Princeton U., 1974; A.M., Harvard U., 1975, Ph.D. in Physics, 1979. Grad. research asst. and teaching fellow dept. physics Harvard U., 1974-79; research assoc. dept. physics SUNY-Stony Brook, 1979-80, U. Minn., 1981-83; research physicist Energy Conversion Devices, Troy, Mich., 1983—. Contbr. articles to profl. jours. NSF fellow, 1974-77. Mem. Am. Phys. Soc., Am. Vacuum Soc., AAAS, Materials Research Soc. Current work: Superconductivity, including materials, effects of low dimensionality and layering, nonequilibrium effects and disorder. Subspecialties: Condensed matter physics; Low temperature physics. Office: Energy Conversion Devices 1675 W Maple Rd Troy MI 48084

KADISH, KARL MITCHELL, chemistry educator, consultant; b. Detroit, Feb. 4, 1945; m. Mary Ludo Frevel, 1968; children—Lesley, Laura. B.S., U. Mich., 1967; Ph.D., Pa. State U., 1970. Vis. asst. prof. U. New Orleans, 1970-71; researcher U. Paris, 1971-72; asst. prof. chemistry Calif. State U.-Fullerton, 1972-76; asst. prof. chemistry U. Houston, 1976-78, assoc. prof., 1978-81, prof., 1981—; vis. prof. U. Strasbourg, France, 1982, U. Lyon, France, 1984, U. Dijon, France, 1985; pres. Intersci. Cons., U.S.A., Midland, Mich. and Houston, 1978—. Editor: Electrochemical and Spectroelectrochemical Studies of Biological Redex Components, 1984. Contbr. articles to profl. jours. Mem. Am. Chem. Soc., Electrochem. Soc., Internat. Union of Pure and Applied Chemistry. Current work: Electrochemistry and spectroelectrochemistry of compounds of biological interest; porphyrin, coordination, spectroelectro and analytical chemistry. Subspecialty: Analytical chemistry. Office: Dept Chemistry U Houston Houston TX 77004

KADUK, JAMES ALBERT, research chemist; b. Cleve., June 21, 1952; s. Edward Eugene and Patricia Ann (Getts) K.; m. Catherine Ann Goodnetter, Aug. 27, 1978; children—Anne Elizabeth, Benjamin James. B.S., U. Notre Dame, 1973; M.S., Northwestern U., 1975, Ph.D., 1977. Staff research chemist Amoco Chems. Corp., Naperville, Ill., 1977-85, Amoco Corp., Naperville, 1985—. Contbr. articles to profl. jours. Patentee in field. Treas., Naperville Community Chorus, 1981-83, pres., 1983-84. Served as 1st lt. USAF, 1979. Mem. Am. Chem. Soc. (co-chmn. coll. edn. com. Chgo. sect. 1983—), Am. Crystallographic Assn., AAAS, Catalysis Soc., Phi Beta Kappa, Sigma Xi, Phi Lambda Upsilon. Republican. Roman Catholic. Current work: Catalysis, minerals, zeolites. Subspecialties: Crystallography; Inorganic chemistry. Home: 423 E Chicago Ave Naperville IL 60540 Office: Amoco Corp Box 400 Naperville OH 60566

KADUSHIN, PHINEAS, psychotherapist, researcher; b. N.Y.C., Oct. 18, 1925; s. Max and Evelyn (Garfiel) K. B.A., Columbia U., 1945; rabbi, M.H.L., Jewish Theol. Sem., 1950; M.S. in Psychology, Yeshiva U., 1961. Psychology intern N.J. Dept. Instns. and Agencies, Bordentown, 1960-61; sr. psychologist Mental Health Ctr., Perth Amboy, N.J., 1961-66; research assoc. Family Treatment and Study Unit dept. psychiatry N.Y. Med. Coll., 1966-70, psychotherapist in pvt. practice, N.Y.C., 1971—. Mem. Am. Psychol. Assn. (assoc.), Am. Group Psychotherapy Assn. (assoc.), Eastern Group Psychotherapy Assn. (assoc.), Rabbinical Assembly Am. Current Work: Dyadic group therapy, a method of improving the man-woman relationship by therapy in a group of two people previously unknown to each other. Subspecialty: Psychiatry.

KAESZ, HERBERT DAVID, chemist; b. Alexandria, Egypt, Jan. 4, 1933; naturalized U.S. citizen; m. 1958. B.A., NYU, 1954; M.A., Harvard U., 1956, Ph.D., 1959. Fellow inorganic chemistry and adviser program high sch. tchrs., Harvard U., 1958-60, from asst. prof. to assoc. prof., 1960-68; prof. inorganic chemistry UCLA, 1968—. Subspecialty: Organometallics. Office: Dept Chemistry ULCA Los Angeles CA 90024

KAFATOS, MINAS, physicist, consultant, educator; b. Irakleion, Crete, Greece, Mar. 25, 1945; came to U.S., 1963; s. Constantine and Helen (Xiroudakis) K.; m. Thalia Loukidou, Aug. 10, 1971; children—Lefteris, Stefanos, Alexios. B.A. in Physics, Cornell U., 1967; Ph.D. in Physics, MIT, 1972. Research assoc. NRC-Nat. Acad. Sci., NASA, Goddard Space Flight Ctr., Greenbelt, Md., 1973-75; asst. prof. dept. physics George Mason U., Fairfax, Va., 1975-79, assoc. prof., 1979-84, prof. dept. physics, 1984—. Author: Astronomy Laboratory Manual, 1984; Crab Nebula and Related Remnants, 1985; contbr. articles to profl. jours. NASA grantee, 1978-84. Mem. Am. Astron. Soc., Am. Phys. Soc., Internat. Astron. Union, Royal Astronom. Soc. Current work: Active galactic nuclei, black holes, symbiotic stars, star formation, ultraviolet rays, supernova remnants, stellar jets, quantum theory, atomic physics, X-rays. Subspecialties: High energy astrophysics; Theoretical astrophysics. Office: Dept Physics George Mason U Fairfax VA 22030

KAFKA, MARIAN ADELE STERN, research physiologist; b. Richmond, Va., Mar. 30, 1927; d. Henry S. and Adele (Lewit) Stern; m. John S. Kafka, Oct. 3, 1952; children: David Egon, Paul Henry, Alexander Charles. A.B., Conn. Coll., 1948; Ph.D., U. Chgo., 1952. Research asst. dept. physiol. chemistry Emory U., Atlanta, 1952-53; research ass. Ill. Neuropsychiat. Inst., U. Ill. Sch. Medicine, 1953-54; research asst. dept. internal medicine Yale U., 1954-57; USPHS fellow Nat. Heart, Lung and Blood Inst., 1965-68, physiologist, 1968-74; physiologist adult psychiatry br. NIMH, Bethesda, Md., 1974-82, physiologist clin. neurosci. br., 1982—. Contbr. chpts. to books and articles in field to profl. jours. Marie J. Mergler fellow U. Chgo., 1950. Mem. Am. Physiol. Soc., Endocrine Soc., Biophys. Soc., Soc. for Neurosci., AAAS, Phi Beta Kappa, Sigma Xi. Current Work: Neurotransmitter receptors; molecular interaction between neurotransmitters, receptors and cell membranes; central nervous system control of circadian rhythms. Subspecialties: Chronobiology; Neurobiology.

KAFRAWY, ADEL, polymer chemist; b. Cairo, Egypt, Oct. 15, 1943; s. Fouad Kamel and Boussaina Murad; m. Maria Lidia Rodriguez, Dec. 5, 1975; children—Laila Nelly, Eric Adel. B.S. in Chemistry, Cairo U., 1964; M.S. in Phys. Organic Chemistry, U. Rochester, 1971; Ph.D. in Organic Chemistry, U. Mo.-Columbia, 1974; M.B.A., Syracuse U., 1983. Research chemist ITT Rayonier, Inc., Whippany, N.J., 1977-81; sr. scientist Ethicon, Inc. div. Johnson & Johnson, Somerville, N.J., 1981—. Contbr. articles to sci. jours. Patentee in field. Mem. Am. Chem. Soc., N.Y. Acad. Scis., Sigma Xi, Phi Lambda Upsilon. Current work: The application of polymers in medicine. Subspecialties: Polymer chemistry; Drug delivery systems. Home: 20 Hickory Trail Flemington NJ 08822 Office: Ethicon Inc Route 22 Somerville NJ 08876

KAGAN, FRED, pharmaceutical company executive; b. Chgo., Dec. 24, 1920; s. Joseph F. and Doris Helen (Franklin) K.; m. Rhoda Gollay, Feb. 17, 1957; children—Laurie, Glenn, Richard, Carolyn, Cathy, James; m. Rochelle Busch, Oct. 21, 1945 (dec. July 1953). B.S., U. Ill., 1942; Ph.D., MIT, 1949. Chemist, Standard Oil Co. Ind., Whiting, 1949-53; with Upjohn Co., Kalamazoo, 1953—, group mgr. therapeutics, 1978-81, dir., v.p. pharm. research div., 1981—. Patentee in field. Co-editor Hypnotics, 1975. Contbr. articles to profl. jours. Trustee Kalamazoo Symphony Orch., 1982—. Mem. Am. Chem. Soc. (chmn. Kalamazoo sect. 1956), AAAS, Am. Coll. Neuropsychopharmacology (corp. mem.), Sigma Xi. Current work: Therapeutics; biotechnology; central nervous system diseases research. Subspecialties: Organic chemistry; Medicinal chemistry. Office: Upjohn Co 301 Henrietta St Kalamazoo MI 49001

KAGEY-SOBOTKA, ANNE, immunologist, researcher; b. Atlanta, June 11, 1940; d. Isaac Benjamin and Eugenia (Roberts) K.; m. John Robert Sobotka, July 18, 1964 (div. 1979). B.A., Vanderbilt U., 1962; Ph.D., John Hopkins U., 1977. Med. tech. Emory U., Atlanta, 1962-64; research assoc. Johns Hopkins Sch. Med., Balt., 1964-77, instr. medicine, 1977-78, asst. prof., 1979-85, assoc. prof., 1985—. Contbr. articles to profl. jours. Mem. New Democratic Club, Balt., 1970—; Charles Village Civic Assn., Balt., 1971—. Fellow Am. Acad. Allergy and Immunology, 1979—; mem. Am. Assn. Immunologists, Collegium Internationale Allergologicum. Methodist. Current work: Research in immediate hypersensity-insect allery, mediator release from human basophils/mast cells, arachidonic acid, leukotrienes. Subspecialties: Immunology (medicine); Allergy. Office: Johns Hopkins U Sch Med 5601 Loch Raven Blvd Baltimore MD 21239

KAHN, CAROLYN ROBIN, immunologist; b. Bklyn., Apr. 24, 1952; d. Nathaniel and Celia (Stashin) Kahn; m. Leslie James Krueger, June 29, 1971 (div. June 1976); m. James Anthony Wilkins, Mar. 6, 1982; children—Philip Nathaniel, Sarah Elizabeth. A.B., Johns Hopkins U., 1974, Ph.D., 1979. Postdoctoral fellow Johns Hopkins U., Balt. 1980-85. Contbr. articles to profl. jours. Mem. Democrats for Action, Mem. Sigma Xi. Jewish. Current work: Basic research involving regulation of autoimmune response through the establishment of anti idiotype network. Subspecialties: Immunobiology and immunology; Developmental biology. Office: Neuromuscular Div 600 N Wolfe St Meyer 5-140 Baltimore MD 21205

KAHN, ROBERT ELLIOT, federal government information processing executive; b. Bklyn., Dec. 23, 1938; s. Lawrence and Beatrice Pauline (Tashker) K.; m. Patrice Ann Lyons, Sept. 13, 1980. B.E.E., CCNY, 1960; M.A., Princeton U., 1962, Ph.D., 1964. Registered profl. engr., N.Y., N.J. Mem. tech. staff Bell Labs., N.Y.C. and Murray Hill, N.J., 1960-62; asst. prof. MIT, Cambridge, Mass., 1964-66; sr. scientist Bolt Beranek Newman, Cambridge, 1966-72; dir. info. processing research Def. Advanced Research Projects Agy., Arlington, Va., 1972—. Editor: Electronic Manuals, 1981. Contbr. articles to profl. jours. Recipient Meritorious Civilian Service medal Dept. Def., 1981. Fellow IEEE; mem. Assn. Computing Math., Math. Assn. Am. Subspecialties: Computer engineering; Research administration. Home: 4819 Reservoir Rd NW Washington DC 20007 Office: IPTO/Def Advanced Research Projects Agy 1400 Wilson Blvd Arlington VA 22209

KAHN, STEPHEN ELLSWORTH, clinical chemist, chemistry educator, researcher; b. Chgo., Oct. 23, 1950; s. Irving and Adeline Ruth (Harker) K.; m. Kristine Elizabeth Rafac, Mar. 30, 1974; children—Rebecca Elizabeth, Matthew Stephen. B.S. in zoology with honors, Mich. State U., 1972; Ph.D. in Biol. Chemistry, U. Ill. Med. Ctr., 1979; postgrad. in bus. adminstrn., Ill. Benedictine Coll., 1983—. Diplomate Am. Bd. Clin. Chemistry. Grad. asst. U. Ill. Med. Ctr.-Chgo., 1972-78; postdoctoral fellow in clin. chemistry Loyola U. Med. Ctr., Maywood, Ill., 1978-80, asst. prof. pathology, 1980—, asst. prof. biochemistry and biophysics, 1980—, asst. dir. clin. chemistry, 1980-81, assoc. dir. clin. chemistry, 1981—, clin. chemistry teaching coordinator, 1980—; instr. biochemistry Ill. Coll. Podiatric Medicine, Chgo., 1978-79. Contbr. articles to profl. jours. Author sci. abstracts. Recipient Research Forum award Sigma Xi, 1977; biomed. research grantee Loyola U. Med. Ctr., 1982, 83. Mem. AAAS, Am. Chem. Soc., Am. Assn. for Clin. Chemistry (corr. 1981, Accent 1982, corr. sec. 1983-85, Clin. Chemists Recognition award 1981), Clin. Lab. Mgmt. Assn., Assn. of Clin. Lab. Scientists (membership com. 1983-84). Roman Catholic. Current work: calcium homeostasis; biochemical alterations in uremia; diagnostic enzymology and clinical laboratory utilization. Subspecialties: Clinical chemistry; Biochemistry (medicine). Office: Loyola U Med Ctr 2160 S 1st Ave Maywood IL 60153

KAHN, THOMAS, nephrologist, medical center administrator, educator; b. Offenburg, Germany, June 23, 1938; came to U.S., 1947, naturalized, 1952; s. Ludwig and Helen (Kaufman) K.; m. Si Mi Park, Nov. 16, 1968; children: Diana, David, Philip. B.A., NYU, 1958, M.D., 1962. Mem. faculty Mt. Sinai Sch. Medicine, N.Y.C., 1969 , assoc. prof. medicine, 1977 ; chief renal sect. Bronx VA Med. Ctr., N.Y.C., 1979 . Contbr. articles to profl. jours. Served to maj. U.S. Army, 1967-69, Korea. N.Y. State Dept. Health grantee, 1975-77; VA grantee, 1981 . Fellow ACP; mem. N.Y. Soc. Nephrology (grantee 1972-74, sec.-treas. 1982-83, pres.-elect 1983-84, pres. 1984-85), Am. Physiol. Soc., Am. Soc. Nephrology, Am. Soc. Artificial Internal Organs. Jewish. Current Work: Electrolyte and acid-base physiology and pathophysiology. Subspecialties: Nephrology; Internal medicine. Home: 511 E 80th St New York NY 10021 Office: Bronx VA Med Center 130 W Kingsbridge Rd Bronx NY 10021

KAHNE, STEPHEN JAMES, systems engineer, educator; b. N.Y.C., Apr. 5, 1937; s. Arnold W. and Janet (Weatherlow) K.; m. Irena Nowacka, Dec. 11, 1970; children: Christopher, Katarzyna. B.E.E., Cornell U., 1960; M.S., U. Ill., 1961, Ph.D., 1963. Asst. prof. elec. engring. U. Minn., Mpls., 1966-69, asso. prof., 1969-76; dir. Hybrid Computer Lab., 1968-76; founder, dir., cons. InterDesign Inc., Mpls., 1968-76; prof. dept. systems engring. Case Western Res. U., Cleve., 1976-83, chmn. dept., 1976-80; dir. div. elec., computer and systems engring. NSF, Washington, 1980-81; dean engring. Poly. Inst. N.Y., Bklyn., 1983-84; pres. Oreg. Grad. Ctr., 1985—; cons. in field; exchange scientist Nat. Acad. Scis., 1968, 75. Editor: IEEE Transactions on Automatic Control, 1975-79; hon. editor: Internat. Fedn. of Automatic Control, 1975-81; editorial bd.: IEEE Spectrum, 1979-82; dep. chmn. editorial bd.: Automatica, 1976-82; dep. chmn. mng. bd.: Internat. Fedn. Automatic Control Publs, 1976—; contbr. articles to sci. jours. Active Mpls. Citizens League, 1968-75. Served with USAF, 1963-66. Recipient Amicus Poloniae award POLAND Mag., 1975; John A. Curtis award Am. Soc. Engring. Edn.; Case Centennial scholar, 1980. Fellow AAAS, IEEE (pres. Control Systems Soc. 1981, bd. dirs. 1982-85, v.p. tech. 1984-85, Centennial medal 1984). Subspecialty: Systems engineering. Home: 10835 NW Brooks Rd Portland OR 97231 Office: 19600 NW Von Neumann Dr Beaverton OR 97006

KAISER, ARMIN DALE, biochemist; b. Piqua, Ohio, Nov. 10, 1927; s. Armin Jacob and Elsa Catherine (Brunner) K.; m. Mary Eleanor Durrell, Aug. 9, 1953; children: Jennifer Lee, Christopher Alan. B.S., Purdue U., 1950; Ph.D., Calif. Inst. Tech., 1955. Postdoctoral research fellow Inst. Pasteur, Paris, 1954-56; asst. prof. microbiology Washington U., St. Louis, 1956-59; mem. faculty Stanford U., 1959—, prof. biochemistry. Served with AUS, 1945-47. Recipient molecular biology award U.S. Steel Corp., 1971; Lasker award in basic med. sci., 1980. Mem. Nat. Acad. Scis., Am. Acad. Arts and Scis., Am. Soc. Biochemists, Genetic Soc. Am. Research on virus multiplication, microbial devel. Subspecialties: Genetics and genetic engineering (biology); Biochemistry (biology). Office: Biochemistry Dept Stanford Univ Stanford CA 94305

KAISER, EMIL THOMAS, chemist. Prof., head lab. bioorganic chemistry and biochemistry Rockefeller U., N.Y.C. Subspecialty: Bio-organic chemistry. Office: Rockefeller U Lab of Bioorganic Chemistry and Biochemistry New York NY 10021

KAISTHA, KRISHAN, KUMAR, toxicologist, pharmacist, clinical chemist; b. Sulah (Kandgra), Himachal Pradesh, India, Apr. 6, 1926; came to U.S., 1959, naturalized, 1974; s. Mangat Ram and Tara Devi (Mahajan) K.; m. Swarn Lata, Feb. 22, 1948; children: Anita, Vivek, Vinek. B.S. in Chemistry, Punjab (India) U., 1947, B.S. in Pharmacy with honors, 1951, M.S., 1955; Ph.D., U. Fla., 1962. Diplomate: Am. Bd. Forensic Toxicology; cert. clin. chemist Nat. Registry Clin. Chemistry registered pharmacist, Ill. Analytical chemist Punjab govt. Med. Directorate, 1952-57, chief pharmacist, 1957-59; research fellow SUNY, Buffalo, 1962-63; head pharm. services and phytochem. research lab. Punjab Govt. Postgrad. Med. Research Inst., 1964-66; research scientist food and drug directorate Dept. Nat. Health and Welfare, Ottawa, Ont., Can., 1966-69; research assoc. dept. psychiatry U. Chgo., 1969-75; dir. toxicology labs. State of Ill. Dept. Mental Health Drug Abuse Programs, Chgo., 1969-74; chief toxicologist State of Ill. Dangerous Drugs Commn., 1974-84, acting adminstr., 1981-84; chief toxicologist State of Ill. Dept. Alcoholism and Substance Abuse, 1984—. Contbr. numerous articles on toxicology and analytical methodology to profl. jours. Recipient 1st Prize Lunsford-Richardson award, 1962; Gov.'s Economy Incentive award State of Ill., 1973. Fellow N.Y. Acad. Scis., Am. Acad. Forensic Scis., Nat. Acad. Clin. Biochemistry; mem. Am. Acad. Clin. Toxicology, Am. Assn. Clin. Chemists, Am. Soc. Pharmacology and Exptl. Therapeutics, Rho Chi, Rho Pi Phi, Phi Kappa Phi, Gamma Sigma Epsilon.; Mem. Vivekanada Vedanta Soc. Current Work: Analytical methodology in toxicology, clinical chemistry and pharmaceutical dosage forms, development of analytical techniques for the detection of drugs and toxic chemicals in biological specimens, applications of thin-layer chromatography. Subspecialties: Toxicology (medicine); Biochemistry (medicine). Home: 542 N Ashbury Ave Bolingbrook IL 60439 Office: I I T Research 10 W 35th St Chicago IL 60616

KAITA, ROBERT, physicist; b. Tokyo, Sept. 2, 1952 (parents Am. citizens); s. Reiichi and Midori (Kokita) K.; m. Chiu-Tze Lin, Apr. 19, 1980. B.S., SUNY-Stony Brook, 1973; Ph.D., Rutgers U., 1978. Research assoc. Princeton U., N.J., 1978-80, research staff, 1980-84, research physicist, 1984—. Contbr. articles to profl. jours. Starr Found scholar, 1969-73. Mem. Am. Phys. Soc., AAAS, Sigma Xi. Democrat. Baptist. Current work: Basic research in controlled nuclear fusion (particle confinement and heating processes in toroidal magnetic confinement devices), plasma physics. Subspecialties: Plasma physics; Fusion. Home: RD 2 80 LaValley Rd Manalapan NJ 07726 Office: Plasma Physics Lab Princeton U PO Box 451 Princeton NJ 08544

KALBACH, CONSTANCE, nuclear physics researcher, educator; b. Chgo., Jan. 12, 1944; d. John Colahan and Mary (Millitch) K.; m. William Delany Walker, Oct. 10, 1975. B.S., U. Rochester, 1965, Ph.D., 1970. Lectr. chemistry Nazareth Coll., Rochester, N.Y., 1970-71; postdoctoral fellow U. Rochester, N.Y., 1971-73; sr. research collaborator C.E.N. Saclay, Gif-Sur-Yvette, France, 1973-74; asst. prof. physics U. Tenn., Knoxville, 1974-76; vis. asst. prof. N.C. State U., Raleigh, 1977; vis. scholar dept. physics Duke U., Durham, N.C., 1981-85, sr. research scientist, 1985—; cons. nuclear physics, Durham, 1978—; research cons. Oak Ridge Nat. Labs., 1974-76. Contbr. articles to profl. jours. Mem. energy task force Presbyterian Ch. in U.S., Atlanta, 1980. Mem. Am. Chem. Soc., Phi Beta Kappa, Sigma Xi. Current Work: statistical models for nuclear reactions. Subspecialties: Nuclear physics; Nuclear chemistry. Office: Physics Dept Duke U Durham NC 27706

KALITA, CHABI CHANDRA, organic and analytic biochemist; b. Jhanjimukh, Sibsagar, Assam, India, May 1, 1935; s. Sondhor and Golapi (Kalita) K.; came to U.S., 1965; children—Ranjita, Chiranjit. B.S. with distinction, Gauhati U., 1957, M.S. with 1st class honors, 1962; M.S., St. John's U., 1968, Ph.D., 1972. Asst. prof. chemistry J.B. Coll., Jorhat, Assam, India, 1961-62, Assam Med. Coll., Dibrugarh, India, 1962-65; instr. chemistry Manhattan Coll., Bronx, N.Y., 1968-69; research assoc. Albert Einstein Coll., Bronx, 1972-75; scientist FCRC/NIH, Fredrick, Md., 1976-82; patent examiner Patent and Trademark Office, Arlington, Va., 1983; chemist Bur. of Engraving and Printing, Washington, 1984—. Author papers on peptides, proteins, antibiotics and analytical chemistry; contbr. chpt. to Am. Chem. Soc. book, 1985. NSF fellow, 1969; NIH fellow, 1971; recipient Merit scholarship Govt. of Assam, India, 1952-61. Mem. Am. Chem. Soc., AAAS, N.Y. Acad. Sci. Subspecialties: Organic chemistry; Analytical chemistry. Home: 10919 Rawley Rd Mount Airy MD 21771 Office: Bur of Engraving and Printing Washington DC 20228

KALLMAN, MARY JEANNE, psychology educator; b. Alexandria, Va., May 27, 1948; d. Ira Semon and Carol Louise (Gardinier) Davis; m. William Michael Kallman, Dec. 20, 1969. B.S., Lynchburg Coll., 1970; M.S., U. Ga., 1974, Ph.D., 1976. Postdoctoral fellow Med. Coll. Va., Commonwealth U., Richmond, 1976-79, adj. asst. prof., 1976-77, research assoc., 1979-80, asst. prof., 1980-83; asst. prof. psychology U. Miss., University, 1983—. Contbr. articles to profl. jours., chpts. to books. Recipient research award U. Miss., 1984; grantee NIH, Nat. Inst. Drug Abuse, 1982-85. Mem. Am. Psychol. Assn., Soc. for Neurosci., AAAS, Behavioral Pharmacology Soc., Southeastern Psychology Assn. Methodist. Current work: Sites of action for drugs of abuse and behavioral pharmacology; behavioral and CNS drugs; brain mechanisms for various behavioral responses. Subspecialties: Neuropharmacology; Environmental toxicology. Home: 2918-A Old Taylor Rd Oxford MS 38655 Office: Dept Psychology U Miss University MS 38677

KALRA, SATYA PAUL, obstetrics and gynecology educator, researcher; b. Mari Indus, India, Jan. 1, 1939; came to U.S., 1968; s. Ishar Dass and Sushila (Malik) K.; m. Pushpa Seth, Sept. 14, 1969; 1 son, Anjay N. B.S., U. Delhi, India, 1960, M.S., 1962, Ph.D., 1966. Research assoc. U. Delhi, 1966-68; postdoctoral fellow UCLA, 1968-69, U. Tex.-Dallas, 1969-71; asst. prof. U. Fla., Gainesville, 1971-76, assoc. prof., 1976-82, prof. ob-gyn, 1982—. Grantee Population Council, 1971-74; Grantee NIH, 1975—. Mem. Endocrine Soc., Internat. Neuroëndocrine Soc., Am. Physiol. Soc., Soc. for Study Reprodn., Soc. for Gynecol. Investigation, Am. Soc. Andrology, Soc. Neurosci. Current Work: Neuroëndocrine control of gonadotropin secretion gonadal feedback; neurotransmitter —neuropeptide interaction, hypothalamus. Subspecialties: Neuroëndocrinology; Reproductive biology. Office: Dept Ob-Gyn U Fla Box J-294 J Hillis Miller Health Ctr Coll Medicine Gainesville FL 32610

KALRA, VIJAY KUMAR, biochemistry educator; b. Multan, Pakistan, Aug. 26, 1942; came to U.S., 1967; naturalized, 1982; s. Sada Nand and Gian Devi (Makhija) K.; m. Prem Jamie Sikka, Nov. 10, 1971; children—Billy-Ashish,

Ruben. B.S. with honors, Delhi U., New Delhi, India, 1961, M.S., 1963, Ph.D., 1967. Postdoctoral fellow U. So. Calif., Los Angeles, 1967-71, asst., then assoc. prof. biochemistry, 1971-84, prof., 1984—, mem. senate, 1976—. Contbr. articles to profl. jours. Mem. Am. Soc. Biol. Chemists, N.Y. Acad. Scis. Democrat. Hindu. Current work: Structure and function membranes; bacterial and mammalian cells, sickle cell anemia; biology endothelial cells. Subspecialties: Biochemistry (biology); Biochemistry (medicine). Home: 2012 Terra Ln Arcadia CA 91006 Office: U So Calif 2025 Zonal Ave Los Angeles CA 90033

KALSNER, STANLEY, educator, pharmacologist; b. N.Y.C., Aug. 21, 1936; s. William Louis and Sadie (Feldman) K.; m. Jenny Book, Aug. 4, 1963; children—Lydia, Pamela, Louisa. A.B., N.Y. U., 1958; postgrad., SUNY Downstate Med. Center, 1959-62; Ph.D., U. Man., Can., 1966, Cambridge (Eng.) U., 1966-67. Asst. prof. pharmacology U. Ottawa, Ont., Can., 1967-72, assoc. prof., 1972-77, prof., 1977-85, prof., chmn. dept. physiology CUNY Med. Sch., 1985—; also med. research scientist; sci. referee Med. Research Council Can., Can. Heart Found. Editor, contbr. chpts. to books, articles to jours.; asso. editor: Can. Jour. Physiology and Pharmacology; mem. editorial bd.: Jour. Autonomic Pharmacology, Blood Vessels. USPHS fellow, 1960-67; Med. Research Council-NRC and Ont. Heart Found. grantee, 1970—. Mem. AAAS, Can. Pharmacology Soc., Am. Soc. Pharmacology and Therapeutics, AAUP. Current work: Mechanics of coronary artery spasm; sudden death, neurotransmitter mechanisms in the autonomic and central nervous systems. Home: 4 Conrad Ln New City NY Office: CUNY Med Sch Dept Physiology 138th St and Convent Ave New York NY 10031

KALTENBACH, JOHN PAUL, biochemist, researcher, educator, retired; b. Rockford, Ill., Feb. 28, 1920; s. John and Anna (Kruger) K.; m. Merle H. Kaltenbach, Oct. 15, 1923; 1 son, John C. B.S., Beloit Coll., 1944; M.S., U. Iowa, 1947, Ph.D., 1950. Chief cell metabolism VA Research Hosp., Chgo., 1954-56, sr. biochemist, 1956-57; Prof. pathology Northwestern U., 1957-83; acting dir. admissions Northwestern U. (Dental Sch.), 1978-79; affiliated profl. staff Northwestern U. (Meml. Hosp.), 1973-82. Contbr. articles to profl. jours. Brittingham fellow, 1950-52; USPHS fellow Karolinska Inst., Stockholm, 1953-54. Mem. AAAS, Am. Assn. Cancer Research, Am. Soc. Exptl. Pathology. Current Work: Induction and protection of D-serine kidney tubular necrosis, pathogenesis of irreversible myocardial injury. Subspecialties: Biochemistry (medicine); Cell biology (medicine).

KALU, DIKE NDUKWE, physiology educator and researcher; b. Abiriba, Imo, Nigeria, Jan. 1, 1938; came to U.S., 1971; s. Ndukwe and Oyediya K.; m. Carolyn A. Rotibi, Aug. 24, 1967; children: Nneji, Ngozi, Ndukwe. B.Sc., U. London, 1967; Ph.D., 1971. Fellow Johns Hopkins U., Balt., 1972-75; sci. officer U. London, 1967-71; asst. prof. U. Tex. Health Sci. Ctr., San Antonio, 1975-79, assoc. prof. physiology, 1979—. NIH grantee, 1979, 80. Mem. AAAS, Endocrine Soc., Am. Physiol Soc., Fedn. Am. Soc. Exptl. Biology, N.Y. Acad. Scis. Current Work: Influence of the endocrines and aging on the regulation of calcium and skeletal metabolism. Subspecialties: Physiology (medicine); Endocrinology. Home: 6822 Brookvale St San Antonio TX 78238 Office: U Tex Health Sci Ctr Dept Physiology 7703 Floyd Curl Dr San Antonio TX 78284

KAM, SHEUNG-TSAM, medicinal chemist; b. Hong Kong, Aug. 10, 1948; came to U.S., 1972; s. Sing-Man and Wai-Hing K.; m. Maria Veng-Nga, Sept. 17, 1974. B.Pharm., Nat. Def. Med. Ctr., Taiwan, 1971; Ph.D., U. Minn., 1979. Research investigator, Am. Critical Care, McGaw Park, Ill., 1979-81, sr. research investigator, 1981-82; medicinal chemist Sch Medicine U. Ill., Chgo., 1982—. Mem. Am. Chem. Soc., AMA. Current work: Medicinal chemistry; design and synthesis of new drugs, especially as related to cardiovascular area; drug metabolism. Subspecialties: Organic chemistry; Molecular pharmacology. Home: 1554 W Harrison St #3C Chicago IL 60607 Office: Sch Med Univ Ill Chicago IL 60612

KAMB, WALTER BARCLAY, educator, geologist; b. San Jose, Calif., Dec. 17, 1931; s. Karl Walter and Eleanor (Williams) K.; m. Linda Helen Pauling, Sept. 8, 1957; children: Barclay James, Carl Alexander, Anthony Pauling, Linus Peter. B.S. in Physics, Calif. Inst. Tech., 1952, Ph.D. in Geology, 1956. Mem. faculty Calif. Inst. Tech., 1956—, prof. geology and geophysics, 1961—, chmn. div. geol. and planetary scis., 1972-83. Guggenheim fellow, 1960; Sloan fellow, 1964. Fellow Geol. Soc. Am., Mineral. Soc. Am. (award 1968); mem. Am. Geophys. Union, Am. Assn. Petroleum Geologists. Glaciology; Subspecialties: Glaciology; Geophysics. Home: 3500 Fairpoint St Pasadena CA 91107

KAMBACK, MARVIN CARL, psychologist; b. Yankton, S.D., July 15, 1939; s. Carl Melvin and Pauline Elizabeth (Albrecht) K.; m. Genevieve Lowthian, Sept. 2, 1962 (div. 1971); children—Elizabeth Farrell, Christopher John. B.A., U. S.D., 1961, M.A., 1962; Ph.D., Vanderbilt U., 1965. Lic. psychologist, Md., Wyo., Calif. Postdoctoral fellow Stanford U. Med. Sch., 1965-66; lectr. U. Calif., Santa Barbara, 1966-67; instr. psychology U. S.D., Vermillion, 1962, asst. prof., 1967-71; asst. prof. psychology Johns Hopkins U. Med. Sch.; sr. clin. psychologist Balt. City Hosps., 1971-74; assoc. prof. U. Md. Med. Sch., Balt., 1974-78; dir. Washakie County (Wyo.) Mental Health Services, 1978-79; dir. psychol. services Alcohol Care Center, Buena Park (Calif.) Hosp., 1979—, Raleigh Hills Hosps., Newport Beach, Calif., 1979—; clin. psychologist Behavior Therapy and Research Inst., 1979-82; dir. psychol. services alcoholism program Advanced Health Systems, Newport, Beach, 1979-82, pvt. practice clin. psychology, San Clemente and Buena Park, 1979—. Contbr. chpts. to books, articles to profl. jours. Mem. Am. Psychol. Assn., AAAS, Md. Psychol. Assn., Soc. for Gen. Systems Research, Sigma Xi. Republican. Lodge: Rotary. Current Work: Addictions research. General systems theory as it applies to health care. Brain function research. Subspecialties: Behavioral psychology; Neuropsychology. Home: 372 Calle Guymas San Clemente CA 92672 Office: Buena Park Community Hosp 6850 Lincoln Ave Buena Park CA 90620

KAMEDA, TIKO, computer science educator; b. Shimonoseki, Japan, Feb. 10, 1939; s. Gengo and Mitsue Kameda. B.S., Tokyo Univ., 1961, M.S., 1963; Ph.D., Princeton Univ., 1968. Asst. to assoc. prof. U. Waterloo, Ont., Can., 1967-79; prof. Simon Faser U., 1981—, dir. Lab. for Computer & Communications Research, Burnaby, Can., 1982—. Author: Introduction to Coding Theory, 1971. Contbr. articles to profl. jours. Mem. Assn. Computing Machinery. Current work: Database systems, computer algorithms, computer-communication protocols, distributed computing. Subspecialties: Algorithms; Database systems. Office: Simon Fraser Univ Lab for Computer & Communications Research Burnaby BC V5A 136 Canada

KAMENTSKY, LOUIS AARON, biophysicist; b. Newark, July 28, 1930; s. Harry and Etta (Brodsky) K.; m. Marcia Alpern, Aug. 28, 1955; children—Lee, Howard, Ellen. B.S.E.E., N.J. Inst. Tech., 1952; Ph.D., Cornell U., 1956. Mem. staff Columbia U. ERL, N.Y.C., 1954-55, Bell Telephone Labs., Murray Hill, N.J., 1956-60, IBM Research, N.Y.C., 1960-68; pres. Biophysics Systems, Mahopac, N.Y., 1968-76; v.p. research Ortho Diagnostics Systems, Cambridge, Mass., 1976—; mem. staff Colombia U. ERL, N.Y.C., 1954-55; sr. research scientist MIT, Cambridge, 1981—. Patentee in field; contbr. articles to profl. jours. Current work: Invitro and invivo diagnostics technology. Home: 180 Beacon St Boston MA 02116 Office: Ortho Diagnostic Systems 195 Albany St Cambridge MA 02139

KAMERLING, STEVEN GLENN, pharmacologist, researcher, educator; b. Chgo., Oct. 20, 1950; s. Leon Martin and Rita Sandra (Azeff) K. B.S. in Pharmacy, Drake U., 1973; Ph.D. in Pharmacology, U. Ill-Chgo., 1979. Registered pharmacist, Ill., Iowa. Intern in pharmacy Borovik Drug Co., Chgo., 1969-73; pharmacist N.W. Hosp., Chgo., 1973; postdoctoral scholar U. Ky., Lexington, 1979-82, research assoc., 1982-84; asst. prof. vet. physiology, pharmacology and toxicology La. State U.-Baton Rouge, 1985—. Contbr. articles, revs. to profl. jours. Recipient Bristol Lab. award, Leadership Recognition award, USPHS award U. Ill.-Chgo., 1977-79; predoctoral fellow U. Ill.-Chgo., 1973-79. Mem. Soc. for Neurosci., AAAS, Am. Pain Soc., Am. Soc. Pharmacology and Exptl. Therapeutics, Lexington Musicians Assn. Current work: Pharmacologic studies of effects of opioids and non-steroidal anti-inflammatory analgesics on pain perception; central nervous system effects of opiates, cholinomimetrics, and monamines. Subspecialties: Pharmacology; Neuropharmacology. Home: 5150 Capital Heights Ave Baton Rouge LA 70806 Office: Dept Vet Physiology La State U Baton Rouge LA 70803

KAMIENIECKI, EMIL, physicist, researcher; b. Warsaw, Poland, June 17, 1938; came to U.S., 1979; s. Jakub and Antonina (Lenga) K.; m. Grazyna Teresa Bienkowska, July 7, 1970; children—Krzysztof Emil, Anna Grazyna. M.S., Warsaw U., 1961; Ph.D., Polish Acad. Scis., 1970, Dr. Sci., 1976. Mem. research staff Inst. Physics Polish Acad. Sci., Warsaw, 1962-79, assoc. head Semiconductor div., 1975-76, acting dep. dir. sci. affairs, head surface physics group, 1977-79; mem. tech. staff GTE Labs., Waltham, Mass., 1980-83, prin. mem. tech. staff, 1983-84; pres. Optical Diagnostic Systems, Inc., Cambridge, Mass., 1984—. Contbr. articles to profl. jours. Recipient awards Sec. Sci. Polish Acad. Scis., 1974, dept. math.-physics, 1978; Von Humboldt-Stiftung fellow, 1972. Mem. Am. Phys. Soc., Electrochem. Soc., Material Research Soc. Current work: Electronic properties of semiconductor surfaces and interfaces especially semiconductor/insulator structures, photo-electrical properties of semiconductors, characterization method. Subspecialties: Condensed matter physics; Electronic materials. Home: 30 Carville Ave Lexington MA 02173

KAMIYAMA, MIKIO, immunochemist; b. Kyoto, Japan, Mar. 25, 1936; came to U.S., 1967; s. Seiryo and Tome (Watanabe) K.; m. Minako Toyoguchi, Sept. 30, 1971; children: Eugene, Kay, June. B.S., Kyoto Prefectural U., 1962; D.M.Sc., Ph.D., U. Tokyo, 1967. Postdoctoral fellow Princeton U., 1967-68; research assoc. SUNY-Buffalo, 1969-70; sr. researcher Institut de Puthologie Moléculaire, U. Paris, 1971-72, 73-74; vis. lectr. U. Marburg., W. Ger., 1972-73; attending staff St. Luke's-Roosevelt Hosp. Center, Columbia U. Coll. Physicians and Surgeons, N.Y.C., 1974—. Contbr. articles to profl. jours. Mem. Am. Assn. Immunologists, Am. Fedn. for Clin. Research (sr.), N.Y. Acad. Sci., Harvey Soc., Japanese Biochem. Soc. Current Work: Immunological and biochemical characterization of tumor-associated antigens, cell membrance markers and receptors. Subspecialties: Cancer research (medicine); Immunology (medicine). Home: 560 Riverside Dr New York NY 10027 Office: St Luke's-Roosevelt Hosp Center/Columbia U 421 W 113th St New York NY 10025

KAMM, ROGER DALE, engineering educator, consultant; b. Superior, Wis., Oct. 10, 1950; s. Rudolph Wilhelm and Betty Jane (White) K.; m. Judith Mary Brown, Sept. 1, 1974; 1 child, Meredith. S.M., MIT, 1973, Ph.D., 1976. Asst. prof. engring. MIT, Cambridge, 1977-80, assoc. prof., 1981—; cons. Brookhaven Nat. Lab., Islip, N.Y., Brown & Williamson Corp., Louisville. Contbr articles to profl. jours. Mem. ASME, Assn. Research in Vision and Ophthalmology. Unitarian-Universalist. Current work: Biomedical fluid mechanics, mass transport. Subspecialty: Fluid mechanics. Office: MIT 77 Massachusetts Ave Cambridge MA 02139

KAMMERAAD, JUDITH ELLEN, physicist; b. Kalamazoo, Jan. 18, 1954; d. Howard W. and Shirley (Lemmen) K. B.A., Hope Coll., 1976; Ph.D., U. Wis., 1983. Physicist, Lawrence Livermore Nat. Lab., Calif., 1983—. Mem. Am. Phys. Soc. Current work: Measurement of cross section for deuteron-triton radiactive capture reaction; observation of gamma-ray-generated plasma effects; neutron pinhole camera. Subspecialties: Nuclear physics; Plasma physics. Office: Lawrence Livermore Nat Lab L-43 PO Box 808 Livermore CA 94550

KAMPER, ROBERT A., government laboratory director. Dir, Nat. Bur. Standards Boulder Labs., Colo. . Office: Nat Bur Standards Boulder Labs 325 S Broadway Boulder CO 80303

KAN, JOSEPH R., geophysics educator; b. Shanghai, China, Feb. 10, 1938; s. John H. S. and Mary (Chen) K.; m. Rosalind J. Chen, May 18, 1961; children: Christina, Deborah, Steven. B.S., Nat. Cheng-Kung U., Taiwan, 1961; M.S., Wash. State U., 1966; Ph.D., U. Calif.-San Diego, 1969. Postdoctoral fellow radiophysics lab. Dartmouth Coll., Hanover, N.H., 1970-72; asst. prof. Geophys. Inst., U. Alaska, Fairbanks, 1972-76, assoc. prof., 1976-81, prof., 1981—; cons. space physics lab. Aerospace Corp., Los Angeles, 1980-81; vis. assoc. geophysicist UCLA, 1980-81. Editor: Physics of Auroral Arc Formation, 1981. Mem. Am. Geophys. Union, Am. Phys. Soc. Current Work: Space plasma physics, magnetaspheric physics and auroral physics. Subspecialties: Solar physics; Plasma physics. Home: 2568 Talkeetna Ave Fairbanks AK 99701 Office: Geophys Inst U Alaska Fairbanks AK 99701

KAN, YUET WAI, physician, educator; b. Hong Kong, June 11, 1936; married, 1964. M.B., B.S., U. Hong Kong, 1958, D.Sc., 1980; M.D. (hon.), U. Cagliari, Italy, 1981; D.Sc. (hon.), Chinese U. Hong Kong, 1981. Asst. prof. pediatrics Harvard Med. Sch., 1970-72; chief hematology service San Francisco Gen. Hosp., 1972-79; assoc. prof. medicine and lab medicine U. Calif.-San Francisco, 1972-77, prof. medicine and lab. medicine, 1977—, prof. biochemistry and biophysics, 1979—, Harvey Soc. lectr., 1980-81; investigator Howard Hughes Med. Inst. Lab., 1976—. Recipient Damashek award Am. Soc. Hematology, 1979; Stratton lectr. Internat. Soc. Hematology, 1980; Gairdner Found. internat. award, Allan award, Lita Annenberg Hazen award, 1984. Fellow Royal Soc. London; mem. Am. Soc. Hematology, Am. Fedn. Clin. Research, Am. Soc. Clin. Investigation, Assn. Am. Physicians. Subspecialties: Genetics and genetic engineering (medicine); Hematology. Office: Univ Calif Dept Med U-426 San Francisco CA 94143

KANA, TIMOTHY WILLIAM, consulting scientist, coastal oceanography educator; b. Glen Cove, N.Y., Mar. 28, 1949; s. Milan and Nancy (Austin) K.; m. Patricia May, Dec. 30, 1972 (div. 1976); 1 son, Christopher Townsend; m. Julia Lucas Lumpkin, May 9, 1981. B.A., Johns Hopkins U., 1971; M.S., U. S.C., 1976, Ph.D., 1979. Open water scuba instr. Research assoc. Chesapeake Bay Inst., Balt., 1969-73; research asst. Geology Dept, U. S.C., Columbia, 1974-78; founding ptnr. Research Planning Inst., Inc., Columbia, 1977-84, dir. coastal dynamics div., 1979-84; pres. Coastal Sci. and Engring., Inc., Columbia, 1984—; adj. prof. U. S.C., Columbia, 1981—; scuba instr., Fla., S.C., 1972—. Co-editor: Classtc Depositional Environments, 1976; designer oceanographic sampler, 1976; contbr. writings in field to profl. publs. Served with USNR, 1966-72. Research scholar Amoco Oil Co., 1977; research grantee Army Research Office; research grantee U.S. Army, C.E.; research grantee NOAA; research grantee USCG; research grantee UN. Mem. ASCE (affiliate), Am. Shore and Beach Preservation Soc., Profl. Assn. (Scuba) Diving Instrs., Coastal Soc., Sigma Xi. Current Work: Innovative soft engineering solutions to beach erosion, shore protection planning and design, surf zone dynamics and sedimentation, prediction of shoreline change. Subspecialty: Oceanography. Home: 1386 Kathwood Dr Columbia SC 29206 Office: Coastal Sci and Engring Inc PO Box 8056 Columbia SC 29202

KANAMORI, HIROO, educator; b. Tokyo, Japan, Oct. 17, 1936; came to U.S., 1972; s. Tokujiro and Saki (Sakurai) K.; m. Keiko Ihara, Apr. 21, 1964; children—Atsushi, Tadashi. B.S., Tokyo U., 1959, M.S., 1961, Ph.D., 1964. Research fellow Calif. Inst. Tech., Pasadena, 1965-66, prof. geophysics, 1972—; asso. prof. geophysics Tokyo U., 1966-69, prof., 1970-72; vis. asso. prof. Mass. Inst. Tech., 1969-70. Author: (with Hitoshi Takeuchi, Seiya Uyeda) Debate About the Earth, 1967. Fellow Am. Geophys. Union; mem. Seismol. Soc. Am. (pres. 1985—), Sigma Xi. Current Work: Seismology. Subspecialty: Geophysics. Home: 375 S Bonnie Ave Pasadena CA 91106

KANDEL, ERIC RICHARD, neurobiologist; b. Vienna, Austria, Nov. 7, 1929; came to U.S., 1939, naturalized, 1945; s. Harris Z. and Charlotte (Zimels) K.; m. Denise Bystryn, June 10, 1956; children: Paul Iser, Michelle Deborah. B.A., Harvard U., 1952; M.D., N.Y. U., 1956. Intern Montefiore Hosp., N.Y.C., 1956-57; resident psychiatry Mass. Mental Health Center, 1960-62, 63-64; instr. psychiatry Harvard U. Med. Sch., 1964-65; asso. prof., then prof. physiology and psychiatry N.Y. U. Med. Sch., 1965-74; chief dept. neurobiology and behavior Pub. Health Research Inst. City N.Y., 1969-74; prof. physiology and psychiatry, dir. Ctr. Neurobiology and Behavior, Columbia Coll. Physicians and Surgeons, 1974—; Univ. prof. Columbia U., 1983—; sr. investigator Howard Hughes Med. Inst., 1984—. Author: Cellular Basis of Behavior, 1976, A Cell Biological Approach to Learning, 1978, Behavioral Biology of Aplysia, 1979, Principles of Neural Science, 1981; also articles. Served to sr. asst. surgeon USPHS, 1957-60. Recipient Career Devel. and Scientist awards NIMH, 1967—, Hofheimer award, 1977, Lucy G. Moses prize, 1977, Karl Spencer Lashley prize, 1981, Dickson prize in biology and medicine, 1982, N.Y. Acad. Scis. award in biology and medicine, 1982, Lasker basic med. research award, 1983; Rosenstiel award, 1984; Harry Crosby Warren medal, 1984. Mem. Nat. Acad. Scis., Am. Acad. Arts and Scis., Soc. Neurosci. (pres. 1980-81), Neurosci. Research Program, Am. Physiol. Soc., IBRO, Am. Psychiat. Assn., Psychiat. Research Orgn., Harvey Soc., Am. Philos. Soc. Subspecialties: Psychiatry; Neurobiology. Home: 9 Sigma Pl Riverdale NY 10471 Office: Coll Physicians and Surgeons Columbia U New York NY 10032

KANDIL, OSAMA ABDEL-MOHSIN, engineering educator, researcher; b. Cairo, Oct. 10, 1944; came to U.S., 1971, naturalized, 1977; s. Abdel-Mohsin Moses and Attiat (Sayed) K.; m. Rawia Ahmed Fouad, Oct. 20, 1968; children—Dalya Osama, Tarek Osama. B.S. with honors, Cairo U., 1966; M.S., Villanova U., 1972; Ph.D., Va. Poly. Inst., 1974. Instr. mech. engring. Cairo U., 1966-70; teaching asst. Villanova U., 1971-72; research asst. Va. Poly. Inst., Blacksburg, 1972-74, asst. prof., 1975-78; assoc. prof. mech. engring. Old Dominion U., Norfolk, Va., 1978-84, prof., 1985—; vis. prof. King Saud U., Riyadh, Saudi Arabia, 1983-84; Contbr. articles to profl. jours. NASA grantee, 1975-78, 78-83, also others. Mem. AIAA (sr. mem.; fluid dynamics tech. com. 1974—), Am. Soc. Engring. Edn., Soc. Engring. Scis., Soc. Indsl. and Applied Math., AAUP, Phi Kappa Phi, Sigma Xi. Current work: Aeronautics; fluid mechanics; numerical analysis; theoretical and applied mechanics; computer-aided design, high angle of attack aerodynamics; vortex flows. Subspecialties: Aerospace engineering and technology; Fluid mechanics. Home: 7212 Midfield St Norfolk VA 23505 Office: Old Dominion U Norfolk VA 23508

KANE, GORDON L., physics educator; b. St. Paul, Jan. 19, 1937; s. Harry and Mary (Millunchick) K.; m. Lois Elizabeth Kliffer, Sept. 9, 1958; children—Hal, Mollie. Ph.D., U. Ill., 1963. Research assoc. physics dept. Johns Hopkins U., Balt., 1963-65; asst. prof. physics U. Mich., Ann Arbor, 1965-69, assoc. prof., 1969-75, prof., 1975—; cons. Brookhaven Nat. Lab., Upton, N.Y., 1982—, mem. high-energy physics adv. com. 1983-85. Mem. editorial bd. Phys. Rev., 1981—; corr. for Comments on Nuclear and Particle Physics, 1984—. Contbr. articles to profl. jours. Guggenheim fellow, 1971-72. Fellow Am. Phys. Soc.; mem. Johns Hopkins Soc. Scholars. Current work: Particle physics beyond standard model, Higgs physics, predictions of guage theories, supersymmetry, physics justification of future facilities. Subspecialty: Particle physics. Home: 1611 Wells St Ann Arbor MI 48104 Office: Randall Lab Physics U Mich Ann Arbor MI 48109

KANE, SHARAD RAMCHANDRA, research physicist; b. Banda, India, Sept. 23, 1935; came to U.S., 1961; s. Ramchandra G. and Indumati (Marathe) K.; m. Kunda B. Kawle, Dec. 20, 1967; children—Vandana, Avinash. B.Sc., Victoria Coll., Gwalior, India, 1954; B.Sc. with honors, U. Poona, India, 1956; M.S.c., Phys. Research Lab., Ahmedabad, India, 1960; Ph.D., U. Minn.-Mpls., 1967. Research assoc., U. Minn., Mpls., 1967-68; asst. research physicist Space Scis. Lab. U. Calif., Berkeley, 1969-75, assoc. research physicist, 1975-82, research physicist, 1982—; vis. scientist Ctr. for Astrophysics, Cambridge, Mass., 1974-75; vis. astronomer Observatoire de Paris, Meudon, France, 1980; vis. scientist dept. physics U. N.H., 1982-83; mem. U.S. del. to Indo-U.S. Workshop on Solar Terrestrial Physics for the Solar Maximum Year, 1979; numerous research positions. Editor: Solar Gamma-, X- and EUV Radiation, 1975. Prin. editor: Recent Advances in the Understanding of Solar Flares, 1983. Contbr. numerous articles to profl. jours. Scholar Karmakshetra Edn. Soc., Ahmedabad, India, 1956-57; scholar Phys. Research Lab., Ahmedabad, 1959-60; recipient Cert. of Recognition NASA, 1979. Mem. Internat Astron Union, Am. Astron Soc., Am. Geophys Union. Current work: Solar physics (solar activity), solar-terrestrial relationship, cosmic radiation. Subspecialties: Solar physics; Gamma ray high energy astrophysics. Office: Space Scis Lab Univ Calif Berkeley CA 94720

KANEMASU, EDWARD TSUKASA, agronomy educator; b. Hood River, Oreg., Nov. 16, 1940; s. George K. and Mary (Okamura) K.; m. Karen Annette Christenot; children—Deborah, Pam, Richard. B.S., Mont. State U., 1962, M.S., 1964; Ph.D., U. Wis.-Madison, 1969. Asst. prof. Kans. State U., Manhattan, 1969-74, assoc. prof., 1974-78, prof. agronomy, 1978—, lab. leader, 1981—. Fellow Am. Soc. Agronomy; mem. Am. Soc. Meteorology, Phi Kappa Phi, Sigma Xi. Current work: Water use efficiency, remote sensing. Subspecialties: Micrometeorology; Remote sensing (atmospheric science). Office: Kans State U Manhattan KS 66506

KANG, JUNG WONG, chemist, researcher; b. Tokyo, July 25, 1933; s. Myung-Yul and Kap-son (Son) Kang; came to U.S., 1963; m. Yoshimi Nishimura, Oct. 23, 1956; children—Masahide, Leo, Mary. B.S., Kinki U., 1956; M.S., Osaka U., 1958, Ph.D., 1962; postgrad. Harvard U., 1963-64, U. N.C., 1964-66. Research assoc. McMaster U., Hamilton, Ont., Can., 1966-70; research and sr. research scientist Firestone Tire & Rubber Co., Akron, Ohio, 1970-79, assoc. scientist, 1979-82, research assoc., 1982—. Contbr. articles to profl. jours. Patentee in field. Mem. Am. Chem. Soc. (inorganic chemistry, organometallic sect, polymer sect., rubber sect.). Current work: Homogeneous catalysts, synthesis of new elastomers. Subspecialties: Organometallics; Polymer chemistry. Home: 6150 Terrace Hills Clinton OH 44216 Office: Central Research Labs Firestone Tire and Rubber Co 1200 Firestone Pkwy Akron OH 44317

KANG, MANJIT SINGH, geneticist, plant breeder, educator; b. Khamanon Kalan, India, Mar. 3, 1948; came to U.S., 1969, naturalized, 1976; s. Gurdit Singh and Parminder Kaur (Brah) K.; m. Georgia Anna Crocker, Feb. 13, 1971. B.S. with honors, Punjab Agrl. U., 1968; M.S. in Plant Genetics, So. Ill. U., 1971, M.A. in Botany, 1977; Ph.D. in Crop Sci., U. Mo., 1977. Teaching asst. So. Ill. U., Edwardsville, 1969-71; research asst., So. Ill. U., Carbondale, 1971-72, preceptor, 1972-74; grad. research asst. U. Mo., Columbia, 1974-77, research assoc., 1980; plant breeder, sta. mgr. Cargill, Inc., St. Peter, Minn., 1977-79; asst. prof. U. Fla., Belle Glade, 1981—. Contbr. articles to profl. jours. Mem. Am. Genetic Assn., AAAS, Internat. Soc. Plant Molecular Biology, Am. Soc. Agronomy, Crop Sci. Soc. Am., Am. Soc. Sugar Cane Technologists, Sigma Xi, Gamma Sigma Delta. Current work: Crop improvement through genetic means; crop physiology; quantitative genetics. . Home: 1221 Bacom Point Rd Pahokee FL 33476 Office: Inst Food and Agrl Sci Everglades Research and Edn Ctr U Fla PO Drawer A Belle Glade FL 33430

KANG, MIN HO, optical scientist, educator; b. Kyungnam Province, Korea, July 20, 1946; s. Ji Sung and Ok Hee (Lee) K.; m. Ae Soon Choi, July 10, 1971; children: Jeannie, Soo Young. B.S.E.E., Seoul Nat. U., 1969; M.S.E.E., U. Mo.-Rolla, 1973; Ph.D., U. Tex.-Austin, 1977. Research asst. U. Tex., 1973-77; mem. tech. staff Bell Telephone Labs., Holdel, N.J., 1977-78; head lab. Korea Electrotech. and Telecommunication Research Inst., Seoul, 1978-82, head opto-electronics research sect., 1982—; lectr. Grad. Sch., Seoul Nat. U., 1979—. Contbr. articles to profl. jours. Recipient Nat. Medal of Honor Govt. of Korea, 1982. Mem. IEEE, Optical Soc. Am., Korean Inst. Electronic Engrs., Korean Inst. Elec. Engrs., Phi Kappa Phi, Eta Kappa Nu. Current Work: High speed optical fiber communication systems; research including optoelectronics, telecommunication systems. Subspecialties: Fiber optics; Electronics. Home: 6 Dong-512 Mizu Apt Chongryang Ri Seoul Korea Office: KPO Box 125 Gwanghwamoon Seoul Korea

KANG, SUNGZONG, biochemist, educator, researcher; b. Puyo, Korea, Mar. 1, 1937; s. Sukzung and Kyung Sook (Lee) K.; m. Nakcheung Paik, Dec. 17, 1965. B.S., U. Seoul, 1959, M.S., 1961; Ph.D., U. Tubingen, Fed. Republic Germany, 1964. Research assoc. U. Tubingen, 1964-66, U. Notre Dame, Ind., 1966-67; research scientist NYU, 1967-68; assoc. prof. Mt. Sinai Med. Sch., N.Y.C., 1968—; research scientist VA Med. Ctr., Bronx, N.Y., 1982—. Contbr. articles to sci. jours. Named AID prof., 1978; NIH/Fogarty fellow 1976; Humboldt Soc. fellow, 1977; Mem. Am. Soc. Pharmacology and Exptl. Therapeutics, N.Y. Acad. Scis., AAAS, Harvey Soc. Current work: Purification, characterization, mechanism and clinical application of blood factors and related proteins. Subspecialties: Biochemistry (biology); Hematology. Home: 104 Wainwright Ave Closter NJ 07624 Office: Mt Sinai Sch Medicine 100th and Fifth Ave New York NY 10029

KANNAN, RAVINDRAN, computer science educator; b. Madras, India, Mar. 12, 1953; s. Seshadri and Mythili K. B.Tech., Indian Inst. Tech., 1974; Ph.D., Cornell U., 1979. Sci. asst. U. Bonn, 1978; postdoctoral fellow U. Calif.-Berkeley, 1979-80; asst. prof. MIT, Cambridge, 1980-83, assoc. prof., 1983-84; assoc. prof. Carnegie Mellon U., Pitts., 1983—. Editor Soc. Indsl. and Applied Math. Jour., 1984; assoc. editor Assn. Computing Machinery Jour. on Math. Software, 1984. Mem. Am. Math. Soc., Assn. Computing Machinery, N.Y. Acad. Scis. Current work: Theoretical computer science: algorithms, computational complexity, mathematics of computation-operations research; combinatorial optimization. Subspecialties: Theoretical computer science; Operations research (mathematics). Office: Dept Computer Sci Carnegie Mellon U Pittsburgh PA 15213

KANNEL, WILLIAM BERNARD, cardiovascular epidemiologist; b. Bklyn., Dec. 13, 1923; s. Joseph M. and Sarah M. (Golden) K.; m. Rita R. Lefkowitz, May 29, 1943; children: Linda J. Kannel Isaacson, Steven Michael, Patricia M.

Kannel Hoffman, Forrest S. M.D., Ga. Med. Coll., 1949; M.P.H., Harvard U., 1959. Intern, resident internal medicine S.I. Pub. Health Hosp., 1949-50, 53-56; asso. dir. Framingham (Mass.) Heart Study, Nat. Heart and Lung Inst., 1950-53, 56-67, dir., 1967-79; cons. Framingham Union Hosp., Cushing Hosp.; asso. medicine Boston U. Med. Sch.; lectr. preventive medicine Harvard U. Med. Sch.; prof. medicine, head sect. epidemiology and preventive medicine Boston U. Med. Center; med. dir. USPHS, 1949—. Contbr. med. jours.; mem. editorial bd.: Am. Heart Jour. Served with AUS, 1943-49. Recipient Gairdner Found. award, 1976; Einthoven award Leiden U., Netherlands, 1974; Francis medal U. Mich. Med. Sch., 1975; Polish Copernicus award, 1977; Dana award, 1972; Soc. Prospective Medicine award, 1979. Fellow Am. Coll. Cardiology, Am. Coll. Epidemiology; mem. Am. Heart Assn. (fellow council epidemiology, former chmn. council epidemiology), Assn. Commd. Officers USPHS, Alpha Omega Alpha. Democrat. Jewish. Current Work: Cardivascular epidemiology; preventive cardiology. Subspecialties: Epidemiology; Cardiology. Home: 30 Eliot St South Natick MA 01760 Office: Boston U Med Center 80 E Concord St Boston MA 02118

KANT, GLORIA JEAN, neurochemist; b. Chgo., June 6, 1944; d. Hans Georg and Jo Sefa (Pick) K.; m. Philip H. Balcom, July 1, 1967 (div. 1976). B.S., Mich. State U., 1965; Ph.D., U. Wis., 1969. Fellow dept. food sci. U. Wis., 1969-70; research chemist dept. psychiatry Walter Reed Army Inst. Research, Washington, 1970-71, dept. microwave research, 1971-76, dept. med. neuroscis., 1976-78, asst. chief neurochemistry and neuroendocrinology br. dept. med. neuroscis., 1978—. Contbr. articles to profl. jours. Mem. Soc. for Neurosci., AAAS, Internat. Chronobiology Soc., Sigma Xi, Sigma Delta Epsilon. Current work: Study of neurochemical and neuroendocrine responses to stress, trauma and centrally acting drugs. Subspecialties: Neurochemistry; Neuroendocrinology. Home: 1124 Dennis Ave Silver Spring MD 20901 Office: Dept Med Neurosciences Walter Reed Army Inst Research Washington DC 20307

KANTROWITZ, ADRIAN, surgeon, educator; b. N.Y.C., Oct. 4, 1918; s. Bernard Abraham and Rose (Esserman) K.; m. Jean Rosensaft, Nov. 25, 1948; children—Niki, Lisa, Allen. A.B., N.Y.U., 1940; M.D., L.I. Coll. Medicine, 1943; postgrad. physiology, Western Res. U., 1950. Diplomate: Am. Bd. Surgery, Am. Bd. Thoracic Surgery. Gen. rotating intern Jewish Hosp. Bklyn., 1944; asst. resident, then resident surgery Mt. Sinai Hosp., N.Y.C., 1947; asst. resident Montefiore Hosp., N.Y.C., 1948, asst. resident pathology, 1949, fellow cardiovascular research group, 1949, chief resident surgery, 1950, adj. surg. service, 1951-55; USPHS fellow cardiovascular research, dept. physiology Western Res. U., 1951-52, teaching fellow physiology, 1951-52; instr. surgery N.Y. Med. Coll., 1952-55; cons. surgeon Good Samaritan Hosp., Suffern, N.Y., 1954-55; asst. prof. surgery State U. N.Y. Coll. Medicine, 1955-56, asso. prof. surgery, 1957-64, prof., 1964-70; dir. cardiovascular surgery Maimonides Med. Center, Bklyn., 1955-64, dir. surgery, 1964-70; chmn. dept. surgery Sinai Hosp. Detroit, 1970—; prof. surgery Wayne State U. Sch. Medicine, 1970—. Contbr. articles profl. jours. Served from 1st lt. to capt., M.C. AUS, 1944-46. Recipient H.L. Moses prize to Montefiore Alumnus for outstanding research accomplishment, 1949; 1st prize sci. exhibit Conv. N.Y. State Med. Soc., 1952; Gold Plate award Am. Acad. Achievement, 1966; Max Berg award for outstanding achievement in prolonging human life, 1966; Theodore and Susan B. Cummings humanitarian award Am. Coll. Cardiology, 1967. Fellow N.Y. Acad. Sci., A.C.S.; mem. Internat. Soc. Angiology, Am. Soc. Artificial Internal Organs (pres. 1968-69), N.Y. County Med. Soc., Harvey Soc., N.Y. Soc. Thoracic Surgery, N.Y. Soc. Cardiovascular Surgery, Am. Heart Assn., Am. Physiol. Soc., Am. Coll. Cardiology, Am. Coll. Chest Physicians, Bklyn. Thoracic Surgery Soc. (pres. 1967-68), Pan Am. Med. Assn., Soaring Soc. Am., Am. Ski Assn. Pub. pioneer motion pictures taken inside living heart, 1950; contbr. to devel. pump- oxygenators for human heart surgey; pioneer devel. mech., artificial hearts; performed 1st permanent partial mech. heart surgery in humans, 1966; 1st use phase-shift intra-aortic balloon pump in patient in cardiogenic shock; 1st human heart transplant in U.S., Dec. 1967. Current Work: Research in area of a practical partial artificial heart. Subspecialties: Cardiac surgery; Artificial organs and prostheses. Home: 70 Gallogly Rd Pontiac MI 48053 Office: 6767 W Outer Dr Detroit MI 48253

KANTROWITZ, ARTHUR, physicist; b. N.Y.C., Oct. 20, 1913; s. Bernard A. and Rose (Esserman) K.; m. Rosalind Joseph, Sept. 12, 1943 (div.); children: Barbara, Lore, Andrea; m. Lee Stuart, Dec. 25, 1980. B.S., Columbia U., 1934, M.A., 1936, Ph.D., 1947; Dr.Engring. (hon.), Mont. Coll. Mineral Sci. and Tech., 1975; D.Sc. (hon.), N.J. Inst Tech., 1981. Physicist NACA, 1935-46; prof. aero. enging. and engring. physics Cornell U., 1946-56; dir. Avco-Everett Research Lab., Everett, Mass., 1955-72, chmn., chief exec. officer, 1972-78; sr. v.p., dir. Avco Corp., 1956-79; prof. Thayer Sch. Engring., Dartmouth Coll., 1979—; vis. lectr. Harvard, 1952; Fulbright and Guggenheim fellow Cambridge and Manchester univs., 1954; fellow Sch. Advanced Study, Mass. Inst. Tech., 1957, vis. inst. prof., from 1957; Messenger lectr. Cornell U., 1978; hon. prof. Huazhong Inst. Tech., Wuhan, China, 1980; mem. Presdl. Adv. Group on Anticipated Advances in Sci. and Tech., 1975-76; mem. tech. adv. bd. U.S. Dept. Commerce, 1974-77; mem. adv. panel NOVA, Sta. WGBH-TV; mem. bd. overseers Center for Naval Analyses, 1973-83; adv. council Israel-U.S. Binational Indsl. Research and Devel. Found.; Hon. trustee, past mem. mech. engring. adv. com. U. Rochester; mem. adv. council dept. aero. and mech. scis. Princeton U., 1959-77; mem. engring. adv. council Stanford U., 1966-82; mem. adv. bd. engring. Rensselaer Poly. Inst., 1982—. Contbr. articles to profl. jours. Recipient Kayan medal Columbia U., 1973, MHD Faraday Meml. medal, 1983, Theodore Roosevelt medal of honor for Distinguished Service in Sci. Fellow Am. Acad. Arts and Scis., Am. Phys. Soc., AAAS, AIAA, Am. Astronautical Soc.; mem. Internat. Acad. Astronautics, Nat. Acad. Scis., Nat. Acad. Engring., Am. Inst. Physics, Sigma Xi. Current Work: Interaction of science and technology with society. Subspecialties: Fluid mechanics; High energy lasers. Office: Dartmouth Coll Thayer Sch Engring Hanover NH 03755

KANURY, (ANJANEYA) MURTY, mechanical engineering educator, combustion researcher; b. Kavutaram, Andhra, India, Aug. 28, 1940; came to U.S., 1961, naturalized, 1973; s. Seshayya and Punnamma (Vellanki) K.; m. Kathleen Scheurer, Oct. 11, 1969; children—Sesh Marshall, Perry Ananth. B.Engring., Andhra U., Waltair, 1961; M.S., U. Minn., 1964, Ph.D., 1968. Sr. research scientist F.M. Research Corp., Norwood, Mass., 1969-73; sr. mech. engr. SRI Internat., Menlo Park, Calif., 1973-75; assoc. prof. mech. engring. U. Notre Dame, Ind., 1975-84; prof. mech. engring. Oreg. State U., Corvallis, 1985—; mem. ferrous metal fires panel Nat. Acad. Scis., 1980-81. Author: Introduction to Combustion Phenomena, 1975; also numerous tech. papers, research reports. Mem. editorial bd. Jour. Fire Safety, 1979—. Named Outstanding Tchr., U. Notre Dame Coll. Engring., 1980, recipient Faculty award dept. mech. engring., 1983; numerous grants. Mem. Combustion Inst., ASME (chmn. com. on environ. heat transfer 1981-84), Am. Soc. Engring. Educators (Western Electric Fund award 1982), Sigma Xi, Pi Tau Sigma. Current work: Fundamental research in heat and mass transfer and thermodynamics in the context of combustion in furnaces, engines and fires; application of engineering methodologies to social, economic and biological systems. Subspecialties: Combustion processes; Heat and mass transfer. Office: Dept Mech Engring Oreg State U Corvallis OR 97331

KAO, CHARLES KUEN, electrical engineer; b. Shanghai, China, Nov. 4, 1933; s. Chun-Hsien and Tsing-Fong K.; m. May Wan Wong, Sept. 19, 1959; children—Simon M. T., Amanda M.C. B.Sc. in Elec. Engring, U. London, 1957, Ph.D. in Elec. Engring, 1965. Devel. engr. Standard Telephones & Cables, Ltd., London, 1957-60; prin. research engr. Standard Telecommunications Lab., Ltd., Harlow, Eng., 1960-70; prof. electronics, chmn. dept. Chinese U. Hong Kong, 1970-74; chief scientist ITT Electro Optical Products div. ITT, Roanoke, Va., 1974-81, v.p., dir. engring., from 1981; now exec. scientist ITT Advanced Tech. Ctr., Shelton, Conn. Author: Optical Fiber Technology II; Optical Fiber Systems. Contbr. articles to profl. jours. Recipient Morey award Am. Ceramic Soc., 1976; Stewart Ballantine medal Franklin Inst., 1977; Rank prize Rank Trust Funds, 1978; Morris Liebmann Meml. award IEEE, 1978, Alexander Graham Bell medal, 1985; L.M. Ericsson Internat. prize, 1979; Gold medal Armed Forces Communications and Electronics Assn., 1980. Fellow IEEE, Inst. Elec. Engrs. (U.K.); mem. Optical Soc. Am. Patentee in field (29). Subspecialty: Fiber optics.

KAO, FA-TEN, geneticist; b. Hankow, China, Apr. 20, 1934; s. Ling-mai and Hang-seng (Feng) K.; m. Betty Chia-mai Tang, Dec. 17, 1960; 1 son, Alan S. B.S., Nat. Taiwan U., 1955; Ph.D., U. Minn., 1964. Nat. Cancer Inst. postdoctoral fellow, fellow dept. biophysics, instr. U. Colo. Med. Ctr., Denver, 1965-67, asst. prof., 1967-70, assoc. prof., 1970-81, prof., 1981—; sr. fellow Eleanor Roosevelt Inst. Cancer Research, Denver, 1965—; vis. scientist Sir William Dunn Sch. Pathology, U. Oxford, Eng., 1973-74. Eleanor Roosevelt Internat. Cancer fellow/Internat. Union Against Cancer, 1973-74. Mem. Genetics Soc. Am., Am. Soc. Cell Biology, Am. Soc. Human Genetics, Am. Assn. Cancer Research, Tissue Culture Assn., AAAS, Sigma Xi. Current Work: Researcher genetic studies of somatic mammalian cells, somatic cell and molecular genetic analysis of the human genome, mapping of human genes in the human genome, recombinant DNA and genetic engineering studies in mammalian cells. Subspecialties: Genome organization; Genetics and genetic engineering (biology). Home: 305 Leyden St Denver CO 80220 Office: Eleanor Roosevelt Inst for Cancer Research 4200 E 9th Ave B129 Denver CO 80262

KAO, RACE L., medical educator; b. Chunking, Sechun, China, Dec. 1, 1943; came to U.S., 1967; s. Yu-Ho and Tsing (Tsou) K.; m. Lidia Wei Liu, Aug. 18, 1969; children: Elizabeth C., Grace W. B.S., Nat. Taiwan U., 1965; M.S., U. Ill., 1971, Ph.D., 1972. Research assoc. dept. animal sci. U. Ill., Urbana, 1972; research assoc. dept. physiology Pa. State U.-Hershey, 1972-75, asst. prof., 1976-77; dir. cardiothoracic research U. Tex. Med. Branch-Galveston, 1977-82, asst. prof. surgery, physiology, 1977-82; asst. prof. dept. surgery Washington U., St. Louis, 1982—. Author: Cardiac Adaptation, 1977. Pres. U. Tex. Chinese Assn., 1981. Served to lt. U.S. Army, 1965-66. NIH grantee, 1982—; Washington U. grantee, 1982—; Am. Heart Assn. grantee, 1983—. Mem. Am. Physiol. Soc., Internat. Soc. for Heart Research, Nat. Soc. Med. Research, Nutrition Today Soc. Current Work: Myocardial metabolism under ischemic, anoxic and hypertrophying conditions; protection of myocardium during cardiopulmonary by-pass; regulation of isolated cardiomyocyte metabolism. Subspecialties: Cardiac surgery; Physiology (medicine). Home: 812 Haverton Dr Saint Louis MO 63141

KAO, WINSTON WHEI-YANG, biochemist, educator; b. Tainan, Taiwan, Mar. 3, 1941; came to U.S., 1970; s. Bin-Wu and Pao-Tsu (Sun) K.; m. Candace Whei-Cheng, May 10, 1970; 2 sons, Edward Chung-Peng, Charles Chung-L. B.S., Nat. Taiwan U., 1966, M.S., 1970; Ph.D., U. Pa., 1974. Teaching asst. Nat. Taiwan U., 1967-68; research and teaching specialist III Rutgers U. Med. Sch., Piscataway, N.J., 1974-76; research asst. prof. U. Pitts., 1976-78, asst. prof., 1978-82; assoc. prof., dir. ophthal. research U. Cin., 1982—. Served to 2nd lt. AUS, 1966-67. Mem. Assn. Research in Vision and Ophthalmology, Am. Soc. Biol. Chemists, Chinese Soc. Biochemists. Current Work: regulation of collagen gene expression in ocular tissues. Subspecialties: Biochemistry (medicine); Cell biology (medicine). Home: 10343 Peachtree Ln Cincinnati OH 45242 Office: Dept Ophthalmolog U Cincinnati Coll Medicine Cincinnati OH 45267

KAPLAN, ALAN MARC, immunologist, educator; b. Bklyn., Dec. 10, 1940; s. Albert J. and Esther (Warshaw) K.; m. Eva Ruzickova, Mar. 18, 1972; 1 dau., Ali Michelle. B.S., Tufts U., 1963; Ph.D., Purdue U., 1969. Postdoctoral fellow U. Toronto Sch. Medicine, 1969-72; asst. prof. depts. microbiology and surgery Med. Coll. Va., Richmond, 1972-75, assoc. prof., 1975-79, prof., 1979-82; assoc. dir. research Med. Coll. Va./Va. Commonwealth U. Cancer Center, Richmond, 1980-82, dep. chmn. dept. microbiology, 1981-82; prof., chmn. dept. med. microbiology and immunology U. Ky. Sch. Medicine, Lexington, 1982—; mem. exptl. immunology study sect. NIH, 1978-82. Named Outstanding Grad. Faculty Mem. Med. Coll. Va., 1978; Med. Research Council Can. postdoctoral fellow, 1969-72. Mem. Am. Assn. Immunologists, Am. Soc. Microbiology, Reticuloendothelial Soc. Explt. Biology and Medicine, Am. Assn. Cancer Research, N.Y. Acad. Scis. Democrat. Jewish. Current Work: Cellular immunology, tumor immunology, macrophage immunology, hybridoma technology. Subspecialties: Immunobiology and immunology; Immunogenetics. Home: 3434 Brandon Dr Lexington KY 40502 Office: U Ky Med Center 800 Rose St MS 409 Lexington KY 40356-0084

KAPLAN, ANN ESTHER, chemist; b. N.Y.C., Dec. 28, 1926; d. Julius Jacob and Vera Deborah (Dentschman) K. B.A., Hunter Coll., 1947; M.A., Mt. Holyoke Coll., 1949; Ph.D., U. Pa., 1959. Postdoctoral fellow Med. Sch., NYU, N.Y.C., 1959-60; sr. postdoctoral fellow, instr. Albert Einstein Coll. Medicine, Bronx, N.Y., 1960-63; research assoc. Rockefeller U., N.Y.C., 1963-65; asst. prof. grad. faculty CUNY, N.Y.C., 1965-67; sr. research assoc. Salk Inst., La Jolla, Calif., 1967-72; chemist, research chemist Nat. Cancer Inst., NIH, Bethesda/Frederick, Md., 1972—. Contbr. articles to profl. jours. Mem. Am. Soc. Biol. Chemists, Biophys. Soc., Am. Chem. Soc., Am. Physiol. Soc., Soc. Gen. Physiology, Am. Soc. Cell Biology, Sigma Xi. Club: Chemists (N.Y.C.). Current work: Molecular modifications in chemically-transformed neoplastic cells, including enzymes and kinetic changes, cytoskeletal proteins and cell ultrastructure. Subspecialties: Biochemistry (medicine); Cancer research (medicine). Office: Nat Cancer Inst Frederick Cancer Research Facility Bldg 560 Frederick MD 21701

KAPLAN, HENRY JERROLD, physician, ophthalmology educator, researcher; b. N.Y.C., Dec. 29, 1942; s. Ralph and Henrietta (Davis) K.; m. Adele Lotner, June 26, 1966; children—Wendi Suzanne, Todd Daniel, Ariane Dev. A.B., Columbia U., 1964; M.D., Cornell U., 1968. Intern Lakeside Hosp., Case Western Res. U., Cleve., 1968-69; resident in surgery Bellevue Hosp., NYU Med. Ctr., N.Y.C., 1969-70; NIH research fellow in immunology dept. cell biology U. Tex.-Dallas, 1972-74; resident in ophthalmology U. Iowa Hosps. and Clinics, Iowa City, 1975-78; retina-vitreous fellow Med. Coll. Wis., Milw., 1978-79; asst. prof. dept. cell biology U. Tex.-Dallas, 1974-75; assoc. prof. dept. ophthalmology Emory U. Sch. Medicine, Atlanta, 1979-84, prof., 1984—. Contbr. articles and abstracts to profl. jours. Served to maj. USAF, 1970-72. Cornell U. scholar, 1964-68; travelling fellow Assn. Research Vision and Ophthalmology, 1975; Olga Keith Wiess scholar Research to Prevent Blindness, Inc., 1984. Fellow Am. Acad. Ophthalmology; mem. Assn. for Research Vision and Ophthalmology, Am. Assn. Ophthalmology, AAAS, AMA, N.Y. Acad. Scis., Am. Assn. Immunology, DeKalb County Med. Soc., Ga. Ophthalmic Soc., Macula Soc., Am. Uveitis Soc. Republican. Jewish. Current work: Ocular immunology of retinal, uveal and vitreous disease; specifically, uveitis, choroidal melanoma and optic nerve regeneration. Subspecialty: Ophthalmology. Office: Emory Clinic 1327 Clifton Rd NE Atlanta GA 30322

KAPLAN, KENNETH CHARLES, physician; b. N.Y.C., Apr. 8, 1937; s. Bernard I. and Helen R. (Gardner) K.; m. Rebecca C. Hall, Oct. 20, 1979; children: Jessica, Jeremy, Miriam, Jonah E., Sarah Christine. A.B., Dartmouth Coll., 1958; M.D., NYU, 1962. Diplomate: Am. Bd. Internal Medicine, Am. Bd. Cardiovascular Diseases. Intern, resident Bellevue Hosp., N.Y.C.; resident Univ. Hosp., N.Y.C.; sr. attending physician Phelps Meml. Hosp., North Tarrytown, N.Y., 1969—, assoc. dir. electrocardiology, 1974—, dir. specialty care units, 1974—; cons. in cardiology Peekskill Community Hosp., 1970—, Ossining Correctional Facility, 1969—. Bd. dirs., pres. area 9 Profl. Standards Rev. Orgn., Westchester and Putnam Counties, 1976-82, sec. exec. com., Purchase, N.Y., 1980-82. Served to lt. comdr. USPHS, 1963-68. Fellow ACP, Am. Coll. Cardiology; mem. Am. Heart Assn. (fellow council on clin. cardiology), Am. Fedn. for Clin. Research. Subspecialties: Cardiology; Internal medicine. Home: Teatown Rd Croton-on-Hudson NY 10520 Office: 100 S Highland Ave Ossining NY 10562

KAPLAN, MARTIN LOUIS, research chemist, lawyer; b. N.Y.C., Dec. 27, 1935; s. Irving and Molly K.; m. Frances Fisher, Dec. 30, 1964; 1 child, Jason. B.S., CCNY, 1956; M.S., Fla. State U., 1960; J.D., Seton Hall U., 1970. Bar: N.J. 1970. Research chemist Richfield Oil Corp., Anaheim, Calif., 1960-62; vol. U.S. Peace Corps, Somali Republic, 1962-64; mem. tech. staff AT&T Bell Labs., Murray Hill, N.J., 1964—. Contbr. articles to profl. jours. Patentee in field. Mem. Am. Chem. Soc., London Chem. Soc. Current work: Electrical and optical properties of organic thin films and polymers. Subspecialties: Organic chemistry; Polymer chemistry. Office: AT&T Bell Labs Murray Hill NJ 07974

KAPLAN, MELVIN H., immunologist, rheumatologist, educator, researcher, clinician; b. Malden, Mass., Dec. 23, 1920; s. Harry and Rena (Chernoff) K. A.B., Harvard U., 1942, M.D., 1952. Intern, Boston City Hosp., 1952-53; research fellow and assoc. Children's Med. Ctr., Boston, 1953-58; asst. instr., assoc. dept. bacteriology and immunology Harvard U., Boston, 1953-58; from asst. prof. to prof. medicine Case-Western Res. U., Cleve., 1958-74; prof. medicine U. Mass., Worcester, 1974—, dir. div. rheumatology and immunology, 1974-82; assoc. mem. commn. streptococcal diseases Dept. Def., 1958-71; established investigator Am. Heart Assn., Boston and Cleve., 1954-61; mem. allergy and immunology study sect. NIH, Washington, 1965-69; mem. research merit rev. VA, Washington, 1972-76; advisor WHO, Africa, 1965; mem. exec. bd., med. adv. bd. Arthritis Found., Mass., 1976—; mem. med. adv. com. Lupus Found., New England, 1978—. Served with AUS, 1942-46. Assoc. editor med. and immunology jours. Contbr. articles and book chpts. to profl. publs. Recipient research career award USPHS, Cleve., 1964-74. Mem. Am. Assn. Immunologists, Am. Soc. Clin. Investigation, Am. Rheumatism Assn., Infectious Disease Soc. Am. Current work: Pathogenesis of rheumatic fever, systemic lupus, and autoimmunity mechanisms; C-reactive protein. Subspecialties: Immunology (medicine); Rheumatology. Home: 1500 Worcester Rd Apt 605E Framingham MA 01701 Office: Dept Immunology and Rheumatology Univ Mass Med Sch 55 Lake Ave N Worcester MA 01605

KAPLAN, MICHAEL, chemist; b. N.Y.C., Nov. 7, 1937; s. Samuel and Ruth (Sarapin) K.; m. Bette Kerr, June 18, 1961 (div. June 1967); m. Ellen Phyllis Max, May 26, 1968. B.S., Rensselaer Polytech. Inst., 1959; M.A., Columbia U., 1961, Ph.D., 1965. Mem. tech. staff RCA Labs., Princeton, N.J., 1965—. Contbr. papers to profl. publs. Patentee in field. Pres., Franklin Twp. Bd. Edn., N.J., 1981-82; pres. Community Jewish Sch., New Brunswick, N.J., 1982-85. Mem. Am. Chem. Soc. Democrat. Jewish. Current work: Interation of radiation with matter, as applied to resist technology. Subspecialties: Physical chemistry; Photochemistry. Home: 645 Copper Mine Rd Princeton NJ 08540 Office: RCA Labs Princeton NJ 08540

KAPLAN, RICHARD STEPHEN, research physician, educator; b. Pitts., Aug. 24, 1945; s. Simon H. and Virginia L. (Mann) K.; m. Laurelynn M. Smith, Aug. 21, 1970. B.A., U. Pitts., 1966; M.D., U. Miami, 1970. Diplomate: Am. Bd. Internal Medicine, Am. Bd. Med. Oncology. Clin. assoc. Nat. Cancer Inst., NIH, Balt. Cancer Research Center, 1971-73, sr. investigator, 1979-81; asst. prof. U. Miami and Comprehensive Cancer Center of Fla., 1975-79; assoc. prof. U. Md. Cancer Center, 1981—. Contbr. chpts. to books, articles to jours. Served with USPHS, 1971-73, 79-81. Fellow ACP; mem. Am. Assn. Cancer Research, Am. Soc. Clin. Oncology, N.Y. Acad. Scis., AAAS. Current Work: Clinical trials of investigational drugs and treatments in lymphomas and brain tumors. Subspecialties: Cancer research (medicine); Oncology. Home: 3806 Greenway Baltimore MD 21218 Office: 22 S Greene St Room S9D05 Baltimore MD 21201

KAPLAN, SANFORD SANDY, geologist; b. N.Y.C., Oct. 2, 1950; s. Lawrence J. and Jeanne (Leon) K.; m. Joanne Mandel, June 5, 1975; children—Elicia Anne, Shira Frieda. A.B., Lafayette Coll., 1971; M.S., Lehigh U., 1976; postgrad. U. Nebr., 1976-79; Ph.D., U. Pitts., 1981. Vis. lectr. Northampton County Community Coll., Bethlehem, Pa., 1974-75; geologist Wyo. Geol. Survey, Laramie, 1975; Coal mining engr. U.S. Steel, Monroeville, Pa., 1976; lectr. U. Nebr., Lincoln, 1976-79; vis. lectr. U. Pitts., 1979; coal geologist U.S. Dept. Energy, Bruceton, Pa., 1979-80; geol. specialist Pennzoil Exploration and Prodn., Denver, 1980—; Co-editor: Cenozoic Paleogeography of the Rocky Mountain Area, 1985. Contbr. articles to profl. jours. Composer mus. Composition and dance, 1979. Chmn. Citizens Against Jewell Ave. Overpass, Aurora, Colo., 1983—; scoutmaster Denver Area council Boy Scouts Am., Aurora, 1983—; vol. pub. radio, Denver, 1982—. Served with USNR, 1969—, lt. comdr. Res. Recipient 2d prize U.S. Naval Inst. Essay Contest, 1984; L. Dyson Meml. scholar, 1970. Mem. Am. Assn. Petroleum Geologists, Geol. Soc. Am., Soc. Econ. Paleontologists and Mineralogists (editor newsletter Rocky Mountain sect. 1982-84, reviewer, 1979—), Naval Res. Assn., Res. Officer Assn., U.S. Naval Inst. Democrat. Jewish. Current work: Relationships between tectonics and sedimentation in North America; coal geology depositional environments and paleotectonic implications; geochemistry of trace elements in coals and nearshore sediments; global tectonics. Subspecialties: Sedimentology; Tectonics. Home: 11761 E Asbury Pl Aurora CO 80014 Office: Penzoil Exploration and Prodn 1600 Broadway Suite 1800 Denver CO 80014

KAPLAN, STANLEY ALBERT, pharm. research co. exec.; b. N.Y.C., Sept. 23, 1938; s. Martin and Sara (Meszel) K.; m. Lois E., Sept. 11, 1960; children: Lisa, Michelle, Martin. B.S., Columbia U., 1959, M.S., 1961; Ph.D. in Pharm. Chemistry, U. Calif., San Francisco, 1965. Postdoctoral fellow NIH, St. Mary's Hosp. Med. Sch., London, Eng., 1965-66; sr. biochemist dept. clin. pharmacology Hoffmann-LaRoche, Inc., Nutley, N.J., 1966-70, research group chief, 1971-73, asst. dir. dept. biochemistry and drug metabolism, 1964-65, assoc. dir., 1976-78, dir. dept. pharmacokinetics and biopharms., 1979. Editorial bd.: Jour. Biopharmacoutics and Drug Disposition; Contbr. numerous articles to profl.jours. Fellow Acad. Pharm. Scis., Am Coll. Clin. Pharmacology; mem. Am. Pharm. Assn., Acad. Pharm. Scis., N.Y. Acad. Scis., AAAS (leader pharm. scis. sect. 1983—), Am. Soc. Pharmacology and Exptl. Therapeutics. Lodge: B'nai B'rith. Current Work: Physiol. dispostion of drugs, pharamacodynamics. Subspecialties: Pharmacokinetics; Biochemistry (biology). Home: 24 Erli St Wayne NJ 07470 Office: Hoffmann LaRoche Inc Nutley NJ 07110

KAPOOR, ASHOK KUMAR, electrical engineer; b. Allahabad, India, Feb. 7, 1952; came to U.S., 1976; s. Ram Nath and Sarla (Tandon) K.; m. Nisha Malhotra, May 1, 1984. B.Tech., Indian Inst. Tech., Kanpur, 1973; M.S., U. Cin., 1979, Ph.D., 1981. Illumination engr. Philips India Ltd., Bombay, 1973-76; mem. research staff Fairchild Research Ctr., Palo Alto, Calif., 1981—; key technologist Fairchild Camera and Instrument Corp., Palo Alto, 1983—. Contbr. articles to profl. jours. Patentee in field. Mem. Electron Devices Soc. of IEEE, Sigma Xi. Current work: High speed semiconductor switching devices and circuits; conduction mechanism between metal and semiconductor (mono and polycrystalline); semiconductor integrated circuit technology; defects in electronic materials; social impact of technology. Subspecialties: Semiconductors; Microchip technology (engineering). Home: 3353 Alma St Apt 145 Palo Alto CA 94306 Office: Fairchild Research Ctr 4001 Miranda Ave Palo Alto CA 94304

KAPP, JOHN PAUL, neurosurgeon, educator; b. Galax, Va., Feb. 22, 1938; s. Paul Homer and Katherine (Vass) K.; m. Emily Lurleese Evans, June 23, 1961; children—Paul Hardin, Emily Camille. M.D., Duke U., 1963, B.S., 1966, Ph.D., 1967. Diplomate: Am. Bd. Neurol. Surgery. Asst. prof. neurosurgery U. Tenn., Memphis, 1971-72; attending neurosurgeon Bapt. Hosp., Memphis, 1972, Bay Med. Ctr., Panama City, Fla., 1972-80; assoc. prof. neurosurgery U. Miss. Med. Ctr., Jackson, 1980-83, prof. neurosurgery, 1983-85; prof., chmn. dept. neurosurgery SUNY-Buffalo, 1985—; pres. Coast Research Found., Panama City, 1978—. Author: The Cerebral Venous System and Its Disorders, 1984. Recipient Research award Am. Acad. Neurol. Surgery, 1967; NIH fellow, 1965-67. Mem. Am. Heart Assn. (stroke council), S.W. Oncology Group (brain com.), Am. Assn. Neurol. Surgeons, ACS, Phi Beta Kappa, Sigma Xi, Alpha Omega Alpha. Democrat. Methodist. Current Work: Drug Sensitivity testing in brain tumor chemotherapy. Venous disease in the brain. Subspecialties: Neurosurgery; Cancer research (medicine). Home: 215 Woodbridge Ave Buffalo NY 14214 Office: 50 High St Buffalo NY 14203

KAPP, JOSEPH ALEXANDER, materials engineer, researcher, educator; b. Troy, N.Y., July 22, 1953; s. Fred G. and Lourdes A. (Duncan) K.; m. Nancy A. Murphy, Oct. 10, 1981. Student, Clarkson Coll, 1971-73, Hudson Valley Community Coll., 1973; B.S.M.E., Union Coll., 1975, M.S.E., 1977; Ph.D., Rensselaer Poly. Inst., 1982. Process engr. processes unit Watervliet (N.Y.) Arsenal, 1975-78; research materials engr. materials engring. sect. Benet Weapons Lab., Watervliet, 1978—; instr. in materials engring. Hudson Valley Community Coll., 1981—; sec. Army fellow and acad. visitor mech. engring. dept. Imperial Coll., London, 1985-86; adj. assoc. prof. Union Coll., 1982—. Contbr. articles to profl. jours. Mem. ASME, ASTM, Soc. Exptl. Mechanics. Roman Catholic. Current Work: Basic research interests in mechanical behavior of materials, fatigue and fracture, including environmental effects; applied research interests in thick walled pressure vessel technology. Subspecialties: Fracture mechanics; Materials (engineering). Home: 25 Elmhurst Ave Rensselaer NY 12144 Office: Research Br Benet Weapons Lab Watervliet NY 12189

KAPPENBERG, RICHARD PAUL, neuropsychologist, clinical psychologist; b. Jamaica, N.Y., Feb. 5, 1944; s. John William and Cornelia (Taylor) K.; m. Judith Nakashima, Nov. 26, 1970; children—Erin, Lee. B.A., Fairfield U., 1965, M.A., 1966; Ph.D., U. Hawaii, 1973. Diplomate Am. Acad. Behavioral Medicine; lic. psychologist, Hawaii; cert. mental health care provider; cert. health care provider in marital and family therapy; cert. disability determination examiner, Hawaii. Dir. rehab. services Salvation Army Men's Soc. Services Ctr., Honolulu, 1967-68; dir. guidance The Acad., Honolulu, 1968-69; counseling intern Counseling and Testing Ctr., U. Hawaii, Honolulu, 1969-70, clin. intern. 1970-72; clin. intern Tripler Army Med. Ctr., Honolulu, 1970-71; psychologist Dept. Army, Schofield Barracks, Hawaii, 1972-73; asst. prof. dept. human devel. U. Hawaii, 1973-79, chmn. dept. human devel., 1980; self-employed psychologist, Honolulu, 1974-80; chief psychologist Rehab. Hosp of Pacific, Honolulu, 1974—; practicum supr. ednl. psychology Sch. Nursing Social Work, U. Hawaii, 1971-73; cons. psychologist Ctr. Psychol.

Service, Tng. and Research, Honolulu, 1970-72; psychologist Model Cities Program, Kuhio Park Terr., Honolulu, 1971; psychologist Met. Counseling Ctr., 1971-72; clin. cons. in psychology div. vocat. rehab. Central sect. State of Hawaii, 1975—; cons. St. Timothy's Preschool, 1978—; peer reviewer Office of Civilian Health and Med. Plan for Uniformed Service, 1978—; conducted over 30 workshops in communication skills for mil. and civilian groups; asst. developer and assessor new criteria for hiring of police officers; mem. Joint. Com. on Continuing Edn. for Psychologists, 1977, Continuing Edn. for Psychologists Com., 1979, Sunset Legis. and Psychol. Licensing Com., 1980, 81. Contbr. articles to profl. publs. Mem. AAAS, Am. Assn. Marriage and Family Therapists, Am. Psychol. Assn., Western Psychol. Assn., Hawaii Psychol. Assn. (profl. affairs com. 1976, 83-85, conv. com. 1977, pres. 1978, ad hoc com. on lic. legis. 1983), Hawaii Council on Family Relations (v.p. 1977, 78, 79, 80), Hawaii Assn. Marriage and Family Therapists. Current work: Brain injury and its rehabilitation. Office: Rehab Hosp of Pacific 226 N Kuakini St Honolulu HI 96817

KAPP-PIERCE, JUDITH ANNE, immunologist, educator; b. Akron, Ohio, July 28, 1943; d. Walter and Dorothy Gwendolyn (Hower) Kapp; m. Carl W. Pierce, Dec. 1, 1973. B.A., Miami U., Oxford, Ohio, 1965; M.S., Ind. U., 1969; Ph.D., Harvard U., 1976. Research asst. Harvard U., Boston, 1969-73; assoc. staff Jewish Hosp., St. Louis, 1976—; asst. prof., then assoc. prof. Washington U., St. Louis, 1976-84, prof., 1984—. Editor; Ir Genes Past, Present, and Future, 1983. Mem. editorial bd. Jour. Immunology, 1979-83. Contbr. chpts. to books, articles to profl. jours. NIH grantee, 1977—. Mem. Am. Assn. Immunologists, Am. Assn. Pathologists, Sigma Xi. Current work: Cellular Immunology; immunoregulation; autoimmunity. Subspecialties: Immunobiology and immunology; Immunogenetics. Office: Jewish Hosp CSB-7 216 S Kingshighway Saint Louis MO 63110

KAPRON, FELIX PAUL, physicist. Sr. tech. cons. ITT Electro-Optical Products Div., Roanoke, Va. Subspecialty: Fiber optics. Office: ITT Electro-Optical Products Div 7635 Plantation Rd Roanoke VA 24019

KAPUR, KAILASH CHANDER, industrial engineering educator, consultant; b. Rawalpindi, Pakistan, Aug. 17, 1941; came to U.S., 1965; s. Gobind Ram and Vidya Vanti (Khanna) K.; m. Geraldine Palmer, May 15, 1969; children: Anjali Joy, Jay Palmer. B.S.M.E., Delhi U., 1963; M. Tech., Indian Inst. Tech., 1965; M.S., U. Calif.-Berkeley, 1967, Ph.D., 1969. Registered profl. engr., Mich. Sr. research engr. Gen. Motors Research Labs., Warren, Mich., 1969-70; mem. faculty Wayne State U., Detroit, 1970—, prof., 1980—; vis. scholar Ford Motor Co., Dearborn, Mich., summer 1973; vis. prof. U. Waterloo, Ont., Can., 1977-78; sr. reliability engr. TACOM, U.S. Army, summer 1978; cons. Author: Reliability in Engineering Design, 1977, also articles.; Assoc. editor: Jour. Reliability and Safety, 1982—. Grantee Gen. Motors Corp., 1974-77; Grantee U.S. Army, 1978; Grantee U.S. Dept. Transp., 1980-82. Mem. Inst. Indsl. Engrs. (assoc. editor 1980—), IEEE (sr.), Ops. Research Soc. Am. (sr.). Current Work: Research in area of reliability engineering, design reliability, transportation systems, quality control and optimization. Subspecialties: Industrial engineering; Operations research (engineering). Home: 17291 Jeanette Southfield MI 48075 Office: Wayne State U 640 Putnam Detroit MI 48202

KARABATSOS, GERASIMOS JOHN, educator, chemist; b. Chomatada, Greece, May 17, 1932; came to U.S., 1950, naturalized, 1963; s. John P. and Athena (Papadopoulou) K.; m. Marianna Marris, Dec. 16, 1956; children—Lelena, Yanna, Jason, Byron. B.A. magna cum laude, Adelphi Coll., 1954; M.A., Harvard, 1956, Ph.D., 1959. Asst. prof. Mich. State U., East Lansing, 1959-63, asso. prof., 1963-65, prof. chemistry, 1966—, chmn. dept., 1975—; NSF sr. postdoctoral fellow U. Calif., Berkeley, 1965-66; Ford Found. vis. prof. San Marcos U., Peru, 1967; sci. dir. Greek Atomic Energy Commn., 1974—. Editor: Advances in Alicyclic Chemistry, 1966; Contbr. articles profl. jours. Sloan Found. fellow, 1962-66; Recipient Sigma Xi Jr. Research award, 1970, Am. Chem. Soc. award in petroleum chemistry, 1971; Distinguished Faculty award Mich. State U., 1971. Mem. Greek Acad. of Athens (corr.), Am. Chem. Soc., Chem. Soc. London, Sigma Xi. Current Work: NMR, isotope effects; stereochemistry; stereochemistry of some biochemical reactions. Subspecialties: Nuclear magnetic resonance; Organic chemistry. Home: 1623 Old Mill Rd East Lansing MI 48823

KARACHEWSKI, JOHN ANDREW, geoscientist, researcher; b. Chgo., Dec. 7, 1957; s. Mike and Helen (Szkodyn) K. B.S. in Geol. Scis., U. Ill.-Chgo., 1980; M.S. in Geology and Geophysics, Western Wash. U., 1983. Teaching asst. Western Wash. U., 1981-83; teaching asst. Colo. Sch. Mines, Golden, 1983-84, ARCO teaching fellow, 1984—. Author: (abstract) Geology of Lincoln Creek Formation Washington, 1984. Mem. Geol. Soc. Am., Am. Geophys. Union. Club: Outdoor Program (Golden). Current work: Paleomagnetism and structural analysis of Brooks Range, Alaska; analysis of clastic-carbonate shorelines. Subspecialty: Tectonics. Office: Dept Geology Colo Sch Mines Golden CO 80401

KARAGUEUZIAN, HRAYR SEVAG, pharmacologist; b. Damascus, Syria, June 30, 1946; came to U.S., 1970, naturalized, 1977; s. Anania Dirkran and Sona (Bedrossian) K.; m. Lena Vahan Demirjian, Feb. 20, 1982; 1 child: Saro. B.Sc., Damascus U., 1969; M.Sc., Columbia U., 1972, M.Phil., 1975, Ph.D., 1978. Research assoc. U. Paris, 1978-79; postdoctoral fellow U. Calif., San Francisco, 1979-80; dir., asst. prof. Cedars-Sinai Med. Ctr., Los Angeles, 1980—. Contbr. articles to profl. jours. Recipient Research Career Devel. award NIH, 1984—; Los Angeles Heart Assn. grantee, 1980-82; Cino-Del-Duca research award Paris, 1978. Mem. Cardiac Electrophysiology Assn. (sec.), Western Pharmacology Soc., Am. Fedn. Clin. Research, Am. Heart Assn., AAAS. Democrat. Christian Orthodox. Current Work: Study of the mechanism and site of origin of cardiac arrhythmias associated with ishcemic heart disease and determination of mode of action of drugs. Subspecialties: Physiology (biology); Pharmacology. Home: 12601 Miranda St North Hollywood CA 91607 Office: Cedars Sinai Med Center 8700 Beverly Blvd Los Angeles CA 91607

KARANTINOS, ANDREW E., mathematics educator; b. Langa, Kastoria, Greece, June 24, 1935; came to U.S., 1951, naturalized, 1956; s. Elias and Vasiliki (Eliades) K.; m. Effie Stergios, June 26, 1960; children: Nick, Chris. B.S., Morningside Coll, Sioux City, Iowa, 1959; M.S., SUNY-Buffalo, 1963; Ph.D., U. S.D., 1973; postgrad., Mich. State U., 1980, U. Wis.-Madison, Rutgers U. Tchr. Paullina (Iowa) High Sch., 1959-61, chmn. math. dept., 1959-61; tchr. Central High Sch., Sioux City, 1961-65, chmn. math. dept., 1961-65; prof. math. U. S.D., Vermillion, 1965—, chmn. sci. and math. div., 1985—, chmn. math contest, 1965—. Author: Math. Sci. Newsletter, 1981-83. Recipient Outstanding Prof. award U. S.D., 1979-80, Outstanding Tchr. of Yr., 1985; Outstanding Tchr. of Yr. award U. S.D. Students, 1985. Mem. Am. Hellenic Ednl. Progressive Assn. (dist. gov. 1976, supreme gov. 1979-80, chmn. edn. found. 1981-83), Math. Assn. Am., Nat. Council Tchrs. Math., Acad. Sci., Pi Mu Epsilon, Sigma Pi Sigma, Phi Delta Kappa, Omicron Delta Kappa. Greek Orthodox. Club: Math. and Computer Sci. (adv. 1970—). Lodges: Lions; Masons. Current Work: Mathematics education; theory of learning mathematics; mathematics curriculum. Subspecialty: Statistics. Home: 1019 Crestview St Vermillion SD 57069 Office: Univ SD Dakota Hall 315 Vermillion SD 57069

KARAS, BRADLEY ROSS, research chemist; b. Milw., Apr. 13, 1955; s. Howard R. and Rollyn (Agulnick) K.; m. Pamela Lynn McCreadie, Apr. 24, 1983. B.A. with honors, U. Pa., 1977; Ph.D., U. Wis.-Madison, 1981. Chemist, Corp. Research and Devel. Ctr., Gen. Electric Co., Schenectady, 1981—. Contbg. author: Faraday Discussion, 1980; Advanced Chemistry Series, 1980. Tng. council mem. Schenectady Day Tng. Club, 1984. Mem. Am. Chem. Soc. (contbg. author symposia series 1981), Electrochem. Soc., (Joseph W. Richards summer fellow 1979), Phi Lambda Upsilon. Current work: Electrochemistry, energy storage, high temperature batteries, electroless metals deposition, organometallic and photochemistry, photoelectrochemistry. Subspecialties: Inorganic chemistry; Electrochemistry. Office: Corp Research and Devel Ctr General Electric Co PO Box 8 Schenectady NY 12301

KARASIK, MYRON SOLOMON, systems and software engineer, consultant; b. N.Y.C., June 3, 1950; s. Jack and Bertha Clara (Shapiro) K.; m. Sara Louise Lieber, Aug. 29, 1976; 1 child, Ruth Jacqueline. M.S.E.E., Purdue U., 1972; M.Mgmt., Northwestern U., 1975. Cert. mgmt. cons.; C.P.A. Mem. tech. staff Bell Telephone Labs., Piscataway, N.J., 1972-73; cons. Deloitte, Haskins and Sells, Chgo., 1975-78; v.p. J.P. Walsh and Co., Chgo., 1979; prin. cons. MWS Cons., Chgo, 1980; ptnr. Veatch, Rich and Nadler, Northbrook, Ill., 1981-83; pres. Orgn., Automation Support & Assurance Services, Ltd., Chgo., 1984—; dir. B.L. Rosenberg and Co., Chgo., Author various software products; co-author: ANSI/IEEE Guidelines for Software Quality Assurance, 1983. Contbr. articles to profl. jours. Austin scholar, 1973-75; Northwestern U. disting. scholar, 1975. Mem. IEEE (tech. com. on software standards), Assn. Computing Machinery, Ill. C.P.A. Soc. (mgmt. adv. service com. 1983—), Am. Inst. CPAs. Jewish. Current work: Development of theoretical foundations of dynamics of complex socio-economic systems and application through simulation models; development of comprehensive system testing techniques using formal languages and expert systems. Subspecialties: Software engineering; Systems engineering. Office: OASAS Suite 2300 180 N LaSalle St Chicago IL 60601

KARAVOLAS, HARRY J(OHN), biochemist; b. Peabody, Mass., Feb. 21, 1936; s. John Louis and Maria (Kayavas) K.; m. Barbara A. Katsaras, Aug. 26, 1962; 1 son, Christian Mark. B.S., Mass. Coll. Pharmacy, 1957, M.S. (Am. Found. Pharm. Edn. fellow), 1959; Ph.D. (USPHS fellow), St. Louis U., 1963; postgrad., Harvard U., 1963-66. Research fellow in biol. chemistry Harvard U. Med. Sch., 1963-66, research asso., instr. biol. chemistry, 1966-68, vis. lectr. biol. chemistry, 1975; tutor biochemical scis. Harvard Coll., 1966-68; asst. prof. physiol. chemistry and endocrinology U. Wis., Madison, 1968-72, mem. endocrinology-reproductive physiology program, 1968—, asso. dir., 1974—, asso. prof. physiol. chemistry, 1972-75, prof., chmn. dept., 1975—; sect. head neuroendocrinology Waisman Center on Mental Retardation and Human Devel., 1972-83; mem. study sect. biochem. endocrinology NIH, 1979—. Editorial bd.: Endocrinology, 1974-78; bd. reviewers: Federation Proceedings, 1972-77; contbr. sci. articles to profl. jours. Recipient Borden award; Merck award; Rexall award, 1957; Amoco Distinguished Teaching award U. Wis., 1977; Ford Found. research grantee, 1970; NICHD research career devel. awardee, 1972-75; NIH research grantee, 1972. Mem. Am. Assn. Biol. Chemists, Endocrine Soc., Soc. Neuroscience, AAAS, Sigma Xi. Subspecialty: Biochemistry (biology). Home: 2 Regis Circle Madison WI 53711 Office: Univ Wisconsin 591 Med Scis Bldg 1215 Linden Dr Madison WI 53706

KARAWYA, ESSAM MOHAMED, biochemist, researcher; b. Mansora, Egypt, Sept. 25, 1944; came to U.S., 1974; s. Mohamed A. and Zainab A. K.; m. Nahed Mahmoud, Feb. 12, 1970; 1 child, Iman Essam. B.Sc., Coll. Scis., Alexandria, Egypt, 1965, M.Sc., 1972; Ph.D., U. Louisville, 1978. Asst. prof. biochemistry Coll. Medicine, Alexandria, 1979-81; vis. fellow Nat. Cancer Inst., NIH, Bethesda, Md., 1981-83, vis. assoc. Nat. Inst. Arthritis, Diabetes and Digestive and Kidney Diseases, 1984—. Current work: DNA replication. Subspecialties: Gene actions; Molecular biology. Office: NIH Nat Inst Arthritis Diabetes and Digestive and Kidney Diseases Bldg 2 Room 214 Bethesda MD 20205

KARBAN, RICHARD, ecology and entomology educator; b. N.Y.C., Dec. 1, 1954; s. Sidney and Sarah (Tobias) K. B.A. in Environ. Sci., Haverford Coll., 1977; Ph.D., U. Pa., 1982. Lectr., Haverford Coll., Pa., 1982; asst. prof. ecology and entomology U. Calif.-Davis, 1982—. Mem. Ecol. Soc. Am., Entomol. Soc. Am., Kans. Entomol. Soc., Phi Beta Kappa. Current work: Organization of herbivore communities; immune-like responses of plants to herbivore attack. Subspecialties: Ecology (biology); Integrated pest management. Office: Dept Entomology U Calif Davis CA 95616

KARDAR, MEHRAN, physicist; b. Tehran, Iran, Aug. 1, 1957; came to U.S., 1979, s. Shokrollah and Ghodsi (Motamen) K. B.A., Cambridge U., Eng., 1979, M.A., 1982; Ph.D., MIT, 1983. Jr. fellow Harvard U. Soc. Fellows, Cambridge, Mass., 1983—. Contbr. articles to sci. jours. IBM grad. fellow MIT, 1981-82. Mem. Am. Phys. Soc. Current work: Phase transitions in adsorbed layers, disordered materials and systems with competing interactions. Subspecialties: Condensed matter physics; Statistical physics. Office: Physics Dept Harvard U Cambridge MA 02138

KARGOL, JOSEPH ANTHONY, JR., chemist; b. Somerville, N.J., Jan. 12, 1952; s. Joseph Anthony and Irene (Walker) K. B.S. in Chemistry, Lebanon Valley Coll., 1974; Ph.D., U. Del., 1979. Postdoctoral fellow Iowa State U., Ames, 1978-79; research chemist Rohm & Haas Co., Spring House, Pa., 1979—. Contbr. articles to profl. jours. Mem. Am. Chem. Soc., N.Am. Thermal Analysis Soc., Internat. Conf. Thermal Analysis, Thermal Analysis Forum Del. Valley, Phila. Catalysis Club, Sigma Xi. Democrat. Roman Catholic. Current work: Thermal analysis, polymerization kinetics, hazard analysis of industrial chemical processes, chemical quenching of runaway reactions. Subspecialties: Inorganic chemistry; Physical chemistry. Home: 2740 Valley Woods Rd Hatfield PA 19440 Office: Rohm & Haas Co 727 Norristown Rd Spring House PA 19477

KARK, PIETER ROBERT ADRIAAN, neurologist, educator; b. Boston, Dec. 3, 1940; s. Robert Manoah and Julia (Reich) K.; m. Spring Verity, Mar. 30, 1963 (div. 1978); children—Colin, Candance, Rebecca; m. Dori Urch, July 28, 1978; children—Marci, Aimee. B.A., Oxford U., 1962, M.A., 1967; M.D., Harvard U., 1965. Diplomate Am. Bd. Psychiatry and Neurology. Intern Harvard med. service Boston City Hosp., 1965-66, resident, 1966-67; resident neurology service Mass. Gen. Hosp., Boston, 1967-68; clin. assoc. NIH, Bethesda, Md., 1968-70, assoc. physician, 1970-71; resident neurology dept. UCLA Hosp., 1971-72; asst. prof. neurology UCLA, 1972-79, assoc. prof., 1979-83; assoc. prof. La. State U.-Shreveport, 1983—; chief neurol. service VA Med. Ctr., 1983—. Editor: Inherited Ataxias, 1978. Contbr. articles to profl. jours. Fellow ACP; mem. Am. Fedn. Clin. Research, Internat. Soc. Neurosci., Am. Assn. Neurology. Democrat. Jewish. Current work: Biochemistry, pharmacology and natural history of inherited ataxias alcoholism and the nervous system. Subspecialties: Genetics and genetic engineering (medicine); Neurochemistry. Home: 7327 S Lakeshore Dr Shreveport LA 71119 Office: Neurology Service (127) VA Med Ctr 510 E Stoner Ave Shreveport LA 71130

KARL, ROBERT RAYMOND, JR., chemist; b. Sewickley, Pa., June 15, 1945; s. Robert Raymond and Sarah Elizabeth (Hagerman) K.; m. Sheila Kay Sims, Aug. 3, 1982; children—Phillip, Sean; children by previous marriage—Heather, Sarah. B.S., Pa. State U., 1967; Ph.D., Cornell U., 1971. Research asst. Cornell U., Ithaca, N.Y., 1971-74; research assoc. SUNY-Binghamton, 1974-76; mem. staff laser photochemistry dept. Los Alamos Nat. Lab., 1976-78, staff mem. atomospheric scis. group, 1978—. Contbr. articles to sci. jours. Mem. Am. Chem. Soc., Am. Phys. Soc. Current work: Remote sensing by optical methods-LIDAR and fluorescence of atmospheric and mesopheric perturbations. Subspecialties: Physical chemistry; Remote sensing (atmospheric science). Office: Atmospheric Scis Group ESS-7 MS-D466 Los Alamos Nat Lab Los Alamos NM 87544

KARLE, ISABELLA LUGOSKI, scientist; b. Detroit, Dec. 2, 1921; married 1942; 3 children. B.S., U. Mich., 1941, M.S., 1942, Ph.D. in Phys. Chemistry (Rackham fellow), 1942-43; Ph.D. (AAUW fellow 1943), 1944, D.Sc. (hon.), 1976, Wayne State U., 1979; L.H.D. (hon.), Georgetown U., 1984. Assoc. chemist U. Chgo., 1944; instr. U. Mich., 1944-46; physicist U.S. Naval Research Lab., Navy Dept., Washington, 1946-59, head X-ray sect., 1959—; Mem. U.S. Nat. Com. on Crystallography; adv. bd. Office Chemistry and Chem. Tech., NRC; mem. bd. on internat. orgns. and programs Nat. Acad. Scis., 1980-83; mem. exec. com. Am. Peptide Symposium, 1975-81. Mem. editorial bd. Polymers, 1975—, Internat. Jour. Peptide and Protein Research, 1981—. Recipient Superior Civilian Service award Navy Dept., 1965, Ann. Achievement award Soc. Women Engrs., 1968; Hillebrand award, 1970; Fed. Woman's award, 1973; Dexter Conrad award Office of Naval Research, 1980; Pioneer award Am. Inst. Chemists, 1984. Mem. Nat. Acad. Scis., Am. Phys. Soc., Am. Biophys. Soc., Am. Crystallographic Assn. (pres. 1976), Am. Chem. Soc. (Garvan award 1976). Research in application of electron and x-ray diffraction to structure problems in chemistry and biology. Current Work: Establishing the molecular formula and geometry of biologically important substances; establishing precise conformations of oligopeptides,solving crystal structures of complex molecules. Subspecialties: X-ray crystallography; Biophysics (biology). Office: Naval Research Lab Laboratory for Structure of Matter Code 6030 Washington DC 20375

KARLE, JEROME, research physicist; b. N.Y.C., June 18, 1918; married, 1942; 3 children. B.S., CCNY, 1937; A.M., Harvard U., 1938; M.S., U. Mich., 1942, Ph.D. in Phys. Chemistry, 1943. Research asso. Manhattan project, Chgo., 1943-44, U.S. Navy Project, Mich., 1944-46; head electron diffraction sect. Naval Research Lab., Washington, 1946-58, head diffraction br., 1958, now head lab. for structure matter; mem. NRC, 1954-56, 67-75, 78—; chmn. U.S. Nat. Com. for Crystallography, 1973-75. Recipient Nobel prize, 1985. Fellow Am. Phys. Soc.; mem. Am. Chem. Soc., Crystallograph. Assn. (treas. 1950-52, pres. 1972), Internat. Union Crystallography (exec. com. 1978—, pres. 1981-84), Am. Math. Soc., AAAS, Nat. Acad. Scis. Research in structure atoms, molecules, crystals, solid surfaces. Current Work: Theory for interpretation of isomorphous replacement and multiple wavelength anomalous dispersion experiments on crystals with objective of enhanced facility in macromolecular structure determination. Subspecialties: Crystallography; Diffraction physics. Office: US Naval Research Lab Lab for Structure of Matter Code 6030 Washington DC 20375

KARLICEK, ROBERT FRANK, JR., chemist, semi-conductor researcher; b. Pitts., Oct. 10, 1952; s. Robert Frank and Jeanine Ann (Lukes) K.; m. Jennifer Irene Edwards, Dec. 22, 1973; children—Kristen, Erin, Robert. B.S., Elmhurst Coll., 1973; Ph.D. U. Pitts., 1979. Postdoctoral fellow U. Pitts., 1979-80; mem. tech. staff AT&T Bell Labs, Murray Hill, N.J., 1980—. Contbr. articles to profl. jours. Co-patentee laser field. Ctr. of Excellence fellow U. Pitts., 1973. Mem. Am. Chem. Soc., Materials Research Soc. Mem. Christian Ch. Current work: Chemical thermodynamics, physics and chemistry of crystal growth; optical spectroscopy, laser photochemistry, computer process control. Subspecialties: Physical chemistry; Electronic materials. Home: 170 Sprague Ave South Plainfield NJ 07080 Office: AT&T Bell Labs 600 Mountain Ave Murray Hill NJ 07974

KARMARKAR, NARENDA, mathematician. Mem. staff AT&T Bell Labs., Murray Hill, N.J. Subspecialty: Algorithms. Office: AT&T Bell Labs Murray Hill NJ 07974

KARO, ARNOLD MITCHELL, physicist; b. Wayne, Nebr., May 14, 1928; s. Henry Arnold and Ethel Leila (Mitchell) Maynard; m. Daniella Thea Cassvan, July 1, 1966; children—Barbara Melissa, Stephen Arnold. B.S. in Chemistry, Stanford U., 1949, B.S. in Physics, 1949; Ph.D. in Chem. Physics, MIT, 1953. Teaching fellow MIT, Cambridge, 1949-51; staff physicist Lincoln Lab., Lexington, Mass., 1952; teaching assoc. dept. chemistry U. Utah, Salt Lake City, 1953-54; research assoc. Solid State Molecular Group, MIT, Cambridge, 1955-58; vis. research scientist European Ctr. Atomic and Molecular Theory U. Paris, Orsay, France, 1975; sr. scientist U. Calif. Lawrence Livermore Nat. Lab., 1958—; cons. in field. Author: (with others) The Lattice Dynamics and Statics of Alkali Halide Crystals, 1979. Contbr. articles to profl. jours. Mem. rev. com. City Pleasanton, Calif., 1973-74. Served with Chem. Corps AUS, 1953-55. Nat. Coffin fellow Gen. Electric Co., 1951-52. Fellow Am. Phys. Soc., AAAS, Am. Inst. Chemistry, N.Y. Acad. Scis.; mem. Calif. Inst. Chemists, (charter), Calif. Acad. Scis., Am. Chem. Soc., Phi Theta Kappa, Phi Lambda Upsilon, Sigma Xi. Presbyterian. Current work: Atomic and molecular physics; theoretical solid state physics; lattice and molecular dynamics; quantum chemistry; application of computer simulation techniques for obtaining equations of state of solids; application of molecular dynamics to shock and detonation phenomena in condensed matter. Subspecialties: Condensed matter physics; Atomic and molecular physics. Office: Lawrence Livermore Nat Lab PO Box 808 Livermore CA 94550

KARPETSKY, TIMOTHY PAUL, biological chemist, developer; b. Torrington, Conn., Apr. 21, 1944; s. Anthony and Mary (Kuretz) K.; m. Anita Susan Harbison, Sept. 25, 1965. B.S. in Chemistry, Mass. Inst. Tech., 1966; Ph.D. in Organic Chemistry, Johns Hopkins U., 1970. Postdoctoral researcher Johns Hopkins U. Sch. Medicine, Balt., 1970-73; staff lab. molecular biology div. cancer treatment Balt. Research Cancer Inst., 1973-81; acting chief lab. molecular biology Nat. Cancer Inst., NIH, Balt., 1981-82; chief toxin def. tech. group. Chem. Research & Devel. Ctr., Aberdeen Proving Ground, Md., 1982—. Contbr. articles to profl. jours. and book chpts. Patentee in field. Recipient Exceptional Performance and Research and Devel. award Chem. Research & Devel. Ctr., 1984, Inventor's award NIH, 1984. Mem. Am. Soc. Biological Chemists, Am. Assn. Cancer Research, Md. Entomology Soc. (v.p. 1981, pres. 1982). Current work: Responsible for planning, designing and developing high tech. point detectors for chemicals and biologicals for joint service use, uses latest advances in sample acquisition tech., fluid flow, microsensor tech., biotech., mass-spectrometry and signal processing to fabricate such detectors. Subspecialties: Materials; Systems engineering. Office: Chem Research & Devel Ctr ATTN: SMCCR-DDT Aberdeen Proving Ground MD 21010-5423

KARPICKE, JOHN ARTHUR, experimental psychologist; b. Saginaw, Mich., Nov. 26, 1945; s. Herbert A. and Eleanor (Stafford) K.; m. Susan G. Denyes, Aug. 9, 1950; children—Jeffrey Denyes, Jennifer Denyes. B.S., Mich. State U., 1972; Ph.D., Ind. U., 1976. Postdoctoral fellow psychobiology research group Fla. State U., Tallahassee, 1976-77; asst. prof. Valparaiso (Ind.) U., 1977-81; mem. tech. staff Bell Labs., Indpls., 1981-83, Am. Bell, Inc., Indpls., 1983, AT&T, Indpls., 1984—. Contbr. articles to profl. jours. NIH fellow, 1976; NIMH grantee, 1979. Mem. AAAS, N.Y. Acad. Scis. Current Work: Telecommunications systems engineering; home information systems; home communication systems; synthetic speech quality/applications; human factors engineering. Subspecialties: Cognition; Learning. Office: AT&T Info Systems Labs PO Box 1008 Indianapolis IN 46206

KARR, JAMES RICHARD, ecologist, educator; b. Shelby, Ohio, Dec. 26, 1943; s. Rodney Joll and Marjorie Ladonna (Copeland) K.; m. Kathleen Ann Reynolds, Mar. 23, 1963 (div. 1983); children: Elizabeth Ann, Eric Leigh; m. Helen Marie Serrano, 1984. B.Sc., Iowa State U., 1965; M.Sc., U. Ill., 1967, Ph.D., 1970. Postdoctoral fellow Princeton U., 1970-71; postdoctoral research assoc. Smithsonian Instn., Balboa, C.Z., 1971-72; asst. prof. biology Purdue U., West Lafayette, Ind., 1972-75; prof. ecology U. Ill., Urbana, 1975-84; dep. dir. Smithsonian Tropical Research Inst., Balboa, Panama, 1984—; mem. evaluation panels NSF, 1975, 76, Energy Research and Devel. Adminstrn., 1976, Instream Flow Group, Office Biol. Services, 1978; condr. workshops U.S. EPA, 1979, 80, 85, U.S. Fish and Wildlife Service, 1979; cons. OAS, 1980. Mem. editorial bd. Tropical Ecology, 1977-81, Ecology, 1981-84, Biosci., 1985—. Contbr. articles, papers, monographs, revs. to profl. jours. Recipient numerous research grants. Fellow Am. Ornithologists Union, AAAS; mem. Ecol. Soc. Am. (mem. council 1982-84), Am. Soc. Naturalists, Cooper Ornithol. Soc., Wilson Ornithol. Soc. (mem. exec. council 1976-79), Assn. for Tropical Biology, Internat. Soc. for Tropical Ecology, Wildlife Soc., Am. Inst. Biol. Scis., Am. Fisheries Soc., Sigma Xi. Current Work: Community ecology of birds and stream fishes, application of ecological principles to management of natural resource systems. Subspecialties: Theoretical ecology; Resource management. Office: Smithsonian Tropical Research Inst PO Box 2072 Balboa Panama Smithsonian Tropical Research Inst APO Miami FL 34002

KARRER, RATHE STEVENS, psychophysiologist, educator; b. Cleve., Mar. 8, 1930; s. Enoch and Ethel (Walther) K.; m. Nancy Donaldson, Apr. 15, 1951 (div. June 1971); children—Dana, Tana; m. Betty MacKune, Aug. 15, 1971; 1 child, Phillip. Research psychologist Tng. Sch. at Vineland, N.J., 1957-66; lectr. Roosevelt U., Chgo., 1968-70; sr. research scientist Ill. Inst. Development Disabilities, Chgo., 1964-79, assoc. research dir., 1979—; asst. prof. U. Ill.-Chgo., 1974-80, prof., 1980—; cons. NIH, March of Dimes, J.D. MacArthur Found. Editor author: Developmental Psychophysiology of Mental Retardation, 1976; Brain and Information, 1983; also numerous articles. Nat. Inst. Inst. Child Health and Devel. grantee, 1974—. Mem. Am. Psychol. Assn., Soc. Psychophysiol. Research, Am. Acad. Mental Retardation, AAAS, Soc. Neurosci., Biofeedback Soc. Am., Ill. Biofeedback Soc. (bd. dirs. 1981-83), Sigma Xi. Current work: Development of brain electrical activity and behavior. Subspecialties: Developmental psychology; Neuropsychology. Home: 411 Woodland Rd Highland Park IL 60035 Office: Ill Inst Developmental Disabilities 1640 Roosevelt Rd Chicago IL 60608

KARROLL, JOSEPH E., research company executive, consultant; b. N.Y.C., Mar. 24, 1922; s. Morris and Lillian (Lerman) K.; m. Zena Muriel Gelernter, Apr. 20, 1947 (div. Feb. 1979); children: Jonathan, Jaimee, Jodee. B.S., NYU, 1950, M.A., 1951; postgrad., 1954. Registered rep. Shearson Am. Express, Los Angeles, 1978-79; pres. Alternative Research Corp., Los Angeles, 1976—; v.p. Crescent Corp., Las Vegas, Nev., 1981—, Karroll Weller & Co., Inc., Los Angeles, 1982—, Karwell Corp., Phoenix, 1982—; pres. Digital Research Corp., Reno, Nev., 1982—; dir. Nat. Safety Inst., Los Angeles, 1979—. Served with U.S. Army, 1942-45, PTO. Mem. Am. Psychol. Assn. Current Work: research, consulting, management. Subspecialties: Operations research (engineering); Systems engineering. Home: 15445 Ventura Blvd Suite 10-311 Sherman Oaks CA 91413 Office: Karwell Corp PO Box 15586 Phoenix AZ 85060

KASAI, GEORGE JOJI, microbiologist, virologist, consultant, researcher; b. Los Angeles, Apr. 8, 1917; s. Araji and Kichino (Miura) K.; m. Tama Katako, July 7, 1946; children: Margaret L. Kasai Freeburg, Elizabeth J. Kasai Collins, Patricia J. A.A., Los Angeles Jr. Coll., 1936; S.B., UCLA, 1942; S.M., U. Chgo., 1945, Ph.D., 1952. Research asst., bacteriologist dept. microbiology U. Chgo., 1945-52; spl. fellow Zoller Dental Clinic, 1950-51, research assoc. in oral bacteriology, 1952-64, research asso. cholera research, asst. prof. univ., 1964-69; supervisor microbiologist in bacteriology Camp Zama, Sagami-Ono, Japan, 1969-75; immunology subsect Brooke Army Med. Center, Ft. Sam Houston, Tex., 1975—; Cons. Swiss Serum and Vaccine, Berne, 1967, WHO Cholera Panel, 1967, John Hopkins Hosp., 1967; Joint investigator, epidemiology Vibrio parahemolyticus, Indonesia, 1972-73. Contbr. articles to profl. jours. Recipient Spl. recognition Swiss Serum and Vaccine Inst., Berne, 1967, Commendation award Japanese Ground Self Def. Forces, Tokyo, 1975, Outstanding award Dept. Army, 1973, 80, Spl. Service award, 1984; Sigma Xi fellow, 1967; AAAS fellow, 1967. Mem. Am. Soc. Microbiology, Soc. Gen. Microbiology, AAAS, N.Y. Acad. Sci., Sigma Xi. Current Work: Viral serology; enzyme immuno assay; serology of infectious diseases; clinical virology (viral identification); electron microscopy. Subspecialties: Virology (medicine); Microbiology. Home: 4807 El Gusto San Antonio TX 78233 Office: Bldg 2830 Room 250 Fort Sam Houston TX 78234

KASAI, PAUL HARUO, physical chemist; b. Osaka, Japan, Jan. 30, 1932; came to U.S., 1950; s. Shunki and Chiyo (Kobayashi) K.; m. Toko Masako Hatori, Nov. 22, 1959; children—Yumi, Miki. B.S. in Chemistry, U. Denver, 1955; Ph.D. in Chemistry, U. Calif.-Berkeley, 1959. Mem. research staff Hitachi Ctr. Research, Tokyo, 1959-62, Union Carbide, Tarrytown, N.Y., 1962-66; assoc. prof. U. Calif.-Santa Cruz, 1966-67; sr. scientist Union Carbide, Tarrytown, N.Y., 1967-79; sr. scientist, mgr. IBM Instruments, Danbury, Conn., 1979—. Contbr. articles to profl. jours. Mem. Am. Chem. Soc. Current work: Matrix isolation ESR study of metal atom-organic and inorganic complexes, MAS-NMR and ESR study of molecular dynamics and chemistry in intracrystalline environments. Subspecialties: Electron spin resonance; Catalysis chemistry. Home: 29 Wintergreen Hill Danbury CT 06811 Office: IBM Instruments Inc Orchard Park Danbury CT 06810

KASARDA, DONALD DAVID, research chemist; b. Kingston, Pa., Oct. 12, 1933; s. John and Mary Kasarda; m. Ferne Johnson, Nov. 27, 1964; 1 child, Amy Elise. B.S., King's Coll., 1955; M.S., Boston Coll., 1957; M.A., Princeton U., 1959, Ph.D., 1961. Mem. tech. staff Bell Telephone Labs., Murray Hill, N.J., 1961-63; cardiovascular research inst. fellow U. Calif.-San Francisco, 1963-64; research chemist Western Regional Research Ctr., USDA, Albany, Calif., 1964—. Author book chpts. Contbr. numerous articles to profl. jours. Competitive research grantee USDA, 1980, NSF, 1977. Mem. AAAS, Am. Chem. Soc., Am. Assn. Cereal Chemists, Western Soc. Crop Sci., Sigma Xi. Current work: structure, interactions, and genetic relationships of wheat and other cereal grain proteins; molecular basis of wheat quality. Subspecialties: Biochemistry (biology); Biophysical chemistry. Office: 800 Buchanan St Albany CA 94710

KASARSKIS, EDWARD JOSEPH, physician, neurochem. researcher; b. Chgo., Oct. 9, 1946; s. Edward J. and Valeria T. (Krauchunas) K.; m. Mary Lenroot, Aug. 30, 1969; children: Andrew J., Peter E., Larisa J., Irina M. B.A., Coll. St. Thomas, St. Paul, 1968; Ph.D., U. Wis., 1975, M.D., 1974. Diplomate: Am. Bd. Psychiatry and Neurology, North Bd. Med. Examiners. Med. intern U. Wis. Ctr. Health Scis., Madison, 1974-75, resident in medicine, 1974—76; resident in neurology U. Va. Hosp., Charlottsville, 1976-79; asst. prof. neurology La. State U., Shreveport, 1979-80; staff neurologist VA Med Ctr., Shreveport, 1979-80; asst. prof.neurology U. Ky., Lexington, 1980-85, assoc. prof. neurology and toxicology, 1985—; staff neurologist VA Med. Ctr., Lexington, 1980—. NIH grantee, 1968-74; grantee VA Research Service, 1979, 81; grantee Distilled Spirits Council of U.S., 1981. Mem. AMA, Am. Acad. Neurology, Soc. Neurosci., AAAS, Am. Soc. Neurochemistry, Internat. Soc. Neurochemistry, Sigma Xi. Current Work: Clinical neurology; vitamin and trace metal nutrition of the developing and mature central nervous system; regulation of cerebrospinal fluid pressure. Subspecialties: Neurology; Neurochemistry. Home: 305 Glendover Rd Lexington KY 40503 Office: Dept Neurology 800 Rose St Lexington KY 40536

KASDAN, HARVEY LEE, imaging scientist; b. Bklyn., July 31, 1940; s. Selig David and Reba (Lesches) K.; m. Judith Sperman, Sept. 2, 1962; 1 child, Sheldon David. B.S.E.E., MIT, 1963, M.S.E.E., 1963; Ph.D. in Engring., UCLA, 1971. Mem. tech. staff Hughes Aircraft Co., Los Angeles, 1963-67; sr. engring. specialist Litton Industries, Van Nuys, Calif., 1967-71; v.p. Recognition Systems, Inc., Van Nuys, 1971-82; dir. product devel. Internat. Remote Imaging Systems, Chatsworth, Calif., 1982—; cons. photo research div. Kollmorgen Corp., Burbank, Calif., 1982-83. Patentee in optics field. Mem. IEEE, Optical Soc. Am., Soc. Photo-Optical Instrumentation Engrs. (editor procs. 1979-80), Tau Beta Pi, Eta Kappa Nu, Sigma Xi. Current work: Image processing system development, pattern recognition applications, artificial intelligence applications, electro-optical system design and development, clinical lab instrument development. Subspecialties: Graphics, image processing, and pattern recognition; Artificial intelligence. Home: 5414 Sunnyslope Ave Van Nuys CA 91401 Office: Internat Remote Imaging Systems 9825 De Soto Ave Chatsworth CA 91311

KASEL, JULIUS ALBERT, virologist, educator; b. Homestead, Pa., Dec. 7, 1923; s. Julius and Anna (Kudis) Kaselonis; m. Nan Elizabeth Cleghon, Sept. 29, 1950; children: Gary Lee, John Foster, Patricia Joyce. B.S., U. Pitts., 1949; M.S., Georgetown U., 1958, Ph.D., 1960. Head med. virology sect. Nat. Inst. Allergy and Infectious Diseases, 1950-72; prof. microbiology and immunology Baylor Coll. Medicine, Houston, 1972—. Served with USAF, 1942-45; served with USPHS, 1958-72. Decorated Air medal; recipient meritorious medal for research USPHS. Fellow Am. Acad. Microbiologists; fellow Infectious Diseases Soc. Am.; mem. Am. Assn. Immunologists, Soc. Exptl. Biology and Medicine. Roman Catholic. Current Work: Immunology of respiratory virus infections in man. Subspecialties: Virology (biology); Immunology (agriculture). Home: 1926 Country Club Dr Sugarland TX 77478 Office: Baylor Coll Medicine Houston TX 77030

KASHA, KENNETH JOHN, crop scientist, educator; b. Lacome, Alta., Can., May 6, 1933; s. John Clarence and Mary Jennette (Proudfoot) K.; m. Marion Eileen Lenz, Aug. 14, 1958; children: Lorelei Marion, David John. B.Sc., U. Alta., 1957, M.Sc., 1958; Ph.D., U. Minn., 1962. Teaching asst./research fellow U. Minn., Mpls., 1960-62; research scientist Agr. Can., Ottawa Research Sta., 1962-66; asst. prof. crop sci. dept. U. Guelph, Ont., 1966-69, assoc. prof., 1969-74, prof., 1974—, dir. Plant Biotech. Ctr., Guelph-Waterloo Biotech. Ctr., 1984—; cons. CIBA-Geigy Seeds, 1974-81. Contbr. articles to profl. jours. U. Alta. research scholar; J.E. Olson prize in botany and lst class standing prize, 1957; Guelph Sigma Xi award for excellence in research, 1974; Grindley award Agr. Inst. Can., 1977; E.C. Manning award for innovation by a Can., 1983; OAC Alumni Disting. Researcher award, 1984. Ont. Agrl. Coll., 1984. Mem. Genetics Soc. Can., Genetics Soc. Am., Am. Soc. Agronomy, Internat. Plant Cell and Tissue Culture Assn., Sigma Xi. Current Work: Plant cytogenetics, genome organization, gene gransfer, chromosome elimination, barley, wheat, cell and tissue culture, linkage mapping. Subspecialties: Plant genetics; Plant cell and tissue culture. Home: 21 Glenburnie Dr Guelph ON N1E 4C4 Canada Office: Crop Sci Dept Univ Guelph Guelph ON N1G 2W1 Canada

KASHGARIAN, MICHAEL, physician; b. N.Y.C., Sept. 20, 1933; s. Toros and Arax (Almasian) K.; m. Jean Gaylor Caldwell, July 2, 1960; children—Michaele, Thea. A.B., NYU, 1954; M.D., Yale U., 1958. Diplomate Am. Bd. Pathology. Intern Barnes Hosp., St. Louis, 1958-59; asst. resident in pathology Yale New Haven Med. Ctr., 1959-61, resident in pathology, 1962-63; research fellow in renal physiology U. Goettingen, Fed. Republic Germany, 1961-62; practice medicine specializing in pathology, New Haven, 1962; instr. Yale U., 1962-64, asst. prof., 1964-67, assoc. prof., 1967-74, prof., 1974, vice chmn. dept., 1976; assoc. pathologist Yale New Haven Hosp., 1964-66, asst. attending physician, 1966-69, attending pathologist, 1969—, pres. med. staff, 1983-84; cons. in pathology, 1962—. Author: (with J.P. Hayslett and B.H. Spargo) Renal Disease, 1974; (with G.N. Burrow) The Endocrine Glands. Mem. editorial bd. Nephron, 1970; Am. Jour. Pathology, 1975; Am. Jour. Kidney Disease. Contbr. articles to profl. jours. Chmn. ednl. adv. council North Haven Bd. Edn., 1971, Christian edn. chm. Ch. of Christ, Yale, 1970. Served to 1st lt. M.C., USAR, 1954-65. Recipient research career devel. award, 1965-75. Fellow Am. Soc. Clin. Pathologists; mem. AMA, Am. Assn. Pathologists and Bacteriologists, Am. Soc. Nephrology, Internat. Acad. Pathology, Conn. Med. Assn., New Haven County Med. Assn., Am. Assn. Pathologists (pres. 1945), Am. Heart Assn., AAAS, Am. Physiol. Soc., Sigma Xi, Alpha Omega Alpha, Alpha Kappa Kappa. Current work: monoclonal antibodies to transport proteins; progression of glomerular sclerosis. Subspecialties: Pathology (medicine); Physiology (medicine). Home: 22 Old Orchard Rd North Haven CT 06473 Office: PO Box 3333 New Haven CT 06510

KASHKET, EVA RUTH, microbiology educator, researcher; b. Zagreb, Yugoslavia, Mar. 1, 1936; came to U.S., 1957; d. Felix M. and Gertrude (Specht) Kraus; m. Shelby A. Kashket, Sept. 8, 1957; children—Michael B., Julie E. B.Sc., McGill U., 1956, M.Sc., 1957; Ph.D., Harvard U., 1963. Postdoctoral fellow Tufts U. Sch. Medicine, Boston, 1963-65; research assoc. Harvard Med. Sch., Boston, 1967-68, prin. research assoc., 1968-74; asst. prof. (part-time) Northeastern U., Boston, 1974-76; assoc. prof. Boston U. Sch. Medicine, 1974-82, prof. microbiology, 1982—; cons. CPC Internat., Summit-Argo, Ill., 1982—. Contbr. articles to sci. jours., chpts. to books. NSF, Dept. Agr. grantee, 1974—. Mem. Assn. for Women in Sci., Am. Soc. Microbiology, Am. Soc. Biol. Chemists. Current work: Bacterial physiology, bacterial bioenergetics, membrane transport, fermentation products. Subspecialty: Microbiology. Office: Boston U Sch Medicine 80 E Concord St Boston MA 02118

KASHMIRI, SYED V.S., molecular biologist, educator; b. Lucknow, India, July 5, 1937; came to U.S., 1964, naturalized, 1980; s. Syed M. and Shandar (Begum) Kazim; m. Rafia Mehdi, Oct. 23, 1969; 1 son, Syed Tabish. Ph.D., Duke U., 1968. Research assoc. Rockefeller U., N.Y.C., 1968-72, U. Md. Sch. Medicine, Balt., 1972-73, Wistar Inst., Phila., 1973-74; sr. scientist Litton Bionetics, Kensington, Md., 1974-77; research assoc. Johns Hopkins U. Sch. Medicine, Balt., 1977-79; asst. prof. molecular biology U. Pa. Sch. Vet. Medicine, Kennett Square, 1979—. Contbr. articles to profl. jours. Mem. Genetics Soc. Am., Am. Soc. Microbiology, Am. Soc. Virology. Current work: Molecular mechanism of leukemogenesis induced by retroviruses. Model system under study is bovine leukosis induced by bovine leukemia virus. Studying the genome organization of the virus. Subspecialties: Molecular biology; Oncology. Home: 16 Glen View Ln Downingtown PA 19335 Office: Leukemia Studies Unit New Bolton Center Kennett Square PA 19348

KASHYAP, RANGASAMI L., electrical engineering educator; b. Mysore, India, Mar. 28, 1938; s. Rangasame Sargur and Sreerangamma Kashyap. M.Engring., Indian Inst. Sci., Bangalore, 1962; Ph.D., Harvard U., 1965. Research asst. Harvard U., Cambridge, Mass., 1963-65, research fellow, 1965-66; faculty mem. Purdue U., West Lafayette, Ind., 1966—, prof. elec. engring., 1966—. Author: Stochastic Dynamic Systems, 1976. Contbr. numerous articles to profl. jours. Bd. dirs., v.p. India Devel. Service, Chgo., 1979—. Recipient Best Research Paper award Nat. Electronic Conf., Chgo., 1967; NSF research grantee, 1967-82. Fellow IEEE; mem. Assn. for Computing Machinery. Current work: Pattern recognition, image processing, control system design, artificial intelligence. Subspecialties: Graphics, image processing, and pattern recognition; Information systems (Information science). Office: Dept Electrical Engring Purdue U West Lafayette IN 47909

KASIMIS, BASIL SPIROS, physician, educator; b. Athens, Greece, June 19, 1946; s. Spiros Dimitrios and Theoni (Stefanides) K.; m. Katherine Markantonis Rukensteiner, July 10, 1975; children: Anne-Theoni, Elizabeth-Jennifer. M.D., Nat. U. Athens, 1970, Dr. Med. Sci., 1974. Intern, South Balt. Gen. Hosp., 1974-75, jr. asst. med. resident, 1975-76, chief resident, 1976-77; fellow in med. oncology Boston U. Hosp., 1977-79, fellow in hematology, 1979-80; asst. prof. medicine U. Calif., Irvine, 1980—; sr. staff physician Long Beach (Calif.) VA Med. Center, 1980—; attending physician U. Calif.-Irvine Med. Center, 1981-84; asst. prof. medicine, chief med. oncology U. Medicine and Dentistry N.J.-Rutgers Med. Sch., 1984—; attending physician Middlesex Gen. Hosp., St. Peter's Med. Ctr., both New Brunswick, N.J., 1984—. Contbr. articles to profl. jours. Served with Greek Armed Forces, 1970-72. Mem. AMA, Am. Soc. Clin. Oncology, ACP, Am. Soc. Internal Medicine. Greek Orthodox. Current Work: Prostate cancer chemotherapy, intra-arterial hepatic infusions of chemotherapy. Subspecialties: Oncology; Hematology. Office: 254 Easton Ave New Brunswick NJ 08901

KASLICK, RALPH SIDNEY, dentist, educator; b. Bklyn., Oct. 17, 1935; s. John J. and Dorothy K.; m. Jessica Hellinger, Oct. 24, 1976. A.B., Columbia U., 1956, D.D.S., 1959, cert. in periodontology, 1962. Instr. Fairleigh Dickinson U. Sch. Dentistry, Hackensack, N.J., 1965-67, asst. prof., 1967-70, asso. prof., 1970-74, prof., 1974—, asst. dean for acad. affairs, 1973-75, acting dean, 1975-76, dean, 1976—; cons. in field. Contbr. chpts. to textbooks, articles to profl. jours. Served to capt. U.S. Army, 1962-64. Recipient Stanley S. Bergen award for contbn. to dental edn. Seton Hall U., 1982. Fellow Am. Coll. Dentists, N.Y. Acad. Dentistry; mem. Council Deans Am. Assn. Dental Schs., Internat. Assn. Dental Research (past pres. N.J. sect.), Am. Acad. Periodontology, ADA, Sigma Xi, Omicron Kappa Upsilon. Current Work: Role of host and genetic factors in rapidly progressive periodontal diseases, especially in young adults; examination of crevicular gingival fluid and defective in vivo leukocyte migration and metabolism for diagnostic and preventive purposes. Subspecialties: Periodontics; Preventive dentistry. Office: 110 Fuller Pl Hackensack NJ 07601

KASPER, BRYON LYNN, electrical engineer; b. Eckville, Can., Sept. 28, 1951; s. August Bruno and Fannie Marie (Tuisku) K.; m. Vicky Jene Woods, May 16, 1980. B.S.E.E., U. Alta., Can., 1973, Ph.D., 1981. Registered profl. engr., Can. Engr. Alta. Govt. Telephones, Edmonton, Can., 1973-75; mem. tech. staff AT&T Bell Labs., Holmdel, N.J., 1981—. Contbr. articles to profl. jours. Mem. IEEE. Current work: Receivers and systems for high speed optical telecommunications. Subspecialties: Fiber optics; Telecommunications. Home: 6 Majestic Ave Lincroft NJ 07738 Office: AT&T Bell Labs Crawford Hill Lab Holmdel NJ 07733

KASPER, RAPHAEL GOLDSMITH, physicist, administrator; b. N.Y.C., Sept. 2, 1942; s. Philip and Rachel (Goldsmith) K.; m. Susan Feller, June 14, 1964 (div. July 1983); children—Lynn, Gabriel. B.A. in Engring. Physics, Cornell, U., 1964; M.S., U. Calif., 1966, Ph.D., 1971. Research Sci. George Wash. U., Washington, 1968-73; staff officer Nat. Acad. Scis., Washington, 1973-77, staff dir., mem. environ. studies bd, 1977-82, exec. dir. commn. on phys. scis., 1982—; sr. policy analyst Office Sci. & Tech. Policy, 1977; dir. of studies Nuclear Safety Oversight Com., 1979-80. Author: Citizen Groups and the Nuclear Power Controversy, 1973; Editor: Technology Assessment, 1972. Mem. Am. Phys. Soc., AAAS. Current work: Direct advisory activities in physics, chemistry, mathematics, earth sciences, natural resources Res: Neutron scattering. Subspecialties: Nuclear physics; Nuclear fission. Office: Nat Acad Scis 2101 Constitution Ave NW Washington DC 20418

KASS, EDWARD HAROLD, physician; b. N.Y.C., Dec. 20, 1917; s. Hyman A. and Ann (Selvansky) K.; m. Fae Golden, 1943 (dec. 1973); children: Robert, James, Nancy; m. Amalie Moses Hecht, 1975; stepchildren: Anne, Robert, Thomas, Jonathan, Peter. A.B. with high distinction, U. Ky., 1939, M.S., 1941; Ph.D., U. Wis., 1943; M.D., U. Calif., 1947; M.A. (hon.), Harvard U., 1958; D.Sc. (hon.), U. Ky., 1962. Diplomate: Am. Bd. Pathology, Am. Bd. Microbiology, Am. Bd. Preventive Medicine. Grad. asst., instr. bacteriology U. Ky., 1939-41; research asst., instr. U. Wis. Med. Sch., 1941-43, immunologist dept. phys. chemistry, 1944, grad. asst. dept. pathology, 1944-45; intern Boston City Hosp., 1947-48, resident, 1948-49; research fellow Thorndike Meml. Lab., 1949-52; sr. fellow in virus diseases NRC, 1949-52; instr. in medicine Harvard Med. Sch., 1951-52, assoc. in medicine, 1952-55, asst. prof. medicine, 1955-58, assoc. prof. bacteriology and immunology, 1958-62, assoc. prof. medicine, 1969-69; asst. physician Thorndike Meml. Lab., 1951-58; assoc. dir. bacteriology Mallory Inst. Pathology, 1957-63; dir. Channing lab., dept. med. microbiology Boston City Hosp., 1963-77; dir. Channing lab. and physician Peter Bent Brigham Hosp., Boston, 1977—; prof. medicine Harvard U., 1969-73, William Ellery Channing prof. medicine, 1973—; Macy Faculty Scholar Oxford U., 1974-75; vis. prof. Hebrew U.-Hadassah Med. Sch., Jerusalem, 1974; vis. prof. community medicine St. Thomas Hosp., London, 1982-83; vis. prof. med. microbiology Royal Free Hosp., London, 1982-83; lectr. London Sch. Hygiene and Tropical Medicine, London; cons. in field. Author 8 books; editor: Jour. Infectious Diseases, 1968-79, Revs. Infectious Diseases, 1979—; mem. editorial bds. profl. jours.; contbr. articles to med. jours. Recipient Public Service award NASA; spl. award Nat. Heart, Lung and Blood Inst.; Pioneer in Antibiotic Therapy award. Fellow Am. Coll. Epidemiology, ACP (Rosenthal award), Coll. Am. Pathologists, Am. Heart Assn., N.Y. Acad. Scis., Am. Coll. Epidemiology, Royal Soc. Medicine (London), Royal Coll. Physicians (London); fellow Infectious Diseases Soc. Am. (sec. 1962-68, pres. 1970, Bristol award 1980); mem. Internat. Epidemiol. Assn. (treas. 1977-81), Internat. Congress for Infectious Disease (pres. 1983—), Mass. Soc. Pathologists, New Eng. Soc. Pathologists, Soc. Exptl. Biology and Medicine, Am. Acad. Arts and Scis., AAAS, Am. Epidemiol. Soc., Am. Fedn. Clin. Research, Pan Am. Infectious Disease Soc., AMA, Am. Pub. Health Assn., Am. Soc. Clin. Investigation, Am. Soc. Microbiology, Soc. Epidemiol. Research, Am. Soc. Nephrology, Am. Thoracic Soc., Assn. Am. Physicians, Infectious Disease Soc. Mex. (hon.), Pan Am. Infectious Diseases Soc. (hon.), Phi Beta Kappa, Sigma Xi, Alpha Omega Alpha. Jewish. Club: Harvard (Boston, N.Y.C.). Current Work: Infectious disease, epidemiology. Subspecialties: Infectious diseases; Epidemiology. Home: Todd Pond Rd Lincoln MA 01773 Office: 180 Longwood Ave Boston MA 02115

KASSAN, STUART S., rheumatologist; b. White Plains, N.Y., Nov. 19, 1946; s. Robert J. and Rosalind (Suchin) K.; m. N. Gail Karesh, Apr. 4, 1971. B.A., Case Western Res. U., 1968; M.D., George Washington U., 1972. Diplomate: Am. Bd. Internal Medicine, 1975 (subcert. in rheumatology). Intern, resident Grady Meml. Hosp., Atlanta, 1972-74; clin. assoc. NIH, Bethesda, Md., 1974-76; fellow in rheumatic diseases Hosp. for Spl. Surgery and N.Y. Hosp., Cornell Med. Ctr., N.Y.C., 1976-78; asst. clin. prof. medicine U. Colo. Health Scis. Ctr., Denver, 1978-84, assoc. clin. prof. medicine, 1984—; attending physician Colo. Gen. Hosp., Denver, 1978—; head rheumatology clinic VA Hosp., Denver, 1978-80; med. dir. Luth. Med. Ctr. Rehab. Ctr., Wheatridge, Colo. Contbr. chpts. to books, articles in field to profl. jours. Served as surgeon USPHS, 1976-78, NIH. N.Y. Arthritis Found. fellow, grantee, 1977; George Washington U. Med. Sch. alumni scholar, 1982. Fellow ACP; mem. Am. Fedn. Clin. Research, Harvey Soc., Am. Rheumatism Assn. Jewish. Current Work: Sjogren's syndrome, central nervous system lupus erythematosus; polymyaglia rheumatica; cyclic nucleotides in the central nervous system in systemic lupus erythematosus; clinical teaching; clinical research. Subspecialties: Rheumatology; Internal medicine. Home: 8101 E Dartmouth Denver CO 80231 Office: Colo Arthritis Associates 4200 W Conejos Pl Denver CO 80204

KASSOY, DAVID R., mechanical engineering educator; b. Bklyn., Jan. 29, 1938; s. Isaac and Sarah (Hadelman) K.; m. Carol Ann Fuchs, Dec. 26, 1964; children—Andrew, Erin. B.A.E., Bklyn. Poly. Inst., 1959; M.S.A.E., U. Mich., 1961, Ph.D., 1965. Asst. prof. U. Colo., Boulder, 1969-75, assoc. prof., 1975-77, prof., 1977—; vis. lectr. U. East Anglia, Norwich, Eng., 1973, sr. vis. fellow, 1982-83; Fulbright visitor Tech. U. Delft (Netherlands), 1983; cons. Sci. Applications, Inc., La Jolla, Calif., 1977-78, Johnson, Mahoney & Scott, Denver, 1980-82. Contbr. articles to profl. jours. Guggenheim Found. fellow, 1972-73; Japan Soc. Promotion of Sci. fellow Nagoya U., 1985. Mem. Am. Phys. Soc., Soc. Indsl. and Applied Math., Combustion Inst., Am. Geophys. Union, Pi Tau Sigma. Current work: Gasdynamics of reactive systems, flame and detonation initiation and evolution, natural convection phenomena in porous media and geothermal systems. Subspecialties: Fluid mechanics; Combustion processes. Home: 2000 Kohler Dr Boulder CO 80303 Office: Dept Mech Engring U Colo Boulder CO 80309

KASTURI, RANGACHAR, engineering educator, researcher; b. Bangalore, Karnataka, India, June 4, 1949; came to U.S. 1978; s. T.M. Rama and Kanakamma Swamy; m. Mrinalini Prasad, Feb. 8, 1974; children—Tejaswi, Kavya. B.S.E.E., Bangalore U., India, 1968; M.S.E.E., Tex. Tech U., 1980. Ph.D., 1982. Grad. trainee Mysore Elecs., Bangalore, 1968-69; research engr. Bharat Electronics, Bangalore, 1969-76; engring. officer Visvesvaraya Mus., Bangalore, 1976-78; research asst. Tex. Tech U., Lubbock, 1978-82, part time instr., 1980-82; asst. prof. Pa. State U., University Park, 1982—. Contbr. articles to profl. jours. NSF grantee, 1983-85, Applied Research Lab grantee, 1984; Digital Equipment Corp. grantee, 1985. Mem. IEEE, Optical Soc. Am., Soc. Photo Optical Instrumentation Engrs., Sigma Xi, Eta Kappa Nu. Hindu. Current work: Image analysis, pattern recognition, speech recognition and text processing for Indian languages, computer vision, robotics, artificial intelligence, restoration of landsat images. Subspecialties: Graphics, image processing, and pattern recognition; Artificial intelligence. Home: 419 Canterbury Dr State College PA 16803 Office: Dept of Elec Engring Pa State U University Park PA 16802

KASZNIAK, ALFRED WAYNE, clinical neuropsychologist, educator, researcher; b. Chgo., June 2, 1949; s. Alfred Herbert and Ann Virginea (Simonsen) K.; m. Mary Ellen Beaurain, Aug. 26, 1973; children—Jesse, Elizabeth. B.S., U. Ill.-Chgo., 1970, M.A., 1973, Ph.D., 1976. Lic. psychologist, Ariz. Instr. Rush Med. Coll., Chgo., 1974-76, asst. prof., 1976-79; asst. prof. U. Ariz., Tucson, 1979-82, assoc. prof., 1982—; Gerontol. Soc. Am. research fellow, 1980; cons. NIH, Washington, 1981—; mem. adv. bd. Alzheimer's Disease and Related Diseases Assn., Chgo., 1981-85; dir. Ariz. Head Injury Found., Tucson, 1983—. Contbr. articles to profl. jours. Contbr. chpts. to Neuropsychology of Dementia, 1985, Depression in the Elderly, 1985. Mem. editorial bd. Psychology of Aging, 1984—. Bd. dirs. S.H.A.R.E. of Ariz., Tucson, 1982—; trustee Nat. Multiple Sclerosis Soc., Tucson, 1980-82; mem. adv. bd. Fan Kane Fund for Brain Injured Children, Tucson, 1980—. NIH grantee. Mem. Am. Psychol. Assn. (disting. contbn. award, 1978), Internat. Neuropsychol. Soc. (program com. 1982-83), Gerontol. Soc. Am. Soc. for Neurosci., Nat. Multiple Sclerosis Soc. (outstanding contbn. award So. Ariz. chpt. 1981). Current work: Human brain/behavior relationships; neuropsychology of age-related degenerative disorders of the central nervous system; behavioral medicine. Subspecialties: Neuropsychology; Gerontology. Home: 7630 N Chapala Pl Tucson AZ 85704 Office: Dept Psychiatry Univ of Arizona 3301 N Campbell Tucson AZ 85724

KATHREN, RONALD LAURENCE, health physicist, educator; b. Windsor, Ont., Can., June 6, 1937; s. Ben and Sally (Forman) K.; m. Susan Krafft, Dec. 24, 1964; children: SallyBeth, Daniel. B.S., UCLA, 1957; M.Sc., U. Pitts., 1962. Diplomate: Am. Bd. Health Physics, Am. Acad. Environ. Engrs.; cert. in applied health physics, U.K.; registered profl. engr., Calif. Supervisory health physicst Mare Island Naval Shipyard, Vallejo, Calif., 1959-61; health physicist U. Calif. Radiation Lab., Livermore, 1962-67; sr. research scientist, sect. mgr. Battelle Pacific N.W. Labs., Richland, Wash., 1967-72; staff scientist, 1978—; corp. health physicist Portland Gen. Electric Co., Oreg., 1972-78; assoc. prof. radiol. scis. Joint Center for Grad. Study, U. Wash., Richland, 1978—, program coordinator, 1980-82; health physicist Reed Coll., 1973-78; cons. in field; adj. prof. Oreg. State Div. of Continuing Edn., 1972-77; Mem. Oreg. State Radiation adv. com., 1977-78; mem. noise adv. com. Oreg. Dept. Environ. Quality, 1976. Editor: Health Physics Jour, 1975-80; adv. editorial bd.: Handbook of Radiation Protection and Measurement, 1978—; Contbr. articles to profl. jours.; author: Radiation Protection, 1985; Health Physics: A Backward Glance, 1980; Ionizing Radiation: Tumorigenic and Tumoricidal Effects, 1983; Radioactivity in the Environment, 1984; Radiation Protection, 1985. Recipient Elda Anderson award Health Physics Soc., 1977, Founders award, 1985; USPHS fellow, 1961-62. Mem. Health Physics Soc., Am. Acad. Environ. Engrs., AAAS, Am. Assn. Physicists in Medicine, Am. Acad. Health Physics, Soc. Radiol. Protection, Am. Nuclear Soc. Current Work: Research in health physics, radiological measurement, history of science. Subspecialties: Health physics; Environmental engineering. Office: Battelle Blvd Richland WA 99352

KATNER, ALLEN SAMUEL, chemist; b. London, Dec. 26, 1938; came to U.S., 1964, naturalized, 1983; s. Joseph Abraham and Gertie Lilly (Nadwick) K.; m. Ruth Madeline Ellen Brown, May 18, 1963; children—Simon Nicholas, Jason Spencer, Clare Madeline. B.Sc. with honors, Nottingham U., Eng., 1958-61, Ph.D. in Organic Chemistry, 1964. Research assoc. Stanford U., Calif., 1964-66; sr. organic chemist Eli Lilly & Co., Indpls., 1966-80, research scientist, 1980—. Contbr. articles to profl. jours. Patentee in Heterocyclic chemistry and biologically active compounds. Fellow Royal Soc. Chemistry; mem. Am. Chem. Soc. Current work: Medicinal chemistry, B-lactam antibiotics; heterocyclic chemistry. Subspecialties: Medicinal chemistry; Synthetic chemistry. Home: 219 W 81st St Indianapolis IN 46260 Office: Eli Lilly and Co Dept MC705 Bldg 88/2 Indianapolis IN 46260

KATZ, ALAN R., physicist, educator, computer scientist; b. Middletown, Conn., Dec. 19, 1955; s. Edmund and Esther K. B.S. in Physics, U. So. Calif., 1977; M.S. in Physics UCLA, 1978, postgrad., 1978—. Research asst. dept. physics, U. So. Calif., Los Angeles, 1973-75, systems programmer learning systems, 1974-77, researcher, programmer Info. Sci. Inst., 1978—; teaching assoc. UCLA, 1979-83, instr. physics, researcher, 1983—; lectr., guide Calif. Mus. Sci. and Industry, Los Angeles, 1976-78; dir. Oasis/L5, Los Angeles, 1978—. Mem. Am. Phys. Soc., Am. Astronautics Soc., AIAA, L-5Soc. Current work: Supersymmetry, classical and quantum field theory, Grassman algebras, computer networks, protocols, internetworking, multimedia mail. Subspecialties: Theoretical physics; Distributed systems and networks. Office: U So Calif Info Scis Inst 4676 Admiralty Marina Del Rey CA 90291

KATZ, ANN HARRIS, college dean, biology educator, biological consultant; b. Long Branch, N.J. B.S., Ursinus Coll., 1966; M.S., U. Mass., 1974, Ph.D., 1976. Biology tchr. Middletown High Sch., N.J., 1967-69; instr. biology Holyoke Community Coll., Mass., 1969-70; research assoc. U. Mass., Amherst, 1970-76; asst. prof. Fordham U., N.Y.C., 1977-83; asst. dean of studies Coll. St. Elizabeth, Convent Station, N.J., 1983-85; co-dir. Great Swamp Research Inst., Basking Ridge, N.J., 1981—; vis. scholar Drew U., 1984—; tech. adv. N.J. Dept. Environ. Protection, 1983—; mem. master plan com. Great Swamp Nat. Wildlife Refuge, U.S. Dept. Interior, 1982—. Contbr. articles to profl. jours. Grantee Earthwatch, 1982, Geraldine Dodge Found., 1982, 83, 84, N.J. Dept. Environ. Protection, 1983; Fordham U. fellow, 1979, 81. Mem. AAAS, Am. Inst. Biol. Sci., Soc. Study of Reproduction, Assn. Women in Sci., Sigma Xi. Current work: Effects of urbanization on natural ecosystems, especially on ecosystems analysis and on reproductive physiology and ecology of white tail deer and other vertebrates. Subspecialties: Physiology (biology); Ecosystems analysis.

KATZ, DONALD L., chemical engineering consultant, author; b. nr. Jackson, Mich., Aug. 1, 1907; m. L. Maxine Crull, 1932 (dec. Mar. 1965); children: Marvin L., Linda M. Katz Cantrell; m. Elizabeth Harwood Correll, Nov. 26, 1965. B.S. in Chem. Engring, U. Mich., 1931, Ph.D. in Chem. Engring, 1933. Research engr. Phillips Petroleum Co., Bartlesville, Okla., 1933-36; mem. faculty U. Mich., Ann Arbor, 1936-77, prof. former chmn. dept. chem. and metall. engring., Alfred Holmes White Univ. prof. chem. engring., from 1966, prof. chem. engring. emeritus, 1977—; cons. engr. on petroleum tech. and underground storage of natural gas to numerous cos. and govtl. orgns. organizer adv. com. on hazardous materials for U.S. Coast Guard, Nat. Acad. Sci., 1964, chmn., 1964-72; mem. task force on info. system World Energy Conf., 1970-71; mem. sci. adv. com. U.S. Coast Guard, 1972-75; chmn. new com. on hazardous material for U.S. Coast Guard, Nat. Acad. Sci.-Nat. Acad. Engring., 1977-79; chmn. com. on air quality and power plant emissions Nat. Acad. Engring.-Nat. Acad. Sci.-NRC, 1974-75; mem. tech. assessment of pollution control adv. com. EPA, 1976-79; lectr. South China Inst. Tech., Ckekeang U., 1982. Co-author: Compressed Air Storage; author: The Settling of Waterloo-Schnackenberg-Katz Families (award of merit Mich. Hist. Soc. 1979); contbr. over 285 articles on heat transfer, fluid dynamics and use of computers in engring. edn. to profl. jours. Former mem., pres. Ann Arbor Bd. Edn.; pres. Ann Arbor Council of Chs., 1944-45; former chmn. ofcl. bd., lay leader 1st United Meth. Ch., Ann Arbor. Recipient Hanlon award Natural Gasoline Assn. Am., 1950, Disting. Faculty Achievement award U. Mich., 1964, Disting. Pub. Service award U.S. Coast Guard, 1972, Gas Industry Research award Am. Gas Assn., 1977; recipient Nat. Medal of Science, 1983; named Mich. Engr. of Year, 1959; Donald L. Katz lectureship in chem. engring. established at U. Mich., 1971. Fellow Am. Inst. Chem. Engrs. (former mem. council, pres. 1959, Founders award 1964, Warren K. Lewis award 1967, Walker award 1968, Anthony F. Lucas god medal 1979), AAAS; mem. Am. Chem. Soc. (E.V. Murphree award indsl. and engring. chemistry div. 1975), ASME, AIME (Mineral Industry's Edn. award 1970), Soc. Petroleum Engrs. of AIME (disting. lectr. 1961-62, John Franklin Carll award 1964; named eminent chem. engr. 1983, disting. mem. 1983), Am. Soc. for Engring. Edn., Am. Assn. Petroleum Geologists, Nat. Acad. Engring., Phi Lambda Upsilon (hon.). Subspecialty: Chemical engineering. Home: 2011 Washtenaw Ann Arbor MI 48104 Office: Dow Bldg Dept Chem Engring U Mich Ann Arbor MI 48109*

KATZ, HYMAN BERNARD, manufacturing company executive; b. Czenstochowa, Poland, Apr. 13, 1945; came to U.S., 1946, naturalized, 1952; s. Israel and Sally (Hertzberg) K.; m. Rose Gisele Gastwirth, Nov. 22, 1969; children: Samuel, Sharon. B.Sc., Poly. Inst. N.Y., 1966; M.Sc., Purdue U., 1968; Ph.D. in Chemistry, Brandeis U., 1973. Group leader quality control Damon corp./Ortho Diagnostics Instruments subs. Johnson & Johnson, Westwood, Mass., 1973-74; quality assurance mgr. Pall Biomed. Products Corp., Glen Cove, N.Y., 1975-76; mgr. quality assurance and regulatory affairs, Pall Corp., Glen Cove, 1976-82, corp. dir. quality assurance and regulatory affairs, 1982—. Contbr. articles to profl. jours. Recipient Interchem. Found. award, 1965-66; USPHS research grantee, 1971-72. Mem. Am. Soc. for Quality Control (bd. dirs., exec. com. v.p., chmn. gen. tech. council, McDermond award 1978), Assn. for Advancement of Med. Instrumentation (bd. dirs. standards council), Parenteral Drug Assn. (regulatory affairs com.), Cosmetic Toiletry and Fragrance Assn. (quality assurance com.), Am. Chem. Soc., Health Industry Mfrs. Assn. Current Work: Contamination control, particulate analysis, fluid clarification, sterile products, statistical sampling, operations research, information systems. Subspecialties: Analytical chemistry; Industrial engineering. Office: 30 Sea Cliff Ave Glen Cove NY 11542

KATZ, I. NORMAN, mathematician, educator; b. N.Y.C., Apr. 14, 1932; s. Oscar A. and Gussie (Glick) K.; m. Judith Batt; children—Avi, Maidi. B.A., Yeshiva U., 1952, M.A. in Math., 1954; Ph.D. in Math., MIT, 1959. Sr. scientist Avco/Research and Advanced Devel., Wilmington, Mass., 1959-62, sect. chief, 1962-64, dept. mgr., 1965-67; assoc. prof. math. Washington U., St. Louis, 1967-75, prof., 1975—; cons. McDonnell Aircraft Corp., St. Louis, 1980—. Contbr. articles to profl. jours. Mem. Soc. Indsl. and Applied Math, Math. Assn. Am., Am. Math. Soc., Ops. Research Soc. Am., Assn. Computing Machinery. Current work: Finite element analysis, numerical algorithms for parallel computations, optimal facility location, Kalman estimation. Subspecialties: Numerical analysis (mathematics); Applied mathematics. Home: 8330 Stanford Ave Saint Louis MO 63132 Office: Washington U Campus Box 1042 Saint Louis MO 63130

KATZ, J. LAWRENCE, educator, biophysicist, biomedical engineer; b. Bklyn., Dec. 18, 1927; s. Frank and Rose (Eidenberg) K.; m. Gertrude Seidman, June 17, 1950; children: Robyn Laurie, Andrea Lee, Talbot Michael. B.S. in Physics, Poly. Inst. Bklyn., 1950, M.S., 1951, Ph.D., 1957. Teaching fellow physics, research fellow, instr. math. Poly. Inst. Bklyn., 1950-56; mem. faculty Rensselaer Poly. Inst., Troy, N.Y., 1956—, prof. physics, 1967—, prof. biophysics and biomed. engring., 1971—, chmn. dept. biomed. engring., 1982, dir. Center for Biomed. Engring., 1974—; summer research asso. Wright Aero. Co., 1956; Summer research asso. Knolls Atomic Power Lab., Schenectady, 1957; hon. research asst. crystallography Univ. Coll., London, 1959-60; vis. prof. biomed. engring., oral biology U. Miami, Fla., 1969-70; vis. prof. biomechanics Chengdu U. Sci. and Tech., China; vis. scientist program Am. Assn. Physics Tchrs.-Am. Inst. Physics, 1970-72; vis. prof. orthopaedics and rehab. U. Miami, summer 1974; cons. in field, 1950—; dir. Bioanalytical Labs., Inc., Troy; adj. prof. orthopaedics Albany Med. Coll., 1972-77, prof. surgery, 1977—; vis. prof. dept. orthopedic surgery Harvard U. Med. Sch., 1978; vis. biophysicist Children's Hosp., Boston, 1978; E. Leon Watkins vis. prof. Wichita (Kans.) State U., 1978; vis. prof. biophysics and biomed. engring. Inst. de Fisica e Quimica de São Carlos, U. São Paulo, Nov. 1978; mem. engring. biology and medicine tng. com. NIH, 1968-71; mem. U.S. Standards Inst. Com. N44; chmn. subcom. diagnostic radiology; mem. VA sci. rev. and evaluation bd. for rehab. engring. research and devel., 1981-83. Editor: (with Robert Plonsey) Marcel Dekker Series on Biomedical Engineering and Instrumentation; contbr. papers to profl. lit., chpts. to books. Mem. organizing com. Black Arts Council, 1969-70; mem. exec. com. Schenectady County Liberal party, 1963—; chmn. 4th jud. dist. nominating conv. Liberal party, 1967-68; Liberal party candidate for U.S. Congress, 1968; committeeman Liberal party, 1968-71; asst. chmn. Schenectady County Liberal party, 1969-71; nat. bd. dirs. Ams. for Democratic Action, 1977—, N.Y. state bd. dirs., 1978—; sponsor tri-city div. United Negro Coll. Fund, 1967-68; mem. Schenectady Light Opera Co., 1964—. Served with USNR, 1946-48. NSF sci. faculty fellow, 1959-60; Guggenheim fellow, 1977-78; NIH Sr. Internat. fellow, 1985-86. Fellow Am. Phys. Soc.; mem. Am. Crystallographic Assn. (chmn. crystal data com.), AIME (chmn. dental med. tech. com.), AAUP (pres. Rensselaer chpt. 1974-75), Biophys. Soc., Orthopaedic Research Soc. (mem. program com. 1973-75, chmn. 1975, exec. com. 1975), Internat. Assn. Dental Research, Am. Soc. Engring. Edn. (chmn. biomed. engring. div. 1978-79, chmn. elect and program chmn. 1977—), Soc. Biomaterials (v.p. 1977-78, pres. 1978-79), Biomed. Engring. Soc. (dir. 1981-84, pres. elect 1982-83, pres. 1983-84), ASTM (chmn. composites subcom. of com. med. implants and devices), IEEE (chmn. ednl. com.), Fedn. Am. Scientists, Sigma Xi, Sigma Pi Sigma. Jewish (trustee temple 1962-63, 63-64, mem. social action com. 1968-69). Patentee pretensioned prosthetic device for skeletal joints. Subspecialties: Biomedical engineering; Biophysics (physics). Home: 838 Maxwell Dr Schenectady NY 12309 Office: Rensselaer Poly Inst Troy NY 12181

KATZ, JAY, physician, educator; b. Zwickau, Germany, Oct. 20, 1922; came to U.S., 1940, naturalized, 1945; s. Paul and Dora (Ungar) K.; m. Esta Mae Zorn, Sept. 13, 1952; children: Sally Jean, Daniel Franklin, Amy Susan. B.A., U. Vt., 1944; M.D., Harvard U., 1949. Intern Mt. Sinai Hosp., N.Y.C., 1949-50; resident Northport (N.Y.) VA Hosp., 1950-51; resident Yale U., 1953-55, instr. psychiatry, New Haven, 1955-57, asst. prof., 1957-58, asst. prof. psychiatry and law, 1958-60, assoc. prof. law, assoc. clin. prof. psychiatry, 1960-67, adj. prof. law and psychiatry, 1967-79, prof., 1979-81, John A. Garver prof. law and psychoanalysis, 1981—; tng. and supervising psychoanalyst Western New Eng. Inst. for Psychoanalysis, 1972—; cons. to asst. sec. health and sci. affairs HEW, 1972-73, mem. artificial heart assessment panel, 1972-73. Author: (with Joseph Goldstein) The Family and the Law, 1964, (with Joseph Goldstein and Alan M. Dershowitz) Psychoanalysis, Psychiatry and Law, 1967, Experimentation with Human Beings, 1972, (with Alexander M. Capron) Catastrophic Diseases—Who Decides What? , 1975; The Silent World of Doctor and Patient, 1984. Bd. dirs. Family Service of New Haven. Served to capt. M.C. USAF, 1951-53. John Simon Guggenheim Meml. Found. fellow, 1981. Fellow ACP (William C. Menninger award 1983), Am. Psychiat. Assn. (Isaac Ray award 1975), Am. Orthopsychiat. Assn., Am. Coll. Psychiatry, Center for Advanced Psychoanalytic Studies; mem. Inst. Medicine, Nat. Acad. of Scis., Group for Advancement of Psychiatry, Am. Psychoanalytic Assn. Jewish. Subspecialty: Psychiatry. Home: 27 Inwood Rd Woodbridge CT 06525 Office: 127 Wall St New Haven CT 06520

KATZ, JOSEPH JACOB, chemist, educator; b. Apr. 19, 1912; s. Abraham and Stella (Asnin) K.; m. Celia S. Weiner, Oct. 1, 1944; children—Anna, Elizabeth, Mary, Abram. B.Sc., Wayne U., 1932; Ph.D., U. Chgo., 1942. Research asso. chemistry U. Chgo., 1942-43, asso. chemist metall. lab., 1943-45; sr. chemist Argonne (Ill.) Nat. Lab., 1945—; Tech. adviser U.S. delegation UN Conf. on Peaceful Uses Atomic Energy, Geneva, Switzerland, 1955; chmn. AAAS Gordon Research Conf. on Inorganic Chemistry, 1953-54. Am. editor: Jour. Inorganic and Nuclear Chemistry, 1955-82. Recipient Distinguished Alumnus award Wayne U., 1955, Profl. Achievement award U. Chgo. Alumni Assn., 1983; Guggenheim fellow, 1956-57. Mem. Am. Chem. Soc. (award for nuclear applications in chemistry 1961, sec.-treas. div. phys. chemistry 1966-76), Nat. Acad. Scis., Am. Nuclear Soc., Phi Beta Kappa, Sigma Xi. Current Work: Chorophyll function in photosynthesis; laser photochemistry of chlorophyll; Synthesis of Chlorophyll model systems. Subspecialty: Physical chemistry. Home: 1700 E 56th St Chicago IL 60637 Office: 9700 S Cass Ave Argonne IL 60439

KATZ, JULIAN, gastroenterologist, educator; b. N.Y.C., Apr. 3, 1937; s. Abraham M. and Fay (Sher) K.; m. Sheila Moriber, Aug. 18, 1963; children—Jonathan Peter, Sara Katherine. A.B., Columbia U., 1958; M.D., U. Chgo., 1962. Diplomate: Am. Bd. Internal Medicine. Intern U. Chgo. Hosps., 1962-63; resident in medicine Duke U., 1963-65; fellow in gastroenterology Yale U., 1965-67; practice medicine specializing in gastroenterology, internal medicine, Phila., 1969—; prof. medicine, lectr. in physiology and biochemistry Med. Coll. Pa., 1970—, also lectr. local and nat. groups; chief clin. gastroenterology Med. Coll. Pa. Editor profl. jours.; Contbr. articles to profl. jours. and books. Served with USN, 1967-69. Fellow ACP; mem. Am. Soc. Gastrointestinal Endoscopy, Am. Soc. Study Liver Disease, Am. Gastroenterological Assn., others. Current Work: Immunologic aspects of gastroenterology, research in nutrition and endoscopy clinical pharmacology. Subspecialty: Gastroenterology. Home: 701 Dodds Ln Gladwyne PA 19035 Office: Gastrointestinal Specialists 555 City Ave Bala-Cynwyd PA 19004

KATZ, MANFRED, polymer chemist, researcher; b. Giesen, Fed. Republic Germany, Feb. 16, 1929; came to U.S., 1938; s. Karl and Jettchen (Oppenheimer) K.; m. Edith Schiff, Mar. 21, 1953 (dec. 1958); 1 child, Harold; m. Barbara A. Ehrlich, Apr. 4, 1965; children—Anita, Carl, Daniel. B.S., Okla. State U., 1950, M.S., 1951; Ph.D., U. Del., 1961. Research chemist E.I. DuPont de Nemours, Wilmington, Del., 1951-54, sr. research chemist, 1955-61, research assoc., 1961-65, research supr., Kinston, N.C., 1965-72, sr. research assoc., Wilmington, 1972—. Author, patentee in field. Served with U.S. Army, 1954-55. Mem. Am. Chem. Soc., N.Y. Acad. Scis., Sigma Xi. Current work: Macromolecular chemistry, synthetic fibers and composites. Subspecialties: Polymer chemistry; Composite materials. Home: 310 Brockton Rd Wilmington DE 19803 Office: EI DuPont de Nemours Inc Wilmington DE 19898

KATZ, MARTIN, research firm executive, marketing executive, scientist; b. N.Y.C., May 16, 1927; s. David and Fannie (Miller) K.; m. Lee Nesenblatt, Dec. 21, 1947; children—Beth, Hallie Michelle. B.S., St. John's Coll. Pharmacy, N.Y.C., 1947; M.S., Columbia U., 1948, M.A., 1951; D.Sc., Phila. Coll. Pharmacy and Sci., 1954; postgrad. Stanford Bus. Sch., 1974. Registered pharmacist, Calif., N.Y. Asst. prof. Columbia U., N.Y.C., 1948-53; group leader Pfizer, N.Y.C., 1953-55, Revlon Corp., N.Y.C., 1955-60; sr. v.p. Syntex, Palo Alto, Calif., 1960-85; sr. v.p. Advanced Polymer Systems, Inc., Redwood City, Calif., 1985—, also dir. Contbr. articles to profl. jours. and chpts. to books. Fellow Acad. Pharm. Scis., Soc. Cosmetic Chemists (N.Y. chmn. 1962), Am. Found. Pharm. Edn. (scholar 1948, 52-54), Am. Pharm. Assn., Am. Chem. Soc. Jewish. Current work: Polymeric entrapment systems for analytical, diagnostic, pharmaceutical, cosmetic and household product applications. Subspecialties: Drug delivery systems; Polymer chemistry. Home: 5 Whitney Ct Menlo Park CA 94025 Office: Advanced Polymer Systems Inc 3696-C Haven Ave Redwood City CA 94063

KATZ, MICHAEL, pediatrician, educator; b. Lwow, Poland, Feb. 13, 1928; came to U.S., 1946, naturalized, 1951; s. Edward and Rita (Gluzman) K. A.B., U. Pa., 1949, postgrad. (Harrison fellow), 1950-51; M.D., SUNY, Bklyn., 1956; M.S., Columbia U. Sch. Public Health, 1968. Intern UCLA Med. Center, 1956-57; resident Presbyterian Hosp. (Babies Hosp.), N.Y.C., 1960-62, dir. pediatric service, 1977—; hon. lectr. in pediatrics Makerere U. Coll., Kampala, Uganda, 1963-64; instr. in pediatrics Columbia U., 1964-65, prof. tropical medicine Sch. Public Health, 1971—, prof. pediatrics Coll. Physicians and Surgeons, 1972-77, Reuben S. Carpentier prof., chmn. dept. pediatrics, 1977—; asso. mem. Wistar Inst., Phila., 1965-71; asst. prof. pediatrics U. Pa., 1966-71; cons. WHO Regional Offices and Guatemala, Venezuela, Egypt, Yemen; mem. U.S. del. 32d World Health Assembly, Geneva, 1979; cons. UNICEF, N.Y.C. and Tokyo., USAID, Egypt, 1982. Contbr. articles to profl. jours.; author: (with others) Parasitic Diseases, 1982; editor: (with Volker ter Meulen) Slow Virus Infections of the Central Nervous System, 1977; editorial bd.: Med. Microbiology and Immunology, 1975—, Pediatric Infectious Diseases, 1981—, Vaccines, 1983—; also co-editor Manuals in Pediatrics. Served to lt. M.C., USNR, 1957-59. NIH grantee, 1968-76; WHO grantee, 1972-76; recipient Jurzykowski Found. award in Medicine, 1983. Fellow Infectious Diseases Soc. Am., AAAS, Am. Acad. Pediatrics; mem. Soc. Pediatric Research, Am. Pediatric Soc., Harvey Soc., Am. Soc. Microbiology, Deutsche Gesellschaft fur Neuropathologie und Neuroanatomie E.V. (corr.), Am. Soc. Tropical Medicine and Hygiene, N.Y. Soc. Tropical Medicine (pres. 1976-77), Royal Soc. Tropical Medicine and Hygiene (London), Inst. Medicine of Nat. Acad. Scis., Sigma Xi. Current Work: Malnutrition infection complex; latent viral infections. Subspecialties: Pediatrics; Tropical medicine. Home: 930 Fifth Ave New York NY 10021 Office: Coll Physicians and Surgeons Columbia U 630 W 168th St New York NY 10032

KATZ, SAMUEL LAWRENCE, medical educator, pediatrician; b. Manchester, N.H., May 29, 1927; s. Morris and Ethel (Lawrence) K.; m. BetsyJane Cohan, 1950 (div. 1970); 7 children; m. Catherine Minock Wilfert, 1971. A.B. magna cum laude, Dartmouth Coll. 1949; M.D. cum laude, Harvard U., 1952. Diplomate Nat. Bd. Med. Examiners, Am. Bd. Pediatrics; lic. physician, Mass., N.C. Intern Beth Israel Hosp., Boston, 1952-53, pediatrician-in-chief, 1958-61, vis. pediatrician, 1961-68; resident Children's Hosp. Med. Ctr., Boston, 1953-54, 55, Mass. Gen. Hosp., Boston, 1954-55; instr. pediatrics Sch. Medicine, Harvard U., Boston, 1958-59, assoc. in pediatrics, 1959-63, asst. prof., 1963-68; co-dir. infectious disease career tng. program Combined Beth Israel Hosp.-Children's Hosp. Med. Ctr., Boston, 1967-68; prof., chmn. dept. pediatrics Sch. Medicine, Duke U., Durham, N.C., 1968—, Wilburt C. Davison prof. pediatrics, 1972—; lectr., vis. prof. various hosps. and univs.; bd. dirs. Nat. Found. for Infectious Diseases, 1980—; chmn. adv. com. on immunization practices Centers for Disease Control, USPHS, 1985—. Contbr. to publs. in field. Served with USN, 1945-46. Rufus Choate scholar, 1947-48; Nat. Found. Infantile Paralysis fellow, 1956-58; research career devel. award NIH, 1965-68; recipient Golden Apple award Duke U. Med. Students, 1969, 78. Fellow Am. Acad. Pediatrics (Grulee award 1975), Infectious Diseases Soc. Am.; mem. New Eng. Pediatric Soc. (sec.-treas. 1963-68), N.Y. Acad. Scis., Soc. for Pediatric Research, AAAS, Am. Soc. for Microbiology, Am. Assn. Immunologists, Am. Pub. Health Assn., Am. Soc. for Clin. Investigation, AAUP, N.C. Pediatric Soc., Soc. Soc. for Pediatric Research, Am. Pediatric Soc. (v.p. 1985—), Am. Epidemiological Soc., Am. Soc. for Virology, Am. Fed. for Clin. Research, Phi Beta Kappa, Alpha Omega Alpha, Sigma Xi. Current work: Immunization studies of new vaccines. Subspecialties: Pediatrics; Infectious diseases. Office: Duke U Med Ctr Box 2925 Pediatrics Durham NC 27710 27710

KATZ, THOMAS JOSEPH, chemistry educator; b. Prague, Czechoslovakia, Mar, 21, 1936; s. Francis and Ida (Jungmann) K.; m. Meta Oehmsen, Dec. 27, 1963; 1 son, Joshua. B.A., U. Wis., 1956; M.A., Harvard U., 1957, Ph.D., 1959. Instr. Columbia U., N.Y.C., 1959-61, asst. prof., 1961-64, asst. prof., 1964-68, prof., 1968—. Contbr. numerous articles on chemistry to profl. jours. Alfred P. Sloan Found. fellow, 1962-66; John Simon Guggenheim Meml. Found. fellow, 1967-68. Mem. Am. Chem. Soc., Royal Soc. of Chemistry (U.K.). Current Work: Organometallic chemistry, catalysis by metals, organic synthesis,organometallic chemistry. Subspecialties: Organic chemistry; Catalysis chemistry. Home: 445 Riverside Dr Apt 82 New York NY 10027 Office: Dept Chemistry Columbia U New York NY 10027

KATZ, WILLIAM, materials scientist, educator; b. Dayton, Ohio, Dec. 10, 1953; s. Murray Louis and Anita Jean (Feller) K.; m. Patricia Valerie Powers, Aug. 12,1979. B.A., Earlham Coll., 1975; M.S. in Analytical Chemistry, U. Ill, Urbana, 1977, Ph.D., 1979; M.B.A. candidate, SUNY, 1986. Research chemist Exxon Research and Devel. Lab., Baton Rouge, 1979-80; materials scientist Gen. Electric Corp. Research and Devel. Center, Schenectady, 1980-84, mgr. chemistry, 1984—; adj. prof. SUNY, Albany. Contbr. numerous articles to profl. jours. Mem. Am. Inst. Physics, Am. Chem. Soc., Am. Vacuum Soc., Materials Research Soc., Phi Lambda Upsilon. Current Work: Materials characterization; surface analysis; sputtering and ionization phenomenon. Subspecialties: Electronic materials; Surface chemistry. Home: 46 Fredericks Rd Scotia NY 12302 Office: Gen Electric Co Bldg K-1 Room 2C27 PO Box 8 Schenectady NY 12301

KAU, SEN T., pharmacologist; b. Taiwan, Dec. 25, 1942; s. Hsing-Jung and Yu Lan (Liau) K.; m. Praphaisri Lee, Dec. 23, 1971; children: Eric, Ryan. B.S. in Pharmacy, Nat. Taiwan U., 1967; Ph.D. in Pharmacology, Vanderbilt U., 1974. Research asso. Vanderbilt U., Nashville, 1974-75; research fellow physiology Cornell U. Med. Coll., N.Y.C., 1975-77; biologist ICI Ltd., Eng., 1977-78; sr. research pharmacologist ICI Ams. Ltd., Wilmington, Del., 1978-80, prin. pharmacologist, 1980—, sect. mgr. biomed. research dept., 1981—. Contbr. articles to profl. jours. NIH grantee, 1971-75; NSF fellow, 1975-77. Mem. Am. Soc. Pharmacology and Exptl. Therapeutics, Am. Soc. Nephrology, Brit. Pharmacol. Soc., N.Y. Acad. Scis., Physiol. Soc. Phila., Am. Physiol. Soc., High Blood Pressure Council. Current Work: Renal biochemistry, physiology, pharmacology and toxicology. Subspecialties: Pharmacology; Renal physiology. Office: ICI Americas Inc New Murphy Rd and Concord Pike Wilmington DE 19897

KAUER, JAMES CHARLES, chemist; b. Cleve., Jan. 17, 1927; s. James George and Lenore Marie (Hess) K.; m. Elisabeth Sophie Dressler, July 10, 1954; children—Julie, Catherine, James, Frederick, Susanne. B.S., Case Inst. Tech., Cleve., 1951; Ph.D., U. Ill., Urbana, 1955. Research chemist DuPont Central Research Dept., Wilmington, Del., 1955—. Contbr. articles on organic chemistry to profl. jours. Patentee organic chemistry field. Served with USN, 1945-47. Mem. Am. Chem. Soc., Soc. for Neurosci., Internat. Occulation Timing Assn. Current work: Synthesis of peptides, heterocycles, neurotransmitter analogs; neurotransmitter receptors. Subspecialties: Organic chemistry; Neurochemistry. Home: 605 Willow Glen Rd Kennett Square PA 19348 Office: DuPont Central Research Dept DuPont Experimental Station Wilmington DE 19898

KAUFMAN, CHARLES, physicist, educator; b. Bklyn., June 4, 1937; s. Irving and Lillian (Greenbaum) K.; m. Carol DeAcutis, June 12, 1967; children—Eleanor, Amelia. B.S., U. Wis., 1956; M.S., Pa. State U., 1959, Ph.D., 1963. Instr. Pa. State U., State College, 1963, 64; prof. physics U. R.I., Kingston, 1964—; vis. asst. prof. U. Wis., Madison, 1966, 67; physicist U.S. Naval Underwater Systems Ctr., Newport, R.I., 1969-71; guest lectr. U. Vienna, Austria, 1971-72; cons. Raytheon Co., Portsmouth, R.I., 1978-83. Contbr. articles to profl. publs. Mem. Am. Phys. Soc., Acoustical Soc. Am. (chmn. Narragansett chpt. 1981-83), N.Y. Acad. Scis. Current work: Underwater acoustics, turbulent flow, particle physics, chaos in deterministic systems. Subspecialties: Acoustics; Theoretical physics. Office: Physics Dept U RI East Hall Kingston RI 02881

KAUFMAN, DONALD WAYNE, ecologist, educator; b. Abilene, Tex., June 7, 1943; s. Leo Fred and Marcella Genevieve (Hobbie) K.; m. Glennis Ann Schroeder, Aug. 5, 1967; 1 child, Dawn. B.S., Ft. Hays State Coll., 1965, M.S., 1967; Ph.D., U. Ga., 1972. Postdoctoral fellow U. Tex.-Austin, 1971-73; vis. scientist Savannah River Ecology Lab., Aiken, S.C., 1973-74; asst. prof. U. Ark., Fayetteville, 1974-75, SUNY-Binghamton, 1975-77; assoc. program dir. NSF, Washington, 1977-80; asst., then assoc. prof. biology Kans. State U., Manhattan, 1980-84, 84—; grant rev. panelist EPA, 1981-85; cons. NSF, 1984. Contbr. articles to profl. jours. NDEA fellow, 1967-69; NIH predoctoral trainee, 1969-70; NIH postdoctoral trainee, 1971-73; NSF grantee, 1981—. Mem. Am. Soc. Mammalogists (award 1972), Ecol. Soc. Am., Soc. for Study Evolution, Am. Inst. Biol. Scis., AAAS. Current work: Population and community ecology of mammals, grassland ecology, ecology of disturbance, ecological and evolutionary genetics of mammals and gastropods. Subspecialties: Ecology (biology); Evolutionary biology. Office: Div Biology Ackert Hall Kans State U Manhattan KS 66506

KAUFMAN, EDWIN H., JR., mathematics educator; b. Decatur, Ill., June 23, 1943; s. Edwin H. and Ada Rose (Parsinger) K. B.A., Millikin U., 1965; M.S., U. Ill.-Urbana, 1967, Ph.D., 1970. Vis. asst. prof. Mich. State U., East Lansing, 1970-72; asst. prof. math. Central Mich. U., Mt. Pleasant, 1972-74, assoc. prof., 1974-78, prof., 1978—. Co-author articles in field. Recipient Scovill award Millikin U., 1964, Univ. fellow, 1965-66; NSF trainee, 1966-70. Mem. Am. Math. Soc., Math. Assn. Am., Soc. Indsl. and Applied Math., Mensa, Sigma Xi. Republican. Current Work: Approximation theory; numerical analysis. Subspecialty: Numerical analysis (computer science). Office: Central Mich U Dept Math Mount Pleasant MI 48858

KAUFMAN, LEO, microbiologist; b. N.Y.C., Jan. 20, 1930; s. David and Dora (Stalbow) K.; m. Renee Ellen Dreyfus, Jan. 19, 1952; children: Jennifer, Gary, Steven. B.S., Bklyn. Coll. of CCNY, 1952; M.S., U. Ky., 1955, Ph.D., 1958. Diplomate: Am. Bd. Microbiology, Am. Acad. Microbiology. Instr. U. Ky., 1958-59; med. research microbiologist, bateriology div. (Communicable Disease Center), 1959-60; with div. mycotic diseases Centers for Disease Control, Atlanta, 1960—, chief fungus immunology br., 1967—; adj. assoc. prof. Sch. Public Health, U. N.C.; adj. prof. Ga. State U., 1976, Emory U., 1982—. Contbr. numerous articles to profl. jours. Recipient Disting. Service award HEW, 1980; Meridian award Med. Mycological Soc. Ams., 1983; Kimble methodology research award Conf. Pub. Health, 1985; Internat. Soc. for Human and Animal Mycology award, 1985. Mem. Am. assn. Immunologists, Am. Soc. Microbiology, Sigma Xi. Current Work: Development and provision of tests for serodiagnosis of systemic mycotic infections. Subspecialties: Immunobiology and immunology; Medical mycology. Office: Centers for Disease Control Bldg 5 Room B13 Immunology Br Div Mycotic Diseases Atlanta GA 30333

KAUFMAN, PETER BISHOP, biologist, plant physiologist, educator; b. San Francisco, Feb. 25, 1928; s. Earle Francis and Gwendolyn Bishop (Morris) K.; m. Hazel Snyder, Apr. 5, 1958; children: Linda Myrl, Ryan, Laura Irene. B.S., Cornell U., 1949; Ph.D. in Botany, U. Calif.-Davis, 1954; Ph.D. Muellhaupt postdoctoral fellow in research, Ohio State U., summer 1955. Research investigator Calif. Rice Growers Assn., 1951-53; instr. dept. botany U. Mich., Ann Arbor, 1956, asst. prof., 1957-62, assoc. prof., 1962-72, prof., 1972—; agrl. research scientist Shell Devel. Co., Modesto, Calif., summer 1959; vis. NSF research scholar Lund (Sweden) U., 1964-65; chmn. Mich. Natural Areas Council, 1972-74; vis. prof. depts. chemistry and molecular, cellular and developmental biology U. Colo., Boulder, 1973, 74; vis. research scientist Prairie Regional Lab., NRC Can., Saskatoon, Sask., 1973; research scientist NASA Space Biology Program, 1979—; author TV series House Botanist,

1977; vis. research scientist U. Calgary, Alta., Can., 1979, Mich. State U., East Lansing, 1980; hon. staff mem. Faculty Agr., Nagoya (Japan) U.; vis research scientist Rice Research Inst., Los Banos, Philippines; speaker numerous symposia and confs. Editorial bd.: Plant Physiology, 1976—; author: Laboratory Experiments in Plant Physiology, 1975, Plants, People and Environment, 1979; also numerous articles. Served with U.S. Army, 1954-56. Fellow AAAS; mem. Mich. Bot. Club (pres. 1963-64), Bot. Soc. Am. (chmn. edn. com.; vice-chmn, developmental sect. 1975-77), N.Y. Acad. Scis., Am. Soc. Plant Physiologists, Scandinavian Soc. Plant Physiologists, Internat. Soc. Plant Morphologists, Soc. Developmental Biology, Am. Soc. Electron Microscopy, Tissue Culture Assn., Am. Inst. Biol. Scis., Nature Conservancy, Internat. Assn. Plant Tissue Culture, Sigma Xi. Democrat. Presbyterian. Current Work: Plant hormones, gravity responses in plants, silicification in plants, growth responses of plants in space shuttle and space stations, rice seed proteins. Subspecialties: Plant physiology (biology); Gravitational biology.

KAUFMAN, RICHARD GILBERT, research scientist; b. Washington, Apr. 18, 1933. A.B. in Chemistry, Catholic U. of America, 1956, Ph.D. in phys. chemistry, 1962. Research assoc. U. Notre Dame Radiation Lab., South Bend, Ind., 1961-63; sr. research physicist Zenith Corp., Glenview, Ill., 1963-78; sr. research chemist Amoco Corp., Naperville, Ill., 1978—. Contbr. articles to profl. jours.; patentee in field. Mem. Am. Phys. Soc., Am. Chem. Soc., Electrochem. Soc., Soc. Photo-optical Instrumentation Engrs. Current work: Solid state luminescence; phosphors display tech.; color measurement tech.; applied optics. Home: 715 S May St Chicago IL 60607 Office: AMOCO Research Ctr Box 400 MS/F-4 Naperville IL 60566

KAUFMAN, SEYMOUR, biochemist; b. Bklyn., Mar. 13, 1924; s. Charles and Anna Kaufman; m. Elaine Elkins, Feb. 6, 1948; children—Allan, Emily, Leslie. B.S., U. Ill., 1945, M.S., 1946; Ph.D., Duke U., 1949. Instr. dept. pharmacology NYU Med. Sch., 1951-52, asst. prof., 1953-54; sect. chief Lab. Gen. Comparative Biochemistry, NIMH, 1954-68, chief Lab. Neurochemistry, 1968—. Contbr. articles to books and profl. jours. Mem. Am. Soc. Biol. Chemists, Am. Chem. Soc., Am. Soc. Neurochemistry, Internat. Soc. Neurochemistry. Current work: Enzymology, phenylketonuria, pterin coenzymes. Subspecialties: Biochemistry (biology); Neurochemistry. Office: Lab Neurochemistry Mental Health Intramural Research Div 3D30 NIH Bldg 36 Bethesda MD 20205

KAUFMANN, JOHN HENRY, zoology educator, researcher; b. Balt., Jan. 7, 1934; B.S., Cornell U., 1956; Ph.D., U. Calif.-Berkeley, 1961. Biologist NIH, San Juan, P.R., 1961-63; asst. prof. zoology U. Fla., Gainesville, 1963-67, assoc. prof., 1967-74, prof., 1974—. Author 2 monographs. Contbr. numerous articles to sci. jours. Chmn. sci. adv. com. Fla. Defenders of Environ., Gainesville, 1970—; mem. Fla. Non-game Wildlife Adv. Council, Tallahassee, 1983—. Mem. Ecol. Soc. Am., Am. Soc. Mammalogists, Animal Behavior Soc. Current work: Research on evolution and ecology of vertebrates, especially mammals, with emphasis on social behavior. Subspecialties: Behavioral ecology; Sociobiology. Office: Dept Zoology U Fla Gainesville FL 32611

KAUSEL, EDUARDO, civil engineering educator, researcher, consultant; b. Santiago, Chile, Feb. 14, 1943; came to U.S., 1970; s. Eberhard and Margarita (Bolt) K.; m. Cecilia Paulina Lewis, Apr. 4, 1967; 1 child, Christoph. Ingeniero Civil, U. Chile, Santiago, 1966; student Tech. Hochschule, Darmstadt, Federal Republic Germany, 1969-70; M.S., MIT, 1971, D.Sc., 1973. Registered profl. engr., Mass. Engr. Endesa, Santiago, 1967-69; research asst. MIT, Cambridge, 1970-73, assoc. prof. civil enginrg., 1978—; cons. Stone & Webster, Boston, 1973-78 cons. various cos., 1978—. Editor: Structural Engineering: Research, Education and Practice, 1983; mem. editorial bd. Soil Dynamics and Earthquake Engrng. Jour., 1984—, Jour. Microsoftware for Engrs., 1985—. Contbr. articles to profl. jours. Scholar Deutscher Akademischer Austauschdienst, W. Ger., 1969; travel grantee, research grantee NSF. Mem. ASCE (coms. 1975—), Earthquake Engrng. Research Inst., Seismological Soc. Am., Internat. Assn. Structural Mechanics in Reactor Tech., Sigma Xi. Current work: Vibrations of foundations and soil-structure interaction, spatial variations of earthquake ground motions, waves in layered media. Subspecialties: Civil engineering; Theoretical and applied mechanics. Home: 22 Heckle St Wellesley MA 02181 Office: MIT Room 1-271 Cambridge MA 02139

KAUTZ, DAVID JOHNATHAN, mechanical design engineer, consultant; b. Youngstown, Ohio, Feb. 28, 1954; s. Henry George and Barbara Jean (Hollingsworth) K.; m. Judith Anne Larkin, Jan. 8, 1977; children—Branden Alexis, Christopher Robert. B.S.M.E., SUNY-Buffalo, 1976. Registered profl. engr., N.Y. Field engr. BASIC Constrn. Co., Richmond, Va., 1976-77; project engr. TAM Ceramics (subs. NL Industries-Indsl. Chem. Devel.), Niagara Falls, 1978-80; project design engr. Battery Disposal Tech., Clarence, N.Y., 1980-81; sr. project engr. Buffalo Color Corp., 1981—; cons. failure analysis. Served to lt. USNR, 1981—. Mem. ASME (assoc., chmn. nat. legal consequences com. 1981-83), Nat. Soc. Profl. Engrs., Am. Soc. Naval Engrs. (assoc.). Club: University (Buffalo). Patentee method, equipment to neutralize high-energy-density lithium batteries. Current Work: Plant facilities planning, design and construction; building rehabilitation; pollution control systems. Subspecialties: Mechanical engineering; Metallurgy. Office: 340 Elk St Buffalo NY 14240

KAUZMANN, WALTER JOSEPH, chemistry educator; b. Mt. Vernon, N.Y., Aug. 18, 1916; s. Albert and Julia Maria (Kahle) K.; m. Elizabeth Alice Flagler, Apr. 1, 1951; children: Charles Peter, Eric Flagler, Katherine Elizabeth Julia. B.A., Cornell U., 1937; Ph.D., Princeton U., 1940. Westinghouse research fellow Westinghouse Mfg. Co., E. Pittsburgh, Pa., 1940-42; mem. staff Explosives Research Lab., Bruceton, Pa., 1942-44, Los Alamos Lab., 1944-46; asst. prof. Princeton U., 1946-51, asso. prof., 1951-60, prof. chemistry, 1960-82, chmn. dept., 1964-68, David B. Jones prof. chemistry, 1963-82, chmn. biochem. sci. dept., 1980-81; vis. scientist Atlantic Research Lab., NRC Can., 1983; vis. lectr. Kyoto U., 1974; vis. prof. U. Ibadan, 1975. Author: Quantum Chemistry, 1957, Kinetic Theory of Gases, 1966, Thermal Properties of Matter, 1967, (with D. Eisenberg) Structure and Properties of Water, 1969. Jr. fellow Soc. Fellows, Harvard, 1942; Guggenheim fellow, 1957, 74-75; Recipient Linderstrom-Lang medal, 1966. Fellow Am. Acad. Arts and Scis.; mem. Nat. Acad. Scis., Am. Soc. Biol. Chemists, Am. Chem. Soc., Am. Phys. Soc., A.A.A.S., Fedn. Am. Scientists, Sigma Xi. Current Work: Physical chemistry of molten silicates, water and aqueous solutions. Subspecialties: Geochemistry; Physical chemistry. Home: 4 Newlin Rd Princeton NJ 08540 Frick Chem Lab Princeton NJ 08540

KAVIPURAPU, KRISHNA M., computer science educator, researcher; b. Telaprolu, India, Apr. 22, 1952; s. Rangarad and Kousalya (Gudipaty) K.; m. Lisa M. McDonald, Dec. 28, 1981. B.E., Indian Inst. Sci., 1975; M.S., So. Meth. U., 1977, Ph.D., 1980. Grad. teaching and research asst. So. Meth. U., 1976-80; asst. prof. dept. computer sci. U. So. La., 1980-82, U. Tex.-Arlington, 1982—. Contbr. articles to profl. jours. Indian Inst. Sci. merit scholar awardee, 1972-75; Indian Nat. Merit Scholarship awardee, 1972; recipient F. E. Terman award So. Meth. U., 1979; Tex. Instruments grantee, 1981-82. Mem. IEEE, Assn. for Computing Machinery. Current Work: New and innovative high-level computer architecture; software development to develop a distributed operating system; model ultra-reliable fault tolerant computers using data flow models. Subspecialties: Computer architecture; Software engineering. Home: 712 Lincoln Green Apt 2103 Arlington TX 76011 Office: U Tex Dept Computer Sci Engring PO Box 19015 Arlington TX 76019

KAWALEK, JOSEPH CASIMIR, federal government chemist; b. Stockton, Calif., Dec. 21, 1945; s. Joseph Casimir and Ann Pauline (Schindler) K.; m. Rosella Mae Seckel, Aug. 12, 1972; children—Kiera Ann, James Andrew. B.S., St. Francis Coll., Loretto, Pa., 1967; Ph.D., U. Pitts., 1973. Research assoc. dept. biochemistry Hoffmann-LaRoche, Inc., Nutley, N.J., 1974-76; staff scientist Frederick Cancer Research Ctr., Md., 1976-80; research chemist Ctr. Vet. Medicine, Div. Vet. Med. Research, FDA, Beltsville, Md., 1980—. Contbr. articles, abstracts to profl. lit. Served with AUS, 1968-70. Grantee NSF, 1967-68, NIH, 1970-73. Mem. Soc. Toxicology, N.Y. Acad. Scis., Am. Soc. Study Xenobiotics, Am. Chem. Soc., Am. Inst. Biol. Scis., AAAS, Sigma Xi. Democrat. Roman Catholic. Current work: Determining factors necessary to ensure safe and effective use of drugs in veterinary animals; factors affecting drug metabolism. Subspecialties: Toxicology (agriculture); Drug metabolism in food producing animals. Office: FDA Ctr Vet Medicine Div Vet Med Research Bldg 328-A Agrl Research Ctr-East Beltsville MD 20705

KAWAMURA, KAZUHIKO, electrical engineering educator, consultant; b. Nagoya, Aichi, Japan, Feb. 4, 1939; came to U.S., 1964, naturalized, 1981; s. Eizo and Nobuko (Tani) K.; m. Ethel Ruth Perisho, Jan. 2, 1971. B.E. in Elec. Engring., Waseda U., Tokyo, 1963; M.S. in Elec. Engring., U. Calif.-Berkeley, 1966; Ph.D. in Elec. Engring., U. Mich., 1972. Teaching fellow U. Mich., Ann Arbor, 1967-72, lectr., U. Mich., Dearborn, 1972-73; research specialist Ford Motor Co., Dearborn, summer 1972; research scientist Battelle Columbus Lab., Ohio, 1973-81; assoc. prof. elec. engrng. and mgmt. of tech., Vanderbilt U., Nashville, 1981—; invited prof. Kyoto U., Japan, 1980; adviser Saudi Arabian Ctr. for Sci. and Tech., Riyadh, 1980-83; assoc. dir. designate Vanderbilt U. Ctr. for Intelligent Systems, 1984—. Editor, contbg. author: Participatory Systems Approach, 1981. Sr. research fellow Japan Soc. for Promotion Sci., Tokyo, 1980. Mem. Am. Assn. Artifical Intelligence, AAAS (com. mem. 1984-87), Soc. Gen. Systems Research. Club: YMCA (Nashville). Current work: Research and development of intelligent robots through application of artificial intelligence techniques; research on expert systems and PROLOG. Subspecialties: Artificial intelligence; Robotics. Home: 1608 S Observatory Dr Nashville TN 37215 Office: Vanderbilt U PO Box 1674 Sta B Nashville TN 37235

KAY, ALAN, computer scientist. Formerly chief scientist Atari, Inc.; now Apple fellow Apple Computer, Inc., 1984—. . Office: Apple Computer Inc 12212 Octagon St Brentwood CA 90049*

KAY, MARGUERITE M. BOYLE, physician, scientist, educator; b. Washington, May 13, 1947; s. Murray and Ann Margot (Boyle) K. A.B. summa cum laude, U. Calif.-Berkeley, 1970; M.D., U. Calif.-San Francisco, 1975. Staff fellow Gerontology Research Ctr., NIH, 1974; chief high resolution membrane lab. NIH, 1975-77; intern, resident Wadsworth VA Med. Ctr., UCLA, 1977-79, fellow in geriatric medicine, 1979-81, chief lab. molecular and clin. immunology, 1977-81, dir. electron microscopy facility, 1977-81, practice medicine specializing in internal medicine, Los Angeles, 1977-81; assoc. chief of staff for research Olin E. Teague Vets. Ctr., Temple, Tex., 1981—; dir. div. geriatric medicine Tex. A&M U. Med Sch, Temple, 1981—. Editor: Biological Sciences, 1981; mem. editorial bd.: Mechanism of Aging and Devel, 1979, Comprehensive Gerontology, 1985, Gerontology (spl. issue), 1985. contbr. articles to profl. jours. Served with USPHS, 1975-77. Mem. Am. Soc. Cell Biology, Gerontological Soc., Am. Geriatrics Soc., Am. Assn. Immunologists, Am. Soc. Hematology, Am. Assn. Biol. Chemists, Am. Fedn. Clin. Research. Current Work: Molecular aging; senescent cell antigen; immune restoration, molecular and cell biology. Subspecialties: Internal medicine; Gerontology. Office: Olin E Teague Veterans Ctr 1901 S First St Temple TX 76501

KAY, STEVEN MICHAEL, electrical engineering educator, consultant; b. Newark, Apr. 5, 1951; s. Jack and Phyllis (Adler) K.; m. Cynthia Anne Mielke, Aug. 18, 1973; children—Lisa Meryl, Ashley Beth. B.S. in Elec. Engring., Stevens Inst. Tech., 1972; M.S. in Elec. Engring., Columbia U., 1973; Ph.D. in Elec. Engring., Ga. Inst. Tech., 1980. Mem. tech. staff Bell Labs., Holmdel, N.J., 1972-75; sr. engr. Raytheon Co., Portsmouth, R.I., 1977-80; assoc. prof. elec. engring. U. R.I., Kingston, 1980—; cons. Sanders Assocs., Nashua, N.H., 1980—, Lear Siegler, Inc., Grand Rapids, Mich., 1983—. Patentee spectrum analyzer and doppler detector. Contbr. articles to profl. jours. Fellow NSF, 1972, Ga. Inst. Tech., 1975, IEEE, 1976; Office Naval Research grantee, 1984. Mem. IEEE (sr.). Current work: Research in spectral analysis, detection and estimation theory, statistical signal processing. Subspecialties: Telecommunications; Statistics. Home: 37 Conant Ln Kingston RI 02881 Office: Elec Engring Dept U RI Kingston RI 02881

KAYE, JACK ALAN, atmospheric chemist, researcher; b. Nov. 3, 1954; s. Ira Stanley and Gloria May (Goldner) K.; m. Dawn Sherry Bressler, May 13, 1984. B.A. in Chemistry, Adelphi U., 1976; Ph.D. in Chemistry, Calif. Inst. Tech., 1982. Participant NSF program dept. chemistry Rensselaer Poly. Inst., Troy, N.Y., 1975; summer intern Monsanto Co., St. Louis, 1976; research and teaching asst. Calif. Inst. Tech., Pasadena, 1976-82; research assoc. Naval Research Lab., Washington, 1982-83; space scientist NASA/Goddard Space Flight Ctr., Greenbelt, Md., 1983—. Contbr. articles to profl. jours. Recipient Herbert Newby McCoy award, 1981; NRC/NRL assoc. award, Nat. Acad. Sci., 1983. Mem. Am. Chem. Soc., Chem. Soc. Washington (vice chmn. younger chemists com. 1984, acting chmn. 1984—), Am. Phys. Soc., Am. Geophys. Union, Am. Astron. Soc. (div. planetary sci.). Jewish. Current work: Chemistry of the Earth's upper atmosphere, analysis and interpretation of satellite data of atmospheric composition, photochemical modeling, planetary atmospheres, chemical reaction rate theory. Subspecialties: Atmospheric chemistry; Theoretical chemistry. Home: 803 N Howard St Apt 133 Alexandria VA 22304 Office: NASA Goddard Space Flight Ctr Code 616 Greenbelt MD 20771

KAYKATY, MAURICE, chemist, pharmaceuticals manufacturing company executive; b. Aleppo, Syria, Sept. 27, 1939; s. George and Camille (Shaben) K.; m. Frances Rose Barone, Aug. 18, 1962; children—Maurice George, Francine Rose, Victor Anthony. B.S., Bklyn. Coll., 1962; M.S., L.I. U., 1969. Analytical chemist quality control Charles Pfizer & Co., Bklyn., 1963-64, asst. supr. analytical research, 1964-69; sr. chemist animal sci. research Hoffmann-LaRoche Inc., Nutley, N.J., 1969—. Contbr. chpt. to book, articles to profl. jours. Mem. Am. Chem. Soc., AAAS. Current work: Analytical method development for drugs in animal tissue; elucidate metabolic fate of drugs in food producing animals. Subspecialties: Analytical chemistry; Drug metabolism. Office: Hoffmann-LaRoche Inc Kingsland St Nutley NJ 07110

KAYLOR, FRANK BAAD, environmental engineer; b. Ashland, Ohio, Feb. 7, 1935; s. John Frederick and Harriett Baad (Metham) Hamlen; m. Suzanne Olton Aungst, Aug. 7, 1958; children—Scott Olton, Carolyn Peirce. B.C.E., U. Akron, 1958; M.S. in San. Engring., MIT, 1961. Registered profl. engr. Ohio, Mass. Construction project engr. Ohio Edison Co., Arkon, 1958-60; civil and sanitary engr. Allied Chem. Co., Syracuse, N.Y., 1961-65; chief environ. engr. Stone & Webster Engring. Corp., Boston, 1965—. Contbr. articles to profl. jours. Adv. Greater Boston Council Boy Scouts Am., Acton and Brookline, Mass., 1972-75; bd. dirs. Acton Solid Waste Study Program, 1972-73, Mass. Siting Council, Boston, 1779-82. Served to 1st lt. U.S. Army, 1958-60. Mem. ASME (cert. of appreciation 1977, 78, Centennial award, 1980), Am. Assn. Engring Socs. (cert. of Appreciation award 1982, chmn. 1979-84), ASCE, Water Pollution Control Fedn., Air Pollution Control Assn., Am. Acad. Environ. Engrs. (diplomate), Sigma Tau, Sigma Xi. Republican. Unitarian. Current work: Manages environmental engineers and scientists on siting studies, impact assessments, feasibility studies, and pollution control projects. Subspecialties: Environmental engineering; Resource management. Home: 37 Weybridge Ln Brookline MA 02146 Office: Stone & Webster Engring Corp PO Box 2325 Boston MA 02107

KAYS, JAMES LEE, mathematics educator, army officer; b. Rogers, Ark., Jan. 2, 1941; s. Lee George and Helen Agnes (Erickson) K.; m. Jeane Gayle Wotherspoon, June 10, 1962; children—Christine Leigh, Michael James, John Michael. B.S., U.S. Mil. Acad., 1962; M.S., Rensselaer Poly. Inst., 1969, Ph.D., 1980. Commd. 2d lt. U.S. Army, 1962, advanced to col., 1982; with Army Gen. Staff, Pentagon, Washington, 1974-76; prof. math U.S. Mil. Acad., West Point, N.Y., 1978—. Contbr. articles to profl. jours. Leader, Cub Scouts, 1981; coach Little League West Point, 1981-85. Decorated Bronze Star; recipient Joaquin B. Diaz award Rensselaer Poly. Inst., 1980. Mem. Assn. Grads. U.S. Mil. Acad. (trustee 1982-83), Acoustical Soc. Am., Soc. Indsl. and Applied Math. Math. Assn. Am., Sigma Xi, Phi Kappa Phi. Current work: Underwater sound transmission; acoustical effects of environmental variations; ocean Doppler effects; acoustic signal processing; simulation modeling and analysis. Subspecialties: Applied mathematics; Acoustics. Home: 122 B Washington Rd West Point NY 10996 Office: Dept Math US Mil Acad West Point NY 10996

KAYS, M(ARVIN) ALLAN, geology educator, researcher; b. Princeton, Ind., May 13, 1934; s. John L. and Mary Ellen (Newberry) K.; m. Dorothy Alice Tucker, June 11, 1955; children—David Allan, Timothy Tucker, Mary Elizabeth. B.A. in Geology, So. Ill. U., 1956; M.A. in Geology, Washington U., St. Louis, 1958, Ph.D. in Geology, 1961. Cert. geologist, Oreg. Teaching asst. in geology Washington U., 1956-58, Wheeler fellow, 1958-60; mem. faculty geology dept., researcher U. Oreg., Eugene, 1961-70, 71—, prof., 1980—; geologist Precambrian div. Dept. Mineral Resources, Regina, Sask., Can., 1970-71; temporary geologist U.S. Geol. Survey, Eugene, 1979-80. Contbr. articles to profl. jours. Fulbright travel award, Copenhagen, 1982; Penrose Fund grantee Am. Philos. Soc., Klamath Mountains, Oreg.-Calif., 1964, Skaergaard, East Greenland, 1974; NSF grantee, Skaergaard, 1976, 79, 82. Mem. Am. Geophys. Union, Geol. Soc. Am., Sigma Xi. Current work: Petrology/geochemistry xenoliths-granophyres associated with partial melting; petrology, structures, fabrics Archean metamorphic rocks, Greenland; mapping metamorphic surfaces and tracing metamorphic chronologies through metamorphic belts. Subspecialty: Petrology. Home: 2260 E 15th St Eugene OR 97403 Office: Dept Geology Univ Oreg Eugene OR 97403

KAZACOS, KEVIN ROBERT, veterinary parasitology educator, researcher, parasitologist; b. Syracuse, N.Y., June 20, 1949; s. Nicholas James and Frances Doris (Hass) K.; m. Evelyn Anne Sofolarides, July 8, 1972. B.S. cum laude, SUNY-Albany, 1971; Ph.D., U. Notre Dame, 1974; D.V.M., Purdue U., 1979. Lic. veterinarian, Ind. NIH predoctoral fellow U. Notre Dame, Ind., 1972-74, grad. instr., 1972-74; instr. Purdue U., West Lafayette, Ind., 1974-79, asst. prof., 1979-82, assoc. prof., 1982-85, prof., 1985—, dir. parasitology diagnostic lab., 1979—; cons. human clin. parasitology local hosps. and clinics, 1975—. Author: (monograph) Raccoon Roundworms-A Cause of Disease, 1983; also articles. Recipient Norden Disting. Tchr. award Norden Pharm. Co. and Purdue U. Sch. Vet. Medicine, 1984. Mem. Am. Soc. Parasitologists, Am. Assn. Vet. Parasitologists, Am. Soc. Tropical Medicine and Hygiene, Helminthological Soc. Washington, Wildlife Disease Assn., AVMA, Conf. Research Workers Animal Disease. Current work: Zoonotic Helminth diseases; especially ascarid infections from wildlife; visceral and ocular migrans, cerebrospinal nematodiasis. Subspecialties: Parasitology; Pathology (veterinary medicine). Office: Dept Vet Microbiology Pathology and Pub Health Purdue U West Lafayette IN 47907

KAZAM, ABDUL RAOOF, veterinarian; b. Chak, Punjab, Pakistan, Mar. 3, 1940; came to U.S., 1973; s. Hadayat-Ullah and Iqbal (Baigum) Malik; m. Attia Nusrut, Nov. 25, 1971; children—Imrana Gulbadan, Irfaan Raoof. B.Sc. in Vet. Sci. and Animal Husbandry, Coll. Animal Husbandry, Lahore, Pakistan, 1962; M.Sc. in Vet. Sci. and Parasitology, U. Agr., Lyallpur, Pakistan, 1969. Lic. vet. practitioner, N.J. Veterinarian in charge vet. hosp., also disease investigation lab. dept. animal husbandry, Peshawar Region, Pakistan, 1962-67, 69-70; instr. parasitology and pathology Faculty Vet. Sci., U. Agr., 1970-73; vet. specialist Vet. Clinic U.S. Army, Aberdeen Proving Ground, Md., 1974-77; vet. med. officer food safety and quality service for meat and poultry U.S. Dept. Agr., 1977-78, supervisory vet. med. officer, food safety and inspection service, meat and poultry inspection program northeastern region, 1979—. Recipient Superior Service award U.S. Dept. Agr. (5). Contbr. articles to profl. jours. Served with U.S. Army, 1974-77. Mem. AVMA. Muslim. Current work: If I have the opportunity, I would like to conduct research on relationship of table eggs from layers with cancer and incidence of cancer in the consumers of these eggs. Office: care B&B Poultry Co Almond Rd Norma NJ 08347

KAZEK, GREGORY JOSEPH, applied physicist; b. Cleve., Oct. 26, 1947; s. Stanley and Irene Martha (Lake) K.; m. Deanne Joan, Sept. 3, 1981; children: Gregory Joseph, Geoffrey S, Rachel E. B.S. in Physics, Case Inst. Tech., 1969; M.S. in Physics, John Carroll U., 1971; Ph.D. in Elec. Engring, Case Western Res. U., 1974. Engr. Lamp Bus. Group, Gen. Electric Co., Cleve., 1969-72; sr. engr. Lamp Bus. Group, Gen. Electric Co. (Lamp Bus. Group), 1972-75; research physicist Lamp Bus. Group, Gen. Electric Co. (Lamp Phenomena Research Lab.), 1975-79; sr. project engr. Reliance Electric Co., Euclid, Ohio, 1979-83; advanced research and devel. engr. GTE Corp., Salem, Mass., 1983—. Contbr. numberous articles to profl. jours. Mem. Am. Phys. Soc., IEEE, Assn. Iron and Steel Engrs. Democrat. Patentee radiation dominated gaseous condrs. applied as lighting sources and circuit components; numerous world-wide installations of digital systems integrating peripherals of great variety. Current Work: Energy conversion applied to product and process design; project mgmt. and engrng. of digital systems to control materials processing for all aspects of arc lamp technology. Subspecialties: Electrical engineering; Plasma engineering. Office: 60 Boston St Salem MA 01970

KEARFOTT, RALPH BAKER, industrial mathematician, educator; b. Salt Lake City, Jan. 27, 1954; s. William Edward and Edith (Chamberlin) K.; m. Ruth Constance Mentley, May 24, 1976; 1 child, Frances Marie. B.A., U. Utah, 1972, M.A., 1974, Ph.D., 1977. Asst. prof. math. U. S.W. La., Lafayette, 1977-82, assoc. prof., 1982-84; sr. mathematician Exxon Research and Engring. Co., Clinton Twp., N.J., 1984—; Referee various scholarly jours.; contbr. articles to profl. jours. Grantee modelling of evoked potentials NIH, 1981. Mem. Am. Math. Soc., Soc. Indsl. and Applied Math., Assn. for Computing Machinery, N.Y. Acad. Scis., Phi Beta Kappa. Current work: Nonlinear algebraic systems, interval mathematics, mathematical software, sparse nonlinear systems, homotopy methods and numerical methods for bifurcation problems; numerical techniques for partial differential equations. Subspecialties: Numerical analysis (mathematics); Numerical analysis (computer science). Office: Exxon Research and Engring Co Computing Tech and Services Clinton Twp Route 22 E Annandale NJ 08801

KEARNS, DAVID TODD, duplicating machine manufacturing company executive; b. Rochester, N.Y., Aug. 11, 1930; s. Wilfred M. and Margaret May (Todd) K.; m. Shirley Virginia Cox, June 1954; children—Katherine, Elizabeth, Anne, Susan, David Todd, Andrew. B.S., U. Rochester, 1952. With IBM Corp., 1954-71, v.p. mktg. ops., data processing div., until 1971; with Xerox Corp., Stamford, Conn., 1971—, group v.p. for info. systems, 1972-75; group v.p. charge Rank Xerox and Fuji Xerox, 1975-77, exec. v.p. internat. ops., 1977, pres., chief exec. officer, 1977—, also dir.; dir. Rank Xerox Ltd., Time Inc., Fuji Xerox, Chase Manhattan Corp., Chase Manhattan Bank N.A., Crum's Foster, Time Inc.; mem. Pres.'s Commn. on Exec. Exchange; mem. adv. council Grad. Sch. Bus., Stanford U. Bd. visitors Grad. Sch. Bus., Duke U.; chmn. bd. trustees U. Rochester; trustee Stamford Hosp., Inst. Aerobics Research; chmn. nat. bd. dirs. Jr. Achievement; bd. dirs. Nat. Urban League, Nat. Action Council for Minority Engrs., Com. Econ. Devel.; trustee Health Corp. Greater Stamford, Inst. Aerobics Research, U.S. Council Internat. C. of C. Served with USNR, 1952-54. Mem. Council Fgn. Relations. Address: Xerox Corp Stamford CT 06904

KEATING, KATHLEEN IRWIN, limnologist, educator; b. Jersey City; d. William Richard and Alda Vogt (Madden) Irwin; m. Martin John Keating, Dec. 21, 1962; 1 child, Sean Michael. B.A., Cornell U., 1960; M.S., William Paterson Coll., 1970, M.Ph., Yale U., 1972, Ph.D., 1975. Prof. Rutgers U., New Brunswick, N.J., 1974—. Contbr. articles to profl. jours. Author: (monograph) EPA, 1976. Cornell U. scholar, 1970; Yale fellow, 1970; NSF grantee, 1978-82. Mem. Ecol. Soc. Am., Internat. Soc. Theoretical Limnology, Am. Soc. Limnology and Oceanography, Internat. Soc. Chem. Ecology, Soc. Environ. Toxicology and Chemistry, N.Y. Acad. Scis., Yale Sci. and Engring. Assn., AAAS, N.J. Acad. Sci., Crustacean Soc., Sigma Xi. Current work: Interplay of allelochemistry and nutrition in plankton community structure; development of functional chronic toxicity tests. Subspecialties: Animal nutrition; Limnology. Home: 6 Webb Ct Park Ridge NJ 07656Office: Rutgers U Cook Campus New Brunswick NJ 08903

KEEFER, DONALD ASHBY, neuroendocrinologist; b. Balt., Jan. 8, 1946; s. William Hobart and Florence (Roughton) K.; m. Mandy Hutson, Aug. 3, 1966; children: Deborah, Mark. B.A., Western Md. Coll., 1968; Ph.D., U.N.C., 1974. Neurobiology fellow U.N.C., Chapel Hill, 1974; guest scientist Max-Planck Inst. for Brain Research, Frankfurt, W. Ger., 1975-76; asst. prof. anatomy U.Va., Charlottesville, 1976-82; assoc. prof., 1982-83; assoc. prof., chmn. dept. biology Loyola Coll.-Balt., 1983—. Current Work: Teaching, modulation of estrogen receptor levels and cellular processing. Subspecialties: Neuroendocrinology; Receptors. Office: Loyola Coll Dept Biology Baltimore MD 21210

KEEHN, NEIL FRANCIS, aerospace company executive, systems engineer, strategic analyst; b. Massillon, Ohio, Oct. 24, 1948; s. Russell Earl and Mary Leona (Danner) M. B.S., Ariz. State U., 1970, M.S., 1970. Mem. tech. staff Tech. Services Corp., Santa Monica, Calif., 1972-74; Hughes Aircraft, El Segundo, Calif., 1974-77; assoc. program mgr. TRW, Inc., Redondo Beach, Calif., 1977-79; mgr. advanced concepts, mil. systems div. Sci. Applications, Inc., El Segundo, 1979-80; pres. Strategic Systems Scis., Santa Monica., Calif., 1980—. Recipient Bd. Govs. citation IEEE Aerospace and Electronic Systems Soc., 1977; Ariz. State U. scholar, 1967. Mem. IEEE (vice chmn. Aerospace Def. Systems Panel 1972-76, chmn. 1976-79, chmn. membership aerospace def. systems com. 1974, Winter Conv. Outstanding Service citation 1974), AIAA, U.S. Strategic Inst. Democrat. Roman Catholic. Inventor in real time processing of pulse compression waveforms (Hughes award 1977). Current Work: Professional activities centered on advanced planning for national security space systems; major portion of work concentrated in development of advanced strategic/systems concepts relating to exploitation of space to enhance national security; several of these efforts have resulted in presentations throughout defense establishment and at the White House. Subspecialties:

National security space systems; Systems engineering. Home: 2603 3d St Santa Monica CA 90405 Office: Strategic Systems Scis 2603 3d St Santa Monica CA 90405

KEEHN, PHILIP MOSES, chemist, educator, cons.; b. Bklyn., Mar. 22, 1943; s. Louis and Frances (Mamches) K.; m. Lillian Brody, June 19, 1966; 4 children. B.A., Yeshiva U., 1964; M.A., Yale U., 1967, Ph.D., 1969. Research assoc. Harvard U., 1969-71; asst. prof. chemistry Brandeis U., 1971-78, assoc. prof., 1978—; vis. assoc. prof. Weizmann Inst. Sci., Rehovot, Israel, 1979-80, cons. in field. Author, editor 2 books. Contbr. numerous articles to chem. jours. Recipient Sir Isaac Wolfson award Brandeis U., 1979-80; Tchr.-Scholar award Camille and Henry Dreyfus Found., 1979-84; Alfred Bader Found. award, 1980; Nat. Acad. Scis. East European exchange fellow, Yugoslavia, 1985. Mem. Am. Chem. Soc. Current Work: Organic synthesis of strained rings and theoretically interesting molecules; synthetic methods; photooxidatiion; host-guest chemistry of tri-o-thymotide; pure and applied laser chemistry. Subspecialties: Organic chemistry; Laser-induced chemistry. Office: Dept Chemistry Brandeis U Waltham MA 02254

KEEL, WILLIAM CLIFFORD, astronomer; b. Jackson, Miss., Sept. 22, 1957; s. Pinckney Durham and Gloria Virginia (Barnes) K. B.A., Vanderbilt U., 1978; Ph.D., U. Calif.-Santa Cruz, 1982. Research assoc. Kitt Peak Nat. Obs., Tucson, 1982—. Contbr. articles to profl. jours. NSF fellow. Mem. Am. Astron. Soc., Astron. Soc. Pacific, Am. Sci. Affiliation. Baptist. Current work: Relationships between events in galactic nuclei and their surroundings; extragalactic jets. Subspecialties: Optical astronomy; High energy astrophysics. Office: Sterrewacht Leiden PO Box 9513 Leiden 2300 RA Netherlands

KEELER, KATHLEEN HOWARD, ecology research educator; b. Hackensack, N.J. Jan. 17, 1947; d. James Howard and Irene (Krantz) K.; m. Richard Karl Anderson, Dec. 24, 1975. B.S. with honors in Anthropology-Zoology, U. Mich., 1969; Ph.D., U. Calif.-Berkeley, 1975. Asst. prof. U. Nebr., Lincoln, 1975-81, assoc. prof. ecology, 1981—, sect. chmn. Sch. Biol. Scis., 1982—, chmn. greenhouse com., 1982—; tchr. field course for Earlham Coll. in Jamaica, 1977. Fellow Ctr. for Great Plains Studies; mem. Soc. for Study Evolution, Ecol. Soc. Am., Bot. Soc. Am., Sigma Xi, others. Current work: Ant-plant interactions; chromosomal polymorphism in plants; ecology of mutualism. Subspecialties: Genetics and genetic engineering (biology); Ecology (biology). Office: U Nebr Sch Piol Scis 348 Manter Hall Lincoln NE 68588

KEELEY, STERLING CARTER, botanist, museum curator, educator, cons.; b. San Francisco, Oct. 23, 1948; d. John Frederick and Star (Steel) Carter; m. Jon Edward Keeley, June 23, 1973. A.B., Stanford U., 1970; M.S. in Biology, San Diego State U., 1973; Ph.D. in Botany, U. Ga., 1977. Lectr. U. Ga., Athens, 1976-77; Lectr. Calif. State U., Northridge, 1977, Long Beach, 1978-79; research assoc.-curator Mus. Natural History Los Angeles, 1978—; asst. prof. biology Whittier (Calif.) Coll., 1979—; reviewer NSF; cons. congl. program low-coast shoreline erosion, 1978-80, Port of Los Angeles, 1978-80. Reviewer: Systematic Botany; editorial bd.: Madrono; contbr. articles to sci. jours. NSF grantee, 1974-76, 79-81, 82-85; Whittier Coll. faculty research grantee, 1980—. Mem. Soc. Study of Evolution, Am. Soc. Plant Taxonomists, AAAS, Inst. Ecology U. Ga., Bot. Soc. Am., Assn. So. Calif. Botanists, Calif. Native Plant Soc., Sigma Xi. Current work: Systematics of neotropical Vernonia; germination of herb species of California chaparral and desert communities. Subspecialties: Systematics; Ecology (environmental science). Office: Whittier Coll Whittier CA 90608

KEEN, NOEL THOMAS, plant pathologist, educator; b. Marshalltown, Iowa, Aug. 13, 1940; s. Walter T. and Evelyn Mae (Mayo) K.; m. Esther M., Apr. 6, 1974. B.S., Iowa State U., 1963, M.S., 1965; Ph.D., U. Wis., 1968. Asst. prof. plant pathology U. Calif., Riverside, 1968-72, asso. prof., 1972-78, prof., 1978—, chmn. dept., 1983—. Contbr. articles in field to profl. jours. Mem. AAAS, Am. Soc. Plant Physiologists, Am. Phytopath. Soc., Am. Inst. Biol. Scis., Sigma Xi, Gamma Sigma Delta. Current Work: Research in mechanisms of disease resistance in plants. Subspecialties: Plant pathology; Biochemistry (biology). Home: 5617 Via Junipero Serra Riverside CA 92506 Office: University of California Dept Plant Pathology Riverside CA 92521

KEENMON, KENDALL ANDREWS, petroleum geologist consultant; b. Detroit, Sept. 13, 1920; s. Fred B. and Myrtie M. (Andrews) K.; m. Elizabeth Ann Pedersen, Aug. 22, 1942; children—Janet, John, Joanne, Judith. B.S., U. Mich., 1947, M.S., 1948, Ph.D., 1950. Div. geologist Shell Oil Co., Wichita, Kans., 1950-60, sr. geologist, Okla. City, 1960-61, Houston, 1961-72; staff geologist Pecten Internatl. Co., Houston, 1972-85; cons. petroleum geology, Houston, 1985—. Served to 2nd lt. USAF, 1943-45. Fellow Geol. Soc. Am.; mem. Am. Assn. Petroleum Geology, Houston Geol. Soc. Subspecialties: Geology; Remote sensing (geoscience).

KEFALIDES, NICHOLAS ALEXANDER, biochemist, educator, physician; b. Alexandroupolis, Greece, Jan. 17, 1927; came to U.S., 1947, naturalized; s. Athanasios K. and Alexandra (Aematidou) K.; m. Eugenia Georgia Kutsunis, Nov. 24, 1949; children: Alexandra, Patricia, Paul. B.A., Augustana Coll., 1951; M.S., U. Ill.-Chgo., 1956, M.D., 1956, Ph.D., 1965; M.A. (hon.), U. Pa., 1971. Asst. prof. medicine U. Ill. Sch. Medicine, Chgo., 1964-65; asst. prof. U. Chgo., 1965-69, assoc. prof., 69-70; assoc. prof. U. Pa. Sch. Medicine, Phila., 1970-74, assoc. prof. biochemistry, 1973-75, prof. medicine, 1974—, prof. biochemistry and biophysics, 1975—; dir. U. Pa. Sch. Medicine (Connective Tissue Research Inst.), 1972—. Contbr. numerous articles on chemistry and metabolism of connective tissues to profl. jours.; author: Biology and Chemistry of Basement Membranes, 1978. Recipient Borden award in medicine Borden Co., 1956; Guggenheim fellow, 1977. Mem. Am. Soc. Biol. Chemists, Am. Soc. for Clin. Investigation, Am. Chem. Soc., Am. Soc. for Cell Biology, Am. Assn. Pathologists. Current Work: Chemistry and metabolism of connective tissue and basement membranes, metabolism of vascular cells. Subspecialties: Internal medicine; Biochemistry (medicine). Office: Connective Tissue Research Inst U Pa 3624 Market St Philadelphia PA 19104

KEIL, ALFRED ADOLF HEINRICH, engineering educator; b. Konradswaldau, Germany, May 1, 1913; came to U.S., 1947, naturalized, 1954; s. Kurt Alfred and Marie (Berger) K.; m. Ursula Leppelt, Oct. 15, 1943; children: Michael G., Juergen G. Dr. nat. sc., U. Breslau, Germany, 1939. Research asst. U. Breslau, 1939-40; research asso. Chem.-Phys. Research Establishment, Kiel, Germany, 1940- 45; chief scientist underwater explosive research div. Norfolk Naval Shipyard, Portsmouth, Va., 1947-59; tech. dir. structural mech. lab. David Taylor Model Basin, 1959-63, tech. dir. basin, 1963-66; prof., head dept. naval architecture and marine engring. MIT, 1966-71, dean Sch. Engring., 1971-77, Ford prof. engring., 1977-78, prof. emeritus, 1978—; mem. Nat. Adv. Com. on Oceans and Atmosphere, 1977-79. Contbr. articles to profl. jours. Served with German Army, 1939-40. Recipient Civilian Disting. Service award Navy Dept., 1963; Gibbs Bros. gold medal for naval architecture Nat. Acad. Scis., 1967, Gold Cross 1st class Fed. Republic Germany. Mem. Nat. Acad. Engring., Am. Soc. Naval Engrs. (Gold Medal award 1964), Verein Deutscher Ingenieure (corr. mem.), Marine Tech. Soc. (Lockheed award 1979). Current Work: Development of ocean uses; advancing engineering education. Subspecialties: Systems engineering; Theoretical and applied mechanics. Home: 39 Hillside Terr Belmont MA 02178 Office: Mass Inst Tech Cambridge MA 02139

KEIL, KLAUS, geology educator, consultant; b. Hamburg, Ger., Nov. 15, 1934; s. Walter and Elsbeth K.; m. Rosemarie, Mar. 30, 1961; children: Kathrin R., Mark K.; m. Linde, Jan. 28, 1984. M.S., Schiller U., Jena, Ger., 1958; Ph.D., Gutenberg U., Mainz, W.Ger., 1961. Research assoc. Mineral. Inst., Jena, 1958-60, MaxPlanck-Inst. Chemistry, Mainz, 1961, U. Calif.-San Diego, 1961-63; research scientist Ames Research Center NASA, Moffett Field, Calif., 1964-68; prof. geology, dir. Inst. Meteoritics, U. N.Mex., Albuquerque, 1968—; cons. Sandia Labs., others. Contbr. over 350 articles to sci. jours. Recipient Apollo Achievement award NASA, 1970; recipient George P. Merrill medal Nat. Acad. Scis., 1970, Exceptional Sci. Achievement medal NASA, 1977, Regents Meritorious Service medal U. N.Mex., 1983, numerous others. Fellow Meteoritical Soc., AAAS, Mineral. Soc. Am.; mem. Am. Geophys. Union, German Mineral. Soc., others. Current Work: Origin of the solar system and evolution of the planets based on studies of meteorites, lunar samples, Mars (Viking) terrestrial volcanology, electron beam microanalysis. Subspecialties: Cosmochemistry; Meteoritics. Office: Dept Geology U N Mex Albuquerque NM 87131

KEISER, BERNHARD EDWARD, consulting engineer; b. Richmond Heights, Mo., Nov. 14, 1928; s. Bernhard and Helen Barbara Julia (Buerkle) K.; m. Florence Evelyn Koenig, Jan. 22, 1955; children: Sandra, Carol, Nancy, Linda, Paul. B.S.E.E., Washington U., St. Louis, 1950, D.Sc.E.E., 1953. Registered profl. engr., Va., Md., D.C. Adminstr., advanced system planning RCA, Moorestown, N.Y., 1967-69; v.p., tech. dir. Page Communications Engrs., Washington, 1969-70; dir. advanced engring. Atlantic Research Corp., Alexandria, Va., 1971-72; dir. analysis Fairchild Space and Electronics Co., Germantown, Md., 1972-75; pres. Keiser Engring., Inc., Vienna, Va., 1975—. Author: EMI Control in Aerospace Systems, 1979, Principles of Electromagnetic Compatilibility, 1979; co-author: Digital Telephony and Network Integration, 1985. RCA fellow, 1951-53. Fellow IEEE (chmn. No. Va. sect. 1980-81), Washington Acad. Scis., Radio Club Am. Republican. Lutheran. Patentee delay line time compressor and expander. Current Work: Feasibility studies in microwave communication systems, communication satellite transmission and wideband cable technology. Subspecialties: Electronics; Telecommunications. Office: 2046 Carrhill Rd Vienna VA 22180

KEISER, GERD EMDO, communications engineer, applied physicist; b. Burlington, Wis., Oct. 8, 1944; s. Hans and Hertha Louise (Klattenhoff) K.; m. Helen Ching-yun Wang, Sept. 4, 1971; 1 child, Nishla Helen. B.A., U. Wis.-Milw., 1966, M.S., 1968; Ph.D., Northeastern U., 1973. Sr. engr. Honeywell, Lexington, Mass., 1973-74; engring. mgr. GTE, Needham Heights, Mass., 1974—. Author: Optical Fiber Communications, 1983. Mem. IEEE, Am. Phys. Soc. Current work: Optical fiber communications and local area networks. Subspecialties: Telecommunications; Fiber optics. Home: 65 Rachel Rd Newton Centre MA 02159 Office: GTE 77 A St Needham Heights MA 02194

KELLAR, KENNETH JON, pharmacologist, educator; b. Balt., Feb. 13, 1944; s. Joseph Aaron and Faye E. (Terkowitz) K.; m. Elizabeth Kaenzig, Sept. 24, 1972; children: Joshua Aaron, Amanda Marin. B.S., Johns Hopkins U., 1966; Ph.D., Ohio State U., 1974. Postdoctoral fellow NASA Ames Research Center, 1974-76; prof. dept. pharmacology Georgetown U. Sch. Medicine, Washington, 1976—. Contbr. articles to sci. jours. Mem. Am. Soc. Pharmacology and Exptl. Therapeutics, Soc. for Neurosci. Current Work: Neuropharmacology. Subspecialties: Molecular pharmacology; Neuropharmacology. Office: Dept Pharmacology Georgetown U Sch Medicine Washington DC 20007

KELLEN, JOHN ANDREW, biochemist; b. Vienna, Austria, July 18, 1928; emigrated to Can., 1968, naturalized, 1972; s. Charles F. and Josepha (Kellen) Koch; m. Marta Hornakova, Jan. 17, 1959; children: Charles, John. M.D., U. Bratislava, Czechoslovakia, 1952; Ph.D., U. Brno, 1963. From intern to sr. resident in medicine and endocrinology Lubochna (Czechoslovakia) Hosp., 1951-56; head biochemistry dept. Levoca and Dun Streda, Czechoslovakia, 1956-63; research fellow Research Inst. Hygiene, Bratislava, 1963-66; lectr. Inst. Postgrad. Med. Edn., U. Bratislava, 1964-68; head dept. biochemistry Cancer Inst. Bratislava, 1966-68; mem. faculty U. Toronto Faculty Medicine, 1968—; prof. clin. biochemistry, 1980—; mem. staff dept. clin. biochemistry Sunnybrook Med. Ctr., Toronto, 1968—. Med. editor: Modern Medicine Can, 1969—; Author papers in field. Mem. Can. Fedn. Biol. Soc., N.Y. Acad. Scis. Current Work: Tumor markers in clinical practice, ectopic hormones and polypeptides in tumors, tumor immunology. Subspecialties: Cancer research (medicine); Immunology (medicine).

KELLER, GEORGE HENRIK, marine geologist, administrator; b. Hartford, Conn., Sept. 9, 1931; s. George and Eva (Damschneider) K.; m. Suzanne Bray, Sept. 10, 1955; children—Mark, Lauri. A.B., U. Conn., 1954; M.S., U. Utah, 1956; Ph.D., U. Ill., 1966. Marine geologist U.S. Navy, Washington, 1959-64; dir. Marine Geology and Geophysics Lab., NOAA, Miami, Fla., 1966-75; assoc. dean oceanography Oreg. State U., Corvallis, 1975-82, acting dean oceanography, 1978, acting dean research, 1981-82, dean research, 1983-85, v.p. research and grad. studies, 1985—; rep. Univ. Corp. for Atmospheric Research, Boulder, Colo., 1982—; mem. council Ctr. for Research Libraries, Chgo., 1984—; dir. Marine div. Nat. Assn. for Univs. and Land-grant Colls., Washington, 1983—. Mem. editorial bd. Marine Geotech. Mag., 1974—. Contbr. articles to profl. jours. Recipient C.A. Hogentolger award ASCE, 1973. Fellow Geol. Soc. Am.; mem. Am. Geophys. Union, Internat. Sedimentological Soc., AAAS, Sigma Xi. Current work: Engineering and mass physical properties of deep-sea and continental margin sediments; sedimentary processes, bottom and near bottom dynamics on the continental shelf and margin. Subspecialties: Sedimentology; Ocean engineering. Home: 3360 NW Witham Hill Dr Corvallis OR 97330 Office: Research Office Oreg State U Corvallis OR 97331

KELLER, JAIME, theoret. chemist, physicist; b. Mexico, D.F., Mexico, Nov. 10, 1936; s. Arturo and Rosario (Torres) K.; m. Cristina Perez, Apr. 29, 1943; children: Cristina, Alejandro, Roberto. B.S. in Chem. Engring, Universidad Nacional Autonoma de Mexico, 1950; Ph.D. in Physics, U. Bristol, 1971. Registered Profl. Engr., Mexico. Project engr. Industrial Quimica Pensalt, Mexico, 1959-61; tech. dir. Derivados Macroquimicos, Mexico, 1961; lectr. Universidad Nacional Autonoma de Mexico, 1961-72, prof., 1972-76, heat theoret. chemistry dept., 1974-76, prof. physics, 1976—, mem. acad. council. Contbr. numerous articles to sci. jours. Mem. Am. Phys. Soc., Societa Italiana di Fisica, European Phys. Soc., Internat. Soc. Quantum Biology, Sociedad Quimica de Mexico, Sociedad Mexicana de Fisica, Academia de la Investigacion Cientifica de Mexico, Hydrogen Energy Soc. Roman Catholic. Developer chem. industry processes. Current Work: The chemistry of condensed matter physics specially metals in the liquid, amorphous and crystalline state and the fundamental theory behind chemistry and condensed matter physics; appplications to actual technological problems. Subspecialties: Condensed matter physics; Theoretical chemistry. Home: 64 Fuente de la Juventud Mexico 11000 Mexico Office: Faculty de Quimica Ciudad Universitaria Universidad Nacional Autonoma de Mexico Mexico Mexico

KELLER, JOHN MAHLON, biochemistry educator; b. Sussex, N.J., Mar. 10, 1939. A.B., Princeton U., 1961; Ph.D., MIT, 1966. Postdoctoral fellow U. Calif.-Berkeley, 1966-68, U. Chgo., 1968-70; asst. prof. U. Wash., Seattle, 1970-76; assoc. prof. U. Health Sci., Chgo. Med. Sch., 1977-82, prof. biochemistry, 1982—; vis. scientist Max Plank Inst. for Biochemistry, Fed. Republic Germany, 1983-84. Am. Cancer Soc. scholar, 1983-84; established investigator Am. Heart Assn., 1971-75. Mem. Am. Soc. Biol. Chemistry, Am. Soc. Cell Biology, Am. Soc. Microbiology, Am. Chem. Soc. Subspecialty: Biochemistry (biology). Office: Dept Biol Chemistry and Structure U Health Scis Chgo Med Sch 3333 Green Bay Rd North Chicago IL 60064

KELLER, JOSEPH BISHOP, mathematician, educator; b. Paterson, N.J., July 31, 1923; s. Isaac and Sally (Bishop) K.; m. Evelyn Fox, Aug. 29, 1963 (div. Nov. 17, 1976); children—Jeffrey M., Sarah N. B.A., N.Y.U., 1943, M.S., 1946, Ph.D., 1948. Prof. math. Courant Inst. Math. Scis., N.Y.U., 1948-79; chmn. dept. math. Univ. Coll. Arts and Scis. and Grad. Sch. Engring. and Sci., 1967-73; prof. math. and mech. engring. Stanford U., 1979—. Contbr. articles to profl. jours. Mem. Nat. Acad. Scis., Am. Acad. Arts and Scis., Am. Math. Soc., Am. Phys. Soc., Soc. Indsl. and Applied Math. Home: 820 Sonoma Terr Stanford CA 94305 Office: Dept Math Stanford U Stanford CA 94305

KELLER, OSWALD LEWIN, JR., chemist, researcher; b. N.Y.C., May 24, 1930; s. Oswald Lewin and Katherine Doris (Leiding) K.; m. Oct. 9, 1953; children—Christopher, Claire, Elaine, Elizabeth. B.S., U. of South, 1951, Ph.D., MIT, 1959. Research staff mem. Oak Ridge Nat. Lab., 1960-65, dir. transuranium lab., 1965-74, 84—, dir. chem. div. 1974-84; mem. Nuclear physics panel Nat. Acad. Scis., 1969-72; chmn. bd. visitors dept. chemistry U. Tenn., Knoxville, 1983-84, mem. dept. energy transplutonium program com., 1966-74, 1980—, mem. sci. alliance faculty adv. com., 1985; exchange scientist U.S. Nat. Acad. Sci. and Acad. Scis. USSR, 1972; invited speaker Robert A. Welch Found, 1969, 75, 78. Contbr. articles to profl. jours. Served with U.S. Army, 1954-56. Fellow Rockefeller Found., MIT, 1951. Fellow AAAS; mem. Am. Chem. Soc. (councillor 1984—), Am. Phys. Soc., Phi Beta Kappa. Current work: Experimental and theoretical studies of elements 101 and above with emphasis on relativistic effects in electronic and chemical behavior. Subspecialties: Inorganic chemistry; Nuclear chemistry. Home: 101 Morgan Rd Oak Ridge TN 37830 Office: Oak Ridge Nat Lab PO Box X Oak Ridge TN 37831

KELLEY, ALBERT JOSEPH, management executive; b. Boston, July 27, 1924; s. Albert Joseph and Josephine (Sullivan) K.; m. Virginia Marie Riley, June 7, 1945; children: Mark, Shaun, David. B.S., U.S. Naval Acad., 1945; B.S. in Elec. Engring., MIT, 1948, Sc.D. in Instrumentation and Control Engring., 1956; postgrad., U.S. Naval Postgrad. Sch., 1953-54. Commd. ensign USN, 1945, advanced through grades to comdr.; fire control officer U.S.S. Rochester, 1946-47; carrier squadron pilot, electronics officer USN Carrier Air Group 2, 1950-51; exptl. test pilot, project dir. U.S. Naval Air Test Center, Patuxent River, Md., 1951-53, asst. head guided missile guidance br. Bur. Weapons, 1956-58, project dir. Eagle missile system Bur. Weapons, 1958- 60; program mgr. Agena launch vehicle NASA, 1960-61, dir. electronics and control, 1961-64; dep. dir. Electronics Research Center, Cambridge, Mass., 1964-67; dean Sch. Mgmt., Boston Coll., 1967-77; pres. Arthur D. Little Program Systems Mgmt. Co., 1977—; cons. Dept. Def.; dir. State St. Bank and Trust, State St. Fin Corp., Perini Corp., Nat. Space Inst., C.S. Draper Lab. Author: Venture Capital, A Guidebook for New Enterprises, New Dimensions of Project Management, State St. Boston Corp., State St. Bank and Trust, Perini Corp., Nat. Space Inst.; mem. C.S. Draper Lab. Corp. Recipient NASA Exceptional Service medal, 1967. Fellow AIAA (assoc.), IEEE; mem. Internat. Acad. Astronautics, Sigma Xi, Tau Beta Pi, Eta Kappa Nu, Sigma Gamma Tau, Beta Gamma Sigma. Current Work: Systems engineering and technology consultant; tollarge, complex projects in communications, command and control FAA, defense, internat. telecommunications, major construction projects and international telecommunications. Subspecialties: Systems engineering; Aerospace engineering and technology. Home: 351 Atherton St Milton MA 02186 Office: Arthur D Little Inc Acorn Park Cambridge MA 02140

KELLEY, MICHAEL STEPHEN, computer consultant; b. Chgo., Feb. 8, 1949; s. Kenneth G. and Alice S. (Wisowaty) K.; m. Kathryn L. Ratiu, Apr. 24, 1982. B.S. in Psychology, U. Ill., 1971. Various tech. positions and employers assoc. with Illiac IV Computer, 1969-77; dir. software devel. Microcomputer Systems Corp., Sunnyvale, Calif., 1977-80; pres. Symbionics, San Jose, Calif., 1980—. Mem. Assn. Computing Machinery. Current Work: Developing graphics processing hardware and software. Developing fax subsystems for teleconferencing. Operating systems. Subspecialties: Operating systems; Graphics, image processing, and pattern recognition. Home and Office: 24505 Loma Prieta Ave Los Gatos CA 95030

KELLEY, NEIL DAVIS, environmental scientist; b. Clayton, Mo., Jan. 8, 1942; s. Davis Franklin and Louise Minnie (Zager) K.; m. Jean Irish, Jan. 14, 1967 (div. June 1977). B.S., St. Louis U., 1963; M.S., Pa. State U., 1968. Staff meteorologist Meteorology Research Inc., Altadena, Calif., 1963-67; project supr. Exxon Research & Engring. Co., Linden, N.J., 1967; instr. Pa. State U., University Park, 1967-72; group chief Nat. Center Atmospheric Research, Boulder, Colo., 1972-77; prin. scientist Solar Energy Research Inst., Golden, Colo., 1977—; tech. reviewer Am. Wind Energy Assn., Washington, 1982—. Recipient Spl. Achievement award Nat. Center, Atmospheric Research, 1974, Outstanding Achievement award Solar Energy Research Inst., 1982. Mem. Instrument Soc. Am. (sr.), Am. Meteorol. Soc., AIAA, AAAS, Sigma Xi. Current Work: Environmental compatibility research of wind energy conversion systems; acoustical, electromagnetic, turbulence-induced fatigue. Subspecialties: Micrometeorology; Wind power. Home: 605 S 42d St Boulder CO 80303Office: Solar Energy Research Inst 1617 Cole Blvd Golden CO 80401

KELLNER, RICHARD GEORGE, computer scientist, consultant; b. Cleve., July 10, 1943; s. George Ernest and Wanda Julia (Lapinski) K.; m. Charlene Ann Zajc, June 26, 1965; children: Michael Richard, David George. B.S. in Math, Case Inst. Tech., 1965; M.S. in Math, Stanford U., 1968, Ph.D. in Math, 1969. Staff mem. Los Alamos Nat. Lab., 1969-79, 83—; dir. software devel. KMP Computer Systems, Los Alamos, 1979-84; spl. projects mgr KMP Computer systems div. First Data Resources, 1984—; co-owner Computer-Aided Communications, Los Alamos, 1982-84, cons., 1979—. Mem. IEEE, AAAS, Assn. for Computing Machinery. Republican. Developer microdelivery option cable TV computer program, 1984, cable star computer program, 1982 co-developer Common Graphics System, computer program, 1979. Current Work: Computer-aided communications, multi-processor computer systems. Subspecialties: Database systems; Distributed systems and networks. Home: 4496 Ridgeway Dr Los Alamos NM 87544 Office: KMP Computer Systems Inc 135 Longview Dr Los Alamos NM 87544

KELLOGG, GARY LEE, physicist; b. Cambridge Springs, Pa., Jan. 16, 1950; s. Richard and Elizabeth Noreen (Collen) K.; m. Susan Jean Lechefsky, June 26, 1971; children—Brian Richard, Justin Mark. B.S., Pa. State U., 1971, Ph.D., 1976. Staff physicist Sandia Nat. Labs., Albuquerque, 1976—. Contbr. articles to profl. jours. Mem. Am. Physical Soc., Am. Vacuum Soc. (chmn. N.Mex. chpt. 1981-82, vice chmn. 1980-81), Sigma Xi. Current work: Experimental research to investigate fundamental atomic and molecular processes of surface reactions using field ion microscope and atom probe. Subspecialties: Condensed matter physics; Surface chemistry. Home: 917 LaCharles Dr NE Albuquerque NM 87112 Office: Sandia Nat Lab PO Box 5800 Albuquerque NM 87185

KELLOGG, HERBERT HUMPHREY, educator, metallurgist; b. N.Y.C., Feb. 24, 1920; s. Herbert H. and Gladys (Falding) K.; m. Jeanette Halstead, July 20, 1940; children—Thomas Bartlett, Jane Falding, David Humphrey, Elizabeth Ann. B.S., Columbia, 1941, M.S., 1943. Asst. prof. mineral preparation Pa. State U., State Coll., 1942-46; faculty Columbia, N.Y.C., 1946—, Stanley-Thompson prof. chem. metallurgy, 1968—; Chmn. titanium adv. com. Office Def. Mblzn., 1954-58. Research; contbr. numerous articles to publs. Recipient Best Paper award extractive metals div. Am. Inst. Mining., Metall. and Petroleum Engrs.; James Douglas Gold medal Am. Inst. Mining, Metall. and Petroleum Engrs., 1973. Fellow Am. Inst. Mining, Metall. and Petroleum Engrs. (chmn. extractive metallurgy div. 1958), Metall. Soc., Instn. Mining and Metallurgy (London); mem. Am. Chem. Soc., Nat. Acad. Engrs., Sigma Xi, Tau Beta Pi. Current Work: Thermodynamic behavior of liquid slags, alloys and sulfide solutions (mattes) in metal production; energy utilization in metal production. Subspecialties: Metallurgical engineering; Thermodynamics. Home: Closter Rd Palisades NY 10964 Office: Columbia New York NY 10027

KELLOGG, RALPH HENDERSON, physiologist; b. New London, Conn., June 7, 1920; s. Edwin Henry and Constance Louise (Henderson) K. B.A., U. Rochester, N.Y., 1940, M.D., 1943; Ph.D., Harvard U., 1953. Intern, Univ. Hosps., Cleve., 1944; investigator physiology U.S. Naval Med. Research Inst., Bethesda, Md., 1946; teaching fellow physiology Harvard Med. Sch., Boston, 1946-47, instr., 1947-53; asst. prof. physiology U. Calif.-Berkeley, 1953-58; asst. prof. physiology U. Calif.-San Francisco, 1958-59, assoc. prof., 1959-65, prof., 1965—, lectr. history of health scis., 1978—, acting chmn. history of health scis., 1984-85, acting chmn. physiology, 1966-70; mem. physiology study sect. NIH, 1966-70; physiology test com. Nat. Bd. Med. Examiners, 1966-73, chmn., 1969-73; com. respiration nomenclature Internat. Union Physiol. Scis., 1970-77, commn. respiratory physiology, 1975-81; editorial com. U. Calif. Press, 1972-76. Physiology editor: Stedman's Med. Dictionary, 1972—; joint editorial bd.: Am. Jour. Physiology and Jour. Applied Physiology, 1962-66; editorial bd.: Jour. Applied Physiology, 1977-79; contbr. articles to profl. publs.; contbg. author books on physiology of saline and urea diuresis, respiration, high-altitude acclimatization, history of physiology. Served with M.C., USNR, 1943-46. Sr. research fellow Harvard U., 1962-63; vis. fellow Corpus Christi Coll. Univ. Lab. Physiology, Oxford (Eng.) U., 1970-71; vis. scientist Laboratoire de Physiologie Respiratoire, Centre National de la Recherche Scientifique, Strasbourg, France, 1977; NIH research grantee, 1962-76. Mem. AAAS, Am. Physiol. Soc., AAUP, Am. Assn. History of Medicine, History of Sci. Soc., Phi Beta Kappa, Sigma Xi, Alpha Omega Alpha. Clubs: Roxburghe, Harvard. Current Work: Professional research publications on respiratory physiology, high altitude acclimatization, history of physiology. Teaching organ system physiology to medical students, Doctor of Pharmacy students, and Ph.D. students. Subspecialty: Physiology (medicine). Home: 601 Noriega St San Francisco CA 94122 Office: Dept Physiology U Calif San Francisco CA 94143

KELLOGG, SCOTT THOMAS, microbial geneticist, researcher; b. San Francisco, Aug. 29, 1947; s. Thomas Joseph and Patricia Ruth (Holt) K.; m. Marilyn Avra Levine, June 20, 1976. B.S., Calif. State U.-Hayward, 1971; M.S., San Diego State U., 1974; Ph.D., U. Hawaii, 1979. Research asst. NOAA, 1974; staff scientist Bethesda Research Labs., Gaithersburg, Md., 1981-83; staff scientist Salk Inst. Biotech., La Jolla, Calif., 1983—. Fellow NSF, 1980, EPA, 1981. Mem. Am. Soc. for Microbiology, Am. Chem. Soc., AAAS, Soc. Gen. Microbiology, Agrl. Chem. Soc. Japan. Democrat. Current work: Microbial genetics and evolution with special reference to extrachromosomal elements and their relationships to population biology and quantitative ecology. Subspecialties: Microbiology; Genome organization. Home: 3505-D Monair Dr San Diego CA 92117 Office: SIBIA PO Box 85200 San Diego CA 92138

KELLOGG, WILLIAM WELCH, meteorologist; b. New York Mills, N.Y., Feb. 14, 1917; s. Frederick S. and Elizabeth (Walcott) K.; m. Elizabeth Thorson, Feb. 14, 1942; children: Karl S., Judith Liebert, Joseph W., Jane K. Holien, Thomas W. B.A., Yale U., 1939; M.A., U. Calif. at Los Angeles, 1942, Ph.D., 1949. With Inst. Geophysics, U. Calif. at Los Angeles, 1946-52, asst. prof., 1950-52; with Rand Corp., Santa Monica, Calif., 1947-64, head planetary scis. dept., 1959-64; asso. dir. Nat. Center Atmospheric Research, Boulder, Colo., also dir. lab. atmospheric scis., 1964-73, sr. scientist, 1973—; Mem. earth satellite panel IGY, 1956-59; mem. space sci. bd. Nat. Acad. Scis., 1959-68, mem. com. meteorol. aspects of effects of atomic radiation, 1956-58, mem. com. atmospheric scis., 1966-72, mem. polar research bd., 1972-77; mem. Rocket and Satellite Research Panel, 1957-62; mem. adv. group supporting tech. for operational meteorol. satellites NASA-NOAA, 1964-72; rapporteur meteorology of high atmosphere, commn. aerology World Meteorol. Orgn., 1965-71; chmn. internat. commn. meteorology upper atmosphere Internat. Union Geodesy and Geophysics, 1960-67, mem., 1967-75; mem. internat. com. climate Internat. Assn. Meteorology and Atmospheric Physics, from 1978; mem. sci. adv. bd. USAF, 1956-65; chmn. meteorol. satellite com. Advanced Research Projects Agy., 1958-59; mem. panel on environment President's Sci. Adv. Com., 1968-72; mem. space program adv. council NASA, 1976-77; chmn. meteorol. adv. com. EPA, 1970-74, mem. nat. air quality criteria adv. com., 1975-76, air pollution transport and transformation adv. com., 1976-78; mem. council on carbon dioxide environ. assessment Dept. Energy, 1976-78; adv. to sec. gen. on World Climate Program, World Meteorol. Orgn., 1978-79; sr. advisor to dir. research Naval Environ. Prediction Research Facility, Monterey, Calif., 1983-84; chmn. adv. com. div. polar programs NSF, from 1983. Served as pilot-weather officer USAAF, 1941-46. Co-recipient spl. award pioneering work in planning meteorol. satellite Am. Meteorol. Soc., 1961; recipient Risseca award contbn. human relations in scis. Jewish War Vets. U.S.A., 1962-63; Exceptional Civilian Service award Dept. Air Force, 1966; award for pioneering first meteorol. satellite Dept. Commerce, 1985. Fellow Am. Geophys. Union (pres. meteorol. sect. 1972-74), Am. Meteorol. Soc. (council 1960-63, pres. 1973-74); mem. AAAS (chmn. atmospheric and hydrospheric sect. 1984), Sigma Xi. Club: Cosmos (Washington). Current Work: Research on meterology, dynamics and turbulence of upper atmosphere, use rockets and satellites for atmospheric research; prediction radioactive fallout and dispersal; applications of infrared techniques; atmospheres of Mars and Venus; theory of climate and causes of climate change. Subspecialties: Meteorology; Climatology. Office: Nat Center Atmospheric Research PO Box 3000 Boulder CO 80307

KELLY, MAHLON GEORGE, JR., environmental biologist; b. Plymouth, N.H., Mar. 24, 1939; s. Mahlon George and Emma (Mehren) K.; m. Gretchen Wagner Leigh, Jan. 23, 1970. A.B., Harvard U., 1960, Ph.D., 1968; M.S., U.N.H., 1962. Asst. prof. NYU, N.Y.C., 1969-70; asst. prof. dept. environ. scis. U. Va., Charlottesville, 1970-75, assoc. prof., 1975—; cons. in field. Author: Biology, Evolution and Adaptation to the Environment, 1973. Contbr. articles to profl. jours. NSF grantee, 1972, 78; NATO grantee, 1975, 77, 79, 81. Mem. AAAS, Am. Soc. Limnology and Oceanography, Ecol. Soc. Am., Freshwater Biol. Assn. U.K., Scottish Marine Biol. Assn., Sigma Xi. Current work: Photosynthesis light relationships of aquatic plants, nutrient-growth relationships of phytoplanketon, numerical analysis of aquatic ecosystem dynamics. Subspecialty: Limnology. Home: 268 Turkey Ridge Rd Charlottesville VA 22901 Office: Dept Environ Scis Clark Hall U Va Charlottesville VA 22903

KELLY, NELSON ALLEN, research scientist; b. Lakewood, Ohio, Aug. 6, 1951; s. John Louis and Laura Katherine (Nelson) K.; m. Suzanne May Gerou, Sept. 4, 1982; 1 child, Benjamin. B.S., Miami U., Oxford, Ohio, 1973; Ph.D., Pa. State U., 1977. Sr. research scientist Gen. Motors Corp., Warren, Mich., 1977-82, staff research scientist, 1982—. Contbr. articles to profl. jours. Sci. reader Rec. for the Blind, Inc., Bloomfield Hills, Mich., 1982—. Harvey Clayton Brill scholar, 1972. Mem. Air Pollution Control Assn., Am. Chem. Soc., Inter-Am. Photochem. Soc., Sigma Xi. Current work: Chemistry of ozone formation in photochemical smog. Subspecialties: Atmospheric chemistry; Photochemistry. Home: 11722 Fairview Sterling Heights MI 48077 Office: Gen Motors Research Labs Environ Sci Dept 12 Mile and Mound Rds Warren MI 48090

KELLY, WILLIAM EDWARD, civil engineering educator; b. Bronxville, N.Y., June 25, 1942; s. William Adrian and Mary (Barrett) K.; m. Carolyn Young, Sept. 9, 1967; 1 child, Susanna. B.S., U. Notre Dame, 1965, M.S., 1969, Ph.D., 1972. Registered profl. engr., R.I., Nebr. Faculty dept. architecture U. Notre Dame, Rome, Italy, 1970-71; faculty civil engring. U. R.I., Kingston, 1972-76, prof., chmn., 1976-82, dir. Water Ctr., 1980-82; prof., chmn. dept. civil engring. U. Nebr., Lincoln, 1982—; cons. in field. Contbr. articles to profl. jours. Mem. Zoning Bd. Rev., South Kingstown, R.I., 1978-82. Served to 1st lt. USMC, 1965-67. NSF grantee, 1974-78. Mem. ASCE, Am. Geophys. Union. Current work: Groundwater pollution, modeling, geophysics. Subspecialties: Civil engineering; Hydrology. Home: 14901 Plum Ridge Rd Lincoln NE 68257 Office: Dept Civil Engring U Nebr W348NH Lincoln NE 68588-0531

KELM, DONALD LEWIS, geophysicist; b. Lamont, Alta., Can., Oct. 12, 1939; s. Henry and Eunice Hilda (Biech) K. A.A., Santa Monica Coll., 1960; B.A., San Diego State Coll., 1963, M.S., 1971. Asst. dean, lectr. in geology San Diego State Coll., 1964-71; geophysicist Texaco, Inc., Los Angeles, 1971-73; chief geophysicist BP Can., Calgary, Alta., 1973-80; v.p. GeoQuest Internat. Inc., Houston, 1980-84; pres. Seismography Internat., Inc., Houston, 1984—. Contbr. articles to profl. jours. Chevron Oil Co. scholar San Diego State U., 1970. Mem. Am. Assn. Petroleum Geologists (commn. astrogeology, geophysics), Geol. Soc. Am., Soc. Exploration Geophysicists, Houston C. of C. Republican. Lutheran. Club: Bachelor (San Diego). Current work: Conducting advanced, state-of-the-art geophysical consulting and interpretations, teaching industry courses, development of advanced techniques. Subspecialties: Geophysics; Tectonics. Office: Seismography Internat Inc 12012 Wickchester Ln Suite 290 Houston TX 77079

KELMAN, ARTHUR, educator, plant pathologist; b. Providence, Dec. 11, 1918; s. Philip and Minnie (Kollin) K.; m. Helen Moore Parker, June 22, 1949; 1 son, Philip Joseph. B.S., U. R.I., 1941, D.Sc. (hon.), 1977; M.S., N.C. State U., 1946; Ph.D., 1949; postgrad., U. Wis., 1947-48. Faculty N.C. State U., Raleigh, 1948-65, prof., 1957-65, W.N. Reynolds distinguished prof. plant pathology, 1961-65; chmn. dept. plant pathology U. Wis., Madison, 1965-75, L.R. Jones disting. prof., 1975—, prof. bacteriology, 1977—, Wis. Alumni Research Found. sr. research prof., 1984—; vis. investigator Rockefeller Inst., 1953-54; vis. lectr. Am. Inst. Biol. Sci., 1961-62; chmn. div. biol. sci. Assembly Life Sci. chmn. bd. basic biology Commn. Life Scis., NRC, 1980-82. Author: The Bacterial Wilt Caused by Pseudomonas solanacearum, 1953. Chmn. div. biol. scis. NRC, 1979-82; chmn. sect. applied biology Nat. Acad. Scis., 1981-84. Served with AUS, 1942-45. NSF sr. postdoctoral fellow Cambridge (Eng.) U., 1971-72. Fellow Am. Phytopath. Soc. (chmn. sourcebook com., councilor-at-large, v.p. 1965-66, pres. 1966-67), AAAS; mem. Internat. Soc. Plant Pathology (v.p. 1968-73, pres. 1973-78), Am. Acad. Arts and Scis., Soc. Gen. Microbiology, Am. Soc. Microbiology, Am. Inst. Biol. Sci., Sigma Xi, Alpha Zeta, Gamma Sigma Delta, Phi Kappa Phi, Phi Sigma, Xi Sigma Pi. Current Work: Bacterial diseases of plants; mechanisms of pathogenesis; tissue maceration; post harvest pathology; calcium nutrition and soft rot resistance, monoclonal antibodies for pectic enzymes. Subspecialties: Plant pathology; Microbiology. Home: 234 Carillon Dr Madison WI 53705

KELMAN, BRUCE JERRY, toxicologist, researcher; b. Chgo., July 1, 1947; s. LeRoy Rayfield and Louise (Rosen) K.; m. Jacqueline Anne Clark, Feb. 5, 1972; children: Aaron Wayne, Diantha Renee, Coreyanne Louise. B.S., U. Ill.-Urbana, 1969, M.S., 1971, Ph.D., 1975. Diplomate: Am. Bd. Toxicology. Research asst. Coll. Vet. Medicine, U. Ill.-Urbana, 1969-74; postdoctoral research assoc. Comparative Animal Research Lab., Oak Ridge, 1974-76, asst. prof., 1976-78; sr. research scientist devel. toxicology sect. biology dept. Battelle Pacific N.W. Labs., Richland, Wash., 1979-80, assoc. mgr., 1980-81, mgr., 1981-83, assoc. mgr. biology, biology and chemistry dept., 1983-84, mgr., 1985—. Contbr. numerous articles on toxicology to profl. jours. Recipient Award of Merit Northwest Sect. Soc. for Exptl. Biology and Medicine, 1979. Current Work: Scientific Management, research in transplacental movements and prenatal effects of toxic materials, metabolism of toxic materials. Subspecialties: Toxicology (medicine); Teratology. Office: Battelle NW PO Box 999 Richland WA 99352

KELSEN, STEVEN GUS, respiratory physiologist, pulmonary disease specialist; b. Phila., Jan. 19, 1943; s. Henry and Hilda (Herbst) K.; m. Rhena Joyce Chazin, Sept. 8, 1963; children—Francine Deborah, Michael Robert. B.A., LaSalle Coll., 1964; M.D., Hahnemann Med. Coll., 1968. Diplomate Am. Bd. Internal Medicine, Am. Bd. Pulmonary Medicine. Intern, Boston City Hosp., 1968-69, med. resident N.Y. Hosp.-Cornell Med. Ctr., 1970-72, postdoctoral research fellow Hosp. U. Pa., 1971-73, med. dir. inhalation therapy service, 1973-77; attending physician dept. of medicine Phila. Gen. Hosp., 1973-77, chief pulmonary service, 1974-77; assoc. of medicine U. Pa., Phila., 1973, asst. prof. of medicine, 1974-77; dir. pulmonary fellowship tng. program Case Western Res. U., Cleve., 1977—, asst. prof. of medicine, 1977-79, assoc. prof. of medicine, 1979-85, prof., 1985—, co-dir. pulmonary div. dept. of medicine, 1983—; dir. pulmonary function lab. Univ. Hosps., Cleve., 1977—. Contbr. articles to profl. jours., also book chpts. Recipient Upjohn Excellence award Upjohn Corp., 1968, Pulmonary Acad. award NIH, 1978-83, VA Clin. Investigator award, 1984-87. Mem. Am. Thoracic Soc. (sec. 1981-83), Am. Soc. Clin. Investigation, Am. Phys. Soc., Am. Fedn. Clin. Research, N.Y. Acad. Scis., Central Soc. Clin. Investigation, Exec. Com. Pulmonary Sect. Jewish. Current work: Investigation of mechanisms regulating motor outflow to the muscles of respiration; effects of lung disease on structure and function of the respiratory muscles. Subspecialties: Pulmonary medicine; Physiology (biology). Home: 16810 Holbrook Rd Shaker Heights OH 44120 Office: Dept of Medicine Pulmonary Div Case Western Res Univ 2074 Abington Rd Cleveland OH 44106

KELSEY, DONALD ROSS, research chemist; b. Windsor, Mo., Sept. 30, 1945; s. H. Ross and Lois Ethyl (Ballinger) K. B.S., Central Mo. State U., 1968; Ph.D., Calif. Inst. Tech., 1973. Postdoctoral fellow Yale U., New Haven, Conn., 1972-74; sr. chemist Union Carbide Corp., Bound Brook, N.J., 1974-76, project scientist, 1976-78, research scientist, 1978-84, sr. research scientist, 1984—. Contbr. articles to profl. jours. Patentee in field. Mem. Am. Chem. Soc., Sigma Xi. Current work: High performance aromatic polymers, reaction mechanisms, orbital topology of concerted thermal reactions, nucleophilic displacement, radicals, computer modeling. Subspecialties: Organic chemistry; Polymer chemistry. Office: Union Carbide Corp Box 670 Bound Brook NJ 08805

KELSOE, LYNDA CAROL, aerospace engineer, computer scientist; b. Birmingham, Ala., Apr. 5, 1943; d. Johnny Willard Simmons and Marjorie Nanette (Wallace) Jones; m. Michael Lawson Pierson, Dec. 20, 1968 (div. Oct. 1978); m. Neal Marshall Kelsoe, July 18, 1981. B.A. in English, U. Montevallo, 1966; B.S. in Econs, 1966; B.S. in Computer Sci, Stevens Inst. Tech., 1970; M.A. in Lit, U. Houston, 1977, M.A. in Humanities, 1979. Programmer Bell Labs., Whippany, N.J., 1970-74; programmer/analyst IBM, Houston, 1974-77; sr. programmer/analyst Lockheed Co., Houston, 1977-78; sr. systems analyst Computer Scis. Corp., Houston, 1978-82; sr. staff analyst Jefferson Assocs., Houston, 1982; sr. aerospace scientist Intermetrics, Houston, 1982—. Author: Heraldry—Study of Coats of Arms, 1969. Councilwoman El Lago City Govt., Seabrook, Tex., 1983—. Mem. Nat. Mgmt. Assn., Assn. for Computing Machinery, Nat. Assn. Female Execs., Am. Businesswoman's Assn. Current Work: Manage a research and technology group working on the space shuttle and related projects; designer, builder and maintain compilers in HAL and Ada. Subspecialties: Aerospace engineering and technology; Software engineering. Home: 206 Yacht Club Ln Seabrook TX 77586 Office: Intermetrics 17625 El Camino Houston TX 77058

KEMELHOR, ROBERT ELIAS, laboratory executive; b. N.Y.C., May 19, 1919; s. Louis and Rebecca (Edelson) K.; m. Shirley Tennen, June 28, 1947; children: Judith Ellen Bielecki, Joel Martin, Barry Alan. B.S. in Mech. Engring, George Washington U., 1949. Design engr. Bur. Aeros. and Ordnance, Washington, 1940-53; chief engr. McLean Devel. Lab., Copiague, L.I., N.Y., 1953-57; dir. research and devel. Pesco div. Borg Warner Corp., Cleve., 1957-59; program mgr. Applied Physics Lab., Johns Hopkins U., Laurel, Md., 1959-82, br. supr., 1982—; cons. TRW, Cleve., 1963-64, Cleve. Pneumatic, Washington, 1959-60, Allied Research Assn., Concord, Mass., 1966. Served with USN, 1943-46. Fellow AIAA (assoc.); mem. Soc. Mfg. Engrs. (sr.). Patentee in field. Current Work: Design and fabrication of spacecraft and underwater sensor devices, supervisor and manager of above articles. Subspecialties: Mechanical engineering; Ocean engineering. Home: 6211 Redwing Ct Bethesda MD 20817 Office: Applied Physics Lab Johns Hopkins U Johns Hopkins Rd Laurel MD 20707

KEMP, MARWIN KING, chemist, oil company scientist; b. Strong, Ark., Nov. 23, 1942; s. Elbert L. and Elvie R. (King) K.; m. Linda Jean Shoemaker, Jan. 9, 1976; children: Kirk, Heather. B.S., U. Ark., 1964; M.S., U. Ill., 1966, Ph.D., 1968. Assoc. prof. U. Tulsa, 1968-81; sr. research scientist Amoco Prodn. Co., Tulsa, 1982—. Author: Physical Chemistry - A Step-By-Step Approach, 1979. Mem. Am. Chem. Soc., AAAS, Phi Beta Kappa, Tau Beta Pi. Current Work: Petroleum geochemistry. Subspecialties: Geochemistry; Physical chemistry. Office: PO Box 591 Tulsa OK 74102

KEMPE, LLOYD LUTE, chemical engineering educator; b. Pueblo, Colo., Nov. 26, 1911; s. Henry Edwin and Ida Augusta (Pittelkow) K.; m. Barbara Jean Bell, June 27, 1938; 1 dau., Marion Louise (Mrs. Steven Sanford Palmer). B.S. in Chem. Engring, U. Minn., 1932, M.S., 1938, Ph.D., 1948. Registered profl. engr., Minn., Mich. Research asst. in soils U. Minn., 1934-35, research asso., 1940-41, asst. in chem. engring., 1946-48; asst. san. engr. Minn. Dept. Health, 1935-40; instr. bacteriology U. Mich., Ann Arbor, 1948-49, asst. prof., 1949-50, asst. prof. chem. engring. and bacteriology, 1952-55, asso. prof., 1955-58, prof., 1958-60, prof. chem. engring. and san. engring., 1960-64, prof. chem. engring., 1964-67, prof. chem. engring. and microbiology, 1967-76; asst. prof. food tech. U. Ill., 1950-52. Mem. editorial bd.: Biotech. and Bioengring, 1959-70, Applied Microbiology, 1964—, Food Tech, 1967-69, Jour. Food Sci, 1967-69. Mem. adv. com. on food irradiation Am. Inst. Biol. Scis./AEC; adv. com. on microbiology of foods Nat. Acad. Scis./NRC; adv. com. on botulism hazards HEW/FDA; adv. com. on mil. environ. research Nat. Acad. Scis./NRC. Served to col. AUS, 1941-45. Decorated Bronze Star. Mem. Am. Inst. C.E., Am. Chem. Soc., Am. Soc. Microbiology, Inst. Food Technologists, A.A.A.S., Am. Acad. Environ. Engrs., Water Pollution Control Fedn., Soc. Indsl. Microbiology, Sigma Xi, Phi Lambda Upsilon, Tau Beta Pi, Alpha Chi Sigma. Lodges: Kiwanis, Masons. Subspecialties: Chemical engineering; Enzyme technology. Home: 3020 Exmoor St Ann Arbor MI 48104 Office: Dept Chem Engring U Mich Ann Arbor MI 48104

KEMPE, ROBERT ARON, scientific instrument manufacturing executive; b. Mpls., Mar. 6, 1922; s. Walter A. and Madge (Stoker) K.; m. Virginia Lou Wiseman, June 21, 1946; children: Mark A., Katherine A. B.Chem. Engring., U. Minn., 1943; postgrad. in metallurgy and bus. adminstrn, Case Western Res. U., 1946-49. Div. sales mgr. TRW, Inc., Cleve., 1943-53; v.p. Metalphoto Corp., Cleve., 1954-63, pres., 1963-71, Allied Decals, Inc. (affiliate Metalphoto Corp.), 1963-68; v.p., treas. Horizons Research, Inc., Cleve., 1970-71; pres. Reuter-Stokes, Inc., affiliate of Gen. Electric Co., Twinsburg, Ohio, 1971—. Contbr. articles profl. jours. Served to lt. (j.g.) USN, 1944-46, PTO. Mem. Am. Nuclear Soc. (exec. officer No. Ohio sect.), Chemists Club N.Y.C. Club: Country of Hudson (Ohio). Patentee in field. Current Work: General manager of high technology business, conversion of innovations and good technical ideas into profitable realities. Subspecialties: Nuclear fission; Integrated pest management. Home: 242 Streetsboro St Hudson OH 44236 Office: Edison Park Twinsburg OH 44087

KEMPF, GARY WILLIAM, mech. engr.; b. Ann Arbor, Mich., Jan. 22, 1940; s. Theodore B. and Cora B. (Shafer) K.; m. Lettie L. Staples, Aug. 8, 1964; children: Karl L., Marcus B., Hans W. B.S.M.E., U. Mich., 1963. Registered profl. engr., Mich., Ohio. Project engr. John G. Hoad & Assocs., Ypsilanti, Mich., 1965-71; assoc., chief mech. engr. Ayres, Lewis, Norris & May, Inc., Ann Arbor, 1971-78; pres. Kempf Engring. and Research, Inc., Milan, Mich., 1978—. Scoutmaster Boy Scouts Am., 1980-82. Served to 1st lt. U.S. Army, 1963-65. Mem. ASME, Instrument Soc. Am., Am. Wind Energy Assn. Lutheran. Lodge: Masons. Current Work: Research in 1 to 10 kilowatt wind energy systems and components; manufacturer of wood blades, feathering blade holders for wind systems. Subspecialties: Wind power; Mechanical engineering. Office: PO Box 84 Milan MI 48160

KENAGA, EUGENE ELLIS, entomologist, ecologist; b. Midland, Mich., July 15, 1917; s. Ivan Arthur and Margaret Lena (Supe) K.; m. Joan Elisabeth Bailey, Oct. 12, 1940 (div.); m. Kathleen Virginia Walker, Oct. 20, 1979; children—Dennis K., Marcia B. Davis, David E. B.S., U. Mich., 1939; M.A., U. Kans., 1940; Ph.D., Tokyo U. Agrl., 1977. Entomologist, Dow Chem. Co., Midland, 1940-44, 46-54, group leader, 1954-66, environ. toxicologist, 1966-84, assoc. scientist, 1960-79, research scientist, 1979-82; cons. in field. Author: Commercial and Experimental Insecticides, 1957-85; Birds, Birders and Birding in the Saginaw Bay Area, 1984; Avian and Mammaliam Wildlife Toxicology, 1979, 81. Contbr. articles to profl. publs. Patentee in field. Founding pres. Midland Nature Club, 1953-55; Chippewa Nature Ctr., Midland, 1966-70; pres. Mich. Nat. Resources Council, 1972-73. Served to lt. USN, 1946-48. Recipient award creative advances Am. Chem. Soc., 1985. Mem. Soc. Environ. Toxicology and Chemistry (founding pres., Service award 1982; Founders award 1985), Am. Inst. Biol. Scis. (bd. dirs. 1981-83), Mich. Audubon Soc. (pres. 1962-64), Am. Ornithologist Union, Entomol. Soc. Am. (emeritus), Wilson Soc. Republican. Methodist. Club: Explorers' (N.Y.C.). Current work: Correlation of chemical structure with biological activity and environmental dissipation, wildlife toxicology, consulting. Subspecialties: Environmental toxicology; Environmental chemistry. Home: 1584 E Pine River Rd Midland MI 48640

KENAKIN, TERRENCE PETER, pharmacologist, research scientist; b. Drumheller, Alta., Can., July 13, 1949; came to U.S., 1978; s. Peter and Anne (Kostewich) K.; m. Marlene Sharon Fick, Dec. 21, 1972; children—Leanne Paula, Andrew Peter. B.S. in Chemistry, U. Alta., 1971, Ph.D. in Pharmacology, 1975. Research fellow Univ. Coll., London, Eng., 1975-78; sr. research pharmacologist Burroughs Wellcome Co., Research Triangle Park, N.C., 1978—; ind. assessor Nat. Health and Med. Research Council Australia, 1983. Field editor: Jour. of Cardiovascular Pharmacology, 1984, Jour. Autonomic Pharmacology, 1984; contbr. articles to sci. jours. Prof. Osman James Walker Meml. scholar, 1971. Mem. Brit. Pharmacol. Soc., Am. Soc. Pharmacology and Exptl. Therapeutics. Current work: quantification of parameters which describe drug and drug-receptor interaction (drug receptor theory). Subspecialties: Drug design; Drug receptor kinetics. Home: 5308 Kirkwood Ct Raleigh NC 27609 Office: Dept Pharmacology Wellcome Research Labs 3030 Cornwallis Rd Research Triangle Park NC 27709

KENDRICK, DAVID RICHARD, agricultural engineer, farm manager; b. Champaign, Ill., June 14, 1951; s. Ted Linn and Dorothy Catherine (Quinlan) K.; m. Carol Ann Weinberg, Aug. 20, 1972; children—Colleen Suzanne, Natalie Beth. B.S. in Agrl. Engring., U. Ill., 1973, M.S., 1975. Registered profl. engr., Mich., Ill. Teaching and research asst. U. Ill., Champaign, 1973-75; farm mngr., engr. Muskegon County Wastewater, Mich., 1975—. Contbr. articles to profl. jours. Mem. Am. Soc. Agrl. Engrs. (chmn. SW-263 com. 1984-85), Nat. Soc. Profl. Engrs., Mich. Farm Bur., U. Ill. Alumni Assn. (life), Theta Xi. Lodge: Lions (pres. Fruitport, Mich. 1982-83). Current work: Crop drainage irrigation problems with high application rates of wastewater, multiple land use for land treatment sites, treatability of toxics and organics in wastewater by land application. Subspecialties: Agricultural engineering; Water supply and wastewater treatment. Home: 2071 Marva St Muskegon MI 49444 Office: Muskegon County Wastewater 8301 White Rd Muskegon MI 49442

KENNEDY, BYRL JAMES, physician, oncologist; b. Plainview, Minn., June 24, 1921; s. Arthur Sylvester and Anna Margaret (Fassbender) K.; m. Margaret Bradford Hood, Oct. 21, 1950; children: Sharon Lynn, James Bradford, Scott Douglas, Grant Preston. B.S., B.A., U. Minn., 1943, B.M., 1945, M.D., 1946; M.Sc., McGill Med. Sch., 1951. Diplomate: Am. Bd. Internal Medicine. Intern Mass. Gen. Hosp., 1945-46, asst. resident, 1946, resident, 1951-52, research fellow in medicine, 1947-49; research fellow McGill Med. Sch., 1949-50, Cornell Med. Sch.-N.Y. Hosp., 1951; asst. prof. U. Minn., 1952-57, assoc. prof., 1957-67, prof., 1967—, Masonic prof. oncology, 1970—. Chmn. bd. dirs. Presbyn. Homes of Minn.; Lucius Littauer fellow, 1947, Damon Runyan Clin. fellow, 1949-51. Contbr. articles to profl. jours. Recipient Am. Cancer Soc. Nat. award, 1975; Outstanding Achievement award Assn. Community Cancer Ctrs., 1985. Mem. AMA, Am. Soc. Clin. Oncology, Am. Assn. Cancer Research, Am. Soc. Hematology, Central Soc., Am. Fedn. Clin. Research, ACP, Am. Assn. Cancer Edn., Alpha Omega Alpha. Presbyterian. Clubs: Town and Country (St. Paul), Campus (Mpls.). Current Work: Medical oncology. Subspecialties: Oncology; Cancer research (medicine). Home: 1949 E River Rd Minneapolis MN 55414 Office: Box 286 Univ Hosps Minneapolis MN 55455

KENNEDY, CHARLES, pediatrician, neurologist, educator, researcher; b. Buffalo, Aug. 27, 1920; s. Charles Morehouse and Florence Louise (Chandler) K.; m. Evelyn Clarke, Mar. 9, 1946; children: Allen C., Jacqueline C., Carol M.; m. Eulsum Ko, Aug. 27, 1968. B.A., Princeton, U., 1942; M.D., U. Rochester, 1945. Diplomate: Nat. Bd. Med. Examiners, Am. Bd. Pediatrics, Am. Bd. Psychiatry and Neurology. Intern New Haven Hosp., 1945-46; resident Childrens Hosp., Buffalo, 1948-51; fellow dept. physiology and pharmacology Grad. Sch. Medicine, U. Pa., Phila., 1951-53; asst. prof. pediatrics Sch. Medicine, U. Pa., 1958-62, asso. prof., 1962-67; resident in neurology Hosp. of U. Pa., 1953-54; fellow in neurology Columbia-Presbyn. Med. Center, N.Y.C., 1957-58; guest worker Lab. Cerebral Metabolism, NIHM, 1967—, sr research scientist, 1980—; prof. pediatrics and neurology Georgetown U. Sch. Medicine, Washington, 1971—, chief div. child neurology dept. pediatrics, 1971—. Contbr. numerous articles to profl. jours. Served to lt. (j.g.) USNR, 1946-48. Life Ins. Med. Research fellow, 1951-53. Mem. Am. Pediatric Soc., Am. Neurol. Assn., Child Neurology Soc., Soc. for Neurosci., Am. Soc. for Neurochemistry. Current Work: Contributions to cerebral circulation and metabolism, energy metabolism of developing brain, funcional pathways of vision. Subspecialties: Neurology; Brain energy metabolism. Office: Dept Pediatrics Georgetown U Sch Medicine 3800 Reservoir Rd Washington DC 20007

KENNEDY, CLIVE DALE, psychologist; b. Los Angeles, Mar. 23, 1953; s. Argustus Kennedy and Gussie (Johnson) Ford; m. Lynda Dianne Jones, June 24, 1978; children—: Marc Antony, Ravel Nicole. A.A., Los Angeles City Coll., 1972; B.A., U. Calif.-Santa Barbara, 1975; Ph.D., U. Wash., 1981. Lic. psychologist, Calif., Tex. Mental health technician VA, Los Angeles, 1971-72; peer counselor U. Calif.-Santa Barbara, 1974-75; teaching/research asst. U. Wash., Seattle, 1976-78; clin. psychologist Titus Harris Clinic, Galveston, Tex., 1979-82; clin. asst. prof. U. Tex., Galveston, 1982; clin. psychologist Ortho Indsl. Med. Ctr., Los Angeles, 1982—; clin. psychologist UCLA Student Psychol. Services, 1983—; mem. staff Las Encinas Hosp., Pasadena, 1985—; Bd. dir. Operation PUSH, Galveston, 1981-82; Pres. bd. ushers Shiloh A.M.E. Ch., 1981, 82, UCLA Med. Aux., 1971-72. UCLA Med. Aux. scholar, 1972; Am. Psychol. Assn. fellow, 1975-76; NIMH fellow, 1975; U. Calif.-Santa Barbara Letters and Sci. scholar, 1974. Mem. Am. Psychol. Assn., So. Calif. Assn. Black Psychologists (pres.), Assn. Black Psychologists., Alpha Phi Alpha. Current Work: Behavioral and personality factors in hypertension and other med. problems, behavioral factors in children with learning disabilities, hypertension and other health problems. Subspecialties: Health services research; Behavioral psychology. Office: 2595 E Washington Blvd Suite 101 Pasadena CA 91107

KENNEDY, ELDREDGE JOHNSON, engineering educator, consultant, researcher; b. Fayetteville, Tenn., Sept. 19, 1935, B.S.E.E., U. Tenn., 1958, M.S.E.E., 1959; Ph.D. in Engring. Sci., 1967. Registered profl. engr., Tenn. Devel. engr. Oak Ridge Nat. Lab, Tenn., 1963-70; assoc. prof. of elec. engring. U. Tenn., Knoxville, 1970-75, Fulton prof. of elec. engring., 1975—; cons. Oak Ridge Nat. Lab., 1970—; project dir. NASA Research, U. Tenn., Knoxville, 1975-77, ORNL Research, 1974-77, Navy Research, 1976-77. Author: Operational Amplifiers, 1985. Patentee in field. Contbr. articles to profl. jours. Mem. IEEE, Sigma Xi, Tau Beta Pi, Eta Kappa Nu. Current work: High temperature electronics, radiation—hardened electronics, low-noise design, nuclear instrumentation. Electronics Edn. Subspecialties: Integrated circuits; Electronics. Office: U Tenn Elec Engring Dept Knoxville TN 37996-2100

KENNEDY, EUGENE PATRICK, educator; b. Chgo., Sept. 4, 1919; s. Michael and Catherine (Frawley) K.; m. Adelaide Majewski, Oct. 27, 1943; children—Lisa Kennedy Helprin, Sheila, Katherine. B.Sc., De Paul U., 1941; Ph.D. (Nutrition Found. fellow), U. Chgo., 1949, Sc.D. (hon.), 1977; A.M. (hon.), Harvard, 1960. Research chemist chem. research dept. Armour & Co., 1941-47; postdoctoral fellow Am. Cancer Soc., U. Calif. at Berkeley, 1949-50; with Ben May Lab. Cancer Research, dept. biochemistry U. Chgo., 1950-56, prof. biochemistry, 1956-60; sr. postdoctoral fellow NSF, Oxford (Eng.) U., 1959-60; Hamilton Kuhn prof. biol. chemistry Harvard Med. Sch., 1960—, head dept., 1960-65; Macy scholar Cambridge, 1976. Recipient Glycerine research award, 1955; Am. Oil Chemist Soc. Lipid Research award, 1970; Gairdner Found. award, 1976; Ledlie prize, 1976, Alexander von Humboldt prize, 1984. Mem. Am. Chem. Soc. (Paul Lewis award 1958), Nat. Acad. Sci., Am. Soc. Biol. Chemists (pres. 1970-71), Am. Acad. Arts and Scis. Current Work: Membrane function; transport in bacterial systems; biosynthesis of membrane lipids. Subspecialties: Biochemistry (biology); Membrane biology. Home: 63 Buckminster Rd Brookline MA 02146 Office: Dept Biol Chemistry Harvard Med Sch Boston MA 02115

KENNEDY, JAMES VERN, research chemist; b. Jessup, Pa., May 4, 1934; s. Ray Vern and Ruth (Ready) K.; m. Patricia Martin, Aug. 4, 1962; children—Lisa Catherine, Vern Martin. A.A., Keystone Jr. Coll., 1953; B.S. in Chemistry, Pa. State U., 1955; Ph.D., U. Pitts., 1972. Research assoc. Mellon Inst., Pitts., 1955-63; tech. mgr. Baroid div. NL Industries, Pitts., Houston, 1963-73; dir. research Min. and Chem. div. Engelhard, Menlo Park, N.J., 1973-80; dir. catalyst research Gulf Research & Devel. Co., Pitts., 1980-85; sr. research assoc. Chevron Research Co., 1985—. Editor The Crucible, 1967-69. Patentee in field. Contbr. articles to profl. jours. Active Boy Scouts Am., 1975—. Fellow Am. Inst. Chemists, N.Y. Acad. Scis., mem. Pitts. Catalysis Soc. (pres. 1967-69), Houston Catalysis Soc. (pres. 1973), Am. Chem. Soc. (bd. dirs. Pitts. sect. 1968-70), Clay Minerals Soc. Episcopalian. Club: Coll. Men's (pres. 1978-79). Current work: Design and commercialization of fluid cracking catalysts, materials research as applied to oil field chems.; synthesis, alteration of clay minerals refining and petrochemical catalysis research and development. Subspecialties: Catalysis chemistry; Physical chemistry. Home: 135 Corte Anita Greenbrae CA 94904 Office: Chevron Research Co PO Box 1627 Richmond CA 94802

KENNEDY, JOHN FISHER, engineering educator; b. Farmington, N.Mex., Dec. 17, 1933; s. Angus John and Edith Wilma (Fisher) K.; m. Nancy Kay Grogan, Nov. 21, 1959; children: Suzanne Marie, Sean Grogan, Brian Matthew Fisher, Karen Lynn. B.S. in Civil Engring., U. Notre Dame, 1955; M.S., Calif. Inst. Tech., 1956, Ph.D., 1960. Research fellow Calif. Inst. Tech., Pasadena, 1960-61; asst. prof. MIT, Cambridge, 1961-64, asso. prof., 1964-66; dir. Iowa Inst. Hydraulic Research; prof. fluid mechanics U. Iowa, Iowa City, 1966—; chmn. div. energy engring. U. Iowa, 1974-76; Fulbright scholar, vis. prof. U. Karlsruhe, Germany, 1972-73; Erskine fellow U. Canterbury, Christchurch, N.Z., 1976; Carver disting. prof. engring., 1981—; cons. to govt. agys., indsl. firms, engring. cons. offices, 1960—; vis. assoc. in hydraulics Calif. Inst. Tech., 1977; ASCE Hunter Rouse lectr., 1981; gastdozent Swiss Fed. Inst. Tech., Zurich, 1985. Served to 2d lt. C.E., U.S. Army, 1957. Recipient J.C. Stevens award ASCE, 1959; W.L. Huber Research prize, 1964; Karl Emil Hilgard Hydraulic prize, 1974, 78; Engring. Honor award U. Notre Dame, 1978; Corning Glass Works fellow, 1959-60; Iowa Gov.'s medal for sci., 1983. Iowa Hon. fellow Inst. Water Conservancy and Hydroelectric Power Research (Beijing, China); mem. Nat. Acad. Engring., ASCE, ASME, Am. Soc. Engring. Edn., Internat. Assn. Hydraulic Research (mem. council 1972-76, v.p. 1976-80, pres. 1981-84), Hungarian Hydrol. Soc., Sigma Xi, Chi Epsilon (hon.), Tau Beta Pi. Roman Catholic. Current work: River mechanics and management; ice and arctic engineering; hydraulic structures. Subspecialties: Hydrology; Fluid mechanics. Home: 2 Ashwood Dr Iowa City IA 52240

KENNEDY, LINDA MANN, neurobiologist, researcher, educator; b. Malden, Mass., July 29, 1939; d. Alfred William and Etta May (Maglue) Mann; m. Richard Dearman Kennedy, Apr. 15,1961; children: Pamela Lea, Ruth Alexander. Diploma in nursing, New Eng. Deaconess Hosp., Boston, 1959; A.B. (New Eng. Psychol. Assn. fellow), Simmons Coll., 1975; Ph.D. (Danforth fellow 1975-79, NSF dissertation grantee 1979), Harvard U., 1980, cert. in bus. mgmt, 1982. Registered nurse, Mass. Staff nurse Lahey Clinic, Boston, 1959-61, and various hosps., Mass. and Ga., 1962-72; teaching asst. Simmons Coll., 1972-75, spl. instr., 1982-83; vis. fellow Cornell U., 1977-81, lectr., 1978-79; NIH postdoctoral research fellow Worcester Found. Exptl. Biology, Shrewsbury, Mass., 1980-83; lectr. Clark U., 1983, research asst. prof., 1983-84, asst. prof., 1984—; cons. Gen. Goods Corp., 1980-81. Contbr. articles for profl. jours. Mem. Framingham (Mass.) Conservation Council, NOW, Soc. Neurosci., Assn. Chemoreception Scis., Eastern Psychol. Assn., AAAS, N.Y. Acad. Scis., European Chemoreception Orgn., European Brain Research Orgn., Assn. Women in Sci., Soc. for Values in Higher Edn. Current Work: Physiol. mechanisms for transduction in taste receptor cell membranes; cellular and molecular processes in chemoreception; action of taste-altering drugs. Subspecialties: Neurobiology; Sensory processes. Office: Dept Biology Clark U Worcester MA 01610

KENNEDY, MICHAEL CRAIG, neurobiologist, educator, researcher; b. Buffalo, Dec. 5, 1946; s. Daniel Francis and Katherine Kinsella (Lawsing) K.; children: David Shawn, Matthew Eric, Catherine Megan. B.A., William Marsh Rice U., Houston, 1968; M.S., U. Rochester, N.Y., 1971, Ph.D., 1974. Fellow dept. cell biology N.Y.U. Med. Coll., 1974-76, asst. prof. biology, 1976-81; assoc. prof. dept. anatomy Hahnemann U. Sch. Medicine, Phila., 1981—; cons. coll. div. Harper & Row, Pubs., Inc. Contbr. articles in field to profl. jours. NIH fellow, 1974-76; NIH grantee, 1978-81; NSF grantee, 1981-82. Mem. Am. Assn. Anatomists, Cajal Club, Soc. Neurosciences. Democrat. Roman Catholic. Current Work: Neurobiological studies of auditory communication; neuroanatomical and developmental studies of auditory system; nerve regeneration. Subspecialties: Comparative neurobiology; Anatomy and embryology. Office: Dept Anatomy MS 408 Hahnemann U Sch Medicine Broad and Vine Sts Philadelphia PA 19102

KENNEDY, PHILIP RICHARD, neuroscientist, neurophysiologist; b. Sussex, Eng., Nov. 7, 1947; s. Dermot Patrick and Andree (Hetzel) K.; m. Eimear Mary Campbell, July 16, 1976; children—Dermot Philip, Finian Patrick, Naomi Eimear. Diploma in Edn., Council for Fgn. Med. Grads., 1972; M.D., Nat. U. Ireland, 1972; Ph.D. in Physiology, Northwestern U., 1983. Resident in neurosurgery U. Western Ont., Can., 1976-78; postdoctoral fellow Muscular Dystrophy Assn. Can., 1978-80; research assoc. Emory U., Atlanta, 1983—; clin. investigator Alta. Heritage Found., 1985. Author book chpt., 1980. Author numerous tech., sci. papers, also abstracts. Recipient Sheppard Meml. prize, 1975; Northwestern U. scholar, 1980-83. Fellow Royal Coll. Surgeons Ireland; mem. N.Y. Acad. Scis., Soc. for Neurosci. Current work: Parvocellular red nucleus' role in motor control and motor learning. Subspecialty: Neurophysiology. Office: Dept Physiology Emory U Med Sch Atlanta GA 30322

KENNEDY, ROBERT ALAN, horticulturist, educator, researcher; b. Benson, Minn., Sept. 29, 1946; s. William Henry and Mary Rose (Pothen) K.; m. Lonnie M. Eisenreich, Aug. 3, 1968; children: Caleb John, Alex E. B.S., U. Minn., 1968; Ph.D., U. Calif.-Berkeley, 1974. Asst. prof. botany U. Iowa, Iowa City, 1974-78; assoc. prof. horticulture Wash. State U., Pullman, 1979-82, prof., 1983—. Contbr. articles on plant physiology to profl. jours. Served with U.S. Army, 1969-71. NSF grantee, 1975—; U.S. Dept. Agr. grantee, 1979—. Current Work: Plant physiology, carbon metabolism, photosynthesis, stress physiology. Subspecialty: Plant physiology (biology). Office: Dept Horticulture Wash State U Pullman WA 99164

KENNEDY, THOMAS ALBERT, JR., physicist; b. Erie, Pa., June 11, 1943; s. Thomas Albert and Jeanne Marie (Nuber) K.; m. Virginia Doyle, June 14, 1969; children—Ellen, Matthew, Steven. B.S., Seton Hall U., 1965; Ph.D., Brown U., 1972. Postdoctoral fellow Rutgers U., New Brunswick, N.J., 1971-74; research assoc. Naval Research Lab., Washington, 1974-76, research physicist, 1976—. Author jour. articles (Naval Research Lab. award 1978); patentee. Soccer coach Camp Springs Boys and Girls Club, 1984. Vis. scientist grantee, Fraunhofer Inst., W.Ger., 1979; travel grantee NATO, U. Hull, U.K., 1982-84. Mem. Am. Phys. Soc., Sigma Xi. Roman Catholic. Current work: Defects in semiconductors with emphasis on optical and structural properties of defects in III-V materials. Subspecialties: Condensed matter physics; Electronic materials. Home: 4104 Maidstone Pl Oxon Hill MD 20744 Office: Code 6871 Naval Research Lab Washington DC 20375

KENNEDY, WILBERT KEITH, JR., electrical engineer, electronics company executive; b. Phoenix, Sept. 19, 1943; s. W. Keith, Sr. and Barbara (Barber) K.; m. Carolyn Ann Arvanites, June 19, 1965; children—Matthew, Mark. B.S.E.E., Cornell U., 1966, M.S., 1966, Ph.D., 1968. Mem. tech staff Watkins-Johnson, Palo Alto, Calif., 1968-70, sect. head, 1970-72, dept. mgr., 1972-74, div. mgr., 1974-78, group v.p., 1978—. Contbr. articles to profl. jours. Patentee in field. Post adviser Stanford Area council Boy Scouts of Am., Palo Alto, 1970-71; adviser Microwave Tng. Inst., Mountain View, Calif., 1984—; dir. Superschs. Found., Sunnyvale, Calif., 1984—. NSF fellow, 1965-68. Mem. IEEE (sr. mem.), Assn. of Old Crows., Sigma Xi. Republican. Episcopalian. Current work: Technical work has focused on GaAs and its use at microwave frequencies. Subspecialties: Electrical engineering; Semiconductors. Home: 10165 McLaren Pl Cupertino CA 95014 Office: Watkins-Johnson 3333 Hillview Ave Palo Alto CA 94304

KENNETT, ROGER HOWARD, geneticist, educator; b. Lakewood, N.J., Dec. 27, 1940; s. R. Howard and Henrietta (Truex) K.; m. Carol Lundberg, June 8, 1966; children: Edward, David, Timothy. A.B., Eastern Coll.; Ph.D. in Biomed. Scis, Princeton U., 1969. Postdoctoral fellow U. Calif., San Diego, 1970-71; research officer genetics labs. dept. biochemistry Oxford (Eng.) U., 1972-76; asst. prof. U. Pa. Sch. Medicine, 1976-79; assoc. prof. human genetics, 1979—; dir Human Genetics Cell Center, 1976—. Editor: (with others) Monoclonal Antibodies and Hybridomas: A New Dimension in Biological Analyses, 1980. Mem. Am. Assn. Immunologists, Genetics Soc. Am., AAAS. Current Work: Molecular basis of human genetic diseases and of human oncogenesis. Subspecialties: Genetics and genetic engineering (medicine); Cancer research (medicine). Office: Dept Human Genetics Med Labs 196 U Pa Sch Medicine Philadelphia PA 19104

KENNEY, JOHN WILLIAM, III, chemistry educator; b. Long Beach, Calif., Aug. 15, 1950; s. John William Jr. and Janice (Kendrick) K.; m. Margaret Inga Samuelsen, Sept. 11, 1982. B.S. with high distinction, U. Nev., 1972; Ph.D. in Chemistry, U. Utah, 1979. Acting dir. sci. learning and instructional ctr. Wash. State U., Pullman, 1979-80, postdoctoral research assoc. chem. physics program, 1979-81; asst. prof. chemistry dept. phys. scis., Eastern N.Mex. U., Portales, 1982—. Contbr. articles to profl. jours. Named to Outstanding Young Men of Am., Jaycees, 1982, 84; grantee Am. Vacuum. Soc., 1983-84. Mem. Am. Chem. Soc. (faculty adviser to student affiliate group Eastern N.Mex. U. 1983—, grantee 1984), Am. Phys. Soc., AAAS, Sigma Xi, Phi Kappa Phi. Democrat. Lutheran. Current work: Synthesis and characterization of novel air-sensitive transition metal complexes; variable temperature (300-10 K) electronic absorption and luminescence spectroscopy; transient photophysical measurements. Subspecialties: Inorganic chemistry; Physical chemistry. Home: 1112 Leo Dr Portales NM 88130 Office: Dept Phys Scis-Chemistry Eastern NMex U Stat 33 Portales NM 88130

KENNEY, RICHARD ALEC, medical educator; b. Coventry, Eng., Oct. 4, 1924; came to U.S., 1967; s. Alec and Dorothy Ada (Cooke) K.; m. Doreen Heather Clift, June 10, 1946 (div. 1959) 1 son, Michael Alec; m. Bette Gladys Green, Aug. 8, 1959. B.Sc., U. Birmingham, Eng., 1945, Ph.D., 1947. Project officer WHO, S.E. Asia, 1955-60; chmn. physiology U. Singapore, 1960-65; reader U. Melbourne, Australia, 1965-67; prof. physiology George Washington U. Med. Ctr., 1968—, chmn. dept. physiology, 1972—. Author: Physiology of Aging, 1982. Mem. Physiol. Soc. London, Am. Physiol. Soc., N.Y. Acad. Scis. Club: Cosmos. Current work: Physiology of the aging worker, toxicology. Subspecialties: Physiology (medicine); Gerontology. Home: 4424 Reservoir Rd NW Washington DC 20007 Office: George Washington U Med Ctr 2300 Eye St NW Washington DC 20037

KENNISH, MICHAEL JOSEPH, environmental scientist; b. Vineland, N.J., Apr. 23, 1950; s. John W. and Ida M. (Dente) K.; m. Jo-Ann C. Castone, July 29, 1973; children—Shawn M., Michael C. B.A. in Geology, Rutgers U., 1972, M.S. in Geology, 1974, Ph.D. in Geology, 1977. Environmental scientist Jersey Central Power & Light Co., Morristown, N.J., 1977-81; sr. environ. scientist GPU Nuclear, Forked River, N.J., 1982—. Author: Ecology of Estuaries, 1985; Editor: Ecology of Barnegat Bay, N.J., 1984. Author chpts. in books, jour. articles. Research grantee The Geol. Soc. Am. Mem. Estuarine Research Fedn., Estuarine and Brackish-Water Scis. Assn., Am. Fisheries Soc., Nat. Shellfisheries Assn., Sigma Xi (research grantee). Current work: Estuarine ecology; marine ecology, marine geology, fisheries science, assessment of power plant impacts on the marine environment. Subspecialties: Ecology (environmental science); Oceanography. Home: 521 Shawnee Dr Toms River NJ 08753 Office: GPU Nuclear PO Box 388 Forked River NJ 08731

KENNY, ALEXANDER DONOVAN, pharmacologist, endocrinologist, educator, research institute director; b. London, Mar. 4, 1925; came to U.S., 1947, naturalized, 1956; s. Alexander and Alice Astley (Barton) K.; m. Dorothy Marie LeTang, Aug. 19, 1950; children: Alexander Leo, Mary Alice Kenny Sinton, Virginia Ann Kenny Drawe, Peter Donovan. B.Sc., U. London, 1945, D.Sc., 1982; Ph.D. (fellow), Athenaeum of Ohio, 1950. Sr. chemist Univ. Coll. Hosp., London, 1950-51; chief Chemistry Lab., Mass. Gen. Hosp., Boston, 1951; asst. Sch. Dental Medicine, Harvard U., 1952-54, instr., 1954-55, assoc. Med. Sch., 1955-59, assoc. prof. Med. Sch., 1959-65; prof. W.Va. U. Med. Ctr., 1965-67, U. Mo. Med. Ctr., 1967-74; U. Tex. Med. Br., Galveston, 1974-75; prof.pharmacology Tex. Tech U. Health Scis. Ctr., Lubbock, 1976—, chmn. dept. pharmacology, 1976—; dir. Tarbox Parkinson's Disease Inst., 1976—. Author: Intestinal Absorption of Calcium and its Regulation, 1981; contbr. numerous articles to sci. jours. Mem. Amarillo Catholic Diocesan Sch. Bd., 1980-84, v.p., 1981-82, pres., 1982-83; pres. Thomas More Cath. High Sch. Bd., 1981-83; mem. Found. for Thomas More, 1984—; mem. sch. bd. Thomas More Prep. Sch., 1985—. USPHS spl. fellow London, 1967-68. Mem. Am. Chem. Soc., Am. Inst. Nutrition, Am. Soc. Bone and Mineral Research, Am. Soc. Pharmacology and Exptl. Therapeutics, Biochem. Soc. (U.K.), Brit. Pharm. Soc., Endocrine Soc., Soc. Endocrinology (U.K.), Soc. Exptl. Biology and Medicine, Bone and Tooth Soc. (U.K.), Sigma Xi. Roman Catholic. Club: University City (Lubbock), Current Work: Endocrine aspects of calcium and bone metabolism; calcemic hormones; parathyroid hormone; Vitamin D; calcitonin. Subspecialties: Pharmacology; Endocrinology. Home: 6606 Oxford Ave Lubbock TX 79413 Office: Dept Pharmacology Tex Tech U Health Scis Ctr Lubbock TX 79430

KENSHALO, DANIEL RALPH, psychology educator; b. West Frankfort, Ill., July 27, 1922; s. Daniel R. and Edith (Schroeder) K.; m. Mary Janice Gordon, Aug. 28, 1970; children—Daniel Ralph, Rebecca Carolyn, Mark Hoyt, Janice Machelle. B.A., Washington U., St. Louis, 1947, Ph.D., 1953. Part-time instr. Washington U., St. Louis, 1948-49; from acting asst. prof. to assoc. prof. psychology Fla. State U., Tallahassee, 1950-59, prof. 1959—; vis. prof. U. Marburg, Fed. Republic Germany, summer 1969, U. Claude Bernard, France, summer 1973, U. Edinburgh, Scotland, fall 1984. Author: The Skin Senses, 1968; Sensory Functions of the Skin of Humans, 1980. Served with USNR, 1943-45, comdr. Res. ret. Grantee NSF, 1955-79, NIH, 1961—, Nat. Inst. Aging, 1979—; named disting. prof. and outstanding educator Fla. State U., 1975. Fellow Am. Psychol. Assn., AAAS, N.Y. Acad. Scis., Soc. Neurosci.; mem. South Soc. Philosophy of Psychology (sec. 1959-64, pres. 1963). Current work: Basic and applied research in cutaneous sensitivity using psychophysical and electrophysiological methods. Subspecialties: Psychophysics; Sensory processes. Home: 2414 Delgado Dr Tallahassee FL 32304 Office: Dept Psychology Fla State U Tallahassee FL 32306

KENYON, ALLEN STEWART, polymer physical chemist; b. Constance, Ky., Mar. 6, 1916; s. Thomas S. and Alice (Tupman) K.; m. Elizabeth Wallace, Apr. 4, 1942; children—Margaret, Barbara, Elizabeth, Thomas. B.S., U. Ky., 1938, M.S., 1939; Ph.D., Columbia U., 1947. Instr. chemistry U. Ky., Lexington, 1940; chemist Monsanto Co., Dayton, Ohio, 1947-61, group leader, fellow, St. Louis, 1961—; vis. prof. chem. engring. Washington U., St. Louis, 1974. Contbr. articles to profl. jours. Patentee in field. Served to maj. USAF, 1942-47. Monsanto Co. sci. fellow, 1980. Mem. Am. Chem. Soc. (past chmn. Dayton sect. 1955, polymer div.), Sigma Xi, Pi Mu Epsilon, Phi Lambda Epsilon. Republican. Presbyterian. Current work: Polymer characterization, structure and properties of polymers, mechanical and solution properties, light scattering, physical chemistry of biological molecules, polymers and fibers. Subspecialties: Polymer chemistry; Physical chemistry. Home: 1318 Londgate Dr Kirkwood MO 63122

KEPLINGER, MORENO L., toxicologist; b. Ulysses, Kans., May 25, 1929; s. Wilbur and Mary (Pudge) K.; m. Barbara Ann Evans, July 22, 1967; children: Kerry, Steven, Robert, Cory, Janice. B.S., U. Kans., 1951, M.S., 1952; Ph.D., Northwestern U., 1956. Diplomate: Am. Bd. Toxicology. Asst. prof. U. Miami Med. Sch., Coral Gables, Fla., 1956-60, 64-68; toxicologist Hercules Med. Dept., Wilmington, Del., 1960-64; mgr. toxicology Ind. Biotest Labs., Northbrook, Ill, 1968-77; cons. toxicologist, Hilltop Lakes, Tex., 1978—; pres. M.L. Keplinger, Inc., 1978—. Contbr. articles and book chpts. to profl. lit. Fulbright scholar, 1952-53; Parke-Davis fellow in pharmacology, 1953-56. Mem. Am. Soc. Toxicology, European Soc. Toxicology, Am. Soc. Pharmacology and Exptl. Therapeutics, Am. Indsl. Hygiene Assn. Lodge: Masons. Current Work: Industrial, environmental and general toxicology including research in cancer, teratology genetics and neurotoxicology. Subspecialties: Toxicology (medicine); Pharmacology. Home and Office: PO Box 1299 Hilltop Lakes TX 77871

KERAN, DOUGLAS CHARLES, wildlife educator; b. Mpls., Nov. 12, 1943; s. Philip L. and Charlotte V. (Hogland) K.; m. Julie D. Godtland, May 12, 1979; children—Douglas B., Kevin M., Shane P., Brianna J. B.S., U Minn., 1965; M.A., St. Cloud State U., 1976. Cert. wildlife biologist. Researcher, Minn. Mus. Natural History, Mpls., 1964-65; dir. Crow Wing Natural History Area, Brainerd, Minn., 1969-73; instr. natural resources Brainerd Tech. Inst., 1973—; pres. Kerdolian, Inc., Brainerd, 1981—; wildlife cons., 1973—. Contbr. articles to profl. jours. Mem. Crow Wing County Wildlife Mgmt. Commn., 1982—; wildlife ecologist Paul Bunyan Arboretum, 1980—; chair Minn. Environ. Commn., 1980-82. Served with USCG, 1965-69. Recipient Minn. Environ. Quality award, 1984. Mem. Wildlife Soc. (state pres. 1980-82; nat. coms.), Am. Fisheries Soc., Raptor Research Found., N.Am. Nongame Wildlife Assn., Minn. Earth Assn. (hon.), Soc. Natural Resource Technicians (hon.). Club: Benayshee Council (program chair 1976-79) (Brainerd). Current work: Nesting habitat for birds of prey; urban wildlife projects; eagle/osprey nest survey and ecology. Subspecialties: Resource conservation; Resource management. Home: Route 7 Box 14 Brainerd MN 56401 Office: Brainerd Tech Inst 300 Quince St Brainerd MN 56401

KERFOOT, WILLIAM BUCHANAN, JR., research corporation, executive, consultant; b. S.I., N.Y., Mar. 13, 1944; s. William Buchanan Kerfoot and Marguerite (Myers) Baumgartel; m. Patricia Hoffmann, Aug. 21, 1965; children: Christopher Alexander, Kerry Ann. B.A. in Entomology, U. Kans., 1966; Ph.D. in Biology, Harvard U., 1970. Asst. scientist Woods Hole (Mass.) Oceanographic Instn., 1970-75; dir. Environ. Mgmt. Inst. div., Environ. Devices Corp., Marion, Mass., 1975-78; pres. K-V Assocs., Inc., Falmouth, Mass., 1978—. Bd. dirs. dir. Assn. for Preservation of Cape Cod., Orleans, Mass., 1975—; mem. water resources council Cape Cod Planning and Econ. Devel. Commn., Barnstable, Mass., 1978—; citizens adv. com. Dept. Environ. Quality Engring., Boston, 1979—. IR 100 Indsl. Research awardee, 1977; NSF postdoctorate award, 1970; hon. Woodrow Wilson fellow Woodrow Wilson Found., 1966. Mem. Nat. Water Well Assn., ASTM, Film Soc. Woods Hold (treas. 1974-75). Episcopalian. Inventor Laminate membrane, septic leachate detector, groundwater flowmeter. Current Work: Development of groundwater treatment and control technology for subsurface engineering. Subspecialties: Water supply and wastewater treatment; Hydrology. Home: 49 Ransom Rd Falmouth MA 02540 Office: K-V Assos Inc 281 Main St Falmouth MA 02540

KERFOOT, WILSON CHARLES, aquatic ecologist, researcher; b. N.Y.C., Mar. 13, 1944; s. William Buchanan Kerfoot and Marguerite Susan (Myers) Kerfoot Baumgartel; m. Marianne Ellen Bettesworth, Aug. 20, 1971 (div. 1975); m. Lucille Marie Zelazny, Aug. 5, 1978; children—Alexander Lee, Katherine Stephanie. B.A. in Zoology and Geology, U. Kans., 1966; M.S., Ph.D. in Zoology, U. Mich., 1972. NSF postdoctoral fellow U. Wash., Seattle, 1972-73, research assoc., 1973-76; asst. prof. Dartmouth Coll., Hanover, N.H., 1975-82, research assoc. prof., 1982-83, adj. assoc. prof., 1984—; assoc. research scientist U. Mich., Ann Arbor, 1984—; vis. sr. scientist Cornell U., Ithaca, N.Y., 1981-83; Editor: Evolution and Ecology of Zooplankton Communities, 1980. Contbr. articles to profl. jours. Recipient numerous grants NSF; hon. Woodrow Wilson scholar, 1969. Mem. Ecol. Soc. Am. (publs. com. 1981—), Am. Soc. Naturalists, Am. Soc. Limnology and Oceanography, Internat. Soc. Limnology, Phi Beta Kappa, Sigma Xi. Democrat. Episcopalian. Current work: Influence of predation in structuring freshwater and marine communities; chemical defenses of freshwater organisms against fishes; predictability of divergence. Subspecialties: Ecology (biology); Paleontology, paleoecology. Office: Great Lakes Research Div 2200 Bonisteel Blvd Ann Arbor MI 48109

KERNS, WILLIAM DAVID, veterinary pathologist; b. Urbana, Ohio, June 20, 1949; s. William Philip and Martha (Wing) K.; m. Sharon Ropp, Sept. 11, 1971; children—Joshua, Heather, Joe. B.S., Wilmington Coll., 1971; D.V.M., Ohio State U., 1975, M.Sc., 1976. Diplomate Am. Coll. Vet. Pathologists. Pathologist Battelle Columbus Co., Columbus, Ohio, 1979-81, DuPont Corp., Newark, 1981-82, Smith, Kline & French, Phila., 1982—. Contbr. articles to profl. jours. and books. Mem. AVMA, AAAS, Soc. Toxicologic Pathologists, Am. Assn. Pathologists, Internat. Acad. Pathologists. Current work: Mechanisms of atherosclerosis. Subspecialties: Pathology (veterinary medicine); Vascular disease, atherosclerosis. Office: Smith Kline & French L60 PO Box 7929 Philadelphia PA 19101

KERR, DONALD MACLEAN, JR., physicist; b. Phila., Apr. 8, 1939; s. Donald MacLean and Harriet (Fell) K.; m. Alison Richards Kyle, June 10, 1961; 1 dau., Margot Kyle. B.E.E. (Nat. Merit scholar), Cornell U., 1963, M.S., 1964, Ph.D. (Ford Found. fellow, 1964-65, James Clerk Maxwell fellow 1965-66), 1966. Staff Los Alamos Nat. Lab., 1966-76, group leader, 1971-72, asst. div. leader, 1972-73, asst. to dir., 1973-75, alt. div. leader, 1975-76; dep. mgr. Nev. ops. office Dept. Energy, Las Vegas, 1976-77, acting asst. sec. def. programs, Washington, 1978, dep. asst. sec. def. programs, 1977-79, dep. asst. sec. energy tech., 1979; dir Los Alamos Nat. Lab., 1979—; mem. Navajo Sci. Com., 1974-77; mem. sci. adv. panel U.S. Army, 1975-78; mem. engring. advs. bd. U. Nev.-Las Vegas, 1976-78; chmn. com. research and devel. Internat. Energy Agy., 1979; mem. nat. security adv. council SRI Internat., 1980—; mem. adv. bd. U. Alaska Geophys. Inst., 1980—; Mem. sci. adv. group Joint Strategic Planning Staff, 1981—; Mem. Naval Research Adv. Com., 1982—; adv. bd. Georgetown U. Center Strategic and Internat. Studies, 1981—; Mem. corp. Charles Stark Draper Lab., 1982—. Mem. AAAS, Am. Phys. Soc., Am. Geophys. Union, Southwestern Assn. Indian Affairs, Sigma Xi, Tau Beta Pi, Eta Kappa Nu. Club: Cosmos (Washington). Research, publs. on plasma physics, microwave electronics, ionospheric physics, energy and nat. security policy. Subspecialties: Physics research and development administration; Energy research and development administration. Office: Los Alamos Sci Lab Los Alamos NM 87545

KERR, JANET SPENCE, pulmonary physiologist; b. New Haven, Conn., May 30, 1942; d. Alexander Pyott and Janet Blake (Conley) Spence; m. Thomas Albert Kerr, Jr., July 24, 1965; children—Sarah Patterson, Matthew Spence, Timothy Marden. B.A., Beaver Coll., 1964; M.S., Rutgers U., 1969, Ph.D., 1973. Asst. prof. Rutgers U., Camden, N.J., 1973-76; research assoc. U. Pa. Sch. Medicine, Phila., 1976-79; adj. asst. prof. U. Medicine and Dentistry N.J.-Rutgers Med. Sch., New Brunswick, 1980-84; sr. research pharmacologist E.I. duPont de Nemours & Co., Wilmington, Del., 1985—. Contbr. articles to profl. jours. Bd. dirs. Delaware-Raritan Lung Assn., Princeton, N.J., 1983—; class agt. Beaver Coll., Glenside, Pa. Busch fellow Rutgers U., 1972. Mem. AAAS, Am. Heart Assn., Am. Fedn. Clin. Research, Am. Physiol. Soc., Am. Thoracic Soc. (council mem. eastern sect. 1984—), N.Y. Acad. Scis., Sigma Xi. Current work: Role of connective tissue in models of lung injury, including oxidant injury, fibrosis, nutritional restrictions and pulmonary hypertension. Subspecialties: Physiology (biology); Physiology (medicine). Home: 111 Canterbury Dr Wilmington DE 19803 Office: E I duPont de Nemours & Co Exptl Sta Wilmington DE 19898

KERR, WILLIAM, nuclear engineering educator; b. Sawyer, Kans., Aug. 19, 1919; s. William and Mary Louise (Gill) K.; m. Ruth Duncan, Apr. 28, 1945; children: William Duncan, John Gill, Scott Winston. B.S. in Elec. Engring, U. Tenn., 1942, M.S., 1947; Ph.D., U. Mich., 1954. Instr., then asst. prof. U. Tenn., 1942-44, 46-48; mem. faculty U. Mich., Ann Arbor, 1948—, prof. nuclear engring., 1958—, chmn. dept., 1961-74, acting dir. Mich. Meml.-Phoenix Project, 1961-65, dir., 1965—, dir. Office Energy Research, 1977—, project supr. AID Nuclear Energy Project, 1956-65; Cons. Atomic Power Devel. Assos., 1954—, Argonne Nat. Lab., Colo. Commn. on Higher Edn.; chmn. nuclear engring. edn. com. Asso. Midwest Univs., 1961-62, pres., 1966-67, bd. dirs., 1965-67; trustee Argonne Univs. Assn., 1965-71; adv. com. reactor safeguards Nuclear Regulatory Commn., 1972—. Mem. Am. Soc. Engring. Edn., IEEE, Am. Nuclear Soc., Sigma Xi, Eta Kappa Nu, Phi Kappa Phi, Tau Beta Pi. Current Work: Reactor safety analysis; radiation shielding; energy production, distribution and consumption. Subspecialties: Nuclear engineering; Nuclear fission. Home: 2009 Hall St Ann Arbor MI 48104

KERREBROCK, JACK LEO, aeronautics and astronautics educator; b. Los Angeles, 1928; s. Oscar A. and Florence (Hoy) K.; m. Bernice May Veverka, Apr. 11, 1953; children—Christopher, Nancy, Peter. Student U. Ore., 1946; B.S., Oreg. State U., 1950; M.S., Yale U., 1951; Ph.D., Calif. Inst. Tech., 1956. Sr. research fellow Calif. Inst. Tech., Pasadena, 1958-60; prof. MIT, Cambridge, 1960—, Maclaurin prof., 1975—, head dept. aeronautics and astronautics, 1978-81, 83—; assoc. administr. NASA, Washington, 1981-83; bd. dirs. Aerodyne Research Inc., Billerica, Mass., 1984—, Orbital Scis. Corp., Vienna, Va., 1984—, ETA Systems Inc., Mpls., 1984—. Author: Aircraft Engines and Gas Turbines, 1977. Contbr. articles to profl. jours. Patentee in field (engine), 1984. Fellow AIAA, Am. Acad. Arts and Scis.; mem. Nat. Acad. Engring.

Current work: Education (engineering), propulsion, power generation. Subspecialties: Aerospace engineering and technology; Aeronautical engineering. Office: MIT 77 Massachusetts Ave Cambridge MA 02139

KERWIN, LARKIN, physics educator; b. Quebec, Que., Can., June 22, 1924; s. Timothy and Catherine (Lonergan) K.; m. Maria G. Turcot, June 10, 1950; children: Lupita, Alan, Larkin, Terrence, Rosa Maria, Gregory, Timothy, Guillermina. B.S., St. Francis Xavier U., 1944, LL.D., 1970; M.S., M.I.T., 1946; D.Sc., Laval U., 1949; D.Sc. (hon.), U. B.C., 1973, McGill U., 1974, Meml. U. Nfld., 1978, U. Ottawa, 1981, Royal Mil. Coll., Kingston, 1982, U. Winnipeg, 1983, U. Windsor, 1984, U. Moncton, 1985; LL.D. (hon.), U. Toronto, 1973, U. Alta., 1983, Dalhousie U., 1983; D.L., Concordia U., 1976; D.C.L. (hon.), Bishop's U., 1978. Asst. prof. physics Laval U., 1948-51, assoc. prof., 1951-56, prof., 1956—, chmn. dept., 1961-67, vice-dean faculty scis., 1967-69, vice-rector, 1969-72, rector, 1972-77; v.p. Natural Scis. and Engring. Council Can., 1978-80; pres. Nat. Research Council Can., 1980—; dir. Cape Breton Devel Corp.; research physicist Geotech. Corp., Cambridge, 1945-46. Author: Atomic Physics, an Introduction, 1963; also articles. Decorated Lt. Gov.'s medal; Gov. Gen. medal; Pariseau medal, 1965; Centenary medal, 1967; Prix David, 1951; Jubilee medal, 1977; knight comdr. Equestrian Order Holy Sepulchre Jerusalem; also knight grand cross; officer Order of Can.; also companion; Laval Alumni medal, 1978; Gold Medal Can. Council Profl. Engrs., 1982. Fellow Royal Soc. Can. (pres. 1976), Royal Soc. Arts, AAAS, Am. Inst. Physics; mem. Internat. Union Pure and Applied Physics (sec.-gen.), Assn. Canadienne-Francaise pour l'avancement des sciences, Assn. Univs. and Colls. Can. (pres. 1974-75), Am. Phys. Soc., Corp. Profl. Engrs. Quebec, Sociedad Mexicana Fisica, Canadian Assn. Physicists (pres. 1955, medal 1969), Sigma Xi. Club: Cercle Universitaire (Quebec). Subspecialty: Atomic and molecular physics. Home: 2166 Parc Bourbonniere Sillery PQ G1T 1B4 Canada

KESLER, CLYDE ERVIN, engineering educator; b. Dewey, Ill., May 7, 1922; s. Roy Francis and Helen (Deffenbaugh) K.; m. Mary Anne Kirk, July 20, 1947; children: Philip Roy, David Clyde. B.S. in Civil Engring., U. Ill., 1943, M.S. in Structural Engring., 1946. Engr. aide I.C.R.R., Champaign, Ill., 1946-47; faculty U. Ill., Urbana, 1947—, prof. mechanics and civil engring., 1962—; pres. Am. Concrete Inst., Detroit, 1967-68; cons. concrete and reinforced concrete problems to pvt. cos., govt. agys., 1949—. Author: (with Taylor, Corten and Wetenkamp) Mechanical Behavior of Solids, 1959; also articles. Served to maj. C.E., U.S. Army, 1943-46. Recipient Alfred E. Lindau award Am. Concrete Inst., 1970, Halliburton Engring. Edn. Leadership award U. Ill., 1982. Fellow ASCE, Ill. Acad. Engring. Anglers; mem. ASTM (Sanford E. Thompson award 1958), Wire Reinforcing Inst. (hon.), Am. Concrete Inst. (hon.), Nat. Acad. Engring., Chi Epsilon, Tau Beta Pi, Phi Kappa Phi, Sigma Xi. Current Work: Research covers the behavior of concrete under various loadings and environments with current emphasis on fracture and fiber reinforcement. Subspecialties: Civil engineering; Materials (engineering). Home: RFD 3 Box 314 Champaign IL 61821 Office: Newmark Lab Civil Engring 208 N Romine St U Ill Urbana IL 61801

KESLER, STANISLAV BRANKO, electrical engineering educator, consultant; b. Valjevo, Serbia, Yugoslavia, July 3, 1942; came to U.S., 1982, naturalized, 1983; s. Branko D. and Bosiljka (Blagojevic) K.; m. Jelisaveta Vlatkovic, May 17, 1967; children—Branko, Olivera. Diploma Engring., U. Belgrade, Yugoslavia, 1965, M.Engring., 1973; Ph.D., McMaster U., Hamilton, Can., 1977. Research engr. Inst. M. Pupin, Belgrade, 1966; research and teaching asst. U. Belgrade, 1966-73; teaching asst. elec. engring. dept. McMaster U., 1973-77, research engr. Communications Research Lab., 1977-82; assoc. prof. elec. engring. Drexel U., Phila., 1982—; cons. Flam & Russell, Inc., Horsham, Pa., 1984—, Interspec Inc., Conshohocken, Pa., 1984—. Reviewer books McMilliam Publs., 1983—; contbr. articles to profl. jours. Mem. IEEE (sr.), Sigma Xi. Current work: Research in adaptive and nonadaptive signal processing; antenna array signal analysis. Subspecialties: Computer engineering; Algorithms. Home: 8508 Elliston Dr Wyndmoor PA 19118 Office: Dept Elec and Comp Engring Drexel Univ 32d & Chestnut Philadelphia PA 19104

KESSEL, DAVID, biochemistry educator; b. Monroe, Mich., Jan. 8, 1931; s. Harry and Gertrude (Herman) K.; m. Elizabeth Sykes, Sept. 8, 1979. B.S. in Chemistry, M.I.T., 1952; Ph.D. in Biol. Chemistry, U. Mich., 1959. Research fellow in pharmacology Harvard U. Sch. Medicine, 1959-63, research assoc. in pathology, 1963-67; assoc. prof. pharmacology U. Rochester, N.Y., 1967-74; prof. medicine and pharmacology Wayne State U., Detroit, 1974—. Contbr. articles to profl. jours. Mem. AAAS, Am. Soc. Biol. Chemists, Am. Soc. for Photobiology, Biochem. Soc., N.Y. Acad. Scis. Current Work: Mode of action of anti-tumor agents; porphyrin photosensitization; circumvention of drug resistance. Subspecialties: Cancer research (medicine); Biophysics (biology).

KESSEN, WILLIAM, educator, psychologist; b. Key West, Fla., Jan. 18, 1925; s. Herman Lowry and Maria Angela (Lord) K.; m. Marion Lord, June 10, 1950; children: Judith, Deborah, Anne, Peter Christopher, Andrew Lord, John Michael. B.S., U. Fla., 1948; Sc.M., Brown U., 1950; Ph.D., Yale U., 1952. Postdoctoral fellow Child Study Center, Yale U., 1952-54, faculty depts. psychology and pediatrics, 1954-76, Eugene Higgins prof. psychology, 1976—, chmn. dept. psychology, 1977-80, prof. pediatrics, 1978—, acting univ. sec., 1980-81; mem. intellective processes research com. Social Sci. Research Council, 1959-63, chmn., 1961-63. Author: (with G. Mandler) The Language of Psychology, 1959, The Child, 1965, Childhood in China, 1975, (with M.H. Bornstein) Psychological Development from Infancy, 1979; editor: Mussen's Handbook of Child Psychology, vol. 3, 1983; contbr. articles to profl. jours. Mem. Carnegie Council on Children, 1973-77. Fellow Center Advanced Study Behavioral Sciences, 1959-60; Guggenheim fellow, 1970-71. Fellow AAAS, Am. Psychol. Assn. (pres. div. 7 1979-80); mem. Soc. Research Child Devel., Am. Acad. Arts and Scis., Soc. Exptl. Psychologists. Current Work: Visual perception in human infants; history of children. Subspecialties: Developmental psychology; Cognition. Home: 30 Halstead Ln Branford CT 06405 Office: Dept Psychology Yale U Box 11A Yale Sta New Haven CT 06520

KESSLER, DONALD JOE, space scientist; b. Houston, Jan. 30, 1940; s. Joseph Valentine and Mazie Irene (Doegen) K.; m. Mary Frances Lawrence, Jan. 26, 1963 (div. 1969); m. Mary Susan Cain, Dec. 31, 1969 (div. 1978). Student, Lamar State Coll., 1961-62; B.S. in Physics, U. Houston, 1965, postgrad., 1966. Student trainee physics NASA Johnson Space Ctr., Houston, 1962-65, aerospace technologist meteroid studies, 1965-69, aerospace technologist flight mission ops., 1969-74, aerospace technologist aeronomy, 1974-78, aerospace technologist flight mechanics, 1978-79, space scientist, 1979—; space debris program chmn. Com. Sci. Research, Paris, France, 1984, 86. Contbr. articles to profl. jours. Served with U.S. Army, 1958-61. Recipient Superior Performance award NASA, 1977, Quality Increase award, 1980, Outstanding Performance Awards, 1983, 84. Mem. Sigma Pi Sigma, Phi Kappa Phi. Current Work: Direct research with objectives to define the orbital debris environment; to predict the effects of this environment on spacecraft and discover preferred techniques to minimize the hazard of orbital debris to spacecraft. Subspecialty: Orbital debris studies. Home: 10822 Kirktown Houston TX 77089 Office: NASA Johnson Space Ctr NASA Rd 1 Houston TX 77058

KESSLER, EDWIN, meteorologist, nat. lab. adminstr.; b. N.Y.C., Dec. 2, 1928; s. Edwin and Marie Rosa (Weil) K.; m. Lottie Catherine Menger; children: Austin Rainier, Thomas Russell. A.B., Columbia Coll., 1950; S.M., MIT, 1952, Sc.D., 1957. Research scientist USAF Cambridge Research Labs., Bedford, Mass., 1954-61; dir. atmospheric physics div. Travelers Research Center, Hartford, Conn., 1961-64; dir. Nat. Severe Storms Lab., Norman, Okla., 1964—; adj. prof. U. Okla., 1964—; vis. prof. M.I.T., 1975-76. Past asso. editor: Jour. Applied Meteorology; Contbr. articles to profl. jours. Served with U.S. Army, 1947-48. Recipient award for outstanding authorship NOAA, 1971. Fellow Am. Meteorol. Soc. (past pres. Greater Boston br., nat. councilor 1966-69, past mem. com. on severe local storms, past chmn. com. on weather radar, cert. cons. meteorologist), AAAS; mem. Royal Meteorol. Soc. (fgn.), Weather Modification Assn., Am. Geophys. Union, Sigma Xi. Current Work: Editor of 3-volume work on thunderstorms, published in 1981-82. Subspecialty: Meteorology. Office: 1313 Halley Circle Norman OK 73069

KESSLER, KARL G., physicist, researcher; b. Hamburg, W. Ger., Aug. 21, 1919; came to U.S., 1927, naturalized 1933; s. Gunther and Anna (Schneider) K.; m. Elizabeth L. Kefgen, June 28, 1944; children—Heidi Ann, Susan Mary. A.B., U. Mich., 1941, M.S., 1942, Ph.D. in Physics, 1947. Research physicist U. Mich., Ann Arbor, 1941-48; physicist Nat. Bur. Standards, Washington, 1948, sect. chief, 1959-62, div. chief, 1962-77, ctr. dir., 1977—. Contbr. articles to profl. jours. Recipient Gold medal Dept. Commerce, 1962; Astin award Nat. Bur. Standards, 1984. Fellow Optical Soc. Am. (pres. 1969-70, Disting. Service award 1985), Am. Phys. Soc.; mem. AAAS, Am. Astron. Soc., Washington Acad. Sci. Current work: Atomic Physics and Spectroscopy. Subspecialty: Atomic and molecular physics. Office: Nat Bur Standards B164 Physics Bldg Gaithersburg MD 20899

KESTENBAUM, AMI, researcher; b. Petach Tikva, Israel, June 7, 1941; came to U.S., 1958, naturalized, 1963; s. I. K. and Regina (Lewit) K.; m. Sylvia W. Kestenbaum, Sept. 5, 1971; children: Robyn, Michael. B.E.E., CCNY, 1963; M.S. in E.E, Poly. Inst. N.Y., 1965, Ph.D., 1969. Sr. mem. tech. staff AT&T Techs., Princeton, N.J., 1969—. Contbr. articles to profl. jours. Mem. Material Research Soc., IEEE, Laser Inst. Am. Patentee in field. Current Work: Laser applications to electronic technology. Subspecialties: Laser applications; Microchip technology (engineering).

KESTIN, JOSEPH, mechanical engineer, educator; b. Warsaw, Poland, Sept. 18, 1913; came to U.S., 1952, naturalized, 1960; s. Paul and Leah K.; m. Alicja Wanda Drabienko, Mar. 12, 1949; 1 dau., Anita Susan. Dipl. Ing., Engring., U. Warsaw, 1937; Ph.D., Imperial Coll., London, 1945; M.A. ad eundem, Brown U., 1955; D.Sc., U. London, 1966; Dr. h.c., Universite Claude Bernard (Lyon I). Sr. lectr. dept. mech. engring. Polish U. Coll., London, 1944-46, dept. head, 1947-52; prof. engring., dir. Center for Energy Studies, Brown U., Providence, 1952—; vis. prof. Imperial Coll., London, 1958, 83—, Summer Sch. in Jablonna, Warsaw Polish Acad. Scis., 1973, U. Md., 1984—; professeur associé U. Paris, 1966, Université Claude Bernard (Lyon I) and Ecole Centrale de Lyon, 1974; Fulbright lectr. Instituto Superior Tecnico, Lisbon, 1972; spl. lectr. Norges Tekniske, Hogskole, Trondheim, Norway, 1963, 71; lectr. Nobel Com. Berzelius Symposium, 1979; fellow Inst. Advanced Studies, West Berlin; spl. adv. on engring. edn. to Chancellor of U. Tehran, Iran, 1968; chmn. NRC Eval. Panel for Office of Standard Ref. Data of Nat. Bur. Standards, 1976-80; mem. Eval. Panel for Nat. Measurement Lab. of Nat. Bur. Standards, 1978-80, Numerical Data Adv. Bd., Nat. Acad. Scis., 1976-80; cons. Nat. Bur. Standards, NATO, Rand Corp.; Mem. vis. com. U. Va., Charlottesville, 1964; mem. exec. com. Nat. Bur. Standards Evaluation Panels, 1974-78. Author 4 books on thermodynamics; editor-in-chief: Dept. Energy Sourcebook on Production of Electricity from Geothermal Energy; tech. editor: Jour. Applied Mechanics, 1956-71; mem. editorial bd.: Internat. Jour. Heat and Mass Transfer, 1961-71, Heat Transfer-Soviet Research, 1968—, Heat Transfer-Japanese Research, 1972—, Mechanics Research Communications, 1973—, Jour. Non-Equilibrium Thermodynamics, 1976—, Revue Generale de Thermique, 1975—, Physica A, 1978—, Internat. Jour. Thermophysics, 1979—, Jour. Chem. and Engring. Data, 1980—; contbr. articles to profl. jours. Fellow Inst. Mech. Engrs. (London) (Water Arbitration prize 1949), ASME (task group on energy 1974-76, applied mechanics div. 1967-78, chmn. 1978, nat. nominating com. 1976-78, Centennial medals for research achievements and disting. service, James Harry Potter Gold medal 1981); mem. Am. Soc. Engring. Edn. (chmn. Curtis W. McGraw Research award com. 1976-78), Internat. Assn. Properties of Steam (U.S. del. exec. com. 1954—, chief of del. 1972—, pres. 1974-76), Internat. Union Pure and Applied Chemistry (chmn. subcom. transport properties 1981—), U.S. Acad. Engring., Sigma Xi (pres. Brown U. chpt. 1979-84), Tau Beta Pi. Clubs: Univ. (Providence), Faculty Brown U. (Providence). Current Work: Energy research, thermophysical properties, thermodynamics. Subspecialty: Mechanical engineering. Home: 140 Woodbury St Providence RI 02906 Office: Brown U Providence RI 02912

KETCHUM, MILO SMITH, civil engineer; b. Denver, Mar. 8, 1910; s. Milo Smith and Esther (Beatty) K.; m. Gretchen Allenbach, Feb. 28, 1944; children—David Milo, Marcia Anne, Matthew Phillip, Mark Allen. B.S., U. Ill., 1931, M.S., 1932; D.Sc. (hon.), U. Colo., 1976. Asst. prof. Case Sch. Applied Sci., Cleve., 1937-44; engr. F.G. Browne, Marion, Ohio, 1944-45; owner, operator Milo S. Ketchum (Cons. Engr.), Denver, 1945-52; partner, prin. Ketchum, Konkel, Barrett, Nickel & Austin (Cons. Engrs. and predecessor firm), Denver, from 1952; prof. civil engring. U. Conn., Storrs, 1967-78, emeritus, 1978—; mem. Progressive Architecture Design Awards Jury, 1958, Am. Inst. Steel Constrn. Design Awards Jury, 1975, James F. Lincoln Arc Welding Found. Design Awards Jury, 1977; Stanton Walker lectr. U. Md., 1966. Author: Handbook of Standard Structural Details for Buildings, 1956; Editor-in-chief: Structural Engineering Practice; Contbr. engring. articles to tech. mags. and jours. Recipient Disting. Alumnus award U. Ill., 1979. Fellow Am. Concrete Inst. (dir., Turner medal 1966), ASCE (pres. Colo. sect., hon.), Instn. Structural Engrs. (London), Am. Cons. Engrs. Council; mem. Nat. Acad. Engring., Am. Soc. Engring. Edn., Internat. Assn. Shell and Space Structures, Structural Engrs. Assn. Colo. (pres.), Cons. Engrs. Council Colo. (pres.), Old Saybrook (Conn.) Hist. Soc., Sigma Xi, Tau Beta Pi, Chi Epsilon, Phi Kappa Phi, Alpha Delta Phi. Club: North Cove Yacht. Subspecialty: Structural engineering. Home: 13527 W 67th Way Arvada CO 80004

KETTLEWELL, NEIL MACKEWAN, neuroscience educator, researcher; b. Evanston, Ill., May 27, 1938; s. George Edward and Barbara Sidney (Kidde) K.; m. Phyllis Ann Miller, Jan. 30, 1965 (div. Sept. 1976); 1 son, Brant Regnar; m. Toni Ann Gianoulias, June 2, 1978. B.S., Kent State U., 1962; M.A., U. Mich., 1965, Ph.D., 1969. Research asst. in psychology U. Mich., 1963-69; programmer U. Mich. (Inst. Social Research), 1966-69, systems analyst time scheduling office, 1967-69; lectr. U. Mont., 1969-70, asst. prof. psychology, 1970-75, assoc. prof., 1976—; cons. in field. Served with USAR, 1958-66. U. Mich. Presdl. scholar, 1964. Mem. Soc. Neurosci., N.Y. Acad. Scis., Pi Mu Epsilon, Psi Chi, Phi Eta Sigma. Current Work: Ultrastructural synaptic changes in brain as result of experience. Subspecialties: Neuropsychology; Molecular biology. Home: 172 Fairway Dr Missoula MT 59803 Office: Dept Psychology U Mont Missoula MT 59801

KETY, SEYMOUR S(OLOMON), physiologist, psychobiologist, emeritus educator; b. Phila., Aug. 25, 1915; s. Louis and Ethel (Snyderman) K.; m. Josephine R. Gross, June 18, 1940; children: Lawrence Philip, Roberta Frances. A.B., U. Pa., 1936, M.D., 1940, Sc.D. (hon.), 1965; Sc.D. (hon.), Loyola U., 1969, U. Ill., 1981; M.D. (hon.), U. Copenhagen, 1979. NRC fellow Harvard, 1943-44; from instr. to asst. prof. pharmacology U. Pa. Sch. Medicine, 1943-48; prof. clin. physiology Grad. Sch. Medicine, 1948-51; sci. dir. Nat. Insts. Mental Health and Neurol. Diseases and Blindness, 1951-56; chief Lab. Clin. Sci., NIMH, 1956-61, 62-67; Henry Phipps prof., dir. dept. psychiatry Johns Hopkins Sch. Medicine, 1961-62; prof. psychiatry Harvard Med. Sch., 1967-83, prof. neurosci. in psychiatry, 1983, prof. emeritus, 1983—; dir. psychiat. research labs. Mass. Gen. Hosp., Boston, 1967-77, Mailman Research Center (McLean Hosp.), Belmont, Mass., 1977—; sr. sci. advisor Office of Adminstr., Alcohol Drug Abuse and Mental Health Adminstrn., Rockville, Md.; Thomas Dent Mütter lectr., 1951, Eastman lectr., 1957, NIH lectr., 1960, Thomas William Salmon lectr., 1961, Alvarenga Prize lectr., 1961; Acad. lectr. Am. Psychiat. Assn., 1961; Saul Korey lectr., 1964, James Arthur lectr., 1966, 3d Mental Health Research Fund. lectr., London, 1965, Benjamin Musser lectr., 1970, Edward Mapother lectr., London, 1974, George Bishop lectr., 1975, Harvey lectr., 1975, Grass Found. lectr., 1975; Henry Maudsley lectr. Editor-in-chief: Jour. Psychiat. Research, 1959-82; contbr. sci. articles to profl. publs. Organizing com. Internat. Neuro-chem. Symposia, 1952-60; sci. advisory com. Mass. Gen. Hosp., 1956-60; dir. Found. Fund Research in Psychiatry, 1962-65; assoc. Neuroscis. Research Found., 1962—; trustee Rockefeller U., 1976—. Recipient Theobold Smith award AAAS, 1949, Max Weinstein award, 1954; Distinguished Service award HEW., 1958; Stanley Dean award, 1962; McAlpin award Nat. Assn. for Mental Health, 1972; Intra-Sci. award, 1975; William C. Menninger award A.C.P., 1976; Fromm-Reichman award, 1978; Founds. Fund award, 1979; Passano award, 1980. Disting. fellow Am. Psychiat. Assn. (Disting. Service award 1980); hon. fellow Royal Coll. Psychiatrists; mem. Nat. Acad. Scis. (Kovalenko award 1973), Am. Acad. Arts and Scis., Am. Philos. Soc., Assn. Research Nervous and Mental Disease (trustee, pres. 1965, 80, Research Achievement award 1980), Am. Psychopath. Assn. (pres. 1965, Paul Hoch award 1973), Soc. for Psychiat. Research, Am. Soc. Clin. Investigation, Am. Soc. Pharmacology and Exptl. Therapeutics, Soc. for Neurosci. (Grass Found. award 1975), Phi Beta Kappa, Sigma Xi, Alpha Omega Alpha. Current Work: Cerebral circulation and metabolism; psychiatric genetics; biological psychiatry. Subspecialties: Psychophysiology; Psychopharmacology. Office: Alcohol Drug Abuse and Mental Health Adminstrn 5600 Fishers Ln Rockville MD 20852

KEVAN, PETER GRAHAM, biologist, educator, researcher; b. Edinburgh, Scotland, June 17, 1944; s. Douglas Kieth and Kathleen Edith (Luckin) K.; m. Sherrene Dawn; children: Colin Douglas, Kathleen Hannah. B.Sc. in Zoology with honors, McGill U., Montreal, Que., Can., 1965; Ph.D. in Entomology, U. Alta. (Can.), Edmonton, 1970. Nat. coordinator IBP-Conservation, Can., Edmonton, 1969-70; contract biologist Can. Wildlife Service, Inuvik, N.W.T., 1970-71; Nat. Research Council postdoctoral fellow Can. Agr., Ottawa, Ont., 1971-72; project mgr. Meml. U., St. John's, Nfld., Can., 1972-75; asst. prof. biology U. Colo., 1975-82; assoc. prof. environ. biology U. Guelph, Ont., 1982—; cons. internat. devel. agys.; invited lectr. univs. and sci. meetings N.Am., Europe and Asia. Contbr. chpts. to books, articles to profl. jours. NSF grantee; Nat. Research and Engring. Research Council grantee, 1982; also various other grants. Mem. Am. Bot. Soc., Brit. Ecol. Soc., Entomol. Soc. Can., Entomol. Soc. Ont. (assoc. editor procs.) Inst. Arctic and Alpine Research, Internat. Bee Research Assn., Internat. Ecol. Soc., Sigma Xi. Current Work: Pollination and apiculture: palaeontology, ecology, botany, zoology, evolution, co-evolution, insect behavior, plant reproduction. Subspecialties: Ecology (environmental science); Evolutionary biology. Home: Rural Route 3 Aberfoyle Guelph ON N1H 6H9 Canada Office: Environ. Biology U Guelph Guelph ON N1G 2W1 Canada

KEY, MICHAEL LEON, systems engineer, consultant; b. Joplin, Mo., Nov. 14, 1942; s. Sydine Leon and Laberta Emileen (Ensley) K.; m. Linda Gail Greathouse, Sept. 30, 1962; children—Kimberly Lynn, Kristen Michelle. A.A. cum laude, Pensacola Jr. Coll., 1974; B.S. cum laude, U. Md., 1982. Commd. seaman U.S. Navy, 1960; served in various tech. mgmt. positions, 1960-79; resigned, 1979; sr. mem. tech. staff Computer Scis. Corp., Falls Church, Va., 1979-80, Processing Research Inc., Falls Church, 1980-82; mem. tech. staff/mgr. systems devel. and design E-Systems div. Melpar, Falls Church, 1982—. Pres. Escambia Bay Jaycees, Pensacola, Fla., 1973-74; mem. Fla. Bicentennial Commn., 1973-74; Fla. state chmn. Fla. Jaycees, 1973-75 (named Outstanding State Chmn. 1973, Jaycee of Yr., Escambia Bay Jaycees, 1973); internat. pres. Internat. Jaycees, Scotland, 1977-79. Decorated Navy Commendation medal, Navy Achievement medal. Mem. Am. Security Council, IEEE, IEEE Info. Theory Soc., IEEE Aerospace and Electronics Soc., IEEE Communications Soc., IEEE Acoustics, Speech and Signal Processing Soc., IEEE Antennas and Propagation Soc., IEEE Microwave Theory and Techniques Soc., Armed Forces Communications and Electronics Assn., U.S. Naval Inst., Assn. Old Crows, Nat. Rifle Assn. (life), Phi Theta Kappa, Alpha Sigma Lambda. Republican. Lodge: Masons. Current work: Development of processing technology for frequency agile spread spectrum communications; signal analysis and processing; electronic threat/weapon system assessment and projection. Subspecialties: Systems engineering; Information systems (Information science). Home: 4996 Kurt Ct Woodbridge VA 22193 Office: E-Systems Melpar Div 7700 Arlington Blvd Falls Church VA 22046

KEYES, ROBERT WILLIAM, physicist; b. Chgo., Dec. 2, 1921; s. Lee P. and Katherine K.; m. Sophie Skadorwa, June 4, 1966; children—Andrew, Claire. B.S., U. Chgo., 1942, M.S., 1949, Ph.D., 1953. With Argonne Nat. Lab., 1946-50; staff mem. Westinghouse Research Lab., Pitts., 1953-60; mem. research staff IBM Research Lab., Yorktown Heights, N.Y., 1960—; vis. physicist Am. Phys. Soc. Vis. Indsl. Physicists Program, 1974-75, 77; vice chmn. Gordon Conf. on High Pressure Physics, 1970; chmn. Gordon Conf. on Chemistry and Physics of Microstructure Fabrication, 1976, Nat. Materials Adv. Bd. (ad hoc com. on ion implantation as a new surface treatment tech.), 1978; mem. Nat. Acad. Scis.-NAE-NRC evaluation panel Nat. Bur. Standards, 1970-73; cons. physics survey com., mem. statis. data panel Nat. Acad. Sci.-NRC Council Physics Survey Com., 1972; mem. data and info. panel Nat. Acad. Sci.-NRC Com. on Survey of Materials Sci. and Engring., 1974. Assoc. editor: Revs. Modern Physics, 1976—; corr.: Comments on Solid State Physics, 1970—. Served with USN, 1944-46. Recipient Outstanding Contbn. award IBM, 1963. Fellow Am. Phys. Soc., IEEE (chmn. subcom. cultural and sci. relations 1976, mem. del. to USSR 1975, W.R.G. Baker prize 1976); mem. Nat. Acad. Engring. Current Work: Heavily-doped semiconductors; physical limits in information processing. Subspecialties: Condensed matter physics; Computer engineering. Office: IBM PO Box 218 Yorktown Heights NY 10598

KEYWORTH, GEORGE A., II, physicist; b. Boston, Nov. 30, 1939; s. Robert Allen and Leontine (Briggs) K.; m. Polly Lauterbach, July 28, 1962; children: Deirdre, George III. B.S., Yale U., 1963; Ph.D., Duke U., 1968; D.Sc. (hon.), Rensselaer Poly. Inst., 1982; D.Engring. (hon.), Mich. Technol. U. Mem. staff Los Alamos Sci. Lab., 1968-78; head exptl. physics div., 1978-81; sci. advisor to the Pres. White House, and dir. Office of Sci. and Tech. Policy, Washington, 1981—. Trustee N.C. Sch. Sci. and Math.; bd. govs. Nat. Space Club. Recipient Chmn.'s award Am. Assn. Engring. Socs., 1982; hon. prof. Fudan U., Peoples Republic of China. Fellow Am. Phys. Soc., AAAS; mem. Air Force Assn. (life patron), Sigma Xi. Club: Cosmos (Washington). Subspecialty: Nuclear physics. Office: Office Sci and Tech Policy Executive Office of the President Washington DC 20506

KHACHATURIAN, HENRY, neuroanatomist, neuroendocrinologist; b. Tehran, Iran, Oct. 19, 1951; came to U.S., 1970, naturalized, 1983; s. Shahen and Emma (Babayan) K.; m. Ellen C. Quinn, June 24, 1983. B.S. in Biology and Chemistry, SUNY-Brockport, 1974, M.S. in Biol. Sci., 1976; Ph.D. in Anatomy, U. Rochester, 1981. Postdoctoral fellow Mental Health Research Inst., U. Mich., Ann Arbor, 1980-83, research investigator, 1983—. Author book chpts., articles and abstracts. Recipient John R. Bartlett prize in neurosci. Ctr. Brain Research, U. Rochester, 1979, outstanding research award, 1980, Mem. Soc. Neurosci., Internat. Narcotic Research Conf., Internat. Brain Research Orgn., World Fedn. Neuroscientists. Current work: Immunocytochemical/anatomical localization of opioid and related peptides in brain. Ontogenetic development of opioid and related peptides in brain. Subspecialties: Neurobiology; Immunocytochemistry. Office: Mental Health Research Inst U Mich Ann Arbor MI 48109

KHADDURI, FARID MAJID, mechanical engineer; b. Baghdad, Iraq, Aug. 10, 1945; came to U.S., 1947, naturalized, 1954; s. Majid and Majdia (Dawaff) K.; m. Alicia Basiliko, Nov. 18, 1973; children: Alexandra, Justine. B.A. in Physics, Amherst Coll., 1967; M.S. in Engring. Sci, George Washington U., 1976. Analytical engr. Atlantic Research Corp., Gainesville, Va., 1968-72, sr. design engr., 1972-73; chief engr. Trident I Missile Post Boost Control System, 1973-78; program mgr. MX programs, 1979-81, Trident II Post Boost Control System, 1981-83, mgr. Trident Project Office, 1983-85, mgr. strategic systems, 1985—. Mem. Am. Phys. Soc., ASME. Republican. Club: Kenwood Country (Bethesda, Md.). Current Work: Program management solid rocket propulsion. Subspecialties: Aerospace engineering and technology; Solid rocket propulsion. Home: 5526 Westbard Ave Bethesda MD 20816 Office: 7511 Wellington Rd Gainesville VA 22065

KHAMBATTA, HOSHANG JAL, anesthesiology educator, anesthesiologist, researcher; b. Bombay, India, Mar. 30, 1931; came to U.S. 1968, naturalized 1976; s. Jal Faramji and Jer Jal (Unwala) K.; m. Renate Friederike Krause, Jan. 4, 1963; children—Sonja, Gustav. M.B., B.S., Dow Med. Coll., Karachi, Pakistan, 1956; M.D., Nat. Bds. in Med. for Fgn. Grads., 1970. Diplomate in Anaesthesia, Royal Coll. Surgeons, Eng., 1967. Instr. anesthesiology Coll. Physicians and Surgeons, Columbia U., N.Y.C., 1971-73, assoc., 1973-74, asst. prof., 1974-82, assoc. prof., 1982—; asst. attending anesthesiologist Columbia-Presbyterian Med. Ctr., N.Y.C., 1972-82, assoc. attending anesthesiologist, 1982—. Contbr. articles to profl. jours. Research fellow in anesthesiology Columbia U., 1970-71; NIH grantee, 1973-79. Mem. Am. Physiol. Soc., Royal Coll. Surgeons Faculty Anesthesia, Am. Coll. Anesthesiologists, Am. Soc. Anesthesiologists, Soc. Neurosurg., Anesthesia and Neurol. Supportive Care (founding mem.), Soc. Cardiovascular Anesthesiologists. Current work: Oxygen consumption of the body, carbon dioxide stores of the body, deliberate hypotension during anesthesia, hypoxia; coronary blood flow during anesthesia and after bypass surgery. Subspecialties: Anesthesiology; Physiology (medicine). Home: 291 Audubon Rd Englewood NJ 07631 Office: Columbia U Coll Physicians and Surgeons 630 W 168th St New York NY 10032

KHAN, ABDUL AZIM, electrical engineering educator, researcher, consultant; b. Sehore, India, Jan. 14, 1950; came to U.S., 1974; s. Abdul Aziz and Wahida Begum K. B.S. with honors, U. Karachi (Pakistan), 1972; M.S. in Physics, U. Nebr., 1976, M.A. in Applied Math., 1979, M.S. in Elec. Engring., 1980, Ph.D. in Engring. Sci., 1983. Lectr., U. Baluchistan, Quetta, Pakistan, 1972-74; grad. asst. U. Nebr., Lincoln, 1974-83; asst. prof. elec. engring. Wash. State U., Pullman, 1983—; cons. Crystal Specialties, Inc., Tigard, Oreg., 1983—; mem. tech. adv. bd. dirs. Yea Assocs., Inc., Beaverton, Oreg., 1984—. Contbr. articles to engring. jours. Mem. Am. Phys. Soc., IEEE, Am. Vacuum Soc. Moslem. Current work: Bridgman growth of electronic and optical materials, epitaxy of II-VI and III-V semiconductors and alloys; GaAs integrated circuits, infra red detectors. Subspecialties: Semiconductors; Electronic materials. Office: Dept Elec and Computer Engring Wash State U Pullman WA 99164

KHAN, MOHAMMAD ASAD, geophysicist, educator; b. Aima, Lahore, Pakistan, Aug. 13, 1940; came to U.S., 1964, naturalized, 1975; s. Ghulam Qadir and Hajira (Karim) K.; m. Tahera Pathan, Jan. 4, 1974; 1 dau., Shehzi Samira. B.S., U. Punjab, Lahore, Pakistan, 1957, M.S., 1963; postgrad., Harvard U., 1964-65; Ph.D. (East West Center scholar), U. Hawaii, 1967. Forecaster Pakistan Meteorol. Dept., Lahore, 1958-63; lectr. in geophysics U. Punjab, 1963-64; asst. prof. geophysics and geodesy U. Hawaii, 1967-71, asso. prof., 1971-74, prof., 1974—; geophysicist, geodesist Hawaii Inst. Geophysics, 1967—; NSF and NASA fellow Summer Inst. Dynamical Astronomy at Mass. Inst. Tech., 1968-69; sr. vis. scientist geodynamics Goddard Space Flight Center NASA, Greenbelt, Md., 1972-74; sr. scientist Computer Scis. Corp., Silver Spring, Md., 1974-76, sr. cons., 1976-77; diplomatic minister/adviser Resource Survey and Devel. Pakistan, 1974-76; sr. resident asso. Nat. Acad. Scis., 1972-74; leader Am. Asian Studies and Contemporary Social Problems Seminar Series, Honolulu, 1968-69. Contbr. articles to profl. publs. Chmn. East and West: A Perspective for the 80's; mem. Hawaii Environ. Council, 1979—, chmn. exec. com., 1979—, vice chmn., 1981—; chmn. Pakistan Relief Fund, Honolulu, 1971. Fellow Explorers Club; mem. Geol. Soc. U. Punjab (pres. 1962-63), Am. Geophys. Union, Pakistan Assn. Advancement Sci., Am. Geol. Inst., Am. Geophys. Union, East West Center Alumni Assn. (dir. 1976—), Internat. Alumni of East West Center (exec. com., chmn. 1977-80). Research in geophys., geodetic and oceanographic applications of satellites, geodynamics, planetary interiors, global tectonics, global correlations, core-mantle boundary problems, gravity, isostasy, satellite altimetry, geodesy, earth models, geophys. exploration, charting and hydrography, ocean dynamics. Current Work: Geophysical geodetic, oceanographic and geodynamical applications of satellites, geodynamics, planetary interiors, global tectonics, global correlations, core-mantle boundary problems, gravity and isostasy, satellite altimetry, geodesy, earth models, geophysical exploration; ocean dynamics, hydrography. Subspecialty: Geophysics. Office: Hawaii Inst Geophysics U Hawaii 2525 Correa Rd Honolulu HI 96822

KHAN, WINSTON, mathematics and physical science educator; b. Port-of-Spain, Trinidad, Mar. 12, 1934; s. Amarnath and Safeeran K.; m. Joan Acklima Aziz, Dec. 22, 1961; children: Alima, Selina, Shereeza, Winston, Alim. B.Sc., London U., 1956, M.Sc., 1958; Dip.Mat.Phys., Birmingham U., 1961, Ph.D., 1964. Asst. lectr. math. London U., 1958-59; asst. prof., dir. math. U. West Indies, Trinidad, 1964-69; asst. prof., dir. math. U. P.R., Cavey, 1969-72, assoc. prof., 1972-74, prof. physics, Mayaguez, 1974—; cons. NSF, 1982-83. Author: Turbulence Phenomena, 1972; contbr. articles to profl. jours. Recipient numerous honors. Grantee U.S. Army, 1982—. Mem. Am. Math. Soc., Soc. Indsl. and Applied Math., N.Y. Acad. Scis., AAAS, Am. Phys. Soc., Internat. Math. Modelling, Smithsonian Instn. Current Work: Fluid mechanics, turbulence phenomena, physics and mathematics of fluids, engineering science. Subspecialties: Applied mathematics; Physics of fluids. Home: Calle Uroyan AD4 Mayaguez PR 00709 Office: U PR Mayaguez PR 00709

KHANNA, PYARE LAL, bio-organic chemistry educator, researcher; b. Lahore, India, Mar. 28, 1945; came to U.S., 1974; s. Chaman Lal and Satya Vati (Malhotra) K.; m. KaPoor Swatanter, Oct. 4, 1973; children—Sonia, Pavan. M.Sc., Delhi U., India, 1967, Ph.D., 1970. Prof. chemistry Delhi U., 1970-74; research assoc. Columbia U., N.Y.C., 1974-77; research scientist Syva, Palo Alto, Calif., 1977-80, research mgr., 1980-83, asst. dir. research, 1983—. Author: College Chemistry, 1974. Inventor Med. Diagnostics (Syntex Sci. award 1984). Patentee in field. Contbr. articles to profl. jours. Mem. AAAS, Am. Chem. Soc., Am. Assn. Clin. Chemistry, N.Y. Acad. Scis. Current work: Research and development management in medical diagnostics. Subspecialties: Organic chemistry; Immunology (medicine). Office: Syva 900 Arastradero Palo Alto CA 94304

KHARE, ASHOK K., metallurgical engineer; b. Kanpur, India, Aug. 7, 1948; came to U.S., 1969; s. Bhagwan Prashad and Krishna (Kumari) K.; m. Poornima Chand, Nov. 18, 1974. B.S.c., Agra U., India, 1964; B. Tech., Indian Inst. Tech., 1969; M.S., Stevens Inst. Tech., 1971. Devel. metallurgist Nat. Forge Co., Irvine, Pa., 1975—; lectr. in field. Contbr. articles to profl. jours. Mem. exec. com. Warren County Republican Com. Mem. Am. Soc. Metals (Presidents' sponsor award 1978-82, editor tech. book), ASME. Republican. Hindu. Clubs: Warren Art League, Warren Players. Lodges: Masons; Shriners. Developer of patent in field. Current Work: Heavy steel forgings, high temperature alloys and some nickel and copper base alloys; product and process development applications and failure analysis; formulation and establishment of standards. Subspecialties: Metallurgical engineering; Metallurgy. Home: 5 Leslie Blvd Warren PA 16365 Office: Nat Forge Co Irvine PA 16329

KHARE, BISHUN NARAIN, physicist; b. Varanasi, India, June 27, 1933; d. Dwarka Nath and Ram (Pyari) Srivastava; m. Jyoti Rani Khare, Dec. 7, 1962; children: Reena, Archana. B.Sc., Banaras Hindu U., India, 1953, M.Sc., 1955; Ph.D., Syracuse U., 1961. Research assoc. U. Toronto, 1961-62; research assoc. SUNY, Stony Brook, 1962-64; assoc. research scientist Ont. Research Found., Can., 1964-66; physicist Smithsonian Astrophys. Obs., 1966-68; sr. research physicist Ctr. for Radiophysics and Space Research, Cornell U., 1968—; assoc. Harvard Obs., 1966-68. Contbr. numerous articles to profl. jours. Mem. Am. Phys. Soc., AAAS, Am. Astron. Soc., Am. Chem. Soc., Internat. Astron. Union, Internat. Soc. for Study of Origin of Life, Astron. Soc. India, Planetary Soc., Sigma Xi. Current Work: Molecular structure and spectroscopy, applications of spectroscopic technques to the study of compounds synthesized in primitive terrestrial and contemporary planetary atmospheres by photochemical reaction, hydrogen bonding among molecules of biological interest, planetary surfaces and atmospheres, and interstellar chemistry. Subspecialties: Planetary science; Space chemistry. Office: 306 Space Scis Cornell U Ithaca NY 14853

KHAVARI, KHALIL AKHTAR, psychology educator; b. Tehran, Iran., Nov. 10, 1932, came to U.S., 1956, naturalized, 1965; s. Ardeshir and Rouhanghiz (Khalili) Akhtarkhavari; m. Sue Williston, June 6, 1959; children—Paul, Katherine. B.S., Bradley U., 1960, M.A., 1963; Ph.D., Ind. U., 1967. Asst. prof. U. Wis., Milw., 1967-70, assoc. prof., 1970-75; prof. psychology, 1975—; dir. Midwest Inst. on Drug Use, Milw., 1974-77. Recipient Teaching Excellence award U. Wis., 1980, research awards NIH, NSF, Nat. Inst. Drug Abuse. Mem. Soc. for Neuroscience, Research Soc. on Alcoholism, Baha'i Internat. Health Agency, Midwestern Psychol. Assn. Mem. Baha'i Faith. Current work: Study psychol. factors in health, alcoholism and drug dependence. Subspecialties: Physiological psychology; Neuropharmacology. Home: 910 E Wahner Pl Milwaukee WI 53217 Office: U Wis Psychology Dept PO Box 413 Milwaukee WI 53201

KHAZAN, NAIM, pharmacologist; b. Baghdad, Iraq, Feb. 15, 1921; came to U.S., 1966, naturalized, 1973; s. Rahmin and Tova (Eleazer K.; m. Evelyn Moulem, Nov. 2, 1952; children—Uri, Ron. Ph.C., Coll. Pharm. Chemistry, Baghdad, 1943; Ph.D. in Pharmacology, Hadassah U., Jerusalem, 1960. Assoc. prof. pharmacology Mt. Sinai Sch. Medicine, N.Y.C., 1967-72; chmn. dept. pharmacology Merrell Nat. Lab., Cin., 1972-74; dept. chmn. pharmacology U. Md. Sch. Pharmacy, Balt., 1974—, Emerson prof. pharmacology, 1980—. Contbr. over 150 articles on drugs of abuse to sci. jours. Reviewer, editor pharmacology related jours. NIH fellow, 1962-63; USPHS internat. fellow, 1968; grantee NIMH, 1967, NIDA, 1968—. Mem. N.Y. Acad. Scis., AAAS, Am. Pharm. Assn., Am. Pharm. Assn. Acad. Sci., Am. Soc. Pharm. Exptl. Therapeutics, Soc. for Neurosci. Current work: Pharmacology of opioids, drug dependence and withdrawal, CNS active agents. Subspecialty: Neuropharmacology. Home: 2126 Caves Rd Owings Mills MD 21117 Office: Univ Md Sch Pharmacy 20 N Pine St Baltimore MD 21201

KHORANA, HAR GOBIND, chemist, educator; b. Raipur, India, Jan. 9, 1922; s. Shri Ganpat Rai and Shrimati Krishna (Devi) K.; m. Esther Elizabeth Sibler, 1952; children: Julia, Emilie, Dave Roy. B.S., Punjab U., 1943, M.S., 1945; Ph.D., Liverpool (Eng.) U., 1948; D.Sc., U. Chgo., 1967. Head organic chemistry group B.C. Research Council, 1952-60; vis. prof. Rockefeller Inst., N.Y.C., 1958—; prof. co-dir. Inst. Enzyme Research, U. Wis., Madison, 1960-70, prof. dept. biochemistry, 1962-70, Conrad A. Elvehjem prof. life scis., 1964-70; Alfred P. Sloan prof. biology and chemistry MIT, Cambridge, 1970—; vis. prof. Stanford U., 1964; mem. adv. bd. Biopolymers. Author: Some Recent Developments in the Chemistry of Phosphate Esters of Biological Interests, 1961; Mem. editorial bd.: Jour. Am. Chem. Soc, 1963—. Recipient Merck award Chem. Inst. Can., 1958, Gold medal Profl. Inst. Pub. Service Can., 1960, Dannie-Heinneman Preiz Göttingen, Germany, 1967, Remsen award Johns Hopkins U., 1968, Am. Chem. Soc. award for creative work in synthetic organic chemistry, 1968, Louisa Gross Horwitz prize, 1968, Lasker Found. award for basic med. research, 1968, Nobel prize in medicine, 1968; elected to Deutsche Akademie der Naturforscher Leopoldina HalleSaale, Germany, 1968; Overseas fellow Churchill Coll., Cambridge, Eng., 1967. Fellow Chem. Inst. Can., Am. Acad. Arts and Scis.; mem. Nat. Acad. Sci. Research and numerous publs. on chem. methods for synthesis of nucleotides, coenzymes and nucleic acids; elucidation on the genetic code, lab. synthesis of genes, biol. membrane, light-transducing pigments. Subspecialties: Organic chemistry; Biochemistry (biology). Office: Dept Biology and Chemistry MIT Cambridge MA 02139

KIANG, YUN-TZU, genetics educator; b. Taiwan, Feb. 1, 1932; m. Ming, May 12, 1957; children: Wailey, Waisen, Phine. B.S., Taiwan Normal U., 1956; M.S., Ohio State U., 1962; Ph.D., U. Calif.-Berkeley, 1970. Asst. prof. genetics U. N.H., Durham, 1970-75, assoc. prof., 1975-83, prof., 1983—, chmn. genetics program, 1980-83, summer faculty fellow, 1971-72. Contbr. articles to profl. jours., also monograph on plant isozymes. Central Univ. Research Funds grantee, 1981-82; N.H. Hwy. Dept. grantee, 1972-74; U.S. Dept. Agr. grantee, 1982—. Mem. Genetics Soc. Am., Am. Soc. Naturalists, Soc. Study of Evolution, Am. Soc. Agronomy. Current Work: Researcher in population, ecological and evolutionary genetics; plant breeding and plant tissue culture. Subspecialties: Genetics and genetic engineering (biology); Evolutionary biology. Office: Dept Plant Sci Univ NH Durham NH 03824

KICLITER, ERNEST EARL, JR., neuroanatomist, educator; b. Ft. Pierce, Fla.; s. Ernest Earl and Betty Lloyd (Winn) K.; m. Veronica Pelaez Herran, Oct. 7, 1967 (div. 1978). A.B. in Psychology, U. Fla., 1968; Ph.D. in Anatomy, SUNY Upstate Med. Ctr., Syracuse, 1973. Predoctoral fellow anatomy SUNY Upstate Med. Ctr., 1969-72; postdoctoral fellow neurosurgery U. Va., Charlottesville, 1972-74; asst. prof. neuroanatomy U. Ill., Urbana, 1974-77; assoc. prof. anatomy U. P.R., San Juan, 1977-84, prof. anatomy, 1984—. Contbr. articles to profl. jours. Fellow Ford Found., 1967-68; Fellow NIH, 1968-74; grantee NIH, 1976—; Nat. Acad. Scis., 1976—. Mem. Am. Assn. Anatomists, AAAS, Assn. Research in Vision and Ophthalmology, Soc. Neurosci (pres. P.R. chpt. 1979-80), Sigma Xi. Clubs: Garcia y Vega (St. Louis); Cajal, J.B. Johnston. Current Work: Neuroanatomy of visual systems, color vision, comparative neuroanatomy. Subspecialties: Comparative neurobiology; Psychophysics. Home: Avenida Wilson 1367 Apt 203 Condado PR 00907 Office: Blvd del Valle 201 San Juan PR 00901

KIECKHEFER, ROBERT WILLIAM, research entomologist; b. Milw., Mar. 13, 1933; s. William Otto and Dorothea Evelyn (Tews) K.; m. Janice Arlene Kadlec, June 7, 1969; children—Karla J., Jon. R., Joel F. B.S., U. of Wis., 1955, Ph.D., 1962; M.S., U. of Minn., 1958. Research entomologist Agrl. Research Service, U.S. Dept. of Agrl., Brookings, S.D., 1963—. Contbr. articles to prof. jours. Mem. Entomological Soc. of Am., Ecological Soc. of Am., Internat. Org. for Biological Control. Unitarian. Current work: Biology, ecology of cereal insects; biological control of cereal insects; insect transmission of plant virues of cereal crops. Subspecialties: Integrated pest management; Ecology (biology). Home: RR3 Sunnyview Brookings SD 57006 Office: Northern Grain Insects Research Lab RR3 Brookings SD 57006

KIEFHABER, NIKOLAUS JOSEF, software engineer, researcher; b. Munich, W. Ger., July 29, 1954; came to U.S., 1977; s. Robert Paul and Gisela (Heidtmann) K.; m. Sarah Hildebrandt, Oct. 18, 1980. Vordiplom Physics, U. Regensburg, Ger., 1977; M.S. in Computer Sci, U. Colo., 1980. Mem. sr. tech. staff Precision Visuals Inc., Boulder, Colo., 1980-82, dir. research, 1982—. Mem. Assn. for Computing Machinery. Current Work: Graphics standards, graphics software, graphics hardware. Subspecialties: Graphics, image processing, and pattern recognition; Software engineering. Office: Precision Visuals Inc 6260 Lookout Rd Boulder CO 80301

KIEHL, RICHARD ARTHUR, electrical engineer, physicist; b. Akron, Ohio, Feb. 14, 1948; s. Arthur Harold and Katherine Mary (Kehl) K. B.S.E.E., Purdue U., 1970, M.S.E.E. 1970, Ph.D., 1974. Mem. tech. staff Sandia Nat. Labs., Albuquerque, 1974-80, AT&T Bell Labs., Murray Hill, N.J., 1980—. Author Numerous tech. presentations. Mem. IEEE (chmn. Albuquerque sect. 1979-80), Sigma Xi, Sigma Pi Sigma. Current work: Research on high-speed electronic and optoelectronic devices, especially in group III-V semiconductors. Subspecialties: Semiconductors; Condensed matter physics. Office: AT&T Bell Labs 600 Mountain Ave Murray Hill NJ 07974

KIELMEYER, WILLIAM HENRY, ceramic engineer; b. Columbus, Ohio, Jan. 6, 1943; s. Peter Henry and Dorothy Ruth (Potts) K.; m. Marjorie Elaine Kaufman, Oct. 5, 1968; children—Cheryl Ann, Thomas Wayne. B. Ceramic Engring., Ohio State U., 1966; M.S. in Ceramic Engring., 1973. Project engr. Owens-Corning Fiberglass, Granville, Ohio, 1968-72; research engr. Johns-Manville Corp., Toledo, 1973-78; sr. research engr. Manville Corp., Denver, 1978—. Patentee in field, group leader and co-inventor silica fiber for space shuttle exterior insulation. Mem. Am. Ceramic Soc. Republican. Lutheran. Current work: Development of next-generation insulations and insulation systems. Subspecialties: Ceramic engineering; Ceramics. Home: 3374 W Chenango Ave Englewood CO 80110 Office: Manville Research and Devel 10100 W Ute Ave Littleton CO 80127

KIER-SCHROEDER, ANN B., comparative pathologist; b. Littlefield, Tex., June 26, 1949; d. Robert Merlin and Martha Ann (Bond) Yarbrough; m. Friedhelm Schroeder, Dec. 9, 1978. B.A., U. Tex., 1971; B.S., Tex. A&M U., 1973, D.V.M., 1974; Ph.D., U. Mo.-Columbia, 1979. Diplomate: Am. Coll. Lab. Animal Medicine. NIH postdoctoral fellow in lab. animal medicine and comparative pathology U. Mo.-Columbia, 1976-79, asst. prof. vet. pathology, 1979-84, assoc. prof. vet. pathology and vet. microbiology, 1984—; supr. histopathology lab., 1980—. Author book chpts., Contbr. articles to profl. jours. Mem. Am. Assn. Pathologists, Am. Coll. Lab. Animal Medicine, Am. Assn. Lab. Animal Sci., AVMA, Reticuloendothelial Soc., Sigma Xi, Phi Zeta, Mortar Board. Current Work: Chemotaxis (neutrophils and macrophages), chemiluminescence, immunopathology, diagnostic laboratory animal pathology, animal models for human health related diseases. Subspecialties: Pathology (veterinary medicine); Immunology (medicine). Home: RD 2 Carter School Rd Columbia MO 65201 Office: Dept Vet Pathology VMDL U Mo Columbia MO 65211

KIERSZENBAUM, FELIPE, microbiologist, educator; b. Cordoba, Argentina, Jan. 1, 1940; s. Nachman and Ester (Niestenpower) K.; children: Martin, Marina. Pharmacist U. Buenos Aires, Argentina, 1961, Biochemist, 1963, Ph.D., 1966, Asst. prof., 1971-74; sr. research scientist Wellcome Research Labs., Eng., 1974-75; research staff Yale U. Sch. Medicine, New Haven, 1975-77; assoc. prof. Mich. State U., East Lansing, 1977-82, prof. microbiology and pub. health, 1982—. Contbr. articles to profl. jours. Mem. Am. Assn. Immunologists, Am. Soc. Microbiology, Reticuloendothelial Soc., AAAS, Soc. Protozoologists, Am. Soc. Tropical Medicine and Hygiene, Am. Soc. Parasitologists. Current Work: The mechanisms of host defense against infection with Trypanosoma cruzi; cellular immunology. Subspecialties: Immunology (medicine); Parasitology. Office: Mich State U Dept Microbiology East Lansing MI 48824

KIESLER, CHARLES ADOLPHUS, psychologist, university administrator; b. St. Louis, Aug. 14, 1934; divorced; children: Tina, Thomas, Eric, Kevin. B.A., Mich. State U., 1958, M.A., 1960; Ph.D. (NIMH fellow), Stanford U., 1963. Asst. prof. psychology Ohio State U., Columbus, 1963-64; asst. prof. psychology Yale U., New Haven, 1964-66, asso. prof., 1966-70; prof., chmn. psychology U. Kans., Lawrence, 1970-75; exec. officer Am. Psychol. Assn., Washington, 1975-79; Walter Van Dyke Bingham prof. psychology Carnegie Mellon U., Pitts., 1979-85, head psychology, 1980-82, acting dean, 1981-82, dean Coll. Humanities and Social Scis., 1983-85; provost Vanderbilt U., Nashville, 1985—. Author: (with B.E. Collins and N. Miller) Attitude Change: A Critical Analysis of Theoretical Approaches, 1969, (with S.B. Kiesler) Conformity, 1969, The Psychology of Commitment: Experiments Linking Behavior to Belief, 1971, (with N. Cummings and G. Vanden Bos) Psychology and National Health Insurance: A Sourcebook, 1979. Served with Security Service USAF, 1952-56. Fellow Am. Psychol. Assn., AAAS; mem. AAUP, Eastern Psychol. Assn., Soc. Exptl. Social Psychology, Midwestern Psychol. Assn., Assn. for Advancement of Psychology, Psychonomic Soc., Council Applied Social Research, Sigma Xi, Psi Chi, Phi Kappa Phi. Current Work: Mental health policy; systems research related to health and mental health. Subspecialties: Social psychology; Cognition. Office: Office of Provost Vanderbilt U Nashville TN 37240

KIESLING, RICHARD LORIN, plant pathologist, educator; b. Rockford, Ill., Nov. 20, 1922; s. Earl Leon and Edith Eugenia (Gorball) K.; m. Frances Mae Groth, June 22, 1947; children: Faye, Gregory, Frances, Richard. B.Sc., U. Wis., 1949, M.S., 1951, Ph.D., 1952. Asst. prof. Mich. State U., 1952-57, assoc. prof., 1957-60; prof. plant pathology, chmn. dept. plant pathology N.D. State U., 1960—. Served with Signal Corps U.S. Army, 1942-46, ETO. Mem. Am. Phytopath. Soc., Am. Inst. Biol. Scis., Sigma Xi. Methodist. Lodge: Lions. Current Work: Research on genetics of barley and barley smut interactions; genetics of virulence and aggressiveness in Ustilago hordei; genetics of resistance in barley to Ustilago hordei, Ustilago nigra, and Ustilago nuda. Subspecialties: Plant pathology; Genetics and genetic engineering (agriculture). Office: Dept Plant Pathology ND State U PO Box 5012 Fargo ND 58105

KIIL, DAVE AIN, Canadian government forestry official; b. Lumanda, Estonia, May 7, 1936; came to Can., 1951, naturalized, 1958; s. Edmund and Leena K.; m. Betty Ann Moulton, Mar. 3, 1962; children—Glenn, Monica, Lisa, Diana. B.Sci. Forestry, U. Toronto, 1960; M.Sc., U. Mont., 1967. Fire research officer Can. Dept. Forestry, Ottawa, Calgary, 1960-67; fire researcher Can. Dept. Environment, Edmonton, Alta., 1967-72, fire protection advisor, Ottawa, Ont., 1972-75, program mgr., Edmonton, 1975-80; regional dir. Can. Forestry Service, Edmonton, 1981—. Contbr. research articles to profl. jours. Mem. Can. Inst. Forestry (chmn. Rocky Mountain sect. 1970-71), Alta. Forestry Assn. (pres. 1984-85), Xi Sigma Pi. Lutheran. Current work: Research on forest fire behavior and management practices, research management. Office: Canadian Forestry Service 5320 122d St Edmonton AB T6H 3S5 Canada

KIKKAWA, YUTAKA, pathologist, educator; b. Oita City, Japan, Jan. 30, 1932; came to U.S., 1958; s. Watari and Chika (Kuroda) K.; m. Helen Mary Zak, June 27, 1964; children—Rita Marie, Denise, Sumiko, James Makoto, Carol Jean. B.S., U. Tokyo, 1953, M.D., 1957. Instr. Albert Einstein Coll., N.Y.C., 1963-65, asst. prof., 1965-70, assoc. prof., 1970-74, prof., 1974-76; prof., chmn. dept. pathology, N.Y. Med. Coll., Valhalla, 1976—; mem. adv. council Nat. Heart, Lung and Blood Inst., NIH, Bethesda, Md., 1972-76, pathology A study sect., 1980-84. Contbr. numerous articles to profl. jours. Fulbright Commn. scholar, 1958; NIH grantee, 1965-84. Mem. Japanese Med. Soc. U.S.A. (pres. 1983), Fedn. Am. Socs. for Exptl. Biology, Am. Thoracic Soc., Internat. Acad. Pathology, Harvey Soc. Club: Scarsdale Golf (Hartsdale, N.Y.). Current work: Pulmonary pathobiology. Subspecialties: Cell biology; Pathology (medicine). Home: 78 Greenacres Ave Scarsdale NY 19583 Office: New York Med Coll Dept Pathology Basic Sci Bldg Valhalla NY 19595

KIKUCHI, CHIHIRO, nuclear engineer, educator; b. Seattle, Sept. 26, 1914; s. Naoki and Mitsue (Ichinomiya) K.; m. Grace Keiko Fujii, June 9, 1946; children: Naomi, Carl, Gary. B.S. in Physics, U. Wash., 1939, Ph.D., 1944; M.A., U. Cin., 1943. Mem. faculty Haverford (Pa.) Coll., 1943-44, Mich. State U., East Lansing, 1944-53; assoc. prof. physics U.S. Naval Research Lab., Washington, 1953-55; mem. faculty dept. nuclear engring. U. Mich., Ann Arbor, 1955—, prof. nuclear engring., 1982—; tech. specialist IAEA, 1964, Brookhaven Nat. Lab., 1951-52; vis. prof. Kyoto (Japan) U., 1976-77; cons., Sao Paulo, Brazil, 1976-77. Mem. Am. Phys. Soc., Am. Nuclear Soc. Democrat. Congregationalist. Current work: Nuclear power and energy alternatives. Subspecialties: Nuclear fission; Magnetic physics. Office: Dept Nuclear Engrin U Mich Ann Arbor MI 48109

KILBOURNE, EDWIN DENNIS, virologist, educator; b. Buffalo, July 10, 1920; s. Edwin I. and Elizabeth (Alward) K.; m. Joy Schmid, Dec. 20, 1952; children: Edwin Michael, Richard Schmid, Christopher Norton, Paul Alward. A.B., Cornell U., 1942, M.D., 1944. Asst. Rockefeller Inst., 1948-51; mem. faculty Tulane U., 1951-55; mem. faculty Cornell U. Med. Coll., N.Y.C., 1955-68, prof. pub. health, dir. div. virus research, 1961-68; prof., chmn. dept. microbiology Mt. Sinai Sch. Medicine, City U. New York, 1968—. Author: (with Wilson G. Smillie) Human Ecology and Public Health, 4th edit, 1968; Editor: The Influenza Viruses and Influenza, 1975. Mem. Health Research Council N.Y.C., 1968-75. Recipient R.E. Dyer Lectureship award NIH, 1973, Borden award Assn. Am. Med. Colls., 1974, Dowling Lectureship award, 1976, Thomas Francis Lectureship award, 1976; Harvey Lectureship award, 1978; award of distinction Cornell U. Med. Alumni Assn., 1979; academy medal N.Y. Acad. Medicine. Fellow N.Y. Acad. Scis.; mem. Nat. Acad. Sci., Harvey Soc., So. Soc. Clin. Research, Central Soc. Clin. Research (emeritus), AAAS, Am. Assn. Immunologists, Am. Acad. Microbiology, Soc. Exptl. Biology and Medicine, Am. Soc. Clin. Investigation (emeritus), N.Y. Acad. Medicine, Am. Pub. Health Assn., Assn. Am. Physicians, Am. Soc. Microbiology, Infectious Diseases Soc. Am. Research and publs. on hormonal influences, genetic studies and exptl. transmission of viruses, recombinant virus vaccines especially influenza. Current Work: Lifetime research and specialization in infectious diseases, including the clinical epidemiological and molecular biological aspects of human viruses, especially influenza; viral genetics, vaccine development. Subspecialties: Microbiology (medicine); Virology (medicine). Home: 446 Hillcrest Rd Ridgewood NJ 07450 Office: City U New York Mt Sinai Sch Medicine Dept Microbiology Fifth Ave at 100th St New York NY 10029

KILBY, JACK ST. CLAIR, inventor; b. Jefferson City, Mo., Nov. 8, 1923; s. Hubert St. Clair and Vina (Freitag) K.; m. Barbara Annegers, June 27, 1948; children: Ann, Janet Lee. B.S. in Elec. Engring, U. Ill., 1947; M.S., U. Wis., 1950. Program mgr. Globe-Union, Inc., Milw., 1948-58; asst. v.p. Tex. Instruments, Inc., Dallas, 1958-70; self-employed inventor, Dallas, 1970—; disting. prof. elec. engring. Tex. A & M U., 1978—, inventor monolithic integrated circuit, others; cons. to govt. and industry. Served with AUS, 1943-45. Recipient Nat. Medal Sci., 1969; Ballentine medal Franklin Inst., 1967; Distinguished Alumni award U. Ill., 1974; named to Holley medal ASME, 1982, Nat. Inventors Hall of Fame U.S. Patent Office, 1981. Fellow IEEE (Sarnoff medal 1966, Brunetti award 1978); mem. Nat. Acad. Engring. (Zworkin medal 1975). Current Work: Integrated circuit technology. Subspecialty: Microchip technology (engineering). Home: 7723 Midbury St Dallas TX 75230 Office: 5924 Royal Ln Suite 150 Dallas TX 75230

KILHAM, PETER, limnologist, biology educator; b. Salisburg, Wiltshire, Eng., June 26, 1943; came to U.S., 1944; s. Lawrence and Mary Jane (Kaufholz) K.; m. Susan Kae Soltau, Sept. 4, 1967. A.B., Dartmouth Coll., 1965; Ph.D., Duke U., 1972. Guest investigator, Woods Hole Oceanographic Inst., Mass., 1972; asst. prof. biology U. Mich., Ann Arbor, 1972-77, assoc. prof., 1977-85, prof., 1985—. Contbr. chpts. to books and articles to profl. jours. NASA trainee, 1965-68; NSF fellow, 1972; NSF grantee, 1974—, others. Mem. Am. Soc. Limnology and Oceanography, Ecol. Soc. Am., AAAS, Societas Internationalis Limnologiae, Internat. Assn. Great Lakes Research. Democrat. Current Work: The biogeochemistry of African lakes and rivers, the physiological ecology of freshwater planktonic diatoms, the neutralization of acid precipitation by aquatic ecosystmes, the limnology of the Great Lakes of North America and similar lakes in other parts of the world. Subspecialty: Limnology. Office: Div Biol Scis U Mich Ann Arbor MI 48109

KILLE, JOHN WILLIAM, toxicologist; b. Tampa, Fla., June 17, 1943; s. John William and Myrtle (Sellers) K.; m. Elaine Martha Anderson, Nov. 30, 1974; children—Amy Catherine, Lindsey Clare, Thomas Andrew. A.B., Lafayette Coll., 1965; M.S., Villanova U., 1968; Ph.D., U. Va., 1972. Lalor Found. fellow Cambridge U., Eng., 1972-73; lectr., research assoc. Northwestern U., Evanston, Ill., 1974-78; scientist Ortho Pharm. Corp., Raritan, N.J., 1978-82, group leader, 1982—; adviser, reviewer Office of Tech. Assessment, U.S. Congress, 1984—. Contbr. articles to profl. jours. Election judge Democratic Party, Evanston, Ill., 1976; vol. worker United Way, Raritan, 1978; chmn. Family Life Edn. Com., Bloomsbury, N.J., 1982-83. Mem. Teratology Soc., Soc. for Study of Reprodn., Genetic Toxicology Assn., Behavioral Teratology Soc., Mid-Atlantic Reprodn. and Teratology Assn., Sigma Xi. Current work: Design, conduct, manage and report scientific studies to determine the potential for general, reproductive, or genetic toxicity of experimental pharmaceutical compounds. Subspecialties: Teratology; Toxicology (medicine). Office: Ortho Pharmaceutical Corp Route 202 Raritan NJ 08869

KILLIAN, BARBARA GERMAIN, aeronautical engineer; b. San Diego, Nov. 25, 1935; d. John Koschka and Martha (Stachwick) K.; m. W. Patrick Crowley, Aug. 11, 1957; m. Lawrence Seymour Germain, June 5, 1975. B.A., San Diego State U., 1957; postgrad., Stanford U., 1960-61, U. Calif.-Berkeley, 1963-64;

M.H. U. N.Mex., 1983. Mem. staff Lawrence Livermore (Calif.) Lab., 1958-71, group leader, 1971-76; mem. staff Los Alamos Nat. Lab., N.Mex., 1976-79, asst. div. leader, 1979-84; mem. staff Calif. Research & Tech., Inc., 1985—; cons. Sci. Applications, Inc., La Jolla, Calif., 1976-80. Contbr. articles to profl. jours. Dept. of Energy rep. to UN Conf. of Com. on Disarmament, 1978, 79. Mem. Seismol. Soc. Am., Am. Geophys. Union, Am. Nuclear Soc. (sec.-treas. div. alternative energy techs. 1975-76, vice chmn. 1976-77, chmn. 1977-78). Current Work: Shock wave and stress wave propagation-numerical modeling experimental and theoretical work with shock waves and shock tubes. Subspecialties: Theoretical computer science; Aeronautical engineering. Home: PO Box 9232 ATO Albuquerque NM 87119 Office: Calif Research and Tech Inc 1900 Randolph Rd SE Suite B Albuquerque NM 87106

KILLINGER, DENNIS KARL, research physicist; b. Boone, Iowa, Sept. 23, 1945; s. Karl H. and Evelyn (Johnson) K.; m. Rose L. Egger, June 15, 1969; children: Laura, Robert. B.A., U. Iowa, 1967; M.A., DePauw U., 1969; Ph.D. in Physics, U. Mich., 1978. Research physicist Naval Avionics Facility, Indpls., 1968-74; research assoc. physics U. Mich., 1974-78; quantum electronics staff and program mgr. laser remote sensing Lincoln Lab., M.I.T., 1979—; Conf. chmn. Workshop on Optical and Laser Remote Sensing, Monterey, 1982; program chmn. Optical Soc. Am. Topical Meeting on Remote Probing of the Atmosphere, Lake Tahoe, 1983. Contbr. articles to profl. jours. Mem. Am. Phys. Soc., Optical Soc. Am. Current Work: Physics of new optical and laser sources, quantum electronics and nonlinear optical techniques with applications toward laser remote sensing. Subspecialty: Remote sensing (atmospheric science). Office: MIT Lincoln Lab Lexington MA 02173

KILMAN, JAMES WILLIAM, surgeon, educator; b. Terre Haute, Ind., Jan. 22, 1931; s. Arthur and Irene (Piker) K.; m. Priscilla Margaret Jackson, June 20, 1968; children: James William, Julia Anne, Jennifer Irene. B.S., Ind. State U., 1956; M.D., Ind. U., 1960. Intern Ind.U. Med. Ctr., Indpls., 1960-61; resident surgery Ind.U. Med. Center, 1961-66, asst. prof., 1966-69, assoc. prof., 1969-73; prof. surgery Ohio State U. Coll. Medicine, 1973-; chmn. dept. thoracic surgery Children's Hosp.; attending surgeon Univ. Hosp., Columbus, Ohio; attending staff Children's Hosp., Columbus, pres. staff, 1978; attending staff Grant Hosp., Riverside Hosp.; cons. surgeon VA Hosp., Dayton; pres. Columbus Acad. Medicine, 1977. Trustee Central Ohio Heart Assn., Acad. Medicine Edn. Found., Children's Hosp., 1978—. Served with USNR, 1951-55. USPHS Cardiovascular fellow, 1963-64. Mem. Columbus Surg. Soc. (pres. 1973-74), Columbus Acad. Medicine (council 1971-73), Am. Surg. Assn., Soc. U. Surgeons, Am. Assn. Thoracic Surgery, Am., Central, Western surg. assns., Soc. Vascular Surgery, Internat. Cardiovascular Soc., Internat. Soc. Surgeons, Chest Club, Cardiovascular Surgery Club, Sigma Xi, Alpha Omega Alpha. Research, articles infant cardiopulmonary bypass and surgery for congenital heart lesions. Current Work: Clinical cardiac surgery for adults and children. Research in vascular heart disease, pericardial disease and congenital heart anomalies. Subspecialty: Cardiac surgery. Home: 4231 Jackson Pike Grove City OH 43123 Office: 410 W 10th Ave Columbus OH 43210

KILMANN, RALPH HERMAN, educator; b. N.Y.C., Oct. 5, 1946; s. Martin H. and Lilli (Loeb) K.; m. Audrey Ann Sabol, July 7, 1977; children: Christopher Martin, Catherine Mary. B.S., Carnegie-Mellon U., 1970, M.S., 1970; C.Phil., UCLA, 1971, Ph.D., 1972. Research asst. Carnegie-Mellon U., 1969-70; teaching asso. UCLA, 1970-72; instr. U. Pitts., 1972, asst. prof., 1972-75, assoc. prof., 1975-79, prof. bus. adminstrn., 1979—; pres. Orgnl. Design Cons., Inc., Pitts., 1975—; coordinator Orgnl. Studies Group, U. Pitts., 1981-84, dir. Program Corporate Culture, 1983—. Author: Social Systems Design, 1977; (with I. I. Mitroff) Methodological Approaches, 1978; Beyond the Quick Fix, 1984; (with I.I. Mitroff) Corporate Tragedies, 1984; (with M.J. Saxton and R. Serpa) Gaining Control of the Corporate Culture, 1985. Recipient 1st Prize Inst. Mgmt. Sci., 1976. Mem. Acad. Mgmt., Inst. Mgmt. Sci., Am. Psychol. Assn. Developer computer-based design MAPS Design Tech., 1975; co-developer personality assessment: The Thomas-Kilmann Conflict Mode Instrument, 1974; Kilmann-Saxton Culture-Gap Survey, 1983. Current Work: Developing social sci. tech. to define/solve complex orgnl. problems. Subspecialties: Organizational sciences; Social psychology. Home: 110 Weir Dr Pittsburgh PA 15215 Office: Univ Pitts Grad Sch Bus Pittsburgh PA 15260

KILNER, SUZANNE MIILLER, environmental planner; b. Evanston, Ill., Dec. 10, 1951; d. Walter Thomas and Suzanne Wiley (Sutherland) Miiller; m. John Frederic Kilner, Dec. 27, 1975; 1 child, Elizabeth Laura. B.A., Duke U., 1973; M. in Forest Sci., Yale U., 1975. Prin. planner Mass. Dept. Environ. Mgmt., Boston, 1976-78; water resource planner Mass. Dept. Environ. Quality Engring., Boston, 1978-82; cons. Nat. Environment Secretariat, Nairobi, Kenya, 1981; project planner Metcalf & Eddy, Inc., Boston, 1982-83; aide to commr. Dept. Pub. Works, Lexington, Ky., 1983—. Contbr. articles to profl. jours. Mem. Cambridge Conservation Commn., Mass., 1979-80; treas. United Presbyterian Ch., Cambridge, 1980-83; advisor Hazardous Materials Task Force, Lexington, 1984; city rep. Citizen's Water Task Force, Frankfort, Ky., 1984-85. Mem. Am. Planning Assn. (cert.), Ecol. Soc. Am. (cert.), Chi Alpha (advisor Wilmore chpt. 1983—). Club: Toastmasters (Lexington). Current work: Water resources management, particularly surface and groundwater drinking supplies, wastewater treatment and watershed/aquifer protection. Subspecialties: Resource management; Water supply and wastewater treatment. Home: 451 Retrac Rd Lexington KY 40503 Office: Dept Pub Works 200 E Main St Lexington KY 40507

KIM, BYUNG SUK, microbiology educator; b. Yosu, Korea, Mar. 20, 1942; s. Young Taik and Gwee Yup Jung; m. Oak Cho Kim, Apr. 19, 1967; children: Peggy, Charles. B.S., Seoul Nat. U., 1967; M.S., Va. State U., 1969; Ph.D., U. Ill., 1973. Sr. research technologist U. Chgo., 1969-70; sr. staff assoc. Inst. Cancer Research, Columbia U., 1973-74; research asst. prof. U. Chgo., 1974-76; asst. prof. Northwestern U., Chgo., 1976-81, assoc. prof., 1981—; mem. study sect. NIH, 1985—. Contbr. articles to profl. jours. Mem. Am. Soc. Microbiology, Am. Assn. Immunologists. Current Work: Regulation of antibody synthesis and tumor immunity. Subspecialties: Immunobiology and immunology; Cellular engineering. Home: 421 Hibbard Rd Wilmette IL 60091 Office: 303 E Chicago Ave Chicago IL 60611

KIM, CHARLES WESLEY, medicine and microbiology educator, researcher; b. Nashville, Tenn., Mar. 20, 1926; s. Herbert Hyungsik and Kyung Sook (Lee) K.; m. Soo J. Kim, June 9, 1956; 1 child, Charles W. Jr. Student, U. Mich., 1944-46; B.A., U. Calif.-Berkeley, 1948; postgrad. UCLA, 1948-49; Ph.D., U. N.C., 1956. Asst. prof. N.Y. Med. Coll., N.Y.C., 1956-64; assoc. scientist Brookhaven Nat. Lab., Upton, N.Y., 1965-68, scientist, 1968-70; assoc. vice provost SUNY-StonyBrook, 1974-83, microbiology assoc. prof., 1970—, assoc. prof. medicine, 1984—; vis. prof. Inst. Pathology, Bern, Switzerland, 1977, Chonnam U. Med. Sch., Korea, 1984, Downstate Med. Ctr., Bklyn., 1984. Author: Microbiology Rev., 1962, 65, 68, 70, 73, 77, 80, 84; Basis Sciences, 1962, 64, 68, 72, 74, 81; (with others) Trichinella & Trichinosis, 1983. Editor: Trichinellosis, 1974, 78, 81, 85. Program chmn. Friends of Sunwood, StonyBrook, 1973-79, Suffolk Symphonic Soc., N.Y., 1975-77; devel. com. Mus. at StonyBrook, 1983—. Fellow La. State U. Med. Sch., 1958, USPHS 1964-65. Fellow Royal Soc. Tropical Medicine and Hygiene; mem. Internat. Commn. Trichinellosis (exec. com. v.p. 1984—), N.Y. Soc. Tropical Medicine (v.p. 1973-74), Northeastern Assn. Grad. Schs., (exec. com. 1981-83), Am. Assn. Immunologists, AAAS, Am. Inst. Biol. Scis., Am. Soc. Microbiologists, Am. Soc. Parasitology, Am. Soc. Tropical Medicine and Hygiene. Democrat. Presbyterian. Current work: Relationship between cholangiocarcinoma and clonorchiasis; chemotherapy of cryptosporidiosis; immune mechanism of Trichinella spirals. Subspecialties: Parasitology; Microbiology (medicine). Office: SUNY Health Scis Ctr StonyBrook NY 11794

KIM, GEUNG-HO, statistician; b. Seoul, South Korea, July 25, 1945; came to U.S., 1969, naturalized, 1980; s. Ki-duk and Duk-bo (Lim) K.; m. Jae Oak Lee, Aug. 19, 1972; children: Jeannie, Benjamin. B.A. in Bus. Administrn, Seoul Nat. U., 1967; M.S. in Stats, Iowa State U., 1971, Ph.D., 1978. Software cons. Iowa State U., Ames, 1971-77, research asst., 1977-78; asst. prof. stats. SUNY, Amherst, 1978-80; statistician U.S. Dept. Commerce, Highlands, N.J., 1980—, cons. EEO matters, 1981—. Reviewer: Math Revs, 1980—; contbr. articles to profl. jours. Fellow Royal Statis. Soc.; mem. Inst. Math. Stats., Am. Statis. Assn. Current Work: Data analysis and model building in terms of multivariate statistical and/or stochastic process techniques pertinent to the marine environmental monitoring and related problems. Subspecialties: Statistics; Environmental engineering. Home: 120 Riveredge Rd Tinton Falls NJ 07724 Office: US Department Commerce Sandy Hook Laboratory Highlands NJ 07732

KIM, HAE SOO, material scientist; b. Chunnam, Kwang Ju, Korea, Oct. 15, 1940; came to U.S., 1967; m. Youn Sook Kim, Feb. 15, 1968; children—Terry, Eugene. B.S., Seoul Nat. U., 1964; M.S., Case Western Res. U., 1969, Ph.D., 1972. Chief petrographic lab. Master Builders Co., Cleve., 1972-75; sr. scientist Tech. Ctr., Owens-Corning Fiberglas, Granville, Ohio, 1975—. Served to 2d lt. Korean Mil., 1964-66. Mem. Am. Ceramic Soc., ASTM, Korean Sci. and Tech. Soc. (U.S.), Korean Assn. Columbus (pres. 1984-85). Presbyterian. Current work: Material characterization by using x-ray diffraction, scanning electron microscopy and optical microscopy. Subspecialties: Ceramics; Mineralogy. Office: Tech Ctr Owens-Corning Fiberglas Granville OH 43023

KIM, HYUN YOUNG, veterinary pathologist; b. Seoul, Korea, Sept. 12, 1939; came to U.S., 1970, naturalized, 1976; s. Kyung S. and Yoon H. K.; m. Duck Jo Kim, Dec. 25, 1967; children: Daniel, Eugene. B.A., Korean Union Coll.; D.V.M., Seoul Nat. U., 1962, M.P.H., 1969; M.S., U. Ga., 1973; D.D., I.B.I.S., 1982. Lic. veterinarian, Pa., Mass. Asst. prof. Korean Union Coll., 1967-70; grad. research asst. U. Ga., 1971-72; research investigator U. Pa., 1973-74; vet. pathologist, head virology lab. Pa. State Vet. Labs., Harrisburg, 1974—. Elder Market Square Presbyterian Ch., Harrisburg; evangelism cons. Presbyn. Ch. U.S.A. UN/FAO fellow, 1969. Mem. AVMA, Pa. Vet. Med. Assn., Tissue Culture Assn., Am. Assn. Vet. Lab. Diagnosticians, Korean-Am. Vet. Soc. (pres.). Current Work: Development of laboratory diagnosis of viral infection in animals; immunofluorescent antibody tissue cultrue system, tissue culture viral-serum neutralization test or ELISA test are employed. Subspecialties: Pathology (veterinary medicine); Virology (veterinary medicine). Office: PO Box 1430 Harrisburg PA 17105

KIM, JAE HO, clin. investigator, radiologist; b. Daegu, Korea, Dec. 17, 1935; came to U.S., 1959, naturalized, 1971; s. Sa Yeup and Moo Sun (Yoo) K.; m. Johni Kim, Sept. 14, 1963; children: Alberta, Lena. M.D., Kungpook Nat. U., Daegu, 1959; Ph.D., U. Iowa, 1963. Intern Montefiore Hosp., N.Y.C., 1968-69; resident in radiology Meml. Hosp., N.Y.C., 1969-72; research assoc. Sloan-Kettering Inst. Cancer Research, 1963-66, assoc., 1966-68; asst. prof. radiology Cornell U. Med. Coll., N.Y.C., 1968-72, assoc. prof., 1974-80, prof., 1980—. Mem. AMA, Radiation Research Soc., Radiol. Soc. N.Am., Am. Radium Soc., Am. Assn. Cancer Research. Current Work: Radiobiology, radiotherapy, hyperthermia. Subspecialty: Cancer research (medicine). Office: 1275 York Ave R101 New York NY 10021

KIM, JIN KOO, engineer; b. Seoul, Republic of Korea, Feb. 17, 1950; came to U.S. 1974; naturalized 1980; s. Choo Pyung and Ok Ran (Lee) K.; m. Ihn Hee, Oct. 26, 1973; children—Karen, Alex. B.S.E.E., Seoul Nat. U., 1972; M.S.E.E., Rutgers U., 1976, Ph.D. in Elec. Engring., 1979. Mem. tech. staff RCA Labs., Princeton, N.J., 1979-81; sr. engr. RIXON Inc., Silver Spring, Md., 1981-83; sr. mem. tech. staff, GTE, Reston, Va., 1983-84; mgr. Gould AMI, Santa Clara, Calif., 1984—. Patentee in field. Served to 1st lt. Korean Army, 1972-74. Hamchoon scholar Seoul Nat. U., 1968. Mem. IEEE, Sigma Xi. Methodist. Current work: Research and development work on advanced computer-aided design for VISI applications. Subspecialties: Computer-aided design; Integrated circuits. Office: Gould AMI Semiconductors 3800 Homestead Rd Santa Clara CA 95051

KIM, JIN KYUNG, medical researcher; b. Seoul, Korea, Dec. 13, 1939; came to U.S., 1969, naturalized, 1979; d. Yong Jo and Chun Ki (Jung) K. B.S., Ewha Woman's U., Korea, 1961; M.S., Mich. State U., 1972; Ph.D., U. Colo., 1975. Research asst. Yonsei U., Seoul, 1961-69, Mich. State U., East Lansing, 1970-72; research assoc. U. Colo., Boulder, 1972-75; postdoctoral fellow Mayo Clinic, Rochester, Minn., 1975-78; assoc. prof. medicine U. Colo. Health Sci. Ctr., Denver, 1978—. Minn. Heart Assn. fellow, 1976-77. Mem. Am. Fedn. for Clin. Research, Internat. Soc. Nephrology, Am. Soc. for Nephrology, Sigma Xi, Rho Chi. Current Work: Cellular action of vasopressin using isolated nephrons from normal and diseased kidney. Subspecialties: Nephrology; Biochemistry (medicine). Home: 7032 E 4th Ave Denver CO 80220 Office: U Colo Health Sci Center 4200 E 9th Ave Denver CO 80262

KIM, JINCHOON, scientist; b. Korea, Mar. 5, 1943; came to U.S., 1966, naturalized, 1976; s. Kyu-Koo and Kyung Hee (Lee) K.; m. Yoonchung Park, Apr. 10, 1970; children—Nina, Margaret, Angela, B.S., Seoul Nat. U., Seoul, Korea, 1965; M.S., U. Calif.-Berkeley, 1968, Ph.D., 1971. Physicist, The Cyclotron Corp., Berkeley, 1971-74; research staff Oak Ridge Nat. Lab., 1974-80; staff scientist GA Tech. Inc., San Diego, 1980—. Patentee in field. Contbr. articles to prof. jours. Mem. IEEE, Am. Phys. Soc., Am. Vacuum Soc., Korean Nuclear Soc. Current work: Heating of thermonuclear fusion plasmas, particle accelerators. Subspecialties: Nuclear fusion; Plasma physics. Home: 12920 Sundance Ave San Diego CA 92129

KIM, JONATHAN JANG-HO, engineering company executive; b. Kwang Ju, Chollanamdo, Korea; June 11, 1932; came to U.S., 1959, naturalized, 1972; s. Jae Yi and Soon Sam (Cho) K.; m. Kunai Chu Kim, Oct. 28, 1958; 1 child, David. B.S. in Metall. Engring., Seoul Nat. U., Korea, 1955; M.S. in Metall. Engring., Carnegie-Mellon U., 1961; Ph.D., U. Okla., 1966. Process design engr. Lummus Co., Bloomfield., N.J., 1965-67; prin. engr., Kennectoo Corp. Lexington Devel. Ctr., Mass., 1967-80; mgr. process tech. Sohio Engring. Materials Co., Niagara Falls, N.Y., 1980—. Patentee in field. Mem. Am. Inst. Metall., Mining and Petroleum Engrs., Am. Ceramic Soc. Subspecialties: High-temperature materials; Materials processing. Home: 79 Brandywine Dr Williamsville NY 14221

KIM, KWANG-SEOK, physicist; b. Kyung Ju, Kyung-Puk, Korea; Dec. 3, 1944; s. Gu-Do and Mal-Sun (Ju) K.; m. Wi Lee, May 1, 1970; children—Nicholas, Susan. B.S., Kyung-Puk Nat. U., 1968; M.S., NYU, 1975, Ph.D., 1983. Sci. tchr. Kimcheon Girls High Sch., Korea, 1970-72; research asst. NYU, N.Y.C., 1975-82, research scientist, 1982-83; mem. tech. staff Bell Communication Research, West Long Branch, N.J., 1983-85; mem. tech. staff Bell Labs., Holmdel, N.J., 1985—. Mem. Am. Phys. Soc. (author bulls. ann. meetings 1980, 81, 82, 83). Current work: optical fiber communications. Subspecialties: Plasma physics; Fiber optics. Home: 8 Fowler Ct Middletown NJ 07701 Office: Bell Labs Crawford Corner Rd Holmdel NJ 07733

KIM, KYUNG-SUK, applied mechanics educator; b. Champaign, Ill.; b. Seoul, Korea, Mar. 29, 1952; s. Sang-Hyun and Ae-Da (Chung) K.; m. Saeja Oh Kim/Oh, Apr. 10, 1976; 1 child, Irene S. B.S., Seoul Nat. U., Korea, 1974, M.S., 1976; Ph.D., Brown U., 1980. Teaching asst. Seoul Nat. U., Korea, 1974-75; research asst. Brown U., Providence, 1976-79; research fellow Calif. Inst. Tech., Pasadena, 1979-80; mem. faculty U. Ill., Urbana, 1980—, asst. prof. dept. theoretical and applied mechanics, 1980—; cons. SRI, Palo Alto, Calif., 1979-80, Calif. Inst. Tech., Pasadena, 1983; vis. asst. prof. Brown U., Providence, 1982. Contbr. articles to various publs. Mem. AAUP, ASME (Melville medal 1981). Current work: Dynamic fracture, Dynamic plasticity, viscoelasticity, peeling, solid mechanics, applied optics. Subspecialties: Theoretical and applied mechanics; Solid mechanics. Home: 2108 Clover Ct West Champaign IL 61821 Office: U of Ill Dept Theoretical and Applied Mechanics 104 S Wright St Urbana IL 61801

KIM, S. PETER, psychiatry educator, researcher; b. Seoul, Korea, Oct. 8, 1939; s. Chongsoon and Soonbok (Rim) K.; m. O. Mary Lee, Mar. 30, 1963; children: John, Kathy. C.P.M., Seoul Nat. U., 1959; M.D., 1963, M.M.S., 1967. Cert. specialist Am. Bd. Psychiatry, Neurology. Instr. psychiatry NYU, 1972-74, clin. asst prof., 1974-76, asst. prof., 1976-79, assoc. prof., 1979—, assoc. attending physician, 1979—; dir. Ctr. Transcultural Devel. Study, N.Y. U.; cons. liaision in pediatrics N.Y. U.-Bellevue Med. Ctr. Author: Transcultural Adoption, 1981. Bd. dirs. Korean Community Service Met. N.Y., 1982—, Asian Am. Community Mental Health Ctr., N.Y., 1981—. Served with Army Republic of Korea, 1963-67. Fellow Am. Acad. Child Psychiatry (chmn. com. transcultural child), Am. Psychiat. Assn., Am Soc. Social Psychiatry; mem. AAAS, Soc. Adolesant Psychiatry. Roman Catholic. Current Work: Trans-/cross-cultural psychiatry, psychosomatic medicine and pediatrics, social psychiatry, stress and emotional-physical illness. Subspecialties: Psychopharmacology; Trans/cross-cultural medical psychology. Home: 7 Pine Terrace Bronxville NY 10708 Office: NYU Sch Medicine 550 First Ave NY NY 10016

KIM, SUNG-HOU, biophysical chemist, educator, molecular biologist; b. Taegu, Korea, Dec. 12, 1937; came to U.S., 1962; s. Yong-Tai and Ok-Kum (Choi) K.; m. Rosalind Yuan, July 27, 1968; children—Christopher Sang-Jai, Jonathan Sang-Joon. B.S., Seoul Nat. U., Korea, 1960, M.S., 1962; Ph.D., U. Pitts., 1966. Research assoc. MIT-Cambridge, 1966-70, sr. research scientist, 1970-72; asst. prof. biochemistry Duke U., Durham, N.C., 1972-73, assoc. prof., 1974-78; faculty sr. scientist Lawrence Berkeley Lab., Calif., 1979—; prof. biophys. chemistry U. Calif.-Berkeley, 1978—, Miller prof., 1983-84 mem. adv. group NIH, Bethesda, Md., 1976-80; co-chmn. Nucleic Acids Gordon Research Conf., 1983. Contbr. numerous articles to sci. jours.; mem. editorial bd. Jour. Biol. Chemistry, 1979-83, Nucleic Acid Research, 1983—. Bd. dirs. Korean Community Ctr. of the East Bay, Oakland, Calif., 1983—. Recipient Sidhu award Pitts. Diffraction Conf., 1970; fulbright Found. fellow, 1962; NIH Research Career Devel. awardee, 1976-79; Guggenheim fellow, 1985-86 Mem. Am. Soc. Biol. Chemists, Am. Chem. Soc., Am. Crystallographic Assn., Korean Scientists and Engrs. in Am., AAAS. Current work: Structure-function relationship of nucleic acids and proteins. Subspecialty: Biophysical chemistry. Home: 1100 Larch Ave Moraga CA 94556 Office: Dept Chemistry U Calif Berkeley CA 94720

KIM, YONGMIN, electrical engineering educator; b. Cheju, Korea, May 19, 1953, came to U.S., 1976; s. Ki-Whan and Yang-Whi (Kim) K.; m. Eunai Yoo, May 21, 1976; children—Janice, Christine. B.E.E., Seoul Nat. U., Korea, 1975; M.E.E., U. Wis.-Madison, 1979, Ph.D., 1982. Grad. asst. U. Wis.-Madison, 1976-82; asst. prof. U. Wash., Seattle, 1982—; cons. Empirical Research Group, Federal Way, Wash., 1984—; cons. D.P.M.S., Kirkland, Wash., 1984—; dir. Minicomputer Lab., Seattle, 1983—; cons. Physio Control, Redmond, Wash., 1984—, Samsung Electronics, Suwon, Rep. Korea, 1985—. Contbr. articles to profl. jours., chpts. in books. Recipient Career Devel. award Physio Control Corp., 1982; NIH grantee, 1984. Mem. IEEE, Assn. Computing Machinery, Tau Beta Pi. Presbyterian. Subspecialties: Computer engineering; Graphics, image processing, and pattern recognition. Home: 2828 NE 203rd St Seattle WA 98155 Office: U Wash Dept Elec Engring Seattle WA 98195

KIM, YOON BERM, immunologist, educator, cancer researcher; b. Sainchang, Soon Chun, Korea, Apr. 25, 1929; came to U.S., 1959, naturalized, 1975; s. Sang Sun and Yang Rang (Lee) K.; m. Soon Cha Kim, Feb. 23, 1959; children: John, Jean, Paul. M.D., Seoul (Korea) U., 1958; Ph.D., U. Minn., 1965. Intern Seoul Nat. U. Hosp., 1958-59; mem. faculty U. Minn. Sch. Medicine, Mpls., 1959-73, assoc. prof. microbiology, 1970-73; prof. immunology Cornell U. Grad. Sch. Med. Scis., N.Y.C., 1973 , chmn. immunology unit, 1980-82; mem., head Lab. Ontogeny of Immune System, Sloan-Kettering Inst. Cancer Research, Rye, N.Y., 1973 ; chmn. credentials review and fellowship subcom. Cornell U. Grad. Sch. Med. Sci., 1976-80; mem. sci. adv. com. Internat. Symposium Gnotobiology, Ulm, Ger. and Tokyo, 1977-81; mem. Lobund Adv. Bd., U. Notre Dame, Ind., 1977 . Contbr. numerous articles to profl. publs. Recipient Research Career Devel. award USPHS, 1968-73, grantee, 1960 ; Am. Cancer Soc. grantee, 1979 . Mem. Am. Assn. Immunologists, Am. Soc. Microbiology, Am. Assn. Pathologists, Assn. Gnotobiotics (bd. dirs. 1975-79, pres. 1979-80), Reticuloendothelial Soc., Internat. Soc. Dwvel. Comparative Immunology, Korean Med. Assn. Am. (sci. edn. com. 1975 , chmn. 1980), N.Y. Acad. Scis., AAAS. Harvey Soc., Sigma Xi. Current Work: Ontogeny and regulation of immune system including T/B lymphocytes, NK/K cells and monocytes/macrophages; immunochemistry and biology of bacterial toxins; gnotobiotics and host-parasite relationships. Subspecialties: Immunobiology and immunology; Cancer research (medicine). Office: Sloan-Kettering Inst Cancer Research 145 Boston Post Rd Rye NY 10580

KIM, YOUNG HWA, physicist, researcher; b. Seoul, Korea, May 8, 1940; came to U.S., 1970; s. Jin Hee and Yong Sook (Choi) K.; m. Myong Yon Park, Apr. 19, 1969; children: Grace Sung, Steven Sung, Julie. B.S., Korean Mil. Acad., Seoul, 1963, Seoul Nat. U., 1967; M.S. in Physics, U. Houston, 1971; Ph.D. in Physics, UCLA, 1980. Teaching fellow U. Houston, 1970-71; teaching assoc. UCLA, 1975-78, research asst., 1978-80; research assoc. U. Ill.-Urbana, 1980-81, vis. asst. prof., 1981-82; sr. physicist 3M Co Central Research Lab., St. Paul, 1982—. Contbg. author: Journal de physique, 1982, Macromolecules, 1983; contbr. articles to profl. jours. Served to capt. Korean Army, 1963-68. Mem. Am. Phys. Soc. Methodist. Current Work: Piezo- and pyroelectricity of polymers, electronic states of polymers, polymer diffusion, nematic polymers, organic conductors. Subspecialties: Condensed matter physics; Polymer physics. Home: 7465 Columbia Ct Woodbury MN 55125 Office: 3M Co Central Research Lab 208-1 3M Center Saint Paul MN 55144

KIM, YUNG DAI, senior scientist; b. Seoul, Korea, Mar. 24, 1936; came to U.S., 1957, naturalized, 1973; s. Ik Soo and Jung Hui (Juhn) K.; m. Young Sook, June 17, 1967; children: Jean, Sue. Ph.D., U. Minn., Mpls., 1968. Vis. scientist Kettering Lab., Yellow Springs, Ohio, 1968-69; NIH postdoctoral fellow Northwestern U., Evanston, Ill., 1969-71; NIH research fellow U. Pa., Phila., 1971-73; sr. scientist Worthington Biochem. Corp., Freehold, N.J., 1973-74, Abbott Labs., North Chicago, Ill., 1974—. Contbr. articles to profl. jours. Mem. Am. Assn. Immunologists, Am. Chem. Soc., Sigma Xi, Phi Lambda Upsilon. Patentee in field. Current Work: Immunochemistry, protein chemistry, enzymology, cancer diagnostics research, clin. diagnostic tests. Subspecialties: Immunology (medicine); Cancer research (medicine). Home: 75 N Rolling Ridge Lindenhurst IL 60046 Office: Abbott Labs D-90C North Chicago IL 60064

KIMELBERG, HAROLD KEITH, neurobiologist, educator; b. Hertford, Eng., Dec. 5, 1941; came to U.S., 1963; s. Morris and Sarah (Cohen) K.; m. Pamela Cheryl Ahrens, July 14, 1966; children: David, Michael. B.Sc., Kings Coll., U. London, 1963; Ph.D., SUNY-Buffalo, 1968. Research assoc. U. Pa. Med. Sch., Phila., 1968-69; sr. cancer research scientist Roswell Park Meml. Inst., Buffalo, 1969-74; assoc. prof. div. neurosurgery Albany (N.Y.) Med. Coll., 1974-80, prof., 1980—; reviewer numerous scholarly jours.; mem. rev. bds. NIH. Contbr. numerous articles and revs. to research jours., also chpts. to books. Mem. Am. Soc. for Neurochemistry, Soc. for Neurosci., Am. Soc. Biol. Chemists. Current Work: Functions and roles of astroglial cells in the mammalian central nervous system concentrating on their ion transport and interactions with transmitters, principally using cell cultures. Subspecialties: Neurobiology; Membrane biology. Home: 11 Candlewood Ln Delmar NY 12054 Office: Div Neurosurgery Albany Med Coll Albany NY 12208

KIMLER, BRUCE FRANKLIN, radiation biologist, medical educator; b. St. Paul, Minn., Sept. 23, 1948; s. Benjamin Franklin and Ruth Ivy (Landis) K.; m. Susan Catherine Watson, Jan. 1975; children—Laura Jean and Britton Franklin. B.A., U. of Tex., 1970, M.A., 1971, Ph.D., 1973. Postdoctoral fellow Argonne Nat. Lab., Argonne, Ill., 1973-75, Thomas Jefferson Hosp., Phila., 1975-77; asst. prof. U. of Kans. Med. Ctr. 1977-80, assoc. prof., 1980-84, prof., 1984—; prof. Instituto Investigaciones Cytologicas, Valencia, Spain, 1984—; adj. prof. U. Kansas, Lawrence, 1977—; assoc. scientist Mid-Am. Cancer Ctr., Kansas City, 1977-81. Contbr. articles to prof. jours. Recipient Faculty Research award U. of Kansas Med. Ctr., 1982. Mem. Cell Kinetics Soc. (sec. 1981-83, councilor 1984-86), Am. Assn. for Cancer Research, Am. Soc. Therapeutic Radiology and Oncology, Radiation Research Soc. Current work: Pre-clinical and clinical evaluation of the effects and interractions of therapeutic modalities for the treatment of cancer. Subspecialties: Radiation biology; Cancer research (medicine). Office: Dept Radiation Oncology U Kans Med Ctr Rainbow Blvd at 39th St Kansas City KS 66103

KIMME, ERNEST GODFREY, mathematician; b. Long Beach, Calif., June 7, 1929; s. Ernest Godfrey and Lura Elizabeth (Dake) K.; m. Carolyn McComas Smith/Rice, Aug. 29, 1952 (div. May 1975); children: Ernest G., Elizabeth E., Karl F.; m. Jeanne Bolen, Dec. 20, 1978. B.A. magna cum laude, Pomona Coll., 1952; M.A., U. Minn., 1954, Ph.D., 1955. Mem. grad. faculty math. Oreg. State U., Corvallis, 1955-57; mem. tech. staff Bell Telephone Labs., Murray Hill, N.J., 1957-65; head applied scis. Collins Radio Co., Newport Beach, Calif., 1965-72; research engr. Northrop Electronics, Hawthorne, Calif., 1972-74; sr. staff engr. Interstate Electronics, Anaheim, Calif., 1974-79; dir. advanced systems Gould Navcomm Systems, El Monte, Calif., 1979-82; pres. Cobit, Inc., Costa Mesa, Calif., 1982-84; mem. tech. staff Gen. Research Corp., 1984—. Mem. Soc. Indsl. and Applied Math., Am. Math. Soc., IEEE (chmn. Saddleback sect. 1977-78). Republican. Club: Old Crows. Current Work: Communications technology, especially redundant time-bandwidth systems and signalling, signal processing and analysis. Subspecialties: Probability; Applied mathematics. Home: 301 Starfire St Anaheim CA 92807 Office: Gen Research Corp 5383 Hollister St Santa Barbara CA 93160

KIND, PHYLLIS DAWN, immunologist, educator; b. Sidney, Mont., July 31, 1933; d. Dan E. and Margaret A. (Erickson) K. B.A. in Bacteriology, U. Mont., 1955; M.S. in Microbiology, U. Mich., 1956, Ph.D. in Immunology, 1960. Postdoctoral fellow dept. dermatology U. Mich., Ann Arbor, 1960-63; instr. dept. pathology U. Colo. Med. Ctr., Denver, 1963-65, asst. prof., 1965-71; research microbiologist Nat. Cancer Inst., NIH, 1971-74; assoc. prof. dept. microbiology George Washington U. Med. Ctr., 1974-79, prof., 1979—, assoc. dir. Tissue Typing Lab., 1978—; ad hoc mem. immunol. scis. study sect. NIH, 1982; mem. grad. fellowship evaluation panel NRC, 1978-80, chmn., 1982. Contbr. articles to profl. jours. NSF fellow, 1955-59; NIH spl. fellow, 1963-64; NIH grantee, 1964-71, 75-78, 82—. Mem. AAAS, Am. Soc. Microbiology, Am. Assn. Immunologists, Soc. Exptl. Biology and Medicine, Assn. Women in Sci., Am. Assn. Clin. Histocompatibility Testing, Sigma Xi, Phi Sigma, Phi Kappa Phi. Current Work: Regulation of immune response; regulation of interferon production. Subspecialty: Immunology (medicine). Office: 2300 Eye St NW 727 Microbiology Washington DC 20037

KINDINGER, PAUL EUGENE, state official; b. Adrian, Mich., Nov. 5, 1946; s. Robert Paul and Evelyn Clara (Heldt) K.; m. Susan Beth Smalley; 1 child, Sarah Marie. B.S. in Agrl. Econs., Mich. State U., 1970, M.S. in Agrl. Econs., 1971; Ph.D. in Agrl. Econs., Cornell U., 1975. Dir. mktg. devel. and research div. Mich. Farm Bur., Lansing, 1975-79; dir. mktg. and internat. trade Mich. Dept. Agr., Lansing, 1979-81, asst. dir., 1981, asst. dir. Coop. Ext. Service, Mich. State U., East Lansing, 1981-83, dir. Mich. Dept. Agr., 1983—; mem. Gov.'s China Commn., 1983—, Gov.'s Exec. Corp., 1983—. Contbr. articles to profl. agrl. jours. Served in USNR, 1967-68. Recipient State Farmer award Future Farmers Assn., 1964. Mem. Mich. State U. Alumni Assn. Current work: Industrial organization, marketing and farm management and production economics; currently directing the Michigan Department of Agriculture. Office: Mich Dept Agr PO Box 30017 Lansing MI 48909

KINDT, THOMAS JAMES, immunologist, educator; b. Cin., May 18, 1939; s. James Michael and Barbara Katherine (Mayer) K.; m. Marie Robinson, Sept. 4, 1964; children: Rachel, James. A.B., Thomas More Coll., 1963; Ph.D., U. Ill.-Urbana, 1967. Ad. assoc. prof. dept. medicine Cornell U. Med. Coll., N.Y.C., 1973-78; assoc. prof. Rockefeller U., N.Y.C., 1973-77, acting head lab. immunology and immunochemistry, 1975-77; chief Lab. Immunogenetics Nat. Inst. Allergy and Infectious Disease NIH, Bethesda, Md., 1977—; adj. prof. Georgetown U. Sch. Medicine and Dentistry, Washington, 1981—; vis. scientist Inst. Pasteur, Paris, 1982-83. Co-author: The Antibody Enigma, 1984; also articles. Mem. editorial bd. Jour. Exptl. Medicine, Jour. Biol. Chemistry, Jour. Immunology. Served with USN, 1957-59. Am. Heart Assn. Investigator, 1970-75; NIH fellow, 1967-70. Mem. Am. Assn. Immunologists, Am. Soc. Biol. Chemists, Harvey Soc., Sigma Xi. Current Work: Research on molecules and genes that are important in immune functions, immunogenetics and biochemistry of histo-compatibility antigens and immunoglobulins. Subspecialties: Immunogenetics; Biochemistry (biology). Office: Bldg 5 Room Bl-04 Bethesda MD 20205

KINDWALL, ERIC POST, physician, hyperbaric medicine educator; b. N.Y.C., Jan. 17, 1934; s. Josef Alfred and Anna Linnea (Post) K.; m. Betsy Fernald, Sept. 12, 1964; children: Kristina, Alexander; m. Marilyn Laurie MacArthur, Aug. 5, 1978. B.A., U. Wis., 1956; M.D., Yale U. Sch. Medicine, 1960. Rotating intern U. Va. Hosp., Charlottesville, 1961-62; resident in psychiatry Mass. Mental Health Ctr.-Harvard U., Boston, 1962-65; asst. dir. U.S. Navy Sch. Submarine Medicine, New London, Conn., 1967-69; asst. clin. prof. pharmacology Med. Coll. Wis., Milw., 1969—; dir. hyperbaric medicine St. Luke's Hosp., Milw., 1969—; cons. diving and hyperbaric medicine Indonesian Navy, 1981-82; hyperbaric cons. Republic of China Navy, 1976—; cons. WHO, Geneva, Switzerland, 1981-82. Contbr. articles to profl. jours.; Editor: Hyperbaric Oxygen Rev. Jour, 1979—. Mem. Undersea Med. Soc. (pres. 1981-82), Am. Occupational Med. Assn., Aerospace Med. Assn., AAAS. Current Work: Clinical hyperbaric medicine research and practice; research on the decompression of deep sea divers and compressed air caisson workers. Subspecialty: Hyperbaric medicine. Home: 13020 Oriole Ln Brookfield WI 53005 Office: St Luke's Hosp 2900 W Oklahoma Ave Milwaukee WI 53215

KING, CARY JUDSON, III, chemical engineer, educator; b. Ft. Monmouth, N.J., Sept. 27, 1934; s. Cary Judson and Mary Margaret (Forbes) K., Jr.; m. Jeanne Antoinette Yorke, June 22, 1957; children: Mary Elizabeth, Cary Judson IV, Catherine Jeanne. B. Engring., Yale, 1956; S.M., Mass. Inst. Tech., 1958, Sc.D., 1960. Asst. prof. chem. engring. Mass. Inst. Tech., Cambridge, 1959-63; dir. Bayway Sta. Sch. Chem. Engring. Practice, Linden, N.J., 1959-61; asst. prof. chem. engring. U. Calif. at Berkeley, 1963-66, asso. prof., 1966-69, prof., 1969—, vice chmn. dept. chem. engring., 1967-72, chmn., 1972-81, dean Coll. Chemistry, 1981—; cons. Procter & Gamble Co., 1969—, CPC Internat., 1982—. Author: Separation Processes, 1971, 80, Freeze Drying of Foods, 1971; Contbr. numerous articles to profl. jours. Active Boy Scouts Am., 1947—; pres. Kensington Community Council, 1972-73, dir., 1970-73. Named Inst. Lectr. Am. Inst. Chem. Engrs., 1973, Food, Pharm. and Bioengring. Div. award, 1975, William H. Walker award, 1976. Mem. Nat. Acad. Engring., Am. Inst. Chem. Engrs., Inst. Food Tech., Am. Soc. Engring. Edn. (George Westinghouse award 1978), Am. Chem. Soc., AAAS. Patentee in field. Current Work: Seperation processes, including dehydration and concentration, extraction, adsorption, distillation, spray drying and freeze drying. Subspecialty: Chemical engineering. Home: 7 Kensington Ct Kensington CA 94707 Office: Coll Chemistry U Calif Berkeley CA 94720

KING, DENNIS R., clinical psychologist; b. Cin., July 22, 1947; s. Granville P. and Loretta (Tirey) K. B.A., U. Cin., 1969; M.S. in Clin. Psychology, Calif. State U.-San Diego, 1973. Diplomate: Internat. Acad. Prof. Counseling and Psychotherapy.; Lic. psychol. examiner, Tenn. Psychol. examiner Hiwassee Mental Health Ctr., Cleveland, Tenn., 1973-77, programs dir., 1977-78, exec. dir., 1978-80; biomed. dir. Cleveland Pain Clinic, 1980-82, Pain Mgmt. Services, Chattanooga, 1982—, Health Mgmt. Services, Cleveland, 1980—; instr. Cleveland State Community Coll., 1975—; exam. cons. Disability Determinations sect. Social Security, Cleveland, 1974—; dir. Behavorial Research Inst., Cleveland, 1981—. Contbr. articles to profl. jours. Bd. dirs. Child Shelter, Inc., Cleveland, 1974-78; mem. policy council Headstart S.E. Tenn., 1982. Tenn. Dept. Human Services grantee, 1980, 82. Fellow Internat. Council Sex. Edn.; mem. Am. Psychol. Assn., Tenn. Psychol. Assn., Biofeedback Soc. Am., Am. Assn. Sex Educators, Counselors and Therapists, Council for Exceptional Children. Republican. Baptist. Current Work: Treatment of chronic pain through biofeedback, visual imagery, hypnosis and relaxation training. Treat low back pain, tension and migraine headache, arthritis, muscle spasm. Child abuse treatment. Subspecialties: Pain management; Biofeedback. Home: 750 Beech Circle NW Cleveland TN 37311 Office: Health Mgmt Services 2850 Westside Dr Suite I PO Box 2965 Cleveland TN 37311

KING, IVAN ROBERT, astronomy educator; b. Far Rockaway, N.Y., June 25, 1927; s. Myram and Anne (Franzblau) K.; children: David, Lucy, Adam, Jane. A.B., Hamilton Coll., 1946; A.M., Harvard U., 1947, Ph.D., 1952. Instr. astronomy Harvard U., 1951-52; mathematician Perkin-Elmer Corp., Norwalk, Conn., 1951-52; methods analyst U.S. Dept. Def., Washington, 1954-56; with U. Ill., 1956-64; assoc. prof. astronomy U. Calif. at Berkeley, 1964-66, prof., 1966—, chmn. astronomy dept., 1967-70. Contbr. numerous articles to sci. jours. Served with USNR, 1952-54. Mem. Soc. of Fellows Harvard, 1947-51. Mem. Nat. Acad. Scis.; Mem. Am. Acad. Arts and Scis., Am. Astron. Soc. (councillor 1963-66, chmn. div. dynamical astronomy 1972-73, pres. 1978-80), AAAS (chmn. astronomy sect. 1974), Internat. Astron. Union. Current Work: Structure and dynamics of star clusters and galaxies. Subspecialty: Optical astronomy. Office: Dept Astronomy U Calif Berkeley CA 94720

KING, JAMES CLAUDE, physicist; b. St. Joseph, Mo., Oct. 2, 1924; s. Oppie Irl and Isla Dessie (Wertenberger) K.; m. Martha Helen Dawson, Sept. 10, 1949; children—Elizabeth, Kathleen, Helen, Robert. B.A., Amherst Coll., 1949; M.S., Ph.D., Yale U., 1953. Mgr. dept. Bell Telephone Co., Whippany, N.J., 1953-65; div. dir. Sandia Nat. Labs., Albuquerque, 1965—. Author books in field. Guest editor Radiation Effects jour. Patentee in field. Served to 1st lt. USAAF, 1942-46, ETO. Recipient Baldwin Sawyer award, 1973. Fellow Am. Phys. Soc.; mem. Phi Beta Kappa, Sigma Xi. Episcopalian. Current work: Materials process engineering and fabrication. Subspecialties: Low temperature physics; Condensed matter physics. Home: 7832 Academy Trail NE Albuquerque NM 87109

KING, JAMES ROGER, biology educator, research physiologist; b. San Jose, Calif., Mar. 12, 1927; s. James Raymond and Dorothy Lydia (Donnelley) K.; m. Eleanor May Porter, June 16, 1950; children—Julia, Robert, Joanna. B.A. in Biology, San Jose State U., 1950; M.S. in Zoology, Wash. State U, 1953, Ph.D. in Physiology, 1957. Asst. prof. exptl. biology U. Utah, Salt Lake City, 1957-60; assoc. prof. physiology Wash. State U., Pullman, 1960-67, prof. physiology, 1967—, chmn. dept. zoology, 1972-78; cons. NSF, Washington, 1973-76, 83-84, NRC, Washington, 1973-76, Ministry Edn., Beijing, China, 1983. Editor: (with others) Avian Biology, 1968—. Contbr. articles to profl. jours. Served with AUS, 1945-46. Recipient Brewster Meml. medal Am. Ornithol. Union, 1974; Guggenheim fellow, 1969; named Hon. Prof. E. China U., 1984, Maytag Vis. Prof. Ariz. State U., 1979. Fellow Am. Ornithologists Union (pres. 1980-82), AAAS; mem. Cooper Ornithol. Soc. (pres. 1977-78, editor 1965-69, hon.), Am. Physiol. Soc. (elected), also many others. Current work: Research in avian energy metabolism and nutrition; graduate teaching in comparatvie vertebrate physiology. Subspecialties: Comparative physiology; Nutrition (biology). Office: Dept Zoology Wash State U Pullman WA 99164

KING, JAMES WESLEY, medicinal and organic chemist; b. Gainesville, Fla., Dec. 21, 1933; s. Clifford Leroy and Lessie Estelle (Hodge) K.; m. Mary Frances Riley, Apr. 23, 1953; children—Clifford Riley, Ramona Leigh. B.S. in Chemistry, Fla. So. Coll., 1955; Ph.D. in Medicinal Chemistry, U. Md.-Balt., 1975. Chemist, F.S. Royster Guano Co., Mulberry, Fla., 1955-56; research chemist Army Chem. Ctr., Edgewood, Md., 1958-60; chemist V-C Chem. Co., Nichols, Fla., 1961-62; research chemist U.S. Army Chem. Research and Devel. Ctr., Aberdeen Proving Ground, Md., 1962—; adj. assoc. prof. medicinal chemistry and pharmacognosy Sch. Pharmacy, U. Md., Balt., 1985—. Contbr. articles to sci. jours. and govtl. reports. Mem. Am. Chem. Soc., N.Y. Acad. Scis., Acad. Pharm. Scis., AAAS, Sigma Xi. Republican. Current work: Design, synthesis, structure-activity and structure-property relationships of bioactive compounds; mathematical modeling of biological systems. Subspecialties: Drug design; Medicinal chemistry. Home: 13 Colonial Rd Bel Air MD 21014 Office: US Army Chem Research and Devel Ctr Edgewood Area Aberdeen Proving Ground MD 21010-5423

KING, (MARY) MARGARET, medical research scientist, research lab. adminstr.; b. Oklahoma City, May 26, 1946; d. James Dean and Mary Bell (Gregory) K. B.S. in Biology and Edn, Central State U., Edmond, Okla., 1969; Ph.D. in Med. Physiology and Biophysics, U. Okla., 1975. Tchr. pub. schs., Oklahoma City, 1969-71; postdoctoral fellow Biomembrane Research Lab., Okla. Med. Research Found., Oklahoma City, 1973-76, research assoc., 1976-77, staff scientist, 1977-80, asst. mem., 1980—; NIH Cardiovascular Physiology and Pharmacology Tng. grantee U. Okla. Health Scis. Ctr., Oklahoma City, 1971-73, assoc. in research biochemistry, 1977-81, asst. prof. research biochemistry and molecular biology, 1981—; asst. prof. U. Okla. Coll. Medicine, 1981—; cons., lectr. in field. Contbr. numerous sci. articles and abstracts to profl. publs. Nat. Inst. Environ. Health Scis. young investigator grantee, 1978-80; NIH grantee, 1978-84. Mem. Am Assn. for Cancer Research, Am. Inst. Nutrition, Am. Assn. Lab. Animal Scis., Soc. for Exptl. Biology and Medicine, N.Y. Acad. Scis., Sigma Xi, Alpha Chi, Kappa Delta Pi. Current Work: Dietary fat and antioxidant influences on breast cancer. Subspecialties: Cancer research (medicine); Pharmacology. Office: 825 NE 13th St Oklahoma City OK 73104

KINGERY, WILLIAM DAVID, educator, ceramist; b. N.Y.C., July 7, 1926; s. Lisle B. and Margaret (Reynolds) K.; m. Gertrude Phillips, Nov. 22, 1965; children—William David, Peter (dec.), Rebekah, Andrew. Grad., Taft Sch., Watertown, Conn., 1943; S.B., MIT, 1950, Sc.D., 1952; Dr. (hon.), Tokyo Inst. Tech., 1982. Mem. faculty MIT, 1951—, prof. ceramics, 1960—, Orton lectr., 1980, Kyocera chair in ceramics sci. and engring., 1985—; vis. prof. Ecole Poly. Fed. de Lausanne, Switzerland, 1980; Mem. materials adv. bd. Nat. Acad. Sci., 1960-68. Author: Property Measurements at High Temperatures, 1959, Introduction to Ceramics, 1960, 2d edit., 1976; Editor: Ceramic Fabrication Process, 1958, Kinetics of High-Temperature Process, 1959, Ice and Snow, 1963; editor-in-chief: Cerammgia Internat, 1976—; Contbr. profl. jours. Chmn. Marion-Bermuda Cruising Yacht Race, 1977-79; chmn. bd. trustees, 1980—; treas. East Marion Steamship Authority. Fellow Am. Ceramic Soc (Ross Coffin Purdy award 1952, John Jeppson award 1958, outstanding service award New Eng. sect. 1957, 1st Distinguished Sosman Meml. lectr. 1973, A.V. Bleininger award 1976, F.H. Norton award 1977, hon. life mem. 1983), Keramos (hon.), Am. Chem. Soc., Glaciological Soc.; mem. Nat. Acad. Engring. Current Work: Structure and properties of ceramics, physical ceramics, inferences from ceramic artifacts. Subspecialties: Ceramics; Ceramic engineering. Office: MIT 77 Massachusetts Ave Cambridge MA 02139

KINGSBURY, WILLIAM DENNIS, bio-organic chemist; b. Buffalo, Nov. 21, 1941; s. William H. and Irene (Hoskinson) K.; m. Lilliam Fajardo, May 20, 1967; children—William Scott, William Lawrence, William Russell. B.A., SUNY-Buffalo, 1964; Ph.D., Wayne State U., 1970. Sr. investigator Smith Kline Beckman, Phila., 1971—. Contbr. articles to profl. jours. Patentee in field. Mem. Am. Chem. Soc., AAAS, Phila. Organic Chemists Club, Sigma Xi. Current work: Antimicrobial chemotherapy; medicinal chemistry. Subspecialties: Organic chemistry; Synthetic chemistry. Home: 865 Babb Circle Wayne PA 19087 Office: Smith Kline Beckman 1500 Spring Garden Philadelphia PA 19101

KING-SMITH, ERIC ALFRED, biomedical engineer, consultant; b. Melbourne, Australia, Mar. 3, 1926; came to U.S., 1965; s. Frederick and Irene Victoria (Harlem) K-S.; m. Ruth Ethel Lustig, Aug. 8, 1950 (div. 1980); children—Judith Elaine, Bernard Alan, Naomi Louise; m. Roxie Harriet Freedman, Jan. 7, 1985. B.E.E., U. Melbourne, 1947, M.Eng. Sc., 1949, Ph.D., 1970. Sr. lectr. elec. engring. U. Melbourne, 1958-65; research assoc., spl. lectr. U. Mich., Ann Arbor, 1966-67, NIH spl. fellow in bioengring., 1968-70; new product devel. mgr. Medtronic, Inc., Mpls., 1971-74; electronic design specialist 3M Detection Systems, St. Paul, 1974-76; sr. product devel. specialist 3M Health Care Spltys., St. Paul, 1976—; adj. prof. mech. engring. U. Minn., Mpls., 1980—; research collaborator Brookhaven Nat. Labs., 1972-76; bioengring. cons. Dorland's Med. Dictionary, 1970-74. Author: Mudpac Manual, 1962; also articles. Grad. scholar, 1947-48; NIH spl. fellow, 1968-70. Fellow Instn. Elec. Engrs. (U.K.), Instn. Engrs. (Australia) (aero. com. 1955-57); mem. IEEE (sr. mem.; chpt. chmn. 1977-78), Australian Computer Soc. (founding mem.; editor Victoria div. 1962-65, sec. 1961-62); mem. N.Y. Acad. Scis., AAAS, Biol. Engring. Soc. (U.K.), Internat. Soc. Chronobiology, Internat. Continence Soc. Current work: Design and development of neural and neuromuscular stimulators, including the associated physiology of biosystems; development of high-technology prostheses and aids to the disabled; integrated man-machine systems. Subspecialties: Bioinstrumentation; Chronobiology. Home: 3430 Boone Ave S Minneapolis MN 55426 Office: 3M Med Products 3M Ctr 270-2N-5 Saint Paul MN 55144

KINNARD, WILLIAM JAMES, JR., pharmacologist, educator; b. Wilmington, Del., Apr. 18, 1932; s. William J. and Helen F. (Ossenkemper) K.; m. Dolores F. Malia, July 18, 1959. B.S., U. Pitts., 1953, M.S., 1955; Ph.D., Purdue U., 1957. From instr. to prof. U. Pitts., 1957-68; prof. pharmacology, dean Sch. Pharmacy, U. Md., Balt., 1968—; dean Grad. Sch., U. Md., 1976-79; Chmn. bd. U.S. Pharmacopeial Conv., 1975—. Contbr. jours. in field. Fellow Am. Found. Pharm. Edn., 1954-57; recipient Honors Achievement award Angiology Research Fedn., 1960-65, Distinguished Alumnus award U. Pitts. Sch. Pharmacy, 1973. Fellow Am. Coll. Clin. Pharmacology, AAAS, Acad. Pharm. Sci.; mem. Am. Soc. Pharmacology and Exptl. Therapy, Am. Pharm. Assn., Inst. Medicine of Nat. Acad. Scis., Am. Assn. Coll. of Pharmacy (pres. 1976-77), Rho Chi. Lutheran. Subspecialty: Pharmacology. Office: U Md Sch Pharmacy 20 N Pine St Baltimore MD 21201

KINNEY, TERRY B., JR., geneticist, government agricultural research administrator; b. Norfolk, Mass., Sept. 12, 1925; widowed; 2 children. B.S., U. Mass., 1955, M.S., 1956; Ph.D., U.Minn., 1963. Research asst. poultry U. Mass., 1955-56; geneticist Hubbard Farms, Inc., N.H., 1956-57; instr. poultry U. Minn., 1957-62; biometrician Dept. Agr., Md., 1963-65, research geneticist, Ind., 1965-69; asst. dir. animal sci. research div. Agrl. Research Service, 1969-72; assoc. dep. adminstr. Agrl. Research Service North Central Region, 1972-73, asst. adminstr. livestock vet. sci., 1974-79, assoc. adminstr., 1979-80, adminstr. Agrl. Research Service, 1980—. Mem. Poultry Sci. Assn. Subspecialties: Population biology; Animal research administration. Office: Agrl Research Service Dept Agr Room 302 Adminstrn Bldg Washington DC 20250*

KINNIER, WILLIAM JAMES, biochemist, researcher; b. Balt., Dec. 23, 1950; s. Robert Joseph and Agnes Rose (Josephs) K.; m. Vickey Kissinger, Oct. 28, 1978. Ph.D., U. N.C., Chapel Hill, 1977. Post doctoral researcher U. N.C., Chapel Hill., 1977-78; mem. staff fellow NIMH, 1978-80; sr. research biochemist A.H. Robins Co., Richmond, Va., 1980—. Contbr. articles in field to profl. jours. Mem. Soc. Neurosci. Current Work: Mechanism of action of receptors beta adrenergic, alpha adrenergic, dopamine, diazepam, muscarinic receptor. Subspecialties: Neuropharmacology; Neurochemistry. Office: 1211 Sherwood Ave Richmond VA 23102

KINNISON, WILLARD WAYNE, physicist; b. Little Rock, Feb. 11, 1948; s. Willard Charles and Lois Ree (Eidson) K.; m. Nancy Kay Schaefer, Dec. 29, 1968; 1 child, Sondra Shannon. B.S. in Physics, U. Tex.-Arlington, 1971, M.A. in Physics, 1972; Ph.D. in Physics, U. Chgo., 1979. Postdoctoral fellow Los Alamos Nat. Lab., 1979-82, staff mem., 1982—. Contbr. articles to profl. jours. Mem. Am. Phys. Soc. Lutheran. Current work: Studying the weak interaction via normal muon decays at LAMPF and rare kaon decays at Brookhaven. Subspecialty: Particle physics. Home: 2236 A 38th St Los Alamos NM 87544 Office: Los Alamos Nat Lab Mail Stop D443 Los Alamos NM 87545

KINSELLA, JOHN EDWARD, food science educator, food chemist, biochemist; b. Wexford, Ireland, Feb. 22, 1938; married, 1965; 4 children. B.S., Nat. U. Ireland, 1961; M.S., Pa. State U., 1965, Ph.D. in Food Sci, 1967. Tchr. zoology, Latin and chemistry CKC Onitsha, Nigeria, 1961-63; asst. prof. food sci. Cornell U., Ithaca, N.Y., 1967-73, assoc. prof., 1973-77, prof. food sci. and chemistry, chmn. dept. food sci., 1977-85, Gen. Foods Disting. prof. food sci., 1985—; dir. Cornell U. (Inst. Food Sci.), 1980—, Liberty Hyde Bailey prof. food sci., 1981—. Recipient Borden award for research, 1976. Mem. Am. Inst. Nutrition, AAAS, Am. Chem. Soc., Am. Dairy Sci. Assn., Inst. Food Tech. Subspecialty: Food science and technology. Office: Dept Food Sci Cornell U Ithaca NY 14850

KINSEY, JAMES LLOYD, chemistry educator; b. Paris, Tex., Oct. 15, 1934; s. Lloyd King and Elaine (Mills) K.; m. Berma McDowell, July 28, 1962; children—Victoria, Samuel, Adam. B.A., Rice U., 1956, Ph.D., 1959. Asst., then assoc. prof. MIT, Cambridge, 1962-74, prof., 1974—, head dept., 1977-82; cons. Los Alamos Sci. Lab., 1974—vis. com. chemistry div., 1983—; adv. com. Army Research Office NRC, 1981-84, steering com., 1983—; mem. bd. chem. scis. and tech., Nat. Acad. Scis.-NRC, 1980-83, chmn., 1982-83. Assoc. editor Jour. Chem. Physics, 1981-84; adv. bd. Jour. Phys. Chemistry, 1985—; mem. editorial adv. bd. Ann. Revs. Phys. Chemistry, 1985—. Contbr. articles to profl. jours. Miller Research Inst. fellow, U. Calif.-Berkeley, 1960-62; J.S. Guggenheim fellow, 1969-70; A.P. Sloan Found. fellow, 1964-68. Fellow Am. Phys. Soc.; mem. Am. Chem. Soc., AAAS, Sigma Xi. Subspecialties: Physical chemistry; Laser spectroscopy. Home: 44 Lombard St Newton MA 02158 Office: MIT 77 Massachusetts Ave Cambridge MA 02139

KINSMAN, DONALD MARKHAM, animal scientist, educator; b. Framingham, Mass., May 20, 1923; s. Joshua Starr and Florence Ruby (Markham) K.; m. Helen Katharine Bailey, Aug. 28, 1949; children: Elizabeth Lee Kinsman Keefe, David Bailey, Martha Jean. B.S., U. Mass., 1949; M.S., U. N.H., 1951; Ph.D., Okla. State U., 1964. Instr. U. N.H., Durham, 1949-51, U. Vt., Burlington, 1951-52; asst. prof. U. Mass., Amherst, 1952-56; prof. animal sci. U. Conn., Storrs, 1956—. Author, editor: International Meat Science Dictionary, 1978; author, editor: International Sausage Book, 1981; contbr. over 75 articles to profl. jours. Bd. dirs. Mansfield (Conn.) Retirement Community, 1976—. Served with USMC, 1942-46. Decorated Purple Heart; NSF teaching fellow, 1959-60. Mem. Am. Soc. Animal Sci. (Disting. Service award 1976), Am. Meat Sci. Assn. (Signal Service award 1975, Disting. Tchr. award 1981, R. C. Pollock award 1985). Republican. Congregationalist. Current Work: Humane slaughter, animal welfare, meat quality, animal stress. Subspecialty: Food science and technology. Home: 45 Moulton Rd Storrs CT 06268 Office: Dept Animal Sci U Conn Storrs CT 06268

KIPLINGER, GLENN FRANCIS, pharmaceutical company executive; b. Indpls., Sept. 29, 1930; s. Glenn DeArmand and Iva Frances (Smoot) K.; m. Martha Lee Peterson, June 13, 1953; children—Jeffrey P., Jonathan D., Jason G., Jennifer G. B.S. in Pharmacy, Butler U., 1953; Ph.D., U. Mich., 1959; M.D., U. Tex.-Galveston, 1967. Asst. prof. pharmacology Boston U. Med. Sch., 1958-62; asst. prof. pharmacology U. Tex. Med. Br., Galveston, 1962-67; clin. pharmacologist Eli Lilly & Co., Indpls., 1967-72, dir. to exec. dir. to v.p. research, 1972-77, mng. dir. Lilly Research Lab., Windlestham, Surrey, Eng., 1977-80; v.p. research and devel. Ortho Pharm. Corp., Raritan, N.J., 1980—. Contbr. articles to profl. jours. Mem. Am. Soc. Clin. Pharmacology and Therapeutics (dir.), Am. Soc. Pharmacology and Exptl. Therapeutics, Soc. Toxicology. Current work: Clin. pharmacology of CNS active compounds; clin. trial methodology; research mgmt. Subspecialty: Pharmacology. Home: 55 Philip Dr Princeton NJ 08540 Office: Ortho Pharm Corp Route 202 Raritan NJ 08869

KIPP, JOHN EDWARD, mechanical engineering educator; b. Lincoln, Nebr., Jan. 5, 1930; s. Harold L. and Constance (Almy) K.; m. Mary C. Lackey, May 9, 1958; children—Jennifer, Stephanie, Charles, Glenn. B.S. M.E., U. Kans.-Lawrence, 1951, M.S.M.E., 1955; Ph.D., Okla. State U., 1968. Registered profl. engr., Kans. Instr. applied mechanics U. Kans.-Lawrence, 1953-56; asst. prof. applied mechanics Kans. State U.-Manhattan, 1956-68, assoc. prof., 1968-74, assoc. prof. mech. engring., 1974-80, prof. mech. engring., 1980—; research assoc. Environ. Research Inst., Manhattan, 1970—; engring. cons. Amoco Oil Co., Whiting, Ind., 1974, Naperville, Ill., 1980-83. Contbr. articles to tech. jours. Served with USAF, 1951-53. NSF Sci. Faculty Fellow awardee, 1963-64. Mem. ASME, Pi Tau Sigma, Sigma Tau, Pi Mu Epsilon. Current work: Pipe Flow, drag reduction, structure of branching flows. Subspecialties: Fluid mechanics; Biomedical engineering. Home: 2416 Wilmar Dr Manhattan KS 66502 Office: Dept Mech Engring Durland Hall 152 Kans State Univ Manhattan KS 66506

KIRK, JAMES ALLEN, mech. engr., educator; b. Lakewood, Ohio, Nov. 3, 1944; s. Charles James and Helen Sophie (Tulas) K.; m. Cynthia Ambler, Feb. 6, 1976; 1 dau., Heather Elizabeth. B.S.E.E., Ohio U., 1967; M.S.M.E., M.I.T., 1969, Ph.D., 1972. Registered profl. engr., Ohio, Md. Vehicle devel. engr. Ford Motor Co., Dearborn, Mich., 1966-67; research asst. M.I.T., Cambridge, 1967-72; asst. prof. mech. engring. U. Md., College Park, 1972-77, assoc. prof., 1977—; owner, dir. J.A. Kirk Cons. Co.; cons. in accident reconstrn., product liability, failure analysis. Contbr. articles to profl. jours.; author: Mechanical Measurements Laboratory Manual, 1979. Mem. Soc. Automotive Engrs. (Ralph Teetor award 1975), ASME, Am. Soc. for Metals, Am. Soc. for Engring. Edn. (Dow Outstanding Young Faculty award 1977). Current Work: Mathematical techniques for vehicular accident reconstruction and vehicle dynamics (emphasis on programmable calculator and personal computer programs). Machine design and manufacturing processes. Tribology. Subspecialties: Mechanical engineering; Automobile accident reconstruction. Home: 7210 Windsor Ln Hyattsville MD 20782 Office: Dept Mech Engring U Md College Park MD 20742

KIRK, JAMES ROBERT, nutritionist. Vice pres. for research Campbell Soup Co., Camden, N.J. Subspecialties: Nutrition (biology); Food science and technology. Office: Campbell Soup Co Campbell Pl Camden NJ 08101*

KIRKIEN-RZESZOTARSKI, ALICJA MARIA, chemistry educator; d. Leszek Tadeusz and Francesca Irena (Mortkowicz) K.; m. Zygmunt Marian Konasiewicz, Aug. 18, 1948; m. Waclaw Janusz Rzeszotarski, Dec. 14, 1972. M.Sc. in Chem. Engring, Polish U. Coll., London, 1951; Ph.D. in Phys. Organic Chemistry, Univ. Coll., London, 1955. Asst. prof. chemistry U. W.I., Jamaica, 1956-59, assoc. prof., 1959-61, Trinidad, 1961-65; prof., chmn. dept. chemistry Trinity Coll., Washington, 1965—. Contbr. articles in field to profl. jours. Treas. Polish Veterans Assn., U.S.A., 1979. Served with Polish Underground, WW II. Fellow Royal Inst. Chemistry; mem. Am. Chem. Soc., Chem. Soc. Great Britain, Polish Inst. Art and Scis., Phi Beta Kappa. Republican. Roman Catholic. Current Work: Kinetics in solutions, high resolution mass spectrometry, history of science, high performance liquid chromatography. Subspecialties: Physical chemistry; Kinetics. Home: 407 Buckspur Ct Millersville MD 21108 Office: Michigan Ave Washington DC 20017

KIRKMAN, HADLEY, anatomist, researcher; b. Richmond, Ind., Mar. 14, 1901; s. Madison Lee and Leila Piety (Hadley) K.; m. Gladys L. Tracy, Apr. 5, 1942; 1 dau., Tracy Leigh Kirkman-Liff. A.B., Iowa U., Iowa City, 1925; student, Bradley U., Peoria, Ill, 1923-24; M.S., U. Chgo., 1929; Ph.D.,

Columbia U., 1937. Acting asst. prof. zoology Ohio U., 1928-29; instr. anatomy N.Y. Med. Coll., 1929-32, Columbia U., 1934-36; instr. anatomy Stanford (Calif.) U., 1936-38, asst. prof., 1938-43, assoc. prof., 1943-59, prof., 1949-65, active prof. emeritus, 1965—. Contbr. numerous articles to profl. jours. NSF, sr. fellow, 1957-58; USPHS, spl. fellow, 1958-59; research grantee Am. Cancer Soc., Jane Coffin Childs Meml. Fund, Yale U., USPHS, 1948-76. Fellow N.Y. Acad. Scis., AAAS; mem. Am. Assn. Anatomists, Am. Assn. Cancer Research, AAUP, Gamma Alpha, Sigma Xi. Democrat. Current Work: Endocrine factors in carcinogenesis and cancer cell growth, effect of steroidal hormones on thymus. Subspecialties: Cancer research (medicine); Cytology and histology. Home: 623 Cabrillo Ave Stanford CA 94305 Office: Stanford University Room 8 Old Anatomy Bldg Stanford CA 94305

KIRKPATRICK, CHARLES HARVEY, clin. immunologist; b. Topeka, Nov. 5, 1931; s. Hazen Leon and Clarice Opal (Privott) K.; m. Janice F. Kirkpatrick, July 11, 1959; children: Heather, Michael, Brian. B.A., U. Kans., 1954, M.D., 1958. Intern U. Ill. Research and Edn. Hosp., Chgo., 1958-59; resident U. Kans. Med. Ctr., Kansas City, 1959-62; asst. prof. medicine U. Kans. Sch. Medicine, Kansas City, 1965-68, assoc. prof., 1968; sr. investigator, head div. clin. allergy and sensitivity Lab. Clin. Investigation, Nat. Inst. Allergy and Infectious Diseases, NIH, Bethesda, Md., 1968-79; head div. clin. immunology Nat. Jewish Hosp. and Research Ctr., Denver, 1979—; prof. medicine U. Colo. Sch. Medicine, 1979—. Contbr. over 100 articles to sci. jours. NIH grantee. Mem. Am. Soc. Clin. Investigation, Am. Acad. Allergy, Am. Fedn. Clin. Research, Western Assn. Physicians, AAAS, Transplant Soc. Episcopalian. Current Work: Host defense mechanisms and resistance to infectious diseases; pathogenesis of immune deficiency diseases, pathogenesis of interstitial lung disease, transfer factor. Subspecialties: Allergy; Infectious diseases.

KIRKPATRICK, FRANCIS H(UBBARD), JR., technical management executive, researcher; b. Laurel Hill, N.C., Nov. 7, 1943; s. F(rancis) Hubbard and Jean Orr (Murray) K.; m. Cornelia Ewart Goodreds, Aug. 30, 1969; 1 child, Adam B. B.A. in Physics, Harvard Coll., 1964; Ph.D. in Biophysics, Stanford U., 1970. Postdoctoral fellow Washington State U., Pullman, 1969-71; postdoctoral fellow U. Rochester, N.Y., 1972-74, asst. prof., 1974-80; lab. mgr. Pall Corp., Glen Cove, N.Y., 1980-84; tech. dir. F.M.C. BioProducts, Rockland, Maine, 1984—. Contbr. articles to profl. jours. Mem. Biophys. Soc., Optical Soc. Am. Current work: Creation of novel/improved materials for biotechnology research, related areas; previous work on membranes and physical biochemistry. Subspecialties: Biotechnology research and development; Biophysics (biology). Home: Woods Rd Owls Head ME 04854 Office: FMC BioProducts 5 Maple St Rockland ME 04841

KIRSCH, RUSSELL ANDREW, computer scientist; b. N.Y.C., June 20, 1929; s. Sol and Lillian K.; m. Joan Levin, Mar. 6, 1955; children—Walden, Peter, Lindsey, Gordon. B.E.E., N.Y. U., 1950; S.M., Harvard U., 1952; postgrad. MIT, Am. U. With U.S. Nat. Bur. Standards, Gaithersburg, Md., 1951-85. dir. research Sturvil Corp., Clarksburg, Md., 1985—. Mem. IEEE, AAAS, Assn. Computing Machinery. Subspecialties: Artificial intelligence; Graphics, image processing, and pattern recognition. Office: Sturvil Corp Box 157 Clarksburg MD 20871

KIRSCHBAUM, THOMAS HARRY, obstetrician and gynecologist; b. Mpls., Apr. 22, 1929; s. Murray M. and Ella A. (Anderberg) K.; children—Steven, Kristin. B.A., U. Minn., 1949, B.S., 1951, M.D., 1953. Intern U. Minn. Hosps., Mpls., 1953-54; resident in obstetrics and gynecology U. Minn. Hosp., 1956-59; asst. prof. U. Utah Med. Sch., 1959-64; asso. prof., then prof. U. Calif. Med. Sch., Los Angeles, 1964-71; prof. obstetrics and gynecology, chmn. dept. Mich. State U. Med. Sch., East Lansing, 1971-84; prof. ob-gyn U. So. Calif., 1985—; cons. RAND Corp., 1964-71; spl. expert Reproductive Service Br. Center Population Research NICHD, 1983-85. Co-editor: Seminars in Perinatology, 1977—. Served with USNR, 1954-56. Mem. Am. Coll. Obstetricians and Gynecologists, Perinatal Research Soc., Soc. Gynecol. Investigation, Am. Gynecol. Soc., Residency Rev. Com. Obstetrics and Gynecology, Central, Pacific Coast obstet. and gynecol. socs., Phi Beta Kappa, Alpha Omega Alpha. Subspecialty: Obstetrics and gynecology. Home: 620 Stone Canyon Rd Los Angeles CA 90077 Office: Los Angeles County/U So Calif Med Ctr Women's Hosp 1240 N Mission Rd Los Angeles CA 90033

KIRSCHSTEIN, RUTH L., physician, administrator; b. Bklyn., Oct. 12, 1926; d. Julius and Elizabeth (Berm) K.; m. Alan S. Rabson, June 11, 1950; 1 child: Arnold Rabson. B.S. magna cum laude, LIU, 1947; M.D., Tulane U., 1951; D.Sc. (hon.), Mt. Sinai Sch. Medicine, CUNY, 1984. Cert. Am. Bd. Pathology. Acting chief pathology lab. DBS, NIH, Bethesda, 1964-65, chief pathology lab., 1965-72, asst. dir. div. biologic standards NIH, 1971-72; acting dep. dir. Bur. Biologics, FDA, Rockville, Md., 1972-73, dep. assoc. commr. for sci. FDA, 1973-74; dir. Nat. Inst. Gen. Med. Sci., NIH, USPHS, Bethesda, 1974—. Author, editor: NIH Grants Peer Review Study Team Report, 1976. Recipient Superior Service award Dept. HEW, 1971; USPHS Superior Service award, 1978; Presdl. Meritorious Exec. Rank award, 1980; USPHS Equal Opportunity Achievement award, 1983. Mem. Am. Assn. Immunologists, Am. Assn. Pathologists, Am. Soc. Microbiology. Current work: Research on health science administration; pathogenesis of viral diseases; viral oncogenesis. Subspecialty: Pathology (medicine). Office: Dir NIGMS Bldg 31 Rm 4A52 Bethesda MD 20205

KIRSNER, JOSEPH BARNETT, physician, educator; b. Boston, Sept. 21, 1909; s. Harris and Ida (Waiser) K.; m. Minnie Schneider, Jan. 6, 1934; 1 son, Robert S. M.D., Tufts U., 1933; Ph.D. in Biol. Scis., U. Chgo., 1942. Intern Woodlawn Hosp., Chgo., 1933-34, resident, 1934-35; asst. in medicine U. Chgo., 1935-37, mem. faculty, 1937—, asso prof., 1946-51, prof., 1951—, Louis Block Distinguished Service prof. medicine, 1968—, chief of staff, also dep. dean for med. affairs, 1970-76; Cons. NIH, 1956-69; hon. pres. Gastrointestinal Research Found., 1961—; Mem. drug efficacy adv. com. to NRC; chmn. adv. group Nat. Commn. on Digestive Diseases, 1978; chmn. emeritus sci. adv. com. Nat. Found. Ileitis and Colitis. Author: also 650 articles. Gastrointestinal Exfoliative Cytology; Editorial bd.: Médecine et Chirurgies Digestives. Served with M.C. AUS, 1943-46, ETO; PTO. Recipient Julius Friedenwald medal disting. work gastroenterology, 1975; Horatio Alger award, 1979; hon. Gold Key for Disting. Service U. Chgo. Med. Alumni Assn., 1979. Mem. Am. Assn. Physicians, ACP (master, John Phillips award), Am. Gastroent. Assn. (past pres., governing bd.), Am. Gastroscopic Soc. (past pres.), Am. Soc. Gastrointestinal Endoscopy (Rudolf Schindler award), Am. Soc. Clin. Investigation, Central Soc. Clin. Research, Chgo. Soc. Internal Medicine (past pres.), Inst. Medicine Chgo. (George H. Coleman medal). Research in gastrointestinal disorders, inflammatory disease of gastrointestinal tract. Current Work: All aspects of infammatory bowel disease (ulcerative colitis and Crohn's disease). Subspecialties: Gastroenterology; Internal medicine. Home: 5805 Dorchester Ave Chicago IL 60637

KIRTLEY, DAVID WARREN, geologist; b. Enid, Okla., Nov. 6, 1927; s. Edwin Lankford and Olina (Talla) K.; m. Marilyn J. Crabtree, June 11, 1947 (div. Oct. 29, 1976); m. Sandra Lee, July 3, 1977; 1 son, Dean Aaron. B.A., Phillips U., 1950; M.S., Fla. State U., 1966, Ph.D., 1974. Vice pres. exploration Amstar Oil Inc., Oklahoma City, 1981-83; pres. D.W. Kirtley and Assocs., Inc., Oklahoma City, 1983—; ptnr. River Resources, Oklahoma City, 1984—. Served with USNR, 1943-46, PTO, 1951-52. Mem. Am. Inst. Profl. Geologists, Geol. Soc. Am., Am. Assn. Petroleum Geologists, Biol. Soc. Washington, Soc. Econ. Paleontologists and Mineralogists, Sigma Xi. Current work: Oil and gas exploration. Subspecialties: Geology; Systematics. Home: 7912 Curtis Terr Oklahoma City OK 73132 Office: D W Kirtley and Assocs Inc Oil Center Bldg Suite 101-E 2601 Northwest Expressway Oklahoma City OK 73112

KISTNER, DAVID HAROLD, biology educator; b. Cin., July 30, 1931; s. Harold Adolf and Hilda (Gick) K.; m. Alzada A. Carlisle, Aug. 8, 1957; children—Alzada H., Kymry Marie Carlisle. A.B., U. Chgo., 1952, B.S., 1956, Ph.D., 1957. Instr. U. Rochester, 1957-59; instr., asst. prof. Calif. State U., Chico, 1959-64, assoc. prof. biology, 1964-67, prof., 1967—; research assoc. Field Mus. Natural History, 1967—, Atlantica Ecol. Research Sta., Salisbury, Zimbabwe, 1970—; dir. Shinner Inst. Study Interrelated Insects, 1968-75. Author: (with others) Social Insects, Vols. 1-3; Biology of Termites, Vol. 1; editor: Sociobiology, 1975—; contbr. articles to profl. jours. Life mem. Republican Nat. Com., 1980—. Recipient Outstanding Prof. award Calif. State Univs. and Colls., Los Angeles, 1976; John Simon Guggenheim Meml. Found. fellow, 1965-66; NSF grantee, 1960—; Am. Philos. Soc. grantee, 1972. Fellow Explorers Club, Calif. Acad. Scis.; mem. Entomol. Soc. Am., Pacific Coast Entomol. Soc., Kans. Entomol. Soc., AAUP, AAAS, Soc. Study of Evolution, Am. Soc. Naturalists, Am. Soc. Zoologists, Soc. Study of Systematic Zoology, Chico State Coll. Assocs. (charter), Council Biology Editors, Am. Mus. Natural History (patron 1985—, life mem.). Research trips to Africa, Orient, Europe, S.Am., Australia, China. Current Work: Interactions of myrmecophiles and termitophiles with their social insects hosts. Origin of social parasitism. Evolution of social parasites coevolution of foreign insects in social insects societies. Subspecialties: Ecology (environmental science); Sociobiology. Home: 3 Canterbury Circle Chico CA 95926

KITE, JOSEPH HIRAM, JR., microbiologist, educator, researcher; b. Decatur, Ga., Nov. 11, 1926; s. Joseph Hiram and Lulie (Hatch) K.; m. Jane Pascale, Aug. 6, 1970. A.B., Emory U., 1948; M.S., U. Tenn., 1954; Ph.D., U. Mich., 1959. Med. technician in bacteriology Communicable Disease Ctr., Atlanta, 1950-51, VA Hosp., Atlanta, 1951-52; research assoc. U. Buffalo, 1958-59, instr., 1959-63; asst. prof. bacteriology and immunology SUNY-Buffalo, 1963-68, assoc. prof. microbiology, 1968-72, prof. microbiology, 1972—. Contbr. articles to med. jours., chpts. to med. textbooks. Served with AUS, 1945-46. Mem. Am. Assn. Immunologists, Am. Soc. Microbiology, Tissue Culture Assn., AAAS, N.Y. Acad. Scis. Methodist. Current Work: Autoimmune diseases; teaching medical, dental and graduate students; research in mechanisms of autoimmune disease and regulation of immune response. Subspecialties: Immunology (medicine); Microbiology (medicine). Home: 108 Chasewood Ln East Amherst NY 14051 Office: Dept Microbiology Med Sch SUNY Buffalo NY 14214

KITHIER, KAREL, physician, researcher; b. Prague, Czechoslovakia, Dec. 6, 1930; s. Karel and Marie (Bohackova) K.; m. Viktorie Svecova, May 6, 1961; 1 son: Karel. M.D., Charles U., Prague, 1962, Ph.D., 1967. Diplomate: Med. diplomate Charles U., Prague, 1962. Resident in pediatrics J. Hradec, Czechoslovakia, 1962-64; research scientist Research Inst. Child Devel., Prague, 1967-68; research assoc. Child Research Ctr. of Mich., Detroit, 1968-71; research scientist Mich. Cancer Found., Detroit, 1972-74; asst. prof. Wayne State U. Sch. Medicine, 1974-78, assoc. prof. pathology, 1978—. Contbr. articles to profl. jours. Served with Czechoslovakian Army, 1951-53. Mem. Am. Assn. Cancer Research, Am. Assn. Immunologists, Am. Assn. Clin. Chemistry, N.Y. Acad. Scis. Current Work: Pathology and clinical aspects of proteins, tumor-associated antigens, tumor markers, specific fetal proteins, oncofetal antigens. Subspecialties: Cancer research (medicine); Pathology (medicine). Office: 540 E Canfield St Room 9231 Detroit MI 48201

KLAHR, SAULO, medical researcher, educator; b. Santander, Colombia, June 8, 1935; came to U.S., 1961, naturalized, 1970; s. Herman and Rachel (Konigsberg) K.; m. M. Carol Declue, Dec. 29, 1965; children—James H., Robert D. B.A., Santa Librada U., Colombia, 1954; M.D., U. Nacional, Colombia, 1959. Resident in medicine Universidad del Valle, 1959-61, asst. prof. medicine, 1964-66; postdoctoral fellow in nephrology Washington U., St. Louis, 1961-63, instr. medicine, 1963-64, asst. prof. medicine, 1966-69, assoc. prof. medicine, 1969-72, prof. medicine, 1972—; chmn. sci. adv. bd. Nat. Kidney Found., N.Y.C., 1983-84. Editor: Differential Diagnos Renal, 1978, 84; Contemporary Nephrology, 1981, 83; Chronic Renal Disease, 1985. USPHS grantee, 1972—. Fellow ACP; mem. Am. Soc. Nephrology (councilor, pres.-elect), Am. Physiol. Soc., Am. Soc. Clin. Investigation, Assn. Am. Physicians, Biophys. Soc., Soc. Gen. Physiologists. Jewish. Current work: Pathophysiology urinary tract obstruction, arachidonic acid metabolism diet and progression of renal disease; ion transport and coupling to metabolism; action of hormones at the cellular level. Subspecialties: Nephrology; Physiology (medicine). Office: Washington U Sch Medicine 660 S Euclid Ave Saint Louis MO 63110

KLAIBER, ROBERT, laser and optics research administrator; b. N.Y.C., Apr. 22, 1936; s. Fredrich and Anna (Blados) K.; m. Janeth Arlene Norman, June 5, 1958; children—James, Jeanne, Karen. B.S. in Physics, Hofstra U., 1960; M.S. in Physics, NYU, 1963. Mem. tech. staff Bell Labs., N.Y.C., 1960-64; research physicist Office Naval Research, Sands Point, N.Y., 1964-67; sr. research engr. Western Elec. Co., Princeton, N.J., 1967-69, research leader, 1969-79; asst. dir. laser and optics research AT&T Techs., Princeton, 1979-85; dept. head lasers, optics Lightguide Research AT&T Engring. Research Ctr., Princeton, 1985—; self-employed cons., New Hyde Park, N.Y., 1966-67. Author: Lasers in Industry, 1972. Contbr. articles to profl. jours. Inventor laser beam deflector, 1975. Mem. IEEE, Optical Soc. Am., Princeton Classical Guitar Soc. (pres. 1975-77), Sigma Xi (exec. com. Princeton chpt. 1980-81). Current work: Lightguide (optical fiber) process and measurement research and development; optical measurement of semiconductors; applications of lasers. Subspecialties: Laser applications; Applied optics. Office: AT&T Engring Research Ctr PO Box 900 Princeton NJ 08540

KLARREICH, SAMUEL HENRY, psychologist; b. Nuremburg, Ger., Oct. 10, 1947; emigrated to Can., 1949; s. Josef and Regina (reiter) K.; m. Penny Ruth Schwartz, June 8, 1969. B.A., U. toronto, 1970, M.A., 1972, Ph.D., 1975. Registered psychologist, Ont. Chief psychologist Scarborough Centenary Hosp., Toronto, 1974-80; lectr. U. Toronto, 1973-77, supr. doctoral students, 1976-80, cons. bus. and industry, Toronto, 1974-80; instr. Ont. Soc. Clin. Hypnosis, 1977-80; dir. employee assistance program Imperial Oil Ltd., Toronto, 1980—; instr. Inst. Rational-Emotive Therapy; cons. Ont. Probation Services, 1973-75. Author: Teaching Interpersonal Skills, 1975, The Employee Assistance Program and the Supervisor, 1982, The Human Resources Management Handbook: Principles and Practice of Employee Assistance Programs, 1985, Health Education and Fitness in the Workplace. Bd. dir., mem. profl. adv. bd. Freedom from Fear Found., Toronto, 1982—; bd. dirs. East Scarborough Boys Club, 1975-76; mem. Scarborough Agy. Fedn., 1979-80. Ministry of Correctional Services grantee, 1973. Mem. Am. Psychol. Assn., Can. Psychol. Assn., Am. Orthopsychiat. Assn., Assn. for Advancement Behavioral Therapy, Am. Soc. Clin. Hypnosis, Ont. Psychol. Assn. (chmn. benefits com. 1975-78, dir. div. pvt. practive 1977-79). Current Work: Cognitive behavioral therapy in industry; cost effectiveness in using short-term psychotherapy in industry; employee productivity as influenced by counselling in industry. Subspecialties: Behavioral psychology; Cognition. Home: 370 Hounslow Ave Toronto ON M2R 1H6 Canada Office: Imperial Oil Ltd 111 St Clair Ave W Toronto ON M5W 1K3 Canada

KLASSEN, KLAAS BEREND, electronics and instrumentation scientist, consultant; b. Bellingwolde, Groningen, Netherlands, Sept. 10, 1941; came to U.S., 1983; s. Sebo and Jantje (Zuiderveen) K.; m. Maria Van der Velden, June 21, 1968; children—Erno Hilbrand, Alwin Helmer. B.S., M.S., Delft U. Tech., 1967, Ph.D., 1978. Registered profl. engr. Research trainee Gen. Electric Co., Utica, N.Y., 1966; scientist Delft U., 1967-79, prof., 1979-83; mem. research staff Research div. IBM, San Jose, Calif., 1983—, cons., 1981-83; ct.-appointed tech. expert, Holland, 1975-80. Author: Measurement Technology, 1977; Analogue Electronic Systems Reliability, 1984. Patentee in field. Contbr. numerous articles to sci. jours. Served to lt. Royal Dutch Air Force, 1960-62. IBM fellow, 1979. Mem. IEEE (sr.), Royal Dutch Inst. Engrs., Dutch Electronics and Radio Soc. Current work: Studies the limits of magnetic recording and the impact of electronics thereon. Subspecialties: Computer engineering; Integrated circuits. Office: IBM Research Lab 5600 Cottle Rd San Jose CA 95193

KLATT, DENNIS H., speech synthesis researcher. Sr. research scientist dept. elec. engring. and computer sci. MIT, Cambridge. . Office: MIT Dept Elec Engring and Computer Sci Cambridge MA 02139

KLAUSMEIER, WILLIAM HILTON, chemical executive, researcher; b. Bangor, Maine, Aug. 6, 1947; s. Robert Louis and Marie Adeline (Hilton) K.; m. Linda Kay Powell, Mar. 11, 1977; children—Jessica Hope, Virginia Marie, Charles Robert. B.S. in Biochemistry, Pa. State U., 1969; M.S. in Organic Chemistry, U. Maine, 1976; Ph.D. in Medicinal Chemistry, U. Mich., 1979. Cert. tchr., Maine. Research chemist Diamond Shamrock, Franklin Park, Ill., 1979-81; systems analyst Argonne Nat. Lab., Ill., 1981-82, research mgr., 1982-83; pres. Sylvatex, Burke, Va., 1983—; exec. dir. Biomass Energy Research, Washington; tech. cons. World Bank, Washington; mem. adv. panel NSF, Washington. Author: Principals of Radiopharm, 1979; Wood and Agricultural Residues, 1983; Advances in Cellulose, 1984. Patentee Synthesis of 1-hydroxy, 1981. Chmn. Com. on Drug Edn., Balt., 1970; asst. scoutmaster Troop 77 Boy Scouts Am., Elmhurst, Ill., 1981; vol. leader Nation's Capitol council Girl Scouts U.S., Burke, Va., 1984. NIH graduate trainee, 1976. Mem. TAPPI, Am. Chem. Soc., Biomass Energy Research Assn. (bd. dirs. 1982-84), Phi Eta Sigma, Phi Kappa Phi, Phi Lambda Upsilon. Republican. Unitarian. Current work: president of new venture developing aquaculture, fermentation and pulping technology; specialty chemicals and other biotechnology products of interest, lecturing, writing and promoting international collaboration. Subspecialties: Biomass (energy science and technology); Chemical engineering. Home: 10708 Burr Oak Way Burke VA 22015 Office: Biomass Energy Research Assn Suite 218 1825 K St NW Washington DC 20006

KLAUSNER, STEVEN CHARLES, cardiologist, educator; b. N.Y.C., Dec. 19, 1941; s. Solomon and Rose (Cohen) K.; m. Jill Ann Hekelburg, Aug. 14, 1965; 1 son, Joshua Charles. B.S. in Engring., Princeton U., 1963; M.D., NYU, 1968. Diplomate: Am. Bd. Internal Medicine. Intern U. Chgo. Hosps., 1968-69, resident, 1969-70, Stanford U., 1972-73; staff cardiologist Latter-day Saints Hosp., Salt Lake City, 1976-81; chief cardiologist sect. Martinez VA Hosp., (Calif.), 1981—; asst. prof. medicine U. Utah, Salt Lake City, 1976-81; assoc. prof. U. Calif.-Davis, 1981—. Contbr. articles to profl. jours. Served to maj. AUS, 1970-72. Fellow Am. Heart Assn. (fellow council on clin. cardiology); mem. ACP, Alpha Omega Alpha. Current Work: Ventricular function; cardiac imaging. Subspecialties: Cardiology; Internal medicine. Office: Martinez VA Med Center 150 Muir Rd Martinez CA 04553

KLAYMAN, DANIEL LESLIE, chemist; b. N.Y.C., Feb. 28, 1929; s. Harry and Clara (Nachmanoff) K.; children—Wanda, Elliot. B.S., Columbia U., 1950; M.S., Rutgers U., 1952, 54, Ph.D., 1956. Asst. prof. Hofstra Coll., Hempstead, N.Y., 1958-59; head organic syntheses sect. Walter Reed Army Inst. of Research, Washington, 1959—. Author, editor: Organic Selenium Compounds, 1973. Patentee in field (9). Contbr. numerous sci. articles to profl. jours. Fulbright grantee, 1956; mem. U.S.-USSR Scientist Exchange program, 1969, U.S.-India Exchange of Scientists and Engrs., 1972. Mem. Am. Chem. Soc. Current work: Involved in antimalarial and antiradiation drug development; has specialized in organic nitrogen, sulfur, selenium chemistry; natural products. Subspecialties: Medicinal chemistry; Organic chemistry. Office: Walter Reed Army Inst Research Div Exptl Therapeutics Washington DC 20307

KLEBAN, PETER HENRY, physicist, educator; b. N.Y.C., May 15, 1942; s. Bernard and Sylvia Lillian (Rod) K.; m. Eloise Alice Rigby, Sept. 23, 1964; children—Rachel, Matthew. B.S., Antioch Coll., 1964; M.A., Brandeis U., 1967, Ph.D., 1970. Research physicist Inst. Laue-Langevin, Grenoble, France, 1970-73; research assoc., vis. asst. prof. U. Minn., Mpls., 1973-77; asst. prof. U. Maine, Orono, 1977-81, assoc. prof., 1981-85, prof., 1985—. Contbr. articles to profl. jours. Mem. Am. Phys. Soc., Am. Vacuum Soc., Sigma Xi. Current work: Theory of phase transitions expecially in two dimensions; finite size effects at phase transitions; surface physics expecially chemisorption systems. Subspecialties: Condensed matter physics; Statistical physics. Home: 23 Hill St Orono ME 04473 Office: Physics Dept U Maine Orono ME 04469

KLEBANOFF, PHILIP SAMUEL, scientist, researcher; b. N.Y.C., July 21, 1918; s. Morris and Celia (Solowey) K.; m. Angelyn Calvo, Dec. 23, 1950; children: Steven Michael, Susan Marian, Leonard Elliott. B.S., Bklyn. Coll., 1939; postgrad., George Washington U., 1942-43, 44-45; Dr. Engring., Hokkaido U., Sapporo, Japan, 1979. Mem. staff Nat. Bur. Standards, Gaithersburg, Md., 1941-83, asst. chief mechanics div., 1969-75, chief aerodynamics sect., 1969-75, asst. chief mechanics div., 1975-78, chief fluid mechanics sect., 1975-78, sr. scientist, 1978-83, cons., 1983—; mem. NRC/NAS U.S. Nat. Commn. Theoretical and Applied Mechanics, 1970-74; mem. indsl. profl. adv. com. Dept. Aerospace Engring. Pa. State U., 1970-75. Bd. editors: Physics of Fluids, 1970-73; contbr. articles to profl. jours. Recipient Ordnance Devel. award U.S. Navy, 1945; cert. of commendation Nat. Bur. Standards, 1968; Gold medal U.S. Dept. Commerce, Washington, 1975. Fellow AIAA, AAAS, Washington Acad. Sci., Am. Phys. Soc. (chmn, exec. com. div. fluid dynamics 1969, vice chmn. 1968, recipient fluid dynamics prize 1981); mem. Philos. Soc. Washington, Nat. Acad. Engring. Current Work: Research in turbulence, boundary layers flows, flow stability and fluid mechanical measurements. Subspecialty: Fluid mechanics. Home: 6412 Tone Dr Bethesda MD 20817

KLEENE, STEPHEN COLE, mathematician, retired educator; b. Hartford, Conn., Jan. 5, 1909; s. Gustav Adolph and Alice Lena (Cole) K.; m. Nancy Elliott, Sept. 21, 1942 (dec. 1970); children—Paul Elliott, Kenneth Cole, Bruce Metcalf, Pamela Lee; m. Jeanne Marie Steinmetz, Mar. 19, 1978. A.B. summa cum laude, Amherst Coll., 1930, Sc.D. (hon.), 1970; Ph.D., Princeton U., 1934. Teaching and research math. Princeton U., 1930-35, vis. prof., 1956-57; mem. Inst. Advanced Study, 1939-40, 65-66; assoc. prof. Amherst Coll., 1941-42; instr. math., U. Wis., 1935-37, asst. prof. 1937-41, assoc. prof., 1946-68, prof., 1948-64, Cyrus C. MacDuffee prof. math., chmn. dept. math., 1957-58, 60-62, chmn. dept. numerical analysis, 1962-63, acting dir. Math Research Ctr., U.S. Army, 1966-67, dean Coll. Letters and Sci., 1969-74, emeritus prof. math and computer sci., emeritus dean letters and sci., 1979—; mem. div. math. NRC, 1956-58, 69-73, chmn. designate div. math. sci., 1969-72; pres. Internat. Union History and Philosophy Sci., 1961, div. Logic, Methodology and Philosophy Sci., 1960-62. Author: Introduction to Metamathematics, 1952; (with Richard E. Vesley) The Foundations of Intuitionistic Matheematics, 1965; Mathematical logic, 1967. Cons. editor Jour. Symbolic Logic, 1936-42, 46-49, editor, 1950-62. Contbr. articles to profl. jours. Guggenheim fellow, 1950; NSF grantee U. Marburg, 1958-59. Served to ltcomdr. USNR, 1942-46. Fellow AAAS; mem. Audubon Soc., Nature Conservancy, Am. Math. So., Assn. Symbolic Logic (mem. exec. com. 1939-41, v.p. 1942, 47-49, pres. 1956-58), Nat. Acad. Sci., Am. Acad. Arts Sci., Phi Beta Kappa, Sigma Xi, Sierra Club. Democrat. Current work: Higher type recursion theory, history of logic in this century. Office: Van Vleck Hall U Wis Madison WI 53706

KLEIMAN, HOWARD, mathematics educator; b. N.Y.C., Apr. 15, 1929; s. Louis and Molly (Blefeld) K.; m. Edna Madge Benjamin, July 26, 1956; children: Michele, Jeffrey, Daniel. B.A., NYU, 1950, M.S., 1961; M.A., Columbia U., 1954; Ph.D., Kings Coll., U. London, 1969. Tchr. N.Y.C. Bd. Edn., 1955-56, Bur. Edn. of Physically Handicapped, N.Y.C., 1956-67; asst. prof. math. Queensborough Community Coll., CUNY, 1967-70, assoc. prof., 1970-75, prof., 1978—. Contbr. articles to profl. jours. Music scholar Met. Music Sch., N.Y.C., 1951; Music scholar Bershire Music Ctr., Tanglewood, 1954. Mem. Math. Assn. Am. (vice chmn. 2-yr. coll. Met. N.Y. sect. 1971-73, treas. 1973-79), Am. Math. Soc., Soc. Indsl. and Applied Math. Current Work: Asymptotic polynomal algorithm for obtaining a hamiltan circuit in a directed graph, probabilistic polynomial algorithms, bounds for the solutions of a new class of diophantine equations. Subspecialties: Algorithms; Algebra and number theory. Home: 188 83 85th Rd Holliswood NY 11423 Office: Queensborough Community College Bayside NY 11364

KLEIN, CORNELIS, mineralogist, petrologist, Precambrian geologist, educator; b. Haarlem, Netherlands, Sept. 4, 1937; came to U.S., 1960, naturalized, 1973; s. Cornelis and Wilhelmina (Van't Hoen) K.; m. Angela Mary Nobbs, Sept. 14, 1960; children—Marc A., Stephanie W. B.S. with honors in Geology, McGill U., 1958, M.S., 1960; Ph.D., Harvard U., 1965. Lectr. mineralogy Harvard U., Cambridge, Mass., 1965-69, sr. tutor, asst. dean, 1966-70, assoc. prof., 1969-72; prof. mineralogy Ind. U., Bloomington, 1972-84; prof. geology U. N.Mex., Albuquerque, 1984—, chmn. dept., 1984—. Author: (with C.S. Hurlbut) Manual of Mineralogy 19th edition, 1977; Manual of Mineralogy 20th edition, 1984. Contbr. articles to profl. jours. Fellow Harvard U., 1962; Guggenheim fellow, 1977. Fellow Geol. Soc. Am., Mineral. Soc. Am. (council 1985—); mem. Mineral. Assn. Can. (exec. com. 1980-81). Current work: Mineralogy, petrology and sedimentology of Precambrian iron-formations worldwide. Subspecialties: Mineralogy; Petrology. Office: Dept Geology U NMex Albuquerque NM 87131

KLEIN, GEORGE DEVRIES, geologist; b. Den Haag, Netherlands, Jan. 21, 1933; came to U.S., 1947, naturalized, 1955; s. Alfred and Doris (deVries) K.; m. Chung Sook Kim Chung, May 23, 1982; children: Richard L., Roger N. B.A., Wesleyan U., 1954; M.A., U. Kans., 1957; Ph.D., Yale U., 1960. Research sedimentologist Sinclair Research Inc., 1960-61; asst. prof. geology U. Pitts., 1961-63; asst. prof. to assoc. prof. U. Pa., 1963-69; prof. U. Ill., Urbana, 1970—; vis. fellow Wolfson Coll. Oxford U., 1969; vis. prof. geology U. Calif., Berkeley, 1970; vis. prof. oceanography Oreg. State U., 1974, Seoul Nat. U., 1980, U. Tokyo, 1983; CIC vis. exchange prof. geophys. sci. U. Chgo., 1979-80; chief scientist Deep Sea Drilling Project Leg 58, 1977-78; continuing edn. lectr.; asso. Center Advanced Studies U. Ill., 1974, 83. Author: Sandstone Depositional Models for Exploration for Fossil Fuels, 2d edit, 1980, 3d edit., 1985, Clastic Tidal Facies, 1977, Holocene Tidal Sedimentation, 1975; asso. editor: Geol. Soc. Am. Bull., 1975-81; cons. editor: McGraw-Hill Ency. of Sci. and Yearbook, 1977—; chief cons. adv. editor: CEPCO div. Burgess Pub. Co, 1979-81; series editor: Geol. Sci. Monographs, 1982—. Recipient Outstanding

Paper award Jour. Sedimentary Petrology, 1970; Erasmus Haworth Disting. Alumnus award in geology U. Kans., 1980; Outstanding Geology Faculty Mem. award U. Ill. Geology Grad. Student Assn., 1983; NSF grantee. Fellow AAAS, Geol. Soc. Am. (chmn. div. on sedimentary geology 1985-86), Geol. Assn. Can.; mem. Am. Geophys. Union, Am. Inst. Profl. Geologists, Soc. Exploration Geophysicists, Soc. Econ. Paleontologists and Mineralogists, Internat. Assn. Sedimentologists, Am. Assn. Petroleum Geologists, Netherlands Geol. and Mining Soc., Sigma Xi. Current Work: Sedimentary geology, basin analysis; sedimentology - tidal sediments, deep-ocean sediments, sediments, sedimentation processes, sandstone diagenesis, sandstone reservoirs, sedimentation patterns and plate tectonics, Sediments from continents to oceans. Subspecialties: Sedimentology; Oceanography. Office: Dept Geology Univ Ill 245 Natural History Bldg 1301 W Green St Urbana IL 61801

KLEIN, HILTON JAMES, veterinarian, research microbiologist; b. Rochester, Pa., Dec. 6, 1950; s. Hilton G. and Jennie (Inman) K.; m. Charlotte Barchet, June 30, 1973; children—Alyssa B., Meghann E. B.S., Rutgers U., 1972; M.S., Pa. State U., 1976; V.M.D., U. Pa., 1980. Head quality control Microbiol. Assocs., Walkersville, Md., 1974-76; mgr. vet. medicine Whittaker M.A. Bioproducts, Walkersville, 1980-82, dir. vet. medicine, 1982—; cons. Harlan-Sprague Dawley, Indpls., 1981-83. Patentee detection of antibiotics in biol. fluids. Mem. AVMA, Am. Assn. Lab. Animal Sci., Phi Sigma, Phi Zeta. Current work: Infectious disease pathophysiology and diagnosis. Subspecialties: Laboratory animal medicine; Microbiology (veterinary medicine). Home: 11316 Hessong Bridge Rd Thurmont MD 21788 Office: Whittaker MA Bioproducts Inc 100 Biggs Ford Rd Walkersville MD 21793

KLEIN, JACK S., research pharmacologist; b. Liverpool, Eng., Dec. 25, 1916; came to U.S., 1921, naturalized, 1924; married; children: Terrence, Susann, Sandra, James. B.Sc., St. John's U., 1941; Ph.B., L.I. U., 1939; M.S., Columbia U., 1943; M.D., United Med. Coll., 1975. Intern Canoga Rehab. Hosp., Canoga Park, Calif., 1975-76; resident Cornell U. Med. Ctr., N.Y.C., 1977; dept. exptl. surgery N.Y. U. Coll. Medicine, N.Y.C., 1943-44; asst. surgeon Columbia U. Aviation Research Lab., 1944; high altitude research Dept. Hosps. City N.Y., 1944-45; pharmacy dept. S. B. Penick Drug Co., 1945-49; chief drug research Meer Corp., North Bergen, N.J., 1950—. Mem. Am. Assn. Physicists in Medicine, Am. Pharm. Assn., AAAS, Am. Chem. Soc.; mem. N.Y. Acad. Sci.; Mem. Am. Police Hall of Fame, N.J. Acad. Sci., Nat. Police and Fire Fighters Assn. Jewish. Current Work: Drug research and elucidation on synthetic organic structures. Subspecialty: Organic chemistry. Home: 1810 Riverside Dr E Bradenton FL 33508 Office: Meer Corp North Bergen NJ 07047

KLEIN, RALPH, physical chemist; b. Pitts., Jan. 24, 1918; s. Benjamin and Rena (Heilbron) K.; m. Joyce Gale, Feb. 3, 1947 (dec. Oct. 31, 1963); children—Kenneth, Douglas; m. Anne Siegel, Feb. 25, 1973. B.S., Carnegie Inst. Tech., 1938; M.S., U. Minn., 1940; Ph.D., U. Pitts., 1950. Chemist Chem. Warfare Service, Edgewood Arsenal, Md., 1940-41, U.S. Bur. Mines, Pitts., 1947-55, Olin-Mathieson, New Haven, Conn., 1955-60, Nat. Bur. Standards, Washington, 1960—. Contbr. numerous articles to profl. jours. Patentee in field. Served to 1st lt. U.S. Army, 1941-45, ETO, PTO. Sci. and Tech. fellow U.S. Dept. Commerce, 1964-65; recipient Meritorious Suprs. award U.S. Dept. Commerce, 1964. Mem. Am. Chem. Soc., Am. Physical Soc., AAAS. Current work: Field electron and ion microscopy, atom probe surface analysis, surface ionization, surface reactions, gas phase kinetics, coal aging. Subspecialties: Physical chemistry; Surface chemistry. Home: 7105 Plantation Ln Rockville MD 20852 Office: Nat Bur Standards Gaithersburg MD 20899

KLEINBERG, ROBERT LEONARD, experimental physicist; b. San Francisco, Aug. 3, 1949; B.S. in chemistry, U. Calif.-Berkeley, 1971; Ph.D. in Physics, U. Calif.-La Jolla, 1978. Postdoctoral physicist Exxon Research and Engring. Co., Linden, N.J., 1978-80; research physicist Schlumberger-Doll Research, Ridgefield, Conn., 1980—, program leader electromagnetics, 1985—. Contbr. articles to profl. jours. Patentee in field. Regents fellow, 1971. Mem. Am. Phys. Soc., Am. Geophys. Union. Current work: Development of electromagnetic and sonic instrumentation for characterization of subsurface geological formations. Subspecialties: Geophysics; Petroleum engineering. Office: Schlumberger-Doll Research Old Quarry Rd Ridgefield CT 06877

KLEINERT, HAROLD EARL, hand surgeon; b. Sunburst, Mont., Oct. 7, 1922; s. Amil and Christine K.; children: Harold, Robert, Christine, James, Jeanne. Student, No. Mont. Coll., 1941, U. Mich., 1941-43; M.D., Temple U., 1946. Diplomate: Am. Bd. Surgery, 1955. Rotating intern Grace Hosp., Detroit, 1946-47, resident in surgery, 1949-53; instr. in surgery U. Louisville, 1954-57, asst. prof. surgery, 1957-62, asso. prof., 1962-69, clin. prof., 1969—; asso. prof. Ind. U., 1967-73, clin. prof., 1973—; nat. cons. to Surgeon Gen. U.S. Air Force, 1973—; mem. staff Jewish Hosp., Louisville, 1955—, pres., 1972; mem. staff Sts. Mary and Elizabeth Hosp., Norton-Kosair-Children's Hosp., Methodist Hosp., Baptist Hosp., Suburban Hosp., Baptist East Hosp., St. Anthony Hosp., Clark County Meml. Hosp., Floyd County Meml. Hosp., North Clark Community Hosp., Audubon Hosp.; Cons. to hosps. Contbr. numerous articles to profl. pubs.; author profl. movies, videotapes. Served with USAAF, 1947-49; with Air N.G., 1953-65. Fellow A.C.S.; mem. Am. Soc. Surgery of the Hand (pres. 1976), AMA (Sci. Achievement award 1980), Am. Assn. Surgery of Trauma, Am. Soc. Plastic and Reconstructive Surgeons, Am. Acad. Orthopedic Surgeons, Am. Assn. Plastic Surgeons (Hon. Award medal 1980), Ohio Valley Soc. Plastic and Reconstructive Surgery, Am. Rheumatism Assn., So. Med. Assn., Ky. Med. Assn., So. Surg. Assn., Am. Trauma Soc., Jefferson County Med. Soc., Aerospace Med. Assn., French Soc. Surgery of Hand, Italian Soc. for Surgery of Hand, Can. Soc. for Surgery of Hand, Colombia Soc. for Surgery of Hand, Louisville Surg. Soc. (pres. 1972), Ky. Surg. Soc. Club: Rotary. Research in microsurgery Research in microsurgery. Subspecialty: Microsurgery. Office: 250 E Liberty St Louisville KY 40202

KLEINROCK, LEONARD, computer scientist; b. N.Y.C., June 13, 1934; s. Bernard and Anne (Schoenfeld) K.; m. Stella Schuler, Dec. 1, 1967; children—Nancy S., Martin C. B.S. in Elec. Engring, CCNY, 1957; M.S., MIT, 1959, Ph.D., 1963. Asst. elec. engr. Photobell Co. Inc., 1951-57; research engr. Lincoln Labs., M.I.T., 1957-63; mem. faculty UCLA, 1963—, prof. computer sci., 1970—; pres. Linkabit Corp., 1968-69, Tech. Transfer Inst., 1976—; cons. in field, prin. investigator govt. contracts. Author: Queueing Systems, Vol. I, 1975, Vol. II, 1976, Communication Nets: Stochastic Message Flow and Delay, 1964, Solutions Manual for Queueing Systems, Vol. I, 1982; also articles. Recipient Best Paper award ICC, 1978, Leonard G. Abraham paper award Communications Soc., 1975, Outstanding Faculty Mem. award UCLA Engring. Grad. Students Assn., 1966, Townsend Harris medal CCNY, 1982, L.M. Ericsson Prize Sweden, 1982; Guggenheim fellow, 1971-72. Fellow IEEE; mem. Nat. Acad. Engring., Ops. Research Soc. Am. (Lanchester prize 1976), Assn. Computing Machinery, Internat. Fedn. Info. Processes Systems, Amateur Athletic Union. Jewish. Subspecialty: Distributed systems and networks. Office: Boelter Hall 3732 UCLA Los Angeles CA 90024

KLEINSORGE, WILLIAM PETER, metallurgical engineer; b. San Francisco, Feb. 10, 1941; s. William Phillip K.; m. Kathryn Deane Vincent, Nov. 14, 1966; children—Elizabeth Louise, Victoria Anne. B.S. in Metall. Engring., U. Nev., 1964. Registered profl. engr., S.C., Calif. Welding engr. U.S. Naval Base, Mare Island, Calif., 1966-69, nuclear welding engr., U.S. Naval Base, Charleston, S.C., 1969-70, supr. welding engr. U.S. Naval Base, Subic Bay, Phillippines, 1970-72, project engr., U.S. Naval Base, Charleston, 1972-78, chief welding engr., 1978-79; metall. engr. U.S. Nuclear Regulatory Commn., Atlanta, 1979—; cons. WPK Engring., Vallejo, Calif., 1966-69, Charleston, 1972-79. Contbr. articles to profl. jours. Mem. Am. Soc. Metals, Am. Welding Soc., Am. Mil. Engrs. Club: Vallejo Yacht. Lodges: Masons, Elks. Current work: Metallurgical consultant; failure analysis and destructive testing and welding with Nuclear Regulatory Commission for nuclear power plant construction and operation. Subspecialties: Metallurgical engineering; Non-destructive testing. Home: 2809 Meadow Dr Marietta GA 30062 Office: US Nuclear Regulatory Commn 101 Marietta St #2900 Atlanta GA 30303

KLEMA, ERNEST DONALD, engineering science educator, physicist; b. Wilson, Kans., Oct. 4, 1920; s. William Wensleau and Mary Bess (Vopat) K.; m. Virginia Clyde Carlock, May 23, 1953; children: Donald David, Catherine Marion. A.B., U. Kans., 1941, M.A., 1942; Ph.D., Rice U., 1951. Staff scientist Los Alamos Sci. Lab., 1943-46; physicist, sr. physicist, prin. physicist Oak Ridge Nat. Lab., 1950-58; assoc. prof. nuclear engring. U. Mich., Ann Arbor, 1956-58; faculty Northwestern U., Evanston, Ill., 1958-68, chmn. dept. engring. scis., 1960-66; faculty Tufts U., Medford, Mass., 1968—; prof. engring. sci. Tufts U. (Coll. Engring.), 1968—, dean coll., 1968-73; adj. prof. internat. politics Fletcher Sch. Law and Diplomacy Tufts U., 1973-83; vis. scholar dept. physics Harvard U., 1985; chmn. neutron measurement and standards NRC, Washington, 1958-63; cons. Gen. Atomic Corp., La Jolla, Calif., 1967, Tech. Edn. Research Ctr., Cambridge, Mass., 1970, Oak Ridge Tech. Enterprises, 1972. Author: manual A Laboratory Course in Reactor Physics, 1953. Mem. exec. com. Winsor Sch., Boston, 1973-76. Fellow Am. Phys. Soc., Am. Nuclear Soc.; sr. mem. IEEE. Clubs: Princeton of N.Y. (N.Y.C.); Harbor (Seal Harbor, Maine). Patentee hydrogen purification method. Current Work: Production of silicon surface-barrier detectors and measurement of their energy resolution for alpha particles, heavy ions, and fission fragments; policy questions related to technological development. Subspecialties: Nuclear physics; Nuclear engineering. Home: 53 Adams St Medford MA 02155 Office: Coll Engring Tufts U Medford MA 02155

KLEMA, VIRGINIA C., numerical analyst; b. Atlanta, Mar. 13, 1929; d. John A. and Mamie C. (Bugg) Carlock; m. Ernest D. Klema, May 23, 1953; children—Donald D., Catherine M. B.A., LaGrange Coll., Ga., 1949; M.S., Auburn U., 1951. Mathematician Oak Ridge Nat. Lab, 1951-56; instr. Kendall Coll., Evanston, Ill., 1959-61; lectr. Northwestern U., Evanston, 1962-68; research assoc., cons. Argonne Nat. Lab., Ill., 1967-76; sr. research assoc. Nat. Bur. Econ. Research, Cambridge, Mass., 1972-78; prin. research scientist Lab. for Info. and Decision Systems, MIT, Cambridge, 1978-83, MIT Stats. Ctr., Cambridge, 1983—. Editor, ACM Trans. on Math. Software, 1976-82. Contbr. sci. articles to profl. jours. Mem. Soc. Indsl. and Applied Math. (trustee 1981-84), Assn. Computing Machinery, IEEE Computer Soc., AAAS. Club: Harbor (Seal Harbor, Maine). Current work: Concurrent computing on microprocessor based systems with emphasis on applications for scientific computing. Subspecialties: Algorithms; Numerical analysis (mathematics). Home: 53 Adams St Medford MA 02155 Office: MIT Stats Ctr E40-131 77 Massachusetts Ave Cambridge MA 02139

KLENKE-HAMEL, KARIN EDDA, industrial organizational psychologist, educator; b. Saarbruecken, W.Ger., May 16, 1947; came to U.S., 1965, naturalized, 1983; d. Herbert and Kaethe (Peters) K.; m. Willem Hamel, Sept. 9, 1970; children: Katja, Max. B.S. summa cum laude, Old Dominion U., 1974, M.S. in Psychology, 1977, Ph.D., 1982. Grant coordinator Southeastern Va. Tng. Ctr., Chesapeake, 1975-77; instr. psychology Old Dominion U., 1977-80, asst. prof., 1982—; pres. Dr. Karin Hamel, Ph.D. & Assocs./Indsl./Organizational Cons., Virginia Beach, 1981—; cons. in field. Author: Human Sexuality, 1980, Exploring Human Sexuality, 1981, Psychology: Its Study and Uses, 1982. Recipient Van Haller Gilmer award Va. Poly. Inst., 1981. Mem. Acad. Mgmt., Am. Psychol. Assn., Assn. Women in Psychology, Cheiron Internat. Soc. History of Behavioral and Social Scis., Southeastern Psychol. Assn. Current Work: Effects of affirmative action programs on employee attitudes and performance, applied theory-building using confirmatory factor analysis and structural equation modeling, organizational life cycles impact of technology on social fabric of organizations, work-family interdependencies. Home: 5309 Sidney Ct Virginia Beach VA 23464 Office: Department Psychology Old Dominion University Norfolk VA 23508

KLEPPNER, DANIEL, physicist. Prof. dept. physics MIT, Cambridge. Subspecialty: Atomic and molecular physics. Office: MIT Dept Physics Cambridge MA 02139

KLESIUS, PHILLIP HARRY, immunologist; b. Bryn Mawr, Pa., Mar. 1, 1938; s. Phillip M. and Mary H. K.; m. Patricia A. Wood, Oct. 28, 1968; children: Stephen, Patrick. B.S., Fla. So. Coll., 1961; M.S., Northwestern State U. La., 1963; Ph.D., U. Tex., 1966. Asst. prof. U. Tex., Austin, 1968; asst. prof. U. Ariz., 1969-72; asst. chief Ctr. for Disease Control, Ft. Collins, Colo., 1973; research leader Agrl. Research Service, U.S. Dept. Agr., Auburn, Ala., 1973—; assoc. prof. Sch. Vet. Medicine, Auburn U., 1973—; vis. prof. Sch. Vet. Medicine Tuskegee Inst.; assoc. prof. Sch. Medicine Med. U. S.C., 1975—. Contbr. articles to profl. jours. Mem. Am. Assn. Immunologists, Am. Assn. Vet. Immunologists, Am. Soc. Microbiology. Methodist. Patentee in field. Current Work: Veterinary Immunology of infectious diseases. Subspecialties: Microbiology (veterinary medicine); Immunology (agriculture). Office: US-DA-ARS PO 952 Auburn AL 36830

KLIBANOV, ALEXANDER MAXIM, biotechnologist, researcher, educator; b. Moscow, July 15, 1949; came to U.S., 1977, naturalized, 1983; s. Maxim and Eugenia (Tomas) K.; m. Margarita Romanycheva, Apr. 21, 1972; 1 dau., Tanya. M.S., Moscow U., 1971, Ph.D., 1974. Research chemist Moscow U., 1974-77; postgrad. research chemist U. Calif., San Diego, 1978-79; asst. prof. dept. applied biol. scis. MIT, 1979-83, assoc. prof., 1983—, E.L. Doherty prof.; cons. in field. Contbr. over 80 articles to profl. jours.; mem. editorial bd.: Applied Biochemistry and Biotech, 1981—, Advances in Biochemical Engring./Biotech., 1985—. Recipient numerous research grants. Mem. Am. Chem. Soc., Am. Soc. Microbiology. Jewish. Current Work: Enzyme Stability and stabilization, immobilized enzymes and cells, enzymes as catalysts in organic chemistry, enzymes for wastewater treatment. Subspecialties: Enzyme technology; Biochemistry (biology). Home: 705 Washington St Boston MA 02135 Office: MIT Bldg 16-209 Cambridge MA 02139

KLIDE, ALAN MARSHALL, veterinary anesthesiologist; b. Bklyn., Aug. 25, 1939; s. Herman and Adele (Silverman) K. Student, CCNY, 1957-60, U. Ga., 1960-61; V.M.D., U. Pa., 1965. Diplomate: Am. Coll. Vet. Anesthesiologists. Postdoctoral trainee dept. anesthesia U. Pa. Sch. Medicine, Phila., 1965-67, U. Pa. Sch. Medicine (dept. pharmacology), 1965-66; instr. anesthsia U. Pa. Sch. Medicine (Sch. Vet. Medicine), 1967-69, asst. prof., 1969-72, assoc. prof., 1972—, chief sect. anesthesia, 1972-80; sec. U. Pa. Sch. Medicine (Small Animal Hosp. Adv. Bd.), 1968. Author: Veterinary Acupuncture, 1977; contbr. articles to profl. jours. Recipient John E. McCoy Meml. award Wash. State U., 1978. Mem. Internat. Vet. Acupuncture Soc. (dir. 1975-81), Am. Soc. Vet. Anesthesia (chmn. program com. 1979-80), Vet. Anesthesia Soc. Am. (editorial rev. bd. 1977-78), Am. Soc. Anesthesiologists, Am. Soc. Pharmacology and Exptl. Therapeutics, Assn. Vet. Anesthetists Gt. Britain and Ireland, Am. Assn. Zoo Veterinarians, Am. Coll. Vet. Pharmacology and Therapeutics, Internat. Vet. Acupuncture Soc., Am. Soc. Regional Anesthesia, Pa. Soc. Anesthesiologists, Phi Zeta. Current Work: Veterinary acupuncture, anesthesia, closed circuit, clin. pharmacology of narcotics, narcotic antagonists, narcotic agonist/antagonist analgesics. Subspecialty: Veterinary Anesthesiology. Office: U Pa Sch Vet Medicine 3850 Spruce St H1 VHUP 3006 Philadelphia PA 19104

KLIEJUNAS, JOHN THOMAS, plant pathologist; b. Sheboygan, Wis., May 4, 1943; s. Anton and Janet (Lamb) K.; m. Barbara Anderson, June 22, 1968; children: Trina Mae, Mary Margaret. B.S., Wis. State U., Stevens Point, 1965; M.F., U. Minn., 1967; Ph.D., U. Wis.-Madison, 1971. Research asso. U. Wis., Madison, 1971-72; plant pathologist U. Hawaii, Hilo, 1972-79; plant pathologist forest pest mgmt. Forest Service, U.S. Dept. Agr., San Francisco, 1979—. Contbr. articles to profl. jours. Mem. Am. Phytopath. Soc. Current Work: Development and implementation of integrated pest management strategies for reducing losses from pests; advising on pest preventive and suppressive actions. Subspecialties: Plant pathology; Integrated pest management. Home: 5305 Lightwood Dr Concord CA 95421 Office: 630 Sansome St San Francisco CA 94111

KLIEM, PETER OTTO, photographic science company executive; b. Berlin, May 13, 1938; children—Peter, John, Eric. B.S., Bates Coll., 1960; M.S., Northeastern U., 1965; postgrad. MIT, 1974. Scientist Polaroid Corp., Waltham, Mass., 1960-70, sr. mgr., 1970-75, div. v.p., 1975-80, v.p. research, Cambridge, Mass., 1980-84, sr. v.p., asst. dir., 1984-85, sr. v.p., dir. research, 1985—. Mem. Am. Chem. Soc., Soc. Photograph. Scientists and Engrs., Indsl. Research Inst. Subspecialty: Photographic science. Office: Polaroid Corp 2 Osborn St Cambridge MA 02139

KLIEWER, KENNETH LEE, research administrator; b. Mountain Lake, Minn., Dec. 31, 1935; s. Henry Gerhard and Susan (Epp) K.; m. Kathleen Kay Zimmermann, Aug. 30, 1959; children—Steven Anthony, Lisa Jo, Christopher Lee. B.E.E., U. Minn., 1957, M.E.E., 1959; Ph.D. in Physics, U. Ill., 1964. Asst. prof. physics Iowa State U., Ames, 1963-66, assoc. prof. physics, 1966-69, prof. physics, 1969-81; program dir. for solid state physics Ames Lab., 1973-78, assoc. dir. sci. and tech., 1978-81; assoc. lab. dir. for physical research Argonne Nat. Lab., Ill., 1981—; guest prof. U. Hamburg, Germany, 1972-73, Free U. Berlin, 1974, Fritz-Haber Inst., Berlin, 1975; vis. scientist Rockwell Internat. Sci. Ctr., Thousand Oaks, Calif., 1976; temporary officer Dept. Energy, Washington, 1979-80. Co-editor: Non-traditional Approaches to the Study of the Solid/Electrolyte Interface, 1980; contbr. articles to tech. jours. Fellow Am. Physical Soc. (exec. com. 1979-81 div. condensed matter physics), AAAS, Sigma Xi, Tau Beta Pi, Eta Kappa Nu. Current work: Electromagnetic theory: nonlocal aspects, collective excitations in solids: plasmons, polaritons and their surface counterparts, electrochemistry. Subspecialties: Condensed matter physics; Theoretical physics. Home: 714 S Charles St Naperville IL 60540 Office: Argonne Nat Lab 9700 S Cass Ave Argonne IL 60439

KLIGER, DAVID SAUL, chemist, educator; b. Newark, Nov. 3, 1943; s. William D. and Natalie K.; m. Rachel Rina, Nov. 24, 1979. B.S., Rutgers U., 1965; Ph.D., Cornell U., 1970. Postdoctoral fellow Harvard U., 1970-71; asst. prof. chemistry U. Calif.-Santa Cruz, 1971-76, assoc. prof., 1976-83, prof., 1983—; mem. molecular and cellular biophysics study sect. NIH, 1980-84. Research, publs. in field. Mem. Interam. Photochem. Soc., Am. Assn. Photobiology, Am. Chem. Soc., Biophys. Soc., AAAS. Current Work: Laser photochemistry, molecular biophysics. Subspecialties: Laser photochemistry; Laser spectroscopy. Home: 546 Arroyo Seco Santa Cruz CA 95060 Office: Natural Sci II U Calif Santa Cruz CA 95064

KLINE, ELLIS LEE, microbiologist, researcher, consultant; b. West Palm Beach, Fla., July 12, 1941; s. George Ellis and Jean Adela (Ross) K.; m. Priscilla Alden Mackenzie, June 12, 1965; children: Heather Jean, Heidi Brooks. B.S. in edn, Greenville (Ill.) Coll., 1964; M.S., No. Ill. U., 1968; Ph.D., U. Calif.-Davis, 1972. Fellow Purdue U., 1972-74; asst. prof. Edinboro (pa.) State Coll., 1974-76, assoc. prof., 1976-78; asst. prof. Clemson U., 1978-79, assoc. prof., 1979-82, prof. microbiology, 1982—; vis. research scientist NIH, Bethesda, Md., 1980; cons. in field. Contbr. articles to profl. jours. USPHS grantee, 1968-72; Clemson U. grantee, 1979, 80. Mem. Am. Soc. Microbiology. Presbyterian. Patentee methods and materials for detection of multiple sclerosis. Current Work: Molecular biology, recombinant DNA in procaryotic and eucaryotic systems; MGR - metabolite gene regulation. Subspecialties: Genetics and genetic engineering (biology); Microbiology. Home: 203 N Elm St Pendleton SC 29670 Office: Clemson University Clemson SC 29631

KLINE, STEPHEN JAY, mechanical engineer; b. Los Angeles, Feb. 25, 1922; s. Eugene Field and Sheda (Lowman) K.; m. Naomi Jeffries, July 11, 1977; children: David M., Mark D., Carolyn R. B.A., Stanford U., 1943, M.S., 1949; Sc.D., M.I.T., 1952. Research analyst N. Am. Aviation, 1946-48; mem. faculty Stanford (Calif.) U., 1952—, prof. mech. engring., 1961—, chmn. thermoscis. div., 1961-73, prof. values, technology, sci. and society, 1970—; cons. Gen. Electric, Gen. Motors, United Technology, DuPont, Brown Boveri. Author: Similitude and Approximation Theory, 1965, Computation of Turbulent Boundary Layers, 1968; editor: Evaluation of Complex Turbulent Flows, 1981. Served with AUS, 1943-46. Recipient Melville medal ASME, 1959, Fluids Engring. award, 1975, Centennial award, 1980; George Stephenson medal Inst. Mech. Engrs. Britain; Bucraino medal Italian Film Soc., 1965. Fellow ASME (past chmn. fluid mechanics com. Fluids Engring. Div.); mem. Nat. Acad. Engring. Current Work: Fluid mechanics of combustion processes; turbulence modelling. Subspecialties: Mechanical engineering; Fluid mechanics. Office: Dept Mech Engring Stanford U Stanford CA 94305

KLINGMAN, GERDA ISOLDE, biochem. pharmacologist, educator; b. Berlin, May 6, 1924; d. Norman Ellsworth and Margarete Luise (Eipel) Schultz; m. Jack Dannis Klingman, May 29, 1953; 1 dau., Karin Louise. B.S., Fordham U., 1952; Ph.D. in Pharmacology, Med. Coll. Va., 1956. Postdoctoral fellow Duke U. Med. Center, 1955-57; asso. in pharmacology dept. pharmacology and exptl. therapeutics Johns Hopkins U. Sch. Medicine, 1957-59, instr., 1959-61; instr. biochem. pharmacology SUNY-Buffalo, 1961-63, asst. prof., 1963-67, asso. prof., 1967-73, prof., 1973—; mem. grant rev. com. NIMH. Contbr. chpts. to books, articles to profl. jours. Commonwealth of Va. Dept. Health predoctoral fellow, 1952-55; USPHS/NIH research career awardee, 1962-67; NIH grantee, 1962-72, 82-83. Mem. Am. Soc. for Pharmacology and Exptl. Therapeutics. Current Work: Neuropharmacology and neurochemistry of the adrenergic nervous system, immunosympathectomy (nerve growth factor antiserum), body temperature regulation, ontogenesis of the adrenergic nervous system, dopamine receptors, acute and chronic tolerance and physical dependence, acute lethal and sublethal alcohol intoxication. Subspecialties: Neurochemistry; Neuropharmacology. Office: Dept Biochem Pharmacology SUNY Buffalo 447 Hochstetter Hall Buffalo NY 14260

KLINGMAN, JACK DENNIS, biochemistry educator; b. Johnson City, N.Y., Apr. 21, 1927; s. Lewis R. and Pearle (Dennis) K.; m. Gerda I. Schultz, 1953; 1 dau., Karin L. B.A., Syracuse U., 1951; M.S., Med. Coll. Va., 1953; Ph.D., Duke U., 1957. Teaching asst. Med. Coll. Va., Richmond, 1951-53, research assoc. in pharmacology, 1953; research asst. Duke U., Durham, N.C., 1954-57; research assoc. Johns Hopkins U., Balt., 1957-61; instr. to prof. biochemistry SUNY-Buffalo, 1961—. Assoc. editor: Preparative Biochemistry, 1975—; mem. editorial bd.: Neurotoxicology, 1980—. Served with U.S. Army, 1945-47, ETO. NIH fellow, 1974-77, 79. Mem. Am. Soc. Biol. Chemistry, Am. Soc. Neurochemistry, Am. Inst. Chemists, Am. Chem. Soc., Internat. Neurochemistry Soc., AAAS, Sigma Xi. Clubs: Nat. Wildlife, Internat. Wildlife. Current Work: Control, metabolism in autonomic ganglia; membrane matrix metabolism; neurogrowth factors; metabolism and control of amino acid and lipid metabolism. Subspecialties: Biochemistry (medicine); Neurochemistry. Office: Dept Biochemistry Sch of Medicine SUNY Buffalo NY 14214

KLIORE, ARVYDAS JOSEPH, space scientist; b. Kaunas, Lithuania, Aug. 5, 1935; came to U.S., 1948, naturalized, 1954; s. Bronius J. and Antonia (Valaitis) K.; m. Birute Anna Ulenas, Sept. 3, 1960; children: Saule Andrea, Rima Birute. B.S.E.E., U. Ill., Urbana, 1956; M.S.E., U. Mich., 1957; Ph.D., Mich. State U., East Lansing, 1962. Engr. Armour Research Found., Chgo., 1957-59; teaching asst. Mich. State U., East Lansing, 1961-62; sr. engr. Jet Propulsion Lab., Calif. Inst. Tech., Pasadena, 1962-66, mem. tech. staff, 1966-81, research scientist, 1981—; co-chmn. Venus Internat. Reference Atmosphere Task Group, COSPAR, 1982—, chmn. sub commn. on planetary atmospheres and aeronomy, 1984—. Editor: The Mars Reference Atmosphere, 1982; contbr. articles to profl. jours. Recipient medal NASA, 1972, Group Achievement award, 1968, 69, 75, 80; Henry Earle Riggs fellow; Bendix fellow, 1962, 1962. Mem. Internat. Astron. Union, Internat. Com. Space Research (exec. mem.), Am. Astron. Soc., Am. Geophys. Union, AAAS, Sigma Xi. Clubs: Backa Athletic (Los Angeles), Lithuanian American Community (Los Angeles). Current Work: Radio propagation studies planetary atmospheres, conduct radio sci. expts. with spacecraft to study planetary atmospheres and ionospheres. Subspecialties: Planetary science; Radio and microwave astronomy. Home: 1475 Scenic Dr Pasadena CA 91103 Office: 4800 Oak Grove Dr 161-228 Pasadena CA 91109

KLITZMAN, BRUCE MAURICE, physiologist, educator, researcher; b. Dayton, Ohio, Nov. 4, 1951; s. Maurice Herman and Mary Ann (Sipek) K.; m. Hardee Burt Brown, Sept. 6, 1980; 1 child, Rachel Hardee. B.S.E., Duke U., 1974; Ph.D., U. of Va., 1979. Research assoc. dept. of physiology U. of Arizona, Tucson, 1979-81; asst. prof. dept. of physiology La. State U., Shreveport, 1982, adj. prof., 1983—, assoc. prof. physiology, 1985—; ad hoc pub. adv. group NIH, 1985; cons. Optech Instruments, Inc., Shreveport, 1984—; adj. asst. prof. dept. biomed. engring. La. Tech. U., Ruston. Contbr. articles to prof. jours. V.P., Timberline Homeowners Assn., Shreveport, 1983—. Research grantee Am. Heart Assn., 1982, Nat. Inst. of Health, 1984, spl. fellow NATO, 1980. Fellow Am. Heart Assoc. (mem. council on circulation, 1984—); mem. Microcirculatory Soc., Inc. (mem. program com. 1983—, mem. com. 1984—), European Soc. for Microcirculation (travel award 1980), Am. Physiol. Soc. (travel award 1983), Biophys. Soc., Am. Fedn. Clin Research. Current work: Physiological regulation of oxygen transport to tissue; Hemorheology; Mathematical modelling of oxygen transport; Neural control of microcirculation; Electron microscopy; regulation of microvasculature. Subspecialties: Physiology (medicine); Biomedical engineering. Office: Dept Physiology & Biophysics LSU Sch Med PO Box 33932 Shreveport LA 71130

KLOCK, BENNY L., astronomer, geodesist; b. Washington, Oct. 29, 1934; s. Leroy and Ertie (Crouse) K.; m. Mildred Olivia Burgess, May 10, 1976; children: Mark, Lorri, Brian. B.A., Cornell U., 1956, M.S., 1960; Ph.D., Georgetown U., 1964. Tech. asst. dir. six-inch Transit Circle Div. U.S. Naval Obs., Washington, 1965-69; dir. U.S. Naval Obs. (No. Transit Circle Div.), 1969-76; chief U.S. Naval Obs. (Instrumentation Br., Astrometry Div.), 1976-84; chief techniques office, geodesy and surveys dept. Def. Mapping Agy., 1984—; cons. astrometry. Contbr. articles in field to astronomy and high precision metrology to profl. jours. Com. chmn. Troop 493 Boy Scouts Am., Rockville, Md., 1970-73. Served to capt. USAF, 1957-59. NSF grantee, 1974-75. Mem. Internat. Astron. Union, Am. Astron. Soc. Republican.

Episcopalian. Current Work: High precision instrumentation for the measurement of small angles. Home: 6601 S Homestake Dr Bowie MD 20715 Office: Defense Mapping Agency Bldg 56 US Naval Obs Washington DC 20305-3000

KLOCK, PETER ILLITCH, JR., energy conservation co. exec.; b. Pitts., Feb. 24, 1940; s. Peter Illitch and Lillian Buchanan (Gresham) K.; married; 1 dau., Holly Alexis. B.S.M.E., Calif. State U., San Jose, 1964; M.S.M.E., Stanford U., 1966. Registered profl. engr., Calif. Energy project mgr. Kaiser Engrs., Oakland, Calif., 1970-74; v.p. environ. affairs URS Corp., San Mateo, Calif., 1974-76; pres. ESC Energy Corp., San Mateo, 1976—. Mem. ASME, Assn. Energy Engrs. Current Work: To apply cogeneration technology to commercial and industrial applications by means of innovative design and financing. Subspecialty: Energy conservation. Home: 494 El Granada Blvd El Granada CA 94018 Office: 1611 Borel Pl Suite 222 San Mateo CA 94402

KLOCKZIEN, VERNON GEORGE, aerospace company executive, consultant; b. Chgo., Sept. 22, 1921; s. George Anthony and Esther Marie (Otto) K.; m. Virginia Rose Mikkola, Aug. 1, 1953; children: Alice, George, Bettina, Charlene. B.S. in Aero. Engring, U. Ill., 1948; M.S. in Aero. Engring, Purdue U., 1950. Research engr. Boeing Co., Seattle, 1950-53; supr. air systems Northrop Aircraft Co., Hawthorne, Calif., 1953-59; dir. thermophysics lab. Lockheed Missile & Space Co., Sunnyvale, Calif., 1959-65; with (Boeing Aerospace Co.), Seattle, 1965—, mgr. propulsion and mech. systems, 1975—. Chmn. Queen Anne Community Council, Seattle, 1969-79; vice chmn. King County Assn. Community Councils, 1972-76, Seattle Center Commn., 1976-82; trustee Seattle Mental Health, 1975-78. Served to 2d lt. USAAF, 1942-45, PTO. Assoc. fellow AIAA; mem. Acad. Polit. Sci., Assn. Am. Historians. Democrat. Current Work: Aerospace propulsion including solid rockets, cryogenic, ramjets and electric propulsion, spacecraft thermal control, thermophysics. Subspecialties: Aerospace engineering and technology; Cryogenics. Home: 1635 Sunset Ave SW Seattle WA 98116 Office: Boeing Aerospace Co PO Box 3999 Seattle WA 98124

KLOTZ, IRVING MYRON, educator, scientist; b. Chgo., Jan. 22, 1916; s. Frank and Mollie (Nasatir) K.; m. Mary Sue Hanlon, Aug. 7, 1966; children: Edward, Audie Jeanne, David. B.S., U. Chgo., 1937, Ph.D., 1940. Research asso. in chemistry Northwestern U., 1940-42, instr., 1942- 46, asst. prof., 1946-47, asso. prof., 1947-50, prof., 1950-63, Morrison prof. chemistry, 1963—; Lalor fellow Marine Biol. Lab., Woods Hole, Mass., 1947-48, corp. mem., 1947—, trustee, 1957-65. Author: Chemical Thermodynamics, 3d rev. edit., 1972, Energies in Biochemical Reactions, rev. edit., 1967; articles sci. jours. Recipient Army-Navy cert. of appreciation for wartime research, 1948. Fellow Royal Soc. Medicine, Am. Acad. Arts and Scis.; mem. Nat. Acad. Scis., Am. Soc. Biol. Chemists, Am. Chem. Soc. (Eli Lilly award 1949, Midwest award 1970), AAAS, Phi Beta Kappa, Sigma Xi, Phi Lambda Upsilon, Alpha Chi Sigma. Current Work: Molecular structure and function of biomacromolecules, thermodynamics. Subspecialties: Biophysical chemistry; Catalysis chemistry. Home: 2515 Pioneer Rd Evanston IL 60201

KLUTH, CHARLES FREDERICK, geologist; b. Rockford, Ill., June 15, 1949; s. Everett Willard and Mary Elizabeth (Haye) K.; m. Mary Jo Anne Morgan, Aug. 28, 1971; children—Mary Anne, Rebecca Lynn. B.A. in Bus. Adminstrn., Augustana Coll., 1971; B.S. cum laude in Geology, No. Ariz. U., Flagstaff, 1973, M.S. in Geology, 1974; Ph.D. in Geology, U. Ariz., Tucson, 1982. Geologist, Chevron USA Inc., Denver, 1974-77, 80-82, sr. geologist, 1982—; dist. supr. Appalachians and Mich. Basin, 1985—. Contbr. articles to profl. jours. Chmn., Bonfils-Chevron Semi-Ann. Blood Drives, Denver, 1982—. Mem. Geol. Soc. Am., Am. Assn. Petroleum Geologists, Rocky Mt. Assn. Geologists, Colo. Sci. Soc. (treas. 1985—). Episcopalian. Club: Rocky Mt. Oyster (Denver). Current work: Structural geology, tectonics, sedimentology. Subspecialties: Tectonics; Geology. Home: 9035 W Geddes Pl Littleton CO 80123 Office: Chevron USA Inc PO Box 599 Denver CO 80201

KNAPP, EDWARD ALAN, government adminstrator; b. Salem, Oreg., Mar. 7, 1932; s. Gardner and Lucille (Moore) K.; m. Jean Elaine Hartwell, June 27, 1954; children—Sandra, David, Robert, Mary. A.B., Pomona Coll., 1954; Ph.D., U. Calif.-Berkeley, 1958. With Los Alamos Sci. Lab., U. Calif., 1958-82, dir. accelerator tech. div., 1977-82; asst. dir., then dir. Nat. Sci. Found., Washington, 1982-84; research adviser, sr. fellow Los Alamos Sci. Lab., 1984-85; pres. Univs. Research Assn., Washington, 1985—; cons. in field. Contbr. articles to profl. jours. Fellow Am. Phys. Soc.; mem. IEEE, AAAS, Sigma Xi. Methodist. Office: Univs Research Assn 1111 19th St Suite 400 Washington DC 20036

KNIGHT, WALTER DAVID, physicist. Prof. dept. physics U. Calif., Berkeley. Elected mem. Nat. Acad. Scis., 1985. Subspecialties: Condensed matter physics; Atomic and molecular physics. Office: U Calif Dept Physics Berkeley CA 94720

KNIGHT, WILBUR HALL, petroleum geologist, consultant; b. Denver, May 8, 1921; s. Samuel Howell and Edwina Gazzem (Hall) K.; m. Elizabeth Lee Fath, Dec. 26, 1941; 1 child, Ernest Emery. B.A., U. Wyo., 1940, M.A., 1945. From geologist to dist. geologist Union Producing Co., Jackson, Miss., 1941-55; chief geologist Larco Drilling Co., Jackson Miss, 1955-60; cons. geology, Jackson, 1960—. Served to 1st lt. U.S. Army, 1941-45. Fellow Geol. Soc. Am.; mem. Am. Assn. Petroleum Geologists (bd. cert., cert. petroleum geologist), Miss. Geol. Soc. (pres. 1950-51), Soc. Petroleum Engrs., Soc. Exploration Geophysicists. Republican. Episcopalian. Club: Jackson Petroleum (pres. 1950-52). Current work: Petroleum geology of Mississippi and Alabama. Subspecialties: Geology; Petroleum engineering. Home: 2030 Southwood Rd Jackson MS 39211 Office: 428 First Nat Bank Bldg Jackson MS 39201

KNIPLING, EDWARD FRED, entomologist; b. Port Lavaca, Tex., Mar. 20, 1909; s. Henry John and Hulda L. (Rasch) K.; m. Phoebe Rebecca Hall, July 21, 1934; children—Edwina H., Anita A., Edward B., Gary D., Ronald R. B.S., Tex. A&M U., 1930; M.S., Iowa State U., 1932, Ph.D., 1947; D.Sc. (hon.), Satawba Coll., 1962, N.D. State U., 1970, Clemson U., 1972. With U.S. Dept. Agr., 1931—, dir. entomology research div., Washington, 1953-71, collaborator, 1972—. Author: Basic Principles of Insect Population Supervision and Management, 1979. Recipient medal of Merit, Pres. U.S., 1948, Disting. Fed. Civil Service award Pres. U.S., 1971, Nat. medal of Sci., U.S. Pres., 1966, Disting. Service award U.S. Dept. Agr., 1960, Rockefeller Disting. Service award Princeton U., 1966, others. Fellow Entomol. Soc. Am. (pres. 1952, Meml. award 1965); mem. Nat. Acad. Scis., Am. Acad. Arts and Scis. Democrat. Lutheran. Club: Cosmos (Washington). Current work: Research on methods of control for insects affecting srops and the health of man and animals. . Home: 2623 Military Rd Arlington VA 22207

KNOBLOCH, CHERYL PORTER, veterinary pathologist; b. Oklahoma City, Nov. 25, 1944; s. Denver Mac and Johnny Alyene (Sapp) P.; m. Robert Elmer Knobloch, June 8, 1967; 1 child, Linnea Alyene. B.S., Okla. State U., 1967, D.V.M., 1970; M.S., U. Ill., 1977. Diplomate Am. Coll. Vet. Pathologists. Pvt. practice vet. medicine, Tucson and Tempe, Ariz., 1970-74; equine extension veterinarian U. Ill., Urbana, 1974-77; vet. communications officer Bur. Vet. Medicine, FDA, Rockville, Md., 1978-80; resident in vet. pathology Armed Forces Inst. Pathology, Washington, 1980-82; research pathologist FDA, Ctr. for Vet. Medicine, Beltsville, Md., 1982-85; prin scientist in pathology Hazleton Labs., Vienna, Va., 1985—; cons. in field. Contbr. articles to profl. jours. FDA grantee, 1980-82; Tex. A&M grad. asst., 1967-68. Mem. AVMA, D.C. Vet. Med. Assn. (exec. bd. 1980-84, pres. 1984, alt. del. to AVMA 1985), Am. Assn. Equine Practitioners, Phi Zeta. Republican. Roman Catholic. Club: Pohick Valley Hunt (exec. bd.). Subspecialty: Pathology (veterinary medicine). Home: 12950 Ford Rd Catharpin VA 22018 Office: Hazleton Labs Am Inc 9200 Leesburg Pike Vienna VA 22180

KNOEBEL, SUZANNE BUCKNER, physician; b. Ft. Wayne, Ind., Dec. 13, 1926; d. Doster and Marie (Lewis) Buckner. A.B., Goucher Coll., 1948; M.D., Ind. U., 1960. Diplomate: Am. Bd. Internal Medicine. Intern Ind. U. Med. Ctr., Indpls., 1960-61, resident, 1961-62; asst. prof. medicine Ind. U. Sch. Medicine, 1966-69, assoc. prof., 1969-72, prof., 1972-77, Krannert prof. medicine, 1977—, asst. dean research, 1975-85; asst. chief cardiology sect. Richard L. Roudebush VA Med. Center, Indpls., 1982-85; assoc. dir. Krannert Inst. Cardiology, Indpls., 1974—. Mem. Am. Fedn. Clin. Research, Assn. Univ. Cardiologists, Am. Coll. Cardiology (pres. 1982-83). Current Work: Clinical coronary heart disease, ischemia, myocardial blood flow, clinical arrhythmias and computer analysis of cardiovascular data. Subspecialty: Cardiology. Office: Ind U Sch Medicine 1100 W Michigan St Indianapolis IN 46223

KNOLL, ANDREW HERBERT, paleontologist, educator; b. W. Reading, Pa., Apr. 23, 1951; s. Robert Samuel and Anna Augusta (Meyer) K.; m. Marsha Craig, June 22, 1974. B.A. with highest honors, Lehigh U., 1973; A.M., Harvard U., 1974, Ph.D., 1977. Asst. prof. Oberlin (Ohio) Coll., 1977-81, assoc. prof., 1982; assoc. prof. Harvard U., Cambridge, Mass., 1982-85, prof., 1985—, curator Bot. Mus., 1985—; mem. Com. on Planetary Biology and Chem. Evolution, U.S. Space Sci. Bd, 1981—, Am. Inst. Biol. Scis. adv. panel to NASA exobiology program, 1980—. Contbr. articles on early evolution of life on earth and evolution of land plants to profl. jours. Active choral groups Boston, Oberlin. NSF grantee, 1980—. Mem. Bot. Soc. Am., Geol. Soc. Am., Paleontol. Soc., AAAS, Soc. Econ. Paleontol. Mineralogy, Internat. Soc. Study Origins of Life, Phi Beta Kappa, Sigma Xi. Democrat. Current Work: Field and laboratory research on the early evolution of life and the fossil record of land plants. Subspecialties: Paleontology; Evolutionary biology. Office: Bot Mus Harvard U Cambridge MA 02138

KNOLL, GLENN FREDERICK, nuclear engineering educator; b. St. Joseph, Mich., Aug. 3, 1935; s. Oswald Herman and Clara Martha (Bernthal) K.; m. Gladys Hetzner, Sept. 7, 1957; children: Thomas, John, Peter. B.S., Case Inst. Tech., 1957; M.S. in Chem. Engring., Stanford, 1959; Ph.D. in Nuclear Engring., U. Mich., 1963. Asst. research physicist U. Mich., Ann Arbor, 1960-62, asst. prof. nuclear engring., 1962-67, asso. prof., 1967-72, prof., 1972—, chmn. dept. nuclear engring., 1979—, also mem. bioengring. faculty.; Vis. scientist Institut für Angewandte Kernphysik, Kernforschungszentrum Karlsruhe, Germany, 1965-66; sr. vis. fellow dept. physics U. Surrey, Guildford, Eng., 1973; summer cons. Electric Power Research Inst., Palo Alto, Calif., 1974; cons. in field. Author: Radiation Detection and Measurement, 1979, Principles of Engineering, 1982. NSF fellow, 1958-60; Fulbright travel grantee, 1965-66; Sci. Research Council sr. fellow, 1973. Fellow Am. Nuclear Soc.; mem. Am. Assn. Engring. Edn. (Glenn Murphy award 1979); Mem. IEEE (nuclear and plasma soc., chmn. tech. com. on nuclear med. sci. 1977-79), Soc. Nuclear Medicine, Sigma Xi, Tau Beta Pi. Patentee in field. Current Work: Radiation detection and spectroscopy, engineering aspects in nuclear medicine and radiology. Subspecialties: Nuclear engineering; Bioinstrumentation. Office: Dept Nuclear Engring 119 Cooley Bldg U Mich Ann Arbor MI 48109

KNOOT, PETER ANTON, semiconductor process engineering manager; b. Vlaardingen, The Netherlands, Dec. 4, 1952; came to U.S., 1969; s. Jacob and Marlene (Capriles) K.; m. Laurie Lynn Winston, Mar. 17, 1980; 1 child, Tyler Alexander. B.S. in Chemistry, Rensselaer Polytechnic Inst., 1974, Ph.D. in Phys. Chemistry, 1978. Process engr. Nat. Semiconductor, Hawthorne, Calif., 1980-81, engring. mgr., 1981-83, Hewlett-Packard, San Jose, Calif., 1983—. Mem. Am. Chem. Soc., Am. Vacuum Soc., Inst. Elec. and Electronic Engrs., Am. Assn. Crystal Growth. Current work: Sub-micron lithography and dry etching; III-V materials growth and epitaxy, GaAs Fets. Subspecialties: Physical chemistry; Integrated circuits. Office: Hewlett-Packard 350 W Trimble Rd San Jose CA 95131

KNOPOFF, LEON, educator; b. Los Angeles, July 1, 1925; s. Max and Ray (Singer) K.; student Los Angeles City Coll., 1941-42; B.S. in Elec Engring., Calif. Inst. Tech., 1944, M.S. in Physics, 1946, Ph.D. in Physics, 1949; m. Joanne Van Cleef, Apr. 9, 1961; children—Katherine Alexandra, Rachel Anne, Michael Van Cleef. Asst., then asso. prof. physics Miami U., Oxford, Ohio, 1948-50; mem. faculty UCLA, 1950—, prof. physics, 1961—, prof. geophysics, 1959—, research musicologist, 1963—, asso. dir. Inst. Geophysics and Planetary Physics, 1972—; prof. geophysics Calif. Inst. Tech., 1962-63, research asso. seismology, 1963-64; vis. prof. Technische Hochschule, Karlsruhe, Germany, 1966, Harvard, 1972, U. Chile, Santiago, 1973. Chmn. U.S. Nat. Upper Mantle Com., 1963-71; sec. Internat. Upper Mantle Com., 1963-71; chmn. com. math. geophysics Internat. Union Geodesy and Geophysics, 1971-75, mem. U.S. nat. com., 1973-75. Recipient Wiechert medal German Geophys. Soc., 1978; Gold medal Royal Astron. Soc., 1979; NSF sr. postdoctoral fellow Cambridge (Eng.) U., 1960-61, Guggenheim Found. fellow, 1976-77. Fellow Am. Acad. Arts and Scis.; mem. Nat. Acad. Scis., Am. Phys. Soc., Am. Geophys. Union, Seismol. Soc., Royal Astron. Soc. (Jeffreys lectr. 1976), AAAS. Current work: Earthquake seismology and seismicity; fracture mechanics; structure of the earth's interior. Office: U Calif Los Angeles CA 90024

KNOTT, DOUGLAS RONALD, crop scientist, educator; b. New Westminster, B.C., Can., Nov. 10, 1927; s. Ronald David and Florence Emily (Keeping) K.; m. Joan Madeline Hollinshead, Sept. 2, 1950; children: Holly Ann, Heather Lynn, Ronald Kenneth, Douglas James. B.S.A. in Agr, U. B.C., 1948; M.S., U. Wis., 1949, Ph.D., 1952. Asst. prof. field. husbandry U. Sask., 1952-56, assoc. prof., 1956-65, prof., head crop sci. dept., 1965-75, prof. crop sci., 1975—. Contbr. research papers to profl. lit. Fellow Am. Soc. Agronomy, Agrl. Inst. Can., Can. Soc. Agronomy, Genetics Soc. Am., Can. Soc. Genetics, Sigma Xi. Liberal. Mem. United Ch. Current Work: Wheat cytogenetics and wheat breeding. Subspecialties: Plant genetics; Plant pathology. Home: 2002 14th St E Saskatoon SK S7H OB2 Canada Office: Crop Sci Dept U Sask Saskatoon SK S7N OWO Canada

KNOWLDEN, NORMAN FRANCIS, mathematical statistician; b. Newburgh, N.Y., Apr. 6, 1925; s. Benjamin Walter and Mabel Leona (Lockwood) K.; m. Gloria Caren Bush; children: Erik Kristin, Ethan Konrad. B.A. (Council scholar), N.Y.U., 1946; postgrad., Columbia U., 1949-51; M.S., Stevens Inst. Tech., 1953. Research chemist Maltbie Chem. Co., Newark, 1946-47; analytical statistician Burroughs-Wellcome Co. Inc., Tuckahoe, N.Y., 1947-54; statis. group leader Am. Cyanamid Co. Lederle Labs., Pearl River, N.Y., 1954-61; mgr. corp. mgmt. scis. Allied Chem. Corp., Morristown, N.J., 1961-68, 69-79, research assoc. in math. scis., 1979—; v.p. Telos Sci. Co., N.Y.C., 1969; mem. vis. faculty mgmt. sci. dept. Stevens Inst. Tech. Grad. Sch., 1957-72. Contbr. articles to sci. jours. Mem. Am. Statis. Assn., Am. Soc. for Quality Control (cert. quality engr. and reliability engr.; edn. com. 1982-85), Zeta Psi. Lutheran. Current Work: Process operations analysis; epidemiology; environmental control procedures; application of mathematical science and statistics in areas of process yield and quality improvement; epidemiological studies; environmental and industrial safety controls. Subspecialties: Statistics; Operations research (mathematics). Home: Brockden Pl Mendham NJ 07945 Office: PO Box 1087R Morristown NJ 07960

KNOWLES, BARBARA B., microbiologist, geneticist, educator; b. N.Y.C., Feb. 27, 1937; d. Christian J. and Undine G. Bang; divorced; children: Jared Appleton, Amanda Gaylord. A.B., Middlebury Coll., 1958; M.S., Ariz. State U., 1963, Ph.D., 1965. Postdoctoral trainee dept. genetics U. Calif., Berkeley, 1965-66; assoc. prof. Wistar Inst., Phila., 1967-82, prof., 1983—; assoc. prof. U. Pa. Coll. Arts and Scis., 1977-84, prof. dept. pathology and lab. medicine and microbiology, 1984—; mem. cancer research manpower com. NIH-Nat. Cancer Inst. Mem. editorial bd. Immunogenetics, 1978-82, Molecular and Cellular Biology, 1983—. Contbr. articles to profl. publs. Recipient USPHS research career devel. award, 1975-80, numerous research grants, 1972—. Mem. Genetics Soc. Am., Am. Soc. Human Genetics, AAAS. Current Work: Description and genetic control of normal, tumor-specific and embryonic cell surface molecules. Subspecialties: Immunogenetics; Cell biology (medicine). Office: Wistar Inst 36th St and Spruce St Philadelphia PA 19104

KNOWLES, JEREMY RANDALL, chemist, educator; b. Rugby, Eng., Apr. 28, 1935; came to U.S., 1974; s. Kenneth Guy Jack Charles and Dorothy Helen (Swingler) K.; m. Jane Sheldon Davis, July 30, 1960; children: Sebastian David Guy, Julius John Sheldon, Timothy Fenton Charles. B.A., Balliol Coll., Oxford (Eng.) U., 1958; M.A., D.Phil., Christ Ch., 1961. Research fellow Calif. Inst. Tech., 1961-62; fellow Wadham Coll., Oxford U., 1962-74, univ. lectr., 1966-74; vis. prof. Yale U., 1969, 71; Sloan vis. prof. Harvard U., 1973, prof. chemistry, 1974—, Amory Houghton prof. chemistry and biochemistry, 1979—; Newton-Abraham vis. prof. Oxford U., 1983-84; hon. fellow Balliol Coll., Oxford, Eng., 1984. Author papers, revs. bioorganic chemistry. Served as pilot officer RAF, 1953-55. Fellow Royal Soc., Chem. Soc. London, Am. Acad. Arts and Scis.; mem. Biochem. Soc. London, Am. Chem. Soc., Am. Soc. Biol. Chemists. Subspecialties: Biochemistry (biology); Organic chemistry. Home: 44 Coolidge Ave Cambridge MA 02138 Office: Dept Chemistry Harvard Univ Cambridge MA 02138

KNOWLES, LLOYD GEORGE, electrical engineering educator; b. Pottsville, Pa., Jan. 27, 1934; s. William George and Thelma May K.; married; children: David Lloyd, Carolyn Anne, Raymond William. Sr. engr. Applied Physics Lab., Johns Hopkins U., Laurel, Md., 1961—; asst. prof. Johns Hopkins U., Balt., 1974—. Contbr. articles to tech. jours., chpts. in books. Mem. Howard County (Md.) County Council, 1974—, Howard County Planning Bd., 1969-74. Served in USN, 1955-57. Mem. Am. Assn. Physicists in Medicine, Soc. Nuclear Medicine, Soc. Photo-optical Instrumentation Engrs. Democrat. Unitarian. Clubs: Columbia (Md.) Democratic, Ellicott City (Md.) Democratic. Current Work: Specialist in evaluation of images in photon-limited situations, evaluating map-matching techniques in missile navigation. Subspecialties: Biomedical engineering; Systems engineering. Home: 10850-617 Green Mountain Circle Columbia MD 21044 Office: Johns Hopkins U Applied Physics Lab Johns Hopkins Rd Laurel MD 20707

KNOWLES, RICHARD JAMES ROBERT, medical physicist, researcher, educator; b. McPherson, Kans., Aug. 2, 1943; s. Richard E. and Pauline H. (Worland) K.; m. Stephanie R. Closter, May 14, 1970; 1 dau., Guenevere Regina. B.S., St. Louis U., 1965; M.S., Cornell U., 1969; Ph.D., Poly Inst. N.Y., 1979. Cert. scientist in nuclear medicine Am. Bd. Sci. in Nuclear Medicine cert. radiol. physicist Am. Bd. Radiology. Research asst. Wilson Synchrotron Lab., Cornell U., Ithaca, N.Y., 1967-70; research asst. Ward Reactor Lab., 1970-72; sr. technologist in nuclear medicine N.Y. Hosp., N.Y.C., 1972-77; chief med. physicist L.I. Coll. Hosp., Bklyn., 1977-81; dir. Radiation Physics Lab., Downstate Med. Center, SUNY, Bklyn., 1981-82; sr. med. physicist N.Y. Hosp. Cornell Med. Ctr., N.Y.C., 1982 ; adj. asst. prof. physics York Coll., CUNY, Jamaica, 1982—. Contbr. articles to profl. publs. Mem. Am. Phys. Soc., Am. Assn. Physicists in Medicine, Soc. Nuclear Medicine, Health Physics Soc., Soc. Magnetic Resonance in Medicine, N.Y. Acad. Scis., Soc. Magnetic Resonance in Medicine. Current Work: Medical imaging, image processing, pattern recognition. Subspecialties: Imaging technology; Graphics, image processing, and pattern recognition. Office: 525 E 68th St New York NY 10021

KNUDSON, ALFRED GEORGE, JR., medical geneticist; b. Los Angeles, Aug. 9, 1922; s. Alfred George and Mary Gladys (Galvin) K.; m. Anna T. Meadows, June 20, 1977; children by previous marriage: Linda, Nancy, Dorene. B.S., Calif. Inst. Tech., 1944, Ph.D. (Guggenheim fellow), 1956; M.D., Columbia U., 1947. Chmn. dept. pediatrics City of Hope Med. Center, Duarte, Calif., 1956-62, chmn. dept. biology, 1962-66; assoc. dean Health Sci. Center, SUNY, Stony Brook, 1966-69; dean Grad. Sch. Biomed. Scis., U. Tex. Health Sci. Center, Houston, 1970-76; dir. Inst. Cancer Research, Fox Chase Cancer Center, Phila., 1976-83, sr. mem., 1976—, pres., 1980-82; mem. Assembly Life Scis., NRC, 1975-81. Author: Genetics and Disease, 1965. Recipient Disting. Alumni award Calif. Inst. Tech., 1978. Mem. Am. Soc. Human Genetics (pres. 1978), Assn. Am. Physicians, Am. Pediatrics Soc., Am. Assn. Cancer Research. Research, publs. in genetics of human cancer. Subspecialties: Genetics and genetic engineering (medicine); Cancer research (medicine). Office: Inst Cancer Research 7701 Burholme Ave Philadelphia PA 19111

KNUDSON, GREGORY BLAIR, geneticist, researcher, educator, army res. officer; b. Salina, Kans., Aug. 9, 1946; s. Cecil C. and Dorothy A. (Hamilton) K.; m. Kathryn H. Malloy, Oct. 21, 1972; 1 son, Todd C. B.A. in Biology, Calif. State U.-Fullerton, 1969, M.A. in Biology, 1971; Ph.D. in Genetics, U. Calif.-Riverside, 1977. Commd. 2d lt. U.S. Army Res., 1970, advanced through grades to capt., 1977; research officer Biomed. Lab., Chem. Corps, Edgewood Arsenal, Md., 1970-73; res. capt. Med. Service Corps., 6252d USAR Hosp., San Bernardino, Calif., 1973-78; research geneticist U.S. Army Med. Research Inst. Infectious Diseases, Ft. Detrick, Md., 1978-81; bacterial geneticist U.S. Army Med. Research Inst. Infectious Diseases (G-12), 1981—; mem. faculty Calif. State Coll., 1976-77; instr. recombinant DNA tech. Hood Coll., Md., 1980. Mem. Genetics Soc. Am., Am. Soc. Microbiology, AAAS, N.Y. Acad. Scis. Republican. Methodist. Current Work: Role of plasmids in pathogens; recombinant DNA technology; mechanisms of DNA repair. Subspecialties: Genetics and genetic engineering (biology); Molecular biology. Office: USAMRIID Ft Detrick Frederick MD 21701

KNUTH, DONALD ERVIN, computer scientist; b. Milw., Jan. 10, 1938; s. Ervin Henry and Louise Marie (Bohning) K.; m. Nancy Jill Carter, June 24, 1961; children: John Martin, Jennifer Sierra. B.S., Case Inst. Tech., 1960, M.S., 1960; Ph.D., Calif. Inst. Tech., 1963. Asst. prof., then asso. prof. math. Calif. Inst. Tech., 1963-68; prof. computer sci. Stanford U., 1968—; guest prof. math. U. Oslo, 1972-73; cons. Burroughs Corp., 1960-68. Author: The Art of Computer Programming series, vol. 1, 1968, vol. 2, 1969, vol. 3, 1973, Surreal Numbers, 1974, Mariages Stables, 1976, Tex and Metafont, 1980; Editor jours. Recipient Nat. Medal of Sci., 1979; Guggenheim fellow, 1972-73. Fellow Am. Acad. Arts and Scis., Brit. Computer Soc; mem. Nat. Acad. Scis., Nat. Acad. Engring., Assn. Computing Machinery (Grace Murray Hopper award 1971, Alan M. Turing award 1974), Math. Assn. Am. (Lester R. Ford award 1975), IEEE Computer Soc. (McDowell award 1980, Computer Pioneer award 1982), Am. Math. Soc., Soc. Indsl. and Applied Math., Am. Guild Organists. Lutheran. Patentee in field. Current Work: Analysis of algorithms, digital typography, combinatorial mathematics. Subspecialties: Algorithms; Programming languages. Office: Computer Sci Dept Stanford Univ Stanford CA 94305

KNUTSON, CARROLL FIELD, geologist, consultant; b. Santa Monica, Calif., Mar. 14, 1924; s. Andrew J. and Harriet K. (Field) K.; m. Jeanne Y. Kennedy, Aug. 20, 1948; children—Craig F., Melanie J., Keith A., Eric M. A.A., Santa Monica City Coll., 1948; B.S., Stanford U., 1950, M.S. 1951; Ph.D., UCLA, 1959. Various positions with various cos., Okla., Calif., Tex., Nev., 1951-74; cons. geologist, Las Vegas, 1974-76; exec. v.p. C.K. GeoEnergy, Las Vegas, 1976-84, pres., 1984—; dir. CKM Resources Inc., Evergreen, Colo., 1981—. Contbr. articles to profl. jours. Patentee in field. Served to lt. USAF, 1942-46. Decorated Air Medal with oak leaf cluster. NSF fellow, 1954. Mem. Geol. Soc. Am., Am. Geophys. Union, Soc. Econ. Paleontologists & Mineralogists, Soc. Ind. Earth Scientists, Am. Assn. Petroleum Geologists, AIME, Soc. Petroleum Geologists. Republican. Presbyterian. Current work: Geologic modeling, petroleum reservoir evaluation, oil shale resource, hydrology geoenvironmental impacts. Subspecialties: Geology; Hydrology. Home: 3714 E Harmon St Las Vegas NV 89121 Office: CK GeoEnergy Corp 4055 S Spencer Suite 228 Las Vegas NV 89109

KNUTZEN, VICTOR FRANCIS, manufacturing company executive; b. Burlington, Wash., Dec. 11, 1914; s. William J. and Helena (Anenson) K.; m. Margaret Elizabeth Carlson, Aug. 31, 1940; children—John A., James V., Gerald C., Ingrid M. Student, Pacific Luth. Coll., 1932-33, Wash. State Coll., 1933-34; B.A., U. Wash., 1936. With Boeing Co., Seattle, 1941-81; successively exec. accounting positions, controller Boeing Co. (Seattle div.), asst. corp. controller, 1941-61, corporate controller, 1961-75, v.p., controller, 1975-81. Mem. Washington Soc. C.P.A.'s, Seattle C. of C., Fin. Execs. Inst., Beta Gamma Sigma, Beta Alpha Psi. Presbyterian. Lodges: Masons, Rotary. Home: 2649 S 304th St Federal Way WA 98003

KO, CHE MING, physics educator; b. Szechuan, China, Jan. 7, 1943; came to U.S., 1968, naturalized, 1980; s. Shu Ping and Kuang Hwa (Liu) K.; m. Shiao Yen Chou, Nov. 3, 1973; children—Shan Wei, Kevin. B.Sc., Tunghai U., Taichung, Republic of China, 1965; M.Sc., McMaster U., Hamilton, Ont., Can., 1968; Ph.D., SUNY-Stony Brook, 1973. Postdoctoral fellow McMaster U., 1973-74; vis. scientist Max-Planck Inst., Heidelberg, Fed. Republic Germany, 1974-77; research assoc. Mich. State U., East Lansing, 1977-78, Lawrence Berkeley Lab, Calif., 1978-80; asst. prof. physics Tex. A&M U., College Station, 1980-84, assoc. prof., 1984—; research assoc. prof. Joint Inst. for Heavy Ion Research, Oak Ridge, 1984-85. Contbr. articles to profl. jours. Mem. Am. Phys. Soc. Current work: Theoretical studies of heavy ion reactions. Subspecialty: Nuclear physics. Home: 2508 Merrimac Ct College Station TX 77840 Office: Physics Dept Tex A&M U College Station TX 77843

KO, WEN-HSIUNG, electrical engineering educator; b. Shang-Hong, Fukien, China, Apr. 12, 1923; came to U.S., 1954, naturalized, 1963; s. Sing-Ming and Sou-Ye (Kao) K.; m. Christina Chen, Oct. 12, 1957; children—Kathleen, Janet, Linda, Alexander. B.S. in E.E. (Tan-Ka-Kee fellow), Nat. Amoy U., Fukien, China, 1946; M.S., Case Inst. Tech., 1956, Ph.D., 1959. Engr., then sr. engr. Taiwan Telecommunication Adminstrn., 1946-54; mem. faculty Case Inst. Tech., Cleve., 1956—, prof. elec. engring., 1967—, prof. elec. and biomed. engring., 1970—, dir. engring. design center, 1970-83; cons. Conoflow Corp., IBM, Diamond Alkali, NIH, 1966-76. Fellow IEEE; mem. Instrument Soc. Am., Bio-Med. Engring. Soc., Sigma Xi, Eta Kappa Nu. Current work: Solid state transducers; integrated circuits; biomedical instrumentations. Home: 1356 Forest Hills Blvd Cleveland Heights OH 44118 Office: Electronics Design Center Case Western Res U Cleveland OH 44106

KOBAYASHI, ALBERT S., mechanical engineer, educator; b. Chgo., Dec. 9, 1924; m. Elizabeth Midori, Sept. 24, 1953; children: Dori Kobayashi Ogami, Tina, Laura. B.Engring., U. Tokyo, 1947; M.S. in Mech. Engring., U. Wash., 1952; Ph.D., Ill. Inst. Tech., 1958. Tool engr. Konishiroku Photo Industry, Tokyo, 1947-50; design engr. Ill. Tool Works, Chgo., 1953-55; research engr. Armour Research Found., Ill. Inst. Tech., Chgo., 1955-58; Coll. faculty cons. Boeing Co., Seattle, 1958-76; asst. prof. mech. engring. U. Wash., Seattle, 1958-61, assoc. prof., 1961-65, prof., 1965—; cons. Mathematical Sci. N.W., 1962—; vis. scholar strength of materials lab., dept. naval architecture U. Tokyo, 1969, 77. Contbr. articles to profl. jours. Fellow ASME, Soc. Exptl. Stress Analysis (F.G. Tatnall award 1973, B.J. Lazan award, 1982); mem. Soc. Engring. Sci. Presbyterian. Current Work: Two and three dimensional fracture mechanics, stable crack growth and dynamic fracture mechanics. Subspecialties: Fracture mechanics; Theoretical and applied mechanics. Office: Dept Mech Engring U Wash FU-10 Seattle WA 98195

KOBAYASHI, HESTER ATSUKO, environmental scientist; b. Honolulu, Oct. 4, 1938; s. Henry T. and Kinuyo (Shinkawa) K. B.A., U. Hawaii, 1960, M.S., 1963; M.S. in Pub. Health, UCLA, 1976; Dr. P.H., 1981. Mgr. Arctic research U. So. Calif., Los Angeles, 1968-72; marine environmentalist Port of Los Angeles, Calif., 1972-73; research assoc. U. So. Calif., Los Angeles, 1973; researcher UCLA, Calif., 1976-81; research assoc. Ill. Dept. Civil Engring. and sci., Urbana, 1980-82; environ. researcher Sohio Research Ctr., Cleve., 1982—; cons. Office Toxic Substances, Washington, 1984—. Contbg. author: Genetic Control of Environ. Pollutants, 1984. Contbr. articles to profl. jours. Mem. Soc. for Environ. Toxicology and Chemistry, Am. Soc. for Microbiology, ASTM, Am. Chem. Soc., Internat. Assn. Water Pollution Research and Control, Water Pollution Control Fedn., Sigma Xi. Subspecialties: Hazardous waste disposal; Waste and waste water treatment. Office: Standard Oil of Ohio Research Ctr 4440 Warrensville Ctr Rd Cleveland OH 44128

KOBAYASHI, HISASHI, computer scientist, computer manufacturing executive; b. Tokyo, June 13, 1938; U.S., 1965; s. Kyuzo and Yoshie (Obi) K.; m. Masaye Okubo. B.S., U. Tokyo, 1961, M.S., 1963; M.A., Princeton U., 1966, Ph.D., 1967. Radar system designer Toshiba, Kawasaki, Japan, 1963-65; mem. research staff IBM, Yorktown Heights, N.Y., 1967—; dir. Japan Sci. Inst. IBM Japan Ltd., 1982—; vis. asst. prof. UCLA, 1969-70; vis. prof. U. Hawaii, 1975, Tech. U. Darmstadt, W. Ger., 1979-80; cons. prof. Stanford U., 1976; Internat. prof. U. Libre de Bruxelles, Belgium, 1980; mem. computer sci. panel NRC, 1981—. Author: Modeling and Analysis, 1978; editor-in-chief: Performance Eval., 1981—; asso. editor: IEEE Trans Infor. Theory, 1980-83; contbr. articles to profl. jours. Recipient David Sarnoff Award; RCA, 1960; IBM Invention award, 1971, 73; Outstanding Contbn. award, 1975; Humboldt award, 1979; IFIP Silver Core award, 1980. Fellow IEEE; mem. Assn. Computing Machinery, Internat. Union Radio Sci. (vice chmn. Commn. C 1978-81), Internat. Fedn. Info. Processing (chmn. working group 1982—). Patentee communication systems. Subspecialty: Research administration. Home: 1323 Judy Rd Mohegan Lake NY 10547 Office: IBM Research Center PO Box 218 Yorktown Heights NY 10598

KOBAYASHI, SHIRO, mechanical engineer, educator; b. Gotsu, Japan, Feb. 21, 1924; s. Toraji and Chisao (Shimizu) K.; m. Suzue Yamaguchi, May 15, 1961. B.S., Tokyo U., 1946; M.S., U. Calif., Berkeley, 1957, Ph.D., 1960. Mem. faculty dept. mech. engring. U. Calif., Berkeley, 1960—, prof., 1968—; vis. prof. Ohio State U., 1967; Miller Research prof. U. Calif., 1977. Contbr. numerous articles to profl. jours.; mem. editorial bd. profl. jours. Recipient Blackall award ASME, 1962. Mem. ASME, Nat. Acad. Engring., Am. Soc. Metals, Soc. Mfg. Engrs. (Gold Medal 1983), Internat. Instn. for Prodn. Engring. Research. Subspecialty: Mechanical engineering. Home: 414 Sea View Dr El Cerrito CA 94530 Office: Dept Mech Engring Univ of Calif Berkeley CA 94720

KOBE, DONALD HOLM, physics educator; b. Seattle, Jan. 13, 1934; s. Kenneth Albert and Jeneva Catherine (Holm) K. B.S., U. Texas-Austin, 1956; M.S., U. Minn., 1959; Ph.D., 1961. Vis. asst. prof. Ohio State U., Columbus, 1961-63; research assoc. Quantum Chemistry Group, Uppsala, Sweden, 1964-66; vis. asst. prof. H.C. Oersted Inst., Copenhagen, Denmark, 1966-67, Northeastern U., Boston, 1967-68; prof. No. Texas State U.-Denton, 1968—; Fulbright lectr., Taipei, Taiwan, 1963-64, Nat. Acad. Sci. lectr., Yugoslavia, 1973. Contbr. articles to profl. jours. Fellow Am. Sci. Affiliation; mem. Am. Phys. Soc., Am. Assn. Physics Tchrs., AAAS. Current Work: I have developed with others a manifestly gauge-invariant formulation of quantum mechanics for the interaction of electromagnetic radiation and charged matter. Subspecialties: Theoretical physics; Atomic and molecular physics. Home: 1704 Highland Park Rd Denton TX 76205 Office: Dept of Physic North Texas State Univ Denton TX 76203

KOBER, CARL LEOPOLD, physicist, mineral exploration company executive; b. Vienna, Austria, Nov. 22, 1913; came to U.S., 1949, naturalized, 1958; s. Leopold and Maria Anna (Cremer) K.; m. Christiana Futschig, Mar. 26, 1942; children—Wolfgang, Peter Christian. Ph.D., U. Vienna, 1935; Ph.D. habilitation Tech. U., Vienna, 1939. Asst. prof. physics Tech. U., Vienna, 1950-54; chief engr. GEMA GmbH, Berlin, 1940-45; cons. Armament Lab., U.S. Air Force, Dayton, Ohio, 1949-55; tech. dir. Gen. Mills, Mpls., 1955-58; v.p., tech. dir. AVCO, Cin., 1958-61; dir. advanced programs Martin-Marietta Corp., Denver, 1961-74; pres. Denver Mineral Exploration, Littleton, Colo., 1974—; prof. Colo. State U., Fort Collins, 1969-79; cons. Martin-Marietta, Denver, 1980-81. Patentee radar, infrared, geophys. instrumentation. Chmn. Scientists and Engrs. for Lyndon Johnson in Colo., Denver, 1964. Fellow IEEE, AAAS, Explorers Club. Club: Columbine Country (Littleton). Current work: Remote sensing instrumentation for geophysical (mineral and hydrocarbon) exploration. Subspecialties: Geophysics; Remote sensing (geoscience). Home: 605 Front Range Rd Littleton CO 80120 Office: Denver Mineral Exploration Corp 1100 W Littleton Blvd Suite 103 Littleton CO 80120

KOBILINSKY, LAWRENCE, immunology and forensic science, educator, forensic science consultant, researcher; b. N.Y.C., Nov. 7, 1946; s. Abraham and Sophie (Selkow) K.; m. Estelle Kartagener, June 10, 1971; 1 dau., Hayley. B.S., CCNY, 1969, M.A., 1971; Ph.D., CUNY, 1977. Research asst. Columbia Presbyn. Med. Ctr., N.Y.C., 1969-70; lectr. City Coll., CUNY, 1970-71; adj. lectr. Bklyn. Coll., 1972-74, Hunter Coll., 1974-75, John Jay Coll., 1975-77; research asst. U. Pa. Johnson Research Found., Phila., 1971; research fellow Complement and Effector Biology Lab. Sloan-Kettering Inst., 1977-79, vis. investigator, 1980-82; research assoc. Sloan-Kettering Inst. (Steroid Binding Protein Lab.), 1979-80; adj. asst. prof. biology John Jay Coll., CUNY, 1977-80; instr. Cornell Grad. Sch. Med. Scis., Sloan-Kettering Div., N.Y.C., 1979-80; attending staff research scientist Animal Med. Center, N.Y.C., 1979-81; mem. biochemistry doctoral faculty CUNY Grad. Center, N.Y.C., 1981—; asst. prof. immunology and forensic sci. John Jay Coll. Criminal Justice, N.Y.C., 1980-84, assoc. prof. immunology and forensic sci., 1984—. Contbr. articles to profl. jours. Served to 1st lt. U.S. Army, 1971-72. Mem. AAAS, Am. Chem. Soc., Am. Assn. Immunologists, Am. Acad. Forensic Sci., N.Y. Acad. Scis., Electron Microscopy Soc. Am., N.Y. Micros. Soc. (bd. mgrs., v.p., assoc. editor newsletter), Northeastern Assn. Forensic Scientists.; mem. Sigma Xi. Current Work: Development of new techniques for forensic serology, teaching graduate and undergraduate students, consulting on criminal cases, research. Subspecialties: Immunobiology and immunology; Immunology (medicine). Home: 504 Rebecca Ln Oceanside NY 11572 Office: John Jay Coll Criminal Justice 445 W 59th St New York NY 10019

KOBLER, VIRGINIA PONDS, research and development administrator; b. Carlsbad, N. Mex., Oct. 8, 1937; d. William Edward and Magnolia Serena (Dryden) Ponds; m. Bobby Sandlin Woodruff, June 1, 1957 (div. 1972); m. Julian S. Kobler, Aug. 18, 1974; children: George Ponds, Jonathan Ponds. B.S., U. Ala., 1964, M.S., 1976, Ph.D., 1979. Research physicist U.S. Army Missile Command, Redstone Arsenal, Ala., 1967-80; mgr. research and devel. U.S. Army Ballistic Missile Def. Advanced Tech. Ctr., Huntsville, Ala., 1980-84, U.S. Army Strategic Def. Command, 1984—; reviewer Army Research Office, Durham, N.C., 1979—. Contbr. articles to profl. jours. Mem. IEEE (reviewer 1979—), Ops. Research Soc., Am. Phys. Soc. Democrat. Mem. Ch. of Christ. Current Work: Research and development in data processing systems; decentralized control algorithms for distributed computer systems and command, control and communications utilizing artificial intelligence techniques. Subspecialties: Algorithms; Artificial intelligence. Home: 5802 Macon Dr Huntsville AL 35802 Office: US Army Strategic Def Command PO Box 1500 Huntsville AL 35807

KOCAOGLU, DUNDAR F., engineering educator, consultant; b. Turkey, June 1, 1939; came to U.S., 1960; s. Irfan and Meliha (Uzay) K.; m. Alev Baysak, Sept. 17, 1968. B.S.C.E., Robert Coll., Istanbul, Turkey, 1960; M.S.C.E., Lehigh U., 1962; M.S.I.E., U. Pitts., 1972, Ph.D. in Ops. Research, 1976. Registered profl. engr., Pa. Structural engr. United Engrs., 1963-71; lectr. U. Pitts., 1973-75, vis. asst. prof., 1975-76, dir. engring. mgmt. program, 1976—; engring. and mgmt. cons., Pitts, 1971—; ednl. cons. various univs.; tech. mgmt. cons. UN, 1979-80; founding chmn. TIMS Coll. on Engring. Mgmt., 1979-81. Author: Engineering Management, 1981; editor series: Engring. Mgmt., 1981—; contbr. articles to profl. jours. Pres. Pitts. Turkish-Am. Assn., 1977-79. Served to lt., C.E. Turkish Army, 1966-68. Mem. Am. Soc. for Engring. Edn. (pres. engring. mgmt. div.), Am. Soc. for Engring. Mgmt. (regional dir.), IEEE Engring. Mgmt. Soc. (publs. dir.), Omega Rho (pres.-elect). Current Work: Engineering management, technological innovations, resource optimization, hierarchical decisions, multicriteria decisions, participative management, project management, program evaluations. Subspecialties: Operations research (engineering); Engineering management. Home: 125 Highvue Dr Venetia PA 15367 Office: 1037 Benedum Hall U Pitts Pittsburgh PA 15261

KOCH, H(ERMAN) WILLIAM, institute administrator; b. N.Y.C., Sept. 28, 1920; m. Margaret Giles, Feb. 3, 1945; children—John, Kathleen, Donald, Robert, Russell. B.S., Queens Coll., 1941; M.S., U. Ill.-Champaign, 1942, Ph.D., 1944. Research asst. U. Ill.-Champaign, 1941-44, asst. prof., 1944-49; chief high energy radiation sect. Radiation Physics div. Nat. Bur. Standards, Washington, 1949-62, chief Radiation Physics div., 1962-66; dir. Am. Inst. Physics, N.Y.C., 1966—, mem. exec. com., governing bd., 1966—; mem. U.S. Laison com. to Internat. Union Pure and Applied Physics, 1973—; pres. Council of Engring. and Sci. and Soc. Presidents, 1982-83. Recipient Gold Medal Meritorious Service award U.S. Dept. Commerce, 1962; named First Alumnus of Yr. Queens Coll., 1961. Fellow Am. Phys. Soc., Optical Soc. Am.; mem. Am. Assn. Physics Tchrs., Acoustical Soc. Am., Soc. Rheology, Am. Astron. Soc., Am. Crystallographic Soc., Am. Assn. Physicists in Medicine, AAAS, Nat. Acad. Sci. (exec. com. div. Phys. Scis., 1972-81, numerical data adv. bd., 1975-80, Nat. Fedn. Abstracting and Info. Services, (pres. 1978-79), Sigma Xi, Phi Kappa Phi. Gamma Alpha, Sigma Pi Sigma (hon.). Subspecialties: Nuclear physics; Medical physics. Office: Am Inst Physics 335 E 45th St New York NY 10017

KOCHER, CARL ALVIN, physicist; b. Seattle, Feb. 14, 1942; s. Paul Harold and Annis Adelle (Cox) K.; m. Marilyn Aleta Tennant Kocher, June 24, 1968; children: Suzanne, Paul, Scott. A.B., U. Calif.-Berkeley, 1963, Ph.D., 1967. Postdoctoral fellow Oxford (Eng.) U., 1967-68; vis. scientist M.I.T., Cambridge, 1968-69; lectr. physics Columbia U., N.Y.C., 1969-73; asst. prof. physics Oreg. State U., Corvallis, 1973-78, assoc. prof., 1978—; prin. investigator U.S. Dept. Energy, 1978—. Contbr. articles in field to profl. jours. Woodrow Wilson fellow, 1963; NSF grad. fellow, 1963-67; NSF postdoctoral fellow, 1967-69. Mem. Am. Phys. Soc., Am. Assn. Physics Tchrs., Fedn. Am. Scientists, Phi Beta Kappa, Sigma Xi. Current Work: Experimental atomic physics; atomic collisions, radiative and ionization processes, laser spectroscopy, high Rydberg states, computer instrumentation. Subspecialties: Atomic and molecular physics; Laser spectroscopy.

KOCHMAN, RONALD LAWRENCE, neuroscientist; b. Rome, N.Y., Apr. 7, 1946; s. Frank Joseph and Connie Rose (Catanzaro) K.; m. Sandra Jean Sturbin, Dec. 21, 1968; children—Collin Frank, Andrew Michael. B.S., Pa. State U., 1968; M.S., Northeastern U., 1974. Research biologist G.D. Searle & Co., Skokie, Ill., 1975-79, research assoc., 1979-82, research investigator, 1982—. Contbr. articles to profl. jours. Mem. Mental Health Adv. Bd., New Trier Twp., 1983-85. Served to sgt. U.S. Army, 1969-71. Mem. Soc. for Neurosci., Am. Soc. Neurochem., N.Y. Acad. Sci., Am. Soc. Pharmacology and Exptl. Therapeutics. Current Work: Neurochemistry memory and learning; analgesia; neurotransmitter and drug receptors; cerebral ischemia. Subspecialties: Neurochemistry; Neuropharmacology. Office: GD Searle & Co 4901 Searle Pkwy Skokie IL 60077

KOCI, BRUCE R., senior engineer, researcher; b. St. Paul, Jan. 10, 1943; s. Raymond Emil and Hazel Johana Augusta (Bauman) K.; m. Ann Irene Guhman, June 15, 1980. B.S., U. Minn., 1966, M.S. in Wildlife Mgmt., 1975. Project engr. Rosemont, Inc., Bloomington, Minn., 1966-72; research asst. geology U. Minn., Mpls., 1974-79; sr. engr. Polar Ice Coring Office U. Nebr., 1979—. Recipient Polar Ice NSF Polar Ice Coring contract U. Nebr., 1983—, Antartic Service medal NSF, 1979. Mem. AIAA, Glaciological Soc. Am., Ecol. Soc. Am., Am. Inst. Biol. Scis. AAAS. Democrat. Mem. United Church of Christ. Current work: Design and development of drills for arctic regions which run on solar or standard electrical power, structures and camp design. Subspecialties: Arctic studies; Systems engineering. Home: 4300 Holdridge St Lincoln NE 55105 Office: Polar Ice Coring Office 329 N 12th St Lincoln NE 68508

KOCKINOS, CONSTANTIN NEOPHYTOS, mathematical scientist, researcher; b. Cairo, Egypt, Oct. 14, 1926; came to U.S., 1947; s. Dimitri and Irene (Sovrani) K.; m. Jean Freeman Lincoln, Aug. 12, 1952 (div. 1962); 1 son, Marc Demetrius. Student, Am. U., Cairo, 1944-47; B.A., U. Calif.-Berkeley, 1950, 1954, M.A., 1956; Ph.D., Stanford U., 1972. Instr. U. Calif.-Berkeley, 1958-62; sr. scientist EGG, Las Vegas, Nev., 1962-64; research mathematician Stanford Research Inst., Menlo Park, Calif., 1964-72; vis. prof. Aristotelian U., Thessaloniki, Greece, 1972-76; San Jose (Calif.) State U., 1976-79; math. scientist Lockheed Missiles & Space Div., Sunnyvale, Calif., 1979—; asst. protocol officer Greek Diplomatic Service, Cairo, Egypt, 1944-45; sec. to King George of the Hellenes; mem. U.S. Senatorial Adv. Bd., Washington. Contbr. writings to publs. Mem. Senatorial Inner Circle, 1983. Fellow Explorers Club; mem. Internat. Platform Assn., U.S. Naval Inst., Am. Math. Soc., Tensor, AIAA, Sigma Xi, Pi Mu Epsilon. Republican. Greek Orthodox. Club: Athletic. Patentee. Current Work: Fluid mechanics; aerodynamics, adaptive grid generation; nonlinear problems; applications of modern mathematics and of geometry to engineering and physics. Subspecialties: Applied mathematics; Theoretical physics. Home: 2121 Creeden Ave Mountain View CA 94040 Office: Lockheed Missiles & Space Co Lockheed Way 81-10 PO Box 504 Sunnyvale CA 94086

KODAMA, TOSHIKO, endocrinologist; b. Kobe, Japan, Sept. 8, 1928; s. Yukichi and Yoshiko (Inagaki) Iida; m. Mitsuo Kodama, Nov. 15, 1963. M.D., Nagoya City U. Sch. Medicine, 1954, Ph.D., 1962. Rotating intern Mt. Sinai Hosp., Chgo., 1954-55; pediatric resident West Suburban Hosp., Oak Park, Ill., 1955-57; assoc. prof. Nagoya City U. Sch. Medicine, Japan, 1961-65; sr. researcher Aichi Cancer Ctr., Nagoya, 1965—. Contbr. articles to profl. jours. Mem. Am. Assn. Cancer Research, Internat. Soc. Preventive Oncology. Current work: Cancer and hormone; chemotherapy (carcinogenesis, environment, nutrition, epidemiology). Subspecialties: Cancer research (medicine); Endocrinology. Home: 1-11-1 Mikagecho Chikusaku Nagoy Japan 464 Office: Aichi Cancer Ctr Research Inst Chikusaku Nagoya Japan 464

KODANAZ, HATICE ALTAN, neuropsychologist, educator; b. Tire, Turkey, July 20, 1930; came to U.S., 1957; d. M. Haydar and A. Sacide (Sandikoglu) K.; m. A. Aytekin, May 9, 1957; children: Ahmet, Taner. B.S., U. Istanbul, Turkey, 1955, M.A., 1956; M.S., U. Kans., 1964; Ph.D., U. Ankara, Turkey, 1976. Psychologist U. Istanbul Med. Sch., 1956-57; research coordinator U. Kans. Med. Ctr., Kansas City, 1966-70, research assoc., 1975-76, instr. dept. neurology, 1976-79, asst. prof., 1979—; founder, chief clin. psychology U. Ankara, 1970-74, cons. dept. psychiatry, 1979-82. Pres. Turkish Am. Assn., Kansas City, 1980-82; area rep. Mini-Mundo, 1980-83; treas. Neighborhood Homes Assn., Fairway, Kans., 1981-82. Fulbright scholar, 1957-58; Smith Mundt grantee, 1958. Mem. Kans. Psychol. Assn., Am. Pain Soc., Turkish-Am. Physicians Assn., Turkish-Am. Neuropsychiat. Assn. Current Work: Brain behavior relationship; dementia; psychological and cultural aspects of headaches; neuropsychological evaluation and diagnosis. Subspecialties: Neuropsychology; Clinical-behavioral studies. Office: Kans Univ Med Center 39th and Rainbow Kansas City KS 66103

KOEHLER, WALLACE CONRAD, physicist, facility administrator; b. Chgo., Aug. 25, 1920; m. Mirjam Stohl, Sept. 7, 1943; children—Wallace William. B.S., U. Chgo., 1943, M.S., 1948; Ph.D., U. Tenn., 1953; hon. doctorate U. Grenoble, France, 1979. Asst. prof. physics Va. Poly Inst., Blacksburg, 1948-49, staff scientist, 1949—; dir. nat. ctr. small-angle scattering research Oak Ridge Nat. Lab., Tenn, 1978—. Contbr. articles to prof. jours. Served with U.S. Army, 1942-45. Fellow Union Carbide Corp., 1979; Fulbright fellow, 1958; Guggenheim fellow, 1958; recipient Spedding award Rare Earth Research Soc., 1983. Fellow Am. Phys. Soc.; mem. Am. Crystallographic Assn. Current work: Direct national user facility for neutron small angle scattering. Research in magnetism, solid state physics. Subspecialties: Condensed matter physics; Neutron scattering. Office: Oak Ridge Nat Lab Oak Ridge TN 37830

KOENIG, JACK LEONARD, educator; b. Cody, Nebr., Feb. 12, 1933; s. John and Lucille May K.; m. Jeanus Brosz, July 5, 1953; children—John, Robert, Stanley, Lori. B.A., Yankton Coll., 1955; M.S., U. Nebr., 1957, Ph.D., 1959. Research chemist plastics dept. DuPont, Wilmington, Del., 1959-63; asst. prof. polymer sci. div. Case Inst. Tech., Cleve., 1963-66; asso. prof. dept. macromolecular sci. Case Western Res. U., Cleve., 1966-70, prof., 1970—; dir. Molecular Spectroscopy Lab., 1974—; co-dir. Materials Research Lab., 1974—; program dir. solid state chemistry and polymer sci. div. materials research NSF, Washington, 1972-73. Author: Chemical Microstructure of Polymer Chains, 1980, (with others) Introduction to Vibrational Spectroscopy With Applications to Polymers, 1981; contbr. (with others) articles to profl. jours. Served with U.S. Army, 1953-55. Grantee NSF; Grantee Army Research Office; Grantee NASA; Grantee Naval Research Office. Current Work: Sturctural characterization of polymeric materials. Subspecialties: Polymer chemistry; Surface chemistry. Home: 15503 Dale Rd Chagrin Falls OH 44022 Office: Case Western Res U Cleveland OH 44106

KOENIG, JOHN RICHARD, materials engineer; b. New Brunswick, N.J., Apr. 29, 1946; s. John Henry and Shirley Ann (Smith) K.; m. Carol Lee Heckman, Feb. 14, 1974; children—Jason John, Justin Richard, Kristin Lee. B.S. in Ceramic Engring., Rutgers U., 1968; M.S. in Ceramic Engring. Ohio State U., 1974. Research engr. So. Research Inst., Birmingham, Ala., 1973-77, div. head, 1980—; materials engr. Air Force Materials Lab., Dayton, Ohio, 1977-80. Inventor high precision dilatometer. Served to capt. USAF, 1969-73. Recipient Tech. Achievement award USAF, 1971, Swartz Engring. award Air Force Materials Lab., 1979. Current work: Head research on nondestructive testing, thermal testing and modeling, and mechanics of composites. Subspecialties: Materials (engineering); Non-destructive testing. Home: 1925 Mission Rd Vestaria Hills AL 35216 Office: So Research Inst 2000 Ninth Ave S Birmingham AL 35255

KOENIG, KARL ERIC, research chemist; b. Washington, Dec. 27, 1947; s. Earl T. and Iris F.M. (Woodhouse) K.; m. JoAnn Weber, Feb. 18, 1983; B.S. in Chemistry summa cum laude, U. Tex., 1970; Ph.D. in Chemistry, U. So. Calif., 1974. Chem. technician San Antonio Coll., Tex., 1966-68; postdoctoral fellow UCLA, 1974-76; sr. research chemist Monsanto Indsl. Chems. Co., 1976-78; research specialist Monsanto Corp. Research Lab., 1978-82; sr. research specialist Nutrition Chem. div. Monsanto Co., St. Louis, 1982—; chmn. Tech. Community of Monsanto, St. Louis, 1982-83. Author: Catalysis in Organic Synthesis, 1982; (with others) Catalytic Aspects of Metal Phosphine Complexes, 1982. Served to capt. USAF, 1970-72. NSF fellow; Stauffer fellow. Mem. Am. Chem. Soc., AAAS, Mo. Whitewater Assn. (pres. 1983—), Graham Partners Investment Club (sec. 1983-85), Phi Beta Kappa, Phi Kappa Phi. Episcopalian. Current work: Organic synthesis chemist in life sciences; animal nutrition via regulation of hormones; development drugs and amino acids via new processes and synthetic routes. Subspecialties: Synthetic chemistry; Animal nutrition. Home: 809 Renee Ln Creve Coeur MO 63141 Office: Monsanto 700 Chesterfield Village Pkwy BB3I Chesterfield MO 63198

KOERNER, ERNEST LEE, technical company executive, environmental engineer; b. Cleve., Mar. 17, 1931; s. Ernest L. and Mary Bridget (McGovern) K.; m. Barbara Jean Payne, Aug. 8, 1953; children: Susan, Patrick, Karen, Sally, Joan, Mary. B.Ch.E., U. Dayton, 1953; M.S. in Chem. Engring, Iowa State U., 1955, Ph.D. in Chem. Engring, 1956. Registered profl. engr., Okla. Research sect. leader Union Carbide Metals, Inc., Niagara Falls, N.Y., 1957-59; research specialist Monsanto Co., St. Louis, 1959-67; sr. research group leader Kerr-McGee Corp., Oklahoma City, 1967-70; pres. Tech. Research & Devel., Inc., Oklahoma City, 1970-83; owner, pres. Techrad Inc., Oklahoma City, 1983—. Contbr. articles on metal recovery to profl. jours. Mem. Am. Inst. Chem. Engrs., AIME, Nat. Soc. Profl. Engrs., Okla. Soc. Profl. Engrs., Am. Inst. Plant Engrs., Nat. Assn. Environ. Profls. Holder 14 patents in metal recovery processes, phosphoric acid purification. Current Work: Recovery of energy from solid wastes, hazardous waste permits and treatment, wastewater pollution control, extractive metallurgy. Subspecialties: Water supply and wastewater treatment; Chemical engineering. Home: 12721 Saint Andrews Terr Oklahoma City OK 73120 Office: 4619 N Santa Fe St Oklahoma City OK 73118

KOESTNER, ADALBERT, pathologist, scientist, educator; b. Hatzfeld, Roumania, Sept. 10, 1920; came to U.S., 1955, naturalized, 1960; s. Johann and Gertraut (Gruber) K.; m. Adelaide Wilma Wacker Koestner, Jan. 20, 1951; children: George, Alexander (dec.), Rosemarie Kathrin. D.V.M., U. Munich, Ger., 1951; M.Sc., Ohio State U., 1957, Ph.D., 1959. Diplomate: Am. Coll. Vet. Pathologist. Gen. practice vet. medicine, Untergriesbach, Ger., 1951-55; instr. Ohio State U., 1955-59, asst. prof., 1959-61, assoc. prof., 1961-64, prof., 1964-81, acting chmn., 1971-72, chmn. vet. pathobiology, 1972-81; prof., chmn. dept. pathology Mich. State U., East Lansing, 1981—. Contbr. chpts. to books and articles to profl. jours. Mem. AVMA (Gaines award 1979), Am. Coll. Vet. Pathologists, Internat. Acad. Pathology, Am. Assn. Pathologists, Am. Assn. Neuropathologists (Weil award 1971), Soc. Neurosci., Am. Assn. Cancer Research. Current Work: Two major areas of current research deal with carcinogenesis of tumors of the nervous system and animal models for demyelinating diseases such as multiple sclerosis. Subspecialties: Pathology (medicine); Comparative neurobiology. Home: 2578 Woodhill Dr Okemos MI 48864 Office: Michigan State University E Fee Hall East Lansing MI 48824

KOETZLE, THOMAS FREDERICK, chemist, researcher; b. Bklyn., Oct. 15, 1943; s. Walter Frederick and Viola May (Schubart) K.; m. Carole Eileen Peltz, Dec. 3, 1967; children—Laura Elizabeth, John Harrison. B.A., Harvard Coll., 1964, M.A., 1965, Ph.D., 1970. Research assoc. Brookhaven Nat. Lab., Upton, N.Y., 1970-73, assoc. chemist, 1973-76, chemist, 1976—; dir. The Protein Data Bank, 1973—; mem. U.S.A. Nat. Com. Crystallography, 1984—. Editor: Structure and Bonding: Relationships between Quantum Chemistry and Crystallography, 1980. Contbr. numerous articles to profl. jours. Mem. Am. Crystallographic Assn., Am. Chem. Soc. (symposium chmn. 1981), AAAS, N.Y. Acad. Scis. Democrat. Club: Harvard-Radcliffe (Long Island) (bd. dirs. 1984—). Current work: Applications of neutron and x-ray diffraction to the analysis of molecular structure and bonding. Subspecialties: Crystallography; Physical chemistry. Home: 35 Arista Dr Dix Hills NY 11746 Office: Chemistry Dept Brookhaven Nat Lab Upton NY 11973

KOFORD, JAMES SHINGLE, semiconductor company executive, electrical engineer; b. Cheyenne, Wyo., July 26, 1938; s. Glenn Wesley and Ella Jane (Shingle) K. B.S.E.E., Stanford U., 1959, M.S.E.E., 1960, Ph.D. in Elec. Engring., 1964. Mem. tech. staff component div. IBM, Fishkill, N.Y., 1964-66, Fairchild Semicondr., Mountain View, Calif., 1966-72; v.p. software Packet Communications Inc., Waltham, Mass., 1973-75; mgr. devel. lab. Boeing Computer Services, Waltham, 1975-81; v.p. design automation LSI Logic, Inc., Milpitas, Calif., 1981—. Developer early adaptive speech recognition, early graphic CAD system, FAIRSIM Logic Simulator. Mem. IEEE. Subspecialty: Computer-aided design. Home: 1480 Chukar Ct Sunnyvale CA 94087 Office: LSI Logic Inc 1551 McCarthy Blvd Milpitas CA 95035

KOGA, ROKUTARO, physicist; b. Nagoya, Japan, Aug. 18, 1942; came to U.S., 1961; s. Toyoki and Emiko (Shinra) K.; m. Cordula Rosow, May 5, 1981; 1 child, Evan A. B.A., U. Calif.-Berkeley, 1966; Ph.D., U. Calif.-Riverside, 1974. Research fellow U. Calif.-Riverside, 1974-75; research physicist Case Western Res. U., Cleve., 1975-79, asst. prof., 1979-81; physicist Space Scis. Lab. Aerospace Corp., El Segundo, Calif., 1981—. Contbr. articles to sci. jours. Mem. Am. Phys. Soc., Am. Geophys. Union, IEEE, N.Y. Acad. Scis., Sigma Xi. Current work: Work in cosmic and solar gamma-ray observation, and solar and atmospheric neutron observation; studies include charged particles in space and the effect of cosmic-rays on microcircuits in space. Subspecialties: High energy astrophysics; Solar physics. Home: 8005 Stewart Ave Los Angeles CA 90045Office: Space Scis Lab Aerospace Corp PO Box 92957 Los Angeles CA 90009

KOGAN, RICHARD JAY, See *Who's Who in America*, 43rd edition.

KOGOMA, TOKIO, molecular genetics educator, researcher; b. Tokyo, Dec. 5, 1939; came to U.S., 1968; s. Kunizo and Kiwa (Kogoma) Yoshimura; m.

Fusae Kogane, Dec. 2, 1966; 1 child: Takeshi. B.S., Chiba (Japan) U., 1963; M., U. Tokyo, 1965, Ph.D., 1968. Lic. pharmacist, Japan. Instr. U. Tokyo, 1968; research assoc. Kans. State U., 1968-70; research assoc. U. Utah, Salt lake City, 1970-71, asst. research prof., 1972-74; asst. prof. molecular genetics U. N.Mex., Albuquerque, 1974-80, assoc. prof., 1980—; vis. prof. Poly. U., Copenhagen, 1982; adj. assoc. prof. cell biology U. N.Mex., 1983—. Contbr. articles to profl. jours. NIH grantee, 1975, 78, 82, 85; NSF grantee, 1977, 79. Mem. Am. Soc. Microbiology, Sigma Xi. Current Work: Bacteria, regulation, DNA replication, mutants, plasmids, restriction endonucleases, gene expression, genetic recombination. Subspecialty: Genetics and genetic engineering (biology). Office: U N Mex Albuquerque NM 87131

KOGOWSKI, GARY JOHN, polymer scientist, researcher; b. Detroit, Nov. 23, 1951; s. John Joseph and Lottie Mary (Cach) K.; m. Cynthia Ann Crocker, July 14, 1984. B.S., Eastern Mich. U., 1973, M.S., 1979; Ph.D., U. Mich., 1984. Teaching asst. Eastern Mich. U.; Ypsilanti, 1976-79, U. Mich., Ann Arbor, 1979-83; sr. research engr. Allied Automotive Tech. Ctr., Troy, Mich., 1984—. Mem. Am. Chem. Soc. (Outstanding Research award 1979), Am. Phys. Soc., Soc. Plastics Engrs., Soc. Automotive Engrs., Soc. Rheology. Roman Catholic. Current work: Physical aging of glassy polymers, calorimetry, computer modeling. Subspecialty: Polymer physics. Home: 14154 Whitcomb Detroit MI 48227 Office: Allied Automotive 900 W Maple Troy MI 48083

KOHEN, ELLI, biology; physics and pathology educator; b. Istanbul, Turkey, Oct. 2, 1930; came to U.S., 1969, naturalized, 1983; s. Yasef and Vida (Bennun) K.; m. Cahide Bahar, June 21, 1957; 1 child, Dahlia Victoria. Student Faculty Sci., U. Istanbul, 1948-49, M.D., 1954; Ph.D. in Microspectrofluorometry, Karolinska Inst., Stockholm, 1973. Lic. physician, Turkey. Intern U. Istanbul Hosps., 1955; resident pathology Springfield Hosp. (Mass.), 1956-59; house physician in pathology Assaf Harofe Govt. Hosp., Tel Aviv, 1957-58; resident pathology Westfield State Sanatorium (Mass.), 1959-60; research asst. dept. pharmacology Baylor U., Houston, 1960-61; research fellow U. São Paulo (Brazil), 1961-62, 63-64; postdoctoral fellow, research assoc. biophysics U. Pa., 1962-63, 64-66; research fellow, vis. scientist dept. pathology Karolinska Inst., 1966-69, 72-73; sr. scientist Papicolaou Cancer Research Inst., Miami, Fla., 1969-80, disting. scientist, 1980; prof. biology U. Miami, Coral Gables, Fla., 1981—, fellow Ctr. for Theoretical Studies, 1984. Editor: Cell Biochemistry and Function, 1983. Contbr. chpts. to books, articles to profl. jours. Served as 1st lt. M.C., Turkish Army, 1954-55. Fellow Anna Fuller Fund, New Haven, 1966-68; research grantee Am. Cancer Soc., 1966—, also NIH, NSF, 1966—; vis. scientist Swedish Med. Research Council, Stockholm, 1972-73; vis. fellow Institut National de la Santé et de la Recherche Médicale and Internat. Cancer Research Tech. Transfer, 1980-82. Mem. Am. Soc. Biol. Chemists, Biochem. Soc. (London), Histochem. Soc., Colombian Soc. Cancerology (hon.). Jewish. Current work: Applications of optical microscopic methods (microspectrofluorometry) and micromethods (microinjection) to study of metabolic regulation, organelle function and interactions in single living cells as well as metabolic cooperation in cell clusters, with applications to study of physiopathological processes. Subspecialties: Cell biology; Biophysics (biology). Home: 9410 SW 53d St Miami FL 33165 Office: Dept Biology Coll of Arts & Scis U Miami Cox Sci Bldg PO Box 249118 Coral Gables FL 33124

KOHL, PAUL ALBERT, chemist; b. Buffalo, Aug. 6, 1952; s. Paul Bernard and Kathleen (Buchinger) K.; m. Elizabeth Ann Proctor, July 27, 1974; children—Abbe Theresa, Alexander Daniel. B.S., Bethany Coll., 1974; Ph.D., U. Tex.-Austin, 1978. Chemist Nuclear Radiation Devel., Grand Island, N.Y., 1974-75; supr. AT&T Bell Labs., Murray Hill, N.J., 1978—. Contbr. articles to profl. jours. Patentee in field. Bd. dirs. Parent Tchr. Orgn., Chatham, N.J., 1985. Recipient G. Ayres award U. Tex.-Austin, 1977; Weston fellow, 1977. Mem. Am. Chem. Soc., Electrochem. Soc. Republican. Roman Catholic. Current work: Photoelectrochemistry of semiconductors; analysis of semiconductors; electrodeposition. Subspecialties: Analytical chemistry; Photochemistry. Home: 67 Fuller Ave Chatham NJ 07928 Office: AT&T Bell Labs 600 Mountain Ave Murray Hill NJ 07974

KOHL, STEVE, physician, researcher; b. N.Y.C., Aug. 13, 1945; s. Moses J. and Dorothy (Weisenfeld) K.; m. Sybil Janice Kohl, June 11, 1967; 1 dau., Gwynne Odette. B.S. magna cum laude, CCNY, 1966; M.D., Columbia U., 1970. Diplomate: Nat. Bd. med. Examiners, 1973, Am. Bd. Pediatrics, 1976; lic. physician, N.Y., Ga., Tex. Trainee in ob-gyn Columbia Presbyn. Med. Ctr., N.Y.C., 1970-71, vis. fellow, 1971, research assoc. pediatrics, 1971; intern in pediatrics Babies Hosp., Children's Med. and Surg. Ctr., N.Y.C., 1972, resident, 1972-74; fellow in pediatric infectious disease and immunology Emory U. Sch. Medicine, Atlanta, 1974-76; asst. prof. infectious diseases, dept. pediatrics M.D. Anderson Hosp. and Tumor Inst., U. Tex. Cancer Ctr., Houston, 1976-81, assoc. prof., prof. pediatrics, program infectious diseases and clin. microbiology U. Tex. Med. Sch., Houston, 1976-79, asst. prof., 1979-84, assoc. prof. pediatrics, program immunology, 1981-84, prof. pediatrics program infectious diseases Program of Immunology, 1984—; attending Hermann Hosp., Houston; pediatric courtesy staff Meml. Hosp. System, Houston; mem. infection control com. Elks Aidemore Hosp., Atlanta, 1974-76, Hermann Hosp., Houston, 1978—; mem. adv. bd. Houston chpt. Nat. Found. March of Dimes, 1978-79. Contbr. articles to profl. jours. Recipient John H. Freeman Outstanding Teaching award U. Tex., 1981; NIH grantee, 1978—; James Donovan scholar, 1966; N.Y. State Med. Regents scholar, 1966-70; Nat. Cancer Inst. fellow, 1975-76. Fellow Infectious Diseases Soc. Am.; mem. Soc. Pediatric Research, Am. Soc. Microbiology, Am. Assn. Immunologists, Am. Acad. Pediatrics, Am. Fedn. Clin. Research, So. Soc. Pediatric Research, N.Y. Acad. Sci., Houston Pediatric Soc., Harris County Med. Soc., Houston Infectious Disease Soc., Pediatric Infectious Disease Soc., Physicians for Social Responsibility, Alpha Omega Alpha, Phi Beta Kappa, Sierra Club. Current Work: Immunology of herpes simplex virus infection; cellular cytotoxicity. Subspecialties: Pediatrics; Infectious diseases. Office: PO Box 20708 Houston TX 77025

KOHLHEPP, SUE JOANNE, life sciences researcher, molecular biology educator; b. Kittaning, Pa., July 15, 1939; d. Bruce Cook and Martha Eunice (Meyers) K. B.S., W.Va. Wesleyan Coll., 1961; M.S., Pa. State U., 1963, Ph.D., 1969. Tchr. Margle/Newtown Schs., Newtown Square, Pa., 1963-66; researcher med. lab. research and devel. St. Anthony Hosp., Louisville, 1969-74; postdoctoral researcher Oreg. State U., Corvallis, 1974-77; research assoc. in infectious diseases Providence Med. Ctr., Portland, Oreg., 1977-78, 79—; research assoc. lipid disorders Presbyn. Hosp., Pitts., 1978-79. Contbr. articles to profl. jours. Chmn. refurbishing East Vancouver United Methodist Ch., Wash., 1984. Fellow N.Y. Acad. Scis., Am. Inst. Chemists mem. Bio-phys. Soc., Am. Soc. Microbiology, AAAS, Assn. for Women in Sci., Iota Sigma Pi. Current work: Mechanism of aminoglycoside nephrotoxicity; antibiotic efficacy; prevention of aminoglycoside nephrotoxicity. Subspecialties: Molecular biology; Microbiology. Home: 11704 NE 70th Ave Vancouver WA 98686 Office: Providence Med Ctr/Infectious Disease Lab 4805 NE Glisan St Portland OR 97213

KOHLI, JAI DEV, pharmacologist, educator; b. Jullundur City, India, Dec. 27, 1918; came to U.S., 1975; s. Kripa R. and Maya D (Chadda) K.; m. Pushpa Sahney, Nov. 28, 1946; children: Atul, Tanuj,. Vandana. M.S., U. Chgo., 1952; Ph.D., U. Man., Can., 1965. Diplomate: Dip. Med., India, 1940. Fellow Indian Council Med. Research, 1942-50; sci. officer Drug Research Inst., India, 1951-61; asst. prof. Faculty Medicine, U. Man., 1961-65; scientist Food and Drug Directorate Can., 1965-70; asst. dir. Indsl. Toxicology Research, India, 1970-75; assoc. research prof. U. Chgo., 1975-79, research prof. pharmacology, 1979—. Contbr. articles to profl. jours. Recipient Drewery award U. Man., 1964; Fulbright fellow, 1951-52; Wellcome Research fellow, 1961-65. Mem. Am. Soc. Pharmacology and Exptl. Therapeutics, Pharm. Soc. Can., N.Y. Acad. Scis., Sigma Xi. Current Work: Autonomic pharmacology, cardiovascular pharmacology drug receptor interactions, Dopamine agonists and antagonists. Subspecialties: Pharmacology; Cardiovascular pharmacology. Office: 947 E 58th St Room 506 Chicago IL 60637

KOHN, ALAN JACOBS, zoology educator; b. New Haven, July 16, 1931; s. Curtis I. and Harriet M. (Jacobs) K.; m. Marian S. Adachi, Aug. 28, 1959; children: Lizabeth, Nancy, Diane, Stephen. A.B., Princeton U., 1953; Ph.D., Yale U., 1957. Asst. prof. Fla. State U., Tallahassee, 1958-61; asst. prof. U. Wash., Seattle, 1961-63, assoc. prof., 1963-67, prof. zoology, 1967—; program officer NSF, 1985-86. Contbr. articles in field to profl. jours. NRC sr. postdoctoral research assoc., 1967; John Simon Guggenheim Meml. fellow, 1974; NSF research grantee, 1959. Fellow AAAS; mem. Am. Soc. Zoologist (treas. 1971-74), Am. Malacological Union (pres. 1982-83). Current Work: Marine invertebrate zoology and ecology, functional morphology, biology and paleobiology of marine molluscs. Subspecialties: Ecology (environmental science); Systematics. Home: 18300 Ridgefield Rd NW Seattle WA 98177 Office: Dept Zoology U Wash Seattle WA 98177

KOHN, DENNIS FREDRICH, veterinarian, microbiologist; b. Toledo, Mar. 8, 1940; s. Ronald Frank and Gertrude (Fredrich) K.; m. Judith Ann Eisenmann, June 9, 1962; children—Denise, Scott, Douglas. D.V.M., Ohio State U., 1964; M.S., W. Va. U., 1970, Ph.D., 1975. Diplomate Am. Coll. Lab. Animal Medicine. Coordinator lab animal resources W.Va. U. Med. Ctr., Morgantown, 1964-74, dir. comparative pathology, 1975-76; assoc. prof., chmn., dept. comparative medicine U. Tex., Houston, 1976-83, prof., chmn. 1983—. Contbr. chpts. to books, articles to profl. jours. Pres. Suncrest Kiwanis, Morgantown, 1972, lt. gov., 1975. Mem. Am. Coll. Lab. Animal Medicine (pres. 1983-84), Am. Soc. Lab. Animal Pratitioners (pres.-elect 1984-85), Am. Soc. Microbiology, AVMA, Am. Assn. Accreditation Lab. Animal Care (council mem. 1976-82). Republican. Lutheran. Current work: Pathogenesis of hydrocephalus, tissue tropisms of mycoplasma. Subspecialties: Laboratory animal medicine; Microbiology (medicine). Home: 3315 Robinson Rd Missouri City TX 77459 Office: U Tex Med Sch 6431 Fannin St Houston TX 77030

KOHN, JAMES PAUL, chemical engineering educator; b. Dubuque, Iowa, Oct. 31, 1924; s. Harry Theodore and Kathryn (Piepel) K.; m. Mary Louise McGovern, Aug. 30, 1958; children—Kathleen Anne, Keven Patrick, Mary Louise. B.S. in Ch.E., U. Notre Dame, 1951; M.S., U. Mich.-Ann Arbor, 1952; Ph.D., U. Kans.-Lawrence, 1956. Chem. engr. Reilly Chem. Corp., Indpls., 1946-51; asst. prof. chem. engring. U. Notre Dame, 1955-60, assoc. prof., 1960-64, prof., 1964—, dir. Solar Lab., 1973—. Contbr. articles to profl. jours. Patentee cyrogenic separations. Mem. City South Bend (Ind.) Energy Commn., 1983—. Served with AUS, 1943-46. Mem. Am. Chem. Soc., Am. Inst. Chem. Engrs., AAAS, Sigma Xi. Republican. Current work: Phase equilibria and solution thermodynamics of multicomponent systems; cryogenics; high pressure properties; solar energy. Subspecialties: Chemical engineering; Solar engineering. Home: 17684 Waxwing Ln South Bend IN 46635 Office: U Notre Dame 178 Fitzpatrick Hall Notre Dame IN 46556

KOHN, STANLEY ERWIN, physicist; b. Mpls., Apr. 4, 1947; s. Sigmund and Bessie (Winker) K. B.A. with honors, U. Chgo., 1969; Ph.D., U. Calif.-Berkeley, 1977. Postdoctoral fellow Hebrew U., Jerusalem, 1977, Los Alamos Nat. Lab., 1978-79; staff scientist Lawrence Berkeley Lab., Calif., 1979-81; mem. tech. staff Aerospace Corp., El Segundo, Calif., 1981—. Mem. Am. Phys. Soc. Current work: Photo acoustic spectroscopy; infrared detectors. Subspecialty: Condensed matter physics. Office: Aerospace Corp Box 92957-MI 109 Los Angeles CA 90009

KOHUT, WILLIAM, ceramic engineer; b. Cleve., Sept. 5, 1928; s. Michael and Dorothy Kohut; m. Julie Ruth Strieter, Dec. 17, 1949; children: William Michael, Alec Matthew, David Mitchell. B.A. in Ceramic Engring., Ohio State U. Research grantee Am. Mineral Co., Los Angeles, 1955-56; dir research and devel. Westwood Ceramic Supply, Los Angeles, 1957-62; gen. foreman Am. Standard, San Pablo, Calif., 1962-67; salesman O. Hommel Co., Memphis, 1967-72; tech. sales mgr. Cyprus Indsl. Minerals, Sandersville, Ga., 1972-83; tech. dir. H.C. Spinks Clay Co., Paris, Tenn., 1984—. Contbr. articles to profl. jours. Founder Drug and Alcohol Abuse Commn., Austintown, Ohio, 1982, Crime Watch Com., Austintown. Served with USMC, 1947-48. Named Father of Yr., Graceland YMCA, Tenn., 1982. Mem. Am. Ceramic Soc., ASTM, Nat. Inst. Ceramic Engrs. (dir. research in rheology and rheometry of clay-water systems). Current work: Direct activities researching clay mineral properties in colloidal suspension including chemistry, mineralogy, particle size distribution. Subspecialties: Ceramic engineering; Ceramics. Home: 1889 Lancaster Dr Austintown OH 44511 Office: HC Spinks Clay Co PO Box 820 Paris TN 38242

KOKATNUR, MOHAN GUNDO, biochemist, researcher; b. Belgaum, Karnataka, India, Mar. 19, 1930; s. Gundo R. and Shanta (Kumthekar) K.; m. Saroj Saraf, Aug. 4, 1963; children—Sharmila, Vinita. B.S., Poona U., 1951; B.S. in Chem. Tech., Nagpur U., 1953; Ph.D., U. Ill., 1959. Research assoc. U. Ill., Urbana, 1959-61, 63-66, research fellow Food Research Inst., Mysore, India, 1961-63; asst. prof. biochemistry La. State U. Med. Ctr., New Orleans, 1966-71, assoc. prof., 1971—; assoc. dir. Charity Hosp. Chemistry Lab., New Orleans, 1978—. Mem. Am. Inst. Nutrition, Am. Assn. Clin. Chemistry, Am. Coll. Nutrition, Sigma Xi. Current work: Lipid biochemistry; lipid metabolism; nutritional biochemistry; clinical biochemistry. Subspecialties: Nutrition (medicine); Biochemistry (medicine). Office: Dept Pathology La State U Med Ctr 1901 Perdido St New Orleans LA 70112

KOKOROPOULOS, PANOS, civil engineer; b. Thessaloniki, Greece, Aug. 10, 1927; came to U.S., 1958, naturalized, 1965; s. Constantine and Mary (Carvonides) K.; m. Carolyn A. Curran, Mar. 26, 1960; children: Mary, Constantine, George. B.S. in Chemistry, U. Thessaloniki, 1955; M.S. in Chemistry, U. Dayton, 1964; Ph.D., U. Akron, 1972. Research chemist U. Dayton Research Inst., 1963-65; asst. prof. chem. tech. U. Akron, 1965-71; dir. U. Akron (Ctr. for Info. Systems), 1965-69, mgr. acad. systems and programming, 1969-71, research asso. dept. civil engring., 1971-72; prof. civil engring. So. Ill. U., Edwardsville, 1973-83; prof. environ. engring. Air Force Inst. Tech., 1985—; cons. in field; tech. reviewer Appropriate Tech. Program, Dept. Energy, 1980—, Engring. Edn. Author: (with A. Fatemi, A. Amirie) Political Economy of the Middle East, 1970; also articles. Asst. dist. commr. Greek Boy Scouts, 1945-56; mem. troop com. Cahokia Mounds council Boy Scouts Am., 1976-79. Served to 2d lt. Greek Army, 1950-52. Fulbright-Smith-Mundt grantee, 1959-60; Guggenheim grantee, 1959-60; Ford Found. grantee, 1959-60. Mem. Solar Energy Soc., Am. Chem. Soc., ASCE, Am. Soc. Engring. Edn. (exec. bd. Ind.-Ill. sect. 1980-83, program chmn. and chmn. div. environ. engring. 1983-85). Democrat. Greek Orthodox. Current Work: Treatment of wastes and resource recovery, energy from wastes, energy auditing, solar energy, math. modeling, domestic applications, retrofitting, hazardous waste management. Subspecialties: Environmental engineering; Solar energy. Home: 45 Old Yellow Springs Rd Apt G Fairborn OH 45324 Office: Air Force Inst Tech Sch Civil Engring Wright Patterson AFB OH 45433

KOLAZ, DAVID JAMES, environmental engineer; b. Springfield, Ill., May 5, 1949; s. James Joseph and Jeanne (White) K.; m. Catherine Sue Mernin, July 17, 1971; children—Nicole, Krista, James, Laura. B.S. in Aero. and Astron. Engring., U. Ill., 1971; M.S. in Environ. Engring., So. Ill. U., 1984. Registered profl. engr., Ill. With Ill. Environ. Protection Agy., Springfield, 1971—, supr. data analysis, 1974-77, mgr. air monitoring programs, 1977—. Contbr. articles to profl. jours. Pres. bd. edn. Athens Unit Sch. Dist. 213, Ill., 1984—. Fellow Air Pollution Control Assn., Ill. Soc. Profl. Engrs. Roman Catholic. Current work: Statewide air sampling for gaseous and particulate air contaminants; toxic organis and metal species; small particle quanification. Subspecialties: Environmental engineering; Ambient air sampling and measurement. Home: 6 Allen Dr Athens IL 62613 Office: Ill Environ Protection Agy 2200 Churchill Rd Springfield IL 62613

KOLB, CHARLES EUGENE, physical chemist, researcher; b. Cumberland, Md., May 21, 1945; s. Charles Eugene and Doris Helen (McFarl) K.; m. Susan Foote, Aug. 19, 1965; children: Craig E., Amy C. S.B. in Chemistry, MIT, 1967; M.A. in Phys. Chemistry, Princeton U., 1968, Ph.D. in Phys. Chemistry, 1971. Sr. research scientist Aerodyne Research Inc., Billerica, Mass., 1971-75, prin. research scientist, 1975—, dir.Center for Chem. and Environ. Physics, 1977-79, tech. dir.Applied Sci. div., 1979-80, v.p., dir. Applied Scis. div., 1981-83, exec. v.p., dir. research, 1984-85, pres., 1985—; research assoc. in atmospheric chemistry div. applied sci. Harvard U., 1976—; research affiliate Spectroscopy Lab., M.I.T., 1981—; mem. adv. bd. Regional Laser Center MIT, 1981—. Contbr. 35 articles to sci. jours. Mem. Am. Chem. Soc., Am. Phys. Soc., Optical Soc. Am., AAAS, Combustion Inst. Current Work: Chemical kinetics and spectroscopy of combustion systems, planetary atmospheres, environmental problems, and gas laser systems; laser and spectroscopic measurements of trace species. Subspecialties: Physical chemistry; Atmospheric chemistry. Home: 51 Woodmere Dr Sudbury MA 01776 Office: 45 Manning Rd Billerica MA 01821

KOLDOVSKY, OTAKAR, pediatrics and physiology educator; b. Olomouc, Czechoslovakia, Mar. 31, 1930; came to U.S. 1968, naturalized 1976; s. Kvetoslav and Marie (Loukotska) K.; m. Eva Libicka, May 6, 1971. M.D., Charles U., Prague, Czechoslovakia, 1955; Ph.D., Czechoslovakian Acad. Sci., 1962; M.A. (hon.) U. Pa., 1974. Resident internal med., gen. practice, balneology, Carlsbad, Czechoslovakia, 1955-57; postgrad. training physiology Inst. Physiology Czechoslovakia Acad. Sci., Prague, 1959-62; pediatric intern Children's Hosp., Phila., 1976-78; scientist Inst. Physiology Czechoslovakia Acad. Sci., Prague, 1962-66, sr. scientist, 1966-68; external mem. dept. pathophysiology Sch. Pediatric Med., Charles U., Prague, 1962-68; vis. scientist Inst. Physiology Acad. Sci., Leningrad, USSR, 1962, Inst. Nutrition, Berlin, 1963, dept. clin. biochem. U. Lund, Sweden, 1967-68; research assoc. pediatrics, Stanford U., 1965, 68-69; asst. prof. pediatrics U. Pa., 1969-73, assoc. prof., 1973-76, prof. research pediatrics, 1976-79; prof. pediatrics, head perinatal and nutritional scis. sect. dept. pediatrics, Ariz. Health Scis. Ctr., Tucson, 1980—, prof. physiology, 1980—. Author: (with P. Hahn) Utilization of Nutrients during Post-natal Period, 1967; Development of the Small Intestinal Functions in Mammals and Man, 1969. Editor: (with P. Hahn) Development of Metabolism as Related to Nutrition, 1966. Contbr. numerous articles to profl. jours. and books. Served with Czechoslovakian Army and Air Force, 1957-59. Grantee NIH, 1971—, Nestle, 1984—. Mem. Internatl. Soc. Human Devel., Am. Inst. Nutrition, Am. Physiol. Soc., Perinatal Research Soc., Soc. Exptl. Biology and Med., North Am. Soc. Pediatric Gastroenterology, Am. Pediatric Soc., Am. Gastroenterology Assn. Current work: Development of gastrointestinal functions in mammals, including man, role of genetic, hormonal and nutritional factors. Subspecialties: Nutrition (biology); Physiology (biology). Office: Dept Pediatrics Univ Ariz Health Scis Ctr Tucson AZ 85724

KOLFF, WILLEM JOHAN, surgeon, educator; b. Leiden, Holland, Feb. 14, 1911; came to U.S., 1950, naturalized, 1956; s. Jacob and Adriana (de Jonge) K.; m. Janke C. Huidekoper, Sept 4, 1937; children: Jacob, Adriana P., Albert C., Cornelis A., Gualtherus C.M. Student, U. Leiden Med. Sch., 1930-38; M.D. summa cum laude, U. Groningen, 1946; M.D. (hon.), U. Turin, Italy, 1969, Rostock (Germany) U., 1975, U. L'Aquila, Italy, 1981, Allegheny Coll., Meadville, Pa., 1960, Tulane U., 1975, CUNY, 1982, Temple U., 1983, U. Utah, 1983, U. Bologne, Italy, 1983. Internist, head med. dept. Mcpl. Hosp., Kampen, Holland; staff research div. Cleve. Clinic Found., 1950-67; privaat docent, dept. medicine U. Leiden, Nether-Bunts Ednl. Inst., Cleve., 1950-67, head dept. artificial organs, 1958-67; Disting. prof. medicine and surgery, head div. artificial organs dept. surgery U. Utah Sch. Medicine, Salt Lake City, 1967—, prof. internal medicine, 1981—; research prof. engring. Inst. Biomed. Engring., 1967—. Decorated commandeur Orde Van Oranje Netherlands, 1970; Orden de Mayo al Merito en el Grado de Gran Official Argentina, 1974; recipient Landsteiner medal for establishment blood banks during war in Holland Netherlands Red Cross, 1942; Cameron prize U. Edinburgh (Scotland), 1964; 5,000 award Gairdner Found., 1966; Valentine award N.Y. Acad. Medicine, 1969; 1st Gold medal Netherlands Surg. Soc., 1970; Leo Harvey prize Technion, Israel, 1972; Sr. U.S. Scientist award Alexander Von Humboldt Found., 1978; Austrian Gewerbeverein's Wilhelm-Exner award, 1980. Mem. AMA (Sci. Achievement award 1982), AAUP, Am. Physiol. Soc., Soc. Exptl. Biology and Medicine, AAAS, N.Y. Acad. Scis., Am. Soc. Artificial Internal Organs, Nat. Kidney Found., European Dialysis and Transplant Assn., ACP, Austrian Soc. Nephrology (hon.), Academia Nacional de Medicina (Colombia) (hon.). Developed artificial kidney for clin. use, 1943; oxygenator, 1956; co-inventor intra-aortic balloon pump, 1961; research on artificial heart, 1957—. Subspecialty: Artificial organs and prostheses. Address: Div of Artificial Organs Univ of Utah Medical Center Bldg 535 Salt Lake City UT 84112

KOLLER, LOREN D., veterinary pathologist, immunotoxicologist, researcher; b. Pomeroy, Wash., June 16, 1940; s. Edwin E. and Doris K. (Shelton) K.; m. Kathleen N. Ringness, Sept. 7, 1963; children: Susan, Michael, Christopher. D.V.M., Wash. State U., Pullman, 1965; M.S., U. Wis., Madison, 1969, Ph.D., 1971. Lic. veterinarian, Oreg., Wash., Idaho. Pvt. vet. practice, Corvallis, Oreg., 1965-66; with Nat. Inst. Environ. Health Scis., Research Triangle Park, N.C., 1971-72, Oreg. State U., Corvallis, 1972-78, WOI Regional Program in Vet. Medicine, U. Idaho, Moscow, 1978-85, Coll. Vet. Medicine, Corvallis, 1985—; cons. EPA, Life Systems, Inc.; mem. grant rev. panel of sci. rev. panel health research EPA. Editorial bd.: Fundamental Applied Toxicology, 1982—; cons. U.S. Dept. Justice; cons. editor: Jour. Reticuloendothelial Soc, 1982—; contbr. articles to sci. jours. Served to capt. M.C., AUS, 1966-68. Grantee NIH; EPA; Dept. Agr.; Dow Chem. Soc.; Merck, Sharp & Dohme; Pacific N.W. Region Commn., FDA. Mem. AVMA, Idaho Vet. Med. Assn., Soc. Toxicol. Pathology, Soc. Toxicology, Am. Coll. Vet. Toxicologists, Reticuloendothelial Soc., Conf. Research Workers in Animal Disease, Assn. Vet. Med. Colls., Am. Assn. Vet. Immunologists. Baptist. Current Work: Study of pathological, immunological, toxicological and oncogenic effects of drugs and chemicals in laboratory animals. Subspecialties: Cancer research (veterinary medicine); Pathology (veterinary medicine). Office: Coll Vet Medicine Oreg State U Corvallis OR 97331

KOLM, HENRY HERBERT, physicist; b. Vienna, Austria, Sept. 10, 1924, came to U.S., 1939, naturalized, 1941; s. Richard and Ella (Jellenik) K.; m. Elizabeth Olmstead Cushing, June 6, 1953; children—Margaret, Juliet, Edna, Cornelia. B.S., in physics, MIT, 1950, Ph.D., 1955. Research staff MIT Lincoln Lab., Lexington, Mass., 1955-60; sr. sci. MIT Nat. Magnet Lab., Cambridge, Mass., 1960—; v.p. research Piezo Elec. Products, Cambridge, 1979—; pres. Electromagnetic Launch Research Inc., Cambridge, 1981—; pres. Kolm Air Transport, Cambridge, 1981—; cons. numerous organizations, 1970-80. Editor: High Magnetic Fields, 1962. Contbr. articles to profl. jours. Patentee in field. Mem. Conservation Commn. Com., Wayland, Mass., 1972. Served to sgt. U.S. Army, 1943-46, World War II. Recipient Peter Mark Medal Dept. of Defense, Boston, 1983; named Entrepreneur of the Year Money Mag., 1981; mem. IEEE (sr.), Am. Inst. Physics, AIAA, AAAS, Nat. Pilots Assn. Current work: Electromagnetic launch technology; pulsed power engineering; cryogenics; magnetically levitated transportation; piezoceramic technology; magnetic separation and filtration. Subspecialties: Applied magnetics; Aerospace engineering and technology. Home: Weir Meadow Wayland MA 01778 Office: Electromagnetic Launch Research Inc 625 Putnam Ave Cambridge MA 02139

KOLODNY, ABRAHAM LEWIS, rheumatologist, clinical researcher; b. Norfolk, Va., July 2, 1917; s. William and Jennie (Eisenberg) K.; m. Mildred A. Fiske, Aug. 10, 1942; children: William (dec.), David, Suki McCormick, Douglas, Peggy. M.D., U. Va., 1941. Intern South Balt. Gen. Hosp., 1941-42; resident in rheumatology Ashburn Army Hosp., McKinney, Tex., 1945-46; rheumatologist N. Charles Gen. Hosp., Balt., 1946—, now chief rheumatology; rheumatologist Franklin Square Hosp., Balt., 1946—, now chief rheumatology, pres. staff, 1981-83; chief rheumatology Children's Hosp., Balt.; lectr. Essex Community Coll., Balt.; mem. Md. Gov.'s Task Force for Arthritis, 1981-83; mem. Md. State Arthritis Commn., cons. to drug coms. Author: Comprehensive Approach Therapy Pain, 1961; contbr. chpts. to books, articles to profl. jours. Bd. dirs. Md. chpt. Arthritis Found., Md. chpt. Lupus Found. Served to maj. U.S. Army, 1942-46. Decorated Bronze Star; recipient Arthritis Found. Disting. Service award, 1981, 82. Fellow Royal Soc. Health, Internat. Acad. Law and Sci., Am. Geriatric Soc., Internat. Coll. Angiology; mem. Am. Fedn. Clin. Research, Am. Rheumatism Assn., Md. Soc. Rheumatic Diseases, Baltimore County Med. Soc., Med. and Chirurg. Faculty Md., AMA, So. Med. Soc., Am. Soc. Clin. Pharmacology and Therapeutic. Club: Hopkins (Balt.). Current Work: Clinical pharmacology, analgesics, anti-rheumatics. Subspecialties: Internal medicine; Immunopharmacology. Home: PO Box 70 Brooklandville MD 21022 Office: Franklin Square Medical Arts Bldg Franklin Square Dr Baltimore MD 21237

KOMANICKY, PAVEL, medical educator, researcher; b. Habura, Czechoslovakia, June 28, 1943; came to U.S., 1969; s. Stefan and Maria e6(Milanova) K. M.D., Šafarik U., Košice, Czechoslovakia, 1966. Diplomate: Am. Bd. Internal Medicine. Intern Univ. Hosp., Košice, 1965-66; research fellow, assoc. Czechoslovak Acad. Scis., 1966-69; resident in medicine Carney Hosp., Boston U., 1970-73; research fellow Univ. Hosp., Boston U., 1973-76, staff physician, 1976-81; asst. prof. medicine Tex. Tech. U. Health Scis. Ctr., Amarillo, 1981—; instr. medicine Boston U., 1975-81; attending physician Univ. Hosp., Boston, 1976-81, Boston City Hosp., 1976-81, Amarillo Med. Ctr., 1981—. Research grantee Univ. Hosp., Boston U., 1976, 78; Research grantee Tex. Tech. U., 1982. Fellow ACP; mem. AMA (Physician Recognition award 1975, 78, 81), Am. Heart Assn., Endocrine Soc., Am. Fedn. Clin. Research. Current Work: Role of humoral factors in etiology of hypertension; role of adrenal hormones in hypertension; pathophysiology of hypertension; study of receptors for adrenal hormones; pathophysiology of cardiomegaly. Subspecialties: Endocrinology; Internal medicine. Home: 6040 Belpree Dr C225 Amarillo TX 79106 Office: Texas Tech University Health Sciences Center 1400 Wallace Blvd Amarillo TX 79106

KOMECHAK, MARILYN GILBERT, psychologist; b. Wabash, Ind., Aug. 28, 1936; d. Russell and Evelyn (Snyder) Gilbert; m. George J. Komechak, Aug. 23, 1936; children: Kimberly, Gilbert. B.S., Purdue U., 1958, Tex. Christian U., 1966; M.Ed., Tex. Christian U., 1968; Ph.D., North Tex. State U., 1975. Staff Child Study Ctr., Diagnostic Clinic, Ft. Worth, 1968-74; assoc. dir. behavioral studies Sch. Community Service, North Tex. State U., 1974-77, pvt. practice psychology, Ft. Worth, 1977—; adj. prof. Tex. Christian U., Ft. Worth, 1977-79, U. Tex.-Arlington, 1977-80; cons. in field; mem. bus. women's bd. Sanger-Harris Dept Stores. Author: Getting Yourself Together, 1982; contbr. articles to profl. jours. Bd. dirs. Jon Pierce, Inc., Ft. Worth, 1980-82; adv. bd. Trinity Valley Mental Health/Mental Retardation, 1980, Mental Health Assn. Tarrant County, 1980; active Easter Seal Soc., 1977. Mem. Am. Psychol. Assn., Tarrant County Psychol. Assn. (sec. 1980), Am. Soc. Clin. Hypnosis, Tex. Psychol. Assn. Episcopalian. Current Work: Psychohistorial research in life problems, hypnosis and psychotherapy. Subspecialty: Psychotherapy. Office: 5280 Trail Lake Dr Fort Worth TX 76133

KOMINZ, MICHELLE ANNE, geophysicist; b. Washington, Apr. 19, 1953; d. David Richard Kominz and Eleanor Hart Condliffe. B.A., Colby Coll., 1975; M.S., U. R.I., 1978. Marine geologist II Grad. Sch. Oceanography U. R.I., Narragansett, 1978-79; geophysicist Lamont Doherty Geol. Obs. Columbia U., Palisades, N.Y., 1979—. Contbr. articles to profl. jours. Mem. Am. Assn. Petroleum Geology, AAAS, Am. Geophys. Union, Geol. Soc. Am. Current work: Geophysical modeling (heat flow, subsidence history, flexure) of compressional and extensional basins. Subspecialty: Geophysics. Office: Lamont-Doherty Geol Obs Palisades NY 10964

KOMMEDAHL, THOR, plant pathology educator; b. Mpls., Apr. 1, 1920; s. Thorbjorn and Martha (Blegen) K.; m. Faye Lillian Kommedahl, Aug. 5, 1951; children: Kris Alan, Siri Lynn, Lori Anne. Student, Bethel Coll., St. Paul, 1938-39; B.S., U. Minn., 1945, M.S., 1947, Ph.D., 1951. Instr. U. Minn., St. Paul, 1946-51; asst. prof. Ohio Agrl. Research and Devel. Ctr., Wooster, 1951-53, Ohio State U., Columbus, 1952-53, U. Minn., St. Paul, 1953-57, assoc. prof., 1957-63, prof. dept. plant pathology, 1963—; cons. botanist and taxonomist Minn. Dept. Agr., 1954-60. Sr. editor: Challenging Problems in Plant Health, 1983; editor-in-chief: Phytopathology, 1964-67; cons. editor: McGraw-Hill Ency. Sci. and Tech, 1972-78; editor: Internat. Congress Plant Protection, 2 vols, 1981; Contbr. articles to profl. jours. Fulbright grantee Iceland, 1968; Guggenheim fellow Australia, 1961-62. Fellow AAAS, Am. Phytopath. Soc. (pres. 1971, coordinator publs. 1978-84, Disting. Service award 1984); mem. Weed Sci. Soc. Am. (award of excellence 1966), Am. Inst. Biol. Scis., Bot. Soc. Am., Council Biology Editors, Internat. Soc. Plant Pathology (councillor 1971-78, sec.-gen., treas. 1983-88), Mycological Soc. Am., Soc. Scholarly Publ., N.Y. Acad. Sci. Baptist. Current Work: Biol. control of plant disease by application of antagonistic microorganisms to seeds, ecology of root disease fungi. Subspecialties: Plant pathology; Biological control. Home: 1840 W Roselawn Ave Falcon Heights MN 55113 Office: Univ Minn 495 Borlaug Hall 1991 Buford Circle St Paul MN 55108

KOMOREK, MICHAEL, JR., health physicist; A.S., Genesee Community Coll., 1974; B.A., SUNY Buffalo, 1977; postgrad., 1980. Research asst. SUNY - Buffalo, 1976-78; health physicist Sch. Medicine and VA Hosp., 1978-82, clin. instr., 1979—; sr. health physicist Alara Mgmt. Co., Elma, N.Y., 1980—; cons. VA Hosp., 1980—, Wyoming County Community Hosp., 1980—. Contbr. articles to profl. jours. Mem. Health Physics Soc. (pres. chpt. 1981-82), Am. Assn. Physicists in Medicine, Nuclear Medicine Soc., Laser Inst. Am. (assoc.). Subspecialty: Nuclear physics. Office: Alara Mgmt Co 2125 Transit Rd Elma NY 14059

KOMOROSKI, RICHARD ANDREW, chemist, educator; b. St. Louis, Feb. 4, 1947; s. Andrew John and Frances Mae (Estermann) K.; m. Eva Maria Marczewski, May 12, 1979. B.S. in Chemistry, St. Louis U., 1969; Ph.D., Ind. U.-Bloomington, 1973. Chemist, Mo. Analytical Labs, St. Louis, 1967-69; postdoctoral fellow Fla. State U., 1973-76; sr. research chemist Diamond Shamrock Corp., Painesville, Ohio, 1976-79; research and devel. assoc. B.F. Goodrich Co., Brecksville, Ohio, 1979—; instr. dept. chemistry John Carroll U., Cleve., 1977, 84. Editor: High Resolution NMR of Synthetic Polymers in Bulk, 1985. Contbr. numerous articles to profl. jours. Swedish Nat. Scis. Research Council grantee, 1976. Mem. Am. Chem. Soc. (chmn. pub. affairs Cleve. sect. 1982-84), Sigma Xi. Roman Catholic. Current work: Applications of nuclear magnetic resonance to chemistry, biology and polymer science; molecular structure of polymers; high resolution nuclear magnetic resonance of solids; nuclear magnetic resonance of surface species. Subspecialties: Nuclear magnetic resonance; Polymer chemistry. Office: BF Goodrich Research Ctr 9921 Brecksville Rd Brecksville OH 44141

KONDILIS, FRANCIS NICHOLAS, JR., engineer; b. Tucson, Dec. 10, 1956; s. Francis Nicholas and Barbara Anne (Stahl) K. B.S.E.E., Ariz. State U., 1979; M.S.E.E., U. Md.-College Park, 1982. Registered profl. engr. assoc., Ariz., 1980. Sr. engr. E-O systems Nat. Security Agency, Ft. Meade, Md., 1980-84; program mgr., digital and A-O systems ESL Inc., Sunnyvale, Calif., 1984—. Served to capt. USAF 1980-84. Mem. IEEE, Nat. Soc. Profl. Engrs., Eta Kappa Nu. Republican. Roman Catholic. Current work: Digital signal processing systems, integration of light and sound, computer modeling of the propagation of monochromatic radiation through the atmosphere, study of open-beam laser communication systems. Subspecialties: Optical signal processing; Algorithms. Home: 160 E Remington Dr #C 149 Sunnyvale CA 94087 Office: ESL Inc M/S 405 PO Box 3510 Sunnyvale CA 94088

KONDO, YOJI, astrophysicist, educator; b. Hitachi, Japan, May 26, 1933; came to U.S., 1960, naturalized, 1968; s. Tsuneo and Hama (Yamada) K.; m. Ursula Tuetermann, Sept. 10, 1965; children: Beatrice, Cynthia, Angela. B.A., Tokyo U. Fgn. Studies, 1958; M.A., U. Pa., 1963, Ph.D., 1965. Asst. prof. U. Pa., Phila., 1965; NAS-NRC fellow NASA Goddard Space Flight Ctr., Greenbelt, Md., 1965-68; astronomer, chief astrophysics sect. Johnson Space Ctr., 1968-77; astrophysicist Goddard Space Flight Ctr., 1978—, project scientist Internat. Ultraviolet Explorer satellite, 1982—; adj. assoc. prof. U. Okla., 1971-72, prof., 1972-77, U. Houston, 1974-77, U. Pa., 1978—. Editor: Earth & Extraterestrial Sci., 1974-79, Comments on Astrophysics, 1979—; contbr. articles to profl. jours.; editor: X-Ray Binaries, 1976, Advances in UV Astronomy, 1982; Local Interstellar Medium, 1984; Future of UV Astronomy, 1984. Recipient Cert. of Commendation, NASA Johnson Space Ctr., 1975. Fellow AAAS; mem. Am. Astron. Soc., Internat. Astron. Union (acting pres. Commn. on Astronomy from Space 1982, v.p. 1982-85), U.S. Judo Assn. Current Work: Research of evolutional processes in interacting binary stars, study of interstellar medium, study of energy generation mechanism in BL Lacertae objects and quasars. Subspecialties: Ultraviolet high energy astrophysics; Satellite studies. Office: NASA Goddard Spaceflight Ctr Greenbelt MD 20771

KONECKY, MILTON STUART, chemist; b. Omaha, July 29, 1922; s. Eugene Max and Eve (Lipp) K.; m. Naomi Marie Schipporeit, Oct. 9, 1948; children—Mark, Chad. B.S., Creighton U., 1944, M.S., 1948; Ph.D., U. Ill., 1958. Cereal chemist Omaha Grain Exchange Labs., Nebr., 1947-50; chemist entomology research div. USDA, Beltsville, Md., 1950-54; sr. chemist Exxon Research and Engring. Co., Linden, N.J., 1957-61; research assoc., 1961-63, sect. head, 1963-69, sr. staff adv., 1969—. Contbr. articles to profl. jours. Patentee fuels and petrochemicals. Adv. sci. curriculum Old Turnpike Sch., Tewksbury, N.J., 1978-80; adv. mock trial team Voorhees High Sch., Glen Gardner, N.J., 1982-84. Served with USN, 1944-46, PTO. Texaco fellow, 1956-57. Mem. Am Chem. Soc., AAAS, N.Y. Acad. Sci., Sigma Xi, Phi Lambda Upsilon. Current work: Research, planning and patent activities in technical fields. Subspecialty: Organic chemistry. Home: Dryden Rd Box 307 Pottersville NJ 07979 Office: Exxon Research and Engring Co PO Box 121 Linden NJ 07036

KONG, JIN AU, elec. engr., educator; b. Kiangu, China, Dec. 27, 1942; came to U.S., 1965, naturalized, 1975; s. Chin Hwu and Shiu C. (Chao) K.; m. Wen Yuan Yu, June 27, 1970; children: Shing David. Ph.D., Syracuse U., 1968. Postdoctoral research engr. Syracuse (N.Y.) U., 1968-69; mem. faculty M.I.T., 1969—, now prof. elec. engring.; cons. N.Y. Port Authority, 1971, Lunar Sci Inst., 1972, Army Engring. Topographical Lab., 1979, Lincoln Lab., 1979-82, Hughes Aircraft Co., 1981; interregional advisor UN Dept. Tech. Coop. for Devel., 1978-80. Author: Theory of Electromagnetic Waves, 1975; editor: Research Topics in Electromagnetic Wave Theory, 1981; contbr. articles to profl. jours. Vinton Hayes postdoctoral fellow, 1969. Mem. Am. Geophys. Union, Am. Phys. Soc., IEEE, Internat. Union Radio Sci., Optical Soc. Am., Sigma Xi, Phi Tau Phi, Tau Beta Pi. Current Work: Remote sensing and electromagnetic wave theory. Subspecialties: Electrical engineering; Remote sensing (geoscience). Home: 72 Hillcrest Ave Lexington MA 02173 Office: 36-383 MIT Cambridge MA 02139

KONISHI, MASAKAZU, biologist. Bing prof. behavioral biology Calif. Inst. Tech. Elected mem. Nat. Acad. Scis., 1985. Subspecialty: Behaviorism. Office: Calif Inst Tech Dir of Biology Pasadena CA 91125

KONOPNICKI, MAREK JAN, optical scientist; b. Warsaw, Poland, Jan. 31, 1947; came to U.S., 1972; s. Wladyslaw and Janina (Musial) K.; m. Barbara Elizabeth Pawlowski, Mar. 1975; 1 child, Camille Maria. B.S. in Elec. Engring., Warsaw Poly., 1968, M.S. in Elec. Engring., 1970; M.A. in Physics, U. Rochester, 1975, Ph.D. in Physics, 1980. Research asst. U. Rochester, 1974-79; vis. lectr. Rochester Inst. Tech., 1974-75; spl. lectr. St. John Fisher Coll., Rochester, 1978; research assoc. U. Rochester, 1980; research scientist U.S. Air Force Weapons Lab., Kirtland AFB, N.Mex., 1980-82, Lockheed Missiles and Space Co., Sunnyvale, Calif., 1982—. Guest co-editor Optical Engring., 1982. Contbr. articles to sci. jours. Patentee optical transmission system. Mem. Am. Phys. Soc., Optical Soc. Am., Soc. Photo-Optical Instrumentation Engrs., AIAA (tech. com. on plasmadynamics and lasers 1984—). Republican. Roman Catholic. Current work: Research and development of high energy laser systems, interaction of short intense laser pulses with matter, propagation, optical solitons, photon echoes. . Home: 1704 Austin Ave Los Altos CA 94022 Office: Lockheed Missiles and Space Co 0/51-20 B/586 PO Box 3504 Sunnyvale CA 94086

KONOWALOW, DANIEL DIMITRI, chemistry educator; b. Cleve., Apr. 28, 1929; s. Dimitry and Mary (Ehnatt) K.; m. Marcy Ellen Rosenkrantz, July 24, 1978. B.Sc., Ohio State U., 1953; Ph.D., U. Wis.-Madison, 1961. Chemist E.I. duPont de Nemours, Wilmington, Del., 1960-62; asst. dir. U. Wis. Theoretical Chemistry Inst., Madison, 1962-65; asst. prof. chemistry SUNY-Binghamton, 1965-70, assoc. prof., 1970-80, prof., 1980—; cons. to industry. Contbr. numerous articles on atomic and molecular interactions to profl. jours. Served with Chem. Corps U.S. Army, 1953-55. Current Work: Molecular structure and spectra; lasers; intermolecular forces; research on electronic structure and spectra of excited states of small molecules; long-range interactions of molecular fragments. Subspecialties: Theoretical chemistry; Atomic and molecular physics. Home: Box 473A Roberts Rd RD 1 Binghamton NY 13903 Office: SUNY Binghamton NY 13901

KOO, PETER HUNG-KWAN, immuno-biochemistry educator, researcher; b. Shanghai, China, Aug. 10, 1940; came to U.S., 1959, naturalized, 1975; s. Yung-Foo and Shun-Wa (Ko) K.; m. Alice Hotapichayawivat, Dec. 23, 1967; children: David G., Christopher G. B.A., U. Wash., 1964; Ph.D., U. Md., 1970. Research assoc. Johns Hopkins U., 1970-74, asst. prof., 1975-77; staff fellow NIH, Balt., 1974-75; asst. prof. microbiology and immunology N.E. Ohio U. Coll. Medicine, 1977-83, assoc. prof., 1983—; adj. assoc. prof. dept. biology and chemistry Kent State U.; lectr. in immunology, biochemistry, microbiology, cancer biology at various univs., 1974—; bd. dirs., mem. profl. edn. com. Portage County (Ohio) chpt. Am. Cancer Soc., 1982—, chmn. profl. edn. com., 1985—. Contbr. articles to profl. publs., 1970—. Deacon First Christian Ch., Kent, Ohio, 1978-81, 82—, mem. fin. com., 1981—. NIH grantee, 1978-82; Am. Cancer Soc. Ohio grantee, 1978, 82; Cystic Fibrosis Care Fund grantee, 1979, 82; United Way Health Found. grantee, 1982; MEFCOM Fund grantee, 1982—; NSF grantee, 1984—. Mem. Am. Assn. Immunologists, Johns Hopkins Immunology Council, Johns Hopkins Med. and Surg. Assn., N.Y. Acad. Scis., Am. Chem. Soc., AAAS, Am. Soc. Microbiology, Sigma Xi. Current Work: Cancer immunology and bilogy: roles of lymphokines, cytokines and interferon inducers in tumor-host interactions; natural immune defense systems; mechanism of spontaneous cancer regression; structure and function of alpha-2-macroglobulin and its interactions with hormones (particularly nerve growth factor). Subspecialties: Immunobiology and immunology; Cancer research (medicine). Office: NE Ohio U Coll Medicine SR 44 Rootstown OH 44272

KOOMANOFF, FREDERICK ALAN, energy research scientist, government agency administrator; b. N.Y.C., Sept. 2, 1926; m. Lora Gahimer, May 27, 1955; children—Vivre, Heather, Elena. B. Engring., NYU, 1952, M.Engring., 1954; postgrad. Ohio State U. Chief systems planning Battell Meml. Inst., Columbus, Ohio, 1958-67; dir. planning and diversification Eastern Airlines Inc., N.Y.C. and Washington, 1969-72; pres., chief exec. officer Stentran Systems Inc., Vienna, Va., 1972-76; mgr. environ. and resources, solar energy Dept. Energy, Washington, 1976-78, dir. solar power satellite Basic Energy Sci. Div., 1978-81, dir. CO2 research, 1981—; cons. Pres.'s Adv. Com. on Mgmt. Improvement, 1970-72. Contbr. articles to profl. jours., chpts. to books. Served with USAAC, 1945. Recipient Exceptional Service medal Dept. Energy, 1984, Outstanding awards Dept. Def. and Dept. Energy. Mem. Soc. of Friends. Current work: Science policy and management, technology forecasting, management of science, systems analysis, computer systems application, earth science. . Home: 10700 Montrose Ave Garrett Park MD 20896 Office: Carbon Dioxide Research Div ER-12 Dept Energy Washington DC 20525

KOONSE, HOWARD JOSEPH, microbiologist, researcher; b. Kansas City, Kans., Feb. 17, 1924; s. Aaron Edward and Elsie Victoria (Haab) K.; m. Bettie Jane McChristy, Mar. 13, 1947. B.A. in Microbiology, Kans. U., 1950, M.S. in Virology, 1952. Research scientist Jefferson Med. Coll., Phila., 1951-52; dir. biol. prodn. Dow Chem. Co., Zionsville, Ind., 1952-72; dir. biol. research and prodn. Fort Dodge Labs., Iowa, 1972-82, v.p. research, 1982-84, sr. v.p. tech. ops., 1984—; cons. Argentine Govt., Buenos Aires, 1958-61. Contbr. articles to profl. jours. Served with USAF, 1942-45. Decorated Bronze Stars (5), 1945. Mem. Am. Soc. Microbiologists, Vet. Biol. Com. Am. Health Inst. Republican. Unitarian. Club: P.M. Gun pres. Zionsville 1968-71). Lodge: Elks. Current work: Virological vaccine production. Subspecialty: Medicinal chemistry. Office: Fort Dodge Labs 800 5th St NW Fort Dodge IA 50501

KOOS, GREGORY LEE, condensed matter physicist; b. Davenport, Iowa, Dec. 3, 1953; s. Carl Henry and Rosemary (Tritz) K. B.S., U. Notre Dame, 1976; M.S., U. Ill., 1978, Ph.D., 1984. Mem. tech. staff AT&T Technologies, Princeton, N.J., 1983—. Mem. Am. Phys. Soc. Subspecialties: Condensed matter physics; Infrared spectroscopy. Home: 1-24 Quail Ridge Plainsboro NJ 08536 Office: Engring Research Ctr AT&T Technologies PO Box 900 Princeton NJ 08540

KOOTSEY, JOSEPH MAILEN, physiologist, computer scientist; b. Houston, Sept. 3, 1939; s. Joseph Steven and Esther Irene (Johnson) K.; m. Lynne Diane Wiles, Aug. 20, 1961; children—Brenden Lamont, Sean Alexander. B.A. in Physics, Pacific Union Coll., 1960; ScM. in Physics, Brown U., 1964, Ph.D., 1966. Asst. prof. physiology Loma Linda U., Calif., 1966-69; asst. prof. physiology Duke U., Durham, N.C., 1969-76, 79-82, assoc. prof., 1982—; cons. Am. Edwards Labs., Santa Ana, Calif., 1980-83; dir. nat. biomed. simulation resource Duke U. Med Ctr., Durham, 1983—. Contbr. articles to profl. jours. Patentee in field. NIH grantee Duke U., 1973—. Mem. Am. Physical Soc., Am. Assn. Physics Tchrs., Biophysical Soc., AAAS, Am. Physiological Soc., N.Y. Acad. Sci., Am. Heart Assn., IEEE, Soc. Computer Simulation, Am. Sci. Affiliation, Sigma Xi. Democrat. Adventist. Current work: Cardiac electrophysiology, biomedical computer simulation. Subspecialties: Physiology (medicine); Mathematical software. Home: 2800 DeKalb St Durham NC 27705 Office: Box 3709 Dept Physiology Duke Univ Med Ctr Durham NC 27710

KOPECKO, DENNIS J., research microbiologist, consultant; b. Ironwood, Mich., Jan. 14, 1947; s. Norbert Robert and Dorothy Eileen (La Chapelle) K.; m. Patricia Guerry, Dec. 10, 1977. B.S. in Biology (U.S. Army scholar, 1966-68), Va. Mil. Inst., 1968; Ph.D. in Microbiology (Va. State Council for Higher Edn. Scholar, 1969-72), Med. Coll. Va., 1972. Predoctoral fellow dept. microbiology Med. Coll. Va., Richmond, 1968-72; postdoctoral fellow dept. medicine Stanford (Calif.) U. Med. Sch., 1972-76, C.F. Aaron fellow, 1972-73; sr. research microbiologist Dept. Def., Walter Reed Army Inst. Research, Washington, 1979—; adj. prof. dept. microbiology U. Md., College Park, 1985—; cons., acting sci. dir. Genetic Research Corp., Columbia, Md.; vis. lectr. genetics Georgetown U., Uniformed Services U., NIH; vis. lectr. in microbial genetics Va. Commonwealth U., Richmond, 1979-80; continuing edn. lectr. Am. Coll. Vet. Microbiologists, Chgo., 1979; invited lectr. symposium on Mil. Vet. Medicine, Washington, 1980-82; vis. lectr. U. Mich., Ann Arbor, 1981; coorganizer ann. Mid-Atlantic Regional Conf. on Extrachromosomal Genetic Elements, 1977—; co-organizer, instr. grad. microbiol. course NIH, Bethesda, Md., 1980-84; exec. sec. Walter Reed Instl. Biosafety Com., 1981—. Co-editor: Progress in Molecular and Subcellular Biology; mem. editorial bd.: Jour. Bacteriology; reviewer for profl. jours.; contbr. articles to profl. publs. in field, papers to profl. confs., U.S., W. Ger., Switzerland, Can., Czechoslovakia, Dominican Republic, Japan, India, Australia. Served to capt. U.S. Army, 1976-79. Va. Heart Assn. fellow, summers 1967-68; Bank Am.-Giannini Med. Research Found. fellow, 1973-75; recipient honors Alpha Sigma Chi, 1971-72; Paul A. Siple medal for outstanding research U.S. Army Sci. Conf., 1984. Mem. Genetics Soc. Am., Am. Soc. Microbiology, Mid-Atlantic Regional Extrachromosomal Genetic Elements Group, Fed. Exec. and Profl. Assn., Sigma Xi. Roman Catholic. Patentee oral vaccine for immunization against enteric disease, method for the rapid detection of typhoid fever bacteria. Current Work: Molecular genetic analysis of enteric bacterial pathogens; molecular genetics of bacteria, genetic engineering of bacterial vaccine strains, rapid diagnosis of bacterial pathogens, genetic manipulations of bacteria. Subspecialties: Genetics and genetic engineering (medicine); Molecular biology. Home: 4601 Flower Valley Dr Rockville MD 20853 Office: Walter Reed Army Inst Research Washington DC 20307

KOPELMAN, RICHARD ERIC, management educator, consultant; b. N.Y.C., May 31, 1943; s. Seymour Harold and Leona Libby (Quint) K.; m. Carol Fran Fialkov, June 7, 1970; children: Joshua Marc, Michael Adam. B.S. in Econs, U. Pa., 1965, M.B.A., 1967; D.B.A., Harvard U., 1974. Diplomate: Accredited personnel diplomate. Instr. mgmt. Baruch Coll., N.Y.C., 1973-74, asst. prof. mgmt., 1974-77, assoc. prof. mgmt., 1978-80, prof. mgmt., 1981—; acad. co-dir. Baruch-Cornell M.S. in Indsl. and Labor Relations Program, 1985—; dir. sec. Aleph Null Corp., Carle Place, N.Y., 1981—; mgmt. cons. Citibank, Lopez & Assocs., Forest Engring. Research Inst., 1976-77, Bendix Corp. Bd. dirs. Day Care Council Nassau County, Inc., Hempstead, N.Y., 1979-82; tech. reader Recs. for the Blind, Inc., N.Y.C., 1976-77; cons. Vol. Urban Cons. Group, Inc., 1975-78. William B. Harding fellow Harvard U., 1972-73; Yoder-Heneman personnel awardee Am. Soc. Personnel Adminstrn., 1982. Mem. Acad. of Mgmt., Am. Arbitration Assn. (panelist), Am. Psychol. Assn., Am. Inst. Decision Scis., Am. Compensation Assn. Current Work: Theoretical and applied research on work motivation; surveyed demonstrated effectiveness of ten prominent behavioral science techniques used to improve productivity; originated return on effort version of expectancy theory; developed model and scales to measure work, family and interrole conflicts. Subspecialty: Industrial and organizational psychology. Home: 65 Colgate Rd Great Neck NY 11023 Office: Baruch Coll 17 Lexington Ave New York NY 10010

KOPIN, IRWIN JEROME, physician, pharmacologist; b. N.Y.C., Mar. 27, 1929; s. Jacob and Eva (Resnick) K.; m. Rita Brownstein; children—Judith R., Alan S., Gail A. B.Sc., McGill U., Can., 1951, M.D., 1955. Diplomate Am. Bd. Internal Medicine. Intern, then resident in medicine Boston City Hosp., 1955-57; research asso. NIH, 1957-60; resident in medicine, Columbia Presbyn. Med. Center, N.Y.C., 1960-61; commd. corps NIMH, USPHS, Bethesda, Md.; chief sect. medicine LCS, NIMH, 1961—; chief Lab. Clin. Sci., NIMH, 1968-83, assoc. dir. clin. research IRP, 1982-83; dir. intramural research program Nat. Inst. Neurol. and Communicative Disorders and Stroke NIH, 1983—. Co-editor-in-chief: Advances in Pharmacology/Chemotherapy, 1968—; editor: Neurosci. Research, 1971-73; asso. editor: Pharmacol. Rev., 1977—; editorial bd. other jours. Recipient Superior Service award HEW, 1970; Pub. Service award NASA, 1974; Disting. Service medal USPHS, 1980; 1st prize Anna Monika Found. Fellow Am. Coll. Neuropsychopharmacology, Soc. Neurosci., Assn. Am. Physicians, AAAS; mem. Am. Soc. Biol. Chemists. Soc. Pharmacology and Exptl. Therapeutics, Assn. Research Nervous and Mental Disease (pres. 1970). Office: NIH Bldg 10 5N 214 Bethesda MD 20205

KOPP, ROGER ALAN, physicist, researcher; b. Detroit, Feb. 17, 1940; s. Walter John and Dena Blanche (Hill) K.; m. Joyce Elizabeth Schrage, June 23, 1962; children: Gregory, Lorene, Duane. B.S. in Astronomy, U. Mich., 1961; M.A., Harvard U., 1963, Ph.D. in Astronomy, 1968. Staff scientist Nat. Ctr. Atmospheric Research, Boulder, Colo., 1966-76; vis. scientist Max Planck Inst. Physics and Astrophysics, Munich, W.Ger., 1979-80, 71-72; physicist Los Alamos Nat. Lab., 1976—; vis. scientist Osservatorio Astrofisico di Arcetri, Florence, Italy, 1982, 84. Contbr. articles to profl. jours. Parker scholar, 1963. Mem. Internat. Astron. Union, Am. Astron. Soc., Am. Geophys. Union. Current Work: Inertial confinement fusion; theoretical physics and target design for CO-2- lasers and heavy ion drivers; solar physics MHD flows in the solar atmosphere; solar wind expansion theory. Subspecialties: Laser fusion; Solar physics. Home: 1104 Paseo Barranca Santa Fe NM 87501 Office: Los Alamos National Lab MS E531 Los Alamos NM 87545

KOPPLE, KENNETH DAVID, chemistry educator, researcher; b. Phila., Oct. 21, 1930; s. Harry N. and Sara M. (Silverstein) K.; m. Frances Marie Hopkins, Apr. 30, 1960. S.B. in Chem. Engring., MIT, 1951, Ph.D. in Chemistry, 1954. Instr., asst. prof. U. Chgo., 1954-62; research chemist Gen. Electric Research Co., Schenectady, 1962-65; assoc. prof. chemistry Ill. Inst. Tech., Chgo., 1965-70, prof., 1970—, chmn. dept. chemistry, 1982—; cons. in field; dir. Am. Peptide Symposium, Inc., 1972—. Author: Peptides and Amino Acids, 1966. Contbr. articles to profl. jours. Recipient Career Devel. award NIH, 1970-75; Guggen heim Found. fellow, 1964; grantee NIH, NSF. Fellow AAAS; mem. Am. Chem. Soc., Am. Soc. Biol. Chemists, Royal Soc. Chemistry. Current work: Chemistry of peptides, Nuclear Magnetic resonance, peptide conformation. Subspecialties: Biophysical chemistry; Nuclear magnetic resonance. Home: 175 E Delaware Pl Chicago IL 60611 Office: Ill Inst Tech Dept Chemistry Chicago IL 60616

KOPPLIN, JULIUS OTTO, electrical engineer; b. Appleton, Wis., Feb. 6, 1925; s. Julius O. and Renata A. (Peters) K.; m. Lola Mae Boldt, Sept. 16, 1950 (dec.); children: William J., John D., Mary Susan, James R.; m. Elizabeth A. Dutmer, Feb. 5, 1983. B.S.E.E., U. Wis., 1949; M.S.E.E., Purdue U., 1954, Ph.D., 1958. Corrosion engr. No. Ind. Public Service Co., 1949-53; asst. prof. elec. engring. U. Ill., 1958-61, asso. prof., 1961-68; prof., chmn. dept. elec. engring. U. Tex., El Paso, 1968-75, Iowa State U., Ames, 1975—. Contbr. articles to profl. jours. Served with USAAC, 1943-45. Decorated Air medal, Purple Heart. Mem. IEEE, Am. Soc. Engring. Edn., Sigma Xi, Eta Kappa Nu, Sigma Pi Sigma. Subspecialties: Electrical engineering; Computer engineering. Home: 241 Trail Ridge Rd Ames IA 50010 Office: Elec Engring Dept Iowa State U Ames IA 50011

KOPROWSKI, HILARY, medical scientist; b. Warsaw, Poland; came to U.S., 1944, naturalized, 1950; s. Paul and Sarah (Berland) K.; m. Dr. Irena Grasberg, July 14, 1938; children: Claude Eugene, Christopher Dorian. B.A., Mikolaj Rej Gymnasium of Luth. Congregation, Warsaw; M.D., U. Warsaw, grad., Warsaw Conservatory Music and Santa Cecilia Acad., Rome; Doctor honoris causa, Widener Coll., Phila., Ludwig-Maximilian U., Ger., U. Helsinki, U. Uppsala (Sweden). Research asst. dept. exptl. and gen. pathology U. Warsaw, 1936-39; staff Yellow Fever Research Service, Rio de Janeiro, 1940-44; staff research div. Am. Cyanamid Co., 1944-46; asst. dir. viral and rickettsial research Lederle Lab., Pearl River, N.Y., 1946-57; dir. Wistar Inst., Phila., 1957—; prof. microbiology Faculty Arts and Scis., U. Pa., 1957—; Wistar prof. research medicine U. Pa., 1957—; cons. WHO, Nat. Cancer Inst., NIH, USPHS, 1962-70. Co-editor: Methods in Virology, Viruses and Immunity, Current Topics in Microbiology and Immunology, 1965—, Cancer Research. Decorated Commandeur Ordre du Mérite pour la Recherche et l'Invention; Chevalier Order Royal De Lion Belgium; recipient Alvarenga prize. Coll. Physicians Phila., 1959; Alfred Jurzykowski Found Polish Millenium prize, 1966; Felix Wankel Tierschutz prize, 1979; Alexander Von Humboldt Sr. U.S. Scientist award; Fulbright Scholar Max Planck Inst. für Verhaltensphysiologie, Seewiesen, Germany, 1971. Fellow N.Y. Acad. Medicine, Phila. Coll. Physicians; mem. Am. Acad. Arts and Scis., Nat. Acad. Scis., N.Y. Acad. Scis. (pres. 1959, trustee 1960-72). Research cell biology, virology and immunology; vaccine against poliomyelitis, hog cholera, rabies. Subspecialties: Immunobiology and immunology; Virology (biology). Home: 334 Fairhill Road Wynnewood PA 19096 Office: Wistar Inst 36th and Spruce Streets Philadelphia PA 19104

KORDONOWY, RHODA KLEMPEL, cereal chemist; b. Lemmon, S.D., July 23, 1956; d. Walter Hugo and Eunice Jeanette (Prang) Klempel; m. Charles Micheal Kordonowy, June 21, 1979; stepchildren—Stuart, Wade, Shawn, Alicia. B.A. in Chemistry, Dickinson State Coll., 1978; Ph.D. in Cereal Chemistry, N.D. State U., 1984. Production engr. Continental Oil Co., Dickinson, N.D., 1978-84; assoc. research chemist Kellogg Co., Battle Creek, Mich., 1984—. Contbr. articles to profl. jours. Chorus mem., dancer Dickinson State Coll. Swing Choir, 1977. Nat. Pasta Assn. fellow, 1979-84. Mem. Am.

Assn. Cereal Chemists, Am. Chem. Soc., Inst. Food Technologists, Sigma Xi (assoc. mem.). Current work: Cereal and other food related carbohydrates in functionality, enzymes, pasta functionality nutrition. Subspecialties: Food science and technology; Biochemistry (biology). Office: Kellogg Co Chemistry Div 235 Porter St Battle Creek MI 49016

KORENYI-BOTH, ANDRAS LEVENTE, pathologist, educator; b. Budapest, Hungary, Mar. 30, 1937; came to U.S. 1974, naturalized, 1984; s. Erno and Maria (Korody-Katona) Korenyi-Both; m. Ildiko Orlos, June 18, 1964; children—Andras, Gyorgy, Adam. M.D., Szeged Med. U., 1962; Cand.Sci., Hungarian Acad. Sci., 1972. Diplomate Hungarian Bd. Pathology, Am. Bd. Pathology. Internist, Szeged Med. U., Hungary, 1961-62; resident dept. pathology Town Council Hosp., Hodmezovasarhely, Hungary, 1962-63; resident dept. pathology Postgrad. Med. Sch., Budapest, 1963-65, research assoc., 1965-68; asst. prof. 1st Inst. of Pathology, Semmelweis Med. U., Budapest, 1968-70, sr. lectr., 1970-74, acting chmn., 1972-73; dir. 8th County Cytodiagnostic Ctr., Budapest, 1972-74; Whipple fellow dept. pathology Genessee Hosp., Rochester, N.Y., 1974-75; research asst. prof. dept. pathology Med. Sch., SUNY-Buffalo, 1975-77, Busell fellow, 1977-78; assoc. dir. dept. pathology Erie County Labs., Buffalo, 1975-76; dir. Neuromuscular Lab., dept. neurology Erie County Med. Ctr., Buffalo, 1976-78; assoc. researcher dept. research Lankenau Hosp., Phila., 1978-81, pathologist, 1978-81; adj. prof. dept. microbiology and cell biology Coll. Sci., Pa. State U., University Park, 1978-83; assoc. prof. dept. pathology Jefferson Med. Coll., Thomas Jefferson U., Phila., 1979—; chief lab. services 348th Gen. Hosp., U.S. Army Res., Folsom, Pa., 1982-83, comdr. 718th Med. Detachment, Folsom, 1983—; pathologist in pvt. practice, Havertown, Pa., 1981—; cons. Sidney Hillman Med. Ctr., Phila., 1981—. Author: Muscle Pathology in Neuromuscular Disease, 1983. Contbr. articles to profl. jours. Served to maj. M.C., USAR, 1982—. Decorated Army Commendation medal. Fellow Am. Coll. Pathologists, Coll. Physicians of Phila.; mem. Soc. Hungarian Pathologists, Soc. Hungarian Immunologists, Soc. Hungarian Human Geneticians, Soc. Hungarian Physiologists, Western N.Y. Soc. Pathologists, European Cancer Soc., Internat. Acad. Pathology, Hungarian Med. Assn. Am., Am. Assn. Neuropathologists, Am. Assn. Pathologists, Pathology Soc. Phila., European Soc. Pathologists, N.Y. Acad. Sci., Fedn. State Med. Bds. U.S., AAAS, Internat. Platform Assn., AMA, Assn. Mil. Surgeons of U.S., Nat. Rifle Assn., Res. Officers Assn., Nat. Geographic Soc., Smithsonian Instn. Clubs: Phila. and Vicinity Hungarian Sportsmen, Delaware County Field and Stream, Safari. Current work: Service/research/teaching in good balance of pathology; electromicrsocopy, immunopathology; field of interest; muscle pathology. Subspecialties: Pathology (medicine); Neuroimmunology. Home: 202 Wickford Rd Havertown PA 19083 Office: Thomas Jefferson Univ 1020 Locust St Philadelphia PA 19107

KORF, RICHARD PAUL, mycology educator; b. Bronxville, N.Y., May 28, 1925; s. Frederick and Evelyn Frederick (Krug) K.; m. Kumiko Tachibaba, June 27, 1959; children: Noni, Mia, Ian Frederick, Mario Takechi. B.Sc., Cornell U., 1946, Ph.D., 1950. Asst. prof. plant pathology Cornell U., Ithaca, N.Y., 1951-55, assoc. prof., 1955-61, prof. mycology, dir. plant pathology herbarium, 1961—; prof. botany Cornell U. (L. H. Bailey Hortorium), 1982—, prof. theatre arts, 1985—, chmn. dept., 1985-86; dir. Exe Island Biol. Sta., Portland, Ont., Can., 1973—. Mng. editor: Mycotaxon, 1974—; contbr. articles to sci. jours. Vice chmn. N.Y. State Liberal Party, 1967-68. NSF systematics program research grantee, 1959-79. Mem. Mycol. Soc. Am., Internat. Assn. Plant Taxonomists, Am. Soc. Plant Taxonomists, Bot. Soc. Am., Mycol. Soc. Britain, Mycol. Soc. France, Mycol. Soc. Japan. Republican. Mem. Universal Life Ch. Current Work: Taxonomy of discomycetes, botanical nomenclature, microanatomy, code of nomenclature. Subspecialties: Mycology; Taxonomy. Home: 316 Richard Pl Ithaca NY 14850 Office: Dept Plant Pathology Cornell U Ithaca NY 14853

KORFMACHER, WALTER AVERILL, analytical chemist, educator; b. St. Louis, Nov. 6, 1951; s. William Charles and Louise (Averill) K.; m. Madeleine Marie Deutsch, June 1, 1974; 1 child, Mary Averill. B.S. in Chemistry, St. Louis U., 1973; M.S. in Analytical Chemistry, U. Ill., 1975, Ph.D., 1978. Chemist Nat. Ctr. for Toxicological Research, Jefferson, Ark., 1978-83, research chemist, 1983—; adj., asst. prof. chemistry U. Ark., Little Rock, 1982—. Contbr. articles to profl. jours. Union Carbide fellow. Mem. Am. Chem. Soc., AAAS, Am. Soc. for Mass Spectrometry, Internat. Assn. Environ. Analytical Chemists, Phi Beta Kappa, Sigma Xi, Alpha Sigma Nu. Roman Catholic. Clubs: Sierra, Audubon. Current Work: Environmental analytical methodology in trace organic analysis by gas chromatography/mass spectrometry. Subspecialties: Analytical chemistry; Mass spectrometry. Office: Chem Div NCTR HFT-154 Jefferson AR 72079

KORI, SHASHIDHAR HALAPPA, neuro-oncologist, educator, researcher; b. Shimoga, India, June 18, 1949; came to U.S., 1974, naturalized, 1980; s. Halappa M. and Rudramma K.; m. Shylaja Rajashekarappa, Nov. 27, 1977; 1 son, Ajay. M.B., B.S., Mysore (India) U., 1971, M.D., 1974. Diplomate: Am. Bd. Psychiatry and Neurology. Intern, Govt. Hosp., Mangalore, India, 1970-71, resident in medicine, 1971-74, VA Hosp., N.Y.C., 1974-75; resident in neurology St. Vincent's Hosp., N.Y.C., 1975-78; fellow in neuro-oncology Meml. Sloan Kettering Cancer Ctr., N.Y.C., 1978-80, pain fellow, 1978-80; postdoctoral fellow in immunobiology Sloan Kettering INst., N.Y.C., 1979-80; asst. prof. neurology Case Western Res. U., 1980-84; chief neuro-oncology div. Univ. Hosps., Cleve., 1980-84, dir. Neuro-Oncology Clinic, 1980-84, dir. Pain Clinic, 1980-84; co-dir. neuro-oncology div. U. South Fla., Tampa, 1984—, med. dir. chronic pain program Tampa Gen. Hosp., 1985—, chief neurology service VA Hosp., Tampa, 1984—; cons. in field. Contbr. articles, chpt. to profl. publs. Recipient Nat. Research Service award USPHS, 1979; USPHS postdoctoral grantee, 1979; Am. Cancer Soc. grantee, 1981. Mem. Am. Acad. Neurology, Am. Soc. Neurol. Investigations, Am. Soc. Neuroscis., AMA, Am. Soc. Internal Medicine, Internat. Assn. Study Pain, Am. Pain Soc., Eastern Pain Assn. Hindu. Inventor approach to treating malignant brain tumors. Current Work: New treatment for brain tumors; biology of brain tumors; immune responses to herpes. Subspecialties: Cancer research (medicine); Neuroimmunology. Home: 4302 Gainsborough Ct Tampa FL 33624 Office: U South Fla Coll Medicine Dept Neurology Box 55 12901 N 30th St Tampa FL 33612

KORN, EDWARD DAVID, biochemist, government research administrator; b. Phila., Aug. 3, 1928; s. Joel and Carrie (Goldman) K.; m. Muriel Evelyn Fisher, June 23, 1950; children: Elizabeth Gail, Sarah Harris. A.B., U. Pa., 1949, Ph.D., 1954. Biochemist Nat. Heart, Lung, and Blood Inst., NIH, Bethesda, Md., 1954—, chief Lab. Cell Biology, 1975—; dep. sci. dir. Nat. Heart, Lung, and Blood Inst. NIH, 1982—. Contbr. numerous articles to profl. jours.; assoc. editor: Jour. Biol. Chemistry, 1977—. Served with USPHS, 1954-56. Mem. Am. Soc. Biol. Chemists, Biophysics Soc., Am. Soc. Cell Biology. Current Work: Biochemistry of cell motility. Subspecialties: Biochemistry (biology); Biochemistry (medicine). Office: NIH Bldg 3 Room B1-22 Bethesda MD 20925

KORN, JOSEPH H., physician; b. Augsburg, Germany, Jan. 31, 1947; s. Leo and Rose (Mann) K.; m. Paulette M. Jeremias, June 26, 1971; children: Naomi, Jerald, Joshua. B.S., CCNY, 1968; M.D., Columbia U., 1972. Diplomate: Am. Bd. Internal Medicine. Intern, resident U. N.C., Chapel Hill, 1972-75; fellow, instr., then asst. prof. medicine and immunology Med. U. S.C., Charleston, 1975-78; asst. prof. U. Conn., 1978-84, assoc. prof., 1984—; assoc. chief staff for research VA Med. Ctr., Newington, Conn., 1982—. Contbr. chpt. to book; articles to profl. jours. VA awardee, 1979-81. Current Work: Immunology of connective tissue. Subspecialties: Immunology (medicine); Cell biology (medicine). Home: 1910 Asylum Ave West Hartford CT 06117 Office: 263 Farmington Ave Farmington CT 06032

KORNBERG, ARTHUR, biochemist; b. N.Y.C., Mar. 3, 1918; s. Joseph and Lena (Katz) K.; m. Sylvy R. Levy, Nov. 21, 1943; children—Roger, Thomas Bill, Kenneth Andrew. B.S. (N.Y. State scholar), CCNY, 1937, LL.D., 1960; M.D. (Buswell scholar), U. Rochester, 1941, D.Sc., 1962; L.H.D., Yeshiva U., 1963; D.Sc., U. Pa., U. Notre Dame, 1965, Washington U., 1968, Princeton U., 1970, Colby Coll., 1970; M.D. (h.c.), U. Barcelona, Italy, 1970. Intern in medicine Strong Meml. Hosp., Rochester, N.Y., 1941-42; commd. officer USPHS, 1942, advanced through grades to med. dir., 1951; mem. staff NIH, Bethesda, Md., 1942-52, nutrition sect., div. physiology, 1942-45; chief sect. enzymes and metabolism Nat. Inst. Arthritis and Metabolic Diseases, 1947-52; guest research worker depts. chemistry and pharmacology coll. medicine N.Y. U., 1946; dept. biol. chemistry med. sch. Washington U., 1947; dept. plant biochemistry U. Calif., 1951; prof., head dept. microbiology, med. sch. Washington U., St. Louis, 1953-59; prof., biochemistry Stanford U. Sch. Medicine, 1959—, chmn. dept., 1959-69; Mem. sci. adv. bd. Mass. Gen. Hosp., 1964-67; bd. govs. Weizmann Inst., Israel. Contbr. sci. articles to profl. jours. Served lt. (j.g.), med. officer USCGR, 1942. Recipient Paul-Lewis award in enzyme chemistry, 1951; co-recipient of Nobel prize in medicine, 1959; Max Berg award prolonging human life, 1968; Sci. Achievement award AMA, 1968; Lucy Wortham James award James Ewing Soc., 1968; Borden award Am. Assn. Med. Colls., 1968. Mem. Am. Soc. Biol. Chemists (pres. 1965), Am. Chem. Soc., Harvey Soc., Am. Acad. Arts and Scis., Royal Soc., Nat. Acad. Scis. (mem. council 1963-66), Am. Philos. Soc., Phi Beta Kappa, Sigma Xi, Alpha Omega Alpha. Office: Dept Genetics Stanford Univ Sch Medicine Stanford CA 94305*

KORNEL, LUDWIG, endocrinology, biochemistry educator, physician; b. Jaslo, Poland, Feb. 27, 1923; came to U.S., 1958, naturalized, 1970; s. Ezriel Edward and Ernestine (Karpf) K.; m. Esther Muller, May 27, 1952; children—Ezriel Edward, Amiel Mark. Student U. Kazan, USSR, 1943-45; M.D., U. Wroclaw, Poland, 1950; Ph.D., U. Birmingham, England, 1958; postdoctoral fellow, Utah, 1959-61. Resident in medicine Hadassah U. Hosp., Jerusalem, 1950-55; Brit. Council research fellow U. Birmingham, 1955-58; asst. prof., assoc. prof., prof. Med. Ctr., U. Ala., Birmingham, 1961-67; prof. medicine Sch. Medicine, U. Ill., Chgo., 1967-71; sr. attending physician, sr. biochemist sci. staff Presbyterian-St. Luke's Hosp., Chgo., 1967—, dir. steroid unit, 1967—; prof. medicine and biochemistry Rush Med. Coll., Chgo., 1971—; hon. guest lectr. Polish Acad. Scis., Warsaw, 1965; vis. prof. U. Kanazawa Sch. Medicine, Japan, 1973, 82; sci. advisor Univ. Without Walls, Northeastern Ill. U., 1974-77; mem. adv. com. med. assts. program Triton Community Coll., River Grove, Ill., 1974—. Editorial bd. Jour. Clin. Physiology and Biochemistry, 1982—. Contbr. articles, reviews to profl. jours. Recipient Outstanding New Citizen award Citizenship Council, Met. Chgo., 1970; Brit. Council scholar, 1955; various grants NIH, 1960—. Fellow Nat. Acad. Clin. Biochemistry (bd. dirs. 1982—), Royal Soc. Health; mem. Endocrine Soc., Am. Physiol. soc., Am. Fedn. Clin. Research, AMA (Physician's Recognition award 1969, 73, 76, 81, 85), Chgo. Endocrine Club, Assn. Brit. Council Scholars (pres. Jerusalem chpt. 1957-58), Sigma Xi. Current work: Metabolism and mechanism of action of steroid hormones; molecular mechanism of mineralocorticoid-induced hypertension; hormone-induced changes in cell membranes. Subspecialties: Receptors; Membrane biology. Home: 6757 LeRoy Ave Lincolnwood IL 60646 Office: Rush Presbyn St Luke's Med Ctr 1753 W Congress Pkwy Chicago IL 60612

KORNETSKY, CONAN, psychologist; b. Portland, Maine, Feb. 9, 1926; s. Alex and Ida (Rosenberg) K.; m. MarciaKornetsky, June 5, 1949; children: David, Lisa. B.A., U. Maine, 1948; M.S., U. Ky., 1951, Ph.D., 1952. Asst. research psychologist Drug Addiction Research Ctr., Lexington, Ky., 1949-52; research scientist NIMH, Bethesda, Md., 1952-59; assoc. research prof. pharmacology Boston U. Med. Sch., 1959-63, prof. div. psychiatry and dept. pharmacology, 1963—; cons. Nat. Inst. Drug Abuse, NIMH, VA, FDA. Author: Pharmacology: Drugs Affecting Behavior, 1976; contbr. articles to profl. jours.; editorial bd. Internat. Rev. Neurobiology, 1975—, Jour. Abnormal Psychology, 1980—; editorial bd. Psychopharmacology, 1964—, U.S. editor, 1970-74. Served with AUS, 1944-45. USPHS sr. fellow, 1959-60. Fellow Am. Coll. Neuropsychopharmacology, Am. Psychol. Assn. (pres. div. psychopharmacology); mem. Am. Soc. Pharmacology and Exptl. Therapeutics, (editorial bd. jour. 1974—), Soc. Neuroscis., Sigma Xi. Current Work: Neurobehavioral basis of rewarding effects of abuse substances, e.g., heroin, cocaine, amphetamine, brain-stimulation reward, pain, animal models of mental illness. Subspecialties: Physiological psychology; Neuropharmacology. Home: 7 Rumford Rd Lexington MA 02173 Office: Boston U Sch Medicine 80 E Concord St L-602 Boston MA 02118

KORNFELD, ITZCHAK E., geologist, oil company executive; b. Tel-Aviv, Israel, Feb. 21, 1953; came to U.S., 1962; s. Abraham Moshe and Helena (Rozdzial) K.; m. Maria Linda Barracca, June 14, 1981. B.S., Bklyn. Coll., 1976, M.S., 1980. Research scientist Research Council of N.Y., N.Y.C., 1976-78, Bur. Econ. Geology, State of Tex., Austin, 1978-79; cons. EPA, N.Y.C., 1980; adj. lectr. S.I. Coll., N.Y., 1980-81; sr. geologist Fred C. Hart Assoc., Newark, 1980-81; geologist Texaco, Inc., New Orleans, 1981—. Bd. dirs. Congregation Beth Israel, New Orleans, 1983—; coordinator United Way, New Orleans, 1983—; bd. dirs. Young Leadership Conf., 1984; vol. Sta. WWNO Pub. Radio, 1984. Research grantee Geol. Soc. Am., 1977, Sigma Xi, 1977. Mem. Am. Assn. Petroleum Geologists, Am. Geophys. Union, Geol. Soc. Am., Internat. Assn. Sedimentologists, Soc. Econ. Mineralogists and Paleontologists, New Orleans Geol. Soc. (chmn. computer applications com.), Sigma Xi. Current work: Continental and rift basin sedimentation and petroleum exploration; fluid flow, toxic and hazardous waste management; geological statistical and computer applications. Subspecialties: Sedimentology; Hydrology. Office: Texaco Inc PO Box 60252 New Orleans LA 70160

KORNGUTH, STEVEN EDWARD, physiological chemist; b. N.Y.C., Dec. 1, 1935; s. Eugene I. and Helen (Pardes) K.; m. Margaret Livens, Aug. 29, 1958; children—Ingrid, David. B.A., Columbia Coll., 1957; M.S., U. Wis., 1959, Ph.D., 1961. Mem. staff N.Y. State Psychiat. Inst., N.Y.C., 1961-63; asst. prof. neurology, physiol. chemistry U. Wis., Madison, 1963-68, asso. prof., 1968-72, prof., 1972—; program dir. neurobiology sect BNS, NSF, Washington, 1981—. NIH research tng. grantee in neurochemistry, 1968-73. Mem. Am. Soc. Biol. Chemists, Am. Neurosci. Soc., Internat. Brain Research Orgn. Subspecialty: Neurobiology. Home: 1114 Shorewood Blvd Madison WI 53705

KORNSTEIN, EDWARD, technical company executive; b. N.Y.C., Sept. 7, 1929; s. Max and Margit (Stahl) K.; m. Marion Beatrice Stein, Dec. 20, 1958; children: Sandra P., Martin R. B.A., NYU, 1951; M.S., Drexel U., 1954. Engr., optics RCA, Camden, N.J., 1951-57, group leader optical physics, Burlington, Mass., 1960-66, mgr. optical physics, 1966-70; cons. optics Phys. Research Lab., Boston U., 1958, Boston, 1959-60; v.p. OPTEL Corp., Princeton, 1970-72; pres. Kortron, Princeton, 1972-78; v.p. Object Recognition Systems, Princeton, 1978—; cons. electro-optics. Contbr. articles to profl., trade jours. Active Boy Scouts Am., 1973—; mem. Princeton C. of C. NSF travel grantee, 1959; Optical Soc. Am. travel grantee, 1959. Mem. Soc. Info. Display, Optical Soc. Am., IEEE, Soc. Motion Picture and TV Engrs. Patentee in field. Current Work: Application of electro-optical techniques to automatic inspection systems, robotics and optical data processing; electro-optical displays. Subspecialties: Optical engineering; Optical image processing.

KORR, IRVIN MORRIS, physiologist, medical educator; b. Phila., Aug. 24, 1909; s. Samuel Pincus and Anna (Goldberg) K.; m. Margot Lindsay, June 13, 1939 (dec. Jan. 1975); 1 child, David L. B.A., U. Pa., 1930, M.A., 1931; Ph.D., Princeton U., 1935; D.Sc. (hon.), Kirksville Coll. Osteo. Medicine, 1976. Instr. physiology NYU Coll. Medicine, N.Y.C., 1936-42; sr. physiologist U.S. War Dept., 1942-45; prof. physiology Kirksville Coll. Osteo. Medicine, Mo., 1945-75; prof. biomechanics Mich. State U., East Lansing, 1975-78; prof. med. edn. Tex. Coll. Osteo. Medicine, Fort Worth, 1978—. Author: (with E.L. Hix and K.A. Buzzell) Physiological Basis of Osteopathic Medicine, 1970; Collected Papers of I.M. Korr, 1979. Editor: Neurobiologic Mechanisms in Manipulative Therapy, 1978. Contbr. articles to profl. jours. Bd. dirs. Fed. Correction Inst. Children's Ctr., Fort Worth. Recipient Founder's medal Tex. Coll. Osteo. Medicine, 1982, Kistner award Am. Assn. Colls. Osteo. Medicine, 1983. Fellow AAAS; mem. Am. Physiol. Soc., Soc. Neurosci., Am. Soc. Neurochemistry, Harvey Soc. (life), ACLU, Common Cause, Sierra Club. Current work: Autonomic nervous system, somato-autonomic relations, trophic function of nerves; curricular design in medical education. Subspecialties: Physiology (biology); Neurobiology. Home: 740 Oakwood Trail Forth Worth TX 76112 Office: Tex Coll Osteo Medicine Camp Bowie at Montgomery Fort Worth TX 76107

KORTAN, AHMET REFIK, physicist; b. Istanbul, Turkey, May 26, 1952; came to U.S., 1975, naturalized, 1985; s. Yusuf Kenan and Bakiye (Gurol) K.; m. Vildan Gul, Nov. 11, 1981; children—Burcu, Kobli. B.S., Middle East Tech. U. (Turkey), 1975; M.S., U. Md., 1976, Ph.D., 1980. Postdoctorate MIT, Cambridge, 1980-81, research assoc., 1981-84; mem. tech. staff AT&T Bell Labs., Murray Hills, N.J., 1984—. Contbr. articles to profl. jours. Mem. Am. Phys. Soc., Materials Research Soc., Am. Vacuum Soc. Current work: Phase transitions in two dimensional systems. Subspecialty: Condensed matter physics. Office: AT&T Bell Labs 600 Mountain Ave Murray Hill NJ 07974

KORWIN, PAUL, consulting mechanical engineer; b. Cracow, Poland, Jan. 5, 1914; came to U.S., 1956, naturalized, 1962; m. Yala Meisels, Oct. 22, 1949; children: Danielle, Robert. M.E., State Engring. Coll., Cracow, Poland, 1934. Registered Profl. Engr., Mass. With Chem. Constrn. Corp., N.Y.C., 1956-67; with Stone & Webster Engring. Co., Boston, 1967-68, Lummus Engring., Bloomfield, N.Y., 1968-74, Heater Cons. Services, Flushing, N.Y., 1974—, cons. engr.; refractory cons. Mem. ASME, Am. Inst. Chem. Engrs. Patentee in field. Current Work: Hydrogen steam-hydrocarbon reformers; high temperature refractory linings for hydrocarbon heaters. Subspecialties: Mechanical engineering; High-temperature materials. Address: 150-09-77th Ave Flushing NY 11367

KORYTNYK, WSEWOLOD, medicinal chemist, educator; b. Caslav, Czechoslovakia, Apr. 21, 1929; came to U.S., 1958, naturalized, 1965; s. Luka and Valentyna (Makarenko) K.; m. Olena Kozak, Sept. 1, 1957; children: Natalie, Christine, Peter. B.Sc., U. Adelaide, Australia, 1953, B.Sc. with 1st class honors in Organic Chemistry, 1954, Ph.D. in Carbohydrate Chemistry, 1957, D.Sc. in Medicinal Chemistry, 1973. Postdoctoral research fellow U. Adelaide, 1957-58, Purdue U., Lafayette, Ind., 1958-59; research chemist U.S. Dept. Agr., Pasadena, Calif., 1959-60; research prof. Niagara U., Buffalo, 1976—; asst. research prof. SUNY, Buffalo, 1968-72, assoc. research prof., 1972-81, research prof., dir. med. chemistry program, 1981—; sr. cancer research scientist, dept. exptl. therapeutics Roswell Park Meml. Inst., Buffalo, 1960-68, 76-80, assoc. cancer research scientist, 1968-76, cancer research scientist G35, 1980—; research assoc. U. Calif., Berkeley, 1967-68. Contbr. articles to profl. jours. and books. Am. Cyanamid fellow, 1957; Sci. Exchange visitor to Poland, 1970; USPHS grantee, 1965-82; other grants. Mem. AAAS, Am. Chem. Soc., Chem. Soc. (London), N.Y. Acad. Sci., Am. Soc. Biol. Chemists, Am. Assn. Cancer Research, Shevchenko Sci. Soc. Ukrainian Catholic. Current Work: Cell surfaces of cancer cells; carbohydrate chemistry, biochemistry and pharmacology; conformational analysis; nuclear magnetic resonance spectroscopy; medicinal chemistry of Vitamin B6; anticancer agents; rational design of drugs. Subspecialties: Medicinal chemistry; Chemotherapy.

KOSCHIER, FRANCIS JOSEPH, III, toxicologist; b. N.Y.C., June 16, 1950; s. Francis Joseph and Mary Frances (Schaefer) K. A.B., Bard Coll., 1972; postgrad., Dartmouth Coll. Grad. Sch., 1972-74; Ph.D., U. Miss., 1976. Diplomate: Am. Bd. Toxicology. Research asst. prof. SUNY-Buffalo, USPHS grantee, 1976-79; toxicologist Food and Drug Research Labs., Waverly, N.Y., 1979-80; staff toxicologist Am. Cyanamid Co., Wayne, N.J., 1980-83; mgr. toxicology, safety, health and ecology dept. CIBA-GEIGY Corp., 1983—. Mem. adv. bd. Jour. Applied Toxicology. Contbr. articles on toxicology to profl. jours. Mem. Soc. Toxicology, Am. Soc. Pharmacology and Exptl. Therapeutics, Phi Kappa Phi. Roman Catholic. Current Work: Industrial toxicology. Subspecialties: Toxicology (medicine); Environmental toxicology. Office: CIBA-GEIGY Corp. Ardsley NY 10502

KOSERSKY, DONALD S., pharmacologist, consultant; b. Waterbury, Conn., Oct. 16, 1932; s. William and Sally (Hanken) K.; m. Marcelle S. Manet; 1 dau., Nicole E. M.S. in Pharmacology, U. Conn., 1968; Ph.D. in Pharmacology, U. of Pacific, 1971. Research assoc. dept. pharmacology U. N.C. Med. Sch., Chapel Hill, 1971-73; assoc. prof. pharmacology Northeastern U., Boston, 1973-80; assoc. prof. pharmacology and physiology, coordinator grad. programs Mass. Coll. Pharmacy and Allied Health Scis., Boston, 1980—, pharmacol. research cons. Contbr. articles to profl. jours. Mem. Am. Soc. Pharmacology and Exptl. Therapeutics, Fedn. Am. Socs. Exptl. Biology, Neurosci. Soc. Current Work: Pharmacology of tolerance and dependence to narcotics and other drugs of abuse. Subspecialties: Pharmacology; Neuropharmacology. Office: Mass Coll Pharmacy and Allied Health Sciences 179 Longwood Ave Boston MA 02115

KOSHLAND, DANIEL EDWARD, JR., educator, biochemist; b. N.Y.C., Mar. 30, 1920; s. Daniel Edward and Eleanor (Haas) K.; m. Marian Elliott, May 25, 1945; children: Ellen, Phyllis, James, Gail, Douglas. B.S., U. Calif., Berkeley, 1941; Ph.D., U. Chgo., 1949; Ph.D. (hon.), Weizmann Inst., 1984, Carnegie Mellon U., 1985. Chemist Shell Chem. Co., Martinez, 1941-42; research asso. Manhattan Dist. U. Chgo., 1942-44; group leader Oak Ridge Nat. Labs., 1944-46; postdoctoral fellow Harvard, 1949-51; staff Brookhaven Nat. Lab., Upton, N.Y., 1951-65; affiliate Rockefeller Inst., N.Y.C., 1958-65; prof. biochemistry U. Calif. at Berkeley, 1965—, chmn. dept., 1973-78; Leo Marion lectr. Nat. Research Council Can., 1972; Harvey lectr., 1969; fellow All Souls, Oxford U., 1972; Phi Beta Kappa lectr., 1976; John Edsall lectr. Harvard U., 1980. Author: Bacterial Chemotaxis as A Model Behavioral System, 1980; mem. editorial bds.: jour. Accounts Chem. Research; editor: jour. Procs. Nat. Acad. Scis, 1980-84; editor Sci. Mag., 1985—. Recipient T. Duckett Jones award Helen Hay Whitney Found., 1977; Guggenheim fellow, 1972. Mem. Nat. Acad. Scis., Am. Chem. Soc. (Edgar Fahs Smith award 1979, Pauling award 1979, Rosenstiel award), Am. Soc. Biol. Chemists (pres.), Am. Acad. Arts and Scis. (council), Academy Forum (chmn.), Japanese Biochem. Soc. (hon.), Royal Swedish Acad. Scis. (hon.). Current Work: Enzymology of behavior, regulatory processes. Subspecialties: Biophysical chemistry; Enzyme technology. Office: Biochemistry Dept U Calif Berkeley CA 94720

KOSHLAND, MARIAN ELLIOTT, immunologist, educator; b. New Haven, Oct. 25, 1921; d. Waller Watkins and Margaret Ann (Smith) Elliott; m. Daniel Edward Koshland, Jr., May 25, 1945; children—Ellen R., Phyllis A., James M., Gail F., Douglas E. B.A., Vassar Coll., 1942, M.S., 1943; Ph.D., U. Chgo., 1949. Research asst. Manhattan Dist. Atomic Bomb Project, 1945-46; fellow dept. bacteriology Harvard Med. Sch., 1949-51; asso. bacteriologist biology dept. Brookhaven Nat. Lab., 1952-62, bacteriologist, 1963-65; asso. research immunologist virus lab. U. Calif., Berkeley, 1965-69, lectr. dept. molecular biology, 1966-70, prof. dept. microbiology and immunology, 1970—, chmn. dept., 1982—; mem. Nat. Sci. Bd., 1976-82; mem. adv. com. to dir. NIH, 1972-75. Contbr. articles to profl. jours. Mem. Nat. Acad. Scis., Am. Acad. Microbiology, Am. Assn. Immunologists (pres. 1982-1983), Am. Soc. Biol. Chemists, Phi Beta Kappa, Sigma Xi. Subspecialty: Immunobiology and immunology. Office: Dept Microbiology and Immunology U Calif Berkeley CA 94720

KOSINSKI, ROBERT JOSEPH, biology educator, aquatic ecologist; b. Montclair, N.J., Jan. 8, 1949; s. Edward Valentine and Alice Mary (Cole) K. B.S. in Biology, Seton Hall U., 1972; Ph.D. in Ecology, Rutgers U., 1977. Asst. prof. Texas A&M U., College Sta., Tex., 1977-84, Clemson U., S.C., 1984—. Contbr. articles to profl. jours. Pres. Condominium Homeowners' Assn., Bryan, Tex., 1981-84. Served to staff sgt. USNG, 1971-78. Research grantee NIH, 1979, EPA, 1980, NSF, 1982, 85. Mem. Ecol. Soc. Am., Am. Soc. Limnology and Oceanography, AAAS, Nat. Sci. Tchrs. Assn., North Am. Benthological Soc. Democrat. Roman Catholic. Current work: Computer-assisted instruction for biology laboratories, ecology of periphytic algae, stream productivity, stream ecology, population ecology of parasites. Subspecialties: Ecology (environmental science); Limnology. Office: Biology Program Clemson Univ Clemson SC 29631

KOSKELO, MARKKU JUHANI, software engineer; b. Turku, Finland, Feb. 11, 1951; came to U.S., 1982; s. Tauno Juhani and Tuija Inkeri (Malmio) K.; m. Pirkko Tellervo (Willberg), Oct. 14, 1972; children: Ilkka Juhani, Antti Ilmari. M.Sc., Helsinki (Finland) U. Tech., 1976, D.Tech., 1981; postgrad., U. Toronto, 1977-78. Asst. Helsinki U. Tech., Espoo, 1975-78, lab. engr., 1978-81, acting assoc. prof., 1981-82; sr. software engr. Canberra Industries, Meriden, Conn., 1982, group leader sci. software devel., 1983, software project mgr., 1983—; assoc. CERN, Geneva, 1977. Contbr. articles to profl. jours. Mem. Finnish Nuclear Soc., Am. Nuclear Soc. Current Work: Computerized gamma spectrum analysis, special nuclear measurement systems. Subspecialties: Nuclear engineering; Algorithms. Office: Canberra Industries Inc One State St Meriden CT 06450

KOSLOW, STEPHEN HUGH, government agency administrator, pharmacologist; b. N.Y.C., Oct. 14, 1940; s. Julius and Lillian (Kaye) K.; m. Diane Heisler, June 18, 1962; children—Karin, James. B.S., Columbia U., 1962; Ph.D., U. Chgo., 1967. Internat. postdoctoral fellow Swedish Med. Research Council, Karolinski Inst., 1968-69; staff fellow, chief unit neurobiol. applications of Mass Spectrometry Research Assn. Lab. Preclin. Pharmacology, NIMH, St. Elizabeth's Hosp., Washington, 1970-77; chief biol. research sect. Clin. Research Bur., NIMH, Rockville, Md., 1975-81, chief Neuroscis. Research Br., 1981—, project dir. Collaboration Program on Phychobiology of Depression, Rockville, 1975—; mem. med. adv. bd. Tourette Syndrome Assn., Bayside, N.Y., 1984—. Contbr. articles to profl. publs. NATO fellow, 1969; recipient Quality Increase award NIMH, 1977,78, Meritorious Achievement award NIMH, 1979. Mem. AAAS, Am. Soc. Neurochemistry, Am. Soc.

Pharmacology and Exptl. Therapeutics, Soc. for Neurosci., Am. Coll. Neuropsychopharmacology, Soc. Biol. Psychiatry. Current work: Brain Neurotransmission, neuropsychopharmacology and biological bases of depression. Subspecialties: Psychopharmacology; Neurochemistry. Office: Neuroscis Research Br DERP NIMH 5600 Fishers Ln Room 9C-09 Rockville MD 20857

KOSS, LEOPOLD G., physician; b. Danzig, Poland, Oct. 2, 1920; came to U.S., 1947, naturalized, 1952; s. Abram and Rose (Merenholc) K.; m. Lydia Palla; children: Michael S., Andrew C., Richard P. M.D., U. Berne, Switzerland, 1946. Intern, Lincoln Hosp., N.Y.C., 1947-48; tng. pathology, St. Gallen, Switzerland, 1946-47, Kings County Hosp., Bklyn., 1949-51; instr. pathology L.I. Coll. Medicine, 1949-51; mem. staff Meml. Hosp. Cancer and Allied Diseases, N.Y.C., 1952-70, attending pathologist, 1961-70, chief cytology service, 1961-70; pathologist-in-chief Sinai Hosp. Balt., 1970-73; prof., chmn. dept. pathology Montefiore Hosp., Med. Center Albert Einstein Coll. Medicine, 1973—; assoc. mem. Sloan-Kettering Inst. Cancer Research, N.Y.C., 1957-70; assoc. prof. pathology Sloan-Kettering div. Postgrad. Sch. Med. Scis., Cornell U., 1957-70; prof. pathology Jefferson Med. Coll., Phila., 1970-73; clin. prof. pathology U. Md. Med. Sch., 1971-73; vis. pathologist James Ewing Hosp., N.Y.C., 1952-60; cons. pathologist N.Y. State Dept. Health, Hosp. Spl. Surgery, N.Y.C.; cons. pathologist Walter Reed Army Med. Center, Nassau County Med. Ctr. Author: Diagnostic Cytology and Its Histopathologic Bases, 3d edit., 1979, Tumors of the Urinary Bladder, 1975; editor: Advances in Clinical Cytology, Vol. I, 1981, Vol. II, 1984; also monographs, chpts. and articles. Served to maj. M.C., AUS, 1955-57. Recipient Wien award Papanicolaou Cancer Inst., 1963, Alfred P. Sloan award cancer research, 1964; Stewart award Meml. Sloan Kettering Cancer Ctr., 1984; Vanden-berghe-Hill award M.D. Anderson Cancer Ctr., 1984; hon. prof. pathology Severance Med. Coll., Seoul, Korea, 1956. Fellow Am. Soc. Clin. Pathology, Coll. Am. Pathologists, Internat. Acad. Cytology (Goldblatt award 1962); mem. Am. Soc. Path. Bacteriologists, James Ewing Soc., AMA, Am. Soc. Cytology (pres. 1962, Papanicolaou award 1966), Internat. Acad. Pathology; corr. mem. Royal Acad. Medicine Spain; hon. mem. Brit. Soc. Clin. Cytology, Korean Med. Assn., Mex., Argentinian socs. cytology, Japanese Soc. Pathology, Polish Soc. Pathology, Peruvian Soc. Obstetrics and Gynecology. Current Work: Computer image analysis of cancer cells; flow cytometry in cancer; papillomaviruses in cancer; bladder cancer. Subspecialties: Pathology (medicine); Cytology and histology. Office: 111 E 210th St Bronx NY 10467

KOSTEM, CELAL NIZAMETTIN, civil engineering educator, structural and software engineering researcher; b. Ankara, Turkey, Feb. 8, 1939; came to U.S., 1963; s. H(alil) Naki and Suada (Nuzam) K.; m. Kathy Michele Nieuwenhuis, Aug. 30, 1966. B.S.C.E., Istanbul Tech. U., Turkey, 1960, M.S.C.E., 1961; Ph.D., U. Ariz., 1966. Cert. fallout shelter analyst, civil engr., Turkey. Asst. engr. Istanbul Harbor Constrn. Co., Turkey, 1960-61; postdoctoral research assoc. Lehigh U., Bethlehem, Pa., 1966-68, asst. prof. civil engring., 1968-72, assoc. prof., 1972-78, prof., 1978—; structural cons., Bethlehem, 1966—; mem. Transp. Research Bd., 1970—. Editor: Computer Aided Design in Civil Engineering, 1984; assoc. editor Civil Engring. for Practising and Design Engring. Jour., 1981—. Contbr. articles to profl. jours. Served to 1st lt. Turkish Army, 1961-63. Fulbright fellow Inst. Internat. Edn. and U.S., Tucson, 1963-66, fellow UN Agy. for Internat. Devel., 1979. Mem. ASCE (chmn. state-of-the-art computer tech. com. 1981—, pres. Lehigh Valley sect. 1983-84, recipient presdl. citation 1984), Internat. Assn. Bridge and Structural Engrs. Current work: Overloading of highway bridges; static and dynamic response prediction of bridges; software design for structural engineering; seismic response of structural systems. Subspecialties: Structural engineering; Computer-aided design. Home: 3520 Chippendale Circle Bethlehem PA 18017 Office: Lehigh U Fritz Engring Lab 13 Bethlehem PA 18015

KOSTOULAS, IOANNIS GEORGIOU, aerospace company physicist; b. Petra, Pierias, Greece, Sept. 12, 1936; came to U.S., 1965, naturalized, 1984; s. Georgios Ioannou and Panagiota (Zarogiannis) K.; m. Katina Sioras Kay, June 23, 1979; 1 child, Alexandra. Diploma in physics, U. Thessaloniki, 1963; M.S., U. Ala.-Tuscaloosa, 1967; M.A., U. Rochester, 1969, Ph.D., 1972. Instr., U. Thessaloniki, Greece, 1963-65; guest jr. research assoc. Brookhaven Nat. Lab., Upton, L.I., N.Y., 1968-72; research physicist, lectr. U. Calif.-San Diego and UCLA, 1972-76; sr. research assoc. Mich. State U., East Lansing, also Fermi Nat. Accelerator Lab., Batavia, Ill., 1976-78; research staff mem. MIT, Cambridge, 1978-80; sr. systems engr., physicist Hughes Aircraft Co., El Segundo, Calif., 1980—. Contbr. articles to profl. jours. Mem. Save Cyprus Council, Los Angeles, 1980—. Served with Greek Army, 1961-63. Mem. Am. Phys. Soc., Los Alamos Sci. Labs. Exptl. Users Group, Fermi Nat. Accelerator Lab. Users Group, Brookhaven Nat. Lab. High Energy Discussion Group, Am. Hellenic Ednl. Progressive Assn., Sigma Pi Sigma. Greek Orthodox. Hellenic Univ. (Los Angeles). Current work: Microelectronics solid state technology as related to device physics and radiation detection including infrared radiation. Subspecialties: Particle physics; Aerospace engineering and technology. Home: 2016 Vanderbilt Ln Unit 7 Redondo Beach CA 90278 Office: Hughes Aircraft Co Bldg E51/A264 PO Box 902 El Segundo CA 90245

KOSTYO, JACK LAWRENCE, physiology educator; b. Elyria, Ohio, Oct. 1, 1931; s. Louis and Matilda (Thomasko) K.; m. Shirlianne Guth, June 10, 1953; children: Cecile A., Louis C. A.B., Oberlin Coll., 1953; Ph.D., Cornell U., 1957; M.D. (hon.), U. Göteborg, 1978. NRC fellow Harvard Med. Sch., Boston, 1957-59; asst. prof., then prof. physiology Duke, 1959-68; prof., chmn. dept. physiology Emory U., Atlanta, 1968-79; prof. U. Mich. Med. Sch., Ann Arbor, 1979—, chmn. dept., 1979-85; mem. endocrinology study sect. NIH, USPHS, 1967-71; mem. physiology test com. Nat. Bd. Med. Examiners, 1974-77; mem. adminstrv. bd. Council Acad. Socs., 1983—. Editor-in-chief: Endocrinology, 1978-82; sect. editor Ann. Rev. of Physiology, 1982—; contbr. articles to profl. jours. Mem. adv. bd. Searle Scholars. Recipient Lederle Med. Faculty award, 1961; Ernst Oppenheimer Meml. award Endocrine Soc., 1969. Mem. Endocrine Soc. (mem. editorial bd., council), Am. Physiol. Soc. (mem. editorial bd., chmn. standing com. on edn., mem. council), Soc. for Exptl. Biology and Medicine (editorial bd.), Internat. Union Physiol. Scis. (commn. on med. edn.), Assn. Chmn. Depts. Physiology (pres. 1979, council), Sigma Xi. Current Work: Research on the structure-function relationships of pituitary growth hormone. Subspecialty: Endocrinology.

KOTAS, ROBERT VINCENT, critical care physician, medical consultant; b. Buffalo, Nov. 26, 1938; s. Vincent John and Regina Agnes (Hadynka) K.; m. Ilona Rae Fielding, Mar. 2, 1968; children: Nicole, Timothy, Robert A., Rebecca. B.S., Canisius Coll., 1959; M.D., U. Buffalo, 1963. Diplomate Am. Bd. Pediatrics. Intern Buffalo Children's Hosp., 1963-64; resident Johns Hopkins Hosp., Balt., 1964-66; neonatology fellow Johns Hopkins Med. Sch., 1968-69; research assoc. McGill U. Med. Sch., Montreal, Que., Can., 1969-70; dir. neonatology U. Okla. Med. Sch., Oklahoma City, 1970-72; dir. physiology Warren Research Ctr., Tulsa, 1972-76, dir., 1976-83, William and Natalie Warren Med. Inst., Tulsa, 1977-83; pulmonary cons. Tulsa Pediatric Edn. Trust, 1972—; cons. perinatologist, attending physician Eastern Okla. Regional Perinatal Ctr., 1972-83; guest scientist Nat. Inst. Child Health and Human Devel., Bethesda, Md., 1975-77, cons., 1979—; clin. assoc. prof. pediatrics U. Okla. Health Scis. Ctr., 1975-77; interim dir. neonatal services St. Francis Hosp., Tulsa, 1977, interim chmn. neonatology div., 1977, instl. rev. bd., 1977-83; clin. prof. U. Okla., Tulsa Med. Coll., 1977-85; chmn. research com. U. Okla., Tulsa Med. Coll. (Tulsa Med. Coll.), 1977-83; pediatric dept. adv. council U. Okla., Tulsa Med. Coll., 1978-85; assoc. prof. U. Tex. Health Sci. Ctr., San Antonio, 1983—; cons. Nat. Heart and Lung Inst., NIH, Bethesda, 1975-78, Am. Lung Assn. Hosp. Respiratory Care Rev. Team Program, 1976—, Nat. Inst. Child Health and Human Devel., Bethesda, 1979—; sect. cons. human embryology and devel. study HHS, NIH, Bethesda, 1981—; reviewer, site visitor, mem. coms. profl. projects in field. Contbr. sects. to books in field, articles to profl. publs. Served to capt. USAF, 1966-68. Recipient award best physician written book Am. Med. Writers Assn., 1980. Fellow Am. Acad. Pediatrics, Am. Thoracic Soc., Soc. for Pediatric Research, Am. Physiol. Soc., Soc. for Gynecologic Investigation; mem. Johns Hopkins Med. and Surg. Assn., So. Soc. Pediatric Research, Central Okla. Pediatric Soc., AAAS, Am. Coll. Obstetricians and Gynecologists, Soc. Exptl. Biology and Medicine. Roman Catholic. Club: Tulsa Computer Soc. (v.p. 1979-80). Current Work: Pulmonary surfactant, pediatric respiratory disease therapy, lung physiology and morphology, diabetes, histocompatibility linked disorders, tumor stem cell drug susceptibility, computer information processing, pediatric research. Subspecialties: Pulmonary medicine; Neonatology. Office: U Tex Health Scis Ctr at San Antonio 7703 Floyd Curl Dr San Antonio TX 78284

KOTTLOWSKI, FRANK EDWARD, geologist, state official; b. Indpls., Apr. 11, 1921; s. Frank Charles and Adella Maria (Markworth) K.; m. Florence Jean Chrisco., Sept. 15, 1945; children: Karen Harvey, Janet Wallace, Dianna Schoderbek. Student, Butler U., 1939-42; A.B., Ind. U., 1947, M.A., 1949, Ph.D., 1951. Grad. fellow Ind. U. Bloomington, 1947-51; geologic party chief Ind. Geol. Survey, Bloomington, 1948-50; instr. geology Ind. U., 1950; econ. geologist N.Mex. Bur. Mines, Socorro, 1951—, dir. div. mineral resources, 1974—; adj. prof. geosci. dept. N.Mex. Tech. Coll., Socorro, 1970—; geologic cons. Sandia Corp., 1965-72; chmn. N.Mex. Mines Safety Adv. Bd., Santa Fe, 1974—. Author: Measuring Stratigraphic Sections, 1955, Paleozoic and Mesozoic Strata on Southwestern New Mexico, 1963, (with others) Strippable Low-Sulfur Coal in San Juan Basin, 1971, Coal Resources of the Americas, 1978. Sec. Socorro County Democratic Com., 1964-68; chmn. Socorro Planning Commn., 1960-68, 71-75. Served to 1st lt. USAAF, 1942-45. Fellow Geol. Soc. Am. (exec. com.), AAAS; mem. Am. Assn. Petroleum Geologists (hon., Disting. Service award 1981, editor 1971-75), Soc. Econ. Geologists, Am. Commn. on Stratigraphic Nomenclature (chmn. 1968-70), Assn. Am. State Geologists (pres. 1985-86). Lutheran. Current Work: Mineral resources, particularly energy resources, coal, uranium, geothermal, petroleum; stratigraphy; areal geology; strategic minerals. Subspecialties: Geology; Coal. Home: 703 Sunset Dr Socorro NM 87801 Office: N Mex Bur Mines and Mineral Resources Campus Station Socorro NM 87801

KOTTMAN, ROY MILTON, college dean; b. Thornton, Iowa, Dec. 22, 1916; s. William D. and Millie J. (Christensen) K.; m. Wanda Lorraine Moorman, Dec. 31, 1941; children: Gary Roy, Robert William, Wayne David, Janet Kay. B.S. in Agr, Iowa State U., 1941, Ph.D., 1952; M.S. in Genetics, U. Wis., 1948; LL.D. (hon.), Coll. Wooster, 1972. Asst. prof. animal husbandry Iowa State U., 1946-47; grad. research asst. U. Wis., 1947-48; mem. faculty Iowa State U., 1949-58, prof. animal husbandry, assoc. dean agr., 1954-58; dean Coll. Agr., Forestry and Home Econs.; dir. Agrl. Expt. Sta., W.Va. U., 1958-60; dean Coll. Agr. and Home Econs., Ohio State U., v.p. agrl. adminstrn. emeritus, also dir. Ohio Agrl. Research and Devel. Center, 1960—; dir. Ohio Coop. Extension Service, 1964-82; acting assoc. dir. Nev. Agr. Expt. Sta., 1982-83; cons. to chancellor U. P.R., Mayaguez, 1984-85; dir. Swift Ind. Corp., 1981-85; mem. exec. com. sci. adv. bd. DNA Plant Tech. Corp., 1981—. Mem. Ohio Soil and Water Conservation Commn., 1960-82; mem. Central Ohio Water Advisory Council, 1976-82; bd. dirs. Ohio 4-H Found., 1964-82, Farm Film Found., 1973-80; mem. Agr. Higher Edn. Projects Com., 1975-80, Friends NACAA Scholarship Com., 1976-80, Ohio Agrl. Mus. Com., 1977-82, Gov.'s Task Force on Gasohol, 1979-80; bd. dirs. Farm Found., 1978—; v.p. Agrl. Research Inst., 1980-81. Recipient FFA degree Am. Farmer, 1977; named to Ohio Agr. Hall of Fame, 1983. Mem. Exec. Order Ohio Commodores, Sigma Xi, Gamma Sigma Delta, Alpha Gamma Sigma (hon.), Alpha Zeta, Phi Kappa Phi, Pi Kappa Phi (future policy com. 1976-80), Phi Zeta (hon.), Alpha Gamma Rho (hon.). Presbyterian. Clubs: Rotary (hon.), Nat. Dairy Shrine. Current Work: Agricultural research administration. Subspecialties: Animal breeding and embryo transplants; Genetics and genetic engineering (agriculture).

KOUCKY, FRANK LOUIS, geologist, educator; b. Chgo., June 24, 1927; s. Frank Louis and Ella (Harshman) K.; m. Virginia Ruhl, Sept. 10, 1949; children: Frank, David, Walter, Jonathan. Ph.B., U. Chgo., 1949, M.S., 1953, Ph.D., 1956. Instr. U. Ill., Chgo., 1949-55; asst. prof. geology Mont. Sch. Mines, Butte, 1955-58, U. Ill.-Urbana, 1958-60; assoc. prof. U. Cin., 1960-72; prof. geology Coll. Wooster, Ohio, 1972—, geologist Middle East excavations. Contbr. articles on geology and archeology to profl. jours. Served with U.S. Army, 1945-47. Danforth fellow, 1967—; Bucher fellow Swansea, Wales, 1968; research assoc. M.I.T., 1978. Fellow Geol. Soc. Am., AAAS, Ohio Acad. Sci.; mem. Soc. Econ. Geologists, Geochem. Soc., Mineral Soc. Am., Can. Mineral Assn., Phi Gamma Delta. Current Work: Archeogeology, acnient mining and metallurgy, research in archeogeology of Middle West archeological sites. Subspecialties: Archaeogeology; Metallurgy. Home: 122 W Easton Rd Burbank OH 44224 Office: Dept Geolog Coll Wooster Wooster OH 44691

KOUSSA, HAROLD ALAN, nuclear engineer; b. Central Falls, R.I., June 20, 1947; s. Harold Albert and June Joann (John) K.; m. Marsha Lynn Heidenis, Dec. 1, 1973. B.S. in Engring. Sci., U. R.I., 1969; M.B.A., U. Hartford, 1975; M.S. in Engring. Sci., Rensselaer Poly. Inst., 1977. Reactor engring. asst. Conn. Yankee Atomic Power Co., East Hampton, 1969-75, reactor engr., 1975-77; staff nuclear engr. Am. Nuclear Insurers, Farmington, Conn., 1977-79, sr staff nuclear engr., 1979-81, prin. engr., 1981-82, ops. mgr., 1982—. Mem. Republican Town Com., East Hampton, 1982—; mem. Water Pollution Control Authority, 1982—, vice chmn., 1984-85, chmn., 1985—; mem. East Hampton Charter Revision Com., 1982. Served to ensign USNR, 1982—. Mem. Am. Nuclear Soc., ASME. Club: U. R.I. Fast Break (Kingston, R.I.). Lodge: Masons. Current Work: Manage activities of engineering staff in regard to nuclear safety inspections of commercial nuclear power reactors and related projects. Subspecialties: Nuclear engineering; Nuclear fission. Home: 73 Childs Rd East Hampton CT 06424 Office: Am Nuclear Insurers 270 Farmington Ave Farmington CT 06032

KOUTNIK, DARYL LEE, bot. systematist, bot. cons.; b. Burbank, Calif., Dec. 22, 1951; s. Robert James and Alta Maria (Raville) K. B.A. in Biology and Math, Calif. State U., Northridge, 1977; M.S. in Botany, U. Calif., Davis, 1981, Ph.D. (Chubb Found. Scholar, Pacific Tropical Bot. Garden grantee), 1982. Research asst. U. Calif., Davis, 1979-80, teaching asst., 1980-82; sci. officer Bolus Herbarium, U. Capetown, South Africa, 1982—, cons. endangered species and environ. impact. Contbr. articles to profl. jours. Mem. Bot. Soc. Am., Am. Soc. Plant Taxonomists, Soc. Study of Evolution, Bot. Soc. South Africa, Sigma Xi. Democrat. Current Work: Systematics of the euphorbieae (euphorbiaceae) with special reference to the genera Euphorbia and Chamaesyce. Subspecialties: Systematics; Morphology. Home: 6922 Hesperia Ave Reseada CA 91335 Office: Bolus Herbarium U Capetown Rondebosch 7700 South Africa

KOUTS, HERBERT JOHN CECIL, physicist; b. Bisbee, Ariz., Dec. 18, 1919; s. Oliver Allen and Lillian (Niemeyer) K.; m. Hertha Pretorius, Feb. 2, 1942; children: Anne Elizabeth, Catherine Jennifer; m. Barbara Stokes, Mar. 27, 1974; stepchildren: Francis Spitzer, Michael Spitzer, Daniel Spitzer. B.S., La. State U., 1941, M.S., 1946; Ph.D., Princeton U., 1952. With Brookhaven Nat. Lab., Upton, L.I., N.Y., 1950-73, 77—, sr. scientist, assoc. div. head, 1958-73, chmn. dept. nuclear energy, 1977—; dir. div. reactor safety research AEC, Washington, 1973-75; dir. Office Nuclear Regulatory Research, U.S. Nuclear Regulatory Commn., Washington, 1975-76; mem. advisory com. reactor physics AEC, 1956-63, mem. adv. com. reactor safeguards, 1962-66; mem. European Am. Adv. Com. for Reactor Physics to European Nuclear Energy Agency, 1962-68; mem. internat. nuclear safety adv. group Internat. Atomic Energy Agy. Served with USAAF, 1942-45. Recipient E. O. Lawrence award AEC, 1963, Disting. Service award, 1975; Disting. Service award NRC, 1976. Mem. Am. Nuclear Soc. (Theos Thompson award in nuclear reactor safety 1983), Center Moriches Audubon Soc., Nat. Acad. Engring. Current Work: Nuclear reactor safety, nuclear reactor development, neutron physics, energy economy. Subspecialties: Nuclear engineering; Nuclear fission. Home: 249 S Country Rd Brookhaven NY 11719 Office: Brookhaven Nat Lab Upton NY 11973

KOUVEL, JAMES SPYROS, physics educator, researcher; b. Jersey City, May 23, 1926; s. Spyros James and Iphegenia (Cassianos) K.; m. Audrey Lumsden, Mar. 28, 1953; children—Diana, Alexander. B.Eng., Yale U., 1946, Ph.D., 1951. Research fellow U. Leeds, Eng., 1951-53, Harvard U., Cambridge, Mass., 1953-55; research physicist Gen. Electric Research Lab., Schenectady, 1955-69; prof. physics U. Ill.-Chgo., 1969—; vis. prof. U. Paris, Orsay, France, 1981; cons. Argonne Nat. Lab., Ill., 1969—; mem. adv. com. NSF, Washington, 1980-82, NRC, Washington, 1982—. Editorial bd. Jour. Magnetism, 1975—. Contbr. numerous articles to profl. publs. Served to lt. (j.g.) USN, 1944-46. Guggenheim fellow, 1967-68; NSF grantee, 1973—. Fellow Am. Phys. Soc., AAAS. Current work: Phase transitions in magnetic materials, including disordered systems such as spin glasses; structural instabilities in intermetallic compounds. Subspecialty: Condensed matter physics. Home: 223 N Euclid Ave Oak Park IL 60302 Office: U Ill Dept Physics PO Box 4348 Chicago IL 60680

KOVAC, PAVOL, research chemist; b. Trencin, Czechoslovakia, Dec. 6, 1938; came to U.S., 1981; s. Vojtech and Judita (Trebitsch) K.; m. Eva Gross, Nov. 24, 1962; 1 son, Roman. M.A. in Chemistry, Slovak Tech. U., 1962; Ph.D. in Organic Chemistry, Slovak Acad. Scis., 1967. Sr. research chemist Slovak Acad. Scis., Bratislava, Czechoslovakia, 1963-81; postdoctoral fellow dept. biochemistry Purdue U., Lafayette, Ind., 1967-68; prodn. chemist and group leader Bachem Inc., Torrance, Calif., 1981-82; vis. scientist NIH, Bethesda, Md., 1983—. Contbr. numerous articles on chemistry to profl. jours.; mem. editorial bd.: Jour. Carbohydrate Chemistry, 1982—; mem. editorial adv. bd.: Jour. Carbohydrates, Nucleosides, Nucleotides, 1974-81. Mem. Am. Chem. Soc. Patentee in field. Current Work: Synthesis of oligosaccharides and oligodeoxy nucleotides. Subspecialties: Organic chemistry; Synthetic chemistry. Office: NIH Rockville Pike Bldg 4 Room 208 Bethesda MD 20892

KOVACH, BELA JOSEPH, electrical engineering executive; b. Krusevlje, Yugoslavia, Jan. 20, 1930; came to U.S., 1975; s. Joseph and Gizella (Horn) K.; m. Almast N. Bedrosian, July 13, 1957; children—Ildi, Aram. B.S. in Elec. Engring., Tech. Coll. Subotica, Yugoslavia, 1973. Postgrad in isotope handling Nat. Research Council of Yugoslavia, Belgrade, 1974; Group leader Inst. of Nuclear Scis. B. Kidric, Belgrade, 1951-75; mgr. Nuclear Cons. Service, Columbus, Ohio, 1975—. Contbr. articles to profl. jours. Patentee in field. Recipient golden award Internat. Inventors Exhbn., Brussels, 1964, Boris Kidric award Inst. Nuclear Sci., 1968; M. Pupin award Inventor Council Yugoslavia, 1969. Mem. Health Physics Soc. Ohio. Current work: Detection of nuclear radiation, isotop identification, nuclear air cleaning on power reactors. Subspecialties: Environmental engineering; Nuclear engineering. Home: 1453 Burnley Square N Columbus OH 43229 Office: Nuclear Consulting Services Inc PO Box 29151 NUCON Columbus OH 43229

KOVACH, JOSEPH K., ethologist, research and evaluation administrator; b. Godollo, Hungary, Feb. 1, 1929; came to U.S., 1957, naturalized, 1962; s. Akos K. and Karolin (Kovats) K.; m. Magdalene Hamel, Mar. 10, 1975; children: Ian, Tobias, Ilsabe, Christopher. A.B., Elmhurst (Ill.) Coll., 1959; Ph.D., U. Chgo., 1963. Russian-Hungarian interpreter Bur. Tech. and Sci. Trans., Budapest, 1953-56; research asst. U. Chgo., 1959-63; NSF fellow U. Stockholm, 1963-64; research scientist U. Ill., 1964-66; research scientist, dir. animal behavior lab. Menninger Found., Topeka, Kans., 1966—, dir. research and evaluation, 1972—, dir. research tng., 1981—; mem. peer rev. com. Biopsychology study sect. NIH, Bethesda, Md., 1981—. Author: (with Gardner Murphy) Historical Introduction to Modern Psychology, 1972; mem. editorial bd.: Applied Animal Ethology, 1975—; cons. editor: Jour. Comparative Psychology, 1982—; contbr. articles to profl. jours. Nat. Inst. Child Health and Human Devel. grantee, 1972; recipient Research Career Devel. award NIH, 1970-80; Research Career Scientist award NIMH, 1980—. Mem. Am. Psychol. Assn., Animal Behavir Soc., AAAS, Internat. Soc. Devel. Psychobiology. Current Work: Behavior—genetics; early development and perceptual learning. Subspecialties: Ethology; Gene actions. Home: 3122 Westover Rd Topeka KS 66604 Office: The Menninger Foundation PO Box 829 Topeka KS 66601

KOVACH, PAUL JOSEPH, emergency planner; b. Colver, Pa., Feb. 7, 1956; s. Paul P. and Shirley (Jackson) K. B.S., St. Francis Coll., Loretto, Pa., 1977; M.S., U. Cin., 1979. Radiol. engr. Rockwell Internat., Hanford, Wash., 1979-81; staff engr. Gen. Physics Corp., Columbia, Md., 1981-82; emergency planner GPU Nuclear, Middletown, Pa., 1982—. Mem. N.Y. Acad. Scis., Health Physics Soc. Current Work: Contingency planning to minimize environmental and social impact of incidents at nuclear power plants. Subspecialty: Applied health physics. Office: GPU Nuclear-Three Mile Island PO Box 480 Middletown PA 17057

KOVACS, EVE VERONIKA ELIZABETH, physicist; b. Melbourne, Australia, Nov. 12, 1954; came to U.S., 1980; d. Joszef Stefan and Eve (Pazar) Kovacs; m. Keith Raymond Thulborn, Feb. 9, 1974 (div. Sept. 1981); Geoffrey Thomas Bodwin, Oct. 30, 1982. B.Sc. with honors, U. Melbourne, 1975, Ph.D. in Physics, 1980. Diploma in Computing Studies, 1980. Vis. scientist Stanford Linear Accelerator Ctr., Calif., 1980-81; research assoc. Rockefeller U., N.Y.C., 1981-82, Argonne Nat. Labs., Ill., 1983—. Contbr. articles to profl. jours. Mem. Am. Inst. Physics. Current work: Theoretical particle physics specializing in Monte Carlo simulations of lattice gauge theories. Subspecialties: Particle physics; Theoretical physics. Office: Argonne Nat Lab 9700 Cass Ave Argonne IL 60439

KOVACS, GYULA, engring. educator, robotics and fiber optics cons.; b. Nagykutas, Hungary, Apr. 22, 1941; came to U.S., 1973; s. Imre and Anna (Gorza) K.; m. Judy G. Kovacs, Dec. 4, 1976; 1 dau., Nicola Ashley. B.Sc., U. Manchester, Eng., 1965, M.Sc., 1971; M.S., Okla. State U., 1977. Registered profl. engr. Inst. Mech. Engring. (Eng.). Engring. trainee, tool maker, Eng., 1957-65; research and devl. engr. U. Manchester, 1965-76; design engr. Fenix & Scissons, Inc., Tulsa, 1976-82; assoc. prof. engring., program dir. U. Ark., Little Rock, 1982—; cons., researcher. Author: Guidelines for the Application of Robots and Automated Processes, 1982. Mem. Am. Inst. Indsl. Engrs., ASME, Am. Soc. Engring. Edn., Soc. Mfg. Engrs., Soc. Die Casting Engrs. Current Work: Robotics, optical signal processing, automation. Subspecialties: Fiber optics; Mechanical engineering. Home: 1624 S Taylor St Little Rock AR 72204 Office: U Ark Sch Engring Technology Little Rock AR 72204

KOVACS, STEPHEN GABRIEL, bio-physicist, cardiac prostheses consultant; b. Montreal, Ont., Can., Jan. 7, 1928; came to U.S., 1929, naturalized, 1958; s. Edmund and Helen (Korossy) K.; m. Mary Kretecos, Aug. 29, 1950 (div. 1964); children—James, Steven, Michael; m. Barbara J. Stubbs, Oct. 2, 1983. B.S. in Physics, U. Ala., 1950, M.S. in Physics, 1968; postgrad. U. South Fla., 1970-72. Lab. engr. Weston Electronic Instruments, Newark, 1950-53; lab. engr. Boeing Aircraft Co., Seattle, 1953-57; sr. cons. Thikol Chem. Corp., Huntsville, Ala., 1957-58; sr. staff engr Sperry Microwave Electronics Co., Clearwater, Fla., 1958-67; sr. design and devel. engr. Gen. Electric/AEC Neutron Devices Div., St. Petersburg, Fla., 1967-73; ind. investigator U. South Fla., 1973-78, research assoc., biophysicist dept. surgery Coll. Medicine, 1977-81, 83—; biophysicist James A. Haley VA Med. Ctr., 1981—. Contbr. articles to profl. jours. Mem. Am. Phys. Soc., Am. Instrument Soc., ASME, Am. Soc. Metals, Am. Vacuum Soc., U.S. Naval Inst., IEEE, Magnetics Soc. of IEEE, Engring. in Medicine and Biology Soc. of IEEE, Artificial Intelligence Soc. of IEEE, Am. Soc. for Artificial Internal Organs. Current work: Myocardial protection and left ventricular assist devices. Office: Dept Surgery Univ South Fla Coll of Medicine Box 16 Tampa FL 33612

KOWAL, CHARLES THOMAS, astronomer; b. Buffalo, Nov. 8, 1940; s. Charles Joseph and Rose (Myszkowiak) K.; m. Maria Antonietta Ruffino, Oct. 17, 1968; 1 dau., Loretta. B.A., U. So. Calif., 1963. Research asst. Mt. Wilson and Palomar obs.'s, 1961-63, Calif. Inst. Tech., Pasadena, 1963-65, 66-75, U. Hawaii, 1965-66; assoc. scientist Calif. Inst. Tech., 1976-78, scientist, 1978-81, mem. profl. staff, 1981—; staff asso. Hale Obs., 1979-80; lectr. in field. Recipient James Craig Watson award Nat. Acad. Scis., 1979. Mem. Am. Astron. Soc., Internat. Astron. Union. Discovered bright supernova, 1972, 13th satellite of Jupiter, 1974, large planetoid between orbits of Saturn and Uranus, 1977, also asteroids and comets; recovered lost comets and asteroids. Current Work: Searching for, and studying, asteroids and comets. Investigating the motion of Neptune. Subspecialty: Optical astronomy. Office: Dept Astrophysics Calif Inst Tech Pasadena CA 91125

KOWALSKI, MICHAEL PAUL, astrophysicist; b. Berwyn, Ill., Nov. 9, 1955; s. Joseph C. and Cecilia D. (Jumbalo) K.; m. Ellen M. Toomey, Apr. 13, 1985. B.S., Ill. Benedictine Coll., 1977; M.S., Northwestern U., 1979, Ph.D., 1982. NRC/Naval Research Lab. coop. associateship Naval Research Lab., Washington, 1982-84; astrophysicist Naval Research Lab., 1984—. Contbr. articles to sci. jours. NRC coop. fellow, 1982-84. Mem. Am. Astron. Soc. (high energy astrophysics div.). Current work: Development of high performance imaging X-ray detectors, physics of clusters of galaxies. Subspecialties: X-ray high energy astrophysics; Optical astronomy. Home: 839 4th St Laurel MD 20707 Office: Naval Research Lab Code 4129 2 Washington DC 20375

KOZLOFF, LLOYD M., university dean, scientist; b. Chgo., Oct. 15, 1923; s. Joseph and Rose (Hollowbow) K.; m. Judith Bonnie, June 16, 1947; children: James, Daniel, Joseph, Sarah. B.S., U. Chgo., 1943, Ph.D. in Biochemistry, 1948. Asst. prof. U. Chgo., 1949-58, assoc. prof., 1958-61, prof., 1961-64; prof. microbiology, chmn. dept. microbiology U. Colo., 1964-80, assoc. dean faculty affairs, 1976-80; dean grad. div. U. Calif.-San Francisco, 1981—, prof., 1981—. Research numerous publs. in field; contbr. chpts. to books. Bd. dirs. Proctor Found., San Francisco, 1982—; trustee U. Calif.-San Francisco Found., 1984—. Served with USN, 1944-46. Lederle fellow, 1954. Fellow AAAS (hon.); mem. Am. Soc. Biol. Chemistry, N.Y. Acad. Scis., Am. Chem. Soc. Current Work: Viral morphogenesis: use of folate and folate enzymes in virus assembly; biogenic origin of ice: ice nucleating site in bacteria. Subspecialties: Virology (biology); Population biology. Home: 2940 Fillmore St San Francisco CA 94123 Office: U Calif S-140 Grad Div San Francisco CA 94143

KOZLOWSKI, THEODORE THOMAS, botany educator; b. Buffalo, May 21, 1917; s. Theodore and Helen (Zamiara) K.; m. Maude Peters, June 29, 1954. B.S., Syracuse U., 1939; M.A., Duke U., 1941, Ph.D., 1947; postgrad., MIT, 1942-43; D.Sc. honoris causa, U. Catholique de Louvain, Belgium, 1978. Asst. prof. botany U. Mass., 1947-48, asso. prof., 1948-50, prof., head dept. botany, 1950-58; prof. forestry U. Wis., 1958-72, A.J. Riker prof., 1972—, sr. disting. prof., 1984—, chmn. dept., 1961-64, dir. biotron lab., 1977—; cons. NSF, Stanford Research Inst., Nat. Park Service, FAO, Oak Ridge Nat. Lab., Malaysian Govt., Mont. Univ. System, Internat. Found. for Sci., Academic Press, Time-Life Books, various comml. firms; vis. biologist Am. Inst. Biol. Scis., 1969-72; vis. scientist Soc. Am. Foresters, 1963-71; vis. prof. U. Pa., 1954; George Lamb lectr. U. Nebr., 1974; George S. Long lectr. U. Wash., 1978; Rapporteur World Consultation on Tree Improvement, 1963. Author: (with P.J. Kramer) Physiology of Trees, 1960; (with P.J. Kramer) Physiology of Woody Plants, 1979; Water Metabolism in Plants, 1964; Growth and Development of Trees, 2 vols., 1971; Tree Growth and Environmental Stresses, 1979; editor: Tree Growth, 1962, Water Deficits and Plant Growth, 7 vols., 1968-83, Seed Biology, 3 vols., 1971, Shedding of Plant Parts, 1973, (with G.C. Marks) Ectomycorrhizae, 1973, (with C.E. Ahlgren) Fire and Ecosystems, 1974, (with J.B. Mudd) Responses of Plants to Air Pollution, 1975, (with P. de T. Alvim) Ecophysiology of Tropical Crops, 1977, (with T.W. Tibbitts) Controlled Environment Guidelines for Plant Research, 1979; Flooding and Plant Growth, 1984; editorial bd.: Forest Sci., Ecology, BioSci.; Tree Physiology; assoc. editor: Can. Jour. Forest Research, Am. Midland Naturalist; editor: (book series) Physiol.-Ecology. Served to capt. USAAF, 1942-46. Sr. Fulbright research scholar Oxford (Eng.) U., 1964-65; recipient Author's award Internat. Shade Tree Conf., 1971. Mem. Am., Scandinavian socs. plant physiologists, Bot. Soc. Am. (merit award 1984), Ecol. Soc. Am., Soc. Am. Foresters (Barrington Moore biol. research award 1974), Internat. Soc. Arboriculture (Arboricultural research award 1976), Societas Forestalis Fenniae (Finland) (hon.), Societas Botanicorum Poloniae (hon.), Am. Inst. Biol. Scis., Phi Beta Kappa, Sigma Xi, Phi Kappa Phi, Phi Sigma. Subspecialty: Plant physiology (agriculture). Home: 10 S Rock Rd Madison WI 53705

KRACHMAN, HOWARD ELLIS, research and development executive; b. Phila., June 12, 1938; s. Albert and Sarah (Linetsky) K.; m. Betty Gurtoff, Feb. 23, 1974; children: Adam, Gower Alexis. B.S. in Mech. Engring, Drexel U., 1961; M.S. in Mech. Engring, U. So. Calif., 1964; diploma, Von Karman Ins., Brussels, 1963. Assoc. Douglas Co., Santa Monica, Calif., 1961-63; mem. tech. staff TRW, Redondo Beach, Calif., 1963-70; dir. engring. Developmental Scis., Industry, Calif., 1970—. Mem. AIAA, ASME, Assn. Unmanned Vehicle Systems. Current Work: Remote piloted vehicles. Subspecialties: Aerospace engineering and technology; Energy management. Home: 2120 San Pasqual Pasadena CA 91107 Office: Devel Scis 15757 E Valley Dr City of Industry CA 91744

KRAEMER, ARTHUR ROBERT, laser systems engineer, corporate executive; b. Montclair, N.J., Nov. 8, 1936; s. Alfred Robert and Estelle Rose (Baran) K.; m. Helena Chmura Aug. 17, 1962; children—Arthur Robert, Jr. (dec.), Stacey Anne, Karen Leah. B.E.E., Cornell U., 1959; M.S., Stanford U., 1961, postgrad., 1962-64. Sr. Scientist Lockheed Missiles and Space, Palo Alto, Calif., 1959-68; mgr. elec. optics orgn. GTE Sylvania Mountain View, Calif., 1969-80; v.p., gen. mgr. fiber optis GTE Lenkurt, Mountain View, 1980-83; v.p. ops. XMR Inc., Santa Clara, Calif., 1983—. Contbr. articles to profl. jours. Patentee in field. Coach, umpire Girls Softball League, Palo Alto, 1975-80; 80; ofcl. U.S. Swimming, Palo Alto, 1980—. Mem. IEEE (sr. mem.), Laser Inst. Am., Phi Kappa Phi, Tau Beta Pi, Eta Kappa Nu. Current work: Development of laser systems, particularly excimer lasers-for semiconductor manufacturing. Subspecialties: Excimers; Fiber optics. Home: 1116 Forest Ave Palo Alto CA 94301 Office XMR Inc: 5403 Betsy Ross Dr Santa Clara CA 95054

KRAEUTER, JOHN NORMAN, marine biologist, invertebrate zoologist; b. Glen Gardner, N.J., Mar. 26, 1942; s. Norman P. and Florence B. (Shaw) K.; m. Carol Irene Foster, Apr. 1, 1970; children—Kirtis R., Kristopher E. B.S., Fla. State U., 1964; M.S., Coll. William and Mary, 1966; Ph.D., U. Del., 1966-71; postgrad. U. Ga., Sapelo Island, 1971-72. Asst. prof. Marine Inst., U. Ga., Sapelo Island, 1972-73, U. Ga. and Skidaway Inst. Oceanography, Savannah, 1973-74; asst. prof. Va. Inst. Marine Sci., Coll. William and Mary, Wachapreasue, 1974-81, assoc. prof., 1981-82; sr. aquaculturist Balt. Gas & Electric Co., Balt., 1982—; mem. outer continental shelf sci. adv. com. Minerals Mgmt. Service, 1982—. Mem. Estaurine Research Fedn. (bus. mgr. jour. 1978—, treas. 1983-85), Am. Malacological Union (editorial bd. 1982—), Nat. Shellfisheries Assn., Am. Fisheries Soc., Malacological Soc. London. Current work: Culture of striped bass and clams; animal sediment relationships. Subspecialty: Aquaculture. Office: Crane Aquaculture Baltimore Gas & Electric Co PO Box 1475 Baltimore MD 21203

KRAFT, DONALD H., computer science educator; b. Omaha, Dec. 21, 1943; s. Hyman and Lillian (Miller) K.; m. Linda Gail Ohlbaum, Dec. 29, 1968; children—Elizabeth R., Suzanne M. B.S. in Indsl. Engring., Purdue U., 1965, M.S., in Indsl. Engring., 1966, Ph.D., 1971. Asst. prof. U. Md., College Park, 1970-75, vis. asst. prof. U.Calif.-Berkeley, 1975-76; assoc. prof. La. State U., Baton Rouge, 1976-82, prof. computer sci., 1982—, adj. prof. library and info. sci., 1984—. Editor Jour. Am. Soc. for Info. Scis., 1985—. Bd. dirs. Liberal Synagogue, Baton Rouge, 1982—; sec. Jewish Fedn. Greater Baton Rouge, 1984—. NSF grantee, 1980-82, 82, 84. Mem. Assn. for Computing Machinery (treas. 1980-82, sec. spl. interest group for info. retrieval 1984-85. Ops. Research Soc. Am. (Newsletter editor 1981-84; sec.-treas. computer sci. tech. sect. 1985), Am. Soc. for Info. Sci. Democrat. Jewish. Current work: Fuzzy subset theory applied to information retrieval, operations research models of information systems. Subspecialties: Information systems, storage, and retrieval (computer science); Information systems (Information science). Office: La State U Dept Computer Sci Baton Rouge LA 70803

KRAG, MARTIN HANS, orthopaedic surgeon, biomechanics researcher; b. St. Louis, Aug. 17, 1949. Student, Calif. Inst. Tech., 1966-67; B.A., Stanford, 1970; M.D., Yale U., 1975. Diplomate Am. Bd. Orthopaedic Surgeons. Intern U. Wash., Seattle, 1975-76; resident Yale-New Haven Hosp., 1976-79; research fellow Yale U., New Haven, 1979-80; clin. fellow Rancho Los Amigos Hosp., Downey, Calif., 1980-81; asst. prof. U. Vt., Burlington, 1981—. Contbr. articles to prof. jours. Recipient Spinal Research award Eastern Orthopaedic Assn., 1984. Mem. Orthopaedic Research Study, Internat. Soc. for Study of Lumbar Spine, Cervical Spine Research Soc., Rehab. Engrs. Soc. of No. Am. Current work: Spine, biomechanics, spine and spinal cord injury treatment, low back pain biomechanics and treatment; rehabilitative orthopaedic surgery. Subspecialties: Orthopedics; Biomedical engineering. Office: Dept Orthopaedics & Rehav Univ Vt Given Bldg Burlington VT 05405

KRAIG, RICHARD PAUL, neurologist, neuroscientist, educator; b. Chgo., Feb. 1, 1949; s. Harry J. and Adelaide (Farnaus) K.; m. Marcia P. Stachura, June 13, 1971; 2 daus., Jenna L., Marisa A. B.A. in Chemistry, Cornell Coll., Mt. Vernon, Iowa, 1971; Ph.D. in Physiology and Biophysics, U. Iowa, 1976; M.D., NYU, 1978. Diplomate: Nat. Bd. Med. Examiners. Grad. research asst. U. Iowa, 1974-76; intern in medicine U. Chgo. Hosp., 1978-79; resident in neurology Cornell U. Med. Coll., N.Y.C., 1979-82, clin. assoc. in neurology, 1979-81, instr., 1981-82, asst. prof. neurology, 1982—. Contbr. numerous articles on micro ion electrodes and their use in study of nervous system physiology and pathophysiology to sci. jours. Grass Found. fellow, 1975; Rockefeller Bros. clin. scholar, 1982-83; Tchr.-Investigator Devel. awardee NIH, 1983—. Mem. Soc. for Neurosci., Am. Acad. Neurology. Current Work: Microphysiology and biochemistry of brain and brain cell microenvironment in the study of stroke; ion microsensors. Subspecialties: Neurology; Neurophysiology.

KRAKAUER, RANDALL SHELDON, physician; b. N.Y.C., Apr. 25, 1949; s. Henry Robert and Violet (Tallmadge) K.; m. Marcia Sue Katcher, June 15, 1969; children: Meryl Lucille, Ari Martin, Barak Lee. B.S., Rensselaer Poly. Inst., 1972; M.D., Albany Med. Coll., 1972. Diplomate: Am. Bd. Internal Medicine and Rheumatology. Med. intern, resident U. Minn. Hosps., 1972-74; clin. assoc. immunology NIH, 1974-76; fellow rheumatology Mass. Gen. Hsop. Harvard U. Med. Sch., Boston, 1976-77; head sect. clin. immunology Cleve. Clinic Found., 1978-83; mem. exec. com. Study Group for Lupus Nephritis, 1981—; chmn. med. adv. bd. Ohio Lupus Found. Served to lt. comdr. USPHS, 1974-76. Fellow ACP; mem. Am. Soc. Clin. Pharmacology and Therapeutics (chmn. immunotherapy sect.), Am. Rheumatism Assn., Am. Assn. Immunologists, Am. Fedn. Clin. Research, Central Soc. Clin. Research. Current Work: Pathogenesis of and immunotherapy for autoimmune disease. Subspecialty: Rheumatology. Office: 900 W Main St Freehold NJ 07728

KRALL, NICHOLAS ANTHONY, physicist; b. Kansas City, Kans., Feb. 16, 1932; s. Nicholas Joseph and Catherine Elizabeth (Carr) K.; divorced; children—Carolyn, Laura, Nicholas, Teresa, Jonathan, Elizabeth; m. Diane C. Miller, July 4, 1985. B.S. in Physics, Notre Dame U., 1954; Ph.D. in Physics, Cornell U., 1959. Staff scientist Gen. Atomic, San Diego, 1959-62, mgr. fusion theory, 1963-67; prof. physics U. Md., College Park, 1967-73; v.p. fusion Sci. Application Inc., San Diego, 1973-78; v.p. plasma scis. Jaycor, Inc., San Diego, 1978—. Author: Shock Waves in Collisionless Plasmas, 1971; Principals of Plasma Physics, 1973; also articles. Fellow Am. Phys. Soc. (exec. com. 1978-83, vice chmn. 1981, chmn. div. plasma physics 1982), Sigma Xi. Clubs: U.S. Tennis, S.W. Yacht. Current work: Plasma physics, particularly theoretical physics relating to controlled thermonuclear research. Subspecialty: Plasma physics. Office: Jaycor Inc Box 85154 San Diego CA 92138

KRALL, RONALD LEE, pharmaceutical clinical researcher, neuropharmacologist; b. Balt., June 24, 1947; s. Melvin and Vivian (Lowy) K.; m. Susan Jane Doerner, Nov. 22, 1975; 2 sons, Joshua Andrew, Benjamin Eric. B.A., Swarthmore Coll., 1969; M.D., U. Pitts., 1973. Diplomate: Am. Bd. Neurology and Psychiatry. Intern Los Angeles County Harbor Gen. Hosp., 1973-74; staff assoc. Epilepsy br. NIH, Bethesda, Md., 1974-77; resident, fellow U. Rochester, N.Y., 1977-80, asst. prof., 1980-83; dir. clin. research Lorex Pharms., Skokie, Ill., 1983—. Recipient Commendation Medal USPHS, 1977. Mem. Epilepsy Found. Am., Am. Acad. Neurology, Am. Epilepsy Soc., Am. Soc. Clin. Pharmacology, Sigma Xi. Current Work: interest: clinical research in neuropharmacology; mechanism of action of neuroactive drugs, especially antiepileptic drugs. Subspecialties: Neurology; Neuropharmacology. Office: Lorex Pharmaceuticals 5200 Old Orchard Rd Skokie IL 60077

KRAMARSKY, BERNHARD, cell biologist; b. Hamburg, Germany, Dec. 27, 1924; s. Felix and Gutta (Nachemson) K.; m. Marion Bienes, Apr. 1946; m. Lea DellaRiccia, Apr. 20, 1951; children: Esther Winter, Jonathan Felix. B.Sc., Cornell U., 1950; D.Sc., U. Florence, Italy, 1963. Instr. microbiology U. So. Calif. Med. Sch., 1964-66; research asst., electron microscopist Albert Einstein Med. Center, Phila., 1966-67; assoc. mem., electron microscopist Inst. Med. Research, Camden, N.J., 1967-74; supervisory electron microscopist, cell biologist Cell Sci. Lab., Electro-Nucleonics, Inc., Silver Spring, Md., 1974—. Served with AUS, 1943-45. Mem. Am. Assn. Cancer Research, Am. Soc. Microbiology, Chesapeake Soc. Electron Microscopy. Current Work: Ultrastructural and immunoelectron microscopic studies of human T-cell lymphotropic viruses. Subspecialties: Cell biology; Virology (biology). Home: 11313 Baroque Rd Silver Spring MD 20901 Office: 12050 Tech Rd Silver Spring MD 20904

KRAMER, FRED RUSSELL, molecular biologist; b. N.Y.C., July 7, 1942; s. Paul Marvin and Janet (Mendelson) K.; m. Janet Retzker, June 20, 1965; children—Jennifer, Jordan. B.S., U. Mich., 1964; Ph.D., Rockefeller U., 1969. Postdoctoral fellow Inst. Cancer Research Columbia U. Coll. Physicians and Surgeons, N.Y.C., 1969-71, research assoc., 1971-72, instr. dept. human genetics and devel., 1972-73, asst. prof., 1973-80, sr. research assoc. Inst. Cancer Research, 1980-83, research scientist, 1983—. Am. Cancer Soc. fellow, 1969-71; grantee Am. Cancer Soc., 1977-78, 84—, NIH, 1984—. Mem. Am. Soc. Biol. Chemists, N.Y. Acad. Scis., Bermuda Biol. Sta., Sigma Xi. Democrat. Jewish. Current work: Recombinant RNA, nucleic acid replication. Subspecialty: Molecular biology. Home: 561 W 231st St New York NY 10463 Office: Inst Cancer Research 701 W 168th St New York NY 10032

KRAMER, LOIS BETH, health center administrator, research dietitian; b. Orange City, Iowa, Feb. 27, 1944; d. Lawrence and Johanna (Punt) VandeBerg; m. Gary Eugene Kramer, Aug. 17, 1963 (div. Mar. 26, 1984); 1 child, Brent Alan. Student Central Coll., 1961-63; B.S., Mundelein Coll., 1965; R.D., Hines VA Hosp., 1966. Clin. dietitian Hines VA Hosp., Ill., 1966-67, research dietitian, 1968-73, cons., research dietitian, 1973—; clin. dietitian St. Vincent Hosp., Sioux City, Iowa, 1974-77; mgr., clin. dietetics Marian Health Ctr., Sioux City, 1977—; mem. speakers bur. nutrition div. Mead Johnson, Evansville, Ind., 1978—. Contbr. articles to profl. jours. Mem. Am. Soc. Clin. Nutritionists, Am. Inst. Nutrition, Am. Dietetic Assn., Iowa Dietetic Assn. (treas. 1983—). Republican. Current work: Mineral and trace element metabolism in man, i.e., calcium in aging, zinc in relation to weight loss, and the availability of minerals and trace elements in vegetarian diets. Subspecialty: Nutrition (medicine). Home: 2300 Indian Hills Dr Apt 302 Sioux City IA 51104 Office: Marian Health Ctr 801 5th St Sioux City IA 51101

KRAMER, PAUL JACKSON, plant physiologist, educator; b. Brookville, Ind., May 8, 1904; s. LeRoy and Minnie (Jackson) K.; m. Edith Vance, June 24, 1931; children: Jean, Richard V. A.B., Miami U., Ohio, 1926, D.Litt., 1966; Ph.D., Ohio State U., 1931, D.Sc. (hon.), 1972; D.Sc. (hon.), U. N.C., 1966; Dr. h.c., U. Paris VII, 1975. Mem. Faculty Duke U., Durham, N.C., 1931—, James B. Duke prof., 1954-74, emeritus, 1974—; program dir. NSF, 1960-61; vis. investigator Calif. Inst. Tech., 1953; vis. lectr. Cornell U., spring 1976; vis. prof. U. Tex., fall 1976; Walker Ames vis. prof. U. Wash., 1977. Author: Plant and Soil Water Relationships, 1949, (with T.T. Kozlowski) Physiology of Trees, 1960, Plant and Soil Water Relationships: A Modern Synthesis, 1969, Physiology of Woody Plants, 1979, (with T.T. Kozlowski) Water Relations of Plants, 1983, A Collection of Lectures in Tree Physiology, 1982; contbr. articles to profl. jours. Recipient Soc. Am. Foresters award for achievement in biology, 1961; AEC grantee, 1949-71; NSF grantee, 1955-85. Mem. AAAS, Am. Inst. Biol. Scis. (pres. 1964, Disting. Service award 1977), Am. Soc. Plant Physiologists (pres. 1945), Bot. Soc. Am. (award of merit 1956, pres. 1964), Nat. Acad. Scis., Am. Philos. Soc., Am. Acad. Arts and Scis., Phi Beta Kappa, Sigma Xi. Republican. Methodist. Club: Cosmos. Current Work: Effects of chilling and water deficits on physiological processes and growth of plants. Subspecialties: Plant physiology (agriculture); Physiology of plant stress. Home: 23 Stoneridge Cir Durham NC 27705 Office: Dept Botany Duke University Durham NC 27706

KRAMER, STEVEN DAVID, physicist; b. Lakewood, N.J., Aug. 27, 1948; s. George and Pearl (Mohel) K. A.B., Cornell U., 1970; A.M., Harvard U., 1971, PH.D., 1976. Research asst. Harvard U., 1972-76; staff scientist Oak Ridge (Tenn.) Nat. Lab., 1976—; cons. Atom Scis., Inc. Contbr. articles to profl. jours. NSF fellow, 1970-74; Dept. Energy grantee. Mem. Am. Phys. Soc., Optical Soc. Am., Archaelol. Inst. Am. (exec. com. E. Tenn.). Current Work: Nonlinear optics, laser spectroscopy, one atom detection, resonance ionization spectroscopy. Subspecialties: Laser spectroscopy; Atomic and molecular physics. Home: 226 Countryside Circle Knoxville TN 37923 Office: PO Box X 5500 Bldg Oak Ridge TN 37830

KRAPCHEV, VLADIMIR BOGDANOV, physicist; b. Sofia, Bulgaria, Mar. 21, 1946; came to U.S., 1971, naturalized, 1979; s. Bogdan Milanov and Evdokia Stefanova (Balamezova) K.; m. Tania Atanassova Kobarelov, June 24, 1972; 1 child, Philip. M.S., U. Sofia, 1969; Ph.D., MIT, 1976. Physicist, Physics Inst., Sofia, Bulgaria, 1969-71; teaching asst. MIT, Cambridge, 1972-76, research scientist Plasma Fusion Ctr., 1977-84, staff mem. Lincoln Lab., 1984—. Contbr. articles to profl. jours. Mem. Am. Phys. Soc. Eastern Orthodox. Current work: Nonlinear waves; scattering of radio frequency waves by turbulent plasmas. Subspecialties: Plasma physics; Theoretical physics. Home: 80 Park St Brookline MA 02146 Office: MIT Lincoln Lab 244 Wood St Lexington MA 02173

KRAPU, GARY LEE, avian ecologist; b. Oakes, N.D., Mar. 12, 1944; s. Jalmer Oscar and DeLores Amber (Aune) K. B.S. in Zoology, N.D. State U., 1966; M.S. in Zoology, Iowa State U., 1968, Ph.D. in Animal Ecology, 1972. Research biologist U.S. Fish and Wildlife Service, Jamestown, N.D., 1971—; adj. prof. U. N.D., Grand Forks, 1974—. Author: Ecology of Platte River, 1981; contbr. articles to profl. publs. Mem. Am. Ornithologists Union (life), Wilson Soc. (life), Ecol. Soc. Am., Wildlife Soc., Natural Sci. Soc. (pres. 1977). Current work: Factors regulating waterfowl reproduction, role of nutrient reserves in life cycles of migratory birds. Subspecialties: Ecology (biology); Reproductive biology. Office: No Prairie Wildlife Research Ctr PO Box 1747 Jamestown ND 58401

KRASNY, HARVEY CHARLES, research scientist; b. High Point, N.C., July 27, 1945; s. Morris Theodore and Elizabeth (Nurkin) K.; m. Maria Cristina Ramirez, Apr. 9, 1979; 1 dau., Pamela Marie. B.S., Lynchburg Coll., 1967; M.S., U. N.C., 1969, Ph.D., 1976. Sr. research scientist Burroughs Wellcome Co., Research Triangle Park, N.C., 1969—. Contbr. articles on antiviral and cancer chemotherapy to sci. jours. Mem. Am. Soc. Clin. Pharmacology and Therapeutics, Am. Soc. Pharmacology and Exptl. Therapeutics, Soc. Toxicology, N.Y. Acad. Sci., Sigma Xi. Current Work: Drug dispositon, pharmacokinetics and biochemistry of nucleic acid antagonist. Subspecialties: Pharmacokinetics; Biochemistry (medicine). Home: 120 Woodbridge Ln Chapel Hill NC 27514 Office: Dept Exptl Therapy Burroughs Wellcome Co Triangle Park NC 27709

KRASS, ALVIN, psychologist, test development company executive; b. Bklyn., Sept. 14, 1928; s. Nathan M. and Nora (Feigels) K.; m. Suzanne Myra Freiwirth, Sept. 5, 1954; children: Peter, Adam, Michael. B.A., Bklyn. Coll., 1951; M.A., NYU, 1952, Ph.D., 1965. Lic. psychologist, N.J.; diplomate marital and family therapy Am. Bd. Family Psychology. Staff psychologist Brisbane Child Treatment Center, Allaire, N.J., 1955-58; chief psychologist Monmouth Med. Center, Long Branch, N.J., 1958-62, pvt. practice psychology, Monmouth County, N.J., 1955—; pres. Key Edn., Inc., Shrewsbury, N.J., 1958—; cons. Monmouth County Parks System, 1977—, N.J. Div. Vocat. Rehab., Red Bank, 1980-82. Author: Mechanisms of the Mind, 1972, also vocat. and learning potential tests. Served with U.S. Army, 1952-54. Recipient Founders' Day award N.Y.U., 1965. Mem. Am. Psychol. Assn., N.J. Psychol. Assn., Am. Acad. Psychotherapists, Monmouth-Ocean County Psychol. Assn. (pres. 1978-79). Jewish. Patentee computer integrated vocat. testing devices. Current Work: Computer integrated test system development for vocational assessment in special populations (handicapped, socially disadvantaged, special needs). Subspecialties: Behavioral psychology; Learning. Home: 205 Holland Rd Holmdel NJ 07733 Office: Key Edn Inc 673 Broad St Shrewsbury NJ 07701

KRATZ, LAWRENCE JOHN, mathematician, educator; b. Detroit, Oct. 7, 1943; s. Lawrence John and Bertha (Fecteau) K.; m. Catherine Alice Foster, Oct. 10, 1970; children: Luke, John, Anne, Mary. B.A., Xavier U., Cin., 1963; M.A., U. Wis., 1966; Ph.D., U. Utah, 1975. Instr. Idaho State U., 1966-70; asst. prof. math U. Ky., Lexington, 1975-76; asst. prof. Idaho State U., Pocatello, 1976-81, assoc. prof., 1981—; engr. EG & G, Inc., Idaho Falls, 1978-79; dir. Student Sci. Tng. Program, NSF, Pocatello, 1981. Mem. Soc. Indsl. and Applied Math, Assn. Computing Machinery, Am. Math. Soc., IEEE. Current Work: Multi-dimensional quadrature; efficient algorithms in computer graphics. Subspecialties: Numerical analysis (computer science); Graphics, image processing, and pattern recognition. Home: 1414 Ammon St Pocatello ID 83201Office: Dept Math Idaho State U Pocatello ID 83201

KRATZER, REINHOLD HERMANN, chemist; b. Kaaden, Czechoslovakia, Nov. 14, 1928; s. Reinhold R. and Johanna M. (Maehner) K. Dr.rer.nat. in Inorganic Chemistry, U. Munich, 1960. Research asst. U. So. Calif., 1960-62; research chemist Naval Ordnance Lab., Corona, Calif., 1962-64; sr. scientist MHD Research, Inc., Hercules Powder Co., 1964-66; mgr. chem. research Marquardt Corp., 1966-70; mgr. chemistry dept. Ultrasystems, Inc., Irvine, Calif., 1970—. Contbr. articles profl. jours. Mem. Am. Chem. Soc., Chem. Soc. London, German Chem. Soc., AAAS, N.Y. Acad. Scis. Patentee in field. Current Work: Mine drainage; coal and oil shale; geothermal brine; perfluorinated ethers; high viscosity index fluids; fluid-seal interactions; flammability and combustion toxicology; boron nitride. Subspecialties: Polymer chemistry; Fuels. Home: 17 Shooting Star St Irvine CA 92714 Office: 2400 Michelson Dr Irvine CA 92715

KRAUS, MARJORIE PATT, biophysicist, researcher, cons.; b. Granville, Mass., Mar. 29, 1913; d. Hermann G. and Mary A. (Wackerbarth) Patt; m. Philip B. Kraus, June 28, 1940; children: Patricia, John, Robert, Deborah, Betsy, Kathryn. Ph.B., Brown U., 1933; A.M. (Royall Victor fellow), Stanford U., 1936. Resident, tutor Sch. Nursing, Springfield (Mass.) Hosp., 1934; bacteriologist St. Lukes Hosp., N.Y.C., 1937-39; research assoc. in biophysics Columbia U., 1936-39; chem. research asst. to v.p. Nat. Oil Products, Harrison, N.J., 1939-41; instr. in chemistry U. Del., 1965, research assoc. dept. civil engring., 1965-67, sr. research assoc. in radiation chemistry, 1969-76, program dir. on blue-green algal studies, 1971-76; guest research assoc. in biophysics Pa. State U., 1976; research dir. Algal Reasearch Ctr., Landenberg, Pa., 1976—; expert witness on aquatic virus for litigation over EPA permits. Contbr numerous articles, including some on cyanophages of blue-green algae, virus problems in sludge disposal and water renovation, molecular biochem. approach to aquatic toxicology, to profl. jours. Workshop leader Chester County Soil Conservation. Grad. Women in Sci. Gerry fellow, 1975-76. Mem. Am. Chem. Soc., Phycological Soc. Am., Radiation Reseaarch Soc., Am. Soc. Photobiology, Am. Soc. Microbiology, ASTM (Virology Task Force), Phi Beta Kappa, Sigma Xi. Current Work: Environmental virology, photosynthesis, nitrogen fixation, genetic engineering water quality and wastewater treatment, resource conservation, environmental toxicology. Subspecialties: Biophysical chemistry; Water supply and wastewater treatment. Home and Office: 317 London Tract Landenberg PA 19350

KRAUS, MENAHEM ALFRED, polymer chemist, researcher; b. Nanking, China, June 1, 1942; came to U.S., 1980; s. Egon and Anna K.; m. Ora Cohen, Feb. 9, 1969; children—Alon, Nirit, Oded. B.S., Hebrew U., Jerusalem, 1964, M.S., 1966; Ph.D., Weizmann Inst., Rehovot, Israel, 1974. Sr. researcher Hydronautics, Israel, 1973-74; mgr. research A.T. Ramot Plastics, Tel Aviv; group leader Monsanto, St. Louis, 1980-83, sr. group leader, 1983-85; v.p. research and devel. Gelman Scis., Ann Arbor, Mich., 1985—. Co-editor Israel Jour. Chemistry, 1978. Patentee in field. Inventor of artificial kidney, 1980. Contbr. articles to profl. jours. Mem. Am. Chem. Soc., Israel Chem. Soc. Jewish. Current work: Artificial membranes; thin films; polymer modification; polymeric reagents; transport phenomena. Subspecialties: Polymer chemistry; Artificial organs and prostheses. Office: Gelman Sciences 600 S Wagner Rd Ann Arbor MI 48106

KRAUSE, CHARLES JOSEPH, otolaryngologist; b. Des Moines, Apr. 21, 1937; s. William H. and Ruby I. (Hitz) K.; m. Barbara Ann Steelman, June 14, 1962; children—Sharon, John, Ann. B.A., State U. Iowa, 1959, M.D., 1962. Diplomate: Am. Bd. Otolaryngology. Intern Phila. Gen. Hosp., 1962-63; resident in surgery U. Iowa, 1965-66, resident in otolaryngology, 1966-69; fellow dept. plastic surgery Marien Hosp., Stuttgart, W. Ger., 1970; asst. prof. otolaryngology U. Iowa, 1969-72, asso. prof., 1972-75, vice chmn. dept. otolaryngology, 1973-77, prof., 1975-77; prof., chmn. dept. otolaryngology U. Mich. Med. Sch., Ann Arbor, 1977—. Author book in field; contbr. chpts. to books, articles to profl. jours. Served to capt. USAF, 1963-65. Fellow Am. Soc. Head and Neck Surgery (Council 1980-83, chmn. research com. 1980-83); Mem. AMA, Am. Acad. Ophthalmology and Otolaryngology, Am. Acad. Facial Plastic and Reconstructive Surgery (regional v.p. 1977-80, chmn. research com. 1977-80, pres. 1981-82), A.C.S. (adv. council otolaryngology 1979-83), Assn. Head and Neck Oncologists Gt. Britain (corr. mem.), Am. Assn. Cosmetic Surgeons, Assn. Research in Otolaryngology, Washtenaw County Med. Soc. (exec. com. 1979-82), Mich. State Med. Soc., Mich. Otolaryngol. Soc., Assn. Acad. Depts. Otolaryngology, Soc. Univ. Otolaryngologists, Walter P. Work Soc., Am. Cancer Soc. (med. adv. com. Washtenaw County unit), Am. Laryngol., Rhinol. and Otol. Soc., Am. Laryngol. Assn., Centurions of Deafness Research Found. Republican. Presbyterian. Current Work: Cancer of the head and neck; rehabilitation of head and neck cancer patients; plastic and reconstructive surgery of the head and neck; tumor immunology. Subspecialties: Otorhinolaryngology; Cancer research (medicine). Home: 3100 Hunting Valley Dr Ann Arbor MI 48104 Office: Dept Otolaryngology U Mich Hosp Ann Arbor MI 48109

KRAUSE, JAMES EDWARD, neurobiologist, biochemist; b. Beaver Dam, Wis., Feb. 1, 1952; s. Edward Norman and Lucille (Hoinacki) K.; m. Kathleen Mary English, June 28, 1980. B.S. with high honors, U. Wis.-Stevens Point, 1974; Ph.D., U. Wis., Madison, 1980. Research assoc. U. Pitts., 1980-81; research assoc. SUNY-Stony Brook, 1981-82, research asst. prof., 1982-83; asst. prof. neurobiology Washington U. Sch. Medicine, St. Louis, 1984—, mem. neurosci. steering com., 1984—; mem. biochem. subcom. study sect. Nat. Inst. on Drug Abuse, Washington, 1984—. Contbr. articles to sci. jours. Recipient New Investigator Research award NIH, 1982, grantee, 1984. Mem. AAAS, Soc. for Neurosci., Sigma Xi, Lambda Omicron (award 1974). Current work: Molecular neurobiology, role of brain peptides in neuronal function, peptide and gene families. Subspecialties: Neurobiology; Molecular biology. Office: Washington U Sch Medicine Dept Anatomy and Neurobiology 660 S Euclid Ave Saint Louis MO 63110

KRAUSE, MANFRED OTTO, physicist, educator; b. Stuttgart, Germany, Mar. 11, 1931; came to U.S., 1960; s. Friedrich B. and Friedel E. (Mann) K.;

m. Josephine C., Dec. 26, 1963. B.S., Tech. Universitat, Stuttgart, 1954, M.S., 1957, Ph.D., 1960. Sr. physicist William M. Johnston Lab., Balt., 1960-63; sr. scientist Oak Ridge Nat. Lab., Tenn., 1963—; professeur d'echange Universite Paris VI, 1975. Author monograph. Contbr. articles to profl. jours., chpt. to books. Discoverer X-ray spectrometry based on photoelectric effect, 1971. Recipient Alexander von Humboldt award, 1976. Fellow Am. Phys. Soc.; mem. AAAS, Sigma Xi. Current work: atomic electron spectrometry with synchrotron radiation. Subspecialty: Atomic and molecular physics. Home: 125 Baltimore Dr Oak Ridge TN 37830

KRAUSE, RICHARD MICHAEL, immunologist, educator, government official; b. Marietta, Ohio, Jan. 4, 1925; s. Ellis L. and Jennie (Waterman) K. B.A., Marietta Coll., 1947, D.Sc. (hon.), 1978; M.D. Case Western Res. U, 1952; D.Sc. (hon.), U. Rochester, 1979, Med. Coll. Ohio, Toledo, 1981. Research fellow dept. preventive medicine Case Western Res. U., 1950-51; intern Ward Med. Service, Barnes Hosp., St. Louis, 1952-53, asst. resident, 1953-54; asst. physician to hosp. Rockefeller Inst., 1954-57, asst. prof., asso. physician to hosp., 1957-61, asso. prof., asso. physician to hosp., 1961-62; prof. epidemiology Sch. Medicine, Washington U., St. Louis, 1962-66, asso. prof. medicine, 1962-65, prof. medicine, 1965-66; asso. prof., physician to hosp. Rockefeller U., 1966-68, prof., sr. physician, 1968-75; dir. Rockefeller U. (Animal Research Center), 1974-75, Nat. Inst. Allergy and Infectious Diseases, NIH, HEW, Bethesda, Md., 1975-84, USPHS surgeon, 1975-77, asst. surgeon gen., 1977-84; now dean Emory U. Sch. Medicine, Atlanta. Bd. dirs. Mo.-St. Louis Heart Assn., 1962-66, mem. research com., 1963-66; mem. exec. com. council on rheumatic fever and congenital heart disease Am. Heart Assn., 1963-66, chmn. council research study com., 1963-66, mem. assn. research com., 1963-66, mem. policy com., 1966-70; mem. commn. streptococcal and staphylococcal diseases U.S. Armed Forces Epidemiol. Bd., 1963-72, dep. dir., 1968-72; bd. dirs. N.Y. Heart Assn., 1967-73, chmn. adv. council on research, 1969-71, mem. dirs. council, 1973-75; cons., mem. coccal expert com. WHO, 1967—; mem. steering com. Biomed. Sci. Scientific Working Group, WHO, 1978; mem. infectious disease adv. com. Nat. Inst. Allergy and Infectious Disease, NIH, 1970-74; bd. dirs. Royal Soc. Medicine Found., Inc., 1971-77, treas., 1973-75; bd. dirs. Allergy and Asthma Found. Am., 1976-77, Lupus Found. Am., 1977—. Assoc. editor: Jour. Immunology, 1963-71; sect. editor: Viral and Microbial Immunology, 1974-75; editor: Jour. Exptl. Medicine, 1973-75; adv. editor, 1976—; mem. editorial bd.: Bacteriological Revs, 1969-73, Infection and Immunity, 1970-78, Immunochemistry, 1973, Clin. Immunology and Immunopathology, 1976, 1978—; Contbr. numerous articles to profl. jours. Served with U.S. Army, 1944-46. Decorated Gumhuria medal Egypt; recipient Disting. Service medal HEW, 1979; C. William O'Neal Disting. Am. Service award. Mem. U.S. Nat. Acad. Scis., Inst. Medicine, Assn. Am. Physicians, Am. Acad. Allergy, Am. Soc. Biol. Chemists, Am. Soc. Clin. Investigation, Am. Assn. Immunologists, Am. Soc. Microbiology, Harvey Soc., Am. Venereal Diseases Soc., Am. Coll. Allergists, AAAS, Infectious Diseases Soc. Am., Royal Soc. Medicine, Am. Rheumatism Assn., Practitioner's Soc. N.Y., Am. Thoracic Soc., Am. Epidemiol. Soc. Clubs: Century Assn. (N.Y.C.); Cosmos (Washington). Research on pathogenesis and epidemiology of streptococcal diseases; immunochem. studies on streptococcal antigens; immunogenetics; recognition of rabbit antibodies with molecular uniformity, genetics of immune response. Subspecialty: Immunogenetics. Office: Emory U Sch Medicine Atlanta GA 30322

KRAUSE, RICHARD THEODORE, analytical research chemist; b. Springfield, Minn., May 26, 1936; s. Alvin Arnold and Mary Dorothea (Martius) K.; m. Marlene Louise Kronbach, Aug. 11, 1962; children—Mark Alan, Lori Kay. B.A., Mankato State Coll., 1960; postgrad., U. N.D., 1962-63. Chemist FDA, Mpls., 1960-72, Washington, 1972-83, research chemist, 1984—; cons. Pan Am. Health Org., Mexico City, Mex., 1984, WHO, Bangkok, Thailand, 1985. Contbr. articles to profl. jours. Recipient Commendable Service award FDA 1981, Mem. Assn. Ofcl. Analytical Chemists (Assoc. Referee of Year award 1984), Am. Chem. Soc. (pesticide sect.). Lutheran. Current work: Development of multresidue methods for determination of organonitrogen pesticides using various high performance liquid chromatographic techniques. Subspecialties: Analytical chemistry; Environmental chemistry. Home: 12015 Wayland St Oakton VA 22124 Office: FDA HFF-426 200 C St SW Washington DC 20204

KRAUSHAAR, JACK JOURDAN, physics educator; b. Newark, N.J., Sept. 6, 1923; s. Lester Adam and Helen (Osterhoudt) K.; m. Nancy W. Curtis; children—Jeffrey Curtis, Steven Lester, Matthew Jourdan. B.S., Lafayette Coll., 1944; M.S., Syracuse U., 1948, Ph.D., 1951. Research assoc. Brookhaven Nat. Lab., Upton, N.Y., 1950-53; instr. Stanford U., 1953-56; from asst. to prof. physics U. Colo., Boulder, 1956—. Author: Energy and Problems of a Technical Society, 1984. Contbr. numerous articles to profl. jours. Served to lt. (j.g.) USNR, 1943-46, PTO. Fellow Am. Phys. Soc.; mem. AAAS, Am. Fedn. Scientists. Democrat. Mem. Soc. of Friends. Current work: Intermediate energy nuclear physics, pion scattering, charge exchange, (p,d) reactions at energies over 100 meV. Subspecialties: Nuclear physics; Energy and society. Office: Dept Physics U Colo Campus Box 390 Boulder CO 80309

KRAUSHAAR, WILLIAM LESTER, educator, physicist; b. Newark, Apr. 1, 1920; s. Lester A. and Helen (Osterhoudt) K.; m. Margaret Freidinger, Feb. 27, 1943 (div. 1980); children—Mark Jourdan, Susan, Andrew Woolman; m. Elizabeth D. Rodgers, Aug. 9, 1980. B.S., Lafayette Coll., 1942; Ph.D., Cornell U., 1949. Physicist Nat. Bur. Standards, Washington, 1942-45; asso. prof. physics Mass. Inst. Tech., Cambridge, 1956-62, prof., 1962-65; prof. physics U. Wis.-Madison, 1965—. Author: (with Uno Ingard) Introduction to Mechanics, Matter and Waves, 1960. Fellow Am. Phys. Soc., Am. Astron. Soc., Internat. Astron. Union, Am. Acad. Arts and Scis., Nat. Acad. Sci. Research and publs. on astrophysics; study of cosmic X and gamma radiation. Subspecialty: High energy astrophysics. Home: 318 S Yellowstone Dr Madison WI 53705

KRAUSS, ALAN ROBERT, physicist; b. Chgo., Oct. 3, 1943; s. Paul and Shirley (Shapiro) K.; m. Julie Emelie Rosado, Aug. 28, 1965; 1 dau., Susan. B.S. in Physics (Nat. Merit scholar), U. Chgo., 1965; M.S., Purdue U., 1968, Ph.D., 1972. Research assoc. U. Chgo., 1972-74; physicist Argonne Nat. Lab., Ill., 1974—. Contbr. chpts. to books, articles to profl. publs. Hon. 2d lt. Ill. N.G. Recipient research award Dept. Energy, 1984. Mem. Am. Phys. Soc., Am. Vacuum Soc. (publicity chmn. fusion tech. div., adv. com. fusion tech. div.), Sigma Xi, Sigma Pi Sigma. Club: Downers Grove (Ill.) Camera. Inventor. Current Work: Surface physics, sputtering, secondary ion emission, interaction of energetic particles with solid surfaces, fusion-related materials problems. Subspecialties: Nuclear fusion; Surface chemistry. Office: Argonne Nat Lab Bldg 200 Argonne IL 60439

KRAUSZ, JOSEPH PHILIP, plant pathologist; b. Flushing, N.Y., May 31, 1948; s. Joseph M. and Elenor M. (Lonergan) K.; m. Cheryl A. Parker, Aug. 14, 1971; 1 son, Thomas. B.A., SUNY-New Paltz, 1971; M.S., Cornell U., 1973, Ph.D., 1976. Research fellow Internat. Center Tropical Agr., Cali, Colombia, 1974-75; sr. research plant pathologist H.J. Heinz Co., Cleveland, Miss., 1975-76; research plant pathologist FMC Cor., Davis, Calif., 1977-78; asso. prof. plant pathology Clemson U., Florence, S.C., 1978—. Contbr. articles in field to profl. jours. Served with USNR, 1966-68. Mem. Am Phytopath. Soc., Sigma Xi, Phi Kappa Phi. Roman Catholic. Current Work: Conduct research and ednl. activities to develop, improve and disseminate disease control practices for tobacco, corn and turfgrass. Subspecialty: Plant pathology. Office: Clemson University Box 5809 Florence SC 29502

KRAUTHAMER, GUNTER MICHAEL (GEORGE), neural science educator; b. Chemnitz, Germany, Sept. 14, 1926; came to U.S., 1942, naturalized, 1945; s. Michael and Ellen (Muller) K.; m. Eleanor Watkins, 1953 (div.); children—Michele, Peter; m. Carole McIntosh, 1966 (div.); children—Barbara, Stephanie, Christina, Michael. B.S., CCNY, 1952, M.S., 1953; Ph.D., NYU, 1958. Research scientist Hillside Hosp., N.Y.C., 1958-60; postdoctoral fellow U. Paris and Centre National de la Recherche Scientifique, Paris, 1960-63, research assoc., 1963-67; asst. prof. Columbia U., N.Y.C., 1967-69; prof. neural sci Rutgers U. Med. Sch., Piscataway, N.J., 1969—; vis. sr. scientist Miles Labs., Elkhart, Ind., 1965, 1966; asst. exec. sec. Internat. Brain Research Orgn., UNESCO, Paris, 1966-68. Editor: Lateralization in Nerve System, 1977. Contbr. articles to profl. jours. Served with U.S. Army, 1944-47, ETO. Fels fellow; NIH fellow. Mem. Soc. for Neurosci. (pres. N.J. chpt. 1972—), AAAS, Internat. Assn. Study of Pain, Internat. Basal Ganglia Soc. Current work: Neuroanatomy and neurophysiology, central integrative mechanisms, basal ganglia, pain, somatosensory functions. Subspecialties: Neurophysiology; Anatomy and embryology. Home: 47 Broadripple Dr Princeton NJ 08540 Office: UMDNJ-Rutgers Medical School PO Box 101 Piscataway NJ 08854

KRAVITZ, DAVID WILLIAM, electronic engineer, mathematician; b. N.Y.C., Apr. 26, 1956; s. Sam and Frances Adeline (Liebowitz) K. B.S. in Math. with highest honors, Rutgers U., 1977; M.A. in Math. Sci, Johns Hopkins U., 1978; M.S. in Elec. Engring, U. So. Calif., 1980, Ph.D. in Elec. Engring, 1982. Teaching asst. Johns Hopkins U., Balt., 1977-78; research asst. Chesapeake Bay Inst., Balt., summer 1978; teaching and research asst. U. So. Calif., Los Angeles, 1978-82; fellow Woods Hole Oceanographic Instn. (Mass.), summer 1976-77; mem. tech. staff Hughes Aircraft Co., El Segundo, Calif., summers 1979-81; electronic engr. Dept. Def., Linthicum, Md., 1982. Contbr. articles to profl. jours. George H. Cook scholar, 1976-77. Mem. Math. Assn. Am., IEEE, Johns Hopkins Alumni Assn., Rutgers U. Alumni Assn., U. So. Calif. Engring. Alumni Assn., Pi Mu Epsilon. Democrat. Jewish. Clubs: Howard County Striders (Columbia, Md.); Tompkins Karate Assn. Current Work: Cryptographic systems design. Subspecialties: Electronics; Applied mathematics. Home: 5656 Stevens Forest Rd Apt 148 Columbia MD 21045

KRAVITZ, LAWRENCE CHARLES, electrical engineer. Sector dir. tech. Bendix Aerospace, Arlington, Va. Subspecialty: Electronics. Office: Bendix Aerospace 1000 Wilson Blvd Arlington VA 22209*

KRAWARIK, PETER HEINZ, physicist; b. Vienna, Austria, Mar. 13, 1939; came to U.S., 1970; s. Franz Johann and Olga (Winckler) K.; m. Maria Pitka, Sept. 24, 1965; children—Carolina, Alexander. Ph.D. in Physics and Math., U. Vienna, 1965. Asst. to dir. Impulsphysik GmbH, Hamburg, Fed. Republic Germany, 1965-70; research staff Western Electric Co., Princeton, N.J., 1970-78, dept. chief, Holmdel, N.J., 1979-82; dist. mgr. 195 Broadway Corp., Piscataway, N.J., 1983; gen. mgr. AT&T Resource Mgmt. Corp., Piscataway, 1984—; owner, dir. Systems Physics, Hopewell, N.J., 1980—. Mem. IEEE (sr.), Ops. Soc. Am., Am. Mgmt. Assn., Soc. Motion Picture and TV Engrs. Current work: Design, implementation and operation of advanced communications systems with emphasis on market/needs directions, human factors, executive use. Subspecialties: Information systems (Information science); Telecommunications. Home: 93 E Prospect St Hopewell NJ 08525 Office: AT&T 30 Knightsbridge Rd Piscataway NJ 08854

KREBS, HELMUT WALDEMAR GRAF VON THORN, research scientist; b. Memel, Germany, June 2, 1942; s. Samuel Graf von Thorn and Else Gräfin (von Keyserling) K.; m. Carol Washington-Bennett, Dec. 24, 1963 (div.); m. Jean Miles Lauder, Nov. 24, 1974. B.A., Sir George Williams U., 1967; M.A., McGill U., 1968, Ph.D., 1971. Research assoc. dept psychology McGill U., Montreal, 1971; Can. Med. Research Council postdoctoral fellow St. Elizabeths Hosp., NIMH, Washington, 1971-73, Fogarty Internat. vis. fellow, 1973-74; ind. writer-in-residence Mansfield Center, Conn., 1974-78, Chapel Hill, N.C., 1982—; research asst. prof. anatomy U. N.C. Sch. Medicine, Chapel Hill, 1981—; cons. in field. Contbr. articles to profl. jours. Miles fellow, 1974—. Mem. Soc. for Neurosci., N.C. Soc. for Neurosci., Internat. Soc. for Developmental Neurosci., AAAS. Current Work: Neuroscience; developmental neurobiology; immunocytochemistry; experimental creative writing; germanistic; theory of modern 20th century novel; the concept of relativity theory in creative writing; philology. Subspecialties: Neurobiology; Regeneration. Home: 106 Marion Way Robin's Wood Chapel Hill NC 27514 Office: 330 Swing Bldg Dept Anatomy U NC Med Sch Chapel Hill NC 27514

KREBS, HERMAN ALLEN, chemist; b. Louisville, Jan. 27, 1953; s. Adolph William and Delores (Young) K.; m. Pamela Renee Ortmann, June 5, 1982; stepchildren—Wendy E. Hixson, Gina R. Hixson. B.S., U. Louisville, 1975. Chemist Nat. Inst. Drug Abuse Addiction Research Ctr., Lexington, KY., 1975-79; research chemist EPA, Research Triangle Park, N.C., 1979-81; chemist A.H. Robins, Richmond, Va., 1981—. Mem. Am. Chem. Soc. Current work: Developing analytical methods for the determination of drugs and their metabolites in biological fluids and tissues. Subspecialty: Analytical chemistry. Home: 950 Bramwell Rd Richmond VA 23225 Office: AH Robins 1211 Sherwood Ave Richmond VA 23211

KREFT, ANTHONY FRANK, III, medicinal chemist; b. Detroit, May 28, 1948; s. Anthony Frank Jr. and Jane Teresa (Miedlar) K.; m. Margaret Mary Doyle, Aug. 26, 1979. B.S., U. Mich., 1970; M.S., Columbia U., 1973, Ph.D., 1976. Postdoctoral research fellow Stanford U., Calif., 1976-78; supr., med. chemist Wyeth Labs, Phila., 1978—. Patentee in field. Mem. Am. Chem. Soc., Phila. Organic Chemists Club. Democrat. Roman Catholic. Clubs: Lower Providence Rod and Gun (Audubon, Pa.); Trout Unltd. Current work: Design and synthesis of compounds which modulate the synthesis or effects of the arachidonic acid cascade. Subspecialties: Medicinal chemistry; Immunology (medicine). Home: Apt 466 1027 Valley Forge Rd Devon PA 19333 Office: Wyeth Labs PO Box 8299 Philadelphia PA 19101

KREH, RICHARD EDWARD, forester, researcher; b. Waterbury, Conn., Dec. 22, 1941; s. Walter Edward and Adeline J. (Vigna) K.; m. Connie Louise Tobias, June 9, 1970; children—Melissa Ann, Richard Edward Jr. B.S., U. Conn., 1969; M.S., Va. Poly. Inst. and State U., 1974. Research assoc. Reynolds Homestead Research Ctr. Va. Poly. Inst. & State Univ., Critz, Va., 1969—. Contbr. articles to profl. jours. Coach, Little League, Critz, 1981-83; asst. scoutmaster council Boy Scouts Am., Critz, 1983-84; pres. Athletic Booster Club High Sch., Stuart, Va., 1984-85. Served with USNR, 1962-66; Pacific. Decorated Vietnam Service medal, Nat. Def. medal. Mem. Soc. Am. Foresters, Va. Acad. Sci., Sigma Xi. Democrat. Current work: Forest soil productivity as affected by harvest techniques; forest watershed studies on eroision and nutrient dynamics; forest nursery quality. Subspecialties: Forestry; Soil science. Office: Reynolds Homestead Research Ctr Va Poly Inst & State U Critz VA 24082

KREID, DENNIS KARL, mechanical engineer; b. Austin, Minn.; s. Otto Fredrick Karl and Dorothy Helen (Christensen) K.; m. Sherilyn K. Griffel, Sept. 14, 1963 (dec. 1968); m. Susan Elizabeth Nelson, June 20, 1970; children—Elizabeth Ann, Jennifer Dorothy. B.S.M.E., U. Minn., 1964, M.S.M.E., 1966, Ph.D. in Mech. Engring., 1970. Asst. prof. mech. engring. Wash. State U., Pullman, 1970-72, Tenn. Tech. U., Cookeville, 1972-75; staff scientist Battelle Northwest Lab., Richland, Wash., 1975—; sr. postdoctoral fellow Nat. Ctr. Atmospheric Research, Boulder, Colo., 1974-75; ASME Congl. fellow, legis. asst. sci./energy to Sen. S. Gorton of Wash., Washington, 1980. Contbr. articles to profl. jours. Mem. ASME (fluid mechs. com. 1973—, pub. affairs governing bd. 1984—), Columbia Basin Flycasters (treas. 1983-84, pres. 1985). Lutheran. Club: Richland Rod and Gun. Current work: Heat transfer, fluid mechanics, thermodynamics, nuclear waste management. Subspecialties: Mechanical engineering; Nuclear fission. Office: Battelle Northwest Battelle Blvd Richland WA 99352

KREIMER-BIRNBAUM, F, biochemist, researcher, director; b. Buenos Aires, Argentina, Aug. 6, 1937; came to U.S., 1964; d. Isaac and Sarah (Katz) K.; m. Abraham S. Birnbaum, Dec. 30, 1958; children—A. Edward, Ron A. B.S., Nat. U. Buenos Aires, 1960, M.S., 1961, Ph.D., 1964; postgrad. SUNY-Buffalo, 1964-66. Research instr. SUNY, Buffalo, 1964-66, research assoc., 1966-68, research asst. prof., 1969-75; assoc. prof. Med. Coll. Ohio, Toledo, 1975-78; dir. research dept. St. Vincent Med. Ctr., Toledo, 1979—; mem. sci. adv. bd. Am. Porphyria Found., Marion, Ohio, 1982—. Albert Einstein Found. fellow, 1960; Nat. U. Buenos Aires fellow, 1960; NRC Argentina fellow, 1961-63. Mem. Am. Chem. Soc., AAAS, Am. Soc. Hematology, Am. Soc. Human Genetics, Am. Fedn. Clin. Research, Ohio Acad. Scis. (v.p. elect med. scis. sect.). Current work: Biochemical and genetic studies in Porphyrias; lead poisoning; Porphyrins as tumor localizers and photosensitizers. Subspecialties: Biochemistry (biology); Cancer research (medicine). Office: St Vincent Med Center 2213 Cherry St Toledo OH 43608

KREISLER, MICHAEL NORMAN, physicist, educator; b. N.Y.C., Oct. 30, 1940; s. Sol and Florence Dorothy (Korn) K.; m. Barbara Hope Laurence, Aug. 24, 1963; children—David Paul, Michele Ann, Jeffrey Scott. A.B., Princeton U., 1962; M.S., Stanford U., 1963, Ph.D. in Physics, 1966. Instr. dept. physics Princeton U., N.J., 1966-68, asst. prof., 1969-72; assoc. prof. dept. physics, U. Mass., Amherst-1972-76, prof., 1976—, assoc. dean Grad. Sch., 1975-77, dir. Marine Sta. Research Facility, chmn. marine scis. program, dir. office of research services; sci. assoc. elem. particles div. CERN, Geneva, Switzerland, 1978-79; cons. Lawrence Livermore Labs., Calif., Los Alamos Nat. Labs., N.Mex. Contbr. numerous articles to profl. publs. NSF grantee. Mem. Am. Phys. Soc., Phi Beta Kappa, Sigma Xi. Current work: Experimental elementary particle physics; search for rare phenomena; development of new approaches to data analysis and acquisition; macron accelerators; impact fusion. Subspecialties: Particle physics; Nuclear fusion. Office: Dept Physics GRC Tower C U Mass Amherst MA 01003

KREMKAU, FREDERICK W., medical researcher, educator; b. Mechanicsburg, Pa., Apr. 30, 1940; s. Ward Joseph and Alice Melda (Wineberg) K.; m. Lillian Ruth Beasley, Sept. 2, 1967; 1 son, Jonathan Stephen. B.E.E., Cornell U., 1963; M.S., U. Rochester, 1969, Ph.D., 1972. Registered profl. engr., N.C., Conn. Research instr. medicine Bowman Gray Sch. Medicine, Wake Forest U., Winston-Salem, N.C., 1971-74, research asst. prof., 1974-80, assoc. prof., 1980-81; assoc. prof. diagnostic radiology Yale U. Sch. Medicine, 1981-85; prof., dir. Ctr. for Med. Ultrasound, Bowman Gray Sch. Medicine, 1985—. Author: Diagnostic Ultrasound: Principles, Instrumentation and Exercises, 1980, 84; also articles. Served to lt. U.S. Navy, 1963-67. NDEA fellow, 1968-69. Am. Coll. Radiology, Radiol. Soc. N.Am.; Fellow Am. Inst. Ultrasound in Medicine (dir., Presdl. recognition award 1981). Acoustical Soc. Am., mem. IEEE (sr.), N.Y. Acad. Scis., AAAS, Am. Assn. Physicists in Medicine, Sigma Xi. Current Work: Ultrasonic molecular absorption mechanisms; acoustic properties of tissues; biological effects of ultrasound; safety of diagnostic ultrasound. Subspecialties: Imaging technology; Acoustical engineering. Home: 5104 Huntcliff Trail Winston-Salem NC 27104 Office: Ctr Med Ultrasound Bowman Gray Sch Medicine Winston-Salem NC 27103

KRENKEL, PETER ASHTON, engineer, educator, university dean; b. San Francisco, Jan. 3, 1930; s. Harry Nichols and Daisy Genevieve (Ashton) K.; m. Jessica Ann Jones, 1985. A.A., Coll. City San Francisco, 1952; B.S. U. Calif.-Berkeley, 1956, M.S., 1958, Ph.D., 1960. Registered profl. engr., Ga., Tenn., Nev., N.C. Instr. U. Calif.-Berkeley, 1958-60; founder Assoc. Air and Water Resources Engrs., Inc., Nashville, 1968—; prof., chmn. dept. environ. and water resources engring. Vanderbilt U., Nashville, 1960-73; dir. div. environ. planning TVA, 1974-78; exec. dir. Water Resources Ctr., U. Nev.-Reno, 1978-82, dean Coll. Engring., 1982—; disting. lectr. Am. Inst. Chem. Engrs.; cons. WHO, Internat. Joint Commn. Gt. Lakes Water Quality, EPA, U.S. Dept. Energy, Roy F. Weston Inc.; chmn. thermal pollution panel Nat. Water Commn., Washington, 1970—, Tenn. Air Conservation Commn., 1971—. Author: (with V. Novotny) Water Quality Management, 1980. Editor: (with F.L. Parker) Thermal Pollution Biological Aspects, 1970; Thermal Pollution Engineering Aspects, 1970; Water Quality Monitoring in Europe, 1972; Heavy Metals in the Aquatic Environment, 1974. Contbr. numerous articles on environ. control to profl. jours. Pres. Tenn. Lung Assn., 1974-75. Served with AUS, 1953-55. Recipient Skill, Integrity and Responsibility award Am. Gen. Contractors, 1984; USPHS fellow, 1963. Mem. Am. Water Works Assn., Water Pollution Control Fedn. (bd. control), Air Pollution Control Assn., Am. Pub. Health Assn., Am. Inst. Chem. Engrs., ASCE (Outstanding Research San. Engring. award 1963), Internat. Assn. Water Pollution Research (governing bd.), Am. Acad. Environ. Engring., Sigma Xi, Tau Beta Pi, Chi Epsilon. Home: 3500 Cashill Blvd Reno NV 89509

KRESGE, EDWARD NATHAN, research scientist; b. Noxen, Pa., Aug. 14, 1935; s. Dolores E. DeYoung, Apr. 11, 1961; children—John E., Susan E. B.S., U. Tampa, 1957; Ph.D., U. Fla.-Gainesville, 1961. Chemist Esso Research & Engring., Linden, N.J., 1961-68; research assoc. Enjay Polymer Labs., Linden, 1968-72; sr. research assoc. Exxon Chem. Co., Linden, 1972-78, chief polymer scientist, 1978—; lectr. Ctr. for Profl. Advancement, East Brunswick, N.J., 1980—. Chmn. editorial bd. Rubber Chemistry and Tech., 1981—. Contbr. articles to profl. jours., Patentee in field. Vice-pres. Watchung Sch. Bd., N.J., 1979. Recipient Inventors award U.S. Patent Office, 1976. Mem. Am. Chem. Soc. (councilor rubber div. 1979—), AAAS, N.Y. Acad. Scis. Current work: Research on new elastomers and polymer blends and composites. Subspecialties: Polymer chemistry; Polymers (materials science). Office: Exxon Chem Co PO Box 45 Linden NJ 07036

KRESSE, HERMAN JOSEPH, chemist, toxicologist; b. Luxora, Ark., Apr. 9, 1929; s. Herman Joseph and Felicia Emma (Paramore) K.; m. Patricia Ann Bridges, June 12, 1950; children—Mark, Joe, John, Matthew, Susan, Stephen, Geoffrey, Margaret. B.S., U. Central Ark., 1951; M.S., U. Tex., 1977. Chemist, Internat. Creosoting Co., Texarkana, Tex., 1951-55, St. Regis Paper Co., Dallas, 1955-60; sales dir. Conoco Corp., Houston, 1960-69; tech. dir. Chemola Corp., Houston, 1970-74; pres. M.B.A. Labs., Houston, 1974—. Patentee in field. Served to 1st lt. USAR, 1951-68. Mem. Am. Chem. Soc., Assn. Ofcl. Analytical Chemists, Am. Pub. Health Assn., Water and Wastewater Analysts Assn. (pres. 1983-84, cert. chief chemist). Democrat. Roman Catholic. Current work: Environmental chemical hazard testing. Subspecialties: Environmental chemistry; Environmental toxicology. Home: 7602 Marinette St Houston TX 77074 Office: MBA Labs 340 S 66th St Houston TX 77011

KRESSEL, HENRY, electronic company executive; b. Vienna, Jan. 24, 1934; came to U.S., 1946, naturalized, 1955; s. Aaron and Hudi (Zauderer) K.; m. Bertha Horowitz, Sept. 16, 1956; children—Aron, Kim. B.S. magna cum laude, Yeshiva U., 1955; M.S., Harvard U., 1956; M.B.A., U. Pa., 1959, Ph.D. (David Sarnoff fellow), 1965. Engr. Solid State div. RCA, 1959-61, engring. leader, 1961-63, 65-66; mem. tech. staff RCA David Sarnoff Research Center, 1966-70, head semicondr. device research, 1970-78, dir. materials research lab., 1978-79, staff v.p. solid state research, Princeton, N.J., 1979-83; mng. dir. E.M. Warburg, Pincus & Co., N.Y.C., 1983—; regents' lectr. U. Calif., San Diego, 1978-79; bd. dirs. Yeshiva U. Research Inst., 1979-84; cons. solar energy U.S. ERDA, 1975. Author: Semiconductor Lasers and Heterojunction LED's, 1977; editor: Characterization of Epitaxial Semiconductor Films, 1976, Semiconductor Devices for Optical Communication, 1980; asso. editor: IEEE Jour. Quantum Electronics, 1978-81; Contbr. numerous articles to sci. jours. Served with Fin. Corps U.S. Army, 1959. Recipient David Sarnoff award RCA, 1974, Bevel award Yeshiva U., 1980. Fellow IEEE (David Sarnoff award 1985, pres. Quantum Electronics and Applications Soc. 1978-79), Am. Phys. Soc.; mem. AIME, Nat. Acad. Engring. Patentee in field. Current Work: Management of electronic corporations. Subspecialties: Superconductors; Microchip technology (engineering). Home: 529 Riverside Dr Elizabeth NJ 07208 Office: E M Warburg Pincus & Co 466 Lexington Ave New York NY 10017

KRETCHMER, NORMAN, pediatrician, nutritional science educator; b. N.Y.C., Jan. 20, 1923; s. Emanuel and Sue (Gross) K.; m. Muriel Reiter, Sept. 10, 1942; children—Pamela Sue, Paul Jay, Steven David. B.S., Cornell U., 1944; M.S., U. Minn., 1945, Ph.D., 1947; M.D., SUNY, N.Y.C., 1952, U. Bern, Switzerland, 1978. Diplomate: Am. Bd. Pediatrics. Teaching asst. U. Minn., 1944-47; asst. prof. pathology and biochemistry U. Vt., 1947-48; fellow, research asso. pathology L.I. Coll. Medicine, 1947-52; lectr. biology Bklyn. Coll., 1950-55; intern Montefiore Hosp., N.Y.C., 1952-53; mem. faculty Cornell U. Med. Sch., N.Y.C., 1953-59, assoc. prof. pediatrics, 1958-59; mem. faculty Stanford U., Palo Alto, Calif., 1959-74, prof. pediatrics, 1959-74, exec. head dept., 1959-69, chief div. devel. biology, 1969-72, chmn. program human biology, 1969-72, chief sect. developmental medicine, 1972, clin. prof. pediatrics, 1974; acting dir. Nat. Inst. Aging, NIH, Bethesda, Md., 1974-75; dir. Nat. Inst. Child Health and Human Devel., 1974-81; prof. dept nutritional scis. U. Calif., Berkeley, 1981—, chmn. dept. nutritional scis., 1983—, prof. pediatrics and obstetrics, San Francisco, 1981; mem. nat. bd. Ben Gurion U. of the Negev; mem. sci. council Inst. de la Vie, Paris, 1974—; mem. bd. U.S.A.-Israel Sci. Found., 1974—; mem. Aide Pour la Recherche Medicale á l'Enfance; cons. NSF; mem. numerous adv. and sci. coms. Author, editor publs. in field. Served with USAAF, 1942-43. Commonwealth Fund fellow, 1952-54, 57, 65-66; Guggenheim fellow, 1973-74; recipient Superior Service award HEW, 1977. Fellow Am. Acad. Pediatrics (E. Mead Johnson award 1958, Borden award 1969), AAAS; mem. Inst. of Medicine of Nat. Acad. Sci., AAUP, Am. Chem. Soc., Am. Pediatrics Soc. (pres. 1979), Am. Soc. Biol. Chemists, Am. Soc. Human Genetics, Am. Soc. Clin. Investigation (council 1964-67), Assn. Am. Med. Colls., Harvey Soc., Soc. Growth and Devel., Soc. Pediatric Research (pres. 1967-68), Western Soc. Pediatric Research (pres. 1966-67), Internat. Orgn. Study Human Devel. (pres. 1970—), Am. Inst. Biol. Scis., Am. Soc. Clin. Investigation, Perinatal Research Soc., Internat. Pediatric Assn. (exec. com. 1974-77), Sigma Xi, Alpha Omega Alpha; hon. mem. numerous fgn. med socs. Current work: Enzymatic adaptations to nutrients with an emphasis on intestinal enzymes; nutritional assessment and status of immigrant school children. Subspecialties: Pediatrics; Maternal and fetal medicine. Office: Dept of Nutritional Sciences Univ of California Morgan Hall Room 309C Berkeley CA 94720

KREVANS, JULIUS RICHARD, university chancellor, physician; b. N.Y.C., May 1, 1924; s. Sol and Anita (Makovetsky) K.; m. Patricia N. Abrams, May 28, 1950; children: Nita, Julius R., Rachel, Sarah, Nora Kate. B.S. Arts and Scis, N.Y. U., 1943, M.D., 1946. Diplomate: Am. Bd. Internal Med. Intern, then resident Johns Hopkins Med. Sch. Hosp., mem. faculty, until 1970, dean acad. affairs, 1969-70; physician in chief Balt. City Hosp., 1963-69; prof. medicine U. Calif. at San Francisco, 1970—, dean Sch. Medicine, 1971-82, chancellor. Contbr. articles on hematology, internal med. profl. jours. Served with M.C. AUS, 1948-50. Mem. A.C.P., Assn. Am. Physicians. Subspecialty: Educational administration. Office: U Calif San Francisco CA 94143

KRIBEL, ROBERT EDWARD, physics educator, consultant; b. Pitts., Sept. 17, 1937; s. Joseph P. and Helen M. (Rausch) K.; m. Ruth Ann Gropelli, June 11, 1959; children—Karen Ann, Robert E., Jr., Mark P., Gary P. B.S., Notre Dame U., 1959; M.S., U. of Calif.-San Diego, 1966, Ph.D., 1968. Staff assoc. Gen. Atomic Inc., San Diego, 1963-65, 68-70; asst. prof. Drake U., Des Moines, Iowa, 1970-73; vis. assoc. prof. Cornell U., Ithaca, N.Y., 1973-74; head physics dept. James Madison U., Harrisonburg, Va., 1974-78, Auburn U., Auburn, Ala., 1978—; cons., Los Alamos Nat. Lab., 1983—, Sandia Nat. Lab. Contbr. articles to prof. jours. Served to lt., USN, 1959-62. Mem. Am. Physical Soc., AAAS, Sigma Xi. Subspecialties: Nuclear fusion; Plasma physics. Home: 408 Dixie Dr Auburn AL 36830 Office: Physics Dept Auburn Univ Auburn AL 36849

KRICKA, HANNA HALYNA, pharmaceutical company executive; b. Czestochowa, Poland, Jan. 1, 1939; came to U.S., 1950, naturalized, 1957; d. Leonid and Helena (Sachnovska) Kryckyj. B.S., Drexel Inst. Tech., 1962; M.S. in Info. Scis, Drexel U., 1971; M.S. in Bus. Policy, Columbia U., 1981. Lit. scientist Merck Sharp & Dohme Research Labs., 1963-64; sr. lit. scientist Merrell-Nat., 1964-69; registration and info. scientist E.R. Squibb & Co. Inc., 1970; assoc. dir. clin. info., sr. info. scientist Hoechst Pharms. Inc., 1971-73; dir. sci. info. Bristol Myers Internat., 1973—. Mem. Am. Chem. Soc., N.Y. Acad. Scis., Am. Soc. for Info. Sci., Assn. for Computing Machinery, Drug Info. Assn., Am. Mgmt. Assn., Nat. Ukrainian Engrs. Soc. Am. (exec. bd.), Assoc. Info. Mgrs. Republican. Byzantine Catholic. Club: Columbia (N.Y.C.). Current Work: Build customized data bases for information storage and retrieval in response to global regulatory and registrational requirements in the pharmaceutical industry. Subspecialties: Information systems, storage, and retrieval (computer science); Information systems (Information science). Home: 215 E 80th St Penthouse J New York NY 10021 Office: 345 Park Ave New York NY 10154

KRIEGER, ALLEN STEPHEN, physicist, researcher; b. N.Y.C., Feb. 23, 1941; s. Georege and Minna (Berkman) K.; m. Jeanne Arnolde Kann, Feb. 25, 1966; children—Sara, Ruth. B.S., MIT, 1962, Ph.D., 1967. Sr. scientist Am. Sci. and Engring. Inc., Cambridge, Mass., 1968-72, sr. staff scientist, 1973-79, acting dir. research, 1971-73, dir. research, 1974-76, v.p. space systems div., 1979-84, sr. v.p., 1984—. Contbr. articles to profl. jours. Mem. Am. Phys. Soc., Internat. Astrophys. Union, Am. Astron. Soc., (chmn. solar physics div. 1982-84). Current work: X-ray imaging solar physics; computer tomography for non-destructive examination. Subspecialty: Solar physics. Office: Am Sci and Engring Inc Fort Washington Cambridge MA 02139

KRIKORIAN, ABRAHAM DER, plant physiologist-biochemist, educator, researcher; b. Worcester, Mass., May 5, 1937; s. Abraham Der and Tarquohie Tashjian K. B.S., Mass. Coll. Pharmacy, 1959; Ph.D., Cornell U., 1965. Assoc. prof. biology SUNY-Stony Brook, 1971-81, assoc. prof. biochemistry, 1981—. Contbr. numerous articles to profl. jours.; Western Hemisphere editor: Annals of Botany, 1976-82; mem. editorial bd.: Jour. Ethnopharmacology, 1979—; plant sci. book rev. cons.: Quar. Rev. Biology, 1979—. Recipient Cosmos Achievement award NASA, 1975, 81. Mem. Beneficial Plant Assn. (adv. bd. 1979—), Soc. Econ. Bontany (mem. council 1975-80, v.p. 1981-82, pres. 1982-83), AAAS, Internat. Council Sci. Unions (subcom. on gravitational biology of com. space research), Am. Soc. for Gravitational and Space Biology (bd. govs. 1984—), Am. Soc. Pharmacognosy, Bot. Soc. Am., Am. Soc. Plant Physiologists, Scandanavian Soc. Plant Physiology, Internat. Soc. Plant Morphologists, Soc. Developmental Biology, Internat. Assn. Plant Tissue Culture. Current Work: Clonal stability; totipotency of higher plant cells in terms of morphogenesis and biochemical competence; plant space biology. Subspecialties: Plant cell and tissue culture; Plant physiology (agriculture). Office: Dept Biochemistry SUNY Stony Brook NY 11794

KRIKORIAN, OSCAR HAROLD, chemist; b. Fresno, Calif., Nov. 22, 1930; s. Hagop Bedros and Aghavnie (Mardirosian) K.; m. Marilyn Ann Kooyumjian, July 18, 1953; children: Deborah, Cheryl Krikorian Scolari. B.S. in Chemistry, Calif. State U.-Fresno, 1952; Ph.D. in Chemistry, U.Calif.-Berkeley, 1955. Chemist Lawrence Livermore (Calif.) Nat. Lab., 1955—. Contbr. over 60 sci. and tech. articles to profl. publs. Fellow Am. Inst. Chemists; mem. Am. Chem. Soc. Patentee in field. Current Work: Development of processes and technology for applications to magnetic fusion and hydrogen production. Subspecialties: High temperature chemistry; Thermodynamics. Office: Lawrence Livermore Nat Lab PO Box 808 L-369 Livermore CA 94550

KRIMIGIS, STAMATIOS MIKE, physicist, researcher, consultant; b. Chios, Greece, Sept. 10, 1938; s. Michael and Angeliki (Tsetseris) K.; m. Evangelia Kantas, Feb. 11, 1968; children: Michael, John. B.S., U. Minn., 1961; M.S., U. Iowa, 1963, Ph.D., 1965. Research assoc. and asst. prof. physics U. Iowa, Iowa City, 1965-68; supr. space physics sect. Applied Physics Lab., Johns Hopkins U., Balt., 1968-74, supr. space physics and instrumentation group, 1974-81, chief scientist space dept., 1980—; mem. Space Sci. Bd., Nat. Acad. Scis. NRC, 1983—, cons.; mem. steering com. space sci. working group Assn. Am. Univs., 1982—. Contbr. over 130 articles to sci. jours.; author books on solar, interplanetary and magnetospheric plasma physics, cosmic rays, magnetospheres of Jupiter and Saturn. Recipient Exceptional Sci. Achievement medal NASA, 1981. Fellow Am. Geophys. Union; mem. Am. Phys. Soc., AAAS. Greek Orthodox. Current Work: Physics of Earth and planetary magnetospheres, the interplanetary medium, and the sun. Subspecialties: Space plasma physics; Planetary science. Home: 613 Cobblestone Ct Silver Spring MD 20904 Office: Applied Physics Lab Johns Hopkins U Laurel MD 20707

KRIMM, SAMUEL, physicist, educator; b. Morristown, N.J., Oct. 19, 1925; s. Irving and Ethel (Stein) K.; m. Marilyn Marcy Neveloff, June 26, 1949; children: David Robert, Daniel Joseph. B.S., Poly. Inst. Bklyn., 1947; M.A., Princeton U., 1949, Ph.D., 1950. Postdoctoral fellow U. Mich., Ann Arbor, 1950-52, mem. faculty, 1952—, prof. physics, 1963—, chmn. biophysics research div., 1976—, dir. program in protein structure and design, 1985—, assoc. dean research Coll. Lit., Sci. and Arts, 1972-75; mem. materials research adv. com. NSF, 1981—, chmn., 1984; cons. to industry. Author papers on vibrational spectroscopy, x-ray diffraction studies of natural and synthetic polymers. Served with USNR, 1944-46. Recipient Humboldt award, 1983; Textile Research Inst. fellow, 1947-50; NSF sr. postdoctoral fellow, 1962-63; sr. fellow U. Mich. Soc. Fellows, 1971-76. Fellow Am. Phys. Soc. (High Polymer Physics prize 1977, chmn. div. biol. physics 1979, div. councilor 1981, exec. com. 1983); mem. AAAS, Am. Chem. Soc., Am. Crystallographic Assn., Biophys. Soc., N.Y. Acad. Scis. Subspecialty: Biophysics (physics). Address: Dept Physics Univ Mich Ann Arbor MI 48109

KRINSKY, JEFFREY ALAN, systems engineer, educator; b. N.Y.C., Sept. 9, 1955; s. Dan and Phyllis (Chinsky) K. B.S. with honors, Fla. Inst. Tech., 1976, M.S. in Physics, 1979. Electronics design engr. Telephonics, Huntington, N.Y., 1977; project engr. Martin Marietta, Kennedy Space Center, Fla., 1979-80; sr. systems engineer Harris Corp., Melbourne, Fla., 1980-85; sr. specialist engr. physics tech. group Boeing Co., Seattle, 1985—; adj. prof. math., computer sci., physics and mech. engring. Fla. Inst. Tech., Melbourne, 1979-85; vis. indsl. prof. math., sci. and elec. engring. Brevard Community Coll., 1983-85; sci. fair judge Fla. Jr. Acad. Scis., 1983—. Mem. AIAA, Am. Optical Soc., Am. Inst. Physics, Laser Inst. Am., Sigma Pi Sigma. Current Work: Using computers to control experiments, collect data, and perform sophisticated data reduction in experiments that would be impractical to do by hand. Subspecialties: Integrated circuits; Laser efficiency. Home: 16630 126th St Renton WA 98058 Also: 65 Devon Rd Bethpage NY 11714 Office: Boeing Co PO Box 3707 Seattle WA 98124

KRIPPNER, STANLEY CURTIS, psychologist, educator; b. Edgerton, Wis., Oct. 4, 1932; s. Carroll Porter and Ruth Genevieve (Volenberg) K.; m. Lelie Anne Harris, June 25, 1966; stepchildren—Caron, Robert. B.S., U. Wis., 1954; M.A., Northwestern U., 1957, Ph.D., 1961; Ph.D. (hon.), U. Humanistic Studies, 1982. Dir. Child Study Ctr., Kent (Ohio) State U., 1961-64; dir. Dream Lab., Maimonides Med. Ctr., Bklyn., 1964-73; faculty Saybrook Inst., San Francisco, 1973—, dean of faculty, 1980-83, dir. Ctr. for Consciousness Studies, 1983—; vis. prof. U. P.R., 1972, Sonoma State U., 1972-73, U. Life Scis., Bogotá, Colombia, 1974, Inst. Psychodrana and Humanistic Psychology, Caracas, Venezuela, 1985. Author: Song of the Siren, 1975, Human Possibilities, 1980, (with M. Ullman) Dream Telepathy, 1973, (with A. Villoldo) The Realms of Healing, 1976; editor: Advances in Parapsychol. Research, 1977, 78, 82, 84. Mem. adv. bd. A.R.E. Clinic, 1970, Found. for Mind Research, 1967; bd. dirs. Acad. Religion and Psychical Research, Washington, 1972. Recipient award for service to youth YMCA, 1959; citation of merit Nat.Assn. Gifted Children, 1972; cert. of recognition U.S. Office Edn., 1976; colleague Creative Problem-Solving Inst., 1980. Fellow Am. Soc. Clin. Hypnosis, Am. Psychol. Assn., Soc. Sci. Study Sex; mem. Am. Soc. Psychical Research, Am. Acad. Social and Polit. Scis, Nat. Assn. Gifted Children (dir. 1965-84), Nat. Assn. Creative Children and Adults (dir. 1975—), AAAS, Am. Ednl. Research Assn., Assn. for Counseling and Devel., Assn. for Transpersonal Psychology, Assn. for Psychophysiol. Study of Sleep, Biofeedback Soc. Am., Council for Exceptional Children, Internat. Soc. Gen. Semantics, Menninger Found., Nat. Soc. for Study of Edn., Soc. for Study of Religion, Soc. for Clin. and Exptl. Hypnosis, World Future Soc., InterAm. Psychol. Assn., Parapsychol. Assn. (pres. 1982-83), Assn. for Humanistic Psychology (pres. 1974-75). Presbyterian. Current Work: Study of parapsychological phenomena in relation to altered states of consciousness; study of possible parapsychological aspects of unorthodox healing. Subspecialty: Cognition. Home: 79 Woodland Rd Fairfax CA 94930 Office: 1772 Vallejo St San Francisco CA 94123

KRISHNA, NEPALLI RAMA, biophysicist, educator; b. Masulipatam, India, Nov. 20, 1945; came to U.S., 1971; s. Nepalli Gopala Krishna and Nepalli Jayaprada Potharaju Murthy. B.Sc. with honors, Andhra U., India, 1965, M.Sc., 1966; Ph.D., Indian Inst. Tech., 1972. Postdoctoral fellow Ga. Inst. Tech., Atlanta, 1972-74; research assoc. U. Alta. (Can.), Edmonton, 1974-76; assoc. scientist Cancer Center, U. Ala., Birmingham, 1976—, asst. prof. physics, 1977—, asst. prof. biochemistry, 1979-85, assoc. prof. biochemistry, 1985—, dir. NMR Core Facility, 1984—; cons. Ortho Pharm. Corp., Raritan, N.J., 1981—. Contbr. articles to profl. jours. Recipient Rao Meml. prize Andhra U., 1966, Metcalfe Gold metal, 1966; Scholar award Leukemia Soc. Am., 1982. Mem. Am. Phys. Soc., Biophys. Soc., Smithsonian Instn. Current Work: Structure-function studies of peptide hormones, proteins and nucleic acids; immunoregulatory peptides; neurotoxins; biomolecular conformational studies by nuclear magnetic resonance spectroscopy; development of NMR techniques; protein dynamics. Subspecialties: Biophysics (biology); Nuclear magnetic resonance. Office: Dept Biochemistry U Ala in Birmingham Univ Sta CHSB-Room B31 Birmingham AL 35294

KRISHNAN, PALLASSANA NARAYANIER, chemistry, educator; b. Edapal, India, Nov. 1, 1941; came to U.S., 1962; s. Pallassana Subramainam Narayanan and C.P. Ananda Lakshmi; m. Padma Srinivas, Sept. 2, 1971; 1 child, Rajesh. B.S., Victoria Coll., India, 1962; Ph.D., Temple U., 1968. Research assoc. U. Ariz., Tucson, 1968-69, So. Ill. U., Carbondale, 1969-70; prof. Coppin State Coll., Balt., 1970—; cons. Nat. Bur. Standards, 1978-79, Naval Research Lab., 1983. Vice pres. Kerala Cultural Assn., Washington Balt. and Md., 1982. NSF research grantee, 1976-78. Mem. Am. Chem. Soc. Current Work: Raman spectroscopy; optical fibers; lasers; high temperature spectroscopy. Subspecialties: Physical chemistry; Laser spectroscopy. Home: 1 Dakin Ct Baltimore MD 21234 Office: Coppin State College 2500 W North Ave Baltimore MD 21216

KRISNAMOORTHY, MUKKAI SUBRAMANIAM, computer science educator; b. Nagerkoil, Madras, India, Jan. 20, 1948; came to U.S., 1979; s. Mukkai Subramaniam and Parvathi Rajam. M.S., Indian Inst. Tech., Kanpur, 1971, Ph.D., 1976. Asst. prof. Indian Inst. Tech., Kanpur, 1977-80; asst. prof. computer sci. Rensselaer Poly. Inst., Troy, N.Y., 1980—. Mem. IEEE, Assn. for Computing Machinery, Am. Math. Soc., Soc. Indsl. and Applied Math. Current Work: Design and analysis of algorithms for different models of computation. Subspecialties: Algorithms; Foundations of computer science.

KRISTAL, MARK BENNETT, psychology researcher, educator; b. N.Y.C., Apr. 19, 1944; s. Emanuel E. and Helen B. (Goldin) K.; m. Tova Iskovits, Oct. 8, 1967; 1 child, Morgan H. B.A., Rutgers U., 1965; M.S., Kans. State U., 1970, Ph.D., 1971. Postdoctoral trainee Jackson Lab., Bar Harbor, Maine, 1971-73; asst. prof. SUNY-Buffalo, 1973-77, assoc. prof. psychology, 1978—; B.A., B.S. faculty com. Regents Coll. Degrees, Albany, N.Y., 1979—; dir. biopsychology program SUNY, Buffalo, 1978—. Contbr. articles to profl. jours. Grantee NSF, NIH, SUNY. Mem. Eastern Psychol. Assn., Animal Behavior Soc., Soc. for Neuroscience, AAAS. Current work: Physiol. bases (endocrine and neural) for maternal behavior, sexual behavior, aggression, pain, ingestion. Subspecialties: Psychobiology; Behaviorism. Home: 122 Old Farm Circle Williamsville NY 14221 Office: Dept Psychology State Univ NY 4230 Ridge Lea Amherst NY 14226

KRITCHEVSKY, DAVID, educator, biochemist; b. Kharkov, Russia, Jan. 25, 1920; came to U.S., 1923, naturalized, 1929; s. Jacob and Leah (Kritchevsky) K.; m. Evelyn Sholtes, Dec. 21, 1947; children—Barbara Ann, Janice Eileen, Stephen Bennett. B.S., U. Chgo., 1939, M.S., 1942; Ph.D., Northwestern U., 1948. Chemist Ninol Labs., Chgo., 1939-46; postdoctoral fellow Fed. Inst. Tech., Zurich, Switzerland, 1948-49; biochemist Radiation Lab., U. Calif. at Berkeley, 1950-52, Lederle Labs., Pearl River, N.Y., 1952-57, Wistar Inst., Phila., 1957—; prof. biochemistry Sch. Vet. Medicine, U. Pa., Phila., 1965—; prof. biochemistry Sch. Medicine, U. Pa., 1970—, chmn. grad. group molecular biology, 1972-84; Mem. USPHS study sect. Nat. Heart Inst., 1964-68, 72-76; chmn. research com. Spl. Dairy Industry Bd., 1963-70; mem. food and nutrition bd. Nat. Acad. Sci., 1976-82. Author: Cholesterol, 1958, also numerous articles.; Editor: (with G. Litwack) Actions of Hormones on Molecular Processes, 1964; co-editor: (with R. Paoletti) Advances in Lipid Research, 1963—, (with P. Nair) The Bile Acids, 1971; Western Hemisphere editor Atherosclerosis. Recipient Research Career award Nat. Heart Inst., 1962, award Am. Coll. Nutrition, 1978. Mem. Am. Inst. Nutrition (Borden award 1974, pres. 1979), Am. Soc. Biol. Chemists, AAAS, Am. Chem. Soc. (award Phila. sect. 1977), Soc. Exptl. Biology and Medicine (pres. 1985-86), Arteriosclerosis Council, Am. Heart Assn., Am. Soc. Oil Chemists (chmn. methods com. 1963-64), Internat. Soc. Fat Research. Research on role vehicle when cholesterol and fat produces atherosclerosis in rabbits, effects saturated and unsaturated fat, deposition orally administered cholesterol in aorta man and rabbit Research on role vehicle when cholesterol and fat produces atherosclerosis in rabbits, effects saturated and unsaturated fat, deposition orally administered cholesterol in aorta man and rabbit. Current Work: Lipid metabolism; experimental atherosclerosis: cholesterol metabolism; nutrition; aging. Subspecialties: Biochemistry (biology); Nutrition (biology). Home: 136 Lee Circle Bryn Mawr PA 19010 Office: Wistar Inst 36th and Spruce Sts Philadelphia PA 19104

KRNJEVIC, KRESIMIR IVAN, neurophysiologist; b. Zagreb, Croatia, Yugoslavia, Sept. 7, 1927; s. Juraj and Nada (Hirsl) K.; m. Jeanne Bowyer, Sept. 27, 1954; children—Peter Juraj, Nicholas John. M.B., Ch.B., Edinburgh U., 1949, B.Sc. in Physiology, 1951, Ph.D., 1953. Demonstrator in physiology Edinburgh U., 1950-54; research assoc., asst. prof. physiology and biophysics U. Wash., 1954-56; vis. fellow, John Curtin Sch. Med. Research, Australian Nat. U., Canberra, 1956-58; prin. then sr. prin. Sci. Research Officer, A.R.C. Inst. Animal Physiology, Babraham, Cambridge, Eng., 1959-65; vis. prof., McGill U., Montreal, Que., Can., 1964-65, prof. physiology and anaesthesia research, 1965—, Joseph Morley Drake prof. physiology, chmn. dept. anaesthesia, dir. anesthesia research, 1978—; mem. council Internat. Union Physiol. Socs., 1983—; Forbes lectr., Woods Hole, 1978. Contbr. articles to profl. jours. Recipient Ellis prize, Edinburgh U., 1951, Sarrazin award Can. Physiol. Soc., 1984, Gairdner Found. Internat. award, 1984. Club: McGill Faculty. Current work: Electrophysiological investigations on chemical and electrical interactions between nerve cells in the brain and spinal cord. Subspecialties: Neurophysiology; Neuropharmacology. Home: 653 Belmont Ave Westmount PQ H3Y 2W3 Canada Office: 3655 Drummond St Montreal PQ H3G 1Y6 Canada

KROGH, LESTER CHRISTENSEN, chemist; b. Ruskin, Nebr., Aug. 22, 1925; s. Jens Clarence and Clara Elizabeth (Christensen) K.; m. Rosa Christina Knickrehm, Dec. 23, 1946; children—Christine Krogh Brown, Charles John. B.S. in Chem. Engring., U. Nebr., 1945, M.S. in Organic Chemistry, 1948; Ph.D. in Organic Chemistry, U. Minn., 1952. Sr. research chemist 3M, St. Paul, 1952-54, supr., mgr., asst. tech. dir., tech. dir., 1954-64, dir., corp. tech. planning and coordinating, 1964-69, gen. mgr. new bus. bentures div., 1969-70, exec. dir. central research labs., 1970-73, dir. v.p. comml. chemistry, research and devel. v.p., indsl. and comml. sector research and devel., 1981-82, v.p. research and devel., 1982—; dir. Eastern Heights State Bank; adviser Denver Research Inst., 1970-78; mem. study on exptl. incentive program NSF, 1972, mem. indsl. panel on sci. and tech., 1983—; chmn. bd. advisers grad. sch. U. Minn., 1984; mem. adv. council task force on comml. use of space NASA, 1984; mem. tech. adv. bd. MCC-Micro electronics and Computer Ctr., 1985. Patentee in field. Bd. dirs. Nat. Home Fashions League, Edn. Found., Inc., 1979-79, mem. adv. council, 1979-81, chmn. bd. dirs., 1979-81; chmn. Roseville PTA Area Council Curriculum Subcom., 1961-62; chmn. bd. dirs. Centennial United Methodist Ch., 1969-70, chmn. adminstrv. bd., 1981-84; mem. regional devel. com. TV Presence and Ministry Campaign of United Meth. Ch., 1981-82; mem. bd. regents Milw. Sch. Engring., 1984; bd. dirs. Sci. Mus. Minn., 1984. Served with USNR, 1944-46. Recipient Outstanding Achievement award U. Minn., 1984. Mem. Am. Chem. Soc. (chmn. centennial fin. com. 1972-76, mem. constitution and bylaws com. 1965-70, chmn., 1969-70, councilor Minn. sect. 1961-72; mem. council policy com. 1971-73, vice chmn. centennial coordinating com. 1972-76, mem. joint bd. council long range planning com. 1972-73, ad hoc adv. com. on property devel. 1979-80, chmn. ChemTech task force 1981-82, other coms.), AAAS, Am. Inst. chem. Engrs., Minn. Acad. Sci. (bd. dirs. 1971-75), Chem. Mfrs. Assn., Am. Indsl. Hygiene Found., Sigma Xi, Sigma Tau. Current work: General research administration, promotion of entrepreneurship and innovation, research in microgravity environment. Subspecialty: Research and development management. Office: 3M Ctr 220 14W Saint Paul MN 55144

KROHMER, JACK STEWART, radiological physicist, educator; b. Cleve., Nov. 7, 1921; s. Jacob and Violet Isabel (Armstrong) K.; m. Doris Elaine Lyman, Sept. 14, 1946; chlidren: Karen Elise Krohmer Carr, Jack Lyman, Candace Lynn Krohmer Blanchard. B.S., Western Res. U., Cleve., 1943, M.A., 1947; Ph.D., U. Tex., 1961. Diplomate: Am. Bd. Radiology, Am. Bd. Health Physics. Assoc. physics Western Res. U., Clev., 1947-57; prof. radiol. physics U. Tex. Southwestern Med. Sch., Dallas, 1957-63; chmn. dept. physics Roswell Park Meml. Inst., Buffalo, 1963-66; chief radiol. physics Geisinger Med. Center, 1966-72; mem. Radiol. Assocs. of Erie, Pa., 1972-79; prof. radiology and radiation oncology, dir. div. radiol. physics Wayne State U., Detroit, 1979-84; cons. in uses of radiation in treatment and diagnosis of disease and in biol. effects of radiation; pres. J.S. Krohmer, Ph.D., Inc.; Trustee Am. Bd. Radiology. Contbr. articles to profl. jours. Served to 1st lt. Chem. Warfare Service U.S. Army, 1943-46. Fellow Am. Coll. Radiology; mem. Am. Assn. Physicists in Medicine (pres. 1974-75, William D. Coolidge award 1985), Radiation Research Soc., Radiol. Soc. N.Am., Health Physics Soc. (Marie Curie award Gt. Lakes chpt. 1985), Am. Roentgen Ray Soc., Mich. Radiol. Soc. Republican. Presbyterian. Clubs: Grosse Pointe (Mich.) Yacht; Ill. Athletic (Chgo.). Current Work: Radiationimaging; low level effects of radiation; radiological shielding research, teaching and service functions in all aspects of the uses of radiation in the treatment and diagnosis of disease. Subspecialties: Imaging technology; Biophysics (biology). Home: 117 Highview Rd Georgetown TX 78628

KROMER, LAWRENCE FREDERICK, neurobiologist, educator; b. Sandusky, Ohio, Sept. 1, 1950; s. Rolland Frederick and Geraldine Susan (Bolish) K.; m. Tanya Marie Sandros, Apr. 2, 1977. B.A., U. Chgo., 1972, Ph.D., 1977. NIH fellow in histology U. Lund, Sweden, 1977-79; asst. research neuroscientist dept. neuroscis. U. Calif.-San Diego, 1979-81; asst. prof. anatomy and neurobiology U. Vt., Burlington, 1981-85; assoc. prof. dept. anatomy Georgetown U., Washington, 1985—. Alfred P. Sloan Found. fellow, 1980-84; Charles E. Culpepper fellow, 1983-84. Mem. Internat. Soc. for Developmental Neurosci., Am. Assn. Anatomists, AAAS, Soc. for Neurosci. Current Work: Teaching and research to analyze development and regeneration in the mammalian central nervous system using the intracephalic transplantation technique which allows the transplantation of embryonic neural tissue into the brain of adult and neonatal rodents. Subspecialties: Regeneration; Neurodevelopment. Office: Dept Anatomy Georgetown U Sch Medicine 3900 Reservoir Rd NW Washington DC 20007

KRONBERG, PHILIPP PAUL, astronomy and astrophysics educator, consultant; b. Toronto, Ont., Can., Sept. 16, 1939; s. Philipp and Jean Stewart (Davidson) K.; m. Roberta Beatrice Secord, Aug. 3, 1963; children: Paul Andrew, Martin Thomas, Michael Philipp Robert. B.Sc. in Engring. Physics, Queen's U., Kingston, Ont., 1961; M.Sc., Queen's U., 1963; Ph.D., U. Manchester, Eng., 1967. Lectr. physics U. Manchester and Jodrell Bank, U.K., 1966-68; asst. prof. astronomy U. Toronto, 1968-73, assoc. prof., 1973-78, prof., 1978—; sr. von Humboldt fellow and guest scientist Max-Planck Inst. Radioastronomie, Bonn, W. Ger., 1975-77; mem. NRC Assoc. Commn. on Astronomy, 1971-74, mem. grants com., 1974-78; mem., adv. com. for VLA Project in N.Mex. U.S. Nat. Radio Astronomy Obs., 1978-82, chmn., 1980; chmn. Assoc. U., Inc.; vis. com. Nat. Radio Astronomy Obs., 1981-82; von Humboldt fellow Max Planck Inst., 1980; mem. U. Toronto Research Bd., 1982—. Contbr. numerous articles on astronomy and astrophysics to profl. jours. Alexander von Humboldt fellow, 1975-77; Guggenheim fellow, 1985-86. Mem. Am. Astron. Soc., Can. Astron. Soc., Internat. Astron. Union. Anglican. Club: Boulevard. Current Work: Galactic and extragalactic astrophysics research, radio astronomy, consulting, research in astrophysics. Subspecialties: Radio and microwave astronomy; High energy astrophysics. Home: 33 Boarhill Dr Toronto (Agincourt) ON M1S 2L9 Canada Office: Dept Astronomy U Toronto 60 St George St Toronto ON M5S 1A7 Canada

KROON, PAULUS ARIE, biochemist; b. Rotterdam, Netherlands, June 1, 1945; came to U.S., 1968; s. Frederik Willem and Elisabet (Visser) K.; m. Lois Eileen Ferguson, Dec. 23, 1968; children—Lisa Michelle, Natasha Kristine, Joanna Elisabeth. B.S., U. Auckland, N.Z., 1967, M.S., 1968; M.S., Calif. Inst. Tech., 1970, Ph.D., 1974. Research assoc. U. Pitts., 1975-77; sr. research biochemist Merck, Sharp & Dohme Research Labs., Rahway, N.J., 1977-82, research fellow, 1982—. Contbr. articles to sci. jours. Mem. Fanwood Rescue Squad, N.J. Mem. Am. Heart Assn. (fellow council arteriosclerosis), Am. Soc. Biol. Chemists, Biophys. Soc., Biochem. Soc. (London). Presbyterian. Current work: Structure and function of plasma lipoproteins, molecular cloning and sequence determination of proteins involved in lipoprotein metabolism. Subspecialties: Molecular biology; Biophysics (biology). Home: 101 North Ave Fanwood NJ 07023 Office: Merck Sharp & Dohme Research Labs PO Box 2000 Rahway NJ 07023

KROTHAPALLI, RADHA KRISHNA, internist; b. Amarthalur, India, May 4, 1951; came to U.S., 1975; s. Raghavaiah and Lakshmi Narasamma (Parvathaneni) K.; m. Shirley Marie Hunt, Jan. 24, 1981. M.B.B.S., Guntur Med. Coll., India, 1973. Diplomate: Am. Bd. Internal Medicine, Am. Bd. Nephrology. Rotating intern Mo. Bapt. Hosp., St. Louis, 1976-77; resident in medicine Montgomery (Ala.) Internal Medicine Residency Program, 1977-80; fellow in nephrology Baylor Coll. Medicine, Houston, 1980-83, practice medicine specializing in nephrology, Montgomery, Ala. Author: Pseudomonas Peritonitis, 1982; contbr. chpts. to books, articles to profl. jours. Nat. Kidney Found. fellow, 1982-83. Mem. ACP, Am. Soc. Nephrology, Internat. Soc. Nephrology, Am. Fedn. for Clin. Research, Am. Soc. Artificial Internal Organs, N.Y. Acad. Scis., Nat. Kidney Found. Current Work: Clinical research in nephrology; basic renal physiology research in field of water transport in the cortical collecting tubule. Subspecialties: Internal medicine; Nephrology. Home: 2746 Baldwin Brook Dr Montgomery AL 36116 Office: 303 S Ripley Montgomery AL 36197

KROWN, SUSAN ELLEN, physician; b. Bronx, N.Y., Sept. 8, 1946; d. Frederick B. and Paula (Hauser) K.; m. Roger Edward Pitt, May 18, 1980; 1 dau., Catherine Krown Pitt. A.B., Barnard Coll., 1967; M.D., SUNY, Bklyn., 1971. Diplomate: Am. Bd. Internal Medicine (subspecialty in med. oncology). Intern, resident in internal medicine Mt. Sinai Hosp., N.Y.C., 1971-74; fellow in med. oncology and clin. immunology Meml. Sloan-Kettering, N.Y.C., 1974-77; research asso. Sloan-Kettering Inst. for Cancer Research, N.Y.C., 1977-84; clin. asst. physician, asst. attending physician Meml. Hosp., N.Y.C., 1977-81, assoc. attending physician, 1982—; asst. prof. medicine Cornell U. Med. Coll., 1977-83, assoc. prof. clin. medicine, 1983—, assoc. mem. (clin.) Meml. Sloan-Kettering Cancer Ctr., 1984—. Contbr. chpts. to books, articles to profl. jours. Am. Cancer Soc. fellow, 1978-81; Nat. Cancer Inst. grantee, 1979-84. Mem. Am. Soc. Clin. Oncology, Am. Assn. Cancer Research, AAAS, Soc. Biol. Therapy, Internat. Soc. Interferon Research. Current Work: Use of biological response modifiers, particularly interferons, in cancer treatment and their role in regulating immune responses. Subspecialties: Cancer research (medicine); Immunology (medicine). Office: 1275 York Ave New York NY 10021

KROWNE, CLIFFORD MITCHELL, electrical engineer, physics researcher; b. N.Y.C., Oct. 2, 1948; s. Philip William and Frances Crystal (Sendrow) K.; m. Rose Lea Smarra, May 28, 1978; children—Aaron, Sandra, Elizabeth. Student Stanford U., 1970; B.S. in Physics with honors, U. Calif.-Davis, Berkeley, 1970; M.S. in Elec. Engring. with honors, U. Calif.-Los Angeles, 1972, Ph.D. in Elec. Engring., 1975. Assoc. engr. Lockheed Missiles & Space Co., Sunnyvale, Calif., 1970; mem. tech. staff Watkins-Johnson Co., Palo Alto, Calif., 1976-78; cons. elec. engring., physics, Raleigh, N.C., 1978-81; asst. prof. in elec. engring., N.C. State U., Raleigh, 1978-81; supervising engr., scientist Naval Research Lab., Washington, 1981—. Contbr. numerous articles and papers to tech. and profl. jours. Founder Research Inst. for Mayan Archaeo-economics, early 1970's. Summer Faculty fellow NASA/ASEE, 1980; fellow Am. Soc. Engrs. in Edn., Johnson Space Center, 1980. Mem. IEEE (sr., chmn. various coms.), Am. Phys. Soc., Tau Beta Pi, Phi Kappa Phi. Current work: Carrier transport in semiconductors and semiconductor devices; microwave/-millimeter wave circuits (integrated, hybrid, monolithic); electromagnetics. Subspecialties: Semiconductors; Integrated circuits. Office: Naval Research Lab Electronic Tech Div Code 6851 Washington DC 20375

KRUG, HARRY EVERISTUS PETER, JR., nuclear engineer; b. Kearney, N.J., Aug. 1, 1932; s. Harry Everistus and Helen (Miliski) K.; m. Madonna Eileen Martin, Nov. 23, 1977 (div. Mar. 1982); children: by previous marriage: Kirk Stanley, Karen Helen, Lynne Allison. B.S., U.S. Mcht. Marine Acad., 1955; M.Nuclear Engring., NYU, 1961. Registered profl. engr., Calif. Fellow engr. Atomic dept. Westinghouse, Pitts., 1961-68; v.p., gen. mgr. NCI, Pitts., 1969-70; nuclear engr. Exxon Nuclear Co., Richland, Wash., 1971; industry mgr. Control Data Corp., Mpls., 1972-73; supr. nuclear engring. Ill. Power Co., Decatur, 1974-75; nuclear engr. U.S. Nuclear Regulatory Commn., Atlanta, 1975—, expert witness, Bethesda, Md., 1975-82. Contbr. articles to profl. jours. Served to lt. USNR, 1956-58. Mem. Am. Nuclear Soc. (pres. Midwest chpt. 1972). Roman Catholic. Current Work: Application of artificial intelligence to the operations and design of nuclear power stations and other complex systems. Subspecialties: Nuclear engineering; Artificial intelligence. Home: 207 14th St Apt E-7 Hartsville SC 29550 Office: Resident Inspection Office Route 5 Box 413 Hartsville SC 29550

KRUGER, CHARLES HERMAN, JR., mechanical engineer; b. Oklahoma City, Oct. 4, 1934; s. Charles H. and Flora K.; m. Nora Nininger, Sept. 10, 1977; children—Sarah, Charles III, Elizabeth, Ellen. S.B., M.I.T., 1956, Ph.D., 1960; D.I.C., Imperial Coll., London, 1957. Asst. prof. M.I.T., Cambridge, 1960; research scientist Lockheed Research Labs., 1960-62; prof. mech. engring. Stanford (Calif.) U., 1962—, chmn. dept. mech. engring., 1982—; vis. prof. Harvard U., 1968-69, Princeton U., 1979-80; mem. Environ. Studies Bd. Nat. Acad. Scis.; mem. hearing bd. Bay Area Air Quality Mgmt. Dist., 1969-83. Co-author: Physical Gas Dynamics, 1965, Partially Ionized Gases, 1973, On the Prevention of Significant Deteriorization of Air Quality, 1981; asso. editor: AIAA Jour, 1968-71; contbr. numerous articles to profl. jours. NSF sr. postdoctoral fellow, 1968-69. Mem. AIAA (medal, award 1979), Combustion Inst., ASME, Am. Phys. Soc., Air Pollution Control Assn., Engring. Aspects of Magnetohydrodynamics. Current Work: Combustion; partially ionized plasma; air pollution; magneto hydrodynamics; diagnostics. Subspecialties: Combustion processes; Plasma engineering. Office: Dept Mech Engring Stanford U Stanford CA 94305

KRUGMAN, SAUL, physician, educator; b. N.Y.C., Apr. 7, 1911; s. Louis and Rachel (Cohen) K.; m. Sylvia Stern, Feb. 18, 1940; children—Richard David, Carol Lynn. Student, Ohio State U., 1929-32; M.D., Med. Coll. Va., 1939. Intern, then resident Cumberland, Willard Parker and Bellevue hosps., N.Y.C., 1939-41, 46-48; teaching and med. research N.Y. U.-Bellevue Med. Center, 1948—, asso. prof. pediatrics, 1954-60, prof., 1960—, chmn. dept., 1960-75; dir. pediatric service Bellevue Hosp., 1960-75, Univ. Hosp., 1960-75; Mem. Commn. Viral Infections, 1960-72; mem. nat. adv. council Nat. Inst. Allergy and Infectious Diseases, 1965-69, chmn. infectious disease adv. com., 1971-73; mem. com. on viral hepatitis NRC, 1973-76; chmn. panel on viral and rickettsial vaccines Bur. Biologies, FDA, 1973-79. Co-author: Infectious Diseases of Children, 1981; contbr. articles on infectious diseases to med. jours. NIH research fellow, 1948-50. Fellow Am. Acad. Pediatrics; mem. Am. Pediatric Soc. (pres. 1972-73), Soc. Pediatric Research, N.Y. Acad. Medicine (chmn. pediatric sect. 1960-61), Am. Epidemiol. Soc., Harvey Soc., Assn. Am. Physicians, Nat. Acad. Scis. Subspecialties: Pediatrics; Infectious diseases. Home: 300 E 33d St New York NY 10016 Office: 550 1st Ave New York NY 10016

KRULL, IRA STANLEY, chemist, researcher, educator, cons.; b. N.Y.C., Oct. 21, 1940; s. Arthur and Anne (Nadelman) K.; m. Erica Krull, Mar. 1, 1973; 1 son, Marc Arthur. B.S. cum laude, CCNY, 1962; M.S. (teaching fellow, NIH predoctoral fellow), N.Y. U., 1966, Ph.D. (NIH postdoctoral fellow), 1968. Fellow Weizmann Inst. Sci., Israel, 1970-73; asst. scientist Boyce Thompson Inst., Yonkers, N.Y., 1973-77, Thermo Electron Corp., Waltham, Mass., 1977-79; sr. scientist Inst. Chem. Analysis, Applications and Forensic Sci., Northeastern U., Boston, 1979—, assoc. prof. chemistry and faculty fellow, 1984—; tchr. Center Profl. Advancement, N.J.; cons. FDA, pvt. indsl. firms, Center Profl. Advancement. Contbr. articles and revs. to profl. jours. Union Carbide postdoctoral fellow, 1968-70; NIH postdoctoral fellow U. Wis., 1967-68; recipient Founders Day award N.Y. U., 1968. Mem. Am. Chem. Soc., Chem. Soc. London, Assn. Ofcl. Analytical Chemists, Sigma Xi, Phi Lambda Upsilon. Current Work: Development of improved trace assays for organic/i-norganic materials, environ. trace analysis, analytical instrumentation development, application of analytical instrumentation for trace analysis, analytical toxicology. Subspecialties: Analytical chemistry; Organic chemistry. Office: Northeastern U 360 Huntington Ave Boston MA 02115

KRUMHANSL, JAMES ARTHUR, physicist, educator, industrial consultant; b. Cleve., Aug. 2, 1919; s. James and Marcella (Kelly) K.; m. Barbara Dean Schminck, Dec. 26, 1944 (div. 1983); children: James Lee, Carol Lynne, Peter Allen.; m. Marilyn Cupp Dahl, Feb. 19, 1983. B.S. in Elec. Engring, U. Dayton, 1939; M.S., Case Inst. Tech., 1940, D.Sc. (hon.), 1980; Ph.D. in Physics, Cornell U., 1943. Instr. Cornell U., 1943-44; physicist Stromberg-Carlson Co., 1944-46; mem. faculty Brown U., 1946-48, asso. prof., 1947-48; asst. prof., then asso. prof. Cornell U., 1948-55; asst. dir. research Nat. Carbon Co., 1955-57, asso. dir. research, 1957-58; prof. physics Cornell U., 1959—, Horace White prof., 1980; dir. Lab. Atomic and Solid State Physics, 1960-64; adj. prof. U. Pa., 1979; fellow Los Alamos Lab., 1980; asst. dir. for math., phys. sci. and engring. NSF, 1977-79; cons. to industry, 1946—; Adv. com for AEC, Dept. Def., Nat. Acad. Sci., from 1956; vis. fellow All Souls Coll., Oxford U., 1977, Gonville and Caius Coll., Cambridge U., 1983, Royal Soc. London, 1983. Editor: Jour. Applied Physics, 1957-60; assoc. editor: Solid State Communications, from 1963, Rev. Modern Physics, 1968-73; editor: Phys. Rev. Letters, from 1974, physics Oxford U. Press; Contbr. articles to profl. jours. Guggenheim fellow, 1959-60; NSF sr. postdoctoral fellow Oxford U., 1966-67. Fellow Am. Phys. Soc. (chmn. div. solid state physics 1968, councillor 1970-74), AAAS, Am. Inst. Physics (governing bd. from 1973); mem. AAUP, Am. Assn. Physics Tchrs., Sigma Xi, Phi Kappa Phi. Republican. Presbyn. Club: Ithaca Yacht. Current Work: Conducting polymers; molecular biophysics of proteins and DNA. Subspecialties: Condensed matter physics; Applied mathematics. Office: Cornell U Dept Physics Ithaca NY 14853

KRUMRINE, PAUL HENRY, III, chemical engineer, researcher; b. Hanover, Pa., Nov. 28, 1951; s. Paul Henry Jr. and Evelyn Jane (Walter) K.; m. Susan Lynn Waybright, Oct. 21, 1978; children—Jodi Danielle, Kelly Nicole. B.S., Lehigh U., 1973, M.S., 1976, Ph.D., 1978; M.B.A., Temple U., 1984. Research engr. Westvaco, Laurel, Md., 1978-79; chemist PQ Corp., Lafayette Hill, Pa., 1979-82, sr. chem. engr., 1982-84, research assoc., 1984—; com. mem. Internat. Oil Field & Geothermal Chem. Symposium, 1982—. Author: (with others) Electrokinetic Separation Methods, 1979, Soluble Silicates, 1982. Patentee in field. Contbr. articles to profl. jours. Mem. Am. Chem. Soc., Am. Inst. Chem. Engrs., Soc. Petroleum Engrs. (jr.), Alpha Sigma Phi. Current work: Research on applications of alkaline chemicals in enhanced oil recovery and waste containment. Subspecialties: Chemical engineering; Petroleum engineering. Home: 1229 Hatfield Valley Rd Hatfield PA 19440 Office: PQ Corp Research & Devel Ctr PO Box 258 Lafayette Hill PA 19444

KRUPP, MARCUS ABRAHAM, physician; b. El Paso, Tex., Feb. 12, 1913; s. Maurice and Esther (Siegel) K.; m. Muriel McClure, Aug. 9, 1941 (dec. Oct. 1954); children: Michael, David (dec.), Peter, Sara; m. Donna Goodheart Millen, Feb. 28, 1958. A.B., Stanford U., 1934, M.D., 1939. Diplomate: Am. Bd. Internal Medicine. Intern Stanford U. Hosp., Calif., 1938-39, resident in internal medicine, 1939-42; chief clin. pathology VA Hosp., San Francisco, 1946-50; dir. Palo Alto Med. Research Found., Calif., 1950—; dir. labs. Palo Alto Med. Clinic, 1950-80; asst. clin. prof. medicine Stanford U., 1946-56, asso. clin. prof., 1956-65, clin. prof., 1965—; mem. med. tech. adv. com. Public Employees Retirement System Calif., 1972—. Editor: (with Milton Chatton) Current Diagnosis and Treatment, ann., 1971-85, (with others) Physicians Handbook, 7th-20th edits., 1981. Vice pres. bd. dirs. Calif. Heart Assn., 1974-75; pres. bd. trustees Channing House, Palo Alto. Served to capt. U.S. Army, 1942-46. Fellow ACP; mem. Western Soc. Clin. Research, Calif. Acad. Medicine (pres. 1966), Pacific Interurban Clin. Club (pres. 1977), AAAS, AMA, N.Y. Acad. Scis., Assn. Ind. Research Insts. (pres. 1966-67), Phi Beta Kappa, Alpha Omega Alpha. Current Work: Nephrology; endocrinology, physiology. Subspecialty: Internal medicine. Home: 195 Ramoso Rd Portola Valley CA 94025 Office: 860 Bryant St Palo Alto CA 94301

KRUSKAL, MARTIN DAVID, mathematical physicist; b. N.Y.C., Sept. 28, 1925; married, 1950; 3 children. B.S., U. Chgo., 1945; M.S., NYU, 1948, Ph.D. in Math, 1952. Asst., instr. dept. math. NYU, 1946-51; research scientist Plasma Physics Lab., Princeton U., 1951—, sr. research assoc., 1959—, prof. astrophys. sci., 1961—, prof. math., 1981—; cons. Los Alamos Sci. Lab., 1953-59, radiation lab. U. Calif., 1954-57, Oak Ridge Nat. Lab., 1955-58, 63—, Radio Corp. Am., 1960-62, IBM Corp., 1963—; lectr. in field. Recipient Dannie Heineman prize in math. physics, 1983; NSF sr. fellow, 1959-60. Mem. Am. Math. Soc., Math. Assn. Am., Am. Phys. Soc. Subspecialty: Applied mathematics. Office: Dept Astrophysics Princeton U Princeton NJ 08540*

KRUTZ, RONALD L., computer engineer; b. Duquesne, Pa., Aug. 27, 1938; s. Louis J. and Rose M. Cardamone; m. Hilda M. Mapolitano, Apr. 29, 1961; children—Sheri R., Lisa M. B.S.E.E., U. Pitts., 1960, M.S.E.E., 1967, Ph.D. in Elec. Engring., 1972. Registered profl. engr., Pa. Sr. engr. Gulf Research, Harmanville, Pa., 1964-74; div. dir. Singer Corp. for Research and Devel., Fairfield, N.J., 1974-75; prof. elec. engring. Carnegie Mellon U., Pitts., 1975-78, dir. computer engring. ctr., 1978—; cons. in field. Author: (textbooks) Microcomputor and Logic Desihn, 1980; Microcomputers for Managers, 1983. Patentee digital systems. Served to 1st lt. U.S. Army, 1961-64. Mem. IEEE, Am. Inst. for Artificial Intelligence, Eta Kappa Nu. Club: University (Pitts.). Current work: Microcomputer hardware and software, distribuer systems, expert systems, process control. Subspecialties: Computer engineering; Distributed systems and networks. Home: 11956 McKee Rd North Huntingdon PA Office: Carnegie-Mellon U Computer Engring Ctr 4616 Henry St Pittsburgh PA 15213

KU, HARRY HSIEN H., statistician, mathematician; b. Beijing, China, Var. 3, 1918; came to U.S., 1938, naturalized, 1958; m. Rubye Mark, Dec. 13, 1942 (dec. 1978); 1 child, Richard; m. Helen H. Hamstra, July 2, 1981. B.S.C.E., Purdue U., 1940, M.S. in Engring., 1941; Ph.D., George Washington U., 1968. With M.W. Kellogg Co., Houston and Balt., 1942-45; with Chinese Gov. Supply Agy., Ottawa, Ont., Can., 1946-50; with Chinese Tech. Mission, Washington, 1950-58; with statis. engring div. Nat. Bur. Standards, Gaithersburg, Md., 1958—. Editor: Precision Measurements and Callibration-Statistical Concepts and Procedures, 1969. Contbr. articles to profl. publs. Fellow Am. Statis. Assn., AAAS; mem. Internat. Statis. Inst. Current work: Precision and accuracy in measurements, analysis of contingency tables. Subspecialty: Statistics. Home: 9608 Glencrest Ln Kensington MD 20895 Office: Nat Bur Standards Gaithersburg MD 20899

KUAN, SHIA SHIONG, bioanalytical chemist, research center administrator; b. Canton, China, Oct. 18, 1933; came to U.S., 1963; s. Chung Liu and Akunt (Lin) K.; m. Rae Juichang Wang, Oct. 20, 1973; 1 child, Nolan. Ph.D., W.Va. U., 1968. Postdoctoral fellow La. State U. New Orleans, 1968-70, research assoc., 1970-80; adj. prof. U. New Orleans, 1980—, dir. Natural Toxins Research Ctr., FDA, New Orleans, 1980—. Mem. Am. Chem. Soc., N.Y. Acad. Sci., AAAS, Am. Ofcl. Analytic Chemists, Am. Oil Chemists Soc., Inst. Food Technologists, Sigma Xi. Current work: Development of new methods for isolation, identification and quantitation of natural toxins using TLC, HPLC, GC, GPC, IR, NMR, MS and immunochemical techniques. Subspecialties: Analytical chemistry; Enzyme technology. Home: 3020 Transcontinental Dr Metairie LA 70006 Office: FDA 4298 Elysian Fields Ave New Orleans LA 70122

KUBITSCHEK, HERBERT ERNEST, biophysicist; b. Oak Park, Ill., June 9, 1920; s. Ernst M. and Anna A. (Nebel) K.; m. Jenny G., June 26, 1943; children: Carolyn, Craig, Warren, Wendy. Ph.D., U. Ill., 1949. Postdoctoral fellow Inst. Radiobiology and Biophysics, U. Chgo., 1949-51; assoc. physicist Argonne (Ill.) Nat. Lab., 1951, sr. biophysicist, 1970, genetics group leader, 1972—; adj. prof. No. Ill. U. Author: Introduction to Research with Continuous Cultures, 1970. USPHS fellow, 1949-51; Minna-James Heineman fellow, 1974. Mem. AAAS, Am. Assn. Physics Tchrs., Am. Soc. Microbiology, Am. Soc. Photobiology, Biophys. Soc., Environ. Mutagen Soc., Genetics Soc. Am., Sigma Xi. Current work: Cell growth, mutagenesis. Office: Argonne Nat Lab 9700 S Cass Ave Argonne IL 60439

KUCK, DAVID JEROME, educational administrator, computer science educator; b. Muskegon, Mich., Oct. 3, 1937; s. Oscar Ferdinand and Alyce (Brems) K.; m. Sharon McCure, July 16, 1977; 1 child, Julianne. B.S.E.E., U. Mich., 1959; M.S., Northwestern U., 1960, Ph.D., 1963. Asst. prof. dept. elec. engring. MIT, Cambridge, 1963-65; asst. prof. dept. computer sci. U. Ill.-Urbana, 1965-68, assoc. prof., 1968-72, prof., 1972—, dir. Ctr. for Supercomputing Research and Devel., 1984—; pres. Kuck and Assocs., Inc., Savoy, Ill., 1979—; cons. Los Alamos Nat. Lab., N.Mex., 1979—, Alliant Computer Systems, Acton, Mass., 1982—. Author: Structure of Computers and Computations, vol. 1, 1978. Editor jour. IEEE Transactions on Computers, 1973-75. Patentee in field. Assoc. mem. Ctr. for Advanced Studies, U. Ill., 1982-83. Fellow IEEE; mem. Assn. Computing Machinery (editor jour.). Current work: Principles of high-speed computer systems, their applications to real system design, algorithms for their use, program restructuring techniques to exploit supercomputer systems, performance analysis. Subspecialties: Computer architecture; Software engineering. Home: 405 Yankee Ridge Ln Urbana IL 61801 Office: Ctr for Supercomputing Research and Devel U Ill 104 S Wright 305 Talbot Lab Urbana IL 61801

KUEHN, THOMAS HOWARD, mechanical engineering educator, thermal science researcher; b. Mpls., Sept. 7, 1949; s. Jerome Henry and Ruth (Sprung) K.; m. Linda Ann Rust, Nov. 28, 1980. B.M.E., U. Minn., 1971, M.S., 1973, Ph.D., 1976. Asst. prof. Iowa State U., Ames, 1976-81, assoc. prof. mech. engring., 1981-83; assoc. prof. U. Minn., Mpls., 1983—; cons. Arkae Devel., Inc., Ames, 1980-81, Engelbrecht & Griffin Architects, Des Moines, 1979-80, Air Conditioning, Inc., Marshalltown, Iowa, 1977-78. Pres. Long Lake Park Assn., 1984—; mem. White Bear Lake Conservation Dist. Bd., 1985—. Served to 1st lt. U.S. Army, 1973-74. NSF grantee, 1978, 80, 83. Mem. Am. Underground Space Assn., ASME (assoc.), AIAA (assoc.), ASHRAE (assoc., student avd. Iowa State U. 1979-82), Ames Folk Dancers Club (pres. 1977-79). Current Work: Heating, ventilating, air conditioning of buildings; natural convection heat transfer; solar thermal energy conversion and utilization. Subspecialties: Environmental engineering; Mechanical engineering. Home: 4 William Woods Mahtomedi MN 55115 Office: Mech Engring Dept U Minn Minneapolis MN 55455

KUEMMERLE, NANCY BENTON STEVENS, research microbiologist; b. Marshall, Minn., Mar. 6, 1948; d. Ralph Brookmeyer and Barbara Annette (Burton) Stevens; m. Edgar W. Kuemmerle, Jr., May 15, 1971. B.S. in Chemistry, U. Iowa, 1970; M.S., U. Tex. Health Scis. Ctr., Houston, 1975; postgrad., Ill. State U., 1972-73, U. Tenn.-Oak Ridge Grad. Sch. Biomed. Scis., 1978—. Microbiology technician Ill. State U., Normal, 1972-73; microbiology technologist U. Ill. Med. Center, Peoria, 1973-74; sr. research asst. U. Tenn.-ERDA Comparative Animal Research Lab., Oak Ridge, 1974-76; research assoc. Biology Div. Oak Ridge Nat. Lab., 1976-82. Rosalie B. Hite fellow in cancer chemotherapy M.D. Anderson Hosp. and Tumor Inst., Houston, 1971-72. Mem. AAAS, Am. Chem. Soc., Am. Soc. Microbiology, Assn. Women in Sci. Current Work: Studies of mechanisms and enzymology of DNA repair, replication and recombination. Subspecialties: Molecular biology; Gene actions. Home: PO Box 126 Seymour TN 37865 Office: Biology Div Oak Ridge Nat Lab PO Box Y Oak Ridge TN 37830

KUESEL, THOMAS ROBERT, engineering company executive, civil engineer; b. Richmond Hill, N.Y., July 30, 1926; s. Henry N. and Marie D. (Butt) K.; m. Lucia Elodia Fisher, Jan. 31, 1959; children—Robert Livingston, William Baldwin. B.Engring. with highest honors, Yale U., 1946, M.Engring., 1947. With Parsons, Brinckerhoff, Quade & Douglas, 1947—, project mgr., San Francisco, 1967-68, partner, sr. v.p., dir., N.Y.C., 1968-83, chmn. bd., dir., 1983—; asst. mgr. engring. Parsons Brinckerhoff-Tudor-Bechtel, San Francisco, 1963-67; vice chmn. OECD Tunneling Conf., Washington, 1970; mem. U.S. Nat. Com. on Tunneling Tech., 1972-74. Contbr. numerous articles to profl. jours.; designer: over 120 bridges, 90 tunnels, numerous other structures in 36 states and 20 fgn. countries, including Newport Suspension Bridge, R.I., 1959-63, NORAD Combat Ops. Center, Colorado Springs, Colo., 1962, San Francisco Bay Area Rapid Transit System, 1963-68, Hampton Roads (Va.) Bridge-Tunnel, 1969-77, Ft. McHenry Tunnel, Balt., 1978-85, Hood Canal Bridge, Washington, 1980-82, subways, Boston, N.Y., Balt., Washington, Atlanta, Pitts., Singapore, Caracas, Niagara Falls power plant expansion, 1984—. Fellow ASCE, Am. Cons. Engrs. Council; mem. Nat. Acad. Engring., Internat. Assn. Bridge, Structural Engring., Brit. Tunnelling Soc., Yale Sci. and Engring. Assn., The Moles, Sigma Xi, Tau Beta Pi. Clubs: Yale (N.Y.C.); Wee Burn (Darien, Conn.). Current Work: Tunnel design and construction, bridge design and construction, engineering and construction management, rapid transit systems, major project development, earthquake engineering. Subspecialty: Civil engineering. Office: One Penn Plaza 250 W 34th St New York NY 10119

KUFFNER, ROY JOSEPH, chemistry educator; b. N.Y.C., Mar. 15, 1922; s. Joseph and Mae (Fernholz) K.; m. Noel Worrell, Oct. 11, 1947; children: Karl, Leslie, Nicola, Greg; m. Marilyn Adair Langer, July 7, 1978. B.S., Coll. Ozarks, 1944; Ph.D., Vanderbilt U., 1955. Asst. prof. Emory U., 1953-54; prof. chemistry Lowell (Mass.) U., 1956-67; prof. Chgo. State U., 1967-70; prof., chmn. dept. chemistry Alverno Coll., Milw., 1970-84; vis. prof. U. Wis.-Milw., 1981-82. Served with M.C. U.S. Army, 1946-49. Mem. Am. Chem. Soc., AAAS, AAUP, Sigma Xi. Current Work: Rate of decay of surface tension at air/solution interface of solutions of slightly soluble solutes. Subspecialties: Physical chemistry; Surface chemistry. Home: 2782 S 60th St Apt 4 Milwaukee WI 53219 Office: 3401 S 39th S Suite 226 Milwaukee WI 53215

KUH, ERNEST SHINU-JEN, engineering educator; b. Beijing, China, Oct. 2, 1928; s. Zone S. and Tsia (Chu) K.; m. Bettine Chow, Aug. 4, 1957; children: Anthony, Theodore. B.S., U. Mich., 1949; M.S., M.I.T., 1950; Ph.D., Stanford U., 1952. Mem. tech. staff Bell Telephone Labs., Murray Hill, N.J., 1952-56; prof. elec. engring. U. Calif-Berkeley, 1956—, chmn. elec. engring. and computer scis., 1968-72; dean U. Calif-Berkeley (Coll. Engring.), 1973-80; hon. prof. Shanghai Jiao Tong U., 1979—, Tsinghua U., 1985—, Tianjin U., 1985—. cons. IBM Research Lab., San Jose, Calif., 1957-62. Co-author: Principles of Circuit Synthesis, 1959, Theory of Linear Active Networks, 1967, Basic Circuit Theory, 1969; contbr. over 70 tech. articles to profl. publs. Recipient Lamme medal Am. Soc. Engring. Edn., 1981; Brit Sci. and Engring. fellow. Fellow IEEE (Edn. medal 1981, Centennial medal 1983), AAAS; mem. Nat. Acad. Engring., Academia Sinica. Current Work: Microelectronics and computer-aided design. Subspecialty: Electrical engineering. Office: Univ Calif Elec Engring and Computer Scis Dept Berkeley CA 94720

KUHN, ALAN KARL, geological engineer; b. Columbus, Ohio, Oct. 8, 1941; s. Karl Earl Kuhn and Margaret Lavada (Andre) Kuhn Hogg; m. Kathy Marie Long, Sept. 3, 1983; children—Keith, Andrew; 1 stepchild, Kelly Long. B.S. in Geology Duke U., 1963; M.S. in Hydrogeology, Colo. State U., 1968; Ph.D. in Engring. Geology, U. Ill., 1973; Registered profl. engr., registered geologist. Sr. engring. geologist DeLeuw Cather Co., N.Y.C., 1973-74; sr. geotechnical engr. Stone & Webster, Denver, 1974-77; project mgr. D'Appolonia Cons. Engrs., Albuquerque, 1977-84; prin. engr. Applied Research Assocs., Albuquerque, 1984; pvt. practice, Albuquerque, 1984—; peer reviewer Office of Nuclear Waste Isolation, Columbus, Ohio, 1984; cons., advisor Waste Isolation Pilot Plant Project, Albuquerque, 1981—. Contbr. articles to profl. jours. Mem. Environ. Commn., Somerset, N.J., 1974. Served to capt. USMC, 1963-66. Mem. Geol. Soc. Am., Assn. Engring. Geologists, Am. Soc. Civil Engrs., Soc. Mining Engrs. of AIME, Internat. Soc. Rock Mechanics, Underground Tech. Research Council. Current work: Nuclear and toxic hazardous waste disposal, energy resource development, development of underground space for energy and civil works. Subspecialties: Geological engineering; Hazardous waste disposal. Home and Office: 13212 Manitoba Dr NE Albuquerque NM 87111

KUHN, HOWARD ARTHUR, consulting metal engineer; b. Pitts., Dec. 6, 1940; s. Howard E. and Selma (Schulze) K.; m. Beverly A. Burke, Dec. 23, 1961; children: Amy, Jeffrey, David, Stephen. B.S., Carnegie Mellon U., 1962, M.S., 1963, Ph.D., 1966. Registered profl. engr. Pa. Mem. faculty Drexel U., Phila., 1966-74, prof. materials engring, 1966-74; prof. metall. engring., prof. mech. engring. U. Pitts., 1975—; pres. Deformation Control Tech., Pitts., 1980—. Author: Powder Metallurgy Processing, 1978; contbr. articles to profl. jours. Mem. citizens adv. com. Babcock Sch. Dist., 1977-80; pres. Richland Athletic Assn., 1978-81. Fellow Am. Soc. Metals; mem. ASME, Am. Powder Metal Inst. Republican. Methodist. Patentee process and apparatus for forging gears from powdered metals. Current Work: Metalworking, powder metallurgy, computer-aided design and computer-aided manufacturing. Subspecialties: Powder metallurgy; Materials processing. Home: 5408 Peach Dr Gibsonia PA 15044 Office: 848 Benedum Hall Pittsburgh PA 15261

KUHN, WILLIAM RICHARD, atmospheric science educator; b. Columbus, Ohio, May 7, 1937; s. Marvin Jacob and Esther M. (Hartranft) K.; m. Dorothy K. Kuhn; children: Jeffrey Richard, Timothy Scott, Tracy Lynn. Ph.D., U. Colo., 1967. Mem. faculty dept. atmospheric and oceanic sci. U. Mich., Ann Arbor, 1967—, chmn. dept., 1980—. Mem. Am. Geophys. Union, Am. Astron. Soc. Current Work: Climate of early earth, influence of water vapor and carbon dioxide on earth's temperature, evolution of Mars atmosphere. Subspecialties: Climatology; Aeronomy. Office: Dept Atmospheric and Oceanic Sci U Mich Space Physics Bldg Ann Arbor MI 48109

KUHNS, JOHN FARRELL, aquatic research company executive, chemist; b. Albuquerque, Mar. 2, 1947; s. Farrell Wayne Kuhns and Rowena Young (Garrison) Earle; m. Carol Lee Johnson, Aug. 5, 1967; 1 child, Ginger Heather Rene. B.S., U. Mo.-Kansas City, 1969. Owner, Mid-Continent Fish, Ltd., Kansas City, Mo., 1969-71; owner, pres. Montserrat Ednl. & Sci. Co., Kansas City, 1971-73; research dir. Gen. Drug & Chem. Corp., North Kansas City, 1974-82; owner, pres. AquaSci. Research Group, Inc., North Kansas City, 1982-84, Owner, corp. sec., 1984—; owner, editor The Written Word, Kansas City, 1979—. Editor, contbr. Codex of Fishery Chemicals, 1983—; editor Jour. Aquariculture and Aquatic Scis., 1979—. Contbr. papers, articles to profl. lit. Patentee aquarium water conditioners. Founder, pres. Friends of the Aquarium, Kansas City, 1977-78, v.p., 1979-84, treas., 1984—. Mem. Am. Fisheries Soc., AAAS, Am. Soc. Ichthyologists and Herpetologists, Fedn. Am. Aquarium Socs. (pres. 1972-73), Am. Chem. Soc., Heart of Am. Aquarium Soc. (v.p. Kansas City 1969-70), Am. Philatelic Soc. Current work: Development of water conditioner for neutralizing chloramines and ammonia in fish culture water; oral therapeutics for fish; synthetic sea salt mixes; fish anesthetics. Subspecialties: Fisheries science; Environmental chemistry. Office: AquaScience Research Group Inc 1100 Gentry St North Kansas City MO 64116

KUKULKA, CARL GEORGE, neurophsiologist, educator; b. Olean, N.Y., Mar. 3, 1949; s. Edward Karl and Mary Ann K.; m. Nancy Landfear, Sept. 11, 1971; children—Erica, Anna. B.S., Ithaca Coll., 1971; Ph.D. (scholar), Med. Coll. Va., Va. Commonwealth U., 1979. Lic. phys. therapist, N.Y. State, Iowa. Vis. asst. fellow John B. Pierce Found., New Haven, 1979-81; asst. prof. dept. phys. therapy Ithaca (N.Y.) Coll., 1981-82, U. Iowa Med. Coll., Iowa City, 1982—. Contbr. articles and abstracts to sci. jours. Muscular Dystrophy Assn. fellow, 1979-81. Mem. Soc. for Neuroscis., AAAS, N.Y. Acad. Scis., Sigma Xi. Current Work: Human motor control, neural control of skeletal muscle. Subspecialty: Neurophysiology. Office: 2600 Steindler Bldg Iowa City IA 52242

KULCZYCKI, ANTHONY, JR., medical researcher; b. Easton, Pa., Dec. 17, 1944; s. Anthony and Mae (Yaworski) K.; m. Judith Mary Brokaw, May 31, 1969; children: Alexander, Amy-Elizabeth. A.B., Princeton U., 1966; M.D., Harvard U., 1970. Diplomate: Am. Bd. Internal Medicine, Am. Bd. Allergy and Immunology. Intern, resident Buffalo Gen. and E.J. Meyer hosps., 1970-72; research assoc. NIAMDD, NIH, 1972-74; NIH research fellow, 1974-76; asst. prof. medicine Washington U., St. Louis, 1977-82, assoc. prof., 1982—; assoc. investigator Howard Hughes Med. Inst., 1978-84. Contbr. articles to profl. jours. Served as lt. comdr. USPHS, 1972-74. Recipient J.D. Lane award. Mem. Am Assn. Immunologists, Am. Acad. Allergy, Am. Soc.

Clin. Investigation, Collegium Internationale Allergologicum, Ethical Soc. St. Louis. Clubs: Princeton (St. Louis), Harvard (St. Louis). Current Work: Allergic diseases and other immunologic diseases. Subspecialties: Immunology (medicine); Allergy. Office: Box 8122 660 S Euclid Washington U Sch Medicine Saint Louis MO 63110

KULICKE, CHARLES SCOTT, equipment engineering company executive; b. Phila., Sept. 28, 1949; s. Frederick William and Ruth (West) K., Jr.; m. Danielle Volckmar, Aug. 1, 1980; 1 child, Ruth. B.S. in Econs., U. Pa., 1972. Internat. mktg. mgr. Kulicke and Soffa Industries, Inc., Horsham, Pa., 1973-75, product mgr., 1975-77, gen. mgr., 1977-79, pres., chief exec. officer, 1979-84, chmn., chief exec. officer, 1984—. Mem. Semiconductor Equipment and Materials Inst. (bd. dirs., treas.). Republican. Subspecialty: Equipment engineering company management. Office: Kulicke and Soffa Industries Inc 507 Prudential Rd Horsham PA 19044

KULKARNI, PRASAD SHRIKRISHNA, eye research educator; b. India, May 22, 1943; came to U.S., 1966, naturalized, 1980; s. Shrikrishna M. and Kamal S. (Kulkarni) K. M.S., SUNY Downstate Med. Ctr., N.Y.C., 1971, Ph.D., 1974. Teaching asst. Downstate Med. Ctr., 1968-74; fellow dept. pharmacology Washington U., St. Louis, 1974-76; research assoc. eye research div. Columbia U., N.Y.C., 1976-78; asst. prof. ocular pharmacology Columbua U., 1978—. Contbr. articles to profl. jours. Nat. Inst. for Eye Research grantee, 1979—. Mem. Am. Soc. for Pharmacology and Exptl. Therapeutics, Assn. for Research in vision and Ophthalmology, Internat. Soc. for Eye Research. Current Work: Mediators of ocular inflammaton, development and mechanism of action of anti-inflammatory drugs, pharmacology of coronary blood vessels. Subspecialties: Pharmacology; Ophthalmology.

KULLE, THOMAS JOHN, medical researcher, environmental health scientist; b. Cin., Aug. 20, 1932; s. Henry Frank and Hermina (Lamott) K.; m. Barbara Ann See, Aug. 18, 1956; children—Donald Gerard, Janice Ann. B.E.E., U. Cin., 1955, Ph.D. in Environ. Health, 1972; M. Applied Sci., Adelphi U., 1961. Design engr. Sperry Rand Corp., Great Neck, N.Y., 1955-63, sr. engr., 1963-68; asst. prof. occupational medicine Johns Hopkins U., Balt., 1972-81, assoc. prof., 1981—; asst. prof. epidemiology U. Md., Balt., 1981—, asst. prof. medicine, 1980-83, research assoc. prof. medicine, 1983—; environ. chamber tech. dir., 1980—; cons. ozone criteria document EPA, 1983-84; active in air pollution control edn. Contbr. articles to profl. jours. NIH fellow, 1968. Mem. Am. Thoracic Soc., Am. Lung Assn., Am. Indsl. Hygiene Assn., IEEE (biomed. group), Am. Chem. Soc., Eta Kappa Nu. Club: Recreation Council (Edgewood, Md.). Current work: Principal investigator in chamber studies of respiratory function in humans with exposure to low levels of air pollutants. Subspecialties: Environmental toxicology; Pulmonary medicine. Home: 1475 Charlestown Dr Edgewood MD 21040 Office: U Md 29 S Greene St GSB-414 Baltimore MD 21201

KUMAR, ANANDA HOSAKERE, materials engineer; b. Bangalore, India, Nov. 29, 1940; came to U.S., 1970; m. Shantha Arakere, Feb. 1, 1969; children—Srinivas, Aparna. M.S., U. Mysore, India, 1961; B.S. in Engring., Indian Inst. Sci., 1963; Ph.D., U. Ill., Urbana, 1974. Foreman, Ally Steels Project, Durgapur, India, 1963-66; sr. metallurgist United Aircraft Ltd., Longueoil, Que., Can., 1966-70; sr. engr. Gen.-Tech. div. IBM, Hopewell Junction, N.Y., 1974—. Contbr. articles to tech. jours. Patentee in field ceramics packaging. Mem. Am. Ceramic Soc., Internat. Soc. Hybrid Microelectronics, Internat. Electronics Packaging Soc. Current work: High density electronic packaging and materials; processes for fabrication. Subspecialties: Ceramics; Microchip technology (materials science). Home: 6 Dorett Dr Wappingers Falls NY 12590 Office: Gen Tech Div IBM Route 52 Hopewell Junction NY 12533

KUMAR, BINOD, materials scientist; b. Jamalpur, India, Jan. 13, 1946; came to U.S., 1971, naturalized, 1981; s. Rambaran and Ramsunder (Roy) Singh; m. Shyama Thakur, May 23, 1969; children—Vineet, Sunita. B.Tech., Banaras U., 1967; M.S., Pa. State U., 1973, Ph.D., 1976. Research engr. Anchor Hocking Corp., Lancaster, Ohio, 1976-79; research scientist U. Dayton, Ohio, 1980—. Contbr. articles to profl. jours. Mem. Am. Ceramic Soc., Nat. Inst. Ceramic Engrs., Indian Ceramic Soc., Keramos. Current work: Research and development of glass and ceramic materials for bio-applications, high energy laser optics and optical wave guides. Subspecialties: Biomaterials; Ceramics. Office: U Dayton 300 College Park Ave Dayton OH 45469

KUMAR, KAPLESH, materials scientist; b. Lucknow, India, Nov. 9, 1947; came to U.S., 1970; s. Shiam and Vidya (Devi) Sunder; m. Savinder Kaur, May 27, 1974; children—Priyadarshini, Ruchira. B.Tech., Indian Inst. Tech., 1969; M.S., Stevens Inst. Tech., 1971; Sc.D., MIT, 1975. Mem. tech. staff Charles Stark Draper Lab., Inc., Cambridge, Mass., 1975-80, chief materials devel. sect., 1980—. Patentee in materials processing. Contbr. articles to profl. publs. Recipient Patent award Charles Stark Draper Lab., Inc., 1982, Invention Disclosure award NASA, 1983. Mem. MIT Sangam Club for India Affairs (pres. 1972-73). Current work: Permanent and soft magnetic materials; structural materials; friction and wear in sliding contacts and surfaces. Subspecialties: Materials; Ceramics. Office: Charles Stark Draper Lab Inc 555 Technology Sq Cambridge MA 02139

KUMAR, KRISHNA, physics educator; b. Meerut, India, July 14, 1936; came to U.S., 1956, naturalized, 1966; s. Rangi and Sushelia (Devi) Lal.; m. Katharine Louise Johnson, May 1, 1960; children—Jai Robert, Raj David. B.Sc., Meerut Coll., India, 1953; M.Sc. in physics, Agra U., India, 1955; M.S., Carnegie Mellon U., 1959, Ph.D., 1964. Postdoctoral fellow Niels Bohr Inst., Copenhagen, 1967-69; research physicist Oak Ridge Nat. Lab., 1969-71; assoc. prof. Vanderbilt U., Nashville, 1971-77; collaborateur etranger AEC, Paris, 1977-79; Nordita prof. U. Bergen, Norway, 1979-80; prof. physics Tenn. Tech. U., Cookeville, 1980—, Univ. prof. physics, 1983—; vis. prof. U. Sussex, Eng., 1983; vis. physicist Lawrence Livermore Lab., Calif., summers 1981-82; Nordita prof. Research Inst. Physics, Stockholm, 1973-74; speaker in field. Author: Nuclear Models and the Search for Unity in Nuclear Physics, 1984. Contbr. articles to profl. jours. Mem. Republican Presdl. Task Force, 1982—; co-chmn. Internat. Host Family Program, Cookeville, 1983—. Fellow Indian Phys. Soc.; mem. AAAS, Am. Phys. Soc., European Phys. Soc., Scis. Inst. for Pub. Info. Hindu. Club: India Assn. (Pitts.) (sec. 1958-59). Lodge: Rotary. Current work: Research of the unified theory of nuclear structure, fission and reactions; developer of dynamic deformation model of atonomic nuclei. Subspecialties: Nuclear physics; Theoretical physics. Home: 1248 N Franklin Cookeville TN 38501 Office: Tenn Tech U Dixie Ave Cookeville TN 38505

KUMAR, MAHESH, electrical engineer, researcher; b. Mathura, India, Dec. 3, 1951; came to U.S., 1978; s. Ramji Das and Somvati Devi; m. Rekha Jain, Mar. 24, 1980; 1 child, Vivek. B.Sc., Agra U., India, 1969, M.Sc. in Physics, 1971; M.Sc. in Tech., Birla Inst. Tech. and Sci., India, 1973; Ph.D., Indian Inst. Tech., 1977. Lectr. India Inst. Tech., Kharagpur, 1976-78; tech. staff RCA David Sarnoff Research Ctr., Princeton, N.J., 1978—. Patentee in field. Contbr. articles to profl. jours. Sr. mem. IEEE (chmn. Princeton sect. 1983-84, chmn. met. sect. activities council 1984-85). Current work: Microwave solid state device circuits and monolithic microwave integrated circuits. Subspecialties: Electrical engineering; Microchip technology (engineering). Home: 16 Miriam Ct Dayton NJ 08810 Office: RCA David Sarnoff Research Ctr 201 Washington Rd Princeton NJ 08540

KUMAR, PRASANNA K., physicist; b. Bangalore, India, Oct. 23, 1937; came to U.S., 1965, naturalized, 1980; d. Krishnamurthy Seshappa and Nagarathna (Krishnamurthy) Vastare; m. Savitri Kumar, Aug. 22, 1971; children—Monisha Anjali, Pratima Valli. B.Sc., Mysore U., Bangalore, India, 1956, B.Sc. with honors, 1958, M.Sc., 1959; M.A., Temple U., Phila., 1967, Ph. D., 1973. Physicist U. Calif., Lawrence Berkeley Lab., Berkeley, 1974-75; asst. prof. physics Spring Garden Coll., Phila., 1975-76; research assoc. physics Drexel U., Phila., 1976-78, adj. assoc. prof. physics, 1978-80; asst. prof. med. physics U. Pa. Med. Sch., Phila., 1980—; cons. physicist. Contbr. articles to profl. jours. Mem. Am. Inst. Physics, Am. Assn. Physicists in Medicine, AAUP, Sigma Xi, Sigma Pi Sigma. Hindu. Current Work: Medical research involving powerful (mega volt) X-rays in the treatment of cancer by radiotherapy techniques. Subspecialties: Nuclear physics; Cancer research (medicine). Home: 55 Lakeview Dr Cherry Hill NJ 08003 Office: Dept. Radiation Therapy Hosp U Pa 3400 Spruce St Philadelphia PA 19104

KUMAR, SHAILENDRA, mechanical engineer, consultant; b. Agra, India, July 2, 1941; came to U.S., 1961, naturalized, 1982; s. Ram Babu and Sushila (Gupta) Gupta; m. Shashi Kala Gupta, Jan. 16, 1967; children—Sanchay, Pankaj, Neil. I.Sc. in Sci. and Math., Agra Coll. Agra U., 1961; B.S. in Mech. Engring., Am. Inst. Engring. and Tech., 1965; cert. in engring. mgmt. George Washington U., 1967; cert. in air conditioning Trane Co., 1966. Registered profl. engr., Wis.; cert. plant engr. Am. Inst. Plant Engrs. With various cons. engring., archtl./engring. and contracting firms, Ill., Mich., N.Y., Washington areas, 1965-82; pres., cons. Shail & Assocs., Inc. Energetic Building Systems, Flossmoor, Ill., 1982—. Contbr. articles to profl. publs. Fellow Inst. Diagnostic Engrs. (founding); mem. ASME, ASHRAE, Assn. Energy Engrs. (cert. energy mgr.). Current work: Heating, ventilation, air conditioning, plumbing/piping, fire protection, utilities, energy conservation studies and system planning for various projects, including commercial, institutional, industrial, hospital and school projects; consulting engineering and construction management services in building environmental systems. Subspecialties: Mechanical engineering; Water supply and wastewater treatment. Home: 18701 S Cypress Ave Country Club Hills IL 60477 Office: Shail & Assocs Inc/Energetic Building Systems PO Box 421 Flossmoor IL 60422-0421

KUMAR, SUDHIR, clinical laboratory director, researcher, educator; b. Anjhi, India, Sept. 16, 1942; came to U.S., 1965, naturalized, 1982; s. Sita Ram and Sarla (Agarwal) Jain; m. Nilima Jain, Jan. 5, 1969; children—Avanti, Anjali. B.S. in Biology, U. Rajasthan, 1959, M.S. in Biochemistry and Chemistry, 1961; Ph.D. in Biochemistry and Neurochemistry, U. Lucknow, 1966; postdoctoral trainee Baylor Med. Sch., 1965-67. Cert. dir. clin. lab., N.Y., Ill. Sr. research scientist N.Y. State Research Inst. Neurochemistry, Wards Island, N.Y., 1967-69; chief biochemist pediatrics, Meth. Hosp., Bklyn., 1969-73; biochemist hematology, VA Hosp., Bklyn., 1973-75; dir. perinatal lab. and research Christ Hosp., Oaklawn, Ill., 1975-82; assoc. prof. biochemistry and neurochemistry, Rush Med. Coll., Chgo., 1979-83, prof. biochemistry and neurol. scis., 1983—; dir. and pres. Clin. Diagnostics, Hazel Crest, Ill., 1982—; cons. scientist medicine dept. VA Hosp., Hines, Ill., 1977-80; dir. Avanti Enterprises, Inc., Hazel Crest, 1982—, Ednl. Services, Inc., Flossmoor, Ill., 1982—. Editor: Biochemistry of Brain, 1980; Perinatal Medicine, vols. 1 to 3, 1979-82; Advances in Brain Research, 1984; contbr. articles to profl. publs.; inventor serum free culture media. Pres. Assn. Indians in Am., Ill. Chpt., 1983—, nat. v.p., 1982—; pres. Lucknow U. Alumni Assn. U.S.A., 1976-78, 82—; mem. bd. Festival of India, Inc., Ill., 1984—. Recipient Honor award, Jaswant Coll., Jodhpur, India, 1957; research fellow Council Sci. and Indsl. Research India, 1962-65; UNESCO fellow, Paris, 1971-73; Dreyfus Found. fellow, 1971, 73; recipient Inserm fellowship award, Govt. France, 1971-73; named Outstanding New Citizen, Citizenship Council Chgo., 1983. Fellow N.Y. Acad. Scis., Nat. Acad. Clin. Biochemists, Royal Inst. Chemistry; mem. Am. Soc. Biol. Chemists, Am. Inst. Nutrition, Am. Soc. Clin. Nutrition, Soc. Pediatric Research, Am. Soc. Neurochemistry, Am. Soc. Microbiologists, Soc. Exptl. Biology and Medicine, Sigma Xi. Jain Hindu. Club: Flossmoor Country. Lodge: Rotary. Current work: Research on enzymes of purine metabolism in developing brain, effect of malnutrition on developing fetus, tissue culture in diagnosis of metabolic disorders, vitamin B12 binding proteins in human tissues, amino acid metabolism and invorm errors of metabolism. Subspecialties: Neurochemistry; Biochemistry (medicine). Home: 18901 Springfield Flossmoor IL 60422 Office: Clin Diagnostics 3611 W 183rd St Hazel Crest IL 60429

KUMAR, VIJAYA BUDDHIRAJU, microbiologist, educator; b. India, May 2, 1945; s. Rajabhushana Rao Buddhiraju and Manorama (Sankara) Rao; m. Vijaya Mysore Lakshmi, Oct. 26, 1971; children: Mamokiran, Chakradhar. B.S., Osmania U., Hyderabad, India, 1963, M.S., 1965, Ph.D., 1972. Postdoctoral fellow Washington U., St. Louis, 1972-74, research coordinator, 1974-75; research asst. prof. infectious disease div. Washington U. Sch. Medicine, 1975-84, assoc. scientist Howard Hughes Med. Ctr., 1984—. Mem. Assn. Mycologists Am., AAAS, Am. Soc. Microbiology. Current Work: Evaluation of molecular events accompnaying dimorphism in microbes; dimorphism genetic-variations in strains of fungi, mechanism of fungal infection; molecular cloning of complement receptors. Subspecialties: Biochemistry (medicine); Microbiology (medicine). Home: 2725 Creekmont Ln Saint Louis MO 63125 Office: Howard Hughes Med Ctr Box 8045 Washington U Sch Medicine Saint Louise MO 63110

KUN, LUIS GUILLERMO, strategic planner, biomedical engineering educator, research anesthesiologist; b. Montevideo, Uruguay, Feb. 5, 1947; came to U.S., 1970; s. Ladislao and Francisca (Roth) K.; m. De Anna Trail, July 29, 1973 (div. 1976). B.S. in Nautical Sci., Merchant Marine Naval Acad., Uruguay, 1969; B.E.E., UCLA, 1972, M.E.E., 1974, Ph.D. in Biomed. Engring., 1978. Research assoc. Jules Stein Eye Inst., Los Angeles, 1972-73; research asst. dept. elect. engring. UCLA, 1973-74; biomed. engr. pacemakers LAC-USC Med. Ctr., Los Angeles, 1974-78; industry specialist sci. IBM-Data Processing, Los Angeles, 1978-82; strategic planner IBM-Health Devel., Irving, Tex., 1983—; mem. exec. com., adv. bd. Rehab. Engring. Ctr., Dallas, 1983—. Contbr. articles to profl. jours. Patentee in field. Nat. champion, Nat. Assn. Track and Field, Uruguay, 1968, 69, 70; qualifier for Munich Olympics, 200 meters, Internat. Olympic Com., Uruguay, 1972. Mem. IEEE (sr., chmn. indsl. relations 1983—, assoc. editor EMBS Mag. 1983—), Biomed. Engring. Soc. (charter founder), Sigma Xi. Current work: Cardiology, pacemakers, signal and image processing, artificial intelligence, expert systems, pattern recognition cardiovascular and neuromuscular physiology, exercise physiology, monitoring devices, computer workstations, health information systems. Subspecialties: Biomedical engineering; Cardiology. Home: 3824 Double Oak Irvine TX 75061 Office: IBM Health Devel 15-04-40 220 Las Colinas Irving TX 75062

KUNAR, ROY RAJPAUL, structural and earthquake engineer, consultant; b. Zorg, Essequibo, Guyana, Nov. 7, 1949; s. David Prem and Irene (Jagnandan) K.; m. Eleanor Marie Martin, Aug. 17, 1974; children—Melina Arianne, Darren Mitra. B.Sc. with 1st class honors in Aeronautical Engring., U. London, 1972, Ph.D. in Structural Mechanics, 1974. Sr. engr. in earthquake engring. Dames & Moore, London, 1974-79; prin. engr., dir. Principia Mechanica, London, 1980-84; sr. tech. cons. Structural Dynamics Research Corp. Engring., Hitchin, Hertsfordshire, Eng., 1985; dir. engring. services Impell Corp. U.K., 1985—. Contbr. articles to profl. jours. Recipient scholarship Guyana Govt., 1969, London U., 1972, prize Royal Aeronautical Soc., England, 1972. Mem. Seismological Soc. Am., Earthquake Engring. and Research Inst., Brit. Nuclear Energy Soc., Soc. Earthquake and Civil Engring. Dynamics (com. 1982—, exec. sub-com. 1983—; vice chmn. 1984—). Presbyterian. Club: Whitton Bridge (London) (com. 1983-84). Current work: Consultant and development and application of computer software for application to linear and non-linear solid dynamics engineering problems. Subspecialties: Nuclear engineering; Theoretical and applied mechanics. Home: 8 Mayfields Iveldale Dr Sheffield Bedfordshire SG17 5AD England Office: Impell Corp UK Genesis Centre Risley Warrington England

KUNCL, RALPH WILLIAM, physician, educator; b. Glendale, Calif., July 15, 1948; s. William J. and Lois (Mears) K.; m. Bonnie Sugar, June 21, 1975; children: Parker R.S., Margaux A. S. A.B. magna cum laude, Occidental Coll., 1970; Ph.D., U. Chgo., 1975, M.D., 1977. Diplomate: Am. Bd. Psychiatry and Neurology. Resident in medicine U. Chgo., 1977-78, in neurology, 1978-80; Muscular Dystrophy Assn. neuromuscular fellow Johns Hopkins U., 1980-83, asst. prof., 1983—. Contbr. articles to profl. jours. Haines scholar, 1967; Med. Scientist tng. program fellow, 1970-77. Mem. Soc. Neurosci., Am. Acad. Neurology, Am. Soc. Neurol. Invstigation, N.Y. Acad. Scis., Sigma Xi, Psi Chi. Current Work: Muscular dystrophy. Subspecialty: Neurology.

KUNDU, MUKUL R., astronomer, educator; b. Calcutta, India, Feb. 10, 1930; s. Makhan L. and Monoroma K.; m. Ranu Paul, Sept. 9, 1958; children: Krishna, Rina, Sanjit. B.S., Calcutta U., 1949, M.S., 1951; D.Sc., U. Paris, 1957. Research assoc. Paris Obs., 1956-58; sr. research fellow Nat. Phys. Lab., Delhi, India, 1958-59; research assoc. U. Mich., 1959-62; assoc. prof. Cornell U., Ithaca, N.Y., 1962-65, Tata Inst. Fund Research, Bombay, 1965-68; prof. astronomy U. Md., College Park, 1968—, dir. astronomy, 1978-85. Contbr. articles to profl. jours.; author: Solar Radio Astronomy, 1965; editor: Radio Physics of the Sun, 1980, Unstable Current Systems and Plasma Instabilities in Astrophysics, 1984. Recipient Anantha Kr. Meml. prize Calcutta U., 1958, Krishna Lal de Gold medal, 1959; NRC fellow, 1968, 74; Humboldt Found. U.S. Sr. Scientist awardee, 1978; Smithsonian Instn. awardee, 1980, 82. Mem. Am. Astron. Soc., Internat. Astron. Union, Internat. Radio Sci. Union, IEEE, Astron. Soc. India. Subspecialties: Radio and microwave astronomy; Solar physics. Home: 9013 Gettysburg Ln College Park MD 20740 Office: Astronomy Program U Md College Park MD 20742

KUNG, PATRICK CHUNG-SHU, biotechnology executive; b. Nanjing, China, July 10, 1947; s. Tao and Yuing (Li) K.; m. Rita W. Wu, Feb. 11, 1980; children—Julia, Calvin. B.S., FuJen U., Taiwan, 1968; Ph.D., U. Calif.-Berkeley, 1974. Research fellow M.I.T., 1974-77; staff scientist DuPont Co., Wilmington, Del., 1977-78; sr. research fellow Ortho Pharm. Co., Raritan, N.J., 1978-81; v.p. research Centocor, Malvern, Pa., 1982-83; co-founder, dir., v.p. research and devel. T Cell Scis., Inc., Cambridge, Mass., 1984—; vis. prof. Columbia U., N.Y.C., 1981—. Contbr. articles to profl. jours. Recipient Philip Hoffman award Johnson & Johnson Co., 1979. Mem. Am. Assn. Immunologists, N.Y. Acad. Scis., Sigma Xi. Roman Catholic. Subspecialties: Immunology (medicine); Transplantation. Office: T Cell Scis Inc 840 Memorial Dr Cambridge MA 02173

KUNG, SHAIN-DOW, plant molecular biologist; b. Shandong, China., Mar. 14, 1935; s. Chao-tzen and Chih (Zhu) K.; m. Helen C. C. Fu, Sept. 5, 1964; children: Grace, David, Andrew. Ph.D., U. Toronto, 1968. Research fellow Hosp. for Sick Children, Toronto, 1968-70; biologist UCLA, 1971-74; asst. prof. biology U. Md. Balt. County, Balt., 1974-77, assoc. prof., 1977-82, prof., 1982—, acting chmn., 1982-84, assoc. dean arts and scis., 1985—. Contbr. chpts. to books, articles to profl. jours. Recipient Philip Morris award for Disting. Achievement in tobacco sci., 1979; disting. scholar Nat. Acad. Sci., 1981; Fulbright awardee, 1982-83; NSF, NIH grantee. Mem. Am. Soc. Plant Physiologists, AAAS. Current Work: Studying the genetics, evolution, structure and function of RuBPCase and the organization, structure, evolution, expression of higher plant chloroplast genome using the recombinant DNA technology. Subspecialties: Genetics and genetic engineering (biology); Molecular biology. Office: Dept Biol Scis U Md Baltimore County Baltimore MD 21228

KUNIN, ISAAK A., mechanical engineering educator; b. Kharkow, USSR, Sept. 11, 1924; s. Abraham L. and Sarra B. (Rosetshtein) K.; m. Inessa M. Dvoskina; 1 son, Boris. M.S., Poly. Inst., Leningrad, USSR, 1952, Ph.D., 1958; D.Scis., Inst. Thermophysics, Acad. Sci. USSR, 1968. Engr. turbogenerator factory, USSR, 1952-56; researcher Mining Inst., Novosibirsk, USSR, 1956-63; prof., chmn. dept. physics Inst. Thermophysics, Acad. Sci., Novosibirsk, 1963-74; prof., chmn. dept. math. Electrotech. Inst., Novosibirsk, 1974-79; prof. dept. mech. engring. U. Houston, 1979—. Author 6 books in field; contbr. articles to profl. jours. Recipient award of excellence Halliburton Edn. Found., 1982. Mem. ASME, Acad. Mechanics, Soc. Indsl. and Applied Math. Patentee in field. Current Work: Continuum mechanics, elasticity, media with microstructure, linear and nonlinear waves, defects in solids, dislocations, quantization, lie groups and their representations, gauge theories, boundary value problems. Subspecialties: Solid mechanics; Applied mathematics. Home: 8219 Twin Tree Houston TX 77071 Office: Dept Mech Engring U Houston Houston TX 77004

KUNTZMAN, RONALD GROVER, pharmaceutical researcher; b. Bklyn, Sept. 17, 1933; s. Herman and Fanny (Brand) K.; m. Bernice Russman, May 29, 1955; children: Fred, Gary. B.S., Bklyn. Coll., 1955; M.S., George Washington U., 1957; Ph.D. in Biochemistry, 1962. Biochemist lab. chem. pharmacology Nat. Heart Inst., NIH, Bethesda, Md., 1955-62; sr. biochemist Wellcome Research Labs., Burroughs Wellcome & Co. (U.S.A.) Inc., Tuckahoe, N.Y., 1962-66, dep. head biochem. pharmacology dept., 1967-70; asso. dir. dept. biochemistry and drug metabolism Hoffmann-La Roche Inc., Nutley, N.J., 1970-71, asso. dir. biol. research, 1972-73, dir. therapeutics research, 1973-79, asst. v.p., 1974-81, dir. pharm. research and devel., 1980-81, v.p. pharm. research and devel., 1981-84, v.p. research and devel., 1984—. Mem. editorial bd.: Biochem. Pharmacology, 1966-68, Jour. Pharmacology and Exptl. Therapeutics, 1968-75, Neuropharmacology, 1970—, Xenobiotica, 1970-84, Archives Biochemistry and Biophysics, 1971-78, Life Scis., 1973-78; contbr. numerous articles to sci. jours. Mem. Am. Soc. Pharmacology and Exptl. Therapeutics (John Jacob Abel award 1969, nominating com. 1972, exec. com. div. drug metabolism 1973-76, chmn. nominating com. div. drug metabolism 1977, chmn. div. 1978-81, sec.-treas. 1981-83, mem. council 1981-83), Am. Soc. Biol. Chemists, Am. Coll. Neuropsychopharmacology, Soc. Toxicology, AAAS, Sigma XI. Current Work: Directs the discovery and development of novel therapeutics; individual research on metabolism of drugs, steroids and carcinogens; biogenic amine metabolism; pharmocokinetics. Subspecialties: Pharmacology; Biochemistry (medicine). Home: 12 Augustine Ave Ardsley NY 10502 Office: 340 Kingsland St Nutley NJ 07110

KUNZ, THOMAS HENRY, biology educator; b. Kansas City, Mo., June 11, 1938; s. William Henry and Edna Johanna (Dornfield) K.; m. Margaret Louise Brown, Dec. 27, 1962; children: Pamela Lyn, David Thomas. B.S., Central Mo. State U., 1961, M.S., 1962; M.A., Drake U., 1968; Ph.D., U. Kans.-Lawrence, 1971. Instr. biology Shawnee Mission (Kans.) Schs., 1962-67; asst. prof. biology Boston U., 1971-77, assoc. prof., 1977-84, prof., 1984—, dir. grad. studies, 1978-81, assoc. chmn. biology, 1981-85, chmn., 1985—. Editor: Ecology of Bats, 1982; Ecological and Behavioral Methods for the Study of Bats, 1986; contbr. over 50 articles in field to profl. jours. Adv. bd. Sch. for Field Studies, Boston, 1982. NSF grantee, 1973-81, 84-86; EPA contract, 1979. Mem. Am. Soc. Mammalogists, Ecol. Soc. Am., AAAS, Sigma Xi. Current Work: Research on the behavorial and physiological ecology of temperate and tropical bats, life history strategies, energy allocation, social behavior, feeding ecology. Subspecialties: Ecology (environmental science); Behavioral ecology. Office: Boston U 2 Cummington St Boston MA 02215

KUNZE, WALTER EDWARD, JR., civil engineer; b. St. Paul, Jan. 3, 1924; s. Walter Edward and Carolina Frieda (Brenning) K.; m. Frances Anne Halverson, June 20, 1947; children—Anne Catherine, Jean Marie, Elizabeth Joan. B.S. in Civil Engring., The Citadel, 1949; S.M. in Civil Engring., MIT, 1950. Registered profl. engr., Fla., S.C. Structural engr. Metcalf & Eddy, Boston, 1950-52, Toltz, King and Day, St. Paul, 1952; structural engr. Portland Cement Assn., Skokie, Ill., 1952-65, regional mgr., 1965-70, v.p. regional ops., 1970-71, group v.p., research and devel. Constrn. Tech. Labs., 1971—. Contbr. articles to profl. jours. Served to 1st lt. U.S. Army, 1943-46, ETO. Decorated Silver Star, Bronze Star, Purple Heart. Fellow Am. Concrete Inst. (v.p. 1984—), ASCE; mem. ASTM (com. chmn. 1982—), Prestressed Concrete Inst. Subspecialties: Civil engineering; Structural engineering. Home: 530 S Newbury Pl Arlington Heights IL 60005 Office: Portland Cement Assn 5420 Old Orchard Rd Skokie IL 60077

KUNZLER, JOHN EUGENE, physicist; b. Willard, Utah, Apr. 25, 1923; s. John Jacob and Freida (Meier) K.; m. Lois McDonald, Dec. 29, 1950; children: Carol Kunzler Blaine, Marilyn, Bonnie, Kim Kunzler Tomeo. B.S. in Chem. Engring, U. Utah; Ph.D., U. Calif., Berkeley. With AT & T Bell Labs., Murray Hill, N.J., 1952—, dir. electronic materials lab., 1969-73, dir. electronic materials and device lab., 1973-79, dir. electronic materials, processes and devices lab., 1979-83, dir. magnetic bubble subsystems and common tech. support lab., 1983-85, dir. future devices study ctr., 1985—. Contbr. articles to profl. jours. Recipient John Price Wetherill medal Franklin Inst., 1964; Internat. prize for new materials Am. Phys. Soc., 1979; Kamerlingh Onnes medal, 1979. Fellow Am. Phys. Soc., AAAS; mem. Am. Chem. Soc., Nat. Acad. Engring., Sigma Xi, Tau Beta Pi, Alpha Chi Sigma. Patentee in field. Subspecialty: Physical chemistry. Home: Route 2 Box 130 Port Murray NJ 07865 Office: AT & T Bell Labs 600 Mountain Ave Murray Hill NJ 07974

KUO, CHENG-YIH, polymer scientist, researcher; b. Tainan, Taiwan, Apr. 2, 1942; came to U.S., 1967, naturalized, 1977; s. Chih and Yueh-Chia (Wong) K.; m. Chiung-Yueh Chang, Jan. 16, 1978; 1 child, Annie. B.S., Nat. Taiwan U., 1966; M.S., U. Akron, 1969, Ph.D. in Polymer Sci., 1973. Postdoctoral fellow Inst. of Polymer Sci., U. Akron, Ohio, 1973-75; sr. chemist Glidden Coatings and Resins div. SCM Corp., Strongsville, Ohio, 1975-80, assoc. scientist, 1980-82, scientist, 1982—. Contbr. articles to profl. jours. Mem. Am. Chem. Soc. Current work: Fundamental research on solution properties of polymers and characterization of organic coatings. Subspecialty: Polymer physics. Office: Glidden Coatings & Resins div SCM Corp 16651 Sprague Rd Strongsville OH 44136

KUO, CLINTON CHANG-KIANG, electrical engineer; b. Hsin-Ying, Taiwan, China, Nov. 27, 1935; came to U.S., 1960, naturalized, 1972; s. Wen Yu and Shien (Liu) K.; m. Mary Ann Blasingame, Aug. 6, 1966; children—Debbie, Andy. B.S. in Elec. Engring., Cheng-Kong U., Taiwan, 1958; M.S. in Elec. Engring., Ga. Inst. Tech., 1962, Ph.D., 1968. Research engr. Ga. Inst. Tech., Atlanta, 1967-68; project leader Texas Instruments Inc., Houston, 1968-79; project mgr. Motorola Inc., Ausin, Tex., 1979—. Patentee in field (29). Author numerous tech. papers. Mem. IEEE, Eta Kappa Nu, Sigma Xi. Current work:

VLSI MOS Memory IC design and development. Subspecialties: Integrated circuits; Microelectronics. Home: 9639 Vista View Austin TX 78750 Office: 3501 Ed Bluestein Austin TX 78721

KUO, JYH-FA, pharmacologist, biochemist, educator; b. Taiwan, May 19, 1933; s. Shine-Fu and Mong (Huang) K.; m. Alexandra W. H. Lou, June 22, 1965; children: Calvin, Frances. B.S., Nat. Taiwan U., 1957; M.S., S.D. State U., 1961; Ph. D., U. Ill., 1964; M.D. (hon.), Linkoping (Sweden) U., 1980. Research biochemist Lederle Labs., Am. Cyanamid Co., Pearl River, N.Y., 1964-68; asst. prof. pharmacology Yale U. Sch. Medicine, New Haven, 1968-71; assoc. prof., 1971-72; assoc. prof. pharmacology Emory U. Sch. Medicine, Atlanta, 1972-76, prof., 1976—, prof. biochemistry, 1985—; mem. study sect. USPHS, NIH, 1982—. Contbr. articles to profl. jours. USPHS research career devel. awardee, 1971-76; USPHS grantee, 1970—; vis. scientist fellow Swedish Med. Research Council, 1979. Mem. AAAS, Am. Soc. Biol. Chemists, Am. Soc. Pharmacology and Exptl. Therapeutics. Current Work: Mechanisms of actions of calcium and cyclicnucleotides (intracellular messengers) and their roles in pathophysiology of cardiovascular system, brain, endocrine system and in cancer. Subspecialties: Molecular pharmacology; Biochemistry (medicine). Home: 2978 Greenbrook Way NE Atlanta GA 30345 Office: Dept Pharmacology Emory Univ Sch Medicine Atlanta GA 30322

KUO, PAO-TSIN, engineer; b. Shanghai, China, Aug. 28, 1938; came to U.S., 1965, naturalized, 1975; s. Ching-Lu and Yuan-Shen (Li) K.; m. Huey-Ching Chen, Dec. 10, 1966; children—Belinda, Ava, Cynthia. Engring. diploma Taipei Inst. Tech. Republic of China, 1958; M.S., N.D. State U., 1966; Ph.D., Rice U., 1974. Asst. engr. Taiwan Water Conservancy Bur., 1960-61, Keelung Harbor Bur., Republic of China, 1961-65; designer John A. Mackel Assocs., Los Angeles, 1965; sr. design engr. Cushing & Nevell Corp., N.Y.C., 1966-67; engring. specialist Bechtel Power Corp., Gaithersburg, Md., 1971-75; sect. leader Nuclear Regulatory Commn., Bethesda, Md., 1975—; com. mem. Am. Inst. Steel Constrn.-Nuclear Specification, N.Y.C., 1978-80; div. rep. Bechtel Seismic Task Force, Gaithersburg, 1972-75. Contbr. papers and reports to profl. publs. Treas. Orgn. Chinese Ams., Washington, 1977. Rice fellow, 1967-71. Mem. Earthquake Engring. Research Inst., ASCE. Current work: Development and application of the latest technology in earthquake and structural engineering to the design and construction of nuclear power plants. Subspecialty: Structural engineering. Home: 10 Thorburn Ct Gaithersburg MD 20878 Office: Nuclear Regulatory Commn 7920 Norfolk Ave Bethesda MD 20814

KUPERSMITH, JOEL, physician, researcher, educator; b. N.Y.C., Nov. 26, 1939; s. Charles Douglas and Sally (Schulz) K.; m. Judith Rose Friedman, June 15, 1969; children: David Z., Rebecca J., Adam J. B.S., Union Coll., Schenectady, 1960; M.D, N.Y. Med. Coll., 1964. Diplomate: Am. Bd. Internal Medicine, Sub-Bd. Cardiovascular Disease. Intern Kaiser Found. Hosp., San Francisco, 1964-65; resident and chief resident in internal medicine N.Y. Med. Coll., 1967-70; fellow in cardiology Beth Israel Hosp.-Harvard U. Med. Sch., Boston, 1970-72; research assoc. in pharmacology, asst. physician in medicine Columbia-Presbyn. Med. Center, N.Y.C., 1972-74, asst. prof. medicine, 1974-78, dir. electrocardiography and clin electrophysiology, 1975-77; chief Columbia-Presbyn. Med. Center (Arrhythmia Clinic), 1977; chief clin. pharmacology Mt. Sinai Sch. Medicine, N.Y.C., 1978-85, assoc. prof. medicine and pharmacology, 1979—, chief Arrythmia Clinic, 1977-85, chief cardiology Beth Israel Med. Ctr., 1985—. Contbr. numerous articles to sci jours. Served with M.C. USN, 1965-67. NIH grantee, 1978—; N.Y. Heart Assn. grantee, 1978-83; Hearst Found. grantee, 1979-82. Mem. Am. Soc. Clin. Investigation, Am. Soc. Pharmacology and Exptl. Therapeutics, Am. Soc. Clin. Pharmacology and Therapeutics, Am. Fedn. Clin. Research. Current Work: Cellular and clinical effects of antirrhythmic drugs: ion sensitive microelectrodes, cellular electrophysiology, antirhythmic drugs, clinic electrophysiology, electrical cardiac mapping, cardiac arrhythmias. Subspecialties: Cardiology; Pharmacology. Home: 16 Courseview Rd Bronxville NY 10708 Office: Beth Israel Med Ctr 10 Nathan D Perlman Pl New York NY 10003

KUPFER, CARL, ophthalmologist; b. N.Y.C., Feb. 9, 1928; s. James and Hannah (Goldwasser) K.; m. Muriel Kaiser, Dec. 9, 1969; children—Charles David, Sarah Delia. A.B., Yale U., 1948; M.D., Johns Hopkins U., 1952. Diplomate: Am. Bd. Ophthalmology. Intern, asst. resident Wilmer Eye Inst., Johns Hopkins Hosp., 1952-54; lab. asst. biostatistics Johns Hopkins Sch. Medicine, 1953-54; research fellow in ophthalmology Wilmer Eye Inst., 1957-58, Harvard Med. Sch., 1958-60, instr., 1960-62, asst. prof. ophthalmology, 1962-66; prof., chmn. dept. ophthalmology U. Wash. Sch. Medicine, 1966-70; dir. Nat. Eye Inst., NIH, Bethesda, Md., 1970—; pres. Internat. Agy. for Prevention of Blindness, 1982—. Mem. editorial bd.; Investigative Ophthalmology, 1969-78, Am. Jour. Ophthalmology, 1971-82; contbr. articles to med. jours. Bd. dirs. Helen Keller Internat. Served with USAF, 1954-56. Mem. Am. Physiol. Soc., Assn. Research in Vision and Ophthalmology, Am. Acad. Ophthalmology, Am. Ophthalmology Soc., Pan Am. Ophthalmol. Soc. Subspecialty: Ophthalmology. Office: Nat Eye Inst NIH Bethesda MD 20205

KUPFERBERG, LENN CARL, physicist; b. N.Y.C., July 27, 1951; s. Jack and Dorothy (Silbermann) K.; m. Karen Frances Fink, June 12, 1976; 1 son, David Charles. B.S., Trinity Coll., 1973; M.A., U. Rochester (N.Y.), 1975, Ph.D., 1979. Postdoctoral assoc. MIT, Cambridge, 1978-80; asst. prof. Worcester Poly. Inst., Mass., 1980-84; sr. scientist research div Raytheon Co., Lexington, Mass., 1984—. Contbr. articles to physics jours. Eastman Kodak fellow, 1974-76. Mem. Am. Phys. Soc., AAAS, Magnetics Soc. of IEE, Sigma Xi, Sigma Pi Sigma. Republican. Jewish. Current work: Orientational order disorder transitions, magnetic, eliastic, dielectric and thermal properties of solids; experimental physics; ferro-and anti-ferro magnetism; ferro and anti-ferro electrics; piezoelectrics. Subspecialties: Condensed matter physics; Magnetic physics. Home: 1239 Edgell Rd Framingham MA 01701 Office: Research Div Raytheon Co 131 Spring St Lexington MA 02173

KUPPER, ROBERT JOE, chemist; b. York, Nebr., Jan. 5, 1950; s. Bernard Charles and Betty Jean (Pickrel) K.; m. Susan Gwen Maley, June 1, 1974; 1 child, Gwendolyn Sue. B.S., Kearney State Coll., 1973; Ph.D., U. Nebr.-Lincoln, 1982; postgrad. U. Calif.-Berkeley, 1980. Sci. staff Eppley Inst., U. Nebr., Omaha, 1974-77; research assoc. Frederick Cancer Research Facility, Md., 1978-80, scientist I, 1982-83, scientist II, 1983-84; research chemist/chemist W.R. Grace & Co., Columbia, Md., 1984-85, sr. research chemist, 1985—; adj. asst. prof. Western Med. Coll., Westminster, 1983-84. Contbr. articles to jours., chpts. to books. Mem. Am. Chem. Soc., AAAS Phi Lambda Upsilon. Current work: Synthetic method development, enantioselective transformations of prochiral materials, enzymatic synthesis, chemistry of amino acids and peptides, chemical carcinogenesis. Subspecialties: Organic chemistry; Enzyme technology. Home: 110 Village Way Mount Airy MD 21771 Office: W R Grace & Co 7379 Rt 32 Columbia MD 21044

KUPST, MARY JO, psychologist, researcher; b. Chgo., Oct. 4, 1945; d. George Eugene and Winifred Mary (Hughes) K.; m. Alfred P. Stresen-Reuter, Jr., Aug. 21, 1977. B.S., Loyola U., Chgo., 1967, M.A., 1969, Ph.D., 1972. Lic. psychologist, Ill. Postdoctoral fellow U. Ill, Med. Center, Chgo., 1972—; research psychologist assoc. prof. in psychiatry and pediatrics Northwestern U. Med. Sch., 1981—. Editor: (with J.L. Schulman) The Child with Cancer, 1980. Contbr. articles to profl. jours. Mem. Am. Psychol. Assn. Current Work: Research in coping with physical illness (especially leukemia) in children. Subspecialty: Psychological aspects of illness. Home: 7920 Howe Rd Ringwood IL 60072 Office: Dept Child Psychiatry Children's Meml Hosp 2300 Children's Plaza Chicago IL 60614

KUROIWA, JULIO, civil engineering educator; b. Canete, Lima, Peru, Apr. 22, 1936; s. Juan and Elvira (Horiuchi) K.; m. Gloria Ana Zevallos, July 24, 1965; children—Julio Martin, Hector Eduardo. Civil Engr. Nat. U. Engring., Lima, 1959; diploma Internat. Inst. Seismology and Earthquake Engring., Toyko, 1962; M.S., Calif. Inst. Tech., 1966, Engr., 1967. Asst. prof. civil engring. Nat. U. Engring., Lima, 1962-65, assoc. prof., 1965-69, prof., 1969—; pres. Kuroiwa-Kogan-Valdiva Cons. Engrs., 1970—; lectr. in field; mem. ad-hoc expert group UN-HABITAT; mem. sci. com. Peru Civil Def., 1973—, chmn., 1978-80; mem adv. comes. for reconstrn. of affected areas by natural disasters, 1970-73. Contbr. articles to profl. jours. Named Disting. Latin-Am. lectr. Fulbright Commn., 1978; grantee, UN Disaster Relief Office, 1981, UN Ctr. for Human Settlements, 1983. Mem. Internat. Assn. for Earthquake Engring. (bd. dirs. 1980—), Peruvian Assn. for Earthquake Engring. (pres. 1976—), Peruvian Assn. Engrs. (bd. dirs. 1970-72), Peruvian Assn. Cons. (bd. dirs. 1984—), U.S. Earthquake Engring. Research Inst., Sigma Xi. Roman Catholic. Club: Real Country (Lima). Current work: Microzonation; multidisciplinary approach, to study all natural disasters threating an area for disaster mitigation planning for human settlements and civil works. Subspecialties: Civil engineering; Geology. Home: Ave Del Parque sur 442 Lima Peru 27 Office: Nat U Engring Ave Tupac Amaru s/n PO Box 1301 Lima Peru 1

KURSUNOGLU, BEHRAM N., physicist. Prof. physics, dir. Ctr. for Theoretical Studies, U. Miami, Coral Gables, Fla. Subspecialty: Theoretical physics. Office: U Miami Ctr Theoretical Studies PO Box 249055 Coral Gables FL 33124*

KURTZ, THEODORE STEPHEN, psychoanalyst, consultant; b. N.Y.C., Apr. 25, 1944; s. Maxwell Arthur and Reba Evelyn (Rosenberg) K.; m. Maritza J. Zurita, Sept. 12, 1975. A.B., Boston U., 1964; M.A., N.Y. U., 1966; tng. psychoanalysis, N.Y. Soc. Freudian Psychologists, N.Y.C., 1968-74. Diplomate: Am. Inst. Counseling and Psychotherapy. Pvt. practice psychoanalysis, Cold Spring Harbor, N.Y., 1966—, tchr.-coordinator classes for emotionally disabled, Northport, N.Y., 1966-70; prin. Woodward Mental Health Center, Freeport, N.Y., 1970-74; asst. prof. C.W. Post Coll., L.I. U., 1974-81, cons. to industry, 1975—. Contbr. articles to profl. jours. Fellow Am. Orthopsychiat. Assn.; mem. Acad. Psychologists in Marriage, Sex, and Family Therapy (clin.), Am. Assn. Marriage and Family Therapists (clin.), Nassau County Psychol. Assn. (exec. bd. 1978), Am. Acad. Psychotherapists, Am. Psychol. Asn., Soc. Psychoanalytic Psychotherapy. Jewish. Current Work: Theory and modification of psychoanalytic technique; application of psychoanalytic theory to industry; organizational and group dynamics theory; research on causes, cults, and terrorism. Subspecialty: Developmental psychology. Home: Willow Brook Rd PO Box 529 Cold Spring Harbor NY 11724 Office: 145 E 74th St New York NY 10021

KURTZE, DOUGLAS ALAN, physics educator; b. Mt. Vernon, N.Y., Oct. 15, 1954; s. Robert Benjamin and Murielee (Brown) K. B.A., Lehigh U., 1974, B.S., 1974; M.S., Cornell U., 1978, Ph.D., 1980. Research physicist Carnegie-Mellon U., Pitts., 1979-82; resident visitor Bell Labs., Murray Hill, N.J., summer 1983, AT&T Bell Labs., summer 1984; asst. prof. physics Clarkson U., Potsdam, N.Y., 1982—. Contbr. papers to profl. lit. Mem. Am. Phys. Soc., Phi Beta Kappa, Sigma Pi Sigma. Bahá'í. Current work: Instabilities, mode selection and pattern formation in solidification and related processes. Subspecialties: Condensed matter physics; Statistical physics. Home: RD 4 Box 169 Canton NY 13617 Office: Dept Physics Clarkson U Potsdam NY 13676

KURTZMAN, RALPH HAROLD, JR., research mycologist; b. Mpls., Feb. 21, 1933; s. Ralph Harold and Susie Marie (Elwell) K.; m. Nancy Virginia Leussler, Aug. 27, 1955; children: Steven Paul, Sue. B.S., U. Minn., 1955; M.S., U. Wis., 1958; Ph.D., 1959. Asst. Prof. plant pathology U. R.I., Kingston, 1959-62; asst. Prof. biology U. Minn., Morris, 1962-65; biochemist Western Regional Research Labs., U.S. Dept. Agr., Albany, Calif., 1965—; guest scientist Tech. Research Center Finland, 1980; inst. mushroom cultivation U. Calif. Extension, Berkeley, 1981. Contbr. chpts. to books, articles to profl. jours. Chmn. camp com. Berkeley YMCA, 1970-80. Mem. Am. Chem. Soc., Mycological SSoc. Am., Am. Soc. Plant Physiologists, Am. Mushroom Inst., Mushroom Growers Assn. Gt. Britain, Calif. Native Plant Soc. (treas. 1971-72). Patentee in field. Current Work: Biology and cultivation of mushrooms, atlatoxin in corn. Subspecialties: Mycology; Plant physiology (agriculture). Home: 445 Vassar Ave Berkeley CA 94708 Office: 800 Buchanan St Berkeley CA 94720

KURZWEIL, RAYMOND C., computer scientist, entrepreneur; b. N.Y.C., Feb. 12, 1948; s. Fredric and Hannah K.; m. Sonya Rosenwald, Aug. 3, 1975; 1 child, Ethan. B.S., MIT, 1970; Ph.D., Hofstra U., 1982. Chmn., Kurzweil Computer Products, Inc./Xerox, Cambridge, Mass., 1974—; pres. Kurzweil Music Systems, Inc., Waltham, Mass., 1982—, Kurzweil Applied Intelligence, Inc., Waltham, 1982—. Recipient Grace Murray Hopper/Outstanding Young Computer Scientist of Yr. award Assn. Computing Machinery, 1978; Nat. award Personal Computing to Aid the Handicapped Johns Hopkins U., 1981; named to Computer Design Hall of Fame, Computer Mag., 1982; recipient Francis Joseph Campbell award Am. Library Assn., 1983. Subspecialty: Artificial intelligence. Office: Kurzweil Applied Intelligence Inc 411 Waverley Oaks Rd Waltham MA 02154

KUSCH, POLYKARP, physicist, educator; b. Blankenburg, Germany, Jan. 26, 1911; came to U.S., 1912, naturalized, 1923; s. John Matthias and Henrietta (van der Haas) K.; m. Edith Starr McRoberts, Aug. 12, 1935 (dec. 1959); children—Kathryn, Judith, Sara; m. Betty Jane Pezzoni, 1960; children—Diana, Maria. B.S., Case Inst. Tech., 1931, D.Sc., 1956; M.S., U. Ill., 1933, Ph.D., 1936, D.Sc. (hon.), 1961; D.Sc. (hon.), Ohio State U., 1959, Colby Coll., 1961, Gustavus Adolphus Coll., St. Peter, Minn., 1962, Yeshiva U., 1976, Coll. of Incarnate Word, 1980, Columbia U., 1983. Engaged as teaching asst. U. Ill., 1931-36; research asst. U. Minn., 1936-37; instr. Columbia U., 1937-41, assoc. prof. physics, 1946-49, prof., 1949-72, chmn. dept. physics, 1949-52, 60-63, acad. v.p. and provost, 1969-72; engr. Westinghouse, 1941-42; research asso. Columbia U., 1942-44; mem. tech. staff Bell Telephone Labs., 1944-46; prof. physics U. Tex.-Dallas, 1972—, Eugene McDermott prof., 1974-80, Regental prof., 1980-82, Regental prof. emeritus, 1982—. Recipient Nobel prize in physics, 1955, Ill. Achievement award U. Ill., 1975; Fellow; Center for Advanced Study in Behavioral Sciences, 1964-65. Fellow Am. Phys. Soc., AAAS; mem. Am. Acad. Arts and Scis., Am. Philos. Soc., Nat. Acad. Scis. Democrat. Research in atomic and molecular beams and optical molecular spectroscopy. Subspecialty: Atomic and molecular physics. Office: Univ Tex-Dallas PO Box 688 Richardson TX 75083

KUSHNER, HAROLD JOSEPH, educator; b. N.Y.C., July 29, 1933; s. Hyman and Harriet (Messing) K.; m. Linda Jane Rosen, Sept. 18, 1960; children—Diana Jeanne, Nina Joanne. B. Elec. Engring, Coll. City N.Y., 1955; M.S., U. Wis., 1956, Ph.D., 1958. With Lincoln Lab., Mass. Inst. Tech., 1958-63, Research Inst. Advanced Studies, Balt., 1963-64; prof. applied math. and engring. Brown U., 1964—; cons. to govt. and industry, 1963—. Contbr. monograph, text, articles. Fellow IEEE; mem. Inst. Math. Statistics, Soc. Indsl. and Applied Math., Ops. Research Soc. Am. Fields: Control and Communication theory; stochastic systems theory. Current work: Stochastic control theory. Home: 560 Lloyd Ave Providence RI 02906

KUSHNER, HARVEY DAVID, research and systems engineering firm executive; b. N.Y.C., Dec. 28, 1930; s. Morris and Hilda (Zweibel) K.; m. Roe Rehert, Jan. 14, 1951; children: Gantt A., Todd R., Lesley K. B.S. in Engring, Johns Hopkins U., 1951. Assoc. engr. Bur. Ships, U.S. Navy, Washington, 1951-52; mem. tech. staff Melpar, Inc., Falls Church, Va., 1953-54; staff and mgmt. positions ORI, Inc. (formerly Ops. Research, Inc.), Silver Spring, Md., 1955—, exec. v.p., 1963-68, pres, 1969—, chmn. bd., 1977—; v.p. Reliance Group, Inc., N.Y.C., 1971-77; pres. Disclosure, Inc., Silver Spring, 1972-77; cons. Applied Physics Lab., Johns Hopkins U., 1960-64, Com. on Undersea Warfare, Nat. Acad. Sci., 1963-64; trustee, mem. exec. com. Nat. Security Indsl. Assn., Washington, from 1963; dir. Profl. Services Council, Washington, 1974—. Mem. Montgomery County Econ. Adv. Council, Rockville, Md., 1981—, chmn., 1983—; campaign chmn. Montgomery County United Way, Rockville, 1980, exec. bd., 1981—; chmn. Montgomery County Commn. on Higher Edn. in High Tech., 1983-84, mem. (Md.) Gov's High Tech. Roundtable, 1983—. Fellow N.Y. Acad. Scis.; mem. IEEE (sr.), Nat. Space Club (bd. govs.), ASME, AIAA, AAAS, Ops. Research Soc. Am., Armed Forces Communications and Electronics Assn., Inst. Mgmt. Scis., Navy League of U.S. Club: Cosmos (Washington). Current Work: Operations research and system engineering. Subspecialties: Operations research (engineering); Systems engineering. Office: ORI Inc 1375 Piccard Dr MD 20850

KUSHNER, IRVING, rheumatologist, immunobiologist, educator; b. N.Y.C., Jan. 16, 1929; s. Boris and Rose (Klosner) K.; m. Enid Pearl Lupeson, Jan. 2, 1955; children: Ellen Ruth, Philip Seth, David Micah. B.A., Columbia U., 1950; M.D., Washington U., St. Louis, 1954. Diplomate: Am. Bd. Internal Medicine and subsplty. in rheumatology. Intern Yale-New Haven Hosp., 1954-55; clin. assoc. clin. center NIH, Bethesda, Md., 1955-57; asst. resident Harvard U. Med. Services, Boston City Hosp., 1957-58; instr. to assoc. prof. medicine Case Western Res. U., 1958-73, prof. medicine, 1974—; med. dir. Highland View Rehab. Hosp., 1985—. Contbr. over 160 publs. to profl. jours.; editor books. Served with USPHS, 1955-57. Recipient Nat. Vol. Service citation Arthritis Found. Mem. Am. Rheumatism Assn., Am. Assn. Immunologists, N.Y. Acad. Sci., AAAS, ACP, Central Soc. Clin. Research. Current Work: Studies of the regulation of biosynthesis of C-reactive protein. Subspecialties: Internal medicine; Rheumatology. Home: 22149 Rye Rd Shaker Heights OH 44122 Office: 3395 Scranton Rd Cleveland OH 44109

KUSKO, ALEXANDER, electrical engineer; b. N.Y.C., Apr. 4, 1921; s. Theodore and Judith (Kulchinsky) K.; m. Isadora Sloan, July 7, 1940; children—Andrea Lee, Jonathan Sloan. B.S.E.E., Purdue U., 1942; S.M.E.E., MIT, 1944, Sc.D., 1951. Registered profl. engr., Mass., Calif. Asst. MIT, Cambridge, 1942-44, successively instr., asst. prof., assoc. prof., 1946-59, lectr., 1959-84; pres. Alexander Kusko, Inc., Needham Heights, Mass., 1957-84, sr. cons., 1957—; dir. Isoreg Corp., Littleton, Mass. Author 3 books on elec. engring. Editor MIT Press monographs on elec. engring. Contbr. articles to profl. jours. Served to lt. (j.g.) USN, 1944-46, PTO. Recipient Disting. Alumnus award Purdue U., 1979. Fellow IEEE (William E. Newell award 1980). Club: Chemists (N.Y.C.). Current work: Power electronics, emphasis on electric motor drives and controls. Subspecialties: Electrical engineering; Electronics. Home: 80 Doublet Hill Rd Weston MA 02193 Office: 161 Highland Ave Needham Heights MA 02194

KUSSE, BRUCE RAYMOND, applied and engineering physics educator, plasma physics; b. Rochester, N.Y., Aug. 10, 1938; s. Clarence Raymond and Laura (Tellier) K. S.B., MIT, 1960, S.M., 1964, Ph.D., 1969. Sr. scientist Edgerton, Germerhauser & Grear, Bellford, Mass., 1970-71; faculty Cornell U., Ithaca, N.Y., 1971—; vis. scientist fusion ctr. MIT, 1978-79; cons. Lawrence Livermore Labs., 1971—, Naval Research Lab., 1971—. Contbr. articles to prof. jours. Served to lt. comdr., USNR, 1960-63. Mem. Am. Physical Soc., Univ. Fusion Assn. Current work: Intense electron and ion beams, plasma fusion. Subspecialties: Plasma physics; Fusion. Home: 144 N Sunset Dr Ithaca NY 14850 Office: Cornell U Ithaca NY 14851

KUSUDA, TAMAMI, government official, mechanical engineer; b. Seattle, June 24, 1925; s. Torao and Mine (Kawahara) K.; m. Tomoko Ishikawa, Nov. 5, 1955; children—Leo, Kay; Yuri; m. Selma Teresa Myers, May 13, 1982. B.S., Tokyo U., 1947; M.S., U. Wash., 1952; Ph.D., U. Minn., 1955. Instr., Okayama U., Japan, 1948-50; research asst. U. Minn.-Mpls., 1952-55; staff engr. Worthington Corp., East Orange, N.J., 1955-62; research engr. Nat. Bur. Standards, Gaithersburg, Md., 1962-70, sect. chief, 1970-82, div. chief, 1982—. Author: Handbook of Building Heat Transfer, 1985. Editor: Use of Computers for Building, 1972; Underground Heat Dispersal Systems, 1975. Fellow ASHRAE; mem. ASME, Automated Procedures for Engring. Cons. (hon.). Democrat. Unitarian. Club: Wanderbirds Hiking (treas. 1981-84) (Washington). Current work: Building physics; use of computers for environmental engineering related to buildings. Subspecialty: Mechanical engineering. Office: National Bur of Standards Gaithersburg MD 20899

KUSWA, GLENN WESLEY, physicist; b. Milw., Dec. 12, 1940; s. Webster S. and Elvira (Lipman) K.; m. Patricia Sue Bedwell, June 6, 1965; children—Kevin, Erika. B.S., U. Wis.-Madison, 1962, M.S. in Physics, 1963, Ph.D., 1970. Mem. tech. staff Sandia Nat. Labs., Albuquerque, 1970-74; project mgr. AEC, Washington, 1974-75; supr. beam physics Sandia Nat. Labs., Albuquerque, 1975-78, mgr. particle beam fusion research dept., 1978-82, mgr. future options group, 1984—; tech. adv. to asst. sec. energy Dept. Energy, Washington, 1982-84. Contbr. numerous articles to sci. jours. Treas., Bear Canyon Neighborhood Assn., Albuquerque, 1979—; bd. dirs. Rio Grande Planned Parenthood Assn., 1982—. Mem. Am. Phys. Soc., Sigma Xi. Democrat. Unitarian. Current work: Plasma physics, fusion energy, pulsed power applications, defende sciences, technological futures study. Subspecialty: Plasma physics. Home: 7538 Bear Canyon Rd NE Albuquerque NM 87109 Office: Sandia Nat Labs Kirtland AFB Albuquerque NM 87109

KUTINA, JAN, educator; b. Prague, Czechoslovakia, July 23, 1924; came to U.S., 1969, naturalized, 1980; s. Jan and Amalie (Tauberova) K.; m. Irena Kutinova, Apr. 10, 1950; children: Irene, Jan. PhMr., Charles U., 1948, RNDr., 1949, C.Sc., 1956, Docent, 1954. Asso. prof. geochemistry Charles U., Prague, 1954-68; vis. prof. econ. geology Lehigh U., Bethlehem, Pa., 1968-69; research scientist Geol. Survey of Can., Ottawa, Ont., 1969-70; sr. research scientist Am. U., Washington, 1977-79, 80, research prof., geologist, 1980—; cons. geologist Bethlehem Steel Corp., 1974-75, UN, 1970-74, W.A. Bowes, Inc., 1976—. Chief editor: Global Tectonics and Metallogeny, 1978—. Mem. Internat. Assn. on Genesis of Ore Deposits (sec. gen. 1964-69), Am. Geol. Soc., others. Club: e de Mineralogia (hon. mem. Brazil). Current Work: Global tectonics/metallogeny; geochemistry & mineralogy of ore deposits. Subspecialties: Geochemistry; Mineralogy. Office: Dept Chemistry Am Univ Washington DC 20016

KUTZ, NANCY ANN, research chemist; b. Youngstown, Ohio, Sept. 15, 1953; d. Dane James and Evelyn RoJean (Pearce) Lobaugh; m. William James Kutz, Nov. 1, 1975. B.Sc., Ohio U., 1975; Ph.D., U. Ill.-Chgo., 1981. Researcher, Argonne Nat. Lab. (Ill.), summer 1976; teaching asst. U. Ill.-Chgo., 1977-78, coordinator freshman chemistry, 1978-81; research chemist Amoco Chems Corp., Naperville, Ill., 1981—. Contbr. articles to profl. jours. Active local YMCA. Mem. Am. Chem. Soc., Internat. Zeolite Assn., Brit. Zeolite Assn., Chgo. Catalysis Club, Iota Sigma Pi. Club: Scubaneers (treas. 1982-84) (Glen Ellyn, Ill.). Current work: Synthesis, characterization and catalytic properties of molecular sieves and zeolites, with applications to hydrocarbon conversion processes. Subspecialties: Catalysis chemistry; Inorganic chemistry. Office: Amoco Chems Corp PO Box 400 Naperville IL 60566

KUTZSCHER, EDGAR WALTER, cons. physicist; b. Leipzig, Germany, Mar. 21, 1906; s. Arno Fritz and Maria Helene K.; m. Edith Hildgard Wagner, Nov. 22, 1919; children: Detlef, Bernd. Ph.D., U. Berlin, 1931; D.Sc., Inst. Tech. Berlin, 1935; D.Eng. (hon.), U. Hannover, 1963. Research and teaching asst. U. Berlin, Inst. Tech. Berlin, 1930-33; physicist German War Dept., 1933-37; research physicist, then asst. prof. Inst. Tech. Berlin, 1936-46; dir. research Electroacustic Co., Kiel, Germany, 1937-45; dir. Univ. Ext., Flensburg, W.Ger., 1945-47; physicist U.S. Navy, 1947-51, Santa Barbara (Calif.) Research Ctr., 1951-53; dept. mgr. Lockheed Aircraft Co., Burbank, Calif., 1954-72, cons. physicist, 1972—. Contbr. articles to profl. jours. Recipient Todt prize Govt. Ger., 1944. Mem. Optical Soc. Am. Presbyterian. Patentee in field. Current Work: Research and development of infrared sensors and devices. Subspecialty: Infrared detectors and technology. Home: 15450 Briarwood Dr Sherman Oaks CA 91403

KUYPER, LEE FREDERICK, medicinal chemist, researcher; b. Madison, S.D., Feb. 28, 1949. B.S., Ouachita U., 1971; Ph.D., U. Ark., 1977. Research assoc. U. N.C., Chapel Hill, 1976-77; research scientist Burroughs Wellcome Co., Research Triangle Park, N.C., 1977—. Contbr. articles to profl. jours. Mem. Am. Chem. Soc., Drug Info. Assn. Current work: Computer based molecular modeling of enzyme inhibitor complexes; design and synthesis of enzyme inhibitors. Subspecialties: Drug design; Medicinal chemistry. Office: 3030 Cornwallis Rd Research Triangle Park NC 27709

KVICK, ÅKE HARRY, chemist; b. Bollnas, Sweden, May 29, 1942; came to U.S., 1980; s. Anders Ivar and Anna Lisa (Martinsson) K.; m. Karin Mona-Britt Wiklöf, Mar. 18, 1967; children—Karin Annelie, Lars Andreas. B.Sc., U. Uppsala, Sweden, 1967, M.Sc., 1970, Ph.D., 1974. Research asst. U. Uppsala, 1965-75, research prof., 1975-80; assoc. chemist Brookhaven Nat. Lab., Upton, N.Y., 1980-83, chemist, 1983—; cons. Exxon, N.J., 1983. Contbr. articles to profl. publs. Recipient Letterstedt award Royal Swedish Acad. Sci., 1980. Mem. Am. Chem. Soc., Am. Crystallographic Assn. Lutheran. Current work: Application of neutrons and synchrotron radiation in structural studies, chemistry physics and structure of zeolites and dielectric materials, instrumentation. Subspecialties: Crystallography; Inorganic chemistry. Home: 6 Evans Ct Huntington NY 11746 Office: Brookhaven Nat Lab Dept Chemistry Bldg 555 Upton NY 11973

KVIST, TAGE NIELSEN, anatomy educator; b. Copenhagen, Denmark, Jan. 17, 1942; came to U.S., 1969; s. Kai and Alma (Nielsen) K.; m. Sharon Lea Armstrong, May 8, 1965; children: Lea-Ann, Lisa Joy, Charlene Tia. B.Sc., U. B.C., Can., 1966, M.SC., 1969; Ph.D., U. Pa., 1973. Teaching fellow U. Pa., Phila., 1969-73, research assoc., 1973-76; lectr. Rosemont (Pa.) Coll., 1972; chief neurosurgery research Joseph Stokes Jr. Research Inst., Phila., 1973-76; asst. prof. anatomy Phila. Coll. Osteo. Medicine, 1976-80, assoc. prof., 1980—; cons. in field. Contbr. articles to profl. jours. Treas. Garfield Park PTO, Willingboro, N.J., 1979-81, pres., 1981-82. Recipient Humanitarian award V.J. Sarte Nat. Hydrocephalus Research Found., 1976; March of Dimes grantee, 1973-75; NIH grantee, 1979-83; Spina Bifida grantee, 1982-83. Mem. Soc. Devel. Biology, Teratology Soc., Humanity Gifts Registry, Am. Assn.

Anatomists, Spina Bifida Assn. Am. (del. 1981—), Spina Bifida Assn. Delaware Valley (dir. 1978—, pres. 1981—). Club: Willingboro Atheltic. Current Work: Development anomalies, teratology. Subspecialties: Developmental biology; Neurobiology. Home: 32 Globe Ln Willingboro NJ 08046 Office: Phila Coll Osteo Med Dept Anatomy 4150 City Ave Philadelphia PA 19131

KWIATKOWSKI, GEORGE THOMAS, polymer chemist; b. Paterson, N.J., Nov. 14, 1940; s. Edward Joseph and Nell Kwiatkowski; m. Mary Anne DiNapoli, Nov. 21, 1964. B.S., Rutgers U., 1962; M.S., Columbia U., 1963, Ph.D., 1965; postdoctoral Harvard U., 1965-66. Dir. research and devel. Union Carbide Corp., Bound Brook, N.J., 1966—. Patentee polymers. Current work: Engineering polymers, composites, cycloaliphatic epoxides, specialty polyurethanes. Subspecialty: Polymer chemistry. Office: Union Carbide Corp Splty Polymers and Composites Div Bound Brook NJ 08805

KWIK, ROBERT JULIUS, engineering consultant; b. Newark, Jan. 6, 1936; s. Julius and Frieda Rose (Schilling) K.; m. Jean Agnes Chown, Sept. 12, 1958; children: Kenneth Lawrence, Karen Elizabeth, Jeanne Frieda. M.E., Stevens Inst. Tech., 1958; M.S., Calif. Inst. Tech., 1959; B.D., Princeton Theol. Sem., 1962, Th.M., 1966; Ph.D., U. Pa., 1974. Ordained minister Presbyterian Ch., 1962; pastor 1st Presbyn. Ch., Steelton, Pa., 1962-65; instr. math. U. Vt., Burlington, 1965-55; prof. physics Coll. de Libamba, Makak, Cameroon, 1967-70; engr. Gibbs & Hill, Inc., N.Y.C., 1974-82, Stone & Webster Engring. Co., N.Y.C., 1982—. Contbr. articles to profl. jours. Mem. Soc. for Risk Analysis, Am. Nuclear Soc., ASME, AAAS. Democrat. Current Work: Application of probabilistic risk assessment fo improvement of nuclear plant reliability. Subspecialties: Nuclear engineering; Mechanical engineering. Home: 50 Terrace Ave Nutley NJ 07110 Office: Stone and Webster Engring Co 250 W 34th St New York NY 10019

KWIRAM, ALVIN L., physical chemist; b. Riverhills, Man., Can., Apr. 28, 1937; came to U.S., 1954; s. Rudolf and Wilhelmina A. (Bilske) K.; m. Verla Rae Michel, Aug. 9, 1964; children: Andrew Brandt, Sidney Marguerite. B.S. in Chemistry; B.A. in Physics, Walla Walla (Wash.) Coll., 1958; Ph.D. in Chemistry, Calif. Inst. Tech., 1963. Alfred A. Noyes instr. Calif. Inst. Tech., Pasadena, 1962-63; research asso. physics dept. Stanford (Calif.) U., 1963-64; instr. chemistry Harvard U., Cambridge, Mass., 1964-67, lectr., 1967-70; asso. prof. chemistry U. Wash., Seattle, 1970-75, prof., 1975—, chmn. dept. chemistry, 1977—. Contbr. numerous articles to sci. jours. Co-founder, 1st pres. Assn. Adventist Forums, 1967-72; chmn. bd. editors, co-editor quar. jour. Spectrum, 1975-77. Recipient Eastman-Kodak Sci. award, 1962; Woodrow Wilson fellow, 1958; Alfred P. Sloan fellow, 1968-70; Guggenheim Meml. Found. fellow, 1977-78. Fellow AAAS; mem. Am. Phys. Soc., Am. Chem. Soc., Council Chem. Research (dir. 1981-84, chmn. 1982-83), Sigma Xi. Current Work: Magnetic resonance in the solid state: crystals, glasses, matrix isolated species. Optical detection of magnetic resonance in photo-excited states of aromatic molecules and biomolecules. Subspecialties: Physical chemistry; Biophysical chemistry. Home: 5639 NE Keswick Dr Seattle WA 98105 Office: Dept Chemistry Univ Washington Seattle WA 98195

KWOK, HOI-SING, electrical engineering educator; b. Hong Kong, Mar. 1, 1951; came to U.S. 1970, naturalized 1985; s. Yung-cheong and Kam-lin (Law) K.; m. Ying-hung Tung; Sept. 12, 1978; 1 child, Theresa. B.A., Northwestern U., 1973; M.S., Harvard U., 1974, Ph.D., 1978. Research fellow Lawrence Berkeley Lab., Berkeley, Calif., 1978-80; asst. prof. SUNY-Buffalo, 1980-83, assoc. prof. elec. engring., 1983-85, prof., 1985—; sci. adviser Photochem. Research Assocs., London, Ont., Can., 1981—. Contbr. articles to profl. jours. Recipient Presdl. Young Investigator award NSF, 1984. Mem. IEEE (sr. mem.), Am. Phys. Soc. Current work: Laser technology, generation and applications of ultrashort laser pulses. Subspecialties: Semiconductors; Laser-induced chemistry. Home: 158 Presidio Pl Williamsville NY 14221 Office: SUNY Bonner Hall Buffalo NY 14260

KWOK, SUN, astronomer; b. Hong Kong, Sept. 15, 1949; s. Chuen-Poon and Pui-Ling (Chan) K.; m. Shiu-Tseng Emily, June 16, 1973; children: Roberta Wing-Yue, Kelly Wing-Hang. B.Sc., McMaster U., 1970; M.S., U. Minn., 1972; Ph. D., 1974. Postdoctoral fellow dept. physics U.B.C., 1974-76; asst. prof. dept. physics U. Minn., 1976-77; research assoc. Center Research in Exptl. Space Sci., York U., Toronto, Ont., Can., 1977-78, Herzberg Inst. Astrophysics, NRC, Ottawa, Ont., 1978-83; asst. prof. physics U. Calgary, (Alta.), 1983-85, assoc. prof., 1985—. Contbr. articles to profl. jours. Mem. Internat. Astron. Union, Am. Astron. Soc., Can. Astron. Soc. Current Work: Stellar winds, planetary nebulae, novae, interstellar molecules, stellar evolution. Subspecialties: Theoretical astrophysics; Radio and microwave astronomy. Home: 139 Edgeland Rd NW Calgary AB T3A 2Y3 Canada Office: Dept Physics U Calgary Calgary AB T2N 1N4 Canada

KWOK, THOMAS YU-KIU, materials scientist, researcher; b. Hong Kong; came to U.S., 1972; s. Kwong-Chio and Shiu-Chun (Lai) K.; m. Lily Fong, Oct. 3, 1981. B.S., MIT, Cambridge, 1976, M.S., 1978, Sc.D., 1981. Mem. research staff IBM Research Ctr., Yorktown Heights, N.Y., 1981—. Contbr. articles to profl. jours. Mem. Am. Phys. Soc., Am. Soc. Metals, IEEE, Sigma Xi, Tau Beta Pi, Eta Kappa Nu. Current work: Electromigration, grain boundary structure and diffusion; thin film metallurgy and interconnection; interface sciences; reliability physics. Subspecialties: Microchip technology (materials science); Condensed matter physics. Office: IBM Thomas J Watson Research Ctr PO Box 218 Yorktown Heights NY 10598

KWOK, WO KONG, chemist, fiber researcher; b. Hong Kong, Jan. 13, 1936; came to U.S., 1961, naturalized, 1972. B.S., Nat. Taiwan U., Taipei, 1958; M.S., E. Tenn. State U., 1963; Ph.D., Ill. Inst. Tech., 1966. Research chemist, sr. research chemist E.I. duPont de Nemours & Co., Inc., Wilmington, Del., also Kinston, N.C., 1966-84, research assoc., Wilmington, 1984—. Contbr. papers to tech. jours. Patentee in field of polymers. Fellow Ill. Inst. Tech. Research Inst., 1965-66. Mem. Am. Chem. Soc. Subspecialties: Polymer chemistry; Polymers (materials science). Office: EI duPont de Nemours & Co Chestnut Run Wilmington DE 19898

KWOLEK, STEPHANIE LOUISE, research chemist; b. New Kensington, Pa., July 31, 1923; d. John and Nellie (Zajdel) Kwolek. B.Sc., Carnegie Mellon U., 1946; D.Sc. (hon.), Worcester Poly. Inst., 1981. Chemist, DuPont Co., Wilmington, Del., 1946-58, research chemist, 1959-66, sr. research chemist, 1967-73, research assoc., 1974—. Author publs. on polymers and fibers (Am. Chem. Soc. Best Publ. award 1960). Patentee in polymers, fibers, polycondensation processes, and liquid crystalline solutions and polymers. Recipient citation for devel. and application of KEVLAR. Am. Soc. Metals, 1980; Carnegie Mellon U. Almuni Assn. Merit award, 1983, Engring. and Tech. award Soc. Plastics Engrs., 1985. Mem. Am. Chem. Soc. (Creative Invention award 1980), Am. Inst. Chemists (Chem. Pioneer award 1980), Franklin Inst. (Howard N. Potts medal 1976), Sigma Xi, Phi Kappa Phi. Club: DuPont Country (Wilmington). Current work: Polymers and fibers; liquid crystalline fibers and polymers, high temperature polymers; condensation polymerization. Subspecialty: Polymer chemistry. Home: 312 Spalding Rd Wilmington DE 19803 Office: DuPont Co Experimental Station Pioneering Research Lab Wilmington DE 19898

KWON, YOUNG DOO, chemical engineer; b. Kyung-gi, Korea, Feb. 18, 1930; came to U.S., 1962; s. Tai Soon and Ryu See K.; m. Kyungha Park, Mar. 5, 1959; children—Euna, Robert Osong, Ronald Oyoung. B.S. in Chem. Engring., Seoul U., Korea, 1955; M.S. in Chem. Engring., MIT, 1964, Sc.D. in Chem. Engring., 1970. Chief engr. Chinahae Battery Co., Seoul, 1961-62; systems engr. Dow Chem. Co., Midland, Mich., 1964-67; sr. research assoc. Allied Corp., Morristown, N.J., 1970—. Patentee in field; contbr. articles to profl. jours. Served lt. Korean Navy, 1955-61. Mem. Am. Chem. Soc., Am. Inst. Chem. Engrs., Tire Soc., Fiber Soc. Current work: Synthetic fibers research related to the making and application (high strength/modulus fibers, their making and uses in composites such as tires). Subspecialties: Materials (engineering); Polymer engineering. Home: 432 Sussex Ave Morristown NJ 07960 Office: Corp Tech Allied Corp PO Box 1021R Morristown NJ 07960

KYDD, GEORGE HERMAN, physiologist; b. Eagle Rock, Va., Aug. 20, 1920; s. George Herman and Nellie Glare (Marshall) K.; m. Mary Louise Penman, Apr. 15, 1944; children: Brenda, Jean, George Herman, Richard Adrian. B.S., W. Va. State Coll.-Institute, 1942; M.S., Ohio State U.-Columbus, 1950, Ph.D., 1955. Research physiologist Aviation Med. Acceleration Lab., Warminster, Pa., 1955-70; with U.S. Naval Air. Devel. Ctr., Warminster, 1971—; phys. sci. adminstr. U.S. Naval Air. Devel. Ctr. (Planning Assessment and Resources Staff), 1977-81; research physiologist U.S. Naval Air. Devel. Ctr. (Aircraft and Crew Systems Directorate), 1981—. Served to 1st lt. U.S. Army, 1942-46. Recipient 1st ann. Aerospace award Nat. Med. Assn., 1970. Fellow Aerospace Med. Assn. (mem. sci. program com. 1965); mem. Am. Physiol. Soc., N.Y. Acad. Scis., Aerospace Physiol. Soc. (Fred Hitchcock award 1972), Sigma Xi. Unitarian. Current Work: Physiological regulation in temperature extremes by integrating experimental results into models that elucidate systems and enable one to predict the behavior of the system in untested conditions. Subspecialties: Integrated systems modelling and engineering; Biomedical engineering. Home: 6631 Boyer St Philadelphia PA 19119 Office: US Naval Air Devel Center Warminster PA 18974

KYLAFIS, NIKOLAOS DIMITRIOU, astrophysicist, educator; b. Nea-Avorani, Trihonidos, Greece, Jan. 1, 1949; came to U.S., 1972; s. Dimitrios K. and Alexandra G. (Katsampas) K.; m. Ekaterini G. Tsoni, Jan. 24, 1957. Ph.D., U. Ill., Urbana-Champaign, 1978. Research assoc U. Ill., Urbana-Champaign, 1979; research fellow Calif. Inst. Tech., Pasadena, 1979-81; mem. Inst. Advanced Study, Princeton, 1981-84; asst. prof. Columbia U., N.Y.C., 1984-85, U. Crete, 1985—. Contbr. articles to profl. jours. Served with Greek Army, 1978. U. Patras (Greece) nat. scholar, 1967-71. Mem. Am. Astron. Soc., Internat. Astron. Union. Current Work: Compact X-ray sources, interstellar medium, astrophysical plasma, transfer of radiation, applied atomic and molecular physics. Subspecialties: X-ray high energy astrophysics; Radio and microwave astronomy. Home: Finikos 3 Iraklion Crete Greece Office: Dept Physics U Crete PO Box 470 Iraklion Crete Greece

KYLE, ROBERT ARTHUR, physician, educator; b. Bottineau, N.D., Mar. 17, 1928; s. Arthur Nichol and Mabel Caroline (Crandall) K.; m. Charlene Mae Showlater, Sept. 11, 1954; children: John, Mary, Barbara, Jean. B.S., U. N.D., 1948; M.D., Northwestern U., 1952; M.S., U. Minn., 1959. Diplomate: Am. Bd. Internal Medicine. Intern Evanston (Ill.) Hosp., 1952-53; fellow internal medicine Mayo Grad. Sch., 1953-55, 57-59, William. H. Donner Prof. medicine and lab. medicine Med. Sch., 1961—; cons. Mayo Clinic, 1961—; research fellow Tufts U., 1960-61; vis. prof. U. Sherbrooke, P.Q., Queen's U., U. Calif., U. B.C., U. Ariz., U. Fla. Author: Monoclonal Gammonpathies, 1976, Medicine and Stamps Volume I, 1970, Volume II 1980; contbr. chpts. to books and articles in field to profl. jours. Pres. Folwell PTA, Rochester, Minn.; chmn. troop com. Gamehaven Council Boy Scouts Am.; bd. trustees First Presbyterian Ch., also elder. Served with USAF, 1955-57. Mem. AMA, Am. Soc. Hematology, Am. Fedn. Clin. Research, N.Y. Acad. Sci., Am. Soc. Clin. Oncology, AAAS, Minn. State Med. Assn., Am. Assn. Cancer Research, Minn. Soc. Internal Medicine, Internat. Soc. Hematology, A.C.P., Sigma Xi, Phi Beta Kappa, Pi Kappa Epsilon. Republican. Current Work: Multiple myeloma and related disorders; identification of monoclonal gammopathies in lab., prospective chemotherapeutic programs of multiple myeloma, amyloidosis and macroglobulinemia. Subspecialties: Hematology; Immunology (medicine). Home: 1207 6th St SW Rochester MN 55901 Office: 200 1st St SW Rochester MN 55901

KYRALA, ALI, astrogeophysicist, educator; b. N.Y.C., Dec. 14, 1921; s. George Abu-Ali and Mildred Frances (Walsh) Kheirallah; m. Judith Anne Wood, Dec. 16, 1966; children: Lawrence Benali, Cadmus Kamal, Andrea Abla. B.Sc., MIT, 1947; M.Sc., Stanford U., 1948; M.S., Harvard U., 1957; Dr.Sc., U. Vienna, 1960. Instr. math. U. Mass., Amherst, 1951-53; math. physicist Lessell & Assocs., Boston, 1953-58, Goodyear Aerospace, Litchfield Park, Ariz., 1958-60; staff scientist Motorola Semiconductor, Phoenix, 1960-62; Fulbright prof. U. Alexandria, Egypt, 1963-64; prof. math. Am. U. Beirut, 1968-70, UPM, Dhahran, Saudi Arabia, 1975-77; prof. physics Ariz. State U., Tempe, 1964—; cons. Author: Applied Functions of a Complex Variable, 1972, Theoretical Physics, 1967. NASA faculty fellow, 1968; NSF faculty fellow, 1965; Am. Cancer Soc. scholar, 1973; CNES scholar, 1980; NASA-ASEE fellow, 1981-82. Mem. Am. Phys. Soc., Am. Math. Soc., Am. Astron. Soc., European Phys. Soc., Assn. Computing Machinery, IEEE, Brit. Interplanetary Soc., Sigma Xi. Muslim. Current Work: Space plasma under high voltage, planetary astrophysics, relativity, statistical physics via Markov chains, theory of galactic spirals, explanation of persistence of great red spot of jupiter. Subspecialties: Theoretical astrophysics; Geophysics. Home: 2309 S Cottonwood St Tempe AZ 85282 Office: Dept Physics Ariz State Univ Tempe AZ 85287

KYRALA, GEORGE AMINE, physicist; b. Bhamdoun, Lebanon, Apr. 20, 1946; s. Amine Asaad and Moura (Habib) Khayrallah; m. Trish Mylet, Nov. 18, 1973; children: Michaelene, Kamaal. B.S., Am. U. Beirut, 1967; M. Phil, Yale U., 1969, Ph.D., 1974. Fellow physics Joint Inst. Lab. Astrophysics, U. Colo., 1974-76; research assoc. Optical Sci. Center, 1976-78; research fellow lasers and molecular spectroscopy U. Ariz., 1976-78; staff mem., project leader Los Alamos Nat. Lab., 1978—; vis. faculty, cons. AL-HAZEN Research Center, Baghdad, Iraq, 1975. Contbr. articles to profl. jours. Recipient Michael Chiha prize, 1964; Rockefeller fellow, 1967; Gibbs fellow, 1967-68. Mem. Am. Phys. Soc., Arab Phys. Soc. Current Work: Inertial confinement fusion and x-ray lasers. Subspecialties: Laser fusion. Office: Los Alamos Nat Lab Box 1663 MS-E526 Los Alamos NM 87545

LAANE, JAAN, chemistry educator; b. Paide, Estonia, June 20, 1942; s. Robert Friedrich and Linda (Treufeldt) L.; m. Tiiu Virkhaus, Sept. 14, 1966; children: Christina, Lisa. B.S. (Agnes Sloan Larsen scholar, Sloan scholar, James scholar), U. Ill., 1964; Ph.D. (Woodrow Wilson fellow, NSF fellow), M.I.T., 1967. Asst. prof. Tufts U., Medford, Mass., 1967-68; asst. prof. Tex. A&M U., College Station, 1968-72, assoc. prof., 1972-76, prof., chmn. div. phys. chemistry, 1976—, speaker faculty senate, 1985-86; vis. scientist Los Alamos Sci. Labs., summers 1964, 65, 68; vis. prof. U. Bayreuth, W.Ger., 1979-80, summer 1981. Contbr. articles to profl. jours. NSF fellow, 1964-67; recipient Alexander von Humboldt U.S. Sr. Scientist award, 1979, Kendall award, 1964, Kodak award, 1967. Mem. Am. Chem. Soc., Am. Phys. Soc., Soc. Applied Spectroscopy, Coblentz Soc. Current Work: Infrared and Raman spectroscopy, nitrogen oxides, research on vibrational spectroscopy. Subspecialties: Physical chemistry; Laser spectroscopy. Home: 1906 Comal Circle College Station TX 77840 Office: Dept Chemistry Tex A&M U College Station TX 77843

LA BARBERA, ANDREW RICHARD, educator; b. Teaneck, N.J., Oct. 6, 1948; s. Mario Richard and Georgine (Mart) LaB. B.S. cum laude, Iona Coll., 1970; M.Phil., Columbia U., 1974, M.A., 1974, Ph.D., 1975. Instr. dept. biology Iona coll., New Rochelle, N.Y., 1970; staff asso. Center for Reprodn. Sci., Columbia U., N.Y.C., 1975-77; research fellow Mayo Grad. Sch. Medicine, Rochester, Minn., 1977-80; asst. prof. physiology Northwestern U., Chgo., 1980—, asst. prof. ob-gyn, 1985—; dir. In Vitro Fertilization Labs., Northwestern Meml. Hosp., 1985—; dir. RIA Lab., CEMN, 1980-85. Contbr. articles to profl. jours. USPHS-NIH predoctoral traineeship, 1971-75; Population Council grantee, 1972-75; Northwestern U. grantee, 1980-81, 81; NIH grantee, 1982—; recipient New Investigator award Am. Diabetes Assn., 1981-82. Mem. AAAS, Am. Inst. Biol. Scis., Am. Physiol. Soc., Am. Soc. Zoologists, Chgo. Assn. Reproductive Endocrinologists, Endocrine Soc., Soc.Exptl. Biology and Medicine, Soc. for Study of Reprodn., Tissue Culture Assn, Beta Beta Beta. Current Work: Mechanism of action of glycoprotein hormones; ovarian cellular physiology; cell membrane biology; follitropin receptor-adenylyl cyclase interactions; stimulus-secretion coupling. Subspecialties: Physiology (biology); Receptors. Home: 913 W Van Buren 4D Chicago IL 60607 Office: Prentice Women's Hosp and Maternity Ctr 333 E Superior St Room 1180 Chicago IL 60611

LABEN, ROBERT COCHRANE, animal scientist, educator; b. Darien Center, N.Y., Nov. 16, 1920; s. Victor L. and Ruth (Cochrane) L.; m. Dorothy Lobb, Nov. 29, 1946; children: John V., Robert J., Elizabeth J. Laben Cunningham, Catherine L. B.S., Cornell U., 1942; M.S., Okla. State U., 1947; Ph.D., U. Mo., 1950. Research and teaching asst. Okla. State U., 1946-47, U. Mo., 1947-50; instr. animal husbandry U. Calif., Davis, 1950-52, asst. prof., 1952-58, assoc. prof., 1958-64, prof., 1964—, prof. animal sci., 1964—, asst. assoc. animal husbandman expt. sta., 1950-64, geneticist, 1964—; dir. U. Calif. (Computer Center), 1964-69, master advisor in animal sci., 1970-84, vice chmn. dept. animal sci., 1977-82. Contbr. articles on dairy breeding, genetics and husbandry to profl. jours. Elder, deacon Davis Community Presbyn. Ch.; hunter safety vol. instr. Calif. Fish and Game Dept., 1962—; com. mem. Boy Scouts Am., 1955-56. Served from 2d lt. to capt. U.S. Army, 1942-46. Decorated Bronze Star, Purple Heart with oak leaf cluster; recipient Outstanding Advisor award U. Calif. at Davis Coll. Agr., 1982. Mem. Am. Dairy Sci. Assn., Am. Soc. Animal Sci., Biometric Soc., Am. Genetic Assn., Sigma Xi, Alpha Zeta. Republican. Current Work: Animal breeding and genetics, with emphasis on productive and reproductive traits of dairy cattle, milk yield and composition, lactation stress. Subspecialties: Animal genetics; Animal production. Home: 502 Oak Ave Davis CA 95616 Office: Dept Animal Sci U Calif Davis CA 95616

LABINGER, JAY ALAN, research scientist; b. Los Angeles, July 6, 1947; s. Harry and Dorothy (Fryer) L.; m. Andrea Graubart, May 31, 1970; 1 child, Barbara. B.S., Harvey Mudd Coll., 1968; Ph.D., Harvard U., 1974. Research assoc. Princeton U., N.J., 1973-74, instr., 1974-75; asst. prof. U. Notre Dame, Ind., 1975-81; sr. research chemist Occidental Research Corp., Irvine, Calif., 1981-83; sr. research scientist Atlantic Richfield Co., Chatsworth, Calif., 1983-84, prin. research scientist, 1984—. Contbr. articles to profl. jours. Sect. editor Dictionary of Organometallic Compounds, 1984. NSF grantee, 1977, 80; Petroleum Research Fund grantee, 1975. Mem. Am. Chem. Soc. Current work: Synthetic and mechanistic study of heterogeneous and homogenous catalysis; oxidation chemistry and catalysis. Subspecialties: Catalysis chemistry; Organometallics. Home: 2204 Villa Maria Rd Claremont CA 91711 Office: Atlantic Richfield Co 20717 Prairie St Chatsworth CA 91311

LABONTE, ANTON EDWARD, computer scientist; b. Mpls., May 6, 1935; s. Anton Ernest and Ruth Eileen (Williams) L.; m. Ana Mae Pelak, June 27, 1959. B.S. in Elec. Engring., U. Minn., 1957, M.S., 1960, Ph.D., 1966. Instr., research fellow U. Minn., Mpls., 1959-65; sr. scientist Control Data Corp., Mpls., 1966-69, mgr. systems analysis, 1969-75, sr. engr. cons., 1975—. Developer micro-adaptive picture sequencing digital image representation technique, Trifacet quadtree scene coding technology. Contbr. articles to profl. jours. Mem. Am. Assn. Artificial Intelligence, IEEE, AAAS, Soc. Photo-Optical Instrumentation Engrs., Am. Phys. Soc., Sigma Xi, Tau Beta Pi, Eta Kappa Nu. Methodist. Current work: Artificial intelligence with focus on knowledge-based systems and computer vision; astronomical data analysis. Subspecialties: Artificial intelligence; Graphics, image processing, and pattern recognition. Home: 4729 30th Ave S Minneapolis MN 55406 Office: Control Data Corp 2800 E Old Shakopee Rd Minneapolis MN 55420

LABUZA, THEODORE PETER, food scientist, educator, cons.; b. Perth Amboy, N.J., Nov. 10, 1940; s. Theodore and Cathrine Julia (Stycheck) L. S.B., MIT, 1962, Ph.D., 1965. Asst. prof. food sci. and nutrition M.I.T., 1965-68, assoc. prof., 1968-71, U. Minn., St. Paul, 1971-73, prof., 1973—; cons. to food cos.; tchr. short courses on phys. chemistry of foods, food law. Author: books including Shelf Life Testing of Foods, 1982; Food Science and Nutritional Health, 1985; Moisture Sorption Isotherms: Theory and Applications, 1985; contbr. 150 articles to profl. and popular publs. Recipient Teaching award M.I.T., 1970, cert. merit NASA, 1973, 74, 76. Fellow Inst. Food Tech. (Samuel Cate Prescott Research award 1972, William V. Cruse Teaching award 1979); mem. Am. Chem. Soc., Am. Inst. Chem. Engring., Am. Soc. Agrl. Engring., Inst. Food Technologists, Am. Assn. Cereal Chemistry, Assn. Food and Drug Ofcls., Sigma Xi, Gamma Sigma Delta, Phi Kappa Phi. Patentee in field. Current Work: Physical chemistry of food stability; water activity; kinetics; nutritional stability; shelf life; computer modeling; biotechnology applications in food processing and packaging. Subspecialties: Food science and technology; Nutrition (biology). Home: 1870 Stowe Arden Hills MN 55112 Office: Dept Food Sci and Nutrition U Minn Saint Paul MN 55108

LACAVA, ALBERTO IGNACIO, chemical engineering educator, process control and catalysis consultant; b. Santa Fe, Argentina, July 27, 1944, came to U.S., 1977; s. Alberto Orlando and Ignacia Delfina (Doldan) L.; m. Lidia Acuna, Jan. 5, 1967 (div. 1980); 1 child, Guillermo Demian; m. Kathy Leong, May 31, 1984. B.Engring., U. Litoral, Santa Fe, 1970; M.Sc., Imperial Coll., London, 1974; Ph.D., U. London, 1976. Research engr., U. Litoral, 1969-73; research fellow Imperial Coll. U. London, 1976-77; assoc. prof. chem. engring. CUNY, 1977—; cons. in field. Contbr. articles to profl. jours. Mem. Am. Inst. Chem. Engrs., Am. Chem. Soc., Couvocation of U. London, The Catalysis Soc., Internat. Research Council Rose-Croix U., Sigma Xi. Current work: Real time control and simulation, conversion of waste to energy by pyrolysis; deactivation of metal catalysts by carbon deposition. Subspecialties: Chemical engineering; Catalysis chemistry. Home: 173 Oak Tree Ave South Plainfield NJ 07080 Office: City Coll CUNY Dept Chem Engring New York NY 10031

LA CELLE, PAUL LOUIS, physician, educator; b. Syracuse, N.Y., July 4, 1929; s. George Clarke and Marguerite Ellen (Waggoner) La C.; m. June Dukeshire, May 23, 1953; children: Andrea Jean, Peter Theodore, Kristina Marie, Erik Clarke. A.B., Houghton Coll., 1951; M.D., U. Rochester, 1959. Intern U. Rochester Med. Center-Strong Meml. Hosp., 1959-60, resident, 1960-62; asst. prof. medicine U. Rochester, 1967-70, asso. prof., 1970-74, prof., 1974—, chmn. dept. radiation biology and biophysics, 1977—; cons. to govt. Mem. Gates-Chili Sch. Bd., Rochester, 1964-72; trustee Houghton Coll., 1976—. Served to lt. (j.g.) USNR, 1952-55. NIH spl. fellow, 1965-66; recipient von Humboldt Sr. Scientist award, 1982-83. Mem. Biophys. Soc., Microcirculation Soc., European Microcirculation Soc., Am. Soc. Hematology, AAAS, Sigma Xi, Alpha Omega Alpha. Research in biophysics of blood cells, physiology of microcirculation. Current Work: Research: Investigation of rheologic properties of normal and pathologic blood cells in the microcirculation. Subspecialties: Biophysics (biology); Hematology. Office: Box RBB Med Center 601 Elmwood Ave Rochester NY 14642

LACH, JOSEPH T(HEODORE), physicist; b. Chgo., May 12, 1934; s. Joseph Lach and Kate Lach Ziemba; m. Barbara Ryan, June 26, 1965; children—Michael, Elizabeth. A.B., U. Chgo., 1953, M.S., 1956; Ph.D., U. Calif.-Berkeley, 1963. Research assoc. Yale U., New Haven, 1963-65, asst. prof., 1965-69; staff physicist Fermilab, Batavia, Ill., 1969—. Contbr. numerous articles to profl. jours. Mem. exec. com. Chgo. chpt. Physicians for Social Responsiblity, 1983—. Mem. Am. Phys. Soc. Roman Catholic. Current work: Small angle scattering; hyperon physics; long-term joint experimental program with Leningrad Nuclear Physics Institute. Subspecialty: Particle physics. Home: 28 W 364 Indian Knoll Tr West Chicago IL 60185 Office: Fermilab PO Box 500 Batavia IL 60510

LA CHANCE, DAVID JOSEPH, petroleum geologist; b. Nashua, N.H., Aug. 14, 1951; s. Leopold A. and Betty L. (Terry) L.; m. Lucille Carol Tamm, Apr. 1, 1979; children—Pepin Leopold, Eric Heinz. B.A., in Geology, U. N.H., 1973; M.S., Eastern Wash. U., 1978. Cert. petroleum geologist. Petroleum geologist U.S. Geol. Survey, Dept. Interior, Metairie, La., 1975-76, Washington, 1976-82, Mineral Mgmt. Service, Vienna, Va., 1982-83, Bur. Land. Mgmt., Milw., 1983—. Contbr. articles to profl. jours. Mem. Geol. Soc. Am., Am. Assn. Petroleum Geologists. Republican. Lutheran. Home: 1722 N 58th St Milwaukee WI 53208 Office: Bur Land Mgmt 310 W Wisconsin Ave Suite 220 Milwaukee WI 53203

LACHANCE, LEO EMERY, geneticist; b. Brunswick, Maine, Mar. 1, 1931; s. Emery and Edwidge (Pouliot) LaC.; m. P. Joan Favreau, Aug. 6, 1955; children: Lois Anne, Marc Hunter, Matthew S. B.S., U. Maine, 1953; M.S., N.C. State U., 1955, Ph.D., 1958. Research asso. biology Brookhaven Nat. Lab., Upton, N.Y., 1958-60; research geneticist Entomology Research div. USDA, Kerville and Mission, Tex., 1960-63; research leader, radiation biology and insect genetics sect. Metabolism and Radiation Research Lab., USDA, Fargo, N.D., 1964-69, 71-76, lab. dir., 1977-82; nat. tech. adv. insect genetics, research geneticist Agrl. Research Service, 1982—; head pest control sect. FAO/IAEA, Vienna, 1969-71. Contbr. articles to profl. jours. Served with USAR, 1953-56. NIH fellow, 1956-58; NRC Nat. Acad. Scis. travel grantee, 1962; vis. lectr. Purdue U., 1972. Fellow AAAS; mem. Genetics Soc. Am., Entomol. Soc. Am., Am. Inst. Biol. Scis., Fedn. Am. Scientists, Sigma Xi. Current Work: Researcher in sterile male technique of insect control, radiation biology, insect reproduction, hybrid sterility, genetics of insect populations, cytology. Subspecialties: Genetics and genetic engineering (agriculture); Cell biology. Home: 77 21st Ave N Fargo ND 58102 Office: Metabolism and Radiation Research Lab PO Box 5674 State Univ Sta Fargo ND 58105

LACKS, SANFORD ABRAHAM, geneticist; b. N.Y.C., Jan. 28, 1934; s. Charles Jonas and Goldie Rose (Dranoff) L.; m. Elaine Rose Norris, Nov. 22, 1959; children: Jennifer, Daniel, Julia. B.S., Union Coll., 1955; Ph.D., Rockefeller U., 1960. Instr., Harvard U., Cambridge, 1960-61; guest investigator Pasteur Inst., Paris, 1957-58, Hebrew U., Jerusalem, 1970-71; sr. geneticist Brookhaven Nat. Lab., Upton, N.Y., 1961—. Contbr. articles to profl. jours. NIH grantee, 1978—, 81—. Mem. Am. Soc. Biol. Chemists, Am. Soc. Microbiology, Genetics Soc. Am. Current Work: Microbial genetics; recombinant DNA, bacterial transformation, DNA repair; biochemistry, deoxyribonucleases. Subspecialties: Genetics and genetic engineering (biology); Biochemistry (biology). Office: Biology Dept Brookhaven Nat Lab Upton NY 11973

LA CLAIRE, JOHN WILLARD, II, botanist, educator; b. Utica, N.Y., July 1, 1951; s. John Willard and Mary Magdelene (Smith) La C. B.S. in Biology, Cornell U., Ithaca, N.Y., 1973; M.A., U. South Fla., 1975; Ph.D. in Botany, U. Calif.-Berkeley, 1979. Asst. prof. botany U. Tex.-Austin, 1979-85, assoc. prof., 1985—. Editorial bd.: J. Phycology, 1985-87; contbr. articles to sci. jours. NSF grantee, 1982-88. Mem. AAAS, Am. Soc. Cell Biol., Bot. Soc. Am. (sec. phycol. sect. 1984-86), Brit. Phycol. Soc., Internat. Phycol. Soc., Phycol. Soc. Am., Sigma Xi. Current Work: Plant cell motility phenomena; cellular wound healing utilizing giant algal cells as model systems; ultrastructure/electron microscopy of marine algae (cell division, cytoskeleton, protoplasts). Subspecialties: Cell biology; Marine phycology. Office: Dept Botany U Texas Austin TX 78713

LACY, LEWIS LEE, physicist; b. Bluefield, W.Va., Mar. 25, 1941; s. Delbert N. and Beulah Virginia (Perkins) L.; m. Peggy Anne Lark, Mar. 19, 1964; children—Gregory Scott, Robert Lewis. B.S., Va. Poly. Inst., 1963, M.S., 1965; Ph.D. in Physics, U. Tenn., 1971. Research assoc. Los Alamos Nat. Lab., 1964; space sci. G.C. Marshall Space Flight Ctr., NASA, Huntsville, Ala., 1965-77, br. chief, 1977-81; sr. research specialist Exxon Prodn. Research, Houston, 1981-84, research assoc. 1984—; mem. physics staff U. Ala., Huntsville, 1977-81. Author: (with others) Apollo-Soyuz Summary Science, 1977, AIAA Material Sciences in Space, 1977, SPE Hydraulic Fracturing, 1986. Patentee drop tube technique for supercooling and solidifying. Nation chief YMCA Indian Guides, Huntsville, 1976. Recipient NASA Manned Flight award, 1974; NASA Tech. award, 1984; NASA fellow, 1967. Mem. Am. Phys. Soc., Soc. Petroleum Engrs., Sigma Pi Sigma (pres. 1964-65), Phi Kappa Phi. Current work: Hydraulic fracturing geometry; subsurface and reservoir engineering; petroleum diagnostic technology; materials processing and characterization; space technology; low temperature physics; rock physics. Subspecialties: Petroleum engineering; Materials processing. Home: 6 Postvine Ct The Woodlands TX 77381 Office: Exxon Production Research Co PO Box 2189 Houston TX 77252-2189

LACY, PRITI SHEILA, neuroscience and anatomy educator, researcher; b. Patna, Bihar, India, June 18, 1942; came to U.S. 1970, naturalized 1980; d. Roger Clifton and Nora Phulmani (Das) L. B.S., Ewing Christian Coll., Allahabad, India, 1962; M.S., Lucknow U., India, 1964; Ph.D. in Biochemistry, Allahabad U., 1968; Ph.D. in Anatomy, U. Nebr., 1980. Cert. biochemist, anatomist. Sr. research fellow Council of Sci. and Indsl. Research, Allahabad U., India, 1969; research assoc. pharmacology U. Nebr. Med. Ctr., Omaha, 1971-75; NIH postdoctoral research assoc. in neurology Cornell Med. Ctr.,-N.Y. Hosp., N.Y.C., 1980-81; lectr. anatomy and cell biology U. Mich. Med. Sch., Ann Arbor, 1981—. Dudgeon Meml. scholar Ewing Christian Coll., Allahabad, 1961; Coondoo Meml. scholar, 1962; M.S. scholar, 1962; Regents fellow U. Nebr. Med. Sch., 1976-79. Mem. N.Y. Acad. Scis., AAAS, Soc. Neurosci., Am. Assn. Anatomists. Current work: Effects of subarachnoid hemorrhage on cardiovascular system, cerebral circulation, renin-angiotensin system, mechanisms of neuronal damage in brain following ischemia. Subspecialties: Physiology (medicine); Neural aspects of stroke. Home: 1315 Astor Apt 4732 Ann Arbor MI 48104 Office: Dept Anatomy and Cell Biology Med Sci II Bldg Catherine St Ann Arbor MI 48109

LADANYI, BRANKA MARIA, chemistry educator; b. Zagreb, Yugoslavia, Sept. 7, 1947; Can. citizen, 1967; permanent resident U.S., 1974; d. Branko and Nevenka (Zilic) L.; m. Marshall Fixman, Dec. 7, 1974. B.S., McGill U., 1969; M.Phil., Yale U., 1971, Ph.D., 1973. Vis. prof. chemistry U. Ill.-Urbana, 1974; postdoctoral research assoc. Yale U., New Haven, 1974-77, research assoc., 1977-79; asst. prof. chemistry Colo. State U., Ft. Collins, 1979-85, assoc. prof. chemistry, 1985—. Contbr. articles to profl. jours., U.S., Can. Active NOW. Sloan Found. fellow, 1982-85; Dreyfus tchr.-scholar, 1983-87; NSF grantee, 1980-87; Am. Chem. Soc. Petroleum Research Fund grantee, 1979-82. Mem. Am. Chem. Soc., Am. Phys. Soc., Sigma Xi. Current Work: Molecular theory of liquids; theory of light scattering in fluids and polymer solutions; theory of solvent effects on chemical reactions. Subspecialties: Physical chemistry; Statistical mechanics. Home: 1100 E Pitkin St Fort Collins CO 80524 Office: Dept Chemistry Colo State U Fort Collins CO 80523

LADD, CHARLES CUSHING, III, civil engineering educator; b. Bklyn., Nov. 23, 1932; s. Charles Cushing and Elizabeth (Swan) L.; m. Carol Lee Ballou, June 11, 1954; children—Melissa, Charles IV, Ruth, Matthew. A.B., Bowdoin Coll., 1955; S.B., MIT, 1955, S.M., 1957, Sc.D., 1961. Asst. prof. civil engring., MIT, Cambridge, 1961-64, assoc. prof. civil engring., 1964-70, prof., 1970—; gen. reporter 9th Internat. Conf. Soil Mechanics and Found. Engring., Tokyo, 1977. Contbr. articles to profl. jours. Mem. Concord (Mass.) Republican Town com., 1968-82; commr. Concord Dept. Pub. Works, 1965-78, chmn., 1972-74. Recipient Civil Engring. Effective Teaching award MIT, 1980. Fellow ASCE (research prize 1969, Croes medal 1973, Norman medal 1976); mem. Boston Soc. Civil Engrs. (bd. govt. 1972-81, pres. 1977-78), ASTM, Nat. Acad. Engring., Transp. Research Bd., Internat. Soc. Soil Mechanics and Found. Engring. Subspecialty: Civil engineering. Office: Dept Civil Engring MIT Cambridge MA 02139

LADDU, ATUL RAMCHANDRA, clinical researcher, physician; b. Poona, India, Aug. 23, 1940; came to U.S., 1968, naturalized, 1972; s. Ramchandra Dnyneshwar and Sarojini (Ramchandra) L.; m. Jayashree Atul, June 19, 1965; children: Prashanta Atul, Abhay Atul. M.B., B.S., G.R. Med. Coll., Gwalior, India, 1962; M.D., Delhi U., 1967. Instr. pharmacology Maulana Azad Med. Coll., New Delhi, India, 1963-68; postdoctoral fellow dept. pharmacology Med. Coll. Wis., Milw., 1968-71; instr., asst. prof., 1971-73; group leader cardiovascular div. Lederle Labs. div. Am. Cyanamid Co., Pearl River, N.Y., 1973-75; sr. clin. investigation assoc. CIBA-GEIGY Corp., Summit, N.J., 1975-76; asst. med. dir. Ives Labs. Inc. div. Am. Home Products Inc., N.Y.C., 1976, assoc. med. dir., 1976-78, project leader, 1978-82; dir. clin. research Am. Critical Care, McGaw Park, Ill., 1982—. Mem. editorial bd.: Jour. Clin. Pharmacology, Am. Heart Jour; Contbr. articles to profl. jours. Fellow Am. Coll. Clin. Pharmacology, Am. Soc. Clin. Pharmacology and Therapeutics, Am. Soc. for Pharmacology and Exptl. Therapeutics, Am. Coll. Cardiology; mem. Am. Fedn. Clin. Research, N.Y. Acad. Scis., Soc. for Exptl. Biology and Medicine, Internat. Study Group for Research in Cardiac Metabolism, Indian Coll. Allergy and Applied Immunology, Sigma Xi. Current Work: Clinical research in broadest sense, cardiovascular drugs in particular Subspecialties: Cardiology; Internal medicine. Office: 1600 Waukegan Rd McGaw Park IL 60085

LADISCH, MICHAEL R., biochemical engineer, educator, researcher; b. Upper Darby, Penn., Jan. 15, 1950; s. Rolf Karl and Brigitte Marie (Gehreis) L.; m. Christine Marie Schmitz, June 25, 1951; children—Sarah Elizabeth, Mark Daniel. B.S. in Chem. Engring., Drexel U., 1973; M.S. in Chem. Engring., Purdue U., 1974, Ph.D. in Chem. Engring., 1977. Research engr. Purdue U., West Lafayette, Ind., 1977-78, asst. prof., 1978-81, assoc. prof., 1981—, group leader, 1978—; librarian microbial and biochem. tech. div. ACS, Washington, 1981-84, chmn. elect. program chmn., 1984—. Contbr. articles to profl. jours. Recipient U.S. Presdl. Young Investigator award NSF, White House, 1984. Mem. Am. Chem. Soc. (microbial and biochem. tech. div., librarian microbial and biochem. tech. div. 1981-84, chmn.-elect program chmn. 1984—, W.H. Peterson award 1977), Am. Inst. Chem. Engrs., Am. Soc. Agrl. Engrs. (assoc.), AAAS, Am. Soc. Biol. Chemists. Current work: Bioseparations: liquid chromatography, adsorption, membrane, chromatographic support; bioreactors: anaerobic bacterial fermentation, process control; kinetics of biological systems. Subspecialties: Chemical engineering; Enzyme technology. Office: Lab of Renewable Resources Engring Potter Bldg Purdue Univ West Lafayette IN 47907

LADISCH, STEPHAN, medical researcher, pediatrician, educator; b. Garmisch-Partenkirchen, W.Ger., July 18, 1947; came to U.S., 1948, naturalized, 1959; s. Rolf Karl and Brigitte (Gareis) L.; m. b. Brigitte Bidault, May 22, 1974; children: Gwenola, Virginie. B.S. in Chemistry, U. Pa., 1969, M.D., 1973. Diplomate: Am. Bd. Pediatrics; subcert. in pediatric hematology/oncology. Intern Children's Hosp. Med. Ctr., Boston, 1973-74, resident, 1974-75; clin. assoc. pediatric oncology br. Nat. Cancer Inst., Bethesda, Md., 1975-77, investigator, 1977-78; asst. prof. pediatrics, sr. mem. human immunobiology group UCLA Sch. Medicine, 1978-82, assoc. prof., 1982—. Contbr. articles to profl. jours. NSF grantee, 1968-69, 72; Von L. Meyer travel fellow, 1975; NIH grantee, 1980—; Research career devel. awardee, 82—; Leukemia Soc. Am. scholar, 1982—; Am. Cancer Soc. grantee, 1985—. Mem. Am. Assn. Immunologists, Am. Soc. Hematology, Western Soc. for Pediatric Research, Am. Fedn. for Clin. Research, Soc. for Pediatric Research, AAAS, Soc. Complex Carbohydrates, Phi Beta Kappa, Alpha Chi Sigma, Phi Lambda Upsilon. Current Work: Functional and marker properties of gangliosides, including modulation of immune responses. Subspecialties: Immunobiology and immunology; Cancer research (medicine). Home: 650 Via de la Paz Pacific Palisades CA 90272 Office: Dept Pediatrics UCLA Sch Medicine Los Angeles CA 90024

LA FARGE, CHRISTOPHER GRANT C., cardiologist; b. N.Y.C., Sept. 14, 1928; s. Christopher Grant and Louisa Ruth (Hoar) La F.; m. Maria Boissevain, Dec. 29, 1952 (div. 1978); children—Christopher, Antoinette, Ian, Gedeon; m. Patricia Arscott, June 27, 1978. B.A., Harvard U., 1951; M.D., Yale U., 1955. Diplomate Am. Bd. Med. Examiner. Intern then resident Grace New Haven Hosp., Conn., 1955-57; pediatrician USAF Med. Corps, Colo. Springs., 1957-61, dep. comdr. chief Ambulatory Inpatient Services, 1958-61; research fellow Children's Hosp., Boston, 1961-63, clin. fellow, 1963-64, asst. then assoc. cardiology, 1964-68, sr. assoc., 1968-79, dir. research catheterization lab., 1968-74, sr. cons., 1979—; research fellow in pediatrics Harvard U., 1961-64, asst., 1964-65, instr., 1965-67, assoc., 1967-70, asst. prof., 1970-74; assoc. prof. Pediatrics Mass. Inst. Tech., 1970-79; cons. in field; vis. prof. Children's Hosp., Boston, 1982—. Contbr. articles to profl. jours. Vice pres. Boston Prof. Standards Bur. Orgn., 1977-79; mem. council Central Metro, Health Planning, Boston, 1976-79, com. Case Mix Mass. Rate Setting Commn., Utilization Review Accreditation Hosps. Commn.; bd. dirs. El Paso County Tuberculosis Assn., Canyon Rd. Homeowner's Assn. NIH grantee. Fellow Am. Soc. Artificial Organs, Am. Physiol. Soc., Am. Coll. Angiology, Am. Acad. Med. Dirs. (charter), Am. Coll. Utilization Review Physicians, Am. Coll. Cardiology, Internat. Soc., Artificial Organs; mem. El Paso County Med. Soc., Mass. Med. Soc., Am. Heart Assn., AAAS, Assn. Advancement Med. Instrumentation, Mass. Hosp. Assn., Am. Inst. Biol. Scis., Soc. Computer Medicine; Alpha Kappa Kappa. Episcopal. Clubs: Harvard, Tavern (Boston). Current work: Cardiac physiology; ventricular function, prosthetic heart devices; pediatric cardiology. Subspecialties: Cardiology; Physiology (biology). Home and Office: PO Box 6132 Santa Fe NM 87502 Office: 1651 Galisteo St #2 Santa Fe NM 87501

LA FERNEY, PRESTON E., agricultural research administrator; b. Griffithville, Ark., July 14, 1935; s. William E. and Vera A. (Jackson) La F.; m. Johnnie V. Vaughn, Nov. 28, 1958 (dec. 1982); children—Pamela L. La Ferney Smith, Scott C.; m. Ellen B. Wilkerson, Sept. 30, 1983. Student Harding U., 1953-55; B.S. U. Ark., 1958, M.S., 1960; Ph.D., Okla. State U., 1962; postdoctorate Stanford U., 1970. Agrl. economist Econ. Research Service, Dept. Agr., Clemson, S.C., 1962-71, Washington, 1972-73; with Agrl. Research Adminstrn., Washington, 1973-80; assoc. dir. Ark. Agrl. Exptl. Sta., Fayetteville, 1980-83, dir., 1983—; chmn., dir. So. Rural Devel. Ctr., Starkeville, Miss. Contbr. articles to profl. jours. Fellow, Dept. Agrl, 1969-70, Congl., 1975-76. Mem. Am. Agrl. Econs. Assn., So. Agrl. Econs. Assn., Gamma Sigma Delta. Mem. Ch. of Christ. Lodge: Rotary. Current work: Agricultural research administration. Subspecialties: Agricultural research administration; Agricultural economics. Office: Ark Agrl Experiment St Room 217 Agr Bldg Fayetteville AR 72701

LAFFERTY, JAMES FRANCIS, biomechanical engineering educator, consultant; b. Pampa, Tex., Dec. 23, 1927; s. John Patrick and Melvina Frances (Gaines) L.; m. Vivian Long, June 30, 1956; children—James Earl, Laura Elaine. B.S. in Mech. Engring., U. Ky., 1955; M.S. in Mech. Engring., U. Southern Calif., 1957; M.S. in Nuclear Engring., U. Mich., 1966, Ph.D. in Nuclear Engring., 1967, Registered prof. engr., Ky. Design engr. Hughes Aircraft Co., Culver City, Calif., 1955-57; prof. biomech. engring. U. Ky., Lexington, 1957—; dir. Wenner-Gren Research Lab., Lexington, 1969—; dir. Biomed. Engring. Ctr., Lexington, 1985—; staff engr. Argonne Nat. Lab., Ill., summer 1958; cons. Oak Ridge Nat. Lab., summer 1967; bd. dirs. U. Ky. Research Found., 1983—. Contbr. articles to profl. jours. Served to cpl. U.S. Army, 1950-53, Korea. Recipient Outstanding Tchr. award U. Ky., 1975; NSF fellow, 1962, 65; Hughes Aircraft fellow, 1955. Mem. ASME, Orthopaedic Research Soc., Neuroelectric Soc. Lodge: Rotary. Current work: Musculoskeletal biomechanics; response of biomaterials to impact, vibration and acceleration; vehicle occupant kinematics restraint systems; protective sports equipment. Subspecialties: Biomedical engineering; Mechanical engineering. Office: Wenner-Gren Research Lab U Ky Rose St Lexington KY 40506

LAFFERTY, JAMES MARTIN, physicist; b. Battle Creek, Mich., Apr. 27, 1916; s. James V. and Ida M. (Martin) L.; m. Eleanor J. Currie, June 27, 1942; children: Martin C., Ronald J., Douglas J., Lawrence E. Student, Western Mich. U., 1934-37; B.S. in Engring. Physics, U. Mich., 1939, M.S. in Physics, 1940, Ph.D. in Elec. Engring, 1946. Physicist Eastman Kodak Research Lab., Rochester, N.Y., 1939; physicist Gen. Electric Research Lab., Schenectady, 1940, 42-81, mgr. power electronics lab., 1972-81; with Carnegie Instn., Washington, 1941-42; Pres. Internat. Union Vacuum Sci. Technique and Applications, 1980-83. Editor, contbg. author: Scientific Foundations of Vacuum Technique (Dushman), 1962; editor: Vacuum Arcs, Theory and Applications, 1980; asso. editor: Jour. Vacuum Sci. and Tech, 1966-69; Editorial bd.: Internat. Jour. Electronics, 1968—; Contbr. articles to profl. jours. Mem. greater consistory Ref. Ch.; trustee Schenectady Museum, 1967-73, sec., 1971-72, pres., 1972-73. Recipient Devel. award Bur. Naval Ordnance, 1946; Distinguished Alumnus citation U. Mich., 1953; IR-100 award, 1968. Fellow Am. Phys. Soc., IEEE (Lamme medal 1979), AAAS (hon. life); mem. Am. Vacuum Soc. (dir. 1962-70, sec. 1965-67, pres. 1968-69), U.S. Power Squadrons (comdr. Lake George squadron 1975-76, comdr. Dist. 2 1981-82), Sigma Xi, Phi Kappa Phi, Iota Sigma, Tau Beta Pi. Patentee in field; inventor lanthanum boride cathode, 1950, hot cathode magnetron ionization gauge, 1961, triggered vacuum gap, 1966. Current Work: Consultant, Electric vehicles. Subspecialties: Electrical engineering; Electronics. Office: PO Box 8 Schenectady NY 12301

LAFFERTY, KEVIN J, physician, medical researcher. Prof. microbiology, immunology, pediatrics U. Colo. Sch. Medicine. Subspecialty: Transplantation. Office: B140 U Colo Sch Medicine 4200 E 9th Ave Denver CO 80262

LAGALLY, MAX GUNTER, materials science educator, consultant; b. Darmstadt, Germany, May 23, 1942; came to U.S., 1953, naturalized, 1960; s. Paul and Herta (Rudow) L.; m. Shelley Tod Meserow, Feb. 15, 1969; children—Eric, Douglas, Karsten. B.S. in Physics, Pa. State U., 1963; M.S. in Physics, U. Wis.-Madison, 1965, Ph.D. in Physics, 1968. Registered profl. engr., Wis. Asst. prof. materials sci. U. Wis.-Madison, 1971-74, assoc. prof., 1974-77, prof., 1977—, dir. thin film ctr., 1982—; vis. scientist Sandia Nat. Lab., Albuquerque, 1975; cons. to various cos., 1976—. Co-editor: Experimental Methods of Physics—Surfaces, 1985; editor spl. issue Jour. Vacuum Sci. and Tech., 1978, editorial bd., 1978-81. Contbr. numerous articles to profl. publs. Co-patentee field emission electron gun. Recipient Best Paper award Naval Research Lab., Conf., 1975, Best Paper award Phys. Electronics 1978; Max Planck Gesellschaft fellow, Berlin, 1968; Alfred P. Sloan Found. fellow, 1972; grantee Research Corp., 1973, also various fed. agys., industry; U. Wis.-Madison H. I. Romnes fellow, 1976. Fellow Am. Phys. Soc.; mem. Am Vacuum Soc. (mem. program and exec. coms. 1974—), Electrochem. Soc., Am. Chem. Soc. (div. colloid and surface chemistry). Current work: Structural and electronic properties of surfaces and thin films; thin film growth; thin film processing and deposition; electronic materials. Subspecialties: Electronic materials; Condensed matter physics. Home: 5110 Juneau Rd Madison WI 53705 Office: U Wis Metall and Mineral Engring Dept 1509 University Ave Madison WI 53706

LAGARIAS, JOHN SAMUEL, environmental engineer; b. Rochester, N.Y., July 4, 1921; s. Samuel Nicholas and Aspacia (Basu) L.; m. Virginia Jane Clark, June 16, 1947; children—Jeffrey, Peter, Clark. B.S., Rensselaer Poly. Inst., 1948; student in Physics, Oak Ridge Sch. Reactor Tech., 1956. Registered profl. engr., Md. Engr. Westinghouse Electric Co., Pitts., 1948-51; mgr. metal products Koppers Co., Inc., Pitts., 1951-63; mgr. research and devel. Am. Ins. Co., Silver Spring, Md., 1963-65; pres. Resources Research, Reston, Va., 1965-71; dir. environ. quality Raymond Kaiser Engrs., Oakland, Calif., 1971-84; pres. Lagarias Assocs., Inc., Moraga, Calif., 1984—. Contbr. articles to profl. jours. Patentee in field. Commr. Parks and Recreation, Moraga, Calif., 1984—. Mem. Am. Inst. Mining and Metall. Engrs., Am. Phys. Soc., IEEE (sr.), Am. Acad. Environ. Engrs., Air Pollution Control Assn. Republican. Club: Cosmos (Washington). Current work: Technology assessment utilization of environ. control systems including air, water and solids control. . Home: 276 Donald Dr Moraga CA 94556

LAGUNAS-SOLAR, MANUEL CLAUDIO, radiochemist; b. Valparaiso, Chile, Dec. 23, 1941; came to came to U.S., 1970; s. Manuel L. and Alejandrina Solar; m. Patricia Isabel Lagunas-Solar, Dec. 27, 1968; children: Claudio, Rodrigo. Licenciate in Chemistry and Edn. summa cum laude, Catholic U., Valparaiso, 1968; M.S. magna cum laude, U. P.R., 1970; Ph. D. in Chemistry, U. Calif.-Davis, 1974. Asst. prof. chemistry Catholic U., Valparaiso, 1965-69; teaching asst. U. P.R., Mayaguez, 1968-69, instr. phys. chemistry, 1969-70; research asst. P.R. Nuclear Ctr., Mayagyez, 1968-70; research asst. U. Calif.-Davis, 1970-73, asst. research radiochemist, 1973-81, assoc. research radiochemist, 1982—, chief radioisotope program, 1973—; cons. in field. Co-patentee: continuous flow radioactive iodine prodn. Mem. Am. Chem. Soc., Soc. Nuclear Medicine, Am. Nuclear Soc., Sigma Xi. Roman Catholic. Current Work: Development of medical radionuclides and radiopharmaceuticals for diagnostic and/or therapeutic nuclear medicine; radiation chemistry; applications of radiation technology (food irradiation, radiation dosimetry, system design and engineering). Subspecialty: Physical chemistry. Home: 2721 Hatteras Pl Davis CA 95616 Office: Crocker Nuclear Lab U Calif Davis CA 95616

LAGUNOFF, DAVID, pathology educator, researcher; b. N.Y.C., Mar. 14, 1932; s. Robert and Cicele (Lipman) L.; m. Susan Powers, Mar. 8, 1958; children—Rachel, Liza, Michael. M.D., U. Chgo., 1957. Intern, U. Calif., San Francisco, 1957-58; mem. faculty U. Wash., Seattle, 1960-79, assoc. prof., 1965-69, prof., 1969-79; prof, chmn. dept. pathology St. Louis U., 1979—. Mem. adv. com. clin. investigation III Am. Cancer Soc., 1980-84. Editorial bd. Lab. Investigation, 1975—, Inflammation, 1980—, Am. Jour. Pathology, 1985—. Spl. fellow Nat. Heart Inst., Copenhagen, 1964, Nat. Cancer Inst., Oxford, Eng., 1970. Mem. Am. Soc. Cell Biology, Am. Assn. Pathologists, Assn. Pathology Chmn., AAUP, AAAS. Cellular pathology, mast cell structure and function, inflammation. Subspecialties: Pathology (medicine); Cell biology (medicine). Home: 23 Southmoor St Saint Louis MO 63105 Office: St Louis U Sch Medicine Dept Pathology 1402 S Grand Blvd Saint Louis MO 63104

LAHART, MARTIN JOSEPH, physicist, researcher; b. St. Paul, July 1, 1938; s. Martin Joseph Lahart and Dorothy Mary (Isett) Lahart Hauck. B.S. in Elec. Engring., Princeton U., 1960; M.S. in Physics, U. Mich., 1962; Ph.D., in Optical Sci., U. Ariz., 1975. Sr. physicist Xerox Corp., Rochester, N.Y., 1969-71; staff Los Alamos Nat. Lab., N.Mex., 1975-81; research physicist Naval Research Lab., Washington, 1981-83; electronics engr. NIH, Bethesda, 1983-85, NVEOL, Ft. Belvoir, Va., 1985—. Contbr. articles to profl. jours. Mem. Optical Soc. Am., IEEE, Soc. Photo Optical Instrumentation Engrs. Current work: Digital image processing, including image enhancement, restoration, pattern recognition, image compression. Subspecialties: Graphics, image processing, and pattern recognition; Optical image processing. Home: 5850 Cameron Run Terr Apt 1103 Alexandria VA 22303 Office: NVEOL Fort Belvoir VA 22060

LAHERU, KEN LIEM, structural engineer, researcher; b. Kuningan, West Java, Indonesia, Aug. 23, 1935; came to U.S., 1969; m. Hilda Djaladhi, Dec. 16, 1963; children: Joshua, Daniel, Suenya. Diploma in Engring, Rhine-Westfalia Tech. U. Aachen, W.Ger., 1960; Ph.D., U. Utah, 1973. Research assoc. Tech. U. Berlin, West Berlin, Ger., 1960-62; univ. lectr. Inst. Tech., Bandung, Indonesia, 1962-69; lectr. Air Force Acad., Bandung, 1963-66; rocket scientist Nat. Inst. for Aero. and Space, Bandung, 1963-67; research assoc. U. Utah, Salt Lake City, 1973-74; assoc. scientist, solid rocket structural engr. Morton Thiokol, Brigham City, Utah, 1974—, pvt. practice cons. wind energy exploration and distillation project, Bandung, 1965-68. Contbr. articles to profl. publs., Ger., U.S. Com. chmn. Lake Bonneville council Boy Scouts Am. troop 322, Brigham city, 1980—. Ministry of Edn. scholar Indonesia, 1954-60. Mem. Soc. Engring. Sci, Joint Army-Navy-NASA-Air Force Interagy. Propulsion Com. Mem. Christian Ref. Ch. Club: Tennis/Ski (Brigham City). Current Work: Material stress-strain relation, material strength, failure and aging characteristics; layered composite material bond. Subspecialties: Aerospace engineering and technology; Theoretical and applied mechanics. Home: 851 South Law Dr Brigham City UT 84302 Office: Morton Thiokol PO Box 524 Brigham City UT 84302

LAHOTI, GOVERDHAN DAS, mechanical engineer, researcher; b. Jaipur, India, May 4, 1948; came to U.S., 1969, naturalized, 1976; s. Ram Kumar and Rukmani Devi (Maloo) L.; m. Sarala Devi, Feb. 17, 1975; children—Parul, Shimul, Ablushek. B.Engring., Burdwan (India) U., 1969; M.S., U. Calif., Berkeley, 1970, Ph.D. in Mech. Engring, 1973. Cons. metalworking tech., Columbus, Ohio, 1973-74; sr. scientist Battelle-Columbus, 1974-81; sr. research specialist Timken Research, Canton, Ohio, 1982—, research scientist, 1982—. Contbr. numerous articles to profl. jours. Mem. ASME, Am. Soc. Metals, N. Am. Metalworking Research Inst. Current Work: Computer-aided modeling of metalworking processes, optimization of mfg. processes, metalworking equipment and processes (forging, rolling, extrusion, etc). Subspecialties: Mechanical engineering; Solid mechanics. Home: 3977 Bramshaw Rd NW Canton OH 44718 Office: 1835 Dueber Ave Canton OH 44706

LAI, CARL MINGTAN, plant pathologist; b. Taiwan, Dec. 11, 1934; came to U.S., 1962; s. Sui and Tou L.; m. Martha L., Jan. 10, 1939; children: Mark, James. Ph.D., U. Calif., Berkeley, 1966. Plant pathologist, plant disease clinic lab. Calif. Dept. Food & Agr., Sacramento, 1969—. Contbr. articles to profl. jours. Mem. Am. Phytopath. Soc. Current Work: Research in plant diseases incited by bacteria and fungi. Subspecialty: Plant pathology. Office: Calif Dept Food and Agr 1220 N St Sacramento CA 95804

LAI, CHING-SAN, biophysicist, educator, researcher; b. Keelung, Taiwan, Nov. 27, 1946; came to U.S., 1974; s. Dong-Cheng and Shay (Wu) L.; m. Shan-Lan Liu, Sept. 9, 1972; children—Yeu-Jeng, Shien-Don. B.S. in Zoology, Taiwan Normal U., Taipei, 1970; Ph.D. in Biophysics, U. Hawaii, 1978. Research assoc. Med. Coll. Wis., Milw, 1979-80, asst. prof. biophysics, 1981-84, assoc. prof., 1985—. Contbr. chpts. to books. NIH grantee, 1982—. Mem. Biophys. Soc., Magnetic Resonance in Medicine. Current work: Electron spin resonance spectroscopy of protein mobility; development of electron spin resonance methodologies for biomedical research. Subspecialties: Biophysics (biology); Biochemistry (biology). Home: 210 N 110th Pl Wauwatosa WI 53226 Office: Med Coll Wis 8701 Watertown Plank Rd Milwaukee WI 53226

LAI, JAMES SHAU-YAN, structural engineer, consultant; b. Hong Kong, May 9, 1940; came to U.S., 1959, naturalized, 1979; s. Chau Kwong and Sui Wen (Fung) L.; m. Yim Fong Leung, Dec. 26, 1966; children—Raymond, Clement, Theodore, Calvin. B.S., Calif. State U.-Chico, 1963; M.S., U. So. Calif., 1965. Registered profl. engr., Ariz., Calif., Fla., N.Mex., Okla., Utah. Structural designer Wilson & Wilson, Los Angeles, 1963-66, Paul Y. Koshi Assocs., Beverly Hills, Calif., 1971-73; project engr. Neptune & Thomas Assocs., Pasadena, Calif., 1966-71; v.p. Johnson & Nielsen Assocs., Los Angeles, 1973—, dir. Applied Tech. Council, Palo Alto, Calif., 1982-85. Author: (with others) Report of Slender Wall Panels (S.B. Barnes award 1983), 1982. Sustaining mem. Republican Nat. Com., 1984. Fellow Am. Concrete Inst. (pres. So. Calif. chpt. 1982-83); mem. ASCE (chmn. joint Am. Concrete Inst.-ASCE com. 421, Slabs 1984-86), Structural Engrs. Assn. So. Calif. (chmn. bldg. code com. 1983-85, chmn. seismology com. 1986-88, bd. dirs. 1979-81), Structural Engrs. Assn. Calif. (bd. dirs. 1983-85), Earthquake Engring. Research Inst., Internat. Conf. Bldg. Officials, Phi Kappa Phi, Chi Epsilon. Club: Univ. (Pasadena). Current work: Consultation and structural design for structures of all types including industrial, residential, commercial and public buildings, schools, universities, offices, shopping centers, department stores, parking structures and recreational facilities. Subspecialties: Civil engineering; Structural engineering. Home: 5151 La Canada Blvd La Canada CA 91011 Office: Johnson & Nielsen Assocs 7462 N Figueroa St Los Angeles CA 90041

LAI, POR-HSIUNG, genetic engineering scientist company executive, biotechnologist; b. Chiy-I, Taiwan, Jan. 21, 1948; came to U.S., 1973, naturalized, 1981; s. Sun-Chang and Su-Lan Lai L.; m. Yun-Ling Chen, Sept. 20, 1975; children—Otto, Angela, Henry. B.S., Kaohsiung Med. Coll., 1970; M.S., Mass. Coll. Pharmacy, 1975, Ph.D., 1977. Asst., investigator Def. Med. Ctr., Taipei, Taiwan, 1971-73; research fellow Mass. Coll. Pharmacy, Boston, 1973-77, mem. adv. com., 1981-82; research assoc. U. Iowa, Iowa City, 1977-81; dir. Sequemat, Inc., Boston, 1981-82; prin. scientist Amgen, Thousand Oaks, Calif., 1982—. Contbr. articles to profl. jours. Research fellow Mass. Coll. Pharmacy,

1973-77, NIH fellow, 1977-81. Mem. AAAS, N.Y. Acad. Scis., Am. Chem. Soc., Kaohsiung Med. Coll. Alumni Assn., Rho Chi. Republican. Current work: Protein engineering; protein chemistry for biotechnology; characterization, purification, scale-up and production of recombinant DNA derived proteins; process automation; automated chemistry systems; quality control of pharmaceutical proteins. Subspecialties: Chronobiology; Bioinstrumentation. Office: Amgen Inc 1900 Oak Terrace Ln Thousand Oaks CA 91320

LAI, YING-SAN, valve company executive; b. Chutung, Taiwan, Sept. 9, 1937; came to U.S., 1962; s. Jung-Lai and Ching-Mei (Chien) L.; m. Nancy Pui-Chin Tom, Feb. 26, 1966; children: Nolan, Ormond, Lynna. B.S. in Mech. Engring, Nat. Taiwan U., 1960; M.S., U. Iowa, 1963; Ph.D., Northwestern U., 1973. Registered profl. engr., Ill., La., Wash. Design engr. CBI Industries, Oak Brook, Ill., 1963-69, stress analyst, 1972-73; chief engr. Dresser Industries, Alexandria, La., 1973-83, engring. dir., 1984—; engring. dir. Dresser Dewrance & Co., Skelmersdale, Eng., 1983-84. Contbr. tech. papers to profl. lit. Mem. ASME, Am. Nuclear Soc., La. Engring. Soc. Current Work: Managing engineering design, research, and development on pressure relief valves and line valves for industrial applications. Subspecialty: Mechanical engineering. Home: 4806 Westgarden Blvd Alexandria LA 71301 Office: Dresser Industries PO Box 1430 Alexandria LA 71301

LAIDLAW, HARRY HYDE, JR., entomologist, geneticist, emeritus educator; b. Houston, Apr. 12, 1907; s. Harry Hyde and Elizabeth Louisa (Quinn) L.; m. Ruth Grant Collins, Oct. 26, 1946; 1 child, Barbara Scott Laidlaw Murphy. B.S., La. State U., 1933, M.S., 1934; Ph.D., U. Wis.-Madison, 1939. Prof. biology Oakland City Coll., Ind., 1939-41; apiarist Ala. Dept. Agr. and Industry, Montgomery, 1941-42; entomologist 1st U.S. Army, N.Y.C., 1946-47; asst. prof. entomology U. Calif., Davis, 1947-53, assoc. prof., 1953-60, prof., 1960-74, prof. emeritus, 1974—, assoc. dean Coll. Agr., 1960-64, coordinator Egypt Agr. Devel. Program-AID, 1979-83. Author: Queen Rearing, 1950, 62, Contemporary Queen Rearing, 1979; Instrumental Insemination of Honey Bee Queens, 1977. Contbr. numerous articles to profl. jours. Served to capt. AUS, 1942-46. Recipient Cert. of Merit Am. Bee Jour., 1957; Spl. Merit award U. Calif., Davis, 1959; Merit award Western Apicultural Soc., 1980; Rockefeller Found. grantee, 1954-55, 67. Fellow AAAS; mem. Entomol. Soc. Am. (C.W. Woodworth award 1981), Am. Soc. Naturalists, Zool. Soc. Am., Internat. Bee Research Assn. Democrat. Presbyterian. Club: Commonwealth (San Francisco). Current work: Honey bee genetics and breeding. Subspecialty: Genetics and genetic engineering (biology).

LAING, FREDERICK MITCHELL, botanist; b. Barre, Vt., Nov. 29, 1919; s. George F. and Margaret (Horne) L.; m. Barbara Bixby; children: Wendy Laing Brown, John M. B.S. in Edn, U. Vt., 1951; M.S., 1953. Mem. faculty U. Vt., Burlington, 1953—, now emeritus research assoc. prof. botany and plant physiology. Served to 1st lt. U.S. Army, 1941-45. Mem. Bot. Soc. Am., Am. Soc. Plant. Physiology, AAAS, Forest Products Research Soc., Can. Soc. Plant Physiol., Council Agrl. Sci. and Tech. Current Work: Plant physiology and development of sugar maple. Intensive culture of native hardwoods for energy. Subspecialties: Biomass (agriculture); Plant physiology (agriculture).

LAING, RONALD ALBERT, physicist; b. Seattle, Dec. 9, 1933; s. Philip V. and Esther L. Laing. B.A., Reed Coll., 1956; M.A., Rice U., 1958, Ph.D., 1960. Assoc. prof. ophthalmology and physiology Boston U. Sch. of Medicine, 1969—. Contbr. articles to profl. jours. Mem. Assn. for Research in Vision and Ophthalmology, Internat. Soc. for Eye Research, Optical Soc. Am., AAAS, Sigma Xi. Current work: Non-invasive, diagnostic ophthalmic instrumentation, cellular wound healing mechanisms. Subspecialties: Biomedical engineering; Ophthalmology. Home: 1024 Massachusetts Ave Lexington MA 02173 Office: Boston U Sch Medicine 80 E Concord St Boston MA 02118

LAITINEN, HERBERT AUGUST, chemistry educator, researcher; b. Ottertail City, Minn., Jan. 17, 1915; s. Nestor A. and Minnie (Nikkari) L.; m. Marjorie Gorans, June 15, 1940; children—Kenneth, Richard, Roger. B.Chem., U. Minn., 1936, Ph.D., 1940. From instr. to prof. U. Ill., Urbana, 1940-74, prof. emeritus, 1974—; grad. research prof. U. Fla., Gainesville, 1974—. Author: Chemical Analysis, 1960, 1975. Author: (with others) pH & Electrotitrations, 1941. Co-editor: History of Analytical Chemistry, 1978. Contbr. articles to profl. jours. Guggenheim fellow, 1953, 62; recipient Gadolin Gold medal Finnish Chem. Soc., Helsinki, 1984. Fellow Royal Soc. Chemistry (hon.); mem. Am. Chem. Soc. (Fisher award in analytical chemistry 1961, editor jour. 1966-79), Electrochem. Soc., AAAS, Japan Soc. Analytical Chemistry (hon.), Finnish Acad. Arts & Scis. (hon.). Current work: Improved battery materials, heterogeneous catalysis. Subspecialties: Analytical chemistry; Electrochemistry. Office: Dept Chemistry U Fla Gainesville FL 32611

LAJTHA, ABEL, neurochemist researcher, educator; b. Budapest, Hungary, Sept. 22, 1922; came to U.S., 1948, naturalized, 1954; s. Laszlo and Rozsa (Hollos) L.; m. Marie Snyder, Nov. 25, 1953; children: Terry, Kathryn. Ph.D., U. Budapest, 1945. Asst. prof. Biochem. Inst., U. Budapest, 1945-47; fellow Stazione Zoologica, Naples, Italy, 1947-48, Royal Instn. Gt. Britain, 1948-49; asst. prof. Inst. Muscle Research, Woods Hole, Mass., 1949-50; research assoc., asst. prof. Columbia U. Coll. Phys. & Surgeons., N.Y.C., 1950-66; sucessively research scientist, sr. research scientist, assoc. research scientist N.Y. State Psychiat. Inst., N.Y.C., 1950-63; prin. research scientist N.Y. State Research Inst. Neurochemistry and Drug Addiction, N.Y.C., 1963-66; research prof. psychiatry NYU Sch. Medicine, 1971—; dir. Center Neurochemistry, Ward's Island, N.Y., 1966—; cons. NIH, NSF, VA. Editor: Brain Barrier Systems, 1968, Handbook of Neurochemistry, 1969-72, 2d edit., 1982-85 , Protein Metabolism of the Nervous System, 1969, Transport Phenomena of the Nervous System, 1976, Mechanisms of Protein Synthesis in the Brain, 1977, Clinical Neurology and Neurochemistry, 1980, Peripheral Nerve Diseases, 1983; editor-in chief: Neurochem. Research, 1975—; editor: Jour. Neurochemistry, 1962-71, Brain Research, 1966-77, Jour. Neurobiology, 1968-77, Internat. Rev. Neurobiology, 1965—, Advances in Experimental Medicine and Biology, 1967—, Biological Psychiatry, 1969—, Internat. Jour. Neurosci, 1970-74, Perspectives in the Brain Sciences, 1972—, Revs. of Neurosci, 1976—, Jour. Neurosci. Research, 1976—. Contbr. chpts. to books, numerous articles to profl. jours. Mem. Am. Acad. Neurology, Am. Soc. Biol. Chemists, Biochem. Soc., AAAs, Internat. Brain Research Orgn., Internat. Soc. Neurochemistry (pres. 1975-77), Am. Soc. Neurochemistry (pres. 1979-81), Internat. Soc. Psychoneuroendocrinology, Found. Mental Hygiene (pres. 1977—), Soc. Neurosci., N.Y. Acad. Sci., Am. Soc. Cell Biology, Soc. Biol. Psychiatry, Collegium Internationale Neurospychologicum, Am. Chem. Soc., Italian Soc. Neurology, Sigma Xi. Current Work: Brain protein metabolism, breakdown, regeneration, peptide metabolism. Subspecialty: Neurochemistry. Home: 75 Orlando Ardsley NY 10502 Office: Center for Neurochemistry Ward's Island NY 10035

LAKE, CHARLES RAYMOND, psychiatrist, pharmacologist, educator; b. Nashville, July 6, 1943; s. Charles Raymond and Vera (Shute) L.; m. Susan Frances de la Houssaye, Aug. 12, 1967; children: Reagan Anne, Craig Anne. B.S. in Zoology, Tulane U., 1965, M.S. in Biology, 1966, Ph.D. in Physiology and Pharmacology, 1971; M.D., Duke U., 1972. Resident in psychiatry Duke U. Med. Ctr., Durham, N.C., 1972-74; research assoc. lab. clin. sci. NIMH, Bethesda, Md., 1974-77; staff psychiatrist sect. exptl. therapeutics, 1977-79; prof. psychiatry and pharmacology Uniformed Services U. Health Scis. Sch. Medicine, Bethesda, 1979—. Contbr. articles to med. jours. Served with USPHS, 1974-79. Mem. Am. Psychiat. Assn., Soc. Neuroscience, Soc. Biol. Psychiatry, Am. Acad. Clin. Psychiatry, Internat. Soc. Hypertension, Am. Coll. Neuropsychopharmacology, Endocrine Soc. Oxford-Cambridge Univ. (London). Current Work: Research in biogenic amine metabolism, amphetamine 'look-alikes,' and 'over-the-counter' speed. Subspecialties: Psychopharmacology; Neuropharmacology. Office: 4301 Jones Bridge Rd Bethesda MD 20814

LAKE, DAVID ALLEN, physical therapy educator, clinician, researcher; b. Ypsilanti, Mich., Feb. 10, 1951; s. Gordon Franklin and Marion Gertrude (Govan) L.; m. Linda L. Wright, May 13, 1978. B.S. in Biology, U. Calif.-Irvine, 1972; M.S. in Physiology, Ind. State U., 1975; Ph.D. in Physiology, Tex. Tech U. Sch. Medicine, 1978; cert. in phys. therapy U. Medicine and Dentistry of N.J., Newark, 1985. Research assoc. Duke U. Med. Sch., Durham, N.C., 1979-80; asst. prof. biol. scis. Kean Coll. of N.J., Union, 1980-84; asst. prof. phys. therapy Northeastern U., Boston, 1984—; vis. asst. prof. N.C. State U., Raleigh, 1978-80; vis. prof. St. George's Sch. Medicine, Grenada, Wis., 1981-82; adj. faculty mem. U. Medicine and Dentistry of N.J., Newark, 1982-83. Author: Laboratory Workbook Human Anatomy and Physiology, 1974; contg. author: Alcoholism: A Perspective; contbr. articles on effect of ethanol on heart and effect of change in osmolarity on nervous system activity to profl. jours. Mem. Soc. for Neurosci., Am. Physiol. Soc., Am. Phys. Therapy Assn., Internat. Brain Research Orgn., Am. Soc. Exptl. Biology, Sigma Xi. Current work: Effects of sensory input on motor control; neurophysiological basis of neurological rehabilitation treatment techniques. Subspecialties: Physical medicine and rehabilitation; Neurobiology. Home: 31 Winchester Ln Plymouth MA 02360 Office: Dept Phys Therapy Northeastern U 308 Robinson Hall Boston MA 02115

LAKES, RODERIC STEPHEN, biomedical and mechanical engineering educator; b. N.Y.C., Aug. 10, 1948; s. Eric A. and Dorothy E. (Hollweg) L.; m. Diana M. Lakes, Aug. 14, 1971. Student, Columbia U., summers 1964-65; B.S. in Physics, Rensselaer Poly. Inst., 1969, Ph.D., 1975; postgrad., U. Md., 1969-70. Research assoc. in engring. and applied sci. Yale U., 1975-77; asst. prof. physics Tuskegee Inst., 1977-78; asst. prof. biomed. and mech. engring. U. Iowa, 1978-82, assoc. prof., 1982—; dir. U. Iowa (Applied Mechanics Lab., Coll. Engring.), 1980—; vis. asst. prof. biomed, engring Rensselaer Poly. Inst., summer 1978, vis. assoc. prof., summer 1982; vis. prof. dept. materials Queen Mary Coll., London, spring 1985. Contbr. articles on bone biomechanics, composite material mechanics and bioelectricity to profl. jours. NIH grantee, 1979-82; NIH Biomed. Research Support grantee, 1979, 80. Mem. Am. Phys. Soc., ASME, Orthopaedic Research Soc., AAAS, Sigma Xi. Inventor device for remote detection of stress waves in bone. Current Work: Bone biomechanics, biophysics, bioelectricity, experimental generalized continuum mechanics. Subspecialties: Biomedical engineering; Solid mechanics. Office: Coll Engring U Iowa Iowa City IA 52242

LAKOSKI, JOAN MARIE, neuropharmacology and neuroendocrinology educator; b. Poughkeepsie, N.Y., Mar. 28, 1953; s. Theodore J. and Vera (Andruson) Lakoski; m. Paul M. Mayercik; 1 child, Vera Ann. A.B. cum laude, Mt. Holyoke Coll., 1975; Ph.D., U. Iowa, 1981. Biologist, Nat. Inst. Neurol., Communicative Disorders and Stroke, NIH, Bethesda, Md., 1975-77; research tchg. fellow U. Iowa, Iowa City, 1977-81; postdoctoral research fellow Yale U., New Haven, Conn., 1981-84; asst. prof. U. Tex. Med. Br., Galveston, 1984—. Contbr. articles to profl. jours. Mem. Soc. Neurosci., Endocrine Soc., AAAS, Sigma Xi. Current work: Neuropharmacology of histamine, GABA and serotonin in mammalian central nervous system, effect of gonadal steroids on neurotransmission. Subspecialties: Neuropharmacology; Neurophysiology. Office: Dept Pharmacology and Toxicology J31 U Tex Med Br Galveston TX 77550

LAKS, MICHAEL MILTON, cardiologist; b. Cleve., July 25, 1928; s. Alexander and Helen (Klein) L.; m. Sandra Beller, June 13, 1959; children: Helaina, Alexander. B.A., UCLA, 1951; M.D., U. So. Calif., 1956. Diplomate: Am. Bd. Internal Medicine (cardiovascular disease). Intern Cedars of Lebanon Hosp., Los Angeles, 1956-57, resident, 1957-59, chief med. resident, 1959-60, research fellow in medicine, 1960-61, spl. NIH cardiac fellow, 1964-65, asst. dir. dept. medicine, 1961-64, dir. dept., 1964-65, physician in charge cardiovascular research lab., 1965-71; research assoc. Cedars-Sinai Med. Ctr., Los Angeles, 1962-69, sr. research scientist, 1969—; dir. heart sta. and cardiovascular research lab. Harbor-UCLA Med. Ctr., 1971—, assoc. chief div. cardiology, 1975—; prof. medicine UCLA, 1975—; vis. internist UCLA Hosp. and Clinics, 1975—; cons. Wadsworth VA Hosp., Hewlett Packard Corp.; lectr. Assoc. editor Jour. Electrocardiography. Contbr. 200 articles and abstracts to profl. jours. Served with USN, 1948-53. Am. Chem. Soc. scholar, 1947; recipient prize for sci. paper ACP, 1961. Fellow Am. Coll. Cardiology, ACP, Am. Geriatrics Soc. (founding), Am. Coll. Chest Physicians, Council Clin. Cardiology of Am. Heart Assn., Royal Soc. Medicine; mem. AMA, Am. Fedn. Clin. Research, Am. Heart Assn., Am. Soc. Nephrology, AAAS, Am. Physiol. Soc., Pan Am. Med. Assn., Western Soc. Clin. Research, Los Angeles County Heart Assn., Calif. Med. Assn., Nat. Assn. Para-Cardiac Specialists (chmn. med. adv. com.), Internat. Study Research in Cardiac Metabolism, Am. Inst. Biol. Scis., Calif. Thoracic Soc., N.Y. Acad. Scis., Western Assn. Physicians, Internat. Soc. Computerized ECG (pres.), Phi Beta Kappa, Alpha Omega Alpha, Phi Kappa Phi. Current Work: Cardiovascular research - ventricular failure and hypertrophy; computerized ECG. Subspecialty: Cardiology. Home: 1939 Edgemont Los Angeles CA 90027 Office: 1000 W Carson St Torrance CA 90509

LAKSHMIKANTHAM, MADURAIVAS VENUGOPAL, chemist; b. Madras, India, Jan. 28, 1930; came to U.S., 1971; d. M.S. and M. (Kanakam) Venugopal; m. J. Sadasivan, Feb. 10, 1958; children—Nandini Prasad, Venkat S. B.Sc., U. Madras, 1950, M.Sc., 1954, Ph.D., 1958, Diplomas in German and French, 1952, 54. Sci. pool officer Govt. India, Madras, 1965-66; research assoc. Va. Poly. Inst. and State U., Blacksburg, 1967-68, Wayne State U., Detroit, 1968-69; sr. research fellow Monash U., Melbourne, Australia, 1969-71; research assoc. U. Pa., Phila., 1971-74, research specialist in chemistry, 1974-85; research specialist chemistry dept U Ala, Tuscaloosa, 1985—. Contbr. articles to profl. jours. Mem. Am. Chem. Soc., Royal Soc. Chemistry. Hindu. Current work: Natural product synthesis, heterocyclic chemistry, organochalcogen chemistry, synthetic materials with unusual solid-state properties e.g. one dimensional conductors, elec. conducting polymers. Subspecialties: Organic chemistry; Synthetic chemistry. Home: 1900 Riceman Road North Tuscaloosa AL 35406

LAKSHMIVARAHAN, SIVARAMAKRISHNAN, computer science educator, consultant; b. Karaikurichi, India, June 12, 1944; came to U.S., 1975, naturalized; s. S. Sivaramakrishnan and Subbulakshmi Iyer; m. Shantha Sitaram, Feb. 5, 1973; children—Subha, Bharathram. B.Sc., Madras U. (India), 1964; B.E., Indian Inst. Sci., 1967, M.E., 1969, Ph.D., 1973. Asst. prof. Indian Inst. Tech., Madras, 1973-75; vis. asst. prof. Brown U., Providence, 1975-76, Yale U., New Haven, 1976-78; assoc. prof. computer sci. U. Okla., Norman, 1978-84, prof., 1984—; vis. prof. U. Bonn, Fed. Republic Germany, 1981, 82, U. Laval, Que., Can., 1982. Author: Learning Algorithms; Theory and Applications. Contbr. articles to profl. jours. Recipient Regents award for research and creative activities U. Okla., 1982, Halliburton Disting. Lectr. award, 1984. Mem. IEEE (sr.), Assn. for Computing Machinery. Current work: Parallel algorithm design, computer interconnection networks, learning algorithms, cryptography and security. Subspecialties: Algorithms; Distributed systems and networks. Office: Sch Elec Engring and Computer Sci U Okla Norman OK 73019

LAL, BRIJ BIHARI, materials engineering administrator; b. Surajpur, Azamgarh, India, Aug. 12, 1944; came to U.S., 1976; s. Kamata Lal and Champa (Champa) Lal Devi; m. Kusum Srivastava, June 14, 1974; 1 child, Prateek. B.Sc. in Physics and Math., Banaras Hindu U., India, 1965, M.Sc. in Physics, 1967, Ph.D. in Physics, 1971. Scientist, Nat. Phys. Lab., New Delhi, 1974-75; postdoctoral fellow SUNY-Stony Brook, 1976-77; research assoc. Colo. State U., Fort Collins, 1977-79, Syracuse U., N.Y., 1979-81; sr. chemist Exxon Enterprises, San Jose, Calif., 1981-83; materials engring. mgr. Info. Memories Corp., Santa Clara, Calif., 1983—. Contbr. articles to profl. jours. Recipient award Nat Phys. Lab., New Delhi, India, 1976. Mem. IEEE, Magnetic Soc. of IEEE, Am. Electroplaters Soc., Am. Vacuum Soc. Current work: Thin film technology, materials development, magnetic recording technology, physics of magnetism, product and process development, process control. Subspecialties: Materials; Materials (engineering). Home: 5916 Southbrook Ct San Jose CA 95138 Office: Info Memories Corp 2875 Northwestern Pkwy Santa Clara CA 95051

LAL, HARBANS, pharmacology educator; b. Harikur, Pakistan, Jan. 8, 1931; came to U.S., 1955; naturalized, 1968; m. Amrit Weber, Sept. 6, 1964; children—Sophia, Ravinder, Ronjeet, B.S., Punjab U., India, 1952; M.S., U. Kans., 1958; Ph.D., U. Chgo., 1962. Assoc. prof. U. Kans., Lawrence, 1965-67; prof. U. R.I., Providence, 1967-80; prof., chmn. Tex. Coll. Osteo. Medicine, Ft. Worth, 1980—; adj. prof. U. R.I., 1980—, Tex. Christian U., 1980—, North Tex. State U., 1980—. Author: (with others) Drug Addiction Experimental Pharmacology and Clinical Toxicology, 1980. Editor Drug Devel. Research profl. jour., 1981—; (with others) GABA Neurotransmission: Current Developments in Physiology and Neurochemistry, 1980; Psychopharmacology of Clonidine, 1981. Contbr. numerous research papers to profl. lit. Mem. Assn. Med. Sch. Pharmacology, Fedn. Am. Socs. Exptl. Biology, Soc. Neuroscis., Soc. Pharmacology and Exptl. Therapeutics, Tex. Osteo. Med. Assn. Current work: Study of pharmacology with emphasis on neuropharmacology and psychopharmacology. Subspecialties: Psychopharmacology; Neuropharmacology. Office: Tex Coll Osteo Medicine Camp Bowie at Montgomery St Fort Worth TX 76107

LAL, JOGINDER, chemist; b. Amritsar, Punjab, India, July 2, 1923; came to U.S., 1947; s. Khem Singh and Champa Devi Mahajan; m. Ardyce Mae Lundenburg, Mar. 24, 1951; children—Anjana Lal Pettigrew, Rajinder K. B.Sc. with honors, U. Punjab, India, 1944, M.Sc., 1946; M.S., Poly. Inst. Bklyn., 1949, Ph.D. in Polymer Chemistry, 1951. Prof. chemistry Hindu Coll., Amritsar, Punjab, 1951-52; head polymer research H.D. Justi & Son, Inc., Phila., 1952-56; research scientist Goodyear Tire & Rubber Co., Akron, 1956-66, sect. head, 1967-75, mgr. polymer research, 1975-82, sr. research and devel. assoc., 1983—; mem. adv. com. Chem. Tech. program U. Akron, 1976—. Mem. adv. bd. Jour. Polymer Sci., chemistry edit., 1967—; mem editorial bd. Macromolecular Syntheses, Inc., John Wiley, N.Y.C., 1981—; co-editor: Am. Chem. Soc. symposium series Elastomers and Rubber Elasticity, 1982. Contbr. numerous articles to sci. jours.; patentee polymer sci. field; prin. inventor Hexsyn rubber. Congl. sci. counselor Congressman John F. Seiberling, 1974—. Recipient Govt. India Merit Scholarship for Advanced Studies award, 1947-50; chmn. elastomer conf. Gordon Research Confs., 1983. Mem. Am. Chem. Soc. (rep. rubber div. macromolecular secretariat 1983—, Disting. Service award Akron Sect. 1976, chmn. awards com. polymer div. 1979-82, polymer div.'s First Service award for exceptional service 1983, First award as moderator of best symposium of rubber div. 1984), Akron Polymer Conf. (chmn. 1976), Akron Polymer Lectr. Group (chmn. 1961-62), Democrat. Hindu. Current work: Sturcture-property relationship of elastomers; mechanisms of vulcanization and reinformcement. Subspecialty: Polymer chemistry. Office: The Goodyear Tire & Rubber Co 142 Goodyear Blvd Akron OH 44316

LAM, HON WAI, electronics engineering executive; b. Hong Kong, Mar. 18 1951; s. Tak Man and So Ha (Chang) L.; m. Katherine Chang, May 15, 1979. B.S., MIT, 1975, M.S., 1975, Ph.D., 1979; M.B.A., So. Meth. U., 1983. Mem. tech. staff Hewlett Packard Co., Palo Alto, Calif., 1979; mem. tech. staff Tex. Instruments, Dallas, 1979-82, sr. mem. tech. staff, 1982—, mgr. advanced device tech. br., 1982—. Patentee magnetic bubble detector, method of producing monocrystal on insulator, retaining wall tech. to maintain phys. shape of material during transient radiation annealing, method of fabricating display with semicondr. circuits on monolithic structure and flat panel display produced thereby; contbg. author articles in field; author presentations to profl. confs. U.S., France, Ca., Japan, Belgium. Organizer Neighborhood Watch, 1980—. Finalist Outstanding Young Elec. Engr. award, Eta Kappa Nu, 1984. Mem. IEEE, Materials Research Soc. Current work: Pioneer for silicon-on-insulator materials development for CMOS and bipolar device applications, also pioneer in three dimensional integrated circuit development. Subspecialties: Microelectronics; Electronic materials. Home: 12906 Jennifer Pl Dallas TX 75243 Office: LAM Assocs PO Box 742943 Dallas TX 75374

LAM, KUI-CHUEN, aerospace engineer, researcher; b. Hong Kong, Sept. 22, 1943; came to U.S., 1968, naturalized, 1978; s. King-Wah and Kam-Lin (Tsang) L.; m. Dorothea M. Heede, July 12, 1974. B.Sc. with honors, U. Hong Kong, 1967, B.Sc. with spl. honors, 1968; M.S., U. Oreg., 1971, Ph.D., 1974. Research assoc. U. Ga., Athens, 1974-75; asst. prof. Shiraz U., Iran, 1975-76; lab. supr. Western Carolina U., Cullowhee, N.C., 1976; research specialist U. Mo.-Rolla, 1976-79, research assoc. MIT, Cambridge, 1979-80, tech. staff C.S. Draper Lab., 1980—. Author tech. papers. Mem. Am. Phys. Soc., N.Y. Acad. Scis. Current work: Astronautical science, computational science, guidance and control, theoretical physics, information theory. Subspecialties: Aerospace engineering and technology; Theoretical physics. Office: MIT Br PO Box 172 Cambridge MA 02139

LAM, TSIT-YUEN, mathematics educator, researcher; b. Hong Kong, Feb. 6, 1942; came to U.S., 1963; s. Shiu-Fan and Sau-Hah (Tsui) L.; m. Chee-King, Dec. 1970; children—Juwen, Fumei, Juleen. B.A., U. Hong Kong, 1963; Ph.D., Columbia U., 1967. Postdoctoral fellow U. Ill., Urbana, 1967; instr. U. Chgo., 1967-68; prof. math. U. Calif., Berkeley, 1968—. Author: Algebraic Theory of Quadratic Forms (Am. Math. Soc. Steele prize 1982); Serre's Conjecture (Am. Math. Soc. Steele prize 1982); Offerings, Valuations and Quadratic Forms, 1984; Editor Communications in Algebra Jour., 1982—. Mem. Am. Math. Soc. Current work: Research in quadratic forms over fields, field-theory, arithmetic of fields, and noncommutative ring theory. Subspecialty: Algebra and number theory. Office: Dept Math U Calif Berkeley CA 94720

LAMATTINA, JOHN LAWRENCE, medicinal chemist; b. Bklyn., Jan. 22, 1950; s. John Anthony and Agnes Marie (Shannon) LaM.; m. Mary Lorraine Boyle, Dec. 18, 1971; children—John Curtis, David Shannon, Kara Christian. B.S. cum laude, Boston Coll., 1971; Ph.D., U. N.H., 1975. Cert. organic chemist. Vis. fellow Princeton U., N.J., 1975-77; research chemist Pfizer, Inc., Groton, Conn., 1977—, mgr., 1984. Contbr. articles to profl. jours. Patentee in field. Mem. Am. Chem. Soc. (medicinal chem. div., organic chemistry div.). Democrat. Roman Catholic. Current work: Drug discovery, medicinal chemistry, organic synthesis including novel synthetic methods and heterocyclic chemistry. Subspecialties: Medicinal chemistry; Organic chemistry. Home: 13 Huntington Way Ledyard CT 06339 Office: Pfizer Inc Eastern Point Rd Groton CT 06340

LAMB, DONALD QUINCY, physicist, researcher; b. Manhattan, Kans., June 30, 1945; s. Donald Quincy and Helen Letson (Keithley) L.; m. Linda Gilkerson, Sept. 23, 1978; 1 son, Michael. B.A., Rice U., Houston, 1967; M.Sc., U. Liverpool, Eng., 1969; Ph.D., U. Rochester, N.Y., 1974. Research asst. prof. physics U. Ill., 1973-75, asst. prof., 1975-77, assoc. prof., 1977-79, prof., 1979-80; vis. assoc. prof. M.I.T., 1978-79; vis. scientist dept. astronomy Harvard U., 1978-80; physicist Harvard-Smithsonian Center for Astrophysics, Cambridge, Mass., 1980-85; prof. astron. astrophysics U. Chgo., 1985—. Editor: (with D. Sugimoto, D. Schramm) Fundamental Problems in Theory of Stellar Evolution, 1981; contbr. articles to profl. jours. Woodrow Wilson fellow, 1967; NSF fellow, 1971-73; Guggenheim fellow, 1978-79; Nat. Merit scholar, 1963-67; Marshall scholar, 1967-69. Mem. Am. Phys. Soc, Am. Astron. Soc., Royal Astron. Soc. (London), Inst. Physics (London), European Phys. Soc., Internat. Astron. Union. Current Work: Stellar evolution, especially evolution of degenerate dwarfs and neutron stars, x-ray astronomy, esp x-ray emission from compact stars. Subspecialties: Theoretical physics; Theoretical astrophysics.

LAMB, RICHARD COMPTON, physicist, astrophysicist; b. Lexington, Ky., Sept. 8, 1933; s. J. C. and Frances (Roberts) L.; m. Jane Oldham, Aug. 29, 1959; children—Cheryl, Richard Jr., David, Wayne. B.S., MIT, 1955; M.S., U. Ky., 1960, Ph.D., 1963. Research assoc. Argonne Nat. Lab., Ill., 1963-64; asst. scientist, 1964-67; assoc. prof. Iowa State U., Ames, 1967-72, prof. physics, 1972—. Contbr. articles to profl. jours. Served to SP3 U.S. Army, 1955-57. Recipient Sr. Research associateship Nat. Research Council, 1982-83. Mem. Am. Phys. Soc., Am. Astron. Soc. Republican. Current work: Observational high energy astrophysics with emphasis on gamma ray astronomy. Subspecialties: Gamma ray high energy astrophysics; Particle physics. Home: 1908 Northwestern Ames IA 50010 Office: Physics Dept Iowa State U Ames IA 50011

LAMB, WILLIS EUGENE, JR., physicist, educator; b. Los Angeles, July 12, 1913; s. Willis Eugene and Marie Helen (Metcalf) L.; m. Ursula Schaefer, June 5, 1939. B.S., U. Calif., 1934, Ph.D., 1938; D.Sc., U. Pa., 1953, Gustavus Adolphus Coll., 1975; M.A., Oxford (Eng.) U., 1956, Yale, 1961; L.H.D., Yeshiva U., 1965. Mem. faculty Columbia, 1938-52, prof. physics, 1948-52, Stanford, 1951-56; Wykeham prof. physics and fellow New Coll., Oxford U., 1956-62; Henry Ford 2d prof. physics Yale, 1962-72, J. Willard Gibbs prof. physics, 1972-74; prof. physics and optical scis. U. Ariz., Tucson, 1974—; Morris Loeb lectr. Harvard, 1953-54; cons. Philips Labs., Bell Telephone Labs., Perkin-Elmer, NASA.; Vis. com. Brookhaven Nat. Lab. Recipient (with Dr. Polycarp Kusch) Nobel prize in physics, 1955; Rumford premium Am. Acad. Arts and Scis., 1953; Research Corp. award, 1955; Guggenheim fellow, 1960-61; recipient Yeshiva award, 1962. Fellow Am. Phys. Soc., N.Y. Acad. Scis.; hon. fellow Inst. Physics and Phys. Soc. (Guthrie lectr. 1958), Royal Soc. Edinburgh (fgn. mem.); mem. Nat. Acad. Scis., Phi Beta Kappa, Sigma Xi. Subspecialty: Theoretical physics. Office: Dept of Physics U Ariz Tucson AZ 85721

LAMBE, THOMAS WILLIAM, civil engineer, educator; b. Raleigh, N.C., Nov. 28, 1920; s. Claude Milton and Mary (Habel) L.; m. Catharine Canby Cadbury, Sept. 13, 1947; children—Philip Cadbury, Virginia Habel, Richard Lee, Robert Henry, Susan Elizabeth. B.S., N.C. State Coll., 1942; S.M., MIT, 1944, Sc.D., 1948. With Standard Oil Co. Calif., 1944, Dames & Moore, 1945; mem. faculty MIT, 1945-81, prof. civil engring., 1958-69, Edmund K. Turner prof., 1969-81, Edmund K. Turner prof. emeritus, 1981—, head soil mechanics div., 1958-69, 72-81, head geotech. div., 1972-81; cons. geotech. engring., 1945—, NASA, 1965—; Rankine lectr., 1973, Kapp Meml. lectr., 1980. Author books, numerous articles. Recipient Desmond Fitzgerald medal Boston Soc. Civil Engring., 1954, 56, Disting. Engring. Alumnus award N.C. State U., 1982. Fellow ASCE (Collingswood prize 1951, Wellington prize 1961, Norman medal 1964, Terzaghi lectr. 1970, Terzaghi award 1975, G. Brooks Earnest award 1982); mem. Internat. Soc. Soil Mechanics and Found. Engring., Nat. Acad. Engring. Subspecialty: Civil engineering. Home: 1641 Harbor Cay Ln Longboat Key FL 33548

LAMBERT, JOHN VINCENT, astronomer; b. Pittsburg, Kans., July 28, 1945; s. Jack Leeper and Beatrice Cecilia (Holub) L.; m. Joan Bollinger, Dec. 30, 1967; 1 dau., Vanya Marie. B.S., Kans. State U., Manhattan, 1967; M.S., Air Force Inst. Tech., 1971; M.S., N. Mex. State U., 1982, Ph.D., 1985. Commd. 2d lt. U.S. Air Force, 1967, advanced through grades to capt., 1967-78, physicist, Wright-Patterson AFB, Ohio, 1967-71, Cloudcroft, N. Mex., 1971-76, project mgr., Griffis AFB, N.Y., 1976-78, astronomer, cons., Alamogordo, N. Mex., 1979-84; orbital analyst TRW, White Sands Missile Range, N. Mex., 1984; laser system engr. Kentron Internat., Maui, Hiwaii, 1984—. Mem. Am. Astron. Soc., Sigma Xi. Roman Catholic. Current Work: Non-imaging techniques for shape/surface property determination; computer simulation of physical processes; applications of advanced electo-optical sensors; automated sensor systems; space def. system devel. Subspecialties: Planetary science; Satellite studies.

LAMBERTS, ROBERT LEWIS, optical engr., researcher; b. Fremont, Mich., Sept. 8, 1926; s. Lambertus and Anna (Dick) L.; m. Margaret Elizabeth Van Mouwerik, Aug. 1, 1951; children: Ruth Lamberts DuMont, Margaret Lamberts Bendroth, Nancy Lamberts Black, William, Robert, Peter. A.B., Calvin Coll., Grand Rapids, Mich., 1949; M.S. in Physics, U. Mich., 1951; Ph.D. in Optics, U. Rochester, 1969. With research labs. Eastman Kodak Co., Rochester, N.Y., 1951-83, sr. research assoc., 1981-83. Contbr. articles to sci. jours. Served with USN, 1944-46. Recipient best paper award Soc. Motion Picture and TV Engrs., 1962. Fellow Optical Soc. Am.; mem. Soc. Photog. Scientists and Engrs. (Charles E. Ives award 1966), Soc. Photog. Instrumentation Engrs. Patentee in field. Current Work: Photographic image structure. Subspecialties: Optical engineering; Holography. Home: 236 Henderson Dr Penfield NY 14526

LAMBETH, VICTOR NEAL, horticulturist, educator; b. Sarcoxie, Mo., July 5, 1920; s. Odus Huston and Carrie (Belle) L.; m. Sarah Katherine Smarr, May 24, 1946; children: Victoria Kay, Debra Jean. B.S. in Agr, U. Mo.-Columbia, 1942, M.S. in Horticulture, 1948, Ph.D., 1950. Asst. prof. horticulture U. Mo., 1950-51, assoc. prof., 1951-59, prof., 1959—. Contbr. articles to profl. jours. Served to lt. USN, 1943-46, PTO. Recipient awards for teaching; NSF grantee, 1982. Mem. Am. Soc. Hort. Sci., Am. Soc. Plant Physiologists, Sigma Xi, Gamma Sigma Delta. Methodist. Patentee in field. Current Work: Tomato genetics and breeding, plant growth media. Subspecialties: Plant genetics; Plant physiology (agriculture). Home: 1327 Lambeth Dr Columbia MO 65202 Office: Dept Horticulture U Mo 1-40 Agr Bldg Columbia MO 65211

LAMBIRD, PERRY ALBERT, pathologist; b. Reno, Nev., Feb. 7, 1939; s. C. David and Florence (Knowlton) L.; m. Mona Sue Salyer, July 30, 1960; children: Allison Thayer, Jennifer Salyer, Elizabeth Gard, Susannah Johnson. B.A., Stanford U., 1958; M.D., Johns Hopkins U., 1962; M.B.A., Okla. City U., 1973. Diplomate: Am. Bd. Pathology. Fellow in internal medicine Johns Hopkins Hosp., Balt., 1962-63, resident pathologist, 1965-68, chief resident, 1968-69; med. cons. USPHS, Washington, 1963-65; pathologist Med. Arts Lab., Oklahoma City, 1969—, Presbyn. Hosp., South Community Hosp., 1974—, Nat. Cancer Inst., 1974-81; propr. Lambird Mgmt. Cons. Service, Oklahoma City, 1974—; cons. in field. Reviewer: Jour. Am. Med. Assn, 1983—; contbr. articles to profl. jours. Pres. Okla. Symphony Orch., 1974-75, Ballet, Okla., 1978-79; del. Republican Nat. Conv., 1976, alt. del., 1984. Served to lt. comdr. USPHS, 1963-65. Recipient Exec. Leadership award Oklahoma City U., 1976; Physician's Recognition award AMA, 1969-83; Outstanding Pathologist award Am. Pathology Found., 1984. Fellow Am. Soc. Clin. Pathologists, Coll. Am. Pathologists, Internat. Coll. Surgeons; mem. AMA (ho. of dels., council med. services 1985—), Okla. Med. Assn. (ho. of dels., trustee), Okla. County Med. Soc. (pres.), Okla. Soc. Cytopathology (pres.), Am. Pathology Found. (pres.), Okla. Found. for Peer Rev. (dir.), Arthur Purdy Stout Soc. Surg. Pathologists, Am. Assn. Pathologists, Okla. Assn. Pathologists (pres.), So. Med. Assn., N.Y. Acad. Sci., Am. Soc. Cytology, Olser Soc., Okla. City Clin. Soc., Phi Beta Kappa, Alpha Omega Alpha. Republican. Methodist. Current Work: Applied anatomic and clinical pathology including management and administration, quality control, cost benefit analysis and efficiency measures in clinical medicine. Subspecialties: Pathology (medicine); Health services research. Home: 419 Northwest 14th St Oklahoma City OK 73103 Office: Med Arts Lab 100 Pasteur 1111 N Lee St Oklahoma City OK 73103

LAMBORG, MARVIN R., biochemistry educator, researcher; B.S., U. Rochester, 1951, Ph.D., 1958. Research fellow in medicine Mass. Gen. Hosp./Harvard Med. Sch., 1958-61; tutor Harvard Coll., 1960-65; research assoc. in medicine Mass. Gen. Hosp., 1961-62, asst. biochemist, 1962-65; investigator Charles F. Kettering Research Lab., Yellow Springs, Ohio, 1965-70, sr. investigator, mission mgr., 1970-83, mgr. internat. food productivity program, 1983-84, assoc. dir. program devel. Battelle Kettering Lab., 1984—; assoc. prof. biochemistry Antioch Coll., Yellow Springs, Ohio, 1967—. Cons. to India, 1981-82; mem. adv. com. pathogenesis of cancer Am. Cancer Soc., 1967-72. Contbr. articles to profl. jours. Mem. Subspecialties: Food science and technology; Plant genetics. Office: Battelle Kettering Lab Yellow Springs OH

LAMBRECHT, RICHARD M(ERLE), chemistry researcher, consultant; b. Salem, Oreg., Apr. 8, 1943; s. Bernard Henry and Eulina Elizabeth (Neal) L.; children—Curtis, Lars, Luke. B.S., Oreg. State U., 1965; Ph.D., U. Nebr., 1969. Research assoc. Eastman Kodak Co., Rochester, N.Y., 1968; research assoc. Brookhaven Nat. Lab., Upton, N.Y., 1969-70, assoc. scientist, 1970-74, scientist, 1974—; vis. scholar Deutsches Krebsforschungzentrum, Heidelberg, King Faisel Specialist Hosp. and Research Ctr., Saudi Arabia; cons. to various orgns., 1975—. Author: Exotic Atoms, 1984; Positions and Positronium, 1986. Editor: Animal Models in Radiotracer Design, 1983; Tracer Kinetics and Physiologic Modeling, 1983; Applications of Nuclear and Radiochemistry, 1982. Patentee in field. Contbr. numerous articles to profl. jours. Pres. Bd. Educ., Quoque, N.Y., 1983-84. Recipient IR-100 Research and Development award, 1984, 85. Mem. Am. Chem. Soc., Soc. Nuclear Med. (pres. Radiopharm. Sci. Council 1983-84). Current work: Radiopharmaceutical science, biomedical research-nuclear medicine, cyclotron, isotope production, PET. Subspecialty: Physical chemistry. Home: 77 Old Depot Rd Quoque NY 11959 Office: Brookhaven Nat Lab Chem Dept Upton NY 11973

LAMBRIS, JOHN DIMITRIOS, immunologist; b. Rodavgi, Greece, June 3, 1954; came to U.S., 1979; s. Dimitrios and Agathi (Phyhogios) L.; m. Rodothea Kokkinou, July 7, 1976; children—Agatha, Dimitrios. B.S., U. Patras, Greece, 1976, Ph.D., 1979. Research asst. Hellenic Anticancer Inst., Athens, Greece, 1976-79; postdoctoral fellow U. N.C., Chapel Hill, 1979-80, research assoc., 1980-81, asst. prof. immunology, 1981-82; vis. prof. Inst. Medical Micro., Mainz, Fed. Republic Germany, 1982-83; asst. mem. Scripps Clinic and Research Found., La Jolla, Calif., 1983—. Contbr. articles to profl. publs. Grantee Am. Cancer Soc., 1982, NIH, 1984; recipient New Investigator award NIH, 1982. Fellow European Molecular Biology Orgn., Alexander Von Humboldt, Fed. Republic Germany; mem. Am. Soc. Immunologists, British Soc. Biochemists. Current work: Functional and structural characterization of human complement components and complement receptors. Subspecialty: Immunocytochemistry. Home: 3839 Camino Lindo San Diego CA 92122 Office: Scripps Clinic and Research Found 10666 N Torrey Pines Rd La Jolla CA 92037

LAMBUTH, ALAN LETCHER, chemist; b. Seattle, Jan. 5, 1923; s. Benjamin Letcher and Olive Serena (Schram) L.; m. Susan Jane DeMelt, Aug. 19, 1944; children: Wendy Lambuth Trudgian, Peter, John, Douglas. Student, U. Wash., 1940-42, Yale U., 1942-43; student, U. Santa Clara, 1944; B.S. in Chemistry, U. Wash., 1947. Research chemist Monsanto Co., Seattle, 1947-57, research leader 3 groups, 1958-69; product devel. mgr. Boise Cascade Corp., Boise, Idaho, 1970-75, research and devel. mgr., 1976-81, mgr. product and process devel., 1981—, also cons. overseas wood products cos.; guest lectr., reviewer research proposals and papers U.S. Dept. Agr. Forest Products Lab., NSF, univs. Publs. in polymer, adhesives and wood structural design fields.; patentee in field. Served with Signal Corps U.S. Army, 1943-46. Recipient Monsanto award for research innovation, 1969; FPRS-Borden award for contbns. to forest products adhesives, 1984. Mem. Forest Products Research Soc. (pres. 1982-83), Am. Chem. Soc., Am. Inst. Timber Constrn., Am. Plywood Assn., ASTM, Nat. Forest Products Assn., Nat. Paint and Coatings Assn., Western Wood Products Assn., Internat. Union Forestry Research Orgns. Republican. Congregationalist. Club: Hillcrest Country. Current Work: Innovative uses for wood, especially underutilized species and waste materials; biomass as a chem. resource; wood treatment or modification for improved performance; new polymers and adhesive concepts; wood structural design; new converting and manufacturing processes. Subspecialties: Polymer chemistry; Wood treatment, modification. Home: 7240 Cascade Dr Boise ID 83704 Office: Boise Cascade Corp 220 S 3d St Boise ID 83702

LAMEY, HOWARD ARTHUR, plant pathologist; b. Bloomington, Ind., Dec. 20, 1929; s. Carl Arthur and Mary Lucile (Seaman) L.; m. Cynthia Joan Huenink, Aug. 22, 1956; children: Timothy, Thaddeus, Linda, Suzan, Laura. B.A., Ohio Wesleyan U., 1951; Ph.D., U. Wis.-Madison, 1954. Project assoc. U. Wis., Madison, 1954-55, 57-58; research plant pathologist U.S. Dept. Agr., Camaguey, Cuba, 1958-59, Baton Rouge, La., 1960-69; plant pathologist Internat. Inst. Tropical Agr., Ibadan, Nigeria, 1969-71; project mgr. food and agr. orgn. UN, Seoul, Korea, 1971-75; extension plant pathologist N.D. State U., Fargo, 1977—. Contbr. numerous articles to profl. jours. Patron Fargo-Moorhead Civic Opera, 1981-85. Served with AUS, 1955-57. Fellow AAAS; mem. Am. Phytopath. Soc., AAAS., Mycol. Soc. Am., N.Y. Acad. Sci., Phi Beta Kappa, Sigma Xi, Gamma Sigma Delta. Current Work: Diseases of cereals, row crops, vegetables, fruits and ornamentals. Subspecialty: Plant pathology. Home: 1517 8th St N Fargo ND 58102 Office: Dept Plant Pathology ND State U Fargo ND 58105

LAMM, MICHAEL EMANUEL, pathologist, immunologist; b. Bklyn., May 19, 1934; s. Stanley S. and Rose (Lieberman) L.; m. Ruth Audrey Kumin, Dec. 16, 1961; children: Jocelyn, Margaret. Student, Amherst Coll., 1951-54; M.D., U. Rochester, 1959; M.S., Western Res. U., 1962. Diplomate: Am. Bd. Pathology. Resident pathology U. Hosp., Cleve., 1959-62; research assoc. NIH, Bethesda, Md., 1962-64; asst. prof. pathology N.Y.U. Sch. Medicine, N.Y.C., 1964-68, assoc. prof., 1968-73, prof., 1973-81; prof., chmn. pathology Case Western Res. U., Univ. Hosps., Cleve., 1981—; mem. cancer spl. program adv. com. Nat. Cancer Inst., Bethesda, Md., 1976-79; mem. sci. adv. com. Damon Runyon-Walter Winchell Cancer Fund, N.Y.C., 1978-82. Editorial bd.: Procs. Soc. Exptl. Biology and Medicine, 1973-82, Molecular Immunology, 1979-82, Jour. Immunological Methods, 1980—, Jour. Immunology, 1981-85, Am. Jour. Pathology, 1982—; contbr. articles in field to profl. jours. Named Career Scientist Health Research Council City N.Y., 1966-75; NIH research grantee, 1965—. Mem. Am. Assn. Pathologists, Am. Assn. Immunologists, Am. Soc. Biol. Chemists, N.Y. Acad. Scis., Coll. Am. Pathologists, Internat. Acad. Pathology, Soc. Exptl. Biol. Medicine. Current Work: Mucosal immunity, immunopathology of renal disease. Subspecialties: Immunobiology and immunology; Pathology (medicine). Office: Inst Pathology Case Western Res U 2085 Adelbert Rd Cleveland OH 44106

LAMON, EDDIE WILLIAM, immunologist; b. Yuba City, Calif., Aug. 30, 1939; s. James Hilyer and Annie Louise (Hannah) L.; m. Bodil I.M. Lidin, June 17, 1973; children: Eddie Wiliam, Cynthia Ann Bently, Leif Christopher. B.S., U. North Ala., 1961; M.D., U. Ala., 1969; D.Sc. with highest honors, Karolinska Inst., Stockholm, 1974. Diplomate: Am. Bd. Med. Examiners, 1970. Asst. biologist So. Research Inst., Birmingham, Ala., 1964-65; intern, resident in surgery U. Ala., Birmingham, 1969-71, asst. prof. surgery, assoc. scientist, cancer research and tng ctr., 1974-75, assoc. prof. surgery, scientist, 1975-79, asst. prof. microbiology, 1974-77, assoc. prof. microbiology, 1977-82, prof. microbiology, 1982—, prof. surgery, sr. scientist, 1979—; chief tumor immunology research Birmingham VA Hosp., 1974—; guest investigator in tumor immunology dept. tumor biology Karolinska Inst., Stockholm, 1971-73. Served with USNR, 1961-63. Nat. Cancer Inst. career devel. awardee, 1975-80; Josiah Macy, Jr. Found. faculty scholar awardee, 1980-81. Mem. Am. Assn. Immunologists, Am. Assn. Pathologists, Am. Assn. Cancer Research, Am. Soc. Microbiologists, AAUP, Sigma Xi. Current Work: Characterization of immune responses to virus induced tumors; studies of antibody-dependent cell-mediated cytotoxicity; studies of immune complex receptors on lymphocytes. Subspecialties: Cancer research (medicine); Immunology (medicine). Home: 3569 Hampshire Dr Birmingham AL 35223 Office: Dept Surgery U Ala School Medicine Birmingham AL 35294

LA MOTTA, ENRIQUE JAIME, environmental engineering educator, consultant; b. Guayaquil, Ecuador, July 8, 1940; s. Ricardo and Eloisa (Diaz) La M.; m. Maria Elena Rueda, June 11, 1971; children: Lorena, David, Ivan. Civil engr., U. Central del Ecuador, 1965; M.S.S.E., U. N.C., 1969, Ph.D., 1974. Sanitary engr. IEOS, Quito, Ecuador, 1965-71; assoc. prof. U. Mass., Amherst, 1976-80; asst. prof. U. Miami, Coral Gables, Fla., 1974-76; prof. prin. Esc. Poli. Nac., Quito, Ecuador, 1980—; cons., Quito, 1980—. Contbr. numerous articles to profl. jours. Recipient Bunker award U.N.C., 1969. Mem. Am. Soc. Civil Engrs., Am. Water Works Assn., Water Pollution Control Fed., Assn. Environmental Engring. Profs., Internat. Assn. Water Pollution Research, Sigma Xi. Current Work: Interest: Kinetics of Biological processes, Eutrophication, Biological films, organics removal. Subspecialty: Water supply and wastewater treatment. Home: Pesantesco 100 Y Manosca Quito Ecuador Office: Escuela Politecnica Nacional Facultad de Ingenieria Civil Quito Ecuador

LAMPE, FREDERICK WALTER, chemist, educator; b. Chgo., Jan. 5, 1927; s. Joseph Dell and Christine Wood (Phillips) L.; m. Eleanor Frances Coffin, Mar. 26, 1949; children: Joan Dell Wakeling, Kathy Lee Wakeling, Erik Steven, Beth Ann, Kristina Jean. B.S., Mich. State Coll., 1950; A.M., Columbia U., 1951, Ph.D., 1953. Research chemist Humble Oil and Refining Co., Baytown, Tex., 1953-56, sr. research chemist, 1956-60; assoc. prof. chemistry Pa. State U., 1960-65, prof., 1965—, head dept. chemistry, 1983—; sci. cons. Author: (with W. R. Allcock) Contemporary Polymer Chemistry, 1981; contbr. (with W. R. Allcock) numerous articles to sci. jours. Served with USN, 1944-46. Recipient U.S.Sr. Scientist award Alexander Von Humboldt Found., 1973; NSF sr. postdoctoral fellow, 1966-67. Fellow Am. Phys. Soc.; mem. Am. Chem. Soc., Am. Soc. Mass Spectrometry, Inter-Am. Photochem. Soc., Sigma Xi. Methodist. Patentee in field. Current Work: Chem. kinetics of free radical and ionic reactions in gas-phase; multiphoton infrared laser induced chemistry; vacuum ultraviolet photochemistry; mass spectrometry. Subspecialties: Kinetics; Laser photochemistry. Home: 542 Ridge Ave State College PA 16801 Office: Pa State U 152 Davey Lab University Park PA 16802

LAMPERT, SEYMOUR, mechanical engineer, educator; b. Bklyn., Mar. 5, 1920; s. Max and Esther (Bakst) L.; m. Shirley Ruth (Axelrod), Mar. 21, 1948; children: Rachel Beth, David Aaron, Martin Daniel. B.S., Ga. Tech. Inst., 1943; M.S., Calif. Inst. Tech., 1947, Ph.D., 1954. Instr. Ga. Tech. Inst., Atlanta, 1943-44; aero. research scientist Ames Lab., Calif Inst. Tech., 1944-51, research engr. Jet Propulsion Lab., 1951-54; chief engr. Odin Assocs., Pasadena, Calif., 1956-57; dept. mgr. Ford Aeronutronic, Newport Beach, Calif., 1957-62; dir. advanced systems research N.Am. Aviation Space Div., 1962-67; v.p. SAI, Long Beach, Calif., 1967-71; prof. dir. solar research dept. mech. engring. U. So. Calif., Los Angeles, 1975—; dir. Davato Corp., Energy Fair Found. Editor-in-chief: Solar Scis., 1982—; contbr. articles to profl. jours. Served to lt. USNR, 1944-54. Mem. Internat. Solar Energy Soc. Patentee in field. Current Work: Solar research and development; educational programs in solar sciences, photovoltaics. Subspecialties: Solar energy; Fluid mechanics. Office: U So Calif Los Angeles CA 90089

LAMPKIN, CURTIS MAGILL, physicist; b. Cin., May 4, 1938; s. Eugene Edelin and Edith Margaret (Magill) L.; m. Joan Carol Bruns, Sept. 1959; children—Michael, Mark, Carol, Theresa, Ellen, Martin. B.S. in Physics, U. Cin., 1960; M.S. in Physics, Xavier U., 1970. Asst. project engr. D. H. Baldwin, Cin., El Paso, Tex., 1959-77; chief research scientist Photon Power, Inc., El Paso, 1977-81, mgr. tin oxide products, 1981-83; chief scientist Martin-Marietta Aerospace, Albuquerque, 1983—. Patentee in field. Mem. IEEE, Am. Inst. Physics, Am. Vacuum Soc., Soc. Photoptical Instrumentation Engrs., Southwest Area Sq. Dance Assn. (pres. 1979-80). Roman Catholic. Current work: Single point diamond turning of optical surfaces; laser metrology; computer controlled optic fabrication. Subspecialty: Solar energy. Office: Martin-Marietta Aerospace PO Box 9316 Albuquerque NM 87119

LAMPORT, LESLIE, computer scientist; b. N.Y.C., Feb. 7, 1941; s. Benjamin and Hannah (Lasser) L.; m. Carol Dahl Crum (div.); 1 child, Jason. B.S., MIT, 1960; M.S., Brandeis U., 1963, Ph.D., 1972. Computer scientist Marlboro Coll., Vt., 1965-69, Mass. Computer Assocs., Wakefield, 1970-77, SRI Internat., 1977-85, Digital Equipment Corp., Palo Alto, Calif., 1985—. Subspecialty: Theoretical computer science. Office: Care SRI Internat 333 Ravenswood Ave Menlo Park CA 94025

LAMVIK, MICHAEL KASPER, anatomy educator; b. Portland, Oreg., June 26, 1946; s. Kasper O. and Marjorie M. (Casper) L. B.S., U. Portland, 1968; Ph.D., U. Chgo., 1976. Postdoctoral fellow Brandeis U., Waltham, Mass., 1976-79, U. Trondheim, Norway, 1979-80; scientist Max-Planck-Soc., Berlin, 1980-82; asst. prof. anatomy Duke U. Med. Ctr., Durham, N.C., 1982—. Contbr. articles to profl. jours. Research grantee. Mem. Biophys. Soc., Electron Microscopy Soc. Am., Scandinavian Soc. Electron Microscopy. Current work: Substructure of protein assemblies; mass measurement by electron scattering; low temperature microscopy and superconducting lenses; electron spectroscopy; cross-correlation image averaging. Subspecialty: Biophysics (biology). Office: Dept Anatomy Duke Univ Med Ctr Box 3011 Durham NC 27710

LANCASTER, ARTHUR LEWIS, electronics engineer; b. St. Louis, May 9, 1950; s. Elroy Bryant and Evelyn Ruth (Scott) L.; m. Mary Ellen Klenk, May 20, 1972. B.S. in Elec. Engring. cum laude, U. Mo.-Columbia, 1972; M.S. in Elec. Engring., U. So. Calif., 1977. Mem. tech. staff Hughes Research Labs., Newport Beach, Calif., 1972-77; sect. mgr. Nat. Semicondr., Santa Clara, Calif., 1977-79; sr. design engr. Inmos Corp., Colorado Springs, Colo., 1979-83; mgr. dept. memory design engring RCA Solid State, Somerville, N.J., 1983-85; v.p., gen. mgr. Design Ctr., RCA Sharp Microelectronics, Camas, Wash., 1985—. Hughes Aircraft Co. fellow, 1972. Mem. IEEE (guest editor Jour. of Solid State Circuits 1984), Tau Beta Pi, Eta Kappa Nu. Club: El Paso County Obedience (pres. Colorado Springs 1981-83). Current work: Management of design and development of CMOS very large scale integrated circuits including memories, microprocessors and logic. Subspecialties: Integrated circuits; Microchip technology (engineering). Home: NW 30th Ct Vancouver WA Office: RCA Sharp Microelectronics PO Box 1044 Camas WA 98607

LANCASTER, PETER, See *Who's Who in America,* 43rd edition.

LAND, EDWIN HERBERT, physicist, inventor; b. Bridgeport, Conn., May 7, 1909; s. Harry M. and Martha F. L.; m. Helen Maislen, 1929; children: Jennifer, Valerie. Ed., Norwich Acad.; student, Harvard, Sc.D. hon., 1957; Sc.D. hon., Tufts Coll., 1947, Poly. Inst. Bklyn., 1952, Colby Coll., 1955, Northeastern U., 1959, Carnegie Inst. Tech., 1964, Yale U., 1966, Columbia U., 1967, Loyola U., 1970, NYU, 1973; LL.D., Bates Coll., 1953, Wash. U., 1966, U. Mass., 1967, Brandeis U., 1980; L.H.D., Williams Coll., 1968. Founder Polaroid Corp., Cambridge, Mass., 1937, chmn. bd., cons. dir. basic research, 1937-82, dir. basic research, 1937-80, pres., 1937-80; founder, dir. research, scientist Rowland Inst. Sci., Cambridge, Mass., 1981—; William James lectr. psychology Harvard, 1966-67, Morris Loeb lectr. physics, 1974; vis. Inst. prof. Mass. Inst. Tech., 1956—; mem. Pres.'s Sci. Adv. Com., 1957-59, cons.-at-large, 1960-73; mem. Pres.'s Com. Nat. Medal of Sci., 1969-72, Carnegie Commn. on Ednl. TV, 1966-67, Nat. Commn. on Tech., Automation and Econ. Progress, 1964-66. Trustee Ford Found., 1967-75. Recipient numerous awards including; recipient Presdl. Medal of Freedom, 1963, Nat. Medal of Sci., 1967, Hood medal Royal Photog. Soc., 1935, Cresson medal, 1937, Potts medal, 1956, Vermilye medal Franklin Inst., Phila., 1974, John Scott medal and award, 1938, Rumford medal Am. Acad. Arts and Scis., 1945, Holley medal Am. Soc. M.E., 1948, Duddell medal Brit. Phys. Soc., 1949, Progress medal Soc. Photog. Engrs., 1955, Albert A. Michelson award Case Inst. Tech., 1966, Kulturpreis Photog. Soc. Germany, 1967, Perkin medal Soc. Chem. Industry, 1974, Proctor award, 1963, Photographic Sci. and Engring. Jour. award, 1971, Progress medal Photog. Soc. Am., 1960, Kosar Meml. award, 1973, Golden Soc. medal Photog. Soc. Vienna, 1961, Interkamera award, 1973, Cosmos Club award, 1970, NAM award, 1940, 66, Jefferson medal N.J. Patent Law Assn., 1960, Indsl. Research medal, 1965, Diesel medal in gold, 1966; named Nat. Inventors Hall of Fame, 1977. Fellow Nat. Acad. Scis., Photog. Soc. Am., Am. Acad. Arts and Scis. (pres. 1951-53), Royal Photog. Soc. Gt. Britain (Progress medal 1957), Royal Micros. Soc. (hon.), Soc. Photog. Scientists and Engrs. (hon., Lieven-Gevaert medal 1976); mem. N.Y. Acad. Scis., Nat. Acad. Engring. (Founders medal 1972), Optical Soc. Am. (hon. mem. 1972, dir. 1950-51, Frederick Ives medal 1967, Dudley Wright prize 1980), Royal Instn. Gt. Britain (hon.), Am. Philos. Soc., German Photog. Soc. (hon.), Soc. Photog. Sci. and Tech. Japan (hon.), IEEE (hon.), Sigma Xi. During coll. years invented 1st light-polarizer in form of an extensive synthetic sheet; developed a sequence of subsequent polarizers, theories and applications of polarized light, including automobile headlight system, 3 dimensional pictures, camera filters; during World War II developed optical, other systems for mil. use; created cameras, films that give instantaneous dry photographs in black and white and color; proposed Retinex Theory for mechanism of color perception and designed series of supporting expts. Subspecialty: Photographic science. Home: 163 Brattle St Cambridge MA 02138 Office: Rowland Inst Sci 100 Cambridge Pkwy Cambridge MA 02142

LAND, MARGARET F., statistics educator, consultant; b. Norman, Okla., Feb. 20, 1939; m. Hugh C. Land, May 24, 1957 (dec. 1968); children—Peter Colman, David Foster, Stephanie Ruth. B.S., N.W. La. State U., 1963, M.S., 1967; Ph.D., Okla. State U., 1981. Asst. prof. math., N.W. La. State U., Natchitoches, 1967-70; asst. prof. and statistics cons. N.Mex. State U., Las Cruces, 1977-80; teaching assoc. Okla. State U., Stillwater, 1970-77, 80-81; asst. prof., cons. Tex. A&I U., Kingsville, 1981—; pvt. practice cons. statistician, 1979—; Fulbright vis. fellow, Venezuela, Author jour. articles. State del. Tex. Republican Party, 1984; county del. Tex. Med. Assn. Aux., 1983-85. Mem. Am. Statis. Assn. (subcom. on statis. cons. edn. 1984-85), Biometric Soc., Soc. for Indsl. and Applied Math., Am. Assn. Quality Control. Lutheran. Clubs: Mensa, Intertel, Triple Nine, Audubon Soc. Research or work interests: Consulting, experimental design, quality control, regression, sample surveys. Subspecialties: Statistics; Quality control. Home: 1800 Newell St Alice TX 78332 Office: Dept Math Tex A&I Univ Box 172 Kingsville TX 78363

LANDAU, HENRY J., communication laboratories mathematician; b. Feb. 11, 1931; s. Majer and Edda (Thaler) L.; m. Julie Weill, Nov. 1, 1960; children—Jennifer, Zeph. A.B., Harvard U., 1953, A.M., 1955, Ph.D., 1957. Mem. tech. staff AT&T Bell Labs., Murray Hill, N.J., 1957—; assoc. mem. Inst. for Advanced Study, Princeton, N.J., 1959-60, 66-67; adj. prof. CUNY, 1966; vis. prof. Chinese U. Hong Kong, 1967-68. Contbr. articles to profl. jours. Mem. Am. Math. Soc., IEEE. Democrat. Jewish. Subspecialty: Harmonic analysis. Home: 90 Charles St New York NY 10014 Office: AT&T Bell Labs 2C-375 Murray Hill NJ 07974

LANDAUER, ROLF WILLIAM, physicist; b. Stuttgart, Germany, Feb. 4, 1927; came to U.S., 1938, naturalized, 1944; s. Karl and Anna (Dannhauser) L.; m. Muriel Jussim, Feb. 26, 1950; children—Karen, Carl, Thomas. S.B., Harvard U., 1945, A.M., 1947, Ph.D., 1950. Solid state physicist Lewis Lab., NACA (now NASA), Cleve., 1950-52; with IBM Research (and antecedent groups), 1952—; asst. dir. research IBM Research (T. J. Watson Research Center), Yorktown Heights, N.Y., 1966-69, IBM fellow, 1969—. Contbr. articles on solid state theory, computing devices, statis. mechanics of computational process to profl. jours.; asso. editor: Rev. Modern Physics, 1973-76. Served with USNR, 1945-46. Fellow IEEE, Am. Phys. Soc.; mem. Nat. Acad. Engring. Initiated IBM programs leading to injection laser, large scale integration. Subspecialties: Condensed matter physics; Computer engineering. Office: IBM Research Center PO Box 218 Yorktown Heights NY 10598

LANDAUER, THOMAS K., research psychologist; b. Highland Park, Ill., Apr. 25, 1932; s. Robert S. and Ruth (Kronthal) L.; m. Cynthia Almy, June 15, 1956 (div. 1976); children—Katherine R., Deborah. B.A., U. Colo., 1954; M.A., Harvard U., 1958, Ph.D., 1960. Instr. Harvard U., Cambridge, Mass., 1959-60; asst. prof. psychology Dartmouth Coll., Hanover, N.H., 1960-64; asst. prof. Stanford U., Calif., 1964-69; lectr. Princeton U., N.J., 1979-82; mem. tech. staff AT&T Bell Labs., Murray Hill, N.J., 1969-84; research mgr. Bell Communications Research, Morristown, N.J., 1985—. Author: Psychology: A Brief Overview, 1974. Contbr. articles to profl. jours. Mem. NRC Com. on Human Factors, Washington, 1984. Ctr. for Advanced Study in the Behavior Scis. fellow, 1964. Fellow Am. Psychol. Assn., AAAS; mem. Psychonomic Soc. Current work: Experimental and theoretical investigaitns of humanmemory; psychologyoofhhuman-computer interaction, especially information retrieval.

Subspecialties: Cognition; Human factors psychology. Office: Bell Communications Research 435 South St Morristown NJ 07960

LANDECKER, PETER BRUCE, physicist; b. N.Y.C., Oct. 1, 1942; s. Louis and Mildred (Nesson) L. A.B., Columbia U., 1963; Ph.D., Cornell U., 1967. Instr. physics Cornell U., 1967-68; asst. research physicist U. Calif., Irvine, 1968-70; research assoc. Columbia U., 1970-74, cons., N.Y.C., 1974-75; mem. tech. staff Aerospace Corp., El Segundo, Calif., 1974-82, cons., 1982-83; sr. scientist Space and Communications Group, Hughes Aircraft Co., El Segundo, 1982—; instr. physics El Camino Coll, 1977. Contbr. articles to profl. jours. N.Y. State teaching fellow, 1963-65; NSF Summer Inst. fellow, 1959; N.Y. State Regents scholar, 1959-63; N.Y. State scholar, 1959-63; NASA trainee fellow, 1965-67; recipient Hughes Aircraft Div. Invention award, 1983. Mem. Am. Phys. Soc., Internat. Astron. Union. Unitarian-Universalist. Club: Hughes Scuba (El Segundo). Mem. Beach Cities Symphony Orch., Redondo Beach, Calif. Current Work: Design of remote sensing satellites and payloads. Subspecialties: Satellite studies; Solar physics. Home: 1736 Nelson Ave Manhattan Beach CA 90266 Office: Hughes Space and Communications Group Bldg S41 Mail Stop B322 PO Box 92919 Airport Sta Los Angeles CA 90009

LANDEL, ROBERT FRANKLIN, physical chemist; b. Pendleton, N.Y., Oct. 10, 1925; s. Carlisle Oscar and Grace Elisabeth (McEachren) L.; m. Aurora Salazar Mamauag, Aug. 1, 1953; children—Carlisle P., Grace P., Han F., Robert Franklin, Kevin L., Matthew N. B.A. cum laude, U. Buffalo, 1949; M.A., 1950; Ph.D., U. Wis., 1954. Research assoc. U. Wis., Madison, 1954-55; sr research engr. Jet Propulsion Lab., Pasadena, Calif., 1955-59, sect. mgr., 1959—, sr. research scientist, 1980—; vis. prof. Ecole Polytech. Federale, Lausanne, Switzerland, 1984; cons. Sandia Nat. Lab., Albuquerque, 1983; mem. various U.S. govt. panels and bds., 1959—. Mem. editorial bd. various polymer jours. Contbr. articles to profl. jours. Patentee on test equipment, novel polymers. Served with inf., AUS, 1943-46. Fulbright fellow, 1971-72; French Govt. fellow, 1972; Recipient Exceptional Sci. Achievement medal NASA, 1976; Fellow Am. Phys. Soc.; mem. Soc. Rheology (v.p., pres. elect 1984—), Am. Chem. Soc., Am. Phys. Soc. (high polymer physics div., exec. com. 1968-70). Current work: Rheology; dynamic mechanical properties of polyers: solids, solutions and composites; finite deformation and ruture of elastomers; lifetime of polymers; filled systems; skin mechanics. Subspecialties: Polymers (materials science); Polymer physics. Office: Jet Propulsion Lab 4800 Oak Grove Dr Pasadena CA 91109

LANDER, GERARD H., physicist. Dir. Inrense Pulsed Neutron Source program Argonne Nat. Lab., Ill. Subspecialty: Condensed matter physics. Office: Argonne Nat Lab 9700 S Cass Ave Argonne IL 60439*

LANDERS, ROY ESLYN, JR., therapeutic radiol. physicist; b. Milledgeville, Ga., Aug. 4, 1944; s. Roy Eslyn and Mildred McNair (Jones) L.; m. Carol Hill, Sept. 13, 1969; children: Kimberly Diane, James Jefferson. B.S. in Physics, Ga. Inst. Tech., 1966, M.S. in Physics, 1968, Ph.D., 1974. Diplomate: Am. Bd. Radiology, 1980. Instr. Devry Inst. Tech., Atlanta, 1973-75, chmn. basic studies, 1975; cons. math. and computer models Varian Assocs., Atlanta, 1974-76; therapeutic radiol. physicist, cons. Sarasota Oncology Center, Fla., 1976—. Contbr. sci. articles to profl. publs. NDEA fellow, 1969. Mem. Am. Assn. Physicists in Medicine, Health Physics Soc., Sigma Xi, Sigma Pi Sigma. Current Work: Physics of therapeutic radiology; computer software development. Subspecialty: Therapeutic radiological physics.

LANDGREBE, DAVID ALLEN, elec. engr.; b. Huntingburg, Ind., Apr. 12, 1934; s. Albert E. and Sarah A. L.; m. Margaret Ann Swank, June 7, 1959; children—James David, Carole Ann, Mary Jane. B.S. in Elec. Enging, Purdue U., 1956, M.S. in Elec. Enging, 1958, Ph.D., 1962. Mem. tech. staff Bell Telephone Labs., Murray Hill, N.J., 1956; electronics engr. Interstate Electronics Corp., Anaheim, Calif., 1958, 59, 62; mem. faculty Purdue U., West Lafayette, Ind., 1962—, dir. lab. for applications of remote sensing, 1969-81, prof. elec. engring., 1970—, asso. dean engring., 1981-84; research scientist Douglas Aircraft Co., Newport Beach, Calif., 1964; dir. Univ. Space Research Assn., 1975-78. Author: (with others) Remote Sensing: The Quantitative Approach, 1978. Recipient medal for exceptional sci. achievement NASA, 1973. Fellow IEEE; mem. Am. Soc. for Enging. Edn., AAAS, Am. Soc. Photogrammetry, Sigma Xi, Tau Beta Pi, Eta Kappa Nu. Club: Rotary. Current Work: Information representation, image processing and pattern recognition. Subspecialties: Graphics, image processing, and pattern recognition; Information systems (Information science). Office: Purdue U Dept Elec Engring West Lafayette IN 47907

LANDIS, MICHAEL EUGENE, industrial chemist, researcher; b. Woodbury, N.J., Oct. 15, 1948; s. Phillip Sherwood and Vivian (Center) L.; m. Bernadette Gale, Aug. 7, 1971; children—Patrick, Jeremy. B.S. in Chemistry, Duke U., 1970; M.A., Harvard U., 1972, Ph.D. in Organic Chemistry, 1974. Asst. prof. phys. organic chemistry So. Ill. U., Edwardsville, 1976-79, assoc. prof., 1979-80; sr. research chemist Mobil Research and Devel. Corp., Paulsboro, N.J., 1980-82, assoc., 1982—. Recipient Outstanding Tchr. award, So. Ill. U., 1980; grantee Petroleum Research Fund, 1976-80, Research Corp., 1978-80. Mem. Am. Chem. Soc., Sigma Xi. Current work: Catalyst synthesis for petroleum and petrochemical processes. Subspecialties: Organic chemistry; Inorganic chemistry. Home: 26 N Horace St Woodbury NJ 08096 Office: Mobil Research and Devel Corp Billingsport Rd Paulsboro NJ 08096

LANDIS, WAYNE G., research scientist; b. Washington, Jan. 20, 1952; s. James G. and Harriet E. L. B.A. cum laude with honors in Biology (Hankins scholar), Wake Forest U., 1974; M.A. in Biology, Ind. U., 1978, Ph.D. in Zoology, 1979. Environ. and health scientist Franklin Research Ctr., Silver Spring, Md., 1979-81; research biologist environ. toxicology br. toxicology div. Chem. Research and Devel. Ctr., Aberdeen Proving Grounds, Md., 1982—. Contbr. articles on ecology, population genetics and evolution of Paramecium, revs. of toxicol. properties of monohaloacetic acids and secondary and tertiary amines to sci. jours. NSF grantee, 1972. Mem. Genetics Soc. Am., Soc. for Study Evolution, Soc. Protozoologists, Soc. Environ. Toxicology and Chemistry, ASTM, AAAS, Sigma Xi. Current Work: Aquatic toxicology, population and community ecology, risk analysis, breeding systems and evolution of protozoa, enzymatic degradation of organophosphates. Subspecialties: Environmental toxicology; Ecology (environmental science). Office: Environ Toxicology Br Toxicology Div Chem Research and Devel Ctr Aberdeen Proving Grounds MD 21010

LANDO, JEROME B., macromolecular scientist, educator; b. Bklyn., May 23, 1932; s. Irving and Ruth (Schwartz) L.; m. Geula, Dec. 2, 1962; children: Jeffrey, Daniel, Avital. A.B. in Chemistry, Cornell U., 1953; Ph.D. in Phys. Chemistry, Poly. Inst. Bklyn., 1963. Chemist, Camille Dreyfus Lab., Research Triangle Inst., Durham, N.C., 1963-65; asst. prof. polymer sci. and engring. Case Inst. Tech., Cleve., 1963-65; assoc. prof. macromolecular sci. Case Western Res. U., Cleve., 1965-68, prof., 1974—, chmn. dept. macromolecular sci., 1978-85; vis. prof. U. Mainz, W.Ger., 1974. Author: (with S. Maron) Fundamentals of Physical Chemistry, 1974; contbr. articles to profl. jours. Alexander von Humboldt sr Am. scientist awardee, 1974. Fellow Am. Phys. Soc.; mem. Am. Chem. Soc., Am. Crystallographic Assn., Sigma Xi. Current Work: Solid state reactions, polymer crystal structure, electrical properties of polymers. Subspecialties: Polymers (materials science); Polymer physics. Home: 21925 Byron Rd E Shaker Heights OH 44122 Office: Dept Macromolecular Sci Case Western Res U Cleveland OH 44106

LANDOLL, LEO M., polymer scientist; b. Cleve., Oct. 11, 1950; s. Leo E. and Margaret Ann (Quinn) L.; m. Mary F. Bissler, Aug. 7, 1971; children—Allison, Christopher. B.A. in Chemistry, Kent State U., 1970; Ph.D. in Polymer Sci., U. Akron, 1975; M.B.A., U. Del., 1983. Research chemist Hercules, Inc., Wilmington, Del., 1974-78, sr. research chemist, 1979-81, research scientist, Oxford, Ga., 1982—. Mem. Am. Chem. Soc. Current work: Fiber melt rheology; water-soluble polymers; polymer microstructure. Subspecialty: Polymer chemistry. Office: Hercules Inc PO Box 8 Oxford GA 30267

LANDOLT, GEORGE ROBERT, research chemist; b. Camden, N.J., Apr. 17, 1927; s. George Theodore and Florence (Saylor) L.; m. Eleanor Dorothy Genzano, Apr. 3, 1948; children—David Robert, Dale Alan, Donald James. A.S., Camden County Coll., 1980. Lab. technician Mobil Research and Devel. Corp., Paulsboro, N.J., 1953-63, sr. lab. technician, 1963-74, staff chemist, 1974-78, sr. staff chemist, 1978-83, research chemist, 1983—. Contbr. chpt. to book. Patentee in field. Scoutmaster Camden County council Boy Scouts Am., Audubon, N.J., 1960-70; mem. chem. adv. bd. Burlington County Coll., 1969-84. Recipient Contbns. to Chemistry award Burlington County Coll., 1974. Mem. Am. Chem. Soc., Del Val Thermal Analysis Assn., N.Am. Thermal Analysis Soc., Democrat. Lutheran. Current work: Zeolite synthesis and characterization as related to separation, petroleum and petrochemical refining processes. Subspecialties: Physical chemistry; Inorganic chemistry. Home: 108 Tweed Ave Audubon NJ 08106 Office: Mobil Research and Devel Corp Paulsboro NJ 08066

LANDRUM, PETER FRANKLIN, environmental toxicologist, environmental chemist; b. Scotia, Calif., Oct. 15, 1947; s. William Weesner and Juanita Jane (Lair) Landrum; m. Fawn Marie Atkinson, June 24, 1972. B.S., Calif. State Coll.-San Bernardino, 1974; Ph.D., U. Calif.-Davis, 1979. Research asst. Calif. State U.-San Bernardino, 1972-73, U. Calif.-Davis, 1974-75, Savannah River Ecology Lab., Aiken, S.C., 1979-81; research chemist NOAA, U.S. Dept. Commerce, Ann Arbor, Mich., 1981—; instr. Eastern Mich. U., Ypsilanti, Mich., 1984—. Served with U.S. Army, 1968-72. NIH grantee, 1975. Mem. Am. Chem. Soc., Calif. Assn. Toxicologists, Soc. Environ. Toxicology and Chemistry (charter mem.), Internat. Soc. Study of Xenobiotics (charter mem.), Internat. Assn. Great Lakes Research. Current work: Fate and effects of organic xenobiotics in aquatic systems with emphasis on the toxic Cokinetics of xenobiotics in invertebrates. Subspecialties: Environmental toxicology; Environmental chemistry. Office: Great Lakes Environ Research Lab 2300 Washtenaw Ave Ann Arbor MI 48104

LANDS, WILLIAM EDWARD MITCHELL, biochemistry educator; b. Chillicothy, Mo., July 22, 1930; s. Alonzo M. and Bernice (Rubenstein) L.; children—Susan Lands Monet, Karen Lands Keech, Edward M., Todd W. B.S. in Chem., U. Mich., 1951; Ph.D. in Biol. Chem., U. Ill., 1954. Research fellow Calif. Inst. Tech., Pasadena, 1954-55; instr. U. Mich. Med. Sch., Ann Arbor, 1955-58, asst. prof., 1958-63, assoc. prof., 1963-67, prof. dept. biochemistry, 1967-80; head dept. biochemistry U. Ill. at Chgo., 1980-85, prof., 1980—; mem. Research Adv. Bd. Chgo. Heart Assn., 1981—; biochem. test com. Nat. Bd. Med. Examiners, 1982—. County commnr. Washtenaw County, Mich., 1969-73. Recipient Glycerine Research award, 1969; Pfizer Biomed. Research award, 1985. Mem. Am. Oil Chemists Soc. (Gold Medal Bond award 1965), Am. Chem. Soc., AAAS, Am. Soc. Biol. Chemists. Current work: Phospholipid metabolism, metabolism of glycerides and long-chain aliphatic acids and aldehydes, formation of membranes and regulation of membrane function; special features of polyunsaturated fatty acids and essential fatty acids; prostaglandin biochemistry. Subspecialties: Biochemistry (medicine); Nutrition (medicine). Home: 901 S Ashland Apt 408A Chicago IL 60607

LANDSBERG, HELMUT E(RICH), meteorologist; b. Frankfurt/Main, Ger., Feb. 9, 1906; came to U.S., 1934, naturalized, 1938; s. Georg Julius and Klara (Zedner) L.; m. A. Frances Simpson; 1 son, Bruce S. Ph.D., U. Frankfurt, 1930. DCert. cons. meteorologist Am. Meteorol. Soc. 1960. Supr. Taunus Obs., 1931-34; asst. prof. geophysics Pa. State U., State College, 1934-41; assoc. prof. meteorology U. Chgo., 1941-43; exec. dir. com. geophysics Research and Devel. Bd., 1946-51; dir. geophys. research Air Force Cambridge Research Ctr., 1951-54; dir. Office Climatology U.S. Weather Bur., Washington, 1954-65, Environ. Data Service, Environ. Sci. Services Adminstrn., 1965-66; vis. prof. Inst. for Fluid Dynamics and Applied Math.; vis. prof. U. Md., College Park, 1964-67, research prof., 1967-76; acting dir. U. Md. (Inst. for Fluid Dynamics and Applied Math.), 1974-76, prof. emeritus, 1976; ops. analyst, cons. USAAF, 1942-45; mem. Nat. Adv. Com. on Oceans and Atmosphere, 1975-77; trustee Univ. Corp. for Atmopheric Research, 1968-72. Author: Physical Climatology, 1941, Weather and Health, 1969, The Urban Climate, 1981: (with S.G. Brush) The History of Geophysics and Meteorology, 1985. Editor: Advances in Geophysics, 1951-76; editor-in-chief World Survey of Climatology. Contbr. articles on meteorology to profl. jours. Recipient Internat. Meteorol. Orgn. prize, 1979; William F. Peterson Found. medal, 1982; Dept. Commerce Exceptional Service award, 1960, Nat. Medal Sci., 1985; Tromp award Enviroscis. Found., 1985. Fellow AAAS (v.p. sect. E 1972), Am. Acad. Arts and Scis., Am. Geophys. Union (pres. meteorology sect. 1956-59, v.p. 1966-68, pres. 1968-70, Bowie medal 1978), Am. Meteorol. Soc. (councilor 1952-60, v.p. 1962-63, Bioclimatology award 1964, C.F. Brooks award 1972, Cleveland Abbe award 1983), Washington Acad. Sci.; mem. Am. Inst. for Med. Climatology (pres. 1967-81, bd. dirs. 1981), N.Y. Acad. Scis. (hon.), World Meteorol. Orgn. (pres. commn. for climatology 1969-78), Nat Acad. Engring., Ger. Meteorol. Soc. (Wegener medal 1980), Phi Beta Kappa, Sigma Xi, Sigma Pi Sigma, Sigma Gamma Epsilon. Clubs: Explorers (N.Y.C.); Cosmos (Washington). Current Work: Climate trends and fluctuations, anthropogenic influences on climate. Subspecialties: Climatology; Micrometeorology. Office: Univ Md College Park MD 20742

LANDSBERG, JOHANNA DOBROT, research chemist; b. Medford, Oreg., July 15, 1940; d. Julius G. and Thelma B. (Ellestad) Dobrot; m. Arne Landsberg, Sept. 2, 1961 (div. Apr. 1977); children—Karin Joan, Eric Arne. B.S. Oreg. State U., Corvallis, 1962, M.S., 1964. Prof. chemistry U. de Costa Rica, San Jose, 1964-66; research asst. Oreg. State U., Corvallis, 1966-67, research assoc., 1976-77; research chemist Bend Research Inc., Bend, Oreg., 1977-78; research chemist Forest Service, USDA, Bend, 1979—, prin. investigator, Spain, 1985. Contbr. articles to profl. jours. Inst. Food Tech. prof. mem., 1977. Mem. AAAS, Am. Chem. Soc., Inst. Food Technologists, Sigma Xi. Democrat. Unitarian. Current work: Research on the effect of prescribed fire on soil fertility, tree growth, and nutrient levels; analytical laboratory supervisor. Subspecialties: Environmental chemistry; Analytical chemistry. Office: Silviculture Lab 1027 NW Trenton Ave Bend OR 97701

LANDSTREET, JOHN DARLINGTON, astrophysicist, educator; b. Phila., Mar. 13, 1940; s. Barent French and Louise (Darlington) L.; 1 son, David Roger. B.A., Reed Coll., 1962; M.A., Columbia U., 1963, Ph.D., 1966. Instr. physics Mt. Holyoke Coll., South Hadley, Mass., 1965-66, asst. prof., 1966-67; research assoc. astronomy Columbia U., N.Y.C., 1967-70, asst. prof., 1970; asst. prof. astronomy U. Western Ont., London, Can., 1970-72, assoc. prof., 1972-76, prof. astronomy, 1976—; vis. scientist Institut für Theoretische Astrophysik, U. Heidelberg, Germany, 1984-85; mem. Nat. Scis. and Engring. Research Council Can. grant selection com. for space and astronomy, 1980-83, chmn., 1982-83; mem. Sci. Adv. Council, Can.-France-Hawaii Telescope Corp., 1980-83, chmn., 1982-83; mem. sci. adv. com. Can. Centre for Space Sci., 1981-83. Contbr. profl. papers in field to publs. Ann. research grantee Nat. Scis. and Engring. Research Council Can., 1970—. Mem. Can. Astron. Soc., Internat. Astron. Union, Royal Astron. Soc. Clubs: University Club of London (Ont.); Bayfield Yacht. Current Work: Measurement of magnetic fields in stars; modelling of magnetic star atmospheres and line profiles; development new astronomical measuring instruments. Subspecialty: Optical astronomy. Home: 10 Silverbrook Dr #5 London ON N5X 2V6 Canada Office: Dept Astronom Univ Western Ont London ON N6A 3K7 Canada

LANDWEBER, LOUIS, educator; b. N.Y.C., Jan. 8, 1912; s. Joseph and Lena (Rosenbush) L.; m. Mae Herschfeld, Apr. 7, 1935; children—Peter Steven, Victor Allen. B.S., CCNY, 1932; M.A., George Washington U., 1935; Ph.D., U. Md., 1951. Physicist, head hydrodynamic div. David Taylor Model Basin, Washington, 1932-54; prof. U. Iowa, research engr. Inst. Hydraulic Research, 1954—; cons. Westinghouse and Davidson Lab. of Stevens Inst. Tech., NRC, referee jours. in field of fluid mechanics. Author: (with others) Advanced Mechanics of Fluids, 1959; editor of: (with others) translation Theory of Ship Motions (Blagoveshchensky), 1962, Theory of Ship Waves and Wave Resistance (A.A. Kostyukov), 1968; contbr. (with others) articles to profl. jours., chpt. to book. Recipient Ward medal and Beldon prize CCNY, 1932, Worthington prize, 1977. Fellow Japan Soc. Promotion of Sci., Soc. Naval Architects and Marine Engrs. (Davidson medal 1978), Am. Acad. Mechanics; mem. Assn. Technique Maritime et Aeronautique (U.S. corr. mem.), Nat. Acad. Engring., Phi Beta Kappa, Sigma Xi, Sigma Pi Sigma, Tau Beta Pi. Current Work: Mathematical and numerical predictions of flow about and forces acting on ship forms (ship hydrodynamics). Subspecialties: Fluid mechanics; Theoretical and applied mechanics. Home: 323 Post Rd Iowa City IA 52240 Office: Inst Hydraulic Research Iowa City IA 52242

LANE, ALEXANDER ZUCHLEWSKI, pharmaceutical company executive; b. Detroit, July 22, 1929; s. Alexander Francis and Bernice Rose (Kurzynski) Z; m. Linda Joan Ford, June 16, 1956. B.S., U. Detroit, 1950; Ph.D. (Edsel B. Ford Inst. research fellow 1951-54), Wayne State U., Detroit, 1954; M.D., 1958. Diplomate: Am. Bd. Clin. Chemistry. Intern Bon Secours Hosp., Grosse Pointe, Mich., 1958-59; trainee Nat. Cancer Inst., 1959-60; dir. clin. pharmacology Parke-Davis & Co., Ann Arbor, Mich., 1960-66; dir. med. research, then v.p., med. dir. Bristol Labs., Syracuse, N.Y., 1966-77; sr. v.p. research ops. Schering Labs., Bloomfield, N.J., 1977-79, pres. pharm. research div., 1979—. Author articles in field. Fellow Am. Coll. Clin. Pharmacology and Chemotherapy; mem. AMA, Am. Soc. Microbiology. Roman Catholic. Field: Pharmaceutics. Current work: Pharmaceutical industry research and development. Home: 110 Ridgewood Ave Glen Ridge NJ 07028 Office: 2000 Galloping Hill Rd Kenilworth NJ 07033

LANE, BERNARD PAUL, pathologist, educator; b. Bklyn., June 27, 1938; s. Jack R. and Rose L. (Weiss) L.; m. Dorothy S. Lane, Aug. 5, 1962; children: Erika, Andrew, Matthew. A.B., Brown U., 1959; M.D., N.Y.U., 1963. Diplomate: Am. Bd. Pathology. Asst. prof. N.Y.U., 1963-69, assoc. prof., 1969-71, SUNY-Stony Brook, 1971-76, prof., 1976—. Contbr. articles in field to profl. jours. Bd. dirs. Am. Cancer Soc., L.I., N.Y., 1979—, v.p., 1980-82, pres., 1983-84. Served with USAF, 1962-84. NIH fellow, 1963-65; NIH grantee, 1973-82. Fellow Am. Soc. Clin. Pathology, Coll. Am. Pathology; mem. N.Y. Acad. Sci., Am. Assn. Cancer Research, Am. Assn. Pathology, Internat. Acad. Pathology, Am. Soc. Cell Biology, Current Work: Cell differentiation and injury; cancer biology. Subspecialty: Pathology (medicine). Address: 6 Intervale Rd Setauket NY 11733

LANE, DANIEL MCNEEL, hematologist, biochemist; b. Fort Sam Houston, Tex., Jan. 25, 1936; s. Samuel Hartman and Mary Maverick (McNeel) L.; m. Carolyn Ann Spruell, Nov. 28, 1958; children: Linda Ann, Daniel M. Jr., Maury S., Oleta K. M.D., U. Tex.-Dallas, 1961; M.S., U. Tenn., 1967; Ph.D., U. Okla., 1973. Head pediatric hematology/oncology U. Okla. Med. Ctr., Oklahoma City, 1966-70; research fellow Okla. Med. Research Found., Oklahoma City, 1969-72; Head pediatric hematology/oncology Tulane Med. Sch., New Orleans, 1972-73; head hematology/oncology Oklahoma City Clinic, 1973-79, Presbyn. Hosp., Oklahoma City, 1979—; dirs. Poplar Pike Realtors, Memphis, 1978—; pres. Samuel Maverick Interests, Inc., Oklahoma City., 1976—. Fin. chmn Dunlap for Congress, 1976; head Physicians for Gov. Nigh, 1978; Democratic candidate for Congress, 5th Dist., 1982. USPHS fellow, 1964-66; spl. research fellow Nat. Heart-Lung Inst., 1969-72. Fellow Am. Acad. Pediatics; mem. Am. Soc. Clin. Oncology, Am. Soc. Hematology, AMA. Democrat. Episcopalian. Current Work: Plasma lipids and apolipoproteins; clinical hematology and oncology (chemotherapy); pediatrics (consultative). Subspecialties: Oncology; Biochemistry (medicine). Home: 1504 Guilford Ln Oklahoma City OK 73120

LANFORD, WILLIAM ARMISTEAD, physics educator, consultant; b. Albany, N.Y., Nov. 15, 1944; s. Oscar Erasmus and Caroline (Sherman) L.; m. Cynthia Smith, Aug. 27, 1966; children—Catherine, William, Anne. B.S. in Physics, U. Rochester, 1966, Ph.D. in Physics, 1972. Asst. prof. physics Mich. State U., East Lansing, 1972-73; asst. prof. physics Yale U., New Haven, 1973-78, assoc. prof., 1978-79; assoc. prof. physics SUNY-Albany, 1979-83, prof., 1983—; cons. IBM, Yorktown and Fishkill, N.Y., 1979—, Exxon Research and Devel., Annandale, N.J., 1980—. Editor: Ion Beam Analysis, 1983; Jour. Radiation Effects, Confs. and Revs., 1983—. Contbr. articles to profl. jours. Alfred P. Sloan Found. fellow, 1979-83. Fellow Inst. Study Defects in Solids, Inst. Archaeol. Studies; mem. Am. Ceramic Soc., Metall. Soc. of AIME, Am. Phys. Soc. (exec. com. N.Y. state sect. 1981-85, vice chmn. 1985-87). Current work: Study hydrogen in materials, thin film characterization and modification, cosmic ray effects on microelectronics, glass surface reactions, archaeological chemistry. Subspecialties: Ceramics; Microchip technology (materials science). Home: Box 51 Malden Bridge NY 12115 Office: Physics Dept SUNY-Albany 1400 Washington Ave Albany NY 12222

LANG, CONRAD MARVIN, chemist, educator; b. Chgo., July 1, 1939; s. Arne Conrad and Myrtle Oliva (Erickson) L.; m. Louise June Swanson, June 17, 1961; children: Kevin Alan, Kurtis Erik, Kenneth Marvin. B.S., Elmhurst (Ill.) Coll., 1961; M.S., U. Wis.-Madison, 1964; Ph.D., U. Wyo., 1970. Instr. U. Wis.-Stevens Point, 1964-66, asst. prof., 1966-70, assoc. prof., 1970-78, prof., 1978—; W.B. King vis. prof. Iowa State U., 1976-77; cons. in field. Contbr. articles to profl. jours. Grantee in field. Mem. Am. Chem. Soc. (Outstanding Service award 1979 and Outstanding Contbns. to Chemistry award 1983 Central Wis. sect.). Current Work: Electron spin resonance application to spin labeled fluids; chemical philately; chemical demonstrations. Subspecialties: Physical chemistry; Electron spin resonance. Home: 3015 Cherry St Stevens Point WI 54481 Office: Dept Chemistry U Wis Stevens Point WI 54481

LANG, JAMES EDWARD, ceramic engineer; b. Buffalo, Mar. 20, 1939; s. Edward Allen and Grace Dorothy (Schiersing) L.; m. Patricia Ann Zmuda, July 22, 1961; children—Dennis, Sherri, Timothy, Kevin, Jason. A.A.S., Erie Tech. Coll., 1958; B.S., Alfred U., 1963; M.S., Rensselaer Poly. Inst., 1965, Ph.D., 1968. Ceramist Gen. Electric Co., Schenectady, 1963-66; supr. Northrop Corp., Palos Verdes, Calif., 1968-73; mgr. RCA Selectavision, Indpls., 1973-80; dir. CBS Tech. Ctr., Stamford, Conn., 1980—. Contbr. articles to profl. jours. Patentee in field. Cubmaster Nutmeg council Boy Scouts Am., 1984. Recipient Outstanding Paper award Soc. Info. Display, 1972. Mem. Am. Ceramic Soc., Soc. Photog. and Instrumentation Engrs., IEEE. Current work: Development of mastering system for RCA videodisc; research and development on magneto-optical data storage materials. Subspecialties: Ceramics; Laser data storage and reproduction. Office: CBS Tech Ctr 227 High Ridge Rd Stamford CT 06905

LANG, JOHN CALVIN, chemist; b. Montclair, N.J., May 6, 1942; s. J. Calvin and Dorothy L. (Davenport) L.; m. Elizabeth Anne Houghton, June 25, 1966; 1 child, Phebe Davenport. B.A., Wesleyan U., 1964; M.S., Cornell U., 1968; Ph.D., 1972. Postdoctoral assoc., Cornell U., Ithaca, N.Y., 1972, Cornell U., 1974-75; postdoctoral fellow U. Reading, Eng., 1972-73; research chemist Procter and Gamble, Cin., 1975-84; research assoc. ARCO Oil and Gas Co., Plano, Tex., 1984—. Contbr. articles to profl. jours. Mem. Am. Chem. Soc., Am. Phys. Soc., Soc. Francaise de Physique, Sigma Xi. Episcopalian. Current work: Thermodynamics, phase transitions, and critical phenomena, especially in multicomponent surfactant mixtures; dynamic light scattering from colloids and surfactant solutions. Subspecialties: Physical chemistry; Thermodynamics. Home: 3412 Omar Ln Plano TX 75023 Office: ARCO Oil and Gas Co 2300 W Plano Pkwy Plano TX 75075

LANG, SERGE, mathematician. Prof. dept. math. Yale U., New Haven, Conn. Elected mem. Nat. Acad. Scis., 1985. . Office: Yale U Dept Math New Haven CT 06520

LANG, WILLIAM WARNER, physicist; b. Boston, Aug. 9, 1926; s. William Warner and Lilla Gertrude (Wheeler) L.; m. Asta Ingard, Aug. 31, 1954; 1 son, Robert. B.S., Iowa State U., 1946, Ph.D., 1958; M.S., M.I.T., 1949. Acoustical engr. Bolt Beranek and Newman, Inc., Cambridge, Mass., 1949-51; instr. in physics U.S. Naval Postgrad. Sch., Monterey, Calif., 1951-55; cons. engr. E.I. du Pont de Nemours & Co., Wilmington, Del., 1955-57; mem. research staff M.I.T., 1958; physicist IBM, Poughkeepsie, N.Y., 1958—, program mgr. acoustics tech., 1976—. Editor: Designing for Noise Control, 1978. Pres. Noise Control Found., Poughkeepsie, 1975—; adj. prof. physics Vassar Coll., 1978—; chmn. working group Internat. Orgn. Standardization, 1969—; tech. com. 29 Internat. Electrotech. Commn., 1975-83. Served with USN, 1944-47, 52. Decorated Meritorious Service medal. Fellow Audio Enging. Soc., IEEE (Group on Audio and Electroacoustics Achievement award 1970, dir. 1970-71), Acoustical Soc. Am.; mem. Nat. Acad. Enging., Inst. Noise Control Enging. (pres. 1978), AAAS. Episcopalian. Club: Rotary (pres. local club 1975-76). Current Work: Noise control engineering. Subspecialties: Acoustical engineering; Acoustics. Office: IBM Acoustics Lab C18/704 PO Box 390 Poughkeepsie NY 12602

LANGE, EUGENE ALBERT, metallurgical engineer, cons.; b. Stevens Point, Wis., Oct. 22, 1923; s. Albert Gustav and Linda (Thalacker) L.; m. Lois June, Feb. 8, 1951. B.S. in Chem. Enging, U. Wis., 1945, M.S. in Metall. Enging, 1951. Registered profl. engr., Wis., 1951. Research metallurgist U. Wis., Madison, 1951-53; research engr. Gray Iron Research Inst., Columbus, Ohio, 1953-56; supervising research metallurgist Naval Research Lab., Washington, 1956-80, cons. metall. engring., 1980—; tchr. short courses on structural integrity tech. Union Coll., Schenectady, U. Wis., Madison. Contbr. numerous articles to profl. jours. Recipient Research Publ. award Naval Research Lab., 1968, Outstanding Performance award USN, 1969, 70. Mem. Am. Soc. Metals, ASME (cert. appreciation 1975), ASTM, Am. Welding Soc. Club: Bolling Air Force Officers. Patentee dynamic tear tes; developed double cantiliver split-pin displacement gauge, high-strength, non-magnetic alloy for steel castings, fluidity test. Current Work: Engring. applications of fracture mechanics tech.;

dynamic fracture mechanics; structural integrity; fracture-safe design; criteria for fracture toughness. Subspecialties: Fracture mechanics; Metallurgical engineering. Home and Office: 5101 River Rd Bethesda MD 20816

LANGE, KLAUS ROBERT, research administrator; b. Berlin, Jan. 15, 1930; came to U.S. 1948, naturalized 1952; s. Horst and Gertrud (Rabinowitcz) L.; m. Sylvia Pollack, June 17, 1951; children—Stephen Mark, Karen Judith. A.B., U. Pa., 1952; M.S., U. Del., 1954, Ph.D., 1956. Research chemist Arco, Phila., 1955-59; sr. research assoc. PQ Corp., Phila., 1959-69; research mgr. Betz Lab., Trevose, Pa., 1969-75; mgr. group lab Quaker Chem. Corp., Conshohoken, Pa., 1975—; dir. Chem. Data Systems, Oxford, Pa., 1971-76. Contbr. articles to profl. jours. Patentee in field. Vice pres. Congregation Beth Chaim, Trevose, Pa., 1975-79. Fellow Am. Inst. Chemists; mem. Am. Chem. Soc. (sr. mem.), TAPPI. Jewish. Current work: Paper chemistry, organic synthesis, water treatment, silicates, silica, catalysis. Subspecialties: Physical chemistry; Surface chemistry. Home: 3929 Sheffield Dr Huntingdon Valley PA 19006 Office: Quaker Chem Corp Elm and Lime Sts Conshohoken PA 19428

LANGELAND, WILLIAM ENBERG, pharmaceutical company executive; b. Massillon, Ohio, July 5, 1923; s. Oscar William and Elizabeth (Enberg) L.; m. Eleanor Seltzer, Jan. 5, 1960 (dec. Dec. 1972); m. Rita Ann Dacey, Sept. 8, 1974. Assoc. prof. chemistry St. Lawrence U., Canton, N.Y., 1950-52; research chemist Penwalt Corp., Phila., 1952-54, sr. devel. rep., 1954-58; project coordinator Wyeth Labs., Phila., 1958-63, dir. project coordination, 1963-77, dir. lab. coordination, 1977—. Twp. supr. East Norriton Twp., Pa., 1966-70; chmn. twp. bd. East Norriton Twp. Bd. Suprs., 1970-72; mem. exec. com. Montgomery County Local Govt. Adv. Council, Norristown, Pa., 1970-72. Served to lt. USN, 1944-50, PTO. Mem. N.Y. Acad. Scis., Am. Chem. Soc., Sigma Xi. Republican. Episcopalian. Current work: Direction and oversight of multidisciplinary research activities in the pharmaceutical area. Subspecialty: Medicinal chemistry. Home: Sunset Ave RD 3 Norristown PA 19403 Office: Wyeth Lab PO Box 8299 Philadelphia PA 19101

LANGENBERG, DONALD NEWTON, physicist, educational administrator; b. Devils Lake, N.D., Mar. 17, 1932; s. Ernest George and Fern (Newton) L.; m. Patricia Ann Warrington, June 20, 1953; children—Karen Kaye, Julia Ann, John Newton, Amy Paris. B.S., Iowa State U., 1953; M.S., UCLA, 1955; Ph.D., U. Calif.-Berkeley, 1959. Electronics engr. Hughes Research Lab., Culver City, Calif., 1953-55; acting instr. U. Calif.-Berkeley, 1958-59; mem. faculty U. Pa., Phila., 1960-83, prof., 1967-83, dir. Lab. for Research on Structure of Matter, 1972-74, vice provost for grad. studies and research, 1974-79; chancellor U. Ill.-Chgo., 1983—; maitre de conference associe Ecole Normale Superieure, Paris, 1966-67; vis. prof. Calif. Inst. Tech., Pasadena, 1971; guest researcher Zentralinstitut für Tieftemperaturforschung der Bayerische Akademie der Wissenschaften and Technische Universitat Munchen, 1974; dep. dir. NSF, 1908-82. Recipient John Price Wietherill medal Franklin Inst., 1975; fellow NSF, 1959-60, Alfred P. Sloan Found., 1962-64, Guggenheim Found., 1966-67. Fellow Am. Phys. Soc., AAAS, Sigma Xi. Current work: Research and publications on solid state and low temperature physics including electronic band structure in metals and semicondrs., quantum phase coherence and nonequilibrium effects in supercondrs. Subspecialties: Condensed matter physics; Low temperature physics. Office: U Ill-Chgo Box 4348 Chicago IL 60680

LANGENHEIM, RALPH LOUIS, JR., geology educator, consultant; b. Cin., May 26, 1922; s. Ralph Louis and Myrtle Rosalia (Helmers) L.; m. Jean Cloteal Harmon, Dec. 23, 1946 (div.); m. Virginia Amelia McCutcheon, June 5, 1962 (div.); children—Victoria Elizabeth, Ralph Louis III; m. Shirley Louise Blair, May 1, 1970. B.S. in Geol. Engring., U. Tulsa, 1943; M.S. in Geology, U. Colo., 1947; Ph.D. in Geology, U. Minn., 1951. Teaching asst. U. Tulsa, 1941-43, U. Colo., Boulder, 1946-47; teaching asst., fellow U. Minn., Mpls., 1948-50; asst. prof. geology Coe Coll., Cedar Rapids, Iowa, 1950-52; asst. prof. paleontology, curator Paleozoic invertebrates Mus. of Paleontology, U. Calif.-Berkeley, 1952-59; from asst. prof. to prof. geology U. Ill., Urbana, 1959—; ptnr. Lanman Assocs., Urbana, 1974—; cons., expert various fgn. geol. surveys. Co-author: Correlations of Great Basin Stratigraphic Units, 1973; Cenozoic Reef Biofacies, 1974. Editor: Handbook of Paleontological Techniques, 1965. Served to lt. comdr. USNR, 1943-46; ETO, PTO. Fellow Geol. Soc. London, Geol. Soc. Am.; mem. Paleontol. Soc. (sec. 1963-71), Am. Assn. Petroleum Geologists, Société Geolgique Suisse. Democrat. Presbyterian. Current work: Stratigraphy, biostratigraphy and field geology of southern Nevada, Big Horn Mountains of Wyoming and Illinois Basin; concentration in problems of Carboniferous, especially boundary stratotype designation and development. Subspecialty: Paleontology. Home: 401 W Vermont St Urbana IL 61801 Office: Dept Geology U Ill 245 NHB 1301 W Green St Urbana IL 61801

LANGER, JAMES S., physicist. Dept. dir. Inst. Physics, U. Calif., Santa Barbara. Elected mem. Nat. Acad. Scis., 1985. Subspecialty: Theoretical physics. Office: U Calif Inst Physics Santa Barbara CA 93106

LANGFORD, WILLIAM FINLAY, mathematics educator, researcher; b. Thunder Bay, Ont., Can., Sept. 11, 1943; s. William Everett and Mary Pearl (Finlay) L.; m. Grace Ann Cooper, Aug. 1, 1970; children: Cathena Dionne, Anne Elisabeth. B.S. with honors, Queen's U., Kingston, Ont., 1966; Ph.D., Calif. Inst. Tech., Pasadena, 1971. Asst. prof. McGill U., Montreal, Que., Can., 1970-78, assoc. prof., 1978-82; assoc. prof. math. U. Guelph, Ont., 1982—; research visitor Inst. de Math. et Scis. Physiques, Nice, France, 1979-80; U. Victoria, B.C., Can., summer 1978; adj. prof. applied math. U. Waterloo, 1983—; vis. prof. dept. math. U. Houston, 1985. Mem. editorial bd. Dynamics and Stability of Systems: an Internat. Jour. Nat. Scis. and Engring. Council Can. grantee, 1971-82; Que.-France travel grantee Nice, France, 1979-80. Mem. Soc. Indsl. and Applied Math., Can. Math Soc (bd. dirs. 1985—), Can. Applied Math. Soc., Am. Math. Soc. Mem. United Ch. of Canada. Current Work: Numerical analysis of bifurcation problems; classification and unfoldings of degenerate bifurcations. Subspecialty: Applied mathematics. Home: 959 Gordon St Guelph ON NIH 6H9 Canada Office: U Guelph Dept Math & Stats Guelph ON NIG 2W1 Canada

LANGHOFF, PETER WOLFGANG, physicist, theoretical chemist, educator, researcher; b. N.Y.C., Jan. 19, 1937; s. Joachim and Frieda A. (Damm) L.; m. Judith Dianna Perrotta, June 30, 1962; children: Lisa M., Kristen D., Allison K. B.S. in Physics, Hofstra U., 1958; Ph.D. in Physics, SUNY, Buffalo, 1965. Research physicist Cornell Aero. Labs., Buffalo, 1962-65; research fellow Harvard U., 1967-69; asst. prof. chemistry Ind. U. Bloomington, 1969-73, assoc. prof., 1973-77, prof., 1977—, chmn. program in chem. physics, 1977-83; cons. MIT Lincoln Lab., 1967-69, Lawrence Livermore (Calif.) Lab., 1977-83; Inst. fellow in physics Brandeis U., 1961; vis. research scientist dept. chemistry Harvard U., 1970, Harvard U. (Harvard Coll. Obs.), 1971; vis. research scientist dept. chemistry Stanford U., 1975, Stanford-Ames faculty fellow dept. aeros. and astronautics, 1976; vis. fellow Joint Inst. for Lab. Astrophysics, Nat. Bur. Standards and U. Colo., Boulder, 1976-77; sr. NRC resident research asso. NASA Ames Research Center, Mountain View, Calif., 1978-79; vis. research scientist Max Planck Inst. for Physics and Astrophysics, Munich, W.Ger., 1980—; vis. fellow theoretical chemistry U. Sydney, Australia, 1981; professeur associé U. Paris, Orsay Cedex, France, 1981; vis. prof. U. B.C., 1983. Contbr. numerous articles to sci. jours. Served to capt. U.S. Army, 1965-67. Decorated Army Commendation medal; NSF grantee, 1980—; Petroleum Research Found. grantee, 1971—; NASA grantee, 1978—. Mem. Am. Phys. Soc. Current Work: Studies of atomic and molecular photoexcitation and ionization. Subspecialties: Theoretical chemistry; Atomic and molecular physics. Office: Dept Chemistry Ind U Bloomington IN 47405

LANGLANDS, ROBERT PHELAN, mathematician; b. New Westminster, Can., Oct. 6, 1936; came to U.S., 1960; s. Robert and Kathleen (Phelan) L.; m. Charlotte Lorraine Cheverie, Aug. 13, 1956; children: William, Sarah, Robert, Thomasin. B.A., U. B.C., 1957, M.A., 1958; Ph.D., Yale U., 1960. From instr. to asso. prof. Princeton (N.J.) U., 1960-67; prof. math. Yale U., New Haven, 1968-72, Inst. Advanced Study, Princeton, 1972—. Editor: Annals of Math., 1979—; author: Euler Products, 1971, (with H. Jacquet) Automorphic Forms on GL(2), 1970, On the Functional Equations Satisfied by Eisenstein Series, 1976, Base Change for GL(2), 1980. Recipient Wilbur Lucius Cross medal Yale U., 1975. Fellow Royal Soc. London, Royal Soc. Can.; mem. Am. Math. Soc. (Cole prize 1982), Can. Math. Soc. Current Work: Automorphic forms, group representations, number theory. Subspecialty: Parasitology. Office: Inst Advanced Study Princeton NJ 08540

LANNING, HOWARD HUGH, astronomer; b. El Centro, Calif., May 26, 1946; s. James Clyde and Ethel Mary (Malan) L.; m. Sheryl Marie Falgout. A.A. in Astronomy, Imperial Valley Jr. Coll., 1966; M.S. in Astronomy, San Diego State U., 1969, M.S., 1974. Research asst. Hale Obs., Pasadena, Calif., 1970-72; grad. teaching asst. San Diego State U., 1972-73; research asst. NASA Ames Research Center at San Diego State U., 1973-74; night asst., astronomer Mt. Wilson Obs., 1974—; sci. writer Calipatria Herald, Mt. Wilson Obs. Assn. Contbr. articles to profl. jours. Mem. Am. Astron. Soc., Royal Astron. Soc., Astron. Soc. Pacific. Current Work: Observation and discovery of variable stars including photometric and spectroscopic studies of white dwarf binaries, cataclysmic variables and novae. Subspecialty: Optical astronomy. Office: Mt Wilson Obs Mount Wilson CA 91023

LANSDELL, HERBERT CHARLES, neuroscience administrator; b. Montreal, Que., Can., Dec. 22, 1922; came to U.S., 1954, naturalized, 1961; s. Archibald and Emma Maude (Leonard) L.; m. Judith Purnell, Oct. 5, 1963 (div.); children: Grant, Bret. B.Sc., Sir George Williams Evening Coll., Montreal, 1944; Ph.D., McGill U., 1950. Asst. prof. McGill U., Montreal, 1949-50; def. service sci. officer Def. Research Med. Lab., Toronto, Ont., Can., 1950-54; asst. prof. U. Buffalo, 1954-58; research psychologist Nat. Inst. Neurol. and Communicative Disorders and Stroke, Bethesda, Md., 1958-70, health scientist adminstr., 1970—. Editor: Physiol. and Comparative Psychology Newsletter, 1979-84; contbr. articles on human brain function, including sex differences to profl. jours. Served with Royal Can. Navy, 1944-45. Fellow Am. Psychol. Assn., AAAS; mem. Acad. Aphasia, Eastern Psychol. Assn., Internat. Brain Research Orgn., Internat. Neuropsychol. Soc., Psychometric Soc., Soc. for Neurosci., Soc. for Philosophy and Psychology, Sigma Xi. Democrat. Designer more legible numbers design. Current Work: Administration of grants and contracts in neuroscience; analysis and publication of neuropsychological data. Subspecialties: Neuropsychology; Physiological psychology. Office: NIH Room 916 Fed Bldg Bethesda MD 20892

LANZKRON, ROLF WOLFGANG, electrical engineer, manufacturing company executive; b. Hamburg, West Germany, Dec. 9, 1929; m. Amy Virginia Yarri, Mar 3, 1961; children: Paul, Sophie and Lisa. B.S. in Elec. Engring, Milw. Sch. Engring., 1953; Ph.D. in Elec. Engring, U. Wis.-Madison, 1955, 1956. Registered profl. engr. Chief systems integration br. Martin-Marietta Co., Balt., 1960-62; div. chief Apollo program NASA, Houston, 1962-68; program mgr. Computer Display Channel, Raytheon Corp., Sudbury, Mass., 1968-73; program mgr. Raytheon Corp. (TPN-19 program), 1973-78, mgr. graphic systems, 1978-79; program mgr. Washington Post/Rayedit, 1979-80, mgr. graphic systems, 1980-82, mgr. radar displays, 1982, dep. dir. air traffic control, 1973—. Mem. AIAA, IEEE, Am. Math. Soc. Current Work: Advanced technology, computers, radar display and graphics. Subspecialty: Electrical engineering. Home: 35 Gardner Rd Brookline MA 02146 Office: Raytheon Co 528 Boston Post Rd Box 4-1-650 Sudbury MA 01776

LAPATOVICH, WALTER PETER, physicist; b. Shenandoah, Pa., July 12, 1953; s. Walter Joseph and Martha Theresa L.; m. Penny Louise, Apr. 24, 1982; 1 dau., Erika. S.B., M.I.T., 1975, Ph.D., 1980. Research asst. dept. physics and research lab. electronics M.I.T., Cambridge, 1975-80, teaching asst. dept. physics, 1974-75; sr. mem. tech. staff GTE Labs., Inc., Waltham, Mass., 1980—. Contbr. writings to profl. publs. in field. Mem. Am. Phys. Soc. (div. electron and atomic physics), Electrochem. Soc., Sigma Xi. Current Work: Molecular spectroscopy of plasmas and vapors, plasma discharges, laser spectroscopy, molecular discharges. Subspecialties: Atomic and molecular physics; Laser spectroscopy. Office: GTE Labs Inc 40 Sylvan Rd Waltham MA 02254

LAPEN, ROBERT JOSEPH, automation engineer, system designer; b. Chgo., May 13, 1953; s. Alex and Julia (Kusmider) L. B.S., M.S., Stanford U., 1975; M.B.A., Harvard U., 1979. Project engr. Westinghouse Electric Co., Westboro, Mass., 1975-77; cons. Ill. Inst. Tech. Research Inst., Chgo., 1979-81; ind. cons., Chgo., 1981-83; sr. systems engr. GCA Corp., Naperville, Ill., 1983—. Patentee insulator. Bd. dirs. Chgo. Assn. Retarded Citizens, 1983—. Mem. IEEE, Am. Assn. Artificial Intelligence. Current work: Developing designs and implementation plans for factory-of-the-future in high technology industries (i.e. integrated circuits, electronics). Subspecialties: Systems engineering; Artificial intelligence. Office: GCA Corp 1 Energy Center Naperville IL 60566

LAPEYRE, JEAN-NUMA, molecular biologist, cancer researcher, consultant; b. Los Angeles, Oct. 17, 1945; s. Jean-Louis and Bonnie Lee (McCall) L.; m. Elizabeth Ealy, Oct. 16, 1968 (div. 1978); children—Alexander Numa, Gavin Keith; m. Adrianne Hurndell, Feb. 15, 1983. B.S. in Physics and Biology, UCLA, 1968; Ph.D. in Molecular and Cellular Biology, U. So. Calif., 1975. Research assoc. M.D. Anderson Hosp. and Tumor Inst., Houston, 1977-79, asst. prof. pathology, 1979—; Nat. Cancer Inst. vis. exchange scientist CNRS Inst. Molecular Biophysics, 1982. Contbr. chpts. to books, articles to profl. jours. Fogarty Internat fellow, 1975-77; Nat. Cancer Inst. grantee, 1980—. Mem. Am. Assn. Cancer Research, Biophys. Soc., AAAS, Nature Conservancy. Club: Hustonian. Current work: Analysis of gene expression, gene rearrangements and DNA methylation during carcinogenesis; studies on the regulation and enzymology of DNA methyltransferse reactions. Subspecialties: Cancer research (medicine); Molecular biology. Office: MD Anderson Hosp and Tumor Inst 6723 Bertner Ave Houston TX 77030

LAPICKI, GREGORY, physicist, educator; b. Warsaw, Poland, Feb. 14, 1945; s. Andrzej and Zofia (Chrzaszczewska) L.; m. Carin Alton; 1 son, Jeremy. Magister Fizyki, Warsaw U., 1967; Ph.D. in Physics, NYU, 1975. Postdoctoral trainee dept. physics NYU, N.Y.C., 1975-76, research scientist Radiation and Solid State Lab., 1977-78; vis. asst. prof. dept. physics Tex. A&M U., College Station, 1979-80; asst. prof. dept. chemistry and physics Northwestern State U., Natchitoches, La., 1980-81; assoc. prof. dept. physics East Carolina U., Greenville, N.C., 1981—; participant in research, nuclear physics div. Oak Ridge Nat. Lab., 1981—. Contbr. articles to profl. jours. Nat. Bur. Standards grantee, 1982-84. Mem. Am. Phys. Soc., N.C. Acad. Sci., Sigma Xi. Current Work: Inner shell ionization; stopping power problems; theory of penetration of charged particles through matter. Subspecialties: Atomic and molecular physics; Theoretical physics. Office: Dept Physics East Carolina U Greenville NC 17834

LAPORTE, DANIEL D'ARCY, physicist; b. Oakland, Calif., Jan. 26, 1934; s. Rollo Collett and Erma Jean A. (Todd) LaP.; m. Carole M. Morrison, June 22, 1957; children: Kristine, Brock, Shareen. B.S., Lewis and Clark Coll., 1956. With Naval Weapons Ctr., Pasadena, Calif., 1956-57; mem. tech. staff Jet Propulsion Lab., Pasadena, 1957-71, supr.IR Instruments Group, 1961-68; staff physicist Jet Propulsion Lab. (IR Instruments Group), 1968-71; mem. tech. staff Santa Barbara Research Ctr., Goleta, Calif., 1971—, staff physicist, 1971-82, sr. staff physicist space sensors lab., systems div., 1982—; lectr. Santa Barbara Sch. Dist. Gifted and Talented Program; bd. dirs. Santa Barbara Intra-Sch. Sci. Fair; co-investigator Mars atmospheric water vapor detection and mapping expt. Viking Mars Mission, NASA, 1967-77. Named to Outstanding Young Men Am. U.S. Jaycees, 1969; NASA grantee, 1967. Mem. Optical Soc. Am., Soc. Applied Spectroscopy. Republican. Mem. United Churches of Christ trustee. Club: Santa Barbara Sailing. Current Work: Design of optical instruments for measurements from spacecraft. Subspecialties: Remote sensing (atmospheric science); Infrared spectroscopy. Office: 75 Coromar Dr Goleta CA 93117

LARACH, SIMON, physical chemist, medical researcher; b. N.Y.C., Apr. 21, 1922; s. David and Beckie (Mose) L.; m. Sarah Romaner, Oct. 31, 1946; children—David Ross, Richard Lloyd. B.S., CCNY, 1943; postgrad. Harvard U., 1944; A.M., Princeton U., 1951, Ph.D., 1955. Research chemist NYU Coll. Med., N.Y.C., 1943, 46; research chemist RCA Labs., Princeton, 1946-61, assoc. lab. dir., 1961-67, fellow, 1967—; vis. prof. physics and chemistry Hebrew U. of Jerusalem, 1969-70; adj. prof. Materials Sci., 1971-74; UN expert, 1971; NATO lectr., 1971; vis. prof. applied physics Ecole Poly. Fédérale, Lausanne, Switzerland, 1972; vis. prof. chem. Princeton U., N.J., 1973; research prof. radiology Hahnemann Med. Coll. and Hosp., Phila., 1974-79; adj. prof. radiology Columbia U., N.Y.C., 1979—. Editor, contbr.: Photo-electronic Materials and Devices, 1965. Numerous patents in field. Served to 1st lt. USAAF, 1943-46, USAF, 1951. Recipient David Sarnoff Gold medal RCA, N.Y.C., 1966, Outstanding Achievement award, Princeton. Designer U.S. Solid State Exhibit, Brussels World Fair, 1958. Fellow Am. Phys. Soc., Am. Inst. Chemists; mem. Electrochem. Soc. (div. editor), Am. Chem. Soc., Sigma Xi. Current work: Surface and interfacial studies of adhesion. Subspecialties: Surface chemistry; Diagnostic radiology. Home: 139 Sycamore Rd Princeton NJ 08540 Office: RCA Labs Princeton NJ 08540

LARAGH, JOHN HENRY, physician, scientist, educator; b. Yonkers, N.Y., Nov. 18, 1924; s. Harry Joseph and Grace Catherine (Coyne) L.; m. Adonia Kennedy, Apr. 28, 1949; children—John Henry, Peter Christian, Robert Sealey; m. Jean E. Sealey, Sept. 22, 1974. M.D., Cornell U., 1948. Diplomate: Am. Bd. Internal Medicine. Intern medicine Presbyn. Hosp., N.Y.C., 1948-49, asst. resident, 1949-50; fellow cardiology, trainee Nat.. Heart Inst., 1950-51; research fellow N.Y. Heart Assn., 1951-52; asst. physician Presbyn. Hosp., 1950-54, asst. attending, 1954-61, asso. attending, 1961-69, attending physician, 1969—, pres. elect med. bd., 1972-74; dir. cardiology Delafield Hosp., N.Y.C., 1954-55; mem. faculty Columbia Coll. Phys. and Surg., 1950—, prof. clin. medicine, 1967—, spokesman exec. com. faculty council, 1971-73; Hilda Altschul Master prof. medicine, dir. Cardiovascular Center and Hypertension Center N.Y. Hosp.-Cornell Med. Center, 1975—, chief Cardiology div., 1976—; dir. Hypertension Center and Nephrology div. Columbia-Presbyn. Med. Center, 1971; cons. USPHS, 1964—. Editor-in-chief: Cardiovascular Reviews and Reports; Editor: Hypertension Manual, 1974, Topics in Hypertension, 1980; Editorial bd.: Am. Heart Jour. Mem. policy adv. bd. detection and follow-up program Nat. Heart and Lung Inst., 1971, bd. sci. counselors, 1972-78; Vice chmn. bd. trustees for profl., scientific affairs Presbyn. Hosp., 1974-75; chmn. U.S.A.-USSR Joint Program in Hypertension, 1977. Served with AUS, 1943-46. Recipient Stouffer prize med. research, 1969. Fellow A.C.P., Am. Coll. Cardiology; mem. Am. Heart Assn. (chmn. council high blood pressure research 1968-72), Am. Soc. Clin. Investigation, Assn. Am. Physicians., Am. Soc. Contemporary Medicine and Surgery (adv. bd.), Internat. Soc. Hypertension (sci. council), Harvey Soc., Kappa Sigma, Nu Sigma Nu, Alpha Omega Alpha. Clubs: Winged Foot (Mamaroneck, N.Y.); Shinnecock Hills Golf (Southampton). Research on hormones and electrolyte metabolism and renal physiology, on mechanisms of edema formation and on the causes and treatment of human high blood pressure. Subspecialty: Physiology (medicine). Home: 435 E 70th St New York NY 10021 Office: NY Hosp-Cornell Med Center 525 E 68th St New York NY 10021

LARDNER, THOMAS JOSEPH, engineering educator; b. Bklyn., July 19, 1938; s. Thomas J. and Anne (Boyhan) L.; m. Anne Jeanne Porter, Nov. 28, 1964; children—Joseph, Theresa, Deborah. B.S., N.Y. Poly. Inst., 1958, M.S., 1959, Ph.D., 1961. Instr., asst. prof. applied math. MIT, 1963-71, assoc. prof. mech. engring., 1971-73; prof. applied mechanics U. Ill., Urbana, 1973-78; prof. civil engring. U. Mass., Amherst, 1978—; cons. Editor: Introduction to Mechanics of Solids, 1978. Contbr. numerous articles to engring. publs. Trustee Jones Library, Inc., Amherst; mem. Amherst Zoning Bd., 1982—. Fulbright award, 1965-66. Fellow ASME; mem. Am. Acad. Mechanics, Soc. Indsl. and Applied Math. Subspecialties: Theoretical and applied mechanics; Solid mechanics. Office: Dept Civil Engring U Mass Amherst MA 01003

LARDY, HENRY ARNOLD, biological sciences educator; b. Roslyn, S.D., Aug. 19, 1917; s. Nick and Elizabeth (Gebetsreiter) L.; m. Annrita Dresselhuys, Jan. 21, 1943; children: Nick, Diana, Jeffrey, Michael. B.S., S.D. State U., 1939, D.Sc. (hon.), 1979; M.S., U. Wis., 1941, Ph.D., 1943. Mem. faculty U. Wis.-Madison, 1945—, asso. prof. biochemistry, 1947-50, prof., 1950—, Vilas prof. biol. scis., 1966—. Co-editor: The Enzymes. Pres. Citizens vs. McCarthy, 1952. Recipient Paul-Lewis award enzyme chemistry Am. Chem. Soc., 1949, Neuberg medal Am. Soc. European Chemists, 1956, award in Agr. Wolf Found., 1981; Nat. award for agrl. excellence, 1982; Amory prize Am. Acad. Arts and Scis., 1984; Carl Hartman award. Mem. Nat. Acad. Scis., Am. Chem. Soc. (chmn. biol. div. 1958), Am. Soc. Biol. Chemists (pres. 1964), Am. Philos. Soc., Golden Retriever Club Am. (pres. 1962), Am. Acad. Arts and Scis., Endocrine Soc., Japanese Biochem. Soc. (hon.). Current Work: Sperm metabolism and functions, regulation of gluconeogenecis by hormones, enzymology, intermediary metabolism. Subspecialty: Behavioral psychology. Home: Thorstrand Rd Madison WI 53705

LARGMAN, KENNETH, strategic analyst, strategic defense analysis company executive; b. Phila., Apr. 7, 1949; s. Franklin Spencer and Roselynd Marjorie (Golden) L.; m. Suzanna Forest, Nov. 7, 1970 (div. Nov. 1978); 1 child, Jezra. Student, SUNY-Old Westbury, 1969-70. Ind. strategic analyst, 1970-77; chmn., chief exec. officer World Security Council, San Francisco, 1980—. Author: research documents Space Peacekeeping, 1978, Preventing Nuclear Conflict: An International Beam Weaponry Agreement, 1979, Space Weaponry: Effects on the International Balance of Power and the Prevention of Nuclear War, 1981, Preventing Nuclear War: Coordinating U.S. and Soviet Space Defense Against Nuclear Attack, 1982; 14 vols. on threats, vulnerabilities and safeguards of coordinated U.S./Soviet Space def. system, 1983; Coordinating U.S. and Soviet Defenses Against Nuclear Attack, 1985; Defense Against Nuclear Attack: U.S./Soviet Interactions, Moves, and Countermoves, 1985. Mem. Air Force Assn., Am. Astron. Soc., AIAA, World Affairs Council. Club: Commonwealth. Current Work: Use of military space systems to prevent nuclear war; design of space-based laser defense system able to destroy nuclear missiles and bomber attacks, yet leaving opposing nations unable to attack each other or Earth targets with system. Subspecialties: Satellite studies; Military space systems. Office: World Security Council 303 World Trade Center San Francisco CA 94111

LAROCCA, JOSEPH PAUL, educator; b. La Junta, Colo., July 5, 1920; s. Vito Michael and Mary (Parlapiano) LaR.; m. Blair Camak, Apr. 19, 1947; children—Carl Anthony, Mary Blair, Charlotte Ann, Elizabeth. B.S., U. Colo., 1942; M.S. (Nat. Formulary fellow), U. N.C., 1944; Ph.D., U. Md., 1948. Research chemist U.S. Naval Research Lab., Washington, 1947-49; asso. prof. medicinal chemistry U. Ga., 1949-50, prof., 1950—, head dept., 1968—; lectr. Oak Ridge Asso. Univs. Mobile Radioisotope Program, 1965, 66; cons. physician manpower USPHS, 1967. Author research papers, reports. Bd. dirs. Am. Assn. Colls. Pharmacy, 1974-76; Chmn. bd. Clark County unit Am. Cancer Soc., 1965-66, pres., 1964-65; chmn. bd. Clark County Community Chest, 1963-64, pres., 1962-63; pres. Athens Assn. Retarded Children, 1960-61. Served with AUS, 1944-46. Gustavus A. Pfeiffer Meml. Research fellow, 1964-65; Orins Research participant, 1964, 65, 66. Fellow A.A.A.S.; mem. Am. Pharm. Soc., Am. Chem. Soc., Ga. Pharm. Assn., Ga. Acad. Sci., Sigma Xi, Phi Kappa Phi, Rho Chi, Phi Delta Chi. Club: Rotarian. Subspecialty: Medicinal chemistry. Home: 115 Fortson Circle Athens GA 30606

LAROCHE, GERMAIN, terrestrial ecologist; b. Lowell, Mass., Sept. 25, 1926; s. Amedee O. and Annette (Germain) LaR.; m. Lorraine Y. Vincent, Feb. 3, 1951; 1 child, Robert A. Diploma, Stockbridge Sch. Agr., U. Mass., 1950, Ph.D., 1969; B.A., Cath. U. of Am., 1957, M.S., 1958. Asst. prof. SUNY-New Paltz, 1968-70, assoc. prof., 1970-73; adj. prof. Empire State Coll., Albany, N.Y., 1973-74; assoc. environ. scientist Environ. Analysts, Garden City, N.Y., 1973-74; dir. terrestrial ecology Equital Environ. Health, Woodbury, N.Y., 1974-77; sr. land use analyst U.S. Nuclear Regulatory Commn., Washington, 1977—; chmn. session conf. Energy Facility Siting, 1982; com. mem. Conf. Resource Mgmt. Applications: Energy and Environment, 1983. Contbr. articles to profl. jours. Served with USN, 1944-46. SUNY grantee, 1969. Mem. Ecol. Soc. Am., Soc. Am. Foresters, Sigma Xi. (Manhattan Coll. sec. 1962-65). Roman Catholic. Current work: The use of remote sensing in the evaluation of large energy related facilities, e.g. nuclear power plants and nuclear waste repositories. The effect of cooling tower drift on terrestrial ecosystems. Subspecialties: Ecology (biology); Ecology (environmental science). Home: 16919 Glen Oak Run Rockville MD 20855 Office: US Nuclear Regulatory Commn P-314 Washington DC 20555

LARRABEE, MARTIN GLOVER, educator; b. Boston, Jan. 25, 1910; s. Ralph Clinton and Ada Perkins (Miller) L.; m. Sylvia Kimball, Sept. 10, 1932 (div. 1944); 1 son, Benjamin Larrabee Scherer; m. Barbara Belcher, Mar. 25, 1944; 1 child, David Belcher Larrabee. B.A., Harvard U., 1932; Ph.D., U. Pa., 1937; M.D. (hon.), U. Lausanne, Switzerland, 1974. Research asst., fellow U. Pa., Phila., 1934-40, asso. to asso. prof., 1941-49; asst. prof. physiology Cornell U. Med. Coll., N.Y.C., 1940-41, asso. prof., Johns Hopkins, Balt., 1949-63, prof. biophysics, 1963—. Contbr. articles to scientific jours. Mem. Am. Physiol. Soc., Biophys. Soc., Am. Soc. Neurochemistry, Internat. Neurochem. Soc., Nat. Acad. Scis., Soc. for Neurosci. (treas. 1970-75), Physiol. Soc. (asso., Eng.), Phi Beta Kappa. Clubs: Appalachian Mountain, Sierra, Mountain of Md. Research on circulatory, respiratory and nervous systems of animals, especially on synaptic and metabolic mechanisms in sympathetic ganglia, 1934—; wartime research on oxygen lack, decompression sickness, nerve injury, infrared viewing devices, 1941-45. Current Work: Research on developmental changes in metabolism in sympathetic and sensory ganglia of chicken embryos.

Subspecialties: Neurophysiology; Neurochemistry. Home: 4227 Long Green Rd Glen Arm MD 21057 Office: Biophysics Dept Johns Hopkins Univ Baltimore MD 21218

LARRABEE, ROBERT DEAN, physicist, educator; b. Flushing, N.Y., Nov. 29, 1931; s. William Morse and Dorothy Dean (Smock) L.; m. Ramona Allien Rogers, Aug. 29, 1953; children—David Allan, Susan Kay. B.S. in Elec. Engring., Bucknell U., 1953; M.S. in Math., 1953; S.M. in Sci., MIT, 1955, Sc.D. in Physics, 1957; M.B.A., Rider Coll., 1976. Regis. profl. engr., N.J., N.Y., Md. Mem. tech. staff RCA Labs., Princeton, N.J., 1957-72; sr. engr. RCA Advanced Tech. Lab., Camden, N.J., 1972-76; physicist Nat. Bur. Standards, Gaithersburg, Md., 1976-80, supervisory physicist, group leader, 1980—; lectr. U. Md., College Park, 1982, 83. Editor: Neutron Transmutation Doping of Semiconductor Materials, 1984; patentee (8); contbr. articles to profl. jours. Dir. local Civil Def. Orgn., West Windsor, N.J., 1960's; advisor, leader Explorer Post Boy Scouts Am., Princeton, 1966-72; advisor, judge local sci. fairs, Gaithersburg, 1982—. Recipient Achievement awards RCA Labs., 1964, 68. Sr. mem. IEEE (local dir. devices sect. 1980); mem. Am. Phys. Soc., AAAS. Current work: Development of new or improved techniques for characterizing and measuring the electrical properties of semiconductor materials. Subspecialties: Microchip technology (materials science); Semiconductors. Office: Nat Bur Standards Bldg 225 Room A-331 Gaithersburg MD 20899

LARRIMORE, JAMES ABBOTT, nuclear engineer; b. San Francisco, Aug. 18, 1934; s. James and Dorothy Elisabeth (Martin) L.; m. Irene Maria Kalbfleisch, Mar. 6, 1965; children: Mark Joseph, Corinne Marilou. B.Eng. Physics, Cornell U., 1957; Ph.D. in Nuclear Engring, M.I.T., 1963. Dir. M.I.T. Engring. Practice Sch., Oak Ridge, 1960-62; asst. prof. nuclear engring. M.I.T., Boston, 1960-63; mem. vis. com. nuclear engring. dept., 1976-78; asst. to head reactor physics dept. Euratom Research Center, Ispra, Italy, 1963-69; br. chief, dept. head Gen. Atomic Co., San Diego, 1969-76, sr. staff adviser, 1979-80; sr. officer div. nuclear power and reactors IAEA, Vienna, Austria, 1976-78; dir. internat. programs GA Techs. Inc., San Diego, 1980-85; sr. officer dept. safeguards IAEA, Vienna, Austria, 1985—. Ford Found. fellow, 1962-63. Mem. Am. Nuclear Soc., Sigma Xi. Republican. Current Work: International nuclear safeguards implementation. Subspecialties: Nuclear fission; Nuclear engineering. Office: IAEA Wagramerstrasse 5 PO Box 200 A-1400 Vienna Austria

LARSEN, JAMES ARTHUR, ecologist, writer, editor; b. Rhinelander, Wis., Mar. 14, 1921; s. Richard Elsmer and Mattie Margaret (McLaughlin) L.; m. Roberta Ann Luers, Dec. 30, 1948 (div. 1965); children—Kirstie, Wendy; m. Marlette Elizabeth Swenson, June 15, 1968; children—Lisabeth, Timothy. B.A., U. Wis., 1946, M.S., 1956, Ph.D., 1968. Research program assoc. U. Wis., Madison, 1958-77, sci. editor, 1946-81; ret.; now profl. writer. Author: The Boreal Ecosystem, 1980; Ecology of the Northern Coniferous Forests and Lowland Bogs, 1982. Mem. Ecol. Soc. Am., Am. Bot. Soc., Arctic Inst., Nat. Assn. Sci. Writers, Am. Meteorol. Soc. Current work: Ecology and bio-climatology of northern continental forest border, boreal forest, and northern tundra; writer on major issues in environmental scis. and public policy. Subspecialties: Ecology (biology); Climatology. Home and office: 2415 Adler Circle Middleton WI 53562

LARSEN, JON THORSTEN, scientist; b. Denver, Feb. 11, 1942; s. Richard Thorsten and Elizabeth Jane (Hughart) L. B.S., Colo. State U., 1964; Ph.D., Iowa State U., 1970. Staff scientist Lawrence Livermore Lab., Calif., 1970-80; sr. scientist Physics Internat. Co., San Leandro, Calif., 1980-81; primary scientist KMS Fusion, Inc., Ann Arbor, Mich., 1981—. Contbr. articles to profl. jours. Mem. Am. Phys. Soc., AAAS, Sigma Xi. Current work: Inertial fusion theory, numerical simulations, hydrodynamics and atomic physics of dense plasmas, x-ray lasers, advanced computational techniques. Subspecialties: Laser fusion; Atomic and molecular physics. Office: KMS Fusion Inc PO Box 1567 Ann Arbor MI 48106

LARSON, BRUCE L., biochemist, educator; b. Mpls., June 24, 1927; married, 1954; 3 children. B.S., U. Minn., 1948, Ph.D. in Biochemistry, 1951. Mem. faculty U. Minn., 1948-51; from instr. to assoc. prof. U. Ill., 1951-66, prof. biol. chemistry, 1966—, mem. staff nutrition sci. faculty, 1972—, Fulbright lectr., 1965. Mem. AAAS, Am. Chem. Soc. (award 1966), Am. Soc. Biol. Chemists, Am. Dairy Sci. Assn. Subspecialty: Biochemistry (biology). Office: U Ill 328 Animal Scis Lab 1207 W Gregory Dr Urbana IL 61801*

LARSON, CLARENCE EDWARD, energy consultant; b. Cloquet, Minn., Sept. 20, 1909; s. Louis Ludwig and Caroline Hilda (Ullman) L.; m. Gertrude Ellen Ruben, Apr. 20, 1935 (dec. May 1953); 1 child, Robert Edward; m. Jane Ritchie Warren; children—Lawrence Ernest, Lance Stafford. B.S., U. Minn., 1932; Ph.D., U. Calif.-Berkeley, 1937. Chmn. chemistry dept. Coll. of Pacific, Stockton, Calif., 1937-41; dir. chem. research, plant mgr. Electro-magnetic Plant, Oak Ridge, 1942-50; dir. Oak Ridge Nat. Lab., 1950-55; mgr. corp. research Union Carbide Corp., N.Y.C., 1955-61, pres. nuclear div., Oak Ridge, 1961-69; mem. AEC, Washington, 1969-74; energy cons., Washington, 1974-85; dir. Pioneers of Sci. and Tech. Hist. Assn., Washington, 1983—. Inventor process for isolation of uranium, 1945. Fellow Am. Nuclear Soc., Am. Inst. Chemists; mem. Nat. Acad. Engring., Tau Beta Pi. Republican. Club: Cosmos (Washington). Current work: Separations technology; isotope separation; electrochemical research; electric car research. Subspecialty: Engineering consulting.

LARSON, DENNIS L., agricultural engineer, educator; b. Mason City, Iowa, Feb. 3, 1940; s. Vernon C. and Adelaide L. (Wamstad) L.; m. Cheryl A. Davisson, June 1, 1963; children: Scott, Kristine, Steven, Kathryn. B.S., Iowa State U., Ames, 1963; M.S., U. Ill., Urbana, 1964; Ph.D., Purdue U., Lafayette, Ind., 1971. Registered profl. engr., Ill, Calif., Ariz. Product engr. John Deere Planter Works, Moline, Ill, 1966-68; asst. prof., tech. advisor in Colombia for U. Nebr.-Lincoln, 1970-73; food engr. Mich. State U., East Lansing, 1973; engr. Chrysler Def. Products, Detroit, 1973; asst. prof. agrl. engring. U. Ariz., Tucson, 1973-79, assoc. prof., 1979—. Served to 1st lt. AUS, 1964-66. Mem. Am. Soc. Agr. Engrs., Am. Soc. Engring. Edn., Am. Solar Energy Soc., Sigma Xi. Current Work: Energy use in agriculture and energy alternatives, use of solar energy to drive irrigation pumps, agricultural systems analysis. Subspecialty: Agricultural engineering.

LARSON, DONALD CLAYTON, physicist, educator, cons.; b. Wadena, Minn., Jan. 29, 1934; s. Clyde Melvin and Selma L. Engen; m. Susan Dunnet, July 17, 1960; children: Tor, Jon, Erika. B.S., U. Wash., 1956; M.S., Harvard U., 1957, Ph.D., 1962. Asst. prof. U. Va., 1962-67; assoc. prof. physics Drexel U., Phila., 1967-83, prof. phsics, 1983—; cons. Mem. Am. Phys. Soc., ASTM, Internat. Solar Energy Soc., Phi Beta Kappa, Sigma Xi, Tau Beta Pi. Democrat. Current Work: Mirror-boosted solar collectiors, field techniques for insulation thermal testing, optical waveguides, semiconductors, optical and electrical properties of films, solar energy, thermal insulation. Subspecialties: Condensed matter physics; Semiconductors. Office: Dept of Physics and Atmospheric Sci Drexel U Philadelphia PA 19104

LARSON, PHILIP RODNEY, research plant physiologist; b. N. Branch, Minn., Nov. 26, 1923; s. Eric Gunnar and Anna Ruth (Fagerstrom) L.; m. Yvonne Evelyn Sybrant, Sept. 3, 1948; children: Cynthia Marie, Paula Rae. B.S., U. Minn., 1949; M.S., 1952; Ph.D., Yale U., 1957. Research forester Southeastern Forest Exptl. Sta., Lake City, Fla., 1952-56; plant physiologist North Central Forest Exptl. Sta., Rhinelander, Wis., 1957—, leader pioneering research unit. Contbr. numerous articles to profl. jours. Served to lt. USNR, 1942-46. Recipient Disting. Service award U.S. Dept. Agr., 1975; N.Y. Bot. Garden Research award, 1977. Fellow Internat. Acad. Wood Sci.; mem. Soc. Am. Foresters (Barrington Moore award 1975), Bot. Soc. Am., Am. Soc. Plant Physiologists. Current Work: Physiology of wood formation, structure and function of the vascular system of trees, relation of primary to secondary vasculature in all aerial organs of trees. Subspecialties: Plant physiology (agriculture); Plant growth.

LARSON, RICHARD BONDO, astronomy educator; b. Toronto, Ont., Can., Jan. 15, 1941; came to U.S., 1963; s. Carl Johan and Elsie (Bondo) L. B.Sc., U. Toronto, 1962, M.A., 1963; Ph.D., Calif. Inst. Tech., 1968. Asst. prof. astronomy Yale U., New Haven, 1968-73, assoc. prof., 1973-75, prof., 1975—, chmn. dept. astronomy, 1981—. Contbr. articles to profl. jours. Mem. Am. Astron. Soc., Royal Astron. Soc., Internat. Astron. Union, Sigma Xi. Current Work: Research on formation of stars, galaxies. Subspecialty: Theoretical astrophysics. Address: Dept Astronomy Yale U PO Box 6666 New Haven CT 06511

LARSON, VIVIAN M., virologist, researcher; b. Erie, N.D., Oct. 3, 1931; d. Orlando C. and Alice M. (Port) L. B.S., N.D. State Coll., 1953; M.P.H., U. Mich., 1958; Ph.D., 1963. Cert. med. technologist Am. Soc. Clin. Pathology. Bacteriologist Detroit Dept. Health Labs., 1953-59; research fellow Merck Sharp & Dohme Research Labs., West Point, Pa., 1963-69, Sr. research fellow, 1969-71, dir. Herpes virus research, 1980—; dir. NIH Virus Lab., 1971-80. Contbr. articles on bacteriology, virology, cancer immunology and viral vaccine devel. to sci. jours. Mem. Am. Soc. for Microbiology, Am. Acad. Microbiology, AAAS, Phi Kappa Phi, Delta Omega. Lutheran. Patentee Herpes subunit vaccine. Current Work: Research on the development of herpes virus vaccines for human use by genetic engineering. Subspecialties: Virology (medicine); Infectious diseases. Home: 362 Park Dr Harleysville PA 19438 Office: Merck Sharp & Dohme Research Labs West Point PA 19486

LARTER, RAIMA MARZEE, chemistry educator, researcher; b. Kingsville, Tex., May 1, 1955; d. Gary Duane and Edith Marie (Carpenter) L.; m. Kenneth Barry Lipkowitz, June 12, 1977; children—Nathan Larter Lipkowitz, Benjamin Larter Lipkowitz. B.S. in Chemistry with honors, Mont. State U., 1976; Ph.D. in Phys. Chemistry, Ind. U.-Bloomington, 1980. Research assoc. Princeton U., 1980-81; instr. Ind.-Purdue U., Indpls. 1981-82, vis. asst. prof., 1982-83, asst. prof. chemistry, 1983—. Contbr. articles to profl. jours. Research Corp. grantee, 1984. Mem. Assn. Women in Sci. (founder, pres. Ind. chpt. 1982—), Am. Chem. Soc., Am. Phys. Soc., Am. Inst. Chem. Engrs., Internat. Soc. Bioelectricity, Ind. Acad. Sci., Hoosier Assn. Sci. Tchrs., Phi Kappa Phi. Current work: Computer modeling of chemical reaction kinetics; applied mathematics for the study of chemical kinetics; studies of self-organization, chemical oscillations. Subspecialties: Theoretical chemistry; Kinetics. Home: 4506 Dickson Rd Indianapolis IN 46226 Office: Ind Univ-Purdue Univ Dept Chemistry 1125 E 38th St Indianapolis IN 46223

LASAGNA, LOUIS CESARE, physician, educator; b. N.Y.C., Feb. 22, 1923; s. Joseph and Carmen (Boccignone) L.; m. Helen Chester Gersten, July 20, 1946; children—Nina, David, Maria, Kristin, Lisa, Peter, Christopher. B.S., Rutgers U., 1943; M.D., Columbia, 1947. Intern Mt. Sinai Hosp., N.Y.C., 1947-48; resident Maimonides Hosp., Bklyn., 1948-50; instr. pharmacology and exptl. therapeutics Johns Hopkins Med. Sch., 1950-52, asst. prof. medicine, 1954-57, asso. prof. medicine, 1957-70, asst. prof. pharmacology and exptl. therapeutics, 1954-59, asso. prof. pharmacology and exptl. therapeutics, 1959-70; prof. pharmacology and toxicology, prof. medicine U. Rochester Sch. Medicine, 1970—; research asso. Harvard, 1953-54, 67-68. Author: The Doctors' Dilemmas, 1962, Life, Death, and the Doctor, 1968, The VD Epidemic, 1975, Controversies in Therapeutics, 1980. Served with USNR, 1943-46; with USPHS, 1952-54. Mem. Am. Soc. Pharmacology and Exptl. Therapeutics, Am. Soc. Clin. Investigation, Assn. Am. Physicians, Inst. Medicine, Phi Beta Kappa, Sigma Xi, Alpha Omega Alpha. Research on placebos, clin. pharmacology. Subspecialty: Pharmacology. Home: 465 Clover Hills Dr Rochester NY 14618

LASHOF, JOYCE R. COHEN, physician, university dean; b. Phila., Mar. 27, 1926; d. Harry and Rose (Brodsky) Cohen; m. Richard Kenneth Lashof, June 11, 1950; children—Judith, Carol, Dan. A.B., Duke U., 1946; M.D., Woman's Med. Coll., Pa., 1950. Diplomate: Am. Bd. Internal Medicine. Intern Bronx Hosp., N.Y.C., 1950-51; resident, 1951-52, Montefiore Hosp., N.Y.C., 1952-53; fellow Yale U., 1953-54; USPHS fellow U. Oxford, Eng., 1964-65; practice medicine specializing in preventive medicine, Chgo., 1954-73; dep. asst. sec. for health programs HEW, Washington, 1977-78; asst. dir. Office Tech. Assessment, U.S. Congress, Washington, 1978-81; dean Sch. Pub. Health, U. Calif.-Berkeley, Washington, 1981—; dir. sect. community medicine Presbyn.-St. Luke's Hosp., Chgo., 1967-71, chmn. dept. preventive medicine, 1971-73; project dir. Mile Sq. Health Center, Chgo., 1967-71; instr. medicine U. Chgo., 1956-58; asst. prof., 1958-60; clin. asst. prof. preventive medicine U. Ill., 1960-61, asst. prof., 1961-64, asso. prof., 1964-68, prof. preventive medicine and community health, 1968-71; prof. preventive medicine Rush Med. Coll., Chgo., 1971-73; dir. pub. health, State of Ill., Springfield, 1973-77; research dir. Chgo. Bd. Health, 1965. Contbr. articles to profl. jours. Fellow Am. Pub. Health Assn., ACP; mem. Am. Assn. Tchrs. of Preventive Medicine. Subspecialties: Preventive medicine; Health services research. Office: Univ of Calif 19 Earl Warren Hall Berkeley CA 94720

LASKER, LESLIE, mathematical physicist; b. Johannesburg, South Africa, Oct. 29, 1944; came to U.S., 1969; s. Helmuth and Eva (Kalischer) L.; m. Carrol Gafin, Feb. 24, 1970; 1 child, Andrea. B.S., U. Witwatersrand, South Africa, 1967; M.S. in Physics, U. Minn., 1971; postgrad. U. Calif.-Berkeley, 1971; M.A. in Math., SUNY-Stony Brook, 1972, Ph.D. in Physics, 1979. Programmer-/analyst Brookhaven Nat. Lab., Upton, N.Y., 1974-84; physicist Fonar Corp., Melville, N.Y., 1985—; adj. faculty Suffolk County Community Coll., 1984—. Served with South African Army, 1963. Mem. Am. Phys. Soc., Math. Assn. Am., Assn. Computing Machinery, IEEE Computer Soc. Jewish. Lodge: B'nai B'rith (Stony Brook). Current work: Applications of computers to physics and biology—cellular automata, nuclear magnetic resonance imaging. Subspecialties: Theoretical physics; Magnetic resonance imaging. Home: 5 Deer Ln East Setauket NY 11733 Office: Fonar Corp 110 Marcus Ave Melville NY 11747

LASKIN, DANIEL M., oral and maxillofacial surgeon, researcher; b. N.Y.C., Sept. 3, 1924; s. Nathan and Flora (Kaplan) L.; m. Eve Pauline Mohel, Aug. 25, 1945; children—Jeffrey, Gary, Marla. B.S., Ind. U.-Bloomington, 1947, D.D.S., Indpls., 1947; M.S., U. Ill.-Chgo., 1951. Diplomate Am. Bd. Oral and Maxillofacial Surgery. Intern oral surgery Jersey City Med. Ctr., N.J., 1947-48; resident in oral surgery Cook County Hosp., Chgo., 1950-51; asst. dept. oral and maxillofacial surgery Coll. Dentistry, U. Ill., 1949-50, research asst., 1950-51, instr., 1951-53, asst. prof., 1953-55, assoc. prof., 1955-60, prof., 1960-83, assoc. head dept., 1962-73, head dept., 1973-83; prof., chmn. dept. oral and maxillofacial surgery Sch. Dentistry, Med. Coll. Va., Va. Commonwealth U., 1984—; dep. chmn. div. oral surgery, attending oral surgeon Cook County Hosp., 1967-83; attending oral surgeon Edgewater Hosp., Skokie Valley Community Hosp., Swedish Covenant Hosp.; cons. oral surgeon Bethany Meth. Hosp., Ill. Masonic Hosp. Author: Oral and Maxillofacial Surgery, Vol. I, 1980, Vol. II, 1985; Management of Oral Emergencies, 1964; co-author: The Temporomandibular Joint, 1980; Diagnosis and Surgical Management of Diseases of the Temporomandibular Joint, 1962. Served with AUS, 1942-44. Recipient numerous awards, including Nell Snow Talbot Instructorship award, U. Ill. Coll. Dentistry, Am. Soc. Oral Surgeons Disting. Service award, Ind. U. Disting. Alumni Service award, Simon P. Hullihen Meml. award, William J. Gies Editorial award, 1978, 79, 84, Heidbrink award, Disting. Alumni award Ind. U. Sch. Dentistry. Fellow Am. Coll. Dentists, AAAS, Internat. Coll. Dentists, Am. Dental Soc. Anesthesiology, Royal Coll. Surgeons (Eng.); mem. Am. Dental Assn., Am. Assn. Oral and Maxillofacial Surgeons (past pres., Research Recognition award), Internat. Assn. Oral and Maxillofacial Surgeons (pres. 1983—), Chgo. Soc. Oral and Maxillofacial Surgeons (past pres.), Great Lake Soc. Oral and Maxillofacial Surgeons, Ill. Soc. Oral and Maxillofacial Surgeons (past pres.), Am. Assn. Dental Research, Internat. Assn. Dental Research, Am. Dental Soc. Anesthesiology (past pres.), Omicron Kappa Upsilon, Sigma Xi. Current work: Pathology of temporomandibular joint; facial growth and development; facial pain. Subspecialty: Oral and maxillofacial surgery. Office: Med Coll Va Box 566 MCV Sta Richmond VA 23298

LASKIN, OSCAR LARRY, clinical pharmacology educator, virologist; b. Phila., Sept. 11, 1951; s. Bernard and Blanche (Friedman) L.; m. Christine Ann Goril, Apr. 4, 1981. A.B. summa cum laude, Temple U., 1972, M.D. with honors, 1976. Diplomate: Am. Bd. Internal Medicine. Intern Johns Hopkins Hosp., Balt., 1976-77, resident in medicine, 1977-79, fellow in medicine, 1979-82, fellow in pharmacology, 1981-82; asst. prof. clin. pharmacology Cornell U. Med. Coll., N.Y.C., 1982—, asst. prof. pharmacology and medicine, 1982—; asst. attending physician N.Y. Hosp., 1982—. Contbr. articles to profl. jours. NIH fellow, 1981; clin. scholar Rockefeller Bros. Fund, 1982; Hartford Found. fellow, 1983; recipient research prize Am. Heart Assn., 1975, Andrew W. Mellon Tchr.-Scientist award. Fellow ACP; mem. Am. Fedn. Clin. Research, Am. Soc. Microbiology, Am. Soc. for Clin. Pharmacology and Therapeutics, Am. Soc. for Pharmacology and Exptl. Therapeutics, Alpha Omega Alpha. Current work: Clinical pharmacology of antiviral drugs, rapid viral diagnosis and therapy of viral diseases especially herpesviruses. Subspecialties: Internal medicine; Pharmacology. Home: 6 Prides Crossing New City NY 10956 Office: Cornell Med Coll 1300 York Ave New York NY 10021

LASKOWSKI, MICHAEL, JR., chemistry educator; b. Warsaw, Poland, Mar. 13, 1930; came to U.S., 1947, naturalized, 1955. B.S., Lawrence Coll., 1950; Ph.D., Cornell U., 1954. Instr. Cornell U., Ithaca, N.Y., 1956-57; asst. prof. chemistry, Purdue U., West Lafayette, Ind., 1957-61, assoc. prof., 1961-65, prof., 1965—; chmn. Gordon Confs., 1966, 82. Contbr. articles to profl. jours. Recipient McCoy Research award Purdue U., 1975, Alfred Jurzykowski Found. award, 1977. Mem. Am. Soc. Biol. Chemists, Am. Chem. Soc., Biophys. Soc. Current work: Protein chemistry, effect of single amino acid replacements upon reactivity of globular proteins. Subspecialties: Biophysical chemistry; Biochemistry (biology). Home: 222 E Navaho West Lafayette IN 47906 Office: Dept Chemistry Purdue U West Lafayette IN 47907

LASOSKI, BERNARD ALBERT, analytical chemist; b. Alden Sta., Pa., Aug. 27, 1929; s. Stanley William and Florence Evelyn (Gommer) L.; m. Ann Lipinski, Aug. 30, 1952; children—Carol, Bernard Jr., David, Janet. B.S. in Chemistry, King's Coll., 1953; M.S. in Chemistry, St. Joseph's U., 1960. Chemist Dupont, Chambers Works, Deepwater, N.J., 1953-56, research chemist, 1956-59, sr. research chemist, 1959-71, research assoc., 1971—; lectr. in chemistry, St. Joseph's U., Phila., 1960-80. Contbr. articles to profl. jours. Patentee in field. Served to 1st lt. USAF, 1953. Mem. Am. Chem. Soc., ASTM, Formaldehyde Inst. Lodge: Lions. Current work: Determining trace concentrations of carcinogenics and toxic compounds in environmental matrices. Subspecialties: Analytical chemistry; Organic chemistry. Home: 1 Cortland Way Mantua NJ 08051 Office: DuPont Jackson Lab Chambers Works Deepwater NJ 08023

LASRY, JEAN-CLAUDE MAURICE, psychologist, educator; b. Casablanca, Morocco, July 21, 1937; emigrated to Can., 1957; s. Marcel and Violette (Leon) L.; children: Eytan, Arielle. B.A., U. Montreal, Que., 1965, M.A., 1966, Ph.D., 1968. Lectr. U. Montreal, 1966-68, asst. prof., 1968-75, assoc. prof., 1975-81, prof. psychology, 1981—; research assoc. Jewish Gen. Hosp., Montreal, 1969—. Editor: quar. Cross-Cultural Psychol Bull, 1980—; contbr. chpts. to books, articles to profl. jours. Founding pres. Ecole Maimonide, Montreal, 1969-71, pres., 1976-80; pres. Assn. Sepharade Francophone, Montreal, 1972-74; officer Can. Jewish Congress, 1975—. Can. NRC scholar, 1964-68; recipient Barkoff Leadership award Allied Jewish Community, Montreal, 1972. Mem. Can. Psychol. Assn., Que. Corp. Psychologists (award 1966), Am. Psychol. Assn., Internat. Assn. for Cross-Cultural Psychology, Que. Family Therapy Assn. (founding pres. 1979-82). Current Work: Cross-cultural psychology; mental health; immigrants' adaptation and identity; family structure and power. Subspecialties: Social psychology; Psychotherapy. Home: 406 Ellerton Ave Mount Royal PQ H3P 1E4 Canada Office: Jewish Gen Hosp 4333 Cote Ste Catherine Montreal PQ H3T 1E2 Canada

LASSETTRE, EDWIN NICHOLS, emeritus chemical physics educator; b. Ga., Oct. 26, 1911; s. Carlos E. and Jennie J. (Nichols) L.; m. Ilse R. Sturies, Dec. 22, 1951. B.S. in Chemistry, Mont. State Coll., 1933; Ph.D., Calif. Inst. Tech., 1938; Dr. Tech. (hon.), Royal Inst. Tech., Stockholm, Sweden, 1977. Faculty dept. chemistry Ohio State U., Columbus, 1937-62; staff fellow Mellon Inst., Pitts., 1962-67; prof. chem. physics Carnegie-Mellon U., Pitts., 1967-73, univ. prof. chem. physics, 1973-77, univ. prof. chem. physics emeritus, 1977—. Contbr. articles to profl. jours. Fellow Am. Phys. Soc.; mem. Am. Chem. Soc., Optical Soc. Am. Current work: Electron impact spectroscopy; theory of analytic behavior of collision amplitudes and electron momentum eigenfunctions. Subspecialties: Physical chemistry; Theoretical chemistry. Home: 224 E Waldheim Rd Pittsburgh PA 15125 Office: Dept Chemistry Carnegie-Mellon U 4400 5th Ave Pittsburgh PA 15213

LASSLO, ANDREW, medicinal chemist, educator; b. Mukacevo, Czechoslovakia, Aug. 24, 1922; came to U.S., 1946, naturalized, 1951; s. Vojtech Laszlo and Terezie (Herskovicova) L.; m. Wilma Ellen Reynolds, July 9, 1955; 1 dau., Millicent Andrea. M.S., U. Ill., 1948, Ph.D., 1952, M.S. in Library Sci., 1961. Research chemist organic chems. div. Monsanto Chem. Co., St. Louis, 1952-54; asst. prof. pharmacology, div. basic health scis. Emory U., 1954-60; prof., chmn. dept. medicinal chemistry Coll. Pharmacy, U. Tenn. Center for Health Scis., 1960—; cons. Geschickter Fund for Med. Research Inc., 1961-62; dir. postgrad. tng. program sci. librarians USPHS, 1966-72; chmn. edn. com. Drug Info. Assn., 1966-68, bd. dirs., 1968-69; dir. postgrad. tng. program organic medicinal chemistry for chemists FDA, 1971; exec. com. adv. council S.E. Regional Med. Library Program, Nat. Library of Medicine, 1969-71; chmn. regional med. library program com. Med. Library Assn., 1971-72; mem. pres.'s faculty adv. council U. Tenn. System, 1970-72; chmn. energy authority U. Tenn. Center for Health Scis., 1975-77, chmn. council departmental chmn., 1977, 81; chmn. Internat. Symposium on Contemporary Trends in Tng. Phamacologists, Helsinki, 1975. Producer, moderator: TV and radio series Health Care Perspectives, 1976-78; Editor: Surface Chemistry and Dental Integuments, 1973, Blood Platelet Function and Medicinal Chemistry, 1984; Contbr. numerous articles in sci. and profl. jours.; Mem. editorial bd.: Jour. Medicinal and Pharm. Chemistry, 1961, U. Tenn. Press, 1974-77; Composer: piano Synthesis in C Minor, 1968. Served to capt. M.S.C. U.S. Army Res., 1953-62. Recipient Sigma Xi Research prize, 1949, Honor Scroll Tenn. Inst. Chemists, 1976; Americanism medal D.A.R., 1976; U. Ill. fellow, 1950-51; Geschickter Fund Med. Research grantee, 1959-65; USPHS Research and Tng. grantee, 1958-64, 66-72, 82—; NSF research grantee, 1964-66; Pfeiffer Research Found. grantee, 1981—. Fellow AAAS, Acad. Pharm. Scis., Am. Inst. Chemists (nat. councillor for Tenn. 1969-70); mem. ALA (life), Am. Chem. Soc. (sr.), Am. Pharm. Assn., Am. Soc. Pharmacology and Exptl. Therapeutics (chmn. subcom. pre-and postdoctoral tng. 1974-78, exec. com. ednl. and profl. affairs 1974-78), Sigma Xi (pres. elect U. Tenn. Center for Health Sci. chpt. 1975-76, pres. 1976-77), Beta Phi Mu, Phi Lambda Sigma, Rho Chi. Methodist (past trustee, ofcl. and adminstrv. bd., chmn. com. edn. and social concerns). Club: Health Scis. Center Faculty Club (charter bd. dirs. 1966-68, exec. com. 1967-68). Inventor, patentee. Current Work: Relationships between chemical constitution, physicochemical characteristics and biodynamic response; development of novel antithrombotic agents; science information and library resources. Subspecialties: Medicinal chemistry; Molecular pharmacology. Home: 5479 Timmons Ave Memphis TN 38119 Office: 26 S Dunlap St Memphis TN 38163

LATA, GENE FREDERICK, biochemist, educator; b. N.Y.C., May 17, 1922; s. Louis F. and Tessie (Greco) L.; married; children: Paul, Matthew, Thomas, Catherine, Mary. B.S., CCNY, 1942; M.S., U. Ill., 1948, Ph.D., 1950. Lab. asst. CCNY, 1941-42; jr. chemist Gen. Foods Central Research Labs., 1942, 1946-47; teaching asst. U. Ill.-Champaign, 1947, research fellow, 1947-50, instr., 1950-53, asst. prof., 1953-63; assoc. prof. U. Iowa, Iowa City, 1963—; traveling fellow U. Iowa (Coll. Medicine), 1965-66; vis. lectr. Scientist Harvard U., 1965-69. Contbr. articles on biochemistry to profl. jours. State del. dist. conv. Democratic Party, 1982, 84. Served with AUS, 1942-46. Mem. Am. Soc. Biol. Chemistry, Am. Chem. Soc., AAAS, N.Y. Acad. Scis., Iowa Acad. Sci., Sierra Club, Sigma Xi, Phi Sigma, Phi Lambda Upsilon, Omicron Kappa Upsilon. Roman Catholic. Current Work: Physical chemical character of steroid solutions, steroid-protein binding, inter-relationships of retinal angiogensis and steroid hormones. Subspecialties: Biochemistry (biology); Receptors. Office: Dept Biochemistry U Iowa Iowa City IA 52242

LATHAM, ALLEN, JR., manufacturing company executive; b. Norwich, Conn., May 23, 1908; s. Allen and Caroline (Walker) L.; m. Ruth Nichols, Nov. 11, 1933; children: W. Nichols, Harriet (Mrs. William S. Robinson), David W., Thomas W. B.S. in Mech. Engring, MIT, 1930, Sloan fellow, 1936. Devel. engr. E.I. duPont, Belle, W.Va., 1930-35; engr., treas. Polaroid Corp., Cambridge, Mass., 1936-41; engr., v.p. Arthur D. Little, Cambridge, 1941-66; pres. Cryogenic Tech., Waltham, Mass., 1966-71; chmn. bd. Haemonetics, Braintree, Mass., 1972-83, also dir.; corporator Eliot Savs. Bank, Boston. Named Engr. of Yr. Socs. New Eng. Engring., 1970. Mem. ASME, Am. Inst. Chem. Engrs., Instrument Soc. Am., AAAS, Nat. Acad. Engring. Club: Country (Brookline, Mass.). Patentee in blood processing equipment and processes. Current Work: Development of centrifugal separation systems with disposable fluid pathways for therapeutic application in human blood disorders. Subspecialties: Mechanical engineering; Biomedical engineering. Home: 143 Whitcomb Ave Jamaica Plain MA 02130 Office: 400 Wood Rd Braintree MA 02184

LATTA, JOHN NEAL, research scientist; b. Ottumwa, Iowa, Apr. 11, 1944; s. Oris N. and Edna M. (Hanna) L.; m. Karen N. Jamison, June 10, 1966; children: J. Neal, Mark R. B.E.S., Brigham Young U., 1966; M.S.E.E., U. Kans., 1969; Ph.D. in Elec. Engring., 1971. Mem. tech. staff RCA Labs., Princeton, N.J., 1967; Bell Telephone Labs., Murray Hill, N.J., 1969; sr. engr. U. Mich., Ann Arbor, 1969-77; sr. scientist Sci. Applications, Inc., Falls

Church, Va., 1977-83; pres. Adroit Systems, Inc., Alexandria, Va., 1983—; cons. holographic optics. Mem. IEEE (sr. mem.), Soc. Automotive Engring., Assn. Computing Machinery, Optical Soc. Am., Soc. Photo-Optical Instrumentation Engrs., Pattern Recognition Soc., Am. Underground Space Assn., Air Force Assn., Sigma Xi. Current Work: Design of large image processing systems using distributed network concepts. Subspecialties: Holography; Graphics, image processing, and pattern recognition. Home: PO Box 6547 Alexandria VA 22306 Office: PO Box 6547 Alexandria VA 22306

LAU, ALBERT MAN-FAI, physicist; b. Hong Kong, Aug. 22, 1947; came to U.S., 1966, naturalized, 1982; s. Kwong Ming and Bik Wah (Lau) L.; m. Winnie Kwok-Yee Siu, June 16, 1971; children—Scott Bokhay, Winita Vinkay. B.S., Yale U., 1970; M.A., U. Calif.-Berkeley, 1972, Ph.D., 1975. Postdoctoral physicist Stanford Research Inst., Menlo Park, Calif., 1975-77; staff physicist Exxon Research and Engring. Co., Linden, N.J., 1977-82; mem. tech. staff Sandia Nat. Labs., Livermore, Calif., 1983—; vis. prof. U. Paris VI, 1979; assoc. prof. Univ. Paris-Sud, Orsay, France, 1980, Univ. d'Orleans, France, 1982. Contbr. articles to profl. jours. Mem. Am. Physical Soc., Phi Beta Kappa. Current work: Laser interaction with atoms and molecules, laser-induced collisions, multiphoton excitations, dissociation and ionization, the photon-as-catalyst effect. Subspecialties: Atomic and molecular physics; Laser-induced chemistry. Office: Sandia Nat Labs Livermore CA 94550

LAU, HENRY, mechanical engineer, consultant; b. Hong Kong, Feb. 4, 1941; s. Mo Ngok and Julia (Ha) L.; m. Bing Sin, June 6, 1970; children—Ryan. B.S., U. Tenn., 1966; M.S., Duke U., 1969, Ph.D., 1973. Research assoc. Duke U., Durham, N.C., 1973-74, Ayres & Hayakawa Energy Mgmt., Los Angeles, 1974-77; tech. dir. Ayres Assocs., Los Angeles, 1977-85; prin. and tech. dir. Ayres, Ezer, Lau Inc., 1985—; Martin Marietta, Los Angeles, 1981, Rockwell Internat., Canoga Park, Calif., 1982, Lawrence Berkeley Lab., Calif., 1978-84. Contbr. articles to profl. jours. Grantee Dow Chem. Co., 1965, ASHRE, 1974, U.S. Army, 1969. Mem. ASHRAE ASME, Sigma Xi. Roman Catholic. Current work: Energy conservation, solar energy, thermal storage, computer simulation, instrumentation systems, load mgmt. Subspecialties: Mechanical engineering; Solar engineering. Home: 1948 Crest Dr Los Angeles CA 90034 Office: Ayres Ezer Lau Inc 1180 S Beverly Dr Los Angeles CA 90035

LAUB, RICHARD JAMES, chemist, educator; b. San Francisco, Aug. 4, 1945; s. Samuel H. and Marie E. (Roumasette) L.; B.S., Regis Coll., 1967; M.S., UCLA, 1971; Ph.D., U. Hawaii, 1974. Postdoctoral researcher U. Waterloo, Ont., Can., 1973, U. Coll. Swansea, Wales, 1974, Sci. Research Council fellow, 1975-78; asst. prof. Ohio State U., Columbus, 1978-82; prof. chemistry San Diego State U., 1982—; cons. Dow Chem. Co., Midland, Mich., 1980-82, Instruments div. IBM, San Jose, Calif., 1980-82, Hoover Universal Plastics, Columbus, 1980-81. Author: Physicochemical Applications of Gas Chromatography, 1978. Contbr. articles to profl. jours. Served with USMC, 1969-71, Vietnam. Grantee NSF, 1979—, Dept. Energy, 1980—, Alcoa, 1983-85, U.S. Air Force, 1984—. Fellow Sigma Xi; mem. Am. Chem. Soc., Royal Soc. Chemistry (chartered). Current work: Separations science; chromatography; nonelectrolyte solutions; thermodynamics; virial effects. Subspecialties: Analytical chemistry; Physical chemistry. Office: Dept Chemistry San Diego State U San Diego CA 92182

LAUBER, JACK DAVID, air pollution control engineer, environmental engineer; b. Yonkers, N.Y., July 14, 1937; s. Benjamin and Elaine (Moskowitz) L.; m. Ruth Meyer, Jan. 12, 1963; children—Evan, Renee. B. Chem. Engring., NYU, 1959. Diplomate Am. Acad. Environ. Engring. Registered profl. engr., N.Y. Asst. engr. N.Y.C. Dept. Air Pollution Control, 1962; indsl. hygiene engr. N.Y. State Dept. Labor, Div. Indsl. Hygiene, 1962-66; sr. san. engr. Bur. Air Quality Control, N.Y. State Dept. Health, Div. Air Resources, Albany, 1966-68; regional air pollution control engr. N.Y. State Dept. Health, N.Y. State Dept. Environ. Conservation, Albany, 1968-71; assoc. air pollution control engr. N.Y. State Dept. Environ. Conservation, Div. Air Resources, Albany, 1971-76; assoc. air pollution control engr., chief toxic materials and effects sect. N.Y. State Dept. Environ. Conservation, Albany, 1976-80; chief toxic tech. devel. sect., assoc. air pollution control engr. spl. projects sect. toxic bur. N.Y. State Dept. Environ. Conservation, Air Div., Albany, 1980—; environ. lectr. to numerous colls. and orgns.; environ. cons. to Israel Ministry of Health, also various orgns. co-author: PCB's in The Environment. Contbr. articles to profl. publs. Mem. Air Pollution Control Assn. (sect. chmn. 1972-73, chmn. solid waste com.), Am. Acad. Environ. Engrs. (multimedia concept group on waste disposal), U.S. Com. for Israel Environment (vice chmn.), Nat. Fedn. Jewish Men's Clubs (regional v.p.). Club: Camera (mem. exec. bd.) (Albany, N.Y.). Lodge: B'nai B'rith. Current work: Expert on best available control technology for resource recovery incineration processes, hazardous waste disposal, incineration technologies, control of industrial process toxic air contaminants. Subspecialties: Environmental engineering; Hazardous waste disposal. Home: 53 Fairlawn Dr Latham NY 12110

LAUBSCHER, ROY EDWARD, astronomer; b. Cleve., May 13, 1944; s. William John and Florence (Huge) L.; m. Mayumi Aono, Dec. 31, 1980. B.S., Case Inst. Tech., 1966; Ph.D. in Astronomy, Yale U., 1970. Analyst Computer Scis. Corp., Silver Spring, Md., 1973-78; sr. analyst Gen. Dynamics Corp., Vandenberg AFB, Calif., 1978-80; mem. prof. staff Geodynamics Corp., Santa Barbara, Calif., 1980—; astronomer Astronomisches Rechen-Institut, Heidelberg, W.Ger., 1970-72. Contbr. articles to profl. jours. Mem. Am. Astron. Soc., German Astron. Soc., Sigma Xi. Current Work: Analysis of satellite geodetic data. Subspecialties: Satellite studies; General relativity. Home: 7321 Padova Goleta CA 93117

LAUDENSLAYER, WILLIAM FRANKLIN, JR., wildlife ecologist; b. Reading, Pa., May 23, 1948; s. William Franklin and Isabel (Tewkesbury) L.; m. Donna Louise Slocum, Aug. 28, 1971; children—Amanda Lynn, Sara Eileen. A.B. in Biology, Eastern Baptist Coll., 1970; M.S. in Biology, No. Ariz. U., 1973; Ph.D. in Zoology, Ariz. State U., 1981. Cert. wildlife biologist; cert. ecologist, Wildlife biologist Bur. Land Mgmt., U.S. Dept. Interior, Riverside, Calif., 1977-80, regional wildlife ecologist forest service U.S. Dept. Agr., San Francisco, 1981—. Editor: Guide to Wildlife Habitats of California, 1985; editor newsletter Western sect. Wildlife Soc., 1982-83, assoc. editor trans., 1983-84. Recipient spl. achievement award, Bur. Land Mgmt., 1981. Mem. Am. Soc. Naturalists, Am. Ornithologists Union, Cooper Ornithol. Soc., Wilson Ornithol. Soc., Am. Soc. Mammalogists, Cactus and Succulent Soc. Am., Calif. Native Plant Soc., Ecol. Soc. Am., Western Field Ornithologists, Heppetologists League, Wildlife Soc. (editor Transactions 1985). Current work: Developing models and other tools to assist in making informed land management decisions. Subspecialties: Ecology (biology); Wildlife management. Home: 105 Names Dr Grass Valley CA 95949 Office: R-5 Tahoe Nat Forest Hwy 49 and Coyote St Nevada City CA 95959

LAUDISE, ROBERT ALFRED, research chemist; b. Amsterdam, N.Y., Sept. 2, 1930; s. Anthony Thomas and Harriette Elizabeth (O'Neil) L.; m. Joyce Elizabeth DeSilvia, Aug. 24, 1957; children: Thomas Michael, Margaret Joyce, John David, Mary Elizabeth, Edward Robert. B.S. in Chemistry, Union Coll., Schenectady, 1952; Ph.D. in Chemistry (A.D. Little fellow), M.I.T., 1956. Mem. Tech. staff Bell Telephone Labs., Murray Hill, N.J., 1956-60, head crystal chemistry research dept., 1960-72, asst. dir. materials research lab., 1972-74, dir. materials research lab., 1974-77, dir. phys. and inorganic chemistry research lab., 1977—; vis. prof. U. Aix, Marseilles, France, 1971, Hebrew U., Jerusalem, 1972, Shandong U., China, 1980; cons. Pres.'s Sci. Com., 1960-64; adv. com. Nat. Bur. Standards, 1970-78; solid state scis. com. NRC, 1977-81; adv. com. NASA, 1977-83. Author: The Growth of Single Crystals, 1970; editor: Jour. Crystal Growth, 1978—; contbr. articles to sci. jours. Recipient Sawyer award, 1974. Fellow Am. Mineral. Soc.; mem. Nat. Acad. Engring., Internat. Orgn. Crystal Growth (pres., award 1981), Am. Assn. Crystal Growth (pres. 1971-77), Am. Chem. Soc., Am. Ceramic Soc., AAAS, Electrochem. Soc., IEEE, Am. Crystall. Soc., Kappa Sigma. Roman Catholic. Clubs: Twin Lakes (Pa.); Sailing. Patentee in field. Current Work: Crystal growth of electronic materials; connection between chemical bonding, structure and useful electronic properties. Subspecialties: Electronic materials; Solid state chemistry. Home: 65 Lenape Ln Berkeley Heights NJ 07922 Office: Bell Telephone Labs 600 Mountain Ave Murray Hill NJ 07974

LAUER, JAMES LOTHAR, chemical physicist, mechanical engineering educator; b. Vienna, Austria, Aug. 2, 1920; came to U.S., 1938, naturalized, 1943; s. Max and Friederike (Rappaport) L.; m. Stefanie D. Blank, Sept. 5, 1955; children—Michael, Ruth. A.B., Temple U., 1942, M.A., 1944; Ph.D., U. Pa., 1948. Scientist, Sun Oil Co., Marcus Hook, Pa., 1944-52, spectroscopist, 1952-64, sr. scientist, 1965-77; research prof. mech. engring. Rensselaer Poly. Inst., Troy, N.Y., 1978-84, prof. mech. engring., 1985—; asst. prof. physics U. Pa., Phila., 1952-55; adj. prof. chemistry U. Del., Newark, 1952-58; postdoctoral fellow U. Calif., San Diego, 1964-65; Coblentz Soc. lectr., Cleve., 1978; cons. Sun Co., Exxon Corp., SKF Inc., Alcan Corp., IBM, 3M Co., Texaco, Torrington Corp. of Ingersoll Rand, Gen. Electric Co., U.S. Navy, NASA. Author: Fourier Transform Infra-red Spectroscopy, 1978. Contbr. numerous articles to profl. jours. Grantee U.S. Air Force, U.S. Navy, NASA. Mem. Penn Wynne Civic Assn., Pa., 1959-77, Country Knolls Civic Assn., Ballston Lake, N.Y., 1978—. Mem. Soc. for Applied Spectroscopy (pres. 1977), Am. Chem. Soc., Am. Phys. Soc., Optical Soc. Am., Spectroscopy Soc. Can. Republican. Jewish. Current work: Tribology, the science of friction and wear, and surface analysis. Subspecialties: Infrared spectroscopy; Surface chemistry. Home: 7 North East Ln Ballston Lake NY 12019 Office: Dept Mechanical Engring Rensselaer Poly Inst Troy NY 12181

LAUGHLIN, ALEXANDER WILLIAM, geologist; b. Hot Springs, Ark., Nov. 9, 1936; s. William Edward and Dorothy Alice (Woodcock) L.; m. Yvonne Odile Corne, Nov. 26, 1959; children—Nicole Yvonne, Deborah Jane, Stephen Edgar. B.Sc., Mich. Technol. U., 1958; M.Sc., U. Ariz., 1960, Ph.D., 1969. Postdoctoral fellow U. Ariz., Tucson, 1969, U. N.Mex., Albuquerque, 1969-70; assoc. prof. geology Kent State U., Ohio, 1970-74; geologist Los Alamos Nat. Lab., 1974—. Contbr. chpts. to books, articles to profl. publs. Bd. dirs. Los Alamos Sportsman Club, 1982-84. Served to lt. USN, 1960-63. Grantee Nat. Geog. Soc., 1973-74. Mem. Geol. Soc. Am., Am. Geophys. Union. Current work: Paleostress in western U.S.A., geothermal geology, geochemistry of alkalic igneous rocks. Subspecialties: Geochemistry; Tectonics. Home: 2336 46th St Los Alamos NM 87544 Office: Los Alamos Nat Lab ESS-1 MSD462 Los Alamos NM 87545

LAURENCE, GEOFFREY CAMERON, biologist; b. Quincy, Mass., Mar. 24, 1943; s. Sidney Frederick and Roslyn (Mignault) L.; div.; children—Robyn, Andrea. B.S., U. Maine, 1965; M.S., Fla. State U., 1967; Ph.D., Cornell U., 1971. Research biologist Bur. Sport Fisheries and Wildlife, Narragansett. R.I., 1970-72; supervisory biologist NOAA/Nat. Marine Fisheries Service, Narragansett, 1972—; mem. working group Internat. Council for Exploration of Sea, 1978—. Contbr. articles to profl. jours. Recipient Spl. Achievement award Nat. Marine Fisheries Service, 1976, Superior Performance award, 1978; gold medal U.S. Dept. Commerce, 1981. Mem. Am. Fisheries Soc. (cert. fisheries scientist; assoc. editor 1983—), Am. Inst. Fisheries Research Biologists, Am. Soc. Limnology and Oceanography. Current work: Ecology and population dynamics of the early life stages of fishes as influenced by environmental and man-induced factors with reference to fisheries management. Subspecialties: Marine biology; Ecosystems analysis. Home: 19B Pier Village Narragansett RI 02882 Office: NOAA/Nat Marine Fisheries Service S Ferry Rd Narragansett RI 02882

LAURENSON, ROBERT MARK, engineer; b. Pitts., Oct. 25, 1938; s. Robert Mark and Mildred Othelia (Frandsen) L.; m. Alice Ann Scroggins, Aug. 26, 1961; children: Susan Elizabeth, Shari Lynn. Student, Drury Coll., 1956-58; B.S., Mo. Sch. Mines, 1961; M.S.E., U. Mich., 1962; Ph.D., Ga. Inst. Tech., 1968. Registered profl. engr., Mo. Dynamics engr. McDonnell Douglas Corp., St. Louis, 1962-64, sr. dynamics engr., 1968-71, group engr., 1971-74, staff engr., 1974-75, tech. specialist, 1975-78, sr. tech. specialist, 1978-81, sect. chief, 1981—; lectr. St. Louis U., 1969-71; adj. assoc. prof. U. Mo.-Rolla, 1980—; participant, session chmn. various confs. and symposia. Contbr. articles, reviewer papers for profl. jours.; editor: 1982 Advances in Aerospace Structures and Materials. NASA tng. grantee. Mem. AIAA (sr., gen. chmn. dynamics specialist conf. 1981), ASME (gen. chmn. conf. 1981, chmn. exec. com. aerospace div. 1983-84, accreditation bd. for engring. and tech. 1985—, planning com. 1986 edn. conf., organizing com. 1986 symposium), Sigma Xi, Pi Tau Sigma, Tau Beta Pi, Phi Kappa Phi, Sigma Phi Epsilon. Current Work: Dynamic analysis of missile and space vehicle structures. Subspecialties: Mechanical engineering; Aerospace engineering and technology. Home: 349 Beaver Lake Dr Saint Charles MO 63303 Office: PO Box 516 Saint Louis MO 63166

LAUTH, ROBERT EDWARD, geologist; b. St. Paul, Feb. 6, 1927; s. Joseph Louis and Gertrude Francis (Stapleton) L.; m. Suzanne Janice Holmes, Apr. 27, 1947; children—Barbara J., Robert E. II, Elizabeth S., Leslie M. Student St. Thomas Coll., 1944; B.A. in Geology, U. Minn., 1952. Geologist Columbian Carbon Co., Houston, 1951-52; dist. geologist Witco Oil and Gas Co., Amarillo, Tex. and Durango, Colo., 1952-55; geologist Reynolds Mining Corp., Durango, 1955; geol. cons., Durango, 1955—; dir. Raisebor, Inc., Durango. Contbr. articles to profl. jours. Served with USNR, 1944-45, PTO. Mem. Four Corners Geol. Soc. (past pres., v.p., treas.), Rocky Mountain Assn. Geologists, Am. Inst. Profl. Geologists, AIME, N.Mex. Geol. Soc., Am. Assn. Petroleum Geologists (So. Colo. communicator 1983—, rep. div. profl. affairs 1983—), Geol. Soc. Am., Soc. Econ. Paleontologists and Mineralogists, N.Y. Acad. Scis., Soc. Econ. Geologists, Explorers Club. Republican. Roman Catholic. Club: Petroleum (Denver). Lodge: Elks. Subspecialties: Geology; Fuels. Home: 2020 Crestview Dr Durango CO 81301 Office: LAMA Corp 555 S Camino del Rio Suite A-4 Durango CO 81301

LAUTZENHEISER, CLARENCE ERIC, research and development institute administrator, metallurgist; b. Lincoln, Nebr., May 21, 1921; s. Delbert L. and Emma (Semler) L.; m. Audrey Aileen Bayliss, Jan. 1, 1948; children: Clarence Eric, John Andrew, Ann. B.S., M.I.T., 1952. Registered profl. engr., Tex., 1961. Flight instr. Moore's Flying Service, Corpus Christi, Tex., 1940-42, Cal-Aero Flight Acad., Ontario, Calif., 1942-43; owner, operator Gulf Coast Flying Service, Kingsville, Tex., 1946-49; with Dow Chem. Co., Freeport, Tex., 1952-62, research engr., 1952-54, maintenance specialist, 1954-62; with S.W. Research Inst., San Antonio, 1962—, dir., 1971-74, v.p. quality assurance systems and engring. div., 1974-85, v.p. emeritus, 1985—; pvt. cons. in field. Contbr. articles to profl. jours. Served to 1st lt. USAAF, 1943-46; to lt. col. USAAFR, 1946-81. Fellow Am. Soc. Nondestructive Testing; mem. Am. Welding Soc., Am. Soc. Metals, Nat. Assn. Corrosion Engrs., ASME (chmn. NDE engring. div. 1984-85, Centennial award 1980). Current Work: Engineering problem solutions through nondestructive testing technologies; structured integrity assessments using nondestructive testing technologies; materials evaluations utilizing destructive and nondestructive testing technologies. Subspecialties: Metallurgical engineering; Systems engineering. Home: Route 1 Box 58 Medina TX 78055 Office: 6220 Culebra Rd San Antonio TX 78238

LAUX, DAVID CHARLES, microbiologist, immunologist, educator; b. Sarver, Pa., Jan. 1, 1945; s. Charles L. and Margaret (Klein) L.; m. Sara E. Pollen; 1 son, Benjamin. B.A., Washington and Jefferson Coll., 1966; M.S., Miami U., Oxford, Ohio, 1968; Ph.D., U. Ariz., 1971. Postdoctoral fellow Pa. State U., 1971-73; faculty U. R.I., 1973—, assoc. prof., 1978-84, prof., 1984—. Contbr. articles to profl. jours. NIH grantee, 1973—. Mem. Am. Assn. Cancer Research, Am. Assn. Immunology, Am. Soc. Microbiology. Current Work: Immunobiology and microbiology. Subspecialties: Immunobiology and immunology; Microbiology. Office: 318 Morrill Microbiology U RI Kingston RI 02881

LAUZON, THOMAS ANDREW, naval officer, naval engineering educator; b. Hackensack, N.J., Oct. 10, 1956. B.S.E.E., U.S. Naval Acad., 1978. Commd. ensign U.S. Navy, 1978, advanced through grades to lt., 1982; asst. engr. in U.S.S. Lafayette, 1980-83; asst. prof. naval sci. Va. Poly. Inst. and State U., Blacksburg, 1980—, mem. reactor safety com., 1984—. Recipient letter of commendation Comdr. Submarine Force Atlantic, 1983. Mem. IEEE, U.S. Naval Inst. Current work: Control systems with applications to nuclear power plants and naval weapons systems. Subspecialties: Nuclear fission; Electrical engineering. Office: Navy ROTC 425 Femoyer Hall Va Poly Inst and State U Blacksburg VA 24061

LAUZZANA, RAYMOND GUIDO, computer scientist; consultant, artist; b. Detroit, Aug. 22, 1941; s. Guido Giovanni and Clara Anna (Baronovski) L.; m. Gail Peterson, 1965 (div. 1972); children—Emile August, Julian Guido. B.Arch., U. Mich., 1965; M.F.A., Calif. Coll. Arts and Crafts, 1971; M.Sc. in Computer Sci., U. Mass., 1976. Research assoc. Geophys. Lab., U.S. Air Force Astronomy Research Facility, Amherst, Mass., 1972-77; computer scientist CALMA Corp., Sunnyvale, Calif., 1978-79; editor Computer Graphics World, San Francisco, 1979-82; v.p. engring. Image Graphix, San Francisco, 1982-84; graphic prodn. mgr. Horizon Software, San Francisco, 1984; mgr. computer graphics facility U. Mass., Amherst 1985—; dir. Onexeno Research, San Francisco, 1981-82; cons. U.S. Library of Congress, McGraw-Hill, Universal Studios, Edison Electric Inst., others; artist, printmaker. Work represented in mus. including Mus. Modern Art, N.Y.C.; exhbn. coordinator Western Assn. Art Mus., Oakland, Library of Congress, Washington, Italian Am. Mus., San Francisco. Mem. Assn. Computing Machinery, Spl. Interest Group in Graphics, IEEE, Optical Soc. Am., Inter Soc. Color Council, Internat. Soc. Artists and Scientists. Republican. Roman Catholic. Current work: Computer graphics, natural scene analysis, natural languages, image semantics, color theory, color semantics, aspects of appearance, image segmentation, graphic expert systems. Subspecialties: Graphics, image processing, and pattern recognition; Artificial intelligence. Office: U Mass Computer Graphics Facility Amherst MA 01020

LAVAIL, MATTHEW MAURICE, researcher, anatomy educator; b. Abilene, Tex., Jan. 7, 1943; s. Matthew Maurice and Edna Chambers (Stevens) LaV.; m. Jennifer Ruth Hart, July 25, 1970; children—Matthew Hart, Katherine Hart. Student So. Methodist U., 1963; B.A., North Tex. State U., 1965; Ph.D., U. Tex., Galveston, 1969. Research fellow in neuropathology Harvard U. Med. Sch., Boston, 1969-73, asst. prof., 1973-76; assoc. prof. anatomy U. Calif.-San Francisco, 1976-82, prof. anatomy and ophthalmology, 1982—, vice chmn. anatomy dept., 1978—; mem. sci. adv. bd. Retinitis Pigmentosa Found. Fighting Blindness, Balt., 1976—. Recipient Fight for Sight citation Fight for Sight, Inc., 1976, Sundial award Retina Found., 1976, Jules Stein Living Tribute award Retinitis Pigmentosa Internat., 1983. Mem. Assn. for Research in Vision and Ophthalmology (sect. chmn. 1976-77, 84—; Friedenwald award 1981), Soc. for Neurosci., Am. Assn. Anatomists, Am. Soc. Cell Biology, Internat. Soc. Eye Research (council 1985—). Current work: Inherited and environmentally induced retinal degenerations; retinal development; photoreceptor-pigment epithelial cell interactions. Subspecialties: Ophthalmology; Cell biology (medicine). Home: 249 Edgewood Ave San Francisco CA 94117 Office: Dept Anatomy Sch Medicine Univ Calif San Francisco CA 94143

LAVERY, JOHN EDWARD, mathematician, educator; b. Columbus, Ohio, Nov. 23, 1945; s. Thomas Francis and Evelyn (Brown) L. Student U. Akron, 1962, U. Cologne, Fed. Republic Germany, 1965-66, U. Würzburg, Fed. Republic Germany, 1966, U. Strasbourg, France, 1966-67; B.A. in Russian, Mich. State U., 1965; M.S. in Math, U. Akron, 1968; Ph.D. in Math, U. Md., 1973. Aerospace technologist NASA Goddard Space Flight Ctr., Greenbelt, Md., 1968-73; assoc. prof. Tunghai U., Taichung, Republic of China, 1973-74, Case Western Res. U., Cleve., 1982—; prof., assoc. prof. Soochow U., Taipei, Republic of China, 1975-79, math. researcher Acad. Scis. of USSR, Novosibirsk, 1979-80, Tech. U. Munich, 1980-82; Chinese and Russian translator Plenum Pub. Corp., N.Y.C., 1975-76; Russian translator Am. Math. Soc., Providence, 1972-76; exchange scientist Acad. Scis. U.S.A. and Czechoslovakia, Brno, 1974, Acad. Scis. U.S.A. and USSR, Novosibirsk, 1979-80. Contbr. numerous articles to profl. jours. Humboldt fellow Alexander von Humboldt Stiftung, 1980-82. Mem. Soc. for Indsl. and Applied Math. Roman Catholic. Clubs: HiRise Ski, Edelweiss Ski, Clevelander Schuhplattler Verein, Cleve. West Road Runners. Current work: Development of numerical methods for the solution of strongly nonlinear partial differential equations, including Navier-Stokes equations, semiconductor problems and nonlinear diffusion. Subspecialties: Applied mathematics; Numerical analysis (mathematics). Home: 13654 Fairhill Rd Apt 304 Shaker Heights OH 44120 Office: Dept of Math and Statistics Case Western Reserve University Cleveland OH 44106

LAVOND, DAVID GERARD, psychobiologist; b. Sacramento, Dec. 21, 1952; s. Raymond Eugene and Dawn Laureen (Rader) L. B.S. magna cum laude, U. Santa Clara, 1975; M.A., Ohio State U., 1976, Ph.D., 1979. Lectr. U. Calif.-Riverside, 1979-80; postdoctoral fellow Stanford U., Calif., 1980-84, research assoc., 1984—. Contbr. articles to profl. jours. Recipient Eagle Scout award Golden Empire council Boy Scouts Am., 1967. Mem. Soc. for Neurosci., Psychonomic Soc. Democrat. Current work; Research on the neural basis of learning and memory in the mammalian brain; effects of aging on learning and memory; recovery of behavorial functioning following injury to the brain. Subspecialties: Psychobiology; Physiological psychology. Office: Dept Psychology Stanford U Bldg 420 Jordan Hall Stanford CA 94305

LAW, HSIANG-YI DAVID, optoelectronics engineer; b. Hong Kong, Feb. 12, 1949; came to U.S., 1969, naturalized, 1978; s. Wan Hei and Yee Hwui (Lin) Lo; m. Ruby Harr Yee, June 16, 1973; 1 son, Jeremy Philbert. B.S.E.E., U. Wash., 1972; M.S.E.E., Cornell U., 1975, Ph.D., 1977. Mem. tech. staff Rockwell Sci. Str., Thousand Oaks, Calif., 1977-80; lab. mgr. TRW Tech. Research Ctr., El Segundo, Calif., 1980-84; v.p. PlessCor Optronics Inc., Chatsworth, Calif., 1984—. Contbr. articles to profl. jours. Patentee monolithic intergrated receiver, 1980. Mem. IEEE (sr. mem.), Am. Phys. Soc., Tau Beta Pi. Current work: III-V Semiconductor, optoelectronics, semiconductor lasers, detectors, semiconductors interface, photovoltaic, material processing, material growth. Subspecialties: Fiber optics; Microchip technology (engineering). Home: 29014 W Saddlebrook Dr Agoura Hills CA 91301 Office: PlessCor Optronics Inc 20200 Sunburst St Chatsworth CA 91311

LAW, KOCK-YEE, chemist; b. Hong Kong, China, Jan. 3, 1952; came to U.S., 1981; s. To and Ching (Lee) Lo; m. Foon-Yee Fung, Aug. 1, 1977; children—Jethro, Alvin. B.Sc., Chinese U., 1974; Ph.D., U. Western Ont., 1978. NRC fellow Xerox Research Ctr of Can., Mississauga, Ont., 1979-81; research scientist Xerox Webster Research Ctr., N.Y., 1981—. Contbr. articles to profl. jours. Mem. Am. Chem. Soc., Inter-Am. Photochem. Soc. (treas. 1984—). Current work: Current research interests are in the areas of design and synthesis of photoconductive squaraines for photoreceptor application and studies of the fundamental properties of squaraines. Subspecialties: Organic chemistry; Photochemistry. Home: 17 Red Post Crescent Fairport NY 14450 Office: Xerox Corp 800 Phillips Rd 0114-39D Webster NY 14580

LAW, STEPHEN LEROY, research chemist, government research administrator; b. Cheyenne Wells, Colo., Apr. 21, 1939; s. Edgar LeRoy and Lucy Ellen (Ault) L.; m. Donna Lee Harris, Apr. 24, 1964; children—Eric, Michael, Christina, Vincent, Teresa, Daniel, Brian, Amanda, Joshua, Jennifer, Kimberly. A.S., Ft. Lewis A&M Coll., 1959; B.S., Ft. Lewis Coll., 1964; M.S., U. Hawaii, 1967; Ph.D., U. Md., 1976. Tchr. pub. high sch., Bayfield, Colo., 1964-65; research and teaching asst. U. Hawaii, Honolulu, 1965-67; research chemist U.S. Bur. Mines, College Park, Md., 1967-81, research supr., Avondale, Md., 1981—, radiation safety officer, College Park, 1971-82. Author: Pocketbook of Calculator Riddles. Contbr. articles to profl. jours., 1967—. Judge various sci. fairs, Washington area; bishop Ch. of Jesus Christ of Latter-Day Saints, College Park, 1977-82, stake pres., 1982—. Dept. Interior LEGIS fellow U.S. Congress, Washington, 1983-84. Mem. Soc. Applied Spectroscopy (Washington area Outstanding Mem. award 1982, 1982 tour speaker), AIME (com. chmn.), Am. Chem. Soc., AAAS. Republican. Current work: Ocean minerals; particulate mineralogy; resources from waste; trace metals determination. Subspecialties: Analytical chemistry; Environmental chemistry. Home: 7925 Hammond Pkwy Laurel MD 20707 Office: US Bur Mines 4900 LaSalle Rd Avondale MD 20782

LAWLER, GEORGE HERBERT, fisheries department administrator, research scientist; b. Kingston, Ont., Can., June 13, 1923; s. William Herbert and Mary Ann (Sexsmith) L., m. Elizabeth Margaret Heffernan, Aug. 2, 1947; children—John, David, Ann, Elizabeth, Jane. B.A., Queen's U., 1946; M.S., U. Western Ont., London, Ont., Can., 1948; Ph.D., U. Toronto, Ont., 1959. Research scientist Fisheries Research Bd. Can., London, Ont., 1950-66; research scientist Freshwater Inst., Winnipeg, Man., Can., 1966-75, dir., 1971-75; dir. gen. Dept. Fisheries and Oceans, Winnipeg, 1975—. Fellow Am. Inst. Fishery Research Biology (sec. 1982—); mem. Am. Fisheries Soc. (chmn. internationalism com. 1982—), Am. Soc. Limnology Oceanography. Royal Lake of Woods Yacht Club. Roman Catholic. Club: Highland Golf and Country. Current work: Administration of region with multi-disciplinary research interests. Subspecialty: Fisheries science. Office: Dept Fisheries Oceans 501 University Crosc Winnipeg MB R3T 2N6 Canada

LAWLER, JAMES EDWARD, physics educator; b. St. Louis, June 29, 1951; s. James Austin and Dolores C. (Krull) L.; m. Katherine Ann Moffatt, July 21, 1973; children—Emily Christine, Catherine Marie. B.S. in Physics, U. Mo.-Rolla, 1973; M.S., U. Wis., 1974, Ph.D., 1978. Research assoc. Stanford U., 1978-80; asst. prof. physics U. Wis., Madison, 1980-85, assoc. prof., 1985—. Contbr. articles to profl. jours. Schlumberger Found. scholar, 1970-73; fellow Wis. Alumni Research Found., 1973-74, NSF, 1974-77. Mem. Am. Phys. Soc., Optical Soc. Am., Sigma Xi. Current work: Physics of gas discharges, laser interactions with gas discharges (optogalvanic effects), laser spectroscopy, laboratory astrophysics. Subspecialties: Atomic and molecular physics; Laser spectroscopy. Office: Dept Physics Univ Wis 1150 University Ave Madison WI 53706

LAWLOR, EVELYN DAVIS, psychologist; b. Hartford, Conn.; d. Frank Wilbert and Adelaide (Byrd) Davis; m. Ignatius E. Lawlor, Aug. 20; 1960; widowed (dec. 1978). R.N., Lincoln Sch. Nursing, 1930; B.S., N.Y.U., 1940, M.A., 1944; M.S.S., New Sch. Social Research, 1953; Ph.D., Yeshiva U., 1960. Diplomate: Am. Bd. Profl. Psychology, Internat. Acad. profl Counseling and Psychotherapy.; Registered psychologist, N.Y. Asst. prof. Yeshiva U., N.Y.C., 1959-61; adj. asst. prof. Queens coll, 1965-74; clin. psychologist B.A.R.O. Clinic, Bklyn., 1954-57; ednl./psychol. cons. Title I Dist. 8, N.Y.C., 1970-71; sch. psychologist Bur. Child Guidance, Bd. Edn., N.Y.C., 1960-70; staff therapist Postgrad. Center for Mental Health, N.Y.C., 1962-76; supr. Postgrad. W., N.Y.C., 1978-80; cons. in field; conductor seminars in field. Recipient Achievement awards Phi Delta Kappa, 1958, 59, 60, 75, 79, 80; Service award P.G.C. for Mental Health, 1972; Grace Humanitarian award Grace Bapt. Ch., 1977; others. Fellow Internat. Council Psychologists; mem. Am. Psychol. Ass., N.Y. Vocational Guidance Assn., Am. Assn. Vocat. Guidance, N.Y. Psychol. Assn., Am. Personnel and Guidance Assn., Am. Group Psychotherapy Assn., Soc. for Clin. and Exptl. Hypnosis, others. Democrat. Presbyterian. Clubs: League Women Voters, Manhood Found, others. Current Work: Hypnosis with symptom of epileploid states - defense stress mgmt. and relaxation; burn out; transcendental meditation; autogenic tng. . Address: 706 S. 6th Ave Mount Vernon NY 10550

LAWRASON, F. DOUGLAS, physician, drug company executive; b. St. Paul, July 30, 1919; s. Joseph F. and Clara (Mueller) L.; m. Elaine J. Wilson, Mar. 18, 1944; children—Peter D., Jock D., Susan E. Student, U. Chgo., 1937-40; B.A., U. Minn., 1941, M.A., 1944; M.D., 1944. Intern, resident, fellow Yale Sch. Medicine and New Haven Hosp., 1944-49; instr., asst. prof. medicine Yale, 1949-53; profl. asso. NRC, 1950-53; asst. prof. medicine, asst. dean Sch. Medicine, U. N.C., 1953-55; prof. medicine, provost U. Ark.; dean U. Ark. Sch. Medicine, 1955-61; exec. dir. med. research Merck Sharp & Dohme Research Labs., West Point, Pa., 1961-66, v.p. med. research, 1966-69; prof. medicine, dean acad. affairs U. Tex. Southwestern Med. Sch., Dallas, 1969-72, dean, 1972-73; sr. v.p. sci. affairs Schering-Plough Corp., 1973-75, pres. research div., 1975-81, sr. v.p. sci., 1981—, also corporate dir. Served with M.C. USNR, 1946-47. Mem. N.Y. Acad. Sci., AAAS, Fedn. for Clin. Research, Nat. Soc. Med. Research (dir. 1981—), Am. Heart Assn., Acad. Hematology, Am. Coll. Cardiology, Sigma Xi. Current Work: Physician (internal medicine, hematology, oncology, chemotherapy) and executive in sciences, mainly in new biotechnology (molecular biology, genetic engineering, etc.). Subspecialties: Internal medicine; Hematology. Home: 53 Spring Valley Rd Convent NJ 07961

LAWRENCE, DAVID A., immunologist; b. Paterson, N.J., Jan. 9, 1945; s. J. Arthur and Doris Helen (Graf) L.; m. Georgia Lawrence, Dec. 29, 1967. A.B., Rutgers U., 1966; M.S., Boston Coll., 1968; Ph.D., 1971. Research fellow Scripps Clinic and Research Found., LaJolla, Calif., 1971-74; mem. faculty dept. microbiology and immunology Albany (N.Y.) Med. Coll., 1974—, assoc. prof., 1977-84, prof., 1984—, assoc. prof. dept. medicine, 1984—, dir. cellular immunology lab., 1984—. Sinsheimer Trust awardee, 1976-78; NIH grantee, 1976—; Am. Cancer Soc. grantee, 1976-78. Mem. Am. Assn. Immunologists, Am. Soc. Microbiologists, N.Y. Acad. Sci. Current Work: Immunotoxicology of heavy metals and chemical carcinogens; reactivities of T-lymphocyte subsets. Subspecialties: Immunobiology and immunology; Immunotoxicology. Office: Dept Microbiology and Immunology Albany Med Coll Albany NY 12208

LAWRENCE, DAVID DELBERT, biomathematician; b. North Tonawanda, N.Y., June 4, 1947; s. Delbert and Louise (Price) L. B.S. in Physics, U. Rochester, 1969; M.S. in Physics, U. Mich., 1972. Cancer research scientist Roswell Park Meml. Inst., Buffalo, 1980—. Contbr. articles to profl. publs. Mem. Assn. Computing Machinery, Am. Phys. Soc., IEEE. Current work: Construction and analysis of databases correlating clinical and laboratory parameters for understanding cancer. Subspecialties: Database systems; Cancer research (medicine). Office: Roswell Park Meml Inst Dept Biomath 666 Elm St Buffalo NY 14263

LAWRENCE, GARY WRIGHT, plant pathologist, technical supervisor; b. Charlotte, N.C., June 24, 1954; s. Ernest Grey and Opal Pauline (Wright) L.; m. Amanda Minix, Nov. 26, 1954. B.A., Greensboro Coll., 1976; M.S., N.C. State U., 1979; Ph.D., La. State U., 1984. Grad. research asst. dept. plant pathology N.C. State U., 1976-78; grad. research asst. dept. plant pathology La. State U., 1979-82; tech. supr. Pennwalt Corp. (AgChem. Div.), Baton Rouge, 1982-85; research nematologist plant pathology dept. Miss. State U., 1985—. Contbr. articles to tech. jours. Mem. Am. Phytopath. Soc., Soc. Nematologists, Gamma Sigma Delta, Beta Iota Omega. Baptist. Current Work: Vegetable crop disease; nematode management; assaying resistance-breaking races of nematodes; nematode population dynamics; pesticide research on agrinomic crops. Subspecialties: Plant pathology; Integrated systems modelling and engineering.

LAWRENCE, HENRY SHERWOOD, physician, educator; b. N.Y.C., Sept. 22, 1916; s. Victor John and Agnes (Whalen) L.; m. Dorothea Wetherbee, Nov. 13, 1943; children—Dorothea, Victor, Geoffrey. A.B., N.Y. U., 1938, M.D., 1943. Diplomate: Am. Bd. Internal Medicine. Mem. faculty N.Y. U. Sch. Medicine, N.Y.C., 1947—, John Wyckoff fellow in medicine, 1948-49, dir. student health, 1950-57, head infectious disease and immunology div., 1959—, prof. medicine, 1961-79, Jeffrey Bergstein prof. medicine, 1979—, co-dir. med. services, 1964—, dir. cancer center, 1974-78; vis. physician Univ. Hosp., Bellevue Hosp., 1964—; cons. medicine Manhattan VA Hosp., 1964—; infectious disease program com. VA Research Service, 1960-63; cons. allergy and immunology study sect. USPHS, 1960-63, chmn., 1963-65; assoc. mem. commn. on streptococcal and staphylococcal diseases Armed Forces Epidemiol. Bd., Dept. Def., 1956-74; mem. coms. Nat. Acad. Scis.-NRC, 1957-65, chmn. com. transplantation, 1963-65; mem. NRC, 1970-72; mem. allergy and infectious disease panel Health Research Council, N.Y.C., 1962-75, co-chmn., 1968-75; mem. sci. adv. council Am. Cancer Soc., 1973-77. Editor: Medical Clinics of North America, 1957, Cellular and Humoral Aspects of Hypersensitive States, 1959, (with M. Landy) Mediators of Cellular Immunity, 1969; (with Kirkpatrick and Burger) Immunobiology of Transfer Factor, 1983. Editorial bd.: Transplantation, Ann. of Internal Medicine; founder, editor-in-chief: Cellular Immunology. Served to lt. M.C. USNR, World War II. Commonwealth Found. fellow Univ. Coll., London, Eng., 1959; recipient Research Career Devel. award USPHS, 1960-65; prize Alpha Omega Alpha, 1943; Meritorious Sci. Achievement award N.Y. U. Alumni Assn., 1970; von Pirquet Gold medal Ann. Forum on Allergy, 1972; award A.C.P., 1973; Sci. Achievement award Am. Coll. Allergists, 1974; Sci. medal N.Y. Acad. Medicine, 1974; Bristol Sci. award Infectious Diseases Soc. Am., 1974; Charles V. Chapin medal, 1975; Lila Gruber honor award Am. Acad. Dermatology, 1975; Alumni Achievement award N.Y. U. Washington Sq. Coll., 1979. Fellow A.C.P. (Bronze medal 1973), Am. Acad. Allergy (hon.), Royal Coll. Physicians and Surgeons Glasgow (hon.); mem. Nat. Acad. Scis., Assn. Am. Physicians, Am. Soc. for Clin. Investigation, Am. Assn. Immunologists, Soc. for Exptl. Biology and Medicine (editorial bd. procs.), Interurban Clin. Club, Harvey Soc. (sec. 1957-60, lectr. 1973—, councillor 1974-77), Peripatetic Clin. Soc., Infectious Diseases Soc. (charter, councillor 1970-72), Royal Soc. Medicine (affiliate) (Eng.), Internat. Transplantation Soc. (chmn. constn. com., councillor), Société Française d'Allergie (corr.), Alpha Omega Alpha. Research, publs. on characterization transfer factor in cellular immunity, mechanisms tissue damage and homograft rejection in man. Current Work: Characterization and purification of antigen specific inducer factor and suppressor factor in lymphocyte dialysates containing transfer factor. Subspecialties: Infectious diseases; Transplantation. Home: 343 E 30th St New York NY 10016

LAWRENCE, MERLE, medical educator; b. Remsen, N.Y., Dec. 26, 1915; s. George William and Alice Rutherford (Bowne) L.; m. Roberta Ashby Taylor Harper, Aug. 8, 1942; children—Linda Alice, Roberta Harper Lawrence Henderson, James Bowne. A.B., Princeton, 1938, M.A., 1940, Ph.D., 1941. NRC fellow Johns Hopkins Hosp., 1941, asst. prof. psychology, Princeton, 1946-50, assoc. prof., 1950-52; assoc. research Lempert Inst. Otology, N.Y.C., 1946-52; asso. prof. dept. otolaryngology U. Mich. Med. Sch., 1952-57, prof. otolaryngology, 1957-85; research assoc. Inst. Indsl. Health, 1952-85; prof. psychology U. Mich. Coll. Lit. Sci. and Arts, 1957-85, prof. emeritus, 1985—; dir. Kresge Hearing Research Inst., 1961-84; mem. Nat. Adv. Neurol. and Communicative Disorders and Stroke Council, 1976-79; mem. communicative disorders research tng. com. Nat. Inst. Neurol. Diseases and Blindness, 1961-65; mem. communicative scis. study sect. div. research grants NIH, 1965-69, chmn., 1967-69, mem. communicative disorders rev. com., 1972-76. Served as naval aviator USNR, 1941-46, 50-51, PTO; Served as naval aviator USNR, Korean conflict, PTO. Decorated Purple Heart, Air medal with nine gold stars; recipient Sec. Navy Commendation, award merit Am. Acad. Ophthalmology and Otolaryngology, 1965, award merit Assn. Research in Otolaryngology, 1979, award merit Am. Otol. Soc., 1967, Distinguished Service award Princeton Class of 1938.; NRC fellow, 1941. Fellow Am. Laryngol., Rhinol. and Otolaryngol. Soc.; mem. AAAS, Acoustical Soc. Am., Mich. Acoustical Soc. (pres. 1956), Am. Acad. Ophthalmology and Otolaryngology, Am. Otol. Soc., Collegium Oto-Rhino-Laryngologicum Amicitiae Sacrum, Soc. U. Laryngologists, Assn. Research Otolaryngology, Am. Auditory Soc. (council 1978-82), Am. Tinnitus Assn., Quarter Century Wireless Assn. Clubs: Rotary (pres. 1978-79), Centurion, Mich. Masters Swim. Current Work: Auditory physiology especially micro circulation of blood and lymph in the ear. Subspecialties: Neurophysiology; Sensory processes. Home: 2029 Vinewood Blvd Ann Arbor MI 48104

LAWRENCE, WILLIAM THOMAS, JR., plant ecophysiologist, ecologist; b. San Fernando, Calif., Jan. 11, 1949; s. William Thomas and June Margarite (Couchey) L.; m. Mercedes Quiroga, Apr. 3, 1975. B.A., U. Calif.-Santa Barbara, 1970; M.S., San Diego State U., 1975; Ph.D., U. Calif.-Davis and San Diego State U., 1983. Asst. prof. Catholic U., Santiago, Chile, 1973-74; research assoc. San Diego State U., 1975-79; research scientist Ctr. Energy and Environ. Research, San Juan, P.R., 1983—. Contbr. articles to profl. jours. and books. Mem. Am. Soc. Plant Physiologists, Assn. Tropical Biology, Ecol. Soc. Am. (vice chmn. internatl. affairs 1984—), AAAS, Internatl. Assn. Ecology. Current work: Plant ecophysiology in general, currently that of the tropical rainforest, photoinhibition, soil respiration, atmospheric CO2 enhancement, carbon balance, microclimate. Subspecialties: Ecology (biology); Photosynthesis. Office: Ctr Energy and Environment Research GPO Box 3682 San Juan PR 00936

LAWSON, DAVID F., research chemist; b. Chgo., June 24, 1945; s. Wilson Charles and Lillian M. (Kolar) L.; m. Nel Walker, 1985; children—Amy Nicole, David Andrew. B.A. in Chemistry, Lewis U., 1967; Ph.D. in Organic Chemistry, Iowa State U., 1971. Instr. in chemistry Iowa State U., Ames, 1969; research scientist Central Research Labs, Firestone Tire and Rubber Co., Akron, Ohio, 1970-75, sr. research scientist, 1975-81, assoc. scientist, 1982—. Contbr. articles to profl. jours and book. Patentee polymers, flame retardants. Mem. Community Council, Uniontown, Ohio, 1978. NDEA fellow Iowa State U., 1967-68; Mobil summer fellow Iowa State U., 1969. Mem. Am. Chem. Soc., Adhesion Soc. Current work: Adhesion and surface modification of polymers, polymer combustion and flammability, polymer-organic chemistry. Subspecialties: Organic chemistry; Polymer chemistry. Office: Central Research Labs Firestone Tire & Rubber Co 1200 Firestone Pkwy Akron OH 44317

LAWSON, EDWARD EARLE, neonatologist, educator; b. Winston-Salem, N.C., Aug. 6, 1946; s. Robert Barrett and Elsie Chatterton (Earle) L.; m. Rebecca Fitts, June 21, 1969; children—Katherine Tabor, Robert Barrett. B.A., Harvard U., 1968; M.D., Northwestern U., 1972. Intern Children's Hosp. Med. Ctr., Boston, 1972-73, resident in pediatrics, 1973-75; fellow in neonatology Harvard Med. Sch., Boston, 1975-78, instr. Harvard U., Boston, 1977-78; asst. prof. dept. pediatrics, U. N.C., Chapel Hill, 1978-82, assoc. prof., 1982—; chmn. research grants com. Am. Lung Assn., N.Y.C., 1982-85. Contbr. numerous articles to sci. jours. Sidney Farber Meml. Research award United Cerebral Palsy, 1982, Research Career Devel. award NIH, 1982—. Fellow Am. Acad. Pediatrics; mem. Am. Thoracic Soc., Am. Physiol. Soc., Soc. Pediatric Research. Current work: Neurobiological aspects of control of breathing in newborns. Subspecialties: Physiology (medicine); Neonatology. Office: Dept Pediatrics 509 Burnett Womack Bldg U NC Chapel Hill NC 27514

LAWSON, KENNETH ROBERT, chemical company executive; b. San Francisco, Apr. 18, 1936; s. Win and Thelma Florence (Surguine) L.; m. Barbara Jean Wunch, Oct. 23, 1954; children—Lucinda, Celeste, Esther. B.S. in Chemistry, U. Calif.-Berkeley, 1958; M.B.A., Ill. Benedictine Coll., 1977. Chemist DeSoto, Inc., Berkeley, Calif., 1958-62, group leader, 1962-65, adminstrv. mgr., 1965-74, market devel. mgr., 1975-83, new ventures mgr., Des Plaines, Ill., 1984—. Contbr. articles to profl. jours. Mem. Assn. Finishing Processes of Soc. Mfg. Engrs. (pres. 1982-84, chmn. radiation curing div.), Optical Soc. Am., Fedn. Coating Socs. (Golden Gate chpt. tech. com. chmn. 1963-65). Republican. Current work: Manages programs in radiation curing of polymers for optical fiber telecommunications and optical and magnetic recording. Subspecialties: Polymers (materials science); Polymer engineering. Office: DeSoto Inc 1700 Mt Prospect Rd Des Plaines IL 60018

LAWSON, WILLIAM BRADFORD, psychiatry researcher, hospital administrator; b. Richmond, Va., Nov. 27, 1945; s. Thomas Henry and Violet Serena (Ronane) L.; m. Rosemary Jackson, Aug. 6, 1983. B.S., Howard U., 1966; M.A., U. Va., 1969; Ph.D., U. N.H., 1972; M.D., U. Chgo., 1978. Diplomate Am. Bd. Psychiatry and Neurology. Asst. prof. psychology U. Ill., Urbana, 1971-73; intern Stanford U. Med. Ctr., Calif., 1979-80, resident, 1980-81; clin. research fellow NIMH, Washington, 1981-84; research dir. Met. State Hosp., Norwalk, Calif., 1984—; asst. prof. psychiatry U. Calif., Irvine, 1984—. Contbr. articles to profl. jours. Chmn. bd. dirs. Hillcrest Children's Ctr., Washington, 1984; bd. dirs. D.C. Mental Health Assn., 1984. Recipient research fellow Chgo. Diabetic Soc., Am. Psychiatric Assn. minority fellow; Service award Alcohol, Drug Abuse and Mental Health Assn. Mem. Black Psychiatrists Am. (v.p. 1982-84), Assn. Black Psychologists (chpt. pres. 1984—), Am. Psychiat. Assn., Soc. Neuroscis., AMA, Omega Psi Phi. Democrat. Baptist. Current work: Racial issues mental health diagnosis and treatment; eating and drinking behavior; biological mechanisms, schizophrenia. Subspecialties: Psychopharmacology; Psychobiology. Home: 12300 4th St #100 Norwalk CA 90650 Office: Met State Hosp 11400 S Norwalk Blvd Norwalk CA 90650

LAWTON, RICHARD GRAHAM, organic chemistry educator, researcher; b. Berkley, Aug. 29, 1934; s. John Hoxie and Dorothy (Hoffman) L.; m. Anne Bender, June 14, 1958; children—Stephen, John, Eric, David, Deborah. B.S. in Chemistry, U. Calif.-Berkeley, 1956; Ph.D. in Organic Chemistry, U. Wis.-Madison, 1962. Chemist, Merck Research, Rahway, N.J., 1956-57; grad. asst. U. Wis.-Madison, 1959-62; prof. organic chemistry U. Mich., Ann Arbor, 1962—; cons. in field. Served with U.S. Army, 1957-59. Guggenheim fellow, 1978-79; Academic Partnerships fellow, 1983. Mem. Am. Chem. Soc., AAAS. Current work: Bioorganic chemistry; peptide and protein reagents; cross-linking reagents and selective cleavage reagents. Subspecialties: Organic chemistry; Biochemistry (biology). Home: 2888 Daleview Dr Ann Arbor MI 48103 Office: U Mich Chemistry Dept Ann Arbor MI 48109

LAX, BENJAMIN, physicist, physics educator; b. Miskolz, Hungary, Dec. 29, 1915; came to U.S., 1926, naturalized, 1940; s. Louis and Amelia (Grosswirth) L.; m. Blossom Cohen, Feb. 11, 1942; children—Daniel, Robert. B.S., Cooper Union, 1941; Ph.D., MIT, 1949; Sc.D. (hon.), Yeshiva U., 1975. Radar officer MIT Radiation Lab., Cambridge, 1944-46; staff mem. Air Force Cambridge Research Ctr., 1946-51, MIT Lincoln Lab., 1951-53, head Ferrites group, 1953-55, head solid state group, 1955-57, assoc. head communications div., 1957-58, head solid state div., 1958-74, assoc. dir. lab., 1964-65, dir. Francis Bitter Nat. Magnet Lab., 1960-81, prof. physics, 1965—; dir. Infrared Inds., Cambridge, 1973-76, Barnes Engring Co., Stamford, Conn., 1978—; cons. in field. Assoc. editor Jour. Applied Physics, 1957-59, Microwave Jour., 1960-63, Phys. Rev., 1960-63. Sr. contbg. editor Laser Focus, 1981-83. Contbr. articles to profl. jours. Patentee in field. Author: (with others) Microwave Ferrites and Ferrimagnetics, 1962. Co-editor: High Magnetic Fields, 1962; Physics of Quantum Electronics, 1966. Mem. adv. com. Am. Friends of Jerusalem Coll. Tech., 1982-83. Served to capt. USAF, 1943-46. Recipient Cooper Union Disting. Profl. Achievement award, 1964; Citation Outstanding Achievement USAF, 1965; Gano Dunn medal, Cooper Union, 1965; Outstanding Achievement award USAF Office Aerospace Research, 1970; Guggenheim fellow, 1981. Fellow Am. Acad. Arts and Scis., Am. Phys. Soc. (exec. com. 1963-67, Buckley Price award 1960), Optical Soc. Am., AAAS; mem. Nat. Acad. Scis., N.Y. Acad. Scis., Sigma Xi, Tau Beta Pi. Current work: Theoretical and experimental research on nonlinear effects on solids and plasmas, interaction of submillimeter radiation with plasmas and solids, laser produced plasmas, semiconductors and ferrites, radaraand millimeter waves. Subspecialties: Condensed matter physics; Semiconductor lasers. Home: 25 Audubon Dr Chestnut Hill MA 02167 Office: MIT Francis Bitter Nat Magnet Lab 170 Albany St Room NW14-4104 Cambridge MA 02139

LAX, PETER DAVID, mathematics educator; b. Budapest, Hungary, May 1, 1926; came to U.S., 1941, naturalized, 1944; s. Henry and Klara (Kornfeld) L.; m. Anneli Cahn, 1948; children: John, James D. B.A., N.Y. U., 1947, Ph.D., 1949; D.Sc. (hon.), Kent State U., 1976; D. honoris causa, U. Paris, 1979. Asst. prof. N.Y. U., 1949-57, prof., 1957—; dir. Courant Inst. Math. Scis., 1972-80. Author: (with Ralph Phillips) Scattering Theory, 1967, Scattering Theory for Automorphic Functions, 1976, (with A. Lax and S.Z. Burstein) Calculus with applications and computing), 1976, Hyperbolic Systems of Conservation Laws and the Mathematical Theory of Shock Waves, 1973. Mem. Pres.'s Com. on Nat. Medal of Sci., 1976, Nat. Sci. Bd., 1980-86. Served with AUS, 1944-46. Recipient Semmelweis medal Semmelweis Med. Soc., 1975. Mem. Am. Math. Soc. (pres. 1979-80, Norbert Wiener prize), Nat. Acad. Scis. (applied math. and numerical analysis award 1983), Am. Acad. Arts and Scis., Math. Assn. Am. (bd. govs., Chauvenet prize), Soc. Indsl. and Applied Math.; fgn. asso. Académie des Scis. (France). Subspecialties: Numerical analysis (computer science); Applied mathematics. Home: 300 Central Park W New York NY 10024 Office: 251 Mercer St New York NY 10012

LAXER, CARY, computer science educator; b. Bklyn., July 16, 1955; s. Stanley and Harriet (Greenbaum) L. B.A., N.Y.U., 1976; Ph.D., Duke U., 1980. Research asst. prof. computer engring. Duke U., Durham, N.C., 1980-81; asst. prof. computer sci. and elec. engring. Rose-Hulman Inst. Tech., Terre Haute, Ind., 1981-84, assoc. prof. computer sci. and elec. engring., 1984—. Mem. Big Bros., Durham County Social Services, Durham, N.C., 1976-81, Big Bros./Sisters Vigo County, Terre Haute, Ind., 1981—; religious sch. tchr. United Hebrew Congregation, Terre Haute, 1982-84. Mem. IEEE, Assn. Computing Machinery, Biomed. Engring. Soc., Am. Soc. Engring. Edn. (sect. treas. Ind./Ill. sect. 1982-83), AAUP. Jewish. Current Work: Computer analysis of cardiac electrical potentials to determine presence of myocardial disease. Subspecialty: Biomedical engineering. Home: 17 Greywing Ct Terre Haute IN 47803 Office: Rose-Hulman Inst Tech 5500 Wabash Ave Terre Haute IN 47803

LAY, KENNETH WILBUR, ceramist; b. Mount Ayr, Iowa, Feb. 4, 1939; s. Wilbur Lee and Madelyn (Keplinger) L.; m. Anita Rollins, Mar. 21, 1964; children—Douglas, Marla, Kathleen. B.S. in Chem., Iowa State U., 1961; Ph.D. in Materials Sci., Northwestern U., 1966. Ceramist Gen. Electric Corp. Research and Devel. Ctr., Schenectady, 1965-73, mgr. communications and admin., 1973-75, mgr. ceramics processing unit, 1975—. Editor: Fundamental Property of Nuclear Fuel Assemblies, 1969; Processing of Metal and Ceramic Powders, 1982. Contbr. articles to tech. jours. Patentee nuclear fuel. Fellow Am. Ceramic Soc. Current work: Ceramic processing and properties. Subspecialty: Ceramics. Office: Gen Electric Corp Research and Devel PO Box 8 Schenectady NY 12301

LAY, MING-MUH, plant biochemist, researcher; b. Chiayi, Taiwan, China, Nov. 30, 1941, came to U.S., 1968; s. Ho-tan and Puh-tsan (Loh) L.; m. Li-chu Hung, June 12, 1968; children—Betty F.S., Cynthia Y.F. B.S., Nat. Taiwan U., Taipei, 1965, M.S., 1968; Ph.D., Rutgers U., 1973. Research scientist U. Calif.-Berkeley, 1973-75; sr. research biochemist Stauffer Chem. Co., Richmond, Calif., 1975—. Contbr. articles to profl. jours. Mem. Am. Chem. Soc., Am. Soc. Plant Physiologists, Weed Sci. Soc. Am. Current work: Mode of action and metabolism of pesticides in plants and animals; plant physiology and biochemistry; design biochemical assays. Subspecialties: Plant physiology (agriculture); Biochemistry (biology). Home: 1050 Rudgear Rd Walnut Creek CA 94596 Office: Stauffer Chem Co 1200 S 47th St Richmond CA 94804

LAYCHOCK, SUZANNE GALE, pharmacologist, educator; b. N.Y.C., Apr. 28, 1949. B.S., Bklyn. Coll., 1971; Ph.D., Med. Coll. Va., 1976. Research assoc. Vanderbilt U., Nashville, 1977-78; asst. prof. pharmacology Med. Coll. Va., Richmond, 1978-85, assoc. prof., 1985—; organizer, advisor Math. and Sci. Ctr., Richmond, 1979—; NIH new investigator, 1979. Mem. Am. Soc. Pharmacology and Exptl. Therapeutics, Am. Diabetes Assn. Current work: Insulin secretion, phospholipids, cyclic nucleotides, calcium, phospholipases. Subspecialties: Cellular pharmacology; Endocrinology. Office: Med Coll of Va Box 524 Dept Pharmacology Richmond VA 23298

LAYCOCK, WILLIAM ANTHONY, range management educator, researcher; b. Fort Collins, Colo., Mar. 17, 1930; s. John and Caroline (Freudenthal) L.; m. Charlotte Elizabeth Pulscher, June 19, 1955; children—Cody, Donice. B.S., U. Wyo., 1952, M.S., 1953; Ph.D., Rutgers U., 1958. Range scientist U.S. Forest Service, Dubois, Idaho, 1958-61, Provo, Utah, 1961-64, Logan, Utah, 1964-74; asst. dir. Rocky Mt. Exptl. Sta., Fort Collins, 1974-76; research leader U.S. Dept. Agr. Agrl. Research Service, Ft. Collins, 1976-85; head dept. range mgmt. U. Wyo., Laramie, 1985—; coordinating site dir. U.S. Internat. Biol. Program, Seattle, 1972. Contbr. articles to profl. jours. Served to 1st lt. U.S. Army, 1953-55; Korea. New Zealand Nat. Resource Adv. Council fellow, 1969-70. Fellow Soc. Range Mgmt. (dir. 1978-81); mem. Ecol. Soc. Am. (cert. sr. ecologist, council 1980-82). Current work: Ecology and management of arid and semi-arid rangelands. Subspecialties: Range management; Resource conservation. Office: Univ Wyo Dept Range Mgmt Box 3354 Univ Sta Laramie WY 82071

LAYDON, JAMES ROBERT, mechanical engineer; b. Iron Mountain, Mich., Aug. 7, 1957; s. Gordon Roy and Delores Rosemary (Rubbo) L.; m. Melany Elizabeth Applin, Aug. 6, 1977; children—Ashlie Elizabeth, Adam James. B.S., Lake Superior State Coll., 1979; M.B.A., Calif. Poly. U., Pomona, 1985. Chief engr. Eagle Tool Co., Iron Mountain, 1979-81, Pioneer Broach Co., Los Angeles, 1981-84; pres. Laydon Tech., Inc., Glendora, Calif., 1984—. Mem. Am. Soc. Mfg. Engrs., Am. Soc. Metals, ASME, Delta Mu Delta. Republican. Roman Catholic. Current work: broachability of ferrous and non-ferrous materials. Subspecialties: Mechanical engineering; Solar engineering. Home: 2329 Greenview Dr Glendora CA 91740 Office: Laydon Tech Inc PO Box 1608 Glendora CA 91740

LAYNE, JAMES NATHANIEL, biologist, mammalogist, research administrator; b. Chgo., May 16, 1926; s. Leslie Joy and Harriet Barbara (Hausman) L.; m. Lois Virginia Linderoth, Aug. 26, 1950; children—Linda Carrie, Kimberly, Jamie Linderoth, Susan Nell, Rachel Pratt. Student, Chgo. City Jr. Coll., 1946-47; B.A., Cornell U., 1950, Ph.D., 1954. Grad. asst. Cornell U., 1950-54; asst. prof. zoology So. Ill. U., 1954-55; asst. prof. biology U. Fla.-Gainesville, 1955-59, assoc. prof. biology, 1959-63; assoc. prof. zoology Cornell U., 1963-67; dir. research Archbold Biol. Sta., Lake Placid, Fla., 1967-76, exec. dir., 1976-85, sr. research biologist, 1976—; cons. WHO, 1969; adj. prof. biol. sci. Fla. Atlantic U., 1980—; adj. prof. zoology U. South Fla., 1968—. Contbr. numerous articles to sci. jours., chpts. to books on life history, ecology, morphology and behavior of mammals and other vertebrates. Served with USAAF, 1944-46. Fellow AAAS; mem. Am. Soc. Mammalogists (pres. 1970-72, C. Hart Merriam award 1976), Fla. Acad. Scis. (pres. 1984-85), Orgn. Biol. Field Stas. (v.p. 1984-85). Current work: Life history and ecology of Florida mammals and other vertebrates. Subspecialties: Behavioral ecology; Species interaction. Home: PO Box 1022 Lake Placid FL 33852 Office: Archbold Biol Sta PO Box 2057 Lake Placid FL 33852

LAZAR, NORMAN H(ENRY), physicist, researcher; b. Bklyn., June 21, 1929. B.S., CCNY, 1949, M.S., 1951; Ph.D., Ind. U., 1953. Physicist Oak Ridge Nat. Lab., 1953-78; sr. scientist TRW, Redondo Beach, Calif., 1978—. Fellow Am. Phys. Soc., AAAS. Subspecialties: Plasma physics; Fusion. Office: TRW One Space Park Redondo Beach CA 90278

LAZARUS, ALLAN K., chemist, educator; b. Bangor, Maine, May 20, 1931; s. Julius E. and Ruth (Hecht) L.; m. Gloria Berkowitz, Dec. 24, 1957; children: Carol R., Martin C., Warren R. B.A., N.Y.U., 1952, M.S., 1955, Ph.D., 1957. Group leader Cities Service Research & Devel. Co., Cranbury, N.J., 1957-59; chemist FMC Corp., Princeton, 1959-65, Esso Research & Enging. Co., Linden, N.J., 1965-66; group leader Tenneco Chems. Inc., Piscataway, N.J., 1966-71; asst. prof. chemistry Trenton (N.J.) State Coll., 1972—. Contbr. articles to profl. jours. Allied Chem. and Dye Corp. fellow, 1956. Mem. Am. Chem. Soc., Phi Beta Kappa, Sigma Xi, Phi Lambda Upsilon. Patentee in field. Current Work: Synthesis of high-molecular-weight monomeric esters of potential utility as base fluids for synthetic lubricating oils and greases. Subspecialties: Organic chemistry; Synthetic lubricants. Home: 149 Lawrenceville Rd Lawrenceville NJ 08648 Office: Dept Chemistry Trenton State Coll CN 550 Ewing Township NJ 08625

LAZARUS, ARNOLD ALLAN, clinical psychologist, educator; b. Johannesburg, South Africa, Jan. 27, 1932; came to U.S., 1966, naturalized, 1976; s. Benjamin and Rachel Leah (Mosselson) L.; m. Daphne Ann Kessel, June 10,

1956; children: Linda Sue, Clifford Neil. B.A. with honors, U. Witwatersrand, Johannesburg, 1956, M.A., 1957, Ph.D., 1960. Diplomate: Am. Bd. Profl. Psychology. Pvt. practice clin. psychology, South Africa, 1959-63; vis. asst. prof. dept. psychology Stanford U., 1963-64; prof. psychology Temple U. Med. Sch., 1967-70; dir. clin. tng. Yale U., 1970-72; disting. prof. psychology Rutgers U., New Brunswick, N.J., 1972—; founder Multimodal Therapy Inst., N.J., Ill., N.Y., Pa., Ohio, Va.; pvt. practice psychotherapeutics, Princeton, N.J., cons. in field. Author: 10 books including Behavior Therapy and Beyond, 1971; Multimodal Behavior Therapy, 1976, The Practice of Multimodal Therapy, 1981; Casebook of Multimodal Therapy, 1985; Marital Myths, 1985; editorial bd. profl. jours.; contbr. articles to profl. jours. Recipient Disting. Service award Am. Bd. Profl. Psychology. Fellow Am. Psychol. Assn.; mem. Am. Orthopsychiat. Assn., Nat. Acads. of Practice, Am. Acad. Psychotherapy, Assn. Advancement Behavior Therapy (past pres.), Assn. Advancement Psychotherapy., Internat. Acad. Profl. Counseling and Psychotherapy (diplomate). Current Work: Discovering rapid and durable methods of psychotherapy in the traeatment of anxiety, depression and marital family discord. Subspecialties: Behavioral psychology; Cognition. Home: 56 Herrontown Circle Princeton NJ 08540 Office: Psychology Bldg Busch Campus Rutgers Univ New Brunswick NJ 08903

LAZARUS, STEVEN, pharmaceutical company executive; b. May 31, 1931; married, 3 children. A.B., Dartmouth Coll. with honors in English Lit., 1952; M.B.A., Harvard Grad. Sch. Bus. Adminstrn., 1965. Exec. asst. to asst. Sec. of Def., Office Sec. Def., 1965-69; dep. asst. sec. commerce for internat. planning U.S. Dept. Commerce, 1972, dept. asst. sec. commerce for East-West trade, 1972-74; exec. v.p. internat. div. Baxter Travenol Labs., Inc., 1974-75, pres. artificial organs div., 1975-78, v.p., 1978-81, sr. v.p., Deerfield, Ill., 1974—; lectr. mgmt. control systems Harvard U. Grad. Sch. Bus. Adminstrn., George Washington U., Indsl. Coll. Armed Forces, others. Author: Resolving Business Disputes; The Future of Commercial Arbitration, 1965. Contbr. articles to profl. jours. Mem. Council on Fgn. Relations, N.Y.C., Chgo., mem. exec. bd. Com. on Fgn. Affairs; mem. spl. study group on East-West Trade, Atlantic Council of U.S.; mem. Bd. Edn., Glencoe, Ill.; chmn. Village Elections Com., Glencoe, Ill.; dir. Am. Arbitration Assn., 1975-76. . Address: Baxter Travenol Labs Inc 1 Baxter Pkwy Deerfield IL 60015

LAZER, EDWARD STEPHEN, medicinal chemist; b. Hartford, Conn., Sept. 19, 1951; s. Philip and Bessie S.; m. Joan Lazer, June 16, 1974; 1 child, Molly Ellen. B.A., Clark U., 1973; Ph.D., U. Conn., 1978. Lectr., U. Conn.-Storrs, 1976; postdoctoral fellow Schering Corp., Bloomfield, N.J., 1978-80; research scientist Clairol Inc., Stamford, Conn., 1980-81; sr. chemist Boehringer Ingelheim Pharms., Inc., Ridgefield, Conn., 1981-85, prin. chemist, 1985—. Contbr. articles to tech. jours. Mem. Am. Chem. Soc., Sigma Xi, Phi Kappa Phi, Rho Chi. Current work: Design and synthesis of disease modifying anti-rheumatic drugs; allergy and CNS fields; drug design QSAR. Subspecialties: Medicinal chemistry; Drug design. Home: 280 Beacon Hill Rd Trumbull CT 06611 Office: Boehringer Ingelheim Pharms Inc 90 East Ridge PO Box 368 Ridgefield CT 06877

LAZICKI-LAKSHMANAN, FLORENCE MARY, chemist; b. N.Y.C., Nov. 20, 1928; d. Charles Stanley and Lillian Mary (Svekus) Lazicki; m. Sitarama Lakshmanan, Dec. 27, 1952 (div. Nov. 1978); children—Mark, Monica, Carl, Linus, Joseph, Leela Ann. B.S., Coll. Mt. St. Vincent, 1950; Ph.D., U. Md., 1958. Research chemist Beltsville Human Nutrition Research Ct., Agrl. Research Service, U.S. Dept Agr., Md., 1958—. Contbg. author chpts. in book, 1981. Mem. Am. Chem. Soc., Am. Inst. Nutrition, N.Y. Acad. Sci., Sigma Xi, Sigma Delta Epsilon. Democrat. Roman Catholic. Current work: Lipid carbohydrate protein nutrition using the rat; amino acid protein mineral requirements of adults children bone status. Subspecialties: Nutrition (medicine); Biochemistry (medicine). Home: 1604 Palace Ln Bowie MD 20716 Office: Energy Protein Nutrition Lab Bldg 308 Room 205 BARC East Beltsville MD 20705

LAZO, JOHN STEPHEN, pharmacology educator, scientist; b. Phila., Dec. 15, 1948; s. John and Mildred Doris (Popowich) L.; m. Jacqui Lynne Fiske, Oct. 12, 1974; 1 dau., Jacquelyn Kristina Fiske. A.B. in Chemistry, Johns Hopkins U., 1971; Ph.D. in Pharmacology, U. Mich., 1976. USPHS-NIH predoctoral research trainee dept. pharmacology U. Mich., Ann Arbor, 1971-76; Am. Cancer Soc. postdoctoral fellow, dept. pharmacology Yale U. Sch. Medicine, New Haven, 1976-78, asst. prof., 1978-83, assoc. prof., 1983—. Author: (with A.C. Startorelli and J.R. Bertino) Molecular Actions and Targets for Cancer Chemotherapeutic Agents, 1981, (with P.S. Dannies and J. W. Kozarich) Pharmacology: Pretest Self-Assessment and Review; contbr. numerous articles on pharmacology to profl. jours. NIH fellow, 1978. Mem. N.Y. Acad. Scis., Am. Soc. for Pharmacology and Exptl. Therapeutics, AAAS, Am. Assn. Cancer Research, Tissue Culture Assn. Current Work: Pharmacology of anticancer agents, cancer, drugs, biochemical, treatment. Subspecialties: Pharmacology; Cancer research (medicine). Home: 262 Stonehedge Ln Guilford CT 06437 Office: 333 Cedar St New Haven CT 06510

LE, HUNG VAN, biochemist; b. Ho Chi Minh City, Vietnam, Nov. 13, 1951; came to U.S., 1969, naturalized, 1983; s. Tan Van and Tinh Thi (Dinh) L.; m. Hoa Thi Nguyen, Jan. 20, 1976 (div. Nov. 1976); m. Thai-Phuong Thi Nguyen, June 12, 1980. B.S., SUNY-Buffalo, 1973, Ph.D., 1978. Cancer research scientist Roswell Park Meml. Inst., Buffalo, N.Y., 1978-80; sr. scientist Schering-Plough Corp., Bloomfield, N.J., 1980-82, prin. scientist, 1982—. Author: Current Chemotherapy and Infectious Diseases, 1980; Interferon: Properties and clinical Uses, 1980; Interferon: Research Clinical Applications, 1984; also articles. fellow in biochem. pharmacology SUNY, 1973-77; biomed. research support grantee NIH, 1980. Mem. Am. Chem. Soc., Am. Soc. Microbiology, N.Y. Acad. Sci. Clubs: White Meadow, Lake Country. Chemistry of Genetically engineered proteins; protein engineering; fermentation, extraction, purification, characterization and formulation. Subspecialties: Biochemistry (medicine); Genetics and genetic engineering (medicine). Home: 75 Valley View Dr Rockaway NJ 07866 Office: Schering-Plough Corp 60 Orange St Bloomfield NJ 07003

LEACH, DAVID GOHEEN, geneticist, researcher, author; b. New Bethlehem, Pa., Jan. 18, 1913; s. Andrew Steelman and Nellie (Goheen) L.; married; children: Robin, David Goheen, Brian. B.S., Coll. Wooster, Ohio, 1934; D.Sc., Coll. Wooster, 1966. Engaged in research and hybridization of ornamental plants, 1953—, subsidiary research, nutrition pathology, entomology, physiology and propagation of ericaceous plants, 1953—, research, toxicology of ericaceous plants, 1966-68, 80-83; dir. expt. sta. for hybridization of woody plants, Brookville, Pa., then Madison, Ohio, 1972—, extensive overseas plant exploration; lectr., U.S., overseas.; chmn. Internat. Conf. Chemotaxonomy, N.Y. Bot. Garden, 1978; co-chmn. Internat. Conf. Taxonomy, Royal Bot. Garden, Edinburgh, Scotland, 1982. Author: Rhododendrons of the World, 1961, Hybrids and Hybridizers, 1978; contbr. numerous articles to profl. jours. and encys. Bd. dirs. Western Res. Fine Arts Assn., East Suburban Concerts, Met. Outdoor Family Ctr., YMCA, all Northeastern Ohio. Gold medal of honor Garden Club Am., 1969; Cert. of Merit, Pa. Hort. Soc., 1970; Jackson Dawson Meml. medal Mass. Hort. Soc., 1972; Research award Nurserymen's Assn., 1980. Mem. Am. Soc. Hort. Sci., Am. Hort. Soc. (pres. 1970-74, recognition award 1974, award for sci. achievement 1985), Am. Assn. Bot. Gardens and Arboreta, Am. Rhododendron Soc. (Gold medal 1965), Internat. Plant Propagators Soc., Royal Hort. Soc. (Loder Gold Cup award 1969), Australian Rhododendron Soc., others. Current Work: Research in gamma radiation effects, induced mutations, cytoplasmic inheritance, pigment inheritance and other characteristics for improved hybrids of ornamental plants. Subspecialty: Plant genetics.

LEAF, ALEXANDER, physician, educator; b. Yokohama, Japan, Apr. 10, 1920; came to U.S., 1922, naturalized, 1936; s. Aaron L. and Dora (Hural) L.; m. Barbara Louise Kincaid, Oct. 1943; children—Caroline Joan, Rebecca Louise, Tamara Jean. B.S., U. Wash., 1940; M.D., U. Mich., 1943; M.A., Harvard, 1961. Intern Mass. Gen. Hosp., Boston, 1943-44, mem. staff, 1949—, physician-in-chief, 1966-81; resident Mayo Found., Rochester, Minn., 1944-45; research fellow U. Mich., 1947-49; practice internal medicine, Boston, 1949—; faculty Med. Sch., Harvard, 1949—, Jackson prof. clin. medicine, 1966-81, Ridley Watts prof. preventive medicine, 1980—, chmn. dept. preventive medicine and clin. epidemiology, 1980—. Served to capt. M.C. AUS, 1945-46. Recipient Outstanding Achievement award U. Minn., 1964; vis. fellow Balliol Coll., Oxford, 1971-72; Guggenheim fellow, 1971-72. Fellow Am. Acad. Arts and Scis.; mem. Am. Soc. Clin. Investigation (past pres.), Am. Physiol. Soc., Biophys. Soc., Assn. Am. Physicians, Nat. Acad. Sci., Inst. Medicine, A.C.P. (master). Current Work: Renal physiology and ion transport; cardiovascular risk factor reduction. Subspecialties: Internal medicine; Nephrology. Home: 1 Curtis Circle Winchester MA 01890 Office: Mass Gen Hosp Boston MA 02114

LEAKE, DONALD LEWIS, oral and maxillofacial surgeon; b. Cleveland, Okla., Nov. 6, 1931; s. Walter Wilson and Martha Lee (Crow) L.; m. Rosemary Dobson, Aug. 20, 1964; children: John Andrew Dobson, Elizabeth, Catherine. A.B., U. So. Calif., 1953, M.A., 1957; D.M.D., Harvard U., 1962; M.D., Stanford U., 1969. Intern Mass. Gen. Hosp., Boston, 1962-63, resident, 1963-64; postdoctoral fellow Harvard U., 1964-66; practice medicine specializing in oral and maxillofacial surgery; asso. prof. oral and maxillofacial surgery Harbor-UCLA Med. Center, Torrance, 1970-74, dental dir., chief oral and maxillofacial surgery, 1970—, prof., 1974—; asso. dir. UCLA Dental Research Inst., 1979-82, dir., 1982—; cons. to hosps.; dental dir. coastal health services region, Los Angeles County, 1974-81. Contbr. articles to med. jours. Recipient 1st prize with greatest distinction for oboe and chamber music Brussels Royal Conservatory Music Belgium, 1956. Fellow ACS; mem. Internat. Assn. Dental Research, So. Calif. Soc. Oral and Maxillofacial Surgeons, Internat. Assn. Oral Surgeons, AAAS, Soc. for Biomaterials, Los Angeles County Med. Assn., Los Angeles Acad. Medicine, ASTM, European Assn. Maxillofacial Surgeons, Brit. Assn. Oral Surgeons, Internationale Gesellschaft fur Kiefer-Gesichts-Chirurgie, Phi Beta Kappa, Phi Kappa Phi. Club: Harvard of Boston. Current Work: Biomarerials for reconstructive surgery. Subspecialties: Oral and maxillofacial surgery; Biomaterials. Home: 2 Crest Rd W Rolling Hills CA 90274 Office: Harbor-UCLA Med Center 1000 W Carson St Torrance CA 90509

LEAMNSON, ROBERT NEAL, biology educator, researcher, cons.; b. Evansville, Ind., July 16, 1932; s. Robert Clinton and Mary Catherine (Farley) L. B.S., U. Notre Dame, 1955; M.S., 1965; Ph.D., U. Ill., 1973. Tchr. secondary schs., Ind., Ohio, 1955-65; research project chemist CTS Research, West Lafayette, Ind., 1966-67; asst. chemist Ill. State Geol. Survey, Urbana, 1967-69; asst. prof. research Wistar Inst., Phila., 1974-77; asst. prof. biology Southeastern Mass. U., 1978—; researcher, cons. Children's Hosp., Boston, Brown U. Contbr. articles to profl. publs. Mem. AAAS, Am. Soc. Microbiology, N.Y. Acad. Sci. Current Work: Molecular biology of viral proteins and nucleic acids; isoelectric points of viral proteins; functional sequences of nucleic acids of retroviruses. Subspecialties: Virology (biology); Molecular biology. Office: Southeastern Mass U Dept Biology North Dartmouth MA 02747

LEARY, DAVID JOSEPH, engineer, consultant; b. Wilmington, Del., Nov. 6, 1954; s. Joseph Rhodes and Marjorie E (Lake) L. B.S. in Elec. Engring. with honors, U. Del., 1975; M.S., Carnegie-Mellon, 1976, Ph.D., 1979. Mem. tech. staff Hewlett-Packard, Fort Collins, Colo., 1979—; dir. Airtech, Inc., Fort Collins. Patentee in field. Contbr. numerous articles to profl. jours. Volunteer Am. Heart Assn., Fort Collins, 1982—. Mem. IEEE, Tau Beta Pi, Eta Kappa Nu. Current work: Integrated circuit process development for VLSI computer circuits, semiconductor device physics characterisation and reliability analysis, semiconductor sensor development. Subspecialties: Integrated circuits; Solid state chemistry. Home: 555 Spindrift Court-Landings Fort Collins CO 80525 Office: Hewlett Packard Corp 3404 E Harmony Rd Fort Collins CO 80525

LEARY, RICHARD LEE, geologist, paleobotanist, museum curator; b. Portsmouth, Va., Sept. 19, 1936; s. Wilbur Talmadge and Mary Katherine (Lee) L.; m. Eleanor Marie Riehl, June 18, 1961; children: Seth Richard, Sara Marie. B.S. in Geology (Inst. scholar), Va. Poly. Inst., 1959; M.S. in Geology (Univ. fellow), U. Mich., 1961; Ph.D. in Geology, U. Ill., 1980. Summer field asst. Calif. Oil Co., Colo., 1959; field asst. Mobil Oil Co., N. Mex., 1960; asst. Kelsey Mus., Ann Arbor, 1960-61; mus. apprentice Newark Mus., 1961-62; curator geology Ill. State Mus., Springfield, 1962—; mem. environ. geology faculty Sangamon State U., 1973-78; mem. faculty The Clearing, Ellison Bay, Wis., alt. summers 1975—. Contbr numerous articles to sci. and non-tech. jours., papers to profl. confs.; research in paleobotany, geology. Deacon, Westminster Presbyn. Ch., Springfield. Ill. State Acad. Sci. grantee, 1975; NSF grantee, 1981, 84, 85. Mem. Geol. Soc. Am., Bot. Soc. Am., Internat Orgn. Paleobotany, Ill. State Acad. Sci. (v.p. 1975-76, pres. 1976-77), Sigma Gamma Epsilon. Discoverer new species of fossil plants, new genus and species of fossil scorpion. Current Work: Carboniferous (Pennsylvanian/Mississippian) non-swamp paleoenvironments; paleobotany, paleoecology, sedimentation, paleotopography. Subspecialties: Paleobiology; Paleontology, paleoecology. Office: Ill State Mus Springfield IL 62706

LEATH, KENNETH THOMAS, research plant pathologist; b. Providence, Apr. 29, 1931; s. Thomas and Elizabeth (Wootten) L.; m. Marie Lorraine, Aug. 6, 1955; children: Kenneth, Steven, Kevin, Maria. B.S., U. R.I., 1959; M.S., U. Minn., 1966, Ph.D., 1966. Research technician Coop. Cereal Rust Lab., St. Paul, 1959-66; research plant pathologist Pasture Research Lab., U.S. Dept. Agr., University Park, Pa., 1966—, adj. prof., 1966—. Contbr. articles in field to profl. jours. Bd. dirs. Pa. Forage and Grassland Council, 1976-82. Served with USN, 1951-55. Mem. Internat. Soc. Plant Pathology, Am. Phytopath. Soc., Am. Soc. Agronomy, Am. Forage and Grassland Soc., Pa. Forage and Grassland Soc. Lodge: Elks. Current Work: Researcher in forage legume diseases. Subspecialties: Plant pathology; Microbiology. Office: US Dept Agriculture Pasture Research Lab University Park PA 16802

LEATHERMAN, STEPHEN PARKER, coastal geomorphologist, educator; b. Charlotte, N.C., Nov. 6, 1947; s. John Fearl and Mary Evelyn (Parker) L. B.S. in Geosci., N.C. State U., 1970; Ph.D. in Environ. Sci., U. Va., 1976. Petroleum geologist Texaco, Inc., Houston, 1970-72; asst. prof. Boston U., 1975-77; dir. research unit U. Mass., Amherst, 1977-81; asst. prof. dept. geography, U. Md., College Park, 1981-83, assoc. prof., 1983—; cons. U.S. Dept. Interior, Washington, 1977-81; alt. dir. Potomac River Basin Consortium, Washington, 1984—; com. mem. Marine Bd., Nat. Acad. Scis., Washington, 1984—; field leader Earthwatch, Belmont, Mass., 1976-79; state coordinator Barrier Island Coalition, Washington, 1977-81; pub. lectr. Chappaquiddick Beach Club, Martha's Vineyard, Mass., 1978; judge Mass. State Sci. Fair, Cambridge, 1978. Author: Barrier Island Handbook, 1982. Editor: Barrier Islands, 1979; other books. Contbr. articles to sci. jours. Served with U.S. Army, 1970-72. Fellow Geol. Soc. Am.; mem. Soc. Econ. Paleontologists and Mineralogists (pres. eastern sect. 1979-80), AAAS, Blue Key, Sigma Xi. Current work: Computer mapping of coastal environments; coastal storm-generated processes. Subspecialties: Coastal zones; Oceanography. Home: 8242 Canning Terr Greenbelt MD 20770 Office: 1113 LeFrak Hall U Md College Park MD 20742

LEBER, RALPH ERIC, science policy adminstr.; b. Seattle, Nov. 30,1949; s. Ralph Theodore and Ann Elisa (Ellsworth) L.; m. Lori Marie Ramonas, Apr. 28, 1979; 1 child, R. Christopher Tyler. Student, Lycee de Math et Sciences, Lyon, France, 1966-67; B.A., Reed Coll., Portland, Oreg., 1972; M.S., Yale U., 1973, M.Ph., 1974, Ph.D. in Chemistry, 1975. Sr. reactor operator, supr. Reed Coll. Nuclear Reactor Facility, 1969-72; summer trainee Pacific N.W. Nat. Labs., 1970, Brookhaven Nat. Lab., 1971; research assoc., teaching asst. Yale U., 1972-75; postdoctoral research fellow Lawrence Berkeley Lab., 1975-77; AAAS Congressional Sci. fellow U.S. Congress, 1977-78; dir. energy research, dir. Demonstration of Energy-Efficient Devels., asst. dir. tech. services Am. Public Power Assn., Washington, 1978-84, exec. com. Fuel Cell Users Group; supervisory com. Intgrated Energy Systems Group; synthetic fuels rev. panel U.S. Synthetic Fuels Corp. Editor: Public Power mag, 1978-84, DEED Digest, 1980-84; contbr. articles tech. jours. Mem. U.S. del. U.S./USSR exchange fields of housing and other constrn.; Advisor Washington Internships for Students in Engring. Program; judge Washington Area High Sch. Sci. Fairs; nat. chmn. Reed Coll. Alumni Fund Drive; bd. dirs. Spring Lake Condominium Assn., Bethesda, Md.; steering and ann. fund coms. Reed Coll. Bd. Trustees. Recipient Richard Wolfgang prize Yale U. Chemistry Dept., 1976; nat. finalist White House Fellowship, 1975. Mem. AAAS, Am. Chem. Soc. (dir. pub. policy and communication 1984—, Coryell Undergrad. award 1972), Am. Nuclear Soc. (award of merit 1972), Am. Phys. Soc., Am. Wind Energy Assn., ASME, Internat. Cogeneration Soc., Internat. Dist. Heating Assn., Women in Energy, Phi Beta Kappa, Sigma Xi. Clubs: Wash. State Soc. (Washington), Yale (Washington). Current Work: Facilitate the development and ennunciation of policy relating to science and technology with emphasis on the chemical sciences. Subspecialties: Fuels and sources; Systems engineering. Home: 11425 Running Cedar Rd Reston VA 22091

LEBLANC, ROBERT BRUCE, chemist, research co. exec.; b. Alexandria, La., Jan. 28, 1925; s. Moreland Paul and Carmen Mary (Haydel) LeB.; m. Barbara Ann Sanders, Oct. 11, 1968. B.S. in Chemistry, Loyola U., 1947; M.S., Tuland U., 1949, Ph.D., 1950. Diplomate: Am. Bd. Bioanalysts, 1976. Asst. prof. chemistry Tex. A&M U., College Station, 1950-52; group leader research Dow Chem. Co., Freeport, Tex., 1952-63, sect. head, Midland, Mich., 1963-67; mgr. textile chem. devel. Ashland Chem. Co., Charlotte, N.C., 1967-68; research mgr. Nat. Cotton Council, Memphis, 1968-70; pres. LeBlanc Research Corp., North Kingstown, R.I., 1970—. Editor 6 books; contbr. articles to profl. jours. Served to lt. USNR, 1943-46. Republican. Roman Catholic. Lodge: Rotary. Patentee in field. Current Work: Textile chemistry, flammability and flame retardance of textiles. Subspecialties: Polymer chemistry; Clinical chemistry. Home: 99 Main St Wickford RI 02852 Office: 6172 Post Rd North Kingstown RI 02852

LEBLANC, ROGER MAURICE, biophysics educator, researcher; b. Trois-Rivières, Que., Can., Jan. 5, 1942; s. Henri and Rita (Moreau) L.; m. Micheline Veillette, June 26, 1965; children: Nancy, Hugues, Daniel. B.Sc. in Chemistry, U. Laval, 1964, D.Sc. in Phys. Chemistry, 1968. Postdoctoral fellow Davy Faraday Research Lab., Royal Instn., London, 1968-70; mem. faculty U. Que., Trois-Rivières, 1970—, prof. phys. chemistry, 1970—, chmn. chemistry-biology dept., 1971-75, dir. biophysics research group, 1978-81; chmn. Photobiophysics Research Ctr., 1981—; vis. prof. INRS-Energie, 1972—, U. Sherbrooke, 1977—; vis. scientist U. Liège, Belgium, 1977, 78, 79. Contbr. articles to sci. jours. Recipient prix du Govt. France, 1962-63; prize Allied Chem. Corp., 1962-63; Sir William Price award, 1963-65; Noranda prize Chem. Inst. Can., 1982; Barringer prize Spectroscopy Soc. Can., 1983; others. Mem. Assn. Canadienne Française pour l'Avancement des Sciences (Vincent prize 1978), Chem. Inst. Can., Am. Chem. Soc., Biophys. Soc., N.Am. Photochem. Soc., Brit. Photobiology Soc., Brit. Biophys. Soc., Am. Soc. Photobiology, European Photochem. Assn. Current Work: Photovoltaic properties of chloroplast pigments; optical properties of chlorophylls in artificial biological membranes; electrical properties of the mixtures phospholipids and retinals in bilayer models; interactions phospholipids and rhodopsin. Subspecialties: Biophysics (biology); Surface chemistry.

LEBLOND, CHARLES PHILIPPS, educator; b. Lille, France, Feb. 5, 1910; s. Oscar and Jeanne (Desmarchelier) L.; m. Gertrude Elinor Sternschuss, Oct. 22, 1936; children: Philippe Louis, Pierre Francis, Paul Noel, Marie-Pascale Murphy. M.D., U. Paris, 1934; Ph.D., U. Montreal, 1942; Dr.Sc., Sorbonne U., 1945; D.Sc. (hon.), McGill U., 1982. Rockefeller fellow Yale U., 1935; in charge biology sect. Lab. Synthese Atomique, Paris, 1937; lectr. history McGill U., Montreal, Que., Can., 1941-46, assoc. prof. anatomy, 1946-48, prof., 1948—, chmn. dept., 1957-74. Contbr articles in field to profl. jours. Served with Free French Army, 1944-45. Named Prix Saintour French Acad., 1935; NATO prof. U. Louvain, Belgium, 1959; recipient award Gairdner Found., 1965; Biology Prize Province of Que., 1968. Fellow Royal Soc. Can., Royal Soc. London.; Mem. Am. Assn. Anatomist (exec. 1954-58, pres. 1962-63), Am. Soc. Cell Biology (mem. council 1968-71), Can. Assn. Anatomists (pres. 1965), Histochem. Soc. (pres. 1956). Club: Faculty (Montreal, Que.). Current Work: The work done on the microscopic localization of biological substances by radioautography has added dynamic features to classical histology. Subspecialties: Microscopy; Cell biology (medicine).

LEBO, ROGER VAN, molecular biologist, geneticist; b. Pottsville, Pa., Mar. 1, 1948; s. Stanley E. and Irene M. (Bush) L.; m. Susan Thelma Southard, Apr. 3, 1972; children: Frank, Paul. A.B., Chaffey Coll., Alta Loma, Calif., 1968; B.S., Pa. State U., 1970; Ph.D., Duke U., 1974. Diplomate: Am. Bd. Med. Genetics. NIH trainee Duke U., 1970-74; postdoctoral fellow U. Calif.-San Francisco, 1974-76, asst. research biochemist, 1976-83, assoc. research biochemist, 1983—; assoc. Howard Hughes Med. Inst., San Francisco, 1979—; prin. project investigator gene mapping by chromosome sorting, 1979, gene mapping by spot blot analysis, 1984. Recipient research award Duke U., 1974. Mem. Am. Soc. Human Genetics, Soc. Analytical Cytometry, Am. Genetic Assn., Am. Fedn. Clin. Research. Republican. Inventor optical bench of dual laser chromosome sorter. Current Work: Human genetic disease, further dissection of human genome, gene expression using chromosome-specific recombinant DNA libraries. Subspecialties: Genetics and genetic engineering (medicine); Cell biology (medicine). Home: 588 Miramar Ave San Francisco CA 94112 Office: U Calif U-426 Health Sciences E San Francisco CA 94143

LEBOFSKY, LARRY ALLEN, planetary astronomer; b. Bklyn., Aug. 31, 1947; s. Harry and Clara (Goodman) L.; m. Marcia J. Lebofsky, July 15, 1973; m. Nancy R. Lebofsky, May 9, 1980; 1 dau., Miranda B. B.S., Calif. Inst. Tech., 1969; Ph.D., MIT, 1974. Cons. Sci. Applications, Inc., 1975; NRC resident research assoc. Jet Propulsion Lab., 1975-77; cons., 1981—; research assoc. Lunar and Planetary Lab., U. Ariz., 1977-80, sr. research assoc., 1980-82, research fellow, 1982-83, assoc. research scientist, 1983—; cons. Infrared Astron. Satellite Sci. Team, 1981—. Contbr. chpts. to books and articles to profl. jours. Mem. Am. Astron. Soc., Internat. Astron. Union, Sigma Xi. Democrat. Jewish. Current Work: Visual and infrared telescopic and satellite observations of asteroids, satellites and planets. Subspecialties: Planetary science; Infrared astronomy. Home: 2333 E 7th St Tucson AZ 85719 Office: Lunar and Planetary Lab U Ariz Tucson AZ 85721

LEBOWITZ, JOEL LOUIS, physicist, educator; b. Taceva, May 10, 1930; came to U.S., 1946, naturalized, 1951; m. Estelle Mandelbaum, June 21, 1953. B.S., Bklyn. Coll., 1952; M.S., Syracuse U., 1955; Ph.D., 1956; Ph.D. hon. doctorate, Ecole Polytechnique Federale, Lausanne, Switzerland, 1977. NSF postdoctoral fellow Yale, 1956-57; mem. faculty Stevens Inst. Tech., 1957-59; mem. faculty Yeshiva U., N.Y.C., 1959-77, prof. physics, 1965-77; acting chmn. dept. physics Belfer Grad. Sch. Sci., 1964-67, chmn. dept., 1967-76; prof. math. and physics, dir. Ctr. for Math. Scis., Rutgers U., New Brunswick, N.J., 1977—, George William Hill prof. math., 1980—; mem. Commn. Thermodynamics and Statis. Mechanics, Internat. Union Pure and Applied Physics, 1979-81, sec., 1982-84, pres., 1985—. Editor: Jour. Statis. Physics, 1975—, Studies in Statis. Mechanics, 1973—, Com. Math. Physics, 1973—; contbr. articles to profl. jours. Guggenheim fellow, 1976-77. Fellow Am. Phys. Soc., AAAS; mem. Nat. Acad. Scis., N.Y. Acad. Scis. (pres. 1979), AAUP, Am. Math. Soc., Phi Beta Kappa, Sigma Xi. Subspecialties: Probability; Statistical physics. Office: Dept Math Hill Center Busch Campus Rutgers U New Brunswick NJ 08903

LEDBETTER, MARY LEE STEWART, cell biologist; b. Monterrey, Nuevo Leon, Mex., Aug. 30, 1944; d. William Sheldon and Maria Rosalind (Markham) Stewart; m. Steven John Ledbetter, Sept. 10, 1966; children: William John, Joanna Marie. B.A., Pomona Coll., 1966; Ph.D., Rockefeller U., 1972. Research assoc. dept. microbiology Dartmouth Med. Sch., Hanover, N.H., 1972-75, instr., 1975-77, research assoc. in psychiatry, 1977-78, research asst. prof. biochemistry, 1978-80; asst. prof. biology Coll. Holy Cross, Worcester, Mass., 1980-85, assoc. prof., 1985—. Contbr. articles to sci. jours. Damon Runyon-Walter Winchell Cancer Research Fund fellow, 1972-73; Leukemia Soc. Am. fellow, 1973-75, 77; Nat. Cancer Inst. fellow, 1975-77. Mem. Am. Soc. Cell Biology, AAAS, Genetics Soc. Am., Assn. Women in Sci., Sigma Xi. Democrat. Current Work: Regulation of growth and development as exhibited in cultured mammalian cells; control of cell communication; control of protein degradation. Subspecialties: Cell and tissue culture; Membrane biology. Office: Dept Biology Coll Holy Cross Worcester MA 01610

LEDBETTER, MYRON CALVERT, cell biologist, electron microscopist; b. Ardmore, Okla., June 25, 1923; s. Robert Hamilton Ledbetter and Nora A. (Moore) Ledbetter Simank. B.S., Okla. StateU., 1948; M.A., U. Calif., Berkeley, 1951; Ph.D., Columbia U., 1958. Tchr. Blackwell (Okla.) Pub. Schs., 1951-52; fellow in plant physiology Boyce Thompson Inst. Plant Research, Yonkers, N.Y., 1952-57, plant anatomist, 1957-60; guest investigator Rockefeller U., N.Y.C., 1960, research assoc., 1961, Harvard Biol. Labs., Cambridge, Mass., 1961-65; guest assoc. Brookhaven Nat. Lab., Upton, N.Y., 1958-60, cell biologist, 1965-74, sr. cell biologist, 1974—; cons. Celanese Research Corp., 1981-82; bd. mgrs. N.Y. Bot. Garden, 1982-84. Author: (with Keith R Porter) Introduction to the Fine Structure of Plant Cells, 1970; Contbr. articles to sci. jours. Served to lt. (j.g.) USNR, 1943-46. USPHS fellow, 1960. Mem. Electron Microscopy Soc. Am. (pres. 1978), N.Y. Soc. Electron Microscopists (pres. 1972-73), AAAS, Am. Inst. Biol. Sci., Am. Soc. Cell Biology, Bot. Soc. Am., Torrey Bot. Club (pres. 1984-85), N.Y. Acad. Sci., Sigma Xi. Co-inventor thin foil apertures for electron microscopes. Current Work: Fine structure of plant cells; microtubules in relation to cell wall formation in plants, plant cell development, transfer of bacterial DNA, morphology of plant pigment complexes, macromolecular structure by cluster ion impact. Subspecialties: Cell biology; Plant growth. Home: PO Box 145 Port Jefferson NY 11777 Office: Brookhaven Nat Lab Dept Biology Upton NY 11973

LEDDICK, GEORGE RUSSELL, psychology educator, therapist; b. Newman, Calif., Apr. 6, 1948; s. Kenneth L. and Ann (Karl) L. B.A., DePauw U., 1970; M.A., Fisk U., 1977; Ph.D., Purdue U., 1980. Instr. Purdue U., 1979-80; prof. counseling psychology and ednl. psychology Ind. U.-Purdue U., Ft. Wayne, 1980—; pres. Ind. Specialists in Group Work, 1982-84. Cons. editor: Jour. for Specialists in Group Work, 1982-85, The Clinical Supervisor jour, 1982-85; Contbr. chpts. to books, ency., articles to profl. jours. Fellow Internat. Council Parenthood Edn.; mem. Am. Assn. Counseling and Devel., Am. Psychol. Assn., Am. Assn. Marriage and Family Therapy, Assn. Specialists in Group Work, Assn. Counselor Edn. and Supervision (chmn. supervision com.), Ind. Assn. Counseling and Devel. (pres.-elect), Ind. Assn. Counselor Edn. and Supervision (pres.), Am. Mental Health Counseling Assn. (del. to China and USSR 1985), Phi Delta Kappa. Current Work: Psychotherapy supervision; marriage and family therapy; group work; organizational development; microcomputer applications. Subspecialty: Counseling psychology. Office: Indiana-Purdue U 2101 Coliseum Blvd E Fort Wayne IN 46815

LEDEEN, ROBERT WAGNER, neurochemist, educator; b. Denver, Aug. 19, 1928; s. Hyman and Olga (Wagner) L.; m. Lydia Rosen Hailparn, July 2, 1982. B.S., U. Calif., Berkeley, 1949; Ph.D., Oreg. State U., 1953. Postdoctoral fellow in chemistry U. Chgo., 1953-54; research assoc. in chemistry Mt. Sinai Hosp., N.Y.C., 1956-59; research fellow Albert Einstein Coll. Medicine, Bronx, N.Y., 1959, asst. prof., 1963-69, assoc. prof., 1969-75, prof., 1975—. Contbr. articles to profl. jours.; mem. editorial bd. Jour. Neurochemistry, Jour. Lipid Research. Mem. neurol. scis. study sect. NIH. Served with U.S. Army, 1954-56. NIH grantee, 1963—; Nat. Multiple Sclerosis Soc. grantee, 1967-74. Mem. Internat. Soc. Neurochemistry, Am. Soc. Neurochemistry, Am. Chem. Soc., Am. Soc. Biol. Chemists, N.Y. Acad. Sci., AAAS. Jewish. Current Work: Research on gangliosides and other glycolipids of nervous system; biochemistry of myelin. Subspecialty: Neurochemistry. Home: 8 Donald Ct Wayne NJ 07470 Office: 1300 Morris Park Ave Bronx NY 10461

LEDER, PHILIP, geneticist, educator; b. Washington, Nov. 19, 1934; married; 3 children. A.B., Harvard U., 1956, M.D., 1960. Research assoc. Nat. Heart Inst., Nat. Cancer Inst.; lab chief molecular genetics Nat. Inst. Child Health and Human Devel., NIH, 1972-80; prof. genetics Harvard U. Med. Sch., Boston, 1980—, now John Emory Andrus prof. genetics. Fields: Genetics, genetic engineering. Current work: Molecular genetics. Mem. Nat. Acad. Scis. Office: Dept Genetics Harvard U Med Sch 25 Shattuck St Boston MA 02115

LEDERBERG, JOSHUA, university president, geneticist; b. Montclair, N.J., May 23, 1925; s. Zwi Hirsch and Esther (Goldenbaum) L.; m. Marguerite S. Kirsch, Apr. 5, 1968; children: David Kirsch, Anne. B.A., Columbia U., 1944; Ph.D., Yale U., 1947, Sc.D. (hon.), 1960; Sc.D. (hon.), U. Wis., 1967, Columbia U., 1967, Yeshiva U., 1970, Mt. Sinai Coll. Medicine, 1979, Rutgers U., 1981, NYU, 1984; M.D. (hon.), U. Turin, 1969; Tufts U., 1985; Litt.D. (hon.), Jewish Theol. Sem., 1979; LL.D. (hon.), U. Pa., 1979. With U. Wis., 1947-58; prof. genetics Stanford Sch. Medicine, 1959-78; pres. Rockefeller U., N.Y.C., 1978—; mem. bd. sci. advisers Cetus Corp., Berkeley, Calif.; mem. study sects. NSF, NIH; cons. NASA; mem. U.S. Def. Sci. Bd.; cons. ACDA; chmn. Pres.'s Cancer Panel, 1979-81; dir. Inst. Sci. Info. Inc., Phila., Procter & Gamble Co., Cin., Ann. Revs., Inc., Palo Alto, Calif.; mem. adv. com. med. research WHO, 1971-76. Bd. dirs. Conservation Found., Washington, Chem. Industry Inst. Toxicology, N.C.; mem. Pres.'s Panel on Mental Retardation, 1961-62; mem. nat. mental health adv. council NIMH, 1967-71. Recipient Nobel prize in physiology and medicine for research genetics of bacteria, 1958. Mem. Nat. Acad. Scis., Royal Soc. London (fgn.). Current Work: Strategies of biomedical research; inculcating and sustaining scientific creativity. Subspecialties: Genetics and genetic engineering (biology); Molecular biology. Office: Office of Pres Rockefeller U 1230 York Ave New York NY 10021

LEDERER, JEROME FOX, aeronautical engineer, advisor; b. N.Y.C., Sept. 26, 1902; s. Sigmund and Sophie (Fox) L. B.S. in M.E., NYU, 1924, M.E., 1925. Registered profl. engr., N.Y. Aero. Engr., U.S. Air Mail Service, Maywood, Ill., 1926-27; chief engr. Aero Ins. Underwriters, 1929-40, 45-47; dir. safety bur. CAB, Washington, 1940-42; dir. Flight Safety Found., N.Y.C., 1947-67; dir. Office Manned Space Flight Safety NASA, Washington, 1967-70, dir. safety, 1970-72; advisor Flight Safety Found., 1972—; adj. prof. Inst. Safety and System Mgmt. U. So. Calif., 1974-82. Author: Safety in the Operation of Air Transport, 1938; Perspectives in Aviation Safety, 1982. Contbr. numerous articles to profl. jours. Recipient David Orr prize NYU, 1924; Von Baumhauer medal Royal Dutch Aero. Soc., 1954; Aviation Safety award Aviation Writers Assn.; Daniel Guggenheim medal, 1961; Exceptional Service medal NASA, 1969. Fellow AIAA, Royal Aero. Soc., Human Factors Soc., Am. Astron. Soc.; mem. Air Traffic Controllers Assn. (hon.), Nat. Acad. Engrng. Club: Wings (N.Y.C.). Subspecialties: Aeronautical engineering; Aerospace safety.

LEDERMAN, LEON MAX, physicist, educator; b. N.Y.C., July 15, 1922; s. Morris and Minna (Rosenberg) L.; m. Florence Gordon, Sept. 19, 1945; children: Rena S., Jesse A., Heidi R. B.S., Coll. City N.Y., 1943; A.M., Columbia, 1948, Ph.D., 1951. Asso. in physics Columbia, N.Y.C., 1951, asst. prof., 1952-54, asso. prof., 1954-58, prof., 1958—, Eugene Higgins prof. physics, 1973—; dir. Fermi Nat. Accelerator Lab., Batavia, Ill., 1979—; Dir. Nevis Labs., Irvington, N.Y., 1960-67, 69—; guest scientist Brookhaven Nat. Labs., 1955—; cons., nat. accelerator lab. European Orgn. for Nuclear Research (CERN), 1970—; mem. high energy physics adv. panel AEC, 1966-70; mem. adv. com. to div. math. and phys. scis. NSF, 1970-72. Contbr. articles to profl. jours. Served to 2d lt. Signal Corps, AUS, 1943-46. Recipient Nat. Medal of Sci., 1965, Wolf Prize, 1983; NSF fellow, 1967; Guggenheim fellow, 1958-59; Ford Found. fellow European Center For Nuclear Research, Geneva, 1958-59; recipient Townsend Harris medal City U. N.Y., 1973; Elliot Cresson medal Franklin Inst., 1976. Fellow AAAS, Am. Phys. Soc.; mem. Italian Phys. Soc., Nat. Acad. Sci. Subspecialty: Nuclear physics. Office: Fermi Nat Accelerator Lab PO Box 500 Batavia IL 60510

LEDINKO, NADA, biologist, educator; b. Girard, Ohio, Dec. 16, 1924; d. John Daniel and Zora Maria (Valencic) L. Ph.d., Yale U., 1952. Scientist Pub. Health Research Inst., N.Y.C., 1956-62; spl. fellow Nat. Cancer Inst., Cold Spring Harbor Lab. and Salk Inst., 1963-65; chief virologist Putnam Meml. Hosp., Research Inst., Bennington, Vt., Putnam, 1965-71; prof. biology U. Akron, 1971—. Contbr artcles to profl. jours. Mem. Am. Soc. Microbiology, Am. Assn. Cancer Research, Tissue Culture Assn., Phi Beta Kappa, Sigma Xi, Phi Kappa Phi. Current Work: Molecular biology of cancer cells; biochemistry of transferred cell phenotype. Subspecialties: Molecular biology; Cell and tissue culture. Office: Dept Biology U Akron Akron OH 44325

LEE, BERNARD SHING-SHU, research institute executive, chemical engineer; b. Nanking, China, Dec. 14, 1934; came to U.S., 1949, naturalized, 1956; s. Wei-Kuo and Pei-Fen (Tang) L.; m. Pauline Pan, Sept. 7, 1963; children: Karen, Lesley, Tania. Student, U. Va., 1952-54; B.Ch.E., Poly. Inst. Bklyn., 1956, D.Ch.E., 1960. Registered profl. engr., N.Y., Ill. Mem. staff Arthur D. Little, Inc., Cambridge, Mass., 1960-65; successively supr., mgr., asst. dir., asso. dir., dir. coal gasification research Inst. Gas Tech., Chgo., 1965-75, v.p. process research, 1976, exec. v.p., 1977, pres., 1978—, trustee, 1978—; dir. GDC, Inc., Hycrude Corp., Peerless Mfg. Co. Contbr. articles to profl. jours. Westinghouse fellow, 1957; recipient Personal Achievement award Chem. Engrng. mag., 1978; Disting. Alumnus award Poly. Inst. N.Y., 1980; Gas Industry research award, 1984. Fellow Am. Inst. Chem. Engrs. (33d Ann. Inst. lectr. 1981); mem. Am. Chem. Soc., AIME, AAAS, Am. Gas Assn. Methodist. Subspecialty: Energy research management. Home: 6900 N Kilpatrick Ave Lincolnwood IL 60646 Office: 3424 S State St Chicago IL 60616

LEE, CHARLES YING-CHEUNG, research engineer, chemist; b. Hong Kong, Nov. 1, 1947; came to U.S., 1966; naturalized, 1980; s. Man-Tai and Sui-Ying (Yeong) L.; m. Cecilia Lanfong Hsu, Oct. 2, 1971; children—Jensiong, Cindy. B.S., Western Ill. U., 1969; Ph.D., U. Wis., 1976. Research assoc. U. So. Calif., Los Angeles, 1977-78; assoc. chemist U. Dayton Research Inst., Ohio, 1978-79; material research engr. Materials Lab. Wright Patterson AFB, Ohio, 1979—, group leader, 1981—, research contract engr., 1980—, road map mgr., 1984—. Contbr. articles to profl. jours. Contbg. author to various books, 1978—. Mem. Am. Chem. Soc., Soc. for Advancement Material and Process Engrng. Current work: Processing and mechanical properties of polymers, especially for applications as matrices for advanced composites; molecular composites; precessing science advanced composites and microwave processing of polymers. Subspecialties: Polymers (materials science); Composite materials. Home: 3094 Village Ct Dayton OH 45432 Office: Materials Lab AFWAL/MLBC Wright Patterson AFB OH 45433

LEE, CHENG-CHUN, pharmacologist, toxicologist, researcher; b. Chiangtu, Chiangsu, China, May 24, 1922; m. Janice Y. C. Wang, Feb. 9, 1959; children: James P., Ray W. D.V.M., Nat. Central U., China, 1945, M.S., 1948; M.S., Mich. State U., 1950, Ph.D., 1952. Teaching asst. Nat. Central U. Nanking, China, 1945-48; research pharmacologist Lilly Research Lab., Indpls., 1952-63; sr. prin. pharmacologist Midwest Research Inst., Kansas City, Mo., 1963-67, head pharmacology and toxicology, 1967-76, asst. dir., assoc. dir., dept. dir. biol. sci. div., 1976-79; sr. sci. adv. health and environ. rev. div. EPA, Washington, 1979—; lectr. Sch. Pharmacy U. MO.-Kansas City, 1965-66; dept. pharmacology Kans. U. Med. Sch., 1966-79; professorial lectr. dept. pharmacology George Washington Med. Sch., Washington, 1981—; cons. Sci. Working Group on Chemotherapy of Malaria WHO, 1980, 81. Contbr. numerous articles on pharmacology and toxicology to profl. jours. Recipient Prin. Adv. award Midwest Research Inst., 1979; recipient Bronze medal EPA, 1979, Award for Spl. Achievement and Contbn., 1981. Mem. Am. Physiol. Soc., Am. Soc. for Pharmacology and Exptl. Therapeutics, Soc. Toxicology, N.Y. Acad. Scis., Am. Soc. for Exptl. Biology and Medicine, Chinese Physiol. Soc., Chinese Animal Husbandry and Vet Med. Assn., Am. Coll. Toxicology. Current Work: Drug metabolism and safe evaluation, health effects of chemicals, toxicology, pharmacology, hazard assessment. Subspecialties: Pharmacology; Toxicology (medicine). Home: 1351 Snow Meadow Ln McLean VA 22102 Office: HERD (TS-796)/OTS/EPA 401 M St SW Washington DC 20460

LEE, CHIN OK, physiology educator; b. Tanyang, Choongbuk, Korea, June 8, 1939; came to U.S., 1968; s. Yoon Hee and Kyung Duk (Song) L.; m. Kwanghee Kim, Sept. 20, 1969; children: Albert S., Daniel S. B.S., Seoul Nat. U., 1965, M.S., 1967; Ph.D., Ind. U., 1973. Research asst. Atomic Energy Research Inst., Seoul, 1967-68; postdoctoral fellow U. Chgo., 1973-76; asst. prof. Cornell U. Med. Coll., N.Y.C., 1976-81, assoc. prof., 1981—. Recipient L.N. Katz Basic Sci. Research prize Am. Heart Assn., 1974, established investigator, 1976; Pfizer award for outstanding research Internat. Soc. for Heart Research, 1986. Mem. Am. Physiol. Soc. (mem. editorial bd. 1981-87), Biophys. Soc., Am. Heart Assn., N.Y. Acad. Scis., Korean Scientists and Engrs. Assn. Am. (pres. N.Y. chpt. 1980-81). Current Work: Electrophysiology and contractility of heart muscle cells, ion transport, mechanism of cardiac glycoside action, application of ion-selective microelectrodes, teaching physiology. Subspecialties: Physiology (medicine); Biophysics (biology). Home: 1161 York Ave New York NY 10021 Office: Dept Physiology Cornell U Med Coll 1300 York Ave New York NY 10021

LEE, CHING Y., geneticist, researcher, educator; b. Peking, China, Sept. 15, 1935; d. Ting P. and Wei H. (Wong) L.; 1 son, Norman. B.S. in Genetics, Taiwan Chung-Hsing U., 1957; M.S. in Microbial Genetics, Bishop's U., Que., Can., 1972. Asst. prof. genetics Taiwan Chung-Hsing U., 1963-67; sr. microbial geneticist Sch. Medicine, U. Ottawa, Ont., Can., 1970-73; research scientist Ill. State Psychiat. Inst., Chgo., 1976—; cons. Contbg. author: Biological Markers in Psychiatry and Neurology, 1981. Mem. Am. Genetics Soc., N.Y. Acad. Scis. Republican. Current Work: Neurochemical and genetic approach to schizophrenia. Subspecialties: Neurochemistry; Genetics and genetic engineering (medicine). Home: PO Box 487 Palos Park IL 60464 Office: 1601 W Taylor St Room 222W Chicago IL 60612

LEE, CHING-LI, research chemist, educator; b. Chia-Yi, Taiwan, Mar. 30, 1942; came to U.S., 1970; s. Yuan-Chi and Liung-Chu (Chang) L.; m. Ming-Lea Liao, Jan. 6, 1972; children: Thomas, George, Jenny. B.S., Chung-Hsing U., Taiwan, 1969; M.S., Wayne State U., 1972-, Ph.D., 1975. Research assoc. dept. immunology Mayo Clinic, Rochester, Minn., 1975-77; research scientist Roswell Park Meml. Inst., Buffalo, 1977-79, sr. research scientist, 1979—; asst. prof. research SUNY-Buffalo, 1981—. Mem. Am. Assn. Immunology, Am. Assn. Cancer Research, Am. Chem. Soc. Current Work: isolation and characterization of human tumor antigens (or enzymes) and their clinical application; studying antigenic structure of globular proteins. Subspecialties: Immunology (medicine); Cancer research (medicine). Home: 184 Cimarand Dr Williamsville NY 14221 Office: Roswell Park Memorial Institute 666 Elm St Buffalo NY 14263

LEE, CHUAN-PU, biochemistry educator; b. Tsingtao, China, Sept. 24, 1931, came to U.S., 1956, naturalized, 1972; s. Fang-Hua and Wei-Pin (Liu) L. B.S., Nat. Taiwan U., China, 1954; Ph.D., Oreg. State U., 1961; M.A. (hon.), U. Pa., 1971, D. Phil. (hon.), U. Stockholm, Sweden, 1978. Asst. prof. phys. biochemistry U. Pa., Phila., 1966-69, assoc. prof., 1970-75, prof., 1975, prof. biochemistry Wayne State U., Detroit, 1975—; mem. adv. panel NSF, Washington, 1975-78; mem. U.S. Nat. Commn. Internat. Congress Biochemistry, Washington, 1978-84. Editor: Biochim. Biophys. Acta, Biochim. Biophys. Acta Rev. on Bioenergetics, 1973-81, Current Topics in Bioenergetics, 1982—; (with others) Probes and Membrane Functions, 1971; Membrane Bioenergetics, 1979, Mitochondria & Microsomes, 1982. Recipient Career Devel. award NIH, 1968-73; grantee NIH, NSF, Muscular Dystrophy Am., Jane Coffin Child Meml. Funds for Med. Research. Mem. Am. Soc. Biol. Chemists, Biophys. Soc., AAAS, Sigma Xi, Iota Sigma Pi. Current work: Mitrochondrial bioenergetics; neuromuscular diseases and mitchondrial energy metabolism; structure and function relationship of biomembranes. Subspecialties: Biochemistry (biology); Biophysics (biology). Office: Wayne State U Sch Medicine 540 E Canfield St Detroit MI 48201

LEE, CHUNG, med. researcher, educator; b. Shanghai, China, Sept. 18, 1936; s. Ho Chaung and Hwy Chi (Pao) L.; m. Daphne Chin-Quee, Aug. 21, 1966; children: Michael, Traci. B.S., Nat. Taiwan U., 1959; M.S., W.Va. U., 1966; Ph.D., 1969. USPHS postdoctoral fellow Albany (N.Y.) Med. Coll., 1969-71; assoc. Northwestern U. Med. Sch., Chgo., 1971-74, asst. prof., 1974-78, assoc. prof., 1979-85, prof., 1985—, dir. urology research labs.; assoc. research dept. Evanston (Ill.) Hosp., 1974—. Contbr. chpts. to books, articles to profl. jours. NIH fellow, 1969-71; Am. Cancer Soc. grantee, 1973-74; NIH grantee, 1974—. Mem. Am. Physiol. Soc., Endocrine Soc., Am. Assn. Cancer Research, Am. Soc. Andrology, Soc. Study Reproduction. Current Work: Laboratory research toward a better understanding in the physiology and pathology of the prostate. Subspecialties: Physiology (biology); Receptors. Home: 3406 Seine Ct Hazel Crest IL 60429 Office: 303 E Chicago Ave Chicago IL 60611

LEE, DAVID MORRIS, physics educator; b. Rye, N.Y.; s. Marvin and Annette (Franks) L.; m. Dana Thorangkul, Sept. 7, 1960; children—Eric Bertel, James Marvin. A.B. cum laude, Harvard U., 1952; M.A. in Physics, U. Conn., 1955; Ph.D. in Physics, Yale U., 1959. Instr. Cornell U., Ithaca, N.Y., 1959-60, asst. prof., 1960-63, assoc. prof., 1963-69, prof. physics, 1969—; vis. scientist Brookhaven Nat. Lab., Upton Long Island, N.Y., 1966-67; vis. prof. U. Fla., Gainesville, 1974-75; vis. lectr. Beijing U., Republic of China, 1981. Co-discoverer of various mixtures. Contbr. articles to profl. jours. Served to cpl. U.S. Army, 1952-54. Recipient Sir Francis Simon Meml. prize British Inst. Physics, 1976, Oliver E. Buddey Solid State Physics prize Am. Phys. Soc., 1981; Japan Soc. for Promotion of Sci. fellow, 1977, Guggenheim fellow, 1966-67, 1974-75. Fellow Am. Phys. Soc., AAAS; mem. N.Y. Acad. Scis. Current work: Research in low temperature physics with special interest in superfluid 3He, solid 3He, superconductivity and spin polarized atomic hydrogen gas. Subspecialty: Low temperature physics. Office: Cornell U Physics Dept Clark Hall Ithaca NY 14853

LEE, EDWARD YUE SHING, computer systems engineer, cons. data base management systems; b. Hong Kong, Aug. 1, 1937; came to U.S., 1957, naturalized, 1971; s. George Arthur and King Won (Lo) L.; m. Esther K. C. Ng, July 3, 1963; children: Philip S.W., Christina K. Y. B.S., Portland State U., 1961; M.S., Purdue U., 1963, Ph.D., 1971. Physicist, engr. Tektronix, Inc., Beaverton, Oreg., 1963-66; research asst. Purdue U., 1966-71; prin. investigator U.S. Army Constrn. Research Lab., Champaign, Ill., 1971-74; mem. tech. staff (Jet Propulsion Lab.), Pasadena, Calif., 1974-77; staff engr. Electronic Systems Group, TRW, Redondo Beach, Calif., 1977-80, sr. project engr., 1980—, lectr. database system, 1979-81. Bd. dirs. Chevy Chase Estate Home Owner Assn., 1976-78. Mem. Assn. Computing Machinery (recipient outstanding mem. award 1978-79; chmn. Los Angeles chpt. 1981-82), IEEE Computer Soc., Am. Phys. Soc. Current Work: Research and development on time critical distributed data processing system; distributed database management systems and information systems; storage and retrieval. Subspecialties: Distributed systems and networks; Database systems. Home: 30675 Via La Cresta Rancho Palos Verdes CA 90274 Office: TRW Electronic Systems Group One Space Park Dr Redondo Beach CA 90278

LEE, EUN SOO, biomaterial scientist; b. Korea, Sept. 26, 1945; came to U.S., 1974; s. Chong and Bong (Ihm) L.; m. Chunok Im, Dec. 22, 1974; children—Spencer, Edward. B.S., Seoul Nat. U., 1970, M.S., 1972; Ph.D., U. Utah, 1979. Instr. Korean Mil. Acad., Seoul, 1972-74, Gook Min. U., Seoul, 1974; research asst. U. Utah, Salt Lake City, 1975-79, research assoc., 1979-80, asst. research prof., 1980-81; sr. chemist Alza Co., Palo Alto, Calif., 1981—. Author articles in profl. jours. U. Utah fellow, 1977; Seoul Nat. U. fellow, 1971. Mem. Am. Chem. Soc., Controlled Release Soc., AAAS, Korean Chem. Soc., Am. Pharm. Assn., Rho Chi. Current work: Novel drug delivery system. Subspecialties: Drug delivery systems; Biomaterials. Home: 258 Elwood St Redwood City CA 94062 Office: Alza Co 950 Page Mill Rd Palo Alto CA 94304

LEE, FRANCIS HIM, clinical pharmacologist; b. Swatow, China, Nov. 11, 1948; came to U.S., 1967, naturalized, 1978; s. Y.T. and C.M. (Lam) L.; m. Sheila W. Cheng, Jan. 10, 1974; children—Rebecca, Moses. B.A., U. Oreg., 1971; Ph.D., SUNY-Buffalo, 1975. Assoc. biologist to sr. scientist Sterling Winthrop Research Inst., Rensselaer, N.Y., 1975-77; sr. scientist to asst. clin. research dir. Bristol-Myers Co., Syracuse, N.Y., 1977-82; assoc. clin. research dir. DuPont Co., Wilmington, Del., 1983—. Author abstracts, also articles. Recipient NSF award, 1968. Mem. Am. Assn. Cancer Research, Am. Soc. Clin. Oncology, Am. Soc. Clin. Pharmacology and Therapeutics (manuscript reviewer 1983—). Republican. Baptist. Current work: Clinical cancer research, cytotoxic drugs, cancer biotechnology, cancer diagnosis licensing (technology transfer), clinical pharmacology, phase I-III clinical studies. Subspecialties: Pharmacology; Cancer research (medicine). Office: DuPont Co Barley Mill Plaza Wilmington DE 19898

LEE, GARRETT, physician, researcher; b. San Francisco, June 23, 1946; s. Frederick B. and Josephine (Woo) L. B.A. in Genetics, U. Calif.-Berkeley, 1968; M.D., U. Calif.-Davis, 1972. Med. intern Duke U. Med. Ctr., 1972; med. resident U. Calif.-Davis, 1973, cardiac fellow, 1974, asst. prof. medicine, 1975; dir. U. Calif.-Davis (Cardiac Catherization Lab.), 1977-83, Cardiovascular Laser Research Lab., Cedars Med. Ctr., Miami, Fla., 1983-84; dir. research Western Heart Inst., San Francisco, 1984—. Contbr. articles to profl. jours. Recipient Med. Student Research award U. Calif.-Davis, 1972. Fellow Am. Coll. Clin. Pharmacology, Am. Soc. Laser Medicine and Surgery; mem. Am. Heart Assn. (dir. Golden Empire chpt.), Alpha Omega Alpha. Current Work: Use of laser in the treatment of cardiovascular diseases, cardiovascular laser research, cardiologist, cardiac catheterization. Subspecialties: Cardiology; Laser medicine. Office: 450 Stanyan St San Francisco CA 94117

LEE, GEORGE C., civil engineering educator, university dean; b. Beijing, China, July 17, 1933; came to U.S., 1956; s. Shun C. and J. T. (Chang) L.; m. Grace S. Su, July 29, 1961; children—David S., Kelvin H. B.S.E., Nat. Taiwan U., 1955; M.S.C.E., Lehigh U., 1958, Ph.D., 1960. Research assoc. Lehigh U., Bethlehem, Pa., 1960-61; asst. prof. civil engrng. SUNY-Buffalo, 1961-63, assoc. prof., 1963-67, prof., 1967—, chmn. dept., 1974-77, dean engrng., 1977—; sr. research fellow Harvard U., 1969-70; head engrng. mechanics NSF, 1977-78; assoc. dir. Calspan-UB Research Ctr., Buffalo, 1983—. Author: Structural Analysis and Design, 1979; Design of Single Story Rigid Frames, 1981. Contbr. articles to profl. jours. Recipient Superior Accomplishment award NSF, 1977; Engrng. Accomplishment award Chinese Inst. Engrs., 1979. Mem. ASCE, Am. Welding Soc. (Adams Meml. award 1974), Welding Research Council, Structural Stability Research Council, Am. Soc. Engrng. Edn., AAAS, Sigma Xi, Tau Beta Pi. Current work: Structural analysis and design; nonlinear structural mechanics; biomechanics of soft tissue; engineering administration. Subspecialties: Structural engineering; Biomedical engineering. Home: 288 Countryside Ln Williamsville NY 14221 Office: Faculty of Engrng and Applied Scis SUNY Buffalo Buffalo NY 14260

LEE, GRIFF CALICUTT, civil engineer; b. Jackson, Miss., Aug. 17, 1926; s. Griff and Lida (Higgs) L.; m. Eugenia Humphreys, July 29, 1950; children: Griff Calicutt III, Robert H., Carol E. B.E., Tulane U., 1948; M.S., Rice U., 1951. Civil engr. Humble Oil & Refining Co., New Orleans, Houston, 1948-54; design engr. J. Ray McDermott & Co., Inc., New Orleans, 1954-66, chief engr., 1966-75, group v.p., 1975-80, v.p., group exec., 1980-83; cons. engr. Griff C. Lee Inc., 1983—; mem. vis. com. dept. civil engrng. U. Tex.; mem. adv. bd. Tulane U., Rice U., MIT; mem. marine bd. NRC. Contbr. articles to profl. jours. Served with USN, 1944-46. Mem. Nat. Acad. Engrng., Am. Bur. Shipping, Am. Concrete Inst., ASCE, Am. Welding Soc., Soc. Petroleum Engrs., Am. Petroleum Inst. Presbyterian. Clubs: International House, City, Petroleum of New Orleans, Bienville, Vista Shores Country. Subspecialty: Civil engineering. Home: 6353 Carlson Dr New Orleans LA 70122 Office: 1010 Common St New Orleans LA 70112

LEE, HARRY WILLIAM, forest engineering educator, researcher; b. Bonners Ferry, Idaho, Sept. 26, 1938; s. Robert Edward and Laura Rhoda (Knowles) L.; m. Evelyn Louise Robinson, Aug. 7, 1962; children: Larissa Dawn, Branda Carol. B.S. in Chem. Engrng, U. Idaho, 1972, M.S. in Chem. Engring, 1977, Ph.D. in Agrl Engring, 1982. Asst. county planner, Latah County, Moscow, Idaho, 1972-74; regional planner State Idaho, Moscow, 1974-79; research assoc. Agrl. Engrng. U. Idaho, Moscow., 1979-80, instr. forest products., 1980-82. Author: Latah County Flood Plain Analysis, 1973, Flood Insurance Brochure, 1976. Planning Commn. Latah County, 1980; study com. Sch. Facilities, Moscow, 1978. Served with U.S. Army, 1961-63. Recipient outstanding civil engrng. student ASCE, 1972. Mem. Nat. Audubon Soc., Am. Soc. Agrl. Engrs. Republican. Current Work: Primary interests are in soil and water conservation applied to forest harvesting schedules; forest harvesting equipment research and development. Subspecialties: Resource conservation; Civil engineering. Home: 1017 N Almon Moscow ID 83843 Office: Dept Forest Products U Idaho Moscow ID 83843

LEE, HAZEL ANN, veterinarian, educator; b. Pitts., Jan. 31, 1952; d. Otis and Grace Lovina (Garner) L. B.A., U. Pa., 1973; B.S., Tuskegee Inst., 1975, D.V.M., 1977. Research asst. Am. Cyanamid Co., Princeton, N.J., 1975; large animal clinic asst., sci. tutor, Tuskegee Inst., Tuskegee, Ala., 1975-77; resident in equine medicine and surgery Wash. State U., Pullman, 1977-79; instr. Harcum Jr. Coll., Bryn Mawr, Pa., 1980-82; free-lance vet. researcher, Phila., 1982—. Vol. Phila. Democratic Com., 1982—. Mem. AVMA, Tuskegee Vet. Alumni Assn., Assn. Women Veterinarians, NAACP, Wash. State Black Women's Orgn., Nat. Flute Assn., Phi Zeta, Beta Kappa Chi. Presbyterian. Current work: Physiological assessment of cardiac and pulmonary diseases in large animals. Subspecialties: Internal medicine (veterinary medicine); Surgery (veterinary medicine). Address: PO Box 2074 Philadelphia PA 19103

LEE, HENRY JOUNG, biological chemist, educator; b. Seoul, Korea, Nov. 17, 1941; s. Hun-Sang and Chung-ok (Kim) L.; m. Hyoja Sue, July 11, 1969; children: Lois, Angie, Jenny. B.S., Seoul Nat. U., 1964, M.S., 1966; Ph.D., Okla. State U., 1971. Research assoc. Mt. Sinai Sch. Medicine, N.Y.C., 1971-73; asst. prof. Fla. A&M U., Tallahassee, 1973-79, assoc. prof., 1979-82, prof., 1982—; head Fla. A&M U. (Center Anti-inflammatory Research), 1982—; vis. scientist Rockefeller U., N.Y.C., 1979; NSF grant reviewer. Editor: Progress in Research and Clinical Application of Corticosteroids, 1982. NIH grantee, 1978—; recipient Fla. A&M U. research award, 1981, service award, 1982. Mem. Am. Soc. Biol. Chemistry, Am. Chem. Soc., Sigma Xi. Democrat. Baptist. Current Work: chemical synthesis and evaluation of new corticosteroids for the development of new anti-inflammatory steroids without side effects. Subspecialty: Medicinal chemistry. Home: 2521 Harriman Circle Tallahassee FL 32312 Office: Fla A&M U Tallahassee FL 32307

LEE, INSU PETER, pharmacologist; b. Kaesong, Korea, Dec. 25, 1935; came to U.S., 1956, naturalized, 1965; s. C.S. and J.S. L.; m. Chong W. Lee, Mar. 11, 1962; children: Deborah, Frederick, Michelle, Jacqueline. B.A., Pacific Luth. U., 1959; Ph.D., U. Wash., 1969. Pharmacologist Nat. Cancer Inst., Bethesda, Md., 1969-72; sr. staff fellow Nat. Inst. Environ. Health Sci., Research Triangle Park, N.C., 1972-74, pharmacologist, 1974—. Contbr. numerous articles to U.S. and internat. sci. jours. Am. Cancer Soc. research grantee Sch. Medicine, U. Wash., 1968-69; NIH predoctoral trainee, 1968-69; fellow Japan Soc. Promotion Sci., 1981. Mem. Am. Soc. Microbiology, AAAS, Soc. Toxicology, European Soc. Toxicology, Am. Soc. Pharmacology and Exptl. Therapeutics, Internat. Union Toxicology, Sigma Xi. Republican. Current Work: Reproductive and developmental toxicology, enzyme induction, gene expression, PAH metabolism, DNA repair, mutagenesis and carcinogenesis. Subspecialties: Cellular pharmacology; Toxicology (medicine).

LEE, JAMES TRAVIS, JR., surgeon; b. Wichita Falls, Tex., Apr. 20, 1943; s. James Travis and Mary Ann (Walker) L. B.A., U. Tex., 1964; M.S., U. Ill., 1966; Ph.D., 1968; M.D., U. Minn., 1975. Diplomate: Am. Bd. Surgery. Chemist Phillips Petroleum Co., Bartlesville, Okla., 1964; sr. chemist 3M Co., St. Paul, 1968-72; research fellow U. Minn., Mpls., 1975-81, asst. prof. surgery, 1981—; staff surgeon VA Hosp., Mpls., 1981—. Mem. Am. Fedn. Clin. Research, Sigma Xi, Alpha Chi Sigma, Phi Lambda Upsilon, Phi Kappa Phi. Republican. Club: Rattlesnake Lodge. Current Work: Surgical infections in compromised hosts. Subspecialties: Surgery; Organic chemistry. Home: 2085 Dotte Dr White Bear Lake MN 55110 Office: Mpls VA Hosp Surg-012 Minneapolis MN 55417

LEE, JOHN FRANCIS, management consulting company executive; b. Boston, Sept. 19, 1918; s. Michael Francis and Catherine Mary (Arrigal) L.; m. Helene Zinka Comes, May 15, 1946 (div. 1972); children: Anne-marie Lee Dorman, Robert Paul, Virginia Louise Lee Linden, Jacqueline. S.B., The Citadel, Charleston, S.C., 1947; S.M., Harvard U., 1948; Sc.D., U. London, 1968; Litt.D. (hon.), U. Malaga, Spain, 1972. Registered profl. engr., D.C., Maine. Asst. prof. engring. U. Maine, Orono, 1948-50, assoc. prof., 1950-52; Broughton prof. engring. N.C. State U., 1952-61; pres. SUNY-Stony Brook, 1961-62; spl. adviser NSF, Washington, 1962; pres., chief exec. officer Internat. Devel. Services, Inc., Washington, 1962-71, Promotorco (S.A.), Luxembourg, 1971-79, Intercontinental Mgmt. Consultants, Inc., Torrance, Calif., 1979—; participant White House Conf. on Internat. Coop., Washington, 1965; personal rank of ambassador Intergovtl. Com. European Migration-Argentina Negotiations, Washington, Buenos Aires, 1968. Author: Theory & Design of Steam & Gas Turbines, 1961, Thermodynamics, 1962, Statistical Thermodynamics, 1973; contbr. numerous articles to profl. jours. Served to maj. U.S. Army, 1941-45. Named Ambassador of Goodwill State of N.C., 1961; decorated Order So. Cross Govt. of Brazil, Order Bernardo O'Higgins Govt. of Chile, Chevalier Legiond'Honeur Govt. of France. Mem. IEEE, AIAA, Optical Soc. Am., Internat. Soc. Hybrid Microelectronics, Soc. Photo-Optical Instrumentation Engrs., Am. Fgn. Service Assn. Unitarian. Clubs: Cosmos (Washington), Internat. (Washington); Jockey (Paris). Current Work: Communication theory; ballistic missile defense; high technology management. Subspecialties: Thermodynamics; Statistical mechanics. Home: 6702 Los Verdes Dr NUM*2 Rancho Palos Verdes CA 90274 Office: Intercontinental Management Consultants Inc 3838 Carson St #110 Torrance CA 90503

LEE, JOHN JOSEPH, marine microbiologist, educator, researcher; b. Phila., Feb. 23, 1933; s. Herbert L. and Janet (Strouse) L.; m. Judith Gail Raskin, May 27, 1956; children—Monica Jane and James Mathew. B.A., Queens Coll., 1955; M.S., U. Mass., 1956; Ph.D., NYU, 1960. Instr., Queens Coll., N.Y.C., 1959-61; asst. prof. NYU, 1961-66; assoc. prof. to prof. dept. biology CUNY, 1966-71, 72—, radiation safety officer, 1980—; research assoc. fellow Am. Mus. Natural History, N.Y.C., 1957—; research assoc. Haskins Labs., N.Y.C., 1957—, Lamont-Doherty Geol. Obs., Palisades, N.Y., 1961-82. Author: Microbiology, 1983; Author, editor: Illustrated Guide to Prototoa, 1984. Contbr. articles to profl. jours. Bd. dirs. Ridgewood YMCA, N.J., 1970—; pres. bd. edn. Hillsdale Schs., N.J., 1974—. Recipient Man of Yr. award B'nai B'rith Women, 1979; Meads award Ridgewood YMCA, 1982. Mem. Soc. Protozoologists (editorial bd., membership sec., chmn. various coms.), Internat. Commn. on Protzoology (sec. 1974-81), Am. Soc. Microbiologists, Am. Soc. Limnologists and Oceanographers, Am. Micros. Soc. Current work: Protozology, foraminifera, micropaleontology, marine food webs, diatoms, meiofauna, intestinal flagellates, symbiosis. Subspecialties: Marine biology: Ecology (environmental science). Home: 61 Hopper St Hillsdale NJ 07642 Office: Dept Biology CUNY Convent Ave at 138 St New York NY 10031

LEE, JOHN YUCHU, research chemist; b. Tai-Ho, An-Huei, China, Jan. 25, 1948; came to U.S., 1971, naturalized, 1981; s. Tzu-Ching and Hua-Yin (Liao) L.; m. Sheila Yunchi Tsai, May 1, 1976; children—Gary Chiaray, Jenny Chianing. B.S., Nat. Cheng-Kung U., Taiwan, 1970; M.S., S.D. State U., 1974; Ph.D., Vanderbilt U., 1978. Teaching asst. S.D. State U., Brookings, 1973-74; grad. asst. Vanderbilt U., Nashville, 1974-78; research assoc. chemistry dept. Tex. A&M U., College Station, 1978-79, Welch research fellow chemistry dept., 1979-80; research chemist Ethyl Corp., Baton Rouge, La., 1980—. Contbr. articles to profl. jours. Patentee in field. Active in Chinese Assn. Baton Rouge, 1980—; spl. mem. Chinese Student Assn. Tex. A&M U., College Station, 1978-80; chmn. Chinese Student Assn. Nashville, 1975-76. Served to 2d lt. Chinese Air Force, 1970-71. Fellow Am. Inst. Chemists; mem. Am. Chem. Soc., Royal Soc. Chemistry (assoc.), Japanese Chem. Soc., S.D. Acad. Sci., Chinese Am. Chem. Assn., Sigma Xi, Phi Lambda Upsilon. Roman Catholic. Clubs: Ethyl Mgmt., Kenilworth (Baton Rouge). Current work: Synthesis, isolation and characterization of pharmaceutical, agricultural, surfactant, and detergent intermediates, as well as process improvement. Subspecialties: Organic chemistry; Synthetic chemistry. Home: 1524 Stoneliegh Dr Baton Rouge LA 70808 Office: Ethyl Corp Central Research Lab Box 341 Baton Rouge LA 70821

LEE, LIHSYNG STANFORD, cancer researcher, geneticist, engineer; b. China, Oct. 28, 1945; came to U.S., 1969, naturalized, 1980; s. Honping and Kuorung (Shea) L.; m. Alice S.F. Chang, Sept. 8, 1974; 1 child, Jenny. B.S. B.S. (Tyen-yu-tan scholar), Nat. Taiwan U., 1968; M.Phil. (fellow), Yale U., 1971, M.S. (fellow), 1972, Ph.D. (fellow), 1974. Postdoctoral fellow Roswell Park Meml. Inst., Buffalo, 1974-76; staff assoc. Columbia U. Coll. Physicians and Surgeons, N.Y.C., 1976-79; mem. staff Gen. Electric Research Center, Schenectady, 1979-84; prin. scientist Cytogen Corp., Princeton, N.J., 1984—. Contbr. numerous articles to sci. jours. Served to 2d lt. Taiwan Army, 1968. NIH grantee, 1976-79. Mem. Am. Soc. Pharmacology and Exptl. Therapeutics, Am. Soc. Cell Biology, Am. Soc. Microbiology, Am. Assn. Cancer Research, Am. Coll. Toxicology, N.Y. Acad. Sci., Sigma Xi. Current Work: Cell culture, biotechnology, hybridoma, transgenic mice, recombinant DNA, gene cloning, cellular pharmacology, biochemistry molecular biology, membrane biology, immunoradio-technology, computer technology. Subspecialties: Genetics and genetic engineering (biology); Cancer research (medicine). Home: 22 Van Wyck Dr Princeton Junction NJ 08550 Office: 201 College Rd East Princeton NJ 08540

LEE, LONG C., electrical engineering educator; b. Taiwan, Oct. 19, 1940; s. Chin L. and Wang (Wen) L.; m. Laura M. Cheng., Dec. 1, 1967; children: Gloria, Thomas. B.S., Taiwan Normal U., 1964; A.M., U. So. Calif., 1967, Ph.D., 1971. Research assoc. U. So. Calif., 1971-77; sr. physicist SRI Internat., Menlo Park, Calif., 1977-81; prof. elec. and computer engring. San Diego State U., 1982—. Contbr. articles to profl. jours. NASA grantee, 1979—; NSF grantee, 1980—; Air Force Office of Sci. Research grantee, 1980—. Mem. Am. Phys. Soc., Interam. Photochemistry Soc., IEEE, Am. Geophys. Union. Current Work: Photoabsoprtion, photonization, and photodissociation processes of molecules, radicals and aerosols. Subspecialties: Atomic and molecular physics; Laser spectroscopy. Office: Dept Elec and Computer Engring San Diego State U San Diego CA 92182

LEE, MARTIN ALAN, space physicist; b. Bromley, Eng., Oct. 9, 1945; came to U.S., 1948, naturalized, 1955; s. Erastus H. and Shirley (Wilson) L. B.S. in Physics, Stanford U., 1966; Ph.D. in Physics, U. Chgo., 1971. Research assoc. Max-Planck-Inst. Extraterrestrial Physics, Munich, W.Ger., 1971-73, U. Chgo., 1973-74; asst. prof. physics Washington U., St. Louis, 1974-79; sr. research scientist U. N.H., Durham, 1979—. Contbr. articles to profl. jours. NASA grantee; recipient Mark Perry Geller prize U. Chgo., 1971; NATO postdoctoral fellow, 1971. Member. Am. Geophys. Union, Am. Astron. Soc. Current Work: Theoretical plasma astrophysics: energetic particle transport, shock acceleration of energetic particles, plasma waves, cosmic ray physics. Subspecialties: Theoretical astrophysics; Solar physics. Home: N River Rd RFD 1 Newmarket NH 03857 Office: Space Sci Ctr DeMereitt Hall U NH Durham NH 03824

LEE, MARY BRONWYN, clinical neuropsychologist, consultant; b. Atlanta, July 29, 1957; d. Joseph Merrill and Mary Isabella (Nichols) B. B.S., Georgetown U., 1978; Ph.D., U. Tex.-Austin, 1981. Postdoctoral research fellow NIMH, Princeton, N.J., 1981; clin. neuropsychologist John F. Kennedy Med. Center, Edison, N.J., 1981-82; dir. cognitive rehab. and research The Head Injury Center Lewis Bay, Hyannis, Mass., 1982-83; dir. Neurologic Ctr. at Forest Manor, Middleboro, Mass., 1982 ; cons. Center for Battered Women, Austin, Tex., 1979-81, Assn. Advancement of Mentally Handicapped, Princeton, N.J., 1981-82; also pvt. practice, Alpine, Calif. Editor: Jour. Community Psychology, 1980-81. U. Tex.-Austin research grantee, 1980. Mem. Am. Psychol. Soc., Internat. Neuropsychol. Soc. Democrat. Methodist. Current Work: Research in cognitive rehabilitation, restitution of function, research in etiology of the psychoses, epidemiology of mental illness. Subspecialties: Neuropsychology; Neurophysiology. Office: Alpine Med Ctr 2065 Arnold Way Suite 103 Alpine CA 92001

LEE, MICHAEL CHING HSUEH, material engineering scientist; b. Taipei, Republic of China, Oct. 3, 1949; came to U.S. 1972; s. Jen Hsuan and Pei Chang (Chao) L; m. Amy Hsuan Yi Hsu, July 20, 1972; children—Benjamin, Josephine, David. B.S.E., Nat. Taiwan Cheng Kung U., 1970; M.S., U. Calif.-Berkeley, 1974; Ph.D., 1977. Postdoctoral research engr. U. Calif.-Berkeley, 1977-78; sr. engr. elastomer group Gen. Motors Research Labs., Warren, Mich., 1978-81; staff engr. reinforced elastomer group, 1981-83, staff engr., group leader engineered polymers, 1983—. Co-author: Adhesive Chemistry-Developments and Trends, 1984. Contbr. articles to profl. jours. Patentee in field. Charles L. McCuen Spl. Achievement award Gen. Motors Research Labs, 1984. Mem. Am. Chem. Soc., Soc. Automotive Engring., Soc. Rheology. Current work: Polymer thermodynamics, rheology, composition-processing-structure-property relationships, polymer mixing and processing, polymer alloys, polymer tribology, automobile elastomers. Subspecialties: Polymers (materials science); Polymer engineering. Office: Twelve Mile and Mound Rds Gen Motors Research Labs Warren MI 48090-9055

LEE, MICKEY MITCHELL, psychological and educational consultant, researcher; b. Erie, Pa., Dec. 20, 1950; s. Mickey Mitchell and Anita L. B.S., Slippery Rock State Coll., 1973; Ed.S. and M.Ed., Edinboro State Coll., 1975; Ph.D., U. Ala., 1977. Cert. ednl. psychology researcher and sch. psychologist. Post-doctoral intern N.W. Regional Edn. Lab., Portland, Oreg., 1978, research assoc., Juneau, Alaska, 1978-79; ednl. psychologist Auburn U., Montgomery, Ala., 1977-78; psychol. and ednl. cons. La. State U. Sch. Dentistry, New Orleans, 1979—; adj. faculty U. New Orleans, 1980-81; cons. Geotrud Bapber Center, Erie, Pa., 1974, Alaska Dept. Edn., Juneau, 1978, La. State U. Sch. Nursing, 1980, La. State U. Med. Center, New Orleans, 1982. Counselor Crisis Line, New Orleans, 1982. Mem. Am. Assn. Cancer Edn., Internat. Assn. Dental Research, Am. Assn. Dental Schs., Am. Ednl. Research Assn., Mid-South Ednl. Research Assn. Russian Orthodox. Current Work: Survey design and analysis; prediction of academic success from non-cognitive variables; evaluation studies. Home: 2719 Ursuline (side) New Orleans LA 70119 Office: La State U Sch Dentistry 1100 Florida Ave New Orleans LA 70119

LEE, MIKE YUAN, nuclear engineer, researcher; b. Chung King, Sichuan, China, June 6, 1941; came to U.S., 1964, naturalized, 1976; s. Chien-nan and Fong-shan (Young) L.; m. Anna Mo-Chee Fung, June 5, 1976; children—Vincent John, Joey John. B.S., Nat. Cheng Kung U., Taiwan, 1963; M.S., N.C. State U., 1966, Nuclear Engr., 1972. Nuclear safety engr. Babcock & Wilcox Co., Lynchburg, Va., 1966-69; sr. nuclear steam supply system engr. Combustion Engring. Co., Windsor, Conn., 1972-76; advanced nuclear physics engr. Westinghouse Hanford Co., Hanford Engring. Devel. Lab., Richland, Wash., 1976-82; sr. core analysis engr., supr. Duquesne Light Co., Pitts., 1982-85, prin. nuclear engr., 1985—. Contbr. articles to profl. jours. Mem. Am. Nuclear Soc. Current work: Work on and supervise: nuclear reactor core analysis, neutron diffusion, neutron transport, hypothetical accident analysis, nuclear safety analysis, thermal reactor and fast breeder reactor physics research. Subspecialty: Nuclear fission. Home: PO Box 14572 Pittsburgh PA 15234 Office: Robinson Plaza #3 Suite 305 Pa Route 60 Pittsburgh PA 15205

LEE, RICHARD M, psychologist; b. Long Beach, N.Y., May 6, 1938; m. Julia Ann Kerstetter, Jan. 30, 1965. B.S., U. Mich., 1959; Ph.D., U. Md., 1966. Lic. psychologist, Mich. USPHS fellow U. Md., College Park, 1963; research assoc. Henry Ford Hosp., Detroit, 1966-67, div. chief, 1967-73; lab. dir. E.B. Ford Inst., Detroit, 1971-78, pvt. practice psychology, Bloomfield Hills, Mich., 1978—; adj. assoc. prof. psychology Wayne State U., Detroit, 1975—; reviewer/cons. NSF, Washington, 1970-78, Science, Washington, 1965-75. Contbr. articles in field to profl. lit. Research grantee NIMH, 1969, 78; Research grantee Mich. Heart Assn., 1973, 76. Mem. Biofeedback Soc. Mich. (pres. 1982—), Am. Psychol. Assn., Biofeedback Soc. Am., Soc. for Neurosci. Inventor, researcher blood pressure tracking system. Current Work: Behavioral science methods for blood pressure control; discrimination (estimation) of blood pressure, self-regulation methods. Subspecialties: Psychophysiology; Psychobiology. Home: 3041 Moon Lake Dr West Bloomfield MI 48033 Office: 2550 S Telegraph St Suite 106 Bloomfield Hills MI 48013

LEE, SI GAPH, obstetrics and gynecology educator, reproductive endocrinologist; b. Seoul, Korea, Jan. 2, 1937; came to U.S., 1965; s. Chang Ran and Sun-Ho L.; m. Esther M Bang, Aug. 29, 1967; children: Susie, Daniel. B.S., Yonsei U., Seoul, 1958, M.D., 1962. Diplomate: Am Coll. Obstetricians and Gynecologists, Am. Bd. Reproductive Endocrinology. Intern Fitkin Meml. Hosp., N.J., 1965-66; resident in ob-gyn Temple U. Hosp., 1966-69; asst. prof. ob.-gyn Temple U. Sch. Medicine, 1971-73; assoc. prof. ob-gyn Sch. Medicine, Sioux Falls, 1974-78, prof. ob-gyn, dir. reproductive endocrinology, 1979—. Contbr. articles to profl. jours. Fellow Am. Coll. Obstetricians and Gynecologists; mem. Endocrine Soc., Am. Fertility Soc., Am. Fedn. Clin. Research. Current Work: Peptides and steroid hormone of the hypothalmic pituitary ovarian feedback system. Subspecialties: Obstetrics and gynecology; Reproductive endocrinology. Home: 2800 Stonehedge Ln Sioux Falls SD 57103 Office: Dept of Obstetrics and Gynecology University of South Dakota 2701 S Spring Ave Sioux Falls SD 57105

LEE, SIN HANG, pathologist, researcher, educator; b. Hong Kong, Nov. 17, 1932; came to U.S., 1963, naturalized, 1976; s. Yat Sun and Siutsing (Wong) L.; m. Kee Hung Hau, Dec. 31, 1958; children—Emil, Karen. M.D., Wuhan Med. Coll., Hankow, Hubei, People's Republic of China, 1956; postgrad. in bacteriology Coll. Medicine, Sichuan Med. Coll., Chengdu, Sichuan, 1956-57. Diplomate Am. Bd. Pathology. Asst. lectr. in bacteriology Sichuan Med. Coll. and bacteriologist Univ. Hosp., 1957-61; demonstrator in pathology U. Hong Kong, 1961-63; rotating intern South Balt. Gen. Hosp., 1963-64; resident N.Y. Hosp., Cornell Med. Ctr., N.Y.C., 1964-65, asst. pathologist, 1965-66, pathologist, 1966-67; fellow in pathology Meml. Hosp. for Cancer and Allied Diseases, N.Y.C., 1967-68; asst. prof. pathology McGill U., Montreal, Que., Can., 1968-71; assoc. prof. pathology Yale U., New Haven, 1971-73, assoc. clin. prof., 1973—; attending pathologist Hosp. St. Raphael, New Haven, 1973—; guest prof. Wuhan Med. Coll., 1984—. Translator into Chinese: Die Praxis der Reistenz und Spiegelbestimmungen zur Antibiotischen Therapie (H-J. Otte and W. Köhler), 1961; also chpts., numerous articles. Patentee cytochem. assay of steroid receptors. Fellow Royal Coll. Physicians and Surgeons Can.; mem. AAAS, Internat. Acad. Pathology, Am. Assn. Pathologists, Pathol. Soc. Great Brit. and Ireland, N.Y. Acad. Scis., Coll. Am. Pathologists. Current work: Actions of steroid hormones at the cellular level, including cancer cells; early detection of mycoplasma infections. Subspecialties: Pathology (medicine); Immunocytochemistry. Office: Hosp of St Raphael 1450 Chapel St New Haven CT 06511

LEE, STUART MILTON, materials scientist; b. N.Y.C., Apr. 14, 1920; s. Herman Bertha (Horowitz) L.; children—Gary, Scott, Randy. B.S. in Chemistry, L.I. U., 1941; M.S. in Chemistry, U. Nev., 1947; Ph.D. in Phys. Organic Chemistry, Fla. State U., 1953. Sr. research chemist Allied Chem. Corp., Hopewell, Va., 1952-59; research chemist Aerojet-Gen., Azusa, Calif., 1959-61; mgr. chem. research and devel. Xerox-Electro-optical Systems, Pasadena, Calif., 1961-64; sr. tech. scientist Rockwell Internat. Corp., Anaheim, Calif., 1964-71; sr. staff scientist Ford Aerospace and Communications Corp., Palo Alto, Calif., 1971-85; cons. SRI Internat., Menlo Park, Calif., 1985—. Assoc. editor Materials and Design Jour., 1981—. Contbr. books on surface analysis, coatings and encapsulants and profl. jours. Patentee in field. Predoctoral fellow Research Corp., 1945. Fellow Soc. Advancement Material and Process Engring. (jour. editor 1979—, Nat. Meritorious Bronze award 1982); mem. Am. Chem. Soc. Subspecialties: Biomaterials; Materials.

LEE, THOMAS HENRY, electrical engineering educator, consultant; b. Shanghai, China, May 11, 1923; s. Y.C. and N.T. (Ho) L.; m. Kim Ping, June 12, 1948; children: William, Thomas Henry, Richard. B.S., Nat. Chiao Tung U., 1946; M.S., Union Coll., 1950; Ph.D., Rensselaer Poly. Inst., 1954. With Gen. Electric Co., 1948-80, mgr. lab. ops., 1967-71, mgr. tech. resources, 1967-71, mgr. strategic planning, 1974-77, staff exec. strategic planning, 1977-78, staff exec., chief technologist, 1978-80; vis. research scientist MIT, 1979-80, prof. elec. engring., 1980-84; assoc. dir. energy lab., Philip Sporn prof. energy processing, 1982—, dir. elec. power systems engring. lab., 1982—; dir. Internat. Inst. Applied Systems Analysis, Vienna, 1984—; exec. com. U.S. Nat. com. CIGRE Internat. Conf. Large High Voltage Electric Systems; lectr. Author: Physics and Engineering of High Power Switching Devices, 1975; contbr. articles to profl. jours. Recipient ann. achievement award Chinese Inst. Engr., 1962; achievement award Chinese Engrs. and Scientists Assn. So. Calif., 1976; meritorious award Power Engring. Soc., 1976; managerial awards Gen. Electric co., 1955-58. Fellow IEEE (pres. Power Engring. Soc.); mem. Nat. Acad. Engring. (founding mem.), Conn. Acad. Sci. and Engring. (chmn.), Am. Phys. Soc., Am. Vacuum Soc., Sigma Xi. Patentee in field. Current Work: Energy systems; energy technology and policy; electric power systems engineering, physical electronics; technology assessment and planning. Subspecialties: Electrical engineering; Energy systems. Home: 33 Chestnut St Boston MA 02108 Office: Massachusetts Institute of Technology Room 10-172 Cambridge MA 02139

LEE, TONY JER-FU, pharmacologist, educator; b. Hualien, Taiwan, Nov. 10, 1942; s. Huo-Yen and Wan L.; m. Mei-shya Su, June 24, 1978; children: Jonathan, Cheryl. B.S., Taipei (Taiwan) Med. Coll., 1967; Ph.D., W.Va. U., 1973. Postdoctoral fellow UCLA, 1973-75; asst. prof. pharmacology So. Ill. U. Sch. Medicine, Springfield, 1975-80, assoc. prof., 1980—. Editorial adv. bd. Jour. Pharmacology and Exptl. Therapeutics. Contbr. articles to profl. jours. Am. Heart Assn. grantee, 1976—; NIH grantee, 1981—. Mem. Am. Soc. Pharmacology and Exptl. Therapeutics, Electron Microscopy Soc. Am., Soc. Neurosci. Current Work: Pharmacology and morphology of blood vessels, cerebral vasodilator and constrictor transmitters, neurogenic control of cerebral and peripheral blood vessel tone in hypertension; immunocytochemistry. Subspecialties: Pharmacology; Microscopy. Home: 61 W Hazel Dell Springfield IL 62707 Office: Dept Pharmacology So Ill Univ Sch Medicine Springfield IL 62702

LEE, TSUNG-DAO, physicist; b. Shanghai, China, Nov. 25, 1926; s. Tsing-Kong L. and Ming-Chang (Chang); m. Jeannette Chin, June 3, 1950; children—James, Stephen. Student, Nat. Chekiang U., Kweichow, China, 1943-44, Nat. S.W. Assoc. U., Kunming, China, 1945-46; Ph.D., U. Chgo., 1950. Research assoc. in astronomy U. Chgo., 1950; research assoc., lectr. physics U. Calif.-Berkeley, 1950-51; mem. Inst. for Advanced Study, Princeton, N.J., 1951-53, prof. physics, 1960-63; asst. prof. Columbia U., N.Y.C., 1953-55, assoc. prof., 1955-56, prof. physics, 1956-60, 63—, Enrico Fermi prof. physics, 1964, adj. prof., 1960-62; Loeb lectr. Harvard U., 1957, 64. Recipient Albert Einstein sci. award Yeshiva U., 1957, Nobel prize in physics (with Chen Ning Yang), 1957. Mem. Nat. Acad. Sci. Subspecialty: Theoretical physics. Office: Dept Physics Columbia U New York NY 10027*

LEE, VAN MING, engineering consultant, educator; b. Shanghai, China, Feb. 17, 1946; came to U.S., 1968; s. Yang Chung and Tsoi Wei (Woo) L.; m. Elizabeth Son-Nuu Tang, June 1, 1973; 1 son, Calvin. B.S., Nat. Taiwan Chung-Hsing U., 1968; M.S., Kans. State U., 1971; Ph.D., NYU, 1978. Cons. Consultants & Designers Inc., Hartford, Conn., 1972-73; environ. engr. Stone & Webster Engring. Corp., Boston, 1973-76; mgr. modeling Equitable Environ. Health, Woodbury, N.Y., 1976-79; project mgr. Parsons Brinckerhoff, N.Y.C., 1979—; adj. asst. prof. CUNY, N.Y.C., 1980-81, SUNY-Old Westbury, 1982-83; asst. prof. computer sci. N.Y. Inst. Tech., 1983—. Mem. ASTM, ASCE (task force, com. 1981—), Acoustical Soc. Am., Soc. Indsl. and Applied Math., Am. Soc. Photogrammetry. Current Work: Application of asymptotic statistics to engineering problems; mathematical modeling and computer simulation; scientific programming and computer graphics. Subspecialties: Programming languages; Integrated systems modelling and engineering. Office: NY Inst Tech Old Westbury NY 11568

LEE, WILLIAM WAI LIM, energy, environmental consultant; b. Shanghai, China, Aug. 6, 1948; came to U.S., 1965; s. Frank H. and Jean (Holt) L. B.S.E., Tulane U, 1969; M.S.E., U. Mich., 1970; S.M.C.E., MIT, 1976, Sc.D., 1977. Cert. civil engr., Calif., N.Y., Pa. Project engr. County Sanitation Dists. Los Angeles, 1970-72; project engr. Woodward-Clyde Cons., San Francisco, 1977-79; asst. prof. dept. civil and urban engring. U. Pa., 1979-82; project dir. R.F. Weston Inc., Rockville, Md., 1982—. Author: Decisions in Marine Mining, 1979; (with M.S. Baram and D.B. Rice) Marine Mining of the Continental Shelf, 1978; editor: Energy '84, Proc. of ASCE Splty. Conf., 1984; contbr. articles in field to profl. jours. Mem. AAAS, ASCE, Soc. Risk Analysis, Ops. Research in Soc. Am., Inst. Mgmt. Scis. Am. Baptist. Current Work: Mathematical modeling of nuclear waste systems; use of quantitative analysis to provide insights into natural resources management and environmental quality problems. Subspecialties: Resource management; Operations research (engineering). Home: 1 Mirrasou Ln Gaithersburg MD 20878

LEE, WYLIE IN-WEI, biomedical engineer; b. Tainan, Taiwan, Aug. 18, 1941; s. Tien-chi and Joan (Huang) L.; m. Nancy Kuo, Jan. 29, 1966; children: Marilyn, Jennifer, Arthur. B.Sc., Taiwan Normal U., 1963; Ph.D., U. Mass., Amherst, 1971. Postdoctoral fellow Manchester (Eng.) U., 1971-72; bioengring. fellow U. Wash., Seattle, 1975-77, asst. prof., 1977-81, assoc. prof., 1981-84; sr. research physicist Syva Co., Palo Alto, Calif., 1984—; cons. Poalyta Co., Taipei, 1982—, Syva Co., Palo Alto, Calif., 1980-81. Pres. Taiwanese Am. Assn., Seattle, 1976. Recipient grants NIH, 1978, 83; Burroughs Wellcome Fund, 1982. Mem. N. Am. Taiwanese Profs. Assn. (dir. 1982-83), Am. Phys. Soc., Biophys. Soc., Am. Fertility Soc. Patentee cilioscope, laser spermometer. Current Work: Biomedical applications of dynamic laser scattering with emphasis on reproductive biology and characterization of biomaterials; development of new clinical instruments using high technology such as microcomputers, lasers optical fibers and fluorescence immunoassays. Subspecialties: Biomedical engineering; Laser medicine. Office: Syva Research Inst 900 Arastradero Rd Palo Alto CA 94303

LEE, YEU-TSU MARGARET, surgeon; b. Sian, Shensi, China, Mar. 18, 1936; d. Kiang-Piao Nee and Lien-Luan Soong; m. Vin-Jang Thomas Lee, Dec. 29, 1962; 1 son, Maxwell Ming-Dao. Student, Nat. Taiwan U., 1953-55; B.A., U. S.D., 1957; M.D. cum laude, Harvard U., 1961. Intern, resident in gen. surgery U. Mich. Hosp., Ann Arbor, 1961-64; sr., chief resident in gen. surgery U. Mo. Hosp., Columbia, 1964-66; post-residency clin. fellow, then cons. surgeon Ellis Fischel State Cancer Hosp., Columbia, 1966-72; asst. prof. UCLA, 1972-73; assoc. prof. surgery U. So. Calif., Los Angeles, 1973-84; head physician Tumor Surgery Service, Los Angeles County-U. So. Calif. Med. Ctr., 1973-84; assoc. clin. prof. Surgery U. Hawaii, 1984—; chief surg. oncology sect. dept. surgery Tripler Army Med. Ctr., Honolulu, 1984—. Author book; contbr. articles to profl. jours. Recipient Service to Humanity award United Chinese-Am. League, 1974; Nat. Cancer Inst. grantee, 1981-84. Fellow ACS; mem. Am. Assn. Cancer Research, AMA, Am. Soc. Clin. Oncology, Soc. Surg. Oncology, Orgn. Chinese-Am. Women. Democrat. Roman Catholic. Current Work: Surgical diagnosis, treatment and clinical research on cancer. Subspecialties: Surgery; Oncology. Home: 1147 Ala Napunani St Apt 605 Honolulu HI 96818 Office: Dept Surgery Tripler Army Med Ctr Honolulu HI 96859

LEE, YONG-JAI, pharmaceutical laboratory administrator, chemist; b. Korea, Nov. 25, 1937; s. Kang-Hee and Ok-Bun (Shin) L.; m. Myung-Ja Oh, Oct. 30, 1964; children—Hyunah, Royce. B.S., Seoul Nat. U., 1960, M.S., 1964; Ph.D., U. N.C., 1972. Instr., Korean Air Force Acad., Seoul, 1960-64; research assoc. U. Rochester, N.Y., 1975-76, U. Okla., 1977-81; group leader Ayerst Lab. Inc., Rouses Point, N.Y., 1982—. Mem. Am. Chem. Soc., N.Y. Acad. Sci., Am. Pharm. Assn., Sigma Xi, Phi Lambda Upsilon. Current work: Physical pharmacy of drug products, preformulation; study of new drug substances, chemical degradation of drugs and reaction kinetics. Subspecialties: Organic chemistry; Drug delivery systems. Home: 45 Trafalgar Dr Plattsburgh NY 12901 Office: Ayerst Labs Inc 64 Maple St Rouses Point NY 12979

LEE, YUAN TSEH, chemist, educator, cons.; b. Hsinchu, Taiwan, China; s. Tsefan and Pei (Tasi) L.; m. Bernice Wu, June 28, 1963; children: Ted, Sidney, Charlotte. B.S., Nat. Taiwan U., 1959; M.S., Nat. Tsinghue U., 1961; Ph.D., U. Calif.-Berkeley, 1965. Asst. prof. to prof. chemistry U. chgo., 1968-74; then prof. U. Calif., Berkeley, 1974—; also prin. investigator U. Calif. (Lawrence Berkeley Lab.). Contbr. numerous articles on chem. physics to profl. jours. Recipient Ernest O. Lawrence award Dept. Energy, 1981; Alfred P. Sloan fellow, 1969-71; Camille and Henry Dreyfus Found. tchr. scholar grantee, 1971-74; John Simon Guggenheim fellow, 1976-77. Fellow Am. Phys. Soc., Am. Acad. Arts and Scis.; mem. Am. Chem. Soc., AAAS, Nat. Acad. Scis. Current Work: Dynamics of elem. chem. reactions and laser photochemistry by crossed molecular beams methods. Subspecialties: Physical chemistry; Kinetics. Office: U Calif Lawrence Berkeley Lab 70A-4414 Berkeley CA 94720

LEE ROARK, CAROL KINDLE, geologist; b. Pitts., Dec. 25, 1957; d. Walter Marston and Donna Mae (Kindle) Lee; m. Timothy Louis Roark, Oct. 4, 1984. B.S., Muskingum Coll., 1979; postgrad. Cornell U., 1984—. Environ. geologist U.S. Geol. Survey, Miami Beach, Fla., 1979; exploration geologist Kerr & Assoc., Denver, 1980-84; cons. CKLR Cons., Lansing, N.Y., 1983—. Nat. Assn. Geology Tchrs. scholar, 1978-79. Mem. Am. Assn. Petroleum Geologists, Geol. Soc. Am., Soc. Econ. Mineralogists and Paleontologists (Rocky Mountain sect.). Current work: Sedimentary basin modelling and analysis; Precambrian geology; eustatic sea level changes and carbonate stratigraphy Subspecialty: Geology. Office: 1142 Snell Hall Cornell U Ithaca NY

LEES, LESTER, aeronautical engineering educator; b. N.Y.C., Nov. 8, 1920; s. Harry and Dorothy (Innenberg) L.; m. Constance Louise Morton, Aug. 30, 1941; 1 son, David Grayson. B.S., M.I.T., 1940, M.S., 1941. Research fellow, instr. math. Calif. Inst. Tech., 1942-44, asso. prof. aeros., 1953-55, prof., 1955-74, dir. environ. quality lab., 1970-74, prof. environ. engring. and aeronautics, mem. sr. staff environ. quality lab., 1974—; aero. engr. Nat. Adv. Com for Aeros., Langley Field, Va., 1944-46; asst. prof. aero. engring. Princeton U., 1946-48, assoc. prof., 1948-53; cons. TRW, 1953—, Aerospace Corp., 1960-65. Contbr. articles to profl. jours. Fellow Am. Acad. Arts and Scis., AIAA (hon.); mem. Nat. Acad. Engring. Democrat. Jewish. Current Work: Effects of carbon dioxide emission from man-made sources on earth's temperature and climate. Subspecialties: Ecology (environmental science); Theoretical ecology. Home: 1911 N Pepper Dr Altadena CA 91001 Office: Calif Inst Tech 1201 E California Blvd Pasadena CA 91125

LEES, MARJORIE BERMAN, biomedical researcher; b. N.Y.C., Mar. 17, 1923; d. Isadore I. and Ruth (Rogal) Berman; m. Sidney Lees, Sept. 17, 1946; children: David, Andrew, Eliot. Ph.D., Radcliffe Coll.-Harvard U., 1951. Asst. and assoc. biochemist McLean Hosp., 1955-62; assoc. biochemist and biochemist, 1966-76; sr. research assoc. in pharmacology Dartmouth Coll. Med. Sch., 1962-66; sr. research assoc., mem. faculty Harvard U. Med. Sch., Boston, 1975—; biochemist E.K. Shriver Center, Mass. Gen. Hosp., Boston, 1976—; mem. nat. adv. council Nat. Inst. Neurol. and Communicative Disorders and Stroke, 1979-82; grant reviewer for NIH and NSF. Contbr. numerous articles to sci. jours.; mem. editorial bd. Jour. Neurochemistry, chief editor, 1986—. Named to Hunter Coll. Hall of Fame, 1982; NIH grantee, 1962—. Mem. Am. Soc. Biol. Chemists, Internat. Soc. for Neurochemistry, Am. Soc. for Neurochemistry (treas. 1975-81, pres. 1982-84), Soc. for Neurosci., Am. Soc. Neuropathologist, N.Y. Acad. Scis. Current Work: Neurochemical research as applied to problems of mental retardation; myelin and demyelinating disorders. Subspecialties: Neurochemistry; Neuroimmunology. Home: 50 Eliot Memorial Rd Newton MA 02158 Office: EK Shriver Center 200 Trapelo Rd Waltham MA 02254

LEEVY, CARROLL MOTON, medical educator, hepatology researcher; b. Columbia, S.C., Oct. 13, 1920; s. Isaac S. and Mary (Kirkl) L.; m. Ruth S. Barboza, Feb. 4, 1956; children: Carroll Barboza, Maria Secora. A.B., Fisk U., 1941; M.D., U. Mich., 1944; Sc.D., N.J. Inst. Tech., 1973; D.Hum., Fisk U., 1981. Intern Jersey City Med. Center, 1944-45, resident, 1945-48, dir. clin. investigation, 1947-57; fellow Banting-Best Inst., U. Toronto, 1953; research assoc. Harvard Med. Sch., 1959; assoc. prof. Univ. Medicine and Dentistry of N.J., 1960-64, prof., 1964; dir. div. hepatology and nutrition N.J. Med. Sch., 1959-75, acting chmn. dept. medicine, 1966-68, chief of medicine, 1968-71, chmn. dept. medicine, 1975—; physician-in-chief Univ. Hosp.; sci. dir. Sammy Davis Jr. Liver Inst., 1985— dir. Liver Center, Univ. Medicine and Dentistry N.J., 1983—; sci. dir. Sammy Davis Jr. Nat. Liver Inst., 1985—; chief of medicine VA Hosp., East Orange, N.J., 1966-71; cons. U.S. Navy, 1956-60, NIH, 1965—, VA, 1966—, FDA, 1970-80; Alcohol and Nutrition Found., 1970-74, Am. Liver Found., 1979-83; mem. expert com. on chronic liver disease Digestive Disease Commn., WHO, 1978. Author: Practical Diagnosis and Treatment of Liver Disease, 1957, Anatomic Diagnosis of Liver Disease, 1970, 2d edit., 1985, Evaluation of Liver Function in Clinical Practice, 1965, 2d edit., 1974, Anatomical Diagnosis of Liver and Biliary Tract Disease, 1968, 2d edit., 1985; Liver Regeneration in Man, 1973, The Liver and Its Diseases, 1973, Diseases of the Liver and Biliary Tract, 1977, Guidelines for Detection of Drug and Chemical-Induced Hepatotoxicity, 1979, Alcohol and the Digestive Tract, 1981; Contbr. numerous articles to med., sci. jours. Served to comdr. USNR, 1954-60. Recipient Edward Ill award, 1973; Modern Medicine award, 1972. Mem. Am. Assn. for Study of Liver Diseases (pres. 1967-68, chmn. steering com. 1968-74), Internat. Assn. for Study of Liver (pres. 1970-74, chmn. criteria com. 1972—), Am. Gastroenterol. Assn. (mem. edn. and tng. com. 1967-71), ACP (mem. publs. com. 1969-74), AMA (vice-chmn., chmn. program com. sect. on gastroenterology 1971-74), Assn. Am. Physicians, Soc. Exptl. Biology and Medicine, Am. Soc. Clin. Nutrition, Am. Inst. Nutrition, AAAS, Nat. Med. Assn., Am. Fedn. Clin. Research, Phi Beta Kappa, Alpha Omega Alpha, Sigma Pi Phi. Current Work: Portal hypertension; liver regeneration; immunologic reactivity in liver disease; drug-induced liver injury; fibrogenesis; hepatocellular cancer. Subspecialty: Hepatology. Home: 35 Robert Dr Short Hills NJ 07078 Office: New Jersey Med Sch Univ Medicine and Dentistry of NJ 100 Bergen St Newark NJ 07103

LEFEBVRE, ARTHUR HENRY, mechanical engineer; b. Long Eaton, Eng., Mar. 14, 1923; came to U.S., 1976; s. Henri and May (Brown) L.; m. Elizabeth Marcella Betts, Dec. 20, 1952; children: David Ivan, Paul Henry, Anne Marie. B.Sc., Nottingham U., 1946; Ph.D., Imperial Coll., London, 1952, D.Sc., 1975. Combustion engr. Rolls Royce, Derby, Eng., 1952-61; prof. aircraft propulsion Cranfield Inst. Tech., Eng., 1961-71, prof., head Sch. Mech. Engring., 1971-76; prof., head Sch. Mech. Engring., Purdue U., West Lafayette, Ind., 1976-80, Reilly prof. combustion engring., 1980—; cons. on combustion to various cos., Britain, Sweden and U.S.A.; mem. propulsion and energetics panel Adv. Group Aero. Research and Devel., 1972-76. Contbr. tech. articles to profl. jours.; author Gas Turbine Combustion, 1983. Recipient Gas Turbine award ASME, 1982, Tom Sawyer award, 1984. Fellow Royal Aero. Soc., Instn. Mech. Engrs., Royal Soc. Arts. Patentee combustion equipment. Current Work: Combustion engineering, fuel atomization, evaporation, flame stabilization, ignition, flame propagation, combustion efficiency, gas turbine combustion. Subspecialties: Combustion processes; Fuels. Home: 1741 Redwood Ln Lafayette IN 47905 Office: Sch Mech Engring Purdue U West Lafayette IN 47907

LEFEBVRE, EUGENE ALLEN, ecologist; b. St. Paul, Oct. 18, 1929; s. Clarence Joseph and Lucille Caroline (Willy) LeF.; m. Mary Ellen Schultz, Aug. 26, 1966; children—Ann-Marie, Charles Allen. B.Sc., U. Minn., 1956, M.S., 1958, Ph.D., 1962. Grad. researcher dept. zoology U. Minn., Mpls., 1952-53, grad. teaching asst., 1953-59, research fellow, 1960-61, research assoc., 1961-66; asst. prof. dept. zoology So. Ill. U., Carbondale, 1966-72, assoc. prof., 1972—; reviewer NSF, The Condor; cons. Prin. Investigators, U. B.C., NPS, Maylansien Agr. Research Inst., 1972-78. Contbr. articles to profl. jours. Chmn. mgmt. adv. com. Nature Conservancy, Mpls., 1962-66, bd. dirs. Minn. chpt., 1964-66; bd. dirs. So. Ill. Bird Obs., Carbondale, 1976-82; chmn., bd. dirs., 1978-82. Grantee NIH, 1960-66, Sigma Xi, 1964, NSF, 1967, 69-73, 80-83, Ill. Dept. Conservancy, 1981, 82. Mem. Am. Ornithologists Union, Brit. Ornithologists Union, Cooper Ornithol. Soc. Ecol. Soc. Am., Wilson Ornithol. Soc. Current work: Bioenergetics of flight, energy expenditure of activity and environmental stress; conservation ecology; age structure analysis of avian population. Subspecialties: Ecology (biology); Resource conservation. Home: Box 112 Route 1 Carterville IL 62918 Office: Dept Zoology So Ill U Carbondale IL 62901

LEGAN, HARRY LEWIS, orthodontic educator, researcher; b. St. Paul, Sept. 16, 1948; s. Leo Theodore and Charlotte June (Most) L.; m. Robertanne Turner, Mar. 27, 1982. B.S., U. Minn-Mpls., 1969, B.A., 1969, D.D.S., 1973; orthodontic cert., U. Conn., 1977. Asst. prof. surgery U. Tex. Southwestern Med. Sch., Dallas, 1977-83, assoc. prof., 1983—, dir. orthodontics, 1977—; guest lectr. Baylor Coll. Dallas, 1980—; research cons. U. Conn.-Farmington, 1982-85; orthodontic cons. Craniofacial Deformities Team, Dallas, 1978—. Contbr. chpts., articles to profl. publs. NIH fellow, 1974-77; U. Tex.-Dallas grantee, 1978. Mem. Am. Assn. Orthodontists, ADA, Southwestern Soc. Orthodontists. Am. Cleft Palate Assn., Internat. Assn. Dental Research, Sadi Fontaine Acad. (hon.), Sociedad Colombiana de Ortodoncia (hon.), Alpha Omega (pres. club 1972-73). Current Work: Clinical and histologic evaluation of temporomandibular joint; planning and stability of maxillofacial surgical procedures; histochemical characterization of head and neck musculature in patients with craniofacial deformities; biomechanics. Subspecialty: Orthodontics. Office: U Tex Southwestern Med Sch 5323 Harry Hines Blvd Dallas TX 75235

LEGTERS, GEORGE RICHARD, physicist, engineer, computer scientist; b. Jamestown, N.Y., Dec. 10, 1951; s. George Richard and Vivian Leita (Paulsen) L.; m. Majel Kaye Smith, May 27, 1979; children—George Richard, Elizabeth Majel. B.S. summa cum laude in Physics, Houghton Coll., 1973; M.S. in Physics, Pa. State U., 1975; M.S.E.E., U. Miami, 1980, Ph.D. in Physics, 1981. Cert. tchr., N.Y. High sch. physics tchr. Broward County, Fort Lauderdale, Fla., 1976-77; research scientist Inst. Acoustical Research, Miami, Fla., 1979-82; assoc. prin. engring. Harris Corp., Melbourne, Fla., 1982-84; sr. scientist DBA Systems, Inc., Melbourne, 1984—; adj. prof. Fla. Inst. Tech., Melbourne, 1982-83. Contbr. articles to profl. jours. Mem. IEEE, Phi Kappa Phi, Sigma Pi Sigma. Republican. Current work: Computer real-time generation of terrain images from digitized ortho photographs digital correlation applied to photogrammetry; data compression techniques on terrain elevation data. Subspecialties: Graphics, image processing, and pattern recognition; Computer engineering. Home: 405 Riverside Dr Melbourne Beach FL 32951 Office: DBA Systems Inc Advanced Programs Box 550 Melbourne FL 32902

LEHENY, ROBERT FRANCIS, electrical engineer physicist; b. N.Y.C., Dec. 8, 1938; s. Vincent Joseph and Frances (Ryan) L.; m. Ann Darlene Lynch, May 26, 1962; children—Ann Rachel, Robert Lynch. B.S., U. Conn., 1960; postgrad. Bklyn. Poly. Inst., 1960-61; M.S., Columbia U., 1963, D.Engring. Sci., 1966. Engr., Sperry Gyroscope Co., Great Neck, N.Y., 1960-61; asst. prof. elec. engring. Columbia U., N.Y.C., 1966-67; mem. tech. staff Bell Labs., Holmdel, N.J., 1967-83; dist. mgr. Bell Communications Research, Murray Hill, N.J., 1983—. Contbr. articles to profl. jours. Mem. Little Silver Bd. Edn., N.J., 1973-79, v.p., 1977-79; chmn. Monmouth Arts Found., 1982-84. Recipient Disting. Tech. Staff award Bell Labs., 1983. Mem. IEEE, IEEE-Electron Device Group, Am. Phys. Soc. Current work: High speed electron devices; integrated opto-electronic devices; highfield transport in semiconductors, optical properties of semiconductors. Subspecialties: Microelectronics; Condensed matter physics. Office: Bell Communications Research Room 6H-318 600 Mountain Ave Murray Hill NJ 07970

LEHMAN, JOHN MICHAEL, experimental pathologist, virologist; b. Abington, Pa., June 19, 1942; s. John Holland and Emily (Doliney) L.; m. Elizabeth Bowen, June 5, 1943; children—Deborah, Eric. B.S., Phila. Coll. Pharmacy and Sci., 1964; Ph.D., U. Pa., 1970. Postdoctoral fellow U. Pa., Phila., 1970-71; asst. prof. pathology U. Colo. Sch. Medicine, Denver, 1971-77, assoc. prof., 1977-80, prof. pathology, 1981—; vis. staff mem. Los Alamos Sci. Lab. 1972—. Research grantee NIH, 1974—, NSF, 1976. Mem. Analytical Cytology Soc., Am. Soc. Microbiology, Tissue Culture Assn. (councillor 1984—), Am. Assn. Cell Biology, Am. Assn. Cancer Research. Presbyterian. Subspecialties: Cell study oncology; Microbiology (medicine). Home: 22 Southwood Dr Slingerlands NY 12159 Office: Albany Med Coll Dept Microbiology and Immunology Albany NY 12208

LEHMANN, ERICH LEO, statistics educator; b. Strasbourg, France, Nov. 20, 1917; came to U.S., 1940, naturalized, 1945; s. Julius and Alma Rosa (Schuster) L.; m. Juliet Popper Shaffer; children: Stephen, Barbara, Fia. M.A., U. Calif.-Berkeley, 1943, Ph.D., 1946; D.Sc.h.c., U. Leiden, 1985. Asst. dept. 1946; D.Sc. h.c., U. Leiden, 1985. U. Calif. at Berkeley, 1942-43, asso., 1943-46, instr., 1946-47, asst. prof., 1947-51, asso. prof., 1951-54, prof., 1954-55, prof. dept. statistics, 1955—, chmn. dept. statistics, 1973-76; vis. assoc. prof. Columbia U., 1950-51, Stanford U., 1951-52; vis. lectr. Princeton, 1951. Author: Testing Statistical Hypotheses, 1959, Basic Concepts of Probability and Statistics, 1964, 2d edit, (with J.L. Hodges, Jr.), 1970, Nonparametrics: Statistical Methods Based on Ranks, 1975, Theory of Point Estimation, 1983. Guggenheim fellow, 1955, 66, 79; Miller research prof., 1962-63, 72-73. Fellow Inst. Math. Statistics, Am. Statis. Assn.; mem. Internat. Statis. Inst., Am. Acad. Arts and Scis., Nat. Acad. Scis. Current Work: Conditional inference, comparison of experiments, multiple comparison problems. Subspecialty: Statistics. Office: Dept Statistics U Calif Berkeley CA 94720

LEHNEN, ALFRED PAUL, mathematics and physics educator, researcher; b. Lafayette, Ind., Apr. 27, 1951; s. Robert Franklin and Lucy Ann (VanVaerenbergh) L.; m. Linda Marie Jordan, June 10, 1972; children—Brian, Rebecca, Sarah. B.S., Purdue U., 1973; M.S., U. Wis., 1975, Ph.D., 1979. Research assoc. U. Wis.-Madison, 1973-79; postdoctoral researcher U. N.C., Chapel Hill, 1979-81; lead engr. Ray-O-Vac Corp., Madison, 1981-83; math., physics instr. Madison Area Tech. Coll., 1983—; cons. Johnson Wax Corp., Racine, Wis., 1980. Contbr. articles to profl. jours. Mem. Am. Phys. Soc., Am. Fedn. Tchrs., Phi Beta Kappa. Roman Catholic. Current work: Theoretical research on ionic and dielectric solids, surface effects and crystal defects; also an interest in areas of applied mathematical methods, statistics, and computer simulations. Subspecialties: Condensed matter physics; Statistical physics. Home: 4124 Winnemac Ave Madison WI 53711 Office: Madison Area Tech Coll 211 N Carroll St Madison WI 53703

LEHNINGER, ALBERT LESTER, biochemistry educator; b. Bridgeport, Conn., Feb. 17, 1917; s. Wally and Selma (Heymer) L.; m. Janet Wilson, Mar. 12, 1942; children: James Wilson, Erika L. Whitmore. B.A., Wesleyan U., 1939; M.S., U. Wis., 1940, Ph.D., 1942. Instr. dept. phys. chemistry U. Wis.-Madison, 1942-45; asst. prof. dept. biochemistry U. Chgo., 1945-49; mem. council biol. scis. Pritzker Sch. Medicine, 1977—; vis. prof. U. Frankfurt, W.Ger., 1951; DeLamar prof., dir. dept. physiol. chemistry Johns Hopkins U., Balt., 1952-78, Univ. prof. med. sci., 1977—; vis. prof. Guy's Hosp., London, 1963; bd. visitors Cornell U. Med. Coll., N.Y.C., 1981-82. Author: The Mitochondrion, 1964, Bioenergetics, 1965, 72, Biochemistry, 1970, 75, Short Course in Biochemistry, 1973, Principles of Biochemistry, 1982; contbr. articles to profl. jours. Mem. Inst. Medicine, Nat. Acad. Sci., Am. Soc. Biol. Chemists, Am. Philos. Soc. (v.p.), Am. Acad. Arts Scis., Am. Soc. Cell Biology, Biochemistry Soc., Biophys. Soc., Phi Beta Kappa, Sigma Xi. Clubs: Green Spring, Hamilton Street, Gibson Island. Current Work: Bioenergetics of normal and cancer cells; mitochondrial activities; biochemistry of calcification. Subspecialties: Biochemistry (biology); Biophysical chemistry. Home: 15020 Tanyard Rd Sparks MD 21152 Office: Johns Hopkins U 725 N Wolfe St Baltimore MD 21205

LEHRER, SAMUEL B., clinical immunologist, educator; b. New Britain, Conn., Apr. 1, 1943; s. Charles Rudy and Nettie (Fleischer) L.; m. Gila Ashinazi, June 20, 1971; children: Rudy, Mark, Sandra, Nicole. B.S., Upsala (N.J.) Coll., 1966; Ph. D., Temple U., 1971. Postdoctoral fellow Scripps Clin. Research Found., LaJolla, Calif., 1971-75; asst. prof. medicine Tulane Med. Sch., New Orleans, 1975-79, assoc. prof., 1979-83, prof., 1983—; adj. prof. microbiology and immunology, 1980—. Nat. Inst. Allergy and Infectious Diseases awardee, 1978-81; Am. Lung Assn. grantee, 1978-80. Mem. Am. Soc. Microbiology, Am. Acad. Allergy, Soc. Exptl. Biology and Medicine, Am. Thoracic Soc., AAAS, Collegium Internat. Allergologicum. Republican. Jewish. Current Work: Isolation and investigation of mechanisms in gastrointestinal and respiratory allergies, IgE biosynthesis. Subspecialty: Immunobiology and immunology. Home: 142 Brockenbrough Ct Metairie LA 70005 Office: Tulane U Med Sch 1700 Perdido St New Orleans LA 70112

LEI, DAVID K.Y., nutrition educator, researcher; b. Macau, July 30, 1944; came to U.S., 1970, naturalized, 1980; s. Sai Lam and Hing Kim (Lau) L.; m. Polin Tong, Dec. 22, 1966; 1 child, Hestia. B.S., U. London, 1968; M.S., U. Guelph, Can., 1970; Ph.D., Mich. State U., 1973. Research assoc. Wayne State U., Detroit, 1973-75; asst. prof. Miss. State U., 1975-78, assoc. prof., 1978-80; assoc. prof. U. Ariz., Tucson, 1980—. Contbr. articles to profl. jours. NIH grantee, 1977; grantee Ariz. Heart Assn., 1981, U.S. Dept. Agr., 1984. Mem. Am. Inst. Nutrition, Am. Dietetics Assn. Roman Catholic. Subspecialties: Nutrition (medicine); Biochemistry (medicine). Office: U Ariz Dept Nutrition and Food Sci 309 Agr Sci Bldg Tucson AZ 85721

LEIB, MICHAEL SAMUEL, veterinary educator; b. N.Y.C., June 21, 1952; s. Aaron and Esther (Sherman) L. B.S., Emory U., 1974; D.V.M., U. Ga., 1979; M.S., Colo. State U., 1983. Pvt. practice vet. medicine, Atlanta, 1979-80; vet. medicine resident Colo. State U., Fort Collins, 1981-83; asst. prof. vet. sci. Va. Poly. Inst. and State U., Blacksburg, 1983—. Contbr. articles to profl. jours. Mem. AVMA, Am. Coll. Vet. Internal Medicine. Gastric emptying and secretion, gastric dilatation volvulus. Subspecialty: Internal medicine (veterinary medicine). Home: 1A Walls Branch Rd Blacksburg VA 24060 Office: Div Pathobiology and Pub Practice VA-Md Regional Col Vet Medicine Blacksburg VA 24061

LEIBHARDT, EDWARD, optics mfg. co. exec., research cons.; b. New Rome, Wis., Oct. 13, 1919; s. Stephan and Roza (Jilling) L.; m. Maidi Wiebe, June 3, 1961; children: Barbara, Leslie. B.A., Northwestern U., 1954; Ph.D. in Astronomy, 1959. Engraver R.R. Donnelly and SonsCo., Chgo., 1937-43; ptnr. Liebhardt Bros., Maywood, Ill., 1943-46; prin. Leibhardt Engring., Maywood, 1946-51; pres. Diffraction Products Inc., Woodstock, Ill., 1951—; cons. optics research and devel. Mem. Optical Soc. Am., Optical Soc. Chgo., Soc. Applied Spectroscopy, Soc. Photo-Optical Instrumentation Engrs., Physics Club Chgo., Sigma Xi. Current Work: Diffraction grating ruling and holography; spectroscopy and photometry research in astronomy. Subspecialties: Diffraction Gratings; Holography. Home: 9416 W Bull Valley Rd Village of Bull Valley IL 60098 Office: PO Box 645 Woodstock IL 60098

LEIBHOLZ, STEPHEN WOLFGANG, engineering company executive; b. Berlin, Jan. 28, 1932; came to U.S., 1936; s. Ernest and Louis Leibholz; m. Ann Esther Greenberg, May 29, 1958; children—Judith, Robert Daniel. A.B. in Physics, NYU, 1952. Prin. engr. Republic Aviation, Farmingdale, N.Y., 1957-60; dir. systems analysis and design Auerbach Corp., Phila., 1960-67; pres. Analytics, Willow Grove, Pa., 1967—; cons. in field. Author, editor 5 books; contbr. articles to profl. jours. Mem. AAAS, IEEE, Ops. Research Soc. Am. (past bd. dirs., monographs editor), Mil. Ops. Research Soc. (bd. dirs. 1979-83). Club: Cosmos (Washington). Current work: Research and development in computer and communications security and in artificial intelligence. Subspecialties: Systems engineering; Artificial intelligence. Office: Analytics 2500 Maryland Rd Willow Grove PA 19090

LEIBOVIC, K. NICHOLAS, neuroscientist, educator; b. Lithuania, June 14, 1921; s. Joseph A. and Chassia (Michailova) L.; m. Marianne Karpf, Aug. 4, 1944; children: David A., Stephen J. B.A. in Engring., Trinity Coll., Cambridge (Eng.) U., 1943; B.Sc. (hon.) in Math, London U., 1952. Sect. leader. math. cons. Brit. Oxygen Co., London, 1956-60; sr. mathematician Westinghouse Research, Pitts., 1960-63; asst. dir., sect. chmn. Ctr. Theoretical Biology, SUNY, Buffalo, 1964-74, prof. dept. biophys. scis., 1965—; vis. prof. U. Calif.-Berkeley, 1968; program dir. neurosci. research program MIT, 1979; cons. NIH, others. Author: Nervous Systems Theory, 1972; editor: Information Processing in the Nervous System, 1969; asso. editor, referee various sci. journ.; contbr. articles to profl. publs. NIH grantee, 1966-70, 82—; NSF grantee, 1966; NRC grantee, 1971, 75; vis. scholar Harvard U., 1980. Mem. AAAS, Biophys. Soc., Brit. Computer Soc., N.Y. Acad. Scis., Ops. Research Soc., Soc. Indsl. and Applied Math., Soc. for Neurosci., Assn. for Research in Vision and Opthalmology. Jewish. Current Work: Informaton processing in nervous system at cellular and systems levels: at former, transduction and transmission of signals, at latter, properties of convergent and divergent pathways. Subspecialties: Neurobiology; Biophysics (biology). Home: 105 High Park Blvd Buffalo NY 14226 Office: Dept Biophysics Cary Hall SUNY Buffalo NY 14214

LEIBOWITZ, LEONARD, physical chemist; b. N.Y.C., Feb. 5, 1931; s. David and Miriam (Sheinbaum) L.; m. Stephanie Malvina Melkin, Sept. 10, 1976; children—Michael G., Naomi C. A.B., NYU, 1951, M.S., 1954, Ph.D., 1956. Chemist, E.I. duPont de Nemours Co., Balt., 1956-58; chemist Argonne Nat. Lab., Ill., 1958—. Mem. editorial bd. Internat. Jour. Thermophysics, 1980—. Contbr. chpts. to books and articles to profl. jours. Mem. Am. Chem. Soc., AAAS, Phi Beta Kappa, Sigma Xi. Current work: Thermodynamic and transport properties of nuclear reactor materials. Subspecialties: Physical chemistry; Nuclear fission. Office: Argonne Nat Lab Chem Tech Div 9700 S Cass Ave Argonne IL 60439

LEIDHEISER, HENRY, JR., chemistry educator, researcher; b. Union City, N.J., Apr. 18, 1920; s. Henry and Margaret (Steinel) L.; m. Virginia Townsend, Feb. 21, 1944; children: Margaret LeBaron, Henry. B.S. in Chemistry, U. Va., 1941, M.S. in Phys. Chemistry, 1944, Ph.D. in Phys. Chemistry, 1946. Research assoc. U. Va., 1946-49; lab. mgr. Va. Inst. Sci. Research, Richmond, 1949-60, dir., chief exec. officer, 1960-68; prof. chemistry Lehigh U., Bethlehem, Pa., 1968-83, Alcoa Found. prof., 1983—, dir. Lehigh U. (Ctr. for Surface and Coastings Research), 1968—; mem. various coms. Nat. Acad. Scis.; bd. dirs. Petroleum Research Fund; cons. industry and govt. Contbr. articles to profl. jours. Recipient numerous awards including Silver medal Am. Electroplaters Soc., 1978, Arch T. Colwell award Soc. Automotive Engrs., 1979, Willis Rodney Whitney award Nat. Assn. Corrosion Engrs., 1983. Fellow AAAS; mem. Am. Chem. Soc., Electrochem. Soc., Nat. Assn. Corrosion Engrs. Republican. Presbyterian. Club: Saucon Valley Country (Bethlehem). Subspecialties: Surface chemistry; Corrosion. Home: RD 7 Pleasant Dr Bethlehem PA 18015 Office: Sinclair Lab 7 Lehigh Univ Bethlehem PA 18015

LEIF, ROBERT CARY, scientist, microbiology educator; b. N.Y.C., Feb. 27, 1938; s. Leonard and Raechel (Fishman) L.; m. Suzanne Bedford, June 23, 1963; children—Liza, Stephanie. B.S., U. Chgo., 1959; Ph.D., Calif. Inst. Tech., Pasadena, 1964. Sr. scientist Papanicolaou Cancer Research Inst., Miami, 1972-81; assoc. prof. microbiology U. Miami, Coral Gables, 1976—; prin. scientist Coulter Electronics, Hialeah, Fla., 1981-84, corp. fellow, 1984—. Contbr. articles to profl. jours. Patentee orifice inside optical element, 1982. Mem. editorial bd. Cell Biophysics, 1979-82, Cytometry, 1980—. NSF fellow, 1959. Mem. Am. Chem. Soc., Biophys. Soc., Analytical Cytology Soc., Sigma Xi. Democrat. Club: P.C. of So. Fla. Current work: The development of cytophysical techniques for the automated flow analysis of cellular sub populations and separation techniques for their purification in order to establish cellular taxonomy and differentiation path waves; clinical chemistry, computer and laboratory instrumentation. Subspecialties: Cell biology; Bioinstrumentation. Home: 1030 Mariposa Ave Coral Gables FL 33146 Office: Coulter Electronics Inc 690 W 20th St Hialeah FL 33010

LEIFER, LARRY, mechanical engineer. Mem. faculty dept. mech. engring. Stanford U., Calif. Subspecialty: Biomedical engineering. Office: Stanford U Dept Mech Engring Stanford CA 94305*

LEIFER, MARK CURTIS, physicist; b. Schenectady, Feb. 23, 1954; s. Herbert N. and Elizabeth Leifer; m. Anne Edith Ginsburg, Nov. 6, 1983. B.S., Stanford U., 1975, Ph.D., 1981. Research and devel. staff Cardio Dynamics Labs., Los Angeles, 1975-76; vis. prof. U. Rome, 1982-83; nuclear magnetic resonance imaging physicist Diasonics Inc., South San Francisco, 1983-85, Varian Assocs., Palo Alto, Calif., 1985—. Contbr. articles to profl. jours. Regents fellow U. Calif.-San Diego, 1976; grantee NIH, 1978, NASA, 1979. Mem. IEEE. Current work: Magnetic resonance imaging of human body tissues and organs; magnetic field systems and digital signal processing. Subspecialties: Medical physics; Magnetic physics. Office: Varian Assocs 1120 Auburn Rd Fremont CA 94538

LEIFMAN, LEV JACOB, mathematician, translator; b. Kiev, Ukraine, Apr. 12, 1929; came to U.S., 1979; s. Jacob Lev and Nina Boris (Tsyrlin) L.; m. Miriam Israel Eidelson, May 16 1962; children: Jacob, Tatyana. M.Sc., Kiev U., 1952; Ph.D., Moscow U., 1962. Research prof. Ukrainian Inst. Trade, Kiev, 1959-63; assoc. prof. Novosibirsk U., USSR, 1963-67; research prof. USSR Acad. Scis., Novosibirsk, 1963-70; assoc. prof. Inst. Civil Engrs., Novosibirsk, 1971-73, Haifa (Israel) U., 1974-78; translation editor Am. Math. Soc., Providence, 1979—; head and sci. supr. lab. exptl. programming Inst. Automated Control Systems, Novosibirsk, 1964-69; faculty R.I. Coll, 1982—. Author: Netzplantechnik bei begrenzten Ressourcen, 1968, Modelling of Private Consumption, 1972; editor: Network Planning under Restraints on Resources, 1971; series Modelling of Control Processes, 1967-73, Theory of Probability and Math. Stats, 1978—, Vestnik of the Leningrad U, 1979-84, Math. of USSR-Sbornik, 1984—, Soviet Math.-Doklady, 1985—. Mem. Internat. Assn. Cybernetics, Math. Programming Soc., Soc. Inds. and Applied Math. Jewish. Current Work: Optimization - development and analysis of methods and algorithms; mathematical models and methods in operations research and economics; mathematical models of translation between natural languages and their implementation on computers. Subspecialties: Algorithms; Operations research (mathematics). Home: 467 Pleasant St Pawtucket RI 02860 Office: PO Box 6248 Providence RI 02940

LEIGH, EGBERT GILES, JR., biologist; b. Richmond, Va., July 27, 1940; s. Egbert Giles and Lucinda Lee (Kinsolving) L.; m. Elizabeth Murray Hodgson, Mar. 21, 1968; children: John Murray, Mary Bruce. A.B., Princeton U., 1962; Ph.D., Yale U., 1966. Asst. prof. biology Princeton (N.J.) U., 1966-72; biologist Smithsonian Tropical Research Inst., Balboa, Panama, 1969—. Author: Adaptation & Diversity, 1971; sr. co-editor: Ecology of a Tropical Forest, 1982. Mem. Am. Soc. Naturalists, Ecol. Soc. Am., Brit. Ecol. Soc., Paleontol. Research Instn., Rocky Mountain Biol. Lab. Subspecialties:

Evolutionary biology; Theoretical ecology. Office: Smithsonian Tropical Research Inst APO Miami FL 34002

LEIGHTON, ALVAH THEODORE, JR., avian reproductive physiologist, educator; b. Portland, Maine, Apr. 17, 1929; s. Alvah Theodore and Margaret Elizabeth (Mogan) L.; m. Frances Blanchard, Dec. 6, 1952; children—Theodore, Thomas, William, Krista. B.S., U. Maine, 1951; M.S., U. Mass., 1952; Ph.D., U. Minn., 1960. Grad. research asst. U. Mass., Amherst, 1951-52, U. Minn., Mpls., 1955-59; prof. poultry sci. Va. Poly. Inst. and State U., Blacksburg, 1959—; cons. Animalens, Inc., Wellesley, Mass., 1979—. Mem. planning commn. Town of Blacksburg, 1972-74, town councilman, 1974—, vice-mayor, 1974-76, 78-80; mem. New River Valley Planning Dist. Commn., Radford, Va., 1974—; chmn. Western Regional Tech. Com., USDA, 1983-85. Served with vet. sect. U.S. Army, 1953-55. U.S. Dept. Agr. grantee, 1982-83, Va. Agrl. Found., 1984-87, Southeastern Poultry and Egg Assn., 1984-87. Mem. Am. Genetics Assn., Poultry Sci. Assn. (assoc. editor 1981—), Va. Acad. Sci., World Poultry Sci. Assn., Sigma Xi (pres. local chpt. 1977-78), Alpha Zeta, Gamma Sigma Delta (pres. local chpt. 1977-78). Republican. Clubs: Blacksburg Country, University (Blacksburg). Lodge: Masons. Current work: Reproductive physiology; genetics behavior and management of turkey populations. Subspecialties: Animal physiology; Animal genetics. Home: 711 Broce Dr NW Blacksburg VA 24060 Office: Dept Poultry Sci Va Poly Inst 2290 Animal Sci Bldg Blacksburg VA 24061

LEIGHTON, MARK, ecologist, anthropology educator; b. Missoula, Mont., Aug. 18, 1951; s. Douglas Frank Leighton and Doris Marjorie (Clay) Glover. B.A., Stanford U., 1973; Ph.D., U. Calif.-Davis, 1981; postgrad., Oxford U., 1982. Asst. prof. Harvard U., Cambridge, 1982—. Contbr. articles to profl. jours. Mem. Ecol. Soc. Am., AAAS, Assn. Tropical Biologists. Current work: Research in tropical forest ecology in Indonesian Borneo; tropical forest conservation, spend part of each year in Borneo directing research site studying ecological interactions between plants and vertebrates. Subspecialty: Ecology (environmental science). Office: Harvard U Dept Anthropology 11 Divinity Ave Cambridge MA 02138

LEIGHTON, MORRIS WELLMAN, geologist, state agency director. Chief Ill. Geol. Survey, Champaign. Subspecialty: Geology. Office: Ill Geol Survey 615 E Peabody Dr Champaign IL 61820

LEIGHTON, ROBERT BENJAMIN, physicist, educator; b. Detroit, Sept. 10, 1919; s. George B. and Olga (Homrig) L.; m. Alice M. Winger, July 31, 1943 (div. 1974); children—Ralph, Alan; m. Margaret L. Lauritsen, Jan. 7, 1977. B.S., Calif. Inst. Tech., 1941, M.S., 1944, Ph.D., 1947. Asst. prof. Calif. Inst. Tech., Pasadena, 1949-53, assoc. prof., 1953-59, prof. physics, 1959-85, prof. emeritus, 1985—, chmn. div. physics, math., astronomy, 1970-75; Prin. investigator TV Expt. Mariner 4, 1964, Mariners 6 and 7, 1969; co-investigator TV Expt. Mariner 9, 1971. Author: Principles of Modern Physics, 1959, (with others) The Feynman Lectures on Physics, 1964. Mem. Am. Phys. Soc., Am. Astron. Soc., Nat. Acad. Sci., Am. Acad. Arts and Scis. Research in cosmic rays, solar physics, space astronomy, infrared astronomy, telescope design. Subspecialties: Cosmic ray high energy astrophysics; Infrared astronomy. Office: Calif Inst Tech Pasadena CA 91125

LEINEN, MARGARET SANDRA, geological oceanographer; b. Chgo., Sept. 20, 1946; d. Earl John and Ester Alphilda (Louis) L.; 1 child, Daniel Whaley. B.S., U. Ill., 1969; M.S., Oreg. State U., 1975; Ph.D., U. R.I., 1979. Marine scientist Grad. Sch. Oceanography, U. R.I., 1980-82, asst. research prof., 1982—. Contbr. numerous articles to profl. jours. Mem. Am. Geophys. Union, Geol. Soc. Am. (assoc. editor Geology 1985—), AAAS, Geochem. Soc. Current work: Paleoceanography, paleochemistry, and paleoclimate inferred from deep sea sediments, ridge crest hydrothermal activity and its history. Subspecialties: Sedimentology; Oceanography. Office: Grad Sch Oceanography U RI Narragansett RI 02882-1197

LEIPHOLZ, HORST HERMANN EDUARD, civil engineer, educator, researcher; b. Plonhofen, Germany, Sept. 26, 1919; s. Ernst and Marta (Wohlfeil) L.; m. Ursula Schlag, May 9, 1942; children: Barbara, Gunthara. Diplom, U. Stuttgart, Germany, 1958, Dr.-Ing., 1959. Asst. U. Stuttgart, 1958-62, docent, 1962-63; prof. U. Karlsruhe, Germany, 1963-69; prof. U. Waterloo, Ont., Can., 1969—, chmn. dept. civil engring., 1982-83, chmn. solid mechanics div., 1971-77; assoc. dean grad. studies U. Waterloo (Faculty of Engring.), 1976-81, dean grad. studies, 1983—. Author: Theory of Elasticity, 1974, Direct Variation Methods, 1977, Stability of Elastic Systems, 1980, others.; Contbr. articles to profl. jours. Recipient Disting. Tchr. award U. Waterloo, 1976. Fellow Engring. Inst. Can., Am. Acad. Mechanics, Royal Soc. Can., Can. Soc. Mech. Engring. (chmn. research and devel. div. 1978-80); mem. German Soc. Engring. Math. and Mechs. (exec. council 1978-81). Current Work: Stability and control of structures. Subspecialties: Theoretical and applied mechanics; Applied mathematics. Home: 401 Warrington Dr Waterloo ON N2L 2P7 Canada Office: Dept Civil Engring Univ Waterloo Waterloo ON N2L 3G1 Canada

LEISS, JAMES ELROY, physicist; b. Youngstown, Ohio, June 2, 1924; s. Paul E. and Virginia C. (Bailey) L.; m. Wilma M. Dindore, June 30, 1945; children—Paul F., Judith A., James D., Susan V. B.S., Case Inst. Tech., 1948; Ph.D., U. Ill., 1955. Physicist, Nat. Bur. Standards, Washington, 1954-72, dir. Ctr. for Radiation Research, 1972-79; assoc. dir. energy research Dept. Energy, Washington, 1979—; mem. numerous adv. and rev. coms. Contbr. articles to sci. publs. Served to sgt. U.S. Army, 1942-45. Mem. Am. Phys. Soc., AAAS. Current work: High energy and nuclear physics, design of particle accelerators. Subspecialty: Nuclear physics. Office: US Dept Energy ER-20 Washington DC 20545

LEITH, EMMETT NORMAN, educator, electrical engineer; b. Detroit, Mar. 12, 1927; s. Albert Donald and Dorothy Marie (Emmett) L.; m. Lois June Neswold, Feb. 17, 1956; children: Kim Ellen, Pam Elizabeth. B.S., Wayne State U., 1950, M.S., 1952, Ph.D., 1978. Mem. research staff U. Mich., 1952—, prof. elec. engring., 1968—; cons. several indsl. corps. Contbr. books, profl. jours. Served with USNR, 1945-46. Recipient Gordon Meml. award S.P.I.E., 1965; citation Am. Soc. Mag. Photographers, 1966; Achievement award U.S. Camera and Travel mag., 1967; Excellence of Paper award Soc. Motion Picture and TV Engrs., 1967; Daedalion award, 1968; Stuart Ballantine medal Franklin Inst., 1969; Distinguished Faculty Achievement award U. Mich., 1973; Alumni award Wayne State U., 1974; cited by Nobel Prize Commn. for contbns. to holography, 1971; Holley medal ASME, 1976; named Man of Year Indsl. Research mag., 1966; Nat. medal of Sci., 1979; Russel lecture award U. Mich., 1981; recipient Dennis Gabor medal Soc. Photo-Instrumentation Engrs., 1983. Fellow Optical Soc. Am. (Wood medal 1975), IEEE (Liebmann award 1967, Inventor of Year award 1976); mem. Nat. Acad. Engring., Sigma Xi, Sigma Pi Sigma. Patentee in field. First demonstrated (with colleague) capability of holography to form high-quality 3-dimensional image. Current Work: White light optical processing and interferometry; optical processing of images. Subspecialties: Holography; Optical image processing. Home: 51325 Murray Hill Canton MI 48187 Office: Univ Mich Inst Sci and Tech PO Box 618 Ann Arbor MI 48107

LEITMANN, GEORGE, mechanical engineer; b. Vienna, Austria, May 24, 1925; s. Josef and Stella (Fischer) L.; m. Nancy Lloyd, Jan. 28, 1955; children: Josef Lloyd, Elaine Michelle. B.S., Columbia U., 1949, M.A., 1950; Ph.D., U. Calif., Berkeley, 1956. Physicist, head aeroballistics sect. U.S. Naval Ordnance Sta., China Lake, 1950-57; mem. faculty U. Calif., Berkeley, 1957—, prof. engring. sci., 1963—, asso. dean grad. affairs, 1981—; cons. to aerospace industry and govt. Author: An Introduction to Optimal Control, 1966, Quantitati ve and Qualitative Games, 1969, The Calculus of Variations and Optimal Control, 1981, others; contbr. articles to profl. jours. Served with AUS, 1944-46, ETO. Decorated Croix de Guerre France; recipient Pendray Aerospace Lit. award, 1979; Von Humboldt U.S. sr. scientist, 1980; Levy medal, 1981; Mech. Contr. Flight award, 1984; Miller Research prof., 1966. Fellow AIAA; mem. Acad. Sci. Bologna, Internat. Acad. Astronautics (corr.), Nat. Acad. Engring. Subspecialty: Mechanical engineering. Office: Coll Engring U Calif Berkeley CA 94720

LELLINGER, DAVID BRUCE, botanist, curator; b. Chgo., Jan. 24, 1937; s. Nicholas Francis and Rose (Kreicker) L.; m. Linda Mae Kuhles, June 15, 1963; children: Richard, Anne. A.B., U. Ill., 1958; M.S., U. Mich., 1960, Ph.D., 1965. Assoc. curator U.S. Nat. Herbarium, Smithsonian Instn., Washington, 1963—. Editor: Am. Fern. Journ, 1966-84; assoc. editor: Pteridologia, 1979-84, editor, 1985—, Nat. Geog. Soc. grantee, 1971; Smithsonian Research Found. grantee, 1971. Mem. Brit. Pterid Soc., Internat. Soc. Plant Taxonomists, Am. Fern. Soc. Current Work: Taxonomy of ferns and fern-allies, especially new world tropics. Subspecialty: Taxonomy. Address: U S Nat Herbarium NHB-166 Smithsonian Instn Washington DC 20560

LEMAY, CHARLOTTE ZIHLMAN, physics educator; b. Fort Worth, June 30, 1919; d. Adam John and Martha Adelia (Darter) Zihlman; m. Jack Evans LeMay, July 29, 1944; children—Douglas Russell, Lawrence Bruce, Caroline Adelia. A.B., Tex. Christian U., 1940; M.A., Mt. Holyoke Coll., 1941; Ph.D., La. State U., 1950. Teaching asst. Barnard Coll., N.Y.C., 1941-43; lectr. Hunter Coll., N.Y.C., summer 1942; engr. Monsanto Chem. Co., Ludlow, Mass., 1943-45; lectr. Mt. Holyoke Coll., South Hadley, Mass., 1945-46; Lectr. La. State U., Baton Rouge, 1946-48, research asst., 1948-50; engr. Tex. Instruments, Inc., Dallas, 1952-53, 55-57; research physicist Stanford Research Inst., Menlo Park, Calif., 1953-54; engr. Westinghouse Electric Co., Pitts., 1958-60; research physicist IBM, Kitchawan, N.Y., 1960-63; prof. physics Western Conn. State U., Danbury, Conn., 1963—, chmn. dept., 1970-78, 85—. Contbr. articles to profl. jours. Patentee in field. Otis Skinner fellow, 1941; NSF grantee, summers 1971, 72; Western Conn. State U. Univ. Faculty scholar, 1983. Mem. Am. Phys. Soc., Am. Assn. Physics Tchrs., Am. Soc. Engring. Edn., IEEE (sr.). Optical Soc., Am., Soc. Women Engrs. (sr.), Soc. Profl. Indsl. Engrs., Soc. for Photog. Edn., DAR (treas. nat. 1980-85), Sigma Xi. Current work: Fiber optics in telecommunication. Subspecialties: Condensed matter physics; Fiber optics. Home: 60 Chestnut Ridge Rd Mount Kisco NY 10549 Office: Western Conn State U 181 White St Danbury CT 06810

LEMBERSKY, MARK RAPHAEL, forest products company executive; b. Pitts., Sept. 30, 1945; s. Herman K. and Alice Lillian (Berger) L.; m. Barbara Jean Diemond, June 6, 1965; 1 child, Carol Sharon. B.S., MIT, 1967; M.S., Stanford U., 1968, Ph.D., 1971, grad. Exec. Program, Grad. Sch. Bus., 1983. Asst. prof. Oreg. State U., Corvallis, 1971-76, assoc. prof., 1976; mgr. merchandising and allocation research and devel. Weyerhaeuser Co., Tacoma, Wash., 1977-79, dir. raw materials research and devel., 1979-81, dir. timberlands research and devel., 1981-83, group systems and fin. dir., 1984-85, gen. mgr. engineered products div., 1985—. Assoc. editor Ops. Research Jour., 1984—. Inventor simulated interactive dividing and allocating process. Trustee Somerset Community Assn., Bellevue, Wash., 1977-79; mem. Edn. Council, MIT, 1983—; bd. dirs. Sci. Affiliates, U. Wash., 1983—; mem. edn. com., chmn. subcom. Wash. Council for Tech. Advancement, 1984—. Recipient Carter award Oreg. State U., 1975; Franz Edelman internat. prize for mgmt. Sci. achievement, 1985. Mem. Mgmt. Scis. Roundtable (exec. bd. 1985—), Ops. Research Soc. Am., Inst. Mgmt. Scis., Computer and Automated Systems Assn. Current work: Effective use of advanced technology, especially computers, graphics, and decision support systems in industrial operations. Subspecialties: Forestry; Operations research (mathematics). Office: Weyerhaeuser Co CH 1B25 Tacoma WA 98477

LEMIEUX, RAYMOND URGEL, chemistry educator, researcher; b. Lac La Biche, Alta., Can., June 16, 1920; s. Octave and Ida (Saint Martin) L.; m. Virginia Marie McConaghie, 1948; children—Laura, Virginia, Michele, Raymond, Andree, Janet. B.Sc., U. Alta., 1943; Ph.D., McGill U., 1946; D.Sc. (hon.) Laval U., 1970, U. Ottawa, 1975, U. Waterloo, 1980, Meml. U., Nfld., 1981, U. Que., 1982, Queen's U., Kingston, 1983, McGill U., 1984. Asst. prof. chemistry U. Sask., Saskatoon, 1947-49; sr. research office Nat. Research Council, Saskatoon, 1949-54; prof., chmn. dept. chemistry U. Ottawa, 1954-61, vice dean Faculty Pure and Applied Sci., 1954-61; prof. organic chemistry U. Alta., Edmonton, 1961-81, univ. prof., 1981—, chmn. div. organic chemistry, 1966-73, 81-83; co-founder, pres., research dir. R & L Molecular Research Ltd., Edmont, 1963-76; founder, pres., research dir. Raylo Chem. Ltd., 1966-76; pres. Chembiomed Ltd., Edmonton, 1977-78, dir., 1983—; lectr. in field. Mem. editorial bd. Nouveau Jour. de Chimie, 1976—; mem. editorial adv. bd. Tetrahedron Letters, 1980—. Contbr. articles to profl. jours. Patentee in field. Recipient Award of Achievement, Province of Alta., 1980; Izaak Walton Killam award, 1981; Research prize U. Alta., 1982; Sir Frederick Haultain prize Govt. of Alta., 1982. Fellow Chem. Inst. Can. (Palladium medal 1964), Royal Soc. Can., Royal Soc. London; mem. Am. Chem. Soc. (C.S. Hudson award 1966). Current work: Synthesis and conformational analysis of cell-surface oligosaccharides and the study of their recognition and binding by lectins and antibodies. Subspecialty: Organic chemistry. Office: Univ Alta Dept Chemistry Edmonton AB T6G 2G2 Canada

LENCHNER, NATHANIEL HERBERT, dentist, consultant; b. N.Y.C., Aug. 28, 1923; s. Edward and Jennie (Reizes) L.; m. Florence Smith; children: Jonathan, Michael, Debra. B.A., N.Y. U., 1943, D.D.S., 1950. Instr. N.Y. U. Coll. Dentistry, 1950-55; dental cons. Whaledent, Internat., N.Y.C., 1977—; pvt. practice dentistry, Forest Hills, N.Y., 1950—; asst. clin. prof. Columbia U. Sch. Dentistry, 1974-80, lectr., 1980—; adj. assoc. prof. biomed. engring. U. Miami Sch. Engring. and Architecture, 1981—; mem. admissions com. NYU Coll. Dentistry, 1982—. Assoc. editor: Jour. Prosthetic Dentistry, 1974—. Fellow Northeastern Gnathological Soc. (pres. 1966-70), Greater N.Y. Acad. Prosthodontics, Acad. Gen. Dentistry; mem. Am. Prosthodontic Soc., ADA. Clubs: Lake Success Golf (Lake Success, N.Y.), Lake Success Tennis (Lake Success, N.Y.); Fountains Country (Lake Worth, Fla.). Current Work: General practice dentistry with strong emphasis in prosthodontics; research in biomedical devices, i.e. electrosurgery. Subspecialties: Prosthodontics; Biomedical engineering. Home: 6 Bridle Path Ln Lake Success NY 11020 Office: PC 104-20 Queens Blvd Forest Hills NY 11375

LENFANT, CLAUDE JEAN-MARIE, physician; b. Paris, Oct. 12, 1928; U.S., 1960, naturalized, 1965; s. Robert and Jeanine (Leclerc) L.; children—Philipe, Bernard, Martine Lenfant Wayman, Brigitte Lenfant Martin, Christine Lenfant Duke. B.S., U. Rennes, France, 1948; M.D., U. Paris, 1956. Asst. prof. physiology U. Lille, France, 1959-60; from clin. instr. to prof. medicine physiology and biophysics U. Wash. Med. Sch., 1961-72; asso. dir. lung programs Nat. Heart, Lung and Blood Inst. NIH, Bethesda, Md., 1970-72, dir. div. lung diseases, 1972-80; dir. Fogarty Internat. Center, NIH and NIH, assoc. dir. internat. research, 1980-82; dir. Nat. Heart, Lung and Blood Inst., 1982—. Assoc. editor: Jour. Applied Physiology, 1976-82, Am. Jour. Medicine, 1979—; mem. editorial bd.: Undersea Biomed. Research, 1973-75, Respiration Physiology, 1971-78, Am. Jour. Physiology and Jour. Applied Physiology, 1970-76, Am. Rev. Respiratory Disease, 1973-79; editor-in-chief: Lung Biology in Health and Disease. Mem. Assn. Am. Physicians, Am. Soc. Clin. Investigation, French, Am. physiol. socs., N.Y. Acad. Scis., Inst. Medicine Nat. Acad. Scis., Undersea Med. Soc. Home: 13201 Glen Rd Gaithersburg MD 20878 Office: Nat Heart Lung and Blood Inst 9000 Rockville Pike Bethesda MD 20014

LENON, RICHARD ALLEN, See *Who's Who in America,* 43rd edition.

LENT, ROBERT WILLIAM, counseling psychologist; b. Bklyn., Apr. 1, 1953; s. Jack Harvey and Gladys (Unger) L. B.A., SUNY-Albany, 1975; M.A., Ohio State U., 1977, Ph.D., 1979. Lic. cons. psychologist. Teaching assoc., Ohio State U., 1976-77, psychology intern, 1978-79, Mpls. VA Hosp., 1977-78; asst. prof. Student Counseling Bur., U. Minn.-Mpls., 1979-84, assoc. prof., 1984-85; asst. prof. counseling psychology Mich. State U., East Lansing, 1985—. Co-editor: Handbook of Counseling Psychology, 1984; behavioral sci. sect. editor: Jour. Minn. Acad. Scis, 1982-85; Contbr. articles to profl. jours. Vol. counselor Walk-In Counseling Center, Mpls., 1977-78, 84-85. Recipient Ohio State U. Fellowship award, 1975-79. Mem. Am. Psychol. Assn., Am. Assn. Counseling and Devel., Phi Beta Kappa. Current Work: Teaching and supervision of counseling, research, consultation, counseling; comparison of anxiety reduction methods; study of placebo control methodology, study of counselor supervision techniques. Subspecialty: Behavioral psychology. Office: Counseling Psychology 513 Erickson Hall Mich State U East Lansing MI 48824

LEON, JUDITH MERER, clinical research coordinator, lecturer; b. N.Y.C.; d. Samuel and Elsie (Streichler) Merer. B.A., CUNY, M.A., McMaster U., Ph.D., 1982. Lectr., U. Calif.-Irvine, 1980-82; clin. research coordinator Allergan Pharms., Irvine, 1983—. Contbr. articles to profl. jours. NSF scholar; N.Y. State scholar; Med. Research Council Can. fellow, 1975-80. Mem. Am. Chem. Soc., Assn. Women in Sci., Assn. Research in Vision and Opthamology, Drug Info. Assn., Soc. Clin. Trials. Current work: Pharmacotherapy of glaucoma, ocular anti-inflammatories, clinical trial management. Subspecialties: Ophthalmology; Pharmacology. Office: Allergan Pharms 2525 Dupont Dr Irvine CA 92715

LEON, SHALOM A., biochemist; b. Jerusalem, Israel, Apr. 7, 1935; came to U.S., 1965, naturalized, 1974; s. Albert S. and Bertha L.; m. Ofra Leon, July 5, 1962; children: Avner, Avital, Iris. M.Sc., Hebrew U., Jerusalem, 1959, Ph.D., 1964. Sr. research asst. pharmacology Hebrew U., 1960-65; postdoctoral research fellow Ind. U., 1965-67; asst. mem. research labs. Albert Einstein Med. Center, Phila., 1968-70, mem. dept. nuclear medicine, 1970—; clin. assoc. prof. radiobiology Temple U. Med. Sch., Phila., 1978—. Author in field. Fellow Am. Cancer Soc., 1980-82. Mem. Radiation Research Soc., N.Y. Acad. Scis., Am. Assn. Cancer Research, Am. Soc. Immunologists, Am. Chem. Soc., Am. Rheumatism Assn., AAAS. Patentee in field. Current Work: Effects of ionizing radiation on DNA and radioprotection, DNA circulation in cancer, rheumatoid diseases, radioimmunotherapy for malignancy. Subspecialties: Cancer research (medicine); Immunology (medicine). Office: Albert Einstein Med Center Philadelphia PA 19141

LEONARD, BENJAMIN FRANKLIN, III, geologist; b. Dobbs Ferry, N.Y., May 12, 1921; s. Benjamin Franklin and Florence J. (Smith) L.; m. Eleanor Vandewater, Mar. 18, 1950; children: Ruth L. O'Neil, William C. B.S., Hamilton Coll., 1942; M.A., Princeton U., 1947, Ph.D., 1951. Geologic field aide Geol. Survey Nfld., 1942; geologist U.S. Geol. Survey, Denver, 1943—; vis. prof. geology Colo. Sch. Mines, Golden, 1967-68. Editor: (with A. E. J. Engel and H. L. James) Buddington Volume, Geological Society America, 1962; editor: (with A. E. J. Engel and H. L. James) Internat. Platinum Symposium Soc. Econ. Geologist, 1976; assoc. editor: (with A. E. J. Engel and H. L. James) Canadian Mineralogist, 1976-78; editorial bd.: (with A. E. J. Engel and H. L. James) Eana. Geology, 1972-73. Fellow Geol. Soc. Am., Mineral. Soc. Am.; mem. Internat. Assn. Genesis Ore Deposits (officer paragenetic commn. 1972-82), Internat. Commn. Ore Microscopy (v.p. 1982—), Mineral. Assn. Can., Soc. Econ. Geologists (councilor 1976-79), Soc. Geology Applied to Mineral Deposits, Colo. Sci. Soc. (pres. 1956), Sigma Xi, Phi Beta Kappa. Current Work: Geology and ore deposits of central Idaho, ore minerals and alteration products, geochemical and biogeochemical exploration. Subspecialties: Mineralogy; Ore or mineral deposits. Home: 2907 Sunset Dr Golden CO 80401 Office: US Geol Survey Mail Stop 905 Box 25046 Federal Center Denver CO 80225

LEONARD, DAVID EDMUND, entomology educator; b. Greenwich, Conn., Dec. 28, 1934; s. James Bernard and Audrey Theresa (Forsberg) L.; m. Donna Kingsbury, Aug. 10, 1957 (div. 1977); children—Linda, Robyn Leonard Franklin; m. Sarah Wyatt Heywood, Sept. 17, 1977. B.S. in Plant Sci., U. Conn., 1956, M.S. in Zoology, 1960, Ph.D. in Zoology, 1964. Asst. then assoc. entomologist Conn. Agrl. Expt. Sta., New Haven, 1960-70; assoc. prof. then prof. U. Maine, Orono, 1970-79, assoc. dir. Expt. Sta., 1979-82; assoc., dir. Expt. Sta., U. Mass., Amherst, 1982-84, prof. entomology, 1984—. Editor sci. jours., 1972-82. Contbr. chpts. to books, articles to profl. jours. Chmn. Park Recreation Commn., Cheshire Court, 1968-70. Served with U.S. Army, 1957-58. Mem. AAAS, N.Y. Acad. Sci., Entomol. Soc. Am., Eastern Branch Entomol. Soc. Am. (pres. 1982-83). Current work: Insect ecology, host-parasite relationships, population biology, population quality, research administration, teaching. Subspecialty: Entomology. Office: U Mass Hatch Lab Amherst MA 01003

LEONARD, NELSON JORDAN, chemistry educator; b. Newark, Sept. 1, 1916; s. Harvey Nelson and Olga Pauline (Jordan) L.; m. Louise Cornelie Vermey, May 10, 1947; children: Kenneth Jan, Marcia Louise, James Nelson, David Anthony. B.S. in Chemistry, Lehigh U., 1937, Sc.D., 1963; B.Sc., Oxford (Eng.) U., 1940, D.Sc., 1983; Ph.D., Columbia U., 1942; D.h.c., Adam Mickiewicz U., Poland, 1980. Fellow and asst. chemistry U. Ill., Urbana, 1942-43, instr., 1943-44, asso., 1944-45, 46-47, asst. prof., 1947-49, asso. prof., 1949-52, prof. organic chemistry, 1952-68, head div. organic chemistry, 1954-63, prof. chemistry, also mem. Center for Advanced Study, 1968—, prof. biochemistry, 1973—; investigator antimalarial program Com. Med. Research, OSRD, 1944-46; sci. cons. and spl. investigator Field Intelligence Agy. Tech., U.S. Army and Dept. Commerce, 1945-46; mem. Can. NRC, summer 1950; Swiss-Am. Found. lectr., 1953, 70; vis. lectr. UCLA, summer 1953; Reilly lectr. U. Notre Dame, 1962; Stieglitz lectr. Chgo. sect. Am. Chem. Soc., 1962; Robert A. Welch Found. lectr., 1964; disting. vis. lectr. U. Calif.-Davis, 1975; vis. lectr. Polish Acad. Scis., 1976; B.R. Baker Meml. lectr. U. Calif., Santa Barbara, 1976; Ritter Meml. lectr. Miami U., Oxford, Ohio; Werner E. Bachman Meml. lectr. U. Mich., Ann Arbor, 1977; vis. prof. Japan Soc. Promotion of Sci., 1978; Arapahoe lectr. U. Colo., 1979; mem. program com. in basic scis. Arthur P. Sloan, Jr. Found., 1961-66; Philips lectr. Haverford Coll., 1971; Baker lectr., Groningen, Netherlands, 1972; FMC lectr. Princeton U., 1973; plenary lectr. Laaxer Chemistry Conf., Laax, Switzerland, 1980, 82; Calbiochem-Behring Corp. U. Calif.-San Diego Found. lectr., 1981; Watkins vis. prof. Wichita State U. (Kans.), 1982; Ida Beam Disting. vis. prof. U. Iowa, 1983; mem. adv. com. Searle Scholars program Chgo. Community Trust, 1982—; ednl. adv. bd. Guggenheim Found., 1969—, mem. com. of selection, 1977—. Editor: Organic Syntheses, 1951-58, mem. adv. bd., 1958—, bd. dirs., 1969—, v.p., 1976-80, pres., 1980—; editorial bd.: Jour. Organic Chemistry, 1957-61, Jour. Am. Chem. Soc, 1960-72; adv. bd.: Biochemistry, 1973-78; contbr. articles to profl. jours. Recipient Am. Chem. Soc. award, 1963; medal Synthetic Organic Chem. Mfrs., 1970; Rockefeller Found. fellow, 1950; Guggenheim Meml. fellow, 1959, 67. Fellow Am. Acad. Arts and Scis.; mem. Polish Acad. Scis. (fgn.), Nat. Acad. Scis., Ill. Acad. Sci. (hon.), Gesellschaft Deutscher Chemiker, Am. Chem. Soc. (Edgar Fahs Smith award and lectureship Phila. sect. 1975, Centennial lectr. 1976, Roger Adams award 1981), Am. Soc. Biol. Chemists, AAAS, Chem. Soc. London, Swiss Chem. Soc., Am.-Can. Soc. Plant Physiologists, Am. Soc. Photobiology, Inter-Am. Photochem. Soc., Phi Beta Kappa, Phi Lambda Upsilon (hon.), Tau Beta Pi, Alpha Chi Sigma. Subspecialty: Organic chemistry. Office: Dept Chemistry U Ill Urbana IL 61801

LEONE, GEORGE FRANK, pharmaceutical executive; b. Astoria, N.Y., Aug. 1, 1926; s. George and Fannie K. (Teano) L.; m. Mary Louise Potts, Dec. 14, 1945; children—Pamela Ann, George Frank. B.S., Tex. Wesleyan Coll., 1949; postgrad., NYU, 1951; grad. Advanced Mgmt. Program, Harvard Bus. Sch., 1959; postgrad., U. Tex., 1977. Chemist, Lederle Labs., Pearl River, N.Y., 1949-50; with Alcon Labs., Inc., Ft. Worth, 1950—, med. sales rep., 1950-54, dist. sales mgr., 1954-58, regional sales mgr., 1958-63, nat. sales mgr., 1963-66, dir. mktg., 1966-69, gen. mgr. domestic, 1969-70, v.p. sci., tech., 1971-81, sr. v.p., 1981—, also dir.; pres. Avicon, Inc., 1972-79. Pres., commr. Erath County Water Control and Improvement, Dist. 1, 1976-80; bd. dirs. Tex. Christian U., Research Found., 1976—; trustee Tex. Wesleyan Coll.; pres., bd. dirs. Yoga Soc. N.Y.; bd. dirs. Tex. Christian U. Research Found., 1976-82; chmn. athletic com. Dan Danciger Jewish Community Center; pres. Peninsula Pecan Growers Assn. Served with USN, 1944-45. Named Disting. Alumnus Tex. Wesleyan Coll., 1979. Mem. Alpha Chi. Club: Fort Worth. Home: 4100 Hildring Dr E Fort Worth TX 76109 Office: 6201 S Freeway Fort Worth TX 76134

LEONE, IDA A., plant pathologist; b. Elizabeth, N.J.; d. Joseph and Josephine (Aprigliano) L. B.S., Douglass Coll., 1944; M.S., Rugters U., 1946. Research asst. Rutgers U., 1946-50, research assoc., 1950-58, asst. research specialist, 1958-70, assoc. research specialist, 1970-76, research prof. plant pathology, 1976—; Bd. mgrs. Central Jersey Regional Air Pollution Control Agy., 1970-81; mem. Elizabeth (N.J.) Mayor's Ad Hoc Com. on Air Pollution, 1965-66. Contbr. numerous articles to profl. jours., chpts. to books. Bd. dirs. Delaware Valley Citizens Council for Clean Air, Union City Tb and Respiratory Disease Assn. EPA grantee, 1975-81. Mem. Am. Soc. Plant Physiologists, Am. Phytopathol. Soc., Air Pollution Control Assn., N.J. Acad. Sci., N.Y. Acad. Scis., Indian Assn. Air Pollution Control. Roman Catholic. Current Work: Air pollution effects on vegetation, re-vegetation of former refuse landfills. Subspecialties: Plant physiology (agriculture); Environmental toxicology. Home: 876 Rayhon Terrace Rahway NJ 07065 Office: Dept Plan Pathology Cook Coll PO Box 231 New Brunswick NJ 08903

LEONG, STANLEY PUI-LOCK, physician, surgeon, researcher; b. Shanghai, China, Sept. 8, 1948; came to U.S., 1967, naturalized, 1985; s. Joseph Yuk-Bor and Maria Yau-Ying (Lam) L.; m. Elizabeth T. Leong, Dec. 7, 1974; 1 son, Benjamin S.T. B.S. in Biology cum laude, Tulane U., 1971, M.D. and M.S. in Immunology and Microbiology, 1974. Lic. physician, La., Mass., Calif., Md. Intern Charity Hosp., New Orleans, 1974-75; fellow surgery and oncology Tulane U., 1975-76; research assoc. Boston U., 1976-78; mem. Hubert H. Humphrey Cancer Research Ctr., 1976-78; resident internal medicine New Eng. Deaconess Hosp., Boston, 1978-79, sr. research assoc. Cancer Research Inst., 1978-79; clin. fellow Harvard U., 1978-79; resident in gen. surgery U. Calif., Irvine 1979-83; research assoc. div. surgery City of Hope Nat. Med Ctr.,

Duarte, Calif., 1979-82; clin. assoc. surgery br. Nat. Cancer Inst., NIH, Bethesda, Md., 1983-85, cancer expert, 1985—. Contbr. articles to profl. jours. Greater New Orleans Cancer Assn. fellow, 1971; Damon Runyon-Walter Winchell Cancer Fund Oncology fellow, 1981-82. Mem. AMA, Mass. Med. Soc., Am. Fedn. Clinic Research, Am. Assn. Cancer Research, AAAS, N.Y. Acad. Sci. Roman Catholic. Current Work: Tumor immunology; melanoma and sarcoma antigens; cytohistochemistry, immunofluorescence; monoclonal antibody; fluorescence activated cell sorter; general surgery. Subspecialties: Immunobiology and immunology; Cancer research (medicine). Office: Surgery Br Bldg 10 Rm 2B42 Nat Cancer Inst NIH Bethesda MD 20205

LEONHARD, WILLIAM EDWARD, engineer. Chmn., The Parsons Corp., Pasadena, Calif. . Office: The Parsons Corp 100 W Walnut St Pasadena CA 91124*

LERCH, IRVING ABRAM, medical physicist; b. Chgo., June 29, 1938; s. Abraham and Rissel (Lutwak) L.; m. Sharon Lerch, Feb. 24, 1963. B.S., U.S. Mil. Acad., 1960; M.S., U. Chgo., 1966, Ph.D., 1969. Research assoc. U. Chgo., 1969-73; first officer IAEA, Vienna, Austria, 1973-76; prof. N.Y. U. Sch. Medicine, N.Y.C., 1976—; tech. asst. expert cons. IAEA, WHO, others. Contbr. articles to profl. jours.; Books and publs. editor: Med. Physics, 1980-82; sci. editor: Biomedical Dosimetry, 1975, Physics, Dosimetry and Biomedical Aspects of Californium, 1976. Served to 1st lt. U.S. Army, 1960-63. USPHS fellow, 1964-69; Nat. Cancer Inst.-USPHS grantee, 1972-73, 69-73; others. Mem. Am. Phys. Soc., Am. Assn. Physicists in Medicine, Radiation Research Soc., Radiol. and Med. Physics Soc. N.Y. Current Work: Radiation dosimetry standardization in use of ionizing radiations in detection and treatment of cancer; computer telecommunications, telematics, and telemedicine. Subspecialties: Cancer research (medicine); Radiology. Home: 146 W 74th St Apt 3 New York NY 10023 Office: 566 First Ave New York NY 10016

LERMAN, MICHAEL ISAAC, molecular biologist, researcher; b. Korosten, Ukraine, USSR, Sept. 21, 1932; came to U.S., 1980, naturalized, 1985; s. Isaac Leyb and Ida (Lerman) L.; m. Svetlana Sno, Mar. 7, 1961 (dec. July 1973); 1 child, Eugene Michael; m. Eugenia Ilya Miniovich, Dec. 5, 1975; 1 child, Leah Victoria. M.D., First Moscow Med. Sch., 1957, M. Biochemistry, 1960; Ph.D., Acad. Scis., Moscow, 1970. Asst. prof. First Moscow Med. Sch., 1960-62; sr. scientist Acad. Scis., Moscow, 1962-68; dir. lab. Acad. Med. Scis., Moscow, 1968-78; vis. scientist Nat. Cancer Inst., NIH, Bethesda, Md., 1980-82, Frederick, Md., 1982—. Mem. Am. Soc. Biol. Chemists, N.Y. Acad. Scis. Jewish. Current work: Molecular biology of cancer; indentification and molecular cloning of cancer genes involved in carcinogenesis and maintenance of malignancy. Subspecialties: Molecular biology; Cancer research (medicine). Home: 261 Congressional Ln Apt 402 Rockville MD 20852 Office: Nat Cancer Inst NIH Bldg 560 Room 32-65 FCRF Frederick MD

LERMAN, SIDNEY, ophthalmology educator; b. nr. Montreal, Que., Can., Oct. 6, 1927; s. Aaron and Rachel L.; m. Marilyn F. Frank, Apr. 14, 1957; children: Lora Rachel, Mark Jonas. B.Sc., McGill U., 1948, M.D.C.M., 1952; M.S. in Biochemistry, U. Rochester, 1961. Diplomate: Am. Bd. Ophthalmology. Intern Montreal Gen. Hosp., 1952, resident, 1953-55; successively instr., asst. prof., assoc. prof and dir. ophthalmology research U. Rochester, 1957-68; prof. ophthalmology and biochemistry, dir. dept. ophthamol. research McGill U., 1968-75; prof. ophthalmology, adj. prof. chemistry Emory U. and Ga. Inst. Tech., 1975—. Author: Glaucoma—Chemical Mechanical, 1961, Cataract Therapy, 1964, Basic Ophthalmology, 1966, Radiant Energy and the Eye, 1980. Fellow Am. Acad. Ophthalmology, Oxford Ophthalmol. Congress, ACS; mem. Am. Soc. Biol. Chemists, Am. Chem. Soc., Am. Soc. Photobiology, Internat. Soc. Eye Research, Assn. Research in Vision and Ophthalmology. Patentee in field. Current Work: Photobiology, photochemistry, pharmacology and toxicology, biologic effects of radiation, biophysical research, optical spectroscopy, NMR spectroscopy. Subspecialties: Biophysical chemistry; Photochemistry. Home: 1648 Musket Ridge Rd NW Atlanta GA 30327 Office: Emory University 1708 Haygood Dr NE Atlanta GA 30322

LERNER, LEONARD JOSEPH, endocrinologist, educator; b. Roselle, N.J., Sept. 26, 1922; s. Hyman and Esther Celia (Honig) L. B.S., Rutgers U., 1943, A.B., 1951, M.S., 1953, Ph.D., 1954; postgrad., N.Y.U., 1951. Registered pharmacist, N.J., Ohio, Calif., N.Y. Research asst. Bur. Biol. Research, Rutgers U., 1952-54; sect. head William S. Merrell Co., Cin., 1954-58; sect. head endocrinology Squibb Inst. Med. Research, New Brunswick, N.J., 1958-65; dir. dept. endocrinology, 1965-70, Lepetit Research Lab., Gruppo Lepetit, Milan, Italy, 1971-77; research prof. Jefferson Med. Coll., Phila., 1977—; adj. prof. Hahnemann Med. Coll., 1971—; cons., lectr. in field. Contbr. numerous articles to profl. jours.; mem. editorial bd. Steroids. Served with AUS, 1944-46. Grantee pharm. co., various agys. Fellow AAAS; mem. Am. Physiol. Soc., N.Y. Acad. Sci., Am. Assn. Cancer Research, Am. Fertility Soc., Soc. Study Reprodn., Soc. Exptl. Biology and Medicine, Internat. Study Group Steroid Hormones, Sigma Xi. Patentee in field. Current Work: Reproductive endocrinology, endocrine pharmacology. Subspecialties: Endocrinology; Reproductive biology. Home: C-5 Windsor Castle Apts Cranbury NJ 08512 Office: 1025 Walnut St Philadelphia PA 19107

LERNER, PAULINE, chemist; b. Balt., July 4, 1948; d. David and Ruth (Marks) Sheplan; m. Melvin Lerner. B.A., Goucher Coll., 1969; Ph.D., U. Md., 1973. Research chemist Nat. Heart, Lung and Blood Inst., NIH, Bethesda, Md., 1974-77, NIMH, NIH, Bethesda, 1977-80; chemist FDA, Washington, 1980—. Mem. AAAS, Assn. Women Scientists, Am. Chem. Soc., Am. Soc. Neurochem., Neurosci. Soc., Phi Beta Kappa, Sigma Xi. Current work: Role of nutrition in health and disease, medical foods, regulation of health aspects of foods. Subspecialties: Biochemistry (biology); Neurochemistry. Home: 1212 Potomac Valley Rd Rockville MD 20850 Office: FDA HFF-204 200 C St SW Washington DC 20204

LERNER, STEPHEN ALEXANDER, microbiology educator; b. Chgo., Oct. 4, 1938; s. David G. and Florence (Trace) L.; m. Ronna Bergman, June 6, 1963; children: Deborah, Daniel, Susan. A.B., Harvard U., 1959, M.D., 1963. Med. intern Peter Bent Brigham Hosp., Boston, 1963-64, resident, 1964-65; research assoc. NIH, Bethesda, Md., 1965-68; postdoctoral fellow Stanford Biochemistry Dept., Palo Alto, Calif., 1968-71; asst. prof. dept. medicine U. Chgo., 1971-78, assoc. prof., 1978—. Editor: Aminoglycoside Ototoxicity, 1981; editorial bd.: Antimicrobial Agents and Chemotherapy, 1981—. Recipient Borden Undergrad. award Harvard U., 1963. Fellow Infectious Diseases Soc. Am; mem. Am. Soc. Microbiology, Phi Beta Kappa, Alpha Omega Alpha. Democrat. Jewish. Current Work: Genetic and physiologic mechanisms of bacterial resistance to antibiotics, antibiotic pharmacology. Subspecialties: Microbiology; Pharmacology. Home: 4918 S Kimbark Ave Chicago IL 60615 Office: U Chgo Sch Medicine 5841 S Maryland Ave Chicago IL 60637

LESCHACK, LEONARD ALBERT, research company executive; b. N.Y.C., Mar. 6, 1935; s. David and Selma (Kaminsky) LeS.; m. Lorraine L., Mar. 3, 1962; children: Christopher E., Adam A. B.S. in Petroleum Geology, Rensselaer Poly. Inst., 1957; diploma in oceanography, Grad. Sch. U.S. Dept. Agr., 1962; postgrad. in geophysics, U. Wis-Madison, 1963-64. Cert. profl. geol. scientist. Geophys. trainee Shell Oil Co., Houston, 1957; asst. seismologist Byrd Sta. Traverse Party, U.S. Nat. Com. Internat. Geophys. Yr., Antarctica, 1957-59; oceanographer Naval Oceanographic Office, Suitland, Md., 1964-65; polar regions project officer EXPO-67, Montreal, Que., Can., 1965-66; pres. LeSchack Assocs., Ltd., Long Key, Fla., 1967—; U.S. rep. Argentine Antarctic Expdn., 1962-63; participant 2d Internat. Permafrost Conf., Siberia, 1973; pres. Trident Arctic Exploration Ltd., Montreal, 1979—. Contbr. chpts. to books, articles to profl. jours. Served to lt. (j.g.) USN, 1959-63; to capt. 1980-81. Decorated Legion of Merit; recipient Antarctica Service medal Nat. Acad. Scis.-NRC, 1966; grantee Arctic Inst. N.Am., 1963. Mem. Am. Geophys. Union, Soc. Exploration Geophysicists, Am. Inst. Profl. Geologists. Patentee graphical data digitizer. Current Work: Collection and analysis of Arctic sea ice data using remote sensing techniques; developing data collection techniques with manned submersibles; exploration for geothermal resources. Subspecialties: Geophysics; Remote sensing (geoscience).

LESKO, ROBERT JOSEPH, mgmt. and tech. cons.; b. Homestead, Pa., Sept. 24, 1942; s. Joseph and Irene Teresa (Anderson) L.; m. Kathleen Menzie, Aug. 7, 1965; children: Mark Joseph, Robert Anderson. B.S. in Mech. Engring, U. Notre Dame, 1964; M.B.A., U. Pa. Wharton Sch., 1967; postgrad., Georgetown U. Law Center, 1966-67; M.F.A., Catholic U. Am., 1979. Mem. tech. staff Computer Scis. Corp., Falls Church, Va., 1967-68; pres. Centaur Mgmt. Cons., Inc., Washington, 1968-72; exec. v.p. Med. Aid Tng. Schs. Inc., Silver Spring, Md., 1972-74; pres. Software Architecture and Engring., Inc., Arlington, Va., 1974-82; v.p. Applied Mgmt. Sci., Inc., Silver Spring, Md., 1982—; mem. faculty Grad. Sch. Bus., George Washington U., 1969-70, Am. U., 1970-71; dir. Knowledge Engring., Inc., Arlington. Bd. dors Oxfam-Am., Washington, 1970-72. Mem. Assn. Energy Engrs. Current Work: Info. systems, energy data systems, advanced data processing systems, strategic planning. Subspecialty: Information systems, storage, and retrieval (computer science).

LESLIE, JOHN FRANKLIN, research microbiologist, educator; b. Dallas, July 2, 1953; s. Frank R. and Peggy J. (Shelton) L.; m. Ingelin Lono, Jan. 10, 1976; children: Timothy Franklin, Inger Joyce. B.A. in Biology, U. Dallas, 1975; M.S. in Genetics, U. Wis., 1977, Ph.D., 1979. Univ. fellow, then NIH trainee Lab. Genetics, U. Wis., Madison., 1975-79; postdoctoral research affiliate dept. biol. sci. Stanford U. Calif., 1979-81; research microbiologist corp. research and devel. Internat. Mineral and Chem. Corp., Terre Haute, Ind., 1981-84; asst. prof. dept. plant pathology Kans. State U., Manhattan, 1984—; tech. adv. Inst. Christian Resources, San Jose, Calif. Contbr. articles to profl. jours. Mem. Genetics Soc. Am., Mycol. Soc. Am., Am. Soc. Microbiology, Soc. Gen. Microbiology, Brit. Mycol. Soc., AAAS, Sigma Xi. Presbyterian. Current Work: Fungal genetics in model and plant pathogenic systems. Genetic enhancement of microbial metabolite production using classical and recombinant DNA techniques. Dissection of fungal development and population structure using chromosome rearrangements and classical genetics. Empirical and theoretical Population genetics. Subspecialties: Genetics and genetic engineering (agriculture); Microbiology. Home: 2921 Hickory Ct Manhattan KS 66502-3115 Office: Kans State U Dept Plant Pathology 418C Throckmorton Hall Manhattan KS 66506

LESTER, DAVID, biochemist, educator, consultant; b. New Haven, Jan. 22, 1916; s. Asher and Esther (Rubin) L.; m. Ruth Weiss, Sept. 18, 1938; children: Anne Deborah Lester Schager, James Matthew. B.S., Yale U., 1936, Ph.D., 1940. Diplomate: Am. Bd. Clin. Chemistry, 1958. Mem. faculty Lab. Applied Physiology, Yale U., 1940-62; prof. biochemistry Rutgers U., New Brunswick, N.J., 1962—; dir. grad. program in pharmacology Rutgers U./U. Medicine and Dentistry N.J., 1980-82; sci. dir. Nat. Alcohol Research Center, 1978-83. Author book in field; contbr. chpts to books, articles to profl. jours.; asso. editor: Jour. Studies on Alcohol, 1950—. Rep. Borough of Princeton to instl. biosafety com. Princeton U. Mem. Am. Chem. Soc., N.Y. Acad. Scis., Am. Soc. Pharmacology and Exptl. Therapeutics, AAAS, Research Soc. Alcoholism. Current Work: Animal models alcoholism, predictive factors alcoholism. Subspecialties: Biochemistry (medicine); Pharmacology. Home: 29 Forester Dr Princeton NJ 08540 Office: Center Alcohol Studies Rutgers Univ New Brunswick NJ 08903

LESTER, JOHN BERNARD, astronomer, educator; b. San Diego, Mar. 11, 1945; s. Bernard Edward and Margaret (Miller) L.; m. Rose Ann Patterson, July 1, 1972; children: Catherine, Margaret. Student, San Diego State U., 1963-65; B.A., Northwestern U., 1967; M.S., U. Chgo., 1969, Ph.D., 1972. Research assoc. Smithsonian Astrophys. Obs., Cambridge, Mass., 1972-76; asst. prof. astronomy U. Toronto, Ont., Can., 1976-81, assoc. prof., 1981—. Contbr.: articles to Astrophys. Jour. Mem. Am. Astron. Soc., Internat. Astron. Union, Astron. Soc. Pacific. Current Work: Stellar atmospheres, chemical compositiopns, ultraviolet astronomy, computer models. Subspecialties: Optical astronomy; Stellar composition. Home: 2581 Barcella Crescent Mississauga ON L5K 1E5 Canada Office: Erindale Coll Mississauga ON L5L 1C6 Canada

LESTER, RICHARD KEITH, engineering educator, consultant; b. Leeds, Eng., Jan. 3, 1954; came to U.S., 1974; s. Bernard and Mona (Smuckler) L.; m. Anne Elizabeth Columbia, Oct. 20, 1979. Sc.B. in Chem. Engring, Imperial Coll., 1974; Ph.D. in Nuclear Engring, M.I.T., 1979. Vis. fellow Rockefeller Found., N.Y.C., 1977-78; instr. M.I.T., Cambridge, 1978-79, asst. prof. nuclear engring., 1979-80, Edgerton asst. prof. nuclear engring., 1980-82, assoc. prof. nuclear engring., 1982-84, Atlantic Richfield assoc. prof. energy studies, 1984—; cons. several U.S. cos. Kennedy scholar, 1974-76. Mem. Am. Nuclear Soc., AAAS. Current Work: Nuclear chemical engineering, nuclear waste management, international nuclear relations, energy policy analysis. Subspecialty: Nuclear engineering. Office: Dept Nuclear Engring MIT 77 Massachusetts Ave Cambridge MA 02138

LESTREL, PETE ERNEST, educator, research anthropologist; b. Quito, Ecuador, Feb. 19, 1938; came to U.S., 1948, naturalized, 1954; s. Hans and Berta (Schwab) L.; m. Dagmar Centa Kowalzyk, Apr. 20, 1968; children: Nicole, Valerie. A.B., UCLA, 1964, M.A., 1966, Ph.D., 1975. Engr. N.Am. Aviation, Los Angeles, 1962-65; instr. Santa Monica (Calif.) Coll., 1967-73; asst. prof. anthropology Case Western Res. U., Cleve., 1973-75, cons. dept. anatomy, 1974-75; asst. prof. UCLA Sch. Dentistry, 1977-80, assoc. prof., 1981—; research anthropologist VA Med. Center, Sepulveda, Calif., 1976—. Editorial bd.: Human Biology Jour, 1980-83; contbr. articles to profl. jours., chpts. in books. Fellow Human Biology Council; mem. Am. Assn. Phys. Anthropologists, Am. Assn. Dental Research, Internat. Assn. for Dental Research. Democrat. Current Work: Quantitative description of complex morphological forms frequently encountered in biology and medicine; computer modelling of growth and devel. and evolutionary processes. Subspecialties: Dental growth and development; Morphometrics. Home: 7327 De Celis Pl Van Nuys CA 91406 Office: 16111 Plummer Ave Sepulveda CA 91343

LETO, SALVATORE, laboratory director, andrologist; b. Borgetto, Sicily, Oct. 28, 1937; came to U.S., 1946; s. Antonino and Elisabetta (Armato) L.; m. Margaret A. Smith, Sept. 12, 1964 (div. July 1970); children: Anthony L., Gerald A.; m. Evelyn H. Brady, Dec. 28, 1973. B.S. in Chemistry, CCNY, 1961; Ph.D. in Biology, Georgetown U., 1967. Cert. clin. lab. supr., N.Y. Staff fellow Nat. Inst. Child Health and Human Devel., NIH, Balt., 1967-71; lab. supr. IDANT Corp., N.Y.C., 1971-72, lab. dir., Balt., 1972-73, Washington Fertility Study Ctr., 1973—; cons., 1980—. Author: Clinical Advances in Andrology, vol. 8, 1982, Male Reproduction and Fertility, 1983; contbr. articles to sci. jours. Served in U.S. Army, 1961-63. Mem. Am. Fertility Soc., Am. Soc. Andrology, Am. Physiol. Soc., AAAS, Am. Assn. Tissue Banks, Pan Am. Congress Andrology, Sigma Xi. Democrat. Roman Catholic. Current Work: Andrology, reproductive biology, cryobiology (human sperm cryo-preservation), immuno-infertility, endocrinology of reproduction. Subspecialties: Andrology; Reproductive biology. Home: 20 Sparrow Hill Ct Baltimore MD 21228 Office: 2600 Virginia Ave Suite 500 Washington DC 20037

LEUNG, BENJAMIN SHUET-KIN, medical educator, researcher; b. Hong Kong, June 30, 1938; s. Yun-Pui and Kan-Yau (Lee) L.; m. Helen Tsan-Fu Hsu, Oct. 19, 1964; children: Kay, Titus, Steven. B.S., Seattle Pacific Coll., 1963; Ph.D., Colo. State U., 1969; postgrad., Vanderbilt U., 1971. Affiliate mem. dept. biochemistry, dir. research, dir. Clin. Research Ctr. Lab., dir. Steroid Receptor Lab. U. Oreg., Portland, 1971-76, asst. prof. dept. surgery, 1971-74, assoc. prof., 1974-76; sr. research scientist Cedars-Sinai Med. Ctr., Los Angeles, 1976-78; assoc. oncologist Med. Sch. UCLA, 1976-78; assoc. prof. dept. ob-gyn U. Minn., Mpls., 1978—; ad hoc cons. NIH, Nat. Cancer Inst., NSF, 1974—; lectr. in field. Reviewer-referee various profl. publs.; editor: Hormonal Regulation of Experimental Breast Tumors, 1982; contbr. articles to sci. jours. Chmn. Dad's Club, Bridlemile Sch., Portland, Oreg., 1975-76; pres. bd. dirs. Ch. in Mpls., 1978—. NIH fellow, 1966-68, 69-71; Ford Found. fellow, 1969-71; numerous research grants. Mem. Am. Soc. Biol. Chemists, Endocrine Soc., Soc. Gynecologic Investigation, AAAS, Minn. Ob-Gyn Soc. Current Work: Mechanism of steroid hormone action; role of hormones in mammary and gynecologic tumors. Subspecialties: Cell and tissue culture; Receptors. Home: 6076 Olinger Blvd Edina MN 55436 Office: University Minn Dept Ob-Gyn Box 395 Mayo 420 Delaware St Minneapolis MN 55455

LEUNG, CHRISTOPHER CHUNG-KIT, anatomist, educator, researcher; b. Hong Kong, Jan. 3, 1939; came to U.S., 1960, naturalized, 1975; s. Nai Kuen and Sau Wah (Chan) L.; m. Stella Tang, May 11, 1970; children: Jacquelyn, Therese. Ph.D., Jefferson Med. Coll., 1969. Instr. Jefferson Med. Coll., 1969-72, asst. prof., 1972-74, U. Kans. Sch. Medicine, 1974-79; assoc. prof. anatomy La. State U. Sch. Medicine, 1979-85; assoc. prof. anatomy Coll. Medicine and Dentistry, N.J. Med. Sch., Newark, 1985—; mem. NIH Ad Hoc Study Sect., 1985. Contbr. numerous articles to profl. jours. NIH grantee, 1978—, mem. ad Loc study sect. human embryology and devel., 1985. Mem. Am. Assn. Anatomists, Soc. Developmental Biology, Am. Soc. Cell Biology, Am. Assn. Immunologists, Soc. Reproductive Biology, Teratology Soc. Democrat. Roman Catholic. Current Work: Embryology, teratology, immunology, pathology. Subspecialties: Anatomy and embryology; Immunology (medicine). Home: 95 Jones Dr New Providence NJ 07974 Office: NJ Med Sch Newark NJ 07103

LEUNG, CHUNG WAI, electrical engineer, researcher; b. Hong Kong, China, Feb. 10, 1945, came to U.S., 1966, naturalized, 1979; s. Nai Kuen and Sau Wah (Chan) L.; m. Wei May Pang, May 18, 1974; children—Andrea Yue-Ting, Dennis Yue-Ping. B.S.E.E., Rutgers U., 1970, M.S.E.E., 1973, Ph.D., 1976. Prin. engr. Honeywell Inc., Mpls., 1974-76; sect. mgr. RCA Corp., Somerville, N.J., 1976-84; mem. tech. staff AT&T Bell Labs., Allentown, Pa., 1984—. Patentee in field. Mem. IEEE, Tau Beta Pi, Eta Kappa Nu. Current work: Advanced CMOS technology development for high speed, high density low power, data communication application. Subspecialties: Integrated circuits; Microelectronics. Home: 1501 Red Maple Ln Allentown PA 18103 Office: AT&T Bell Labs 555 Union Blvd Allentown PA 18103

LEUNG, PHILIP MIN-BUN, nutritionist, researcher; b. Canton, China, July 31, 1932; s. Shiu-Tsze and Yu-Woon (Chu) L; m. Anita Ming-Yuen, Aug. 26, 1962; children—Terence Yin-Nin, Frances Wing-Yee, Stephen Yin-Yam. B.S., Nat. Chung Hsing U., Republic of China, 1956; M.S., McGill U., 1959; Ph.D., MIT, 1965. Demonstrator McGill U., Montreal, Que., Can., 1956-59; research asst. MIT, Cambridge, 1960-65; research biochemist, group leader Miles Labs, Elkhart, Ind., 1965-67; research nutritionist U. Calif.-Davis, 1967—. NIH grantee, 1969—. Mem. Am. Inst. Nutrition. Roman Catholic. Current work: Nutrition and biochemistry of amino acid imbalances and deficiences, influence of amino acid balance on food intake regulation. Subspecialties: Nutrition (medicine); Biochemistry (medicine). Office: Dept Physiological Scis Sch Ved Med U Calif Davis CA 95616

LEUNG, WING HAI, chemistry educator, researcher; b. Hong Kong, July 29, 1937; came to U.S., 1969; s. Ju-Dug and Ping-Fan (Yu) L.; m. Lai-Yin Kwan, Aug. 15, 1965; children: Kar-Woo, Kar-Hong, Kar-Peck. B.Sc., U. Hong Kong, 1963; M.S., U. Miami, 1970, Ph.D., 1974. Research assoc. SUNY-Buffalo, 1974-76; sr. chemist GAF Corp., Binghamton, N.Y., 1976-77; scientist Clinton (Iowa) Corn Corp., 1977-78; asst. prof. chemistry Hampton (Va.) Inst., 1978-82, assoc. prof., 1982—; mem. U.S. Congl. Adv. Bd., Washington, 1982-83. Contbr. articles to profl. jours. NASA grantee, 1981. Mem. Am. Chem. Soc., Am. Geophys. Union, N.Y. Acad. Sci., Sigma Xi. Current Work: Surface phenomena, kinetic studies of crystal growth and the interaction of solid/solution interfaces such as iron oxide and other suspended particles. Subspecialties: Surface chemistry; Physical chemistry. Office: Department of Chemistry Hampton University Hampton VA 23668

LEV, MAURICE, pathologist; b. St. Joseph, Mo., Nov. 13, 1908; s. Benjamin and Rose L.; m. Lesley Beswick, Sept., 1947; children: Benita J., Peter B. B.S., N.Y.U., 1930; M.D., Creighton U., 1934; M.A. in Philosophy, Northwestern U., 1966; H.H.D., DePaul U., 1981. Diplomate: Am. Bd. Pathology. Intern Michael Reese Hosp., Chgo., 1937-38, resident in pathology, 1938-40; instr. pathology U. Ill., Chgo., 1939-46, asst. prof., 1947-48, assoc. prof., 1948-51, lectr., 1963—; pathologist Chgo. State Hosp., 1940-42; asst. prof. Creighton U., 1946-47; assoc. prof. U. Miami, Coral Gables, Fla., 1951-56, prof., 1956-57; pathologist, dir. research labs. Mt. Sinai Hosp. Greater Miami, 1951-57; prof. pathology Northwestern U., 1957-77, prof. emeritus, 1977—; dir. Congenital Heart Disease Research and Tng. Ctr., Chgo. Heart Assn., Hektoen Inst. Med. Research, 1957-82, career investigator and educator, 1966—; professorial lectr. U. Chgo., 1959—; cons. cardiovascular pathology Children's Meml. Hosp., Chgo., 1957—; lectr. pathology Chgo. Med. Sch. U. Health Scis., 1970—; lectr. Loyola U., Maywood, Ill., 1971—; Disting. prof. pediatrics Rush Med. Coll., Chgo., 1974—, Disting. prof. dept. internal medicine, 1975—, Disting. prof. dept. pathology, 1977—; lectr. Cook County Grad. Sch. Medicine, Chgo., 1977—; dir. Clin. Lab. Deborah Heart & Lung Ctr., Browns Mills, N.J., 1982—. Contbr. articles to profl. jours. Served to lt. col. U.S. Army, 1942-46. Recipient Alumni Assn. Michael Reese Hosp. & Med. Ctr. Disting. Alumnus award, 1978; Creighton U. Alumni Achievement award, 1979; named to City of Chgo. Sr. Citizens Hall of Fame, 1980; Brennamen award, 1983; Golden Merit award, 1984. Fellow AMA, Am. Coll. Cardiology (v.p. 1963-64), Am. Soc. Clin. Pathologists, Coll. Am. Pathologists, N.Y. Acad. Sci., Am. Coll. Chest Physicians, Inst. Medicine Chgo., Am. Heart Assn. (award of merit 1977, research achievement award 1980); mem. Am. Soc. Pathologists and Bacteriologists, Am. Assn. Anatomists, Histochem. Soc., Gerontol. Soc., Chgo. Path. Soc. (v.p. 1966-67, pres. 1967-68), Ill. Path. Soc., Midwest Soc. Electron Microscopists, Nashville Cardiovascular Soc., Sigma Xi, Alpha Omega Alpha, Phi Delta Epsilon. Current Work: Congenital heart and conduction system. Subspecialties: Health services research; Pathology (medicine). Office: Deborah Heart & Lung Center Trenton Rd Browns Mills NJ 08015

LEVARY, REUVEN ROBERT, management sciences educator, researcher; b. Bucurest, Romania, Jan. 6, 1944; came to U.S., 1975, naturalized, 1983; s. Jacob and Carola (Fisher) L.; m. Martha Merritt, Dec. 16, 1978 (div.); 1 dau., Sarah. B.Sc., Technion, Haifa, Israel, 1969, M.Sc., 1972; M.S., Case Western Res. U., 1976, Ph.D., 1978. Teaching asst. Technion, 1969-72; grad. asst. Case Western Res. U., 1975-77; asst. prof. mgmt. scis. St. Louis U., 1978-81, assoc. prof., 1981-85, prof., 1985—; vis. scientist Ops. Research Ctr., MIT, 1984-85; vis. assoc. prof. Sloan Sch. Mgmt., MIT, spring 1985; cons. in field. Contbr. articles to profl. jours. Case Western Res. U. travel grantee, 1977; St. Louis U. grantee, 1979; Beaumont Faculty Devel. Fund grantee, 1984. Mem. IEEE (sr.), Ops. Research Soc. Am., Inst. Mgmt. Scis., Omega Rho. Current Work: Applied optimization, computer simulation, production management, distribution systems, energy modeling. Subspecialties: Operations research (engineering); Resource management. Office: Saint Louis U 3674 Lindell Blvd Saint Louis MO 63108

LEVENSON, MILTON, chemical engineer; b. St. Paul, Jan. 4, 1923; s. Harry and Fanny M. L.; m. Mary Beth Novick, Aug. 27, 1950; children: James L., Barbara G., Richard A., Scott D., Janet L. B.Ch.E., U. Minn., 1943. Jr. engr. Houdaille-Hershey Corp., Decatur, Ill., 1944; research engr. Oak Ridge Nat. Lab., 1944-48; with Argonne (Ill.) Nat. Lab., 1948-73, assoc. lab. dir., 1973; dir. nuclear power div. Electric Power Research Inst., Palo Alto, Calif., 1973-80; cons. to pres. Bechtel Power Corp., San Francisco, 1981—; lectr. in field. Contbr. articles to profl. jours., chpts. to books. Served with C.E. U.S. Army, 1944-46. Fellow Am. Inst. Chem. Engrs. (Robert E. Wilson award 1975), Am. Nuclear Soc. (pres. 1983-84); mem. AAAS, Nat. Acad. Engring. Patentee in field. Subspecialty: Nuclear engineering. Office: 50 Beale St San Francisco CA 94119

LEVENTHAL, BRIGID GRAY, research physician; b. London, Eng., Aug. 31, 1935; came to U.S., 1940, naturalized, 1954; d. Hugh Joseph and Barbara Theodora (Church) Gray; m. Carl M. Leventhal, Feb. 4, 1962; children: George Leon, Sarah Elizabeth, Dinah Susan, James Gray. B.A. with highest honors, UCLA, 1955; M.D., Harvard U., 1960. Diplomate: Am. Bd. Pediatrics, Am. Bd. in Pediatric Hematology/Oncology). Intern Mass. Gen. Hosp., Boston, 1960-61, jr. asst. resident in pediatrics, 1961-62; sr. asst. resident in pediatrics Boston City Hosp., 1962-63; USPHS trainee St. Elizabeth's Hosp., Brighton, Mass., 1963-64; postdoctoral fellow leukemia service Nat. Cancer Inst., Bethesda, Md., 1964-65, sr. investigator, 1965-73, head chemoimmunotherapy sect. pediatric oncology br., 1973-76; dir. div. pediatric oncology Johns Hopkins U., Balt., 1976—, assoc. prof. oncology, 1976—, assoc. prof. pediatrics, 1976—; mem. oncology and pediatric staffs Johns Hopkins Hosp., 1976—; mem. bd. sci. counselors div. cancer treatment Nat. Cancer Inst.; sci. adv. bd. St. Jude Hosp. Judge Westinghouse Sci. Talent Search. Editorial bd.: Jour. Nat. Cancer Inst, 1974-76, Leukemia Research, 1977—, Jour. Biol. Response Modifiers, 1981—; contbr. numerous articles and abstracts to profl. jours., chpts. in books. Recipient Fed. Woman's award, 1974; Outstanding Career Woman award Nat. Council Women, 1979; Edward A. Dickson Alumnus of Yr. Achievement award UCLA, 1982. Mem. Am. Fedn. Clin. Research, Am. Soc. Hematology, Am. Assn. Cancer Research, Am. Soc. Clin. Oncology (sec.-treas. 1976-79, dir. 1980-83), Transplantation Soc., AAAS, Internat. Soc. Exptl. Hematology, Soc. Pediatric Research, Am. Soc. Clin. Investigation, Am. Pediatric Soc., Phi Beta Kappa, Alpha Omega Alpha. Democrat. Jewish. Current Work: Clinical research in pediatric cancer patients with emphasis on interaction of drugs and immune system. Subspecialties: Cancer research (medicine); Pediatrics. Home: 9254 Old Annapolis Rd Columbia MD 21045 Office: Oncology Ctr 3 12 Johns Hopkins Hospital Baltimore MD 21205

LEVENTHAL, STEPHEN HENRY, rsearch mathematician, reservoir engineer; b. N.Y.C., Apr. 2, 1949; s. Louis and Sylvia (Miller) L.; m. Ellen Sue Warach, Aug. 29, 1971; children: Daniel Scott, Seth Andrew. B.A. in Math,

Rutgers U., 1969; M.A. in Math, U. Md., 1971, Ph.D. in Math, 1973. Mathematician Naval Surface Weapons Center, Silver Spring, Md., 1973-77; research mathematician Gulf Research and Devel. Co., Pitts., 1977-79, sr. research mathematician, 1979-81, supr. math. research, 1981-83, dir. reservoir simulation, 1983-85; staff research engr. Shell Devel. Co., 1985—. Contbr. articles to profl. jours. Organizer New Leadership of Israel Bonds, Pitts., 1982. NDEA fellow U. Md., 1969-72; NRC Postdoctoral fellow, 1973-74. Mem. Soc. Indsl. and Applied Math., Soc. Petroleum Engrs., N.Y. Acad. Scis., Pi Mu Epsilon. Current Work: Research into new and improved numerical methods for partial differential equations, with principle field of application being petroleum engineering. Subspecialties: Numerical analysis (computer science); Petroleum engineering. Home: 7623 Del Rey Houston TX 77071 Office: Shell Devel Co PO Box 481 Houston TX 77001

LEVICH, BENJAMIN GREGORY, physicist; b. Charkov, USSR, Mar. 30, 1917; s. Gregory and Evgenya (Atlasney) L.; m. Tanya Rubinstein, Nov. 4, 1943; children—Alexander, Evgeny. M.Physics, Kharkov U., USSR, 1937; Ph.D., Moscow Pedagogical Inst., 1940; D.Sc. (hon.), Hebrew U. Jerusalem, Boston U., Carnegie-Mellon U. Sr. researcher Inst. Electrochemistry, USSR Acad. Scis., 1940-58, 72-78, head dept., 1958-72; prof. theoretical physics, head dept. Moscow Inst. Physics and Engring., 1954-65; head dept. chem. mechanics Moscow U., 1964-72; prof. Tel Aviv U., 1978—; Albert Einstein prof. sci. CUNY, 1979—; dep. of sec. gen. Com. on Atomic Energy, USSR, 1946-50. Editorial bd.: Energy Conversion, Physico-Chem. Hydrodynamics; Author: Physico-Chemical Hydrodynamics, 1952, English edit., 1962, Chinese edit., 1952, Hungarian edit., 1952; Statistical Physics, 1949, 53, Theoretical Physics. An Advanced Text, 2 vols, 1962, rev. edit., 1971, English rev. edit., 1972-73, Spanish rev. edit., 1975-78, also articles. Recipient Mendeleev prize in Chemistry, 1960; Palladium medal Am. Electrochem. Soc., 1973; medal Brit. Chem. Soc., 1981. Hon. mem. Imperial Coll., London.; Corr. mem. Acad. Scis. USSR (expelled 1979); mem. Nat. Acad. Engring., Norwegian Acad. Scis. and Letters (fgn.), N.Y. Acad. Scis. (hon.), Nat. Acad. Engring. Office: City College Inst Applied Chem Physics New York NY 10031

LEVIN, FRANK S., physicist, educator; b. N.Y.C., Apr. 14, 1933; s. James J. and Celia A. Levin; m. M. Carol McMurrough, Apr., 1973; 4 children. A.B., Johns Hopkins U., 1955; Ph.D., U. Md., 1961. Prof. physics, Brown U., Providence, R.I., 1977—. Co-author: (lecture notes) Reaction Dynamics, 1973. Co-translator: (text) Introduction to Physics, Vol. I, 1966. Editor: (conf. procs.) The Few Body Problem, 1981. Contbr. articles to profl. jours. Sr. vis. fellow U.S. Sci. Research Council, 1974-75; recipient Sr. U.S. Scientist award Alexander von Humboldt-Stiftung, 1979-80. Fellow Am. Phys. Soc. (founder topical group on few body systems and multiparticle dynamics); mem. AAAS. Current work: Scattering theory, few-body systems, atomic and molecular structure, nuclear reaction theory. Subspecialties: Nuclear physics; Atomic and molecular physics. Home: 625 Angell St Providence RI 02906 Office: Brown U Physics Dept Providence RI 02912

LEVIN, HARVEY STEVEN, neuropsychologist, educator; b. N.Y.C., Dec. 12, 1946; s. Nathan and Mary (Weinberg) L.; m. Ellen Margaret Halliczer, June 23, 1968; 1 son, Marc. B.A., CCNY, 1967; M.A., U. Iowa, 1971, Ph.D., 1972. Lic. psychologist, Tex. Postdoctoral research fellow U. Iowa Hosps., 1972-73; asst. prof. neurosurgery U. Tex. Med. Br., Galveston, 1974-79, assoc. prof., 1979-83, prof., 1983; cons. neuropsychologist U.S. Army Hosp., Landstuhl, W.Ger., 1981. Author: Neurobehavioral Consequences of Closed Head Injury, 1982; cons. editor: Cortex, 1981—, Jour. Clin. and Exptl. Neuropsychology, 1984—. NSF fellow, 1970; Jacob K. Javitz neurosci. investigator awardee NINCDS, 1984—. Fellow Am. Psychol. Assn.; mem. Soc. Neurosci., Internat. Neuropsychol. Soc. (bd. govs. 1984-86), Assn. Nervous and Mental Disease, Acad. Neurology, N.Y. Acad. Sci., Nat. Head Injury Found. (cons.). Current Work: Recovery from traumatic brain injury; neuropsychology and pharmacology of memory disorders; neuropsychological correlates of aging and dementia. Subspecialties: Neuropsychology; Neuropharmacology. Home: 10 Quintana Dr Galveston TX 77551 Office: U Tex Med Br Div Neurosurgery E17 Galveston TX 77550

LEVIN, IRA WILLIAM, chemist; b. Washington, Sept. 20, 1935; s. Samuel S. and Reba (Smelkinson) L.; m. Barbara Chernov, June 18, 1961; children—David, Jordan. B.S., U. Va., 1957; Ph.D., Brown U., 1961. Research instr. U. Wash., Seattle, 1961-62; guest worker NIH, Bethesda, Md., 1963-65, staff fellow, 1965-66, research scientist, 1966-79, acting chief Lab. Chem. Physics, 1984—, chief sect. on molecular biophysics, 1979—; lectr. Georgetown U., Washington, 1964-65, 73-74. Contbr. numerous sci. papers to profl. lit. Served to 1st lt. AUS, 1961-62. Recipient Lippincott award, 1985. Mem. Am. Phys. Soc., Biophys. Soc., Coblentz Soc. (bd. mgrs. 1975-79, pres. 1978-79). Current work: Vibrational spectroscopy of biological membrane assemblies. Subspecialties: Biophysical chemistry; Physical chemistry. Office: Lab Chem Physics NIH Bldg 2 Room B1-27 Bethesda MD 20205

LEVIN, JACK, physician, medical educator, biomedical researcher; b. Newark, Oct. 11, 1932; s. Joseph and Anna (Greengold) L.; m. Francine Corthesy, Apr. 13, 1975. B.A. magna cum laude, Yale Coll., 1953, M.D. cum laude, 1957. Diplomate Am. Bd. Internal Medicine. Chief resident in medicine Yale-New Haven Med. Ctr., 1964-65; prof. medicine Johns Hopkins Med. Sch., Balt., 1978-82; prof. lab. medicine U. Calif., San Francisco, 1982—, prof. medicine, 1982—; dir. Hematology Lab. VA Med. Ctr., San Francisco, 1982—; corp. mem. Marine Biol. Lab., Woods Hole, Mass., 1966—; physician-in-charge hematology clinic Johns Hopkins Hosp., Balt., 1967-82; sr. lectr. U. Melbourne, Australia, 1978-79. Author: (with others) Disorders of Hemostasis, 1976. Contbr. articles to profl. jours. Editor: (with others) Biomedical Applications of Horseshoe Crab, 1979; Endotoxins and Detection with Limulus Lysate Test, 1982; Bacterial Endotoxins: Structure, Biomedical Significance and Detection with Limulus Amebocyk Lystate Test, 1985. Served to lt. (s.g.) USPHS, 1958-60. Recipient Markle Scholarship in Academic Medicine Markle Found., 1968-73, USPHS Research Career Devel. Award, 1970-75, Faculty Scholar Award Josiah Macy Found., 1978-79. Fellow ACP; mem. Am. Soc. Hematology, Am. Fedn. Clin. Research, Internat. Soc. Hematology, Am. Soc. Clin. Investigation, Am. Assn. Pathologists, Western Assn. Physicians, Calif. Acad. Medicine, Soc. Invertebrate Pathology. Jewish. Clubs: Hamilton St., Balt. Blood (pres. 1974-75), Tudor & Stuart (pres. 1977-78) (Balt.); Yale (San Francisco). Current work: Regulation of hematopoiesis; effects of bacterial endotoxins; comparative physiology of hemostasis. Subspecialties: Hematology; Marine biology. Office: VA Hosp 113A 4150 Clement St San Francisco CA 94121

LEVIN, JOSHUA ZEV, computer programmer; b. Cambridge, Mass., Feb. 5, 1949; s. Herschel Levin and Betty Louise (Tennenbaum) Zimmermann; m. Susan Evelyn Goldsmith, Feb. 20, 1982. B.A. in Physics, Queens Coll., 1971; M.S.E.E., NYU, 1974; Ph.D., Rensselaer Poly. Inst., 1980. Sr. engr. Boeing Computer Systems, Seattle, 1979-80; sr. software engr. Gen. Dynamics, E.D.S.C., Groton, Conn., 1980-81; sr. applied mathematician Aydin Controls, Ft. Washington, Pa., 1981-84; systems engr. Aydin Computer Systems, Horsham, Pa., 1984—; cons. Mfg. Data Systems, Inc., Gen. Electric. Contbr. articles to profl. jours. Mem. Assn. for Computing machinery, IEEE, Phi Beta Kappa. Democrat. Jewish. Current Work: Devel. of algorithms in algebraic geometry for application to computer graphics and computer-aided design; avionics displays. Subspecialties: Algorithms; Graphics, image processing, and pattern recognition. Home: Bldg 2 Townhouse 2 English Village Apts North Wales PA 19454 Office: 700 Dresher Rd Horsham PA 19044

LEVIN, MICHAEL HOWARD, environmental scientist, engineer; b. N.Y.C., Sept. 25, 1936; s. Irving and Bess (Ruderman) L.; 1 dau., Eleanor Marie. B.S., U. Vt., 1958; M.S., Rutgers U., 1960, Ph.D., 1964. Cert. sr. ecologist, 1981. Research assoc. N.Y. Bot. Garden, 1964; asst. prof. U. Notre Dame, 1964-66, U. Man., 1966-68, U. Pa., 1968-73; sr. ecologist Delaware River Basin Commn., 1977-78; pres., dir. research Environ. Research Assocs., Inc., Villanova, Pa., 1970—; dir. Ambric Environ. Sci., Inc., 1980—; adj. prof. Del. State Coll., 1980—. Contbr. articles to profl. jours. Served to 1st lt. Med. Service Corps U.S. Army, 1960-61. Fellow AAAS; mem. Ecol. Soc. Am., Sigma Xi, Alpha Zeta. Current Work: Research director of environmental sciences involved in testing of air, land, water and specialty in wood technology and materials testing. Subspecialties: Ecology (environmental science); Systematics. Address: 490 Darby-Paoli Rd Villanova PA 19085

LEVIN, PAUL, environmental engineer; b. Chgo., Nov. 14, 1927; s. Louis and Ida (Boshes) L.; m. Sema Bell, Oct. 8, 1956; children—Mitchell, Amy, Lisa. B.S., U. Ill., 1949; M.P.H., U. Minn., 1955; Ph.D., Ill. Inst. Tech., 1971. Diplomate Am. Acad. Environ. Engrs. Chief san. engr. Dupage County Health Dept., Wheaton, Ill., 1956-67; research engr. Gen. Am. Research Div., Niles, Ill., 1967-72; assoc. prof. U. Ill., Chgo., 1972-74; regional engr. Ill. Dept. Pub. Health, Chgo., 1974—. Patentee sludge dewatering apparatus. Mem. Am. Water Works Assn., Water Pollution Control Fedn. Current work: Hazardous substances and toxic wastes, long-term care sanitation. Subspecialties: Water supply and wastewater treatment; Hazardous waste disposal. Home: 7615 W Davis St Morton Grove IL 60053 Office: Ill Dept of Pub Health Rm 6-600 100 W Randolph Chicago IL 60601

LEVIN, STEPHEN MICHAEL, orthopedic surgeon, researcher; b. Toronto, Ont., Can., July 10, 1932; s. Benjamin and Anabelle (Glassman) L.; m. Patricia R. Rollo, May 27, 1976; children: Leslie, Mindy, Jody, Erin. B.S., CCNY, 1954; M.D., SUNY-Bklyn., 1958; postgrad., U. Pa., 1965-66. Diplomate: Am. Bd. Orthopedic Surgery. Intern Robert Packer Hosp., Sayre, Pa., 1958-59; resident in orthopedic surgery Nat. Orthopedic Hosp., Arlington, Va., 1963-67, pvt. practice medicine, specializing in orthopedic surgery, Alexandria, Va., 1967—, researcher in biomechanics, 1976—; assoc. clin. prof. Mich. State U.; clin. asst. prof. Howard U., Washington; sec. N.Am. Acad. Manipulative Medicine. Contbr. articles to profl. jours. Served to capt. U.S. Army, 1959-62. Fellow ACS, Am. Coll. Orthopedic Surgeons; mem. Eastern Orthopedic Assn., N.Am. Lumbar Spine Assn. Current work: Back pain and biomechanics. Subspecialties: Orthopedics; Biomedical engineering. Office: 5021 Seminary Rd Suite 125 Alexandria VA 22311

LEVIN, STUART, veterinary pathologist; b. Luling, Tex., Aug. 19, 1944; s. Jacob Max Levin and Leona Faye (Kitchner) Levin Millburg; m. Susan Gaye Goldman, Aug. 27, 1967; children—John, Daniel. D.V.M., U. Mo., 1968; Ph.D., U. Chgo., 1972. Pathologist FDA, Washington, 1972, Abbott Labs., North Chicago, Ill., 1972-78, Mich. State U., East Lansing, 1978-82, G. D. Searle & Co., Skokie, Ill., 1982—. Contbr. articles to profl. jours., 1969—. Mem. AVMA, Soc. Toxicologic Pathologists, Am. Coll. Vet. Pathologists (diplomate). Current work: Toxicological evaluation of potential new pharmaceutical products. Subspecialties: Pathology (veterinary medicine); Toxicology (medicine). Home: 1132 Cayuga Dr Northbrook IL 60062 Office: G D Searle & Co 4901 Searle Pkwy Skokie IL 60077

LEVIN, WAYNE, biochemist; b. N.Y.C., Feb. 29, 1940; s. Max H. and Blanche (Bohslav) L.; m. Rosemary Barnello, June 30, 1962; children—Kira J., Darryl K. B.A., Ithaca Coll., 1962; M.S., U. Ill., 1964. Biochemist, Burroughs Wellcome Co., Tuckahoe, N.Y., 1965-69, sr. biochemist, 1969-70; with Hoffmann La Roche Inc., Nutley, N.J., 1970—, group chief, 1974-78, sect. head, dept. exptl. carcinogenesis and metabolism, 1978—. Contbr. articles to profl. jours. Recipient Pharmacology Research Achievement award Acd. Pharm. Scis., 1979. Mem. Am. Soc. Biol. Chemists, Am. Soc. Pharmacology and Exptl. Therapeutics, Soc. Toxicology, Am. Assn. Cancer Research, N.Y. Acad. Sci., Sigma Xi. Lutheran. Metabolism of drugs, steroids and chemical carciogens; induction of microsomal enzymes; heme synthesis and metabolism; chemical carcinogenesis. Subspecialties: Biochemistry (biology); Pharmacology. Home: 181 Werimus Rd Woodcliff Lake NJ 07675 Office: Dept Exptl Carcinogenesis and Metabolism Hoffmann La Roche Inc Nutley NJ 07110

LEVIN, WILLIAM COHN, physician, university president; b. Waco, Tex., Mar. 2, 1917; s. Samuel P. and Jeanette (Cohn) L.; m. Edna Seinsheimer, June 23, 1941; children: Gerry Lee Levin Hornstein, Carol Lynn Cantini. B.A., U. Tex., 1938, M.D., 1941; M.D. (hon.), U. Montpellier, 1980. Diplomate: Am. Bd. Internal Medicine. Intern Michael Reese Hosp., Chgo., 1941-42; resident John Sealy Hosp., Galveston, Tex., 1942-44; mem. staff U. Tex. Med. Br. Hosps., Galveston, 1944—, asso. prof. internal medicine, 1948-65, prof., 1965—; now Warmoth prof. hematology; pres. U. Tex. Med. Br., 1974—; past chmn., past mem. cancer clin. investigation rev. com. Nat. Cancer Inst. Exec. com., mem. nat. bd. Union Am. Hebrew Congregations; trustee Houston-Galveston Psychoanalytic Found., 1975-78, Menil Found., 1976-83. Recipient Nicholas and Katherine Leone award for adminstrv. excellence, 1977; decorated Palmes Académiques France). Fellow A.C.P., Internat. Soc. Hematology; mem. Am. Fedn. Clin. Research, Central Soc. Clin. Research, Am. Soc. Hematology, Phi Beta Kappa, Sigma Xi, Alpha Omega Alpha. Subspecialties: Hematology; Oncology. Office: 301 University Bldg Suite 646 Adminstrn Bldg Galveston TX 77550

LEVINE, ARTHUR SAMUEL, government official, research physician; b. Cleve., Nov. 1, 1936; s. David A. and Ethel S. (Rubenstein) L.; m. Ruth E. Rubin, Oct. 14, 1959; children—Amy, Raleigh, Jennifer. A.B., Columbia U., 1958; M.D., Chgo. Med. Sch., 1964. Diplomate Am. Bd. Pediatrics, Am. Bd. Pediatric Hematology-Oncology. Pediatric intern U. Minn. Hosps., Mpls., 1964-65, resident, 1965-66, USPHS fellow in hematology and biochem. genetics, 1966-67; clin. assoc. medicine br., div. cancer treatment Nat. Cancer Inst., Bethesda, Md., 1967-69, sr. staff fellow, 1969-70, sr. investigator, 1970-73, head sect. infectious disease, pediatric oncology br., 1973-75, chief pediatric oncology br., 1975-82, asst. dir. for sci., div. cancer treatment, 1982; sci. dir. Nat. Inst. Child Health and Human Devel., Bethesda, 1982—; clin. prof. medicine and pediatrics Georgetown U. Sch. Medicine, Washington, 1975—; prof. pediatrics Uniformed Services U. of Health Scis., Bethesda, 1983—; mem. biohazards com. NIH, 1975-78; mem. interferon working group Nat. Cancer Inst., 1976-80, others; vis. prof. Benares Hindu U., India, 1974, U. Minn. Sch. Medicine, 1975, Hebrew U. Jerusalem, 1981; Karon lectr. U. So. Calif., 1983; Scham lectr. U. Minn., 1983; lectr. throughout world. Editor: Cancer in the Young, 1982; assoc. editor Jour. Nat. Cancer Inst., 1976—, Am. Jour. Pediatric Hematology-Oncology, 1982—; contbr. numerous articles to profl. jours. Trustee, Windsor Mountain Sch., Lenox, Mass., 1972-78, Leukemia Soc., 1975-81. Served to capt. USPHS, 1967—. Recipient Disting. Alumnus award Chgo. Med. Sch., 1972, NIH Dirs. award, 1984. Mem. Am. Soc. Clin. Investigation, Soc. Pediatric Research, Am. Assn. Cancer Research, Am. Soc. Hematology, Am. Soc. Clin. Oncology, AAAS, Am. Soc. Microbiology, Am. Fedn. Clin. Research, Internat. Soc. Pediatric Oncology, Am. Soc. Pediatric Hematology-Oncology. Subspecialties: Molecular biology; Oncology. Office: NICHHD NIH Bethesda MD 20205

LEVINE, HOWARD ALLEN, mathematics educator, consultant; b. St. Paul, Jan. 15, 1942; s. Morris B. and Rebbeca (Wernick) L.; m. Elyse M., June 16, 1974; children—Joseph, Margo. B.A., U. Minn.-Duluth, 1964; M.A., Cornell U., 1967, Ph.D., 1969. Prof. math. Iowa State U., Ames, 1980—; cons. Naval Underwater Systems Center, New London, Conn., 1977-79, Ames Lab., Iowa, 1982-83, Lawrence Livermore Nat. Lab., Calif., 1984—. Contbr. articles to profl. jours. Mem. Am. Math. Soc., Soc. for Indsl. and Applied Math., Sigma Xi. Current work: Partial differential equations, numerical analysis of partial differential equations, ill posed problems, transport problems. Subspecialties: Analysis; Applied mathematics. Office: Math Dept Iowa State U Ames IA 50011

LEVINE, JERRY DAVID, nuclear engineer; b. Mount Vernon, N.Y., June 27, 1952; s. Stanley Irwin and Edith (Souberman) L.; m. Ronnie Elaine Freedman, July 31, 1977; 1 child, Audrey Michelle. B.S. in Physics and Earth and Space Sci, SUNY-Stony Brook, 1974; M.S. in Nuclear Engring, Poly. Inst. N.Y., 1976. Asst. engr. Ebasco Services, Inc., N.Y.C., 1976-77, assoc. engr., Princeton, N.J., 1977-78, engr., 1978-80; sr., prin. engr. Envirosphere Co. div., 1980—. Mem. Am. Nuclear Soc. Current Work: Involved in nuclear safety studies for the Tokamak Fusion Test Reactor since 1976. Also involved in regulatory compliance planning for mined geologic repository for high level nuclear wastes since 1982. Subspecialties: Fusion; Nuclear engineering. Home: 1 Ivy Way Dayton NJ 08810 Office: Envirosphere Co div Ebasco Services Inc James Forrestal Campus Princeton NJ 08544

LEVINE, JULES DAVID, electronics company manager; b. N.Y.C., June 24, 1937; s. Hyman Levine and Caroline Antman; m. Marcia Susan Herberg, June 13, 1966; children—Gail Felice, Scott Nathaniel. B.S. in M.E., Columbia U., 1959; Ph.D., MIT, 1963. Scientist, mgr. RCA, Princeton, N.J., 1963-79; mgr. Tex. Instruments, Dallas, 1979—. Editor: Modern Methods of Surface Science, 1970. Contbr. numerous articles to profl. jours. Patentee in field of solar cells and displays. Recipient Outstanding Achievement award RCA Research Lab., 1968, 72, 75. Fellow IEEE (pres. Princeton sect. 1977-78); mem. Power Engring. Soc. (founder, pres. 1975-78). Current work: Specialist in surface science, materials science, crystal growth and photovoltaic solar cells. Subspecialties: Electronic materials; Solar energy. Home: 6931 Flintcove Dr Dallas TX 77248 Office: Tex Instruments PO Box 225936 MS 147 Dallas TX 75265

LEVINE, LEON, chemist; b. Bklyn., Jan. 6, 1934; s. Moe and Sylvia (Zablow) L.; m. Elissa Rosenberg, Sept. 3, 1966; children—Madelon, Stefanie. B.S., Bklyn. Coll., 1956; Ph.D., Polytech. Inst. N.Y., 1963. Chemist, Lactona Corp., Phila., 1968-72, Nat. Patent Devel. Corp., Brunswick, N.J., 1972-76; sr. chemist Loctite Corp., Newington, Conn., 1976-80, Springborn Labs., Enfield, Conn., 1980, Richardson Polymer, Milford, Conn., 1982—; pres. Coats & Levine, Inc., Somers, Conn., 1980-82. Contbr. articles to profl. jours. Patentee in field. Mem. Am. Chem. Soc. Current work: Polymerization, characterization of acrylic and styrenic polymers for molding and coating uses; adhesives; consumer oriented chemical products. Subspecialty: Polymer chemistry. Home: 94 Brewster Rd West Hartford CT 06117 Office: Richardson Polymer Corp 111 Pepes Farm Rd Milford CT 06460

LEVINE, RANDOLPH HERBERT, computer company executive; b. Denver, Nov. 20, 1946; s. Harold and Muriel Faye (Sachs) L.; m. Sarah Loewenberg, June 21, 1970; children: Seth Jason, Johanna Beth. A.B., U. Calif.-Berkeley, 1968; M.A., Harvard U., 1969, Ph.D., 1972. Vis. scientist Nat. Ctr. Atmospheric Research, Boulder, Colo., 1972-74; research assoc., lectr. astronomy Harvard Coll. Obs., Cambridge, Mass., 1974-81; sr. staff scientist, dir. computing AER, Inc., Cambridge, 1981-82; engring. mgr. Ednl. Services, Digital Equipment Corp., Maynard, Mass., 1982-85, tech. dir. high performance sci. computing, 1985—; cons. Univs. Space Research assn., Aerospace Corp., NASA; tchr. astronomy Harvard Coll., 1974-81. Mem. Assn. Computing Machinery, IEEE Computer Soc., Am. Phys. Soc., Am. Astron. Soc., Am. Geophys. Union, Internat. Astron. Union. Current Work: Development of computers in scientific research; research in solar physics. Subspecialties: Computer education; Solar physics. Home: 50 Carver Rd Newton Highlands MA 02161 Office: 12 Crosby Dr Bedford MA 01730

LEVINE, RHEA JOY COTTLER, anatomy educator, muscle biologist; b. Bklyn., Nov. 26, 1939; d. Zachary Robert Cottler and Hildreth (Abramson) Rosenfeld; m. Stephen Maxwell Levine, June 16, 1960; children—Elizabeth, Michael Gordon, Zachary Thomas. A.B. summa cum laude, Smith Coll., 1960; M.S., NYU, 1963, Ph.D., 1966. USPHS postdoctoral fellow Yale U. Sch. Medicine, New Haven, 1966-68; research assoc. U. Pa. Sch. Medicine, Phila., 1968-69; asst. prof. Med. Coll. Pa., Phila., 1969-74, assoc. prof., 1974-80, prof. anatomy, 1980—; outside reviewer grants NSF, Washington, 1975—, VA, 1983—; mem. study sect., div. research grants NIH, Bethesda, Md., 1980-84. Editor, author: Basic Biology of Muscles - A Comparative Approach (symposium vol.), 1982. Contbr. sci. articles to profl. jours. Reviewer manuscripts for profl. jours., 1975—. Class of 1960 fund agt. Smith Coll., Northampton, Mass., 1980-85; trustee Stockton State Coll., Pomona, N.J., 1983—. Recipient Founder's Day award NYU Grad Sch. Arts and Scis., 1966; NSF grantee, 1960-65, NIH grantee, 1972—. Mem. AAAS, N.Y. Acad. Scis., Am. Soc. for Cell Biology, Biophys. Soc., Histochem. Soc., Soc. for Gen. Physiology, Phi Beta Kappa, Sigma Xi. Jewish. Clubs: Woodcrest Country (Cherry Hill, N.J.) (house chmn. 1984-85); Smith Coll. (Phila.). Current work: Structure and function of contractile apparatus (thick filaments, mainly) of muscle fibers (mainly invertebrate); molecular organization of proteins in thick filaments. Subspecialties: Biophysics (biology); Cell biology. Office: Dept Anatomy Medical College of Pa/EPPI Div 3200 Henry Ave Philadelphia PA 19129

LEVINE, ROBERT SIDNEY, chemical engineer; b. Des Moines, June 4, 1921; s. George Julius and Betty (Denner) L.; m. Lillian Kohn, 1947 (div.); children—George, Gail; m. Sharon Lorraine White, Sept. 9, 1970; children—Michelle, James. B.Sc. Chem.E., Iowa State U., 1943; M.S. in Chem. Engring., MIT, 1946, Sc.D., 1949. Assoc. research dir. Rocketdyne Div. Rockwell, Canoga Park, Calif., 1949-66; chief liquid propulsion tech. NASA, Washington, 1966-72, tech. specialist, Langley Research Ctr., Hampton, Va., 1972-77; chief fire research resources Nat. Bur. Standards, Gaithersburg, Md., 1977—. Contbr. articles to profl. jours. Scoutmaster, Boy Scouts Am., 1964. Assoc. fellow AIAA; mem. Am. Chem. Soc., Combustion Inst. (pres. 1974-78), Nat. Fire Protection Assn., Soc. Fire Protection Engrs. Current work: Mathematical modeling of fire growth, fire processes such as combustion and extinction. Subspecialties: Chemical engineering; Combustion processes. Home: 19017 Threshing Pl Gaithersburg MD 20879 Office: Nat Bur Standards Gaithersburg MD 20899

LEVINE, SAMUEL HAROLD, physicist; b. Hazlehurst, Ga., Nov. 30, 1925; s. Abraham and Rebecca (Starr) L.; m. Trudy Foner, Aug. 14, 1955; children: Renee, Lisa, Suzanne. B.S., Va. Poly. Inst. and State U., 1947; M.S., U. Ill., 1948; Ph.D., U. Pitts., 1954. Instr. Va. Poly. Inst. and State U., 1949-50; mgr. Westinghouse Bettis Atomic Plant, Pitts., 1954-59; reactor physicist Gen. Atomic Co., San Diego, 1959-61; group head Rocketydne Co., Canoga Park, Calif., 1961-62; head nuclear sci. lab. Northrop Space Lab., Hawthorne, Calif., 1962-68; prof. physics Pa. State U., University Park, 1968—; dir. Breazeale Nuclear Reactor, 1968—. Served with USAAF, 1943-44. Recipient Invention award NASA, 1973; Westinghouse fellow, 1953; Lady Davis fellow Technion, Haifa, Israel, 1976. Mem. Am. Nuclear Soc., Am. Phys. Soc., Sigma Xi, Phi Kappa Phi. Current Work: In-core fuel management; experimental reactor physics; neutron and beta radiation dosimetry. Subspecialties: Nuclear engineering; Nuclear fission. Home: 528 E Hamilton Ave State College PA 16801 Office: Breazeale Nuclear Pa State U University Park PA 16802

LEVINE, WILLIAM SILVER, engineering educator, researcher; b. N.Y.C., Nov. 19, 1941; s. Louis Nathan and Gertrude (Silver) L.; m. Shirley Ann Johannesen, Feb. 14, 1963; children—Bruce Jonathan, Eleanor Joan. A.B. in Elec. Engring., MIT, 1962, S.M. in Elec. Engring., 1965, Ph.D., 1969. Project engr. Data Tech., Inc., Watertown, Mass., 1962-64; grad. asst. MIT, Cambridge, 1964-69; asst. prof. elec. engring. U. Md., College Park, 1969-73, assoc. prof., 1973-81, prof., 1981—; cons. IBM, Gaithersburg, Md., 1972-75, BTS, Inc., Seabrook, Md., 1980—. Contbr. articles to profl. jours. NASA summer faculty fellow, 1969; grantee NSF, 1970, NIH, 1975, 77, Minta Martin Fund, 1984. Mem. IEEE (sr. mem.; tech. activities bd. 1984, conf. activities bd. 1984, bd. govs. Controls Soc. 1984-86), Internat. Fedn. Automatic Control (vice chmn. biomed. engring. com. 1984-86). Jewish. Current work: Control of movement, computer aided control system design, estimation, control on networks. Subspecialties: Electrical engineering; Computer engineering. Office: Dept Elec Engring U Md College Park MD 20742

LEVINSKY, NORMAN GEORGE, physician, educator; b. Boston, Apr. 27, 1929; s. Harry and Gertrude (Kipperman) L.; m. Elena Sartori, June 17, 1956; children—Harold, Andrew, Nancy. A.B. summa cum laude, Harvard U., 1950, M.D. cum laude, 1954. Diplomate: Am. Bd. Internal Medicine. Intern Beth Israel Hosp., Boston, 1954-55, resident, 1955-56; commd. med. officer USPHS., 1956; clin. asso. Nat. Heart Inst., Bethesda, Md., 1956-58; NIH fellow Boston U. Med. Center, 1958-60; practice medicine, specializing in internal medicine and nephrology, Boston, 1960—; chief of medicine Boston City Hosp., 1968-72; physician-in-chief, dir. Evans dept. clin. research Univ. Hosp., Boston, 1972—; asst. prof., asso. prof. medicine Boston U., 1960-68, Wesselhoeft prof., 1968-72, Wade prof. medicine, 1972—; Mem. drug efficacy panel NRC.; mem. nephrology test com.-Am. Bd. Internal Medicine, 1971-76. Editor: (with R.W. Wilkins) Medicine: Essentials of Clinical Practice, 1978, 2d edit., 1983; Contbr. chpts. to books, sci. articles to med. jours. Mem. AAAS, Am. Fedn. Clin. Research, Am. Soc. Clin. Investigation, Assn. Am. Physicians, Am. Physiol. Soc., Am. Soc. Nephrology, Phi Beta Kappa, Alpha Omega Alpha. Club: Interurban. Current Work: Renal KalliKrein systems; acute renal failure. Subspecialties: Nephrology; Physiology (biology). Home: 20 Kenwood Ave Newton MA 02159 Office: 75 E Newton St Boston MA 02118

LEVINSON, DAVID ALAN, research engineer; b. Meadville, Pa., Apr. 6, 1950; s. Weldon and Jolene Janet (Svirman) L. B.S., Cornell U., 1972; M.S., Stanford U., 1973, Engr. degree, 1975. Sr. assoc. scientist Lockheed Palo Alto Research Lab. (Calif.), 1977-79, scientist, 1979-82, sr. scientist, 1982—; lectr. applied mechanics Stanford U., 1981, 84. Author: (with others) Spacecraft Dynamics, 1983, Dynamics: Theory and Applications, 1985; also articles in tech. jours. Mng. editor Jour. Astronautical Scis., Alexandria, Va., 1984—. Recipient Meritorious Service in Engring. Teaching award U. Tex., 1977. Assoc. fellow AIAA (named Outstanding Young Engr. 1984, mem. Astrodynamics tech. com. 1981-84); mem. Am. Astronautical Soc. (sr.), ASME, Cornell Soc. Engrs., Am. Acad. Mechanics, Sigma Xi. Republican. Jewish. Club: Rinconada Masters Swim (Palo Alto). Current work: Formulation of full nonlinear equations governing attitude motions of complex multibody spacecraft. Subspecialties: Astronautics; Theoretical and applied mechanics. Office: 92-30/205 Lockheed Palo Alto Research Lab 3251 Hanover St Palo Alto CA 94304

LEVINTHAL, CHARLES FREDERICK, research psychologist, educator; b. Cin., July 6, 1945; s. Sam and Mildred Caroline (Greenburg) L.; m. Beth Ellen Kuby, Dec. 16, 1973; children: David, Brian. A.B., U. Cin., 1967; M.A. in Psychology, U. Mich, 1968, Ph.D. in Psychology, 1971. Asst. prof. psychology Hofstra U., 1971-78, assoc. prof., 1978—; dir. Ph.D. program in applied research and evaluation, 1978—. Author: The Physiological Approach in Psychology, 1979, Introduction to Physiological Psychology, 2d edit, 1983; contbr. articles to profl. jours. Served with USAR, 1968-74. Woodrow Wilson fellow, 1967; NSF Found. grad. fellow, 1967-71. Mem. Am. Psychol. Assn., Midwestern Psychol. Assn., Soc. Psychophysiol. Research, Soc. Neurosci., Phi Beta Kappa. Current Work: Research on physiological bases for cognitive activity in the brain, hemispheric specialization in brain, electrophysiology. Subspecialties: Neuropsychology; Physiological psychology. Home: 9 Royal Oak Dr Huntington NY 11743 Office: Hofstra U Hempstead NY 11550

LEVINTHAL, MARK, geneticist, researcher, educator; b. Bklyn., Mar. 3, 1941; s. Louis and Bertha (Nissenbaum) L.; m. Maxine Kassiola, Dec. 23, 1962; children: Peter, Sarita. B.S., Bklyn. Coll., 1962; Ph.D., Brandeis U., 1966. Postdoctoral fellow Johns Hopkins U., Balt., 1966-68; staff fellow lab. molecular biology Nat. Inst. Arthritis, Metabolic and Digestive Diseases, NIH, Bethesda, Md., 1968-72; assoc. prof. biol. sci. Purdue U., West Lafayette, Ind., 1972—. Contbr. articles to profl. jours. Mem. steering com. New Moblzn. to End the War, 1969-71; mem. Vietnam moratorium com. NIH/NIMH, 1969-72. Recipient Biology prize Blkyn. Coll., 1958; NIH fellow, 1966, 66-68; grantee, 1972-74; NSF grantee, 1974-77. Mem. Am. Soc. Microbiology, AAAS, Genetics Soc. Am., AAUP, Italian Molecular Biology Soc., ACLU, Sigma Xi, Darwin Soc., Soc. for Study of Evolution. Mem. Peace and Freedom Party. Zen Buddhist. Club: Brooklyn (Lafayette). Current Work: Experimental molecular evolution of prokaryotes. Genetic engineering; molecular evolution; prokaryotes; genetics evolution; metabolic evolution. Subspecialties: Gene actions; Evolutionary biology.

LEVIS, ALEXANDER HENRY, research scientist; b. Yannina, Greece, Oct. 3, 1940; s. Henry N. and Jeannette (Matathia) L.; m. Ilze E. Sedriks, Mar. 26, 1970; children—Livia, Philip. A.B., Ripon Coll., 1963; B.S., M.S., MIT, 1965, M.E., 1967, Sc.D., 1968. Asst. prof. Bklyn. Poly. Inst., 1968-73, assoc. prof., 1973; mgr. research dept. Systems Control, Inc., Palo Alto, Calif., 1973-79; sr. research scientist MIT, 1979—. Editor: Automatica Jour., 1980—; assoc. editor: IEEE Transactions Automatic Control, 1975-77; contbr. articles to sci., tech. jours. Mem. IEEE, IEEE Control Systems Soc. (v.p. 1984-86), AIAA. Current work: Command and control systems, rehabilitation systems for the disabled, measures of effectiveness of large scale systems. Subspecialties: Systems engineering; Operations research (engineering). Home: 228 Follen Rd Lexington MA 02173 Office: Mass Inst Tech 35-410/LIDS Cambridge MA 02139

LEVITAN, HERBERT, neuroscience educator, researcher; b. Bklyn., Apr. 25, 1939; s. Meyer and Lena (Kohl) L.; m. Karen Brounstein, Aug. 23, 1964; children: James, Danielle. Student, Bklyn. Coll., 1956-58; B.E.E., Cornell U., 1962, Ph.D., 1965. Sr. staff assoc. Lab. Neurobiology Nat. Inst. Child Health and Human Devel., Bethesda, Md., 1970-72; neurophysiologist Lab. Neuroscience, Nat. Inst. Aging, Balt., 1979-82; assoc. prof. dept. zoology U. Md., 1972-83, prof. dept. zoology, 1983—. Contbr. articles in field to profl. jours. NIH fellow, 1965-67, 68-70, 70; named Disting. Scholar-Tchr. U. Md., 1985-86. Mem. Soc. Neuroscience, Am. Physiology Soc., Am. Soc. Cell Biology, Soc. Gen. Physiologist, AAUP, Sigma Xi. Current Work: Biophysical mechanisms underlying the effects of drugs on excitable and inexcitabe cells. Subspecialties: Neurobiology; Neuropharmacology. Home: 212 Dale Dr Silver Spring MD 20910 Office: Department Zoology University Maryland College Park MD 20742

LEVITIN, LEV BEROVICH, engineering educator; b. Moscow, Sept. 25, 1935; came to U.S., 1981; s. Ber L. and Tzetzilia (Gushansky) L.; m. Yulia Shmukler, 1959 (div. 1970); 1 son, Boris. M.Sc., Moscow U., 1960; Ph.D., Acad. Scis. of USSR, 1969. Sr. research scientist Inst. Info. Transmission Problems, Moscow Acad. Scis., 1961-73; sr. lectr. Tel-Aviv U., 1974-80; vis. prof. Bielefeld U., W. Ger., 1980-81, Syracuse (N.Y.) U., 1981-82; prof. engring. Boston U., 1982—; vis. scientist Heinrich-Hertz Inst., Berlin, 1980, Institut für Optoelektronik, Oberpfaffenhofen, W.Ger., 1981; cons. Vishay Israel, Ltd., Tel-Aviv, 1979. Editor: Principles of Cybernetics (in Russian), 1967; contbr. articles sci. jours. Mem. Popov Sci. and Engring. Soc., IEEE, Israel Statis. Assn., AAUP, Am. Math. Soc., Assn. Computing Machinery, Soc. Indsl. and Applied Math., AAAS. Current Work: Information theory and its applications, physical information theory, optical communication, quantum theory of measurements, physics of computation, coding theory, automata theory, statistical physics, computational complexity, VLSI testing. Subspecialties: Applied mathematics; Computer engineering. Home: 11 Monmouth Ct Apt 1 Brookline MA 02146Office: Boston University College of Engineering 110 Cummington St Boston MA 02215

LEVITSKY, SIDNEY, physician, cardiothoracic surgeon; b. N.Y.C., Mar. 3, 1936; s. Max and Sylvia (Stanger) L.; m. Lynne C. Lipton, Apr. 17, 1967; children—Shari E., Jonathan E., Jennifer E. Student, NYU, 1953-56; M.D., Albert Einstein Coll., 1960. Intern Yale-New Haven Med. Ctr., 1960-61; resident gen. thoracic and cardiovascular surgery, 1960-66; chief of surgery Third Surg. Hosp., Vietnam, 1966-67; sr. staff surgeon NIH, 1968-70; chief div. cardiothoracic surgery U. Ill. Med. Ctr., Chgo., 1974—; instr. surgery Yale U., 1964-66; sr. investigator, sr. staff surgeon NIH, 1968-70; assoc. prof. surgery U. Ill. Coll. Medicine, 1970-75; lectr. Cook County Grad. Sch., 1970—; attending surgeon Cook County Hosp., 1973—; assoc. prof. pharmacology in surgery U. Ill. Coll. Med. Scis., 1974-75, prof. pharmacology, 1975—, prof. surgery, 1975—; sr. cons. West Side VA Hosp., 1975—; grad. faculty dept bioengineering U. Ill., 1977—. Contbr. numerous book chapters and articles to profl. jours. Served with U.S. Army, 1966-68. Decorated Bronze Star. Recipient numerous grants in field. Recipient Samuel C. Harvey award, Yale U.; Golden Apple award U. Ill. Coll. Medicine, 1972, Established Investigator, Am. Heart Assn., 1971-75; recipient A.V. Vishnevsky Surg. medal Moscow 1982. Fellow ACS (med. devices com. 1976-80, councilor Met. chgo. chpt. 1980—), Am. Coll. Cardiology (annual sci. sessions program com. 1983-84), Am. Coll. Chest Physicians (chmn. steering com. sect. cardiovascular surgery 1983-84), Am. Heart Assn.; mem. Assn. Acad. Surgery, Soc. Thoracic Surgeons, Internat. Cardiovascular Soc., Soc. Vascular Surgery, Soc. University Surgeons, Am. Assn. Thoracic Surgery, Am. Surgical Assn., Am. Physiol. Soc., Central Surg. Assn., Chgo. Surgical Soc., European Soc. Surg. Research, societe Internationale De Chirurgie, Assn. Clin. Cardiac Surgeons (sec., treas. 1978-80), Soc. Cons. Armed Forces, Pediatric Cardiac Surg. Group, Chgo. Heart Assn. (chmn. cardiovascular surgery com. 1978-80, sec. 1980-83, pres. elect 1983-84, pres. 1984—), A.G. Morrow Soc., W.H. Cole Soc., AAAS, Assn. Am. Med. Colls, Thoracic Surgery Dirs. Assn., Sigma Xi. Subspecialties: Cardiac surgery; Physiology (medicine). Office: Dept Surgery PO Box 6998 Chicago IL 60680

LEVITT, MORTON, pharmacologist; b. N.Y.C., Jan. 4, 1929; s. Abe S. and Nellie (Glass) Leviit; m. Renee Rosenberg, Jan. 5, 1952; children: Ilene, Steven, David. B.S., CCNY, 1951; B.S. in Pharmacy, Fordham U., 1957; M.S., George Washington U., 1959; Ph.D., Howard U., 1966. Research asst. George Washington U., Washington, 1957-59; pharmacologist Nat. Heart Inst., 1962-67; research biologist Sterling Winthrop, Rensselaer, N.Y., 1967-70; sr. research fellow dept. psychiatry Columbia U., N.Y.C., 1970—, N.Y. State Psychiat. Inst., 1970—. Contbr. articles on pharmacology to profl. jours. Served with USMC, 1951-53. Mem. Am. Soc. for Pharmacology and Exptl. Therapeutics, N.Y. Acad. Scis., Sigma Xi. Current Work: Genetics of mental illness, hypertension, advenergic mechanisms, catacholamines, biochemistry of behavior. Subspecialties: Molecular pharmacology; Neurochemistry.

LEVNER, MARK HENRY, microbiologist; b. Milw., Jan. 1, 1941; s. Sidney Aaron and Faye (Bindler) L.; m. Abigail Straus, Nov. 16, 1969; children: Adam Harris, Ethan Straus; married: 1 son by previous marriage, Geoffrey Michael. B.S. in Physics, U. Wis.-Madison, 1963; M.S. in Physics, U. Ill.-Urbana, 1965; Ph.D. in Biophysics, U. Chgo., 1971. Postdoctoral assoc. Inst. Cancer Research, Fox Chase, Pa., 1971-73; research assoc. Haverford (Pa.) Coll., 1973; sr. microbiologist Wyeth Labs., Radnor, Pa., 1973-83, supr. molecular biology unit, 1983-84, mgr. biol. sect., 1984—. Contbr. articles to profl. publs.; patentee processes for enhancing prodn. of enterotoxin. NIH postdoctoral research fellow, 1971-72, 72-73. Patentee enterotoxin. Current Work: Genetic, biochemical studies of bacterial toxins; vaccine development. Subspecialties: Genetics and genetic engineering (biology); Microbiology (medicine). Office: Wyeth Labs PO Box 8299 Philadelphia PA 19101

LEVY, ALAN JOEL, chemist, medical products company executive; b. N.Y.C., July 25, 1937; s. George and Sylvia (Marcus) L.; m. Sharon Ann Rodriguez, Aug. 19, 1962; children—Mitchell, Arden. B.S., CUNY, 1958; Ph.D., Purdue U., 1962. Chemist Allied Chem Co., Morristown, N.J., 1962-66; with Ethicon Inc., Somerville, N.J., 1966—, dir. devel., 1978-80, v.p. research and devel., 1980-84, v.p. new tech., 1984—; bd. sci. advisers Tulane U., New Orleans, 1978-80. Contbr. articles to profl. jours. Patentee chem. mechanisms. Chmn. com. Fair Housing Council, Morristown, N.J.; N.J. pres. United World Federalists. Recipient Philip B. Hoffmann award Johnson & Johnson, New Brunswick, N.J., 1975, Johnson medal, 1980. Mem. Am. Chem. Soc., N.Y. Acad. Sci., AAAS, Polymer Soc., Sigma Xi. Current work: Polymers for bio-medical applications; polymer synthesis. Subspecialty: Polymer chemistry. Office: Ethicon Inc US Route 22 Somerville NJ 08876

LEVY, DAVID ALFRED, research immunologist, educator; b. Washington, Aug. 27, 1930; s. Stanley A. and Blanche Barbara (Berman) L.; m. Annette Badouk, Apr. 26, 1985; children from former marriage—Jill D., William D., Stanley A. B.S. in Zoology, U. Md., 1952, M.D., 1954. Lic. physician Md.; cert. Am. Bd. Internal Medicine, Am. Bd. Allergy and Immunolgy. Intern, Univ. Hosp., U. Md., Balt., 1954-55, asst. resident in medicine, 1955-58, resident in medicine, 1958-59; staff physician VA Hosp., Balt., 1961-62; postdoctoral fellow USPHS dept. microbiology Johns Hopkins U. Sch. Medicine, 1962-66, asst. prof. radiol. scis. Johns Hopkins U. Sch. Hygiene & Pub. Health, Balt., 1966-68, asst. prof. medicine Sch. Medicine, 1966-78, assoc. prof. radiol. scis. and epidemiology Sch. Hygiene & Pub. Health, 1968-72, prof., 1972-73, prof. biochemistry, 1973-82, prof. epidemiology, 1973—, prof. pathobiology, 1980-82, prof. immunology and infectious diseases, 1982—, prof. biochemistry, 1982—; vis. scientist Lab. Exptl. Parasitology, Institut Pasteur, Paris, 1985—; cons. and lectr. in field. Contbr. chpts. to books, articles to profl. jours. Mem. editorial bd.: Clin. Immunology and Immunopathology Reviewer, Jour. Allergy and Clin. Immunology; Jour. Immunology; numerous others. Served to capt. U.S. Army, 1959-61. Fogarty internat. sr. research fellow, Paris, 1976; WHO travel fellow, 1979. Mem. AAAS, Am. Assn. Immunologists, Am. Acad. Allergy, Soc. Exptl. Biology and Medicine, Am. Fedn. Clin. Research, Am. Soc. Tropical Medicine and Hygiene, Md. Thoracic Soc., Md. Soc. Allergy, Helminthological Soc. of Washington, Alpha Omega Alpha, Sigma Xi. Current work: Allergy, asthma and immediate hypersensitivity; parasite immunology, focusing on filarial infections. Home: 11 Quai St Michel Paris 75005 France Office: Johns Hopkins USHPS 615 N Wolfe St Baltimore MD 21205

LEVY, DAVID EDWARD, neurologist, researcher, educator; b. Washington, May 10, 1941; s. Maurice W. and Cele (Blue) L.; m. Ellen K., Jan. 8, 1967. A.B. cum laude, Harvard U., 1963, M.D., 1968. Diplomate: Am. Bd. Inernal Medicine, Am. Bd. Psychiatry and Neurology. Intern in medicine N.Y. Hosp., N.Y.C., 1968-69, resident in medicine, 1969-70, resident in neurology, 1970-73; instr. in neurology Cornell U., N.Y.C., 1973-75, asst. prof. neurology, 1975-80, assoc. prof., 1980—; practice medicine specializing in neurology; mem. staff N.Y. Hosp., N.Y.C.; established investigator Am. Heart Assn., 1978-83; grant reviewer Nat. Inst. Neurol. and Communicative Diseases and Stroke. Contbr. numerous articles, abstracts to profl. jours.; editorial bd.: Stroke. Community rep. N.Y.C. Mayor's com. on subway constrn. Robert Wood Johnson Found. grantee, 1981-87. Mem. Am. Acad. Neurology, Am. Neurol. Assn., ACP, Soc. Neurosci., Stroke Council of Am. Heart Assn., Phi Beta Kappa. Current Work: Mechanisms and prevention of ischemic brain damage, establishment of computer database systems usable for determining prognosis from major illnesses. Subspecialties: Neurology; Database systems. Office: Dept Neurology (A-569 Cornell U Med Col) 1300 York Ave New York NY 10021

LEVY, DAVID HOWARD, astronomy observer; b. Montreal, Que., Can., May 22, 1948; came to U.S., 1979; s. Nathaniel Lewis and Edith (Pailet) L.; B.A., Acadia U., Wolfville, 1972; M.S., Queen's U., Kingston, Ont., 1979. Observer, Planetary Sci. Inst., Tucson, 1982—; research asst. lunar & planetary lab. Internat. Halley Watch; instr. sch. groups Flandrau Planetarium 1980-82, floor mgr., 1981-82; astronomy instr. various children's camps, 1966-70, 76-81; lectr. in field. Editor newsletter Tails and Trails. Contbr. articles to profl. jours. and newsletters. Named Outstanding Young Man Am., 1982. Mem. Astron. League (Messier cert. 1983), Western Amateur Astronomers, Assn. Lunar and Planetary Observers (recorder meteors sect. 1983—, recorder comets sect. 1984—), Royal Astron. Soc. Can. (co-ordinator, tchr. 1978-80, Chent medal for observations of variable stars 1980, Messier cert. 1981), Am. Assn. Variable Star Observers, Tucson Amateur Astronomy Assn. (pres. 1980-83, Bart and Priscilla Bok award 1984), Pi Lambda Theta. Discoverer comet Levy-Rudenko, Nov. 13, 1984. Current work: Writing astronomical books; teaching astronomy to children; observing guides. Subspecialties: Astronomy journalism; Planetary science. Home and Office: Route 7 Box 414 Tucson AZ 85747

LEVY, DONALD HARRIS, chemistry educator; b. Youngstown, Ohio, June 30, 1939; s. Gabriel and Minnie (Lerner) L.; m. Susan Louise Miller, June 14, 1964; children—Jonathan G., Michael A., Alexander B. B.A., Harvard U., 1961; Ph.D., U. Calif.-Berkeley, 1965. Asst. prof. chemistry U. Chgo., 1967-74, assoc. prof., 1974-78, prof., 1978—, chmn. dept. chemistry, 1983—; mem. chemistry adv. com. NSF. Assoc. editor Jour. Chem. Physics, Chgo., 1983—. Fellow Am. Phys. Soc., AAAS; mem. Am. Chem. Soc., Optical Soc. Am. Subspecialty: Physical chemistry. Office: Dept Chemistry U Chgo 5735 S Ellis Ave Chicago IL 60637

LEVY, GERHARD, pharmacologist; b. Wollin, Germany, Feb. 12, 1928; came to U.S., 1948, naturalized, 1953; s. Gotthold and Eliesabeth (Luebeck) L.; m. Rosalyn Mincer, June 8, 1958; children—David, Marc, Sharon. B.S., U. Calif. at San Francisco, 1955, Pharm.D., 1958; Dr. honoris causa, Uppsala (Sweden) U., 1975, Phila. Coll. Pharmacy and Sci., 1979, L.I. U., 1981. Asst. prof. pharmacy U. Buffalo, 1958-60; assoc. prof. pharmacy State U. N.Y. at Buffalo, 1960-64, prof. biopharmaceutics, 1964-72, distinguished prof. pharmaceutics, 1972—, chmn. dept. pharmaceutics, 1966-70; vis. prof. Hebrew U., Jerusalem; cons. WHO, 1966, Bur. Drugs Adv. Panel System, FDA, 1971-74; mem. com. on problems of drug safety NRC, 1971-75; mem. pharmacol.-toxicol. com. NIH, 1971-75. Mem. editorial bd.: Jour. Pharm. Sci, 1970-75, Clin. Pharmacology and Therapeutics, 1969—, Internat. Jour. Clin. Pharmacology, 1968—, Drug Metabolism and Disposition, 1973—; contbr. articles to profl. jours. Served with AUS, 1950-51. Recipient Ebert prize, 1969, Am. Pharm. Assn. Research Achievement award, 1969, McKeen Cattell award Am. Coll. Clin. Pharmacology, 1978, Host-Madsen medal Internat. Pharm. Fedn., 1978, Oscar B. Hunter award in exptl. therapeutics Am. Soc. Clin. Pharmacology and Therapeutics, 1982, Volwiler Research Achievement award Am. Assn. Colls. Pharmacy, 1982; named Alumnus of Year U. Calif. Sch. Pharmacy Alumni Assn., 1970. Fellow Am. Pharm. Assn., Acad. Pharm. Scis. (Takeru Higuchi Research prize 1983), AAAS; mem. Inst. Medicine of Nat. Acad. Scis., Am. Chem. Soc., Am. Soc. Exptl. Pharmacology and Therapeutics, Soc. Exptl. Biology and Medicine. Subspecialties: Pharmacokinetics; Pharmacology. Home: 169 Surrey Run Williamsville NY 14221 Office: Sch Pharmacy State U NY Amherst NY 14260

LEVY, JOHN STUART, dentist, clinical consultant; b. New Haven, Dec. 26, 1946; s. Morton Julian and Pearl Ruth (Brodes) L.; m. Beverly Eileen Eden, Nov. 28, 1971; 1 dau., Perri Melissa. B.S., George Washington U., 1968; D.D.S., Georgetown U., 1976. Registered dentist. Postdoctoral fellow Yale U., New Haven, 1976-78; asst. prof. Georgetown U., Washington, 1976—; pres. Levy-D.D.S., P.C., New Haven, 1976—. Contbr. articles to profl. jours. Bd. dirs. Camp Laurelwood, Madison, Conn., 1979-82; bd. dirs., sec. med. bd. Jewish Home for Aged, New Haven, 1978—; bd. dirs. Jewish Fedn.; cabinet, mem. United Jewish Appeal Nat. Young Leadership, N.Y.C., 1980—. Served with U.S. Army, 1968-71. Recipient Joseph Borkowski award for professionalism Georgetown U., 1976; Nat. Service award NIH, 1977, 78. Mem. Internat. Assn. Dental Research, ADA. Jewish. Current Work: Flouride-dental enamel studies, biomaterials related to dental applications. Subspecialty: Cariology. Home: 37 Spoke Dr Woodbridge CT 06525 Office: John S Levy DDS PC 52 Trumbell St New Haven CT 06510

LEVY, NELSON LOUIS, immunologist, pharmaceutical company executive; b. Somerville, N.J., June 19, 1941; s. Myron and Sylvia (Cohen) L.; m. Louisa Stiles; children: Michael, Andrew; married; children from previous marriage: Scott, Erik, Jonathan. B.A., B.S., Yale U., 1963; M.D., Columbia U., 1967; Ph.D., Duke U., 1973. Diplomate: Am. Bd. Allergy and Immunology. Asst. prof. immunology Duke U., Durham, N.C., 1973-76, assoc. prof., 1976-80, prof., 1980-81; dir. biol. research Abbott Labs., North Chicago, Ill., 1981-82, v.p. pharm. discovery, 1982—; cons. NIH, 1973—, Gen. Motors Cancer Research Found., 1981—. Assoc. editor: Jour. Immunology, 1975—; contbr. articles to profl. jours. Served with USPHS, 1968-70. Mem. Am. Assn. Immunologists, Am. Assn. Cancer Research, Alpha Omega Alpha, Phi Gamma Delta. Club: Yale (Chgo.). Current Work: Directing multidisciplinary program to find new therapeutics entities in the areas of neuroscience, immunology, cardiovascular disease and infectious disease. Subspecialties: Immunology (medicine); Neurobiology.

LEVY, PAUL HENRIE, physicist, researcher, consultant; b. San Pedro, Calif., Sept. 14, 1953; s. Abraham Jack and Naomi Anne (Wehmhoner) L.; m. Christine Marie Infante, June 9, 1980; children—Aaron Paul, Alexia P. B.A., U. Calif.,-San Diego, 1975; Ph.D. candidate, 1975-78. Scientist, Jaycor, San Diego, 1978-80; sr. scientist Sci. Applications Internat. Inc., La Jolla, Calif., 1980-82; dir. electromagnetics technology Physics Internat., San Leandro, Calif., 1982—. Contbr. numerous articles to profl. jours. Mem. Am. Phys. Soc., IEEE, AAAS, Phi Beta Kappa. Democrat. Current work: Transient electromagnetic phenomena; nuclear radiation effects; directed-energy technology. Subspecialties: Nuclear physics; Particle physics. Office: Physics Internat 2700 Merced St San Leandro CA 94577

LEVY, ROBERT ISAAC, physician, university official; b. Bronx, N.Y., May 3, 1937; s. George Gerson and Sarah (Levinson) L.; m. Ellen Marie Feis, 1958; children: Andrew, Joanne, Karen, Patricia. B.A. with high honors and distinction, Cornell U., 1957; M.D. cum laude, Yale U., 1961. Intern, then asst. resident in medicine Yale-New Haven Med. Center, 1961-63; clin. asso. molecular diseases Nat. Heart and Lung Inst., Bethesda, Md., 1963-66; chief resident Nat. Heart, Lung and Blood Inst., Bethesda, 1965-66, attending physician molecular disease br., 1965-80, head sect. lipoproteins, 1966-80, dep. clin. dir. inst., 1968-69, chief clin. services molecular diseases br., 1969-73, chief lipid metabolism br., 1970-74, dir. div. heart and vascular diseases, 1973-75, dir. inst., 1975-81; v.p. health scis., dean Sch. Medicine Tufts U., Boston, 1981-83, prof. medicine, 1981-83; v.p. health scis. Columbia U., N.Y.C., 1983—, prof. medicine, 1983—; attending physician Georgetown U. med. div. D.C. Gen. Hosp., 1966-68; spl. cons. anti-lipid drugs FDA. Editor: Jour. Lipid Research, 1972-80, Circulation, 1974-76, Am. Heart jour, 1980—; contbr. articles to profl. jours. Served as surgeon USPHS, 1963-66. Recipient Kees Thesis prize Yale U., 1961; Arthur S. Flemming award, 1975; Superior Service award HEW, 1975; Research award and Van Slyke award Am. Soc. Clin. Chemists, 1980. Mem. Am. Heart Assn. (mem.-at-large exec. com. council basic sci., mem. exec. council on atherosclerosis), Am. Inst. Nutrition, Am. Fedn. Clin. Research, N.Y. Acad. Scis., Am. Soc. Clin. Nutrition, Am. Soc. Clin. Investigation, Am. Coll. Cardiology, Inst. Medicine of Nat. Acad. Scis., Am. Soc. Clin. Pharmacology and Therapeutics, Assn. Am. Physicians, Phi Beta Kappa, Sigma Xi, Alpha Omega Alpha, Alpha Epsilon Delta, Phi Kappa Phi. Current Work: Lipopreteins; cholesterol; preventive cardiology; nutrition; atherosclerosis; disordrs of lipid transport and lipid metabolism. Subspecialties: Cardiology; Internal medicine. Office: Columbia U Coll Physicians and Surgeons 630 W 168th St New York NY 10032

LEVY, RONALD, medical educator, physician, medical researcher; B.S., Harvard U.; M.D., Stanford U., 1968. Helen Hay Whitney Found. fellow in dept. chem. immunology Weizmann Inst. Sci., Rehovot, Israel, 1973-75; mem. faculty Stanford U., Calif., 1975—, now assoc. prof. dept. medicine-oncology. Co-recipient (with G. Telford) 1st award for cancer research Armand Hammer Found.; diplomate Am. Bd. Internal Medicine. Subspecialty: Cancer research (medicine). Office: Dept Medicine-Oncology Stanford U Sch Medicine Stanford CA 94305

LEVY, SALOMON, mechanical engineer, consultant; b. Jerusalem, Apr. 4, 1926; s. Abraham Isaac and Sultana Claire (Elyachar) L.; m. Eileen D. Smith, Oct. 14, 1951; children—Marshall, Linda. B.S., U. Calif.-Berkeley, 1949, M.S., 1951, Ph.D., 1953. Supr. atomic power Gen. Electric Co., San Jose, Calif., 1954-56, adv. nuclear specialist, 1956-59, mgr. heat transfer, 1959-66, mgr. systems engring., 1966-68, mgr. design engring., 1968-71, gen. mgr. nuclear fuel, 1971-73, gen. mgr. boiling water reactors, 1973-75, gen. mgr. boiling water reactors ops., 1975-77; pres. S. Levy Inc., Campbell, Calif.; Springer prof. U. Calif., Berkeley, 1979; adj. prof. UCLA, 1982—; cons. in field. Mem. editorial com. Internat. Jour. Heat and Mass Transfer, 1965-73. Contbr. articles to tech. jours. Treas., chmn. exec. com. Unitarian Ch., San Jose, 1968-72. Fellow ASME (Heat Transfer Meml. award 1966); mem. Nat. Acad. Engring., Am. Nuclear Soc. Democrat. Current work: Heat transfer, fluid flow, safety analysis, nuclear power plant design. Subspecialties: Nuclear engineering; Heat transfer. Office: S Levy Inc 3425 S Bascom Ave Campbell CA 95008

LEVY, STEPHEN RAYMOND, consultant, research, development and products company executive; b. Everett, Mass., May 4, 1940; s. Robert George and Lillian (Berfield) L.; m. Sandra Helen Rosen, Aug. 26, 1961; children: Phillip, Susan. B.B.A., U. Mass., 1962. Chmn., chief exec. officer, dir. Bolt Beranek & Newman, Inc., Cambridge, Mass. Served with AUS, 1963-66. Decorated Army Commendation medal. Mem. Assn. Computing Machinery, Fin. Execs. Inst. Home: 175 Commonwealth Ave Boston MA 02116 Office: Bolt Beranek & Newman Inc 10 Moulton St Cambridge MA 02138

LEVY, WALTER JOSEPH, JR., neurosurgeon, researcher, educator; b. Balt., Dec. 16, 1947; s. Walter Joseph and Genevieve (Ferguson) L. B.A. in Chemistry, Duke U., 1969; M.D., Med. Coll. Ga., 1973. Diplomate Am. Bd. Neurol. Surgery. Intern. Med. Ctr. Central Ga., Macon, 1974-75; surg. resident Med. Ctr. Western Mass., Springfield, 1975-76; resident in neurosurgery, Cleve. Clinic, 1976-81; chief neurosurgery Harry Truman VA Hosp., Columbia, Mo., 1981—; asst. prof. neurosurgery, U. Mo. Hosps., Columbia, 1981—. Developer clin. test: Motor Evoked Potential, 1981; inventor surg. instruments; author articles in field. Mem. Congress Neurol. Surgeons, Am. Spinal Injury Assn., AMA, IEEE, Soc. for Neurosci. Current work: Spinal cord injury including use of motor evoked potentials, study of axon injury processes, use of microsurgical instruments, pain, stereotaic surgery. Subspecialty: Neurosurgery. Office: U Mo N522 1 Hospital Dr Columbia MO 65212

LEWIN, BENJAMIN, molecular biologist, editor, writer; b. Eng.; s. Sherry and Ann L.; m. Ann; children: Nicholas Sheridan, Jonathan Asher. B.A., Cambridge (Eng.) U., 1967, M.A., 1970, Ph.D., 1976; M.Sc., U. London, 1968. Tutorial fellow U. Sussex, Eng., 1969-70; editor Nature New Biology, 1970-71; vis. scientist Nat. Cancer Inst., NIH, Bethesda, Md., 1972-73. Editor: Cell mag, M.I.T., 1974—; Author: Gene Expression 1: Bacterial Genomes, 1974, Gene Expression 3: Plasmids and Phages, 1977, Gene Expression 2: Eucaryotic Chromosomes, 1980, Genes, 1983. Current Work: Communication in molecular biology. Subspecialties: Gene actions; Genome organization. Office: Cell Offices 292 Main St Cambridge MA 02142

LEWIS, ALAN JAMES, pharmacologist, research exec.; b. Newport, Wales, Sept. 29, 1945; came to U.S., 1979; s. William Tyssul and Elizabeth Ella (Deers) L.; m. Judith Ann Royle, Sept. 14, 1947; children: Nina Francis, Huw Gareth, Victoria Elizabeth. B.S. in Physiology and Biochemistry, Southampton (Eng.) U., 1967; Ph.D., U. Wales, 1970. Postdoctoral fellow research dept. biomed. scis. U. Guelph, Can., 1970-72, Yale U. Lung Research Center, New Haven, 1972-73; group leader Organon Labs., Glasgow, Scotland, 1973-79; assoc. dir. exptl. therapeutics Wyeth Labs., Inc., Phila., 1979—. Contbr. articles to profl. publs. and jours. Mem. Brit. Pharmacol. Soc., Brit. Immunological Soc., Am. Pharmacol. Soc., Reticuloendothelial Soc. Current Work: Pharmacological modulation of autoimmune diseases and allergic diseases. Subspecialties: Immunogenetics; Allergy. Home: 1041 Shearwater Dr Audubon PA 19407 Office: Wyeth Labs Inc PO Box 8299 Philadelphia PA 19101

LEWIS, ANDREW MORRIS, JR., virologist, researcher; b. Cheriton, Va., Nov. 28, 1934; s. Andrew M. and Wilsye H. L.; m. Gladys R. Shorrock, June 8, 1960; children: T. Reid, Andrew M. III. B.A., Duke U., 1956, M.D., 1961. Intern in pediatrics Duke U. Med. Ctr., 1961-62, resident in pediatrics, 1962-63; research virologist USPHS Nat. Inst. Allergy and Infectious Diseases, NIH, Bethesda, Md., 1963—, Lab. Molecular Microbiology, 1981—. Served with USPHS, 1963—. Decorated Commendation medal USPHS. Mem. AAAS, Am. Soc. Microbiology, Am. Assn. Immunologists. Current Work: Mechanisms of viral carcinogenesis; biology of DNA virus transformed mammalian cells; replication of Ad2-SV40 hybrids. Subspecialties: Virology (biology); Cell study oncology. Office: Bldg 5 Rm B1-32 NIH Bethesda MD 20205

LEWIS, BRIAN MURRAY, radio astronomer; b. Oxford, Eng., June 20, 1943; s. Brian Clive and Christina (Murray) L.; m. Dianne Nell Barnett, May 27, 1967; children: Rupert Murray, Penelope Anne. Ph.D., Australian Nat. U., 1970. With Jodrell Bank, Manchester, Eng., 1969-71; dir. Carter Obs.,

Wellington, N.Z., 1973-81; research assoc. Arecibo (P.R.) Obs., 1982—. Contbr. articles to sci. jours. Mem. Royal Astron. Soc., Am. Astron. Soc., Australian Astron. Soc. Current Work: 21 cm observations of external galaxies, structure of clusters of galaxies, missing mass, neutrino mass. Subspecialties: Radio and microwave astronomy; Theoretical astrophysics. Home: 120-122 L St Ramey Aguadilla PR 06006 Office: Box 995 Arecibo PR 06120

LEWIS, DAVID SLOAN, JR., aircraft company executive; b. North Augusta, S.C., July 6, 1917; s. David S. and Reuben (Walton) L.; m. Dorothy Sharpe, Dec. 20, 1941; children: Susan, David Sloan III, Robert, Andrew. Student, U. S.C., 1934-37; B.S. in Aero. Engring, Ga. Inst. Tech., 1939. Aerodynamicist Glenn L. Martin Co., Balt., 1939-46; chief aerodynamics McDonnell Aircraft Corp., St. Louis, 1946-52, chief preliminary design, 1952-55, mgr. sales, 1955-56, mgr. projects, 1956-57, v.p. project mgmt., 1957-59, sr. v.p. ops., 1960-61, exec. v.p., 1961-62, pres., 1962-67, McDonnell-Douglas Co.; also chmn. Douglas Aircraft Co. div., 1967-70; chmn., chief exec. officer Gen. Dynamics Corp., 1970—; dir. Ralston Purina Co., St. Louis, BankAm. Corp., San Francisco; dir. Mead Corp., Cessna Aircraft Co., Wichita, Kans. Alderman, Ferguson, Mo., 1951-54; Trustee Washington U., St. Louis. Fellow AIAA. Episcopalian. Subspecialty: Aeronautical engineering. Office: Pierre Laclede Center Saint Louis MO 63105

LEWIS, DONALD RICHARD, archaeometry educator, consultant, researcher; b. New Leipzig, N.D., May 18, 1920; s. Reuben Benjamin and Mary Isabella (Johnson) L.; m. Evelyn Delores Schwingel, June 21, 1943; children—Donna Diane, Jeffrey Scott. B.S., U. Wis., 1942, M.S., 1947, Ph.D., 1948. Supr. Ballistics Hercules Powder Co., Radford, Va. and Baraboo, Wis., 1942-46; research fellow U. Wis., Madison, 1946-48; staff research chemist Shell Devel. Co., Houston, 1948-80; lectr. U. Tex.-San Antonio, 1980—; also faculty assoc. Ctr. for Archaeol. Research; cons. in field, San Antonio, 1980—; exchange scientist Royal Dutch Shell, Amsterdam, 1956-57; prin. scientist USAF/Advanced Research Projects Agy., San Francisco, 1964-66; dir. Nuclear Monitoring Systems and Mgmt. Corp., Houston, 1980—; nat. chmn. Gordon Research Conf. on Ion Exchange, N.H., 1955, Conf. Chemistry at Interfaces, N.H., 1963. Editor: Clays and Clay Minerals, 1957-59. Contbr. articles to profl. jours. Patentee in field. Fellow AAAS, Mineral. Soc. Am.; mem. Instrument Soc. Am. (sr. mem.), Am. Chem. Soc. (nat. counselor, chmn. local sect. S.E. Tex.), Am. Phys. Soc., Geochem. Soc., Geol. Soc. Am., Soc. for Archeol. Sci., Assn. for Field Archeology, Houston Archaeol. Soc. (life), Phi Beta Kappa, Sigma Xi, Phi Lambda Upsilon. Club: Torch (San Antonio). Current works: Thermoluminescence dating of archaeological artifacts, archaeometry, trace element geochemistry, nuclear waste disposal, laboratory automation with computers. Subspecialties: Archaeological chemistry; Geochemistry. Home: 9219 Lasater San Antonio TX 78250 Office: Earth and Physical Sciences Div Behavioral and Cultural Sciences Ctr for Archaeological Research U Tex San Antonio TX 78285

LEWIS, EDWIN REYNOLDS, biomedical engineering educator, neuroscience researcher; b. Los Angeles, July 14, 1934; s. Edwin McMurtry and Sally Newman (Reynolds) L.; m. Elizabeth Louise McLean, June 11, 1960; children—Edwin Mclean, Sarah Elizabeth. B.A. in Biol. Sci., Stanford U., 1956, M.S. in Elec. Engring., 1957, Ph.D. in Elec. Engring., 1962. Mem. research staff Gen. Precision Co., Glendale, Calif., 1961-67; mem. faculty U. Calif.-Berkeley, 1967—, prof. biomed. engring., 1971—; Jacob Javits neurosci. investigator NIH, 1984. Author: (with others) Neural Modeling, 1977; Network Models in Population Biology, 1977; (with others) The Vertebrate Inner Ear, 1985. Mem. editorial bd. Internat. Jour. Scanning Electron Microscopy, 1977—, Jour. Theoretical Neurobiology, 1981—. Recipient citation for disting. teaching U. Calif.-Berkeley, 1972; Neurosci. Research Program fellow 1966, 69. Fellow IEEE; mem. Assn. Research in Otolaryngology, Acoustical Soc. Am., Soc. for Neuro sci., AAAS. Current work: Research on microanatomy, biophysics and evolution of vertebrate ear; studies of mechanical and physiological bases of senses of hearing and balance. Subspecialties: Neurobiology; Biomedical engineering. Home: 1047 Overlook Rd Berkeley CA 94708 Office: Dept Elec Engring and Computer Sci U Calif Berkeley CA 94720

LEWIS, FRANK LEROY, electrical engineering educator; b. Wurzburg, Germany, May 11, 1949; s. Frank Leroy and Ruth Evangeline (Shirley) L.; m. B.A. in Elec. Engring. and Physics, Rice U., 1971, M.E.E., 1971; M.S. in Aero. Systems, U. Western Fla., 1977; Ph.D. in Elec. Engring., Ga. Tech., 1981. Asst. prof. elec. engring. Ga. Inst. Tech., Atlanta, 1981—; cons. Lockheed-Ga., Marietta, 1983—. Author: Optimal Control, 1985; Optimal Estimation, 1985; contbr. articles to engring. jours. Served to lt. USN, 1971-77. NSF grantee, 1982. Mem. IEEE (Control Systems Soc.), Soc. Indsl. and Applied Math., Sigma Xi (M. Ferst awards 1981, 84). Current work: Generalized state-space systems; adaptive systems. Subspecialty: Systems engineering. Home: 835 Glendale Terr #6 Atlanta GA 30308 Office: Sch Elec Engring Ga Inst Tech Atlanta GA 30332

LEWIS, HAROLD WALTER, physicist, educator; b. Keene, N.H., May 7, 1917; s. Hiram Edwin and Lena (Ashton) L.; m. Mary Anne O'Rourke, June 1, 1946; children—Barbara, Richard. B.S., Middlebury (Vt.) Coll., 1938; M.A., U. Buffalo, 1940; Ph.D., Duke, 1950. Physicist, Naval Ordnance Lab., also Bur. Ordnance, 1941-46; mem. faculty Duke, Durham, N.C., 1949—, prof. physics, 1959—, chmn. dept. physics, 1981—, dean arts and scis., 1963-69, vice provost, 1963-80, dean faculty, 1969-80. Univ. disting. service award, 1980—. Fellow Am. Phys. Soc.; mem. Am. Assn. Physics Tchrs., Nat. Acad. Scis. Research on nuclear physics. Subspecialty: Nuclear physics. Home: 1708 Woodburn Rd Durham NC 27705

LEWIS, JAMES ALEXANDER, neurobiologist, educator; b. Phila., Mar. 7, 1946; s. George Campbell and Elizabeth Glenn (Zipf) L.; m. Anne Sun Wah Kuan, Dec. 27, 1975; children: Diane, Cynthia. B.S. in Chemistry, M.I.T., 1964-68; Ph.D. in Biochemistry, U. Calif.-Berkeley, 1972. Postdoctoral fellow M.R.C. Lab. Molecular Biology, Cambridge, Eng., 1972-74; asst. prof. Columbia U., N.Y.C., 1974-81; research asst. prof. U. Pitts., 1981-82; asst. prof. U. Mo., Columbia, 1982—. Contbr. articles to profl. jours. NSF fellow, 1968-72; Am. Cancer Soc. fellow, 1972-74. Mem. Soc. Neuroscience. Current Work: Genetic and pharmacological characterization of drug-resistant mutants of the nematode Caenorhabditis elegans that appear acetylcholine receptor-deficient; synthesis of a radioactive receptor ligand and demonstration through binding assays of mutant receptor deficiency. Subspecialties: Neurobiology; Gene actions. Office: Division Biological Sciences University Missouri Columbia MO 65211

LEWIS, JAMES BRYSON, maintenance engineer; b. Wyandotte, Mich., July 27, 1950; s. Jack Bryson and Gladys Irene (Forsyth) L.; m. Anna M. Welke, Feb. 28, 1976 (div. July 1981); 1 son, Phillip. B.S., U. Mich.-Ann Arbor, 1972. Registered profl. engr., Mich. Field engr. Gen. Electric Co., Chgo., 1972-76, startup mgr., Platteville, Colo., 1976-77, field engr.-nuclear, Oak Brook, Ill., 1977-78, service supr., 1978-79; sr. engr. Consumers Power Co., Jackson, Mich., 1979-81, gen. supr. mech. maintenance, 1981—. Mem. ASME, Am. Nuclear Soc. Current Work: Failure analysis of steam turbine generators and related mechanical equipment. Subspecialties: Mechanical engineering; Fracture mechanics. Office: Consumers Power Co 1945 W Parnall Rd Jackson MI 49201

LEWIS, JOHN CLARK, JR., See *Who's Who in America,* 43rd edition.

LEWIS, MICHAEL DOLAN, mechanical engineer; b. Houston, Nov. 7, 1952; s. Henry John and Dolores Marie (Barkis) L.; m. Roberta Francis, Oct. 22, 1977; children: Matthew Dolan, Kelli Christine. B.S.M.E., Tex. A&M U., 1975; M.B.A., U. Houston, 1982. Registered profl. engr., Tex. Asst. design engr. subsea drilling equipment Nat. Supply Co., Houston, 1975-77, asso. design engr. standard wellhead, 1977-79, design engr. standard wellhead, 1979-81, product engr. standard wellhead, 1981-82, product supr. standard wellhead, 1982—; v.p. Cornell Ranches Corp., 1976—. Mem. Meadow Brook Civic Club, 1978—. Model for Mgmt. award Armco Inc., 1982; Quality Plus award, 1982. Mem. ASME, Tex. Soc. Profl. Engrs., Tex. A&M U. Former Students Assn. (century). Republican. Roman Catholic. Club: WCS Mgmt. (Houston) (treas.). Inventor metal seal, flow control choke with studded inlet, high temperature casing packoff, hydraulic casing jack. Current Work: Design and devel. of wellhead equipment for critical applications. Subspecialties: Mechanical engineering; Metallurgical engineering.

LEWIS, ROBERT MASON, neurobiologist, molecular biologist; b. N.Y.C., Aug. 19, 1953. B.A., NYU, 1975; Ph.D., U. Wis., 1980. Postdoctoral fellow Yale U. Sch. Medicine, New Haven, 1981-83, Rockefeller U., N.Y.C., 1983—. Contbr. articles to profl. jours. Fellow Epilepsy Found. Am., 1981-83, Am. Cancer Soc., 1982-83, Nat. Inst. Neurol. and Communicative Disorders and Stroke, 1983-85. Mem. N.Y. Acad. Scis., Soc. for Neurosci., AAAS. Current work: Developmental biology of mammalian nervous system at level of gene expression; applications of molecular biology to correcting neurological disorders. Subspecialties: Developmental biology; Molecular biology. Office: Rockefeller U 1230 York Ave New York NY 10021

LEWIS, THOMAS B., See *Who's Who in America,* 43rd edition.

LEY, RICHARD WAYNE, mathematician, software consultant; b. Harrisburg, Pa., Aug. 31, 1947; s. Robert Emil and June Doris (Weaver) L. A.B. in Math, U. Calif.-Berkeley, 1969; M.S. in Math, Stanford U., 1970. Mathematician Dept. Def., Ft. Meade, Md., 1974-81, 82—; assoc. mgr. BDM Corp., Los Angeles, 1981-82; owner, mgr. Minicomputer Software Projects, Silver Spring, Md., 1982-84; ptnr. K Plus L Software, Silver Spring, Md., 1983—. Pres. Citizens for Greenbelt Assn., 1980. Served to lt. USNR, 1971-73. NSF fellow, 1969; recipient Spl. Achievement award Dept. Def., 1981. Mem. Math. Assn. Am., Soc. for Indsl. and Applied Math., Ops. Research Soc. Am. Republican. Roman Catholic. Current Work: Conducting computer-aided research in speech and digital signal processing; writing microcomputer applications software; performing computer systems analysis and simulation testing. Subspecialties: Mathematical software; Probability. Home: 11425 Oak Leaf Dr Silver Spring MD 20901 Office: K Plus L Software PO Box 2303 White Flint Mall Kensington MD 20895-2303

LHOTA, JAMES RAYMOND, II, physicist; b. Canton, Ohio, Jan. 16, 1954; s. James Raymond and Marilyn (McKimm) L.; B.S. in Physics, Wayne State U., Detroit, 1977, Ph.D. in Physics, 1983. Mem. tech. staff Aerospace Corp., Los Angeles, 1983—. Contbr. articles to profl. publs. Recipient Grad. Teaching award Wayne State U., 1983. Mem. Am. Phys. Soc., Soc. Physics Students, Sigma Xi. Current work: Development of materials with large a specific heat peaks at certain low temperatures. Subspecialties: Condensed matter physics; Magnetic physics. Office: Aerospace Corp M2-250 PO Box 92957 Los Angeles CA 90009

LI, CHOH HAO, biochemist, endocrinologist; b. Canton, China, Apr. 21, 1913; came to U.S., 1935, naturalized, 1955; s. Kan-chi Li and Mewching Tsui; m. Annie Lu, Oct. 1, 1938; children: Wei-i Li, Ann-si Li, Eva Li. B.S., U. Nanking, 1933; Ph.D., U. Calif.-Berkeley, 1938; M.D. (hon.), Cath. U. Chile, 1962; LL.D., Chinese U., Hong Kong, 1970; D.Sc., U. Pacific, 1971, Marquette U., 1971, St. Peter's Coll., 1971; hon. doctor, Uppsala U., 1977; D.Sc., U. San Francisco, 1978, L.I. U., 1981, U. Colo., 1981, Med. Coll. Pa., 1982. Instr. chemistry U. Nanking, 1933-35; research asso. U. Calif.-Berkeley, 1938-44, asst. prof. exptl. biology, 1944-47, asso. prof., 1947-49; prof. biochemistry, prof. exptl. endocrinology dir. Hormone Research Lab., Berkeley and San Francisco, 1950—; mem. acad. adv. bd. Chinese U., Hong Kong, 1963—; adv. bd. Chem. Research Center, Nat. Taiwan U., 1964—; vis. scientist Children's Cancer Research Found., Boston, 1955, 63-73; co-chmn. Internat. Symposium on Growth Hormone, Milan, Italy, 1967, Internat. Symposium on Protein and Polypeptide Hormones, Leige, Belgium, 1968; hon. pres. Internat. Symposium on Gonadotropins, Bangalore, India, 1973; chmn. Internat. Symposium on Proteins, Taipei, 1978, Internat. Symposium Growth Hormones and other Biologically Active Peptides, Milan, Italy, 1979; vis. prof. U. Montreal, 1948, Nat. Taiwan U., 1958, Chinese U. Hong Kong, 1967, Marquette U., 1973. Co-editor: Perspectives in the Biochemistry of Large Molecules, Supplement 1, 1962; sect; editor: Chem. Abstracts, 1960-63; co-asso. editor: Internat. Jour. Peptide and Protein Research, 1969-76, editor-in-chief, 1976—; mem. editorial adv. bd.: Family Health, 1969-81, Biopolymers, 1979—; editorial bd.: Current Topics in Exptl. Endocrinology, 1969—, Archives Biochem. Biophysics, 1979—; editor: Hormonal Proteins and Peptides, 1973—, Versatility of Proteins, 1979. Recipient numerous honors, including Ciba award in endocrinology, 1947, Amory prize Am. Acad. Arts and Scis., 1955, Albert Lasker award for basic med. research, 1962, Golden Plate award Am. Acad. Achievement, 1964, Univ. medal Liege, Belgium, 1968; Sci. Achievement award AMA, 1970; Nat. award Am. Cancer Soc., 1971; Nicholas Andry award Assn. Bone and Joint Surgeons, 1972; Lewis prize Am. Philos. Soc., 1977; Nichols medal Am. Chem. Soc., 1979; Sci. award Academia Santa Chicra, Genoa, 1979; Koch award Endocrine Soc., 1981; Heyrovsky Gold medal Czech Acad. Sci., 1982; Harvey lectr., 1951; Faculty Research lectr. U. Calif., San Francisco, 1962-63; Evans lectr., 1976; Pres. Marcos lectr. Manila, 1967; Lasker award lectr. Salk Inst., 1969; Nord lectr. Fordham U., 1972; Geschwind lectr. U. Calif., Davis, 1980; Grattarola lectr. U. Milan, 1981; Guggenheim fellow, 1948. Fellow Am. Acad. Arts and Scis., AAAS, N.Y. Acad. Sci., Am. Inst. Chemists; mem. Am. Chem. Soc. (Calif. sect. award 1951), Am. Soc. Biol. Chemists, Endocrine Soc., Biochem. Soc. London, Soc. Exptl. Biol. Medicine; hon. mem. Harvey Soc., Argentina Soc., Endocrinol. Metabolism Biol. Soc. Chile, Academia Sinica (Republic of China; Hu Shih meml. lectr. 1967), Nat. Acad. Scis.; fgn. mem. Chilean Acad. Scis., Israel Biochem. Soc., Indian Nat. Sci. Acad., Third World Acad. of Sci. Subspecialties: Endocrinology; Biochemistry (biology). Office: Lab of Molecular Endocrinology Univ of Calif-San Francisco Room 1018 Health Scis East San Francisco CA 94143

LI, CHUNG-HSIUNG, engineer, researcher; b. Chia-Yi, Taiwan, May 10, 1939; arrived in U.S., 1967, naturalized, 1978; s. Ten-Song and Huan (Lai) L.; m. Lee-Jung Chang, Nov. 20, 1976; children—Ronald, Grace. B.S. in Chem. Engring., Tunghai U. (Taiwan), 1964; M.S. in Chem. Engring., U. N.H., 1969; Ph.D. in Engring., U. Ill.-Chgo., 1976. Specialist Sargent & Lundy Engrs., Chgo., 1974-79; sr. engr. C-E Air Preheater, Wellsville, N.Y., 1979—. Contbr. articles to Fluids Mechanics, Heat Transfer, and Mass Transfer. Mem. Nat. Soc. Profl. Engrs., Am. Inst. Chem. Engrs., ASME, Soc. Indsl. and Applied Math., Combustion Inst. Current work: Improvement of performance of rotating regenerative heat exchanger and bayonet tube heat exchanger. Subspecialties: Biomass (energy science and technology); Fluid mechanics. Home: 238 School St Wellsville NY 14895 Office: C-E Air Preheater Co Andover Rd Wellsville NY 14895

LI, JONATHAN J., pharmacologist, educator; b. N.Y.C., June 22, 1939; s. Wah O. and Theresa M. Lee; m. Sara Antonia, Aug. 4, 1972; children: Christopher, Stephanie. A.B., Brown U., 1962; postgrad., Columbia U., 1963-64, Stanford U., 1965-67; Ph.D., SUNY-Syracuse, 1972. Research fellow dept biol. chemistry Harvard U., 1971-74; asst. dir. spl. diagnostic. and treatment unit endocrine sec. VA Med. Ctr., Mpls., 1974-76, research scientist, 1976—; asst. prof. dept. urologic surgery U. Minn., Mpls., 1980—, dir. steroid research lab., 1983—; ad hoc mem. clin. cancer program project rev. com. NIH, HHS, 1983; con-founder, co-chmn. Gordon Research Conf. on Hormonal Carcinogenesis, 1985, chmn., 1987. Contbr. numerous articles in field to profl. jours. VA med. research grantee, 1974—; Nat. Cancer Inst. grantee, 1977—. Mem. Assn. VA Scientists (nat. sec. 1980—), Am. Soc. Biol. Chemists, Am Assn. Cancer Research, Endocrine Soc., Histochemical Soc., N.Y. Acad Sci., AAAS. Current Work: Estrogen and chemical carcinogenesis, sex steroid receptors, mechanism of action of steroid hormones; metabolism of natural and synthetic steroids, inhibitors of carcinogenesis, mixed function oxidases, toxicology and drug metabolism. Subspecialties: Cancer research (medicine); Receptors. Office: 54th St and 48th Ave S Med Research Labs Bldg 49 VA Med Ctr Minneapolis MN 55417

LI, MING CHIANG, physicist; b. Ningpo, China, June 18, 1935; s. Yung Fu and Shih Heng (Fei) L.; m. Betty Wang, Jan. 30, 1965. B.S., Peking U., 1958; Ph.D., U. Md., 1965. Mem. Inst. Advanced Study, Princeton, N.J., 1965-67; asst. prof. Va. Poly. Inst. and State U., Blacksburg, Va., 1967-72, assoc. prof., 1972—; system engr. Mitre Corp., McLean, Va., 1983-84; sr. physicist Naval Research Lab., U.S. Dept. Def., Washington, 1984—. Mem. Am. Phys. Soc., Sigma Xi. Current Work: Radar detection and development; computer network; high precision spectroscopy; mathematical modelling; light scattering interferometry; measurement with coherent beams. Subspecialties: Theoretical physics; Atomic and molecular physics. Office: Naval Research Lab Washington DC 20375

LI, TINGYE, electrical engineer; b. Nanking, China, July 7, 1931; came to U.S., 1953, naturalized, 1963; s. Chao and Lily Wei-peng (Sie) L.; m. Edith Hsiu-hwei Wu, June 9, 1956; children: Deborah Chunroh, Kathryn Dairoh. B.Sc. in Elec. Engring, U. Witwatersrand, South Africa, 1953; M.S., Northwestern U., Evanston, Ill., 1955, Ph.D., 1958. Mem. tech. staff Bell Labs., Holmdel, N.J., 1957-67, dept. head repeater techniques research dept., 1967-76, lightwave media research dept., 1976-84, lightwave systems research dept., 1984—. Assoc. editor: Jour. on Lightwave Tech., 1983—; Editorial bd.: Procs. IEEE, 1974-83; contbr. articles on microwave antennas and propagation, lasers, coherent optics, optical communications, optical-fiber transmission to sci. jours., chpts. in books. Recipient Alumni Merit award Northwestern U., 1981. Fellow IEEE (W.R.G. Baker prize 1975, David Sarnoff award 1979), Optical Soc. Am. (chmn. optical communications tech. group 1979-80), AAAS; mem. Chinese Inst. Engrs. U.S.A. (dir. 1974-78, achievement award 1978), Nat. Acad. Engring., Chinese Am. Acad. and Profl. Assn. (bd. dirs. 1985—, achievement award 1985), Sigma Xi, Eta Kappa Nu, Phi Tau Phi. Club: F.F. Fraternity. Patentee in field. Current Work: Optical-fiber communication; optical fiber fabrication; transmission properties; semiconductor lasers and detectors. Subspecialties: Fiber optics; Electrical engineering. Office: AT&T Bell Laboratories Box 400 Holmdel NJ 07733

LI, VICTOR ON-KWOK, electrical engineering educator; b. Hong Kong, Oct. 11, 1954; came to U.S., 1973; s. Chia-Luen and Wai-Ying (Chan) L.; m. Regina Yui-Kwan Wai, Aug. 14, 1977. B.S., MIT, 1977, M.S., 1979, Elec. Engr., 1980, Sc.D., 1981. Cons. Pub. Systems Evaluation, Inc., Cambridge, Mass., 1977-80; teaching asst. MIT Cambridge, 1977-78, research asst., 1979-81; asst. prof. elec. engring. U. So. Calif., Los Angeles, 1981—; founding mem. Communication Scis. Inst., 1982—; cons. Jet Propulsion Lab., Pasadena, Calif., 1983—; joint services elec. program researcher U.S. Dept. Def., 1982—. Contbr. numerous articles to profl. publs. N.Y.C. Urban fellow, 1975; Inst. Advancement Engring. fellow, 1984; NSF grantee, 1982—. Mem. IEEE, IEEE Info. Theory Soc. (chmn. 1983—), IEEE Communications Soc. (tech. com. on computer communications 1983—, conf. coord. 1985—) Ops. Research Soc. Am., Assn. Computing Machinery, Eta Kappa Nu, Tau Beta Pi. Current Work: Performance modeling; distributed databases; communication networks; network reliability analysis, spread spectrum networks. Subspecialties: Database systems; Distributed systems and networks. Home: 3485 Ashwood Ave Los Angeles CA 90066 Office: Elec Engring Dept U So Calif Los Angeles CA 90089

LI, XING ZHONG, plasma physicist; b. Shanghai, China, Nov. 13, 1939; came to U.S., 1979; s. Zhi Cai Li and Yue Ying Ren; m. Chong Xin, Aug. 1, 1972; 1 child, Jian Bing. B.S., Tsinghua U., Beijing, China, 1962, M.S., 1962, Ph.D., 1965; Ph.D., U. Wis.-Madison, 1983. Mem. research staff Southwestern Inst. Physics, Leshan, Sichuan, China, 1972-79, vice head mirror div. Southwestern Inst. Physics, 1983—; vis. scientist U. Wis.-Madison, 1979-83, MIT Plasma Fusion Ctr., Cambridge, 1984—. Inventor in field. Mem. Am. Phys. Soc., Fusion Power Assocs., Am. Nuclear Soc. Current work: Plasma physics; tandem mirror; thermal barrier; high B fusion reactor engineering; MHD theory. Subspecialties: Plasma physics; Nuclear engineering. Home: Dept Physics Tsinghua U Beijing Peoples Republic of China Office: Plasma Fusion Ctr MIT 175 Albany St NW 17-125 Cambridge MA 02139

LI, YING-SING, chemistry educator; b. Kwangtung, China, July 26, 1936; came to U.S., 1963, naturalized, 1977; s. Mu-Sun and Tzu-Chun (Lin) L.; m. Jackie T.L. Tu, Dec. 30, 1968; children: Ming-Po, Ming-Lin, Ming-Way, Ming-Yen Jason. B.S., Cheng Kung U., Taiwan, 1961; Ph.D., U. Kans., 1968. Research asst. Taiwan Sugar Research Inst., 1961-63, U. Kans., Lawrence, 1963-68, Princeton U., 1968-70, U. S.C. Columbia, 1970-82; asst. prof. chemistry Memphis State U., 1982-84; assoc. prof. chemistry Memphis State U., 1984—; vis. prof. Cheng Kung U., 1975-76. Contbr. articles to profl. jours. Mem. Am. Chem. Soc., Sigma Xi, Phi Lambda Upsilon. Roman Catholic. Current Work: Molecular spectroscopy and structural chemistry. Subspecialties: Physical chemistry; Infrared spectroscopy. Office: Dept Chemistry Memphis State U Memphis TN 38152

LIANG, TEHMING, biochemist; b. Tainan, Republic of China, Apr. 14, 1945; came to U.S., 1969, naturalized, 1981; s. I-Fan and Yu-Ying (Wang) L.; m. Abby Tsu-Mei Chang, Aug. 16, 1976; 1 child, Charlene. B.S., Nat. Taiwan U., 1968; Ph.D., U. Chgo., 1973. Research assoc. U. Chgo., 1973-76, research asst. prof., 1976-77; sr. research biochemist Merck Inst, Rahway, N.J., 1977-81, research fellow, 1981—. Contbr. articles to profl. pubs. Mem. Am. Soc. Biol. Chemists, Endocrine Soc., Soc. for Neuroscis., N.Y. Acad. Scis. Current work: Actions of Peptide and steroid hormones. Subspecialties: Biochemistry (biology); Receptors. Home: 11603 SW 90th St Miami FL 33176 Office: Merck Sharp & Dohme Research Labs PO Box 2000 Rahway NJ 07065

LIANG, TOM YUAN-TONG, computer systems architect, consultant; b. Mei-Hsien, China, Aug. 7, 1943; came to U.S., 1968; s. Jing-Kuang and Hsieh-Fei (Hsiung) L.; m. Chu-Ching Wang, Aug. 11, 1974; children—Jungber, Jahming, Jengyee. B.S. in Elec. Engring., Nat. Taiwan U., 1965, M.S. in Elec. Engring., 1967; M.S. in Ops. Research, U. Calif.-Berkeley, 1977; M.Engring., UCLA, 1980; Ph.D. in Applied Math. and Stats., SUNY-Stony Brook, 1973. Cert. elec. and electronic engr., Republic of China. Various teaching positions SUNY, U. Wis., U. Calif.-Berkeley, Nat. Taiwan U., 1967-77; electronic engr. Otis, Material Handling Div., Roanoke, Va., 1975; reliability engr. Lawrence Berkeley Lab. and Xerox, Calif., 1976-79; mgr. systems integration and testing Printing Systems div. Xerox, El Segundo, Calif., 1979-80, mgr. S/W tool devel., 1981-82, systems architect, 1983-84; computer systems architect Hughes Support Systems Group, Long Beach, Calif., 1984—; cons. in field. Co-author: Electrical Machinery, 1968. Contbr. articles to tech. jours. Served to 2d lt. Army of Republic of China, 1966-67. Mem. IEEE (sr. mem.), Reliability Soc., Computer Soc., Communications Soc., Biomed. Engring. Soc., Engring. in Medicine and Biology Soc. Current work: Parallel computer architectures/algorithms, modeling/simulation/performance evaluation distributed systems and networks. Subspecialties: Computer architecture; Operations research (engineering). Office: Hughes Support Systems Group Bldg A1 MS 3C923 Long Beach CA 90810

LIAO, PAUL F(OO-HUNG), physicist; b. Phila., Nov. 10, 1944; s. Tseng Wu and Tung Mei (Lin) L.; m. Karen Ann Pravetz, Aug. 31, 1968; children: Teresa, Joanna. B.S. in Physics, M.I.T., 1966; Ph.D. in Physics, Columbia U., 1973. Research assoc. Columbia U. Radiation Lab., 1972-73; mem. tech. staff Bell Labs., Holmdel, N.J., 1973-80, head dept. quantum electronics research, 1980-83; div. mgr. physics and optical scis. research Bell Communications Research, 1984—; mem. tech. program com. Internat. Quantum Electronics Conf., 1980, tech. program co-chmn. N.Am. subcom., 1982; mem. tech. program com. Conf. on Lasers and Electro Optics, 1981-82, chmn. subcom. on laser spectroscopy, nonlinear optics and phase conjugation, 1983, 85; chmn. Gordon Conf. on Nonlinear Optics and Lasers, 1985. Contbr. numerous articles to profl. jours. and; editor: (with P.L. Kelley) Quantum Electronics series, 1981; mem. adv. bd.: CRC Handbook of Laser Science and Technology, 1982-83. Fellow IEEE. (mem. adminstrv. bd. quantitative elec. application soc.); mem. Am. Phys. Soc. (rep. to Joint Council on Quantum Electronics), Optical Soc. Am., Methodist. Club: Fair Haven (N.J.) Sailing (first officer 1980-81, chief officer 1982). Patentee in nonlinear optics, quantum electronics and laser spectroscopy. Current Work: Quantum electronics, solid state physics, laser spectroscopy. Subspecialties: Laser spectroscopy; Condensed matter physics. Office: Bell Labs Holmdel NJ 07733

LIAO, SHUEN-KUEI, immunology educator; b. Morioka, Japan, June 27, 1940; s. Lung-Sheng and Fa-Mei Liao (Hsu) L.; m. Mary Elizabeth Rumble, Sept. 23, 1972; children: May-Lynn, Nelson G-Y. B.Sc., Tunghai U., 1964; Ph.D., McMaster U., 1971. Demonstrator, fellow, histology U. Toronto, Ont., Can., 1970-73; profl. asst. Ont. Cancer Found., Hamilton, 1973-74, research assoc., 1976—; lectr. to asst. prof. McMaster U., Hamilton, 1974-80, assoc. prof. pathology, pediatrics and immunology, 1980—; mem. staff lab. medicine Henderson Gen. Hosp., Hamilton, 1974—. Contbr. numerous sci. articles to profl. publs. Danish Cancer Soc. fellow, 1970; Med. Research Council Can. grantee, 1976—; Ont. Cancer Treatment and Research Found. grantee, 1978—; Nat. cancer Inst. Can. grantee, 1981—. Mem. AAAS, Am. Assn. Cancer Research, Can. Soc. Immunology, Cancer Soc. Cell Biology, Internat. Pigment Cell. Soc., N.Y. Acad. Sci. Current Work: Work includes cancer immunology, cell biology, monoclonal antibodies, somatic genetics, and gene cloning. Subspecialties: Cancer research (medicine); Immunobiology and immunology. Office: McMaster Univ Pathology Dept Hamilton ON L8N 3Z5 Canada

LIAO, SHUTSUNG, biochemist, educator; b. Tainan, Taiwan, Jan. 1, 1931; came to U.S., 1956, naturalized, 1970; s. Chi-Chun and Chin-Shen L.; m. Shuching Kuo, Mar. 19, 1960; children: Jane Tzufen, Tzuming, May. Ph.D., U. Chgo., 1961. Asst. prof. U. Chgo., 1964-69, assoc. prof., 1969-71, prof. biochemistry/molecular biology, 1972—. Contbr. articles to profl. jours. NIH research grantee, 1965—; Am. Cancer Soc. research grantee, 1975—. Mem.

Am. Soc. Biol. Chemists, Endocrine Soc., Internat. Soc. Biochem. Endocrinolgy. Current Work: Mechanism of action of hormones, regulation of biosynthesis of proteins and nucleic acids. Subspecialties: Biochemistry (biology); Endocrinology. Home: 5632 S Woodlawn Ave Chicago IL 60637 Office: U Chgo 5841 S Maryland Ave Chicago IL 60637

LIBBY, VIBEKE, integrated circuit development scientist; b. Copenhagen, July 29, 1950; came to U.S., 1980, naturalized, 1983; d. Preben Viggo and Lis (Sorensen) Eider; m. Stephen B. Libby, Apr. 27, 1980. Candidatus scientiarum degree in physics and chem, Niels Bohr Inst., U. Copenhagen, 1981. Assoc. scientist Stone & Webster Engring Corp., Boston, 1981-82; sr. scientist Raytheon Research Div., Lexington, Mass., 1982—. Contbr. articles in nuclear engring. to publs. Bd. dirs. Women for Energy, Boston, 1981-82. Mem. Am. Nuclear Soc. Current Work: Semiconductor research: development of integrated circuit processing technology; computer-aided design; ternary logic; nuclear engineering; accident analysis, fission product transport and low level waste disposal. Subspecialties: Condensed matter physics; Integrated circuits. Home: 159 Emeline St Providence RI 02906 Office: Raytheon Research Div 131 Spring St Lexington MA 02173

LICHSTEIN, EDGAR, cardiologist; b. N.Y.C., Nov. 27, 1936; s. Joseph and Ruth (Weisner) L.; m. Marilyn Dorf, June 19, 1966; children: Adam, Amy. B.A., Columbia U., 1957; M.D., SUNY-Downstate Med. Ctr., 1961. Diplomate: Am. Bd. Internal Medicine (subspecialty cardiovascular disease). Intern Lenox Hill Hosp., N.Y.C.; resident in medicine, fellow in cardiovascular disease NYU Med. Ctr.; dir. cardiology Mt. Sinai Hosp. Services, City Hosp. Ctr., Elmhurst, N.Y., 1968-76; dir. div. cardiology Maimonides Med. Ctr., Bklyn., 1976—; chmn. heart info. com. N.Y. Heart Assn., 1979-83, chmn. council on pub. edn., 1983—. Author: Hemodynamics Reference File, 1970; contbr. articles to profl. jours. Mem. New Rochelle (N.Y.) Bd. Edn., 1976-81. Served to capt. USAF, 1966-68. Nat. Heart and Lung Inst. grantee, 1978-82. Fellow Am. Coll. Cardiology, ACP, Am. Coll. Chest Physicians, Am. Council Clin. Cardiology, N.Y. Cardiologic Soc. Jewish. Current Work: Clinical research in the field of cardiovascular medicine. Subspecialty: Cardiology.

LICHTENBERG, BYRON K., biomedical engineer, astronaut; b. Stroudsburg, Pa., Feb. 19, 1948; s. Glenn John and Georgiana (Bierei) L.; m. Roberta Lee; children—Kimberly, Kristin. Sc.B., Brown U., 1969; M.S., MIT, 1975, D.Sc., 1979. Commd. officer U.S. Air Force, 1969, advanced through grades to lt. col.; fighter pilot, 1969-72; research scientist MIT, Cambridge, Mass., 1978-84; pres. Payload Systems, Inc., 1984—. Contbr. articles to profl. publs. Trustee, Brown U., Providence, 1985—. Recipient Haley Space Flight award AIAA, 1984, Flight Achievement award AAAS, 1983, Space Medal NASA, 1984, Space Flight award VFW, 1984. Mem. Tau Beta Pi, Sigma Xi. Subspecialties: Biomedical engineering; Biomedical engineering. Office: Payload Systems Inc 47 Chrush St Wellesley MA 02181

LICHTENBERG, DON BERNETT, physics educator; b. Passaic, N.J., July 2, 1928; s. Milton and Ida (Krulewitz) L.; m. Rita Kalter, Jan. 10, 1954; children—Naomi, Rebecca. B.A., NYU, 1950; M.S., U. Ill., 1951, Ph.D., 1955. Research assoc. Ind. U., Bloomington, 1955-57; vis. prof. U. Hamburg, 1957-58; asst. prof. Mich. State U., East Lansing, 1958-61, assoc. prof., 1961-63; staff physicist Stanford U., Calif., 1962-63; assoc. prof. physics Ind. U., Bloomington, 1963-66, prof., 1966—. Author: Meson and Baryon Spectroscopy, 1965; Unitary Symmetry and Elementary Particles, 1970, 78. Contbr. articles to profl. jours. Sci. Research Council sr. fellow Oxford U., 1979. Fellow Am. Phys. Soc. Current work: theoretical particle physics. Subspecialty: Particle physics. Home: 715 S Fess St Bloomington IN 47401 Office: Dept Physics Ind U Bloomington IN 47405

LICHTMAN, MARSHALL A., physician, educator; b. N.Y.C., June 23, 1934; s. Samuel and Vera L.; m. Alice Jo Maisel, June 23, 1957; children: Susan, Joanne, Pamela. A.B., Cornell U., 1955; M.D., U. Buffalo, 1960. Resident in medicine Strong Meml. Hosp., Rochester, N.Y., 1960-63, chief resident, instr. medicine, 1965-66; USPHS postdoctoral research assoc. Sch. Public Health U. N.C., 1963-65; sr. instr., research trainee in hematology U. Rochester Sch. Medicine, 1966-67, asst. prof. medicine, spl. postdoctoral research fellow in hematology, 1968-70, assoc. prof. medicine and radiation biology, biophysics, 1971-74, prof. medicine and radiation biology and biophysics, 1974—, chief hematology unit dept. medicine, 1975—, assoc. dean acad. affairs and research, 1979, sr. assoc. dean, 1980—. Editor: Abnormalities of Granulocytes and Monocytes, 1975, Hematology for Practitioners, 1978, Hematology and Oncology, 1980; co-editor: Hermatology, 3d edit, 1983; White Cell Mechanics; Basic Science and Clinical Aspects, 1984; contbr. articles to profl jours. Leukemia Soc. Am. scholar, 1969-74; USPHS grantee, 1971—. Fellow ACP; mem. Am. Fedn. Clin. Research, AAAS, Am. Soc. Hematology, Internat. Soc. Hematology, N.Y. Acad. Scis., Am. Soc. Clin. Investigation, Assn. Am. Physicians, Am. Assn. Cancer Research, Am. Physiol. Soc., Reticuloendothelial Soc., Soc. Exptl. Biology and Medicine, Am. Soc. Cell Biology. Current Work: Research interests include physiology and biochemistry of blood cells, hemopolisis and leukemia. Subspecialties: Hematology; Physiology (medicine). Home: 138 Roby Dr Rochester NY 14618 Office: U Rochester Sch Medicine 601 Elmwood Ave Rochester NY 14642

LICHTMAN, ROBERT MARK, psychotherapist; b. Bklyn., Dec. 7, 1937; s. Jack and Matilda (Rubel) L.; m. Florence Pearl Greenstein, Dec. 14, 1958 (div. Sept. 1980); children: Ira Mark, Melissa Joy, Stewart Gordon, Jennifer Beth; m. Virginia Karla Witt, May 1, 1982. A.S. in Psychology, SUNY, N.Y.C., 1976; B.A., New Sch. Social Research, 1978, M.A., 1980; Ph.D. in Psychology, Columbia Pacific U., Calif., 1981. Cert. in behavior therapy L.I.U. Psychotherapist Nassau Hosp., Mineola, N.Y., 1977-82, cons. psychotherapist, 1982—; psychotherapist Nassau Pain & Stress Ctr., L.I., 1980—; psychologist Creedmoor Psychiat. Ctr., N.Y.C., 1982—. Mem. Psychologists for Social Responsibility, Washington, 1982. Served with U.S. Army, 1955-58. Mem. Am. Psychol. Assn. (cert. exptl. psychotherapist), Psychologists in Marital, Sex & Family Therapy, Assn. for Advancement Behavior Therapy, Am. Assn. Artist Therapists, Mensa. Current Work: Program coordinator Seven Communities Counseling Center, Queens, N.Y.; work in marital, sex and family counseling in private practice; consultant in stress management. Subspecialties: Behavioral psychology; Cognition. Home: 48-19 38th St Long Island City NY 11101 Office: The Nassau Pain & Stress Center 222 Station Plaza N Mineola NY 11501

LIDE, DAVID REYNOLDS, JR., physicist, scientific administrator; b. Gainesville, Ga., May 25, 1928; s. David Reynolds and Kate (Simmons) L.; m. Mary Ruth Lomer, Nov. 5, 1955; children: David A., Vanessa G., James H., Quentin R. B.S., Carnegie Inst. Tech., 1949; M.A., Harvard U., 1951, Ph.D., 1952. Research physicist Nat. Bur. Standards, 1954-63, chief molecular spectroscopy sect., 1963-69; dir. Office Standard Reference Data, 1969—. Author research papers on microwave and infrared spectroscopy, high temperature sci., infrared lasers and related areas; also articles. Recipient Samuel Wesley Stratton award Nat. Bur. Standards, 1968; Gold medal Dept. Commerce, 1968. Mem. Am. Phys. Soc., Internat. Council Sci. Unions. (sec. gen., com. on data for sci. and tech.), Internat. Union Pure and Applied Chemistry (pres. phys. chemistry div.), Am. Chem. Soc., AAAS. Current Work: Direct program for developing scientific and engineering data bases with aid of computer and telecommunications technology. Subspecialties: Information systems (Information science); Atomic and molecular physics. Home: 4604 Tournay Rd Bethesda MD 20816 Office: Nat Bur Standards Gaithersburg MD 20899

LIEB, ELLIOTT HERSHEL, physicist, mathematician, educator; b. Boston, July 31, 1932; s. Sinclair M. and Clara (Rosenstein) L.; m. Christiane Fellbaum; children—Alexander, Gregory. B.Sc., M.I.T., 1953; Ph.D., U. Birmingham, Eng., 1956; D.Sc.h.c., U. Copenhagen, 1979. With IBM Corp., 1960-63; sr. lectr. Fourah Bay Coll., Sierra Leone, 1961; mem. faculty Yeshiva U., 1963-66, Northeastern U., 1966-68, M.I.T., 1968-75; prof. physics, 1963-68, prof. math., 1968-73, prof. math. and physics, 1973—, Princeton U., 1975—. Author: (with D.C. Mattis) Mathematical Physics in One Dimension, 1966, (with B. Simon and A. Wightman) Studies in Mathematical Physics; also articles. Recipient Boris Pregel award chem. physics N.Y. Acad. Scis., 1970; Dannie Heineman prize for mathematical physics Am. Inst. Physics and Am. Phys. Soc., 1978; Prix Scientifique Union des Assurances de Paris, 1985. Guggenheim Found. fellow, 1972, 78. Fellow Am. Phys. Soc.; mem. Austrian Acad. Scis., Nat. Acad. Scis. Current work: Statistical physics; condensed matter physics; mathematical analysis. Subspecialties: Theoretical physics; Analysis. Office: Physics Dept Jadwin Hall Princeton U PO Box 708 Princeton NJ 08544

LIEBER, RICHARD LOUIS, medical researcher, medical educator; b. Walnut Creek, Calif., Dec. 14, 1956; s. Richard and Janet Elizabeth (Stone) L.; m. Deborah Jane Chippendale, Nov. 22, 1980; 1 child, Katelyn Suzanne. B.S., U. Calif.-Davis, 1978, Ph.D., 1982. Research assoc. U. Calif.-Davis, 1980-82; postgrad. research physiologist, U. Calif.-San Diego, 1982-85, asst. prof. surgery, 1985—; biomed. engr. VA Med. Ctr., San Diego, 1983—; cons. Mentor Corp., Mpls., Sutter Biomed., Inc., San Diego, 1983—. Contbr. articles to profl. jours. Patentee in field. Recipient Jastro-Shields award U. Calif.-Davis, 1981, Effects of Muscle Stimulation award Mentor Corp., 1983, Effects of Immobilization on Muscle, V.A., 1985. Mem. Rehab. Engr. Soc. N.Am., Orthopaedic Research Soc., IEEE, Biophys. Soc. Democrat. Current work: Study of skeletal muscle properties in normal and diseased muscles. Techniques used involve computer controlled muscle contraction and optical sensors for structure monitoring. Subspecialties: Physiology (biology); Bioinstrumentation. Home: 1624 Glasgow Ave Cardiff-by-the-Sea CA 92007 Office: Orthop Research V-151 VA Med Ctr 3350 La Jolla Village Dr San Diego CA 92161

LIEBERMAN, ALFRED GEORGE, physicist; b. Vienna, Austria, Jan. 17, 1937; came to U.S., 1939, naturalized, 1948; s. Oscar and Gertrude (Riegelhaupt) L.; m. Kari Hoihjelle, Dec. 30, 1965; children—Lisa, Lauri Anne. B.S.E.E., Poly. Inst. Bklyn., 1958; M.S.E.E., Calif. Inst. Tech., 1959, Ph.D., 1964; M.S. in Physics, U. Md., 1972. Elec. engr. ITT Labs., Nutley, N.J., 1959; fellow Hughes Aircraft Co., 1958-59, Consol. Electrodynamics Corp., 1959-60, Am.-Scandinavian Found., 1963-64; research assoc. Chalmers U., Gothenburg, Sweden, 1963-64; sr. research physicist Applied Physics Lab., Johns Hopkins U., Silver Spring, Md., 1965-68; lectr. mechanics U. Va., George Mason Coll., Fairfax, Va., 1968-71; prof. elec. engring. U. Md., College Park, 1968-73; physicist Nat. Bur. Standards, Gaithersburg, Md., 1973—; cons. Aerochem. Research Labs., Princeton, N.J., 1965, Presearch, Inc., Silver Spring, 1972; instr. math. NIH, Found. Advanced Edn., Bethesda, 1966-68; guest worker U. Oslo, U. Trondheim, Norway, 1971. Vice pres., then pres. Goshen Estates Homeowners Assn., Gaithersburg, 1977—; bd. dirs. Goshen Community Assn., 1985—. Dobbins scholar, Calif. Inst. Tech., 1958-59; fellow NASA-ASEE, 1969-70, NATO, 1971. Mem. Am. Phys. Soc., Optical Soc. Am., Sigma Xi, Eta Kappa Nu, Tau Beta Pi, Sigma Pi Sigma, Phi Kappa Phi. Current work: Ultrashort optical pulse phenomena, surface science, integrated circuit processing, plasma fusion, nuclear effects simulation and testing. Subspecialties: Theoretical physics; Optical signal processing. Home: 20804 Apollo Ln Gaithersburg MD 20879 Office: Nat Bur Standards Metrology Bldg A 117 Gaithersburg MD 20899

LIEBERMAN, DIANA DALE, biologist; b. Los Angeles, Jan. 19, 1949; d. John Edwin and Lucille Marie (Tomlin) Smith; m. Milton Eugene Lieberman, 1969; 1 child, Sarah Briseis. B.S., U. Ghana, 1976, Ph.D., 1979. Demonstrator U. Ghana, Legon, 1976-79; vis. asst. prof. U. Va., Charlottesville, 1980-81; asst. prof. U. N.D., Grand Forks, 1981—. Contbr. articles to profl. jours. AAUW fellow, 1979; grantee NSF, 1981—. Mem. Ecol. Soc. Am., Assn. for Tropical Biology, Orgn. for Tropical Studies, Sigma Xi. Current work: Population biology with special interest in population ecology and growth of tropical forest trees. Subspecialties: Population biology; Ecology (biology). Office: Dept Biology U ND Grand Forks ND 58202

LIEBERMAN, HARRIS RITCHIE, research psychologist, consultant; b. Phila., Jan. 14, 1951; s. Jacob and Miriam (Wohlburg) L.; m. Ellice Silver, June 10, 1973; children—Rachel, Daniel. A.B., Franklin and Marshall Coll., 1972; M.A., U. Fla., 1974, Ph.D., 1977. Research assoc. dept. psychology MIT, Cambridge, 1977-78, postdoctoral fellow, 1978-81, research scientist, 1981—, research assoc., dept. nutrition, 1983—, prin. investigator Clin. Research Ctr., 1983—; postdoctoral fellow psychology Harvard U., Cambridge, 1980-83. Guest editor Jour. Psychiat. Research, 1983; Contbg. editor Surgeon Gen.'s Report on Nutrition and Health; contbr. articles to profl. jours. NIH fellow, 1978-81, 73-77. Mem. Soc. for Neurosci., AAAS. Current work: Behavioral effects of foods, hormones and drugs on humans; human neuropsychology, psychophysics and electrophysiology; psychopharmacology. Subspecialties: Neuropsychology; Nutrition (medicine). Office: Dept Psychology MIT E20-1138 Cambridge MA 02139

LIEBERMAN, JOSEPH ABRAHAM, environmental engineer; b. Balt., Oct. 6, 1918; s. David and Rose (Klioze) L.; m. Rita Grace Hackerman, Jan. 6, 1946 (dec. 1975); 1 child, Richard Stuart; m. Tamar Eleanor Friedman, June 18, 1978. B.C.E., Johns Hopkins U., 1938, D. Eng., 1941. Registered profl. engr., D.C. Asst. dir. for nuclear safety AEC, Washington, 1948-68; dep. asst. adminstr. EPA, Washington, 1970-72; sr. specialist energy and environ. Congl. Research Service, Washington, 1972-73; mgr. environ. analysis Gen. Electric Co., Washington, 1973-76; v.p. Nuclear Safety Assocs., Bethesda, Md., 1976-81, now cons.; pres. OTHA, Inc., Glen Echo, Md., 1981—; cons. IAEA, Vienna, Austria, 1959-61, NEA, OECD, Paris, 1983, Nuclear Safety Assoc.; lectr. various Univs. Contbr. articles to profl. jours. Served to maj. C.E., U.S. Army, 1941-46. Decorated Bronze Star with oak leaf cluster. Mem. Am. Acad. Environ. Engrs., Sigma Xi. Jewish. Club: Johns Hopkins (Balt.). Current work: consulting engineer in environmental aspects of nuclear power; management of radioactive wastes from nuclear power generation. Subspecialties: Environmental engineering; Resource management. Home: 6605 Selkirk Dr Bethesda MD 20817 Office: OTHA Inc P O Box 686 Glen Echo MD 20812

LIEBERMAN, MILTON EUGENE, biologist, educator; b. Chgo., Aug. 30, 1934; s. Samuel Mitchell and Reva (Bernstein) L.; m. Diana Dale Smith, 1969; 1 child, Sarah Briseis. A.B., U. Calif.-Berkeley, 1962; M.S., Ariz. State U., 1966; Ph.D., U. Calif.-Irvine, 1969. Lectr. U. of Negev, Beersheva, Israel, 1970-71; asst. prof. Chapman Coll., Orange, Calif., 1972-73, West Ga. Coll., Carrollton, 1973-74; sr. lectr. U. Ghana, Legon, 1974-79; vis. prof. U. Va., Charlottesville, 1980-81; research prof. U. N.D., Grand Forks, 1981—; environ. and statis. cons. Contbr. articles to profl. jours. Recipient Rothschild award U. of Negev, 1971; Ford Found. postdoctoral fellow, 1968-69; NSF research grantee, 1981—. Mem. Ecol. Soc. Am., Assn. for Tropical Biology, Orgn. for Tropical Studies, Sigma Xi. Current work: Population and community ecology of tropical forests; plant-animal interactions; forest structure and dynamics. Subspecialties: Evolutionary biology; Ecology (biology). Office: Dept Biology Univ ND Grand Forks ND 58202

LIEBERMAN, SEYMOUR, educator; b. N.Y.C., Dec. 1, 1916; s. Samuel D. and Sadie (Levin) L.; m. Sandra Spar, June 5, 1944; 1 son, Paul B. B.S., Bklyn. Coll., 1936; M.S., U. Ill., 1937, Ph.D. (Rockefeller scholar 1939-41), Stanford U., 1941; Traveling fellow, U. Basle, Switzerland, Eidgenoess. Tech. Hochschule, Zurich, Switzerland, 1946-47. Chemist, Schering Corp., 1938-39; spl. research asso. Harvard U., 1941-45; asso. mem. Sloan-Kettering Inst., 1945-50; mem. faculty Columbia Coll. Physicians and Surgeons, N.Y.C., 1950—, prof. biochemistry, 1962—; pres. Inst. Health Scis., St. Luke's Roosevelt Hosp. Center, 1981—; mem. subcom. human applications radioactive materials N.Y.C. Health Dept.; Pfizer traveling fellow McGill U., 1968; Syntex lectr. Mexican Endocrine Soc., 1970; mem. Am. Cancer Soc. panel steroids, 1945-49, hormones, 1949-50, mem. com. pathogenesis of cancer, 1957-60; mem. endocrine study sect. NIH, 1959-63, chmn., 1963-65, mem. gen. clin. research centers, 1967-71; mem. med. adv. com. Population Council, 1961-73; mem. endocrinology panel Cancer Chemotherapy Nat. Service Center, 1958-62; cons. WHO human reprodn. unit, 1972-74, Ford Found., 1974-77. Editor: Jour. Clin. Endocrinology and Metabolism, 1963-67, editorial bd., 1958-63, 68-70, Jour. Biol. Chemistry, 1975-80; contbr. articles to profl. jours. Recipient Disting. Alumnus award Bklyn. Coll., 1971. Fellow N.Y. Acad. Scis., Nat. Acad. Scis.; mem. Am. Soc. Biol. Chemists, Am. Chem. Soc., Internat. Soc. Endocrinology (U.S. del. central com.), Endocrine Soc. (Ciba award 1952, Koch award 1970, council 1970-73, pres. 1974-75, Roussel prize 1984, Dale medal 1985), Harvey Soc. Assocs. Current Work: Steroid hormone biochemistry, endocrine biochemistry. Subspecialties: Biochemistry (medicine); Endocrinology. Home: 32-22 163d St Flushing NY 11358 Office: 630 W 168th St New York NY 10032

LIEBIG, WILLIAM JOHN, medical manufacturing company exec.; b. Huntingdon, Pa., Mar. 24, 1923; s. William A. and Gertrude L. (Schierz) L.; m. Suzanne V. King, Nov. 16, 1978; 1 dau.: Barbara. B.S., Juniata Coll., 1943; M.S., Phila. Coll. Textiles, 1949; M.B.A., NYU, 1951. Div. mgr. Susquehanna Mills, Inc., N.Y.C., 1949-54; gen. mgr. Meadox Weaving Co., Waldwick, N.J., 1954-55; pres. Dormeyer Sales Corp., Haledon, N.J., 1955-60; div. sales mgr. Webcor, Inc., Mt. Vernon, N.Y., 1955-60, Camfield, Inc., Mt. Vernon, 1955-60; pres., chief exec. officer Meadox Meds., Inc., Oakland, N.J., 1961—; v.p., dir. Huntingdon Throwing Mills, Mifflinburg, Pa., 1967—; pres., dir. Meadox (U.K.) Ltd., Eng., 1978—; dir. Surgimed, A/S, Denmark, Surgimed, Inc., Meadox France, Meadox do Brasil; chmn. Liebig Found. Contbr. articles to profl. jours. Pres. Harrington Park (N.J.) Bd. Edn., 1957-65; chmn. Tri-County Com. on I287 Alignment, 1965-73. Served with USAAF, 1942-45. Decorated Air medal with 3 oak leaf clusters, D.F.C., Presdl. citation with oak leaf cluster. Mem. Assn. Advancement Med. Instrumentation, Health Industry Mfg. Assn., Asia Soc., Alumni Assn. NYU, Phi Beta Kappa. Lodge: Masons. Subspecialties: Biomedical engineering; Medical instrumentation. Office: 103 Bauer Dr Oakland NJ 07436

LIEBMAN, JON CHARLES, civil engineer, educator; b. Cin., Sept. 10, 1934; s. J. Charles and Joan (Heineman) L.; m. Judith Rae Stenzel, Dec. 27, 1958; children: Christopher Brian, Rebecca Anne, Michael Jon. B.S., U. Colo., Boulder, 1956; M.S., Cornell U., Ithaca, N.Y., 1963, Ph.D., 1965. Asst. prof., then asso. prof. Johns Hopkins U., Balt., 1965-72; prof. civil engring. U. Ill., Urbana, 1972—, head dept., 1978-84. Served from ensign to lt. USN, 1956-61. Mem. Am. Soc. Engring. Edn. (Western Electric Fund award 1969), ASCE, Assn. Environ. Engring. Profs. (dir. 1980-82), Ops. Research Soc. Am. Subspecialties: Environmental engineering; Operations research (engineering). Office: Newmark Lab 208 N Romine St Urbana IL 61801

LIEBOVITCH, LARRY S., scientist; b. N.Y.C.; s. Harry and Florence Ruth (Grossman) L. B.S. in Physics, CCNY, 1972; A.M. in Astronomy, Harvard U., 1973, Ph.D. in Astronomy, 1978. Postdoctoral fellow Mt. Sinai Sch. Medicine, N.Y.C., 1978-79; postdoctoral fellow in ophthalmology Coll. Physicians and Surgeons, Columbia U., N.Y.C., 1979-82, research scientist, 1982—. Contbr. articles to profl. jours. Mem. Am. Astron. Soc., Assn. Research in Vision and Ophthalmology, N.Y. Acad. Sci., Internat. Soc. for Eye Research, AAAS. Current work: How cells and epithelia transport ions and fluid. Subspecialties: Theoretical astrophysics; Physiology (biology). Office: Eye Research Columbia U 630 W 168th St New York NY 10032

LIENHART, DAVID ARTHUR, engineering geologist; b. Cin., Sept. 28, 1939; s. Arthur Carl and Grace Hilda (Burger) L.; m. Donna Paula Klosterman, June 12, 1964; children—Devin Scott, Dana Ann. B.A., U. Cin., 1961, M.S., 1964. Petrographer Ohio River Div. Lab., Cin., 1964-70, staff geologist, 1970-76, lab. dir., supervising geologist, 1976—. Contbr. articles to profl. jours. Patentee strain controlled direct shear device for rock. Agy. chmn. Combined Fed. Campaign, Cin., 1980-84. Fellow Geol. Soc. Am.; mem. Assn. Engring. Geologists, ASTM, Internat. Soc. Rock Mechanics, Soc. Mining Engrs. AIME, Sigma Xi, Sigma Gamma Epsilon. Current work: Delineation of physical and chemical weathering phenomena and application to prediction of weathering durability of construction materials. Subspecialties: Geology; Remote sensing (geoscience). Office: Ohio River Div Lab PO Box 27168 Cincinnati OH 45227

LIENKAEMPER, JAMES JULIUS, geophysicist, earthquake researcher; b. Barstow, Calif., Feb. 11, 1953; s. James Julius and Frances Wilson (Long) L.; m. Valerie Bernadette Hooper, Aug. 14, 1977. B.A. in Geology, U. Calif.-Berkeley, 1976, M.S. in Geol. Engring., 1977. Geophysicist, U.S. Geol. Survey, Menlo Park, Calif., 1978—. Contbr. articles to profl. jours. Mem. Am. Geophys. Union, Am. Seismol. Soc., Geol. Soc. Am. Current work: Geological and geophysical observation of late-Quaternary faulting processes. Subspecialties: Tectonics; Geophysics. Office: Mailstop 977 US Geol Survey 345 Middlefield Rd Menlo Park CA 94025

LIEPMANN, HANS WOLFGANG, aeronautics educator, researcher; b. Berlin, Germany, July 3, 1914; came to U.S., 1939; s. Wilhelm and Emma (Leser) L.; m. Kate Kaschinsky, June 29, 1939; m. Dietlind Goldschmidt, Sept. 27, 1954; children—Till W., Dorian. Ph.D., U. Zurich, 1938. Research fellow U. Zurich, 1938-39; research fellow Calif. Inst. Tech., Pasadena, 1939-45, asst. prof. aeros., 1945-46, assoc. prof., 1946-49, prof., 1949-76, Charles Lee Powell prof. fluid mechanics and thermodynamics, 1976-83, Theodore von Karman prof. aeros., 1983-85, emeritus, 1985—, dir. Grad. Aero. Labs., 1972-85. Author: (with A. Puckett) Introduction to Aerodynamics of a Compressible Fluid, 1947; (with A. Roshko) Elements of Gasdynamics, 1957. Recipient Physics prize U. Zurich, 1939; Worchester Reed Warner medal ASME, 1969, Fluids Engring. award, 1984; Fluid Dynamics prize Am. Phys. Soc., 1980. Fellow Am. Acad. Arts & Scis., Am. Phys. Soc., Indian Acad. Scis. (hon.), AIAA (hon.); mem. Nat. Acad. Scis., Nat. Acad. Engring. Current works: Laminar instability, transition, turbulence, shock wave boundary layer interaction, rarefied gasdynamics, chemical reactions in turbulent mixing, fluid mechanics of helium II. Subspecialties: Aeronautical engineering; Fluid mechanics. Office: Calif Inst Tech Pasadena CA 91125

LIGHT, ALAN RAY, neurophysiologist, educator; b. Tulsa, Mar. 22, 1950; s. Raymond Edmund and Zenobia Rose (Ogle) L.; m. Kathleen C., Dec. 22, 1972. B.A., Hamilton Coll., 1972; Ph.D., SUNY-Syracuse, 1976. Research asst. SUNY-Syracuse, 1972-76; State of N.Y. Research Found. fellow U.N.C., Chapel Hill, 1976-77, research instr. dept. physiology, 1977-79, research asst.prof., 1979—, asst. prof., 1982—. Mem. Soc. for Neurosci. Current Work: Researcher in pain systems and descending control of pain. Subspecialties: Neurobiology; Neurophysiology. Office: U NC Dept Physiology 51 Med Research Bldg 2064 Chapel Hill NC 27514

LIGHT, ALBERT, biochemistry educator, researcher; b. Bklyn., June 19, 1927; s. David and Sarah (Edinoff) L.; m. Tobia L. Lipsher, May 18, 1952; children—Pamela S., Audrey L. B.S. in Chemistry, CCNY, 1948; Ph.D., Yale U., 1955; postdoctoral student Cornell U. Med. Sch., 1955-57. Research instr. U. Utah, 1957-59, asst. research instr., 1959-63; assoc. prof. biochemistry UCLA, 1963-65; assoc. prof. chemistry Purdue U., West Lafayette, Ind., 1965-77, prof., 1977—, head div. biochemistry, 1978-82; vis. scientist NIH, 1972; cons. duPont, 1983, Eli Lilly, 1983-84. Author: Proteins-Structure and Function, 1974. Mem. editorial bd. Jour. Biol. Chemistry, 1982—, Analytical Biochemistry, 1984—. Contbr. articles to sci. jours. Bd. dirs. Ind. Civil Liberties Union, ACLU, 1981-82. NSF research grantee, 1971-74; NIH USPHS research grantee, 1965-83. Mem. Am. Chem. Soc., Am. Soc. Biol. Scis., AAAS. Club: Lafayette Sailing (bd. govs. 1984—). Current work: Protein chemistry and enzymology; protein folding; relationship of structure to function of biologically active proteins. Subspecialties: Biochemistry (medicine); Biochemistry (biology). Home: 2307 Carmel Dr West Lafayette IN 47906 Office: Dept Chemistry Purdue Univ West Lafayette IN 47907

LIGHT, JOHN C., chemistry educator; b. Mt. Vernon, N.Y., Nov. 24, 1934; B.A. with honors, Oberlin Coll., 1956; Ph.D., Harvard U., 1960. Research assoc. U. Libre de Bruxelles, 1959-61; instr. dept. chemistry and James Franck Inst., U. Chgo., 1961-63, asst. prof., 1963-66, assoc. prof., 1966-70, prof. chemistry, 1970—, dir. Materials Research Lab., 1970-73; cons. Inst. Def. Analysis, 1962-65, IBM Research Labs., San Jose, Calif., 1975, Lawrence Livermore Lab., 1979—; vis. prof. Yale U., 1968; research assoc. Argonne Nat. Lab., 1975-80; vis. scientist U. Colo., Boulder, 1976-77; adv. bd. Petroleum Research Fund, 1981—. Editor: Jour. Chem. Physics, 1983—. NSF fellow; Alfred P. Sloan Found. fellow. Am. Phys. Soc.; mem. AAAS, Phi Beta Kappa, Sigma Xi. Subspecialties: Theoretical chemistry; Physical chemistry. Home: 1034 E 49th St Chicago IL 60615 Office: James Franck Inst U Chgo 5640 S Ellis Ave Chicago IL 60637

LIGHT, THOMAS DALE, geologist; b. Dayton, Ohio, Oct. 27, 1947; s. Paul J. and Ruth V. (Lang) L.; m. Frances M. Lang, Dec. 29, 1976. B.S., Bowling Green U., 1969; M.S., No. Ariz. U., 1976. Geologist, U.S. Geol. Survey, Denver, 1981—. Mem. Geol. Soc. Am., Assn. Exploration Geochemists, Soc. Econ. Geologists, Mineralogical Assn. Can. Current work: Research on the geochemistry of mineralized systems; use of trace-element distributions and associations to determine the potential for buried mineral deposits. Subspecialties: Geochemistry; Geology. Home: 3178 29th St Boulder CO 80301 Office: US Geol Survey PO Box 25046 MS 955 Denver Fed Ctr Denver CO 80225

LIGHTY, ROBIN GREG, geology educator; b. Harrisburg, Pa., Nov. 13, 1951; s. Raymond Greek and Dorothy Louise (Pinkerton) L.; m. Kathe Ann Wege, Apr. 30, 1977. B.S. with honors, Fla. Atlantic U., 1975; M.S. in Geology, Duke U., 1977; Ph.D. in Geology, U. N.C., 1985. Field geologist Chevron Resources Co., Denver, 1977; geol. con. Cities Service Co., Belize and Bahamas, 1980; research geologist, Tulsa, Okla., 1980-83; asst. prof. dept. geology Tex. A&M U., College Station, Tex., 1983—, dir. Ctr. for Tropical Marine Research, 1984—. Author: International Reef Symposium Procs., 1977, 83; contbr. articles to profl. jours. Vis. research fellow, Smithsonian Instn., 1976. Mem. Geol. Soc. Am., Am. Assn. Petroleum Geologists, Soc. Econ. Paleontologists and Mineralogists, Internat. Assn. Sedimentologists, Internat. Soc. Reef Studies, Am. Geophys. Union, AAAS, Sigma Xi. Current work: Modern and ancient reefs; sea level history; geology of ooid shoals; submarine cement diagenesis; marine geology of Caribbean petroleum exploration in carbonates rocks. Subspecialties: Sedimentology; Oceanography. Office: Ctr Tropical Marine Research Box E College Station TX 77841

LIGLER, GEORGE TODD, computer graphics co. exec.; b. Gary, Ind., Oct. 4, 1949; s. George Edward and Audrey (Anderle) L.; m. Frances Hart Smith, Aug. 19, 1972; 1 dau., Amy. B.S., Furman U., 1971; M.Sc., Oxford (Eng.) U., 1973, D.Phil., 1975. Asst. prof. U. Tex.-San Antonio, 1975-76; research mgr. Tex. Instruments, Dallas, 1976-80; dep. gen. mgr. Burroughs Corp., Paoli, Pa., 1980-82; pres. Aydin Controls, Ft. Washington, Pa., 1982—; cons. in field; panel chmn. Air Force Studies Bd., Washington, 1981. Rhodes scholar, 1971; Woodrow Wilson fellow, 1971; named to Furman U. Hall of Fame, 1979. Mem. IEEE, Assn. Computing Machinery, Am. Assn. Rhodes Scholars, Am. Trust for Wolfson Coll. (v.p., trustee). Republican. Presbyterian. Current Work: Design, marketing and manufacturing of computer graphics workstations, display generators, high resolution color monitors. Subspecialties: Graphics, image processing, and pattern recognition; Software engineering. Home: 606 Kilburn Rd Wilmington DE 19803 Office: 401 Commerce Dr Fort Washington PA 19034

LIGOMENIDES, PANOS ARISTIDES, electrical engineering educator, consultant; b. Pireus, Greece, Apr. 3, 1928; came to U.S., 1955, naturalized, 1966; s. Aristides and Sonia (Akritides) L.; m. Danae P. Tsarmaklis, Dec. 29, 1973; 1 child, Katerina. B.Sc., U. Athens (Greece), 1951, spl. grad. degree, 1952; M.Sc., Stanford U., 1956, Ph.D., 1958. Prof. San Jose State U., Calif., 1959-61; prof. Santa Clara U., Calif., 1961-64; research staff engr. IBM, San Jose, 1958-64; asst. prof. UCLA, 1964-69; adj. prof. Stanford U., Calif., 1969-71; disting. prof. U. Md., College Park, 1971—; cons. IBM, 1964-69, Control Data Corp., Athens, 1971-74, Greek Govt., Athens, 1969-73. Author: Information Processing Machines, 1969; contbg. Author: Computers: Applications in Industry and Management, 1981; Management and Office Information Systems, 1984; also articles; patentee. Served to lt. Greek Navy, 1952-54. Recipient OECD fellow, 1965, 74; Ford Found. fellow, 1966-68; Fulbright Found. awardee: 1970-71; Salzburg Sem. fellow, 1971; Outstanding Educator Am. award, 1973. Sr. mem. IEEE. Democrat. Current work: Goal-seeking, computer based, cybernetic systems; computer architectures, microcomputers, intelligent machines, VLSI systems. Subspecialties: Artificial intelligence; Information systems, storage, and retrieval (computer science). Home: 8802 Magnolia Dr Lanham MD 20706 Office: U Md Elec Engring Dept College Park MD 20742

LILES, CLIFTON ROY, systems analyst, software designer; b. San Antonio, Jan. 28, 1944; s. Roy Clifton and Lucy Mae (Grier) L. B.S. in Physics, U. Houston, 1974. Software design engr. Tex. Instruments, Dallas, 1978-82, systems engring. analyst, 1982—. Served with U.S. Army, 1967-71. Mem. IEEE, Assn. for Computing Machinery, Am. Geophys. Union, AAAS, Brit. Interplanetary Soc. Current work: Digital signal processing. Subspecialty: Graphics, image processing, and pattern recognition. Home: 1517 N Waterview Richardson TX 75080 Office: Tex Instruments PO Box 22615 Dallas TX 75266

LILJE, KARL DAVID, mech. engr., educator, cons.; b. Scranton, Pa., Aug. 10, 1935; s. Ralph Waldo and Helen Rhoda (Ball) L.; m. Ann Marie Victoria, Nov. 6, 1960; children: Anneliese, Erik. B.S.M.E., Pa. State U., 1957; M.S.M.E., N.Y.U., 1960. Registered profl. engr., Ohio. Instr. in mech. engring. N.Y.U., 1957-60; mfg. engr. Westinghouse Electric Corp., Columbus, Ohio, 1960-63; opto-mech. engr. Kollmorgen Corp., Northampton, Mass., 1963-65; sr. opto-mech. engr. Eastman Kodak Co., Rochester, N.Y., 1965-71; sr.mech. engr. Cogar Corp., Hopewell Junction, N.Y., 1971-72; cons. mech. engring., Sharon, Conn., 1972-76; sr. opto-mech. engr. Perkin Elmer Corp., Danbury, Conn., 1976-81; assoc. prof. engring. tech. Calif. Poly. State U., San Luis Obispo, 1981—; cons. opto-mechanics Perkin Elmer, 1981—. Mem. ASME, Am. Soc. Elec. Engrs. Inventor safety interlock for high-speed centrifuges; co-inventor tape controlled memory clip sorting machine. Current Work: Teaching applied machine design, mechanisms, dynamics, statics, descriptive geometry, sr. design projects. Subspecialties: Mechanical engineering; Opto-mechanics consulting. Home: 251 Del Mar Ct San Luis Obispo CA 93401 Office: Dept Engring Tech Calif Poly State U San Luis Obispo CA 93407

LILLEHOJ, HYUN SOON, immunologist, researcher; b. Seoul, Mar. 1, 1949; came to U.S., 1969, naturalized, 1981; d. Chung H. Kwan; m. Erik P. Lillehoj, June 23, 1980; children—Sylvia, Peter. B.S., U. Hartford, 1974; M.S., U. Conn., 1976; Ph.D., Wayne State U., 1979. Research assoc. Wayne State U., Detroit, 1979-81; staff fellow NIH Lab. Immunology, Bethesda, Md., 1981-84; microbiologist Animal Parasitology Inst., Agrl. Research Service, U.S. Dept. Agr. Beltsville, Md., 1984—. Contbr. articles to profl. jours. Mem. Am. Soc. Immunologists, Helminth Soc., Am. Soc. Microbiologists. Current work: Immunology of avian coccidiosis (parasites). Subspecialty: Immunology (agriculture). Office: USDA ARS API BARC-East Beltsville MD 20705

LILLYWHITE, MALCOLM ALDEN, thermophysical scientist, educator; b. Washington, June 7, 1940; s. Benjamin Alden and Leah (Plowman) L.; m. Lynda Knobloch, May 25, 1979. B.S. in Physics, Coll. William and Mary, 1963; Ph.D., U. Calif., 1970. Registered thermophys. scientist. Physicist NASA-Langly Space Ctr., Hampton, Va., 1958-62; sr. physicist Slumberger Oil Co., Washington, 1964-67; chief engr., supr. Thermophysics Lab., Martin Marietta Corp., Denver, 1967-72; dir. Domestic Tech. Inst., Denver, 1973-80; pres. Domestic Tech. Internat., Inc., Denver, 1982—; prof. tech. mgmt. Grad. Sch. Internat. Studies, U. Denver, 1982—. Author: Solar Simulation Technology, 1967, Thermophysical Properties Handbook, 1968, Passive Solar Greenhouse Design, 1983; contbr. articles to profl. publs. Bd. dirs. Nat. Gasohol Comm., Lincoln, Nebr., 1978-81; chmn. passive solar tax credits com. Internat. Solar Energy Soc., Denver, 1980—. Recipient George Washington Meml. Engring. award Va. Acad. Scis., 1959. Mem. AIAA, IEEE, ASTM, Internat. Solar Energy Soc., Inst. Environ. Scis. Current Work: Third World food and energy technology development; small scale industry decentralized food and energy production; rural techno-economic development; technical manpower development and training; renewable energy technology. Subspecialties: Food science and technology; Solar energy. Office: Domestic Technology International Inc 6726 S Happy Hill Rd Evergreen CO 80439

LIM, CHUN BIN, imaging scientist; b. Seoul, Korea, Feb. 15, 1941; came to U.S., 1966; s. Young-Soon and Ok Nam (Kim) L.; m. Hyang Hy Oh, Dec. 22, 1967; children—Sandra Lim, Grace Lim. B.S., Seoul Nat. U., 1966; M.S., U. Calif.-Berkeley, 1969, Ph.D. in Nuclear Engring., 1972. Asst. prof. U. Calif.-San Francisco, 1974-78; research group leader Searle Diagnostics, Des Plaines, Ill., 1978-79; sr. scientist EMI Med., Northbrook, Ill., 1979-80; group leader Siemens Gammasonics, Des Plaines, 1980-81; dir. nuclear tech. Technicare, Solon, Ohio, 1982—, v.p. nuclear engring., 1984—; lectr. in field. Contbr. articles to profl. jours. Mem. IEEE, Soc. Nuclear Medicine, Am. Nuclear Soc. Current work: Medical diagnostic application of nuclear instrumentation; imaging physics, nuclear engineering for 3D imaging of radioisotopes for SPECT and PET. Subspecialties: PET scan; CAT scan. Home: 5251 Cheswick Dr Solon OH 44139 Office: Technicare Corp 29100 Aurora Rd Solon OH 44139

LIM, DAVID JONG JAI, otolaryngology researcher, educator; b. Seoul, Nov. 27, 1935; s. Yang Sup and Cha Nang (Yoo) L.; m. Young Sook, May 14, 1966; children—Michael, Robert. A.B., Yonsei U., 1955, M.D., 1960. Intern, resident in otolaryngology Nat. Med. Center, Seoul, 1960-64; research assoc. dept. otolaryngology Med. Coll. Ohio State U., Columbus, 1965-67, asst. prof., 1967-71, assoc. prof., 1971-76, prof., 1976—, prof. dept. anatomy, 1977—; dir. Otological Research Labs., dept. otolaryngology, 1967—. Bd. dirs. Deafness Research Found.; mem. nat. adv. neurol. and communicative disorders and stroke council NIH, 1979-83. Fogarty fellow, 1982; Mem. Am. Acad. Ophoathalomology and otolaryngology (Gold award 1972), Am. Acd. Otolaryngology (Merit award 1978), Am. Laryngological, Rhinological and Otological Soc., Assn. Research in Otolaryngology (pres. 1976-77, editor historian 1980—), Collegium Oto-rhinolarynolgoicim Amicitiae Sacrum, Centurions of Deafness Research Found. Club: Contientnal Athletic. Contbr. articles to profl. jours. Current work: Otopathology and electron microscopy, immunology, immuno-cyto-chemistry and microbiology of the ear. Subspecialties: Otorhinolaryngology; Morphology. Office: 456 Clinic Dr Columbus OH 43210

LIM, EDWARD CHOL, chemistry educator; b. Seoul, Nov. 17, 1932, came to U.S., 1952, naturalized, 1965; s. Kwang Un and Chang Soon (Kim) L.; m. Bee Tuan Uy, June 23, 1958; children—Diane Marie, Janice Catherine. B.S., St. Procopius Coll., 1954; M.S., Okla. State. U., 1957, Ph.D., 1959. Instr. chemistry Loyola U., Chgo., 1959-61, asst. prof., 1961-63, assoc. prof., 1963-66, prof., 1966-68; prof. chemistry Wayne State U., Detroit, Mich., 1968—, head dept. phys. chemistry, 1977—. Editor: Excited States, 1974—. Mem. Am. Chem. Soc., Am. Phys. Soc., Sigma Xi. Presbyterian. Current work: Excited-state dynamics and energetics; electronic and vibrational relaxations; molecular electronic spectroscopy. Subspecialty: Physical chemistry. Home: 28758 Oak Point Dr Farmington Hills MI 48018 Office: 75 Chemistry Wayne State U Detroit MI 48202

LIM, TECK-KAH, physics educator, consultant; b. Malacca, Malaysia, Dec. 1, 1942; came to U.S., 1968; S. Chin-Toh and Siew-Leng (Sim) L.; m. Nyok-Kheng Liew, Jan. 28, 1966; children—Kian-Tat, Ai-Li. B.S. with honors, U. Adelaide (South Australia), 1965, Ph.D., 1968. Lectr., U. Malaya, Malaysia, 1968; research assoc. Fla. State U., Tallahassee, 1968-70; asst. prof. physics Drexel U., Phila., 1970-75, assoc. prof., 1975-82, prof., 1982—; referee NSF, Phys. Rev. A., Phys. Rev. C., Phys. Rev. Letters, J. Chem. Phys., Theochem; organizer Symposium on Few-Body Problems, Nanning, P.R.C., 1985. Contbr. articles to physics jours.; editor: Procs. of Symposium on Few-Body Problems, 1985. Pres., Chinese Sch. of Greater Phila., 1980; chmn. Chinese Schs. Conf. northeast U.S., Phila., 1980; mem.-at-large Penn Valley Elem. Sch., 1973; vol. United Way, Phila., 1984. Recipient Legion of Honor Chapel of Four Chaplains, 1982; von Humboldt fellow, 1980; NSF grantee, 1978—. Mem. Am. Phys. Soc., Acad. of Sci. at Phila. (bd. govs. 1978-82), Sigma Xi. Democrat. Club: Lower Merion Aquatic (publicity officer 1980) (Ardmore, Pa.). Subspecialties: Atomic and molecular physics; Theoretical physics. Office: Drexel U 32d and Chestnut Sts Philadelphia PA 19104

LIM, TEONG CHENG, engineering manager; b. Penang, Malaysia, Oct. 4, 1939; came to U.S., 1970; s. Joo-Thye and Quee-Sim (Goh) L.; m. Liliane Chang, June 18, 1966; 1 child, Cliff Shiao. B.Sc. Eng., Nat. Taiwan U., 1963; M.Sc., Ottawa U., 1964; Ph.D., McGill U., 1968; M.B.A., Pepperdine U., 1982. Mgr., Rockwell Research & Devel. Dept., Thousand Oaks, Calif., 1970-83; pres. Amerasia Technology, Westlake Village, Calif., 1984—; cons. in field. Contbr. articles to profl. jours. NRC fellow, 1966-70, studentship, 1966-68. Mem. IEEE (sr.), Soc. for Info. Display. Republican. Roman Catholic. Current work: Device physics, radar signal processing, oscillator and frequency synthesizer and electro luminiscent displays Subspecialties: Microelectronics; Integrated circuits. Home: 368 Venus St Thousand Oaks CA 91360 Office: Amerasia Tech Inc 2239 Townsgate Suite 208 Westlake Village CA 91360

LIN, CHIEN-CHANG, chemist; b. Hsinchu, Taiwan, Republic of China, Feb. 28, 1937; s. Fu-lo and Pao (Chi) L.; m. Jing Jan, Aug. 19, 1967; children—Kelly M., Arthur M., Eunice M. B.S. in Chem. Engring., Tunghai U., Taiwan, Republic of China, 1959; Ph.D. in Chemistry, U. N.Mex., 1968. Research asst. Tsinghua U., Taiwan, Republic of China, 1961-63; postdoctoral research assoc. Washington U., St. Louis, 1967-70; tech. leader Gen. Electric Co., San Jose, Calif., 1971—. Mem. Am. Chem. Soc., Sigma Xi. Current work: Nuclear power reactor chemistry; nuclear and radiochemistry; radiochemical analysis; radiological technology; water treatment. Subspecialties: Nuclear chemistry; Physical chemistry. Home: 4683 Northdale Dr Fremont CA 94536 Office: Gen Electric Co Vallecitos Nuclear Ctr Pleasanton CA 94566

LIN, CHINLON, electronic engr., optical scientist; b. Taiwan, Jan 19, 1945; came to U.S., 1968; s. Bing-Chuan and Shiao-Chi (Tsang) L.; m. Helen C. L., Aug. 10, 1969. B.S., Taiwan U., Taipei, 1967; M.S., U. Ill., 1970; Ph.D., U. Calif.-Berkeley, 1973. Mem. tech. staff Bell Labs., Holmdel, N.J., 1974—; research asst. Electronics Research Labs. U. Calif., 1970-73. Contbr. articles to profl. jours. Recipient Electronics Premium award Inst. Elec. Engrs. London, 1980. Mem. IEEE, Optical Soc. Am. (topical advisor on fiber and integrated optics). Patentee in field. Current Work: Optical electronics and fiber optics; optical fiber communication, laser technology, electro-optical engring. Subspecialties: Fiber optics; Laser technology. Office: Bell Labs Holmdel NJ 07733

LIN, CHIU-HONG, chemist; b. Pingtung, Taiwan, Nov. 25, 1934; s. Chang and Yao-Mei (Su) L.; m. Alice H. Yang, July 3, 1965; children—Emily H., Janet H. B.S., Nat. Taiwan U., Taipei, 1957, M.S., 1960; Ph.D., U. Chgo., 1968. Research assoc. Ben May Lab. for Cancer Research, U. Chgo., 1968-72, asst. prof., research assoc., 1971-72; sr. research scientist Upjohn Co., Kalamazoo, 1973—. Patentee in field of prostaglandins. Mem. Am. Chem. Soc., Sigma Xi. Current work: Synthetic work involves molecules of biological interest, mostly via organic syntheses. Subspecialties: Organic chemistry; Synthetic chemistry. Home: 3720 Pinetree Terr Portage MI 49002 Office: Upjohn Co Henrietta St Kalamazoo MI 49001

LIN, CHUN CHIA, research physicist, educator; b. Canton, China, Mar. 7, 1930; s. Yue Hang Lam and Kin Ng. B.S., U. Calif.-Berkeley, 1951; M.A., 1952; Ph.D., Harvard U., 1955. Asst. prof. physics U. Okla., Norman, 1955-59, assoc. prof. physics, 1959-63, prof. physics, 1963-68, U. Wis., Madison, 1968—; cons., univ. retainee Tex. Instruments Inc., 1960-68; cons. Sandia Labs., 1976-81; sec. Gaseous Electronics Conf., 1972-73. Contbr.: sci. research articles to publs. including Jour. Chemical Physics, Phys. Rev. Sloan Found. fellow, 1962-66; research grantee NSF and Air Force Office Sci. Research. Fellow Am. Phys. Soc. (sec. div. electron and atomic physics 1974-77). Current Work: Atomic and molecular collision processes; radiation of atoms and molecules excited by electron impact and laser irradiation; electronic energy band theory of crystalline solids, impurity atoms in solids, amorphous solids. Subspecialties: Atomic and molecular physics; Condensed matter physics. Home: 1652 Monroe St Apt C Madison WI 53711 Office: Dept Physics Univ Wis Madison WI 53706

LIN, HEH-SEN, elec. engr., biomed. product researcher; b. China, Jan. 3, 1942; came to U.S., 1966, naturalized, 1975; s. Chao-Yuan and Shu-Ying (Shea) L.; m. Alice Ko-Chien Ho, June 8, 1968; children: Andrew Li-Shing, David Li-Wen. Ph.D. in Elec. Engring, Case-Western Res. U., 1968. Project mgr. LFE Corp., Waltham, Mass., 1970-75; sr. staff mem. Medtronic Inc., Mpls., 1975-77; elec. engring. mgr. Edwards Pacemaker div. Am. Hosp. Supply Corp., Los Angeles, 1977-80; mgr. ELA Med. Co., Paris, 1980-82; founder, pres. Lin & Co., Los Angeles, 1982—; assoc. prof. elec. engring. dept. U. Minn., Mpls., 1975-76; cons. on Chinese trade and biomed. products. Contbr. articles to profl. jours. Mem. Pres. Reagan's Task Force. Served as lt. Chinese Air Force, 1965-66. NSF scholar, 1970-73. Mem. IEEE. Patentee pacemaker field. Current Work: Implantable pacemakers in cardiology field; pacemaker, cardiology, EKG,biomaterials. Subspecialty: Biomedical engineering. Office: Lin & Co Los Angeles CA

LIN, HSIU-SAN, cell biologist, radiation oncologist; b. Nagoya, Japan, Mar. 15, 1935; came to U.S., 1962, naturalized, 1976; s. Mao-Sung and Tao L.; m. Su-Chiung Chen, Sept. 22, 1962; children: Kenneth, Bertha, Michael. M.D., Nat. Taiwan U., 1960; Ph.D., U. Chgo., 1968. Cert. Am. Bd. Radiology, 1982. Intern Cook County Hosp., Chgo., 1962-63; resident in internal medicine, 1963-64; resident in therapeutic radiology Mallinckrodt Inst. Radiology, St. Louis, 1979-81; asst. prof. radiology Washington U., St. Louis, 1971-76, assoc. prof., 1976-84, prof., 1984—; vis. scientist U. Oxford, Eng., 1977-78. Cons. editor: Jour. Reticuloendothelial Soc, 1982—; contbr. articles to profl. jours. Recipient Research Career Devel. award NIH, 1974-79. Mem. Am. Soc. Microbiology, Am. Assn. Cancer Research, Reticuloendothelial Soc. Current Work: Differentiation of mononuclear phagocytes. Subspecialties: Cell biology (medicine); Radiology. Office: 510 S Kingshighway Saint Louis MO 63110

LIN, JAMES C., electrical and biomedical engineer, educator; b. Seoul, Korea, Dec. 29, 1942; came to U.S., 1962; m. Mei Fei, Mar. 21, 1970; children—Janet, Theodore, Erik. B.S., U. Wash.-Seattle, 1966, M.S., 1968, Ph.D., 1971. Asst. prof. U. Wash., 1971-74; prof. Wayne State U., Detroit, 1974-80; prof. elec. engring, physiology and biophysics U. Ill.-Chgo., 1980—, prof., head dept. bioengring., 1980—, prof., dir. Robotics and Automation Labs., 1982—; mem. com. Diagnostic Radiology NIH, Washington, 1981—; panelist NSF Presdl. Young Investigator award, Washington, 1984. Author: Microwave Auditory Effects and Applications, 1978. Contbr. over 100 articles to profl. jours. Recipient Nat. Research Services award USPHS, 1982. Mem. Biomed. Engring. Soc., Robotics Internat., Bioelectromagnetics Soc. (bd. dirs. 1979—), IEEE (se.). Current work: Electromagnetic imaging, biomedical instrumentation and measurement, microprocessor-based instrumentation, microwave biological effects, computer aided vision, non-visual sensory information processing. Subspecialties: Biomedical engineering; Electrical engineering. Office: U Ill Dept Bioengring Box 4348 Chicago IL 60680

LIN, JU-CHUI, chemist, consultant; b. Taoyuan, Taiwan, Apr. 25, 1947; came to U.S., 1974; s. Pai-Liang and Mai (Wang) L.; m. Jing-Fang Wang, Dec. 24, 1975. B.S. in Chemistry, Nat. Taiwan Normal U., 1972; M.S. in Chemistry, Southwest Tex. State U., 1977; Ph.D. in Macromolecular Sci., Case Western Res. U., 1985. Tchr. Taipei Gimmei Jr. High Sch., Taiwan, 1971-73; lab. instr. Nat. Central U., Chungli, Taiwan, 1973-74; cons. Polytronics Inc., Cleve., 1983-85; chemist Sohio Research Ctr., Warrensville Heights, Ohio, 1983, DPJ Research Ctr., SCM Corp., Strongsville, Ohio, 1984—; Author youth sci. books Youth Ency., 1970; also papers in field. Inventor in field of resin and coating composition. Mem. Am. Chem. Soc., Soc. Plastics Engring. Current work: Monomer and polymer synthesis; characterizations; catalysts; solution thermodynamics; polymers for electronics; polymer morphology; electrical properties of polymers; high solids coatings; powder coatings; electrodepositions. Subspecialties: Polymer chemistry; Polymer physics. Office: DPJ Research Ctr SCM Corp 16651 Sprague Rd Strongsville OH 44136

LIN, KENNETH SHOU-CHEIN, label company executive; b. Chang-Hua, Taiwan, Republic of China, June 19, 1950; came to U.S., 1977; Li-Chuan and Mei-Lan (Yang) L.; m. Lotus Shing-Er, Dec. 31, 1976. B.S., Nat. Tsing Hua U., Hsinchu, Taiwan, 1972, M.S., 1974; Ph.D., U. So. Calif., 1981. Research chemist Avery Internat., Pasadena, Calif., 1981-82, sr. research chemist, 1982-83, research assoc., 1984; research mgr. Avery Label, Azusa, Calif., 1984—. Contbr. articles to profl. jours. Mem. Am. Chem. Soc. Current work: Polymer viscoelasticity, polymer physics, adhesive research and development, research and developement management, computer aided modeling, polymer chemistry, radiation curing, surface chemistry. Subspecialties: Polymers (materials science); Polymer engineering. Home: 16932 Septo St Sepulveda CA 91343 Office: Avery Label 777 E Foothill Blvd Azusa CA 91702

LIN, LOUIS MIN-TSU, dental educator; b. Tainan, China, Mar. 14, 1939; came to U.S., 1969, naturalized, 1978; s. Chin-Shian and Luan-Tsu (Chen) L.; m. Betty C. Huang, Apr. 23, 1970; 1 son, John Jeffy. B.D.S., Chung Shan Med. and Dental Coll., Taiwan, 1964; Ph.D. in Pathology, U. Okla., 1972; D.M.D., U. Medicine and Dentistry N.J.-Newark, 1976. Diplomate: Am. Bd. Endodontics. Resident in oral pathology La. State U.-New Orleans, 1972-74; chief resident in endodontics U. Conn., Farmington, 1976-79; asst. prof. dentistry Fairleigh Dickinson U., Hackensack, N.J., 1979-80; assoc. prof. dentistry U. Medicine and Dentistry N.J.-Newark, 1983—. La. State U. fellow, 1972; Found. U. Medicine and Dentistry N.J. grantee, 1981. Mem. Internat. Assn. for Dental Research, ADA, Am. Acad. Oral Pathology, Am. Assn. Endodontists. Current Work: Pathogenesis of pulpal-periapical tissue complex; tissue response to viable and killed bacteria. Subspecialties: Endodontics; Oral pathology. Home: 16 Cherry Ln Parsippany NJ 07054

LIN, MING-CHANG, research chemist, educator; b. Hsinpu, Hsinchu, Taiwan, Oct. 24, 1936; came to U.S., 1967, naturalized, 1975; s. Fushin and Tao May (Hsu) L.; m. Juh-Huey Chern, June 26, 1965; children: Karen, Linus H., Ellena J. B.Sc., Taiwan Normal U., Taipei, 1959; Ph.D., U. Ottawa, 1966. Postdoctoral research fellow U. Ottawa, Ont., Can., 1965-67; postdoctural research assoc. Cornell U., Ithaca, N.Y., 1967-69; research chemist Naval Research Lab., Washington, 1970-74, supervisory research chemist, head chem. kinetics sect., 1974-82, Sr. Scientist for chem. kinetics, 1982—; adj. prof. chemistry Cath. U. Am., Washington, 1981—. Contbr. over 140 articles on reaction kinetics, chem. lasers, combustion and planetary atmosphere chemistry and applications of lasers to studying chem. kinetics to profl. jours. Served as 2d lt. Taiwan ROTC, 1960-62. Recipient Hillebrand prize Chem. Soc. Washington, 1975; Navy Civilian Meritorious Service award, 1979; Humboldt award, 1982; Guggenheim fellow, 1982. Fellow Washington Acad. Scis. (Phys. Scis. award 1976); mem. Am. Chem. Soc., Combustion Inst., N. Am. Taiwanese Profs. Assn., Sigma Xi (Pure Sci. award Naval Research Lab. chpt. 1978). Club: Taiwanese Assn. Am. Current Work: Lasers and other modern diagnostic tools are used to study kinetics and mechanisms of homogeneous and heterogeneous (catalytic) chemical reactions Subspecialties: Kinetics; Laser-induced chemistry. Office: Code 6100 Naval Research Lab Washington DC 20375

LIN, MOU-SHIUNG, physicist, electrical engineer; b. Peitou, Changhua, Republic of China, Sept. 15, 1952; came to U.S., 1977; s. Ten-Tsai and Tsai (Liu) L.; m. Shu-Mei Wu, Mar. 28, 1981; children—Marina Tingli. B.S., Nat. Taiwan U., 1975; M.S., Harvard U., 1978, Ph.D., 1982. Scientist, engr. IBM, Essex Junction, Vt., 1982-84; mem. tech. staff AT&T Bell Labs, Murray Hill, N.J., 1984—. Contbr. articles to profl. jours. Served with Republic of China Army, 1975-77. Mem. IEEE, Am. Phys. Soc., Phi Tau Phi. Current work: Process/device design and modeling of VLSI CMOS technology; physical limitations of VLSI technology; advanced VLSI system design and analysis; advanced VLSI packaging; wafer scale integration; optical fiber/VLSI interfaces. Subspecialties: Microchip technology (engineering); Microelectronics. Office: AT&T Bell Labs 600 Mountain Ave Murray Hill NJ 07974

LIN, PEI-JAN PAUL, diagnostic radiologic physicist, consulting radiologic physicist; b. Taipei, Taiwan, China, Aug. 25, 1946; s. Jintoku and Rie Hayashi; m. Keiko M. Lin; children: Rika, Rina. B.S. in Physics, Rikoy U., Tokyo, 1969; M.S. in Physics, De Paul U., 1974; Ph.D. in Sci, U. Tsukuba, Ibaraki, Japan, 1981. Cert. diagnostic radiol. physics Am. Bd. Radiology, 1977. Asst. med. physicist, dept. therapeutic radiology Rush-Presbyterian-St. Luke's Hosp., Chgo., 1971-73; instr. dept. radiology Northwestern U. Med. Sch., Chgo., 1973-76, assoc., 1976-77, asst. prof., 1977-82, assoc. prof., 1982—; radiol. cons. various hosps.; staff physicist, dept. diagnostic radiology affiliated profl. staff Northwestern Meml. Hosp. Contbr. papers to profl. publs. Spl. research grantee Philips Med. Systems, Inc., 1982. Mem. Am. Coll. Radiology, Am. Assn. Physicists in Medicine, Soc. Photo-Optical Instrumentation Engrs., Radiol. Soc. N.Am., Soc. Radiol. Engring. Current Work: Imaging properties in diagnostic radiology; information transfer and mass data storage for radiology; physics and engring. of diagnostic radiol. imaging equipment evaluation, performance evaluation and testing of radiological imaging equipment, including Computed Tomography, Digital Subtraction Angiography and nuclear magnetic resonance imaging equipment. Subspecialties: Imaging technology; Biomedical engineering. Office: Dept Radiology Northwestern Univ Med Sch 303 E Chicago Ave Room 2-307 Chicago IL 60611

LIN, SHAOW BURN, polymer scientist; b. Taipei, Republic of China, Mar. 20, 1953; came to U.S. 1979, naturalized, 1984; s. Chen-Ming and Yu-Hsein (Yeh-Wang) L.; m. Feng Yin, Jan. 14, 1979; children—Karen Y., Alan G. B.S., Cheng Kung U., Republic of China, 1975, M.S., 1979; Ph.D., Case Western Res. U., 1982. Teaching asst. Cheng Kung U., 1977-79; research asst. Case Western Res. U., Cleve., 1979-82; research assoc. U. Wis., Madison, 1982-83; staff researcher Syntex Ophthalmics, Inc., Phoenix, 1983—. Patentee polymer hydrogels. Rotary Found. fellow, 1979. Mem. Am. Chem. Soc., Am. Phys. Soc., Soc. Plastics Engrs. Current work: Synthesis and modification of polymer hydrogels, siloxane copolymers and urethane photoresists, structure-property-morphology of polyurethane copolymers and blends. Subspecialties: Polymers (materials science); Polymer chemistry. Office: Syntex Ophthalmics Inc PO Box 39600 Phoenix AZ 85069

LIN, SHEN, mathematician; b. Amoy, Fukien, China, Feb. 4, 1931; s. Chio-Shih and Shui-Hsian (Wang) L.; m. Jih-Jie Chang, Oct. 23, 1971; m. Mona Lo, Nov. 12, 1956 (div. 1964); children: John, David, Robert. B.S. summa cum laude, U. Philippines, 1951; M.A., Ohio State U., 1953, Ph.D., 1963. Instr. Ohio State U., Columbus, 1956-59, lectr., research assoc., 1962-63; asst. prof. Ohio U., Athens, 1959-62; vis. lectr. Princeton (N.J.) U., 1972; mem. tech. staff Bell Labs., Murray Hill, N.J., 1963—; cons. AT&T Long Lines, Bedminster, N.J., 1976—. Named Disting. mem. tech. staff Bell Labs., 1982. Mem. Am. Math. Soc., Math. Assn. Am., Soc. Indsl. and Applied Math. Current Work: Design of algorithms and mathematical software to perform optimization of telecommunication network. Subspecialties: Mathematical software; Algorithms. Home: 159 Southgate Rd Murray Hill NJ 07974 Office: Bell Labs Inc 600 Mountain Ave Murray Hill NJ 07974

LIN, SHENG HSIEN, chemist, educator, research, cons.; b. Taiwan, Sept. 17, 1937; came to U.S., 1962, naturalized, 1971; s. Ching-Po and Li-Mei (Chow) L.; m. Pearl, Aug. 30, 1970; 1 son, Huie. B.S., Nat. Taiwan U., Taipei, 1959, M.S., 1961; Ph.D., U. Utah, 1964. Postdoctoral fellow Columbia U., 1964-65; asst. prof. chemistry Ariz. State U., 1965-68, assoc. prof., 1968-72, prof., 1972—; vis. prof. U. Cambridge, Eng., 1972-73, Tech. U. Munich, W.Ger., 1978-80; invited lectr. Academia Sinica, 1980-81, Nuclear Research Ctr., Strasbourg, France, 1982. Co-author: books, including Basic Chemical Kinetics, 1980, Multi-photon Spectroscopy of Molecules, 1984; editor: books, including Radiationless Transitions, 1980; Advances in Multiphoton Processes and Spectroscopy, 1984. Contbr. articles to profl. jours. Served to 2d lt. Chinese Air Force, 1961-62. Recipient U.S. Sr. Scientist award Alexander von Humboldt Found., 1979-80, Disting. Research award Ariz. State U., 1983-84; Alfred P. Sloan fellow, 1967-71; Guggenheim fellow, 1971-73. Mem. Am. Chem. Soc., Am. Photochem. Soc., Am. Soc. Photobiology, AAAS, Soc. Columbia Chemists, Academia Sinica, Sigma Xi, Phi Lambda Upsilon, Phi Kappa Phi. Current Work: Multi-photon processes, time-resolved x-ray scattering, ion spattering, solid state chemistry. Subspecialties: Physical chemistry; Photochemistry. Home: 1915 E Calle de Caballos Tempe AZ 85284 Office: Dept Chemistry Ariz State U Tempe AZ 85281

LIN, SHIH-CHIA CHEN, research scientist; b. Ka-Shing, Chekiang, China, Nov. 3, 1917; came to U.S., 1948; d. Tse-kung and Malon (Fong) C.; m. Teh Ping Lin, Sept. 17, 1948; children: Florence Jean, Henry John. B.S. in Chemistry, Central U., Nanjing, China, 1940; M.S. in Oceanography, Scripps Instn.; 1951; Ph.D. in Biochemistry, U. Calif.-Berkeley, 1954. Jr. research pharmacologist U. Calif.-San Francisco, 1960-61, asst. research pharmacologist, 1961-67, 73-84, assoc. research pharamacologist, 1984—; biochem. pharmacologist SRI Internat., Menlo Park, Calif., 1967-68. Mem. Am. Soc. Pharmacology and Exptl. Therapeutics, Internat. Soc. Study of Xenobiotics (charter mem.), Western Pharmacol. Soc., Sigma Xi, Iota Sigma Pi. Current Work: Cation transport at the nerve endings, interaction of Ca 2t-ATPase and the release of neurotransmitter, relation of cation transport to the development of tolerance and physical dependence to CNS depressant agent. Subspecialties: Neurochemistry; Neuropharmacology. Home: 7345 Pebble Beach Dr El Cerrito CA 94530 Office: Univ Calif Dept Pharmacology Parnassus San Francisco CA 94143

LIN, TSAU-YEN, biochemist; b. Taipei, Republic of China, July 18, 1932; came to U.S., 1960, naturalized, 1972; s. S.-P. and S.-C. (Fan) L. B.S., Nat. Taiwan U., 1955, M.S., 1957; Ph.D., U. Calif.-Berkeley, 1965. Lectr. Kaohsiung Med. Coll., Republic of China, 1957-58; chemist China Chem. and Pharm. Co., Republic of China, 1958-59; research assoc. U.S. Naval Med. Research Unit 2, Republic of China, 1959-60; asst. research biochemist U. Calif.-Berkeley, 1965-68; research biochemist Merck Sharp and Dohme Research Lab., Rayway N.J., 1969-81, sr. research fellow, 1981—. Mem. Am. Soc. Biol. Chemists, Am. Chem. Soc., AAAS, N.Y. Acad. Scis. Current work: Enzyme chemical studies on proteinases. Subspecialty: Biochemistry (biology). Office: Merck Sharp & Dohme Research Labs PO Box 2000 Rahway NJ 07065

LIN, TSUNG-I GEORGE, biophysicist; b. Taipei, Taiwan, May 10, 1946; came to U.S., 1969; s. Nai-Min and Ashin (Liu) L.; m. Rachel Tsai, Sept. 15, 1978; children—Alex R., Arthur B. B.S. in Chemistry, Nat. Taiwan U., Taipei, 1968; M.S. in Biophysics, U. Chgo., 1971; Ph.D. in Biophysics, Ohio State U., 1975. Asst. prof. U. Tex., Dallas, 1977-80; med. staff affiliate Baylor U. Med. Ctr., Dallas, 1981-83; sr. chemist Beckman Instruments, Brea, Calif., 1983—; cons. Clin. Diagnostic Reagents, Inc., Dallas, 1980-81. Contbg. author: Excited States of Biopolymer, 1983; Cell and Muscle Motility, Vol. 4, 1983. Grantee Am. Heart Assn., 1977-80, Nat. Heart, Lung and Blood Inst., 1977-83. Mem. Biophys. Soc., Soc. for Exptl. Biology and Medicine, Am. Assn. Clin. Chemists, Am. Soc. Chemists. Subspecialties: Biophysics (physics); Biophysical chemistry. Home: 19941 Crestknoll Dr Yorba Linda CA 92686 Office: Beckman Instruments Inc 200 S Kraemer Blvd Brea CA 92621

LIN, TSUNG-MIN, research scientist; b. Chefoo Shangtung Province, China, Oct. 8, 1916; s. Chiu-Poo and Shu-Ying (You) L.; m. Hsia Lin, July 7, 1943; children: Abraham Tau-Tse, Dora Tao-Loo. B.S., Nat. Tsing Hun U., 1938; M.S., U. Ill., 1952; Ph.D., 1954. Asst. in physiology Tsing Hua U., 1939-41; instr. Peking Union Med. Coll., 1948-51; asst. prof. clin. sci. U. Ill., 1954-56; sr. pharmacologist Lilly Research Labs., Indpls., 1956-60, research scientist, 1960-64, research assoc., 1964—; del. Internat. Physiol. Congress, 1959; U.S. del. Congrss Pharmacology, 1961. China Med. Bd. fellow, 1951-54. Mem. Am. Physiol. Soc., Am. Pharmacol. Soc., Am. Gastroen. Assn., Am. Pancreatic Assn., Parietal Cell Club. Current Work: Histmaine, anti-histamines, gastrointestinal hormones, Glucagon on gastric, pancreatic and bile secretions; pancreatic polypeptide and somatostain on gastrointestinal functions. Subspecialties: Physiology (medicine); Pharmacology. Office: 307 E McCarty St Indianapolis IN 46285

LIN, TUNG YEN, civil engineer, educator; b. Foochow, China, Nov. 14, 1911; came to U.S., 1946, naturalized, 1951; s. Ting Chang and Feng Yi (Kuo) L.; m. Margaret Kao, July 20, 1941; children—Paul, Verna. B.S. in Civil Engring, Tangshan Coll., Chiaotung U., 1931; M.S., U. Calif.-Berkeley, 1933; LL.D., Chinese U. Hong Kong, 1972, Golden Gate U., San Francisco, 1982. Chief bridge engr., chief design engr. Chinese Govt. Rys., 1933-46; asst., then assoc. prof. U. Calif., 1946-55, prof., 1955-76, chmn. div. structural engring., 1960-63, dir. structural lab., 1960-63; chmn. bd. T.Y. Lin Internat. (cons. engrs.), 1953—, Inter-Continental Peace Bridge, Inc., 1968—; cons. to State of Calif., Def. Dept., also to industry; chmn. World Conf. Prestressed Concrete, 1957, Western Conf. Prestressed Concrete Bldgs., 1960. Author: Design of Prestressed Concrete Structures, 1955, rev. edit., 1963, 3d edit. (with N.H. Burns), 1981, (with B. Bresler, Jack Scalzi) Design of Steel Structures, rev. edit, 1968, (with S.D. Statesbury) Structural Concepts and Systems, 1981; contbr. articles to profl. jours. Recipient Berkeley citation award, 1976; NRC Quarter-Century award, 1977; AIA honor award, 1984; Outstanding Alumni of Yr. award U. Calif. Alumni Assn., 1984; named hon. prof. Chiaotung U., Omei, Szechuan, China, 1982, Ging Hua U., Be jing, Tong Ji U., Shanghai. Mem. ASCE (hon., Wellington award, Howard medal), Nat. Acad. Engring., Academia Sinica, Internat. Fedn. Prestressing (Freyssinet medal), Am. Concrete Inst. (hon.), Prestressed Concrete Inst. (medal of honor). Fields: Civil engineering; structural engineering. Current work: Structural engineering in concrete and steel. Home: 8701 Don Carol Dr El Cerrito CA 94530 Office: 315 Bay St San Francisco CA 94133

LIN, WINSTON T., educator, researcher; b. Taiwan, Oct. 16, 1944; came to U.S., in 1970, naturalized, 1977; s. Chang C. and Shian S. (Young) L.; m. Wendy W. Szu, Nov. 6, 1967; 1 son, Paul C. B.A., Nat. Taiwan U., Taipei, 1966; M.A., Northwestern U.-Evanston, Ill., 1972, Ph.D., 1976. Research asst. fellow Academia Sinica, Taipei, Taiwan, 1967-70; sr. economist John Deere & Co., Moline, Ill., 1974-75; asst. prof. SUNY-Buffalo, 1975-80, assoc. prof. mgmt. sci. and fin., 1980—; mem. Orgn. Prin. Investigators, Buffalo, 1983-84. Author: Applied Econometrics for Management, 1986; editor: Readings in Mathematical Finance, 1985; assoc. editor: Advances in Modeling and Simulation, 1983. Recipient award Health Research Council, 1982-83; U. Buffalo Found. grantee, 1978-79; Research Found. SUNY grantee-in-aid, 981-83. Mem. Ops. Research Soc. Am., Am. Statis. Assn., Inst. Mgmt. Scis., Am. Fin. Assn., Western Fin. Assn., Econometric Soc. Clubs: Chinese (Buffalo), Formosan (Buffalo) (com. 1982-83). Current Work: Modeling and decision systems, optimal control optimization, statistical analysis with computers, analytic methods of planning, corporate finance. Subspecialties: Statistics; Operations research (mathematics). Office: SUNY-Buffalo Main St Buffalo NY 14214

LIN, YUE JEE, geneticist, educator; b. China, Oct. 8, 1945; s. Yung C. and Rye M. (Chen) L.; m. Chiu Y. Lin, June 29, 1972; children: Jeffrey, Sarah. B.S., Nat. Taiwan U., 1967; M.S., Ohio State U., 1972; Ph.D., 1976. Research asst. Taiwan Agrl. Research Inst., 1968-69; research asst. Nat. Taiwan U., 1969-70; teaching assoc. Ohio State U., Columbus, 1970-76; asst. prof. St. John's U., Jamaica, N.Y., 1976-82, assoc. prof. genetics, 1982—. Contbr. articles to sci. jours. Mem. Am. Soc. Cell Biology, Genetics Soc. Am., Am. Genetic Assn., Sigma Xi. Current Work: Cytogenetics of complex heterozygotes, of polyploids; cytogenetic effects of mutagens and environmental chemicals. Subspecialty: Genome organization. Office: St John's U Jamaica NY 11439

LINCOLN, WALTER BUTLER, JR., ocean engineer, consultant; b. Phila., July 15, 1941; s. Walter B. and Virginia (Callahan) L.; m. Sharon Platner, Oct. 13, 1979; 1 dau., Amelia Adams. B.S., U. N.C., 1963; Ocean Engr., M.I.T., 1975; M.B.A., Rensselaer Poly. Inst., 1982. Registered profl. engr., N.H. Ops. research analyst applied physics lab. Johns Hopkins U., Silver Spring, Md., 1969-71; research asst. M.I.T., Cambridge, 1971-75; ocean engr. USCG Research and Devel. Center, Groton, Conn., 1975-79; prin. ocean engr. Sanders Assocs., Inc., Nashua, N.H., 1979—, head ocean engring. analysis group, 1982—. Mem. Planning Bd., Town of Brookline, N.H., 1982—. Served to lt. comdr. USN, 1963-70. Mem. Soc. Naval Architects and Marine Engrs., Marine Tech. Soc. (exec. bd. New Eng. sect. 1980—). Clubs: Nat. Assn. Underwater Instrs, Am. Schooner Assn. Current Work: Integrated systems modelling and engineering of deep ocean acoustic systems for U.S. Navy, development of algorithms for simulation of hydromechanics of ocean systems. Subspecialties: Systems engineering; Algorithms. Home: Mason Rd Brookline NH 03033 Office: Sanders Assocs Inc 95 Canal St Nashua NH 03061

LINDAU, INGOLF EVERT, physicist, educator; b. Vaxjo, Sweden, Oct. 4, 1942; came to U.S., 1971; s. Ture Gustav Verner and Siri Syster (Johansson) L.; m. Inge-Britt Elisabeth Lof, Apr. 26, 1980. Civil Engr., Chalmers U. Tech., Gothenburg, Sweden, 1968, Tech. lic., 1970, Ph.D., 1971. Research asst. Chalmers U. Tech., 1968-71; research scientist Varian Assocs., Palo Alto, Calif., 1971-72; research assoc. Stanford U., 1972-74, adj. prof. physics, 1974-81, prof., 1981—; assoc. dir. Synchrotron Radiation Lab., 1980—. Contbr. chpts. to books and articles in field to profl. jours. Served with Swedish Army, 1963-64. Fellow Am. Phys. Soc., Am. Vacuum Soc., Am. Chem. Soc., Electrochem. Soc., Optical Soc., IEEE, AAAS. Current Work: Electron spectroscopy studies of surfaces and interfaces using synchrtoron radiation. Subspecialties: Condensed matter physics; Atomic and molecular physics. Home: 135 Peter Coutts Stanford CA 94305 Office: SEL Stanford U Stanford CA 94305

LINDAUER, MAURICE WILLIAM, chemist, educator, cons.; b. Millstadt, Ill., Sept. 25, 1924; s. Herbert Johann and Pearl (Maserang) L.; m. Janie Ruth Shiver, Feb. 14, 1946; children: Jane E. Lindauer Elder, Rosemary Lindauer Brannen, Maurice Jack. A.B., Washington U., St. Louis, 1949; A.M., 1952; M.Ed., Harvard U., 1962; Ph.D. (Oak Ridge Inst. fellow 1964; NSF fellow 1964-65, Oak Ridge Assn. fellow 1968), Fla. State U., 1970. Research chemist Mallinckrodt Chem. Works, St. Louis, 1952-55; research engr. Am. Zinc Co., Monsanto, Ill., 1955-56; research chemist Allied Chem. & Dye Corp., Hopewell, Va., 1956-57; asst. prof. chemistry Valdosta State Coll., 1957-63, assoc. prof., 1963-71, prof., 1971-84, prof. emeritus, 1984—, head dept. chemistry, 1982-84; with research and devel. Splty. Supply Co., Valdosta, Ga.; participant NSF Summer Programs, 1959-63; NSF Acad. Yr. Inst., 1962. Contbr. articles to profl. jours. Served with USN, 1943-46. AEC grantee, 1959, 61, 63, 67; NEDA equipment grantee, 1966. Mem. Am. Chem. Soc., Sigma Xi. Current Work: History of Chemistry; thermodynamics; electrochemistry. Subspecialties: Analytical chemistry; Physical chemistry. Home: 1401 Miramar St Valdosta GA 31601 Office: Dept Chemistry Valdosta State Coll Valdosta GA 31698

LINDBERG, DONALD A.B., library director. Dir. Nat. Library Medicine, Bethesda, Md., 1984—. Subspecialty: Information systems (Information science). Office: Nat Library Medicine 8600 Rockville Pike Bethesda MD 20209

LINDBERG, ERIC KENT, air force officer; b. Kearney, Nebr., July 18, 1944; s. Oscar and Bess (Svanda) L.; m. Marion Faye Alsup, Apr. 23, 1983; children by previous marriage—Eric, Kent, Hans, Ian. B.S. in Engring. Sci., U.S. Air Force Acad., 1966; M.S., U.S. Air Force Inst. Tech., 1974, Ph.D., 1978. Commd. 2d lt. U.S. Air Force, 1966, advanced through grades to lt. col. 1982; simulation engr. Wright Patterson AFB, Ohio, 1976-77, test mgr. flight dynamics lab., 1977-78, chief aero and airframe br., 1978-80, mgr. civil res. air fleet program Hdqrs. MAC, Scott AFB, Ill., 1980-82; system engr. Milstar Mission Ctr., Space Div., El Segundo, Calif., 1982-84, dir., 1984—. Mem. IEEE, Air Force Assn., Tau Beta Pi. Methodist. Current work: Sattelite control, communications satellite control, survivable satellite control. Subspecialties: Aerospace engineering and technology; Systems engineering. Home: 11560 Panay Cypress CA 90630 Office: Air Force Space Div Milstar Mission Control Los Angeles AFS CA 90009

LINDEN, HENRY ROBERT, chemical engineering research executive; b. Vienna, Austria, Feb. 21, 1922; came to U.S., 1939, naturalized, 1945; s. Fred and Edith (Lermer) L.; m. Natalie Govedarica, 1967; children by previous marriage: Robert, Debra. B.S., Ga. Inst. Tech., 1944; M.Chem. Engring., Poly. Inst. N.Y., 1947; Ph.D., Ill. Inst. Tech., 1952. Chem. engr. Socony Vacuum Labs., 1944-47; with Inst. of Gas Tech., 1947-78, various research mgmt. positions, 1947-61, dir., 1961-69, exec. v.p., dir., 1969-74, pres., trustee, 1974-78; research asso. prof. Ill. Inst. Tech., 1954-62, adj. prof., 1962-78, research prof. chem. engring., prof. gas engring., 1978—; chief operating officer Gas Devels. Corp., 1965-73, chief exec. officer, 1973-78; also dir.; pres., dir. Gas Research Inst., 1976—; dir. Sonat Inc., So. Natural Gas Co., Reynolds Metals Co., UGI Corp.; mem. energy research adv. bd. Dept. Energy. Author tech. articles. Recipient award of merit, operating sect. Am. Gas Assn., Disting. Service award Am. Gas Assn., Gas Industry Research award Am. Gas Assn., 1982; Walton Clark Medal Franklin Inst.; Bunsen-Pettenkofer-Ehrentafel medal Deutscher Verein des Gas- und Wasserfaches.; named to IIT Hall of Fame, 1982. Fellow Am. Inst. Chem. Engrs., Inst. of Fuel; mem. Am. Chem. Soc. (recipient H.H. Storch award, chmn. div. fuel chemistry 1967, councilor 1969-77), Nat. Acad. Engring. Holder U.S. and fgn. patents in fuel tech. Subspecialties: Fuels; Chemical engineering. Home: 1515 N Astor St Chicago IL 60610 Office: 8600 W Bryn Mawr Ave Chicago IL 60631

LINDENBLAD, IRVING WERNER, astronomer; b. Port Jefferson, N.Y., July 31, 1929; s. Nils Erik and Elsie Christine (Lawson) L.; m. Ann Bolling Terry, Dec. 21, 1958; children: Irving Werner, Nils Bolling. A.B., Wesleyan U., Middletown, Conn., 1950; M.Div., Colgate Rochester Div. Sch., 1956; M.A., George Washington U., 1963. Ordained to ministry Baptist Ch., 1956; minister Savannah (N.Y.) Congl. Ch., 1954-55, Market St. Bapt. Ch., Harrisburg, Pa., 1957, Montowese Bapt. Ch., North Haven, Conn., 1961-62; astronomer U.S. Naval Obs., Washington, 1953, 58-60, 63—. Contbr. articles to profl. jours. Founder, pres. local chpt. Nat. Fedn. Fed. Employees, 1967-69, Arlington County Civic Fedn., 1970-71. Served with AUS, 1951-53. Recipient Sustained Superior Performance award U.S. Navy, 1979. Fellow Royal Astron. Soc.; mem. N.Y. Acad. Sci., Am. Astron. Soc., Am. Geophys. Union. Current Work: Operation of largest photographic zenith tube in world. Subspecialties: Geodetic astronomy; Optical astronomy. Home: 4735 Arlington Blvd Arlington VA 22203 Office: US Naval Obs Washington DC 20390

LINDER, GERHARD MARTIN, petroleum geologist; b. Gottwollshausen, Fed. Republic Germany, Sept. 20, 1954; came to U.S., 1957, naturalized, 1965; s. Egon Joseph and Anni Marie (Blaschek) L. Student, Oakland U., 1972-75; B.S., Mich. State U., 1976; M.S., U. Idaho, 1981. Chief engr. Central Metal Products, Warren, Mich., 1972-78; asst. field dir. Juneau Icefield Research, Seattle, Wash., 1975-81; geol. engr. Shell Oil Co., New Orleans, 1981—; geologist, hydrologist Terra Services, Moscow, Idaho, 1979-81; speaker, lectr. Primary Sch. Edn. Program, New Orleans Geol. Soc., 1982-84. Sr. adviser Jr. Achievement, New Orleans, 1982-83. Explorers Club research grantee 1979. Mem. Geol. Soc. Am., Am. Assn. Petroleum Geologists, Internat. Glaciological Soc. Democrat. Current work: Hydrocarbon potential in ice-dominated environments predictive models of sandstone occurance in subsurface. Arctic regions; petroleum exploration in south and east Texas; development of depositional model for South Texas Vicksburg formation. Subspecialties: Arctic studies; Sedimentology. Home: 1930 Prism Houston TX 77043 Office: Shell Oil Co PO Box 576 Houston TX 77001

LINDER, SOLOMON LEON, physicist, educator; b. Bklyn., Mar. 13, 1929; s. Aaron and Miriam Sabena (Stern) L.; m. Barbara Sue German, Nov. 29, 1953; children: Aaron, David, Burton. B.S. in Physics, Rutgers U., 1950; Ph.D. in Physics (NSF fellow), Washington U., St. Louis, 1955. Mem. tech. staff Bell Telephone Labs., Whippany, N.J., 1955-62; sr. group engr. McDonnell Douglas Astronautics Co., St. Louis, 1962-67, 72—, Titusville, Fla., 1967-71, tech. specialist, St. Louis, 1977—; part-time instr. physics and math. Fairleigh Dickinson U., Madison, N.J., 1959-62, Washington U., 1963-67, 76—, U. Central Fla., Orlando, 1970-71, So. Ill. U., Edwardsville, 1973-74. Contbr. articles to tech. jours. Mem. IEEE (sr.), Optical Soc. Am. Patentee in optics and electro-optics fields. Current Work: Applied research and development of optical and electro-optical systems. Subspecialties: Guidance systems; Electro-optical systems. Home: 14571 Coeur D'Alene Ct Chesterfield MO 63017 Office: McDonnell Douglas Astronautics Co PO Box 516 Saint Louis MO 63166

LINDOW, STEVEN E., plant pathologist. Assoc. prof. dept. plant pathology U. Calif.-Berkeley. Recipient Initiatives in Research award Nat. Acad. Scis., 1985. Subspecialty: Plant pathology. Office: Univ Calif-Berkeley Dept Plant Pathology Berkeley CA 94720*

LINDSAY, WILLIAM FRANCIS, project engineer scientist, researcher; b. Marinette, Wis., July 19, 1926; s. Francis William and Mae Sylvia (Scherer) L.; m. Beverly Ann, Apr. 16, 1953; children: Ann, David, Thomas, Michael, Barbara, Maureen, Carole, Janet, Diane. B.S., Marquette U., Milw., 1950; postgrad., Ill. Inst. Tech., 1951-52, U. Calif.-Livermore, 1959-60. Sr. technician Argonne Nat. Lab., 1950-52; research engr. Allis Chalmers Mfg. Co., Milw., 1953-55; staff engr. Boeing Co., Seattle, 1955-56; staff physicist U. Calif., Livermore, 1956-61, EGG, Santa Barbara, Calif. and Albuquerque, 1961-70; sr. engr. KOA Inc., Albuquerque, 1970-77; engr. scientist Sci. Applications, Inc., Albuquerque, 1977-83; prin. engr. Computer Scis. Corp., 1983-85; mem. inst. Spectra Research Inst., 1985—. . Served with USN, 1944-46. Mem. Am. Phys. Soc., Am. Nuclear Soc., Soc. Am. Mil. Engrs., Sigma Xi, Sigma Pi Sigma. Republican. Roman Catholic. Patentee solid state detector. Current Work: Directed energy beams, radiation effects in materials, systems engineering; electromagnetic radiation environment instrumentation design. Subspecialties: Nuclear physics; Particle physics. Home: 641 Stagecoach Rd SE Albuquerque NM 87123 Office: Sci Applications Inc 505 Marquette St NW Albuquerque NM 87102

LINDSLEY, DAN LESLIE, biology educator; b. Evanston, Ill., Oct. 13, 1925; s. Dan Leslie and Ruth Christine (Hubbard) L.; married, Aug. 26, 1947; children—Kathleen Ann, Dale Edward, Jennifer Joyce, Dan Arthur. Student U. Tex., 1943-45, U. Ark., 1946-47; B.A., U. Mo., 1947, M.A., 1949; Ph.D., Calif. Inst. Tech., 1952. Postdoctoral fellow Princeton U., N.J., 1952-53, U. Mo., Columbia, 1953-54; biologist Oak Ridge Nat. Lab., 1954-67; prof. dept. biology U. Calif.-San Diego, La Jolla, 1967—. Author: Genetic Variations of Drosophila melanogaster, 1968. Contbr. articles to sci. jours. Served with USN, 1943-45. Mem. Genetics Soc. Am. (treas. 1975-78, v.p. 1985-86), Lepidopterists Soc., Nat. Acad. Scis., Am. Acad. Arts and Scis. Current work: Genetics of Drosophila melanogaster. Subspecialty: Genetics and genetic engineering (biology). Office: Dept Biology U Calif San Diego La Jolla CA 92093

LINDSLEY, DONALD BENJAMIN, physiological psychologist, educator; b. Brownhelm, Ohio, Dec. 23, 1907; s. Benjamin Kent and Mattie Elizabeth (Jenne) L.; m. Ellen Ford, Aug. 16, 1933; children: David Ford, Margaret, Robert Kent, Sara Ellen. A.B., Wittenberg Coll. (now U.), 1929, D.Sc., 1959; A.M., U. Iowa, 1930, Ph.D., 1932; Sc.D., Brown U., 1958, Trinity Coll., Hartford, Conn., 1965; D.Sc., Loyola U. Chgo., 1969; Ph.D. (hon.), Johannes Gutenberg U., Mainz, W.Ger., 1977. Instr. psychology U. Ill., 1932-33; NRC fellow Harvard U. Med. Sch., 1933-35; research asso. Western Res. U. Med. Sch., 1935-38; asst. prof. psychology Brown U.; also dir. psychol. and neurophysiol. lab. Bradley Hosp., 1938-46; dir. war research project on radar operation Yale, OSRD, Nat. Def. Research Com., Camp Murphy and Boca Raton AFB, Fla., 1943-45; prof. psychology Northwestern U., 1946-51; prof. psychology, physiology, psychiatry and pediatrics UCLA, 1951-77, chmn. psychology dept., 1959-62, prof. emeritus, 1977—, mem. Brain Research Inst., 1951—; William James lectr. Harvard, 1958; Univ. Research lectr. UCLA, 1959; Phillips lectr. Haverford Coll., 1961; Walter B. Pillsbury lectr. psychology Cornell U., 1963; vis. lectr. Columbia U., 1949, U. Hawaii, 1961, Kansas State U., 1966, Tex. A & M U., 1980; Mem. sci. adv. bd. USAF, 1947-49; undersea warfare com. NRC, 1951-64; cons. NSF, 1952-54; mem. mental health study sect. NIMH, 1953-57; neurol. study sect. Nat. Inst. Neurol. Diseases and Blindness, 1958-62; cons. Guggenheim Found., 1963-70, mem. ednl. adv. bd., 1970-78; chmn. behavioral scis. tng. com. Nat. Inst. Gen. Med. Scis., 1966-69; mem. behavioral biology adv. panel AIBS-NASA; mem. space sci. bd. Nat. Acad. Scis., 1967-70; mem. com. space medicine, 1969-71; mem. Calif. Legis. Assembly Sci. and Tech. Council, 1970-71. Cons. editor: Jour. Exptl. Psychology, 1947-68, Jour. Comparative and Physiol. Psychology, 1952-62, Jour. Personality, 1958-62; editorial bd.: Internat. Jour. Physiol. and Behav, 1965—, Exptl. Brain Research, 1965-76, Developmental Psychobiology, 1968-82, Archives for Psychologie, 1978—; Contbr. numerous articles on physiol. psychology, neurosci., brain and behavior to sci. jours., also numerous chpts. in books. Trustee Grass Found., 1958—. Awarded Presdl. Cert. of Merit (for war work), 1948; Guggenheim fellow Europe, 1959; Distinguished Sci. Achievement award Calif. Psychol. Assn., 1977. Mem. Nat. Acad. Scis. (chmn. com. long duration missions in space 1967-72, mem. space sci. board), Am. Psychol. Assn. (Distinguished Sci. Contbn. award 1959), Am. Physiol. Soc., Soc. Exptl. Psychologists, Am. Electroencephalographic Soc. (pres. 1964-65, hon. mem. 1980—), AAAS (v.p., chmn. sect. I 1954, chmn. sect. J 1977), Midwest Psychol. Assn. (pres. 1952), Am. Acad. Cerebral Palsy, Western Soc. Electroencephalography (hon. mem. with great distinction, pres. 1957), Western Psychol. Assn. (pres. 1959-60), Am. Acad. Arts and Scis., Internat. Brain Research Orgn. (treas. 1967-71), Soc. Neuroscis. (Donald B. Lindsley prize in behavioral neurosci. established in his name), Sigma Xi, Alpha Omega Alpha, Gamma Alpha, Phi Gamma Delta. Conglist. Current Work: Electrophysiological studies of brain and behavior in emotion, attention, perception, learning and information processing; studies of spinal cord and brain stem reflexes; electromyographic studies of neuromuscular disorders; electroencephalographic studies of behavior disorders in children and adults. Subspecialties: Neurophysiology; Physiological psychology. Home: 471 23d St Santa Monica CA 90402 Office: Dept Psychology U Calif Los Angeles CA 90024

LINEBACK, DAVID R., food scientist; b. Russellville, Ind., June 7, 1934; married, 1956; 3 children. B.S., Purdue U., 1956; Ph.D. in Organic Chemistry, Ohio State U., 1962. Research chemist Monsanto Chem. Co., 1956-57; fellow U. Alta., 1962-64; from instr. to asst. prof. biochemistry U. Nebr., Lincoln, 1964-69; from assoc. prof. to prof. grain sci. and industry Kans. State U., 1969-76; prof. food sci. and head dept. Pa. State U., 1976-80, N.C. State U., 1980—. Mem. Am. Assn. Cereal Chemists, Inst. Food Technologists, Am. Chem. Soc. Subspecialty: Food science and technology. Office: Dept Food Sci NC State U Box 7624 Raleigh NC 27695*

LINEBERRY, MICHAEL J., nuclear engineer; b. Pomona, Calif., Sept. 11, 1946; s. Harold L. and Lella (Hilliard) L.; 1 child, Gregory. B.S. in Engring., UCLA, 1967; M.S. in Mech. Engring., Calif. Inst. Tech., 1968, Ph.D., 1972. Assoc. dir. REE div. and IFR program Argonne Nat. Lab., Idaho Falls, Idaho, 1972—; adj. faculty Idaho State U., 1984—, U. Idaho, 1973-76. Recipient E.O. Lawrence award U.S. Dept. Energy, 1983. Mem. Am. Nuclear Soc. (chmn. scholarship com.). Republican. Current work: Fast reactor physics; manager fast reactor fuel cycle work within Argonne's integral fast reactor initiative. Subspecialty: Nuclear engineering. Office: Argonne Nat Lab PO Box 2528 Idaho Falls ID 83403

LING, ROBERT F., statistics educator; b. Hong Kong, Apr. 21, 1939; came to U.S., 1957, naturalized, 1968. B.A., Berea (Ky.) Coll., 1961; M.A., U. Tenn., 1963; M.Phil., Yale U., 1968, Ph.D., 1971. Asst. prof. stats. U. Chgo., 1970-75; assoc. prof. math. scis. Clemson (S.C.) U., 1975-77, prof., 1977—; vis. prof. Vanderbilt U., Nashville, 1982, U Chgo., 1983; vis. lectr. Com. of Pres. of Statis. Socs., 1984-86. Co-author: Exploring Statistics with IDA, 1979, IDA: A User's Guide, 1981, Conversational Statistics, 1982; assoc. editor: Am. Statis. Assn, 1977—; mem. editorial bd.: Jour. of Classification, 1983. Office of Naval Research grantee, 1973—; recipient Frank Wilcoxon prize for best practical application paper, 1984. Fellow Am. Statis. Assn.; mem. Internat. Assn. for Statis. Computing, Mensa. Current Work: Applied statistics and data analysis; cluster analysis and classification; numerical approximations of statistical distributions; statistical computing. Subspecialties: Statistics; Mathematical software. Home: 102 Brookwood Dr Clemson SC 29631 Office: Dept Math Scis Clemson U Clemson SC 29631

LINGREL, JERRY B., biochemist, educator, researcher; b. Byhalia, Ohio, July 13, 1935; s. Gaylord and Nancy E. (Bonham) L.; m. Sara Wright, June 14, 1958; children—Douglas, Lynne. B.S., Otterbein Coll., 1957; Ph.D., Ohio State U., 1960. Postdoctoral fellow Calif. Inst. Tech., Pasadena, 1961-62; from asst. prof. to assoc. prof. biol. chemistry dept. U. Cin., 1962-81, prof., 1981—, chmn. dept. microbiology and molecular genetics, 1981—. Contbr. numerous articles to profl. jours. Mem. Am. Chem. Soc., Am. Soc. Cell Biology, Am. Soc. Biol. Chemistry, Am. Soc. Microbiologists, Sigma Xi. Current work: Expression and regulation of genetic information of mammalian cells. Subspecialties: Genome organization; Genetics and genetic engineering (biology). Office: Dept Microbiology and Molecular Genetics U Cin Coll Medicine ML 524 Cincinnati OH 45267

LINIGER, WERNER, mathematician; b. Tschugg, Switzerland, Dec. 22, 1927; came to U.S., 1957; s. Samuel and Mathilde Rosa (Fuerst) L.; m. Margrit Aline Adlung, Nov. 3, 1956; children—Eric G., Stephanie C. Diploma in math. Swiss Fed. Inst. Tech., Zurich, 1951; Sc.D., U. Lausanne, Switzerland, 1955. Research asst. U. Lausanne, 1952-55; statistician Swiss Nat. Accident Ins. Inst., Lucerne, 1955-57; research mathematician Sperry Rand Corp., Phila., 1957-59; mem. research staff IBM Research Ctr., Yorktown Heights, N.Y., 1959—. Contbr. 50 articles to profl. jours. Patentee in field. Mem. Soc. Indsl.

and Applied Math. Current work: Numerical analysis in particular numerical solution of ordinary differential equations, and of elliptic partial differential equations. Subspecialties: Numerical analysis (mathematics); Applied mathematics. Office: IBM Research Ctr PO Box 218 Yorktown Heights NY 10598

LINN, JOHN, computer scientist; b. Ithaca, N.Y., Aug. 8, 1955; s. John Gaywood and Eleanor Morrison (Ringer) L.; m. Eve F.W. Eve Wahrsager, May 15, 1982. B.A., Hampshire Coll., Amherst, Mass., 1977. Programming analyst Data Gen. Corp., Westboro, Mass., 1977-78; computer scientist research staff Bolt Beranek and Newman, and BBN Communications Corp., Cambridge, Mass., 1978—. Mem. Assn. Computing Machinery, IEEE Computer Soc. Current Work: Techniques and architectures to support reliable and secure communication in computer networks; monitoring and control of networks. Subspecialties: Cryptography and data security; Distributed systems and networks. Office: BBN Communications Corp 50 Moulton St Cambridge MA 02238

LINNELL, ALBERT PAUL, physics and astronomy educator; b. Canby, Minn., June 30, 1922; s. Edward Payson and Pearl (Huston) L.; m. Jane Elliott, May 24, 1944; children—Carol Anne, Paul Huston, John Andrew, Barbara Marie, James Scott. B.A., Coll. Wooster, 1944; Ph.D., Harvard U., 1950; M.A., Amherst Coll., 1962. Mem. faculty Amherst Coll. (Mass.), 1949-66, prof. astronomy, 1962-66; prof. Mich. State U., East Lansing, 1966—; dir. at large Assoc. Univs. for Research in Astronomy, Tucson, 1962-65; vis. scholar Cambridge U. (Eng.), 1974-75. Contbr. articles to profl. jours. Served to 1st lt. AUS, 1944-46. Agassiz fellow, 1947; AEC fellow, 1947. Mem. Am. Astron. Soc., AAAS, Internat. Astron. Union, AAUP. Presbyterian. Current work: Structure of contact binary stars. Subspecialties: Optical astronomy; Theoretical astrophysics. Home: 1918 Yuma Trail Okemos MI 48864 Office: Dept Physics and Astronomy Mich State U East Lansing MI 48824

LINSLEY, RAY KEYES, civil engineering educator; b. Hartford, Conn., Jan. 13, 1917; s. Ray Keyes and Flora Madelaine (Ladd) L.; m. Anne Virginia Cutler, Nov. 26, 1937; children: Dianne, Stephen, Alan, Brian. B.S., Worcester Poly. Inst., 1937, D.Engring. (hon.), 1979; D.Sc., U. Pacific, 1973. Engr. TVA, 1937-40; engr. U.S. Weather Bur., Washington, 1941, Sacramento, 1942-44, chief hydrology, Washington, 1945-50; asso. prof. Stanford U., 1950-55, prof., head dept. civil engring., 1956-67, asso. dean School Engring., 1956-58, dir. project engring.-econ. planning School Engring., 1962-71, prof. emeritus, 1975—; Fulbright prof. Imperial Coll., London, 1957-58; v.p. Carroll Bradberry & Assos., 1959-67; pres. Hydrocomp Internat., 1967-78; chmn. Hydrocomp, Inc., 1972-78; pres. Linsley Kraeger Assos. Ltd., 1979—; cons. engr.; with Office Sci. and Tech., Washington, 1964-65. Author: Applied Hydrology, 1949, Elements of Hydraulic Engineering, 1955, Hydrology for Engineers, 1958, 3d edit., 1982, Water-Resources Engineering, 3d edit, 1979. Commr. U.S. Nat. Water Commn., 1968-73. Recipient Meritorious Service award Dept. Commerce, 1949. Fellow Am. Geophys. Union (pres. hydrology sect. 1956-59), ASCE (Collingwood prize 1943, Julian Hinds award 1978); mem. Nat. Acad. Engring., Am. Meteorol. Soc., Nat. Soc. Profl. Engrs., Venezuelan Soc. Hydraulic Engrs. (hon.), Am. Inst. Hydrology (sr. v.p. 1983—), Japan Soc. Civil Engrs. (hon.), Sigma Xi, Tau Beta Pi. Subspecialty: Hydrology. Home: 280 Swanton Blvd Santa Cruz CA 95060 Office: 527 Bayview Dr Aptos CA 95003

LINVILL, JOHN GRIMES, engineering educator; b. Kansas City, Mo., Aug. 8, 1919; s. Thomas G. and Emma (Crayne) L.; m. Marjorie Webber, Dec. 28, 1943; children: Gregory Thomas, Candace Sue. A.B., William Jewell Coll., 1941; S.B., Mass. Inst. Tech., 1943, S.M., 1945, Sc.D., 1949; Dr. Applied Sci., U. Louvain, Belgium, 1966. Asst. prof. elec. engring. Mass. Inst. Tech., 1949-51; mem. tech. staff Bell Telephone Labs., 1951-55; asso. prof. elec. engring. Stanford U., 1955-57, prof., dir. solid-state electronics lab., 1957-64, prof., chmn. dept. elec. engring., 1964-80, co-dir. Center for Integrated Systems, 1980—; co-founder, dir. Telesensory Systems, Inc.; dir. Spectra-Physics, Inc., Cromemco, Inc., Author: (with J.F. Gibbons) Transistors and Active Circuits, 1961, Models of Transistors and Diodes, 1963. Recipient citation for achievement William Jewell Coll., 1963, Medal of Achievement Am. Electronics Assn., 1983. Fellow IEEE (Edn. medal 1976); mem. Nat. Acad. Engring. (John Scott medal 1980), Am. Acad. Arts and Scis. Inventor Optacon, reading aid for blind. Subspecialty: Integrated circuits. Home: 30 Holden Ct Portola Valley CA 94025 Office: Dept Elec Engring Stanford U Stanford CA 94305

LINVILLE, MALCOLM EUGENE, JR., psychology educator; b. Kansas City, Mo., Mar. 30, 1939; s. Malcolm Eugene and Maebell (Reimert) L.; married; children: Douglas, Deborah. B.A. in Psychology, Kansas City U., 1957, M.A. in Edn. and Psychology, 1963; Ph.D. in Counseling, U. Mo.-Kansas City, 1974. Lic. psychologist, Mo. cert. Nat. Bd. Cert. Counselors. Intern Walter Reed Hosp., Los Angeles, 1959; tchr. Consol. Dist. No. 1, Hickmon Mills, Mo., 1962-64; psychologist Prairie Sch. Dist., Prairie Village, Kans., 1964-69; prof. counseling psychology U. Mo.-Kansas City, 1969—, pvt. practice psychology, 1978; cons. Kansas City Sch. Dist., Kansas City Urban Affairs Dept., Menorah Med. Ctr. Speech and Hearing Dept. Editor: The Counseling Interviewer, 1979-82; contbg. editor: Jour. Sch. Psychology, 1975—; contbr. articles to profl. jours. Bd. dirs. New Sch. Human Edn., 1973-79; pres. Booster Club, Kansas City, 1976-79; chmn. Human Resources Corp., 1977. Served to sgt. AUS, 1959-62. Danforth assoc., 1980-84; named Outstanding Tchr. AMOCO Found., Kansas City, 1977. Mem. Am. Psychol. Assn., Am. Personnel and Guidance Assn., Assn. Tchr. Educators, Mo. Guidance Assn. (v.p. 1981-2), Phi Delta Kappa. Current Work: Research dealing with family therapy, especially in outcome studies. Subspecialty: Counseling psychology. Office: University of Missouri 365 Education Bldg Kansas City MO 64110

LINZ, ARTHUR, physicist, researcher; b. Barcelona, Spain, Jan. 30, 1926; s. Arthur and Dorothy (Warnock) L. B.S.E.E., Brown U., 1946; M.S. in Physics, U. N.C., 1950; Ph.D. in Physics, 1952. Physicist Nat. Lead. Co., South Amboy, N.J., 1952-58; sr. research assoc. dept. elec. engring. and computer scis. M.I.T., 1958—; participant summer faculty research program Naval Research Lab., Washington, summers 1980-81. Contbr. articles to profl. jours. Served with USN, 1943-45. Mem. Am. Phys. Soc., Am. Inst. Physics, Optical Soc. Am., Am. Assn. Crystal Growth, AAAS, Fedn. Am. Scientists, Sigma Xi. Patentee in field. Current Work: Electro-optical materials; new solid state tunable laser materials; application of computer control techniques to crystal growth of high optical quality laser crystals; tailored band gap oxides for solar photolysis. Subspecialty: Laser research. Office: Room 13-3154 MIT Cambridge MA 02139

LIOTINE, FRANK JAMES, JR., electrical engineer; b. Chgo., Oct. 25, 1950; s. Frank and Ida (Angiolo) L.; m. Bernadette I. Lester, Oct. 26, 1979. B.S.E.E., Rose-Hulman Inst., 1973. Sr. project engr. Motorola, Inc., Schaumburg, Ill., 1973-75, project leader, 1975-77; engring. mgr. Chamberlain Corp., Elmhurst, Ill., 1977-81, mgr., research and devel., electronics div., 1981—, tech. tchr., 1984—; tech. cons. Elmhurst Coll., U. Ill.-Chgo., 1981; consumer adv. bd. Crown Internat. Corp., Elkhart, Ind., 1980-83. Author: Financial Budget Analysis, 1979. Editor: New Technology S.M.T., 1984. Patentee in field. Mem. adv. bd. 2d Legis. Dist., Bartlett, Ill., 1982. Rose-Hulman scholar, 1969-73. Mem. Engring. Mgmt. Soc. of IEEE, Microelectronics Soc. of IEEE, Am. Mgmt. Assn., Internat. Soc. Hybrids Microelectronics. Republican. Roman Catholic. Club: Bartlett Country. Current work: Electronic design using new technology surface mounted devices, S.M.T.; apply said technology to micro processor and radio remote control products. Subspecialties: Electronics; Software engineering. Home: 1128 Monroe Dr Bartlett IL 60103 Office: Duchossois Industries Chamberlain Electronics Div 845 Larch Ave Elmhurst IL 60126

LIOTTA, LANCE A., pathologist. Head pathol. anatomy dept. NIH Clin. Ctr., Bethesda, Md. Subspecialty: Pathology (medicine). Office: NIH Clin Ctr Pathol Anatomy Dept 9000 Rockville Pike Bethesda MA 20205

LIOU, KUO-NAN, atmospheric scientist, educator; b. Taiwan, China, Nov. 16, 1943; came to U.S., 1966, naturalized, 1976; s. and S. Y. (Yang) L.; m. Agnes L. Y., Aug. 4, 1968; 1 child, Julia C. C. B.S., Taiwan U., Taipei, 1965; M.S., N.Y. U., 1968; Ph.D., 1970. Research asst. N.Y. U., 1966-70; research assoc. Goddard Inst. Space Studies, N.Y.C., 1970-72; asst. prof. U. Wash., 1972-74; assoc. prof. U. Utah, 1975-79, prof., 1980—; dir. grad. studies in meteorology, 1981—. Mem. adv. panel for ISCCP, climate research com. Nat. Acad. Scis., 1984—. Author: An Introduction to Atmospheric Radiation, 1980. Editor: Archives for Meteorology, Geophysics and Bioclimatology, 1985—; mem. editorial com. Advances in Atmospheric Sciences, 1985—. Contbr. numberous articles, chpts. to profl. pubs. Recipient Founders Day award N.Y. U., 1971; David P. Gardner Fellow award U. Utah, 1978. Fellow Optical Soc. Am., mem. Am. Meteorol. Soc. (chmn. radiation energy com. 1982-84), Am. Geophys. Union, AAAS, N.Y. Acad. Scis. Current Work: Radiation and climate modelling, remote sensing from satellites, light scattering by nonspherical particles. Subspecialties: Meteorology; Remote sensing (atmospheric science). Office: Dept Meteorology U Utah Salt Lake City UT 84112

LIPKIN, GEORGE, physician; b. N.Y.C., Dec. 31, 1930; s. Samuel and Celia (Greenfield) L.; m. Sari Berger, June 16, 1957; children: Michael David, Lisa Susan. A.B., Columbia Coll., 1952; M.D., SUNY Downstate Med. Ctr., 1955. Diplomate: Am. Bd. Dermatology, 1961. Intern Montefiore Hosp., Bronx, N.Y., 1955-56; resident in dermatology NYU Med. Center, 1956-57, 59-61; mem. faculty dept. dermatology NYU Sch. Medicine, 1961—, assoc. prof., 1967-74, prof. dermatology, 1974—; dir. Berger Found. Cancer Research; vis. scientist U. Zurich, 1972-73. Contbr. chpts. to books, articles to profl. jours. Served to capt. M.C. U.S. Army, 1957-59. Mem. Am. Acad. Dermatology, Soc. Investigative Dermatology, Am. Assn. Cancer Research, Harvey Soc., AAAS, Fedn. Am. Scientists, Union Concerned Scientist. Current Work: Cancer research, emphasis on study of growth inhibitors, their identification, purification, application to control of tumor growth. Subspecialties: Dermatology; Cancer research (medicine). Home: 61 Virginia Ave Clifton NJ 07012 Office: 530 1st Ave New York NY 10016

LIPMAN, NEIL SCOTT, veterinarian, researcher and clinician laboratory animal medicine; b. New Bedford, Mass., Sept. 23, 1958; s. Aron and Roberta Faith (Gofman) L. B.A. magna cum laude, Boston U., 1980; V.M.D. magna cum laude, U. Pa., 1984; postgrad., MIT, 1984—. Postdoctoral assoc. MIT, Cambridge, 1984—. Mem. AVMA, Phi Zeta, Alpha Epsilon Delta. Current work: Laboratory animal medicine including research activity in virology, animal models of human disease. Subspecialty: Laboratory animal medicine. Office: MIT 37 Vassar St Cambridge MA 02129

LIPMANN, FRITZ (ALBERT), biochemist; b. Koenigsberg, Germany, June 12, 1899; came to U.S., 1939, naturalized, 1944; s. Leopold and Gertrud (Lachmanski) L.; m. Elfreda M. Hall, June 23, 1931; 1 son, Stephen. Student, U. Koenigsberg, 1917-22, U. Munich, 1919; M.D., U. Berlin, 1924, Ph.D., 1928; M.D. (hon.), U. Marseilles, 1947, U. Copenhagen, 1972; M.A. (hon.), Harvard, 1949; D.Sc. (hon.), U. Chgo., 1953, U. Paris, 1966, Harvard, 1967, Rockefeller U., 1971; L.H.D., Brandeis U., 1959, Yeshiva U., 1964. Research asst. Prof. Meyerhof's Lab., Kaiser Wilhelm Inst., Berlin and Heidelberg, 1927-30; Dr. A Fischer's Lab., Berlin, 1930-31; Rockefeller fellow Rockefeller Inst. Med. Research, N.Y.C., 1931-32; research asso. Biol. Inst. Carlsberg Found., Copenhagen, Denmark, 1932-39; dept. biochemistry Med. Sch. Cornell U., 1939-41; research chemist, head biochem. research lab. Mass. Gen. Hosp., Boston, 1941-57; prof. biol. chemistry Med. Sch. Harvard, 1949-57; prof. Rockefeller U., 1957—. Author: Wanderings of a Biochemist, 1971; sci. papers. Recipient Carl Neuberg medal, 1948; Mead Johnson & Co. award for outstanding work on Vitamin B-complex, 1948; Nobel prize for medicine and physiology, 1953; Nat. Medal Sci., 1966. Fellow N.Y. Acad. Sci., Danish Royal Acad. Scis.; fgn. mem. Royal Soc.; mem. Nat. Acad. Scis., Am. Chem. Soc., Am. Soc. Microbiology, Biochem. Soc., A.A.A.S., Am. Soc. Biol. Chemists, Harvey Soc., Am. Philos. Soc. Current Work: Phospho-proteinkinase, malignant transformation, sulfo proteinkinase. Subspecialties: Biochemistry (biology); Microbiology. Home: 201 E 17th St New York NY 10003 also RD 2 Box 347 Rhinebeck NY 12572 Office: Rockefeller University New York NY 10021

LIPNICK, ROBERT LOUIS, research chemist; b. Balt., Sept. 9, 1941; s. David Aaron and Dorothy (Moss) L.; m. Anne Ruth Goldberg, June 11, 1967; children—Deborah Ellen, David Henry. B.S. in Chemistry, U. Md., 1963; Ph.D. in Organic Chemistry, Brandeis U., 1969. Postdoctoral fellow U. Minn., Mpls., 1968-73; research assoc. Sloan-Kettering Inst., Rye, N.Y., 1974-79; leader structure activity group EPA, Washington, 1980—; speaker and panelist profl. confs.; jour. referee. Contbr. articles to profl. jours., chpts. to books. Bd. dirs., v.p. Friends of Marshlands, Rye, 1977-79. Recipient Bronze medal EPA, 1982, Commendable Service award, 1983; NIH grantee, 1978, 80. Mem. Am. Chem. Soc., AAAS, N.Y. Acad. Scis., Soc. Environ. Toxicology and Chemistry, Chemometrics Soc. Club: Dowden Terrace Recreation Assn. (Alexandria, Va.) (bd. dirs. 1984—). Current work: Development of quantitative structure activity relationships for predictive toxicology; molecular mechanism of biochemical action. Subspecialties: Environmental toxicology; Toxicology (medicine). Home: 5308 Pender Ct Alexandria VA 22304 Office: EPA 401 M St SW Washington DC 20460

LIPPARD, STEPHEN JAMES, chemist, educator; b. Pitts., Oct. 12, 1940; s. Alvin I. and Ruth (Green) L.; m. Judith Ann Drezner, Aug. 16, 1964; children—Andrew (dec.), Joshua, Alexander. B.A., Haverford Coll., 1962; Ph.D. (NSF fellow), MIT, 1965. Postdoctoral research asso. chemistry MIT, Cambridge, 1965-66, prof. chemistry, 1983—; asst. prof. chemistry Columbia U., N.Y.C., 1966-69, asso. prof., 1969-72, prof., 1972-83; mem. study sect. medicinal chemistry NIH, 1973-77. Editor: Progress in Inorganic Chemistry, 1967—, Chemistry Concepts; mem. editorial bd.: Inorganic Chemistry, 1981—; contbr. articles to profl. jours. Coach Demarest Borough Soccer Team, 1975-82, league adminstr., 1979-82. Alfred P. Sloan fellow, 1968-70; Guggenheim fellow, 1972; recipient Tchr.-Scholar award Camille and Henry Dreyfus Found., 1971-76; sr. internat. fellow John E. Fogarty Internat. Center, 1979. Fellow AAAS; mem. Am. Chem. Soc., Am. Crystallographic Assn., Am. Soc. Biol. Chemists, Chem. Soc. (London), Biophys. Soc., Phi Beta Kappa. Subspecialty: Inorganic chemistry. Office: Dept Chemistry Room 18-207 MIT Cambridge MA 02138

LIPPINCOTT, JAMES ANDREW, biochemist, educator; b. Cumberland County, Ill., Sept. 13, 1930; s. Marion Andrew and Esther Oral (Meeker) L.; m. Barbara Sue Barnes, June 2, 1956; children: Jeanne Marie, Thomas Russell, John James. A.B., Earlham Coll., 1954; A.M., Washington U., St. Louis, 1956; Ph.D., 1958. Lectr., research assoc. Washington U., 1958-59; postdoctoral fellow Centre National de la Recherche Scientifique, Gif-sur-Yvette, France, 1959-60; asst. prof. biol. scis. Northwestern U., Evanston, ILL., 1960-66, assoc. prof., 1966-73, prof., 1973-81, prof. biochemistry, molecular biology and cell biology, 1981—, assoc. dean biol. scis., 1980-83. Contbr. articles to profl. jours. Recipient Tanner-Shaughnessy merit award Ill. Soc. for Microbiology, 1981; Jane Coffin Childs fellow, 1959-60. Mem. Am. Soc. Biol. Chemists, Am. Soc. Microbiology, Am. Soc. Plant Physiologists, Am. Soc. Phytopathology, Bot. Soc. Am., Scandinavian Soc. Plant Physiologists, Japanese Soc. Plant Physiologists. Current Work: Plant tumorigenesis and development. Subspecialties: Plant physiology (biology); Microbiology. Office: Dept Biochemistry Molecular Biology and Cell Biology Northwestern U Evanston IL 60201

LIPPINCOTT, SARAH LEE, astronomer; b. Phila., Oct. 26, 1920; d. George E. and Sarah (Evans) L.; m. Dave Garroway. Student, Swarthmore Coll., 1938-39, M.A., 1950; B.A., U. Pa., 1942; D.Sc., Villanova U., 1973. Research asst. Sproul Obs., Swarthmore (Pa.) Coll., 1941-50, research asso., 1951-72, dir., 1972-81, prof., 1977-81, prof. and dir. emeritus, 1981—, research astronomer, 1981—. Author: (with Joseph M. Joseph) Point to the Stars, 1963, 3d edit., 1977, (with Laurence Lafore) Philadelphia, the Unexpected City, 1965; Contbr. articles to profl. jours. Mem. Savoy Opera Co., Phila., 1947—; bd. mgrs. Societe de Bienfaisance de Philadelphie, 1966-69. Recipient achievement award Kappa Kappa Gamma, 1966; Distinguished Daus. of Pa. award, 1976; Fulbright fellow Paris, 1953-54. Mem. Rittenhouse Astronom. Soc., Am. Astronom. Soc. (lectr. 1961—), Internat. Astron. Union (v.p. commn. 26 1970-73, pres. 1973-76), Sigma Xi (nat. lectr. 1971-73). Current Work: Study of stars in vicinity of the sun: distances, stellar mases; search for low mass unseen companions, plants, other solar systems. Subspecialty: Optical astronomy. Home: 507 Cedar Ln Swarthmore PA 19081 Office: Sproul Observatory Swarthmore Coll Swarthmore PA 19081

LIPSCHUTZ, BRUCE HOWARD, chemistry educator; b. N.Y.C., Dec. 10, 1951; s. Emanuel and Muriel (Towbin) L.; m. Charlene Debby Daly, June 24, 1979; children—Abbey Faith, Douglas Ryan. B.A., SUNY-Binghampton, 1973; M.S., Yale U., 1974, Ph.D., 1977. Postdoctoral research fellow Harvard U., Cambridge, Mass., 1977-79; asst. prof. U. Calif., Santa Barbara, 1979-84, assoc. prof., 1984—. Contbr. articles to profl. jours. Am. Cancer Soc. postdoctoral fellow, 1977-79, jr. faculty research award, 1981-83; A.P. Sloan Found. fellow, 1984-86; Camille & Henry Dreyfus Tchr./Scholar, 1984—; Harold J. Plous Meml. Teaching award U. Calif., Santa Barbara, 1984. Mem. Am. Chem. Soc., Sigma Xi. Democrat. Jewish. Current work: Synthetic methods development and applications of syntheses of molecules of biological activity, including antibiotics, antifungal agents and antitumor agents. Subspecialties: Synthetic chemistry; Organic chemistry. Home: 6284 Marlborough Dr Goleta CA 93117 Office: Dept Chemistry Univ Calif Santa Barbara CA 93106

LIPSCHUTZ, MICHAEL ELAZAR, chemistry educator; b. Phila., May 24, 1937; s. Maurice and Anna (Kaplan) L.; m. Linda Jane Lowenthal, June 21, 1959; children: Joshua Henry, Mark David, Jonathan Mayer. B.S., Pa. State U., 1958; S.M., U. Chgo., 1960, Ph.D., 1962. Gastdocent U. Bern, Switzerland, 1964-65; asst. prof. chemistry Purdue U., West Lafayette, Ind., 1965-68, assoc. prod., 1968-73, prof., 1973—; vis. assoc. prof. Tel Aviv (Israel) U., 1971-72; cons. NASA, 1973-75, 77-79, Lunar and Planetary Inst., 1980—. Assoc. editor: Proc. 11th Lunar and Planetary Sci. Conf., 3 vols, 1980; contbr. articles to profl. jours. NSF-NATO fellow, 1964-65; Fulbright fellow, 1971-72; NASA grantee; NSF grantee. Fellow Meteoritical Soc. (treas. 1978-84); mem. Am. Chem. Soc., AAAS, Geochem. Soc., Am. Geophys. Union. Democrat. Jewish. Current Work: Geo- and cosmochemistry; trace and ultra-trace element analysis; high temperature and high pressure chemistry; solid state chemistry; cosmic ray-induced nuclear reactions. Subspecialties: Space chemistry; High temperature chemistry. Home: 2900 Henderson Ave West Lafayette IN 47906 Office: Dept Chemistry Purdue U West Lafayette IN 47907

LIPSCOMB, WILLIAM NUNN, JR., educator, physical chemist; b. Cleve., Dec. 9, 1919; s. William Nunn and Edna Patterson (Porter) L.; m. Mary Adele Sargent, May 20, 1944; children: Dorothy Jean, James Sargent; m. Jean Craig Evans, 1983. B.S., U. Ky., 1941, D.Sc. (hon.), 1963; Ph.D., Calif. Inst. Tech., 1946; Dr.h.c., U. Munich, 1976; D.Sc. (hon.), L.I. U., 1977, Rutgers U., 1979, Gustavus Adolphus Coll., 1980, Marietta Coll., 1981. Phys. chemist OSRD, 1942-46; with U. Minn., 1946-59, successively asst. prof., asso. prof. and acting chief phys. chemistry div., prof. and chief phys. chemistry div., 1954-59; prof. chemistry Harvard U., 1959-71, Abbott and James Lawrence prof., 1971—, chmn. dept. chemistry, 1962-65; dir. Dow Chem. Co.; Mem. U.S.A. Nat. Com. for Crystallography, 1954-59, 60-63, 65-67; chmn. program com. Fourth Internat. Congress of Crystallography, Montreal, 1957; mem. sci. adv. bd. Robert A Welch Found.; mem. adv. com. Inst. for Amorphous Studies. Author: The Boron Hydrides, 1963, (with G.R. Eaton) NMR Studies of Boron Hydrides and Related Compounds, 1969; Asso. editor: (with G.R. Eaton) Jour. Chemical Physics, 1955-57; contbr. (with G.R. Eaton) articles to profl. jours.; Clarinetist, mem. (with G.R. Eaton), Amateur Chamber Music Players. Guggenheim fellow Oxford U., Eng., 1954-55; Guggenheim fellow Cambridge U., Eng., 1972-73; NSF sr. postdoctoral fellow, 1965-66; Overseas fellow Churchill Coll., Cambridge, Eng., 1966, 73; Robert Welch Found. lectr., 1966, 71; Howard U. distinguished lecture series, 1966; George Fisher Baker lectr. Cornell U., 1969; centenary lectr. Chem. Soc., London, 1972; lectr. Weizmann Inst., Rehovoth, Israel, 1974; Evans award lectr. Ohio State U., 1974; Gilbert Newton Lewis Meml. lectr. U. Calif., Berkeley, 1974; also lectureships Mich. State U., 1975; also lectureships U. Iowa, 1975; also lectureships Ill. Inst. Tech., 1976; also lectureships numerous others; also speaker confs.; Recipient Harrison Howe award in Chemistry, 1958; Distinguished Alumni Centennial award U. Ky., 1965; Distinguished Service in advancement inorganic chemistry Am. Chem. Soc., 1968; George Ledlie prize Harvard, 1971; Nobel prize in chemistry, 1976; Disting. Alumni award Calif. Inst. Tech., 1977; sr. U.S. scientist award Alexander von Humboldt-Stiftung, 1979; award lecture Internat. Acad. Quantum Molecular Sci., 1980. Fellow Am. Acad. Arts and Scis., Am. Phys. Soc.; mem. Am. Chem. Soc. (Peter Debye award phys. chemistry 1973, chmn. Minn. sect. 1949-50), Am. Crystallographic Assn. (pres. 1955), Nat. Acad. Sci., Netherlands Acad. Arts and Scis. (fgn.), Math. Assn. Bioinorganic Scientists (hon.), Academie Europeenne des Sciences, des Arts et des Lettres, Royal Soc. Chemistry (hon.), Phi Beta Kappa, Sigma Xi, Alpha Chi Sigma, Phi Lambda Upsilon, Sigma Pi Sigma, Phi Mu Epsilon. Subspecialty: Physical chemistry. Office: Dept Chemistry Harvard U 112 Oxford St Cambridge MA 02138

LIPSETT, MORTIMER BROADWIN, physician; b. N.Y.C., Feb. 20, 1921; s. Theodore and Gertrude (Broadwin) L.; m. Lois Friedman, Mar. 10, 1974; children—Roger, Edward. A.B., U. Calif., 1943; M.S., U. So. Calif., 1947, M.D., 1951. Diplomate: Am. Bd. Internal Medicine. Research asso. U. So. Calif., 1947; intern Los Angeles County Hosp., 1951-52; resident in internal medicine Sawtelle VA Hosp., Los Angeles, 1952-54; USPHS fellow, asst. mem. Sloan-Kettering Inst., N.Y.C., 1954-57; mem. staff NIH, 1957-74, 76—, asso. sci. dir. intramural research, chief reprodn. research br., 1970-74; asso. dir. clin. care, dir. Clin. Center, NIH, 1976-82; dir. Nat. Inst. Child Health and Human Devel., NIH, 1982-85, Nat. Inst. Arthritis, Digestive and Kidney Diseases, Bethesda, Md., 1985—; dir. Cancer Center N.W. Ohio, Cleve.; also prof. medicine Case Western Res. U. Med. Sch., 1974-76. Served with AUS, 1944-46. Decorated Bronze Star with oak leaf cluster; recipient Alfred P. Sloan award cancer research Sloan-Kettering Inst., 1955; Superior Service Honor award HEW, 1969; Disting. Service award Dept. Health and Human Services, 1981; Presdl. Meritorious Rank award, 1982. Fellow ACP; mem. Endocrine Soc. (sec.-treas. 1974-78, pres. 1979-80, Disting. Leadership award 1976), Internat. Soc. Endocrinology (sec.-gen. 1976—), AAAS, Am. Assn. Cancer Research, Am. Fedn. Clin. Research, Am. Soc. Andrology (named Disting. Andrologist 1984), Am. Soc. Clin. Investigation, Assn. Am. Physicians, Harvey Soc., Soc. Study Reprodn., German Endocrine Soc. (corr.), Japan Endocrin Soc. (hon.). Subspecialty: Endocrinology. Office: NIH Bldg 31 9000 Rockville Pike Bethesda MD 20205

LIPSKY, STEPHEN EDWARD, electronics company executive; b. N.Y.C., Jan. 18, 1932; s. Arthur Arnold and Sophie (Malsbrook) L.; m. Laura Roher, May 11, 1958 (div. 1978); children—Janice, Sharon, David; m. Hyla Schaffer, Apr. 7, 1979. B.E.E., N.Y. Poly. Inst., 1953, M.E.E., 1962. Project engr. Fisher Radio Corp., 1957-58; div. mgr., staff scientist Loral Electronics, Yonkers, N.Y., 1958-63; corp. v.p. Polarad-Radiometrics, Lake Success, N.Y., 1963-70; dir. advanced systems Gen. Instrument Corp., Hicksville, N.Y., 1970-79; sr. v.p. Govt. Ops. Group, Am. Electronic Labs., Lansdale, Pa., 1979—. Subspecialty: Electronics. Office: Am Electronic Labs Govt Ops Group PO Box 552 Lansdale PA 19446

LIPTON, ALLAN, physician; b. N.Y.C., Dec. 29, 1938; s. Murray and Rutb L.; m. Nancy Whitcomb; children: Samuel, Joshua A., Sarah Jan. A.B., Amherst Coll., 1959; M.D., N.Y.U., 1963. Intern Bellevue Hosp., N.Y.C., 1963-64; resident, 1964-65; fellow in hematology-oncology Meml. Hosp., 1967-69; mem. staff Hershey (Pa.) Med. Center, 1971—, chief div. oncology, 1972—, prof. medicine, 1979—. Served with USPHS, 1965-67. Mem. Am. Soc. Clin. Oncology, Am. Assn Cancer Research. Current Work: Cancer research and treatment, cell growth. Subspecialties: Cell biology; Chemotherapy. Address: Hershey Med Center Hershey PA 17033

LIPTON, JAMES ABBOTT, federal health executive, dental educator, researcher; b. N.Y.C., July 24, 1946; s. Benjamin M. and Ann (Rappaport) L.; m. Jill Friedman, Oct. 8, 1978. B.S., CCNY, CUNY, 1967; D.D.S., Columbia U., 1971, M.Phil., 1974, Ph.D., 1980. Trainee USPHS, N.Y.C., 1971-74, dental cons., 1976-77, commd. dental officer, 1976—; chief Nat. Health Service Corps, Region II, N.Y.C., 1977—; asst. clin. prof. Dental Sch. Columbia U., N.Y.C., 1976-83; asst. prof. Sch. Pub. Health Columbia U., N.Y.C., 1983—. Contbr. articles to profl. jours. Recipient commd. officer plaque USPHS, 1980. Mem. ADA, Am. Pub. Health Assn., Internat. Assn. Dental Research, Internat. Assn. for Study of Pain, Am. Sociol. Assn. Jewish. Current Work: Psychosocial and linguistic aspects of facial pain patients; sociocultural dimensions of health and illness behavior. Subspecialties: Facial pain; Medical sociology. Office: USPHS 26 Federal Plaza Room 3304 New York NY 11278

LIS, ADAM WIKTOR, biochemist; b. Przemysl, Poland, Jan. 5, 1925; came to U.S., 1947; s. Piotr E. Emilia L. (Samborski) L.; children—; Richard A., Janina D., Victoria M. B.S., U. Ark.-Fayetteville, 1949; B.A., U. Calif.-Berkeley, 1954, Ph.D., 1960. Lectr. U. Calif. Sch. Medicine, San Francisco, 1960-62; fellow Nat. Cancer Inst., U. Uppsala, Sweden, 1962-63; assoc. prof. U. Oreg. Med. Sch., Portland, 1963-77, dir. Intermediate Metabolism Lab., 1977-82; prof. biochemistry Wash. (Western) U., Bellingham, 1982—. Founder, editor Physiol. Chemistry & Physics jour., 1969-83. Pres. Polish Am. Congress, N.W. Div., Portland, 1975-83. Served with Polish Army, 1943-45. Recipient Copernican medal, Jagiellonian U., 1973. Mem. Am. Chem. Soc., Biophysic Soc., Radiation Research Soc., Biochem. Soc., AAAS. Democrat. Roman Catholic. Current work: Characterization of primary structure of nucleic acids as pertaining to minor bases. Application of basic research techniques to clin. and environ. problems. Non-ionizing and ionizing radiation effects on genetic material. Subspecialties: Biochemistry (medicine); Biophysics (physics). Office: Huxley Coll Western Wash Univ Bellingham WA 98225

LISAK, ROBERT PHILIP, physician, educator; b. Bklyn., Mar. 17, 1941; s. Irving Arthur and Sylvia Lillian (Kadish) L.; m. Deena Freda Penchansky, Aug. 2, 1964; children: Ilene Ann, Michael. A.B. cum laude with highest honors in History, NYU, 1961; M.D., Columbia U., 1965. Diplomate: Nat. Bd. Med. Examiners, Am. Bd. Neurology. Intern Montefiore Hosp. and Med. ctr., Bronx, N.Y., 1965-66; research assoc. NIMH, Bethesda, Md., 1966-68; resident in medicine Bronx Mcpl. Hosp. Ctr., 1968-69; resident in neurology Hosp. U. Pa., Phila., 1969-72; asst. prof. neurology U. Pa. Sch. Medicine, 1972-76, assoc. prof., 1976-80, prof., 1980—; hon. vis. fellow Univ. Coll. London, 1978-79, Inst. Neurology, London, 1978-79; cons. Co-author: Myasthenia Gravis, 1982; contbr. articles to sci. jours., chpts. to books. Served as sr. asst. surgeon USPHS, 1966-68. Recipient Helen M. Jones award NYU, 1961; Founders Day award, 1961; USPHS-Nat. Inst. Neurol. Communicative Disease and Stroke tchr.-investigator award, 1972-77; Fulbright-Hays scholar, 1978-79. Fellow Am. Acad. Neurology; mem. AAAS, Am. Neurol. Assn., N.Y. Acad. Scis., Am. Assn. Immunologists, Am. Fedn. Clin. Research, Soc. Neurosci., Med. Soc. London, Phila. Neurol. Soc. Current Work: Neuroimmunology: study of experimental and human disorders of possible immunopathogenesis, including multiple sclerosis Guillian-Barre Syndrome, myasthenia gravis; neurology: clinical and teaching; cell and tissue culture; neurobiology and immunology of cultured oligodendrocytes and Schwann cells. Subspecialties: Neuroimmunology; Neurology. Office: U Pa Sch Medicine 3400 Spruce St Philadelphia PA 19104

LISCHER, LUDWIG FREDERICK, consultant, former utility company executive; b. Darmstadt, Germany, Mar. 1, 1915; came to U.S., 1923, naturalized, 1933; s. Ludwig J. and Paula (Stahlecker) L.; m. Helen Lucille Rentz, Oct. 1, 1938; 1 dau., Linda Sue. B.S. in Elec. Engring, Purdue U., 1937, D.Eng. (hon.), 1976. Registered profl. engr., Ill. With Commonwealth Edison Co., Chgo., 1937-80, v.p. charge engring., research and tech. activities, 1964-80, ret., 1980; cons. and mem. adv. com. to engring. tech. div. Oak Ridge Nat. Lab., 1980—; cons. energy and electric utility fields; mem. various tech. adv. coms. to fed. agys. and Edison Electric Inst.; chmn. research adv. com. Electric Power Research Inst. Contbr. articles to profl. jours. Bd. dirs. Chgo. Engring. and Sci. Center; trustee Ill. Inst. Tech. Served to lt. col. AUS and USAAF, 1941-45. Fellow IEEE; mem. ASME, Nat. Acad. Engring., Am. Nuclear Soc., Tau Beta Pi, Eta Kappa Nu. Current Work: Energy conversion and electric power generation and transmission. Subspecialties: Electrical engineering; Nuclear engineering. Home: 441 N Park Blvd Glen Ellyn IL 60137

LISH, PAUL MERRILL, scientific consultant, pharmacist, researcher; b. McCammon, Idaho, Feb. 2, 1921; s. Marion M. and Viola (Davis) L.; m. Irene Howe, Nov. 17, 1960 (dec.); children: Michael, Marilyn, Gloria, Carol; m. Grete Enderweit, Oct. 27, 1978. B.S. in Pharmacy, U. Idaho, 1949; M.S., U. Nebr., 1951; Ph.D. in Pharmacology, St. Louis U. Med. Sch., 1955. Pharmacologist, dept. head, v.p. biol. scis. Mead Johnson Co., 1955-69; dir. research and devel. Chromalloy Am. Corp., 1969-78; sci. advisor on pharmacology, and regulatory affairs toxicology Ill. Inst. Tech., Chgo., 1978—. Author. Served as 1st petty officer USN, 1943-46. Recipient Mead Johnson Presdl. award for meritorious research, 1960. Mem. Am. Soc. Pharmacology and Exptl. Therapeutics, Soc. Exptl. Biology and Medicine, Sigma Xi, Rho Chi. Mormon. Patentee in field. Current Work: Testing toxicity of munitions; FDA liaison work in new drug development. Subspecialties: Pharmacology; Toxicology (medicine). Office: Ill Inst Tech Research Inst 10 W 35th St Chicago IL 60616

LISIECKI, JERRY BOYD, limnologist; b. Vallejo, Calif., Sept. 10, 1948; s. Clarence Chester and Olga (Pavkovic) L.; m. Connie Ann McNabb, Dec. 20, 1969; 1 child, Chad Edward. B.S., Ohio State U., 1970, M.S., 1972; Ph.D., Mich. State U., 1977. Gen. mgr., gen. ptnr. Grand Valley Farms, Ltd., Orwell, Ohio, 1976-84; Ohio dir. Midwest Water Resources Mgmt., Charlotte, Mich., 1983—. Author monthly column Habitat Mgmt., 1983—. Contbr. articles to profl. jours. Coach, Little League Baseball, North Bloomfield, Ohio, 1981-82, 7th and 8th grade basketball, 1982. Mem. Am. Fisheries Soc., Am. Soc. Limnology and Oceanography. Republican. Lutheran. Lodge: Rotary (treas. 1982-84). Current work: Attempting domestication of yellow perch for aquaculture; heavy metal dynamics in water; consultant for industrial waste water disposal and monitoring. Subspecialties: Limnology; Animal genetics. Home: 9830 Penniman Rd NW Orwell OH 44076 Office: Grand Valley Farms Ltd Route 1 Box 121A Orwell OH 44076

LISK, ROBERT DOUGLAS, biology educator, researcher; b. Pembroke, Ont., Can., Nov. 10, 1934; came to U.S., 1960; s. Robert Leslie and Elsie Agnes (Yandt) L. B.A. in Biology and Chemistry, Queens U., Kingston, Ont., 1957; A.M. in Biology, Harvard U., 1959, Ph.D. in Biology, 1960. Mem. faculty Princeton U., N.J., 1960—, prof. biology, 1970—, dir. program in neurosci., 1983—. Contbr. chpts. to books, articles to profl. jours. Fellow AAAS; mem. Endocrine Soc., Animal Behavior Soc., Soc. for Study Reprodn., Sigma Xi (pres. Princeton chpt. 1983-84). Democrat. Current work: Neuroendocrine regulation of reproduction in mammals, hormone effects on brain in regulation of social and sexual behaviors. Subspecialties: Neuroendocrinology; Psychobiology. Home: 376 Walnut Ln Princeton NJ 08540 Office: Dept of Biology Princeton U Princeton NJ 08544

LISSANT, KENNETH JORDAN, chemist; b. London, Aug. 6, 1920; came to U.S., 1926; s. Alfred Herbert and Florence Ada (Giles) L.; m. Ellen Marie Kern, June 14, 1947; children—Joyce Ellen, Keith Jordan, Nathan Kern. B.A., Ottawa U., 1941; M.S., Washington U., 1943; Ph.D., Stanford U., 1947. Research chemist Petrolite Corp., St. Louis, 1944-81, prin. investigator surface chemistry, 1981—. Editor/author: Emulsions and Emulsion Technology, vol. 1, 2, 3, 1977, 84. Contbr. articles to profl. jours. Patentee in field. Author: Demulsification, 1983. Mem. Am. Chem. Soc., AAAS. Current work: Demulsification, emulsions, liquid-liquid systems, computer graphics Subspecialties: Surface chemistry; Physical chemistry. Office: Route 1 Box 251A Clever MO 65631

LISTER, RICHARD MALCOLM, plant virologist; b. Sheffield, Eng., Nov. 14,1928; s. Francis William and Frances May (Scotrick) L.; m. Jean Isabel Mills, May 19, 1953; children: Susan, Christina, Rosalind, John. B.Sc., Sheffield (Eng.) U., 1949; Dip. Agrl. Sci., Cambridge (Eng.) U., 1951; Dip. Trop. Agr., Imperial Coll. Trop. Agr., Trinidad, W.I., 1952; Ph.D., St. Andrews (Scotland) U., 1964. Scientist West African Cocoa Research Inst., Ghana and Nigeria, 1952-56; princ. scientist Scottish Hort. Research Inst., Invergowrie, 1956-66; prof. dept. botany and plant pathology Purdue U., West Lafayette, Ind., 1966—. Contbr. chpts. to books, articles to profl. jours. NSF grantee; U.S. Dept. Agr. grantee; Ind. Crop Improvement Soc. grantee; Am. Phytopath. Soc., fellow, 1973. Mem. Assn. Applied Biologists, Am. Phytopath. Soc., AAUP. Current Work: Mission-oriented virological problems of crop plants. Subspecialties: Plant virology; Plant pathology. Office: Dept Botany and Plant Pathology Purdue U West Lafayette IN 47907

LISZCZAK, THEODORE MICHAEL, neuroanatomist, consultant; b. Meriden, Conn., May 29, 1942; s. Michael Ambrose and Sophie (Laskowski) L.; m. Elizabeth Hazaltine Crocker, Sept. 12, 1964 (dec. Aug. 1978); m. Elizabeth Ann Young, Feb. 24, 1979; children—Kristin, Caitlin. B.A., U. Conn., Storrs, 1965; M.A., Montclair State Coll., Upper Montclair, N.J., 1973; Ph.D., Tufts U., 1981; M.B.A., Suffolk U., Boston, 1986. Cert. tchr., N.J., Mass. Research assoc. Yale U., 1965-68; electron microscopist Pfizer Inc., Maywood, N.J., 1968-73; research assoc. Mass. Gen. Hosp., Boston, 1973-81, asst. neuroanatomist, 1981—; dir. Mixter Lab. Ultrastructural Research, Boston, 1965-81. Contbr. articles to profl. jours. Mem. exec. bd. Barnstable Village Civic Assn., Mass., 1980—, recording sec., 1982—. Mem. Am. Assn. Anatomists, N.Y. Soc. Electronmicroscopists, Electron Microscopt Soc. Am. Republican. Episcopalian. Clubs: Computer Soc. (Boston); Cruising Cape Cod (Mass.); Barnstable Yacht. Current work: Cerebral arterial anatomy and pathology; choroid plexus, pituitary anatomy and physiology, immunohistochemistry, electron microscopy. Subspecialties: Anatomy and embryology; Neurosurgery. Home: 107 Mill Way Barnstable MA 02630 Office: Mass Gen Hosp Neurosurg Service Warren 459 Boston MA 02114

LISZEWSKI, MARY KATHRYN, technician, medical science writer; b. St. Louis, Sept. 29, 1948; d. Stanley Louis and Margaret Mary (Dubin) Myers; children—Jason, Julie. B.S. in Biology, U. Mo., 1971. Research asst. St. Louis U. Med. Sch., 1971-79; sr. technician Washington U. Med. Sch., St. Louis, 1979-83, head technician, 1983—. Author: (with others) Antibodies Specific for Modified Nucleosides, 1980. Contbr. articles to profl. jours. Recipient Curator's award U. Mo., 1967. Home: 49 Graeler Dr St Louis MO 63146

LIT, ALFRED, psychologist; b. N.Y.C., Nov. 24, 1914; s. Zachary Oscar and Elsie (Jaro) L.; m. Imogene Speegle, Jan. 27, 1947. B.S., Columbia U., 1938; M.A., 1943, Ph.D., 1948. Lic. optometrist, N.Y., psychologist, N.Y. Lectr. optometry Columbia U., N.Y.C., 1946-48, asst. and assoc. prof., 1949-56; staff, research project dept. psychology and U.S. Office Naval Research, 1949-56; research psychologist Vision Research Labs., U. Mich., Ann Arbor, 1956-59; head human factors engring. staff Bendix Systems Div., Ann Arbor, 1959-61; prof. psychology, prof. elec. scis. and systems engring., prof. engring. biophysics program and prof. molecular sci. doctoral program So. Ill. U., Carbondale, 1961-85; research prof. SUNY/State Coll. Optometry, N.Y.C., 1984—; mem. com. on vision NRC, Nat. Acad. Sci., Washington, 1965—. Contbr. articles to profl. jours.; sci. referee: Am. Jour. Optometry, 1975—. Served to 1st lt. USAAF, 1943-46. Recipient Kaplan Research award Sigma Xi, 1971; Ill. Dept. Mental Health grantee, 1962-65; NSF grantee, 1965-69, 76-78; USPHS grantee, 1967—. Fellow Am. Psychol. Assn., Am. Acad. Optometry, Optical Soc. Am., Psychonomic Soc., AAAS, N.Y. Acad. Sci., Soc. Engring. Psychology; mem. Human Factors Soc., Assn. for Research in Vision and Ophthalmology, Eastern Psychol. Assn., Midwestern Psychol. Assn., N.Y. County Optometric Soc. (pres. 1954-55). Current Work: Psychophysiological and electrophysiological studies on spatio-temporal factors in monocular and binocular perception, the visual latent period, and their applications to clinical practice. . Home: 321 E 45th St New York NY 10017 Office: SUNY Coll Optometry 100 E 24th St New York NY 10010

LITCHFIELD, JOHN HYLAND, microbiologist; b. Scituate, Mass., Feb. 13, 1929; s. Frank Albert and Alma (Hyl) L.; m. Dianne Chappell, Apr. 15, 1966; 1 son, Robert Chappell. S.B., MIT, 1950; M.S., U. Ill., 1954, Ph.D., 1956. Chief chemist Searle Food Corp., Hollywood, Fla., 1950-51; research scientist Swift & Co., Chgo., 1956-57; asst. prof. Ill. Inst. Tech., Chgo., 1957-60; research leader Battelle Meml. Inst., Columbus, Ohio, 1960—; adj. assoc. prof. human nutrition and food mgmt. Ohio State U., 1977-78. Contbr. articles to profl. jours. Served to 1st lt. AUS, 1951-53, ETO. Recipient Disting. Inventor award Battelle Meml. Inst., 1977. Fellow AAAS, Am. Acad. Microbiology, Inst. Food Technologists (Outstanding Service award 1980), Am. Inst. Chemists, Am. Pub. Health Assn., Royal Soc. Health; mem. Soc. Indsl. Microbiology (pres. 1971, Charles Porter award 1977). Patentee in field. Current Work: Applied and industrial microbiology, food science and technology. Subspecialties: Food science and technology; Microbiology. Home: 255 Bryant Ave Worthington OH 43085 Office: Battelle Memorial Institute 505 King Ave Columbus OH 43201

LITCHFIELD, WILLIAM JOHN, biochemistry researcher; b. Waukegan, Ill., Feb. 28, 1950; s. John Wilfied and Jeane Lenore (Emmerich) L.; m. Marilyn Elizabeth Kammlade, June 24, 1972; children—Brian John, David William. B.S., U. Ill., 1972, M.S. in Biochemistry, 1973; Ph.D. in Biochemistry, Mich. State U., 1976. Postdoctoral fellow Johnson Research Found. U. Pa., Phila., 1976-77; research biochemist E.I. duPont de Nemours & Co., Wilmington, Del., 1977-82, supr. research, 1983-84, research supr., 1984—. Contbr. articles to profl. jours. and ency. Patentee in field. NIH grantee, 1972-76; Ill. State scholar. Mem. Am. Assn. Immunologists, Am. Assn. Clin. Chemists, Am. Chem. Soc., Del. Chem. Soc., Sigma Xi, Phi Eta Sigma, Pi Kappa Alpha. Republican. Methodist. Club: Planetary Soc. (Pasadena, Calif.) Current work: Immunodiagnostic methods for detecting and measuring polypeptide hormones, viral and bacterial antigens, therapeutic drugs, etc. Subspecialties: Biochemistry (medicine); Immunology (medicine). Office: E I DuPont De Nemours & Co Inc Glasgow Research Lab Wilmington DE 19898

LITKE, ALAN MICHAEL, physicist, educator; b. New Haven, Dec. 22, 1943; s. Abraham Herbert and Ruth Beatrice (Calegman) L.; m. Maryse Patricia Mazal Douek, Jan. 20, 1983; 1 dau., Rachel Renee. B.A., Johns Hopkins U., 1964; M.A., Harvard U., 1966, Ph.D., 1970. NSF postdoctoral fellow Harvard U., 1970-73; research fellow Lawrence Berkeley Lab., Calif., 1973-75; asst. prof. physics Stanford U., Calif., 1975-83; sci. assoc. on leave from Stanford U., Centre Européen de Recherche Nucléaire, Geneva, 1981-82; assoc. research physicist, adj. prof. physics U. Calif.-Santa Cruz, 1984—. Contbr. articles to sci. jours. Mellon fellow, 1978-79, Alfred P. Sloan Found. fellow, 1978-82. Mem. AAAS, Am. Phys. Soc. Jewish. Club: Commonwealth of Calif. (San Francisco). Current work: Research in exptl. high energy physics: electron-positron colliding beam experiments on charmonium (at SLAC) and bottomium (at DESY); future experiment on the Z degree at the SLAC Linear Collider; development of silicon micro-strip detectors. Subspecialty: Particle physics. Home: 1524 8th Ave San Francisco CA 94122 Office: Inst for Particles Physics U Calif Santa Cruz CA 95064

LITLE, PATRICK ALAN, psychologist; b. Pomona, Calif., Nov. 14, 1946; s. Ralph and Doris Elizabeth (Little) L. B.Music, U. Redlands, Calif., 1968; M.A., Calif. State U.-Long Beach, 1982; postgrad., U. Del., 1979—. Registered music therapist, Calif., Va. Music therapy intern Lanterman State Hosp., Pomona, Calif., 1977; music tchr. Pomona City Schs., 1977; music therapist Coll. Hosp., Cerritos, Calif., 1977-78; therapist trainee Community Psychology Clinic, Long Beach, Calif., 1978-79; psychology trainee VA, Perry Point, Md., 1980-82; psychology intern VA Outpatient Clinic, Los Angeles, 1982-83; health sci. specialist VA Med. Ctr., Perry Point, Md., 1984—; psychology technician VA Med. Ctr., Coatesville, Pa.; psychology cons. Wilmington (Del.) City Schs., 1980-81. Served with USN, 1969-72. Calif. State scholar, 1964-68, 69. Mem. Am. Psychol. Assn. (assoc.), Nat. Assn. Music Therapy, Psychomusicology Soc., Phi Kappa Phi, Phi Mu Alpha Sinfonia (chpt. pres. 1967-68). Current Work: Psychology of music: psychophysiological aspects of musical rhythms, role of personality factors and musical preferences in psychophysiological responses to music; hypnosis. Subspecialties: Behavioral psychology; Neuropsychology. Home: 4 Forest Creek Dr Hockessin DE 19707 Office: VA Med Ctr Perry Point MD 21902

LITOV, RICHARD EMIL, nutritionist, researcher; b. N.Y.C., Sept. 28, 1953; s. Tzvetan A. and Alice V. L. B.S., U. Calif., Davis, 1975, Ph.D., 1980. Sr. scientist Mead Johnson & Co., Evansville, Ind., 1980—. Recipient Edward Frank Kraft award U. Calif., Davis, 1972. Mem. Am. Inst. Nutrition, Inst. Food Technologists. Methodist. Current Work: Trace mineral bioavailability in infant and adult enteral formulas, appetite-weight Control, physiological evaluation of dietary fiber. Subspecialties: Nutrition (biology); Biochemistry (biology). Office: Nutritional Sci Dept Mead Johnson & Co Evansville IN 47721

LITOVCHENKO, VLADIMIR ALEXEI, physicist, chemist, mathematician, researcher, educator; b. Makhachkala, USSR, Nov. 15, 1934; came to U.S., 1981; s. Alexei Z. and Alexandra P. (Shepetkova) L.; m. Irina A. Poletaieva, July 28, 1957 (div. 1964); m. Olga Aroseva., Nov. 10, 1978; children: Ioann, Anastasia-Christine, Porphyry Basil. B.Sc. in Physics and Math., U. Moscow, 1956; M.Sc. in Theoretical Physics, 1958; Ph.D., Lebedev Inst. Physics, USSR Acad. Sci., 1967. Predoctoral fellow Lebedev Inst. Physics, USSR Acad. Sci., 1958-61; asst., then assoc. prof. dept. applied math. Faculty of Sci., People's Friendship U., Patrice Lumumba U., 1961-73; chief pharmacopoeia dept. Inst. antibiotics, Moscow, 1973-74; adj. assoc. prof. dept. quantum theory Faculty Physics U. Moscow, 1971-81; research assoc. prof. dept. phys. chemistry, 1977-81; vis. asst. prof. dept. math. and research assoc. dept. chemistry U. Okla., Norman, 1982-83, adj. asst. prof. dept. physics, 1983-84, adj. assoc. prof. depts. chemistry and math., 1984—. Contbr. articles to Soviet and U.S. profl. publs. Mem. Am. Phys. Soc., Am. Math. Soc., European Phys. Soc., N.Y. Acad. Scis. Current Work: Theoretical physics: interaction of polarized radiation with chiral media, statistical physics of chiral media, theoretical solid state physics. Physical chemistry: solubilization and micellization study by fluorescence, Raman and infrared spectroscopy. Optics: Polarization of fluorescence, synchrotron radiation. Subspecialties: Theoretical physics; Physical chemistry. Office: 620 Parrington Oval Norman OK 73019

LITROWNIK, ALAN JAY, educator; b. Los Angeles, June 25, 1945; s. Irving and Mildred Mae (Rosin) L.; m. Hollis Merle Glazer, Aug. 20, 1967; children: Allison Brook, Jordan Michael. B.A., UCLA, 1967; M.A., U. Ill., 1969, Ph.D., 1971. Asst. prof. psychology San Diego State U., 1971-75, assoc. prof., 1975-78, prof., 1978-81, prof., chmn. dept. psychology, 1981—; cons. San Diego County Dept. Edn., 1975-81, Jay Nolan Ctrs., 1981-82; exec. bd. Ctr. for Behavioral Medicine, San Deigo, 1982—. Contbr. articles to profl. jours. U.S. Office Edn. grantee, 1975-78, 80-81. Mem. Am. Psychol. Assn., Assn. for Advancement Behavior Therapy. Democrat. Jewish. Current Work: Application of social learning and information processing approaches to understanding and treatment of disturbed and/or handicapped children. Subspecialties: Behavioral psychology; Cognition. Office: Dept Psychology San Diego State Univ 5300 Campanile Dr San Diego CA 92182

LITT, MORTON HERBERT, polymer science educator, researcher, consultant; b. Bklyn., Apr. 10, 1926; s. Samuel Bernard and Minnie (Hertz) L.; m. Lola Natalie Abrahamson, July 7, 1957; children—Jonathan Samuel, Jennifer Anne. B.S., City Coll. N.Y., 1947; M.S., Poly. Tech. Bklyn., 1953, Ph.D., 1956. Postdoctoral fellow Manchester U., Eng., 1956-57; sr. postdoctoral fellow N.Y. State Coll. Forestry, Syracuse, 1958-60; sr. scientist Allied Chem. Corp., Morristown, N.Y., 1960-64, assoc. dir. research, 1964-67; assoc. prof. Case Western Res. U., Cleve., 1967-75, prof. polymer sci., 1975—; cons. Allied Chem. Corp., Morristown, 1967—, Lawrence Livermore Lab., Calif., 1984—, Church & Dwight, Piscattaway, N.J., 1978—, Air Products, Pa., 1974—. Author numerous sci. papers. Patentee in field. Manchester U. Turner Newall Fellow 1956, 57. Fellow Am. Phys. Soc., AAAS; mem. Am. Chem. Soc., Chem. Soc. London, N.Y. Acad. Scis. Jewish. Subspecialties: Polymer chemistry; Kinetics. Home: 2575 Charney Rd University Heights OH 44118 Office: Case Western Res U 713 Olin Cleveland OH 44106

LITTAUER, ERNEST LUCIUS, electrochemist, metallurgist, materials sciences administrator; b. London, Mar. 8, 1936; came to U.S., 1963; s. Heinz Ludwig and Esther Ruth (Felsenstein) L.; m. Deveda Merrilyn McDonough, Aug. 10, 1969. B.Sc., U. London, Eng., 1958, Ph.D., 1961. Mgr. electrochemistry dept. Lockheed Aircraft Service Co., Ont., Calif., 1967-72, mgr. chemistry lab. Lockheed Palo Alto Research Lab., Palo Alto, Calif., 1972-84, dir. materials scis. research and devel. div., 1984—; lectr. electrochemistry U. Santa Clara, Calif., 1974-75; invited lectr. Stanford U., U. Calif.-Berkeley. Contbr. numerous articles to sci. jours.; patentee in field. Recipient Nat. Assn. Corrosion Engrs. Recognition award, 1968; Outstanding Metallurgy Grad. award U. London, 1958. Mem. The Electrochem. Soc. (mem. fin. and contbg. membership coms. 1977-80, chmn. new tech. subcom. 1981—). Current work: Direct multidisciplinary research organization, covering wide spectrum of aerospace-related advanced materials technologies. Subspecialties: Physical chemistry; Metallurgy. Office: Lockheed Palo Alto Research Lab 3251 Hanover St Palo Alto CA 94304

LITTLE, ELBERT LUTHER, JR., botanist, dendrologist; b. Ft. Smith, Ark., Oct. 15, 1907; s. Elbert Luther and Josephine (Conner) L.; m. Ruby Rema Rice, Aug. 14, 1943; children: Gordon Rice, Melvin Weaver, Alice Conner. B.A., U. Okla., 1927, B.S., 1932; M.S., U. Chgo., 1929, Ph.D., 1929; postgrad., U. Mich., 1927, Utah State U., 1928. Asst. prof. biology Southwestern Okla. State U., 1930-33; asst. to assoc. forest ecologist Forest Service, U.S. Dept. Agr., Tucson, 1934-41; dendrologist Forest Service, Washington, 1942-67, chief dendrologist, 1967-76; botanist Fgn. Econ. Adminstrn., Bogota, Colombia, 1943-45; prodn. specialist U.S. Comml. Co., Mexico City, 1945; cons. FAO, Cost Rica, 1964-65, 67, Ecuador 1965, 75, Nicaragua 1971, Peace Corps, 1984-85; collaborator dept. botany Nat. Mus. Natural History, Smithsonian Inst., Washington, 1965-76, research asso., 1976—; vis. prof. Universidad de Los Andes, Merida, Venezuela, 1953-54, 1960, Va. Poly. Inst. and State U., 1966-67, U. D.C., 1979; forester Okla. Forestry Div., 1930, 77-78. Author: Checklist of U.S. Trees, 1979, Atlas of U.S. Trees, 1971-81, Trees of Puerto Rico and the Virgin Islands, 1964-74, Alaska Trees and Shrubs, 1972, Arboles Commes de Esmeraldas, 1969, Audubon Society Field Guide to North American Trees, Eastern Region and Western Region, 1980, Forest Trees of Oklahoma, 1981; Contbr. articles to profl. jours. Recipient Superior Service award U.S. Dept. Agr., 1960, Disting. Service award, 1973, Outstanding award, 1975; Disting. Service award Am. Forestry Assn., 1981; Profl. Achievement award U. Chgo., 1982. Fellow Soc. Am. Foresters, Washington Acad. Sci., Okla. Acad. Sci., AAAS; mem. Bot. Soc. Am., Am. Soc. Plant Taxonomists, Ecol. Soc. Am., Internat. Soc. Plant Taxonomy, Am. Inst. Biol. Sci. (governing bd. 1956-60), Internat. Soc. Tropical Foresters, Sociedad Botanica de Mexico, Explorers club. Current Work: Research on trees of U.S. and tropical America; preparation of references for tree identification. Subspecialties: Taxonomy; Ecology (biology). Home: 924 20th St S Arlington VA 22202 Office: Dept Botan Smithsonian Inst Washington DC 20560

LITTLE, GORDON RICE, physicist, optical engineer; b. Mexico City, Oct. 22, 1945; came to U.S., 1945; s. Elbert L. Jr. and Ruby R. (Rice) L.; m. Vicki Lynn Cosner, Mar. 21, 1970; children—Chandra Noel, Jason Patrick. B.S. in Physics, Ohio State U., 1966, M.S. in Physics, 1970, Ph.D. in Physics, 1973. Research physicist Systems Research Labs., Inc., Dayton, Ohio, 1973-78; sr. analyst Sci. Applications, Inc., Dayton, 1978-79; sr. physicist Systems Research Labs., Inc., 1975-85; research optical physicist U. Dayton Research Inst., 1985—. Active Kettering Civic Band, Ohio, 1973-85, Wright State Community Orch., Dayton, 1982-83. Mem. Optical Soc. Am., Soc. Photo-Optical Instrumentation Engrs. Club: Miami Valley Horn (treas. 1984). Current work: Modern applied optics including development of schemes for laser detection, optical computing. Subspecialties: Composite materials; Optical engineering. Home: 2637 Oak Park Ave Kettering OH 45419 Office: Univ Dayton Research Inst 300 College Park Ave Dayton OH 45469

LITTLE, ROBERT COLBY, physiologist, educator; b. Norwalk, Ohio, June 2, 1920; s. Edwin Robert and Eleanor Thresher (Colby) L.; m. Claire Campbell Means, Jan. 20, 1945; children—William C., Edwin C. A.B., Denison U., 1942; M.D., Western Res. U., 1944, M.S., 1948. Intern Grace Hosp., Detroit, 1944-45; USPHS postdoctoral research fellow Western Res. U., 1948-49; resident internal medicine Crile VA Hosp., Cleve., 1949-50; asst. prof. physiology, then asso. prof. physiology and medicine U. Tenn. Sch. Medicine, 1950-54; research participant Oak Ridge Inst. Nuclear Studies, 1952; dir. clin. research Mead Johnson & Co., 1954-57; lectr. medicine U. Louisville, 1955-57; dir. cardio pulmonary labs. Scott Sherwood and Brindley Found., Temple, Tex., 1957-59; prof. physiology, asst. prof. medicine Seton Hall Coll. Medicine and Dentistry, 1957-64; prof. physiology, chmn. dept., also asst. prof. medicine Ohio State U. Sch. Medicine, 1964-73; prof. physiology, chmn. dept., prof. medicine Med. Coll. Ga. Sch. Medicine, Augusta, 1973—; Cons. in field. Author: Physiology of the Heart and Circulation, 1977, 3d edit., 1985; editor: Physiology of Atrial Pacemakers and Conductive Tissues, 1980; contbr. articles to profl. jours. Served to capt. M.C. AUS, 1945-47. Mem. Am. Physiol. Soc., So. Soc. Clin. Investigation, Am. Heart Assn., Assn. Chmn. Depts. Physiology, Soc. Exptl. Biology and Medicine, Am. Fedn. Clin. Research, Sigma Xi, Sigma Chi, Alpha Kappa Kappa. Current Work: Cardiovascular physiology, cardiology. Subspecialties: Physiology (medicine); Cardiology. Home: 44 Plantation Hills Dr Evans GA 30809

LITTLE, ROBERT JOHN, JR., botanist; b. Oceanside, Calif., July 8, 1946; s. Robert John and E. Ruth (Price) L.; m. Cynthia L. Haugen, June 11, 1968; children—Jeffery, Branden. B.S. in Botany, U. Utah, 1968; M.A. in Biology, Calif. State U., 1977; Ph.D. in botany, Claremont Grad. Sch., 1980. Lectr. in botany Calif. State U.-Fullerton, 1977-80; instr. biology Saddleback Coll., Mission Viejo, Calif., 1977-80; terrestrial ecologist Envirosphere Co., Santa Ana, Calif., 1980—; dir. Calif. Native Plant Soc., Sacramento, So. Calif. Botanists, Claremont. Co-author: A Dictionary of Botany, 1980. Editor: (with others) Handbook of Experimental Pollination Biology, 1983. Contbr. articles to profl. jours. Served to lt. USN, 1968-72. Grantee Audubon Soc., Sigma Xi. Mem. Botanical Soc. Am., Am. Soc. Plant Taxonomists; Ecological Soc. Am., AAAS. Current work: Floral mimicry in desert annuals; pollination and plant reproductive biology; ecology of solitary bees; ecology of southwestern deserts. Subspecialties: Botany; Reproductive biology. Home: 16 Pebble River Circle Sacramento CA 95831 Office: Envirosphere Co 555 Capitol Mall Suite 215 Sacramento CA 95814

LITTLE, ROBERT NARVAEZ, JR., physicist, physics educator; b. Houston, Mar. 11, 1913; s. Robert Narvaez and Lillian Forrest (Kinney) L.; m. Betty Jo Browning, June 1, 1942; children—Scott Robert, Emily Browning. B.A., Rice U., 1935, M.A., 1942, Ph.D., 1943. Seismologist Shell Oil Co., Houston, 1936-40; asst. prof. physics U. Oreg., Eugene, 1943-44; research sci. prof. U. Tex., Austin, 1944—; chief nuclear physics Gen. Dynamics, Ft. Worth, 1953-55; prof. visitante Universidad del Valle Guatemala, 1971; catedrático ad honorem U. Nacional de Educación a Distancia, Madrid, 1981; cons. Gen. Dynamics, Ft. Worth, 1955-65, Sandia Corp., Albuquerque, 1955, Bendix Corp., Detroit, 1955. Author: Motion and Matter, 4th edition, 1983. Contbr. articles to profl. jours. Fellow Tex. Acad. Sci., Am. Phys. Soc.; mem. Am. Assn. Physics Tchrs. (pres. 1970, Disting. Service award 1973), Groupe Internat. des Recherches sur l'Enseignement de la Physique, Sociedad de Fisicade Centroamericano y del Caribe. Current work: Experimental techniques for neutron detection and use of neutron scattering to study nuclear structure. Subspecialties: Nuclear fission; Nuclear physics. Home: 3928 Balcones Dr Austin TX 78731 Office: U Tex Physics Dept Austin TX 78712

LITTLE, TERRY WILLIAM, wildlife biologist; b. Preston, Minn., Nov. 13, 1946; s. Frank Harlow and Myrna Annette (Storhoff) L.; M. Cheryl Louise Southern, June 1, 1968; children—Heather Elizabeth, Sarah Jeanne, Emily Annette. B.A. in Biology, Luther Coll., 1968; M.S. in Wildlife Biology, Iowa State U., 1972; Ph.D. in Wildlife Biology, U. Minn.,-St. Paul, 1978. Wildlife biologist Iowa Conservation Commn., Boone, 1975-84, wildlife research supr., 1984—; mem. tech. com. Nat. Wild Turkey Fedn., 1977—. Contbr. sci. and popular articles to various publs. Served with USMC, 1968-70; Vietnam. Mem. Wildlife Soc. (cert. wildlife biologist), Wildlife Soc. (North Central sect.), Wildlife Soc. (Iowa chpt. pres. 1980-82), Am. Ornithologists Union, Nat. Wildlife Fedn., Gamma Sigma Delta, Phi Kappa Phi. Republican. Lutheran. Current work: Population ecology of game animals, specifically wild turkey, deer, ruffed grouse; habitat requirements of forest wildlife; management-research interface for wildlife populations. Subspecialties: Resource conservation; Population biology. Home: 1716 Marshall St Boone IA 50036 Office: Iowa Conservation Commission Wallace Office Bldg Des Moines IA 50319

LITTLEFIELD, JOHN WALLEY, geneticist, educator, pediatrician; b. Providence, Dec. 3, 1925; s. Ivory and Mary Russell (Walley) L.; m. Elizabeth Legge, Nov. 11, 1950; children: Peter P., John W., Elizabeth L. M.D., Harvard U., 1947. Diplomate: Am. Bd. Internal Medicine. Intern Mass. Gen. Hosp., Boston, 1947-48, resident in medicine, 1948-50, staff, 1956-74, chief genetics unit children's service, 1966-73; asso. in medicine Harvard U. Med. Sch., 1956-62, asst. prof. medicine, 1962-66, asst. prof. pediatrics, 1966-69, prof. pediatrics, 1970-73; prof., chmn. dept. pediatrics Johns Hopkins U. Sch. Medicine, Balt., 1974-85, prof., chmn. dept. physiology, 1985—; pediatrician-in-chief Johns Hopkins U. Hosp., 1974-85. Author: Variation, Senescence and Neoplasia in Cultured Somatic Cells, 1976. Served with USNR, 1952-54. Guggenheim fellow, 1965-66; Josiah Macy Jr. Found. fellow Oxford U., 1979. Mem. Am. Acad. Arts and Scis., Nat. Acad. Scis., Am. Soc. Biol. Chemists, Am. Soc. Clin. Investigation, Tissue Culture Assn., Soc. Pediatric Research, Am. Soc. Human Genetics, Am. Pediatric Soc., Am. Acad. Pediatrics, Assn. Am. Physicians, Phi Beta Kappa, Alpha Omega Alpha. Current Work: Developmental biology, molecular genetics, medical genetics. Subspecialties: Genetics and genetic engineering (medicine); Pediatrics. Home: 304 Golf Course Rd Owings Mills MD 21117 Office: Children's Medical and Surgical Center 2-116 Johns Hopkins Hosp Baltimore MD 21205*

LITTLER, MARK MASTERTON, botany curator, educator; b. Athens, Ohio, Sept. 24, 1939; s. Robert Howe and Alice Pauline (Masterton) L.; m. Diane Irene Scullion, Aug. 15, 1966. B.S., Ohio U., 1961, M.S., 1966; Ph.D., U. Hawaii, 1971. Prof. U. Calif.-Irvine, 1970-82; curator of botany Smithsonian Instn., Washington, 1982—; vis. prof. Stanford U., Monterey, Calif., 1973, U. So. Calif., Santa Catalina Island, 1973, 75; adj. prof. George Mason U., Fairfax, Va., 1984—. Contbr. numerous articles to profl. jours. Recipient numerous grants from govtl. agys.; Earle C. Anthony innovative research grantee U. Calif.-Irvine, 1973; recipient Darbaker prize Bot. Soc. Am., 1984, Exceptional Service award Smithsonian Instn., 1983; named Disting. Vis. Scientist, Northeastern U., 1981. Mem. Japanese Phycol. Soc., Phycol. Soc. Am. (assoc. editor 1984—), Ecol. Soc. Am., So. Calif. Acad. Sci., Internatl. Phycol. Soc. (com. 2nd internatl. symposium 1983-84), Western Soc. Naturalists, Internatl. Soc. Reef Studies, Brit. Phycol. Soc. Current work: Seaweed and seagrass experimental taxonomy, functional morphology, natural history; effects of disturbance on marine ecosystems, variability in standing stocks of temperate and tropical reef algae, productivity, evolution, biosystematics. Subspecialties: Systematics; Marine biology. Office: Dept Botany Smithsonian Instn NHB 166 Washington DC 20560

LITTLETON, JESSE TALBOT, III, radiology educator; b. Corning, N.Y., Apr. 27, 1917; s. Jesse Talbot and Bessie (Cook) L.; m. Martha Louise Morrow, Apr. 17, 1943; children: Christine, Joanne, James, Robert, Denise. Student, Emory (Va.) and Henry Coll., 1934-35, Johns Hopkins U., 1935-39; M.D., Syracuse U., 1939-43. Lic. physician N.Y., Pa., Fla., Ala. cert. Am. Bd. Radiology. Intern Buffalo Gen. Hosp., 1943; resident in medicine, surgery, radiology Robert Packer Hosp., Sayre, Pa., 1946-51, assoc. radiologist, 1951-53, chmn. dept. radiology, 1953-76; prof. radiology U. S. Ala., Mobile, 1976—; cons. in field. Author textbooks (2); contbr. chpts. to books and 80 articles to profl. jours., sci. exhibits to profl. confs. Served to capt. U.S. Army MC, 1944-46, Pacific. Fellow Am. Coll. Radiology; mem. AMA, N.Y. Acad. Scis., Am. Roetgen Soc., Ala. Acad. Radiology, Med. Assn. Ala., Sigma Xi, Alpha Omega Alpha. Republican. Methodist. Club: Country of Mobile (Ala.). Current Work: Conventional tomography, physical principles, equipment development and testing and clinical applications; transportation and radiology of the acutely ill and traumatized patient; angiography, development of equipment for sectional radiographic anatomy. Subspecialty: Radiology. Home: 5504 Churchill Downs Ave Theodore AL 36582 Office: U S Ala Med Ctr 2451 Fillingim St Mobile AL 36617

LITTLETON, JOHN EDWARD, educator, astrophysicist; b. Ballston Spa, N.Y., July 28, 1943; s. Clarence Eugene and Anna Lucy (Seeley) L. B.S. in Engring. Physics, Cornell U., 1965; Ph.D. in Astrophysics, U. Rochester, 1972. Research assoc. Belfer Grad. Sch. Sci., Yeshiva U., N.Y.C., 1972-73; research fellow Harvard Coll. Obs., Cambridge, Mass., 1973-75; asst. prof. physics W.Va. U., Morgantown, 1975-81, assoc. prof. physics, 1981—; vis. assoc. research astronomer U. Calif.-Berkeley, summer 1984, 85; vis. scientist dept. astronomy Ind. U., 1984. Contbr.: research articles to sci. publs. including Astrophys. Jour. Mem. Am. Astron. Soc., AAAS, Internat. Astron. Union, Am. Assn. Physics Tchrs., Sigma Xi. Current Work: Astrophysical fluid mechanics and astrophysical plasma processes; atomic and molecular processes in atmospheres of cool stars. Subspecialties: Theoretical astrophysics; Atomic and molecular physics. Home: 1432 Dorsey Ave Morgantown WV 26505 Office: Dept Physics WVa U PO Box 6023 Morgantown WV 26506

LITTMAN, MICHAEL GEIST, research scientist, educator; b. Washington, Mar. 29, 1950; s. Maxwell Leonard and Mildred (Geist) L.; m. L. Marion Katz Littman, Aug. 29, 1971. B.A., Brandeis U., 1972; Ph.D., M.I.T., 1977. Postdoctoral assoc. M.I.T., 1977-79; asst. prof. dept. mech. and aero. engring. Princeton U., 1979-85, assoc. prof., 1985—. Contbr. articles in field to profl. jours. Co-recipient Alfred Rheinstein Faculty award Princeton U., 1981. Mem. Am. Phys. Soc., Optical Soc. Am., Phi Beta Kappa, Sigma Xi. Jewish. Current Work: Effects of external fields on excited atoms; Stark effect, spectroscopy of alkali atoms, atomic beams, pulsed tunable lasers. Subspecialties: Atomic and molecular physics; Laser spectroscopy. Office: Princeton U D418 EQ Princeton NJ 08544

LITTON, COLUMBUS C., research agronomist; b. Shoopman, Ky., Nov. 21, 1921; s. John Sherman and Mary Ann (Blevins) L.; m. Neva Sue Miller, Dec. 25, 1954; 1 son, Thomas Christopher. B.S. in Agr. U. Ky., 1949, M.S. in Agr, 1952. Asst. prof. U. Ky., 1952-53; agt. Agrl. Research Service, U.S. Dept. Agr., U. Ky., 1953-55; research agronomist West Ky. Substation, Princeton, 1955-60, Agrl. Research Service, U. Ky., Lexington, 1960-85; ret. Contbr. articles to profl. jours. Served with U.S. Army, 1942-46. Mem. Am. Phytopath. Soc. Republican. Baptist. Current Work: Breeding for disease resistance in burley and dark air and dark fire cured tobaccos. Subspecialty: Plant pathology. Home: 2024 Bellefonte Dr Lexington KY 40503 Office: Dept Plant Pathology U Ky Lexington KY 40546

LITTON, STEPHEN FREDERICK, orthodontist, anatomist, educator; b. Bklyn., Jan. 8, 1943; s. Murray A. and Eda (Schwartz) L.; m. Bonnie Tarnoff, July 4, 1965; children: Jeremy, Jonathan. B.A., U. Minn., 1965; B.S. with distinction, 1965, D.D.S., 1967, Ph.D., 1972. Research fellow, teaching asst. U. Minn., 1966-72, asst. prof. dept. anatomy, 1972—; cons. orthodontics Pilot City Health Ctr., Mpls., 1972-73; dir. orthodontics Children's Health Ctr., Mpls., 1972-83; chief dentistry Mt. Sinai Hosp., Mpls., 1980—; cons. orthodontics State of Minn., St. Paul, 1979—. Named Tchr. of Year Sch. Dentistry, U. Minn., 1979. Mem. Internat. Assn. Dental Research (W.H. Crawford award Minn. sect. 1965), ADA, Minn. Dental Assn., Mpls. Dist. Dental Soc., Am. Assn. Orthodontists, Minn. Soc. Orthodontists (award 1967), Midwestern Soc. Orthodontists, Omicron Kappa Upsilon, Alpha Omega (scholarship 1967, pres. 1966-67). Current Work: collagen connective tissue, orthodontic tooth movement. Subspecialties: Orthodontics; Anatomy and embryology. Home: 1850 Kelly Dr Golden Valley MN 55427

LITVAK, BORIS LVOVICH, petroleum engineer; b. Tashkent, USSR, Nov. 25, 1943; came to U.S., 1979, naturalized, 1985; s. Lev E. and Dora M. Litvak; m. Alla P. Danilova, Nov. 5, 1968; 1 child, Maxim B. M.S., Oil and Gas Inst., USSR, 1964, Ph.D., 1969. Sr. research assoc. Oil and Gas Inst., Moscow, 1965-78; sr. petroleum engr. Texaco Inc., Houston, 1979—. Author: Optimization of Multivariable Systems, 1972; Optimization of Water Flooding Processes, 1977; Theory and Numerical Methods of Optimization, 1977; also articles. Mem. Soc. Petroleum Engrs., Soc. Indsl. and Applied Math. Current work: Reservoir engineering; numerical simulators development and application; primary, secondary and enhanced oil recovery; study of naturally fractured reservoirs. Subspecialties: Petroleum engineering; Mathematical software. Office: Texaco Inc PO Box 430 Bellaire TX 77401

LITWAK, PHILIP, veterinarian, researcher; b. Bklyn., Feb. 4, 1942; s. Hyman and Rita (Akivis) L.; m. Maxine L. Groten, Feb. 27, 1966; children—Kenneth N., Jeffrey B., Alan E. B.S., Kans. State U., 1962, D.V.M., 1964; Ph.D., Colo. State U., 1976; M.B.A., Pepperdine U., 1981. Diplomate Am. Coll. Vet. Surgeons. Assoc. veterinarian Ann Arbor Animal Hosp., Mich., 1966-67; staff veterinarian Hempstead Hosp. for Animals, Uniondale, N.Y., 1967-72; vet. project mgr. Inst. Med. Sci., San Francisco, 1976-79; project mgr. Vet. Thoratec Labs., Berkeley, Calif., 1980-82, v.p., 1982—; cons. NASA, Palo Alto, Calif., 1984—, Coll. of Pacific, San Francisco, 1979-80. Contbr. chpts. to books, articles to profl. jours. Patentee wound closure device, 1984. Treas. Lake Sherwood Homeowner's Assn., Fort Collins, Colo., 1975; mem. Bel Marin Keys Bd. Edn., Calif., 1978. Served to 1st lt. U.S. Army, 1965-66. NIH fellow, 1964-65, 72-76. Fellow Am. Coll. Vet. Surgery; mem. AVMA, Acad. Surg. Research. Jewish. Current work: Circulatory support devices; blood vessel prostheses. Subspecialties: Surgery (veterinary medicine); Artificial organs and prostheses. Home: 164 Caribe Isle Novato CA 94947 Office: Thoratec Labs Corp 2023 8th St Berkeley CA 94710

LITZENBERG, DAVID P., nuclear engineer, business, executive; b. Llanarch, Pa., Aug. 5, 1924; s. Charles C. and Elisabeth (Parker) L.; m. Pat Vickers, Sept. 1, 1979; m. Jeanne Carpenter, Feb. 27, 1947 (dec. Aug. 1977). B.S., U. Pa., 1946; M.B.A., Harvard U., 1952; Ph.D. in Nuclear Sci. Calif. Inst. Tech., 1958. Registered profl. engr., Ill. Chief engr. Zenith Engring. Corp., Phila., 1958-62; pres. Chempump Corp., Phila., 1958-65; chmn. bd. Powerdyne Corp., Phila., 1965—, Scottsdale, Ariz., 1965—; owner Litzenberg Engring. Soc., Phila., 1965—; chmn. bd. Pioneer Industries, Inc., Hayden Corp.; dir. L.A. Mitchell Ltd., Gt. Britain, N.K.K.K. Ltd., Japan, Heinze Fabrikat, Germay. Mem. Regional Econ. Council, 1957-62; chmn. United Fund, 1965, Am. Assn. Grad. Schs., 1969. Served to col. U.S. Army, 1947-52. Recipient Thomas awrad Am. Inst. Mgmt., 1965; Cutler award Inernat. Mktg. Soc., 1962. Mem. Am. Nuclear Soc. (chmn.), Am. Ordnance Assn. (life), Soc. Am. Mil Engrs. (dir.), Navy League (dir.), Franklin Inst., Pa. C. of C., Pa. Mfrs. Assn., Am. Nuclear Soc., Am. Inst. Mgmt. Patentee process equipment (3). Subspecialties: Industrial engineering; Mechanical engineering. Home: 8638 N 84th Pl Scottsdale AZ 85258

LITZENBERGER, LEONARD NELSON, research physicist; b. East Macungie, Pa., Oct. 15, 1945; s. Nelson George and Cora Maggie (Hausman) L.; m. Anne Fabiola Ward, Oct. 19, 1974; 1 child, Julie Beth. B.S. in Engring. Physics with highest honors, Lehigh U., 1967; S.M. in Physics, MIT, 1969, Ph.D. in Physics, 1971. Prin. research scientist Avco Everett Research Lab., Inc., Mass., 1971—. Contbr. articles to profl. jours. Patentee in field of laser isotope separation. Mem. Am. Phys. Soc., Sigma Xi, Phi Beta Kappa, Tau Beta Pi. Current work: Development of technology needed to scale e-beam pumped excimer lasers to high energy and high average power levels. Subspecialty: Excimers. Office: Avco Everett Research Lab Inc 2385 Revere Beach Pkwy Everett MA 02149

LIU, CHANG YU, mechanical engineer; b. Potin, Hopei, China, June 21, 1935; s. Tien-fu and Cherish (Pei-chang) L.; m. Wu peng yun, Aug. 13, 1968; children: Zeh-chen, Zeh-Wen. B.S., Chinese Naval Coll. Tech., Tsoying, 1958; M.S., Colo. State U., 1965, Ph.D., 1967. Design engr. Chinese 1st Naval Shipyard, Tsoying, 1959-60; instr. Chinese Naval Acad., Tsoying, 1961-63; assoc. prof. mech. engring. and naval architecture Nat. Taiwan U., Taipei, 1967-75; assoc. prof. Singapore U., 1975-78; prof. mech. engring. Unicamp, Campinas, Brazil, 1978—. Author: Principles of Naval Architecture, 1974. Ministry Edn. Taiwan scholar, 1976. Mem. AIAA, Aeros. and Astronautics Soc. Republic China. Patentee semibalanced rudder, twin-wire resistance probe manometer. Current Work: Instrumentations, theoretical and experimental study of boundary layer, heat transfer and energy storage; flow through porous medium. Subspecialties: Fluid mechanics; Wind power. Home: Rua Luiz Vicentin 144 Barao Geraldo Campinas Sao Paulo 13100 Brazil Office: DEM FEC Unicamp Barao Geraldo Campinas Sao Paulo 13100 Brazil

LIU, CHEN-HUEI, aerospace engineer, researcher; b. Hsing Ling, Kwangtung, China, June 29, 1941; came to U.S., 1966, naturalized, 1975; s. Hsiang-Hsien and Lin (Teng) L.; m. Grace Chi-Kun, Feb. 9, 1968; children: Edwin, Gene, Eric. B.S., Cheng Kung U., Tainan, Taiwan, 1963; M.S., NYU, 1968, Ph.D., 1971. Sr. analyst Computer Sci. Corp., Hampton, Va., 1972-73; research scientist NRC, NASA-Langley, Hampton, Va., 1973-75, aerospace engr., 1975—. Mem. Am. Phys. Soc., ASME, AIAA, Sigma Gamma Tau. Current Work: Computational fluid dynamics, aerodynamics, vortex flows. Subspecialties: Fluid mechanics; Aeronautical engineering. Home: 128 Macaulay Rd Williamsburg VA 23185 Office: NASA Langley Research Center Mail Stop 128 Hampton VA 23665-5225

LIU, CHING-TONG, research physiologist, educator; b. Kiangsu, China, Oct. 19, 1931; s. Lien Yi and Su Ju (Ku) L.; m. In-May Hsin, Feb. 28, 1970; children: Rex, Grace, Jeannette, Christine. M.S., U. Tenn., Memphis, 1959, Ph.D., 1963. Assoc. research biologist Sterling-Winthrop Research Inst., Renssalaer, N.Y., 1965-66; asst. prof. physiology Baylor Coll. Medicine, Houston, 1966-73, adj. prof., 1979—; research physiologist, chief dept. clin. and exptl. physiology U S. Army Med. Research Inst. Infectious Diseases, Ft. Detrick, Md., 1973—. Contbr. numerous articles to profl. jours. Mem. Soc. Exptl. Biology and Medicine, Am. Physiol. Soc., Am. Soc. Pharmacology and Exptl. Therapeutics, Am. Soc. Nephrology. Current Work: Dynamic functional changes and systematically integrated responses to certain viral infections in animals. Subspecialties: Physiology (medicine); Pharmacology. Home: 7915 W 7th St Frederick MD 21701 Office: Disease Assessment Div USAMRIID Fort Detrick Frederick MD 21701

LIU, HAN-SHOU, space scientist, researcher; b. Hunan, China, Mar. 9, 1930; came to U.S., 1960, naturalized, 1972; s. Yu-Tin and Chun-Chen (Yeng) L.; m. Sun-Ling Yang Liu, May 2, 1957; children: Michael Fu-Yen, Peter Fu-Tze. Ph.D., Cornell U., 1963. Research asst. Cornell U., 1962-63; research assoc. Nat. Acad. Sci., Washington, 1963-65; scientist NASA Goddard Space Flight Center, Greenbelt, Md., 1965—; Pres. Mei-Hwa Chinese Sch., 1980-81. Contbr. articles to profl. jours. Fellow AAAS; mem. Am. Astron. Soc., Am. Geophys. Union, Planetary Soc., AIAA. Current Work: Dynamics of the earth and planets. Subspecialties: Tectonics; Geophysics. Home: 2301 Laurelwood Terr Silver Spring MD 20904 Office: Code 621 NASA Goddard Space Flight Center Greenbelt MD 20771

LIU, HSIANG MEI, neurobiology educator; b. Leeshan, China, Nov. 19, 1929; came to U.S., 1953, naturalized, 1962; s. Shan-Tung and Shee-Chou (Hsia) L; m. Tieh Chun Wang, June 6, 1953 (div. 1970); children—Pamela, Peter, Deborah. M.D., Taiwan U., 1953; M.D., Brown U., 1979. Asst. prof. pathology U. Chgo., 1969-71, Northwestern U., Chgo., 1971-77; neuropathologist Miriam Hosp., Providence, 1977—; assoc. prof. Brown U., Providence, 1977—. Author: Biology and Pathology of Nerve Growth, 1981. Fellow Am. Assn. Pathologists; mem. Am. Assn. Neuropathologists, Soc. for Neurosci., Sigma Xi. Current work: Using experimental tissue culture and chemical methods, I study the mechanisms involved in the maintenance of the neural circuitry and in the growth and regeneration. Subspecialties: Neurobiology; Regeneration. Home: 106 John St Providence RI 02906 Office: Miriam Hosp 164 Summit Ave Providence RI 02906

LIU, HUA-KUANG, electrical engineer, scientist, educator; b. Kueilin, Kwangsi, China, Sept. 2, 1939; s. Shui-chien and Cheng-Hsia (Fang) L.; m. Shao-Fen Liu; children: Tien-Wen, Ren-Wen. B.S.E.E., Nat. Taiwan U., 1962; M.S.E.E., U.Iowa, 1965; Ph.D., Johns Hopkins U., 1969. Jr. instr. Johns Hopkins U., 1965-69; mem. faculty dept. elec. engring. U. Ala., 1969-84, prof., 1977-84; sr. scientist Jet Propulsion Lab., Calif. Inst. Tech., Pasadena, 1984—; vis. assoc. prof. Stanford U., 1975-76; vis. prof. Nat. Taiwan U., 1982-83, U. Wis., Madison, 1983; cons. to industry U.S. Army Missile Command. Whitehead fellow, 1965-69; NSF grantee, 1970-73, 75-77. Fellow Optical Soc. Am.; mem. IEEE, Sigma Xi. Patentee in field. Current Work: Optical image processing, holography and printing. Subspecialties: Optical engineering; Semiconductors. Office: Observational System Div Jet Propulsion Lab Calif Inst Tech 4800 Oak Grove Dr Pasadena CA 91109

LIU, KEH-FEI FRANK, physicist, physics educator; b. Beijing, China, Jan. 11, 1947; came to U.S., 1969, naturalized, 1983; s. Hsien-Chang and Jui-Hua (Wang) L.; m. Yao-Chin Ko, Apr. 6, 1974; 1 child, Helen. B.S. with honors, Tunghai U. (Taiwan), 1968; M.S., SUNY-Stonybrook, 1972, Ph.D., 1975. Vis. scientist CEN Saclay, France, 1974-76; research assoc. UCLA, 1976-78, asst. prof., 1978-80; assoc. prof. physics U. Ky., Lexington, 1980—. Assoc. editor Internat. Review Nuclear Physics World Sci. Pub. Co., Singapore, 1983—. Contbr. articles to profl. jours. Fellow Assoc. Western U. 1981; Dept. of Energy grantee 1982—. Mem. Am. Phys. Soc., European Phys. Soc., Phi Tau Phi. Current work: Hadron spectroscopy, lattice gauge theory, chiral solutions, quark model, Fermi liquid theory of nuclei, nuclear force. Subspecialties: Nuclear physics; Particle physics. Home: 309 Atwood Dr Lexington KY 40503 Office: Dept Physics U Ky Lexington KY 40506

LIU, KOU-CHANG, chemist; b. Chunking, China, Dec. 30, 1939, came to U.S., 1964; s. Ping-yu and Tuan-bon (Cheng) L.; m. Lie-ming Lee, Oct. 17, 1971; children—Josephine, Raymond. B.S., Tunghai U., Taiwan, 1963; Ph.D., NYU, 1973. Research assoc. Mich. State U., East Lansing, 1973-74, Columbia U., N.Y.C., 1974-76; sr. chemist Monsanto Co., St. Louis, 1976-79; sr. research chemist GAF Corp., Wayne, N.J., 1979-81, sr. staff chemist, 1982-83, tech. assoc., 1983—. Contbr. articles to profl. jours. Patentee in field. Mem. Am. Chem. Soc., Catalysis Soc. N.Y., Sigma Xi. Current work: Heterocyclic compounds; photochemistry; micellar phenomena; acetylenic chemicals and reaction mechanisms. Subspecialties: Organic chemistry; Photochemistry. Office: GAF Corp Central Research 1361 Alps Rd Wayne NJ 07470

LIU, PAUL CHI, oceanographer; b. Chefoo, Shuntung, China, June 18, 1935; came to U.S., 1959, naturalized, 1972; s. Joseph T. C. and Agatha I. M. (Wang) L.; m. Teresa Sheau-mei Wang, Jan. 30, 1965; 1 dau., Christina P. B.S., Nat. Taiwan U., 1956; M.S., Va. Poly. Inst., 1961; Ph.D., U. Mich.-Ann Arbor, 1977. Research phys. scientist U.S. Lake Survey, U.S. Army C.E., Detroit, 1965-71; research phys. scientist Nat. Ocean Survey, NOAA, Detroit, 1971-74; oceanographer Great Lakes Environ. Research Lab., NOAA, Ann Arbor, Mich., 1974—; vis. scholar U. Mich., 1978—. NOAA fellow, 1971-72. Mem. Am. Acad. Mechanics, Am. Geophys. Union, Am. Meteorol. Soc., ASCE, Soc. Indsl. and Applied Math., Sigma Xi, Phi Kappa Phi. Roman Catholic. Current Work: Wind-generated waves, coastal engineering, physical oceanography. Subspecialties: Ocean engineering; Fluid mechanics. Home: 2939 Renfrew St Ann Arbor MI 48105 Office: Great Lakes Environ Research Lab NOAA 2300 Washtenaw Ave Ann Arbor MI 48104

LIU, SAMUEL HSI-PEH, physicist; b. Taiyuan, China, Apr. 17, 1934; came to U.S., 1955; m. Annabel Liu, 1961; children—Andrea, Clifton. B.A., Nat. Taiwan U., 1954; M.S., Iowa State U., 1958, Ph.D., 1960. Research staff IBM Research Ctr., Yorktown Heights, N.Y., 1960-64; assoc. prof. Iowa State U., Ames, 1964-67, prof., 1967-81; sr. research staff mem. Oak Ridge Nat. Lab., 1981—. Contbr. articles to profl. jours. Fellow Am. Phys. Soc. (exec. com. div. condensed matter physics 1985-88); mem. Sigma Xi, Eta Kappa Nu. Current work: Theoretical condensed matter physics, including magnetism, lattice dynamics, surface physics, mixed valence, fractals. Subspecialties: Condensed matter physics; Theoretical physics. Office: Oak Ridge Nat Lab PO Box X Oak Ridge TN 37830

LIU, YET-ZEN, electrical engineer, researcher; b. Cheng-tu, China, June 29, 1940; came to U.S., 1963; s. Hsun-wu and T.S. (Yao) L.; m. Katherine June Chang; children—Alan, Laura. B.S. in Elec. Engring., Nat. Taiwan U., Republic of China, 1962; M.S. in Elec. Engring., U. Calif.-Berkeley, 1965; Ph.D. in Elec. Engring., Stanford U., 1969. Research asst. dept. elec. engring. Stanford U., 1965-69; research scientist Electro-Nuclear Labs; Menlo Park, Calif., 1969-71; mgr. compound materials and devices ITT, Ind. and Va., 1971-78; mem. tech. staff Rockwell Internat. Sci. Ctr., Thousand Oaks, Calif., 1978-82; dir. research Fermionics Corp., Chatsworth, Calif., 1982—. Patentee light emitting diode fabrication process, current confining light emitting diode, backside illuminated imaging charge couple device, w-shaped diffused strip laser. Contbr. articles to profl. jours. Mem. IEEE, Electrochem. Soc. Current work: Developing high performance semiconductor lasers and marketing them. Subspecialties: Semiconductor lasers; Semiconductors. Office: Fermionics Corp 9555 Owensmouth Ave Chatsworth CA 91311

LIU, YUNG SHENG, scientist; b. Anhwei, China, Sept. 23, 1944; came to U.S., 1967, naturalized, 1982; s. Hsing Chi and Li Wen (Wang) L.; m. Ming Lee, Jan 20, 1945; children: Alan, Jenny. B.S., Nat. Taiwan U., 1966; Ph.D., Cornell U., 1972. Research asst. Cornell U., 1968-72, teaching asst., 1968; physicist Gen. Electric Research Center, Schenectady, 1972—; vis. scientist UCLA, 1969; cons. in field; mem. U.S. Congressional Adv. Bd., 1982—. Contbr. articles to profl. jours. AVCO fellow, 1970; USAF grantee, 1975—; recipient Gen. Electric Outstanding Achievement award, 1977, Publ. award, 1982. Mem. Am. Phys. Soc., Optical Soc. Am., IEEE, Sigma Xi. Current Work: Laser physics and nonlinear optical devices; high power solid state lasers; laser processing of semiconductors, microelectronics. Subspecialties: Laser optics; Microelectronics. Home: 101 Woodhaven Dr Scotia NY 12302 Office: KWB-1307 PO Box 8 Schenectady NY 12345

LIU, YUNG YUAN, materials and energy research engineer; b. Taipei, Taiwan, Mar. 20, 1950; came to U.S., 1973, naturalized, 1982; s. Kan C. and Mon W. (Chou) L.; m. Teresa L. Ngai, Jan. 4, 1975; children: Sharon H.Y., Alvin H.L. B.S., Nat. Tsing-Hua U., Taiwan, 1971; M.A., MIT, 1976, Sc.D., 1978. Staff engr. Entropy Ltd., Lincoln, Mass., 1977-78; asst. nuclear engr. Argonne (Ill.) Nat. Lab., 1978-81, nuclear engr., 1981—; mem. life code com. U.S. Dept. Energy, 1978-81, mem. fuel performance evaluation task force, 1978-81; cons. Los Alamos Nat. Lab., 1982-83. Contbr. articles to profl. jours.; editor-in-chief: Free Chinese Monthly, Cambridge, Mass., 1973-75. Mem. Am. Nuclear Soc., Am. Soc. Metals. Baptist. Current Work: Energy technology related materials, high temperature materials behavior; radiation damage; physics of deformation and fracture; computer simulation of materials behavior. Subspecialties: Nuclear fission; Nuclear fusion. Home: 333 Hampton Pl Hinsdale IL 60521 Office: Materials Sci and Tech Argonne Nat Lab 9700 S Cass Ave Argonne IL 60439

LIU, YUNG-PIN, biochemist; b. Tao-Yuan, Taiwan, Aug. 26, 1937; came to U.S., 1963, naturalized, 1975; s. A-Yen and Kan-Mei (Hsu) L.; m. Mei-Shiang Sung, July 10, 1967; 1 dau., Bo-May. B.S., Chung-Yuan U., 1960; M.S., Lowell Tech. U., 1967; Ph.D., Baylor U., 1970. Teaching asst. Lowell Tech. U., Lowell, Mass., 1965-67; research asst. Wadley Inst. Molecular Medicine, Dallas, 1967-69; postdoctoral fellow Yale U., New Haven, 1969-72; research assoc. St. Jude Children's Hosp., Memphis, 1972-75; asst. prof. U. Tenn., Memphis, 1973-75; cancer expert NIH, Bethesda, Md., 1975-82; research biochemist Walter Reed Army Inst. Research, Washington, 1982—. Contbg. author: Cyclic Nucleotides in Disease, 1975, Ocular Pathology Update, 1980, Molecular Mechanics Photoreceptor Transduction, 1981, Structure of the Eye, 1982, Pharmacologic Principles Cancer Treatment, 1982. Named Outstanding Supr. NIH, 1979; recipient Outstanding Achievement award Fight for Sight, Inc., 1980. Mem. Am. Soc. Biol. Chemists, Chinese Biochem. Soc. Current Work: Isolation, identification, and characterizations of plasminogen activator and plasminogen inhibitor in the human promyelocytic leukemia cell line. Subspecialties: Biochemistry (biology); Hematology. Home: 9723 Singleton Dr Bethesda MD 20817 Office: Walter Reed Army Inst Research 14th St and Dahlia Washington DC 30207

LIVE, DAVID HARRIS, chemist; b. Phila., Apr. 3, 1946; s. Israel and Anna (Harris) L. B.S., U. Pa., 1967; Ph.D., Calif. Inst. Tech., 1974. Research assoc. Rockefeller U., N.Y.C., 1974-78, asst. prof. dept. phys. biochemistry, 1978-84; sr. research assoc. Jet Propulsion Lab., Calif. Inst. Tech., 1984-85; assoc. prof. dept. chemistry Emory U., Atlanta, 1986—. Mem. Am. Chem. Soc., AAAS, N.Y. Acad. Sci. Subspecialties: Biophysical chemistry; Polymer chemistry. Office: Emory U Dept Chemistry Atlanta GA 30322

LIVINGSTON, CLARK H., plant pathologist; b. Eau Claire, Wis., Nov. 25, 1920; s. George Wallace and Helen Louise (Holcomb) L.; m. Ann Jean Garney, June 9, 1947; children: Kay Ann, Thomas Clark. B.S., Colo A&M U., 1951,

M.S., 1953; Ph.D., U. Minn., 1966. Mem. faculty Colo. State U., Ft. Collins, 1955—, now plant pathologist, prof. botany plant pathology. Contbr. articles in field to profl. jours. Active Boy Scouts Am. Served with U.S. Army, 1943-46. Mem. Am. Phytopath. Soc., Potato Assn Am. Republican. Current Work: Potato, bean and tree viruses and their related diseases. Subspecialties: Plant pathology; Plant virology. Home: 3008 Shore Rd Fort Collins CO 80524 Office: 113 Potato Virus Research Lab Fort Collins CO 80523

LIVINGSTON, DAVID MORSE, physician, molecular biologist; b. Cambridge, Mass., March 29, 1941; s. Arthur Joshua and Phyllis Freda (Kanters) L.; m. Jacqueline Sue Gutman, June 23, 1963; children: Catherine Ellen, Julie. A.B., Harvard U., 1961; M.D. Magna Cum Laude, Tufts U., 1965. Diplomate: Am. Bd. Internal Medicine. Intern, resident in medicine Peter Bent Brigham Hosp., Boston, 1965-67; research fellow NIH, Bethesda, Md., 1967-69, sr. staff fellow, 1971-72, scientist, 1972-73; research fellow in biochemistry, fellow Helen Hay Whitney Found. Harvard Med. Sch., Boston, 1969-71, asst. prof., 1973-1976, assoc. prof., 1976-82, prof. medicine, 1982—; mem. virology study sect. NIH, 1979-83. Mem. editorial bd.: Virus Research, Virology, Jour. Virology, 1976-79, Cell, 1976-79, Archives of Virology, 1977-79. Served with USPHS, 1967-69, 1971-73. Mem. Am. Soc. Biol. Chemists, Am. Soc. Clin. Investigation, Am. Soc. Microbiology. Current Work: molecular biology of tumor viruses, molecular genetics and biology of blood clotting proteins, cancer medicine. Subspecialties: Molecular biology; Cancer research (medicine). Office: Dana Farber Cancer Inst Harvard Med Sch Boston MA 02115

LIVINGSTON, JAMES DUANE, physicist; Bklyn., June 23, 1930; s. James Duane and Florence J. (Boullee) L.; m. Nancy Lee Clark, June 26, 1953 (div. 1976); children—Joan, Susan, Barbara; m. Sherry Hood Penney, Mar. 30, 1985. B.S. in Engring. Physics, Cornell U., 1952; M.S., Harvard U., 1953, Ph.D., 1956. Physicist Gen. Electric Corp. Research and Dev. op., Schenectady, 1956—; guest prof. Göttingen U., Fed. Republic Germany, 1970. Author: (with H.W. Schadler) The Effect of Metallurgical Variables on Superconducting Properties, 1964. Contbr. articles to profl. jours. Fellow Am. Soc. for Metals, Am. Phys. Soc.; mem. AAAS, AIME, Magnetics Soc. of IEEE. Democrat. Unitarian. Current work: Research relations between metallurgical microstructure and ferromagnetic, superconducting and mechanical properties. Subspecialties: Metallurgy; Condensed matter physics. Office: Gen Elec Co Corp Research and Dev Schenectady NY 12301

LIVINGSTON, JOHN DAVID, computer consultant; b. Jefferson City, Mo., Apr. 16, 1928; s. Joseph Hall and Laura Mae (Terrill) L.; m. Rachel Ann Jennings, Dec. 27, 1952; children: David Hall, Jennie Ann, Francis Joseph. B.S. in Indsl. Edn., Ind. State U., 1954; postgrad., Purdue U., 1954. With U.S. Bur. Census, Suitland, Md., 1960-64; mgr. computer test facility Bunker Ramo, Ft. Huachuca, Ariz., 1964-65; mgr. computation Lab. Electronic Assocs., Inc., Princeton, N.J., 1965-68; computer ctr. mgmt. expert UN, Bucharest, Romania, 1969-70, prof. info. tech., Turin, Italy, 1970-79; UN chief tech. advisor Egyptian Fgn. Ministry, Cairo, 1979—. Author: What is a Computer? , 1971, Computer Operations Management, 1969. Served in U.S. Army, 1945-49. Fellow Inst. Prodn. Control, Visible Record Soc.; mem. IEEE, Assn. Computing Machinery, Data Processing Mgmt. Assn., Nat. Micrographics Assn. Current Work: Computer assisted instruction research; current information retrieval and management systems; special interests computers in aid to developing countries. Subspecialties: Information systems, storage, and retrieval (computer science); Information systems (Information science). Home: Rt 6 Box 171 Mountain Home AZ 72653 Office: UN-Cairo PO Box 20-Grand Central New York NY 10163

LIVINGSTON, WILLIAM CHARLES, astronomer; b. Santa Ana, Calif., Sept. 13, 1927; s. William Charles and Ada Markley (Parvin) L.; m. Dorothy Wingate Newell, June 22, 1957; children: Ann, Peter. Student, Los Angeles City Coll, 1946-49; A.B., UCLA, 1952; Ph.D., U. Calif.-Berkeley, 1959. Observing asst. Mt. Wilson Obs., 1950-52, 57-58; jr. astronomer Kitt Peak Nat. Obs., Tucson, 1959-60, asst. astronomer, 1960-65, asso. astronomer, 1965-69, astronomer/tenure, 1969—, researcher meterol. optics. Served with USAF, 1945-46. Mem. Am. Astron. Soc., Internat. Astron. Union (pres. com. 9 instruments), Astron. Soc. India. Current Work: Solar instruments and telescopes, solar magnetic fields, solar eclipses, observations of solar spectrum, solar variability. Subspecialties: Optical astronomy; Solar physics.

LJUNG, DONOVAN ALLEN, physicist; b. Alexandria, Minn., July 16, 1943; s. Allen Latimer and Irene Margaret (Hanson) L.; m. Ellen Jo Szabad, Sept. 5, 1968; children—Michael Allen, David Jeffrey. Diploma, Phillips Exeter Acad., N.H., 1958-61; B.A. in Physics, Carleton Coll., 1965; M.A. in Physics, U. Wis., 1966, Ph.D., 1972. Research assoc. Fermi Nat. Accelerator, Batavia, Ill., 1972-74; instr. in physics Yale U., New Haven, 1974-75, asst. prof., 1975-79; physicist Fermi Nat. Accelerator, Batavia, 1979-81; mem. tech. staff AT&T Bell Labs., Naperville, Ill., 1981—, supr., 1985—. Contbr. articles to tech. jours. Sec., bd. dirs. Temple B'Nai Israel, Aurora, Ill., 1981—; founder, pres. Blackberry Homeowners Assn., Geneva, Ill., 1980-81, 85. Mem. Am. Phys. Soc., IEEE. Jewish. Current work: software development for central office switching systems. Subspecialties: Telecommunications; Software engineering. Home: 2257 Clover Ln Geneva IL 60134 Office: AT&T Bell Labs Indian Hill Room 2B-268 Napierville-Wheaton Rd Naperville IL 60566

LLAURADO, JOSEP G., nuclear medicine physician, scientist; b. Barcelona (Catalonia), Spain, Feb. 6, 1927; s. Jose and Rosa (Llaurado) Garcia; m. Deirdre Mooney, Nov. 9, 1966; children: Raymund, Wilfred, Mireya; m. Catherine D. Entwistle, June 28, 1958 (dec.); children: Thadd, Oleg, Montserrat. B.S., B.A., Balmes Inst., Barcelona, 1944; M.D., Barcelona U., 1950; Ph.D., 1960; M.Sc. Biomed. Engring., Drexel U., 1963. Diplomate: Am. Bd. Nuclear Medicine. Resident Royal Postgrad Sch. Medicine, Hammersmith Hosp., London, 1952-54; fellow M.D. Anderson Hosp. and Tumor Inst., Houston, 1957-58, U. Utah Med. Coll., Salt Lake City, 1958-59; asst. prof. U. Otago Dunedin, N.Z., 1954-57; sr. endocrinologist Pfizer Med. Research Lab., Groton, Conn., 1959-60; assoc. prof. U. Pa., 1963-67; prof. Med. Coll. Wis., Milw., 1970-82, Marquette U., Milw., 1967-82; clin. dir. nuclear medicine service VA Med. Ctr., Milw., 1977-82; chief nuclear medicine service VA Hosp., Loma Linda, Calif., 1983—; prof. dept. radiation scis. Loma Linda U. Sch. Medicine, 1983—; U.S. rep. symposium on dynamic studies with radioisotopes in clin. medicine and research IAEA, Rotterdam, 1970, Knoxville, 1974. Contbr. numerous articles to profl. jours. Merit badge counselor Boy Scouts Am., 1972—; pres. Hales Corners (Wis.) Hist. Soc., 1981-83. Recipient Commendation cert. Boy Scouts Am., 1980. Fellow Am. Coll. Nutrition; mem. Soc. Nuclear Medicine (computer and acad. councils), IEEE (sr.), Biomed. Engring. Soc. (charter), Am. Physiol. Soc., Am. Soc. Pharmacology and Exptl. Therapeutics, Soc. Math. Biology (founding), Endocrine Soc., Royal Soc. Health, Soc. Catalana de Biologia. Roman Catholic. Current Work: Cardiac nuclear medicine; phosphorus-32 therapy of cancer; computer applications to biomedicine; compartmental analysis. Subspecialties: Nuclear medicine; Biomedical engineering. Office: VA Hosp 115 Loma Linda CA 92357

LLINAS, RODOLFO RIASCOS, medical educator, researcher, physician; b. Bogotá , Colombia, Dec. 16, 1934; came to U.S., 1960, naturalized, 1973; s. Jorge Enrique and Bertha (Riascos) L.; m. Gillian Kimber, Dec. 24, 1965; children: Rafael Hugo, Alexander Jorge. B.S., Gimnasio Moderno, Bogotá , 1952; M.D., Universidad Javeriana, Bogotá , 1958; Ph.D., Australian Nat. U., Canberra, 1965. Rotating intern Hosp. San José , Bogotá , 1959; postdoctoral research fellow Stanley Cobb Lab., Mass. Gen. Hosp., Harvard U. Med. Sch., Boston, 1959-61; NIH researchfellow in physiology U.Minn., Mpls., 1961-63, assoc. prof. physiology, 1965-66; assoc. mem. AMA Inst. Biomed. Research, Chgo., 1966-68, mem., 1970, head neurobiology unit, 1967-70; assoc. prof. neurology and psychiatry Northwestern U., 1967-71; professorial lectr. in pharmacology U. Ill. Coll. Medicine-Chgo., 1967-68, clin. prof. pharmacology, 1968-72; prof. physiology, head neurobiology div. U. Iowa Sch. Medicine, 1970-76; prof. physiology and biophysics, chmn. dept. physiology and biophysics NYU Med. Sch., 1976—; guest prof. physiology Wayne State U. Sch. Medicine, 1967-74; professorial lectr. College de France, Paris, 1979; mem. neurol. sci. research tng. com. Nat. Insts. Neurol. Diseases and Stroke NIH, 1971-73; assoc. neurosci. research program MIT, 1974-83; mem. neurology study sect. div. research grants NIH, 1974-78; mem. panel on basic neurosci. research Nat. Acad. Sci. Task Force, 1978; mem. sci. adv. bd. for basic research Max-Planck Inst. Psychiatry, Munich, W.Ger., 1979-83. Authors: (with Hubbard and Quastel) Electrophysiological Analysis of Synaptic Transmission, 1969; editor: (with Hubbard and Quastel) Neurobiology of Cerebellar Evolution and Development, 1969, (with W. Precht) Frog Neurobiology: A Handbook, 1976; chief editor: (with W. Precht) Neurosci, 1974—; editorial bd.: (with W. Precht) Jour. Neurobiology, 1980—, Pfluegers Archiv, 1981—, Jour. Theoretical Neurobiology, 1981—. Recipient John C. Krantz award U. Md. Sch. Medicine, 1976. Mem. Soc. Neurosci. (council 1974-78), Am. Physiol. Soc. (Bowditch lectr. 1973, mem. task force on neurophysiology 1974), Am. Soc. Cell Biology, Biophys. Soc., Harvey Soc., Internat. Brain Research Orgn. (mem. U.S. nat. com. 1978-81, acting chmn. com. 1982, chmn. com. 1983-84), N.Y. Acad. Scis., Tensor Soc., Alpha Omega Alpha. Current Work: Synaptic transmission in vertebrates and invertebrates; single cell electrophysiology; neuronal nets; cerebellar function; mathematical modelling. Subspecialties: Neurophysiology; Biophysics (biology). Office: NYU Med Ctr 550 1st Ave New York NY 10016

LLORCA, ARTHUR LEE, psychologist; b. Chgo., Sept. 21, 1940; s. Arthur Edward and Zelia (Collebrusco) L.; m. Rita Mary Pedretti, Oct. 31, 1964 (div. Dec. 1979); children: Raymond, Michael, Robert; m. Ann Elise Aucker, May 7, 1980. M.A., U. N.C., Greenville, 1980; M.T.I.D., N.C. State U., Raleigh, 1975. Staff psychologist Sandhills Ctr., Pinehurst, N.C., 1981—; staff psychologist S.E. Mental Health, Wilmington, N.C., 1985—; adj. faculty Campbell U., Buies Creek, N.C., 1976—; cons. N.C. Headstart Program, Raleigh, 1982—. Served to majr., inf. U.S. Army, 1960-78. Mem. Am. Psychol. Assn., Internat. Soc. Polit. Psychology, Pinehurst Clinic Group. Roman Catholic. Current Work: International relations/human behavior. Subspecialty: Clinical psychology. Home: Box 1074 Wrightsville Beach NC 28480

LLOYD, EVAN ELLIOTT MORGAN, engineering company exec.; b. New Haven, Oct. 16, 1945; s. David P.C. and Kathleen Mansfield (Elliott) L.; m. Cathy Ann Disque, Sept. 5, 1965; children: Steven Kenneth Elliott, Melissa Kim. A.A.S., Capitol Inst. Tech., 1968, B.S. E.T., 1968. Customer engr. IBM Corp., Arlington, Va., 1966-68; instr. Capitol Inst. Tech., Kensington, Md., 1968-69; sr. engr. Link div. Singer Co., Silver Spring, Md., 1969-75, mgr.bus. devel., 1976-80; group mgr. Quadrex Corp., Campbell, Calif., 1980-82; v.p. Interfacts, Inc., San Jose, Calif., 1982—. Recipient Ann. Research and Devel. award Singer Co., 1975. Mem. Am. Assn. Engring. Edn., IEEE, Am. Nuclear Soc. (standards com. 1980—). Current Work: Directing development of new power generation simulation systems and training data base systems for power utility applications. Subspecialties: Distributed systems and networks; Theoretical computer science.

LLOYD, JAMES EDWARD, entomology educator; b. Oneida, N.Y., Jan. 17, 1933; s. Harry Austin and Ann Lucille (Lynch); m. Dorothy June Pafka, Aug. 16, 1958; children: Robert Stanley, Kyle Anne. B.S., SUNY-Fredonia, 1960; M.A., U. Mich., 1962; Ph.D., Cornell U., 1966. Sci. tchr. Dunkirk (N.Y.) pub. schs., 1960; prof. U. Fla., Gainesville, 1966—. Contbr. sci. articles to profl. jours. Served with USN, 1951-55. Recipient Disting. Alumni award SUNY, Fredonia, 1982. Fellow AAAS; mem. Fla. Entomol. Soc., Coleopterists Soc., Animal Behavior Soc. Current Work: Systematics and behavior of fireflies (lampyridae), evolution of insect communication systems, insect behavioral ecology. Subspecialties: Evolutionary biology; Ethology. Home: 915 NW 40th Terr Gainesville FL 32605Office: Dept Entomology U Fla Gainesville FL 32611

LLOYD, JOHN TRACY, psychologist, consultant; b. Astoria, Oreg., Dec. 20, 1946; s. Fred. H. and Alice Rose (Baker) L.; m. Susan Lynn Quackenbush, Aug. 20, 1970. B.A., U. Oreg., 1969; M.S., U. Idaho, 1972, Ph.D., 1977. Lic. psychologist, Wash. Instr. U. Idaho, Moscow, 1972-73, 75-77; research faculty Whitman Coll., Walla Walla, Wash., 1973-75; psychologist OUI: Rehab. Ctr., Lewiston, Idaho, 1976-77; asst. prof. Wash. State U., Pullman, 1977-82; psychologist Spokane Behavioral Medicine, Wash., 1982—; cons. psychologist Eptom Soc., Pullman, 1976-82, supt. pub. instrn., Olympia, Wash., 1979-82; text rev. cons. Random House, Inc., N.Y.C., 1981-82; field supr./cons. Psychol. Corp., N.Y.C., 1981. Contbr. articles to profl. jours. Mem. Am. Psychol Assn., Wash. State Psychol. Assn., Western Assn. for Counselor Edn. and Supervision, Southeastern Wash. Counselor Edn. Consortium (co-dir. 1981). Current Work: Closed head brain trauma and its effects; learning disability and neuroeducation. Subspecialties: Cognition; Neuropsychology. Home: South 1249 Wall Spokane WA 99204

LO, KWOK-YUNG, radio astronomer, educator; b. Nanking, China, Oct. 19, 1947; came to U.S., 1965, naturalized, 1980; m. Helen Chen, Jan. 1, 1973; children: Jan Hsin, Pei Hsin. S.B., M.I.T., 1969; Ph.D., 1974. Research fellow radio astronomy Calif. Inst. Tech., Pasadena, 1974-76, sr. research fellow radio astronomy, 1978-80, asst. prof., 1980—; Miller fellow basic research in sci. U. Calif.-Berkeley, 1976-78, asst. research astronomer, 1978. Contbr. articles in field to profl. jours. Mem. Internat. Astron. Union, Internat. Union Radio Sci., Am. Astron. Soc. Current Work: The galactic center, star formation, intergalactic hydrogen, dwarf galaxies, very long baseline interferometry. Subspecialties: Radio and microwave astronomy; Infrared astronomy. Office: Dept Astronomy Calif Inst Tech 105-24 Pasadena CA 91125

LOATMAN, ROBERT BRUCE, computer scientist; b. Washington, Aug. 23, 1945; s. Paul John and Miriam Joyce (Barna) L.; m. Carol Anne Chalmers, June 6, 1969; children: Thomas, Cynthia, Ryan, Michael. B.A., Fordham U., 1967, M.A., 1972, Ph.D., 1976. Programmer Gen. Electric Co., Schenectady, 1968-69; instr. math. Fordham U., Bronx, N.Y., 1972-73, Georgetown U., Washington, 1973-76; info. systems engr. Mitre Corp., McLean, Va., 1978; sr. assoc. Killalea Assocs., Inc., Alexandria, Va., 1976-80; computer scientist Planning Research Corp., McLean, Va., 1980-84, dir. artificial intelligence dept., 1984—; cons. Phonic Ear, Palo Alto, Calif., 1980; NSF trainee, 1970-73. Recipient Medals of Achievement Math. Assn. Am., 1963, Medals of Achievement Rensselaer Poly. Inst., 1963; NSF research grantee, 1965. Mem. Am. Assn. Artificial Intelligence, Am. Math. Soc., Soc. Indsl. and Applied Math., Assn. Computing Machinery, Spl. Interest Group in Artificial Intelligence, AAAS, Cognitive Sci. Soc., Assn. Computational Linguistics. Roman Catholic. Current Work: Knowledge representation, knowledge-based systems, knowledge acquisition, natural language interface. Subspecialty: Artificial intelligence. Home: 9903 Snowbound Ct Vienna VA 22180 Office: Artificial Intelligence Dept Planning Research Corp 1500 Planning Research Dr McLean VA 22102

LOBO, PETER ISAAC, physician, educator; b. Kabale, Uganda, Apr. 11, 1943; s. Leonard Luciano and Carmen Isabelle L.; m. Monica Lobo, May 5, 1971; children: Toinette Carmen, Ingrid Elizabeth, Leonard Jason. M.B.Ch.B., Makerere U., Kampala, Uganda, 1966. Diplomate: Am. Bd. Internal Medicine, Am. Bd. Nephrology. Resident in internal medicine and nephrology U. Va. Sch. Medicine, Charlottesville, 1971-76, instr., 1976-77, asst. prof., 1977-81, assoc. prof. medicine, 1981—, dr. tissue typing lab., 1978—. Contbr. articles to sci. jours. Fellow ACP; mem. Am. Assn. Immunologists, Am. Histocompatibility Soc., Internat. Transplantation Soc., So. Soc. Clin. Investigatio. Roman Catholic. Current Work: Function of human lymphocyte subsets, immune-regulation, studies on formation and role of alloantibodies pre- and post-transplantation. Subspecialties: Nephrology; Transplantation. Home: 348 Keywest Dr Charlottesville VA 22901 Office: U Va Med Center Box 133 Charlottesville VA 22908

LOCHER, PAUL JOHN, psychology educator; b. Allentown, Pa., Sept. 27, 1941; s. Paul Otto and Teresa (Bedics) L. Ph.D., Temple U., 1972. Assoc. prof. Montclair State Coll., Upper Montclair, N.J., 1972—. NSF grantee, 1967. Mem. Am. Psychol. Assn., Jean Piaget Soc., Eastern Psychol. Assn., Psychonomic Soc. Current Work: Using several techniques to record eye movements, relation between visual encoding strategies and higher cognitive processes. Subspecialty: Cognition. Home: 586 Upper Mountain Ave Upper Montclair NJ 07043 Office: Montclair State Coll Upper Montclair NJ 07043

LOCHTE, GLEN ELGIN, mechanical engineer, consultant; b. Fredericksburg, Tex., Sept. 27, 1947; s. Elgin Harry and Lorraine Thirza (Fiedler) L.; m. Carolyn Louise Stephenson, May 13, 1972; children—Glen Ernst, Jeremy Elgin. B.S.M.E., U. Houston, 1970. Registered profl. engr., Tex. Engr., FMC Corp., Houston, 1970-72, mgr. research project, Oslo, Norway/Houston, 1975-79; research and devel. project mgr. Hydrotech Inc., Houston, 1973-74; v.p. H.O. Mohr & Assocs., Houston, 1980-84, pres., 1985—; officer, ptnr. Sea Troll Engring., Inc., Houston, 1984-85; lectr. subsea prodn. systems Continuing Edn. Inst., Los Angeles, 1977—, dir. subsea pipelines, 1980—. Patentee in field. Mem. ASME. Republican. Lutheran. Current work: Mechanical equipment-oriented solutions to petroleum-related problems. Subspecialties: Mechanical engineering; Petroleum engineering. Home: 4907 Wind Chimes Houston TX 77066 Office: 2707 N Loop West Suite 200 Houston TX 77008

LOCICERO, JOSEPH, III, cardiothoracic surgeon, educator, researcher; b. Chgo., Nov. 1, 1948; s. Joseph Jr. and Inez (Touzet) L.; m. Martha Slater, M.D., June 19, 1971; children—Joseph IV, John Paul. B.S. in Mech. Engring., Tulane U., 1970, M.D., 1973. Diplomate Am. Bd. Surgery, Am. Bd. Thoracic Surgery; engr.-in-tng. Intern Charity Hosp. La., New Orleans, 1974-75, resident in surgery, 1977-81; resident in cardiothoracic surgery Northwestern Meml. Hosp., Chgo., 1981-83; research fellow Northwestern U. Med. Sch., Chgo., 1983-84, assoc. in surgery, 1984—. Contbr. numerous articles to profl. jours. Served as capt. U.S. Army, 1975-77. Mem. ASME, ASHRAE, IEEE, So. Med. Assn., Southeastern Surg. Congress, Assn. for Acad. Surgery. Current work: Laser usage in cardiothoracic surgery, mathematical modelling of cardiac electrophysiology, hemodynamics of right ventricular failure. Subspecialties: Cardiac surgery; Laser medicine. Home: 1 East Schiller St Chicago IL 60610 Office: Div Cardiothoracic Surgery Northwestern U Medical Sch 303 E Chicago Ave Ward 9-105 Chicago IL 60611

LOCICERO, JOSEPH LAWRENCE, electrical engineering educator; b. N.Y.C., Sept. 18, 1947; s. Lawrence Augustus and Anne Marie (Cario) L.; m. Sandra Sorin, Oct. 24, 1976; 1 child, Jennifer Suzane. B.E.E., CCNY, 1970, M.E.E., 1971, Ph.D., 1976. Grad. teaching asst. CCNY, N.Y.C., 1971-72, part-time lectr., 1972-75, grad. research assoc. NASA grant, 1975-76; asst. prof. elec. engring. Ill. Inst., Chgo., 1976-82, assoc. prof., asst. chmn. dept. elec. and computer engring., 1982—; cons. Ill. Tool Works, 1978-80, AT&T Bell Labs., Naperville, 1982—; lectr. Info Gate Keepers, Boston, 1977-78. Editor: Tutorial in Modern Communications, 1982, Today's Television Technology, 1985. Contbr. articles to profl. jours. VA grantee, 1978, 78-79; Engring. Found. grantee, 1978-79; NSF grantee, 1978-81; AT&T Bell Labs. grantee, 1982—. Mem. IEEE Communications Soc., Info. Theory Group of IEEE, Acoustics Speech and Signal Processing Soc. of IEEE, N.Y. Acad. Sci., Soc. Motion Picture and TV Engrs., Sigma Xi. Current work: Communications (electrical) theory and systems, digital and data communications, digital signal processing, digital encoding of speech, high definition television. Subspecialties: Electrical engineering; Computer engineering. Home: 559 E Parkway Rd Riverside IL 60546 Office: Ill Inst Tech Dept Elec and Computer Engring 3301 S Dearborn St Chicago IL 60616

LOCKHART, JAMES ARTHUR, botanist, educator; b. Grand Rapids, Mich., June 7, 1926; s. Arthur John and Ruth Laura (Eyles) L.; m. Donna Margaret; m. Joan Conway, June 6, 1943; 1 dau., Joan Elizabeth. B.S., Mich. State Coll., M.S., 1952; Ph.D. (NSF fellow), UCLA, 1954. NSF postdoctoral fellow U. Pa., Phila., 1954-55; postdoctoral fellow Calif. Inst. Tech., 1955-60; assoc. plant physiologist U. Hawaii, 1960-65; prof. botany U. Mass., Amherst, 1965—. Research publs. in field. Served to sgt. U.S. Army, 1944-46, 50-51. NSF grantee, 1960-72. Mem. AAAS, Am. Soc. Plant Physiologists, Bot. Soc. Am., Am. Inst. Biol. Scis., VFW, Sigma Xi. Current Work: Analyses of integration of plant functions to define alternative survival strategies as functions of different environments. Subspecialties: Plant physiology (biology); Population biology. Home: 294 Puffton Village Amherst MA 01002 Office: Dept Botany U Mass Amherst MA 01003

LOCKWOOD, JOHN ALEXANDER, physics educator; b. Easton, Pa.; s. Harold J. and Elizabeth L.; m. Jean E. Manville, Mar. 28, 1942; children—Elizabeth, Nancy, Jane. B.A., Dartmouth Coll., 1941; M.S., Lafayette Coll., 1943; Ph.D., Yale U., 1948. Assoc. prof. physics U. N.H., Durham, 1953-59, prof., 1959—, chmn. dept. physics, 1963-65, assoc. dir. research, 1975-80, dir. research, 1980-82; chmn. N.H. State Radiation Adv. Com., 1973—. Trustee, Mt. Washington Obs., 1974—. Fellow Am. Phys. Soc.; mem. AAAS, Am. Geophys. Union, Sigma Xi, Sigma Pi Sigma. Current work: Cosmic radiation studies; atmospheric neutron studies; gamma-ray astrophysics. Subspecialties: Satellite studies; Solar physics. Office: Physics Dept U New Hampshire Durham NH 03824

LODHI, SATTAR KHAN, physics educator, researcher; b. Sohagpur, India, Apr. 4, 1937; came to U.S., 1962; s. Abdul Gnafoor Khan and Massom (Begum) L.; m. Mariam Rahimi, Dec. 5, 1969 (div. Apr. 1980); m. Lily Manou, May 23, 1980; children—Paimaan Khan, Naseem Lily. Diploma in sci. D.J. Govt. Sci. Coll., Karachi, Pakistan, 1957; B.S. with honors, U. Karachi, 1960, M.S. in Applied Math., 1962; M.S. in Physics, U. Houston, 1969; Ph.D. in Physics, Baylor U., 1974. Cert. energy auditor, Tex. Lectr. physics Adamjee Sci. Coll., Karachi, 1962-63; teaching fellow U. Houston, 1963-66; asst. prof. Paul Quinn Coll., Waco, Tex., 1966-68; research and teaching asst. Baylor U., Waco, 1968-74; lectr. physics McLennen Community Coll., Waco, 1968-69; research scientist Atomic Energy Orgn., Tehran, Iran, 1974-79; asst. prof. physics Pa. State U., Erie, 1981-84, Sam Houston State U., Huntsville, Tex., 1984—; head div. nuclear physics Atomic Energy Orgn. of Iran, 1979. Contbr. articles to profl. jours. Fulbright scholar, 1963. Mem. Am. Phys. Soc., Sigma Xi, Sigma Pi Sigma. Muslim. Lodge: Sertoma (Erie). Current work: Stopping powers of various elements and compounds for alpha particles, environmental pollution and effects, molecular structures of simple organic compounds, X-ray spectroscopy. Subspecialties: Atomic and molecular physics; Nuclear physics. Home: PO Box 2012 Sam Houston State U Huntsville TX 77341 Office: Sam Houston State U Dept Physics Huntsville TX 77341

LODISH, HARVEY FRANKLIN, cell biologist, educator; b. Cleve., Nov. 16, 1941; s. Nathan H. and Sylvia B. (Friedman) L.; m. Pamela Chentow, Dec. 29, 1963; children: Heidi, Martin, Stephanie. A.B., Kenyon Coll, 1962; D.Sc. (hon.), 1982; Ph.D., Rockefeller U., 1966. Postdoctoral fellow MRC Lab. Molecular Biology, Cambridge, Eng., 1966-68; asst. prof. biology M.I.T., 1968-71, assoc. prof., 1971-76, prof., 1976—; mem. Whitehead Inst. Biomed. Research, 1982—; cons. scientist Children's Hosp., Boston, 1979—; mem. sci. bd. Damon Biotech Inc., Med. Found., Am. Cancer Soc. Contbr. articles to profl.jours. Am Cancer Soc. fellow, 1966-68; Guggenheim fellow, 1977-78. Mem. Am. Chem. Soc., Am. Soc. Biol. Chemists, AAAS, Am. Soc. Microbiology, Am. Soc. Cell Biologists, Phi Beta Kappa. Current Work: Research on cell biology; synthesis and function of membrane proteins; regulation of gene expression. Consultant biotechnology. Subspecialties: Cell biology; Biochemistry (biology).

LODWICK, GWILYM SAVAGE, radiologist, educator; b. Mystic, Iowa, Aug. 30, 1917; s. Gwylim S. and Lucy A. (Fuller) L.; m. Maria Antonia De Brito Barata; children by previous marriage: Gwilym Savage III, Philip Galligan, Malcolm Kerr, Terry Ann. Student, Drake U., 1934-35; B.S., State U. Iowa, 1942, M.D., 1943. Resident pathology State U. Iowa, 1947-48, resident radiology, 1948-50; fellow, sr. fellow radiologic and orthopedic pathology Armed Forces Inst. Pathology, 1951; asst., then asso. prof. State U. Iowa Med. Sch., 1951-56; prof. radiology, chmn. dept. U. Mo. at Columbia Med. Sch., 1956-78, research prof. radiology, 1978—, interim chmn. dept. radiology, 1980-81, chmn. dept. radiology, 1981-83, prof. bioengring., 1969-83, acting dean, 1959, assoc. dean, 1959-64; assoc. radiologist Mass. Gen. Hosp., 1983—; vis. prof. dept. radiology Harvard Med. Sch., 1983—; cons. in field; vis. prof. Keio U. Sch. Medicine, Tokyo, 1974; chmn. sci. program com. Internat. Conf. on Med. Info., Amsterdam, 1983; trustee Am. Registry Radiologic Technologists, 1961-69, pres., 1964-65, 68-69; mem. radiology tng. com. Nat. Inst. Gen. Med. Scis., NIH, 1966-70; com. radiology Nat. Acad. Scis.-NRC, 1970-75; chmn. com. computers Am. Coll. Radiology, 1965, Internat. Commn. Radiol. Edn. and Information, 1969—; cons. to health care tech. div. Nat. Center for Health Services, Research and Devel., 1971—; dir. Mid-Am. Bone Tumor Diagnostic Center and Registry, 1971—; adv. com. mem. NIH Biomed. Image Processing Grant Jet Propulsion Lab., 1969-73; nat. chmn. MUMPS Users Group, 1973-75; mem. radiation study sect. div. research grants NIH, 1976-79, mem. study sect. on diagnostic radiology and nuclear medicine div. research grants, 1979—, chmn. study sect. on diagnostic radiology div. research grants, 1980-82; mem. bd. sci. counselors Nat. Library of Medicine, 1985—, adv. editorial bd. Radiology, 1965—, assoc. editor, 1985; adv. bd. Current/Clin. Practice, 1972—; mem. editorial bd. Jour. Med. Systems, 1976—, Radiol. Sci. Update div. Biomedia, Inc, 1975—; mem. cons. editorial bd. Skeletal Radiology, 1977—, Contemporary Diagnostic Radiology, 1978-80. Served to maj. AUS, 1943-46. Decorated Sakari Mustakallio medal Finland; named Most Disting. Alumnus in Radiology, State U. Iowa Centennial, 1970; recipient Sigma Xi Research award U. Mo., Columbia, 1972, Gold medal XIII Internat. Conf. Radiology, Madrid, 1973; named Disting. Practitioner, Nat. Acad. Practice, 1984. mem. Fellow AMA (radiology rev. bd. council med. edn., council rep. on residency rev. com. for radiology 1969-74), Am. Coll. Med. Informatics (founding), Am. Coll. Radiology, European Soc. Radiology (European steering com. on computers), Radiol. Soc. N.Am. (3d v.p. 1974-75, chmn. ad hoc com. representing assoc. scis. 1979—, chmn. assoc. scis. com. 1981—), Assn. Univ. Radiologists, Mo. Radiol. Soc. (1st pres.

1961-62), Salutis Unitas, Alpha Omega Alpha; hon. mem. Portuguese Soc. Radiology and Nuclear Medicine, Tex. Radiol. Soc., Ind. Roentgen Soc., Phila. Roentgen Ray Soc., Finnish Radiol. Soc. Current Work: Modeling and analysis; bone images, automated image analysis; medical decision making; radiology information systems. Subspecialties: Diagnostic radiology; Imaging technology.

LÖE, HARALD, dentist, educator; b. Steinkjer, Norway, July 19, 1926; s. Haakon and Anna (Bruem) L.; m. Inga Johansen, July 3, 1948; children—Haakon, Marianne. D.D.S., U. Oslo, 1952; Dr. Odont., 1961; hon. degrees, U. Gotherburg, 1973, Royal Dental Coll., 1980, U. Athens, 1980, Catholic U., Leuven, 1980, U.Lund, 1983, Georgetown U., 1983, U. Bergen, 1985. Instr. Sch. Dentistry, Oslo U., 1952-55; research assoc. Norwegian Inst. Dental Research, 1956-62; Fulbright research fellow, research asso. dept. oral pathology U. Ill., Chgo., 1957-58; Univ. research fellow Oslo U., 1959-62, asso. prof. dept. periodontology, 1960-61; prof. dentistry, chmn. dept. periodontology Royal Dental Coll., Aarhus, Denmark, 1962-72, asso. dean, dean-elect, 1971-72; prof., dir. Dental Research Inst. U. Mich., Ann Arbor, 1972-74; dean, prof. periodontology Sch. Dental Medicine U. Conn., Farmington, 1974-82; dir. Nat. Inst. Dental Research, Bethesda, Md., 1983—; vis. prof. periodontics Hebrew U., Jerusalem, 1966-67; cons. WHO, NIH. Served with Norwegian Army, 1944-48. Recipient Aalborg Dental Soc. prize, Denmark, 1965; Wm. J. Gies Periodontology award, 1978; numerous others. Mem. AAAS, ADA, Danish Dental Assn., Am. Acad. Periodontology, Am. Assn. Dental Research, Am. Soc. Preventive Dentistry (internat. award), Mass. Dental Soc. (internat. award), Internat. Assn. Dental Research (award for basic research in periodontology 1969, pres. 1980), Internat. Coll. Dentists, Scandinavian Assn. Dental Research, Scandinavian Soc. Periodontology. Subspecialties: Periodontics; Dental research institute administration. Office: Nat Inst Dental Research 9000 Rockville Pike Bethesda MD 20892

LOEB, MELVIN LESTER, industrial chemical research executive; b. N.Y.C., Jan. 20, 1943; s. Walter and Bertha Loeb; m. Anne Loeb; children—Jason, Andrea. B.S., CCNY, 1964; S.M., MIT, 1967, Ph.D., 1969; M.B.A., U. Chgo., 1976. Mgr. indsl. chem. research Kraft, Inc., Glenview, Ill., 1969-78; dir. research Stepan Co., Northfield, Ill., 1978—. Mem. Am. Chem. Soc., Am. Oil Chem. Soc. Current work: Synthesis, process development, analytical research in surfactants and urethane/isocyanurate technology, sulfonation and sulfation technology. Subspecialty: Organic chemistry. Home: 1830 Larkdale Rd Northbrook IL 60062 Office: Stepan Co Edens Expressway at Winnetka Rd Northfield IL 60093

LOEB, ROBERT ELI, ecology researcher, environmental educator; b. Bronx, N.Y., Aug. 7, 1955; s. Karl and Blanche Carmen (Alvarez) L. B.S., C.W. Post Coll., 1977; Ph.D., NYU, 1984. Instr. N.Y. Botanical Gardens, Bronx, 1972-78, research asst., 1972-78; environ. cons. pvt. practice, N.Y.C., 1979—; edn. dir. Inwood Parks Alliance, N.Y.C., 1984—; dir. N.Y.C. Audubon Soc., 1982—, Bronx Council Environ. Quality, N.Y., 1982—; instr. Pa. State U., 1985—, faculty devel. officer Altoona Campus, 1985—. Editor: Inwood Park, 1985. Contbr. articles to profl. jours. Sec. Community Planning Bd., Bronx, 1983—; chmn. Parks Com. Planning Bd., Bronx, 1979—; pres. Seton Falls Neighborhood Assn., Bronx, 1979-81. Recipient Mayor's Community Assistance award N.Y.C., 1982; fellow NYU, 1977-84; scholar NSF, Student Conservation Assn. Mem. Am. Quaternary Assn., Geol. Soc. Am., Torrey Bot. Club, Nat. Audubon Soc., Am. Assn. Stratagraphic Palynologists, Phi Beta Kappa. Democrat. Current work: Tracing history, development and changes in ecological systems during historical period in urban environment. Subspecialties: Ecology (biology); Paleontology, paleoecology. Home: 1005-G E Atlantic Ave Altoona PA 16602 Office: Continuing Edn Dept Pa State U Altoona Campus Altoona PA 16602

LOEB, WILLIAM A., mechanical engineer; b. N.Y.C., Sept. 7, 1924; s. Samuel L. and Ethel (Kossman) L.; m. Marion Conrad, May 26, 1971; children: David, Jonathan, Suzanne. B.S., MIT, 1945, M.S., 1947. Registered profl. engr., Mass., N.Y., Alaska. Research engr. Delaval Steam Turbine Co., Trenton, N.J., 1947-51; v.p. engring. United Nuclear Corp., White Plains, N.Y., 1951-65; pres. Iso Nuclear Corp., N.Y.C., 1965-67; v.p. research Tech. Investors Corp., N.Y.C., 1967-71; dir. spl. projects Combustion Engring., Windsor Locks, Conn., 1971-75; pres. West Stockbridge Enterprises, Inc., Mass., 1975—; cons. U.S. Dept. Energy, Washington, 1976-78. Served to lt. (j.g.) USN, 1942-46, PTO. Mem. ASME, Nat. Soc. Profl. Engrs., Am. Congress Surveying and Mapping, Am. Nuclear Soc., Internat. Solar Energy Soc., Sigma Xi, Tau Beta Pi. Current Work: Small hydroelectric plants, computer-based facility control systems, economic small energy systems. Subspecialties: Solar energy; Systems engineering. Home: Austerlitz Rd West Stockbridge MA 01266 Office: West Stockbridge Enterprises Inc Box 100 West Stockbridge MA 01266

LOEFFLER, WILLIAM ROBERT, quality productivity engineer, engineering educator; b. Cleve., Aug. 31, 1949; s. Harry T. and Frances R. (Pearson) L.; m. Beth Ann Manderfield, Dec. 1978; children—Lindsay Brooke, Kelly Lynn, Robert Jason. B.A., Wittenberg U., 1971; M.A., SUNY-Stony Brook, 1972; Ed. Specialist, U. Toledo, 1979; Ph.D., U. Mich., 1984. Dir. alternate learning ctr. Lucas County Schs., Toledo, 1977-79; dir. chem. and metall. services Toledo Testing Lab., 1979-82; pres. Chem. Resources, Lambertville, Mich., 1982-83; div. mgr. Benchmark Techs., Toledo, 1983—; pres. Tech. Soc. Toledo, 1985-86; conf. chmn. Am. Soc. Quality Control. Deming Conf., Toledo, 1984; mem. Nat. Task Force ALARA Atomic Indsl. Forum, Washington; congl. sci. counselor PACCOS, Ohio. Editor Jour. Toledo Tech. Topics 1982—; asst. editor Jour. English Quarterly, 1976-77. Contbr. articles to profl. jours. Vice chmn. Pvt. Industry Council, Monroe County, Mich., 1983, 84; chmn. Bus.-Industry-Edn. Day Toledo C. of C., 1984; trustee Bedford Pub. Schs., Mich., 1982-85; chmn. Robotics Internat., 1985. Fellow SUNY-Stony Brook 1975-76, Cambridge U. 1976-77. Recipient Harvard Book award 1967. Mem. Am. Chem. Soc. (chmn. Toledo chapt. 1984), Am. Soc. Non-Destructive Testing, Phi Delta Kappa, Phi Kappa Phi. Methodist. Club: U. Mich. (Toledo). Lodge: Rotary. Current work: Development of research on ambiguity in language and decision making in the human factors engineering context; analysis of quality productivity matrices. Subspecialties: Human factors engineering; Materials. Office: Benchmark Technologies Corp 1995 Tremainsville Rd Toledo OH 43613

LOEPPKY, JACK ALBERT, physiologist, researcher; b. Saskatoon, Sask., Can., Jan. 14, 1944; came to U.S., 1967; s. George and Sarah (Martens) L.; m. Janet Sue By, Nov. 22, 1974; children—Kristopher, Ninya. B.A. with distinction, U. Sask., 1966; M.S., U. N.Mex., 1969, Ph.D., 1973; postgrad., Colo. State U., 1969-70. Instr. U. Sask., Saskatoon, 1966-67; technician Lovelace Med. Found., Albuquerque, 1966-69, research assoc., 1970-75, assoc. scientist, 1975—, head dept. cardiopulmonary physiology, 1981-83; head respiratory technologist Wellington (N.Z.) Hosp., 1975; adj. asst. prof. U. N.Mex., Albuquerque, 1982—; Max-Planck fellow, Gottingen, Fed. Republic Germany, 1983-84. Editor: Oxygen Transport to Human Tissues, 1982; contbr. articles to profl. jours. Scholar, 1962-66. Mem. Am. Physiol. Soc. Club: N.Mex. Mountain (Albuquerque). Current Work: Pulmonary gas exchange, exercise physiology, cardiopulmonary effects of gravitational stress. Subspecialties: Physiology (medicine); Gravitational biology. Office: Research Div Lovelace Med Found 5400 Gibson Blvd SE Albuquerque NM 87108

LOEW, FRANKLIN MARTIN, veterinary scientist, university dean; b. Syracuse, N.Y., Sept. 8, 1939; s. David Franklin and Sarah (Adelaide) L.; m. Mary Elizabeth Moffatt, Sept. 9, 1964; children—Timothy, Andrew. B.S., Cornell U., 1961, D.V.M., 1965; Ph.D., U. Sask., Can., 1971. Research asst. Reynolds Tobacco Co., Winston-Salem, N.C., 1965-66, Tulane U., New Orleans, 1966-67; from lectr. to prof. U. Sask., Saskatoon, 1967-77; dir. comparative medicine Johns Hopkins U., Balt., 1977-82; dean vet. medicine Tufts U., Boston, 1982—; chmn. Inst. Lab. Animal Resources, Nat. Acad. Sci., 1981—; mem. Commn. on Life Scis., 1981—; N.B. lectr. Am. Soc. for Microbiology, 1984; pres. Assn. Am. Veterinary Med. Colls., 1985-86. Trustee, Worcester Acad., 1984—. Author: Vet in the Saddle, 1978. Editor: Laboratory Animal Medicine, 1984; Contbr. articles to profl. jours. Chmn. bd. trustees Boston Zool. Soc., 1984—. Recipient Queen's Jubilee medal Gov.-Gen. of Can., 1977. Fellow Am. Acad. Vet. and Comparative Toxicology, mem. Am. Coll. Lab. Animal Medicine (diplomate; bd. dirs. 1978-81), Am. Inst. Nutrition, Soc. Toxicology. Current work: Nutritional toxicology, thiamin deficiency, diseases of laboratory animals, humane care of laboratory animals. Subspecialties: Laboratory animal medicine; Animal nutrition. Office: Tufts U Sch Vet Medicine 200 Westboro Rd North Grafton MA 01536

LOEWENSTEIN, WERNER RANDOLPH, physiologist, biophysicist; b. Spangenberg, Germany, Feb. 14, 1926; came to U.S., 1957, naturalized, 1965; s. Siegfried and Adele (Muller) von Loewenstein; m. Birgit Rose, Oct. 7, 1971; children: Claudia, Patricia, Harriett, Stewart. B.S., U. Chile, 1945, Ph.D., 1950. Instr. physiology U. Chile, Santiago, 1951-53, asso. prof., 1955-57; fellow in residence Wilmer Inst., Johns Hopkins U., Balt., 1953-54; research zoologist U. Calif., Los Angeles, 1954-55; asst. prof. physiology Columbia U. Coll. Physicians and Surgeons, N.Y.C., 1957-59, asso. prof., 1959-66, prof., dir. cell physics lab., 1966-71; prof. physiology and biophysics, chmn. dept. U. Miami (Fla.) Sch. Medicine, 1971—; Block lectr. U. Chgo., 1960; lectr. Royal Swedish Acad. Sci., 1966; Max Planck lectr., 1967, Fulbright disting. prof., 1970, USSR Acad. Sci. lectr., Leningrad, 1975; mem. Pres.'s Biomed. Research Adv. Panel, 1975-77, USAF Sci. Adv. Panel, 1982—. Author, editor several books; editor: Biochimica et Biophysica Acta, 1967-74; editor-in-chief: Jour. Membrane Biology, 1969—; editor: Handbook of Sensory Physiology, 12 vols., 1971-77; contbr. numerous articles on membrane biophysics, physiology of intercellular communication, and neurophysiology to profl. jours. Kellogg internat. fellow in physiology, 1953-55; Commonwealth Fund internat. fellow, 1967; NSF, NIH research grantee. Fellow N.Y. Acad. Scis.; mem. Am. Physiol. Soc., Biophys. Soc., Marine Biol. Lab. Woods Hole (corp. mem.). Clubs: Woods Hole Yacht, Coconut Grove Sailing, Royal Kev Biscayne Tennis and Racquet. Current Work: Intercellular communication. Subspecialties: Biophysics (biology); Neurobiology. Home: 1090 Mariner Dr Key Biscayne FL 33149 Office: Dept Physiology and Biophysics Univ Miami Sch Medicine PO Box 520875 Miami FL 33152

LOEWY, ROBERT GUSTAV, engineering educator, consulting engineer; b. Phila., Feb. 12, 1926; s. Samuel N. and Esther (Silverstein) L.; m. Lila Myrna Spinner, Jan. 16, 1955; children—David G., Esther Elizabeth, Joanne Victoria, Raymond M. B.Aero. Engring., Rensselaer Poly. Inst., 1947; M.S., MIT, 1948; Ph.D., U. Pa., 1962. Sr. vibrations engr. Martin Co., Balt., 1948-49; asso. research engr. Cornell Aero. Lab., Buffalo, 1949-52; staff stress engr. Piasecki Helicopter Co., Morton, Pa., 1952-53; prin. engr. Cornell Aero. Lab., 1953-55; chief dynamics engr., also chief tech. engr. Vertol div. Boeing Co., 1955-62; faculty U. Rochester, 1962-74, prof. mech. and aerospace scis., 1965-74; dir. Space Sci. Center, 1966-71; dean Coll. Engring. and Applied Sci., 1967-74; v.p., provost Rensselaer Poly. Inst., 1974-78; Inst. prof. Rensselaer Poly Inst., 1978—; chief scientist USAF, 1965-66; cons. govt. and industry, 1959—; Mem. aircraft panel Pres.'s Sci. Adv. Council, 1968-72; mem. Air Force Sci. Adv. Bd., 1966-75, 78-85, vice chmn., 1971, chmn., 1972-75, chmn. aero. systems adv. group, 1978-84; mem. Post Office Research and Engring. Adv. Council, 1966-68; mem. research and tech. adv. com. on aeros. NASA, 1970-71, mem. research and tech. adv. council, 1976-77, chmn. aero. adv. com., 1978-83; mem. aerospace engring. bd. NRC, 1972-78; mem. naval studies bd. Nat. Acad. Scis., 1979-82; chmn. tech. adv. com. FAA, 1976-77. Contbr. articles to profl. jours. Served with USNR, 1944-46. Gotshall-Powell scholar Rensselaer Poly. Inst.; USAF Exceptional Civilian Service awards, 1966, 75, 85; NASA Disting. Pub. Service award, 1983. Hon. fellow Am. Helicopter Soc. (tech. dir. 1963-64); fellow AIAA (Lawrence Sperry award 1958), AAAS; mem. Am. Soc. Engring. Edn., Nat. Acad. Engring., Sigma Xi, Sigma Gamma Tau, Tau Beta Pi. Current Work: Structural dynamics, unsteady aerodynamics, aeroelasticity. Subspecialties: Aeronautical engineering; Aerospace engineering and technology. Home: Dutch Village Menands NY 12204

LOFGREN, GARY ERNEST, federal government space center geologist; b. Los Angeles, Apr. 17, 1941; m. Kenneth Gordon and Mildred Edith (Johnson) L.; m. Ellen Much, June 22, 1965. B.S., Stanford U., 1963, Ph.D., 1969; M.A., Dartmouth Coll., 1965. Space geoscientist NASA Johnson Space Ctr., Houston, 1968—; adj. prof. geology U. Houston, 1976—; team leader Basaltic Volcanism Study Project, Lunar and Planetary Inst., Houston, 1976-81. Author/editor: Basaltic Volcanism, 1981; contbr. articles to profl. jours.; editor: Lunar Sci. Conf. Procs, 1968; assoc. editor: Geophys. Research Letters, 1972-76. Recipient Superior Achievement award NASA Johnson Space Ctr., 1978; NDEA fellow, 1965-68. Fellow Mineral. Soc. Am., Geol. Soc. Am. (Spl. commendation 1973); mem. Internat. Union Geol. Socs. (com. on igneous rocks 1976-80), Am. Geophys. Union, Am. Assn. Crystal Growth, Houston Philos. Soc., Sigma Xi. Current Work: Nucleation and crystallization in natural rock forming silicate melts and synthetic analogs; experimental igneous petrology. Subspecialties: Petrology; Geochemistry. Home: Route 1 Box 510 Hillister TX 77624 Office: NASA Johnson Space Ctr Mail Code SN4 Houston TX 77058

LOFQUIST, LLOYD HENRY, psychology educator; b. Mpls., June 11, 1917; s. Frederick G. and Hilma B. (Lundin) L.; m. Lillian Mary Holm, Nov. 1, 1941; children—Mary Lillian, Mark Frederick. B.A., U. Minn., 1940, M.A., 1941, Ph.D., 1955. Chief psychology service Mpls. VA Hosp., 1948-56; asso. prof. psychology dept. U. Minn., Mpls., 1956-60, prof. psychology, 1960—, asso. dean social scis., 1967-69, asst. v.p., acad. adminstrn., 1969-73, chmn. dept. psychology, 1975-85; chmn. Minn. Bd. Examiners of Psychologist, 1960-65; cons. VA, 1957-79; prin. investigator various HEW research and tng. grants. Author: Vocational Counseling with the Physically Handicapped, 1957, Egyptian transl, 1961, Psychological Research and Rehabilitation, 1960, Problems in Vocational Counseling, 1961, Adjustment to Work, 1969; A Psychological Theory of Work Adjustment, 1984. Mem. editorial bds.: Rehab. Counseling Bull, 1975-80, Jour. Vocat. Behavior, 1970-75. Served to capt. U.S. Army, 1942-46. Decorated Bronze Star. Fellow Am. Psychol. Assn.; mem. Am. Personnel and Guidance Assn. (research award 1967), Am. Rehab. Counseling Assn. (pres. 1968, research awards 1960, 65). Democrat. Lutheran. Current Work: Adjustment to work. Subspecialties: Behavioral psychology; Vocational psychology.

LOFTFIELD, ROBERT BERNARD, biochemistry educator, researcher; b. Detroit, Dec. 15, 1919; s. Sigurd and Katherine Maria (Roller) L.; m. Ella Bradford, Aug. 24, 1946; children: Lore, Eric, Linda, Norman, Bjorn, Curtis, Katherine, Earl, Allison, Ella-Kari. B.S., Harvard U., 1941, M.A., 1942, Ph.D., 1946. Research assoc. physics MIT, 1946-48; research assoc. medicine Mass. Gen. Hosp., 1948-64; tutor biochemistry sci. Harvard U., 1950-64, asst. prof. biochemistry, 1959-64; prof., chmn. biochemistry U. N.Mex., Albuquerque, 1964—. Contbr. articles to profl. jours. Served with U.S. Army, 1945-46. Recipient Warren Triennial prize, 1956; Damon Runyon fellow, 1952-53; Guggenheim fellow, 1961-62; NIH fellow, 1971-72; Fulbright fellow, 1977; NATO fellow, 1983. Current Work: Mechanisms of enzymic rate enhancement and specificity, synthesis of protein, aminoacyl tRNA; biochemistry of burn and trauma. Subspecialties: Biochemistry (medicine); Enzyme technology. Home: 707 Fairway St NW Albuquerque NM 87107 Office: Department Biochemistry University of New Mexico Albuquerque NM 87131

LOFTING, EVERARD MERVYN, economist; b. Toronto, Ont., Can., Nov. 14, 1922; came to U.S., 1952; s. Charles Lindsay and Helen Florence (Matthews) L. B.S. in Gen. Sci., Sir George Williams U., Montreal, Que., 1951; M.A. in Econs., Wayne State U., 1960; Ph.D., in Engring. Sci., U. Calif.-Berkeley, 1968. Acting assoc. prof. Civil Engring., UCLA, 1968-69; regional economist U.S. Army Corps Engrs., San Francisco, 1969-71; economist energy and environ. div. Lawrence Berkeley Lab., Calif., 1973-75; research economist dry lands research inst. U. Calif.-Riverside, 1972-75; economist Engring.-Econ. Assocs., Berkeley, 1975—. Served with USN, 1943-44. Mem. ASCE, Am. Water Resources Assn., Am. Agrl. Econs. Assn., Am. Econ. Assn. Office: Engring-Econs Assocs Inc 1700 Solano Ave Suite F Berkeley CA 94707

LOFTUS, ELIZABETH F., psychology educator; b. Los Angeles, Oct. 16, 1944; d. Sidney A. and Rebecca (Breskin) Fishman; m. Geoffrey R. Loftus, June 30, 1968. B.A., UCLA, 1966; M.A., Stanford U., 1967, Ph.D., 1970; D.Sc. (hon.), Miami U., Oxford, Ohio, 1982. Asst. prof. New Sch. Social Research, N.Y.C., 1970-73; asst. prof. to prof. psychology U. Wash., Seattle, 1973—; cons. Gen. Services Adminstrn., FTC, Dept. of Justice, numerous corps. Author: Eyewitness Testimony, 1979 (Am. Psychol. Found. Disting. Contbn. award 1980), Memory, 1980; 9 other books. Fellow Ctr. Advanced Study in Behavioral Scis., 1978-79. Fellow Am. Psychol. Assn. (council reps.); mem. Western Psychol. Assn. (pres. 1984), Am. Psychology-Law Soc. (pres. 1985), Psychonomic Soc. Current Work: Experimental research on human memory. Subspecialties: Cognition; Learning. Home: 1221 22d Ave E Seattle WA 98112 Office: Psychology Dept University of Washington Seattle WA 98195

LOFTUS, MARGARET A., computer scientist. Vice pres. software devel. Cray Research, Inc., Mpls. Subspecialty: Software engineering. Office: Cray Research Inc 608 2d Ave S Minneapolis MN 55402

LOGAN, KATHRYN VANCE, research engineer, consultant; b. Atlanta, June 12, 1946; d. Charles Monroe and Lucille (James) Vance; m. William Stephen Logan, Sept. 9, 1967; children—Stephanie, Bill. B.Ceramic Engring., Ga. Inst. Tech., 1970; M.S. in Ceramic Engring., 1980. Registered profl. engr., Ga. Student asst. geophys. sci. Ga. Tech. Inst., Atlanta, 1965-68, research engr. I engring. experiment sta., 1970-76, research engr. II energy and materials scis. lab., 1976-85, sr. research engr., 1985—, head thermite processing group, 1985—. Contbr. articles to profl. jours. Recipient Outstanding Achievement award Soc. Women Engrs., 1980. Mem. Am. Ceramic Soc., Nat. Inst. Ceramic Engrs., Ceramic Ednl. Council, Materials Research Soc., Sigma Xi. Current work: Thermite reactions, materials characterization, manufacturing technology of ferrites, processing and fabricating techniques of ceramic materials. Subspecialties: Ceramic engineering; Ceramics. Home: 295 Junction Track Roswell GA 30075 Office: Ga Tech Research Inst Ga Inst Tech Atlanta GA 30332

LOGAN, RALPH ANDRE, physicist; b. Cornwall, Ont., Can., Sept. 22, 1926; came to U.S., 1948; s. Joseph Alexander and Lucy Theresa (Carter) L.; m. Ann Sheila Garvey, Aug. 26, 1950; children—Howard, Mary, Marguerite, Anthony, Enid, Alisa, Ruth, John, Thomas. B.Sc., McGill U., 1947, M.Sc., 1948; Ph.D., Columbia U., 1952. Mem. tech. staff AT&T Bell Labs, Murray Hill, N.J., 1952—. Sir Edward Beatty scholar, McGill U., 1943-47. Fellow Am. Phys. Soc.; mem. IEEE. Current work: Crystal growth of semiconductor communication devices. Subspecialties: Semiconductor lasers; Electronic materials. Home: 179 Mills St Morristown NJ 07960

LOGULLO, FRANCIS MARK, chemist; b. Wilmington, Del., Dec. 19, 1939; s. John J. and Helen (Yorksiatis) L.; m. Despiona Hadzoglo, July 29, 1962; children—Francis, Christopher, Michael. B.S., U. Del., 1961; Ph.D., Case Inst. Tech., Cleve., 1965. Research chemist, EI duPont de Nemours Co., Wilmington, 1961-66, sr. research chemist, 1966-72, research assoc., 1972—. Contbr. articles to profl. jours. Mem. Am. Chem. Soc. Republican. Roman Catholic. Current work: Organic polymer chemistry; textile fibers; science of adhesion; fiber reinforced plastics. Subspecialties: Organic chemistry; Polymer chemistry. Home: Route 5 Box 160C Hockessin DE 19707 Office: EI DuPont de Nemours Co E302210 Wilmington DE 19898

LOH, YOKE PENG, neurobiologist; b. Singapore, July 27, 1947; s. Poon Lip and Sue Heng L. B.Sc., Univ. Coll. Dublin, 1969; Ph.D., U. Pa., 1973. Vis. fellow Lab. Devel. Neurobiology, NIH, Bethesda, Md., 1973-76, sr. staff fellow, 1976-79, research chemist, 1979-83; chief sect. cellular neurobiology Lab. Neurochemistry and Neuroimmunology, NIH, 1983—. Contbr. articles to profl. jours. Fogarty Internat. Postdoctoral fellow, 1973-76; recipient Deutscher Akademischer Austauschdienst award, 1978. Mem. Soc. Neurosci. Neurochemistry Soc., N.Y. Acad. Sci., Biochem. Soc. Gt. Britain. Current Work: Biosynthesis of neuropeptides and their role in neuronal functions; neuropeptide biosynthesis; nerve regeneration and protein synthesis. Subspecialties: Neurobiology; Neuroendocrinology. Office: NIH Bldg 36 Rm 2A-21 Bethesda MD 20205

LOHSE, DAVID JOHN, physicist; b. N.Y.C., Sept. 14, 1952; s. Edward and Mildred Edna (Hofmeister) L.; m. Maria I.M. Garcia, Sept. 2, 1978. B.S. in Physics and Computer Sci, Mich. State U., 1974; Ph.D., U. Ill., 1978. Research assoc. U. Ill., 1974-78; research engr. Exxon Chem. Co., Linden, N.J., 1980—. NRC fellow, 1978-80. Mem. Am. Phys. Soc., Am. Chem. Soc. Lutheran. Current Work: Theoretical statistical mechanics of polymer solutions and polymer blends; use of small angle neutron scattering on polymer solutions and blends. Subspecialty: Polymer physics. Home: 556 Stony Brook Dr Bridgewater NJ 08807 Office: Exxon Chemical Company PO Box 45 Linden NJ 07036

LOKEN, MERLE KENNETH, radiologist, educator; b. Hudson, S.D., Jan. 21, 1924; s. Albert R. and Emma T. (Lunder) L.; m. Fern Mae Buhler, June 1, 1947; children—Allen, Evonne, Gwenda, Lynette, Warren. B.A., Augustana Coll., Sioux Falls, S.D., 1946; B.S., Mass. Inst. Tech., 1948, M.S., 1949; Ph.D., U. Minn., 1956, M.D., 1962. Diplomate: Am. Bd. Nuclear Medicine. Asst. prof. Augustana Coll., 1949-50; mem. faculty U. Minn. Sch. Medicine, 1953—, prof. radiology, 1969—, dir. div. nuclear medicine, 1963—, faculty rep. to Big 10 Intercollegiate Conf., 1974-81. Contbr. numerous sci. papers. Served with USNR, 1943-46, 51-52. Fellow Am. Coll. Radiology; mem. Soc. Nuclear Medicine (pres. central chpt. 1972-74, nat. treas. 1972-75, trustee 1976-80, nat. pres. 1983-84), Minn. Radiol. Soc., Radiol. Soc. N.Am., Sigma Xi. Republican. Lutheran. Current Work: Development and evaluation of techniques utilizing radioactive materials in the practice of medicine. Subspecialties: Nuclear medicine; Radiology in nuclear medicine. Home: 16 Park Ln Minneapolis MN 55416

LOKENSGARD, JERROLD PAUL, chemistry educator and researcher; b. Saskatoon, Sask., Can., July 30, 1940; came to U.S., 1943; s. Bernhard Oliver and Eleanor Ruth (Bensen) L.; m. Elizabeth Ann Hopkins, Aug. 14, 1965; children: Michael John, Ann-Marie. B.A., Luther Coll., 1962; M.A., U. Wis., 1964; Ph.D., 1967. NIH postdoctoral fellow Iowa State U., Ames, 1967; asst. prof. Lawrence U., Appleton, Wis., 1967-76, assoc. prof. chemistry, 1976—; research assoc. U. Toronto, Ont., Can., 1973-74; vis. assoc. prof. Cornell U., Ithaca, N.Y., 1980-81. Contbr. articles to profl. jours. Danforth grad. fellow, 1962; NSF grad. fellow, 1962, 63. Mem. Am. Chem. Soc. (local sect. chmn. 1970), AAAS, AAUP. Lutheran. Current Work: Organic synthesis, insect defensive substances, strained hydrocarbons. Subspecialties: Organic chemistry; Synthetic chemistry. Office: Lawrence Univ PO Box 599 Appleton WI 54912

LOLLEY, RICHARD NEWTON, vision scientist, researcher, anatomy educator; b. Blaine, Kans., May 25, 1933; s. Loran Newton and Catherine Agnes (Caffrey) l.; m. Hazel Bauerrichter, June 4, 1959; children—Emily Ruth, Melissa Ann, Cybil Marie. B.S. in Pharmacy, U. Kans., 1955, Ph.D. in Physiology, 1961. Registered pharmacist. Postgrad. fellow U. London, Maudsley Hosp., London, 1961-62, Harvard U., McLean Hosp., Boston, 1962-64; research pharmacologist VA Med. Ctr., Sepulveda, Calif., acting assoc. chief of staff research, 1978-80; asst. prof. UCLA Sch. Med., Los Angeles, 1966-70, assoc. prof., 1970-76, prof. anatomy, 1976—; cons. mem. Jules Stein Eye Inst., UCLA Sch. Med., Los Angeles, 1972-78, mem., 1981—; mem. Nat. Adv. Eye Council, Nat. Eye Inst., NIH, Bethesda, Md., 1979-84; research scientist promotion com. VA, Washington, 1981-84. Editor: Neurochemistry of the Retina, 1980; mem. editorial bd. Investigative Ophthalmology and Visual Sci., 1983—. Research grantee Nat. Eye Inst. NIH, 1966—, NSF, 1975—, Nat. Retinitis Pigmentosa Found.; recipient Research Career Scientist award VA, 1979; Outstanding Profl. Employee award Los Angeles Fed. Exec. Bd., 1985; Jules Stein living tribute award PR Internat., 1985. Mem. Assn. Research in Vision and Ophthalmology, Am. Soc. Neurochemistry, Internat. Soc. Neurochemistry, Soc. Neurosci., Am. Assn. Anatomists. Current work: Identification of the biochemical mechanisms that act in the perception of light by retinal photoreceptor cells and specification of which of these biochemical specializations is responsible for causing photoreceptor degeneration in diseases, causing blindness. Subspecialty: Neurochemistry. Home: 1107 Vallejo Ave Simi Valley CA 93065

LOMBARDI, FABRIZIO, electrical and computer engineering educator; b. Formia, Italy, Aug. 6, 1955; s. Enezio and Anna (Tatta) L.; m. Maryam Jalali, Oct. 14, 1983. B.Sc. in Elec. Engring. with honors, U. Essex, Eng. 1977; Diploma in Microwave Engring., U. Coll., London, 1978, M.Sc., 1978, Ph.D., 1982. Research asst. Microwave Research unit, Univ. College, London, 1978-82; asst. prof. elec. engring. and computer sci. Tex. Tech U., Lubbock, 1982-84; asst. prof. elec. and computer engring. U. Colo, Boulder, 1984—; cons. IBM, Austin, Tex., 1983—. Contbr. numerous articles to profl. jours. Scholar Cardiothoracic Inst., London, 1978-79, Nat. Research and Devel. Corp., London, 1979-80. Mem. IEEE, European Assn. Microprocessing and Microprogramming, Assn. for Computing Machinery, Soc. for Applied and Indsl. Math., Eta Kappa Nu. Current work: Fault tolerant computing, supercomputing, system-level diagnosis, parallel and distributed processing. Subspecialties: Computer-aided design; Computer architecture. Home: 4700 W Moorhead Circle Boulder CO 80303 Office: Dept Elec and Computer Engring U Colo Campus Box 425 Boulder CO 80309

LOMEN, DAVID ORLANDO, mathematics educator, consultant; b. Decorah, Iowa, May 11, 1937; s. Erlin Rueben and Ellen Dorthea (Jensen) L.; m. Constance Sylvia Trecek, Dec. 25, 1961; 1 dau., Catherine Ellen. B.A., Luther Coll., 1959; M.S., Iowa State U., 1962, Ph.D., 1964. Design specialist Gen. Dynamics/Convair, San Diego, 1963-66; prof. math. U. Ariz., 1966—; vis.

scientist Cambridge U., 1972; research scientist ICW, Wageningen, Netherlands, 1978; vis. prof. U. Oslo, 1980; cons. to industry. Contbr. articles to math. jours. Bd. dirs. Tucson Cystic Fibrosis Found., 1974-80. Recipient Creative Teaching award Univ. Found., Tucson, 1978; sr. scientist NTNF of Norway, Oslo, 1980; Marshall Fund award Norway Am. Found., 1980, 84. Mem. Am. Math. Soc., Soc. Indsl. and Applied Math., Soil Sci. Soc. Am., Am. Geophys. Union. Republican. Lutheran. Club: Norsemen Fedn. of Tucson (treas.). Current Work: Research in soil physics and other areas applied mathematics; development of computer-aided instruction materials in mathematics. Subspecialties: Applied mathematics; Soil science. Office: Dept Mathematics University of Arizona Tucson AZ 85721

LONDON, EDYTHE DANICK, neuropharmacologist; b. Rome, Italy, Sept. 14, 1948. B.S. in Zoology, George Washington U., 1969; M.S. in Biol. Scis, Towson State U., 1973; Ph.D. in Pharmacology, U. Md., 1976. NIMH postdoctoral fellow dept. pharmacology and exptl. therapeutics Johns Hopkins U. Sch. Medicine, Balt., 1976-78; staff fellow Lab. of Neuroscis. Gerontology Research Center Nat. Inst. on Aging, Balt. City Hosps., Balt., 1979-80, pharmacologist, 1981-82, Gerontology Research Center, Nat. Inst. Aging, NIH, pharmacologist, 1982-1985, chief Neuropharmacology lab. NIDA: 1982, NIDA Addiction Research Ctr., 1985—. Contbr. articles on neuropharmacology, neurochemistry to prof. jours. Mem. Am. Soc. for Pharmacology and Exptl. Therapeutics, Am. Soc. for Neurochemistry, Soc. for Neurosci, AAAS, Am. Aging Assn., Internat. Soc. fo Cerebral Blood Flow and Metabolism, Current Work: Neuropharmacology, neurochemistry of development aging and substance abuse. Subspecialties: Neurochemistry; Neuropharmacology. Office: NIDA Addiction Research Ctr Francis Scott Key Med Ctr Baltimore MD 21224

LONDON, IRVING MYER, physician, educator; b. Malden, Mass., July 24, 1918; s. Jacob A. and Rose (Goldstein) L.; m. Huguette Piedzicki, Feb. 27, 1955; children: Robert L.J., David T. A.B., Harvard U., 1939, M.D., 1943; D.Sc., U. Chgo., 1966. Sheldon Traveling fellow Harvard U., 1939-41, Delamar research fellow med. sch., 1940-41; intern Presbyn. Hosp., N.Y.C., 1943, asst. resident, 1946-47, asst. physician, 1946-52, asso. attending physician, 1954-55; Rockefeller fellow in medicine Coll. Physicians and Surgeons, Columbia U., 1946-47; instr. Columbia U., 1947-49; asso. in medicine Coll. Phys. and Surg., Columbia U., 1949-51; asst. prof. Coll. Phys. and Surg., Columbia, 1951-54, asso. prof., 1954-55; prof., chmn. dept. medicine Albert Einstein Coll. Medicine, N.Y.C., 1955-70, vis. prof. medicine, 1970—; prof. biology M.I.T., 1969—; vis. prof. medicine Harvard Med. Sch., 1969-72; dir. div. health scis. and tech. Harvard and M.I.T., 1969-85, prof. medicine, 1972—, Grover M. Hermann prof. health scis. and tech., 1977—; dir. Whitaker Coll. Health Scis., Tech. and Mgmt., M.I.T., 1978-83; dir. med. service Bronx Mcpl. Hosp. Center, 1955-70; Roger Morris lectr. U. Cin., 1958; Stuart McGuire lectr. Med. Coll. Va., 1960; Phi Delta Epsilon lectr. U. Colo., 1962, Harvey lectr., 1961; Jacobaeus lectr., Stockholm, Sweden, 1964; vis. scientist Pasteur Inst., Paris, 1962-63; Commonwealth Fund fellow, 1962-63; Alpha Omega Alpha lectr. Yale, Boston U., Columbia, SUNY Downstate Med. Center, U. Chgo.; Harry L. Alexander vis. prof. Washington U., St. Louis, 1968; Alpha Omega Alpha vis. prof. Johns Hopkins U., 1970; Eugene A. Stead Jr. vis. lectr. Duke Med. Center, 1970; Cons. to Surgeon Gen., AUS, 1957-60; chmn. metabolism study sect. USPHS, 1961-63; Med. fellowship bd. Nat. Acad. Scis., NRC, 1955-64; mem. bd. sci. cons. Sloan Kettering Inst., 1960-72; bd. sci. counselors Nat. Heart Inst., 1964-68; exec. com. Health Research Council, City N.Y., 1958-63; mem. sci. adv. council Pub. Health Research Inst., N.Y.C., 1958-63; mem. adv. com. to dir. NIH, 1966-70, nat. cancer adv. bd., 1972-76; chmn. research group Nat. Commn. on Arthritis, 1975-76; chmn. adv. com. Div. Health Scis., Inst. Medicine, 1979-82; mem. Bd. Sci. Counselors, NIH, 1979-83. Asso. editor: Jour. Clin. Investigation, 1952-57; mem. editorial bd.: Am. Jour. Medicine, 1965-79. Served as capt. AUS, 1944-46. Recipient Theobald Smith award in med. scis. AAAS, 1953. Fellow Am. Acad. Arts and Scis.; mem. Am. Soc. Biol. Chemists, Am. Soc. Clin. Investigation (pres. 1963-64), Nat. Acad. Scis. (mem. bd. medicine 1967-70, mem. exec. com. Inst. Medicine 1970-72), Internat. Soc. Hematology, Soc. Exptl. Biology and Medicine, Assn. Am. Physicians, Nat. Acad. Scis., Phi Beta Kappa, Alpha Omega Alpha. Current Work: Research, teaching, academic medicine. Subspecialties: Hematology; Internal medicine. Office: Harvard-Mass Inst Tech Div Health Scis and Tech 77 Massachusetts Ave Cambridge MA 02139

LONDON, MARK DAVID, environmental scientist; b. Bklyn., May 24, 1947; s. Julius William and Caroline Janet London; m. Helen Louise Hollander, Jan. 25, 1970; children—Tracie Gayle, Jill Whitney. B.S., C.W. Post Coll., 1970, M.S., 1974. Biologist, Engrng. Sci., Inc., Great Neck, N.Y., 1969-72; scientist Woodward-Clyde, Clifton, N.J., 1972-76; systems analyst Tymshare, Inc., Fair Lawn, N.J., 1976; prin. staff scientist Pub. Service Electric & Gas Co., Newark, 1976—. Editor: Statistics in Environmental Science, 1984. Chmn. Denville Twp. Environ. Commn., 1980—. Mem. Am. Inst. Biol. Sci., Am. Soc. Limnology and Oceanography, Am. Fisheries Soc., N.Y. Acad. Sci. Republican. Current work: Application of statistics to environmental science-creating useful, informative data sets oriented towards problem solving. Subspecialties: Ecology (environmental science); Statistics. Home: 107 West Shore Rd Denville NJ 07834 Office: Pub Service Electric & Gas Co 80 Park Plaza (T22A) Newark NJ 07101

LONDON, RAY WILLIAM, clinical, consulting and medical psychologist, researcher; b. Burley, Idaho, May 29, 1943; s. Loo Richard and Maycelle Jerry (Moore) L. A.S., Weber State Coll., 1965, B.Sc., 1967; M. S.W., U. So. Calif., 1973, Ph.D., 1976. Diplomate: Am. Bd. Psychol. Hypnosis, Am. Acad. Behavioral Medicine, Am. Bd. Psychotherapy, Internat. Bd. Medicine and Psychology. Congl. asst. U.S. Ho. of Reps., 1964-65; research assoc. Bus. Advs., Inc., Ogden, Utah, 1965-67; dir. counseling and consultation services Meaning Found., Riverside, Calif., 1966-69; mental health and social service liaison San Bernardino County (Calif.) Social Services, 1968-72; clin. trainee VA Outpatient Clinic, Los Angeles, 1971-72; clin. trainee Children's Hosp., Los Angeles, 1972-73, clin. fellow, 1973-74; clin. trainee Reiss Davis Child Study Ctr., Los Angeles, 1973-74, Los Angeles County-U. So. Calif. Med. Center, 1973; psychotherapist Benjamin Rush Neuropsychiat. Ctr., Orange, Calif., 1973-75; clin. psychology postdoctoral trainee Orange County (Calif.) Mental Health, 1976-77; postdoctoral fellow U. Calif.-Irvine Coll. Medicine, 1978; now clin. faculty; clin. psychologist Orange Police Dept., 1974-80, pvt. practice consultation and psychotherapy, Santa Ana, Calif., 1974—; cons. to public schs., hosps., bus., nationally and internationally, 1973—; pres. bd. govs. Human Factor Programs, Ltd., 1976—; pres. Internat. Bd. Medicine and Psychology, 1980—; mem. faculty Internat. Congress of Hypnosis and Psychosomatic Medicine, Soc. Clin. and Exptl Hypnosis, Internat. Adv. Bd. European Congress Hypnosis and Psyhcosomatic Medicine; research assoc. Nat. Commn. for Protection of Human Subjects of Biomed. and Behavioral Research, 1976; fellow Inst. for Social Scientists on Neurobiology and Mental Illness, 1978. Editor: Internat. Bull. Medicine and Psychology, 1980; assoc. editor: Australian Jour. Clin. Hypnotherapy and Hypnosis, 1980; editorial cons.: Internat. Jour. Clin. and Exptl. Hypnosis, 1981; pub.: London Behavioral Medicine Assessment, 1982; producer: TV series Being Human, 1980. Recipient Congl. recognition U.S. Ho. of Reps., 1978; named scholar laureate Erickson Advanced Inst., 1980. Fellow Internat. Acad. Medicine and Psychology (dir. 1981—), Soc. Clin. Social Work (dir. 1979-80), Royal Soc. Health; mem. Acad. Psychosomatic Medicine, Am. Assn. Social Psychiatry, Am. Assn. Marriage and Family Therapy, Am. Psychology-Law Soc., Am. Psychol. Assn., CAlif. Psychol. Assn., Am. Group Psychotherapy Assn., Am. Orthopsychiat. Assn., Am. Soc. Clin. Hypnosis, Am. Soc. Psychosomatic Dentistry and Medicine, Biofeedback Soc. Am., Internat. Soc. Hypnosis, N.Y. Acad. Sci., Soc. Behavioral Medicine, Soc. Clin. and Exptl. Hypnosis, World Assn. Social Psychiatry, Phi Delta Kappa, Delta Sigma Rho, Tau Kappa Alpha, Pi Rho Phi, Lambda Iota Tau. Club: Toastmasters. Current Work: Medical psychology; behavioral medicine; biofeedback and hypnosis; research and clinical application of behavioral, cognitive, psychophysiology, cancer, nephrology, immunology, pain, pediatrics, phobias, neuropsychology and cardiology problems. Subspecialties: Psychophysiology; Cognition. Office: 1125 E 17th St Suite E-211 Santa Ana CA 92701

LONDON, WILLIAM THOMAS, research physician; b. N.Y.C., Mar. 11, 1932; s. William Wolf and Lillian (Mann) L.; m. Linda Jane Greenman, June 23, 1957; children: Barbara, Katharine, Emily, Nancy. B.A., Oberlin Coll., 1953; M.D., Cornell U., 1957. Postdoctoral research fellow in endocrinology Sloan-Kettering Inst., N.Y.C., 1960-62; sr. surgeon USPHS NIH, Bethesda, Md., 1962-66; research epidemiologist Inst. Arthritis and Metaboloic Disease, 1962-66; research physician Inst. Cancer Research, Phila., 1966-67, sr. research physician, 1978—; adj. prof. U. Pa. Sch. Medicine, 1977—. Contbr. articles to profl. jours. Bd. dirs. Cheltenham Twp. Adult Sch. Nat. Cancer Inst. grantee, 1966—; Nat. Inst. Arthritis, Metabolic and Digestive Diseases grantee, 1978-81. Fellow ACS; mem. AMA, ACP, Endocrine Soc., Am. Assn. Cancer Research, Am. Soc. Preventive Oncology, Soc. Epidemiol. Research. Democrat. Jewish. Current Work: Hepatitis B virus, hepato cellular carcinoma; chronic hepatitis, cirrhosis. Subspecialties: Cancer research (medicine); Epidemiology. Office: 7701 Burholme Ave Philadelphia PA 19111

LONG, DAVID AINSWORTH, environmental engineering educator, consultant; b. Reinbeck, Iowa, Aug. 17, 1933; s. Wilbur McKinnis and Lora Myrtle (Ainsworth) L.; m. Marilyn Jane Norris, Aug. 8, 1954; children: Jeffrey, James and Joan (triplets), Thomas. B.S.C.E., State U. Iowa, 1957, M.S., 1959; Ph.D., Pa. State U., 1971. Diplomate: Am. Acad. Environ. Engrs.; Registered profl. engr., Iowa, Pa. Research assoc. State U. Iowa, Iowa City, 1957-59; drainage basin engr. Wis. Commn. Water Pollution, Wisconsin Rapids, 1959-61; project engr. Baxter & Woodman, Inc., Crystal Lake, Ill., 1961-64; civil environ. engrng. Pa. State U., University Park, 1964—; cons. Gilbert Assocs., Reading, Pa., 1978-80, Lyco Systems, Williamsport, Pa., 1979—, Sweetland Engrng., State College, Pa., 1977—. Chmn. State Coll. Boro Water Authority, State College, Pa., 1977—; commr. Juniata Valley council Boy Scouts Am., State College, 1972—. Mem. Water Pollution Control Fedn. (bd. dirs. 1976-79, Philip F. Morgan award 1973, Arthur Sidney Bedell award 1975), ASCE, Am. Water Works Assn., Assn. Environ. Engrng. Profs. Republican. Episcopalian. Current Work: Operation and management of water and wastewater treatment utilities. Subspecialty: Water supply and wastewater treatment. Home: 1009 Metz Ave State College PA 16801 Office: Pa State U 212 Sackett Bldg University Park PA 16802

LONG, FRANKLIN A., emeritus chemistry educator; b. Great Falls, Mont., July 27, 1910; s. F.A. and Ethel (Beck) L.; m. Marion Thomas, 1937; children: Franklin, Elizabeth. A.B., U. Mont., 1931, M.A., 1932; Ph.D., U. Calif., 1935. Instr. chemistry U. Calif., 1935-36, U. Chgo., 1936-37; instr. chemistry Cornell U., 1937-38, prof., 1939-79, prof. emeritus, 1979—, chmn. dept., 1950-60, v.p. research and advanced studies, 1963-69, Henry Luce prof. sci. and society, 1969-79, dir. program on sci., tech. and society, 1969-73, dir. peace studies program, 1976-79; Dir. United Tech. Corp., Exxon Corp., 1969-81, cons., 1970-82; Mem. President's Sci. Adv. Com., 1961-66; asst. dir. U.S. Arms Control and Disarmament Agy., 1962-63, cons., 1963-73, 77-79; dir. Arms Control Assn., 1971-77; mem. adv. com. for planning and instnl. affairs NSF, chmn., 1973-74, mem. adv. panel for policy research analysis, 1976-80; co-chmn. Am. Pugwash Steering Com., 1974-79; mem. Indo-U.S. subcom. for ednl. and cultural affairs, 1974-82, co-chmn., 1977-82; bd. dirs. Associated Univs., Inc., 1947-74, hon. bd. dirs., 1975—; bd. dirs. Council Sci. and Tech. for Devel., 1977—, Albert Einstein Peace Prize Found., 1979—. Mem. editorial bd.: Am. Scientist, 1974-81; Contbr. articles on chemistry, sci. policy and pub. affairs and arms control and disarmament to books, jours., encys. and reference works. Trustee Cornell U., 1956-57, Alfred P. Sloan Found., 1970-83, Fund for Peace, 1981—. Guggenheim fellow, 1970. Fellow Am. Acad. Arts and Scis. (v.p. 1976-80); mem. Nat. Acad. Scis., AAAS, Council on Fgn. Relations, Am. Chem. Soc. (Charles Lathrop Parsons award 1985). Current Work: Policies for hazardous chemical wastes; military technology; Science and technology for development. Subspecialty: Physical chemistry. Home: 429 Warren Rd Ithaca NY 14850

LONG, GARY JOHN, chemist, educator; b. Binghamton, N.Y., Dec. 3, 1941; s. Clifford J. and Margaret B. (Goodnow) L.; m. Audrey A. Ristway, Aug. 24, 1963; 1 son, Jeffrey R. B.S., Carnegie-Mellon U., 1964; Ph.D., Syracuse U., 1968. Prof. chemistry U. Mo.-Rolla, 1968—. Contbr. numerous articles on chemistry to profl. jours. Fellow Royal Soc. Chemistry, Am. Chem. Soc., Sigma Xi. Current Work: Solid state and physical inorganic chemisry, Mossbauer effect spectroscopy, magnetic susceptibilities, X-ray and neutron diffraction, synthetic inorganic chemistry. Subspecialties: Inorganic chemistry; Solid state chemistry. Office: Dept Chemistry U Mo-Rolla Rolla MO 65401

LONG, HARRY JOSEPH, medical oncologist; b. Natrona Heights, Pa., Dec. 23, 1946; s. Harry Joseph and Iva Mae (Elliott) L.; m. Louise Mary Parten, June 24, 1967; children—Lara Louise, Kristin Mary, Harry Joseph, IV. B.S., U. Pitts., 1967; M.D., Temple U., 1971. Diplomate Am. Bd. Internal Medicine. Resident in internal medicine Naval Regional Med. Ctr., Phila., 1971-74, fellow in med. oncology, 1974-76, staff hematology/oncology, Naval Regional Med. Ctr., San Diego, 1976-81; asst. prof. oncology Mayo Grad. Sch. Medicine, Rochester, Minn., 1981—, cons. in oncology Mayo Clinic, 1981—. Served to capt. USNR, 1968—. Fellow ACP; mem. Am. Soc. Clin. Oncology, Am. Soc. Hematology, Am. Assn. Cancer Research, Am. Cancer Soc. (bd. dirs. Minn. div. 1984—). Current work: Development of new approaches to cancer treatment with chemotherapy. Subspecialties: Chemotherapy; Oncology. Office: Mayo Clinic 215 2d St SW Rochester MN 55905

LONG, JOHN PAUL, pharmacologist, educator; b. Albia, Iowa, Oct. 4, 1926; s. John Edward and Bessie May L.; m. Marilyn Joy Stookesberry, June 11, 1950; children: Jeff, John, Jane. B.S., U. Iowa, 1950, M.S., 1952, Ph.D., 1954. Research scientist Sterling Winthrop Co., Albany, N.Y., 1954-56; asst. prof. U. Iowa, Iowa City, 1956-58, assoc. prof., 1958-63, prof., 1963—, head dept. pharmacology, 1970-83. Author 288 research publs. in field. Served with U.S. Army, 1945-46. Recipient Abel award Am. Pharm. Assn., 1958; Ebert award Pharmacology Soc., 1962. Mem. Am. Soc. Pharm. Exptl. Therapy, Soc. Exptl. Biol. Medicine. Republican. Current Work: Structure-activity relationships of dopamine receptor agonist. Subspecialties: Neuropharmacology; Molecular pharmacology. Home: 1817 Kathlin Dr Iowa City IA 52240 Office: Dept Pharmacology Coll Medicine Iowa City IA 52242

LONG, LEONARD MICHAEL, engineering consultant; b. New Orleans, July 6, 1955; s. William Anthony and Joyce (Eiserloh) L. B.S. in Mech. Engrng, La. State U., Baton Rouge, 1977, M.S. in Mech. Engring, 1979. Project/maintenance engr. Vulcan Materials Co., Geismar, La., 1979-80; mech. engr. Beard Engrng., Inc., Baton Rouge, 1980—. Contbr. articles to profl. jours. Mem. ASME (treas. Baton Rouge chpt.). Republican. Roman Catholic. Current Work: Innovative technology for treatment of industrial wastes. Subspecialty: Mechanical engineering. Home: 3030 Congress Blvd Number 69 Baton Rouge LA 70808

LONG, LYLE NORMAN, aeronautical engineer; b. Fergus Falls, Minn., Apr. 7, 1954; s. Norman Laverne and Shirley Ann (Leeman) L.; m. Laura Jean Greuel, July 11, 1981. B.M.E. with distinction, U. Minn., 1976; M.S., Stanford U., 1978; D.Sc., George Washington U., 1983. Engr. Donaldson Co., Inc., Mpls., 1974-76; research asst. Stanford (Calif.) U./NASA-Ames, 1977-78; research assoc. Joint Inst. for Advancement Flight Scis., NASA-Langley Research Center, Hampton, Va., 1979-83; research specialist Lockheed Advanced Aero. Co., Valencia, Calif., 1983—. Mem. AIAA (chmn. Langley student br. 1978-80), Am. Soc. Engrng. Edn., Soc. Indsl. and Applied Math., Sigma Xi, Pi Tau Sigma. Club: Sierra (San Francisco). Current Work: Unsteady nonlinear aerodynamics, aerodynamics of rotating blades using an acoustic formulation in the time domain, computational aerodynamics. Subspecialties: Aeronautical engineering; Fluid mechanics. Home: 25688 Dorado Dr Valencia CA 91355 Office: PO Box 551 Burbank CA 91520

LONG, ROBERT B., chemical consulting company executive; b. Annville, Pa., Feb. 18, 1923; s. Morris Miller and Elizabeth Catherine (Fencil) L.; m. Marie Nellie Parker, June 24, 1944; children—Gretchen, Gilbert, Robin, Kate, James, Bonnie. B.S. in Chem. Engring., Pa. State U., 1944, M.S., 1947, Ph.D., 1951. Sr. engr. Exxon Research, Linden, N.J., 1952-57, research assoc., 1957-64, sr. research assoc., 1964-69, sci. advisor, 1969-84; pres. Long Cons., Inc., Atlantic Highlands, N.J., 1984—. Contbr. articles to profl. jours. Patentee in field. Mem. Am. Chem. Soc., Am. Inst. Chem. Engrs., AAAS. Republican. Presbyterian. Lodges: Masons, Lions. Current work: Separation processes, petroleum and synthetic fuel processing. Subspecialties: Chemical engineering; Petroleum engineering. Home: 60 Ocean Blvd Atlantic Highlands NJ 07716

LONG, ROBERT RADCLIFFE, educator; b. Glen Ridge, N.J., Oct. 24, 1919; s. Clarence D. and Gertrude (Cooper) L.; m. Cristina Nersing, 1962; children: John Radcliffe, Robert W. A.B. in Econs, Princeton, 1941; M.S. in Meteorology, U. Chgo., 1949, Ph.D., 1950. Meteorologist U.S. Weather Bur., Paris, France, 1946-47; asst. prof. Johns Hopkins, 1951-56, asso. prof., 1956-59, prof. fluid mechanics, 1959—, dir. hydrodynamics lab., 1951—. Author: also articles in field. Engineering Science Mechanics; Editor: Tellus, 1966—, Jour. Geophys. Research, 1968—. Served from aviation cadet to capt. USAAF, 1942-45. Mem. Am. Meteorol. Soc. Current Work: Fluid mechanics with application to meteorological and oceanographic systems. Subspecialties: Meteorology; Fluid mechanics. Home: 802 Beaverbank Circle Towson MD 21204 Office: Johns Hopkins U Baltimore MD 21218

LONGENECKER, GESINA (LOUISE) LIZANA, pharmacology researcher, medical educator; b. New Orleans, June 25, 1945; d. Florian Joseph and Shirley Louise (White) Lizana; m. Herbert Eugene Longenecker, June 12, 1965; children: Lani Louise, Herbert Eugene, Aimee Lee. B.S. with honors in Chemistry, Tulane U., 1965; Ph.D. in Pharmacology, Cornell U. Grad Sch. Med. Scis., N.Y.C., 1971. Postdoctoral fellow in pharmacology Cornell U. Grad. Sch. Med. Scis., 1971-72; postdoctoral fellow in biochemistry U. South Ala. Coll. Medicine, 1972-74, instr. pharmacology, 1974-75, asst. prof. pharmacology, 1975-81, assoc. prof., 1981—; mem. environ. biology rev. panel EPA, 1981—; mem. study sects. on use perfluorochems., sickle cell disease, coronamy vasospasm NIH; cons. Gulf States div. ARC, 1975—. Contbr. numerous articles, abstracts to profl. publs.; trainee editor: Clin. Pharmacology and Therapeutics, 1971-72; editor: Jour. Electrophysiol. Techniques, 1974-79. U. South Ala. Intramural grantee, 1975-78; Am. Lung Assn. grantee, 1978-80; NIH grantee, 1980-83; Council Tobacco Research—U.S.A., Inc. grantee, 1981-84; Upjohn Co. grantee, 1981-82. Mem. Neurosci. Soc., Soc. Exptl. Biology and Medicine, N.Y. Acad. Scis., Southeastern Pharmacology Soc., AAAS. Current Work: Platelet-endothelial interactions; prostaglandins; free radicals. Subspecialties: Pharmacology; Hematology. Home: 3728 Claridge Rd S Mobile AL 36608 Office: Pharmacology-MSB Coll Medicin U South Al Mobile AL 36688

LONGEWAY, PAUL ALLEN, physical chemist; b. Washington, Jan. 31, 1947; s. Leroy I. and Mary C. (Stein) L. B.A., Messiah Coll., 1968; M.S., Shippensburg U., 1979; Ph.D., Pa. State U., 1982. High sch. chemistry tchr., 1969-76; mem. tech. staff RCA-David Sarnoff Research Ctr., Princeton, N.J., 1981—. Contbr. articles to profl. jours. Patentee in field. Active Big Brothers of Mercer County, N.J., 1981—; karate instr. Nat. Am. TaeKwonDo Assn., 1984—. Mem. Am. Chem. Soc. Democrat. Lodge: Masons. Current work: Vapor phase epitaxial growth of III-V compounds for use in semiconductors; chemistry of silanes; deposition of amorphous Si:H; plasma kinetics; semiconductor properties of III-V materials. Subspecialties: Solid state chemistry; Physical chemistry. Office: RCA-David Sarnoff Research Ctr Princeton NJ 08540

LONGHI, RAYMOND, chemical and engineering company executive; b. Plymouth, Mass., Nov. 14, 1935; s. Henry Joseph and Hazel M. (Raymond) L.; m. Betty Helen Johnson, Sept. 2, 1961; children—Jon, Michael, Jennifer. B.S. in Chemistry, U. Mass., 1957; A.M. in Chemistry, Dartmouth Coll., 1959; Ph.D. in Chemistry, U. Ill., 1962. Research chemist, sr. research chemist, E.I. DuPont, Waynesboro, Va., 1962-65, research supr., Wilmington, Del., 1966-68, sr. research supr., Chattanooga, 1969-74, tech. supt., Martinsville, Va., 1974-78, tech. supt., Seaford, Del., 1978-82, site research and devel. mgr., 1982—. Contbr. articles to profl. jours. Mem. Am. Chem. Soc., Am. Assn. Textile Chemists and Colorists, Sigma Xi. Current work: Coordination chemistry-reactions, structure, mechanisms polymers chemistry, reactions mechanisms, computer and engineering applications. Subspecialties: Inorganic chemistry; Polymer chemistry. Office: E I du Pont de Nemours Seaford DE 19973

LONGNECKER, DANIEL SIDNEY, pathologist, educator; b. Omaha, June 8, 1931; s. Walter Winfield and Hope Aline (Ranney) L.; m. Louise Elizabeth Miller, June 22, 1952; children: Matthew Paul, Daniel Alan, Jane Aline, Thomas Winfield. A.B., U. Iowa, 1954; M.D., 1956, M.S., 1962. Diplomate: Am. Bd. Pathology. Asst. prof., then assoc. prof. pathology U. Iowa, 1962-69; assoc. prof. St. Louis U. Med. Sch., 1969-72; prof. pathology Dartmouth Coll. Med. Sch., 1972—; mem. Nat. Adv. Envron. Health Scis. Council, 1978-81. Author papers in field. Served to lt USNR. Research grantee NIH, 1974—. Mem. Am. Assn. Cancer Research, Am. Assn. Pathologists, Am. Pancreatic Assn., Soc. Exptl. Biology and Medicine, Common Cause. Current Work: Experimental carcinogenesis, carcinoma of the pancreas. Subspecialties: Pathology (medicine); Cancer research (medicine). Office: Dept Pathology Dartmouth Med Sch Hanover NH 03756

LONGWELL, JOHN PLOEGER, chemical engineering educator; b. Denver, Apr. 27, 1918; s. John Stalker and Martha Dorothea (Ploeger) L.; m. Marion Reed Valleau, Dec. 11, 1945; children: Martha Reed, Elizabeth Ann, John Dorney. B.S. in Mech. Engrng, U. Calif., Berkeley, 1940; Sc.D. in Chem. Engrng, M.I.T., 1943. With Exxon Research & Engrng. Co., Linden, N.J., 1943-77; dir. Exxon Research & Engrng. Co. Central Basic Research Lab., 1960-69; sr. sci. adv. Exxon Research & Engrng. Co. (Central Basic Research Lab.), 1969-77; prof. chem. engrng. M.I.T., Cambridge, 1977—; chmn. NRC Com. on Advanced Energy Storage Systems, 1979. Contbr. articles to profl. jours. Recipient Sir Alfred Egerton medal for contbns. to combustion Nat. Acad. Engrng., 1976. Mem. Am. Chem. Soc., Combustion Inst. (past pres.), Am. Inst. Chem. Engrs. (award 1979), Sigma Xi, Tau Beta Pi. Republican. Patentee in field. Current Work: High temperature fuel conversion processes-combustion, gasification pyrolysis; control of pollutants from combustion. Subspecialties: Combustion processes; Fuels. Home: 22 Follen St Cambridge MA 02138 Office: Mass Inst Tech Room 66-350 Cambridge MA 02139

LONNGREN, KARL ERIK, electrical and computer engineer, educator; b. Milw., Aug. 8, 1938; s. Bruno Leonard and Edith Irene (Osterlund) L.; m. Vicki Mason, Feb. 16, 1963; children: Sondra Lyn, Jon Erik. B.S., U. Wis.-Madison, 1960, M.S., 1962, Ph.D., 1964. Asst. prof. elec. and computer engrng. U. Iowa, Iowa City, 1965-67, assoc. prof., 1967-72, prof., 1972—; vis. scientist, Sweden, 1964, Japan, 1972, 81, Denmark 1982, Oak Ridge, 1967-69, Los Alamos, 1979-80, Can., 1971, Wis., 1976-77. Co-author: Introduction to Wave Phenomena. Contbr. numerous articles to profl. jours.; co-editor: Solitons in Action, 1978. Fellow Am. Phys. Soc., IEEE. Current Work: Research in nonlinear waves, solitons and shocks, nonlinear mathematics with emphasis in plasma physics. Subspecialties: Electrical engineering; Plasma physics. Office: Elec and Computer Engring Dept U Iowa Iowa City IA 52242

LONSDALE, HAROLD KENNETH, high tech. co. exec.; b. Westfield, N.J., Jan. 19, 1932; s. Harold K. and Julia (Papandrea) L.; m. Constance Kerr, June 20, 1953; children: Karen Anne, Harold Kenneth. B.S. in Chemistry, Rutgers U., 1953; Ph.D. in Phys. Chemistry, Pa. State U., 1957. Staff mem. Gen. Atomic Co., San Diego, 1959-70; prin. scientist Alza Corp., Palo Alto, Calif., 1970-72; vis. scientist Max Planck Inst. for Biophysics, Frankfurt, W.Ger., 1973-74, Weizmann Inst. Sci., Rehovot, Israel, 1973-74; pres. Bend Research, Inc., Bend, Oreg., 1975—. Editor: Reverse Osmosis Membrane Research, 1972; contbr. articles to profl. jours. Served to 1st lt. USAF, 1957-59. Named Small Bus. Entrepreneur of Yr. Oreg. Bus. Mag., 1982. Mem. Am. Chem. Soc. Patentee in field. Current Work: Founder, pres. high technology co.; membrance science and technology; water desalination and purification by membrane processes; controlled release products; gas separations. Subspecialty: Physical chemistry. Office: Bend Research Inc 64550 Research Rd Bend OR 97701-8599

LONTZ, JOHN FRANK, biophysicist, educator; b. Bridgeport, Pa., Oct. 14, 1909; s. Frank Jacob and Mary Anna (Weinczyk) L.; m. Alexandra Elizabeth Gorzelska; children: Robert Jan., John F. B.S., Rutgers U., 1931; A.M., Temple U., Phila., 1933; Ph.D., Yale U., 1936; L.H.D., Holy Family Coll., 1971. Research chemist E. I. du Pont de Nemours, Wilmington, Del., 1936-41, research supr., 1950-60, research assoc., 1960-72; prof. biophysics Holy Family Coll., Torresdale, Pa., 1959-72; adj. prof. Temple U. Sch. Dentistry, Phila., 1972—; assoc. dir. maxillofacial clinic VA Med. Ctr., Wilmington, 1972—; cons. UN Indsl. Devel. Orgn., 1962-72, NIH, 1964-72. Bd. dirs., pres. Cath. Social Services, Wilmington, 1954-62. Served to lt. col. AUS, 1941-46; to col. USAR, 1960-70. Mem. Am. Chem. Soc., Am. Phys. Soc., AAAS, Soc. Biomaterials, Tissue Culture Assn., ASTM, Res. Officers Assn. Roman Catholic. Club: Athenaeum (Wilmington). Patentee plant growth stimulants, new structures, Teflon. Current Work: Polymer structure, molecular viscoelasticity, biological cell activity, toxicity and tumorigenicity, safe and effective prosthetics. Subspecialties: Polymer physics; Biophysics (biology). Home: 515 Eskridge Dr Wilmington DE 19809 Office: VA Med Ctr 1601 Kirkwood Hwy Wilmington DE 19805

LOOK, DAVID CHARLES, physicist; b. St. Paul, Dec. 19, 1938; s. Oliver Ardell and Hyacinth Harriet (Hansen) L.; m. Rita Marie Beatty, Oct. 19, 1968; children—James Wesley, Christine Marie. B.Physics, U. Minn., 1960, M.S., 1962; Ph.D., U. Pitts, 1966; M.S., U. Dayton, 1978. Research physicist U.

Dayton, Ohio, 1969-71, sr. research physicist, 1971-80; sr. research physicist Wright State U., Dayton, 1980—; pres. DCL Semicondr. Co., Dayton, 1984—; dir. Systems for Sci., Cleve.; cons. Keithley Inc., Cleve., 1981—. Patentee toneburst NMR relaxation. Contbr. articles to profl. jours. Leader Spinning Road Bapt. Ch., 1972—. Mellon fellow, 1962; NSF fellow, 1963. Served to capt. USAF, 1966-69. Fellow Am. Phys. Soc.; mem. Am. Sci. Affiliation. Current work: Electrical measurements on III-V semiconducting materials and devices especially gallium arsenide. Subspecialties: Condensed matter physics; Semiconductors. Home: 1851 Stonewood Dr Dayton OH 45432 Office: Wright State U Research Center Dayton OH 45435

LOOK, DWIGHT CHESTER, JR., mechanical engineering educator, researcher; b. Smith Center, Kans., Aug. 25, 1938; s. Dwight C. and Margery Rae (Bash) L.; m. Patricia A. Wellbaum, June 4, 1960; children: Dwight, Douglas. B.A., Central Coll., Fayette, Mo., 1960; M.S., U. Nebr., 1962; Ph.D., U. Okla., 1969. Teaching asst. dept. physics U. Nebr., Lincoln, 1960-63; aerosystems engr. Ft. Worth div. Gen. Dynamics, 1963-67; instr. evening coll. Tex. Christian U., Ft. Worth, 1967; spl. instr. mech. engring. U. Okla., Norman, 1969; from asst. prof. to prof. mech. engring. U. Mo.-Rolla, 1969—. Author: Thermodynamics, 1982; contbr. articles to profl. jours. NDEA fellow U. Okla., 1967-69; recipient Ralph R. Teetor award Soc. Automotive Engrs., 1978. Mem. ASME, AIAA, Am. Soc. Engring. End., Mo. Acad. Sci. Current Work: Research project dealing with two-dimensional electromagnetic scattering. Subspecialty: Mechanical engineering. Office: Univ Mo Rolla 204 Mech Engring Bldg Rolla MO 65401

LOOMIS, HAROLD GEORGE, mathematics educator, researcher; b. Erie, Pa., Apr. 22, 1925; s. Harold Lloyd and Mildred Elsie (Backstrom) L.; m. Phyllis Goodrich Wright, Nov. 26, 1947 (div. 1972); children: Thomas P., Richard W., Nancy A., Mary S.; m. Robin Uluwehi Fern, Feb. 15, 1972. B.S., Stanford U., 1950; M.A., Pa. State U., 1952, Ph.D., 1957. Scientist HRB Singer, State College, Pa., 1952-55; instr. Pa. State U., State College, 1955-57; asst. prof. Amherst (Mass.) Coll., 1957-62; asst. prof. U. Hawaii, Honolulu, 1963-66, prof., 1981—; scientist NOAA, Honolulu, 1966-81; sec. tsunami commn. Internat. Union Geodesy and Geophysics, 1979—. Contbr. chpt. to book, articles to profl. jours. Served with USMC, 1942-46. Mem. Math. Assn. Am., Soc. Indsl. and Applied Math. Democrat. Unitarian. Current Work: Generation, propagation and terminal effects of tsunamis. Numerical hydrodynamics of long waves. Subspecialties: Oceanography; Applied mathematics. Home: 1125 B 9th Ave Honolulu HI 96816 Office: Univ Hawaii 2540 Dole St Honolulu HI 96822

LOOMIS, TED ALBERT, physician, toxicologist; b. Spokane, Apr. 24, 1917; s. George and Sadie (Turner) L.; m. Marion Adams, Aug. 19, 1923; children: Bonnie, Becky. B.S., U. Wash., 1939; M.S., U. Buffalo, 1941; Ph.D., 1943; M.D., Yale U., 1946. Prof. pharmacology and toxicology U. Wash., Seattle, 1947—. Contbr. numerous articles to sci. jours. Mem. Soc. Pharmacology and Exptl. Therapeutics, Soc. Toxicology, Soc. Exptl. Biology and Medicine. Current Work: Mechanisms of chemical induced toxicity; clinical toxicology. Subspecialty: Toxicology (medicine). Address: Dept Pharmacology U Wash Sch Medicine Mail Stop SJ-30 Seattle WA 98195

LOOR, RUEYMING, cancer researcher, biochemist, immunologist, clinical chemist; b. Kaohsiung, Republic of China, Aug. 16, 1948; came to U.S., 1973, naturalized, 1985; s. Ho and Kang (Huang) L.; m. Chungpei Wang, Aug. 28, 1976; 1 child, Jeffrey. B.S., Nat. Chungshing U., 1970; M.S., U. Wis.-Superior, 1974; Ph.D., SUNY-Buffalo, 1978. Research assoc. U. Chgo., 1978-80; sr. cancer research scientist Roswell Park Meml. Inst., Buffalo, 1980-82; sr. research chemist BIORAD Lab., Richmond, Calif., 1982; scientist, project leader Cetus Corp., Emeryville, Calif., 1982—. Patentee automated assay tray, 1984; monoclonal antibody, 1984; simultaneous assays, 1984. Contbr. articles to profl. jours. Roswell Park Meml. Inst. grantee, 1981; Nat. Cancer Inst. grantee, 1982. Mem. Am. Soc. Cell Biology, Am. Assn. Clin. Chemistry, Am. Assn. Cancer Research, AAAS, Fedn. Am. Socs. Exptl. Biology (affiliate), N.Y. Acad. Scis. Current work: Cancer research, tumor immunology, immunodiagnosis of cancer, monoclonal antibody to cancer marker, clinical chemistry. Subspecialties: Cancer research (medicine); Clinical chemistry. Home: 8 Pinnacle Ct Hercules CA 94547 Office: Cetus Corp 1400 53rd St Emeryville CA 94608

LOOSEN, PETER THOMAS, psychiatrist, researcher, educator; b. Freiburg, Germany, Mar. 19, 1944; s. Otto Willi and Olga Maria (Hiener) L.; m. Laura Jeanne d'Angelo, Apr. 10, 1982. M.D., Ludwig Maximilian-U., Munich, W.Ger., 1970; Dr.med., 1974. Diplomate: German Bds. Psychiatry and Psychoanalysis, Am. Bd. Psychiatry and Neurology. Resident in psychiatry Psychiat. Hosp., U. Munich, 1972-74; psychiat. research fellow, resident dept. psychiatry U. N.C. Sch. Medicine, Chapel Hill, 1975-79, assoc. prof. psychiatry, dir. clin. research unit, 1979-83; prof., dir. affective disorders clin. Duke U. Med. Ctr., 1983—. Contbr. articles to profl. jours. Mem. Am. Psychiat. Assn., Internat. Soc. Psychoneuroendocrinology, N.Y. Acad. Scis., Collegium Internationale Neuropsychopharmacologicum, Am. Coll. Neuropsychopharmacology, Soc. Biol. Psychiatry, Soc. Neuroscience. Current Work: Psychoneuroendocrinology. Subspecialties: Psychiatry; Neuroendocrinology. Office: Department Psychiatry Box 3857 Duke U Med Ctr Durham NC 27710

LOPATIN, DENNIS EDWARD, immunologist; b. Chgo., Oct. 26, 1948; s. Leonard Harold and Cynthia (Shifrin) L.; 1 child, Jeremy G.; m. Constance M. McLeod, July 24, 1983. B.S., U. Ill, Urbana, 1970; M.S., 1972, Ph.D. in Microbiology, 1974. Postdoctoral fellow Northwestern U. Med. Sch., Chgo., 1974-75; research scientist U. Mich., Ann Arbor, 1976—, assoc. prof., 1982—. Contbr. articles to sci. jours. Mem. Am. Assn. Immunologist, Am. Soc. Microbiology, Internat. Assn. Dental Research, Sigma Xi. Current Work: Evaluation of the influence of microorganisms on immunoregulatory mechanisms and the influence of immunoregulatory mechanisms on response to certain microorganisms. Subspecialties: Immunology (medicine); Periodontics. Office: U Mich Ann Arbor MI 48109

LOPEZ, HECTOR, physicist, researcher; b. El Paso, Tex., Sept. 6, 1947; s. Isidro E. and Victoria C. L. B.S., U. Tex.-El Paso, 1970; M. Engring., U. Va., 1976. Radiol. physics cons. Physics Control, Inc., 1976-77; with Ctr. for Devices and Radiol. Health, FDA, USPHS, 1977—. Contbr. articles to profl. jours. Served with USAF, 1970-74. Recipient Commendation award USAF, 1974; USPHS unit commendation, 1981; IEEE Sonics and Ultrasonics award for best sci. paper, 1983. Mem. Am. Assn. Physicists in Medicine, Am. Inst. Ultrasound in Medicine. Democrat. Roman Catholic. Patentee in field. Current Work: Ultrasound image analysis; ultrasound signal processing and analysis. Subspecialties: Graphics, image processing, and pattern recognition; Optical signal processing. Office: Nat Ctr for Devices and Radiol Health HFZ-132 5600 Fishers Ln Rockville MD 20857

LOPEZ, ORLANDO, electrical engineer; b. Aguadilla, P.R., May 17, 1945; s. Galileo and Lucila (Jimenez) L.; m. Elizabeth Jane Barrows, June 15, 1968; children—Gwendolyn L., Hannah M., Robert O. B.E.E., U. P.R., 1965; M.S., MIT, 1967; M.Phil., Yale U., 1972; Ph.D., U. Colo., 1981. Mem. tech. staff N.Am. Rockwell, Anaheim, Calif., 1971-72; research sci. Kaman Scis. Corp., Colorado Springs, Colo., 1972-74; staff physicist Physics Internat., San Leandro, Calif., 1976-79; sr. adv. engr. Shugart Assocs. (Xerox), Sunnyvale, Calif., 1979-81; sr. cons. Magnetic Peripherals/Control Data, Bloomington, Mass., 1981—; cons. Sci. Applications, Colorado Springs, 1976; instr. San Jose State U., Calif., 1979-81; adj. asst. prof. U. New Haven, 1970-71. Contbr. articles to profl. jours. Mem. IEEE, Am. Phys. Soc., Sigma Xi. Current work: Theory of reproduce and record process in perpendicular magnetic recording, application of magnetic recording theory to the design of magnetic rotating shorage devices (disk drives). Subspecialties: Applied magnetics; Magnetic physics. Home: 18555 13th Ave N Plymouth MN 55447 Office: Magnetic Peripherals Inc 7801 Computer Ave South Bloomington MN 55435

LOPEZ-OVEJERO, JORGE ANDRES, physician, researcher, educator, consultant; b. San Pedro, Jujuy, Argentina, Oct. 16, 1938; came to U.S., 1966; s. Andres Isidoro Lopez-Ovejero and Delia Murguiondo; m. Linda Marie Krieger; 1 son, Andres. M.D., U. Buenos Aires, Argentina, 1965. Jr. resident in medicine Research Inst., U. Buenos Aires Sch. Medicine, 1965-66; research fellow dept. nephrology Research Inst., U. Buenos Aires Sch. Medicine (Research Inst. of Sch. Medicine), 1966; intern Elmhurst (N.Y.) div. Mt. Sinai Hosp. Services, 1967-68; resident in medicine Manhattan VA Hosp., N.Y.C., 1969-70; resident in medicine Coney Island Hosp.-Maimonides Downstate Sch. Medicine, Bklyn., 1970-71, chief resident in medicine, 1971-72; attending physician Columbia U., Presbyterian Hosp., N.Y.C., 1972-73; asst. attending physician N.Y. Hosp., Cornell Med. Center, N.Y.C., 1973—; instr. in medicine Cornell U., N.Y.C., 1973-77, asst. prof. medicine, 1977—; cons. reviewer med. jours. Contbr. articles to profl. jours. Recipient Virginia Nash award Virginia Nash Fund, 1971; N.Y. Heart Assn. research fellow Columbia U., 1972-73. Mem. Am. Fedn. Clin. Research. Roman Catholic. Current Work: Clinical research/treatment of hypertension; nutritional factors in the development and treatment of various chronic diseases. Subspecialty: Internal medicine. Office: 525 E 68th St Room k 400 New York NY 10021

LORANCE, ELMER DONALD, chemistry educator; b. Tupelo, Okla., Jan. 18, 1940; s. Elmer Dewey and Imogene (Triplett) L.; m. Phyllis Ilene Miller, Aug. 30, 1969; children: Edward Donald, Jonathan Andrew. B.A., Okla. State U., 1962; M.S., Kans. State U., 1967; Ph.D., Okla. U., 1977. Asst. prof. chemistry So. Calif. Coll., Costa Mesa, 1970-73, assoc. prof., 1973-80, prof., 1980—. Contbr. articles in chemistry to profl. jours. Mem. Am. Chem. Soc., AAAS, Phi Lambda Upsilon, Phi Theta Kappa. Republican. Current Work: Research in chemotaxonomical studies of populations of desert plants at different elevations. Subspecialties: Organic chemistry; Biochemistry (biology). Home: 3101 S Sycamore St Santa Ana CA 92707 Office: Southern California College Dept Chemistry Costa Mesa CA 92626

LORENZ, PHILIP BOALT, chemist; b. Dayton, Ohio, Aug. 14, 1920; s. Karl Kumler and Caroline (Boalt) L.; m. Irene McNeil, June 2, 1946; children—Douglas M., Eugene M., David R. B.A., Swarthmore Coll., 1941; M.A., Harvard U., 1946, Ph.D., 1949. Research asst. Princeton U., N.J., 1942-43, SAM Labs. (Columbia U./Carbide), N.Y.C., 1943-45; research chemist Bur. Mines, Dept. Energy, Bartlesville, Okla., 1949-83; sci. adviser Nat. Inst. Petroleum Energy Research, Bartlesville, 1983—. Contbr. articles to profl. jours. Mem. editorial bd. Jour. Colloids and Surfaces. Pres. Chs. United for Community Concern, 1972, 84, Scenic Rivers Assn. of Okla., 1982—; treas. Bartlesville br. NAACP, 1970. Mem. Am. Chem. Soc. (treas. chpt. 1979), Soc. Petroleum Engrs. (officer chpt. 1982—), Sigma Xi (pres. chpt. 1972). Democrat. Presbyterian. Club: Toastmasters. Current work: Enhanced oil recovery by chemicals. Subspecialties: Surface chemistry; Petroleum engineering. Home: 1541 Keeler Ave Bartlesville OK 74003 Office: Nat Inst for Petroleum and Energy Research PO Box 2128 Bartlesville OK 74005

LORENZEN, ROBERT T., agricultural engineering educator; b. New Leipzig, N.D., Feb. 16, 1917; s. Theodore and Hattie (Marek) L.; m. Mary K. Junkman, Feb. 6, 1954. B.S. in Agr, N.D. State U., 1943; B.S. in Civil Engring, U. Wis., 1954; M.S. in Agrl. Engring, U. Calif., Davis, 1957. Registered profl. engr., N.Y. Constrn. foreman Nat. Park Service, Mt. Rainier, Wash., 1936-39; constrn. supr. U. Wis., Madison, 1946-54; instr. U. Calif., Davis, 1954-56; asst.prof. agrl. engring. Colo. State U., Ft. Collins, 1956-59; from asst. prof. to prof. agrl. engring. Cornell U., Ithaca, N.Y., 1959-82, prof. emeritus, 1982—; design engr. Potlatch Forest, Lewiston, Idaho, 1978-79. Served to lt., inf. U.S. Army, 1943-46, ETO. Mem. Am. Soc. Agrl. Engring., Forest Products Research Soc., ASTM, ASHRAE, Sigma Xi, Chi Epsilon. Republican. Lutheran. Current Work: Consultant on safety, farm structures and production systems. Subspecialties: Agricultural engineering; Solar energy. Office: Cornell U Riley-Robb Hall Ithaca NY 14853

LORENZINI, PAUL GILBERT, nuclear engineer; b. Portland, Oreg., Apr. 16, 1942; s. Gilbert Henry and Viola P. (Gates) L.; m. Janet Grace Jesperson, Aug. 19, 1967; children: Christy, Michael. B.S., U.S. Mcht. Marine Acad., 1964; Ph.D., Oreg. State U., 1969; J.D., Loyola U., Los Angeles, 1975. Cert. nuclear engr., Calif. Project engr. Atomics Internat., Canoga Park, Calif., 1973-74, program mgr., 1974-76; assoc. Tooze, Kerr, et al., Portland, 1976-79; asst. chief counsel Rockwell Hanford Ops., Richland, Wash., 1979, dir. health, safety, environment, 1979-82, asst. gen. mgr., 1982-84, v.p., gen. mgr., 1984—. Founder, pres. Washington Voice Energy, Oreg. Voice Energy; chmn. fundraising bd. dirs. United Way, 1985; v.p. comp. devel. Boy Scouts Am., 1985; trustee Kadlee Hosp.; bd. dirs. Tri-City Indsl. Devel. Council. Named Tri-Cities Engr. of Yr., 1983. Mem. Am. Nuclear Soc. (dir. Oreg. sect. 1978-79, fuel cycle/waste mgmt. exec. com. 1981-84, rules and by laws com. 1982—), Health Physics Soc., Calif. Bar. Assn., Oreg. Bar. Assn. Republican. Presbyterian. Subspecialties: Nuclear fission; Nuclear engineering. Home: 121 W Orchard Way Richland WA 99352 Office: Rockwell Hanford Ops PO Box 800 Richland WA 99352

LORING, THOMAS JOSEPH, ecologist, consultant; b. Hailaybury, Ont., Can., May 27, 1921; s. Ernest Moore and Eva Margaret (Bachallor) L.; m. Beth Rogers McLaughlin, Oct. 29, 1966; children—John Francis, Christopher Thomas. B.Sc. in Forestry, Mich. Technol. U., 1946; M.F., N.Y. State Coll. Forestry, 1951. Forester McCormick Estates, Champion, Mich., 1946-48, logging boss, Penokee, Veneer and Mellon, Mich., 1951-52; forester U.S. Forest Service, Albuquerque, 1956-66, sect. head S.W. region, 1966-81; cons., Shawnigan Lake, B.C., Can., 1981—. Co-editor: Ecology, Uses and Management of Pinyon Juniper Woodlands, 1977; compiler Fuelwood Dealers in Arizona and New Mexico, 1981. Bd. dirs. Shawnigan Lake Community Ctr., 1982-85; chmn. Shawnigan Lake Residents and Ratepayers, 1984. Mem. Forest Products Research Soc. (regional bd. 1980-81, sect. chmn. 1978, outstanding service award 1979). Soc. Am. Foresters (sect. chmn. 1961-62), Ecol. Soc. Am., Can. Inst. Forestry, Shawnigan/Malahat Dist. C. of C. (bd. dirs. 1983-84). Roman Catholic. Current work: Urban forestry, land management and uses; part-time instructor basic ecology. Subspecialties: Ecology (biology); Fuels and sources. Home: 2700 Walbank Rd Shawnigan Lake BC VOR 2WO Canada

LORION, RAYMOND PAUL, psychologist, educator; b. Worcester, Mass., May 19, 1946; s. Edmond Gerard and Irene Agnes (Brodeur) L.; m. Sheila Catherine O'Connor, Nov. 24, 1967; children—Jennifer Irene, Matthew Raymond. B.S., Tufts U., 1968; Ph.D., U. Rochester, 1972. Research assoc., then asst. prof. dept. psychology U. Rochester, N.Y., 1972-74; assoc. prof. dept. psychology Temple U., Phila., 1974-79; prof. psychology U. Tenn.-Knoxville, 1979-85; prof. psychology, dir. clin.-community psychology U. Md.-College Park, 1985—; clin. psychologist in pvt. practice, Rochester, Phila., Knoxville, 1972—; vis. scientist NIMH, Rockville, 1982—; acting assoc. adminstr. for prevention Alcohol Drug Abuse and Mental Health Adminstrn., Rockville, 1983—, sr. cons. Office of Adminstr.; clin. psychologist dept. psychiatry Park West Hosp., Knoxville, 1982—; cons., lectr. in field. Author: Effective Behavior and Human Development, 1977. Editor: Ajuriaguerra's Handbook of Child Psychiatry and Psychology, 1980. Assoc. editor Am. Jour. Community Psychology, 1983—; editorial bd. Am. Jour. Community Psychology, 1974-82, Internat. Jour. Mental Health, 1978—, Paraprofl. Jour., 1980-81. Book rev. editor Internat. Jour. Mental Health, 1976—; editorial cons. Contbr. articles to profl. jours. Pres. Gulf Park Recreation Assn., Knoxville, 1982; mem. Foster Care Rev. Bd., Knoxville, 1981-85; cons. Council on Adoptable Children, 1980-85, Tenn. Dept. Corrections, 1980-85; mem. Tenn. & Gov.'s Task Force on Youth, Alcohol and Drug Abuse, 1984-85. Fellow Am. Psychol. Assn. (mem. task force on prevention, promotion and intervention alts. 1983—). mem. Soc. for Research in Child Devel., Southeastern Psychol. Assn., Eastern Psychol. Assn., Sigma Xi, Phi Beta Kappa. Roman Catholic. Current work: Prevention of emotional and behavioral dysfunction in preschool and primary grade children; delivery of human services to disadvantaged. Subspecialty: Developmental psychology. Home: 12111 Mt Pleasant Dr Laurel MD 20708 Office: Dept Psychology 1123 E Psychology-Zoology Bldg U Md College Park MD 20742

LORNITZO, FRANK ADAM, researcher, biochemist; b. N.Y.C., Dec. 18, 1926; s. Frank Charles and Michaela Marie (Krupicka) L.; m. Elspeth Mary Colwell, July 12, 1958 (div. Mar. 1983); children—Steven, Morris, Hannahjan. B.S. in Chem., U. R.I., 1955; M.S. in Organic Chem., U. Wis., 1956, M.S. in Philosophy, 1958. Research chemist, project assoc. U. Wis. Enzyme Inst. and TB Research Lab., V.A. Hosp., Madison, 1958-64; research chemist V.A. Hosp., Madison, 1964—, lipid metabolism lab, 1972—. Patentee Mycoribnin T-6-P. Contbr. numerous articles to profl. jours. Active mem. Citizens Concerned for Human Rights, Milw., 1982—; bd. dirs. Welfare Advocacy Center, Milw., 1983—. Mem. Am. Chem. Soc., AAAS, Sigma Xi. Quaker. Current work: Enzymology; fatty acid synthetase; hormonal control and activators; immunoaffinity chromatography and immunotitration; analytical techniques; enzymatic conversion of toxic cholesterol derivatives. Subspecialties: Biochemistry (biology); Immunobiology and immunology. Home: 1557 N Farwell Ave #204 Milwaukee WI 53202 Office: VA Med Center Overlook Terrace Madison WI 53705

LORTIE, JOHN WILLIAM, solar mktg. specialist, research corp. execl, solar cons., phys. sci. researcher; b. Chgo., July 11, 1920; s. William Arthur and Alice Marie (McNamee) L.; m. Mary Elaine Sullivan, Sept. 21, 1946; children: Colleen, Kevin, Timothy. Student in radar sci, Ill. Inst. Tech., 1940-42; Student in edn, U. Ala., 1976. Radar technician Western Electric Co., 1946-50; pres. Wm. A. Lortie & Sons, Westchester, Ill., 1950-65, Monark Instant Homes, Ocean Springs, Miss., 1965-75; exec. officer Energy Research Corp., Mobile, Ala., 1975-82, dir. research, 1980-85; head dept. solar tech. Carver State Tech. Coll., 1976-81; pres. Essential Solar Products, Mobile, 1980—, solar cons. Served in U.S. Army, 1942-46. Mem. Ala. Solar Energy Assn. (state chmn.), Ala. Solar Industries Assn. (pres.), Internat. Solar Energy Soc., Nat. Assn. Solar Contractors. Republican. Roman Catholic. Current Work: Patent research; laser guidance systems; solar ponds; sol desalination. Subspecialties: Combustion processes; Fuels and sources. Home: 4774 Bit and Spur Rd Mobile AL 36608 Office: 1508 Government St Suite 1C Mobile AL 36604

LOSIN, EDWARD THOMAS, research scientist; b. Racine, Wis., July 9, 1923; s. John and Sophia (Jamroz) L.; m. Laura Joy Soderstrom, June 10, 1950; children—Peter Thomas, Eric Barclay, Martha Sophia. B.S. in Chemistry, U. Ill., 1948; A.M. in Chemistry, Columbia U., 1950, Ph.D. in Chemistry, 1955. Postdoctoral fellow U. Mich., Ann Arbor, 1954-57; research chemist Union Carbide Corp., Tarrytown, N.Y., 1957-61; mgr. chemistry dept. Isomet Corp., Palisades Park, N.J., 1961-63; sr. research scientist Allis Chalmers Corp., Milw., 1963—. Contbr. articles to profl. jours. Patentee hydrazine process. Served with USN, 1943-46, ETO, PTO. Mem. Am. Chem. Soc., AAAS, N.Y. Acad. Scis., Combustion Inst., Sigma Xi. Congregationalist. Current work: Chemical reaction mechanisms; discharge plasma chemistry; pulverized coal combustion; coal desulferization; coal-water slurry properties and combustion. Subspecialty: Coal. Home: 10000 N Sheridan Dr Mequon WI 53092 Office: Allis Chalmers Corp PO Box 512 Milwaukee WI 53201

LOSS, FRANK J., mechanical engineer; b. Homestead, Pa., May 14, 1936. B.S., Carnegie-Mellon U., 1958, M.S., 1959, Ph.D., 1961. Registered profl. engr., Calif. Engr. Westinghouse Bettis Atomic Power Lab., Pitts., 1961-62; head mechanics of materials br. U.S. Naval Research Lab., Washington, 1964-82; tech. dir. Materials Engring. Assocs., Lanham, Md., 1982—. Contbr. numerous articles on engring. to profl. jours. Served to 1st lt., C.E. U.S. Army, 1962-64. Mem. ASTM, ASME. Current Work: Director of research and engineering, structural integrity technology development, fracture mechanics assessment of structural steels, corrosion fatigue, assessment of nuclear structural steels, radiation embrittlement, failure analysis. Subspecialties: Fracture mechanics; Materials (engineering). Home: 10318 Royal Rd Silver Spring MD 20903 Office: 9700-B Palmer Hwy Lanham MD 20706

LOSTROH, ARDIS JUNE, physiology educator; b. Malcolm, Nebr., Dec. 21, 1925; d. Louis Henry and Huldah (Larson) L.; m. Maurice Edward Krahl, Feb. 4, 1967. A.B. with distinction, U. Nebr.-Lincoln, 1950, M.A., 1952; Ph.D., U. Calif.-Berkeley, 1956. Postdoctoral fellow USPHS, U. Chgo., 1959-61; asst. prof. exptl. endocrinology U. Calif.-San Francisco, 1961-65, assoc. prof., 1965-77; vis. assoc. prof. physiology Stanford U., 1970-77; prof. dept. physiology Med. Coll. Va., Richmond, 1977-78; cons., 1978—. Nat. Found. Infantile Paralysis Postdoctoral fellow Paris, 1957-58; USPHS Postdoctoral fellow, 1959-61. Mem. Am. Phyiol. Soc., Phi Beta Kappa, Sigma Xi, Alpha Lambda Delta. Republican. Lutheran. Club: Catalina Racquet and Swim (Tucson). Current Work: Mammalian models; cellular-organ functions: regulation by hormones, ions, etc.; gonadal-pituitary hormones; control of reproduction; pituitary hormones: general metabolic effects; pituitary hormones and insulin: growth/diabetes. Subspecialties: Endocrinology; Cell and tissue culture. Home: 2783 W Casas Circle Tucson AZ 85741

LOTH, JOHN LODEWYK, aerospace engr., educator; b. The Hague, Netherlands, Sept. 14, 1933; s. Julius Edward and Fyna Johanna (Van de Berg) L.; m. Harriet H. Huffman; children by previous marriage: Eric, Frank, Marianne. B.A., U. Toronto, 1957, M.A. Sc., 1958, Ph.D. in Mech. Engring, 1962. Research fellow Centre National de Recherche Scientifique, Paris, 1958-59; lectr. U. Toronto, 1961-62; asst. prof. aero. engring. U. Ill., Urbana, 1962-67; prof. aerospace engring. W.Va. U., Morgantown, 1967—; pres. Dynamic Flow, Inc. (Engring. Cons.), 1972—. Contbr. articles to profl. jours. Mem. AIAA, Am. Soc. Engring. Edn., Combustion Inst., Profl. Engrs. Soc. W. Va., Sigma Xi, Sigma Gamma Tau. Current Work: Vertical axis wind turbine optimization and aerodynamic automatic speed control; powered high lift wing development, designed and tested the first circulation controlled stol aircraft. Subspecialties: Aerospace engineering and technology; Combustion processes. Home: PO Box 4094 Morgantown WV 26505 Office: Engring Sci Bldg W Va U Morgantown WV 26506

LOTLIKAR, PRABHAKAR DATTARAM, biochemist, educator; b. Shirali, Karnatak, India, May 21, 1928; came to U.S., 1955, naturalized, 1966; s. Dattaram Vithalrao and Laxmibai Dattaram (Kamath) L.; m. Faye Lun Chin, June 17, 1960; 1 son, Jeffrey. B.S., Bombay U., 1950, M.S., 1954; Ph.D., Oreg. State U., 1960. Asst. chemist Raptakos Brett & Co., Bombay, 1950-55; postdoctoral fellow, then project assoc. McArdle Lab. Cancer Research, U. Wis.-Madison, 1960-65, instr., 1965-66; research instr. biochemistry Fels Research Inst., Temple U. Med. Sch., Phila., 1967-68, asst. prof. biochemistry, 1968-75, assoc. prof., 1975—. Recipient USPHS Career Devel. award, 1969-73; Nat. Cancer Inst. grantee, 1968—. Mem. Am. Chem. Soc., AAAS, Am. Assn. Cancer Research, Am. Soc. Biol. Chemists., Soc. Exptl. Biology and Medicine, Biochem. Soc., N.Y. Acad. Scis. Current Work: Mechanisms of chemical carcinogenesis. Subspecialties: Cancer research (medicine); Oncology. Home: 1042 Randolph Dr Yardley PA 19067 Office: 3420 N Broad St Philadelphia PA 19140

LOTT, FREDRICK WILBUR, III, physicist, physics educator; b. San Mateo, Calif., Aug. 21, 1943; s. Fred W. and Kathryn (Deever) L.; m. Marilyn Claire Spear, Jan. 28, 1984. B.A. in Physics, Carleton Coll., 1964; M.A. in Physics, U. Calif.-Berkeley, 1966, Ph.D. in Physics, 1978. Computer programmer ATC Med. Tech., Sunnyvale, Calif., 1979-80; instr. physics Coll. San Mateo, Calif., 1980-81; asst. prof. physics Wilkes Coll., Wilkes-Barre, Pa., 1982-84; asst. prof. physics Weber State Coll., Ogden, Utah, 1984—. Nat. Merit scholar, 1961; Woodrow Wilson fellow, 1964. Mem. Am. Phys. Soc., Am. Assn. Physics Tchrs., Math. Assn. Am., Sigma Xi, Phi Beta Kappa. Current work: Particle physics, relativity and gravitation, physics in general; college physics teaching. Subspecialties: Particle physics; Relativity and gravitation. Home: 2108 Jefferson #D Ogden UT 84401 Office: Weber State Coll Ogden UT 84408

LOTTI, VICTOR JOSEPH, pharmacologist, pharm. co. exec., researcher; b. Trenton, Jan. 6, 1938; s. Joseph Anthony and Elizabeth (Persiano) L.; m. JoAnna Pitcock, Sept. 7, 1960; m. Barbara M., Nov. 17, 1976; children: Lynn E., Victor J., Lisa A. B.S. in Pharmacy, U. Conn., 1959; M.S. in Pharmacology, U. Mo., 1961; Ph.D. in Pharmacology (NIH fellow), UCLA, 1965. Registered pharmacist, Mo. With Merck & Co., 1967—, sr. dir. research coordination, Rahway, N.J., 1975-77, sr. dir. pharmacology, Chibret, France, 1977-79, dir. microbial pharmacometrics, West Point, Pa., 1980—. Contbr. numerous articles, abstracts, chpts. to profl. publs. NIH postdoctoral fellow, 1966. Mem. Am. Soc. Pharmacology and Exptl. Therapeutics, Am. Chem. Soc., Western Pharmacol. Soc., Soc. Neuroscis., Assn. Research Vision and Ophthalmology. Roman Catholic. Patentee composition and method of treatment of dopamine deficiency, methods of treating hypertension. Current Work: Ocular pharmacology; glaucoma; ocular and CNS neurotransmitters; ocular and CNS receptor mechanism; drug mechanisms of action; microbial natural product interaction with mammalian enzymes and receptors. Subspecialties: Ophthalmology; Neuropharmacology. Home: 214 Brookside Circle Harleysville PA 19438 Office: Merck Sharp and Dohme West Point PA 19486

LOTZE, MICHAEL THOMAS, surgical oncologist, tumor immunologist; b. Pasadena, Calif., July 11, 1952; s. Thomas Hilary and Joanne Bernice (Bellas) L.; m. Joan Harvey, June 25, 1977; children—Thomas, Anna, Michael. B. in Med. Sci., Northwestern U., 1973, M.D., 1974. Diplomate Am. Bd. Surgery. Intern in surgery U. Rochester, N.Y., 1975-76, resident in surgery, 1976-77, sr. resident, chief resident, 1980-82; practice medicine specializing in oncology and tumor immunology Nat. Health Service Corps, Region V, Onamia, Minn., 1977-78; clin. assoc. surgery br. div. cancer treatment Nat. Cancer Inst., Bethesda, Md., 1978-80, sr. staff surgery br., 1982—; assoc. prof. surgery Uniformed Services U. Health Scis., Bethesda 1984—. Contbr. articles to profl. jours. Mem. com. Unitarian Ch. of River Road, Bethesda, 1984. Served with USPHS, 1977-78. Recipient Myron White Med. Teaching award U. Rochester, 1982. Mem. AMA, Am. Assn. Immunology, Am. Assn. Cancer Research.

Subspecialties: Surgery; Cellular engineering. Office: Nat Cancer Inst NIH Bldg 10 Room 2B56 Surgery Br Bethesda MD 20205

LOU, JACK YUNG KIA, engineering educator; b. ChiChang, China, Oct. 11, 1931; came to U.S., 1961, naturalized, 1970; s. Yeh-Ting and Mo-kuang (Hu) L.; m. Shirley S.C. Sun, Sept. 1962; children—Richard C.H., Linda M.C. B.S. in Naval Architecture, Chinese Naval Coll. Tech., Republic of China, 1955; M.S. in Naval Architecture and Marine Engring., MIT, 1962; Ph.D. in Applied Mechanics, Poly. Inst. Bklyn., 1969. Naval architect George Sharp, Inc., N.Y.C., 1962-63; dynamics engr. Republic Aviation Co., Farmingdale, N.Y., 1963-65, Litton Industries Co., Paramus, N.J., 1965-66; staff engr. Hydrosystems, Inc., Farmingdale, 1966-68; assoc. prof. ocean engring. Columbia U., N.Y.C., 1968-74; prof., head ocean engring. program Tex. A&M U., College Station, 1974—; research cons. Nat. Sci. Council, Republic of China, 1972—. Editor Proc. Deep Water Mooring and Drilling, 1979; assoc. editor Jour. Energy Resources Tech., 1979-83. Recipient disting. teaching award Tex. A&M U., 1985. Fellow ASME (golden cert. award 1983, Bd. Govs. award 1984), Soc. Naval Architects and Marine Engrs. Current work: Naval architecture, ocean vehicle dynamics, offshore structures, fluid-structure interactions. . Home: 1004 Rose Circle College Station TX 77843 Office: Ocean Engring Program Tex A&M U College Station TX 77843

LOUCKS, VERNON REECE, JR., medical products and service company executive; b. Kenilworth, Ill., Oct. 24, 1934; s. Vernon Reece and Sue (Burton) L.; m. Linda Kay Olson, May 12, 1972; children—Charles, Greg, Suzy, David, Kristi, Eric. B.A. in History, Yale U., 1957; M.B.A., Harvard U., 1963. With Baxter Travenol Labs., Inc., Deerfield, Ill., 1966—, exec. v.p., 1973-76, dir., 1975—, pres., chief exec. officer, 1976—; dir. Dun & Bradstreet Corp., Emerson Electric Co., Quaker Oats Co.; mem. sr. council James S. Kemper & Co.; mem. adv. com. NIH. Bd. dirs. Lake Forest Hosp., Protestant Found., Econ. Club of Chgo.; trustee Rush, Presbyn. St. Lukes Med. Center; asso. Northwestern U.; alumni trustee Yale Corp. Served to 1st lt. USMC, 1957-60. Mem. Health Industry Mfrs. Assn. (chmn. 1983). Subspecialty: Medical products research and development management. Office: One Baxter Pkwy Deerfield IL 60015

LOUD, WARREN SIMMS, mathematics educator; b. Boston, Sept. 13, 1921; s. Roger Perkins and Esther (Nickerson) L.; m. Mary Louise Strasburg, Dec. 27, 1947; children—Margaret Loud McCamant, Elizabeth Ann Loud Liebman, John Alden. S.B., MIT, 1942, Ph.D., 1946. Instr. MIT, Cambridge, 1943-47; asst. prof., U. Minn., Mpls., 1947-56, assoc. prof., 1956-59, prof., 1959—. Contbr. articles to profl. jours. Mem. Am. Math. Soc., Math. Assn. Am. (bd. govs. 1960-62, 76-79), Soc. Indsl. and Applied Math. (editor 1961-75), U. Minn. Alumni Assn. (Outstanding Tchr. award 1979). Congregationalist. Current work: Research in ordinary differential equations. Subspecialties: Analysis; Applied mathematics. Office: Sch Math U Minn 206 Church St SE Minneapolis MN 55410

LOUGHMAN, BARBARA ELLEN EVERS, research immunologist; b. Frankfort, Ind., Oct. 26, 1940; d. Jimmie and Ruth (Hoyer) Evers; m. Terry B. Loughman, June 28, 1962; children: Lance Evers, Chad Elliott. B.S., U. Ill., 1962; Ph.D., U. Notre Dame, 1972. With Ames Research Labs., Miles Labs., Inc., Elkhart, Ind., 1962-72; NIH staff fellow Gerontology Research Center, Balt., 1972-74; research scientist hypersensitivity diseases research Upjohn Co., Kalamazoo, 1974-78, sr. research scientist, 1978-79, reserach head, 1979-84, research mgr., 1985; dir. immunology research Monsanto Co., 1985—; mem. study sect. NIH, 1982-85. Contbr. articles to sci. jours. Mem. AAAS, Am. Assn. Immunologists, Assn. Gnotobiology. Patentee in field. Current Work: Research administration; cellular immunology; somatic cell hybridization; clinical pharmacology of biologicals; immune pharmacology. Subspecialties: Immunobiology and immunology; Immunopharmacology. Home: 1522 Timber Point Ct Chesterfield MO 63017 Office: Monsanto Co Life Scis Research Ctr 700 Chesterfield Village Pkwy Chesterfield MO 63198

LOUI, MICHAEL CONRAD, engineering educator; b. Phila., June 1, 1955. B.S., Yale U., 1975; S.M., MIT, 1977, Ph.D., 1980. Vis. asst. prof. elec. engring., vis. research asst. prof. Coordinated Sci. Lab., U. Ill., Urbana-Champaign, 1981-82, asst. prof. elec. engring., research asst. prof., 1982—. Fannie and John Hertz Found. grad. fellow, 1975-80. Recipient Everitt award for Teaching Excellence, Coll. Engring. U. Ill.-Urbana-Champaign, 1984; Dow Outstanding Young Faculty award Am. Soc. Engring. Edn., 1985. Mem. Assn. Computing Machinery, IEEE, Math. Assn. Am., Soc. Indsl. and Applied Math., Sigma Xi, Phi Beta Kappa, Tau Beta Pi. Current Work: Analysis of algorithms, automata, computational complexity, data structures, distributed computation. Subspecialty: Theoretical computer science. Office: Coordinated Sci Lab U Ill 1101 W Springfield Ave Urbana IL 61801

LOUIS, JOHN, hematologist; b. Chgo., June 21, 1924; s. Demitrios John and Artemis (Halkiopolous) L.; m. Priscilla Humay, July 5, 1975; children: Priscilla Artemis, Demitrios John. B.S., U. Ill., 1948, M.S., 1950, M.D., 1950. Diplomate: Am. Bd. Internal Medicine, Am. Bd. Pathology. Instr., research assoc. U. Ill., 1951-65; asst. prof. medicine Loyola U., Chgo., 1965-70; pvt. practice medicine, 1970-75; prof. medicine VA Med. Center North Chgo./Chgo. Med. Sch., 1975—; cons. in field. Contbr. articles to profl. jours. Served with AUS, 1942-44. NIH grantee, 1958-65, 60-65. Fellow ACP; mem. Am. Soc. Clin. Oncology, Am. Assn. Cancer Research, Am. Soc. Hematology, Internat. Soc. Hematology. Greek Orthodox. Current Work: Clinical pharmacology. Subspecialties: Hematology; Chemotherapy. Address: 347 Circle Ln Lake Forest IL 60045

LOUTTIT, RICHARD TALCOTT, behavioral sciences administrator; b. Bloomington, Ind., Dec. 5, 1932; s. Chauncey McKinley and Laura Talcott L.; m. Carolyn Mae Creviston, June 20, 1954; children—Robert Scofield, Cathy Ann. A.B., DePauw U., 1954; M.A., U. Mich., 1959, Ph.D., 1961. Asst. prof. U. Pacific, Stockton, Calif., 1961-64; health scientist-adminstr. NIMH, Bethesda, Md., 1965-70; prof., head dept. psychology U. Mass., Amherst, 1970-75; dir. div. behavioral and neural scis. NSF, Washington, 1975—. Editor: Research in Physiological Psychology, 1965. Served to lt. (j.g.) USN, 1954-57. Fellow AAAS. Subspecialty: Behavioral sciences program administration. Office: National Science Foundation 1800 G St NW Washington DC 20550

LOVE, JERRY THORTON, biomedical engineer, researcher; b. Kress, Tex., Jan. 10, 1940; s. Hubert Alexander and Callis Henrietta (Goss) L.; m. Martha Carol Butler, Apr. 17, 1959 (div. Apr. 20, 1981); children—Lori LeAnn, Lisa DeAnn, Jerisa Kalene; m. Patricia Ann Harrer, Jan. 1, 1982. A.S., Central Tech. Inst., 1961. Co-investigator grant NIH, Bethesda, Md., 1979-84; mem. staff Sandia Nat. Labs., Albuquerque, 1961—; sci. review bd. VA, Washington, 1982; cons. Naval Intelligence Service Ctr., 1983. Recipient Outstanding Paper award Govt. Microcircuit Applications Conf., Houston, 1980. Mem. IEEE, N.Mex. Watercolor Soc. (Albuquerque) (vice pres. 1981, pres. 1982). Current work: Developed electronic controls for implantable insulin delivery system, first programmable system to be implanted in humans; completed technology transfer to industry; developed electronic controls for urinary and fecal incontinence. Subspecialties: Artificial organs and prostheses; Biomedical engineering. Office: Sandia Nat Labs Div 2335 PO Box 5800 Albuquerque NM 87185

LOVE, TOM JAY, JR., engineer, educator; b. Jonesboro, Ark., Oct. 2, 1923; s. Tom Jay and Tomazine (Stephens) L.; m. Georgia Lee Mathis, Dec. 2, 1945; children—Tom Jay III, Deborah Lee, Nancy Ruth. B.S., U. Okla., 1948; M.S., U. Kans., 1956; Ph.D., Purdue U., 1963. Project engr. Colgate Palmolive Co., Kansas City, Kans., 1947-52; sr. research engr. Midwest Research Inst., Kansas City, Mo., 1952-56; asst. prof. mech. engring. U. Okla., Norman, 1956-60, asso. prof., 1960-64, prof. dept. aerospace, mech. and nuclear engring., 1964—, dir., 1963-72, Halliburton prof. engring., 1972, George Lynn Cross research prof., 1973; dir. Local Fed. Savs. & Loan Assn., Oklahoma City, Sverdrup ARO, Inc., Tullahoma, Tenn. Author: Radiative Heat Transfer, 1968. Bd. dirs. U. Okla. Research Inst., 1969—, v.p., 1970-72; bd. dirs. U. Okla. Univ. Devel. Fund, 1970-73. Served with USAAF, 1943-45. Mem. AIAA (asso. editor jour. 1972-75; Thermophysics award 1984), ASME, Am. Soc. for Engring. Edn., Am. Thermographic Soc., Sigma Xi, Tau Beta Pi, Pi Tau Sigma, Sigma Gamma Tau. Subspecialty: Heat transfer. Office: U Okla Dept Aerospace Mech and Nuclear Engring Norman OK 73019

LOVE, WARNER EDWARDS, biophysics educator; b. Phila., Dec. 1, 1922; s. J. Warner E. and Elizabeth (Ford) L.; m. Lois Jane Hosbach, Dec. 26, 1945; children: Rebecca Edwards, Michael Warner. B.A. in Zoology, Swarthmore Coll., 1946; Ph.D. in Physiology, U. Pa., 1951. Fellow, then asso. biophysics U. Pa., 1951-55; research fellow, then research asso. physics Inst. Cancer Research, Fox Chase, Pa., 1955-57; faculty Johns Hopkins, 1957—, prof. biophysics, 1965—, dept. chmn., 1971-74, 80-83. Served with Am. Field Service, 1943-45; Served with AUS, 1945-46. Mentioned in despatches. Research on x-ray crystal structure analysis of biol macro-molecules, particularly hemoglobins. Subspecialty: X-ray crystallography. Home: 1419 Eutaw Pl Baltimore MD 21217

LOVECCHIO, PAUL, infrared detector scientist; b. Syracuse, N.Y., Nov. 5, 1942; s. Cosmo and Mary Rosario (Falso) LoV.; m. Mary Lou Reese, Nov. 29, 1969; children—Christine M., David P. B.S. in Physics, Syracuse U., 1964, Ph.D. in Physics, 1971. Research physicist, team chief Night Vision and Electro-Optics Lab., Ft. Belvoir, Va., 1971-79; research physicist, group leader Honeywell Electro-Optics Div., Lexington, Mass., 1979—. Contbr. articles to profl. jours. Patentee in field. Vol. community orgns. Recipient Tech. Achievement award Honeywell Electro-Optics Div., 1982. Mem. Am. Phys. Soc., IEEE. Current work: Research in infrared detectors. Subspecialty: Semiconductors. Home: 20 Winslow St Concord MA 01742 Office: Honeywell Electro-Optics Div 2 Forbes Rd Lexington MA 02173

LOVEJOY, THOMAS EUGENE, biologist, association executive; b. N.Y.C., Aug. 22, 1941; s. Thomas Eugene and Audrey Helen (Paige) L.; m. Charlotte Seymour, 1966 (div. 1978); children—Elizabeth Paige, Katherine Seymour, Anne Williams. B.S. in Biology, Yale U., 1964, Ph.D., 1971. Research assoc. in biology U. Pa., 1971-74; exec. asst. to sci. dir. Acad. Natural Scis., Phila., 1972, asst. to v.p. for resources and planning, 1972-73; program dir. World Wildlife Fund-U.S., Washington, 1973-78, v.p. for sci., 1979—, exec. v.p., 1985—; research assoc. in ornithology Acad. Natural Scis., 1971—; chmn. Wildlife Preservation Trust Internat., 1974—; treas. Pan Am. Sect. Internat. Council for Bird Preservation, 1973-84; co-prin. investigator Minimum Critical Size of Ecosystems Project, Brazil, 1980—; prin. adviser WNET Pub. TV series, Nature, 1980—; vis. lectr. on tropical ecology Yale U. Sch. Forestry and Environ. Studies, 1982; trustee Rocky Mountain Biol. Lab., Crested Butte, Colo., 1984—; mem. com. on biol. diversity Nat. Acad. Scis., 1985—; mem. adv. council Ctr. Plant Conservation, Arnold Arboretum, Harvard U., 1984—; research assoc. Internat. Ctr. African, Near Eastern and Asian Cultures, Smithsonian Instn., 1984—, also mem. council, 1982—; dir. Manhattan Life Corp., also chmn. exec. com., 1982—. Contbr. articles to profl. jours. Trustee Millbrook Sch., N.Y., 1971—, Henry Found. for Bot. Research, 1975—, St. Timothy's Sch., Stevenson, Md., 1984—. Fellow Linnean Soc. London, Am. Ornithologists Union, N.Y. Zool. Soc. (sci.); mem. AAAS, Am. Inst. Biol. Scis., Ecol. Soc. Am. Clubs: New Haven Lawn; Knickerbocker, Century Assn. (N.Y.C.); Cosmos (Washington). Current work: Conservation biology, tropical biology. . Home: 8526 Georgetown Pike McLean VA 22102 Office: World Wildlife Fund 1255 23d St NW Washington DC 20036

LOVELESS, SCOTT EDWARD, immunopharmacologist; b. Wilmington, Del., Nov. 20, 1951; s. Harry Edward and Edith (Erdossy) L.; m. Laurel Constance Plumstead, Dec. 29, 1973; children—Marian Laurel, Sara Elizabeth, Daniel Edward, Luke Earl. B.S., Duke U., 1973; Ph.D., Med. Coll. Va., 1980. Scientist, Mich. Cancer Found., Detroit, 1980-83; research toxicologist DuPont Co., Newark, 1983-84, research immunopharmacologist, Glenolden, Pa., 1984—. Contbr. articles to profl. jours. Active PTA, Newark, 1984—, Fairfield Civic Assn., 1984. Damon Runyon Walter Winchell fellow, 1980-82; NIH Research Service award, 1977-79; Am. Cancer Soc. grantee, 1978-79; Comprehensive Cancer Ctr. Met. Detroit grantee, 1982-83. Mem. Am. Assn. Cancer Research, Am. Assn. Immunologists, Reticuloendothelial Soc. Presbyterian. Club: Fairfield. Current work: Biological response modifiers; immunology and metastasis; role of macrophages in host defense against neoplasia, immunotoxicology. Subspecialties: Immunopharmacology; Chemotherapy. Home: 119 Country Club Dr Newark DE 19711 Office: DuPont Pharmaceuticals 500 S Ridgeway Glenolden PA 19036

LOVELL, JAMES FREDERICK, university dean; b. Lovell, Okla., June 9, 1934; s. James Wood Lovell and Ruth Louise (Newbold) Anderson; m. Janis K. Crall, May 30, 1954; children—Ralph, Randall, Rhonda, Diana Ruth. B.S., Okla. State U., 1956, M.S., 1958; Ph.D., Kans. State U., 1963. Coordinator life sci. Pa. State U., 1963-66; exec. dir. Okla. Acad. Sci., Weatherford, 1972-79; chmn. life services S.W. Okla. State U., Weatherford, 1966-79; asst. dir. dept. allied health accreditation MAM, Chgo., 1979-82; asst. dean adminstrv. services Tex. Tech U., Lubbock, 1982—; chmn. State Pollution Control Bd., Oklahoma City, 1975-79; accreditation surveyor Com. on Allied Health Edn. and Accreditation, Chgo., 1979—; mem. family health adv. com. Tex. Edn. Agy., Austin, 1984—. Author Acad. Sci. Newsletter, 1973-79; accredited survey manuals, 1979-80. Editor: Diagnostic Code Manual CPT-4, 1982. Contbr. articles to profl. publs. Vol. Gen. Hosp., Lubbock, Tex., 1982—. Served with M.C., U.S. Army, 1958. Recipient Outstanding Educator award Am. Council Edn., 1971, 72; NSF grantee, 1973-78. Fellow AAAS; mem. Am. Soc. Allied Health Profls. (nat. program com. 1984—), Tex. Soc. Allied Health Profls. (treas. 1984), Ecol. Soc. Am., Am. Soc. Human Genetics, Okla. Med. Record Assn. (hon.), Ranching and Heritage Assn., Lubbock C. of C. (health com. 1982—). Methodist. Lodge: Rotary (exec. council 1972-74). Current work: Interdisciplinary approach to teaching health care/patient management, computer simulations and production of health-oriented enrichment modules, human genetics, environmental science. Subspecialties: Information systems (Information science); Health services research. Office: Tex Tech U Health Scis Ctr Sch Allied Health 4th and Indiana Lubbock TX 79430

LOVEN, ANDREW WITHERSPOON, engring. co. exec.; b. Crossnore, N.C., Jan. 31, 1935; s. Andrew W. and Annie Laura (Crowell) L.; m. Elizabeth Joann De Groot, June 20, 1959; children: Laura Elizabeth, James Edward. B.S., Maryville (Tenn.) Coll., 1957; Ph.D. (NSF fellow), U. N.C., Chapel Hill, 1962. Diplomate: Am. Acad. Environ. Engrs.; P.E., Va., Ga., S.C., N.C., Md. Fla. Research assoc. U. N.C., 1962-63; sr. research chemist Westvaco Corp., Charleston, S.C., 1963-66, Covington, Va., 1963-66, mgr. carbon devel., 1966-71; mgr. Westvaco Cons. Service, 1968-71; project mgr. and mgr. product devel. Engring.-Sci., Inc., Washington and Atlanta, 1971-74, v.p., regional mgr., 1974-80, sr. v.p. engring., 1980-81, group v.p. and dir., 1981—. Mem. Am. Inst. Chem. Engrs., Water Pollution Control Fedn., Am. Pub. Works Assn., ASTM. Patentee and publs. in environ sci. and engring. fields. Current Work: All phases of environmental science and engineering. Subspecialties: Environmental engineering; Chemical engineering. Home: 1941 Huntington Hall Ct Atlanta GA 30338 Office: Engring Sci Inc 57 Executive Park S Suite 590 Atlanta GA 30329

LOVETT, PAUL SCOTT, biol scientist, educator, researcher, cons.; b. Phila., Dec. 14, 1940; s. Paul Joseph and Kathleen Jean (Mulhern) L.; m. Patricia Elene, Jan. 5, 1982; children: Beth A., Mark S. B.S. in Biology, Delaware Valley Coll., 1964; Ph.D. in Microbiology, Sch. Medicine, Temple U., 1968. Postdoctoral fellow Scripps Clinic and Research Found., La Jolla, Calif., 1968-70; asst. prof. dept. biol. scis. U. Md. Baltimore County, Catonsville, 1970-74, assoc. prof., 1974-78, prof. biol. scis., 1978—; cons., researcher in field. Mem. Am. Soc. Microbiology. Current Work: Gene cloning and expression in Bacillus subtilis. Subspecialties: Genetics and genetic engineering (biology); Molecular biology. Office: 5401 Wilkens Ave Catonsville MD 21228

LOW, FRANCIS EUGENE, physics educator; b. N.Y.C., Oct. 27, 1921; s. Bela and Eugenia (Ingerman) L.; m. Natalie Sadigur, June 25, 1948; children—Julie, Peter, Margaret. B.S., Harvard, 1942; M.A., Columbia, 1947, Ph.D., 1949. Mem. Inst. Advanced Study, 1950-52; asst. prof. U. Ill., Urbana, 1952-55, asso. prof., 1955-56; prof. physics MIT, 1957-67, Karl Taylor Compton prof., 1968—, dir. Center for Theoretical Physics, 1973-76, dir. Lab. for Nuclear Scis., 1979-80, provost, 1980-85, inst. prof., 1985—; cons. in field. Contbr. articles to profl. jours. Served with USAAF, 1942-43; Served with AUS, 1944-46. Mem. Nat. Acad. Scis., Phys. Soc. (chmn. div. particles and fields 1974, councillor-at-large 1979-82), Fedn. Am. Scientists (mem. nat. council 1973-77), ACLU, Am. Acad. Arts and Scis., Union Concerned Scientists (chmn. 1969). Subspecialty: Theoretical physics. Home: 28 Adams St Belmont MA 02178 Office: Room 6-301 Mass Inst Tech Cambridge MA 02139

LOW, KENNETH BROOKS, JR., molecular geneticist; b. New Rochelle, N.Y., Jan. 19, 1936; s. Kenneth Brooks and Elizabeth (Hammond) L.; m. Elise Langworthy, Aug. 21, 1960; children: Kennan, David. A.B., Amherst Coll., 1958; M.S., U. Pa., 1960, Ph.D., 1965. Postdoctoral fellow N.Y.U. Med. Center, 1966-68; mem. faculty Yale U. Sch. Medicine, 1968—, asst. prof., 1968-73, assoc. prof., 1973-78, sr. scientist, 1978-84, prof., 1984—. Contbr. articles to profl. jours.; Mem. editorial bd.: Jour. of Bacteriology, 1973-78. Mem. Am. Soc. Microbiology. Current Work: Mechanisms of genetic recombination, DNA repair and gene transfer in microorganisms. Subspecialties: Gene actions; Genetics and genetic engineering (medicine). Office: Radiobiol Labs Yale U 333 Cedar St New Haven CT 06510

LOW, WALTER CHENEY, neurophysiologist, researcher; b. Madera, Calif., May 11, 1950; s. George Chen and Linda Quan (Gong) L. B.S., U. Calif., Santa Barbara, 1972; M.S., U. Mich., 1974, Ph.D. (NIH fellow), 1979. NSF fellow Cambridge U., U.K., 1979-80; AGAN fellow U. Vt., Burlington, 1980—. Contbr. articles to profl. jours. Recipient Nat. Research Service award Nat. Inst. Neurol. and Communicative Disorders and Stroke, 1979, Nat. Research Service award Nat. Heart, Lung and Blood Inst., 1981—. Mem. AAAS, Soc. Neurosci., N.Y. Acad. Scis., Sigma Xi, Eta Kappa Nu. Current Work: Research in structure and function of central nervous system, and use of neural transplants in recovery of function. Subspecialties: Neurophysiology; Neural transplantation. Office: Dept Physiology and Biophysics U Vt Burlington VT 05405

LOWE, DONALD RAY, geology educator; b. Sacramento, Sept. 22, 1942; s. Ray C. and Mary F. (Thomas) Veach; m. Necla Aytug, Sept. 6, 1964; children—Nina, Deniz. B.Sc. with honors, Stanford U., 1964; Ph.D., U. Ill., 1967. Postdoctoral research assoc. U.S. Geol. Survey, Menlo Park, Calif., 1968-70; from asst. prof. to prof. geology La. State U., Baton Rouge, 1970—. Contbr. articles to profl. jours. NSF grantee, 1977—. Mem. Geol. Soc. Am., Internat. Assn. Sedimentologists, Soc. Econ. Paleontologists and Mineralogists. Current work: Characteristics and interpretation of Precambrian sedimentary systems; Archean paleobiology and paleoecology; clastic sedimentology; sedimentology of cherts. Subspecialty: Sedimentology. Home: 724 Rue Crozat Baton Rouge LA 70810 Office: Dept Geology La State U Baton Rouge LA 70803

LOWE, JAMES EDWARD, cardiovascular surgeon and researcher; b. Brunswick, Ga., Dec. 27, 1946; s. Gordon E. and Elsie Muriel (Foster) L.; m. Lorraine Elizabeth Sassone, Sept. 7, 1969; children: Summer Elizabeth, Natalie Susanne. B.A., Stanford U., 1969; M.D., UCLA, 1973. Diplomate: Am. Bd. Surgery. Resident in surgery Duke U., Durham, N.C., 1973-81, NIH surg. scholar, 1975-81, research fellow in pathology, 1975-77, asst. prof. surgery and pathology, 1981—, dir. surg. electrophysiology service; asst. dir. cardiovascular surgery Durham VA Med. Center, 1981—; established investigator Am. Heart Assn., 1981—. Mem. Alpha Omega Alpha. Current Work: Pathogenesis of reversible and irreversible ischemic myocardial injury (metabolic, ultrastructural and electrophysiological alterations). Subspecialty: Cardiac surgery. Home: 23 Surrey Ln Durham NC 27707 Office: Dept Surger Duke Univ Med Center Erwin Rd Durham NC 27710

LOWE, PHILLIP A(RNOLD), oil company executive, energy consultant; b. Salt Lake City, Feb. 25, 1939; s. Ellis Edward and Elinor (Havus) L.; married; 1 dau., Susan. B.S., U. Utah, 1961; M.S., U. R.I., 1964; Ph.D., Carnegie-Mellon U., 1968. Registered profl. engr., Pa. Sr. engr. Westinghouse Electric Co., Pitts., 1964-70; mgr. prodn. devel. Combustion Engring., Windsor, Conn., 1970-74; dep. asst. ins. gen. Dept. Energy, Washington, 1974-80; dir. advanced tech. NUS Corp., Gaithersburg, Md., 1980—; chief exec. officer B & P Energy Inc., Potomac, Md., 1982—, also dir. Editor: Jour. Fluid Mechanics, 1964-66. Served to lt. USN, 1962-64. Recipient Superior award Dept. Energy, 1979. Mem. ASME (dir. chpt. 1972-74), Am. Petroleum Engrs., Am. Nuclear Soc. Current Work: Consulting on use of coal and synthetic fuels; production of oil and gas. Subspecialties: Fuels; Mechanical engineering. Home: 11316 Rouen Dr Potomac MD 20854 Office: B & P Energy Inc 11316 Rouen Dr Potomac MD 20854

LOWE, SUNNY KEN, plant pathologist; b. 1930, m. Helena; children—Mayette, Cyrus. B.S., U. Hawaii, 1955; M.S., U. Calif.-Davis, 1962. Research assoc. plant pathology U. Calif.-Davis, 1957—. Contbr. articles to profl. jours. Recipient Sears Roebuck Found. scholarship award, 1951-55. Mem. Am. Phytopath. Soc., AAAS, Alpha Beta. Current Work: Stone fruit virus and mycoplasma diseases, electronmicroscopy, indexing, thermal and chemo-therapy, detection and diagnosis of plant diseases. Subspecialty: Plant pathology. Office: Plant Pathology Dept U Calif Davis CA 95616

LOWINGER, THOMAS, physicist, educator; b. Cell, Hungary, Apr. 18, 1949; came to U.S., 1962, naturalized, 1967; s. Eugene and Charlotte (Blumenthal) L. B.S., Bklyn. Coll., 1970; M.A., Columbia U., 1972; Ph.D., SUNY-Bklyn., 1980. Instr. SUNY-Bklyn., 1980-81; systems analyst R.R. Donnelley Co., N.Y.C., 1981-84; asst. prof. physics Mt. Sinai Med. Ctr., N.Y.C., 1984—; cons. scientist Antares Co., Lake Elmo, Mich., 1984—. Contbr. articles to profl. jours. Mem. N.Y. Acad. Scis., IEEE, Soc. Nuclear Medicine, Am. Assn. Physicists in Medicine. Current work: Image processing applications in nuclear medicine, single photon emission computed tomography. Subspecialties: Graphics, image processing, and pattern recognition; Medical physics. Home: 1325 52d St Brooklyn NY 11219 Office: Mt Sinai Med Ctr/Nuclear Medicine 1 Gustave L Levy Pl New York NY 11219

LOWY, DOUGLAS RONALD, physician, researcher; b. N.Y.C., May 25, 1942; s. Milton M. and Frances (Siegel) L.; m. Lyndia, Dec. 15, 1968; children: Stephanie, Diane, Matthew. A.B., Amherst Coll., 1964; M.D., NYU, 1968. Diplomate: Am. Bd. Internal Medicine, Am. Bd. Dermatology. Intern in internal medicine Stanford U. Med. Center, 1968-69, resident in internal medicine, 1969-70; resident in dermatology Yale-New Haven Med. Center, 1973-75; commd. lt. comdr. USPHS, 1970, advanced through grades to med. dir., 1980; research assoc. Lab. Viral Diseases, Nat. Inst. Allergy and Infectious Diseases, Bethesda, Md., 1970-73; sr. investigator dermatology br. Nat. Cancer Inst., Bethesda, 1975-82, dep. chief dermatology br., 1982-83, chief lab. cellular oncology, 1983. Editorial bd.: Jour. Virology, 1980—, Archives of Virology, 1983—, Jour. Investigative Dermatology, 1981—, Leukemia Research, 1985—, Jour. Nat. Cancer Inst., 1985—. Mem. Am. Acad. Dermatology, Soc. Investigative Dermatology, Am. Soc. Microbiology, AAAS. Current Work: Retroviruses, papillomaviruses, oncogenes, dermatology. Subspecialties: Virology (medicine); Genetics and genetic engineering (medicine). Office: Bldg 37 Rm 1B-26 Nat Cancer Inst Bethesda MD 20205

LOZANO-ALARCON, FERNANDO, veterinary pathologist, researcher, educator; b. Neiva, Huila, Colombia, May 30, 1943; came to U.S., 1982; s. Luis Emilio and Susana (Alarcon) L. D.V.M., Nat. U., Bogota, Colombia, 1967, M.S., 1971; Ph.D., Tex. A&M U., 1979. Dir. pathology sect. Colombian Agr., Bogota, 1976-78, dir. drug control, 1980-82; sci. dir. Byala Labs., Bogota, 1978-80; vet. pathologist La. Vet. Med. Diagnostic Lab., La. State U., Baton Rouge, 1982-84, mem. ad hoc organizing com. on parasitology, 1983, asst. prof. Sch. Vet. Medicine, 1984—; prin. investigator Colciencias, Bogota, 1976-82. Contbr. articles to profl. jours. Worker St. Jude Catholic Ch., Baton Rouge, 1983-84; Grantee bovine lymphosarcoma Colciencias, 1977, 79; awardee bovine lymphosarcoma, Bogota, 1978, bovine tuberculosis, Villavicencio, Colombia, 1980. Mem. AVMA, Colombian Soc. Human Pathology, Colombian Vet. Assn., Tex. A&M Alumni Assn., Phi Zeta. Liberal Party Colombia. Current work: Understanding of naturally occurring disease of domestic animals including bovine babesiosis, bovine lymphosarcoma, bovine brucellosis, bovine tuberculosis and domestic animal mycotic infections. Subspecialties: Pathology (veterinary medicine); Cancer research (veterinary medicine). Home: 326 Rue de la Place Baton Rouge LA 70810 Office: Dept Vet Pathology La State Univ Baton Rouge LA 70803

LU, ALLEN AN-HUA, hydrologist; b. Hankow, Hubei, China, Dec. 29, 1934; came to U.S., 1964, naturalized, 1973; s. Shu-Chih and Hsiu Wen (Chu) L.; m. Caroline An-Chun Lu/Li, June 18, 1972; children: Janice Hsin-Min, Irene Ya-Min. B.S., Chinese Naval Acad., 1958; M.S., Tsin-Hua U., 1964; Ph.D., Rensselaer Poly. Inst., 1969. Asst. prof. Siena Coll., Loudonville, N.Y., 1969-76; research scientist N.Y. State Dept. Health, Albany, 1976-78, sr. research scientist, 1978-79; staff scientist Rockwell Hanford Operation, Richland, Wash., 1979-81, staff hydrologist, 1981—. Mem. Am. Physics Soc., Am. Nuclear Soc., Sigma Pi Sigma. Current Work: Develop and apply computer models for predicting the gaseous and liquid radioactive waste transport and assessing the impact on the environment. Subspecialties: Hydrology; Numerical analysis (computer science). Home: 2237 Carriage Ave Richland WA 99352 Office: Rockwell Hanford Operation PO Box 800 Richland WA 99352

LU, CHIH-YUAN, electronic scientist, physicist; b. Canton, China, Aug. 13, 1950; came to U.S., 1983; s. Shan-Tung and You-Chen (Tang) L.; m. Fen-Fen

Chang, Apr. 3, 1978; children—Jim Kuan-chi, Charlin Chia-Ning. B.S., Nat. Taiwan U., 1972; M.S., Columbia U., 1974, Ph.M., 1975, Ph.D., 1977. Assoc. prof. electronics and physics Nat. Chiao-Tung U., Hsin-Chu, Taiwan, 1978-81, prof., 1981-83; vis. assoc. prof. N.C. State U., Raleigh, 1983-84; mem. tech. staff AT&T Bell Labs, Reading, Pa., 1984—; research mem. Energy Com. of Ministry of Econs, Taipei, Taiwan, 1978-83; pres., editor Sci. Monthly Mag. Taipei, 1978-83; research advisor Sci. Tech. Adv. Group, Taipei, 1981-83. Contbr. articles to profl. jours. Mem. IEEE (sr.), Phys. Soc. Republic China (exec. bd. dirs. 1981-84), Chinese Inst. Engring., Am. Phys. Soc., Electro-Chem. Soc., Sigma Pi Sigma, Phi Tau Phi, Phi Lambda. Current work: Semiconductor device technology research and development; material research and device physics. Subspecialties: Integrated circuits; Electronic materials. Office: AT&T Bell Labs 2525 N 12th St Reading PA 19603

LU, CHUN CHIAN, physicist; b. Taiwan, China, May 15, 1938; came to U.S., 1964, naturalized, 1975; s. Wen-Lai and Gue-Mei (Yeh) L.; m. Ann S.C. Liu, Dec. 14, 1968; 1 child, Ja. B.S., Nat. Taiwan U., 1962; Ph.D., U. Tenn., 1969. Postdoctoral fellow Oak Ridge Nat. Lab., 1969-71, Ctr. Theoretical Studies, Coral Gables, Fla., 1971-73; engr. Fla. Power & Light Co., Miami, 1973-78; sr. engr. Westinghouse Research/Devel. Ctr., Pitts., 1978-80; princ. engr. Racal Milgo Inc., Miami, 1980—; v.p. Sci. Programming, Inc. Contbr. articles to profl. jours. Mem. Am. Phys. Soc. Current Work: High speed communication networks, digital sigmal processing; symmetry principles in matter, microprocessor applications. Subspecialties: Atomic and molecular physics; Distributed systems and networks. Office: 8600 NW 41 St Miami FL 33166

LU, JOHN KUEW-HSIUNG, ob-gyn educator, endocrinologist; b. Miaoli, Taiwan, Sept. 16, 1937; came to U.S., 1967, naturalized, 1980; s. En-Gie and Jan-Mei (Wu) L.; m. Marianne Mann Wang, Dec. 29, 1969; children: Judith Maria, John Lawrence. B.Sc., Nat. Taiwan Normal U., 1961; M.Sc., Nat. Taiwan U., 1967; Ph.D., Mich. State U., 1972. Postdoctoral fellow U. Pitts., 1972-74; research assoc. Mich. State U., East Lansing, 1974-75; asst. prof. U. Calif.-San Diego, La Jolla, 1975-77; asst. prof. UCLA, 1977-82, assoc. prof. ob-gyn and anatomy, 1982—. Author: Progress in Prolactin Physiology, 1978, Parkinson's Disease II, 1978, Dynamics of Ovarian Function, 1981, Neuroendocrinology of Aging, 1983. Recipient Disting. Research award Sigma Xi, 1970; Nat. Cancer Inst. research grantee, 1977; Nat. Inst. Aging research grantee, 1980, 84, 85. Mem. Soc. Gynecol. Investigation, Am. Physiol. Soc., Endocrine Soc., Soc. Study Reproduction, N.Y. Acad. Scis., Sigma Xi. Current Work: Changes in ovarian folliculogenesis during aging, relationship between ovarian steroids and neuroendocrine regulation of gonadotropin and prolactin secretion. Subspecialties: Neuroendocrinology; Reproductive biology. Home: 1129 Iliff St Pacific Palisades CA 90272 Office: Dept Ob-Gyn Sch Medicine UCLA 405 Hilgard Ave Los Angeles CA 90024

LU, KAU U., mathematics educator; b. Canton, China, July 10, 1939; came to U.S., 1963; s. Shuk-to and Shon (Haung) L.; m. Huey Mei Lee, Sept. 12, 1968; 1 dau., Pamela. B.S. E.E., Nat. Taiwan U., 1961; Ph.D. in Math, Calif. Inst. Tech., 1968. Asst. prof. Calif. State U.-Long Beach, 1968-75, assoc. prof., 1975-79, prof. math., 1979—; cons. Tridea Electronics, El Monte, Calif., 1969-70; research assoc. U. Calif.-Berkeley, 1981. Contbr. articles to publs. in field. Mem. Am. Math. Soc., Pacific Astronomy Soc., Soc. for Indsl. and Applied Math. Democrat. Current Work: Applied mathematics, mathematical analysis, astronomy, astrophysics, solar physics, analytic number theory. Subspecialty: Applied mathematics. Office: Calif State Univ Dept Math Long Beach CA 90840

LU, PONZY, molecular biologist, educator; b. Shanghai, China, Oct. 7, 1942; came to U.S., 1949, naturalized, 1963; s. Abraham and Beth (Chou) L.; m. Heidi Fahl, Jan. 13, 1975; 1 child, Kristina. B.S., Calif. Inst. Tech., 1964; Ph.D., M.I.T., 1970. Postdoctoral fellow Arthritis Found., Max Planck Inst., Goettingen, W.G., U. Geneva, 1970-73; asst. prof. dept. chemistry U. Pa., Phila., 1973-78, assoc. prof., 1978-82, prof., 1982—; mem. study sect. NIH, 1982-86. Recipient Career Devel. award NIH, 1977-82. Mem. Am. Soc. Biol. Chemists, Biophys. Soc., Sigma Xi. Current Work: Gene regulation studied by NMR spectroscopy, use of modern spectroscopic and genetic methods to look at the molecules involved in gene regulation. Subspecialties: Molecular biology; Biophysical chemistry. Office: Dept Chemistry U Pa Philadelphia PA 19104

LUBAR, JOEL FREDRIC, psychologist, clinical psychophysiologist, educator; b. Washington, Nov. 16, 1938; s. Raymond and Barbara Frances (Pollak) L.; m. Judith Ostrovsky, June 18, 1961; children: Sandra Gita, Edward Justin. B.S. (scholar), U. Chgo., 1960, Ph.D., 1963; Sr. postdoctoral fellow, UCLA, 1976. Asst. prof. psychology U. Rochester, N.Y., 1963-67; assoc. prof. U. Tenn., Knoxville, 1967-71, prof., 1971—; cons. VA; pvt. practice physiol. psychology and biofeedback Southeastern Biofeedback Inst.; Bd. dirs., mem. profl. adv. bd. Knox Area Epilepsy Found., 1978—; research dir. Chileda Inst. Ednl. Devel., LaCrosse, Wis., 1976—; profl. adv. bd. Epilepsy Found. Am., 1979-83. Author: Biological Foundations of Behavior, 1969, A Primer of Physiological Psychology, 1971, (with Isaacson, Schmaltz and Douglas) Study Guide to Accompany a Primer of Physiological Psychology, 1971, A First Reader in Physiological Psychology, 1972, Biological Foundations of Behavior, 1974, Brain and Behavior, 1975, (with W.M. Deering) Behavioral Approaches to Neurology, 1981; regional editor: Physiology and Behavior, 1970—; contbr. articles to profl. jours. NIMH grantee, 1964-75; NSF grantee, 1975-76. Fellow N.Y. Acad. Scis.; mem. Am. Psychol. Assn., AAAS, AAUP, Southeastern Psychol. Assn., Soc. Neurosci., European Brain Research Orgn., Biofeedback Soc. Am., Biofeedback Soc. Tenn. (pres. 1977-78, 81), Sigma Xi. Current Work: Biofeedback research in regard to epilepsy, learning disorders and psychophysiol. disorders. Subspecialties: Neuropsychology; Physiological psychology. Office: Dept Psychology U Tenn Knowville TN 37916

LUBATTI, HENRY JOSEPH, physics educator; b. Oakland, Calif., Mar. 16, 1937; s. John and Pauline (Massimino) L.; m. Catherine Jeanne Berthe Ledoux, June 29, 1968; children: Karen E., Henry J., Stephen J.C. M.S., U. Ill., 1963; A.A., U. Calif.-Berkeley, 1957, A.B., 1960, Ph.D., 1966. Research assoc. U. Paris, Orsay, France, 1966-68; asst. prof. physics M.I.T., Cambridge, 1968-69; mem. faculty U. Wash., Seattle, 1969—, prof. physics, 1974—; sci. dir. U. Wash. (Visual Techniques Lab.), 1969—; vis. staff Los Alamos Nat. Lab. Mem. phys. editorial adv. com. World Sci. Pub. Co., Ltd., 1983—. Contbr. over 60 articles to sci. publs. Alfred P. Sloan fellow, 1971-75. Fellow Am. Phys. Soc.; mem. Sigma Xi, Tau Beta Pi. Current Work: Experimental: rare decays of K-mesons; deep inelastic lepton scattering (neutrinos and muons). Subspecialty: Particle physics. Office: Physics Dept Univ Wash FM-15 Seattle WA 98195

LUBELL, MICHAEL STEPHEN, educator; b. N.Y.C., Mar. 25, 1943; s. Richard M. and Lillian (Aronoff) L.; m. Ellen Bloom, June 29, 1969; 1 dau., Karina Bloom. B.A., Columbia U., 1963; M.S., Yale U., 1965, Ph.D., 1969. Instr. physics Yale U., New Haven, 1971-72, asst. prof., 1972-77, assoc. prof., 1977-80; assoc. prof. physics CCNY, 1980-82, prof., 1983—; NRC steering com. for Army Basic Research, 1980-83; sci./tech. adv. to Senator Chistopher J. Dodd, 1980—; mem. exec. com. Internat. Conf. Physics of Elec. and Atomic Collisions, 1983—. Contbr. articles to profl. jours. NSF fellow, 1965-67; AEC fellow, 1969-70; Sloan fellow, 1979-83; NSF grantee, 1974—; Dept. of Energy grantee, 1980—; Office Naval Research grantee, 1983—. Mem. Am. Phys. Soc. (panel on pub. affairs 1982-84), AAAS, N.Y. Acad. Sci. Democrat. Current Work: Experimental studies of parity violation effects in neutral weak currents, spin-dependence in electron-hydrogen scattering, spin structure of nucleons, laser cooling of atomic beams. Subspecialties: Atomic and molecular physics; Particle physics. Home: 171 Bayberry Ln Westport CT 06880 Office: Convent Ave at 138th St New York NY 10031

LUBIN, BERTRAM HAROLD, physician; b. N.Y.C., Jan. 21, 1939. B.A., Washington & Jefferson Coll., 1960; M.D., U. Pitts., 1964. Diplomate Am. Bd. Pediatrics. Intern, Children's Hosp. Phila., 1964-65, asst. chief resident, 1965-66, assoc. hematologist, 1970-71, coordinator Clin. Labs., 1971-73, dir. Hematology Lab., 1971-73, dir. Sickle Cell Anemia project, 1971-73; fellow hematology Children's Hosp. Med. Ctr., Boston, 1968-70; asst. prof. pediatrics Hosp. U. Pa., Phila., 1972-73; chief hematology-oncology service Children's Hosp. Med. Ctr., Oakland, Calif., 1973—, dir. Sickle Cell Screening Counseling and Edn. program, 1973-77, dir. Spl. Hematology Lab., 1973—, chief dept. medicine, 1980-81, dir. med. research, 1980—; asst. clin. prof. pediatrics U. Calif. Med. Ctr., San Francisco, 1973-77, adj. assoc. clin. prof. pediatrics, 1977-84, research assoc. Cancer Research Inst., 1979—, adj. prof. pediatrics, 1984—; co-dir. No. Calif. Sickle Cell Ctr., Oakland, 1977—; vis. scientist Lawrence Berkley Lab. U. Calif., Berkeley, 1980—; clin. prof. dept. pediatrics U. Nev., 1983—. Contbr. numerous articles to profl. jours. Served with U.S. Army, 1966-68; Vietnam. Recipient Outstanding Tchr. award Children's Hosp. Phila. Mem. Am. Fedn. Clin. Research, East Bay Pediatric Soc., Am. Soc. Hematology (chmn. sci. subcom. on pediatric hematology), N.Y. Acad. Scis., Western Soc. Pediatric Research (mem. exec. com. 1982-85), Soc. Pediatric Research, Assn. for Care of Children in Hosps., Am. Soc. Parental and Enteral Nutrition, Am. Pediatric Soc. Inc. Subspecialties: Pediatrics; Hematology. Office: Bruce Lyon Meml Research Lab Children's Hosp Med Ctr 51st St and Grove St Oakland CA 94609

LUBINIECKI, ANTHONY STANLEY, microbiologist; b. Greensburg, Pa., Oct. 4, 1946; s. Stanley Anthony and Helen Marie L.; m. Robin Lea Brudowsky, June 8, 1968; 1 son, Gregory. B.S., Carnegie-Mellon U., 1968; Sc.D. in Microbiology, U. Pitts., 1972. Research asst. U. Pitts., 1971-72, asst. research prof., 1972-74; prin. scientist Meloy Labs., Inc., Springfield, Va., 1974-78, mng. dir., 1979-80; tech. dir. biol. products Flow Labs., Inc., McLean, Va., 1980-82; mgr. cell culture ops. Genentech Inc., South San Francisco, 1982-83, dir. cell culture R&D, 1983—. Contbr. articles to profl. jours. Mem. Reston Community Assn., 1976—. NIAID/NIH grantee, 1973-74, 74-82; other grants. Mem. Am. Soc. Microbiology, Am. Assn. Immunologists, N.Y. Acad. Scis., Soc. Gen. Microbiology, Tissue Culture Assn., Soc. Exptl. Biology and Medicine. Roman Catholic. Current Work: Development and production of human biological products for clinical trials; large-scale cell culture; cell culture studies of human cancer risk and genetics. Subspecialties: Genetics and genetic engineering (medicine); Cell biology (medicine). Office: Genentech Inc 460 Point San Bruno Blvd South San Francisco CA 94080

LUBLIN, FRED DAVID, neurologist, researcher, educator; b. Phila., Sept 28, 1946; s. P. Paul and Sara (Raynes) L.; m. Barbara H. Swartz, June 11, 1969; children: Alex, Derek. A.B. magna cum laude, Temple U., 1968; M.D. summa cum laude, Jefferson Med. Coll., 1972. Diplomate: Am. Bd. Med. Examiners, Am. Bd. Psychiatry and Neurology. Intern Albert Einstein Med. Ctr., Bronx, N.Y., 1972-73; resident in neurology N.Y. Hosp.-Cornell Med. Ctr., N.Y.C., 1973-76; instr. neurology Cornell Med. Ctr., 1975-76; instr. neurology Thomas Jefferson U., Phila., 1976-78, asst. prof. neurology and biochemistry, 1978-82, assoc. prof. neurology and biochemistry, 1982—; attending neurologist Thomas Jefferson U. Hosp., 1976—, also co-dir. Multiple Sclerosis Comprehensive Clin. Ctr.; cons. neurologist Wilmington and Coatesville VA Hosps., 1978—; dir. Kensington Hosp., 1980—. Recipient Tchr.-Investigator award NIH, 1978; Nat. Multiple Sclerosis Soc. research grantee, 1981, 83, 85. Mem. Am. Assn. Neurology, Soc. Neurosci., N.Y. Acad. Scis., AAAS, Assn. Research in Nervous and Mental Diseases, Am. Assn. Immunology, Sigma Xi, Alpha Omega Alpha. Current Work: Neuroimmunologic research utilizing animal models of multiple sclerosis and other demyelinating disorders, studies of lymphocyte activity and immunomodulation in neuroimmunologic disorders. Subspecialties: Neuroimmunology; Neurology. Office: Thomas Jefferson University Medical College 1025 Walnut St Philadelphia PA 19107

LUBORSKY, FRED EVERETT, research chemist; b. Philadelphia, May 14, 1923; s. Meyer and Cecelia (Miller) L.; m. Florence Rosalee, Aug. 28, 1946; children—Judith Lee, Mark Robert, Rhoda Susan. B.S. in Chemistry, U. Pa., 1947; Ph.D. in Phys. Chemistry, Ill. Inst. Tech., Chgo., 1952. Researcher Gen. Electric Co., Schenectady, 1951-52, mgr. applied physics, West Lynn, Mass., 1952-58, researcher, Schenectady, 1958—. Editor: Amorphous Metallic Alloys, 1983; mem. editorial adv. bd. Internat. Jour. Magnetism, 1972—, Internat. Jour. Rapid Solidification, 1982—. Contbr. numerous articles to profl. jours. Patentee in field. Served with USN, 1944-46. Brit. Sci. Council fellow, 1977. Fellow IEEE (pres. Magnetics Soc. 1975-77, Centennial medal 1984, Achievement award Magnetics Soc. 1981), Am. Inst. Chemists; mem. Am. Chem. Soc., Am. Inst. Physics, AAAS, Nat. Acad. Engring. Current work: Magneto-optic mass memory materials; amorphous magnetic materials; magnetic separation; thin magnetic films; permanent magnet materials; soft magnetic materials. Subspecialties: Materials; Applied magnetics. Home: 1162 Lowell Rd Schenectady NY 12308 Office: Gen Electric Co PO Box 8 Schenectady NY 12301

LUCANTONI, DAVID MICHAEL, operations research scientist; b. Balt., Aug. 31, 1954; s. Vincent Michael and Marie (Fitzpatrick) L. B.S. in Math, Towson State U., 1976; M.S. in Stats, U. Del., 1978, Ph.D. in Ops. Research, 1981. Mem. tech. staff Bell Labs., Holmdel, N.J., 1981—. Author: An Algorithmic Analysis of A Communication Model, 1983; contbr. articles to sci. jours. Mem. Ops. Research Soc. Am., Math. Assn. Am. Current Work: Algorithmic methods in stochastic modelling; performance analysis of computer systems and data communication networks. Subspecialties: Operations research (mathematics); Probability. Home: 37 Victoria Dr Eatontown NJ 07724 Office: Bell Laboratories Crawfords Corner Rd Holmdel NJ 07733

LUCAS, MYRON CRAN, geneticist; b. Cin., Nov. 15, 1946; s. Ralph Frank and Dallace Fair (Coberly) L. B.S., Lewis and Clark Coll., 1969; Ph.D., Wash. State U., 1974. Postdoctoral research assoc. botany U. Ill., 1973-75, U. Ga., 1975-76; adj. asst. prof. biol. scis. Fla. State U., 1977; postdoctoral research asso. U. Idaho, Moscow, 1977-78; assoc. prof. biol. scis. La. State U., Shreveport, 1978—. La. State U. grantee, 1981; Magale Found. grantee, 1982; NDEA fellow, 1969-71. Mem. Am. Soc. Microbiology, Genetics Soc. Am., AAAS, N.Y. Acad. Sci., Sigma Xi. Current Work: Researcher in gene regulation and devel. in fungi; structure and function of messenger RNA. Subspecialty: Gene actions. Office: Dept Biol Scis La State U Shreveport LA 71115

LUCAS, ROBERT ELMER, retired soil scientist; b. Manila, Philippines, June 27, 1916 (parents Am. citizens); s. Charles Edmond and Harriet Grace (Deardorff) L.; m. Norma Emma Schultz, Apr. 27, 1941; children—Raymond, Richard, Milton, Keith, Charles. B.S. in Agr., Purdue U., 1939, M.A., 1941; Ph.D., Mich. State Coll., 1947. Research asst. Va. Agr. Research Sta., Norfolk, 1941-42; farmer, Culver, Ind., 1943-44; grad. asst. Mich. State Coll., East Lansing, 1945-46, soil scientist, 1951-77, 1981; agronomist William Gehring, Inc., Rensselaer, Ind., 1946-51, 77-78; soil scientist U. Fla., Belle Glade, 1979-80; tester, sampler peat soils ASTM, 1966-70. Assoc. editor, reviewer Agronomy Jour., 1967-70. Contbr. articles to profl. jours., chpts. to books. Leader Chief Okemos council Boy Scouts Am., 1961-72, dist. chmn., 1965-66. Fellow Am. Soc. Agronomy, Soil Sci. Soc. Am., Mich. Extension Specialist Assn. (Outstanding Specialist 1967), Internat. Peat Soc., U.S. Peat Soc. Republican. Lutheran. Current work: Alternative management systems in vegetable and field crop production, organic soils-properties and management for plant production. Subspecialties: Agronomy; Soil science. Home: 3827 Dobie Rd Okemos MI 48864 Office: Dept Crop and Soil Scis Mich State U East Lansing MI 48824

LUCAS, WILLIAM JOHN, botanist, educator; b. Adelaide, S. Australia, Feb. 23, 1945; came to U.S., 1977; s. Robert Bruce and Thelma Rose (Packer) L.; m. Diana Kristine Gorny, Dec. 17, 1966; children: Jessica Kristine, Judith Margret, Joanna Ruth, Julian Keith. B.S. with honors, U. Adelaide, 1971, Ph.D. in Plant Physiology, 1975. Postdoctoral fellow and research assoc. dept. botany U. Toronto, Ont., Can., 1975-77; asst. prof. botany U. Calif., Davis, 1979-80, assoc. prof., 1980-83, prof., 1983—, dir. lab. research program. Contbr. articles on plant physiology and plant biophysics to profl. jours. NSF grantee, 1978—. Mem. Am. Soc. Plant Physiologists, Bot. Soc. Am., Can. Soc. Plant Physiologists, Soc. for Exptl. Biology. Current Work: Regulation of plant membrane transport systems with special emphasis on plasmalemma transport, photosynthetic assimilation of exogenous HCO3 by Chara Corallina, K influx into corn roots-mechanisms and site of entry, phloem physiology; loading phenomena and regulation of long-distance translocation. Subspecialties: Plant physiology (biology); Biophysics (biology). Home: 1001 Deodara Ct Davis CA 95616 Office: Dept Botany U Calif Davis CA 95616

LUCAS, WILLIAM RAY, official NASA; b. Newbern, Tenn., Mar. 1, 1922; m. 1948; 3 children. B.S., Memphis State U., 1943; M.S., Vanderbilt U., 1950, Ph.D. in Chem. Metallurgy, 1952; L.H.D. (hon.), Mobile Coll., 1977; D.Sc. (hon.), Southeastern Inst. Tech., 1980, U. Ala., Huntsville, 1981. Instr. chemistry Memphis State U., 1946-48; chemist guided missile devel. div. Redstone Arsenal, 1952-54, chief chem. sect., 1954-55; chief engr. material sect. Army Ballistic Missile Agy., 1955-56, chief engr. material br., 1956-60; with Marshall Space Flight Center, NASA, 1960—, material div., 1963-66, dir. propulsion and vehicle engring. lab., 1966-68, dir. program devel., 1968-71, dep. dir., 1971-74, dir., 1974—. Served as lt. USNR, 1943-46. Recipient Exceptional Sci. Achievement medal NASA, 1964, 2 Exceptional Service medals, 1969, Distinguished Service medal, 1972; Presdl. rank disting. exec., 1980; Roger W. Jones award for outstanding exec. leadership Am. U., 1981; NASA Disting. Service medal, 1981; Space Flight award Am. Astronautical Soc., 1982; Disting. Alumni award Memphis State U., 1984; Space award for outstanding contbns. in field of space VFW, 1983. Fellow Am. Soc. Metals, Am. Astronautical Soc., AIAA (Oberth award 1965, Holger N. Toftoy award 1976); mem. Nat. Acad. Engring., Am. Chem. Soc., Sigma Xi, Tau Beta Pi. Research in materials engring. metallurgy, inorganic chemistry, environ. effects on materials, especially space environ. effects. Current Work: Research and development of space launch vehicles and spacecraft. Subspecialties: Aerospace engineering and technology; Metallurgy. Office: NASA Marshall Space Flight Center AL 35812

LUCATORTO, THOMAS BENJAMIN, research physicist; b. N.Y.C., May 9, 1937; s. Benjamin and Faye (Mautone) L.; m. Kathleen Gross, Aug. 5, 1966 (div. Feb. 1979); children: Theresa, Rachael; m. Linda Bryson, Apr. 7, 1979. B.S. in Physics, CCNY, 1960; M.S., Columbia U., 1964, Ph.D., 1968. Postdoctoral fellow Columbia U., 1968-69; physicist Nat. Bur. Standards, Washington, 1969—. Contbr. articles to profl. jours. Recipient Silver medal Dept. Commerce, 1981. Mem. Am. Phys. Soc. Current Work: Shell collapse in atoms, atomic autoionization, atomic effects in solids, resonant laser-vapor interactions. Subspecialties: Atomic and molecular physics; Plasma physics. Home: 3600 Van Ness St Washington DC 20008 Office: Nat Bur Standards A251-Physics Gaithersburg MD 20899

LUCCHITTA, BAERBEL KOESTERS, geologist; b. Muenster, Germany, Oct. 2, 1938; d. Bernhard and Frida Koesters; m. Ivo Lucchitta, Apr. 17, 1964; 1 child, Maya. B.S., Kent State U., 1961; M.S., Pa. State U., 1963, Ph.D., 1966. German instr. Kent State U., 1960-61; research and teaching asst. Pa. State U., University Park, 1961-65, lab. technician, 1965-66; phys. sci. technologist U.S. Geol. Survey, Flagstaff, Ariz., 1967-68, geologist, 1968—, coordinator Jupiter Moon Geol. Mapping Program, U.S. Geol. Survey and NASA, 1980—. Author jour. papers, abstracts, maps. Fulbright scholar, 1960; recipient Spl. Recognition awards NASA, 1979, U.S. Geol. Survey, 1983. Mem. Geol. Soc. Am. (assoc. editor 1982-83), Assn. for Woman in Sci., Assn. Women Geoscientists, Planetary Soc., Am. Geophys. Union (assoc. editor 1981-83). Democrat. Current work: Coordinator Jupiter Moon Geological Mapping Program; geology of Europa and Ganymede; mass wasting, periglacial and glacial processes, channel development, tectonics and volcanism on Mars; remote sensing of Antarctica. Subspecialties: Geology; Planetology. Office: US Geol Survey 2255 N Gemini Dr Flagstaff AZ 86001

LUCE, JAMES KENT, physician, research oncologist; b. Le Mars, Iowa, May 11, 1922; s. Ernie LeRoy and Gladys (Knapp) L.; m. Joan Larpenter, Mar. 31, 1967; children: Holly, Laura, Douglas, Gregory; m. Candace Ann Myers, Feb. 14, 1981. A.B. in Geology (James Monroe MacDonald scholar), U. Calif.-Berkeley, 1948; M.D., Yale U., 1952. Intern Tripler Army Hosp., Honolulu, 1952-53; resident in internal medicine VA Hosp., Iowa City, 1958-60, U. Calif.-San Francisco, 1962-63; asst. prof. medicine U. Tex.-M.D. Anderson Hosp., Houston, 1966-71; dir. clin. research and med. dir. Mountain States Tumor Inst., Boise, Idaho, 1971-77; dir. div. community and clin. activities West Coast Cancer Fedn., San Francisco, 1977-78; dir. clin. oncology Adria Labs. Inc., Dublin, Ohio, 1978—. Contbr. articles to profl. jours. Mem. bd. dirs. Thomas A. Dooley Found., N.Y.C., 1964—. Served with USNR, 1943-45; with USAF, 1952-54. Mem. Am. Assn. Cancer Research, Am. Soc. Clin. Oncology. Democrat. Current Work: Clinical research in medical oncology; development of new or improved cancer chemotherapeutic agents. Subspecialty: Chemotherapy. Home: 343 W Main St Plain City OH 43064 Office: 5000 Post Rd Dublin OH 43017

LUCE, (ROBERT) DUNCAN, educator; b. Scranton, Pa., May 16, 1925; s. Robert R. and Ruth Lillian (Downer) L.; m. Gay Gaer, June 5, 1950 (div. 1967); m. Cynthia Newby, Oct. 2, 1967 (div. 1977); 1 dau., Aurora Newby. B.S. in A.E, M.I.T., 1945, Ph.D. in Math, 1950; M.S. (hon.), Harvard U., 1976. Asst. prof. sociology and math stats. Columbia U., N.Y.C., 1953-57; lectr. social relations Harvard U., Cambridge, 1957-59, Alfred N. Whitehead prof. psychology, 1976-81, prof. psychology, 1981-83, Victor S. Thomas prof. psychology, 1984—, chmn., 1981-84; prof. U. Pa., Phila., 1959-69; vis. prof. Inst. for Advanced Study, Princeton, N.J., 1969-72; prof. social scis. U. Calif-Irvine, 1972-75; chmn. sect. psychology Nat. Acad. Scis., Washington, 1980-83. Author: (with H. Raiffa) Games and Decisions, 1957, Individual Choice Behavior, 1959; co-editor: (with H. Raiffa) Handbook Math. Psychology, 1963, 65 (3 vols); author: (with D.H. Krantz, P. Suppes, A. Tversky) Foundations of Measurement, 1971. Chmn. Assembly of Behavioral and Social Sci. NRC, 1976-79. Served with USNR, 1942-45. Guggenheim fellow, 1980-81; NSF fellow, 1966-67. Fellow AAAS, Am. Psychol. Assn. (Disting. Sci. Contbrs. award 1971); mem. Psychonomic Soc., Soc. for Math. Psychology (pres. 1979), Psychometric Soc. (pres. 1976), Am. Math. Soc., Am. Acad. Arts and Scis., Nat. Acad. Scis. Current Work: Axiomatic measurement (conjoint, non-associative, utility), reaction time models, psychophysical models, choice behavior. Subspecialty: Psychophysics. Home: 33 Washington St Cambridge MA 02140 Office: Harvard U William James Hall Cambridge MA 02138

LUCE, WILLIAM GLENN, animal science educator; b. Beaver Dam, Ky., Mar. 21, 1936; s. William Horton and Annie Elizabeth (Shultz) L.; m. Dorcas Linda Ward, Dec. 20, 1957; m. Nancy Ebey Ballard, Nov. 24, 1970; children: William Glenn, Bryan Ward. B.S. in Animal Husbandry, U. Ky., 1958; M.S. in Animal Sci, U. Nebr., 1964, Ph.D. in Animal Nutrition, 1965. Cert. animal scientist Am. Registry Profl. Animal Scientists. Co-mgr. Kroger Co., Louisville, 1958-62; research asst. U. Nebr., 1962-65; extension animal scientist U. Ga., 1965-68; prof. dept. animal sci., extension livestock specialist Okla. State U., 1968—. Served with USAR, 1958—. Recipient Outstanding Service award Okla. Swine Breeders Assn., 1977; Tyler award Okla. State U., 1980. Mem. Am. Soc. Animal Sci. (Outstanding Animal Sci. Extension Specialist), Sigma Xi, Sigma Phi Epsilon, Gamma Sigma Delta. Democrat. Methodist. Current Work: Swine nutrition and management; swine extension specialist for State Oklahoma; utilization of cereal grain by swine. Subspecialty: Animal nutrition. Home: 2817 W 17th Ave Stillwater OK 74074 Office: Animal Sci Dept Okla State U Stillwater OK 74078

LUCEY, ROBERT FRANCIS, educator; b. Worcester, Mass., Mar. 13, 1926; s. Cornelius Joseph and Mary (Shea) L.; m. Marie E. Lemire, Sept. 27, 1952; children—Robert Francis, Eileen, Jeanne-Marie, Mary, James, Elizabeth, Cornelius J., II, Brian. B.Vocat. Agr., U. Mass., 1950; M.S., U. Md., 1954; Ph.D., Mich. State U., 1958. Asst. prof. agronomy U. N.H., Durham, 1958-61; asst. prof. field crops Cornell U., 1961-67, asso. prof., 1967-70, prof., 1970—, chmn. dept. agronomy, 1975—. Recipient N.Y. Farmers award, 1968; highest achievement certificate Epsilon Sigma Phi, 1968. Mem. Am. Soc. Agronomy, Crop Sci. Soc. Am., N.Y. Acad. Scis., AAAS, Am. Grassland Council. Home: RD 2 Ithaca NY 14850 Office: Dept Agronomy Cornell U Ithaca NY 14850

LUCHSINGER, DONALD WAYNE, veterinary laboratory diagnostician, administrator; b. Milaca, Minn., Dec. 7, 1935; s. Clarence Melvin and Lucille (Stadig) L.; m. Judith Lorraine Jacobsen, Nov. 23, 1962; children—Daniel William, Thomas Allan, James Harold. Student Macalester Coll., 1953-55; B.S., U. Minn., 1957, D.V.M., 1961, M.P.H., 1966. Regional epidemiologist Animal and Plant Health Inspection Service, U.S. Dept. Agr., St. Paul, 1967-73, staff veterinarian export animals, Hyattsville, Md., 1978, sect. head Diagnostic Bacteriology Lab., Nat. Vet. Services Lab., Ames, Iowa, 1979-80, area veterinarian in charge, St. Paul, 1980-84, chief fgn. animal disease, diagnostic lab., Plum Island, N.Y., 1984—; chief tech. advisor Pan Am. Health Orgn., Kingston, Jamaica, 1973-77, cons., 1980, 82. Contbr. articles to profl. jours. Recipient awards U.S. Dept. Agr., 1965, 72, 84. Mem. AVMA, U.S. Animal Health Assn., Minn. Veterinary Med. Assn. (chmn. com. 1970-72), Am. Assn. Veterinary Lab. Diagnosticians, Phi Zeta. Current work: Diagnostic evaluation for foreign animal diseases from domestic and zoo animals being imported into the United States; training of veterinarians in foreign animal disease diagnosis. Subspecialties: Diagnostic veterinary medicine; Virology (veterinary medicine). Office: Fgn Animal Disease Diagnostic Lab US Dept Agr PO Box 848 Greenport NY 11944

LUCHTERHAND, KUBET EMIL, physical anthropologist; b. Marshfield, Wis., Mar. 17, 1945; s. Emil Arthur and Mary Arvella (Barrett) L.; m. Karen Saxon Heller, Feb. 22, 1970 (div. May 1972); m. Jean Anne Seiler, Mar. 8, 1985. B.S., Northwestern U., 1966; M.A., U. Chgo., 1968, Ph.D., 1974. Asst. prof. Roosevelt U., Chgo., 1970-74, assoc. prof., 1974-82, prof. anthropology, 1982-84; research assoc. Field Mus. Natural History, Chgo., 1980—; tech. cons. Wenner-Gren Found., N.Y.C., 1969-74; lectr. Ill. Inst. Tech. Chgo., 1982—. Contbr. articles to sci. jours. Woodrow Wilson Found. fellow, 1966-67;

grantee Nat. Geog. Soc., 1980, Am. Philos. Soc., 1982, Am. Council Learned Socs., 1982. Mem. Soc. for Study of Evolution, Am. Assn. Phys. Anthropologists, Soc. Vertebrate Paleontology, AAAS, Assn. Tropical Biologists, Sigma Xi. Current work: Evolution and paleoecology of mammalian communities during the Cenozoic, especially of small mammals. Subspecialties: Evolutionary biology; Paleontology, paleoecology. Office: Field Mus Natural History Roosevelt Rd at Lake Shore Dr Chicago IL 60605

LUCK, DAVID JONATHAN LEWIS, educator, biologist; b. Milw., Jan. 7, 1929; s. Max. and Sarah (Plonsker) L. S.B., U. Chgo., 1949; M.D., Harvard, 1953; Ph.D., Rockefeller U., 1962. House officer Mass. Gen. Hosp., Boston, 1953-54, resident physician, 1957-58; research asso. Rockefeller U., 1962—, mem. faculty, 1964—, prof. biology, 1968—. Editor: Jour. Cell Biology, 1968-74. Served to capt. USAF, 1955-57. Decorated Commendation medal with oak leaf cluster. Mem. Am. Soc. Biol. Chemists, Am. Soc. Cell Biologists, Nat. Acad. Sci. Club: University (N.Y.C.). Fields: Cell biology, genetics and gene actions. Current work: Biochemistry and genetics of eukaryotic flagellar function and assembly. Home: 205 E 78th St New York NY 10021

LUCKENBILL-EDDS, LOUISE, biologist; b. Lebanon, Pa., Nov. 19, 1936; d. Fred E. and Anna M. (Luckenbill). B.A., Oberlin Coll., 1958; postgrad., Washington U., St. Louis, 1958-61; Ph.D., Brown U., 1964. Postdoctoral fellow, research instr. Boston U. Med. Sch., 1964-68; sci. fellow Hubrecht Lab., Utrecht, Netherlands, 1968-69; asst. prof. Smith Coll., Northampton, Mass., 1969-75; instr. neuropathology Harvard U. Med. Sch., 1975-77; research assoc. Boston Children's Hosp. Med. Ctr., 1975-77; now assoc. prof. zoology and biomed. sci. Coll. Osteo. Medicine, Ohio U.; vis. asst. prof. Harvard U., 1973-74; guest scientist Lab. Devel. Biology and Anomalies, Nat. Inst. Dental Research, NIH, 1985-86. Mem. Soc. Devel. Biology, Am. Soc. Cell Biology, Soc. Neurosci., AAAS. Current Work: Development of neural crest and sympathetic neurons. Subspecialties: Developmental biology; Neurobiology. Office: Ohio U Coll Osteopathic Medicine Irvine Hall Athens OH 45701

LUCKETT, LARRY WAYNE, medical physicist, army officer; b. San Antonio, Oct. 8, 1948; s. Robert Miles and Murriel Mae (Stearns) L.; m. Judith Ann Blodgett, June 2, 1972. B.S. cum laude, Trinity U., San Antonio, 1971; M.S., Tex. A&M U., College Station, 1973; postgrad., Rensselaer Poly. Inst., 1980—. Cert. Am. Bd. Health Physics. Commd. 1st lt. M.S.C. U.S. Army, 1973, advanced through grades to maj., 1983; cons. physicist U.S. Army Environ. Hygiene Agy., Aberdeen, Md., 1973-76; radiation protection officer Tripler Army Med. Center, Honolulu, 1977-80; now with dept. radiology Walter Reed Army Med. Center, Washington. Chmn. subcom. on environ. factors and cancer Am. Cancer Soc., Honolulu, 1978-80. Mem. Health Physics Soc., Am. Assn. Physicists in Medicine, Soc. Nuclear Medicine, Am. Nuclear Soc. (assoc.), Tau Beta Pi, Alpha Nu Sigma, Sigma Pi Sigma. Baptist. Current Work: Quantitative nuclear image analysis; computed tomography; population exposures to environmental radiation sources. Subspecialties: Nuclear medicine; Imaging technology. Home: 17224 Hobble Bush Ct Rockville MD 20855 Office: Dept Radiology Walter Reed Army Med Center Washington DC 20307

LUCKINBILL, LEO STEPHEN, biology educator, researcher; b. Fort Smith, Ark., Feb. 29, 1944; s. Lawrence Benedict and Agnes Sarah (Nulph) L.; m. Sandra Marian Tanzillo, Sept. 16, 1967; 1 child, Gregory. B.S., St. Mary's Coll., Moraga, Calif., 1966; M.S., San Diego State U., 1968; Ph.D., UCLA, 1971. Postdoctoral research fellow U. Calif.-Santa Barbara, 1971-72; asst. prof. biology Rutgers U., Newark, 1972-74; asst. prof. biology Wayne State U., Detroit, 1974-77, assoc. prof., 1978—. Contbr. articles to profl. jours., chpts. to books. Grantee NIH, 1979, NSF, 1974, 78, 85. Mem. AAAS, Ecol. Soc. Am. Democrat. Current work: Population genetics, ecology, genetics of life span. Subspecialties: Radiation biology; Gene actions. Office: Dept Biol Scis Wayne State Univ Detroit MI 48202

LUCKY, ROBERT WENDELL, electrical engineer; b. Pitts., Jan. 9, 1936; s. Clyde Arthur and Grace Katherine (Luck) L.; m. Joan Miriam Jackson, Aug. 19, 1961; children: David William, Karen Joan. B.S. in Elec. Engring, Purdue U., 1957, M.S., 1959, Ph.D., 1961. With Bell Telephone Labs., Holmdel, N.J., 1961—, supr. signal theory, 1964-65, head dept. advanced data communications, 1965-76, dir. Electronic and Computer Systems Research Lab., 1977-81, exec. dir. research Communications Scis. Div., 1982—; Mem. engring. adv. bd. Purdue U., 1973-75; mem. USAF Sci. Adv. Bd., 1979—, vice chmn., 1983—; mem. adv. com. NSF, 1983—. Author: Principles of Data Communication, 1968; Editor: Proc. of IEEE, 1974-76, Computer Communication, 1975; cons. editor: Plenum Press, 1979—. Named Distinguished Alumnus Purdue U., 1969. Fellow IEEE (v.p. 1978-79, exec. v.p. 1980—, publs. bd. 1970-76, bd. govs. info. theory group 1969-74); mem. Nat. Acad. Engring., Communications Soc. (pres. 1977—, Achievement award 1975), Eta Kappa Nu (nat. dir. 1974-76). Patentee in field. Current Work: Telecommunications systems; computer communications; computer science. Subspecialty: Computer engineering. Home: 238 Kemp Ave Fair Haven NJ 07701 Office: Room 4E605 Bell Telephone Labs Holmdel NJ 07733

LUCOT, JAMES BERNARD, pharmacologist, educator; b. McKeesport, Pa., Aug. 17, 1951; s. Joseph Bernard and Florence Patricia (Greger) L.; m. Katherine Ann Lucot, May 22, 1982. B.S. magna cum laude, U. Pitts., 1973; Ph.D., U. N.C.-Chapel Hill, 1977. Grad. research asst. neurobiology U. N.C., 1976-77; postdoctoral fellow U. Chgo., 1977-80; asst. prof. depts. pharmacology and toxicology, psychiatry Wright State U., Dayton, Ohio, 1980—; researcher; community resource person for info. on central nervous system pharmacology. Contbr. articles to profl. jours. Recipient Wright State U.seed grant Dayton, Ohio, 1980—. Mem. AAAS, Soc. Neurosci., N.Y. Acad. Scis., Soc. Stimulus Properties of Drugs. Democrat. Current Work: Categorization of serotonin receptors and serotonin antagonists, mechanism of action of antidepressants, mechanism of motion sickness. Subspecialties: Psychopharmacology; Neuropharmacology. Office: Wright State U Dept Pharmacology and Toxicology Sch Medicine Dayton OH 45435

LUDERER, ALBERT AUGUST, medical research scientist; b. Jersey City, May 23, 1948; s. Albert Frank and Hilda Marie (Koenig) L.; m. Margaret Annetta Diaz, June 27, 1970; children: Hilary Faye, Albert William. A.B., Drew U., 1970; M.S., Rutgers U., 1973, Ph.D., 1975. With Corning Glass Works, N.Y., 1976 , sr. research scientist and tech. dir. cancer research div., 1979-83, mgr. biomed. research health and sci. group, 1983—; Co-chmn. 3d Internat. Conf. Diagnostic Immunology, Henniker, N.H., 1981. Contbr. numerous sci. articles to profl. publs. Postdoctoral fellow Jefferson Med. Coll. Pa., Phila., 1974-76. Mem. Am. Assn. Immunologists, N.Am. Hyperthermia Group, Am. Genetic Assn., N.Y. Acad. Sci., Tissue Culture Assn. Current Work: Early diagnosis and therapy of cancer. Application of hybridoma and DNA technology of the diagnosis and therapy of neoplastic diseases. Subspecialties: Cancer research (medicine); Immunology (medicine). Office: Corning Glass Works Sullivan Research Park FR-64 Corning NY 14831

LUDINGTON, JOHN SAMUEL, See *Who's Who in America,* 43rd edition.

LUDLOW, CHRISTY LESLIE, speech pathologist; b. Montreal, Que., June 7, 1944; d. Forester Wilcox and Margaret Helen (Sweet) Leslie; m. Gregory Ludlow, Sept. 7, 1968. B.Sc., McGill U., 1965, M.Sc., 1967; Ph.D., NYU, 1973. Staff speech pathologist, research asst. NYU Med. Ctr., 1967-70; Walter A. Anderson fellow, 1970-72; project mgr. Am. Speech and Hearing Assn., Washington, 1973-74; research speech pathologist, communicative disorders program, chief speech pathology unit, intramural research program. Nat. Inst. Neurol. and Communicative Disorders and Stroke, NIH, Bethesda, Md., 1974—; cons. Vietnam head injury study Walter Reed Army Med. Ctr., 1980—. Assoc. editor: Jour. Speech and Hearing Research, 1981-84. Recipient Dir.'s award NIH, 1977. Fellow Internat. Acad. Research in Learning Disabilities, Am. Speech and Hearing Assn. (chmn. sci. affairs com. 1978-82); mem. Internat. Assn. Research in Otolarnyngology, Internat. Neuropsychol. Soc., Acad. Aphasia, N.Y. Acad. Sci., Soc. Neurosci. Am. Assn. Phonetic Sci. Current Work: Speech motor control and phonation, neurolinguistics, brain injury and language function. Subspecialties: Neuropsychology; Otorhinolaryngology. Home: 8801 Garfield St Bethesda MD 20817 Office: 7550 Wisconsin Ave Bethesda MD 20892

LUDLUM, DAVID BLODGETT, medical scientist, clinical pharmacologist; b. N.Y.C., Sept. 30, 1929; s. C. Daniel and Elsie B. (Blodgett) L.; m. Carlene L. Dyke, Dec. 23, 1952; children: Valerie Jean Ludlum Wright, Kenneth David. B.A., Cornell U., 1951; Ph.D., U. Wis., 1954; M.D., NYU, 1962. Research scientist DuPont Co., Wilmington, Del., 1954-58; intern Bellevue Hosp., N.Y.C., 1962-63; asst. prof. pharmacology Yale U. Sch. Medicine, New Haven, 1963-68; assoc. prof. pharmacology U. Md. Sch. Medicine, Balt., 1968-70, prof., 1970-76; prof., chmn. dept. pharmacology Albany (N.Y.) Med. Coll, 1976-80, prof. pharmacology and medicine, dir. oncology research, 1980—; cons. indsl. exposure; adj. prof. chemistry Rensselaer Poly. Inst., Troy, N.Y., 1977—; vis. prof. oncology Johns Hopkins U., 1973-76; vis. prof. Courtauld Inst., London, summer, 1970. Contbr. articles to profl. jours.; assoc. editor: Cancer Research, 1980—. WARF fellow, 1951-52; Am. Heart Assn. fellow, 1960-62; NIH Research Career Devel. awardee, 1968; Markle scholar, 1967; NIH grantee, 1963—; Am. Cancer Soc. grantee, 1981-82. Mem. Am. Soc. Pharmacology and Exptl. Therapeutics, Am. Soc. Clin. Pharmacology and Therapeutics, Am. Assn. Cancer Research, Am. Soc. Biol. Chemists, Am. Chem. Soc., Phi Beta Kappa, Phi Kappa Phi, Sigma Xi, Alpha Omega Alpha. Current Work: Pharmacology of antineoplastic agents, clinical pharmacology, molecular pharmacology, mutagenesis and carcinogenesis. Subspecialties: Pharmacology; Cancer research (medicine). Home: 24 Linda Ct Delmar NY 12054 Office: Albany Med Coll 47 New Scotland Ave Albany NY 12208

LUDWIG, JOHN HOWARD, environ. engr.; b. Burlington, Vt., Mar. 7, 1913; s. Rudolf Frederick and Emily Henrietta (Sikora) L.; m. Gilda Mary Silva, Nov. 9, 1946; children—Howard Russell, Robert William. B.S. in Engring, U. Calif., Berkeley, 1934; M.S. in Engring, U. Colo., 1941; M.S. in Indsl. Hygiene, Harvard, 1956, Sc.D., 1958. Registered profl. engr., Calif., Oreg. Engr. Bur. Reclamation, Denver, 1936-39; Engr. C.E., Portland, 1939-43, Sacramento, 1949-51; engr. water pollution USPHS, Washington, 1951-55; dir. research and devel. EPA, Washington, 1955-69; asst. commr. Nat. Air Pollution Control Adminstrn., 1969-70, asso. commr., 1970-72, cons. environ. engring. to fgn. and internat. agys., 1972—; U.S. del. Econ. Commn. for Europe, Geneva, 1969-72, Orgn. for Econ. Co-op. and Devel., Paris, 1969-72, NATO Com. on Challenges of Modern Soc., Brussels, 1969-72. Contbr. articles to profl. jours. Mem. Santa Barbara Environ. Quality Bd., 1973-75. Served to capt. USAAF, 1943-46. Recipient Commendation medal HEW, 1963, Superior Service award, 1967; Gold medal for Exceptional Service EPA, 1971; Gordon Fair award Am. Acad. Environ. Engrs., 1973; named Distinguished Engring. Alumnus U. Colo., 1976. Mem. Nat. Acad. Engrs., Cosmos Club, ASCE, Am. Meteorol. Soc., Am. Acad. Environ. Engrs., Phi Beta Kappa, Sigma Xi, Tau Beta Pi, Chi Epsilon, Delta Omega. Current Work: Consulting in administrative and technical aspects of air pollution control programs. Subspecialties: Environmental engineering; Water supply and wastewater treatment. Home and Office: 43 Alston Pl Santa Barbara CA 93108

LUEHRS, DEAN CARL, chemistry educator; b. Fremont, Nebr., Apr. 20, 1939; s. Glen C. and Louise A. (Haebler) L.; m. Joan Marie Moege, June 14, 1969; 1 dau., Janine. B.S., Mich. State U., 1961; Ph.D., U. Kans., 1965. Asst. prof. Mich. Technol. U., Houghton, 1965-70, assoc. prof. chemistry, 1970—. NSF fellow, 1961-64; NIH fellow, 1964-65. Mem. Am. Chem. Soc., Am. Pomological Soc. Baptist. Patentee in field. Current Work: Reactions in nonaqueous solvents, kinetics of multidentate substitution reactions, synthesis of one-dimensional electrically conducting solids. Subspecialty: Inorganic chemistry. Office: Dept Chemistry Mich Technol U Houghton MI 49931

LUERSSEN, FRANK WONSON, steel company executive; b. Reading, Pa., Aug. 14, 1927; s. George V. and Mary Ann (Swoyer) L.; m. Joan M. Schlosser, June 17, 1950; children: Thomas, Mary Ellen, Catherine, Susan, Ann. B.S. in Physics, Pa., State U., 1950; M.S. in Metall. Engring, Lehigh U., 1951; LL.D. hon., Calumet Coll. Metallurgist research and devel. div. Inland Steel Co., East Chicago, Ind., 1952-54, mgr. various positions, 1954-64, mgr. research, 1964-68, v.p. research, 1968-77, v.p. steel mfg., 1977-78, pres., 1978—, chmn., 1983—; dir. Continental Ill. Corp. Author various articles on steelmaking tech. Trustee Calumet Coll., Whiting, Ind., 1972-80, Northwestern U., 1980—; trustee, sec., treas. Munster Sch. Bd., 1957-66. Served with USNR, 1945-47. Named disting. alumnus Pa. State U. Fellow Am. Soc. Metals, Nat. Acad. Engring.; mem. Am. Inst. Mining, Metall. and Petroleum Engrs., Am. Iron and Steel Inst., Metals Soc. Gt. Britain. Subspecialty: Metallurgical engineering. Home: 8226 Parkview Ave Munster IN 46321 Office: 30 W Monroe St Chicago IL 60603

LUFT, HERBERT ARTHUR, amateur astronomer; b. Breslau, Germany, May 19, 1908; came to U.S. 1946, naturalized, 1950; s. Arthur and Elise (Laqueur) L.; m. Hilde Dreyfuss, May 17, 1949; 1 child, Lillian Eve. Student pub. schs. Bank clk., Breslau, Germany, 1924-30; jr. bus. exec., Germany, 1931-39; bus. exec., Brazil, 1940-46; import-export asst. to customs house broker J.E. Bernard & Co., Inc., N.Y.C., 1950-65; owner Mail Order Sci. Books Sale, Oakland Gardens, N.Y., 1950—; amateur astronomer reporting astron. observations to Swiss Fed. Obs., Zurich, 1925-80, Royal Obs., Brussels, 1980—; past cons. Royal Greenwich Obs., U.S. Naval Obs. Contbr. articles, papers to various profl. mags. Mem. Am. Assn. Variable Star Observers, Amateur Astronomers Assn. (Silver medal 1977). Lodge: Masons. Jewish. Current work: Observation of sun spots. Subspecialty: Optical astronomy. Home: 69-11 229th St Oakland Gardens Bayside NY 11364

LUGO, ARIEL EMILIO, ecologist; b. Mayaguez, P.R., Apr. 28, 1943; s. Herminio and Ramonita (Álvarez) L.; m. Alma Guzmán (div. 1979); children—Alma Veronica, Ariel A.; m. Helen A. Nunci, Sept. 1, 1984. B.S. in Biology, U. P.R., 1963, M.S. in Biology, 1965; Ph.D. in Ecology, U. N.C., 1969. Gen. zoology lab. asst. U. P.R., 1962, cell psysiology lab. asst., 1963; gen. botany lab. asst. U. N.C.-Chapel Hill, 1967; asst. prof. dept. botany U. Fla.-Gainesville, 1969-73, 75-76, assoc. prof., 1976-79, acting dir. Ctr. for Wetlands, 1977-78; asst. sec. for planning and resource analysis Dept. Natural Resources, 1973-74, asst. sec. for sci. and tech., 1974-75; staff mem. Council on Environ. Quality, Exec. Office of Pres., Washington, 1978-79; supervisory research ecologist, project leader USDA Forest Service, Inst. Tropical Forestry, Rio Piedras, P.R., 1979—; cons. in field; lectr. in biol. scis. and ecology numerous univs.; expert witness to fed. cts. Contbr. articles to profl. publs. Fellow NIH, 1965-68, Fulbright-Hayes Found., 1978; grantee U. Fla., 1969, 71-72, 72, NSF, 1974, EPA, 1977-79, Conservation Found., 1977, U.S. Dept. Energy, 1978-82, 83-85, U.S. Man and the Biosphere Consortium, 1980-83, 81-83, 80-84, IAD, 1983, U.S. Nat. Oceanographic Adminstrn., 1984-85, others. Mem. Ecol. Soc. Am., Assn. Tropical Biologists, Soc. Limnology and Oceanography, Internat. Assn. Ecology, Inst. Caribbean Studies, Fla. Acad. Scis., Internat. Soc. Tropical Ecology, Internat. Soc. for Vegetation Scis. (mem. editorial bd. 1981—), Internat. Soc. Tropical Foresters, Sigma Xi. Subspecialty: Ecosystems analysis. Home: 1528 Tamesis St El Paraiso Rio Piedras PR 00926 Office: USDA Forest Service ITF PO Box AQ Rio Piedras PR 00926

LUKASIK, STEPHEN JOSEPH, aerospace company executive; b. S.I., N.Y., Mar. 19, 1931; s. Stephen Joseph and Mildred F. (Tynan) L.; m. Marilyn B. Trappiel, Jan. 31, 1953; children: Carol J., Gregory C., Elizabeth A., Jeffrey P.; m. Virginia Dogan Armstrong, Feb. 11, 1983; stepchildren: Elizabeth L. Armstrong, Alan D. Armstrong. B.S., Rensselaer Poly. Inst., 1951; M.S., MIT, 1953, Ph.D., 1956. With Advanced Research Projects Agy., Dept. Def., Washington, 1966-74; v.p. Xerox Corp., Rochester, N.Y., 1974-76; chief scientist, sr. v.p. Rand Corp., Santa Monica, Calif., 1977-79; chief scientist FCC, Washington, 1979-82; with Northrop Corp., Los Angeles 1982—, v.p., mgr. Northrop Research and Tech. Ctr., 1985—; cons. to govt. Trustee Stevens Inst. Tech.; mem. adv. com. Stanford U. Computer Center; assoc. editor The Info. Soc. Author: Some Relations between Technology and Arms Control, 1983, The 1979 WARC - Its Results and Subsequent FCC Actions, 1981, Military Research and Development, 1977, Technology, Transfer and National Security, 1976. Served to capt. USAR, 1951-66. Recipient Disting. Civilian Service medal Sec. Def., 1973, 74. Mem. Am. Phys. Soc., AAAS. Club: Cosmos. Current Work: Direct corporate research laboratory in areas of microelectronics, image processing and manufacturing productivity Subspecialties: Fluid dynamics; Information systems (Information science). Office: 1840 Century Park E Los Angeles CA 90067

LUKEZIC, FELIX LEE, plant pathologist, educator; b. Florence, Colo., May 27, 1933; s. Felix and A. and Irene (Wands) L.; m. Arlene Claire, Aug. 18, 1955; children: Bret, Craig, Susan. B.S., Colo. State U., 1956, M.S., 1958; Ph.D., U. Calif. Davis, 1963. Lab. technician II U. Calif. Davis, 1958-63; asst. plant pathologist United Fruit Co., LaLima, Honduras, 1963-65; asst. prof. plant pathology Pa. State U., University Park, 1965-70, assoc. prof., 1970-75, prof., 1975—. Contbr. articles in field to profl. jours. Danforth Found. fellow, 1969. Mem. Am. Phytopath. Soc., Am. Soc. Plant Physiologists. Democrat. Methodist. Club: Nittany Valley Sailing. Current Work: Researcher in physiological interaction between the host and pathogens. Subspecialties: Plant pathology; Microbiology. Home: 531 Hillside Ave State College PA 16801 Office: Pa State U Dept Plant Pathology 211 Buckhout Lab University Park PA 16802

LUM, LAWRENCE GEORGE, immunologist; b. Sacramento, Calif., June 28, 1947; s. George Wai and Nellie (Quan) L.; m. Carol Ann Lee, June 17, 1973; children: Hillary Eileen, Amanda Renee. B.S., U. Redlands, 1969; M.D., U. Calif., San Francisco, 1973. Diplomate Am. Bd. Pediatrics. Intern pediatrics dept. pediatrics U. Calif., San Francisco, 1973-74, resident pediatrics, 1974-75, U. Colo., Denver, 1975-76; clin. asso., fellow immunology, cellular immunology sect., metabolism br. Nat. Cancer Inst., NIH, Bethesda, Md., 1976-78, expert cons., 1978-79; asst. prof. pediatrics U. Wash., Seattle, 1979-85, assoc. prof., 1985—; assoc. mem. Fred Hutchinson Cancer Research Center, Seattle, 1979-85; assoc. mem., 1985—; mem. staff Children's Orthopedic Hosp. Med. Center, Seattle, 1979—. Contbr. articles in field to profl. jours. Recipient awards Bank Am., 1965, awards Optimist Club, 1965, Outstanding Alumnus award U. Redlands.; Am. Bapt. nat. scholar, 1965-69. Mem. Am. Assn. Immunologists, Am. Fedn. Clin. Research, Soc. Pediatric Research, Am. Soc. Hematologists, Phi Delta Epsilon. Current Work: Human T cell subpopulations, the regulation of specific antibody prodn. in bone marrow transplant recipients and immunodeficiency disorders; discoverer and delineated the function of Fe-IgA receptors on human lymphocytes transfer of antigen specific immunity from donor to recipient. Subspecialties: Immunology (medicine); Transplantation. Office: Fred Hutchinson Cancer Research Center Room 785 1124 Columbia St Seattle WA 98104

LUMB, RALPH FRANCIS, physical chemist, consultant; b. Worcester, Mass., May 27, 1921; s. Irving E. and Clara L. (Bunker) Clapp; m. Phyllis M. Wetherbee, Feb. 11, 1941; Sandra Lumb Eddy, Joy Lumb Gardner, Cheryl Lumb Drescher, Randall W., Richard I., Linda Lumb Warner, Steven R., Bonnie S. Lumb Lillis. A.B., Clark U., 1947, Ph.D. in Phys. Chemistry, 1951. Cert. safeguards specialist. Chief physics and chemistry br. AEC, Washington, 1951-56; v.p. Quantum, Wallingford, Conn., 1956-60; dir. Western N.Y. Nuclear Research Center; SUNY, Buffalo, 1960-68; pres. Advanced Tech. Cons. Corp., Wallingford, 1968-71, NASAC, Inc., Reston, Va., 1971—. Editor: Management of Nuclear Materials, 1960. Mem. Gov.'s Com. on Western N.Y. Devel., 1962-64; chmn. N.Y. State Adv. Com. on Radiation Utilization, 1962-64. Served with USAF, 1943-45. Fellow Am. Inst. Chemists, AAAS; mem. Inst. Nuclear Materials Mgmt., Am. Nuclear Soc. Patentee in field. Current Work: Nuclear fuel consulting; measurement and control of nuclear materials; development and evaluation of systems for measurement and control of nuclear materials and for quality assurance for nuclear fuel. Subspecialties: Fuels and sources; Nuclear engineering. Office: 1850 Samuel Morse Dr Reston VA 22090

LUMLEY, JOHN LEASK, physicist, educator; b. Detroit, Nov. 4, 1930; s. Charles S. and Jane Anderson Campbell (Leask) L.; m. Jane French, June 20, 1953; children: Katherine Leask, Jennifer French, John Christopher. B.A., Harvard, 1952; M.S. in Engring, Johns Hopkins, 1954, Ph.D., 1957. Postdoctoral fellow Johns Hopkins, 1957-59; mem. faculty Pa. State U., 1959-77, prof. aerospace engring., 1963-74, Evan Pugh prof. aerospace engring., 1974-77; Willis H. Carrier prof. engring. Cornell U., 1977—; prof. d'echange U. d'Aix-Marseille, France, 1966-67; Fulbright sr. lectr. U. Liege; vis. prof. U. Louvain-La-Neuve, Belgium; Guggenheim fellow U. Provence (Ecole Centrale de Lyon), France, 1973-74. Author: (with H.A. Panofsky) Structure of Atmospheric Turbulence, 1964, Stochastic Tools for Turbulence, 1970, (with H. Tennekes) A First Course in Turbulence, 1971; also articles.; Tech. editor: Statistical Fluid Mechanics, 1971, 75, Variability of the Oceans, 1977; assoc. editor Physics of Fluids, 1971-73, Ann. Rev. of Fluid Mechanics, 1976-85, co-editor, 1985—; chmn. tech. editorial bd.: Izvestiya: Atmospheric and Oceanic Physics, 1971—; editorial bd.: Fluid Mechanics: Soviet Research, 1972—; Prin.: films Deformation of Continuous Media, 1963, Eulerian and Lagrangian Frames in Fluid Mechanics, 1968. Recipient medallion U. Liege, Belgium, 1971. Fellow Am. Acad. Arts and Scis., Am. Acad. Mechanics, Am. Phys. Soc. (exec. com. div. fluid dynamics 1972-75, 81-84, chmn. exec. com. div. fluid dynamics 1982); mem. Soc. Natural Philosophy, N.Y. Acad. Scis., AAAS, Am. Geophys. Union, AIAA (fluid and plasmadynamics award 1982), Johns Hopkins Soc. Scholars (charter), Sigma Xi. Current Work: Turbulence modeling in geophysical flows and in technology and biology. Subspecialties: Fluid mechanics; Micrometeorology. Home: 743 Snyder Hill Rd Ithaca NY 14850 Office: 238 Upson Hall Cornell U Ithaca NY 14853

LUND, ARNOLD MILTON, JR., human factors engineer, researcher; b. Seattle, July 21, 1950; s. Arnold Milton and Alice Elizabeth (Locke) L.; m. Marlene Mildred Meland, Aug. 18, 1973. B.A. in Chemistry, U. Chgo., 1972; postgrad. Trinity Evangelical Div. Sch., Deerfield, Ill, 1972-73; M.A. in Exptl. Psychology, Calif. State U.-Fullerton, 1977; Ph.D. in Exptl. Psychology, Human Learning and Memory, Northwestern U., 1980. Lectr. personality theory Calif. State U., Fullerton, 1976-77; research asst. Northwestern U., 1977-80, instr., 1979; mem. tech. staff AT&T Bell Labs, Holmdel, N.J., 1980-85, supr., 1985—, editor Behavioral Sci. Newsletter, 1983-85, mem. behavioral sci. liaison com., 1983-85. Contbr. articles to profl. jours. Mem. Human Factors Soc., IEEE. Presbyterian. Current work: Systems engineering of human-computer interfaces, problem solving. Subspecialties: Human factors engineering; Cognition. Home: 5 Johnny Ct Red Bank NJ 07701 Office: AT&T Bell Labs Crawfords Corner Rd Holmdel NJ 07733

LUND, CHARLES EDWARD, stress engineer; b. Fremont, Mich., Apr. 4, 1946; s. Henry Knute and Dorothy Carol (Beatty) L.; m. Sandra Leaha Ruff, July 30, 1967; 1 dau., Deanna Marie. B.S.E., U. Mich., 1968, M.S.E., 1970; postgrad., Stanford U., 1972-77. Assoc. engr. McDonnell-Douglas Astron. Co., Culver City, Calif., 1968-69; structures engr. Lockheed Missiles & Space Co., Sunnyvale, Calif., 1970-77; stress engr. II NWL Control Systems, Kalamazoo, 1977—. Treas. Angling Rd. Sch. Parent Tchr. Orgn., Portage, Mich., 1981-82, chmn. carnival, 1981-83. Mem. AIAA. Club: Mood Makers Band (dir. 1979—). Patentee digital plotter pen caddy; co-inventor composite cylinder closure. Current Work: Finite element analysis. Subspecialties: Aeronautical engineering; Mechanical engineering. Home: PO Box 3335 Kalamazoo MI 49003 Office: NWL Control Systems 2220 Palmer Ave Kalamazoo MI 49001

LUND, MELVIN ROBERT, dental educator; b. Siren, Wis., Oct. 17, 1922; s. Alexander and Emelia (Hamson) L.; m. Margaret Elizabeth Reith, Nov. 10, 1946; children: Mark, Kristine, Kelly. D.M.D., U. Oreg., 1946; M.S., U. Mich., 1954. Mem. restorative faculty Loma Linda (Calif.) U. Sch. Dentistry, 1954-56, chmn. restorative faculty, 1956-69, mem. faculty, 1969-71; chmn. operative dentistry Ind. U. Sch. Dentistry, Indpls., 1971—. Author: Operative Dentistry, 4th edit, 1982; Textbook of Operative Dentistry, 2d edit; contbr. articles to profl. jours. Served to capt. U.S. Army, 1946-48, Korea. Mem. Internat. Assn. Dental Research, Am. Acad. Restorative Dentistry, Am. Assn. Dental Schs. Republican. Seventh-day Adventist. Lodge: Lions Internat. Current Work: By controlling the technical and manipulative procedures for purpose of observing effects on the restorative material. Subspecialty: operative dentistry. Office: Ind U Sch Dentistry 1121 W Michigan St Indianapolis IN 46202

LUNDBLAD, ROGER LAUREN, biochemist, educator; b. San Francisco, Oct. 31, 1939; s. Lauren Alfred and Doris Ruth (Peterson) L.; m. Susan Taylor, Oct. 15, 1966; children: Christina Susan, Cynthia Karin. B.S., Pacific Luth. U., 1961; Ph.D., U. Wash., 1965. Research assoc. biochemistry U. Wash., 1965-66, Rockefeller U., 1966-68; asst. prof. to prof. depts. pathology, biochemistry and periodontics U. N.C., Chapel Hill, 1968—; assoc. dir. adminstrn. Dental Research Center, U. N.C., 1968—; assoc. dir. program devel. Center Thrombosis and Hemostasis, U. N.C., 1968—. Contbr. articles to profl. jours. Mem. Am. Heart Assn., Am. Soc. Biol. Chemists, Am. Chem. Soc., AAAS, Internat. Soc. Thrombosis and Hemostasis, Sigma Xi. Democrat. Lutheran. Current Work: Thrombosis and hemostasis, regulation of gene expression in eukaryotic systems, recombinant DNA. Subspecialties: Biochemistry (biology); Genetics and genetic engineering (biology). Home: 638 Wellington Dr Chapel Hill NC 27514 Office: Dental Research Center 210H U NC Chapel Hill NC 27514

LUNDEEN, GERALD WAYNE, information and library studies educator; b. Moose Lake, Minn., June 5, 1937; s. Wayne Oscar and Alma Lidia (Siiro) L.; m. Carol Tenopir, Aug. 7, 1979. B.S., U. Wis.-Madison, 1959; Ph.D., U. Minn., 1964; A.M.L.S., U. Mich., 1972. Postdoctoral fellow Battelle Lab., Columbus, Ohio, 1966-68, sr. chemist, 1968-71; asst. sci. tech. librarian Eastern Mich. U., Ypsilanti, 1972-74; asst. prof. info. and library studies U. Hawaii, Honolulu, 1974-80, assoc. prof., 1980—. Author: (with others) Illustrated Computer

Program, 1981. Contbr. articles to profl. jours. Woodrow Wilson fellow, 1959, NSF fellow, 1965; Margret Mann scholar, 1971. Mem. Am. Soc. Info. Sci. Current work: Information storage and retrieval, personal information systems, microcomputer applications. Subspecialty: Information systems (Information science). Home: 308 Opihikao Pl Honolulu HI 96825 Office: GSLS U Hawaii 2550 the Mall Honolulu HI 96822

LUNDGREN, JAMES REINHOLD, civil engr.; b. Vancouver, B.C., Can., Jan. 11, 1945; s. Nels Reinhold and Agnes May (Fulton) L.; m. Angela Andrian Plaza, Nov. 24, 1973; children: Steven, Douglas, Mary. B.A.Sc., U. B.C., 1968; M.S., U. Ill., 1970. Registered profl. engr., Que. Project dir. Can. Nat. Rys., Edmonton, Atla., Montreal, 1971-73, sr. project engr., Montreal, 1973-76; mgr. Fast Project Assn. Am. R.R.s, Pueblo, Colo., 1976-77, mgr. track research div., Chgo., 1977-78, dir. research and test ops., Pueblo, 1978-82; exec. dir. Transp. Test Center, Pueblo, 1982-83, asst. v.p., 1983—. Contbr. articles to profl. jours. Mem. ASME; mem. Locomotive Maintenance Officers Assn.; Mem. Am. Ry. Engring. Assn., Roadmasters and Maintenance of Way Assn., Car Dept. Officers Assn., Ry. Fuel and Operating Officers Assn. Presbyterian. Current Work: Management of rail transportation related hardware research and test activities. Subspecialties: Civil engineering; Mechanical engineering. Office: PO Box 11130 Pueblo CO 81001

LUNDIN, BRUCE THEODORE, energy tech. adminstr., cons.; b. Alameda, Calif., Dec. 28, 1919; s. Oscar L. and Elizabeth E. (Erickson) L.; m. Barbara A. Bliss, July 27, 1946; children: Dianne, Robert, Nancy; m. Jean A. Oberlin, Mar. 20, 1982. B.S. in Mech. Engring, U. Calif.-Berkeley, 1942; D.Eng. (hon.), U. Toledo, 1975. Assoc. dir. NASA Lewis Research Center, Cleve., 1961-68, dep. assoc. adminstr., 1968-70, dir., 1970-77; cons. EPRI, others; staff dir. Pres.'s Commn. on Accident at Three-Mile Island. Contbr. articles on aircraft propulsion to profl. jours. Pres. Westshore Unitarian Ch.; trustee Southwest Gen. Hosp. Recipient NASA medal for Outstanding Leadership, 1965, Public Service medal, 1971, 79; Disting. Service medal, 1971, 77; named Nat. Space Club Engr. of Yr., 1976. Fellow AIAA, AAAS, Royal Aero. Soc.; mem. Nat. Acad. Engring. Current Work: Safety advisory board, recovery of Three Mile Island. Subspecialties: Aerospace engineering and technology; Nuclear engineering.

LUNDIN, ROBERT WILLIAM, psychologist; b. Chgo., Apr. 28, 1920; s. Adolph Eugene and Agnes (King) L.; m. Margaret Waitt, Aug. 8, 1952; children: Sara Jane, Robert King. A.B., DePauw U., 1942; M.A., Ind. U., 1943, Ph.D., 1947. Asst. prof. Denison U., Granville, Ohio, 1947-49; assoc. prof. Hamilton Coll., Clinton, N.Y., 1949-64; prof. U. of South, Sewanee, Tenn., 1964—, Kenan prof., 1981—. Author: Psychol. Music, 1967, Personality: Behavioral Analysis, 1974, Personality: Experimental Approach, 1961, Theories and Systems of Psychology, 1985. Fellow Am. Psychol. Assn. (sec.-treas. 1969-76); mem. Southeastern Psychol. Assn., Sigma Xi. Club: Ecce Quo Bonum. Current Work: Experimental psychologist: psychological theory, personality studies, psychology of music, history of psychology. Subspecialties: Behavioral psychology; Learning. Home: Greens View Rd Sewanee TN 37375 Office: Univ Of South Sewanee TN 37375

LUNSFORD, CARL DALTON, pharmaceutical company executive; b. Richmond, Va., Feb. 11, 1927; s. Edward Burpee and Mabel Louise (Harris) L.; m. Audrey Strong, Jan. 11, 1947; children—Bonnie Kay Moyer, Jan Dalton Major, Debra Ann Webb. Student, Coll. William and Mary, 1944-45; B.S., U. Richmond, 1949, M.S., 1950; Ph.D., U. Va., 1953. Instr. chemistry U. Va., 1952-53; research chemist A. H. Robins Co., Inc., Richmond, 1953-57, asso. dir. chem. research, 1957-59, dir. chem. research, 1959-62, dir. labs. and chem. research, 1962-64, dir. research, 1964-66, asst. v.p., 1966-73, v.p., 1973-78, v.p. research and devel., 1978-80, sr. v.p. research and devel., 1980—; chmn. bd. Lee Labs., Inc., Petersburg, Va., 1976-84. Treas. U.S. Power Squadrons, 1976, sec., 1977, adminstrv. officer, 1978, exec. officer, 1979, comdr., 1980. Served with U.S. Army, 1945-46. Fellow AAAS, Am. Inst. Chemists; mem. Am. Chem. Soc., Va. Acad. Sci. (chmn. chemistry sect. 1965-66), N.Y. Acad. Sci., Sigma Xi, Sigma Pi Sigma, Gamma Sigma Epsilon, Phi Beta Kappa. Republican. Patentee in field. Subspecialties: Pharmaceutical research; Medicinal chemistry. Home: 904-A Palace Way Richmond VA 23233 Office: 1211 Sherwood Ave Richmond VA 23220

LUNT, OWEN RAYNAL, educator, biologist; b. El Paso, Tex., Apr. 8, 1921; s. Owen and Velma (Jackson) L.; m. Helen Hickman, Aug. 8, 1953; children: David, Carol, Janet. B.A. in Chemistry, 1947, Ph.D. in Agronomy, 1951. Mem. faculty UCLA, 1951—, prof. plant nutrition, 1964-72, prof. biology, 1972—, acting chmn. dept. biophysics, 1965-70; dir. Lab. Biomed. and Environ. Scis., 1968—. Served with USN, 1944-46. Fellow Am. Soc. Agronomy, Soil Sci. Soc. Am.; mem. Am. Soc. Plant Physiologists, Internat. Soc. Soil Sci., AAAS, Am. Nuclear Soc. (Los Angeles chpt.), Sigma Xi. Research in soil chemistry, fertility, plant physiology. Current Work: Research administration; soil chemistry, fertility and managemant. Subspecialties: Soil science; Plant physiology (biology). Home: 1200 Roberto Ln Los Angeles CA 90077 Office: 900 Veteran Ave Los Angeles CA 90024

LUO, REN-CHYUAN, engineering educator, researcher; b. Taoyuan, Republic of China, Sept. 8, 1949; came to U.S., 1982, naturalized, 1984; s. Chi-Hsin and I-Mei (Tsao) L.; m. Lan-Chien Hsueh, Sept. 5, 1976; children—Alice Luo. B.S., Feng-Chia U., Republic of China, 1973, M.S., 1975; M.S., Technische U., Berlin, 1980, Ph.D., 1982. Registered profl. engr., Berlin. Chief engr. Taichung Machinery Co., Republic of China, 1974-76; sci. research fellow Fraunhofer Inst., IPA, Berlin, 1977-80, Technische U., Berlin, 1980-82; project leader U. R.I., Kingston, 1982-83; asst. prof. elec. engring. U. Ill.-Chgo., 1983-84, N.C. State U., Raleigh, 1984—. Contbr. numerous articles to sci. jours. Recipient China-Germany Tech. Cooperative Research award Bundesministerium für Forschungs und Tech., 1976; research grantee Deutsche Forschungs Gemeinschaft, 1980. Mem. Chinese Soc. Engrs., Verein Deutsche Inginieure, Robotics Internat. Soc. Mfg. Engrs., IEEE. Subspecialties: Robotics; Sensory processes. Home: 1121 Ivy Ln Cary NC 27511 Office: Dept Electrical and Computer Engring NC State U PO Box 7911 Raleigh NC 27695

LUPASH, LAWRENCE O(VIDIU), computer analyst, researcher; b. Bucharest, Romania, May 29, 1942; came to U.S., 1980; s. Ovidiu N. and Stefania (Lebu) L.; m. Corina Constantineanu, Dec. 26, 1975. M.S., Poly. Inst. Bucharest, 1965, Ph.D., 1972. Project engr. Inst. for Automation, Bucharest, 1965-68, sr. engr., 1971-72; researcher Romanian Acad. Scis., Bucharest, 1968-71; sr. researcher/lectr. U. Bucharest, 1972-79; sr. analyst Intermetrics, Inc., Huntington Beach, Calif., 1980—; asst. prof. Poly. Inst. Bucharest, 1966-68, 71-72; vis. lectr. U. Tirana, Albania, 1973. Author: (with V. Ionescu) Numerical Techniques in System Theory, 2 vols, 1974; Contbr. articles to profl. publs. Mem. IEEE, Soc. Indsl. and Applied Math., Orange County Philatelic Soc., Am. Philatelic Soc. Greek Orthodox. Current Work: Numerical methods in system theory, mathematical software, computer-aided design of control systems, numerical analysis, simulations. Subspecialties: Mathematical software; Computer-aided design. Office: Intermetrics Inc 5312 Bolsa Ave Huntington Beach CA 92649

LUPIANI, DONALD ANTHONY, psychologist; b. N.Y.C., June 7, 1946; s. Louis and Josephine (Boccia) L.; m. Linda Moyik, June 1970; 1 dau., Jennifer. B.A., Iona Coll., 1968; M.A., Columbia U., 1971, Ph.D., 1973. Diplomate Am. Bd. Profl. Psychology, Am. Acad. Behavioral Medicine, Am. Bd. Profl. Psychotherapy. Postdoctoral Behavior Therapy Inst., White Plains, N.Y., 1974-76; Clin. intern Psychiat. Service Center, White Plains, 1974-76; adj. assoc. prof. Iona Coll., New Rochelle, N.Y., 1973—; psychologist Kaliski Sch., Bronx, 1979-80; clin. assoc. Tchrs. Coll. Columbia U., 1975—; psychologist Franciscans, N.Y.C., 1979—; dir. psychology and spl. edn. services Riverdale Country Sch., Bronx, 1973—. NIMH fellow, 1968-73. Fellow Am. Orthopsychiat.Assn., Am. Coll. Psycology; mem. Am. Psychol. Assn., Westchester Psychol. Assn., (chmn. ethics com.), N.Y. State Psychol. Assn., Nat. Assn. Sch. Psychologists; Mem. Am. Orthopsychiatry Assn. Roman Catholic. Current Work: Diagnosis and treatment of psychological disorders and learning difficulties. Subspecialties: Behavioral psychology; Clinical psychology. Home: 227 Square Mile Rd Yonkers NY 10701 Office: Riverdale Country Sch W 253d St and Fieldston Rd Riverdale NY 10471

LUPO, MICHAEL VINCENT, aeronautical engineer; b. St. Louis, May 6, 1952; s. Vincent Joseph and JoAnn Marie (Macke) L.; m. Marilyn Kay Kern, June 5, 1976; 1 dau., Maria Christine. B.S. in Aero. Engring, U. Mo., Rolla, 1975, M.S. in Engring. Mgmt, 1982. Gen. engr. U.S. Army, Texarkana, Tex., 1975-76, U.S. Army (U.S. Army Aviation Systems Command), St. Louis, 1976—. Mem. AIAA (sec. Rolla br. 1975), Planetary Soc. (founding mem.), Soc. Reliability Engring., Am. Helicopter Soc., Army Aviation Assn. Am., Am. Soc. for Engring. Mgmt. Roman Catholic. Current Work: Work in reliability and maintainability of aircraft; study political aspects of space enterprise. Subspecialties: Reliability and maintainability; Satellite studies. Home: 9332 Talbot St Saint Louis MO 63123 Office: US Army Aviation Systems Command 4300 Goodfellow St Saint Louis MO 63120

LUPULESCU, AUREL PETER, medical educator, researcher, physician; b. Manastiur, Banat, Romania, Jan. 1, 1923; came to U.S., 1967, naturalized, 1973; s. Peter Vichentie and Maria Ann (Dragan) L. M.D. magna cum laude, Sch. Medicine, Bucharest, Romania, 1950; Ph.D. in Biology, Faculty of Scis., U. Windsor, Ont., Can. Diplomate: Am. Bd. Internal Medicine. Chief Lab. Investigations, Inst. Endocrinology, Bucharest, 1950-67; research assoc. SUNY Downstate Med. Ctr., 1968-69; asst. prof. medicine Wayne State U., 1969-72, assoc. prof., 1973—; vis. prof. Inst. Med Pathology, Rome, 1967; cons. VA Hosp., Allen Park, Mich, 1971-73. Author: Steroid Hormones, 1958, Ultrastructure of Thyroid Gland, 1968, Hormones and Carcinogenesis, 1983; contbr. chpts., numerous articles to profl. publs. Mem. N.Y. Acad. Sci., AMA, Am. Soc. Cell Biology, Soc. Exptl. Biology and Medicine, AAAS. Republican. Current Work: Hormones and tumor biology; studies regarding role of hormones in carcinogenesis. Subspecialties: Endocrinology; Cancer research (medicine). Office: Wayne State U Sch Medicine 540 E Canfield Ave Detroit MI 48201

LURIA, SALVADOR EDWARD, biologist; b. Turin, Italy, Aug. 13, 1912; came to U.S., 1940, naturalized, 1947; s. David and Ester (Sacerdote) L.; m. Zella Hurwitz, Apr. 18, 1945; 1 son, Daniel. M.D., U. Turin, 1935. Research fellow Curie Lab., Inst. of Radium, Paris, 1938-40; research asst. surg. bacteriology Columbia U., 1940-42; successively instr., asst. prof., assoc. prof. bacteriology Ind. U., 1943-50; prof. bacteriology U. Ill., 1950-59; prof. microbiology M.I.T., 1959-64, Sedgwick prof. biology, 1964—, Inst. prof., 1970—, dir. center cancer research, 1972—; non-resident fellow Salk Inst. Biol. Studies, 1965—; lectr. biophysics U. Colo., 1950; Jesup lectr. zoology Columbia U., 1950; Nieuwland lectr. biology U. Notre Dame, 1959; Dyer lectr. NIH, 1963; with OSRD, Carnegie Instn., Washington, 1945-46. Author: A Slot Machine, a Broken Test Tube, 1984. Assoc. editor: Jour. Bacteriology, 1950-55; editor: Virology, from 1955; sect. editor: Biol. Abstracts, 1958-62; editorial bd.: Exptl. Cell Research Jour, 1948—; adv. bd.: Jour. Molecular Biology, 1958-64; hon. editorial adv. bd.: Jour. Photochemistry and Photobiology, 1961—. Guggenheim fellow Vanderbilt U. and Princeton U., 1942-43; Guggenheim fellow Pasteur Inst., Paris, 1963-64; Co-recipient Nobel prize for medicine, 1969. Mem. Am. Philos. Soc., Am. Soc. Microbiology (pres. 1967-68), Nat. Acad. Scis., Am. Acad. Arts and Scis., AAAS, Soc. Gen. Microbiology, Genetics Soc. Am., AAUP, Sigma Xi. Subspecialty: Microbiology. Home: 48 Peacock Farm Rd Lexington MA 02173 Office: Dept Biology MIT Cambridge MA 02139

LURIA, SAUL MARTIN, research psychologist, educator; b. Athol, Mass., Dec. 24, 1929; s. Maurice and Florence (Shefts) L.; m. Honi Surnamer, Apr. 7, 1963; children: David, Steven. B.S., U. Richmond, 1949; M.S., U. Pa., 1951, Ph.D., 1955. Dir. vision dept. Naval Submarine Med. Research Lab., Groton, Conn., 1957—; instr. U. New Haven, 1971-82. Served with U.S. Army, 1954-57. Current Work: Vision research. Subspecialties: Psychophysics; Behavioral psychology. Home: 35 Beacon Hill Dr Waterford CT 06385 Office: Naval Submarine Med Research Lab Submarine Base Groton CT 06349

LURIX, PAUL LESLIE, JR., chemist; b. Bridgeport, Conn., Apr. 6, 1949; s. Paul Leslie and Shirley Laurel (Ludwig) L.; m. Cynthia Ann Owens, May 30, 1970; children—Paul Christopher, Alexander Tristan, Einar Gabrielson. B.A., Drew U., 1971; M.S., Purdue U., 1973; postgrad., 1973—. Tech. dir. Analysts, Inc., Linden, N.J., 1976-77; chief chemist Caleb Brett USA, Inc., Linden, 1977-80; v.p. Tex. Labs., Inc., Houston, 1980-82; pres. Lurix Corp., Fulshear, Tex., 1982—; cons. LanData, Inc., Houston, 1980—, Nat. Cellulose Corp., Houston, 1981—, Met. Transit Authority, Houston, 1981—; v.p. Diesel King Corp., Houston, 1980-82. Contbr. article to profl. jour. Patentee distillate fuel additives. Mem. Am. Chem. Soc., ASTM, AAAS, Soc. Applied Spectroscopy, N.Y. Acad. Sci., Phi Kappa Phi, Phi Lambda Upsilon, Sigma Pi Sigma. Lodge: Kiwanis (pres., 1970-71). Current work: Infrared spectroscopy; data base programming for science and industrial applications. Subspecialties: Infrared spectroscopy; Information systems, storage, and retrieval (computer science). Home: 32602 Hepple White Dr Fulshear TX 77441 Office: Lurix Corp PO Box 148 Fulshear TX 77441

LUSAS, EDMUND WILLIAM, research food scientist, consultant; b. Woodbury, Conn., Nov. 25, 1931; s. Anton Frank and Damicele Anna (Kasputis) L.; m. Jeannine Marie Muller, Feb. 2, 1957; children—Daniel, Ann, Paul. B.S. in Dairy Product Mfg., U. Conn., 1954; M.S. in Food Tech., Iowa State U., 1955; Ph.D. in Food Tech., U. Wis.-Madison, 1958; M.B.A. in Exec. Programming, U. Chgo., 1972. Project leader cereal mixes Quaker Oats Co. Research Labs., Barrington, Ill., 1958-61, sect. mgr. canned pet foods, 1961-65, mgr. pet foods, 1965-72, mgr. sci. services, 1972-77; assoc. dir. food protein research devel. Ctr., Tex. A&M U., College Station, 1977-78, dir., 1978—. Contbr. articles to books and profl. jours. Fund raiser, exec. v.p., Lake Region YMCA, Crystal Lake, Ill., 1968-77. Gen. Foods Corp. grad. fellow, 1956, 57. Mem. Am. Oil Chemists' Soc. (assoc. editor jour. 1980—), Am. Chem. Soc., Inst. Food Technologists, Am. Assn. Cereal Chemsits, Am. Soc. Agrl. Engrs., Nutrition Today Soc., Guayule Soc. Am., Sigma Xi, Phi Tau Sigma. Current work: Processing and utilization research of agriculture crops, including process, quality and quality improvement, energy reduction, automation and sensors. Subspecialty: Food science and technology. Office: Food Protein Research Devel Ctr Tex A&M U FM-183 College Station TX 77843

LUST, ROBERT MAURICE, physiologist, educator; b. Rantoul, Ill., Aug. 20, 1955; s. Robert Maurice and Margaretta Regina (McLaughlin) L.; m. Carol Ann White, June 26, 1978; children—Catherine Colleen, Jennifer Ann. B.A., Hamilton Coll., 1977; Ph.D., Tex. Tech. U., 1981. Research asst. Tex. Tech. U., Health Scis. Ctr., Lubbock, 1977-79, cardiology research fellow, 1981-83, asst. prof. internal medicine, asst. prof. physiology, 1983—, dir. cardiology research labs., 1983—. Head coach Tex. Tech. U. Soccer Team, 1978—; coaching tchr. North Tex. State Soccer assn., 1980—, staff coach state amateur teams, 1980—. NIH fellow, 1979-81; Inst. Biomed. Research grantee, 1982, 83, 84. Mem. Am. Physiol. Soc., Shock Soc. (Young Investigator 1982), AAAS (sec. biomed. sect. southwestern and Rocky Mountain div. 1984-86), Sigma Xi. Current work: Relationship between changes in rate and strength of cardiac function; responses of cardiac muscle to stresses, including altitude, shock and ischemia. Subspecialties: Physiology (medicine); Cardiology. Home: 4412 17th St Lubbock TX 79416 Office: Tex Tec U Health Scis Ctr Dept Internal Medicine Lubbock TX 79430

LUSTIG, STANLEY, chemist; b. Bklyn., Feb. 23, 1933; s. Sam and Edna (Solomon) L.; m. Delores Goldberg, Feb. 21, 1960; children—Rochelle, Mark. B.S., U. Toledo, 1958. Chemist Save Electric Co., Toledo, 1958; research chemist Union Carbide Corp., Chgo., 1959-72, mgr. research and devel., 1973—. Contbr. articles to profl. jours. Patentee in field. Served with U.S. Army, 1954-56. Mem. Am. Chem. Soc., Soc. Plastic Engrs., Packaging Inst. Am. Current work: Research and development plastic packaging; product and process design and manufacturing. Subspecialties: Polymer engineering; Polymers (materials science). Home: 561 Lakewood Blvd Park Forest IL 60466 Office: Union Carbide Corp Films Packaging Div 6733 W 65th St Chicago IL 60638

LUSZTIG, GEORGE, mathematician. Prof. math. MIT, Cambridge. Recipient Cole prize in algebra Am. Math. Soc., 1985. Subspecialty: Algebra and number theory. Office: MIT Dept Math Cambridge MA 02139

LUTAS, ELIZABETH M., physician, educator; b. N.Y.C., Oct. 2, 1951; d. Michael and Maria (Dano) L. B.A., N.Y.U., 1972, M.D. with honors, 1976. Diplomate: Am. Bd. Internal Medicine, Nat. Bd. Med. Examiners. Intern N.Y.U. Med. Center, N.Y.C., 1976-77, resident, 1977-79, instr. medicine, 1977-81, fellow in cardiology, 1979-81; research fellow in cardiology, instr. medicine N.Y. Hosp-Cornell U. Med. Center, N.Y.C., 1981-82, asst. prof. internal medicine, 1982—. Mem. ACP, Am. Coll. Cardiology, Am. Fedn. Clin. Research. Current Work: Extensive research on hypertension, mitral valve prolapse. Subspecialties: Cardiology; Internal medicine. Office: NY Hosp-Cornell Med Ctr 525 E 68th St New York NY 10021

LUTH, WILLIAM CLAIR, geoscience administrator, researcher; b. Winterset, Iowa, June 28, 1934; s. William Henry Luth and Ora Anna (Klingaman) Sorenson; m. Betty Lou Heubrock, Aug. 23, 1953; children: Linda Diane, Robert William, Sharon Jean. B.A., U. Iowa, 1958; M.S., 1960; Ph.D., Pa. State U., 1963. Research assoc. Pa. State U., 1963-65; asst. prof. MIT, 1965-68; assoc. prof. geology Stanford U., 1968-77, prof., 1977-79; geoscientist Dept. Energy, 1976-78; div. supr. Sandia Nat. Labs., Albuquerque, 1979-82, mgr. geoscis. dept., 1982—; Alfred P. Sloan research fellow MIT, 1966-68; cons. Council on Environ. Quality, Washington, 1978; mem. vis. staff Los Alamos Labs., 1978. Contbr. chpts. to books, articles to profl. jours. Served to cpl. U.S. Army, 1953-56. Fellow Geol. Soc. Am., Mineral. Soc. Am.; mem. Am. Geophys. Union, Geochem. Soc., Sigma Xi. Republican. Current Work: Crystallization of the igneous rocks, experimental petrology, radioactive waste disposal, geochemical aspects of in situ fossil fuel utilization. Subspecialties: Geochemistry; Geothermal power. Home: 1600 La Cabra Dr SE Albuquerque NM 87123 Office: Sandia Nat Labs Geosci Dept 1540 Albuquerque NM 87185

LUTHY, RICHARD GODFREY, civil engineering educator, b. Buffalo, June 11, 1945; s. Robert Godfrey Luthy and Marian (Ireland) Haines; m. Mary Frances Sullivan, Nov. 22, 1969; children—Matthew Robert, Mara Catherine, Jessica Bethlin. B.S. in Chem. Engring., U. Calif.-Berkeley, 1967; M.S. in Ocean Engring., U. Hawaii, 1969; M.S. in Civil Engring., U. Calif.-Berkeley, 1974, Ph.D. in Civil Engring., 1976. Registered profl. engr., Pa. Resident aide Stanford U., Calif., 1967; grad. asst. IBM, Honolulu, 1968; research asst. dept. ocean engring. U. Hawaii, Honolulu, 1968-69, dept. civil engring. U. Calif., Berkeley, 1974-75; asst. prof. to assoc. prof. Carnegie-Mellon U., Pitts., 1975-83, prof. civil engring., 1983—; cons. Dept. Energy, Washington, 1976—, EPA Sci. Adv. Bd., Washington, 1983, various corps., 1978—. Contbr. articles to profl. jours. Tech. advisor Allegheny County Health Dept., Pitts., 1977—. Served to lt. USN, 1969-72. Mem. Water Pollution Control Fedn. (Eddy medal 1980), Assn. Environ. Engring. Profs. (Nalco award 1978, 82), Am. Water Works Assn., Internat. Assn. Water Pollution Research, ASCE. Republican. Presbyterian. Current work: Industrial water and waste water treatment; aquatic chemistry; environmental engineering problems in groundwater contamination. Subspecialties: Water supply and wastewater treatment; Hazardous waste disposal. Home: 7001 Reynolds St Pittsburgh PA 15208 Office: Dept Engring Carnegie-Mellon U Pittsburgh PA 15208

LUTTRELL, ERIC MARTIN, geologist; b. Wheeling, W.Va., May 12, 1941; s. L. Robert and Gertrude D. (Olson) L.; m. Janet Marie Quigg, June 8, 1963; children—Dawn A., Brooke C. B.S. in Geology, U. Wis.-Madison, 1963, M.S. in Geology, 1965; Ph.D. in Geology, Princeton U., 1967. Research geologist Texaco Inc., Houston, 1969-76, asst. supr., 1976-79, sr. exploration geologist, New Orleans, 1979-80; div. geologist Sohio Petroleum Co., Dallas, 1980-82, asst. exploration mgr., 1982-84, project mgr.-exploration, 1984—, Mem. Am. Assn. Petroleum Geologists, Geol. Soc. Am., Soc. Econ. Paleontologists and Mineralogists, Dallas Geol. Soc. Lutheran. Current work: Exploration and development of stratigraphically entrapped petroleum accumulations utilizating advanced techniques of stratigraphic seismic. Subspecialties: Sedimentology; Petroleum engineering. Office: Sohio Petroleum Corp 5420 LBJ Freeway Dallas TX 75240

LUTZ, BARRY LAFEAN, research astronomer, educator; b. Windsor, Pa., Jan. 2, 1944; s. Ray D. and Nina C. (Bull) L.; m. Karen L. Witman, Sept. 3, 1966 (div.); m. Mary Susanna Maxwell, July 25, 1981. B.S. magna cum laude, Lebanon Valley Coll., 1965; A.M., Princeton U., 1965, Ph.D., 1968. Postdoctoral fellow Nat. Research Council Can., Ottawa, 1968-70; research astronomer Lick Obs., U. Calif.-Santa Cruz, 1970-71; sr. research assoc., adj. asst. prof., then adj. asso. prof. SUNY-Stony Brook, 1971-77, adj. asso. prof., 1977-81; astronomer Lowell Obs., Flagstaff, Ariz., 1977—; adj. assoc. prof. physics Ariz. State U., 1981-83, adj. prof., 1983—. Contbr. articles to profl. publs. Democratic town committeeman, 1972-78; nat. del. Dem. Conv., 1974. NSF grantee, 1972, 74, 76, 77, 78, 80, 82, 84, 85; NASA grantee, 1977-85. Mem. Am. Astron. Soc., Astron. Soc. Pacific, Internat. Astron. Union, Sigma Xi. Subspecialties: Optical astronomy; Planetary science. Home: 3330 Gillenwater Dr Flagstaff AZ 86001 Office: Lowell Obs Mars Hill Rd 1400 W Flagstaff AZ 86001

LUTZ, JULIE HAYNES, astronomy educator; b. Mount Vernon, Ohio, Dec. 17, 1944; d. Willard Damon and Julia Awilda (Way) Haynes; m. Thomas Edward Lutz, July 8, 1966; children—Melissa, Clea. B.A., San Diego State U., 1965; M.S., U. Ill., 1968, Ph.D., 1971. Prof. Astronomy Wash. State U., Pullman, 1984—. Contbr. articles to profl. jours. Fellow Royal Astron. Soc.; mem. Internat. Astron. Union, Am. Astron. Soc., Astron. Soc. of Pacific. Current work: Optical and satellite ultraviolet observations of planetary nebulae and symbiotic stars. Subspecialty: Optical astronomy. Office: Program in Astronomy Wash State U Pullman WA 99164-2930

LUTZ, PAUL EUGENE, Invertebrate ecologist, biology educator; b. Hickory, N.C., June 25, 1934; s. Cy Emmet and Ruth May (Karriker) L.; m. Alice Patterson, June 8, 1957 (div. Oct. 1977); 1 child, Carol S. Lutz Freyermuth. A.B., Lenoir-Rhyne Coll., 1956, L.H.D. (hon.), 1983; M.S., U. Miami, 1958; Ph.D., U. N.C., 1962. Faculty mem. U. N.C., Greensboro, 1961—, assoc. prof., 1966-70, prof. invertebrate ecology, 1970—. Author: (with Paul Santmire) Ecological Renewal, 1972. Contbr. articles to profl. jours. Trustee Lenoir-Rhyne Coll., Hickory, N.C., 1963-81, 84—; mem. mgmt. com., div. for mission in N.Am., Lutheran Ch. in Am., 1972-80, mem. mgmt. com. div. parish services, 1980—; NSF grantee, 1965, 69. Mem. Ecol. Soc. Am., Assn. Southeastern Biologists, Am. Inst. Biol. Sci., N.C. Acad. Sci., Sigma Xi. Democrat. Current work: Effects of light (photoperiod) and temperature as they affect the rates of growth and maturity (seasonal regulation) in Odonata nymphs. Subspecialties: Ecology (biology); Population biology. Office: Dept Biology U NC-Greensboro 1000 Spring Garden St Greensboro NC 27412

LUUS, REIN, chemical engineer, educator; b. Tartu, Estonia, Mar. 8, 1939; emigrated to Can., 1949, naturalized, 1955; s. Edgar and Aili (Prakson) L.; m. Taina Hilkka Inkeri Jaakola, June 17, 1973; children—Brian Markus, Kristina Annika. B.A., M.A. in Sci, U. Toronto, 1962; A.M., Princeton U., 1963, Ph.D., 1964. Fellow in chem. engring. Princeton U., 1964-65; asst. prof. chem. engring. U. Toronto, Ont., 1965-68, assoc. prof., 1968-74, prof., 1974—; dir. Chem. Engring. Research Cons. Ltd., Toronto, Ont., Can., 1966—; cons. in field.; Nat. Research Council Can. sr. fellow Steel Co. Canada, 1972-73; vis. assoc. Calif. Inst. Tech., 1979-80. Author: (with L. Lapidus) Optimal Control of Engineering Processes, 1967. Recipient E.W. R. Steacie prize NRC, Can., 1976. Fellow Chem. Inst. Can.; mem. Can. Soc. for Chem. Engring. (ERCO award 1980), Assn. Profl. Engrs. Ont., Sigma Xi. Lutheran. Club: Hart House Squash. Current Work: Optimization of engineering processes,suboptimal control, model reduction and parameter estimation. Subspecialties: Chemical engineering; Operations research (engineering). Home: 65 Laurentide Dr Don Mills ON M3A 3E1 Canada Office: Dept Chem Engring U Toronto Toronto ON M5S 1A4 Canada

LUVALLE, JAMES ELLIS, chemistry educator, consultant, researcher; b. San Antonio, Nov. 10, 1912; s. James A.G. and Isabel (Ellis) LuV.; m. Jean Long, Feb. 2, 1946; children—John Vernon, Phyllis Ann, Michael James. B.S., UCLA, 1936, M.S., 1937; Ph.D., Calif. Tech. Inst., 1940. Instr. Fisk U., Nashville, 1940-41; sr. chemist, research assoc., Eastman Kodak, Rochester, N.Y., 1941-53; head photog. research Tech. Ops. Aytington, Burlington, Mass., 1953-59; dir. phys. and chem. research Fairchild Camera, Syosset, N.Y., 1959-68; tech. dir., research dir. S.C.M. Labs., Chgo., Palo Alto, Calif., 1968-69, 1969-75; dir. undergrad. labs. Stanford U. Chemistry Dept., Calif., 1975-82. Patentee in photog. field. Chmn. Boy Scout Troop Com. Syosset, N.Y., 1962-68; pres. Town Meeting Members, Lexington, Mass., 1957-59. Fellow Royal Chem. Soc., Am. Inst. Chemists; mem. Am. Chem. Soc., Soc. Neurosci., Am. Physiol. Soc. Democrat. Clubs: Cosmopolitan (Rochester, N.Y.) (pres. 1944-46), Eichler Swim and Tennis (Palo Alto) (pres. 1974-79). Current work: Neurobiology, graphics modeling (simulation). Subspecialties: Physical chemistry; Kinetics. Home: 3580 Evergreen Dr Palo Alto CA 94303 Office: Dept Chemistry Stanford Univ Stanford CA 94305

LUYENDYK, BRUCE PETER, marine geophysics educator; b. Freeport, N.Y., Feb. 23, 1943; s. Peter John and Francis Marie (Blakeney) L.; m. Linda Kay Taylor, Sept. 7, 1967 (div. Aug. 1979); children—Loren Taylor; m. Jaye Ellen Updegraff, Oct. 13, 1984. B.S., San Diego State U., 1965; Ph.D., Scripps Inst. Oceanography, 1969. Asst. scientist Woods Hole Oceanographic Instn., Mass., 1969-73; prof. marine geophysics U. Calif., Santa Barbara, 1973—. Contbr. articles to profl. jours. Recipient Newcomb Cleveland prize AAAS,

1980. Fellow Geol. Soc. Am.; mem. Am. Geophys. Union, Soc. Exploration Geophysicists. Democrat. Club: Coast Geol. Soc. (Ventura, Calif.) (treas. 1980-81). Current work: Paleomagnetic analysis of the tectonics of the western U.S. and New Zealand; structure of offshore California; sea floor spreading centers; Rio Grande rift. Subspecialties: Geophysics; Sea floor spreading. Home: 5245 James Rd Santa Barbara CA 93111 Office: U Calif Dept Geol Scis Santa Barbara CA 93106

LVOVSKY, EDWARD ABRAHAM, physician, researcher; b. Jassy, Romania, Jan. 17, 1937; came to U.S., 1974, naturalized, 1980; s. Abracham Boruch and Beila (Partugeis) L.; m. Valentina Geogia Deomichieva, Oct. 17, 1969; children: Boris, Paul. M.D., Leningrad (USSR) Med. Sch., 1961; Ph.D., Radiology Inst., Leningrad, 1967. Practice medicine, Inta, USSR, 1961-63, Leningrad, 1964; research scientist Radiology Inst., 1967-74; vis. scientist NIH, Bethesda, Md., 1974-79; house staff Md. U. Hosp., 1980, George Washington U. Hosp., Washington, 1981-83; asst. prof. radiation medicine Georgetown U., Washington, 1983—. Contbr. chpts. to books and articles to profl. jours. Fogarty fellow, 1974-76. Mem. Am. Soc. Therapeutic Radiologists, AMA, Am. Tissue Culture Assn. Democrat. Jewish. Current Work: Synthesis and biological effects of interferon inducers; patient care, reseach in field of interferon. Subspecialties: Immunopharmacology; Cancer research (medicine). Home: 1100 W Side Dr Gaithersburg MD 20878

LYGRE, DAVID GERALD, chemistry educator, administrator; b. Minot, N.D., Aug. 10, 1942; s. C. Gerald and Esther R. (Fossum) L.; m. Laurae Y. Johnson, Aug. 20, 1966; children—Jedd, Lindsay. B.A., Concordia Coll., 1964; Ph.D., U. N.D., 1968. Postdoctoral fellow Case Western Res. U., Cleve., 1968-70; asst. prof. chemistry Central Wash. U., Ellensburg, 1970-73, assoc. prof., 1973-80, prof., 1980—, asst. dean Coll. of Letters, Arts and Scis., 1981-83, assoc. dean, 1983—. Author: Life Manipulation, 1979. Contbr. numerous articles to profl. jours. Research Corp. research grantee, 1970; Am. Cancer Soc. fellow, 1969-70, NIH fellow, 1966-68. Mem. AAAS, Am. Chem. Soc., Sigma Xi. Current work: Enzymology of carbohydrate metabolism; biochemistry of aging; implications of new reproductive and genetic techniques. Subspecialty: Biochemistry (biology). Home: 805 B St Ellensburg WA 98926 Office: Central Wash U Dept Chemistry Ellensburg WA 98926

LYLE, ROBERT EDWARD, JR., chemistry research administrator; b. Atlanta, Jan. 26, 1926; s. Robert Edward and Adaline (Cason) L.; m. Gloria Gilbert, Aug. 28, 1947. B.A., Emory U., 1945, M.S., 1946; Ph.D., U. Wis.-Madison, 1949. Asst prof. chemistry Oberlin Coll., Ohio, 1949-51; asst. prof. then prof. U. N.H., Durham, 1951-77; prof., chmn. dept. chemistry North Tex. State U., Denton, 1977-78; v.p. div. chemistry and chem. engring. Southwest Research Inst., San Antonio, 1979—. Co-editor: Organic Electronic Spectral Data, 1969. Contbr. numerous articles to profl. jours. Patentee in field. Mem. Am. Chem. Soc. (councillor 1968-84, 86-88), Chem. Soc. (Eng.), AAAS, Am. Assn. Cancer Research, Phi Beta Kappa, Sigma Xi, Alpha Chi Sigma. Methodist. Subspecialties: Organic chemistry; Medicinal chemistry. Home: 12814 Kings Forest San Antonio TX 78230 Office: Southwest Research Inst 6220 Culebra Rd San Antonio TX 78284

LYMAN, GARY HERBERT, cell biologist, cancer researcher, educator; b. Buffalo, Feb. 24, 1946; s. Leonard Samuel and Beatrice Louise L.; m. Carolyn Gertrude Zalewski, Nov. 21, 1979; children by previous marriage: Stephen Leonard, Christopher Henry, Robert Dean. B.A., SUNY-Buffalo, 1968, M.D., 1972; M.P.H., Harvard U., 1982. Diplomate: Am. Bd. Internal Medicine (med. oncology, hematology). Resident in medicine U. N.C.-Chapel Hill, 1972-74; fellow in oncology Roswell Park Meml. Inst., Buffalo, 1974-77; research instr. medicine SUNY Med. Sch.-Buffalo, 1974-77; mem. faculty U. South Fla. Coll. Medicine, Tampa, 1977—, assoc. prof. medicine, 1980—, dir. div. med. oncology, 1979—. Co-author: Cancer Chemotherapy Therapeutics Agents: Handbook of Clinical Data, 2d edit, 1982; Contbr. articles to profl. jours., chpts. to books. Spl. fellow Leukemia Soc. Am., 1976-77; postdoctoral fellow biostats. Harvard U., 1981-82; spl. clin. fellow Roswell Park Meml. Inst., Buffalo, 1975-76. Fellow ACP, Am. Coll. Preventive Medicine, Am. Coll. Clin. Pharmacology; mem. Physicians for Social Responsibility. Current Work: Cancer clinical trials, biostatistics, epidemiology, clinical decision analysis. Subspecialties: Oncology; Epidemiology. Office: 12901 N 30th St Tampa FL 33549

LYMAN, JOHN, psychology and engineering educator; b. Santa Barbara, Calif., May 29, 1921; s. Oren Lee and Clara Augusta (Young) L. A.B. in Psychology and Math., UCLA, 1943, M.S., 1950, Ph.D. in Psychology, 1951. Research technician Lockheed Aircraft Corp., Burbank, Calif., 1940-43, mathematician, 1943-44; with dept. psychology UCLA, 1947—, asso. prof., 1957-63, prof., 1963—, from instr. to assoc. prof. Sch. Engring. and Applied Sci., 1950-63, prof. Sch. Engring. and Applied Sci., 1963—, chmn. engring. systems dept., 1978-84, head Biotech. Lab., 1958—; research engr. Inst. Traffic and Transp., 1967-73; vis. prof. bioengring. Technol. Inst., Delft, Netherlands, 1965; spl. cons. Nat. Acad. Scis., Washington, 1973; cons. VA, Los Angeles, 1962-66, 67-80, NIH, 1963-66, 68-73, med. devices div. FDA, 1976-79; dir. Perceptronics, Inc., Woodland Hills, Calif., other agys. and cos. Author chpts. in books, articles in profl. jours.; editor in field. Served to lt. (j.g.) U.S. Navy, 1944-46. Recipient numerous fellowships and grants. Fellow Am. Psychol. Assn., Soc. Engring. Psychologists, AAAS, Human Factors Soc. (Paul Fitts award 1971, pres. 1967-68); mem. Biomed. Engring. Soc. (pres. 1980-81), IEEE, Am. Soc. Engring. Edn., Sigma Xi, Tau Beta Pi. Subspecialties: Human factors engineering; Biomedical engineering. Office: UCLA 6532 Boelter Hall U Calif Los Angeles CA 90024

LYMAN, JOHN LESLIE, physical chemist, researcher; b. Delta, Utah, June 16, 1944; s. Frank Anderson and Virginia (Porter) L.; m. Jean Eliason, Aug. 9, 1968; children—Michael, Roger, Katherine, Jared, Jeanette. B.S., Brigham Young U., 1968, Ph.D., 1973. Staff mem. Los Alamos Nat. Lab, 1973-83, fellow, 1983—; guest prof. U. Bielefeld, Fed. Republic of Germany, summer 1980; vis. scientist Max Planck Inst. for Quantam Optics, summers 1982, 1984. Patentee Laser Isotope Separation, 1977. Contbr. numerous articles to profl. jours. Served with U.S. Army, 1969-71. Fellow NDEA, 1969, Associated Western Univs., 1971. Mem. Am. Chem. Soc., Optical Soc. Am. Republican. Mormon. Current work: Research on photochemical applications of lasers and basic research on laser-molecule interactions. Subspecialties: Laser-induced chemistry; Laser photochemistry. Home: 270 Donna Ave Los Alamos NM 87544 Office: Los Alamos Nat Lab MSJ567 PO Box 1663 Los Alamos NM 87545

LYNCH, DAVID WILLIAM, physicist; b. Rochester, N.Y., July 14, 1932; s. William Joseph and Eleanor Elizabeth (Fouratt) L.; m. Joan Noanie Hill, Aug. 29, 1954; children—Jean Louise, Richard William, David Allan. B.S., Rensselaer Poly. Inst., 1954; M.S., U. Ill., 1955, Ph.D., 1958. Asst. prof. physics Iowa State U., Ames, 1959-63, assoc. prof., 1963-66, prof., 1966—, chmn., 1985—; sr. physicist Ames Lab., U.S. Dept. Energy, 1966—; vis. scientist Italian Nat. Research Council, Rome, 1969; vis. prof. U. Hamburg, Federal Republic Germany, 1974; acting. assoc. dir. Synchrotron Rediation Ctr., U. Wis.-Stoughton, 1984. Contbr. articles to profl. jours., chpts. to books. Fulbright fellow, 1959. Fellow Am. Phys. Soc.; mem. Optical Soc. Am., AAAS. Current work: Experimental solid-state physics, optical properties of solids, photoemission spectroscopy, uses of synchrotron radiation. Subspecialty: Condensed matter physics. Home: 3315 Ross Rd Ames IA 50010 Office: Iowa State U Physics Dept Ames IA 50011

LYNCH, DENIS PATRICK, pathologist, educator; b. Kansas City, Kans., Oct. 5, 1951; s. Patrick Edward and Helen Mary (Dragastin) L.; m. Monica Colosimo, June 29, 1973; children: Sydney Alexis, Shannon Meredith. D.D.S., U. Calif.-San Francisco, 1976; cert. oral pathology, U. Ala.-Birmingham, 1978, postgrad., 1977—. Sr. intern in oral medicine U. Calif.-San Francisco, 1975-76; resident in anatomic pathology U. Ala.-Birmingham, 1976-77, chief resident in oral pathology, 1977-78, NIH-Nat. Inst. Dental Research postdoctoral fellow, 1977-80; asst. prof. pathology and radiology U. Tex. Dental Br., Houston, 1981—. Editorial bd.: Jour. Dental Edn, 1978-81; cons. editor: Dental Student Mag, 1981—. Tchr. Confrat. of Christian Doctrine, Birmingham, Ala., 1978-81, Houston, 1981—. U. Calif.-San Francisco Pres.'s scholar, 1972; Regent's scholar, 1973-76; named Outstanding Instr. U. Ala.-Birmingham, 1977. Mem. Am. Assn. Dental Schs. (v.p. and mem. exec. com. 1977-79, Recognition award 1981), Internat. Assn. Dental Research, Houston Soc. Clin. Pathology, Omicron Kappa Upsilon. Roman Catholic. Current Work: Immunopathology and treatment of mucocutaneous disease; nutritional effects on immune response; secretory immunology and dental caries, diagnosis and treatment of oral manifestations of AIDS. Subspecialties: Oral pathology; Pathology (medicine). Home: 10923 Atwell Houston TX 77096 Office: U Tex Dental Br PO Box 20068 Houston TX 77225

LYNCH, FRANK WILLIAM, aerospace company executive; b. San Francisco, Nov. 26, 1921; s. James Garfield and Med (Kelly) L.; m. Marilyn Leona Hopwood, June 24, 1950; children—Kathyn Leona, Molly Louise. A.B., Stanford U., 1943, postgrad., 1946-48.; LL.D. (hon.), Northrop U., 1984. Research engr. Boeing Airplane Co., Seattle, 1948-50; with Northrop Corp., Hawthorn, Calif., 1950-57, Los Angeles, 1959—, sr. v.p. ops. corp. hdqrs., 1974-78, sr. v.p. and group exec. Tactical and Electronic Systems Group, 1978-82, pres., chief operating officer, 1982—; div. v.p. engring. Lear-Siegler Corp., Anaheim, Calif., 1957-59. Served with AC U.S. Army, 1942-46. Mem. IEEE, AIAA, Assn. U.S. Army, Navy League, Air Force Assn., Am. Def. Preparedness Assn. Clubs: Balboa Yacht (Newport Beach, Calif.); Regency (Los Angeles). Home: 1933 Altura Dr Corona Del Mar CA 92625 Office: 1840 Century Park E Los Angeles CA 90067

LYNCH, JOHN PATRICK, computer analyst; b. Morgantown, W.Va., Aug. 29, 1956; s. George Lamont and Marian (Cira) L. B.S., George Mason U., Fairfax, Va., 1979. Sr. mem. tech. staff Computer Scis. Corp., Silver Spring, Md., 1979—. Mem. Am. Astron. Soc. (assoc.), Am. Inst. Aeros. Astronautics, Sigma Pi Sigma, Alpha Chi. Republican. Current work: mission analysis, launch operations support, attitude and orbit control of geosynchronous meteorological satellites. Subspecialty: Satellite studies. Home: 2805 Hunter Mill Rd Oakton VA 22124 Office: Computer Scis Corp 8728 Colesville Rd Silver Spring MD 20910

LYNCH, NANCY ANN, computer scientist; b. Bklyn., Jan. 19, 1948; d. Roland David and Marie E. Evraets. B.S., Bklyn. Coll., 1968; Ph.D., MIT, 1972. Ellen Swallow Richards assoc. prof. computer sci. and engring. MIT, Cambridge, NSF fellow, 1972. Office: MIT Dept Computer Sci Cambridge MA 02139*

LYNCH, ROBERT EMMETT, JR., chemistry educator, educational and psychological consultant; b. Ridgewood, N.J., Sept. 1, 1955; s. Robert Emmett and Kathryn (Duncan) L. B.S. in Behavioral Sci., U. Houston-Clear Lake, 1982, postgrad., 1983; postgrad. William Paterson Coll., 1984. Adolescent milieu therapist Baytown Med. Ctr., Tex., 1979-82, summer 1983; psychiat. technician Deer Park Hosp., Tex., 1981-82; tchr. sci. and math. St. Joseph's Sch., Baytown, 1982-83; tchr. sci. Devonshire Sch., Mahwah, N.J., 1983—; psychol. and ednl. cons., 1983—. Chmn. acad. subcom. U. Houston-Clear Lake, 1982. Mem. N.Y. Acad. Scis., Southwestern Psychol. Assn., Nat. Sci. Tchrs. Assn., Nat. Council Tchrs. Math., Am. Psychol. Assn. (assoc.), Phi Theta Kappa. U.S. Tennis Assn. Club: Chess (pres., founder 1982-83). Current work: Educator in the field of biology and chemistry; educational and psychological consulting with students that are good students with one area of difficulty; studying adolescent suicide, causes and intervention strategies; analgesic effect of D-Phenylalanine in relation to Endorphines. Subspecialties: Learning; Neurobiology. Home: 76 N Franklin Turnpike Ho-Ho-Kus NJ 07423

LYNDS, CLARENCE ROGER, astronomer; b. Kirkwood, Mo., July 18, 1928. A.B., U. Calif., 1952, Ph.D. in Astronomy, 1955. Asst., Lick Obs., 1952; astronomer U. Calif., 1953-54, jr. research astronomer, assoc. astronomer, 1955-58; NRC Can. fellow Dominion Astrophys. Obs. Can., 1958-59; asst. astronomer Nat. Radio Astron. Obs., 1959-61; asst. astronomer Kitt Peak Nat. Obs., Tucson, after 1961—, assoc. astronomer, to 1968, astronomer, 1968—. Mem. Nat. Acad. Sci., Am. Astron. Soc., Royal Astron. Soc., Internat. Astron. Union. Subspecialty: Optical astronomy. Office: Kitt Peak Nat Obs PO Box 26732 Tucson AZ 85726

LYNDS-CHERRY, PATRICIA GAIL, psychologist; b. Woodlake, Calif., Feb. 7, 1950; d. Edgar David and Frances Jean (Eberle) L.; m. Albert Lee Cherry, Nov. 13, 1982. B.A., Calif. State U., 1972; M.A., U. Nebr., 1975, Ph.D., 1977; postgrad., U. Calif.-Davis, 1978-81. Project coordinator U. Calif.-Davis, 1979-80; psychologist Sacramento County Office Edn., 1980-81, Kings County Supt. of Schs., Hanford, Calif., 1981—. Contbr. articles to profl. jours. Chmn. Kings County Child Abuse Com., 1982. Maude Hammond Fling fellow U. Nebr., 1973-74. Mem. Am. Psychol. Assn., Calif. Assn. Sch. Psychologists and Psychometrists, Assn. Women in Sci., Women in Neursci. Club: VA-25 Officers Wives. Current work: Child abuse prevention and intervention, genetic bases of learning disabilities, spl. edn. for bilingual/bicultural students. Subspecialties: School psychology; Psychobiology. Office: Kings County Supt of Schools Government Center Hanford CA 93230

LYNN, GEORGE LESLIE, psychologist; b. N.Y.C., Oct. 4, 1947; s. Fred H. and Nellie K. (Riszcerles) L.; m. Cynthia Chase, June 1, 1985. B.A., Hunter Coll., 1971; M.A., Columbia U., 1972; Psy.D., Ill. Sch. Profl. Psychology, 1981. Diplomate: Am. Acad. Behavioral Medicine.; lic. psychologist, N.Y. Cert. psychotherapist. Counselor Bellevue Hosp., N.Y.C., 1973-74; psychologist South Beach Psychiat. Ctr., S.I., 1974-75; psychotherapist L.I. Consultation Ctr., Rego Park, 1975-76; counselor Northwestern U. Med. Ctr., Chgo., 1977-78; psychology intern Manhattan Psychiat. Ctr., Ward's Island, 1978-79; supr., psychotherapist Community Guidance Service, N.Y.C., 1975-84; supr., faculty Postgrad. Ctr. for Mental Health, N.Y.C., 1980-83; supr. Inst. for Human Identitiy, 1982-83; clin. instr. psychiatry New Sch. for Social Research, 1982-83; psychologist Metro. Hosp.-N.Y. Med. Coll., 1982—; supr. psychologist Inwood Community Services, 1983—. Contbr. articles to profl. jours.; commentator, WOR-Radio, Nighttalk Show, N.Y.C., 1980—. Cons. psychologist Lenox Hill Neighborhood Assn., N.Y.C., 1972-73; bd. govs. Commn. on Consumer and Patient Rights, 1979—. L.I. Cons. Center fellow, 1973-75. Fellow Am. Orthopsychiatric Assn., Am. Inst. Psychotherapy & Psychoanalysis; mem. Acad. Psychosomatic Medicine, Am. Acad. Psychotherapists, Am. Group Psychotherapy Assn., Am. Psychol. Assn., AAAS, N.Y. Acad. Sci., Biofeedback Soc. Am., Soc. Personality Assessment, Soc. Behavioral Medicine, Soc. Pediatric Psychology, Assn. for Birth Psychology, Assn. Applied Psychoanalysis. Inventor Draw-A-Group Test (personality assessment), 1981, Psychosomatic Therapy (psychol. treatment), 1975. Current Work: Research activities as relates to psychotherapy, psychosomatic disorders, and personality assessment. . Address: 165 E 89th St #3D New York NY 10128

LYNN, JEFFREY WHIDDEN, physics educator; b. Hackensack, N.J., Mar. 2, 1947; s. Theodore John and Francis (Whidden) L.; m. Linda Mayo, Dec. 23, 1964; children—Robert William, Heather Diane. B.S., Ga. Tech. Inst., 1969, M.S., 1970, Ph.D., 1974. Research asst. Oak Ridge Nat. Lab., 1972-74, guest scientist, 1983-84; research assoc. Brookhaven Nat. Lab., Upton, N.Y., 1974-76; invited researcher Institut Laue Langevin, Grenoble, France, 1983-84; prof. associe Universite de Grenoble, 1983-84; asst. prof. physics U. Md., College Park, 1976-79, assoc. prof., 1979—; cons. Nat. Bur. Standards, Gaithersburg, Md., 1976—; guest scientist CNRS, Grenoble, 1983-84. Contbr. numerous articles to physics jours. Recipient Creativity award NSF, 1981, grantee, 1976—; recipient U. Md. research award, 1978; Nat. Bur. Standards grantee, 1984—. Mem. Am. Phys. Soc., Am. Inst. Physics, AAAS, Greater Washington Colloquium Com. (sec. 1979-80). Republican. Presbyterian. Current work: Neutron scattering measurements to determine the microscopic properties of matter, especially magnetic phenomena; fundamental properties of the neutron. Subspecialties: Condensed matter physics; Particle physics. Office: Dept Physics U Md College Park MD 20742

LYNN, JESSE LYNCH, JR., chemist, technology development manager; b. Shelbyville, Tenn., July 19, 1944; s. Jesse Lynch and Olive Jean (Paty) L.; m. Ann Rucker, June 15, 1966 (dec. 1982); m. Mary Martha Dofflemyer, May 31, 1983; children—Jesse Lynch, III, Nathan Bradley; stepchildren—Philip Andes, Michael Richards, Sharon O'Dell Baugh. B.S., Davidson Coll., 1966; Ph.D., Ohio State U., 1971. NIH predoctoral fellow Ohio State U., Columbus, 1967-71; NIH postdoctoral fellow Harvard U., Cambridge, Mass., 1971, Dartmouth Med. Sch., Hanover, N.H., 1972; asst. prof. Ga. State U., Atlanta, 1974-75; Sci. Research Council fellow Oxford U., Eng., 1975-76; research scientist Lever Bros., Edgewater, N.J., 1977-81, mgr. phys. chemistry, 1981-82, mgr. laundry detergent, 1982—. Contbr. articles to profl. jours. and revs. to ency. Reviewer Jour. Organic Chemistry, 1971-73. Assoc. editor Jour. Am. Oil Chemists Soc., 1984—. Vice pres. PTA, Englewood, N.J., 1979. Mem. Am. Chem. Soc., Sigma Xi, Gamma Sigma Upsilon. Democrat. Episcopalian. Clubs: Les Amis du Vin (Closter, N.J.); Applachian Trail Conf. Current work: Surfactants and detergency; kinetics and reaction mechanisms. Subspecialty: Surface chemistry. Home: 140 Cambridge Ave Englewood NJ 07631 Office: Lever Bros Research & Devel Ctr 45 River Rd Edgewater NJ 07020

LYNN, WALTER ROYAL, civil engineering educator, university administrator; b. N.Y.C., Oct. 1, 1928; s. Norman and Gussie (Gdalin) L.; m. Barbara Lee Campbell, June 3, 1960; children: Michael Drew. B.S., U. Miami, 1950; M.S., U. N.C., 1955; Ph.D., Northwestern U., 1963. Registered profl. engr., N.Y. State registered land surveyor, Fla. Land surveyor Ehly Constrn. Co., Miami, Fla., 1950-51; chief party Rader Engring. Co., Miami, 1951; supt. sewage treatment, lectr. civil engring. U. Miami, 1951-53, asst. prof. mech. engring., 1954-55, asst. prof. civil engring., 1955-57, research asst. prof. marine lab., 1957-58, assoc. prof. civil and indsl. engring., 1959-61; dir. research Ralph B. Carter Co., 1957-58; assoc. prof. san. engring. Cornell U., Ithaca, N.Y., 1961-64, prof. civil and environ. engring., 1964—, dir. Center Environ. Quality Mgmt., 1966-76, dir. Sch. Civil and Environ. Engring., 1970-78, dir. Program on Sci., Tech. and Society, 1980—, adj. prof. pub. health Med. Coll., 1971—; mem. spl. adv. commn. solid wastes NRC, 1968-76; com. to rev. Washington met. water supply study Nat. Acad. Engring., 1976-84, chmn., 1980-84; chmn. Bd. Water Sci. and Tech. NRC, 1982-85; cons. WHO, 1969—, Rockefeller Found., 1976—, SEARO, 1978. Editor: (with A. Charnes) Mathematical Analysis of Decision Problems in Ecology, 1975; assoc. editor: Jour. Ops. Research, 1968-76, Jour. Environ. Econs. and Mgmt, 1972—; Contbr.: chpt. to Human Ecology and Public Health, 1969; author articles. Chmn. Ithaca Mayor's Citizens Adv. Com., 1964-65, Ithaca Urban Renewal Agy., 1965-68; trustee Cornell U., 1980—; bd. dirs. Cornell Research Found., 1978—. Served with AUS, 1946-48. Fellow ASCE; mem. AAAS, Inst. Mgmt. Sci., Ops. Research Soc. Am., Nat. Acad. Engrs. Mex. (corr.), Sigma Xi, Phi Kappa Phi., Chi Epsilon. Current Work: Analysis of university /industrial research. Subspecialties: Civil engineering; Operations research (engineering). Home: 102 Iroquois Pl Ithaca NY 14850

LYNN, YEN-MOW, mathematics educator, researcher; b. Shanghai, China, Jan. 17, 1935; came to U.S., 1956; s. Thuinli and Pao-Chiung (Tcheng) L.; m. Helen Han, Sept. 5, 1964; children—Edward, Kirk, Genevieve. B.S., Nat. Taiwan U., 1955; M.S., Calif. Inst. Tech., 1957, Ph.D., 1961. Asst. then assoc. research scientist Courant Inst. Math. Sci., NYU, N.Y.C., 1960-64; assoc. prof. Ill. Inst. Tech., Chgo., 1964-67; assoc. prof. then prof. math. U. Md., Baltimore County, 1967—, chmn. dept. math., 1976-82; cons. NASA Ames Research Ctr., Moffett Field, Calif., 1966, sr. resident research assoc. Nat. Acad. Sci.-NRC, NASA Ames Research Ctr., summers, 1966, 67; cons. U.S. Army Ballistic Research Lab., Aberdeen, Md., 1969-75. Contbr. articles to profl. jours. Mem. Am. Math. Soc., Soc. Indsl. and Applied Math., Math. Assn. Am., Am. Phys. Soc., AAAS. Current work: Applied mathematics; magnetogasdynamics; rotating fluids; plasma physics. Office: U Md Baltimore County 5401 Wilkens Ave Baltimore MD 21228

LYON, L. JACK, wildlife research biologist, research administrator; b. Sterling, Colo., Oct. 31, 1929; s. Leslie and Pauline (Krambeck) L.; m. Natalie S. Allen, Nov. 23, 1956; children—Kendal, Kerry. B.Sc., Colo. State U., 1951, M.Sc., 1953; Ph.D., U. Mich., 1960. Cert. wildlife biologist, Wildlife Soc. Research biologist Colo. Game Dept., Fort Collins, 1955-62; project leader U.S. Forest Service, Missoula, Mont., 1962—. Assoc. editor Jour. Wildlife Mgmt., 1983-85. Contbr. articles to profl. jours. Served to cpl. U.S. Army, 1953-55. Current work: Wildlife habitat. Subspecialty: Ecology (environmental science). Office: U S Forest Service Forestry Sci Lab Box 8089 Missoula MT 59807

LYON, WALTER ALPHONS, engineering educator, consultant; b. Cologne, Germany, June 26, 1924; came to U.S., 1939, naturalized, 1944; s. Ludwig Paul and Otilie (David) L.; m. Ann Durr, May 19, 1951; children—Nancy, Clifford, Paul, James. B.E., Johns Hopkins U., 1947, M.S.E. in San. Engring., 1948; postgrad. Am. U., Washington, 1950-53. Registered profl. engr., Pa. With USPHS, Washington, 1950-54; asst. chief environ. health sect. Phila. Dept. Pub. Health, 1954-57; asst. dir. Div. San. Engring., Pa. Dept. Health, 1957-58, dir. Div. San. Engring, 1958-70; dir. Bur. Water Quality Mgmt., Pa. Dept. Environ. Resources, 1971-79, dep. sec. planning, 1979-83; adj. prof. civil engring. U. Pa., 1983—; cons. environ. and water resources, 1983—; mem. sci. adv. bd. Internat. Joint Commn., 1983—; v.p. Law and Planning Inst., 1984—. Contbr. articles to profl. jours. Trustee Unitarian Ch. Harrisburg, Pa., 1966-68; pres. Conodoquinet Civic Assn., 1967-78, Central Pa. Internat. Ctr., 1979-81; bd. dirs. Mus. Sci. Discovery, 1981—, pres., 1983-84. Served with U.S. Army, 1944-46. Recipient Karl M. Mason award for creativity in environ. mgmt., 1980. Fellow ASCE (numerous coms.), Am. Pub. Health Assn.; mem. Am. Acad. Environ. Engrs., Assn. State and Interstate Water Pollution Control Adminstrs. (bd. dirs. 1977-79), Conf. State San. Engrs., Water Pollution Control Fedn., Pa. Pub. Health Assn., Am. Water Works Assn., Am. Soc. Pub. Adminstrn., Am. Pub. Works Assn. (pres. central Pa. chpt. 1965-66), AAAS, Pa. Soc. Profl. Engrs., Pa. Water Works Operators Assn., Caribbean Conservation Assn. Unitarian. Club: Torch (Harrisburg). Current work: Water quality management, water resources management, environmental management. Subspecialty: Environmental engineering.

LYONS, JOHN W(INSHIP), government agency administrator, chemist; b. Reading, Mass., Nov. 5, 1930. A.B. in Chemistry, Harvard U., 1952; A.M. in Phys. Chemistry, Washington U., St. Louis, 1963, Ph.D. in Phys. Chemistry, 1964. With Monsanto Co., 1955-73, group leader, sect. mgr. research dept., inorganic chems. div., 1962-69, mgr. comml. devel., head fire safety center, 1969-73; mem. ad hoc panel on fire research Nat. Bur. Standards, Washington, 1971-73, dir. Center for Fire Research, 1973-77, Inst. Applied Tech., 1977-78, Nat. Engring. Lab., 1978—, acting dep. dir. Nat. Bur. Standards, 1983; chmn. Products Research Com. (trust which adminstrs. fire research funds), 1974-79; bd. dirs. Nat. Fire Protection Assn., 1978; vis. lectr. various univs.; co-chmn. U.S.-Japan Natural Resources Panel on Fire Research, 1975-78; mem. adv. com. on engring. NSF, 1981—; mem. adv. council U. Md. Coll. Engring., 1980—. Author: Viscosity and Flow Measurement, 1963, The Chemistry and Uses of Fire Retardants, 1970; Fire, 1985; contbr. numerous articles to profl. publs. Served with U.S. Army, 1953-54. Recipient Gold medal Dept. Commerce, 1977, Pres.'s Mgmt. Improvement award White House, 1978, Pres.'s Disting. Exec. Rank award, 1981. Fellow AAAS, Washington Acad. Sci.; mem. Nat. Acad. Engring., Am. Chem. Soc. (chmn. St. Louis sect. 1971-72), Am. Inst. Chem. Engrs., Sigma Xi. Current Work: Director National Engineering Laboratory, National Bureau of Standards. Subspecialty: Engineering research administration. Office: Nat Engring Lab Nat Bur Standards Gaithersburg MD 20899

LYONS, KENNETH PAUL, nuclear medicine physician and, educator; b. Worcester, Mass., Nov. 12, 1938; s. William Patrick and Jean (Mattson) L.; m. Joanna Harris, Sept. 5, 1975; children: James, Kathleen, Kevin, Michael. B.S., Loyola U., Los Angeles, 1961; M.D., Creighton U., 1965. Diplomate: Am. Bd. Nuclear Medicine. Intern St. Joseph Hosp., Omaha, 1965-66; resident in internal medicine Harbor Gen. Hosp., Los Angeles, 1968-71; instr., fellow in nuclear medicine UCLA, 1971-73; asst. prof. radiol. scis. U. Calif.-Irvine, 1973-81, assoc. prof., 1981—; chief nuclear medicine Long Beach VA Med. Ctr., 1973—; dept. assoc. dir. 1982; prin. investigator VA, 1981—. Author: Cardiovascular Nuclear Medicine, 1981; editor: Atlas of Nuclear Medicine, 1981, Jour. Clin. Nuclear Medicine, 1975—; contbr. over 100 articles to med. jours. Served to capt. USAF, 1966-68. Research fellow USPHS, 1962-66. Mem. Soc. Nuclear Medicine (sec./treas. So. Calif. chpt. 1982-83, pres. elect 1983-84, pres. 1984), Am. Coll. Nuclear Physicians (sec.-treas. 1984-85). Republican. Roman Catholic. Current Work: Detection and assessment of coronary artery disease; development of miniature avalanche radiation detectors. Subspecialties: Nuclear medicine; Internal medicine. Office: Long Beach VA Med Ctr 5901 E 7th St Long Beach CA 90822

LYONS, MICHAEL JOSEPH, microbiologist, virologist, educator; b. Cork, Ireland, Sept. 16, 1930; came to U.S., 1960, naturalized, 1973; s. Michael J. and Margaret M. (Hopkins) L.; m. Yvonne J. T. Barnett, Sept. 7, 1960; children: Fiona, Conor, Patricia, Desmond. B.S., Nat. U. Ireland, 1953, M.S., 1954; Ph.D., U. Glasgow, Scotland, 1959. Research assoc. Rockefeller Univ., N.Y.C., 1961-66; asst. prof. dept. microbiology Sch. Medicine, U. Pa., Phila., 1966-68; asst. prof. Cornell U. Med. Coll., N.Y.C., 1968-76; adj. assoc. prof. Lab of Bacteriology and Immunology Rockefeller U., N.Y.C.; assoc. dir. Center for Natural Scis., N.Y. Inst. Tech., Old Westbury, N.Y. Contbr. articles on microbiology/virology and chem. carcinogenesis to profl. jours. USPHS fellow, 1961-63; NIH grantee, 1969-73; Nat. Multiple Sclerosis Soc. grantee, 1978-82. Mem. Harvey Soc., Am. Soc. for Microbiology, Sigma Xi. Club: Brit. Schs. and Univs. (N.Y.C.). Current Work: Virus-induced obesity, pathogenesis of multiple sclerosis. Subspecialties: Neuroimmunology; Virology (medicine). Home: 53 Eiler Ln Irvington NY 10533 Office: Rockefeller U 1230 York Ave New York NY 10021

LYONS-RUTH, KARLEN, research psychologist, educator; b. Sheffield, Ala., Aug. 21, 1945; d. Vernon Everett and Helen (Karlen) L.; m. William Atkinson Ruth, Aug. 11, 1973; children: Adrienne, Gregory. B.A., Duke U., 1967; Ph.D., Harvard U., 1974. Fellow Boston U. Med. Sch., 1974-77; instr. psychology Harvard U. Med. Sch., Cambridge, Mass., 1977—; psychologist Cambridge Hosp., 1977-80, prin. investigator social devel. project, 1981—; dir. Family Support Project, Somerville, Mass., 1980—. Research grantee NIMH, 1977, 80; recipient New Investigator award Nat. Inst. Child Health and Human Devel., 1981. Mem. Am. Psychol. Assn., Soc. for Research in Child Devel. Current Work: Social development, developmental psychopathology, effectiveness of prevention services for infants at risk for emotional disorder. Subspecialty: Developmental psychology. Office: Dept Psychology Cambridge Hosp 1493 Cambridge St Cambridge MA 02139

LYTLE, JAMES MARK, electronic kits and educational products company executive, consultant; b. Pitts., Sept. 16, 1939; s. William Allen and Mary Elizabeth (Leahey) L.; m. Katherine Martha Rausch, Feb. 21, 1964; children: Mark, David, Susan. B.S., Capitol Inst. Tech., 1968. Engr. RCA Service Co., Bendix, McGraw Hill, 1967-79; design engr. Heath Co., St. Joseph, Mich., 1979-82, product line mgr., 1982—. Served with USN, 1957-67. Current Work: Defining hi-technology electronic products to be used for educational purposes. Subspecialties: Electronics; Robotics. Home: 5780 Echo Ridge Stevensville MI 49127 Office: Heath Co Hilltop Rd St Joseph MI 49085

MA, DAVID I., research physicist; b. Taipei, Taiwan, June 14, 1952; came to U.S., 1977, naturalized, 1985; s. Peter P.Y. and Iris (Di) M.; m. Josephine Yung, Oct. 24, 1981; 1 child, Peter H. B.S. in Physics, Tung Hai U., 1975; M.S. in Physics, U. Md., 1981. Teaching asst. U. Md., 1977-81; research physicist Sachs Freeman Assoc. Inc., Bowie, Md., 1981—. Mem. Am. Phys. Soc. Mem. Christian Ch. Current work: Device and circuit modeling for both MOSFET and MESFET; design test pattern and test results; x-ray lothography. Subspecialties: Microelectronics; Condensed matter physics. Home: 975 N Quantico St Arlington VA 22205 Office: Naval Research Lab Code 6804 4555 Overlook Ave SW Washington DC 20375

MA, TSO-PING, electrical engineering educator, researcher; b. Lan-Chou, Kan-Su, Republic of China, Nov. 13, 1945; came to U.S., 1969, s. Liang-Kway and Zwui-Yuen (Liu) M.; m. Pin-fang Lin, June 10, 1972; children—Hau, Jasmine Y. B.S., Nat. Taiwan U., Taipei, 1968; M.S., Yale U., 1972, Ph.D., 1974. Research asst. Yale U., New Haven, 1970-74, vis. lectr., 1976-77, asst. prof. elec. engring., 1977-80, assoc. prof., 1980-85, prof., 1985—; sr. assoc. engr. IBM Corp., Hopewell Junction, N.Y., 1974-75, staff engr., 1975-77; cons. Burroughs Corp., San Diego, 1978-79, Rockwell Internat., Anaheim, Calif., 1979-83; session chmn. Semiconductor Interface Specialist Conf., 1979, 83. Contbr. articles to profl. jours., chpt. to book. Inventor MOS processes, 1975. Pres. Yale Chinese Student Assn., 1972; faculty advisor Yale Chinese Student Service, 1980-84; bd. dirs. New Haven Chinese Culture Assn., 1983-84. Recipient Harding Bliss award Yale U., 1975; Cottrell research grantee, 1978. Mem. IEEE (sr.), Am. Phys. Soc., Electrochem. Soc., Sigma Xi. Club: Yale Figure Skating. Subspecialties: Semiconductors; Microchip technology (materials science). Office: Yale Univ Dept Elec Engring 15 Prospect St New Haven CT 06520

MAACK, THOMAS MICHAEL, physiologist, medical educator; b. Insterburg, Germany, July 17, 1935; came to U.S., 1965; s. Hans H. and Kate (Maligson) M.; m. Isa Tavares, Jan. 13, 1962; children: Marisa Tavares, Marcia Tavares. M.D., Escola Paulista de Medicina, Brazil, 1961, hon. doctorate in nephrology, 1981. Intern Hosp. das Clinicas, São Paulo, 1961-62; instr. physiology Faculdade de Medicina da Universidade de Sao Paulo, 1963-64; instr. to asst. prof. physiology SUNY-Upstate Med. Ctr., Syracuse, 1965-69; mem. faculty Cornell U. Med. Coll., N.Y.C., 1969—, prof. physiology, 1976—; investigator Mt. Desert Island Biol. Lab., Salisbury, Cove, Maine, 1966-72. Mem. editorial bd.: Am. Jour. Physiology, 1971-82; contbr. sci. articles to profl. publs. Recipient Associação prize Faculdade de Medicina, Universidade de São Paulo, 1961; Am. Heart Assn. Advanced Research fellow, 1966. Mem. Am. Physiol. Soc., Am. Soc. Nephrology, Internat. Soc. Nephrology, Sociedade Brasileira Para o Progresso de Ciencia, Salt and Water Club. Current Work: Renal physiology; filtration, transport and metabolism of proteins and peptide hormones; mechanisms and regulation of fluid and electrolyte transport; isolated kidney preparation; lysosomal physiology and endocytosis in epithelial tissues and cells. Subspecialties: Physiology (biology); Nephrology. Home: 1161 York Ave New York NY 10021 Office: Cornell U Med Coll Physiology Dept 1300 York Ave New York NY 10021

MAAHS, HOWARD GORDON, research chemist; b. Los Angeles, May 16, 1939; s. Willis George and Katherine Louise (Melvin) M.; m. Carol Jean Larson, May 10, 1962 (div. Apr. 1978); children—Kendra Louise, Jennifer Paige, Cynthia Jean, Gordon Lewis; m. Dola Jean Haracivet, Jan. 27, 1979. B.S., Stanford U., 1959; Ph.D., U. Wash., 1964. Chem. engr. U. Wash., Seattle, 1960-61; research chemist NASA Langley Research Ctr., Hampton, Va., 1964—. Contbr. articles to profl. jours. Fellow Hooker Chem. Co., 1963, Rayonier Inc., 1962, Standard Oil Calif., 1961; Stanford U. scholar, 1954. Current work: Research into the understanding and fabrication of carbon fiber reinforced carbon matrix composites for high temperature structural applications in oxidizing and non-oxidizing environments. Subspecialties: High-temperature materials; Physical chemistry. Home: 22 Ridgewood Pkwy Newport News VA 23602 Office: NASA Langley Research Ctr Mail Stop 191 Hampton VA 23665

MAAS, DANA JON, research scientist; b. Dickinson, N.D., Mar. 8, 1956; s. Waldemar Walter and LaVerna Marie (Hinsz) M. B.S. in Chemistry, N.D. State U., 1978; M.S. in Chem. Engring., 1983. Cert. secondary tchr., N.D. Educator, Milnor Pub. Schs., N.D., 1978-80; lectr. U. N.D., Grand Forks, 1982-83, research sci. energy research ctr., 1983—. Mem. Am. Chem. Soc., Am. Inst. Chem. Engrs. (assoc. mem.). Club: Minn. Bluegrass and Old Time Music Assn. (St. Paul). Current work: Preparation of concentrated low-rank coal-water slurries. Hot-water drying studies of low-rank coals and biomass. Subspecialty: Coal. Home: 523 North 6th St Grand Forks ND 58201 Office: Univ ND Energy Research Ctr 15 North 23rd St Grand Forks ND 58201

MAAS, JAMES WELDON, physician, psychiatrist; b. St. Louis, Oct. 16, 1929; s. James Werner and Agnes (Weldon) M.; m. Joanne Henderson, Dec. 13, 1953; 1 dau., Elizabeth; m. Marilyn L. Loren, Oct. 12, 1972; children—James, Jonathan. B.A., Washington U., St. Louis, 1950, M.D., 1954; M.A., Yale U., 1972. Diplomate Am. Bd. Psychiatry and Neurology. Med. intern Grade Meml. Hosp., Emory U. Med. Sch., Atlanta, 1954-55; resident gen. psychiatry Cin. Gen. Hosp., 1955-56, resident gen. psychiatry, 1958-59, fellow psychosomatic medicine, 1959-60; chief psychiatry 5040th USAF Hosp., Anchorage, 1956-58; attending physician NIMH, 1960-66, chief sect. psychosomatic medicine, adult psychiatry br., 1961-66; acting chief adult psychiatry br. NIMH, 1963-64; prof. psychiatry U. Ill. Med. Sch., Chgo., 1966-72; dir. research Ill. Stat Psychiat. Inst., Chgo., 1966-72; mem. faculty Yale Univ. Sch. Medicine, New Haven, 1972-82; prof. psychiatry U. Ill., Abraham Lincoln Sch. Medicine, Chgo., 1981-82; prof. psychiatry and pharmacology U. Tex. Health/Sci. Center, San Antonio, 1982—; cons. to govt. agys., 1968—; lectr. to various univs., 1966—; chmn. NIMH Six-Univ. Collaborative Study of Psychobiology Depressive Illness, 1983-84; mem. treatment devel. and assessment research rev. com. TDAC, 1983-84; mem. research scientist devel. award com. NIMH, 1975-79. Recipient C. V. Mosby Book award, Washington U. Med. Sch., 1954; Tchr. of Yr. award Ill. State Psychiat. Inst., 1970; 2d prize Anna-Monika Stiftung, 1973. Mem. editorial bd. Psychosomatic Medicine, 1971-82, Psychopharmacology Communications, 1973-81, Jour. Affective Disorders, 1978—. Contbr. articles to numerous publs. Served to maj. USAF, 1956-58. Fellow Am. Psychiat. Assn., Am. Psychosomatic Soc. (mem. council 1967-70), Am. Coll. Neuropsychopharmacology; mem. Psychiat. Research Soc., Conn. Psychiat. Soc., Am. Psychopath. Soc., Am. Soc. Pharmacology and Exptl. Therapeutics, Soc. Neurosci. (mem. steering com. 1971), Internat. Soc. Neurochemistry, AAAS, Sigma Xi. Current Work: Biology of psychiatric disorders. Subspecialties: Psychopharmacology; Neuropharmacology. Office: U Tex Health Sci Center 7703 Floyd Curl Dr San Antonio TX 78284

MAAS, SYNTHEA JEAN, veterinary microbiologist, veterinarian; b. Williamsburg, Iowa, Dec. 22, 1947; d. Willard Albert and Annabelle Mae (Holden) M.; m. Gerald T. Wedemeyer, Dec. 18, 1976; children—Zachary A., Jacob T., Micah A.Z. B.S. in Nursing, Cornell U., 1971; D.V.M., Iowa State U., 1978; postgrad. U. Mo., 1982—. Registered staff nurse pub. hosps., 1971-74; gen. practice vet. medicine, Solon, Iowa and Hershey, Pa., 1978-82; acad. research in vet. med. U. Mo., Columbia, 1982—. Quaker liaison Columbia Peace Ctr., 1984—; class parent rep. PTA, 1983—; bd. dirs. United Way Funded Day Care, Columbia, 1983-84. Iowa State U. and Alpo Corp. scholar, 1976. Mem. AVMA, Iowa Vet. Med. Assn., Am. Soc. Microbiology, Iowa State U. Vet. Med. Alumni Assn., Christian Vet. Mission (charter), Am. Assn. Vet. Immunologists, Phi Zeta. Democrat. Society of Friends. Club: Suzuki Music Educ. Assn. (Columbia). Current work: The bovine immune response to Fusobacterium Necrophorum, the infectious agent with a primary virulence role in bovine and ovine foot rot and liver abscess. Subspecialties: Microbiology (veterinary medicine); Infectious diseases. Home: 2712 Braemore Rd Columbia MO 65203 Office: U Mo Dept Vet Microbiology 101 Connaway Hall Columbia MO 65211

MABRY, PAUL DAVIS, JR., psychobiologist, research scientist, educator; b. Meridian, Miss., Sept. 28, 1943; s. Paul Davis and Frances Elizabeth (Thigpen) M. B.S., Millsaps Coll., Jackson, Miss., 1965; M.S., U. Miss., 1967, Ph.D., 1970. Predoctoral fellow neurosurgery U. Miss. Med. Center, 1969-70; research assoc. neurosci. and behavior program Princeton U., 1970-76; assoc. prof., chmn. psychology dept., head behavioral and phys. scis. Sacred Heart Coll., Belmont, N.C., 1976—. Contbr. articles to profl. jours. Mem. Soc. Neurosci., Am. Psychol Assn., Eastern Psychol. Assn., AAAS, Sigma Xi. Current Work: Functional devel. of brain, research, education, psychobiology. Subspecialty: Neuropharmacology. Home: 6500 Carsdale Pl Charlotte NC 28210 Office: Dept Psychology Sacred Heart Coll Belmont NC 28012

MACARA, IAN GREGORY, biochemistry educator, researcher; b. Derby, Derbyshire, Eng., Jan. 28, 1949; came to U.S., 1977; s. Robert and Mary (Webster) M.; m. Margaret Evans, July 31, 1971. B.Sc. (spl. honors) U. Sheffield, Eng., 1970, Ph.D., 1974. Lectr., asst. prof. U. Nairobi, Kenya, 1974-77; postdoctoral fellow Brandeis U., Waltham, Mass., 1977-79, Harvard U., Cambridge, Mass., 1979-82; research assoc. Harvard U., 1982-83; asst. prof. Rochester U. Med. Ctr., N.Y., 1983-85, assoc. prof., 1985—. Contbr. articles to profl. jours. Mem. AAAS, Biophys. Soc., Sigma Xi. Current work: Functions of oncogene proteins; mechanisms of transformation; growth factor regulation of phosphatidylinositol turnover; ion transport. Subspecialties: Biochemistry (biology); Cancer research (medicine). Office: Rochester Univ Med Ctr PO Box RBB Rochester NY 14642

MACARAEG, MICHELE GAY, research scientist, aerospace engineer; b. Norfolk, Va., Oct. 10, 1956; d. G.E. and S.I. (Roccia) M. B.S. in Chemistry and Math., Coll. William and Mary, 1978; M.S. in Chem. Engring., U. Tenn. Space Inst., 1980, Ph.D. in Computational Fluid Dynamics, 1984. Lab. instr. Coll. William and Mary, Williamsburg, Va., 1975, researcher, 1977-78; grad. research asst. U. Tenn. Space Inst., Tullahoma, 1978-84; NASA Marshall research fellow Marshall Space Flight Ctr., Huntsville, Ala., 1981-84; NASA Langley research scientist NASA Langley Research Ctr., Hampton, Va., 1984—; seminar lectr. on research on aerospace scis. NASA Langley Research Ctr., MIT, Harvard U., 1984—; computational fluid researcher for Inst. for Computer Applications in Sci. and Engring., Hampton, 1984—. Contbr. articles to sci. jours. NASA fellow, 1981-84. Mem. Assn. Sci. Mech. Engrs., AIAA, Sigma Xi, Alpha Lambda Delta. Roman Catholic. Current work: Mathematical models of flows around space structures and supersonic aircraft (with chemistry), atmospheric models for future shuttle experiment. Subspecialties: Numerical analysis (mathematics); Chemical engineering. Home: 37 Wendfield Circle Newport News VA 23601 Office: NASA Langley Research Ctr MS 395 Hampton VA 23665

MACARTHUR, DUNCAN WHITTEMORE, physicist; b. Fort Huachuca, Ariz., Feb. 23, 1956; s. Robert Helmer and Elizabeth Bayles (Whittemore) MacA.; m. Nancy Jean Uhlenhopp, June 12, 1977. B.A., Carleton Coll., 1977; M.A., Princeton U., 1979, Ph.D., 1982. Postdoctoral fellow Los Alamos Nat. Lab., 1982-85, mem. staff, 1986—. Contbr. articles to profl. publs. Mem. Am. Phys. Soc., Phi Beta Kappa, Sigma Xi, Pi Mu Epsilon. Unitarian. Current work: Use of the intersection of laser beams and particle beams in order to study the atomic physics of Ho and H- and medium energy physics. Subspecialties: Atomic and molecular physics; Nuclear physics. Office: MS J562 Los Alamos National Lab Los Alamos NM 87545

MACASAET, FRANCISCO FRIGINAL, pathologist, army officer; b. Infanta, Quezon, Philippines, Mar. 19, 1939; came to U.S., 1965, naturalized, 1979; s. Ricardo Orozco and Juliana (Friginal) M.; m. Evelyn Paralejas, Mar. 9, 1946; children: Eloise, Joel, David, Alan. A.A., Far Eastern U., Manila, 1958, M.D., 1963. Diplomate: Am. Bd. Pathology. Intern Far Eastern Univ. Hosp., 1962-63; resident Silliman U. Med. Ctr., Philippines, 1963-65; fellow in virus research Kans. U. Med. Ctr., 1965-67; research physician Silliman U. Med. Center, 1967-70; resident in pathology Cleve. Met. Gen. Hosp., 1970-73; fellow in microbiology Mayo Clinic, Rochester, Minn., 1974; asst. prof. pathology Case Western Res. U. and Met. Gen. Hosp., Cleve., 1975-78; maj. U.S. Army, 1978, advanced through grades to lt. col., 1982; clin. pathologist U.S. Army Research Inst. Infectious Diseases, Ft. Detrick, Md., 1978—. Contbr. articles to profl. jours. Recipient Spl. award Nat. Sci. Devel. Bd., Philippines, 1974. Fellow Am. Soc. Clin. Pathologists; Mem. Coll. Am. Pathologists, Am. Soc. Microbiology, N.Y. Acad. Sci. Current Work: Clinical pathology, virology, rapid diagnosis, enzyme-linked immunospecific assay. Subspecialties: Microbiology (medicine); Pathology (medicine). Home: 920 Conjurers Dr Colonial Heights VA 23834 Office: Kimbrough Army Hosp Fort Meade MD 20755

MACBRYDE, BRUCE, plant conservationist; b. St. Louis, May 21, 1941; s. Cyril M. and Anita E. (Koehler) MacB.; m. Olga S. Herrera Carvajal, Aug. 24, 1968; 1 son, Brendon Douglas. A.B., Washington U., St. Louis, 1963, Ph.D., 1970. Founder herbarium, researcher Pontificia Universidad Catolica del Ecuador, Quito, 1970-72; extramural asst. prof. St. Louis U., 1970-72; postdoctoral fellow Mo. Bot. Garden, 1970-72; research assoc. U. B.C. Bot. Garden, Vancouver, Can., 1972-75; botanist Office Endangered Species, U.S. Fish and Wildlife Service, Dept. Interior, Washington, 1975-84, Office Sci. Authority, 1984—; chmn. plant working group Conv. on Internat. Trade in Endangered Species Wild Fauna and Flora; mem. Fed. Working Group on Biol. Control of Weeds; chmn. Bot. Soc. Am., 1976, 77. Co-author: Prevalent Weeds of Central America, 1975, Vascular Plants of British Columbia, 1977; co-editor: Genetics and Conservation, 1983; contbr. articles to sci. and popular mags. Grantee Ga. Pacific Corp., Gulf Oil Co., Nat. Acad. Scis. Sigma Xi. Mem. Internat. Assn. Plant Taxonomy, Biol. Inst. Tropical Am. (bd. dirs.), Ctr. for Plant Conservation (adv. bd.), Flora of North Am. (editorial bd.). Unitarian. Current work: Threatened plants in trade; conservation in Latin America; plant taxonomy synthesis and outreach. Subspecialty: Taxonomy. Office: US Fish and Wildlife Service Office Sci Authority Washington DC 20240

MACCALLUM, CRAWFORD JOHN, physicist; b. N.Y.C., May 28, 1929; s. Ian Crawford and Lucile Annette (Heath) MacC.; m. Reut Leah Ran, July 13, 1981; children: John, Bruce, Reid, Taber, Ari. B.A., Princeton U., 1951; Ph.D., U. N.Mex., 1962. Mem. tech. staff Sandia Nat. Labs., Albuquerque, 1957—. Contbr. articles to profl. jours. Fulbright fellow Ain Shams U., Cairo, Egypt, 1964-65. Mem. Am. Phys. Soc., Am. Astron. Soc. Current Work: Gamma ray line astronomy, high energy electron transport. Subspecialty: Gamma ray high energy astrophysics.

MACCHETTO, FERDINANDO DUCCIO, astrophysicist; b. Biella, Italy, Oct. 4, 1942; came to U.S. 1983; s. Leonida and Vera (Borrino) M.; m. Ana Maria Urioste, Feb. 3, 1968; 1 child, Claudio. Licenciado in Physics, U. Córdoba, Argentina, 1963; Ph.D. in Physics, U. Rome, 1965. Astronomer NRC, Rome, 1965-68, Sci. Research Council, Abingdon, Eng., 1968-71; sr. astronomer NRC, 1971-73; project scientist European Space Agy., Noordwijk, Netherlands, 1973-76, project scientist space telescope, 1976-83; chief instrument br. Space Telescope Sci. Inst., Balt., 1983—. Editor: Astronomical Uses of Space Telescope, 1979; Dwarf Galaxies, 1980; Optical Jets in Galaxies, 1981. Mem. Internat. Astron. Union, Dutch Astron. Soc., Italian Astron. Soc., Am. Astron. Soc. Current work: Space research, space instrumentation for astronomy detector development, research on supernovae, jets from galaxies, active galactic nuclei. Subspecialties: Ultraviolet high energy astrophysics; Optical astronomy. Home: 6001 Tilden Ln Rockville MD 20852 Office: Space Telescope Sci Inst 3700 San Martin Dr Baltimore MD 21218

MACCHIA, DONALD DEAN, physiology educator, freelance writer, consultant; b. Gary, Ind., May 17, 1948; s. Mike D. and Elizabeth (Pilla) M.; children—Anthony, Marianne. A.B., Ind. U., Bloomington, 1971; M.A., Ball State U., 1972; M.S., U. Ill., Urbana, 1974, Ph.D., 1977; postgrad. U. Chgo., 1976-79. Chemist U.S. Steel, Gary, Ind., 1970-71; teaching asst. U. Ill., Urbana, 1972-74, USPHS fellow, 1975-76; postdoctoral fellow U. Chgo., 1976-79, asst. prof., 1979-80; asst. prof. Ind. U. Sch. Medicine, Gary, 1980-84, assoc. prof., 1984—; instr. Columbia U., N.Y.C., 1974-75. Author: various books. Contbr. articles to various publs. Fellow NIH, 1977-79, USPHS, 1975-76. Mem. Am. Physiol. Soc., Soc. Gen. Physiologists, Biophys. Soc., Am. Heart Assn., Internat. Soc. Heart Research, AAAS, ABA, Chgo. Bar Assn., Sigma Xi. Home: 7434 Grand Blvd Hobart IN 46342 Office: Indiana U Sch Medicine 3400 Broadway Gary IN 46408

MACCOBY, ELEANOR EMMONS, psychology educator; b. Tacoma, May 15, 1917; d. H. Eugene and Viva (Johnson) Emmons; m. Nathan Maccoby, Sept. 16, 1938; children: Janice B. Maccoby Carmichael, Sarah Maccoby Bellina, Mark. Student, Reed Coll., 1934-35, 36-37; B.A., U. Wash., 1939; M.A., U. Mich., 1949, Ph.D., 1950. Study dir., div. program surveys Dept. Agr., 1942-46, Survey Research Center, U. Mich., 1946-48; lectr. social relations Harvard U., 1950-58; faculty Stanford U., 1958—, prof. psychology, 1958—, chmn. dept., 1973-76. Author: (with R.R. Sears, H. Levin) Patterns of Child Rearing, 1957, (with M. Zellner) Experiments in Primary Education, 1970, (with C.N. Jacklin) The Psychology of Sex Differences, 1974, Social Development: Psychological Growth and the Parent-Child Relationship, 1980; Editor: (with Newcomb and Hartley) Readings in Social Psychology, 1957, Development of Sex Differences, 1966; Contbr. articles to profl. jours. Center for Advanced Study in Behavioral Sci. fellow, 1969-70. Fellow Am. Psychol. Assn. (div. pres. child psychology); mem. Soc. Research Child Devel. (gov. council 1963, pres. 1981-83), Social Sci. Research Council (chair 1983-85), Western Psychol. Assn. (pres. 1974-75). Subspecialty: Developmental psychology. Home: 729 Mayfield Ave Stanford CA 94305

MACCOLL, ROBERT, chemist, educator; b. Bklyn., Mar. 27, 1942; s. Robert and Mildred P. (Lanigan) M.; children—R. Michael, Daniel, Laurie. B.A., Queens Coll., 1963; M.S., U. Miss., 1967; Ph.D., Adelphi U., 1969. Postdoctorial fellow N.Y. State Dept Health Wadsworth Ctr., Albany, 1969-70, research scientist, 1979—; adj. assoc. prof. Albany Med. Ctr. Dept. Microbiology and Immunology, N.Y., 1984—. Contbr. articles to profl. jours. Mem. Am. Chem. Soc., Am. Soc. Photobiology. Republican. Roman Catholic. Current work: Research on proteins functioning as antenna pigments in photosynthesis of algae. Subspecialties: Physical chemistry; Biochemistry (biology). Home: 357 Morris St Albany NY 12208 Office: N Y State Dept Health Wadsworth Ctr ESP Albany NY 12201

MACCOSS, MALCOLM, organic chemist, researcher; b. Cleator, Cumbria, U.K., June 2, 1947; came to U.S., 1976; s. John MacDonald and Ruth Victoria (Bibby) MacC.; m. Sandra Eve Bramwell; children—Michael J., Rachel N. B.S., U. Birmingham, U.K., 1968, Ph.D., 1971. Postdoctoral fellow U. Alta., Edmonton, 1972-76; asst. scientist Argonne Nat. Lab., Ill., 1976-80, scientist, 1980-82; research fellow Merck & Co., Rahway, N.J., 1982—; adj. assoc. prof. U. Ill. Med. Ctr., Chgo., 1981-82. Contbr. articles to profl. jours. and chpts. to books. Recipient County Major scholarship, Cumbria (U.K.), 1965-68, Brit. Empire Cancer Campaign, 1968-71, U. Chgo. Disting. Scientist award, 1980. Assoc. mem. Royal Chem. Soc.; mem. Am. Chem. Soc., N.Y. Acad. Scis. Current work: Medicinal chemistry of nucleosides and nucleotides, chemistry and biochemistry of nucleic acids, antiviral agents, chemotherapy of cancer. Subspecialties: Organic chemistry; Biochemistry (biology). Office: Merck Sharp & Dohme Research Labs P O Box 2000 Rahway NJ 07065

MACCOY, DOUGLAS MAIDLOW, veterinary surgeon, educator; b. Washington, Aug. 15, 1947; s. Edgar Milton and Charlotte (Maidlow) MacC. B.S., Purdue U., 1969; D.V.M., U. Ga., 1973. Diplomate: Am. Coll. Vet. Surgeons. Intern N.Y. State Coll. Vet. Medicine, Cornell U., Ithaca, 1973-74, resident in surgery, 1974-76, asst. prof., 1976-82, Coll. Vet. Medicine, U. Ill., Urbana, 1982—. Contbr. articles to profl. jours. Mem. AVMA, Am. Coll. Vet. Surgeons, Vet. Cancer Soc., Am. Assn. Vet. Clinicians. Democrat. Episcopalian. Current Work: Application of advanced surgical techniques to animal disease (reconstructive and microsurgery); fracture repair in birds; clinical treatment of animal cancer; development of implantable insulin pumps; research of human obesity. Subspecialties: Surgery (veterinary medicine); Cancer research (veterinary medicine). Office: Dept Clin Scis Coll Vet Medicine U Ill Urbana IL 61801

MAC CREADY, PAUL BEATTIE, aeronautical engineer; b. New Haven, Sept. 29, 1925. B.S. in Physics, Yale U., 1947; M.S., Calif. Inst. Tech., 1948, Ph.D. in Aeros. cum laude, 1952. Founder, pres. Meteorology Research, Inc., 1951-70, Atmospheric Research Group, 1958-70; founder, 1971, since pres., now also chmn. AeroVironment, Inc., Pasadena, Calif.; cons. in field, 1951—, mem. numerous govt. tech. adv. coms. Author research papers in field. Recipient Collier trophy Nat. Aero. Assn., 1979, Edward Longsreth medal Franklin Inst., 1979, Gold Air medal Fedn. Aero. Internat., 1981, Inventor of Year award Assn. Advancement Innovation and Invention, 1981; named Engr. of Century ASME, 1980. Mem. Nat. Acad. Engring., Am. Acad. Arts and Scis., Am. Meteorol. Soc. (chmn. com. atmospheric measurements 1968-69, councilor 1971-74), AIAA (Reed Aero. award 1979). Leader team that developed Gossamer Condor (Kremer prize 1977), 1976-77, Gossamer Albatross (Kremer prize 1979) for human-powered flight across English channel, 1979, Solar Challenger, ultralight aircraft powered by solar cells, 1981, Gossamer Penguin. Address: AeroVironment Inc 145 Vista Ave Pasadena CA 91107

MACDERMOTT, RICHARD PRATT, gastroenterology educator, researcher; b. Wellington, Ohio, Nov. 16, 1943; m. Martha Elizabeth Ryan, Dec. 11, 1971; children—Sean Michael, Kara Renee, Kevin Patrick, Kristen Elizabeth. B.A., Oberlin Coll., 1965; M.D., Ohio State U., 1969. Diplomate Am. Bd. Internal Medicine, Diplomate Am. Bd. Allergy and Immunology, Am. Bd. Gastroenterology. Internship and residency in medicine Peter Bent Brigham Hosp., Boston, 1969-71; fellow Boston U., 1971-73; Sidney Farber Cancer Ctr., Boston, 1973-74; with dept. immunology and gastroenterology Walter Reed Army Inst. Research, Washington, 1974-77; investigator Howard Hughes Med. Inst., 1977-81; asst. prof. medicine Wash. U. Sch. Medicine, St. Louis, 1977-82, assoc. prof. medicine, 1982—, asst. physician dept medicine, div. gastroenterology Barnes Hosp., St. Louis, 1977-82, assoc. physician, 1982—; mem. grants rev. com. Nat. Found. Ileitis and Colitis, 1980—; NIH, 1982—. Mem. editorial bd. Jour. Immunology 1982, Quar. Rev. of Gastroenterology 1982. Contbr. articles to profl. jours. Served to maj. U.S. Army, 1974-77. Recipient Ind. Research award Nat. Found. Ileitis and Colitis, 1983-85. NIH grantee, 1983—. Mem. Am. Fedn. Clin. Research, Am. Assn. Immunologists, AAAS, Am. Gastroent. Assn., Reticuloendothelial Soc., Am. Soc. Clin. Investigation, Alpha Omega Alpha. Roman Catholic. Current work: The immunology of inflammatory bowel disease. Subspecialties: Immunology (medicine); Gastroenterology. Office: Wash U Med Sch 660 S Euclid Ave St Louis MO 63110

MACDONALD, DONALD MACKENZIE, chemist, researcher; b. Newark, July 26, 1928; s. J.E. Robertson and Andrea Marie (Olson) MacD.; m. Christine M. Bennett, July 28, 1960; children—Sandra, Kevin. B.Sc., Mt. Allison U., Sackville, N.B., Can., 1949; M.Sc., U. N.B., 1951, Ph.D., 1953. Postdoctoral fellow NRC, Ottawa, Ont., Can., 1953-54; sci. service officer Naval Research Establishment, Dartmouth, N.S., 1954-60; research assoc. CIP Research Ltd., Hawkesbury, Ont., 1960-69; sr. research and devel. assoc. Internat. Paper Co., Tuxedo Park, N.Y., 1969—. Contbr. articles to profl. jours. and books; patentee (8) in field. Mem. Am. Chem. Soc., Tech. Assn. Pulp and Paper Ind. Current work: Chemistry and techology of cellulose, hemicelluloses, and lignin. Subspecialties: Polymer chemistry; Organic chemistry. Home: 147 Cromwell Hill Rd Monroe NY 10950 Office: Corp Research Ctr Long Meadow Rd Tuxedo NY 10987

MACDONALD, G(EORGE) WAYNE, psychologist; b. Sydney, N.S., Nov. 6, 1945; s. John George and Winnifred Evelyn (MacMillan) MacD.; m. Susan Elizabeth Barrett, May 9, 1970; children: Josh, Scott, Lindsay. B.A. magna cm laude, St. Francis Xavier U., 1967; M.A., U. Windsor, 1969, Ph.D., 1974. Registered psychologist, N.S. Intern Windsor Western Hosp., 1969-72; asst. prof. St. Francis Xavier U., Antigonish, N.S., 1972-73; chief psychologist Sarnia Lambton Centre, Sarnia, Ont., 1973-76; staff psychologist I.W.K. Hosp. for Children, Halifax, N.S., 1976; dir. Dept. Psychology, 1976—; cons. in clin.

neuropsychology; profl. adv. bd. Canadian Assn. for Children with Learning Disorders, 1982—. Fellow Assn. Psychologists of N.S. (pres. 1980-81); mem. Internat. Neuropsychology Soc., Am. Psychol. Assn., Canadian Psychol. Assn. Roman Catholic. Current Work: Neuropsychological correlates of dietary phenylalanine restriction in older children with phenylketonuria; elucidation of neuropsychological deficits in wide variety of pediatric conditions. Subspecialties: Neuropsychology; Behavioral psychology. Home: 2541 Westmount St Halifax NS B3L 3G7 Canada Office: PO Box 3070 Halifax NS B3J 3G9 Canada

MAC DONALD, GORDON JAMES FRASER, geophysicist; b. Mexico City, July 30, 1929; s. Gordon and Josephine (Bennett) MacD.; m. Marcelline Kuglen (dec.); children: Gordon James, Maureen, Michael; m. Betty Ann Kipniss; 1 son, Bruce. A.B. summa cum laude, Harvard U., 1950, A.M., 1952, Ph.D., 1954. Asst. prof. geology, geophysics Mass. Inst. Tech., 1954-55, asso. prof. geophysics, 1955-58; staff asso. geophysics lab. Carnegie Inst. Washington, 1955-58; cons. U.S. Geol. Survey, 1955-60; prof. geophysics UCLA, 1958-68, dir. atmospheric research lab., 1960-66, assoc. dir. Inst. Geophysics and Planetary Physics, 1960-68; v.p. research Inst. for Def. Analyses, 1966-67, exec. v.p., 1967-68, trustee, 1966-70; vice chancellor for research and grad. affairs U. Calif. at Santa Barbara, 1968-70, prof. physics and geophysics, 1968-70, mem. council on Environ. Quality, Washington, 1970-72; Henry R. Luce prof. environ. studies and policy, dir. environ. studies program Dartmouth, 1972-79; trustee Mitre Corp., 1968-70, 72-77, mem. exec. com., 1972-77, disting. vis. scholar, 1977-79, chief scientist, 1979-83, v.p., chief scientist, 1983—; cons. NASA, 1960-70, mem. lunar and planetary missions bd., 1967-70; mem. def. sci. bd. Dept. Def., 1966-70; cons. Dept. State, 1967-70; mem. Pres.'s Sci. Adv. Com., 1965-69; adv. panel on nuclear effects Office Tech. Assessment, 1975-77. Author: The Rotation of the Earth, 1960; co-author: Sound and Light Phenomena: A Study of Historical and Modern Occurrences, 1978; Contbr. articles to sci., tech. jours. Fellow Am. Acad. Arts and Scis., AAAS; mem. Am. Math. Soc., Nat. Acad. Scis. (chmn. environmental studies bd. 1970, 72-73, chmn. commn. on natural resources 1973-77), Am., Royal astron. socs., Am. Mineral. Soc., Am. Geophys. Union., Geochem. Soc. Am., Geol. Soc. Am., Am. Meteorol. Soc., Am. Philos. Soc., Seismol. Soc. Am., Soc. Indsl. and Applied Math., Council Fgn. Relations, Sigma Xi. Subspecialties: Geophysics; Statistics. Address: MITRE Corp 1820 Dolley Madison Blvd McLean VA 22102

MACDONALD, JAMES ROSS, physicist, educator; b. Savannah, Ga., Feb. 27, 1923; s. John Elwood and Antonina Jones (Hansell) M.; m. Margaret Milward Taylor, Aug. 3, 1946; children: Antonina Hansell, James Ross, William Taylor. B.A., Williams Coll., 1944; S.B., Mass. Inst. Tech., 1944, S.M., 1947; D.Phil. (Rhodes scholar), Oxford (Eng.) U., 1950, D.Sc., 1967. Mem. staff Digital Computer Lab., Mass. Inst. Tech., 1946-47; physicist Armour Research Found., Chgo., 1950-52; asso. physicist Argonne Nat. Lab., 1952-53; with Tex. Instruments Inc., Dallas, 1953-74, v.p. corporate research and engring., 1968-73, v.p. corporate research and devel., 1973-74, cons., 1974—; dir. Simmonds Precision Products Inc., 1979-83; William Rand Kenan Jr. prof. physics U. N.C., Chapel Hill, 1974—; mem. editorial bd. Jour. Applied Physics, 1984—; adj. prof. biophysics U. Tex. Med. Sch., Dallas, 1954-74; mem. solid state scis. panel NRC, 1965-73; mem. adv. com. for sci. edn. NSF, 1971-73; mem. vis. com. physics Mass. Inst. Tech., 1971-74; mem. external adv. com. Engring. Expt. Sta., Ga. Inst. Tech., 1976-79. Contbr. articles to profl. jours. Mem. Dallas Radio Commn., 1967-71; mem. sci. adv. council Callier Hearing and Speech Center, Dallas, 1974-78; bd. dirs. League for Ednl. Advancement in Dallas, 1965-70. Fellow Am. Phys. Soc. (com. on edn. 1973-75, com. on applications of physics 1975-78, George E. Pake prize 1985), IEEE (awards 1962, 74, asso. editor Transactions of Profl. Group on Audio 1961-66, Transactions on Audio and Electroacoustics 1966-73), AAAS; mem. Nat. Acad. Engring. (exec. com. assembly of engring. 1975-78, council 1971-74), Nat. Acad. Scis. (chmn. numerical data adv. bd. 1970-74, com. on motor vehicle emissions 1971-74, chmn. com. on motor vehicle emissions 1973-74, mem. com. on satellite power systems 1979-81, mem. com. on sci., engring., and pub. policy 1981-83, commn. on phys. scis., math. and resources 1985—), Am. Inst. Physics. (governing bd. 1975-78, chmn. com. on profl. concerns 1976-78, editorial bd. Jour. Applied Physics, Applied Physics Letters, Applied Physics Revs. 1983—), Electrochem Soc., Audio Engring. Soc., Phi Beta Kappa, Sigma Xi. Patentee in field. Current Work: Analysis of the electrical response of solids and liquids, especially solid and liquid electrolytes. Subspecialties: Condensed matter physics; Analytical chemistry. Office: Dept Physics and Astronomy U NC Chapel Hill NC 27514

MACDONALD, JOHN STEPHEN, oncologist, educator; b. Bklyn., June 2, 1943; s. John Stephen and Margaret (Martin) M.; m. Mary Suzanne Stock, July 11, 1964; children: Margaret Wilson, John Stephen, Kathleen Lenore, Frederick Stock. A.B., Dartmouth Coll., 1965, B.M.S., 1967; M.D., Harvard U., 1969. Intern and resident in medicine Beth Israel Hosp., Boston, 1969-71; clin. assoc. immunology and med. oncology Nat. Cancer Inst., Bethesda, Md., 1971-74, assoc. dir. cancer therapy evaluation program, div. cancer treatment, 1979-82, med. oncologist Washington Clin., 1982-84; instr., asst. prof., then assoc. prof. medicine Georgetown U., Washington, 1974-79, clin. assoc. prof., 1979-84, George Washington U., 1980-84; prof. medicine, chief dir. hematology-oncology U. Ky., Lexington, 1984—, assoc. dir. Markey Cancer Center, 1984—. Editor-in-chief: Cancer Treatment Reports, 1979-83; contbr. over 100 articles to med. jours. Bd. mgmt. YMCA, 1979-84; bd. dirs. CYO, 1979-84. Served with USPHS, 1971-74. Jr. faculty clin. fellow Am. Cancer Soc., 1974-76. Fellow ACP; mem. Am. Fedn. Clin. Research, Am. Soc. Clin. Oncology, Am. Assn. for Cancer Research, AMA, So. Med. Assn. Current Work: Clinical cancer treatment and research. Subspecialties: Chemotherapy; Internal medicine. Home: 719 Brookhill Dr Lexington KY Office: Albert Chandler Med Center U Ky Lexington KY

MACEDA, EDWARD LOUIS, nuclear engineer; b. Bklyn., Sept. 5, 1948; s. Joseph Edward and Eileen Louise (Sheffer) M.; m. Elizabeth Ann Kronenthal, Sept. 1, 1972; children—Steven Edward, Jason Michael, Elizabeth Ann, Edward Louis, Gregory James. B.S., Manhattan Coll., 1970; M.S., U. Ill., 1972, Ph.D., 1977. Teaching asst. physics dept. U. Ill., Urbana, 1970-72, research asst. nuclear engring. program, 1972-77; research engr. Babcock and Wilcox, Lynchburg, Va., 1977-80, sr. research engr., 1980-82; lectr. physics dept. Lynchburg Coll., Va., 1979-82; nuclear engr. U.S. Dept. Def., Washington, 1982—. Contbr. articles to profl. jours. Served to capt. USAR, 1973-1982, capt. Res., ret. Mem. Am. Phys. Soc., Am. Nuclear Soc. (Criticality Safety Div. Best Paper award, 1979, 81), Sigma Xi. Lodge: Optimists. Subspecialties: Nuclear fission; Nuclear fusion. Home: 1538 Stuart Rd Herndon VA 22070 Office: Dept Defense DT-1A Washington DC 20301-6111

MACFADDEN, KENNETH ORVILLE, research and development company executive, analytical chemist; b. Phila., Sept. 5, 1945; s. Kenneth Pennel and Alice Amelia (Whitehorn) MacF.; m. Lois Nellie Rierson, June 8, 1968; children—Michelle, Kira. B.S., Juniata Coll., 1966; Ph.D., Georgetown U., 1972. Sect. mgr. Air Products Co., Allentown, Pa., 1978-80, mgr. analytical service, 1980-82, mgr. chem. research, 1982-84; dir. analytical research W.R. Grace Co., Columbia, Md., 1984—; postdoctoral fellow U. Calgary, Alta., Can., 1972-73; asst. prof. Stockton State Coll., Pomona, N.J., 1973-75. Contbr. articles to profl. jours. Mem. Am. Chem. Soc., AAAS, Sigma Xi. Current work: Applications of analytical chemistry to industrial problem solving especially in the area of mass spectrometry. Subspecialties: Analytical chemistry; Physical chemistry. Office: W R Grace Co 7379 Route 32 Columbia MD 20144

MACFARLANE, MALCOLM DAVID, pharmacologist; b. Cambridge, Mass., Sept. 26, 1940; s. Robert Malcolm and Elizabeth Agnes (Hennessey) MacF.; m. Mary Kay Allen, Mar. 8, 1975. B.S. in Pharmacy, Northeastern U., 1962; Ph.D. in Pharmacology, Georgetown U., 1967. Instr. pharmacology Kirksville (Mo.) Coll. Osteo. Medicine, 1967-69; Assoc. prof. pharmacology U. So. Calif., 1969-74; dir. research Meyer Labs., Ft. Lauderdale, Fla., 1974-78; v.p. profl. services Glaxo Inc., Research Triangle Park, N.C., 1978-81, dir. regulatory affairs, 1981—. Contbr. articles to numerous profl. publs. Pres Oakland Shores Condominium Assn. Kappa Psi scholar, 1961; Rho Chi scholar, 1961. Fellow Am. Coll. Clin. Pharmacology; mem. Am. Soc. Pharmacology and Exptl. Therapeutics, Am. Soc. Clin. Pharmacology, Regulatory Affairs Professionals Soc., Sigma Xi, Rho Chi, Kappa Psi, U.S. Power Squadron. Current Work: Pharmacotherapy of aging. Subspecialty: Pharmacology. Office: Glaxo Inc 5 Moore Dr Research Triangle Park NC 27709

MACFARLANE, ROBERT BRUCE, biological oceanographer, researcher; b. Greensburg, Pa., Jan. 24, 1947; s. Samuel and Elizabeth Mae (Ramsey) M.; m. Christine Anne Stuart, Dec. 10, 1968. B.S., Pa. State U., 1968; M.S., Fla. State U., 1970, Ph.D., 1980. Research asst. dept. food and dairy sci. Pa. State U., University Park, 1967-68; research asst. dept. oceanography Fla. State U., 1968-70, researcher, teaching asst. instr., 1975-77, 78-80; oceanographer NOAA, Tiburon, Calif., 1980—; tech. advisor Calif. Water Resources Control Bd., Oakland, 1982—. Contbr. articles to profl. jours. Served to capt. USAF, 1970-75. Recipient Quality Step Increase award NOAA, Dept. Commerce, 1984. Mem. AAAS, Am. Chem. Soc., Am. Fisheries Soc., Am. Inst. Fisheries Research Biologists, Am. Soc. Zoologists, Sigma Xi. Democrat. Club: Sierra (San Francisco). Current work: Biochemistry of fishes; stress physiology; bioenergetics; reproductive physiology and biochemistry of fishes; environmental physiology of fishes. Subspecialties: Marine biology; Biochemistry (biology). Office: 3150 Paradise Dr Tiburon CA 94920

MACGREGOR, IAN DUNCAN, geologist; b. Calcutta, India, Jan. 5, 1935; came to U.S., 1965, naturalized, 1985; s. David Duncan and Marjorie Joan (Prike) M.; m. Katherine Ann Hay, Aug. 1, 1956 (div. Nov. 1975); children—Duncan David, Caroline Janet, Andrew Ian, Jennifer Kate; m. Susan Garbini, Apr. 25, 1975; 1 child, Glenna Yvonne. B.Sc. with honors, Aberdeen U., Scotland, U.K., 1957; M.Sc., Queens U., Kingston, Ont., Can., 1960; Ph.D., Princeton U., 1963. Geologist, Geol. Survey of Can., Ottawa, 1957-63; fellow Geophys. Lab., Carnegie Inst., Washington, 1963-65; assoc. prof. S.W. Ctr. Advanced Studies, Dallas, 1965-69; prof. geology U. Calif.-Davis, 1969-81; geoscientist U.S. Dept. of Energy, Washington, 1978-80; dep. div. dir. earth sci. Nat. Sci. Found., Washington, 1981—; advisor in field. Contbr. articles to profl. jours. Mem. Geol. Soc. Am., Mineral. Soc. Am. (council mem. 1978-80), Am. Geophys. Union, AAAS, Potomac Geophys. Soc. (pres. 1983-84). Current work: Study of petrology and geochemistry of the upper mantle; geology of oceans; uranium resource studies. Subspecialties: Geology; Geochemistry. Home: 5005 River Hill Rd Bethesda MD 20816 Office: Div Earth Scis Nat Sci Found 1800 G St NW Washington DC 20550

MACHLIN, LAWRENCE JUDAH, nutritionist, biochemist, educator; b. Bklyn., June 24, 1927; s. Morris Louis and Lilly (Manevitz) M.; m. Ruth Beerman, May 30, 1953; children—Marc David, Steve Richard, Paul Jeffrey. B.S., Cornell U., 1948, M.S. in Nutritional Sci., 1949; Ph.D., Georgetown U., 1953. Nutritional biochemist USDA-AEC, Beltsville, Md., 1949-56; group chief Monsanto Co., St. Louis, 1956-73; mgr. Hoffman-LaRoche Inc., Nutley, N.J., 1973—; lectr. nutrition Washington U., St. Louis, Mo., 1969-72; adj. prof. nutrition NYU, N.Y.C., 1977-82; adj. assoc. prof. nutrition in med. Cornell U., N.Y.C., 1979—. Editor: Vitamin E, A Comprehensive Treatise, 1980; Handbook of Vitamins, 1984. Contbr. numerous articles to profl. jours. Mem. Am. Inst. Nutrition, Am. Soc. Clin. Nutrition, N.Y. Acad. Scis., Soc. Exptl. Biology and Medicine, N.Y. Lipid Club. Democrat. Jewish. Current work: Vitamin research with particular emphasis on vitamins E, C, A, beta-carotene, their metabolism, cellular function, and role in human nutrition. Subspecialties: Nutrition (biology); Biochemistry (biology). Office: Hoffmann-LaRoche Inc 340 Kingsland St Nutley NJ 07110

MACHOVEC, GEORGE STEPHEN, information specialist, editor, consultant; b. Columbus, Ohio, June 10, 1952; s. Charles R. and Geraldine (Elieff) M. B.S. in Physics and Astronomy, U. Ariz., 1974, M.L.S., 1977. Solar energy librarian, coordinator computer reference service for sci. and engring. Ariz. State U. Library, Tempe, 1977—; cons. Info. Intelligence, Inc., Phoenix, 1980—. Author: Solar Energy Index, 1980, Supplement I, 1982; editor: Info. Intelligence Online Newsletter, 1981—, Info. Intelligence Online Hotline, 1982—; mng. editor: Online Libraries and Microcomputers, 1983—. Mem. Am. Soc. Info. Sci., ALA., Spl. Libraries Assn., Am. Solar Energy Soc., Internat. Solar Energy Soc., Ariz. Online User Group (chmn. 1979-81). Democrat. Current Work: Have developed computerized index to solar energy publications, involved with solar energy, information storage and retrieval, online systems, database systems. Subspecialties: Solar energy; Information systems (Information science). Home: PO Box 785 Tempe AZ 85281 Office: Arizona State U Library Tempe AZ 85287

MACHTA, LESTER, meteorologist; b. N.Y.C., Feb. 17, 1919; s. Nathan and Bertha (Leavitt) M.; m. Phyllis Meryl Margaretten, Jan. 27, 1947; children—Jonathan, Deborah. B.S., Bklyn. Coll., 1939; M.A., NYU, 1947; Sc.D., MIT, 1948. With ESSA, NOAA, Washington, 1948—, now dir. air resources lab. Contbr. articles to profl. jours. Served with USAAF, 1943-45. Fellow AAAS, Am. Meteorol. Soc. (councilor), Am. Geophys. Union; mem. Royal Meteoroll Soc. Current work: Atmospheric sciences; air pollution; atmospheric chemistry. Subspecialty: Atmospheric chemistry. Office: NOAA Air Resources Labs 8010 13th St Silver Spring MD 20910

MACHTIGER, HARRIET GORDON, psychotherapist; b. N.Y.C., July 27, 1927; d. Michael J. and Miriam D. (R) Gordon; m. Sidney Machtiger, Feb. 7, 1948; children: Avram Coleman, Marcia Gordon, Bennett Rand. B.A., Bklyn. Coll., 1947; diploma with distinction, U. London, 1966, Ph.D., 1974. Lic. clin. psychologist, Pa. cert. psychoanalyst, Jungian analyst. Tchr. Phila. Pub. Schs., 1962-64; ednl. therapist Child Guidance Tng. Ctr., London, 1966-68; specialist Sch. Psychol. Service, Inner London Ednl. Authority, 1968-70; psychotherapist Paddington Day Hosp., London, 1970-71, London Ctr. Psychotherapy, 1971-74, Staunton Clinic U. Pitts., 1974-78, pvt. practice psychotherapy and psychoanalysis, Pitts., 1976—; pres. C.G. Jung Ctr., Pitts., 1975-80. Recipient Disting. Contbn. to Edn. award Commonwealth of Pa., 1962. Fellow Am. Orthopsychiat. Assn.; mem. Am. Psychol. Assn., Brit. Psychol. Soc., Inter-Regional Soc. Jungian Analysts (tng. com. 1979-81), Brit. Assn. Psychotherapists. Democrat. Jewish. Current Work: Psychotherapeutic techniques, particularly transference/counter transference issues; working with difficult and handicapped patients; teaching. Subspecialties: Psychotherapy; Developmental psychology. Home: 207 Tennyson Ave Pittsburgh PA 15213 Office: 110 The Fairfax 4614 5th Ave Pittsburgh PA 15213

MACINNES, DAVID FENTON, JR., chemistry educator; b. Abington, Pa., Mar. 19, 1943; s. David F. and Kathleen (O'Neill) MacI.; m. Barbara Hardy MacInnes, June 22, 1974; children: Colin, Breanyn. B.A., Earlham Coll., 1965; M.A., Princeton U., 1968, Ph.D., 1972. Tchr. chemistry, head dept. sci. Westtown Sch., Pa., 1970-73; asst. prof. chemistry Guilford Coll., 1973-81, assoc. prof., 1982—; fellow U. Pa., 1980-81; summer research assoc. Brookhaven Nat. Lab., Upton, N.Y., 1982; adv. Toxic Waste Task Force, Greensboro, 1979-82. Contbr. articles in field to profl. jours. Mem. Am. Chem. Soc. (Dolittle award 1981), N.C. Acad. Arts and Scis. Quaker. Current Work: Conductive polymers, organic batteries, photovoltaic cells, computers in chemical education. Subspecialties: Inorganic chemistry; Polymer chemistry. Office: Dept Chemistry Guilford Coll Greensboro NC 27410

MACINTYRE, WILLIAM JAMES, physicist; b. Canaan, Conn., Nov. 26, 1920; s. William M. and Helen (Hoyt) MacI.; m. Patricia Nelle Grossman, Sept. 16, 1947; children: Kathleen S., Steven J. B.S., Western Res. U., 1943, M.A., 1947; M.S., Yale U., 1948, Ph.D., 1950. Prof. biophysics Sch. Medicine, Case Western Res. U., Cleve., 1949-72; staff physicist Cleve. Clinic Found., 1972—; cons. in field. Contbr. articles to profl. jours.; author: Quantitative Nuclear Cardiology, 1975. Served with U.S. Army, 1943-46. Mem. Soc. Nuclear Medicine, Am. Phys. Soc., Biophys. Soc., Am. Assn. Physicists in Medicine, Central Research Soc., Am. Heart Assn., Physiol. Soc., Soc. Magnetic Resonance in Medicine, Soc. Magnetic Resonance Imaging, Am. Coll. Nuclear Physicians, Am. Coll. Radiology. Current Work: Emission tomography, applications of nuclear magnetic resonance to cardiac studies, cardiovascular nuclear medicine. Subspecialties: Nuclear medicine; Imaging technology. Home: 3108 Huntington Rd Shaker Heights OH 44120 Office: 9500 Euclid Ave Cleveland OH 44106

MACK, MARK PHILIP, chemistry researcher; b. Buffalo, Jan. 14, 1950; s. Stanley Joseph and Florence Matilda (Kopacz) M.; m. Jean Ann Merrick, June 2, 1984. B.A., SUNY-Buffalo, 1971, Ph.D., 1975. Research assoc. Duke U., 1975-77; research chemist exploratory research Conoco Inc., Ponca City, Okla., 1977-80, group supr., 1980-81, group leader plastic research, 1982—. Contbr. articles to profl. jours. Patentee in field. Samuel B. Silbert fellow SUNY, Buffalo, 1974. Mem. Am. Chem. Soc., N.Y. Acad. Scis., Soc. Plastics Engrs., AAAS, Sigma Xi. Republican. Roman Catholic. Current work: Discovered new polymers and plastics; developed a drug reducing agent for the Aleyska pipeline; developed catalysts for polymerization reactions. Subspecialties: Polymer chemistry; Catalysis chemistry. Home: 536 N 13th St Ponca City OK 74601 Office: Conoco Inc PO Box 1267 Ponca City OK 74603

MACK, MICHAEL EDWARD, physicist; b. Poughkeepsie, N.Y., May 28, 1939; s. Edward Joseph and Anita Eleanor (Barton) M.; m. Sarah Marie McManus, July 20, 1963; children: Patrick E., Michael P., Kathleen E., Maura A. B.S. in Physics, M.I.T., 1961, Ph.D., 1967. Prin. research scientist United Technologies Research Ctr., East Hartford, Conn., 1967-73; dir. laser systems, measurements, tech. and systems group Avco Everett Research Labs., Revere Beach, Everett, Mass., 1973-81; tech. dir. Eaton Ion Implantation Div., Beverly, Mass., 1981—; fellow Ctr. Advanced Engring. Studies, M.I.T., 1981. Contbr. articles to prof. jours. Mem. Manchester Harbor Adv. Com., 1978—. Mem. Optical Soc. Am., Am. Phys. Soc., Laser Inst. Am. Club: Manchester Yacht. Current Work: Wafer cooling and dosimetry in ion implantation; charge neutralization during ion implantation; high power ion sources. Subspecialties: Atomic and molecular physics; Laser spectroscopy. Home: 7 Hidden Ledge Rd Manchester MA 01944 Office: 16 Tozer Rd Beverly MA 01915

MACK, RICHARD NORTON, botany educator; b. Providence, R.I., July 31, 1945; s. Samuel Norton and Elizabeth (Dryman) M.; m. Nancy Lee Stack, June 17, 1972; 1 child, Lauren Hilary. B.A., Western State Coll. Colo., 1967; Ph.D., Wash. State U., 1971. Asst. prof. Kent State U., Ohio, 1971-75; asst. prof. Wash. State U., Pullman, 1975-79, assoc. prof., 1979-83, prof. botany, 1983—; mem. ecology panel NSF, Washington, 1982-85. Contbr. articles to profl. jours. NSF research grantee, 1974, 77, 80, 82, 84. Mem. Ecol. Soc. Am. (council 1982-85, editor ecology and ecol. monographs 1982-85), Brit. Ecol. Soc., Am. Quaternary Assn., Sigma Xi. Current work: The ecology of plant invasions; plant demography and competition; evolutionary interactions between plants and their grazers; the Quaternary vegetation history of the Pacific Northwest. Subspecialties: Ecology (biology); Population biology. Office: Dept Botany Wash State U Pullman WA 99164

MACKANESS, GEORGE BELLAMY, pharmaceutical company executive; b. Sydney, Australia, Aug. 20, 1922; came to U.S., 1965, naturalized, 1978; s. James Vincent and Eleanor Frances (Bellamy) M.; m. Gwynneth Patterson, May 5, 1945; 1 son, Miles Philip. M.B. B.S. with honors U. Sydney, 1945; D.C.P., London U., 1949; M.A. with honors, U. Oxford, 1949, D.Phil., 1953. Demonstrator, tutor in pathology Sir William Dunn Sch. Pathology, Oxford, 1949-53; sr. fellow Australian Nat. U., 1954-58, asso. prof., 1958-60, professorial fellow, 1960-63; prof. microbiology U. Adelaide, 1963-65; dir. Trudeau Inst., 1965-76; pres. The Squibb Inst. for Med. Research, Princeton, N.J., 1976—; clin. prof. dept. medicine Coll. of Medicine and Dentistry of N.J.; adj. prof. pathology N.Y. U. Author articles in field. Recipient Paul Ehrlich-Ludwig Darmstaedter prize, 1975. Fellow Royal Soc. London; mem. Am. Assn. Immunologists, AAAS, Am. Soc. Microbiologists, Internat. Soc. Immunopharmacology. Subspecialty: Medical research management. Home: 1515 Rolling Green Rd Yardley PA 19067 Office: PO Box 4000 Princeton NJ 08540

MACKAY, G. DAVID MACIVOR, university administrator, educator; b. Antigonish, N.S., Can., May 4, 1933; s. George Kenneth and Malcena Grace (MacIvor) MacK.; m. Ethel Kristine Saxhaug, Aug. 15, 1959; children—Ross D., Janet L., James E., Robin K., Bjarne P. B. Engring., Tech. U. N.S. (Can.), 1955, M. Engring., 1959; Ph.D., McGill U. (Can.), 1963. Registered profl. engr., N.S. Research officer Can. Dept. Forestry, Ottawa, Can., 1963-65; asst. prof. Tech. U. N.S., Halifax, 1965-66, assoc. prof., 1966-68, prof., head dept., 1968-79, dir. Ctr. Energy Studies, 1979—. Served to lt. Can. Air Force, 1950-53. Recipient Nat. Research Council fellow, 1973; Queens medal Govt. Can., 1976. Fellow Chem. Inst. Can. (dir. 1982-83); mem. Can. Soc. Chem. Engring. (pres. 1982-83). Current work: Combustion of wood and biomass-fluidized bed combustion. Subspecialties: Biomass (energy science and technology); Chemical engineering. Office: Tech U NS PO Box 1000 Halifax NS B3J 2X4 Canada

MACKAY, KENNETH DONALD, chemical company executive, chemist; b. Detroit, July 18, 1942; m. Bonnie Young, Aug. 12, 1964; children—Heather, Laurel. B.S., U. Mich., 1964; Ph.D., U. Minn., 1968. With Henkel Corp., Mpls., 1968—, assoc. dir. research, 1980-82, dir. research, 1982-83, v.p., 1983—. Contbr. articles to profl. jours. Patentee in field. Mayor, City of Circle Pines, Minn., 1971-77. Mem. Am. Chem. Soc., Am. Mgmt. Assn., Indsl. Research Inst. Subspecialty: Chemistry research administration. Office: Henkel Corp 2010 E Hennepin St Minneapolis MN 55413

MACKE, HARRY JERRY, mechanical engineer; b. Newport, Ky., Aug. 26, 1922; s. Harry Jerome and Mildred Ruth (Rauch) M.; m. Virginia Heinlein, Apr. 1, 1948; children: Janice, Jennifer. B.S. in Mech. Engring, U. Ky., 1947; M.S. in Mech. Engring, Harvard U., 1948, S.D. in Applied Mechanics, 1951. Registered profl. engr., Ohio. Instr. applied mechanics U. Ky., 1947; teaching fellow in civil engring. Harvard U., 1948-50; mech. engr. Aircraft Engine Bus. Group, Gen. Electric Co., Boston, 1951-52, Cin., 1952-71, cons. engring. mechanics, 1971-77, mgr. applied exptl. stress, 1977—; adj. assoc. prof. aerospace engring. U. Cin., 1961-66, 83. Contbr. articles to profl. jours. Served to 1st lt. Signal Corps U.S. Army, 1943-46. Mem. ASME, Soc. Exptl. Mechanics, Sigma Xi, Tau Beta Pi. Current Work: Exptl. mechanics, stress analysis, photoelasticity, aircraft gas turbines. Subspecialties: Mechanical engineering; Theoretical and applied mechanics. Home: 7305 Drake Rd Cincinnati OH 45243 Office: 1 Neumann Way Mail Drop G60 Cincinnati OH 45215

MACKENZIE, JOHN DOUGLAS, educator; b. Hong Kong, Feb. 18, 1926; came to U.S., 1954, naturalized, 1963; s. John and Hannah (Wong) MacK.; m. Jennifer Russell, Oct. 2, 1954; children—Timothy John, Andrea Louise, Peter Neil. B.Sc., U. London, 1952, Ph.D., 1954. Research asst., lectr. Princeton U., 1954-56; ICI fellow Cambridge (Eng.) U., 1956-57; research scientist Gen. Electric Research Center, N.Y.C., 1957-63; prof. materials sci. Rensselaer Poly. Inst., 1963-69; prof. engring. U. Calif., Los Angeles, 1969—; U.S. rep. Internat. Glass Commn., 1964-71. Author books in field (6); editor: Jour. Non-Crystalline Solids, 1968—; contbr. articles to profl. jours. Fellow Am. Ceramic Soc., Royal Inst. Chemistry; mem. Nat. Acad. Engring., Am. Phys. Soc., Electrochem. Soc., ASTM, Am. Chem. Soc., Soc. Glass Tech. Patentee in field. Subspecialty: Ceramics. Office: 6531 Boelter Hall Univ of Calif Los Angeles CA 90024

MACKERER, CARL ROBERT, oil co. exec., research scientist; b. Jersey City, Sept 2, 1940; s. Carl Joseph and Kathryn Anna M.; m. Marie Elizabeth Kempster, Dec. 3, 1946; children: Mary Ann, Carl William, Linda Marie. A.B., Rutgers U., 1963, postgrad., 1967-68; Ph.D. in Med. Biochemistry, U. Nebr., 1971. Cardiovascular pharmacologist Hoffmann-La Roche, Nutley, N.J., 1963-67; instr. biochemistry U. Nebr. Coll. Medicine, Omaha, 1971; research investigator G.D. Searle, Inc., Skokie, Ill., 1971-73, sr. research investigator, 1973-75, research scientist, 1975-77, sr. research scientist, 1978; mgr. biochem. toxicology Toxicology div. Mobil Oil Corp., Princeton, N.J., 1978—. Contbr. 76 articles to sci. jours. Mem. Am. Coll. Toxicology, Am. Soc. for Pharmacology and Exptl. Therapeutics, Biochem. Soc., Am. Chem. Soc. Current Work: Manager of a section working in fields of genetic toxicology, pharmacokinetics, analytical chemistry, clinical chemistry, pharmacology attempting to determine and explain toxic effects of chemicals. Subspecialties: Pharmacology; Toxicology (medicine). Home: 5 Blue Spruce Dr Pennington NJ 08536 Office: PO Box 1029 Princeton NJ 08540

MACKIE, RICHARD JOHN, wildlife management educator; b. Foster City, Mich., July 6, 1933; s. Arvid Axel and Ruth Hildegard (Rein) M.; m. Barbara Ann Rye, June 22, 1957; children—Bryan, Alan, Leann, Lorelyn. B.S., Mich. State U., 1958; M.S., Washington State U., 1960; Ph.D., Mont. State U., 1965. Cert. wildlife biologist. Research biologist Mont. Dept. Fish and Game, Lewistown and Bozeman, 1960-65, research coordinator, Bozeman, 1965-66; asst. prof., then assoc. prof. wildlife U. Minn., St. Paul, 1966-70; prof. wildlife mgmt. Mont. State U., Bozeman, 1970—; big game range project leader Mont. Dept. Fish and Game, Bozeman, 1970-75, statewide deer research leader, 1975—; mem. Mont. Rangeland Resources Council, 1977-80. Author: wildlife monographs Deer, Elk, Cattle Relations, 1970; Moose Ecology Northeast Minnesota, 1974. Contbr. articles to profl. jours., chpts. to books. Served with U.S. Army, 1953-55. Mem. Wildlife Soc. (Northwest sect. rep. 1980—, pres. Northwest. sect. 1976-77, pres. Mont. chpt. 1973-74), Soc. Range Mgmt., Western Deer Workshop (chmn. 1984-85), Phi Sigma (Biologist of Yr. 1965). Presbyterian. Current work: Population ecology and habitat relationships of deer, habitat ecology, interspecific relations among ungulates/ between wild ungulates and domestic livestock. Subspecialties: Ecology (biology); Ecology (environmental science). Home: 1312 Cherry Dr Bozeman MT 59715 Office: Dept Biology Mont State U Bozeman MT 59717

MACKWORTH, ALAN KEITH, computer scientist, educator, researcher; b. Cambridge, Eng., Oct. 18, 1945; came to Can., 1958; s. Norman Humphrey and Jane Felicity (Thring) M.; m. Marian Elizabeth Fry, Apr. 30, 1969; 1 child, Bryn Sarah. B.A.Sc., U. Toronto, 1966; A.M., Harvard U., 1967; Ph.D., Sussex U., 1974. Lectr. U. Toronto, 1967-70; asst. prof. dept. computer sci. U. B.C., Vancouver, 1974-79, assoc. prof., 1979-84, prof., 1984—. Contbr. chpts. books and articles to profl. jours. Killam Found. fellow, 1980-81, Canadian Inst. Advanced Research fellow, 1984—. Mem. Can. Soc. Computational Studies of Intelligence (v.p. 1978-80, pres. 1980-82), Internat. Joint Confs. on Artificial Intelligence, Inc. (chmn. bd. trustees 1983-84). Current work: Artificial intelligence, knowledge representation, computational vision, remote sensing, applications to resource management, computer graphics. Subspecialty: Artificial intelligence. Office: Univ BC Dept Computer Sci 2075 Wesbrook Mall Vancouver BC V6T 1W5 Canada

MACLACHLAN, JAMES ANGELL, physicist; b. Cambridge, Mass., May 18, 1938; s. James Angell and Mary Jane (Carrier) MacL.; m. Patricia Ann Petruschke, June 25, 1960; children—Beryl Z., Jared T. A.B., U. Mich., 1959; M.S., Yale U., 1962, Ph.D., 1967. Cons. programmer Yale Computer Ctr., New Haven, 1967-68; physicist Fermi Nat Accelerator Lab., Batavia, Ill., 1968—; dir. Endura Plastics Inc., Kirtland, Ohio. Contbr. articles to sci. jours. Mem. Am. Phys. Soc., ACLU (former chmn., treas., fin. chmn. Kane County, Ill. chpt. 1982—), Phi Beta Kappa, Sigma Xi (chmn. Amoco/Fermilab awards com. 1984). Current work: R F systems for proton-antiproton colliding beam facillities, especially low level and control; hadron physics, scattering and decays; production. Subspecialty: Particle physics. Home: 318 S 5th St Geneva IL 60134 Office: Fermi Nat Accelerator Lab PO Box 500 Batavia IL 60510

MACLACHLAN, JAMES MORRILL, educator; b. Geneva, Ill., Mar. 21, 1934; s. John Andrew and Gladys (Morrill) MacL.; m. Sally Gerig, Oct. 21, 1978; children: Sheila, Carolyn, Laura. B.S., Carnegie Inst. Tech., 1956; M.B.A., Harvard U., 1971; Ph.D., U. Calif.-Berkeley, 1975. Pubr. The Tri-Town News, Sidney, N.Y., 1958-69; asst. prof. NYU, N.Y.C., 1975-79; assoc. prof. Columbia U., N.Y.C., 1980, Rensselaer Poly. Inst., Troy, N.Y., 1981—; pres. Timely Decisions, Inc., Delmar, N.Y., 1978—, Biblical Films, Inc., Delmar, 1981—. Author: Response latency: New Measure of Advertising, 1977. Served with U.S. Army, 1956-58. Mem. Am. Psychol. Assn., Soc. Motion Picture and TV Editors, Nat. Assn. Religious Broadcasters. Club: Harvard. Current Work: Developed process for time compression of TV; developing advanced chroma-key system for TV. Subspecialty: Cognition. Home: 310 Elm Ave S Delmar NY 12054 Office: Rensselaer Poly Inst Lally Mgmt Bldg Troy NY 12181

MAC LAREN, MALCOLM DONALD, computer scientist; b. Tarrytown, N.Y., Aug. 5, 1936; s. Malcolm Neil and Grace Margaret (Du Bois) MacL.; m. Cecilia Marie Flynn, Apr. 20, 1968. A.B. magna cum laude, Harvard U., 1958, M.A. in Math., 1960, Ph.D., in Math., 1962. Mem. staff Boeing Sci. Research Labs., Seattle, 1960-64; asst., then assoc. mathematician Argonne Nat. Labs., Ill., 1964-72; cons. engr., then mgr. Advance Lang. Systems Devel., Cambridge Info. Systems Lab., Honeywell, Cambridge, Mass., 1972-76; sr. cons. engr. Digital Equipment Corp., Bellevue, Wash., 1976—; vis. prof. Northwestern U., Evanston, Ill., 1969; vice chmn. Am. Nat. Standards Inst. com. X3J1, Evanston, 1971-72. Author: Engineering A Compiler, 1982. Contbr. articles to profl. jours. Mem. Assn. Computing Machinery (Nat. Lectr. award 1968-69), Am. Math. Soc., Soc. Indsl. and Applied Math. Current work: Design of programming languages; compilers and related software; related problems in computer architecture. Subspecialties: Programming languages; Computer architecture. Home: 4910 E Mercer Way Mercer Island WA 98040 Office: Digital Equipment Corp 2265 116 Ave NE Bellevue WA 98004

MACLAY, WILLIAM NEVIN, physical chemist, manufacturing company executive; b. Belleville, Pa., Dec. 30, 1924; s. Robert B. and Grace V. (Royer) M.; m. Betty Jane Boucher, June 4, 1949; children: Gary L., Dennis K., Rebekah L., Bonnie L., Beth S. B.S. magna cum laude, Juniata Coll, Huntingdon, Pa., 1947; Ph.D. in Phys. Chemistry, Yale U., 1950. Assoc. prof. chemistry Davis and Elkins Coll., 1950-51; research scientist B.F. Goodrich Co., 1951-59; with Koppers Co., Inc., Monroeville, Pa., 1959-85, asst. mgr. research dept., 1968, v.p., mgr. research and devel., 1968-84, v.p., mgr. external research, 1984-85; ret., 1985; dir. Ceramatec Corp., Kopvenco, Inc., Advanced Refractories Tech. Inc.; bd. dirs. Indsl. Health Found., 1974-77; mem. materials adv. panel State of Pa., 1974-77, mem. indsl. panel on sci. and tech. NSF, 1973—. Contbr. articles to profl. jours. Trustee Juniata Coll., 1971-74; chmn. Pres.'s Devel. Council, 1969; deacon, elder United Presbyn. Ch. Served with USN, 1944-46. Mem. Am. Chem. Soc. Patentee in field. Current Work: Emulsion polymerization, suspension polymerization, surface and colloid chemistry. Subspecialties: Physical chemistry; Polymer chemistry. Home: 539 Greenleaf Dr Monroeville PA 15146 Office: 440 College Park Dr Monroeville PA 15146

MACLEOD, LLOYD BECK, Canadian government agriculture official; b. Grand View, P.E.I., Can., Apr. 27, 1930; s. Angus Bruce and Mary Myrtle (Beck) MacL.; m. Audrey Page Lawrence, Aug. 20, 1955; children—Susan Margaret, Kathryn Ann, David Lloyd. Student, Prince of Wales Coll., 1949-50; B.Sc., McGill U., 1952, M.Sc., 1953; Ph.D., Cornell U., 1962. Registered profl. agrologist. Research officer Agr. Can., Nappan, N.S., 1953-59, 62-65, research scientist, Charlottetown, P.E.I., 1965-70, dir. research sta., 1970—. Recipient Premier's Disting. Citizenship award Govt. P.E.I. Can., 1975. Fellow Can. Soc. Soil Sci.; mem. P.E.I. Inst. Agrologists (pres. 1969-70), Agrl. Inst. Can., Can. Soc. Agronomy, Am. Soc. Agronomy. Mem. United Ch. of Can. Lodge: Charlottetown Rotary (sec. 1984-85, pres.-elect 1985-86). Current work: Soil science, plant physiology; research on cereal, forage potato management and production, livestock feed systems. Subspecialties: Soil science; Agronomy. Office: Agr Can Research Sta PO Box 1210 440 University Ave Charlottetown PE C1A 7M8 Canada

MACMILLAN, JOHN HARRY, chemist, technologist; b. Peabody, Mass., May 22, 1944; s. John Henry and Enid Marjorie (Corpe) MacM.; m. Lynn Woltemate, May 22, 1981. B.S., Tufts U., 1966; Ph.D., Northeastern U., 1970. Research assoc. U. Utah, Salt Lake City, 1970-71; asst. prof. chemistry Eureka Coll., Ill., 1971-72; asst. prof., research assoc. Temple U., Phila., 1972-80; sr. chemist Thiokol Corp., West Trenton, N.J., 1980-83; dir. Homasote Co., West Trenton, 1983—; cons. in field. Contbr. articles to profl. jours. Mem. Am. Chem. Soc., Sigma Xi. Current work: Rigid urethane foams, insulating materials high performance materials; specialty chemicals; liquid crystals. Subspecialties: Polymer chemistry; Organic chemistry. Home: 324 Beechmont Rd Ambler PA 19002 Office: Homasote Co PO Box 7240 West Trenton NJ 08628

MACMILLEN, RICHARD EDWARD, biological sciences educator, researcher; b. Upland, Calif., Apr. 19, 1932; s. Hesper Nichols and Ruth Henrietta (Golder) MacM.; m. Barbara Jean Morgan, Oct. 23, 1980; 1 child, Ian Richard. B.A. in Zoology, Pomona Coll., 1954; M.S. in Zoology, U. Mich., 1956; Ph.D. in Zoology, UCLA, 1960. From instr. to assoc. prof. Pomona Coll., Claremont, Calif., 1960-68; from assoc. prof. to prof. U. Calif.-Irvine, 1968—, chmn. ecology and evolutionary biology dept., 1972-74, 84—; vis. prof. U. New South Wales, Kensington, Australia, 1974-75; vis. curator Australian Mus., Sydney, New South Wales, 1983; chmn. president's adv. com. White Mountain Research Sta., U. Calif., 1980—. Assoc. editor Jour. Mammalogy, 1979-81. Contbr. articles to profl. jours. Fulbright-Hays sr. research fellow Monash U., Victoria, Australia, 1966-67; grantee NSF Biotic Resources, 1962-83, panel mem. 1978-80. Fellow AAAS; mem. Cooper Ornithol. Soc. (bd. dirs. 1980-83), Am. Ornithologists Union, Ecol. Soc. Am. Democrat. Current work: The ecology of energy and water regulation in higher vertebrates, ecological energetics. Subspecialties: Ecology (biology); Evolutionary biology. Home: 31871 8th Ave South Laguna CA 92677 Office: Dept Ecology and Evolutionary Biology U Calif Irvine CA 92717

MACNAIR, RICHARD NELSON, research chemist; b. Newton, Mass., Oct. 19, 1929; s. Luther Knight and M. Louise (Hawkins) M.; m. Wanda Mae Decker, Jan. 2, 1960; 1 child, Douglas Cameron. B.A., Middlebury Coll., 1952; Ph.D., U. Del., 1960. Chemist Arthur D. Little, Inc., Cambridge, Mass., 1960-63; sr. organic chemist Tracer Lab div. Lab. for Electronics, Waltham, Mass., 1964; supervisory research chemist U.S. Army Natick Research and Devel. Ctr., Natick, Mass., 1964—. Contbr. articles to profl. jours. and book. Patentee in field. Served with U.S. Army, 1952-54, Korea. Fellow Am. Inst. Chemists, Mass. Inst. Chemists (pres. elect. 1976-78, pres. 1978-80, councilor 1980—); mem. Am. Chem. Soc., Am. Carbon Soc., Sigma Xi (pres. elect Natick chpt. 1972-73, pres. 1973-74). Democrat. Clubs: Boston Mineral; MIT Pistol and Rifle (Cambridge). Current work: Textile research, protective clothing, flame resistance, activated carbon preparation and properties. Subspecialties: Organic chemistry; Polymer chemistry. Home: 177 Hancock St Cambridge MA 02139 Office: US Army Natick Research and Devel Ctr Kansas St Natick MA 01760-5019

MACOVSKI, ALBERT, electrical engineering educator, researcher; b. N.Y.C., May 2, 1929; s. Philip and Rose (Wionogr) M.; m. Adelaide Paris, Aug. 5, 1950; children: Michael, Nancy. B.E.E., CCNY, 1950; M.E.E., Poly. Inst. Bklyn., 1953; Ph.D., Stanford U., 1968. Engr. RCA Lab., Princeton, N.J., 1950-57; assoc. prof. Poly. Inst. Bklyn., 1957-60; staff scientist Stanford Research Inst., Menlo Park, Calif., 1960-71; fellow U. Calif. Med. Center, San Francisco, 1971-72; prof. elec. engring. and radiology Stanford U., 1972—, cons., researcher med. imaging. Author: Medical Imaging Systems, 1983; contbr. numerous articles to profl. jours. Recipient RCA achievement awards, 1952, 54; NIH spl. fellow, 1972. Fellow IEEE (Zworykin award 1973, Profl. Group on BTR award 1957), Ops. Soc. Am.; mem. Am. Assn. Physicists in Medicine, Sigma Xi, Tau Beta Pi. Democrat. Jewish. Holder more than 100 patents in field. Current Work: Med. imaging using x-ray and ultrasound, multiple energy x-ray imaging, NMR imaging. Subspecialties: Biomedical engineering; Imaging technology. Home: 2505 Alpine Rd Menlo Park CA 94025 Office: Stanford University Electrical Engineering Dept Durand Bldg Stanford CA 94305

MACPHAIL, RICHARD ALLYN, chemistry educator, researcher; b. Midland, Mich., Jan. 27, 1953; s. Arthur Allyn and Barbara (Schumacher) MacP. B.A., Oberlin Coll., 1977; Ph.D., Univ. Calif.-Berkeley, 1981. Postdoctoral scholar UCLA, 1981-84; asst. prof. chemistry Duke U., Durham, N.C., 1984—. Contbr. articles to profl. jours. Mem. Am. Phys. Soc., Coblentz Soc., AAAS, Am. Chem. Soc., Sigma Xi. Current work: Vibrational spectroscopy and vibrational dephasing of non-rigid molecules in condensed phases; light scattering from viscous fluids and glasses. Subspecialties: Physical chemistry; Condensed matter physics. Office: Dept Chemistry Duke Univ Durham NC 27706

MAC QUEEN, ROBERT MOFFAT, solar physicist; b. Memphis, Mar. 28, 1938; s. Marion Leigh and Grace (Gilfillan) MacQ.; m. Caroline Gibbs, June 25, 1960; children: Andrew, Marjorie. B.S., Rhodes Coll., Southwestern U., Memphis, 1960; Ph.D., Johns Hopkins U., 1968. Asst. prof. physics Rhodes Coll., Southwestern U., Memphis, 1961-63; instr. physics and astronomy Goucher Coll., Towson, Md., 1964-66; sr. research scientist Nat. Center for Atmospheric Research, Boulder, Colo., 1967—, dir. high altitude obs., 1979—; prin. investigator NASA Apollo program, 1971-75, NASA Skylab program, 1970-76, NASA Solar Maximum Mission, 1976-79, 83—, NASA/ESA Internat. Solar Polar Mission, 1978-83; lectr. U. Colo., 1968-79, adj. prof., 1979—; mem. com. on space astronomy Nat. Acad. Scis., 1973-76, mem. com. on space physics, 1977-79; mem. Space Sci. Bd., 1983—; dir. Assoc. Univ. for Research in Astronomy, 1984—. Recipient NASA Exceptional Sci. Achievement medal, 1974. Fellow Optical Soc. Am.; mem. Am. Astron. Soc. (chmn. solar physics div. 1976-78), Am. Assn. Physics Tchrs., Sigma Xi. Current Work: Solar Coronal processes, space instrumentation. Subspecialty: Solar physics. Home: 1366 Northridge Ct Boulder CO 80302 Office: Box 3000 Nat Center for Atmospheric Research Boulder CO 80307

MACSWAN, IAIN CHRISTIE, plant pathologist; b. Ocean Falls, C., Can., Apr. 15, 1921; s. John and Catherine Rintoul (Kennedy) MacS.; m. Helen Constance White, Feb. 17, 1943; children: Neil, Catherine, Margot. B.S.A., U. B.C., 1942, M.S.A., 1961. Prin. research asst. Dominion Lab. Plant Pathology, U. B.C. (Can.), Vancouver, 1946-47; asst. provincial plant pathologist B.C. Dept. Agr., Vancouver, 1947-55; extension plant pathologist Oreg. State U., Corvallis, 1955—, asst. prof., 1955-61, assoc. prof., 1961-67, prof., 1967—. Contbr. articles to profl. jours. Served with RCAF/RAF, 1942-46. Mem. Am. Phytopathol. Soc., Can. Phytopathol. Soc. Republican. Lodge: Elks. Current Work: Fungicide testing and pear storage rots. Subspecialty: Plant pathology. Home: 1629 NW 14th ST Corvallis OR 97330 Office: Oreg State U Cordley Hall 1089 Corvallis OR 97331

MADAN, ARUN, physicist, consultant; b. New Delhi, India; came to U.S., 1977; s. Mohan Lal and Krishna (Varma) M.; m. Angela Turnell, May 8, 1970; children—Nadia, Damian. B.Sc., Reading U., Eng., 1967; M.Sc., London U., 1968; Ph.D., Dundee U., Scotland, 1973. Postdoctoral fellow Sheffield U., Eng., 1973-75; lectr. physics U. W.I., Trinidad, 1975-77; mgr. research and devel. Energy Conversion Devices, Troy, Mich., 1977-82; mgr. amorphous sci. Chevron Research, Richmond, Calif., 1982-83; head amorphous silicon Seri, Golden, Colo., 1983-85; v.p. Glasstech Solar, Inc., Wheat Ridge, Colo., 1985—; cons. energy conversion devices, 1983—. Contbr. chpts. to books, articles to profl. jours. Mem. Am. Phys. Soc., IEEE, Am. Vacuum Soc. Current work: Amorphous semiconductors, photovoltaics, thin film transistors, electronic devices. Subspecialties: Condensed matter physics; Solar energy. Office: Glasstech Solar Inc 12441 W 49th Ave Wheat Ridge CO 80033

MADERAK, MARION LOUIS, petroleum engineer, hydrologist; b. Kansas City, Kans., Apr. 25, 1933; s. George John and Anna Marie (Jaskot) M.; m. Catherine Ruth Steinauer, Sept. 16, 1961; 1 child, Michelle Lynn. B.S. in Geology, Kans. State U., 1958, M.S., 1960. Watershed geologist U.S. Geol. Survey, Lincoln, Nebr., 1960-65, hydrologist, Wichita Falls and Austin, Tex., 1967-79; exploration geologist Pan Am. Oil Corp., Oklahoma City, 1965-67; petroleum geology engr. James E Russell Petroleum & Engring, Chanute, Kans., 1979-80; petroleum cons., Chanute, 1980-84; petroleum engr. Bur. Land Mgmt., Cheyenne, Wyo., 1984—; subdist. chief U.S. Geol. Survey, Austin, 1974-79; div. geol. mgr. James E. Russell Petroleum & Engring., Chanute, 1979-80; dir. Marmaton Oil & Gas Co., Denver, 1980-82. Contbr. articles to profl. jours. Mem. Am. Assn. Petroleum Geologists, Am. Inst. Profl. Geologists, Geol. Soc. Am., Kans. Geol. Soc., Eastern Kans. Oil and Gas Assn. (dir. 1980), Chanute C. of C., Sigma Gamma Epsilon. Republican. Roman Catholic. Current work: Petroleum reservoir evaluation, enhanced oil recovery and petroleum geology, hydrology, ground water, surface water, chemical quality, sediment transport. Subspecialties: Petroleum engineering; Hydrology. Home: 422 Dalcour Cheyenne WY 82009-3516 Office: Bur Land Mgmt 2515 Warren Ave Cheyenne WY 82001

MADEY, THEODORE EUGENE, surface science researcher; b. Wilmington, Del., Oct. 24, 1937; s. Eugene and Lucy E. (Wojcik) M.; m. Jane Mary Gunn, Sept. 3, 1960; children—Timothy Francis, Doretta Marie, Maureen Anne, Daniel Andrew. B.S. in Physics, Loyola Coll., Balt., 1959; Ph.D. in Physics, U. Notre Dame, 1963. Physicist, Nat. Bur. Standards, Washington, 1965-83, fellow and group leader, 1983—; Chevron vis. prof. Calif. Inst. Tech., Pasadena, 1981. Co-editor: Desorption Induced by Electronic Transitions, 1983; History of Vacuum Science and Technology, 1984. Contbr. numerous articles to sci. jours., chpts. to books. Pres., Boyds Fed. Credit Union, Md., 1969-71; mem. Burkittsville Town Council, Md., 1974-80. Recipient Silver medal Dept. Commerce, 1973, Gold medal, 1981; Stratton award Nat. Bur. Standards, 1978. Fellow Am. Phys. Soc.; mem. Am. Vacuum Soc. (pres. 1981, bd. dirs. 1978-82, M.W. Welch award 1985), Am. Inst. Physics (exec. com. of governing bd. 1982-85). Roman Catholic. Current work: Physics and chemistry of surfaces, chemisorption, catalysis, electron spectroscopy of surfaces, electron and photon-stimulated desorption. Subspecialties: Surface chemistry; Condensed matter physics. Office: Nat Bur Standards Gaithersburg MD 20899

MADISON, DON HARVEY, physicist, educator; b. Pierre, S.D., Jan. 4, 1945; s. Walter Leon and Marguerite M.; m. Lina Erika Madison, Aug. 27, 1966; children: Lisa, Kristina. B.A. with highest honors in Math., Sioux Falls (S.D.) Coll., 1967; M.S. in Physics, Fla. State U., Tallahassee, 1970, Ph.D. in Physics, 1972. Admissions counselor Sioux Falls Coll, 1967-68; research assoc. U. N.C.-Chapel Hill, 1972-74; asst. prof. physics Drake U., Des Moines, 1974-77, assoc. prof., 1977-81, prof., 1981—, Ellis and Nelle Levitt prof. physics, 1984—; sci. adv. com. for profl. meetings; referee profl. jours. Contbr. articles to profl. jours., chpts. to books. Bd. dirs. Home, Inc. Served with Army N.G., 1962-70. Recipient Disting. Alumni award Sioux Falls Coll., 1982; Centennial Scholar award Drake U., 1981. Mem. Am. Phys. Soc., Am. Assn. Physics Tchrs. Baptist. Current Work: Atomic excitation and ionization by charged particle impact, research in theoretical aspects of atomic scattering. Subspecialty: Atomic and molecular physics. Office: Dept Physics Drake U Des Moines IA 50311

MADISON, VINCENT STEWART, chemist; b. Adrian, Minn., Feb. 10, 1943; s. Ray Vincent and Bessie Irene (Downes) M.; m. Susan Virginia Nelson, July 26, 1970; children—Cecelia, Jane, Nicholas Elmer. B.Chemistry, U. Minn., 1965; Ph.D. in Chemistry, U. Oreg., 1969. Research fellow U. Calif. Med. Sch., San Francisco, 1970-71, Harvard U. Med. Sch., Boston, 1971-74; asst. to assoc. prof. U. Ill. Med. Ctr., Chgo., 1975-82; research fellow Hoffman-La Roche Inc., Nutley, N.J., 1982—; cons. Abbott Labs., North Chicago, Ill., 1978-81. Contbr. articles to profl. jours. Mem. Am. Chem. Soc., Current work: Molecular modeling, computer graphics, computational chemistry, NMR spectroscopy. Subspecialties: Biophysical chemistry; Theoretical chemistry. Home: 12 Ronarm Dr Mountain Lakes NJ 07046 Office: Hoffman-La Roche Inc 340 Kingsland St Nutley NJ 07110

MADISSOO, HARRY, veterinarian, research executive; b. Paide, Estonia, July 4, 1924; came to U.S., 1951; s. August and Alide (Vimberg) M.; m. Leida Rossman, Sept. 26, 1964; children—Tiina, Andres. Dipl. Veterinarian, Vet. Coll., Hannover, Fed. Republic Germany, 1958, Dr. Med. Vet., 1960. Research asst. Cornell U. Med. Coll., N.Y.C., 1952-54, 55-57; sr. research scientist E.R. Squibb & Co., New Brunswick, N.J., 1960-64; dir. toxicology Bristol-Myers Co., Syracuse, N.Y., 1964—. Contbr. articles to profl. jours. Mem. Soc. Toxicology, AVMA, European Soc. Toxicology, N.Y. Acad. Scis., Am. Assn. for Lab. Animal Sci. Lutheran. Current work: pharmaceutical pathology and toxicology. Subspecialties: Toxicology (medicine); Pathology (veterinary medicine). Office: Bristol-Myers Co Thompson Rd Syracuse NY 13221

MADRI, JOSEPH ANTHONY, pathologist; b. N.Y.C., May 16, 1946; s. Vito and Anna (Melfi) M.; m. Lucille Katherine Gallo, June 28, 1969; children—Daniel Joseph, Jessica Lynn. B.S., St. John's U., 1967, M.S., 1969; Ph.D., Ind. U., 1973, M.D., 1974. Diplomate Am. Bd. Pathology. Intern, Yale-New Haven Hosp., 1975-76, resident, 1976-77; asst. prof. pathology Yale U., New Haven, 1980—; co-dir. immunochemistry lab., 1981-84; reviewer NIH, NCI, Bethesda, Md., 1981—. Contbr. articles to profl. jours. NIH grantee, 1981, 84. Mem. Am. Soc. Cell Biology, Am. Assn. Pathologists, N.Y. Acad. Scis. Democrat. Current work: Cell matrix interactions in angiogenesis and neovascularization. Subspecialty: Cell biology (medicine). Office: Dept Pathology Yale U 310 Cedar St New Haven CT 06510

MADURA, JAMES ANTHONY, surgery educator; b. Campbell, Ohio, June 10, 1938; s. Anthony Peter and Margaret Ethel (Sebest) M.; m. Loretta Jayne Sovak, Aug. 8, 1959; children: Debra Jean, James Anthony II, Vicki Sue. B.A., Colgate U., 1959; M.D., Western Res. U., 1963. Diplomate: Am. Bd. Surgery. Intern, resident in surgery Ohio State U., 1963-71; asst. prof. surgery Ind. U.-Indpls., 1971-76, assoc. prof., 1977-80, prof., 1980—. Contbr. articles profl. jours., chpts. in books. Chmn. ad hoc com. redistricting Washington Twp. Sch. Bd., Indpls., 1979-80; safety dir. Indpls. Youth Hockey League, 1975-77. Served to capt. U.S. Army, 1964-66, Vietnam. Fellow ACS (pres. Ind. chpt. 1982-83); mem. Central Surg. Assn., Western Surg. Assn., Soc. Surgery Alimentary Tract, Midwest Surg. Soc., Assn. Acad. Surgery, Assn. Surg. Edn., ASTM, Sigma Xi. Republican. Roman Catholic. Club: Columbia. Lodge: Elks (Indpls.). Current Work: Education of medical students and surgical residents; nutritional treatment of critically ill patients. Subspecialties: Surgery; Nutrition (medicine). Home: 9525 Copley Dr Indianapolis IN 46260 Office: Dept of Surgery Indiana University Medical Center 545 Barnhill Dr Indianapolis IN 46223

MAGAR, SURENDAR SINGH, electronic engineer; b. Dehradun, India, Mar. 1, 1949; came to U.S., 1980; s. Karam Singh and Surjit (Kaur) M.; m. Nirmal Jit, Oct. 22, 1975; children—Jigeesh, Gireesh. B.Sc. in Elec. Engring. with 1st class honors, U. Aston, Ph.D. in Elec. Engring. Chartered engr., Eng. Research assoc. U. Birmingham, Eng., 1975-76; sr. scientist Plessey Research Ltd., Northampton, Eng., 1976-79; tech. mgr. digital signal processing Tex. Instruments Co., Houston, 1979—, sr. mem. tech. staff, 1984—. Contbr. articles to profl. jours. Patentee in field. Mem. IEEE, Instn. Elec. Engrs. Current work: Research and development in area of digital signal processing hardware, computer architectures and integrated circuit technology. Subspecialties: Integrated circuits; Computer architecture. Home: 2115 Green Cove Sugarland TX 77479 Office: Tex Instruments Co PO Box 1443 M/S 6400 Houston TX 77001

MAGE, ROSE GOLDMAN, immunologist; b. N.Y.C., Oct. 8, 1935; d. Abraham and Augusta (Wagner) Goldman; m. Michael Gordon Mage, June 12, 1955; children—Dan, Gene, Anita. B.S., Cornell U., 1956; Ph.D., Columbia U., 1963. Postdoctoral fellow Lab. Immunology, Nat. Inst. Allergy and Infection, NIH, Bethesda, Md., 1963-65, sr. investigator, 1965—. Contbr. articles to profl. jours., chpts. to books. Mem. Am. Assn. Immunologists, Am. Soc. Microbiology (chmn. div. immunology 1982-84), Sigma Xi. Current work: Genetics; organization and regulated expression of genes for antibody heavy and light chains and belated structures on lymphocytes. Subspecialties: Immunobiology and immunology; Genome organization. Home: 7008 Wilson Ln Bethesda MD 20817 Office: Lab Immunology Nat Inst Allergy and Infectious Diseases NIH Bethesda MD 20205

MAGEE, JOHN FRANCIS, research company executive; b. Bangor, Maine, Dec. 3, 1926; s. John Henry and Marie (Frawley) M.; m. Dorothy Elma Hundley, Nov. 19, 1949; children—Catherine Anne, John Hundley, Andrew Stephen. A.B., Bowdoin Coll., 1946; M.S., U. Maine, 1952; M.B.A., Harvard U., 1948. With Arthur D. Little, Inc., Cambridge, Mass., 1950—, v.p., 1961-72, pres., 1972—, chief exec. officer, 1974—, also dir.; dir. John Hancock Mut. Life Ins. Co., Boston, Houghton-Mifflin, Inc., Bank of New Eng. Corp., Boston. Author: Physical Distribution Systems, 1967, Industrial Logistics: Analysis and Management of Physical Supply and Distribution Systems, 1968, (with D. M. Boodman) Production Planning and Inventory Control, 1968. Trustee New Eng. Aquarium, Boston, Univ. Med. Center, Boston, U.S.S. Constitution Mus., Boston, Bowdoin Coll., Woods Hole Oceanographic Instn. Served with USNR, 1944-46. Mem. Ops. Research Soc. Am. (pres. 1966-67), Inst. Mgmt. Scis. (pres. 1971-72), Phi Beta Kappa, Phi Kappa Psi. Clubs: Concord (Mass.) Country (gov. 1971—); The Country (Brookline, Mass.); Somerset (Boston). Office: 25 Acorn Park Cambridge MA 02140

MAGEE, JOHN LAFAYETTE, radiation chemist; b. Franklinton, La., Oct. 28, 1914; s. John Lafayette and Edith (Jenkins) M.; m. Priscilla Williams, Jan. 1, 1948; children—Lawrence Edward, Linda Sue, John Bradley. A.B., Miss. Coll., Clinton, 1935; M.S., Vanderbilt U., 1936; Ph.D., U. Wis., 1939. NRC fellow Princeton U., N.J., 1939-40, research assoc., 1940-41; research chemist B.F. Goodrich Co., Akron, Ohio, 1941-43; staff mem. Los Alamos Sci. Lab., 1943-45; group leader Naval Ordinance Test Sta., Calif., 1945-46; sr. scientist Argonne Nat. Lab., Ill., 1946-48; asst. prof. chemistry U. Notre Dame, Ind., 1948-49, assoc. prof., 1949-53, prof., 1953-79, prof. emeritus, 1979—, assoc. dir. radiation lab., 1954-71, dir. radiation lab., 1971-75, chmn. chem. physics program, head chemistry dept., 1967-70, vis. staff sr. scientist Lawrence Berkeley Lab., Calif., 1976-77, staff sr. scientist, 1977—; observer atomic testing, Bikini, South Pacific, 1946; project dir. Weapons Evaluation Group, Dept. Def., 1955-57; cons AEC, 1946-70; cons. Argonne Nat. Lab., Oak Ridge Nat. Lab., Brookhaven Nat. Lab.; cons. Rand Corp., 1952-55, Lockheed Missiles and Space Co., 1957-67. Co-editor: Comparative Effects of Radiation, 1960; Advances in Radiation Chemistry, 1969-76. Contbr. numerous articles on reaction rate theory and chem. effects of radiation to sci. jours. Fellow Am. Phys. Soc.; mem. Am. Chem. Soc., Radiation Research Soc. (council 1957-60, 66-69, pres. 1967-68), Faraday Soc., AAAS, AAUP (pres. Notre Dame chpt. 1959-61), Sigma Xi. Current work: Radiation chemical effects of heavy particle irradiation of DNA in aqueous solution. Home: 6 Dorothy Pl Berkeley CA 94705 Office: Lawrence Berkeley Lab 1 Cyclotron Rd Berkeley CA 94720

MAGLICH, BOGDAN C., physicist; b. Yugoslavia, Aug. 5, 1928; came to U.S., 1956, naturalized, 1967; s. Cveta and Ivanka (Bingulac) M.; m. Elowyn Castle Westervelt, 1959 (div. 1969); children: Marko Castle, Ivanka Taylor; m. Sharon Bundy Chagnaud, 1970 (div. 1977); 1 dau., Roberta Cveta.; m. Shelia Sanders Aldrich Mosler, 1982. Diploma physics, U. Belgrade, 1951; M.S., U. Liverpool, Eng., 1955; Ph.D., MIT, 1959. Staff mem. Lawrence Berkeley Lab., 1959-62; dep. group leader Brit. group CERN European Orgn. Nuclear Research, Geneva, 1962-63, leader Swiss group, 1964-67; vis. prof., joint faculty mem. Princeton U.-U. Pa. accelerator U. Pa., 1967-69; prof. physics, prin. investigator high energy physics Rutgers U., 1969-74; chmn. Migma Inst. High Energy Fusion, 1974—; pres., chmn. Fusion Energy Corp., Princeton, N.J., 1972-81, Aneutronix Inc., 1982-83, Sci. Transfer Assocs., Inc., 1981—, United Scis. Inc., 1984—; dir. Nat. Computer Analysts, Princeton.; Resident scientist UN-ILO Seminar Econ. Devel. East Africa, Kenya, 1967; lectr. Postdoctoral Sch. Physics, Yerevan, USSR, 1965, Internat. Sch. Majorana, Italy, 1969; mem. U.S. delegation Internat. Conf. High Energy Physics, Vienna, 1968, Kiev, 1970;

spl. rep. of U.S. Pres. to Yugoslavia, 1976; sci. project dir. Univ. Research Ctr., King Abdulaziz U., Saudi Arabia, 1981-82; vis. prof. elec. engring. Poly. Inst. N.Y., 1981. Editor: Adventures in Experimental Physics. Chmn. Yugoslav-Am. Bicentennial Com., 1975-76, Sheila and Bogdan Maglich Found., 1983—. Recipient White House citation, 1961; Bourgeois d'honneur de Lens Switzerland, 1973; UNESCO fellow, 1957-58. Fellow Am. Phys. Soc.; mem. Ripon Soc. (bd. govs.), Sigma Xi. Clubs: Nassau (N.Y. and Princeton), Mass. Inst. Tech. (N.Y. and Princeton). Current work: Research and development of aneutronic energy (fission of light elements) as space power source. Discoverer omega-meson, 1961, missing-mass spectrometer, 1964, delta-meson, 1963, g-meson, S, T, U-mesons, 1965, precetron, 1969, migma-cell, 1972, aneutronic energy process, 1982. Patentee in field. Subspecialties: Nuclear fusion; Relativity and gravitation. Office: 20 Nassau St Princeton NJ 08542

MAGNANTI, THOMAS LEE, management educator; b. Omaha, Oct. 7, 1945; s. Lee A. and Florence L. (Lindquist) M.; m. Beverly A. McVinney, June 10, 1967; 1 son, R. Randall. B.S. summa cum laude, Syracuse U., 1967; M.S. in Stats, Stanford U., 1969, M.S. in Math, 1971, Ph.D., 1972. Asst. prof. Sloan Sch. Mgmt., MIT, Cambridge, 1971-75, assoc. prof., 1975-79, prof., 1979—, head mgmt. sci. area, 1982—; vis. fellow CORE, Leuven, Belgium, 1976 77; vis. scientist Grad. Sch. Bus., Harvard U., Cambridge, Mass., 1980-81. Author: (with S. Bradley, A. Hax) Applied Mathematical Programming, 1977; editor in chief: (with S. Bradley, A. Hax) Ops. Research, 1983—; co-editor: (with S. Bradley, A. Hax) Math. Programming, 1981-83; assoc. editor: (with S. Bradley, A. Hax) Mgmt. Sci, 1978-81, Soc. Indsl. and Applied Math. Jour. on Applied Math, 1976-81, Jour. on Algebraic and Discrete Methods, 1981—. Com. chmn. Cub Scouts, Holliston, Mass., 1981—. Mem. Ops. Research Soc. Am. (com. chmn. 1978-82), Inst. Mgmt. Scis., Soc. Indsl. and Applied Math., Math. Programming Soc. Current Work: Research in theoretical and applied optimization, particularly network optimization, transportation and distribution planning. Subspecialties: Operations research (engineering); Operations research (mathematics). Home: 616 Prentice St Holliston MA 01746 Office: Sloan Sch Mgmt MIT Bldg E53-350 Cambridge MA 02139

MAGNUSON, GUSTAV DONALD, physicist; b. Chgo., Aug. 22, 1926; s. Gust and Anna (Sjostrand) M.; m. Phyllis Elaine Mason, Mar. 18, 1950; children: Randal B., Donald G., Erik J., Scott K. Ph.B., U. Chgo., 1949, B.S., 1950; M.S., U. Ill., 1952, Ph.D., 1957. Lifetime teaching cert., Calif. Sr. staff scientist Gen. Dynamics/Convair, San Diego, 1957-66; now staff scientist; research assoc. prof. U. Va., Charlottesville, 1966-69; staff scientist Gulf Gen. Atomic, San Diego, 1969-72, IRT Corp., San Diego, 1972-76; instr. San Diego Community Coll, San Diego State U.; judge San Diego Sci. Fair. Contbr. papers to profl. jours.; speaker profl. confs. Served with U.S. Army, 1946-47. Mem. Am. Phys. Soc., Am. Assn. Physics Tchrs., AAAS, Sigma Xi. Republican. Roman Catholic. Club: Nat. Assn. Clock and Watch Collectors. Current Work: Calculation of radar cross sections. Subspecialties: Atomic and molecular physics; Magnetic physics. Home: 1755 Catalina Blvd San Diego CA 92107 Office: Gen Dynamics/Convair PO Box 80847 MZ 41-6850 San Diego CA 92138

MAGRATH, IAN TREVOR, cell biologist, physician; b. Isle of Man, U.K., Oct. 31, 1944; s. Albert Ernest and Ivy Gladys (Myers) M.; m. Pamela Vera Green, Mar. 4, 1943; children: Samantha, James, Simon. M.B., B.S., London U., 1967. Intern Charing Cross Hosp., London, 1967-68; resident in medicine-/oncology, also Royal Postgrad. Med. Sch., 1968-70; Research fellow in immunology Kennedy Inst. Rheumatology, 1970-71; hon. lectr. Inst. Diseases of the Chest, London U., 1970-71; dir. Lymphoma Treatment Ctr., Kampala, Uganda, 1971-74; sr. investigator and vis. scientist pediatric oncology Nat. Cancer Inst., Bethesda, Md., 1974—. Editor: The Pathogenesis of Leukemias and Lymphomas: Environmental Influences; contbr. chpts. to books, sci. articles to profl. publs. Recipient Gov.'s Clin. Gold medal Charing Cross Hosp., London, 1967; Llewellyn scholar, 1967; Cancer Research Campaign grantee, 1971-74. Mem. Am. Soc. Clin. Oncology, Am. Assn. Cancer Research, Royal Coll. Physicians, Royal Coll. Pathologists. Current Work: Major interest is lymphoid neoplasia, especially Burkitt's lymphoma; studies involve pathogenesis, cell biology and treatment; the geography of lymphoid neoplasia. Subspecialties: Chemotherapy; Cell study oncology. Home: 814 Patton Dr Silver Spring MD 20901 Office: NIH Bldg 10 Room 13N240 Bethesda MD 20205

MAGUIRE, GERALD QUENTIN, JR., computer scientist, educator; b. Indiana, Pa., Jan. 6, 1955; s. Gerald Quentin and Lois Margaret (Clark) M. B.A., Indiana U. of Pa., 1975; M.S., U. Utah, 1981, Ph.D., 1983. Asst. prof. computer sci. Columbia U., N.Y.C., 1983—; research collaborator NYU, 1976—, Brookhaven Nat. Lab., Upton, N.Y., 1981—. Author: Radiation Protection in the Radiologic and Health Sciences, 2d edit., 1985. Contbr. articles to profl. jours. Fulbright-Hayes fellow U. Utah; grantee AEC, ERDA, NSF. Mem. IEEE, Assn. for Computing Machinery, N.Y. Acad. Scis., Am. Phys. Soc., Sigma Xi. Current work: Programming environments for parallel processors; hardware and software for non-textual data. Subspecialties: Computer architecture; Graphics, image processing, and pattern recognition. Office: Computer Sci Dept Columbia U 520 W 120th St New York NY 10027

MAGUIRE, MARJORIE PAQUETTE, geneticist, educator; b. Pearl River, N.Y., Sept. 2, 1925; d. Percy Carlton and Pearl Ella (Phillips) P.; m. Bassett Maguire, Jr., June 13, 1950; children: William C., David J. B.S., Cornell U., 1947, Ph.D., 1952. Research assoc. U. Tex., Austin, 1958-64, research scientist, 1964-75, assoc. prof., 1975-81, prof., 1981—. Contbr. articles to profl. jours. NIH career devel. awardee, 1965-75; grantee NSF; grantee NIH. Mem. Genetics Soc. Am., Am. Genetic Assn., Am. Soc. Cell Biology, Bot. Soc. Am., Internat. Soc. Plant Molecular Biology, Sigma Xi. Current Work: Researcher in genetic recombination, meiotic chromosome structures, nuclear ultrastructure, interrelationships of synapsis, crossing over and chromosome disjunction. Subspecialties: Gene actions; Cell biology. Home: 2702 Valley Springs Rd Austin TX 78746 Office: Dept Zoology U Tex Austin TX 78712

MAHAN, GERALD D., physicist. Prof. physics U. Tenn., Knoxville, disting. scientist Oak Ridge Nat. Lab., Tenn. Subspecialty: Condensed matter physics. Office: U Tenn Dept Physics Knoxville TN 27916

MAHAN, HARRY CLINTON, psychologist, consulting statistician in neuropsychology; b. Ashtabula, Ohio, Mar. 14, 1909; s. Ray Noble and Jennie (Strickler) M.; m. Eleanor Gearhart, Apr. 20, 1944; 1 son, Michael G. A.B., Ohio U., 1931; M.A., Ohio State U., 1932, Ph.D., 1940. Psychologist Warren (Pa.) State Hosp., 1932-35, Warren (Pa.) State Hosp. (Ind. Div. Corrections), 1938-41; pvt. practice indsl. psychology, Wichita, Kans., 1946-50; assoc. prof. psychology U. Wichita, 1947-50; head dept. social sci. Oceanside (Calif.) Coll., 1954-57; head behavioral sci. dept. Palomar Coll., San Marcos, Calif., 1957-76, cons. neuropsychology statistician, Oceanside, Calif., 1977—; dir. Project Socrates, 1965—; 1st chmn. Calif. State Psychology Examining Com., 1957-60. Author: The Interactional Psychology of J.R. Kantor, 1968, A Primer of Interactional Psychology, 1970. Served to col. USMCR, 1943-69. Fellow Am. Psychol. Assn. (life); mem. Nat. Acad. Neuropsychologists (life), Blue Key, Phi Delta Theta. Presbyterian. Current Work: Statistical consulting and computational assistance. Subspecialties: Statistics; Neuropsychology. Home: 811 Leonard Ave Oceanside CA 92054

MAHAPATRA, RAJAT KANTI, cardiologist; b. Sautia, West Bengal, India, Aug. 6, 1943; s. Naba K. and Mohamaya (Bhattacha Riva) M.; m. Dipta Panda, May 19, 1973; children: Anirban Gora, Rita. B.S., Govt. Med. Coll., India; M.D. in Internal Medicine, Post Grad. Med. Inst., India, 1971; M.D. in Cardiology, All India Med. Inst., 1976. Bd. cert. in Internal Medicine and Cardiology, India. Fellow in hepatology Postgrad. Med. Inst., Chandigarh, India, 1971-72; registrar in cardiology All India Med. Inst., New Delhi, India, 1973-76; chief cardiology Safdar Jang Hosp., New Delhi, 1976-77; cardiology fellow Maimonides Med. Ctr., Bklyn., 1977-78, SUNY-Downstate Med. Ctr., Bklyn., 1978-79; fellow in hypertension U. Louisville, 1979-80; chief cardiologist USAF Carswell AFB Hosp., Ft. Worth, 1980-82, civilian cardiologists, 1983—, dir. cardiology. Served to maj. USAF, 1980-82. Recipient All India Med. Inst. Benjamin Castleman award, 1974. Fellow Am. Coll. Angiology; mem. Am. Fedn. Clin. Research. Current Work: investigate work in clinical pharmacology, drug trials, non-invasive cardiology and hypertension. Subspecialties: Cardiology; Internal medicine. Home: 1200 Mesquite Trail Benbrook TX 76126 Office: Carswell AFB Hosp Ft Worth TX 76127

MAHBOUBI, EZZAT OLLAH, physician; b. Dargaz, Iran, Apr. 21, 1929; s. Abbas and Khadijah M.; m. Pouran Minou, Apr. 12, 1957; children: Arta, Artin. M.D., U. Teheran, 1961; M.P.H., UCLA, 1964; cert. in cancer epidemiology, communications sci., preventive medicine and epidemiology. Dir. Babol Med. Research Sta.; head Internat. Agy. Research on Cancer, Teheran, Iran; acting chief epidemiology Am. Health Found., N.Y.C., 1980-81; prof. epidemiology Eppley Cancer Inst., U. Nebr. Med. Ctr., Omaha, 1973—; mem. grad. faculty U. Nebr., 1976—. Contbr. numerous articles to profl. jours., chpts. to books. Mem. Am. Assn. Cancer Research, Am. Public Health Assn., Internat. Epidemiol. Assn. Republican. Current Work: Causation of cancer; etiological factors in cancer. Subspecialties: Epidemiology; Preventive medicine. Home: 9933 Devonshire Dr Omaha NE 68114 Office: Eppley Cancer Inst UNMC Omaha NE 68105

MAHLBERG, PAUL GORDON, botanist, educator; b. Milw., Aug. 1, 1928; s. Paul Rudolph and Antoinette Marie (Heinkel) M.; m. Marilyn Margaret Waite, Aug. 14, 1954; children: Melinda Sue, Heidi Margaret. B.S., U. Wis., 1950; Ph.D., U. Calif.-Berkeley, 1958. Asst. prof. botany U. Pitts., 1958-65; prof. biology Ind. U., Bloomington, 1965—; cons. to cos. engaged in plant tissue culture to produce secondary products, rubber, alkaloids, in a culture system. Author: Laboratory Program in Plant Anatomy, 1971; editor 8 books; Contbr. articles to profl. jours. Recipient numerous grants from nat. agys. Current Work: Laticifer cell, glandular cells. Subspecialties: Plant cell and tissue culture; Cell and tissue culture.

MAHLER, INGA R., molecular biologist, educator; b. Beuthen, Germany, Sept. 13, 1925; d. Julius and Margarete (Goldstein) Ring; m. Donald L. Mahler, May 28, 1950. B.A., U. Pa., 1947, M.S., 1949; Ph.D., Brandeis U., 1961. Researcher dental bacteriology Tufts U. Dental Sch., 1950-57; postdoctoral fellow dept. biochemistry Brandeis U., Waltham, Mass., 1961-63, jr. research assoc., 1963-70; sr. scientist Rosenstiel Biomed. Research Ctr., Waltham, 1970—; cons. in field. Contbr. writings to profl. publs. Active NOW, LWV, World Wildlife Fund. Career devel. grantee Nat. Health Found., 1957-59. Mem. Am. Soc. Microbiology. Current Work: EPA sponsored research on metal resistant bacteria in polluted soil and water. Subspecialty: Molecular biology. Home: 36 Boulder Rd Newton Center MA 02159 Offic: Rosenstiel Research Ct Brandeis U Waltham MA 02154

MAHONEY, JOHN JAMES, aerospace executive; b. Boston, July 22, 1931; s. William Daniel and Margaret Ann M.; m. Barbara Cudworth, June 2, 1956; children—Mark, Brian, Lisa, John, Christopher. B.S.E.E., Northeastern U., 1954, M.S.E.E., 1962; M.S. in Mgmt., MIT, 1975. Dir. engring. Avco Systems Div., Wilmington, Mass., 1966-74, v.p. ops., 1975-77, v.p., gen. mgr., 1977-82; sr. v.p., group exec. Avco Corp., Wilmington, 1982—. Served with U.S. Army, 1954-57. Sloan fellow, 1975. Mem. Associated Industries Mass. (dir.), Nat. Security Indsl. Assn. (trustee). Home: 168 Elm St Byfield MA 01922 Office: Avco Corp 201 Lowell St Wilmington MA 01887

MAHOWALD, ANTHONY P., genetics educator; b. Albany, Minn., Nov. 24, 1932; s. Aloys and Cecelia (Maus) M.; m. Mary Briody, Apr. 11, 1971; children: Maureen, Lisa, Michael. B.S., Spring Hill Coll., 1958; Ph.D., Johns Hopkins U., 1962. Asst. prof. Marquette U., 1966-70; asst. mem. Inst. Cancer Research, 1970-72; asso. prof. biology Ind. U., Bloomington, 1972-76, prof., 1976-82; prof., chmn. dept. devel. genetics and anatomy Case Western Res. U., Cleve., 1982—. Editor-in-chief: Developmental Biology, 1980-85. Mem. Am. Soc. Cell Biology, Am. Soc. Genetics, (sec.), Soc. Devel. opmental Biology, Am. Soc. Zoology. Current Work: Analysis of oogenesis and early development, utilizing mutations, recombinant DNA and hybridoma approaches. Subspecialties: Developmental biology; Gene actions. Office: Dept Devel Genetics and Anatomy Case Western Res Cleveland OH 44106

MAHY, TYLER XEREZ, power sources development engineer, physical chemist; b. Augusta, Maine, Jan. 7, 1941; s. Andrew Xerez and Helen Jeanette (Hoag) M.; m. Marylou Ellen Kelly, Nov. 23, 1968; children—Helen, Andrew II, Richard II. A.B. in Chemistry, U. Pa., 1965; M.S. in Chemistry, Northeastern U., 1972, Ph.D. in Chemistry, 1979. Lithium battery chemist Livingston Electronic, Montgomeryville, Pa., 1963-66; phys. chemist research and devel. Norton Co., Newton, Mass., 1968-72; grad. student, tchr. Northeastern U., Boston, 1972-75; sr. engr. power sources CIA, Washington, 1975-80, dep. chief power sources br., 1980—. Patentee in field. Served to 1st lt. U.S. Army, 1966-68. Recipient Spl. Tech. Achievement award CIA, 1983. Mem. Am. Chem. Soc., Electrochem. Soc., Am. Soc. Metals, AAAS. Republican. Unitarian. Current work: Lithium/Thionyl-chloride, Lithium/-Sulfur-dioxide, Lithium/Carbon-fluoride, Nickel-Cadmium, and Alkaline-Manganese electrochemical cells and batteries Non-destructive measurements on cells. Subspecialties: Electrochemical energy storage and conversion; Physical chemistry. Home: 130 Duvall Ln Apt T-1 Gaithersburg MD 20877 Office: CIA care OTS Washington DC 20505

MAI, CHAO CHEN, engineer; b. Kwangchow, Canton, China, Feb. 26, 1936; came to U.S. 1962, naturalized 1973; m. Shao Shen Yam; children—Glenn, Kenneth. M.S.E.E., Oreg. State U., 1964; Ph.D. in E.E., Utah State U., 1967. Project engr. Sylvania Electric Co., Woburn, Mass., 1967-70; mgr. research and devel. Mostek Corp., Carrollton, Tex., 1970-76, v.p. research and devel., 1976-84; founder v.p. engring. Dallas Semiconductor Corp., 1984—. Patentee Silicon gate combined with depletion load process, 1974, MOSFET Fabrication Process, 1984. Mem. IEEE, Electrochem. Soc. Current work: Advanced processing technology in integrated circuits. Subspecialties: Integrated circuits; Microchip technology (engineering). Office: Dallas Semiconductor Corp 4350 Beltwood Pkwy So Dallas TX 75244

MAIBACH, HOWARD I., dermatologist; b. N.Y.C., July 18, 1929; s. Jack Louis and Sidonia (Fink) M.; m. Siesel Wile, July 8, 1953; children—Lisa, Ed, Todd. A.B., Tulane U., 1950, M.D., 1955. Diplomate: Am. Bd. Dermatology. Intern William Beaumont Army Hosp., El Paso, Tex., 1955-56; resident, fellow in dermatology USPHS, Hosp. of U. Pa., 1959-61; asst. instr. U. Pa., 1958-61, lectr., 1960-61; practice medicine specializing in dermatology U. Calif. Hosps., San Francisco, 1961—; asst. prof. dermatology U. Calif. Sch. Medicine, San Francisco, 1961-63, asso. prof., 1967-73; research asso. Cancer Research Inst., 1967—; mem. staff U. Calif.-H.C. Moffitt Hosps., 1961—; cons. Laguna Honda Hosp., 1962-66, chief dermatology service, 1963-67; cons. Letterman Gen. Hosp., San Francisco Gen. Hosp., Stanford Research Inst., Menlo Park, Calif., Calif. Dept. Public Health, Berkeley, David Grant USAF Hosp. of Travis AFB, Naval Hosp., San Diego, Wilford Hall AFB, Tex., Army Environ. Health Agy., Md.; mem. Internat. Contact Dermatitis Research Com. Editor: Animal Models in Dermatology, 1965; co-editor: Dermatotoxicology and Pharmacology, 1977, Skin Microbiology, 1981; bd. editors: Internat. Jour. Dermatology, 1974—; editorial bd.: Contact Dermatitis: Environ. Dermatology, 1974—, Clin. Toxicology, 1976—; internat. editorial bd.: Excerpta Media, 1976—; contbr. numerous articles to profl. jours. Served to capt. M.C. U.S. Army, 1955-58. Recipient awards Soc. Cosmetic Chemists, 1970, 71, 73. Fellow A.C.P.; mem. Am. Acad. Dermatology (award for essay 1961), San Francisco Dermatol. Soc. (pres. 1970-71), Pacific Dermatol. Assn., Soc. Investigative Dermatology, N.Y. Acad. Scis., Calif. Med. Assn., Am. Fedn. Clin. Research, AMA, San Francisco Med. Soc., Am. Dermatol. Assn., Internat. Soc. Tropical Dermatology, Am. Soc. Clin. Pharmacology and Therapeutics, Am. Coll. Toxicology; hon. mem. Swedish Dermatol. Soc., Am. Vet. Dermatol. Assn., Am. Acad. Vet. Dermatology, Danish Dermatol. Soc., German Dermatol. Soc. Subspecialties: Dermatology; Toxicology (medicine). Office: University of California Hospital San Francisco CA 94143

MAICKEL, ROGER PHILIP, pharmacologist, educator; b. Floral Park, N.Y., Sept. 8, 1933; s. Philip Vincent and Margaret Mary (Rose) M.; m. Lois Louise Pivonka, Sept. 8, 1956; children: Nancy Ellen Maickel Ward, Carolyn Sue. B.S., Manhattan (N.Y.) Coll., 1954; postgrad., Poly. Inst. Bklyn., 1954-55; M.S., Georgetown U., 1957, Ph.D., 1960. Biochemist Nat. Heart Inst., Bethesda, Md., 1955-65; assoc. prof. pharmacology Ind. U., 1965-69, prof., 1969—, head sect. pharmacology med. scis. program, 1971-77; prof. pharmacology and toxicology, head dept. Sch. Pharmacy and Pharmacal Scis. Purdue U., West Lafayette, Ind., 1977-83; acting v.p. product acquisition and devel. BetaMED Pharms., Inc., Indpls., 1982-84. Adv. editor: Pergamon Press, 1970—; adv. editorial bd.: Neuropharmacology, 1974—. Bd. dirs. TEAMS, Inc., 1981—. Recipient Alumni award in medicine Manhattan Coll., 1972. Fellow AAAS, Am. Coll. Neuropsychopharmacology, Am. Inst. Chemists, Royal Soc. Chemistry, Collegium Internat. de Neuro-Psychopharmacologicum; mem. Am. Chem. Soc., Am. Soc. Pharmacology and Exptl. Therapeutics, Am. Soc. Clin. Pharmacology and Therapeutics, ASTM, Soc. Forensic Toxicologists, Internat. Assn. Chiefs Police, Internat. Soc. Psyconeuroendocrinology, N.Y. Acad. Scis., Soc. Neurosci., Soc. Toxicology, Sigma Xi, Rho Chi. Subspecialty: Pharmacology. Home: 3567 Canterbury Dr Lafayette IN 47905 Office: Pharmacy Bldg Purdue U West Lafayette IN 47907

MAIER, LEO ROBERT, JR., mechanical engineering educator; b. Allentown, Pa., Oct. 23, 1939; s. Leo Robert and Dorothy Smith (Grim) M.; m. Marilyn Kater, Dec. 27, 1969; 1 child, Clifford John. B.S., Purdue U., 1961; M.Engring., Pa. State U., King of Prussia, 1967; Ph.D., Iowa State U., 1972. Registered profl. engr., Ohio, N.J. Sr. mech. engr. Power Generators, Inc., Trenton, N.J., 1961-69; tchr., research grad. asst. Iowa State U., Ames, 1969-72; sr. mech. design engr. United Aircraft Corp., Norwalk, Conn., 1972-73; sr. analytical engr. Atlantic Research Corp., Alexandria, Va., 1973-75; assoc. prof. mech. engring. Ohio No. U., Ada, 1975—; cons. in field, 1977—. Active United Way, 1979-84, ARC, 1978-84. Grantee NSF-Def. Civil Preparedness Agy.-Am. Soc. for Engring. Edn., 1976; NASA-Am. Soc. for Engring. Edn. summer faculty fellow, 1977; USAF-Am. Soc. for Engring. Edn. summer faculty fellow, 1978. Mem. ASME, Am. Soc. for Engring. Educators. Current Work: Failure analysis, polymers, fracture mechanics, robotics. Subspecialties: Mechanical engineering; Solid mechanics. Office: Dept Mech Engring Ohio No U Ada OH 45810

MAIER, ROBERT JAMES, microbiology educator, researcher; b. Detroit, July 1, 1951; s. William Frederick and Helen Viola (Mount) M.; m. Susan Elaine Johnson, Aug. 11, 1973; children—Robin, Cheryl. B.S., Mich. State U., 1973; M.S., U. Wis., 1975, Ph.D., 1977. research asst. U. Wis., Madison, 1973-77; post-doctoral fellow Oreg. State U., Corvallis, 1977-79; asst. prof. Johns Hopkins U., Balt., 1979-84, assoc. prof., 1984—; editorial bd. mem. Applied Environ. Microbiology Jour., 1982—; cons. Allied Chem. Corp., Syracuse, N.Y., 1982-83. Mem. Am. Soc. for Microbiology, Am. Soc. Biol. Chemists. Current work: Biochemistry, physiology and genetics of nitrogen-fixing bacteria. Subspecialties: Biochemistry (biology); Microbiology. Home: 1908 Fairbank Rd Baltimore MD 21209 Office: Johns Hopkins Univ 34th & Charles St Baltimore MD 21218

MAIMAN, THEODORE HAROLD, physicist; b. Los Angeles, July 11, 1927. B.S. in Engring. Physics, U. Colo., 1949; M.S. in Elec. Engring, Stanford U., 1951, Ph.D. in Physics, 1955. Sect. head Hughes Research Labs., 1955-61; pres., founder Korad Corp., Santa Monica, Calif., 1961-68, Maiman Assos., Los Angeles, 1968-76; v.p., founder Laser Video Corp., Los Angeles, 1972-75; v.p. advanced tech. and new ventures TRW Inc. Electronics and Def. Sector, Los Angeles, 1976-83; prin. Maiman Assocs., 1984—. Author papers in field.; Adv. bd.: Indsl. Research mag. Served with USNR, 1945-46. Recipient award Fannie and John Hertz Found., 1966; Ballantine award Franklin Inst., 1962; award for devel. laser Aerospace Elec. Soc.-Am. Astron. Soc., 1965; Light award Braille Inst., 1982; named Alumni of Century U. Colo., 1976; named to Nat. Inventors Hall of Fame, 1984. Fellow Soc. Motion Picture and TV Engrs., Am. Phys. Soc. (Oliver E. Buckley prize 1966), Optical Soc. Am. (R.W. Wood prize 1976), Soc. Photog. and Instrumentation Engrs. (Pres.'s award 1985); mem. Nat. Acad. Engrs., Nat. Acad. Scis., IEEE, Am. Soc. Laser Medicine and Surgery, Soc. Info. Display, Sigma Xi, Sigma Pi Sigma, Sigma Tau, Pi Mu Epsilon. Responsible devel. 1st laser. Subspecialties: Graphics, image processing, and pattern recognition; Laser data storage and reproduction.

MAISH, F(REDERIC) MICHAEL, engineer, administrator; b. Bedford, Ind., Sept. 28, 1943; s. Frederic F. and Helen L. (Robinette) M.; m. Melanie L. Barnes, June 24, 1972; children—Scott, Lara. B.S. in Elec. Engring., Purdue U., 1965; M.S. in Elec. Engring., Colo. U., 1973. Registered profl. engr., Colo. Elec. engr. Emerson Electric, St. Louis, 1965-66; research scientist U.S. Dept. Commerce, Boulder, 1967-83; mgr. Nat. Bur. Standards, Boulder, 1984—. Contbr. chpt. to Frozen Future. Founding bd. dirs. Hist. Boulder Inc., 1973—; trustee St. Paul's United Meth. Ch., Boulder, 1984-86. Recipient Soviet-Am. Exchange Scientist award Office Polar Research, NSF, 1969, Soviet 150th Antarctic Anniversary medal Artic and Antarctic Inst., Leningrad, 1970. Mem. IEEE, Assn. Computing Machinery, Theta Xi, Theta Alpha Phi. Current work: Scientific computing: computer standards, interconnection standards, algorithms for information interchange; computer networking standards and implementation. . Office: Nat Bur Standards 325 Broadway Boulder CO 80303

MAJEWSKI, FRANK THOMAS, mechanical and industrial engineer, automation and robotics consultant; b. Newark, Dec. 12, 1920; s. Thomas Michael and Mary (Gleba) M.; m. Adele J. Poznanski, Nov. 26, 1950; 1 dau., Patricia A. A.A., Seton Hall U., 1956, B.S., 1958, M.B.A., 1965; D.B.A., Heed U., 1983. Lic. profl. engr., N.J., Calif. Vice pres. Pullman Kellog, Inc., Jersey City, 1955-58; exec. v.p. Astrotherm Corp., Indpls., 1958-60; pres. RMF, Inc., King of Prussia, Pa., 1960-66, dir., 1960-67; v.p. MAI Corp., N.Y.C., 1966-67; cons. in automation and robotics IBM, Boca Raton, Fla., 1967-83; mem. adv. com. W.Va. Inst. Tech., 1960-64, Seton Hall U., 1960-67. Recipient U.S. Naval Ordnance award, 1945; Outstanding Contbn. award IBM, 1968; Inventions award, 1981, 82, 83. Mem. ASME, Soc Mfg. Engrs. (cert. mfg. engr.), Am. Inst. Indsl. Engrs., Soc. Advancement Mgmt., Robot Inst. Am., Alpha Kappa Psi. Inventor high altitude pressure suits, 1956, wrist joint for robots, 1979. Current Work: Industrial robots and robotic applications, plant automation. Subspecialties: Mechanical engineering; Industrial engineering. Home: 2551 NE 35th St Lighthouse Point FL 33064

MAJIDI-AHY, GHOLAMREZA, engineer, university lecturer. Student U. Tex.; B.S.E.E., M.S.E.E., U. Calif.-San Diego. Former teaching asst. and programmer U. Calif., San Diego; then sr. design engr. Harris Microwave Semiconductors, Milpitas, Calif.; now with Microwave Tech. Inc., Fremont, Calif.; also adj. lectr. U. Santa Clara, Calif. Contbr. articles to profl. jours. U. Calif. scholar. Mem. IEEE. Current work: GaAs discrete devices and monolithic microwave intergrated circuits; applied electromagnetic theory for microwave and milimeter waves devices. Subspecialties: Semiconductors; Integrated circuits. Home: PO Box 5071 Stanford CA 94305

MAK, SIOE THO, electrical engineer, researcher; b. Medan, N. Sumatra, Indonesia, Sept. 3, 1932; came to U.S., 1967, naturalized, 1976; s. Boen Kit and Tjioe Nio (Tjoa) M.; m. Jeanne Giok Nio, June 12, 1959; children—Sharleen, Shanta. Engring. degree, U. Indonesia, 1958; M.S. in Elec. Engring., Ill. Inst. Tech., 1961, Ph.D. in Elec. Engring., 1970. Sr. scientist Joslyn Mfrs. & Supply Co., Woodstock, Ill., 1972-76, research project mgr., 1976-78; sr. staff engr. TWACS program Emerson Electric, St. Louis, 1978-80, sr. staff scientist, 1980-82; mgr. advanced systems Chance Load Mgmt. Systems div. Emerson Electric, St. Louis, 1982—; sr. lectr. elec. engring. Bandung Inst. Tech., Indonesia, 1961-67; instr. elec. engring. Ill. Inst. Tech., Chgo., 1967-78, Washington U., St. Louis, 1982. Patentee in field. Contbr. articles to tech. jours. AID Jr. fellow, 1959. Mem. IEEE (sr. power system engring. com. 1984—). Current work: 10100 distributed systems and networks, power system control, powerline carrier on distribution networks, load management reliability. Subspecialties: Systems engineering; Composite materials. Office: Chance Load Mgmt Systems div Emerson Electric 5657 Campus Pkwy Hazelwood MO 63042

MAKAR, ADEEB BASSILI, pharmacology educator, researcher; b. Alexandria, Egypt, Dec. 2, 1936, came to U.S., 1980; s. Bassili E. and Sesil A. (Habib) M.; m. Zeizaf I. Saleeb, July 14, 1968; children—Mina A., George A. B.S. in Pharmacy, Alexandria U., 1958; Ph.D. in Pharmacology, U. Minn., 1966. Asst. prof. U. Alexandria, 1966-1972, assoc. prof., 1972-77; prof. pharmacology, 1977-80; vis. prof. U. Iowa, Iowa City, 1980-82; assoc. prof. U. Osteo. Medicine, Des Moines, 1983—; research cons. Alexandria Drug Co., 1972-74. Contbr. articles to profl. jours., chpt. to book. Internat. research fellow U. Iowa, 1974-76; grantee NIH, 1977-80, U. Osteo. Medicine, 1983—. Mem. Am. Soc. Pharmacology and Exptl. Therapeutics, N.Y. Acad. Scis., Iowa Acad. Sci., Am. Chem. Soc., Am. Coll. Toxicology. Current work: Biochemical basis of methanol toxicity in humans and experimental animals; role of glutathione in chemical toxicology. Subspecialties: Molecular pharmacology; Toxicology (medicine). Home: 2450 E Shawnee Ave Des Moines IA 50317 Office: U Osteopathic Medicine and Health Sci 3200 Grand Ave Des Moines IA 50312

MAKAR, BOSHRA HALIM, mathematics educator; b. Sohag, Egypt, Sept. 23, 1928; came to U.S., 1966, naturalized, 1971; s. Halim and Hakima (Khair Mikhail) M.; m. Nadia E. Eissa, Jan. 1, 1960; children: Ralph, Roger. B.Sc., Cairo U., 1943-47, M.Sc., 1952, Ph.D., 1955. Mem. faculty Cairo U., 1948-65; vis. assoc. prof. Am. U., Beirut, Lebanon, 1966, Mich. Tech. U., Houghton, 1967; prof. math. St. Peter's Coll., Jersey City, 1967—. Mem. Am. Math Soc., Math. Assn. Am., AAUP. Republican. Roman Catholic. Clubs: Poetry Soc. London; United Poets Internat. (Philippines) (v.p. 1971-76). Current Work: Mathematical analysis, functions of a complex variable and functional analysis, and cryptology. Subspecialties: Theory of functions and functional analysis; Cryptography and data security. Home: 410 Fairmount Ave Jersey City NJ 007306 Office: St Peter's Coll Math Dept Kennedy Blvd Jersey City NJ 07306

MAKAREWICZ, JOSEPH CHESTER, limnologist, educator; b. Attleboro, Mass., Aug. 5, 1947; s. Chester and Sophie Ann (Gawlik) M.; m. Joyce Ann Barac, July 31, 1971; children—Cheryl, Karen. B.S., Southeastern Mass. U., 1969; Ph.D., Cornell U., 1974. Research asst. U. Ga. Marine Inst., Sapelo Island, 1969; instr. Bristol Community Coll., Fall River, Mass., 1969-70; instr. Southeastern Mass. U., North Dartmouth, 1969-70; grad. asst. Cornell U., Ithaca, N.Y., 1970-74; prof. limnology SUNY-Brockport, 1974—; cons. Malcolm Pirnie, Inc., White Plains, N.Y., 1983, Saiki Inc., Pittsford, N.Y., 1982-84. Contbr. articles to profl. jours. Grantee EPA, NSF, NOAA. Mem. AAAS, Gt. Lakes Research Assn., Limnology and Oceanography Assn., Sigma Xi (Outstanding Researcher award 1983). Roman Catholic. Current work: Ecosystem approach to environmental analysis; nutrient cycling; zooplankton-phytoplankton interactions; toxic chemicals. Subspecialties: Limnology; Ecology (biology). Office: Biology Dept SUNY Brockport NY 14420

MAKAROWITZ, LLOYD, physics educator, administrator; b. Bronx, N.Y., Jan. 16, 1947; s. Sol and Frances (Levinson) M.; m. Kay Kramer, Aug. 10, 1969; children—Jonathan Michael, Seth Mathew. B.S., CCNY, 1967; M.A., Columbia U., 1969; Ph.D., CUNY, 1974. Instr. Kean Coll. of N.J., Union, 1974-75; asst. prof. St. John's U., N.Y.C., 1975-78; project dir. N.Y.C. Sch. Dist. 6, 1978-79; asst. prof., assoc. prof. SUNY-Farmingdale, 1979—, chmn. dept. physics, 1981—, mem. ednl. adv. group, 1983—, chmn. computer lit. com., 1984, mem. admissions and acad. standards com., 1983—. Editor brochure: Physical Sciences at Farmingdale, 1983; author, co-author jour. articles; lectr. civic orgn. Regents scholar, 1963-67; grad. faculty fellow Columbia U., 1967-69; teaching and research fellow, CUNY, 1969-74. Mem. N.Y. Acad. Scis., Am. Phys. Soc., Am. Assn. Physics Tchrs., AAAS, AAUP. Democrat. Jewish. Current work: Administrator physics education and research. Subspecialties: Particle physics; Physics education. Home: 8 Putnam Ave Jericho NY 11753 Office: Dept Physics SUNY Farmingdale NY 11735

MAKDISI, FAIZ ISBIR, civil engineer; b. Rashaya, Labanon; Aug. 24, 1948; came to U.S., 1970; s. Isbir Yousef and Naceema (Nemr) M.; m. Rima Yazigy, June 23, 1984. B.Sc. in Engring., Am. U., Beirut, 1970; M.Sc. in Civil Engring., U. Calif.-Berkeley, 1971, Ph.D. in Civil Engring., 1976. Registered profl. engr., Calif.; registered civil engr., Beirut. Grad. research asst. U. Calif.-Berkeley, 1973-76, asst. research engr., 1976-78; project engr. Woodward-Clyde Cons., San Francisco, 1976-78; v.p. MIDCO, Jeddah, Saudi Arabia, 1978—. Contbr. articles to profl. jours. Mem. ASCE (Norman medal 1976), Nat. Soc. Profl. Engrs., Inst. Civil engrs., Seismol. Soc. Am., Earthquake Engring. Research Inst. Current work: Geotechnical studies and pile foundations, earthquake engineering of earth structures, dynamic studies of earth dams and seismically induced deformations. Subspecialty: Civil engineering. Home: 6766 Snowdon Ave El Cerrito CA 94530 Office: MIDCO Saudi Arabia PO Box 75 Jeddah Saudi Arabia 21411

MAKI, KAZUMI, physics educator, researcher; b. Takamatsu, Japan, Jan. 27, 1936; came to U.S., 1974; s. Toshio and Hide (Shibata) M.; m. Masako Tanaka, Sept. 21, 1969. B.S. Kyoto U. (Japan), 1959, Ph.D., 1964. Research assoc. Inst. Math. Scis., Kyoto U., 1964-67; research assoc. U. Chgo., 1964-65; asst. prof. U. Calif., San Diego, 1965-67; prof. Tohoku U., Sendai, Japan, 1967-74; prof. physics U. So. Calif., Los Angeles, 1974—; vis. prof. Université Paris-Sud, Orsay, France, 1969-70, 79-80, Laue-Langevin Inst., Grenoble, France, 1979-80. Assoc. editor Jour. Low Temperature Physics, 1969—. Fulbright fellow, 1964; Guggenheim fellow, 1979-80; NSF grantee, 1975—; recipient Nishina prize Nishina Meml. Found., 1972. Fellow Am. Phys. Soc.; mem. Phys. Soc. Japan, AAAS. Current work: Theory of quantum liquid-like superconductivity and superfluid 3He; theory of topological defects, such as solitons, vortices and dislocations in condensed state. Subspecialties: Condensed matter physics; Low temperature physics. Home: 2615 33d St Santa Monica CA 90405 Office: Dept Physics Univ of So Calif Los Angeles CA 90098

MAKI, TAKASHI, surgery educator, physician; b. Tokyo, Sept. 18, 1940; came to U.S., 1971; s. Toru and Umeko (Kato) M.; m. Teruko Okumura, Oct. 9, 1966; children: Hisako, Reiko, Keiko, Satoshi. M.D., U. Tokyo, 1966; Ph.D., SUNY-Downstate Med. Ctr., 1977. Intern U. Tokyo Hosp., 1966-67, resident, 1967-71; asst. prof. surgery SUNY-Downstate Med. Ctr., 1977-78; assoc. mem. Cancer Research Inst., New Eng. Deaconess Hosp., Boston, 1978—; asst. prof. surgery Harvard Med. Sch., 1979-83, assoc. prof. surgery, 1983—. Contbr. numerous articles to sci. jours. Whitaker Health Scis. Fund grantee, 1979-80; William F. Milton Fund grantee, 1982. Mem. Am. Assn. Immunologists, N.Y. Acad. Sci., Transplantation Soc., Am. Soc. Transplant Surgeons, Sigma Xi. Congregationalist. Clubs: Cambridge Boat, Harvard. Current Work: Immunological studies of specific unresponsiveness; suppressor cells in allograft system; immunological studies of spontaneous mammary tumors. Subspecialties: Transplantation; Cancer research (medicine). Home: 17 Redwood Rd Westwood MA 02090 Office: Cancer Research Inst 185 Pligrim Rd Boston MA 02215

MAKINEN, MARVIN WILLIAM, educator; b. Chassell, Mich., Aug. 19, 1939; s. William John and Milga Katarina (Myllyla) M.; m. Michele de Groot, July 30, 1966; children: Eric William, Stephen Matthew. B.A., U. Pa., 1961; postgrad., Free U. Berlin, 1960-61; M.D., U. Pa., 1968; D.Phil., U. Oxford, Eng., 1976. Diplomate: Am. Bd. Med. Examiners. Intern dept. pathology Coll. Physicians and Surgeons, Columbia U., 1968-69; vis. fellow Lab. Molecular Biophysics, U. Oxford, 1971-74; asst. prof. dept. biophysics and theoretical biology U. Chgo., 1974-80, assoc. prof., 1980-84, assoc. prof. biochemistry and molecular biology, 1984—. Contbr. articles to profl. jours. Served with USPHS, 1969-71. NIH spl. fellow, 1971-74; established investigator Am. Heart Assn., 1975-80; John E. Fogarty sr. internat. fellow, 1984-85. Mem. Am. Chem. Soc., Biophys. Soc., Am. Soc. Biol. Chemist. Current Work: Enzyme structure and function, physical chemistry of biological macromolecules, molecular spectroscopy. Subspecialties: Biophysics (biology); Inorganic chemistry. Office: Dept Biochemistry and Molecular Biology U Chicago 920 E 58th St Chicago IL 60637

MAKINODAN, TAKASHI, biologist; b. Hilo, Hawaii, Jan. 19. 1925; s. Shinsuke and Mitsuyo (Haitani) M.; m. Jane Oganeku, Dec. 19. 1954; 1 dau., Ann. B.S., U. Hawaii, 1949; M.S., U. Wis.-Maidson, 1950, Ph.D., 1953. Assoc. biologist biology div. Oak Ridge Nat. Lab., 1955-57, biologist, head immunology group, 1957-72; prof. Oak Ridge Grad. Sch. Biomed. Scis., U. Tenn., 1968-72; dir. Oak Ridge Grad. Sch. Biomed. Scis., U. Tenn. (Tng. Program in Research on Aging), 1968-72; chief Lab. Cellular and Comparative Physiology Gerontology Research Ctr., Nat. Inst. Aging, NIH, Balt. City Hosps., 1972-76; prof. medicine in residence UCLA, 1976—, mem. exec. com. multi-campus div. geriatric medicine, 1981—; dir. geriatric research Edn. and Clin. Ctr. VA Wadsworth Med. Ctr., Los Angeles, 1976—; adj. prof. biology U. So. Calif., 1982—; mem. microbioloby fellowship rev. com. NIH, 1967-70; mem. adv. panel regulatory biology program NSF, 1971-73; mem. study sect. immunolo. scis. NIH, 1978-82; mem. adv. com. Andrew Norman Inst. Advanced Study in Gerontology and Geriatrics, U. So. Calif., 1981—; cons. Radiation Effects Research Found., Hiroshima, Japan., 1976—; mem. sci. council Intra-Sci. Research Found., 1980—; cons. White House Conf. Aging, 1970, 80 U.S. assoc. editor Mechanisms of Ageing and Devel., 1980—; editorial bd. Jour. Gerontology, 1976-80, Jour. Am. Geriatric Soc., 1982-85, Exptl. Gerontology, 1984—. Contbr. articles to profl. jours. Recipient Biomed. Scis. award ethel Percy Andrus Gerontology Ctr., Los Angeles, 1976; NSF fellow, 1961-62. Mem. Am. Assn. Immunologists, AAAS, Am. Chem. Soc., Gerontological Soc., Soc. Exptl. Biology and Medicine, Internat. Assn. Gerontology (U.S. rep. council 1975-78). Current Work: Aging and the immune system; late radiation effects onimmune function. Subspecialties: Immunobiology and immunology; Gerontology. Office: VA Wadsworth Med Ctr Wilshire and Sawtelle Blvds Los Angeles CA 90037

MAKOFSKE, WILLIAM JOSEPH, environmental physicist, educator; b. Bklyn., July 27, 1943; s. Harold A. and Amelia (Heinz) M.; m. Mary Frances Morris, June 10, 1967; children: David, Adam. B.S. in Physics, Pratt Inst., Bklyn., 1964; M.S. (teaching fellow, research fellow), Rutgers U., 1966, Ph.D. in Physics, 1968. Postdoctoral fellow Rutgers U., 1968; research assoc., lectr. U. Minn., Mpls., 1968-71, Columbia U., 1971-74; prof. physics Ramapo Coll. N.J., Mahwah, 1974—, dir. Alt. Energy Ctr., 1975—, dir. Inst. Environ. Studies, 1985—; vis. research scientist Bldg. Research Establishment, Garston, Eng., 1984. Contbr. articles profl. jours. Co-chmn. Warwick Conservation Bd., 1978-82; mem. Westchester Scientists for Environ. Info., 1972-74. Recipient award Pratt Inst. Engring. Alumni Assn., 1964, Thomases award Ramapo Coll., 1975, 83. Faculty Research grantee Ramapo Coll., 1985; NSF grantee, 1978. Mem. Am. Phys. Soc., Am. Assn. Physics Tchrs., Met. Solar Energy Soc., Tau Beta Pi. Current Work: Nuclear structure physics, solar greenhouse and passive solar research, design and devel. Subspecialties: Nuclear physics; Solar energy. Office: 505 Ramapo Valley Rd Mahwah NJ 07430

MAKOUS, WALTER, visual scientist, educator; b. Milw., Nov. 22, 1934; s. Lawrence and Ruth Lorraine (Luehring) M.; m. Marilyn Ann Carlson, Feb. 2, 1958; children: Ann Louise, James Carl, Matthew Lloyd; m. Barbara Anne Duggins, Apr. 29, 1982. B.S., U. Wis., 1958; M.Sc., Brown U., 1961, Ph.D., 1964. Staff mem. IBM Research Center, Yorktown Heights, N.Y., 1963-66; asst. prof. psychology, lectr. physiology and biophysics U. Wash., Seattle, 1966-69; vis. scientist IBM Research Center, 1970-71; assoc. prof. to prof. psychology U. Wash., 1969-79; prof. psychology and ophthalmology, dir Center Visual Sci., U. Rochester, N.Y., 1979—; cons. Served in USNR, 1953-55. NIH and NSF grantee and fellow. Fellow AAAS, Optical Soc. Am.; mem. Assn. Research in Vision and Ophthalmology, Neurosci. Soc., Psychonomic Soc., Human Factors Soc., Am. Psychol. Assn. Current Work: Research in visual psychophysics. Subspecialties: Psychophysics; Sensory processes. Office: Center for Visual Science U Rochester Rochester NY 14627

MAKOWSKI, ARMAND MAURICE, electrical engineering educator; b. Watermael-Boitsfort, Belgium, Oct. 9, 1953; came to U.S., 1975; s. Idel and Roszja (Wolf) M. Lic. Sc. Math., Free U. Brussels, Belgium, 1975; M.S. in Engring., UCLA, 1976; Ph.D. in Math., U. Ky., 1981. Vis. grad. student U. B.C., Can., 1978; vis. instr. U. Ky., Lexington, 1980-81; asst. prof. elec. engring. U. Md., College Park, 1981-85, assoc. prof., 1985—; cons. Naval Surface Weapons Ctr., White Oak, Md., 1983—, Bus. Tech. Systems, Seabrook, Md., 1984—. Contbr. articles to profl. jours. Recipient Presdl. Young Investigator award NSF, 1984; fellow Belgian-Am. Edn. Found., 1975. Mem. IEEE. Current work: Applications of stochastic processes to engineering including stochastic control, dynamical estimation and filtering, queueing systems. Subspecialties: Operations research (engineering); Telecommunications. Office: U Md Elec Engring Dept College Park MD 20740

MALAMED, SASHA, cell biologist; b. Bklyn., May 6, 1928; s. Harry and Fannie (Felman) M.; m. Lyanne Schneider, July 30, 1931; 1 child, David. B.A., U. Pa., 1948, M.S., 1950, Ph.D., 1955. Instr., Cornell Coll., Mt. Vernon, Iowa, 1955; postdoctoral fellow Western Res. U., Cleve., 1956-58; instr. anatomy Albert Einstein Coll. Medicine, Bronx, 1958-59, asst. prof., 1959-67; assoc. prof. anatomy U. Medicine and Dentistry N.J.-Rutgers Med. Sch., Piscataway, N.J., 1967-74, prof. anatomy, 1974—. Contbr. articles to profl. jours. NIH fellow, 1952-54, postdoctoral fellow, 1956-58; Lederle Med. Faculty awardee, 1961-64. Mem. Am. Assn. Anatomists, Am. Soc. Cell Biology, Am. Physiol. Soc., Biophys. Soc., Am. Soc. Zoologists. Current work: Ultrastructure and function of the adrenal cortex. Subspecialties: Cell biology; Endocrinology. Home: 900 Timber Ln Bridgewater NJ 08807 Office: Dept Anatomy UMDNJ Rutgers Med Sch Piscataway NJ 08854

MALAMUD, ERNEST I., physicist, science education consultant; b. N.Y.C., May 8, 1932; s. Nathan and Rita (Kayser) M. A.B. with highest honors in Physics, U. Calif.-Berkeley, 1954; Ph.D. in Physics, Cornell U., 1959. Physicist Fermilab, Batavia, Ill., 1968—. Contbr. articles to profl. jours. Mem. Warrenville Bicentennial Celebration Commn., Ill., 1976, mem. Sesquicentenial Commn., 1983-84. Mem. IEEE, Am. Phys. Soc. Current work: Particle physics: experiments, experimental apparatus, accelerators. Subspecialty: Particle physics. Home: 3S710 River Rd Sarrenville IL 60555 Office: Fermilab Box 500 Batavia IL 60510

MALAMUD, HERBERT, physicist, medical and health physicist, consultant; b. N.Y.C., June 28, 1925; s. Max and Anna (Mintzer) M.; m. m Sylvia, Oct. 27, 1951; children: Ronni Sue, Marc David, Kathi Jan. B.S. in Physics, CCNY, 1949; M.S. in Physics, U. Md., 1952; Ph.D. in Physics, N.Y. U., 1957; M.S. in Mgmt. Sci. and Engring, L.I. U., 1976. Diplomate: Am. Bd. Sci. in Nuclear Medicine. Various indsl. research positions, 1957-70; sr. physicist dept. nuclear medicine Queens Hosp., N.Y.C., 1970-79; tech. dir. Nuclear Assos./Victoreen, Carle Place, N.Y., 1979—, cons. med. physics, 1976—; adj. prof. various conns. and univs., 1955—. Contbr. articles to profl. publs. Served with Signal Corps U.S. Army, 1943-46. Mem. Am. Phys. Soc., AAAS, Soc. Nuclear Medicine, Am. Assn. Physicists in Medicine, Health Physics Soc., Am. Inst. Ultrasound in Medicine. Current Work: Physics of radiology, nuclear medicine, radiotherapy, ultrasound, med. nuclear magnetic resonance, health (radiation) physics; nuclear and atomic physics. Subspecialties: Imaging technology; Nuclear medicine. Home: 30 Wedgewood Dr Westbury NY 11590 Office: 100 Voice Rd Carle Place NY 11514

MALANGA, CARL JOSEPH, pharmacist, educator, researcher; b. N.Y.C., Aug. 26, 1939; s. Joseph John and Carolina J. (Graziano) M.; m. Mary Louise Villano, July 30, 1966; 1 son, Carl Joseph III. B.S. in Pharmacy, Fordham U., 1961, M.S., 1967, Ph.D., 1970. Registered pharmacist, N.Y., W.Va. Lab. instr. Coll. Pharmacy, Fordham U., 1964-67, instr., 1967-70; asst. prof. Sch. Pharmacy, W.Va. U., Morgantown, 1970-73, assoc. prof., 1973-78, prof., 1978—, chmn. basic pharm. scis., 1978—. Contbr. articles to profl. jours. Served to 1st lt., inf. U.S. Army, 1962-64. Decorated U.S. Army Commendation medal; recipient Borden prize, 1961, Merck award, 1961, Bristol award, 1961, Outstanding Tchr. award W.Va. U., 1975-82; N.Y. State scholar, 1957-61. Mem. Am. Pharm. Assn., Am. Soc. for Pharmacology and Exptl. Therapeutics, Am. Assn. Colls. Pharmacy, Rho Chi. Democrat. Roman Catholic. Lodge: Kiwanis. Current Work: Pharmacological control of ciliary activity and mucociliary transport. Subspecialties: Pharmacology; Comparative physiology. Home: 2202 Surrey Dr Morgantown WV 26505 Office: Sch Pharmacy WVa U Med Ctr Morgantown WV 26506

MALBICA, JOSEPH ORAZIO, research biochemist; b. N.Y.C., Apr. 6, 1925; s. Orazio and Venera (Strano) M.; m. Joanne Ruth Craft, July 30, 1947; children: Colleen Malbica Hewes, Kathryn Malbica, Joseph O., Suzanne Malbica Miller. B.S., Bklyn. Coll., 1949; M.S., Fordham U., 1954; Ph.D., Rutgers U., 1967. Med. service rep. E.L. patch, 1949-52; research biochemist Hoffman-LaRoche, Inc., 1954-65; Hess & Clark Div. Richardson-Merrill, Inc., 1967-69; mgr. drug metabolism Stuart Pharms. div. ICI Americas Inc., Wilmington, Del., 1969—. Contbr. articles to sci. publs. Served with M.C. U.S. Army, 1943-46. Mem. Am. Chem. Soc., N.Y. Acad. Scis., Am. Soc. Pharmacology and Exptl. Therapeutics, Am. Soc. Mass Spectrometry, AAAS, Am. Pharmacology Assn. Sigma Xi. Mormon. Current Work: Drug metabolism, pharmacokinetics, biotransformation, drug protein binding kinetics. Subspecialties: Biochemistry (medicine); Analytical chemistry. Home: 1039 Carolyn Dr West Chester PA 19380 Office: Concord Pike and Murphy Rd Wilmington DE 19897

MALCOLM, JOHN LOWRIE, soil and fertilizer specialist, agronomist; b. Westfield, N.J., July 30, 1920; s. John Lowery and Adelaide Gregory (Allardice) M.; m. Janet A. May, Nov. 27, 1946; children—Martha Jean, Frieda Louise, David Lowrie. B.S., Rutgers U., 1943, M.S., 1945, Ph.D., 1948. Research asst. Rutgers U., New Brunswick, N.J., 1943-48; assoc. soil chemist U. Fla., Homestead, Fla., 1948-59; soils advisor Int. Cooperation Adminstrn., Santa Tecla, El Salvador, 1959-63; fertilizer specialist AID, New Delhi, India, 1963-68, soil and Fertilizer specialist, Washington, 1979—; project mgr. FAO, Accra, Ghana, 1969. Fellow AAAS; mem. Am. Soc. Agronomy, Am. Chem. Soc. (councilor 1958-59). Democrat. Episcopalian. Current work: Primary focus is on soil fertility management supported by analysis; selection and recommendation of appropriate fertilizers for use in tropical agriculture. Subspecialties: Soil science; Agronomy. Home: 1607 Kirby Rd McLean VA 22101 Office: Agency Internat Devel Washington DC 20523

MALCOLM, RONALD LEE, organic hydrogeochemistry and chemisty researcher; b. Huntington, W.Va., Oct. 6, 1937; s. Norman Lee and Elizabeth (McKeand) M.; m. Mollie Jane Sellards, May 30, 1958; children—Gregory Lee, Susan Jane, Jeffery Dale, Janel Eleen. B.S., W.Va. U., 1959, M.S., 1961; Ph.D., N.C. State U., 1964. Soil scientist U.S. Geol. Survey, Denver, 1964-66, research hydrologist, 1966—, researcher cons., 1964—. Author, editor: Humic Substances in Water, 1984. Contbr. articles to profl. jours. Mem. Jefferson County Bd. Health, Lakewood, Colo., 1976-81. Recipient best paper of yr. award Groundwater Jour., 1974, Outstanding Performance award U.S. Geol. Survey, 1970. Mem. Internat. Humic Substances Soc. (pres. 1983-85), Am. Chem. Soc., Soil Sci. Soc. Am., Internat. Clay Mineral Soc., Am. Geophys. Union. Mem. Ch. of Christ. Current work: Research in humic substances, waste disposal, reverse osmosis, clay mineralogy lake and stream hydrology, government consulting on these research topics. Subspecialties: Hydrology; Geochemistry. Home: Route 1 Box 612 Morrison CO 80465 Office: US Geol Survey WRD Box 25046 MS 408 Denver Fed Ctr Denver CO 80225-0046

MALEY, TERRY SAMUEL, geologist; b. Portland, Oreg., Feb. 9, 1942; s. Max and Pearl Irene (Aerni) M.; m. Louise Gulick Overstreet, Nov. 11, 1967; children—Reading Gulick, Blaine Clift. B.S., Oreg. State U., 1964, M.S., 1965; Ph.D., U. Idaho, 1974. Registered profl. geologist, Idaho. Oceanographer Naval Oceanographic Office, Washington, 1965-72; geologist Bur. Land Mgmt., Elko, Nev., 1972-74; adminstr. Idaho Div. Earth Resources, Boise, 1974-78; cons., Boise, 1978-79; geologist Bur. Land Mgmt., Boise, 1979—; chmn. Idaho Earthquake Hazards Panel, Boise, 1975-77, Idaho Tech. Adv. Council, Boise, 1980. Author: Handbook of Mineral Law, 1983; Mineral Title Examination, 1984; Mining Law, 1985. Contbr. articles to profl. jours. Recipient Gold Quill award Soc. Farm Mgrs. and Rural Appraisers, 1982; Outstanding Performance award Naval Oceanographic Office, 1970; named Keynote speaker Women in Mining Ann. Meeting, 1979; NASA research fellow, 1969. Mem. Am. Land Forum, Am. Inst. Profl. Geologists (pres. Idaho sect. 1982-84), Idaho Assn. Profl. Geologists (chmn. 1976-78), Geol. Soc. Am., Soc. Mining Engrs. of AIME. Current work: Serve as Bureau of Land Management's senior field advisor in earth resources management; guidance is provided to all field offices nationwide; present several seminars on minerals management yearly. Subspecialties: Geology; Resource management. Home: 1608 N 9th St Boise ID 83702 Office: Bur Land Mgmt Americana Terr Boise ID 83706

MALFARA, DAVID JOSEPH, electronic engineer, telecommunication consultant; b. Marblehead, Ohio, Dec. 27, 1954; s. Joseph John and Dorothy Jean (Thomas) M.; m. Deborah Lynn Diddle, Oct. 16, 1981; 1 child, David Joseph Jr. Degree in Elec. Engring., ITT Tech. Inst., 1974; postgrad. U. Toledo, 1977. Engring. asst. Gould OSD ATG, Cleve., 1974-75; communications mgr. JP Levis Computer Ctr., Perrysburg, Ohio, 1975-78; dir. telecommunications Vector Group, Washington, 1978-80; tech. advisor Honeywell Info. Systems, Pitts., 1980-82; sr. engr. GTE Telenet, Pitts., 1982-83; pres., dir. Pa. Alternative Communications, Inc., Jeannette, Pa., 1983—; cons. United Food and Comml. Workers, Washington, 1980—, Bowling Green State U., Ohio, 1984—. Patentee Life PAC life safety system, 1983; contbr. articles to profl. jours. Sponsor Assn. Chiefs of Police, Greensburg, Pa., 1984. Mem. IEEE (chmn. Pitts. sect. communications soc. 1984—, chmn. Pitts. vehicular tech. soc., mem. Pitts. exec. com. 1984—). Current work: Integration of voice and computer data information achieved through digitizing; introduction of this information to a transmission medium capable of transport without degradation; digital decoding upon reception. Subspecialties: Telecommunications; Distributed systems and networks. Office: Pa Alternative Communications Inc 601 Michigan Ave Jeannette PA 15644

MALHOTRA, MANOHAR LAL, metallurgist, dental gold co. exec.; b. Multan, West Pakistan, Sept. 12, 1939; came to U.S., 1968, naturalized, 1977; s. Chetan Dass and Prakash Wati (Khanna) M.; m. Usha Kapoor, June 6, 1966; children: Dinesh K., Arun K. B.Sc. with honors in Physics, Delhi (India) U., 1961, M.Sc. in Physics, 1963; M.S. magna cum laude in Physics, Fairleigh Dickinson U., 1970; Ph.D. in Physics, Banaras Hindu U., 1972; Ph.D. in Materials Sci, U. Va., 1974. Scientist Nat. Phys. Lab., New Delhi, 1965-68; teaching cum research fellow dept. physics Fairleigh Dickinson U., Teaneck, NJ., 1968-70; NIH predoctoral research fellow in materials sci. dept. U.Va., 1970-74; NSF postdoctoral research fellow in chem. engring. SUNY, Buffalo, 1974-75; NIH postdoctoral research fellow dept. dental materials U. Mich., Ann Arbor, 1975-77; metallurgist Degussa Dental Inc., Long Island City, N.Y., 1977—. Contbr. articles on dental research to profl. jours. Mem. Internat. Assn. for Dental Research, Am. Assn. for Dental Research, Am. Soc. Metals, Am. Def. Preparedness Assn., Internat. Precious Metals Inst., Sigma Xi. Democrat. Current Work: Reseach and development of low-gold dental alloys with higher tarnish and corrosion resistance in the oral environment. Subspecialties: Dental materials; Metallurgy. Home: 104-07 Weside Ave Corona NY 11368 Office: Degussa Dental Inc 21-25 44th Ave Long Island City NY 11101

MALHOTRA, SHYAM KUMAR, orthodontist; b. Lahore, Pakistan, Apr. 1, 1942; came to U.S., 1970; s. Som Nath and Tara M.; m. Veena Malhotra, Nov. 20, 1969; children: Rachna, Rishi. B.Sc., U. Lucknow, India, 1960, B.D.S., 1964, M.D.S., 1968; D.D.S., Meharry Med. Coll., 1982. Lectr. K. G. Med. Coll., Lucknow, 1968-70; research assoc. Meharry Med. Coll., Nashville, 1970-73, instr., 1973-76, asst. prof., 1976-84, assoc. prof., 1984—. Contbr. sci. articles to profl. jours. Mem. ADA, Internat. Assn. Dental Research, Am. Assn. Dental Research, Tenn. Dental Assn., Nashville Dental Soc. Current Work: Human growth and development. Subspecialties: Orthodontics; Dental growth and development. Office: Meharry Med Coll Box 33-A 1005 18th Ave N Nashville TN 37208

MALIK, MAZHAR NASIR, research scientist, biochemistry educator; b. Jhang, Punjab, Pakistan, Aug. 19, 1940; came to U.S., 1969; s. Ghafoor Ul Haq and Surriya (Begum) M.; m. Shahnaz Begum, Apr. 11, 1973; children—Sadia, Rabia, Sarah. B.S. with hons., Forman Christian Coll., Lahore, Pakistan, 1963; M.S., Punjab U., 1964; Ph.D., U. Strathclyde, Glasgow, Scotland, 1969. Lic. dir. clinical lab., N.Y. Asst. prof. biochemistry SUNY Downstate Med. Ctr., Bklyn., 1975-77; vis. prof. cell biology Rockefeller U., N.Y.C., 1977-79; research scientist V N.Y. State Inst. Basic Research in Devel. Disabilities, State Island, 1979-82, research scientist VI, 1982—; chmn. dept. pathology, biochemistry, 1984—, dir. biochemistry/hematology inst. basic research-consolidated clin. labs, 1982—. Contbr. articles (37) to profl. jours. Grantee Am. Heart Assn., 1976, NIH, 1976-85, N.Y. Heart Assn., 1984-87. Fellow N.Y. Heart Assn.; mem. Am. Heart Assn. (e. investigator 1975-80). Current work: Biochemistry of neuronal proteases and cytoskeletal proteins. Subspecialty: Biochemistry (medicine). Office: New York State Inst Basic Research in Devel Disabilities 1050 Forest Hill Rd Staten Island NY 10314

MALIN, SHIMON, physicist, educator; b. Tel Aviv, July 21, 1937; came to U.S., 1965; s. Menashe and Ita (Cohen) M.; m. Tova Borkovsky, June 9, 1960; children—Nadav, Jonathan, Daniella. M.Sc., Hebrew U. Jerusalem, 1961; Ph.D., U. Colo., 1968. Asst. prof. physics Colgate U., Hamilton, N.Y., 1968-76, assoc. prof., 1976-84, prof., 1984—. Author: (with M. Carmeli) Representations of the Rotation and Lorentz Groups: an Introduction, 1976. Contbr. articles to profl. jours. Mem. Am. Phys. Soc. Current work: Foundations of quantum mechanics; general relativity and cosmology; quantum gravity. Subspecialties: Relativity and gravitation; Theoretical physics. Home: 21 W Kendrick Ave Hamilton NY 13346 Office: Dept Physics and Astronomy Colgate U Hamilton NY 13346

MALINA, ROGER FRANK, astronomer, editor; b. Paris, July 6, 1950; came to U.S., 1968; s. Frank Joseph and Marjorie (Duckworth) M. B.Sc. in Physics, M.I.T., 1972; Ph.D. in Astronomy, U. Calif.-Berkeley, 1979. Research asst. Univ. Coll., London, 1979-81; asst. research astronomer U. Calif.-Berkeley, 1980—; project scientist U. Calif.-Berkeley (Extreme Ultraviolet Explorer project), 1981—. Contbr. articles to profl. jours. Mem. Brit. Interplanetary Soc., Royal Astron. Soc., Am. Astron. Soc., Internat. Soc. Arts Sci. and Tech. (dir. 1982—), Sigma Xi. Current Work: Project scientist, extreme ultraviolet explorer, exec. editor Leonard Jour. Internat. Soc. Arts, Sci. and Tech. Subspecialty: X-ray high energy astrophysics. Home: 508 Connecticut St San Francisco CA 94107 Office: Space Science Lab U Calif Berkeley CA 94720

MALINCONICO, LAWRENCE LORENZO, JR., geologist, educator; b. Hartford, Conn., Apr. 24, 1952; s. Lawrence Lorenzo and Doris Marie (Patenaude) M.; m. Mary Ann Love, Aug. 17, 1974; 1 child, Megan. A.B. cum laude, Dartmouth Coll., 1974, A.M., 1978, Ph.D., 1982. Research asst. Mineralogy Mus., Oslo, 1974-76; teaching asst. Mich. Technol. U., Houghton, 1978-79; guest investigator Hawaiian Volcano Obs., U.S. Geol. Survey, 1979; geologist Climax Molybdenum Co., Battle Mountain, Nev., 1980, Anaconda Copper Co., Mont. and Idaho, 1981; research asst. dept. earth scis. Dartmouth Coll., Hanover, N.H., 1976-82; asst. prof. geology So. Ill. U., Carbondale, 1982—; cons. in field. Contbr. articles to profl. jours. First aid instr. ARC. Grantee NSF, ARCO Found., AID. Mem. Geol. Soc. Am. (dept. rep.), Am. Geophys. Union, Am. Assn. Petroleum Geologists, Sigma Xi (com.). Current work: Applied geophysical modelling in the Himalaya in northern Pakistan; detecting and defining seismicity patterns and structure of southern Illinois. Subspecialty: Geophysics. Office: Dept Geology So Ill U Carbondale IL 62901

MALINOWSKI, EDMUND ROBERT, chemist, educator, consultant; b. Mahanoy City, Pa., Oct. 16, 1932; s. Francis and Stella (Pieczul) M.; m. Helen Devcich, Sept. 6, 1958; children: Paul, Robert. B.S., Pa. State U., 1954; M.S., Stevens Inst. Tech., 1956, Ph.D. (Robert-Crooks-Stanley fellow), 1961. Research assoc. Stevens Inst. Tech., 1960-63, asst. prof. chemistry, 1963-66, assoc. prof., 1966-70, prof., 1970—, cons. in field. Author: (with D. Howery) Factor Analysis in Chemistry, 1980; research numerous publs. in chemistry. Recipient Jess H. Davis Research award Stevens Inst. Tech., 1977. Mem. Am. Chem. Soc. Roman Catholic. Current Work: Computer analysis of chem. data. Subspecialties: Physical chemistry; Analytical chemistry. Home: 49 New England Dr Lake Hiawatha NJ 07034 Office: Dept Chemistry and Chem Engring Stevens Inst Tech Hoboken NJ 07030

MALINOWSKI, KENNETH CHESTER, hazardous waste management company executive; b. Buffalo, July 22, 1947; s. Chester Edward and Helen (Walenka) M.; m. Rona Julie Starr, July 2, 1972; children—Rachel Helene, Danielle Starr. B.A., SUNY-Buffalo, 1969; M. Phil., Yale U., 1972, Ph.D., 1974. Sr. scientist SCA Services, Inc., Buffalo, 1974-77; v.p. Recra Research, Inc., 1977-80, pres., 1980-81; v.p. research and devel. CECOS Internat., Inc., 1981—. Vice chmn. Niagara County Environ. Mgmt. Council, Lockport, 1975—. Mem. Am. Chem. Soc., Nat. Assn. Environ. Profls., AAAS, Water Pollution Control Fedn., N.Y. Acad. Scis. Current work: Application of biological systems for hazardous waste treatment; development of novel thermal oxidation systems; solidification, encapsulation and stabilization of organic hazardous wastes. Subspecialties: Hazardous waste disposal; Water supply and wastewater treatment. Home: 419 Harper Dr Lewiston NY 14092 Office: CECOS Internat Inc 2321 Kenmore Ave Buffalo NY 14207

MALINS, DONALD CLIVE, marine biochemist, educator, research center director; b. Lima, Peru, May 19, 1931; came to U.S., 1947, naturalized, 1953; s. Richard Henry and Mabel Madeline (Warner) M.; m. Mary Louise Leiren, Jan. 27, 1962; children: Christopher, Gregory, Timothy. B.A., U. Wash., 1953; B.S., Seattle U., 1956; Ph.D., U. Aberdeen, Scotland, 1967, D.Sc., 1976. Research chemist N.W. and Alaska Fisheries Center, Seattle, 1956-74; research prof. Seattle U., 1972—; affiliate prof. U. Wash., Seattle, 1974—; dir. environ. conservation div. N.W. and Alaska Fisheries Ctr., Seattle, 1974—; cons. UN Environ. Program, Nairobi, Kenya, 1980—. Editor: (with J.R. Sargent) Effects of Petroleum on Arctic and Subarctic Marine Environments and Organisms, Vols. I and II, 1977; editor-in-chief Aquatic Toxicology, Seattle, 1979—. Recipient gold medal Dept Commerce, 1982, spl. achievement award, 1975, 80; superior performance award Dept. Interior, 1960, 61; Bond award cert. Am. Oil Chemists Soc., 1961. Mem. Am. Soc. Biol. Chemists, Am. Chem. Soc. Clubs: Wash. Athletic (Seattle), Sand Point Golf and Country (Seattle). Current Work: Marine biochemistry and toxicology, studies on marine pollutants and pollutant related diseases in marine life, biochemistry of porpoise sonar. Subspecialties: Environmental toxicology; Biochemistry (medicine). Office: Environ Conservation Div NW and Alaska Fisheries Center 2725 Montlake Blvd E Seattle WA 98112

MALITZ, SIDNEY, physician; b. N.Y.C., Apr. 20, 1923; s. Benjamin and Etta (Cohen) M. Student, N.Y. U., 1940-42, Tulane U., 1942-43; B.M., Chgo. Med. Ch., 1946, M.D., 1947. Diplomate: Am. Bd. Psychiatry and Neurology. Intern St. Mary's Hosp., Huntington, W.Va., 1946-47; sr. intern Bethesda, Hosp., Cin., 1947-48; resident N.Y. State Psychiat. Inst., N.Y.C., 1948-51, sr. research psychiatrist, 1954-56, acting prin. research psychiatrist, 1956-58, acting chief psychiat. research, chief dept. exptl. psychiatry, 1958-64, chief psychiat. research dept. exptl. psychiatry, 1964-72, chief dept. biol. psychiatry, 1984—, dep. dir., 1972-75, acting dir., 1975-76, 81-84, dep. dir., 1976-78; in charge psychiat. drug clinic Vanderbilt Clinic, Presbyn. Hosp., N.Y.C., 1956-75, asst. attending psychiatrist, 1960-66, asso. attending psychiatrist, 1966-71, attending psychiatrist, 1971—, acting dir. psychiatry service, 1975-76, 81-84; asst. dept. psychiatry Coll. Physicians and Surgeons, Columbia U., N.Y.C., 1955-57, asso., 1957-59, asst. clin. prof., 1959-65, asso. prof., 1965-69, prof., 1969—, vice chmn. dept. psychiatry, 1972-75, acting chmn., 1975-76, 81-84, vice chmn., 1976-78; mem. panel impartial psychiat. experts N.Y. State Supreme Ct., 1960—; mem. adv. com. subcom.; cons. U.S. Pharmacopeia; mem. adv. com. subcom. health N.Y. State Constl. Conv.; cons. div. med. scis. NRC, Washington, 1967-70; cons. Rush Found., Los Angeles, 1968—; mem. ad hoc rev. com. to select Nat. Drug Abuse Research Centers, Center Studies Narcotic and Drug Abuse, NIMH, 1972. Contbr. numerous articles to profl. jours. Life fellow Am. Psychiat. Assn. (chmn. com. biol. psychiatry 1961-62, program com. 1961-62, sec-treas. chpt. 1962-63, mem. com. research 1966-68, pres. chpt. 1969-70, chmn. Council Research and Devel. 1971-73); fellow N.Y. Acad. Medicine, AAAS (council 1969—), Am. Coll. Neuropsychopharmacology, Collegium Internationale Neuropsychopharmacologicum, Am. Coll. Psychiatrists (archivist-historian 1978—), Royal Coll. Psychiatrists, Am. Coll. Psychoanalysts, N.Y. Soc. Clin. Psychiatry, Assn. Research Newvous and Mental Disease, N.Y. State, N.Y. County med. socs., AMA (cons. council drugs 1960—), N.Y. Acad. Scis, N.Y. Psychiat. Soc., Am. Psychopath. Assn., Soc. Biol. Psychiatry. Current Work: Lateralization of brain function; regional cerebral blood flow as it relates to mental illness; brain metabolism; cognitive and affective changes with electroconvulsive therapy. Subspecialties: Psychopharmacology; Neuropsychology. Address: Coll Physicians and Surgeons Columbia U Dept Psychiatry 161 Fort Washington Ave New York NY 10032

MALKAN, MATTHEW ARNOLD, astronomy educator; b. N.Y.C., June 4, 1956; s. Arnold George and Audrey Jane (Hubbard) M. A.B. summa cum laude, Harvard U., 1977, A.M., 1977; Ph.D., Calif. Inst. Tech., 1983; C.P.G.S., U. Cambridge, Eng., 1978. Research assoc. Calif. Inst. Tech., Pasadena, 1983; research assoc. U. Ariz., Tucson, 1983-84; asst. prof. astronomy UCLA, 1984—. Contbr. articles to profl. jours. Marshall scholar, 1977-78; fellow NSF, Hertz Found. Mem. Am. Astron. Soc., Phi Beta Kappa, Sigma Xi. Current work: Observational and theoretical study of active galactic nuclei and quasars emphasizing the nature of their enormous energy source. Subspecialty: Optical astronomy. Office: U Calif Dept Astronomy Los Angeles CA 90024

MALKINSON, ALVIN MAYNARD, biochemist, educator; b. Buffalo, Jan. 5, 1941; s. Irving nd and Ida (Gitin) M.; m. Lynn Ellen Reynolds, Dec. 26, 1967; children: Sabra E., Zachary D. B.A., U. Buffalo, 1963; Ph.D., Johns Hopkins U., 1968. Served with US. Peace Corps, 1968-72; postdoctoral fellow U. Leicester, Eng., 1971-72; lectr. U. Nairobi, Kenya, 1969-71; postdoctoral Yale U. Med. Sch., New Haven, 1972-74; asst. prof. U. Minn. Med. Sch., Mpls., 1975-78, U. Colo., Boulder, 1978—. Author: Hormone Action, 1975; also articles. White House summer fellow, 1964; Minn. Med. Found. grantee, 1975; NIH fellow, 1975-78; grantee, 1980—; Nat. Found.-March of Dimes Basil O'Connor fellow, 1976-78; Colo. Heart Assn. grantee, 1979. Mem. Assn. Advancement of Cancer Research, Am. Soc. Pharmacology and Exptl. Therapeutics, Rho Chi. Current Work: Role of protein phosphorylation in regulation normal and neoplastic lung development in mice. Subspecialties: Cancer research (medicine); Biochemistry (medicine). Home: 3855 Broadway Boulder CO 80302 Office: U Colo Boulder CO 80309

MALKOFF, DONALD BURTON, computer systems analyst; b. Pitts., July 10, 1935; s. Louis and Shirley Malkoff; m. Margaret Ellen Aldridge, June 16, 1980. Student Harvard U., 1953-56; M.D., U. Pitts., 1960; M.S. in Computer Sci., U. Calif.-San Diego, 1983. Diplomate Am. Bd. Psychiatry and Neurology. Intern, then resident U. Mich., Ann Arbor, 1960-66; researcher USPHS-NIH, Balt., 1961-63; practice medicine specializing in neurology, Fort Myers, Fla., 1973-79; pres. Lodos Oil Corp., Europe, 1979-80; assoc. in computer sci. U. Calif.-San Diego, LaJolla, 1981-83; computer systems analyst Navy Personnel Research and Devel. Ctr., San Diego, 1983—. Contbr. articles to profl. jours. Recipient citations for outstanding and sustained superior performance Navy Personnel research and Devel. Ctr., 1984. Mem. Am. Acad. Neurology, Am. Assn. Artificial Intelligence, Assn. Computing Machinery, Soc. Neurosci., Am. Soc. Naval Engrs. Club: Harvard (San Diego). Current work: Artificial intelligence applications to ship control and fault handling; real-time, learning expert systems; man-machine interfaces. Subspecialties: Artificial intelligence; Neurology. Home: 10960 Worthing Ave San Diego CA 92126 Office: Navy Personnel Research and Devel Ctr San Diego CA 92152

MALL, VANCE AUSTIN, computer software executive, former air force officer; b. Lawrence, Kans., Mar. 14, 1942; s. Oscar Austin and Leonice Ruth (Wadhams) M.; m. Mary Everitt Hilton, Mar. 27, 1967; children—Catherine, Courtney, Matthew, Allison. A.B. cum laude in Math., Princeton U., 1964; M.S., NYU, 1967; M.S. in Computer Sci., Cornell U., 1973. Commd. 2d lt. U.S. Air Force, 1964, advanced through grades to lt. col., 1980; asst. chief data automation England AFB, La., 1964-66, chief data automation U-Tapao Airfield, Thailand, 1967-68; assoc. prof. computer sci. U.S. Air Force Acad., Colorado Springs, Colo., 1968-70, 73-80; air force dep. dir. Ada Joint Program Office, U.S. Dept. Def., Washington, 1981-84, acting dir. STARS program, 1983-84, ret. 1984; research staff Inst. Def. Analyses, Alexandria, Va., 1984—. Decorated Air Force Commendation medal with one oak leaf cluster, Air Force Meritorious Service medal with one oak leaf cluster. Mem. IEEE, IEEE Computer Soc., Assn. Computing Machinery. Democrat. Club: Princeton. Current work: Practical applications of computer technology. Subspecialties: Programming languages; Software engineering. Home: 3301 Edenvale Rd Fairfax VA 22031 Office: Inst Def Analyses 1801 N Beauregard St Alexandria VA 22311

MALLATT, MARK EDWARD, dental researcher and educator, consulting clinical examiner; b. Gary, Ind., July 6, 1950; s. Russell Clayton and Marjorie May (Hoagl) M.; m. Kathleen Ann Quill, Aug. 21, 1976. B.S., Ind. U.-Bloomington, 1972; D.D.S., Ind. U.-Bloomington (Sch. Dentistry), Indpls., 1975. Cert. dentist, Ind. Clin. research assoc. Oral Health Research Inst., Indpls., 1975-77, assoc. dir. clin. research, 1978—; instr. Ind. U. Sch. Dentistry, 1977-78, asst. prof. preventive dentistry, 1978—; cons. clin. examiner for pvt. industry, Ind., Ohio, Tex., 1977-85. Pvt. industry grantee, 1977-82. Mem. Am. Assn. Dental Research (v.p. Ind. sect. 1981-82, pres. sect. 1982-83), Am. Assn. Dental Schs., ADA, Ind. Dental Assn., Omicron Kappa Upsilon, Psi Omega (Achievement award 1974). Republican. Current Work: Clinical investigations in assessing the efficacy and safety of oral health products and procedures relative to: dental caries, gingivitis, plaque, calculus, pellicle, and oral soft tissue pathology. Subspecialties: Preventive dentistry; Cariology. Home: 1753 Esther Ct Plainfield IN 46168 Office: Oral Health Research Inst 415 Lansing St Indianapolis IN 46202

MALLINGER, ALAN GARY, psychiatrist, psychopharmacologist; b. Pitts., July 29, 1947; m. Joan Ellen Mallinger, Aug. 20, 1972; children: Julie Beth, Daniel Todd. B.S., U. Pitts., 1969, M.D., 1973. Diplomate: Am. Bd. Psychiatry and Neurology. Resident in gen. psychiatry Univ. Health Center, Pitts., 1973-75, 79-81; instr. psychiatry and pharmacology U. Pitts., 1975-76, asst. prof., 1976—; attending psychiatrist Western Psychiat. Inst. and Clinic, Pitts., 1981—. Contbr. chpt. to books, articles to profl. jours. Laughlin fellow, 1981; Mead Johnson travel fellow, 1982. Mem. Am. Soc. for Clin. Pharmacology and Therapeutics, Am. Coll. Clin. Pharmacology, Soc. for Neurosci., Am. Psychosomatic Soc., AAAS, Phi Beta Kappa, Alpha Omega Alpha. Current Work: Research on cell membrane transport processes in relation to mood disorders and the mechanisms of action of psychotherapeutic drugs. Subspecialties: Psychopharmacology; Psychiatry. Office: 3811 O'Hara St Pittsburgh PA 15213

MALLMANN, ALEXANDER JAMES, physicist, educator; b. Sheboygan, Wis., Dec. 8, 1937; s. Alexander Bernard and Anne Frances (Govek) M.; m. Jean Louise, Aug 10, 1968 (div.); children: James, David. B.S. in Physics, U. Wis.-Milw., 1965, M.S., 1968; Ph.D. in Materials Sci, Marquette U., 1977. Mem. faculty Milw. Sch. Engring., 1968—, prof. physics, 1979—; cons. in optics and acoustics. Contbr. articles to profl. jours. Served with USAF, 1955-59. Recipient Outstanding Teaching award Inland Steel-Ryerson Found., 1983. Mem. Optical Soc. Am., Am. Assn. Physics Tchrs. (pres. Wis. sect. 1981-82), Internat. Solar Energy Soc., Physics Club Milw. (pres. 1982-83). Current Work: Computer simulation of optical phenomena of the atmosphere. Subspecialty: Solar energy. Home: 20250 Jeffers Dr New Berlin WI 53151 Office: Dept Physics PO Box 644 Milwaukee WI 53201

MALLORY-BARKLEY, BARBARA ZOMMER, psychologist; b. New Haven., Conn., May 25, 1936; d. Peter and Estelle (Serba) Zommer; m. George Boudreau, Apr. 11, 1955 (div. 1969); children: Deborah Boudreau, George Boudreau, Scott Boudreau.; m. Hunter Mallory, May 25, 1972 (div. 1976). B.A., So. Conn. State Coll., New Haven, 1968; M.A., U. Conn.-Storrs, 1972; postgrad., Harvard U., 1974-76. Supr. research program Mass. Gen. Hosp., Boston, 1972-74; edn. dir. Sch. for Learning Disabled, Beacon Sch., Brookline, Mass., 1973-74; assoc. dir. clinic Eagle Hill Sch., Greenwich, Conn., 1974-76; assoc. to pres., dir. New Eng. div. Ednl. Records Bur., Wellesley, Mass., 1978—; lectr. Harvard U., 1972-73. Author: Developmental Implications of Iconic Memory, 1972; test battery Objectives per Item of Comprehensive Testing Program, 1980. State of Conn. grantee, 1972. Mem. Internat. Neuropsychology Assn., Am. Psychol. Assn., Power Squadron (asst. edn. dir. 1983-84), World Affairs Council (mem. council Forum II 1983—), Phi Delta Kappa. Republican. Episcopalian. Clubs: Harvard Faculty, Newport (R.I.) Yacht. Current Work: Director diagnostics and evaluation. Subspecialties: Cognition; Learning. Home: 411 Marrett Rd Lexington MA 02173 Office: Educational Records Bureau 37 Cameron St Wellesley MA 02181

MALLOY, JR. DONALD EDWIN, chemist; b. Boston; Mar. 31, 1952; s. Donald Edwin and Gloria Loretta (LoPilato) M.; m. Diane Marie Houle, Mar. 27, 1977; children—Jessica Anne, Valerie Dawn, Tiffany Glo. B.S. in Chemistry, Lowell Tech. Inst., 1974; M.S. in Organic Chemistry, U. Lowell, 1977; M.B.A. in Mktg. Mgmt., N.Y. Inst. Tech., 1984. Lab. asst. Lowell Tech. Inst., Mass., 1972-74, researcher, 1975-76; chemist Boston Chem. Industries, 1976-77, Brookhaven Nat. Lab., Upton, N.Y., 1977-79, Monsanto, Melville, N.Y., 1979-81; mgr. indsl. tech. Thomas and Betts, Raritan, N.J., 1981—; mem. mgmt. adv. panel Chem. Week, Highstown, N.J., 1982—; cons., pres. DMA Assn., Milford, N.J., 1983—. Contbr. articles to profl. jours. Patentee in field. Mem. Am. Chem. Soc., Soc. Plastics Engrs., Am. Soc. Metals, Instrument Soc. Am., Am. Mgmt. Assn., Chemist's Club. Current work: Fiber optic LAN system development; compounding of polymers for electron beam crosslinking. Subspecialties: Polymer engineering; Electronic materials. Home: RD 1 Box 444 Milford NJ 08848 Office: Thomas and Betts Corp 920 Route 202 Raritan NJ 08869

MALLUCHE, HARTMUT HORST, nephrologist, educator; b. Breslau, Germany, Jan. 1, 1943; came to U.S., 1975, naturalized, 1985; s. Harald E. and Renate (Muenzberg) M.; m. Gisela Gleich, Dec. 19, 1975; children—Nadine, Danielle, Tiffany. Abitur, Albertus Magnus Coll., Koenigstein, Germany, 1963; postgrad. Phillips U., Marburg/Lahn, Fed. Republic of Germany, 1963-65, U. Innsbruck, Austria, 1965-66, U. Vienna, Austria, 1966; M.D., J. W. Goethe U., Frankfurt, Fed. Republic of Germany, 1969. Diplomate German Bd. Internal Medicine. Intern, County Hosp., Aichach, Fed. Republic of Germany, 1969-70; resident in internal medicine and fellow in nephrology Ctr. Internal Medicine, Univ. Hosp., Frankfurt am. Main, 1970-75, asst. prof. medicine U. So. Calif., Los Angeles, 1975-78, assoc. prof., 1978-81; prof., dir. div. nephrology U. Ky. Med. Ctr., Lexington, 1981—; cons. NIH; grant reviewer NYU, Kidney Found. Can. Contbr. articles to profl. jours. Grantee NIH, 1982, 84, Shriner's Hosp. for Crippled Children, Lexington, 1982. Fellow ACP; mem. Am. Soc. Nephrology, Am. Soc. Bone and Mineral Research, Am. Fedn. Clin. Research, Internat. Soc. Nephrology, AAAS. Subspecialty: Nephrology. Office: U Ky Med Ctr Div Nephrology 800 Rose St Lexington KY 40536

MALMGREN, LESLIE THEODORE, JR., biomed. researcher, educator; b. Brockton, Mass., Mar. 28, 1946; s. Leslie Theodore and Abbie H. (Denson) M.; m. Kathleen A. A.B., Bridgewater (Mass.) State Coll., 1968, M.A., 1972; Ph.D., Clark U., 1975. Asso. prof. otolaryngology Upstate Med Center, Syracuse, N.Y. Grantee NIH, 1971-73, 76-78, 82—; Grantee Swedish Med. Research Council, 1977-78; Grantee Hendircks Fund, 1978-80; Grantee Voice Found., 1978-79, 80-81; Grantee Deafness Research Found., 1980—. Mem. Am. Assn. Anatomists, Assn Research in Otolaryngology, Soc. Neurosci. Current Work: Histochemistry and electron microscopy of head and neck muscles and their innervation. Experimental neuropathology of head and neck muscles. Subspecialties: Otorhinolaryngology; Neurobiology. Office: Otolaryngology Research Labs SUNY Upstate Med Center Weiskotten Hall Rm 89 7600 Irving Ave Syracuse NY 13210

MALOFF, BRUCE L, research pharmacologist; b. Syracuse, N.Y., Aug. 26, 1953; s. Paul and Leah (Gilot) M.; m. Amy Beth Miller, Aug. 14, 1976. B.S., Syracuse U., 1973; Ph.D., SUNY-Albany, 1977. Research assoc. SUNY Upstate Med. Sch., Syracuse, 1977-78; instr., fellow U. Rochester Sch. Medicine, 1978-81, sr. instr., 1981; research pharmacologist E.I. DuPont Co., Wilmington, Del., 1981—. Contbr. articles to profl. jours. Mem. Am. Diabetes Assn. (profl. sect.), Endocrine Soc., AAAS. Jewish. Current work: Development of pharmaceutical agents in metabolic diseases targeted toward defects at the receptor and cellular levels, especially in anti-inflammatory and hypoglycemic drugs. Subspecialties: Cellular pharmacology; Endocrinology. Home: 13 Devon Ct Wilmington DE 19810 Office: EI DuPont Co Experimental Station Wilmington DE 19898

MALONE, MARVIN HERBERT, pharmacologist, educator, researcher; b. Fairbury, Nebr., Apr. 2, 1930; s. Herbert August Frederick and Elizabeth Florinda (Torrey) M.; m. Shirley Ruth Cane, Dec. 21, 1952; children: Carla Margaret, Gayla Christa. B.S. in Pharmacy, U. Nebr., 1951, M.S. in Physiology and Pharmacology, 1953; Ph.D. in Pharmacology and Pharm. Scis, 1958; postgrad., Rutgers U., 1954-55. Asst. U. Nebr., Lincoln, 1951-53, 1956-58; research ast. Squibb Inst. Med. Research, New Brunswick, N.J., 1953-56; asst. prof. U. N. Mex., Albuquerque, 1958-60; assoc. prof. U. Conn., Storrs, 1960-69; prof. physiology and pharmacology U. of Pacific, Stockton, Calif., 1969-84, Disting. prof. pharmacology and toxicology, 1984—; cons. Drug Plant Labs., U. Wash., 1960-64, Research Pathology Assoc., 1967-70, Amazon Natural Drug Co., 1967-70, ICI USA Inc., 1968-78, SISA Inst. Research, 1977-82; mem. task force on plants for fertility regulation WHO Spl. Program for Research, Devel. and Research Tng. in Human Reproduction, 1982—; mem. State of Calif. Med. Therapeutics and Drug Adv. Com., 1985—. Author: Experiments in the Pharmaceutical Biological Sciences, 1973; editorial bd.: Jour. Natural Products: Lloydia, 1971—, Jour. Ethnopharmacology, 1978-84; editor: Am. Jour. Pharm. Edn, 1974-79, Pharmat, 1984—, Jour. Ethnopharmacology, 1985—; contbr. articles on pharmacology to profl. jours. Recipient U. Pacific Distinction of Merit, 1980, Mead Johnson Labs. award, 1964; USPHS grantee., 1960-63, 1968-73; U.S. Army grantee, 1962-63; U. Conn. research Found. grantee, 1964-68. Fellow Am. Found. Pharm. Edn., Am. Inst. Chemists, AAAS; mem. Acad. Pharm. Scis. (sr.), Am. Soc. Pharmacology and Exptl. Therapeutics, Western Pharmacology Soc., Am. Soc. Pharmacognosy, Am. Pharm. Assn., Am. Assn. Colls. Pharmacy, Acad. Pharm. Scis., Soc. Econ. Botany, Sigma Xi, Rho Chi, Phi Lambda Upsilon, Phi Kappa Phi. Current Work: Screening and assay of natural products, pharmacology of inflammation and anti-inflammation, pharmacodynamics of psychotropic and autonomic agents, biometrics, fertility regulation. Subspecialties: Pharmacology; Toxicology (medicine). Home: 722 Bedford Rd Stockton CA 95204 Office: Dept Physiology and Pharmacology Univ Pacific Sch Pharmacy Stockton CA 95211

MALONEY, TIMOTHY JAMES, electrical engineer; b. Dayton, Ohio, Aug. 11, 1949; s. Edward James and Anita Merceda (Spieler) M. S.B. in Physics, MIT, 1971; M.S. in Physics, Cornell U., 1973, Ph.D. in Elec. Engring., 1976. Postdoctoral assoc. Cornell U., Ithaca, N.Y., 1976-77; engr. Varian Assocs., Inc., Palo Alto, Calif., 1977-80, sr. engr., 1980-84; staff engr. Intel Corp., Santa Clara, Calif., 1984—. Contbr. articles in applied physics and elec. engring. to profl. jours. NSF grad. fellow Cornell U., 1971-74. Mem. IEEE (sr.), Electrochem. Soc., Elec. Overstress/Electrostatic Discharge Soc., Phi Kappa Phi. Club: MIT of No. Calif. Current work: Semiconductor device physics and technology, microchip component reliability, electrostatic discharge phenomena in semiconductor components. Subspecialties: Microchip technology (engineering); Semiconductors. Office: Intel Corp SC2-05 3065 Bowers Ave Santa Clara CA 95051

MALOSH, JAMES BOYD, mechanical engineer, educator; b. Licking, Ill., July 30, 1943; s. John Andrew and Nadean (Crandall) M.; m. Sandra Sue Browne, June 22, 1963 (div. 1971); 1 son, Ronald; m. Helen Faye Kangas, Oct. 22, 1973; children: Jeffrey, Brian, Ronald, Melanie. B.S., Wayne State U., Detroit, 1966; M.S., Mich. Tech. U., Houghton, 1969; Ph.D., 1980. Registered profl. engr., Mich., Ohio, Pa. Acoustical engr. Walker Research Labs., Grass Lake, Mich., 1969-70; research engr. Lawrence Livermore Labs., Livermore, Calif., summers 1971, 72; research assoc. Mich. Tech. U., 1970-75; sr. research engr. U.S. Steel Research Labs., Monroeville, Pa., 1975-80; prin. research scientist Battelle Meml. Labs., Columbus, Ohio, 1980-81; assoc. prof. mech. engring. U. Alaska, Fairbanks, 1981—; cons. Arctic Designers, Fairbanks, 1982, Cowper and Madson Attys., Fairbanks, 1982; prin. investigator Alaska Dept. Transp., Fairbanks, 1982. Mem. ASME, Nat. Soc. Profl. Engrs., Sigma Xi, Tau Beta Pi, Pi Tau Sigma. Patentee automotive silencer, blast furnace stove burner. Current Work: Application of experimental and theoretical dynamic analysis with computers to the solution of problems in noise, vibration and pulsation control. Particular interests are in transient fluid flow, finite waves and energy system pulsation and control. Subspecialties: Acoustical engineering; Theoretical and applied mechanics. Home: 717 Chandalar Univ Alaska Fairbanks AK 99701 Office: U Alaska Fairbanks AK 99701

MALSKY, STANLEY JOSEPH, physicist; b. N.Y.C., July 15, 1925; s. Joseph and Nellie (Karpinski) M.; m. Gloria E. Gagliardi, Oct. 15, 1965; 1 son, Mark A. B.S., NYU, 1949, M.A., 1950, M.S., 1953, Ph.D., 1963. Nuclear physicist Dept. Def., 1950-54; chief physicist VA, 1954-63; adj. asso. prof., then prof. radiol. sci. Manhattan Coll., Bronx, N.Y., 1960-74; non-resident research collaborator med. div. Brookhaven Nat. Labs., Upton, N.Y., 1964-69; research prof. radiology NYU Sch. Medicine, N.Y.C., 1975-77; pres. Radiol. Physics Assn., White Plains, N.Y., 1965—. Contbr. chpts. to books. Served with U.S. Army, 1945-46. Recipient James Picker Found. award, 1963-67; Founder's Day award NYU, 1964; Leadership award Manhattan Coll., 1969. Fellow Am. Pub. Health Assn., AAAS, Royal Soc. Health; charter mem. Am. Assn. Physicists in Medicine, Health Physics Soc.; mem. Sigma Xi, Sigma Pi Sigma, Phi Delta Kappa. Roman Catholic. Current Work: Radiation doismetry; radiation exposures; med.physics applied to diagnostic radiology; nuclear medicine; radiation therapy and tng. of staffs;legal aspects. Subspecialties: Cancer research (medicine); Biophysics (physics). Address: 119 Lansdowne Westport CT 06880

MALVERN, DONALD, aircraft manufacturing company executive; b. Sterling, Okla., Apr. 22, 1921; s. George Michael and Anna Francesca (Elsass) M.; m. Ruth Marie Vogler, June 4, 1949; 1 son, Michael John. B.S., U. Okla., 1946. Engr. Victory Architects and Engrs., Clinton, Okla., 1943, Douglas Aircraft Co., Santa Monica, Calif., 1943; with McDonnell Aircraft Co., St. Louis, 1946—, exec. v.p., 1973-82, pres., 1982—; v.p. McDonnell Douglas Corp., 1973—; pres. McDonnell Douglas Services, Inc., 1978-82. Trustee Falcon Found., 1983—. Served to 1st lt. USAAF, 1943-46. Fellow AIAA (Tech. Mgmt. award 1968, Reed Aeros. medal 1980); mem. Am. Def. Preparedness Assn. (pres. St. Louis chpt. 1979-80), Navy League U.S. (life), Nat. Aeros. Assn., Air Force Assn., Armed Forces Mgmt. Assn., Pi Tau Sigma, Tau Beta Pi, Tau Omega. Clubs: Bellerive Country, St. Louis. Current Work: General management. Subspecialty: Aeronautical engineering. Home: 37 Baron Ct Rural Route 2 Florissant MO 63034 Office: PO Box 516 Saint Louis MO 63166

MALY, EDWARD JOHN, aquatic population ecologist, educator; b. Troy, N.Y., Nov. 10, 1942; s. Dis and Janet Adelaide (Brown) M.; m. Mary Temple Porter, June 13, 1967; children—Kenneth Edward, Elizabeth Anne. B.S., U. Rochester, 1964; postgrad., U. Pa., 1964-65; Ph.D., Princeton U., 1968. Asst. prof. biology Tufts U., Medford, Mass. 1968-75; asst. prof. biology Concordia U., Montreal, Que., Can., 1975-77, assoc. prof., 1977—, assoc. chmn., grad. program dir., 1983-85, acting chmn., 1985—; trustee Rocky Mountain Biol. Lab., Crested Butte, Colo., 1974-78, sec. 1976-78. Contbr. articles to profl. jours. Grantee Natural Sci. and Engring. Research Council, 1976—, NSF, 1971-73. Mem. Ecol. Soc. Am., Am. Soc. Limnology and Oceanography, Sigma Xi. Current work: Factors affecting distribution and abundance of aquatic invertebrates. Subspecialties: Ecology (biology); Limnology. Home: 115 Coolbreeze Ave Pointe-Claire PQ H9R 3S8 Canada Office: Biology Dept Concordia Univ 1455 Demaisonneuve Blvd W Montreal PQ H3G 1M8 Canada

MAN, CHI-SING, mechanics educator, researcher; b. Hong Kong, Aug. 23, 1947; emigrated to Can., 1981; s. Yip and Sau-Ying (Leung) M.; m. May Lai-Ming Chan, July 5, 1973; children: Li-Xing, Yi-Heng. B.Sc. with honors, U. Hong Kong, 1968, M.Phil., 1976; Ph.D., Johns Hopkins U., 1980. Tutor in math. and physics Hong Kong Bapt. Coll., 1970-72, asst. lectr. in physics, 1972-76; postdoctoral fellow Johns Hopkins U., Balt., 1980-81; asst. prof. U. Man., Winnipeg, Can., 1981-85, U. Ky., Lexington, 1985—. Editor: jour. Dousou, 1974-76. Natural Sci. and Engring. Research Council Can. grantee, 1982-85. Mem. Soc. for Natural Philosophy. Current Work: Subsea permafrost; in-situ pressuremeter tests; settlement of artificial islands; creep of ice and frozen soils; foundations of continuum thermomechanics; continuum theories of phase transitions; frozen soils as multiphase mixtures. Subspecialties: Theoretical and applied mechanics; Offshore technology. Home: 709 Old Dobbin Rd Lexington KY 40502 Office: Dept Math U Ky Lexington KY 40506

MANALIS, MELVYN SAMUEL, research physicist, educator; b. Los Angeles, Oct. 16, 1939; s. Barney M. and Kathryn (Swiler) M.; m. Marilyn Jean White, June 21, 1965; children: Andrew, Scott, Jeremy. B.A. in Math, Calif. State U.-Northridge, 1961; M.S. in Physics, U. N.H., 1964; Ph.D. in Physics, U. Calif.-Santa Barbara, 1970. Instr. dept. physics Colby Coll., Waterville, Maine, 1963-64; scientists Jet Propulsion Lab., Calif. Inst. Tech., Pasadena,

1965; research scientist II U. Colo., Boulder, 1966; physicist Nat. Bur. Standards, Washington, 1967; scientist The Te Co., Santa Barbara, Calif., 1970-72; research physicist U. Calif.-Santa Barbara, 1972-79, lectr., 1975, adj. lectr. environ. studies, 1975—, research physicist, 1975—. Contbr. articles on physics to profl. jours. Cons. Santa Barbara County Bd. Suprs. Gen. Motors fellow, 1967-68; U. Calif. Sea grantee, 1977-78, 1978-79. Mem. Am. Inst. Physicists, Am. Assn. Physics Tchrs., Sigma Xi. Club: Friends of the Earth. Current Work: Directing one of the largest wind energy assessment programs in the state of California, recent results of this work were presented at the first U.S.-China Conference on energy resources and the environment. Subspecialties: Wind power; Solar energy. Office: Dept Environ Studies U Calif Santa Barbara CA 93106

MANDAL, ANIL KUMAR, physician, researcher; b. West Bengal, India, Nov. 12, 1935; came to U.S., 1967, naturalized, 1978; s. Nirmal C. and Kamala B. M.; m. Pranati Ganguly, June 18, 1964; children: Aditi, Atashi. Intermediate sci., Suri Vidyasagar Coll., West Bengal, India, 1953; M.D., Calcutta Nat. Med. Coll., 1959. Diplomate: Am. Bd. Internal Medicine. Research fellow in nephrology West Suburban Hosp., Oak Park, Ill., 1962-63; med. officer med. research Inst. Postgrad. Medicine, Calcutta, India, 1963-66; registrar in medicine R.G. Med. Coll. Hosps., Calcutta, 1966-67; lectr. dept. pathology U. Edinburgh, 1968-69; research fellow in nephrology U. Ill. Hosps., Chgo., 1969-70, resident in internal medicine, 1970-71; chief resident, instr. medicine and phys. diagnosis U. Ill., Chgo., 1971-72; staff physician, asst. and assoc. prof. medicine VA Med. Ctr., U. Okla. Health Sci. Ctr., Oklahoma City, 1972-82; staff physician, prof. medicine VA Med. Center, Med. Coll. Ga., Augusta, 1982—; prof., head dept. nephrology Sanjay Gandhi Postgrad. Inst. Med. Scis., Lucknow, India. Author: (with James E. Wenzl) Electron Microscopy of the Kidney in Renal Disease and Hypertension - A Clinicopathological Approach, 1979; editor: (with Sven O. Bohman) The Renal Papilla and Hypertension, 1980. Recipient Outstanding Service award West Suburban Hosp., Oak Park, Ill., 1970, Physicians Recognition award AMA, 1972. Fellow ACP; mem. Internat. Soc. Nephrology, Am. Soc. Nephrology, So. Soc. Clin. Investigation, Central Soc. Clin. Research. Current Work: The spleen and acute renal failure: an experimental model, protection is afforded against acute renal failure by splenectomy, mechanisms of protection are studied. Subspecialties: Nephrology; Pathology (medicine). Office: Nephrology Sect VA Med Center Augusta GA 30910

MANDAVA, NAGA BHUSHAN, chemist, environmental scientist; b. Bhushanagulla, India, Oct. 14, 1934; came to U.S. 1963, naturalized 1978; s. Krishnaiah and Sampurnamma (Yalamanchili) M.; m. Leela Kumari Yalamanchili, June 15, 1957; children—Santi, Srinivas, Madhu. B.S., Andhra U., India, 1955; M.S., Banaras U., India, 1957; Ph.D., Indian Inst. Sci., India, 1962. Cert. profl. chemist. Research assoc. Okla. State U., Stillwater, 1963-65, SUNY-Stony Brook, 1965-66; sr. research assoc. Laval U., Que., Can., 1966-68; research chemist U.S. Dept. Agr., Beltville, 1968-82; sr. scientist EPA, Washington, 1982—; sr. research assoc. Nat. Acad. Sci., 1968-70. Editor: Plant Growth Substances, 1979; Natural Pesticides: Methods, 1985; Naturally Occurring Pesticides, 1982-86. Contbr. articles to profl. jours. Patentee in field. Recipient Publ. award Naval Research Lab, 1981, Superior Service award U.S. Dept. Agr., 1984. Fellow Am. Inst. Chemists (bylaws com. 1982—), mem. Am. Chem. Soc. (councilor 1977—), Chem. Soc. Wash. (pres. 1984), AAAS, Sigma Xi, Phi Lambda Upsilon. Current work: Pesticides, plant growth and development, biotechnology, health and environment, natural products, analytical chemical-methods devel. and applications, agriculture for developing countries. Subspecialties: Integrated pest management; Organic chemistry. Home: 15404 Tindlay St Silver Spring MD 20904 Office: EPA 401 M St SW Washington DC 20460

MANDEL, H(AROLD) GEORGE, pharmacologist; b. Berlin, June 6, 1924; came to U.S., 1937, naturalized, 1944; s. Ernest A. and Else (Crail) M.; m. Marianne Klein, July 25, 1953; children: Marcia Vivian, Audrey Lynn. B.S., Yale U., 1944, Ph.D., 1949. Lab. instr. in chemistry Yale U., 1942-44, 47-49; research assoc. dept. pharmacology George Washington U., 1949-50, asst. research prof., 1950-52, assoc. prof. pharmacology, 1952-58, prof., 1958—, chmn. dept. pharmacology, 1960—; Advanced Commonwealth Fund fellow Molteno Inst. Cambridge (Eng.) U., 1956; Commonwealth Fund fellow U. Auckland (N.Z.) and U. Med. Scis., Bangkok, Thailand, 1964; Am. Cancer Soc. Eleanor Roosevelt Internat. fellow Chester Beatty Research Inst. London, 1970-71; Am. Cancer Soc. scholar U. Calif., San Francisco, 1978-79; mem. cancer chemotherapy com. Internat. Union Against Cancer, 1966-73; mem. external rev. com. Howard U. Cancer Research Center, 1972—; cons. Bur. Drugs, 1975-79, EPA, 1978-82; mem. toxicology adv. com. FDA, 1975-78; mem. med. research service merit rev. bd. in alcoholism and drug dependence VA, 1975-78; mem. cancer spl. program adv. com. Nat. Cancer Inst., 1974-78, chmn., 1976-78; mem. Nat. Large Bowel Cancer Project Working Cadre, 1980-84; mem. com. on toxicology NRC-Nat. Acad. Sci., 1978-82; mem. Kettering award selection com. Gen. Motors Cancer Research Found., 1979-81; FASEB Com. on Pub. Affairs, 1984—. Mem. editorial bd. Jour. Pharmacology and Exptl. Therapeutics, 1960-65; field editor, 1978—; mem. editorial bd. Molecular Pharmacology, 1965-69, Research Communications in Chem. Pathology, Pharmacology, 1972—, mem. editorial bd. Cancer Research, 1974-76; assoc. editor, Cancer Drug Delivery, 1983—. Served with AUS, 1944-46. Recipient John J. Abel award in pharmacology Eli Lilly and Co., 1958, Distinguished Achievement award Washington Acad. Scis., 1958, Golden Apple Teaching award Student AMA, 1969, 85. Mem. Am. Chem. Soc., Am. Soc. Biol. Chemists, Am. Soc. Pharmacology and Exptl. Therapeutics (pres. 1973-74), Am. Assn. Cancer Research, AAAS, Assn. Med. Sch. Pharmacology (pres. 1976-78), Internat. Soc. Biochem. Pharmacology, Alpha Omega Alpha, Sigma Xi. Democrat. Club: Cosmos (Washington). Research, numerous publs. on cancer chemotherapy, mechanism of growth inhibition, antimetabolites, drug disposition. Subspecialty: Pharmacology. Home: 5500 Christy Dr Bethesda MD 20816 Office: 2300 Eye St NW Washington DC 20037

MANDEL, LEONARD, physicist; m. Jeanne Elizabeth Kear, Aug. 20, 1953; children: Karen Rose, Barry Paul. B.Sc., U. London, Eng., 1947, 1948, Ph.D., 1951. Tech. officer Imperial Chem. Industries, 1951-54; lectr., sr. lectr. Imperial Coll., U. London, 1954-64; prof. physics U. Rochester, N.Y., 1964—, prof. optics, 1977-80; joint sec. Rochester Confs. on Coherence and Quantum Optics, 1966, 72, 77, 83. Editor books; asso. editor: Optics Letters, 1977-79; Contbr. numerous sci. articles to profl. jours. First recipient Max Born prize Optical Soc. Am., 1982. Fellow Am. Phys. Soc., Optical Soc. Am. (asso. editor jour. 1970-76, 82—, chmn. com. for soc. objectives and policy 1977, bd. dirs. 1985—). Current Work: Research on lasers and quantum optics, both experimental and theoretical,particularly interactions between atoms and light, photon statistics, phase transitions in lasers. Subspecialties: Atomic and molecular physics; Laser optics. Office: Dept Physics and Astronomy U Rochester Rochester NY 14627

MANDELBAUM, DAVID MICHAEL, electrical engineer; b. Tel Aviv, Israel, Dec. 28, 1933; came to U.S. 1941, naturalized 1944; s. Isaac and Jean M.; m. Stefanie Singer, Apr. 4, 1965; children—Andrew, Richard. A.B. in Math., Princeton U., 1956; M.A. in Math., Harvard U., 1957; M.E.E., Columbia U., 1960. Engr. ITT, Nutley, N.J., 1960-65, Communication Systems, Inc., Paramus, N.J., 1965-68, U.S. Army Avionics Research and Devel., Ft. Monmouth, N.J., 1968—. Contbr. articles to profl. jours. Mem. IEEE, Sigma Xi, Phi Beta Kappa. Current work: Error correcting codes and decoding algorithms resulting in 40 published papers. Subspecialties: Electrical engineering; Algorithms. Home: PO Box 645 Eatontown NJ 07724 Office: US Army Avionics Research and Devel Activity SAVAA-F Ft Monmouth NJ 07703

MANDELBROT, BENOIT B., mathematician, educator, scientist; b. Warsaw, Poland, Nov. 20, 1924; came to U.S., 1958; s. Charles and Belle (Lourie) M.; m. Aliette T. Kagan, Nov. 5, 1955; children—Laurent M., Didier A.J. Diploma Ecole Polytechnique, Paris, 1947; M.S., Calif. Inst. Tech., 1948; Ph.D. in Math., U. Paris, 1952. Mem. Inst. for Advanced Study, Princeton, N.J., 1953-54; jr. prof. math. U. Geneva, 1955-57, U. Lille, France, 1957-58, Ecole Polytechnique, Paris, 1957-58; research staff mem. IBM Research Ctr., Yorktown Heights, N.Y., 1958-74; IBM fellow T.J. Watson Research Ctr., Yorktown Heights, 1974—; vis. prof. econs. Harvard U., Cambridge, Mass., 1962-63, vis. prof. applied physics, 1963-64, vis. prof. math., 1979-80, prof. dept. math., 1984—; vis. inst. lectr. MIT, Cambridge, 1967-72. Author: Les Objets Fractals, 1974, 85; Fractals: Form, Chance and Dimension, 1977; The Fractal Geometry of Nature, 1982; (with others) Logique, Langage et Theorie de l'Information, 1957. Recipient Barnard medal for meritorious service to sci. Nat. Acad. Scis., 1985; Rockefeller Found. scholar, 1954; Guggenheim Found. fellow, 1968. Fellow Am. Acad. Arts and Scis., IEEE, Inst. Math. Stats., Econometric Soc.; mem. Am. Math. Soc. Current work: Conceived, developed, and continues to develop the fractal geometry of nature, an inter-disciplinary enterprise concerned with shapes and phenomena that are rough, irregular and broken up. Subspecialties: Applied mathematics; Condensed matter physics. Office: Dept Math Harvard U 1 Oxford St Cambridge MA 02138 Also: T J Watson Research Ctr PO Box 218 Yorktown Heights NY 10598

MANDELKERN, LEO, physical chemistry educator, researcher; b. N.Y.C., Feb. 23, 1922; s. Israel and Gussie (Krostich) M.; m. Berdie Medvedoff, May 1946; children—Irwin Paul, Marshal, David. B.A., Cornell U., 1942, Ph.D., 1952. Research chemist Nat. Bur. Standards, Washington, 1952-62; prof. chemistry Fla. State U., Tallahassee, 1962—, disting. prof., 1984—. Author: Crystallization of Polymers, 1964; An Introduction to Macromolecules, 1973, rev. edit., 1983. Contbr. articles to profl. jours. Served to 2d lt. USAAF, 1942-46, PTO. Recipient Arthur S. Fleming award Jaycees, 1958, Meritorious award, 1959; Witco Chem. award, 1975, Mettler award NATAS, 1984; NIH grantee, 1962-67. Fellow Am. Phys. Soc.; mem. AAAS, Biophysics Soc., Am. Chem. Soc. (Fla. award 1984), Sigma Xi, Alpha Epsilon Pi. Club: Cosmos (Washington). Current work: Physical properties of polymers, phase transition. Subspecialties: Physical chemistry; Polymer chemistry. Home: 1503 Old Fort Dr Tallahassee FL 32301 Office: Fla State U Tallahassee FL 32301

MANESS, LINDSEY VANCE, JR., exploration geologist; b. Jacksonville, N.C., May 24, 1946; s. Lindsey Vance Maness and Fannie Irene (Griffin) Hill; m. Pin-Ching Chen, June 21, 1980; 1 child, Lee Van. B.S. in Geology, N.C. State U., 1974; M.A. in Geology, Ind. State U., 1977. Remote sensing specialist Goddard Space Flight Ctr., NASA, Greenbelt, Md., 1977-79, sr. remote sensing specialist Ames Research Ctr., Moffett Field, Calif., 1979-80; pres. Remote Sensing Cons., Fremont, Calif., 1980; dir. remote sensing lab. Barringer Resources, Inc., Golden, Colo., 1981-82; pres. PetroImage Corp., Golden, Colo., 1982—, chmn. bd. dirs. Assoc. editor State Sentinel, N.C. State U., 1973-74. Contbr. papers on remote sensing to profl. publs. Active Boy Scouts Am., 1968-70, 78. Served with. USAF, 1966-71. Mem. Am. Assn. Petroleum Geologists, Rocky Mountain Assn. Geologists, Geosat Com., Am. Soc. Photogrammetry (mem. hydrospherics com. 1978-79), Geol. Soc. Am., W4ATC Amateur Radio Club, Sigma Gamma Epsilon, Gamma Theta Upsilon. Republican. Current work: Digital image enhancement for mapping faults and geological structures, lithology, geochemistry and geobotany; exploration applications of space technology. Subspecialties: Geology; Remote sensing (geoscience). Office: PetroImage Corp 12875 W 15th Dr Golden CO 80401

MANGANO, RICHARD MICHAEL, scientist; b. Mt. Vernon, N.Y., Mar. 2, 1950; s. Frank G. and Louise (Amoruso) M.; m. Patricia B. Siuta. B.S. in Chemistry, Iona Coll., New Rochelle, N.Y., 1972; Ph.D. in Biochemistry, Fordham U., 1980. Instr. dept. chemistry Manhattan Coll., Riverdale, N.Y., 1977-79; faculty research assoc. Md. Psychiat. Research Center, 1979-81; dept. psychiatry U. Md., Balt., 1979-81; fellow Hoffmann-LaRoche, Inc., Nutley, N.J., 1981-82, sr. scientist dept. pharmacology, 1982—. Contbr. articles to profl. jours. Mem. N.Y. Acad. Sci., Soc. Neurosci., Phi Lambda Upsilon, Sigma Xi. Current Work: Research interests in biochemistry and biochemical pharmacology include investigations of cellular metabolism, toxicity and cellular degeneration, regulation of ligand receptor interactions as pertains to drug devel. Subspecialties: Biochemistry (biology); Neurochemistry.

MANGER, WILLIAM MUIR, physician, research scientist; b. Greenwich, Conn., Aug. 13, 1920; s. Julius and Lilian B. (Weissinger) M.; m. Lynn Seymour Sheppard, Jan. 14, 1942; children: William, Lilian, Shep, Charles. B.S., Yale U., 1944; M.D., Columbia U., 1946; Ph.D., Mayo Clinic, 1959. Diplomate: Am. Bd. Internal Medicine. Intern Presbyn. Hosp., N.Y.C., 1946-47, resident, 1949-50; fellow in internal medicine Mayo Clinic, 1950-57; successively instr., assoc., asst. attending physician, lectr. in medicine Columbia U. Med. Center, 1957—; dir. Manger Research Found., 1960-77; asst. clin. prof. medicine NYU Med. Ctr., 1968-75, assoc. clin. prof. medicine, 1975-83; clin. prof. medicine N.Y.U. Med. Ctr., 1983—; cons. in internal medicine Southampton (L.I.) Hosp., 1972—; asst. attending physician Bellevue Hosp., 1969-77, assoc. attending physician, 1977-83. Univ. Hosp., 1977—; attending Bellevue Hosp., 1983—. Author: Chemical Quantitation of Epinephrine and Norepinephrine in Plasma, 1959, Pheochromocytoma, 1977, Catecholamines in Normal and Abnormal Cardiac Function, 1982; editor: Hormones and Hypertension, 1966; contbr. articles to profl. jours. Trustee Thyroid Found., 1979-85; bd. dirs. Found. for Depression and Manic Depression, Inc., 1978—, pres., 1979—; trustee Found. for Advancement Internat. Research in Microbiology; Trustee St. Albans Sch., Washington, 1958-64, 67-74, 83—, chmn. bd., 1967-69; trustee Buckley Sch., N.Y.C., 1975—; former deacon, elder, trustee Fifth Ave. Presbyn. Ch. Served to lt. (j.g.) USNR, 1947-49. Recipient Mayo Alumni award for meritorious research, 1955. Fellow Am. Heart Assn. (council high blood pressure research, council circulation), ACP, Am. Physiol. Soc., Am. Coll. Cardiology, N.Y. Acad. Medicine (admission and edn. coms. Acad. Psychosomatic Medicine, Am. Inst. Chemists, Royal Soc. Health, Am. Coll. Clin. Pharmacology, Am. Geriatrics Soc., mem. AMA, Am. Thoracic Soc., N.Y. Acad. Scis., AAAS, Am. Chem. Soc., Am. Soc. Pharmacology and Exptl. Therapeutics, Endocrine Soc., Pan Am. Med. Assn., Soc. Exptl. Biology and Medicine, Harvey Soc., Am. Soc. Internal Medicine, Physicians and Surgeons Alumni Soc., Soc. Alumni Presbyn. Hosp., Mayo Fellow Assn. (past pres.), Mayo Alumni Assn. (pres. elect.), Internat. Soc. Hypertension, Inter-Am. Soc. Hypertension, Am. Fedn. Clin. Research, Catecholamine Club (founder; pres. 1981), Research Discussion Group (founder) Am. Soc. Nephrology, Med. Strollers (past exec. com.), Nat. Hypertension Assn. (founder, chmn. 1977—), Internat. Med. Council Drug Use, Sigma Xi, Nu Sigma Nu. Clubs: Yale, University, N.Y. Athletic, Meadow, Southampton Bathing Corp, Devon. Current Work: Hypertension; catecholamines; pheochromocytoma; endocrinology; research concerns studies on human and experimental pheochromocytoma and prevention of tumor development. Subspecialties: Cardiology; Neuroendocrinology. Office: 324 E 30th St NYU Med Ctr New York NY 10016

MANGUS, ALFRED RING, structural engineer; b. Washington, July 2, 1953; s. Marvin Dale and Jane (Gray) M. B.Archtl.Engring., Pa. State U., 1976; M.S.C.E., U. Calif.-Berkeley, 1977. Registered civil engr., Alaska, Calif., Wash., Oreg. Structural engr. Tryck Nyman & Hayes, Anchorage, 1977-81; sr. engr. Peratrovich, Nottingham & Drage, Anchorage, 1983-84; structural engr. Frank Moolin & Assocs., Anchorage, 1983; sr. civil structural engr. Arctic Slope Cons. Engrs., Anchorage, 1983; structural engr. Architects GDM & Assocs., Anchorage, 1984-85, Goentzel Builders Inc., Anchorage, 1985—. Contbr. articles to profl. publs. Mem. ASCE, Earthquake Engring. Research Inst. (v.p. Alaska chpt. 1984), Nat. Soc. Profl. Engrs., Internat. Assn. Bridge and Structural Engrs., Am. Concrete Inst., Structural Engrs. Assn. Alaska, Am. Inst. Steel Constrn., Am. Inst. Timber Constrn., Am. Welding Soc., Profl. Engrs. in Pvt. Practice, Am. Engring. Modeling Soc., Masonry Soc. (founding mem.), Concrete Reinforcing Steel Inst., Internat. Assn. Shell and Space Structures, Canadian Soc. Civil Engring., Deep Founds. Inst., Capt. Cook Jaycees. Republican. Methodist. Clubs: Nordic Ski, Anchorage Corvette, Single Support Network. Current work: Timber structures; buildings; earthquake resistance design; marine structures (docks, dolphins and fender systems); Arctic structures (ice loads, snow loading and foundations in permafrost). Subspecialties: Civil engineering; Structural engineering. Home: 4805 Mills Dr Anchorage AK 99508 Office: Goentzel Builders Inc 2418 E 86th Ct Anchorage AK 99507

MANIATIS, THOMAS PETER, biology educator; b. Denver, May 8, 1943; s. Peter T. and Jane V. (Swearingen) M.; m. Jessie Marion Klyce, Aug. 27, 1968; children—Ethan David, Silas Dana. B.A., U. Colo., 1965, M.A., 1967; Ph.D., Vanderbilt U., 1971. Asst. prof. Harvard U., Cambridge, Mass., 1975-77, prof. molecular biology, 1981—; sr. staff investigator Cold Spring Harbor, N.Y., 1975-77; assoc. prof. Calif. Inst. Tech., Pasadena, 1977-79, prof., 1979-81; co-founder, sci. adviser Genetics Inst., Cambridge, 1981—; chmn. molecular biology study sect. NIH, 1982; mem. Searle Scholars Adv. Com., 1985. Author: Molecular Cloning Manual, 1982. Assoc. editor Cell, 1978. Recipient Rita Allen Found. award, 1978; Eli Lilly research award Am. Soc. Microbiology, 1981. Fellow Am. Acad. Arts and Scis.; mem. Nat. Acad. Scis. (Richard Lounsbery award 1985). Current work: Control of gene expression; molecular basis of human genetic diseases. Subspecialties: Biochemistry (medicine); Genetics and genetic engineering (medicine). Office: Dept Biochemistry Harvard U 7 Divinity Ave Cambridge MA 02138

MANILOFF, JACK, biophysicist; b. Balt., Nov. 6, 1938; s. Boris and Edith (Cohen) M.; m. Sandra Sue Steele, Dec. 22, 1960; children—Beth Susan, Eric Steele. B.A., Johns Hopkins U., 1960; M.S., Yale U., 1964, Ph.D., 1965. Research assoc. Brown U., Providence, 1964-66; asst. prof., then assoc. prof. dept. microbiology U. Rochester, N.Y., 1966-79, prof., 1979—; vis. scientist John Innes Inst., Norwich, Eng., 1972-73. Contbr. articles to profl. jours. Recipient Research Career Devel. award USPHS, 1970. Mem. Biophys. Soc., Am. Soc. Microbiology, AAAS, Internat. Orgn. Mycoplasmology, Sigma Xi. Current work: Research on molecular events in virus infection of cells; evolution of small cells and their genetic information; new methods for studying biological supermolecular structures. Subspecialties: Molecular biology; Virology (biology). Office: Dept Microbiology U Rochester Med Ctr 601 Elmwood Ave Rochester NY 14642

MANION, DAVID EDWARD, spaceflight orbit computation operations specialist; b. Pitts., Aug. 25, 1953; s. David Thomas Manion and Constance Jean (Ross) Manion Berry; m. Karen Lynn Komisak, Nov. 20, 1976 (div. Feb. 1982); m. Carrie Jane Mauck, Oct. 16, 1982. B.S. in Indsl. Arts Edn., California State Coll., Pa., 1975. Apprenticeship instr. Jones & Laughlin Steel Corp., Aliquippa, Pa., 1975-77; tech. instr. Bendix Field Engring., Greenbelt, 1977-82, project systems analyst, 1982-84; sr. tech. trainer MA-COM/DCC, Germantown, Md., 1984; sr. tech. specialist Computer Scis. Corp., Beltsville, Md., 1984—. Author/editor: TDRSS Orientation Course (NASA Documentation), 1981. Mem. speakers bur. Pub. Affairs Office, NASA, Goddard Space Flight Ctr., 1981. Served with USNR. Mem. Am. Astronautical Soc., IEEE. Current work: Spaceflight systems support, flight dynamics computation facility operations, space shuttle mission planning, tracking and data relay satellite system support operations. Subspecialty: Astronautics. Home: 2290 Four Seasons Dr Gambrills MD 21054 Office: Computer Scis Corp Bldg 12 Room E135A Goddard Space Flight Ctr Greenbelt MD 20771

MANITIUS, ANDRZEJ ZDZISLAW, mathematician, engineer; b. Warsaw, Poland, June 9, 1938; came to U.S., 1972; s. Jan Stefan and Alina (Lada) M.; m. Jolanta Maria Manitius, July 17, 1965 (div. 1983); 1 son, Michal; m. Barbara M. Kielczewska, Apr. 20, 1985. M.S., Acad. Mining and Metallurgy, Cracow, 1960; Ph.D., Poly. Schs. of Warsaw, 1968. Asst., adj. Poly. Schs. Warsaw, Poland, 1961-72; vis. prof. U. Minn., Mpls., 1972-73; researcher Université de Montreal, Que., Can., 1974-83; prof. math. scis. dept. Rensselaer Poly. Inst., Troy, N.Y., 1981—; mem. pure and applied math. grant com. Nat. Scis. and Engring. Research Council Can., 1979-82. Co-author: Principles of Automation (in Polish), 1974; assoc. editor SIAM Rev., IEEE Trans. Automatic Control, 1979-80; contbr. over 50 articles to sci. jours. Recipient prize Polish Acad. Scis., 1972. Mem. Soc. Indsl. and Applied Math. Lutheran. Current work: Mathematical control theory, delay-differential equations. Subspecialties: Applied mathematics; Electrical engineering. Office: Math Scis Dept Rensselaer Poly Inst Troy NY 12180-3590

MANLEY, DONALD GENE, entomology educator; b. Monterey Park, Calif., Sept. 15, 1946; s. Maurice Emerson and LaVada Louise (Bryant) M.; m. Julia Ann Beaver, Feb. 15, 1969; children: Stephanie Suzanne, Christine Louise. B.A., UCLA, 1973; M.A., Calif. State U.-Long Beach, 1975; Ph.D., U. Ariz., 1978. Asst. prof. entomology Clemson (S.C.) U., 1978-82, assoc. prof., 1982—. Assoc. editor Jour. Agrl. Entomology; mem. editorial bd. Jour. Entomol. Sci., Tobacco Sci. Active Boy Scouts Am. Mem. Entomol. Soc. Am., AAUP, Entomol. Soc. S.C., Am. Registry Profl. Entomologists, Ga. Entomol. Soc., Phi Kappa Phi, Kappa Delta Pi, Alpha Zeta. Republican. Roman Catholic. Current Work: Developed and coordinated integrated pest management program on tobacco in South Carolina; research on biology, ecology and taxonomy of velvet ants. Subspecialties: Integrated pest management; Taxonomy. Office: Pee Dee Expt Sta Clemson U PO Box 5809 Florence SC 29502

MANLEY, DONALD MARK, physicist; b. Columbia, La., Sept. 1, 1954; s. Leslie Earl and Mabel (Lee) M.; m. Mari Takai, July 23, 1977. B.S., N.E. La. U., 1975; Ph.D., U. Wyo., 1981. Research assoc. Va. Poly. Inst. and State U., Blacksburg, 1981-84; postdoctoral research assoc. Lawrence Livermore Nat. Lab., Calif., 1984—. Contbr. articles to profl. jours. Mem. Am. Phys. Soc., LAMPF Users Group. Current work: Nuclear structure studies of light nuclei by inelastic electron and pion scattering, partial-wave analysis of pion-induced single-pion production on protons. Subspecialties: Nuclear physics; Particle physics. Office: Lawrence Livermore Nat Lab L-405 Livermore CA 94550

MANLEY, MARTIN HAROLD, electrical engineer; b. Norwich, Norfolk, Eng., Sept. 12, 1952; came to U.S. 1980; s. Harold and Margaret (Oscroft) M. B.Sc., Southampton U., Eng., 1974, Ph.D., 1978. Prin. engr. GEC Research Labs., London, 1978-80; mem. tech. staff Philips Research Labs., Signetics, Sunnyvale, Calif., 1980-83; mgr. device engring. Exel Microelectronics, San Jose, Calif., 1983—. Contbr. articles to profl. jours. Patentee carrier domain devices. Mem. IEEE. Current work: Development and characterization and modelling of MOS integrated circuits. Subspecialties: Semiconductors; Integrated circuits. Office: Exel Microelectronics 2150 Commerce Dr San Jose CA 95128

MANLULU, HIGINIO Y(ABUT), physicist, consultant; b. Calauag, Quezon Province, Philippines, Jan. 11, 1927; came to U.S., 1973, naturalized, 1978; s. Jesus Ramirez and Bernardita Yabut (Zablan) M.; m. Leticia Josue Malubag, Mar. 27, 1960; children—Christine, Catherine, Constantine-Eugene. B.S.E.E., Mapua Inst. Tech., Manila, 1952; postgrad. U. Gottingen, 1957-58. Cert. plant mechanic, lic. elec. engr., Philippines. Mem. faculty dept. physics Sch. Mech. Engring., Mapua Inst. Tech., 1954-73; radiation safety/regulations officer S.S. White Dental of Pennwalt Corp., Holmdel, N.J., 1973-75; regulatory affairs adminstr. Philips Med. Systems, Shelton, Conn., 1975-82; indsl. engring. mgr. Haake Buchler, Fort Lee, N.J., 1982-83; dir-regulatory Biosearch Inc., Somerville, N.J., 1983—; mem. faculty depts. physics and elec. engring. Bridgeport Engring. Inst., Conn., 1979-82; cons. in field. Co-author faculty jour. Far Eastern U., 1952. Mem. choir St. Lawrence Ch., Lawrence Harbor, N.J. Mem. IEEE, Regulatory Affairs Profl. Soc., Assn. for Advancement Med. Instrumentation, N.Y. Acad. Scis., Philippine Amat Judo Assn. Roman Catholic. Current work: Biomedical engineering; forensics/criminalistics. Subspecialties: Nuclear physics; Medical physics. Home: 244 Betsy Ross Dr Freehold NJ 07728

MANN, JOHN BUNYAN, electrical engineering company executive; b. Lawrence, Kans., June 17, 1949; s. William Aden and Mary Nell (Lynch) M.; m. Martha Caroline Michalski, May 25, 1985. B.S.E.E., Princeton U., 1972; M.S.E.E., Columbia U., 1975. Sr. assoc. Booz-Allen & Hamilton, Bethesda, Md., 1974-82; dir. MCI Corp., Washington, 1982-84; pres., chief exec. officer Spectrum Digital Corp., Herndon, Va., 1984—, also dir.; dir. TechTel Corp., Rockville, Md., Digital TranService Corp., Paramus, N.J. Mem. IEEE, AAAS, Eta Kappa Nu. Democrat. Club: Princeton (Washington). Current work: Telecommunications system design, detection and estimation. Subspecialties: Telecommunications; Computer engineering. Office: Spectrum Digital Corp Herndon VA 22070

MANN, MICHAEL DAVID, neurobiologist, researcher, educator; b. Gold Beach, Oreg., May 20, 1944; s. Merrill Gordon and Geraldine Avis (Erickson) M.; m. Sally Lee Pingleton, Aug. 19, 1966; children—Koren Kathleen, Aaron Michael. A.B., U. So. Calif., 1966; Ph.D., Cornell U., 1971. Asst. prof. U. Nebr. Med. Ctr., Omaha, 1973-77, assoc. prof., 1977—. Author: The Nervous System and Behavior, 1981. Contbr. articles to profl. jours. Vol. tchr. Omaha Pub. Schs., 1976—, curriculum rev. com., 1980—. Grantee NSF, 1976-82, NIMH, 1976-77. Mem. Am. Physiol. Soc., Soc. for Neurosci. Democrat. Club: Cajal. Current work: Development, evolution, anatomy and physiology of motor systems in mammals and reptiles. Subspecialties: Neurobiology; Comparative neurobiology. Office: U Neb Med Ctr Dept Physiology 42d St and Dewey Ave Omaha NE 68105

MANN, ROBERT WELLESLEY, educator, engineer; b. Bklyn., Oct. 6, 1924; s. Arthur Wellesley and Helen (Rieger) M.; m. Margaret Ida Florencourt, Sept. 4, 1950; children: Robert Wellesley, Catherine Louise. S.B., Mass. Inst. Tech., 1950, S.M., 1951, Sc.D., 1957. With Bell Telephone Labs., N.Y.C., 1942-43, 46-47; research engr. Mass. Inst. Tech., 1951-52, research supr., 1952—, mem. faculty, 1953—, prof. mech. engring., 1963-70, Germeshausen prof., 1970-72, prof. engring., 1972-74, Whitaker prof. biomed. engring., 1974—, head systems and design div., mech. engring. dept., 1957-68, 82-83, founder, engring. projects lab., 1959-62; founder, chmn. steering com. Center Sensory Aids Evaluation and Devel., 1964—, chmn. div. health scis., tech., planning and mgmt., 1972-74, founder biomechanics and human rehab. lab., 1975—; lectr. engring. in faculty of medicine Harvard U., 1973—; exec. com. program in health scis. and tech. Harvard-Mass. Inst. Tech., 1972—; research assoc. in orthopedic surgery Children's Hosp. Med. Center, 1973—; cons. in engring. sci. Mass. Gen. Hosp., 1969—; cons. in field, 1953—; mem. Commn. Engring. Edn., 1962-69; com. prosthetics research and devel. Nat. Acad. Scis., 1963-69, chmn. sensory aids subcom., 1965-68, com. skeletel system, 1969; mem. com. interplay engring. with biology and medicine Nat. Acad. Engring., 1969-73, chmn. sensory aids subcom., 1968-73; mem. com. sci. policy for medicine and health Inst. Medicine, 1973-74, 84-86; mem. com. on nat. needs for rehab. physically handicapped Nat. Acad. Scis., 1975-76; mem.-at-large confs. com. Engring. Found., 1975-81. Author numerous articles in field.; Cons. editor: Ency. Sci. and Tech.; editorial bd.: Jour. Visual Impairment and Blindness, 1976-80; assoc. editor: IEEE Trans. in Biomed. Engring, 1969-78; asso. editor: ASME Jour. Biomed. Engring, 1976-82. Pres., trustee Amanda Caroline Payson Scholarship Fund, 1965—, Nat. Braille Press, 1982—; bd. dirs. Carroll Rehab. Center, 1967-74, pres., 1968-74; mem. corp. Perkins Sch. for Blind, 1970—, Mt. Auburn Hosp., 1972—. Served with AUS, 1943-46. Recipient Sloan award for outstanding performance, 1957; Talbert Abrams photogrammetry award, 1962; award Assn. Blind of Mass., 1969; IR-100 award for Braillemboss, 1972; Bronze Beaver award Mass. Inst. Tech., 1975; J.R. Killian faculty achievement award Mass. Inst. Tech., 1983; UCP Goldenson Research for Handicapped award, 1976; H.R. Lissner award, 1977; New Eng. award, 1979. Fellow Am. Acad. Arts and Scis., IEEE (chmn. group on engring. in biology and medicine 1974-78), AAAS; mem. Nat. Acad. Engring., Nat. Acad. Scis., Inst. Medicine of Nat. Acad. Scis., ASME (gold medal 1977), AAAS, Biomed. Engring. Soc. (dir. 1981-84), M.I.T. Alumni Assn. (pres. 1983-84), Sigma Xi (nat. lectr. 1979-81), Tau Beta Pi, Pi Tau Sigma. Roman Catholic. Patentee in field. Current Work: Human musculo-skeletal-joint biomechanics, osteoarthritis; human rehabilitaion; computer-aided surgical simulation. Subspecialty: Biomedical engineering. Home: 5 Pelham Rd Lexington MA 02173 Office: 77 Massachusetts Ave Cambridge MA 02139

MANNING, IRWIN, physicist; b. Bklyn., Mar. 7, 1929; s. Louis and Nettie (Jaffee) M.; m. Amelia Ann Young, May 24, 1964; children: Emily, Sarah. B.S. in Math, M.I.T., 1951, Ph.D. in Physics, 1955. Research assoc. Syracuse U., 1955-57, U. Wis., 1957-59; research physicist Naval Research Lab., Washington, 1959—. Mem. Am. Phys. Soc. Current Work: Materials modification by ion implantation. Subspecialty: Theoretical physics. Home: 1801 Courtland Rd: Alexandria VA 22306 Office: Condensed Matter and Radiation Scis Div Naval Research Lab Washington DC 20375

MANNING, RUTH ANN, supercomputer consultant, mathematician; b. Middlesboro, Ky., Feb. 21, 1951; d. John Thomas and Elsie Lorene (Rowland) Williams; m. Douglas Eugene Manning, Oct. 3, 1982; children—Martha Ruth, John Douglas. B.S. in Math., U. Tenn.-Knoxville, 1972, M.S., 1974, Ph.D., 1979. Computer programmer Clinch Powell Ednl. Coop., Harrogate, Tenn., 1974; math. coordinator and cons. Claiborne County Schs., Tazewell, Tenn., 1974-75; grad. teaching asst. U. Tenn., Knoxville, 1972-74, 75-76; asst. prof. math. Lincoln Meml. U., Harrogate, Tenn., 1976-78; programming asst. Union Carbide Corp., Oak Ridge, Tenn., 1979; supercomputer cons. Control Data Corp., Knoxville, 1979—. Author: (with J.A. Carpenter) keyword in Context Index for Numerical Algebra, 1980. Area coordinator Dulin Gallery of Art, Knoxville, 1976-78. Hilton A. Smith grad. fellow, 1978-79. Mem. Soc. for Indsl. and Applied Math., Knoxville Assn. Women Execs. Republican. Baptist. Current work: Applied math and numerical algorithm devel. for vector computers. Subspecialties: Algorithms; Numerical analysis (computer science). Home: 7300 Rule Rd Knoxville TN 37920 Office: Control Data Corp 9041 Executive Park Dr Suite 100 Knoxville TN 37923

MANOR, ROBERT EDWARD, physicist, consultant; b. Whitehouse, Ohio, Dec. 3, 1937; s. Clifford William and Emily Melissa (Bradford) M. B.S., U. Toledo.; M.S., Kent State U., 1969. Devel. physicist LOF Glass Co., Toledo, 1964-65; math. physicist Toledo Engring. Co., Inc., 1965-67; devel. physicist Haughton Elevator Co., Toledo, 1969-70; cons. math., devel. physicist laser-energy beam systems Energystics, Inc., Toledo, 1976-77; owner, chief physicist REM Agy., Whitehouse, Ohio, 1970—Current Work: Development mathematics and quantum optics for a continuous laser fusion of deuterium and tritium pellets; solid state computer with digital electronic readout system; development of math and physics of plasma fusion system for commercial use. Subspecialties: Integrated circuits; Laser fusion.

MANSFIELD, JOHN EDWARD, physicist; b. Cleve., July 2, 1938; s. John Edward and Loretta Agnes (Martis) M.; m. Karen Marie Beakey, May 25, 1968; children—Clare Marie, Keyne Catherine. A.B., U. Detroit, 1960; licentiate in philosophy St. Louis U., 1963, M.S., 1963; A.M., Harvard U., 1966, Ph.D., 1970. Postdoctoral fellow U. Notre Dame, South Bend, Ind., 1968-71; sr. scientist Sci. Applications, McLean, Va., 1971-76; div. chief Def. Intelligence Agy., Washington, 1976-82; asst. def. dir. Def. Nuclear Agy., Washington, 1982-84; mem. profl. staff Armed Services Com., U.S. Ho. of Reps., Washington, 1984—. Author numerous tech. reports. Recipient Exceptional Civilian Service award U.S. Dept. Def., 1980. Fellow Harvard, 1963, NSF, 1964-68. Mem. Am. Phys. Soc. Club: Harvard (Washington). Current work: Applied physics as related to national defense. Subspecialty: Theoretical physics. Office: Armed Services Com US House of Reps Washington DC 20515

MANSON, STEVEN TRENT, physics educator; b. Bklyn., Dec. 12, 1940; s. Henry Joshua and Rosalind (Frey) M.; m. Bettye Bonds, July 17, 1944; children: Jonathan, Andrew. B.S., Rensselaer Poly. Inst., 1961; M.A., Columbia U., 1963, Ph.D., 1966. NAS-NRC postdoctoral fellow Nat. Bur. Standards, Washington, 1966-68; asst. prof. Ga. State U., Atlanta, 1968-72, assoc. prof., 1972-77, prof., 1977—; cons. Oak Ridge Nat. Lab., Argonne Nat. Lab., Batelle Meml. Inst. Editorial bd.: Jour. Electron Spectroscopy and Related Phenomena; Contbr. articles to profl. jours. Active Winnona Park Neighbors Assn., 1977—, Decatur Neighborhood Alliance, 1977—; mem. Decatur Community Goals Com., 1980—. NSF grantee, 1973—; U.S. Army Research Office grantee, 1974—; recipient Alumni Disting. Prof. award Coll. Arts and Scis., Ga. State U., 1977. Fellow Am. Phys. Soc.; mem. Inst. Physics (London), Sigma Pi Sigma. Current Work: Theoretical studies of atomic collisions and photoabsorption. Subspecialties: Atomic and molecular physics; Theoretical physics. Home: 463 Kirk Rd Decatur GA 30030 Office: Dept Physics and Astronomy Ga State Univ Atlanta GA 30303

MANSOUR, TAG ELDIN, pharmacologist; b. Belkas, Eqypt, Nov. 6, 1924; came to U.S., 1951, naturalized, 1956; s. Elsayed and Rokaya (Elzayat) M.; m. Joan Adela MacKinnon, Aug. 6, 1955; children—Suzanne, Jeanne, Dean. B.Sc., Cairo U., 1946; PH.D., U. Birmingham, Eng., 1949, D.Sc., 1974. Lectr. U. Cairo, 1950-51; Fulbright instr. physiology Howard U., Washington, 1951-52; sr. instr. pharmacology Western Res. U., 1952-54; asst. prof., assoc. prof. pharmacology La. State U. Med. Sch., New Orleans, 1954-61; assoc. prof., prof. pharmacology Stanford U. Sch. Medicine, 1961—, Donald E. Baxter prof., chmn. dept. pharmacology, 1977—; cons. USPHS, WHO, Nat. Acad. Scis.; Mem. adv. bd. Med. Sch., Kuwait U.; Heath Clarke lectr. London Sch. Hygiene and Tropical Medicine, 1981. Contrbr. sci. articles to profl. jours. Commonwealth Fund fellow, 1965; Mercy Found. scholar NIMR, 1982. Fellow AAAS; mem. Am. Soc. Pharmacology and Exptl. Therapeutics, Am. Soc Biol. Chemists, Am. Heart Assn., World Affairs Council, Sierra Club, Sigma Xi. Club: Stanford Faculty. Current Work: Regulation of enzymes and effect of hormones on regulatory enzymes-biochemistry and pharmacology of parasitic worms. Subspecialties: Molecular pharmacology; Biochemistry (medicine). Office: 300 Pasteur Dr Stanford CA 94305

MANTIONE, CHARLES ROSS, pharmacologist; b. Pittston, Pa., Oct 6, 1951; s. Patrick and Marie T. (Shandra) M.; m. Jacquelyn Ann Toth, May 12, 1973 (div. Aug. 1983); 1 child, Lianne Renae. B.S., Pa. State U., State College, 1973; M.S., Fairleigh-Dickenson U., 1978; Ph.D., U. Pitts., 1983. Research pharmacologist Hoechst-Russell Pharm. Co., Somerville, N.J., 1974-78; Prat fellow NIH, Bethesda, Md., 1983-85; pharmacologist Miami Valley Labs., Procter & Gamble Co., Cin., 1985—. Mem. Soc. for Neurosci., Am. Soc. Pharm. and Exptl. Therapeutics (travel award 1982), N.Y. Acad. Sci. Current work: Research on the pharmacological role of benzodiazepines in the central and peripheral nervous system. Subspecialties: Neuropharmacology; Molecular pharmacology. Home: 473 G Dewdrop Circle Forest Park OH 45240 Office: Miami Valley Labs Procter & Gamble Co Cincinnati OH 45247

MANUS, ANDREW THEODORE, marine research administrator, marine science educator; b. Concord, N.H., Feb. 18, 1952; s. Mark Eletherios and Bessie Andrea (Rouvalis) M. B.S., U. N.H., 1974; M.S., Tex. A&M U., 1976. Area marine advisor Marine Adv. Service Sea Grant Coll. Program, U. Calif., San Francisco, 1976-78, coastal resources specialist, 1978-80; dir. marine adv. service Sea Grant Coll. Program, U. Del., Lewes, 1980—, asst. sea grant dir., 1981-84, exec. dir., Lewes/Newark, 1984—; functional group leader Sea Grant Coll. Program, U. Del., 1980—; chmn. report drafting com. Gov.'s Task Force on Inland Bays, Dover, Del., 1983-84, chmn. Finfish Adv. Council, Dover, 1984—. Contbr. articles to profl. jours., chpt. to book. Vice chmn. Calif. State Parks and Recreation Adv. Bd., San Mateo, 1978-80; mem. Provost's Ad-hoc Com. on Ednl. Services for Lower Del., Newark, 1980-81. Recipient Dean's award for research Coll. Marine Studies, U. Del., 1984; grantee NOAA, 1982-84, 84—. Mem. Nat. Assn. Environ. Profls. (cert. environ. profl.), Am. Acad. Polit. and Soc. Sci., Nature Conservancy. Current work: Environmental conflict resolution, marine resource management, natural resources decision-making. Subspecialties: Resource management; Coastal zones. Home: 129 Laurel Rd Millsboro DE 19966 Office: Sea Grant Coll Program 700 Pilottown Rd Lewes DE 19958

MANVI, RAMACHANDRA, engineering educator, systems engineer; b. Hyderabad, India, Jan. 26, 1939; came to U.S. 1971, naturalized 1977; s. Narsinga Rao and Pramila (Bupuji) M.; m. Sati R. Puhuja, Nov. 27, 1963. B.S., Osmania U., Hyderabad, 1958; Ph.D., Washington State U., 1968. Registered profl. mech. engr. Sci. officer Atomic Energy, Bombay, India, 1958-64; asst. prof. engring. Pahlavi U., Shiraz, Iran, 1969-71; asst. prof. engring. Calif. State U., Los Angeles, 1974-79, assoc. prof., 1979-81, prof., 1981—, dean engring., 1981—; mem. tech. staff Jet Propulsion Lab., Pasadena, Calif., 1974—; bd. dirs. Productivity Council of Pacific Southwest, Los Angeles, 1981—. Contbr. articles to profl. jours. Mem. Am.-India Soc. Grantee NASA, 1978-80, 82, Dept. Energy, 1979-81. Mem. ASME, Am. Soc. Engring. Educ. Democrat. Hindu. Club: Calif. State U. Los Angeles Faculty. Subspecialties: Mechanical engineering; Systems engineering. Office: Calif State Univ 5151 State University Dr Los Angeles CA 90032

MANYAM, BALA VENKTESHA, neurologist, researcher; b. Bangalore, India, Oct. 15, 1942; d. Kolar and Swarnam Venktesier; m. Rani C. Manyam, June 10, 1970; 1 child, Shaila. M.B., B.S., Bangalore Med. Coll., 1967. Diplomate Am. Bd. Psychiatry and Neurology. Resident internal medicine Dalhousie U., 1972; resident in neurology Med. Coll. Wis. Hosp., Milw., 1972-75; Thomas Jefferson U. Hosp., Phila., 1972-75; asst. research officer Nat. Inst. Nutrition, Hyderabad, India, 1970; staff neurologist VA Med. Center, Wilmington, Del., 1975-81, asst. chief neurology service, dir. movement disorders clinic, 1981-84; instr. Thomas Jefferson U., Phila., 1975-81, asst. prof. depts. neurology and pharmacology, 1981-84; assoc. prof. div. neurology, dir. Parkinson's Disease and Movement Disorders Clinic, So. Ill. U. Sch. Medicine, Springfield, 1984—. Contbr. articles to profl. jours., chpts. to books. Recipient Spl. Performance award VA, 1977; VA grantee, 1980-84. Mem. Am. Acad. Neurology, Am. Soc. Pharmacology and Exptl. Therapeutics, World Fedn. Neurology (research com. neuroepidemiology), Soc. Neurosci., AMA, Assn. Research in Mental and Nervous Diseases, AMA, Sigma Xi. Hindu. Current Work: Biochemical and pharmacological alterations of central nervous system in movement disorders and the effect of various drugs. Subspecialties: Neurology; Neuropharmacology. Home: 49 Frontier Lake Dr Springfield IL 62707 Office: Div Neurology So Ill U Sch Medicine PO Box 3926 Springfield IL 62708

MAO, CHUNG-LING, chemist; b. Nanking, China, Apr. 21, 1936; came to U.S., 1962, naturalized, 1976; s. Hong and Ying-Hwa (Su) M.; m. Leanne Hai-ping Chou, Dec. 31, 1966; children—Kelvin K., Vivian H. B.Sc., Cheng-Kung U., Tainan, Taiwan, 1959; M.S., Tex. Tech. U., 1964; Ph.D., Va. Tech. and State U., 1967. Research assoc. Duke U., 1967-69; research chemist Uniroyal, Inc., Wayne, N.J., 1969-72, sr. research scientist, Middlebury, Conn., 1973-80; sr. research assoc. Avery Internat., Pasadena, Calif., 1980-83; research assoc. Air Products and Chems., Inc., Allentown, Pa., 1983—. Contbr. articles on organic chemistry to profl. jours. Patentee in field of polymer chemistry. Mem. Am. Chem. Soc. Current work: Polymer chemistry, emulsion polymerization, pressure sensitive adhesives, polyurethane chemistry, olefin chemistry, organic chemistry, process engineering. Subspecialties: Polymer chemistry; Organic chemistry. Home: 4696 Sweetbriar Circle Emmaus PA 18049 Office: Air Products and Chems Inc PO Box 538 Allentown PA 18105

MAO, CHUNG-REI, chemist, researcher, consultant; b. Nanking, China, Sept. 9, 1948; came to U.S., 1972, naturalized, 1983; s. Cheng and Hsiu-Ying (Lu) M.; m. Hsien-Chueh Hwang Mao, June 14, 1980; 1 child, Michael Anyeu Mao. B.S., Tamkang U., 1971, M.S., U. Rochester, 1974, Ph.D., 1976. Research assoc. SUNY-Syracuse, 1976-77, U. Ill.-Chgo., 1977-79; research chemist Argonne Nat. Lab., Ill., 1979-81; research engr. InterNorth Inc., Omaha, 1981-84, prin. research scientist, 1984—; cons. InterNorth Inc., Omaha, 1982-83, project leader, 1984—. Author: Molecular Orbital Theory, 1971. Patentee in field. Fellow Gro-Fu Chen Found., 1971, U. Rochester, 1972-74, Uniroyal Inc., 1975. Mem. Am. Chem. Soc., AAAS, Omaha Chinese Assn. (chmn. 1982-84), Sigma Xi. Republican. Current work: Research and development and photoelectrochemical catalysis system for chemical synthesis and process gas cleanup; catalytic pyrolysis of natural gas and sonochemistry. Subspecialties: Catalysis chemistry; Electron spin resonance. Home: 13527 Jefferson Circle Omaha NE 68137 Office: Research Ctr InterNorth Inc 4840 F St Omaha NE 68117

MAPLESDEN, DOUGLAS CECIL, former college administrator, consultant; b. Sandhurst, Eng., Oct. 30, 1919; came to U.S., 1963, naturalized, 1975; s. Cecil Walker Maplesden and Frances (Pantry) Maplesden Cutts; m. Elizabeth Rawlings, Nov. 23, 1940 (div. 1981; children—Anne Elizabeth, John Douglas, Mary Jane, Joann Margaret; m. Joan Duda, May 27, 1984. D.V.M., Ont. Vet. Coll., 1950; M.S.A., U. Toronto, 1957; Ph.D., Cornell U., 1959. Prof. Ont. Vet. Coll., Guelph, Can., 1953-60; v.p. Stevenson, Turner & Boyce, Guelph, 1960-63; gen. mgr. animal health CIBA, Three Bridges, N.J., 1963-69; dir. animal health research E.R. Squibb & Sons, Three Bridges, 1969-79; dean Ont. Vet. Coll., Guelph, 1980-84. Author: Handbook of Nutrition, 1962; The Universal Diet, 1985. Pres. Hunterton County C. of C., Flemington, N.J., 1972-73. Served with Royal Can. Air Force, 1942-45. Mem. N.Y. Acad. Sci., AVMA, Can. Vet. Med. Assn., Nutrition Soc. Can., Nutrition Research Council. Current work: Consulting on pharmaceutical and biological research and biotechnology. Subspecialties: Internal medicine (veterinary medicine); Animal nutrition. Home and Office: RD 1 Box 282B Flemington NJ 08822

MAPOTHER, DILLON EDWARD, physicist, academic administrator, consultant; b. Louisville, Aug. 22, 1921; s. Dillon Edward and Edith (Rubel) M.; m. Elizabeth Beck, June 29, 1946; children—Ellen, Susan, Anne. B.S. in M.E., U. Louisville, 1943; D.Sc. in Physics, Carnegie-Mellon U., 1949. Engr., Westinghouse Research Labs., Pitts., 1943-46; instr. Carnegie Inst. Tech., Pitts., 1946; mem. faculty U. Ill., Urbana, 1949—, prof. physics, 1959—, dir. Computing Services Office, 1971-76, assoc. vice chancellor for research, 1976—, acting dean Grad. Coll., acting vice chancellor for research, 1977-78, assoc. dean Grad. Coll., 1979—; cons. in field. DuPont fellow, 1947-49; Sloan fellow, 1958-61; Guggenheim fellow, 1960-61. Fellow Am. Phys. Soc.; mem. Am. Assn. Physics Tchrs., AAAS, Soc. Univ. Patent Adminstrs., Sigma Xi. Current work: Solid state diffusion; superconductivity; higher order phase transitions, thermodynamics; academic research administration. Subspecialties: Low temperature physics; Mechanical engineering. Office: Univ Ill Grad Coll 107 Coble Hall 801 S Wright St Champaign IL 61820

MARAMOROSCH, KARL, virologist, educator; b. Vienna, Austria, Jan. 16, 1915; came to U.S., 1947, naturalized, 1952; s. Jacob and Stefanie Olga (Schlesinger) M.; m. Irene Ludwinowska, Nov. 15, 1938; 1 dau., Lydia Ann. M.S. magna cum laude in Entomology, Agrl. U., Warsaw, Poland, 1938; student, Poly. U. Bucharest, Rumania, 1944-46; fellow, Bklyn. Bot. Garden, 1947-48; Ph.D. (predoctoral fellow Am. Cancer Soc. 1948-49), Columbia, 1949. Civilian internee in, Rumania, 1939-46; asst., then asso. Rockefeller Inst., N.Y.C., 1949-61; sr. entomologist Boyce Thompson Inst., Yonkers, N.Y., 1961-74, program dir. virology and insect physiology, 1962-74; prof. microbiology Waksman Inst., Rutgers U., New Brunswick, N.J., 1974-85, prof. entomology dept., 1985—, Robert L. Starkey prof., 1983; vis. prof. agr. U. Wageningen, Netherlands, 1953, Cornell U., 1957, Rutgers U., 1967-68, Fordham U., 1973, Sapporo U., Japan, 1980, Fudan U., Shanghai, 1982, Justus Liebig U., Giessen, 1983; Mendel lectr. St. Peters Coll., Jersey City, 1963; virologist FAO to Philippines, 1960; cons. World-wide survey, 1963; chmn. U.S.-Japan Coop. Seminar, 1965, 74, 85; mem. panel food and fiber Nat. Acad. Scis., 1966; cons. rice virus diseases AID-IRRI, Hyderabad, India, 1971; cons. UNDP, Bangalore, India, 1978-79; virologist FAO/UNDP, Sri Lanka, 1981, 82, 83, Mauritius, 1985; Am. Inst. Biol. Scis. lectr., 1970-72, Found. Microbiology Nat. lectr., 1972-73, Fulbright disting. prof., Yugoslavia, 1972, 78; mem. tropical medicine and parasitology study sect. NIH, 1972-76; chmn. 1st-3d Internat. Confs. Comparative Virology, 1969, 73, 76. Author: Comparative Symptomatology of Coconut Diseases of Unknown Etiology, 1964; Editor: Biological Transmission of Disease Agents, 1962, Insect Viruses, 1968, Viruses, Vectors and Vegetation, 1969, Comparative Virology, 1971, Mycoplasma Diseases, 1973, Viruses, Evolution and Cancer, 1974, Invertebrate Immunity, 1975, Legume Diseases in the Tropics, 1975, Invertebrate Tissue Culture: Research Applications, 1976, Invertebrate Tissue Culture: Applications in Medicine, Biology and Agriculture, 1976, Aphids as Virus Vectors, 1977, Insect and Plant Viruses: An Atlas, 1977, Viruses and Environment, 1978, Practical Tissue Culture Applications, 1979, Leafhopper Vectors and Plant Disease Agents, 1979, Vectors of Plant Pathogens, 1980, Invertebrate Systems in Vitro, 1980, Vectors of Disease Agents, 1981, Mycoplasma Diseases of Trees and Shrubs, 1981, Invertebrate Cell Culture Applications, 1982, Subviral Pathogens of Plants and Animals: Viroids and Prions, 1985, Viral Insecticides for Biological Control, 1985, Methods in Virology, 1964—, Advances in Virus Research, 1972—, Archives of Virology, 1973—, Intervirology, 1973—, Advances in Cell Culture, 1979—, In Vitro, 1981—; editor-in-chief Jour. N.Y. Entomol. Soc, 1972-83; asso. editor: Virology, 1964-68, 75-79. Recipient sr. research award Lalor Found., 1957; Nat. Ciba-Geigy award in agr., 1976; Wolf prize in agr., 1980; Jurzykowski prize in biology, 1980; Disting. Service award Am. Inst. Biol. Scis., 1983. Fellow N.Y. Acad. Scis. (A. Cressy Morrison prize natural sci. 1951, chmn. div. microbiology 1956-60, rec. sec. 1960-61, v.p. 1962-63), Nat. Acad. Scis. India (hon.), AAAS (Campbell award 1958); mem. Harvey Soc., Growth Soc., Phytopath. Soc. (councellor), Entomol. Soc. Am., Indian, Japan, Can. phytopath. socs., Leopoldina Acad., Internat. Com. Virus Nomenclature, Electron Microscope Soc., Am. Soc. Microbiology (Waksman award 1978), Tissue Culture Assn. (pres. N.E. br. 1978-81), Sigma Xi (pres. Rugers chpt. 1978). Subspecialty: Microbiology. Home: 17 Black Birch Ln Scarsdale NY 10583 Office: Entomology Dept Rutgers U New Brunswick NJ 08903

MARAN, JANICE WENGERD, pharmacologist; b. Balt., June 30, 1942; d. Edgar Arthur and Mildred Ilease (Laughter) Wengerd; m. Anthony J. Maran, Apr. 29, 1966. B.S., Juniata Coll., 1964; Ph.D. (NIH fellow, George D. and Grace H. Shafer fellow), Stanford U., 1974. Research asst. Stanford (Calif.) U., 1964-66, research asso., 1966-69; research scientist McNeil Labs., Ft. Washington, Pa., 1977-78; sr. scientist McNeil Pharm., Spring House, Pa., 1978—, project mgr., 1980—; NATO postdoctoral fellow in sci. U. Bristol, Eng., 1974-75; NIH postdoctoral fellow Johns Hopkins U. Med. Sch., 1975-77. Contbr. articles to sci. publs., chpts. to books. NSF award for summer study in chemistry, 1960. Mem. Am. Physiol. Soc., Biomed. Engring. Soc., Soc. for Neurosci., N.Y. Acad. Scis., AAAS, Internat. Platform Assn., Sigma Xi. Current Work: Discovery of novel psychotrophic drugs and the eleucidation of the mechanism of action of novel and existing central nervous system drugs through electrophysiological techniques; project management of drug development of a cerebral vasodilator. Subspecialties: Neuropharmacology; Neurophysiology. Home: 106 Anton Rd Wynnewood PA 19096 Office: McNeil Pharmaceutical Spring House PA 19477

MARAN, STEPHEN PAUL, astronomer; b. Bklyn., Dec. 25, 1938; s. Alexander P. and Clara F. (Schoenfeld) M.; m. Sally Ann Scott, Feb. 14, 1971; children: Michael Scott, Enid Rebecca, Elissa Jean. B.S., Bklyn. Coll., 1959; M.A., U. Mich., 1961, Ph.D., 1964. Astronomer Kitt Peak Nat. Obs., Tucson, 1964-69; project scientist for orbiting solar observatories NASA-Goddard Space Flight Center, Greenbelt, Md., 1969-75, head advanced systems and ground observations br., 1970-77, mgr. operation Kohoutek, 1973-74, sr. staff scientist, 1977—; Cons. Westinghouse Research Labs., 1966; vis. lectr. U. Md., College Park, 1969-70; sr. lectr. U. Calif. at Los Angeles, 1976. Author: (with John C. Brandt) New Horizons in Astronomy, 1972, 2d edit., 1979, Arabic edit., 1979; Editor: Physics of Nonthermal Radio Sources, 1964, The Gum Nebula and Related Problems, 1971, Possible Relations Between Solar Activity and Meteorological Phenomena, 1975, New Astronomy and Space Science Reader, 1977, A Meeting with the Universe, 1981; assoc. editor: Earth, Extraterrestrial Scis, 1969-79; editor: Astrophys. Letters, 1974-77, assoc. editor, from 1977; Contbr. articles on astronomy, space to popular mags. Named Distinguished Visitor Boston U., 1970; recipient Group Achievement awards NASA, 1969, 74, Hon. Mention AAAS-Westinghouse Sci. Writing Award, 1970. Mem. Internat. Astron. Union, AAAS, Am. Astron. Soc. (Harlow Shapley vis. lectr. 1981), Royal Astron. Soc., Am. Phys. Soc., Am. Geophys. Union, Am. Inst. Aeros. and Astronautics. Current Work: Observations of nebulae from space; space telescope research. Subspecialties: Ultraviolet high energy astrophysics; Optical astronomy. Office: Code 680 NASA-Goddard Space Flight Center Greenbelt MD 20771

MARANGOS, PAUL JEROME, neurochemist, researcher; b. Bklyn., July 2, 1947; s. Peter John and Ann (Ventra) M.; m. Maia Doumato, Aug. 18, 1968; children: Peter Jerome, Victoria Ann. B.A., R.I. Coll., 1969; Ph.D., U. R.I., 1973. Postdoctoral fellow Roche Inst. Molecular Biology, Nutley, N.J., 1973-76; sr. staff fellow NIMH, Bethesda, Md., 1976-79, chief unit on neurochemistry, 1979—; adj. professorial lectr. George Washington U. Sch. Medicine. Editor: Neurobiological Research, 1983; Contb. articles to profl. jours. Recipient Bennett award in biol. psychiatry Soc. Biol. Psychiatry, 1980. Mem. AAAS, Am. Soc. Neurochemistyr, Soc. Neurosci. Current Work: Brain specific proteins, neurotransmitters and drug receptors in brain. Mechanism of benzodiazepine action, adenosine receptors. Subspecialties: Neuropharmacology; Neurochemistry. Home: 18409 Kingshill Rd Germantown MD 20874 Office: 9000 Rockville Pike Bldg 10 Room 3D-48 Bethesda MD 20205

MARASH, STANLEY ALBERT, statistical consultant; b. N.Y.C., Dec. 18, 1938; s. Albert and Esther (Cunio) M.; m. Muriel Sylvia Sutchin, Dec. 9, 1941; children: Judith Ilene, Alan Scott. B.B.A., CCNY, 1961; M.B.A., Bernard M. Baruch Coll., 1970. Registered profl. engr., Calif. Statistician Gen. Dynamics/Electric Boat, Groton, Conn., 1961-62, Idaho Nuclear Energy Lab., Idaho Falls, 1962-63; statistician RCA Memory Products Operation, Needham, Mass., 1963-64, engr. quality assurance, 1964-65; cons. engr. (RCA Astro Electronics div.), Princeton, N.J., 1965-66; corp. mgr. quality assurance Ideal Corp., Bklyn., 1966-68; mgr. quality assurance Gen. Instrument SignaLite, Neptune, N.J., 1968; pres. Stat-A-Matrix Group, Edison, N.J., 1968—; p. Stat-A-Matrix, Internat., Inc., Edison, n.j., 1975—; trustee, mng. dir. Stat-A-Matrix Inst., 1975—; adj. prof., indsl. adv. com. Middlesex County Coll., Edison, N.J., 1971—; vis. prof. U. Sao Paulo, 1974, 75, 77, Madrid Poly U., 1975; mem. exec. standards council Am. Nat. Standards Inst. Author: Quality Assurance for the Nuclear Power Industry, 1972, Statistical Quality Control, 1972; editor: Industrial Quality Programs, 1976, Managing Quality Costs, 1975, Nuclear Quality Assurance, 1976, Auditing Nuclear Quality Assurance, 1975, (with Louis I. Korn) Reliability in Nuclear Power Generating Stations, 1974. Fellow Am. Soc. Quality Control (cert. quality engr., cert. reliability engr., Ellis R. Ott award 1981); mem. IEEE, Am. Statis. Assn., Am. Soc. Tng. and Devel., ASTM, ASME. Subspecialties: Statistics; Quality assurance. Office: 2124 Oak Tree Rd Edison NJ 08820

MARAVOLO, NICHOLAS C., biology educator; b. Chgo., Dec 4, 1940; s. Nicholas and Mary A. (Plonis) M. S.B., U. Chgo., 1962, S.M., 1964, Ph.D., 1966. Asst. prof. biology Lawrence U., Appleton, Wis., 1966-75, assoc. prof., 1975-83, prof., 1983—. Mem. Bot. Soc. Am., Am. Soc. Bryology and Lichenology, Am. Soc. Plant Physiology. Current Work: Developmental physiology of growth regulators in hepatics. Subspecialty: Plant growth. Home: 845 E Alton St Appleton WI 54911 Office: Dept Biology Lawrence U PO Box 599 Appleton WI 54912

MARCELLA, KENNETH LOUIS, veterinarian; b. Waterbury, Conn., Mar. 27, 1957; s. Albert Joseph and Alfonsina (Mazzini) M.; m. Jane Tracy Horton, May 14, 1983. B.A., Dartmouth Coll., 1979; D.V.M., Cornell U., 1983. Clin. veterinarian, asst. prof. dept. comparative medicine U. Va. Med. Ctr., Charlottesville, 1983—; team veterinarian Polo Ctr., U. Va., 1983—; mem. anesthesia crew Vet. Sch. Cornell U., Ithaca, N.Y., 1982-83. Contbr. articles to profl. jours., gen. interest mags. Mem. AVMA, Va. Vet. Med. Assn., Am. Assn. Lab. Animal Medicine, Blue Ridge Veterinary Assn. Roman Catholic. Current work: Clinical evaluation and management of animal pain; clinical veterinary anesthesiology; equine surgery. Subspecialties: Laboratory animal medicine; Anesthesiology. Home: Panorama Farms Route 2 Box 82A Earlysville VA 22936 Office: U Va Med Ctr Dept Comparative Medicine Box 450 Charlottesville VA 22936

MARCH, ROBERT HERBERT, physicist; b. Chgo., Feb. 28, 1934; s. Herbert and Jacinta Virgilia (Grbac) M.; m. Kathryn Ann Holtgraver, Dec. 15, 1979; m. Georgianna Bennington Pugh, Jan. 5, 1953 (div. 1972); 1 son, Thomas. B.A., U. Chgo., 1952, M.S., 1955, Ph.D., 1960. Instr., U. Chgo., 1959-60; lectr. Midwest U. Research Assn., Madison, Wis., 1960-61; mem. faculty U. Wis.,-Madison, 1961—, assoc. prof. physics, 1965-71, prof., 1971—; vis. scientist European Orgn. Nuclear Research, Geneva, 1965, 68, Lawrence Berkeley Lab., 1966, 1969, Fermilab, Batavia, Ill., 1969, 73. Author: Physics for Poets, 1970 (award from Am. Inst. Physics and U.S. Steel Found.); contbr. articles to profl. jours. Mem. Am. Phys. Soc., AAAS, AAUP. Democrat. Current work: High energy astrophysics with gamma rays and neutrinos; structure of subatomic particles; cosmology. Subspecialties: Particle physics; Gamma ray high energy astrophysics. Home: 1217 N Wingra Dr Madison WI 53715 Office: Dept Physics Univ Wis Madison WI 53706

MARCHAJ, TADEUSZ JOZEF, cryogenics engineer; b. Kielce, Poland, Dec. 12, 1924; came to U.S., 1969, naturalized, 1976; s. Michal Antoni and Stanislawa (Mulewicz) M.; m. Irena Maliszewska, Dec. 25, 1972; children—Konrad, Dorothy, Jan. B.Mech. and Aeros., Wawelberg and Rotwand Sch. Engring., Warsaw, Poland, 1950; M.Mech. in Indsl. Energetics and Aeronautics, Warsaw Poly., 1966. Registered profl. engr., D.C. Asst. to prof. Warsaw Poly., 1950-54; designer test equipment Polish Office Standards, Warsaw, 1955-57; head cryogenic dept. Inst. Physics, Polish Acad. Sci., Warsaw, 1957-69; sr. cryogenics research and devel. engr. Preload Tech., Inc., Garden City, N.Y., 1969—; lectr. Inst. Gas Tech., Chgo., 1977-83, U. Boumerdes, Algiers, Algeria, 1978, Japan Bus. Related to LNG, Tokyo, Osaka, and Fukuoka, 1982. Contbr. papers to profl. publs. Patentee in field. Served with Underground Polish Army, 1940-45, World War II. Recipient award of merit Concrete Industry Bd. N.Y., 1975. Mem. Earthquake Engring. Research Inst. Republican. Roman Catholic. Current work: Dynamic response of liquid containing tanks to the vertical acceleration of the earthquake phenomenon. Subspecialties: Cryogenics; Fuels and sources. Home: 6 Ivy Way Port Washington NY 11050 Office: Preload Tech Inc 839 Stewart Ave Garden City NY 11530

MARCHANT, DAVID DENNIS, scientist, researcher; b. Murray, Utah, May 1, 1943; s. David Jenson and Elizabeth (Harding) M.; m. Shanna Dean Jacobs, Sept. 1, 1966; children—David, Tamara, Robert, John, Jennifer, Stephen, Bradley. B.S. in Ceramic Engring., U. Utah, 1967; Sc.D. in Ceramics, MIT, 1974. Research scientist Argonne Nat. Lab., Ill., 1974-77; sr. research scientist Battelle Pacific NW Labs., Richland, Wash., 1977-85; research assoc. Standard Oil Co. (Ohio), Cleveland. Contbr. articles to profl. jours. Patentee in field. Chmn. Tri-Cities Tech. Council, Richland, 1982. Served to capt. USPHS, 1968-70. Spl. fellow AEC, 1970. Mem. Am. Ceramic Soc. (sect. chmn. 1979-80), Soc. Photo-Optical Instrument Engrs. Republican. Mormon. Current work: Development of high technology ceramics and materials; electrochemical testing of ceramics in molten salts and silicates, measurement of thermal-physical properties; development of ceramic fabrication processes. Subspecialties: Ceramics; High-temperature materials. Home: 7077 Longview Dr Solon OH 44139 Office: Standard Oil Co (Ohio) 4440 Warrensville Center Rd Cleveland OH 44139

MARCHATERRE, JOHN FREDERICK, nuclear engineer; b. Hermansville, Mich., Aug. 28, 1932; s. Frederick Joseph and Louise Marie (Boucher) M.; m. Joan Patricia Konvalinka, Sept. 14, 1957; children: Mary, Ann, Madeleine. B.S.Ch.E., Mich. Tech. U., 1954, M.S.Ch.E., 1956; M.S.Ch.E. Engr, 1960; M.B.A., U. Chgo., 1980. Registered profl. engr., Ill. Asst. engr. Argonne Nat. Lab., Ill., 1955-58, group leader, 1956-62, project mgr., 1962-69, assoc. div. dir., reactor analysis and safety div., 1969—; invited lectr. Advanced Summer Inst., Kjeller, Norway, 1959; tech. advisor City of Chgo., 1966-70; cons. Adv. Com. Reactor Safeguards, 1980—; mem. nuclear engring. edn. com. U. Chgo., 1976—. Mem. elec. adv. bd. City of Naperville, 1972-80, precinct committeeman, DuPage County, Ill., 1970-78. Mem. Am. Nuclear Soc., Sigma Xi. Republican. Roman Catholic. Current work: Heat transfer and hydrodynamics; nuclear reactor safety. Subspecialties: Nuclear engineering; Chemical engineering. Home: 1209 Atlas Ln Naperville IL 60540Office: 9700 S Cass Ave Bldg 208 Argonne IL 60439

MARCHETTA, FRANK CARMELO, surgeon, cancer researcher, educator; b. Utica, N.Y., Apr. 28, 1920; s. Donato Anthony and Teresa Maria (Romano) M.; m. Jean Elenor Cile, Apr. 30, 1949; children: Linda Marchetta Wild, Charles, Joanne. Student, Cornell U., 1938-41; M.D., U. Buffalo, 1944. Diplomate: Am. Bd. Surgery. Intern Deaconess Hosp., Buffalo, 1944-45, resident in surgery, 1947-50, Roswell Park Meml. Inst., Buffalo, 1950-51, assoc. cancer research head and neck surgeon, 1951-54, assoc. chief cancer research head and neck surgeon, 1954-56, chief cancer research head and neck surgeon sect. A, 1956-75, cons., 1975—; assoc. clin. prof. head and neck surgery Dental Sch. SUNY-Buffalo, 1958—, SUNY-Buffalo (Med. Sch.), 1962—; cons. VA Hosp., Buffalo. Contbr. articles to sci. jours. Served to capt. M.C. AUS, 1945-47. Recipient award Roswell Park Meml. Inst., 1975. Mem. N.Y. State Med. Soc., New York County Med. Soc., ACS, Soc. Head and Neck Surgeons (sec.), Soc. Surg. Oncology, Am. Assn. for Cancer Research. Current Work: Clinical research in head and neck tumors; laboratory experiments related to problems in head and neck surgery. Subspecialties: Surgery; Oncology. Home: 180 High Park Blvd Eggertsville NY 14226 Office: 2804 Main St Buffalo NY 14214

MARCHETTI, ALFRED PAUL, chemist; b. Bakersfield, Calif., Feb. 16, 1940; s. Fred and Antoinette Rose (Wegis) M.; m. Elaine Caroline Brinker, Aug. 17, 1963; children—Maria Patrice, Michael Paul, David William. B.A., U. Calif.-Riverside, 1961, Ph.D., 1966; M.S., U. Calif.-Berkeley, 1963. NASA fellow U. Calif.-Riverside, 1965-66; NIH postdoctoral fellow U. Pa., Phila., 1966-69; sr. research chemist Eastman Kodak Co., Rochester, N.Y., 1969-75, research assoc., 1975—; adj. prof. U. Rochester, 1981, 82. Contr. articles to profl. jours. Patentee organic photovoltaic. Mem. Am. Phys. Soc., Soc. Photographic Sci. and Engring., Sigma Xi, Phi Lambda Upsilon. Current work: Photophysics of silver halides, photographic emulsion design and sensitization. Subspecialties: Physical chemistry; Condensed matter physics. Office: Eastman Kodak Research Labs 2000 Lake Ave Rochester NY 14650

MARCHIN, GEORGE L., microbiologist, educator; b. Kansas City, Kans., July 12, 1940; s. George Leonard and Ann Maria (Hanis) M.; m. Anne S., July 20, 1974; children: Melissa Ann, Katherine Louise, Madelaine Christine. A.B., Rockhurst Coll., 1962; Ph.D., U. Kans., 1967. Grad. teaching asst., grad. research asst. U. Kans. Med. Center, Kansas City, 1962-67; research assoc. Purdue U., West Lafayette, Ind., 1967-70; asst. prof. Kans. State U., Manhattan, 1970-77, assoc. prof. microbiology, 1978—; researcher bacteriophage T4, giardiasis; vis. scientist, Swedish exchange grantee Umea (Sweden) Universitet, 1977-78. Contbr. articles in field to profl. publs. NIH postdoctoral fellow, 1968-70; NIH research grantee, 1972-75, 75-78. Mem. AAAS, Am. Soc. Microbiology. Democrat. Roman Catholic. Club: Optimist. Lodge: Jednota Lodge. Current Work: Modification of protein synthesis in Escherichia coli by bacteriophage T4; inactivation and pathogenesis of giardia lamblia. Subspecialties: Microbiology; Molecular biology. Home: Route 4 Box 43 Driftwood Estates Manhattan KS 66502 Office: Div of Biolog Kans State U Manhattan KS 66506

MARCOT, BRUCE GREGORY, research ecologist, researcher; b. Lynchburg, Va., Aug. 31, 1953; s. Guy C. and Olga (DeMartin) M. B.S., Humboldt State U., 1977, M.S., 1978; Ph.D., Oreg. State U., 1985. Contract ecologist USDA Forest Service, Eureka, Calif., 1976-78, biol. tech., 1978-79; research asst. Oreg. State U., Corvallis, 1979-84, instr. Humboldt State U., Arcata, Calif., 1980-81; contract ecologist Fish and Wildlife Service, Corvallis, 1983-84; wildlife ecologist U.S. Forest Service, Portland, Oreg., 1985—. Editor: Wildlife Habitat Relations, 1979. Contbr. articles to profl. jours. Vol. U.S. Forest Service, Eureka, 1976-77, 79. Recipient Performance award U.S. Forest Service, 1979, Woolford Scholastic award Rotary Club, 1977, Headlee Scholastic award Young Republicans, 1971. Mem. Ecol. Soc. Am., The Wildlife Soc. (chmn. 1975-77, vol. 1975-79, cert. appreciation 1977), Am. Assn. Artificial Intelligence, Northwest Sci. Assn., Sigma Xi, Phi Kappa Phi, Xi Sigma Pi (acad. achievement award 1976). Current work: Integration of wildlife management with multiple resource uses, wildlife habitat modelling, application of expert system technology to wildlife and vegetation management. Subspecialties: Ecology (environmental science); Artificial intelligence. Home: 4308 SE Ash Portland OR 97215 Office: USDA Forest Service 319 SW Pine Portland OR 97208

MARCOTT, CURTIS ALLEN, chemist, researcher; b. Mpls., Apr. 8, 1952; s. Allen Henry and Marion Lorraine (Grahl) M.; m. Susan Frances Marshall, Apr. 28, 1984. B.A., Concordia Coll., 1974; Ph.D., U. Minn., 1979. Research chemist Procter & Gamble Co., Cin., 1979—. Contbr. articles to profl. jours. Mem. Am. Chem. Soc., Soc. for Applied Spectroscopy, Coblentz Soc., Optical Soc. Am., Sigma Xi. Current work: Infrared spectroscopy. Subspecialties: Physical chemistry; Analytical chemistry. Office: Procter & Gamble Co Miami Valley Labs Cincinnati OH 45247

MARCOULLIS, GEORGE PANAYIOTIS, physician, biochemist, medical educator, biochemical science researcher; b. Limassol, Cyprus, Apr. 4, 1949; s. Panayiotis Stylianou and Ageliki (Joannou) M.; m. Erato Kozakou, Aug. 20, 1970; 1 son, Panos. M.D., Athens U., 1974; Ph.D., Helsinki U., 1978. Lic. in medicine, Greece, Finland, N.Y. Jr. researcher Athens U., 1971-73; biomed. researcher Minerva Inst., Helsinki, 1973-77; mem. staff Maria Hosp., Helsinki, 1976-77; asst. prof. medicine N.Y. Med. Coll., 1977-79; vis. asst. prof. U. Nancy (France) Faculty of Scis., 1979-80; vis. assoc. prof. Nancy Med. Sch., 1981-82; assoc. prof. medicine SUNY-Downstate Med. Center, Bklyn., 1980-83, N.Y. Med. Coll., Valhalla, 1984—; med. resident Washington VA Hosp., 1983; chief med. resident Mt. Vernon Hosp., (N.Y.), 1983-84; fellow in hematology N.Y. Med. Coll., 1984, 85. Author: (with others) Contemporary Issues in Clinical Nutrition, 1983, Progress in Gastroenterology, Vol. IV, 1983; Contbr. articles to profl. jours. Recipient medal award Nancy U., 1980; grantee Athens U., 1971-74; grantee WHO, 1975-77; grantee INSERM, 1977-79; grantee NIH, 1979-82; grantee VA, 1982—. Mem. Am. Fedn. Clin. Research, Soc. for Exptl. Biology and Medicine, ACP, N.Y. Acad. Scis. Current Work: Use of protein chemistry techniques to delineate the structure and role of membrane receptors and transport proteins in cellular recognition, in hormone, drug and nutrient metabolism, and in receptor-related diseases. Subspecialties: Biochemistry (biology); Hematology. Home: 453 E 14th St Apt 11C New York NY 10009 Office: NY Med Coll Dept Medicine Sect Hematology-Hemostasis Valhalla NY 10595

MARCUS, FRANK, biochemistry educator; b. Berlin, July 27, 1933; came to U.S., 1974; s. Heinz and Feiga (Wolf) M.; m. Marietta Munoz, Sept. 12, 1959; children—Claudio, Daniel, Andres. Ph.C. (Pharm. Chemist), U. Chile, 1958; postgrad. Australian Nat. U., 1962-63, U. Wis., 1964. Asst. prof. biochemistry U. Chile, Santiago, 1965-68. Prof. biochemistry, chmn. dept. Inst. Biochemistry, So. U., Valdivia, Chile, 1968-74; vis. prof. U. Wis.-Madison, 1974-77; assoc. prof. biochemistry U. Health Scis., Chgo. Med. Sch., North Chicago, Ill., 1977-81, prof. biochemistry, 1981—. Contbr. articles to sci. jours. Recipient Morris L. Parker Research award Chgo. Med. Sch., 1982; grantee NIH, 1977—, USDA, 1983—; Fulbright travel awardee, 1968; Rockefeller Found. fellow, 1962-64. Mem. Am. Soc. Biol. Chemists, Am. Chem. Soc., Am. Soc. Plant Physiologists, Sigma Xi, Alpha Omega Alpha. Current work: Structure and function of enzymes, regulation of gluconeogenesis. Subspecialty: Biochemistry (biology). Home: 634 Dunsten Circle Northbrook IL 60062 Office: Health Scis Chgo Med Sch 3333 Green Bay Rd North Chicago IL 60064

MARCUS, HARRIS LEON, materials science and engineering educator, metallurgist; b. Ellenville, N.Y., July 5, 1931; s. David and Bertha (Messite) M.; m. Leona Gorker, Aug. 28, 1962; children—Leland, M'Risa. B.S., Purdue U., 1963; Ph.D., Northwestern U., 1966. Mem. tech. staff Tex. Instruments, 1966-68; mem. tech. staff Rockwell Sci. Center, Thousand Oaks, Calif., 1968-70, group leader, 1971-75; prof. mech. engring. U. Tex., Austin, 1975-79, H.L. Kent Jr. prof., 1979—, dir. Center for Materials Sci. Engring., 1975—; Krengel lectr. Technion, Haifa, 1983. Contbr. articles to tech. jours. Treas., Reed PTA, Austin. Recipient profl. achievement award U. Tex. Engring. Found., 1983. Fellow Am. Soc. Metals; mem. Metall. Soc. (bd. dirs.), AIME, ASTM, Am. Phys. Soc. Current work: Fracture and fatigue of environment sensitive structural materials; applications of Auger and ESCA spectroscopy; microelectronic packaging. Subspecialties: Metallurgy; Composite materials. Home: 4102 Hyridge Austin TX 78759 Office: Dept Mech Engring U Tex Austin TX 78712

MARCUS, RUDOLPH ARTHUR, chemist; b. Montreal, Que., Can., July 21, 1923; came to U.S., 1949, naturalized, 1958; s. Myer and Esther (Cohen) M.; m. Laura Hearne, Aug. 27, 1949; children: Alan Rudolph, Kenneth Hearne, Raymond Arthur. B.S., McGill U., 1943, Ph.D., 1946; D.Sc. (hon.), U. Chgo., 1983. Postdoctoral research asso. NRC of Can., Ottawa, 1946-49, U. N.C., 1949-51; asst. prof. Poly. Inst. Bklyn., 1951-54, asso. prof., 1954-58, prof., 1958-64, U. Ill., Urbana, 1964-78; Arthur Amos Noyes prof. chemistry Calif. Inst. Tech., Pasadena, 1978—; temp. mem. Courant Inst. Math. Scis., N.Y. U., 1960-61; trustee Gordon Research Confs., 1966-69, chmn. bd., 1968-69, mem. council, 1965-68; mem. rev. panel Argonne Nat. Lab., 1966-72, chmn., 1967-68; mem. rev. panel Brookhaven Nat. Lab., 1971-74; mem. adv. council in chemistry Princeton U., 1972-78; mem. rev. com. Radiation Lab., U. Notre Dame, 1975-80; mem. panel on atmospheric chemistry climatic impact com. Nat. Acad. Scis.-NRC, 1975-78, mem. com. kinetics of chem. reactions, 1973-77, chmn., 1975-77, mem. com. chem. scis., 1977-79, mem. com. to survey opportunities in chem. scis., 1982—; vis. com. div. chemistry and chem. engring. Calif. Inst. Tech., 1977-78; adv. council chemistry Poly. Inst. N.Y., 1977-80; adv. com. for chemistry NSF, 1977-80; vis. prof. theoretical chemistry U. Oxford, Eng., 1975-76; also professorial fellow Univ. Coll. Mem. editorial bd.: Jour. Chem. Physics, 1964-66, Ann. Rev. Phys. Chemistry, 1964-69, Jour. Phys. Chemistry, 1968-72, 80-84, Accounts of Chem. Research, 1968-73, Internat. Jour. Chem. Kinetics, 1976-80, Molecular Physics, 1977-80, Chem. Physics Letters, 1980—, Laser Chemistry, 1982—; Advances in Chemical Physics, 1984—; Theoretica Chimica Acta, 1985—; contbr. articles to profl. jours. Recipient Anne Molson prize in chemistry McGill U., 1943, Alexander von Humboldt Found. Sr. U.S. Scientist award, 1976, Robinson medal Faraday div. Royal Soc. Chemistry, 1982, Chandler medal Columbia U., 1983, Wolf prize in chemistry, 1984; Alfred P. Sloan fellow, 1960-63; NSF sr. postdoctoral fellow, 1960-61; sr. Fulbright-Hays scholar, 1972. Fellow Am. Acad. Arts and Scis. (exec. com. Western sect., Co-chmn. 1981-84); mem. Nat. Acad. Scis., Am. Chem. Soc. (past div. chmn., mem. exec. com., mem. adv. bd. petroleum research fund, Irving Langmuir award Chem. Physics 1978), Am. Phys. Soc. (exec. com. div. chem. physics), AAUP, Alpha Chi Sigma. Current Work: Theories of electron transfer reactions, unimolecular reactions, and intra-molecular dynamic. Subspecialties: Kinetics; Theoretical chemistry. Home: 331 S Hill Ave Pasadena CA 91106

MARCUSE, DIETRICH, physicist; b. Koenigsberg, Germany, Feb. 27, 1929; s. Richard and Gertrud (Solty) M.; m. Haide Schwarz, Sept. 18, 1934; children: Christina, Mikel. Diplom physiker, Freie Universitaet Berlin, 1954; Doktor Ingenieur, Universitaet Karlsruhe, Germany, 1962. Physicist Central Lab. Siemens und Halske, Berlin, 1954-57; mem. tech. staff Bell Labs., Holmdel, N.J., 1957—. Author 4 books; contbr. articles to profl. jours. Fellow Optical Soc. Am., IEEE (Quantum Electronics award 1981). Patentee in field. Current Work: Fiber optic communications theory; semiconductor lasers. Subspecialties: Fiber optics; Electrical engineering. Office: Bell Labs Holmdel NJ 07733

MARCUVITZ, NATHAN, educator; b. Bklyn., Dec. 29, 1913; s. Samuel and Rebecca (Feiner) M.; m. Muriel Spanier, June 30, 1946; children—Andrew, Karen. B.E.E., Poly. Inst. Bklyn., 1935, M.E.E., 1941, D.E.E., 1947. Engr. RCA Labs., 1936-40; research asso. Radiation Lab., Mass. Inst. Tech., 1941-46; asst. prof. elec. engring. Poly. Inst. Bklyn., 1946-49, asso. prof., 1949-51, prof., 1951-65; dir. Poly. Inst. Bklyn. (Microwave Research Inst.), 1957-61; v.p. research, acting dean Poly. Inst. Bklyn. (Grad. Center), 1961-63, prof. electrophysics, 1961-66, dean research, dean, 1964-65; asst. dir. def. research and engring. Dept. Def., Washington, 1963-64; prof. applied physics N.Y.U., 1966-73; prof. electrophysics Poly. Inst. N.Y., 1973—, inst. prof., 1978—; vis. prof. Harvard U., spring 1971. Author: Waveguide Handbook, Vol. 10, 1951, (with L. Felsen) Radiation and Scattering of Waves, 1973; also numerous articles. Recipient Microwave Career award IEEE Microwave Theory and Techniques Soc., 1985. Fellow IEEE; mem. Nat. Acad. Engring., Am. Phys. Soc., Sigma Xi, Tau Beta Pi, Eta Kappa Nu. Subspecialties: Electrical engineering; Plasma physics. Home: 7 Ridge Dr E Great Neck NY 11021 Office: Poly Inst NY Grad Center Rt 110 Farmingdale NY 11735

MARDEN, MICHAEL CHARLES, biophysicist; b. Elmhurst, Ill., Aug. 12, 1953; s. James C. and Olga A. (Laho) M.; m. Francoise Stetzkowski, Nov. 26, 1983. B.S., U. Mo., Rolla, 1975; M.S., U. Ill., 1975, Ph.D., 1980. Asst. assoc. Inst. de Biologie Physico-Chimique, Paris, 1980-84; fellow European Molecular Biology Lab., Hamburg, Germany, 1981; postdoctoral assoc. Cornell U., Ithaca, N.Y., 1984—. Contbr. articles to profl. jours., chpt. to book. Mem. Biophys. Soc., Am. Phys. Soc. Current work: Kinetics of ligand binding to heme proteins. Subspecialty: Biophysics (physics).

MARDER, TODD BENJAMIN, research chemist; b. Bklyn., Nov. 14, 1955; s. Harold S. and Evelyn Marder. B.S. in Chemistry, MIT, 1976; Ph.D., UCLA, 1981. Postdoctoral fellow U. Bristol, Eng., 1982-83; vis. research scientist DuPont Central Research, Wilmington, Del., 1983—. Contbr. articles to profl. jours. Regents fellow UCLA, 1976-80. Mem. Am. Chem. Soc., Royal Soc. Chemistry (London), AAAS, N.Y. Acad. Scis., Sigma Xi. Current work: Synthesis, structure, bonding and dynamic properties of organometallic complexes, mechanisms of catalytic reactions, design of homogeneous catalysts. Subspecialties: Organometallics; Catalysis chemistry. Home: 131 Scarborough Park Dr Wilmington DE 19804 Office: DuPont Central Research and Devel Dept Exptl Sta 328/325 Wilmington DE 19898

MAREK, MIROSLAV I., materials educator, researcher; b. Prague, Czechoslovakia, Jan. 3, 1934; came to U.S., 1966; naturalized, 1976; s. Frantisek Marek and Gisela (Mirovska) Markova; m. Anna L. Ledecka, July 14, 1958. Ing., Czechoslovak Tech. U., Prague, 1957; Ph.D., Ga. Inst. Tech., 1970. Instr. Czechoslovak Tech. U., 1957-60, asst. prof., 1960-66; sr. research scientist Ga. Inst. Tech., Atlanta, 1973-76, assoc. prof., 1976—. Contbr. numerous articles to sci. jours. Grantee NIH Nat. Inst. Dental Research, 1973—, NATO, 1974-76, Nat. Bur. Standards, 1983—. Mem. Internat. Assn. for Dental Research, Nat. Assn. Corrosion Engrs., Am. Soc. Metals (chmn. Atlanta chpt. 1980-81). Current work: Corrosion, biomaterials (research). Subspecialties: Metallurgy; Corrosion. Office: Sch Materials Engring Ga Inst Tech Atlanta GA 30332-0100

MARES, FRANK, chemist; b. Porici n/Sazavou, Czechslovakia, Nov. 1, 1932; came to U.S., 1969; s. Antonin and Anna (Smejkalova) M.; m. Jirina Chocholous, July 12, 1958; children—Peter J., Marie P. B.S., Tech. U., Prague, Czechoslovakia, 1957; Ph.D., Czechoslovak Acad. Scis., 1960. Postdoctoral fellow U. Calif.-Berkeley, 1965-67; staff mem. Acad. Scis., Prague, 1960-65, editor Collection Czechoslovak Chem. Communications, 1961-68, leader research group, 1967-68; sci. asst., lectr. U. Tübingen, Inst. für Organische Chemie, Tubingen, W.Ger., 1968-69; lectr. dept. chemistry U. Calif.-Berkeley, 1969-70; sr. research assoc. to scientist, research supr., group leader, sr. research chemist Allied Corp. Corporate Research and Devel., Morristown, N.J., 1970—, mgr., 1983—. Contbr. articles to profl. jours. Patentee in field. Recipient Chmn.'s award Allied Corp., 1981. Mem. Am. Chem. Soc. Roman Catholic. Subspecialties: Catalysis chemistry; Polymer chemistry. Home: 32 Valley Forge Dr Whippany NJ 07981 Office: Allied Corp Corp Research and Devel PO Box 1021R Columbia Rd Morristown NJ 07960

MARES, MICHAEL ALLEN, vertebrate ecologist, educator, museum director; b. Albuquerque, Mar. 11, 1945; s. Ernesto Gustavo and Rebecca (Devine) M.; m. Lynn Ann Brusin, Aug. 27, 1966; children—Gabriel Andres, Daniel Alejandro. B.S., U. N.Mex., 1967; M.S., Fort Hays State U., 1969; Ph.D., U. Tex., 1973. Adj. prof. Nat. U. Cordoba, Argentina, 1971, Nat. U. Tucuman, Argentina, 1972; asst. assoc. prof. U. Pitts., 1973-81; vis. prof. U. Ariz., Tucson, 1981; nat. Chicano postdoctoral fellow Nat. Council for Chicanos in Higher Edn., Mus. No. Ariz., Flagstaff, 1981; Ford Found. Minority fellow U. Ariz., Tucson, 1981; assoc. prof. U. Okla., Norman, 1981-85, prof., 1985—, dir. Stovall Mus., 1983—; cons. on tropical ecology NUS Corp., Pitts., 1980-81; cons. on desert ecology Argentina Nat. Sci. Found., Mendoza, 1983; research assoc. Carnegie Mus., Pitts., 1973—; mem. adv. bd. Council for Internat. Exchange of Scholars (Fulbright Commn.), Washington, 1981—; mem. research bd. Okla. City Zoo, 1981—; mem. rev. panels in sci. edn. NSF, 1980, mem. grad. fellowship panel, 1984, 85. Editor: Mammalian Biology in South America, 1982; Search for Purebloods, 1983; mem. editorial bd. Acta Zoologica Mexicana, Current Mammalogy. Contbr. numerous articles to profl. jours. NSF research grantee Brazil Nat. Acad., 1975—; Fulbright research award, 1976. Mem. Am. Inst. Biol. Sci., Ecol. Soc. Am., Am. Soc. Mammalogists (editor 1983—), Soc. Study Evolution, Interam. Assn. Advancement Sci. Current work: Biogeography, tropical ecology, desert studies, community structure, conservation, museology, faunal studies, population ecology, evolution of biotas. Subspecialties: Evolutionary biology; Ecology (biology). Home: 2632 Trenton Rd Norman OK 73069 Office: Stovall Mus Univ Okla 1335 Asp Ave Norman OK 73019

MARFAT, ANTHONY, research scientist, chemist; b. Zadar, Croatia, Yugoslavia, Sept. 8, 1951; came to U.S., 1968, naturalized, 1975; s. Svetko and Ljubica (Alavanja) M.; m. Katica Rimanic, Dec. 17, 1977; children—Eric A., Melina A. B.A., CUNY, 1974, M.S., SUNY-Stony Brook, 1977, Ph.D., 1978. NIH postdoctoral fellow Harvard U., Cambridge, Mass., 1978-81; sr. research scientist Pfizer Co., Groton, Conn., 1981—. Contbr. articles to profl. jours. Mem. Am. Chem. Soc. Roman Catholic. Current work: Chemistry and biology of leukotrienes and their roles in various inflammatory diseases. Subspecialties: Organic chemistry; Medicinal chemistry. Home: 568-F Shennecossett Rd Groton CT 06340 Office: Pfizer Central Research Eastern Point Rd Groton CT 06340

MARGARITONDO, GIORGIO, physics educator; b. Rome, Italy, Aug. 24, 1946; s. Giuseppe and Maria Luisa (Averardi) M.; came to U.S., 1978; m. Marina Savalli, Sept. 1, 1971; children—Laura, Francesca. Laurea in Fisica, U. Rome, 1969. Postdoctoral fellow U. Rome, 1969-71; mem. research staff Italian Nat. Research Council, Rome, 1971-78; asst. prof. U. Wis.-Madison, 1978-80, assoc. prof., 1980-83, prof., 1983—; resident visitor Bell Labs., Murray Hill, N.J., 1975-77; assoc. dir. research Synchrotron Radiation Ctr., Stoughton, Wis., 1984—. Contbr. articles to profl. jours. Grantee NSF, Office Naval Research; Romnes Found. fellow, 1983. Mem. Am. Phys. Soc., Am. Vacuum Soc. Roman Catholic. Current work: Semiconductor interfaces; electronic structure of surfaces; electron spectroscopy; stimulated desorption spectroscopy; synchrotron radiation techniques. Subspecialties: Condensed matter physics; Electronic materials. Home: 2728 Tami Trail Madison WI 53711 Office: Dept Physics U Wis Madison WI 53706

MARGERUM, DALE WILLIAM, chemistry educator; b. St. Louis, Oct. 20, 1929; s. Donald C. and Ida Lee (Nunley) M.; m. Sonya Lora Pedersen, May 16, 1953; children: Lawrence Donald, Eric William, Richard Dale. B.A., S.E. Mo. State U., 1950; Ph.D., Iowa State U., 1955. Research chemist Ames Lab., AEC, Iowa, 1952-53; instr. Purdue U., West Lafayette, Ind., 1954-57, asst. prof., 1957-61, assoc. prof., 1961-65, prof., 1965—, head dept. chemistry, 1978-83; phys. chemist, vis. scientist Max Planck Inst., 1963, 70; vis. prof. U. Kent, Canterbury, Eng., 1970; mem. med. chem. study sect. NIH, 1965-69; mem. adv. com. Research Corp., 1973-78; mem. chemistry evaluation panel Air Force Office Sci. Research, 1978-82. Cons. editor: McGraw Hill, 1962-72; editorial bd.: Jour. Coordination Chemistry, 1971-81, Analytical Chemistry, 1967-69, Inorganic Chemistry, 1985. Recipient Grad. Research award Phi Lambda Upsilon, 1954; Sigma Xi research award Purdue U., 1973; Herbert C. McCoy research award Purdue U., 1983; NSF sr. postdoctoral fellow, 1963-64. Fellow AAAS; mem. Am. Chem. Soc. (chmn. Purdue sect. 1965-66), AAUP, Sigma Xi, Phi Lambda Upsilon. Subspecialties: Inorganic chemistry; Analytical chemistry. Office: Dept Chemistry Purdue U West Lafayette IN 47907

MARGOLIASH, EMANUEL, biochemist, educator; b. Cairo, Feb. 10, 1920; s. Wolf and Bertha (Kotler) M.; m. Sima Beshkin, Aug. 22, 1945; children: Reuben, Daniel. B.A., Am. U., Beirut, 1940, M.A., 1942, M.D., 1945. Research fellow, lectr., acting head cancer research labs. Hebrew U., Jerusalem, 1945-58; research assoc. U. Utah, Salt Lake City, 1958-60, McGill U., Montreal, Que., Can., 1960-62; research fellow Abbott Labs., North Chicago, Ill., 1962-69, sr. research fellow, 1969-71, head protein sect., 1962-71; prof. biochemistry and molecular biology Northwestern U., Evanston, Ill., 1971—; mem. com. on cytochrome nomenclature Internat. Union Biochemistry, 1962—; mem. adv. com. Plant Research Lab., Mich. State U./AEC, 1967-72; co-chmn. Gordon Research Conf. on Proteins, 1967. Editorial bd.: Jour. Biol. Chemistry, 1966-72, Biochem. Genetics, 1966—, Jour. Molecular Evolution, 1971-82; contbr. articles and revs. to sci. jours. Rudi Lemberg fellow Australian Acad. Sci., 1981; Guggenheim fellow, 1983. Fellow Am. Acad. Arts and Scis.; mem. Nat. Acad. Scis., Biochem. Soc. (Keilin Meml. lectr. 1970), Harvey Soc. (lectr. 1970-71), Am. Soc. Biol. Chemists (publs. com. 1973-76), Am. Chem. Soc., Can. Biochem. Soc., Soc. Developmental Biology, Biophys. Soc. (exec. com. U.S. bioenergetics group 1980—), N.Y., Ill. acads. scis., Am. Soc. Naturalists, Sigma Xi (nat. lectr. 1972-73, 74-77). Current Work: Structure-function relations, molecular biology and evolution of respiratory proteins; cytochrome as a model antigen. Subspecialties: Biochemistry (biology); Molecular biology. Office: Dept Biochemistry Molecular Biology and Cell Biology Northwestern U Evanston IL 60201

MARGOLIS, DONALD LEE, mechanical engineering educator; b. Washington, Nov. 13, 1945; s. Joel and Jeanette (Lowenwirth) M.; children—Scott Alan, David Andrew. B.S. in M.E., Va. Poly. Inst. and State U., 1967; M.S. in M.E., MIT, 1969, Ph.D., 1971. Coordinator engrng. project lab. MIT, Cambridge, 1968-70, instr. mech. engrng., 1968-71; prof. mech. engrng. U. Calif., Davis, 1971—; cons. Lord Corp., Erie, Pa., 1979—, Welch-Allyn Corp., 1983—, Lawrence Livermore Lab., 1980—; book reviewer Franklin Inst., Phila., 1978—. Contbr. articles to profl. jours. German Govt. invited lectr., 1984, Tech. U. Netherlands invited lectr., 1984. Mem. ASME, Soc. Auto. Engrng. Current work: Research and advanced development in area of modelling, simulation and automatic control of engineering systems. Subspecialties: Mechanical engineering; Robotics. Office: Univ Calif Dept Mech Engring Davis CA 95616

MARGOLIS, FRANK LEONARD, research biochemist; b. Bklyn., Jan. 21, 1938; m. Joyce Weisman; children: Jonathan, Peter, Michael. B.S., Antioch Coll., 1959; Ph.D. in Biochemistry, Columbia U., 1964. NIH postdoctoral trainee Columbia U., 1964-65; NIH fellow U. Paris, 1965-66; asst. research microbiologist UCLA Sch. Medicine, 1966-69; research assoc. Roche Inst. Molecular Biology, Nutley, N.J., 1969-71, asst. mem., 1971-73, assoc. mem., 1974-80, mem., 1981—; adj. prof, grad. program in biochemistry CUNY, 1972—. Contbr. papers, chpts and abstracts to profl. lit. Recipient S. Freeman award for innovative research in chem. senses, 1985. Mem. AAAS, Am. Soc. Biol. Chemists, Am. Soc. Pharmacology and Exptl. Therapeutics, Am. Soc. Neurochemistry, Internat. Soc. Neurochemistry, Soc. Neurosci., Sigma Xi, Phi Lambda Upsilon. Current Work: Biochemistry of olfaction, neurochemistry, regulation of mammalian gene expression. Subspecialties: Biochemistry (medicine); Neurochemistry. Office: Roche Inst Molecular Biology Nutley NJ 07110

MARGOLIS, SAM AARON, biochemist, educator; b. Cambridge, Mass., Nov. 17, 1933; s. Abraham and Rose (Huberman) M.; m. Evelyn Gertrude Meltzer, Aug. 7, 1960; children: Laura Beth, Daniel Abraham. A.B., Boston U., 1955; Ph.D., 1963; M.S., U. R.I., 1957; postgrad., Yale U., 1957-59. Fellow Enzyme Inst., U. Wis., 1964-66; pharmacologist FDA, Washington, 1966-68; microbiologist NIH, 1968-70, Nat. Cancer Inst., 1970-72; research chemist Nat. Bur. Standards, Washington, 1972—; instr. pharmacology and biochemistry U.S. Dept. Agr. Contbr. articles to profl. jours. Mem. Am. Chem. Soc., Am. Soc. Microbiology, N.Y. Acad. Sci., Am. Assn. Clin. Chemistry, Sigma Xi. Current Work: Methods development and preparation of standards for clinical chemistry and food analysis (nutrients) using HPLC, NMR. amino acid analysis and other analytical techniques. Subspecialties: Biochemistry (medicine); Analytical chemistry. Office: National Bureau Standards Bldg 222 Washington DC 20234

MARGOLIUS, HARRY STEPHEN, pharmacologist, physician, educator, cons.; b. Albany, N.Y., Jan. 29, 2938; s. Irving and Betty (Zweig) M.; m. Francine Rockwood, May 22, 1964; children: Elizabeth Anne, Craig Matthew. B.S., Union U., 1959; Ph.D., Albany Med. Coll., 1963; M.D., U. Cin., 1968. Diplomate: Nat. Bd. Med. Examiners. NIH postdoctoral fellow U. Cin., 1963-66, instr., 1967; USPHS fellow NIH, Bethesda, Md., 1967; intern, med. resident, clin. fellow in medicine Harvard U. Med. Sch., Boston City Hosp., 1968-70; pharmacology research asso. Nat. Heart, Lung and Blood Inst., NIH, Bethesda, 1970-72, sr. clin. invstigator, 1972-74; asso. prof. pharmacology, asst. prof. medicine Med. U. S.C., Charleston, 1974-77, prof. pharmacology, 1977—, asso. prof. medicine, 1977-80, prof. medicine, 1980—; program dir. Gen. Clin. Research Center, 1974-81; vis. scholar dept. pharmacology Cambridge (Eng.) U., 1980-81; attending staff Med. Univ. Hosp., VA Hosp., Charleston Meml. Hosp., St. Francis Hosp.; mem. research grant rev. com. NIH, NSF, 1976-80, FDA, 1982-86. Contbr. articles to sci. jours., chpts. to books. Served to sr. surgeon USPHS, 1970-74. NIH grantee, 1975—; Burroughs Wellcome scholar, 1976-81; Pfizer lectr., 1976. Mem. AAAS, Am. Soc. Pharmacology and Exptl. Therapeutics, Am. Soc. Clin. Pharmacology and Therapeutics, Am. Fedn. Clin. Research, Am. Soc. Clin. Investigation, So. Soc. Clin. Investigation, Council High Blood Pressure Research of Am. Heart Assn., Alpha Omega Alpha, Pi Kappa Epsilon. Jewish. Club: Hobcaw Yacht. Current Work: Kallikreins, kinins and membrane ion transport in epithelial cells (gastrointestinal, renal). Kallikrein synthesis and activity in cells, organs and secretions of amphibians and mammals; clinical investigation in hypertension, renal, cardiovascular, and diabetic diseases. Subspecialties: Cellular pharmacology; Cell biology (medicine). Home: 645 Molasses Ln Mount Pleasant SC 29464 Office: 171 Ashley Ave Charleston SC 29425

MARGON, BRUCE H., astronomer, educator; b. N.Y.C., Jan. 7, 1948; s. Leon and Maxine E. (Margon) Siegelbaum; m. Carolyn J., May 8, 1976; dau., Pamela. A.B., Columbia U., 1968; M.A., U. Calif.-Berkeley, 1971, Ph.D., 1973. NATO fellow Univ. Coll. London, 1973-74; mem. faculty U. Calif.-Berkeley, 1974-76, UCLA, 1976-80; chmn., prof. astronomy U. Wash., Seattle, 1980—; chmn. bd. dirs. Astrophys. Research Consortium, Inc. Contbr. research articles to profl. jours. Sloan research fellow, 1979-83. Mem. Am. Astron. Soc. (Pierce prize 1981), Internat. Astron. Union, Am. Phys. Soc., Royal Astron. Soc. Current Work: X-ray and ultraviolet astronomy; optical observations of X-ray source counterparts. Subspecialties: X-ray high energy astrophysics; Optical astronomy. Office: Astronomy Dept FM-20 U Wash Seattle WA 98195

MARGULIES, SEYMOUR, physicist, physics educator; b. Jaslo, Poland, Oct. 3, 1933; came to U.S., 1939, naturalized, 1950; s. Morris Hirsch and Ruth (Kalb) M.; m. Cecile Stoller, Jan. 25, 1959; children—Jonathan, Daniel. B.E.E., Cooper Union U., 1955; M.S. in Physics, U. Ill.-Urbana, 1956, Ph.D. in Physics, 1962. Teaching and research asst. U. Ill., Urbana, 1955-61; postdoctoral research fellow Max Planck Inst. for Nuclear Phys., Heidelberg, Germany, 1961-63; research assoc. Nevis Labs. of Columbia U., Irvington-on-Hudson, N.Y., 1963-65; asst. prof. physics U. Ill., Chgo., 1965-69, assoc. prof. physics, 1969—; vis. scientist Argonne Nat. Lab., Ill., 1967, Fermi Nat. Accelerator Lab., Batavia, Ill., 1973. Contbr. articles to profl. jours. Translator (with H.R. Lewis) Pauli Lectures on Physics (6 vols.), 1973. Mem., former chmn. 57th St Art Fair Com., Chgo., 1973—. Fellow Raytheon Corp., 1958-59, Nat. Acad. Sci.-NRC, 1961-63; NSF grantee, 1973—; recipient Silver Circle award for excellence in teaching U. Ill., Chgo., 1975, 77, 78. Mem. Am. Phys. Soc., Sigma Xi. Current work: Experimental investigation of strong interactions of elementary particles, multiparticle production, high-transverse-momentum reactions, jets and particle constituents, detector technology. Subspecialty: Particle physics. Home: 1623 E Hyde Park Blvd Chicago IL 60615Office: U Ill at Chgo Dept Physics Box 4348 Chicago IL 60680

MARGULIS, LYNN, cell biologist, microbiologist; b. Chgo., Mar. 5, 1938; d. Morris and Leone (Wise) Alexander; m. Carl Sagan, June, 1957 (div. 1963); children—Dorion, Jeremy. m. T.N. Margulis, Jan., 1967 (div. 1980); children—Zachary, Jennifer. A.B., U. Chgo., 1957; M.A., U. Wis.-Madison, 1960; Ph.D., U. Calif.-Berkeley, 1965. Cons., mem. staff Ednl. Services, Inc., Mass., 1963-67; adj. prof. Boston U., 1966-67, asst. prof., 1967-71, assoc. prof., 1971-77, prof. biology, 1977—; vis. prof. Calif. Inst. Tech., Pasadena, 1980, Scripps Inst. Oceanography, LaJolla, Calif., 1980; codir., mem. faculty NASA Planetary Biol. and Microbial Ecology 1980, 82, 84; mem. space sci. bd. NASA, Washington, 1977-81, adv. council, 1982—; mem. Commonwealth Book Fund Com., N.Y.C., 1982—. Author: Origin of Eukaryotic Cells, 1970; Symbiosis in Cell Evolution, 1981; (with others) Five Kindgoms, 1982; Early Life, 1982; (with Dorion Sagan) Origins of Sex, 1986. Grantee NASA, 1972—; Sherman Fairchild Disting. Scholar, 1976-77; Guggenheim fellow, 1979. Mem. Nat. Acad. Sci., Internat. Soc. for Study of the Origin of Life, AAAS, Soc. for Evolutionary Protistology, Marine Biol. Lab. (corp. mem.). Current work: Symbiosis in evolution, evolution of cells, protistology, origin of life, early evolution of life on earth, life's regulation of the biosphere, gaia hypothesis. Subspecialties: Microbiology; Evolutionary biology. Home: 401 Lowell Ave Newtonville MA 02160 Office: Boston U Biology Dept 2 Cummington St Boston MA 02215

MARGULIS, THOMAS N., chemistry educator; b. N.Y.C., Sept. 7, 1937; s. William and Sonia (Liff) M.; children—Zachary, Jennifer. B.S., MIT, 1959; Ph.D., U. Calif.-Berkeley, 1962. Asst. prof. Brandeis U., 1962-67; assoc. prof. Chemistry U. Mass., Boston, 1967-74, prof., 1974—; cons. Boston Pub. Library, 1979-80; cons. Ednl. Devel. Corp., 1954-70, Mass. Dept. Edn., 1983-84. Contbr. articles to profl. jours. Grantee Nat. Cancer Inst., NSF. Mem. Am. Chem. Soc., Am. Crystallographic Assn. Subspecialties: X-ray crystallography; Cancer research (medicine). Home: 106 Gibbs St Newton Centre MA 02159 Office: Dept Chemistry U Mass Boston MA 02125

MARHIC, MICHEL EDMOND, electrical engineering educator; b. Ivry, France, June 25, 1945; came to U.S., 1968, naturalized, 1984; s. Jean Marie and Yvonne Marie Renee (Nenez) M. Diplome d'ingenieur, Ecole Superieure d'Electricite, 1968; M.S., Case Western Res. U., 1970; Ph.D., UCLA, 1974. Asst. prof. elec. engring. Northwestern U., Evanston, Ill., 1974-79, assoc. prof., 1980-84, prof., 1984; vis. prof. Stanford U., Calif., 1984—. Contbr. articles to profl. jours. Mem. Optical Soc. Am., IEEE, Soc. Photo-Optical Instrumentation Engrs. Current work: Research on fiber optic local area networks; laser beam delivery through flexible waveguides; free electron lasers, multilayer coatings. Subspecialties: Fiber optics; Laser medicine. Home: 586 Lagunita Dr Apt 22 Stanford CA 94305 Office: Stanford U Stanford CA 94305

MARICQ, HILDEGARD RAND, research medicine educator; b. Rakvere, Estonia, Apr. 23, 1925; came to U.S., 1954, naturalized, 1959; d. August and Elvine Rosalie (Vunderlich) Rand; m. John George Maricq, Oct. 9, 1948; children—Michel Matti, Andres Villu, Peter Toivo. Cand. Nat. and Med. Sci., Free U., Brussels, Belgium, 1949, M.D., 1953; Fellow in dermatology Columbia-Presbyterian Hosp., N.Y.C., 1956; clin. investigator VA Hosp., Lyons, N.J., 1963-65, dir. schizophrenia research sect., 1970-73; postdoctoral fellow in biol. scis. in relation to mental health Columbia U., N.Y.C., 1965-67, research assoc., 1973-75; assoc. prof. research medicine Med. U. S.C., Charleston, 1975-81, prof. research medicine, 1981—. Contbr. articles to profl. jours. Mem. Microcirculatory Soc., Soc. Phychophysiol. Research, Am. Physiol. Soc., Am. Rheumatism Assn., Soc. Biol. Psychiatry. Current work: pathogenesis of rheumatic diseases especially as related to microvasculature; epidemiology of Raynaud phenomenon. Subspecialty: Interdisciplinary clinical research. Office: U SC Div of Rheumatology Med 171 Ashley Ave Charleston SC 19425

MARINE, I. WENDELL, geohydrologist; b. Washington, Apr. 15, 1927; s. Ira M. and Mattie M. (McCready) M.; m. Helen R. Landsman, June 20, 1953; children—Karen L., Andrew C., Kenneth S., Linda C. B.A., St. John's Coll., Annapolis, Md., 1949; postgrad. Johns Hopkins U., 1949-51; Ph.D., U. Utah, 1960. Geologist, hydrologist U.S. Geol. Survey, Salisbury, Md. and Newark, Del., 1951-54, Salt Lake City, 1954-60, Norman, Okla., 1960-61, Aiken, S.C., 1961-71, E.I. Dupont de Nemours & Co., Aiken, 1971—. Contbr. articles to profl. jours. Served with USN, 1945-46. Recipient cert. of appreciation AEC, 1969. Fellow Geol. Soc. Am.; mem. Am. Geophys. Union, Am. Assn. Petroleum Geologists, Nat. Water Well Assn., Seismol. Soc. Am. Current work: Ground water, contaminant transport in the ground, dating ground water, osmosis in geologic materials, geologic storage of high level nuclear waste, hydrology of crystalline rocks, seismology. Subspecialties: Hydrology; Seismology. Home: 1002 Hitchcock Dr Aiken SC 29801 Office: EI Dupont de Nemours & Co Savannah River Lab Aiken SC 29808

MARINI, RICHARD PAUL, horticulturalist, educator; b. Brockton, Mass., Feb. 11, 1952; s. Dominic Alexander and Aida (Duprimio) M.; m. Michele Eva Choma, Aug. 30, 1981. B.S., Univ. Mass., 1974; M.S., Univ. Vt., 1978; Ph.D., Va. Tech. Inst., 1981. Research fellow Univ. Vt., Burlington, 1974-76, research technologist, 1976-78; research asst. Va. Tech. Inst., Blacksburg, 1978-81; asst. prof. Rutgers U., New Brunswick, N.J., 1981-85; assoc. prof. horticulture Va. Tech. Inst., Blacksburg, 1985—. Mem. Sigma Xi (research award 1982). Current work: Physiology and cultural practices of deciduous tree fruit crops. Subspecialty: Plant physiology (agriculture). Office: Va Tech Inst Dept Horticulture Blacksburg VA 06401

MARINO, ANDREW ANTHONY, biophysicist, lawyer; b. Phila., Jan. 12, 1941; s. Frank and Frances M.; m. Linda Lee, Aug. 14, 1965; children: Lawrence, Andrew, Christopher, Lisa. B.S. in Physics, St. Joseph's U., Phila., 1962; M.S. in Biophysics, Syracuse U., 1965, Ph.D., 1968, J.D., 1974. Bar: N.Y. bar 1975. Biophysicist VA Med. Ctr., Syracuse, N.Y., 1964-81; asst. prof. dept. orthopaedic surgery La. State U. Med. Ctr., Shreveport, 1981—; pres. Plastafil Corp. Author: (with R.O. Becker) Electromagnetism and Life, 1982; editor: Jour. Bioelectricity; contbr. articles to profl. publs. Current Work: Biological effects of electromagnetic radiation bioelectricity and therapeutic aspects of electromagnetism. Subspecialty: Biophysics (physics). Home: PO Box 127 Belcher LA 71004 Office: La State U Med Center PO Box 33932 Shreveport LA 71130

MARINO, MARY LOU, environmental policy analyst; b. Pontiac, Mich., Sept. 16, 1950; d. Jack and Grace (Marchiori) M.; m. Stephen Melwood Welch, June 16, 1973; 1 child, Jacob Marino. B.S. summa cum laude, Mich. State U., 1972, M.S., 1974, Ph.D., 1980. Research asst. Mich. Dept. State Hwys., Lansing, 1973-74; teaching asst. dept. botany and plant pathology Mich. State U., 1974-77; research assoc. Devel. Planning & Research Assocs., Manhattan, Kans., 1979-80, assoc., 1980—. Contbr. articles to profl. jours. and chpts. to books. Mem. Manhattan Arts Council, 1980—; mem. LWV Riley County, 1981—. Sigma Xi research grantee, 1977. Mem. Ecol. Soc. Am., Brit. Ecol. Soc., Nat. Assn. Environ. Profls. Assn. for Women in Sci. Roman Catholic. Club: Friends of the Sunset Zoo (bd. dirs.). Current work: Regulatory policy analysis particularly in area of hazardous waste management; research on the regulation of pesticies and water pollution. Subspecialties: Resource management; Ecology (environmental science). Home: 1727 Fairview Rd Manhattan KS 66502 Office: Devel Planning and Research Assocs 200 Research Dr Box 727 Manhattan KS 66502

MARINUCCI, ANDREW CARMEN, microbiologist, ecologist; b. New Brunswick, N.J., Sept. 28, 1950; s. Andrew James and Fannie (Rinaldi) M. A.B. in Biology, Rutgers Coll., 1972, Ph.D. in Ecology, Rutgers U., 1981; M.S. in Marine Sci., U. Del., 1975. Postdoctoral fellow Marine Biol. Lab., Woods Hole, Mass., 1979-82; research assoc. Princeton U., N.J., 1982—; peer reviewer NSF, Washington, D.C., 1982—. Contbr. articles to profl. jours. Fund raiser Rutgers U. Found., 1984—. NSF facilities grantee, research grantee, 1984. Mem. Corp. Marine Biol. Lab., Am. Soc. Microbiology, Am. Soc. Indsl. Microbiology, Am. Soc. Limnology and Oceanography, Ecol. Soc. Am., AAAS, Soc. Environ. Toxicology and Chemistry. Roman Catholic. Current work: Microbial ecology; microbial degradation of leaf litter and other natural substrates; environmental toxicology; ground water pollution; degradation of organic pollutants by microbes; marine biology. Subspecialties: Microbiology; Ecology (biology). Office: Dept Civil Engring Princeton Univ Princeton NJ 08544

MARINUS, MARTIN GERARD, pharmacology educator; b. Amsterdam, Netherlands, June 22, 1944; came to U.S., 1968, naturalized, 1977; m. Isabel Cristina Castro, Dec. 21, 1970; children: Lucinda M., Julian M., Alicia I. B.Sc., U. Otago, N.Z., 1965, Ph.D., 1968. Posdoctoral fellow Yale U. Sch. Medicine, 1968-70; vis. fellow Free U. Amsterdam, 1970-71; research assoc. Rutgers Med. Sch., 1971-74; assoc. prof. pharmacology U. Mass. Med. Sch., 1974—. Contbr. articles to profl. jours. Recipient Faculty Research award Am. Cancer Soc., 1976-81. Mem. Am. Soc. Microbioloby. Current Work: DNA methylation, DNA repair; mutagenesis. Subspecialty: Genetics and genetic engineering (medicine). Home: 58 Newton St West Boylston MA 01583 Office: Dept Pharmacology U Mass Med Sch Worcester MA 01605

MARION, DANIEL FRANCIS, tree and ornamental plant pathologist; b. Washington, May 3, 1944; s. Edmund M. and Marie P. (Pate) M.; m. Dorothy K., Nov. 27, 1965; children: Daniel, Matthew, Meghan. B.Sc., U. Ga., 1966; M.Sc., Ohio U., 1968; Ph.D., U.R.I., 1974. Regional plant pesticide specialist Diamond Shamrock Corp., Cleve., 1968-70; research assoc. instr. plant disease control U. R.I., Kingston, 1970-74; assoc. prof. tree and ornamental plant protection SUNY-Canandaigua, 1974—, pvt. practice tree pathology, Canandaigua, N.Y., 1975—; regional research coordinator, cons. Mauget Co., Burbank, Calif., 1976—. Contbr. articles in field to profl. jours. Mem. Internat. Soc. Arboriculture, Internat. Phytopath. Soc., Am. Forestry Assn., Am. Phytopath. Soc., N.Y. Arborists Assn., Pesticide Assn. N.Y., Soc. Am. Foresters, Gamma Sigma Delta, Phi Sigma. Republican. Roman Catholic. Current Work: Researcher/consultant in chemotherapy for suppression of internal disorders of trees; diseases of turfgrasses. Subspecialties: Plant pathology; Integrated pest management. Home: 3650 Middle Cheshire Rd Canandaigua NY 14424 Office: Dept Environ Conservation/Horticulture SUNY-CCFL Lincoln Hill Campus Canandaigua NY 14424

MARION, WAYNE RICHARD, researcher, ecology educator, consultant; b. Ithaca, N.Y., June 28, 1947; s. Maurice Verne and Doris Grace (Cross) M.; m. Marjorie Anne Durfee, June 7, 1969; children: Julie Lynn, Kristi Jill. B.S., Cornell U., 1969; M.S., Colo. State U., 1970; Ph.D., Tex. A&M U., 1974. Cert. wildlife biologist. Grad. research asst. Tex. A&M U., 1970-74; instr. Cornell U., 1974; asst. prof. U. Fla., Gainesville, 1975-80, assoc. prof., 1980—; cons. Applied Biology, Inc., Decatur, Ga., 1979—; pres. Wildlife Resources Mgmt., Gainesville, 1979—; chmn. edn. com. Morningside Nature Ctr., Gainesville, 1982-84. Contbr. chpts. to books, numerous articles to profl. jours. Bd. dirs. Morningside Nature Ctr., 1982—; ruling elder Westminster Presbyterian Ch. U.S. Forest Service grantee, 1978-83; Occidental Chem. Co., grantee, 1979-81; Fla. Game and Fish Commn. grantee, 1980-82; Fla. Inst. Phosphate research grantee, 1981-85. Mem. Wildlife Soc., Sigma Xi, Xi Sigma Pi, Phi Sigma, Alpha Zeta, Phi Kappa Phi, Gamma Sigma Delta. Republican. Current Work: Currently, I am conducting research on the effects of intensive forest management and intensive phosphate mining activity on wildlife populations with emphasis upon designing and enhancing future reforested and reclaimed areas as wildlife habitats. Subspecialties: Ecology (environmental science); Resource management. Home: 1807 NW 39th Terr Gainesville FL 32605 Office: Dept Wildlife and Range Scis U Fla Gainesville FL 32611

MARIS, HUMPHREY JOHN, physics educator; b. Eng., Apr. 25, 1939; s. John Robert and Ethel Norah (Rudderham) M.; m. Faye Celia Thormodsgard, July 26, 1969. B.Sc., Imperial Coll., London, 1960, Ph.D., 1963. Research assoc. Case Inst., Cleve., 1963-65; asst. prof. physics Brown U., Providence, R.I., 1965-71, assoc. prof., 1971-76, prof., 1976—; sr. vis. fellow U. East Anglea, U.K., 1972-73; vis. fellow CNRS, Grenoble, France, 1973, Chalmers Inst., Sweden, 1973; vis. prof. Centro Atómico, Bariloche, Agrentina, 1982, U. Tokyo, 1982, U. Paris, 1984; vis. scientist Inst. Physical Problems, Moscow, 1983. Contbr. articles to profl. publs. NSF grantee, 1967—. Fellow Am. Phys. Soc. Current work: Low temperature physics, ultrasonics, phonics. Subspecialties: Low temperature physics; Acoustics. Office: Brown U Physics Dept Providence RI 02912

MARK, HERMAN F., See *Who's Who in America,* 43rd edition.

MARK, JAMES EDWARD, chemistry educator; b. Wilkes-Barre, Pa., Dec. 14, 1934; s. Frank Charles and Anna (Raisch) M.; m. Eliza Pollard, Nov. 28, 1964; children: Elizabeth, Eleanor. B.S., Wilkes Coll., 1957; Ph.D. in Chemistry, U. Pa., 1962. Asst. prof. chemistry Poly. Inst. Bklyn., 1964-67; mem. faculty dept. chemistry U. Mich., Ann Arbor, 1967-77, prof., 1972-77; prof. chemistry, dir. polymer research ctr. U. Cin., 1977—; cons. Dow Corning, Midland, Mich., 1981—. Co-editor 1 book in field; contbr. articles to profl. jours. Fellow Am. Phys. Soc., N.Y. Acad. Sci.; mem. Am. Chem. Soc. (best paper award rubber div. 1975-81). Republican. Current Work: Rubberlike elasticity, statistical properties of polymers, polymer-coated electrodes. Subspecialties: Polymer chemistry; Physical chemistry. Home: 5236 Oakhill Ln Cincinnati OH 45239 Office: Dept Chemistry U Cin Cincinnati OH 45221

MARK, WILLIAM DAVID, research mechanical engineer; b. La Oroya, Peru, June 23, 1934; came to U.S., 1934; s. William David and Lauretta (McDonald) M. B.M.E., Catholic U. Am., 1956; M.S., MIT, 1958, Ph.D., 1962. Research asst. MIT, 1958-61; mem. research staff Sperry Rand Research Ctr., Sudbury, Mass., 1964-65; prin. scientist Bolt Beranek & Newman Inc., Cambridge, Mass., 1965—. Author: (with Stephen H. Crandall) Random Vibration in Mechanical Systems, 1963; contbg. author: Engine Noise, 1982. Contbr. articles to profl. jours. Served as 1st lt. USAF, 1961-64. Mem. Acoustical Soc. Am., IEEE, Sigma Xi. Current work: Research in gear system dynamics; characterization of atmospheric turbulence; engineering applications of stochastic processes. Subspecialties: Theoretical and applied mechanics; Mechanical engineering. Office: Bolt Beranek and Newman Inc 10 Moulton St Cambridge MA 02238

MARKATOS, NICOLAS-CHRISTOS GREGORY, educator; b. Athens, Greece, Mar. 1, 1944; s. Gregory Nicolas and Katherine John M. Dipl. Eng., Nat. Tech. U., Athens, 1967, M.Sc., 1967; M.A., Athens Sch. Econs., 1970; DIC, Imperial Coll., London, 1973; Ph.D., 1974. Systems engr. Proctor & Gamble, Athens, 1969-70; research asst. Imperial Coll., London, 1973-74; group leader Concentration, Heat and Momentum Research Ltd., London, 1975-78, tech. mgr., 1978—; co-dir. Centre Math. Modelling and Process Analysis, Thames Poly., London, 1983—; reader Math. Modeling and Computer Simulation, 1983—, lectr. in field; prof. analysis and design of thermophys. processes, Nat. Tech. U., Athens, 1984—. Research numerous publs. in field. Recipient cert. of recognition for creative devel. tech. innovation NASA, 1980. Mem. Chartered Engring. Instn., Instn. Chem. Engrs., Am. Inst. Chem. Engrs., AIAA, Internat. Soc. Computer Simulation, Greek Tech. Chambers. Christian Orthodox. Current Work: Research and teaching in fluid mechanics, heat/mass transfer and combustion; particular interest in mathematical modelling and computer simulation of turbulent fluid flows with special emphasis on flows with chemical reaction, two-phase and compressible supersonic flows; and thermophysical processes in general purpose of work is advancement of computer modelling as powerful tool to scientific research, industry and environment. Subspecialties: Chemical engineering; Mathematical software. Home: 21 Shottfield Ave London SW14 8EA England Office: Faculty Sci and Math Sch Math and Sci Computing Thames Poly London SE18 6PF England

MARKERT, WALLACE, JR., See *Who's Who in America,* 43rd edition.

MARKEY, DAVID JOHN, III, government official, lawyer; b. Frederick, Md., July 25, 1940; s. David John and Mary Alice (Moberly) M.; m. Patricia Elizabeth Markey, Sept. 24, 1977; 1 child, Courtney Anne. B.S., Western Md. Coll., 1963; LL.B., U. Md., 1967. Bar: Md. 1967. Legis. officer Office Gov. Md., Annapolis, 1967-68; adminstrv. asst. to Senator J. Glenn Beall, Washington, 1969-74; v.p. congl affairs Nat. Assn. Broadcasters, Washington, 1974-81; chief of staff Senator Frank Murkowski, Washington, 1981-83; legal asst. to chmn. FCC, Washington, 1983; asst. sec. for communications and info. Dept. Commerce, Washington, 1983—. Served in U.S. Army, 1958. Mem. Md. Bar Assn., ABA. Republican. Office: Nat Telecommunications and Info Adminstrn Dept Commerce 14th and Constitution Ave NW Washington DC 20230

MARKLAND, FRANCIS SWABY, JR., biochemist, educator; b. Phila., Jan. 15, 1936; s. Francis Swaby and Willie Lawrence (Averritt) M.; m. Barbara Blake, June 27, 1959; children: Cathleen Blake, Francis Swaby. B.S., Pa. State U., 1957; Ph.D., Johns Hopkins U., 1964. Postdoctoral fellow UCLA, 1964-66, asst. prof. biochemistry, 1966-74; vis. asst. prof. U. So. Calif., 1973-74, assoc. prof., 1974-83, prof., 1983—; cons. Clin. Lab. Med. Group, Los Angeles. Contbr. numerous articles to profl. jours. Mem. Northridge Masterworks Chorale; asst. coach Pop Warner Football. Recipient NIH research career devel. award, 1968-73; grantee Am. Cancer Soc., Nat. Cancer Inst., 1979—; grantee Nat. Heart, Lung and Blood Inst., 1978—. Mem. Am. Soc. Biol. Chemistry, Am. Chem. Soc., Am. Soc. Hematology, Internat. Soc. Toxinology, Am. Assn. Cancer Research, Endocrine Soc., Am. Heart Assn., Internat. Soc. Thrombosis and Huemostasis, Sigma Xi, Alpha Zeta. Current Work: Protein receptors for steroid hormones, snake venom coagulant and fibrinolytic enzymes. Subspecialties: Biochemistry (medicine); Cancer research (medicine). Office: USC Cancer Center Cancer Research Lab Rm 106 1303 N Mission Rd Los Angeles CA 90033

MARKLEY, JOHN LUTE, biophysicist; b. Denver, Mar. 6, 1941; s. Miles Russell and Winnifred Farrar (Lute) M.; m. Diane A. Sheehan, Aug. 9, 1975; children—Jessamyn Sheehan, Andrew Lute. B.A., Carleton Coll., 1963; Ph.D., Harvard U., 1969. Research chemist Merck Inst. Therapeutic Research, Rahway, N.J., 1966-69; postdoctoral fellow U. Calif.-Berkeley, to 1972; asst. prof. chemistry Purdue U., 1972-76, assoc. prof., 1976-81, prof., 1981-84, dir. Biochem. Magnetic Resonance Lab., 1977-85, chmn. biochemistry div., 1982-83; prof. biochemistry U. Wis.-Madison, 1984—; dir. Biochem. Magnetic Resonance Lab., 1985—. Contbr. articles to profl. jours. NIH fellow, 1970-71; Fogarty fellow, 1980-81; recipient NIH Research Career Devel. award, 1976-80. Mem. AAAS, Am. Soc. Biol. Chemists, Am. Chem. Soc., Biophys. Soc., Internat. Soc. Magnetic Resonance, Soc. Magnetic Resonance in Medicine, Sigma Xi, Phi Beta Kappa. Current Work: Application of nuclear magnetic resonance spectroscopy and bio-technology to biomedical problems, protein chemistry, protein nucleic acid interactions, enzyme mechanisms, in vivo NMR. Subspecialties: Magnetic resonance imaging; Biophysical chemistry. Office: Dept Biochemistry U Wis-Madison 420 Henry Hall Madison WI 53706

MARKS, DENNIS WILLIAM, educator; b. Madison, Wis., Nov. 5, 1944; s. Louis Sheppard and Helen Teresa (Oeters) M.; m. Sita Patricia Smith, Nov. 30,

1968. B.S., Fordham U., 1966; Ph.D., U. Mich., 1970. Postdoctoral fellow, asst. prof. astronomy U. Toronto, Ont., Can., 1970-71; asst. prof. physics and astronomy Valdosta (Ga.) State Coll., 1971-74, dir. Planetarium and Obs., 1973-80, assoc. prof. physics and astronomy, 1974-78, prof., 1978—; vis. prof. physics and astronomy Iowa State U., Ames, 1982-83; NASA trainee, 1966-69; faculty assoc. Advanced Computational Methods Ctr., U. Ga., summer 1985. Author: The Rotation of Viscous Polytropes, 1970. NSF predoctoral fellow, 1969-70; NSF internat. travel grantee, 1978; U.S. Nat. Com.-Internat. Astron. Union travel grantee, 1979; Com. Humanities in Ga. project grantee, 1980. Mem. Internat. Soc. Gen. Relativity and Gravitation, AAUP (nat. council 1978-81), Am. Astron. Soc., Ga. Acad. Sci. (sect. physics, math. and engring. sec. 1984-85, sect. chmn. 1985—). Current Work: Relativistic thermo-hydrodynamics, energy-momentum tensor for radiation, cosmic background radiation, radiative viscosity, differential rotation of stars. Subspecialties: Relativity and gravitation; Theoretical astrophysics. Office: Valdosta State Coll 1500 N Patterson St Valdosta GA 31698

MARKS, LAWRENCE EDWARD, psychologist; b. N.Y.C., Dec. 28, 1941; s. Milton and Anne (Parnes) M.; m. Joya Ellen Cazes, Dec. 24, 1963; children: Liza Robin, Laura Jill. A.B., Hunter Coll., 1962; Ph.D., Harvard U., 1965. Lectr., research asst. Harvard U., 1965-66; asst. fellow John B. Pierce Found. Lab., Yale U., New Haven, 1966-69, asso. fellow, 1969-84, fellow, 1984—, dir., 1985—, research asso., 1966-76, asst. prof., 1970-76, asso. prof., 1976-84, prof., 1984—; cons. Inst. Artificial Organs. Author: Sensory Processes: The New Psychophysics, 1974, The Unity of the Senses, 1978; contbr. articles to profl. jours. Mem. Am. Psychol. Assn., Soc. Neuroscience, Internat. Soc. Artificial Organs, Acoustical Soc. Am., Optical Soc. Am. Current Work: Processes of hearing, vision, touch and sensory perception, development of aids for blind and deaf. Subspecialties: Psychophysics; Sensory processes. Office: 290 Congress Ave New Haven CT 06519

MARKS, NEVILLE, neurochemist, educator; b. Dublin, Ireland, Apr. 10, 1930; s. Rudolf and Freda (Rapp) M.; m. Liliane Dahan, Dec. 31, 1971; children: Timothy Joseph, Lionel Victor. Ph.D., Inst. Psychiatry, U. London, 1960. Research scientist U. Mich., 1960; mem. staff N.Y. State Dept. Mental Hygiene, 1961—, prin. research scientist, 1972—; assoc. prof. psychiatry NYU, 1979—. Editor: Research Methods in Neurochemistry, Vols. 1-5, 1982, Protein Catabolism, 1976; contbr. articles to profl. jours. NIH grantee. Mem. Am. Soc. Biol. Chemists, Internat. Soc. Neurochemistry, Am. Soc. Neurochemistry, Soc. Endocrinology, Biochem. Soc. (U.K.), Council Research Scientists State of N.Y. (past chmn.). Current Work: Purification and assay of enzymes involved in protein turnover and polypeptide metabolism in CNS tissues. Subspecialties: Neurochemistry; Biochemistry (biology). Home: 1 Lincoln Plaza 38N New York NY 10023 Office: Ctr for Neurochemistry Nathan S Kline Research Inst for Psychiat Research New York NY 10035

MARKS, PAUL ALAN, oncologist, cell biologist; b. N.Y.C., Aug. 16, 1926; s. Robert R. and Sarah (Bohorad) M.; m. Joan Harriet Rosen, Nov. 28, 1953; children: Andrew Robert, Elizabeth Susan, Matthew Stuart. A.B. with gen. honors, Columbia U., 1945, M.D., 1949; Doct. Biol. Sci. h.c., U. Urbino (Italy), 1982. Fellow Columbia Coll. Physicians and Surgeons, 1952-53, assoc., 1955-57, mem. faculty, 1956-82, dir. hematology tng., 1961-74, prof. medicine, 1967-82, dean faculty of medicine, v.p. med. affairs, 1970-73, dir. Comprehensive Cancer Ctr., 1973-80, v.p. health scis., 1973-80, prof. human genetics and devel., 1969-82, Frode Jensen prof. medicine, 1974-80; prof. medicine Cornell U. Coll. Medicine, N.Y.C., 1981—; attending physician Presbyn. Hosp., N.Y.C., 1967-83; pres., chief exec. officer Meml. Sloan-Kettering Cancer Center, 1980—; attending physician Meml. Hosp. for Cancer and Allied Diseases, 1980—; mem. Sloan-Kettering Inst. for Cancer Research, 1980—; adj. prof. Rockefeller U., 1980—; vis. physician Rockefeller U. Hosp., 1980—; instr. Sch. Medicine, George Washington U., 1954-55; cons. VA Hosp., N.Y.C., 1962-69; Assoc. investigator Nat. Inst. Arthritis and Metabolic Diseases, NIH, Bethesda, Md., 1953-55; mem. adv. panel hematology tng. grants program NIH, 1969-73, chmn. hematology tng. grants program, 1971-73; vis. scientist Lab. Cellular Biochemistry, Pasteur Inst., 1961-62; vis. prof. 1st di Chemica Biologica, U. Genoa, Italy, 1963; mem. adv. panel on developmental biology NSF, 1964-67; mem. Delos Conf., Athens, Greece, 1971, 72; mem. founding com. Radiation Effects Research Found., Japan, 1975-77; mem. Pres.'s Biomed. Research Panel, 1975-76, Pres.'s Cancer Panel, 1976-79, Pres.'s Commn. on Accident at Three Mile Island, 1979; chmn. exec. com. div. med. scis. Nat. Acad. Scis.-NRC, 1973-76; ad hoc adviser White House Conf. on Aging, 1981; adviser Leopold Schepp Found.; dir. Pfizer, Inc., Dreyfus Mut. Funds. Editor: Monographs in Human Biology, 1963; Contbr. articles to profl. jours.; Mem. editorial bd.: Blood, 1964-71, assoc. editor, 1976-77, editor-in-chief, 1978-82, Jour. Clin. Investigation, 1967-71. Trustee St. Luke's Hosp., 1970-80, Roosevelt Hosp., 1970-80, Presbyn. Hosp., 1972-80; mem. jury Albert Lasker Awards, 1974-76, 80-82; bd. dirs. Pub. Health Research Inst., N.Y.C., 1971-74; bd. govs. Weizmann Inst., 1976—; bd. dirs. Revson Found., 1976—; bd. sci. counselors, div. cancer treatment Nat. Cancer Inst., 1980-83; mem. council div. biol. scis. and Pritzker Sch. Medicine, U. Chgo., 1977—; mem. tech. bd. Milbank Meml. Fund, 1978-85; trustee Metpath Inst. Med. Edn., 1977-79. Recipient Charles Janeway prize Columbia, 1949, Joseph Mather Smith prize, 1959, Stevens Triennial prize, 1960, Swiss-Am. Found. award in med. research, 1965, Columbia U. Coll. Physicians and Surgeons Disting. Service medal, 1980; Commonwealth Fund fellow, 1961-62. Fellow Am. Acad. Arts and Scis.; mem. Inst. Medicine (mem. council 1973-76), Nat. Acad. Scis. (chmn. sect. med. genetics, hematology and oncology 1980-83, chmn. Acad. Forum Adv. Com. 1980-81, mem. council 1984—), Red Cell Club (past chmn.), Am. Fedn. Clin. Research (past councillor Eastern dist.), Am. Soc. Clin. Investigation (pres. 1972-73), Am. Soc. Biol. Chemists, Am. Soc. Human Genetics (past mem. program com.), Am. Assn. Cancer Research, ACP, Am. Soc. Cell Biology, Am. Soc. Hematology (pres.-elect 1983, pres. 1984), Assn. Am. Physicians, Enzyme Club, Harvey Soc., Internat. Soc. Developmental Biologists, Interurban Clin. Club, Soc. for Study Devel. and Growth, World Soc. Ekistics. Research on biochemistry erythrocyte aging, predisposing factors to anemia, messenger RNA for hemoglobin, polyribosomes, molecular defect in thalassemia, erythroid cell differentiation and leukemia. Subspecialty: Oncology. Home: Beach Hill Rd Bridgewater CT 06752 Office: 1275 York Ave New York NY 10021

MARKS, ROBERT JACKSON, II, electrical engineering educator, researcher; b. Sutton, W.Va., Aug. 25, 1950; s. Robert Jackson and Lenore Ethyl (Hersman) M.; m. Connie Lynn Jewett, July 28, 1974; children—Jeremiah Jackson Jewett, Joshua Jackson Jewett. B.S.E.E., Rose-Hulman Inst. Tech., 1972, M.S.E.E., 1973; Ph.D. in Elec. Engring., Tex. Tech U., 1977. Reliability engr. Naval Wepons Ctr., Crane, Ind., 1973-74; research asst. Tex. Tech U., Lubbock, 1974-77; asst. prof. elec. engring. U. Wash., Seattle, 1978-82, assoc. prof., 1982—; cons. Applied Physics Lab., Seattle, 1978-79, Appa Systems Inc., Bellevue, Wash., 1981-82, Tech. Arts Corp., Seattle, 1983-84. Contbr. articles to profl. jours. Mem. IEEE (sr. mem.; Centennial medal and cert. 1984, outstanding br. councilor-advisor award 1982), Optical Soc. Am., Soc. Photo-optical Instumentation Engrs., Sigma Xi, Eta Kappa Nu. Republican. Current work: Signal and image analysis, optical computers, multidimensional signal processing, signal detection. Subspecialties: Systems engineering; Optical signal processing. Home: 16515 Ashworth Ave N Seattle WA 98133 Office: Dept Elec Engring Univ Wash Seattle WA 98195

MARKS, SANDY COLE, JR., anatomy educator, peridontist; b. Wilmington, N.C., Nov. 16, 1937; s. Sandy Cole and Katherine Stuart (Woods) M.; m. Julia Marie Westberg, Aug. 4, 1962; children—Christine, Sandy III. B.S., Washington and Lee U., 1960; D.D.S., U. N.C., 1964; Ph.D. in Anatomy, Johns Hopkins U., 1968. Asst. prof. anatomy dept. U. Mass. Med. Sch., Worcester, 1970-73, assoc. prof., 1973-77, prof., 1977—; periodontist, Westboro, Mass., 1982—. Contbr. articles to profl. jours. Bd. dirs. The Bridge (Halfway House), Westboro, 1971-77; active Boy Scouts Am., Africa, U.S., 1955—. Served with USNR, 1968-70. Mem. Am. Acad. Periodontology, AAAS, Am. Assn. Anatomists, Am. Assn. Clin. Anatomists (founding), Internat. Assn. Dental Research. Current work: Bone metabolism, development and pathology, clinical periodontology, bone lesions in leprosy. Subspecialties: Anatomy and embryology; Periodontics. Office: Anatomy Dept Univ Mass Med Sch 55 Lake Ave Worcester MA 01605

MARKS, TOBIN JAY, chemistry educator; b. Washington, Nov. 25, 1944; s. Eli Sidney and Miriam (Heller) M.; m. Indrani Mukharji, May 19, 1985. B.S., U. Md., 1966; Ph.D., MIT, 1970. Asst. prof. chemistry Northwestern U., 1970-74, assoc. prof., 1974-78, prof., 1978—. Editor: Organometallics of the f-Elements, 1979; Fundamental and Technological Aspects of Organo-f-Element Chemistry, 1985. Sloan Found. fellow, 1974; Dreyfus Found. scholar, 1975. Mem. Am. Chem. Soc. (A.K. Doolitte award 1984), Soc. Applied Spectroscopy, Sigma Xi, Phi Lambda Upsilon (Nat. Fesenius award 1979). Jewish. Subspecialty: Organometallics. Office: Northwestern U Dept Chemistry 2145 Sheridan Rd Evanston IL 60201

MARLOW, WILLIAM HENRY, physicist; b. Beaumont, Tex., Mar. 1, 1944; s. Harry and Gabrielle (Ross) M.; m. Laurine Annette Elkins, July 29, 1972; 1 child, Synnove Laurine. B.S. in Physics, MIT, 1966; Ph.D. in Physics, U. Tex., 1974. Research assoc. U. N.C., Chapel Hill, 1973-74; asst. physicist Brookhaven Nat. Lab., Upton, N.Y., 1975-77, assoc. physicist, 1977-82, physicist, 1982—. Editor: Aersol Microphysics I, 1980, II, 1982. Co-editor: Aersosol Measurement, 1979. Contbr. articles to profl. jours. Mem. Am. Phys. Soc., Am. Assn. Aerosol Research. Current work: Long-range forces involving particles, molecular clusters, or surfaces; applications of aerosol methods in chemistry and materials areas. Subspecialties: Aerosol micro physics; Aerosol applications. Home: 7 Old Post Rd E Port Jefferson NY 11777 Office: Brookhaven Nat Lab Bldg 426 Upton NY 11973

MARONI, GUSTAVO PRIMO, biologist, educator; b. Merlo, Argentina, Nov. 20, 1941; came to U.S., 1968; s. Victor and Iole (Brighi) M.; m. Donna Farolino Kubai, Dec. 16, 1974. Licenciado in Biology, U. Buenos Aires, 1968; Ph.D., U. Wis., 1972. Research assoc. Institut fur Genetik, U. Cologne, 1974-75; asst. prof. dept. zoology U. N.C., Chapel Hill, 1975-80, assoc. prof., 1980-82, assoc. prof. dept. biology, 1982—. Contbr. articles to profl. jours. Mem. Genetics Soc. Am., AAAS. Current Work: Gene control in Drosophila; molecular and genetic analyses of gene-protein systems; metallothioneins; metal-binding proteins. Subspecialties: Gene actions; Genome organization. Home: 412 Landerwood Ln Chapel Hill NC 27514 Office: Dept Biology U NC Chapel Hill NC 27514

MARQUARDT, DONALD WESLEY, statistician, researcher; b. N.Y.C., Mar. 13, 1929; s. Kurt C. and Amelia P. (Moller) M.; m. Margaret E. Rittershaus, Sept. 13, 1952; children: Paul E. (dec.), Joan N. A.B., Columbia U., 1950; M.A., U. Del., 1956. Research engr./mathematician E.I. du Pont de Nemours & Co., Inc., Wilmington, Del., 1953-57, research project engr./sr. mathematician, 1957-64, cons. supr., 1964-72, cons. mgr. engring. dept., 1972—; mem. NRC eval. panel for applied math. for Nat. Bur. Standards; mem. Am. Nat. Standards Inst. com. on quality assurance, vice chmn., 1983, chmn., 1984; rep. to Internat. Standards Orgn. tech. coms. on statis. methods and quality assurance., chmn. coordinating groups. Mem. editorial bd. Communications in Stats.; assoc. editor: Jour. Bus. and Econ. Stats; contbr. articles to profl. jours. Served with U.S. Army, 1951-52. Fellow Am. Statis. Assn.; mem. AAAS, Am. Soc. for Quality Control (sr. mem., Youden prize 1974), Assn. for Computing Machinery, Soc. for Indsl. and Applied Math., Am. Inst. Chem. Engrs., Sigma Xi. Presbyterian. Current Work: Quality mgmt. systems tech.; analysis of unequally-spaced time series for environ. and chronobiology data. Subspecialties: Statistics; Algorithms. Home: 1415 Athens Rd Wilmington DE 19803 Office: Engring Dept EI du Pont de Nemours & Co Inc Wilmington DE 19898

MARQUARDT, WARREN WILLIAM, veterinary scientist, educator; b. Erhard, Minn., Nov. 1, 1930; s. William Gust and Freida Amelia (Neubert) M.; m. Alice Mae Overboe, Sept. 4, 1955; children: Gregory D., Sheila P., Cheryl K., Steven R. B.S., U. Minn., 1959, D.V.M., 1961, Ph.D., 1970. Research fellow Coll. Vet. Medicine, U. Minn., St. Paul, 1962-65, instr., 1965-69; assoc. prof. vet. sci. U. Md., College Park, 1969-80, prof., 1980—, dir. avian disease research sect., 1971—. Contbr. articles to profl. jours. Served as staff sgt. USAF, 1951-55. U.S. Dept. Agr. grantee. Mem. AVMA, Am. Soc. Microbiology, World Vet. Poultry Assn., Am. Assn. Avian Pathologists, Minn. Vet. Med. Assn., Sigma Xi, Phi Zeta, Gamma Sigma Delta.. Lutheran. Current Work: Hybridoma technology—monoclonal antibodies for the antigenic assessment of avian corona viruses; biochemistry of virus antigens; enzyme-linked immunosorbent assays in diagnostic virology. Subspecialties: Virology (veterinary medicine); Infectious diseases. Office: VA-MD Regional Coll Vet Medicine College Park MD 20742

MARQUET, LOUIS CARL, government agency administrator; b. Phila., May 9, 1936; s. Milton Carl and Margaret (Wood) M.; m. Carolou Fidder, Aug. 23, 1958; children—L. David, Christopher T., Michele D., Julianne. B.S., Carnegie Inst. Tech., 1958; M.S., U. Calif.-Berkeley, 1960, Ph.D., 1963. Asst. prof. physics U. Ariz., Tucson, 1965-67; staff mem. laser tech. group MIT Lincoln Lab., Lexington, 1967-73, group leader, applied radiation, 1972-80, assoc. dir. optics div., 1980-83; dir. directed energy office Def. Advanced Research Projects Agy., Arlington, Va., 1983-84, Strategic Def. Initiative Orgn., Washington, 1984—. Contbr. articles to profl. jours. Chmn. Concord-Carlisle Sch. Com., Concord, Mass., 1980-83. Served to capt. U.S. Army, 1963-65. Recipient Meritorious Civilian Service award Sec. Def., 1984. Mem. AAAS, AIAA. Office: Strategic Def Initiative Orgn The Pentagon Washington DC

MARR, JAMES DOUGLAS, electrical engineering educator; b. Howell, Mich., Feb. 16, 1949; s. Douglas Eugene and Mary Frances (Cooper) M. B.E.E., Ga. Inst. Tech., 1971, M.S.E.E., 1972, Ph.D., 1980. Registered profl. engr., Ala. Grad. asst. Ga. Inst. Tech., Atlanta, 1972-80; asst. prof. elec. and computer engring U. Ala., Huntsville, 1980—; cons. Army Missile Command, Huntsville, 1981—, Creative Solutions, Chamblee, Ga., 1977-80. Mem. IEEE, Assn. Computing Machinery, Mensa. Roman Catholic. Club: Twickenham Toastmasters (Huntsville) (pres. 1984). Current work: very high speed integrated circuit (VHSIC); custom hardware and software for digital signal processing; Unix and C; computer graphics. Subspecialty: Computer engineering. Home: 204 Jones Vally Dr SW Huntsville AL 35802 Office: ECE Dept U Ala Huntsville AL 35899

MARRAZZI, MARY ANN, pharmacologist, educator; b. Ann Arbor, Mich., Dec. 22, 1945; d. Amedeo Sorrentino and Rose Florence (Netter) M. B.A., U. Minn., 1966; Ph.D., Washington U., St. Louis, 1972. NIH postdoctoral fellow dept. pharmacology Washington U. Sch. Medicine, 1972-74; vis. investigator Inst. Psychiatry, U. Mo., St. Louis, 1974; asst. prof. pharmacology Sch. Medicine, Wayne State U., Detroit, 1974-78, assoc. prof., 1978—; assoc. dept. psychiatry Harper-Grace Hosps., Detroit, 1981—. Contbr. articles to profl. jours. NSF internat. travel award, 1976. Mem. Am. Soc. Pharmacology and Exptl. Therapeutics, Soc. for Neurosci., Am. Soc. for Neurochemistry, Sigma Xi. Current Work: CNS control of metabolic homeostasis and feeding, hypothalamic glucoreceptors, energy metabolism in brain, metabolic encephalopathies, anorexia nervosa, prostaglandins in brain. Subspecialties: Neuropharmacology; Neurochemistry. Home: 962 Lochmoor Grosse Pointe Woods MI 48236 Office: Dept Pharmacology Sch Medicine Wayne State U Detroit MI 48201

MARRS, BARRY LEE, biochemist, educator; b. Newark, Sept. 23, 1942; s. Donald Lee and Goldie (Mack) M.; m. Barbara Griswold, Aug. 20, 1966; children: Abbe Lea, Gwendolyn Griswold. B.A., Williams Coll., 1963; Ph.D., Case Western Res. U., 1968. NSF postdoctoral fellow U. Ill., 1967-69; Am. Cancer Soc. postdoctoral fellow Stanford U., 1969-71; research assoc. Ind. U., Bloomington, 1971-72; asst. prof. Sch. Medicine St. Louis U., 1972-75, assoc. prof., 1975-78, prof. biochemistry, 1978-83, program dir. cell and molecular biology tng. program, 1977-83; sr. research assoc. Exxon Research and Engring. Co., 1983-85; group head Exxon, 1983-85; research mgr. E.I. duPont de Nemours and Co., 1985—. Research grantee NIH, 1973-83; Research grantee NSF, 1973-83; recipient Career Devel. award Gen. Med. Scis. Inst., NIH, 1975-80. Mem. Am. Soc. Microbiology, Am. Soc. Biol. Chemists. Current Work: Genetics of photosynthetic bacteria; regulation of membrane development; research on structure, function and development photosynthetic membranes using classical genetic and recombinant DNA and biochemical approaches. Subspecialties: Genetics and genetic engineering (biology); Molecular biology. Home: 7 Possum Tree Ln Rennett Square PA 19348 Office: Central Research and Devel Dept Exptl Sta Wilmington DE 19898

MARSDEN, SULLIVAN SAMUEL, JR., petroleum engineering educator, consultant; b. St. Louis, June 3, 1922; s. Sullivan Samuel and Irene Margaret M.; married; children: Sullivan F., Robert S., Mary V. Marsden Hilton, Anastasia E. B.A. in Chem. Engring, Stanford U., 1944, Ph.D. in Phys. Chemistry, 1948. Phys. chemist Tenn. Eastman Corp., Oak Ridge, 1945; with Stanford Research Inst., Menlo Park, Calif., 1947-50; asst. dir. Nat. Chem. Lab. India, Poona, 1950-53; assoc. prof. petroleum and nat. gas engring. Pa. State U., 1953-57; asso. prof. petroleum engring. Stanford (Calif.) U., 1957-62, prof., 1962—; cons. in field. Fulbright awardee U. Tokyo, 1963-64; Fulbright awardee Inst. Petroleum, Ploesti, Romania and Gubkin Inst., Moscow, 1978. Mem. Soc. Petroleum Engrs. Republican. Club: Stanford U. Faculty. Patentee in field. Current Work: Development of use of barge-mounted processing plants for offshore and remote (Arctic) natural gas fields; subsurface hydraulic mining methods for tar sand deposits. Subspecialties: Petroleum engineering; Fuels. Office: Dept Petroleum Engring Stanford U Stanford CA 94305

MARSH, BENJAMIN BRUCE, meat and animal science educator; b. Petone, N.Z., Nov. 15, 1926; came to U.S., 1971, naturalized, 1982; s. Spencer Albon and Thomasina (Leeder) M.; m. Doris Lillian Johannesson, Dec. 6, 1952; children: Richard J., David B. B.Sc., Victoria U., Wellington, N.Z., 1946, M.Sc., 1947; Ph.D., Cambridge (Eng.) U., 1951. Chemist Dominion Lab., 1951-57; biochemist, dep. dir. Meat Industry Research Inst., Hamilton, N.Z., 1957-71; prof. meat and animal sci. U. Wis.-Madison, 1971—; dir. Muscle Biology Lab., 1971—. Contbr. articles to profl. jours. Mem. Am. Meat Sci. Assn. (Disting. Meats Research award 1970), Am. Soc. Animal Sci. (Research award 1978), Inst. Food Technologists. Current Work: Muscle biology and meat science: early postmorten behavior and properties; muscle contraction; muscle metabolism; rigor mortis; meat quality. Subspecialties: Food science and technology; Biochemistry (biology). Office: 1805 Linden Dr Madison WI 53706

MARSH, KENNETH ALBERT, industrial scientist; b. Rochford, Eng., Apr. 1, 1949; came to U.S., 1975; s. Albert Frederick Alexander and Irene Mabel (Emery) M.; m. Lucile Chapman Marsh, Aug. 28, 1976; children: Rhonda, Jessica. B.Sc. with honors, U. Canterbury, N.Z., 1969, M.Sc., 1971; Ph.D., York U., Toronto, Ont., Can., 1975. Research fellow solar astronomy Calif. Inst. Tech., 1975-82; mem. tech. staff Sci. Ctr., Rockwell Internat., Thousand Oaks, Calif., 1982—. Contbr. articles to profl. jours. Mem. Am. Astron. Soc. Current Work: Image reconstruction as applied to passive sonar. Subspecialties: Radio and microwave astronomy; Graphics, image processing, and pattern recognition. Office: 1049 Camino Dos Rios Thousand Oaks CA 91360

MARSH, MAX MARTIN, chemist, pharmaceutical company official; b. Indpls., Feb. 25, 1923; s. Albert E. and Sarah J. M.; m. Mary Midlred Trueblood, Dec. 31, 1941 (div. Mar. 1974); children—Timothy, Deborah, Shawn, Neil. B.S. in Chemistry with high honors, Ind. U., 1947. Lab. asst. Herff-Jones Co., Indpls., 1941-42; lab. asst. Eli Lilly & Co., Indpls., 1942-43, dir. phys. chemistry, 1967-69, research advisor, 1966—; mem. research grants bd. overseers Ind. U., 1979—. Mem. editoral adv. bd. Jour. Computational Chemistry, 1980—. Contbr. chpts. to books, articles to profl. jours. Mem., pres. Town Bd. of Warren Park, Indpls., 1971-75; mem. White House Conf. on Libraries, 1979, Ind. Gov.'s Com. Libraries and Info. Services, 1979-80; mem. adv. bd. Ind. U. Inst. Molecular and Cell Biology, 1985—. Served with U.S. Army, 1943-45, CBI. Recipient Meritorious Service award dept. chemistry Ind. U., 1982. Mem. Am. Chem. Soc., AAAS, Ind. Acad. Sci., Ind. U. Grad. Sch. Alumni Assn. (bd. dirs. 1984—), Alpha Chi Sigma, Phi Lambda Upsilon. Subspecialties: Molecular biology; Physical chemistry. Home: 1511 Foxcliff S Martinsville IN 46151 Office: Lilly Corp Ctr Eli Lilly & Co Indianapolis IN 46285

MARSHAK, MARVIN LLOYD, physics educator; b. Buffalo, Mar. 11, 1946; s. Kalman and Goldie (Hait) M.; m. Anita Sue Kolman, Sept. 24, 1972; children: Rachel, Adam. A.B., Cornell U., 1967; M.S., U. Mich., 1969, Ph.D., 1970. Research assoc. U. Mich., Ann Arbor, 1970; research assoc. U. Minn., Mpls., 1970-74, asst. prof., 1974-78, assoc. prof. dept physics, 1978-83, prof., 1983—; prin. investigator U.S. Dept. Energy contract in elem. particle physics, 1982; project dir. NSF grants, 1979, 81. Contbr. articles to profl. jours. Mem. Am. Phys. Soc. Current Work: Strong interaction experiments, protein decay, experiments in cosmic rays. Subspecialties: Particle physics; Cosmic ray high energy astrophysics. Home: 2855 Ottawa Ave S Minneapolis MN 55416 Office: 116 Church St SE Minneapolis MN 55455

MARSHAK, ROBERT EUGENE, physicist, educator; b. N.Y.C., Oct. 11, 1916; s. Harry and Rose (Shapiro) M.; m. Ruth Florence Gup, Apr. 18, 1943; children—Ann, Stephen. A.B., Columbia U., 1936; Ph.D., Cornell U., 1939; Ph.D. hon. degree, Utkal U., India, 1977, City U. N.Y., 1979, CCNY, 1980. Instr. dept. physics U. Rochester, N.Y., 1939-43, asst. prof., 1943-46, asso. prof., 1946-49, prof., 1949-70, chmn. dept. physics and astronomy, 1950-64, Disting. Univ. prof., 1964-70; pres. CCNY, 1970-79, pres. emeritus, 1979—; Univ. Disting. prof. physics Va. Poly. Inst. and State U., Blacksburg, 1979—; lectr. Harvard Obs., summer 1940; professeur d'Echange (Guggenheim fellow) at Sorbonne, 1953-54; vis. prof. Columbia U., summer 1950, U. Mich., 1952, Tata Inst. Bombay, 1953, French Sch. for Theoretical Physics, 1954, Sch. for Theoretical Physics, Tokyo, 1965, Goteburg, 1970; guest prof. at CERN, Geneva; Ford Found. and Guggenheim fellow, 1960-61, Guggenheim fellow, 1967-68, Nobel Found. prof., Sweden, 1970; mem. Inst. Advanced Study, Princeton, spring 1948; physicist radiation lab. Mass. Inst. Tech., 1942-43, Montreal Atomic Energy project, 1943-44; dep. group leader in theoretical physics Los Alamos Sci. Lab., 1944-46; vice chmn. N.Y. State Adv. Com. on Atomic Energy, 1958; Avco vis. prof. Cornell U., 1959; chmn. vis. physics com. Brookhaven Nat. Lab., 1964-65; Niels Bohr vis. prof. Inst. Math. Sci., Madras, India, 1963; lectr. Yalta Internat. Sch., 1966, Hercig Novi Internat. Sch., 1967; head Nat. Acad. Sci. del. to Poland, 1964, to Yugoslavia, 1965; mem. Sloan Fellowship Com., 1967-73; mem. sci. council Internat. Center of Theoretical Physics, Trieste, 1967-75, 84—; Buhl vis. prof. Carnegie-Mellon U., 1968; distinguished visitor U. Tex., 1970; mem. Solvay Congress, 1967, 82, Pugwash Conf., 1967, U.S.-Japan Com. on Sci.-Cooperation, 1969-72; mem. nat. com. UNESCO, 1970-73; trustee Univ. Research Assn., 1968-70, Atoms for Peace Award, 1958-70; chmn. div. particles and fields, 1970-71; founder Rochester Confs. on High Energy Physics, 1950—; vis. com. physics Carnegie Mellon U., 1967-70; bd. dirs. Internat. Found. for Sci., 1970-75. Author: Meson Physics, 1952, (with L.I. Schiff and E.C. Nelson) Our Atomic World, 1946, (with E.C.G. Sudarshan) Elementary Particles, 1961, (with Riazuddin and C. Ryan) Theory of Weak Interactons, 1969; Assoc. editor: Phys. Rev, 1953-55; editor interscience: Tracts and Monographs in Physics and Astronomy, 1955-70; dir.: Jour. History of Ideas, 1973-80. Recipient A. Cressy Morrison Astron. prize N.Y. Acad. Scis., 1940, J. Robert Oppenheimer Meml. prize, 1982, Alexander von Humboldt award. Fellow Am. Phys. Soc. (exec. com. 1968-69, council 1965-69, pres. 1983), AAAS; mem. AAUP, Fedn. Am. Scientists (chmn. 1947-48), Nat. Acad. Scis. (past chmn. adv. com. on sci. exchanges with USSR and Eastern Europe; council 1971-74), Am. Acad. Arts and Scis. (council 1985—), Am. Philos. Soc., Council Fgn. Affairs, Internat. Union Pure and Applied Physics (past sec. commn. on high energy physics, past vice chmn. nat. commn.), Phi Beta Kappa (Scholar 1982), Sigma Xi (nat. lectr. 1969), Phi Kappa Phi. Researcher in theoretical particle physics. Current Work: Theory of weak interactions in particle physics, grand unified theories, structure of quarks and leptons. Subspecialties: Particle physics; Theoretical physics. Office: Va Poly Inst and State U Dept Physics Blacksburg VA 24061

MARSHAK, ROBERT REUBEN, university dean, veterinarian; b. N.Y.C., Feb. 23, 1923; s. David and Edith (Youselovsky) M.; m. Ruth Emilie Lyons, Dec. 4, 1948; children: William Lyons, John Ball, Richard Best.; m. Margo Post Marshak, June 25, 1983. Student, U. Wis., 1940-41; D.V.M., Cornell U., 1945; D.V.M. (hon.), U. Bern, 1968; M.A. (hon.), U. Pa., 1971. Diplomate: Am. Coll. Vet. Internal Medicine (charter). Practice vet. medicine, Springfield, Vt., 1945-56; prof., chmn. dept. medicine Sch. Vet. Medicine, U. Pa., Phila., 1956-58; prof. medicine Grad. Sch. Medicine, 1957-64; chmn. dept. clin. studies Sch. Vet. Medicine, 1958-73; dir. Bovine Leukemia Research Center, 1965-73; dean Sch. Vet. Medicine, 1973—; co-dir. center on Interactions Animals and Soc., 1975-79; also mem. grad. group com. in comparative med. scis. Center on Interactions Animals and Soc.; dir. Edgewater Corp.; adv. council James A. Baker Inst. and N.Y. State Coll. Vet. Medicine (both Cornell U.); adv. bd. Pa. Dept. Agr.; mem. com. on vet. medicine scis. Nat. Acad. Scis.; chmn. Gov.'s Study Group on Horse Racing Industry in Pa., 1979; mem. del. to evaluate vet. med. and research Chinese Ministry Agr. Mem. editorial bd.: Jour. of Am. Vet. Radiology Soc, 1964—; Contbr. numerous articles to sci. jours. Bd. dirs. Humane Soc. U.S., 1978-82, Bide-a-wee Home Assn. Served with AUS, 1943-44. Fellow N.Y. Acad. Scis., Phila. Coll. Physicians; mem. John Morgan Soc. (pres. 1967-68); AAAS Am. Assn. Cancer Research, Am., Pa. vet. med. assns.; Pa. Livestock Assn. (dir.), Conf. Research Workers in Animal Diseases, Am. Assn. Vet. Med. Colls., Sigma Xi, Phi Zeta. Subspecialty: Internal medicine (veterinary medicine). Office: U Pa Sch Vet Medicine Philadelphia PA 19174

MARSHALEK, ROBERT GERALD, electrical engineering researcher, educator; b. Balt., Nov. 29, 1954; s. Melvin Sylvester and Jean Frances (Ray) M.

B.E.S., Johns Hopkins U., 1976, Ph.D., 1982. Assoc. engr. Westinghouse Electric Corp., Balt., summers 1976-78; instr. elec. engring. Johns Hopkins U., Balt., part-time 1976-78, 80-81, lectr. elec. engring. Applied Physics Lab., Laurel, Md., part-time 1984—; mem. tech. staff COMSAT Labs., Clarksburg, Md., 1981—. Contbr. articles to profl. jours. Mem. IEEE, Phi Beta Kappa, Tau Beta Pi, Eta Kappa Nu. Democrat. Roman Catholic. Current work: Applications of optical methods to all aspects of satellite communications (space and terrestrial segments). Subspecialties: Telecommunications; Fiber optics. Home: 19608 Crystal Rock Dr Apt 22 Germantown MD 20874 Office: COMSAT Labs 22300 COMSAT Dr Clarksburg MD 20871

MARSHALL, DAVID BRUCE, ceramics scientist; b. Melbourne, Australia, Dec. 2, 1950; came to U.S., 1979; s. L. S. and M. E. (Hutchinson) M.; m. Christine J. Lyster, Dec. 9, 1972; children—Andrew, Peter. B.Sc. with honors, Monash U., 1971, Ph.D., 1975. Research fellow U. N.S.W., Australia, 1975-79; research engr. U. Calif.-Berkeley, 1979-83; mgr. ceramics group Rockwell Internat. Sci. Ctr., Thousand Oaks, Calif., 1983—. Contbr. numerous articles to sci. jours., chpts. to books. Mem. Am. Ceramic Soc. (sub editor 1983—). Current work: Fracture mechanics of brittle materials; failure analysis, especially with the aim of relating failure mechanisms and reliability of toughened structural ceramics to microstructural properties. Subspecialties: Ceramics; Fracture mechanics. Home: 3387 Hidden Creek Ave Thousand Oaks CA 91360 Office: Rockwell Internat Sci Ctr 1049 Camino Dos Rios Thousand Oaks CA 91360

MARSHALL, FRANKLIN NICK, pharmacologist; b. Chgo., July 5, 1933; s. John Nick and Elizabeth (Hegel) M.; m. Nancy Rose Emmering, Nov. 25, 1955; 1 son: Nicholas Franklin. B.S., U. Iowa, 1957, M.S. (scholar), 1959, Ph.D., 1961. Instr. pharmacology U. Iowa, Iowa City, 1961; pharmacologist Dow Chem. Co., Indpls., 1961-66, project leader, 1966-72, group leader, 1972-73, assoc. scientist, 1973-80; dir. pharmacology Merrell Dow Pharms. Co., Indpls., 1980—. Contbr. articles to profl. jours. Mem. Am. Soc. Pharmacology and Explt. Therapeutics, Soc. Explt. Biology and Medicine, N.Y. Acad. Scis., Am. Heart Assn., AAAS, Sigma Xi. Current work: Renal, cardiovascular and autonomic pharmacology. Subspecialties: Pharmacology; Cardiology. Home: Route 2 Box 111A Thorntown IN 46071 Office: PO Box 68511 Indianapolis IN 46268

MARSHALL, GAILEN DAUGHERTY, JR., physician, scientist; b. Houston, Sept. 9, 1950; s. Gailen D. and Evelyn C. (Gresham) M.; m. Elizabeth Marie Marek, Nov. 5, 1978; children—Sarah Elizabeth, Jonathan David, Rebecca Marie. B.S., U. Houston, 1972; M.S., Tex. A&M U., 1975; Ph.D., U. Tex.-Galveston, 1979, M.D., 1984. Grad. research asst. Tex. A&M U., College Station, 1973-75; grad. asst. U. Tex.-Galveston, 1975-78, research scientist, 1979-84; grad. asst. George Washington U., 1978-79; instr. biology George Mason U., Fairfax, Va., 1978-79; research resident in internal medicine U. Iowa Hosps., Iowa City, 1984—. Contbr. articles to sci. jours. Mem. So. Med. Assn., AMA, Sigma Xi. Baptist. Subspecialties: Immunology (medicine); Internal medicine. Home: 2031 Southridge Dr Coralville IA 52241 Office: U Iowa Hosps and Clinics Dept Internal Medicine Iowa City IA 52242

MARSHALL, GARLAND ROSS, biomedical scientist, educator; b. San Angelo, Tex., Apr. 16, 1940; s. Garland Ross and Jewel Gray M.; m. Suzanne Russell, Dec. 26, 1959; children: Stuart C., Keith W., Melissa A., Kenneth L. B.S., Calif. Inst. Tech., 1962; Ph.D., Rockefeller U., 1966. Instr. depts. physiology and biophysics and biol. chemistry Washington U., St. Louis, 1966-67, asst. prof., 1967-72, asso. prof., 1972-76, prof., 1976—, prof. dept. pharmacology, 1985—; vis. prof. Massey U., Palmerston North, N.Z., 1975; pres. Tripos Assos., Inc.; mem. sci. council Nelson Research.; Am. Heart Assn. investigator, 1970-75. Mem. Am. Chem. Soc., Endocrine Soc., Biophys. Soc., Am. Phys. Soc., Am. Soc. Biol. Chemistry, Am. Soc. Pharmacology and Exptl. Therapeutics. Current Work: Computer-aided drug design, conformation of peptides receptors, molecular graphics, peptide chemistry, conformational analysis. Subspecialties: Molecular pharmacology; Graphics, image processing, and pattern recognition. Office: Dept Pharmacology Washington Univ Med Sch Saint Louis MO 63110

MARSHALL, GERALD FRANCIS, optical physicist; b. Seven Kings, Essex, Eng., Feb. 26, 1929; came to U.S., 1967; s. Albert Edward and Ethelena Maria (Plaskett) M.; m. Irene Mary Stook, Oct. 11, 1958; children: Clare Marshall De Forge, Mark, Guy, Maria. B.Sc. in Physics, London U., 1952. Mktg. tech. advisor Morganite Internat. Ltd., London, 1954-59; sr. research and devel. engr. Ferranti Ltd., Edinburgh, 1959-67; dir. engring. Med. Lasers, Burlington, Mass., 1969-70; staff cons. Schiller Industries, Warren, Mich., 1971-76; dir. optical engring. Energy Conversion Devices Inc., Troy, Mich., 1976—; cons. physicist, 1967—. Contbr. chpts. to books, articles to profl. jours. Served with RAF, 1947-49. Fellow Inst. of Physics, Internat. Soc. for Optical Engring.; mem. Optical Soc. Am. Roman Catholic. Patentee in optics. Current Work: Editing and writing optical engineering, optical design of flat panel displays, of swimming goggles with prescription lenses and optical instrumentation. Subspecialties: Optical engineering; Laser alignment. Office: 32400 Edward St Madison Heights MI 48071

MARSHALL, HARRY DWIGHT, machine tool company executive; b. Grand Rapids, Mich., Aug. 26, 1915; s. Harry Dwight and Edith Lenore (Butler) M.; m. Judy Corrigan, Dec. 26, 1942; children: Nancy Marshall Taylor, John Stephen. B.S.M.E. in Mech. and Indsl. Engring. U. Mich., 1939. Cost engr. Eastman Kodak Co., Rochester, N.Y., 1939-40; asst. to v.p. mfg. Gallmeyer & Livingston Co., Grand Rapids, 1940-52, v.p., 1952—, treas., 1959—, also dir.; dir. Mut. Home Fed. Savs. & Loan Assn., Grand Rapids, 1964—; dir. Mut. Ins. Co. Grand Rapids, 1964—, v.p., 1967, pres., 1968-74; bd. dirs. Employers Assn. Grand Rapids, 1956—, v.p., 1957, pres., 1958-60. Bd. dirs. Kent County (Mich.) chpt. ARC, 1960-69; elder, trustee Westminster Presbyterian Ch., Grand Rapids. Mem. ASME, Tau Beta Pi, Phi Kappa Phi. Republican. Clubs: Univ. Penninsular. Lodge: Rotary (dir. 1960-62, 69-71, v.p. 1961-62, 69-70) (Grand Rapids). Current Work: Mfg. and fin. responsibilities and decisions of machine tool mfr. Subspecialties: Mechanical engineering; Industrial engineering. Home: 1661 Fisk Rd SE Grand Rapids MI 49506 Office: 336 Straight Ave SW Grand Rapids MI 40504

MARSHALL, LOUISE HANSON, neuro scientist, administrator; b. Perrysburg, Ohio, Oct. 2, 1908; d. Norman Luther and Helen (Vortriede) Hanson; m. Wade Hampton Marshall (dec. 1972); children—Thomas, Alice Martin. A.B., Vassar Coll., 1930, M.A., 1932; Ph.D., U. Chgo., 1935. Instr. physiology Vassar Coll., Poughkeepsie, N.Y., 1937-38; research physiologist NIH, Bethesda, Md., 1943-65; assoc. Nat. Acad. Scis., D.C., 1965-75; mng. editor Exptl. Neurology UCLA, 1975—, administrn. analyst Brain Research Inst., 1975—, assoc. dir. Neurosci. History Program, 1980—. Contbr. articles to profl. jours. Contbng. exhibitor (posters) Neurosci. History, 1980—. Mem. Soc. Neurosci. (editor newsletter), Am. Physiol. Soc. Club: YWCA. Unitarian. Current work: Neurophysiology. Subspecialty: Neurophysiology. Office: Brain Research Inst UCLA Los Angeles CA 90024

MARSHALL, STEVEN EDWIN, engineer, consultant; b. Logansport, Ind., June 20, 1956; s. Philip R. and Phyllis J. (Shaver) M. B.S. in Mech. Engring., U. Cin., 1979; M.S. in Mech. Engring., Purdue U., 1984. Assoc. engr. Delco Products div. Gen. Motors Corp., Dayton, Ohio, 1979—; research asst. Purdue U., West LaFayette, Ind., 1982-84 Contbr. articles to profl. publs. Mem. Soc. Automotive Engrs., ASME, Inst. Noise Control Engring. Club: Amateur Radio (Detroit). Current work: Acoustics, audio, noise control. Subspecialties: Acoustical engineering; Mechanical engineering. Home: 3024 Brickwall Dr Apt 2C Kettering OH 45420 Office: Delco Products Div Gen Motors Corp PO Box 1042 Dayton OH 45401-1042

MARSHALL, WAYNE EDWARD, biochemist, researcher; b. Washington, Dec. 20, 1944; s. Edward Oren and Tania Margaret (Preveden) M.; m. Patricia Margaret Tobin, July 13, 1968; 1 child, Abigail Victoria. B.S., U. Md., 1966; Ph.D., U. Ill.-Chgo., 1970. USPHS-NIH predoctoral trainee, 1966; research assoc. U. Ill. Med. Ctr., Chgo., 1971-77; sr. scientist, group leader Kraft Inc. Research & Devel., Glenview, Ill., 1977-85; research leader Agrl. Research Service, U.S. Dept. Agr., New Orleans, 1985—. Lions Club scholar, 1962. Recipient Outstanding Research Presentation award Am. Oil Chemists Soc., 1984. Contbr. articles to profl. publs. Patentee in field. Mem. Am. Chem. Soc., Sigma Xi. Current work: Investigation of the physicochemical properties of food proteins in order to determine structure-function relationships; protein modification to improve the use of proteins in food. Subspecialties: Food science and technology; Biochemistry (biology). Office: USDA-ARS-SRRC PO Box 19687 New Orleans LA 70179

MARSTEN, RICHARD BARRY, engineering organization executive; b. N.Y.C., Oct. 28, 1925; s. Jesse and Rosalind M.; m. Sarah Betty Jaffe, June 26, 1949; children: Michael Frederick, Jessica Claire. B.S. in Elec. Engring, M.I.T., 1946, M.S., 1946, postgrad., 1946-49; Ph.D., U. Pa., 1951. Registered profl. engr., N.J. With RCA, 1957-69, mgr. radar systems projects Missile and Surface Radar div., 1959-61, mgr. spacecraft electronics, 1961-67, chief engr. Astro Electronics div., 1967-69; dir. communications programs Office of Applications, NASA Hdqrs. Washington, 1969-76; dean Sch. Engring., CUNY, 1975-79, prof. engring., 1979-81; mgr. space program Office of Technology Assessment, U.S. Congress, 1980-81; exec. dir. Bd. on Telecommunications and Computer Applications, Nat. Acad. Engring./NRC, Washington, 1981—; mem. broadcast panel study space applications Nat. Acad. Scis., 1967, chmn. point-to-point communications panel, 1968; mgr., dir. study on communications for social needs Pres.'s Domestic Council, 1971; mem. panel automation opportunities in health care Fed. Council Sci. and Tech., 1972-73; mem. panel on telecommunications research in U.S. and selected fgn. countries, com. on telecommunications Nat. Acad. Engring., 1973-74; chmn. telecommunications adv. panel Office of Technology Assessment, 1979-80; Adv. council Nat. Energy Found. Editor: Communications Satellite Systems Technology, 1966. Recipient Exceptional Service medal, also Group Achievement award NASA, 1974; Sustained Superior Performance award White House, 1972; Educator of Yr., Internat. Women's Yr., 1975; NASA/USSR Apollo-Soyuz Space medal, 1976. Asso. fellow AIAA (chmn. nat. tech. activities com. communications 1967-69, chmn. tech. program 1st Communications Satellite Systems Conf. 1966, chmn. tech. splty. group on info. systems 1970-71); fellow IEEE (com. policy bd. 1972-79, adv. bd. EASCON 1973-75, program chmn. EASCON 1970, bd. govs. com. soc. 1977-80, chmn. com. on telecommunications policy 1978-80, cons. mem. 1980-81, mem. 1981-83, mem. steering com. U.S. Tech. Policy Conf. 1978—, mem. U.S. Tech. Policy Com. 1982—, bd. govs. aero. and elec. systems soc. 1982—, v.p. tech. ops. aero. and elec. systems soc. 1985—, bd. dirs. EASCON 1985—); mem. AAAS, N.Y. Acad. Scis. Club: Cosmos. Current Work: Satellite applications; satellite communications, broadcasting and remote sensing systems; telecommunications and information systems. Address: NAE/NRC 2100 Pennsylvania Ave NW Washington DC 20418

MARSTON, RICHARD ALAN, geography educator, consultant; b. Bethesda, Md., Apr. 6, 1952; s. Alan Douglas and Nancy (Burdick) M.; m. Linda Mary Crowe, July 16, 1977. B.A., UCLA, 1974; M.S., Oreg. State U., 1976, Ph.D., 1980. Environ. scientist V.T.N.-Colo., Denver, 1974-76, EPA, Corvallis, Oreg., 1976-77; hydrologist U.S. Forest Service, Waldport, Oreg., 1978-79; asst. prof. geography U. Tex.-El Paso, 1980—; cons. on environ. geoscis., El Paso, 1980—. Contbr. articles to profl. jours. Recipient spl. achievement award EPA, 1977; A Grantee Assoc. Western Univs., 1984, Horizon Communities Improvement Assn., 1983, Fort Bliss Mil. Reservation, 1981, U.S. Forest Service, 1979. Mem. Assn. Am. Geographers (Warren Nystrom award 1981), Am. Geomorphological Field Group, Am. Soc. Photogrammetry, Am. Water Resources Assn. Geol. Soc. Am. Current work: physical geography, geomorphology, hydrology, remote sensing. Subspecialties: Geology; Hydrology. Office: Dept Geol Scis U Tex at El Paso El Paso TX 79968

MARTEN, GORDON CORNELIUS, research agronomist, educator; b. Wittenberg, Wis., Sept. 14, 1935; s. Clarence George and Cora Levina (Verpoorten) M.; m. Lynette Joy Hanson, Sept. 9, 1961; 1 dau., Kimberly Joy. B.S. with highest honors, U. Wis., 1957; M.S., U. Minn., 1959, Ph.D., 1961. Research agronomist U.S. Dept. Agr.-Agrl. Research Service, St. Paul, 1961-72; asst. prof. U. Minn., St. Paul, 1962-66, assoc. prof., 1966-71, prof. dept. agronomy and plant genetics, 1971—; research leader, research agronomist Agrl. Research Service, U.S. Dept. Agr., St. Paul, 1972—; bd. dirs. Am. Forage and Grassland Council, Lexington, Ky., 1976-79; bd. govs., program chmn. XIV Internat. Grassland Congress, Lexington, 1978-81; bd. dirs. Council for Agrl. Sci. and Tech., 1985—; trustee Agronomic Sci. Found., 1984—. Assoc. editor: Crop Sci, 1972-74; sr. editor USDA handbook Near Infrared Reflectance Spectroscopy: Analysis of Forage Quality, 1985; contbr. articles to profl. jours.; co-breeder low-alkaloid reed canarygrass, 1983. Chmn. Roseville (Minn.) Sch. Dist. Curriculum Com. Recipient Merit Cert. Am. Forage and Grassland Council, 1976; Outstanding Service awards Am. Forage and Grassland Council and U. Ky., 1981; Outstanding Service awards Minn. Forage and Grassland Council, 1982. Fellow Am. Soc. Agronomy; mem. Crop Sci. Soc. Am. (dir. 1975-76, div. chmn. 1976, chmn. Crop Sci. Research award com. 1985), Biol. Club U. Minn. (pres. 1978). Lutheran. Current Work: Evaluation techniques for nutritional value of forage crops, environmental and genetic influences on feed value of forages and grasslands, discovery of antiquality constituents in forage feeds for ruminant animals. Subspecialties: Ecology (environmental science); Animal nutrition. Office: Dept Agronomy and Plant Genetics USDA-ARS 1991 Upper Buford Circle Saint Paul MN 55108

MARTIGNONI, MAURO EMILIO, microbiologist, educator; b. Lugano, Switzerland, Oct. 30, 1926; came to U.S., 1956, naturalized, 1963; s. Angiolo Fedele and Lucia Albina (Rava) M.; m. Marie Louise di Suvero, May 15, 1953; children: Enrico A., Matteo L. Diploma in biol. sci, Fed. Inst. Tech., Zurich, Switzerland, 1950, Ph.D., 1956; postgrad., U. Calif., Berkeley, 1951-52. Asst. Fed. Inst. Tech., Zurich, 1950, 52; Am.-Swiss Found. for Sci. Exchange fellow Inst. Internat. Edn., 1951-52; cons. FAO, UN, Rome, 1952-53; entomologist Swiss Forest Research Inst., Zurich, 1953-56; asst. pathologist, lectr. invertebrate pathology U. Calif., Berkeley, 1956-63, assoc. prof., 1963-65; prin. research microbiologist Forestry Scis. Lab., Dept.Agr., Corvallis, Oreg., 1965-68, chief microbiologist, 1968—; prof. invertebrate pathology Oreg. State U., 1965—; co-coordinator U.S. Working Group in Microbiology U.S./USSR Joint Comm. on Sci. and Tech. Cooperation, 1977-83. Author: Laboratory Exercises in Insect Microbiology and Insect Pathology, 1961; Terms Used in Invertebrate Pathology in Five Languages, 1984; contbr. chpts., numerous articles to profl. publs.; editorial bd.: Jour. Invertebrate Pathology, 1964-67, Current Topics in Comparative Pathobiology, 1970-73. Mem. Sierra Club, Citizens for a Clean Environment of Oreg. Recipient Silver medal and Kern award Fed. Inst. Tech., 1957, Superior Service Unit award Dept. Agr., 1977; USPHS grantee, 1958-64; Dept. Agr. grantee, 1975-80. Mem. AAAS, Am. Soc. Microbiology, Am. Soc. Virology, Entomol. Soc. Am., Schweizerische Entomologische Gesellschaft, Soc. Invertebrate Pathology (founding), Sigma Xi. Democrat. Roman Catholic. Current Work: Etiology, pathogenesis and pathophysiology of viral diseases of insects; current emphasis is in identification of insect-pathogenic viruses, biological assay and standardization of virus preparations, and safety evaluation of insect virus preparations. Subspecialties: Virology (biology); Animal pathology. Office: Forestry Scis Lab 3200 Jefferson Way Corvallis OR 97331

MARTIN, BILLY R., pharmacologist, educator; b. Winston-Salem, N.C., Apr. 25. 1943; s. John Lee and Leva Montrose (King) M.; m. Jean Yarbrough, May 5, 1947; children: Zachary, Lindsay. A.B. in Chemistry, U. N.C., 1965; Ph.D. in Pharmacology, 1974. Asst. prof. pharmacology Med. Coll. Va., Richmond., 1976-82, assoc. prof., 1982—. Contbr. chapts. to books, articles to profl. jours. Swedish Med. Research Council fellow, 1975-76; Wellcome Trust fellow, 1976. Mem. Am. Soc. Pharmacology and Exptl. Therapeutics, Va. Acad. Scis., Sigma Xi. Current Work: Pharmacology. Subspecialty: Pharmacology. Office: Med Coll Va Box 613 MCV Station Richmond VA 23298

MARTIN, BRADFORD DOUGLAS, biology educator; b. Los Angeles, July 14, 1955; s. Russell McCleary and Alberta Joy (Tetz) M.; m. Sherylle Renee Skoretz, Nov. 22, 1981. B.S., Loma Linda U., 1979, M.A., 1981, Ph.D., 1984. Interpreter specialist State of Calif. Dept. Parks, Cuyamaca Rancho State Park, 1979-81; teaching asst. dept. biology Loma Linda U., Riverside, Calif., 1979-81, botany instr., 1983, research asst., 1982-84; research asst. State of Calif., Dept. Parks, 1981-82; asst. prof. biology Calif. Bapt. Coll., Riverside, 1984-85. Contbr. articles to profl. jours. Loma Linda U. fellow, 1982, Edmund C. Jaeger award, 1983, Pres.'s award, 1984. Mem. Calif. Bot. Soc., Calif. Native Plant Soc., So. Calif. Botanists, Soc. for Study of Evolution, Nature Conservancy, Ecol. Soc. Am. Current work: Niche partitioning in Downingia spp. in vernal pools of Calif.; reproductive biology of Croton californicus (Euphorbiaceae). Subspecialties: Ecology (biology); Population biology. Home: 25421B Cole St Loma Linda CA 92354

MARTIN, DAVID LEE, biochemist, research scientist; b. St. Louis, May 30, 1941; s. L. Frederick and Ruth Elma (Wilson) M.; m. Sandra Bloom, Aug. 20, 1966; children: Laura Eleanor, Rachel Kirsten. B.S. (Internat. Milling Co. scholar), U. Minn., 1963; M.S., U. Wis., 1965, Ph.D. (NIH fellow), 1968. Research assoc. U. Wis., 1968; asst. prof. chemistry U. Md., 1968-72, assoc. prof., 1972-80; research chemist Armed Forces Radiobiology Research Inst., Bethesda, Md., 1976; vis. scientist, 1977-80; research scientist Ctr for Labs. and Research, N.Y. State Health Dept., Albany, 1980—, chief Lab. of Neurotoxicology and Nervous System Disorders, 1983—; prof. toxicology and environ. health SUNY, Albany, 1985—; dir. Chemistry Assocs. Md. Inc.; cons. in field. Author: Molecules in Living Systems, 2d edit, 1978, Teacher's Guide to Molecules in Living Systems, 2d edit, 1978. NIH grantee, 1975—. Mem. Am. Soc. Biol. Chemists, Biochem. Soc., Soc. Neurosci., Am. Soc. Neurochemistry, N.Y. Acad. Scis., AAAS, Sigma Xi. Current Work: Neurochemistry, neurotoxicology, especially of synaptic transmission and of glial cells. Subspecialties: Biochemistry (biology); Neurochemistry. Office: Ctr for Labs and Research NY State Dept Health Albany NY 12201

MARTIN, EDITH WAISBROT, corporate executive. Vice pres. tech. assessment Boeing Aerospace, Seattle. . Office: Boeing Aerospace PO Box 3999 Seattle WA 98124*

MARTIN, FREDERICK WIGHT, physicist, educator, consultant; b. Boston, Feb. 16, 1936; s. Frederick E. and Rhoda (Nichols) M.; m. Elizabeth Foltz, Apr. 24, 1965; children: Frederick N., Katharine. A.B., Princeton U., 1957; M.S., Yale U., 1958, PH.D., 1964. Research asst. Yale U., 1959-63; physicist Ion Physics Corp., Burlington, Mass., 1963-64, sr. physicist, 1964-66; amaneunsis I fysik U. Aarhus, Denmark, 1966-68; research assoc., asst. prof. physics U. Ky., Lexington, 1968-70; asst. prof. physics U. Md., College Park, 1970-78; pres. Microscope Assocs., Inc., Dedham, Mass., 1978—; vis. scientist SUNY, Stony Brook, 1975-76; Nat. Acad. Sci.-NRC sr. research assoc., 1978; adj. assoc. prof. physics Worcester Poly. Inst., 1983—. Contbr. articles to profl. publs. Mem. Am. Phys. Soc., IEEE, Sigma Xi. Patentee in field. Current Work: Research on ion implantation and device fabrication in semiconductors; stopping of particles; principal investigator of various grants on X-ray production in single atomic collisions at high velocities; studies on use of ions rather than electrons in microscopy and microfabrication. Subspecialties: Microelectronics; Atomic and molecular physics. Office: 50 Village Ave Dedham MA 02026

MARTIN, GEORGE FRANKLIN, anatomist; b. Englewood, N.J., Feb. 20, 1937; s. George Franklin and Nellie Alamanda (Williams) M.; m. Muriel Joy Brandkamp, Aug. 13, 1960; children: George F., Laurie Lee. B.S. in Biology, Bob Jones U., 1960; postgrad., Emory U., 1956-57; M.S. in Anatomy, U. Ala., Birmingham, 1963, Ph.D. in Anatomy, 1965. Instr. anatomy Ohio State U. Coll. Medicine, Columbus, 1965-67, asst. prof., 1967-69, assoc. prof., 1970-73, prof., 1973—; mem. neurobiology rev. group NIH. Mem. editorial bd.: Jour. Comparative Neurology, 1981—, Anat. Record, 1982—; contbr. articles to profl. jours. NIH grantee, 1967-80; NSF grantee, 1980—. Mem. Am. Assn. Anatomists, Pan Am. Assn. Anatomists, Am. Neurosci. Soc., AAAS, Internat. Soc. Developmental Neurobiology. Current Work: Research in developmental and comparative neuroscience, development of motor systems, development of cerebellum. Subspecialties: Comparative neurobiology; Anatomy and embryology. Office: 1645 Neil Ave Columbus OH 43210

MARTIN, JEFFREY DONALD, hydrologist; b. Omaha, Aug. 25, 1954; s. Donald Francis and Jean Eleanor (Magnuson) M.; m. Kathryn Ann Watson, Aug. 27, 1983. B.A., Ind. U., 1977, M.S., 1981. Hydrologist U.S. Geol. Survey, Indpls., 1980—. Author tech. papers. Mem. Ind. Water Resources Assn., Am. Water Resources Assn., Am. Statis. Assn. Current work: Investigating effects of coal mining on the hydrology and water quality of small watersheds. Subspecialties: Hydrology; Statistics. Office: US Geol Survey 6023 N Gulon Rd Indianapolis IN

MARTIN, JOHN JOSEPH, See *Who's Who in America,* 43rd edition.

MARTIN, JOSE GINORIS, energy engineering educator, consultant, researcher; b. Havana, Cuba, Feb. 4, 1941; s. José and María De La Paz (Ginoris) M.; m. Dagma Faria Neto, Sept. 2, 1975; children: Víctor José Faría, Cassia Inés Faria. B.S. in Engring, Miss. State U., 1964; M.S. in Engring, U. Wis., 1966, Ph.D., 1970. Engr. Theory div. Lawrence Radiation Lab., Livermore, Calif., 1968; prof. Instituto Politecnico Nacional, Mexico City, 1970-75; prof., grad. coordinator dept. energy engring. U. Lowell, Mass., 1975—; vis. prof. Instituto Militar de Engenharia, Rio de Janeiro, 1972-73, U. Mexico, 1976-77; vis. faculty Coll. Architecture Ariz. State U., Tempe, 1983—; prin. investigator Nuclear Regulatory Commn. Project, Lowell, Mass., 1977-80, NSF project, 1981—; mem. internat. test and evaluation team Sandia Nat. Labs./Small Solar Power Systems, Almeria, Spain, 1982-83; Cons. Oak Ridge Nat. Lab, Los Alamos Nat. Lab., N. Mex. Editor: Procs. of Internat. Workshop on Distributed Solar Collectors; Contbr. articles to profl. publs. Bd. dirs. Unitas-Service Orgn., Lowell, 1979-82, Talented and Gifted program Lowell Schs., 1980, Lowell Manpower Bd., 1980-82. Wis. Alumni Research Found. fellow, 1965-66; AEC fellow, 1966-69; NSF grantee, 1978—. Fellow Am. Soc. Engring. Edn.; mem. Internat. Solar Energy Soc., Am. Nuclear Soc., Am. Phys. Soc., AAAS, Mexican Soc. Physics, Sigma Xi, Tau Beta Pi, Phi Kappa Phi. Patentee in field. Current Work: Solar thermal engineering; fusion and fission energy systems; cost of power. Subspecialties: Solar energy; Nuclear engineering. Home: 85 Mansur St Lowell MA 01852 Office: Department of Energy Engineering University of Lowell Lowell MA 01854

MARTIN, L(AURENCE) ROBBIN, research scientist; b. Annapolis, Md., Sept. 21, 1939; s. Lawrence H. and Ethel A. (Robbin) M. B.A., Pomona Coll., 1961; Ph.D., MIT, 1966. Noyes postdoctoral fellow Calif. Inst. Tech., 1966-68; asst. prof. chemistry U. Calif., Riverside, 1968-73; research scientist Aerospace Corp., Los Angeles, 1973—. Author: (with Gokcen) Solution Manual for Thermodynamics, 1978, 'SO2, NO, and NOx Oxidation...' Atmospheric Considerations, 1983; also articles. Grantee Research Corp.; Grantee NSF; Grantee EPA; Grantee Am. Chem. Soc. Mem. Am. Phys. Soc., AAAS, Am. Geophys. Union, Sigma Xi. Current Work: Gas phase and aqueous kinetics, thermodynamics, atmospheric chemistry; research in atmospheric chemistry. Subspecialties: Kinetics; Atmospheric chemistry. Office: Aerophysics Labs Aerospace Corp Los Angeles CA 90009

MARTIN, LAWRENCE LEO, medicinal chemist, pharmacist; b. Charleston, W.V., July 5, 1942; s. Lawrence Leo and Louise Hope (Williamson) M.; m. Arlene Stangs, Nov. 10, 1973; children—Elizabeth Sarah, Lawrence William. B.S., U. Md., 1966; Ph.D., Ohio State U., 1971. Registered pharmacist, Md., Ohio. Sr. research chemist Hoechst-Roussel Pharms., Somerville, N.J., 1972-79; exchange scientist Hoechst A.G., Frankfurt, Fed. Republic Germany, 1976-77, research assoc. Hoechst-Roussel Pharms., Somerville, 1979-81, sr. research assoc., 1981—. Editor Drug Devel. Research, 1985. Contbr. articles to profl. jours. Numerous patents in field. Noxzema Found. Scholar, 1965-66; fellow Ohio State U., 1966-67, Am. Found. Pharm. Edn., 1967-71. Mem. Am. Chem. Soc. (medicinal and organic sects.), Am. Pharm. Assn., Acad. Pharm. Sci., Phi Kappa Phi, Rho Chi. Current work: Design and synthesis of potential therapeutic agents in psychotropic, antiinflammatory and cardiovascular areas; biosynthesis of antibiotics. Subspecialties: Medicinal chemistry; Drug design. Home: Route 3 Box 81 Concord Rd Lebanon NJ 08833 Office: Hoechst-Roussel Pharms Inc Route 202-206 North Somerville NJ 08876

MARTIN, LAWRENCE RONALD, nuclear engineer, aerospace engineer; b. Sterling, Ill., Nov. 22, 1946; s. Arthur Wilford and Dorothy Helen (Snyder) M.; m. Karen Patricia Morgan, Mar. 5, 1982; children: Mary, Benjamin. B.S., U. Kans.-Lawrence, 1972; M.S., Air Force Inst. Tech., 1980. Commd. 2d lt. U.S. Marine Corps, 1972, advanced through grades to maj., 1982; combat engr. firepower div. devel. ctr. (U.S. Marine Corps Devel. and Edn. Command), Quantico, Va., 1972—. Mem. Am. Nuclear Soc., IEEE. Roman Catholic. Current Work: Military applications, nuclear and chemical warfare and directed energy weapons, research and development of offensive and defensive systems, including system survivability design hardening against their effects. Subspecialties: Nuclear engineering; Laser applications.

MARTIN, LEE DAVID, defense electronics scientist, consultant; b. Chillicothe, Mo., June 23, 1923; s. Albert Justin and Matilda (Hankins) M.; m. Betty Jeanne Holmes, Feb. 16, 1946; children: Mary Ann Martin Toohey, William Albert. B.S.E. in Chemistry, George Washington U., 1958; M.S. in Mgmt., Rensselaer Poly. Inst., 1963. Commd. 2d lt. with prior enlisted service U.S. Marine Corps, 1946, advanced through grades to lt. col., 1964, ret., 1966; mem. tech. staff Hdqrs. Marine Corps, Washington, 1953-58; mem. logistics staff

First Marine Aircraft Wing, Iwakuni, Japan, 1958-59; mem. staff F8U aircraft program Marine Corps Air Sta., Beaufort, S.C., 1959-62; officer-in-charge planning office Marine Corps East Coast Logistics Staff, Albany, Ga., 1963-66; advance planner Gen. Electric Fleet Ballistic Missile Support Project, Gen. Electric Co., Pittsfield, Mass., 1966-78; mgr. tech. planning Gen. Electric Ordnance Systems, 1978-83, systems cons., 1983—. Fellow Wildfowl Trust (U.K.); mem. Ops. Research Soc. Am., Am. Geophys. Union, Am. Phys. Soc. Republican. Presbyterian. Current Work: Gravitational physics. Home: 165 Tower Rd Dalton MA 01226 Office: General Electric Company Ordnance Systems 100 Plastics Ave Pittsfield MA 01201

MARTIN, PAUL ALAN, electrical engineer; b. Dearborn, Mich., Jan. 31, 1956; s. James Ralph and Lillian Lee (McClaren) M. B.S., MIT, 1978; M.S., U. Ill., 1981. Teaching asst. elec. engring. dept. U. Ill., Urbana, 1978-79, research asst. coordinated sci. lab., 1979—. Mem. Am. Phys. Soc., IEEE. Current work: Semiconductor heterojunctions, defects in semiconductors. Subspecialties: Semiconductors; Condensed matter physics. Office: Coordinated Sci Lab U Ill 1101 W Springfield Ave Urbana IL 61801

MARTIN, PAUL CECIL, physicist, educator; b. Bklyn., Jan. 31, 1931; s. Harry and Helen (Salzberger) M.; m. Ann Wallace Bradley, Aug. 7, 1957; children: Peter, Stephanie, Daniel. A.B., Harvard U., 1952, Ph.D., 1954. Faculty Harvard U., 1957—, prof. physics, 1964-82, J. H. VanVleck prof. pure and applied physics; chmn. dept. physics Harvard U., 1972-75, dean div. applied scis., 1977—; vis. prof. Ecole Normale Superieure, Paris, 1963, 66, U. Paris (Orsay), 1971. Bd. editors: Jour. Math Physics, 1965-68, Annals of Physics, 1968-82, Jour. Statis. Physics, 1975-80. Bd. dirs. Assoc. Univs. for Research in Astronomy, 1979-85; trustee Assoc. Univs., Inc., 1981—. NSF postdoctoral fellow, 1955; Sloan Found. fellow, 1959; Guggenheim fellow, 1966, 71. Fellow Nat. Acad. Scis., Am. Acad. Arts and Scis., AAAS (chmn. elect physics sect. 1985), Am. Phys. Soc. (Councillor-at-large 1982-84); mem. Inst. Theoretical Physics (chmn. adv. com. 1979). Current Work: Phase transitions, critical phenomena, turbulence and chaos. Subspecialties: Condensed matter physics; Statistical physics. Home: 27 Stone Rd Belmont MA 02178 Office: Lyman Lab Physics Pierce Hall Harvard U Cambridge MA 02138

MARTIN, PAUL JOSEPH, research director, consultant; b. Hammond, Ind., May 22, 1936; s. Joseph Edward and Verna Catherine (Heidgerken) M.; m. Jeanne Therese Oubre, Sept. 10, 1960; children: Mary Kay, Barry, Craig, Colleen. B.S.E.E., U. Tex.-Austin, 1961; M.S., Drexel U., 1962; Ph.D., Case-Western Res. U., 1967. Research fellow Latter-day Saints Hosp., Salt Lake City, 1962-63; research bioengr. Tech., Inc., Dayton, Ohio, 1963-64; research assoc. Mt. Sinai Med. Ctr., Cleve., 1967-75, head bioengring. sect., 1975—; asst. prof. Case-Western Res. U., Cleve., 1967-75, assoc. prof., 1975-83, prof., 1983-; research cons. NIH, NSF, EPA, Cleve. Clinic, 1975—. Assoc. editor: Am. Jour. Physiology, 1975-80; editorial bd.: Circulation Research, 1975-82. Served with USN, 1954-57. Research grantee Am. Heart Assn., 1967-78; Research grantee NIH, 1972—. Fellow Am. Heart Assn. (chmn. research study sect. 1973-76, mem. regional research com. council on circulation 1977—); mem. Am. Physiol. Soc., Biomed. Engring. Soc. (membership com. 1972—), IEEE. Clubs: Classical Guitar Soc. (Cleve.), Western Res. Woodworkers (Cleve.). Current Work: Dynamic and steady-state control of the heart and circulation, cardiovascular pharmacokinetics, laboratory instrumentation and computer control, computers in health care delivery. Subspecialties: Physiology (medicine); Software engineering. Home: 2099 Lamberton Rd Cleveland Heights OH 44118 Office: Mount Sinai Med Center University Circle Cleveland OH 44106

MARTIN, RICHARD DOUGLAS, nuclear engineer, consultant; b. Englewood, N.J., May 17, 1959; s. Douglas Harry and Christine (Jacob) M.; m. JoAnne Diodato, Nov. 21, 1981. B.S. in Nuclear Engring., Pa. State U., 1981; postgrad. Poly. Inst. N.Y., White Plains, 1984. Cert. sr. reactor operator. Staff nuclear engr. Gen. Physics, Linfield, Pa., 1981-83; tng. coordinator PSE&G, Salem, N.J., 1983; tech. dir. LOM-TECH, Inc., Elmsford, N.Y., 1983-85; v.p., dir. CDS Techs., Inc., Elmsford, 1985—. Co-author: Mitigating Core Damage, 1982. Contbr. articles to profl. publs. Mem. alumni admissions bd. Pa. State U., 1983. Mem. Am. Nuclear Soc. (John and Muriel Landis award 1980), IEEE, AAAS. Republican. Presbyterian. Current work: Nuclear power plant operations in the area of emergency condition evaluation and response, operations support, and training. Subspecialties: Plasma engineering; Information systems, storage, and retrieval (computer science). Office: CDS Technologies Inc PO Box 533 Elmsford NY 10523

MARTIN, RICHARD LEE, research chemist; b. Garden City, Kans., Oct. 13, 1950; s. George Abraham and Della Faye (Faulkender) M. B.S. in Chemistry, Kans. State U., 1972; Ph.D. in Chemistry, U. Calif., Berkeley, 1976. Research asso. U. Wash., Seattle, 1977; Chaim Weizman fellow, 1978; mem. staff theoret. div. Los Alamos Nat. Lab., 1979—. Contbr. numerous articles to sci. jours. Mem. Am. Chem. Soc., Am. Phys. Soc. Current Work: Quantum chemistry; ab initio electronic structure of molecules. Subspecialties: Theoretical chemistry; Physical chemistry. Office: Theoretical Div MSJ 569 Los Alamos Nat Lab Los Alamos NM 87544

MARTIN, SCOTT MCCLUNG, biochemist, editor; b. Charleston, W.Va., Mar. 2, 1943; s. Harry Milton and Phyllis Lee (Amos) M. B.S., Marshall U., 1965; M.S., Brigham Young U., 1968; Ph.D., Ohio State U., 1973. Asst. prof. biology Wittenberg U., Springfield, Ohio, 1973-75; postdoctoral study Ohio State U., Columbus, 1975-76; curator Bacillus Genetic Stock Center, 1978-79; postdoctoral study U. Mo., Kansas City, 1976-78, vis. asst. prof. biology, 1978; asso. editor of biochemistry Chem. Abstracts Service, Columbus, 1980—. Contbr. articles to profl. publs. Mem. Am. Soc. Microbiology, Soc. Protozoologists, Am. Inst. Biol. Scis., AAAS, Ohio Acad. Sci. Democrat. Mormon. Subspecialties: Microbiology; Genome organization. Home: 712 Harley Dr Columbus OH 43202 Office: Dept Biochemistry Chem Abstracts Service Columbus OH 43210

MARTIN, TERRY ZACHRY, astronomer; b. N.Y.C., Aug. 7, 1946; s. Edward Berry and Marjorie Mae (Boyd) M.; m. Marcia Baker, May 30, 1982. A.B., U. Calif., Berkeley, 1967; M.S., U. Hawaii, 1969, Ph.D., 1975. Research geophysicist UCLA, 1975-79; mem. tech. staff Jet Propulsion Lab., Pasadena, Calif., 1979—. Mem. Am. Astron. Soc., Common Cause, ACLU, Cousteau Soc., Planetary Soc. Current Work: Planetary atmospheres, infrared detector tech., optics, vacuum tech. Subspecialties: Planetary science; Infrared astronomy. Home: 2031 Ahlin Dr La Canada Flintridge CA 91011 Office: 4800 Oak Grove Dr 11-116 Pasadena CA 91109

MARTIN, THOMAS LYLE, JR., university president; b. Memphis, Sept. 26, 1921; s. Thomas Lyle and Malvina (Rucks) M.; m. Helene Hartley, June 12, 1943; children: Michele Marie, Thomas Lyle. B.E.E., Rensselaer Poly. Inst., 1942, M.E.E., 1948, D.Eng., 1967; Ph.D., Stanford U., 1951. Prof. elec. engring. U. N.Mex., 1948-53; prof. engring. U. Ariz., 1953-63, dean engring., 1958-63, U. Fla., Gainesville, 1963-66, So. Meth. U., Dallas, 1966-74; pres. Ill. Inst. Tech., Chgo., 1974—; dir. Stewart-Warner Co., Inland Steel Co., Amsted Industries, Cherry Elec. Products Corp., Commonwealth Edison Co., Sundstrand Corp., Kemper Funds. Mem. Dallas-Fort Worth Regional Airport Bd., 1970-74; bd. dirs. Museum Sci. and Industry, 1975—. Served to capt. Signal Corps AUS, 1943-46. Decorated Bronze Star. Fellow IEEE; mem. Nat. Acad. Engring. Subspecialties: Electronics; Semiconductors. Home: 990 Lake Shore Dr Apt 19C Chicago IL 60611

MARTINEZ, IRVING RICARDO, JR., dermatologist, anatomist and electron microscopist; b. New Orleans, Apr. 30, 1935; s. I. Ricardo and Amelia (Areces) M.; m. Dolly-Dean Kimball, June 24, 1961; children: Tessa Mariana, I. Ricardo. B.S. in Biology, Loyola U., New Orleans, 1958, M.S. in Physiology, 1960; M.D., La. State U., 1965; Ph.D. in Anatomy, Boston U., 1971. Diplomate: Am. Bd. Dermatology and Dermatopathology. Instr. physiology La. State U., New Orleans, 1959-60; dermatology Boston U., 1969-70; assoc. chmn. dermatology Ochsner Clinic, New Orleans, 1971-74; head electron microscopu lab. Alton Ochsner Med. Found., New Orleans, 1972-74, asst. dir. research, 1973-74, Practice medicine specializing in dermatology, Metairie, La., 1974—; clin. prof. Tulane Med. Sch., New Orleans, 1970—, La. State U., 1970—; cons. E. Jefferson Gen. Hosp., Metairie, 1974—, Lakeside Hosp., Metairie, 1974—. Author: Wound Healing, 1972; editor: Med. Sch. Newspaper, 1963-64, Yearbook, 1963-65. Bd. dirs. New Orleans Opera Assn., 1975, Delta Festival Ballet Co., New Orleans, 1977. Served to capt. M.S.C. U.S. Army, 1958-60. Recipient Russel L. Holman award La. State U. Med. Sch., 1964, Mabel Claire Elmore award, 1965; NIH grantee, 1974-76. Fellow Am. Acad. Dermatology (Bronze award 1971), ACP, Am. Soc. Dermapathology; mem. Am. Assn. Anatomists, Noah Worcester Dermatol. Soc., La. Dermatol. Soc. (sec.-treas. 1972-73). Clubs: Bienville, Pendennis (New Orleans); Metairie Country. Current Work: Dermatology, dermatopathology, electron microscopy, research in normal and abnormal keratinization, wound healing, membrane coating granules, psoriasis, laser surgery. Subspecialties: Dermatology; Cell biology (medicine). Office: Dermatology-Allergy-Dermatologic Surgery 3333 Kingman St Suite M Metairie LA 70006

MARTINEZ-CARRION, MARINO, biochemistry educator; b. Felix, Almeria, Spain, Dec. 2, 1936; came to U.S., 1957; s. Juan Martinez and Maria Carrion; m. Jeanne Larson, Sept. 7, 1957; children: Victoria, Juan. B.A., U. Calif.-Berkeley, 1959, M.A., 1961, Ph.D., 1964. Asst. prof. U. Notre Dame, Ind., 1965-69, assoc. prof., 1969-74, prof., 1974-77; prof., chmn. dept. biochemistry Va. Commonwealth U., Richmond, 1977—; chmn. biophys. chemistry study sect. NIH, 1977-82. Contbr. 96 articles to sci. jours. Bd. dirs. Inst. Biotech., Ctr. for Innovative Tech. Va., 1985—. NIH fellow U. Rome, 1964-65; NIH Research Career awardee, 1972-77; recipient Faculty Excellence award Va. Commonwealth U., 1982. Fellow N.Y. Acad. Scis.; mem. Am. Soc. Biol. Chemists, Pan Am. Assn. Biochem. Socs. (sec. 1981—), Am. Soc. Neurochemistry, Am. Chem. Soc., Spanish Biochem. Soc. Current Work: Neuroreceptors, enzyme structure and function, spectroscopy of macromolecules, membrane function, site specific mutagenesis of proteins. Subspecialties: Biochemistry (biology); Biophysics (biology). Office: Va Commonwealth U Dept Biochemistry Richmond VA 23298

MARTINO, FRANK, physicist, educator; b. Boston, Apr. 10, 1937; s. Giuseppe and Anna (Oster) M.; 1 child, Carlo Bartolomeo. A.B., Harvard Coll., 1959; M.S., U. Ill., 1961; Ph.D., MIT, 1966. Research asst. MIT, Cambridge, Mass., 1961-66; research assoc. U. Uppsala, Sweden, 1967-68; asst. prof. physics CCNY, 1968-73, prof., 1977—, dean sci., 1982—; prof. physics U. Linkoping, Sweden, 1973, 75-76. Contbr. articles to sci. jours., chpts. to books. Mem. Am. Phys. Soc., N.Y. Acad. Scis. Current work: Calculations in electronic structure of large molecules, disordered systems, metal-insulator transitions, compton scattering, biological molecules. Subspecialties: Condensed matter physics; Theoretical physics. Home: 531 Main St New York NY 10044 Office: CCNY Convent Ave at 138th St New York NY 10031

MARTIN-ROBINSON, KERA GAYLE marketing manager; b. N.Y.C., Dec. 13, 1953; d. Sigmund and Pauline Lillian (Saretsky) Schwager; m. William Edward Robinson, July 12, 1981. Systems analyst New Eng. Life Ins. Co., Boston, 1973-77; database analyst Standard Oil of Calif., San Francisco, 1977-79; database tech. rep. Nat. CSS, San Francisco, 1979-82; pres. Softstone Cons., San Francisco, 1980—; tech. cons. info. ctr. Fed Res. Bank, San Francisco, 1982-83; tech. instr. Exploratorium of San Francisco, 1982-83; sr. tech. instr., course designer Fortune Systems, Redwood City, 1983-84; software mktg. mgr. Ducommun Data Systems, Cypress, Calif., 1984—. Mem. Assn. Computing Machinery, Nat. Computer Graphics Assn. Democrat. Current Work: Advances in database technology to enhance user acceptance. Special interests in computer graphics and animation for effective communication and in the arts; in computer aided instrn. for end-user training; integration of applications software to provide complete software systems solutions. Subspecialties: Database systems; Graphics, image processing, and pattern recognition. Home: 540 Stanford Irvine CA 92715 Office: Ducommun Data Systems 10824 Hope St Cypress CA 90630

MARTINSON, CHARLIE ANTON, plant pathology educator, researcher, cons.; b. Orchard, Colo., Sept. 15, 1934; s. George W. and Bertha E. (Wirsing) M.; m. Kathryn A. Reichert, June 9, 1957; children: Gerald, Karen, Nancy, Brian. B.S., Colo. State U., 1957, M.S., 1959; Ph.D., Oreg. State U., 1964. Asst. prof. Cornell U., Ithaca, N.Y., 1963-68; assoc. prof. plant pathology Iowa State U., Ames, 1968—; cons. Corn Prodn. Systems, Chgo., Am. Agrl. Industries, Rosemont, Ill. Research publs. in field. Served to capt. USAR, 1957-63. Mem. Am. Phytopath. Soc., AAAS. Lutheran. Current Work: Physiology and control of corn diseases; biol. control and mgmt. fungal pathogens; resistance and breeding of corn for resistance. Subspecialties: Plant pathology; Integrated pest management. Office: Iowa State U 425 Bessey Hall Ames IA 50011

MARTINSON, IDA MARIE, nurse-physiologist, educator; b. Mentor, Minn., Nov. 8, 1936; d. Oscar and Marvel (Nelson) Sather; m. Paul Varo Martinson, Mar. 31, 1962; children—Anna Marie, Peter. Diploma, St. Luke's Hosp. Sch. Nursing, 1957; B.S., U. Minn., 1960, M.N.A., 1962; Ph.D., U. Ill., Chgo., 1972. Instr. Coll. St. Scholastica and St. Luke's Sch. Nursing, 1957-58, Thornton Jr. Coll., 1967-69; lab. asst. U. Ill. at Med. Center, 1970-72; lectr. dept. physiology U. Minn., St. Paul, 1972—; asst. prof. U. Minn. (Sch. Nursing), 1972-74, asso. prof., research, 1974-77, prof., dir. research, 1977—; vis. research prof. Nat. Taiwan U. Def. Med. Center, 1981. Author: Mathematics for the Health Science Student, 1977; editor: Home Care for the Dying Child, 1976, Women in Stress, 1979; contbr. chpts. to books, articles to profl. jours. Active Am. Cancer Soc., Am. Heart Assn. Recipient Am. Bus. Press award, 1977; recipient various grants. Mem. Council Nurse Researchers, Nat. League for Nursing, Am. Acad. Nursing, Am. Nurses Assn., Inst. Medicine, Sigma Xi, Sigma Theta Tau. Lutheran. Current Work: Block nurse project; home care. Subspecialties: Gerontology; Pediatrics. Office: Dept Family Health Care Nursing U Calif San Francisco CA 94135

MARTON, JOSEPH, chemist; b. Budapest, Hungary, Mar. 5, 1919; came to U.S., 1960; s. Stephan and Rose (Prober) M.; m. Terezia Kellner Marton, Jan. 9, 1949; children—Marianne Evelyn. Ph.D. in Chemistry, Pazmany P. U.-Budapest, 1943. Sr. lectr. Tech. U. Budapest, 1949-56; sect. head Inst. Ind. Organic Chemistry, Budapest, 1948-56; research fellow Chalmers Tech. U., Gothenburg, Sweden, 1956-60; adj. prof. SUNY-Syracuse, 1983—; sr. research assoc. Westvaco Corp., Laurel, Md., 1960—. Contbr. articles to profl. jours. Patentee in field. Fellow TAPPI; mem. Am. Chem. Soc., Can. Chem. Soc., AAAS. Club: Cosmos. Current work: Papermaking science, wet end colloid chemistry, sizing with hydrophobes, wood and fiber chemistry. Subspecialties: Surface chemistry; Biomass (agriculture). Home: 10705 Meadowhill Rd Silver Spring MD 20901 Office: Westvaco Corp 11101 Johns Hopkins Laurel MD 20707

MARTON, LAURENCE JAY, physician, educator; b. Bklyn., Jan. 14, 1944; s. Bernard Dov and Sylvia M.; m. Marlene Lesser, Ju 27, 1967; 1 son, Eric Nolan. A.B., Yeshiva U., 1965; M.D., Albert Einstein Coll. Medicine, 1969. Surg. intern Los Angeles County Harbor Gen. Hosp., 1969-70; resident in neurosurgery U. Calif., San Francisco, 1970-71, resident in lab. medicine, 1973-75, asst. research biochemist dept. neurosurgery, 1973-74, asst. clin. prof. depts. lab. medicine and neurosurgery, 1974-75, asst. prof., 1975-78, assoc. prof., 1978-79, prof., 1979—, asst. dir. div. clin. chemistry dept. lab. medicine, 1974-75, dir., 1975-79, acting chmn. dept. lab. medicine, 1978-79, chmn., 1979—. Editor: (with D.R. Morris) Polyamines in Biology and Medicine, 1981, (with P.M. Kabra) Liquid Chromatography in Clinical Analysis, 1981, Clinical Liquid Chromatography, Vols. I, II, 1984; contbr. articles and abstracts to sci. jours. Served as sr. asst. surgeon USPHS, 1971-73. Nat. Cancer Inst. research career devel. award, 1975-80; research grantee, 1975—; Am. Cancer Soc. research grantee, 1981-82. Mem. Am. Assn. for Cancer Research, Am. Assn. for Clin. Chemistry, AAAS, Acad. Clin. Lab. Physicians and Scientists, Assn. Pathology Chairmen, Am. Assn. Pathologists, Calif. Med. Assn., San Francisco Med. Soc., Alpha Omega Alpha. Current Work: Polyamines and tumors; clinical applications of liquid chromatography; polyamine biosynthesis inhibitors as anti-tumor agents; application of advanced technology to patient diagnosis. Subspecialty: Cancer research (medicine). Home: 69 Aloha Ave San Francisco CA 94122 Office: Dept Lab Medicine U Calif San Francisco CA 94143

MARUYAMA, YOSH, physician, educator; b. Pasadena, Calif., Apr. 30, 1930; s. Edward Yasaki and Chiyo (Sakai) M.; m. Fudeko Tsuji, July 18, 1954; children: Warren H., Nancy C., Marian M., Karen A. A.B., U. Calif.-Berkeley, 1951; M.D., U. Calif.-San Francisco, 1955. Diplomate: Am. Bd. Radiology. Intern San Francisco Hosp., 1955-56; resident Mass. Gen. Hosp., Boston, 1958-61; James Picker advanced acad. fellow Stanford U., 1962-64; asst. prof. radiology Coll. Med. Scis., U. Minn., Mpls., 1964-67, asso. prof., 1967-70, dir. div. radiotherapy, 1968-70; prof., chmn. dept. radiation medicine Coll. Medicine, U. Ky., Lexington, 1970—, dir. Radiation Cancer Ctr., 1975—; bd. dirs. Ephraim McDowell Cancer Ctr.; cons. VA Hosp., Lexington. Author: Cf-252 Neutron Brachytherapy: An Advance for Bulky Localized Cancer Therapy, 1984. Assoc. editor: Applied Radiology; editor: New Methods in Tumor Localization, 1977; Contbr. articles to profl. jours. Served with M.C. AUS, 1956-58. Am. Cancer Soc. fellow, 1960-61. Mem. Am. Coll. Radiology (commn. on radiation therapy and patterns of care study), AAAS, Am. Radium Soc., Cell Kinetics Soc., Ky. Cancer Commn., Nippon Radiol. Soc., Radiation Research Soc., Soc. Exptl. Biol. Medicine, Am. Assn. Cancer Research, Radiol Soc. N.Am., Am. Soc. Therapeutic Radiology, Soc. Chmn. Acad. Radiation Oncology Programs, Am. Assn. Immunologists, Southeastern Cancer Research Assn. (dir.), Southeastern Cancer Group, Southwestern Oncology Group, Ky. Med. Assn., Order Ky. Cols. Minn., N.Y. Acad. Scis., Japan Soc. Ky., Shodan Judoka, Kodokan Inst. (Tokyo), Phi Beta Kappa, Sigma Xi (chpt. pres.), Alpha Omega Alpha. Club: Spindletop Hall (Lexington). Current Work: Neutron brachytherapy; chemo-radiotherapy leukemia/lymphoma. Subspecialties: Oncology; Cancer research (medicine). Home: 1739 Lakewood Dr Lexington KY 40502

MARVASTI, SETAREH ALIM, research and development chemist, chemistry educator; b. Tehran, Iran, June 22, 1952; came to U.S., 1970; d. Abdolhamid Alim Marvasti and Paridokht Khazrai Moghaddam; m. Feraidoon Kanani Kashani, Oct. 1, 1984. B.S. in Chemistry, Russell Sage Coll., 1974; M.S. in Phys. Chemistry, Rutgers U., 1978, Ph.D. in Phys. Chemistry, 1984. Research asst., teaching asst. Rutgers U., New Brunswick, N.J., 1974-81, vis. lectr., 1981, 1983-84; sr. research chemist The Drackett Co., Cin., 1981-83; research and devel. chemist, polymer characterization Tenneco Polymers, Flemington, N.J., 1984—; chemistry and French tutor; Troy, N.Y. and New Brunswick, 1970—; French translator, New Brunswick, 1984—. Named Outstanding Sr. Am. Inst. Chemists, 1974; Russell Sage Coll. scholar, 1970-73; recipient Research Assistantship NIH, 1976-80. Mem. Am. Chem. Soc., AAAS, Soc. Plastics Engrs., Biophys. Soc., ASTM (mem. com. D12 1981-82). Current work: Polymer characterization; polyvinyl chloride technology. Subspecialties: Analytical chemistry; Polymer chemistry. Home: 575 Easton Ave #3R Somerset NJ 08873 Office: Tenneco Polymers River Rd Flemington NJ 08822

MARVIN, JOSEPH GEORGE, research engineer; b. San Jose, Calif., June 9, 1934; s. John and Mary (Thomas) M.; m. Gwendolyn Hoskins, Feb. 21, 1957; children: John, Cheryl, Gregory, Cynthia, Laura. B.S. in Mech. Engring, Santa Clara U., 1956; M.S. in Engring. Mechanics, Stanford U., 1964. Registered profl. engr., Calif. Research scientist Ames Research Ctr., NASA, Moffett Field, Calif., 1956-66, asst. chief fluid mechanics, 1966-71, chief exptl. fluid dynamics, 1971—. Contbr. chpts. to books, articles to profl. jours. Served to 1st lt. U.S. Army, 1956-57. Recipient Shuttle Aerothermo Group award NASA, 1981, Shuttle Aeroheating award, 1982. Fellow AIAA (assoc.); mem. Calif. Soc. Profl. Engrs., Tau Beta Pi. Current Work: Fluid mechanics, turbulent flows, entry heating, facility design, computational fluid dynamics. Subspecialties: Aeronautical engineering; Fluid mechanics. Office: NASA Ames Research Center MS 229-1 Moffett Field CA 94035

MARVIN, RICHARD FREDERICK, geochronologist; b. Bozeman, Mont., May 1, 1926; s. Guy and LaVerne (Birkett) M.; m. Lillian Esther Kabes, Nov. 1, 1955; children—Ellen, Eric. B.S. in Geol. Engring., Mont. Sch. Mines, 1950, M.S. in Geology, 1952. Geologist, U.S. Geol. Survey, Denver, 1952—. Mem Geol. Soc. Am., Am. Geophys. Union, Geol. Soc. of Washington. Current work: Geochronology Subspecialty: Geology. Home: 2470 Miller St Lakewood CO 80215 Office: US Geol Survey MS 963 Denver Fed Ctr Denver CO 80225

MARWAH, JOE, pharmacologist, educator, researcher; b. Uganda, May 27, 1952; came to U.S., 1978, naturalized, 1984; s. Suraj Prakash and Kamla Rani (Kapur) M.; m. Carmen Kim Fonkalsrud, Dec. 20, 1978. B.Sc. with honours, U. London, 1974; Ph.D., U. Alta. Sch. Medicine, 1978. Instr. U. Colo. Health Scis. Center, Denver, 1978-80; scientist Yale U. Sch. Medicine, New Haven, 1980-81; assoc. prof. pharmacology, physiology and neurobiology Ind. U. Sch. Medicine, Terre Haute, 1981—. Contbr. articles to sci. jours. Mem. Soc. for Neurosci., AAAS, Am. Soc. Pharmacology and Exptl. Therapeutics, Am. Physiol. Soc., Soc. Biol. Psychiatry (A.E. Bennet award 1981), N.Y. Acad. Scis., Sigma Xi. Current Work: Neurotransmitters; neuroreceptors; hormones; electrophysiology; monoamines; central nervous system. Subspecialties: Neuropharmacology; Neurology. Office: Dept Pathology U Medicine and Dentistry of NJ 401 Haddon Ave Camden NJ 08103

MARX, DONALD HENRY, plant pathologist; b. Ocean Falls, C., Can., Oct. 3, 1936; s. Edmund N. and Francis (Gorski) M.; m. Selina Van Giesen, Dec. 21, 1957; children: Selina, Teresa, Mary, Donald, Frank. B.S., U. Ga., 1961, M.S., 1962; Ph.D., N.C. State U., 1966. With Forest Service, U.S. Dept. Agr., 1966—, chief plant pathologist, 1973—, dir. inst., 1975—; cons. Internat. Found Sci., Sweden. Contbr. numerous articles to profl. jours. Served with USMC, 1954-57. Recipient U.S. Dept. Agr., Superior Service award, 1970; Ruth Allen award, 1977; Arthur Fleming award, 1975; Barrington Moore award, 1977. Mem. Am. Phytopath. Soc., AAAS, Sigma Xi. Roman Catholic. Current Work: Forest regeneration and reclamation; nursery tree seedling prodn. Subspecialties: Plant growth; Resource management. Home: 1081 Palomino Pass Bogart GA 30622 Office: Inst Mycorrhizal Research and Devel USDA Forest Service Forestry Scis Lab Carlton St Athens GA 30602

MARX, JAMES JOHN, JR., immunologist, researcher; b. Paris, Tex.; s. James John and Grace E. (Beckfeld) M.; m. Mary Alice Kettrick, Aug. 25, 1973; children—Jonathyn Andrew, Christopher James, Scott Michael Civ., St. Vincent Coll., Latrobe, Pa., 1966; M.S. in Immunology, W.Va. U., 1970, Ph.D., 1973. Sr. scientist Marshfield (Wis.) Med. Found., 1973—. Contbr. articles to profl. jours. Mem. nat. Explorer com. Boy Scouts Am.; mem. Wildwood Park Zool. Soc. Served with Med. Service Corps U.S. Army, 1966-68. Mem. Am. Soc. Microbiology, Am. Assn. Clin. Immunology and Allergy, Am. Lung Assn., Am. Acad. Allergy, Reticuloendothelial Soc., Wis. Lung Assn., Am. Assn. Immunologists, Sigma Xi. Roman Catholic. Current Work: Definition of immunologic lung disease - mechanisms of pathogenesis; culture of human tumor cells for defining chemotherapy. Subspecialties: Immunology (medicine); Chemotherapy. Home: M204 Marsh Ln Marshfield WI 54449 Office: 510 N Saint Joseph Ave Marshfield WI 54449

MARX, JAY NEIL, physicist, consultant; b. N.Y.C., Nov. 30, 1945; s. Leo and Lila (Weil) M.; m. Eleanor Fisher, June 4, 1968 (div. June 1975); m. Katya Michele Hope, July 7, 1977; 1 child, Elena Hope. A.B., Columbia U., 1966, M.S., 1969, Ph.D., 1970. Mem. faculty dept. physics Yale U., New Haven, 1969-75; physicist Lawrence Berkeley Lab., Calif., 1976—; cons. U.S. Dept. Energy, Washington, 1983—. Bd. dirs., treas. New Bridge Found., Berkeley, 1976-82; bd. dirs. Safari Sch., Berkeley, 1977-79, Magic Mountain, Sch., Berkeley, 1981-82. Yale U. faculty fellow, 1975. Mem. Am. Phys. Soc., Sigma Xi. Current work: Experiments in study of electron and posiron annihilation at high energy; administration of research in particle physics, accelerator physics and fusion research. Subspecialty: Particle physics. Home: 1821 Delaware St Berkeley CA 94703 Office: Lawrence Berkeley Labs 1 Cyclotron Rd Berkeley CA 94703

MARX, KENNETH ALLAN, chemistry educator; b. Chgo., Mar. 18, 1947; s. Edward Nicholas and Gladys Edith (Fuller) M. B.S. in Chemistry, Calif. State U.-San Diego, 1968; Ph.D. in Chemistry, U. Calif.-Berkeley, 1973. Research assoc. U. Calif.-Berkeley, 1974; postdoctoral fellow U. Edinburgh, Scotland, 1974-76, Worcester Found., Shrewsbury, Mass., 1976-77; prof. chemistry Dartmouth Coll., Hanover, N.H., 1977-84, adj. prof. biochemistry, 1978-84, staff mem. Norris Cotton Cancer Ctr., 1978—; mem. faculty U. Lowell (Mass.), 1984—; cons., reviewer textbook publs. Contbr. articles and revs. to profl. publs. Mem. Nat. Resources Def. Council, N.Y.C., 1981—. Grantee Research Corp., 1979-81, NIH, 1979-83, 81-84. Mem. Am. Soc. Cell Biology, Biophys. Soc. Union Concerned Scientists, Amnesty Internat., Am. Farmland Trust, Common Cause, Am. Chem. Soc., Sigma Xi. Current work: Chromosome structure and function, mitosis, DNA secondary and tertiary structure, DNA-protein interactions, microtubules, virus and bacteriophage structure, transition metal ions, carcinogenesis. Subspecialties: Biophysical chemistry; Molecular biology. Office: Dept Chemistry U Lowell 1 University Ave Lowell MA 01854

MASCARENHAS, JOSEPH PETER, biologist, educator, researcher, consultant; b. Nairobi, Kenya, Nov. 19, 1929; came to U.S., 1957; s. Theotonio C. and Philomena Olive (D'Sousa) M.; m. Patricia Schneider, Jan. 23, 1960; children: Nonika, Shaun. B.Sc. in Agr, U. Poona, India, 1952, M.Sc. in Agr, 1954; Ph.D., U. Calif.-Berkeley, 1962. Research officer Parry & Co., Thiruvalla, India, 1953-56; instr. in biology Amherst Coll., 1962-63; instr. biol. scis. Wellesley Coll., 1963-64, asst. prof. biol. scis., 1964-67; vis. asst. prof. and research assoc. dept. biology M.I.T., 1966-68; assoc. prof. biol. scis.

SUNY-Albany, 1968-74, prof., 1974—; cons. in field. Contbr. numerous articles to sci. jours. Brown Hazen Fund of Research Corp. grantee, 1963-64; NSF grantee, 1965—; Research Found. SUNY grantee, 1969-78; Am. Soybean Assn. grantee, 1980-81; U.S. Dept. Agr. grantee, 1983—. Mem. Am. Soc. Plant Physiologists, Bot. Soc. Am., Soc. Developmental Biology, Am. Soc. Cell Biology, AAAS, Plant Molecular Biology Assn., Internat. Soc. Developmental Biology, Internat. Plant Tissue Culture Assn. Current Work: Molecular regulation of plant development with emphasis on pollen; engineering of plants for heat stress tolerance. Subspecialties: Genetics and genetic engineering (agriculture); Developmental biology. Office: Dept Biol Scis SUNY Albany NY 12222

MASIELLO, RALPH D., electrical engineer; b. N.Y.C., May 5, 1947; s. S. Ralph and Mayo (Groomes) M.; m. Suzanne Perry, Aug. 29, 1970; children—David, Elizabeth. B.S., MIT, 1969, M.S., 1969, Ph.D., 1973. Dir. systems planning projects Control Data, Mpls., 1975—. Mem. Power Engring Soc. of IEEE (vice chmn. power system engring.). Current work: Computer operation of electric power systems. Subspecialty: Computer engineering. Office: Control Data Corp Energy Mgmt Systems div 8100-34th Ave PO Box 0 Minneapolis MN 55440

MASILAMANI, DIVAKAR, chemistry researcher; b. Palayamkottai, Tamil Nadu, India, Dec. 23, 1933; came to U.S., 1962; s. Harry Jesudoss and Anne Cynthia (Devadoss) M.; m. Mary Pluckhahn, Feb. 22, 1971; children—Priya Rebecca, Rachel Padmini. B.Sc. in Chemistry, Am. Coll., Madurai, India, 1954; M.A. in Chemistry, Presidency Coll., Madras, India, 1959; M.A. in Organic Chemistry, Oberlin Coll., Ohio, 1964; Ph.D., U. Notre Dame, 1968. Demonstrator chemistry Am. Coll., 1954-57, lectr., 1959-62; postdoctoral fellow U. Wis., Madison, 1968-70; prof. chemistry Am. Coll., 1970-73; postdoctoral fellow Drexel U., Phila., 1974-75, U. Pa., 1974-75; research assoc. Allied Corp., Morristown, N.J., 1975—. Contbr. articles to profl. jours. Patentee in field. Fulbright grantee, 1962; Lubrizol fellow, 1967. Mem. Am. Chem. Soc., Catalysis Soc. N.Y., Sigma Xi. Democrat. Episcopalain. Current work: Conformational analysis, organic reactions of sulfur dioxide and oxygen, catalysis, electron transfer, reactions in supercritical fluids, organic solvents for gas seperations, photogenic ionophores, carbonium ions, cyclo additions. Subspecialties: Organic chemistry; Catalysis chemistry. Home: 13 Green Hill Rd Morristown NJ 07960 Office: Allied Corp PO Box 1021R Morristown NJ 07960

MASKER, WARREN EDWARD, molecular biologist, research scientist, educator; b. Honesdale, Pa., July 8, 1943; s. Warren Russel and Eva (Chuprevich) M.; m. Aug. 1985. B.S. in Engring. Physics, Lehigh U., 1965; Ph.D. in Physics, U. Rochester, 1970. Postdoctoral fellow dept. radiation biology and biophysics U. Rochester, N.Y., 1969-71; postdoctoral fellow dept. biol. scis. Stanford (Calif.) U., 1971-73; postdoctoral fellow dept. biochemistry Harvard Med. Sch., Boston, 1973-74; mem. research staff biology div. Oak Ridge Nat. Lab., from 1975; prof. grad. sch.biomed. sci. U. Tenn., Oak Ridge, part-time from 1975; now assoc. prof. biochemistry Temple U. Sch. Medicine. Contbr. articles to sci. jours. Am. Cancer Soc. postdoctoral fellow, 1970; Helen Hay Whitney Found. postdoctoral fellow, 1971; USPHS research grantee, 1980. Fellow AAAS; mem. Am. Phys. Soc., Biophys. Soc., Am. Soc. Photobiology, Am. Soc. Microbiology. Current Work: replication, repair, recombination DNA molecular mechanisms of DNA damage and repair, in vitro DNA replication, in vitro packaging of DNA, mutagenesis. Subspecialties: Molecular biology; Microbiology. Home: 22 Mercer Hill Rd Ambler PA 19002 Office: Biochemistry Dept Temple U Med Sch Philadelphia PA 19140

MASLAND, RICHARD HARRY, neurobiologist, neurophysiologist, educator; b. Phila., June 12, 1942; s. Richard Lambert and Mary Hooper (Wootton) M. A.B., Harvard U., 1964; M.S., McGill U., Montreal, Que., Can., 1965, Ph.D., 1968. Fellow Med. Sch., Stanford U., Palo Alto, Calif., 1968-71; research assoc. Med. Sch., Harvard U., Boston, 1971-74, asst. prof. physiology, 1975-80, assoc. prof., 1980—; assoc. neurophysiologist Mass. Gen. Hosp., Boston, 1971—. Author sci. papers. Recipient Career Devel. award NIH, 1975; Woodrow Wilson fellow McGill U., 1965. Mem. Am. Physiol. Soc., Assn. for Research in Vision, Soc. Neurosci. Current work: Cellular physiology of neural interactions. Subspecialties: Neurobiology; Neurophysiology. Office: Mass Gen Hosp 32 Fruit St Boston MA 02114

MASLANSKY, STEVEN PAUL, environmental consultant, educator; b. N.Y.C., Mar. 2, 1948; s. Lawrence and Jean Theda (Brasel) M.; m. Carol Jeanne Lane, Mar. 3, 1949. B.S., Washington and Lee U., 1970; postgrad. SUNY-Cortland, 1971; M.A., Manhattanville Coll., 1976; M.S.C.E., Manhattan Coll., 1982. Cert. geologist Maine, Ind. Chief estimator Griffin Wellpoint, Bronx, N.Y., 1973-74; sr. scientist Malcolm Pirnie Inc., White Plains, N.Y., 1974-81; pres. Geoenviron. Cons. Inc., White Plains, 1982—; adj. asst. prof. SUNY, Purchase, 1982—. Contbr. articles to profl. jours. Served to maj. USAR, 1971-72. Mem. Am. Inst. Profl. Geologists, Assn. Ground Water Sci. and Engrs., Soc. Am. Mil. Engrs., Am. Inst. Hydrology, Nat. Environ. Tng. Assn. Current work: Hazardous materials management, safety training, ground water resource protection and development. Subspecialties: Hydrology; Hazardous waste disposal. Home: 122 Saxon Woods Rd White Plains NY 10605 Office: Geoenvironmental Cons Inc 122 Saxon Woods Rd White Plains NY 10605

MASON, BRIAN HAROLD, geologist, curator; b. N.Z., Apr. 18, 1917; came to U.S., 1947, naturalized, 1953; s. George Harold and Catherine (Fairweather) M. M.Sc., U. New Zealand, 1938; Ph.D., U. Stockholm, 1943. Lectr. geology Canterbury Coll., N.Z., 1944-47; prof. mineralogy Ind. U., 1947-53; chmn. dept. mineralogy Am. Mus. Natural History, N.Y.C., 1953-65; research curator Dept. Mineral Scis. Smithsonian Instn., Washington, from 1965, now curator emeritus. Author: Principles of Geochemistry, 3d edit., 1967, Meteorites, 1962, The Literature of Geology, 1958, (with L. G. Berry) Mineralogy, 1959, (with W.G. Melson) The Lunar Rocks, 1970. Fellow Mineral. Soc. Am., Geol. Soc. Am.; mem. Geochem. Soc., Royal Soc. N.Z., Swedish Geol. Soc. Subspecialty: Geochemistry. Office: Dept Mineral Scis Smithsonian Instn Washington DC 20560

MASON, CAROLINE FAITH VIBERT, chemist; b. Harrogate, England, Feb. 24, 1942; came to U.S. 1967, naturalized 1974; d. Thomas Vibert and Edith Jane Legerton (Smith) Pearce; m. Rodney Jackson Mason, Feb. 1, 1969; children—Vanessa, Rosalind. B.S., London U., England, 1964, Ph.D., 1967. Analytical chemist Ortho Research Found., Raritan, N.J., 1973-74; chemist Los Alamos Nat. Lab., 1975—; cons. Particle Tech., Inc., Los Alamos, 1973-76. Author (with others): Inorganic Reactions and Mechanisms, 1984. Mem. Am. Chem. Soc. Current work: Hydrogen as an energy source, isotope separation. Subspecialties: Inorganic chemistry; Thermodynamics. Home: 148 Piedra Loop Los Alamos NM 87544 Office: Los Alamos Nat Lab IT-3 B231 Los Alamos NM 87545

MASON, CHARLES PERRY, biologist; b. Newport, R.I., Aug. 12, 1932; s. Charles Perry and Bernice Marie (Passmore) M.; m. Harriet Gale, Sept. 7, 1958; children: Grant Vause, Gale Perrie. B.S., U. R.I., 1954; M.S., U. Wis., Madison, 1958; Ph.D., Cornell U., 1961. Asst. prof., then assoc. prof. biology Hamline U., 1961-67; assoc. prof. Gustavus Adolphus Coll., 1967-81, prof., 1981—; vis. scientist Gray Freshwater Biol. Inst., U. Minn., summers 1977-81. Mem. Phycological Soc. Am., Internat. Phycological Soc., Nature Conservancy, Minn. Acad. Sci. Lutheran. Current Work: Physiological ecology of algae. Subspecialties: Ecology (environmental science); Physiology (biology). Home: 905 S 5th St Saint Peter MN 56082 Office: Dept Biology Gustavus Adolphus Coll Saint Peter MN 5608

MASON, DAVID DICKENSON, statistics educator; b. Abingdon, Va., Jan. 22, 1917; s. William Thomas and Eva (Dorton) M.; m. Virginia Louise Pendleton, Oct. 28, 1944; children: Marjorie F., David P. B.A., King Coll., 1936; M.S. (Acad. Merit fellow), Va. Poly. Inst., 1938; postgrad., Ohio State U., 1939-40; Ph.D., N.C. State U., 1948. Asst. soil scientist Va. Poly. Inst., 1938-39; asst. prof. soils Ohio State U., 1947-49; prin. biometrician Dept. Agr., Beltsville, Md., 1949-53; prof. stats. N.C. State U., 1953-62, prof., head dept. stats., 1962-81, emeritus prof. and head, 1981—; head Inst. Stats., 1962-81, emeritus head, 1981—; Sr. cons. United Fruit Co., Boston, 1957—. Contbr. articles to profl. jours. Instl. rep. So. Regional Edn. Bd. com. statistics, 1963—, chmn., 1973-75; Bd. dirs. Triangle Univs. Computation Center Corp., chmn., 1968-70. Served with AUS, 1941-45. Fellow Am. Statis. Assn., Am. Soc. Agronomy, Soil Sci. Soc. Am.; mem. Biometric Soc., Sigma Xi, Phi Kappa Phi, Gamma Sigma Delta. Presbyn. (elder, deacon). Club: Rotarian. Subspecialty: Statistics. Home: 4212 Arbutus Dr Raleigh NC 27612 Office: Dept Statistics Box 8203 NC State U Raleigh NC 27695

MASON, EDWARD ALLEN, scientist, educator; b. Atlantic City, Sept. 2, 1926; s. Edward Paul and Olive Margaret (Lorah), M.; m. Ann Courtenay Laufman, July 6, 1952; children—Catherine Hubbard, Stephen Edward, Elizabeth Margaret, Sarah Lois. B.S., Va. Poly. Inst., 1947; Ph.D., MIT, 1951; A.M., Brown U., 1968. Research assoc. MIT, 1950-52; NRC fellow U. Wis., 1952-53; mem. faculty Pa. State U., 1953-55, U. Md., 1955-67; prof. chemistry and engring. Brown U., Providence, 1967, Newport Rogers prof. chemistry, 1983—; vis. prof. physics Leiden (Netherlands) U., 1981-82. Author: (with J.T. Vanderslice and H.W. Schamp) Thermodynamics, 1966, (with T.H. Spurling) Virial Equation of State, 1969, (with E.W. McDaniel) Mobility and Diffusion of Ions in Gases, 1973, (with A.P. Malinauskas) Gas Transport in Porous Media: The Dusty-Gas Model, 1983; Assoc. editor: Physics of Fluids, 1963-65, Jour. Chem. Physics, 1964-66; adv. editor: Case Studies in Atomic Physics, 1971-75; editoria bd.: Jour. Membrane Sci., 1981. Fellow Am. Phys. Soc., Washington Acad. Scis. (Phys. Scis. award 1962), Random Soc.; mem. AAAS, Am. Assn. Physics Tchrs., Sigma Xi. Subspecialties: Theoretical chemistry; Atomic and molecular physics. Home: 26 Nayatt Rd Barrington RI 02806 Office: Brown Univ Engring Div Providence RI 02912

MASON, EDWARD ARCHIBALD, chemical and nuclear engineer; b. Rochester, N.Y., Aug. 9, 1924; s. Henry Archibald and Monica (Brayer) M.; m. Barbara Jean Earley, Apr. 15, 1950; children—Thomas E., Kathleen M., Paul D., Mark J., Anne M., Mary Beth. B.S., U. Rochester, 1945; M.S., Mass. Inst. Tech., 1948, Sc.D., 1950. Asst. prof. chem. engring. MIT, Cambridge, 1950-53, asso. prof. nuclear engring., 1957-63, prof., 1963-77, dept. head, 1971-75; commr. Nuclear Regulatory Commn., Washington, 1975-77; v.p. research Standard Oil Co. (Ind.) (now Amoco Corp.), Chgo., 1977—; dir. research Ionics, Inc., Cambridge, Mass., 1953-57; sr. design engr. Oak Ridge Nat. Lab., 1957; mem. adv. com. reactor safeguards AEC, 1972-75; cons. other govt. agys., industry; dir. Cetus Corp., Commonwealth Edison Co., MR, Inc. Contbr. articles to profl. jours. Mem. adv. com. M.I.T., U. Chgo., U. Tex., Ga. Inst. Tech.; bd. dirs. John Crerar Library. Served with USNR, 1943-46. NSF Sr. Postdoctoral fellow, 1965-66. Fellow Am. Acad. Arts and Scis., Am. Nuclear Soc., Am. Inst. Chemists; mem. Nat. Acad. Engring. (councilor 1978-84), N.Y. Acad. Scis., Am. Inst. Chem. Engrs. (R.E. Wilson award in nuclear chem. engring. 1978), Western Soc. Engrs., Am. Chem. Soc., AAAS, Phi Beta Kappa, Sigma Xi, Tau Beta Pi. Club: Hinsdale (Ill.) Golf. Patentee in field. Subspecialty: Nuclear engineering. Office: Amoco Corp 200 E Randolph Dr Chicago IL 60601

MASON, GEORGE ROBERT, surgeon, educator; b. Rochester, N.Y., June 10, 1932; s. George Mitchell and Marjorie Louise (Hooper) M.; m. Grace Louise Bransfield, Feb. 4, 1956; children—Douglas, Marcia, David. B.A., Oberlin Coll., 1955; M.D. with honors, U. Chgo., 1957; Ph.D. in Physiology, Stanford U., 1968. Diplomate Am. Bd. Surgery. Teaching asst. in pathology U. Chgo., 1954-56, rotating intern, 1957-58; NIH postdoctoral fellow, USPHS fellow in surgery Stanford Univ. Hosps., Calif., 1960-62, asst. resident in surgery, 1962-63, resident in surgery, 1963-64, sr. and chief resident, 1964-66; teaching asst. in physiology Stanford U., 1960-62, acting instr. surgery, 1965-66, instr., 1966-67, asst. prof., 1967-70, assoc. prof., 1970-71; prof. physiology U. Md., 1971-80, prof., chmn. dept. surgery, 1971-80; prof., chmn. dept. surgery U. Calif.-Irvine, 1980—; staff surgeon VA Hosp., Long Beach, Calif.; attending surgeon Long Beach Meml. Hosp. Contbr. numerous articles to profl. jours. and chpts. to books. Served to capt. M.C., USAFR, 1958-60. Grantee NASA, NIH. Mem. Soc. Clin. Surgery (chmn. membership com. 1977-78), Am. Bd. Surgery (bd. dirs. 1980-86, chmn. examining com. 1983—), ACS (chmn. com. on surg. edn. in med. schs. 1983-85, Balt. Acad. Surgery (pres. 1977-78), U. Md. Surg. Soc. (sec. 1977-80), Am. Acad. Med. Dirs., AMA, Am. Assn. for Thoracic Surgery, AAUP, Am. Coll. Chest Physicians, Am. Gastroent. Assn., Am. Physiol. Soc., Am. Surg. Assn., Calif. Med. Assn., Halsted Soc., Soc. Clin. Surgery, Soc. Univ. Surgeons, Sigma Xi, Alpha Omega Alpha. Current work: Gastrointestinal neurophysiology and neuropharmacology. Subspecialty: Surgery. Home: 18712 Via Torino Irvine CA 92715 Office: U Calif-Irvine Med Ctr 101 City Dr S Orange CA 92668

MASON, JAMES OSTERMANN, public health research center director; b. Salt Lake City, June 19, 1930; s. Ambrose Stanton and Neoma (Thorup) M.; m. Lydia Maria Smith, Dec. 29, 1952; children—James, Susan, Bruce, Ralph, Samuel, Sara, Benjamin. B.A., U. Utah, 1954, M.D., 1958; M.P.H., Harvard U., 1963, Dr. P.H., 1967. Intern, Johns Hopkins Hosp., Balt., 1958-59; resident in internal medicine Peter Bent Brigham Hosp., Harvard Med. Service, Boston, 1961-62; chief epidemic intelligence service CDC, Atlanta, 1959, chief hepatitis surveillance unit, 1960, chief surveillance sect. epidemiology br., 1961, dep. dir. Bur. Labs., 1964-68, dep. dir., 1969-70, dir., 1983—; chief infectious diseases Latter Day Saints Hosp. and asst. prof. dept. medicine and preventive medicine U. Utah, 1968-69; commr. health Services Corp., Ch. of Jesus Christ of Latter Day Saints, 1970-76; dep. dir. health Utah Div. Health, 1976-78; assoc. prof., chmn. div. community medicine, dept. family and community medicine, U. Utah, 1978-79; exec. dir. Utah Dept. Health, 1979-83; physician, cons. to med. services Salt Lake VA Hosp., 1977-83; clin. prof. community health Emory U. Sch. Medicine, 1984—. Assoc. editor Diagnostic Procedures for Bacterial, Mycotic and Parasitic Infections, 5th edit. 1970. Contbr. articles to profl. jours. Mem. recombinant DNA adv. com. NIH, 1979-83; exec. com. Thrasher Research Found. tech. adv. com., 1980—; mem. Robert Wood Johnson Found. program for hosp. initiatives in long-term care, 1982—; bd. dirs. Deseret Mut. Benefit Assn., 1972-79; mem. sci. and tech. adv. com. UNDP/World bank/WHO spl. program for research and tng. in tropical diseases, 1984—, others. Mem. Am. Pub. Health Assn., AMA, Utah Med. Assn. (trustee 1979-83), Utah Acad. Preventive Medicine (pres. 1982-83), Utah Pub. Health Assn. (pres. 1980-82). Lodge: Rotary. Current work: Health promotion, disease prevention, public health. Subspecialty: Preventive medicine. Office: CDC 1600 Clifton Rd NE Atlanta GA 30333

MASON, JOHN MONTGOMERY, JR., marine fisheries biologist; b. Bridgeport, Conn., July 9, 1945; s. John Montgomery and Jayne (Hutton) M.; m. Barrie Orr, June 8, 1974; 1 son, Jeremy M. B.A., DePauw U., 1967; M.S., U. R.I., 1976. Cert. fisheries scientist Am. Fisheries Soc. cert. Am. Inst. Fishery Research Biologists. Research assoc. Woods Hole (Mass.) Oceanographic Instn., 1970-79; sr. fishery biologist Mid-Atlantic Fishery Mgmt. Council, Dover, Del., 1979-80; research scientist N.Y. State Div. Marine Resources, Stony Brook, 1980—; advisor U.S. sect. Internat. Commn. Conservation of Atlantic Tunas, 1979—. Contbr. articles to sci. jours. Vestryman, dir. Sunday Sch., St. Mark's Episcopal Ch., Westhampton, N.Y.; co-founder N.Y. Sport Fishing Fedn., 1982. Rector scholar DePauw U., 1963-67. Mem. Am. Fisheries Soc. (life; cert. fisheries scientist), AAAS, Am. Inst. Fishery Research Biologists, Internat. Game Fish Assn., Babylon Tuna Club (hon.), Va. Bluewater Gamefish Assn. (hon.), Atlantic Tuna Club, Nat. Coalition Marine Conservation (adv. bd. North Atlantic region 1982-83), Phi Sigma. Current Work: Study of marine fish and fisheries for determination of management needs including research on catch and effort, species distribution, behavior and population structure. Subspecialties: Resource management; Marine biology. Home: 8 Annette Ln East Moriches NY 11940 Office: NY State Dept Environ Conservation Bldg 40 SUNY Stony Brook NY 11794

MASON, MARGARET JEANNE, veterinarian, researcher; b. Albuquerque, July 13, 1956; d. Harry and Alice Lee (Sawyers) M. B.S., N.Mex. Tech. Coll., 1977; D.V.M., Colo. State U., 1983. Research asst. N.Mex. Tech. Coll., Socorro, 1975-77; research technologist Med. Sch., U. N.Mex., Albuquerque, 1977-79; veterinarian, immunologist Inhalation Toxicology Research Inst., Albuquerque, 1983—. Pfizer veterinary scholar, 1983. Mem. AVMA, N.Mex. Vet. Med. Assn., Vet. Cancer Soc., Phi Kappa Phi, Phi Zeta. Current work: understanding the role of the immune system in the lung in health and disease; how the immune system is altered by neoplasia and aging. Subspecialties: Clinical veterinary medicine; Immunobiology and immunology. Home: 1304 Kentucky St NE Albuquerque NM 87110 Office: Inhalation Toxicology Research Inst PO Box 5890 Albuquerque NM 87185

MASON, NORMAN RONALD, biochemist; b. Rochester, Minn., Nov. 20, 1929; s. Harold Lawrence and Maude (Mackenzie) M.; m. Nancy M. Bumgarner, June 24, 1953; children—Charles Norman, Susan Elizabeth. B.A., U. Chgo., 1950; M.A., U. Utah, 1956, Ph.D., 1959. Lab. Asst. U. Utah, Salt Lake City, 1954-55; research instr. U. Miami Med. Sch., Fla., 1959-60, research asst. prof., 1960-64; investigator Howard Hughes Med. Inst., Miami, 1959-64; sr. scientist Eli Lilly and Co., Indpls., 1964—. Contbr. articles to profl. jours. Active local United Methodist Ch., Indpls., 1964—. Mem. Endocrine Soc., Am. Chem. Soc., AAAS, Soc. for Neurosci. Current work: Research on serotonin receptors in brain, control of receptors, action of compounds on serotin receptors, development of serotonin agonists and antagonists, effect on serotonergic agents on brain and behavior. Subspecialties: Neurochemistry; Neuropharmacology. Home: 7301 Steinmeier Dr Indianapolis IN 46250 Office: Lilly Research Labs Eli Lilly and Co Indianapolis IN 46285

MASON, RODNEY JACKSON, physicist; b. N.Y.C., Feb. 27, 1939; s. Rodney Jackson and Elizabeth Lorraine (Maher) Weismuller; m. Caroline Faith Vibert Pearce, Feb. 1, 1969; children—Vanessa Jane, Rosalind Jennifer. B.A. in Physics, Cornell U., 1960, Ph.D. in Aerospace Engring., 1964. Fulbright grad. fellow Inst. Plasma Physik, Garching, West Germany, 1964-65; asst. prof. and Ford fellow MIT, Cambridge, Mass., 1965-67; mem. staff Bell Labs., Whippany, N.J., 1967-72, Los Alamos Nat. Lab., 1972—; cons. Canadian Nat. Sci. and Engring. Research Council, 1981—. Jour. referee several profl. jours., 1969—; contbr. articles to profl. jours. Fellow, spl. engring. fellow Cornell U., 1960-62, vis. fellow Imperial Coll., London, 1984; recipient Disting. Performance award Los Alamos Nat. Lab., 1981. Fellow Am. Phys. Soc.; mem. IEEE (sr.), AAAS. Current work: Computational modeling of laser and pulse-power generated collisionless and collisional plasma flows in self-consistent electric and magnetic fields. Subspecialties: Laser fusion; Plasma physics. Home: 148 Piedra Loop Los Alamos NM 87544 Office: Los Alamos Nat Lab X-1 E531 Los Alamos NM 87545

MASORO, EDWARD JOSEPH, physiologist; b. Oakland, Calif., Dec. 28, 1924; s. Edward Joseph and Louise Elizabeth (DePaoli) M.; m. Barbara Muir Weikel, June 25, 1947. A.B., U. Calif.-Berkeley, 1947, Ph.D., 1950. Asst. prof. Queen's U., Kingston, Ont., Can., 1950-52; asst. prof., then assoc. prof. Tufts U. Sch. Medicine, Boston, 1952-62; research assoc. prof. U. Wash., Seattle, 1962-64; prof., chmn. Med. Coll. Pa., Phila., 1964-73; prof., chmn. dept. physiology U. Tex. Health Sci. Ctr., San Antonio, 1973—; mem. aging rev. com. Nat. Inst. Aging, 1981-84, mem. bd. sci. counselors, 1985—. Author: Acid-Base Regulation, 1971; editor: CRC Handbook of Physiology in Aging, 1982; editor biol. scis. Exptl. Aging Research, 1980—; mem. editorial bd. Jour. Gerontology, 1979—; contbr. articles to profl. jours. Nat. Heart Lung, Blood Inst. grantee, 1978—; Nat. Inst. Aging grantee, 1979—. Fellow Gerontol. Soc. Am. (v.p. 1978-79), AAAS; mem. Am. Physiol. Soc. Current work: Study of basic nature of aging process; investigation of role of nutrition as modulator of aging process. Subspecialty: Physiology (biology). Home: 221 E Guenther St San Antonio TX 78204 Office: Dept Physiology U Tex Health Sci Ctr 7703 Floyd Curl Dr San Antonio TX 78284

MASOUREDIS, SERAFEIM P., physician, educator; b. Detroit, Nov. 14, 1922; s. Panagiotis George and Lemonia (Moniodis) M.; m. Marion Helen Mykytew, Oct. 4, 1943; children: Claudia, Linus. A.B., U. Mich., 1943; M.D., 1948; Ph.D. in Med. Physics, U. Calif., Berkeley, 1952. Intern San Francisco Hosp., 1952-53; research asso. Donnor Lab., Berkeley, Calif., 1953-54; resident in medicine U. Calif., San Francisco Gen. Hosp., 1954-55; asst. prof. pathology, asst. dir. central blood bank U. Pitts., 1955-58, assoc. prof., 1958-59; assoc. prof. preventive medicine U. Calif., San Francisco, 1959-62; assoc. prof. medicine, dir. Moffitt Hosp. Blood Bank, 1962-67; exec. dir. Milw. Blood Center, 1967-69; prof. medicine Marquette U. Sch. Medicine, 1967-69; prof. pathology, dir. Univ. Hosp. Blood Bank, U. Calif., San Diego, 1969—; cons. WHO, 1966-67; mem. merit rev. bd. hematology VA, 1969-75; sci. counselor div. biologics standards NIH, 1971-72; bd. dirs. Milw. Blood Center, 1969—, San Diego Blood Bank, 1970-76. Contbr. articles to profl. jours. Mem. Western Soc. Clin. Research, Am. Assn. Blood Banks, Am. Assn. Cancer Research, Am. Fedn. Clin. Research, Am. Assn. Immunologists, Am. Physiol. Soc. Human Genetics, Brit. Soc. Immunology, Central Soc. Clin. Research, Internat. Soc. Blood Transfusion, Internat. Soc. Hematology, Soc. Exptl. Biology and Medicine, Western Assn. Physicians. Greek Orthodox. Current Work: Blood group antigens, red cell membrane biochemistry, hemolytic anemias, blood group antibodies. Subspecialties: Hematology; Immunology (medicine). Office: U Calif Sch Medicine San Diego La Jolla CA 92093

MASSAD, CAROLYN EMRICK, educational psychologist, psychometrician, educator, consultant; b. Cleve., Nov. 24, 1935; d. Steve George and Mary Elizabeth (Evans) Emrick; married; 1 son, Mark Isam. B.S., Kent State U., 1956, M.Ed., 1963, Ph.D., 1967. Tchr., Havana, 1955, Solon (Ohio) Bd. Edn., 1957-67; assoc. examiner Ednl. Testing Service, Princeton, N.J., 1967-74, examiner, 1974-80, sr. examiner, group head test devel., 1980—; cons. La. Dept. Edn., Bermuda Dept. Edn. Internat. Assn. Evaluation of Ednl. Achievement, 1972-83. Author: English as a Foreign Language in 10 Countries, 1975; author, editor: Handbook of Information for Evaluation and Assessment, 1977; rev. editor: Am. Ednl. Research Jour, 1972-75. Spencer Found. postdoctoral fellow Stockholm, 1972-73; NDEA fellow, 1961, 64. Mem. Am. Ednl. Research Assn., Am. Psychol. Assn., Nat. Council Measurement in Edn., Internat. Reading Assn. Republican. Roman Catholic. Current Work: Development of measures for job licensure/selection; development of language skills and how they can be measured/assessed. Subspecialties: Developmental psychology; Psychometrics. Home: 303 Emmons Dr 5B Princeton NJ 08540 Office: Educational Testing Service Rosedale Rd Princeton NJ 08540

MASSARO, EDWARD JOSEPH, biochemist, toxicologist, research scientist; b. Passaic, N.J., June 7, 1933; s. Anthony and Sarah (Topchik) M.; m. Janet Carole Elser, Nov. 23, 1953 (div. 1977); children: David Alan, Anita Diane, Paul Anthony, Steven Joseph; m. Arlene Margaret Mahood, May 31, 1978. A.B., Rutgers U., 1955; M.A., U. Tex., 1958, Ph.D. in Biochemistry, 1962. Instr. Blinn Coll., Brenham, Tex., 1956-57; research assoc. Johns Hopkins U., Balt., 1965, Yale U., 1965-68; asst. prof. biochemistry SUNY, Buffalo, 1968-71, assoc. prof., 1971-75, prof., 1975-78, research prof., 1978-79; dir. chem. carcinogenesis Mason Research Inst., Worcester, Mass., 1977-78, dir. toxicology and chem. carcinogenesis, 1978; dir. Center for Air Environment Studies, Pa. State U., 1978-85, prof. toxicology, dept. vet. sci., 1978—; dir. inhalation toxicology div. EPA Health Effects Research Lab., Research Triangle Park, N.C., 1983-85, sr. research scientist, 1985—; adj. prof. toxicology program U. N.C., 1984—; cons. in field. Contbr. articles to profl. jours. Bd. dirs. Environ. Clearing House, Inc., Buffalo, 1973; bd. dirs. Central Pa. Lung and Health Service Assn., 1979-85, mem. exec. com. of adv. bd., 1981-85, mem. budget and program com., 1981-85, v.p., 1981-84. USPHS fellow, 1960-62, 62-63, 63-65; fellow Rachel Carson Coll., SUNY, Buffalo, 1968-78. Mem. AAAS, Am. Assn. for Lab. Animal Sci., Am. Assn. Pathologists, Am. Coll. Toxicology, Am. Soc. Biol. Chemists, Am. Soc. Icthyologists and Herpetologists, Am. Soc. for Pharmacology and Exptl. Therapeutics, Am. Wildlife Fedn., Behavioral Teratology Soc., Internat. Assn. Bioinorganic Scientists, Internat. Assn. Water Pollution Research, Internat. Soc. for Study of Xenobiolics, Internat. Union Pharmacology, Internat. Soc. for Ectotoxicology and Environ. Safety, Nat. Soc. for Med. Research, N.Y. Acad. Scis., Soc. for Environ. Geochemistry and Health, Soc. Environ. Toxicology and Chemistry, Soc. for Prodn. of Old Fishes, Soc. Toxicology, Teratology Soc., Toxicology Forum, Sigma Xi. Current Work: xenobiotic metabolism, heavy metal toxicology; perinatal toxicology of lead. Subspecialty: Biochemistry (biology). Office: EPA Health Effects Research Lab Triangle Park NC 27711

MASSEY, GAIL AUSTIN, electrical engineering educator; b. El Paso, Tex., Dec. 2, 1936; s. Albert Harley and Mary Frances (Edmondson) M.; m. Barbara Suzanne Koch, July 2, 1960. B.S., Calif. Inst. Tech., 1959; M.S., Stanford U., 1967, Ph.D., 1970. Engr. Raytheon Co., Santa Barbara, Calif., 1959-63; sr. engr. GTE Sylvania, Mountain View, Calif., 1963-72; assoc. prof. Oreg. Grad. Ctr., Beaverton, 1972-74, prof., 1974-80; prof. elec. engring. San Diego State U., 1981—; cons. in field. Contbr. chpts. to books and articles to profl. jours. Fellow Optical Soc. Am.; mem. IEEE, Acoustical Soc. Am., Soc. Photo-Optical Instrumentation Engrs. Current Work: Generation of electron beams and images using laser-excited nonlinear photoelectric emission; laser instrumentation for remote measurement of gas temperature and density. Subspecialties: Laser instrumentation; Nonlinear optics. Home: 7107 Birchcreek Rd San Diego CA 92119 Office: San Diego State Dept Engring San Diego CA 92182

MASSEY, JAMES KENDALL, engineering educator, consultant; b. Daytona Beach, Fla., Jan. 3, 1953; s. James Gerald and Vivian Malinda (Bellamy) M.; m. Karen Lee Parker, Mar. 14, 1974; 1 child, Lee. A.A., U. Fla., 1973, B.S. in Elec. Engring., 1976, M. Engring., 1978. Teaching asst. U. Fla., Gainesville, 1974-76, grad. research asst., 1976-78; cons. engring., Gainesville, 1977-79; prof. engring. U. Fla., Gainesville, 1979—. Contbr. articles to profl. jours.; co-chmn. confs. Recipient Col. Frank Borman Falcon award CAP, 1977; Fla. Regents scholar, 1971; U.S. Air Force scholar, 1971. Fellow Inst. for Advanced

Study of the Communications Processes; mem. IEEE, IEEE Computer Soc., IEEE Engring. in Medicine and Biology Soc., IEEE Acoustics, Speech and Signal Processing Soc., Alpha Epsilon Pi. Democrat. Mormon. Club, U. Fla. Judo. Current work: Principally involved in use of computers to collect, manage and retrieve large free text databases; secondary emphasis on computer communications standards. Subspecialties: Database systems; Information systems, storage, and retrieval (computer science). Home: 3951 SW 1st Ave Gainesville FL 32607 Office: U Fla PO Box J-356 Gainesville FL 32610

MASSEY, ROBERT STEWART, physicist; b. Bartlesville, Okla., Oct. 20, 1950; s. Phillip Stewart and Ruth Ellen (Wright) M.; m. Pamela Sue Wilson, Aug. 21, 1971; B.S. in Physics, U. Okla., 1971; M.S. in Physics, U. Wash.-Seattle, 1973, Ph.D. in Physics, 1976. Staff Los Alamos Nat. Lab., N. Mex., 1976-83, group leader, 1983—. Contbr. articles to profl. jours. Mem. Am. Phys. Soc., Phi Beta Kappa. Current work: Group leader for reversed-field pinch physics; experimental physics research on two reversed-field pinch experiments. Subspecialties: Plasma physics; Nuclear fusion. Office: Los Alamos Nat Lab Los Alamos NM 87545

MASSEY, WALTER EUGENE, physicist, university official; b. Hattiesburg, Miss., Apr. 5, 1938; s. Almar Clevel and Essie (Nelson) M.; m. Shirley Streeter, Oct. 25, 1969; children: Keith Anthony, Eric Eugene. B.S., Morehouse Coll., 1958; M.A., Washington U., St. Louis, 1966, Ph.D., 1966. Physicist Argonne (Ill.) Nat. Lab., 1966-68; asst. prof. physics U. Ill., Urbana, 1968-70; asso. prof. Brown U., Providence, 1970-75; prof., dean Brown U. (Coll.), 1975-79; cons. Argonne Nat. Lab., dir., 1979—; v.p. for research U. Chgo., 1982—; mem. NSB, NSF, 1978—; cons. Nat. Acad. Scis., 1973-76. Contbr. articles on sci. edn. in secondary schs. and in theory of quantum fluids to profl. jours. Trustee Brown U., 1980—, Mus. Sci. and Industry, Chgo., 1980—. NSF fellow, 1962; NDEA fellow, 1959-60. Fellow AAAS (dir. 1981—); Mem. Am. Phys. Soc. (councillor-at-large 1980—), Am. Assn. Physics Tchrs. (Disting. Service award 1975), Sigma Xi. Subspecialties: Condensed matter physics; Theoretical physics. Home: 4950 Chicago Beach Dr Chicago IL 60615 Office: Argonne Nat Lab Argonne IL 60439

MASTERS, ROBERT EDWARD LEE, neural re-education researcher, psychotherapist, human potential educator; b. St. Joseph, Mo., Jan. 4, 1927; s. Robert and Katherine (Leeper) M.; m. Jean Houston, May 8, 1965. B.A. in Philosophy, U. Mo.-Columbia, 1951; Ph.D. in Clin. Psychology, Humanistic Psychology Inst., 1974. Dir. Library of Sex Research, N.Y.C., 1962-66. Dir. Sensory Imagery Program, 1965-68; dir. research Found. for Mind Research, N.Y.C. and Pomona, N.Y., 1968—; dir. Zarathustra Project, Pomona, 1980—; co-dir. Human Capacities Tng. Program, Ramapo, N.J., 1982—; pvt. practice psychotherapy, neural re-edn.; prin. tchr. Psychophys. Method Tchr. Tng. Programs, 1980—; pres. Human Capacities Corp., Pomona, 1982—; prin. tchr. Hypnotherapist Tng., Pomona, 1982—; co-leader seminars U.S. and abroad; pres. Kontrakundabuffer Corp., Pomona, 1983—. Author: books, including Eros and Evil, 1962, (with J. Houston) Varieties of Psychedelic Experience, 1966, Mind Games, 1972, Listening to the Body, 1978; author: books, including Psychophysical Method Exercises Vols. I-VI, 1983. Served with USN, 1945-46, PTO. Grantee Erickson Found, 1966; Kleiner Found, 1968; Babcock Found, 1970; Doris Duke Found., 1972. Mem. Am. Psychol. Assn., Can. Psychol. Assn., Authors League Am., N.Y. Acad. Scis., Am. Assn. Sex Educators, Counselors and Therapists, AAAS, Assn. Humanistic Psychology, Assn. Masters Psychophys. Method (hon. pres.). Current Work: Human potentials; genius and high-level creativity; hypnosis and altered states of consciousness; neural re-education; body image; movement disinhibition; nonverbal communication; parapsychology; sexology; applications of brain research to education. Subspecialties: Gerontology; Neuropsychology. Office: Foundation for Mind Research PO Box 3300 Pomona NY 10970

MASTRONARDI, RICHARD, engineering administrator; b. N.Y.C., Nov. 14, 1947; s. Pasquale Severio and Lucy Lillian (Spoto) M.; m. Susan Elizabeth Kessler, Apr. 25, 1970; 1 child, Sara Elizabeth. B.S. in Aero. Engring, Rensselaer Poly. Inst., 1969; M.B.A., Northeastern U., 1975. Aeroelastic design engr. Boeing Co., Seattle, 1969-70; exptl. flight test engr. Sikorsky Helicopter, Stratford, Conn., 1970; project engr. Atkins & Merrill Inc., Ashland, Mass., 1970-75; pres. Aerowedge Inc., Medfield, Mass., 1975-81; v.p. engring. Am. Sci. and Engring. Inc., Cambridge, Mass., 1975—; cons. various orgns. Co-chmn. New Start Com. (Vietnam refugees), Medfield, 1980—. Mem. AIAA, ASME, Planetary Soc., NASA Get Away Spl. User Com. Inventor proximity rotary table and elevator for CT scanner, hollow electro-less nickle baffle tube, aerowedge truck wind deflector. Current Work: Engineering manager for developing X-ray and higher energy high-resolution digital inspection systems for medical, security, astrophysics and non-destructive testing, medical digital radiography and low dosage systems. Subspecialties: Aerospace engineering and technology; X-ray high energy astrophysics. Home: 55 South St Medfield MA 02052 Office: American Science and Engring Inc Fort Washington Cambridge MA 02139

MASURSKY, HAROLD, geologist; b. Ft. Wayne, Ind., Dec. 23, 1923; s. Louis and Celia (Ochstein) M.; 4 children. B.S. in Geology, Yale U., 1943, M.S., 1951; D.Sc. (hon.), No. Ariz. U., 1981. With U.S. Geol. Survey, 1951—, chief astrogeologic studies br., 1967-71; chief scientist U.S. Geol. Survey (Center Astrogeology), Flagstaff, Ariz., 1971-75, sr. scientist, 1975—; lunar orbiter U.S. Geol. Survey (Surveyor Projects), 1965-67; team leader, prin. investigator TV experiment (Mariner Mars), 1971; co-investigator Apollo field geol. team Apollo 16 and 17, also mem. Apollo orbital sci. photog. team, Apollo site selection group; leader Viking landing site staff, dep. team leader orbiter visual imaging systems (Viking Mars), 1975; mem. Voyager teams (Jupiter, Saturn)), 1977, chmn. mission ops. group Venus Pioneer Mission, 1978, co-chmn. mission operational group Galileo Mission, 1981, mission ops. leader, radar team Venus Orbiting Imaging Radar Mission, 1981; mem. Space Sci. Adv. Com., 1978-81, solar system exploration com., 1980-83; mem. Space Sci. Bd., 1982—; v.p. com. B, COSPAR; sec. Coordinating Com. of Moon and Planets. Asso. editor: Icarus, Geophys. Rev. Letters. Served with AUS, 1943-46. Fellow Geol. Soc. Am. (asso. editor bull., pres. planetary geol. div.), AAAS, Am. Geophys. Union, Internat. Astron. Union (commns.), Am. Astron. Assn., Com. Space Research. Subspecialties: Geology; Satellite studies. Address: US Geol Survey 2255 N Gemini St Flagstaff AZ 86001

MATARAZZO, JOSEPH DOMINIC, psychologist; b. Caiazzo, Italy, Nov. 12, 1925; s. Nicholas and Adeline (Mastroianni) M.; m. Ruth Wood Gadbois, Mar. 26, 1949; children: Harris, Elizabeth, Sara. Student, Columbia U., 1944; B.A., Brown U., 1946; M.S., Northwestern U., 1950, Ph.D., 1952. Fellow in med. psychology Washington U. Sch. Medicine, 1950-51; instr. Washington U., 1951-53, asst. prof., 1953-55; research asso. Harvard Med. Sch., asso. psychologist Mass. Gen. Hosp., 1955-57; prof., head med. psychol. dept. Oreg. Health Scis. U., Portland, 1957—; mem. nursing research and patient care study sect., behavioral medicine study sect. NIH; spl. research com. Am. Cancer Soc.; Bd. regents Uniformed Services U. Health Scis., 1974-80. Author: Wechsler's Measurement and Appraisal of Adult Intelligence, 5th edit., 1972, (with A.N. Wiens) The Interview: Research on its Anatomy and Structure, 1972, (with Harper and Wiens) Nonverbal Communication, 1978; asso. editor: Human Orgn, 1954-66; editorial bd.: Jour. Clin. Psychology, 1962—, Contemporary Psychology, 1962-70, 80—, Jour. Community Psychology, 1974-81, Behavior Modification, 1976—, Intelligence: An Interdisciplinary Jour, 1976, Jour. Behavioral Medicine, 1977—, Profl. Psychology, 1978—, Jour. Cons. and Clin. Psychology, 1978—. Served to ensign USNR, 1943-47; capt. Res. Recipient Hofheimer prize Am. Psychiat. Assn., 1962. Fellow Am. Psychol. Assn. (pres. div. health psychology 1978-79, bd. dirs. 1986—, mem. Council of Reps. 1982—), AAAS; mem. Western (dir., pres. 1986-87), Oreg. psychol. assns., Am. Assn. State Psychology Bds. (pres. 1963-64), Nat. Assn. Mental Health (dir.), Oreg. Mental Health Assn. (dir., pres. 1962-63), Internat. Council Psychologists (dir. 1972-74, pres. 1976-77), Assn. Advancement of Psychology (trustee 1980—, chmn. bd. trustees 1983-85), Sigma Xi. Current Work: Lifestyle risk factors in health and illness; brain-behavior parameters in cognition. Subspecialties: Psychobiology; Neuropsychology. Home: 1934 SW Vista Ave Portland OR 97201

MATCHETT, ARNETT, veterinarian; b. Valdosta, Ga., Oct. 24, 1922; s. Turner and Irene (Wright) M.; m. Irma Brown, Feb. 5, 1948; children—Ronald (Muhammad Abullah), Gerald. Student, Savannah State Coll., 1941-42; B.S., A&T U., 1949; M.S., Iowa State U., 1978; D.V.M., Tuskegee Inst., 1961. Cert. veterinarian Ga., Ala. Tchr. Quitman County Bd. Edn., Georgetown, Ga., 1949-53; lab. asst. Carver Research Found., Tuskegee, Ala., 1953-61; veterinarian U.S. Dept. Agr., Sioux Falls, S.D., 1961-66, sect. head lab. biologics lab., Ames, Iowa, 1967-80; prin. staff officer Emergency Programs, Hyattsville, Md., 1980-81; chief animal med. & tech. Animal Welfare Program, Hyattsville, 1981—; staff cancer research Tuskegee Inst., 1953-57. Contbr. articles to profl. jours. Bd. dirs. Ames-Gilbert United Way, 1974; chmn. religion and race Iowa Methodist Conf., Ames, 1975. Mem. AVMA, Tissue Culture Assn., Am. Assn. Lab. Animal Sci., Am. Soc. Microbiology, Cell Biology/Cryobiology, Omega Psi Phi (Man of Yr. 1976). Democrat. Lodges: Masons, Lions (pres. 1974). Current work: Transformation of cells by oncogenic viruses used for vaccine production; establishment and characterization of cells to be used for vaccine production. Subspecialties: Plant cell and tissue culture; Cell study oncology. Home: 1309 Morningside Dr Silver Spring MD 20904 Office: USDA Animal Care Staff 6505 Belcrest Rd Room 766 Hyattsville MD 20782

MATEKER, EMIL JOSEPH, JR., geophysicist, geophysical company executive; b. St. Louis, Apr. 25, 1931; s. Emil Joseph and Lillian A. (Broz) M.; m. Lolita Ann Winter, Nov. 25, 1954; children: Mark Steven, Anne Marie, John David. B.S., St. Louis U., 1956, M.S., 1959, Ph.D. in Geophysics, 1964. Registered geophysicist, geologist, Calif. Geophysicist Standard Oil Co. Calif., 1957-60; instr. geophysics St. Louis U., 1960-63; asst. prof. geophysics Washington U., 1963-65, assoc. prof., 1965-69, cons. oil cos., 1962-70; mgr. geophysical research Western Geophys. Co. Am., 1969-70, v.p. research and devel., 1970-74; pres. Westrex, 1974-77, Litton Resources Systems, 1977; pres. Aero Service Div., v.p. corp. Western Geophys. Co. Am., 1974—. Author: A Treatise on Modern Exploration Seismology, 2 vols, 1965; contbr. articles to profl. jours. Chmn. bd. dirs. St. Agnes Acad., Houston, 1977—; pres. Strake Jesuit Boosters Club, 1977-78; mem. parish council St. John Vianney Ch., Houston. Served with U.S. Army, 1952-54. Recipient Merit award St. Louis U., 1976. Mem. Soc. Exploration Geophysicists, Am. Geophys. Union, Seismol. Soc. Am., AAAS, Geophys. Soc. Houston, European Assn. Exploration Geophysicists, Sigma Xi. Roman Catholic. Current Work: Exploration geophysics, synthetic aperture radar. Subspecialties: Geophysics; Remote sensing (geoscience). Home: 419 Hickory Post Houston TX 77079 Office: 8100 Westpark Dr Houston TX 77063

MATELES, RICHARD ISAAC, chemical company executive; b. N.Y.C., Sept. 11, 1935; s. Simon and Jean (Phillips) M.; m. Roslyn C. Fish, Sept. 2, 1956; children—Naomi Adeline, Susan Rachel, Sarah Frances. B.S., MIT, 1956, M.S., 1957, D.Sc., 1959. USPHS fellow Laboratorium voor Microbiologie Technische Hogeschool, Delft, Holland, 1959-60; mem. faculty MIT, 1960-70, assoc. prof. biochem. engring., 1965-68, dir. Fermentation unit, Jerusalem, 1968-77; prof. applied microbiology Hebrew U., Hadassah Med. Sch., Jerusalem, 1968-80; vis. prof. dept. chem. engring. U. Pa., Phila., 1978-79; asst. dir. research Stauffer Chem. Co., Westport, Conn., 1980, dir. research, 1980-81, v.p. research, 1981—. Editor: Biochemistry of Some Foodborne Microbial Toxins, 1967, Single Cell Protein, 1968; mem. editorial bd.: Biotech. and Bioengring., 1971—, Jour. Chem. Tech. and Biotech., 1972—; contbr. articles to profl. jours. Mem. Conn. Acad. Sci. Engring., 1981—; mem. vis. com., dept. nutrition and food sci. MIT, 1980—; mem. exec. com. Council on Chem. Research, 1981—. Mem. Am. Chem. Soc., Am. Inst. Chem. Engrs., Am. Soc. Microbiology, Soc. for Gen. Microbiology U.K., Inst. Food Technologists, AAAS, SAR, Sigma Xi. Current work: Research and technology management. Subspecialties: Enzyme technology; Food science and technology. Home: 5 E Meadow Rd Westport CT 06880 Office: Stauffer Chem Co Nyala Farm Rd Westport CT 06881

MATHER, JOHN CROMWELL, physicist; b. Roanoke, Va., Aug. 7, 1946; s. Robert Eugene and Martha Belle (Cromwell) M.; m. Jane Anne Hauser, Nov. 22, 1980. B.A. in Physics with highest honors, Swarthmore Coll., 1968; Ph.D. in Physics (NSF fellow, hon. Woodrow Wilson fellow, 1968, Fannie and John Hertz fellow 1970-74), U. Calif.-Berkeley, 1974. NAS/NRC research assoc. Goddard Inst. Space Studies, N.Y., 1974-76; astrophysicist Goddard Space Flight Center, Greenbelt, Md., 1976—; lectr. in astronomy Columbia U., N.Y.C., 1975-76. Contbr. sci. articles to profl. publs. Mem. Optical Soc. Am., Am. Phys. Soc., Am. Astron. Soc., Soc. Photo-optical Instrumentation Engrs., Sigma Xi, Phi Beta Kappa. Democrat. Unitarian. Current Work: Measurement of cosmic background radiation from the Big Bang using infrared and microwave instruments on NASA Cosmic Background Explorer Satellite planned for 1988 launch. Subspecialties: Cosmology; Infrared astronomy. Home: 4400 Romlon St Beltsville MD 20705 Office: Code 697 NASA Goddard Greenbelt MD 20771

MATHES, STEPHEN JOHN, plastic and reconstructive surgeon, educator; b. New Orleans, Aug. 17, 1943; s. John Edward and Norma (Deutsch) M.; m. Jennifer Wood-Bridge, Nov. 1966; children : David, Brian, Edward. B.S., La. State U., 1964, M.D., 1968. Diplomate: Am. Bd. Surgery, Am. Bd. Plastic and Reconstructive Surgery. Intern U. Va., Charlottesville, 1968-69, resident in gen. surgery, 1969-70, Emory U., Atlanta, 1972-75, resident in plastic surgery, 1975-77; asst. prof. Washington U., St. Louis, 1977-78; assoc. prof. U. Calif.-San Francisco, 1978—. Author: Clinical Atlas of Muscle and Musculocutaneous Flaps, 1979, Clinical Applications for Muscle and Musculocutaneous Flaps, 1982; contbr. articles to profl. jours. Served as maj. U.S. Army, 1970-72. NIH grantee, 1982; recipient best paper award Am. Soc. Aesthetic Plastic Surgery, 1981; 1st prize Plastic Surgery Ednl. Found. Scholarship Contest, 1981. Fellow ACS; mem. Am. Soc. Plastic and Reconstructive Surgeons (James Barrett Brown prize 1982), Am. Burn Assn., Internat. Soc. Reconstructive Microsurgery, Plastic Surgery Research Council, Am. Soc. for Surgery of Hand. Episcopalian. Current Work: Clinical and experimental research in microsurgery, wound healing, wound infections and flap use in reconstructive surgery. Subspecialties: Microsurgery; Surgery. Home: 618 Dorchester Rd San Mateo CA 94402 Office: Dept Surgery U Calif San Francisco CA 94143

MATHESON, ALASTAIR TAYLOR, biochemistry educator, university official; b. Vancouver, B.C., Can., Oct. 10, 1929; s. F. Alexander and Helen Johnson (MacFarlane) M.; m. Betsy Lawrie Auld, July 19, 1959; children—Sarah Marie, Ellen Donna. B.Sc., U. B.C., 1951, M.Sc., 1953; Ph.D., U. Toronto, 1957. Postgrad. fellow NRC Can., Ottawa, Ont., 1958-59; sr. research officer, 1960-77; research assoc. John's Hopkins U., Balt., 1959-60; adj. prof. Carleton U., Ottawa, Ont., 1974-77; prof. biochemistry, U. Victoria, B.C., 1977—, dean of sci., 1985—; vis. prof. U. Mass., Amherst, 1982-83. Contbr. chpts. to books, sci. articles to profl. jours. Fellow Royal Soc. Can.; mem. Can. Biochem. Soc. (pres. 1980-81), Can. Soc. for Cell Biology, Can. Soc. Microbiology, Am. Soc. Biol. Chemists, AAAS. Current work: Use of ribosomal protein sequence data to determine molecular evolution of the ribosome; structure of ribosomal protein genes in Archaebacteria. Subspecialties: Biochemistry (biology); Molecular biology. Home: 1036 Joan Crescent Victoria BC V8W 2Y2 Canada Office: Univ Victoria Dept Microbiology and Biochemistry PO Box 1700 Victoria BC V8W 2Y2 Canada

MATHEWS, GRANT JAMES, nuclear astrophysicist; b. Saginaw, Mich., Oct. 14, 1950; s. Kenneth Ward and Agnes Hazel M. B.S., Mich. State U., 1972; Ph.D., U. Md., 1977. Postdoctoral research assoc. U. Md., 1977, 1977; research assoc. U. Calif. (Lawrence Berkeley Lab.), Berkeley, 1977-79; research fellow Calif. Inst. Tech., Pasadena, 1979-81; physicist U. Calif. Lawrence Livermore Nat. Lab., Livermore, 1981—. Contbr. articles to research jours. Recipient Sigma Xi Research Excellence award, 1976. Mem. Am. Phys. Soc., Am. Astron. Soc., Am. Chem. Soc. Current Work: Nuclear astrophysics, stellar evolution, galactic evolution, cosmological nucleosynthesis, cosmic-ray propagation, explosive nucleosynthesis. Subspecialties: Nuclear astrophysics; Nuclear physics. Office: U Calif Lawrence Livermore Nat Lab Livermore CA 94550

MATHEWS, KENNETH PINE, physician, educator; b. Schenectady, Apr. 1, 1921; s. Raymond and Marguerite Elizabeth (Pine) M.; m. Alice Jean Elliott, Jan. 26, 1952 (dec.); children: Susan Kay, Ronald Elliott, Robert Pine; m. Winona Beatrice Rosenburg, Nov. 8, 1975. A.B., U. Mich., 1941, M.D., 1943. Diplomate Am. Bd. Internal Medicine, subsplty. bd. in allergy. Intern, asst. resident, resident in medicine Univ. Hosp., Ann Arbor, Mich., 1943-45, 48-50; mem. faculty dept. medicine U. Mich. Med. Sch., 1950—, assoc. prof. internal medicine, 1956-61, prof., 1961—, head div. allergy, 1967-83, chmn. residency rev. com. for allergy and immunology; cons. Ann Arbor VA Hosp. Co-author: A Manual of Clinical Allergy, 2d edit, 1967; editor: Jour. Allergy and Clin. Immunology, 1968-72; contbr. numerous articles in field to profl. jours. Served to capt. M.C. AUS, 1946-48. Recipient Disting. Service award Am. Acad. Allergy, 1976; Faculty Disting. Achievement award U. Mich., 1984. Fellow Am. Acad. Allergy (past pres.), ACP; mem. Am. Assn. Immunologists, Central Soc. Clin. Research (emeritus), Am. Fedn. Clin. Research, Am. Thoracic Soc., Mich. Allergy Soc. (past pres.), Washtenaw County Med. Soc., Mich. State Med. Soc., Alpha Omega Alpha, Phi Beta Kappa. Current Work: Mechanisms of urticaria and angioedema; IgE antibodies; mechanisms of drug hypersensitivity. Subspecialties: Allergy; Immunopharmacology. Home: 1145 Aberdeen Dr Ann Arbor MI 48104 Office: Box 27 Univ of Mich Med Center Ann Arbor MI 48109

MATHEWSON, CHRISTOPHER COLVILLE, engineering geologist, educator, researcher, consultant; b. Plainfield, N.J., Aug. 12, 1941; s. George Anderson and Elsa Ray (Shrimpton) M.; m. Janet Marie Olmstead, Nov. 2, 1968; children: Heather Alexis, Glenn George Anderson. B.S. in Civil Engring, Cast Inst. Tech., 1963; M.S. in Geol. Engring, U. Ariz., 1965, Ph.D. in Geol. Engring, 1971. Profl. engr., Tex., Ariz. profl. geologist, Oreg. Asst. prof. Tex. A&M U., College Station, 1971-75, assoc. prof., 1975-81, prof., 1981—, dir. Center for Engring. Geoscis., 1982. Author: Engineering Geology, 1981. Chmn. Planning and Zoning Commn., College Station, 1973-78. Served to lt. NOAA, 1965-70. Fellow Geol. Soc. Am., Geol. Assn. Can.; mem. Assn. Engring. Geologists. (editor 1981—, C.P. Holdredge award), Am. Geophys. Union, ASCE, Internat. Assn. Engring. Geologists. Current Work: Engineering geology applied to coal development, urban planning, coastal and river processes and geomorphic processes. Subspecialties: Geology; Coal. Office: Tex A&M Dept Geology College Station TX 77843

MATHIAS, JOSEPH SIMON, metallurgical engineer; b. Bombay, India, Oct. 28, 1925; came to U.S., 1948, naturalized, 1954; s. Pascal Lawrence and Dulcine Applina (De Souza) M.; m. Anna Katherine Elliott, Nov. 10, 1956. B.S., U. Bombay, 1944, B.A., 1946; Ph.D., Lehigh U., Bethlehem, Pa., 1954; M.Engr., U. Calif., Berkeley, 1951. Research asso. Lehigh U., 1951-54; chief metallurgist Superior Metals, Inc., Bethlehem, Pa., 1954-56; mgr. process metall. research Foote Mineral Co., Easton, Pa., 1956-59; mgr. materials research, then group mgr. physics and materials Sperry Univac Co., Blue Bell, Pa., 1959-67, dir. research, 1967-79, dir. mfg. and systems hardware research, 1979—; mem. program com. Internat. Magnetic Conf., 1969, 70; cons. in field. Author. Fellow Am. Inst. Chemists, N.Y. Acad. Sci.; sr. mem. IEEE; mem. Am. Soc. Electrochemistry, Am. Inst. Mining and Metall. Engrs., Sigma Xi, Tau Beta Pi. Club: Riverton Country. Lodge: Rotary (dir.). Patentee in field. Fields: Materials, data storage and reproduction. Current work: Electronic materials, microchip technology, microelectronics and information systems. Home: 105 Thomas Ave Riverton NJ 08077 Office: Sperry Univac Co PO Box 500 Blue Bell PA 19422

MATHIPRAKASAM, B., research engineer; b. Virudhunagar, Tamilnadu, India, Jan. 3, 1942; came to U.S. 1976; s. G. Balakrishna Nadar and B. Rajammal; m. M. Pavalamani, Sept. 11, 1972; 1 child, Murthy. L.M.E., Virudhunagar Poly. Inst., India, 1961; M.E., Mysore U., Surathkal, India, 1976; Ph.D., Ill. Inst. Tech., 1980. Lectr. Virudhunagar Poly. Inst., 1961-68, shop supt., 1968-74; assoc. energy engr. Midwest Research Inst., Kansas City, Mo., 1980-81, sr. energy engr., 1981-84, prin. engr., 1984—. Contbr. articles to profl. jours. Patentee in field. Mem. ASME, Sigma Xi. Hindu. Current work: Thermoelectric cooling/heating; novel cooling concepts; energy storage; energy system modeling. Subspecialties: Mechanical engineering; Thermoelectrics. Home: 8429 Broadmoor Overland Park KS 66212 Office: Midwest Research Inst 425 Volker Blvd Kansas City MO 64110

MATHIS, JOHN SAMUEL, astronomy educator; b. Dallas, Feb. 7, 1931; s. Forrest and Mattie Mae (Godbold) M.; m. Carol Simpelaar, Sept. 11, 1954; children—Matthew, Alice, Jeffrey, Emily, Sarah. B.S., MIT, 1953; Ph.D., Calif. Inst. Tech., 1956. NSF Postdoctoral fellow Yerkes Obs., U. Chgo., 1956-57; asst. prof. Mich. State U., 1957-59; mem. faculty U. Wis.-Madison, 1959—, prof. astronomy, 1969—. Editor: Astrophys. Jours. Letters, 1971-73. U.S. Sr. Scientist awardee Alexander-von-Humboldt Found., 1975-76. Mem. Am. Astron. Soc. Field: Theoretical astrophysics. Current work: Nature and composition of gaseous nebulae; composition, size distribution and nature of interstellar grains. Home: 1639 Norman Way Madison WI 53705

MATHUR, SUBBI, immunologist, educator; b. Insein, Burma, Oct. 13, 1939; came to U.S., 1969; d. T.A. Ramaswami Pillai and Seethalakshmi Ramaswami; m. Rajesh S. Mathur, May 4, 1968; children: Veena Rani, Arun Kumar. B.A., U. Madras, India, 1957; M.A., 1959, M.S., 1960, Ph.D., 1966. Research asso. Med. U. S.C., Charleston, 1975-81, asst. prof., 1981—. Mem. adv. panel Am. Assn. Minority Women in Science, Washington, 1982. NIH research grantee, 1981; Career Devel. awardee, 1982. Mem. Am. Soc. Microbiologists, Internat. Assn. Reproductive Immunology, Am. Assn. Immunologists, Am. Fertility Soc. Hindu. Current Work: Reproductive immunology; immune mechanisms in infertility and endocrinological disorders; immune mechanisms between mother and fetus; immunology of chronic vaginal candidiasis; human leukocyte antigens and infertility. Subspecialties: Immunology (medicine); Transplantation. Office: BCIM Dept Med U SC 171 Ashley Ave Charleston SC 29425

MATIN, ABDUL, microbiology researcher educator, consultant; b. Delhi, India, May 8, 1941; s. Zohra Begum M.; m. Mimi Keyhan, June 21, 1968. B.S., U. Karachi, Pakistan, 1960. M.S., 1962; Ph.D., UCLA, 1969. Postgrad. in bacteriology UCLA, 1964-69, postdoctoral research assoc., 1969-71; sci. officer 1st class State U. Groningen, Kerklaan, Netherlands, 1971-75; acting asst. prof. Stanford U., Calif., prof., 1975-84, assoc. prof. dept. med. microbiology, 1984—; cons. Enegenics, Inc., Menlo Park, Calif., 1981-83, law firm, Bakersfield, Calif., 1981-83, Stanford Research Inst., Menlo Park, 1985—. Research grantee NSF, 1980-82, Ctr. for Biotech. Research, 1980-85, EPA, 1981—, Alta. Research Council, Can., 1981, 82. Subspecialty: Microbial physiology. Home: 690 Coronado Ave Stanford CA 94305 Office: Dept Med Microbiology Stanford U Sch Medicine Fairchild Sci Bldg Stanford CA 94305

MATKOWSKY, BERNARD JUDAH, applied mathematician, educator; b. N.Y.C., Aug. 19, 1939; s. Morris N. and Ethel H. Matkowsky; m. Florence Knobel, Apr. 11, 1965; children: David, Daniel, Devorah. B.S., CCNY, 1960; M.E.E., N.Y. U., 1961, M.S., 1963, Ph.D., 1966. Fellow Courant Inst. Math. Scis., N.Y. U., 1961-66; mem. faculty dept. math. Rensselaer Poly. Inst., 1966-77; prof. applied math. and math. Northwestern U., Evanston, Ill., 1977—; vis. prof. Tel Aviv U., Israel, 1972-73; vis. scientist Weizmann Inst. Sci., Israel, summer 1976, summer 1980, Tel Aviv U., summer 1980; cons. Argonne Nat. Lab., Sandia Nat. Labs., Lawrence Livermore Nat. Lab., Exxon Research and Engring. Co. Editor: Wave Motion-An Internat. Jour, 1979—; editor: SIAM Jour. Applied Math, 1976; asso. mng. editor, 1978—; mem. editorial adv. bd. Springer Verlag Applied Math. Scis.; contbr. chpts. to books, articles to profl. jours. Fulbright grantee, 1972-73; Guggenheim fellow, 1982-83. Mem. Soc. Indsl. and Applied Math., Am. Math. Soc., AAAS, Combustion Inst., Am. Phys. Soc., Conf. Bd. Math. Scis. (council, com. human rights of math. scientists), Com. Concerned Scientists, Soc. Natural Philosophy, Sigma Xi, Eta Kappa Nu. Current Work: Combustion theory, stochastic differential equations, bifurcation theory, nonlinear stability theory, singular pertubation theory. Subspecialty: Applied mathematics. Home: 3704 Davis St Skokie IL 60076 Office: Technological Inst Northwestern U Evanston IL 60201

MATSON, LAWRENCE ROBERT, geology educator; b. Cortland, N.Y., Feb. 9, 1940; s. Lawrence Donald and Ona Olive (Record) M.; m. Susan Iona Brown, Aug. 22, 1964; children—Lawrence Donald, Robert Michael, Edward Franklin. B.S. in Edn. in Math., SUNY-Cortland, 1961, M.S. in Earth Sci., 1967; M.S. in Geology, Case Western Res. U., 1971 postgrad. Syracuse U., Cornell U., U. Md., Howard U., Goddard Space Flight Ctr. Cert. secondary tchr., N.Y. Tchr. chemistry and physics earth sci., math. secondary pub. schs., N.Y., 1961-71; lab. instr., curator, SUNY-Cortland, 1967; lectr. geomorphology, SUNY-New Paltz, 1981—; lab. instr. geology Case Western Res. U., Cleve., 1969-70; assoc. prof. Ulster County Community Coll., Stone Ridge, N.Y., 1971—; geol. cons. Geosci. Services, Accord, N.Y., 1976—; grant reviewer, panel chmn. sci. edn. div. NSF, Washington, 1976-78; pres. Earth Treasures, Stone Ridge, N.Y., 1977—. Author: Field Guide-Glacial Geology, 1984. Contbr. articles to profl. jours. Past pres. Accord Fire Co. (vol.); past v.p., mgr. Indian Little League Baseball, Kerhonkson, N.Y., 1974—; mem. planning bd. Town of Rochester, Accord, 1983—. Named Fireman of Yr., Accord Fire Co., 1980; grantee Gulf Oil Found, 1974, research fellow NASA and Am. Soc. Engring. Edn., 1978, 79, NSF, 1976. Mem. Geol. Soc. Am., Nat. Assn. Geol. Tchrs. (mem., chmn. com.), Am. Soc. for Photogrammetry and Remote Sensing, NEA (life mem., former state rep.), N.Y. Acad. Scis. Republican. Current work: Lineament and structure analysis by computer enhancement; geomorphology, especially glacial geology, sinkhole formation-detection and groundwater contamination. Subspecialties: Remote sensing (geoscience); Geomorphology. Home: Rural Route 1 Box 296B Accord NY

12404 Office: Ulster County Community Coll Cottekill Rd Stone Ridge NY 12484

MATSUDA, FUJIO, research organization executive; b. Honolulu, Oct. 18, 1924; s. Yoshio and Shimo (Iwasaki) M.; m. Amy M. Saiki, June 11, 1949; children—Bailey Koki, Thomas Junji, Sherry Noriko, Joan Yuuko, Ann Mitsuyo, Richard Hideo. B.S. in Civil Engring., Rose Poly. Inst., 1949; D.Sc., Mass. Inst. Tech., 1952; D. Engring. (hon.), Rose Hulman Inst. Tech., 1975. Research asst. MIT, 1950-52, research engr., 1952-54; research asst. prof. engring. U. Ill., Urbana, 1954-55; asst. prof. engring. U. Hawaii, Honolulu, 1955-57, asso. prof., 1957-62, chmn. dept. civil engring., 1960-63, prof., 1962-65, dir. engring. expt. sta., 1962-63, v.p. bus. affairs, 1973-74, pres., 1974-84; exec. dir. Research Corp. U. Hawaii, 1984—; dir. Hawaii Dept. Transp., Honolulu, 1963-73; v.p. Park & Yee, Ltd., Honolulu, 1956-58; pres. SMS & Assos., Inc., 1960-63; pvt. practice as structural engr., 1958-60; dir. C. Brewer & Co., Ltd., Hawaiian Electric Co., UAL, Inc., First Hawaiian Bank; mem. adv. bd. Duty Free Shoppers Ltd. Mem. Bd. Water Supply, Honolulu, 1963-73; mem. Airport Ops. Council Internat., 1968-73; pres. Pacific Coast Assn. Port Authorities, 1969; mem. sci. bd. Dept. Army, 1978-80; mem. U.S. Army Civilian Adv. Group, 1978—; bd. dirs. Hawaii Inst. Electronic Research; ex-officio mem. bd. govs. East-West Ctr.; mem. exec. com. transp. research bd. NRC, 1982—. Bd. dirs. Aloha United Way, 1973-76; trustee Kuakini Health Systems, 1984-86. Served with AUS, 1943-45. Recipient Honor Alumnus award Rose Poly. Inst., 1971, Disting. Service award Airport Ops. Council Internat., 1973, Disting. Alumnus award U. Hawaii, 1974; named Hawaii Engr. of Yr., 1972. Mem. ASCE, Nat. Acad. Engring., Nat. Soc. Profl. Engrs., ASCE; mem. Social Sci. Assn., Western Coll. Assn. (exec. com. 1977-84, pres. 1980-82), Japanese-Am. Soc. Honolulu (trustee 1976-84, adv. council 1984—); Mem. Beta Gamma Sigma, Sigma Xi, Tau Beta Pi. Home: 1844 Kihi St Honolulu HI 96821 Office: 1110 University Ave Honolulu HI 96826

MATSUMOTO, TERUO, surgeon, medical educator; b. Fukuoka, Japan, Jan. 2, 1929; came to U.S., 1956, naturalized, 1961; s. Yoshinari and Fumie (Hayashi) M.; m. Mary L. Cousino, July 1961; children—Louisa Michi, Maria Chieko, Monica Mieko, Nelson Tateru. B.S., Kyushu U., 1949, M.D., 1953, Ph.D., 1956. Diplomate Am. Bd. Surgery, Am. Bd. Gen. Vascular Surgery. Intern, Cook County Hosp., Chgo., 1956-57; resident in surgery Maumee Valley Hosp., Toledo, 1957-61; assoc. prof., dir. surg. research Hahnemann U. Hosps., Phila., 1969-80, prof., chmn. dept. surgery, 1975—; reviewer Sci. Rev. Com. Study Sect., NIH, 1969—; cons. gen., vascular surgery City of Phila., 1977—. Author: Tissue Adhesive, 1972, Acupuncture, 1974, Vascular Surgery, 1982. Editor: Jour. Internat. Surgery, 1972, Jour. Critical Care, 1979. Served to lt. col. M.C., U.S. Army, 1961-69. Recipient Sir Henry Wellcome award Mil. Medicine Assn., 1965, Gold medal Southeastern Surg. Congress, 1968, Golden Apple award AMA, 1972; Pacer Tech. Research Found. grantee, 1979. Fellow Soc. for Vascular Surgery, Internat. Cardiovascular Soc., Collegium Internationale Chirvigiae Digestivae, Soc. for Surgery Alimentary Tract, Am. Assn. for Surgery of Trauma. Republican. Unitarian. Current work: Vascular surgery, vascular graft; vascular reconstruction, anastomosis, surgery of alimentary tract, stress ulcer, bleeding; critical care, shock, microcirculation; tissue adhesives. Subspecialties: Preventive medicine; Surgery. Home: 515 Fishers Rd Bryn Mawr PA 19010 Office: Dept Surgery Hahnemann U Broad and Vine Sts Philadelphia PA 19102

MATSUZAKI, MASAJI, neuropsychopharmacologist; b. Sanjo Niigata, Japan, Feb. 12, 1933; came to U.S., 1967; m. Keiko Kudo, Dec. 15, 1962. B.E., Niigata U., Japan, 1956; M.A., Tohoku U., Japan, 1958; Ph.D., Tokyo U. Med. Sch., 1967; postgrad. Stanford U. Med. Sch., 1967-68. Sr. research assoc. U. Calif.-Davis Med. Sch., 1968-72; head research scientist Dept. Neuropharmacology, N.Y. State Div. Substance Abuse Services, Research Lab., Bklyn., 1972—; asst. adj. prof. SUNY-Bklyn., 1980—. Contbr. articles to profl. jours. Mem. Am. Soc. Pharmacology and Exptl. Therapeutics, N.Y. Acad. Scis., Japanese Pharm. Soc., Physiol. Soc. Japan, Japanese Psychol. Assn. Current work: Electroneurophysiology and neuropharmacology mechanisms of central nervous systems interactions of drugs of abuse and drug dependence. Subspecialties: Neuropharmacology; Neurophysiology. Home: 92-16 68th Ave Forest Hills NY 11375 Office: NY State Div Substance Abuse Services Research Lab 80 Hanson Pl Brooklyn NY 11217

MATTEI, JANET AKYUZ, astronomer; b. Bodrum, Turkey, Jan. 2, 1943; came to U.S., 1962; d. Baruh and Polise (Isbir) A.; m. Michael Mattei, Dec. 17, 1972. B.A., Brandeis U., 1965; Yuksek Lisans in Astronomy, Ege U., Turkey, 1970; M.S. in Astronomy, U. Va., 1972. Tchr. physics, astronomy, phys. scis. Am. Collegiate Inst., Turkey, 1967-69; teaching asst. astronomy Ege U., Turkey, 1969-70; research asst. astronomy Maria Mitchell Obs. Nantucket, Mass., summer 1969; asst. to dir. Am. Assn. Variable Star Observers, Cambridge, Mass., 1972-73, dir., 1973—; worldwide coordinator variable star observations; cons. dwarf nova type variable stars; speaker colls., high schs. Contbr. articles to sci. jours. Recipient Wien internat. scholarship award; prin. investigator grants made to Am. Assn. Variable Star Observers from NSF; prin. investigator grants made to Am. Assn. Variable Star Observers from NASA Research Corp. Mem. Internat. Astron. Union, Am. Astron. Soc., Am. Assn. Variable Star Observers. Current Work: Visual and photometric studies of variable stars, particularly dwarf novae, long period variables, symbiotic variables. Subspecialties: Optical astronomy; Variable stars. Office: 187 Concord Ave Cambridge MA 02138

MATTEN, LAWRENCE CHARLES, paleobotanist; b. Newark, Sept. 1, 1938; s. Bernard and Florence (Law) M.; m. Marlene Rotbart, Sept. 6, 1959; children: Sharlene, Alan, Sharon, Ronald. B.A., Rutgers U., 1959; Ph.D., Cornell U., 1965. Cert. tchr. gen. sci., biology, physics, chemistry, N.J. Gen. Sci. tchr. Woodstown (N.J.) High Sch., 1959-60; teaching asst., research asst., extension corr. Cornell U., Ithaca, N.Y., 1960-64; instr. biology SUNY, Cortland, 1964-65; asst. prof. dept. botany So. Ill. U., Carbondale, 1965-69, assoc. prof., 1969-77, prof., 1977—; cons., researcher. Contbr. articles on paleobotany to profl. jours. NSF grantee, 1981-85; Am. Philos. Soc. grantee, 1982-84. Mem. Linnean Soc. (London), Bot. Soc. Am., Paleontol. Soc., Torrey Bot. Club, Internat. Orgn. Paleobotany, Ill. Acad. Sci. Current Work: Evolutionary relationships of earliest seed plants and related groups, structure of progymnosperms and Devonian ferns, floras of Ireland, development of techniques for preparing petrified remains. Subspecialties: Evolutionary biology; Paleobiology. Office: Dept Botany So Ill U Carbondale IL 62901

MATTHEWS, BRIAN WESLEY, molecular biologist, educator; b. South Australia, May 25, 1938; s. Lionel and E.L. (Harris) M.; m. Helen F. Denley, Sept. 7, 1963; 2 children. B.Sc., U. Adelaide, 1959, Hons., 1960, Ph.D. (Physics), 1964; Australian Atomic Energy Commn. fellow, 1960. Mem. staff Med. Res. Council Lab. Molecular Biology, Eng., 1963-66; vis. assoc. molecular biologist NIH, Bethesda, Md., 1967-68; prof. physics, mem. Inst. Molecular Biology, U. Oreg., Eugene, 1969—. Imperial Chem. Ind. Australia and N.Z. fellow, 1962; John S. Guggenheim Meml. Found. fellow, 1977; Alfred P. Sloan fellow, 1971. Mem. Am. Crystallographic Assn., Am. Chem. Soc. Current Work: Protein structure and function; crystallography. Subspecialty: Molecular biology. Address: Inst of Molecular Biology Univ Ore Eugene OR 97403

MATTHEWS, DENNIS LEE, laser physicist. Project head x-ray laser devel. Lawrence Livermore Lab., Calif. Subspecialty: X-ray lasers. Office: Lawrence Livermore Lab Y Div PO Box 808 Livermore CA 94550*

MATTHEWS, DWIGHT EARL, internal medicine educator, consultant; b. Greencastle, Ind., Sept. 10, 1951; s. Robert Earl and Madeline Vivian (Huber) M.; m. Ellen Lee Keller, Aug. 2, 1972; children—Thomas Earl, Benjamin Earl. B.A., DePauw U., 1973; Ph.D., Ind. U., 1977. Instr. Washington U. Sch. Medicine, St. Louis, 1977-80, asst. prof., 1977—. Contbr. articles to profl. jours., chpts. in books. Mem. Am. Soc. Clin. Nutrition, Am. Soc. Parenteral and Enteral Nutrition, Am. Inst. Nutrition, Am. Soc. Mass Spectrometers, AAAS. Current work: Stable isotope tracer applications to human metabolic study; physiological biochemistry. Subspecialties: Nutrition (medicine); Analytical chemistry. Home: 6309 Pershing Ave Saint Louis MO 63130 Office: Washington U Sch Medicine Metabolism Div 660 S Euclid Ave Saint Louis MO 63110

MATTHEWS, LESLIE SCOTT, orthopedic surgeon, educator; b. Balt., Sept. 18, 1951; s. Warren Gamelial and Jane (Black) M.; m. Julie Ann Nolan, June 13, 1981. B.A. in Natural Sci, Johns Hopkins U., 1973; M.D., Baylor U., 1976. Intern Johns Hopkins Hosp., Balt., 1976-77, resident in surgery, 1976-78, resident in orthopedics, 1978-81, asst. prof. orthopedic surgery, 1981—; asst. chief orthopedic surgery Union Meml. Hosp., Balt., 1981—; cons. Loch Raven Veterans Hosp., Balt., 1981—, Bethesda (Md.) Naval Hosp. Trustee St. Paul's Sch. Boys, Brooklandville, Md., 1982. Recipient C. Markland Kelly award Johns Hopkins U., 1972, 73, Barton Cup, 1973. Mem. Johns Hopkins Med. and Surg. Soc., Arthroscopy Assn. N.Am. Episcopalian. Current Work: Arthroscopic surgical techniques, particularly involving the shoulder joint. Subspecialty: Orthopedics. Home: 101 Cotswold Rd Baltimore MD 21210 Office: Union Memorial Hospital 201 E University Pkway Baltimore MD 21218

MATTHYSSE, ANN GALE, biologist, educator; b. Chgo., Oct. 25, 1937; d. George W. and Ann (Van Nice) Gale; m. Steven W. Matthysse, Aug. 25, 1962; 1 son, Michael. A.B. in Biochem. Scis. magna cum laude, Radcliffe Coll., 1961; postgrad. in Life Scis., Rockefeller U., 1961-63; Ph.D. in Biology, Harvard U., 1967. Postdoctoral research fellow in molecular biology Calif. Inst. Tech., 1966-69; in bacterial physiology Harvard Med. Sch., 1969-70; lectr. in biology Harvard U., Cambridge, Mass., 1970-71; asst. prof. microbiology Ind. U. Sch. Medicine, Indpls., 1971-75; asst. prof. botany U. N.C., Chapel Hill, 1975-77, assoc. prof., 1977-82, assoc. prof. biology, 1982—; Allen Lectr. in phytobacteriology U. Wis., 1982. Editorial bd.: Jour. Bacteriology, Jour. Microbiol. Methods; contbr. articles to profl. jours. Treas., Orange County Assn. Retarded Citizens, 1976-78. Mem. Am. Soc. Microbiology, Am. Phytopath. Soc., Am. Soc. Plant Physiology, AAAS, Phi Beta Kappa. Quaker. Current Work: Molecular biology of bacterial diseases of plants, crown gall, Agrobacterium, plant pathology, bacterial attachment, plant tissue culture. Subspecialties: Plant pathology; Molecular biology. Office: Coker Hall 010A Univ NC Chapel Hill NC 27514

MATTOX, DONALD M., national laboratory research scientist. Supr. surface metallurgy div., Sandia Nat. Labs., Albuquerque. Pres. Am. Vacuum Soc. Office: Sandia Nat Labs Surface Metallurgy Div Albuquerque NM 87185

MATTSON, MARGARET ELLEN, biologist, government research institute officer; b. Phila., May 13, 1947; d. John C. and Margaret M. (Brazz) M. B.A. magna cum laude, Holy Family Coll., 1969; Ph.D. in Neurobiology and Behavior, Cornell U., 1975. Health scientist/epidemiologist Enviro Control, Inc., Rockville, Md., 1976-78; program scientist Behavioral Medicine br. Nat. Heart Lung and Blood Inst., NIH, Bethesda, Md., 1978-81, project. officer for behavioral studies Clin. Trials br., 1981-83; spl. asst. for research devel. Div. Cancer Prevention and Control, Nat. Cancer Inst., 1983—; guest lectr. Found. Advanced Edn. in Scis., Bethesda, Md. Contbr. articles to profl. jours. Referral coordinator, newsletter editor Women's Center and Referral Service, Adelphi, Md., 1975-77. Recipient Outstanding Alumni award Holy Family Coll., 1981; NDEA grad. fellow Cornell U. Mem. Am. Psychol. Assn., Am. Pub. Health Assn., Soc. Clin. Trials, Grad. Women in Sci. (pres. Washington chpt. 1982—). Subspecialties: Behavioral psychology; Epidemiology. Office: Blair Bldg Room 423 9000 Rockville Pike Bethesda MD 20205

MATZINGER, DALE FREDERICK, geneticist, researcher; b. Alleman, Iowa, Apr. 14, 1929; s. Albert Christian and Violet Marie (Schrumpf) M.; m. Joan Camilla Cox, June 11, 1960; children: Michael, Ellen. B.S., Iowa State U., 1950, M.S., 1951, Ph.D., 1956. Asst. statistician N.C. State U., Raleigh, 1956-57, asst. prof. stats., 1957-60, asso. prof. genetics, 1960-64, prof. genetics, 1964—. Mem. editorial bd. Tobacco Sci, 1964-71, chmn. editorial bd., 1984—; mem. editorial bd. Jour. Heredity, 1981—. Contbr. articles to profl. lit. Served with U.S. Army, 1951-53. Recipient Sigma Xi research award, 1961, Gamma Sigma Delta award of merit, 1970, Philip Morris award for disting. achievement in tobacco sci., 1971; Am. Soc. Agronomy fellow, 1965. Mem. Am. Soc. Agronomy, Biometrics Soc., Genetics Soc. Am., Am. Genetic Assn., AAAS. Methodist. Current Work: Quantitative genetics of nuclear and cytoplasmic organelle variability in self-fertilizing plant species. Subspecialties: Plant genetics; Population biology. Home: 3413 Doyle Rd Raleigh NC 27607 Office: Dept Genetics NC State U Raleigh NC 27695-7614

MAUGHAN, O. EUGENE, fishery biologist; b. Weston, Idaho, Jan. 3, 1943; s. Owen Weston and Ione (Stocks) M.; m. Lu Dean Lewis, Aug. 30, 1962; children: Terry Lynn, Cindy Jean, Kimberly Dene, James Benjamin, Robert Samuel, Summer Nicole. B.S., Utah State U., 1966; M.A., Kans. U., 1968; Ph.D., Wash. State U., 1972. Fishery biologist U.S. Fish and Wildlife Service, Spokane, 1971-72, Blacksburg, Va., 1972-77, Stillwater, Okla., 1977—; leader Okla. Coop. Fishery and Wildlife Research Unit, 1977-84. Contbr. articles to profl. jours. Recipient Commendation award Sport Fishing Inst., 1978. Mem. Am. Fisheries Soc. (Most Significant Paper award 1983), Soc. Herpetologists and Ichthyologists, Okla. Acad. Sci., Okla. Wildlife Fedn., Nat. Wildlife Fedn., Sigma Xi. Mormon. Current Work: Fish culture, fish ecology, reservoir management, stream and riverine management, instream flow methodology, habitat evaluation procedures. Subspecialties: Ecology (environmental science); Theoretical ecology. Office: Okla Coop Fishery Research Unit Okla State U Stillwater OK 74078

MAULIK, DEBABRATA, obstetrician, gynecologist, cons. perinatologist; b. Calcutta, West Bengal, India, Mar. 3, 1939; came to U.S., 1976; s. Ananta Kumar and Tara (Chakrabarti) M.; m. Shibani Mukherji, Aug. 11, 1973; children: Devika, Davesh. M.D., U. Calcutta, 1962; M.R.C.O.G., Royal Coll. Obstetrics/Gynecology, London, 1967; Ph.D., U. London, 1975. Diplomate: Am. Bd. Ob-Gyn. Intern Med. Coll. Hosps., Calcutta, 1962-63, resident, 1963-65, resident various hosps., 1965-69; lectr. Charing Cross, U. London, 1973-76; dir. maternal/fetal dept. Deaconess Hosp., Buffalo, 1976-80; asst. prof. SUNY, Buffalo, 1976-80; asst. prof. dept. ob-gyn U. Rochester (N.Y.) Sch. Medicine, 1980—; assoc. attending ob-gyn Strong Meml. Hosp., Rochester, 1982—, Deaconess Hosp., Buffalo, 1976-80; mem. nat. program com. Assn. Planned Parenthood Physicians Am., 1978-81; mem. orgn. com. 9th Trophoblast Conf., Rochester, 1982. Bd. dirs. Buffalo Council World Affairs, 1979-80. Recipient Gold medal U. Calcutta, 1962; Nuffield Found. fellow, 1970-73; U. Buffalo Found. research grantee, 1978-79; E.R. and M.S. Goode research grantee, 1981-82; NIH research grantee, 1982-85. Fellow Am. Coll. Ob-Gyn; mem. Planned Parenthood Fedn. Am. (program com. 1978—), Royal Coll. Ob-Gyn, AMA, AAAS, Indian Assn. Rochester. Hindu. Developer extracorporeal perfusion of human placenta, 1975. Current Work: Extracorporeal perfusion of human placenta, model system, transport kinetic and toxicologic study, development of doppler flowmetry technology and applications in medicine, computers in perinatal medicine. Subspecialties: Maternal and fetal medicine; Perinatal diagnosis and therapy. Home: 225 Oakdale Dr Rochester NY 14618 Office: U Rochester 601 Elmwood Ave Strong Meml Hosp Rochester NY 14642

MAUSEL, PAUL WARNER, geography educator; b. Mpls., Jan. 2, 1936; s. Paul George and Esther Victoria (Sundstrom) M.; m. Jean Frances Kias, July 2, 1966; children—Paul Brandon, Catherine Suzanne, Justin Thomas. B.A. in Chemistry and Geography, U. Minn., 1958, M.A. in Geography, 1961; Ph.D., U. N.C., 1966. Asst. prof. geography Eastern Ill. U., Charleston, 1965-70, assoc. prof., 1970-71; assoc. prof. geography Ind. State U., Terre Haute, 1971-75, prof., 1975—, dir. Remote Sensing Lab., 1975—; research geographer Lab. Applications of Remote Sensing Purdue U., West Lafayette, Ind., 1972-73; soils geographer cons. U. Mo. at Columbia, summer 1974; lectr. in field. Contbr. articles to profl. jours., Chpts. to textbooks, NSF fellow, 1978; recipient research award Ind. State U., 1983. Mem. Assn. Am. Geographers, Soil Sci. Soc. Am., Am. Soc. Photogrammetry, Sigma Xi. Current work: Computer-aided analysis of 7-band Thematic Mapper satellite data to determine the distribution of selected soil parameters. Subspecialties: Remote sensing (geoscience); Soil science. Home: Rural Route 32 Box 105 Terre Haute IN 47803

MAUTER, WARREN EUGENE, chemist; b. Denver, Aug. 27, 1951; s. Jacob Martin and Harriette June (Kaiser) M.; m. Deborah Lee Long, Jan. 22, 1982. B.S., Met. State Coll., 1977. Research chemist Manville Corp., Denver, 1977-80, task group leader, 1980-83; applications mgr. Cardinal Chem. Co., Columbia, S.C., 1983-84; founding prin. Alpine Cons. Group, Denver, 1984—. Contbr. articles to profl. jours. Mem. Am. Chem. Soc., Am. Mgmt. Assn., ASTM, Soc. Plastics Engrs. Republican. Club: Colo. Mountain. Current work: Stabilization, morphology, characterization, rheology control and properties peformance of thermopolastic polymers. Subspecialties: Polymer chemistry; Polymers (materials science). Home: 1649 S Marion St Denver CO 80210 Office: Alpine Cons Group PO Box 10791 Denver CO 80210

MAVROYANNIS, CONSTANTINE, theoretical physicist; b. Athens, Greece, Nov. 13, 1927; s. George and Paraskevi (Xylas) M.; m. Paraskevi Logothetis, Aug. 30, 1961; children: Maria, Irene. B.S. in Ch.E, Tech. U. Athens, Greece, 1957; Ph.D. in Phys. Chemistry, McGill U., 1961; D.Phil. in Math, Oxford U., Eng., 1963. Postdoctoral fellow NRC Can., Ottawa, Ont., 1963-64, asst. research officer, 1964-65, assoc. research officer, 1966-73, sr. research officer, 1974—. Contbr. numerous articles to sci. jours. Served with Greek Army, 1951-54. NRC Can. Student fellow, 1959-61; NATO Sci. Postdoctoral Overseas fellow, 1961-63; NRC Can. postdoctoral fellow, 1963-64. Fellow Chem. Inst. Can.; Mem. Am. Phys. Soc., Can. Assn. Physicists. Current Work: Many-body theory in solid state physics, collective electronic excitations, optical properties of solids, surface physics, quantum optics and quantum electronics. Subspecialties: Condensed matter physics; Atomic and molecular physics. Home: 2121 Maywood St Ottawa ON K1G 1E8 Canada Office: NRC Can 100 Sussex Dr Ottawa ON K1A OR6 Canada

MAX, STEPHEN RICHARD, biochemist, educator; b. Providence, Dec. 25, 1940; s Leo and Paula (Strasberg) M.; m. Barbara H. Sohmer, Aug. 8, 1976; 1 dau., Paula E. Max-Sohmer. B.S., U. R.I., 1962, Ph.D., 1966. Guest worker NIH, 1968-70; asst. prof. biochemistry Howard U. Sch. Medicine, 1966-70; asst. prof. neurology U. Md., Balt., 1970-74, assoc. prof., 1974-81, prof., 1981—. Contbr. articles to profl. publs. Served to capt. U.S. Army, 1966-68. Research grantee NIH; Research grantee Muscular Dystrophy Assn.; Research grantee Roche Research Found.; Research grantee NASA. Mem. Soc. for Neurosci., Am. Soc. Neurochemistry, Am. Soc. Biol. Chemists, Endocrine Soc., Internat. Soc. Neurochemistry, Internat. Brain Research Orgn., Am. Chem. Soc., Am. Acad. Neurology. Current Work: Neuromuscular biochemistry; endocrinology, neurochemistry, neuroscience, regeneration, denervation. Subspecialties: Biochemistry (biology); Neurochemistry. Office: Dept Neurolog U Md Sch Medicine Baltimore MD 21201

MAXSON, CARLTON JAMES, mathematician, educator; b. Cortland, N.Y., Apr. 19, 1936; s. Edward C. and Eleanor M. (Brooks) M.; m. Carol Y. Maxson, Aug. 31, 1957; children: Debra, James. B.S., SUNY, Abalny, 1958; M.S. (NSF fellow), U. Ill., 1961; Ph.D. (NSF fellow, Faculty fellow), SUNY, Buffalo, 1967. Tchr. high sch. math., Hammondsport, N.Y., 1958-62; asst. prof. to assoc. prof. SUNY, Fredonia, 1962-69; assoc. prof. to prof. Tex. A&M U., 1969-81, prof. math., assoc. dean of sci., 1981—; vis. prof. Teeside Poly., Middlebrough, Eng., 1981. Contbr. articles on algebra and discrete math. to profl. jours. Mem. Am. Math. Soc., Math. Assn. Am., AAAS, Edinburgh Math. Soc., Sigma Xi. Methodist. Current Work: Algebra and discrete math., near-rings, applications of algebra to problems in computer sci.

MAXSON, LINDA ELLEN, genetics and development educator, administrator; b. N.Y.C., Apr. 24, 1943; d. Albert and Ruth (Rosenfeld) Resnick; m. Richard Dey Maxson, June 13, 1964; 1 child, Kevin R. B.S. in Zoology, San Diego State U., 1964, M.A. in Biology, 1966; Ph.D. in Genetics, U. Calif., San Diego State U., 1973. Cert. secondary tchr., Calif. Instr. biology San Diego State U., 1966-68; gen. sci. tchr. San Diego Unified Sch., 1968-69; instr. biochemistry U. Calif., 1974; mem. faculty U. Ill.-Urbana, 1974—, prof., assoc. dir. Sch. Life Scis., 1984—, exec. officer biology, 1981—; curator Mus. Natural History, Urbana, 1983—. Author: Genetics: A Human Perspective, 1985. Judge Sci. Fair, Ill. Acad. Sci., 1976-80. NSF fellow U. Calif.-La Jolla, 1965; NSF research grantee U. Ill., 1976—. Mem. Soc. Study Evolution (v.p. II 1981, councilor 1985—), AAAS, Am. Soc Ichtyologists and Herpetologists (bd. govs. 1985—), Soc. for Study Amphibians and Reptiles (bd. dirs. 1983—), Sigma Xi (speaker 1980—). Democrat. Current work: Reconstruct evolutionary history of living species using molecules as probes of phylogeny, use molecules as clocks to estimate rates of evolutionary change. Subspecialties: Evolutionary biology; Molecular systematics. Home: 612 W Washington Urbana IL 61801 Office: U Illinois 505 South Goodwin St 515 Morrill Hall Urbana IL 61801

MAXSON, STEPHEN CLARK, behavioral geneticist, educator; b. Newport, R.I., Apr. 13, 1938; s. Clark S. and Louise K. (Williams) M.; m. Kathleen N. Wilson, Aug. 28, 1965; m. Susan Irene Wolf, June 21, 1980. S.B., U. Chgo., 1960, Ph.D., 1966. Instr. biology, research assoc. in behavior genetics U. Chgo., 1966-69; asst. prof. depts. biobehavioral scis. and psychology U. Conn., Storrs, 1969-74, assoc. prof., 1974-83, prof., 1984—. Fellow Internat. Soc. Research on Aggression; mem. AAUP, Soc. Neurosci., Behavior Genetics Assn., Sigma Xi. Current Work: Effects of Y-Chromosome on sexually dimorphic behaviors in mammals. Genetics, development, aggression, sexual behavior, inbred mice. Subspecialties: Gene actions; Psychobiology. Office: Dept Behavioral Scis U-154 U Conn Storrs CT 06268

MAXWELL, ARTHUR EUGENE, geophysics institute director, researcher; b. Maywood, Calif., Apr. 11, 1925; s. John Henry and Nelle Irene (Arnold) M.; m. Beulah McKay, 1946 (div. 1963); children: Delle Rae, Eric Arnold, Lynn Marie; m. Rita Louise Johnson, Nov. 23, 1963; children: Brett Alan, Gregory James. B.S. with honors in Physics, N.Mex. State U., 1949; M.S. in Oceanography, Scripps Inst. Oceanography U. Calif.-San Diego, 1952, Ph.D. in Oceanography, 1959. Head oceanographer Office Naval Research, Washington, 1955-60, head grophysics br., 1960-65; assoc. dir., dir. research Woods Hole (Mass.) Oceanographic Inst., 1967-71, provost, 1971-81; dir. Inst. for Geophysics, U. Tex.-Austin, 1982—; mem. corp. Woods Hole Oceanographic Inst., 1971-81, Marine Biol. Lab., Woods Hole, 1973-82, Mus. Sci., Boston, 1972—; bd. dirs. Palisades Geophys. Inst., Nyack, N.Y., 1982—. Editor: The Sea, Vol. IV, 1970; jour. Bolletino de Geofisica, 1968-79. Mem. Nat. Adv. com. on Oceans and Atmosphere, Washington, 1972-76; mem. Mass. Gov.'s Adv. Com. on Sci. and Tech., 1965-71, Mass. Commn. on Ocean Mgmt., 1968-71. Served with USN, 1942-46. Recipient meritorious civilian service award Office Naval Research, 1958; superior civilian service award Asst. Sec. Navy, 1963; disting. civilian service award Sec. Navy, 1964; disting. alumni award N.Mex. State U., 1965. Fellow Am. Geogphys. Union (pres. 1976-78), Marine Tech. Soc. (pres. 1981-82), Internat. Oceanographic Found.; mem. Sigma Xi. Club: Cosmos (Washington). Current Work: Heat flow through ocean floor and other marine geophysical measurements. Subspecialties: Geophysics; Sea floor spreading. Home: 8200 Neely Dr #163 Austin TX 78759 Office: Inst Geophysics U Tex Austin TX 78712

MAXWELL, DONALD LEE, nuclear engineering consultant, consulting firm executive, information management systems consultant; b. Youngstown, Ohio, sept. 14, 1927; s. Jay and Ruth LaRue (Muller) M.; m. Margie Ann Lawton, July 19, 1948; children: Karen Ann, Sharon Lee Terry Lynn. B.S. in Sci, Ohio U., 1951. Registered profl. engr., Calif. Mem. Apollo Support Group, Gen. Electric Corp., 1962 72; mem. quality assurance staff NUS Corp., Clearwater, Fla., 1972 77; mgr. quality assurance Ill. Power Co., Decatur, 1977; cons. corp. staff Black & Veatch, Overland Park, Kans., 1977-79; dir. quality assurance Reliability Engineering Info. Mgmt. Systems, S.W. Research Inst., San Antonio, 1979-81; sr. systems engr. Rockwell Hanford Ops., Richland, Wash., 1981-82; v.p. Project Assistance Corp., San Antonio, 1982—; Dir./developer electronic power plant info. control system and project mgmt. control system, 1980. Served to 1st lt. C.E. U.S. Army, 1946-48, 51-53, Korea. Recipient Apollo award NASA, Houston, 1968. Mem. Am. Soc. Quality Control, Am. Nuclear Soc. Republican. Lodge: Elks. Current Work: Developing large computer-assisted information management control systems for electric power companies and petrochemical industry for productivity improvement. Subspecialties: Information systems, storage, and retrieval (computer science); Nuclear fission. Home and Office: 8618 Timberwilde Dr San Antonio TX 78250

MAXWELL, DONALD ROBERT, pharmaceutical company executive; b. Paris, Mar. 30, 1929; came to U.S., 1974; s. Titus Bonner and Helen Mary Camille M.; m. Catherine Billon, Aug. 16, 1956; children: Monica, Nicholas, Christopher, Caroline, Denis, Dominic, Marie-Claire, Philip. B.A., U. Cambridge, Eng., 1952, M.A., 1956, Ph.D., 1955. Research scholar Med. Research Council, Eng., 1953-55; attaché de récherche Institut Pasteur, Paris, 1955-56; research pharmacologist May & Baker Ltd., Eng., 1957-74; dir. preclin. research Warner-Lambert, Morris Plains, N.J., 1974-77; v.p. preclin. research Warner-Lambert/Parke-Davis, Ann Arbor, Mich., 1977—. Contbr. articles to profl. jours. Mem. Am. Soc. Pharmacology and Exptl. Therapeutics, Brit. Pharmacol. Soc., Physiol. Soc., Biochem. Soc., Internat. Coll. Neuro-Psychopharmacology, Royal Soc. Medicine (Eng.); fellow Inst. Biology (Eng.). Current Work: Direction of drug discovery research in areas of central nervous, cardiovascular and related areas. Subspecialties: Pharmacology; Neuropharmacology. Home: 5621 Navajo Trail Pinckney MI 48169 Office: Warner-Lambert/Parke Davis 2800 Plymouth Rd Ann Arbor MI 48106

MAYER, DAVID JONATHAN, physiologist, educator; b. Mt. Vernon, N.Y., July 18, 1942; s. Jerome Herman and Doris (Cantor) M.; m. Ursula Brigitte Fischer, Aug. 2, 1972. B.A., Hunter Coll., 1966; Ph.D., UCLA, 1971.

Postdoctoral fellow UCLA, 1971-72; asst. prof. Med. Coll. Va., Richmond, 1972-75, assoc. prof., 1975-78, prof., 1978—. Contbr. over 100 articles to profl. jours. NIDA grantee, 1973—. Mem. Soc. Neurosci., Am. Physiol. Soc., Internat. Assn. Study of Pain (founding), Am. Pain Soc. (dir.). Current Work: Neurobiology of pain; endogenous opiates and pain control systems. Subspecialties: Neurophysiology; Psychobiology. Home: 502 Honaker Ave Richmond VA 23226 Office: Med Coll Va Richmond VA 23298

MAYER, DIETER HEINZ HERMANN, electronic engineer; b. Kaiserslautern, Ger., Oct. 25, 1936; came to U.S., 1961; s. August and Elisabeth (Kercher) M.; m. Ute Gisela Wendt, Dec. 30, 1966; children—Gisela, Michael. Dipl. Ing., Fachhochschule, Mannheim, W.Ger., 1960; M.Sc., U. Pa.-Phila., 1965, Ph.D., 1968. Mgr., H. Kuenzig, Kaiserslautern, W.Ger., 1954-56; head Electronic Lab., Johnson Found., U. Pa., Phila., 1961-67, research assoc., 1968-69; researcher BASF AG, Ludwigshafen, Ger., 1970-82, v.p. BASF Systems Corp., Bedford, Mass., 1983—. Contbr. articles to profl. jours.; patentee in field. Mem. IEEE. Current work: Magnetic recording process; automated manufacturing operations. Subspecialty: Information systems, storage, and retrieval (computer science). Home: Hillside Pl Sudbury MA 01776 Office: BASF Systems Corp Crosby Dr Bedford MA 01730

MAYER, JAMES WALTER, materials science educator; b. Chgo., Apr. 24, 1930; s. James Leo and Kathleen (Engels) M.; m. Elizabeth Billmire, June 27, 1952; children—James L., John W., Frank C., Helen K., William A. B.S.M.E., Purdue U., 1952, Ph.D. in Physics, 1960. Tech. staff Hughes Research Labs., Malibu, Calif., 1959-67; prof. Calif. Tech. Inst., Pasadena, 1967-80, master student houses, 1975-80; prof. Cornell U., Ithaca, N.Y., 1980—; scuba instr. Nat. Assn. Underwater Instrs., Los Angeles, 1970-80. Author: Ion Implantation, 1970, Backscattering Spectrometry, 1978; Materials Analysis by Ion Channeling, 1982. Editor: Thin Films, 1978. Bd. dirs. Mayer Sch., Ithaca. Served to capt. U.S. Army, 1952-54. Receipient Von Hippel award Materials Research Soc., Boston, 1981. Fellow Am. Phys. Soc., IEEE; mem. Bohmische Phys. soc., Nat. Acad. Engrs. Current work: Ion implantation, thin film reactions, rapid solidification, ion beam analysis of materials. Subspecialties: Electronic materials; Semiconductors. Home: 416 Cayuga Heights Rd Ithaca NY 14850 Office: Dept Materials Sci Bard Hall Cornell U Ithaca NY 14853

MAYER, RAMONA ANN, quality assurance ofcl., researcher; b. Algona, Iowa, May 9, 1929; d. William John and Esther Theresa (Wolf) M. B.A. in Chemistry, State U. Iowa, 1956; postgrad. in chemistry, Ohio State U., 1960. Lab. asst. Tb Hosp., Iowa City, 1952-53; library asst. State U. Iowa, Iowa City, 1954-56; info. specialist Battelle Meml. Inst., Columbus, Ohio, 1956-59, researcher, 1959-77, dir. quality assurance unit, 1977—; abstractor Chem. Abstracts Service, Columbus, 1958-79. Recipient Achievement award Nat. Aerospace Assn., 1970. Fellow Am. Inst. Chemists; mem. Am. Chem. Soc., Am. Soc. for Quality Control, ASTM, Nat. Soc. for Med. Research. Current Work: Quality assurance on programs dealing with toxicology, pathology, teratology, animal behavior, biochemistry, immunology, chemotherapy, ecology. Subspecialties: Toxicology (medicine); Cancer research (veterinary medicine). Home: 4314 Chaucer Ln Columbus OH 43220 Office: 505 King Ave Columbus OH 43201

MAYER, RICHARD FREDERICK, neurologist, research neurophysiologist; b. Olean, N.Y., June 2, 1929; s. Frank W. and Rosemond F. (Bush) M.; m. Janet R. Bury, Oct. 10, 1959; children: Kathryn, Julianna, Andrea, Christopher, Randall. B.S., St. Bonaventure U., 1950; M.D., SUNY, Buffalo, 1954; postgrad., Mayo Found., U. Minn., 1955-56, Harvard U., 1956-57, 60-62, Neurology Inst., U. London, 1957-58. Diplomate: Am. Bd. Psychiatry and Neurology. Intern Boston City Hosp., 1954-55; resident in neurology Mass. Gen. Hosp., Boston, 1956-60; instr., asso. neurol. unit Harvard U., Boston City Hosp., 1962-66, asso. prof., 1966-68; prof. neurology U. Md. Hosp. and Sch. Medicine, 1968—; dir. EMG Lab., Myasthenia Gravis Clinic and Neuromuscular Service; guest resercher Lab. Neural Control, Nat. Inst. Neurol. and Communicative Disease and Stroke, NIH, Bethesda, Md.; med. adv. bd. Nat. Myasthenia Gravis Found., 1974—; mem. neurobiology merit rev. bd. VA Office, Washington. Contbr. articles profl. jours. Served to lt. USNR, 1958-60. Grantee M.S. Soc.; Grantee NIH; Grantee Myasthenia Gravis Soc. Fellow Am. Acad. Neurology; mem. Am. Neurol. Assn., Soc. Neurosci., N.Y. Acad. Scis., Am. EEG Soc., Am. Assn. Neuropathology, Alpha Omega Alpha. Roman Catholic. Current Work: Studies of diseases of neuromuscular system (Myasthenia gravis, muscular dystrophy), studies of control and orgn. of muscles and motor units. Subspecialties: Neurology; Neurophysiology. Office: U Md Hosp Redwood Greene Baltimore MD 21201

MAYER, WILLIAM JOHN, pharmaceutical company chemist; b. Alliance, Ohio, July 9, 1950; s. John Edward and Mary Louise (DeSimio) M.; m. Kathy Jean Eller, Jan. 8, 1977; children—Mark William, Angela Rae. B.S. in Edn., Kent State U., 1972, M.S., 1976, Ph.D., 1979. Tchr. chemistry Painesville Twp. Bd. Edn., Ohio, 1972-73; research chemist Diamond Shamrock Corp., Painesville, 1979-83; sr. analytical chemist Armour Pharm. Co., Kankakee, Ill., 1983—. Contbr. sci. articles, papers to profl. lit. Mem. Am. Chem. Soc. Current work: Liquid chromatographic separation of desired analytes from sample matrix; use of electrochemical detector for specialized projects; separation and identification of ions by ion chromatography. Subspecialties: Analytical chemistry; Separation science. Home: 8 Emery Dr Bourbonnais IL 60914 Office: Armour Pharmaceutical Co PO Box 511 Kankakee IL 60901

MAYES, LESLIE WILLIAM, computer scientist, educator; b. Thunder Bay, Ont., Can., Dec. 7, 1955; s. Edward Arthur and Marguerite Elizabeth (Blake) M.; m. Martha B. Laking, Sept. 6, 1975. B.S., Queen's U., Kingston, Ont., 1979. Programmer part-time dept. computing and info. sci. Queen's U., 1976-79; systems programmer Lakehead U. Computer Centre, Thunder Bay, 1979—, asst. dir. computer services, 1984—, lectr. dept. math., 1980-85, seminar leader Confedn. Coll., 1984—; cons. computer sci., 1985—. Ont. Ministry of Edn. scholar, 1974. Mem. Assn. Computing Machinery, IEEE. Mem. United Ch. Can. Clubs: Lakehead Toastmasters, Port Arthur Curling and Athletic. Current Work: Enhance and maintain operating systems and programming environments on VAX11/780 and DEC 2020 computers. Subspecialties: Programming languages; Operating systems. Home: 26 Wishart Crescent Thunder Bay ON P7A 6G3 Canada Office: Lakehead U Oliver Rd Thunder Bay ON P7B 5E1 Canada

MAYFIELD, DONALD LEWIS, radiation protection scientist, health physicist; b. Scottsbluff, Nebr., Jan. 20, 1938; s. Lewis Kenneth and Irene Elizabeth (Longstreth) M.; m. Jorlene Lana Schuler, Mar. 22, 1959; children: Brandon James, Christinna Lynne, David Paul, Gail Loraine. B.S., U. Colo., Boulder, 1964; M.P.H., U. Mich., 1969. Radiation protection specialist Batelle-Northwest, Richland, Wash., 1969-70, radiation monitoring supr., 1970-72, devel. engr., 1972-74; mem. staff Health Physics Group, Los Alamos Nat. Lab., 1974-76, Environ. Surveillance Group, 1976—; cons. radiation protection. Mem. Health Physics Soc., Am. Assn. Physicists in Medicine, Am. Phys. Soc. Republican. Lutheran (Mo. Synod). Current Work: Radiation dosimetry, radiation protection instrumentation, radioactive waste disposal, environmental radiation surveillance, alternative fuels, solar energy. Subspecialties: Radiological protection; Health physics. Home: 45 Puye Ct Los Alamos NM 87544 Office: Los Alamos Nat Lab Box 1663 Mail Stop K490 Los Alamos NM 87545

MAYHEW, ERIC GEORGE, cancer research scientist; b. London, June 22, 1938; s. George J. and Doris I. (Tipping) M.; m. Barbara Doe, Sept. 28, 1966; m. Karen Ann Caruana, Apr. 1, 1978; children: Miles, Ian, Andrea. B.Sc., U. London, 1960, M.Sc., 1964, Ph.D., 1967. Research asst. Chester Beatty Research Inst., London, 1960-64; Cancer research scientist Roswell Park Meml. Inst., 1964—; vis. scientist Internat. Inst. Cellular and Molecular Pathology, Brussels, 1977-78; asso. research prof. SUNY, Buffalo, 1979—. Contbr. numerous articles to profl. jours. Mem. N.Y. Acad. Scis., Am. Assn. Cancer Research, AAAS. Current Work: Basis of metastasis, selective delivery of drugs to tumors. Subspecialties: Cancer research (medicine); Pharmacology. Office: Dept Exptl Pathology Roswell Park Meml Inst Buffalo NY 14263

MAYNARD, KENNETH BAKER, automation and systems engineer; b. Birchardville, Pa., Oct. 12, 1933; s. Harry Francis and Edna Frances (Baker) M.; m. Sharon Lee Eddy, June 22, 1957; children—Kevin B., Shari L., Shelley L., Kari B. B.S., M.E., Penn State U., 1960; M.S. in Engring. Adminstrn., Syracuse U., 1969. Registered profl. engr., Calif.; cert. mfg. engr. in robotics and computer-aided mfg. soc. mfg. engrs. Project engr. IBM Corp., Endicott, N.Y., 1960-67, devel. engr., Princeton, N.J., 1967-71, tech asst. to plant mgr., Sherman, Tex., 1971-74, adv. engr., Poughkepsie, N.Y., 1974-76, Austin, Tex., 1976-79, sr. engr., Boca Raton, Fla., 1979-83, Austin, 1983—. Author tech. publs. IBM Products and Processes. Patentee in field. Served with U.S. Army, 1953-55. Recipient IBM Invention Achievement awards, 1968, 72, 73, Tech. Innovation award IBM, 1973. Mem. Nat. Soc. Profl. Engrs., Tex. Soc. Profl. Engrs., Robotics Internat., ASME, Computer and Automated Systems Assn., Soc. Mfg. Engrs., Inst. Indsl. Engrs. (dir. 1972-74), Penn State Alumni Club (v.p. 1982—). Republican. Presbyterian. Current work: Flexible automated manufacturing systems, continuous flow manufacturing processes. Subspecialties: Systems engineering; Robotics. Home: 10204 Vista View Circle Austin TX 78750 Office: IBM Corp 196-007 11400 Burnet Rd Austin TX 78758

MAYO, CLYDE CALVIN, organizational psychologist; b. Robstown, Tex., Feb. 2, 1940; s. Clyde Culberson and Velma (Oxford) M.; m. Jeanne Lynn McCain, Aug. 24, 1963; children: Brady Scott, Amber Camille. B.A., Rice U., 1961; B.S., U. Houston, 1964, Ph.D., 1972; M.S., Trinity U., 1966. Lic. psychologist, Tex. Mgmt. engr. LWFW, Inc., Houston, 1966-72, sr. cons., 1972-78, prin., 1978-81; ptnr. Mayo, Thompson, Bigby, Houston, 1981-83; founder Mgmt. & Personnel Systems, 1983—; counselor Interface Counseling Ctr., Houston, 1976-79; instr. St. Thomas U., Houston, 1979—, U. Houston Downtown Sch., 1972, U. Houston-Clear Lake, 1984—. Co-author: Bi/Polar Inventory of Strengths, 1978. Coach, mgr. Meyerland Little League, 1974-78, So. Belles Softball, 1979-80, S.W. Colt Baseball, 1982-83. Mem. Houston Psychol. Assn. (membership dir. 1978, sec. 1984), Tex. Psychol. Assn., Am. Psychol. Assn., Am. Soc. Tng. and Devel., Houston Area Indsl. Orgnl. Psychologists, Internat. Assn. Quality Circles, Bus. Execs. for Nat. Security. Club: Meyerland. Current Work: Career development within organizations, executive assessment, organization development, management training. Subspecialties: Industrial/organizational psychology; Behavioral psychology. Home: 8723 Ferris St Houston TX 77096 Office: MPS 4545 Bissonnet St Suite 265 Bellaire TX 77401

MAYO, HOWARD ARMSTRONG, JR., mechanical engineer; b. Framingham, Mass., July 30, 1925; s. Howard Armstrong and Dorothy Estelle (Ordway) M.; m. Freddie Lee Dale Kuhne, Nov. 4, 1951; children—Howard Armstrong, III, Lee Dale, Tommi Klare. B.S. in M.E., Worcester Poly. Inst., 1946. Registered profl. engr., Pa. Sales engr., S. Morgan Smith Co., York, Pa., 1946-59; field sales mgr. Allis-Chalmers Corp., York, Pa., 1960-69, sr. staff engr., 1970-76, mgr. customer services, 1976, mgr. standard turbines, 1977-78, mgr. product promotion, 1979-80, mgr. standard turbine market devel., 1981-85; mem. organizing com. Internat. Small Hydro Symposium, Chgo., 1982, New Orleans, 1984; co-chmn. hydroelectric Am. Power Conf., Chgo., 1984, 85; hydro mfg. specialist AID/Stanley Cons., Bangkok, Thailand, 1984. Author: with C.C. Warnick) Hydropower Engineering, 1983. Contbr. articles to profl. jours. Patentee in field. Scout master York-Adams council Boy Scouts Am., York, Pa., 1947-48, commr., 1949—; comdr. U.S. Power Squadron, York, 1973, edn. officer, 1976, 84, 85. Served to lt. (j.g.), USNR, 1943-46. Recipient Scouters award Boy Scouts Am., 1955. Fellow ASME (chmn. hydropower com. Power Div. 1982-83); mem. Nat. Soc. Profl. Engrs., Pa. Soc. Profl. Engrs. (Engr. of Yr. award 1982). Republican. Unitarian. Club: Internat. Equestrian Orgn. (v.p., pres. 1970-73). Current work: Development and promotion of more economical ultra law-head hydro-electric generating systems Subspecialties: Hydro power systems; Mechanical engineering. Home: 2051 Log Cabin Rd York PA 17404

MAYO, JOHN SULLIVAN, communications company executive; b. Greenville, N.C., Feb. 26, 1930; s. William Louis and Mattie (Harris) M.; m. Lucille Dodgson, Apr. 1957; children—Mark Dodgson, David Thomas, Nancy Ann, Lynn Marie. B.S., N.C. State U., 1952, M.S., 1953, Ph.D., 1955. With Bell Telephone Labs., Inc., Murray Hill, N.J., 1955—, exec. dir. toll electronic switching div., 1973-75, v.p. electronics tech., 1975-79, exec. v.p. network systems, 1979—. Contbr. articles to profl. jours. Mem. CAD/CAM policy com., adv. bd. Coll. Engring., U. Calif.-Berkeley; mem. com. Sch. Engring., UCLA; mem. engring. adv. council N.C. State U.; adv. panel Office Tech. Assessment; bd. dirs. Poly Inst. N.Y. Recipient Alexander Graham Bell award; named Outstanding Engring. Alumnus N.C. State U., 1977. Fellow IEEE; mem. Nat. Assn. Engring. Socs. Nat. Acad. Engring. Patentee in field. Current Work: Technology and systems for telecommunications with emphasis on digital approaches for transmssion and switching. Subspecialty: Electrical engineering. Office: AT&T Bell Labs 600 Mountain Ave Murray Hill NJ 07974

MAYOCK, ROBERT LEE, internist; b. Wilkes-Barre, Pa., Jan. 19, 1917; s. John F. and Mathilde M.; m. Constance M. Peruzzi, July 2, 1949; children: Robert Lee, Stephen Philip, Holly Peruzzi. B.S., Bucknell U., 1938; M.D., U. Pa., 1942. Diplomate: Am. Bd. Internal Medicine. Intern Hosp. U. Pa., Phila., 1943-44, resident, 1944-45, chief med. resident, 1945-46, attending physician, 1946—; chief pulmonary disease sect. Phila. Gen. Hosp., 1959-72, sr. cons. pulmonary disease sect., 1972—; asst. prof. clin. medicine U. Pa., 1949-59, assoc. prof., 1959-70, prof. medicine, 1970—; mem. med. adv. com. for Tb Commonwealth of Pa., 1965-74, mem. med. adv. com. on chronic respiratory disease, 1974—, chmn. adv. com., 1981—; cons. Subsplty Bd. Pulmonary Disease Am. Bd. Internal Medicine, 1971-76; bd. dirs. Am. Lung Assn. Contbr. articles in field to med. jours. Served to capt. U.S. Army, 1952-54. Fellow ACP, Am. Coll. Chest Physicians (regent 1972-79); mem. Pa. Med. Soc., Phila. County Med. Soc., Physiology Soc. Phila., Laennec Soc. Phila. (pres. 1963-64), Am. Thoracic Soc., N.Y. Acad. Scis., AMA, Am. Fedn. Clin. Research, Am. Lung Assn. (dir. Phila. and Montgomery County 1961—, pres. 1966-69, dir.-at-large 1983—), Am. Heart Assn., Pa. Lung Assn. (dir. 1976—), Sigma Xi, Alpha Omega Alpha. Clubs: Merion Cricket, Swiftwater Reserve; Westmoreland (Wilkes Barre, Pa.). Current Work: Educator in pulmonary disease. Subspecialties: Pulmonary medicine; Pharmacokinetics. Home: 244 Gypsy Ln Wynnewood PA 19096 Office: Ravdin Bldg 3d Floor Suite 1 U Pa Philadelphia PA 19104

MAYOL, PETE SYTING, biology educator; b. Negros Occidental, Philippines, Aug. 12, 1936; came to U.S., 1963; s. Abundio Y. and Restituta (Syting) M.; m. Flocer Villarente, July 11, 1964; children: Paul A., Virgil A., Jason M. B.S., U. Philippines, 1957; M.S., Okla. State U., 1965; Ph.D., Purdue U., 1968. Plant pathologist Bur. Plant Industry, Manila, 1957; lab. tech. Forest Products Research Inst., Philippines, 1957-58; instr. dept. agronomy U. Philippines, Los Banos, 1958-63; grad. research asst. dept. botany Okla. State U., Stillwater, 1963-65; grad, teaching asst. dept botany and plant pathology Purdue U., West Lafayette, Ind., 1965-66; asst. prof. dept. biol. scis. Calif. State U.-Stanislaus, Turlock, 1968-73, assoc. prof., 1973-81, prof., 1981—; mem. sci. rev. group NIH, Washington, 1981—. Contbr. articles to profl. jours. Entrance scholar U. Philippines, 1953; David-Ross fellow Purdue U., 1966; Danforth Found. assoc., 1980. Mem. AAAS, Calif. Acad. Scis., Filipino-Am. Assn. Stanislaus County (pres. 1976-78), U. Philippines Alumni Assn. Central Calif. (dir. 1982—), Sigma Xi, Phi Sigma. Current Work: Interrelationships between soil microorganisms and plant parasitic nematodes particularly the root-knot nematodes. Subspecialties: Microbiology; Plant pathology. Home: 1620 Carleton Dr Turlock CA 95380 Office: Dept Biol Scis Calif State U Stanislaus 800 Monte Vista Ave Turlock CA 95380

MAYOR, HEATHER DONALD, microbiologist, educator; b. Melbourne, Australia, July 6, 1930; d. Joseph Arthur Lindsay and Elizabeth Emily (Boyd) Donald; m. Richard Blair Mayor, May 28, 1956; children: Diana Boyd, Philip Hastings. B.S., U. Melbourne, 1948, M.S., 1950; Ph.D., U. London, 1954; D.Sc., U. Melbourne, 1970. Walter and Eliza Hall postdoctoral fellow Inst. Med. Research, Melbourne, 1954-56; asst. prof. virology Harvard U. Med. Sch., Cambridge, Mass., 1956-59; assoc. prof. Baylor U. Coll. Medicine, Houston, 1963-75, prof. microbiology and immunology, 1975—; cons. NIH, AEC, U. Tex. Health Sci. Ctr., others. Contbr. over 200 articles to sci. jours. Mem. women's com. Houston Symphony Orch.; mem. Houston Contemporary Arts Mus., Young Women in the Arts, Houston Friends of Music. Recipient Disting. award Center for Interaction: Man. Sci. and Culture, 1971. Mem. Am. Assn. Immunologists, Am. Soc. Virologists, Am. Soc. Microbiology, Biophys. Soc., Electron Microscopy Soc. Am., Am. Soc. Cell Biology, Tissue Culture Assn., Sigma Xi. Episcopalian. Clubs: Tuesday Music (Houston), Doctors (Houston), Houstonian (Houston). Current Work: Defective viruses and cancer, interference and prevention. Subspecialties: Virology (medicine); Genetics and genetic engineering (biology). Home: 226 Pine Hollow Ln Houston TX 77056 Office: Baylor Coll Medicine Houston TX 77030

MAYR, ERNST, zoologist, research scientist; b. Kempten, Germany, July 5, 1904; came to U.S., 1931; s. Otto and Helene (Pusinelli) M.; m. Margarete Simon, May 4, 1935; children: Christa E., Susanne. Cand. med., U. Greifswald, 1925; Ph.D., U. Berlin, 1926; Ph.D. (hon.), Uppsala U., Sweden, 1957; D.Sc. (hon.), Yale U., 1959, U. Melbourne, 1959, Oxford U., 1966, U. Munich, 1968, U. Paris, 1974, Harvard U., 1980, Guelph U., U. Cambridge, 1982, U. Vt., 1984. Asst. curator zool. mus. U. Berlin, 1926-32; mem. Rothschild expdn. to Dutch New Guinea, 1928, expdn. to Mandated Ty. of New Guinea, 1928-29, Whitney Expdn., 1929-30; research asso. Am. Mus. Natural History, N.Y.C., 1931-32, asso. curator, 1932-44, curator, 1944-53; Jesup lectr. Columbia U., 1941; Alexander Agassiz prof. zoology Harvard U., 1953-75, emeritus, 1975—; dir. Harvard (Mus. Comparative Zoology), 1961-70. Author: List of New Guinea Birds, 1941, Systematics and the Origin of Species, 1942, Birds of the Southwest Pacific, 1945, Birds of the Philippines, (with Jean Delacour), 1946, Methods and Principles of Systematic Zoology, (with E. G. Linsley and R. L. Usinger), 1953, Animal Species and Evolution, 1963, Principles of Systematic Zoology, 1969, Populations, Species and Evolution, 1970, Evolution and the Diversity of Life, 1976, (with W. Provine) Evolutionary Synthesis, 1980, Biologie de l'Evolution, 1981, The Growth of Biological Thought, 1982; editor: Evolution, 1947-49. Pres. XIII Internat. Ornith. Congress, 1962. Recipient Leidy medal, 1946; Wallace Darwin medal, 1958; Brewster medal Am. Ornithologists Union, 1965; Daniel Giraud Elliot medal, 1967; Nat. Medal of Sci., 1970; Molina prize Accademia delle Scienze, Bologna, Italy, 1972; Linnean medal, 1977; Gregor Mendel medal, 1980; Balzan prize, 1983. Fellow Linnean Soc. N.Y. (past sec. editor), Am. Ornithol. Union (pres. 1956-59), New York Zool. Soc.; mem. Am. Philos. Soc., Nat. Acad. Sci., Am. Acad. Arts and Scis., Am. Soc. Zoologists, Soc. Systematic Zoology (pres. 1966), Soc. Study Evolution (sec. 1946, pres. 1950); hon. or corr. mem. Royal Australian, Brit. ornithol. unions, Zool. Soc. London, Soc. Ornithol. France, Royal Soc. New Zealand, Bot. Gardens Indonesia, S. Africa Ornithol. Soc., Linnean Soc. London, Deutsche Akademie der Naturforsch Leopoldina., Accad. Naz. dei Lincei. Current Work: Philosophy of biology, intellectual history of biology. Subspecialty: Evolutionary biology. Office: Mus Comparative Zoology Harvard U Cambridge MA 02138

MAYWOOD, PAUL STANLEY, mine geologist; b. Salt Lake City, Sept. 17, 1952; s. Stanley Wallace and Katherine Frances (Forcade) M. B.S., Mesa Coll., 1978; postgrad. Portland State U., 1980-82. Computer operator First Nat. Bank Denver, Grand Junction, 1978-79; drafting technician Agapito & Assocs., Inc., Grand Junction, 1979; computer geologist NERCO, Inc., Portland, 1980-82; staff geologist NERCO Mining Co., Sheridan, Wyo., 1982-84; instr. geology Western Wyo. Coll., Rock Springs, 1985—; mine geologist Bridger Coal Co./Pacific Minerals, Rock Springs, 1984—. Contbr. articles to profl. jours. State of Colo. grantee, 1978; recipient NASA Achievement award, 1970. Mem. Soc. Econ. Paleontologists and Mineralogists, Am. Assn. Petroleum Geologists, Soc. Mining Engrs. of AIME, Geol. Soc. Am., Wyo. Geol. Assn. Democrat. Club: Skyline High Sch. Chess (pres. 1969-70). Current work: Geocharacterization of coal overburden and application of mine-level depositional models to applied mining problems and pit dewatering techniques. Subspecialties: Sedimentology; Geochemistry. Office: Bridger Coal Co PO Box 2068 Rock Springs WY 82901

MAZARAKIS, MICHAEL GERASSIMOS, physicist, researcher; b. Volos, Greece, Apr. 25, 1937; came to U.S., 1966, naturalized, 1980; s. Nikolaos Gerassimos and Anthie Gerassimos (Kappatos) M. B.S. in Physics, U. Athens, Greece, 1960; M.S. in Physics, U. Sorbonne, Paris, 1963, Ph.D. in Physics, 1965; Ph.D. in Physics, U. Pa., 1971; cert. in mgmt., MIT, 1976. Mem. faculty Rutgers U., New Brunswick, N.J., 1971-74; v.p. and dir. exptl. program Fusion Energy Corp., Princeton, N.J., 1974-77, also exec. v.p., 1975-77; research physicist Argonne Nat. Lab., U. Chgo., 1978-81; research physicist Sandia Nat. Lab. Div. 1272, Albuquerque, 1981—. Contbr. articles to profl. jours. Patentee in field. Bd. dirs. Orthodox Ch., Albuquerque, 1981-83; Served to maj. Greek Army, 1960-62. Recipient award Italian. Govt., 1956, Greek Govt., 1956-60, French Govt., 1962-65; Yale U. grantee, 1966. Mem. Am. Phys. Soc., IEEE, Alliance Francaise, N. Mex. Mountain Club, Sigma Xi. Current work: Particle beam physics, accelerator research and development, inertial fusion, pulse power technology, plasma physics. Subspecialty: Nuclear fusion. Office: Sandia Nat Lab Div 1272 PO Box 5800 Albuquerque NM 87185

MAZIA, DANIEL, biologist, educator; b. Scranton, Pa., Dec. 18, 1912; s. Aaron and Bertha (Kurtz) M.; m. Gertrude Greenblatt, June 19, 1938; children: Judith Ann, Rebecca Ruth. A.B., U. Pa., 1933, Ph.D., 1937; Ph.D. h.c, U. Stockholm, 1976. National Research Council fellow in biology sci. Princeton, 1937-38; asst. prof. zoology U. Mo., 1938-41, asso. prof., 1942-47, prof., from 1947; asso. prof. zoology U. Calif., Berkeley, 1951-53; now prof.; prof. biol. scis. Stanford U., 1980—; Mem. corp. Marine Biol. Lab., Woods Hole.; mem. bd. trustees and physiology teaching staff, 1950—. Mem. editorial bd.: Exptl. Cell Research. Served as 1st lt. AAF, 1942-44; capt. aviation medicine 1944-45. Fellow Am. Acad. Arts and Scis.; mem. Am. Soc. Cell Biology (Wilson medal 1981), Soc. Gen. Physiologists, Nat. Acad. Scis. Current Work: Mitosis. Subspecialty: Cell biology. Address: Hopkins Marine Station (Stanford U) Pacific Grove CA 93950

MAZO, ROBERT MARC, chemistry educator, researcher; b. Bklyn, Oct. 3, 1930; s. Nathan and Rose Marian (Mazo) M.; m. Joan Ruth Spector, Sept. 5, 1954; children: Ruth Sara, Jeffrey Alan, Daniel Paul. A.B., Harvard U., 1952; M.S., Yale U., 1953, Ph.D., 1955. NSF postdoctoral fellow U. Amsterdam, Netherlands, 1955-56; research assoc. U. Chgo., 1956-58; asst. prof. Calif. Inst. Tech., 1958-62; assoc. prof. chemistry U. Oreg., 1962-65, prof., 1965—; cons. in field. Author: Statistical Mechanical Theories of Transport Process; contbr. numerous articles to profl. publs. Alfred P. Sloan fellow, 1961-65; NSF sr. postdoctoral fellow, 1968-69; Heinrich Hertz Stiftung fellow, 1981-82; Meyerhof fellow, 1982. Mem. Am. Chem. Soc., Am. Phys. Soc., AAAS, AAUP, Sigma Xi. Patentee in field. Current Work: Theory of irreversible processes; applications of stat.mechanics to varied fields. Subspecialties: Statistical mechanics; Statistical physics. Home: 2460 Charnelton St Eugene OR 97405 Office: Inst Theoretical Sci U Oreg Eugene OR 97403

MAZUR, ALEXANDER, electrical engineer; b. Moscow, USSR, Dec. 23, 1937; came to U.S., 1979; s. Lev and Roza (Surois) Feiman; m. Yelena Mazur, July 18, 1966; 1 son, Dmitry. M.S. in Electromech. and Elec. Engring., Univ. Elec. Engring., Moscow, 1967. Sr. engr. Moscow Electric Plant, Moscow, 1956-79; sr. elec. engr. Internat. Transformer Corp., Montebello, Calif., 1980—. Author: Auxiliaries Transformers, 1978; contbr. articles to tech. jours. Patentee in field. Assoc. mem. IEEE. Current work: Transformer and reactor design; formula deduction; research and development in new field of transformer design. Subspecialty: Applied magnetics. Office: Internat Transformer Corp 6900 E Washington Blvd Montebello CA 90640

MAZUR, PETER, cell physiologist, cryobiologist; b. N.Y.C., March 3, 1928; s. Paul M. and Adolphia (Kaske) M.; m. Drusilla Stevens, May 28, 1953 (dec. May 1982); 1 child, Timothy Stevens; m. Sara Jo Bolling, June 16, 1984. A.B. magna cum laude, Harvard U., 1949, Ph.D., 1953. NSF postdoctoral fellow, Princeton U., N.J., 1957-59; research staff biology div. Oak Ridge Nat. Lab., 1959—, group leader theoretical and applied cryobiology, 1966—, sci. dir. biophysics and cell physiology, biology div., 1974-75; mem. vis. com. biology Harvard U. Bd. Overseers 1972-77; mem. Space Sci. Bd. of Nat. Acad., 1975-77. Contbr. articles to prof. jours. Served to capt. USAF, 1953-57. Recipient Author of Yr. award Martin-Marietta Energy Systems, 1985; Lalor fellow Harvard U., 1952, John Harvard fellow, 1951. Sigma Xi Nat. lectr., 1980. Fellow AAAS; mem. Soc. for Cyrobiology (pres. 1973-74, bd. govs., 1979—). Club: Cosmos (Washington). Current work: Cryobiology mechanisms of freezing injury in living cells and tissues. Subspecialties: Cell biology; Biophysics (biology). Home: 125 Westlook Circle Oak Ridge TN 37830 Office: Biology Div Oak Ridge Lab PO Box Y Oak Ridge TN 37831

MAZUREK, THADDEUS JOHN, physicist, physics and astrophysics educator; b. Tarnogrod, Poland, Aug. 11, 1942; came to U.S., 1951, naturalized, 1962; s. Josef and Marianna (Pavliha) M.; m. Carolyn Bryant, Nov. 30, 1974; children—Fabrienne T., Cassandra L. M.S., Fordham Coll., 1966; M.A., Yeshiva U., 1968, Ph.D., 1973. Research asst. Yeshiva U., 1973; research assoc. Harvard Coll. Obs., Cambridge, Mass., 1973-74; research scientist, lectr. U. Tex.-Austin, 1974-79; asst. prof. SUNY-Stony Brook, 1979-82; sr. physicist Mission Research Corp., Santa Barbara, Calif., 1982—; lectr., guest prof. Nordita, Copenhagen, Denmark, 1979. Contbr. articles to profl. jours. NSF Research grantee, 1978-79; Dept. Energy Research grantee, 1980-82. Mem. Am. Astron. Soc., Internat. Astron. Union, N.Y. Acad. Sci., AAAS. Democrat. Current Work: Theory of fluid and plasma flows in nuclear explosions within the atmosphere; supernova theory, including hydrodynamics and energy transport of stellar explosions. Subspecialties: Theoretical physics;

Theoretical astrophysics. Office: Mission Research Corp 735 State St Santa Barbara CA 93102

MC*KEE, LEWIS WITHERSPOON, mechanical engineer; b. Portsmouth, N.H., Mar. 12, 1923; s. Andrew Irwin and Katherine (Brown) McKee; m. Sophia Kuhlmann Greenstein, June 29, 1946; m. Pat, Oct. 26, 1963; children: Lewis, Sophia, Miriam, Eugenia. B.S.M.E., MIT, 1944. Registered profl. engr., Calif. Chief product engr. Barden Corp., Danbury, Conn., 1947-73; engring. mgr. NMB Corp., Chatsworth, Calif., 1973-74, cons. mech. engring., Westlake Village, Calif., 1974-75, Thousand Oaks, Calif., 1978-80; mgr. bearing engring. W.S. Shamban & Co., Newbury Park, Calif., 1975-77; mgr. engring. Tribotech Corp., Redwood City, Calif., 1977-78; engring. specialist Aerospace Corp., El Segundo, Calif., 1980—. Served with USN, 1942-45. Recipient Project Hindsight award Dept. Def., 1966. Republican. Club: Thousand Oaks Racquet. Patentee ball bearing components and assemblies. Current Work: Consulting activities on bearing applications for satellites. Office: Aerospace Corp El Segundo CA 90009

MCABEE, THOMAS ALLEN, psychologist, consultant; b. Spartanburg, S.C., Mar. 31, 1949; s. Thomas Walker and Doris Lee (Gillespie) McA. Student, Ga. Inst. Tech., 1967-69; B.A., Furman U., 1971; M.A., U. S.C., 1975, Ph.D., 1979. Co-dir. community problems survey Eau Claire Community Project, Columbia, S.C., 1975; instr. U.S.C., Columbia, 1976—; NSF intern S.C. State Legislature, Columbia, 1978; research dir. S.C. Legislative-Gov.'s Com. on Mental Health and Mental Retardation, Columbia, 1979-80; co-dir. Children's TV project Feelings Just Are, Columbia Area Mental Health Center, 1980—; psychologist S.C. Dept. Mental Retardation, Florence, 1982—; chmn. Primary Prevention Public Media Com., S.C. Dept. Mental Health, 1979-81; research cons. S.C. Protection and Advocacy System for Handicapped Citizens, 1980, 81, cons. numerous govtl. and pvt. agys. Recipient Palmetto Pictures Photography award U. S.C., 1977, Gabriel award, 1981; NIMH fellow, 1976-77. Mem. Am. Psychol. Assn. Current Work: Behavior modification for the developmentally disabled; mass media-based community interventions; children's television. Subspecialties: Behavioral psychology; Community psychology. Office: SC Department Mental Retardation PO Box 3209 Florence SC 29502

MC AFEE, JERRY, retired oil company executive, chemical engineer; b. Port Arthur, Tex., Nov. 3, 1916; s. Almer McD. and Marguerite (Calfee) McA.; m. Geraldine Smith, June 21, 1940; children: Joe R., William M., Loretta M., Thomas R. B.S. in Chem Engring, U. Tex. at Austin, 1937; Sc.D. in Chem. Engring, Mass. Inst. Tech., 1940; student, Mgmt. Problems for Execs., U. Pitts., 1952. Research chem. engr. Universal Oil Products Co., Chgo., 1940-43, operating engr., 1944-45; tech. specialist Gulf Oil Corp., Port Arthur, Tex., 1945-50; successively dir. chemistry, asst. dir. research, v.p., asso. dir. research subs. Gulf Research & Devel. Co., Hamarville, Pa., 1950-55, v.p. engring. mfg. dept. of corp., 1955-60, v.p., exec. tech. advisor of corp., 1960-64, also dir. planning and econs., 1962-64; sr. v.p. Gulf Oil Corp., 1964-67, chmn. bd., chief exec. officer, 1976-81; sr. v.p. Gulf Eastern Co., London, 1964-67; exec. v.p. Brit. Am. Oil Co., Ltd., Toronto, Ont., 1967-69; pres., chief exec. officer, dir. Gulf Oil Can. Ltd., 1969-75; dir. McDonnell Douglas Corp. Bd. dirs. Am. Petroleum Inst., MIT Corp.; mem. exec. com. Allegheny Conf. Community Devel. Fellow Am. Inst. Chem. Engring. (v.p. 1959, pres. 1960); Mem. Nat. Acad. Engring., Am. Petroleum Inst., Am. Chem. Soc. Presbyterian. Clubs: Duquesne (Pitts.); Toronto (Toronto), York (Toronto); Fox Chapel Golf; Rolling Rock (Ligonier, Pa.); John 's Island (Vero Beach, Fla.). Patentee in field. Current Work: Petroleum and its products. Subspecialties: Chemical engineering; Fuels. Home: 4 Indian Hill Rd Pittsburgh PA 15238

MCAFEE, KENNETH BAILEY, JR., chemical physics researcher; b. Chgo., June 22, 1924; s. Kenneth Bailey and Ruth G. McAfee; m. Patricia Davis, Dec. 22, 1959; children—Ellen Armstrong, Graham Ashton. B.S., Harvard U., 1946, Ph.D., 1950. Mem. tech. staff AT&T Bell Labs., Murray Hill, N.J., 1949—, dept. head, 1966—; vis. fellow Joint Inst. Lab. Astrophysics, U. Colo., Boulder, 1965-66; mem. def. sci. bd. Dept. Def., Washington, 1967-69, NRC Commn. on Sociotech. Systems, Nat. Acad. Engring., Washington, 1975-78; chmn. sci. adv. com. Gov. State of N.J., Trenton, 1979-83. Patentee in field. Served to lt. (j.g.) USNR, 1943-46; PTO. Recipient Disting. Scientist award AT&T Bell Labs., 1982, Spl. award of Merit, EPA, 1981; Vis. Fellow award U. Colo., 1965. Fellow Am. Phys. Soc. (gaseous electronics conf., exec. com. 1965-66); mem. AIEE. Current work: Studies of charge and energy transfer processes and communications transmission technology. Subspecialties: Physical chemistry; Atomic and molecular physics. Home: 41 Ellis Dr Basking Ridge NJ 07920 Office: AT&T Bell Labs 600 Mountain Ave Murray Hill NJ 07974

MCALLISTER, CHRIS THOMAS, metabolic physiologist, researcher; b. Pine Bluff, Ark., July 26, 1955; s. James Thomas and Mary Ellen (Kober) McA.; m. Elizabeth Ann Mills, Aug. 19, 1978. B.S., U. Ark.-Little Rock, 1978; M.S. in Biology, Ark. State U., 1981. Phlebotomist, med. asst. St. Vincent's Infirmary, Little Rock, Ark., 1974-78; teaching asst. Ark. State U., 1978-80, North Tex. State U., Denton, 1980-82; research mammalian physiologist VA Med. Ctr., Dallas, 1982—; cons. environ. impact statement Techrad, Bald Knob, Ark., 1979. Contbr. numerous articles to tech., ecol., biol. jours. Herpetol. grantee, Ark. Herpetol. Soc., 1979; Sigma Xi grant-in-aid awardee, 1982; Am. Mus. Natural History Theodore Roosevelt Meml. Fund awardee, 1982. Mem. Soc. for Study of Amphibians and Reptiles (grantee 1985), Am. Soc. Ichthyologists and Herpetologists, Nat. Speleol. Soc., Southwestern Assn. Naturalists, Sigma Xi. Lutheran. Current work: Renal-metabolic physiology; natural history; biology of reptiles; cave salamander metabolism; cave community ecology; parasites of herptiles. Subspecialties: Physiology (biology); Herpetology. Office: VA Med Ctr 4500 S Lancaster Rd Dallas TX 75216

MCALLISTER, HAROLD ANTONIO, veterinary pathologist, microbiologist; b. San Juan, P.R., Nov. 1, 1941; s. Claudio Jesus and Tomasa (Charneco) McA.; m. Pamela Kay Walsworth, Mar. 21, 1970. B.S. Magna cum laude, U. P.R., 1961, M.S., Sch. Medicine, 1966; D.V.M., Mich. State U., 1980. Lic. veterinarian Iowa, Mich.; specialist microbiologist in pub. health and med. lab. microbiology Am. Acad. Microbiology. Grad. asst. Mich. State U., East Lansing, 1966-68, asst. instr., 1968-70, microbiologist, 1970-73, research asst., 1973-77; adj. instr. Iowa State U., Ames, 1980—. Author: Procedures for the Identification of Microorganisms from the Higher Animals, 1970; contbg. author chpts. and illustrations: Diagnostic Procedures in Veterinary Bacteriology and Mycology, 1973, 4th edit., 1984. Contbr. articles to profl. jours. Co-discoverer Pasteurella aerogenes, new species of porcine bacteria, 1974. Recipient Alumni Assn. award U. P.R., 1961, cert. of achievement Iowa State U., 1981, 82, 83, 84, 85; Charles L. Davis Found. scholar, 1983. Mem. AVMA, Am. Assn. Vet. Lab. Diagnosticians, Assn. Vet. Microbiologists, Assn. Puerto Ricans in Sci. and Engring., Sigma Xi, Phi Zeta, Gamma Sigma Delta. Current work: Pathology of pseudorabies; pathobiology of herpes viruses; biopsy and necropsy veterinary service; veterinary diagnostic bacteriology and mycology. Subspecialties: Pathology (veterinary medicine); Microbiology (veterinary medicine). Office: Dept Vet Pathology Iowa State U Ames IA 50011

MCARDLE, RICHARD NEFF, horticulturist; b. Columbus, Ohio, July 31, 1956; s. Richard Coppedge and Nancy Lee (Neff) M.; m. Alice Eileen Jacot, Apr. 17, 1982. B.S., Pa. State U., 1977; M.S., U. Md., College Park, 1980, Ph.D., 1983. Staff scientist Dynamac Corp., Rockville, Md., 1983-85; sr. scientist Tech. Resources Inc., Rockville, 1985—. Mem. Am. Soc. Hort. Sci., Biometric Soc., Am. Genetic Assn., Soil Conservation Soc. Am. Current work: Pesticide chemistry research evaluation, analysis of pesticide metabolism in plants and animals. Subspecialties: Environmental chemistry; Plant physiology (agriculture).

MCARTHUR, DAVID ALEXANDER, research engineer, marketing consultant; b. Meridian, Miss., Aug. 14, 1938; s. Robert Stainton and Kathleen Adele (Sanders) McA.; m. Beverley Bogue, Sept. 16, 1961; children: Shirin R., Kara Kay, Paul D. B.S., U. Ariz., Tucson, 1960; postgrad., U. Munich, Ger., 1961; Ph.D., U. Calif.-Berkeley, 1967. Mem. tech. staff Bell Telephone Labs., Holmdel, N.J., 1967-69; with Sandia Nat. Labs., Albuquerque, 1969—, Disting. mem. tech. staff, 1983—. Contbr. articles to profl. jours. Woodrow Wilson fellow, 1962; NSF fellow, 1963-67; Nat. Merit scholar, 1956; Fulbright scholar, 1960-61. Mem. Am. Phys. Soc. Republican. Presbyterian. Patentee reactor excited laser. Current Work: Nuclear reactor safety research; numerical modelling of plasmas, reactor-excited lasers, coded-aperture imaging of fission sources. Subspecialty: Atomic and molecular physics. Office: PO Box 5800 Albuquerque NM 87185

MCARTHUR, ELDON DURANT, research geneticist, botany and range science educator; b. Hurricane, Utah, Mar. 12, 1941; s. Eldon and Denise (Dalton) McA.; m. Virginia Johnson, Dec. 20, 1961; children: Curtis Durant, Monica, Denise, Ted Owen. A.S. with high honors, Dixie Coll., 1963; B.S. cum laude, U. Utah, 1965, M.S., 1967, Ph.D., 1970. Agrl. Research Council postdoctoral fellow U. Leeds, Eng., 1970-71; research geneticist Intermountain Research Sta., Forest Service, U.S. Dept. Agr., Ephraim, Utah, 1972-75, Provo, Utah, 1975-78, prin. research geneticist, 1978—, project leader, 1983—; adj. assoc. prof. dept. botany and range sci. Brigham Young U., 1976-78, adj. prof., 1978—; adj. prof. biol. scis. Wayne State U., 1985—; chmn. Shrub Research Consortium. Contbr. numerous articles to profl. jours., govt. publs., chpts. to books; also book editor. Recipient U.S. Dept. Agr. cert. of Merit, 1979; NDEA fellow, 1965-68; NIH fellow, 1968-70; Sigma Xi grantee, 1970-71; NSF grantee, 1981—. Mem. Soc. Range Mgmt., Soc. Study of Evolution, Bot. Soc. Am., Am. Genetic Assn., Rocky Mountain Forest Genetics Com., Sigma Xi. Mormon. Current Work: Cytogenetics, breeding systems, evolution; improvement of Western wildland shrubs. Subspecialty: Plant genetics. Home: 555 N 1200 E Orem UT 84057 Office: 735 N 500 E Provo UT 84601

MCARTHUR, WILSON COOPER, engineering consultant executive, radiation protection consultant; b. Clinton, N.C., June 28, 1936; s. Charles Dixon and Margaret (McLamb) McA.; m. Robbie Louise Taylor, Aug. 23, 1959; children: Gregory, Suzette, Alexander. B.S., East Carolina U., 1965; M.S., U. N.C., 1967; Ph.D., Purdue U., 1971. Registered profl. engr. cert. hazards control mgr. Prin. engr. Carolina Power and Light Co., Raleigh, N.C., 1971-77; v.p., gen. mgr. Hittman Corp., Columbia, Md., 1977-78; div. mgr. Tera Corp., Berkeley, Calif., 1978-80, EDS Nuclear, Walnut Creek, Calif., 1980-82; pres. KLM Engring., Inc., Walnut Creek, 1982—. Served with USAF, 1955-59. Named Outstanding physics student East Carolina Coll., 1965. Mem. Am. Nuclear Soc. (pres. N.C. chpt. 1977), Health Physics Soc. (pres. N.C. chpt. 1976). Current Work: Development of radiation protection criteria and development of techniques to process, transport and dispose of radioactive waste. Subspecialties: Artificial intelligence; Nuclear fission. Home: 1478 Ramsay Circle Walnut Creek CA 94598 Office: KLM Engring Inc 2700 Ygnacio Valley Rd Suite 160 Walnut Creek CA 94596

MCATEE, JAMES LEE, JR., chemist, educator, cons.; b. Waco, Tex., Aug. 29, 1924; s. James Lee and Edith Beatrice (Smith) McA.; m. Francis Louise Linville, Sept. 6, 1947; children: Susan Monday, James Lee, Rosamonde Slakie, Winfield Linville. B.S., Tex. A&M U., 1947; M.S., Rice U., 1949, Ph.D., 1951. Lab. technician Shell Exploration & Prodn. Research, summers 1948-50; research scientist Barold div. NL Industries, Houston, 1951-59, supvr. tech. service labs., 1954-59; mem. faculty dept. chemistry Baylor U., 1959—, asst. prof. chemistry, 1959-61, assoc. prof., 1961-69, prof., 1969—, chmn. dept., 1981—; cons. chemistry of clays to industry. Contbr. numerous articles on clays, clay minerals, Am. minerals, surface and colloid sci. to profl.jours. Deacon, elder First Presbyterian Ch., Waco. Served to lt. USAAF, 1943-45. Fellow Minerals Soc. Am.; mem. Am. Chem. Soc., Am. Crystollography Soc., Clay Minerals Soc., Tex. Electron Microscopy Soc., N.Am. Thermal Analysis Soc. Club: Kiwanis (Waco) (pres. 1970-71). Current Work: Study of clay minerals and organo-clay complexes; surface and rheology of clays and organo-clays extending to high pressure areas. Subspecialties: Physical chemistry; Surface chemistry. Home: 5625 Oakview Waco TX 76710 Office: Dept Chemistry Baylor U Waco TX 76798

MCAULAY, ALASTAIR D., engineer; b. West Wickham, Kent, England, May 9, 1938; came to U.S. Nov. 1967, naturalized 1973; s. John and Martha (Huni) McA.; m. Carol Julia Saggs, May 27, 1967; 1 child, Alexander Charles Douglas. B.A., Cambridge U., 1961, M.A., 1964; Ph.D., Carnegie-Mellon U., 1974. Researcher Brush Electrical Co., Loughborough, England, 1961-64; research engr. Kodak, Harrow, England, 1964-67; sr. engr. Westinghouse, Pitts., 1967-70; prin. engr. Honeywell, Seattle, 1974-79; mem. tech. staff Tex. Instruments, Dallas, 1979—; adj. prof. Seattle U., 1976-79, So. Meth. U., Dallas, 1982—. Contbr. articles to engring. jours. Kent scholar Kent County, Eng., 1958-61, Victoria scholar Whitgift Found., 1949-56; U. fellow U.S. Dept. Transp., 1971-73. Mem. IEEE (sr. mem.; chmn. Dallas 1983-84, regions rep. 1984—), IEEE Computer Soc. (Outstanding Service award 1983), Internat. Soc. for Optical Engring., Soc. of Exploration Geophysicists, Dallas Geophysicists Soc. Current work: Signal processing and numerical computation with parallel electronic and optical computers. Applications include modeling and inversion in geophysical exploration, NMR modeling and finite elements. Subspecialties: Computer engineering; Optical signal processing. Home: 15808 Nedra Way Dallas TX 75248 Office: Tex Instruments Central Research Labs PO Box 226015 Dallas TX 75266

MCAULEY, VAN ALFON, aerospace mathematician; b. Travelers Rest, S.C., Aug. 28, 1926; s. Stephen Floyd and Emily Floree (Cox) McA. B.A., U. N.C., Chapel Hill, 1951. Mathematician Army Ballistic Missile Agy., Huntsville, Ala., 1956-59; physicist NASA, Marshall Center, Huntsville, 1960-61, research mathematician, 1962-70, mathematician, 1970-81. Served with U.S. Army, 1944-46. Recipient Apollo achievement award NASA, 1969, cost savs. award, 1973, Skylab achievement award, 1974, Outstanding Performance award, 1976. Mem. Am. Math. Soc., Soc. Indsl. and Applied Math., AAAS, N.Y. Acad. Scis., Phi Beta Kappa. Patentee in field, of control system invention. Current Work: Documentation of methods devised for the numerical solution of heat flow equations involving both elliptic and parabolic partial differential equations. Subspecialties: Aerospace engineering and technology; Numerical analysis (computer science). Home: 3529 Rosedale Dr Huntsville AL 35810

MCBAY, HENRY CECIL, chemistry educator; b. Mexia, Tex., May 29, 1914; s. William Cecil and Roberta (Ransom) McB.; children—Michael H.C., Ronald P.W. B.S. in Chemistry, Wiley Coll., 1934; M.S. in Chemistry, Atlanta U., 1936; Ph.D. in Chemistry, U. Chgo., 1945. Instr. chemistry Wiley Coll., Marshall, Tex., 1936-38, Western U., Quindaro, Kans., 1938-39; research fellow Carver Found., Tuskegee Inst., Ala., 1941-42; prof. chemistry Morehouse Coll., Atlanta, 1945-81, Atlanta U., 1981—; tech. expert UNESCO, Paris-Republic Liberia, 1951; vis. prof. U. Minn., Mpls., 1969-70. Contbr. articles to profl. jours. Mem. Am. Chem. Soc. (exec. com. local sect.). Subspecialties: Organic chemistry; Electron spin resonance. Office: Atlanta U 223 Chestnut St SW Atlanta GA 30314

MCBREEN, JAMES, research chemist; b. Cavan, Ireland, Sept. 5, 1938; came to U.S., 1961, naturalized, 1974; s. Bernard and Mary Ellen (Coyle) McB.; m. Elizabeth Ann O'Connor, Apr. 23, 1966; children—Susan E., Brian J. B.S., U. Coll. Dublin (Ireland), 1961; Ph.D., U. Pa., 1965. Chemist Yardney Electric Corp., N.Y.C., 1965-68; sr. scientist Gen. Motors Research Labs., Warren, Mich., 1968-77; chemist Brookhaven Nat. Lab., Upton, N.Y., 1977—. Patentee in field. Mem. Electrochem. Soc. (life, chmn. edn. com. 1981-83, chmn. energy tech. group 1981-83, sec.-treas. battery div. 1984—), AAAS, N.Y. Acad. Scis. Roman Catholic. Current work: Batteries, fuel cells, electrochemical kinetics, electrodeposition, corrosion, hydrogen embrittlement of metals. Subspecialty: Physical chemistry. Home: 24 Bellport Ln Bellport NY 11713 Office: Brookhaven Nat Lab Upton NY 11973

MCBRIDE, RAYMOND ANDREW, physician, educator; b. Houston, Dec. 27, 1927; s. Raymond Andrew and Rita (Mullane) McB.; m. Isabelle Davis, May 10, 1958 (div. 1978); children—James Bradley, Elizabeth Conway, Christopher Ramsey, Andrew Gore. B.S., Tulane U., 1952, M.D., 1956. Diplomate Am. Bd. Pathology. Intern in surgery Baylor Coll. Medicine, Houston, 1956-57, prof. pathology, 1978—; asst. in pathology Peter Bent Brigham Hosp., Boston, 1957-60, sr. resident pathologist, 1960-61; teaching fellow in pathology Harvard U., Boston, 1958-61, NIH research trainee, 1958-61; resident pathologist Free Hosp. for Women, Brookline, Mass., 1959; asst. resident pathologist Children's Hosp. Med. Ctr., Boston, 1960; Nat. Cancer Inst. spl. postdoctoral fellow McIndoe Meml. Research Unit, East Grinstead, Eng., 1961-63; asst. attending pathologist Presbyterian Hosp., N.Y.C., 1963-65; asst. prof. pathology Columbia U., N.Y.C., 1963-65; research assoc. Mt. Sinai Hosp., N.Y.C., 1963-65; assoc. prof. surgery and immunogenetics Mt. Sinai Sch. Medicine, N.Y.C., 1965-68; career scientist Health Research Council City N.Y., N.Y.C., 1967-73; attending pathologist Flower and Fifth Ave. Hosp., N.Y.C., and Met. Hosp. Ctr., N.Y.C., 1968-78; prof. pathology N.Y. Med. Coll., Valhalla, 1968-78, exec. dean, 1973-75; exec. dir., chief operating officer devel. bd. Westchester Med. Ctr., Valhalla, 1974-76; attending pathologist Harris County Hosp. Dist./Ben Taub Gen. Hosp., Houston, 1978—; active staff Methodist Hosp., Houston, 1978—; vis. mem. grad. faculty Tex. A&M U., College Station, 1979—; clin. prof. pathology Grad. Sch. Biomed. Scis., U. Tex.-Galveston, 1982—, U. Tex. Med. Br., Galveston, 1982—; bd. dirs. Westchester div. Am. Cancer Soc., Purchase, N.Y., 1973-78, Westchester Artificial Kidney Found., Inc., Valhalla, 1974-78, Westchester Med. Ctr. Library, Valhalla, 1974-78; co-chmn. Burn Ctr. Tank Force of Westchester County, N.Y., 1974-77. Editorial bd. Jour. Immunogenetics, 1980—, Clin. and Exptl. Immunogenetics, 1984—. Contbr. numerous articles on immunogenetics and exptl. oncology to profl. jours. Sustaining mem. Republican Nat. Com., 1983—; trustee Tuxedo Park Sch., N.Y., 1975-78, Tuxedo Library, N.Y., 1976-78. Fellow Royal Soc. Medicine; mem. Transplantation Soc., AAAS, Am. Assn. Immunologists, AMA, Am. Assn. Clin. Pathologists, Internat. Acad. Pathology, Am. Assn. Pathologists, Houston Soc. Clin. Pathologists, Tex. Med. Assn., Harris County Med. Soc., Houston Acad. Medicine, Fedn. Am. Scientists, N.Y. Cancer Soc., Alpha Omega Alpha. Roman Catholic. Clubs: Tuxedo (Tuxedo Park); U.S. Senatorial. Current work: Influence of the major histocompatibility complex and oncogenic virus on carcinogenesis. Subspecialties: Pathology (medicine); Immunogenetics. Home: 12431 Woodthorpe St Houston TX 77024 Office: Baylor Coll Medicine One Baylor Plaza Houston TX 77030

MCBRIDE, WILLIAM JOSEPH, JR., neurochemist, educator; b. Phila., Dec. 24, 1938; s. William Joseph and Elizabeth (Fantini) McB.; m. Dianne Burnice Stewart, July 14, 1962; children: Vicki, Richard, Rebecca, Andrew. B.A., Rutgers U., 1964; Ph.D., SUNY, Buffalo, 1968. Postdoctoral fellow in neurobiology Ind. U., Bloomington, 1968-71; asst. prof. psychiatry and biochemistry Ind. U. (Sch. Medicine), Indpls., 1971-75, assoc. prof., 1975-79, prof., 1979—; manuscript referee Jour. Neurochemistry and Pharmacology, Biochemistry and Behavior; research proposals evaluator VA Hosp. Contbr. articles to sci. jours. Served with USAF, 1956-60. Recipient Research Scientist Career Devel. award NIMH, 1979—. Mem. Soc. for Neurosci., Am. Soc. for Neurochemistry, Research Soc. on Alcoholism, Internat. Soc. for Neurochemistry. Current Work: Neurochemistry of alcoholism; interactions of neurotransmitter systems; amino acid transmitters and nervous system function. Subspecialties: Neurochemistry; Neurobiology. Home: 7530 Hoover Rd Indianapolis IN 46260 Office: Inst. Psychiatric Research Ind U Sch Medicine Indianapolis IN 46223

MCBRYDE, FELIX WEBSTER, consulting ecologist, thematic cartographer; b. Lynchburg, Va., Apr. 23, 1908; s. John McLaren and Flora O'Neall (Webster) McB.; m. Frances Van Winkle, July 23, 1934; children: Richard Webster, Sarah Elva, John McLaren. B.A., Tulane U., 1930, LL.D. (hon.), 1967; Ph.D., U. Calif.-Berkeley, 1940. Instr. geography Ohio State U., Columbus, 1937-42; geographer U.S. War Dept., Washington, 1942-45; dir. Peruvian Office, Inst. Social Anthropology Smithsonian Instn., Lima, 1945-47; geographer-cons. U.S. Bur. Census, Washington and, Latin Am., 1958-64; field dir. Gordon A. Friesen Assocs., Washington and, Guatemala, 1958-64; chief geography br. Interam. Geodetic Survey, C.Z., 1964-65; field dir. Battelle Meml. Inst., Panama and Colombia, 1965-70; dir. McBryde Ctr. for Human Ecology, Potomac, Md., 1970—; U.S. Census Mission chief 1st Nat. Census of Ecuador, 1949-51; ecologist, expert on tourism UN Devel. Programme, Jamaica, 1971; ecologist, expert on hydrology, Argentina, 1972; census geography cons. U.S. Bur. Census, Honduras, 1972; ecology cons. hydroelectric dam World Bank, Bayano River, Panama, 1973; ecology cons. on transp. Battelle-U.S. Dept. Transp., Panama, 1973; ecology cons. on mining UN, N.Y. and Cerro Colorado, Panama, 1981; dir. geog. research div. Transemantics, Inc., Washington, 1975—. Author: Solola: A Guatemalan Town, 1933, Cultural and Historical Geography of Southwest Guatemala, 1947; founding editor: Bull. Am. Soc. Profl. Geographers (now Profl. Geographer), 1943-45; patentee in field. Election campaign adviser to Pres. Milleda Morales Exec. Research Inc. N.Y., Honduras, 1957; election campaign adviser to Pres. Ydigoras Fuentes F.W. McBryde Assocs., Inc., Guatemala, 1957-58; mem. nat. adv. bd. Am. Security Council, Washington, 1977—. U. Colo. fellow, 1930-31; Clark U. research fellow, 1931-32; U. Calif.-Berkeley teaching fellow, 1933-35, 37; Social Sci. Research Council fellow, 1935-36; NRC fellow, 1940; Pan Am. Airways travel fellow, 1940-41; Ohio State U. Grad. Sch. research grantee, 1940-41. Mem. Ecuadorian Inst. Anthropology and Geography (hon. dir. 1951—), Assn. Am. Geographers (founding pres., sec., treas. 1943-45), Am. Congress Surveying and Mapping, Am. Geophys. Union, Am. Inst. Biol. Scis., Soc. Am. Mil. Engrs., Marine Tech. Soc., AAAS, N.Y. Acad. Scis., Explorers Club. Episcopalian. Club: U.S. Senatorial (Washington). Current Work: World map plottings on original series of equal-area map projections, special interest in all oceanic distributional data. Subspecialty: Geography, space relationship analysis; Thematic cartography, cartographic design. Home: 10100 Falls Rd Potomac MD 20854 Office: McByde Center for Human Ecology 10100 Falls Rd Potomac MD 20854

MC CABE, BRIAN FRANCIS, physician; b. Detroit, June 16, 1926; s. Charles J. and Rosalie T. (Dropiewski) McC.; m. Yvonne L. Fecteau, Sept. 8, 1951; children: Brian F., Bevin E. B.S., U. Detroit, 1950; M.D., U. Mich., 1954. Intern Univ. Hosp., Ann Arbor, Mich., 1954-55; resident U. Mich. Med. Sch., 1955-59; practice medicine specializing in otolaryngology and maxillofacial surgery, Iowa City; mem. staff Iowa City VA Hosp.; prof., head dept. otolaryngology and head and neck surgery U. Iowa, also chmn. residency rev. com. for otolaryngology.; Dir. Bd. Examiners Otolaryngology. Editor: Annals of Otology, Rhinology and Laryngology. Mem. Am. Acad. Ophthalmology and Otolaryngology (sec. for otolaryngology), Am. Laryngol., Rhinol. and Otolaryngol. Soc., Am. Otol. Soc. (editor-librarian), Am. Laryngol. Soc., Otosclerosis Study Group, Galens Hon., Linn County, Am., Iowa med. socs., Collegium Oto-Rhino-Laryngologicum Amicitae sacrum, New Zealand Soc. Otolaryngology, The von Bekesy Soc. (pres. 1981-83), Snipe Class Internat. Racing Assn., Nat. Amateur Yacht Racing Assn., DN Ice Yacht Racing Assn., Alpha Omega Alpha. Clubs: Centurion, Barton Boat, Hawkeye Sailing. Current Work: Vestibular neurophysiology, cochlear electrode inplant physiology. Subspecialties: Otorhinolaryngology; Neurophysiology. Home: 237 Ferson St Iowa City IA 52240 Office: Univ Hosps and Clinics Iowa City IA 52240

MCCALL, EDWARD HUFFAKER, computer scientist; b. Oxford, Miss., Dec. 11, 1938; s. Ephriam Forrest and Mariada (Huffaker) McC.; m. Judith Irene Bohn, Aug. 20, 1960; children—Scott Edward, Cathy Ann, Douglas James. Student in Chem. Engring., U. Ill., 1956-59; B.S. in Chem. Engring., Iowa State U., 1960; M.S. in Computer Sci., U. Minn., 1970; Ph.D. in Computer Sci., 1979. Jr. engr. Panhandle Eastern Pipeline Co., Kansas City, Mo., 1958; chem. engring. researcher 3M Co., Maplewood, Minn., 1960-63, programmer, 1963-68; programmer, mgr. Sperry Univac, Roseville, Minn., 1968-79; adj. asst. prof. U. Minn., Mpls., 1979-84; sci. data processing cons. Sperry Corp., Roseville, Minn., 1979—; mem. fortran standards com. Am. Nat. Standards Inst. Contbr. articles to profl. jours. Asst. scoutmaster Indianhead council Boy Scouts Am., 1974-80; football coach Mounds View Jr. Football League, New Brighton, Minn., 1979-80. Mem. Math. Programming Soc., Ops. Research Soc., Soc. Indsl. and Applied Math., Assn. Computing Machinery, Computer Soc. of IEEE. Republican. Lutheran. Current work: Vectorizers for supercomputers, Fortran standards, numerical algorithms for vector and parallel processors, mathematical software, large scale linear and mixed integer programming. Subspecialties: Mathematical software; Operations research (mathematics). Home: 4710 Debra Ln Shoreview MN 55126 Office: Sperry Corp PO Box 64942 Saint Paul MN 55164

MCCALL, JERRY CHALMERS, government official; b. Oxford, Miss., June 30, 1927; s. E. Forrest and Mariada (Huffaker) McC.; m. Margaret Denton, Nov. 28, 1952; children—Betsy, Lynn, Kim. B.A., U. Miss., 1951, M.A., 1951; M.S., U. Ill., 1956, Ph.D., 1959. Teaching asst. dept. math. U. Miss., 1950-51, instr. math., 1952-53, prof. math., 1973-76, exec. vice chancellor, 1973-76; research assoc. U. Ill., 1953-57; applied sci. rep. IBM, Springfield, Ill., 1957-58, mgr., Bethesda, Md., 1966-68, Huntsville, Ala., 1968-71, Owego, N.Y., 1971-72; exec. v.p. Midwest Computer Service, Inc., Decatur, Ill., 1958-59; mem. sci. staff computation lab. Army Ballistic Missile Agy., Huntsville, 1959-60; asst. to dir. Marshall Space Flight Center, NASA, Huntsville, 1960-63, dep. dir. research and devel. ops., 1963-66; dir. info. research Miss. Test Facility, Bay St. Louis, 1972-73; pres. 1st State Bank and Trust Co., Gulfport, Miss., 1976-77; dir. Nat. Data Buoy Ctr., Bay St. Louis, Miss., 1977—; head math. dept. St. Bernard Coll., Cullman, Ala., part-time, 1960-65; asso. prof. math. U. Ala., Huntsville, 1960-62; pub. speaker, 1960-63; chmn. incorporators First State Bank & Trust Co., Gulfport, Miss., 1973-76; tech. cons. Gen. Electric Co., 1974-75. Editor: (with Ernst Stuhlinger) Astronautical Engineering and Science, 1963, From Peenemunde to Outer Space, 1963. Mem. Miss. Criminal Justice Standards Commn., 1974-75; mem. Miss. Marine Resources Council, 1974-76; bd. dirs. U. Miss. Found.; bd. advisers Sch. Engring., U. Miss., 1965-73; mem. indsl. advisors U. New Orleans; chmn. founders U. Ala. Research Inst., Huntsville, 1960-62. Mem. Am. Judicature

Soc. (lay mem.), U. Miss. Alumni Assn. (dir. 1966-73). . Home: Box 7092 Gulfport MS 39506 Office: NOAA NSTL Sta MS 35929

MCCALLA, THOMAS MARK, JR., electrical engineer, educator, researcher, consultant; b. Corinth, Miss., May 1, 1934; s. Thomas Mark and Virginia Elizabeth (Key) McC.; m. Dora Mae Stamm. B.S. in Elec. Engring., U. Nebr., 1956; M.S. in Elec. Engring., N.Mex. State U., 1965; Ph.D. in Engring., Case Western Res. U., 1969. Registered profl. engr., Ill. Electronic engr. White Sands Missile Range, N. Mex., 1956-63; assoc. prof. engring. So. Ill. U., Carbondale, 1969—; cons. So. Ill. U. Med. Sch., Springfield, Gen. Telephone Co., Ill. Author: Preliminary Candidate Advanced Avionics System for General Aviation, 1977; How to Protect Wind Turbines from Lightning, 1983; also articles. Served with U.S. Army, 1958. NASA grantee, 1978. Mem. IEEE, Am. Soc. for Engring. Edn., Instrument Soc. Am., Am. Tchrs. Tech. Writing. Club: Southwestern Mountaineers (Las Cruces, N.Mex.) (pres. 1959-60). Current work: System design of electronic/electrical systems including reliability, transient protection EMI, RFI, design automation, systems theory. Subspecialty: Systems engineering. Home: 1417 E Grand Ave Carbondale IL 62901 Office: Coll Engring and Tech So Ill U Tech D-47 Carbondale IL 62901

MCCALLEY, RODERICK CANFIELD, physical chemist; b. Portland, Oreg., Aug. 2, 1943; s. Roderick Gilbert and Esther Drew (Canfield) McC.; m. Peggy Ann Hock, Dec. 11, 1976; children—Roderick Hock, Carmody Kathryn. B.S., Calif. Inst. Tech., 1964; Ph.D., Harvard U., 1971. Asst. prof. in chemistry Dartmouth Coll., Hanover, N.H., 1972-79; research scientist Lockheed Research and Devel., Palo Alto, Calif., 1979—. Mem. Am. Chem. Soc., Sigma Xi. Current work: Leak test technology (development and interpretation), magnetic resonance in the solid state (organic free radicals). Subspecialties: Electron spin resonance; Physical chemistry. Home: 3489 Cowper St Palo Alto CA 94306 Office: Lockheed Research and Devel 0/93-50 B/204 3251 Hanover St Palo Alto CA 94304

MCCALMON, ROBERT THOMAS, JR., immunobiologist, researcher; b. Bremerton, Wash., May 5, 1943; s. Robert Thomas and Dorothy Jane (Miller) McC.; m. Sandra Ann Gagnon, Mar. 20, 1976; 1 son, Scott Thomas. B.A., U. Colo., 1967; M.A., Drake U., 1969; Ph.D., U. Ariz., 1973. Postdoctoral fellow Nat. Jewish Hosp. and Research Ctr., Denver, 1973-75; asst. prof. dept. surgery U. Colo. Health Scis. Ctr., Denver, 1975-79; dir. surg. immunology Denver VA Hosp., 1975-79; dir. Immunol. Assocs. Denver, 1979—, pres., 1980-82. Contbr. articles to profl. jours. Pres. bd. trustees Mile High Transplant Bank; mem. utilization com. End-Stage Renal Disease Coordinating Council. NIH grantee. Mem. Am. Assn. Clin. Histocompatibility Testing, Am. Assn. Immunologists, Am. Soc. Microbiology. Club: Denver Athletic. Current Work: Biological significance of lymphocyte surface antigens. Subspecialty: Immunology (medicine). Office: 3570 E 12th Ave #200 Denver CO 80206

MCCAMMON, KENNETH RICHARD, plant geneticist, researcher; b. Mineola, N.Y., Dec. 8, 1951; s. Frederick Von and Mary Joyce (LeBlanc) McC.; m. Mary Elise (Marlise) Lewis, June 22, 1974; children—Margaret Joyce, Colleen Lewis. B.S., Southeastern La. U., 1973; M.S., Mich. State U., East Lansing, 1982, Ph.D., 1983. Plant geneticist Phyto Dynamics, Inc., Lafayette, Ind., 1983—. Contbr. articles to sci. jours. Mem. Am. Soc. Hort. Sci., Am. Genetic Assn. Roman Catholic. Current work: Genetic manipulation and improvement of agronomic and horticultural plant species. Subspecialties: Genetics and genetic engineering (agriculture); Plant genetics. Home: 2219 Sycamore Ln West Lafayette IN 47906 Office: Phyto Dynamics Inc 624 S 775 East PO Box 5418 Lafayette IN 47903

MCCAMPBELL, STANLEY REID, physician; b. Nashville, Dec. 16, 1925; s. Basil Davis and Louise (McCall) McC.; m. Joan F. Garner, Nov. 7, 1953; children: Louise, Robert, James, Kelly. B.A., Vanderbilt U., 1949, M.D., 1952. Intern, resident Cornell/Bellevue Hosp., N.Y.C., 1952-55; fellow in cardiology Cornell Med. Ctr., N.Y.C., 1955-56, U. London, 1956-57, practice medicine, specializing in cardiology, Oklahoma City, 1957—. Contbr. articles to profl. jours. Served with USN, 1943-46. Named Phi Beta Kappa of Yr., 1981. Mem. Okla. County Med. Soc. (pres. 1970), Okla. Med. Assn. (pres. 1972), World Med. Tennis Soc. (pres. 1971-83, Internat. Congress Psychosomatic and Preventive Medicine, pres. 1978—), Okla. Assn. of Phi Beta Kappa (pres. 1975), Am. Med. Tennis Assn. (pres. 1969-71). Republican. Presbyterian. Current Work: Practice of cardiology, pacemaker electronics, physical fitness, coronary artery disease. Subspecialty: Cardiology. Home: 6609 N Hillcrest St Oklahoma City OK 73116 Office: 1211 N Shartel Room 408 Oklahoma City OK 73103

MCCANDLISS, RUSSELL JOHN, molecular biologist, research scientist; b. Pitts., Jan. 18, 1948; s. John H. and Marjorie (Steele) McC.; m. Elizabeth Kajner, Sept. 27, 1973; children—Michelle Lucy, Marianne Frances. B.S., U. Tenn., 1969; M.S., Purdue U., 1972, Ph.D., 1978. Postdoctoral fellow Roche Inst. Molecular Biology, Nutley, N.J., 1978-80; sr. research scientist Genex Corp., Gaithersburg, Md., 1981-82; prin. research scientist IGI Biotech., Columbia, Md., 1982-83, Genex Corp., 1983—. Contbr. articles to profl. book and jours. Served with U.S. Army, 1971-74. Mem. Am. Chem. Soc., AAAS. Current work: Genetic engineering. Subspecialties: Molecular biology; Genetics and genetic engineering (medicine). Office: Genex Corp 16020 Industrial Dr Gaithersburg MD 20877

MCCANN, MARTIN WILLIAM, JR., civil engineer, consultant, researcher; b. Troy, N.Y., Feb. 23, 1953; s. Martin William and Claire (Hientz) McC.; m. Margaret McElduff, Aug. 31, 1975; children—Geoffrey Martin, Kevin Patrick. B.S., Villanova U., 1975; M.S., Stanford U., 1976, Ph.D. in Civil Engring., 1980. Assoc., Jack R. Benjamin & Assocs., Mountain View, Calif., 1979-84, v.p., 1984—; cons. prof. Stanford U., Palo Alto, Calif., 1980—. Contbr. tech. papers to profl. lit. Mem. ASCE (mem. working group on seismic probabilistic risk assessment, 1983—, mem. safety of nuclear structures com. 1984—), Earthquake Engring. Research Inst., Am. Geophys. Union, Seismol. Soc. Am., Structural Engrs. Assn. No. Calif. Roman Catholic. Current work: Earthquake engineering, risk analysis. Subspecialties: Civil engineering; Probability. Home: 241 Marmona Dr Menlo Park CA 94025 Office: Jack R Benjamin & Assocs 444 Castro St Suite 501 Mountain View CA 94041

MCCANN, ROBERT THOMAS, computational physicist; b. Chambersburg, Pa., Apr. 5, 1948; s. George Ambrose and Edith McIlhany (Main) McC. B.A., Shippensburg U., 1970; M.S., Univ. Md., 1973. Computational physicist Science Applications, Inc., Naval Research Lab, Washington, 1976-80, Princeton U., N.J., 1980—. Contbr. articles to profl. jours. Mem. Am. Inst. Physics (div. plasma physics). Current work: Development and implementation of numerical modeling algorythms for tokamak transport analysis. Subspecialty: Plasma physics. Office: Princeton Plasma Physics Lab PO Box 451 Princeton NM 08544

MCCARLEY, ROBERT WILLIAM, neurophysiologist, psychiatrist; b. Mayfield, Ky., Aug. 17, 1937; s. Robert Smith and Mary Agnes (McGill) McC.; m. Alice M. Bowen, Aug. 10, 1968; children: Robby, Scott. A.B. summa cum laude, Harvard U., 1959; postgrad., Gutenberg U., Mainz, W.Ger., 1959-60; M.D., Harvard U., 1964. Diplomate: Am. Bd. Psychiatry and Neurology, 1972. Intern Brigham and Women's Hosp., Boston, 1964-65; psychiat. resident Mass. Mental Health Ctr., Boston, 1965-68; lectr. psychiatry Simmons Coll. Social Work, Boston, 1967; instr. Harvard U. Med. Sch., Boston, 1970-75, asst. prof. psychiatry, 1975-78, assoc. prof., 1978-84, prof., 1984—, co-dir. lab. neurophysiology, 1975-85, dir. neurosci. lab., 1985—; co-dir. clin. research tng. program Mass. Mental Health Ctr., 1980—; cons. Mass. Rehab. Commn.; mem. rev. panel NIMH. Contbr. over 100 articles to sci. jours. Gen. Motors scholar, 1955-59; NIMH grantee, 1968—; NSF grantee, 1974—; others. Mem. AAAS, Sleep Research Soc., Soc. Neurosci., Am. Psychiat. Assn., Mass. Psychiat. Assn., Phi Beta Kappa. Democrat. Clubs: Harvard (Boston); Neighborhood (West Newton, Mass.). Current Work: Neurophysiology of sleep; mathematical and computer modeling of sleep cycle control; computer techniques of neurophysiological cellular data description and display; topographic mapping of human electrical activity during sleep and schizophrenia. Subspecialties: Neurophysiology; Psychiatry. Office: Brockton VAMC Belmont St Brockton MA 02401

MCCARTHY, DENNIS DEAN, astronomer; b. Oil City, Pa., Sept. 22, 1942; s. William Henry and Evelyn Dorothy (Siembida) McC.; m. Diane Kay Wallingford, Sept. 17, 1966; children: Duncan Sean, Deidre Carrie. B.S., Case Inst. Tech., 1960; M.A., U. Va., 1970, Ph.D. in Astronomy, 1972. Astronomer U.S. Naval Obs., 1965-75, project leader, 1975-79, head astron. time and polar motion sect., 1979-82, chief earth orientation parameters div. 1982—; vis. prof. Japan Soc. Promotion of Sci., 1979. Contbr. articles to profl. jours. Fellow Royal Astron. Soc.; mem. Am. Astron. Soc., Am. Geophys. Union, Internat. Astron. Union. Current Work: Orientation and rotation of the earth; modeling and prediction of earth orientation parameters; application of modern technology to the determination of earth orientation. Subspecialties: Astrometry; Geodesy. Home: 2432 Riviera Dr Vienna VA 22180 Office: US Naval Observatory Washington DC 20390

MC CARTHY, JOHN FRANCIS, JR., aeronautical engineer, executive; b. Boston, Aug. 28, 1925; s. John Francis and Margaret Josephine (Bartwood) McC.; m. Camille Dian Martinez, May 4, 1968; children: Margaret I., Megan, Jamie M., Nicole E., John F. S.B., M.I.T., 1950, S.M. in Aero. Engring, 1951; Ph.D. in Aeros. and Physics, Calif. Inst. Tech., 1962. Supr. air/ground communications TWA, Rome, 1946-47; project mgr. aeroelastic and structures research lab. M.I.T., 1951-55, prof. aeros. and astronautics, 1971-78; ops. analyst Hdqrs. SAC, Offutt AFB, Nebr., 1955-59; dir., asst. chief engr. Apollo, Space div. N.Am. Aviation, Inc., Downey, Calif., 1961-66; v.p. Los Angeles div./Space div., Rockwell Internat. Corp., 1966-71; dir. and prof. M.I.T. Center for Space Research, 1974-78; dir. NASA Lewis Research Ctr., Cleve., 1978-82, v.p., gen. mgr. Electromech. div. Northrop Corp., 1982—; mem. Internat. Council Aero. Scis., Koln, Germany, 1978—, USAF Sci. Adv. Bd., Washington, 1970-82; mem. sci. adv. group Joint Chiefs of Staff, Joint Strategic Target Planning Staff, Offutt AFB, 1976-81; com. mem. Energy Engring. Bd., Assembly Engring., NRC, 1979; cons. in field.; cons. Office of Undersec. Def. for Research and Engring. Author numerous tech. reports. Campaign chmn. Downey Community Hosp., 1968-69; bd. govs. Nat. Space Club, Washington, 1978-82, 82-84; chmn. Fed. Exec. Bd., Cleve., 1979-80; mem. adv. bd. for dept. mech. engring., aero. engring. and mechanics Rensselaer Poly. Inst., 1981-84. Served with USAAF, 1944-46. Recipient Apollo Achievement award NASA, 1969, Meritorious Civilian Service medal USAF, 1973, Exceptional Civilian Service medal, 1978, Disting. Service medal NASA, 1982. Fellow Am. Astronautical Soc., AIAA (dir. 1975-76), Royal Aero. Soc. (London); mem. Nat. Acad. Engring., Am. Soc. Engring. Edn. (exec. com. aerospace div. 1969-72), Am. Mgmt. Assn. (pres.'s council 1978—), Sigma Xi, Sigma Gamma Tau. Unitarian. Clubs: Cosmos, 50 of Cleve. Patentee impact landing system. Current Work: Engaged in research, development and manufacture of passive sensors, signal processing, micro-electronics. Subspecialties: Aerospace engineering and technology; Aeronautical engineering. Home: 19171 Via del Caballo Yorba Linda CA 92686 Home: 19171 Via del Caballo Yorba Linda CA 92686 Office: Northrop Electro-Mech Div 500 E Orangethorpe Ave Anaheim CA 92801

MCCARTHY, JOSEPH GERALD, plastic surgeon, surgery educator, investigator; b. Lowell, Mass., Nov. 28, 1938; s. Joseph H. and Eva McC.; m. Karlan L. Sloan, June 6, 1964; children: Cara, Stephen. A.B., Harvard U., 1960; M.D., Columbia U., 1964. Diplomate: Am. Bd. Surgery, Am. Bd. Plastic Surgery. Intern Columbia-Presbyn. Med. Ctr., N.Y.C., 1964-65, resident in surgery, 1967-71; resident in plastic surgery NYU Med. Ctr., N.Y.C., 1971-73; instr. plastic surgery NYU Sch. Medicine, 1973-75, asst. prof. plastic surgery, 1975-78, assoc. prof. plastic surgery, 1978-81, Lawrence D. Bell prof. plastic surgery, 1981—; dir. Inst. Reconstructive Plastic Surgery, NYU Med. Ctr., 1981—; attending plastic surgeon Univ. Hosp.; vis. plastic surgeon, dir. service Bellevue Hosp.; attending surgeon Manhattan Eye, Ear and Throat Hosp.; assoc. attending physician VA Hosp., N.Y.C. Assoc. editor: Reconstructive Plastic Surgery, 7 vols, 1977; assoc. editor: Jour. Plastic and Reconstructive Surgery. Served to lt. comdr. USPHS, 1965-67. Am. Cancer Soc. fellow, 1969-70. Fellow ACS; mem. Am. Soc. Plastic and Reconstructive Surgeons, N.Y. Regional Soc. Plastic and Reconstructive Surgeons, Plastic Surgery Research Council, N.Y. Acad. Scis., Am. Cleft Palate Assn., Am. Assn. Plastic Surgeons. Clubs: Harvard of N.Y.C. (N.J.) Field.), Englewood (N.J.) Field.). Current Work: Principal investigator craniofacial anomalies-etiology and treatment for NIH. Subspecialty: Surgery. Office: Inst Reconstructive Plastic Surgery 560 1st Ave New York NY 10016

MCCARTHY, WILLIAM JAMES, mathematics educator; b. Beverly, Mass., Mar. 14, 1955; s. William Augustus and Mildred (Nadeau) McC. B.S. in Biology, U. Maine, 1977; M.A. in Applied Math., U. Calif.-San Diego, 1983, B.A. in Applied Math., 1985. Research asst. in botany U. Maine-Orono; 1975-77, researcher in physics, 1977-78; assoc. scientist Lockheed, Carlsbad, Calif., 1978-79; teaching asst. U. Calif.-San Diego, 1982-83; lectr. U. Lowell, Mass., 1983—. Contbr. articles to profl. publs. NSF grantee, 1977. Mem. Soc. Indsl. and Applied Math., Am. Phys. Soc., AAAS, New Eng. Estuarine Research Soc. Current work: Numerical analysis, finite element analysis, pollution ecology of aquatic ecosystems, fluid dynamics. Subspecialties: Numerical analysis (mathematics); Ecosystems analysis. Home: 95 Hesperus Ave Gloucester MA 01930 Office: U Lowell Math Dept Lowell MA 01854

MCCARTY, KENNETH SCOTT, biochemist; b. Dallas, June 20, 1922; s. Justine S. and Louisa L. (Kremp) McC.; m. Marketa M. Regan, 1944; children—Kristine M. McCarty Hammatt, Kenneth S., Jr. B.S., Georgetown U., 1944; Ph.D., Columbia U. Coll. Physicians and Surgeons, 1958. Dir. grad. studies Duke U., Durham, N.C., 1967-71, assoc. prof., 1959-68, prof. biochemistry, 1968—; cons. to corps., hosps. Mem. Endocrine Soc., Tissue Culture Assn. (chmn. constn. com. 1981), SE Soc. Exptl. Biology (pres. 1981). Contbr. articles to profl. jours. Subspecialty: Biochemistry (medicine). Office: Duke U Med Ctr Durham NC 27710

MCCARTY, MACLYN, medical scientist; b. South Bend, Ind., June 9, 1911; s. Earl Hauser and Hazel Dell (Beagle) McC.; m. Anita Alleyne Davies, June 20, 1934 (div. 1966); children: Maclyn, Richard E., Dale, Colin; m. Marjorie Steiner, Sept. 3, 1966. A.B., Stanford U., 1933; M.D., Johns Hopkins U., 1937; Sc.D., Columbia, 1976, U. Fla., 1977, Rockefeller U., 1982, Med. Coll. Ohio, 1985. asst. resident physician Johns Hopkins Hosp., 1937-40; asso. Rockefeller Inst., 1946-48, asso. mem., 1948-50, mem., 1950-81, prof., 1957-81, prof. emeritus, 1981—, v.p., 1965-78, phys. in chief to hosp., 1961-74, research in streptococcal disease and rheumatic fever.; Cons. USPHS, NIH. Mem. distbn. com. N.Y. Community Trust, 1966-74; chmn. Health Research Council City N.Y., 1972-75; Mem. bd. trustees Helen Hay Whitney Found.; chmn. bd. Pub. Health Research Inst., N.Y.C., 1984—. Served with Naval Med. Research Unit, Rockefeller Hosp. USNR, 1942-46. Fellow medicine N.Y. U. Coll. Medicine, 1940-41; NRC fellow med. scis. Rockefeller Inst., 1941-42; Recipient Eli Lilly award in bacteriology and immunology, 1946, 1st Waterford Biomed. Research award, 1977, Robert Koch Gold medal, W.Ger., 1981. Mem. Am. Soc. for Clin. Investigation, Am. Assn. Immunologists, Soc. Am. Bacteriologists, Soc. for Exptl. Biology and Medicine (pres. 1973-75), Harvey Soc. (sec. 1947-50, pres. 1971-72), N.Y. Acad. Medicine, Assn. Am. Physicians, Nat. Acad. Scis., Am. Acad. Arts and Scis., N.Y. Heart Assn. (1st v.p. 1967, pres. 1969-71), Am. Philos. Soc. Current Work: Pneumococcal transformation and discovery of genetic role of DNA; streptococcal infections and pathogenesis of rheumatic fever. Subspecialties: Microbiology (medicine); Infectious diseases. Home: 500 E 63d St New York NY 10021 Office: Rockefeller U 66th St and York Ave New York NY 10021

MCCLELLAN, GEORGE BAIRD, physiologist, educator; b. Oneida, N.Y., Apr. 28, 1941; m. Margaret Campbell; children—Marcie, Jean. B.A., U. Wyo., 1964, M.S., 1969; Ph.D., U. Rochester, N.Y., 1975. USPHS postdoctoral fellow U. Pa., Phila., 1975-78; research assoc., 1978-80, research asst. prof. physiology, 1980—. Served to 1st lt. U.S. Army, 1964-66, Vietnam. Named Primary Investigator, NIH, 1984. Mem. Biophys. Soc., Am. Soc. Mammalogists, Sigma Xi. Current work: Mechanisms involved in regulation of cardiac contractility. Subspecialties: Physiology (medicine); Biophysics (biology). Office: Dept Physiology U Pa 37th and Hamilton Walk Philadelphia PA 19104

MCCLELLAND, JABEZ JENKINS, physicist; b. Middletown, Conn., July 31, 1954; s. David Clarence and Mary Warner (Sharpless) McC.; m. Catherine Kai-Ling Chow, Dec. 30, 1978. B.A., Wesleyan U., Middletown, Conn., 1976; M.A., U. Tex., 1980, Ph.D., 1984. Physicist, Nat. Bur. Standards, Gaithersburg, Md., 1984—. Contbr. articles to profl. jours. Robert A. Welch fellow U. Tex., 1978-81; Fulbright grantee, Berlin, 1981-82. Mem. Am. Phys. Soc., Phi Beta Kappa, Alpha Delta Phi. Current work: Electron scattering from atoms and molecules, polarized electron physics, interaction of laser light with atoms and molecules. Subspecialty: Atomic and molecular physics. Office: Nat Bur of Standards MET B206 Gaithersburg MD 20899

MCCLELLAND, JOHN BENJAMIN, nuclear physicist; b. Santa Ana, Calif., Jan. 4, 1950; s. Benjamin William and Rosaria Mary (Sinacori) McC.; m. Linda Sue Dillow, Mar. 21, 1970; children—Benjamin Michael, Amanda Maria. B.S., UCLA, 1973, M.S., 1974, PH.D., 1979. Postdoctoral fellow UCLA, Los Alamos, 1979-80; staff physicist Los Alamos Nat. Lab., 1980—. Mem. Am. Physics Soc. Current work: Nuclear physics research at intermediate energies using high resolution magnetic spectrometers, particular interest in polarization phenomena in proton-nucleus interactions. Subspecialty: Nuclear physics. Office: Los Alamos Nat Lab MS-H 841 Los Alamos NM 87545

MCCLENDON, JOHN HADDAWAY, plant physiologist, educator; b. Mpls., Jan. 17, 1921; s. Jesse Francis and Margaret (Stewart) McC.; m. Betty Morgan, Nov. 16, 1923; children: Susan, Lise, Natalie. B.A., U. Minn., 1942; Ph.D., U. Pa., 1951. Research assoc. Stanford (Calif.) U., 1951-52; U. Minn., Mpls., 1952-53; asst. prof. dept. agrl. biochemistry U. Del., Newark, 1952-64; assoc. prof. dept. botany U. Nebr., Lincoln, 1965—. Contbr. articles to sci. jours. Chmn. Nebr. chpt. Zero Population Growth, 1970-73; mem. Nebr. Environ. Coalition. Served to 1st lt. U.S. Army, 1943-46. NSF grantee, 1960, 65. Mem. Am. Soc. Plant Physiologists, AAAS, Am. Inst. Biol. Scis., Bot. Soc. Am., Sierra Club, Wilderness Soc., Sigma Xi. Democrat. Current Work: Photosynthesis in trees; origin of life. Subspecialties: Plant physiology (biology); Evolutionary biology. Home: 1970 B St Lincoln NE 68502 Office: U Nebr Lincoln NE 68588

MCCLINTOCK, BARBARA, geneticist; b. June 16, 1902. Ph.D. in Botany, Cornell U., 1927; D.Sc. (hon.), U. Rochester, U. Mo., Smith Coll., Williams Coll., Western Coll. for Women. Instr. botany Cornell U., Ithaca, N.Y., 1927-31, research assoc., 1934-36, Andrew D. White prof.-at-large, 1965—; asst. prof. U. Mo., 1936-41; mem. staff Carnegie Instn. of Washington, Cold Spring Harbor, N.Y., 1941-47, Disting. Service mem., 1967—; cons. agrl. sci. program Rockefeller Found., 1962-69. Recipient Achievement award Assn. Univ. Women, 1947, Nat. medal of Sci., 1970, MacArthur Found. prize; Rosenstiel award, 1978; Nobel Prize, 1983; NRC fellow, 1931-33; Guggenheim Found. fellow, 1933-34. Mem. Nat. Acad. Scis. (Kimber genetics award 1967), Am. Philos. Soc., Am. Aad. Arts and Scis., Genetics Soc. Am. (pres. 1945), Bot. Soc. Am. (award of merit 1957), AAAS, Am. Inst. Biol. Sci., Am. Soc. Naturalists. Subspecialty: Gene actions. Office: Carnegie Instn of Washington Cold Spring Harbor NY 11724*

MCCLOY, JAMES MURL, laboratory administrator, marine science educator; b. Hollywood, Calif., Mar. 28, 1934; s. James Isaac and Lucile Jeanett (Phillips) McC.; m. Patricia Mae Mullins, Aug. 8, 1964. B.A., State Coll. at Los Angeles, 1961; Ph.D., La. State U., 1969. Asst. prof. marine sci. U. Mont., Missoula, 1968-71; asst. dean acad. affairs Tex. A&M U., Galveston, 1972-75, head dept. gen. acads., 1975-77; asst. program dir. Sea Grant Coll. Program, Washington, 1977-78; dir. Coastal Zone Lab. Tex. A&M U., 1978—; cons. Council Nat. Coop. Aquatics, Indpls., 1981—; dir. Sci., Inc., Galveston. Contbr. articles to profl. jours. Adv. council Satori Sch., Galveston, 1981-84. Recipient numerous grants for research, 1968—. Mem. Marine Tech. Soc., Nat. Safety Council, Coastal Soc. (bd. dirs. 1982-84), U.S. lifesaving Assn., World Life Saving Assn., Soc. Risk Analysis, Internat. Geog. Union, Assn. Am. Geographers (chmn. coastal and marine group 1983-85). Current work: Epidemiology of water-related fatalities and the risk management of public open-water recreational beaches. Subspecialty: Coastal zones. Home: 3627 Ave Q Galveston TX 77550 Office: Tex A&M U at Galveston Coastal Zone Lab PO Box 1675 Galveston TX 77553

MCCLURE, CARL KENNETH, research scientist, mech. engr.; b. Roaring Spring, Pa., Nov. 23, 1936; s. William Warren and Ida Belle (Kimmel) McC.; m. Joyce Elaine Montgomery, June 22, 1959; children: Susan Amelia, Dean Maurice, Hugh Charles. B.S.M.E., Pa. State U., 1959; Ph.D. in Engring. Mechanics, 1972; M.S.M.E., Drexel U., 1962. Registered profl. engr., Pa. Engr. Philco-Ford Corp., Phila., 1959-62; instr. Pa. State U., University Park, 1964-69; sr. research scientist Armstrong World Industries, Inc., Lancaster, Pa., 1969—. Contbr. articles to profl. jours. Docent North Mus., Franklin and Marshall Coll., Lancaster, Pa., 1979—. Served to capt. U.S. Army, 1962-68. Mem. ASME, Soc. for Exptl. Stress Analysis. Methodist. Current Work: Application of solid mechanics to research directed toward the development of plastic and elastomeric products. Vibrations and impact mechanics of composite materials, and material testing techniques. Subspecialties: Solid mechanics; Mechanical engineering. Office: PO Box 3511 Lancaster PA 17604

MCCLURE, DAVID EARL, medicinal chemist, research administrator; b. Omaha, Apr. 22, 1947; s. Earl Donald and Marian M. (Pasinger) McC.; m. Anne Elizabeth Doyle, July 1, 1972; children—Shannon Elise, Marc David, Katherine Anne. B.S., Nebr. Wesleyan U., 1969; Ph.D., Stanford U., 1973. Research assoc. Columbia U., N.Y.C., 1973-75; Sr. research chemist Merck Sharp & Dohme, West Point, Pa., 1975-79, research fellow, 1979-83, sr. research fellow, 1983; sect. head medicinal chemistry McNeil Pharm., Spring-house, Pa., 1983—; lectr. in field. Contbr. articles to profl. jours. Patentee in field. Recipient Silver Key, Nebr. Wesleyan U., 1969; NSF summer trainee, 1970; Frederick P. Whitaker fellow, 1971-72. Mem. Am. Chem. Soc., Am. chem. Soc. (Phila. sect.), Phila. Organic Chemists Club (chmn.-elect 1984-85, chmn. 1985—), AAAS, Sigma Xi, Phi Kappa Phi. Current work: Synthesis of biologically intersting compounds; synthesis of chiral compounds; interactions of chiral compounds with biological systems; cardiovascular and CNS drugs. Subspecialties: Organic chemistry; Medicinal chemistry. Office: McNeil Pharm R-4 Spring House PA 19477-0776

MCCLURE, HAROLD MONROE, veterinary pathologist, researcher, administrator; b. Hayesville, N.C., Oct. 2, 1937; s. Elmer S. and Willie S. (Davenport) McC.; m. Joan C. Cunningham, June 11, 1958; children—Michael, Michele, Barry. B.S., N.C. State Coll., 1959; D.V.M., U. Ga. 1963. Postdoctoral fellow U. Wis., Madison, 1963-66; pathologist, Yerkes Primate Ctr., Atlanta, 1966—, assoc. dir., 1982—. Assoc. editor: Lab. Animal Sci., Am. Jour. Primatology; author, co-author sci. publs. Asst. scoutmaster Atlanta council Boy Scouts Am., 1976-78; pres. Clairmont Little League, Atlanta, 1973-75. Recipient grants, contracts NIH, NASA, U.S. Dept. Agr., Cystic Fibrosis Found. Mem. AVMA, Internat. Acad. Pathology, Am. Soc. Vet. Clin. Pathologists, Am. Assn. Lab. Animal Sci., Internat. Primatol. Soc., Am. Soc. Primatologists, others, Phi Kappa Phi, Soc. Phi Zeta, Gamma Sigma Delta. Republican. Baptist. Current work: Comparative pathology, diseases of nonhuman primates, animal models of human disease, biomedical research. Subspecialties: Animal pathology; Pathology (medicine). Home: 2301 Poplar Springs Dr Atlanta GA 30319 Office: Emory Univ Yerkes Primate Research Ctr Atlanta GA 30322

MCCLURE, MICHAEL EDWARD, health scientist administrator; b. Goshen, Ind., Aug. 15, 1941; s. Frank E. and Thelma D. (Hahn) McC.; m. Elaine Mabel Adair, Aug. 5, 1962; 1 child, Kelly Denise. B.S., Purdue U., 1963; M.S., U. Tex.-Houston, 1966, Ph.D., 1970. Asst. biochemist U. Tex., Houston, 1972-73; asst. prof. cell biology Baylor Coll. Medicine, Houston, 1973-76; asst. prof. devel. therapy U. Tex., Houston, 1976-79; staff specialist population research grants br. Center for Population Research, Nat. Inst Childhood Diseases, NIH, Bethesda, Md., 1979-81, head biol. chemistry, molecular gen. program reproductive scis. br., 1981-83, head gen. and immmunology program, 1983—. Contbr. articles to profl. jours., chpts. to books. USPHS predoctoral fellow NIH, U. Tex., 1963-68; R.A. Welch predoctoral fellow U. Tex., 1968-69, R.B. Hite postdoctoral fellow, 1969-70, R.A. Welch postdoctoral fellow, 1970-71. Mem. AAAS, Am. Chem. Soc., Am. Soc. Cell Biology, Biochem. Soc. (London), N.Y. Acad. Scis., Sigma Xi. Current work: Molecular biology of hormone action related to reproductive function, immunology of fertility and infertility, biochemistry of nucleoprotein structure and function. Subspecialties: Reproductive biology; Gene actions. Home: 303 Epping Way Annapolis MD 21401 Office: NIH Nat Inst Child Health and Human Devel Landow Bldg Room 7C33 Bethesda MD 20205

MCCOLL, JOHN DUNCAN, pharmacologist, consultant; b. London, Ont., Can., Nov. 11, 1925; s. Gordon and Mary Rosamund (Clunis) McC.; m. Patricia Amy Ridont, May 29, 1954; children: Pamela, Susan, Gordon. B.A., U. Western Ont., 1946, M.S., 1950; Ph.D., U. Toronto, 1953. Asst. dir. research Frank W. Horner Ltd., Montreal, Que., Can., 1950-69; v.p. biol. scis. Mead-Johnson Research Center, Evansville, Ind., 1969-75; v.p., dir. research Chattem Labs., Inc., Chattanooga, 1975-83; pres. McColl & Assocs., Inc., Chattanooga, 1983—. Contbr. numerous articles on pharmacology, toxicology and biochemistry to profl. jours. Served to capt. Can. Armed Forces, 1943-46. Mem. Am. Soc. Pharmacology and Exptl. Therapeutics, Soc. of Toxicology, Am. Chem. Soc., Biochem. Soc. (Gt. Brit.), Am. Soc. Clin. Pharmacology and Therapeutics, Soc. Toxicology of Can., Deutsch Pharmakologische Gesellschaft, European Soc. Study of Drug Toxicity, Pharm. Soc. Can. Episcopalian. Club: Walden (Chattanooga). Patentee in field. Current Work: Clinical pharmacology; consulting. Subspecialties: Pharmacology; Toxicology (medicine). Home and Office: 901 Brynwood Dr Chattanooga TN 37415

MCCOLLOUGH, MICHAEL LEON, astronomy educator; b. Sylva, N.C., Nov. 3, 1953; s. Stribling Mancell and Vivian Hazel (Bradley) McC. B.S., Auburn U., 1975, M.S., 1981; Ph.D. candidate, Ind. U. Lab. instr. Auburn (Ala.) U., 1974-75, grad. asst., 1975-77, lab. technician, 1977-78; assoc. instr. Ind. U., Bloomington, 1978—. Mem. Am. Astron. Soc., Royal Astron. Soc., Astron. Soc. Pacific, Am. Phys. Soc., Optical Soc. Am., Am. Assn. Physics Tchrs., Soc. Physics Students, N.Y. Acad. Scis., AAAS, Sigma Xi, Sigma Pi Sigma. Baptist. Current Work: Reduction of high resolution multiwave length observations of supernova remnant IC443, computer modeling of evolution of supernova remnants in a multiphase interstellar medium. Subspecialties: Optical astronomy; Theoretical astrophysics. Home: 988 Eigenmann Hall Bloomington IN 47406 Office: Dept Astronomy Ind Univ 319 Swain W Bloomington IN 47405

MCCOLLUM, GILBERT DEWEY, JR., research plant geneticist; b. Bellingham, Wash., Aug. 25, 1929; s. Gilbert Dewey and Jennie Marie (Johnson) McC.; B.S., Wash. State U., 1951, M.S., 1953; postgrad. U. Calif.-Berkeley, 1953-55; Ph.D., U. Calif.-Davis, 1958. Research plant geneticist U.S. Dept. Agr., Parma, Idaho, 1958-66, Beltsville, Md., 1966—. Mem. Bot. Soc. Am., Am. Genetic assn., Internat. Assn. Plant Taxonomy. Current work: Genetics, cytogenetics, interspecific hybridization and cytoplasmic male sterility with applications to varietal improvement of vegetables. Subspecialty: Plant genetics. Home: 6142 Springhill Terr Apt 201 Greenbelt MD 20770 Office: US Dept Agr ARS Vegetable Lab Beltsville Agrl Research Ctr-W Beltsville MD 20705

MCCOMBS, HARRIET G., social psychologist, educator; b. Columbia, S.C., Nov. 9, 1954; d. William F. and Harriet C. McC. B.S., U. S.C., 1974; M.A., U. Nebr., 1976, Ph.D., 1978. Instr. U. Nebr., Lincoln, 1975-77; congressional intern U.S. Ho. of Reps., Washington, 1976; asst. prof. Wayne State U., Detroit, 1978-82; asst. prof. psychology Yale U., New Haven, 1983—. Editor: newsletter Sojourner, 1977-82. Evaluator State Crime Commn., Lincoln, 1976-77, Wayne County Children's Center, Detroit, 1979-82. Psychol. Assn. minority fellow, 1975-78. Am. ; Mem. Am. Psychol. Assn., Evaluation Research Soc., Sigma Xi, Sigma Gamma Rho. African Methodist. Current Work: Application of social psychological principles to the study and improvement of the mental health of individuals and communities. Subspecialty: Social psychology. Office: Yale Child Study Center 333 Cedar St New Haven CT 06510

MCCOMBS, ROLLIN KOENIG, radiation oncologist; b. Denver, Aug. 17, 1919; s. Curtis and Emma Elizabeth (Koenig) McC.; m. Judy Louise Bacon, Oct. 22, 1924; children: David, Daniel, Susan, Kathleen, Michael. B.A., U. Colo., 1941, M.A., 1944; M.D., Stanford U., 1954. Diplomate: Am. Bd. Radiology, Am. Bd. Nuclear Medicine; lic. physician, Calif., Ariz., Colo. Instr. physics U. Colo., Boulder, 1942-48; intern in surgery Stanford U. Hosps., San Francisco, 1953-54; research fellow, assoc. physician Donner Lab., U. Calif., Berkeley, 1954-57; resident, staff VA Hosp., Long Beach, Calif., 1957-67; radiation oncologist Long Beach Community Hosp., 1967—; assoc. clin. prof. radiology U. So. Calif., Los Angeles, 1978—; Meml. Fund lectr. Radiol. Soc. N.Am., 1956. Contbr. articles to profl. jours. Mem. Am. Assn. Physicists in Medicine, Brit. Inst. Radiology, Am. Coll. Radiology, Am. Soc. Therapeutic Radiologists, AMA, Phi Beta Kappa, Sigma Xi, Alpha Chi Sigma, Pi Mu Epsilon, Sigma Pi Sigma. Presbyterian. Club: Frank Isaac Meml. Soc. Lodge: Masons. Current Work: Particle radiotherapy, med. physics, radiation dosimetry, ferrokinetics, radionuclide therapy, radiation protection, organ imaging. Subspecialties: Radiology; Nuclear medicine.

MCCONAHEY, PATRICIA JANE, med. research scientist; b. Dover, Ohio, June 9, 1936; d. Wallace Veigh and Edith Elizabeth McC. B.S., Waynesburg (Pa.) Coll., 1958. Sr. Technician dept. pathology U. Pitts. Sch. Medicine, 1958-61; research asst. dept. immunopathology Scripps Clinic and Research Found., La Jolla, Calif., 1961-63, research assoc., 1964-74, asst. mem. dept. immunology, 1974—; cons. Johnson & Johnson Co., 1981—. Contbr. articles to profl. jours. Brown Hazen grantee, 1968. Mem. Am. Assn. Immunologists. Current Work: Genetics influencing autoimmunity as observed in mouse model systems. Subspecialty: Immunology (medicine). Home: 8882 Caminito Primavera La Jolla CA 92137 Office: 10666 N Torrey Pines Rd La Jolla CA 92037

MCCONKEY, JOHN WILLIAM, physicist, educator; b. Portadown, Northern Ireland, Feb. 20, 1937; s. James William and Matilda Jean (Lawson) McC.; m. Maureen Greer, Aug. 31, 1963; children: Ruth, Andrew, Deborah, Christa. B.Sc., Queens U., Belfast, Northern Ireland, 1958, Ph.D., 1962. Lectr. Queen's U., 1962-70; vis. research fellow Sorbonne, Paris, 1964; prof. physics U. Windsor, Ont., Can., 1970—. Contbr. articles to profl. jours. Royal Soc. Commonwealth fellow, 1976-77; NATO sr. fellow, 1976-77; NASA sr. fellow, 1983-84; recipient numerous grants from Can. govt. and industry. Fellow Brit. Inst. Physics; Mem. Can. Assn. Physicists, Am. Phys. Soc. Baptist. Current Work: Electron and photon interactions with atoms and molecules.

MCCONNELL, DENNIS BROOKS, horticulturist, educator; b. Waupun, Wis., Aug. 18, 1938; s. Robert Brooks and Edith Carol (Erickson) McC.; m. Ruth Ann Bickel, Nov. 28, 1964; children: Michael Brooks, Sharon Kay. B.S., U. Wis.-River Falls, 1966; M.S., U. Wis.-Madison, 1968, Ph.D., 1971. State extension foliage specialist Agrl. Research Ctr., U. Fla., Apopka, 1970-73, mem. faculty dept. ornamental horticulture, Gainesville, 1973—, asst. prof. ornamental horticulture, 1970-75, assoc. prof., 1975—. Author: (with C. A. Conover and R. W. Henley) Professional Guide to Green Plants, 1976, The Indoor Gardener's Companion, 1978; contbr. chpts., articles, abstracts to profl. publs.; editor: (with P. L. Neel and J. T. Midcap) Florida Nurserymen's Retail Sales Handbook, 1974, (with G. S. Smith and J. T. Midcap) Florida Landscape Installation Handbook), 1975, Florida Landscape Maintenance Handbook, 1975. Served with U.S. Army, 1960-63. Florist Trans-World grantee, 1975; Dept. Agr. grantee, 1978; Foliage Edn. and Research Found. grantee, 1980; Sea-Land Corp. grantee, 1982. Democrat. Methodist. Club: Gainesville Torch. Subspecialties: Plant growth; Morphology. Home: 3745 SW 3d Pl Gainesville FL 32607 Office: Dept Ornamental Horticulture 1541 HS/PP Bldg U Fla Gainesville FL 32611

MCCONNELL, HARDEN MARSDEN, chemistry educator, researcher; b. Richmond, Va., July 18, 1927; m. Sofia Glogovac, 1956; children—Hunter, Trevor, Jane. B.S., George Washington U., 1947; Ph.D. in Chemistry, Calif. Inst. Tech., 1951. NRC fellow in physics U. Chgo., 1950-52; research chemist Shell Devel. Co., 1952-56; from asst. prof. to prof. chemistry Calif. Inst. Tech., 1956-64; prof. Stanford U., 1964-79, Robert Eckles Swain prof. chemistry, 1979—; founder Molecular Devices Corp., 1983; cons. Exxon Corp., Becton, Dickinson & Co.; Harkins lectr. U. Chgo., 1967; Falk-Plaut lectr. Columbia U., 1967; 21st Renaud Found. lectr., 1971; Debye lectr. Cornell U., 1973; Harvey lectr. Rockefeller U., 1977; A.L. Patterson lectr. Inst. Cancer Research, U. Pa., 1978; 8th Pauling lectr. Stanford U., 1981; 37th Remson Meml. lectr. Md. sect. Am. Chem. Soc., 1982. vis. com. dept. chemistry MIT, 1980-81; vis. com. dept. biology Carnigie-Mellon U., 1983—; Remsen Meml. lectr. Mem. editorial bd.: Bio Organic Chemistry, Jour. Membrance Biology, Jour. Supra Molecular Structure. Recipient Alumni Achievement awrd George Washington U., 1971; recipient Dickson Prize for Science Carnegie-Mellon U., 1982, Disting. Alumni award Calif. Inst. Tech., 1982; ISCO award, 1984. Fellow Am. Phys. Soc., AAAS; mem. Nat. Acad. Sci., Am. Soc. Biol. Chemists, Biophys. Soc., Am. Chem. Soc. (Sect. award 1961; Pure Chemistry award 1962, Harrison Howe award 1968, Irving Langmuir award 1971, Wolf prize 1984), Swedish Biophys. Soc. (hon. mem.). Subspecialty: Biophysical chemistry. Home: 421 El Escarpado Stanford CA 94305 Office: Dept Chemistry Stanford U Stanford CA 94305*

MCCONNELL, WILLIAM RAY, toxicologist; b. Wise, Va., Oct. 15, 1943; s. William and Rebecca Ruth (Stallard) McC.; m. Barbara Hicks, June 24, 1967. B.S., Va. Poly. Inst. and State U., 1965; M.S., Med. Coll. Va., 1973, Ph.D., 1976. Research pharmacologist So. Research Inst., Birmingham, Ala., 1976-79; sr. research toxicologist A.H. Robins Co., Inc., Richmond, Va., 1979—. Contbr. articles to profl. jours. Mem. AAAS, Am. Soc. Pharmacology and Exptl. Therapeutics, Soc. Toxicology. Republican. Baptist. Current Work: Safety testing of pharm. drugs. Subspecialties: Toxicology (medicine); Pharmacology. Office: 1211 Sherwood Ave PO Box 26609 Richmond VA 23261

MCCORKLE, GEORGE MASTON, molecular biologist; b. Wise, Va., Aug. 1, 1921; s. Claiborne Ross and Hazel Stewart (Webb) McC.; m. Harriet List Trees, Apr. 10, 1947 (div. 1972); children: Katharine McCorkle Snyder, Judith McCorkle Cole, James; m. Barbara Swanton Backus, Apr. 13, 1974. B.A., Yale U., 1942, M.Phil., 1973, Ph.D., 1975. With U. S. Dept. State, 1946, Charles Scribner's Sons, N.Y.C., 1947-60, v.p., 1955-60; also dir.; v.p. fin. New Am. Library, Inc., N.Y.C., 1960-67; with R.R. Bowker Co., N.Y.C., 1967-70, pres., 1968-70; research assoc. dept. biol. scis. Purdue U., 1975-79; assoc. research scientist dept. biology Yale U., 1979—. Served to lt. comdr. USNR, 1942-46, 50-52. Mem. Genetics Soc. Am., Soc. Devel. Biology, Phi Beta Kappa, Sigma Xi. Current Work: Bacterial gene regulation and expression; RNA processing; ribonuclease Pstructure and function. Subspecialties: Molecular biology; Gene actions. Home: 45 Mill Rock Rd Hamden CT 06511 Office: Kline Biology Tower Yale U New Haven CT 06520

MCCOWN, BRENT HOWARD, horticulturist, educator, cons.; b. Chgo., Feb. 21, 1943; s. C. Y. and Francis E. (Howard) McC.; m. Deborah D. Donoghue, June 15, 1968; children: Elizabeth, Nevin James. B.S., U. Wis., 1965, M.S., 1967, Ph.D. (U. Wis. Alumni Research Found. 4-Yr. prize fellow), 1969. Asst. prof. plant physiology Inst. Arctic Biology, U. Alaska, Fairbanks, 1970-72; research coordinator Cold Regions Research and Engring. Lab., Hanover, N.H., 1970-72; asst. prof. dept. horticulture U. Wis., Madison, 1972-77, assoc. prof., 1977-82, prof., 1982—, instr. plant prodn. Inst. Environ. Studies, 1972—; bd. dirs. Twyford Plant Labs. Internat.; mem. sci. adv. bd. Plant Resources Venture Fund; cons. on genetic engring. and biotech. applications to agr. Contbr. articles to profl. jours., chpts. to books. Served to capt. Chem. Corps U.S. Army, 1969-72. Recipient Outstanding Teaching award U. Wis., 1977. Mem. Internat. Assn. Plant Tissue Culture, Internat. Plant Propagator's Soc. (Outstanding Research Paper award 1980), Am. Soc. Hort. Sci., Am. Soc. Plant Physiology, Tissue Culture Assn. Am., AAAS, Wis. Acad. Arts and Sci., Sigma Xi, Phi Kappa Phi (pres. Wis. chpt.). Current Work: Micropropagation of crop plants, especially woody; production of secondary products for cell cultures; incorporation of herbicide resistance genes into forest trees via genetic engineering; protoplast culture of tree crops. Subspecialties: Genetics and genetic engineering (agriculture); Plant cell and tissue culture. Home: 236 E Sunset Ct Madison WI 53705 Office: Dept Horticulture U Wis Madison WI 53706

MCCOY, ALEXANDER WATTS, III, petroleum geologist, oil company executive; b. Bartlesville, Okla., Aug. 22, 1918; s. Alexander Watts and Helen Miranda (Aylesbury) McC.; m. Grace Wilkinson, June 12, 1944 (div. 1954); m. Bonnie Jean Weaver, Apr. 22, 1967; children—Anne Aylesbury, Martha Melanie, Alice Lewise, Alexander Watts IV, Bonnie Ann. B.S. in Geology, U. Okla., 1940. Geologist Carter Oil Co., Tulsa, 1940-45; research geologist Phillips Petroleum Co., Denver, 1945-50; asst. exploration mgr. Gulf Oil Co., Tulsa, 1950-53; pres. Alex W. McCoy Assocs., Tulsa, 1953—. Contbr. articles to profl. jours. Served with U.S. Army, 1941. Fellow Geol. Soc. Am.; mem. AAAS, AIME, Am. Petroleum Inst., Am. Assn. Petroleum Geologists. Republican. Episcopalian. Club: So. Hills Country (Tulsa). Current work: Finding oil and gas fields. Subspecialties: Geology; Fuels. Home: 6120 S Harvard Tulsa OK 74136Office: Alex W McCoy Assocs Inc 1 Warren Pl Suite 303 6100 S Yale Tulsa OK 74136

MCCOY, JOHN R(OGER), pathologist, educator, consultant, researcher; b. Trenton, N.J., June 11, 1916; s. George Lambert and Mae Ellen (Rogers) M.; m. Lloma Gregory, Dec. 11, 1945; 1 child, Wayne Douglas. V.M.D., U. Pa., 1940. Research prof. Bur. Biol. Research Rutgers U., New Brunswick, N.J., 1950-70, adj. research prof., 1970—; prof. comparative pathology Rutgers Med. Sch., Piscataway, N.J., 1970-83, emeritus prof. pathology, 1983—; cons., pathologist for various chem. and pharmaceutical cos. Editor: Pathology of Laboratory Animals, 1965. Author: (manual) Continuing Education Program, 1975; contbr. chpts. to books. Served to maj. Vet. Corps., AUS, 1943-46, PTO. Recipient Disting. Service award, N.J. Vet. Med. Assn., 1968, 74, Disting. Alumnus, U. Pa., 1979, Centennial Merit, U. Pa., 1984. Fellow N.Y. Acad. Scis.; mem. N.J. Vet. Med. Assn. (pres. 1971-72), AVMA (AVMA award 1981; mem. exec. bd. 1963-69, chmn. 1966-69, pres. 1971-72), Soc. Toxicological Pathologists (pres. 1977-78), Am. Vet. Med. Assn. Found. (pres. 1966-69). Presbyterian. Current work: Cancer chemotherapy; safety of drugs, cosmetics and food additives, and drinking water; pathology induced by drugs, cosmetics agents and food additives. Subspecialties: Pathology (veterinary medicine); Cancer research (veterinary medicine). Home: 1007 River Rd Piscataway NJ 08854 Office: UMDNJ Rutgers Med Sch PO Box 101 Piscataway NJ 08854

MCCRACKEN, ROBERT HENRY, opto-electronics engineer, nuclear researcher; b. Greensboro, N.C., May 9, 1921; s. John Lavercombe and Mary Jane (Ping) M.; m. Helen Christine Sutton, Apr. 24, 1942 (dec. 1975); children—Helen Jeannette, Nancy Kathryn. Cert. electronics engr. Electronics engr. Sperry Gyroscope Co., Garden City, N.Y., 1943-44, Nat. Bur. Standards, Washington, 1945-54, Harry Diamond Labs., Washington, 1954-78; pres. Hopewell Corp., Alexandria, Va., 1970—; vis. lectr. pub. and pvt. schs., Washington, 1950—; panel mem. U.S. Civil Service Examiners, Washington, 1955-60's; planner, observer optical satellite program Smithsonian Astron. Obs., 1956-60; cons. sci. dept. D.C. Pub. Schs., 1959. Contbr. articles to sci. publs. Project engr. 1st cesium-beam atomic clock, 1950-54; patentee in field; producer, presenter radio and TV programs on sci. and edn., 1958-80. Vol., Nat. Park Service, Washington, 1960—; pres. Green Acres-Glen Cove Citizens Assn., Md., 1950's—; vis. lectr. civic, sch. sci. and other groups, 1956—. Mem. Washington Acad. Scis. (bd. mgrs. 1982—), Optical Soc. Am., Nat. Capital Astronomers (past pres., trustee, editor, Astron. League award), Soc. Photog. Scientists and Engrs., Soc. Photo-Optical Instrumentation Engrs., Astron. Soc. Pacific. Current work: Encouragement of education in sciences and humanities; devise and develop scientific instrumentation for astronomy and related sciences; publishing. Subspecialties: Electronics; Optical astronomy. Home: 5120 Newport Ave Bethesda MD 20816

MCCRAW, RONALD KENT, psychologist; b. Houston, Dec. 6, 1947; s. Leon Frank and Lorna Mae (Bailey) McC. B.A., U. Tex.-Austin, 1970; M.A., U. Tex. Med. Br., Galveston, 1972; Ph.D., U. South Fla., 1981; postgrad. USAF Squadron Officers Sch., Air U., 1983, USAF Air Command and Staff Coll., 1985—. Research technician U. Tex. Med. Br., Galveston, 1972-74; grad. asst. Fla. Mental Health Inst., Tampa, 1975-76; resident in clin. psychology U. Tex. Health Scis. Ctr., San Antonio, 1977-78; psychometrist Hillsborough Community Mental Health Ctr., Tampa, 1978-79; clin. psychologist USAF Hosp., Chanute AFB, Ill., 1982—; commd. capt. U.S. Air Force, 1982; Film/book reviewer Sci. Books & Films. AAAS, 1978—, Jour. Nurse-Midwifery, 1984—, Birth, 1984—. Editorial bd.: Birth Psychology Bull., 1984—, Health Care of Women Internat., 1984—. Contbr. articles to profl. jours. Asst. coach Leaguerettes, Temple Terrace, Fla., 1979; coach Girls Softball Assn., Baytown, Tex., 1980-82; instr. ARC, Baytown, Tampa, 1980—, coach Chanute AFB Varsity Softball League, 1983-84, Rantoul Ponytail League, 1983-85. Fellow Am. Orthopsychiat. Assn.; mem. Am. Psychol. Assn., Ill. Psychol. Assn., Am. Acad. Behavioral Medicine, Internat. Childbirth Edn. Assn. (alt. hour rev. subcom. 1985), Soc. Personality Assessment, Acad. Psychosomatic Medicine, Assn. for Advancement Behavior Therapy, N.Y. Acad. Sci., AAAS, Assn. Birth Psychology, Sigma Xi, Psi Chi, Omicron Delta Kappa. Methodist. Lodges: Masons; Order of Demolay. Current Work: Behavioral medicine, personality assessment, pregnancy and childbirth, individual and family therapy, group therapy with adolescents. Subspecialty: Behavioral psychology. Home: PSC Box 1429 Chanute AFB IL 61868 Office: Mental Health Clinic USAF Hosp Chanute AFB IL 61868

MC CREDIE, KENNETH BLAIR, physician, educator; b. Christchurch, N.Z., July 2, 1935; came to U.S., 1969, naturalized, 1976; s. Gordon Blair and Margaret J. (Stevenson) McCredie; m. Maria Isabel Delgado, Oct. 29, 1980; children: Wendy Jane, Anna Margaret, Jennifer Mary. Student, Canterbury U., 1953-54; M.B., Ch.B., Otago U., 1960. Intern medicine Napier Hosp., N.Z., 1961-62, resident, 1962-65; resident medicine Prince Henry Hosp., Sydney, Australia, 1965-66, sr. fellow hematology, 1966-69; project investigator dept. development therapeutics U. Tex. System Cancer Ctr., M.D. Anderson Hosp. and Tumor Inst., Houston, 1969-70, asst. internist, asst. prof. medicine, 1970-73, assoc. internist, assoc. prof. medicine, 1973-76, chief leukemia service, 1973, internist, assoc. prof. medicine, 1976, prof. medicine, internist, chief leukemia service, 1978, prof. dept. dental oncology, 1979, dep. dept. head, chief leukemia service, 1981—, asst. prof. program in gen. internal medicine Med. Sch., 1973-74, assoc. prof., 1974, assoc. prof. dept. dental oncology Health Sci. Center, Dental br., 1977, prof. medicine, internist, chief leukemia service, dep. chmn. dept. hematology of div. medicine, 1983—; prof. dept. internal medicine U. Tex. Med. Sch., Houston, 1983—; Sir James Wattie vis. prof., N.Z., 1980. Mem. editorial bd.: Exptl. Hematology, 1973-78. Vice-pres. med. and sci. affairs Leukemia Soc. Am., Inc., 1979—, chmn. med. and sci. adv. com., 1979—, v.p. Tex. Gulf Coast chpt., Houston, 1981. Served to capt. Royal N.Z. Army, 1954-65. Recipient Outstanding Service to Mankind award Tex. Gulf Coast chpt. Leukemia Soc. Am., 1981, Dr. John Kenny award Nat. chpt. Tex. Gulf Coast chpt. Leukemia Soc. Am., 1983. Fellow Royal Australasian Coll. Physicians, ACP, Philippine Coll. Physicians (hon.); mem. Royal Soc. Medicine, Haematology Soc. Australia, Am. Fedn. Clin. Research, Am. Soc. Hematology, Am. Assn. Cancer Research, AMA, Am. Soc. Clin. Oncology, Internat. Soc. Exptl. Hematology, Working Group Leukocyte Procurement Nat. Cancer Inst., Tex. Med. Assn., S.W. Cancer Chemotherapy Study Group, Harris County Med. Soc., Internat. Assn. Comparative Research on Leukemia and Related Diseases, N.Y. Acad. Scis. Subspecialties: Cancer research (medicine); Oncology. Office: 6723 Bertner Ave Houston TX 77030

MCCUBBIN, THOMAS KING, JR., physicist, educator; b. Balt., June 1, 1925; s. T. King and Isabella M. McC.; m. Mary Lamb, Jan. 27, 1951; children: Mary Louisa, Thomas, Ruth. B.E.E., U. Louisville, 1946; Ph.D., Johns Hopkins U., 1951. Mem. faculty dept. physics Pa. State U., 1957—, prof., 1964—; mem. research staff M.I.T., 1954-57, Johns Hopkins U., 1951-54; professeur etranger Universite de Dijon, France, 1974. Contbr. articles to profl. jours. Served with USN, 1944-46. NSF grantee; Fulbright grantee, 1983. Fellow Am. Phys. Soc., Optical Soc. Am. (dir.-at-large 1968-70). Democrat. Episcopalian. Current Work: Infrared and Raman and fluorescence spectroscopy of molecules. Subspecialties: Infrared spectroscopy; Atomic and molecular physics. Home: 909 Willard Circle State College PA 16801 Office: 104 Davey Lab University Park PA 16802

MCCULLOUGH, EDWIN CHARLES, medical physicist; b. N.Y.C., June 2, 1942; married; 2 children. B.S., SUNY-Stony Brook, 1964; M.S., U. Md., 1967; Ph.D. in Radiol. Physics, U. Wis.-Madison, 1971. Scientist neutron physics Med. Research Council Cyclotron Unit, Hammersmith Hosp., 1971; research scientist radiation physics U. Wis.-Madison, 1971-73; staff physicist Mayo Clinic, Rochester, Minn., 1973—. Mem. editorial bds. Neuroradiology, Radiology, Jour. Computer Assisted Tomography. Mem. Am. Assn. Physicist in Medicine (pres.-elect), Radiol. Soc. N.Am., Sigma xi. Subspecialty: Medical physics. Office: Mayo Clinic 200 1st St SW Rochester MN 55901

MCCULLY, KILMER SERJUS, pathologist, educator, researcher; b. Daykin, Nebr., Dec. 23, 1933; s. Cyrus Harold and Lulu Viola (Litwinenco) McC.; m. Annina Elena Jacobs, Aug. 14, 1955; children—Michael Kilmer, Martha Elizabeth. A.B. magna cum laude, Harvard U., 1955, M.D. cum laude, 1959; M.A. ad eundum, Brown U., 1983. Diplomate Am. Bd. Pathology. Intern, Mass. Gen. Hosp., Boston, 1959-60, resident in pathology, 1965-68, asst. pathologist, 1968-74, assoc. pathologist, 1974-79; biochemist NIMH, Bethesda, Md., 1960-62; research assoc. in genetics Glasgow U., Scotland, 1963-64; pathologist VA Med. Ctr., Providence, 1981—; vis. prof. lab. medicine U. Conn., Farmington, 1980-81; asst., instr., asst. prof. pathology Harvard U. Med. Sch., Boston, 1965-79; assoc. prof. pathology Brown U., Providence, 1981—. Author: (monograph) Atherosclerosis, Homocysteine Theory of Arteriosclerosis, 1983. Contbr. articles to med. jours. Patentee in field. Served with USPHS, 1960-62. Recipient Faculty Research award Am. Cancer Soc., 1963-68; Career Devel. award NIH, 1971-76; NIH fellow, 1962-63. Mem. Am. Assn. Pathologists, AAAS, R.I. Soc. Pathologists, Harvard Mus. Assn., Phi Beta Kappa, Alpha Omega Alpha. Current work: Enhancement of activity of anti-neoplastic derivatives of homocysteine thiolactone by lipid and lipsome encapsulation, description of mesangial cell origin of erythropoietin and induction of arteriosclerosis by nickel subsulfide. Subspecialties: Pathology (medicine); Cancer research (medicine). Home: 15 Wildwood St Winchester MA 01890 Office: VA Med Ctr Davis Park Providence RI 02908

MC CUNE, WILLIAM JAMES, JR., manufacturing company executive; b. Glens Falls, N.Y., June 2, 1915; s. William James and Brunnhilde (Decker) McC.; m. Janet Waters, Apr. 19, 1940; 1 dau., Constance (Mrs. Leslie Sheppard); m. Elisabeth Johnson, Aug. 8, 1946; children—William Joseph, Heather H.D. S.B., Mass. Inst. Tech., 1937. With Polaroid Corp., Cambridge, Mass., 1939—, v.p. engring., 1954-63, v.p., asst. gen. mgr., 1963-69, exec. v.p., after 1969, pres., chief exec. officer, dir., 1980-82, chmn. bd., pres., chief exec officer, 1982, now chmn. bd., chief exec. officer. Chmn. bd., trustee Mitre Corp.; Trustee Boston Mus. Sci., Mass. Gen. Hosp. Fellow Am. Acad. Arts and Scis.; mem. Nat. Acad. Engring. Subspecialty: Manufacturing, engineering administration. Office: Polaroid Corp 549 Technology Sq Cambridge MA 02139

MCDANIEL, BOYCE DAWKINS, physicist, educator; b. Brevard, N.C., June 11, 1917; s. Allen Webster and Grace (Dawkins) McD.; m. Jane Chapman Grennell, Aug. 3, 1941; children: Gail P., James G. B.S., Ohio Wesleyan U., 1938; M.S., Case Inst. Tech., 1940; Ph.D., Cornell U., 1943. Staff mem. radiation lab. Mass. Inst. Tech., 1943; physicist Los Alamos Sci. Lab., 1943-46; mem. faculty Cornell U., Ithaca, N.Y., 1945—, prof., 1956—, assoc. dir. lab. nuclear studies, 1960-67, dir. lab. nuclear studies, 1967-85, Floyd R. Newman prof. nuclear studies, 1977—; head accelerator sect. Nat. Accelerator Lab., Batavia, Ill., 1972; mem. high energy physics adv. panel ERDA, 1975-78. Contbr. articles to profl. jours. Trustee Associated Univs., Inc., 1962-75. Vis. fellow Brookhaven Nat. Lab., 1966; Fulbright Research grantee Australian Nat. U., 1953; Guggenheim and Fulbright grantee U. Rome and Synchrotron Lab., Frascati, Italy, 1959-60. Fellow Am. Phys. Soc.; mem. Univs. Research Assn. (trustee 1971-77, 83-84), Nat. Acad. Sci. Spl. research neutron spectroscopy, gamma ray spectroscopy, high energy photoprodn. K mesons and hyperons, instrumentation for high energy physics, accelerator design and constrn. Subspecialty: Particle physics. Home: 26 Woodcrest Ave Ithaca NY 14850

MCDANIELS, DAVID KEITH, physicist, educator; b. Hoquiam, Wash., May 21, 1929; s. Forest L. and Grace L. McD.; m. Patricia R. McDaniels, Feb. 9, 1966; children: D. Douglas, Keith A., Kevin P. B.S., Wash. State U., 1951; M.S., U. Wash., Seattle, 1958, Ph.D., 1960. Physicist Hanford Atomic Products Operation, Gen. Electric Co., 1951-54; NSF research fellow Nuclear Research Centre, Saclay, France, 1962; successively asst. prof., assoc. prof., prof. physics U. Oreg., Eugene, 1963—; vis. staff mem. Los Alamos Nat. Lab., 1970-71, Uppsala U., Sweden, 1979. Author: The Sun: Our Future Energy Source, 1979; contbr. numerous articles profl. jours. Served with AUS, 1954-55. Grantee NSF, Bonneville Power Adminstr., 1963—. Mem. Am. Phys. Soc., AAAS, Am. Assn. Physics Tchrs., Internat. Solar Energy Soc. Current Work: Nuclear physics and solar energy, giant resonance studies at intermediate energies, solar radiation. Subspecialties: Solar energy; Nuclear physics. Home: 2365 W 23rd St Eugene OR 97405 Office: Physics Dept U of Oregon Eugene OR 97403

MCDERMOTT, DANIEL JOSEPH, pharmaceutical corporation executive, medical researcher; b. Pitts., May 19, 1936; s. Daniel J. and Anne (Collins) McD.; m. Janet Patricia Duhon, 1979; children: Jennifer, Brian. B.S., Georgetown U., 1958; M.S., U. Minn., 1965; Ph.D., Marquette U., 1969. Postdoctoral fellow Med. Coll. Wis., Milw., 1969-72, asst. prof. physiology, 1972-73; assoc. dir. cardiovascular clin. research G.D. Searle & Co., Chgo., 1973-79; v.p. med. research Smith Labs, Inc., Northbrook, Ill., 1979—. Served to lt. USN, 1959-63; served to capt. USNR. Mem. Am. Soc. Clin. Pharmacology and Exptl. Therapeutics, AAAS, Am. Heart Assn., N.Y. Acad. Scis., Sigma Xi. Current Work: Clinical trials of chymopapain; randomized controlled trials to evaluate new drugs. Subspecialties: Pharmacology; Physiology (medicine). Home: 2525 Telegraph Bannockburn IL 60015 Office: Smith Labs Inc 2215 Sanders Rd Northbrook IL 60062

MCDEVITT, HUGH O'NEILL, immunologist, educator, hospital administrator; b. Cin., 1930. M.D., Harvard U., 1955. Diplomate: Am. Bd. Internal Medicine. Intern Peter Bent Brigham Hosp., Boston, 1955-56, sr. asst. resident in medicine, 1961-62; asst. resident Bellevue Hosp., 1956-57; research fellow dept. bacteriology and immunology; Harvard U., 1959-61; USPHS spl. fellow Nat. Inst. Med. Research, Mill Hill, London, 1962-64; assoc. prof. med. immunology Stanford U., 1969-72, prof., 1972—; chief div. immunology Stanford U. (Univ. Hosp.), from 1970; physician (Univ. Hosp.), from 1966; cons. physician VA Hosp., Palo Alto, Calif., from 1968. Mem. Nat. Acad. Sci., AAAS, Am. Fedn. Clin. Research, Inst. Medicine, Am. Soc. Clin. Investigation, Am. Assn. Immunologists. Subspecialty: Immunology (medicine). Office: Stanford U Sch Medicine Stanford CA 94305*

MCDIARMID, IAN BERTRAND, physicist; b. Carleton Place, Ont., Can., Oct. 1, 1928; s. John and Lillian (Campbell) McD.; m. Dorothy May Folger,

Aug. 18, 1951; children—John Charles, Leslie-Anne. B.A., Queen's U., 1950, M.A., 1951; Ph.D., U. Manchester, 1954. Research officer NRC Can., Ottawa, 1955-75, asst. dir. div. physics, 1970-75; asso. dir. Herzberg Inst. Astrophysics, NRC Can., 1975-80; dir. Can. Centre for Space Sci., NRC, 1980—. Contbr. articles to profl. jours. Mem. Royal Soc. Can., Am. Geophys. Union, Can. Assn. Physicists. Subspecialties: High energy astrophysics; Government space program administration. Office: National Research Council 100 Sussex Dr Ottawa ON K1A 0R6 Canada

MCDONAGH, PAUL FRANCIS, physiology educator, researcher; b. Norwood, Mass., Mar. 25, 1945; s. John J. and Josephine Thomas McD.; m. Jennifer L. Crockett, May 21, 1978; children: John, Denise. B.S., Worcester Poly. Inst., 1967; M.S., Columbia U., 1969; Ph.D., U. Calif.-Davis, 1977; postgrad., U. Ariz.-Tucson, 1979. Research asst. chem. engring. Columbia U., N.Y.C., 1967-68; research assoc. U. Calif.-Davis, 1974-75; postdoctoral fellow U. Ariz., Tucson, 1976-79; asst. prof. Yale U., New Haven, 1979—; mem. research com. Conn. Heart Assn., 1982-84; cons. Miles Inst. Preclin. Pharmacology, 1982. Mem. editorial bd.: Microcirculation, 1983. Served to 1st lt. U.S. Army, 1968-70. Standard Oil fellow, 1970; U. Calif. Chancellor's fellow, 1974; grantee Ariz. Heart Assn.; grantee Yale Fluid Research; grantee NIH; grantee Conn. Heart Assn.; grantee Charles Oshe Fund; grantee Miles Labs. Mem. Am. Physiol. Soc., Microcirculatory Soc., Biomed Engring. Soc., N.Y. Acad. Scis. Current Work: Pathophysiology, coronary microvascular physiology, improved protection and preservation of hearts during surgery. Subspecialties: Physiology (medicine); Biomedical engineering. Office: Dept Surgery Yale U Sch Medicine 333 Cedar St New Haven CT 06510

MCDONALD, FRANK BETHUNE, physicist; b. Columbus, Ga., May 28, 1925; s. Frank B. and Lucy (Kyle) McD.; m. Virginia Ballew, June 15, 1951 (dec. 1977); children—Kyle Louise Jossi, Robert Kyle, Douglas Frank. B.S., Duke U., 1948; M.S., U. Minn., 1951, Ph.D., 1955. Part time prof. U. Md., Balt., 1963—; br. head Goddard Space Flight Ctr., Greenbelt, Md., 1959-70, lab. chief, 1970-82; detailed to Exec. Office of Pres., 1982; chief scientist NASA Hdqrs., Washington, 1982—. Recipient Exceptional Sci. Achievement award NASA, 1964, Presdl. Mgmt. Improvement cert., Outstanding Leadership medal, 1981. Fellow Am. Phys. Soc.; mem. Am. Geophys. Union, Am. Astron. Soc., Internat. Union Pure and Applied Physics (sec. internat. commn. on cosmic rays 1984—). Subspecialties: Cosmic ray high energy astrophysics; X-ray high energy astrophysics. Office: NASA Hdqrs Code P 400 Maryland Ave SW Washington DC 20546

MCDONALD, GERAL IRVING, forest pathologist; b. Wallowa, Oreg., Dec. 31, 1935; s. Harvey Irving and Lola M. (Gorbett) McD.; m. Judy Lynne Manos, Feb. 4, 1962; children: Michele, Scott, Alyssa. B.S. in Forestry, Wash. State U., 1963; Ph.D. in Plant Pathology, 1969. Research plant pathologist Forestry Scis. Lab., U.S. Forest Service, Moscow, Idaho, 1966—. Contbr. articles to profl. jours. Served with Wash. N.G., 1954-61. Mem. Am. Phytopath. Soc., Sigma Xi. Lodge: Lions. Current Work: Genetics of host pest systems, mathematical analysis and computer simulation of disease epidemics, development of integrated pest management. Subspecialties: Plant genetics; Integrated pest management. Office: 1221 S Main Moscow ID 83843

MCDONALD, HEMPROVA GHOSH, pathologist, researcher; b. Habigunj, India, Feb. 24, 1918; came to U.S., 1951, naturalized, 1962; d. Kunja Behari and Kusum Kamini (Ray) Guha; m. Hendley A. McDonald, June 11, 1960. M.D., M.B., Calcutta Med. Coll., India, 1941. Diplomate Am. Bd. Pathologic Anatomy. Fellow div. cancer research Washington U., St. Louis, 1951-52, resident in pathology, 1952-55, instr. surg. pathology, 1956-59; chief lab. services VA Hosp., McKinney, Tex., 1959-65; clin. asst. prof. U. Tex. Med. Sch., Dallas, 1960-68; dir. Diagnostic and Cell Research Inst., Waco, Tex., 1965—; cons. pathologist Hillcrest Bapt. Med. Ctr., Waco, 1966—, Providence Hosp., Waco, 1966—. Contbr. articles to profl. jours. Fellow Coll. Am. Pathologists, Am. Soc. Clin. Pathologists; mem. Indian Med. Assn., AMA, Am. Assn. Cancer Research, AAAS. Current work: Studies of natural processes of transformation of malignant and benign tissues into connective tissue stroma and vascular channels with the possible utilization of these processes in cancer therapy; studies of cellular lysis and regeneration of cardiac muscle in rheumatic fever; possible development of red blood corpuscles from local tissues appearing as hemoglobin globules bypassing nucleated phases of erythropoiesis. Subspecialties: Hematology; Cancer research (medicine). Home: 2713 N 43d St Waco TX 76710 Office: Diagnostic and Cell Research Inst 1206 Speight St Waco TX 76706

MCDONALD, JOHN FRANCIS PATRICK, electrical engineering educator; b. Narberth, Pa., Jan. 14, 1942; s. Frank Patrick and Lulu Ann (Hegedus) McD.; m. Karen Marie Knapp, May 26, 1979. B.S.E.E., MIT, 1963; M.S. in Engring., Yale U., 1965, Ph.D., 1969. Instr. Yale U., New Haven, 1968-69, asst. prof., 1969-74; assoc. prof. Rensselaer Poly. Inst., Troy, N.Y., 1974—. Contbr. articles to profl. publs. Patentee in field. Recipient numerous grants, 1974—. Mem. ACM, IEEE, Optical Soc., Acoustical Soc., Vacuum Soc. Current work: Computer hardward design applied to such areas as medical imaging (ultrasound, NMR); VLSI design automation using computer graphics. Subspecialties: Computer engineering; Computer-aided design. Home: 6 Twilight Dr Clifton Park NY 12065 Office: Rensselaer Poly Inst Ctr for Integrated Electronics Troy NY 12065

MCDONALD, KEITH LEON, theoretical physicist; b. Murray City, Utah, Apr. 20, 1923; s. Thomas Francis and Ada Pearl (Russell) McD. B.S. in Physics, U. Utah, Salt Lake City, 1950, M.S. in Physics, 1951, Ph.D. in Physics, 1956. With research and devel. dept. U.S. Naval Ordnance Test Sta., China Lake, Calif., 1951-52; theoretical grad. researcher U. Utah, 1954-56; mem. staff U. Calif.-Los Alamos Sci. Lab., 1956-57; researcher math. and physics U.S. Army Chem. Corps Proving Ground, Dugway, Utah, 1957-60; mem. faculty Brigham Young U., 1960-62, U. Utah, 1963; with Nat. Bur. Standards, Boulder, Colo., 1963-64, Idaho State U., 1965; theoretical researcher ESSA Environ. Research Labs., Boulder, 1966-68; cons. NOAA, Environ. Research Labs., Boulder, 1969-71, cons., researcher cosmic hydromagnetism, Salt Lake City, 1971—. Contbr. articles to profl. jours. Mem. Am. Phys. Soc., Am. Geophys. Union, Am. Assn. Physics Tchrs., Am. Astron.Soc., Optical Soc. Am., Phi Beta Kappa, Sigma Xi, Sigma Pi Sigma. Current Work: Cosmic hydromagnetism and dynamo theory, solar-terrestrial relations, high speed streams with origin in breaches in the sun's upper magnetic toroid. Subspecialties: Theoretical physics; Theoretical astrophysics. Office: PO Box 2433 Salt Lake City UT 84110

MCDONOUGH, JAMES MICHAEL, engineer, educator; b. Springfield, Ohio, Dec. 10, 1945; s. James Michael and Marjorie Ann (Brandle) McD.; m. Mei Tsuo Huang, Feb. 19, 1983. B. Aero. and Astronautical Engring., Ohio State U., 1968; M.A. in Applied Math., UCLA, 1975, Ph.D. in Engring., 1980. Engr., scientist McDonnell-Douglas Co., Huntington Beach, Calif., 1968-72; staff mathematician Prose, Inc., Los Angeles, 1973-76; mem. tech. staff The Aerospace Corp., El Segundo, Calif., 1980—; vis. lectr. UCLA, 1980-83, adj. asst. prof., 1983—. Contbr. articles to profl. jours. Mem. Am. Math. Soc., Soc. Indsl. and Applied Math., AAAS, N.Y. Acad. Sci. Current work: Numerical analysis of partial differential equations, especially computational fluid dynamics, study of chaotic solutions to deterministic nonlinear dissipative systems, i.e., strange attractors. Subspecialties: Numerical analysis (mathematics); Fluid mechanics. Office: The Aerospace Corp PO Box 92957 M4-964 Los Angeles CA 90009

MCDONOUGH, THOMAS REDMOND, astrophysicist; b. Boston, Oct. 4, 1945; s. Redmond Augustus and Sophie Theresa (Stankewich) McD. B.S. in Physics, M.I.T., 1966; Ph.D., Cornell U., 1973. Postdoctoral researcher Cornell U., Ithaca, N.Y., 1973-75; resident research assoc. Jet Propulsion Lab., Pasadena, 1976-77, cons., 1978-81; lectr. engring. Calif. Inst. Tech., Pasadena, 1979—; coordinator Search for Extraterrestrial Intelligence, Planetary Soc., Pasadena, 1981—; cons. Avco Embassy Pictures, Hollywood, Calif., 1981-82. Contbr. articles to profl. jours.; popular sci./sci. fiction stories pub. in Creative Computing. Recipient citation NASA, 1979. Fellow Brit. Inter-planetary Soc.; mem. Internat. Astron. Union, Am. Astron. Soc., Am. Phys. Soc., AIAA, Authors Guild, Sci. Fiction Writers Am., Internat. Platform Assn. Club: Toastmasters. Current Work: Spacecraft research on giant planets; search for extraterrestrial intelligence. Subspecialties: Planetary science; Search for extraterrestrial intelligence. Home: 500 S Oak Knoll 46 Pasadena CA 91101 Office: 138 78 Calif Inst Tech Pasadena CA 91125

MC DOWELL, CHARLES ALEXANDER, physical chemist, educator; b. Belfast, Ireland, Aug. 29, 1918; s. Charles and Mabel (McGregor) McD.; m. Christine Joan Staddart, Aug. 10, 1945; children—Karen Mary Anne, Christina Anne, Avril Jeanne. B.Sc., M.Sc., Queens U., Belfast, 1942; D.Sc., Queen's U., Eng., 1955; D.Sc. (hon.), U. B.C., 1984. Sr. asst. lectr. Queen's U., 1941-42; sci. officer U.K. Civil Def., 1942-45; lectr. U. Liverpool, 1945-55; prof., head dept. chemistry U. B.C., Vancouver, 1955-81, Univ. prof., 1981—, Killiam sr. research fellow, 1969-70; vis. prof. Kyoto (Japan) U., 1965, 69-70; Disting. vis. prof. U. Fla., Gainesville, 1974; NRC Sr. Research fellow, vis. prof. Cambridge (Eng.) U., 1963-64; W.U.S. cons. U. Honduras, 1975; Disting. vis. prof. U. Capetown, 1975; Frontiers of Chemistry lectr. Wayne State U., 1978; Disting. vis. lectr. Faculty of Sci., U. Calgary, 1978; chmn. Internat. Union Pure and Applied Chemistry Congress, Vancouver, 1981. Editor: Mass Spectrometry, 1963, Magnetic Resonance, 1972; contbr. articles to profl. jours. Recipient Letts Gold medal in theoretical chemistry Queen's U., 1941, Sci. medal Université de Liège, Belgium, 1955; Centennial medal Gov. of Can., 1967; Queen Elizabeth Silver Jubilee medal, 1977; Guggenheim fellow, 1984, 85. Fellow Chem. Soc. London; Mem. Chem. Inst. Can. (medal 1969, Montreal medal 1982, pres. 1979), Royal Soc. Chemistry (U.K.), Royal Soc. Can., Am. Chem. Soc., Am. Mass Spectrometry Soc., Mass Spectrometry Soc. Japan, Am. Phys. Soc. Current Work: Electron spin resonance spectrometry; nuclear magnetic resonance spectroscopy; ENDOR spectrometry; electronic structures of molecules; photoionization and photoelectron spectroscopy; cryogenic studies on chemical substances. Subspecialties: Nuclear magnetic resonance; Physical chemistry. Home: 5612 McMaster Rd Vancouver BC V6T 1JB Canada

MCDOWELL, DAVID JAMISON, clinical psychologist, educator, researcher; b. Pitts., Jan. 11, 1947; s. David Emerson and Auleene Marley (Jamison) McD.; m. Nancy Annis, Jan. 13, 1973; children: Sasha Annis, Christopher Daniel. B.A., Princeton U., 1968; Ph.D., U. Maine-Orono, 1980. Lic. psychologist, Mass. Predoctoral intern Worcester (Mass.) State Hosp., 1976-77, part-time admission officer, 1979-82; instr. Coll. of the Holy Cross, Worcester, 1977-78; clin. dir. Milford (Mass.) Assistance Program, Inc., 1978-80; asst. prof. psychiatry and pediatrics U. Mass. Med. Ctr., Worcester, 1980-83; vis. lectr. Assumption Coll., Worcester, 1979-80; ptnr. Worcester County Counseling Assocs., Bolton, Mass., 1982—; dir. Adolescent Service, Intatient Psychiat. Unit, U. Mass. Med. Ctr., 1982-83; clin. dir. Newton (Mass.) Multi-Service Ctr., 1983-84. Co-author: The Mental Health Industry, 1978; contbr. chpts. to books, articles to ency. State of Maine mental health fellow, 1973-75; Chemstrand Corp. nat. merit scholar, 1964-68. Mem. Am. Psychol. Assn., Mass. Psychol. Assn., Am. Orthopsychiat. Assn., Phi Kappa Phi. Current Work: Cognitive and interpersonal aspects of schizophrenia; identity formation; sociology of mental health consumers and providers; treatment of adolescents and adults; individual and family psychotherapy. Subspecialty: Clinical psychology. Office: Worcester County Counseling Assocs 42 Lake Ave Suite 103-106 Worcester MA 01604

MCDOWELL, LEE RUSSELL, animal nutritionist, nutritional consultant, educator; b. Lyons, N.Y., Apr. 11, 1941; s. Russell Gale and Ida May (Lee) McD.; m. Lorraine Marie Worden, June 19, 1965; children: Suzannah, Joana, Teresa. A.A.S., Alfred (N.Y.) Agr. and Tech., 1961; B.S., U. Ga., 1964, M.S., 1965; Ph.D. in Animal Nutrition, Wash. State U., 1971. Vol Peace Corps, Santa Cruz, Bolivia, 1965-67; asst. prof. dept. animal sci. U. Fla., Gainesville, 1971-77, assoc. prof., 1977-82, prof., 1982—; nutritional cons. in, Latin Am. and, S.E. Asia. Co-author: Latin American Tables of Feed Composition, 1972, 74, Latin American Symposium on Mineral Research with Grazing Ruminants, 1978; contbr. chpts. to books. Mem. Am. Dairy Sci. Assn., Am. Soc. Animal Sci., Am. Inst. Nutrition, Am. Forage and Grassland Council, Council Agrl. Scis. and Tech., Asociación Latinoamericana de Producción Animal. Methodist. Current Work: Research in international animal agriculture: tropical feeds and mineral deficiencies and toxicities for grazing livestock. Subspecialty: Animal nutrition. Home: 13 SW 15B Archer FL 32618 Office: U Fla 125 Animal Sci Bldg Gainesville FL 32611

MCDOWELL, ROBERT E., JR., animal scientist, educator, researcher; b. Charlotte, N.C., June 27, 1921; s. Robert E. and Grace Wilson (Bradford) McD.; m. Dorothy Gill, Dec. 8, 1945; children: Jean, Ann, Robert. B.S., N.C. State U., 1942; M.S., U. Md., 1949, Ph.D., 1955. Tchr. agrl. program VA, 1946; research investigator, program dir. USDA, Beltsville, Md., 1946-67; prof. internat. animal sci. Cornell U., Ithaca, N.Y., 1967—; cons. FAO, U.S. AID, Rockefeller Found., U. P.R., U. Venezuela, U. Dominican Republic, U.S. Peace Corps, U. Calif.-Davis, USDA; chmn. bd. trustees Internat. Livestock Ctr. for Africa; vice chmn. external evaluation panel U.S. AID; chmn. steering com. internat. agr. Cornell U. Author: Improvement Livestock Production in Warm Climates, 1972; Contbr. chpts. to books, articles to profl. jours. Served with USMC, 1942-46. Decorated Bronze Star, Meritorious Commendation medal.; Recipient Superior Service award USDA, 1962; Animal Agr. award in internat. animal agr. Am. Soc. Animal Sci., 1979. Mem. Am. Diary Sci. Assn., Am. Soc. Animal Sci., AAAS, Nat. Dairy Council, Ret. Officers Assn., Alpha Zeta. Current Work: Contributions—animals to support man in developing countries; research, training and development of small farm agriculture in developing countries. Subspecialties: Animal physiology; Animal genetics. Office: Cornell U 131 Morrison Hall Ithaca NY 4853

MCDUFFIE, FREDERIC CLEMENT, physician, foundation administrator; b. Lawrence, Mass., Apr. 27, 1924; m. Isabel Simpson Wiggin, May 31, 1952; children: Elisabeth Wiggin, Joan Selden, Deborah Howard, Charles Dennett. Grad., Harvard U., M.D. cum laude, 1951. Diplomate: Am. Bd. Internal Medicine. Intern Peter Bent Brigham Hosp., Boston, 1951-52, resident, 1952-53, 56-57; tng. in phys. chemistry Harvard U., 1953-54; in immunology Columbia Coll. Physicians and Surgeons, 1954-56; asst. prof. internal medicine U. Miss., Jackson, 1957-62, asst. prof. microbiology, 1957-64, asso. prof., 1964-65; cons. medicine and microbiology Mayo Clinic and Mayo Found., Rochester, Minn., 1965; asst. prof. internal medicine and microbiology Mayo Grad. Sch. Medicine, 1965-69, assoc. prof., 1969-73, Mayo Med. Sch., 1973, prof. internal medicine and immunology, 1974-79; prof. medicine Emory U., Atlanta, 1979—; vis. investigator Center for Disease Control, Atlanta, 1979—; sr. v.p. med. affairs Arthritis Found., Atlanta, 1979—; pres. Miss. chpt. Arthritis Found., 1962-63; bd. dirs., mem. exec. com. Miss. chpt. Arthritis Found. (Minn. chpt.), 1974-79, chmn. med. and sci. com., 1975-79, nat. trustee, 1978-79, chmn. nat. research com., 1978-79. Editorial bd.: Arthritis and Rheumatism, 1976-81, Jour. Rheumatology, 1974—; editor: Jour. Lab. and Clin. Medicine, 1977-79; contbr. articles to profl. jours. Served with U.S. Army, 1943-45. Mem. Am. Assn. Immunologists, Am. Rheumatism Assn., Central Rheumatism Assn. (pres. 1973-74), Central Soc. Clin. Research (council 1977-79), Soc. Exptl. Biology and Medicine, Am. Fedn. Clin. Research, A.C.P., Alpha Omega Alpha. Home: 3155 Arden Rd NW Atlanta GA 30305 Office: Arthritis Found 1314 Spring St NW Atlanta GA 30309

MCELDOWNEY, ROLAND CONANT, geologist, consultant; b. Newton, Mass., Nov. 14, 1940; s. Richard Lancaster and Virginia Davis (Conant) McE.; m. Barbara Lynne Read, Mar. 26, 1966; children—Richard, Scott, Kathryn. B.A., Franklin and Marshall Coll., 1963; M.S., San Diego State U., 1971. Cert. geologist Maine. Geologist U.S. Peace Corps, Ghana, West Africa, 1963-65, Army Corps. Engrs., San Francisco, 1966-68; sr. geologist Geodata Systems Inc., Orange, Calif., 1969-71; assoc. Dames & Moore, Golden, Colo., 1972-79; v.p. Apache Energy & Mineral Co., Lakewood, Colo., 1979-84; pres. Wolf Creek Exploration Co., Evergreen, Colo., 1984—; dir. Apache Energy & Minerals Co., Lakewood, 1979-84. Contbr. articles to profl. jours. Mem. Geol. Soc. Am., Denver Region Exploration Geologists Soc., Colo. Mining Assn., AIME. Republican. Episcopalian. Lodge: Kiwanis (bd. dirs. 1983). Current work: Development of geophysical and geochemical techniques for oil and gas and precious metals exploration; use of remote sensing to enhance this development. Subspecialties: Geology; Fuels and sources. Home: 29434 Greenwood Ln Evergreen CO 80439 Office: Wolf Creek Exploration Co PO Box 3523 Evergreen CO 80439

MCELHANEY, JAMES HARRY, biomedical engr.; b. Phila., Oct. 27, 1933; s. James H. and Olga M. (Lazuk) McE.; m. Eileen M. Esbensen, Nov. 17, 1954; children—Kathy, Amy, Liza. B.S., Villanova U., 1955; M.S., U. Pa., 1960; Ph.D., W.Va. U., 1964. Registered profl. engr., Pa. Mech. engr. Philco Corp., Phila., 1955-59; asst. prof. mech. engring. Villanova (Pa.) U., 1959-62; prof. theoretical and applied mechanics W.Va. U., Morgantown, 1962-69; asso. prof. mech. engring., head biomechanics dept. Hwy. Safety Research Inst., U. Mich., 1969-74; prof. biomechanics Duke U., Durham, N.C., 1974—, dir. grad. studies, 1974-75, chmn. biomed. engring. dept., 1983—; pres. Safety Electronics Corp.; cons. Ford Motor Co., Am. Motors Co., Chrysler Corp., Westinghouse Corp., NIH, others; chmn. com. on indsl. head protection Am. Nat. Standards Inst. Editor: mech. engring. sect. Jour. of Bioengring, 1977—; mem. editorial adv. bd.: mech. engring. sect. Jour. of Biomechanics, 1967—; Contbr. articles on biomechanics to profl. jours. Served with U.S. Army Res., 1955-63. NIH grantee, 1967—. Fellow ASME (chmn. bioengring. div. 1975—, asso. editor Trans. on Biomech. Engring.); mem. Am. Soc. Engring. Edn., Soc. for Exptl. Stress Analysis, Soc. Automotive Engrs. (chmn. anthropometric dummy study com.), Biomedical Engring. Soc., Am. Acad. Mechanics, Sigma Xi, Pi Tau Sigma. Club: Duke Men's. Subspecialty: Biomedical engineering. Home: 3411 Cambridge Rd Durham NC 27707 Office: Biomedical Engring Dept Duke U Durham NC 27707

MC ELLIGOTT, JAMES GEORGE, neuroscientist; b. N.Y.C., June 20, 1938; s. James P. and Mildred C. (Biernesser) McE.; m. Sandra G. Fitzpatrick., Aug. 26, 1967; children: Seamus, Sean. B.S., Fordham Coll., 1960; M.A., Columbia U., 1963; Ph.D., McGill U., 1967. NIH postdoctoral fellow Brain Research Inst. UCLA, 1967-68, research assoc., 1968-71; assoc. prof. pharmacology Temple U., 1971—; cons. in field. Mem. Soc. Neurosci., AAAS, Sigma Xi. Current Work: Neurophysiology, bioengineering, computer science. Subspecialties: Neuropharmacology; Neuropsychology.

MCELLISTREM, MARCUS THOMAS, physics educator; b. St. Paul, Minn., Apr. 19, 1926; s. Marcus Thomas and Loretta Camille (Simard) M.; m. Eleanor DeMeuse, Aug. 17, 1957; children—Mary Ann, Marcus Jr., Rebecca, Joan, Catherine, Deborah. B.A., Coll. St. Thomas, 1950; M.S., U. Wis.-Madison, 1951, Ph.D., 1955. Research asst. U. Wis.-Madison, 1953-55; research assoc. Ind. U., 1955-57; from asst. prof. to prof. physics U. Ky., Lexington, 1957—, acting chmn. physics and astronomy, 1983; cons. in field; pres. Adena Corp., 1970-74. Contbr. articles (60) to profl. jours. Faculty sponsor Newman Ctr., U. Ky., 1964-73, pres., 1978-80; sec. Lexington Cath. High Sch., 1983—. Served with USNR, 1944-46. Named Collaborateur Etranger, Com. Energie Atomique, France, 1974, 75, 83, Disting. Prof., Coll. Arts and Sci., 1981, 82. Fellow Am. Phys. Soc.; mem. Albertus Magnus Guild, Sigma Xi. Roman Catholic. Current work: Mechanisms of neutron induced reactions; nuclear structure studies with neutrons; reaction rates for nuclear astrophysics. Subspecialties: Nuclear physics; Nuclear medicine. Home: 1841 Blairmore Ct Lexington KY 40502 Office: Physics and Astronomy Dept U Ky Chem-Phys Bldg Lexington KY 40506

MC ELROY, WILLIAM DAVID, biochemist; b. Rogers, Tex., Jan. 22, 1917; s. William D. and Ora (Shipley) McE.; m. Nella Winch, Dec. 23, 1940 (div.); children—Mary Elizabeth, Ann Reed, Thomas Shipley, William David; m. Marlene A. DeLuca, Aug. 28, 1967; 1 son, Eric Gene. B.A., Stanford, 1939; M.A., Reed Coll., 1941; Ph.D., Princeton U., 1943; D.Sc., U. Buffalo, 1962, Mich. State U., 1970, Loyola U., Chgo., 1970, U. Notre Dame, 1975, Calif. Sch. Profl. Psychology, 1978; D.Pub. Service, Providence Coll., 1970; LL.D., U. Pitts., 1971, Johns Hopkins U., 1977. War research, com. med. research OSRD, Princeton, 1942-45; NRC fellow Stanford, 1945-46; instr. biology dept. Johns Hopkins, 1946, successively asst. and asso. prof., prof. biology, 1951-69, chmn. biology dept., 1956-69; also dir. McCollum-Pratt Inst., 1949-64; dir. NSF, Washington, 1969-71; chancellor U. Calif., San Diego, 1972-80, prof., 1980—. Author textbook.; Editor: (with Bentley Glass) Copper Metabolism, 1950, Phosphorus Metabolism, 2 vols, 1951, 52, Mechanism of Enzyme Action, 1954, Amino Acid Metabolism, 1955, The Chemical Basis of Heredity, 1957, The Chemical Basis of Development, 1959, Light and Life, 1961, Cellular Physiology and Biochemistry, 1961, (with C.P. Swanson) Foundations of Modern Biology series, 1961-64. Mem. Sch. Bd. Baltimore City, 1958-68. Recipient Barnett Cohen award in bacteriology, 1958; Rumford prize Am. Acad. Arts and Scis., 1964. Mem. Am. Inst. Biol. Scis. (pres. 1968), Am. Chem. Soc., Nat. Acad. Sci., Am. Soc. Biol. Chemists (pres. 1963-64), Soc. Gen. Physiology (pres. 1960-61), Soc. Naturalists, Soc. Zoologists, Am. Acad. Arts and Scis., Am. Soc. Bacteriologists, Am. Philos. Soc., AAAS (pres. 1976, chmn. 1977), Sigma Xi, Kappa Sigma. Current Work: Basic science of bioluminescence-applilcations to clinical, agriculture and industrial problems. Subspecialties: Biochemistry (biology); Microbiology. Office: Univ Calif San Diego La Jolla CA 92093

MC EVILLY, THOMAS VINCENT, seismologist; b. East Saint Louis, Ill., Sept. 2, 1934; s. Robert John and Frances Nathalie (Earnshaw) McE.; m. Dorothy K. Hopfinger, Oct. 23, 1970; children: Mary, Susan, Ann, Steven, Joseph, Adrian. B.S., St. Louis U., 1956, Ph.D., 1964. Geophysicst California Co., New Orleans, 1957-60; engring. v.p. Sprengnether Instrument Co., St. Louis, 1962-67; asst. prof. seismology U. Calif., Berkeley, 1964-68, assoc. prof., 1968-74, prof., 1974—, chmn. dept. geology and geophysics, 1976-80, asst. dir. seismographic sta., 1968—; assoc. dir., head earth sci. div. Lawrence Berkeley Lab., 1982—; chmn. bd. dirs. Inc. Research Inst. Seismology, 1984—; cons. numerous govt. agys., geotech. cos. Contbr. numerous articles to profl. jours. Fellow Am. Geophys. Union; mem. Royal Astron. Soc., Earthquake Engring. Research Inst., Seismol. Soc. Am. (editor bull. 1976-85), Soc. Exploration Geophysicists, AAAS. Current Work: Earthquake processes and crustal structure; applied seismology and seismic instrmentation. Subspecialty: Geophysics. Office: Dept Geology and Geophysics U Calif Berkeley CA 94720

MCEVILY, ARTHUR JOSEPH, metallurgy educator; b. N.Y.C., Dec. 20, 1924; s. Arthur Joseph and Ann Loretta (Leeman) M. B.S., Columbia U., 1945, M.S., 1949, Dr. Engring. Sci., 1959. Registered profl. engr., N.Y., Conn. Research scientist NASA, Langley Field, Va., 1949-61, Ford Motor Co., Dearborn, Mich., 1961-67; prof. metallurgy U. Conn., Storrs, 1967—; Contbr. articles to profl. jours. Served with USN, 1943-46. Fellow Am. Soc. Metallurgy; mem. ASME (tech. editor 1984—), Am. Inst. Metall. Engrs., ASTM. Current work: Fatique and fracture of materials. Subspecialty: Metallurgical engineering. Office: Univ Conn Metallurgy Dept U-136 Storrs CT 06268

MCFADDEN, LESLIE DAVID, soil geomorphologist, geology educator; b. Orlando, Fla., Jan. 11, 1952; s. Lawrence David and Virginia Mae (Maxwell) McF. B.A., Stanford U., 1973; M.S., U. Ariz., 1978, Ph.D., 1982. Geologist U.S. Geol. Survey, Tucson, 1979-81, mem. faculty, staff geologist, Albuquerque, 1982-84; asst. prof. geology U. N.Mex., Albuquerque, 1981—; cons. to industry. Contbr. articles to profl. jours., chpts. to books. Mem. Geol. Soc. Am., Soil Sci. Soc. Am., Am. Quaternary Soc., N.Mex. Geol. Soc. Democrat. Current work: Studies of processes of soil formation and landscape evolution; influences of climate and soil parent material on rates and magnitudes of soil development. Subspecialties: Geology; Soil science. Home: 229 Horton Ln Albuquerque NM 87107Office: Dept Geology U N Mex Albuquerque NM 87131

MCFADDEN, PETER WILLIAM, mechanical engineering educator; b. Stamford, Conn., Aug. 2, 1932; s. Kenneth E. and Marie (Gleason) McF.; children: Peter, Kathleen, Mary. B.S. in Mech. Engring. U. Conn., 1954, M.S., 1956; Ph.D., Purdue U., 1959. Registered profl. engr., Ind., Conn. Asst. instr. U. Conn., 1954-56, dean Sch. Engring., prof. mech. engring., 1971—; mem. faculty Purdue U., 1956-71; prof. mech. engring., head Purdue U. (Sch. Mech. Engring.), 1965-71; postdoctoral research Swiss Fed. Inst., Zurich, 1960-61; cons. to industry, 1959—. Mem. ASME, Am. Soc. Engring. Edn. Research in cryogenics, heat transfer, mass. transfer. Subspecialty: Mechanical engineering.

MCFADDEN, TERRY TED, mechanical engineering educator, Arctic engineering consultant; b. Dillon, Mont., June 28, 1936; s. Everett Kuhle and Eleanor Mae (Baril) M.; m. Loretta Stejer, Dec. 28, 1955 (div. May 1967); children—Tammy Roben, Ronn Kevin, Toni Lynn, Kary Scott; m. Helen Ruth Finlayson, Apr. 6, 1968. B.S., Brigham Young U., 1964; M.S., Stanford U., 1964; Ph.D., U. Alaska, 1974. Registered profl. engr., Alaska. Research and devel. engr. Hewlett Packard Corp., Palo Alto, Calif., 1960-68; research engr. Arctic Health Research, Fairbanks, Alaska, 1968-73; research engr. Cold Regions Engring., Fairbanks, 1973-74, dir., 1974-82; dir. research Shannon and Wilson, Fairbanks, 1982-83; assoc. prof. mech. engring. U. Alaska, Fairbanks, 1983—; v.p. engring. McFadden Engring. Cons., Fairbanks, 1970—; mem. exec. com. Tech. Council for Cold Regions Engring., 1980—. Contbr. articles to profl. jours. Mem. ASCE (vice chmn. tech. council for cold regions engring. 1984-85, pres. Alaska sect. 1982-83), ASME, Nat. Soc. Profl. Engring. Republican. Current work: Research into problems related to living and working in cold regions, including permafrost, ice fog, ice forces and water supply. Subspecialty: Mechanical engineering. Home: 3400 Sandvik Rd Fairbanks AK 99701

MCFALL, ELIZABETH, molecular biologist, educator, cons.; b. San Diego, Oct. 28, 1928; d. C. E. and Teresa (Moore) McF.; m. Andrew L. Floyd. B.S. in Chemistry, San Diego State Coll., 1950; M.A. in Econs, U. Calif., Berkeley, 1954, Ph.D. in Biochemistry, 1957. Research fellow Harvard U., 1957-60; research asso. M.I.T., Cambridge, 1960-61 62-63; NIH spl. research fellow Nat. Inst. Med. Research, London, 1961-62; prof. microbiology Sch. Medicine, N.Y. U., N.Y.C., 1963—. Editor: Jour. Bacteriology. Recipient NIH career devel. award, 1964-74. Mem. Am. Soc. Biol. Chemistry, Am. Soc. Microbiology, AAAS, Am. Acad. Microbiology. Democrat. Current Work: Molecular biology, control of gene expression. Subspecialties: Genetics and genetic engineering (biology); Gene actions. Office: Dept Microbiology Sch Medicine NY Univ New York NY 10016

MCFARLAND, JAMES WILLIAM, medicinal chemist, researcher; b. Sacramento, Nov. 16, 1931; s. Joseph Benjamin and Ruth Leah (Boggs) McF.; m. Leray Lucille Connell, July 1, 1961; children—Lincoln Randall, William Connell, Terri Lucille. B.A., Chico State Coll., 1954; Ph.D., U. Calif.-Berkeley, 1957. Fulbright scholar U. Munich, Fed. Republic Germany, 1957-58; postdoctoral fellow U. Calif.-Berkeley, 1959-60; research chemist Pfizer, Inc. Groton, Conn., 1960—. Contbr. articles to profl. jours., chpts. to books. Patentee in field. Mem. Regional Sch. Dist. 18 Bd. Edn., Old Lyme, Conn., 1975—, chmn., 1981—. Mem. Am. Chem. Soc. Current work: Animal health products; anthelmintic, antibacterial agents, graphical and quantitative structure-activity relationships. Subspecialties: Drug design; Medicinal chemistry. Office: Pfizer Inc Eastern Point Rd Groton CT 06340

MCFARLAND, ROBERT HAROLD, physicist, educator, researcher, administrator; b. Severy, Kans., Jan. 10, 1918; s. Robert Eugene and Georgia Ellen (Simpson) M.; m. Twilah Mae Seefeld, Aug. 28, 1940; children—Robert Alan, Rodney Jon. B.S., B.A., Kans. State Tchrs. Coll., 1940; Ph.M., U. Wis., 1943, Ph.D., 1947. Tchr. sci., coach Chase High Sch., Kans., 1940-41; instr. Navy Radio Sch., U. Wis., Madison, 1943-44; sr. engr. Sylvania Elec. Corp., Salem, Mass., 1944-46; mem. faculty Kans. State U., Manhattan, 1947-60, prof. physics, 1954-60, dir. nuclear labs., 1958-60; physicist Lawrence Radiation Lab., U. Calif., 1960-69; dean grad. sch. U. Mo.-Rolla, 1969-79, prof. physics, 1969-85, prof. emeritus, 1985—, dir. instl. analysis and planning, 1979-82; acting v.p. for acad. affairs; U. Mo. System, Columbia, 1974-75; vis. prof. U. Calif.-Berkeley, 1980-81; intergovernmental personnel act appointee Dept. Energy, Germantown, Md., 1982-84; cons. Well Surveys, Inc., Tulsa, 1953-54, Argonne Nat. Lab., Ill., 1955-59; physicist, regional counselor Office Ordnance Research Durham, N.C., 1955; cons. on radiation legis. Kans. Dept. Pub. Health, Topeka, 1956-57; cons. in residence Lawrence Radiation Lab., U. Calif., summers 1957, 58, 59; mem. Grad. Record Exams. Bd., Princeton, N.J., 1971-75; Council Grad Schs. cons. med. physics U. Okla, Med. Sch., 1971, Council Grad. Schs. cons. Ph.D. physics program Utah State U., 1972; chmn. steering com. Grad. Record Exams. Bd.-Council Grad. Schs., 1972-73. Contbr. articles to profl. jours. Patentee in field. Active Boy Scouts Am. 1952—, mem. exec. bd. San Francisco Bay Area council, 1964-68; chmn. Library Bond Drive, Livermore, 1964. Recipient Community Service award Livermore C. of C., 1965, Silver Beaver award Boy Scouts Am., 1968, Disting. Alumnus award Kans. State Tchrs. Coll., 1969; Mendenhall fellow U. Wis., 1943; WARF fellow, 1946-47; research grantee. Fellow Am. Phys. Soc., AAAS; mem. AAUP (chpt. pres. 1956-57), Mo. Acad. Sci., Sigma Xi, Phi Kappa Phi, Lambda Delta Lambda, Xi Phi, Kappa Mu Epsilon, Kappa Delta Pi, Pi Mu Epsilon, Gamma Sigma Delta. Lodge: Kiwanis (lt. gov. Mo.-Ark. dist. 1984-85). Current work: Atomic and nuclear physics phenomena related to fusion as an energy source. Subspecialties: Atomic and molecular physics; Plasma physics. Home: 309 Christy Dr Rolla MO 65401 Office: Physics Dept U Mo Rolla MO 65401

MCFEE, WILLIAM WARREN, soil scientist; b. Concord, Tenn., Jan. 8, 1935; s. Fred Thomas and Ellen Belle (Russell) McF.; m. Barbara Anella Steelman, June 23, 1957; children—Sabra Anne, Patricia Lynn, Thomas Hallie. B.S., U. Tenn., 1957; M.S., Cornell U., 1963, Ph.D., 1966. Mem. faculty Purdue U., 1965—, prof. soil sci., 1973—, dir. natural resources and environ. sci. program, 1975—; vis. prof. U. Fla., 1972-73; cons. acid rain program Electric Power Research Inst., EPA. Author articles in field, chpts. in books. Served with USAR, 1958-61. Alpha Zeta scholar, 1957; named Outstanding Agr. Tchr. Purdue U., 1972. Fellow Am. Soc. Agronomy, Soil Sci. Soc. Am.; mem. Internat. Soil Sci. Soc., Soc. Am. Foresters, Sigma Xi. Presbyterian. Current Work: Effects of atmosphere depositon on soils; properties of reclaimed minelands. Subspecialties: Soil science; Ecosystems analysis. Home: 709 McCormick Rd West Lafayette IN 47906 Office: Agronomy Dept LILY Purdue U West Lafayette IN 47907

MCGARITY, ARTHUR EDWIN, engineering educator, energy and environmental systems researcher; b. Chgo., Apr. 2, 1951; s. Owen and Lois Wilson (Thomas) McG.; m. Jane Ziegler, June 11, 1977; children: Kate Elizabeth, Owen Carlos. B.S., Trinity U., 1973; M.S.E., Johns Hopkins U., 1978, Ph.D., 1979. Elec. engr. San Antonio Pub. Service, 1973-74; profl. asst. NSF, Washington, summer 1975; summer intern Exec. Office of Pres., Washington, summer 1975; asst. prof. engring. Swarthmore (Pa.) Coll., 1978—; scientist-in-residence Solar Energy Group, Argonne (Ill.) Nat. Lab., 1981-82. Author: Solar Heating and Cooling: An Economic Assessment, 1977. Solar Energy Research Inst. course devel. grantee, 1979; Sigma Xi summer research grantee, 1979; Argonne Nat. Lab. faculty research leave grantee, 1981-82. Mem. Inst. Mgmt. Sci., Internat. Solar Energy Soc. Democrat. Presbyterian. Current Work: Solar energy systems, ops. research, environ. policy, research on solar heating systems design, computer simulation methods, seasonal storage, compound parabolic concentrator solar collectors. Subspecialties: Solar energy; Operations research (engineering). Home: 525 Elm Ave Swarthmore PA 19081 Office: Dept Engring Swarthmore Coll Swarthmore PA 19081

MCGEACHIN, ROBERT LORIMER, biochemistry educator; b. Pasadena, Calif., May 13, 1917; s. William Rankin and Mary Elizabeth (Killian) McG.; m. Margaret Wardell DeLong, May 30, 1947; children—William Thomas, Robert Bruce. B.S., U. Nebr., 1939, M.S., 1940; Ph.D., Washington U., St. Louis, 1942. Research asst. U. Ill., Urbana, 1946-47; asst. prof. biochemistry U. Louisville, 1947-51, assoc. prof. 1951-66, prof., 1966—. Contbr. articles to profl. jours. Served to maj. U.S. Army, 1942-46, PTO. Recipient Silver Beaver award Boy Scouts Am., 1968. Mem. Am. Chem. Soc. (treas. 1963-66), Am. Soc. Biol. Chemists, Soc. for Exptl. Biology and Medicine. Republican. Presbyterian. Current work: Biochemistry and physiology of mammalian amylase enzymes. Subspecialties: Biochemistry (medicine); Biochemistry (biology). Home: 2246 Rutherford Wynd Louisville KY 40205 Office: U Louisville Sch Medicine Louisville KY 40292

MCGEAN, THOMAS JAMES, transp. cons. co. exec.; b. N.Y.C., Apr. 8, 1937; s. James T. and Lilian R. (Sargent) McG.; m. Doris L., Aug., 1962; children: Terence, Cynthia. B.M.E. cum laude, NYU, 1959; M.S.M.E., Calif. Inst. Tech., 1960. Registered profl. engr., Va., Fla. Engr. Bell Telephone Labs., Murray Hill, N.J., 1960-67; engr. Computer Sci. Corp., Falls Church, Va., 1967-69; sr. engr. Mitre Corp., McLean, Va., 1969-74; dir. transp. tech. Deleuw Cather, Washington, 1974-76; cons. transp., Annandale, Va., 1976-81; exec. v.p. N. D. Lea & Assocs., Washington, 1981—; ptnr. Lea, Elliott, McGean and Co., Washington, 1983—; assoc. professorial lectr. George Washington U.; vis. asso. prof. Howard U. Author: Urban Transportation Technology, 1976. Pres. Washington chpt. Vols. for Internat. Tech. Assistance, 1962-73. Recipient William R. Bryan medal in engring. N.Y. U., 1959, David Orr prize in mech. engring., 1959. Mem. Transp. Research Bd., Inst. Transp. Engrs., ASME, Tau Beta Pi, Pi Tau Sigma. Patentee coaxial cable design. Current Work: Advanced automated transit systems and cost/benefit assesment of advanced research and devel. needs. Subspecialties: Systems engineering; Mechanical engineering. Home: 3711 Spicewood Dr Annandale VA 22003 Office: Dulles Internat Airport 600 W Service Rd Suite 32 PO Box 17030 Washington DC 20041

MCGEE, KENNETH A., geologist. Dep. scientist-in-charge Cascades Volcano Obs., U.S. Geol. Survey, Vancouver, Wash. Subspecialty: Volcanology. Office: US Geol Survey Cascades volcano Obs 5400 MacArthur Blvd Vancouver WA 98661

MCGEE, THOMAS DONALD, materials engineering educator; b. Tripoli, Iowa, June 9, 1925; s. Nacy Waters and Maude Sophia (Ridenaur) McG.; m. Avis Ethylin Morse, Dec. 28, 1948 (div.); children—Evelyn Ann, Timothy Morse, James Ridenour, Matthew John; m. Clara Maxine Perdelwitz Thomas, July 5, 1981; stepchildren—Robert, Charles, John Thomas, Susan Lee. Registered ceramic engr., Iowa. Research engr. A.P. Green Refractories Co., Mexico, Mo., 1948-54, research engring. supr., 1954-56; asst. prof. materials engring. Iowa State U., Ames, 1956-61, assoc. prof., 1961-65, prof., 1965—. Contbr. articles to tech. jours. Patentee ceramics and bioceramics fields. Served with USNR, 1944-46. Fellow Am. Ceramic Soc.; mem. Nat. Inst. Ceramic Engrs. (sec.-treas. 1983, v.p. 1984), Am. Soc. Engring. Edn., Soc. Glass Tech. Presbyterian. Lodge: Kiwanis. Current work: Bioceramics, glass technology, refractories, linings for coal gasifying vessels. Subspecialties: Ceramic engineering; Metallurgy. Home: 2924 Woodland St Ames IA 50010 Office: Materials Sci and Engring Dept Iowa State U Ames IA 50011

MCGEHEE, RICHARD PAUL, mathematics educator; b. San Diego, Sept. 20, 1943; s. Maurice Seaton and Edith Marie (Adamson) McG.; m. Tamara Stovall Easton, Feb. 27, 1981; children—Stephanie M.Y. B.S., Calif. Inst. Tech., 1964; M.S., U. Wis.-Madison, 1965, Ph.D., 1969. Vis. mem. Courant Inst. Math. Sci., N.Y.C., 1969-70; asst. prof. dept. math. U. Minn., Mpls., 1970-75, assoc. prof., 1975-79, prof., 1979—. Mem. Am. Math. Soc., Math. Assn. Am., AAAS, Am. Astron. Soc. Current work: Dynamical systems, celestial mechanics, mathematical aspects of digital devices, computer graphis. Subspecialty: Applied mathematics. Office: Sch of Math U Minn Minneapolis MN 55455

MCGHEE, GEORGE RUFUS, JR., paleobiologist, educator; b. Henderson, N.C., Sept. 25, 1951; s. George Rufus and Mary London (Cobb) McG.; m. Marae Wilcox Paschall, Nov. 25, 1971. B.Sc. with honors, N.C. State U., 1973; M.Sc., U. N.C.-Chapel Hill, 1975; Ph.D., U. Rochester, 1978. Hydrologic field asst. U.S. Geol. Survey, Raleigh, N.C., 1972-73; geprüfte wissenschaftliche Hilfskraft U. Tübingen, W.Ger., 1977; asst. prof. geology and ecology Rutgers U.-New Brunswick, 1978-83, assoc. prof., 1983—; vis. scientist Field Mus. Natural History, Chgo., 1981; research assoc. Am. Mus. Natural History, N.Y.C., 1982—; Gastdozent U. Tübingen, 1982, 83, Gastprof., 1984. Assoc. editor: Paleobiology, 1982-85. NSF grantee, 1981-84; Deutsche Forschungsgemeinschaft grantee, 1982, 84; Am. Chem. Soc. grantee, 1982-85. Mem. Internat. Palaeontol. Assn., Paleontol. Soc., Die Paläontologische Gesellschaft, Palaeontol Assn. (Eng.), Soc. Systematic Zoology. Democrat. Quaker. Current Work: Ecosystem evolution, marine paleoecology, evolutionary morphology. Subspecialties: Paleobiology; Paleontology, paleoecology. Home: 23 Courtlandt St New Brunswick NJ 08901 Office: Geol Scis Rutgers U New Brunswick NJ 08903

MCGILL, LAWRENCE DAVID, veterinary pathologist; b. Lincoln, Nebr., Mar. 24, 1944; s. Stanley Raymond and Phyllis Roylene (Quick) McG.; m. Cheryl Lynn Nelson, June 1966 (div. Oct. 1974); m. Marilyn Sue Nyren, June 15, 1975; children—Lorice Annette, Lisa Kay, Marchelle Elizabeth, Mark Stanley John. Student U. Nebr., 1962-64; B.S., Okla. State U., 1966, D.V.M., 1968; Ph.D., Tex. A&M U., 1972. Asst. prof. U. Minn.-St. Paul, 1971-72, U. Nebr., Lincoln, 1972-77; vet. pathologist Vet. Reference Lab., Salt Lake City, 1977-81, chief pathology, 1981—; cons. Shiley Inc., Los Angeles, 1979—, Am. Edwards Labs., Los Angeles, 1979—, Utah Biotech. Lab., Salt Lake City, 1980—. Contbr. articles to profl. jours. Trustee Christ United Methodist Ch., Salt Lake City, 1966, mem. administrv. bd., 1982—; mem. Utah Symphony Chorus, 1978—. NIH fellow, 1968-71. Mem. Am. Coll. Vet. Pathologists (diplomate), AVMA, Utah Vet. Med. Assn., Salt Lake Vet. Med. Assn., Sigma Xi. Republican. Lodge: Masons. Current work: Immunopathology; viral pathology; naturally occuring animal tumors; neuropathology. Subspecialties: Pathology (veterinary medicine); Cancer research (veterinary medicine). Home: 8495 Kings Cove Dr Salt Lake City UT 84121 Office: Veterinary Reference Lab PO Box 30633 Salt Lake City UT 84130

MCGILL, MICHAEL JOHN, computer information scientist, educator; b. Detroit, Oct. 16, 1942; s. John Arthur and Margaret Mary (Woodcock) McG.; m. Jennifer Joan Kuehn, Dec. 2, 1977; children—Erin Kuehn, Andrew Kuehn. B.A., Mich. State U., 1965; M.A., Syracuse U., 1968, Ph.D., 1973. Asst. prof. computer sci. SUNY, Oswego, 1973-74; assoc. prof., asst. dean Sch. Info. Studies, Syracuse U., N.Y., 1974-80; sr. info. computer sci. advisor U.S. EPA, Washington, 1980-81; program dir. for info. sci. NSF, Washington, 1981-83; dir. tech. planning Online Computer Library Ctr., Dublin, Ohio, 1983-85, v.p. research and tech. planning, 1985—; adj. prof. Catholic U., Washington, 1981-83; vis. prof. Cornell U., Ithaca, N.Y., 1978; bd. visitors Sch. Info. Studies, Syracuse U., 1984—. Author: Introduction to Modern Information Retrieval, 1983. Mem. Am. Soc. Info. Sci., Assn. for Computing Machinery, AAAS, IEEE. Current work: Information retrieval, automatic indexing, knowledge based retrieval. Subspecialty: Information systems (Information science). Office: Online Computer Library Ctr 6565 Frantz Rd Dublin OH 43017

MCGILL, SCOTT DOUGLAS, data processing educator, consultant; b. Meadville, Pa., Sept. 24, 1946; s. Gaylord Arthur and Margaret Annetta (Kebert) McG.; m. Cathleen Ann Chaffin, Nov. 28, 1970; children: Kelly Meghan, Kerry Shannon. B.S. in Math, Allegheny Coll., Meadville, 1968; B.S. in Meterology and Oceanography, NYU, 1971; M.A. in Computer Systems Mgmt, U. Nebr., 1972; M.B.A. in Info. Systems, U. Colo., 1985. Cert. in data processing, 1975. Systems analyst Sperry Univac, Washington, 1972-73; sr. systems analyst Colorado Springs, Colo., 1973-75; mgr. programming and design City of Colorado Springs, 1975-76, dir. data processing, 1975—; mem. honorarium faculty U. Colo., Colorado Springs, 1975—; sr. instr. Mgmt. Devel. Found., Colorado Springs, 1978; dir. Cibar Systems Inst., Colorado Springs, 1982—, data processing cons. Mem. bus. adv. council Computer Tng. for Severely Handicapped, Denver, 1982—; bd. dirs. Goodwill Industries, Colorado Springs, 1982—; mem. adv. council U. So. Colo., Pueblo, 1981—; mem. bus. adv. council U. Colo., 1978—; mem. exec. council Pikes Peak council Boy Scouts Am., Colorado Springs, 1979—. Served to capt. USAF, 1968-72. Recipient Disting. Greater Colo. Service award Denver Fed. Exec. Bd., 1980; Silver Individual Service award Data Processing Mgmt. Assn., 1981; Outstanding Contbn. to Data Processing award Colo. Intergovtl. ADP Council, 1978; Outstanding Data Processing Orgn. of Yr. award Rocky Mountain Assn. Local Govt. Computer Users, 1979. Mem. Soc. for Info. Mgmt. (chmn. Rocky Mountain chpt. 1983), Data Processing Mgmt. Assn. (pres. 1978, internat. dir. 1982—), IEEE, Assn. for Computing machinery (chmn. Pikes Peak chpt. 1977-78), Am. Mgmt. Assn. (program chmn. 1983). Republican. Club: Rocky Mountain (dir. 1982). Lodges: Kiwanis (pres. 1983-84); Masons; Shriners; Elks. Current Work: Data processing management (motivation, productivity, system life cycle, government applications). Subspecialties: Software engineering; Information systems (Information science). Home: 4529 Misty Dr Colorado Springs CO 80907 Office: Data Processing Adminstrn 121 E Pikes Peak Ave Suite 335 Colorado Springs CO 80903

MCGINNESS, JOHN EDWARD, III, cancer researcher; b. Houston, Nov. 19, 1943; s. John E. and Fergus (Connell) McG.; m. Barbara Ambrose, June 28, 1968. B.S. in Physics, U. Houston, 1966; Ph.D., Rice U., 1970; M.D., U. Tex.-Houston, 1985. Asst. prof. Youngstown U., Ohio, 1970-72; asst. prof. dept. physics M.D. Anderson Cancer Ctr., Houston, 1972—. Contbr. articles to profl. jours. Patentee in field. Mem. Am. Assn. Cancer Research. Current work: Energy storage in polymer systems; experimental cancer chemotherapy. Address: Univ Tex Cancer Ctr MD Anderson Hosp Houston Med Ctr Houston TX 77025

MCGINNIES, WILLIAM GROVERNOR, research administrator, desert researcher; b. Steamboat Springs, Colo., Aug. 14, 1899; s. William and Ina Lourina (Grow) McG.; m. Rosemary Josephine Almini, Feb. 14, 1925; 1 child, William J. B.S.A., U. Ariz., 1922; Ph.D., U. Chgo., 1932. Asst. prof. U. Ariz., Tucson, 1926-34, dir. Office Arid Land Studies, 1960-71, dir. emeritus, 1972—; dir. Navajo project U.S. Soil Conservation Service, 1935-38; range researcher U.S. Forest Service, Tucson, 1939-42, dir. forest expt. sta., Fort Collins, Colo., 1945-52, Columbus, Ohio, 1953-66; mem. staff Guayule Rubber Project, Los Angeles, 1943-44. Author: Discovering the Desert, 1981. Editor: Deserts of the World, 1968; also articles. Served with SATC, 1918. Recipient Disting. Citizen award U. Ariz. Alumni Assn., 1974; Medallion of Merit U. Ariz., 1966. Fellow AAAS (cert. of merit Southwestern and Rocky Mountain div. 1970), Soc. Range Mgmt. (charter mem., outstanding achievement and service citation 1973, outstanding service award Ariz. sect. 1975), Ariz. Acad. Sci., World Acad. Art and Sci.; mem. Ecol. Soc. Am., Tree-Ring Soc., Sigma Xi, Phi Kappa Phi, Xi Sigma Pi, Alpha Zeta, Gammma Alpha. Democrat. Presbyterian. Current work: Interelation of desert vegetation and climate, conservation and management of deserts. Subspecialties: Resource conservation; Ecology (biology). Home: 530 E Cambridge Dr Tucson AZ 85704

MCGINTY, JACQUELINE FRANCES, neuroscientist; b. Lawrence, Mass., Dec. 1, 1950; d. John Francis and Dorothy Jane (Sprowls) McG.; m. Donald Gordon Smith, Sept. 15, 1972. B.A. cum laude Conn. Coll., 1972; Ph.D., SUNY-Bklyn., 1978. Research fellow Salk Inst., La. Jolla, Calif., 1978-82; asst. research neuroscientist U. Calif.-San Diego, La Jolla, 1982-83; asst. prof. anatomy Sch. Medicine, East Carolina U., Greenville, N.C., 1983—. Producer videotapes: Creation or Evolution: A Debate, 1981; Positive Emotions: A Natural Defense against Disease, 1985. Contbr. numerous articles to profl. jours., chpts. to books. Mem. San Diego Community Video Ctr., 1979-83, NIMH-NIH postdoctoral fellow, 1979-81; grantee NIH, 1983-85, Nat. Inst. Drug Abuse, 1985—. Mem. Soc. for Neurosci., N.Y. Acad. Sci., AAAS, N.C. Soc. Neurosci., So. Soc. Anatomists, Sigma Xi. Current work: Role of opioid peptides in central nervous system, development, distribution and plasticity in response to chemical or electrical perturbation. Subspecialties: Neurobiology; Immunocytochemistry. Home: RD 1 Box 165B Stokes NC 27884 Office: Dept Anatomy Sch Medicine East Carolina U Greenville NC 27834-4354

MC GOON, DWIGHT CHARLES, surgeon, educator; b. Marengo, Iowa, Mar. 24, 1925; s. Charles Douglas and Ada Belle (Buhlman) McG.; m. Betty Lou Hall, Apr. 2, 1948; children: Michael, Susan, Betsy, Sarah. Student, Iowa State U., 1942-43, St. Ambrose Coll., Davenport, Iowa, 1943-44; M.D., Johns Hopkins U., 1948. Intern Johns Hopkins Hosp., 1948-49, resident in surgery, 1949-54; cons. in surgery Mayo Clinic, Rochester, Minn., 1957—; Stuart W. Harrington prof. surgery Mayo Med. Sch., 1975-79. Editor-in-chief: Jour. Thoracic and Cardiovascular Surgery, 1977—; editorial bd.: Circulation, 1970-76, Surgery, 1971-77, Am. Jour. Cardiology, 1969-77, Am. Heart Jour, 1969-76; contbr. numerous articles to profl. jours. Served with USN, 1943-45; with M.C. USAF, 1954-56. Fellow ACS; mem. Am. Assn. Thoracic Surgery (pres. 1983-84), Am. Coll. Cardiology (trustee 1979-83), Am. Surg. Assn., Soc. Clin. Surgery, Soc. Univ. Surgeons, Johns Hopkins Soc. Scholars, Phi Beta Kappa, Alpha Omega Alpha. Presbyterian. Subspecialty: Cardiac surgery. Home: 706 12th Ave SW Rochester MN 55902 Office: Mayo Clinic 200 1st St SW Rochester MN 55905

MCGORRIN, ROBERT JOSEPH, chemist; b. Chgo., Aug. 15, 1951; s. Robert Joseph and Jeanine M. (Jahnke) McG.; m. Barbara Ann Gembala, Oct. 1, 1977. B.S. in Chemistry Northwestern U., 1973; M.S. in Organic Chemistry, U. Ill., 1976, Ph.D. in Organic Chemistry, 1980. Research scientist Quaker Oats Co., Barrington, Ill., 1978-81; sr. research scientist I, Kraft, Inc., Glenview, Ill., 1981-84, sr. research II, 1984—. Mem. Am. Chem. Soc. (sec. 1984—), Chgo. Chemists Club (pres. 1985—), Phi Lambda Upsilon. Current work: Isolation and identification of unique volatile flavor components by GC-MS-MS and GC-FT/IR. Subspecialty: Synthetic chemistry. Office: Kraft Inc 801 Waukegan Rd Glenview IL 60025

MCGOVREN, JAMES PATRICK, pharmacologist; b. Washington, Ind., June 12, 1947; s. Paul Francis and Elizabeth Mary (McCrisaken) McG.; m. Cecilia Marie Shaw, Nov. 28, 1968; children: Laura Elizabeth, Kathryn Susan. Student, U. Notre Dame, 1965-67; B.S. in Pharmacy, Purdue U., 1970; Ph.D. in Pharm. Scis, U. Ky., 1975. Assoc. dir. cancer biology, cancer and viral diseases research Scientist, Upjohn Co., Kalamazoo, 1975-83, assoc. dir. career research, 1983—. NSF trainee, 1970-73; Charles J. Lynn Meml. fellow Am. Found. Pharm. Edn., 1973-75. Mem. Am. Assn. Cancer Research, Am. Pharm. Assn., Acad. Pharm. Scis. Current Work: Pharmacology and pharmacokinetics of antitumor agents. Subspecialties: Cancer research (medicine); Pharmacology. Home: 2239 Crimora Schoolcraft MI 49087 Office: Upjohn Co Kalamazoo MI 49001

MCGOWAN, JON GERALD, mechanical engineer, educator; b. Lockport, N.Y., May 3, 1939; s. Gerald F. and Xenia W. (Guenther) McG.; m. Suzanne Jessop, Sept. 25, 1965; children: Gerald, Edward. B.S., Carnegie Inst. Tech., 1961, Ph.D., 1965; M.S., Stanford U, 1962. Devel. Engr. E.I. DuPont de Nemours, Wilmington, Del., 1965-67; prof. mech. engring. U. Mass., Amherst, 1967—; cons., ptnr. Windpower Assocs. Contbr. articles to profl. jours. Trustee Dickenson Meml. Library, Northfield, Mass., 1975—. Mem. ASME, Internat. Solar Energy Soc., Air Pollution Control Assn., Internat. Hydrogen Energy Soc. Republican. Congregationalist. Current Work: Solar energy research and consulting; wind energy systems research; combustion engineering—applied fluid mechanics and thermodynamics. Subspecialties: Combustion processes; Wind power. Home: 134 Main St Northfield MA 01360 Office: Dept Mech Engring U Mass Amherst MA 01003

MCGRATH, THOMAS JOHN, JR., biomedical engineering educator; b. Waterbury, Conn., Aug. 25, 1948; s. Thomas John and Rosemary Teresa (Cruess) McG.; m. Patricia Marie Shea, June 24, 1977. A.S. in Elec. Engring., Waterbury State Tech. Coll., 1976; B.S. in Elec. Engring., U. New Haven, 1981; M.S. in Biol. Engring., U. Conn., 1982. Elec. technician NAPCO, Terryville, Conn., 1972-75, Gould Inc., Plantsville, Conn., 1976-78; project engr. Lewis Engring. Co., Naugatuck, Conn., 1978-80; asst. prof. Greater New Haven State Tech. Coll., North Haven, Conn., 1981—. Coll. coordinator McGovern for Pres. Campaign, Naugatuck Valley, 1972; singer Waterbury Chorale, 1978—. Served with USAF, 1967-71. Mem. IEEE, Soc. Biomed. Equipment Technicians (founder, pres. Greater New Haven chpt. 1982—), Assn. Advancement Med. Instrumentation, Engring. Medicine and Biology Soc., New Eng. Soc. Clin. Engring., Am. Legion (sgt. at arms 1973-76). Democrat. Roman Catholic. Lodges: K.C. (right to life chmn. 1983—, chancellor 1985—); Ancient Order Hibernians. Current work: Biomedical engineering education based in instrumentation and electronics; research in ultrasound and fiber optics in medicine, insects and infrared electromagnetic energy also noninvasive diagnostic instrumentation, alternative energy and safety. Subspecialties: Biomedical engineering; Electronics. Office: Greater New Haven State Tech Coll 222 Maple Ave North Haven CT 06473

MCGRAW, JOHN THOMAS, astronomer; b. Gaylord, Minn., Mar. 22, 1946; s. Thomas Roger and Grace Ann (Friederichs) McG.; m. Maryann Margaret McDonough, June 23, 1973; 1 child, Thomas Patrick. B.A., St. Olaf Coll., 1968; M.A., U. Tex., 1973, Ph.D., 1977. Research scientist asst. dept. astronomy U. Tex.- Austin, 1970-77, research assoc., 1977-78; research assoc. dept. astronomy U. Cape Town, South Africa, 1975-76; research assoc. Steward Obs., U. Ariz., Tucson, 1979-81, asst. astronomer, 1981-84, assoc. astronomer, 1984—. Contbr. articles in field to profl. jours. NSF research grantee, 1981-85. Mem. Am. Astron. Soc., Royal Astron. Soc., Astron. Soc. Pacific, Sigma Xi, Sigma Pi Sigma. Current Work: Development of automated survey telescope to do observational cosmology. Subspecialties: Optical astronomy; Cosmology. Office: Steward Obs U Ariz Tucson AZ 85721

MCGREGOR, DENNIS NICHOLAS, electrical engineer, researcher; b. Oelwein, Iowa, Nov. 6, 1943; s. Curtis Floyd and Mary Jane (Sykes) McG.; m. Karen Louise McCarthy, Aug. 7, 1965; children—Dennis Nicholas, Michael J. B.E.E., Catholic U. Am., 1965, M.E.E., 1966, postgrad., 1966-69. Mem. tech. staff Computer Scis. Corp., Falls Church, Va., 1966-71; prin. staff ORI, Inc., Silver Spring, Md., 1971-73; assoc. program dir., 1973-75, sr. scientist, 1975-79, prin. scientist, 1979-81; head communication networks sect. Naval Research Lab., Washington, 1981—. Contbr. papers to profl. publs. Baseball and basketball coach Little League, Woodbridge, Va., 1975-76. NSF research grantee Cath. U., 1964. Mem. IEEE (sr.; mem. admissions and advancement com. Washington chpt. 1981-82), Communications Soc. of IEEE (chmn. Washington chpt. 1980-81), Sigma Xi (assoc.). Roman Catholic. Current work: Analysis and design of communication networks; satellite and terrestrial communications; advanced networking techniques; coding and modulation; anti-jam techniques; network simulation. Subspecialties: Electrical engineering; Telecommunications. Home: 5912 Oakland Park Dr Burke VA 22015 Office: Naval Research Lab 4555 Overlook Ave SW Washington DC 20375

MC GREGOR, DOUGLAS HUGH, pathologist; b. Temple, Tex., Aug. 28, 1939; s. Harleigh Heath and Joyce Ellen (Lambert) McG.; m. Mizuki Kitani, July 6, 1969; children: Michelle Sakuya, David Kenji. B.A., Duke U., 1961, M.D., 1966; postgrad., U. Edinburgh, Scotland, 1961-62. Diplomate: Am. Bd. Pathology. Intern and chief resident in pathology UCLA Med. Ctr., Los Angeles, 1966-68; surgeon and lt. comdr. Atomic Bomb Casualty Commn., Hiroshima, Japan, 1968-71; chief resident in pathology Queens Med. Ctr., Honolulu, 1971-73; asst. and assoc. prof. pathology U. Kans. Med. Ctr., Kansas City, 1973-82, prof., 1982—; dir. anat. pathology VA Med. Ctr., Kansas City, Mo., 1975—. Contbr. numerous articles to profl. jours., chpts. to books. Leader YMCA Indian Princess Program, Overland Park, Kans., 1977-79, Indian Guide Program, 1978-80, Cub Scouts Am., Overland Park, 1980-82, Boy Scouts Am., Leawood, Kans., 1982—. Served to lt. comdr. USPHS, 1968-71, Japan. Grantee Merck, Sharp and Dohme, 1980; Grantee NIH, 1980. Fellow Coll. Am. Pathologists, Am. Soc. Clin. Pathologists; mem.

Am. Assn. Pathologists, Internat. Acad. Pathologists, Soc. Exptl. Biology and Medicine, N.Y. Acad. Scis., AAAS, Kansas City Soc. Pathologists (sec.-treas. 1982-83, pres. 1983-84). Club: Leawood Country. Current Work: Biology and pathology of parathyroid hormone secretion; platelet-leukocyte aggregation; ultrastructure and pathobiology of neoplasms; radiation carcinogenesis; morphogenesis of atherosclerosis. Subspecialties: Pathology (medicine); Microscopy. Home: 9400 Lee Blvd Leawood KS 66206 Office: VA Medical Ctr 4801 Linwood Blvd Kansas City MO 64128

MCGREGOR, WHEELER KESEY, JR., physicist; b. Akron, Ohio, Apr. 20, 1929; s. Wheeler Kesey and Emma Zada (Turner) McG.; m. Frankie Marie Simons, Feb. 12, 1930. B.S. in Engrng. Physics, U. Tenn., 1951, M.S. in Engrng. Sci, 1961, Ph.D. in Physics, 1969. With ARO, Inc. (now Sverdrup Tech., Inc.), 1951; at Arnold Engrng. Devel. Center, U.S. Air Force, Arnold AFB, Tenn., 1951—, now sr. tech specialist; sabbatical Rocket Propulsion Lab., Edwards AFB, Calif., 1977-78; adj. faculty U. Tenn. Space Inst. Contbr. articles to profl. jours. Recipient Arnold award for contbns. to aero. and astronautics Am. Rocket Soc., 1961. Mem. AIAA, Am. Phys. Soc., Air Force Assn. Current Work: Plasma physics, combustion technology rocket plume signatures, quantitative spectroscopy. Subspecialties: Atomic and molecular physics; Aerospace engineering and technology. Home: Route 8 Box 8070 Stillwood Dr Manchester TN 37355 Office: Mail Stop 960 Arnold AF Station TN 37389

MCGREGOR-DAWSON, JAMES LINDSAY, geologist; b. Melbourne, Australia, Dec. 9, 1947; came to U.S., 1976; s. John Horace McGregor and Alice Elizabeth (Lindsay) D. Assoc. Diploma, Royal Melbourne Inst. Tech., 1970, Fellowship Diploma (hon.), 1971. Geologist, Kennecott Exploration, Australia, 1971-73, Union Oil Devel. Corp., 1973-76, Molycorp, 1976-81, Bear Creek Mining Co., 1981-82, St. Joe Am. Corp. 1984—; cons. geologist Kennecott Minerals, 1983. Mem. Australasian Inst. Mining and Metallurgy, Geol. Soc. Australia, Soc. Mining Engrs., AIME, Geol. Soc. Am., Assn. Exploration Geochemists, N.W. Mining Assn. Subspecialty: Geology. Home: PO Box 13087 Spokane WA 99213 Office: St Joe Am Corp N 111 Vista St Suite 3F Spokane WA 99212

MCGUIGAN, FRANK JOSEPH, psychologist, clinician, educator; b. Oklahoma City, Dec. 7, 1924; s. Frank Leo and Edith Louise (Whiting-Van Bogaert) McG.; m. Betty J. Spieler; children—Joan, Constance, Richard. B.A., UCLA, 1945, M.A., 1949; postgrad. Harvard U., 1945, Columbia U., 1947, U. Colo.-Boulder, 1951; Ph.D., U. So. Calif., 1950. Lic. clin. psychologist. Asst. prof. U. Nev., Reno, 1950-51; dir. research George Washington U., Fort Knox, Ky., 1951-55; prof., chmn. psychology Hollins Coll., Roanoke, Va., 1955-76; grad. research prof. also prof. psychology and psychiatry U. Louisville, 1976-83; prof. psychology U.S. Internat. U., San Diego, 1983—. Author: Experimental Psychology, 4th edit., 1983; Calm Down, 1981; Cognitive Psychophysiology, 1978; Psychophysiological Measurement of Covert Behavior, 1979. Editor, chmn. publ. bd. Pavlovian Jour. Biol. Sci., 1978—; mem. editorial bd. Biofeedback and Self-Regulation, 1976—; Served with USNR, 1942-46. Mem. English Speaking Union, Am. Psychol. Assn., Am. Physiol. Soc., Inter-Am. Soc. Psychology, Internat. Stress-Tension Control Soc. (exec. v.p. 1972—), Pavlovian Soc. (past pres.), Psychonomic Soc. Current work: Research in cognitive psychophysiology of electrically measuring mental activities; clinical research and practice in clinical progressive relaxation. Subspecialties: Behavioral psychology; Physiological psychology. Home: 2101 1/4 S Beverly Glen Blvd Los Angeles CA 90025 Office: Sch Human Behavior US Internat Univ 10455 Pomerado Rd San Diego CA 92131

MCGUIRE, JAMES HORTON, physicist, educator; b. Canandaigua, N.Y., June 7, 1942; s. Horton E. and Karolyn W. (McGuire); m. V. Jane Rasmussen, Oct. 10, 1981; children: Bruce, Brooke, Carrie, Marti. B.S., Rensselaer Poly. Inst., 1964; M.S., Northeastern U., 1966, Ph.D., 1969. Vis. scientist Hahn Meitner Inst., Berlin, 1980-81; asst. prof. Tex. A&M U., 1969-72; asst. prof. Kans. State U., Manhattan, 1972-76, assoc. prof. physics, 1976-83, prof., 1983—; cons. Picatinny Arsenal, Naval Surface Weapons Lab., White Oak, Md., Lawrence Livermore Lab.; summer fellow Goddard Space Flight Ctr. Contbr. articles to profl. publs. U.S. Air Force grantee, 1970-72; Dept. Energy grantee, 1974—; NSF travel grantee to USSR, 1978. Mem. Am. Phys. Soc. Current Work: Atomic collisions, multiple ionization, electron capture, ionization. Subspecialties: Atomic and molecular physics; Theoretical physics. Office: Physics Dept Kans State U Manhattan KS 66506

MCGUIRE, JOHN L., pharmaceutical company research executive; b. Kittanning, Pa., Nov. 3, 1942; s. Lawrence F. and Florence (Jones) McG.; m. Pamela Hale, Aug. 2, 1969; children: Megan L., Christa H. B.S., Butler U., 1965; M.A., Princeton U., 1968, Ph.D., 1969. Pharmacologist, Ortho Pharm. Corp., Raritan, N.J., sect. head molecular biology, 1972-75, exec. dir. research, basic scis., 1975-80, v.p. pre-clin. research and devel., 1980—; adj. assoc. prof. M.S. Hershey Sch. Medicine, Pa. State U., 1978—; adj. prof. Rutgers U., 1983—; cons. NASA, 1985. Contbr. articles to profl. jours. Mem. exec. bd. Keystone Area council Boy Scouts Am., 1975—, George Washington council, 1980—; trustee Hunterdon Med. Ctr., Flemington, N.J., 1978—, vice chmn., 1984—; bd. dirs. Hunterdon County YMCA, 1982—; bd. dirs. Hunterdon County United Way, 1983—, pres., 1985—; Mem. Am. Soc. Pharmacology and Exptl. Therapeutics, Soc. Exptl Biology and Medicine, Am. Phys. Soc., Endocrine Soc., Am. Soc. Clin. Pharmacology and Therapeutics, Am. Chem. Soc., Am. Fertility Soc., Soc. Adv. Contraception (trustee 1983—), N.J. Health Scis. Group, Royal Soc. Medicine (U.K.), Biochem. Soc. (U.K.). Club: Princeton (N.Y.C.). Patentee in field. Current Work: Management pharmaceutical research and development activies; pharmacology. Subspecialty: Neuroendocrinology. Home: 9 Sunnyfield Dr Whitehouse Station NJ 08889 Office: Research Labs Ortho Pharm Corp Raritan NJ 08869

MCGUIRE, KEVIN MARIAN, research physicist, educator; b. Enniscorty, Ireland, June 2, 1954; came to U.S., 1980; s. Daniel Oliver and Maureen (Buckley) McG.; m. Ann Geraldine Clarke, Dec. 1, 1979; children: Helen Maureen, Brian Patrick. B.Sc., Univ. Coll. Dublin, 1976; M.Sc., Oxford U., 1977, D.Phil., 1979. Mem. postdoctoral staff Culham Lab., Abingdon, Eng., 1979-80; research physicist Plasma Physics Lab., Princeton U., N.J., 1980—. Contbr. articles to profl. jours. Sr. scholar Keble Coll., 1978, 79. Mem. Am. Phys. Soc. Roman Catholic. Current work: Study of magnetohydrodynamic instabilities in large tokamak devices close to thermonuclear conditions; the effects of these instabilities on transport processes in the plasma. Subspecialties: Plasma physics; Nuclear fusion. Home: 4 Penbrook Ct Princeton Junction NJ 08550 Office: Princeton U Plasma Physics Lab PO Box 451 James Forrestal Campus Princeton NJ 08540

MCGUIRE, STEPHEN CRAIG, physics educator, consultant; b. New Orleans, Sept. 17, 1948; s. Harry Stewart and Ruth (Barsock) McG.; m. Saundra Yancy, Aug. 28, 1971; children: Carla Abena, Stephanie Niyonu. B.S., So. U., Baton Rouge, 1970; M.S., U. Rochester, 1974; Ph.D., Cornell U., 1979. Research asst. U. Rochester, N.Y., 1971-74, Cornell U., Ithaca, N.Y., 1975-78; lectr. Stanford (Calif.) U. Linear Accelerator Ctr., 1976; devel. assoc. Oak Ridge Nat. Lab., 1978-82; asst. prof. physics Ala. A&M U., Normal, 1982—; cons. chem. tech. div. Oak Ridge Nat. Lab., 1982—; cons. Los Alamos Nat. Lab., 1984—. John McMullen fellow in nuclear sci. Cornell U., 1977; Crown Zellerbach Found. fellow, 1968. Mem. Am. Phys. Soc., Am. Nuclear Soc., AAAS, Am. Assn. Physics Tchrs., Sigma Xi. Current Work: Nuclear spectroscopy, neutron physics, plasma physics, nuclear waste management. Subspecialties: Nuclear engineering; Nuclear physics. Office: Dept Physics Ala A&M U PO Box 523 Normal AL 35762

MCGURRIN, MICHAEL FRANCIS, physicist; b. Scranton, Pa., Aug. 29, 1956; s. Francis Robert and Irene Viola (Travis) McG.; m. Gena Elaine Cadieux, June 9, 1984. B.S. in Physics, Pa. State U., 1978; M.S. in Physics, U. Mass., 1983. Systems engr. Link div. Singer Corp., Houston, 1978-81; teaching asst. U. Mass., Amherst, 1981-83, research asst., 1981-83; mem. tech. staff MITRE Corp., McLean, Va., 1983—. Contbr. research articles to profl. jours. Mem. Am. Phys. Soc., IEEE (Computer Soc.). Current work: System design of FAA Nat. Airspace System, analytical models of local area networks. Subspecialties: Systems engineering; Low temperature physics. Home: 874 N Arlington Mill Dr Arlington VA 22205 Office: MITRE Corp Mail Stop W 389 1820 Dolley Madison Blvd McLean VA 22102

MCHARRIS, WILLIAM CHARLES, chemistry, physics, astronomy educator; b. Knoxville, Tenn., Sept. 12, 1937; s. Garrett Clifford and Margaret Alice (Zimmerman) McH.; m. Orilla Ann Spangler, Aug. 27, 1960; 1 child, Louise Alice. B.A., Oberlin Coll., 1959; Ph.D., U. Calif., 1965. Summer trainee Oak Ridge Nat. Lab., Tenn., 1957-59; research student Lawrence Berkeley Lab., Calif., 1959-65; vis. prof., scientist, 1970-71, 1981—; asst. prof. Mich. State U., East Lansing, 1965-68, assoc. prof., 1968-70, prof., 1970—; cons. Argonne Nat. Lab., Ill., 1965—. Author: Into the Atom, 1985. Composer organ and choral works. Contbr. articles to popular and profl. jours. Recipient Westinghouse Sci. Talent Search award 1955; Alfred E. Sloan fellow, 1971-75. Mem. Am. Chem. Soc., Am. Phys. Soc., Sigma Xi (Jr. Sci. award 1972). Congregationalist. Current work: Nuclear spectroscopy; application of concepts from particle physics in the field of nuclear physics (neutral weak currents, quarks, etc.). Subspecialties: Nuclear chemistry; Nuclear physics. Home: 512 Beech St East Lansing MI 48823 Office: Nat Superconducting Cyclotron Lab Mich State U East Lansing MI 48824

MCHENRY, HENRY MALCOLM, anthropology educator; b. Los Angeles, May 19, 1944; s. Dean Eugene and Jane (Snyder) McH.; m. Linda Jean Conway, June 25, 1966; children—Lindsay Jean, Annalisa Jane. B.A., U. Calif-Davis, 1966, M.A., 1967; Ph.D., Harvard U., 1972. Asst. prof. anthropology U. Calif.-Davis, 1971-76, assoc. prof., 1976-81, prof., 1981—, dept. chmn., 1984—. Contbr. articles to profl. jours. Fellow Am. Anthropol. Assn.; mem. Am. Assn. Phys. Anthropologists (exec. com. 1982-84), Human Biology Council, Soc. Vertebrate Paleontology, Soc. for Study of Evolution, Phi Beta Kappa, Phi Kappa Phi. Democrat. Current work: Human paleontology, human evolution, primate evolution, human and primate morphology, quantitative analysis of morphology. Subspecialties: Evolutionary biology; Morphology. Home: 330 11th St Davis CA 95616 Office: Dept Anthropology Univ Calif Davis CA 95616

MCHENRY, KEITH WELLES, JR., oil company executive; b. Champaign, Ill., Apr. 6, 1928; s. Keith Welles and Jayne (Hinton) McH.; m. Lou Petry, Aug. 23, 1952; children: John, William. B.S. in Chem. Engrng, U. Ill., 1951; Ph.D. in Chem. Engrng, Princeton U., 1958. With Amoco Corp. (previously Standard Oil Co. Ind.) and affiliates, 1955—; asst. project chem. engr. research and devel. dept. Amoco Oil Co., Whiting, Ind., 1955-58, group leader, 1958-67, research asso., 1967-68, asst. dir. fuels research, 1968-70, dir. process and analytical research, 1970-74, mgr. process research, Naperville, Ill., 1974-75, v.p. research and devel., 1975—; Hurd lectr. Northwestern U., 1981; mem. adv. council Catalysis Center, U. Del., Newark, 1978-83, chmn., 1981-82; mem. adv. council Sch. Engrng. and Applied Sci., Princeton U., 1976—; mem. ind. adv. bd. Coll. Engrng. U. Ill.-Chgo., 1979—, chmn., 1984; Thiele lectr. in fuels engrng. U. Utah, 1983; mem. U.S. Nat. Com. World Petroleum Congress, 1975-83. Trustee North Central Coll., Naperville, 1978—; bd. overseers Sch. Bus. Adminstrn., Ill. Inst. Tech., 1983—; bd. dirs. Ind. Research Inst., 1982—; chmn. area com. Jr. Achievement, 1981-83; ordained elder Presbyn. Ch., 1964. Served with U.S. Army, 1946-47. Gen. Electric fellow, DuPont fellow, 1952-54. Mem. Nat. Acad. Engrng., Am. Inst. Chem. Engrs. (editorial bd. jour. 1974-78), Am. Chem. Soc., AAAS, Am. Petroleum Inst., Sigma Xi, Tau Beta Pi. Subspecialty: Chemical engineering. Office: PO Box 400 Naperville IL 60566

MCHENRY, MARTIN CHRISTOPHER, internist; b. San Francisco, Feb. 9, 1932; s. Merl and Marcella (Bricca) McH.; m. Patricia G. Hughes, Apr. 27, 1957; children: Michael, Christopher, Timothy, Mary Ann, Jeffrey, Paul, Kevin, William, Monica, Martin. Student, U. Santa Clara, 1950-53; M.D., U. Cin., 1957; M.S. in Medicine, U. Minn.-Mpls., 1966. Diplomate: Am. Bd. Internal Medicine. Rotating intern Highland Alameda County Hosp., Oakland, Calif., 1957-58; fellow in internal medicine Mayo Clinic, Rochester, Minn., 1958-61; spl. appointee in infectious diseases, 1963-64; staff physician div. infectious diseases Henry Ford Hosp., Detroit, 1964-67; staff physician Cleve. Clinic, 1967-72, head dept. infectious diseases, 1972—; asst. clin. prof. medicine Case Western Res. U., 1970-77, assoc. clin. prof., 1977—. Contbr. numerous chpts., articles to profl. publs.; co-editor First, Second and Third Cleve. Symposiums on Infectious Diseases, 1974, 75, 78; editorial adv. bd.: Med. Update, 1978-79. Chmn. manpower com. Swine Flu Program, Cleve., 1976. Named Disting. Tchr. of Yr. in Medicine Cleve. Clinic, 1972; 1st Ann. Bruce Hubbard Stewart award Cleve. Clinic Found., 1985. Fellow ACP, Am. Coll Chest Physicians (chmn. com. cardiopulmonary infections 1975-77, 81-83); mem. Infectious Diseases Soc. Am., Am. Thoracic Soc., Am. Fedn. Clin. Research, Am. Soc. Microbiology, N.Y. Acad. Scis., Am. Soc. Tropical Medicine and Hygiene, Am. Soc. Clin. Pharmacology and Therapeutics (chmn. sect. infectious diseases and antimicrobial agts. 1970-77, 80-85, dir. 1972-75), Am. Geriatrics Soc., AAAS, Alumnae Assn. Mayo Clinic Found., AMA, Cleve. Acad. Medicine, Ohio Soc. Internal Medicine, Am. Soc. Clin. Pathology, Royal Soc. Medicine Gt. Brit., Am. Veneral Disease Assn., So. Med. Assn. Current Work: Cooperative study on vertebral osteomyelitis. Subspecialties: Infectious diseases; Internal medicine. Home: 2779 Belgrave Rd Pepper Pike OH 44124 Office: Cleve Clinic Found 9500 Euclid Ave Cleveland OH 44106

MC ILRATH, THOMAS JAMES, physics educator, researcher; b. Dowagiac, Mich., May 10, 1938; s. William Frederick and Leora May (Lewis) McIlrath; m. Valerie Hoy, June 30, 1962; children: Christine, Laura. B.S., Mich. State U., 1960; Ph.D., Princeton U., 1966. Research assoc. Harvard Coll. Obs., Harvard U., 1967-73; prof. U. Md., College Park, 1973—; physicist Nat. Bur. Standards, Gaithersburg, Md., 1974—. Contbr. articles to profl. jours. Patentee capillary array windows. NSF fellow, 1960; Woodrow Wilson fellow, 1960; NATO fellow, 1966-67; recipient Dept. Commerce Silver medal, 1980. Fellow Am. Phys. Soc.; mem. Optical Soc. Am., Current Work: Short wavelength optical radiation; non-liner optics, remote sensing lasers, generation of coherent short wave length radiation, interaction of intense radiation with matter, atmospheric sensing. Subspecialties: X-ray lasers; Atomic and molecular physics. Home: 5944 Westchester Park Dr College Park MD 20740 Office: IPST U Md College Park MD 20742

MCILREATH, FRED J., pharmaceutical company executive; b. Amsterdam, N.Y., Apr. 1, 1929; s. Fred J. and Catherine (Cantwell) McI.; m. Betty Frenette, June 16, 1952; children—David, Fred III, Jeffrey, Heather, Sheila. B.S., Siena Coll.; M.S., U. Ky.; Ph.D., Mcgill U. Pharmacologist, Strasenburgh, Rochester, N.Y., 1959-62; pulmonary physiologist Riker, Los Angeles, 1962-71; dir. regulatory affairs Searle, Chgo., 1971-78; v.p., dir. research and devel. Reed and Carnrick, Piscataway, N.J., 1978—; asst. prof. physiology U. Calif.-Irvine, 1968-71; dir. pulmonary research Sunland Home for Asthmatic Children, Calif., 1969-71. Contbr. articles to profl. jours. Chmn. troop Boy Scouts Am., 6 yrs.; mem. sch. bd. St. Norberts Sch., Northridge, Calif., 2 yrs. Served with U.S. Army, 1951-53. Mem. N.Y. Acad. Scis., AAAS. Republican. Roman Catholic. Subspecialties: Physiology (medicine); Pharmaceutical research and development. Office: Reed and Carnrick Pharms 1 New England Ave Piscataway NJ 08854

MCINTOSH, TRACY KAHL, neuroendocrinologist, educator; b. N.Y.C., May 8, 1953; s. Ezra Albert and Roe McI. A.B., Williams Coll., 1975; Ph.D., Rutgers, U., 1980. Postdoctoral fellow Boston U. Med. Sch., 1980-82, asst. prof., 1982—; spl. scientist Boston City Hosp., 1982—; instr. U. Mass., Boston, 1982—; cons. Surg. Assocs., Boston, 1982—. Mem. Com. for Social Responsibility, Concord, Mass., 1983; mem. Crime Prevention Com., Jamaica Plain, Mass., 1982—. Recipient Hyde Scholarship award Williams Coll., 1975; NIH postdoctoral fellow, 1980-82. Mem. AAAS, Endocrine Soc., Internat. Soc. Psychoneuroendocrinology, Neuroendocrine Soc., N.Y. Acad. Sci., Phi Beta Kappa, Sigma Xi. Unitarian. Current Work: To explore the endocrine response to stress, shock and trauma, particularly endophins and enkephalins, and relationship to development of immunosuppressive syndromes. Subspecialties: Neuroendocrinology; Neuroimmunology. Home: 29 Lakeville Rd Jamaica Plain MA 02130 Office: Boston U Med Center 80 E Concord St Boston MA 02118

MCINTYRE, BRIAN ARCH, mechanical engineer; b. Davenport, Iowa, Apr. 25, 1947; s. Dennis and Yvonne Marie (Wagner) McI. B.S., Purdue U., 1971, M.S., 1972. Registered profl. engr., Pa. Research asst. Purdue U., West Lafayette, Ind., 1970-72; engr. Westinghouse Electric, Pitts., 1972-81, prin. engr., 1981-82, mgr. safeguards analysis, 1982—. Contbr. articles to profl. jours. Mem. ASME. Current work: Analysis of nuclear power plant thermal hydraulic transients; heat transfer and fluid flow computer model development. Subspecialties: Fluid mechanics; Nuclear fission. Home: 11099 Mallard Ln North Huntingdon PA 15642 Office: Westinghouse Electric Corp PO Box 355 Pittsburgh PA 15230

MCINTYRE, GARY ALLEN, plant pathologist, educator; b. Portland, Oreg., July 16, 1938; s. John H. and Onie (Meihoff) McI.; m. Loene, Sept. 1, 1963; children—Paula, Laura. B.S., Oreg. State Coll., 1960, Ph.D., 1964. Faculty U. Maine, Orono, 1969-75; faculty Colo. State U., Fort Collins, 1975—, prof., chmn. dept. botany and plant pathology, 1975-84, prof., head dept. plant pathology and weed sci., 1984—. Contbr. articles in field to profl. jours. NDEA fellow, 1960-63. Mem. Am. Phytopath. Soc., Potato Assn. Am., Sigma Xi, Phi Kappa Phi, Phi Sigma. Current Work: Researcher in skin diseases of potato. Subspecialties: Plant pathology; Integrated pest management. Home: 904 Cheyenne Dr Fort Collins CO 80525 Office: Colorado State Dept Botany and Plant Pathology Fort Collins CO 80523

MCINTYRE, OSWALD ROSS, physician; b. Chgo., Feb. 13, 1932; m. Jean Geary, June 5, 1957; children—Margaret Jean, Archibald Ross, Elizabeth Geary. A.B. cum laude, Dartmouth Coll., 1953, postgrad. 1953-55; M.D., Harvard U., 1957. Intern U. Pa. Hosp., 1957-58; resident in medicine Dartmouth Med. Sch. Affiliated Hosps., 1958-60; instr. medicine Dartmouth Coll., 1964-66; attending physician VA Hosp., White River Junction, Vt., 1964; asst. prof. medicine Dartmouth, 1966-69, asso. prof., 1969-75, prof., 1976—, James J. Carroll prof. oncology, 1980—; dir. Dartmouth (Norris Cotton Cancer Center), 1975—; cons. in hematology, oncology; individual practice medicine specializing in hematology-oncology, Hanover, N.H., 1964—. Served with USPHS, 1961-63. Mem. Am. Fedn. Clin. Research, AAAS, Am. Soc. Hematology, N.Y. Acad. Sci., Internat. Assn. Study Lung Cancer. Subspecialties: Hematology; Oncology. Home: River Rd Lyme NH 03768 Office: Norris Cotton Cancer Center Hanover NH 03755

MCIVER, SAMUEL HODGEDEN, chemical engineer; b. Mpls., May 21, 1919; s. Carl Oscar Ness and Mary Irene (Hodgeden) McI.; m. Emma Jean Ooley, Sept. 21, 1941 (div. 1973); children—Colin, Nancy; m. Wanda Lacinski, Dec. 13, 1973; stepchildren—Gretchen Schaefer, Eric Schaefer. B.Ch.E., U. Minn., 1942. Project engr. Donaldson Co., Inc., St. Paul, 1941-50; sales engr. Hauenstein Co., Mpls., 1950-51; test and field engr. Day Co., Mpls., 1951-57; research scientist Honeywell, Mpls., 1957-60; sr. chem. engr. Carrier, Syracuse, N.Y., 1960-74; devel. engr. Cambridge Filter, Liverpool, N.Y., 1974—. Contbr. articles to profl. jours. Active various councils Boy Scouts Am., 1932—; small craft vol. ARC, Cazenovia and Manlius, N.Y., 1962—. Mem. Am. Inst. Chem. Engrs. (sect. chmn. 1973-74), Fine Particle Soc., Am. Assn. Aerosol Research, N.Y. Acad. Scis., Am. Chem. Soc. Republican. Episcopalian. Clubs: Wooden Boat, Traditional Small Craft. Current work: Fine particle technology, develop air filter test methods; develop and design residential electronic air cleaners. Subspecialty: Gas cleaning systems. Home: 7594 Glencliffe Rd Manlius NY 13104 Office: Cambridge Filter Corp 7645 Henry Clay Blvd Liverpool NY 13008

MCKEE, DOUGLAS WILLIAM, research chemist, b. Toronto, Ont., Can., Oct. 6, 1930; came to U.S., 1955; s. William Campbell and Dorothy (Drinkwater) McK.; m. Rita Yvonne Pothier, Sept. 19, 1959; Marc, Michelle, Nicole, Monique. B.Sc., U. London, 1951, Ph.D., 1954, D.Sc., 1982. Research chemist Linde Co., Buffalo, 1956-60; staff scientist Gen. Electric Co., Schenectady, 1960—. Assoc. editor Carbon, 1983—. Contbr. articles to profl. jours. Patentee in field. Mem. Am. Carbon Soc. (chmn. 1983—), Royal Soc. Chemistry, Am. Chem. Soc. Current Work: High temperature stability of metals, alloys, ceramics and composites; carbon reactivity; surface chemistry and catalysis; corrosion. Subspecialties: Physical chemistry; Surface chemistry. Office: Gen Electric Research and Devel Ctr PO Box 8 Schenectady NY 12301

MCKEE, JAMES STANLEY COLTON, physics educator; b. Belfast, Northern Ireland, June 6, 1930; s. James and Dorothy (Colton) McK.; m. Christine Diane Savage, July 16, 1961; children: James Conor, Sylvia Dorothy Siobhan. B.Sc., Queen's U., Belfast, 1952, Ph.D., 1956; D.Sc., U. Birmingham, Eng., 1968. Asst. lectr. Queens U., Belfast, 1954-56; lectr. Birmingham U., 1956-64, sr. lectr., 1964-74; prof. physics, dir. Cyclotron Lab. U. Man., 1974—; mem. grant selection com. Nat. Scis. and Engrng. Research Council, 1980-83. Contbr. articles to profl. jours. Fellow Inst. Physics, mem., Canadian Assn. Physicists. Liberal. Current Work: Few body problems in nuclear and particle physics; polarisation studies; solar concentrators. Subspecialties: Nuclear physics; Solar energy. Home: 1443 Wellington Crescent Winnipeg MB R3N OB2 Canada Office: U Man Rm 223 Allen Bldg Winnipeg R3T 2N2 Canada

MCKEE, KEITH EARL, civil engr., research center adminstr.; b. Chgo., Sept. 9, 1928; s. Charles Richard and Maude Alice McK.; m. Lorraine Marie Celichowski, Oct. 26, 1957; children: Pamela Ann, Paul Earl. B.S., Ill. Inst. Tech., 1950, M.S., 1956, Ph.D., 1962. Designer Swift & Co., Chgo., 1953-54; research engr. Armour Research Found., Chgo., 1954-63; dir. mech. design and product assurance Andrew Corp., Chgo., 1963-68; dir. engring. Ill. Inst. Tech. Research Inst., Chgo., 1968-80; dir. Ill. Inst. Tech. Research Inst. (Mfg. Productivity Ctr.), 1977—, also adj. prof. Author articles. Served to capt. USMC, 1950-53. Mem. ASME, ASCE, Soc. Mfg. Engrs., Numerical Control Soc., Am. Assn. Engrng. Socs., Am. Def. Preparedness Assn. (pres. Chgo. chpt. 1975—), Navy League, Air Force Assn., Assn. U.S. Army. Current Work: Manufacturing technology and productivity, flexible manufacturing systems, robotics, computer-aided design and manufacturing. Subspecialties: Industrial engineering; Robotics. Home: 608 Burns St Flossmoor IL 60422 Office: 10 W 35th St Chicago IL 60616

MCKELL, CYRUS MILO, crop physiologist, plant scientist; b. Payson, Utah, Mar. 19, 1926; s. Robert D. and Mary C. (Ellsworth) McK.; m. Betty Marie Johnson, June 16, 1947; children—Meredith Sue, Brian Marcus, John Cyrus. B.S., U. Utah, 1949, M.S., 1950; Ph.D., Oreg. State U., 1956; postdoctoral U. Calif.-David, 1957. High sch. prin. Duchesne County Sch. Dist., Utah, 1952-53; teaching asst., then instr. Oreg. State U., Corvallis, 1953-56; research scientist, range plant physiologist USDA-ARS, Davis, Calif., 1956-61; prof., dept. chmn. U. Calif., Riverside, 1961-69; prof., dept. head, inst. dir. Utah State U., Logan, 1969-81; v.p. research NPI, Salt Lake City, 1981—; cons. USAID, Ford Found., FAO, Rockefeller Found., Nat. Acad. Scis. Editor: Grass Biology and Utilization, 1972, Useful Wildland Shrubs: Their Biology, 1972, Paradoxes Western Energy Development, 1984; also articles. Chmn. Cache County Planning Commn., Logan, 1975-81, Utah Energy Conservation and Devel. Council, 1979-81. Served to 1st lt. USAF, 1951-52. Rockefeller study grantee, 1964; Fulbright scholar, 1967-68. Fellow AAAS (chmn. com. arid lands 1980—); mem. Am. Soc. Agronomy, Soc. Range Mgmt. (pres. Calif. sect. 1963, pres. Utah sect. 1983), Soil Conservation Soc. Am. (merit award 1981). Republican. Mormon. Club: Kiwanis. Current work: Presently serve as director of research for NPI, a plant biotechnology company with internat. lab., nursery and seed locations; review research in molecular biology, cell biology, soil microbiology, plant genetics, phytochemistry, and applied ecology. Subspecialty: 15300. Office: NPI 417 Wakara Way Salt Lake City UT 84108

MC KELVEY, JOHN CLIFFORD, research institute executive; b. Decatur, Ill., Jan. 25, 1934; s. Clifford Venice and Pauline Lytton (Runkel) McK.; m. Carolyn Tenney, May 23, 1980; children—Sean, Kerry, Tera, Evelyn, Aaron. B.A., Stanford U., 1956, M.B.A., 1958. Research analyst Stanford Research Inst., Palo Alto, Calif., 1959-60, indsl. economist, 1960-64; with Midwest Research Inst., Kansas City, Mo., 1964—, v.p. econs. and mgmt. sci., 1970-73, exec. v.p., 1973-75, pres., chief exec. officer, 1975—; dir. Yellow Freight System, Inc., Mem. Civic Council of Greater Kansas City; bd. regents Rockhurst Coll., Kansas City, Mo., 1973—; bd. dirs. NCCJ, 1978, Oxford Park Acad.; North Star Found., 1981; trustee Avila Coll., 1974, U. Kansas City, 1982; trustee, mem. exec. com. The Menninger Found., 1975. Clubs: Carriage, Mission Hills. Home: 912 W 121 Terr Kansas City MO 64145 Office: 425 Volker Blvd Kansas City MO 64110

MCKELVY, JEFFREY FORRESTER, neurobiologist, educator; b. Akron, Ohio, Aug. 25, 1938; s. Jack Forrester and Beverly Brickner McK.; m. Linda Mollin, June 7, 1963 (div.); children: Kathleen Forrester, Jill Leslie; m. Mary Louise Tally, Feb. 22, 1977. B.Sc., U. Akron, 1963; Ph.D., Johns Hopkins U., 1968. Asst. prof. anatomy U. Conn. Health Center, 1971-76; assoc. prof. biochemistry U. Tex. Health Sci. Center, Dallas, 1976-79; assoc. prof. psychiatry U. Pitts. Sch. Medicine, 1979-81; prof. neurobiology and behavior SUNY, Stony Brook, N.Y., 1981—; cons. NIH, mem. neurology study sect., 1978-82; mem. NIH Task Force on Research Needs in Endocrinology, 1979—. Contbr. numerous articles to sci. jours.; Editor: Current Methods in Cellular Neurobiology, 1982. Recipient NIH Research Career Devel. award, 1977-82. Mem. Am. Soc. Biol. Chemists, Soc. Neurosci., Am. Soc. Neurochemistry, Endocrine Soc., Internat. Brain Research Orgn. Democrat. Episcopalian. Subspecialties: Neurobiology; Molecular biology. Office: Dept Neurobiology and Behavior SUNY Grad Biol Bldg Stony Brook NY 11794

MCKENNA, GREGORY BORN, rheologist; b. Pitts., Jan. 28, 1949; s. Robert Benedict and Dorothy Ann (Born) McK.; m. Lonna Mary Morris, June 2, 1973; 1 child, Stacey Alexandra. B.S., U.S. Air Force Acad., 1970; S.M., MIT, 1971; Ph.D., U. Utah, 1976. Postdoctoral fellow NRC/Nat. Acad. Sci., Nat. Bur. Standards, 1976; research scientist Nat. Bur. Standards, Gaithersburg, Md., 1977—; vis. scientist Centre de Recherches sur les Macromolecules, Strasbourg, France, 1981-83. Contbr. articles to profl. publs. Served to capt. USAF, 1970-75. Mem. Am. Phys. Soc. (high polymer physics div.), Soc. Rheology, Am. Chem. Soc. (rubber div.), Soc. Plastics Engrs., AAAS. Club: Potomac Tennis (Md.). Current work: Study of the rheological behavior of cyclic macromolecules in the melt, investigation of the strain energy density function of model rubbers, relationship between physical aging and non-linear viscoelastic behavior of polymer glasses. Subspecialty: Polymer physics. Home: 9824 Korman Ct Potomac MD 20854 Office: Nat Bur Standards Polymers Div Gaithersburg MD 20899

MCKENNA, JAMES EMMET, research chemist; b. Bayonne, N.J., Mar. 7, 1947; s. James E. and Mildred E. (Jones) McK.; m. Diane Louise Ashcraft, Aug. 31, 1968; children—James S., Peter, Erin. B.S., St. Peter's Coll., 1968; Ph.D., Fordham U., 1973. Research chemist Research Organic, Belleville, N.J., 1975-76; sr. research chemist Chem-Fleur Inc., Newark, 1977—. Patentee B-Phenethyl alcohol fron styrene oxide, 1983, selective decarbonylation, 1984. Com. chmn. Essex council Boy Scouts Am., 1980—. Served to capt. U.S. Army, 1973-75. Mem. Am. Chem. Soc., Sigma Xi, Phi Lambda Upsilon. Republican. Roman Catholic. Current work: Application of state-of-the-art technology to the commercial synthesis of fragrance compounds, development of clean catalytic processes. Subspecialties: Organic chemistry; Synthetic chemistry. Home: 112 Greenwood Dr Millburn NJ 07041 Office: Chem-Fleur Inc 189 Clifford St Newark NJ 07105

MCKENZIE, ROBERT JAMES, plant physiologist; b. Warrenton, Va., Sept. 8, 1943; s. Charles Robert and Emma Kathleen (Brosius) McK.; m. Linda Rae McKenzie, Apr. 21, 1967 (div. 1980); children: Amanda Brooke, Sean Robert. B.S.B.A., U. Wash., 1970; Ph.D., Wash. State U., 1978. Plant physiology Hawaiian Sugar Planters Assn., Aiea, 1979-82, cons. plant cell and tissue culture, genetic engring., Phila., 1982—; membrane electro-physiology/bioenergetics Hahnemann U., Phila., 1984—. Contbr. articles to sci. jours. Served in U.S. Army, 1965-67, Vietnam. Mem. AAAS, Am. Bot. Soc., Am. Soc. Plant Physiologists, Am. Inst. Biol. Scis. Current Work: Mitochondrial bioenergetics, plant cell and tissue culture; protoplast technology; organelle transfer; organelle genetics. Subspecialties: Plant cell and tissue culture; Genetics and genetic engineering (agriculture). Home: 4252 Terrace St Philadelphia PA 19128 Office: Dept Biol Chemistry Hahnemann U Broad and Vine Sts Philadelphia PA 19102

MCKEON, JAMES EDWARD, chemical company executive; b. Shelton, Conn., June 25, 1930; s. Patrick Diamond and Mary (Keating) McK.; m. Patricia A. Tuttle, June 25, 1953 (div.); children—Timothy, Michael, Brian, Daniel; m. Betty Lou Brauer, Oct. 7, 1978. B.A. in Chemistry, Wesleyan U., 1951, M.A. in Chemistry, 1953; Ph.D. in Chemistry, Yale U., 1959. Research scientist Union Carbide Chemicals and Plastics Corp., So. Charleston, W.Va., 1959-68, asst. dir. research and devel., Tarrytown, N.Y., 1968-77, dir. research and devel., Bound Brook, N.J., 1977-84; v.p. tech. specialty chemistry div. Union Carbide Corp., Danbury, Conn., 1984—. Contbr. articles to profl. publs. Patentee in field. Mem. Am. Chem. Soc., N.Y. Acad. Sci. Roman Catholic. Current work: Oxidation processes, homogeneous catalysis, biochemical conversions. Subspecialty: Organic chemistry. Office: Union Carbide Corp 39 Old Ridgebury Rd Danbury CT 06817

MC KETTA, JOHN J., JR., chemical engineering educator; b. Wyano, Pa., Oct. 17, 1915; s. John J. and Mary (Gelet) McK.; m. Helen Elisabeth Smith, Oct. 17, 1943; children: Charles William, John J. III, Robert Andrew, Mary Anne. B.S., Tri-State Coll., Angola, Ind., 1937; B.S.E., U. Mich., 1943, M.S., 1944, Ph.D., 1946; D.Eng. (hon.), Tri-State Coll., 1965, Drexel U., 1977; Sc.D., U. Toledo, 1973. Diplomate: registered profl. engr., Tex., Mich. Group leader tech. dept. Wyandotte Chem. Corp., Mich., 1937-40, asst. supt. caustic soda div., 1940-41; teaching fellow U. Mich., 1942-44, instr. chem. engring., 1944-45; faculty U. Tex., Austin, 1946—, successively asst. prof. chem. engring., asso. prof., then prof. chem. engring., 1951-52, 54—, E.P. Schoch prof. chem. engring., 1970-81, Joe C. Walter chair, 1981—; asst. dir. Tex. petroleum research com., 1951-52, 54-56, chmn. chem. engring. dept., 1950-52, 55-63, dean Coll. Engring., 1963-69; exec. vice chancellor acad. affairs U. Tex. System, 1969-70; editorial dir. Petroleum Refiner, 1952-54; pres. Chemoil Cons., Inc., 1957-73; dir. Gulf Pub. Co., AID, Inc., Dallas, Dresser Industries, Dallas, Howell Corp., Houston, Commonwealth Refining Co., San Antonio, Tipperary Corp., Midland, Tex., Tesoro Petroleum Co., San Antonio, Vulcan Materials Co., Birmingham, Ala., KINARK Corp., Tulsa.; Chmn. Tex. AEC, So. Interstate Nuclear Bd.; mem. Tex. Radiation Adv. Bd., 1978—; chmn. Nat. Energy Policy Com., 1970-72, Nat. Air Quality Control Com., 1972—; mem. adv. bd. Carnegie-Mellon Inst. Research, 1978—; mem. U.S. Acid Precipitation Task Force. Author: series Advances in Petroleum Chemistry and Refining; Chmn. editorial com.: series Petroleum Refiner; mem. adv. bd.: series Internat. Chem. Engring. mag; editorial bd.: series Ency. of Chem. Tech; exec. editor: series Ency. of Chem. Processing and Design. Bd. regents Tri-State U., 1957—. Recipient Bronze plaque Am. Inst. Chem. Engrs., 1952, Charles Schwab award Am. Steel Inst., 1973; Lamme award as outstanding U.S. educator, 1976; Joe J. King Profl. Engring. Achievement award U. Tex., 1976; Gen. Dynamics Teaching Excellence award, 1979; Triple E award for contbns. to nat. issues on energy, environment and econs. Nat. Environ. Devel. Assn., 1976; Boris Pregal Sci. and Tech. award N.Y. Acad. Scis., 1978; named distinguished alumnus U. Mich Coll. Engring., 1953; named distinguished alumnus Tri-State Coll., 1956; fellow Allied Chem. & Dye, 1945-46; distinguished fellow Carnegie-Mellon U., 1978. Mem. Am. Inst. Mining Engrs., Am. Chem. Soc. (chmn. Central Tex. sect. 1950), Am. Inst. Chem. Engrs (chmn. nat. membership com. 1955, regional exec. com., nat. dir., nat. v.p. 1961, pres. 1962, service to soc. award 1975), Am. Soc. Engring. Edn., Chem. Markets Research Assn., Am. Gas Assn. (adv. bd. chems. from gas 1954), Houston C. of C. (chmn. refining div. 1954, vice chmn. research and statistics com. 1954), Engrs. Joint Council (dir.), Engrs. Joint Countil Profl. Devel. (dir. 1963—), Nat. Acad. Engring., Sigma Xi, Chi Epsilon, Alpha Psi Omega, Tau Omega, Phi Lambda Upsilon, Phi Kappa Phi, Iota Alpha, Omega Chi Epsilon, Tau Beta Pi, Omicron Delta Kappa. Current Work: High pressure thermodynamics; the energy supply and demand. Subspecialties: Chemical engineering; Fuels. Home: 5227 Tortuga Trail Austin TX 78731

MCKEY, PAUL MICHAEL, mechanical engineer; b. Detroit, Apr. 6, 1935; s. Thomas Joseph and Pauline Helen (Feys) McK.; m. Frances Elwart Toelle, Jan. 14, 1961; children—Paul Michael, Ellen Frances, Kristine Lisa. B.S.M.E., Wayne State U., 1960. Devel. engr. Chrysler Corp., Highland Park, Mich., 1962-64; mech. group supr. Bechtel Corp., San Francisco, 1964-67; program mgr. MB Assocs., San Ramon, Calif., 1967-69; sr. mech. engr. Physics Internat., San Leandro, Calif., 1969-71; mgr. dryer engring. Pall Trinity Micro Corp., Cortland, N.Y., 1971-77; chief engr. Niagara Blower Co., Buffalo, 1977—; cons. in field. Patentee increased capacity wet surface air cooling system, adsorbent fractionator with system gas-powered cycle control and process, adsorbent fractionator with fail-safe automatic cycle control and process. Served to pfc. U.S. Army, 1954-56. Mem. ASME, Am. Legion, Nat. Rifle Assn. (life). Subspecialty: Mechanical engineering. Home: 17 Therin Dr Hamburg NY 14075 Office: Niagara Blower Co 673 Ontario St Buffalo NY 14207

MCKILLIP, WILLIAM JAMES, chemical company executive; b. LaCrosse, Wis., Jan. 13, 1935; s. James William and Helen Marie (Sieger) McK.; m. Elizabeth Catherine Poehling, June 8, 1957; children—Mary, Robert, Teresa, Ann, Susan, Martha. B.S., Loras Coll., 1957; Ph.D., U. Iowa, 1962. Sr. research chemist, group leader Archer Daniels Midland, Mpls., 1962-67; group leader, mgr. Ashland Chem. Co., Dublin, Ohio, 1967-74; assoc. dir., v.p. Quaker Oats Co., Barrington, Ill., 1974-84; sr. v.p. QO Chems., Oakbrook, Ill., 1984—. Contbr. articles to profl. jours. Mem. Comml. Devel. Assn., Am. Chem. Soc., Am. Foundry Soc. Democrat. Roman Catholic. Current work: Organic synthesis, polymer applications. Subspecialty: Research and development management. Office: QO Chems 823 Commerce Dr Oakbrook IL 60521

MCKOWN, CORA F., home economics educator; b. Atoka, Okla., Aug. 21, 1943; d. W.F. and Zelma (Minton) McK. B.S., Southeastern Okla. U., 1964; M.S., Okla. State U., 1968; Ph.D., U. Mo., 1972. Instr. U. Okla. Extension, 1965-67; asst. prof. U. Ark., 1972-77; prof., chairperson housing and consumer dept. Tex. Tech U., 1977—; cons.; energy research. Author: Texas, Earth Sheltered, 1982, Residential Energy Alternatives, 1979; author articles on energy and housing. Mem. Am. Soc. Interior Designers, Am. Assn. Housing Educators, Am. Home Econs. Assn., AAUW, LWV. Current Work: Passive solar housing; energy consumption; earth sheltered design. Subspecialties: Solar energy; Behavioral ecology. Office: PO Box 4170 Lubbock TX 79409

MC KUSICK, VICTOR ALMON, physician, geneticist, educator; b. Parkman, Maine, Oct. 21, 1921; s. Carroll L. and Ethel M. (Buzzell) McK.; m. Anne Bishop, June 11, 1949; children: Carol Anne, Kenneth Andrew, Victor Wayne. Student, Tufts Coll., 1940-43; M.D., Johns Hopkins U., 1946; D.Sc., N.Y. Med. Coll., 1974, U. Maine, 1978, Tufts U., 1978; M.D. (hon.), Liverpool U., 1976; Sc.D. (hon.), U. Rochester, 1979, Meml. U. Nfld., 1979; D.Med.Sc., Med. U. S.C., 1979; D.M.Ch., U. Helsinki, 1981. Tng. in clin. medicine, lab. research Johns Hopkins U./USPHS, 1946-52; instr. medicine Johns Hopkins Sch. Medicine, 1952-54, asst. prof., 1954-57, asso. prof., 1957-60, prof. medicine, 1960—, chief div. med. genetics, dept. medicine, 1957-73, prof. epidemiology, biology, 1969-78, William Osler prof. medicine, 1978—, chmn. dept. medicine, 1973—; physician-in-chief Johns Hopkins Hosp., 1973—; mem. research adv. com. Nat. Found., 1959-78; mem. med. adv. bd. Howard Hughes Med. Inst., 1967-83; pres. Internat. Med. Congress, Ltd., 1972-78; mem. Nat. Adv. Research Resources Council, 1970-74; mem. bd. sci. advisers Roche Inst. Molecular Biology, 1967-71; trustee Jackson Lab., 1979—. Author: Heritable Disorders of Connective Tissue, 1956, 60, 66, 72, Cardiovascular Sound in Health and Disease, 1958, Medical Genetics 1958-60, 1961, Human Genetics, 1964, 69, On the X Chromosome of Man, 1964, Mendelian Inheritance in Man, 1966, 68, 71, 75, 78, 83, (with others) Genetics of Hand Malformations, 1978, Medical Genetic Studies of the Amish, 1978; editor med. textbook. Recipient John Phillips award ACP, 1972; Gairdner Internat. award, 1977; Premio Internazionale Sanremo per le Ricerche Genetiche, 1983. Fellow Am. Acad. Orthopedic Surgeons (hon.), Royal Coll. Physicians (London), AAAS; mem. Nat. Acad. Sci., Am. Philos. Soc., Am. Soc. Human Genetics (pres. 1974, Wm. A. Allan award 1977), Assn. Am. Physicians, Am. Soc. Clin. Investigation, Académie Nationale Médecine (France) (corr.), Phi Beta Kappa, Alpha Omega Alpha. Presbyterian. Clubs: West Hamilton Street, St. Andrew's Soc. Balt. Current Work: Delineation of genetic disorders and traits-gene mapping of human chromosomes. Subspecialties: Gene actions; Genome organization. Home: 221 Northway Baltimore MD 21218 Office: Johns Hopkins Hosp Baltimore MD 21205

MCLAFFERTY, FRED WARREN, chemist, educator; b. Evanston, Ill., May 11, 1923; s. Joel E. and Margaret E. (Keifer) McL.; m. Elizabeth E. Curley, Feb. 5, 1948; children: Sara L., Joel E., Martha A., Samuel A., Ann E. B.S., U. Nebr., 1943, M.S., 1947, D.Sc. (hon.), 1983; Ph.D., Cornell U., 1950. Postdoctoral fellow U. Iowa, 1949-50; research chemist, div. leader Dow Chem. Co., 1950-56; dir. Eastern Research Lab., 1956-64; prof. chemistry Purdue U., 1964-68, Cornell U., 1968—; mem. chem. sci. and tech. bd. NRC. Author: Mass Spectrometry of Organic Ions, 1963, Mass Spectral Correlations, 2d edit, 1981, Interpretation of Mass Spectra, 3d edit, 1980, Tandem Mass Spectrometry, 1983, Advances in Analytical Chemistry and Instrumentation, (with C.N. Reilley), Vols. 4-7), 1967-70, Index and Bibliography of Mass Spectrometry, (with J. Pinzelik), 1967, Atlas of Mass Spectral Data, (with E. Stenhagen and S. Abrahamsson), 1969, (with E. Stenhagen and S. Abrahamson) Registry of Mass Spectral Data, 1974; Co-editor: (with E. Stenhagen and S. Abrahamson) Archives of Mass Spectral Data, 1969-72. Served with AUS, 1943-45, ETO. Decorated Purple Heart, Combat Inf. badge, Bronze Star medal with 4 oak leaf clusters; recipient Pitts. Spectroscopy award Spectroscopy Soc. Pitts., 1975; Anachem. award Assn. Analytical Chemists, 1985; J.J. Thomson medal Internat. Mass. Spectrometry Conf., 1985; John Simon Guggenheim fellow, 1972. Fellow N.Y. Acad. Scis., Nat. Acad. Scis., AAAS (chmn. chemistry sect.), Am. Acad. Arts and Scis.; mem. Am. Chem. Soc. (chmn. analytical chem. div. 1969, chmn. Midland sect. 1956, Northeastern sect. 1964, award chem. instrumentation 1971, award analytical chemistry 1981, Nichols medal N.Y. sect. 1984, Oesper award Cin. sect. 1984), Am. Soc. Mass Spectroscopy (founder, sec. 1957-58), Chem. Soc. London, Sigma Xi, Phi Lambda Upsilon, Alpha Chi Sigma. Current Work: Mass spectrometry of molecules, computer identification of unknown spectra. Subspecialty: Analytical chemistry. Home: 110 The Parkway Ithaca NY 14850

MC LAREN, DIGBY JOHNS, geologist, educator; b. Carrickfergus, No. Ireland, Dec. 11, 1919; m. Phyllis Mary Matkin, Mar. 25, 1942; children: Ian, Patrick, Alison. Student, Queens' Coll., Cambridge U., 1938-40; B.A., Cambridge U., 1941, M.A. (Harkness scholar), 1948; Ph.D., Mich. U., 1951; D.Sc. (hon.), U. Ottawa, 1980. Geologist Geol. Survey Can., Ottawa, Ont., 1948-80, dir. gen., 1973-80; sr. sci. advisor Can. Dept. Energy, Mines and Resources, Ottawa, 1981-84; vis. prof. U. Ottawa, 1981—; 1st dir. Inst. Sedimentary and Petroleum Geology, Calgary, Alta., Can., 1967-73; pres. Commn. on Stratigraphy, Internat. Union Geol. Scis., 1972-76; apptd. 14th dir. Geol. Survey Can., 1973; chmn. bd. Internat. Geol. Correlation Program, UNESCO-IGCP, 1976-80. Contbr. memoirs, bulls., papers, geol. maps, sci. articles in field to profl. lit. Served to capt. Royal Arty. Brit. Army, 1940-46. Gold medalist (sci.) Profl. Inst. Pub. Service of Can., 1979. Fellow Royal Soc. Can., Royal Soc. London, European Union of Geoscis. (hon.); fgn. assoc. U.S. Nat. Acad. Scis, Geol. Soc. France; mem. Geol. Soc. London, Geol. Soc. Germany (hon.), Geol. Soc. Am. (pres. 1982), Paleontol. Soc. (pres. 1969), Geol. Assn. Can., Can. Soc. Petroleum Geologists. (pres. 1971). Subspecialties: Geology; Paleontology. Office: Dept Geology Univ Ottawa Ottawa ON K1N 6N5 Canada

MCLAUGHLIN, CALVIN S., biochemist, educator; b. St. Joseph, Mo., May 29, 1936. B.A. magna cum laude; scholar, King Coll., 1958; postgrad. (Rockefeller Bros. fellow), Yale U., 1958-59; Ph.D. in Biochemistry (Upjohn fellow, Nutrition Found. fellow, NIH fellow), M.I.T., 1964. Am. Cancer Soc. postdoctoral fellow Institut de Biologie Physico-chimique, Paris, 1964-66; asst. prof. biochemistry U. Calif., Irvine, 1966-69, asso. prof., 1969-73, prof., 1973-78, vice-chmn. dept. biol. chemistry, 1978-83; dir. Cancer Research Inst., 1981-84; Gabriel Lester Meml. lectr., 1979; chemist Tenn. Eastman. Co., Kingsport, 1957-58; vis. prof. Sch. Botany, Oxford (Eng.) U., 1976, Linacre Coll., Oxford, 1980; mem. sci. adv. bd. Am. Cancer Soc., NSF, NIH; sec.-treas. Pacific Slope Biochem. Conf., 1973-76; participant profl. cons. and seminars. Editorial bd.: Jour. Bacteriology; reviewer: Molecular and Cellular Biology; contbr. articles to sci. jours. Danforth asso., 1976-82; grantee NIH; grantee Burns Family Found.; grantee Nat. Mycology Research Center; grantee Nat. Cancer Inst. Mem. AAAS, Genetics Soc. Am., Am. Soc. Microbiology, Am. Soc. Biol. Chemists, Mycol. Soc. Am. Subspecialties: Genetics and genetic engineering (biology); Biochemistry (biology). Office: Dept Biol Chemistr U Calif Irvine CA 92625

MCLAUGHLIN, DONALD REED, chemist, educator, researcher; b. Los Angeles, Oct. 6, 1938; s. Alfred Reed and Anita Grace (Squires) McL.; m. Linda Irene, June 15, 1964. B.A., UCLA, 1960; Ph.D., U. Utah, 1965. Assoc. prof. chemistry U. N.Mex., 1965—; dir. Los Alamos Center for Grad. Studies. Mem. Am. Chem. Soc., Sigma Xi. Current Work: Quantum chemistry; dynamics and theoretical molecular spectroscopy. Subspecialties: Theoretical chemistry; Laser photochemistry. Office: Dept Chemistry U NMex Albuquerque NM 87131

MCLAUGHLIN, MICHAEL RAY, plant pathologist, researcher; b. Carroll, Iowa, June 20, 1949; s. Harold Eugene and Charlene Martha (Yost) McL.; m. Cindy Lee Richardson, May 30, 1970; children: Erin, Caragh, Mark. B.S., Iowa State U., 1971, M.S., 1974; Ph.D., U. Ill., 1978. Vis. asst. prof. plant pathology and physiology Clemson (S.C.) U., 1978-79; asst. prof. entomology and plant pathology U. Tenn., Knoxville, 1979-82; research plant pathologist USDA Agr. Research Service, Mississippi State, Miss., 1982—; adj. assoc. prof. Miss. State U., Mississippi State, 1982—. Mem. Am. Photopath. Soc., Sigma Xi, Gamma Sigma Delta. Current Work: Viruses and virus desease of forage legumes. Subspecialties: Plant virology; Plant pathology. Office: PO Drawer PG Mississippi State MS 39762

MCLAUGHLIN, WILLIAM LOWNDES, physicist, researcher; b. Stony Point, Tenn., Mar. 30, 1928; s. John Calvin Brown and Fanny Dargen (McCaa) M.; m. Nancy Elizabeth Shepherd, Mar. 27, 1951; children—Peter Shepherd, David Wallace. B.S. summa cum laude, Hampden-Sydney Coll., 1949; M.S. in Physics, George Washington U., 1963. Physicist, Nat. Bur. Standards, Washington, 1951—, Gaithersburg, Md., 1973—; cons. Riso Nat. Lab., Roskilde, Denmark, 1975—, Boris Kidric Inst., Vinca, Belgrade Yugoslavia, 1976—, Internat. Atomic Energy Agy., Vienna, 1977—. Editor: Trends in Radiation Dosimetry, 1982; Author: Dosimetry for Food Irradiation, 1977. Patentee in field. Served with U.S. Army, 1954-56. Recipient Silver medal for research U.S. Dept. of Commerce, 1969, Gold medal, 1979; Tech. Transfer award Fed. Lab. Consortium, 1984; Applied Research award Nat. Bur. Standards, 1985; Rotary Internat. fellow, 1950-51. Mem. St. Andrews Soc., Rockbridge Hist. Soc., N.Y. Acad. Sci., Optical Soc. Am., Am. Phys. Soc., Soc. Photographic Sci. and Engring. (dir. 1964-67), Radiation Research Soc. Presbyterian. Current work: Ionizing radiation; x and gamma ray physics; electron transport; photochemistry of dyes and organic chemicals; fiber optics; optical image processing; radiobiology; macromolecules; physical chemistry; radiological imaging; space chemistry. Subspecialties: Atomic and molecular physics; Nuclear physics. Home: 3901 Albemarle St NW Washington DC 20016 Office: Nat Bur Standards Radiation Physics Lab Gaithersburg MD 20899

MCLEAN, JOHN ROBERT, clinical scientist; b. St. Thomas, Ont., Can., Apr. 15, 1926; came to U.S., 1954; s. John and Dorothy (MacFarlane) McL.; m. Elizabeth Virtue, Sept. 8, 1951; children: Dorothy, Mark. Ph.D., Queen's U., Ont., 1954. Dir. neuropharmacology Parke-Davis & Co., Ann Arbor, Mich., 1972-77, assoc. dir. biochemistry, 1977-82, group leader neurol. diseases, 1982-83, asst. dir. clin. sci., 1983—. Mem. Am. Soc. Pharmacology and Exptl. Therapeutics, Am. Heart Assn. Council on Thrombosis, Am. Epilepsy Soc. Current Work: Development of drugs for the treatment of neurological diseases. Subspecialties: Neurology; Neuropharmacology. Home: 1708 Covington Ann Arbor MI 48103 Office: 2800 Plymouth Rd Ann Arbor MI 48105

MCLENDON, GEORGE LELAND, chemistry educator; b. Fort Worth, June 6, 1952; s. George and Berta (Shaw) McL.; m. Donna Turner, Aug. 31, 1973; children—Heather, Audrey. B.S., U. Tex.-El Paso, 1972, Ph.D., Tex. A&M U., 1976. Assoc. prof. chemistry U. Rochester, N.Y., 1976-81, assoc. prof., 1981—. Contbr. articles to profl. jours. Vestryman St. Stephens Episcopal Ch., A.P. Sloan fellow, 1980; Dreyfus Found. scholar, 1980. Mem. Am. Chem. Soc. (exec. com. Rochester sect. 1980-82). Current work: Inorganic and biochemistry; photochemistry and electron transfer. Subspecialties: Inorganic chemistry; Biophysical chemistry. Office: Dept Chemistry U Rochester Rochester NY 14627

MCLENITHAN, KELLY DANIEL, theoretical physicist, numerical analyst; b. Grand Rapids, Mich., June 11, 1954; s. Earle Chester and Norma Fay (Gierloff) McL.; m. Priscilla Colleen Pflug, Aug. 7, 1976; children: Shannon Leigh, Kevin Daniel. A.B., Ill. Coll., 1976; M.S., U. Ill.-Urbana, 1978, Ph.D., 1982. Research trainee Oak Ridge Nat. Lab., summer 1975; teaching asst. U. Ill.-Urbana, 1976-78, research asst., 1978-82, research assoc., 1982; project assoc. U. Wis.-Madison, 1982-84; mem. tech. staff TRW, Inc., Redondo Beach, Calif., 1984—. Mem. Am. Phys. Soc., Math. Assn. Am., Soc. Indsl. and Applied Math., Phi Lambda Upsilon, Sigma Xi. Current Work: Quantum mechanical scattering problems; magnetohydrodynamic equilibrium and stability of confined fusion plasmas; thermonuclear reaction dynamics, nuclear weapons effects, operations research. Subspecialties: Theoretical physics; Applied mathematics. Home: 9951 Silver Strand Dr Huntington Beach CA 92646 Office: TRW Def Systems Group One Space Park Redondo Beach CA 90278

MCLENNAN, JEAN GLINN, virologist; b. Charlotte, N.C., Feb. 8, 1934; d. John Manning and Irene Mae (Pool) Glinn; m. William Eldon McLennan, Sept. 17, 1961. B.A., U. Pa., Phila., 1955; B.S., U. Nebr.-Omaha, 1983; postgrad., Hunter Coll., 1960-61. Microbiologist Emory U. Sch. Medicine, 1955-57, virologist, 1963-66; microbiologist Cornell U. Sch. Medicine, 1957-61, Ga. Dept. Pub. Health, Atlanta, 1961-62, Cutter Labs., Berkeley, Calif., 1966-75; virologist Burns-BioTec Lab., Elkhorn, Nebr., 1975—. Mem. Am. Soc. Microbiology, N.Y. Acad. Scis., Assn. Vet. Microbiologists (editor newsletter 1982-83). Democrat. Lutheran. Current Work: Quality control and statistical analysis. Subspecialties: Animal virology; Microbiology (veterinary medicine). Home: 1442 S 163d St Omaha NE 68130 Office: PO Box 3113 Omaha NE 68103

MC LERAN, JAMES HERBERT, educational administrator, dentist; b. Audubon, Iowa, Apr. 9, 1931; s. Louis D. and Alma K. (Christensen) McL.; m. Hermine Weinert Hayden, July 15, 1979; 1 son, Stephen Andrew. B.S., Simpson Coll., 1953; D.D.S., U. Iowa, 1957, M.S., 1962. Diplomate: Am. Bd. Oral and Maxillofacial Surgeons. Instr. U. Iowa, 1959-60, asst. prof., 1963-67, asso. prof., 1967-69, prof. oral surgery, 1972—; asso. dean U. Iowa (Coll. Dentistry), 1972-74, dean, 1974—; prof. and chmn. dept. oral surgery U. N.C., Chapel Hill, 1969-72. Served with Dental Corps USN, 1957-59. Recipient Finkbine Leadership award U. Iowa, 1957; named Instr. of Yr. Jr. ADA, 1964, Outstanding Instr. award, 1965. Mem. Am. Assn. Oral and Maxillofacial Surgeons, Iowa Assn. Oral and Maxillofacial Surgeons, Internat. Assn. Dental Research, ADA, Midwestern Assn. Oral and Maxillofacial Surgeons, Am. Dental Soc. Anesthesiology, N.C. Soc. Dental Surgeons, N.C. Dental Soc., Iowa Dental Assn., Univ. Dist. Dental Soc., Johnson County Dental Soc., Am. Coll. Dentists, Internat. Coll. Dentists, Am. Assn. Dental Schs. (pres. 1978-79), Psi Omega (adv.). Republican. Club: Rotary. Subspecialty: Oral and maxillofacial surgery. Office: Coll Dentistry U Iowa Iowa City IA 52242

MCLERRAN, ARCHIE RALPH, mechanical engineer, consultant; b. Milam County, Tex., Aug. 27, 1918; s. Archie Roy and Pearl Marie (Smith) McL.; m. Inez Smith, Aug. 14, 1917; 1 dau., Marilyn McLerran Souchek. B.S. in Mech. Engring, Tex. A&M U., 1939. Registered profl. engr., Tex., La. With Ideco div. Dresser Industries, Beaumont, Tex., 1939-60, chief research and devel. engr., 1939-60; owner, prin. engr. A.R. McLerran & Assocs. (cons. engrs.), Beaumont, 1961-64; mgr. field operation, project mohole NSF, Houston, 1964-68, field ops. officer, deep sea drilling project, La Jolla, Calif., 1968-83; mgr. ops. and engring. ocean drilling program Tex. A&M U., College Station, 1983-85; cons. Bd. dirs. Isla Verde Assn., Inc., Solana Beach, Calif., 1979-81, pres., 1980-81. Recipient Meritorious Service award NSF, 1978, Disting. Service award NSF, 1983. Mem. ASME, Am. Petroleum Inst.; Republican. . Baptist. Club: Lomas Santa Fe Country (Solana Beach). Patentee in field. Current Work: Management of scientific ocean drilling program and development deep sea drilling and coring technology. Subspecialties: Mechanical engineering; Offshore technology.

MCLERRAN, LARRY DEAN, physicist; b. Yakima, Wash., Feb. 24, 1949; s. Stanford John and Geraldine (Meyers) McL.; m. Alice Van Kleeck Enderton, May 8, 1976. B.S., U. Wash., 1971, Ph.D., 1975. Research assoc. MIT, Cambridge, 1975-78, Stanford Linear Accelerator, Calif., 1978-80; asst. prof. U. Wash., Seattle, 1980-84; scientist Fermilab, Batavia, Ill., 1984—. Contbr. articles to profl. jours. Mem. Am. Phys. Soc., AAAS. Club: Sierra. Current work: Theoretical particles physics; ultra-relativistic nulcear collisions. Subspecialties: Theoretical physics; Particle physics. Home: 3 N Jackson St Batavia IL 60510 Office: Fermilab MS106 PO Box 500 Batavia IL 60510

MCLOON, LINDA KIRSCHEN, anatomy researcher, educator; b. N.Y.C., July 28, 1953; m. Steven Charles McLoon. B.S. in Biology, SUNY, Binghamton, 1974; Ph.D. in Anatomy, U. Ill. at Med. Center, Chgo., 1979. Teaching asst. dept. anatomy U. Ill. Med. Center, 1974-79; instr. dept. anatomy Ill. Coll. Podiatric medicine, Chgo., 1975-78; research assoc. dept. biol. structure U. Wash., Seattle, 1979; research assoc. dept. ophthalmology U. Minn. Contbr. articles and abstracts to profl. jours. Mem. Soc. Neurosci., Am. Assn. Anatomists, AAAS. Current Work: Developmental neurobiology; transplantation of nervous tissue; trophic factors in development. Subspecialties: Neurobiology; Developmental biology. Office: Dept Ophthalmology Box 493 U Minn 516 Delaware SE Minneapolis MN 55455

MC MAHON, CHARLES JOSEPH, JR., materials science educator; b. Phila., July 10, 1933; s. Charles Joseph and Alice (Schu) McM.; m. Helen June O'Brien, Jan. 31, 1959; children: Christine, Charles, Elise, Robert, David. B.S., U. Pa., 1955; Sc.D., MIT, 1963. Instr. metallurgy MIT, 1958-62, research asst., 1962-63; postdoctoral fellow U. Pa., 1963-64, asst. prof. dept. materials sci. and engring., 1964-68, assoc. prof., 1968-74, prof., 1974—; cons. in field. Editor: Microplasticity, 1968; Contbr. articles to profl. jours. Served with USN, 1955-58. Churchill Overseas fellow Churchill Coll., Cambridge (Eng.) U., 1973-74. Fellow Am. Soc. Metals, Nat. Acad. Engring., Inst. Metallurgists (U.K.), Metall. Soc. of AIME; mem. AIME, Instn. Metallurgists, Metals Soc. (U.K.), AAAS. Democrat. Roman Catholic. Current Work: Interfacial fracture, solute segregation to surfaces and interfaces. Subspecialty: Metallurgy.

Home: 7103 Sherman St Philadelphia PA 19119 Office: U Pa Philadelphia PA 19104

MCMAHON, DONALD HOWLAND, optical physicist; b. Buffalo, Apr. 18, 1934; s. Arthur Philmore and Elnora Winifred (Langley) McM.; m. Mable Grinnell, Sept. 11, 1954; B.S. in Physics with honors, U. Buffalo, 1957; Ph.D. in Exptl. Physics, Cornell U., 1964. Mem. research staff Sperry Research Ctr., Sudbury, Mass., 1963-71, program mgr. in optics tech., 1971-73, mgr. optics dept., 1973-83; tech. mgr. Polaroid Corp., Cambridge, Mass., 1983—. Contbr. numerous articles, on optics to profl. jours. Fellow Am. Optical Soc.; mem. Am. Phys. Soc., IEEE, Phi Beta Kappa. Patentee in field, mainly in optics. Current Work: Fiber optic sensors, fiber optic communication, optical pattern recognition, electro optics, acousto optics, optical info. processing. Subspecialties: Fiber optics; Optical image processing. Home: 580 West St Carlisle MA 01741 Office: 100 North Rd Sudbury MA 01776

MCMAHON, ROBERT FRANCIS, zoology educator; b. Syracuse, N.Y., June 17, 1944; s. Robert Francis and Rebecca Margret (Meyer) McM.; m. Maria Colette O'Byrne, June 17, 1980. B.A., Cornell U., 1966; Ph.D., Syracuse U., 1972. Asst. prof. zoology U. Tex., Arlington, 1972-78, assoc. prof., 1979-84, prof., 1984—; vis. prof. Trinity Coll., U. Dublin, Ireland, 1978-79. Contbr. articles to profl. jours., chpts. to books. Fulbright-Hayes fellow, 1978-79. Mem. Marine Biol. Lab., Am. Soc. Zoologists, Marine Biol. Assn. of U.K., Scotish Marine Biol. Assn., Malacological Soc. London. Current work: Comparative physiology of fresh water and marine invertebrates, adaptations of aquatic animals to exposure in air, biological effects of thermal effluents, bioenergetics. Subspecialty: Physiology (biology). Office: Dept Biology Box 19498 U Tex Arlington TX 76019

MCMANAMON, PAUL FRANCIS, electronic engr.; b. Cleve., July 1, 1946; s. John and Catherine (Bauman) McM.; m. Laura Sarina (DeDonne), July 5, 1969; children: Joan, Steven, David., Deborah. B.S., John Carroll U., 1968; M.S., Ohio State U., 1973, Ph.D., 1977. Physicist Electronic Warfare Analyses U.S. Air Force, 1968-70, electronics engr., 1970-71, 71-73; tech. specialist Electronic Warfare Avionics, Wright Patterson AFB, Ohio, 1973-79; group leader Passive IR Sensor Group, 1979—. Mem. Am. Phys. Soc., Optical Soc. Am., Assn. Old Crows. Roman Catholic. Current Work: Research on focal plane array infrared sensors. Subspecialty: Thermal imaging.

MCMENAMIN, EDWARD WILLIAM, engring. exec.; b. Phila., Jan. 22, 1928; s. Edward A. and Wilhelmina (Muth) McM.; m. Catherine E. Rowland, May 1, 1954; children: James R., Robert T., Cathy E. B.S.M.E., Drexel U., Phila., 1952. Registered profl. engr., Pa. Successively draftsman, coop. student, design engr., project engr. Proctor & Schwartz, Phila., 1945-59; successively chief engr., v.p. engring. and sales Gimpel Corp., Langhorne, Pa., 1959—. Mem. ch. council, fin. sec., chmn. fin. and bldg. coms. St. John's Lutheran Ch.; adult leader Boy Scouts Am. Served with USAAF, 1946-47. Mem. ASME, Am. Soc. Non-destructive Testing. Republican. Lodges: Odd Fellows; Masons. Current Work: Leading designer and developer trip throttle valves for steam turbines for marine, petro, chem. industries and utilities. Subspecialties: Mechanical engineering; Metallurgy. Home: 680 Mason Dr Warminster PA 18974 Office: 250 Woodbourne Rd PO Box 188 Langhorne PA 18974

MC MILLAN, EDWIN MATTISON, physicist, educator; b. Redondo Beach, Calif., Sept. 18, 1907; s. Edwin Harbaugh and Anna Marie (Mattison) McM.; m. Elsie Walford Blumer, June 7, 1941; children—Ann B., David M., Stephen W. B.S., Calif. Inst. Tech., 1928, M.S., 1929; Ph.D., Princeton U., 1932; D.Sc., Rensselaer Poly. Inst., 1961, Gustavus Adolphus Coll., 1963. Nat. research fellow U. Calif. at Berkeley, 1932-34, research asso., 1934-35, instr. in physics, 1935-36, asst. prof. physics, 1936-41, asso. prof., 1941-46, prof. physics, 1946-73, emeritus, 1973—; mem. staff Lawrence Radiation Lab., 1934—, asso. dir., 1954-58, dir., 1958-73; on leave for def. research at Mass. Inst. Tech. Radiation Lab., U.S. Navy Radio and Sound Lab., San Diego, and Los Alamos Sci. Lab., 1940-45; mem. gen. adv. com. AEC, 1954-58; mem. commn. high energy physics Internat. Union Pure and Applied Physics, 1960-67; mem. sci. policy com. Stanford Linear Accelerator Center, 1962-66; mem. physics adv. com. Nat. Accelerator Lab., 1967-69; chmn. 13th Internat. Conf. on High Energy Physics, 1966; guest prof. CERN, Geneva, 1974. Trustee Rand Corp., 1959-69; Bd. dirs. San Francisco Palace Arts and Scis. Found., 1968—; trustee Univs. Research Assn., 1969-74. Recipient Research Corp. Sci. award, 1951; with Glenn T. Seaborg) Nobel prize in chemistry, 1951; with Vladimir I. Veksler) Atoms for Peace award, 1963; Alumni Distinguished Service award Calif. Inst. Tech., 1966; Centennial citation U. Calif. at Berkeley, 1968; Faculty Research lectr. U. Calif. at Berkeley, 1955. Fellow Am. Acad. Arts and Scis., Am. Phys. Soc.; mem. Nat. Acad. Scis. (chmn. class I 1968-71), Am. Philos. Soc., Sigma Xi, Tau Beta Pi. Subspecialty: Nuclear physics. Address: Lawrence Berkeley Lab Berkeley CA 94720

MC MILLAN, ROBERT SCOTT, astronomer; b. Pitts., Feb. 26, 1950; s. William Robert and Mary Eunice (Amos) McM.; m. Gloria Lee, Dec. 22, 1980; 1 son, Christopher Norman. B.S., Case Inst. Tech., 1972; M.A., U. Tex., 1974, Ph.D., 1977. Research and teaching asst. U. Tex., Austin, 1972-77; research asso. astrophysics br. Space Scis. Labs., NASA Marshall Space Flight Center, Huntsville, Ala., 1977-79; sr. research asso. Lunar and Planetary Lab., U. Ariz., Tucson, 1979—. Mem. Am. Astron. Soc., Soc. Photo-optical Instrumentation Engrs., Current Work: Developer of an optical spectrometer for accurately measuring Doppler shifts of stars and of an electronic camera for detecting nearby asteroids. Subspecialties: Optical astronomy; Optical image processing. Home: 428 E Adams St Tucson AZ 85705 Office: Univ of Arizon Space Science Bldg Tucson AZ 85721

MCMILLAN, ROBERT WALKER, physicist, researcher; b. Sylacauga, Ala., Apr. 18, 1935; s. Robert Thomas and Mary Alma (Bush) McMillan; m. Dorothea Ann Simmons, Sept. 11, 1955; children: Marisa, Robert, Natalie. B.S., Auburn U., 1957; M.S., Rollins Coll., 1966; Ph.D., U. Fla., 1974. Assoc. engr. Westinghouse Electric Corp., Balt., 1960-61; staff engr. Martin Marietta Aerospace Corp., Orlando, Fla., 1961-76; prin. research scientist Ga. Tech. Research Inst., Ga. Inst. Tech., Atlanta, 1976—. Contbr. articles to profl. jours. Served to 1st lt. USAF, 1958-60. Mem. Optical Soc. Am., IEEE. Democrat. Baptist. Patentee in field. Current Work: Millimeter wave systems, spectroscopy, radiometry, atmospheric physics, millimeter wave devices. Subspecialties: Electrical engineering; Condensed matter physics. Home: 6332 Queen View Ln Stone Mountain GA 30087 Office: Ga Inst Tech Research Inst Atlanta GA 30332

MCMILLEN, SANDRA LEE, software engineer; b. Canandaigua, N.Y., Sept. 17, 1960; d. Ivan Leslie and Florence Shirley (Myers) McM. B.S. in Math., Colo. State U., 1982. Avionics software engr. Ford Aerospace & Communications Corp., Houston, 1983—. Mem. Soc. for Indsl. and Applied Math. Current work: Avionics software to support primary onboard Space Shuttle flight operations, particularly in guidance, navigation and control. Subspecialties: Aerospace engineering and technology; Software engineering.

MCMILLIN, DAVID EDWIN, geneticist, educator; b. Pitts., Apr. 16, 1952; s. John Glenn and Dorothy Ruth (Lauterette) McM.; m. Mary Katherine McMillin, Dec. 25, 1974; children: John David, Phillip Matthew. B.S. in Biology, Ga. So. Coll., 1974; M.S. in Plant Genetics, Tex. A & M U., 1977; Ph.D. in genetics, N.C. State U., 1981. Asst. prof. dept. biol. scis. N. Tex. State U., 1981—. Contbr. articles to profl. jours. Recipient Kenneth R. Keller award, 1981. Mem. Genetics Soc. Am., AAAS, Soc. Devel. Biology, Gamma Sigma Delta. Current Work: Devel. genetics, gene regulation; nuclear organelle interactions; crop improvement using choromosome mediated gene transfer. Subspecialties: Gene actions; Plant genetics. Home: 1721 Teasley Ln #271 Denton TX 76203 Office: Dept Biological Science North Texas State U Denton TX 76203

MCMILLIN, JOHN MICHAEL, endocrinology educator and administrator; b. Mpls., Jan. 16, 1940; s. John Dominic and Margaret Dagmar (Marklund) McM.; m. Joan Francis Austin, May 10, 1970; children: J. Andrew, Christy Ann. B.S., U. Minn., 1962, M.D., 1965, postgrad., 1969-73. Diplomate: Am. Bd. Internal Medicine. Intern Parkland Meml. Hosp., Dallas, 1965-66; research fellow, resident in psychiatry Mass. Gen. Hosp., Boston, 1968-69; fellow in medicine U. Minn., Mpls., 1969-71, fellow in endocrinology, 1971-73, asst. prof. medicine, 1973-76; head div. endocrinology U. S.D., Sioux Falls, 1976—; assoc. chief of staff for research devel. VA, Sioux Falls, 1976—. Author: Dissipative Structores and Spatiotemporal Organization in Biomedical Research, 1980; contbr. articles to profl. jours. Served to capt. AUS, 1966-68, Vietnam. Recipient Order of Ski Umah U. Minn., 1965; VA research grantee, 1976—; recipient Faculty Recognition award U. S.D., 1981. Mem. Am. Cancer Soc. (pres. S.D. 1977-81, 82-83, nat. med. del.), Am. Diabetes Assn. (dir. S.D.), Am. Fedn. Clin. Research, Endocrine Soc., Soc. Study of Reprodn., Internat. Soc. Chronobiology, Alpha Omega Alpha. Democrat. Episcopalian. Current Work: Control and function of growth hormone, prolactin and sex steroids. Subspecialty: Neuroendocrinology. Home: 1601 Cedar Ln Sioux Falls SD 57103 Office: U South Dakota Sch of Medicine 2501 W 22d St Sioux Falls SD 57105

MCMORRIS, F(REDERICK) ARTHUR, research biologist, educator; b. Lawton, Okla., Sept. 17, 1944; s. William Arthur and Mary Alfredda (Pope) McM. A.B. with high honors, Brown U., 1966; Ph.D., Yale U., 1972. Research assoc. M.I.T., 1972-74; asst. prof. Wistar Inst., Phila., 1974-84, assoc. prof., 1985—; mem. grad. groups in molecular biology, neurosci. and genetics U. Pa., 1975—. Contbr. articles to profl. jours. Bd. dirs. Spruce Hill Community Assn., 1976—, exec. v.p., 1980—; bd. dirs. Friends of Clark Park, 1978-80. NIH fellow, 1972. Mem. AAAS, Am. Soc. Cell Biology, Am. Soc. Neurochemistry, Am. Soc. Human Genetics, Soc. Devel. Biology, Soc. Neurosci., Sigma Xi. Democrat. Current Work: Gene regulation and biochemical expression in cells of the nervous system. Subspecialties: Neurochemistry; Gene actions. Home: 4333 Larchwood Ave Philadelphia PA 19104 Office: Wistar Institute 36th and Spruce Sts Philadelphia PA 19104

MCMURDIE, DENNIS STODDARD, geologist; b. Logan, Utah, Aug. 16, 1939; s. Neil Hansen and Eva (Riggs Stoddard) McM.; m. Ruth Blanchard, Dec. 27, 1962; children—Neil Deloy, Christina, Celeste, Russell Erick. Student Brigham Young U., 1958-63; B.S., U. Utah, 1967, M.S., 1968; postgrad. U. So. Calif., 1970. Registered geologist, Calif. Devel. geologist THUMS Long Beach Co., Calif., 1967-70, Los Angeles Basin, Union Oil Co., Santa Fe Springs, 1970-74; area geologist Union Oil Co., Santa Rosa, Calif., 1974-78; geothermal geologist Western U.S.A., Southland Royalty Co., Ft. Worth, 1978-80; sr. geologist Geotronics Corp., Austin, Tex., 1980-83; cons., pres. McMurdie Energy Services, Austin, 1984—; instr. Calif. State U., Fullerton, 1973-74. Contbr. articles to profl. jours.; contbr. to U.S. Geol. Survey maps of geysers. Chmn. membership Sonoma-Mendocino council Boy Scouts Am., Santa Rosa, Calif., 1978. Mem. Geol. Soc. Am., Am. Assn. Petroleum Geologists, Geothermal Resource Council, AAAS, Sigma Xi. Republican. Mormon. Current work: Subsurface geology and structural tectonics of geothermal areas; overthrust hydrocarbon potential provinces, basement tectonics, fractured reservoirs and regional thrusts. Subspecialties: Geology; Geothermal power. Office: McMurdie Energy Services 7418 Fire Oak Dr Austin TX 78759

MCMURRY, PETER HOWARD, mechanical engineering educator, aerosol scientist, researcher; b. Palmerton, Pa., July 5, 1947; s. Howard V. and Margaret A. (Gifford) McM.; m. Pamels Schain, May 10, 1969; children—Timothy, Nathaniel. B.A. in Physics, U. Pa., 1969; M.S. in Environ. Engring. Scis., Calif. Inst. Tech., 1973, Ph.D. in Environ. Engring. Scis. and Physics, 1977. Assoc. prof. mech. engring. U. Minn., Mpls., 1977-83, assoc. prof., 1983—; cons. clean air sci. adv. com. EPA, 1981—. Contbr. articles to prof. jours. Mem. Am. Assn. Aerosol Research, AAAS, Am. Chem. Soc., ASME, Air Pollution Control Assn., Sigma Xi. Current work: Gas-to-particle conversion; ultrafine aerosol studies; evaporation and condensation; aerosol coagulation; aerosol dynamics; acid rain, haze. Subspecialties: Atmospheric chemistry; Environmental engineering. Office: Dept Mech Engring Univ Minn 111 Church St SE Minneapolis MN 55455

MCNABB, JOHN LELAND, railroad communications engineer; b. Harvey, Ill., Apr. 19, 1931; s. John Leander and Mary Mildred (Billington) McN.; m. Georgia Diane Propper, June 20, 1953 (div. 1973); children—John Robert, Sharon Diane, Steven James, Thomas Allen. B.S.E.E., Chgo. Tech. Coll., 1959; postgrad. U. Va., 1981. Mechanic Ill. Central RR, Chgo., 1947-51, field signal engr., various locations, 1953-65; engr. communications and signals Assn. Am. RRS, Washington, 1965-72; engr. communications and signals AMTRAK, Washington, 1972-73, asst. chief engr. communications and signals, 1973-83, sr. dir. communications, Phila., 1983—; chmn. Nat. Indsl. Adv. Com. FCC, Washington, 1967-72; dir. Operational Fixed Microwave Council, Washington, 1969-72; pres. Land Mobile Communication Council, Washington, 1971-72. Served with U.S. Army, 1951-53. Mem. IEEE (sr. mem., chmn. land transp. com. Washington sect. 1982-84), ASME, Assn. Am. RRs (com. of direction 1983—). Current work: Installation and maintenance of radio frequency, land line and fiber optic transmission. Subspecialties: Solar engineering; Systems engineering. Home: 11336 Frances Dr Beltsville MD 20705 Office: Nat RR Passenger Corp AMTRAK Room 368 30th St Sta Philadelphia PA 19104

MCNAIR, JOHN WILLIAM, JR, consulting civil engineer; b. Asheville, N.C., June 17, 1926; s. John William and Annie (Woody) McN.; m. June Clemens Kratz, Apr. 8, 1950; children—Jeffry, Marsha, Cathy. B.S. in Forestry, Pa. State U., 1950; B.S. in Civil Engring., Va. Poly. Inst. and State U., 1955; postgrad. in engring. U. Va., 1957-58. Diplomate Acad. Environ. Engrs. Forester, U.S. Forest Service, Flagstaff, Ariz., 1950, U.S. Gypsum Co., Buena Vista, Va., 1951; mem. engring. faculty U. Va., Charlottesville, 1955-58; prin. John McNair & Assocs., cons., Waynesboro, Va., 1958—, Brucheum Group, Multidisciplinary Cons., Waynesboro, 1983—. Author engring. and land mgmt. study reports. Mem. Waynesboro City Council, 1968-72, vice mayor, 1970-72; chmn. Waynesboro Indsl. Devel. Authority. Served to capt. AUS, 1944-46, 51-53, France, Okinawa. Recipient Disting. Service cert. VA. Soc. Profl. Engrs., 1971. Fellow ASCE; mem. Va. State Bd. Architects, Profl. Engrs. and Land Surveyors (v.p. 1977-78, pres. 1978-79), Acad. Ind. Scholars. Republican. Presbyterian. Clubs: Rappahannock Yacht (Irvington, Va.). Lodge: Rotary (Waynesboro) (bd. dirs.). Subspecialties: Civil engineering; Water supply and wastewater treatment. Home: PO Box 1385 1805 W Main St Waynesboro VA 22980 Office: John McNair and Assocs Wayne Ave L B & B Bldg Waynesboro VA 22980

MCNALLY, JAMES HENRY, physicist; b. Orange, N.J., Dec. 18, 1936; s. James Osborne and Edith Maude (Jones) McN.; m. Nancy Lee Eudaley, July 4, 1976. B. Engring. Physics, Cornell U., 1959; Ph.D. in Physics, Calif. Inst. Tech., 1966. Staff mem., program mgr. Los Alamos Nat. Lab., N.Mex., 1965-74, assoc. div. leader, dep. for inertial fusion, asst. for nat. security issues, 1975—; asst. dir. for lasers and isotope separation tech. AEC and ERDA, Washington, 1974-75; U.S. del. mem. Geneva Conf. on Disarmament, 1969, 73, 74, Threshold Test Ban Treaty Negotiations, Moscow, 1974. Contbr. articles in field. Bd. dirs. Wilson Mesa Met. Water Dist., Colo., 1976—. Mem. Am. Phys. Soc., Internat. Inst. Strategic Studies, AAAS, Sigma Xi. Current work: Nuclear weapon technology and implications. Subspecialties: Nuclear physics; Plasma physics. Home: 550 Rim Rd Los Alamos NM 87544 Office: Los Alamos Nat Lab Box 1663 (A-105) Los Alamos NM 87545

MCNALLY, JAMES RAND, JR., fusion energy consultant; b. Boston, Nov. 10, 1917; s. James R and Margaret (Turley) McN.; m. Margaret Anne McKenna, Nov. 26, 1942; children: James Rand, Peter Joseph, Mary Ellen, Francis Edward, Anne Therese, Michael Stephen, Margaret Rose. B.S. in Physics, Boston Coll., 1939; M.S., MIT, 1941, Ph.D. in Physics, 1943. Mem. faculty MIT, 1939-48; with Oak Ridge Nat. Lab., 1948-82, sr. research physicist, until 1982, fusion energy cons., 1982—. Contbr. articles to profl. jours. Trustee Dedham Pub. Library, 1945-48. Recipient Manhattan Dist. award AEC, 1946. Fellow Optical Soc. Am. (charter), AAAS; mem. Am. Phys. Soc., Am. Assn. Physics Tchrs. Republican. Roman Catholic. Club: KC. Current Work: Advanced fuel fusion reactor development utilizing multi-MeV accelerators, interpretation of giant red spots formed in upper atmosphere by nuclear weapons tests or unusual aurora, in fusion-fission breeder prospects, in properties of nuclear dynamos fueled by fusion fuel, safety questions of large or multiple nuclear weapons explosions; aneutronic fusion, Grasers. Subspecialties: Nuclear fusion; Plasma physics. Address: 103 Norman Ln Oak Ridge TN 37830

MCNAMARA, JAMES O'CONNELL, neurologist; b. Portage, Wis., Sept. 25, 1942; s. Louis V. and Lucille M. (O'Connell) McN.; m. Anne M. Niebler, Aug. 15, 1964; children—Dennis, Brigid, James O'Connell, Michael, Brian. A.B., Marquette U., postgrad. Med. Sch., 1964-66; M.D., U. Mich., 1968. Diplomate: Am. bd. Psychiatry and Neurology; cert Am. Bd. Qualification in EEG. Asst. prof. medicine and neurology Duke U. Med. Ctr., 1975-80; dir. Epilepsy Ctr., Durham VA Med. Center-Duke U., 1976—, assoc. prof., 1980-85, prof., 1985—, asst. prof. pharmacology, 1982—; dir. Center Advanced Study of Epilepsy, 1982—; Chmn. profl. adv. bd. Epilepsy Assn. N.C., 1978-80; mem. profl. adv. bd. Epilepsy Found. Am., 1981—; mem. neurology study sect. NIH, 1984—. Contbr. articles to profl. publs. Served to maj. M.C. U.S. Army, 1971-73. NIH, VA research grantee. Mem. Am. Neurol. Assn., Am. Acad. Neurology, Soc. Neurosci., Am. Epilepsy Soc., Am. Soc. Pharmacology and Exptl. Therapeutics, Am. Soc. Clin. Investigation. Roman Catholic. Club: Chapel Hill Country. Current Work: Neurobiologic approach to epilepsy. Clinical and scientific approaches to epilepsy. Scientific disciplines utilized span morphology, pharmacology, biochemistry and physiology. Subspecialties: Neurology; Neurobiology. Office: Dept Neurology Durham VA Hos Duke U Med Center 508 Fulton St Durham NC 27705

MCNAMARA, T(HOMAS) F(RANCIS), microbiologist, immunologist educator; b. Bklyn., Jan. 26, 1928; s. Thomas Francis and Georgiana Regina (Costello) McN.; m. Virginia Anne Daly, June 27, 1953; children: Thomas J. (dec.), Michael A., Mary K., Carolyn V., Georgine T. B.S., Manhattan Coll., 1949; M.A., Hofstra U., 1950; Ph.D., Catholic U. Am., 1959. Sr. scientist Eaton Labs., Norwich, N.Y., 1957-59; sr. research asso. Am. Cyanamid Co., Pearl River, N.Y., 1959-61; asso. dir. research Warner Lambert Co., Morris Plains, N.J., 1961-72; asso. prof. Sch. Dental Medicine, SUNY-Stony Brook, 1972-85, prof., 1985—; cons. Warner Lambert, Morris Plains, 1972—, Richardson-Vick, N.Y.C., 1975-77, Johnson & Johnson, New Brunswick, N.J., 1980—, Am. Cyanamid, Morris Plains, 1982—. Organizer Conservative Party, Rockland County, N.Y.C., 1963-64. Served with U.S. Army, 1950-52. Recipient award Soc. Cosmetic Chemists, 1965, Presdl. citation Sigma Xi, 1979; Cath. U. fellow, 1955-57. Mem. AAAS, Internat. Assn. Dental Research (Leadership award N.J. chpt. 1974), N.Y. Acad. Sci., Sigma Xi. Republican. Roman Catholic. Patentee in biol. field. Current Work: Microbiology of caries and periodontal disease. Subspecialties: Microbiology; Immunobiology and immunology. Home: PO Box 44 Port Jefferson NY 11777

MCNAUGHTON, SAMUEL JOSEPH, botanist, educator; b. Takoma Park, Md., Aug. 10, 1939; s. Frank and Ruth Ellen (Flanders) McN.; m. Margaret M. Smith, Sept. 7, 1959; children: R. Sean, Erin M. B.S., N.W. Mo. State Coll., 1961; Ph.D., U. Tex., Austin, 1964. Asst. prof. biology Portland (Oreg.) State Coll., 1964-65; USPHS postdoctoral trainee Stanford U., 1965-66; asst. prof. botany Syracuse (N.Y.) U., 1966-73, prof., 1973—. Contbr. numerous articles on botany to profl. jours. Recipient Chancellors Citation Syracuse U., 1982; NSF grantee, 1966—. Fellow AAAS, Explorers Club; mem. Bot. Soc. Am., AAUP, Am. Soc. Naturalists, Ecol. Soc. Am., Brit. Ecol. Soc., Sigma Xi (Syracuse U. faculty research award 1980). Current Work: Ecology and ecosystems analysis. Subspecialties: Ecology (environmental science); Ecosystems analysis. Office: 130 College Pl Syracuse NY 13210

MCNEAL, DONALD RICHARD, rehabilitation engineer; b. Lexington, Ky., Mar. 27, 1938; s. Richard Schofield and Esther (Eisenmann) McN.; children—Kelley Jean, Kathryn Lynn. B.S. in Elec. Engring., U. Mich., 1960, M.S. in Elec. Engring., 1962; Ph.D. in Elec. Engring., Stanford U., 1967. Research analyst Lockheed Missile and Space Ctr., Palo Alto, Calif., 1962-68; sr. engr. Rancho REC, Downey, Calif., 1968-79; program mgr. NSF, Washington, 1979-80; co-dir. Rancho Rehab. Engring. Ctr., Downey, 1980—. Mem. Rehab. Engring. Soc. N.Am. (pres. 1981-82), IEEE (assoc. editor 1979—). Current work: Research related to development of neuroprostheses for functional control of extremities. Subspecialties: Biomedical engineering; Physical medicine and rehabilitation. Office: Rancho Rehab Engring Ctr 7601 E Imperial Hwy Downey CA 90242

MCNEAL, LYLE GLEN, animal scientist, educator; b. Calif., May 16, 1942; s. Darrell Glen and Elizabeth Bessie (Mista) McN.; m. Nancy Wilkie, Aug. 10, 1962; children: Tamara, Sean, Joshua, Travis, Susannah, Jenny, Ian, Ilene. B.S., Calif. Poly. State Coll., 1964; M.S., U. Nev., Reno, 1966; Ph.D., Utah State U., 1978. Asst. Mgr. Hidden Trails Ranch, Agoura, Calif., 1960-61; shepherd, dept. animal husbandry Calif. Poly. State Coll., Pomona, 1962-64; grad. research asst., div. animal sci. U. Nev., Reno, 1964-66; county agrl. extension agt. U. Nev. Coop. Extension Service, 1966-68; assoc. prof. animal sci. Calif. Poly. State U., San Luis Obispo, 1969-79; Sheep scientist U.S. Sheep Experiment Sta., DuBois, Idaho, 1974-78; dept. animal, dairy and vet. sci. Utah State U., Logan, 1979—; nat. sheep cons.; dir. Navajo Sheep Project. Active Boy Scouts Am. Recipient Disting. Teaching award Calif. Poly. State U., 1973; Cindy award Informational Film Producers Am., 1975; award of achievement Internat. Audio Visual Competition; award of achievement Soc. for Tech. Competition, 1980. Mem. Am. Soc. Animal Sci., Nat. Wool Growers Assn., Am. Assn. Sheep and Goat Practitioners, Am. Polypay Sheep Assn. (hon. life). Republican. Mormon. Current Work: Sheep production and management—systems and applied approaches; wool production and wool fiber biology; restoration of Navajo sheep germ plasm. Subspecialties: Animal breeding and embryo transplants; Animal physiology. Home: 85 Quarter Circle Dr Nibley UT 84321 Office: UMC 48 ADVS Dept Utah State U Logan UT 84322

MCNEILL, THOMAS HUGH, neuroanatomist; b. Denver, Jan. 1, 1947; s. Virgil Hugh and Gloria (Tenopir) McN.; m. Florence McNeill, July 26, 1980. B.S., Colo. State U., 1971; M.S., Colo. Stae U., 1974; Ph.D., U. Rochester, 1980. USPHS trainee U. Rochester, 1975-79, NIH postdoctoral fellow, 1979-81, research assoc., 1979-81, asst. prof. neurology, 1981—; asst. prof. oncology Cancer Ctr., 1984—. Contbr. articles to profl. jours. NIH postdoctoral fellow, 1979-81; young investigator award, 1982—; Research Career Devel. award, 1985—; Alzheimer's Disease and Related disorders Assn. grantee, 1982-83; United Cancer Council grantee, 1982-83; Nat. Inst. Neurol. Commn. Diseases and Stroke grantee, 1983—; Nat. Inst. Aging grantee, 1982—. Mem. Soc. Neurosci., Am. Aging Assn., Histochem. Soc., Brit. Brain Research Assn., European Brain and Behavioral Soc., Am. Assn. Anatomists, Am. Acad. Neurology. Current Work: Neurobiology of neurotransmitter and neuropeptide systems; immunocytochemistry, fluorescence histochemistry, senile dementia, aging, development, radiation sensitizers, Alzheimer's disease. Subspecialties: Neurobiology; Immunocytochemistry. Home: 15 Alleyn's Rise Fairport NY 14450 Office: Dept Neurology Box 673 U Rochester Rochester NY 14642

MCNULTY, IRVING BAZIL, botany educator; b. Salt Lake City, Jan. 6, 1918; s. Irving Monroe and Svea Melvina (Lindegren) McN.; m. Elizabeth Lund, Dec. 24, 1943 (div. 1967); children—Michael, Marc, Michelle; Joyce Reeder, Mar. 21, 1980. B.A., U. Utah, 1942, M.S., 1947; Ph.D., Ohio State U., 1952. Instr. to prof. U. Utah, Salt Lake City, 1947—. Contbr. articles to profl. jours. Mem. Salt Lake City Shade Tree Commn., 1960-65, Salt Lake County Canyon Planning and Zoning, 1972-81; chmn. adv. State Arboretum, 1974-80, Utah Heritage Found., 1967-73. Served to lt. USAF, 1943-45. Mem. AAAS (chmn. com. 1973, exec. council 1966-70, 78-80, 82-84), Am. Soc. Plant Physiology, Botanical Soc. Am., (chmn. sect. 1973-74), Phi Kappa Phi, Sigma Xi. Club: Lakefront Duck (bd. dirs. 1983-84). Current work: Salt metabolism and cell membrane properties of terrestrial halophytes. Subspecialties: Plant physiology (biology); Plant physiology (agriculture). Home: 4001 Oliver Dr Salt Lake City UT 84124 Office: Biology Dept U Utah Salt Lake City UT 84112

MCPHERSON, DONALD J., metallurgist. Ret. corp. exec., former chmn. Nat. Materials Adv. Bd., Washington. Subspecialty: Metallurgy. Office: care Nat Research Council Nat Materials Adv Bd 2101 Constitution Ave NW Washington DC 20418*

MCPHILLIPS, JOSEPH J(OHN), pharmacologist, clinical research scientist; b. Phila., Oct. 10, 1934; s. Joseph Francis and Anna (Armstrong) McP.; m. Margaret M. McNierney, Nov. 28, 1959; children—Mary Kathleen, Sheila, Patrick, Teresa. B.S. in Biology, St. Joseph's U., 1956; M.S. in Pharmacology, Thomas Jefferson U., 1959, Ph.D. in Pharmacology, 1962. Diplomate Am. Bd. Toxicology. Asst. prof. Med. Coll. Va., Richmond, 1962-67; assoc. prof. pharmacology W.Va. U., Morgantown, 1967-73, adj. prof., 1973—; cons. Astra Pharms., Worcester, Mass., 1966-73, assoc. dir. clin. research, 1973-81; asst. dir. clin. research G. D. Searle and Co., Skokie, Ill., 1981-85; assoc. dir. clin. research Boehringer-Mannheim Corp., Rockville, Md., 1985—. mem publs. com. Fedn. Am. Socs. Exptl. Biology, Bethesda, Md. Author profl. monographs; also chpts., numerous articles, abstracts. Field editor autonomic pharmacology Jour. Pharmacology and Exptl. Therapeutics, 1981-85, mem. editorial bd., 1981—. Recipient Mclachlan Excellence in Teaching award W.Va. U. Students, 1971, Outstanding Tchr. award W.Va. U. Faculty, 1972; grantee USPHS, NIH, 1963-73. Mem. Am. Soc. Pharmacology and Exptl. Therapeutics, Soc. Toxicology. Roman Catholic. Current work: Plan and direct clinical research to evaluate safety and efficacy of new drug products, specifically in areas of cardiovascular and gastrointestinal disease; autonomic pharmacology. Office: Boehringer-Mannheim Corp 1301 Piccard Dr Rockville MD 20850

MCQUARRIE, IRVINE GRAY, neuroscientist, neurosurgeon, educator, consultant; b. Ogden, Utah, June 27, 1939; s. Irwin Bruce and Ruby Loretta (Epperson) McQ.; m. Katharine Gamble Rogers, Mar. 11, 1967 (div.); children: Michael Gray, Mollie m. Maryann Priscilla Kaminski, Aug. 14, 1980; children—Morgan Elizabeth, Gray. B.S. in Biology, U. Utah, 1961; M.D., Cornell U., 1965, Ph.D., 1977. Diplomate: Am. Bd. Neurol. Surgery. Intern, asst. surgeon, surgeon N.Y. Hosp., N.Y.C., 1965-71, 72-73; research fellow dept. physiology Cornell U. Med. Coll., N.Y.C., 1971-72, 74-76, asst. prof. depts. physiology and surgery, 1976-81; vis. asst. prof. dept. anatomy Case-Western Res. U., Cleve., 1979-81, asst. prof. neurosurgery, 1981-85, asst. prof. devel. genetics and anatomy 1981-85, assoc. prof. neurosurgery, developmental genetics and anatomy, 1985—; clin. investigator in neurol. surgery VA Med. Center, Cleve., 1981-84, med. investigator in neurosurgery, 1984—; asst. neurosurgeon Univ. Hosps. of Cleve., 1981—. Contbr. articles to sci. jours. Served to comdr., M.C. UNSR, 1973-74. Recipient Andrew W. Mellon Tchr.-Scientist award, 1977-79; NIH fellow, 1971-72, 74-76, grantee, 1983—; VA career devel. award and individual research grantee, 1981—. Mem. AAAS, Soc. for Neurosci., Am. Soc. for Cell Biology, Am. Assn. Anatomists, Congress Neurol. Surgeons, Am. Assn. Neurol. Surgeons, Internat. Platform Assn., N.Y. Acad. Scis. Democrat. Presbyterian. Current Work: Mechanism of axonal regeneration in the central nervous system; biochemical investigations on the maintenance and replacement of nerve cell processes (called axons and dendrites) by complex intraneuronal transport mechanisms. Subspecialties: Regeneration; Neurosurgery. Office: 2119 Abington Rd Cleveland OH 44106

MCSORLEY, ROBERT, nematologist, educator, researcher; b. Cin., July 23, 1949; s. Robert T. and Mary T. (Creed) McS.; m. Rosario T. Silva, Jan. 17, 1976; 1 child, Teresa. B.S. in chemistry, U. Cin., 1971; M.S. in Biology, 1974; Ph.D. in Entomology, Purdue U., 1978. Asst. prof. nematology U. Fla., Homestead, 1978-83, assoc. prof., 1983—. Editor-in-chief: Nematropica, 1983—; assoc. editor: Hort. Sci., 1984—. Mem. Orgn. Tropical Am. Nematologists, Soc. Nematologists, Am. Soc. Hort. Sci., Fla. State Hort. Soc. Current work: Research on ecology and management of plant-parasitic nematodes. Office: Dept Entomology and Nematology U Fla Gainesville FL 32611

MCSWEENY, AUSTIN JOHN, psychology educator; b. Berwyn, Ill., May 2, 1946; s. Austin John and Erna Elanor (DeSollar) McS.; m. Jane Marilee Erickson, Sept. 28, 1968; children—Andrew John, Patrick Michael. B.A., U. Wis., 1969; M.A., No. Ill. U., 1974, Ph.D., 1975. Lic. psychologist. Intern, Baylor Coll. Medicine, Houston, 1973-74; postdoctoral fellow Northwestern U., Evanston, Ill., 1975-77, lectr., 1977-78; asst. prof. W. Va. U., Morgantown, 1978-81; asst. prof. psychology Med. Coll. Ohio, Toledo, 1981-84, assoc. prof., 1985—; cons. in field. Editor: Practical Program Evaluation, 1982. Com. mem. Am. Lung Assn., Toledo, 1981—, bd. dirs., W. Va., 1978-81. Leslie Holmes fellow, 1972. Mem. Am. Psychol. Assn., Internat. Neuropsychol. Soc., Ohio Psychol. Assn., Ohio Acad. Neuropsychology (pres.), Midwestern Psychol. Assn. Current work: Computer applications in neuropsychology; neuropsychological components of life funcioning; hypoxia and neurospsychology. Subspecialty: Neuropsychology. Home: 4146 Northmoor Rd Toledo OH 43606 Office: Med Coll Ohio CS 10008 Toledo OH 43699

MCVOY, GARY RICHARD, environmental scientist, state government transportation executive; b. Utica, N.Y., Aug. 14, 1951; s. Richard Kenneth and Rita Veronica (Newman) VcV.; m. Elaine Joan Danahy, Aug. 31, 1974; 1 child, Brian Gary. B.S. in Geology, SUNY, 1973; M.Forest Sci., Yale U., 1975, M.S., 1978, M.Phil., Ph.D., 1979. Environ. geologist Cahn Engrs., New Haven, 1974-75; pres. McD Assocs., Inc., Environ. Cons., Hamden, Conn., 1975-78; air quality modeler N.Y. State Dept. Transp., Albany, 1978-80, ecologist/hydrologist, 1980—; cons., Voorheesville, N.Y., 1979—. Author: (with L. Cohn) Environmental Analysis of Transportation Systems, 1982. Yale U. fellow, 1974, 75, 77-79. Current work: Consulting, environmental impact assessment and mitigation, low-tech solar energy applications, computer simulations especially of pollutant dosage and response. Subspecialties: Resource management; Ecology (environmental science). Office: NY State Dept Transportation 5-524 State Campus Albany NY 12232

MCWHIRTER, JAMES HERMAN, electrical engineer; b. Mercer, Pa. July 4, 1924; s. John H. and Blanche Rebecca (Anderson) M.; m. Suzanne Kibler, July 5, 1952; children—Kathleen, Meg Allyn, John R., Thomas C., Robert B. B.S., Columbia U., 1945; M.S., Carnegie Inst. Tech., 1948. Registered profl. engr., Pa. Elec. tester Gen. Electric Co., Erie, Pa., 1946-47; research asst. Carnegie Inst. Tech., Pitts., 1947-48; devel. engr. Westinghouse Co., Sharon, Pa., 1948-65, research engr. Research & Devel. Ctr., Pitts., 1965—. Contbr. articles to profl. jours. Mem. Citizens Adv. Group, Murrysville, Pa., 1975. Served to lt. (j.g.) USNR, 1943-46, PTO. Mem. IEEE (chmn. Sharon sect. 1965-66, dir. Pitts. sect. 1984—). Republican. Presbyterian. Current work: Analysis of semiconductor devices; analysis of electromagnetic fields. Subspecialties: Applied magnetics; Semiconductors. Home: 4047 W Benden Dr Murrysville PA 15668 Office: Westinghouse Research & Devel Ctr 1310 Beulah Rd Pittsburgh PA 15235

MCWRIGHT, GLEN MARTIN, electrical engineer; b. D.C., July 6, 1958; s. Cornelius Glen and Carolyn Marie (Martin) McW. B.S. in Elec. Engring., U. Va., 1980, M.E., 1981, Ph.D., 1983. Research asst. dept. elec. engring. U. Va., Charlottesville, 1980-83, teaching asst., 1983; engr. Laser Program Lawrence Livermore Nat. Lab., Livermore, Calif., 1983—. Contbr. articles to profl. jours. Bd. dirs. Ctr. Counseling and Crisis Intervention, Pleasonton, Calif., 1983—. DuPont fellow, U. Va., 1980; recipient Cert. Intermediate Honas award U. Va., 1978. Mem. IEEE, Optical Soc. Am. Republican. Episcopalian. Current work: Electro optics; quantum electronics; integrated optics. Subspecialties: Electrical engineering; Laser fusion. Home: 9200 Alcosta Bl F-3 San Ramon CA 94583 Office: Laser Program Lawrence Livermore Nat Lab L-494 Livermore CA 94550

MEAGHER, DONALD JOSEPH, engineering administrator, researcher; b. Albany, N.Y., May 2, 1949; s. John J. and Caroline H. (Glatz) M.; m. Linda Jean Stapleton, June 5, 1971; children: Kelly J., Donald F., Sean J. B.S. in Elec. Engring., Rensselaer Poly. Inst., Troy, N.Y., 1971, M.Eng. in Elec. Engring., 1972, M.Eng. in Computer and Systems Engring., 1979, Ph.D. in Elec. Engring., 1982. Assoc. electronics engr. Cornell Aero. Lab., Buffalo, 1972-74; mem. tech. staff Argo Systems, Palo Alto, Calif., 1974-77; mgr. Interactive Computer Graphics Ctr., Rensselaer Poly. Inst., 1978-80, instr., 1980-81; dir. computer graphics devel. Phoenix Data Systems, Inc., Albany, N.Y., 1981—, v.p. tech. Contbr. articles to profl. jours. Mem. IEEE, Assn. Computing Machinery, Sigma Xi. Republican. So. Baptist. Current Work: Development of "Octree" techniques for real-time solid modeling and image generation. Applications in medical imaging, CAD/CAM, simulation, cinematography, etc. Subspecialties: Graphics, image processing, and pattern recognition; Computer-aided design. Home: 18 Lynwood Dr Loudonville NY 12211 Office: Phoenix Data Systems Inc 80 Wolf Rd Albany NY 12205

MECH, LUCYAN DAVID, wildlife research biologist; b. Auburn, N.Y., Jan. 18, 1937; s. Lucyan Frank and Margaret C. (Nade) M.; m. Betty Ann Smith, Aug. 30, 1958; children—Sharon, Stephen, Nicholas, Christopher. B.S. in Conservation, Cornell U., 1958; Ph.D. in Wildlife Ecology, Purdue U., 1962. Research asst. Purdue U., West Lafayette, Ind., 1958-62; research assoc. U. Minn., St. Paul, 1963-66; asst. prof., research assoc. Macalester Coll., St. Paul, 1966-68; wildlife research biologist U.S. Fish and Wildlife Service, St. Paul, 1969—; chmn. Wolf Specialist Group Species Survival Commn., Internat. Union Conservation Nature and Natural Resources, 1978—; cons. No. Rocky Mountain Wolf Recovery Team, 1975—; mem Eastern Timber Wolf Recovery Team, 1975—. Author: Wolves of Isle Royle, 1966; The Wolf: Ecology and Behavior of an Endangered Species, 1970 (Best Wildlife Book award Symposium on Threatened and Endangered Wildlife 1974, Best Terrestnal Wildlife Publ. Wildlife Soc. 1972); Handbook of Animal Radio-Tracking, 1983; (film) Techniques of Animal Immobilization, 1983; Animal Immobilization—Techniques of Drug Delivery, 1984. Contbr. articles to profl. jours. Patentee (with R. C. Chapman and W.W. Cochran) radio-triggered anesthetic dart collar. Recipient Spl. Achievement award U.S. Fish and Wildlife Service, 1970, 81, Civil Servant of Yr. award Region III, U.S. Fish and Wildlife Service, 1973, Disting. Service in Science Edn. and Science Research award Minn. Acad. Scis., 1981, Gulf Oil Conservationist award, 1984. Mem. Am. Soc. Mammalogists, Wildlife Soc., Ecol. Soc. Am., Sigma Xi, Gamma Sigma Delta. Current work: Wolf ecology and behavior; predator-prey relations; population regulation; social ecology. Subspecialties: Wildlife biology; Behavioral ecology. Office: U S Fish and Wildlife Service North Central Forest Exptl Sta 1992 Folwell Ave Saint Paul MN 55108

MECHLIN, GEORGE FRANCIS, See *Who's Who in America,* 43rd edition.

MEDHI, NABEEL ABDEL-QADIR, veterinary pathologist, toxicology researcher; b. Kut, Iraq, July 1, 1951; came to U.S., 1978; s. Abdel Qadir and Kamela A. (Wahed) M.; m. Suha Ahmad, May 13, 1976; children—Anmar, Fadi. B.V.M.&S., Coll. Vet. Medicine, Iraq, 1973; M.S., Purdue U., 1980, Ph.D., 1984. Instr. Baghdad U., Iraq, 1974-78; instr., resident Purdue U., West Lafayette, Ind., 1978-83, prof. asst. Animal Diagnostic Lab., 1983-84; v.p., pathologist Toxicity Research Labs, Muskegon, Mich., 1984—. Contbr. articles to profl. jours. Mem. Am. Coll. Vet. Pathologists (diplomate), AVMA, Midwest Assn. Vet. Pathologists, Iraqi Med. Assn., Iraqi Vet. Med. Assn. Current work: Toxicologic pathology, mycotoxicosis, cancer research mainly long term carcinogenicity studies. Subspecialties: Toxicology (medicine); Mycotoxicosis. Home: 2337 Westwood Dr Musekgon MI 49441 Office: Toxicity Research Labs 510 W Hackley Ave Muskegon MI 49444

MEDHIN, NEGASH GABRE, mathematics educator; b. Addis Ababa, Ethiopia, Sept. 20, 1951; came to U.S. 1970; s. Gabre Medhin Wolde Giorgis and Bekelech Tessema; m. Cheryll Lynn Bowman, Feb. 27, 1983; 1 child, Danye Negash. B.S., Stanford U., 1974; Ph.D., Purdue U., 1980. Asst. prof. math. Addis Ababa U., 1980-82; vis. instr. Purdue U., West Lafayette, Ind., 1982-83; asst. prof. math. No. Ill. U., DeKalb, 1983—. Current work: Partial differential equations, optimal control theory. Subspecialties: Analysis; Applied mathematics. Office: No Ill Univ DeKalb IL 60115

MEDICUS, HEINRICH ADOLF, physicist; b. Zurich, Switzerland, Dec. 24, 1918; came to U.S., 1950; s. Friedrich Georg and Clara Anna (Frey) M.; m. Hildegard Julie Schmelz, June 15, 1961. Diploma in Natural Sci., Swiss Fed. Inst. Tech., Zurich, 1943, D.Sc., 1949. Research assoc. Swiss Fed. Inst. Tech., Zurich, 1943-50; vis. scientist radiation lab. U. Calif.-Berkeley, 1950-51; guest scientist MIT, Cambridge, 1951-52, instr., vis. asst. prof., 1952-55; assoc. prof. Rensselaer Poly. Inst., Troy, N.Y., 1955-72, prof. physics, 1972—; vis. scientist Atomic Energy Research Establishment, Harwell, Eng., 1967-68, Swiss Inst. Nuclear Research, Viligen, 1975-76. Co-author: Fields and Particles, 1973; contbr. articles on physics and history of physics to profl. jours. Swiss Found. fellow, 1950. Served to 1st lt. Swiss Army, 1938-50. Mem. Am. Phys. Soc., Swiss Phys. Soc., Soc. Wine Educators, Swiss-Am. Hist. Soc., Hudson-Mohawk Swiss Soc. (pres. 1974—), Delta Tau Delta. Presbyterian. Club: Swiss Alpine (Zurich). Current work: Experimental nuclear physics at low and intermediate energies, history of modern physics. Subspecialty: Nuclear physics. Home: East Acres Troy NY 12180 Office: Rensselaer Poly Inst Troy NY 12180

MEDITCH, JAMES STEPHEN, electrical engineering educator; b. Indpls., July 30, 1934; s. Vladimir Stephen and Sandra (Gogeff) M.; m. Theresa Claire Scott, Apr. 4, 1964; children: James Stephen, Sandra Anne. B.S. in Elec. Engring, Purdue U., 1956, Ph.D., 1961; S.M., M.I.T., 1957. Registered profl. engr., Calif. Staff engr. Aerospace Corp., Los Angeles, 1961-65; assoc. prof. elec. engring. Northwestern U., 1966-67; mem. tech. staff Boeing Sci. Research Labs., Seattle, 1967-70; prof. U. Calif., Irvine, 1970-77; prof., dept. elec. engring. U. Wash., 1977—, chmn., 1977-85, also adj. prof. computer sci. dept. Author: Stochastic Optimal Linear Estimation and Control, 1969. Editor: Computer Communication Networks, 1983. Editor Proc. proc. IEEE, 1983—. Fellow IEEE (Centennial medal 1984; Disting. mem. Control Systems Soc. 1983 mem. AAAS, Am. Soc. Engring. Edn., Assn. for Computer Machinery. Current Work: Computer-communication systems and networks, local area networks,distributed processing. Subspecialties: Computer engineering; Distributed systems and networks. Office: Dept Elec Engring FT-10 U Wash Seattle WA 98195

MEDZIHRADSKY, FEDOR, biochemist, educator; b. Kikinda, Yugoslavia, Feb. 4, 1932; came to U.S., 1966; s. Miklos and Melanie (Gettmann) M.; m. Anneliese Westmeyer Mechthild, Sept. 13, 1967; children—Sofia, Oliver. M.S. in Chemistry, Technische Hochschule Munich, Fed. Republic Germany, 1961, Ph.D. in Biochemistry, 1965. Instr. biochemistry U. Munich, 1965-66; postdoctoral assoc. U. Wis.-Madison and Washington U., St. Louis, 1966-69; asst. prof. biochemistry U. Mich., Ann Arbor, 1969-73, assoc. prof. biochemistry, 1973-81, assoc. prof. pharmacology, 1975-81, prof. biochemistry and pharmacology, 1981—, supr. biochemistry lab., Upjohn Ctr. Clin. Pharmacology, 1969-76; dir. and co-dir. biochemistry core lab. Mich. Diabetes Research and Tng. Ctr., U. Mich. Med. Ctr. 1977—; vis. assoc. prof. Stanford U., 1975-76; vis. prof. U. Calif.-San Diego, 1983-84. Contbr. articles to profl. jours. and books. Recipient Kaiser Permanente award for excellence in teaching U. Mich. Med. Sch., 1985. NIH postdoctoral fellow, 1966-69; USPHS research fellow, 1975-76. Mem. Soc. Biol. Chemistry of Germany, Am. Soc. Neurochemistry, Am. Soc. Biol. Chemists, Am. Soc. Pharmacology and Exptl. Therapeutics, AAAS. Current work: Neurochemistry; molecular pharmacology; membrane biochemistry. Subspecialties: Biochemistry (medicine); Molecular pharmacology. Office: Dept Biol Chemistry U Mich Med Sch 6440 Med Sci I Ann Arbor MI 48109

MEDZIHRADSKY, JOSEPH LADISLAS, immunologist; b. Levice, Czechoslovakia, Apr. 30, 1924; s. Joseph and Gisela (Dohany) M.; m. Zdenka Helena, Apr. 8, 1967. M.D., Comenius U., Bratislava, Czechoslovakia, 1951. Asst. prof. Comenius U. Med. Sch., 1951-60; sr. scientist Cancer Inst., Bratislava, 1960-75; vis. scientist Roswell Park Meml. Inst., Buffalo, 1974-75; sr. scientist Wellcome Research Labs., Research Triangle Park, N.C., 1975—. Eleanor Roosevelt Internat. Cancer fellow Internat. Union Against Cancer, Geneva, 1973. Mem. Am. Assn. Immunologists, Internat. Soc. Immunopharmacology. Current Work: Cellular immunology and drug interactions: manipulations in immune reactions against cancer. Subspecialties: Immunopharmacology; Transplantation.

MEE, CHARLES DENIS, researcher; b. Quorn, Leicestershire, Eng., Dec. 28, 1927; came to U.S., 1957; m. Molly Orchard, Aug. 9, 1951; 1 child, Robert. B.Sc. in Physics, London U., 1948; Ph.D. in Physics, U. Nottingham, Eng., 1951, D.Sc. in Physics, 1967. Mgmr. magnetic rec. CBS Labs., Stamford, Conn., 1957-62; mgr. magnetic devices IBM Watson Research Ctr., Yorktown, N.Y., 1962-65, mgr. advanced tech., San Jose, Calif., 1965-82, mem. corp. tech. com., Armonk, N.Y., 1976-77, mgr. Magnetic Rec. Inst., San Jose, 1982-84; IBM fellow, 1984—; mem. adv. bd. Ctr. for Magnetic Rec. Research, U. Calif.-San Diego, La Jolla, 1983—. Author: Physics of Magnetic Recording, 1964. Contbr. articles to profl. jours. Fellow IEEE (Achievement award 1964). Current work: Information storage technology; magnetic recording; beam addressable storage; magnetic film memory; magnetic materials. Office: IBM 5600 Cottle Rd San Jose CA 95193

MEEHAN, THOMAS, research biochemist; b. Youngstown, Ohio, May 16, 1942; s. Frank C. and Verona (Zanover) M.; m. Nancy Aherns, Feb. 1967; m. Susan P. Hawkes, Sept. 17, 1978. B.S., U. Akron, 1965; Ph.D., St. Louis U., 1973. Trainee Lawrence Radiation Lab., U. Calif.-Berkeley, 1973-76; biochemist Lawerence Radiation Lab., U. Calif.-Berkeley, 1976-78; research scientist Mich. Molecular Inst., Midland, 1978—; adj. prof. Case Western Res. U., 1978—; cons. in field. Contbr. articles to profl. jours. NIH grantee, 1967-73, 74-76; Nat. Cancer Inst. grantee, 1979—. Mem. AAAS, Am. Assn. Cancer Research, Am. Chem. Soc., Biophys. Soc. Current Work: Molecular mechanisms of tumor initiation by chemical carcinogens. Subspecialties: Cancer research (medicine); Molecular biology. Office: 1910 W St Andrews Rd Midland MI 48640

MEEKER, RALPH DENNIS, physics educator; b. Chgo., Nov. 15, 1945; s. Ralph and Mary (Nobile) M., m. Pamela R. Pulver, Sept. 7, 1968; children—Michelle, Mark. B.S., Ill. Benedictine Coll., 1967; Ph.D., Iowa State U., 1970. Instr. Iowa State U., Ames, 1970; asst. prof., physics Ill. Benedictine Coll., Lisle, 1970-73, assoc. prof., 1973-78, prof., 1978—; pres. Exradin, Inc., Warrenville, Ill., 1978—; vis. prof. Argonne Nat. Lab., 1971-74. Chmn. bldg. com. St. Margaret Mary Ch., Naperville, Ill., 1982-84. Recipient Mgmt. award Chgo. Community Trust, 1980. Mem. Am. Phys. Soc., Am. Assn. Physics Tchrs., Ill. Acad. Sci. Roman Catholic. Current work: Radiation dosimetry; applications of microcomputers. Subspecialties: Nuclear physics; Medical physics. Office: Ill Benedictine Coll 5700 College Rd Lisle IL 60532

MEEKINS, JOHN FRED, astrophysicist; b. Boston, Oct. 4, 1937; s. Donald Fred and Signe (Bjork) M.; m. C. Ann.Turner, Sept. 9, 1961; children: David George, Brian John. B.A., Bowdoin Coll., 1959; Ph.D., Cath. U. Am., 1973. Research physicist Naval Research Lab., Washington, 1959-79, astrophysicist, 1979—. Contbr. articles to profl. jours. Asst. scoutmaster Boy Scouts Am., 1980-82, scoutmaster, 1982—. Mem. Am. Astron. Soc., Sigma Xi. Current Work: Study of high energy astrophys. objects, by means of their radiation, especially X-Ray emission. Subspecialties: High energy astrophysics; X-ray high energy astrophysics. Home: 5674 Ravenel Ln Springfield VA 22151 Office: Code 4125 Naval Research Lab Washington DC 20375

MEEKS, JAMES LAVERNE, chemistry educator, researcher, consultant; b. Harlan, Ky., Oct. 4, 1939; s. James R. and Anna Marie (Brown) M.; m. Peggy L. Taylor, Aug. 10, 1963; 1 child, Suzanne. B.S., Cumberland Coll., 1962; postgrad. Purdue U., 1962-64; Ph.D., La. State U., 1974. Prof., head chemistry dept. Cumberland Coll., Williamsburg, Ky., 1964-78; prof., chmn. chemistry dept. Murray State U., Ky., 1978-82, vis. prof. physics, 1983-84; lectr. dept. chemistry So. Ill. U., Carbondale, 1984—; cons. Triple E Research Inst., Murray, 1978—. Contbr. articles to profl. jours. Mem. Am. Chem. Soc. (chmn. Ky. Lake sect. 1981), Ky. Acad. Sci. (chmn. chemistry div. 1980). Baptist. Club: Optimists (bd. dirs. 1980-85). Current work: Photoelectron spectroscopy, carbonyls, dicarbonyls, transfer of electrons, molecular orbitals, ferroelasticity, theoretical computations. Subspecialties: Physical chemistry; Theoretical chemistry. Home: 1615 Cardinal Dr Murray KY 42071 Office: Dept Chemistry and Biochemistry So Ill U Carbondale IL 62901

MEEKS, MARION LITTLETON, astronomer, physicist, researcher; b. Gainesville, Ga., Oct. 1, 1923; s. Jesse Littleton and Ione (Tumlin) M.; m. Bennie Scurry Stone, May 25, 1944 (div.); children: Marshall, Fleming, Marion; m. Louise Ann Vogt, Aug. 14, 1970; children: Lita, Mariano. B.S., Ga. Inst. Tech., 1943, M.S., 1947; Ph.D., Duke U., 1950. Asst. prof., assoc. prof. physics Ga. Inst. Tech., Atlanta, 1951-59; assoc. Harvard Coll. Obs., Cambridge, Mass., 1959-61; staff MIT Lincoln Lab., Lexington, 1961-70, research staff, 1978—; head radio astronomy ops. Haystack Obs., Westford, Mass., 1970-78; adj. prof. astronomy U. Mass., Amherst, 1971-75; researcher; film maker. Editor: Radio Telescopes and Observations, 1976; author: Radar Propagation at Low Altitudes, 1982; contbr. sci. papers to publs; author computer-generated astronomy films. Served to lt. j.g. USN, 1943-46. Mem. Internat. Astron. Union, Internat. Sci. Radio Union, Am. Astron. Soc., Sigma Xi. Episcopalian. Club: Valley Pond (Lincoln). Current work: Remote sensing from satellites, radio and microwave propagation studies, computer animation for video and films. Subspecialties: Radio and microwave astronomy; Remote sensing (atmospheric science). Home: Stonehenge RFD 4 Lincoln MA 01773 Office: MIT Lincoln Lab PO Box 73 Lexington MA 02173

MEEKS, ROBERT G., toxicologist educator, researcher; b. Columbus, Ohio, Jan. 24, 1942. B.S., Otterbein Coll., Westerville, Ohio, 1972; Ph.D., Ohio State U., 1978. Staff fellow NIH Nat. Cancer Inst., Bethesda, Md., 1978-80; research toxicologist So. Research Inst., Birmingham, 1980-81, head toxicology div., 1981-84; assoc. prof. toxicology U. Ala., Birmingham, 1984—; cons. in field. Mem Soc. Toxicology, Am. Coll. Toxicology, Am. Assn. Cancer Research, Am. Soc. Pharmacology and Exptl. Therapeutics. Subspecialties: Environmental toxicology; Toxicology (medicine). Office: U Ala University Station Birmingham AL 35294

MEEKS, STEVEN WAYNE, research physicist; b. Indpls., Feb. 1, 1952; s. Lloyd Milton and Lois Ann (Burton) M. B.S., U. Central Fla., 1974, M.S., 1977; M.S., Stanford U., 1983, Ph.D., 1985. Phys. sci. aide Naval Research Lab., Orlando, Fla., 1972-74; research physicist, 1974-81, Naval Research Lab. fellow at Stanford U., Calif., 1981—. Contbr. articles to sci. jours. Recipient publ. award Naval Research Lab., 1975, 79, 80, 83, spl. achievement award, 1974. Mem. Am. Phys. Soc., IEEE, Acoustical Soc. Am. Democrat. Current work: Acoustical and optical device applications of ferroelastics, ferroelectrics, and ferromagnetics. Subspecialties: Acoustics; Optical signal processing. Home: 541 Del Medio Ave Apt 238 Mountain View CA 94040 Office: Dept Applied Physics Stanford U Stanford CA 94305

MEEM, JAMES LAWRENCE, JR., nuclear scientist; b. N.Y., Dec. 24, 1915; s. James Lawrence and Phyllis (Deaderick) M.; m. Buena Vista Speake, Sept. 5, 1940; children: James, John. B.S., Va. Mil. Inst., 1939; M.S., Ind. U., 1947, Ph.D., 1949. Aero. research sci. NACA, 1940-46; dir. bulk shielding reactor Oak Ridge Nat. Lab., 1950-53, in charge nuclear operation aircraft reactor expt., 1954-55; chief reactor sci. Alco Products, Inc., 1955-57; in charge startup and initial testing Army Package Power Reactor, 1957; prof. nuclear engring. U. Va., Charlottesville, 1957-81, dept. chmn., dir. reactor facility, 1957-77, prof. emeritus, 1981—; cons. U.S. Army Fgn. Sci. and Tech. Ctr., 1981—; vis. cons. nuclear fuel cycle programs Sandia Labs., Albuquerque, 1977-78; vis. staff mem. Los Alamos Sci. Lab., 1967-68; mem. U.S.-Japan Seminar Optimization of Nuclear Engring. Edn., Tokai-mura, 1973. Author: Two Group Reactor Theory, 1964. Fellow Am. Nuclear Soc. (sec. reactor ops. div. 1966-68, vice chmn. 1968-70, chmn. 1970-71, Exceptional Service award 1980); mem. Am. Phys. Soc., Am. Soc. Engring. Edn., SAR. Subspecialties: Nuclear fission; Nuclear engineering. Home: Mount Airy RFD 12 Box 45 Charlottesville VA 22901

MEENAKSHI SUNDARAM, KANDASAMY, engineer, researcher; b. Tirumangalam, India, Dec. 24, 1949; came to U.S., 1980; s. Kandasamy Muthusamy and Mahamayee Kandasamy; m. Selvamani, Mar. 26, 1979; 1 child, Varuna. B.Tech., Madras U., India, 1972; M.E., Indian Inst. Sci., Bangalore, 1974; Ph.D., State U. Ghent, Belgium, 1977. Research asst. U. Ghent, 1977-79; postdoctoral fellow U. Del.-Newark, 1980-81; prin. engr. Lummus Crest Inc., Bloomfield, N.J., 1981—. Mem. Am. Inst. Chem. Engrs., Am. Chem. Soc. Current work: Reactor design, mathematical modeling of chemical reactors and chemical kinetics, computer control and optimization of chemical plants. Subspecialties: Chemical engineering; Numerical analysis (computer science). Home: 157-H Meriline Ave West Paterson NJ 07424 Office: Lummus Crest Inc 1515 Broad St Bloomfield NJ 07003

MEGEL, HERBERT, toxicologist; b. Newark, Nov. 10, 1926; s. Benjamin Abraham and Anna (Geller) M.; m. Eleanor Sitzman, Jan. 20, 1951; children—Diana, Joseph. B.A., N.Y. U., 1948, M.S., 1950, Ph.D., 1954. Diplomate: Am. Bd. Toxicology. Dir. bioassay Princeton Labs. Inc., 1954-59; sr. research physiologist Boeing Co., Seattle, 1959-62; dir. biochemistry Nat. Drug. Co., Phila., 1962-70; sect. head immunology Merrell-Nat. Labs., Cin., 1970-78; sr. research toxicologist pathology-toxicology dept. Merrell Dow Research Inst., Cin., 1978—. Contbr. articles and book chpts. to profl. lit. Fellow N.Y. Acad. Sci.; mem. Am. Soc. Immunologists, Am. Soc. Pharmacology and Exptl. Therapeutics, Soc. Toxicology, Phi Beta Kappa. Current Work: Immunopharmacology, immunotoxicology, compliance with good laboratory practice. Subspecialties: Pharmaceutical toxicology; Immunotoxicology. Home: 1250 Forest Ct Cincinnati OH 45205 Office: 2110 E Galbraith Rd Cincinnati OH 45215

MEGGET, LESLIE MAKEPEACE, architectural science educator, structural consultant; b. Wellington, N.Z., July 31, 1946; s. Ronald Calverley and Alice Joyce (Weeber) M.; m. Shirley Christine Meikle, Oct. 23, 1976; children—Katrina Joy, Bruce Leslie. B.E. in Civil Engring., Canterbury U., Christchurch, N.Z., 1968, M.E., 1971; diploma Internat. Inst. Seismology and Earthquake Engring., Tokyo, 1972. Registered engr., N.Z. Asst. engr. Ministry Works and Devel., Wellington, 1969-73, sr. engr., 1974-77; sr. lectr. Victoria U., Wellington, 1977—; cons. several archtl. offices, Wellington, 1978—. Editor Bull. N.Z. Nat. Soc. for Earthquake Engring., 1980-84. Contbr. articles to profl. jours. Fellow UNESCO, Tokyo, 1971-72. Fellow N.Z. Nat. Soc. Earthquake Engring. (tech. conf. organizer 1979, mgmt. com. 1979-84, reconnaissance team mem. 1982—, Otto Glogau award 1981); mem. Instn. Profl. Engrs. N.Z. (br. com. 1973-75, Fulton Gold medal 1972; Freyssinet award 1976, 82), N.Z. Timber Soc., N.Z. Concrete Soc. (council 1979). Clubs: Alfa Romeo Owners (com. 1982-85), Austin Healey Car (com. 1979-85). Lodge: Loyal Antipodean. Current work: Base isolation of buildings, structural design of reinforced concrete beam column joints, timber design, general seismic analysis and designs. Subspecialties: Structural engineering; Materials (engineering). Home: 59 Karepa St Wellington 2 New Zealand Office: Victoria U Sch Architecture Private Bag Wellington 1 New Zealand

MEGGS, WILLIAM JOEL, physician, immunologist; b. Newberry, S.C., May 30, 1942; s. Wallace N. and Elizabeth (Pruitt) M.; m. Susan Spring, June 11, 1966; children—Jason, Benjamin, Thomas. B.S., Clemson U., 1964; Ph.D., U. Syracuse, 1969; M.D., U. Miami, 1979. Diplomate Am. Bd. Internal Medicine. Vis. scientist CERN, Geneva, 1969; research scientist U. Rochester, N.Y., 1969-71, McGill U., Montreal, Que., Can., 1971-77; intern Rochester Gen. Hosp., 1979-80, resident, 1980-82; med. staff fellow NIH, Bethesda, Md.,

1982—. Contbr. articles to profl. jours. Mem. ACP, Am. Assn. Immunologists. Subspecialties: Immunobiology and immunology; Immunology (medicine). Office: NIH Bldg 10 Room 11C212 Bethesda MD 20205

MEHENDALE, HARIHARA MAHADEVA, toxicologist, educator; b. Philya, India, Jan 12, 1942; came to U.S., 1963, naturalized, 1969; s. Shinginkodlu Mahadeva Bhat and Narmada (Mahadeva) M.; m. Rekha H. Mehendale, Mar. 5, 1947; children: Roopa, Neelesh. B.Sc., Karnatak U., Dharwar, India, 1963; M.S. in Physiology, N.C. State U., 1966, Ph.D., 1969. Diplomate: Am. Bd. Toxicology, Acad. Toxicol. Scis. Postdoctoral fellow in toxicology U. Ky., 1969-71; vis. fellow Nat. Inst. Environ. Health Scis., 1971-72, staff fellow, 1972-75; asst. prof. dept. pharmacology and toxicology U. Miss. Med. Center, Jackson, 1975-78, asso. prof., 1978-80, prof., 1980—, dir. toxicology tng. program, 1982-; vis. prof. forensic medicine Karolinska Inst., Stockholm, 1983-84; also cons.; mem. adv. panel toxicology study sect. NIH, 1981-85; FASEB vis. prof. for minority instns., 1983—. Contbr. numerous articles and chpts. to sci. lit.; editorial bd.: Fundamental and Applied Toxicology, Jour. Toxicology and Environ. Health; overseas editor Indian Jour. Pharmacology. Pres. India Assn. of Miss. Mem. Am. Soc. Pharmacology and Exptl. Therapeutics, Soc. Toxicology India, Am. Chem. Soc., Internat. Soc. Study Xenobiotics, Am. Thoracic Soc., Internat. Union Pharmacology (sect. toxicology), AAAS, Assn. Scientists of Indian Origin in Am., Indian Sci. Congress Assn., Entomol. Soc. Am., Entomol. Soc. India, Miss. Acad. Scis., Miss. Heart Assn., Sigma Xi (chpt. pres. 1982-83). Current Work: Environmental toxicology. Subspecialties: Toxicology (agriculture); Environmental toxicology. Office: U Miss Med Center Dept Pharmacology/Toxicology 2500 N State St Jackson MS 39216-4505

MEHRA, RAMAN KUMAR, systems company executive, researcher; b. Lahore, Pakistan, Feb. 10, 1943; came to U.S., 1964, naturalized 1978; s. Madan M. and Vidya V. (Khanna) M.; m. Anjoo Talwar, Dec. 13, 1968; children—Archana, Madira, Kunal. B.E.E., Punjab Engring. Coll., Chandigarh, India, 1964; M.S., Harvard U., 1965, Ph.D., 1968. Research assoc. Harvard U., Cambridge, Mass., 1964-67, assoc. prof., 1972-76; mem. tech. staff Analytic Scis., Reading, Mass., 1967-69; sr. research engr., div. mgr. Systems Control, Inc., Palo Alto, Calif., 1969-72; pres., founder Sci. Systems, Cambridge, 1976—. Recipient Eckman award Am. Automatic Control Council, 1971; Automatica prize paper award Internat. Fedn. Automatic Control, 1984. Mem. IEEE, AIAA, Ops. Research Soc. Am./Inst. Mgmt. Scis., Nat. Security Indsl. Assn. (bd. dirs. New Eng. 1981—). Current work: Control system design, computer simulation, stability analysis, optimal control and estimation, numerical solution of optimization problems, adaptive and stochastic control. Subspecialties: Software engineering; Numerical analysis (computer science). Home: 5 Angier Rd Lexington MA 02173 Office: Scientific Systems Inc 54 Cambridge Park Dr Cambridge MA 02140

MEHRABADI, M MORTEZA M., mechanical engineer, educator, researcher; b. Tehran, Iran, July 11, 1947; came to U.S., 1972; s. Ali Mirzaie and Mehri (Alipoor) M.; m. Fatemeh Ashraf Mirahmadi, June 6, 1975; 1 child, Roxana. B.S.M.E., Tehran U., 1969; M.S., Tulane U., 1973, Ph.D., 1979. Research asst. dept. mech. engring. Tulane U., 1973-79, asst. prof. mech. engring., 1982-85, assoc. prof., 1985—; postdoctoral fellow and lectr. dept. civil engring. Northwestern U., Evanston, Ill., 1979-82. Contbr. articles to profl. jours. Mem. Am. Acad. Mechanics, ASME, Soc. Engring. Sci., Sigma Xi, Tau Beta Pi. Current Work: Continuum mechanics, elasticity, plasticity, mechanics of granular materials. Office: Dept Mech Engring Tulane U New Orleans LA 70118

MEHRAN, FARROKH, physicist, researcher; b. Tehran, June 29, 1936; came to U.S., 1955; s. Hossein and Mansoureh (Mashayekhy) M.; m. Mitra Partovi, Feb. 2, 1963; children—Hooman, Reyhan. B.S., U. Calif.-Berkeley, 1959; Ph.D., Harvard U., 1964. Research fellow Harvard U., 1964-65; asst. prof. physics Calif. State U.-Sacramento, 1965-67; staff physicist IBM, Gaithersburg, Md., 1967-69, research staff mem. Watson Research Ctr., Yorktown Heights, N.Y., 1970—. Contbr. articles to profl. jours. Patentee optical logic, 1972. Mem. Am. Phys. Soc. Current work: Molecular beams, quantum electronics, magnetic resonance. Subspecialties: Condensed matter physics; Magnetic physics. Home: 44 Florence Dr Chappaqua NY 10514 Office: IBM Watson Research Ctr Yorktown Heights NY 10598

MEHRAVARI, NADER, electrical engineer, researcher; b. Teheran, Iran, May 15, 1956; came to U.S., 1974, naturalized 1984; s. Ali and Sima (Etminan) M.; m. Judith L. Cosens; 1 child, Peter C. B.S.E.E., George Washington U., 1980; M.S.E.E., Cornell U., 1980, Ph.D., 1982. Lab. technician George Washington U., Washington, 1978; grad. teaching asst. Cornell U., Ithaca, N.Y., 1978-80, grad. research asst., 1980-82, postdoctoral research assoc., 1982; mem. tech. staff Bell Labs., Holmdel, N.J., 1982—. Mem. IEEE (Outstanding Achievement award 1977), Sigma Xi, Eta Kappa Nu, Tau Beta Pi. Current work: Computer communication networks, information theory, applied probability. Subspecialties: Electrical engineering; Probability. Home: 19 Coventry Dr Freehold NJ 07728 Office: Bell Labs Holmdel NJ 07733

MEHRING, JAMES WARREN, electrical engineer; b. Denver, June 15, 1950; s. Clinton Warren and Carol Jane (Adams) M.; B.S., Colo. State U., 1972; M.S., UCLA, 1974; Engr., Stanford U., 1981, Ph.D., 1983. Mem. tech. staff Hughes Aircraft Co., Los Angeles, 1972-77, project engr., Sunnyvale, Calif., 1977-81, sr. project engr., 1981-83, project mgr., 1983—. Author: Satellite Applications of Amplitude Companded Single Sideband, 1983. Mem. IEEE, AIAA, ASME. Republican. Methodist. Current work: Satellite communications systems. Subspecialties: Electronics; Satellite studies. Home: 4005 Old Mill Rd Alexandria VA 22309 Office: Hughes Aircraft Co 1000 Wilson Blvd Arlington VA

MEHROTRA, ASHOK KUMAR, propellant chemist; b. Varanasi, India, Jan. 15, 1949; came to U.S., 1979; naturalized, 1982; s. Hiralal and Vijay (Kumari) M.; m. Vibha, Feb. 15, 1976; children—Meghna, Sunny. M.Sc., Kanpur U., India, 1969; Ph.D., Indian Inst. Tech., Kanpur, 1976. Sr. chemist Indian Drugs and Pharms. Ltd., Hyderabad, India, 1976-79; postdoctoral assoc. Marquette U., Milw., 1979-80, U. So. Calif., Los Angeles, 1980-82; sr. propellant chemist Olin Corp., Marion, Ill., 1982—. Contbr. numerous articles to profl. jours. Recipient Dr. R.R. Agarwal Gold medal Kanpur U., 1969, Mrs. J.D. Jaipuria Gold medal, 1969. Fellow India Assn. So. Ill., Am. Chem. Soc., N.Y. Acad. Sci. Current work: Development of new energetic binder systems and its application to propellant formulations, and new synthetic methods. Subspecialty: Synthetic chemistry. Home: 37 Mockingbird Carterville IL 62918 Office: Olin Corp PO Drawer G Marion IL 61959

MEHTA, BIPIN MOHANLAL, microbiologist; b. Bombay, India, July 25, 1935; s. Mohanlal Jamnadas and Vimala (Harkisondas) M.; m. Varsha Bipin Mehta, May. 8, 1960. Ph.D., U. Bombay, 1963. Lectr. nutrition U. Bombay, 1963-65; research assoc., teaching asst. SUNY Downstate Med. Center, 1965-66; vis. research fellow Sloan-Kettering Inst. Cancer Research, N.Y.C., 1966-69, research assoc., 1972-74, assoc., 1974-81, asst. mem., 1982—; instr. microbiology Grad. Sch. Med. Scis., Cornell U., 1973-75, asst. prof. biology unit, 1975-80, pharmacology and exptl. therapeutics unit, 1980—; research assoc. U. Ottawa, 1969-72; adj. prof. dept. chemistry and phys. scis. Pace U., Pleasantville, N.Y., 1985—. Contbr. articles to profl. jours. Bd. Dirs. Westchester div. Am. Cancer Soc. Mem. Am. Soc. Microbiology, Can. Soc. Cell Biology, Soc. Gen. Microbiology (U.K.), AAAS, N.Y. Acad. Scis., Am. Assn. Cancer Research, Am. Soc. Clin. Oncology. Current Work: Microbial genetics, physiology and nutrition with pharmacology of anticancer agents; molecular biology of cancer cell. Subspecialties: Microbiology; Pharmacokinetics. Office: 145 Boston Post Rd Rye NY 10580

MEHTA, NARIMAN BOMANSHAW, research scientist; b. Bombay, India, Apr. 8, 1920; came to U.S., 1947; s. Bomanshaw Hormazjedi and Dhunbai M.; children—Perrin Lynne, Norman Mehta, Anita June. B.Sc., St. Xavier's Coll., 1941, B.A., 1942; Ph.D., U. Kans., 1952. Lectr. physics U. Bombay, 1941-46; trainee Seagram & Sons, Inc., Louisville, 1947-48; fellow U. Toronto, Ont., Can., 1953-54; prof. chemistry Central State U., Wilberforce, Ohio, 1954-57; sr. research scientist Wellcome Research Labs., Research Triangle Labs., 1957-77, prin. scientist, 1977—; cons. in field. Author: (with K.D. Irani) Theory and Practical Physics for Intermediates, 1948. Contbr. articles to profl. jours. Patentee in field. Am. Inst. Chemists fellow, 1983. Fellow Royal Soc. Chemistry; mem. Am. Chem. Soc. Republican. Current work: Design and research of central nervous system drugs, antidepressents, anti-anxiety and anxiolytics; design of cardiovascular drugs. Subspecialties: Neurochemistry; Organic chemistry. Home: 4207 Union St Raleigh NC 27609 Office: Burroughs Wellcome Co 3030 Cornwallis Rd Research Triangle Park NC 27709

MEHTA, NOSHIR RUSTOM, periodontist, educator; b. Secunderabad, A.P., India, Mar. 5, 1945; came to U.S., 1969, naturalized, 1981; s. Rustom Cawasha and Sooni R. (Darabsha) M.; m. Dara Rosenblatt, Nov. 10, 1977; 1 dau., Larina Noshir. B.D.S., Punjab Govt. Dental Coll. and Hosp., Amritsar, India, 1967; M.D.S. in Periodontics, Govt. Dental Coll., Lucknow, India, 1969; M.S. in Peridontics, Tufts U., 1973, D.M.D., 1976. Research assoc. Dental Sch. Tufts U., 1970-71; clin. instr. 1971-73, asst. prof., 1973-75, clin. instr., 1975-77, asst. clin. prof., 1977-82, assoc. clin. prof., 1983—, co-dir. cranio-mandibular pain dysfunction ctr., 1979—; periodontal cons. USPHS Hosp., Brighton, Mass., 1974-81, Dental Service Corp Mass., Boston, 1980—, Indsl. Accident Bd. Mass., Boston, 1979—. Contbr. articles to profl. jours. Fellow Internat. Acad. Dental Studies (internat. liaison officer 1982—); mem. Mass. Periodontal Soc., Am. Acad. Periodontology, ADA, Mass. Dental Soc., Internat. Assn. Dental Research, Indian Acad. Periodontology (hon.). Zorastrian. Current Work: Research in cranio-mandibular and cervical dysfunctions and research in clinical periodontology and dental occlusion. Subspecialties: Periodontics; Cranio-mandibular cervical pain and dysfunction. Office: 77 Commercial St Boston MA 02181

MEHTA, RAJENDRA G., cell biologist; b.; b. Dabhoi, India, Aug. 31, 1947; s. Govindlal H. and Arvinda G. (Vora) M.; m. Raksha R. Mehta, Feb. 23, 1976; 1 child, Sonkulp. M.Sc., Gujarat U., Ahmedabad, India, 1968; Ph.D., U. Nebr., 1974. Research asst. U. Nebr., Lincoln, 1971-74; research assoc. U. Rochester (N.Y.) Sch. Medicine and Cancer Center, 1974-76, U. Louisville Sch. Medicine, 1976-77; research scientist Ill. Inst. Tech. Research Inst., Chgo., 1978-80, sr. biochemist, 1980—. Contbr. articles to profl. jours. Mem. Am. Assn. Cancer Research. Hindu. Current Work: Mechanism of hormone and retinoid action during normal and neoplastic differentiation of mammary gland. Subspecialties: Cancer research (medicine); Receptors. Home: 16537 S 76th Ave Tinley Park IL 60477 Office: 10 W 35th St Chicago IL 60616

MEIER, MARK FREDERICK, glaciologist; b. Iowa City, Iowa, Dec. 19, 1925; s. Norman Charles and Clea (Grimes) M.; m. Barbara McKinley, Sept. 16, 1955; children—Lauren Gale, Mark Stephen, Gretchen Ann. B.S. in Elec. Engring., State U. Iowa, 1949, M.S. in Geology, 1951; Ph.D. in Geology and Applied Mechanics, Calif. Inst. Tech, 1957. Postgrad. researcher U. Innsbruck, Austria, 1955-56; geol. engr. U.S. Bur. Reclamation, Coulee Dam., Wash., 1948, 49; geologist U.S. Geol. Survey, Big Delta, Alaska, 1951; instr. geology Occidental Coll., Los Angeles, 1952-55; leader Crevasse Study Expedition, North Greenland, 1955; project chief glaciology U.S. Geol. Survey, Tacoma, Wash., 1956-85; dir. Inst. Arctic and Alpine Research, U. Colo., Boulder, 1985—; vis. prof. Dartmouth Coll., Hanover, N.H., 1964; affiliate prof. geophysics U. Wash., Seattle, 1964—; dir. World Data Ctr. A-Glaciology, Tacoma, 1970-75; chmn. com. glaciology Nat. Acad. Scis., Washington, 1981-84, mem. polar research bd., 1981-84. Contbr. articles to profl. jours. Served with USN, 1944-46. Fulbright fellow, 1955-56; recipient Antarctic Service medal, U.S. Govt. Disting. Service award, U.S. Dept. Interior, 1970, 3 medals Acad. Scis. USSR, 1970-85, Sigma Xi award, 1957. Fellow Am. Geophys. Union, AAAS, Geol. Soc. Am., others; mem. Internat. Assn. Hydrol. Scis. (pres. 1979-83), Internat. Commn. Snow Ice (pres. 1969-71), Internat. Glaciol. Soc. (v.p. 1966-69, hon. mem. 1980, Seligman Crystal award 1985). Current work: glaciology, mountain and polar earth sciences. Subspecialty: Arctic studies. Office: Inst Arctic and Alpine Research U Colo Campus Box 450 Boulder CO 80309

MEIER, MICHAEL MCDANIEL, nuclear physicist; b. Chgo., Oct. 14, 1940; s. Albert Hans and Margaret Laura (Toman) M.; m. Frances Colclough Dick, Mar. 7, 1970; children—Margaret Colclough, Albert Paul. B.S., St. Procopius Coll., Lisle, Ill., 1962; Ph.D., Duke U., 1969. Physicist, Nat. Bur. Standards, Gaithersburg, Md., 1970-80; mem. staff Los Alamos Nat. Lab., 1980—. Contbr. articles to profl. publs. Mem. AAAS. Republican. Roman Catholic. Current work: (p,n) reactions, neutron detectors, neutron flux measurements, spallation sources (n,Y) discrimination. Subspecialty: Nuclear physics. Office: Los Alamos Nat Lab Box 1663 MS H805 Los Alamos NM 87545

MEIER, WILBUR LEROY, JR., educator, university dean; b. Elgin, Tex., Jan. 3, 1939; s. Wilbur Leroy and Ruby (Hall) M.; m. Judy Lee Longbotham, Aug. 30, 1958; children: Melynn, Marla, Melissa. B.S., U. Tex., 1962, M.S., 1964, Ph.D., 1967. Planning engr. Tex. Water Devel. Bd., Austin, 1962-66, cons., 1967-72; research engr. U. Tex., Austin, 1966; asst. prof. indsl. engring. Tex. A&M U., College Station, 1967-68, asso. prof., 1968-70, prof., 1970-73, asst. head dept. indsl. engring., 1972-73; prof., chmn. dept. indsl. engring. Iowa State U., Ames, 1973-74; prof., head sch. of indsl. engring. Purdue U., West Lafayette, Ind., 1974-81; dean Coll. Engring., Pa. State U., University Park, 1981—; cons. Indsl. Research Inst., St. Louis, 1979, Environments for Tomorrow, Inc., Washington, 1970—, Water Resources Engrs., Inc., Walnut Creek, Calif., 1969-70, Computer Graphics, Inc., Bryan, Tex., 1969-70, Kaiser Engrs., Oakland, Calif., 1971, Tracor, Inc., Austin, 1966-68; cons. div. planning coordination Tex. Gov.'s Office, 1969; cons. Office of Tech. Assessment, 1982—, Southeast Ctr. for Elec. Engring. Edn., 1978—; mem. rev. team Naval Research Adv. Com. Editor: Marcel Dekker Pub. Co., 1978—; Contbr. articles to profl. jours. Named Outstanding Young Engr. of Year Tex. Soc. Profl. Engrs., 1966; USPHS fellow, 1966. Fellow Inst. Indsl. Engrs. (dir. ops. research div. 1975, pres. Ind. chpt. 1976, program chmn. 1973-75, editorial bd. Trans., publ. chmn., newsletter editor engring. economy div. 1972-73, v.p. region VIII 1977-79, exec. v.p. chpt. ops. 1981-83, pres.-elect 1984-85, pres. 1985-86). Mem. Ops. Research Soc. Am., Inst. Mgmt. Scis. (v.p. S.W. chpt. 1971-72), ASCE (sec.-treas. Austin br. 1965-66, chmn. research com., tech. council water resources planning and mgmt. 1972-74), Nat. Soc. Profl. Engrs. (bd. govs., vice chmn. N.E. div. 1985—), Ind. Soc. Profl. Engrs., Am. Soc. for Engring. Edn. (chmn. indsl. engring. div. 1978-83), Am. Assn. Engring. Socs. (bd. govs.), Am. Soc. for Engring. Edn. (pres. Tex. A&M U. chpt. 1971-72), Nat. Assn. State Univ. and Land Grant Colls. (mem. engring. legis. task force 1983—), Assn. Engring. Colls. Pa. (treas. 1982, v.p. 1984-85, pres. 1985-86), Sigma Xi, Tau Beta Pi, Alpha Pi Mu (asso. editor Cogwheel 1970-75, regional dir. 1976-77, exec. v.p. 1977-80, pres. 1980-82), Phi Kappa Phi, Chi Epsilon. Club: Rotary. Subspecialties: Industrial engineering; Operations research (engineering). Home: 596 Shadow Ln State College PA 16803 Office: Coll Engring 101 Hammond Bldg Pennsylvania State U University Park PA 16802

MEINDL, JAMES DONALD, electrical engineer; b. Pitts., Apr. 20, 1933; s. Louis M. and Elizabeth F. (Steinhauser) M.; m. Frederica Ziegler, May 21, 1961; children: Peter James, Candace Ann. B.S., Carnegie Mellon U., 1955, M.S., 1956, Ph.D., 1958. Engr. Autonetics Co., Downey, Calif., 1957, Westinghouse Co., Pitts., 1958-59; head sect. microelectronics U.S. Army Electronics Command, Ft. Monmouth, N.J., 1959-62, chief br. semicondr. and microelectronics, 1962-65, dir. div. integrated electronics, 1965-67; assoc. prof. elec. engring. Stanford U., 1967-70, prof., 1970—, John M. Fluke prof. elec. engring., 1984—, dir. integrated circuits lab., 1967-84, dir. Electronics Labs., 1972—, dir. Center Integrated Systems, 1981—; dir. Telesensory Systems Inc., Palo Alto, Calif., 1971-84; cons. to govt., industry. Author: Micropower Circuits, 1969; contbr. numerous articles to profl. publs. Served to 1st lt. AUS, 1959-61. Recipient Arthur S. Flemming Commn. award Washington Jr. C. of C., 1967; J.J. Ebers award IEEE Electron Devices Soc., 1980. Fellow IEEE (editor Jour. Solid State Circuits 1966-71, Internat. Solid-State Circuits Conf. Outstanding Paper award 1970, 75, 76, 77, 78), AAAS; mem. Nat. Acad. Engring., Electrochem. Soc., Biomed. Engring. Soc. (co-editor Annals of Biomed. Engring. 1976-80), AAUP, Sigma Xi, Tau Beta Pi, Eta Kappa Nu, Phi Kappa Phi. Patentee integrated circuit field. Current Work: Engineering education, research and development of integrated systems. Subspecialty: Integrated circuits. Office: 106 CIS Bldg Stanford U Stanford CA 94305

MEINEL, ADEN BAKER, optical science and astronomy educator; b. Pasadena, Calif., Nov. 25, 1922; s. John George and Gertrude (Baker) M.; m. Marjorie Pettit, Sept. 5, 1944; children: Carolyn, Walter, Barbara, Edward, Elaine, Mary, David. A.B., U. Calif., Berkeley, 1947, Ph.D., 1949. Asso. prof., asso. dir. Yerkes Obs., U. Chgo., 1950-57; dir. Kitt Peak Nat. Obs., 1958-61; prof. astronomy and optical scis. U. Ariz., Tucson, 1961—, chmn. dept. astronomy, 1961-65; dir. U. Ariz. (Steward Obs.), 1962-65, dir. optical sci. center, 1965-74; cons. Perkin-Elmer Corp., 1961-70, Itek Corp., 1970-75, U.S. Air Force, 1963-76, Sci. Applications, Inc., 1976-82. Author 5 books in field; contbr. chpts. to books, articles to profl. jours. Regent Calif. Luth. Coll., 1963-71. Served with USNR, 1944-46. Mem. Optical Soc. Am. (pres. 1972-73, Adolph Lomb medal 1952, Ives medal 1980), Am. Astron. Soc. (Warner prize 1954), Internat. Astron. Union (pres. Commn. 9 1973-76), Soc. Photo-Optical Instrumentation Engrs. (Goddard award). Lutheran. Current Work: Telescope design, solar energy, atmospheric optics; development of designs for major telescopes for several countries including U.S. Subspecialty: Optical astronomy. Home: 375 San Juan Pl Pasadena CA 91107 Office: JPL MS186-134 4800 Oak Grove Dr Pasadena CA 91109

MEINEL, CAROLYN PETTIT, systems engineer, author; b. Aug. 14, 1946; d. Aden Baker and Marjorie Steele (Pettit) M.; m. Howard Keith Henson, Dec. 25, 1967 (div. July 1982); children—Gale Eden, Windy Morningstar, Valerie Aurora, Virginia Heinlein; m. John Thomas Bosma, May 27, 1983. B.A, U. Ariz., 1981, M.S. in Indsl. Engring., 1983. Gen. mgr. Analog Precision, Tucson, 1973-76; editor L-5 News, L-5 Soc., Tucson, 1975-78, pres., 1977-79, prin. investigator, 1979-80; staff scientist Analytic Decisions, Inc. Arlington, Va., 1983—; cons. NASA/Ames Research Ctr., Moffett Field, Calif., 1975; cons. various pvt. cos., 1980—; lectr. Tucson pub. Library, 1982. Contbr. articles to jours. and mags., tech. papers to profl. confs. Mem. Inst. Indsl. Engrs., AIAA, Am. Astron. Soc., AAAS, L-5 Soc. for Space Devel. (life mem.; pres. 1977-79). Lutheran. Current work: Strategic defense with emphasis on space surveillance; military use of extraterrestrial resources; parallel computer architecture with application to decision problems. Subspecialties: Systems engineering; Theoretical computer science. Home: 742 N Edison Arlington VA 22203 Office: Analytic Decisions Inc 1401 Wilson Blvd Suite 200 Arlington VA 22209

MEINERT, LAWRENCE DAVID, geologist, enologist, educator; b. Cin., July 28, 1953; s. Walter T. and Delores C. (Mengel) M.; m. Georgia Yuan, Nov. 28, 1980. B.A., Carleton Coll., 1975; Ph.D., Stanford U., 1980. Instr. Stanford U., Calif., 1980-81; asst. prof. geology Wash. State U., Pullman, 1981—; cons. ASARCO, Chevron, Falconbridge, U.S. Bur. Mines. Contbr. articles to profl. jours. NSF grantee, 1982. Mem. Soc. Econ. Geologists (assoc. mem.), Soc. Mining Engrs., Geol. Soc. Am., Geol. Assn. Can., N.W. Mining Assn. Current work: Geology and geochemistry of ore deposits, exploration models, mining technology, ore microscopy and fluid inclusion analysis, computer applications, mapping. Subspecialty: Petrology. Home: 435 Gladstone Pullman WA 99163 Office: Geology Dept Wash State U Pullman WA 99164-2812

MEINWALD, JERROLD, chemist, educator; b. Bklyn., Jan. 16, 1927; s. Herman and Sophie (Baskind) M.; m. Yvonne Chu, June 25, 1955 (div. 1979); children: Constance Chu, Pamela Joan; m. Charlotte Greenspan, Sept. 7, 1980; 1 child, Julia Eve. Ph.B., U. Chgo., 1947, B.S., 1948; M.A., Harvard, 1950, Ph.D., 1952. Mem. faculty Cornell U., 1952-72, 73—, Goldwin Smith prof. chemistry, 1980—; research dir. Internat. Centre Insect Physiology and Ecology, Nairobi, 1970-77; prof. chemistry U. Calif. at San Diego, 1972-73; vis. prof. Rockefeller U., 1970; Camille and Henry Dreyfus Disting. scholar Mt. Holyoke Coll., 1981, Bryn Mawr Coll., 1983; cons. to industry; mem. vis. com. chemistry Brookhaven Nat. Lab., 1969-72, chmn., 1972; mem. med. A chemistry study sect. NIH, 1963-67, chmn., 1965-67; mem. adv. bd. Petroleum Research Found., 1971-73; mem. adv. council chemistry dept. Princeton U., 1978-84; mem. adv. bd. Research Corp., 1978-83; mem. adv. bd. chemistry div. NSF, 1979-83; mem. adv. bd. A.P. Sloan Found., 1985—; organizing chmn. Sino-Am. Symposium on Chemistry of Natural Products, Shanghai, 1980. Bd. editors: Jour. Organic Chemistry, 1962-66, Organic Reactions, 1968-78, Organic Syntheses, 1968-72, Jour. Chem. Ecology, 1974—, Insect Sci, 1979—; contbr. articles to profl. jours. Sloan fellow, 1958-62; Guggenheim fellow, 1960-61, 76-77; NIH spl. postdoctoral fellow, 1967-68; NIH Fogarty internat. scholar, 1980-85; Japan Soc. Promotion of Sci. fellow, 1983. Mem. Am. Chem. Soc. (chmn. organic div. 1969), AAAS, Nat. Acad. Sci., Am. Acad. Arts and Scis., Phi Beta Kappa, Sigma Xi. Current Work: Organic chemical defense and communication mechanisms in nature; chemical ecology, isolation, characterization, synthesis and biosynthesis of natural products. Subspecialties: Organic chemistry; Species interaction. Office: Baker Lab Cornell U Ithaca NY 14853

MEIROVITCH, LEONARD, structural engineer; b. Maxut, Romania, Nov. 28, 1928; came to U.S., 1956, naturalized, 1964; s. Carol and Adelle (Schoenfeld) M.; m. Jo Anne Reifer, Oct. 15, 1960. B.Sc. summa cum laude, Technion-Israel Inst. Tech., 1953; M.S. in Engring., UCLA, 1957, Ph.D., 1960. Structural engr. Water Planning for Israel, Tel Aviv, 1953-55, asst. sect. head, 1955-56; asst. research engr., asso. in engring. UCLA, 1956-60; staff engr. IBM, Endicott, N.Y., 1960-62; asso. prof. Ariz. State U., 1962-66; prof. U. Cin., 1967-71, Va. Poly. Inst. and State U., Blacksburg, 1971-79, Reynolds Metals prof., 1979-83, Univ. Disting. prof., 1983—; cons. Goodyear Aerospace, Phoenix, 1962-63; Cons. C.S. Draper Labs., Cambridge, Mass., 1976-78, Naval Research Lab., Washington, 1977-79, Intelsat, 1980-82. Author: Analytical Methods in Vibrations, 1967, Methods of Analytical Dynamics, 1970, Elements of Vibration Analysis, 1975, Computational Methods in Structural Dynamics, 1980; also articles.; asso. editor: Jour. Spacecraft and Rockets, 1971-76, Jour. Optimization Theory and Applications, 1971-76; editor: Mechanics: Dynamical Systems; mem. internat. editorial bd.: Journal de Mécanique Appliquée. Served with Israeli Army, 1948-49. Am. Soc. Engring. Edn.-NASA fellow, 1964; Nat. Acad. Scis. sr. research asso. Langley Research Center, Hampton, Va., 1966-67. Fellow AIAA (Structures, Structural Dynamics and Materials award 1983); mem. ASME, Sigma Xi, Tau Beta Pi. Subspecialty: Structural engineering. Office: Va Poly Inst and State U Dept Engring Sci and Mechanics Blacksburg VA 24061

MEISEL, DAN, chemist; b. Tel Aviv, July 4, 1943; came to U.S., 1974, naturalized, 1981; s. Arie and Miriam (Ribak) M.; m. Osnat Zerubavel, Dec. 30, 1965; children—Einat, Omer. B.Sc., Hebrew U., Jerusalem, 1967, M.S., 1969, Ph.D., 1974. Postdoctoral fellow Carnegie-Mellon U., Pitts., 1974-76; scientist Argonne Nat. Lab., Ill., 1976—. Contbr. numerous papers to sci. jours. Mem. Am. Chem. Soc., Radiation Research Soc., Am. Soc. for Photobiology. Current work: Photochemistry and radiation chemistry, solar energy conversion and storage, free radicals, chemistry in organized systems, colloidal chemistry. Subspecialties: Physical chemistry; Photochemistry. Home: 737 Ash St Flossmoor IL 60422 Office: Chemistry Div Argonne Nat Lab Argonne IL 60439

MEISEL, DAVID DERING, physics and astronomy educator, consultant, researcher; b. Fairmont, W. Va., Mar. 28, 1940; s. Louis David and Dorothy (Dering) M.; m. Carolyn Mae Conrad, Aug. 25, 1962; children—Grace, Catherine. B.S. in Physics, W.Va. U., 1961; M.S., Ohio State U., 1963, Ph.D., 1967. Obs. asst. Ohio State U., Columbus, 1963-65; asst. prof. U. Va., Charlottesville, Va., 1968-70, SUNY-Geneseo, 1970-76; assoc. prof. 1976-82, prof., 1982—; dir. planetarium SUNY-Geneseo, 1970—; assoc. C.E.K. Mees Obs. U. Rochester, N.Y., 1973—; exec. dir. Am. Meteor Soc., 1974; vis. astronomer Kitt Peak Nat. Obs., Tucson, 1976. Contbr. articles to profl. jours. Grantee NASA, 1965-67, 73-78, Fellow AAAS, Royal Astron. Soc.; mem. Am. Astron. Soc., Soc. Photo-optical Instrumentation Engrs., Internat. Sci. Radio Union (U.S. nat. com.) Internat. Astron. Union, Explorers Club, Sigma Pi Sigma. Current work: Fabry Perot interfermetry images processing of astronomical spectra, ionospheric/solar radio astronomy. Subspecialties: Optical astronomy; Mathematical software. Office: Dept Physics Astronomy SUNY Greene 209 Geneseo NY 14454

MEISELS, GERHARD GEORGE, university dean, chemist, educator; b. Vienna, Austria, May 11, 1931; came to U.S., 1951, naturalized, 1961; s. Leo and Adele Josefa Maria (Seehofer) M.; m. Sylvia Claire Knopsnider, June 28, 1958; 1 dau., Laura Germaine. Student, U. Vienna, 1949-51, 52-53; M.S., U. Notre Dame, Ind., 1952, Ph.D., 1956. Postdoctoral research asso. U. Notre Dame, 1955-56; chemist Gulf Oil Corp., Pitts., 1956-59; part time instr. Carnegie Inst. Tech., Pitts., 1956-58; chemist nuclear div. Union Carbide Corp., Tuxedo, N.Y., 1959-63, asst. group leader, 1964-65; asso. prof. U. Houston, 1965-70, prof., 1970-75, dept. chmn., 1973-75; prof., chmn. dept. chemistry U. Nebr., Lincoln, 1975-81, dean Coll. Arts and Scis., 1981—; cons. Union Carbide Corp., Gearhart-Owen Industries. Editor: spl. issue Jour. Radiation Physics and Chemistry, 1980; contbr. writings in field to profl. publs. Sec., pres. Ramsey (N.J.) Jr. C. of C., 1959-64. Fulbright fellow, Smith-Mundt fellow, 1951-52; sr. fellow Sci. Research Council, Eng., 1976. Mem. Am. Chem. Soc. (com. chmn.), Am. Soc. for Mass Spectrometry (charter, com. chmn., v.p. programs, pres. elect), Nebr. Acad. Scis., AAAS, Am. Phys. Soc., Sigma Xi. Clubs: Houston Kennel (dir. 1968-70), Cornhusker Kennel (pres., dir., del. to Am. Kennel Club 1976-81). Current Work: Unimolecular and bimolecular reactions of gaseous ions with well defined internal energies; radiation chemistry and structure of heavy ion tracks. Subspecialties: Physical chemistry; Kinetics. Home: 6001 Frontier Rd Lincoln NE 68516 Office: 1223 Old Father Hall U Nebr Lincoln NE 68588

MEISER, JOHN HENRY, chemist, educator; b. Cin., Nov. 21, 1938; s. Paul M. and Mildred P. (Turck) M.; m. Enya P. Flores, Aug. 12, 1967; children: Cristina, Teresa, Katharina. B.S., Xavier U., 1961; Ph.D., U. Cin., 1966. Asst. prof. U. Dayton, Ohio, 1966-69; asst. prof. Ball State U., Muncie, Ind., 1969-74, assoc. prof., 1974-80, prof. chemistry, 1980—. Author: Physical Chemistry, 1982. Recipient Student award Am. Inst. Chemists, 1961. Mem. Am. Chem. Soc., Am. Phys. Soc., Ind. Acad. Sci. (sec. 1979-82). Current Work: X-ray diffraction, solid-state chemistry, radiocarbon dating. Subspecialties: Physical chemistry; Solid state chemistry. Office: Dept Chemistry Ball State U Muncie IN 47306

MEISNER, JAMES EDWARD, electronics engineer; b. Rifle, Colo., Sept. 7, 1949; s. Edward Henry and Irma Lillian (Hollenbaugh) M.; m. Debra Susan Younger, Jan. 25, 1975; children—Christopher, Melinda. B.S.E.E., Colo. State U., 1971. Field engr. Dresser-Atlas Inc., Long Beach, Calif., 1972-73, field test engr. research and devel., Houston, 1973-76, project engr., 1980-82; research geoscientist Bendix Field Engring., Grand Junction, Colo., 1976-80; chief engr. Exploration Logging, Sacramento, 1982—. Patentee in field. Mem. IEEE (sr.), Soc. Prof. Well Log Analysts. Republican. Episcopalian. Current work: Well logging and measurement-while-drilling, systems, Downhole and surface instrumentation, geophysical instrumentation, nuclear instrumentation. Subspecialty: Systems engineering. Home: 8188 Woodlake Hills Dr Orangevale CA 95662 Office: Exploration Logging Inc 1770 Tribute Rd Sacramento CA 95821

MEISTER, ALTON, biochemist, educator; b. N.Y.C., June 1, 1922; s. Morris and Florence (Glickstein) M.; m. Leonora Garten, Dec. 26, 1943; children: Jonathan Howard, Kenneth Eliot. B.S., Harvard U., 1942; M.D., Cornell U., 1945. Intern, asst. resident N.Y. Hosp., N.Y.C., 1946; head clin. biochem. research sect. Nat. Cancer Inst., NIH, 1951-55; commd. officer USPHS, NIH, 1946-55; prof. biochemistry, chmn. dept. Tufts U. Sch. Medicine, 1955-67; prof., chmn. dept. biochemistry Cornell U. Med. Coll., N.Y.C., 1967—; biochemist-in-chief N.Y. Hosp., 1971—; Vis. prof. biochemistry U. Wash., 1959, U. Calif. at Berkeley, 1961; cons. USPHS, 1964-68; chmn. physiol. chemistry study sect.; cons. com. on growth NRC, 1954; cons. biochemistry study sect. USPHS, 1955-60, cons. biochemistry tng. com., 1961-63; cons. Am. Cancer Soc., 1958-61, 71-74. Author: Biochemistry of Amino Acids; Mem. editorial bd.: Jour. Biol. Chemistry, 1958-64; asso. editor, 1976—; mem. editorial bd.: Biochem. Preparations, 1957-64, Biochemistry, 1962-71, 80—, Methods in Biochem. Analysis, 1963—, Biochimica et Biophysica Acta, 1965-77, Ann. Rev. Biochemistry, 1961-65; asso. editor, 1965—; Editor: Advances in Enzymology, 1969—; Contbr. chpts. to books, articles on enzymes, amino acids and glutathione to sci. jours. Recipient Paul-Lewis award enzyme chemistry Am. Chem. Soc., 1954; chmn. U.S. com. Internat. Union Biochemistry, 1960-65, 79—. Fellow Am. Acad. Arts and Scis.; mem. Nat. Acad. Scis., Inst. of Medicine of Nat. Acad. Sci. (sr.), Biophys. Soc., Biochem. Soc. London, Chem. Soc. London, AAAS, Am. Chem. Soc. (chmn. div. biol. chemistry 1965), Am. Assn. Cancer Research, Am. Soc. Biol. Chemists (pres. 1977, William C. Rose award in biochemistry 1984), Japanese Biochem. Soc. (hon.), Harvey Soc. (hon.), Sigma Xi, Alpha Omega Alpha. Subspecialty: Biochemistry (medicine). Address: 1300 York Ave New York NY 10021

MEITZLER, ALLEN HENRY, research scientist, educator; b. Allentown, Pa., Dec. 16, 1928; s. Herbert Henry and Estella Irene (Wagner) M.; m. Joan Catherine Egan, June 13, 1953; children—Thomas Joseph, Peter Michael, David Christopher. B.S. in Physics, Muhlenberg Coll., 1951; M.S. in Physics, Lehigh U., 1953, Ph.D., 1955. Mem. tech. staff Bell Labs., Murray Hill, N.J., 1955-72; prin. research scientist, research staff Ford Motor Co., Dearborn, Mich., 1972—. Contbr. articles to tech. jours. Patentee ultrasonic and electro-optic devices, automotive electronic devices. Fellow IEEE, Acoustical Soc. Am.; mem. Am. Phys. Soc., Am. Ceramic Soc., Soc. Automotive Engrs. Republican. Current work: Research on silicon-based smart sensors and semiconductor device processing technology. Subspecialties: Electronics; Microelectronics. Home: 3055 Foxcroft Rd Ann Arbor MI 48104 Office: Sci Research Lab Ford Motor Co Box 2053 Dearborn MI 48121

MELANCON, MARK JOHN, pharmacologist, educator; b. Chgo., Sept. 17, 1939; s. Mark John and Margaret (Pleiss) M.; m. Janet Kathleen, Jan. 15, 1966; children—Mark John, Mary Margaret, Paul Matthew. B.A., St. Mary's Coll., Winona, Minn., 1961; M.A., Loyola U., Chgo., 1964, Ph.D., 1966. Instr. Loyola U., Chgo., 1966; research assoc. U. Wis.-Madison, 1968-70; asst. prof. U. Wis.-Milw., 1970-74; research assoc. Med. Coll. Wis., Milw., 1974-83, adj. asst. prof. pharmacology, 1979-85; adj. assoc. prof. pharmacology, 1985—; assoc. scientist U. Wis. Med. Sch., Mt. Sinai Med. Ctr., Milw., 1983—. Contbr. articles to profl. publs., chpts. to books. NIH fellow, 1966-68; grantee Wis. Sea Grant Program, 1973-74, 80-82, EPA, 1984—. Mem. Am. Soc. Pharmacology and Exptl. Therapeutics, Am. Chem. Soc., Soc. Environ. Toxicology and Chemistry, AAAS, Sigma Xi. Current work: Clinical pharmacology, drug metabolism and pharmacokinetics, uptake, effects, metabolism and elimination of pollutants in fish. Subspecialties: Pharmacology; Environmental toxicology. Home: 2941 N Farwell Milwaukee WI 53211 Office: Mt Sinai Med Ctr 950 N 12th St Milwaukee WI 53233

MELBY, EDWARD CARLOS, JR., veterinarian; b. Burlington, Vt., Aug. 10, 1929; s. Edward C. and Dorothy H. (Folsom) M.; m. Jean Day File, Aug. 15, 1953; children: Scott E., Susan J., Jeffrey T., Richard A. Student, U. Pa., 1948-50; D.V.M., Cornell U., 1954. Diplomate: Am. Coll. Lab. Animal Medicine. Practice veterinary medicine, Middlebury, Vt., 1954-62; instr. lab. animal medicine Johns Hopkins U. Sch. Medicine, Balt., 1962-64, asst. prof., 1964-66, asso. prof., 1966-71, prof., dir. div. comparative medicine, 1971-74; prof. medicine, dean Coll. Veterinary Medicine, Cornell U., Ithaca, N.Y., 1974-84; v.p. research and devel. Smith Kline AHP, Smith Kline Beckman Corp., Phila., 1985—; cons. VA, Nat. Research Council, NIH. Author: Handbook of Laboratory Animal Science, Vols. I, II, III, 1974-76. Served with USMC, 1946-48. Mem. AVMA, N.Y. State Veterinary Med. Assn., Am. Assn. Lab. Animal Sci., Am. Coll. Lab. Animal Medicine, Am. Assn. Accreditation Lab. Animal Care, AAAS, Phi Zeta. Subspecialties: Pathology (veterinary medicine); Laboratory animal medicine. Home: 770 Newtown Rd Villanova PA 19085 Office: Smith Kline Beckman Corp PO Box 7929 One Franklin Plaza Philadelphia PA 19101

MELCHER, JAMES RUSSELL, electrical engineering educator; b. Giard, Iowa, July 5, 1936; s. Melvin Charles and Opal Maxine (Getty) M.; m. Janet Louise Damman, June 15, 1957; children: Jennifer, Eric, Douglas. B.S. in Elec. Engring, Iowa State U., 1957, M.S. in Nuclear Engring, 1958; Ph.D., Mass. Inst. Tech., 1962. Mem. faculty Mass. Inst. Tech., 1962—, asst. prof., 1962-66, asso. prof., 1966-69, prof. elec. engring., 1969—, Stratton chair in elec. engring., 1981-84, dir. High Voltage Research Lab., 1980, dir. Lab. for Electromagnetic and Electronic Systems, 1984—; Guggenheim fellow Churchill Coll., Cambridge, Eng., 1972; cons. to industry, 1962—. Author: Field-Coupled Surface Waves, 1963, (with H.H. Woodson) Electromechanical Dynamics, 1969, Continuum Electromechanics, 1981. Recipient first Mark Mills award Am. Nuclear Soc., 1958, Western Electric Fund award New Eng. sect. Am. Soc. Engring. Edn., 1969, Young Alumnus Recognition Ia. State U., 1971; Profl. Achievement citation Iowa State U., 1981. Fellow IEEE, Am. Soc. Engring. Edn., Am. Acad. Engring., Am. Phys. Soc., Am. Chem. Soc., Sigma Xi, Tau Beta Pi. Research and publ. in continuum electromechanics, continuum feedback control, energy conversion, electrohydrodynamics, air-pollution control, electromech. power apparatus, electromechanics of electrochem. and biol. systems. Subspecialties: Electrical engineering; Mechanical engineering. Home: 29 Fairlawn Ln Lexington MA 02173 Office: Mass Inst Tech Cambridge MA 02139

MELICHAR, JOSEPH FRANK, adult development and aging educator, researcher, engineer; b. N.Y.C., Dec. 29, 1937; s. Joseph Thomas and Helen Mary (Broz) M. B.S., Lafayette Coll., 1959; M.S. in Mech. Engring., Lehigh, U., 1960; M.A. in Spl. Edn., San Francisco State U., 1970; Ph.D. in Human Devel. and Aging, U. Calif.-San Francisco, 1982. Research engr. Hamilton Standard div. United Aircraft, Windsor Locks, Conn., 1960-61; physicist Ballistic Research Labs., Aberdeen Proving Ground, Md., 1962-67, sr. analyst, div. dir. URS Systems Corp., San Mateo, Calif., 1967-72; sr. analyst, pres., chmn., dir. Adaptive Systems Corp., San Mateo, 1972—; exec. cons. Ariz. Dept. Health Services, Phoenix, 1983-84; adj. prof. Ariz. State U., Tempe, 1983—; cons. various univs., local and state agys., pvt. industry, 1967—. Contbr. articles to profl. jours. Mem. ASME, Am. Phys. Soc., Am. Assn. Mental Deficiency, Soc. Research Child Devel., Inst. Mgmt. Sci., Soc. Gen. Systems Research, Gerontol. Soc., Western Gerontol. Soc., Council for Exceptional Children, Assn. for Severely Handicapped, Nat. Soc. Study Edn., Assn. Computing Machinery. Current work: Models of human development and aging, chronic disease epidemiology models and methods, applications of information science to health and aging, epidimiology of birth defects, stress and health. Subspecialties: Developmental psychology; Information systems (Information science). Home: 2829 Newlands Ave Belmont CA 94002 Office: Adaptive Systems Corp PO Box 3068 San Mateo CA 94403

MELLIN, THEODORE NELSON, research scientist; b. Paterson, N.J., Dec. 24, 1937; s. Nelson F. and Helen S. (Steib) M.; m. Beverly E. Donahue, July 4, 1959; children: Jennifer, Victoria, Abigail; m. Josephine R. Carlin, June 11, 1977. B.S., U. Vt., 1959; M.S., U. Maine, 1961; Ph.D. (David Ross fellow), Purdue U., 1964. USPHS fellow, postdoctoral trainee in steriod biochemistry Worcester Found. Exptl. Biology, 1964-66; with Merck Inst. Therapeutic Research, Rahway, N.J., 1966, sr. research fellow dept. biochemistry, 1974—, guest lectr. Merck speakers program; reviewer endocrinology sect. Prostaglandin Jour.; presenter papers at profl. meetings. Contbr. articles and abstracts to profl. jours. Mem. Soc. Neurosci., Soc. Study of Reprodn., N.J. Soc. Neurosci., Merck Sci. Club (pres. 1969-71), Sigma Xi, Alpha Zeta. Independent. Presbyterian. Club: Old Straw Hat Ski (pres. 1975-77). Current Work: BPH, hirsutism and acne. Subspecialties: Neuroendocrinology; Neurobiology. Home: 32 Overhill Dr North Brunswick NJ 08902 Office: Merck & Co PO Box 2000 Rahway NJ 07065

MELLINKOFF, SHERMAN MUSSOFF, medical school dean, medical educator, physician; b. McKeesport, Pa., Mar. 23, 1920; s. Albert and Helen (Mussoff) M.; m. June O'Connell, Nov. 18, 1944; children—Sherrill M., Albert J. B.A., Stanford U., 1941, M.D., 1944. Diplomate: Am. Bd. Internal Medicine. Intern, asst. resident Stanford Hosp., Calif., 1944-45; asst. resident Johns Hopkins Hosp., Balt., 1947-49, resident, 1950-51, instr. medicine, 1951-53; fellow in gastroenterology U. Pa., 1949-50; asst. to assoc. prof. medicine UCLA Med. Sch., 1953-62, prof. medicine, dean Med. Sch., 1962—; attending cons. internal medicine Wadsworth Gen. Hosp., VA Ctr., Los Angeles; sr. attending physician Harbor Gen. Hosp., Torrance, Calif. Editor: Differential Diagnosis of Abdominal Pain, 1959, Differentail Diagnosis of Diarrhea, 1964; contbr. numerous articles to med. jours. Capt., M.C. U.S. Army, 1945-47. Mem. Am. Gastroent. Assn., ACP, Assn. Am. Physicians. Western Assn. Physicians, Nat. Acad. Scis. Inst. Medicine, AMA, Am. Soc. Clin. Nutrition, Western Soc. Clin. Research, Am. Fedn. Clin. Research, AAAS. Subspecialty: Gastroenterology. Office: UCLA Med Ctr Los Angeles CA 90024*

MELLORS, ROBERT CHARLES, pathologist; b. Dayton, Ohio, 1916; s. Bert S. and Clementine (Steinmetz) M.; m. Jane K. Winternitz, Mar. 25, 1944; children: Alice J., Robert Charles, William K., John. Ph.D., Western Res. U., 1940; M.D., Johns Hopkins, 1944. Diplomate: Am. Bd. Pathology in path. anatomy. Intern Nat. Naval Med. Center, Bethesda, Md., 1944-45; research fellow medicine Meml. Center Cancer and Allied Diseases, N.Y.C., 1946-50, research fellow pathology, 1950-53, asst. attending pathologist, 1953-57, assoc. attending pathologist, 1957-58; sr. fellow Am. Cancer Soc., 1947-50; sr. clin. research fellow Damon Runyon Meml. Fund, 1950-53; asst. attending pathologist Meml. Hosp., N.Y.C., 1953-57, asso. attending pathologist, 1957-58; asst. attending pathologist Ewing Hosp., N.Y.C., 1953-57, assoc. attending pathologist, 1957-58; instr. biochemistry Western Res. U., 1940-42; research assoc. Poliomyelitis Research Ctr. and Dept. Epidemiology Johns Hopkins U. Sch. Hygiene, 1942-44; asst. prof. biology Meml. Center Cancer and Allied Diseases, N.Y.C., 1952-53; asst. prof. pathology Sloan Kettering div. Cornell U., 1953-57, assoc. prof., 1957-58; prof. pathology Cornell U. Med. Coll., 1961—; assoc. attending pathologist N.Y. Hosp., 1961-72, attending pathologist, 1972—; pathologist-in-chief, dir. labs., 1958-84, emeritus, 1984—, cons., 1984—; assoc. dir. research Hosp. for Spl. Surgery, N.Y.C., 1958-69, dir. research, 1969-84, emeritus, 1984—, cons., 1984—; mem. research adv. com. NIH, 1962-66; adv. com. Nat. Inst. Environ. Health Sci., 1966-69; com. nomenclature and classification of disease Coll. Am. Pathologists, 1960-64. Author: Analytical Cytology, 1955, 2d edit., 1959, Analytical Pathology, 1957. Served as lt. (j.g.), M.C. USNR, 1944-46. Recipient Kappa Delta award Am. Acad. of Orthopedic Surgeons, 1962. Fellow Royal Coll. Pathologists, Am. Soc. Clin. Pathology; mem. Am. Assn. Pathologists, Am. Assn. Immunologists, Am. Soc. Biol. Chemists, Am. Orthopedic Assn. (hon.). Current Work: Immunology or retroviruses; human endogenous retrovirus gene expression; systemic lupus erythematosis and related autoimmune diseases. Subspecialties: Pathology (medicine); Immunology (medicine). Home: 3 Hardscrabble Circle Armonk NY 10504

MELNICK, JOSEPH L., educator, virologist; b. Boston, Oct. 9, 1914; s. Samuel and Esther (Melny) M.; m. Matilda Benyesh, 1958; 1 dau., Nancy. A.B., Wesleyan U., 1936; Ph.D. (Univ. scholar), Yale, 1939; D.Sc., Wesleyan U., 1971. Asst. in physiol. chemistry Yale Sch. Medicine, 1937-39, Asst. in physiol. chemistry, Finney-Howell Research Found. fellow, 1939-41, NRC fellow in med. scis., 1941-42, research asst. in preventive medicine with rank of instr., 1942-44, asst. prof., 1944-48, research asso., 1948-49, asso. prof. microbiology, 1949-54, prof. epidemiology, 1954-57; chief virus labs., div. biologics standards NIH, USPHS, 1957-58; prof. virology and epidemiology Baylor Coll. Medicine, Houston, 1958-74, disting. service prof., 1974—, dean grad. studies, 1968—; Mem. com. virus diseases WHO, 1957—; dir. WHO Internat. Center Enteroviruses, 1963-70, mem. cons. group on poliomyelitis vaccine, 1973—; dir. WHO Collaborating Center for Virus Reference and Research, 1974—; mem. com. on live poliovirus vaccines USPHS, 1959-61; virus reference bd. NIH, 1962-70; mem. human cancer virus task force Nat. Cancer Inst., USPHS, 1962-67; nat. adv. cancer council NIH, 1965-69; adv. com. Nat. Multiple Sclerosis Soc., 1980-83; sec.-gen. Internat. Congresses Virology, 1968-71; chmn. Internat. Conf. Viruses in Water, Mexico City, 1974, Tel Aviv, 1982; mem. exec. bd. Internat. Assn. Microbiol. Socs., chmn. sect. on virology, 1970-75, mem. internat. commn. microbiol ecology, 1972—; mem. research council Am. Cancer Soc., 1971-75; mem. com. on hepatitis Nat. Acad. Sci./NRC, 1972-77; lectr. cons. Chinese Acad. Med. Scis., 1978, 79; mem. adv. com. Comparative Virology Orgn., 1978—. Author: other sci. publs. Textbook of Medical Microbiology; Editor: Monographs in Virology; editor-in-chief: ofcl. jour. virology Intervirology, Internat. Union Microbiol. Socs. Recipient Internat. medal (with Dr. Herids von Magnus of Denmark); award Argentinian Found. Against Infantile Paralysis, for research in immunity to poliomyelitis, 1949; Humanitarian award Jewish Inst. Med. Research, 1964; Modern Medicine Disting. Achievement award, 1965; Eleanor Roosevelt Humanities award, 1965; Indsl. Research-100 award (with Prof. Craig Wallis), 1971, 74; Inventor of Year award Houston Patent Law Assn., 1972; named to Nat. Found.'s Polio Hall Fame, 1958; Gold medal South African Poliomyelitis Research Found., 1979; Maimonides award State of Israel, 1980. Fellow AAAS, Am. Pub. Health Assn., N.Y. Acad. Scis. (Freedman Found. award for research in virology 1973), Am. Acad. Microbiology; mem. Am. Soc. Microbiology, Soc. Exptl. Biol. and Medicine (mem. council 1965-69), Am. Assn. Immunologists, Am. Epidemiol. Soc., Am. Assn. Cancer Research (pres. S.W. sect. 1968), Internat. Com. Taxonomy of Viruses (hon. life), Internat. Union Microbiol. Socs., Microbiol. Soc. Israel (hon.), USSR Soc. Microbiologists and Epidemiologists (hon.), Phi Beta Kappa, Sigma Xi. Current Work: Medical virology including a synthetic vaccine for viral hepatitis, possible viral etiologies of atherosclerosis and chronic diseases of the central nervous system, environmental virology. Subspecialties: Virology (biology); Virology (medicine).

MELOUK, HASSAN ALY, plant pathologist; b. Alexandria, Egypt, May 19, 1941; came to U.S., 1965, naturalized, 1975; s. Aly H. and Hanem M. (Kadour) M.; m. Afaf H. Abo-El-Dahab, Dec. 9, 1964; children: Sammy, Sharif. B.S., Alexandria U., 1962; M.S., Oreg. State U., 1967, Ph.D., 1969. Instr., Alexandria (Egypt) U., 1962-64; grad. research asst. Oreg. State U., Corvallis, 1965-69; postdoctoral research assoc. Wash. State U., Prosser, 1969-70; research assoc. Oreg. state U., Corvallis, 1970-76; plant pathologist, prof. dept. plant pathology U.S. Dept. Agr., Agrl. Research Service, Okla. State U., Stillwater, 1976—. Contbr. articles to profl. jours. Den leader Cub Scouts Am., 1972-74. Nat. Mint Research Council research grantee, 1972-76. Mem. Am. Phytopath. Soc., Am. Peanut Research and Edn. Soc. Republican. Current Work: Development of peanut germplasm with multiple resistance to diseases. Subspecialties: Plant pathology; Plant genetics. Home: 4802 Country Club Ct Stillwater OK 74074 Office: US Dept Agr Agrl Research Service Dept Plant Pathology Okla State U Stillwater OK 74078

MELSA, JAMES LOUIS, electrical engineer, manager, consultant; b. Omaha, July 6, 1938; s. Louis Fred and Ann (Pelnar) M.; m. Katherine Smith, June 25, 1960; children: Susan, Elisabeth, Peter, Jon, Jennifer, Mark. B.S.E.E., Iowa State U., 1960; M.S.E.E., U. Ariz., 1962, Ph.D., 1965. Assoc. mem. tech. staff Radio Corp. Am., Tucson, 1960-61; instr. elec. engring. U. Ariz., 1961-65, Asst. prof., 1965-67; assoc. prof. info. and control scis. So. Meth. U., 1967-69, prof., 1969-73; prof., chmn. dept. elec. engring. U. Notre Dame, 1973-84; v.p. research Tellabs, Inc., 1984—; cons. to industry; cons. Los Alamos Sci. Lab., 1965—. Author-12 books including: (with J.D. Gibson) Nonparametric Detection with Applications, 1975, (with D.L. Cohn) A Step by Step Introduction to 8080 Microprocessor Systems, 1977, Decision and Estimation Theory, 1978; editor: (with M.K. Sain and J.L. Peczkowski) Alternatives for Linear Multivariable Control, 1978; mem. editorial adv. bd.: Jour. Computers and Elec. Engring, 1972—; assoc. editor: Man and Cybernetics, 1972-79; contbr. numerous articles profl. jours. Fellow IEEE; mem. AIAA, Nat. Engring. Consortium (dir. 1975-79), Am. Soc. Engring. Edn. (Western Electric award Gulf S.W. sect. 1973), Sigma Xi, Tau Beta Pi, Pi Mu Epsilon, Eta Kappa Nu, Phi Kappa Phi. Subspecialty: Electrical engineering. Home: 53222 Martin Ln South Bend IN 46635 Office: Tellabs Inc 2012 Ironwood Circle South Bend IN 46635

MELTON, CHARLES ESTEL, educator; b. Fancy Gap, Va., May 18, 1924; s. Charlie Glenn and Ella (Ayers) M.; m. Una Faye Hull, Dec. 7, 1946; children—Sharon (Mrs. Lawrence Husch), Wayne, Sandra (Mrs. Glenn Allen). B.A., Emory and Henry Coll., 1952, D.Sc., 1967; M.S., Vanderbilt U., 1954; Ph.D., U. Notre Dame, 1964. Physicist Oak Ridge Nat. Lab., 1954-67; prof. chemistry U. Ga., Athens, 1967—, head dept., 1972-77. Author: Principles of Mass Spectrometry and Negative Ions, 1970; Ancient Diamond Time Capsules, Secrets of Life and the World, 1985. Contbr. articles to profl. jours. Served with USNR, 1943-46. Recipient DeFriece medal Emory and Henry Coll., 1959; numerous research grants. Fellow AAAS; mem. Am. Phys. Soc., Am. Chem. Soc., Ga. Acad. Sci. Presbyterian. Current Work: Research in the svolution of petroleum, the evolution of the earths atmosphere and oceans, the orgin of the earths magnetic field, and the origin and age of diamonds. Subspecialties: Physical chemistry; Geophysics. Home: Route 2 Box 34 Hull GA 30646 Office: Dept Chemistry Univ Georgia Athens GA 30602

MELVILLE, RICHARD DEVERN SAMUELS, JR., engineering executive; b. Los Angeles, Nov. 10, 1939; s. Richard Devern Samuels and Dorothy Irene (Dorchester) M.; m. Esther Jean Melville, Sept. 1, 1962; children: Richard Devern Samuels, Donald Scott. B.S. in Elec. Engring, U. So. Calif. Elec. Engring, 1960; M.S. in Physics, U.S. Naval Postgrad. Sch., 1967; M.S. in Elec. Engring, Calif. Inst. Tech., 1971, Ph.D., 1975. Commd. ensign U.S. Navy, 1960, advanced through grades to lt. comdr., 1970, served as naval aviator, fighter pilot; resigned, 1970; sr. researcher R & D Assoc., Marina Del Rey, Calif., 1975-81; mgr advanced systems dept TRW, Redondo Beach, Calif., 1981-82; co-founder, dir. advanced tech. programs EOS Technologies Inc., Santa Monica, Calif., 1982—. Contrbr articles to profl. jours. Mem. Optical Soc. Am., Sigma Xi. Current Work: Corporate director advanced technology programs, principally military, infra-red and optical sensor systems and laser systems. Subspecialties: Laser technology; Optical image processing.

MEMON, MUSHTAQ AHMED, veterinary educator, theriogenologist; b. Shikarpur, Pakistan, Aug. 22, 1948; came to U.S., 1975; s. Rahim Bux and Noor Begum Memon; m. Homa Saatara, Dec. 11, 1982. B.V.Sc., B.Sc., U. Punjab, Lahore, Pakistan, 1971; M.Sc. with honors, U. Agr., Faisalabad, Pakistan, 1974; Ph.D., U. Minn., 1980. Diplomate Am. Coll. Theriogenologists. Lectr. Sind Agrl. U., Tandojam, Pakistan, 1972-74; teaching assoc. U. Ill., Urbana, 1979-81; asst. prof. Okla. State U., Stillwater, 1981-83; asst. prof., then assoc. prof. theriogenology La. State U., Baton Rouge, 1983—. Research, publs. on goat and sheep reprodn. U. Ill. biomed. research grantee U. Ill., Urbana, 1978; Sarkey's faculty devel. fellow Okla. State U., 1982; research grantee La. State U., 1983, 84, 85. Mem. AVMA, Am. Soc. Animal Sci., Soc. Theriogenology, Internat. Goat Soc. Moslem. Current work: Semen preservation of cattle, sheep and goats; effects of prostaglandins on reproduction; infertility in male domestic animals; teaching theriogenology to D.V.M.s and graduate students. Subspecialty: Animal physiology. Office: Dept Vet Clin Sci La State U S Stadium Dr Baton Rouge LA 70803

MENDELOFF, ALBERT IRWIN, physician, educator; b. Charleston, W.Va., Jan. 29, 1918; s. Morris Israel and Esther (Cohen) M.; m. Natalie Lavenstein, Dec. 19, 1943; children: Henry, John, Katherine. A.B., Princeton U., 1938; M.D., Harvard U., 1942, M.P.H., 1944. Fellow in nutrition Rockefeller Found., 1943-44; nutrition cons. UNRRA mission to Greece, 1944-46; asst. prof. medicine and preventive medicine Washington U. Med. Sch., 1949-54, asso. prof., 1955; gastroenterology cons. Barnes Hosp., St. Louis, 1952-55; asso. prof. medicine Johns Hopkins Med. Sch., 1955-70, prof., 1970—; physician-in-chief Sinai Hosp., Balt., 1955-80, chief research medicine, 1980-83; Sr. surgeon Res. USPHS. Editor-in-chief: Am. Jour. Clin. Nutrition, 1981—. Mem. Assn. Am. Physicians, Am. Soc. Clin. Investigation, Central Soc. Clin. Research, Am. Fedn. Clin. Research, Am. Gastroent. Assn., Phi Beta Kappa, Alpha Omega Alpha. Subspecialty: Nutrition (medicine). Home and Office: 2109 Northcliff Dr Baltimore MD 21209

MENDELS, JOSEPH, psychiatrist; b. Capetown, South Africa, Oct. 29, 1937; came to U.S., 1964, naturalized, 1975; s. Max and Lily (Turecki) M.; m. Ora Kark, Jan. 17, 1960; children: Gilla Avril, Charles Alan, David Ralph. M.B., Ch.B., U. Capetown, 1960; M.D., U. Witwatersrand, 1965. Intern U. Witwatersrand, 1961; resident in psychiatry U. Witwatersrand and U. N.C., 1964-67; chief depression research program, prof. psychiatry and pharmacology U. Pa. and VA Hosp., Phila., 1973-80; med. dir., v.p. Fairmount Inst., Phila., 1980-81; med. dir. Therapeutics Inc., 1981—, Phila. Med. Inst., 1983—; prof. psychiatry, human behavior and pharmacology Thomas Jefferson Med. Coll., Phila., 1982—; ad hoc cons. NIMH, NIH; dir. Spectrum Publs.; lectr. univs. and hosps. Author, editor: Concepts of Depression, 1971, Biological Psychiatry, 1973, Psychobiology of Affective Disorders, 1981; contbr. articles to med. jours. Grantee NIMH; Grantee VA. Fellow Inst. for Study Human Issues; mem. Am. Psychiat. Assn. (Lester N. Hofheimer award 1976), Psychiat. Research Soc., Am. Coll. Neuropsychopharmacology, Congressium Internationale Neuropsychopharmacologia. Current Work: Clinical pharmacology; psychopharmacology; biology and treatment of depression and mania. Subspecialties: Psychopharmacology; Pharmacokinetics. Office: 1015 Chestnut St Philadelphia PA 19107

MENDELSON, NEIL HARLAND, geneticist, microbiologist, educator; b. N.Y.C., Nov. 15, 1937; s. Michael and Rose (Kutner) M.; m. Joan Rintel, July 30, 1959; children: Debora Cybelle, Marie Dianna. B.S., Cornell U., N.Y., 1959; Ph.D., Ind. U., 1964. NSF postdoctoral fellow Med. Research Council, London, 1965-66; asst. prof. biology U. Md., Catonsville, 1967-69; asso. prof. micro/med. tech. U. Ariz., Tucson, 1969-74, prof., 1974-78, prof. cellular and developmental biology, 1978-83, head dept., 1979-83, prof. molecular and cellular biology, 1983—; vis. scientist Inst. Pasteur, Paris, 1976-77, U. Lausanne, Switzerland, 1979, Cambridge U., Eng., 1984, 86. Contbr. articles to sci. jours. Bd. dirs. Tucson Jr. Strings, 1976-79; mem. So. Ariz. Symphony, treas., 1981-83, pres., 1983—. Served to capt., Chem. Corps U.S. Army, 1963-65. NIH grantee, 1971-82, 84—; NSF grantee, 1968-71, 82-84. Mem. Am. Soc., Microbiolgy, AAAS, Genetics Soc. Am. Jewish. Current Work: Genetic regulation of cell growth and division; helical macrofibers; helix clock theory; cell surface and morphology; biomechanics of bacteria; minicell molecular biology; stress-strain deformations in cell regulation. Subspecialties: Genetics and genetic engineering (biology); Microbiology. Home: 7031 Katchina Ct Tucson AZ 85715 Office: U Ariz Tucson AZ 85721

MENDELSON, THEA, biologist, educator, researcher; b. Durham, N.C., May 5, 1935; d. Carl Williams and Mable Dorothy (Gaiser) Borgmann; m. Martin Mendelson, Mar. 29, 1958 (div.); children: Kathryn, Christopher. B.A., Swarthmore Coll., 1957; postgrad., Cornell U., 1957-58; Ph.D., SUNY-Stony Brook, 1978. Muscular Dystrophy fellow Cornell U., Ithaca, N.Y., 1977-80; asst. prof. biology Wells Coll., Aurora, N.Y., 1980—; lectr. Occidental Coll., Los Angeles, 1958-60. Contbr. articles to profl. jours. Recipient Nat. Research Service award NIH, 1980. Mem. AAAS, Soc. Neurosci., N.Y. Acad. Scis., NOW, Sierra Club, Sigma Xi. Democrat. Current Work: Neurotransmitter uptake at crayfish neuro-muscular junction; role of glial cells. Subspecialties: Neurobiology; Regeneration.

MENDELSON, YITZHAK, biomedical engineer, educator; b. Tel-Aviv, Isarel, Sept. 10, 1949; came to U.S., 1974; m. Lea Bankai, Aug. 28, 1977; children—Karen, Avital. B.S., SUNY-Buffalo, 1975, M.Sc., 1976; Ph.D., Case Western Res. U., 1983. Asst. prof. Worcester Poly. Inst., Mass., 1983—. Recipient Admiral Ralph Earle Medel award Worcester Engring. Soc., 1985.

Mem. IEEE, Biomed. Engring. Soc., Optical Soc. Am. Current work: Invasive and noninvasive blood gas analysis, biosensors, biomedical instrumentation, optics. Subspecialty: Biomedical engineering. Office: Worcester Poly Inst 100 Institute Rd Worcester MA 01609

MENDENHALL, HARLAN VINCENT, surgical researcher, veterinarian; b. Gulfport, Miss., Oct. 21, 1944; s. Harlan Harry Mendenhall and Catherine Rose (Cunningham) Mendenhall Cowell; m. Suzette Joyce Copeland, June 9, 1965 (div.); children—Tai Justin, Tiffany; m. Toni Meglitsch, July 28, 1978. D.V.M., Colo. State U., 1968, Ph.D., 1981. Staff veterinarian Rangitaiki Plains Dairy Co., Edgecumbe, N.Z., 1968-71; staff surgeon Surg. Metabolic Lab. and Vet. Sch., Colo. State U., Ft. Collins, 1971-74; surg. research specialist 3M Co., St. Paul, 1975—; cons. veterinarian St. Paul Ramsey Med. Ctr., 1981—; referral surgeon Vet. Surg. Specialists, Mahtomedi, Minn., 1977—. Editor book General Surgical Considerations in Biomaterial Evaluations, 1985. Mem. AVMA, Soc. Biomaterials (Ph.D. Student award 1982). Current work: Development of animal surgical models to evaluate new artificial organs and prostheses in all areas, primarily orthopedic, ophthalmic and vascular. Subspecialties: Artificial organs and prostheses; Surgery (veterinary medicine). Home: 9150 Lansing Ave N Stillwater MN 55082 Office: 3M Co 270 1S 03 3M Ctr Saint Paul MN 55144

MENDIS, D(EVAMITTA) ASOKA, research physicist; b. Colombo, Sri Lanka, Feb. 13, 1936; came to U.S., 1969; naturalized, 1980; s. Dixon Ashley and Leila Felicia (de Zoysa) M.; m. Janine Peters, May 30, 1975. B.Sc., U. Ceylon, 1960; Ph.D., U. Manchester, Eng., 1967, D.Sc., 1978. Lectr. U. Ceylon, Colombo, 1976-69; asst. research physicist U. Calif.-San Diego, 1969-75, assoc. research physicist, 1975-78, research physicist, 1978—. Contbr. articles to profl. jours. Fellow Royal Astron. Soc. London; mem. Am. Astron. Soc., Am. Geophys. Union, Internat. Astron. Union, Com. Space Research. Current work: Solar system physics; cometary physics; physics of dusty plasmas; interstellar medium. Subspecialties: Solar physics; Cometary physics. Office: U Calif Dept Elec Engring and Computer Sci Ctr Astrophysics and Space Sci San Diego CA 92093

MENINO, ALFRED RODRIGUES, JR., reproductive physiology educator; b. Hilo, Hawaii, Sept. 17, 1954; s. Alfred R. and Gertrude V. (Dias) M.; m. Rebecca Suzanne Whelchel, July 7, 1979; 1 dau., Holly Marie Ann. B.A. in Biology, U. Hawaii, 1976; M.S. in Animal Sci, Wash. State U., 1978, Ph.D. in Animal Sci, 1981. Teaching asst. in animal sci., research asst. in animal sci. Wash. State U., 1977-81; asst. prof. animal sci. U. Hawaii-Hilo, 1981—; cons. in field. Contbr. articles on reproductive physiology to profl. jours. Mem. Sci. Research Soc., Am. Soc. Animal Sci., Internat. Embryo Transfer Soc., Soc. for Study of Reprodn., AAAS, Phi Kappa Phi, Sigma Xi. Roman Catholic. Current Work: Mammalian embryology with emphasis on the domestic species. Subspecialties: Animal physiology; Reproductive biology. Office: 1400 Kapiolani St Hilo HI 96720

MENNINGER, WILLIAM WALTER, psychiatrist; b. Topeka, Oct. 23, 1931; s. William Claire and Catharine Louisa (Wright) M.; m. Constance Arnold Libbey, June 15, 1953; children: Frederick Prince, John Alexander, Eliza Wright, Marian Stuart, William Libbey, David Henry. A.B., Stanford U., 1953; M.D., Cornell U., 1957. Diplomate: Am. Bd. Psychiatry and Neurology, Am. Bd. Forensic Psychiatry. Intern Harvard Med. Service, Boston City Hosp., 1957-58; resident in psychiatry Menninger Sch. Psychiatry, 1958-61; chief med. officer, psychiatrist Fed. Reformatory, El Reno, Okla., 1961-63; asso. psychiatrist Peace Corps, 1963-64; staff psychiatrist Menninger Found., Topeka, 1965—, coordinator for devel., 1967-69, dir. law and psychiatry, 1981-85, dir. dept. edn., 1984—, chief staff, 1984—; clin. supr. Topeka State Hosp., 1969-70, sect. dir., 1970-72, asst. supt., clin., dir. residency tng, 1972-81; clin. prof. U. Kans. Med. Sch.; adj. prof. Washburn U., Wichita State U.; instr. Topeka Inst. for Psychoanalysis; mem. adv. bd. Nat. Inst. Corrections, 1975—, chmn., 1980-84; cons. U.S. Bur. Prisons; mem. Fed. Prison Facilities Planning Council, 1970-73. Syndicated columnist: In-Sights, 1975-83; Author: Happiness Without Sex and Other Things Too Good to Miss, 1976, Caution: Living May Be Hazardous, 1978, Behavioral Science and the Secret Service, 1981; Editor: Psychiatry Digest, 1971-74; mem. bd. editors, 1974-78; Contbr. chpts. to books, articles to profl. jours. Mem. nat. health and safety com. Boy Scouts Am., 1970—, chmn., 1980-85, mem. nat. exec. bd., 1980—; mem. Kans. Gov.'s Adv. Commn. on Mental Health, Mental Retardation and Community Mental Health Services, 1983—; bd. dirs. Nat. Com. for Prevention Child Abuse, 1975-83; mem. nat. adv. health council HEW, 1967-71; mem. Nat. Commn. Causes and Prevention Violence, 1968-69, Kans. Gov.'s Penal Planning Council, 1970. Served with USPHS, 1959-64. Fellow ACP, Am. Psychiat. Assn., Am. Coll. Psychiatrists; mem. AMA, Group for Advancement of Psychiatry (chmn. com. mental health services 1974-77), Inst. Medicine Nat. Acad. Scis., Am. Psychoanalytic Assn., Am. Acad. Psychiatry and Law, AAAS. Current Work: Administration, preventive psychiatry, applications in corrections, law and psychiatry, public education. Subspecialty: Psychiatry. Office: Menninger Found Box 829 Topeka KS 66601

MENON, MADHAVAN KRISHNA, pharmacologist, researcher; b. Trivandrum, India, Dec. 10, 1936; came to U.S., 1969, naturalized, 1979; s. Krishnapillay Madhavan Nayar and Mookambika Rajamma M.; m. Nirmala Krishna Menon, Aug. 27, 1966; children: Murali Madhav, Anupama. B.S., U. Coll., Trivandrum, 1954; B.Pharm., Madras (India) Med. Coll., 1959; M.S., Sawai Man Singh Med. Coll., Jaipur, India, 1964, Ph.D., 1969. Research fellow, research asst. Sawai Man Singh Med. Coll., 1960-64, asst. research officer, 1964-66; asst. prof. U. Saugar, India, 1966-69; postdoctoral research fellow VA Med. Center, Sepulveda, Calif., 1969-72, pharmacologist, 1974-79; chief VA Med. Center (psychoPharmacology Research lab.), 1979—; research pharmacologist Clarke Inst. Psychiatry, Toronto, Ont., Can., 1972-73; pharmacologist dept. pharmacology Sch. Medicine, U. Calif., San Francisco, 1973-74; research psychopharmacologist dept. psychiatry and biobehavioral scis. Neuropsychiat. Inst., UCLA, 1979—. Contbr. articles to sci. jours. Indian Council Med. Research research fellow, 1960-63; Found.'s Fund for Research in Psychiatry fellow, 1969-72; Found. for Vol. Control of Psychophysiol. States fellow, 1972-73. Mem. Am. Soc. Pharmacology and Exptl. Therapeutics, Soc. Neurosci., Soc. Biol. Psychiatry, AAAS, Western Pharmacology Soc., Brit. Brain Research Assn. (hon.), European Brain and Behavior Soc. (hon.), N.Y. Acad. Sci. Patentee antiparkinsonism drug. Current Work: Research on etiological and therapeutic aspects of schizophrenia, alcoholism, and movement disorders such as Parkinson's disease, tardive dyskinesias, myoclonus, attentional deficit disorder, Huntington's disease. Research on pharmacological, neurochemical and behavioral aspects of drugs of abuse, temperature regulation, electromyography and drug-receptor interactions. Subspecialties: Psychopharmacology; Neuropharmacology. Office: 16111 Plummer St Sepulveda CA 91343

MENSAH, THOMAS, chemical engineer; b. Ghana, Jan. 21, 1950; s. John K. and Margaret J. M.; m. R. Lucerchia, Apr. 25, 1983. B.S. in Chem. Engring., U. Sci. and Tech., Ghana, 1974; Ph.D., in Chem. Engring., U. Sci. and Tech., Montpellier, France, 1978; cert. MIT, 1977. Plant engr. Troy Polymers, Newark, 1978-80; sr. reserach engr. Air Products and Chems., Allentown, Pa., 1980-83; tech. leader fiber optics Corning Glass Works, N.Y., 1983—. Contbr. articles to profl. jours. Patentee in field. Invited speaker Engring. Found. Conf., New England, 1983; recipient speaker award Air Products Chems., Allentown, Pa., 1981; Govt. of France fellow, 1974. Mem. Am. Inst. Chem. Engrs. (local chpt. chmn. 1985, session chmn. at nat. confs., San Francisco, 1984, Houston, 1985), N.Y. Acad. Scis., Optical Soc. Am., Soc. Mfg. Engrs., Am. Chem. Soc. Current work: Technical leader fiber draw process, coatings, radiation curing, telecommunications, reactor design, lasers, laser monitoring, glass processing. Subspecialties: Fiber optics; Chemical engineering. Office: Corning Glass Works Sullivan Park Research and Devel DV-18 Corning NY 14831

MENSE, ALLAN TATE, research scientist; b. Kansas City, Mo., Nov. 29, 1945; s. Martin Conrad and Nancy (Tate) M.; m. Ramona Carol Stelford, Aug. 26, 1983; children: by previous marriage: Melanie Georgia, Eileen Madelaine. B.S., U. Ariz., 1968, M.S., 1970; Ph.D., U. Wis., 1977. Research scientist, fusion energy div. Oak Ridge Nat. Lab., 1976-79; sci. cons., sci. and tech. com. U.S. Ho. of Reps., Washington, 1979-81; sr. scientist, fusion sci. dept. McDonnell Douglas Astronautics Co., St. Louis, 1981-85; chief scientist Dept. of Def., 1985—; adj. prof. physics U. Mo., St. Louis, 1982-85. Contbr. articles to profl. jours. Served to capt. USAF, 1975. Mem. Am. Phys. Soc., Am. Nuclear Soc., Am. Vacuum Soc., IEEE (sr.), AIAA, Sigma Xi, Theta Tau. Current Work: Analyze scientific information and programs in areas of strategic defense initiative. Subspecialties: Nuclear fusion; Plasma engineering. Home: 601 Braxton Pl Alexandria VA 22301 Office: Strategic Def Initiative Orgn Office Sec of Def Washington DC 20301

MENYHERT, WILLIAM ROBERT, research and development scientist; b. Budapest, Hungary, Jan. 7, 1935; s. William and Piroska (Muranyi) M.; m. Louisa Guthrie Roach, Oct. 18, 1964; children—William Lansing, Gabriella Anne, Genavieve Gomori. Diploma med. chemistry Med. U. Budapest, 1956, Sc.D., 1964; diploma Georgetown U., 1957; postgrad. Boston U., 1960, Harvard U., 1961. Chemist, Ohio Valley Gen. Hosp., Wheeling, W.Va., 1957-58; biochemist Oscar B. Hunter Meml. Labs., Washington, 1958-60; research scientist Lahey Found., Boston, 1962; research scientist Bionics Systems Research, Alexandria, Va., 1962-63; asst. prof. chemistry U. Md., College Park, 1963-64; asst. prof. pharmacol. chemistry Howard U., Washington, 1964-65; pres. Menyhert Labs., Inc. and Cem-Pox Co., Washington, 1965-73; v.p. research and devel. Superior Polymers Co. Inc., Easton, Md., 1973-76; dir. Environ. Sci. Cons., Nags Head, N.C., 1976-79; v.p., pres. Inovations, Inc., St. Micheals, Md., 1980-82, also dir.; dir. polymer div. Innova, Inc., Clearwater, Fla., 1982-83; head dept. research Security Tag Systems, Inc., St. Petersburg, Fla., 1984—; courtesy prof. chemistry U. South Fla., Tampa, 1983—; cons. U.S. Armed Forces, 1966—, Presdl. Council on Consumer Affairs, 1968-70, Presdl. Council on Environment, 1969-72. Contbr. articles to profl. jours. Patentee in field. Founder, mem. Scientists and Engrs. for Nixon, 1968; mem. nationalities council Nat. Republican Party, 1970—; mem. nationalities sect. Com. to Re-Elect the Pres., 1972. Recipient Presdl. citation White House, 1970. Fellow Am. Inst. Chemists (cert.); mem. Am. Chem. Soc., Am. Def. Preparedness Assn., N.Y. Acad. Scis., Polymer Chemists Inc. Roman Catholic. Current work: Conductive polymers-polymer growth using unique oxi-redox systems; conductive states in semi-crystalline matrixes; new polymers via metal-organo ligands. Subspecialties: Polymer chemistry; Conductive polymers. Office: Security Tag Systems Inc 1615 118th Ave N Saint Petersburg FL 33742

MENZEL, DAVID WASHINGTON, oceanographer; b. Bilaspur, India, Feb. 22, 1928; came to U.S., 1941; s. Emil W. and Ida E. (Thrun) M.; m. Dorothy A. Adamy, Sept. 7, 1951. B.S., Elmhurst Coll., 1949; M.S., U. Ill., 1952; Ph.D., U. Mich., 1958. Marine biologist, Bermuda Biol. Sta., 1957-63; assoc. scientist Woods Hole Oceanographic Inst., Mass., 1963-70; dir. Skidaway Inst. Oceanography, Savannah, Ga., 1970—. Contbr. numerous articles to profl. jours. Served with U.S. Army, 1952-54. Mem. Am. Soc. Limnologist and Oceanography, Am. Geophys. Union. Current work: Oceanography-marine geochemistry, biology. Subspecialty: Oceanography.

MENZEL, RONALD GEORGE, soil scientist, researcher; b. Independence, Iowa, Jan. 23, 1924; s. Raymond Gerald and Amy Bonnie (Dillard) M.; m. Elsie Gray Burke, Feb. 23, 1952; children—Martha Jean, Robert Gray. B.S., Iowa State U., 1947; Ph.D., U. Wis., 1950; Soil scientist U.S. Dept. Agr., Beltsville, Md., 1950-69, Durant, Okla., 1969—. Editor Jour. Environ. Quality, 1977-83. Recipient Outstanding Performance award U.S. Dept. Agr., 1980. Fellow Am. Soc. Agronomy (bd. dirs. 1983—); mem. Soil Conservation Soc. Am., Am. Chem. Soc., AAAS, Okla. Acad. Sci. Methodist. Lodge: Kiwanis (pres. Durant 1979-80). Current work: Water quality from agricultural watersheds; sediment trapping and nutrient enrichment in small impoundments. Subspecialties: Soil science; Environmental chemistry. Home: 1216 Alma Dr Durant OK 74701 Office: Agrl Research Service US Dept Agr PO Box 1430 Durant OK 74702

MERCER, KERMIT RAY, biophysics educator; b. Brockport, N.Y., June 1, 1933; s. Harold R. and Elma H. (Case) M.; m. Janet L. Hollinger, Feb. 28, 1953; children: Deborah L., Susan R. B.S., SUNY-Brockport, 1970. 2Electronics asst. Delco div. Gen. Motors Corp., Rochester, N.Y., 1951-53; research assoc. Gen. Dynamics, Rochester, 1957-70; assoc. tchr. Monroe County BOCES, Spencerport, N.Y., 1970-72; assoc. in biophysics U. Rochester, 1972—; owner Electro-Sci., Brockport, N.Y., 1963—. Chmn. Clarkson (N.Y.) Bd. Appeals, 1963—. Served with USAF, 1953-57. Mem. IEEE, U.S. Power Squadron. Club: Oak Orchard Yacht. Current Work: Radiation damage to DNA constituents using ESR techniques involving magnetic fields, microwaves and cryogenics. Subspecialties: Electron spin resonance; Biophysics (physics). Home: 7816 Ridge Rd Brockport NY 14420 Office: Univ Rochester Dept Biophysics Rochester NY 14642

MERCHANT, MYLON EUGENE, engineer, physicist; b. Springfield, Mass., May 6, 1913; s. Mylon Dickinson and Rebecca Chase (Currier) M.; m. Helen Silver Bennett, Aug. 4, 1937; children—Mylon David, Leslie Ann Merchant Alexander, Frances Sue Merchant Jacobson. B.S. magna cum laude, U. Vt., 1936, D.Sc. (hon.), 1973; D.Sc., U. Cin., 1941, U. Salford, Eng., 1980. Research physicist Cin. Milacron, Inc., 1940-48, sr. research physicist, 1948-51, asst. dir. research, 1951-57, dir. phys. research, 1957-63, dir. sci. research, 1963-69, dir. research planning, 1969-81, prin. scientist, mfg. research, 1981-83; dir. advanced mfg. research Metcut Research Assocs., Inc., 1983—; adj. prof. mech. engring. U. Cin., 1964-69; vis. prof. mech. engring. U. Salford, Eng., 1973—. Contbr. articles to profl. jours. Bd. dirs. Dan Beard council Boy Scouts Am., 1967-80, pres.'s council, 1980—. Recipient Georg Schlesinger prize City of Berlin, 1980; Otto Benedikt prize Hungarian Acad. Scis., 1981. Fellow Am. Soc. Lubrication Engrs. (pres. 1952-53), Am. Soc. Metals, Ohio Acad. Sci.; mem. Nat. Acad. Engring., Soc. Mfg. Engrs. (hon.; pres. 1976-77), ASME (hon.), Internat. Instn. Prodn. Engring. Research (hon.; pres. 1968-69), Engring. Soc. Cin. (pres. 1961-62), Fedn. Materials Socs. (pres. 1974), Phi Beta Kappa, Sigma Xi, Tau Beta Pi. Research on systems approach to mfg. Current Work: Research on computer integrated manufacturing (computer automation, optimization and integration of total system of manufacturing). Subspecialty: Mechanical engineering. Home: 3709 Center St Cincinnati OH 45227 Office: 11240 Cornell Park Dr Cincinnati OH 45242

MERCIER, PAUL, oral and maxillofacial surgeon, researcher; b. Montreal, Que., Can., Mar. 3, 1936; s. Oscar and Jeanne (Bruneau) M.; m. Andree Fernet, Aug. 27, 1960; children: Bruno, Brigitte. B.A., U. Montreal, 1956, D.D.S., 1961; diploma, U. Pa., 1964. Diplomate: Am. Bd. Oral and Maxillofacial Surgeons. Asst. prof. oral surgery Faculty Dental Medicine, U. Montreal, 1964-69, assoc. prof., 1969-73; research assoc. St.-Mary's Hosp., Montreal, 1974—; examiner Royal Coll. Dentists, 1969—; Nat. Bd. Dental Examiners, Can., 1970-73; dir. Clinic for Atrophy of Maxillae, 1974—. Editorial bd.: Internat. Jour. Oral Surgery, 1980. Fellow Royal Coll. Dentists Can.; mem. Internat. Assn. Dental Research, Can. Assn. oral and Maxillofacial Surgeons (pres. 1973), Que. Assn. Oral and Maxillofacial Surgeons, Am. Assn. Oral and Maxillofacial Surgeons. Current Work: Primary activity centered around the rehabilitation of severe masticatory deficits due to atrophy of jaws. Subspecialty: Oral and maxillofacial surgery. Office: St-Mary's Hosp 3830 Lacombe Ave Montreal PQ H3T 1M5 Canada

MEREDITH, ORSELL MONTGOMERY, research administrator; b. Jamestown, N.Y., Oct. 19, 1923; s. Orsell Montgomery and Bernardine Elva (Goggin) Meredith; m. Martha Linnea Helbon, Jan. 29, 1949; 1 son, Michael Wayne. B.S., U. Chgo., 1948; M.S., U. So. Calif., 1951, Ph.D., 1953; M.S., Am. U., 1975. Asst research pharmacologist, asst. prof. biophysics and nuclear medicine UCLA, 1953-61; research scientist Lockheed Palo Alto Research Labs., Calif., 1961-66; ops. research analyst/radiation biologist Naval Radiol. Def. Lab., 1966-69, Naval Ordnance Lab., 1969-75; exec. sec. grants rev. Nat. Cancer Inst., Bethesda, Md., 1976—. Contbr. articles to profl. publs. Served to lt. (j.g.) USNR, 1942-46. Mem. Radiation Research Soc., Am. Soc. Pharmacology and Exptl. Therapeutics, N.Y. Acad. Scis., Soc. Nuclear Medicine, Health Physics Soc. Current Work: Research administration. Subspecialties: Biophysics (physics); Operations research (engineering). Home: PO Box 4135 Rockville MD 20850 Office: 5333 Westbard Ave Room 822 Bethesda MD 20892

MEREWETHER, DAVID EVAN, electromagnetic engineer, researcher; b. Detroit, July 7, 1936; s. Edward Merewether and Mary (Kimball) Merewether McCanless; m. Torksey Ann Ensminger, June 12, 1958; children—Pamalee, Kimball, David Evan. B.S. in Elec. Engring., U. N. Mex., 1960, B.A. in Math., 1960, M.S. in Elec. Engring., 1962, Ph.D. in Elec. Engring., 1968. With Sandia Labs., Albuquerque, 1960-71, Mission Research Corp., Albuquerque, 1971-77, Electro Magnetic Applications Inc., Albuquerque, 1977—; mem. tech. adv. groups Def. Nuclear Agy., Washington, 1969-72, 75-77, 80-85, also various govt. agys. Patentee RFI-EMP Enclosures; contbr. articles to profl. jours. Served with USMC, 1953-57. Recipient Best EMP Paper award Summa Found., 1973-74. Mem. IEEE. Current work: Electromagnetic pulse, electromagnetic interference, electromagnetic compatability, RFI shielding and hardening. Subspecialty: Electrical engineering. Office: Electro Magnetic Applications Inc 1025 Hermosa SE Albuquerque NM 87108

MERGLER, HARRY WINSTON, engineering educator; b. Chillicothe, Ohio, June 1, 1924; s. Harry Franklin and Letitia (Walburn) M.; m. Irmgard Erna Steudel, June 22, 1948; children—Myra A. L., Marcia B. E., Harry F. B.S., M.I.T., 1948; M.S., Case Inst. Tech., 1950, Ph.D., 1956. Aero. research scientist NACA, 1948-56; mem. faculty Case Inst. Tech., 1957—, prof. engring., 1962—, Leonard Case prof. engring., 1973—; dir. Digital Systems Lab., 1959—; vis. scientist, USSR, 1958; vis. prof. Norwegian Tech. U., 1962; cons. to industry, 1957—; editor Control Engring. mag., 1956—; pres. Digital/Gen. Corp., 1968-72; cons. Exploratory Research div. NSF. Author: Digital Systems Engineering, 1961, also articles, chpts. in books. Served with AUS, 1942-45. Recipient Gold medal for sci. achievement Case Inst. Tech., 1980. Fellow IEEE (pres. Indsl. Electronic Soc. 1977-79, Lamme medal 1978); mem. Cleve. Engring. Soc., N.Y. Acad. Scis., Nat. Acad. Engring., Sigma Xi, Tau Beta Pi, Theta Tau, Pi Delta Epsilon, Zeta Psi, Blue Key. Current Work: Robotic vision, in-process ganging. Subspecialties: Computer engineering; Robotics. Home: 1525 Queen Anne's Gate Westlake OH 44145

MERICLE, DAVID ALLEN, clinical chemist, consultant; b. Centerville, Iowa, July 14, 1947; s. Trenton and Lola Ruth (McCannon) M. B.A. in Chemistry, Ariz. State U., 1971. Internat. customer service Motorola Semicondr., Phoenix, 1971—; med. technologist Mesa Luth. Hosp., Ariz., 1974-79, head chemistry and nuclear medicine, 1979—, clin. lab coordinator, 1982—. Mem. Am. Chem. Soc., Am. Soc. Clin. Pathologists. Current work: Evaluating, developing and implementing newtest protocols and quality control procedures for clinical chemistry, therapeutic drug monitoring, toxicology and nuclear medicine. Subspecialties: Clinical chemistry; Nuclear medicine. Home: 429 W Flint Chandler AZ 85224 Office: Mesa Luth Hosp 525 W Brown Mesa AZ 85201

MERIGAN, THOMAS CHARLES, JR., physician, med. researcher, educator; b. San Francisco, Jan. 18, 1934; s. Thomas C. and Helen M. (Greeley) M.; m. Joan Mary Freeborn, Oct. 3, 1959; 1 son, Thomas Charles III. B.A. with honors, U. Calif., Berkeley, 1955; M.D., U. Calif., San Francisco, 1958. Diplomate: Am. Bd. Internal Medicine. Intern in medicine 2d and 4th Harvard med. services Boston City Hosp., 1958-59, asst. resident medicine, 1959-60; clin. asso. Nat. Heart Inst., NIH, Bethesda, Md., 1960-62; asso. Lab. Molecular Biology, Nat. Inst. Arthritis and Metabolic Diseases, NIH, 1962-63; practice medicine specializing in internal medicine and infectious diseases, Stanford, Calif., 1963—; asst. prof. medicine Stanford U. Sch. Medicine, 1963-67, asso. prof. medicine, 1967-72, head div. infectious diseases, 1966—, prof. medicine, 1972—, George E. and Lucy Becker prof. medicine, 1980—; dir. Diagnostic Microbiology Lab., Univ. Hosp., 1966-72, Diagnostic Virology Lab., 1969—; hosp. epidemiologist; mem. microbiology research tng. grants com. NIH, 1969-73, virology study sect., 1974-78; cons. antiviral substances program Nat. Inst. Allergy and Infectious Diseases, 1970—; mem. Virology Task Force, 1976-78, bd. sci. counselors, 1980-84; mem. U.S. Hepatitis panel U.S. and Japan Cooperative Med. Sci. Program, 1979—; co-chmn. interferon evaluation Group Am. Cancer Soc., 1978-81; mem. adv. com. J.A. Hartford Found., 1980—; mem. Albert Lasker awards jury; mem. vaccines and related biol. products adv. com. FDA. Contbr. numerous articles on infectious diseases, virology and immunology to sci. jours.; editor: Antivirals with Clinical Potential, 1976, Antivirals and Virus Diseases of Man, 1979, 2d edit., 1984. Regulatory Functions of Interferon, 1980, Interferons, 1982; asso. editor: Virology, 1975-78; co-editor: monograph series Current Topics in Infectious Diseases, 1975—; editorial bd.: Archives Internal Medicine, 1971-81, Jour. Gen. Virology, 1972-77, Infection and Immunity, 1973—, Intervirology, 1973—, Virology, 1975-78, Proc. Soc. Exptl. Biology and Medicine, 1978—, Reviews of Infectious Diseases, 1979—, Jour. Interferon Research, 1980—, Antviral Research, 1980—, Jour. Antimicrobial Chemotherapy, 1981—, Molecular and Cellular Biochemistry, 1982—, AIDS Research, 1983—, Jour. Virology, 1984—. Recipient Borden award for Outstanding Research Am. Assn. Med. Colls., 1973; Guggenheim Meml. fellow, 1972. Mem. Assn. Am. Physicians, Western Assn. Physicians, Am. Soc. Microbiology, Am. Soc. Clin. Investigation (council 1977-80), Am. Assn. Immunologists, Am. Fedn. Clin. Research, Western Soc. Clin. Research, Soc. Exptl. Biology and Medicine, Infectious Diseases Soc. Am.; mem. Am. Soc. Virology; Mem. Inst. Medicine; mem. Pan Am. Group for Rapid Viral Diagnosis; Mem. AMA; mem. Internat. Soc. Interferon Research (council 1983—); Mem. Calif. Med. Assn., Santa Clara County Med. Soc., Calif. Acad. Medicine, Royal Soc. Medicine, AAAS, Alpha Omega Alpha. Current Work: Host response to viral infections (including interferon); antivirals. Subspecialties: Virology (medicine); Infectious diseases. Home: 148 Goya Rd Portola Valley CA 94025 Office: Div Infectious Diseases Stanford Univ Sch Medicine Stanford CA 94305

MERILAN, CHARLES PRESTON, dairy husbandry scientist; b. Lesterville, Mo., Jan. 14, 1926; s. Peter Samuel and Cleo Sarah (Harper) M.; m. Phyllis Pauline Laughlin, June 12, 1949; children—Michael Preston, Jean Elizabeth. B.S. in Agr, U. Mo., 1948, A.M., 1949, Ph.D., 1952. Mem. faculty U. Mo., Columbia, 1950—, prof. dairy husbandry, 1959—, chmn. dept., 1961-62; asso. dir. Mo. Agrl. Expt. Sta., 1962-63, asso. investigator space sci. research center, 1964-74, exec. sec., dir. grad. studies physiology area, 1969-72, chmn. univ. patent and copyright com., 1963-80. Served with USMC, 1944-45. Decorated Purple Heart. Mem. AAAS, Am. Chem. Soc., Am. Dairy Sci. Assn., Am. Soc. Animal Sci, IEEE (profl. group biomed. electronics), Soc. Cryobiology, Sigma Xi, Alpha Zeta, Gamma Sigma Delta, Phi Beta Pi. Researcher on biol. material preservation. Current Work: Reproductive physiology, cell preservation, bioinstrumentation, biophyscal characterization of cellular response to microenvironmental parameters. Subspecialties: Animal physiology; Biophysics (biology). Home: 1509 Bouchelle Ave Columbia MO 65201 Office: Univ Missouri Columbia MO 65211

MERILO, MATI, research engineer, research administrator; b. Tallinn, Estonia, Jan. 23, 1944; came to U.S., 1977; s. Arkadi and Hermeline (Dampf) M.; m. Kathleen Lorraine Frail, Aug. 21, 1971; children: Erik Grant, Aleksander Evan, Kristi-Anne Merilo. B.Eng., McGill U., Montreal, Que., 1966; M.S., Case Inst. Tech., 1968, Ph.D., 1972. Research engr. Atomic Energy of Can. Ltd., Chalk River, Ont., 1971-77; project mgr. Electric Power Research Inst., Palo Alto, Calif., 1977—. Editor: Thermal-Hydraulics of Nuclear Reactors, 1983; contbr. articles to profl. jours. Mem. ASME, Am. Nuclear Soc. Current Work: Two phase flow and heat transfer, aerosol transport and deposition. Subspecialties: Mechanical engineering; Fluid mechanics. Office: Electric Power Research Inst 3412 Hillview Ave Palo Alto CA 94303

MERLIN, HOWARD ELIOT, information systems company consultant; b. Uniontown, Pa., Apr. 1, 1949; s. David K. and Shirley B. (Nebelkopf) M.; m. Debrah Ann Schenker; 1 child, Jessica. B.S. in Physics with high honors, U. Va., 1970; M.S. in Physics, U. Pa., 1973, M.B.A., Wharton Sch., 1976. C.P.A., Pa. Acct. Ernst and Whinney, Pitts., 1976-78; sr. fin. analyst Rockwell Internat., Pitts., 1978-81; asst. treas. Tasa Corp., Pitts., 1981-84; sr. cons. Corp. Info. Systems, Bridgeville, Pa., 1984—; part time instr. Robert Morris Coll., Pitts., 1977-78. Mem. Pitts. Ctr. Internat. Visitors, 1977—; reader Golden Triangle Radio for Blind, Pitts., 1977. Recipient Nat. Internship, Ernst and Whinney, 1975; U. Pa. fellow, 1970-73; Mem. Am. Phys. Soc., Wharton Alumni Assn. (treas. 1978—), Am. Inst. C.P.A.s, Pa. Inst. C.P.A.s, Nat. Assn. Accts., Sigma Xi, Sigma Pi Sigma, Alpha Phi Omega. Current work: Capture and efficient representation of industrial telemetry for financial and manufacturing data base decision systems, local communications networks. Subspecialty: Software engineering. Home: 5610 Marlborough Rd Pittsburgh PA 15217 Office: Corp Info Systems 850 Boyce Rd Pittsburgh PA 15017

MERMIN, N. DAVID, physicist, physics educator; b. New Haven, Mar. 30, 1935; s, John and Eva (Gordon) M.; m. Dorothy E. Milman, June 9, 1957; children—Jonathan George, Elizabeth Ruth. A.B., Harvard U., 1956, A.M., 1957, Ph.D., 1961. NSF postdoctoral fellow U. Birmingham, Eng., 1961-63; postdoctoral fellow U. Calif., San Diego, 1963-64; from asst. to assoc. prof. physics Cornell U., Ithaca, N.Y., 1964-72, prof., 1972—, dir. Lab. Atomic & Solid State Physics, 1984—; Loeb Lectr. Harvard U., Cambridge, Mass., 1980; Emil Warburg prof. U. Bayreuth, Ger., 1981; Japan Soc. Promotion of Sci. fellow Nagoya U., 1982; Walker Ames prof. U. Washington, Seattle, 1984. Author: Space and Time in Special Relativity, 1968; (with others) Solid State Physics, 1976. Contbr. articles to profl. jours. Sloan Found. fellow, 1966-68; Guggenheim fellow, 1970-71. Fellow Am. Phys. Soc. Subspecialty: Condensed matter physics. Home: 315 The Parkway Ithaca NY 14850 Office: Cornell Univ Lab of Atomic & Solid State Physics Clark Hall Ithaca NY 14853

MERRIAM, DANIEL F(RANCIS), geologist; b. Omaha, Feb. 9, 1927; s. Faye Mills and Amanda Frances (Wood) M.; m. Annie Laura Young, Feb. 12, 1946; children: Beth Ann Merriam Wissman, John Francis, Anita Pauline Merriam Howe, James Daniel, Judith Diane Merriam Palley. B.S., U. Kans., 1949, M.S., 1953, Ph.D., 1961; M.Sc., Leicester U., 1969, D.Sc., 1975. Geologist, Union Oil Co. Calif., Rocky Mountains and W. Tex., 1949-51, summer 1952; asst. instr. U. Kans., 1951-53, instr., 1954, research assoc., 1963-71; geologist Kans. Geol. Survey, 1953-58, div. head basic geology, 1958-63, chief geologic research, 1963-71; Jessie Page Heroy prof. geology Syracuse U., 1971-81, chmn. dept., 1971-80; Endowment Assn. Disting. prof. natural sci., chmn. dept. geology Wichita State U., 1981—; vis. research scientist Stanford U., 1963; Fulbright-Hays sr. research fellow, U.K., 1964-65; dir. Am. Geol. Inst.'s Internat. Field Inst. to Japan, 1967; vis. prof. geology Wichita State U., 1968-70; Am. Geol. Inst. vis. geol. scientist, 1969; U.S. del. UNESCO-IUGS Internat. Geol. Correlations Program, Budapest, 1969; mem. U.S. Nat. Com. for IGCP, 1976-79, 81-83, chmn., 1976-79; participant project COMPUTe, Dartmouth Coll., 1974; Esso disting. lectr. Earth Scis. Found., U. Sydney, Australia, 1979; vis. prof. Centre d'Informatique Geologique, Ecole des Mines de Paris, 1980; mem. U.S. Nat. Commn. for UNESCO, 1979—. Founder, editor-in-chief: Math. Geology, 1968-76, Computers & Geoscis., 1975—; editorial cons.: Geosystems, 1971-83; co-editor: Pacific Geology, 1971-83; founder, editor: Syracuse U. Geology Contbns., 1973-81; editorial rev. bd.: Colo. Sch. Mines Quar., 1974—; editorial com.: Syracuse U. Press, 1978-81; nat. editor: The Compass (Sigma Gamma Epsilon), 1983—; corr.: Open Earth, 1978-83; contbr. articles to sci. jours. Served with USNR, 1945-46. Recipient Erasmus Haworth Grad. award in Geology, U. Kans., 1955. Fellow Geol. Soc. Am., AAAA (chmn. sect. E. 1983-84, chmn. sect. nominating com. 1983-84); mem. Am. Assn. Petroleum Geologists (bus. com. 1956-57, research com. 1964-67, chmn. field trip research and coordination com. 1964-73, assoc. editor 1969-75, Matson Award com. 1970, acad. adv. com. 1973-77, ho. of dels. 1974-76, 84—, computer applications in geology com. 1971-81, membership com. 1980—); Mem. (chmn. tech. program com. regional meeting 1983); mem. Soc. Econ. Paleontologists and Mineralogists (chmn. research group in computer tech. 1970-75, 82-83, nominating com. 1972-73, publs. com. 1980-83, chmn. 1981-82), Classification Soc. (chmn. membership com. 1968-71, dir. 1968-71, council 1968-72); Mem. Geosci. Info. Soc. (program com. 1980-82); mem. Internat. Assn. Math. Geology (council 1968—, sec.-gen. 1972-76, pres. 1976-80, chmn. Pres.'s Prize com. 1981, others, Wm. Christian Krumbein medal 1981); mem. N.Y. State Geol. Assn. (exec. sec. 1972-77, pres. 1977-78, dir. 1978-82), Rocky Mountain Assn. Geologists (research com. 1966-69), Kans. Acad. Sci. (program chmn. geology sect. 1959, mem. council 1983—), Geologists Assn. (Eng.) (field trip dir. 1965), CODATA (ad hoc com. on publs. 1980), Internat. Union Geol. Scis. (chmn. adv. bd. on publs. 1980—, chmn. 1980-84), Kans. Geol. Soc. (mem. coms., dir. 1964), Leicester Geol. Soc. (hon. life), Nat. Assn. Geology Tchrs., Sigma Xi, Sigma Gamma Epsilon (Alpha chpt. pres. 1952-53); Mem. Phi Kappa Phi. Current Work: Developing quantitative techniques for stratigraphic correlation, analyzing cyclic sediments, and plains-type folding; defining similarity functions for comparing thematic maps; study recent sediments in Florida Bay and their analogies in the ancient rock record, especially in the midcontinent. Subspecialties: Geology; Fuels. Office: Dept Geology Wichita State Univ Wichita KS 67208

MERRIFIELD, ROBERT BRUCE, biochemist, educator; b. Ft. Worth, July 15, 1921; s. George E. and Lorene (Lucas) M.; m. Elizabeth Furlong, June 20, 1949; children—Nancy, James, Betsy, Cathy, Laurie, Sally. B.A., UCLA, 1943, Ph.D., 1949. Chemist Park Research Found., 1943-44; research asst. Med. Sch., UCLA, 1948-49; asst. Rockefeller Inst. for Med. Research, 1949-53, asso., 1953-57; asst. prof. Rockefeller U., 1957-58, assoc. prof., 1958-66, prof., 1966—, John D. Rockefeller prof., 1983—. Assoc. editor: Internat. Jour. Peptide and Protein Research; Contbr. aritcles sci. jours. Recipient Lasker award biomed. research, 1969, Gairdner award, 1970, Intra-Sci. award, 1970, Nichols medal, 1973; Alan E. Pierce award Am. Peptide Symposium, 1979; Nobel prize in Chemistry, 1984. Mem. Am. Chem. Soc. (award creative work synthetic organic chemistry 1972), Nat. Acad. Scis., Am. Soc. Biol. Chemists, Sigma Xi, Phi Lambda Upsilon, Alpha Chi Sigma. Developed solid phase peptide synthesis; completed (with B. Gutte) 1st total synthesis of an enzyme, 1969. Subspecialty: Biochemistry (biology). Office: Rockefeller U New York NY 10021

MERRILL, EDWARD WILSON, educator; b. New Bedford, Mass., Aug. 31, 1923; s. Edward Clifton and Gertrude (Wilson) M.; m. Genevieve de Bidart, Aug. 19, 1948; children—Anne de Bidart, Francis de Bidart. A.B., Harvard, 1945; D.Sc., Mass. Inst. Tech., 1947. Research engr. Dewey & Almy div. W.R. Grace & Co., 1947-50; mem. faculty Mass. Inst. Tech., 1950—, prof. chem. engring., 1964—, Carbon P. Dubbs prof., 1973—; cons. in field, 1950—; research asso. in surgery Beth Israel Hosp., Boston, 1969—. Author articles on polymers, rheology, med. engring. Pres. bd. trustees Buckingham Sch., Cambridge, 1969-74; trustee Browne and Nichols Sch., Cambridge, 1972-74, hon. trustee, 1974—. Fellow Am. Acad. Arts and Scis.; mem. Am. Chem. Soc., Am. Inst. Chem. Engrs., Am. Phys. Soc., Am. Soc. Artificial Internal Organs. Episcopalian (vestry 1960-69). Patentee chem. and rheological instruments. Current work: Biopolymer separations and purification; blood viscosity; clinical measurement. Home: 90 Somerset St Belmont MA 02178

MERRILL, MARSHALL LEIGH, software engineer; b. Paducah, Ky., Oct. 23, 1955; s. Glenn Herschel and Perla Dudley (Hudson) M. B.A. in Math./Computer Sci., U. S. Ala., 1977; M.S. in Computer Sci., Northwestern U., 1978. Cons. Computer Cons., Mobile, Ala., 1975-77, Telemed Corp., Hoffman Estates, Ill., 1978-80; research and devel. software engr. Teletype Corp., Skokie, Ill., 1980—; instr. computer sci. Northwestern U., Evanston, Ill., 1978-80, freelance programmer. Mem. Assn. Computing Machinery, IEEE Computer Soc. Baptist. Current Work: Microcomputer networks and operating systems, computer graphics on microcomputers. Subspecialties: Operating systems; Graphics, image processing, and pattern recognition. Home: 8258 Niles Center Rd #20 Skokie IL 60077 Office: 5555 Touhy Skokie IL 60077

MERRILL, ROBERT PERKINS, chemical engineering educator; b. Salt Lake City, Nov. 17, 1934; s. O. . and Ruth (Perkins) M.; m. Oretta Jeanne Cluff; children—Ellen Merrill Fluckeger, Laurie Merrill Grimsman, Lydelle, David, Paul. B. Chem. Engring., Cornell U., 1960; Sc.D., MIT, 1964. Instr. chem. engring. MIT, 1963-64; asst. prof. chem. engring. U. Calif., Berkeley, 1964-70, assoc. prof., 1970-73, prof., 1973-77; H.F. Johnson prof. Cornell U., 1977—; cons. Universal Oil Products, Chgo., E.I. duPont de Neurs, Wilminton, Del. Stake pres. Ch. of Jesus Christ of Latter-Day Saints, Ithaca, N.Y., 1980—. Mem. Am. Chem. Soc., Am. Inst. Chem. Engrs., Am. Phys. Soc., Am. Vacuum Soc. Current work: Molecular surface chemistry and physics of chemically reactive surfaces; molecular beams. Subspecialty: Surface chemistry. Office: Cornell Univ 201 Olin Hall Ithaca NY 14850

MERRIN, CLAUDE EMILE ANDRE, physician, clin. researcher; b. Paris, Apr. 18, 1936; came to U.S., 1966, naturalized, 1975; s. Bernard and Isabelle (Haimo) M. B.S. in Exptl. Sci, U. Paris, 1955; M.D., U. Buenos Aires, 1962. Cert. Am. Bd. Urology. Intern, ACS fellow Cook County Hosp., Chgo., 1966-67, resident in gen. surgery, 1967-68, in urology, 1968-71; cancer research urologist Roswell Park Meml. Inst., Buffalo, 1971-72, sr. cancer research urologist, 1972-73, acting dir. dialysis unit and transplantation, 1973-74, acting chief dept. urologic oncology, 1973-74, dir. dialysis unit and transplantation program, 1973-79, chief dept. urologic oncology, 1974-79; research assoc. in surgery SUNY, Buffalo, 1971-73; urologic oncologist Swedish Covenant Hosp., Chgo., 1979—; assoc. clin. prof. urology Strich Med. Sch., Loyola U., Chgo., 1979—; cons. European Orgn. Research on Treatment of Cancer, Ill. Cancer Council. Contbr. articles to profl. jours. Mem. Am. Assn. Cancer Research, Am. Soc. Clin. Oncology, Am. Urol. Assn. Acad. Surgery, Chgo. Med. Soc., Chgo. Urol. Soc., Ill. State Med. Soc., Ill. State Urol. Soc., N.Y. State Cancer Program Assn., Roswell Park Surg. Soc., Soc. Surg. Oncology. Current Work: Clin. oncological researc; urologic oncology, clin. research. Subspecialties: Chemotherapy; Urology. Office: 5145 N California Ave Chicago IL 60625

MERRITT, DAVID ALAN, computer systems engineer; b. Takoma Park, Md., Aug. 4, 1948; s. Walter David and Mary Sue (Branch) M.; m. Maureen Therese English, May 12, 1983. B.S. in math magna cum laude, Met. State Coll., Denver, 1976. Computer specialist NOAA, Boulder, Colo., 1976-77, computer systems engr., wave propagation labs., 1978—; software engr. Data Gen. Corp., Denver, 1977-78; cons. in field. Served with USAF, 1968-72. Recipient Software Productivity award NOAA, 1976, 77, Software Engring. award, 1981, 82; Tech. Achievement award Data Gen. Corp., 1978. Mem. Assn. for Computing Machinery. Current work: Real-time data acquisition, control, and networking for remote sensing of the atmosphere; operating systems software engineering. Subspecialties: Software engineering; Operating systems. Home: 907 Acadia Ave Lafayette CO 80026 Office: NOAA-WPL-REWP-4 325 Broadway Boulder CO 80303

MERTENS, THOMAS ROBERT, biology educator; b. Ft. Wayne, Ind., May 22, 1930; s. Herbert F. and Hulda C. (Burg) M.; m. Beatrice Janet Abair, Apr. 1, 1953; children: Julia Ann, David Gerhard. B.S., Ball State U., 1952; M.S., Purdue U., 1954, Ph.D., 1956. Research assoc. dept. genetics U. Wis.-Madison, 1956-57; asst. prof. biology Ball State U., Muncie, Ind., 1957-62, assoc. prof., 1962-66, prof., 1966—, dir. doctoral programs in biology, 1974—. Author: Genetics Laboratory Investigations, 1980, 85; co-author: Human Genetics, 1983; contbr. articles to profl. jours. NSF fellow Stanford U., 1963-64; recipient Service award Nat. Assn. Biology Tchrs., 1981, Disting. Alumnus award Ball State U., 1983. Fellow Ind. Acad. Sci., AAAS; mem. Nat. Assn. Biology Tchrs. (pres. 1985), Am. Genetic Assn., Genetics Soc. Am., others. Lutheran. Current Work: Human genetics education, educational needs assessments relative to human genetics and bioethics. Subspecialty: Genetics and genetic engineering (biology). Home: 2506 Johnson Rd Muncie IN 47304 Office: Dept Biology Ball State Univ Muncie IN 47306

MERTON, ROBERT K(ING), sociologist, educator, science historian; b. Phila., July 5, 1910. A.B., Temple U., 1971, LL.D. (hon.), 1956; A.M., Harvard U., 1932, Ph.D., 1936, LL.D. (hon.), 1980; L.H.D. (hon.), Emory U., Loyola U., Chgo., Kalamazoo Coll., Cleve. State U., U. Pa., Brandeis U.; Dr. honoris causa, U.Leyden; LL.D. (hon.), Western Res U., U. Chgo., U., Md.; LItt.D. (hon.), Colgate U., SUNY, Columbia U.; D.Sc.Soc. (hon.), Yale U.; D.Sc. Econ. (hon.), U. Wales; Ph.D. (hon.), Hebrew U. Jerusalem, Tutor, instr. Harvard U., Cambridge, Mass., 1936-39; assoc. prof., prof., chmn. Tulane U., New Orleans, 1939-41; from asst. prof. sociology to prof. Columbia U., N.Y.C., assoc. dir. bur. applied social research, 1942-71, Giddings prof. sociology, 1963-74, Univ. prof., 1974-79, Univ. prof. emeritus, 1979—, Spl. Service prof., 1979-84; adj. prof. Rockefeller U., 1979—; resident scholar Russell Sage Found., 1979—; cons. to numerous companies and orgns. Author: Science, Technology and Society in Seventeenth-Century England, 1938; On the Shoulders of Giants: A Shandean Postscript, 1965, 85; On Theoretical Sociology, 1967; Social Theory and Social Structure, 1968; The Sociology of Science: Theoretical and Empirical Investigations, 1973; Sociological Ambivalence and Other Essays, 1976; The Sociology of Science: An Episodic Memoir, 1979; Social Research and the Practicing Professions, 1982. Editor, co-editor books in field; mem. editorial bd. various jours. Trustee, Inst. for Sci. Info., 1968—. Guggenheim fellow, 1962; MacArthur Prize fellow, 1983—. Mem. Am. Sociol. Assn. (pres. 1957), Eastern Sociol. Soc. (pres. 1969), Internat. Sociol. Assn. (exec. council 1971-73), Sociol. Research Assn. (pres. 1968), Soc. for Study of Social Problems, History of Sci. Soc., History of Tech. Soc., Soc.for Social Studies of Sci. (pres. 1975-76), AAUP, Authors Guild (mem. council 1974-78), The Tocqueville Soc. Club: Century (N.Y.C.). Current work: Sociology of science; history of science; selected problems in the sociology of scientific knowledge; socially expected durations; the self-fulfilling prophecy. . Office: Fayer Weather 415 Columbia U New York NY 10027

MERTZ, DAVID BYRON, biology educator; b. Sandusky, Ohio, July 10, 1934; s. Henry William and Mary (Hettrick) M.; m. Sarah Burnham, Feb. 25, 1961. S.B., U. Chgo., 1960, Ph.D., 1965. NSF postdoctoral fellow U. Calif.-Berkeley, 1965-66; asst. prof. U. Calif.-Santa Barbara, 1966-69; assoc. prof. U. Ill.-Chgo., 1969-74, prof. dept. biol. scis., 1974—. Co-editor: Readings in Ecology and Ecological Genetics, 1970; mem. editorial bds. jours.: Ecology, 1970-71, Evolution, 1979. NSF grantee, 1967-79. Mem. AAAS, Am. Soc. Naturalists, Ecol. Soc. Am., Soc. for Study Evolution, Brit. Ecol. Soc. Democrat. Current Work: Studies in experimental demography, interspecies competition, ecological genetics, population theory. Subspecialties: Ecology (environmental science); Evolutionary biology. Home: 1226 E Madison Park Chicago IL 60615 Office: Dept Biol Scis Univ Ill-Chicago Chicago IL 60680

MERTZ, EDWIN THEODORE, biochemist, educator; b. Missoula, Mont., Dec. 6, 1909; s. Gustav Henry and Louise (Sain) M.; m. Mary Ellen Ruskamp, Oct. 5, 1936; children: Martha Ellen, Edwin T. B.A., U. Mont., 1931, D.Sc. (hon.), 1979; M.S. in Biochemistry, U. Ill., 1933, Ph.D. in Biochemistry, 1935; D.Agr. (hon.), Purdue U., 1977. Research biochemist Armour & Co., Chgo., 1935-37; instr. biochemistry U. Ill., 1937-38; research asso. pathology U. Iowa, 1938-40; instr. agrl. chemistry U. Mo., 1940-43; research chemist Hercules Powder Co., 1943-46; prof. biochemistry Purdue U., West Lafayette, Ind., 1946-76, emeritus, 1976—; vis. prof. U. Notre Dame, South Bend, Ind., 1976-77; cons. in field. Author: Elementary Biochemistry, 1969. Recipient McCoy award Purdue U., 1967; John Scott award City of Phila., 1967; Hoblitzelle Nat. award Tex. Research Found., 1968; Congressional medal Fed. Land Banks, 1968; Disting. Service award U. Mont., 1973; Browning award Am. Soc. Agronomy, 1974; Pioneer Chemist award Am. Inst. Chemists, 1976. Mem. AAAS, AAUP, Nat. Acad. Scis., Am. Soc. Biol. Chemists, Am. Inst. Nutrition (Osborne-Mendel award 1972), Am. Chem. Soc. (Spencer award 1970), Am. Assn. Cereal Chemists. Presbyterian. Co-discoverer high lysine corn, 1963. Current Work: Improvement of nutritional value of cereal grains through genetics and genetic engineering. Subspecialties: Genetics and genetic engineering (agriculture); Plant genetics. Office: Dept Agronomy Purdue U Lafayette IN 47907

MERTZ, WALTER, nutritionist; b. Mainz, Germany, May 4, 1923; s. Oskar and Aenne (Gablemann) M.; m. Marianne C. Maret, Aug. 8, 1953. M.D., U. Mainz, 1951. Lic. physician, W. Ger. Intern County Hosp., Hersfeld, W. Ger., 1952-53; with NIH, Bethesda, Md., 1953-61, Walter Reed Army Inst. Research, Washington, 1961-69; staff Human Nutrition Research Ctr., U.S. Dept. Agr., Beltsville, Md., 1969—; dir. Human Nutrition Research Ctr., U.S. Dept. Agr. (Beltsville Ctr.), 1972—. Served with Germany Army, 1941-42. Recipient Research and Devel. Achievement award Dept. Army, 1969; Superior Service award U.S. Dept. Agr., 1972. Mem. Am. Inst. Nutrition (Osborne and Mendel award 1971, Lederle award 1982), Am. Soc. Clin. Nutrition. Current Work: Trace element nutrition and metabolism. Subspecialty: Nutrition (biology). Office: US Dept Agr Bldg 308 BARC-East Beltsville MD 20705

MESELSON, MATTHEW STANLEY, educator, biochemist; b. Denver, May 24, 1930; s. Hymen Avram and Ann (Swedlow) M.; m. Sarah Page; children: Zoe, Amy Valor. Ph.B., U. Chgo., 1951, D.Sc. (hon.), 1975; Ph.D., Calif. Inst. Tech., 1957; Sc.D. (hon.), Oakland Coll., 1964, Columbia, 1971. From research fellow to sr. research fellow Calif. Inst. Tech., 1957-60; asso. prof. biology Harvard U., 1960—, prof. biology, 1964-76, Thomas Dudley Cabot prof. natural scis., 1976—. Recipient prize for molecular biology Nat. Acad. Scis., 1963, Eli Lilly award microbiology and immunology, 1964, Alumni medal U. Chgo., 1971; Pub. Service award Fedn. Am. Scientists, 1972; Lehman award N.Y. Acad. Scis., 1975; Alumni Distinguished Service award Calif. Inst. Tech., 1975; Leo Szilard award Am. Phys. Soc., 1978, MacArthur Prize fellow, 1984—. Mem. Am. Acad. Arts and Scis., Council Fgn. Relations, Accademia Santa Chiara, Nat. Acad. Scis., Inst. Medicine, Am. Philos. Soc., Royal Soc. London (fgn.), Academie des Sciences (fgn.). Subspecialty: Biochemistry (biology). Address: Fairchild Biochem Bldg 7 Divinity Ave Harvard U Cambridge MA 02138

MESSENGER, GEORGE CLEMENT, engineering consultant; b. Bellows Falls, Vt., July 20, 1930; s. Clement George and Ethel Mildred (Farrar) M.; m. Priscilla Betty Norris, June 19, 1954; children—Michael Todd, Steven Barry, Bonnie Lynn. B.S. in Physics, Worcester Poly. Inst., 1951; M.S. in Elec. Engring., U. Pa., 1957. Engring. mgr. Philco, Phila., 1951-59, Hughes, Newport Beach, Calif., 1959-61; div. mgr. Transitron, Wakefield, Mass., 1961-63; engring. fellow Northrop, Newberry Park, Calif., 1963-67; pvt. practice engring. cons., Las Vegas, Nev., 1967—; lectr. UCLA, 1967-73. Author: (with others) Fundamentals of Nuclear Hardening of Electronic Equipment, 1977. Patentee microwave mixer diode. Contbr. articles to profl. jours. Recipient Spl. Heart award, 1984, Alan Berman Research Publ. award, 1983. Fellow IEEE; mem. Sigma Xi. Congregationalist. Club: Balboa Bay (Newport Beach). Current work: Radiation hardening of satellites and electronic systems; radiation hardening of integrated circuits to reduce single event upset caused by cosmic radiation. Subspecialties: Electronics; Nuclear physics. Home and Office: 3111 Bel Air #7F Las Vegas NV 89109

MESSIHA, FATHY SABRY, biochemical pharmacologist, toxicologist, educator; b. Cairo, Feb. 10, 1936; came to U.S., 1966, naturalized, 1972. Diploma in Pharmacy, U. Basel, Switzerland, 1963; Ph.D. in Physiol. Biochemistry, U. Bern, Switzerland, 1965; postgrad., Med. Chem. Inst., Sch. Medicine, 1965-66, U. Vt. Med. Sch., 1966-67. Research asso. Biochem. Research Lab., Spring Grove State Hosp., Balt., 1967-68; research scientist dept. biochemistry Md. Psychiat. Research Center, Balt., 1968-71, lab. dir. pharmacology unit, 1971-72; asso. prof. pharmacology and therapeutics Tex. Tech. U. Health Sci. Center Sch. Medicine, Lubbock, 1972-77, asso. prof. psychiatry, 1973-80, prof., 1980—, assoc. prof. pathology, 1977-80, prof., 1980—, dir. div. toxicology, 1980—. Editor 7 books, meeting presentations abstracts; contbr. over 150 articles to sci. jours., procs., chapt. to books. Mem. Am. Coll. Toxicology, Am. Soc. Pharmacology and Exptl. Therapeutics, Am. Pharm. Assn., Acad. Pharm. Scis., Soc. for Neurosci., N.Y. Acad. Scis., Collegium Internationale Neuropsychopharmacologicum, Soc. Exptl. Biology and Medicine, Internat. Union Pharmacology (sect. on toxicology), Am. Chem. Soc., Western Pharmacology Soc., AAAS, Research Soc. on Alcoholism. Copt Orthodox. Current Work: Toxicology, psychopharmacology, CNS-pharmacology, clinical pharmacology, biological psychiatry, enzymology, chemotherapy, drug metabolism, alcoholism. Subspecialties: Toxicology (medicine); Psychopharmacology. Office: Dept Pathology Tex Tech U Health Sci Center Sch Medicine Lubbock TX 79430

MESSING, JOACHIM W., molecular biologist, educator; b. Duesburg, W.Ger., Sept. 10, 1946; came to U.S., 1978; s. Heinrich and Martha (Pfeifer) M.; m. Rita C. Stremmer, Sept. 25, 1975; 1 child, Simon. B. Arts & Scis., Mercator Gymnasium, Duisburg, 1966; B.S., in Pharmacy, Apothekerkammer, Dusseldorf, W.Ger., 1968; M.S., Free U. of Berlin, 1971; Dr.rer. nat., LM U., Munich, W.Ger., 1975. Research fellow Max Planck Inst. of Biochemistry, Munich, 1975-78; vis. research assoc. in biochemistry and biophysics U. Calif.-San Francisco, 1978; research assoc. in bacteriology U. Calif.-Davis, 1978-80; asst. prof. biochemistry U. Minn., St. Paul, 1980-82, assoc. prof., 1982-84, prof., 1984-85; prof. Rutgers U., New Brunswick, N.J., 1985—, dir. research Waksman Inst., Piscataway, N.J., 1985—; cons. and lectr. in field. Co-author: An Introduction to Recombinant DNA Techniques, 1984. Contbrs. chpts. to books, articles to profl. jours. Mem. editorial bd.: DNA; Jour. of Biotech. Recipient award 1981 paper in life scis., 1981-82. Research fellow Deutsche Forschungsgemeinschaft, 1978-80. Mem. AAAS, Am. Soc. Biol. Chemists, Internat. Soc. Plant Molecular Biologists, Sigma Xi. Current Work: Regulation of gene expression in higher plants, M13 cloning, sequencing, gene synthesis. Subspecialties: Molecular biology; Gene actions. Office: Rutgers U Waksman Inst Microbiology Hoes Ln PO Box 759 Piscataway NJ 08854

MESSING, RITA BAILEY, pharmacologist; b. Bklyn., July 7, 1945; d. Max and Kate (Katkin) Zimmerman; m. William Messing, June 20, 1965; 1 son, Charles. B.A. magna cum laude, Bklyn. Coll., 1966; Ph.D., Princeton U., 1970. Asst. prof. Rutgers U., Camden, N.J., 1969-72; research asso. M.I.T., 1973-75; asso. research psychobiologist U. Calif., Irvine, 1976-81; Research fellow Organon Pharms, Oss, The Netherlands, 1980; asst. prof. U. Minn., 1981—. Editor: (with others) Endogenous Peptides and Learning and Memory Processes, 1981. NSF fellow, 1966-69; Med. Found. fellow, 1974-75; Organon fellow, 1980. Mem. AAAS, Am. Soc. Pharmacology and Exptl. Therapeutics, Soc. Neursci. Patentee in field. Current Work: Neuropharmacology and Behavioral Toxicology. Subspecialties: Neuropharmacology; Neurobiology. Home: 735 Goodrich Ave St Paul MN 55105 Office: Dept Pharmacology U Minn Minneapolis MN 55455

MESULAM, M. MARSEL, neurologist, medical educator; b. Istanbul, Turkey, Apr. 7, 1945; s. Mose and Fani (Rozanes) M.; married; 1 dau., Semra. B.A., Harvard U., 1968, M.D., 1972. Diplomate: Am. Bd. Psychiatry and Neurology. Assoc. prof. neurology Harvard U. Med. Sch., 1980—; dir. neuroanatomy and behavioral neurology Beth Israel Hosp., Boston, 1979—. Mem. Internat. Brain Research Orgn., Am. Neurol. Assn., Am. Acad. Neurology, Am. Assn. Anatomists, Histochem. Soc., Soc. Neurosci. Current Work: Connections of the brain; behavioral neurology. Subspecialties: Neurology; Neuroanatomy. Home: 15 Desmond Watertown MA 02172 Office: Beth Israel Hosp Boston MA 02215

METCALF, JOHN FRANKLIN, medical educator, researcher; b. Phoenix, Dec. 12, 1944; s. John Allen and Lois McIlwain (Willet) M.; m. Susan Wolschina, Sept. 5, 1974; children: Andrew Allen, Jessica Lynn, Christopher John. B.A., Northwestern U., 1966, M.D., 1969. Diplomate: Am. Bd. Internal Medicine. Intern and jr. resident Cleve. Met. Hosp., 1969-71; resident, fellow Duke U. Med. Ctr., Durham, N.C., 1973-75; postdoctoral fellow U. Calif.-San Diego, 1975-77; asst. prof. dept. medicine Med. U. S.C., Charleston, 1977—; staff physician Univ. Hosp., Charleston, 1977. Served to capt. U.S. Army, 1971-73, Vietnam. USPHS grantee, 1978. Fellow Am. Fedn. Clin. Research; mem. Am. Thoracic Soc., ACP, Am. Coll. Chest Physicians, Phi Beta Kappa, Alpha Omega Alpha. Democrat. Current Work: Pathophysiology of gas exchange in pulmonary disease; inflammatory secretion of proteases by alveolar macrophages. Subspecialties: Physiology (biology); Pulmonary medicine. Office: 171 Ashley Ave Charleston SC 29425

METCOFF, JACK, pediatrician, educator; b. Chgo., Feb. 2, 1917; B.S., Northwestern U., 1938, M.D., 1942, M.S., 1944; M.P.H., Harvard U., 1944. Diplomate Am. Bd. Pediatrics, Am. Bd. Nutrition. Asst. prof. pediatrics Childrens Med. Ctr., Boston, 1953-56; chmn. dept. pediatrics Michael Reese Hosp., Chgo., 1956-70; prof. pediatrics Northwestern U., Chgo., 1956-63; prof. pediatrics U. Okla., Oklahoma City, 1970-76, G.L. Cross research prof., 1976—; cons. in pediatrics to surgeon gen. U.S. Navy, 1966-72, NIH, 1980—; mem. council Nat. Kidney Found., 1950-67. Contbr. articles to profl. jours. Served with USPHS, 1943-45. Grantee NIH, 1948-82, USDA, 1980-84; recipient Alexander von Humboldt prize, 1985. Mem. Am. Coll. Nutrition (council), Internat. Pediatric Nephrology Assn. (council), Am. Inst. Nutrition, Am. Soc. Clin. Nutrition, Am. Physiol. Soc., Am. Pediatric Soc., Am. Soc. Clin. Investigation, Am. Soc. Nephrology, Internat. Soc. Nephrology, Am. Soc. Pediatric Nephrology, Central Soc. Clin. Research, Am. Acad. Cert. Med. Nutritionists. Club: Cosmos (Washington). Current work: Cell biochemistry related to nutrition in pregnancy, neonatology, nephrology, malnutrition. Subspecialties: Nutrition (medicine); Nephrology. Office: Dept Pediatrics Univ Okla Health Scis Center PO Box 26901 Oklahoma City OK 73190

METH, SHELDON ZALMEN, physicist; b. Bklyn., Aug. 28, 1950; s. Irving and Rose (Greenapple) M.; m. Marcia Stark, June 6, 1971; children—Abraham Asher, Rivka Miriam, Nathaniel. B.S., Columbia U., 1971, M.A., 1973, M. Phil., 1974, Ph.D., 1977. Programmer, CCNY, 1970-71; grad. research asst. Columbia Radiation Lab., N.Y.C., 1971-77; mem. tech. staff Inco, Inc., McLean, Va., 1977-78; staff mem. The BDM Corp., McLean, 1978-79, scientist, 1979-80, sr. scientist, 1980-82, mgr. optics expts., 1982-84, dir. directed energy interactions and countermeasures tech., 1984—. Patentee in field. Vice pres. SE Hebrew Congregation, Silver Spring, Md., 1980-81, 84—, bd. dirs., 1981-82, rec. sec., 1982-83; bd. edn. Yeshivah High Sch. of Greater Washington, 1983—; hon. bd. dirs. Hebrew Acad. Greater Washington, Silver Spring, 1980-82. Recipient teaching excellence citation Columbia U., 1973. Mem. Am. Def. Preparedness Assn., Am. Phys. Soc., IEEE (sr.), Optical Soc. Am., Assn Orthodox Jewish Scientists, Assn. Old Crows, Sigma Xi. Current work: Laser countermeasure materials development; directed energy interactions technology; strategic defense technology; fiber optic sensors; laser radar; signal and data processing, systems design and engineering, high performance nuclear power sources and applications. Subspecialties: Military applications of lasers; Advanced technology assessment. Office: The BDM Corp 7915 Jones Branch Dr McLean VA 22102

METSGER, ROBERT WILLIAM, geologist; b. N.Y.C., Apr. 27, 1920; s. William Martin and Mabel (Herbst) M.; m. Sylvia Haff, Mar. 29, 1947 (dec. 1961); children: Mary Gwendolen Metsger Chong, Deborah Anne; m. Barbara Lawrence Holbert, Aug. 2, 1963; 1 son, Robert Lawrence. A.B., Columbia Coll., 1948. Cert. profl. geol. scientist. With N.J. Zinc. Co., Ogdensburg, N.J., 1949—, chief geologist, 1981—. Contbr. numerous geol. articles to profl. publs. Sr. warden Christ Ch., Newton, N.J., 1978-83, vestryman, 1984—; v.p. Western Dist., Episcopal Diocese of Newark, 1972-76, pres, 1976-80, mem. missions dept., 1972-82. Served to lt. comdr. USNR, 1941-46. Fellow Geol. Soc. Am. (chmn. NE sect. 1981-82); mem. Soc. Econ. Geologists, Am. Inst. Profl. Geologists. Republican. Episcopalian. Lodge: Rotary. Current Work: Studies of the genesis and subsequent alteration and tectonic disruption of a Precambrian ore deposit in New Jersey; studies of Earth strain, both as a result of mining activity and as a natural phenomenon. Subspecialties: Geology; Hydrology. Home: 69 Hunters Ln Sparta NJ 07871 Office: NJ Zinc Co Inc Plant St Ogdensburg NJ 07439

METTLER, RUBEN FREDERICK, electronics and engineering company executive; b. Shafter, Calif., Feb. 23, 1924; s. Henry Frederick and Lydia M.; m. Donna Jean Smith, May 1, 1955; children: Matthew Frederick, Daniel Frederick. Student, Stanford, 1941-43; B.S. in Elec. Engring, Calif. Inst. Tech., 1944, M.S., 1947, Ph.D. in Elec. and Aero. Engring, 1949. Registered profl. engr., Calif. Asso. div. dir. systems research and devel. Hughes Aircraft Co., 1949-54; spl. cons. to asst. sec. def., 1954-55; asst. gen. mgr. guided missile research div. Ramo-Wooldridge Corp., 1955-58; pres. Space Tech. Labs., Inc., Los Angeles, 1962-65, TRW Systems Group, 1965-68; exec. v.p., dir. TRW Inc. (formerly Thompson Ramo Wooldridge, Inc.), 1965, asst. pres., 1968-69, pres., 1969-77, chmn. bd., chief exec. officer, 1977—; dir. Bank Am. Corp., Merck & Co.; past vice-chmn. Ind. adv. council Dept. Def. Author reports airborne electronic systems. Nat. campaign chmn. United Negro Coll. Fund, 1980; chmn. Pres.' Sci. Policy Task Force, 1969; mem. Pres.' Blue Ribbon Def. Panel, 1969-70, Emergency Com. for Am. Trade; chmn. Nat. Alliance Business, 1978-79; vice chmn. bd. trustees Calif. Inst. Tech.; trustee Com. Economic Devel.; bd. dirs. Nat. Action Council for Minorities in Engring.; trustee Cleve. Clinic Found. Served with USNR, 1942-46. Named 1 of ten Outstanding Young Men of Am. U.S. Jr. C. of C., 1955; So. Calif.'s Engr. of Year, 1964; recipient Meritorious Civilian Service award Dept. Def., 1969, Nat. Human Relations award NCCJ, 1979; Excellence in Mgmt. award Industry Week mag., 1979. Fellow IEEE, AIAA; mem. Sci. Research Soc. Am., Bus. Roundtable (Chmn. 1982—), Conf. Bd. (trustee 1982—), Bus. Council (vice chmn. 1981-82), Nat. Acad. Engring., Sigma Xi, Eta Kappa Nu (named nation's outstanding young elec. engr. 1954), Tau Beta Pi, Theta Xi. Clubs: Cosmos (Washington); Union (Cleve.), 50 (Cleve.). Patentee interceptor fire control systems. Subspecialties: Aerospace engineering and technology; Electronics, engineering management. Home: 1900 Richmond Rd Cleveland OH 44124 Office: 1 Space Park Redondo Beach CA 90278

METZ, CHARLES EDGAR, medical physics educator; b. Bayshore, N.Y., Sept. 11, 1942; s. Clinton Edgar and Grace Muriel (Schienke) M.; m. Maryanne Theresa Bahr, July 1, 1967; children—Rebecca, Molly. B.A., Bowdoin Coll., 1964; M.S., U. Pa., 1966, Ph.D., 1969. Instr. U. Chgo., 1969-71, asst. prof., 1971-75, assoc. prof., 1976-80, dir. grad. programs in med. physics, 1979-85, prof. radiology, 1980—, prof. structural biology, 1984—; cons. Internat. Atomic Energy Agy., Vienna, Austria, 1976-78; cons. Bolt, Bernek & Newman, Inc., Cambridge, Mass., 1976-79, vis. scientist, 1979; mem. editorial bd. Med. Decision Making, 1980-84. Contbr. articles to profl. jours. Editor: Information Processing in Scintigraphy, 1975. Current work: Development of methodology for the evaluation of diagnostic performance; digital image processing and image reconstruction. Subspecialties: Medical physics; Imaging technology. Office: Box 225 U Chgo 5841 S Maryland Ave Chicago IL 60637

METZGER, ALBERT EMANUEL, space scientist; b. N.Y.C., Sept. 10, 1928; s. Frederic and Hortense (Abrams) M.; married; children: Joslyn Vahni, Loren Frederic. Student, Bethany (W.Va.) Coll., 1946; B.A., Cornell U., Ithaca, N.Y., 1949; M.A., Columbia U., 1951, Ph.D., 1958. Chemist Sylvania Electric Products, Inc., Bayside, L.I., 1951-54; scientist, research group supr. Jet Propulsion Lab., Pasadena, Calif., 1960—. Contbr. articles to profl. jours. Recipient Exceptional Sci. Achievement medal NASA, 1975. Fellow AAAS; mem. Am. Phys. Soc., Am. Geophys. Union, Am. Astron. Soc., Phi Lambda Upsilon. Current Work: Spacecraft expt. design, devel., data reduction and analysis in fields of planetary composition, magnetospheric interactions, and high energy astrophysics. Subspecialties: Planetary science; Gamma ray high energy astrophysics. Office: 4800 Oak Grove Dr Pasadena CA 91109

METZGER, ROBERT MELVILLE, chemistry educator, cons. researcher; b. Yokohama, Japan, May 7, 1940; s. Ferdinand J. and Gabriella J. (Szigeti) M.; m. Christian D. Csoeke-Poeckh, Sept. 12, 1971; 1 son, Gian-Lorenzo. B.S., UCLA, 1962; Ph.D., Calif. Tech. Inst., 1968. Postdoctoral research assoc. Stanford (Calif.) U., 1969-71, 1972; lectr. Italian, 1970-71; asst. prof. chemistry U. Miss., University, 1971-76, assoc. prof., 1976-83, prof., 1983—, Coulter prof., 1984—; vis. prof. U. Heidelberg, W.Ger., 1969-70, Bordeaux U., France, 1969-70. Contbr. articles on chemistry to profl. jours. Mem. Am. Chem. Soc., Am. Phys. Soc., Am. Crystallographic Assn. Current Work: Organic donor-acceptor crystals, cohesion and ionicity, organic unimolecular rectifiers, polarizability calculations. Subspecialties: Theoretical chemistry; Solid state chemistry. Home: 2225 Lee Loop Oxford MS 38655 Office: Dept Chemistry U Miss University MS 38677

METZGER, W. JAMES, physician, educator; b. Pitts., Oct. 30, 1945; s. Walter James and Marion Smith (Vine) M.; m. Carol Louise Hughes, Jan. 17, 1942; children: James Andrew, Joel Robert, Anne Elizabeth. B.A., Stanford U., 1967; M.D., Northwestern U., 1971. Diplomate: Am. Bd. Allergy and Clin. Immunology. Staff allergist David Grant Med. Center, Travis AFB, Calif., 1976-78; asst. prof. internal medicine U. Iowa Med. Sch., Iowa City, 1978-84; assoc. prof. internal medicine East Carolina U. Sch. Medicine, 1984—, also head sect. allergy. Served to maj. USAF, 1976-78. Fellow ACP, Am. Acad. Allergy and Clin. Immunology; mem N. Central Allergy Soc. (pres.), N.C. Soc. Allergy. Current Work: Allergy, immunotherapy, asthma, late asthmatic responses, mediators of late responses. Subspecialties: Internal medicine; Allergy. Office: Dept Internal Medicine East Carolina U Sch Medicine Brody Bldg Greenville NC 27834

METZL, MARILYN NEWMAN, clinical psychologist, educator; b. N.Y.C., Apr. 12, 1938; d. George and Rose (Shanen) Newman; m. Kurt Metzl, June 25, 1961; children: Jonathan, Jordan, Jamie, Joshua. B.A., Queens Coll., CUNY, 1959; M.A., Hunter Coll., 1969; Ph.D., U. Kans., 1978. Therapist Columbia Presbyn. Med. Ctr., N.Y.C., 1960-63; dir. Dependent Clinic, Ismir, Turkey, 1963-65; therapist Menorah Med. Ctr., Kansas City, Mo., 1966-68; dir. Family Devel. Ctr., Spelman Hosp., Smithville, Mo., 1980—; assoc. prof. Avila Coll., Kansas City, 1978—; dir. Psycholednl. Assocs., Kansas City, 1971—; dir. Family Devel. Ctr. Gardner (Kans.) Hosp., 1982—. Mem. Soc. for Research in Child Devel., Am. Psychol. Assn., Council for Exceptional Children (mem. adv. com. div. children with communicative disorders 1980—), Am. Speech and Hearing Assn., NOW. Democrat. Jewish. Current Work: Parent-child interaction, parenting styles and child development, adolescent development, learning disabilities. Subspecialties: Cognition; Developmental psychology. Office: 601 E 63rd St Kansas City MO 64110

MEYER, DALE R., research scientist; b. Cin., Sept. 15, 1946; s. George Ernest and Thelma Louise N.; m. Pamela De Angelo, May 23, 1970; children: Royce J., Justin T. B.A., U. Cin., 1969; Ph.D., U. Louisville, 1975. NIMH research fellow U. Minn., Mpls., 1975-77; sr research toxicologist pathology and toxicology sect. Norwich-Eaton Pharms., Norwich, N.Y., 1977-79; research assoc. dept. ophthalmology U. Louisville, 1979-82; research asst. prof. dept. ophthalmology U. Tex. Health Sci. Center, 1982—; cons. drug safety evaluation. Contbr. articles to profl. jours. NSF fellow, 1969-73. Mem. Internat. Soc. Chronobiology, Soc. Neuroscience, AAAS, Nat. Acad. Sci., N.Y. Acad. Sci., Assn. Research in Vision and Ophthalmology, U. Cin. Alumni Assn., U. Louisville Alumni Assn., Psi Chi. Current Work: Cell biology of ocular and neural tissues; in vitro model development for study of ophthalmic and neurotoxicity; clinical toxicology and pharmacology. Subspecialties: Cell biology; Toxicology (medicine). Office: 5323 Harry Hines Blvd Dallas TX 75235

MEYER, EDMOND GERALD, energy and natural resources educator; b. Albuquerque, Nov. 2, 1919; s. Leopold and Beatrice (Ilfeld) M.; m. Betty F. Knobloch, July 4, 1941; children: Lee Gordon, Terry Gene, David Gary. B.S. in Chemistry, Carnegie Mellon U., 1940, M.S., 1942; Ph.D. (research fellow), U. N.Mex., 1950. Chemist Harbison Walker Refractories Co., 1940-41; instr. Carnegie Mellon U., 1941-42; asst. phys. chemist Bur. Mines, 1942-44; chemist research div. N.Mex. Inst. Mining and Tech., 1946-48; head dept. sci. U. Albuquerque, 1950-52; head dept. chemistry N.Mex. Highlands U., 1952-59; dir. N.Mex. Highlands U. (Inst. Sci. Research), 1957-63; dean N.Mex. Highlands U. (Grad. Sch.), 1961-63; dean Coll. Arts and Sci., U. Wyo., 1963-75, v.p., 1974-80, prof. energy and natural resources, 1981—; exec. cons. Diamond Shamrock Corp., 1980; chmn. Carbon Fuels Corp., 1981—; chmn. Am. Nat. Bank, Laramie.; Sci. adviser Gov. Wyo.; cons. Los Alamos Nat. Lab., NSF, HHS, GAO, Diamond Shamrock Corp., Wyo. Bancorp.; contract investigator Research Corp., Dept. Interior, AEC, NIH, NSF, Dept. Energy, Dept. Edn.; Fulbright exchange prof. U. Concepcion, Chile, 1959. Co-author: Chemistry-Survey of Principles, 1963, Legal Rights of Chemists and Engineers, 1977, Industrial R&D Management, 1982; Contbr. articles to profl. jours. Served with USNR, 1944-46. Recipient Disting. service award Jaycees. Fellow AAAS, Am. Inst. Chemists (dir.); mem. Asso. Western Univs. (chmn. 1973-74), Am. Chem. Soc. (councillor), Chilean Chem. Soc., Biophys. Soc., Council Coll. Arts and Scis. (pres. 1971, sec.-treas. 1972-75, dir. Washington office 1973), C. of C. (pres. 1984), Sigma Xi. Current Work: Invention, development and commercialization of a novel coal based slurry transport and fuel system. Subspecialty: Coal. Home: 1058 Colina Dr Laramie WY 82070 Office: PO Box 3825 University Sta Laramie WY 82071

MEYER, FRED LEWIS, ops. research scientist, naval officer; b. Queens, N.Y., Sept. 8, 1943; s. Henry and Pauline F. (Bauer) M.; m. Patricia Lynn McGrath, Oct. 12, 1968; children: Julie Anne, James Bryant. A.B. in Psychology, U. Rochester, 1965; M.S. in Ops. Research, U.S. Naval Postgrad. Sch., 1973; diploma, Nat. Def. U., 1981. Commd. ensign U.S. Navy, 1965, advanced through grades to comdr., 1979; dep. planning officer Naval Supply Ctr., Charleston, S.C., 1973-75; asst. supply officer USS Saratoga, 1975-77; dir. stock point and afloat systems Naval Supply Systems Command Hdqrs., Washington, 1977-80; dir. fleet non-tactical logistics info. systems Chief of Naval Material Hdqrs., Washington, 1980-81; dir. systems devel., internat. logistics programs Aviation Supply Office, Phila., 1981-83, dep. comptroller, 1982—; Mem. supervisory com. Navy Fed. Credit Union, 1980-81. Writer: Supply Corps Newsletter, 1983—. Cubmaster Boy Scouts Am., 1977-81, asst. scoutmaster, 1981-82. Recipient Leadership award Gen. Dynamics Corp., 1965; Citizenship award B'nai B'rith, 1961; decorated Navy Commendation (2). Mem. Ops. Research Soc. Am., World Future Soc., Theta Chi. Republican. Lutheran. Current Work: Operations research of navy logistics and business systems; comptrollership; information systems functional applications; design; acquisition; planning; inventory and financial systems modelling; strategic planning; futuristics. Subspecialties: Operations research (mathematics); Information systems (Information science). Home: 5314 Stonington Dr Fairfax VA 22032 Office: 700 Robbins Ave Philadelphia PA 19111

MEYER, (LAWRENCE) DONALD, agricultural engineer, researcher; b. Concordia, Mo., Apr. 14, 1933; s. Lawrence Dick and Florence Malinda (Uphaus) M.; m. Loretta Lou Bush, Dec. 26, 1954; children—Dan W., James B., David J. Student Central Coll., Mo., 1950-51; B.S. in Agrl. Engring, U. Mo., 1954, M.S. in Agrl. Engring, 1955; Ph.D., Purdue U., 1964. Registered profl. engr., Ind. Agrl. engr. Agr. Research Service, USDA, West Lafayette, Ind., 1955-73, Sedimentation Lab, Oxford, Miss., 1973—; asst., assoc. prof. agrl. engring Purdue U., West Lafayette, 1965-73; adj. prof. agrl. and biol. engring Miss. State U., Starkville, 1975—. Contbr. articles to profl. jours. Recipient Outstanding Performance award U.S. Dept. Agr.-Agr. Research Service, 1959. Fellow Am. Soc. Agrl. Engrs. (chmn. Soil and Water div. 1972-73, dir. pub. 1968-69, Hancor Soil and Water engring. award 1985); mem. Soil Conservation Soc., Am., Soil Sci. Soc. Am., World Assn. Soil and Water Conservation. Club: Toastmasters (pres. 1982) Lodge: Optimists (Lafayette, Ind.). Current work: Soil erosion and sedimentation processes, erosion control practices, and erosion research technology. Subspecialties: Agricultural engineering; Soil science. Office: USDA Sedimentation Lab PO Box 1157 Oxford MS 38655

MEYER, RALPH ROGER, biological sciences educator; b. Milw., Feb. 18, 1940; s. Ralph George and Geneva Lorna (Schmidt) M.; m. Marjorie Kathleen Stark, Sept. 24, 1960 (div. 1971); children: Christine, Gregory, Lauren; m. Diane Carla Rein, Oct. 26, 1974; 1 child, Jocelyn. B.S., U. Wis.-Milw., 1961; M.S., U. Wis.-Madison, 1963, Ph.D., 1966. Postdoctoral fellow in biochemistry Yale U., 1966-67, SUNY-Stony Brook, 1967-69; asst. prof. biol. sci. U. Cin., 1969-75, assoc. prof., 1975-79, prof., 1979—; vis. prof. biochemistry Stanford U., 1977-78; vis. prof. Molecular biology U. Paris, 1983. Contbr. articles to profl. jours. NSF grantee, 1969-71; Am. Cancer Soc. grantee, 1969-73, 78—; NIH grantee, 1975—. Mem. Am. Soc. Biol. Chemists, Am. Soc. Cell Biology, Am. Soc. Microbiology, AAAS, Ohio Acad. Sci., Sigma Xi. Current Work: Regulation and mechanism of DNA synthesis in normal and turmor cells and in E. Coli. Subspecialties: Biochemistry (medicine); Cancer research (medicine). Home: 4067 Ridgedale Dr Cincinnati OH 45247 Office: Dept Biol Sci U Cin Cincinnati OH 45221

MEYER, WALTER, energy engineer; b. Chgo., Jan. 19, 1932; s. Walter and Ruth (Killoran) M.; m. Jacqueline Miscall, May 8, 1953; children: Kim, Holt, Eric, Leah, Suzannah. B.Chem. Engring., Syracuse (N.Y.) U., 1956, M.Chem. Engring., 1957; postgrad. (NSF Sci. Faculty fellow), M.I.T., 1962; Ph.D. (NSF Sci. Faculty fellow), Oreg. State U., 1964. Registered nuclear engr., Calif. Prin. chem. engr. Battelle Meml. Inst., Columbus, Ohio, 1957-58; instr., then asst. prof. Oreg. State U., 1958-64; research engr. Hanford Atomic Labs., Richland, Wash., 1959-60, Lawrence Radiation Lab., Livermore, Calif., 1964; from asst. prof. to prof. nuclear engring. Kans. State U., Manhattan, 1964-72; prof., chmn. nuclear engring. U. Mo., Columbia, 1972-82, Robert Lee Tatum prof. engring., 1974-82, co-dir. energy systems and resources program, 1974; co-founder Energy and Public Policy Center, 1981-82; 1st Niagara Mohawk Energy prof. Syracuse U., 1982—, dir. Inst. Energy Research, 1984—; adj. prof. nuclear engring. U. Mo.-Columbia; dir. summer insts. NSF-AEC, 1969, NSF, 1972; co-dir. summer instr. AEC, 1972, dir. workshop, 1973; dir. (ERDA workshops), 1975-79; mem. Columbia Coal Gasification Task Force, 1977, Gov. Kans. Nuclear Energy Council, 1971-72; cons. to govt. and industry. Author. Mem. Manhattan Human Relations Orgn., 1966-72; active local Boy Scouts Am.; Mo. co-chmn. No on 11 Com., 1980. Grantee NSF, 1965-67, 73-75, 77-80; Grantee AEC, 1969-71, 73-74; Grantee Dept. Def., 1969-72; Grantee ERDA, 1975, 77—; NRC, 1977-80. Fellow Am. Nuclear Soc. (chmn. pub. info. com. 1975-79, nat. spl. award 1974, outstanding service award 1980, bd. dirs. 1981-84); Mem. Am. Inst. Chem. Engrs. (chmn. nuclear engring. div. 1977-78), Am. Chem. Soc. (touring lectr. 1976-83), Am. Soc. Engring. Edn. (chmn. nuclear div. 1976-77), Am. Wind Soc., Sigma Xi, Tau Beta Pi. Presbyterian. Patentee in field. Subspecialties: Chemical engineering; Nuclear engineering. Home: 17 Horseshoe Ln Chittenango NY 13037 Office: Inst Energy Research B 139 Link Hall Syracuse U Syracuse NY 13210

MEYERAND, RUSSELL GILBERT, JR., scientist; b. St. Louis, Dec. 2, 1933; s. Russell Gilbert and Elsa Louise (Gebhardt) M.; m. Mary Grace Guillemin, June 16, 1956; 1 dau., Mary Elizabeth. B.S. in Elec. Engring, MIT, 1955, M.S. in Nuclear Engring, 1956, Ph.D. in Plasma Physics, 1959. Cons. to atomic power equipment dept. Gen. Electric Co., Schenectady, 1955-56; research asst. MIT, 1957-58; prin. scientist plasma physics United Technologies Research Center, East Hartford, Conn., 1958-64, chief research scientist, 1964-67, dir. research, 1967-79, v.p. tech., 1979—; Mem. vis. com. for sponsored research MIT; mem. adv. com. U. Hartford Sch. Arts and Scis., 1965—; mem. engring. adv. com. Rensselaer Poly. Inst., 1965—; mem. vis. com. Nat. Bur. Standards, 1980—. Contbr. articles to profl. jours., chpts. to books. Bd. dirs. Newington Children's Hosp. Recipient Eli Whitney award Conn. Patent Law Assn., 1979. Fellow AIAA; mem. Nat. Acad. Engring., IEEE, Am. Phys. Soc., Dirs. Indsl. Research, Sigma Xi. Patentee in field. Subspecialty: Plasma physics. Office: United Techs Corp United Techs Research Ctr Silver Ln East Hartford CT 06108

MEYERHOF, WALTER ERNST, physicist, educator; b. Kiel, Germany, Apr. 29, 1922; came to U.S., 1941, naturalized, 1946; s. Otto Fritz and Hedwig (Schallenberg) M.; m. Miriam G. Ruben, Aug. 21, 1947; children: Michael O., David L. Ph.D., U. Pa., 1946; Ph.D. hon. degree, U. Frankfurt, W. Ger., 1980. Asst. prof. U. Ill., Urbana, 1946-49; faculty physics Stanford U., 1949—, prof., 1959—, acting exec. head, 1962-63, chmn. dept. physics, 1970-77. Fellow Am. Phys. Soc. Subspecialty: Atomic and molecular physics. Home: 213 Blackburn Ave Menlo Park CA 94025 Office: Physics Dept Stanford U Stanford CA 94305

MEYERHOFF, ARTHUR AUGUSTUS, consulting companies executive, petroleum geologist; b. Northampton, Mass., Sept. 9, 1928; s. Howard Augustus and Anna Sophia (Theilen) M.; m. Kathryn Eleanor Laskaris, Jan. 2, 1951; children: James Charles, Richard Dietrich, Donna Kathryn. B.A., Yale U., 1947; M.S., Stanford U., 1950, Ph.D., 1952. Geologist U.S. Geol. Survey, Mont., Wyo., 1948-52; geologist Standard Oil Co. Calif., Latin Am., 1952-56, sr. geologist, various fgn. and domestic locations, 1956-65; publs. mgr. Am. Assn. Petroleum Geologists, Tulsa, 1965-74; pres. Meyerhoff & Cox, Inc., Tulsa, 1974—; v.p. for research and devel. Associated Resource Cons., Inc., Tulsa, 1978—; dir. Hagen-Greenbriar Corp., Houston, 1980—, cons. exec. br., Washington, 1976-83; guest lectr. U. Belgrade, 1973, USSR Ministry Oil Industry, 1974, USSR Acad. Scis. Inst. Physics of Earth, 1974, USSR Acad. Scis. Far East Inst., 1977, 78; Disting. lectr. Geol. Assn. Can. and U. Calgary, 1974; guest TV shows; vis. scholar Gonville and Caius Coll., Cambridge (Eng.) U., 1978-79. Contbr. numerous articles on oceanography, sea floor spreading, geology, politics of petroleum to profl. publs. Fellow Geol. Soc. Am., AAAS, Geol. Soc. (London); mem. Geol. Soc. Australia, Am. Assn. Petroleum Geologists (cert. petroleum geologist, Matson award 1969), Can. Soc. Petroleum Geologists (hon. lectr. 1975), Am. Geophys. Union, Soc. Econ. Paleontologists and Mineralogists, Paleontol. Assn., Petroleum Exploration Soc. Australia (Distig. Lectr. from Overseas 1982), Assn. Earth Sci. Editors (pres. 1968-69), Rocky Mountain Assn. Geologists, Tulsa Geol. Soc. (hon.), Lafayette (La.) Geol. Soc., Soc. Ind. Profl. Earth Scientists (cert. profl. geologist), Assn. Ind. Profl. Geologists, S.E. Asia Exploration Soc., Geol. Soc. Malaysia, German Geol. Soc., Okla. City Geol. Soc., Geol. Assn. India, Sociedad Mexicana Geologica, Houston Geol. Soc., Assn. Geoscientists for Internat. Devel., Asociación Mexicana de Geólogos Petroleros, Soc. Exploration Geophysicist, Sociedade Brasileira de Geologia. Club: Cosmos (Washington). Current Work: Earth dynamics—most research directed toward explaining origin of earth; petroleum geology consultant, especially to Third World nations which are energy poor. Subspecialties: Tectonics; Geophysics. Home: 3123 E 28th St Tulsa OK 74114 Office: Associated Resources Cons PO Box 4602 3336 E 32d St Suite 208 Tulsa OK 74135

MEYERHOLZ, GEORGE WILLIAM, veterinary medicine educator; b. Burlington, Iowa, Feb. 22, 1928; s. Earl Raymond and Esther Ella (Huddle) M.; m. Barbara Francis Conley, June 24, 1951 (dec. Oct. 1970); children—Linda Ann, Steven James, Larry Allen. D.V.M., Iowa State U., 1954. Regulatory veterinarian Stephenson County, Freeport, Ill., 1954-63; extension veterinarian U. Ill., Urbana, 1963-68, U. Fla., Gainesville, 1968-81; program leader vet. medicine extension service USDA, Washington, 1981—. Contbr. articles and book chpts. to profl. lit. Served with USN, 1946-48. Recipient awards for outstanding contbns. to vet. medicine Fla. Vet. Med. Assn., 1973, 76; named hon. diplomate Am. Coll. Vet. Preventive Medicine. Mem. Am. Assn. Extension Veterinarians (pres. 1974-75, sec.-treas. 1984—, extension veterinarian of yr. 1981), AVMA (chmn. jour. 1983-84, service plaque 1984), U.S. Animal Health Assn. (salmonella com. 1983—). Republican. Current work: Food-animal herd health management, animal disease prevention programs, animal disease disaster medicine, drug residue prevention. Subspecialty: Preventive medicine (veterinary medicine). Home: 219 Oronoco St Alexandria VA 22314 Office: USDA Extension Service 3334 S Bldg Washington DC 20250

MEYEROWITZ, ELLIOT MARTIN, biol. researcher; b. Washington, May 22, 1951. A.B., Columbia U., 1973; M.Phil., Yale U., 1975, Ph.D., 1977. Research fellow dept. biochemistry Stanford (Calif.) U., 1977-79; asst. prof. biology Calif. Inst. Tech., Pasadena, 1980—. Sloan Found. fellow, 1981-83. Mem. Genetics Soc. Am., AAAS. Current Work: Gene regulation and pattern formation in animal and plant development. Subspecialties: Genetics and genetic engineering (biology); Molecular biology. Office: Div Biology Calif Inst Tech Pasadena CA 91125

MEYERS, ALBERT IRVING, chemistry educator; b. N.Y.C., Nov. 22, 1932; s. Hyman and Sylvia (Greenberg) M.; m. Joan Shepard, Aug. 10, 1957; children—Harold, Jil, Lisa. Research chemist Cities Service Oil Co., Cranbury, N.J., 1957-58; asst. prof. La. State U., New Orleans, 1958-61, assoc. rprof., 1961-65, prof., 1965-70, Boyd prof., 1969; prof. Wayne State U., Detroit, 1970-72; prof. chemistry Colo. State U., Ft. Collins, 1972—; spl. postdoctoral fellow Harvard U., Cambridge, Mass., 1965-66; cons. to govt. agys., also various corps. Editor Jour. Am. Chem. Soc., 1980-85. Contbr. articles to sci. jours. Named Man of Yr., New Orleans Jaycees, 1968; fellowship and research award Japan Chem. Soc., 1979; Alexander von Humboldt sr. scientist award Govt. W.Ger., 1984. Mem. Am. Chem. Soc. (chemistry award Colo. sect. 1983, organic chemistry award, nat. soc. 1985), Royal Inst. Chemistry (silver medal 1982). Current work: New synthetic methods; asymmetric syntheses; synthetic utility of heterocyclic compounds; synthesis of complex natural products; antitumor agents. Subspecialties: Organic chemistry; Synthetic chemistry. Office: Colo State U Dept Chemistry Fort Collins CO 80523

MEYERS, CAL YALE, chemistry educator, researcher; b. Utica, N.Y., Nov. 14, 1927; s. Max and Anna (Bernstein) M.; m. Vera Kolb, Sept. 7, 1976. B.A., Cornell U., 1948; M.S., U. Ill., 1949, Ph.D., 1951; postgrad. Princeton U., 1951-53. Chemist, project leader Union Carbide Corp., Bound Brook, N.J., 1953-60; vis. research prof. U. Bologna, Italy, 1960-63; vis. scholar UCLA, 1963-64; assoc. prof. chemistry So. Ill. U., Carbondale, 1964-68, prof., 1968—; cons. in field. Editor: The Chemistry of Organic Sulfur Compounds, Vol. 2, 1966; mem. editorial bd. Internat. Jour. Sulfur Chemistry, 1971-76, Phosphorus and Sulfur, 1976-83. Contbr. chpts. to books, articles to profl. jours. Patentee in field. Recipient research award Intra-sci. Research Found., 1964; NSF grantee, 1961, 71, 73; Petroleum Research Fund-Am. Chem. Soc. grantee, 1961, 62, 68, 85. Swedish Natural Sci. Research Council grantee 1982. Mem. Am. Chem. Soc., Intra-sci. Research Found., Sigma Xi, Phi Lambda Upsilon. Current work: Electron-transfer mechanisms in organic chemistry; sulfone and carbanion chemistry; coal chemistry/organic sulfur compounds; heat-resistant polyaryl sulfones; doisynolic acid estrogenic mechanisms. Subspecialties: Organic chemistry; Receptors. Home: 112 Hewitt St Carbondale IL 62901 Office: Dept Chemistry and Biochemistry So Ill Univ Carbondale IL 62901

MEYERS, MORTON ALLEN, physician, educator; b. Troy, N.Y., Oct. 1, 1933; s. David and Jeanne Sarah (Dunn) M.; m. Beatrice Applebaum, June 1, 1963; children—Richard, Amy. M.D., SUNY, Upstate Med. Coll., 1959. Diplomate: Am. Bd. Radiology. Intern Bellevue Hosp., N.Y.C., 1959-60; resident in radiology Columbia-Presbyn. Med. Center, N.Y.C., 1960-63; fellow Am. Cancer Soc., 1961-63; prof. dept. radiology Cornell U. Med. Center, N.Y.C., 1973-78; prof., chmn. dept. radiology SUNY Sch. Medicine, Stony Brook, 1978—; vis. investigator St. Mark's Hosp., London, 1976. Author: Diseases of the Adrenal Glands: Radiologic Diagnosis, 1963, Dynamic Radiology of the Abdomen: Normal and Pathologic Anatomy, 1976, 2d edit., 1982, Iatrogenic Gastrointestinal Complications, 1981; series editor: Radiology of Iatrogenic Disorders, 1981—; Founding editor-in-chief: Gastrointestinal Radiology, 1976—; contbr. chpts. to med. textbooks, articles to med. jours. Served to capt. M.C. U.S. Army, 1963-65. Fellow Am. Coll. Radiology; mem. Radiol. Soc. N. Am., Am. Roentgen Ray Soc., Assn. Univ. Radiologists, N.Y. Roentgen Ray Soc., Am. Gastroenterol. Assn., Soc. Gastrointestinal Radiologists, AAAS, Soc. Uroradiology, N.Y. Acad. Gastroenterology, Phila. Roentgen Ray Soc., Harvey Soc., N.Y. Acad. Scis., Soc. Chmn. Acad. Radiology Depts., L.I. Radiologic Soc., Alpha Omega Alpha. Subspecialty: Diagnostic radiology. Home: 14 Wainscott Ln East Setauket NY 11733 Office: Dept Radiology Sch Medicine Health Scis Center SUNY Stony Brook NY 11794

MEYERS, PHILIP ALAN, chemist, educator, consultant; b. Hackensack, N.J., Mar. 3, 1941; s. Harold Grove and Gertrude Myra (Smith) M.; m. Judith Arlene Brown, May 15, 1965; children: Shelley, Suzanne, Christopher. B.S. in Chemistry, Carnegie-Mellon U., Pitts., 1964; Ph.D. in Oceanography, U. R.I., Kingston, 1972. Research chemist Inmont Corp., Nutley, N.J., 1967-68; asst. prof. oceanography U. Mich., Ann Arbor, 1972-77, assoc. prof., 1977-82, prof., 1982—; vis scientist Ind. U., Bloomington, 1979-80; cons. Raytheon Ocean Systems Co., NOAA, UCLA; dir. Gt. Lakes and Marine Waters Center of U. Mich., 1982. Contbr. articles and abstracts to profl. jours. Served to lt. (j.g.) USNR, 1964-67. Recipient Disting. Service award U. Mich. Coll. Engring., 1976; NOAA faculty summer fellow, 1981. Fellow Geol. Soc. Am.; mem. AAAS, Am. Geophys. Union, Am. Soc. Limnology and Oceanography, Internat. Assn. Gt. Lakes Research, Geochem. Soc., Am. Assn. Petroleum Geologists, European Assn. Organic Geochemists. Club: Ann Arbor Country. Current Work: Organic geochemistry of natural waters and sediments, diagenesis and degradation of fatty acids and hydrocarbons and sterols, biomarker and paleoenvironmental studies in Ocean Drilling Program. Subspecialties: Geochemistry; Oceanography. Home: 3580 Stanton Ct Ann Arbor MI 48105 Office: 2455 Hayward Ave Ann Arbor MI 48109

MEYERS, ROBERT ALLEN, scientist, executive; b. Los Angeles, May 15, 1936; s. Jack and Penina (Cassell) M.; m. Ilene Braun, Feb. 27, 1976; children by previous marriage—Tamara Hart, Robert Allen. B.A., San Diego State U., 1959; Ph.D., UCLA, 1963; postgrad. Calif. Inst. Tech., 1963-64. Sr. research chemist Bell & Howell Research Ctr., Sierra Madre, Calif., 1964-65; head organic chemistry sect. TRW, Redondo Beach, Calif., 1966-75, bus. area mgr., 1975—. Author: Coal Desulfurization, 1977. Editor-in-chief: Coal Handbook, 1981, Coal Structure, 1982, Handbook of Energy Technology, 1983, Handbook of Synfuels Technology, 1984, Chemical Process Handbook series and Acad. Press Ency. of Phys. Sci. and Tech., 1985. Chmn. adv. bd. Guide to Nuclear Power, 1984; mem. US-USSR Working Group on Air Pollution Control, 1974-76. Recipient award for distinction in chemistry San Diego State U., 1959. Current work: Coal, petroleum and oil shale processing; new processes for production of organic and inorganic chemicals. Subspecialties: Fuels; Chemical engineering. Home: 3715 Gleneagles Dr Tarzana CA 90278 Office: TRW Electronic and Defense Sector Redondo Beach CA 90278

MEYSTEL, ALEXANDER MICHAEL, electrical engineering educator; b. Leningrad, USSR, Feb. 25, 1935; came to U.S., 1978, naturalized, 1984; s. M.L. and C.S. (Cotliar) M.; m. Marina Selitsky, Feb. 26, 1971; 1 child, Misha. M.S.E.E., Poly. Inst., Odessa, USSR, 1957; Ph.D., ENIMS, Moscow, 1965. Project leader Design Office Machines, Odessa, USSR, 1957-63; sr. researcher Exptl. Sci. Research Inst. Metalcutting Machines, Moscow, 1963-65, head lab., Erevan, 1965-69, sr. scientist, Moscow, 1969-73; head dept. Informelecto, 1973-77; sr. staff scientist Gould, Inc., Chgo., 1978-79; research/devel. dir. Hyperloop, Inc., Chgo., 1980-81; assoc. prof. elec. engring. U. Fla., Gainesville, 1980-84; prof. elec. engring. and computer engring. Drexel U., Phila., 1984—; cons. in field. Contbr. articles to profl. jours.; author: Automated Positioning Controls, 1970, Engineering Computations and Design of Automated Machines, 1976, Computer Aided Decision Making, 1976. Recipient medals for engring. innovations All-Union Exhbn. of Indsl. Achievements, Moscow, 1962-70. Mem. IEEE, N.Y. Acad. Sci., Soc. Indsl. and Applied Math., Am. Assn. Artificial Intelligence, Sigma Xi. Jewish. Patentee in field. Current Work: Control of intelligent machines, optimum control of multilink robot manipulators, intelligent mobile systems, others. Subspecialties: Electrical engineering; Artificial intelligence. Office: Dept Elec Engring Drexel U Philadelphia PA 19104

MICELI, JOSEPH JAMES, JR., physicist; b. Brockton, Mass., Nov. 15, 1954; s. Joseph James and Martha Mary (Zukas) M.; m. Dolores Marie Johnson, Dec. 4, 1982; 1 child, Tia Marie. B.S., Worcester Poly. Inst., 1977; Ph.D., U. Rochester, 1982. Instr. physics Rochester Inst. Tech., N.Y., 1981-82; research scientist Eastman Kodak Research Labs., Rochester, N.Y., 1982—; research staff U. Rochester Inst. Optics, 1982—. Contbr. articles to profl. jours. Current work: Infrared gradientindex, interferometry, optical data storage. Subspecialty: Laser data storage and reproduction. Home: 4196 Cream Ridge Rd Macedon NY 14502 Office: Eastman Kodak Bldg 801 OASIS Rochester NY 14650

MICHA, DAVID ALLAN, chemistry and physics educator, chemical physics researcher; b. Villa Mercedes, San Luis, Argentina, Sept. 12, 1939; s. Simon David and Catherine (Cohen) M.; m. Margaretha Samuelsson, Aug. 26, 1966; children—Michael F., Anna K. M.Sc., U. Cuyo, Argentina, 1962; Ph.D., U. Uppsala, Sweden, 1965, D.Sc., 1966. Research assoc. Quantum Chemistry Group, U. Uppsala, 1965-66, vis. prof., 1977; research assoc. Theoretical Chemistry Inst., U. Wis., Madison, 1966-67; asst. research physicist U. Calif.-San Diego, 1967-69, vis. prof., 1973; assoc. prof. chemistry and physics U. Fla., Gainesville, 1969-74, prof., 1974—, dir. Ctr. for Chem. Physics, 1982—; vis. research assoc. U. Buenos Aires, Argentina, 1966; vis. Lamberg prof. U. Sweden, 1970; vis. prof. Harvard U., 1972, 1973, Max-Planck Inst., Gottingen, Fed. Republic Germany, 1976, Imperial Coll., London, 1977; vis. research physicist U. Calif.-Santa Barbara, 1982; vis. prof. Weizmann Inst. Sci., Rehovot, Israel, 1983; vis. fellow U. Colo., Boulder, 1983; faculty research participant Oak Ridge Nat. Lab., 1984. Recipient Von Humboldt Sr. U.S. Scientist award, 1976; numerous grants including NSF, NASA, NATO, Am. Chem. Soc.; fellow Swedish Internat. Devel. Agy., 1962-65, Alfred P. Sloan Found., 1971-74, Nat. Bur. Standards, 1983. Fellow Am. Phys. Soc.; mem. Am. Chem. Soc., Sigma Xi. Current work: Quantum molecular dynamics; many-body theory of atomic collisions; intermolecular forces; interaction of radiation with molecules (photodissociation, photopolymerization); scattering by solid surfaces and adsorbates; dynamics of stochastic systems; scattering of electrons in magnetic fields; computational methods of scattering and electronic structure. Subspecialties: Theoretical chemistry; Laser photochemistry. Office: 366 Williamson Hall U Fla Gainesville FL 32611

MICHAEL, ALFRED FREDERICK, pediatrician, educator; b. Phila., Aug. 10, 1928; s. Alfred F. Michael and Emma M. Michael Peters; m. Jane Jewson, Dec. 27, 1952; children—Mary, Susan, Carol. M.D., Temple U., 1953. Diplomate Am. Bd. Pediatrics, Am. Bd. Nephrology. Intern Phila. Gen. Hosp., 1953-54; resident in pediatrics Children's Hosp., Cin., 1957-60; USPHS fellow in pediatrics and immunology U. Minn. Med. Sch., Mpls., 1960-63, established investigator, Am. Heart Assn., 1963-68, assoc. prof. pediatrics, 1965-68, chief immunopathology lab., dept. lab. medicine and pathology, 1978—, chief, prof. pediatrics and pediatric nephrology, 1968—; cons. NIH. Mem. editorial bd. Kidney Internat., Am. Jour. Nephrology. Contbr. articles to profl. jours. Served to capt. USAF, 1955-57. Guggenheim fellow, 1965-67; various NIH grants, 1968—. Mem. Assn. Am. Physicians, Am. Soc., Clin. Investigation; Am. Assn. Immunologists, Am. Assn. Pathologists, Soc. Exptl. Biol. and Medicine, Central Soc. Clin. Research, Am. Pediatric Soc., Soc. Pediatric Research, Am. Soc. Nephrology, Internat. Soc. Nephrology, Am. Soc. Pediatric Nephrology. Congregationalist. Current work: Immunopathology, pathogenesis of kidney disease. Subspecialties: Pediatrics; Nephrology. Office: U Minn Hosp Box 491 Minneapolis MN 55455

MICHAEL, JACOB GABRIEL, microbiology educator; b. Rimavska Sobota, Czechoslovakia, July 2, 1931; s. Stephan and Mary (Laszlo) M.; m. Ann Deborah Blumrosen, Aug. 29, 1958; children: Naomi, Ruth, David, Abigail. B.A., Hebrew U., Jerusalem, Israel, 1955, M.S., 1956; Ph.D., Rutgers U., 1959. Vis. scientist Nat. Cancer Inst., Bethesda, Md., 1959-61; assoc. dir. research Children's Hosp., Harvard Med. Sch., Boston, 1961-66; assoc. prof. U. Cin., 1966-70, prof. microbiology and immunology, 1970—; vis. prof. Inst. Pasteur, Paris, 1979, Karolinska Inst., Stockholm, 1973. Contbr. articles to profl. jours. Am. Heart Assn. fellow, 1962; Am. Soc. Microbiology fellow, 1964; Med. Found. Boston fellow, 1966. Fellow Am. Acad. Microbiology; mem. Am. Soc. Microbiology, N.Y. Acad. Scis., Am. Assn. Immunologists, AAAS. Jewish. Current Work: Regulation of immune response; immunology, allergens, autoimmune disease, suppression or enhancement of the response. Subspecialties: Immunobiology and immunology; Allergy. Office: Dept Microbiology U Cin Coll Medicine Cincinnati OH 45267

MICHAELI, DOV, biochemist, physician, educator; b. Ramat Gan, Israel, May 28, 1935; came to U.S., 1960; s. Shaul Michaeli and Cana (Drazne) Weil; m. Adis Erlich, 1963 (div. 1976); children—Karen, Gil, B.Sc., Hebrew U. Jerusalem, 1959; Ph.D., U. Calif.-Berkeley, 1963; M.D., U. Calif.-San Francisco, 1976. Research scientist Kaiser Found. Research Inst., San Francisco, 1963-70; asst. prof. biochemistry U. Calif.-San Francisco Med. Sch., 1970-76, assoc. prof., 1976—. Contbr. articles to profl. jours. Mem. Am. Assn. Immunologists, AAAS, N.Y. Acad. Scis. Current work: Regulatory mechanisms of wound healing Subspecialty: Biochemistry (biology). Office: U Calif 839 HSE San Francisco CA 94143

MICHAELS, ADLAI ELDON, chemistry educator; b. Alma, Wis., Nov. 22, 1913; s. Frederick William and Olga (Wald) M.; m. Josephine Gertrude Blake, Mar. 16, 1940; children: Lee Frederick, Carol Ann Price; m. Opal M. Carfrey, June 4, 1971. B.S., U. Wis., 1935; Ph.D., Ohio State U., 1940. Instr. U. Tenn., Knoxville, 1940-43; research chemist Esso Research & Engring. Co., Elizabeth, N.J., 1949-59; mem. chemistry faculty Washington and Jefferson Coll., Washington, Pa., 1959—, prof. chemistry, 1967—. Sci adviser U.S. Congress. Recipient Arthur Donahue Meml. award Alpha Phi Omega, 1982. Mem. Am. Chem. Soc. Lodge: Elks. Patentee in field. Current Work: Corrosion, air pollution control. Subspecialties: Physical chemistry; Analytical chemistry. Office: Washington and Jefferson Coll Washington PA 15301

MICHAELS, HOWARD BRIAN, medical physicist, educator, hospital administrator; b. Toronto, Ont., Can., May 29, 1949; s. Isaiah and Rosalind (Rosenberg) M.; m. Lois S. Kwitman, Mar. 15, 1980. B.A.Sc., U. Toronto, 1971, M.Sc., 1973, Ph.D. in Med. Biophysics, 1976. Registered profl. engr., Ont. Postdoctoral fellow Ont. Cancer Inst., Toronto, 1976; research fellow in radiation medicine Mass. Gen. Hosp., 1976-78; research fellow in radiation therapy Harvard Med. Sch., Boston, 1976-78; asst. radiation biophysicist and asst. prof. radiation therapy, 1978-81; chief physicist, head div. clin. physics Ont. Cancer Found., Toronto-Bayview Regional Cancer Ctr., 1981—; asst. prof. depts. med. biophysics and radiology, U. Toronto, 1981—; depts. oncology and radiology (Sunnybrook Med. Centre), 1981—. Contbr. articles to profl. jours. Nat. Cancer Inst. Can. K.M. Hunter fellow, 1975-76; Radiation Research Soc. awardee, 1974, 76, 78, 79, 83. Mem. Am. Assn. Physicists in Medicine, Can. Assn. Physicists, Radiation Research Soc., Assn. Profl. Engrs. Ont. Current Work: Medical radiation physics associated with radiotherapy treatment for cancer; radiobiology and radiation chemistry; radiation sensitization by oxygen and chemical radiosensitizers and radioprotectors of mammalian cells; clinical use of radiosensitizers in radiotherapy; chemical modifiers of ionizing radiation damage. Subspecialty: Cancer research (medicine). Office: 2075 Bayview Ave Toronto ON M4N 3M5 Canada

MICHALAK, EDWARD MICHAEL, electrical engineer, industrial automation controls company executive; b. Milw., Oct. 1, 1924; s. Michael and Emily (Bulak) M.; m. Rita Y. Glazewski, May 23, 1953; children—Barbara, Mary, Cynthia, Jean. B.S. in Gen. Engring., U.S. Mil. Acad., 1945; M.E.E., U. Wis., 1952, M.B.A., U. Wis.-Milw., 1976. Registered profl. engr., Wis. Devel. engr. Cutler Hammer and Globe Union Inc., Milw., 1952-57; solid state engr. Allen Bradley Co., Milw., 1958-66, dir. elec. engring., 1967-68, product mgmt., 1969-73, corp. v.p. 1973—; advisor Marquette U., Milw., 1980—, Milw. Sch. Engring., 1983—. Contbr. articles to profl. jours. Served to 1st lt. U.S. Army, 1945-49, PTO. Mem. IEEE, Internat. Inst. (bd. dirs. 1982—, v.p., 1984—), Indsl. Research Inst. (prin.), Wis. Assn. Research Mgmt. (chmn. 1984—). Roman Catholic. Current work: Process control; cermet technology; metallurgy; analytical chemistry; plastics; reliability testing. Subspecialties: Microelectronics; Electronic materials. Home: 3414 W Poe St Milwaukee WI 53215 Office: Allen Bradley Co 1201 S 2nd St Milwaukee WI 53204

MICHALCHIK, MICHAEL, chemist, researcher; b. Chgo., June 9, 1931; s. Trofim Zaharovich and Sophia Emilianova (Boichuk) M.; m. Froughieh Akhavan-e-Safa, Aug. 17, 1957; children—Neda Safa, Vera Safa, Michael Safa. B.S.Ch.E., U. Ill., 1954. Assoc. research engr. Armour Research Found., Chgo., 1956-59; chem. group leader RCA, Camden, N.J., 1959-61; program mgr. Fairchild Camera, Syosset, N.Y., 1961-70; cons., supplier Semi-Alloys, Standard Oil of N.J., West Milford, 1970-72; supplier, inventor Bell Labs./-Gen. Electric, Holmdel, N.J., 1972-75; chief chemist Dynacon, Inc., Leonia, N.J., 1972-75; pres., cons. Internat. Research Union, Santa Ana, Calif., 1975-79; research staff engr. Discovision Assoc., Costa Mesa, Calif., 1979-82; sr. staff engr Optimem/Xerox, Sunnyvale, Calif., 1982-83; founder Chemfield Scientific, Newport Beach, Calif., 1985—. Patentee anti-radar, doping, tranducer, video-laser. Recipient honor Armour Research Found., NASA, 1958; grantee CIA, 1965, Armour Research Found., 1959, Foster & Kleiser, 1963. Mem. Am. Chem. Soc., Instrument Soc. Am. Baha'i. Current work: Laser recording; video and digital data disks; materials and processes including media architecture; tranducers; pressure-conductive coatings. Subspecialties: Electronic materials; Materials processing. Home: 1153 Brucito Ave Los Altos CA 94022

MICHALITSIANOS, ANDREW GERASIMOS, astrophysicist; b. Alexandria, Egypt, May 22, 1947; came to U.S., 1951; s. Gerasimos Andrew and Maria (Soultanakis) M.; m. Kathryn, Mar. 25, 1950. B.S. in Physics, U. Ariz., 1969; Ph.D. in Astrophysics, U. Cambridge, Eng., 1973. Research fellow Calif. Inst. Tech., Pasadena, 1972-75; research assoc. Swiss Fed. Inst. Tech., Zurich, 1976-77; assoc. NRC/ Nat. Acad. Scis., NASA Goddard Space Flight Center, Greenbelt, Md., 1975-77; staff scientist Lab. for Astronomy and Solar Physics, 1977—, head obs. sect., 1981—. Contbr. articles to profl. jours. Recipient NASA Merit Achievement award, 1980. Fellow Am. Astron. Soc., Royal Astron. Soc.; mem. Internat. Astron. Union. Democrat. Greek Orthodox. Current Work: Ultraviolet astronomy mainly with earth orbiting UV astronomical satellites; ground-based observations with radio telescopes and optical instrumentation. Subspecialties: Ultraviolet high energy astrophysics; Optical astronomy.

MICHALSKI, FRANK JOSEPH, lab adminstr., researcher, educator; b. St. Louis, Sept. 28, 1938; s. Frank Joseph and Ann Teresa (Kane) M.; m. Julieta Amy Buera, Aug. 11, 1973. Ph.D. in Biology, U. Notre Dame, 1971. Postdoctoral virus research Wistar Inst. U. Pa., 1971-73, Yale U., 1973-76; dir. diagnostic virology lab. St. Michaels Med. Center, Newark, 1976-85; asst. prof. N.J. Med. Sch., Newark, 1976—; dir. diagnostic virology lab. Metpath, Teteroro, N.J., 1985—. Mem. Am. Soc. Microbiology, Pan Am. Group for Rapid Viral Diagnosis, Infectious Diseases Soc. Am., Am. Soc. Virology, Acad. Medicine of N.J. Democrat. Roman Catholic. Current Work: Rapid virus diagnosis, herpes virus research, oncogenic viruses. Subspecialty: Virology (medicine).

MICHALSKI, RYSZARD SPENCER, computer science researcher, educator; b. Kalush, Poland, May 7, 1937; came to U.S., 1970, naturalized, 1980; s. Jan Stanislaw and Eugenia (Botulinska) M. Cert., Cracow Tech. U., Poland, 1956; B.S., Warsaw Tech. U., Poland, 1959; M.S., Leningrad Poly. Inst., USSR, 1961, cert. in computer sci., 1961; Ph.D., Tech. U. Silesia, Poland, 1969. Prof. computer sci. U. Ill., Urbana, 1982—, dir. Artificial Intelligence Lab., 1983—; vis. scientist Artificial Intelligence Lab., MIT, Cambridge, 1983, 84-85; guest prin. researcher Boeing Computer Service, Seattle, 1983; speaker in field. Author: (with Carbonell and Mitchell) Machine Learning: An AI Approach, Vol. I, 1983, Vol. II, 1986. Subspecialties: Artificial intelligence; Graphics, image processing, and pattern recognition. Office: Dept Computer Sci U Ill 1304 Springfield Ave Urbana IL 61801

MICHAUD, TED CORNEILLE, biology educator; b. Fort Wayne, Ind., Oct. 5, 1929; s. Howard Henry and Ruth Mills (Hefner) M.; m. Jean Helen Mackenzie, Sept. 10, 1955; children—Michael Rene, David Wayne, Susan Lynn. B.S., Purdue U., 1951; M.S., U. Mich., 1954; Ph.D., U. Tex., 1959. Naturalist Ind. State Parks, 1949-54; prof. biology Carroll Coll., Waukesha, Wis., 1959—. Contbr. articles to profl. jours. Served to col., USAR. Mem. Assn. Midwestern Coll. Biology Tchrs. (2d v.p. 1981, pres.-elect 1986), Soc. for Study Evolution, Am. Soc. Ichthyologists and Herpetologists, Am. Inst. Biol. Scis., AAAS, Wis. Ornithol. Soc., Beta Beta Beta (nat. exec. com. 1976—, v.p. north central region 1976—, dist. dir. 1972—), Phi Sigma, Pi Kappa Phi. Presbyterian. Current work: Appalachian studies, recombinant DNA, BBE, AMCBT. Subspecialties: Genetics and genetic engineering (biology); Ecology (biology). Home: 1227 Downing Dr Waukesha WI 53186 Office: Carroll Coll 100 N East Ave Waukesha WI 53186

MICHEL, BERNARD, civil engineering educator; b. Chicoutimi, P.Q., Can., May 31, 1930; s. Joseph-Williams and Jeanne (Tremblay) M.; m. Mariette Boivin, Sept. 9, 1954; children: Marianne, Francois, Luc, Jacques, Charles, Christine. B. Applied Sci., Laval U., 1954; Dr.Engr., Grenoble U., 1962. Profl. engr., P.Q. Research engr. Lasalle Hydraulic Lab., Quebec, 1956-60; head dept. civil engring. Laval U., Quebec, 1960-63, prof. civil engring., 1963—; v.p. Arctec Can. Ltd., Ottawa, 1973-78; cons. Recherches B.C. Michel Inc., Quebec, 1978—. Author: Ice Mechanics, 1978. Recipient Gzowski medal Engring. Inst. Can., 1963. Fellow Royal Soc. Can. (mem. Acad. of Scis.), Engring. Inst. Can., Can. Soc. Civil Engring. (Keefer medal 1977, 81), Internat. Assn. Hydraulic Research (pres. com. on ice problems 1970-76). Inventor, patentee hydraulics and off-shore installations. Current Work: Research and consultations for the development of northern water resources with specialty in ice engineering. Subspecialty: Civil engineering. Home: 739 des Vignes Ste-Foy PQ G1V 2Y1 Canada Office: Universite Laval Dep de Genie civil Ste-Foy PQ G1K 7P4 Canada

MICHEL, MARY ELLEN, neurobiologist; b. Savage, Md., Feb. 26, 1947; d. Fred and Hazel Irene (Akers) M. Ph.D., U. Md. Med. Sch., 1979. Pres. Eastern Lab., Inc., Balt., 1983-84; mgr. clin. and preclin. studies and new drug devel. Key Pharm. Inc., Miami, Fla., 1984—. Contbr. articles to profl. jours. Recipient Nat. Research Service award; fellow U. Md. Med. Sch., NIH. Mem. Soc. for Neurosci., N.Y. Acad. Scis., Am. Diabetes Assn. Democrat. Clubs: Sierra, Audubon (Miami). Current work: Pharmacology of the nervous system; regeneration in the central nervous system; blood brain barrier. Office: Key Pharm Inc 18425 NW 2nd Ave Miami FL 33169

MICHELI, ROGER PAUL, chemist; b. Denver, July 26, 1949; s. Roger Horst and Dorothy Ellen (Waldron) M.; m. Cheryl Lynn Pritchard, July 11, 1969; children—Gwen, Roger, Amee, Adam. B.S., U. Denver, 1971; M.S., U. Colo., 1973, Ph.D., 1975. Postdoctoral fellow Ohio State U., Columbus, 1975-78; analytical research chemist Syntex Chems., Inc., Boulder, Colo., 1978-79, sr. analytical research chemist, 1979-83, mgr. analytical research, 1983—. Contbr. articles to profl. jours. Recipient Syntex Corp. Community Service award, 1983. Mem. Am. Chem. Soc. Republican. Episcopalian. Current work: Enantiomeric separations. Subspecialties: Analytical chemistry; Organic chemistry. Office: Syntex Chemicals Inc 2075 N 55th St Boulder CO 80301

MICHELS, DAVID BARRY, physiologist, engineer; b. Chgo., Feb. 21, 1942; s. Charles Bernard and Ethelyn (Leven) M.; m. Lynnell Roberta Spitza, June 21, 1964; children—Melinda Relayne, Tamara Joy. B.S., UCLA, 1964, M.S., 1967, Ph.D., 1975. Engr. Bendix, North Hollywood, Calif., 1964-65; engr. Hughes Aircraft, Culver City, Calif., 1965-69, sr. staff mem., Canoga Park, Calif., 1980—; research scientist Tech. Service Corp., Santa Monica, Calif., 1969-72; researcher UCLA, 1972-75; faculty researcher U. Calif.-San Diego, 1975-80; cons., 1980—. Contbr. articles to profl. jours. Officer, Nobel Jr. High Adv. Council, Northridge, Calif., 1983-84; bd. dirs. Parents Heart Assn. Childrens Hosp., Los Angeles, 1984. Mem. Am. Physiol. Soc., IEEE. Republican. Jewish. Current work: Effects of weightlessness and gravity on the lung, first chest x-rays and measurements of gas and blood distributions during weightlessness, designing analyser to test astronauts' lungs aboard space shuttle. Subspecialties: Pulmonary medicine; Systems engineering. Home: 10828 Amigo Ave Northridge CA 91326 Office: Hughes Aircraft (B-69) Canoga Park CA 91304

MICHELSON, ERIC LEE, cardiovascular researcher; b. Phila., Sept. 18, 1947; s. Norman George Michelson and Ellin (Karlin) Blumenthal; m. Donna Jean Glover, June 4, 1977. B.A., M.S., U. Pa., 1969; M.D., Columbia U., 1973. Diplomate Am. Bd. Med. Examiners, Am. Bd. Internal Medicine, Am. Bd. Cardiovascular Disease. Med. intern, then resident and fellow in cardiology Hosp. of U. Pa., 1973-79; asst. prof. medicine Jefferson Med. Coll., 1979-82; assoc. prof. medicine Thomas Jefferson U., Phila., 1982—; chief clin. research unit Lankenau Hosp., 1979-83; chief clin. research Lankenau Med. Research Ctr., Phila., 1983—; cons. in field. Co-editor; The Evaluation of New Antiarrhythmic Drugs, 1981; mem. editorial bd., cons. med. jours. Contbr. articles to profl. jours., chpts. to books. Recipient Physicians Recognition award Am. Heart Assn., 1979-82; 85-88; Am. Heart Assn. grantee, 1979-84. Fellow ACP, Am., Coll. Cardiology (course dir., continuing edn. com.); mem. Am. Heart Assn. (bd. govs. Southeastern Pa. chpt.); Am. Physiol. Soc., Cardiac Electrophysiol. Soc., Am. Fedn. Clin. Research. Current work: Cardiac electrophysiology; cardiac electropharmacology; cardiovascular pharmacology; hypertension. Subspecialties: Cardiology; Physiology (biology). Office: Lankenau Med Research Ctr Lancaster Ave West of City Line Philadelphia PA 19151

MICHENER, CHARLES DUNCAN, educator, entomologist; b. Pasadena, Calif., Sept. 22, 1918; s. Harold and Josephine (Rigden) M.; m. Mary Hastings, Jan. 1, 1941; children: David, Daniel, Barbara, Walter. B.S., U. Calif., Berkeley, 1939, Ph.D., 1941. Tech. asst. U. Calif., Berkeley, 1939-42; asst. curator Am. Mus. Natural History, N.Y.C., 1942-46, assoc. curator, 1946-48, research assoc. 1949—; assoc. prof. U. Kans., 1948-49, prof., chmn. dept. entomology, 1949-61, 72-75, Watkins disting. prof. entomology, 1959—, acting chmn. dept. systematics, ecology, 1968-69, Watkins distinguished prof. systematics and ecology, 1969—; dir. Snow Entomol. Museum, 1974-83, sr. curator, 1983—; state entomologist, 1949-61; Guggenheim fellow, vis. research prof. U. Paraná, Curitiba, Brazil, 1955-56; Fulbright fellow U. Queensland, Brisbane, Australia, 1958-59; research scholar U. Costa Rica, 1963; Guggenheim fellow, Africa, 1966-67. Author: (with Mary H. Michener) American Social Insects, 1951, (with S.F. Sakagami) Nest Architecture of the Sweat Bees, 1962, The Social Behavior of the Bees, 1974; also articles; editor: Evolution, 1962-64; Am. editor: Insectes Sociaux, Paris, 1954-55, 62—; assoc. editor: Ann. Rev. of Ecology and Systematics, 1970—. Served from 1st lt. to capt. San. Corps AUS, 1943-46. Fellow Am. Entomol. Soc., Am. Acad. Arts and Scis., Royal Entomol. Soc. London, AAAS; mem. Nat. Acad. Scis., Am. Acad. Arts and Scis., Linnean Soc. London (corr.), Soc. for Study Evolution (pres. 1967), Soc. Systematic Zoologists (pres. 1969), Am. Soc. Naturalists (pres. 1978), Internat. Union for Study Social Insects (pres. 1977-82), Bee Research Assn., Kans. Entomol. Soc. (pres. 1950), Brazilian Acad. Scis. (corr.), Entomol. Soc. Am. Current Work: Origin and evolution of social behavior in insects; kin recognition; ethology of bees; systematics and ecology of bees; principles of systematics. Subspecialties: Sociobiology; Systematics. Home: 1706 W 2d St Lawrence KS 66044

MICHENER, JOHN RUSSELL, research engineer, applied physicist, microstructural analyist; b. Oakland, Calif., Oct. 6, 1951; s. John Harold and Ann (Crabtree) M.; m. Ann Gardner, Dec. 30, 1974; children: Robin Ann, Kristin Lee. B.S. in Physics, U. Md., 1973; M.S. in Materials Sci, U. Rochester, 1979, Ph.D. in Mech. Engring. (Materials), 1983. Research physicist Eastman Kodak Co., Rochester, N.Y., 1974-79; research asst. U. Rochester, 1979-82; microelectronics research engr. Siemens Co., Princeton, N.J., 1982—; cons. on microstructural characterization. Mem. Am. Phys. Soc., Am. Soc. for Metals, AIME, IEEE, AAAS. Patentee in field. Current Work: Failure analysis, testing and evaluation of ULSI devices, microstructural characterization of electronic devices, computer vision, processing of compound semiconducton devices, cryptography and computer security, internal stress effects on materials. Subspecialties: Fracture mechanics; Microelectronics. Home: 177 Moore St Princeton NJ 08540 Office: Siemens Co 105 College Ave Princeton Forestal Center Princeton NJ 08540

MICHL, JOSEF, chemistry educator; b. Prague, Czechoslovakia, Mar. 12, 1939; s. Josef and Vera (Polakova) M.; m. Sara Margaret Allensworth, Mar. 14, 1969; children—Georgina Frances, John Allensworth. M.S., Charles U., Prague, Czechoslovakia, 1961; Ph.D., Czechoslovakia Acad. Sci., Prague, 1965. Postdoctoral fellow U. Houston, 1965-66, U. Tex., Austin, 1966-67; research scientist Czechoslovak Acad. Sci., 1967-68; amanuensis Aarhus U., Denmark, 1968-69; Postdoctoral fellow, U. Utah, Salt Lake City, 1969-70; research assoc. prof., 1970-71, assoc. prof., 1971-75, chmn. dept. chemistry, 1979-84, prof., 1975—; chmn. 19th Conf. Reactive Mechanisms, Salt Lake City, 1982. Editor, Chem. Revs., 1984—, Jour. of Phys. and Chem. Referance Data, 1985—. Mem. editorial adv. bd. Jour. Accounts of Chem. Research, 1984—. Contbr. articles to profl. jours. Recipient Alexander von Humboldt sr. scientist award, 1980; Alfred P. Sloan fellow, 1971-75, Guggenheim fellow, 1984-85. Mem. Am. Chem. Soc. (exec. com. mem. 1982—), Interam. Photochem. Soc. (exec. com. 1977-80), Internat. Union Pure and Applied Chemistry, Commn. on Photochemistry (titular), The Chem. Soc., Am. Soc. Mass Spectrometry. Roman Catholic. Subspecialty: Physical chemistry. Home: 961 Fairview Ave Salt Lake City UT 84105 Office: U Utah Dept Chemistry Salt Lake City UT 84112

MICHNE, WILLIAM FRANCIS, chemist, researcher; b. Albany, N.Y., Dec. 9, 1942; s. Joseph and Edith (Romanowski) M.; m. Carol Joan Eaton, Nov. 16, 1963 (div. 1975); children—William, Michelle; m. Elizabeth Ann DuPont, Mar. 6, 1976; children—Jodi, Gregory. B.S., Siena Coll., 1964; Ph.D., Rensselaer Poly. Inst., 1968. Research chemist Sterling-Winthrop Research Inst., Rensselaer, N.Y., 1964-72, group leader, 1972-80, sect. head, 1980—. Mem. editorial adv. bd. Jour. Medicinal Chemistry, 1983—. Contbr. articles to profl. jours., chpts. to books. Patentee opioid substances. Mem. Nat. Ski Patrol, 1968-79. Mem. Am. Chem. Soc., AAAS, Internat. Narcotic Research Conf., Am. Radio Relay League, U.S. Power Squadron. Current work: Structure activity relationships of analgesics. Subspecialties: Medicinal chemistry; Drug design. Home: RD 2 Box 146 Averill Park NY 12018 Office: Sterling Winthrop Research Inst Columbia Turnpike Rensselaer NY 12144

MICHOD, RICHARD EARL, theoretical population biologist; b. Chgo., May 11, 1951; s. Charles Louis and Florence (Wise) M.; m. Carol Elaine Santich, Mar. 20, 1977; 1 dau., Kristin Olivia. B.S., Duke U., 1973; M.A., U. Ga., 1979, Ph.D., 1979. Asst. prof. dept. ecology and evolutionary biology U. Ariz., Tucson, 1979-82, assoc. prof., 1982—. NSF grantee, 1979-82, 82-85. Mem. Am. Soc. Naturalists, Soc. Study Evolution, Genetics Soc. Am., Ecol. Soc. Am. Current Work: Evolution of social behavior; origin of life. Subspecialties: Evolutionary biology; Sociobiology. Office: Dept Ecology and Evolutionary Biology University of Arizona Tucson AZ 85721

MICKELSON, CLAUDIA A(NN), immunologist, genetic engineer, researcher; b. Detroit, Mar. 8, 1944; d. Gordon Francis and Virginia R. (Randall) Roberts; m. Michael Jay Mickelson, Sept. 17, 1965; 1 son, David Paul. B.Sc. in Biology, Antioch Coll., 1966; Ph.D. in Biology, U. Rochester, 1974. Research scientist Bigelow Labs., Booth Bay Harbor, Maine, 1976-78; sr. research fellow U. Glasgow, Scotland, 1978-80, U. Melbourne, Australia, 1981—. Mem. Am. Soc. Immunologists. Subspecialties: Genetics and genetic engineering (biology); Immunobiology and immunology. Office: Research Center Dept Pathology U Melbourne Melbourne Australia

MICKELSON, KENNETH EUGENE, chemist; b. La Porte, Ind., May 14, 1949; s. Avery Laverne and Naomi Louise (Nelson) M.; m. Claudia Lee Chaney, Aug. 14, 1970; children—Nathan Lee, Andrew Avery. A.B. with honors, Ind. U., 1971; M.S., U. Wash., 1974, Ph.D., 1977. Research assoc. U. Louisville, 1977-79, instr. biochemistry, 1979-80; research scientist Miles Lab., Elkhart, Ind., 1980-81, med. mgr. 1981-82, staff scientist, 1982—. Contbr. articles to profl. jours. NSF fellow, 1970. Mem. Am. Assn. Clin. Chemistry, Am. Chem. Soc., AAAS, N.Y. Acad. Scis., Alpha Chi Sigma. Current work: Development of diagnostic immunoassays; interaction of small molecules with antibodies; dry phase chemistry. Subspecialties: Clinical chemistry; Biochemistry (medicine). Home: 54076 Eastwood Dr Elkhart IN 46514 Office: Miles Labs 1127 Myrtle St Elkhart IN 46515

MICKELSON, ROME HUEBERT, agricultural engineer; b. Twin Valley, Minn., Feb. 16, 1931; s. Roy Ilton and Helen Andora (Johnson) M.; m. Grace C. Andrews, Dec. 20, 1969 (div. Mar. 1984); m. Betty June Higinbotham, Apr. 29, 1984. Student Concordia Coll., Moorhead, Minn., 1949-50; B.S., N.D. State U., 1955. Asst. agrl. engr. N.D. State U., Fargo, 1955; agrl. engr. U.S. Dept. Agr.-Agrl. Research Service, Mandan, N.D., 1955-56, Grand Forks, N.D., 1956-61, Bushland, Tex., 1961, Akron, Colo., 1961—, research leader, location leader, 1967-79, contracting officers rep., 1974-76. Contbr. articles to profl. jours. Recipient merit certs. U.S. Dept. Agr., 1976, 82. Fellow Soil Conservation Soc. Am. (pres. Colo. chpt. 1967-68, Chpt. Commendation award 1974); mem. Am. Soc. Agrl. Engrs., Soil Sci. Soc. Am. (invited reviewer Madison, Wis. 1980, 82), Am. Soc. Agronomy, Am. Soc. Water Resources (charter), Am. Geophys. Union, Akron C. of C. (pres. 1973). Club: Washington County Golf (pres. 1964, 84). Lodges: Lions (dist. gov. 1972-73), Elks (exalted ruler 1981-82). Democrat. Lutheran. Current work: Water conservation and soil erosion control research including landfarming techniques and deep tillage to improve precipitation-use efficiency for dry-land agriculture. Subspecialty: Agricultural engineering. Home: PO Box I Akron CO 80720 Office: US Dept Agr-Agrl Research Service PO Box K Akron CO 80720

MICKENS, RONALD ELBERT, physicist, educator; b. Petersburg, Va., Feb. 7, 1943; s. Joseph and Daisy (Brown) M.; m. Aug. 13, 1977; children—James, Leah. B.A., Fisk U., 1964; Ph.D., Vanderbilt U., 1968. Postdoctoral fellow in physics MIT, Cambridge, 1968-70, vis. prof., 1973-74; asst. prof. then prof. physics Fisk U., Nashville, 1970-81; vis. scholar Vanderbilt U., Nashville, 1980-81; research fellow Joint Inst. for Lab. Astrophysics, Boulder, Colo., 1981-82; prof. physics Atlanta U., 1982—, now Callaway prof. physics and chmn. dept. Author: Nonlinear Oscillations, 1981. Editor: Mathematical Analysis of Physical Systems, 1985. Contbr. articles to sci. publs. Fellow Woodrow Wilson Found., 1964-65, Danford Found., 1965-68, NSF, 1968-70 JILA, 1981-82; grantee NSF, 1971-73, NASA, 1975-81, 83—, Dept. Energy, 1983—. Mem. Am. Phys. Soc., Am. Assn. Physics Tchrs. (chmn. com. on physics in higher edn. 1984—), AAAS. Current work: Construction of exact and approximate analytic solutions to nonlinear differential and difference equations; mathematical physics. Subspecialty: Applied mathematics. Office: Physics Dept Atlanta U Atlanta GA 30314

MICKEY, GEORGE HENRY, cytogeneticist; b. Claude, Tex., Jan. 26, 1910; s. Luke Ross and Clara Alice (Pennington) M.; m. Alwilda Editha Davis, Aug. 20, 1932; children: Wilda Rhea, Don Davis. B.A., Baylor U., 1931; M.S., U. Okla., 1934; Ph.D., U. Tex., Austin, 1938. Cert. clin. lab. dir., Conn. Instr. zoology U. Tex., Austin, 1935-38; instr. La. State U., Baton Rouge, 1938-42, asst. prof., 1942-44, asso. prof., 1944-48; research fellow biology Calif. Inst. Tech., Pasadena, 1948; asso. prof. biology Northwestern U., Evanston, Ill., 1949-56; prin. biologist Oak Ridge Nat. Lab., 1953; prof., chmn. dept. zoology La. State U., 1956-59; dean La. State U. (Grad. Sch.), 1959-60; sr. scientist New Eng. Inst., Ridgefield, Conn., 1960-70; dean (Grad Sch.), 1970-74; clin. asso. and dir. cytogenetics Duke U. Med. Center, Durham, N.C., 1975—; vis. prof. U. Bridgeport, Conn., 1971. Co-author: Manual Studies in General Zoology, 1947; contbr. articles to sci. jours. Guggenheim fellow, 1948; grantee Sigma Xi; grantee Rockefeller Found.; grantee AEC; grantee Wallace Genetic Found.; grantee NSF; grantee Wood Found.; grantee Population Council; grantee Hartford Found.; grantee Office Naval Research. Fellow AAAS; mem. Am. Genetics Assn., Am. Naturalists, Am. Soc. Study Evolution, N.Y. Acad. Scis., Ill. Acad. Sci., La. Acad. Scis. (pres. 1948), Am. Soc. Human Genetics, Am. Inst. Biol. Sci., Am. Soc. Zoologists, AAUP, Genetics Soc. Am., Assn. Southeastern Biologists, Sigma Xi, Beta Beta Beta (nat. pres. 1957-60). Democrat. Methodist. Current Work: Human chromosome analysis; genetic counseling; hazards of genetic damage by environmental agents. Subspecialties: Genome organization; Cytology and histology. Home: 2404 Perkins Rd Durham NC 27706 Office: Duke U Med Center Box 3062 Durham NC 27710

MICKLE, MARLIN HOMER, electrical engineering educator, consultant; b. Windber, Pa., July 5, 1936; s. Howard T. and Ruth Elma (Corle) M. B.S. in Elec. Engring., U. Pitts., 1961, M.S. in Elec. Engring., 1963, Ph.D. in Elec. Engring., 1967. Jr. engr. IBM, Endicott, N.Y., 1962; engr. Westinghouse Electric Co., Lima, Ohio, 1964, 65; vis. assoc. prof. Am. U. of Beirut, Lebanon, 1969-70; program dir. NSF, Washington, 1974-75; prof. elec. engring. U. Pitts., 1962—; pres. Mickle Computer Techs., Inc.; dir. Power Resources, Inc., Pitts., Splty. Phones, Inc., Pitts. Co-author: Optimization in Systems Engring., 1972. Co-editor: Socio Economic Systems and Principles, 1973. Author numerous tech. papers. Bd. dirs. Mount Lebanon United Methodist Home, Pa. Served with USAF, 1954-58. Mem. IEEE, Internat. Tech. Inst., Internat. Platform Assn. Republican. Methodist. Current Work: High technology applications of microprocessors and computer control; design of high technology systems. Subspecialties: Computer engineering; Telecommunications. Home: 1376 Simona Dr Pittsburgh PA 15201 Office: U Pitts 348 Benedum Hall Pittsburgh PA 15261

MICKLEY, HAROLD SOMERS, retired chemical company executive; b. Seneca Falls, N.Y., Oct. 14, 1918; s. Harold Franklin and Marguerite Gladys (Somers) M.; m. Margaret W. Phillips, Dec. 21, 1941; children: Steven P., Richard S. B.S., Calif. Inst. Tech., 1940, M.S., 1941; Sc.D., MIT, 1946. Process engr. Union Oil Co. Calif., 1941-42; civilian project dir. torpedo research U.S. Navy, World War II; mem. faculty Mass. Inst. Tech., 1946-71, Ford prof. engring., 1961-71; dir. Center Advanced Engring., 1963-71; dir. Stauffer Chem. Co., Westport, Conn., 1967-83, v.p., 1971-72, exec. v.p., 1972-81, vice chmn. bd., 1981-83. Co-author: Applied Mathematics in Chemical Engineering, 1957, Recent Advances in Heat and Mass Transfer, 1961; Contbr. articles to profl. jours. Recipient Naval Ordnance Devel. award, 1946; Disting. Alumni award Calif. Inst. Tech., 1973; Corp. Leadership award MIT, 1983. Fellow AAAS, Am. Inst. Chem. Engrs., Am. Acad. Arts and Scis.; mem. Nat. Acad. Engring., Am. Chem. Soc., Soc. Chem. Industry, N.Y. Acad. Scis., Conn. Acad. Sci. and Engring., Sigma Xi, Tau Beta Pi. Club: Silvermine (Norwalk, Conn.). Subspecialties: Chemical engineering; Immunobiology and immunology. Home: 11 Pequot Trail Westport CT 06880

MIDDLEDITCH, BRIAN STANLEY, biochemistry educator; b. Bury St. Edmunds, Suffolk, Eng., July 15, 1945; came to U.S., 1971; s. Stanley Stafford and Dorothy (Harker) M.; m. Patricia Rosalind Nair, July 18, 1970; 1 dau., Courtney Lauren. B.Sc., U. London, 1966; M.Sc., U. Essex, 1967; Ph.D., U. Glasgow, 1971. Research asst. U. Glasgow, Scotland, 1967-71; vis. asst. prof. Baylor Coll. Medicine, Houston, 1971-75; asst. prof. U. Houston, 1975-80, assoc. prof., 1980—. Author: Mass Spectrometry of Priority Pollutants, 1981; editor: Practical Mass Spectrometry, 1979, Environmental Effects of Offshore Oil Production, 1981. Grantee Nat. Marine Fisheries Service, 1976-80; Grantee Sea Grant Program, 1977-81; NASA grantee, 1980-86, IBM grantee, 1985-86. Mem. Am. Chem. Soc., Am. Soc. Mass Spectrometry, World Mariculture Soc. Current Work: Biochemical ecology, mariculture. Subspecialties: Analytical chemistry; Environmental engineering. Home: 4101 Emory Ave Houston TX 77005 Office: U Houston Dept Biochem and Biophys Scis Houston TX 77004

MIDDLETON, DAVID, statistical physics, communication theory, and applied mathematics consultant and educator; b. N.Y.C., Apr. 19, 1920; s. Charles Davies Scudder and Lucile (Davidson) M.; m. Nadea Butler, May 26, 1945 (div. Mar. 1971); children—Susan Terry, Leslie Butler, David Blakeslee, George Davidson Powell; m. Joan Bartlett Reed, Apr. 2, 1971; children—Christopher Hope Reed, Andrew Bartlett Reed, Henry Hope Reed. A.B. summa cum laude, Harvard U., 1942, A.M., 1945, Ph.D. in Physics, 1947. Spl. research assoc. Radio Research Lab., Harvard U., 1942-45, teaching fellow in electronics, 1947-49, asst. prof. applied physics, 1949-54; cons. applied math., statis. physics, statis. communication theory, Cambridge, Mass., 1955—, N.Y.C., 1971—; cons. to industry and U.S. Govt.; adj. prof. communication theory U. R.I., 1966—; adj. prof. math. scis. Rice U., 1979—. Author: Introduction to Statistical Communication Theory, 1960; Topics in Communication Theory, 1965. Sci. editor: (English edit.) Statistical Methods in Sonar (v.v. Olsh'evskii), 1978. Contbr. articles to profl. jours. Recipient various awards, 1952—. Fellow Am. Phys. Soc., IEEE, AAAS, Acoustical Soc. Am.; mem. Am. Math. Soc., Inst. Math. Stats., Optical Soc. Am., Sigma Xi, Phi Beta Kappa. Clubs: Cosmos (Washington); Harvard, Explorers (fellow) (N.Y.C.). Current work: Signal processing, system analysis and electomagnetic compatibility with statistical-physical modeling of man-made and natural environments; scattering from random surfaces and volumes with applications to EM and underwater acoustics; threshold signal algorithms, telecommunications, and remote sensing. Home: 127 E 91st St New York NY 10128 Office: 35 Concord Ave Cambridge MA 02138

MIDDLETON, ELLIOTT, JR, medicine and pediatrics educator; b. Glen Ridge, N.J., Dec. 15, 1925; s. Elliott and Dorothy (Thoman) M.; m. Elizabeth Blackford, Sept. 25, 1948; children—Elliott, Ellen Alice, Blackford, James Jay. B.A., Princeton U., 1947; M.D., Columbia U., 1950. Intern, Presbyn. Hosp., N.Y.C., 1950-51, resident, 1951-52, asst. in medicine Immunochemistry Lab., Columbia U., N.Y.C., 1952-53; clin. fellow NIH, 1953-54; clin. and research fellow Roosevelt Hosp., 1955-56; part-time pvt. practice specializing in allergy, Montclair, N.J., 1955-69; research in biochem. and abnormal pharmacol. mechanisms and allergic diseases Columbia U./Roosevelt Hosp., 1955-69; dir. clin. service and research Children's Asthma Ctr., Denver, 1969-76; prof. medicine and pediatrics, dir. allergy div. SUNY-Buffalo, 1976—, cons., 1976—; cons. VA, 1976—, Children's Hosp. Buffalo, 1976—. Author: Allergy: Principles and Practice, 2nd edit. 1983. Editor Jour. Alergy/Clin. Immunology, 1983—. Contbr. articles to profl. jours. Served with USN, 1944-50. Fogarty Internat. fellow, NIH, 1982-83. Mem. Am. Acad. Allergy (pres. 1972), Fedn. Am. Socs. for Exptl. Biology. Republican. Episcopalian. Current work: Mechanisms and management of allergic diseases; immunopharmacology; effects of plant flavonoids on cell processes. Subspecialties: Allergy; Immunopharmacology. Office: Allergy Div Buffalo Gen Hosp 100 High St Buffalo NY 14203

MIERNYK, WILLIAM HENRY, economist, researcher, educator; b. Durango, Colo., Jan. 4, 1918; s. Andrew Taber and Elizabeth (Sopko) M.; m. Mary Lorraine Davis, Oct. 4, 1940; children: Jan, Judith, Jeanne, James. B.A., U. Colo., 1946; M.A., Harvard U., 1952, Ph.D., 1953. Instr. to prof. econs. Northeastern U., 1952-62; prof. econs., dir. Bur. Econ. Research, U. Colo., Boulder, 1962-65; C.W. Benedum prof. econs. W.Va. U., Morgantown, 1965—; dir. Regional Research Inst. U.Va. U., 1965-83; vis. prof. econs. MIT, 1957-58, Harvard U., 1969-70. Author or contbr.39 books, including: Regional Analysis and Regional Policy, 1982; (with others) Regional Impacts of Rising Energy Prices, 1978, (with John T. Sears) Air Pollution Abatement and Regional Economic Development, 1974; contbr. numerous articles to profl. jours. Served with AUS, 1941-45. Fellow So. Regional Sci. Assn.; mem. Am. Econ. Assn., Regional Sci. Assn., Indsl. Relations Research Assn. Current Work: Regional impacts of energy availability and prices. Subspecialties: Fuels; Coal.

MIERS, RICHARD ERNEST, physics educator, atomic and molecular physics researcher; b. Warrens, Wis., Oct. 29, 1932; s. Edward Charles Miers and Violet Viola (Callaway) Coleman; m. Ruth Merle Hawley, Aug. 28, 1955 (div. 1982); children—Marshall Hawley, Catherine Elizabeth Miers Fisk, Edward Richard. B.S., Wis. State Coll., 1957; M.S., U. Wis., 1961, Ph.D., 1970. Tchr. sci. and math. Cadott High Sch., Wis., 1957-59; teaching and research asst. U. Wis., Madison, 1964-69, vis. asst. prof. physics, summers 1971, 80-83; instr., asst. prof., assoc. prof. physics Purdue U., Fort Wayne, Ind., 1961-74, Ind. U./Purdue U., Ft. Wayne, 1974—; vis. scientist Argonne Nat. Lab., Ill., summer 1973; physicist Monsanto Research Corp., Miamisburg, Ohio, summers 1974-80. cons., 1974-80; summer fellow Air Force Wright Aero. Lab., Wright-Patterson AFB, Ohio, 1984. Contbg. author to profl. publs. Served with U.S. Army, 1953-55. NSF Sci. faculty fellow, 1965; U. Wis. fellow, 1968; cancer research grantee, Purdue U., 1973; grantee univ. research program Monsanto Research Corp. Mound Lab.; summer research fellow Air Force Office Sci. Research, 1984. Mem. Am. Assn. Physics Tchrs., Am. Phys. Soc., Ft. Wayne Engrs. Club, Sigma Xi. Current work: Electron excitation cross section measurements; electron energy distribution functions in thyratron tubes; atomic and molecular collisions. Subspecialty: Atomic and molecular physics. Office: Ind U/Purdue U Ft Wayne 2101 Coliseum Blvd E Fort Wayne IN 46805

MIEYAL, JOHN JOSEPH, biochemistry educator; b. Cleve., Feb. 17, 1944; s. Stanley John and Jennie Ann (Miesowicz) M.; m. Donna Celeste Dobscha, Aug. 20, 1966; children: Thomas Joseph, Paul Anthony, Jennifer Lynn, Angela Marie. B.S., John Carrol U., 1965; Ph.D (USPHS fellow), Case-Western Res. U., 1969. USPHS fellow in biochemistry Brandeis U., 1969-71; asst. prof. pharmacology and biochemistry Northwestern U. Med. Sch., Chgo., 1971-76; assoc. prof. pharmacology Case Western Res. U., Cleve., 1976—, assoc. prof. chemistry, 1981—. Contbr. articles to profl. jours. Mem. parish council St. Ann Catholic Ch. Recipient John S. Diekhoff Teaching award Case-Western Res. U., 1980; Chgo. Heart Assn. grantee, 1972-76; Research Corp. grantee, 1972-75; Nat. Inst. Gen. Med. Scis. grantee, 1974—; Los Alamos Stable Isotope Resource grantee, 1980-83; Am. Heart Assn. of N.E. Ohio grantee, 1977-80; Kidney Found. Ohio grantee, 1981-82. Mem. Am. Soc. Biol. Chemists, Am. Soc. Pharmacology and Exptl. Therapeutics, Am. Chem. Soc., AAAS, AAUP, Sigma Xi. Roman Catholic. Current Work: Molecular basis for differential reactivity of hemoprotein involved in oxygen transport, drug and xenobiotic metabolism, toxic activation of drugs and environmental agents and selective activity of chemotherapeutic agts. Subspecialty: Molecular pharmacology. Home: 2245 Lamberton Rd Cleveland Heights OH 44118 Office: Dept Pharmacology Case Western Res U Med Sch Cleveland OH 44106

MIGLIORE, HERMAN JAMES, mechanical engineering educator, researcher; b. Detroit, July 13, 1946; s. Rose (Montante) M. B.S.M.E., U. Detroit, 1968, M.M.E., 1968, D.Eng., 1975. Registered profl. engr., Oreg., Calif. Coop. engr. Ford Motor Co., Dearborn, Mich., 1966-69; doctoral intern Chrysler Corp., Detroit, 1973-75; research mech. engr. Naval Civil Engring. Lab., Point Hueneme, Calif., 1969-72, 75-77; prof. mech. engring. Portland State U., Oreg., 1977—; vis. research scientist U.S. Navy, Point Hueneme, 1978. Contbr. articles to profl. jours. Chrysler Corp. fellow, 1972; grantee Office Naval Research, NSF. Mem. ASME, Am. Soc. Engring. Edn., Tuyere, Sigma Xi, Pi Tau Sigma, Tau Beta Pi. Current work: Developed numerical techniques for nonlinear mechanical engineering problems; applying microprocessors with intelligent sensors. Subspecialties: Mechanical engineering; Computer-aided design. Home: 4128 SW Hewett Portland OR 97221 Office: Portland State U PO Box 751 Portland OR 97207

MIHALAS, DIMITRI MANUEL, scientist; b. Los Angeles, Mar. 20, 1939; s. Emmanuel Demetrious and Jean (Christo) M.; m. Alice Joelen Covalt, June 15, 1963 (div. Nov. 1974); children—Michael Demetrious, Genevieve Alexandra; m. Barbara Ruth Rickey, May 18, 1975. B.A. with highest honors, UCLA, 1959; M.S., Calif. Inst. Tech., 1960, Ph.D., 1964. Asst. prof. astrophys. scis. Princeton U., 1964-67; asst. prof. physics U. Colo., 1967-68; asso. prof. astronomy and astrophysics U. Chgo., 1968-70, prof., 1970-71; adj. prof. astrogeophysics, also physics and astrophysics U. Colo., 1972-80; sr. scientist High Altitude Obs., Nat. Center Atmospheric Research, Boulder, Colo., 1971-79, 82-85; George C. McVittie prof. astronomy U. Ill., Urbana, 1985—; astronomer Sacramento Peak Obs., Sunspot, N.Mex., 1979-82; cons. Los Alamos Nat. Lab, 1981—; vis. prof. dept. astrophysics Oxford (Eng.) U., 1977-78; sr. vis. fellow dept. physics and astronomy Univ. Coll., London, 1978; mem. astronomy adv. panel NSF, 1972-75. Author: Galactic Astronomy, 2d edit, 1981, Stellar Atmospheres, 1970, 2d edit., 1978, Theorie des Atmospheres Stellaires, 1971; Foundations of Radiation Hydrodynamics, 1984; asso. editor: Astrophys. Jour, 1970-79, Jour. Computational Physics, 1981—, Jour. Quantitative Spectroscopy, 1984—; editorial bd.: Solar Physics, 1981—. NSF fellow, 1959-62; Van Maanen fellow, 1962-63; Eugene Higgins vis. fellow, 1963-64; Alfred P. Sloan Found. Research fellow, 1969-71; Alexander von Humboldt sr. U.S. scientist award, 1984. Mem. U.S. Nat. Acad. Sci., Internat. Astron. Union (pres. commn. 36 1976-79), Am. Astron. Soc. (Helen B. Warner prize 1974), Astron. Soc. Pacific (dir. 1975-77). Current Work: Radiation hydrodynamics; radiation transport and spectral-line formation; stellar pulsation. Subspecialty: Theoretical astrophysics. Home: 308 Pond Ridge Ln Urbana IL 61801 Office: Dept Astronomy U Ill 1011 W Springfield Ave Urbana IL 61801

MIHAS, FAQUIR ULLAH, mathematician, researcher; b. Shadiwal, Pakistan, Dec. 4, 1924; emigrated to Can., 1962; s. Atta and Sakeena Minhas. B.A. in Math, Panjab U., Lahore, Pakistan, 1952, M.A., 1957; M.A.Sc., U. Laval, Que., Can., 1965, D.Sc. in Mech. Engring, 1972; M.Eng. in Elec. Engring, McGill U., Montreal, 1982. Edn. officer Pakistan Air Force, 1957-61; devel. engr. John Inglish Co. Ltd., Toronto, Ont., Can., 1963-64; sr. project engr. Dominion Engring. Works Ltd., Montreal, 1966-74, head transport phenomena br., 1974-80; staff specialist in aerodynamics Canadair Ltd., Montreal, 1980-82, staff specialist in systems, 1982—. Fellow Brit. Interplanetary soc.; mem. Can. Aerospace Inst., ASME, AIAA, Order of Engrs., Que. Current Work: Electrical propulsion; electromagnetic confinement of plasma. Subspecialties: Aerospace engineering and technology; Plasma (energy science and technology). Home: 4000 Maisonneuve West Apt 2404 Westmount Montreal PQ H3Z 1J9 Canada Office: Canadair Ltd 1800 Laurentain Blvd Montreal PQ H3C 3G9 Canada

MIHM, MARTIN CHARLES, JR., dermatopathology administrator, researcher; b. Pitts.; s. Martin Charles and Cecelia Matilda (Hepp) M. A.B., Duquesne U., 1955; M.D., U. Pitts., 1961. Diplomate: Am. Bd. Dermatology, Am. Bd. Pathology, Am. Bd. Dermatopathology. Intern Mt. Sinai Hosp., N.Y.C., 1961-62, resident, 1963-64; resident in dermatology Mass. Gen. Hosp., Boston, 1965-67, resident in pathology, 1969-73; asst. prof. pathology Harvard U., 1972-75, assoc. prof., 1975-79, chief dermatopathology, 1982—, Mass. Gen. Hosp., 1974—; prof. pathology Mass. Gen. Hosp./Harvard Med. Sch., 1980—, chief photopathology, 1985—; pres. Mass. Gen. Hosp./Harvard Med. Sch. (House Officers Assn.), 1982-84; chmn. pathology panel Intergroup Melanoma Study; cons. VA Hosp., Boston, U. B.C., Vancouver. Author: Human Malignant Melanoma, 1979, Pigment Cell, 1981, 1981, Dermatology in General Medicine, 1981, Primer of Dermatopathology, 1983. Served to comdr. USPHS-Coast Guard, 1967-69. Fellow Am. Acad. Dermatology, ACP; mem. New Eng. Pathology Soc., New Eng. Dermatol. Soc., Soc. Investigative Dermatology, Am. Soc. Dermatopathology, Am. Soc. Clin. Oncology, Am. Dermatol. Assn., Alpha Omega Alpha, Pi Gamma Nu. Roman Catholic. Current Work: Malignant melanoma, delayed hypersensitivity studies in man, monoclonal antibody studies of inflammation, allograft rejection, bullous diseases, mechanism and pathogenesis; studies of histology of laser-tissue interactions. Subspecialties: Dermatology; Pathology (medicine). Office: Dermatopathology Unit Mass Gen Hosp Fruit St Boston MA 02114

MIKAT, EILEEN MARIE, medical research scientist; b. Cleve., May 1, 1930; d. Edward and Elizabeth (Seman) M. A.B., Case Western Res. U., 1952; M.A., Duke U., 1969, Ph.D., 1979. Coordinator, supr. med. tech. sch. Cleve. Met. Gen. Hosp., Case Western Res. U., Cleve., 1952-61; research asst. Duke U., Durham, N.C., 1961-69, research assoc., 1969-79; asst. prof. dept. pathology Duke U. (Med. Ctr.), 1979—. Mem. Am. Assn. Pathologists, Am. Soc. Clin. Pathologists. Current Work: Cardiovascular and shock research. Subspecialties: Pathology (medicine); Cardiology. Office: Duke U Med Ctr Pathology Dept Box 3712 Durham NC 27707

MIKSCHE, JEROME PHILLIP, botany educator, researcher, administrator; b. Breckenridge, Minn., June 11, 1930; s. Anton Francis and Clara Gertrude (Braun) M.; m. Betty Jane Logan, May 23, 1953; children: Michael Logan, Elizabeth Clare, James Jerome. B.S., Moorhead State U., 1954; M.S., Miami U., Oxford, Ohio, 1956; Ph.D., Iowa State U., 1959. Postdoctoral assoc. Brookhaven Nat. Lab., Upton, N.Y., 1959-60; asst. botanist, 1960-65; prin. plant cytologist Inst. of Forest Genetics U.S. Dept. Agr. Forest Service, Rhinelander, Wis., 1965-77; prof., head dept. botany N.C. State U., Raleigh, 1977—. Contbr. articles to profl. jours. Chmn. Headwaters dist. Boy Scouts Am., 1965-67; mem. N.C. Bd. Sci. and Tech., 1979-85. Served with USMC, 1948-51. Named Outstanding Alumnus Moorhead State U., 1977. Mem. Am. Soc. for Cell Biology, Am. Soc. Plant Physiology, AAAS, Am. Soc. for Histochemistry, Bot. Soc. Am., Sigma Xi, Gamma Sigma Delta. Democrat. Roman Catholic. Current Work: DNA genome Changes during development in plants. Subspecialties: Genome organization; Developmental biology. Home: 3212 Ruffin St Raleigh NC 27607 Office: Botany Dept NC State U Raleigh NC 27650

MIKULLA, VOLKER, aeronautical engineer; b. Dzieditz, Silesia, Germany, Jan. 5, 1944; s. Hans Joachim and Elfriede (von Gruchalla) M.; m. Jennifer Mary Bartlett, Aug. 19, 1972; children: Christian, Claire, Peter. B.Aero. Engring., Rensselaer Poly. Inst., 1967; M.Engr., U. Liverpool, Eng., 1969, Ph.D., 1973. Research engr. helicopter div. Messerschmitt Boelkow-Blohm, Munich, Bavaria, W.Ger., 1975—. Assoc. fellow AIAA; mem. Deutsche Gesellschaft fuer Luft-und Raumfahrt. Roman Catholic. Patentee. Current Work: Research and development in helicopter aerodynamics, numerical analysis, computational fluid dynamics, turbulence, wind tunnel techniques. Subspecialties: Aeronautical engineering; Fluid mechanics. Home: Hohenbrunnerstrasse 73 8012 Riemerling Federal Republic of Germany Office: Messerschmitt Boelkow-Blohm Postfach 8011 40 8000 Munich 80 Federal Republic of Germany

MILANI, CYRUS SAEED, pathologist; b. Mashad, Iran, May 14, 1941; came to U.S., 1968, naturalized, 1980; s. Boyouk and Habibeh (Sadaghianai) Sadeghi; m. Afsaneh Khavas, Aug. 25, 1966; children: Natalie B., Natasha B. M.D., Pahlavi U., Shiraz, Iran, 1966. Intern Ellis Hosp., Schenectady, 1968-69; resident Hosp. U. Pa., Phila., 1969-73, assoc. pathologist, 1973-74; pathologist Cantonal U. Hosp., Lausanne, Switzerland, 1974-75; asst. prof. Teheran (Iran) U., 1975-77; dir. Central Diagnostic Lab., Tarzana, Calif., 1977—, Preventive Clinic Am., Encino, 1981—, Valley Cryobank div. Tissue Preservation Inst., Woodland Hills, Calif., 1981—. Bd. dirs. French Am. Sch., Van Nuys, Calif., 1979—, Am. Cancer Soc., Van Nuys, 1981-82, Am. Heart Assn., Studio City, Calif., 1982—. Mem. Am. Assn. Immunologists, Coll. Am. Pathologists, Am. Soc. Clin. Pathologists, Soc. Cryobiology, AAAS. Current Work: Tissue banking, autologous cell preservation and use, anatomic pathology and clinical pathology. Subspecialties: Pathology (medicine); Cellular engineering. Office: Valley Cryobank Div Tissue Preservation Inst Topanga Canyon Blvd 508 Woodland Hills CA 91376

MILBURN, RONALD MCRAE, chemistry educator; b. Wellington, N.Z., May 29, 1928; s. Henry Joseph and Sylvia May (Sandlant) M.; m. Josephine Nicholson Fishel, Apr. 26, 1928; children: Rosemary R., Jeffrey R. B.Sc., Victoria U., Wellington, 1949, M.Sc., 1951; Ph.D., Duke U., 1954. Instr., research assoc. Duke U., 1954; lectr. Victoria U., 1955; instr., research assoc. Duke U., 1956; research assoc. U. Chgo., 1956-57; asst. prof. chemistry Boston U., 1957-63, assoc. prof., 1963-68, prof., 1968—; NIH spl. fellow Oxford U., Eng., 1965-66; vis. fellow Australian Nat. U., 1974-75; vis. scientist U. Basel, Switzerland, 1982-83. Contbr. articles to profl. jours. Fulbright grantee, 1952. Mem. Am. Chem. Soc., AAUP. Current Work: Influence of metal centers on reactions of coordinated ligands, phosphate chemistry. Subspecialty: Inorganic chemistry. Office: Dept Chemistry Boston U Boston MA 02215

MILES, EDWARD LANCELOT, marine studies and public affairs educator, consultant; b. Port-of-Spain, Trinidad, West Indies, Dec. 21, 1939; came to U.S., 1959; s. Cecil Bannister and Louise (Dufont) M.; m. Wanda Elaine Merrick, Aug. 24, 1963; children—Anthony Roger, Leila Yvonne. B.A., Howard U., 1962; Ph.D., U. Denver, 1965. Instr. Grad. Sch. Internat. Studies U. Denver, 1965-66, asst. prof., 1966-70, assoc. prof., 1970-74; sr. fellow Woods Hole Oceanographic Inst., Mass., 1973-74; prof. marine studies and pub. affairs, U. Wash., Seattle, 1974—, dir. Inst. Marine Studies, 1982—; joint appointee Micronesian Maritime Authority, Ponape, East Carol Island, 1978-82, chief negotiator, 1981—; task group leader seabed working group NEA/OECD, Paris, 1981-85, chmn. NRC, 1971-79; mem. exec. bd. Law of the Sea Inst., 1971-80, 85—. Author: The Management of Marine Regions: The North Pacific, 1982; Atlas of Marine Use in the North Pacific Region, 1982. Advisor, mem. UN Assn., Seattle, 1975—. Fellow Hill Found., 1962-63, Council on Fgn. Relations, 1972-73; James P Warburg fellow Ctr. Internat. Affairs, Harvard U., 1973-74; grantee Ford Found., 1968-70, NSF, 1980-84. Democrat. Club: Harvard (N.Y.C.). Current work: The management of living resources; radioactive waste management and disposal; the law of the sea and changing ocean regimes; international science and technology policy. Subspecialty: Marine studies. Office: Inst for Marine Studies Hf-05 Univ Wash Seattle WA 98195

MILES, JOHN WILDER, applied mechanics educator; b. Cin., Dec. 1, 1920; s. Harold M. and Cleopatra (Morton) M.; m. Herberta Blight, June 19, 1943; children: Patricia Marie, Diana Catherine, Ann Leslie. B.S., Calif. Inst. Tech., 1942, M.S. in Aero. Engring., 1944; Ph.D., 1944. With research lab. Gen. Electric Co., Schenectady, 1942; instr. Calif. Inst. Tech., 1943-44; with radiation lab. Mass. Inst. Tech., 1944; with Lockheed Aircraft Co., Burbank, Calif., 1944-45; asst. prof. UCLA, 1945-49, assoc. prof., 1949-55, prof., 1955-61; prof. applied math. Australian Nat. U., 1962-64; prof. applied mechanics and geophysics U. Calif. at San Diego, 1965—, chmn. applied mechanics and engring. sci., 1968-72, vice chancellor acad. affairs, 1980-83; cons. Northrop Aircraft Co., 1946-49, N.Am. Aviation Co., 1948-51, U.S. Naval Ordnance Test Sta., 1948-51, Douglas Aircraft Co., 1952-54, Ramo Wooldridge Corp., 1955-60, NASA, 1959-60, Aerospace Corp., 1961-68, Gulf Gen. Atomic Corp., 1965-68, Systems Sci. & Software, 1972-75, Sci. Applications, 1978-80, Gas Centrifuge Theory Cons. Group, 1978-85. Assoc. editor: Jour. Soc. Indsl. and Applied Math, 1958-61, Jour. Fluid Mechanics, 1966—;

co-editor: Cambridge Monographs on Mechanics and Applied Math, 1963-83. Math. Tools for Engrs. Series, 1967-70; bd. editors: U. Calif. Press, 1955-58, Ann. Rev. of Fluid Mechanics, 1967-73, Fluid Mechanics-Soviet Research, 1972—; reviewer: Applied Mechanics Revs, 1947—, Math. Revs, 1946—. Recipient Fulbright awards U. New, Zealand, 1951, Fulbright awards Cambridge U., 1969; vis. lectr. Imperial Coll., London, 1952; recipient Timoshenko Medal ASME, 1982; Guggenheim fellow, 1958-59, 68-69; G.H. Laporte lectr. Am. Phys. Soc., 1983. Fellow AIAA, Am. Acad. Arts and Scis., Am. Acad. Mechs.; mem. Nat. Acad. Scis., AAAS, N.Y. Acad. Scis., Fedn. Am. Scientists, Am. Geophys. Union, Sigma Xi, Tau Beta Pi. Current Work: Water waves, nonlinear dynamics (strange attractors, etc.). Subspecialties: Applied mathematics; Geophysics.

MILES, RICHARD BRYANT, electrical engineer, applied physicist, educator; b. Washington, July 10, 1943; s. Thomas Kirk and Elizabeth (Bryant) M.; m. Susan McCoy; 1 child, Thomas Nelson. B.S., Stanford U., 1966, M.S., 1967, Ph.D., 1972. Postdoctoral assoc. Stanford U., 1972; asst. prof. mech. and aerospace engring. Princeton U., 1972-78, assoc. prof., 1978-82, prof., 1982—. Contbr. articles to profl. jours. Fannie and John K. Hertz fellow, 1969-72. Mem. Am. Inst. Physics, IEEE, Sierra Club, Aircraft Owners and Pilots Assn. Patentee in field. Current Work: Laser diagnostics, molecular dynamics, optics, laser induced fluorescence, nonlinearoptics, laser ranging, picosecond surface spectroscopy, photoacoustics, molecular relaxation. Subspecialties: Optical engineering; Laser spectroscopy. Home: 3 Newlin Rd Princeton NJ 08540 Office: Princeton U D-414 Engring Quardrangle Princeton NJ 08544

MILETICH, DAVID JOHN, medical researcher, educator; b. Akron, Ohio, Feb. 12, 1937; s. John and Katherin (Tressel) M.; m. Marilyn Ellen Schroeder, Mar. 25, 1971; children: Brenna, Elizabeth, Nicklas. B.A. in Biology, Kent State U., 1963; Ph.D. in Physiology, Georgetown U., 1968. Dir. anesthesia research Michael Reese Hosp. and Med. Ctr., Chgo., 1971—; assoc. prof. anesthesiology U. Chgo., 1971—. Served to lt. USN, 1957-61. Mem. Am. Soc. Anesthesiologists, Stroke Council Am. Heart Assn., Am. Physiol. Soc., Internat. Anesthesia Research Soc., N.Y. Acad. Scis. Current Work: Cerebral physiology and drug effects, cerebral blood flow and metabolism anesthetic effects. Subspecialties: Anesthesiology; Physiology (medicine). Office: Michael Reese Hosp and Med Ctr 31st and Lake Shore Dr Chicago IL 60616

MILEY, GEORGE HUNTER, nuclear engineering educator; b. Shreveport, La., Aug. 6, 1933; s. George Hunter and Norma Angeline (Dowling) M.; m. Elizabeth Burroughs, Nov. 22, 1958; children: Susan Elizabeth, Hunter Robert. B.S. in Chem. Engring., Carnegie-Mellon U., 1955; M.S., U. Mich., 1956, Ph.D. in Chem.-Nuclear Engring., 1959. Nuclear engr. Knolls Atomic Power Lab., Gen. Electric Co., Schenectady, 1959-61; mem. faculty U. Ill., Urbana, 1961—, prof., 1967—, chmn. nuclear engring. program, 1975—, dir. Fusion Studies Lab., 1976—, assoc. Ctr. Advanced Study, 1985-86; vis. prof. U. Colo., summer, 1967, Cornell U., 1969-70. Author: Direct Conversion of Nuclear Radiation Energy, 1971, Fusion Energy Conversion, 1976; editor: Jour. Nuclear Tech./Fusion, 1980—; U.S. assoc. editor: Laser and Particle Beams, 1982—. Served with C.E. AUS, 1960. Recipient Western Electric Teaching-Research award, 1977; NATO sr. sci. fellow, 1975-76; Guggenheim fellow, 1985-86. Fellow Am. Nuclear Soc. (dir. 1980-83, Disting. Service award 1980), Am. Phys. Soc.; mem. Am. Soc. Engring. Edn. (chmn. energy conversion com. 1967-70, pres. U. Ill. chpt. 1973-74, chmn. nuclear div. 1975-76, Outstanding Tchr. award 1973), Sigma Xi. Presbyterian. Lodge: Kiwanis. Research on fusion, energy conversion, reactor kinectics Research on fusion, energy conversion, reactor kinectics. Current Work: Fusion plasma engineering; inertial confinement fusion; nuclear pumped lasers; direct energy conversion. Subspecialties: Fusion; Nuclear fusion. Office: 214 Nuclear Engring Lab 103 S Goodwin St U Ill Urbana IL 61801

MILIC-EMILI, JOSEPH, physiologist, educator; b. Sezana, Yugoslavia, May 27, 1931; emigrated to Can., 1963, naturalized, 1969; s. Joseph and Giovanna (Perhavec) Milic-E.; m. Ann Harding, Sept. 2, 1957; four children. M.D., U. Milan, Italy, 1955. Asst. prof. physiology U. Milan, Italy, 1956-58, U. Liège, Belgium, 1958-60; research fellow in physiology Harvard U., Boston, 1960-63; asst. prof. physiology and exptl. medicine McGill U., Montreal, Que., Can., 1963-65, asso. prof., 1965-69, prof. dept. physiology, 1970—, prof. exptl. medicine, 1970—, chmn. dept. physiology, 1973-78; dir. Meakins-Christie Labs., Montreal, 1979—; vis. cons. aeros. Imperial Coll. Tech., London, Eng., 1969-70; vis. cons. medicine Royal Postgrad. Med. Sch., London, 1969-70; cons. Brookhaven Nat. Lab., 1974, Columbia U., 1977. Editorial bds.: American Jour. of Physiology, 1970-76, Jour. of Applied Physiology, 1970-76, Revue Francaise Des Maladies Respiratoires, 1979, Rivista di Biologia, Am. Rev. Respiratory Disease, 1982; assoc. editor: Can. Jour. Physiology and Pharmacology, 1972-76; asso. editor: Jour. Applied Physiology, 1976-78; contbr. over 200 sci. research articles to profl. publs. Fellow Royal Soc. Can.; mem. Association des Physiologistes de Langue Francaise, Am. Physiol. Soc., Can. Physiol. Soc., Can. Soc. Clin. Investigation, Italian Physiol. Soc., Can. Thoracic Soc., Med. Research Council (grants com., heart and lung), Fleischner Soc., Societe Belge de Pneumologie (hon.). Current Work: Respiratory mechanics, control of breathing; respiratory diseases. Subspecialties: Physiology (medicine); Pulmonary medicine. Home: 4394 Circle Rd Montreal PQ H3W 1Y5 Canada Office: Meakins-Christie Labs McGill Univ Lyman Duff Medical Sciences Bldg 3775 University St Montreal PQ H3A 2B4 Canada

MILJANICH, GEORGE PAUL, biochemist, biology educator; b. Watsonville, Calif., Feb. 17, 1950; s. Peter George and Barbara Ann (Eldredge) M.; m. Patricia Ann Henderson, June 6, 1982; children—Nicolene Georgene, Martine Patricia, Peter Ralph. B.S., U. Calif.-Berkeley, 1972; Ph.D., U. Calif.-Santa Cruz, 1978. Postdoctoral scholar U. Calif.-San Francisco, 1978-82; asst. prof. biology U. So. Calif., Los Angeles, 1982—. Contbr. articles to profl. publs. Alumni scholar U. Calif.-Berkeley, 1967-68; predoctoral fellow Fight for Sight, Inc., 1972-76; postdoctoral fellow Muscular Dystrophy Assn., 1978-81; pub. health service grantee NIH, 1984—. Mem. Am. Soc. Cell Biology, U. Calif.-Berkeley Alumni Assn. Current work: Biochemistry, pharmacology and cell biology of nervous system. Subspecialties: Biochemistry (biology); Neurochemistry. Home: 1769 Sherbourne Dr Los Angeles CA 90035 Office: Dept Biol Scis Univ So Calif University Park Los Angeles CA 90089

MILJKOVIC, MOMCILO, chemistry educator, researcher; b. Belgrad, Yugoslavia, Dec. 12, 1931; s. Adam and Dragoslava (Jankovic) M.; m. Irina Beljajev, Oct. 23, 1960; children: Marko, Marija. B.S. in Chemistry, Faculty of Sci., U. Belgrade, 1959; Ph.D. in chemistry, Eidg. Technische Hochschule, Zurich, Switzerland, 1965; M.S., Hershey Med. Center, Pa. State U.-Hershey, 1968. Research assoc. dept. biochemistry Duke U., Durham, N.C., 1967; asst. prof. Hershey Med. Center, Pa. State U., 1968-75, assoc. prof., 1975—. Contbr. articles on chemistry to profl. jours. Mem. Swiss Chem. Soc., Serbian Chem. Soc. Serbian Orthodox. Current Work: Natural product chemistry, carbohydrate chemistry, use of carbohydrate as chiral synthons for synthesis of non-carbohydrate chiral molecules, synthetic reactions, sialic acid chemistry. Subspecialties: Organic chemistry; Synthetic chemistry. Home: 1440 Deerfield Dr Hummelstown PA 17036 Office: 500 University Dr Hershey PA 17033

MILLER, C. ARDEN, physician, educator; b. Shelby, Ohio, Sept. 19, 1924; s. Harley H. and Mary (Thuma) M.; m. Helen Meihack, June 26, 1948; children—John Lewis, Thomas Meihack, Helen Lewis, Benjamin Lewis. Student, Oberlin Coll., 1942-44; M.D. cum laude, Yale, 1948. Intern, then asst. resident pediatrics Grace-New Haven Community Hosp., 1948-51; faculty U. Kans. Med. Center, 1951-66, dir. childrens rehab. unit, 1957-60; dean Med. Sch., dir. U. Kans. Med. Center, 1960-66; prof. pediatrics and maternal and child health U. N.C., Chapel Hill, 1966—, vice chancellor health scis., 1966-71, chmn. dept. maternal and child health, 1977; cons. UNICEF, HEW, World Bank; chmn. exec. com. Citizens Bd. Inquiry into Health Services for Am., 1968—; cons. United Mine Workers Welfare and Retirement Fund, 1973-80; mem. adv. com. on nat. health ins. U.S. Ho. of Reps. Ways and Means Com., 1974-78. Mem. editorial bd.: Jour. Med. Edn, 1960-66; Author numerous articles in field. Trustee Appalachian Regional Hosps., 1974-82. Alan Guttmacher Inst., Planned Parenthood Fedn. Am. Markle scholar in med. scis., 1955-60; Recipient Robert H. Felix Distinguished Service award St. Louis U., 1977. Hon. fellow Royal Soc. Health; mem. Am. Pub. Health Assn. (chmn. action bd. 1972-74, pres. 1974-75, Martha Mae Eleat award 1984), Soc. Pediatric Research, Assn. Am. Med. Colls. (v.p. 1965-66), Inst. of Medicine of Nat. Acad. Sci., Sigma Xi, Alpha Omega Alpha, Delta Omega. Current Work: Public policy for improved maternal and child health outcomes. Subspecialties: Pediatrics; Preventive medicine. Home: 908 Greenwood Rd Chapel Hill NC 27514

MILLER, CARL EDWARD, veterinarian; b. Wapello, Iowa; Nov. 8, 1931; s. Thurimas T. and Christena (Brauns) M.; m. Margery Ann Held, Feb. 6, 1955; children—Carol, David, Linda. D.V.M., Iowa State U., 1955; M.P.H., Johns Hopkins U., 1966. Diplomate Am. Coll. Lab. Animal Medicine. Gen. practice vet. medicine specializing in large animals, Hampton, Iowa, 1955; lab. animal veterinarian Vanderbilt U., Nashville, 1957-59; assoc. veterinarian Tenn. Animal Disease Lab., Nashville, 1959-60; research veterinarian NIH, Bethesda, Md., 1960—; bd. dirs. Assn. for Gnotobiotics, Notre Dame, Ind., 1967-71. Contbr. articles to profl. jours. Advancement chmn. Nat. Capital Area council Boy Scouts Am., Rockville, Md., 1967, asst. scoutmaster, 1965-72; trustee Million Meth. Ch., Rockville, 1974-78; treas. Rockinghouse Elem. Sch. PTA, Rockville, 1964-66. Served with Vet. Corps, U.S. Army, 1955-57. Mem. AVMA, Am. Assn. Lab. Animal Sci. (pres. Nat. Capital area br. 1970), D.C. Vet. Med. Assn. Current work: Laboratory animal science, currently peer review of grants. Subspecialty: Laboratory animal medicine. Home: 11510 Patapsco Dr Rockville MD 20852 Office: NIH 9000 Wisconsin Ave Bethesda MD 20205

MILLER, CARLOS OAKLEY, plant science educator; b. Jackson, Ohio, Feb. 19, 1923; s. William Flay and Marcella (Leach) M. B.S. in Agr, Ohio State U., 1948, M.A., 1949, Ph.D., 1951. Project assoc. U. Wis., Madison, 1951-55, asst. prof., 1955-57, Ind. U., Bloomington, 1957-60, assoc. prof., 1960-63, prof., 1963—. Contbr. articles to profl. jours. Served with AUS, 1943-46. Mem. Bot. Soc. Am., Am. Soc. Plant Physiologists, Japanese Soc. Plant Physiologists, AAAS. Democrat. Current Work: Biosynthesis, action and roles of cytokinins, plant hormones, tissue culture. Subspecialties: Plant growth; Plant physiology (biology). Home: 103 N Glenwood Ave W Bloomington IN 47401 Office: Biology Dept Indiana U Bloomington IN 47405

MILLER, CAROLE ANN, neurosurgeon; b. Kalamazoo, May 7, 1939. A.S., Bay City Jr. Coll., 1959; B.A., Ohio State U., 1962, M.D., 1966. Diplomate: Am. Bd. Neurology. Intern Grad. Hosp. U. Pa., 1966-67; resident Ohio State U. Hosp., 1967-72, instr., 1970-71, asst. prof., 1975, assoc. prof., 1980—; asst. prof. surgery U. Mich., Ann Arbor, 1972-74. Contbr. articles to profl. jours. Ohio Heart Assn. grantee, 1970; NIH grantee, 1973, 75; co-investigator NIH grant, 1984. Mem. ACS, Am. Assn. Neurol. Surgeons, AAUP, Surg. Hist. Soc., Neurosurg. Soc. Am., Congress Neurol. Surgeons, Ohio Neurosurg. Soc., AMA, Ohio Med. Soc. Current Work: Vascular smooth muscle physiology; cerebellar stimulation in cerebral palsy; percutaneous spinal cord stimulation in multiple sclerosis; spinal trauma. Subspecialty: Neurosurgery. Office: 410 W 10th Ave Univ Hosp N-935 Doan Hall Columbus OH 43210

MILLER, CHARLES LESLIE, civil engineer, planner, consultant; b. Tampa, Fla., June 5, 1929; s. Charles H. and Myrle Iona (Walstrom) M.; m. Roberta Jean Pye, Sept. 9, 1949; children—Charles Henry, Stephen, Jonathan, Matthew. B.C.E., Mass. Inst. Tech., 1951, M.C.E., 1958. Registered profl. engr., Mass., Fla., Tenn., N.H., R.I., P.R. Successively field engr., project engr., exec. engr. Michael Baker, Jr., Inc. (cons. engrs.), Rochester, Pa., 1951-55; asst. prof. surveying, dir. photogrammetry lab. Mass. Inst. Tech., 1955-59, asso. prof. civil engring., head data engring. div., 1959-61, prof. civil engring., 1961-77, head dept., 1961-70, dir. urban systems lab., 1968-75, dir. civil engring. systems lab., 1961-65, dir. inter-Am. program civil engring., 1961-65, asso. dean engring., 1970-71; cons. engr., 1955—; chmn. bd., sr. cons., pres. CLM Systems, Inc., C.L. Miller Co., Inc.; adviser Commonwealth of P.R; dir. Geo-Transport Found.; Chmn. Pres.-elect's Task Force on Transp., 1968-69. Author tech. papers. Recipient Outstanding Young Man of Greater Boston award. Fellow Am. Acad. Arts and Scis.; mem. ASCE, N.Y. Acad. Scis., Am. Inst. Cons. Engrs., Am. Soc. Engring. Edn. (George Westinghouse award), Am. Soc. Photogrammetry, Am. Congress Surveying and Mapping, Am. Rd. Builders Assn., Transp. Research Bd., Assn. Computing Machinery, Sigma Xi, Chi Epsilon, Tau Beta Pi. Originator of DTM, COGO and ICES computer systems. Current work: Design and development of CLM COGO/CAD/TOPO software. Home: 6214 Bayshore Blvd Tampa FL 33611 Office: 3654 Gandy Blvd Tampa FL 33611

MILLER, D. MERRILY, educational consultant, therapist; b. Yonkers, N.Y., Mar. 3, 1943; d. Stanley and Pearl (Colin) Dulman; m. Edward Richard Miller, Dec. 24, 1964; children: Logan, Sloan, Dane. A.B. cum laude, Vassar Coll., 1965; M.A., Memphis State U., 1968; Ed.M., Columbia U., 1972, Ed.D., 1974. Tchr. Bd. Edn., Yonkers, N.Y., 1968-72; instr. Fairleigh Dickinson U., Teaneck, N.J., 1972-73; dir. edn. Mend Human Devel. Ctr., N.Y.C., 1973-74; ednl. coordinator The Door, N.Y.C., 1974-75; asst. prof. Fordham U. Grad. Sch. Edn., N.Y.C., 1976-82; ednl. cons. Miller Assocs., Katonah, N.Y., 1981—. Contbr. articles to profl. jours. Columbia U. fellow, 1972-73; Bur. Edn. Handicapped grantee, 1977-80. Mem. Am. Psychol. Assn., Council for Exceptional Children, Assn. Women Administrs. in Westchester, Assn. N.Y. Educators of Emotionally Disturbed. Current Work: Narrowing gap between research/theory and ednl. practice. Subspecialty: Learning. Address: 26 Cherry St Katonah NY 10536

MILLER, DONALD SPENCER, geologist, educator; b. Ventura, Calif., June 12, 1932; s. Spencer Jacob and Marquerite Rachael (Williams) M.; m. Carolyn Margaret Losee, June 12, 1954; children: Sandra Louise, Kenneth Donald, Christopher Spencer. B.A., Occidental Coll., 1954; M.A., Columbia U., 1956, Ph.D., 1960. Asst. prof. Rensselaer Poly. Inst., Troy, N.Y., 1960-64, assoc. prof., 1964-69, prof., 1969—, chmn. dept. geology, 1969-76, 80—; research assoc. geology Columbia U., 1960-63; research fellow geochemistry Calif. Inst. Tech., Pasadena, summer 1963; NSF Sci. Faculty fellow U. Bern, Switzerland, 1966-67; sci. guest prof. Max-Planck Inst. Nuclear Physics, Heidelberg, W. Ger., 1977-78, vis. prof., summer 1979, guest scientist, Aug. 1979, 80, 81, 82; vis. prof. Isotope Geology Lab., U. Berne, summer 1979; participant NATO exchange program Demokritos Inst., Athens, Greece, Sept. 1983, July 1985. Pres., treas. Troy Rehab. and Improvement, Inc., 1968-74; mem. Troy Zoning Bd. Appeals, 1970-85. Fellow Geol. Soc. Am.; mem. Am. Geophys. Union, Geochem. Soc., Nat. Assn. Geol. Tchrs., Sigma Xi, Sigma Pi Sigma. Current Work: Studies of igneous and sedimentary rocks using quantitative age methods to reveal uplift rates and to determine their thermal history. Subspecialty: Geochemistry. Home: 2198 Tibbits Ave Troy NY 12180 Office: Dept Geology Rensselaer Poly Inst Troy NY 12181

MILLER, DUANE DOUGLAS, medicinal chemistry educator, researcher; b. Great Bend, Kans., July 15, 1943; s. Chester W. and Lois E. Miller; m. Nona Kay Anderson, July 26, 1962; children—Ronald Gene, Donald Wayne, Randall Scott. B.S. in Pharmacy with distinction, U. Kans., 1966; Ph.D. in Medicinal Chemistry, U. Wash., 1969. Asst. prof. Coll. Pharmacy, Ohio State U., Columbus, 1966-74, assoc. prof., 1974-80, prof., 1980—, chmn. Coll. of Pharmacy, Div. Medicinal Chemistry and Pharmacognosy, 1983—; ptnr. Lab. Automated Design Group, Columbus, 1983—. Contbr. articles to profl. jours., chpts. to books. Mem. Am. Chem. Soc., AAAS, Sigma Xi, Phi Kappa Phi, Rho Chi, Phi Lambda Upsilon. Baptist. Current work: Synthesis, isolation and characterization of drugs affecting the central nervous and peripheral nervous systems; drugs affecting aldose reductase for diabetes and thromboxane A2 antagonists to be used as antiaggregatory agents. Subspecialties: Medicinal chemistry; Organic chemistry. Home: 218 Colonial Ave Worthington OH 43085 Office: Medicinal Chemistry and Pharmacognosy Coll Pharmacy Ohio State U Div 500 W 12th Ave Columbus OH 43210 Office: Medicinal Chemistry and Pharmacognosy Coll Pharmacy Ohio State U Div 500 W 12th Ave Columbus OH 43210

MILLER, EDWARD PHILLIP, veterinarian, toxicologist; b. Cherryvale, Kans., Mar. 19, 1942; s. Ralph Davidson and Faye Caroline (Smisor) M.; m. Peggy Jean Wise, June 4, 1966; children—Kyle Edward, Trenton Arthur. B.S., Kans. State U., 1964, D.V.M., 1966; M.S., U. Kans., 1983. Diplomate Am. Bd. Vet. Toxicology. Pvt. vet. practitioner, Oskaloosa, Kans., 1968-79; clin. research veterinarian Wellcome Animal Health, Kansas City, Kans., 1979-81, dir. animal services, 1981-82, dir. vet. med. dept., 1982—. Contbr. articles to sci. jours. Mem., past pres. sch. bd. Unified Sci. Dist. 341, Oskaloosa, 1981—; mem. Jefferson County Planning Commn., 1977-80. Served to capt. Vet. Corps, U.S. Army, 1966-68. Mem. AVMA, Indsl. Vet. Assn., Am. Assn. Lab. Animal Sci., Equine Nutrition and Physiology Soc., U.S. Animal Health Assn. Republican. Methodist. Lodge: Rotary (pres. Oskaloosa 1971-72). Current work: Pharmaceutical research and development, descriptive and clinical veterinary toxicology. Subspecialties: Drug design; Toxicology (agriculture). Home: Route 2 Box 73M Oskaloosa KS 66066 Office: Coopers Animal Health Inc 2000 S 11th St Kansas City KS 66103

MILLER, ELIZABETH CAVERT, oncology educator, research laboratory administrator; b. Mpls., May 2, 1920; d. William Lane and Mary Elizabeth (Mead) Cavert; m. James Alexander Miller, Aug. 30, 1942; children: Linda Ann, Helen Louise. B.S., U. Minn., 1941; M.S., U. Wis., 1943, Ph.D., 1945; D.Sc. (hon.), Med. Coll. Wis., 1982. Instr. dept. oncology U. Wis. Med. Center, 1946-48, asst. prof., 1948-58, assoc. prof., 1958-69, prof., 1969—; assoc. dir. McArdle Lab. for Cancer Research, U. Wis., Madison, 1973—; Wis. Alumni Research Found. prof. oncology U. Wis., 1980—, Van Rensselaer Potter prof. oncology, 1982—. Assoc. editor: Cancer Research, 1957-62; contbr. numerous articles on chem. carcinogenesis and microsomal oxidations to profl. jours. Recipient (with J.A. Miller) Langer-Teplitz award for cancer research Ann Langer Cancer Research Found., 1962, Lucy Wortham James award for cancer research James Ewing Soc., 1965, Bertner award M.D. Anderson Hosp. and Tumor Inst., 1971, Wis. div. award Am. Cancer Soc., 1973, Outstanding Achievement award U. Minn., 1973, Papanicolau award for cancer research Papanicolaou Cancer Research Inst., Miami, 1975; Rosenstiel award for basic med. scis. Brandeis U., 1976; Nat. award Am. Cancer Soc., 1977; Bristol-Myers award in cancer research, 1978; Gairdner Found. Ann. award, 1978; Founders award Chem. Industry Inst. Toxicology, 1978; Prix Griffuel Assn. pour Developpement de Recherche sur Cancer, 1978; 3M Life Sci award Fedn. Am. Socs. Exptl. Biology, 1979; Freedman award N.Y. Acad. Sci., 1979; Mott award Gen. Motors Cancer Research Found., 1980. Fellow Am. Acad. Arts and Scis., Wis. Acad. Scis., Arts and Letters; mem. Nat. Acad. Sci., Am. Assn. for Cancer Research, Am. Soc. Biol. Chemists, Japanese Cancer Soc. (hon.). Subspecialty: Oncology. Home: 5517 Hammersley Rd Madison WI 53711 Office: University of Wisconsin McArdle Lab Madison WI 53706

MILLER, FRANCIS PETER, pharmacologist; b. Bklyn., Sept. 5, 1941; s. Milton Peter and Florence Dorothea (Gattavara) M.; m. Marie Suzanne Gaspar, Dec. 24, 1962; m. Jacquelin Joyce McKee, Feb. 25, 1978; children: Marie Suzanne, Francis Peter, Eric Alan, Kristin Elizabeth. B.S. in Chemistry, Manhattan Coll., Riverdale, N.Y., 1959-63; M.S. in Biochemistry, George Washington U., 1965; Ph.D. in Pharmacology, Ind. U., 1968. Chemist NIH, Bethesda, Md., 1963-65; research asst. Ind. U., Bloomington, 1965-68; sr. pharmacologist Lakeside Labs., Milw., 1968-75, Merrell Dow Pharms., Inc., Cin., 1975—. Contbr. articles to profl. jours. Mem. Soc. Neuroscience, N.Y. Acad. Scis., Sigma Xi. Republican. Roman Catholic. Current Work: Study of the effects of drugs on the brain; development of better drugs for treating abnormal behavior. Subspecialties: Pharmacology; Biochemistry (medicine). Home: 336 Broadway Loveland OH 45140 Office: 2110 E Galbraith Rd Cincinnati OH 42515

MILLER, FREEMAN DEVOLD, astronomer, educator; b. Somerville, Mass., Jan. 4, 1909; s. Rasmus Kjeldsberg and Ednah Freeman (Weeks) M.; m. Caroline Marie Dresser, June 27, 1933. S.B., Harvard U., 1930, M.A., 1932, Ph.D., 1934. Dir. Swasey Obs., Denison U., Granville, Ohio, 1934-40; mem. faculty U. Mich., Ann Arbor, 1946—, prof. astronomy, 1956-77, prof. emeritus, 1977—; assoc. dean Rackham Schl. Grad. Studies, 1959-66. Contbr. articles to profl. publs. Served to capt. USNR, 1931-69. Mem. Am. Astron. Soc., Internat. Astron. Union. Episcopalian. Current Work: Study of plasma tails of comets and interaction with interplanetary medium. Subspecialty: Cometary physics. Home: 1614 Shadford Rd Ann Arbor MI 48104 Office: U Mich 1049 Denison Bldg Ann Arbor MI 48109

MILLER, GEORGE ARMITAGE, psychologist, educator; b. Charleston, W.Va., Feb. 3, 1920; s. George E. and Florence (Armitage) M.; m. Katherine James, Nov. 29, 1939; children—Nancy, Donnally James. B.A., U. Ala., 1940, M.A., 1941; Ph.D., Harvard U., 1946; Doctorat honoris causa, U. Louvain, 1976; D.Social Sci. (hon.), Yale U., 1979; D.Sc. honoris causa, Columbia U., 1980, U. Sussex, 1984. Instr. psychology U. Ala., 1941-43; research fellow Harvard Psycho-Acoustic Lab., 1944-48; asst. prof. psychology Harvard U., 1948-51, assoc. prof., 1955-58, prof., 1958-68, chmn. dept psychology, 1964-67; prof. Rockefeller U., N.Y.C., 1968-79, adj. prof., 1979-81; James S. McDonnell disting. univ. prof. psychology Princeton (N.J.) U., 1979—; vis. Inst. for Advanced Study, Princeton, fall 1950, 70-72; assoc. prof. psychology MIT, 1951-55, vis. prof., 1976-79, group leader Lincoln Lab., 1953-55; fellow Center Advanced Study in Behavioral Scis., Stanford U., 1958-59; Fulbright research prof. Oxford (Eng.) U., 1963-64. Author: Language and Communication, 1951, (with Galanter and Pribram) Plans and the Structure of Behavior, 1960, Psychology, 1962, (with Johnson-Laird) Language and Perception, 1976, Spontaneous Apprentices, 1977, Language and Speech, 1981. Mem. Am. Psychol. Assn. (pres. 1968-69), Eastern Psychol. Assn. (pres. 1961-62), Acoustical Soc. Am., Linguistic Soc. Am., Am. Statis. Assn., Am. Philos. Soc., Am. Physiol. Soc., Psychometric Soc., Soc. Exptl. Psychologists, Am. Acad. Arts and Scis., Psychonomic Soc., Nat. Acad. Sci., AAAS (chmn. sect. J 1981), Royal Netherlands Acad. Arts and Scis. (fgn.), Sigma Xi. Home: 478 Lake Dr Princeton NJ 08540 Office: Dept Psychology Green Hall Princeton U Princeton NJ 08544

MILLER, GLENN EDWARD, astronomer, educator; b. Holyoke, Mass., Oct. 2, 1953; s. Ralph August and Mary Louise (Johnston) M.; m. Cherie Vaughn Miller, June 15, 1975; 1 child, Glenn Edward. B.A., Rollins Coll., 1975; M.A., U. Tex.-Austin, 1978, Ph.D., 1981. Asst. prof. astronomy U.Va., Charlottesville, 1981-83; staff astronomer Computer Scis. Corp. Space Telescope Sci. Inst. Johns Hopkins U., Balt., 1983—. Contbr. articles in field to profl. jours. Mem. AAAS, Am. Astron. Soc. Current Work: Galaxies, stellar evolution. Subspecialty: Theoretical astrophysics. Home: 6329 Sun High Pl Columbia MD 21045 Office: Space Telescope Sci Inst Computer Scis Corp Johns Hopkins U Baltimore MD 21218

MILLER, HARVEY PHILIP, engineering educator, consultant; b. N.Y.C., Jan. 18, 1945; s. Samuel Abraham and Lila Dorothy (Discount) M. B.Mech. Engring., Rensselaer Poly. Inst., 1966; M.S. in Mech. Engring, MIT, 1968; M.Phil. in Applied Physics, Columbia U., 1973, Postgrad. in applied physics. Profl. engr., Pa. Research asst. Columbia U., N.Y.C., 1970-72; standards engr. ASME, N.Y.C., 1973-75; research assoc. U. Miami, Coral Gables, Fla., 1975-78; cons. engr. United Engrs., Phila., 1978-82; adj. prof. Drexel U., Phila., 1982—; cons. and Seminar Speaker Energy and Environ. Dynamics, San Juan, P.R., 1981. Contbr. articles to profl. jours. Raytheon Co. fellow, 1966. Mem. Am. Phys. Soc., Am. Nuclear Soc., ASME, Am. Soc. Indsl. and Applied Math., Tau Beta Pi, Pi Tau Sigma. Democrat. Current Work: Mathematical modeling of hydrodynamics and heat transfer of environmental flows. Subspecialties: Fluid mechanics; Applied mathematics. Home: 2400 Chestnut St Apt 1407 Philadelphia PA 19103Office: Drexel U 32nd & Chestnut Sts Philadelphia PA 19103

MILLER, HERBERT IRVING, sanitary and civil engineer; b. Memphis, July 29, 1949; s. Meyer and Marie (Siegel) M.; m. Faye Marie Daube, Mar. 22, 1975; children—Gia Elisa, Cara Dawn. B.S. Civil Engring., Ga. Inst. Tech., 1972, M.S. in San Engring., 1976. Registered profl. engr., Ala., Ga., La., Tex., Miss. Diplomate Am. Acad. Environ. Engrs. Engr., Jordan, Jones & Goulding, Atlanta, 1972-76; chief san. engr. J.J. Krebs & Sons, Inc., New Orleans, 1976-78; dir. sewerage Jefferson Parish, Metairie, La., 1976-81; v.p. Environ. Profls. Ltd., Metairie, 1981—. Mem. La. Water Pollution Control Fedn. (pres. 1983-84), Am. Water Works Assn., La. Engrs. Selection Bd., Nat. Soc. Profl. Engrs., ASCE, Cons. Engring. Council. Jewish. Current work: Solar energy for drying wastewater sludge; bank filtration of raw water sources; concentrations of organics in drinking water. Subspecialties: Water supply and wastewater treatment; Operations research (engineering). Home: 4928 Academy Dr Metairie LA 70003 Office: Environ Profls Ltd 4813 W Napoleon Ave Metairie LA 70001

MILLER, HILLARD CRAIG, physicist; b. Northampton, Pa., Dec. 15, 1932; s. Hillard Alvin and Dorothy (Frantz) M.; m. Ruth Hazel Kingsbury, June 16, 1956; children: Eric, Kent, Curtis, Alice. B.A., Lehigh U., 1954, M.S., 1955; Ph.D., Pa. State U., 1960. Physicist Gen. Electric Co., 1960—, prin. physicist, St. Petersburg, Fla., 1972—; adj. instr. St. Petersburg Jr. Coll., 1974—. Served with C.E. U.S. Army, 1955-57. Mem. AAAS, Am. Phys. Soc., Am Vacuum Soc., IEEE, Royal Astron. Soc. Can., European Phys. Soc. Current Work: Researcher in elec. discharges and breakdown in gases and vacuums. Subspecialty: Plasma physics. Home: 616 Ruskin Rd Clearwater FL 33575 Office: General Electric Co PO Box 2908 Largo FL 34294

MILLER, IRVING FRANKLIN, educator, univ. dean; b. N.Y.C., Sept. 27, 1934; s. Sol and Gertrude (Rochkind) M.; m. Baila Hannah Milner, Jan. 28, 1962; children—Eugenia Lynne, Jonathan Mark. B.S. in Chem. Engring, N.Y. U., 1955; M.S., Purdue U., 1956; Ph.D., U. Mich., 1960. Research scientist

United Aircraft Corp., Hartford, 1959-61; asst. prof. to prof., head chem. engring. Poly. Inst. Bklyn., 1961-72; prof., head bioengring. program U. Ill., Chgo., 1973-79, acting head systems engring. dept., 1978-79; dean U. Ill. (Grad. Coll.), 1979—, asso. vice chancellor for research, 1979—; cons. to industry, also Nat. Acad. Scis., NIH. Editor: Electrochemical Bioscience and Bioengineering, 1973; Contbr. articles profl. jours. Mem. Am. Inst. Chem. Engrs., Am. Chem. Soc., AAAS, Biomed. Engring. Soc., N.Y. Acad Scis. Current Work: Bioelectrochemistry, membrane transport, artificial organs. Subspecialties: Biomedical engineering; Artificial organs and prostheses. Home: 2600 Orrington Ave Evanston IL 60201 Office: Box 4348 Chicago IL 60680

MILLER, JAMES ALEXANDER, oncologist; b. Dormont, Pa., May 27, 1915; s. John Herman and Emma Anna (Stenger) M.; m. Elizabeth Cavert, Aug. 30, 1942; children: Linda Ann, Helen Louise. B.S. in Chemistry, U. Pitts., 1939; M.S., U. Wis., 1941, Ph.D. in Biochemistry, 1943; D.Sc. (hon.), Med. Coll. Wis., 1982. Finney-Howell fellow in cancer research U. Wis., Madison, 1943-44, instr. oncology, 1944-46, asst. prof., 1946-48, asso. prof., 1948-52, prof., 1952—, Wis. Alumni Research Found. prof. oncology, 1980-82, Van Rensselaer Potter prof. on oncology, 1982—; mem. advisory coms. Nat. Cancer Inst., Am. Cancer Soc., 1950—. Contbr. numerous articles on chemical carcinogenesis and microsomal oxidations to profl. jours. Recipient awards (with E.C. Miller); Langer-Teplitz award Ann Langer Cancer Research Found., 1962; Lucy Wortham James award James Ewing Soc., 1965; G.H.A. Clowes award Am. Assn. Cancer Research, 1969; Bertner award M.D. Anderson Hosp. and Tumor Inst., 1971; Papanicolaou award Papanicolaou Inst. Cancer Research, 1975; Rosenstiel award Brandeis U., 1976; award Am. Cancer Soc., 1977; Bristol-Myers award in cancer research, 1978; Gairdner Found. ann. award Toronto, 1978; Founders award Chem. Industry Inst. Toxicology, 1978; 3M Life Sci. award Fedn. Am. Socs. Exptl. Biology, 1979; Freedman award N.Y. Acad. Sci., 1979; Mott award Gen. Motors Cancer Research Found., 1980. Fellow Am. Acad. Arts and Scis., Wis. Acad. Scis., Arts and Letters; mem. Am. Assn. for Cancer Research, Am. Soc. Biol. Chemists, AAAS, Japanese Cancer Soc. (hon.), Am. Chem. Soc., Soc. Toxicology, Soc. for Exptl. Biology and Medicine, Nat. Acad. Scis. Subspecialty: Oncology. Home: 5517 Hammersley Rd Madison WI 53711 Office: McArdle Laboratory University of Wisconsin Madison WI 53706

MILLER, JAMES EDWARD, computer scientist, educator; b. Lafayette, La., Mar. 21, 1940; s. Edward Gustave and Orpha Marie (DeVilbis) M.; m. Diane Moon, June 6, 1964; children: Deborah Elaine, Michael Edward. B.S., U. Southwestern La., 1961, Ph.D., 1972; M.S., Auburn U., 1964. Systems engr. IBM, Birmingham, Ala., 1965-68; asst. prof. U. West Fla., Pensacola, 1968-70, chmn. systems sci., 1972—; grad. researcher U. Southwestern La., Lafayette, 1970-72; computer systems analyst EPA, Washington, 1979; cons., lectr. in field. Author numerous articles for tech. publs. Mem. Assn. Computing Machinery (editor Computer Sci. Edn. spl. interest group bull. 1982—), Data Processing Mgmt. Assn. Democrat. Methodist. Current Work: Computer security/crime computer science education. Subspecialties: Cryptography and data security; Information systems, storage, and retrieval (computer science). Home: 824 N Deerfoot Ln Cantonment FL 32533 Office: U West Fla Pensacola FL 32514

MILLER, JAY, space science consultant; b. Glendale, Calif., July 3, 1955; s. Joseph Carl and Louise Genevieve (Knight) M. A.S., Coll. of Siskiyous, Weed, Calif., 1975; A.B., U. Calif.-Berkeley, 1983; postgrad. Stanford U., 1984—. Data aide Space Scis. Lab., U. Calif., Berkeley, 1976-80; editor Space Age Rev. Mag., Santa Clara, Calif., 1980-82; intern Joint Com. on Sci. and Tech., Calif. Senate, 1983; cons. Stanford U., 1984—; founder, adminstr. U. Calif. Space Working Group, Berkeley, 1978-83; founder, dir. San Francisco Space Frontier Soc., 1980-84; treas., dir. The Space Initiative campaign, 1983; chmn. Calif. Space Program, San Francisco, 1983—, author Calif. Legislature joint resolution to endorse space station program, 1983. Mem. Am. Astronautical Soc., Nat. Space Club, AAAS, Planetary Soc., Nat. Space Inst., AIAA, L5 Soc. Current work: Space science, astronautics. Subspecialty: Astronautics. Address: Calif Space Program PO Box 3573 San Francisco CA 94119

MILLER, KENNETH JOHN, chemist, educator; b. Chgo., Mar. 24, 1939; s. John N. and Elsie M. (Sucic) M.; m. Brunhilde Franziska, June 19, 1964; children: Michael N., John L. B.S., Ill. Inst. Tech., 1960; M.S., Johns Hopkins U., 1964; Ph.D., Iowa State U., 1966. Successively Nat. Acad. Sci.-NRC postdoctoral research assoc., asst. prof., assoc. prof. Rensselaer Poly. Inst., Troy, N.Y., 1967-81, prof. theoretical chemistry, 1981—. Contbr. articles to profl. publs. Faculty adviser local chpt. Pi Kappa Phi, 1980—. Recipient Achievement award Am. Inst. Chemists, 1960; grantee Petroleum Research Found.; grantee NIH. Mem. Am. Inst. Physics, Am. Chem. Soc., AAUP (v.p. 1976-77, pres. 1977-78), Sigma Xi, Phi Eta Sigma, Sigma Pi Sigma, Phi Lambda Upsilon. Current Work: Theoretical chemistry, conformations of DNA, computer assisted drug design and analysis of carcinogenicity, computer graphics, intercalation of molecules with DNA, analysis of carcinogenicity of polynuclear aromatic hydrocarbons, chemical reactivity of sulfur containing systems and diol epoxides of polynuclear aromatic hydrocarbons. Subspecialties: Biophysical chemistry; Molecular pharmacology. Home: 20 Michael St Troy NY 12180 Office: Dept Chemistry Rensselaer Poly Inst Troy NY 12181

MILLER, LARRY LEE, See *Who's Who in America,* 43rd edition.

MILLER, LEE N., editor, plant ecologist; b. Decatur, Ill., July 9, 1930; s. Ben G. and Marguerite (Rosenberg) M.; m. Sylvia D. Dordek, Nov. 29, 1953; children: Benjamin A., Danna Ruth. Student, U. Ill., 1948-52; B.B.A., So. Methodist U., 1953; M.F., Yale U., 1961; Ph.D., Duke U., 1966. Time study engr. Bell & Howell, Lincolnwood, Ill., 1953-54; with Borg-Warner, Decatur, 1954-55; mgr. Ben Miller Jewelers, Decatur, 1955-59; asst. ecologist Brookhaven Nat. Lab., Upton, N.Y., 1961-62; asst. prof. Cornell U., 1966-73, adminstrv. mgr. dept. entomology, 1974-76; vis. prof. SUNY Coll. Environ. Sci. and Forestry, 1978; mng. editor Ecol. Soc. Am., Ithaca, N.Y., 1979—. Author: Psychrometry in Water Relations Research. Contbr. articles to profl. jours. Bd. editors: Who'sWho in Frontiers of Sci. and Tech; mem. publs. com.: Am. Inst. Biol. Scis. Mem. Ecol. Soc. Am., Council Biology Editors. Club: Adirondack Mountain (pres. Finger Lakes chpt.). Current Work: Plant ecology. Subspecialties: Ecology (environmental science); Theoretical ecology. Office: Ecol Soc Am E 139 Corson Hall Cornell U Ithaca NY 14853

MILLER, LEE STEPHEN, engineer; b. Jacksonville, Fla., June 5, 1930; s. Oscar Lee and Elsie (Simpson) M.; m. Diana Sheppard, Aug. 1, 1950; children—Stephen, Jeanette. B.S., Ind. Inst. Tech., 1952; Ph.D., Clemson U., 1967. Sr. scientist Research Triangle Inst., N.C., 1968-72; pres. Applied Sci. Assocs., Inc., Apex, N.C., 1972—; cons. Dept. Def., Washington, 1973—. Contbr. articles to profl. jours. Current work: Research in satellite radar remote sensing. Office: 105 E Chatham St Apex NC 27502

MILLER, LOIS KATHRYN, molecular biologist, educator, researcher, consultant; b. Lebanon, Pa., Oct. 8, 1945; d. Clarence Elmer and Naomi Alice (Gibson) M.; m. Karl Edward Espelie, June 13, 1974; 1 child, Erin Marie. B.S., Upsala Colo., 1967; Ph.D., U. Wis., 1972. Am. Cancer Soc. fellow Calif. Inst. Tech., Pasadena, 1972-74; NIH fellow Imperial Cancer Research Fund, London, 1974-76; prof. U. Idaho, Moscow, 1976—; cons. Genetics Inst., Boston, 1982—; mem. NIH Exptl. Virology, Bethesda, Md., 1982-86, NRC Nat. Strategy Com., Washington, 1985. Contbr. articles to profl. jours. Current work: Molecular biology of insect viruses and development of microbial pesticides; nature of mobile genetic elements/transposons. Subspecialties: Genetics and genetic engineering (agriculture); Virology (biology). Office: U Idaho Dept Bacteriology and Biochemistry 115 Agricultural Sci Moscow ID 83843

MILLER, LYLE DEVON, veterinarian, educator; b. Lebanon, Ind., Dec. 8, 1938; s. Lyle and H. Pauline (Beck) M.; m. Janice M. Lilly, Apr. 18, 1962; children—Donald D., Brenda J. B.S., Kans. State U., 1961, D.V.M., 1963; M.S., U. Wis., 1969, Ph.D., 1971. Diplomate Am. Coll. Vet. Pathologists. Vet. med. officer U.S. Dept. Agr., Ames, Iowa, 1971-81, collaborator, Hyattsville, Md., 1982—; prof. Coll. Vet. Medicine, Iowa State U., Ames, 1981—. Contbr. articles to profl. jours. Troop adv. council Boy Scouts Am., Ames, 1975. Served to capt. U.S. Army, 1963-65. Mem. Am. Coll. Vet. Pathologists, Nat. Assn. Fed. Veterinarians, U.S. Animal Health Assn., AVMA, Iowa Vet. Med. Assn., Sigma Xi, Phi Kappa Phi, Phi Zeta. Club: Toastmasters. Current work: Research on serologic diagnosis and methods of control of bovine leukemia virus infection; pathogenesis of viral diseases including pseudorabies, pathogenesis of mycobacterial infections and microbial virulence. Subspecialties: Pathology (veterinary medicine); Animal pathology. Home: 2803 Northwood Dr Ames IA 50010 Office: Dept Vet Pathology Coll Vet Medicine Iowa State U Ames IA 50011

MILLER, LYNNE CATHY, biological sciences educator; b. Washington, Dec. 25, 1951; d. Albert and Lorraine Shirley (Sweet) M.; m. Gary Franklin Clark, July 25, 1982. B.S. in Pharmacy, U.R.I., 1974; M.S. in Biol. Sci. U. Tex.-El Paso, 1977; Ph.D. in Biology, N. Mex. State U., 1980. Registered pharmacist, Mass., N.Y., R.I., Pa., N. Mex. Clin. pharmacy intern Misericordia Hosp., Bronx, N.Y., 1974-75; grad. teaching asst. dept. biology U. Tex.-El Paso, 1975-77; grad. teaching asst. dept. biology N.Mex. State U., Las Cruces, 1977-80, postdoctoral fellow, 1980-81; clin. pharmacist Meml. Gen. Hosp., Las Cruces, 1979; prof. parasitology Bloomsburg (Pa.) U., 1981—, pre-med. advisor, 1981—, pre-pharmacy advisor, 1981—, dir. internships, 1982—, coordinator honors program, 1981—; sponsor USPHS program, 1981. Contbr. articles to profl. jours. Sponsor Ronald McDonald House, Children's Oncology Services, 1981. Faculty research grantee Pa., 1981—. Fellow Sigma Xi (assoc.); mem. AAAS, Pa. Acad. Sci., Entomol. Soc. Am., Helminthological Soc. Washington, Phi Kappa Phi (pres.-elect), Beta Beta Beta (faculty advisor). Jewish. Club: Biology (Bloomsburg U.) (sponsor); Current Work: Research on the protective mechanism or self-cure reaction elicited by the host-immune response which causes elimination of parasitic worm burden; implications on reduction of anthelmintic dosages. Subspecialties: Parasitology; Pharmacology. Office: Dept Biology and Allied Health Bloomsburg U Bloomsburg PA 17815

MILLER, MICHAEL JAMES, medical educator, research physiologist; b. Iron Mountain, Mich., Oct. 11, 1946; s. Robert J. and Jeanne (Barlement) M. B.S., U. Mich., 1968; Ph.D., Dartmouth Med. Sch., 1974, M.D., 1975. Teaching fellow Dartmouth Med. Sch., Hanover, N.H., 1974-75; clin. fellow in medicine Harvard Med. Sch., Boston, 1975-77, instr. medicine, 1981-83, 83—; instr. Med. U. S.C., Charleston, 1978-80; pulmonary cons. Brockton (Mass.) VA Hosp., 1981-83; v.p. Controls Supply Co., Inc., Kingsford, Mich., 1975—; co-dir. ICU, Brockton VA Med. Ctr. Hosp., 1982—. Contbr. articles to sci. jours. Mem. Republican Nat. Com., 1981-83, Brockton VA Exec. Com., 1982—. State of S.C. grantee, 1980; Parker B. Francis Found. grantee, 1978-80; recipient Alice Ryan award Dartmouth Coll., 1970-73; William Ogden award U. Mich., 1964. Mem. Mass. Med. Soc., Soc. Critical Care Medicine, Am. Thoracic Soc., Am. Fedn. Clin. Research (com. chmn. 1982). Methodist. Club: Newton Yacht. Inventor digital speed limiter and monitor, 1982. Current Work: Examining the physiology of the respiratory muscles in both in vitro studies and in patients with pulmonary disease. Subspecialties: Pulmonary medicine; Physiology (medicine). Home: 45 Mathews Dr Wayland MA 01778 Office: 75 Francis St Boston MA 02115

MILLER, MORTON W(ILLIAM), radiation and cell biology researcher, educator, consultant; b. Neptune, N.J., Aug. 4, 1936; s. Elwood E. and Francis E. (Senkel) M.; m. Marylynn M. Brown, July 13, 1968; children: Marcus, Heath, Carl. B.A. cum laude, Drew U., 1958; M.S., U. Chgo., 1960, Ph.D., 1962. NATO postdoctoral fellow Oxford (Eng.) U., 1962-63; postdoctoral fellow Brookhaven Nat. Lab., Upton, N.Y., 1963-65; sci. officer IAEA, Vienna, Austria, 1965-67; asst. prof. radiation biology and biophysics U. Rochester, 1967-75, assoc, prof., 1975—. Numerous publs. in field. Bd. dirs. Chili (N.Y.) Pub. Library, 1981—. Dept. Energy grantee, 1967—; Office Naval Research grantee, 1969-72; NIH grantee, 1976—; Empire State Electric Energy Research Corp. grantee, 1981—. Mem. Radiation Research Soc., Environ, Mutagen Soc., N.Y. Acad. Scis., AAAS, Am. Inst. Biol. Sci., Council Biology Editors, Am. Inst. Ultrasound Medicine, Bioelectromagnetics Soc. Current Work: Radiation biology of electromagnetic and ultrasonic fields. Subspecialties: Radiation biology; Cell biology. Office: U Rochester Box RBB Rochester NY 14642

MILLER, NANCY E(LLEN), psychopathology clinical researcher, research administrator, psychoanalyst, clinical psychologist, neuropsychologist; b. Long Beach, N.Y., Aug. 20, 1947; d. Jerome H. and Katherine (Pearlman) M.; m. Walter A. Romanek, Aug. 25, 1983. B.A., N.Y. U., 1969; M.A., Harvard U., 1970; postgrad. fellowship program in mental health adminstrn, Washington Sch. Psychiatry, 1977-78; Ph.D., U. Chgo., 1978; postgrad. advanced psychotherapy program, Washington Sch. Psychiatry, 1978-81; candidate, Washington Psychoanalytic Inst., 1981—. Lic. psychologist, D.C. cert. psychologist, Md. Clin. psychologist S.E. Community Mental Health Ctr., Chgo., 1971-77; research assoc. dept. psychiatry U. Chgo. Sch. Medicine, 1972-77; chief clin. research program Ctr. for Studies Mental Health of Aging, NIMH, Rockville, Md., 1977—; exec. sec. aging and mental health initial rev. group NIMH, 1977-79; instr. in clin. psychiatry Georgetown U. Sch. Medicine, 1980—. Editor: (with G.D. Cohen) Clinical Aspects of Alzheimer's Disease and Senile Dementia, 1981, Psychodynamic Research Perspectives on Development, Psychopathology and Treatment in the Elderly, 1983, (with L. Erlenmeyer-Kimling) Longitudinal Predictors of Psychopathology Across the Life Span, 1985, Schizophrenia, Paranoia and Schizophreniform Disorders in Later Life, 1983; spl. edit.: Neurobiology of Aging, winter, 1983; editorial bd.: Jour. Edn. Gerontology, 1976—, Neurobiology of Aging, 1980—, Profl. Psychology, 1980—, Psychoanalytic Psychology, 1982—; contbr. numerous articles to profl. publs. Bd. dirs. Montgomery County Mental Health Assn., 1978-80; bd. dirs. Montgomery County Mobile Med. Free Clinic, 1978—. Current Work: Research on clinical aspects of psychopathology in late adulthood and old age, with special emphasis on late life dementias and major affective disorders, including their etiology and treatment; research administration; clinical assessment and treatment; teaching. Subspecialties: Neuropsychology; Developmental psychology. Home: 10401 Grosvenor Pl Apt 704 Rockville MD 20852 Office: NIMH 5600 Fishers Ln 11-C-03 Rockville MD 20857

MILLER, PATRICIA LYNN, clinical psychologist, consultant; b. Chgo., Jan. 27, 1938; d. Joseph L. and Gertrude R. (Kontek) Lynn; m. Eric E. Miller, Feb. 27, 1960; children: Kurt D., Nathan C., Peter J. A.B., U. Chgo., 1958; M.S., Ill. Inst. Tech., 1971, Ph.D., 1979. Cert. sch. psychologist, Ill. lic. clin. psychologist, Ill. Pub. relations dir. Chgo. Area Council Camp Fire Girls, 1958-68, asst. exec. dir., 1966-68; tchr. Valley View Sch. Dist., Romeoville, Ill., 1968-70; sch. psychologist Lockport (Ill.) Spl. Edn. Dist., 1971-80, clin. psychologist in pvt. practice, specializing in diagnostics and treatment of women and children, part-time, 1977-80, full-time, 1980—; sec./treas., dir. HEM, Inc., Joliet, 1980—; instr., cons. dept. psychology Ill. Inst. Tech., Chgo., 1975-77; field supr. Chgo. Sch. Profl. Psychology, 1981-82. Author: forms Health and Social History of the Child, 1981, Psychological History, 1982. Mem. Citizens' Com. for Wider Use of the Schs., Mayor Daley's Youth Commn., Tribune Charities Youth Commn., all Chgo., 1958-68; active Women's Network for E.R.A., 1970s. Grad. fellow State of Ill., 1970. Mem. Am. Psychol Assn., Ill. Psychol. Assn., Internat. Neuropsychol. Soc., Nat. Assn. Sch. Psychologists, Ill. Sch. Psychologists Assn., Sigma Xi. Club: Zonta. Co-developer Neuropsychological Test Battery, 1980. Current Work: Continuing development of Psy-Dx, electronic version of Halstead Neuropsychological Test Battery with computer administration, scoring, and profile generation plus other neuropsychological tests for computer to yield comprehensive diagnosis; co-developer Psy-Dx. Subspecialty: Neuropsychology. Home: 3510 Bankview Ln Joliet IL 60435 Office: 310 N Hammes Ave Joliet IL 60435

MILLER, PAUL LEROY, JR., mechanical engineering educator; b. Guthrie, Okla., June 27, 1934; married, 1955; 3 children. B.S., Kans. State U., 1957, M.S., 1961; Ph.D. in Mech. Engring, Okla. State U., 1966. From instr. to assoc. prof. Kans. State U., 1957-72, prof. mech. engring., 1972—, head dept. mech. engring., 1975—; cons. in field. Fellow ASHRAE; Mem. ASME., Am. Soc. Engring. Edn. Subspecialty: Mechanical engineering. Office: Dept Mech Engring Durland Hall Kans State U Manhattan KS 66506

MILLER, RAYMOND EARL, JR., chemist; b. Corning, N.Y., Jan. 26, 1956; s. Raymond Earl and Harriet (Mastenbrook) M. B.S. in Chemistry, Mansfield U. of Pa., 1977; M.S. in Chemistry, W.Va. U., 1981. Teaching asst. W.Va. U., Morgantown, 1977-78, research asst., 1978-79, Nat. Steel research fellow, 1979-81; research chemist U.S. Army, Aberdeen Proving Ground, Md., 1982—. Contbr. articles and reports to profl. lit. Recipient letters of recognition and commendation U.S. Army, 1982, 83. Mem. Am. Chem. Soc. (div. phys. chemistry 1978-80, 82—, div. fuel chemistry 1979-82), Sigma Xi, Phi Lambda Upsilon. Current work: Modelling of reactions; thermochemical kinetics; estimation of physical properties; digital electronics; coal conversion technology; FT-IR spectroscopy. Subspecialties: Kinetics; Physical chemistry. Home: 4421 Furley Ave Baltimore MD 21206

MILLER, RAYMOND MICHAEL, microbial ecologist; b. Chgo., July 16, 1945; s. John Michael and Margaret Leona (Courtney) M. B.S., Colo. State U., 1969; M.S., Ill. State U., 1971, Ph.D., 1975. Ext. plant pathologist Colo. State U., Ft. Collins., 1969; postdoctoral fellow Environ. Impact Div., Argonne (Ill.) Nat. Lab., 1975-76; asst. scientist Land Reclamation Program, 1976-80, scientist environ. research div., 1980—. Mem. AAAS, Am. Soc. Microbiology, Mycological Soc. Am., Soil Sci. Soc. Am., Bot. Soc. Am. Roman Catholic. Current Work: Role of mycorrhizae in natural and disturbed ecosystems; effects of acid deposition on soil ecosystems. Subspecialties: Ecosystems analysis; Plant pathology. Home: 16W 731 Mockingbird Ln Apt 105 Hinsdale IL 60521 Office: Argonne Nat Lab Argonne IL 60439

MILLER, REGIS BOLDEN, wood anatomist; b. Meyersdale, Pa., Aug. 29, 1943; s. Elam D. and Rita L. (Bolden) M.; married; children: Kelly, Sean. B.S. in Wood Sci, W.Va. U., 1966; M.S. in Botany, U. Wis., 1968; Ph.D. in Botany, U. Md., 1973. With U.S. Forest Products Lab., Madison, Wis., 1970—, botanist, 1970-80; project leader U.S. Forest Products Lab. (Center for Wood Anatomy Research), 1980—. Mem. Internat. Assn. Wood Anatomists, Internat. Assn. Plant Taxonomists, Am. Soc. Plant Taxonomists, Soc. Tropical Foresters, Bot. Soc. Am. Roman Catholic. Developed chem. spot-test for aluminum and its value for wood identification, 1980, wood identification via computer, 1980, standard list of characters suitable for computerized hardwood identification, 1981. Current Work: Computer-assisted wood identification; wood anatomy of Juglandaceae, Flacourtiaceae and Leguminosae; temperate and tropical wood identification. Subspecialty: Taxonomy. Home: 23 Mountain Ash Trail Madison WI 53717 Office: Forest Products Lab One Gifford Pinchot Dr Madison WI 53705

MILLER, RENE HARCOURT, aeronautical engineering educator, consultant; b. Tenafly, N.J., May 19, 1916; s. Arthur and Elizabeth (Tobin) M.; m. Maureen E. Michael, Nov. 20, 1973; m. Marcelle Hansotte, July 16, 1948; children: Christal L., John J. B.A., Cambridge (Eng.) U., 1937, M.A., 1954. Registered profl. engr., Mass. Aero. engr. G.L. Martin Co., Balt., 1937-39; chief aerodynamics and devel. McDonnell Aircraft, St. Louis, 1939-44; mem. faculty MIT, Cambridge, 1944—, prof., 1957-62, H.N. Slater prof. flight transp., 1962-68, head dept. aeros. and astronautics, 1968-78; dir. Space Systems Lab., 1978—. Contbr. articles to sci. jours. Recipient Meritorious Civilian Service award U.S. Army, 1967, 70; I.B. Laskowitz award N.Y. Acad. Scis., 1976. Mem. Nat. Acad. Engring., AIAA (Sylvanus Albert Reed award 1969), Am. Helicopter Soc. (Klemin award 1968), Royal Aero. Soc. Republican. Club: St. Botolph's (Boston). Current Work: Space systems, transportation systems, VTOL aircraft, rotary wing aerodynamics and dynamics including helicopter and wind turbines. Subspecialties: Aerospace engineering and technology; Wind power. Home: 321 Beacon St Boston MA 02115 Office: 77 Massachusetts Ave Bldg 33-411 Cambridge MA 02139

MILLER, RICHARD KERMIT, medical scientist, educator; b. Scranton, Pa., Oct. 17, 1946; s. Roland Kermit and Vera (Edwards) M.; m. Judith Berens. A.B., Dartmouth Coll., 1968, Ph.D., 1973. Postdoctoral fellow Jefferson Med. Coll., Phila., 1972-74; asst. prof. ob-gyn and pharmacology/toxicology U. Rochester, N.Y., 1974-80, dir. div. research, 1978—, assoc. prof., 1980—; prof. U. Paris VI, 1983. Editor: Trophoblast Research; assoc. editor Teratology, 1979-83. Contbr. articles on pharmacology to profl. jours. Goode Found. grantee, 1976-82; Nat. Cancer Inst. grantee, 1978-84; NIMH grantee, 1979-86; Nat. Insts. Environ. Health Scis. grantee, 1982-86; NIH Fogarty sr. internat. fellow, 1983. Mem. Teratology Soc., Am. Soc. Pharmacology and Exptl. Therapeutics, Soc. Gynecol. Investigation, Behavioral Teratology Soc., Sigma Xi. Current Work: Teratology/transplacental carcinogenesis, reproductive toxicology, diethylstilbestrol, cadmium. tellurium, organ perfusion technology, xenobiotic metabolism, placental function, diazepam, neurochemical/behavior alterations. Subspecialties: Pharmacology; Maternal and fetal medicine. Office: Dept Ob-Gyn 601 Elmwood Ave Rochester NY 14642

MILLER, RICHARD LYNN, microbiologist, researcher; b. Stevens Point, Wis., Sept. 27, 1945; s. Gordon L. and Jean E. (Leary) M.; m. Lisa L., Sept. 15, 1973; children: Analiese, Colin, Autumn. B.S. in Biology, U. Wis., Stevens Point, 1968; Ph.D. in Microbiology, U. Minn., Mpls., 1974. Lab technician in diagnostic virology U.S. Army Med. Lab., 1968-70; teaching asst. in microbiology U. Minn., 1970-74, asst. prof., 1977-80; postdoctoral researcher Pa. State U. Med. Sch., 1975-77; sr. microbiologist, researcher Rike Labs., 3M Co., St. Paul, 1977-79, research specialist, 1979—. Contbr. papers to profl. meetings, jours. Served with U.S. Army, 1968-70. Mem. Am. Soc. Microbiology, AAAS, Henrici Soc. Minn., N.Y. Acad. Sci. Current Work: Antiviral drug research, research and supervision antiviral drug program. Subspecialties: Virology (medicine); Microbiology (medicine). Office: 3M Center Bldg 270-2S-06 Saint Paul MN 55144

MILLER, ROBERT ALAN, senior staff scientist; b. Montclair, N.J., Jan. 30, 1943; s. George Ulmer and Florence Lahoma (Fairchild) M.; m. Mary Kathleen Sheridan, Jan. 30 1971; children: Brendan Alexander, Stacey Ann. B.S., U. Ill.-Urbana, 1965, M.S., 1966, Ph.D. (NSF fellow), 1970. Research assoc. Coll. of William and Mary, 1970-72, Rutgers U., 1972-74; theoretician, dir. theory, program dir. reactor design, mem. mgmt. com. Fusion Energy Corp., 1974-77; applications software group leader Princeton Gamma Tech., 1977-81; v.p. Sci. Transfer Assocs., N.Y.C., 1981-82, pres., 1982-83; sr. staff scientist Princeton Gamma-Tech, 1983-85; mem. tech. staff AT&T Bell Labs., 1985—; cons. Contbr. articles to profl. jours. Mem. Am. Phys. Soc., IEEE, AAAS, U. Ill. Alumni Assn., Sigma Xi, Tau Beta Pi. Current Work: X-ray fluorescence material analysis. Subspecialties: Fusion; Software engineering. Home: 22 Evans Dr Cranbury NJ 08512 Office: 1200 State Rd Princeton NJ 08540

MILLER, SIDNEY ISRAEL, chemist, educator, cons., researcher; b. Saskatoon, Sask., Can., May 22, 1923; s. Max and Esther Herstein (Zuckerman) M.; m. Laura Reznick, Jan. 31, 1950; children: Matthew, Naomi, Joel. B.Sc., U. Man., 1945, M.Sc., 1946; Ph.D., Columbia U., 1951. Lectr. Ill. Inst. Tech., 1951-54, asst. prof., 1954-60, assoc. prof., 1960-64, prof., 1964—; tech. cons., tech. witness, analyst, info. specialist. Contbr. numerous articles on chemistry to profl. jours. Mem. Am. Chem. Soc., AAUP. Current Work: Mechanisms, kinetics, acetylenes, heterocycles, coal chemistry. Subspecialties: Organic chemistry; Analytical chemistry. Office: Dept Chemistry Ill Inst Tech Chicago IL 60616

MILLER, STANLEY FRANK, agricultural economist, plant protectionist; b. Idaho Falls, Idaho, Oct. 13, 1935; s. Odis Lavaughn and Florence (Burtenshaw) M.; m. Catherine Lu Turrentine, Sept. 9, 1960; children—Vaughn, Jamie. B.Sc., Brigham Young U., 1960; M.Sc., Utah State U., 1962; Ph.D., Oreg. State U., 1965. Economist, U.S. Dept. Agr., Corvallis, Oreg., 1961-66, 1968-71; econ. adviser IRI Research Inst., Rio de Janeiro, Brazil, 1966-68, N.Y.C., 1971-73; prof. Oreg. State U., 1973—, dir. Internat. Plant Protection Ctr., 1973—. Contbr. articles to profl jours. Mem. Am. Assn. Agr. Econs., Internat. Assn. Agr. Econs., Western Assn. Agr. Econs., Sigma Xi, Phi Kappa Phi. Republican. Mormon. Subspecialty: Agricultural economics. Office: Internat Plant Protection Ctr Oreg State U Corvallis OR 97331

MILLER, STEWART EDWARD, electrical engineer; b. Milw., Sept. 1, 1918; s. Walter C. and Martha L. (Ferguson) M.; m. Helen Jeanette Stroebel, Sept. 27, 1940; children—Jonathan James, Stewart Ferguson, Chris Richard. Student, U. Wis., 1936-39; B.S., Mass. Inst. Tech., 1941, M.S., 1941. With Bell Labs., N.Y.C., 1941-49, Holmdel, N.J., 1949-80, dir. guided wave research, 1980-83, dir. lightwave telecommunications research, 1983—; cons. in field. Recipient Ballantine medal Franklin Inst., 1977. Fellow IEEE (Liebmann award 1972, Baker prize 1975), Optical Soc. Am.; mem. AAAS, Nat. Acad. Engring. Patentee in field. Current Work: Optical fiber telecommunication. Subspecialties: Fiber optics; Electrical engineering. Home: 67 Wigwam Rd Locust NJ 07760 Office: Bell Communications Research Inc 331 Newman Springs Rd Red Bank NJ 07701

MILLER, THOMAS ALLEN, surgery educator; b. Harrisburg, Pa., July 7, 1944; s. Joseph E. and Marion R. (Corpman) M.; m. Janet Ruth Walters, Dec. 28, 1968; children: David Allen, William James, Laurie Ann. B.S. cum laude, Wheaton (Ill.) Coll., 1966; M.D., Temple U., 1970. Instr. dept. biology Wheaton(Ill.) Coll., 1966; intern in surgery U. Chgo. Hosps., 1970-71; resident in Surgery U. Mich. Hosps., 1971-75; instr. dept. surgery, postdoctoral research fellow in gastrointestinal hormone physiology U. Tex. Med. Branch, Galveston, 1975-76; instr. dept. surgery & physiology, postdoctoral research fellow in gastrointestinal physiology U. Tex. Med. Sch., Houston, 1976-77, asst. prof. surgery, 1977-79, assoc. prof., 1979—, dir. acad. affairs, resident tng., 1981-82, dir. grad. surg. edn., 1982—. Co-editor: (with S.J. Dudrick) The Management of Difficult Surgical Problems, 1981; contbr. articles to profl. jours. Upjohn Co.

grantee, 1977-78; Distilled Spirits Council grantee, 1977-78; U. Tex. grantee, 1978-79; NIH grantee, 1979—. Fellow ACS; Mem. AAAS, Am. Digestive Disease Soc., Am. Fedn. Clin. Research, Am. Gastroent. Assn., AMA, Am. Physiol. Soc., Am. Soc. Parenteral and Enteral Nutrition, Assn. Acad. Surgery (chmn. com. on legis. issues 1978-79, com. on issues 1979-81, nominating com. 1983—), Coll. Internat. Chirugiae Digestivae, Harris County Med. Soc. (cancer com. 1980—), Houston Gastroent. Assn., Houston Surg. Soc., N.Y. Acad. Scis., Pancreatic Club Inc., Soc. Internat. de Chirurgie, Soc. Exptl. Biology & Medicine, Soc. Surgery of Alimentary Tract (nominating com. 1982, auditing com. 1983), Soc. Univ. Surgeons (councilman-at-large 1983-86), Splanchnic Circulation Group, Tex. Med. Assn. Republican. Presbyterian. Current Work: Extensive research on the mechanisms by which prostaglandins mediate their ability to prevent gastric mucosal injury; teaching medical students and residents daily. Subspecialties: Physiology (medicine); Surgery. Home: 10618 Shady River Houston TX 77042 Office: Dept Surgery U Tex Med Sch 6431 Fannin Rm 4266 Houston TX 77030

MILLER, TRUDI CLAIRE, government science administrator, researcher; b. Kingston, N.Y., Feb. 4, 1941; d. Paul Anton and Alice (Heutschi) M. B.A., Cornell U., 1962; Ph.D., U. N.C., 1969. Asst. prof. SUNY-Buffalo, 1969-70; program dir. NSF, Washington, 1972—. Editor: Public Sector Performance, 1984. Contbr. articles to profl. jours. Mem. IEEE, Inst. Mgmt. Scis. (v.p. fin. 1984—), Ops. Research Soc. Am., Am. Polit. Sci. Assn. (Franklin L. Burdette award 1981), Pi Sigma Alpha. Current work: Scientific methods for the study of partly man-made systems. Subspecialty: Operations research (engineering). Office: NSF 1800 G St NW Washington DC 20550

MILLER, WILBUR CHARLES, mathematician; b. Westcliffe, Colo., Nov. 8, 1930; s. Martin and Fredia (Kitzman) M.; m. Marilyn Louise Franz, Aug. 1, 1953; 1 son, Robert. B.A., U. Wash., 1962; M.B.S., U. Colo., 1967; Ph.D., Colo. State U., 1975. Research test designer Boeing Co., Seattle, 1958-63; tchr. Douglas County Schs., Castle Rock, Colo., 1963-65, Fremont County Schs., Florence, Colo., 1965-67; mem. faculty U. So. Colo., Pueblo, 1967—, assoc. prof. math, 1976-79, prof., 1979—. Served as sgt. USAF, 1953-57. Mem. Soc. Indsl. and Applied Math, Am. Soc. Animal Scientists, Am. Soc. Agrl. Cons. Current Work: Mathematical modeling in agricultural small scale hydroelectric power generation. Subspecialties: Integrated systems modelling and engineering; Applied mathematics. Home: Rt 1 Box 48 Westcliffe CO 81252 Office: Dept Math U So Colo Pueblo CO 81001

MILLER, WILLARD, JR., mathematician; b. Ft. Wayne, Ind., Sept. 17, 1937; s. Willard and Ruth (Kemerly) M.; m. Jane Campbell Scott, June 5, 1965; children—Stephen, Andrea. S.B. in Math, U. Chgo., 1958; Ph.D. in Applied Math, U. Calif., Berkeley, 1963. Vis. mem. Courant Inst. Math. Scis., N.Y. U., 1963-65; mem. faculty U. Minn., 1965—, prof. math., 1972—, head Sch. Math., 1978—, co-prin. investigator Inst. Math. and its Applications, 1980—. Author: Lie Theory and Special Functions, 1968, Symmetry Groups and Their Applications, 1972, Symmetry and Separation of Variables, 1977; Asso. editor: Jour. Math. Physics, 1973-75, Applicable Analysis, 1978—. Mem. Soc. Indsl. and Applied Math. (mng. editor Jour. Math. Analysis 1975-81), Am. Math. Soc., AAAS, AAUP, Sigma Xi. Current Work: Relations between the symmetry groups of partial differential equations and the solutions of these equations that arise through variable separation. Subspecialties: Applied mathematics; Group theory. Home: 4508 Edmund Blvd Minneapolis MN 55406 Office: Sch Math U Minn Minneapolis MN 55455

MILLER, WILLIAM FREDERICK, multidisciplinary research institute executive; b. Vincennes, Ind., Nov. 19, 1925; s. William and Elsie M. (Everts) M.; m. Patty J. Smith, June 19, 1949; 1 son, Rodney Wayne. Student, Vincennes U., 1946-47; B.S., Purdue U., 1949, M.S., 1951, Ph.D., 1956; D.Sc., 1972. Mem. staff Argonne Nat. Lab., 1955-64, assoc. physicist, 1956-59, dir. applied math. div., 1959-64; prof. computer sci. Stanford U., Palo Alto, Calif., 1965-79, Herbert Hoover prof. pub. and pvt. mgmt., 1979—, asso. provost for computing, 1968-70, v.p. for research, 1970-71, v.p., provost, 1971-78, mem., 1972—; pres., chief exec. officer SRI Internat., Menlo Park, Calif., 1979—; profl. lectr. applied math. U. Chgo., 1962-64; vis. prof. math. Purdue U., 1962-63; vis. scholar Center for Advanced Study in Behavioral Scis., 1976; Dir. Fireman's Fund Ins. Co., Ann. Revs. Inc., Varian Assos. Inc., 1st Interstate Banks, 1st Interstate Bank of Calif., Pacific Gas and Electric Co.; Mem. computer sci. and engring. bd. Nat. Acad. Sci., 1968-71; mem. corp. com. on computers in edn. Brown U., 1972-79; mem. policy bd. EDUCOM Planning Council on Computing in Edn., 1974-79, chmn., 1974-76; bd. dirs. SIAM Inst. Math. in Society, 1977-79; ednl. adv. bd. Guggenheim Meml. Found., 1976-80; com. postdoctoral and doctoral research staff NRC, 1977-80; bd. dirs. RESOLVE, Center for Environ. Conflict Resolution, 1978-80; mem. Nat. Sci. Bd., 1982—. Asso. editor: Pattern Recognition Jour. 1968—, Jour. Computational Physics, 1970-74. Served to 2d lt. F.A. AUS, 1943-46. Fellow IEEE, Am. Acad. Arts and Scis.; mem. Am. Math. Soc., Am. Phys. Soc., AAAS, Assn. Computing Machinery, Sigma Xi. Office: SRI Internat 333 Ravenswood Ave Menlo Park CA 94025

MILLER, WILLIAM LAWRENCE, metallurgist, chemist, minerals research executive; b. Medford, Oreg., May 12, 1937; s. Oliver William Miller and Ida Lucile (Lowry) Vosburgh; m. Jo Anne Carmen Clifton, Jan. 29, 1961; children—William Scott, Douglas Britton. B.S. in Chemistry, U. Calif.-Davis, 1963, M.S. in Geology, 1967. Assoc. chemist Aerojet Gen. Corp., Sacramento, Calif., 1963-64; program analysis officer Dept. of Interior, Washington, 1970-71; chemist Bur. of Mines, Washington, 1966-70, staff metallurgist, 1971-77, chief div. metallurgy, 1977-79, chief research directorate staff, 1979-82, asst. dir. minerals and materials research, 1982—; alt. mem. coordinating com. on materials research and devel. Fed. Council Sci. and Tech., 1969. Recipient Silver medal and Meritorious Service award U.S. Dept. Interior, 1982. Mem. Am. Chem. Soc., Geol. Soc. Washington, Metall. Soc., Am. Inst. Mining, Metall. and Petroleum Engrs., Sr. Execs. Assn. Subspecialties: Petrology; Metallurgy. Office: U S Bur of Mines 2401 E Street NW Washington DC 20241

MILLER, WILLIAM ROBERT, JR., physicist, educator; b. Balt., June 17, 1934; s. William Robert and Ida Louise (Werner) M.; m. Barbara Ann Flammer, June 21, 1958; children: Robin Louise, Patricia Ann, Jill Elizabeth. B.A., Gettysburg Coll., 1956; Ph.D., U. Del., 1961. Sr. physicist Westinghouse Electric Corp., Balt., 1965-67; physicist RCA Corp., Lancaster, Pa., 1967-68; assoc. prof. physics Pa. State U., Middletown, 1969—; instr. York Coll. Pa., 1969-78. Contbr. articles to profl. jours. Mem. Am. Phys. Soc., Am. Assn. Physics Tchrs., Sigma Xi. Lutheran. Current Work: Experimental solid state physics. Subspecialty: Condensed matter physics. Home: 1029 Preston Rd Lancaster PA 17601 Office: Pa State U Middletown PA 17057

MILLHORN, DAVID EUGENE, physiologist; b. Chattanooga, June 25, 1945; s. Cecil David and Ola (Doggett) M.; m. Sherry Lynn Long, July 5, 1968; children: Amy Lynn, Emily Katherine, Lauren Paige. B.S., U. Tenn., 1974; Ph.D., Ohio State U., 1978. NIH postdoctoral fellow dept. physiology U. N.C., Chapel Hill, 1978-80, Parker B. Francis fellow, 1980-82, asst. prof. physiology, 1980—, asst. prof. neurobiology, 1982—; established investigator Am. Heart Assn., 1982-87. Contbr. articles to profl. jours. NIH grantee, 1982—. Mem. Am. Physiol. Soc., Soc. Neurosci., AAAS, Am. Heart Assn. Current Work: Central neural regulation of respiration and cardiovascular function. Subspecialties: Physiology (medicine); Neurophysiology. Home: 1001 Sedwick W Durham NC 27713 Office: U NC 70 Med Research Wing Dept Physiology Chapel Hill NC 27514

MILLICH, FRANK, chemistry educator; b. N.Y.C., Jan. 31, 1928; s. Frank J. and Frances (Cop) M.; children: Theadocia Fran, Frank Theodore. B.S., CUNY, 1949; M.S., Poly. Inst. N.Y., 1956, Ph.D., 1959; postgrad., Cambridge (Eng.) U., 1958-59, U. Calif.-Berkeley, 1959-60. Asst. prof. chemistry U. Mo.-Kansas City, 1960-64, assoc. prof., 1964-67, prof., 1967—; vis. research scientist Ames Research Center, Moffett Field, Calif., 1964, Jet Propulsion Lab., Calif. Inst. Tech., 1966; cons. in fields of photochemistry, organic chemistry, and polymer sci. Author: (with C.E. Carraher) Interfacial Synthesis, vol. I, II, 1977; Contbr. articles in field to profl. jours. Grantee in field. Mem. Am. Chem. Soc., AAAS, Chem. Soc. London. Current Work: Polymer syntheses and properties, interfacial synthesis, artificial biopolymers, polyisocyanides, viscosity theory. Subspecialties: Polymer chemistry; Organic chemistry. Home: 301 E New Santa Fe Trail Kansas City MO 64145 Office: 5100 Rockhill Rd U Mo-Kansas City Kansas City MO 64110

MILLING, MARCUS EUGENE, geologist; b. Galveston, Tex., Oct. 8, 1938; s. Robert Richardson and Leonora (Currey) M.; m. Sandra Ann Dunlay, Sept. 11, 1959; children: Marcus Eugene. B.S., Lamar U., 1961; M.S., U. Iowa, 1964, Ph.D., 1968; postgrad., U. Tex., Austin, 1964. Registered profl. geologist. Research geologist Exxon Prodn. Research Co., Houston, 1968-75, research supr., 1975-77; prodn. geologist Exxon Co. USA, Kingsville, Tex., 1977-78, dist. geologist, 1978-80; mgr. geol. research ARCO Oil & Gas Co., Dallas, 1980—; dir. GEOSAT, San Francisco, 1980-83. Fellow Geol. Soc. Am.; mem. Am. Assn. Petroleum Geologists (editor 1982-85), Soc. Econ. Geologists and Paleontologists (dir. offshore tech. conf. 1982—). Lutheran. Current Work: Hydrocarbon potential deepwater clastic reservoirs. Subspecialties: Geology; Sedimentology. Home: 2300 Winding Hollow Rd Plano TX 75075 Office: ARCO Oil and Gas Co PO Box 2819 Dallas TX 75221

MILLS, HARRY LEE, JR., psychologist, consultant; b. Huntsville, Ala., Sept. 17, 1944; s. Harry Lee and Florence (Barnett) M.; m. Joyce Reynolds, May 20, 1972; children: Candice Michelle, Courtney Sullivan. B.S., U. So. Miss., 1966; Ph.D., 1973. Lic. clin. psychologist, Tenn., Ala. Research assoc. U. Miss. Med. Ctr., 1972-73; project dir. Youth Achievement House, Gulfport, Miss., 1973-74; unit leader and psychologist Mobile (Ala.) Mental Health Ctr., 1974-75; coordinator adult services Huntsville (Ala.) Mental Health Ctr., 1975-79; assoc. exec. dir. Dede Wallace Ctr., HES, Inc., Nashville, Tenn., 1979—; adj. assoc. prof. Vanderbilt U., 1979-82; clin. dir. Health Edn. Services, Nashville, 1981-82; bd. dirs. Research Rev., Ala. A&M U., Huntsville, 1977-79; chmn. profl. adv. bd. H.E.L.P. Inc., Huntsville, 1975-79. Author Clinical Productivity, 1981. NDEA fellow, 1968; ACTS grantee NIH, 19 77; HEW grantee, 1976. Mem. Am. Psychol. Assn., Assn. Advancement of Behavior Therapy, Tenn. Psychol. Assn., Tenn. Assn. Behavior Therapy. Democrat. Methodist. Current Work: Treatment of compulsive disorders and agoraphobia, applications of behavioral technology to organizational problems; development and supervision. Subspecialties: Behavioral psychology; Learning. Home: 657 Hill Rd Brentwood TN 37027 Office: Dede Wallace Ctr. and HES Inc 700 Craighead Ave Nashville TN 37211

MILLS, JOHN ALEXANDER, physician, educator; b. Montreal, Que., Can., June 5, 1929; s. Edward Sadler and Marion (Baile) M.; m. Nancy Gordon. B.A., McGill U., 1950, M.D., 1954. Diplomate: Am. Bd. Internal Medicine. Intern Montreal Gen. Hosp., 1954-55; resident in medicine Mass. Gen. Hosp., Boston, 1956-58, physician, med. service, 1970—; mem. faculty Harvard Med. Sch., Boston, 1961—, assoc. prof. medicine, 1972—. Fellow Royal Coll. Physicians (Can.); mem. Am. Rheumatism Assn., Am. Assn. Immunologists, Portuguese Soc. Rheumatology (hon.). Current Work: Clinical research relating to rheumatic diseases and immunotherapy of autoimmune disease. Subspecialties: Internal medicine; Immunology (medicine).

MILLS, PATRICK LEO, industrial chemical engineering researcher, chemical engineering educator; b. Quantico, Va., Sept. 24, 1952; s. Robert Arthur and Nellie (Clark) M.; m. Pamela Marie Jackson, Mar. 30, 1974; children: Patrick Leo, Paul Joseph, Robert Edwin. B.S. in Chem. Engring, Tri-State U., 1973; M.S. in Chem. Engring, Washington U., 1980, D.Sc., 1980. Lectr. Tri-State U., 1973-74; process design engr. Monsanto Co., St. Louis, 1974-75; instr. Washington U., 1975-80, adj. prof., 1980—; research engr. Gen. Electric Co., Schenectady, 1980-81, Monsanto Co., St. Louis, 1981—. Contbr. articles to profl. jours., chpts. to books. Recipient Gen. Motors Co. Scholarship award, 1971. Mem. Am. Inst. Chem. Engrs., Am. Chem. Soc., Soc. Indsl. and Applied Math., Internat. Assn. Math. Modelling, Sigma Xi. Roman Catholic. Current Work: Industrial chemical reaction engineering research and development and technology assessment; applied mathematics in chemical engineering; chemical engineering education. Subspecialties: Chemical engineering; Applied mathematics. Home: 1321 Dautel Ln Creve Coeur MO 63146 Office: Monsanto Co 800 N Lindbergh Blvd Saint Louis MO 63167

MILLS, RANDALL ADRAIN, geologist; b. Chattanooga, Sept. 7, 1953; s. Thomas Milton and Maudie Syble (Smith) M.; m. Patricia Carol Stenger, Apr. 8, 1978; children—Tamar Anne, Timothy Ryan. B.S. in Geology, U. Ga., 1976. Hydrocarbon well logger Core Labs., Inc., Oklahoma City, 1977-79; geologist Jim Walter Resources, Brookwood, Ala., 1979-81, strata control engr., 1981-82, methane drainage specialist, 1982—. Mem. Geol. Soc. Am., Soc. Mining Engrs. AIME. Baptist. Current work: Production of unconventional gas, methane, from deep coal seams. Subspecialties: Natural gas from coal seams; Geology. Home: 4037 Windermere Dr Tuscaloosa AL 35405 Office: Jim Walter Resources 4 Mine Brookwood AL 35444

MILMAN, HARRY ABRAHAM, toxicologist, pharmacologist; b. Cairo, May 16, 1943; s. David and Ruth (Manitsky) M.; m. Caren Susan Weisberg, Aug. 5, 1968; children: Deborah, Jennifer. B.S. in Pharmacy, Columbia U., 1966; M.S., St. John's U., 1968; Ph.D. in Pharmacology, George WashingtonU., 1978. Lic. pharmacist, N.Y., Md. Lab. asst. St. John's U., Jamaica, N.Y., 1967-68; chief pharmacist USPHS Indian Health Center, White Earth, Minn., 1968-70; research pharmacist Nat. Cancer Inst., Bethesda, Md., 1970-77; toxicologist nat. toxicology program NIH, Bethesda, 1977-80; sr. toxicologist EPA, Washington, 1980—; with USPHS, 1968—, comdr., 1978—. Contbr. articles to sci. jours. Recipient Commendation medal USPHS, 1980. Mem. Am. Soc. Pharmacology and Exptl. Therapeutics, Soc. Toxicology, Internat. Assn. Comparative Research on Leukemia and Related Diseases, Internat. Soc. Oncodevelopmental Biology and Medicine. Democrat. Jewish. Current Work: Biological markers of carcinogenicity; chemical carcinogenesis; regulatory toxicology. Subspecialties: Toxicology (medicine); Cancer research (medicine).

MILNER, JOHN A., nutritionist, educator; b. Pine Bluff, Ark., June 11, 1947; s. Austin P. and N. Lourena (Briggs) M.; m. Mary Frances Picciano, June 19, 1976; children: Kristina, Matthew. B.S., Okla. State U., 1969; Ph.D., Cornell U., 1974. Teaching asst. Cornell U., Ithaca, N.Y., 1969-73, USPHS postdoctoral fellow, 1974; asst. prof. dept. food sci. U. Ill., Urbana, 1975-79, assoc. prof., 1979—; asst. dir. Ill. Agrl. Expt. Sta., 1981—, dir. div. nutritional scis., 1981—. Author articles. Served to 2d lt. N.Y. State N.G., 1969-75. Recipient Young Investigator award Nutritional Found., 1976, Young Investigator award Am. Diabetes Assn., 1976. Mem. Am. Inst. Nutrition, Am. Assn. for Cancer Reseasrach, Soc. for Nutrition Edn., Inst. Food Technologists, Internat. Assn. Bioinorganic Scientists. Lodge: Rotary. Current Work: Relationship of diet to cancer. Control of intermediary metabolism as it applied to protein metabolism. Subspecialties: Nutrition (medicine); Cancer research (medicine). Home: 2505 Bedford St Champaign IL 61820 Office: U Ill 455 Bevier Hall 905 S Goodwin St Urbana IL 61801

MILUSCHEWA, SIMA, systems engineer; B.S. in Mech. Engring, N.J. Inst. Tech., 1955, M.S. in Mech. Engring, 1955. Design engr. design and dvel. dept. Westinghouse Electric Co., 1951-56; project engr. aero. group research div. Curtiss-Wright Co., Clifton, N.J., 1956-58; space systems specialist advanced systems analysis group Astro-Electronics div. RCA, Princeton, N.J., 1958-68; sr. engr. Grumman Aerospace Corp., Bethpage, L.I., N.Y., 1968—. Recipient Salute to Women in Elec. Living award for space vehicle design work Elec. Women's Round Table, Inc., 1963. Mem. AIAA, Robotics Internat., Soc. Women Engrs. Current Work: Satellite Power Systems; high energy lasers and other space systems. Subspecialties: Solar energy; Robotics.

MIN, KYUNG-WHAN, pathologist, educator; b. Seoul, Korea, May 5, 1937; came to U.S., 1964; s. Chungi and Inyoung (Lee) M.; m. Young-Jin, May 24, 1939; children: K. Christopher, W. David. M.D., Seoul Nat. U., Korea, 1962. Rotating intern Hanil Hosp., Seoul, 1962-63, resident in internal medicine, 1962-64; resident in pathology Balt. City Hosp., 1964-65; resident in pathology Baylor U., 1965-70, asst. instr., 1965-70; assoc. prof. Choson (Korea) U., 1970-71; asst. prof. Baylor U., 1971-78; pathologist Mercy Hosp. Med. Ctr., Des Moines, 1978—; also clin. assoc. prof. Creighton U., Omaha, 1978—. Fellow ACP, Am. Soc. Clin. Pathologists, Coll. Am. Pathologists; mem. Internat. Acad. Pathologists, Am. Assn. Pathologists. Current Work: Ultrastructural cytopathological changes in relation to cancer and other allied diseases for understanding and diagnostic application of electronmicroscopy in cancer diagnosis. Subspecialties: Pathology (medicine); Cancer research (medicine). Home: 5109 Aspen Dr West Des Moines IA 50265 Office: Mercy Hosp Med Ctr 6th and University Sts Des Moines IA 50314

MIN, TONY CHARLES, mechanical engineering educator; b. Shanghai, China, Jan. 5, 1923; came to U.S., 1949, naturalized, 1961; s. Tee and Wei-Inn (Huang) M.; m. Elsie Hui Tan, Dec. 28, 1968; 1 child, C(hristopher) Justus. B.S. in Aero. Engring., Chaio Tung U., 1947; M.S. in Mech. Engring., U. Tenn., 1953, Ph.D. in Engring. Sci., 1969. Mech. design engr. TVA, Knoxville, 1951-54; research engr. ASHRAE Research Lab., Cleve., 1954-57; assoc. prof. mech. engring. Auburn U., Ala., 1957-64; program mgr. U.S. Dept. Energy, Washington, 1978-79; prof. mech. engring. Mich. Tech. U., Houghton, 1968-72; prof. mech. engring., chmn. dept. N.C. A&T State U., Greensboro, 1981—; cons. Oak Ridge Nat. Lab., 1963-68, Power & Energy Inc., Beloit, Wis., 1980-81; cons. Tech. Adv. Services for Attys. Port Washington, Pa., 1983—. Editor, co-editor ASME books, 1977, 84; assoc. editor Jour. Solar Energy Engring., 1977—. Contbr. articles to profl. jours. NSF sci. faculty fellow, 1961-63, internat. travel grantee, 1961. Patentee in field. Fellow ASME (chmn. solar energy div. 1981-82, exec. com. div. 1979-83, at-large mem. energy resources operating bd. 1983—, voting mem. nat. nominating com. 1983-86, Disting. award 1982), Sigma Xi, Phi Tau Phi (nat. v.p. 1974, pres. Mid-Am. chpt. 1974-76), Tau Beta Pi, Pi Tau Sigma. Club: Toastmaster Internat. (pres. Portage Lake 1974, area gov. Dist 35 1974-75). Current work: Fluid mechanics (rod-bundles, two phase, turbulent flow); drag reduction; tribology, aerothermodynamics (gas dynamics, actuator-disk); heat transfer (rod-bundles, cooling of electrophic equipment); solar energy (chiller and irrigation). Subspecialties: Mechanical engineering; Heat transfer. Home: 5121-G Lawndale Dr Greensboro NC 27405 Office: Dept Mech Engring NC A&T State U Greensboro NC 27411

MINASSIAN, DONALD PAUL, mathematical acturial educator, consultant; b. N.Y.C., Dec. 8, 1935; s. George Diran and Lydia (Hartunian) M.; m. Elaine S. Garabedian, Aug. 15, 1964; children—Laura, Valarie. B.A., Fresno State U., 1957; M.A., Brown U., 1964; M.S., U. Mich., 1965, Ph.D., 1967; postgrad. Ind. U. Assoc. prof. Butler U., Indpls., 1967-73, prof., 1974—; acct. George Olive, C.P.A.s, Indpls., 1976-78; actuary Am. States Ins. Co., Indpls., 1979-82, Indpls. Life Ins. Co., 1983—. Contbr. articles to profl. jours. Bd. dirs. Indpls. Symphonic Choir, 1970. Mem. Math. Assn. Am. (past mem. com. on ednl. media), Soc. Indsl. and Applied Math., Soc. Actuaries, Acad. Actuaries, Ind. Assn. C.P.A.s. Current work: Research in mathematics, economics, business and finance. Subspecialties: Algebra and number theory; Actuarial science. Home: 410 Blue Ridge Rd Indianapolis IN 46208 Office: Butler Univ 4600 Sunset Ave Indianapolis IN 46208

MINDLIN, RAYMOND DAVID, educator, civil engineer; b. N.Y.C., Sept. 17, 1906; s. Henry and Beatrice (Levy) M.; m. Elizabeth Roth, 1940 (dec. 1950); m. Patricia Kaveney, 1953 (dec. 1976). Student, Ethical Culture Sch., N.Y.C., 1918-24; B.A., Columbia U., 1928, B.S., 1931, C.E., 1932, Ph.D., 1936; D.Sc. (hon.), Northwestern U., 1975. Research asst. dept. civil engring. Columbia U., N.Y.C., 1932-38, Bridgham fellow, 1934-35, instr. civil engring., 1938-40, asst. prof., 1940-45, assoc. prof., 1945-47, prof. civil engring., 1947-67, James Kip Finch prof. applied sci., 1967-75, prof. emeritus, 1975—; cons. Bell Telephone Labs. Inc., N.Y.C., 1943-51; cons. physicist Dept. Terrestrial Magnetism, Carnegie; cons. Nat. Defense Research Com., 1941-42; sect. T Office Sci. Research and Devel., Applied Physics Lab., Johns Hopkins U., Balt., 1942-45. Mem. adv. bd. Applied Mech. Reviews. Contbr. articles to tech. and sci. jours. Recipient Illig medal Columbia U., 1932; U.S. Naval Ordnance Devel. award, 1945; Presdl. medal for Merit, 1946; Class of 1889 Sch. Mines medal Columbia U., 1947; research prize ASCE, 1958; Great Tchr. award Columbia U., 1960; von Karman medal ASCE, 1961; Timoshenko medal ASME, 1964; ASME medal, 1976; C.B. Sawyer Piezoelectric Resonator award, 1967; Egleston medal Columbia U., 1971; Trent-Crede medal Acoustical Soc. Am., 1971; Frocht award Soc. Exptl. Stress Analysis, 1974; Nat. medal of Sci., 1979. Fellow Acoustical Soc. Am., Am. Acad. Arts and Scis.; mem. Soc. Exptl. Stress Analysis (founding mem.; exec. com. 1943-50, v.p. 1946, pres. 1947), ASCE (sec. com. applied mechanics 1940-42, chmn. 1942-45), Eastern Photoelasticity Conf. (exec. com. 1938-41), Am. Phys. Soc., Nat. Acad. Engring., Nat. Acad. Sci., Conn. Acad. Sci. and Engring., U.S. Nat. Com. Theoretical and Applied Mechanics, Internat. Union Theoretical and Applied Mechanics, ASME (hon.), Tau Beta Pi, Sigma Xi, Columbia Varsity "C". Current Work: Materials Science. Subspecialty: Theoretical and applied mechanics. Home: South Cove Vista Grantham NH 03753

MINEHART, RALPH CONRAD, physicist; b. Mitchell, S.D., Jan. 25, 1935; s. Paul A. and Sybil Nora (Fairley) M.; m. Jean Elizabeth Besse, Aug. 28, 1959; children—Patricia Lynne, Deborah Fairley, Elizabeth Woodward, Stephen James. B.S., Yale U., 1956; M.A., Harvard U., 1957, Ph.D., 1962. Research assoc. Yale U., New Haven, 1962-66; asst. prof. physics U. Va., Charlottesville, 1966-68, assoc. prof., 1968-81, prof., 1981—; chmn.-elect CEBAF Users Group, Newport News, Va., 1984—. Contbr. articles to profl. jours. NSF fellow, 1957-62. Mem. Am. Phys. Soc., Phi Beta Kappa. Democrat. Presbyterian. Current work: Meson interactions with nuclei, properties of particles. Subspecialties: Nuclear physics; Particle physics. Home: 1714 Yorktown Dr Charlottesville VA 22901 Office: U Va Physics Dept McCormick Rd Charlottesville VA 22901

MINER, BRYANT ALBERT, chemist, educator; b. Moroni, Utah, Aug. 9, 1934; s. Glen Bryant and Caroline (Eyring) M.; m. Janice Mabey, June 8, 1960; children: Melanie, JaNae, David, Helen, Heidi, Jason, Jared. B.A., U. Utah, 1961, Ph.D., 1965. Agrl. researcher Am. Smelting & Refining Co., Murray, Utah, summers 1953, 54; chem. researcher U. Utah, summers 1965, 67; prof. chemistry Weber State Coll., Ogden, Utah, 1964—. Served with U.S. Army, 1957-59. Recipient medal Am. Inst. Chemists, 1961. Mem. Am. Chem. Soc., Phi Beta Kappa, Phi Kappa Phi. Mormon. Current Work: Thermodynamics, high pressure electrochemistry. Subspecialties: Physical chemistry; Thermodynamics. Home: 4260 Jefferson Ave Ogden UT 84403 Office: Chemistry Dept 2503 Weber State Coll Ogden UT 84408

MINER, JOHN BURNHAM, psychology research educator, writer, consultant; b. N.Y.C., July 20, 1926; s. John Lynn and Bess (Burnham) M.; married; children by previous marriage: Barbara, John, Cynthia, Frances; m. Barbara Allen Williams, June 1, 1979; children—Jennifer, Heather. A.B., Princeton U., 1950, Ph.D., 1955; M.A., Clark U., 1952. Lic. psychologist, Ga. Research assoc. Columbia U., 1956-57; mgr. psychol. services Atlantic Refining Co., Phila., 1957-60; faculty mem. U. Oreg., Eugene, 1960-68; prof., chmn. dept. organizational sci. U. Md., College Park, 1968-73; research prof. Ga. State U., Atlanta, 1973—; pres. Organizational Measurement Systems Press, Atlanta, 1976—; cons. McKinsey & Co., N.Y.C., 1966-69; vis. lectr. U. Pa., Phila., 1959-60; vis. prof. U. Calif.-Berkeley, 1966-67, U. South Fla., Tampa, 1972. Author: many books and monographs including Personnel Psychology, 1969; (with M.G. Miner) Personnel and Industrial Relations, 1969, 73, 77, 85; The Challenge of Managing, 1975, (with Mary Green Miner) Policy Issues in Personnel and Industrial Relations, 1977, (with George A. Steiner) Management Policy and Strategy, 1977 (James A. Hamilton-Hosp. Adminstrs. Book award), 1982, 86; (with M.G. Miner) Employee Selection Within the Law, 1978, Theories of Organizational Behavior, 1980, Theories of Organizational Structure and Process, 1982; The Practice of Management, 1985; People Problems: The Executive Answer Book, 1985; contbr. numerous articles, papers in field to profl. lit. Served with AUS, 1944-46, ETO. Decorated Bronze Star medal, Combat Infantryman's Badge; named Disting. Prof. Ga. State U., 1974. Fellow Acad. Mgmt. (editor Jour. 1973-75, pres. 1977-78), Am. Psychol. Assn., Soc. for Personality Assessment; mem. Indsl. Relations Research Assn. Republican. Club: Princeton (N.Y.C.). Current Work: Organizational motivation, theories of organization, human resource utilization, personnel management, business policy/strategy. Subspecialty: Organizational psychology. Home: 651 Peachtree Battle Ave NW Atlanta GA 30327 Office: Dept Mgmt Ga State U University Plaza Atlanta GA 30303

MINICHIELLO, LEE P., physicist, government official; b. Concord, N.H., Dec. 25, 1940; s. Lewis Allen and Susan (Walker) M.; m. Lynne Nash Seekamp, May 1, 1976; children—Susanna, Janet. B.A., Johns Hopkins U., 1962, postgrad., 1963; postgrad. George Washington U., 1964-68, Fgn. Sci. Inst. State Dept., 1966, Harvard U., 1981. Mem. staff CIA, Washington, 1963-68; sr. staff mem. Inst. Defense Analysis, Arlington, Va., 1968-78; dep. dir. ISP, Office Sec. Def., Washington, 1978-83, asst. dep. undersec. def. Strategic and Theater Forces, 1983—. Mem. Phi Beta Kappa. Office: Strategic and Theater Nuclear Forces US Dept Defense Pentagon Washington DC 20301

MINISCALCO, WILLIAM JOSEPH, physicist; b. Homewood, Ill., Apr. 28, 1946; s. Bruno and Emma Mary (Ciampa) M.; m. Sarah Morse Guilford, Oct. 6, 1979; children—Emma Louise, Nathalie Emilia. B.S., U. Ill., 1968, M.S., 1972, Ph.D., 1977. Research assoc. U. Wis., Madison, 1977-79; mem. tech. staff GTE Labs Inc., Waltham, Mass., 1979-84, prin. mem. tech. staff, 1984—. Contbr. articles to profl. publs., chpt. to book. Served with U.S. Army, 1969-71. Mem. Am. Phys. Soc., Sigma Xi. Current work: Optical and magneto-optical investigations of electronic structure and dynamical effects in solids, nonlinear optical effects in optical fibers. Subspecialties: Condensed matter physics; Laser spectroscopy. Home: 126 Hemlock Rd Sudbury MA 01776 Office: GTE Labs Inc 40 Sylvan Rd Waltham MA 02254

MINKER, JACK, computer science educator; b. Bklyn., July 4, 1927; s. Harry and Rose (Lapuck) M.; m. Rita Goldberg Minker, June 24, 1951; children—Michael Saul, Sally Anne. B.A. cum laude with honors in math. Bklyn. Coll., 1949; M.S. in Math., U. Wis., 1950; Ph.D. in Math., U. Pa., 1959. Mgr. info. tech. RCA, 1952-63; dir. staff/mgr. Auerbach Corp., 1963-67, tech. cons., 1967-72; prof. computer sci. U. Md., College Park, 1971—, chmn. dept. computer sci., 1974-79; cons. Bell Communications Research. Co-editor: Logic and Databases, 1978; Advances in Databases, Vol. 1, 1981, Vol. 2, 1984; editor: Logic Programming Jour., Info. Systems, Jour. Expert Systems: Research and Applications; editorial advisor Computing Revs. Served with U.S. Army, 1945-46. NSF grantee, 1971-86; Air Force Office Sci. Research grantee, 1981-85; Army Research Office grantee, 1985—. Mem. IEEE (sr. mem.), Soc. Indsl. and Applied Math., Assn. Computing Machinery (vice chmn. com. on sci. freedom and human rights 1980—), Com. Concerned Scientists (vice chmn. 1973—). Current work: Artificial intelligence, logic and databases, logic programming. Subspecialties: Artificial intelligence; Database systems. Home: 6913 Millwood Rd Bethesda MD 20817 Office: Dept Computer Sci U Md College Park MD 20742

MINKOFF, MICHAEL, computer scientist; b. Chgo., Oct. 20, 1944; s. Sol M. and Ann (Grossman) M.; m. Ruth Nadine Rosner, Dec. 5, 1982. B.S., U. Wis., 1966; M.S.E., Princeton U., 1968; M.S., U. Wis., 1970, Ph.D., 1973. Asst. prof. No. Ill. U., DeKalb, 1972-75, adj. asst. prof., 1975-76, adj. assoc. prof., 1976-77; computer scientist Argonne Nat. Lab., Ill., 1975—. Contbr. articles to profl. jours. Mem. Soc. Indsl. and Applied Math., Math. Programming Soc., Am. Math. Soc., Assn. Computing Machinery, Ops. Research Soc. Am., Sigma Xi, Phi Kappa Phi, Phi Eta Sigma. Subspecialties: Mathematical software; Numerical analysis (computer science). Office: Argonne Nat Lab 9700 S Cass Ave Argonne IL 60439

MINKOWYCZ, W(OLODYMYR) J(OHN), mechanical engineering educator, consultant; b. Libokhora, Ukraine, Oct. 21, 1937; came to U.S. 1949, naturalized 1956; s. Alexander and Anna (Tokan) M.; m. Diana Eva Szandra, May 12, 1973; 1 child, Liliana Christine Anne. B.S. in Mech. Engring., U. Minn., 1958, M.S. in Mech., Engring., 1961, Ph.D. in Mech. Engring. Asst. prof. mech. engring. U. Ill.-Chgo., 1966-68, assoc. prof., 1968-78, prof., 1978—; cons. Argonne Nat. Lab., Ill., 1970-82, U. Hawaii, Honolulu, 1974—. Editor: (book series) Computational Methods in Thermal Sciences, 1979—; Rheologically Complex Fluids, 1972; Numerical Heat Transfer, 1978—; assoc. editor Internatl. Jour. Heat and Mass Transfer, 1968—; Internatl. Communications in Heat and Mass Transfer, 1974—; cons. editor Applications of Numerical Heat Transfer, 1978; also articles. Recipient Silver Circle award for excellence in teaching U. Ill.-Chgo., 1975-76, 81. Mem. ASME, Sigma Xi, Pi Tau Sigma. Current work: Fluid mechanics and heat transfer, porous media flows, two-phase flows, numerical heat transfer. Subspecialties: Mechanical engineering; Fluid mechanics. Office: Dept Mechanical Engring Univ Ill Chicago IL 60680

MINOR, JOSEPH EDWARD, structural engineer, educator; b. Corpus Christi, Tex., June 2, 1938; s. William Smoot and Irene (Schiller) M.; m. Treva Ann Edmiston, Sept. 3, 1960; children—Joseph Edward Jr., Sharon Diane. B.S. in Civil Engring., Tex. A & M U., 1959, M.Engring., 1960; Ph.D., Tex. Tech. U., 1974. Registered profl. engr., Tex. Sr. engring. asst. Tex. Hwy. Dept., Houston, 1959; nat. def. fellow Tex. A & M U., College Station, 1959-60; sr. research engr. S.W. Research Inst., San Antonio, 1962-69; P.W. Horn prof. Tex. Tech U., Lubbock, 1969—, dir. Inst. for Disaster Research, 1971—, Glass Research and Testing Lab., 1984—; prin. McDonald, Mehta & Minor Cons. Engrs., Lubbock, 1975—. Contbr. articles to profl. jours., chpts. to books. Served to 1st lt. C.E., U.S. Army, 1960-62. Recipient Excellence in Research award, Tex. Tech U., 1984; Fulbright scholar, 1978. Fellow ASCE (pres. Tex. sect. 1985); mem. Nat. Soc. Profl. Engrs., Am. Meteorol. Soc., Structural Engrs. Assn. Tex. Presbyterian. Current work: Wind engring; tornadoes, hurricanes, wind effects on bldgs., wind resistant construction, window glass research, strength of window glass, cladding performance, failure analysis. Subspecialties: Civil engineering; Structural engineering. Home: 6602 Orlando Ave Lubbock TX 79413 Office: Tex Tech Univ PO Box 4089 Lubbock TX 79409

MINORE, DON, plant ecologist, research forester; b. Chgo., Oct. 31, 1931; s. E. Don and Gertrude L. (Moline) M.; m. Ione M. Bruning, June 22, 1963; children—Anna Miriam, Timothy John. B.S. in Forestry, U. Minn.-St. Paul, 1953; Ph.D., in Botany, U. Calif.-Berkeley, 1966. Research forester U.S. Dept. Agr. Forest Service, Portland, Oreg., 1954, 57-60, plant ecologist, Corvallis, Oreg., 1965—; teaching asst. U. Calif.-Berkeley, 1961-63, teaching fellow, 1963-65. Contbr. articles to profl. jours. Served with U.S. Army Engrs., 1955-57. Wis. Alumni research fellow, U. Wis., 1953, Baker fellow U. Calif., 1960; NSF fellow 1964, 65. Mem. Soc. Am. Foresters, Ecol. Soc. Am., N.W. Sci. Assn. (trustee 1981-84), Republican. Current work: Autecology of trees and shrubs in the Pacific Northwest; forest regeneration and growth. Subspecialties: Ecology (biology); Plant growth. Home: 31750 Peoria Rd Albany OR Office: US Dept Agr Forestry Sciences Laboratory 3200 Jefferson Way Corvallis OR 97331

MINSKY, MARVIN LEE, mathematician, educator; b. N.Y.C., Aug. 9, 1927; s. Henry and Fannie (Reyser) M.; m. Gloria Anna Rudisch, July 30, 1952; children: Margaret, Henry, Juliana. B.A., Harvard U., 1950; Ph.D., Princeton U., 1954. Mem. Harvard Soc. Fellows, 1954-57; with Lincoln Lab., MIT, 1957-58, prof. math., 1958-61, prof. elec. engring., 1961—, Donner prof. sci., 1973, dir. artificial intelligence group MAC project, from 1958, dir. artificial intelligence lab. MAC project, from 1970. Author: Computation, 1967, Semantic Information Processing, 1968, Perceptrons, (with S. Papert), 1968. Served with USNR, 1945-46. Recipient Turing award Assn. for Computing Machinery, 1970. Fellow I.E.E.E., Am. Acad. Arts and Scis., N.Y. Acad. Scis., Nat. Acad. Sci. Subspecialty: Artificial intelligence. Office: Dept Elec Engring-Computer Sci MIT Cambridge MA 02139*

MINTER, JERRY BURNETT, radio and electronics engineer, consultant; b. Fort Worth, Oct. 31, 1913; s. Claude Joe and Roxie (Ayers) M.; m. Monica Hanlon, Feb. 2, 1940; children—Claude J., Mark A., Byron M., Claire L., Maureen R. B.S. MIT, 1934. Radio engr. Boonton Radio Corp., N.J., 1935-36, Radio Frequency Labs., Boonton, 1936-37, Ferris Inst. Co., Boonton, 1937-39; founder, v.p., chief engr. Measurements Corp., Boonton, 1939-53; founder, pres. Components Corp., Denville, N.J., 1946—, also dir. Patentee in field. Mem. CAP, Morristown, 1947. Fellow IEEE (chmn. N.J. sect. 1948-49), Audio engrs. Soc. (life; pres. 1954), Radio Club Am. (pres. 1948-49, Armstrong Medal 1968, Pres. award 1981); mem. Soc. Motion Pictures and TV Engrs. (life), Am. Soc. for Metals (life). Current work: Medical audio-visual diagnostic systems; radio interference instrumentation from 1937-53 concerned with military, radio and broadcast TV interference measurements and standardization on IRE and ASA. Subspecialties: Electronics; Imaging technology. Home: 48 Normandy Heights Rd Morristown NJ 07960 Office: Components Corp 6 Kinsey Pl Denville NJ 07834

MINTZ, BEATRICE, biologist; b. N.Y.C., Jan. 24, 1921; d. Samuel and Janie (Stein) M. A.B. magna cum laude, Hunter Coll., N.Y.C., 1941; postgrad., N.Y. U., 1941-42; M.S., U. Iowa, 1944, Ph.D., 1946; D.Sc. (hon.), N.Y. Med. Coll., 1980, Med. Coll. Pa., 1980, Northwestern U., 1982. Instr. to assoc. prof. biol. scis. U. Chgo., 1946-60; assoc. mem. Inst. Cancer Research, Phila., 1960-65, sr. mem., 1965—. Lalor Found. Research fellow, 1954, 55; recipient Bertner Found. award, 1977, Papanicolaou award, 1979, Lewis S. Rosenstiel award, 1980. Fellow AAAS, Am. Acad. Arts and Scis.; hon. fellow Am. Gynecol. and Obstet. Soc.; mem. Genetics Soc. Am., Soc. Study Developmental Biology, Internat. Soc. Developmental Biology, Am. Soc. Zoologists, Am. Inst. Biol. Scis., Nat. Acad. Scis., N.Y. Acad. Sci. (recipient award in biol. and med. scis. 1979), Sigma Xi, Phi Beta Kappa. Office: 7701 Burholme Ave Philadelphia PA 19111

MINTZER, DAVID, educator, university official; b. N.Y.C., May 4, 1926; s. Herman and Anna (Katz) M.; m. Justine Nancy Klein, June 26, 1949; children: Elizabeth Amy, Robert Andrew. B.S. in Physics, Mass. Inst. Tech., 1945, Ph.D., 1949. Asst. prof. physics Brown U., 1949-55; research asso. Yale U., 1955-56, asso. prof., dir. lab. marine physics, 1956-62; prof. mech. engring., astronautical scis. Northwestern U., Evanston, 1962—, prof. astrophysics, 1968—; asso. dean Technol. Inst., 1970-73, acting dean, 1971-72, v.p. for research, dean sci., 1973—; mem. mine adv. com. Nat. Acad. Sci.-NRC, 1963-73. Trustee EDUCOM, interuniv. communications council, 1975-83, vice chmn., 1977-78, chmn., 1978-81; trustee Adler Planetarium, 1976—. Fellow Am. Phys. Soc., Acoustical Soc. Am.; mem. ASME, Am. Astron. Soc., Sigma Xi, Tau Beta Pi, Pi Tau Sigma. Current Work: Research administration. Subspecialties: Acoustics; Statistical physics. Home: 736 Central St Evanston IL 60201

MIRABEL, IGOR FELIX, astronomer, educator; b. Montevideo, Uruguay, Oct. 23, 1944; s. Mauricio and Zulema (Miquele) M.; m. Silvia Alicia Revora, May 10, 1944; children: Mariana, Paula, Sofia. Ph.D. in Astronomy, Nat. U. La Plata, Argentina, 1974. Researcher NRC Argentina, Buenos Aires, 1974-76; prof. philosophy Nat. U. Buenos Aires, 1975; postdoctoral research fellow Nuffield Radio Astronomy Labs., Jodrell Bank, Eng., 1976-79; research asso. astronomy U. Md., 1979-81; prof., researcher in astronomy, physics dept. U. P.R., 1981—. Contbr. articles to sci. jours. Internat. Astron. Union grantee, 1976; NSF grantee; OCEC U. P.R. grantee, 1981-82. Mem. Internat. Astron. Union, Am. Astron. Soc., Argentine Astron. Soc. Current Work: Scientific research in galactic and extragalactic astronomy. Subspecialty: Radio and microwave astronomy. Office: Dept Physics U PR Box AT Rio Piedras PR 00931

MIRACKY, ROBERT FOSTER, physicist, researcher; b. Milw., May 16, 1955; s. Robert John and Barbara Charlotte (Foster) M. S.B. in Physics, MIT, 1977; M.A. in Physics, U. Calif.-Berkeley, 1980, Ph.D. in Physics, 1984. Research asst. Lawrence Berkeley Lab., Calif., 1978-80, research asst., 1981-84; devel. engr. Advanced Micro Devices, Sunnyvale, Calif., 1980-81; staff scientist Microelectronics and Computer Tech. Corp., Austin, Tex., 1984—; adj. prof. dept. elec. and Computer engring. U. Tex.-Austin, 1985—. Contbr. articles to profl. jours. U. Calif.-Berkeley fellow, 1977; NSF summer scholar, 1982. Mem. Am. Phys. Soc., IEEE. Current work: Interconnection technologies in support of advanced computer architectures; high speed microelectronics; Josephson junctions; nonlinear dynamics. Subspecialties: Microelectronics; Microchip technology (engineering). Home: 415 Cluck Creek Trail Cedar Park TX 78613 Office: Microelectronics and Computer Tech Corp 12100-A Technology Blvd Austin TX 78727

MIRAND, EDWIN ALBERT, cancer scientist; b. Buffalo, July 18, 1926; s. Thomas and Lucy (Papier) M. B.A., U. Buffalo, 1947, M.A., 1949; Ph.D., Syracuse (N.Y.) U., 1951; D.Sc. (hon.), Niagara (N.Y.) U., 1970, D'Youville Coll., Buffalo, 1974. Successively undergrad. asst., grad. asst., instr. U. Buffalo, 1946-48; teaching fellow Syracuse U., 1948-51; instr. Utica (N.Y.) Coll., 1950; mem. staff Roswell Park Meml. Inst., Buffalo, 1951—; head W. Seneca labs., 1961—, asso. inst. dir., head dept. edn., 1967—, dir. cancer research, 1968-73, head dept. viral oncology, 1970-73, head dept. biol. recources, 1973—; research prof. biology Grad. Sch., prof. biochem. pharmacology Sch. Pharmacy, State U. N.Y., Buffalo, 1955—; dean Roswell Park Meml. Inst. grad. div., 1967—; research prof. biology (Grad. Sch.); dean Roswell Park Meml. Inst. grad. div. Niagara U.; mem. human cancer virus task force, clin. cancer edn. com. NIH. Author articles cancer research, endocrinology, hematology, virology.; Editorial bd.: Jour. Surg. Oncology. Mem. U.S. nat. com. Union Internat. Contra Cancer; profl. edn. com. cancer control Nat. Cancer Inst; liaison mem. Pres.'s Nat. Cancer Adv. Bd.; mem. N.Y. State Health Research Council. Recipient Billings Silver medal AMA, 1963; award sci. research mammalian tumor viruses Med. Soc. State N.Y., 1963; citation award in sci. Coll. Arts and Scis., State U. N.Y., Buffalo, 1964. Life mem., fellow N.Y. Acad. Sci.; fellow AAAS; mem. Am. Cancer Soc., Assn. Gnotobiotics (pres. 1968-69, dir. 1975-78), Assn. Am. Cancer Insts. (sec.-treas. 1968—), Am. Assn. Cancer Research, Radiation Research Soc., Am. Soc. Zoologists, Soc. Exptl. Biology and Medicine, Buffalo Acad. Medicine, Animal Care Panel, Internat. Soc. Hematology, Pub. Health Cancer Assn. Am., Internat. Union Against Cancer (chmn. U.S. nat. com. 1979—, sec.-gen. 13th Internat. Cancer Congress), Hematology Soc., Am. Soc. Preventive Oncology, Buffalo Hist. Soc. (life), Buffalo Fine Arts Acad. (life), Sigma Xi. Current Work: Role of viruses in tumors, interferon and role of erythroporetin in regulating erythropoiesis. Subspecialties: Cancer research (medicine); Hematology. Home: 925 Delaware Ave Buffalo NY 14209 Office: 666 Elm St Roswell Park Meml Inst Buffalo NY 14263

MIRCETICH, SRECKO MIRKO, research plant pathologist; b. Skela Kod Obrenovca, Yugoslavia, Sept. 2, 1926; came to U.S., 1957, naturalized, 1960; s. Mirko Srecko and Jelena Rajko (Mircetih) M.; m. Jane Velika, Nov. 16, 1956; children: Jon, Kristofer. Agronomy Engr., U. Sarajevo, 1952; M.S., U. Belgrad, 1954; Ph.D., U. Calif.-Riverside, 1966. Research assoc. dept. plant pathology U. Calif.-Riverside, 1958-66; research plant pathologist Nat. Agrl. Research Ctr., U.S. Dept. Agr., Beltsville, Md., 1966-71, supervisory research plant pathologist, 1971-72; research plant pathologist U.S. Dept. Agr., U. Calif.-Davis, 1973—. Contbr. articles in field to profl. jours. Mem. Internat. Soc. Plant Pathology, Am. Phytopath. Soc. Republican. Serbian Orthodox. Current Work: Researcher in etiology and control of soil-borne diseases of deciduous fruit and nut trees. Subspecialty: Plant pathology.

MISCHKE, RICHARD EVANS, physicist; b. Bristol, Va., Aug. 19, 1940; s. Vernon Evans and Ruth (Shollenberger) M.; m. Alice Ruth Joyce, Dec. 27, 1962; children—Rachel Ellen, Rebecca Elise. B.S., U. Tenn., 1961; M.S., U. Ill., 1962, Ph.D., 1966. Instr. Princeton U., N.J., 1966-68, asst. prof., 1968-71; staff mem. Los Alamos Sci. Lab., 1971-73; asst. group leader Los Alamos Nat. Lab., 1973-75, assoc. group leader, 1975-78, dep. group leader, 1978—; bd. dirs. LAMPF Users Group, Inc., Los Alamos, 1977; guest scientist Swiss Inst. Nuclear Research, Villigen, 1978-79; mem. organizing com. Conf. on Intersects. between particle and Nuclear Physics, 1984. Editor: Procs. of Conf. on Intersects. between Particle and Nuclear Physics, 1984. Contbr. numerous articles to profl. jours. Patroller, Nat. Ski Patrol, 1974—; mem. Los Alamos Democratic Central Com., 1979—, ward chmn., 1981-83; chmn. bicycle subcom. Los Alamos County, 1983—. Nat. scholar United Meth. Ch., 1958-59; grad. fellow U. Ill., 1961-62; NSF fellow, 1962-64. Fellow Am. Phys. Soc. (program com. div. nuclear physics 1978-80); mem. Sigma Pi Sigma, Phi Kappa Phi. Democrat. Mem. Ch. of Christ. Current work: Research in nuclear and particle physics using pions, muons, and protons with an emphasis on weak interactions and symmetry laws; administration of research group. Subspecialties: Particle physics; Nuclear physics. Home: 137 Chamisa Los Alamos NM 87544 Office: Los Alamos Nat Lab MS H846 Los Alamos NM 87545

MISCONI, NEBIL YOUSIF, astronomer; b. Baghdad, Iraq, Dec. 8, 1939; came to U.S., 1970; s. Yousif Yacoub and Kolomba Salim (Dawood) M.; m. Irene Theresa Donohue, Aug. 31, 1972; 1 child, Michael Nebeel. B.Sc., Istanbul (Turkey) U., 1965; Ph.D., SUNY-Albany, 1975. Instr. Physics Lab., U. Baghdad, 1966-70; grad. research asst. Dudley Obs. and SUNY-Albany, 1970-75; postdoctoral research assoc. Space Astronomy Lab., SUNY-Albany, 1975-77, research assoc., 1978-80; asst. research scientist U. Fla., 1980-82; assoc. research scientist U. Fla. (Space Astronomy Lab.), 1982—. Research publs. in field. NASA grantee, 1978-79; NSF grantee, 1982-84; AFOSR grantee, 1984—. Mem. Am. Astron. Soc., Royal Astron. Soc., Internat. Astron. Union (Commns. 21 and 22), Sigma Xi. Current Work: Interplanetary medium; zodiacal light; dynamics of cosmic dust; cometary physics; laser particle dynamics. Subspecialty: Planetary science.

MISER, HUGH JORDAN, operations research and systems analyst, consultant, editor; b. Fayetteville, Ark., May 23, 1917; s. Wilson Lee and Nellie (Pyle) M.; m. Josephine Spence Lehmann, June 24, 1944; children—James Spence, Wendel Lee, Andrew Lehmann, Emily Margaret. B.A. magna cum laude, Vanderbilt U., 1938; M.S., Ill. Inst. Tech., 1940; Ph.D., Ohio State U., 1946. Various teaching positions in math. Ill. Inst. Tech., Chgo., Ohio State U., Columbus, Lawrence Coll., Appleton, Wis., 1938-46, acting chmn. math. dept. Lawrence Coll., Appleton, 1944; ops. analyst Hdqrs. U.S. Air Force, Washington 1945, 1949-59, dep. asst. ops. analysis, 1951-59, acting asst. ops. analysis, 1958-59; asst. prof. math. Williams Coll., Williamstown, Mass., 1946-49; dir. operational scis. lab. Research Triangle Inst., Durham, N.C., 1959-60; dir. applied sci. div. ops. evaluation group MIT, 1960-62; asst. to dir. systems planning and research The Mitre Corp., Bedford, Mass., 1962-65; v.p. Travelers Research Ctr., Inc., Hartford, Conn., 1965-69; prof. indsl. engring. and ops. research U. Mass., Amherst, 1969-80, acting head dept. indsl. engring. and ops. research, 1975-76, head dept., 1976-79, prof. emeritus, 1980—; leader craft of systems analysis Internat. Inst. Applied Systems Analysis, Laxenburg, Austria, 1979-82, exec. editor inst. publs., 1979-82, acting head communications, 1980-81; cons. and editor, Farmington, Conn., 1983—; cons. to sec. and chief of staff U.S. Air Force, 1967-68, with ops. analysis office, 1968-71, with info. systems program Office Sci. Info. Service, NSF, 1969-74, Ctr. Environ. and Man, Inc., Hartford, 1970-79, Rensselaer Poly. Inst. Conn., Hartford, 1970, cons., mem. systems and program analysis panel GAO, Washington, 1972-76; mem. Nat. Acad. Scis. evaluation panel for tech. analysis div. Inst. applied Tech. Nat. Bur. Standards, 1967-69, 72-73, chmn. 1969-72; mem. commerce tech. adv. bd. Panel on Noise Abatement, 1968-71; chmn. research adv. com. Ins. Inst. Hwy. Safety, Washington, 1967-69. Co-author: Basic Mathematics for Engineers, 1944; Basic Mathematics for Science and Engineering, 1955. Co-editor: Handbook of Systems Analysis, vol. 1, 1985. Contbr. numerous articles on ops. research, systems analysis and related subjects to profl. jours. Cons. Am. Acad. Arts and Scis., Cambridge, Mass., 1983—. Recipient Arthur S. Flemming award, 1952, for meritorius civilian service U.S. Air Force, 1954, award for exceptional civilian service U.S. Air Force, 1957. Fellow AAAS; mem. Ops. Research Soc. Am. (sec. 1958-61, v.p. 1961-62, pres. 1960-63, rep. to NRC 1967-73, editor Bull. 1959-61, book rev. editor Ops. Research 1963-68, editor Ops. Research 1968-74, George E. Kimball medal 1975), Inst. Mgmt. Scis., Can. Operational Research Soc., Am. Math. Soc., Math. Assn. Am. Soc. Indsl. and Applied Math., Inst. Math. Statistics, Am. Stat. Assn., Conn. Acad. Sci. and Engring. (founding mem.), Phi Beta Kappa, Sigma Xi. Congregationalist. Current work: Managing and carrying out interdisciplinary research on the operating and policy problems of man-machine-nature systems, that is, systems analysis. Subspecialties: Operations research (engineering); Statistics. Home: 199 South Rd Farmington CT 06032

MISFELDT, MICHAEL LEE, immunologist, educator; b. Davenport, Iowa, June 15, 1950; s. Melvin Lawrence and Wanda Irene (Dee) M.; m. Mary Alice Griffin, Aug. 4, 1973; children—Andrew Michael, Kristin Marie. B.S., U. Ill., 1972; Ph.D., U. Iowa, 1977. Research asst. dept. microbiology U. Iowa, Iowa City, 1973-77; staff fellow Lab. Molecular Genetics, Nat. Inst. Child Health and Devel.; NIH, Bethesda, Md., 1977-81; asst. prof. microbiology U. Mo., Columbia, 1981—. Contbr. articles to profl. jours. Mem. Am. Soc. Microbiology, N.Y. Acad. Scis., Am. Assn. Immunologists, AAAS. Current Work: Immunomodulation by bacterial products, T-lymphocyte differentiation. Subspecialties: Immunopharmacology; Neuroimmunology. Office: U Mo-Columbia M264 Med Scis Bldg Columbia MO 65212

MISKIMEN, GEORGE WILLIAM, neurobiologist; educator; b. Applet., Wis., May 21, 1930; s. George Oscar and Gladys Matilda (Burns) M.; m. Carmen M. Rivera-Batlle, Apr. 19, 1963; children—Kathryn Ann, Teresa Marie, Elizabeth Joan, Carmen Mildred. B.S., Ohio U., 1953, M.S., 1955; Ph.D., U. Fla., 1966. Registered profl. entomologist. Entomologist Agriculture Research Service U.S. Dept. Agriculture, St. Croix, Virgin Islands, 1958-61, investigations leader entomology research div., Mayaguez, P.R., 1962-66; prof. biology U. P.R., Mayaguez, 1966—, dir. research, 1975—; adj. prof. ophthalmology U. Fla. Sch. Medicine, Gainesville, 1981—; dir. biomed. research support program NIH. Contbr. articles to profl. jours. Served with U.S. Army, 1947-52. U. Fla. fellow, 1955-56; grantee NIH, NSF, U.S. Dept. Agr., 1974—. Fellow Explorers Club; mem. Soc. Neuroscis., Assn. Research Vision and Ophthalmology, Assn. Tropical Biology, Internat. Orgn. Biol. Control., Sigma Xi. Republican. Episcopalian. Clubs: Deportivo (Mayaguez), Casino de Mayaguez, Boqueron Yacht. Lodges: Masons, Rotary. Current work: Neurosciences; neurobiology; electrophysiology; environmental stimuli effects on visual receptors; morphology; electron microscopy. Subspecialty: Microscopy. Home: Box 1420 Villa Sonsire Km 4 O Miradero Rd Mayaguez PR 00709 Office: Dept Biology U Puerto Rico Mayaguez PR 00708

MISLANKAR, DATTATRAYA GHANSHYAM, chemist; b. Karwar, India, Dec. 23, 1950; came to U.S., 1974, permanent resident, 1982; s. Ghanshyam Vithoba Mislankar and Tarabai Sheth; m. Praveena Revankar, Dec. 25, 1977. B.Sc., Karnatak U., Dharwar, India, 1970, M.Sc. in Inorganic Chemistry, 1972; M.S. in Organic Chemistry, Akron U., 1977, Ph.D. in Organic Chemistry, 1981. Teaching asst. Akron U., Ohio, 1975-78, Stauffer Chem. research fellow, 1979-81; chemist trainee Am. Xtal Co., Kent, Ohio, 1978; specialist II, Mead Research, Chillicothe, Ohio, 1981-82, research specialist, 1982-83; chief chemist Mead Paper, Chillicothe, 1983—. Mem. mgmt. adv. bd. Chem. Week Jour., N.Y.C., 1984—. Contbr. articles to profl. jours. Mem TAPPI, AM. Chem. Soc. Hindu. Current work: To provide technical expertise and consultative services to manufacturing and marketing deptment of Mead. Subspecialties: Organic chemistry; Inorganic chemistry. Home: 25 Timberlane Dr Chillicothe OH 45601 Office: Mead Paper S Paint St Chillicothe OH 45601

MISLOW, KURT MARTIN, chemist, educator; b. Berlin, Germany, June 5, 1923; came to U.S., 1940, naturalized, 1946; s. Max and Ida (Bingen) M.; m. Jacqueline Ford, 1966; children—Christopher, John. B.S., Tulane U., 1944, D.Sc. (hon.), 1975; Ph.D., Calif. Inst. Tech., 1947; D. honoris causa, Free U., Brussels, 1974, Uppsala U., 1977. Instr. N.Y.U., 1947-51, asst. prof., 1951-56, assoc. prof., 1956-60, prof., 1960-64; Hugh Stott Taylor prof. chemistry Princeton, 1964—, chmn. dept. chemistry, 1968-74; vis. prof. Stanford U., 1960; Univ. lectr. U. London, 1965; J.A. McRae Meml. lectr. Queen's U., 1967; H.A. Iddles lectr. U. N.H., 1972; Solvay lectr. and medalist Free U. Brussels, 1972; E.C. Lee lectr. U. Chgo.; A.A. Vernon lectr. Northeastern U., 1976; PPG lectr. Ohio U., 1977; J. Musher Meml. lectr. Hebrew U. Jerusalem, 1978; North Country lectr., 1978; honor lectr. Ariz. State U., 1981; E. Ritchie meml. lectr. Sydney U., 1983; Fuson lectr. U. Nev., 1983; Research Scholar lectr. Drew U., 1983; McGregory lectr. Colgate U., 1984; Churchill fellow Cambridge U., 1974-75; mem. adv. panel chemistry NSF, 1963-66; mem. panel medicinal and organic chemistry NIH, 1963-66. Author: Introduction to Stereochemistry, 1965; also numerous articles; Bd. editors: Jour. Organic Chemistry, 1965-70; mem. editorial adv. bd.: Monatshefte für Chemie, Topics in Stereochemistry, Accounts of Chem. Research, Chem. and Engring. News, Bull des Sociétés Chimques Belges. Guggenheim fellow, 1957-58, 74-75; Alfred P. Sloan fellow, 1959-63. Fellow Am. Acad. Arts and Scis.; mem. Nat. Acad. Scis., Am. Chem. Soc. (James Flack Norris award 1975), Chem. Soc. London, AAUP, Phi Beta Kappa, Sigma Xi, Phi Lambda Upsilon. Subspecialty: Organic chemistry.

MISRA, ANAND LAL, medicinal chemist, educator; b. Kanpur, India, June 5, 1928; came to U.S., 1969, naturalized, 1977; s. Chotey Lal and Sahodra Ruttondevi (Shukla) M. B.Sc., Allahabad U., 1946, M.Sc., 1948, Ph.D. (Kanta Prasad research scholar), 1950; F.H.-W.C. (Assam Oil Co.-Burmah Shell scholar), Heriot-Watt Coll., Edinburgh (Scotland) U., 1955. Research asst. Allahabad U., 1951-53; sci. officer Nat. Chem. Lab., Poona, India, 1956-57; Smith-Mundt Fulbright research fellow U. Mich., Ann Arbor, 1957-60; research officer Central Drug Research Inst., Lucknow, India, 1960-61; research chemist Ciba Ltd., Basel, Switzerland, 1961-64; head product devel. Ciba of India Ltd., Bombay, 1964-67; research assoc. U. Iowa, Iowa City, 1969-70; research scientist V Research Lab., N.Y. State Div. Substance Abuse Services, Bklyn., 1971—; adj. assoc. prof. dept. psychiatry SUNY Downstate Med. Center, Bklyn., 1980—; participant numerous nat. and internat. sci. confs. Contbr. numerous articles on structure-activity relationships, biopharmaceutics, phytochemistry, pharmacokinetics, biol. disposition and metabolism of drugs subject to human abuse to sci. jours. U.P. Govt. scholar, 1951-53; U.S. Army Med. Research and Devel. Command grantee, 1973-76. Fellow Royal Soc. Chemistry (U.K.), Am. Inst. Chemists; mem. Am. Soc. Pharmacology and Exptl. Therapeutics, Am. Chem. Soc., AAAS, Fedn. Am. Scientists, Assn. for Med. Edn. and Research in Substance Abuse, N.Y. Acad. Scis. Current Work: Radioactive tracer studies; biological disposition, metabolism, pharmacokinetics of drugs subject to human abuse; mechanism of development of tolerance, psychic and physiological dependence on psychoactive drugs. Subspecialties: Pharmacology; Medicinal chemistry. Office: Research Lab NY State Div Substance Abuse Services 80 Hanson Pl Brooklyn NY 11217

MISRA, BALABHADRA, chemical engineer, research consultant; b. Berhampur, India, Apr. 21, 1926; came to U.S., 1949; s. Gopal Bhatta and Malati (Dash) M.; m. Nalini Misra, Apr. 14, 1949; children: Bijoy, Binoy. B.Sc. with honors, Ravenshaw Coll., India, 1947; B.S., Indian Inst. Sci., 1949; M.S., Columbia U., 1951, Ph.D., 1957. Registered profl. engr., Calif. Research assoc. Columbia U., N.Y.C., 1956-58; tech. specialist Aerojet-Gen. Corp., Sacramento, 1958-71; chem. engr. Argonne Nat. Lab., Ill., 1971—, project mgr., 1971-77. Contbr. numerous articles to sci. jours. Fundraiser Sacramento Symphony, 1967-70; troop leader Boy Scouts Am., 1966-68. Recipient Gold medal Utkal U., Orissa, India, 1947. Mem. Am. Inst. Chem. Engrs., AIAA, Am. Nuclear Soc. Republican. Hindu. Current Work: Component development and testing for LMFBR and fusion reactor; safety analysis of nuclear reactors; tritium extraction from fusion reactor breeding blankets. Subspecialties: Nuclear fission; Nuclear fusion. Home: 73 Finch Ct Naperville IL 60565 Office: 9700 S Cass Ave Argonne IL 60439

MISRA, DWARIKA NATH, physical chemist; b. Sarai Miran, India, Mar. 17, 1933, came to U.S., 1958, naturalized, 1974; s. Kanauji Lal and Sanatani Devi (Sukul) M.; m. Chandra Kala, June 10, 1954; children—Sunil, Vinod, Timir. B.S., Lucknow U., India, 1951, M.S., 1953; Ph.D., Howard U., 1963. Sr. scientist Itek Corp., Lexington, Mass., 1966-68; lectr. Howard U., Washington, 1970-72; research assoc. research unit ADA Health Found., Nat. Bur. Standards, Washington, 1972—. Editor: Adsorption on and Surface Chemistry of Hydroxyapatite, 1984. Contbr. articles to profl. jours. NSF fellow, 1963-66. Mem. Am. Chem. Soc., Sigma Xi. Democrat. Current work: Adsorption and kinetics on heterogeneous surfaces; surface chemistry of hydroxyapatite and oxides; reaction mechanisms of adsorbed species; chemical bond between bone material and resins. Subspecialties: Surface chemistry; Dental materials. Home: 13501 Jamieson Pl Germantown MD 20874

MISRA, HARA PRASAD, biochemist, researcher, educator; b. Khallikote, India, June 1, 1940; came to U.S., 1966; s. Jaya Krishna and Baikoli (Rath) M.; m. Bijaya Kumari Mahapatra, July 6, 1962; children—Bhaba, Bibhu, Anoo. D.V.M., Utkal U., Orissa, India, 1962; M.S., Va. Poly. Inst., 1968, Ph.D., 1971. Instr. vet. medicine, officer Orissa Vet. Coll., Bhubaneswar, Orissa, 1962-66; postdoctoral fellow Med. Ctr., Duke U., Durham, N.C., 1971-73, sr. research assoc., 1975-78; asst. prof. Med. Ctr., U. Ala., Birmingham, 1973-75; pulmonary biochemist U. Calif.-Davis, 1978-82; asst. mem. Okla. Med. Research Found., Oklahoma City, 1982-85, assoc. mem., 1985; assoc. prof. Coll. Vet. Medicine, Va. Inst. Tech., Blacksburg, 1985—; cons. U. Md., Balt., 1984—; speaker profl. confs.; prin. investigator NIH, 1984—, Am. Inst. Cancer Research, 1984—. Author articles, papers in field. Mem. Am. Soc. Biol. Chemistry, Am. Toxicol. Soc., N.Y. Acad. Scis., Free Radical Soc. Current work: Free radical tissue injury, membrane biology, enzymology, pulmonary biochemistry, heart reperfusion injury. Subspecialties: Biochemistry (biology); Free radical biology. Home: 1733 Donlee Dr Blacksburg VA 24060 Office: Coll Vet Medicine Va Inst Tech Blacksburg VA 24061

MISRA, RAGHUNATH PRASAD, physician, pathology educator; b. Calcutta, West Bengal, India, Feb. 1, 1928; came to U.S., 1964, naturalized, 1971; s. Guru Prasad and Anandi (Devi) M.; m. Therese Rettenmund, Sept. 12, 1963; children: Sima, Joya, Maya, Tara. B.Sc., Calcutta (India) U., 1948, M.B.B.S., 1954; Ph.D., McGill U., 1965. Diplomate: Am. Bd. Pathology. Intern Med. Coll. Hosps., Calcutta, 1953-54, resident, 1954-56, Univ. Hosps., Cleve., 1973-76; instr., asst. prof. dept. medicine U. Louisville Sch. Medicine, 1966-68; asst., assoc. investigator Mt. Sinai Hosp., Cleve., 1968-73; asst. prof. exptl. pathology Case Western Res. U., Cleve., 1971-76; asst. prof. pathology La. State U. Sch. Medicine, Shreveport, 1976-80, assoc. prof., 1980—, chief renal/immunopathology. 1976—; dir. Kidney Research Lab., U. Louisville Sch. Medicine, 1966-68, Kidney Lab., Mt. Sinai Hosp., Cleve., 1968-73. Author: An Atlas of Skin Biopsy, 1983. Sec. bd. govs. India House Project, Cleve., 1976. Indian Med. Assn. fellow, 1957-60; Can. Heart Found. fellow, 1960-64; Jean Talliamon Meml. fellow, 1971-73. Fellow Coll. Am. Pathologists, Am. Soc. Clin. Pathologists; mem. Am. Assn. Pathologists, Am. Soc. Nephrology, AMA, Sigma Xi. Unitarian-Universalist. Current Work: Molecular pathobiology of Kidney diseases. Subspecialties: Nephrology; Pathology (medicine). Home: 6153 River Rd Shreveport LA 71105 Office: La State Sch Medicine 1501 Kings Hwy Shreveport LA 71130

MISTRY, VITTHALBHAI DAHYABHAI, med. physicist; b. Vesma, India, Sept. 30, 1942; came to U.S., 1965, naturalized, 1976; s. Dahyabhai Jivanji and Jamnaben (Dullabhbhai) M.; m. Padmaben Kalyanji Prajapati, May 18, 1974; children: Vandana, Rohitkumar. B.S. with great distinction, Haile Selassie I U., Addis Ababa, Ethiopia, 1964; Ph.D. in Nuclear Physics, U. Tex.-Austin, 1969. Cert. in therapeutic radiol. physics Am. Bd. Radiology. Asst. prof. Haile Selassie I U., 1964-65; research assoc. U. Tex.-Austin, 1967-69; postdoctoral fellow Tex. Christian U., Ft. Worth, 1969-71; inst. x-ray physics Austin (Tex.) State Hosp., 1974-78; med. physicist Capital Area Radiation and Research Ctr., Austin, 1971—; cons. med. radiation physicist. Mem. Am. Phys. Soc., Am. Assn. Physicists in Medicine, Soc. Tex. Regional Physicists, Am. Soc. Therapeutic Radiology, Sigma Xi, Sigma Pi Sigma. Hindu. Current Work: Biological effect of therapeutic doses of ionizing radiation for different treatment modalities in radiation therapy. Subspecialties: Nuclear physics; Medical physics. Office: Alan Shivers Radiation Therapy Ctr 2600 E Martin Luther King Blvd Austin TX 78702

MITALAS, ROMAS, astronomer, educator; b. Lithuania, Feb. 28, 1933; s. Adolfas and Leonarda (Grigonyte) M.; m. Nancy Louise Callaghan, Sept., 1979. B.A. in Applied Math, U. Toronto, 1957, M.A., 1958; Ph.D. in Theoretical Physics, Cornell U., 1964. Asst. prof. physics U. Western Ont., London, 1964-68, asst. prof. astronomy, 1968-73, asso. prof., 1973—. Mem. Can. Astron. Soc., Am. Astron. Soc. Current Work: Stellar structure and evolution. Subspecialties: Theoretical astrophysics; Nucleosynthesis. Home: 61 Meridene Circle E London ON N5X 2M1 Canada Office: Dept Astronomy U Western Ont London ON N6A 3K7 Canada

MITCHELL, ALBERT WALLACE, III, consulting geologist; b. Brigham City, Utah, Dec. 7, 1945; s. Albert Wallace and Geneva Naomi (Cliff) M.; m. Margaret Elaine Rolfson, June 4, 1970; children—Emily, Kara, Mark, Laurie, Erin, Anna, Kristen. B.S. in Geology, Utah State U., 1970; M.S., in Geology, U. Nev., 1977. Registered profl. geologist, Oreg., Ga. Geologist Milchem Inc., Battle Mountain, Nev., 1972-80, sr. geologist, Houston, 1977-80, chief geologist, Glenwood, Ark., 1980-83; cons. geologist, Glenwood, 1983—. Contbr. articles to profl. jours. vice pres. Pike County Fair Bd., Glenwood, 1981-84; scoutmaster Ouachita Area council Boy Scouts Am., 1982—. Mem. Soc. Mining Engrs., Geol. Soc. Am. Mem. Ch. of Jesus Christ of Latter-day Saints. Current work: Discovery of sedimentary exhalative ore deposits and industrial minerals. Subspecialty: Geology. Home and office: Route 1 Box 43F1 Glenwood AR 71943

MITCHELL, EARL DOUGLASS, JR., biochemistry educator; b. New Orleans, May 16, 1938; s. Earl Douglass and Mary Magdeline Duncan; m. Bernice Compton, Oct. 31, 1959; children—Karen, Earl Douglass III, Michael. B.S., Xavier U., 1960; M.S., Mich. State U., Ph.D., 1966. Research assoc. Okla. State U., Stillwater, 1967-69, asst. prof. biochemistry, 1969-73, assoc. prof., 1973-78; prof., asst. dean., 1978—; research chemist NIH, Bethesda, Md., 1980, mem. biochem. study sect., 1984—; vis. prof. U. Ark., Fayetteville, 1975. Contbr. articles to profl. jours. Pres. Payne County NAACP, Stillwater, 1970-74; vice chmn. Okla. State ACLU, Oklahoma City, 1972-78; chmn. SAC, U.S. Commn. on Civil Rights, Okla., 1978—, Okla. State Personnel Bd. and Ethics and Merit Commn., Oklahoma City, 1980—. Mem. Am. Chem. Soc., Am. Soc. Biol. Chemists, AAAS, Tissue Culture Assn. Democrat. Methodist. Subspecialties: Biochemistry (biology); Plant cell and tissue culture. Office: Dept Biochemistry Okla State Univ Stillwater OK 74078

MITCHELL, GARY EARL, physicist, educator; b. Louisville, July 5, 1935; s. Earl Raymond and Delma Kathlene (Lockard) M.; m. Carolyn Fey Stutz, Aug. 4, 1957; children—Scott Frederick, Karen Lee. B.S. in Physics, U. Louisville, 1956; M.A., Duke U., 1958; Ph.D., Fla. State U., 1962. Research assoc. Columbia U., N.Y.C., 1962-64, asst. prof. physics, 1964-68; assoc. prof. physics N.C. State U., Raleigh, 1968-74, prof., 1974—, assoc. head dept., 1982—. Contbr. articles to profl. jours. Recipient Sr. Scientist award Alexander Von Humboldt-Stiftung, 1975. Fellow Am. Phys. Soc. Current work: Statistical properties of nuclei; nuclear spectroscopy. Subspecialty: Nuclear physics. Home: 2913 Harriman Durham NC 27705 Office: Dept Physics NC State U PO Box 8202 Raleigh NC 27695

MITCHELL, GEORGE BERT, veterinarian, researcher; b. Listowel, Ont., Can., June 2, 1936; s. Bennett A. and Alba M. (Musgrove) M.; m. Mary Margaret Townsend, June 29, 1963; children—Dave, Alan. B.S.A., U. Toronto, 1960, D.V.M., 1964; diploma bus. adminstrn., Washington U., St. Louis, 1968. Vet. pathologist Ralston Purina, St. Louis, 1964-65, mgr. clin. research, 1965-76, dir. health ind. research, 1976-82; dir. Bur. Vet. Drugs, Govt. of Can., Ottawa, Ont., 1982—. Pres. Citizens' Adv. Council, Parkway Sch. Dist., 1982; coach Amateur Hockey, Kirkwood, Mo., 1970-74. Recipient Super Goal award Ralston Purina, 1981; McGillvary award Ont. Vet. Coll., 1964; named Boss of Yr., Profl. Secs. Internat., 1981, Jaycees, 1978. Mem. AVMA, Can. Vet. Med. Assn., Am. Assn. Indsl. Veterinarians (pres. 1974), Am. Assn. Vet. Nutritionists (pres. 1980), Am. Acad. Vet. Pharmacology and Therapeutics, Ont. Vet. Assn. Republican. Methodist. Current work: Consideration of animal drug residues and antibiotic resistance of bacteria in relation to human health; efficacy of drugs used in food producing and companion animals. Subspecialty: Pharmacokinetics. Office: Health and Welfare Can Tunneys Pasture Ottawa ON K1A 1B7 Canada

MITCHELL, GEORGE ERNEST, JR., animal scientist, educator; b. Duoro, N.Mex., June 7, 1930; s. George Ernest and Alma Thyrza (Hatley) M.; m. Billie Carolyn McMahan, Mar. 14, 1952; children: Leslie Dianne, Karen Leigh, Cynthia Faye. B.S., U. Mo., 1951, M.S., 1954; Ph.D., U. Ill., 1956. Asst. prof. animal sci. U. Ill., 1956-60; assoc. prof. U. Ky., Lexington, 1960-67, prof., 1967—, dir. grad. studies in animal scis., 1964—, coordinator beef cattle and sheep, 1974—; mem. com. on animal nutrition NRC. Contbr. articles to profl. jours. Served with USAF, 1951-53. Fulbright research scholar New Zealand, 1973-74. Mem. Am. Soc. Animal Sci. (sec. 1969-70, v.p. 1970-71, pres. So. sect. 1971-72), Am. Dairy Sci. Assn., Am. Inst. Nutrition, AAAS, Am. Assn. Registered Animal Scientists, Council for Agrl. Sci. and Tech., Sigma Xi, Alpha Zeta, Gamma Sigma Delta, Omicron Delta Kappa. Democrat. Methodist. Current Work: Ruminant nutrition, comparative nutrition, vitamin metabolism, starch utilization, digestive physiology. Subspecialties: Animal nutrition; Nutrition (biology). Home: 690 Hill 'n' Dale Lexington KY 40503 Office: 809 Agrl Sci So U Ky Lexington KY 40546

MITCHELL, JAMES KENNETH, civil engineer, educator; b. Manchester, N.H., Apr. 19, 1930; s. Richard N. and Henrietta (Moench) M.; m. Virginia D. Williams, Nov. 24, 1951; children: Richard A., Laura K., James W., Donald M., David L. B.C.E., Rensselaer Poly. Inst., 1951; M.S., M.I.T., 1953; D.Sc., 1956. Mem. faculty U. Calif., Berkeley, 1958—, prof. civil engring., 1968—, chmn. dept., 1979-84; geo tech. cons., 1960—. Author: Fundamentals of Soil Behavior, 1976; contbr. articles to profl. jours. Asst. scoutmaster Boy Scouts Am., 1975-82; mem. Moraga (Calif.) Environ. Rev. Com., 1978-80. Served to 1st lt. AUS, 1956-58. Recipient Exceptional Sci. Achievement medal NASA, 1973. Fellow ASCE (Huber prize 1965, Middlebrooks award 1962, 70, 73, Norman medal 1972, Terzaghi lectr. 1984, Karl Terzaghi award 1985); mem. Nat. Acad. Engring., Am. Soc. Engring. Edn. (Western Electric Fund award 1979), Transp. Research Bd. (exec. com. 1983—), Clay Minerals Soc., Sigma Xi, Tau Beta Pi, Chi Epsilon. Current Work: Ground improvement for engineering works, geotechnical engineering, geotechnical aspects of hazardous waste containment. Subspecialty: Civil engineering. Office: Dept Civil Engring U Calif Berkeley CA 94720

MITCHELL, JAMES THOMAS, electrical engineer, mathematics educator; b. Stilwell, Okla., Dec. 22, 1923; s. Samuel Leonard and Nora Mary (Testerman) M.; m. Mary Martha Morton, July 19, 1952; 1 child, Mary Martha. B.S.E.E., U. Okla., 1950; M.S., U. Pitts., 1955; Ph.D., Ohio State U., 1968. Registered profl. engr., Ohio. Design engr. Westinghouse Elec. Corp., Lima, Ohio, 1950—, fellow engr., scientist, 1958—; lectr. Ohio State Univ., Lima, 1980—. Contbr. articles to profl. jours. Patentee in field; recipient Westinghouse engring. achievement award, 1985. Chmn. Citizens Adv. Com., Elida, Ohio, 1970; treas. Band Boosters, Elida, 1976. Served with U.S. Army, 1943-46. Mem. IEEE (sr. mem.), Internat. Soc. Hybrid Mfrs., Sigma Tau, Tau Beta pi, Eta Kappa Nu, Phi Eta Sigma. Republican. Presbyterian. Current work: Minaturized high capacity film capacitors; radiation hardening of electronic circuits, hybrid microelectronic packaging, failure analysis of components. Subspecialties: Electrical engineering; Microelectronics. Home: 147 Burlington Pl St Lima OH 45805 Office: Westinghouse Elec Corp 1501 South Dixie Lima OH 45806

MITCHELL, JERE HOLLOWAY, research physician, cardiologist; b. Longview, Tex., Oct. 17, 1928; s. William Holloway and Dorthea (Turner) M. m. Pamela Battey, Oct. 1, 1960; children—Wendy Keener, Laurie Clemens, Amy Dewing. B.S., Va. Mil. Inst., 1950; M.D., Southwestern Med. Sch., 1954. Intern, Parkland Med. Hosp., Dallas, 1954-55, resident, 1955-56; cardiac trainee Nat. Heart Inst., Southwestern Med. Sch., Dallas, 1956-57, postdoctoral research fellow, 1957-58; surgeon, NIH, USPHS, Bethesda, Md., 1958-62; asst. prof. medicine and physiology U. Tex. Health Sci. Ctr., Dallas, 1962-66, assoc. prof., 1966-69, prof. medicine and physiology, 1969—, dir. Harry S. Moss Heart Ctr., 1976—, dir. Weinberger Lab. for Cardiopulmonary Research, 1966—; Frank M. Ryburn, Jr. chair in heart research, Harry S. Moss Trust, 1982—. Author chpts. in books in field. Editor monograph. Bd. mem. Dallas Theater Ctr. Recipient Research Career Devel. award USPHS, 1968-73. Fellow Am. Coll. Cardiology (Young Investigator award 1961), ACP, Am. Coll. Sports Medicine (Citation award 1983); mem. Am. Physiol. Soc., Am. Fedn. Clin. Research (emeritus), Assn. Am. Physicians, Assn. Univ. Cardiologists, Am. Soc. Clin. Investigation (emeritus), Am. Heart Assn. (councils: basic sci., circulation, fellow clin. cardiology, established investigator 1962-67, Award of Merit 1984, pres. Tex. affiliate 1983-84). Research or work interests: Neural control of circulation, cardiovascular response and adaptation to exercise, dimensional analysis of ventricular function. Subspecialties: Physiology (medicine); Internal medicine. Office: Harry S Moss Heart Ctr Southwestern Med Sch Univ Tex Health Sci Ctr at Dallas 5323 Harry Hines Blvd Dallas TX 75235

MITCHELL, JOHN MURRAY, JR., climatologist; b. N.Y.C., Sept. 17, 1928; s. John Murray and Lanier (Comly) M.; m. Pollyanne Bryant, May 5, 1956; children: John Murray, Harrison Brian, Katherine Comly, Anne Stuart. B.S., Mass. Inst. Tech., 1951, M.S., 1952; Ph.D., Pa. State U., 1960; postgrad., Nat. War Coll., 1970-71. Research meteorologist Weather Bur., Commerce Dept., Suitland, Md., 1955-65; project scientist environ. data service NOAA, Silver Spring, Md., 1965-74, sr. research climatologist, 1974-79, sci. advisor, 1980—; mem. various coms. and panels Nat. Acad. Scis., NRC; vis. lectr., prof. U. Calif., U. Wash. Contbr. articles to books, encys., tech. jours.; editor: Meteorol. Monographs, 1965-73. Mem. Fairfax County Air Pollution Control Bd. Served with USAF, 1952-55. Recipient Silver and Gold medals Commerce Dept. Fellow AAAS, Am. Meteorol. Soc. (2d Half Century award), Washington Acad. Scis.; mem. Am. Geophys. Union, Royal Meteorol. Soc., Sigma Xi. Current Work: Causes of present-day climatic changes, and assessment of natural and anthropogenic causes of future changes. Subspecialty: Climatology. Home: 1106 Dogwood Dr McLean VA 22101 Office: NOAA 6010 Executive Blvd Rockville MD 20852

MITCHELL, MALCOLM STUART, physician; b. N.Y.C., May 6, 1937; s. Max E. and Sylvia W. M.; m. June Kan, Aug. 14, 1976; children: Jeffrey Scott, Roderick Keith, Derek James. A.B. magna cum laude, Harvard U., 1957; M.D., Yale U., 1962; postgrad. (Fulbright scholar), U. Oxford, Eng., 1959-60. Diplomate: Am. Bd. Internal Medicine. Instr. to asso. prof. medicine Yale U., 1968-78; prof. medicine and microbiology U. So. Calif., 1978—; chief med. oncology, dir. clin. investigations U. So. Calif. (Cancer Center), 1978—; adv. com. NIH, 1975-82, Am. Cancer Soc., 1975-79, U.S. Pharmacopeia, 1975-80; chmn. adv. com. Nat. Cancer Cytology Center, 1981—. Editor in chief: Yale Jour. Biology and Medicine, 1976-78; asso. editor 11 other jours.; contbr. numerous articles to profl. jours.; editor: Hybridomas in Cancer Diagnosis and Treatment, 1982; The Modulation of Immunity, 1985; Immunity to Cancer, 1985. Served with USPHS, 1963-65. Leukemia Soc. scholar, 1968-73; NIH awardee, 1974-79. Mem. Soc. Clin. Investigation, Am. Assn. Cancer Research, Am. Assn. Immunologists, Phi Beta Kappa, Sigma Xi. Current Work: Immunology, immunotherapy. Subspecialties: Oncology; Immunology (medicine). Office: 2025 Zonal Ave Los Angeles CA 90033

MITCHELL, MICHAEL EUGENE, electronics systems engineer, military communications consultant and researcher; b. Kalamazoo, Mich., June 29, 1930; s. Otto Eugene and Helen Elaine (Mullins) M.; m. Joan Hortense Beard, Sept. 13, 1953 (dec. Apr. 1983); children—Michael Thomas, Donald Gregory, Nicole Margaret. B.S.E. in Elec. Engring., B.S.E. in Engring. Math., U. Mich., 1953. Mem. tech. staff Bell Telephone Labs., Whippany, N.J., 1953-57; project engr. advanced electronics ctr., Gen. Elec. Co., Ithaca, N.Y., 1957-62, systems engr. mil. communications dept., Oklahoma City, 1962-66, telecom specialist spl. info. products dept., Syracuse, N.Y., 1966-68, cons. engr. heavy mil. products dept., 1968-75; sr. staff engr. communications systems div. Hughes Aircraft Co., Fullerton, Calif., 1975—; dir. Opportunityland, Inc., Fullerton. Contbr. articles and reports to profl. publs; patentee error correcting decoders. Scholar Jr. C. of C., Kalamazoo, Mich., 1948, Joseph Boyer scholar, 1952; citizen's grantee Kalamazoo C. of C., 1949. Mem. IEEE (chmn. profl. group on info. theory Syracuse chpt. 1974-75), Communications Soc. of IEEE, Computer Soc. of IEEE, Sigma Xi, Phi Kappa Phi, Eta Kappa Nu (v.p. U. Mich. chpt. 1952-53), Tau Beta Pi, Kappa Rho Sigma, Kappa Alpha Psi (treas.). Democrat. Mem. Self Realization Fellowship. Clubs: Camera (Kalamazoo), RESA (hon.) (Ithaca, Syracuse). Current work: Research and development of advanced technology for modulation/demodulation, coding/decoding, correlation and processing for secure and reliable military communications, with the aid of LSI/VLSI/VHSIC and microprocessors. Subspecialties: Telecommunications; Electronics. Home: 147 S Kingsley St Anaheim CA 92806 Office: Hughes Aircraft Co PO Box 2215 Fullerton CA 92633

MITCHELL, NANCY BROWN, human factors engineer; b. Chgo., Mar. 7, 1941; d. Edward Berrien and Jeannette (Landes) Brown; m. James Evans, Jr., July 18, 1961 (dec. 1979); children: James Evans, Thomas Edward, Janet Lucille. B.A., Montevallo U., 1967; M.S., U. Ga., 1974, Ph.D., 1976. Tchr. remedial reading Hannah J. Mallory Sch., Goodwater, Ala., 1967-71; research and teaching asst. U. Ga., Athens, 1971-75; spl. asst. So. Regional Edn. Bd., Atlanta, 1976-77; psychologist Dept. Youth Services, Birmingham, Ala., 1977; human engr. U.S. Army Infantry Sch., Columbus, Ga., 1977-80; human factors engr. Army Research Inst., Alexandria, Va., 1980-84; human factors engr., specialist Lockheed Missiles & Space Inc., Sunnyvale, Calif., 1984-85; sr. tech. analyst Human factors Decisions and Designs Inc., McLean, Va., 1985—. Bd. dirs. PTA, Sylacauga, Ala., 1965. Mem. Am. Psychol. Assn., Human Factors Soc., Women in Sci. and Engrng., Sigma Xi, Kappa Delta Pi. Current Work: Extension of surrogate travel over open terrain; purpose, simulation, tactical training; development and evaluation of displays for use in remotely piloted reconnaissance vehicles and tracked vehicles and human productivity in space. Subspecialties: Graphics, image processing, and pattern recognition; Human factors engineering. Office: Decisions and Designs Inc PO Box 907 McLean VA 22101

MITRA, JYOTIRMAY, biology educator; b. Calcutta, India, Nov. 25, 1921; s. Jnan Chandra and Aruna (Basu) M.; m. Bakul Mitra, Mar. 26, 1970. B.A. with honors, Calcutta U., 1942, M.A., 1944; Ph.D., Cornell U., 1955. Research asst. Bot. Survey of India, Calcutta, 1945-46; lectr. botany Calcutta U., 1948; research fellow Imperial Chem. Industries, Calcutta, 1948-51; research asso. Cornell U., Ithaca, N.Y., 1957-61; cytogeneticist-in-charge Beth Israel Med. Center, N.Y.C., 1961-77; assoc. prof. biology N.Y. U., N.Y.C., 1963-67, prof. biology, 1967—; cons. in field. Contbr. articles to profl. jours. Calcutta U. scholar, 1942-44; Sir R.B. Ghosh Research scholar, 1945; Fulbright and Smith-Mundt research scholar, 1952; NIH grantee, 1975; NSF grantee, 1977-80; Damon Runyon Cancer Research grantee, 1967-69; others. Mem. Genetics Soc. Am., Am. Genetic Assn., AAAS, Sigma Xi, Phi Kappa Phi. Club: Synapsis. Current Work: Cytogenetics and cytotaxonomy of Eukaryotic organisms; cancer genetics/cytogenetics. Subspecialties: Animal genetics; Plant genetics. Home: 4 Washington Square Village 4H New York NY 10012 Office: Dept Biology NY Univ New York NY 10003

MITSCH, WILLIAM JOSEPH, environmental educator, researcher, consultant; b. Wheeling, W.Va., Mar. 29, 1947; s. William Hughes and Evelyn Marie (Glaser) M.; m. Ruthmarie Hamburge, May 28, 1970; children—Rebecca Nell, Jane Frances. B.S., U. Notre Dame, 1969; M.E., U. Fla., 1972, Ph.D., 1975. Environ. specialist Commonwealth Edison, Chgo., 1970-71; grad. asst. U. Fla., Gainesville, 1971-75; asst. prof. Ill. Inst. Tech., Chgo., 1975-79; from asst. to assoc. prof. U. Louisville, Ky., 1979-84, prof. 1984—, acting dir. Ctr. Environ. Sci. and Mgmt., 1984—; cons., pres. Mitsch and Assocs., Louisville, 1979—. Author: Wetlands, 1985. Editor: Energy and Ecological Mod, 1981; Energetics and Systems, 1982. Editor newsletters; contbr. numerous articles to profl. jours. Environ. fellow AAAS, 1983; grantee U.S. Fish and Wildlife, Argonne Nat. Lab., Va. Environ. Endowment. Mem. Internat. Soc. Ecol. Modelling (sec. gen. 1982—), Ecol. Soc. Am. (cert.), AAAS, Sigma Xi (chpt. pres.). Roman Catholic. Current work: Ecology and management of freshwater wetlands, particularly aspects such as primary productivity, modelling, nutrient cycling, and protection techniques. Subspecialties: Ecosystems analysis; Ecology (environmental science). Home: 2238 Strathmoor Blvd Louisville KY 40205 Office: Ctr for Environ Sci and Mgmt U Louisville Louisville KY 40292

MITSCHER, LESTER ALLEN, chemist, educator; b. Detroit, Aug. 20, 1931; s. Lester and Mary Athelda (Pounder) M.; m. Betty Jane McRoberts, May 29, 1953; children: Katrina, Kurt, Mark. B.S., Wayne U., 1953, Ph.D., 1958. Research scientist, group leader Lederle Labs., Pearl River, N.Y., 1958-67; prof. Ohio State U., Columbus, 1967-75; Univ. disting. prof., chmn. dept. medicinal chemistry U. Kans., Lawrence, 1975—; inter-research prof. Victorian Coll. Pharmacy, Melbourne, Australia, 1975—; cons. NIH, Abbott Labs., Searle Labs., Adria Labs. Author: (with D. Lednicer) The Organic Chemistry of Drug Synthesis, Vol. 1, 1976, Vol. 2, 1980, Vol. 3, 1984, The Chemistry of the Tetracycline Antibiotics, 1978; contbr. over 140 articles to profl. jours. Recipient Disting. Alumnus award Sch. Pharmacy, Wayne State U., 1980, Research Achievement award Acad. Pharm. Scis., 1980. Mem. Am. Chem. Soc. (former chmn. and councilor medicinal chemistry div.), Chem. Soc. London, Japanese Antibiotics Assn., AAAS, Soc. Heterocyclic Chemistry, Am. Soc. Pharmacognosy. Presbyterian. Club: Elks. Subspecialty: Organic chemistry. Office: Dept Medicinal Chemistry U Kans Lawrence KS 66045

MITSUMOTO, HIROSHI, neurologist; b. Sapporo, Japan, Mar. 3, 1944; s. Masaji and Etsu M.; m. Chizuko Suzuki, Sept. 26, 1947; children: Ken Joseph, Jun Michael. B.S., Toho U., 1964, M.D., 1968, D. Med. Scis., 1981. Intern Toho U., Tokyo, 1968-69, asst. in internal medicine, 1969-72; intern Balt. City Hosp., 1972-73; resident in neurology Univ. Hosps., Cleve., 1973-76; fellow in neuropathology Cleve. Clinic, 1976-78, assoc. staff, 1978-79; research fellow Tufts-New Eng. Med. Ctr., Boston, 1979-81; asst. prof. neurology and neuropathology Case Western Res. U., Cleve., 1981-83, Cleve. Clinic, 1983—. Contbr. articles to profl. jours. Muscular Dystrophy Assn. Am. fellow, 1979-81; Amyotrophic Lateral Sclerosis Found. grantee, 1979-81, 82—; NIH grantee, 1982. Mem. Am. Acad. Neurology, Soc. Neuroscience, Am. Assn. Neuropathologists, Japanese Soc. Neurology. Current Work: Amyotrophic lateral sclerosis, murine motor neuron disease, neuromuscular diseases, axonal and neuronal regeneration, perhipheral neuropathies. Subspecialties: Neurology; Neuropathology. Home: 3387 Ingleside Shaker Heights OH 44122 Office: Cleve Clinic Cleveland OH 44106

MITTAL, CHANDRA KANT, educator, pharmacologist; b. Aligarh, Uttar Pradesh, India, Aug. 5, 1948; s. Murari Lal and Kanti Devi (Singhal) M.; m. Sarita Dayal, July 6, 1976; children: Richa, Hersh. B.S., U. Lucknow, India, 1967, M.S. in Biochemistry, 1969; Ph.D., All-India Med. Inst., 1975. Research fellow All-India Med. Inst., 1969-72, sr. research fellow, 1972-74; fellow in pharmacology U. Va., Charlottesville, 1974-77, research instr. pharmacology, 1977-80; asst. prof. U. Ill. Coll. Medicine, Peoria, 1980—. Contbr. articles on pharmacology to profl. jours. Am. Heart Assn. grantee, 1981-83, 85—. Mem. Am. Soc. for Exptl. Therapeutic Pharmacology. Current Work: Hypertension, drug receptors, cyclic nucleotides, calcium modulations, smooth muscle pharmacology. Subspecialties: Biochemistry (medicine); Molecular pharmacology. Office: One Illni Dr Peoria IL 61656

MITTLER, SIDNEY, biology educator; b. Detroit, Aug. 2, 1917; s. Max and Ida (Shulman) M.; m. Leonore Broder, Aug. 16, 1942; children: Jeanne, Judith, Michele; m. Judith W. Daskovsky, Aug. 10, 1969. B.S., Wayne U., 1938, M.S., 1939; Ph.D., U. Mich., 1944. Instr. Bowling Green (Ohio) State U., 1945-46; asst. prof. Ill. Inst. Tech., 1946-52; research biologist Armour Research Found., 1952-60; prof. biol. scis. No. Ill. U., DeKalb, 1960—. Contbr. articles to profl. jours. Served with M.C. U.S. Army, 1942-45. Recipient Award of Sci. Merit Morton Salt Co. and Chemistry dept. Armour Research Found., 1955. Fellow AAAS; mem. Radiation Research Soc., Genetics Soc. Am., Environ. Mutagenesis Soc., Am. Genetics Assn. Current Work: Research on effect of hyperthermia upon radiation induced genetic damage. Subspecialty: Radiation biology. Office: Dept Biol Sci No Ill Univ DeKalb IL 60115

MITYAGIN, BORIS SAMUEL, mathematician, researcher, math. educator; b. Voronezh, USSR, Aug. 12, 1937; came to U.S., 1978, naturalized, 1984; s. Samuel Yakov and Vera Alexander (Mityagin) Gasul; m. Sophia A. Katz, July 13, 1962; 1 dau., Xenia. M.S., Moscow State U., 1958, Sc.D., 1963. Asst. lectr. Voronezh State U., USSR, 1961-62, assoc. prof., 1962-64, prof., 1964-67; head lab. sr. researcher Central Econs. - Math. Inst., Acad. Sci., Moscow, USSR, 1967-78; prof. Moscow State U., 1968-73; vis. prof. Purdue U., 1978-79; prof. math. Ohio State U., 1979—, dir. Lab. Math. and Its Applications, 1985—. ; vis. prof. l'Ecole Polytechnique, Paris, 1978; prof. Inst. Math., Bonn (W.Ger.) U., 1979; Rothschild prof. Tel-Aviv (Israel) U., 1980; prof. Central U. Venezuela, Caracas, 1982; Disting. vis. prof. U. Toronto, Ont., Can., 1984; tech. asst. Corna & Co., Columbia, 1984—. Contbr. numerous articles to profl. jours.; mem. editorial bd.: Functional Analysis and Its Applications Jour, 1967-77, Integral Equations and Operator Theory Jour, 1981—; mem. adv. bd.: Jour. Math. Econs, 1973—. NFS grantee, 1979-82. Mem. Moscow Match. Soc.,

Am. Math. Soc., Soc. Indsl. and Applied Match. Club: Ohio State U. Faculty. Current Work: Research to develop general methods of linear and nonlinear functional analysis and apply them in differential equations, numerical analysis and models of economic dynamics. Subspecialties: Functional analysis and its applications; Applied mathematics. Home: 3538 La Rochelle Dr Upper Arlington OH 43221 Office: Ohio State U 231 W 18th Ave Columbus OH 43210

MITZEL, GLENN EARLE, engineer, educator; b. Annapolis, Md., July 5, 1951; s. Robert Earle and Doris Louvenia (Justice) M.; m. Patricia Gale Blanton, Sept. 2, 1973. B.S. in Elec. Engring., Johns Hopkins U., 1973, M.S. in Elec. Engring., 1975, Ph.D., 1977. Engr. Harry Diamond Lab., Washington, 1973; engr. Johns Hopkins U. Applied Physics Lab., Laurel, Md., 1974—; instr. Johns Hopkins Evening Coll., Laurel, 1974-83; instr. Johns Hopkins G.W.C. Whiting Sch. Engring., Balt., 1983—; prof. Chung-Yuan U., Chung-Li, Taiwan, 1983-84. Contbr. articles to profl. jours. William S. Parsons fellow, 1981-82. Mem. IEEE (sr.), Phi Beta Kappa. Presbyterian. Current work: Mathematical modeling and simulation; advanced signal and information processing. Subspecialties: Systems engineering; Applied mathematics. Home: 6706 White Gate Rd Clarksville MD 21029 Office: Johns Hopkins U Applied Physics Lab Johns Hopkins Rd Laurel MD 20707

MIYASHIRO, AKIHO, geologist, educator; b. Okayama Prefecture, Japan, Oct. 30, 1920; came to U.S, 1967; s. Tsuneshi and Hideyo (Shigemasa) M. B.S., U. Tokyo, 1943, Ph.D., 1953. Jr. instr. U. Tokyo, 1946-58, assoc. prof., 1958-67; vis. prof. Columbia U., N.Y.C., 1967-70; prof. SUNY, Albany, 1970—. Author: Metamorphism and Metamorphic Belts, 1973, Orogeny, 1982. Recipient Geol. Soc. Japan prize, 1958; P. Fourmarier prize Royal Acad. Belgium, 1981; P. Bose Meml medal Asiatic Soc., 1984. Fellow Geol. Soc. Am. (Arthur L. Day medal 1977), Mineral. Soc. Am.; hon. mem. Geol. Soc. London, Geol. Sco. France. Current Work: Metamorphic geology, metamorphic minerals, igneous petrology, tectonics. Subspecialty: Petrology. Home: 14 Stonehenge Dr Albany NY 12203 Office: Dept Geol Scis SUNY Albany NY 12222

MOCHIZUKI, LESLIE YASUKO, systems engineer; b. Los Angeles, May 16, 1959; d. Bruce Koji and Chieko (Asano) M. A.B. in Math, U. So. Calif., 1979. Mem. tech. staff Rockwell Internat., Anaheim, Calif., 1979—, mem. youth motivation task force, 1981-82, conservation com., 1982-83. Active Wintersburg Presbyn. Ch., Garden Grove, Calif. Mem. Am. Math. Soc., Soc. Indsl. and Applied Math., Soc. Women Engr. (assoc.), Alpha Epsilon Delta (life). Republican. Current Work: Currently designing and developing operational systems software for the Minuteman missile, designing requirements for code processing systems. Subspecialties: Mathematical software; Software engineering. Home: 3621 S Parton St Santa Ana CA 92707 Office: Rockwell Internat Anaheim CA 92803

MODAK, MUKUND JANARDAN, biochemist, biomedical research scientist; b. Satara, India, Dec. 12, 1942; came to U.S., 1970, naturalized, 1974; s. Janardan B. and Usha J. M.; m. Shanta M. Modak, Oct. 20, 1969; children: Rajiv, Rohit. B.Sc. (hons.), Poona (India) U., 1963; M. Sc., Bombay (India) U., 1965, Ph.D., 1969. NAITO Found. Overseas fellow U. Nagoya (Japan), 1970; research assoc. Columbia U., N.Y.C., 1971-72; research assoc. Sloan Kettering Inst. Cancer Research, N.Y.C., 1972-75, assoc., 1976-79, assoc. mem., 1979-85; assoc. prof. biochemistry, molecular biology and genetics Cornell U., 1979-85; prof. biochemistry U. Medicine and Dentistry N.J., Newark, 1985—. Contbr. articles to sci. jours. Haffkine Inst. of Bombay Diamond Jubilee fellow, 1966-69; Internat. Union Against Cancer vis. fellow, 1975; recipient Research Career Devel. award NIH, 1979. Mem. Am. Soc. Biol. Chemists, Am. Soc. Microbiology, Am. Soc. Virology, Am. Assn. Cancer Research. Current Work: Mechanisms of DNA synthesis, DNA enzymes, T cell differentiation, tumor virus enzymes. Subspecialties: Gene actions; Molecular biology. Office: Dept Biochemistry U Medicine and Dentistry NJ Newark NJ 07103

MODEL, PETER, scientist, researcher, consultant; b. Germany, May 17, 1933; s. Leo and Jane (Ermel) M.; m. Marjorie Russel, June 21, 1981; children: Paul, Sascha. B.A., Stanford U., 1954; Ph.D., Columbia U., 1965. Assoc. prof. Rockefeller U., N.Y.C.; cons. dir. Biotechnica Internat. Inst. for Sci. Info. Assoc. editor: Virology, Jour. Virology; contbr. articles to sci. publs. Served to 1st lt. U.S. Army, 1954-56. Mem. Am. Soc. Microbiology. Current Work: Bacteriophage assembly; assembly of proteins into membranes; structure and function of thioredoxin; translational control. Subspecialties: Molecular biology; Biochemistry (biology). Office: Rockefeller Univ New York NY 10021

MOE, GORDON KENNETH, physiologist, educator; b. Fairchild, Wis., May 30, 1915; s. Sylvester and Ellen Mae (Hanson) M.; m. Janet Woodruff Foster, Aug. 6, 1938; children—Christopher, Melanie, Jonathan, Bruce, Sally, Eric. Student, Virginia (Minn.) Jr. Coll., 1932-34; B.S., U. Minn., 1937, M.S., 1939, Ph.D., 1940; M.D., Harvard, 1943. Instr. Physiology U. Minn., 1939-40; instr. pharmacology Harvard Med. Sch., 1941-44; asst. prof. pharmacology U. Mich. Med. Sch., 1944-46, asso. prof., 1946-50; prof. physiology, chmn. dept. State U. N.Y. Coll. Medicine, Syracuse, 1950-60; dir. Masonic Med. Research Lab., Utica, N.Y., 1960-84; chmn. physiol. test com. Nat. Bd. Med. Examiners, 1956-57; mem. WHO (vis. scientists), Israel, Iran, 1951; cons. Walter Reed Army Med. Center.; Mem. Nat. Heart and Lung Adv. Council, 1970-74. Recipient travel award Internat. Physiol. Congress Oxford, 1947; Outstanding Achievement award U. Minn., 1958; Merit award Am. Heart Assn., 1968; Am. Physiol. Soc. fellow Western Res. U., 1940-41; USPHS fellow Instituto Nacional de Cardiologia, Mexico City, 1948. Fellow AAAS (chmn. sect. 1958), Am. Coll. Cardiology (hon.); mem. Am. Physiol. Soc., N.Y. Soc. Med. Research, Am. Heart Assn. (chmn. basic sci. council 1962-63, chmn. research com. 1959-60), Mexican Acad. Medicine (hon.), Mexican Soc. Cardiology (hon.), Sigma Xi, Alpha Omega Alpha. Club: Mason (33 deg.). Current Work: Cardiac electrophysiology. Subspecialty: Physiology (medicine). Office: Masonic Med Research Lab Utica NY 13503

MOE, JAMES BURTON, army officer, veterinary pathologist; b. Hayfield, Minn., Oct. 4, 1940; s. James Herald and Clara Clemnetine M.; m. Janice Naomi Nackerud, Nov. 27, 1959; children: Carolyn, Alyson, Jennifer, Bryce. B.S., U. Minn., 1962, D.V.M., 1964; Ph.D., U. Calif.-Davis, 1978. Cert. Am. Coll. Vet. Pathologists, 1973. Gen. practice vet. medicine Dodge Center, Minn., 1964-66; practice vet. medicine specializing in preventive vet. medicine, Ft. Bliss, Tex., 1966-68; commd. 2d lt. U.S. Army, 1966, advanced through grade to lt. col., 1979, resident in pathology, Ft. Detrick, Md., 1969-73, microbiol.-path. researcher, 1973-75; 78-80; with research mgmt. div. Walter Reed Army Inst. Research, Washington, 1980—, dir. div. pathology; cons. pathology, cons. to Surgeon Gen. of Army; chmn. instl. Biosafety Com. Contbr. articles on pathology, microbiology and infectious diseases. Decorated Bronze Star.; Calif. Lung Assn. grantee, 1976-77. Mem. Am. Coll. Vet. Pathologists, AVMA, Internat. Acad. Pathology, Am. Assn. Pathologists. Lutheran. Current Work: Experimental pathology, director research division engaged in basic and applied aspects of infectious diseases, toxicology and drug and vaccine development. Subspecialties: Pathology (veterinary medicine); Microbiology (medicine). Office: Walter Reed Army Inst Research Washington DC 20012

MOE, RODERICK DONALD, SR., meteorologist; b. Rochester, Minn., Mar. 29, 1924; s. Carl Oscar and Alice Hildegarde (Carlson) M.; m. Charlene Estelle Martin, Aug. 31, 1951; children—Mary Katherine Yogi, Roderick D. Jr., Erica Lynne. M.S., Tex. A&M U., 1965; B.S., U. Minn., 1949; Ph.B., U. Chgo., 1947. Commd. aviation cadet, U.S. Air Force; 1943, advanced through grades to col., 1970; weather officer, High Wycombe, Eng., 1965-68; intelligence specialist, Saigon and Honolulu, 1968-70; ret., 1970; research coordinator Inst. Storm Research, Houston, 1970-71; environ. health specialist Austin-Travis Co. Health Dept., Tex., 1971-73; air quality specialist State Dept. Hwys. & Pub. Transp., Austin, 1973—. Contbr. articles to profl. jours. Com. mem. Transp. Research Bd., Washington, 1974—; panel mem. Nat. Coop. Hwy. Research Program, 1976-82; mem. task force on environment Clean Air Act Com. Am. Assn. State Hwy. and Transp. Ofcls., 1981—. Mem. Am. Meteorol. Soc. (chpt. pres. 1968), Air Pollution Control Assn. (chpt. pres. 1978). Mem. Christian Ch. Club: Austin Kennel, Austin Bonzai. Current work: Research on air quality modeling along highways and air quality modeling of mobile source emissions in urban areas; effect of gravity waves. Subspecialties: Meteorology; Meteorologic instrumentation. Home: 1502 The High Rd Austin TX 78746 Office: State Dept Hwys & Pub Transp D-8 11th St & Brazos Ave Austin TX 78701-2483

MOEHRING, JOAN MARQUART, microbiology educator; b. Orchard Park, N.Y., Sept. 23, 1935; d. Carl B. and Marjorie H. (Pearson) Marquart; m. Thomas J. Moehring, June 6, 1964. B.S., Syracuse U., 1961; M.S., Rutgers U., 1963, Ph.D., 1965. Postdoctoral fellow Stanford U., 1965-68; research assoc. U. Vt., 1968-73, research prof. dept. med. microbiology, 1973—; cons. in field. Contbr. articles to profl. jours. NIH grantee, 1973—. Mem. Am. Soc. Microbiology, Am. Soc. Cell Biology, Phi Beta Kappa, Sigma Xi. Current Work: Study of action of microbial toxins in mammalian cells, biological research. Subspecialties: Cell and tissue culture; Microbiology. Office: U Vt Dept Med Microbiology B210 Given Bldg Burlington VT 05405

MOELLER, DADE WILLIAM, environmental engineer, educator; b. Grant, Fla., Feb. 27, 1927; s. Robert A. and Victoria (Bolton) M.; m. Betty Jean Radford, Oct. 7, 1949; children: Garland Radford, Mark Bolton, William Kehne, Matthew Palmer, Elisabeth Anne. B.C.E., Ga. Inst. Tech., 1947, M.S. in Civil Engring, 1948; Ph.D., N.C. State U., 1957. Commd. jr. asst. san. engr. USPHS, 1948, advanced through grades to san. engr. dir., 1961; research engr. Los Alamos Sci. Lab., 1949-52; staff asst. Radiol. Health Program, Washington, 1952-54; research asso. Oak Ridge Nat. Lab., 1956-57; chief radiol. health tng. Taft San. Engring. Center, Cin., 1957-61; officer charge Northeastern Radiol. Health Lab., Winchester, Mass., 1961-66; assoc. dir. Kresge Center Environ. Health, Harvard Sch. Pub. Health, 1966-83, prof. engring. in environmental health, head dept. environmental health scis., 1968-83, dir. Office of Continuing Edn., 1982-84, assoc. dean for continuing edn., 1985—; cons. radiol. health Profl. Exam. Service, Am. Pub. Health Assn., 1960-62, WHO, 1965—. Contbr. articles to profl. jours. Chmn. Am. Bd. Health Physics, 1967-70; mem. Nat. Council Radiation Protection and Measurements, 1968—; mem. com. 4 Internat. Commn. on Radiol. Protection, 1978-85; chmn. nat. air pollution manpower devel. adv. com. U.S. Environ. Protection Agy., 1972-75; mem. adv. com. reactor safeguards U.S. Nuclear Regulatory Commn., 1973—, vice chmn., 1975, chmn., 1976. Fellow Am. Pub. Health Assn., Am. Nuclear Soc.; mem. Am. Acad. Environ. Engrs. (bd. dirs. 1968-73), Nat. Acad. Engring., Health Physics Soc. (pres. 1971-72), AAAS. Current Work: Natural background radiation; control of airborne radon decay products inside buildings; planning for nuclear emergencies; nuclear air cleaning; safety of nuclear power plants. Subspecialties: Environmental engineering; Gas cleaning systems. Home: 27 Wildwood Dr Bedford MA 01730 Office: 677 Huntington Ave Boston MA 02115

MOERNER, WILLIAM ESCO, laser research physicist, solid state physicist, laser photochemist; b. Pleasanton, Calif., June 24, 1953; s. William Alfred and Bertha Frances (Robinson) M.; m. Sharon Judith Stein, June 19, 1983. B.S. in Physics, Washington U., St. Louis, 1975, A.B. in Math., 1975, B.S. in Elec. Engring., 1975; M.S. in Physics, Cornell U., 1978, Ph.D. in Physics, 1982. Research asst. Cornell U., Ithaca, N.Y., 1978-81; mem. research staff IBM Research Labs., San Jose, Calif., 1981—. Contbr. articles to tech. jours. Mem., singer Gilbert and Sullivan Soc., San Jose, 1982—; tenor San Jose Symphonic Choir, 1984—. Langsdorff fellow Washington U., 1971, NSF grad. fellow, 1975; research contract Office Naval Research, 1984. Mem. Am. Phys. Soc., Optical Soc. Am., IEEE, Am. Chem. Soc. Current works: Laser-induced processes in condensed matter such as new photo-chemical or photophysical processes in order to find new spectral hole- burning materials for frequency domain optical data storage. Subspecialties: Condensed matter physics; Laser spectroscopy. Office: IBM Research Lab K32/281 5600 Cottle Rd San Jose CA 95193

MOERTEL, CHARLES GEORGE, physician; b. Milw., Oct. 17, 1927; s. Charles Henry and Alma Helen (Soffel) M.; m. Virginia Claire Sheridan, Mar. 22, 1952; children: Charles Stephen, Christopher Loren, Heather Lynn, David Matthew. B.S., U. Ill., 1946-51, M.D., 1953; M.S., U. Minn., 1958. Intern Los Angeles County Hosp., 1953-54; resident in internal medicine Mayo Found., Rochester, Minn., 1954-57; cons. Mayo Clinic, Rochester, 1957—, chmn. dept. oncology, 1975—; dir. Mayo Comprehensive Cancer Center, 1975—; prof. medicine Mayo Med. Sch., 1972-76, prof. oncology, 1976—; mem. oncologic drugs adv. com. FDA; mem. cancer adv. com. AMA; mem. bd. sci. counselors, div. resources, centers and community activities Nat. Cancer Inst. Author: Multiple Primary Malignant Neoplasms, 1966, Advanced gastrointestinal Cancer, Clinical Management and Chemotherapy, 1969; editorial bd.: Cancer, 1974—, Cancer Medicine, 1978—, Current Problems in Cancer, 1978-84, Jour. Soviet Oncology, 1979—, Cancer Research, 1979-84, Cancer Treatment Rep, 1980-82, Internat. Jour. Radiation Oncology Biol. Physics, 1981—. Served with U.S. Army, 1946-47. Walter Hubert lectr. Brit. Assn. Cancer Research, 1976; Ejnar Perman Meml. lectr. Swedish Surg. Assn., 1978. Mem. Am. Soc. Clin. Oncology (pres. 1979-80), Soc. Clin. Trials (dir.), Am. Assn. Cancer Research, Gastrointestinal Tumor Study Group (co-chmn.), A.C.P., Soc. Surg. Oncology, Am. Gastroenterologic Assn., North Central Cancer Treatment Group (chmn.), Sigma Xi. Research in treatment of gastrointestinal cancer, clin. pharmacology. Subspecialties: Cancer research (medicine); Oncology. Home: 1009 Skyline Ln SW Rochester MN 55902 Office: 200 SW 1st St Rochester MN 55905

MOFFAT, ANTHONY FREDERICK JOHN, astronomy researcher and educator; b. Toronto, Ont., Can., Jan. 30, 1943; s. Bryce F. and Margaret E. (Boorman) M.; m. Ruth Ann Huntley, Sept. 10, 1966; children: Bryce A., Lesley A. B.Sc., U. Toronto, 1965, M.Sc., 1966; Dr. rer. nat., Ruhr (W.Ger.) U., 1970, Dr. Habil., 1976. Sci. asst. U. Bonn, W.Ger., 1966-69; sci. asst. Ruhr U., 1970-76; assoc. prof. astronomy U. Montreal, 1977-80, prof., 1981—. Contbr. articles to profl. jours. Recipient Silver medal in physics and math. U. Toronto, 1965; Gold medal Royal Astron. Soc. Can., 1965; Imperial Oil Can. Ltd. fellow, 1966-69; NRC of Can. grantee, 1977—; Alexander von Humboldt research fellow, 1982. Mem. Internat. Astron. Union, Am. Astron. Soc., Can. Astron. Soc., Royal Astron. Soc. Can., Astronomische Gesellschaft. Current Work: The nature of massive stars, young star clusters; structure and dynamics of milky way system. Subspecialty: Optical astronomy. Office: Dept Physique U Montreal CP 6128 Montreal PQ H3C 3J7 Canada

MOFFAT, JOHN WILLIAM, physics educator; b. Copenhagen, Denmark, May 24, 1932; s. George William and Esther (Winther) M. Ph.D., Trinity Coll., Cambridge (Eng.) U., 1958. Sr. research fellow Imperial Coll., London, Eng., 1957-58; scientist Research Inst. Advanced Studies, Balt., 1958-60, prin. scientist, 1961-64; scientist CERN, Geneva, Switzerland, 1960-61; asso. prof. dept. physics U. Toronto, Ont., Can., 1964-67, prof., 1967—. Contbr. articles to profl. jours. Dept. Sci. and Indsl. Research fellow, 1958-60; NRC Can. grantee, 1965. Fellow Cambridge Philos. Soc. (Eng.). Current Work: Theory of gravitation, unified gauge theories, early universe cosmology, astronomy and astrophysics. Subspecialties: Relativity and gravitation; Particle physics. Office: Dept Physics U Toronto Toronto ON Canada

MOHAMMAD, SYED FAZAL, biochemical educator, researcher; b. India, Sept. 2, 1942; came to U.S., 1972; s. Shafi and Nisa (Chaudhry) M.; m. Rani Failbus, Feb. 27, 1969; children—Zeenat, Habeeb. B.S., U. Lucknow, India, 1961, M.S., 1963; Ph.D., All India Inst. Med. Scis., 1972. Postdoctoral fellow U. N.C., Chapel Hill, 1972-75; clin. instr. Brown U., Providence, 1975-77; asst. prof. U. South Fla., Tampa, 1977-79; research asst. prof. pathology, U. Utah, Salt Lake City, 1979-80, research assoc. prof., 1980—. Contbr. articles to sci. jours., chpts. to books. NIH grantee. Mem. Am. Assn. Pathologists, N.Y. Acad. Scis., AAAS, Internat. Soc. Thrombosis and Hemostasis. Democrat. Current work: Biochemistry and pathology of coagulation, hemostasis and thrombosis. Subspecialties: Biochemistry (biology); Hematology. Office: Dept Pathology U Utah 50 N Medical Dr Salt Lake City UT 84132

MOHANTY, NIRODE CHANDRA, electrical engineer; b. Soro, India, Jan. 18, 1937; s. Chakra Dhar and Sabitri (Das) M.; m. Sneha Das, May 21, 1964; children: Bapi, Lisa. M.S., Utkal U., Bhubaneswar, India, 1960, U. So. Calif., 1968; M.S. in Elec. Engring, U. So. Calif., 1971; Ph.D., 1972. Prof. Utkal U., 1960-66; research scholar U. So. Calif., 1966-73; prof. SUNY-Buffalo, 1973-75; research engr. Systems Control Co., 1975-76; sr. engring. specialist Ford Aerospace, Newport Beach, Calif., 1976-81; mgr. communications simulation Aerospace Corp., Los Angeles, 1981—; mem. tech. staff Rockwell Internat., Los Angeles, 1976-79. Contbr. articles to profl. jours. Recipient Excellence in Creativity award Rockwell Internat., 1978. Mem. IEEE (sr. mem. chmn. info. theory div. 1973-75, chmn. nat. aerospace and electronics div. 1979), Internat. Telemetry Conf. (chmn. 1980). Current Work: Signal processing, as related to radar, sonar, electrooptics, speech, music and computer vision, communications systems. Subspecialties: Electrical engineering; Information systems (Information science). Home: 18362 Springtime Huntington Beach CA 92646 Office: Aerospace Corp PO Box 92957 Los Angeles CA 90009

MOHANTY, SASHI B., virologist, educator; b. India, Sept. 4, 1932; came to U.S., 1960, naturalized, 1985; s. Madhu s. and Narayani (Parida) M.; m. Pranoti Samal, July 3, 1957; children: Nibedita, Bibhu, Nihar, Puspa. B.V.Sc., Bihar U., India, 1956; M.S., U. Md., 1961, Ph.D., 1963. Vet. surgeon, Orissa, India, 1956-60; asst. prof. vet. sci. U. Md., College Park, 1963-69, assoc. prof., 1969-74, prof., 1974—; vis. prof. U. Munich, W.Ger., 1972-73; cons. Flow Lab., Rockville, Md., Indsl. Biologic Lab., Rockville. Author: Veterinary Virology, 1981, Electron Microscopy for Biologist, 1982; contbr. chpts. to books, articles to profl.jours. NIH grantee, 1963-65; U.S. Dept. Agr. grantee, 1977—. Mem. AVMA, Am. Soc. Microbiology, Electron Microscopy Soc. Am., Soc. for Exptl. Biology and Medicine, Sigma Xi. Current Work: Pathogenesis and prevention of bovine respiratory viruses; effect of interferon and antiviral drugs on bovine repsitory viruses; electron microscopy of viruses and cells. Subspecialties: Virology (veterinary medicine); Internal medicine (veterinary medicine). Home: 4306 Kenny St Beltsville MD 20705 Office: U Md College Park MD 20742

MOHIUDDIN, SYED MAQDOOM, cardiologist, educator; b. Hyderabad, India, Nov. 14, 1934; came to U.S., 1961, naturalized, 1976; s. Syed Nizamuddin and Amat-Ul-Butool Mahmoodi; m. Ayesha Sultana Mahmoodi, July 16, 1961; children: Sameena J., Syed R., Kulsoom S. M.B., B.S., Osmania U., 1960; M.S., Creighton U., Omaha, 1967; D.Sc., Laval U., Que., Can., 1970. Diplomate: Am. Bd. Internal Medcine (cardiovascular disease). Intern Altoona (Pa.) Gen. Hosp., 1961-62; resident in cardiology Creighton Meml. Hosp., also St. Joseph Hosp., Omaha, 1963-65, mem. staff, 1965—; prof. adjoint Laval U. Med. Sch., 1970; practice medicine specializing in cardiology, Omaha, 1970—; prof. Creighton U. Med. Sch., 1977—, assoc. dir. div. cardiology, 1983—; cons. Omaha VA Hosp. Research fellow Med. Research Council Can., 1968; grantee Med. Research Council Can., 1970; grantee NIH, 1973. Fellow ACP, Am. Coll. Cardiology; mem. Am. Heart Assn. (fellow council clin. cardiology), Am. Fedn. Clin. Research, Nebr. Heart Assn. (chmn. research com. 1974-76, dir. 1973-85), Gt. Plains Heart Com. (Nebr. rep. 1976-85, pres. 1977-78), Nebr. Cardiovascular Soc. (pres. 1980-81), N.Y. Acad. Scis. Democrat. Islam. Current Work: Cardiovascular drugs, cardiac pacemaker, echo-cardiography, cardiovascular education. Subspecialties: Cardiology; Internal medicine. Home: 12531 Shamrock Rd Omaha NE 68154 Office: 601 30th St Omaha NE 68131

MOHLA, SURESH, endocrinologist; b. Calcutta, India, May 5, 1943; came to U.S., 1970, naturalized, 1983; s. Rai Sahib Karam Ch and Shakuntla Devi (Kumaria) M.; m. Chitra Mohla Harisingh, Aug. 31, 1969; 1 dau. Anjali. B.Sc. with honors, U. Delhi, 1963, M.Sc., 1965, Ph.D., 1968. Postdoctoral fellow U. Delhi, India, 1968-70; research assoc. U. Chgo., 1970-75, 75-76; asst. prof. oncology Howard U., Washington, 1977-82, assoc. prof., 1982—; dir. hormone receptor support lab. Howard U. (Cancer Ctr.), 1976—, program dir. endocrinology, 1979—; chmn. research com. Howard U. (Coll. Medicine), 1983—; Mem. adv. com. on anti-smoking Am. Cancer Soc., Washington, 1980-82; mem. speaker's bur. Cancer Coordinating Council and Cancer Info. Service for Met. Washington, 1979—. Recipient Travel award NFS, 1978; NIH research grantee, 1980—. Mem. Am. Assn. Cancer Research, Am. Physiol. Soc., Endocrine Soc., Am. Soc. Cell Biology. Hindu. Current Work: Hormonal control of growth in normal and neoplastic tissues and mechanism of steroid hormone action, clinical significant of steroid hormone receptors in human breast and prostate cancers, androgen regulation of nitrosamine metabolism in the kidney. Subspecialties: Cancer research (medicine); Endocrinology. Home: 6440 Franconia Ct Springfield VA 22150 Office: Howard U Cancer Ctr 2041 Georgia Ave NW Washington DC 20060

MOHLER, ORREN CUTHBERT, educator, astronomer; b. Indpls., July 28, 1908; s. Charles Mikesell and Mary Ann (Culp) M.; m. Helen Jean Beal, June 10, 1935; children—Alice Beal (Mrs. William George DeLana), Jane Radcliffe (Mrs. Jeffery Wessels Barry). A.B., Mich. State Normal Coll., 1929; M.A. (State Coll. fellow 1929), U. Mich., 1930, Ph.D. (Lawton fellow 1930-33), 1933; D.Sc. (hon.), Eastern Mich. U., 1956. Instr. astronomy Swarthmore Coll., 1933-40; astromomer Cook Obs., Wynnewood, Pa., 1933-40; observer McMath-Hulbert Obs., U. Mich., 1933; dir. Obs., 1961—, mem. faculty univ., 1940—, prof. astronomy, 1955-78, emeritus prof. astronomy, 1978—, chmn. dept. astronomy, dir. observatories, 1962-71; adj. prof. physics Oakland U., 1980—; dir. Assn. Univs. Research Astronomy, Tucson, 1961-74, chmn. scientific com., 1965-73; Vice pres. U.S. Nat. Com. Internat. Astron. Union, 1962-65; Bd. govs. Cranbrook Inst. Sci., 1960—. Author: Photometric Atlas of the Near Infrared Solar Spectrum, 1950, Table of Solar Spectrum Wave Lengths, 1955; also articles. Recipient USN award, 1946; Fulbright research scholar Inst. d'Astrophysique, Liege, 1960-61. Mem. Am., Astron. Soc., Royal Astron. Soc. Can., Phi Beta Kappa, Sigma Xi. Clubs: Univ. Research (pres. 1966-67), Sci. Research (pres. 1970-71), Ann Arbor Golf and Outing; Torch (Oakland County). Current Work: Encyclopedic table of wave lengths in solar spectrum; sunspot cycle; design of large solar telescopes, design and development of detectors of radiation. Subspecialties: Optical astronomy; Solar physics. Home: 405 Awixa Rd Ann Arbor MI 48104

MOHNEY, LEONE LAURA, microbiologist; b. Raton, N.Mex., May 29, 1935; d. Curtis Gilliam and Ruth Clara (Jillson) M. B.S., U. Ariz., 1957; M.S., U. Calif., Berkeley, 1961. Research asst. George W. Hooper Found., U. Calif., San Francisco, 1958-60; research assoc. U. Calif. Sch. Pub. Health, Berkeley, 1961-77; research asst. dept. microbiology U. Ariz., Tucson, 1978-81, research asst. Environ. Research Lab., 1983—; research asst. U. Ariz. Health Scis. Center, Tucson, 1981-83. Active LWV, Berkeley, 1963-77. Mem. Am. Soc. for Microbiology, Am. Inst. Biol. Scis., Assn. Women in Sci. Republican. Presbyterian. Current Work: Study of microbial diseases of shrimp. Subspecialty: Microbiology. Office: Dept Aquaculture Pathology Environmental Research Lab Tucson Internat Airport Tucson AZ 85706

MOHR, JOHN LUTHER, marine biologist, consultant, parasitic protozoan researcher; b. Reading, Pa., Dec. 1, 1911; s. Luther Seth and Anna Elizabeth (Davis) M.; m. Frances Edith Christensen, Nov. 23, 1939; children—Jeremy John, Christopher Charles. A.B. in Biology, Bucknell U., 1933; student Oberlin Coll., 1933-34; Ph.D. in Zoology, U. Calif.-Berkeley, 1939. Microtechnician U. Calif.-Berkeley, 1938-42; research assoc. Pacific Islands Project, Stanford U., Palo Alto, Calif., 1942-44, Hancock Found., U. So. Calif., Los Angeles, 1944-47; from asst. prof. to prof. zoology, biology, biol. sci. U. So. Calif., Los Angeles, 1947-77, prof. emeritus, cons., 1977—; prin. investigator harbor surveys, 1948-51, research drifting station projects, Arctic Ocean, 1952-71, Antarctic Research Vessel Eltanin, 1962-65; research assoc. malacology Los Angeles County Mus. Natural History, 1970—; bd. dirs. Calif. Natural Areas Coordinating Council, 1974—. Sci. adv. com. Conception-Arguello problems State Lands Commn., Sacramento, 1983; speaker at workshops Environ. Def. Ctr., 1985—; mem. Biol. Stain Commn., 1948—, trustee, 1971-81, emeritus, 1981—. Guggenheim fellow 1957-58. Fellow AAAS (council mem. 1964-73), So. Calif. Acad. Scis.; Marine Biol. Assn. U.K. (life), mem. Sigma Xi (life; bd. dirs. 1964-67, 68, 69). Democrat. Mem. Huxleyans. Current work: Analysis of industry studies and agency documents, EPA, MMS agents; recommendations to state agencies; study of standards of professional behavior. Subspecialty: Marine biology. Home and Office: 3819 Chanson Dr Los Angeles CA 90043

MOKLER, CORWIN MORRIS, pharmacologist, educator; b. Forsyth, Ill., Dec. 10, 1925; s. Morris Michael and Mary Lois (Goodrich) M.; m. Margaret Mary Costello, Aug. 15, 1950; children: David James, Gregory Alan. B.A., Colo. Coll., 1950; M.S., U. Nev., 1952; Ph.D., U. Ill., 1958. Sr. investigator G.D. Searle & Co., Skokie, Ill., 1958-61; asst. prof. U. Fla. Coll. Pharmacy, Gainesville, 1961-67; assoc. prof. U. Ga. Sch. Pharmacy, Athens, 1967—. Contbr. articles to profl. jours. Served with USNR, 1943-46. Mem. Am. Soc. Pharmacology and Exptl. Therapeutics, Am. Heart Assn., Athens Choral Soc., Internat. Soc. Heart Research, Sigma Xi. Current work: Cardiovascular physiology, pharmacology. Subspecialties: Pharmacology; Physiology (medicine). Office: Sch Pharmacy U Ga Athens GA 30602

MOLDENHAUER, JEANNE ELISABETH, microbiologist, consultant; b. Chgo., July 22, 1951; d. Richard E. and Dorothy C. Gibbons. A.A., Wright Coll., Chgo., 1972; B.A. with honors, U. Mo., St. Louis, 1974; M.S. with honors, Loyola U., Chgo., 1977. Teaching asst. Loyola U., 1976-77; developer quality systems for immunological and microbiol. new product line Lab Tek div. Miles Labs., Naperville, Ill., 1979-80; prin. engr. Travenol Labs., Round Lake, Ill., 1980—. Mem. Am. Soc. Quality Control (cert. quality engr., mem. FDS subdiv.), Am. Soc. Microbiology, Ill. Soc. Microbiology, Tissue Culture Assn., Muscular Dystrophy Assn., South Central Assn. Clin. Microbiology. Mem. Christian Ch. Club: Navigators (Colorado Springs, Colo.). Patentee cell culture media supplement. Current Work: Chemical serum replacements; muscular viral infectivity; diagnostic virology; computer applications for qualification, validation plant assistance, troubleshooting, develop quality systems, and methods of sterilization, improved cycles, trend analysis. Subspecialties: Cell and tissue culture; Operating systems. Office: Travenol Labs Wilson Rd and Belvidere Round Lake IL 60073

MOLDENHAUER, WILLIAM CALVIN, soil scientist; b. New Underwood, S.D., Oct. 27, 1923; s. Calvin Fred and Ida Killam M.; m. Catherine Anne Maher, Nov. 26, 1947; children—Jean Ann Cash, Patricia Bortnem, Barbara Lee, James Alan, Thomas John. B.S., S.D. State U., 1949; M.S., U. Wis., 1951, Ph.D., 1956; Cert. profl. soil scientist; profl. in erosion and sediment control. Soil surveyor S.D. State U., Brookings, 1949-54; soil scientist USDA Agr. Research Sta., Big Spring, Tex., 1954-57, Ames, Iowa, 1957-72, Morris, Minn., 1972-75, supervisory scientist, research leader, West Lafayette, Ind., 1975-81, supervisory soil scientist, research leader Nat. Soil Erosion Lab., 1981—. Contbr. articles to profl. jours. Served with AUS, 1943-46. Fellow Soil Conservation Soc. Am. (pres. 1979), Soil Sci. Soc. Am., Am. Soc. Agronomy; mem. Am. Soc. Agrl. Engrs., World Assn. Soil and Water Conservation (pres. 1983—). Current work: Erosion research; tillage research; soil physical properties. Subspecialties: Soil science; Resource conservation. Home: 400 N River Rd #1140 West Lafayette IN 47906 Office: Nat Soil Erosion Lab Purdue U Bldg Soil West Lafayette IN 47907

MOLINA, LUISA TAN, chemist; b. Manila, Philippines, Jan. 14, 1945; came to U.S., 1966; d. Hay and Dorotea (Yu) Tan; m. Mario Jose Molina, July 12, 1973; 1 child, Felipe Jose. B.Sc. in Chemistry, McGill U., 1966; Ph.D. in Chemistry, U. Calif.-Berkeley, 1970. Research chemist IBM Corp., San Jose, Calif., 1970-71; dir. ednl. opportunity program U. Calif., Berkeley, 1971-72, asst. prof. chemistry, Santa Cruz, 1972-73, lectr. chemistry, Irvine, 1973-76, assoc. specialist, 1976-82; research scientist Jet Propulsion Lab., Pasadena, Calif., 1985—. Nat. Research Council Sr. Research associateship, 1983-85. Mem. Am. Chem. Soc. Democrat. Roman Catholic. Current work: Atmospheric chemistry, molecular spectroscopy, investigate the physical and photochemical changes of molecules of atmospheric interest. Subspecialties: Physical chemistry; Photochemistry. Home: 1415 Sugar Loaf Dr La Canada Flintridge CA 91011 Office: Jet Propulsion Lab 4800 Oak Grove Dr Pasadena CA 91109

MOLL, DON L., ecologist, educator, researcher; b. Peoria, Ill., Oct. 3, 1949; s. Edward and Bessie I. (Kennedy) M.; m. Barbara Kay Rogers, Mar. 17, 1972; children: Jane Elisabeth, Bryan Christopher. B.S., Ill. State U., 1971; M.S., Western Ill. U., 1973; Ph.D., Ill. State U., 1977. Asst. prof. biology Southwest Mo. State U., Springfield, 1977-82, assoc. prof. biology, 1982—; cons. Mo. Dept. Conservation, Jefferson City, 1980-82, U.S. Fish and Wildlife Service, Washington, 1980, World Wildlife Fund, Washington, 1983, Internat. Union Conservation Nature and Natural Resources, Gland, Switzerland, 1981—. Contbr. numerous articles to profl. jours. Southwest Mo. State U. grantee, 1982, 83; World Wildlife Fund grantee, 1984; Fauna and Flora Preservation Soc. grantee, 1984. Mem. Am. Soc. Ichthyologists and Herpetologists, Herpetologists League, Soc. Study Amphibians and Reptiles, Mo. Acad. Sci., Nat. Audubon Soc., Bobby Witcher Soc., Sigma Xi (assoc.). Clubs: Alligator Snapper Soc, Gretna, La. Current Work: Paleoecology of marine turtles, ecology of endangered reptiles and amphibians, foraging ecology and interactions in aquatic vertebrate communities. Subspecialties: Ecology (environmental science); Species interaction. Home: 2455 S Aspen Springfield MO 65807 Office: Dept Biology Southwest Mo State U 901 S National Springfield MO 65804

MOLL, JOHN LEWIS, electronics engineer; b. Wauseon, Ohio, Dec. 21, 1921; s. Samuel Andrew and Esther (Studer) M.; m. Isabel Mary Sieber, Oct. 28, 1944; children: Nicolas Josef, Benjamin Alex, Diana Carolyn. B.Sc., Ohio State U., 1943, Ph.D., 1952; Dr. h.c., Faculty Engring., Katholieke U. Leuven, (Belgium), 1983. Elec. engr. RCA Labs., Lancaster, Pa., 1943-45; mem. tech. staff Bell Telephone Labs., Murray Hill, N.J., 1952-58; mem. faculty Stanford U., 1958-69, prof. elec. engring., 1959-69; tech. dir. optoelectronics Fairchild Camera and Instrument Corp., 1969-74; dir. integrated circuits labs. Hewlett-Packard Labs., Palo Alto, Calif., 1974-80, dir. IC structures research, sr. scientist, 1980—. Author: Physics of Semi Conductors, 1964. Guggenheim fellow, 1964; Recipient Howard N. Potts medal Franklin Inst., 1967, Disting. Alumnus award Coll. Engring., Ohio State U., 1970. Fellow IEEE (Ebers award 1971); mem. Am. Phys. Soc., Nat. Acad. Engring., Sigma Xi, Sigma Pi Sigma. Current Work: Integrated circuits structure research. Subspecialty: Integrated circuits. Home: 4111 Old Trace Rd Palo Alto CA 94306 Office: 3500 Deer Creek Rd Palo Alto CA 94304

MOLLENAUER, LINN FREDERICK, physicist; b. Washington, Pa., Jan. 6, 1937; s. Donley Uhr and Alice (Hartz) M.; m. Marjorie Lynn Trammel, Aug. 4, 1962; children—David E., James E. B.Eng.Physics, Cornell U., 1959; Ph.D. in Physics, Stamford U., 1965. Asst. prof. phsyics U. Calif., Berkeley, 1966-72; mem. tech. staff, staff scientist Bell Labs., Holmdel, N.J., 1972—. Contbr. articles to profl. jours., chpts. to books. Editor: Tunable Lasers, 1985. Recipient R.W. Wood prize, Optical Soc. Am., 1982; Disting. Tech. staff award, Bell Labs., 1982. Fellow Optical Soc. Am., AAAS; mem. IEEE, Am. Phys. Soc. Current work: Lasers: inventor, developer of tunable color center laser; pioneering studies of short pulses and solitons in optical fibers. Subspecialty: Fiber optics. Home: 11 Carriage Hill Dr Colts Neck NJ 07722 Office: Bell Labs Rm 4C-306 Crawford Corner Rd Holmdel NJ 07733

MOLZ, FRED JOHN, III, civil engineering educator, hydrologist; b. Mays Landing, N.J., Aug. 13, 1943; s. Fred John Jr., and Viola Violet (MacDonald) M.; m. Mary Lee Clark, Dec. 17, 1966; children—Fred John IV, Stephen Joseph. B.S. in Physics, Drexel U., 1966, M.S. in Civil Engring., 1968; Ph.D. in Hydrology, Stanford U., 1970. Registered profl. engr., Ala. Asst. prof. civil engring. Auburn U., Ala., 1970-76, alumni assoc. prof., 1976-80, engring expt. sta. dir., asst. dean for research, 1979-84, Feagin Prof., 1984—; vis. prof. Univ. Ill., Urbana, 1977; cons. Elec. Power Research Inst., Palo Alto, Calif., 1984—. Author: (with others) Numerical Methods in Subsurface Hydrology, 1970; Modeling Wastewater Renovation, 1981. Contbr. articles to profl. jours. Recipient S.J. Leonard Meml. award Drexel Univ., 1968; named Moore Lectr. U. Va., 1977; NSF fellow. 1970. Mem. Am. Geophys. Union, Soil Sci. Soc. Am., Am. Soc. Plant Physiologists, Nat. Water Well Assn. Club: Auburn Stating (pres. 1982-83). Current work: Soil-plant-atmosphere system including contaminant dispersion in groundwater and numerical modeling thereof. Subspecialties: Hydrology; Numerical analysis (computer science). Home: 1224 Ferndale Ct Auburn AL 36830 Office: Civil Engring Dept Auburn University Auburn AL 36849

MONAGHAN, LEO JOHN, polymer chemist, engineer; b. South Amboy, N.J., Aug. 14, 1924; s. Leo A. and Catherine (Noble) M.; m. Marilyn Ruth Freeley, Jan. 31, 1948; children—Richard, Karen, Jeanne, Kathleen, John, James, Marilyn, Carol. A.B. in Chemistry, Harvard U., 1947, postgrad. 1952-53; M.S. in Phys. Chem., Boston Coll., 1949. Mgr. research and devel. Shawinigan Corp., Springfield, Mass., 1962-68; sr. group leader research and devel. Monsanto Co., Springfield, 1968-72, sr. engring. specialist, 1972-74, gen. supt. mfg., 1974-80, mgr. research and devel., 1980—; bd. dirs. Formaldehyde Inst., 1979-83. Patentee in field. Chmn. Springfield Lic. Commn., 1960-65; Confraternity Christian Doctrine tchr. Our Lady of Sacred Heart Ch., Springfield, 1955—, mem. parish council, 1970-80, chmn. 1975-76. Served to lt. (j.g.) USN, 1943-46, PTO. Mem. Am. Chem. Soc. Democrat. Roman Catholic. Current work: Polymer processes; properties; structure. Subspecialties: Polymer chemistry; Polymer engineering. Home: 80 Embassy Rd Springfield MA 01119 Office: Monsanto Polymer Products Co 730 Worcester St Springfield MA 01151

MONASH, ELLIS ALAN, geomathematician; b. Phila., Dec. 31, 1938; s. Max and Helen Selma (Streitfeld) M.; m. Carol Joan Bernard, June 11, 1960; children: Temma J., Adam M., Nathan S. A.B., Temple U., 1961; M.Sc., U. Wis., 1962, U. Colo., 1971. Ops research analyst System Devel. Corp., Colorado Springs, Colo., 1968-70; mathematician U.S. Army Air Def. Commn., Ent AFB, Colo., 1970-75; computer systems analyst U.S. Geol. Survey, Lakewood, Colo., 1975-81; engring. cons. Intercomp Resource Devel., Englewood, Colo., 1981-82; sr. research analyst System Tech., Inc., Paonia, Colo., 1982—. Author, editor: Lumped Parameter Models of Hydrocarbon Reservoirs, 1983. Recipient Gubernatorial scholarship State Pa., 1958. Mem. Soc. Computer Simulation (assoc. editor 1980—), Soc. Petroleum Engrs., Soc. Indsl. and Applied Match., Internat. Assn. Match. Geology. Current Work: Research to maximize ultimate recovery of hydrocarbon reservoirs while minimizing thermodynamic waste from them. Subspecialties: Numerical analysis (computer science); Resource management. Home: 2080 Newcombe Dr Lakewood CO 80125 Office: System Tech Inc PO Box 459 Paonia CO 81428

MONDAL, KALYAN, electrical and computer engineer, educator, researcher; b. Calcutta, India, Aug. 17, 1951; came to U.S., 1974; s. Dwijendra Nath and Bijali (Das) M.; m. Chitralekha Mandal, Aug. 5, 1981; 1 dau., Indrani. B.Sc. with honors, U. Calcutta, 1969, B.Tech., 1972; M.Tech., 1974; Ph.D., U. Calif.-Santa Barbara, 1978. Research asst. U. Calif.-Davis, 1975-77; research asst. U. Calif.-Santa Barbara, 1977-78, postgrad. researcher, 1978-79, lectr., 1978-79; asst. prof. Lehigh U., Bethlehem, Pa., 1980-81, adj. asst. prof., 1982-83; mem. tech. staff AT&T Bell Telephone Labs., Allentown, Pa., 1982—. Contbr. research papers to profl. jours. Recipient Gold medal U. Calcutta, 1972, 74; Pa. Power & Lights Co. grantee, 1981. Mem. IEEE, Assn. for Computing Machinery, Sigma Xi, Eta Kappa Nu. Current Work: VLSI system design, digital signal processing, microprocessor-based system design, database systems, and digital image processing. Subspecialties: Integrated circuits; Computer engineering. Office: AT&T Bell Labs 1247 S Cedar Crest Blvd Allentown PA 18104

MONETI, GIANCARLO, physics educator; b. Rome, Nov. 2, 1931; came to U.S., 1968; s. Pietro Moneti and Maria DeAngelis; m. Annamaria Sacchi, June 30, 1955; children—Andrea, Francesca, Filippo, Carlo, Elena. Dr. in Physics, U. Rome, 1954, Libero Docente, 1963. Asst. prof. physics U. Rome, 1954-62, assoc. prof., 1962-68; assoc. physicist Brookhaven Nat. Lab., Upton, N.Y., 1961-62; prof. physics Syracuse U., N.Y., 1968—. Contbr. articles to physics jours., conf. procs. Bd. dirs. Istituto Nazionale Fisica Nucleare, 1966-68. Fellow Am. Phys. Soc.; mem. Societa Italiana di Fisica, European Phys. Soc. Current work: Properties of bottom quark, quark and gluon hadronization. Subspecialty: Particle physics. Office: Syracuse U 201 Physics Bldg Syracuse NY 13210

MONETTE, FRANCIS C., biology educator; b. Lowell, Mass., Aug. 9, 1941; s. Francis L. and Yvonne A. (Payer) M.; m. Yvonne A. Belanger, Apr. 21, 1968; 1 child, Michelle. B.A., St. Anselm's Coll., 1962; M.S., NYU, 1965, Ph.D., 1968. Postdoctoral fellow Tufts U., Boston, 1968-71; asst. prof. biology Boston U., 1971-77, assoc. prof., 1978-82, prof., 1982—. Mem. editorial bd. Exptl. Hematology. Contbr. over 55 articles to profl. jours. Recipient Career Devel. award NIH, 1977-82; numerous research grants NIH, Nat. Leukemia Assn., Am. Cancer Soc. Mem. Internat. Soc. for Exptl. Hematology, Am. Soc. Hematology, Am. Physiol. Soc., Am. Soc. Cell Biology. Current work: Hemopoiesis; erythropoiesis; stem cell biology; biology of the cell cycle. Subspecialties: Cell and tissue culture; Hematology. Office: Dept Biology Boston Univ 2 Cummington St Boston MA 02215

MONISMITH, CARL LEROY, civil engr., educator; b. Harrisburg, Pa., Oct. 23, 1926; s. Carl Samuel and Camille Frances (Geidt) M. B.S. in Civil Engring, U. Calif., Berkeley, 1950, M.S., 1954. Mem. faculty U. Calif., Berkeley, 1951—, prof. civil engring., 1965—, chmn. dept., 1974-79; cons. to govt. and industry. Author numerous papers, reports in field. Served to 2d lt. AUS, 1945-47. Recipient Rupert Meyers medal U. New South Wales, Australia, 1976; Fulbright scholar Australia, 1971. Fellow ASCE (pres. San Francisco sect. 1979-80, State of Art award 1978); mem. Nat. Acad. Engring., Assn. Asphalt Paving Technologists (pres. 1968, Walter J. Emmons award 1961, 65), Transp. Research Bd. o3(asso.) (chmn. pavement design sect. 1973-79, K.B. Woods award 1972), ASTM, Am. Soc. Engring. Edn. Current Work: Pavement design and rehabilitation, including overlay design; asphalt paving technology. Subspecialty: Civil engineering. Office: 115 McLaughlin Hall U Calif Berkeley CA 94720

MONIZ, ERNEST JEFFREY, physics educator; b. Fall River, Mass., Dec. 22, 1944; s. Ernest Perry and Georgina (Pavao) M.; m. Naomi Hoki, June 9, 1973; 1 child, Katya. B.S., Boston Coll., 1966; Ph.D., Stanford U., 1971. Research assoc. SACLAY, Gif-sur-Yvette, France, 1971-72; research assoc. U. Pa., Phila., 1972-73; prof. physics MIT, Cambridge, 1973—; cons. Los Alamos Nat. Lab. Contbr. articles to profl. jours. Current work: Understanding nuclear structure and forces in terms of fundamental constituents. Subspecialties: Theoretical physics; Nuclear physics. Office: Lab for Nuclear Sci 26-567 Mass Inst Tech Cambridge MA 02138

MONJAN, ANDREW ARTHUR, immunologist, psychologist; b. N.Y.C., Feb. 9, 1938; s. Victor and Sonia (Sherinian) M.; m. Susan Vollenweider, Aug. 2, 1962; m. Usha Bose, Aug. 14, 1969; children: Matthew V., Vanessa K. B.S., Rensselaer Poly. Inst., 1960; Ph.D., U. Rochester, 1965; M.P.H., Johns Hopkins U., 1970. Postdoctoral fellow Ctr. Brain Research, U. Rochester, N.Y., 1964-66; asst. prof. depts. psychology and physiology U. Western Ont., London, Ont., Can., 1966-69; asst. prof. dept. epidemiology Johns Hopkins U. Sch. Hygiene and Pub. Health, Balt., 1971-75, assoc. prof., 1975-83; program dir. for AIDS epidemiology Nat. Cancer Inst., NIH, Bethesda, Md., 1983-85, chief immunology and basic neurosci. programs Nat. Inst. Aging, 1985—. Contbr. articles to profl. jours. NIH grantee; Med. Research Can. grantee; Nat. Research Council Can. grantee. Mem. Am. Assn. Immunologists, Am. Assn. Virology, Eastern Psychol. Assn., Teratology Soc, AAAS, Sigma Xi. Democrat. Current Work: Stress and the modulation of immune response; immunopathology due to viruses, AIDS epidemiology. Subspecialties: Infectious diseases; Neurobiology. Home: 7138 Rivers Edge Rd Columbia MD 21044 Office: Physiology of Aging Br Biomed Research and Clin Med Program Nat Inst Aging NIH Bldg 31 Room 5C27 Bethesda MD 20205

MONTAGNA, WILLIAM, scientist; b. Roccacasale, Italy, July 6, 1913; s. Cherubino and Adele (Giannangelo) M.; m. Martha Helen Fife, Sept. 1, 1939 (div. 1975); children: Eleanor, Margaret, James and John (twins); m. Leona Rebecca Swift, Apr. 19, 1980. A.B., Bethany Coll., 1936, D.Sc., 1960; Ph.D., Cornell U., 1944; D. B.S., Università di Sassari, 1964. Instr. Cornell U., 1944-45; asst. prof. L.I. Coll. Medicine, 1945-48; asst., asso. prof. Brown U., 1948-52, prof., 1952-63, L. Herbert Ballou univ. prof. biology, 1960-63; prof., head exptl. biology U. Oreg. Health Scis. Center; dir. Oreg. Regional Primate Research Center, Beaverton, 1963—. Author: The Structure and Function of Skin, 1956, 3d edit., 1974, Comparative Anatomy, 1959, Nonhuman Primates in Biomedical Research, 1976, Science Is Not Enough, 1980; co-author: Man, 1969, 2d edit., 1973, Skin, Your Owner's Manual; editor: The Biology of Hair Growth, 1958, Advances in Biology of Skin, 20 vols, The Epidermis, 1965, Advances in Primatology, 1970, Reproductive Behavior, 1974. Decorated Order di Cavaliere, 1963, Cavaliere Ufficiale, 1969, Commendator della Repubblica Italiana, 1975; Italy; recipient spl. award Soc. Cosmetic Chemists, 1957; Gold award Am. Acad. Dermatology, 1958; Ann. award Consiglio Nazionale delle Ricerche, 1963; gold medal for meritorious achievement Università di Sassari, 1964; Aubrey R. Watzek award Lewis and Clark Coll., 1977; Hans Schwarzkopf Research award German Dermatol. Soc., 1980. Mem. Acad. Dermatology and Syphilology, Soc. Investigative Dermatology (pres. 1969, recipient Stephen Rothman award 1972, ann. William Montagna lectr. 1975—), Sigma Xi (Pres. 1960-62). Research in biology mammalian skin with emphasis on primates. Subspecialty: Dermatology. Office: 3181 SW Sam Jackson Rd Dept Pathology Portland OR 97201

MONTALBANO, FRANK, III, wildlife biologist; b. Beaumont, Tex., Mar. 6, 1948; s. Frank and Tommie Ruth (Messer) M.; m. Nancy Ann Silcox, Nov. 30, 1974; children—Thomas E., Robert S. B.S., Tex. A&M U., 1970. Regional wildlife biologist Fla. Game and Fresh Water Fish Commn., Lakeland, 1974-77, sect. leader Kissimmee Basin Wetlands Investigation, Okeechobee, 1977-80, waterfowl biologist, mgmt. program coordinator, 1980-85, asst. dir. div. wildlife, 1985—; cons. waterfowl biologist. Contbr. articles to profl. jours. Served to capt. USAF, 1970-74. Decorated Air Force Commendation medal; recipient spl. award Ducks Unltd., 1981. Mem. Wildlife Soc. (cert. wildlife biologist; pres. Fla. chpt. 1981-83), Fla. Assn. Wildlife and Aquatic Biologists (pres. 1975-76), Alpha Zeta. Roman Catholic. Current work: Waterfowl ecology/management, wetlands ecosystem ecology/management, wildlife impacts of surface mining, mine reclamation/wildlife habitat. Subspecialties: Resource management; Resource conservation. Office: Fla Game and Fresh Water Fish Commn 620 S Meridian St Tallahassee FL 32301

MONTE, JUDITH ANN, environmental scientist; b. Mt. Holly, N.J., June 18, 1947; d. Michael and Mary (Davison) M. A.B., Douglass Coll., 1969; M.S., Rutgers U., 1971; Ph.D., La. State U., 1978. Vis. asst. prof. geography U. S.C., Columbia, 1974-79; dir. MAST-Baruch Inst., 1977-79; vis. asst. prof. geography San Diego State U., 1979-80; assoc. prof. geography U. Md., College Park, 1982-83; sr. earth scientist Greenhorne & O'Mara, Inc., Greenbelt, Md., 1980—. Author: Manual Landsat and Groundwater Exploration, 1982. Mem. Assn. Am. Geographers, Ecol. Soc. Am., Am. Soc. Photogrammetry, Coastal Soc., LWV. Club: Sierra (College Park). Current Work: Resource assessments; wetlands; groundwater exploration; remote sensing; vegetational succession on dredge spoil; human impact on coastal environments, especially petroleum impacts. Subspecialties: Remote sensing (geoscience); Hydrology. Home: 7815 Enola St #203 McLean VA 22102 Office: Greenhorne & O'Mara Inc 9001 Edmonston Rd Greenbelt MD 20770

MONTEFUSCO, CHERYL MARIE, surgery educator, lung transplantation researcher; b. New Kensington, Pa., May 14, 1948; d. Benjamin Bosco and Edith (Costanzo) Bongiovanni; m. Frank Joseph Montefusco, Nov. 14, 1970 (div. 1982). B.S., St. Francis Coll., 1970; Ph.D., Coll. Medicine and Dentistry of N.J., 1975. Research assoc. Squibb Inst. Med. Research, Lawrenceville, N.J., 1970-71; editor dept. radiology Harrison S. Martland Hosp., Newark, 1972-73; instr. Coll. Medicine and Dentistry N.J., Newark, 1973-74; instr. dept. biology Kean Coll. of N.J., Union, 1974; research assoc. vascular surgery, dir. scanning electron microscopy lab. Newark Beth Israel Med. Ctr., 1975-76; tech. sales rep. W.L. Gore & Assocs., Inc., Newark, Del., 1976-77; instr. physiology Albert Einstein Coll. Medicine, N.Y.C., 1977—, asst. prof. surgery, 1977-83, assoc. prof. surgery, 1983—; co dir. lung transplant research Montefiore Hosp. and Med. Ctr., N.Y.C., 1977—; project leader Exptl. Lung Transplantation, 1980—, clin. co dir. lung transplantation, 1981—; guest lectr. U. Utrecht, Netherlands, 1976. Contbg. author sci. writings in field. Fellow Internat. Coll. Angiology, Am. Coll. Angiology; mem. Am. Physiol. Soc., N.Y. Acad. Scis., N.Y. Transplantation Soc. Republican. Roman Catholic. Current Work: Lung transplantation, mucociliary transport, exercise, physiology, nutrition in health and disease states. Subspecialties: Physiology (medicine); Transplantation. Office: Montefiore Med Ctr 111 E 210th St Bronx NY 10467

MONTESANO, RUGGERO, scientist; b. Alba, Piemonte, Italy, Oct. 4, 1939; s. Giuseppe and Adelina (Vallet) M.; m. Caroline Soden, Feb. 9, 1970; children—Flavia, Clementine. Laurea in Medicine and Surgery, U. Turin, Italy, 1965; Ph.D. in Biochemistry, U. London, 1974. Research assoc. Chgo. Med. Sch., 1966-68; asst. prof. pathology Eppley Inst. Research Cancer, Omaha, 1968-69; research tng. fellow Courtauld Inst. Biochemistry, London, 1969-71; scientist Internat. Agy. for Research of Cancer, Lyon, France, 1971-79, unit chief mechanisms of carcinogenesis, 1979—. Contbr. numerous articles to profl. jours. Mem. Biochem Soc. U.K., Royal Soc. Medicine, Pathol. Soc. Gt. Britain and Ireland, Am. Assn. Cancer Research, Societa Italiana di Cancerologia. Current work: Carcinogenesis; tissue culture. Office: Internat Agy for Research of Cancer 150 Cours Albert Thomas Lyon 69008 France

MONTGOMERY, DEANE, mathematician; b. Weaver, Minn., Sept. 2, 1909; s. Richard and Florence (Hitchcock) M.; m. Katherine Fulton, July 14, 1933; children—Mary, Richard. A.B., Hamline U., 1929; M.S., U. Iowa, 1930; Ph.D., 1933; Ph.D. hon. doctorate, Hamline U., 1954, Yeshiva U., 1961, Tulane U., 1967, U. Ill., 1977. NRC fellow Harvard, 1933-34; NRC fellow Princeton U., 1934-35, vis. assoc. prof., 1943-45; NRC fellow Inst. for Advanced Study, 1934-35, Guggenheim fellow, 1941-42, mem., 1945-46, permanent mem., 1948-51, prof. math, 1951—; asst. prof., prof. Smith Coll., 1935-41, 42-43; asso. prof. Yale, 1946-48. Mem. Am. Math. Soc. (pres. 1961-62), Nat. Acad. Sci., Math. Assn. Am., Am. Philos. Soc., Am. Acad. Arts and Sics., Internat. Math. Union (pres. 1975-78). Current Work: Action of compact lie groups on manifolds. Subspecialty: Topology and foundations. Home: 55 Rollingmead Princeton NJ 08540 Office: Inst for Advanced Study Princeton NJ 08540

MONTGOMERY, DONALD LEE, veterinary pathologist; b. Shamrock, Tex., Nov. 2, 1950; s. Thomas Calvin and Mary Ernestine (Fincher) M.; m. Carol Lynn Gruber, Dec. 27, 1969; 1 child, Jason Lee. B.S., Tex. A&M U., 1975, D.V.M., 1976, Ph.D., 1981. Diplomate Am. Coll. Vet. Pathologists. Asst. prof. Collaborative Radiol. Health Lab., Ft. Collins, Colo., 1981-82; head diagnostic pathology Tex. Vet. Med. Diagnostic Lab., Amarillo, 1982—. Contbr. articles to profl. jours. Recipient Vet. Pathology Scholarship award C.L. Davis Found., 1979, Vet. Jour. Scholarship award, 1984. Mem. AVMA, Am. Coll. Vet. Pathologists, Internat. Acad. Pathology. Republican. Methodist. Current work: Diagnostic veterinary pathology; research interests are development of animal models of human neurodegenerative disease. Subspecialty: Pathology (veterinary medicine). Office: Tex Vet Med Diagnostic Lab PO Box 3200 Amarillo TX 79116

MONTGOMERY, PHILIP O'BRYAN, JR., pathology educator, health center administrator; b. Dallas, Aug. 16, 1921. B.S., So. Meth. U., 1942; M.D., Columbia U., 1945. Diplomate Am. Bd. Pathology, Am. Bd. Pathologic Anatomy, Am. Bd. Clin. Pathology, Am. Bd. Forensic Pathology. Intern, Mary Imogene Bassett Hosp., Cooperstown, N.Y., 1945-46; fellow in pathology Southwestern Med. Sch., Dallas, 1950-51, asst. prof. pathology, 1953-55, assoc. prof., 1955-61, prof., 1961—, assoc. dean, 1968-70; research asst. in pathology and cancer research Cancer Research Inst., New Eng. Deaconess Hosp., Boston, 1951-52; spl. asst. to chancellor U. Tex. System, 1971-75; exec. dir. cancer ctr. U. Tex. Health Sci. Ctr. at Dallas, 1975—; pathologist Parkland Meml. Hosp., Dallas, 1952—, Tex. Children's Hosp., Dallas, 1954-55, Dallas City Zoo, 1955-68; cons. pathologist Navarro County Meml. Hosp., Corsicana, Tex., 1952-53, McKinney VA Hosp., Tex., 1952-65, Lisbon VA Hosp., Dallas, 1953—, St. Paul Hosp., Dallas, 1958—, Flow Meml. Hosp., Denton, Tex., 1958-65; med. examiner Dallas County, 1955-58; pres. dist. med. staff mem. dist. adv. council Dallas County Hosp., 1962-63; mem. pathology study sect. B NIH, 1965-69; mem. sci. adv. com. Damon Runyon Meml. Fund for Cancer Research, 1966-72, med. adviser to bd. dirs., 1973-74; com. mem. Am. Inst. Biol. Scis., 1965-67, Nat. Cancer Plan, 1971-72; adj. prof. biology Sch. Natural Scis. and Math., U. Tex. at Dallas, 1977—. Mem. editorial bd. Space Life Scis. Jour., 1967-69; mem. editorial adv. bd. Cancer Research, 1970-73. Bd. dirs. Vis. Nurses Assn. Dallas, 1957-60, Met. YMCA, 1960-63, Dallas Council on World Affairs, 1962-65, Dallas Mental Health Soc., 1966-67, Dallas County unit, Am. Cancer Soc., 1971-72; bd. dirs. Planned Parenthood Dallas, 1958-63, pres. bd. dirs., 1958-60; trustee St. Mark's Sch. Tex., 1958—, v.p., chmn. exec. com. bd. trustees, 1966-68, v.p., 1968-69, pres., 1974-76; sec. vis. com. for molecular sci. lab. Grad. Research Ctr. of Southwest, 1963-64; founder mem. Met. Philos. Soc., 1963-64; trustee Biol. Humanics Found., 1965-77, 79—, pres., 1974-77; chmn. bd. Restoration of Gillespie County Courthouse, Tex., 1966-67; trustee Lamplighter Sch., 1967-70; chmn. Dallas Area Library Planning Council, 1970-72; bd. dirs. Damon Runyon-Walter Winchell Cancer Fund, 1973—, pres. bd. dirs., 1974-79; regents Uniformed Services U. of Health Scis., Washington, 1974-77, cons., 1977-81; chmn. health task force com. Goals of Dallas, 1975-76; chmn. Fleet Admiral Nimitz Mus. Commn., 1979-81; coordinator Dallas Arts Dist., 1982—. Served to capt. M.C., U.S. Army, 1946-49. Recipient Cancer Devel. award NIH, 1962-68, Astronauts' Silver Snoopy award for Profl. Excellence, 1970, Disting. Service medal Uniformed Services U. of Health Scis., 1980, Gov.'s Cert. of Appreciation for Exceptional and Disting. Vol. Service, 1983, Vol. of Yr. award City of Dallas, 1983, Obelisk award Dallas C. of C., 1983, Linz award, 1984, Dallas Hist. Soc. Award for Excellence in Community Service in Humanities, 1984; named Headliner of Yr., Dallas Press Club, 1984; perpetual fellowship named in his honor Damon Runyon-Walter Winchell Cancer Fund, 1983. Fellow Am. Soc. Clin. Pathologists, Royal Micros. Soc., N.Y. Acad. Scis.; mem. Am. Assn. Pathologists and Bacteriologists, Am. Assn. Cancer Research, Internat. Acad. Pathology, Am. Acad. Forensic Scis., Soc. Exptl. Biology and Medicine, Internat. Soc. Cell Biology, Biophys. Soc., Am. Soc. Cell Biology, Am. Soc. Exptl. Pathology, Tissue Culture Assn., Internat. Fedn. Med. Electronics, Profl. Group for Med. Electronics of Inst. Radio Engrs., AAAS, Optical Soc. Tex. (founding), Optical Soc. Am., Pan Am. Med. Assn. AMA, Aerospace Med. Assn., So. Med. Assn., Tex. Med. Assn., Dallas County Med. Soc., North Tex. Soc. Pathologists, Tex. Soc. Pathologists, Tex. Acad. Sci., AAUP. Office: U Tex 5323 Harry Hines Blvd Dallas TX 75235

MONTGOMERY, ROBERT LEW, psychology educator; b. Grayson, Ky., July 2, 1941; s. Everett DeForest and Ruth Agnes (Glass) M.; m. Sallie Stewart Meier, Sept. 6, 1966 (dec. Feb. 1978); m. Frances Marie Haemmerlie, June 16, 1979; children: Melissa, John. B.A., Bethany (W.Va.) Coll., 1964; M.S., Okla. State U., 1967, Ph.D., 1968. Research asst. Okla. State U., 1964-68; asst. prof. psychology U. Mo.-Rolla, 1968-73, assoc. prof., 1973-78, prof., 1978—, head dept. psychology, 1975-81; vis. prof. U. Fla., 1974-75. Contbr. articles to profl. jours. Recipient Phi Kapp Phi Disting. Service award U. Mo.-Rolla, 1975; Nat. Cambell fellow, 1963-64; NDEA fellow, 1967-68; U. Mo.-Rolla Asst. Prof. grantee, 1969, 71. Mem. Am. Psychol. Assn., Psychonomic Soc., Midwestern Psychol. Assn. (local rep. 1981—), Southwestern Psychol. Assn., Mo. Psychol.

Assn. Episcopalian. Club: Oak Meadows (Rolla). Current Work: Experimental social psychology, industrial/organizational psychology, evaluation research, group dynamics, leadership, attitude test construction, social influence, community psychology, psychology of aging, and person perception. Subspecialties: Social psychology; Behavioral psychology. Home: Route 4 Box 322 Rolla MO 65401 Office: Dept Psycholog U Mo Rolla MO 65401

MOODY, ARNOLD RALPH, plant pathologist; b. Augusta, Maine, Oct. 8, 1941; s. Norman O. and Annie (Bradstreet) M.; m. Donna Rich, June 19, 1965; 1 dau., Sara Ann. B.S., U. Maine, 1963; M.S., U. N.H., 1965; Ph.D., U. Calif.-Berkeley, 1971. Asst. research plant pathologist U. Calif.-Berkeley, 1971-72; research plant pathologist Station Federale de Recherches Agronomiques de Changins, Nyon, Switzerland, 1972-74; assoc. prof. plant pathology Va. State U., Petersburg, 1975—. Contbr. articles to profl. jours. Mem. Am. Phytopath. Soc., Sigma Xi. Presbyterian. Current Work: Vegetable diseases, biol. control, root diseases, soil microbiology, resistance. Subspecialties: Plant pathology; Microbiology. Home: 301 Charlotte Ave Colonial Heights VA 23834 Office: Virginia State U Box 501 Petersburg VA 23803

MOODY, CHARLES EDWARD, JR., immunologist; b. Portsmouth, N.H., Feb. 14, 1948; s. Charles Edward and Doris Mae (Chapman) M.; m. Alexandra C. Soggiu, Feb. 14,1976 (div. 1982). B.A., Providence Coll., 1970; M.Sc., U. R.I., 1973, Ph.D., 1976. Postdoctoral fellow, div. allergy and immunology Cornell U. Med. Coll., N.Y.C., 1976-79, asst. prof. immunology in medicine, div. geriatrics and gerontology, 1979-82; asst. prof. microbiology U. Maine, Orono, 1982—. Contbr. articles to profl. jours. Nat. Inst. on Aging/NIH and NOAA grantee, 1977-79, 81—. Mem. Am. Assn. Immunologists, Harvey Soc., N.Y. Acad. Scis., AAAS, Sigma Xi. Democrat. Roman Catholic. Current Work: Aging and the immune response, immune response of salmonids, immunology education, aging. tolerance, comparative immunology, autoreactivity, self recognition, syngeneic mixed lymphocyte reaction. Subspecialties: Immunobiology and immunology; Microbiology. Home: 11 Fernald Rd Apt 11 Orono ME 04473 Office: Dept Microbiology U Maine Room 262 Hitchner Hall Orono ME 04469

MOODY, DANIEL, world government health official, scientist, consultant; b. Oak Park, Ill., Dec. 4, 1946; s. John Henry and Antoinette (Gentile) M. B.A., U. Western Mich., 1968; M.S., MIT, 1970; Ph.D. in Computer Sci., Calif. Inst. Tech., 1972, D.Sc. in Astronomy, 1972. Instr. Internat. Devel. Agy., Washington, 1972-79; computer scientist U.S. Govt., 1979-82; dir. edn. Fedn. Computer Users in Medicine, 1984—; del. Med. Informatics UN, San Francisco, 1982—; cons. IBM, Med. Systems, AT&T, Expert Systems, Am. Med. Found. Author: (with others) How to Choose the Right Computer for Your Medical Practice, 1985, How to Choose the Right Computer for Your Dental Practice, 1985. Computer cons. San Francisco AIDS Found., 1984; instr. Ctr. for Blind, San Francisco, 1972-84. Served to capt. USAF, 1964-68. Named Computer Scientist of Yr., Internat. Assn. Computer Scientists, Oxford, Eng., 1984. Fellow AAAS (named Most Promising Research Scientist 1979), Am. Computer Assn. (membership com. 1984), Assn. for Med. Systems and Informatics, Assn. for Prospective Medicine. Current work: Inventor of logic gate amplifier switch, a microcircuit that performs one operation every fifty picoseconds, holds 38 patents on computer medical technology. Subspecialties: Artificial intelligence; Information systems, storage, and retrieval (computer science). Office: UN Adv Com UN Plaza Box 15579 San Francisco CA 94115

MOODY, DAVID WRIGHT, hydrologist, administrator; b. Boston, Nov. 23, 1937; s. Robert Earle and Eleanor Newton (Wragg) M.; m. Jeanne Christensen, Dec. 27, 1963; 1 child, Sarah. A.B., Harvard U., 1960; Ph.D., Johns Hopkins U., 1964. Hydrologist U.S. Geol. Survey, Phila., 1964-67, Reston, Va., 1968-73, program analyst, Reston, 1974-76, staff scientist, 1977-82, chief, Office Nat. Water Summary and Long Range Planning, 1983—; mem. geophysics study com. NRC, Washington, 1981-83. Treas. Green Hedges Sch., Vienna, Va., 1978-79. Recipient Meritorious Service award U.S. Dept. Interior, 1982; Am. Polit. Sci. Assn. congl. fellow, 1976-77. Mem. Geol. Soc. Am., Am. Water Resources Assn., Am. Geophys. Union, AAAS. Current work: National water resources assessment, natural resource information systems. Subspecialty: Hydrology. Office: U S Geol Survey 407 Nat Ctr Reston VA 22092

MOODY, ELIZABETH ANNE, physicist; b. Portland, Me., Oct. 29, 1948; d. Earl Louis and Margaret Mary (Downing) M. B.A., Simmons Coll., 1971; postgrad., Harvard U., 1973. Data analyst Smithsonian Astrophys. Obs., Cambridge, Mass., 1969; research cons. M.I.T. Instrumentation Lab., Cambridge, 1973-74, Ind. Cons., Boston, 1975-76; research scientist Aerodyne Research, Burlington, Mass., 1977-78, Sci. Applications, Bedford, Mass., 1979-80, U.S. Air Force Geophysics Lab., Bedford, 1981; design/devel. engr. Raytheon Co., Bedford, 1982—; cons. Contbr. articles to profl. jours. Adviser, counselor Meml. Soc. New Eng., 1981—. Recipient Woman of Future citation Mass. Dept. Edn., 1965, Scholastic Achievement award, 1970; Leadership award Am. Legion, 1970; Community Service commendation United Community Services Mass., 1970. Mem. Am. Astron. Soc., Am. Phys. Soc., Astron. Soc. Pacific, Assn. Women in Sci., ACLU, NAACP, NOW, People Am. Way, Harvard U. Alumni Assn. Kirkland Cosmotology Club (liaison officer 1980—). Mem. Ch. of Larger Fellowship, Unitarian Universalist. Club: Cosmology. Current Work: Energy astrophysics, space telescope instrumentation, signal and image processing. Subspecialties: Cosmology; Aerospace engineering and technology. Home: PO Box 546 Beverly Farms MA 01915 Office: MSD MS M26-4 Hartwell Rd Bedford MA 01730

MOODY, JOHN CHRYSTOR, electro optic engineer, consultant; b. Dinwiddie, Va., May 3, 1928; s. Arthur Maxey and Grace Randolph (Atkinson) M.; m. Elizabeth Louise Harman, Apr. 2, 1955; children—John Chrystor, Lynn Harman, Ellen Grey. B.S. in Physics, Am. U., 1960, postgrad., 1961-66; postgrad. Johns Hopkins U., 1966-78. Electro optic engr. Night Vision Lab. U.S. Army, Fort Belvoir, Va., 1956-62, Goddard Space Flight Ctr. NASA, Greenbelt, Md., 1962-80, OAO Corp., Greenbelt, 1980—; cons. NASA Goddard Space Flight Ctr., 1981—. Author, co-author articles. Served with USCG, 1950-53, Japan. Mem. IEEE, Soc. Photo Optical Instrumentation Engrs. Methodist. Research or work interests: Space optics design and analysis, remote sensing systems and technology for space applications. Subspecialties: Aerospace engineering and technology; Remote sensor optics and systems. Home: 9935 Whiskey Run Laurel MD 20707 Office: OAO Corp 9500 Greenway Ctr Greenbelt MD 20770

MOODY, TERRY WILLIAM, biochemistry educator, researcher; b. Fresno, Calif., Dec. 2, 1949; s. Robert A. and Marie M.; m. Carol D. Linden, July 9, 1977; 1 dau., Elizabeth. B.Sc., U. Calif.-Berkeley, 1972; Ph.D., Calif. Inst. Tech., 1977. USPHS predoctoral trainee Calif. Inst. Tech., 1972-77; research chemist Nat. Inst. Drug Abuse, NIH, Rockville, Md., 1977-79; HEW postdoctoral fellow NIMH, Bethesda, Md., 1979-80; asst. prof. biochemistry George Washington U. Med. Sch., Washington, 1980-83, assoc. prof., 1983—. Contbr. over 30 articles to sci. jours. USPHS grantee, 1981—. Mem. AAAS, N. Y. Acad. Sci., Am. Soc. Biol. Chemists, Soc. Neurosci. Current Work: Neuron and neuroendocrine peptides and their receptors; research concerning the chemistry and biology of bombesin, a peptide present in certain neurons and cancer cells. Subspecialties: Neurochemistry; Biochemistry (biology). Office: George Washington U Med Center Washington DC 20037

MOODY, WILLIS ELVIS, JR., ceramic engineering educator, consultant, lawyer; b. Raleigh, N.C., Mar. 30, 1924; s. Willis Elvis and Inez (McDade) M.; m. Mary Susan McAfee, Mar. 22, 1947 (div. 1967); children—Susan E., Michael T., Peggy A., Willis E. III, William S. B.S. in Ceramic Engring, N.C. State U., 1948, M.S. in Ceramic Engring., 1949, Ph.D. in Ceramic Engring., 1956; J.D., Woodrow Wilson Coll. of Law, 1979. Bar: Ga. 1980. Registered profl. engr., Ga. Ceramic engr. Electric Auto-Lite Co., Fostoria, Ohio, 1949-50, Lab. Equipment Corp., St. Joseph, Mich., 1950-51; instr. metall. and ceramic engring. N.C. State U., Raleigh, 1951-56; research participant Oak Ridge Nat. Lab., Tenn., summer 1954-55; prof. Ga. Inst. Tech., Atlanta, 1956—; cons. to clay and ceramic cos., 1951—. Author book. Contbr. articles to profl. jours. Patentee (with others) dental coupling agt. Served to 1st lt. USAAF, 1943-46, ETO. Decorated Air medal with 2 oak leaf clusters; Orton Ceramic Found. fellow, 1948. Fellow Am. Ceramic Soc. (trustee 1965-68); mem. Am. Assn. Engring. Socs. (bd. govs. 1979-81), Nat. Inst. Ceramic Engrs. (pres. 1980), Ceramic Ednl. Council (pres. 1963), Am. Soc. Engring. Edn. (chmn. materials div. 1971), Clay Minerals Soc. (councilor 1969-71). Current work: Clay mineral deposit evaluation and processing and mining contracts. Subspecialties: Ceramic engineering; Materials processing. Home: Apt 13K 4545 Northside Pkwy Atlanta GA 30339 Office: Dept Materials Engring Ga Inst Tech Atlanta GA 30332

MOERS, CHRISTOPHER NORTHRUP KENNARD, oceanography educator; b. Hagerstown, Md., Nov. 11, 1935; s. Frank Burt and Helen Wakefield (Miner) M.; m. Elizabeth Eva Fauntleroy, June 11, 1960; children—Blaine Hansen, Randall Walden. B.S., U.S. Naval Acad., 1957; M.S., U. Conn.-Storrs, 1964; Ph.D., Oreg. State U., 1969. NATO postdoctoral fellow U. Liverpool, Eng., 1969-70; asst. and assoc. prof. U. Miami, Fla., 1970-76; assoc. and full prof. Coll. Marine studies, U. Del., Newark, 1976-79; prof., chmn. dept. oceanography Naval Postgrad. Sch., Monterey, Calif., 1979—; cons. in field. Contbr. articles to profl. jours. Editor: Springer Verlag's Lecture Notes on Coastal Sci., 1978—, Estuarine Studies, 1978—, others. Active Boy Scouts Am., 1972-76. Served to lt. USN, 1957-64. NSF grad. fellow, 1964-67; Sr. Queen Elizabeth fellow, 1980. Mem. Am. Geophys. Union (pres. ocean sci. sect. 1982-84), Am. Meteorol. Soc., AAAS. Current work: Dynamical and synoptic oceanography; data assimilation; Mesoscale variability (ocean eddies, fronts and meandering jets) in eastern and western boundary currents. . Home: 4 Pinehill Way Monterey CA 93940 Office: Dept Oceanography Naval Postgrad Sch Monterey CA 93943

MOON, THOMAS WILLIAM, biology educator, laboratory administrator; b. Portland, Oreg., June 10, 1944; s. Francis Theodore and Henry-Etta (Lamoree) M.; m. Lou Anne Waln, Mar. 21, 1965; children—Tana Lynn, Anik Michelle. B.Sc., Oreg. State U., 1966, M.A., 1968; Ph.D., U. B.C., 1971. Postdoctoral fellow Meml. U., St. John's, 1971-72; asst. prof. biology U. Ottawa, 1972-76, assoc. prof., 1976-83, prof., 1983—; exec. dir. Huntsman Marine Lab., St. Andrews, N.B., 1983-85; vis. prof. U. Toronto, 1975, U. St. Andrews, 1978-79. Contbr. numerous articles to profl. jours. Recipient Excellence in Teaching award U. Ottawa, 1982; Japna Soc. Promotion of Sci. fellow, 1983. Mem. Am. Soc. Zoologists, Am. Physiol. Soc., Can. Soc. Zoologists (sect. pres. 1970, councilor 1983-86). Current work: Comparative physiology/biochemistry of animals, especially with respect to environmental perturbations; role of the liver in adaptive strategies of animals; hepatocyte biology. Subspecialty: Comparative physiology. Office: Ottawa Dept Biology 30 Somerset E Ottawa ON K1N 6N5 Canada

MOONEY, HAROLD ALFRED, plant ecologist; b. Santa Rosa, Calif., June 1, 1932; s. Harold Walter and Sylvia Anita Stefany; m. Sherry Lynn Gulmon, Aug. 15, 1974; children—Alyssa, Adria. A.B., U. Calif., Santa Barbara, 1957; M.A., Duke U., 1958, Ph.D., 1960. From instr. to assoc. prof. UCLA, 1960-68; asso. prof. Stanford U., 1968-73, prof. biology, 1975—, Paul S. Achilles prof. environ. biology, 1976—; advisor NRC, Dept. Energy, NSF, Electric Power Research Inst., Ford Found. Author: Mediterranean-type Ecosystems, 1973, Convergent Evolution in Chile and California, 1977, Components of Productivity of Mediterranean Climate Regions, 1981, Disturbance and Ecosystems, 1983, Physiological Ecology of North American Vegetation, 1985. Served with AUS, 1953-55. Guggenheim fellow, 1974; Nat. Acad. Scis. fellow, 1982; Am. Acad. Arts and Scis. fellow, 1982. Fellow AAAS; mem. Ecol. Soc. Am. (Mercer award 1961), Brit. Ecol. Soc. Current Work: Carbon balance of plants. Subspecialties: Ecology (environmental science); Photosynthesis. Home: 2625 Ramona St Palo Alto CA 94306 Office: Biology Dept Stanford Univ Stanford CA 94305

MOONEY, JAMES DONALD, computer science educator; b. Jersey City, Nov. 29, 1946; s. Donald J. and Anita M. (Degross) M.; m. Joan Arbogast, Apr. 29, 1972; 1 dau., Tara. B.S.E.E., U. Notre Dame, 1968; M.Sc., Ohio State U., 1969, Ph.D., 1977. Systems programmer Dymo Graphic Systems, Wilmington, Mass., 1971-79; asst. prof. computer sci. W.Va. U., Morgantown, 1979-82, assoc. prof., 1982—. Scoutleader, Boy Scouts Am., 1967-75. Mem. IEEE, Assn. Computing Machinery. Roman Catholic. Current Work: Computer architecture, text processing, operating systems. Subspecialties: Computer architecture; Operating systems. Home: 632 W Virginia Ave Morgantown WV 26505 Office: Dept Stats and Computer Sci W Va U Morgantown WV 26506

MOONEY, JOHN BRADFORD, JR., naval officer; b. Portsmouth, N.H., Mar. 26, 1931; s. John Bradford and Margaret Theodora (Akers) M.; m. Martha Ann Huntley, Dec. 25, 1953; children—Melinda Jean, Pamela Ann, Jennifer Joan. B.S., U.S. Naval Acad., 1953; student, U.S. Naval Submarine Sch., 1954. Commd. ensign U.S. Navy, 1953, advanced through grades to rear adm., 1979; served aboard USS Chilton, 1953-54, USS Burrfish, 1954-56, USS Sarda, 1956-59; instr. advanced tactics U.S. Naval Submarine Sch., 1959-61; asst. tng. officer, mem. staff Comdr. Submarine Forces Atlantic Fleet, 1961-62; exec. officer USS Sea Robin, 1962-64; officer-in-charge Trieste II and U.S. Navy Deep Submergence Group, 1964-66; comdg. officer USS Menhaden, 1966-68; plans and programs officer for deep submergence systems program coordinator Office Chief Naval Ops., Washington, 1968-71; chief staff officer Submarine Devel. Group 1, 1971-73; comdg. officer Naval Sta., Charleston, S.C., 1973-75; dep. dir. deep submergence systems div. Office Chief Naval Ops., Washington, 1975-77; comdr. Naval Tng. Ctr., Orlando, Fla., 1977-78; dir. total force planning div. Office Chief of Naval Ops., Washington, 1978-81, oceanographer of the Navy, 1981-83, now chief naval research. At controls of Trieste II when hull of Thresher was found on floor of Atlantic, 1964; coordinated dept search and recovery of hydrogen bomb lost off coast of Spain, 1966; condr. search and recovery operation from depth of 16,000 feet in Mid-Pacific, 1972. Active various dist. and council positions Boy Scouts Am., 1954-79, dist. chmn. Eastern Dist. Pequot council, 1961, exec. bd. Central Fla. Council, 1978. Decorated Legion of Merit, Meritorious Service medal with 2 gold stars, Navy Commendation medal with 2 gold stars; recipient spl. citation Armed Forces Recreation Assn., 1975. Mem. U.S. Naval Inst., Smithsonian Instn. Assocs., Nat. Geog. Soc., Marine Tech. Soc., Nat. Sojourners. Episcopalian. Club: N.H. Legion of Honor Preceptory. Lodges: Order DeMolay (Legion of Honor 1964); Mason; Shriners. Current work: Naval research and exploratory development. Office: Office of Naval Research Arlington VA 22217

MOONEY, RICHARD T., radiol. physicist, cons.; b. N.Y.C., Jan. 12, 1925; s. Michael J. and Rose G. M.; m. Cecilia G. Powers, Sept. 23, 1950; children: Maureen Rose, Michael Richard. B.S., Pratt Inst., 1944; M.S., N.Y.U., 1952. Diplomate: Am. Bd. Radiology, Am. Bd. Health Physics. Physicist Physics Service, N.Y.C. Dept. Hosps., 1950-60, prin. physicist, 1960-67; dir. physics services N.Y.C. Health and Hosps. Corp., 1967—; asst. prof. clin. radiology Sch. Medicine, SUNY-Stony Brook; cons. radiol. physics. Contbr. articles to profl. publs. Served to ensign USN, 1942-46. Fellow Am. Coll. Radiology; mem. Radiol. Soc. N.Am., Am. Assn. Physicists in Medicine, Am. Physics Soc., N.Y. Acad Scis. Roman Catholic. Inventor in field. Current Work: Research and development in radiology imaging techniques and radiation protection. Subspecialties: Imaging technology; Radiology in nuclear medicine. Home: 4 Edgemont Circle Scarsdale NY 10583 Office: 82-68 164th St Jamaica New York NY 11432

MOORE, ALAN FREDERIC, cardiovascular pharmacologist; b. Birmingham, Eng., Aug. 27, 1948; s. Frederic Hotchin and Olive May (Ballard) M.; m. Valerie Harvey, Dec. 16, 1972; children: Jessica, Eleanor. B.Sc. (hons.), U. Aston, Birmingham, 1970, Ph.D., 1974. Postdoctoral fellow Cleve. Clinic, 1974-76, project research scientist, 1976-77; asst. prof., pharmacology U. Houston, 1977-79; sr. research scientist Norwich Eaton Pharms., N.Y., 1979-82, unit leader, 1982-84, sect. chief research and devel., 1984—, also assoc. dir. product devel. Contbr. articles to profl. jours. Recipient Lower award Cleve. Clinic, 1976. Fellow Am. Heart Assn.; mem. Am. Soc. Pharmacology and Exptl. Therapeutics, N.Y. State Neurosci. Soc., Interam. Soc. Hypertension. Current Work: Etiology and maintenance of hypertension; development of peripherally and centrally acting drugs which regulate cardiovascular system. Subspecialty: Pharmacology. Home: 9 Eric St Norwich NY 13815 Office: Norwich Eaton Pharms Inc Subs Procter & Gamble Co PO Box 191 Norwich NY 13815

MOORE, BARBARA S. P., ocean engineer; b. Phila., July 4, 1942; d. Philip and Eleanor (Eckman) Schneider; m. John Norton Moore, Dec. 12, 1981. B.S. in Chem. Engring, Drexel U., 1965; M.S. Ocean Engring, Cath. U. Am., 1969. U.S. Peace Corps. vol., 1965-66; chem. engr. U.S. Navy, White Oak, Md., 1966, Naval Oceanographic Office, Washington, 1966-69; ocean engr. NOAA, Washington, 1969-83; sr. policy analyst internat. and ocean affairs Office of Sci. and Tech. Policy, White House, 1983—; guest lectr. Georgetown U., 1978-82, Am. U., 1983. Mem. Marine Tech. Soc., Am. Oceanic Orgn. (v.p. 1980-81), Tau Beta Pi. Republican. Episcopalian. Current work: International science policy, marine science policy. Subspecialty: Ocean engineering. Home: 602 Pendleton St Alexandria VA 22314 Office: Office Sci and Tech Policy Exec Office of Pres New Exec Office Bldg Washington DC 20500

MOORE, BENJAMIN L., clinical psychologist; b. Atlanta, Jan. 19, 1940; s. Donald Laverne and Carolyn (Carson) M.; m. Mary Evelyn Ratteree, June 8, 1963; children: Donald Todd, Kevin Carson. B.A., Emory U., 1961, M.Div., 1969; M.S., Fla. State U., 1971, Ph.D., 1973. Registered psychologist, Ill. cert. sch. psychologist, Ill. Child behavior cons. Regional Rehab. Ctr., Tallahassee, Fla., 1971-72; clin. psychology intern W.Va. U. Med. Ctr., Morgantown, 1972-73; asst. prof. dept. psychology Ill. State U., Normal, 1973-80, assoc. prof., 1980—; vis. assoc. prof. dept. psychology Ill. Wesleyan U., Bloomington, 1980; clin. dir. The Baby Fold, Normal, 1976—; impartial due processing hearing officer Ill. Office Edn., 1976-78; cons. several schs. for behavioral and emotionally disordered children, 1974—. Editor: Junction, 1968-69. Mem. pres's sci. adv. com. Ill. Wesleyan U., 1977-80; advisor Gov.'s Commn. on Children and Adolescent Mental Health and Devel. Disabilities, State of Ill., 1979-80; chmn. Council on Ministries, Calvary United Meth. Ch., Normal, 1979-80. Served to 1st lt. USAF, 1962-66. USPHS fellow, 1970-72; decorated Air Force Commendation medal with oak leaf cluster. Mem. Am. Psychol. Assn., Midwestern Psychol. Assn., Southeastern Psychol. Assn., Ill. Psychol. Assn., Assn. Behavior Analysis, Omicron Delta Kappa. Democrat. Current Work: Research on behavior and learning disorders/disabilities in children: Psychological assessment: theory and practice of behavior change and psychotherapy. Subspecialties: Behavioral psychology; Developmental psychology. Home: 14 Briarwood Ave Bloomington IL 61701 Office: The Baby Fold 108 E Willow St Normal IL 61761

MOORE, CARLA JEAN, geologist; b. Mount Morris, Ill., July 10, 1950; d. Vernon Earl and Ula (Rhone) Wilson; m. Ben Allen Potter, May 18, 1974 (div. 1979); m. Gary L. Moore, Aug. 31, 1979. B.S. in Geology, U. Mo., 1972, M.A. in Geology, 1975. Geologic field asst. U.S. Geol. Survey, Denver, 1975-76; geologist U.S. Dept. Commerce, NOAA, Boulder, Colo., 1976—. Mem. Geol. Soc. Am., Sigma Xi. Presbyterian. Current work: Development and implementation of computerized systems for the storge, retrieval and exchange of marine geologic information. Subspecialties: Geology; Geological systems development and data base management. Home: South Star Route Riverside Lyons CO 80540 Office: Word Data Ctr A for Marine Geology and Geophysics Nat Geophys Data Ctr E/GC3 NOAA 325 Broadway Boulder CO 80303

MOORE, CARLETON BRYANT, educator; b. N.Y.C., Sept. 1, 1932; s. Eldridge Carleton and Mabel Florence (Drake) M.; m. Jane Elizabeth Strouse, July 25, 1959; children—Barbara Jeanne, Robert Carleton. B.S., Alfred U., 1954, D.Sc. (hon.), 1977; Ph.D., Cal. Inst. Tech., 1960. Asst. prof. geology Wesleyan U., Middletown, Conn., 1959-61; mem. faculty Ariz. State U., Tempe, 1961—; now prof., dir. Center for Meteorite Studies; vis. prof. Stanford U., 1974; Prin. investigator Apollo 11-17; preliminary exam. team Lunar Receiving Lab., Apollo, 12-17. Author: Cosmic Debris, 1969, Meteorites, 1971; author: Principles of Geochemistry, 1982; Editor: Researches on Meteorites, 1961; editor: Jour. Meteoritical Soc; Contbr. articles to profl. jours. Fellow Ariz.-Nev. Acad. Sci. (pres. 1979-80), Meteoritical Soc. (pres. 1966-68), Geol. Soc. Am., Mineral. Soc. Am., AAAS (council 1967-70); mem. Geochem. Soc., Am. Chem. Soc., Sigma Xi. Current Work: Analytical geochemistry, meteorites, lunar samples, ceramic materials. Subspecialties: Geochemistry; Space chemistry. Home: 507 E Del Rio Dr Tempe AZ 85282

MOORE, DUNCAN THOMAS, optical engineering educator; b. Biddeford, Maine, Dec. 7, 1946; s. Thomas Fogg and Virginia Robinson (Wing) M.; 1 child, Matthew Duncan. B.A., U. Maine, 1969; M.S., U. Rochester, 1970, Ph.D., 1974. Asst. prof. optical engring. U. Rochester, N.Y., 1974-78, assoc. prof., 1978—; mgr. optics Nippon Schlumberger, Tokyo, 1983; pres. Gradient Lens Corp., Rochester, 1980—; cons. on optical engring. and gradient index materials, U.S., Asia, Europe, 1974—. Contbr. articles to profl. jours. Patentee lens systems. Fellow Soc. Photo-Optical Instrument Engrs., Optical Soc. Am.; mem. Am. Ceramic Soc., Soc. for Exploratory Geophysics. Subspecialty: Gradient-index optics. Home: 335 Aberdeen St Rochester NY 14619 Office: U Rochester Inst Optics Wilmot Bldg Rochester NY 14627

MOORE, EARL NEIL, veterinarian, physiology educator; b. Morgantown, W.Va., Dec. 19, 1932; s. Earl and Leola (VonWotring) M.; m. Jane Russell (div.); children—Kimberly K., Candice VonWotring; m. Barbara Jean Bray, May 6, 1977. D.V.M., Cornell U., 1956; B.A. in Physiology with honors, Cambridge U., 1957; Ph.D., SUNY-Syracuse, 1962; M.A. (hon.), U. Pa., 1972. Research asst., then assoc. in physiology Sch. Vet. Medicine, U. Pa., Phila., 1962-70, assoc. prof., 1966-70, prof., 1970—, prof. grad. group Grad. Sch. Arts and Scis., 1970—, prof. dept. medicine, 1971—, prof. grad. group comparative medicine, 1971—; William Daniel Stroud established investigator Am. Heart Assn., 1966-71. Editor: How to Evaluate a New Antiarrhythmic Drug, 1981; Sudden Cardiac Death and Congestive Heart Failure, Diagnosis and Treatment, 1983. Served to 1st lt. Vet. Corps, U.S. Army, 1956. NSF fellow, 1965, Fellow Am. Coll. Cardiology; mem. Southeastern Pa. Heart Assn. (gov. 1980), Cardiac Eletrophysiology Group (pres. 1975-76), Am. Fedn. Clin. Research, Phi Zeta. Presbyterian. Subspecialties: Physiology (biology); Cardiology. Home: 419 Karen Ln Wallingford PA 19104 Office: Sch Veterinary U Pa 3800 Spruce St Philadelphia PA 19104

MOORE, (EDWIN) NEAL, physics educator, consultant; b. Dallas, Aug. 14, 1934; s. Ernest Ethridge and Ruby Aline (Elkins) M.; m. Helen Ruth Blair, Aug. 30, 1962; children—Eric, Julie. B.S., So. Methodist U., 1957; M.S., Yale U., 1958, Ph.D., 1962. Lectr. physics U. Calif.-Santa Barbara, 1961-62; asst. prof. physics U. Nev., Reno., 1962-67, assoc. prof., 1967—. Author: Theoretical Mechanics, 1983. Contbr. articles to profl. jours. Mem. Am. Phys. Soc., Am. Assn. Physics Tchrs. Methodist. Current work: Interested in research and educational applications of personal computers. Subspecialty: Atomic and molecular physics. Home: 1475 Alturas Ave Reno NV 89503 Office: Dept Physics Univ Nev Reno NV 89557

MOORE, F. RICHARD, music educator; b. Uniontown, Pa., Sept. 4, 1944; s. Franklin L. and Anna Jane (White) M.; m. Cynthia Mettge; 1 child, Amanda R. B.F.A. in Performance, Carnegie Mellon U., 1966, B.F.A. in Composition, 1966; postgrad. U. Ill., 1967; M.S.E.E., Stanford U., 1975, Ph.D. E.E., 1977. Assoc. mem. tech. staff Bell Labs., Murray Hill, N.J., 1967-77, mem. tech. staff, 1977-79; prof. music U. Calif.-San Diego, La Jolla, 1979—, dir. computer audio research lab., 1979—, dir. Ctr. for Music Expt., 1982—; mem. editorial adv. bd. Computer Music Jour. MIT Press., 1979—. Author: (with others) Technology of Computer Music, 1969; Programming in C, 1985. Grantee NEA, Rockefeller Found., Ford Found., System Devel. Found., 1979—. Mem. Acoustical Soc. Am., IEEE, Audio Engring. Soc. Current work: Research in the creation of new music, new musical instruments, new knowledge about music through digital technology. Office: Ctr for Music Experiment Q-037 U Calif-San Diego La Jolla CA 92093

MOORE, FRANCIS MEARS, ceramic engineer; b. Cowpens, S.C., July 11, 1936; s. Wilbur Alfred and Annlyn M. (Mears) M.; m. Elaine Frank, Dec. 22, 1961; children—Wendy E., Frank, Eddie. B.S. in Ceramic Engring., Clemson U., 1958. Engr. Gen. Shale, Kingsport, Tenn., 1958-59; research engr. Drakenfeld Colors, Washington, Pa., 1959-62, salesman, 1963-80, mgr. mktg., 1980—. Patentee in field. Mem. Phoenix Award Com. Served to 1st lt. U.S. Army, 1959. Mem. Am. Ceramic Soc., Glass Tempering Assn. Soc. Glass Decorators, Soc. Glass Tech. Democrat. Lutheran. Current work: Ultraviolet applications on glass; automotive windshields; backlites printing; thermoplastic printing on glass; glass enamels. Subspecialties: Ceramic engineering; Ceramics. Home: 627 Murdoch St Washington PA 15301 Office: Drakenfeld Colors Box 519 Washington PA 15301

MOORE, GEORGE EUGENE, surgeon, educator; b. Minn., Feb. 22, 1920; s. Jesse and Elizabeth (MacRae) M.; m. Lorraine Hammell, Feb. 22, 1945; children—Allan, Laurie, Linda, Cathy, Donald. B.A., U. Minn., 1942, M.A., 1943, B.S., 1944, B.M., 1946, M.D., 1947, Ph.D. in Surgery, 1950. Intern, U. Minn. Hosp., Mpls., 1946-47, med. fellow in gen. surgery, 1947, dir. tumor clinic, 1951-53; sr. research fellow U. Minn. Med. Sch., Mpls., 1948-53, cancer coordinator, 1951-53; chief surgery Roswell Park Meml. Inst., Buffalo, 1953-72, dir. surgery, 1953-67; dir. pub. health research N.Y. State Health Dept., Albany, 1967-73; clin. prof. surgery SUNY-Buffalo, 1962-73; dir. surg. oncology Denver Gen. Hosp., 1973—; prof. surgery, U. Colo., 1973—; profl. research biologist, 1955-69; pres. Colo. Oncology Found., Lakewood, 1982—. Author: Diagnosis and Location of Brain Tumors, 1950; Cancerous Diseases, 1970. Contbr. numerous articles to profl. jours. Recipient Outstanding Citizens award Buffalo Evening News, 1958; Outstanding Sci. Achievement award, 1959; Disting. Achievement award Modern Medicine mag., 1962; Chancellor's medal U. Buffalo, 1963; Charles Evans Hughes award in pub. adminstrn. N.Y. State, 1963; Bronfman prize Am. Pub. Health Assn., 1964. Mem. Soc. Univ. Surgeons, Am. Surg. Assn., Halsted Soc. Current work: Practice includes patient care, medical teaching, medical research and cancer education; I hope to see the practical development of cell therapy for the infectious and cancerous diseases and genetic corrections of inherited disorders. Subspecialties: Surgery; Cell and tissue culture. Home: 13755 W Kentucky Dr Lakewood CO 80228 Office: Denver Gen Hosp 645 Bannock St Denver CO 80204

MOORE, GORDON E., electronics company executive; b. San Francisco, Jan. 3, 1929; s. Walter Harold and Florence Almira (Williamson) M.; m. Betty I. Whittaker, Sept. 9, 1950; children: Kenneth, Steven. B.S. in Chemistry, U. Calif., 1950; Ph.D. in Chemistry and Physics, Calif. Inst. Tech., 1954. Mem. tech. staff Shockley Semicondr. Lab., 1956-57; mgr. engring. Fairchild Camera & Instrument Corp., 1957-59, dir. research and devel., 1959-68; exec. v.p. Intel Corp., Santa Clara, Calif., 1968-75, pres., chief exec. officer, 1975-79, chmn., chief exec. officer, 1979—; dir. Micro Mask Inc., Silver King Ocean Farms., Varian Assocs. Inc., Transamerica Corp. Fellow IEEE; mem. Nat. Acad. Engring., Am. Phys. Soc., Electrochem. Soc. Current Work: Electrical, microchip technology; semiconductors. Subspecialties: Microchip technology (engineering); Semiconductors. Office: 3065 Bowers Ave Santa Clara CA 95051

MOORE, GORDON GEORGE, chemistry educator; b. Des Moines, Iowa, Mar. 18, 1935; s. Tolbert Clyde and Gladys Carolyn (Parsons) M.; m. Norma Jean Dillon, Sept. 1, 1956; children—Steven, Ronald, Cynthia. B.S., Iowa State U., 1956; M.S., Yale U., 1958, Ph.D., 1962. Postdoctoral research assoc. Brookhaven, Upton, Long Island, N.Y., 1960-62; asst. prof. Marshall Univ., Huntington, W.Va., 1962-65; asst. prof. Pa. State Univ., Abington, 1965-72, assoc. prof., 1972-77, prof., 1977—; research chemist U.S. Dept. Agr., Wyndmoor, Pa., 1967-83. Contbr. articles to profl. jours. Mem. Am. Chem. Soc., Pa. Acad. of Sci. Republican. Presbyterian. Current work: Synthetic organic chemistry, corrosion, lipids, molecules of biochemical interest. Subspecialty: Organic chemistry. Home: 163 Greyhorse Rd Willow Grove PA 29090 Office: Ogontz Campus Pa State Univ 1600 Woodland Abington PA 19001

MOORE, GREGORY FRANK, geoscience educator, researcher; b. Bismarck, N.D., Sept. 25, 1951; s. Walter Edgar and Mildred F. (Lang) M.; m. Susan K. Heller, Aug. 11, 1974; B.A., U. Calif.-Santa Barbara, 1973; M.A., John Hopkins U., 1974; Ph.D., Cornell U., 1978. Postdoctoral assoc. Cornell U., Ithaca, N.Y., 1977; asst. research geologist Scripps Inst. Oceanography, La Jolla, Calif., 1978-82; research geologist Cities Service Oil Co., Tulsa, 1982-83; assoc. prof. geoscis. U. Tulsa, 1984—. Contbr. articles to profl. jours. NSF grantee, 1979, 80, 81, 84. Fellow Geol. Soc. Am. (assoc. editor 1984); mem. Am. Geophys. Union, Am. Assn. Petroleum Geologists, Soc. Exploration Geophysicists. Current work: Tectonics of convergent margins, marine multichannel seismology, seismic stratigraphy. Subspecialties: Tectonics; Geophysics. Office: Dept Geoscis U Tulsa Tulsa OK 74104

MOORE, HENRY JOHN, II, planetary geologist; b. Albuquerque, Sept. 2, 1928; s. Daniel Chadwick Moore and Marion Elizabeth (Fox) Bryan; m. Patsy Ann Williams, June 14, 1959; children—Daniel Chadwick II, Donald Williams, Laura Elizabeth. B.S. in Minerology, U. Utah, 1951; M.S. in Econ. Geology, Stanford U., 1959, Ph.D., 1965. Geologist U.S. Geol. Survey, Grand Junction, Colo., 1955-57, Menlo Park, Calif., 1967—; sampler Anaconda Co., Butte, Mont., 1957; cons. geologist, Stanford, Calif., 1959-60; geologist Pinnacle Exploration, Salt Lake City, 1960; guest lectr. Menlo Coll., Calif., 1979—. Contbr. articles to profl. jours. Supervisory com. chmn. Menlo Survey Fed. Credit Union, 1984; merit badge counselor Boy Scouts Am., Palo Alto, Calif., 1974; coach Little League Baseball, Girls Softball, Palo Alto, 1970. Served to lt. USN, 1951-54, Korea. Recipient Exceptional Service award NASA, 1977, Group Achievement awards, 1972, 73, 77. Mem. Geol. Soc. Am. (astronaut tng. award 1973), AIME (Old Timer award, 1983), Am. Geophys. Union, AAAS, Sigma Xi. Methodist. Club: University (bd. dirs. 1984) (Palo Alto). Current work: Geology of the moon, mars and earth; geologic mapping of Io. Subspecialties: Planetology; Geology. Home: 528 Jackson Dr Palo Alto CA 94303 Office: US Geol Survey MS-946 345 Middlefield Rd Menlo Park CA 94025

MOORE, JAMES ROBERT, geol. oceanographer; b. Temple, Tex., May 18, 1925; s. James Robert and Mary Louise (Petty) M. B.S. with honors, U. Houston, 1951; M.A., Harvard U., 1954; Ph.D., U. Wales, 1964. Research geologist Standard Oil, Ohio, 1951-52; sr. scientist Texaco Research, 1956-66; chief marine geologist U.K.-Irish Sea Project, 1962-64; prof. U. Wis., Madison, 1966-77; also dir. marine lab.; prof., dir. Marine Sci. Inst., U. Alaska, 1977-79; prof. marine studies, dir. marine sci. inst. U. Tex., Austin, 1979—. Editor: Marine Mining, 1976—; editor-in-chief: Marine Series, 1978—; Contbr. articles to profl. jours. Served with USNR, 1943-46. Mem. Assn. Marine Mining (exec. sec.), Am. Assn. Petroleum Geologists, Soc. Econ. Mineralogists, Geochem. Soc., Challenger Soc. Oceanography, AAAS, Internat. Assn. Sedimentologists, Sigma Xi. Subspecialty: Geology. Home: PO Box 8178 Univ Tex Station Austin TX 78713 Office: Marine Inst Univ Tex Austin TX 78713

MOORE, JERRY LAMAR, nutritional company executive; b. Anderson, S.C., Feb. 28, 1942; s. James Edward and Edith Wilda (Callaham) M.; m. Ann Elizabeth Hamilton, June 25, 1966; children—Kimberly Kay, Karla Renee. B.S. in Dairy Sci., Clemson U., 1963; M.S. in Food Sci., U. Wis., 1965, Ph.D., 1967. Assoc. dir. corp. research and devel. Pillsbury Co., Mpls., 1972-77; v.p. research and devel. Mead Johnson & Co., Evansville, Ind., 1977—; mem. food and nutrition bd. Nat. Acad. Scis., Washington, 1981-84. Served to capt. Biosci. Corps, USAF, 1968-72. Mem. Am. Dietetic Assn., Inst. Food Technologists, Soc. for Nutrition Edn. (nat. officer 1973-77, 81-84), Nat. Nutrition Consortium (pres. 1983-85), Am. Inst. Nutrition, Sigma Xi. Current work: Nutrition products and services. Subspecialties: Food science and technology; Nutrition (biology). Home: 700 Cedar Hill Dr Evansville IN 47710 Office: Mead Johnson & Co 2404 Pennsylvania St Evansville IN 47721

MOORE, JOHN DUAIN, plant science educator; b. Lancaster, Pa., Dec. 11, 1913; s. Willis Duain and Charlotte Blanche (Rote) M.; m. Doris Fretz Blakemore, June 13, 1940; children: Barbara Moore Henderson, John Duain. B.S., Pa. State U., 1939; Ph.D., U. Wis., 1945. Asst. prof. plant pathology U. Wis.-Madison, 1945-49, asso. prof., 1949-54, prof. plant pathology, 1954-80, prof. emeritus, 1980—, dir. Univ. Exptl. Farms, 1974-79; U.S. Dept. Agr. agt., plant pathologist, Madison, 1956-65, collaborator, 1965-71; collaborator U.S. AID/U. Wis. Project, U. Ife, Ile-Ife, Nigeria, 1968-70, head dept. plant sci., 1968-70, dean Grad. Sch., 1969, dean faculty agr., 1969-70; mem. study team Future Nigerian-U.S. Linkages in Higher Edn., Nigeria, 1977. Translator (with R.M.S. Heffner and D.C. Arny), editor: (with D.C. Arny and R.N. Schwebke) Phytopathological Classic No. 11 (Investigations of the Brand Fungi and the diseases of plants caused by them with reference to grain and other useful plants), 1969; co-editor: Virus Diseases and Noninfectious Disorders of Stone Fruits in North America, 1976; contbr. articles profl. jours. Mem. Am. Phytopath. Soc. (asso. editor 1949-51), Bot. Soc. Am., AAAS, Am. Inst. Biol. Sci., Wis. Acad. Scis., Arts and Letters, Sigma Xi, Phi Eta Sigma, Phi Kappa Phi, Gamma Sigma Delta. Clubs: Rotary (Madison), Professional Men's (Madison). Subspecialty: Plant pathology. Home: 2918 Grandview Blvd Madison WI 53713

MOORE, JOHN HAYS, chemist, educator; b. Pitts., Nov. 6, 1941; s. John Hays and Mary Eva (Welfer) M.; m. Judy Williams, Aug. 10, 1963; children: John Hays, Victoria Inez. B.S., Carnegie Inst. Tech., 1963; M.A., Johns Hopkins U., 1965, Ph.D., 1967. Research assoc. Johns Hopkins U., Balt., 1967-79; asst. prof. chemistry U. Md., College Park, 1969-73, assoc. prof., 1973-77, prof., 1977—; vis. fellow Joint Inst. for Lab. Astrophysics, U. Colo.-Boulder, 1975-76; program officer NSF, 1980-81, 85. Author: Building Scientific Apparatus, 1982; Contbr. numerous articles to profl. jours. Mem. Am. Phys. Soc., Am. Chem. Soc., Sigma Xi. Current Work: Electron spectroscopy. Subspecialties: Physical chemistry; Atomic and molecular physics. Office: Chemistry Dept U Md College Park MD 20742

MOORE, JOHN ROBERT, biology educator, researcher; b. Bridgeville, Pa., Mar. 3, 1934; s. Robert Wilson and Edith (Mawhinney) M.; m. Elaine Ernest, Aug. 25, 1955; children—Daniel Robert, Lorna Diane. B.S. in Edn., Clarion State Coll., 1957; M.S. in Botany, U. Pitts., 1962, Ph.D. in Biology, 1965. Cert. sci. tchr., Pa. Tchr. sci. Keystone Joint Schs., Knox, Pa., 1958-62; grad. research asst. U. Pitts., 1962-65; assoc. prof. biology Clarion State Coll., Pa., 1965-67; prof. biology Clarion U. of Pa., 1967—; cons. Pa. Electric Co., Johnstown, 1978—. Vice pres. Clarion Area Authority, 1978—; dep. waterways patrolman Pa. Fish Commn., Harrisburg 1972; bd. dirs. Clarion County Planning Commn., 1983. Mem. Am. Inst. Biol. Scis., Ecol. Soc. Am., Sigma Xi. Republican. Methodist. Clubs: Concerned Sportsmen (Clarion) (del. 1980—), Clarion Rifle and Pistol. Lodge: Moose. Current work: Aquatic ecology, water pollution. Subspecialties: Ecology (biology); Limnology. Home: 526 Wood St Clarion PA 16214 Office: Biology Dept Clarion Univ of Pa Clarion PA 16214

MOORE, LAURENCE D., plant pathologist, educator; b. Danville, Ill., July 12, 1937; s. Jean W. and Marjorie (Spring) M.; m. Mary Ann Pichon, Aug. 16, 1958; children: Jean Martin, Susan Laura, Steven Dale, Ellen Spring. B.S., U. Ill., 1959; M.S., Pa. State U., 1961, Ph.D., 1965. Asst. prof. plant pathology Va. Poly Inst. and State U., Blacksburg, 1965-70, assoc. prof., 1970-84, prof., head dept., 1985—, chmn. interdepartmental grad. curriculum in plant physiology, 1981-83. Contbr. chpts. to books, articles to profl. jours. Mem. exec. bd. Blue Ridge Mountain Council Boy Scouts Am., 1975—, dist. scout chmn., 1976-78, scoutmaster, 1972-76. Recipient Silver Beaver award Boy Scouts Am., 1976. Mem. Am. Phytopath. Soc. (pres. Potomac div. 1982-83, counciler 1984—), Am. Inst. Biol. Scis. (councilor 1984-86), Am. Soc. Plant Physiologist, Va. Acad. Sci. Roman Catholic. Current Work: Disease physiology, mechanism of resistance, role of steroids, effects of pollution stress. Subspecialties: Plant pathology; Plant physiology (agriculture). Home: 615 Broce Dr NW Blacksburg VA 24060 Office: VA Poly Inst and State U 401 Price Hall Blacksburg VA 24061

MOORE, MICHAEL LEE, chemist; b. Tampa, Fla., Sept. 4, 1951; s. Arthur Lee and June Anne (Woitas) M.; m. Rita McLaughlin, Apr. 25, 1981; 1 child, Kevin Lee. B.S. in Chemistry, Furman U., 1973; Ph.D. in Biochemistry, Washington U., St. Louis, 1978. Research asst. Washington U., 1973-78; research assoc. U. Ill., Urbana, 1978-81; assoc. sr. investigator Smith Kline & French Labs., Phila., 1981-85, sr. investigator, 1985—. Contbr. articles to profl. jours. Patentee vasopressin antagonists. Fellow NSF, NIH. Mem. Am. Chem. Soc., AAAS, N.Y. Acad. Scis., Sigma Xi. Current work: Peptide synthesis; peptide conformational analysis; computer aided drug design; design of biologically active peptides and enzyme inhibitors. Subspecialties: Medicinal chemistry; Drug design. Home: 417 S Jackson St Media PA 19063 Office: Smith Kline & French Labs 1500 Spring Garden St Philadelphia PA 19101

MOORE, PATRICK DAVID, chemical researcher, computer scientist; b. Salt Lake City, Apr. 2, 1952; s. James Lowell and Vera (Blake) M.; m. Ann Tobey, Aug. 22, 1978; children—Suzanne, Karen, David. B.S., Calif. State U.-Northridge, 1973; M.A., Johns Hopkins U., 1975, Ph.D., 1977. Postdoctoral fellow MIT, 1978; research chemist Milliken Research Corp., Spartanburg, S.C., 1978-80; devel. chemist Milliken Chem., Spartanburg, 1980-85, devel. mgr., 1985—. Contbr. articles to profl. jours. Patentee in field. Mem. Am. Chem. Soc., Soc. Plastics Industry, Soc. Pulp and Paper. Club: Men's Garden (pres. 1983) (Spartanburg). Current work: Polymeric colorants, anhydride products. Subspecialties: Organic chemistry; Database systems. Office: Milliken Chem M700 PO Box 1927 Spartanburg SC 29304

MOORE, PETER BARTLETT, biophysical chemistry educator; b. Boston, Oct. 15, 1939; s. Francis Daniels and Laura Benton (Bartlett) M.; m. Margaret Sue Murphy, Jan. 30, 1966; children—Catherine, Philip. B.S. in Biophysics, Yale U., 1961; Ph.D., in Biophysics, Harvard U., 1966. Postdoctoral fellow Institut de Biologie Moleculaire, Geneva, 1966-67, M.R.C. Lab. Molecular Biology, Cambridge, U.K., 1967-69; asst. prof. molecular biophysics and biochemistry Yale U., New Haven, 1969-73, assoc. prof., 1973-76, assoc. prof. dept. chemistry, 1976-79, prof., 1979—; guest biophysicist Brookhaven Nat. Lab., Upton, L.I., N.Y., 1972—. Contbr. numerous articles to profl. jours. Guggenheim fellow, 1979-80. Mem. Am. Soc. Biol. Chemists, Biophys. Soc., Am. Chem. Soc., Sigma Xi. Democrat. Unitarian. Current work: Structure and function of nucleoproteins; ribosomes, neutron scattering techniques for structure determination; NMR studies of nucleoproteins. Subspecialties: Biophysical chemistry; Biochemistry (biology). Home: 30 Kent Dr Hamden CT 06517 Office: Dept Chemistry Yale U PO Box 6666 New Haven CT 06511

MOORE, RAYMOND FRANKLIN, research entomologist; b. Fisherville, Va., Dec. 17, 1927; s. Raymond Franklin and Louise (Linhos) M.; m. Verna Caricofe, June 5, 1951 (div. May 1977); children—R. Scott, S. Kent, Kurt E.; m. Barbara White, Sept. 8, 1979. B.S., Bridgewater Coll., 1951; M.A., U. Richmond, 1956; Ph.D., Rutgers U., 1959. Research entomologist Agrl. Research Service, U.S. Dept. Agr., Florence, S.C., 1959-65, 66-78, supervisory research entomologist, 1978—; asst. prof. Coker Coll., Hartsville, S.C., 1964-65, U. S.C.-Columbia, 1965-66, U. S.C.-Florence, 1966-68, 71-73. Co-editor: Handbook of Insect Rearing, 1985. Served with U.S. Army, 1946-48. Mem. Entomol. Soc. Am., Am. Chem. Soc., S.C. Entomol. Soc., Sigma Xi. Methodist. Current work: Rearing insects in laboratory on artificial diet. Subspecialty: Animal nutrition. Home: 851 Championship Dr Florence SC 29501 Office: Cotton Prodn Research Unit Agrl Research Service US Dept Agr PO Box 2131 Florence SC 29503

MOORE, RICHARD HARLAN, college dean, biology researcher; b. Houston, Sept. 16, 1945; s. Russell Lewis and Hazel (Harlan) M.; m. Robin Morris, May 14, 1977; 1 son, Merlin Morris. B.A., Vanderbilt U., 1967; M.A., U. Tex.-Austin, 1970, Ph.D., 1973. Staff scientist Environ. Cons., Inc., Dallas, 1973-74; asst. prof. biology Coastal Carolina Coll., Conway, S.C., 1974-78, assoc. prof., 1978—, chmn. div. sci., 1978-79, dean sch. sci., 1979—. Author: (with H. D. Hoese) Fishes of the Gulf of Mexico, 1977; contbr. articles to profl. jours. Leader Coastal Bend council Boy Scouts Am., Pt. Aransas, Tex., 1970-73; cub scout leader Coastal Carolina council, Pawley's Island, S.C., 1978-82; sec. adv. bd. trustees Waccamaw Sch., Pawley's Island, 1981—; bd. dirs. S.C. Crawfish Festival Assn., Pawleys Island, 1980—, Waccamaw chpt. Nat. Audubon Soc., Myrtle Beach, S.C., 1981—. Mem. Am. Soc. Zoologists, Soc. Systematic Zoology, Am. Soc. Ichthyologists and Herpetologists, Am. Fisheries Soc., Southeastern Fishes Council. Episcopalian. Current Work: Physiological ecology and evolutionary biology of aquatic organisms especially fish. Subspecialties: Marine biology; Evolutionary biology. Home: PO Box 513 Murrell's Inlet SC 29576Office: Coastal Carolina College PO Box 1954 Conway SC 29526

MOORE, RICHARD KERR, electrical and computer engineering educator, researcher; b. St. Louis, Nov. 13, 1923; s. Louis Daniel and Nina (Megown) M.; children—John, Daniel. B.S.E.E., Washington U., St. Louis, 1943; Ph.D., Cornell U., 1951. Registered profl. engr. Research assoc. Cornell U., Ithaca, N.Y., 1949-51; sect. supr. Sandia Corp., Albuquerque, 1951-55; lectr., prof. U. N.Mex., Albuquerque, 1953-56, chmn. elec. engring. dept., 1956-62; disting. prof. elec. and computer engring. U. Kans., Lawrence, 1962—; dir. Remote Sensing Lab, 1964-74, 84—; pres. CADRE Corp., Lawrence, 1968—; chmn. Commn. F, U.S. nat. com. Internat. Sci. Radio Union, 1985—. Author: Traveling Wave Engineering, 1960; (with others) Microwave Remote Sensing, 3 vols., 1982-86. Contbr. articles to engring. jours. Inventor poly-panchromatic target identification, 1971. Served to lt. (j.g.) USNR, 1944-46, PTO. Recipient Alumni Achievement award Sch. Engring, Washington U., 1978; (Outstanding Tech. Achievement award Council on Ocean Engring., 1978; Disting. Achievement award Geosci. and Remote Sensing Soc., Fellow IEEE 1982. Centennial award, 1984); mem. AAUP, Am. Soc. Engring. Edn. Presbyterian. Lodge: Kiwanis. Subspecialty: Electrical engineering. Home: 1620 Indiana St Lawrence KS 66044 Office: Remote Sensing Lab 2291 Irving Hill Dr Lawrence KS 66045-2969

MOORE, RICHARD OWEN, JR., chemical engineer, researcher; b. Columbus, Ohio, Jan. 29, 1956; s. Richard Owen and Marianne Ruth (Daries) M.; m. Susan Ellen Dufficy, May 3, 1980; 1 child, Richard Owen III. B.S., Rice U., 1978, M.Chem. Engring., 1979. Registered profl. engr., Calif. Research engr. Chevron Research Co., Richmond, Calif., 1979—. Mem. Am. Inst. Chem. Engrs. (profl. devel. recognition cert. 1981), Am. Chem. Soc. Current work: Process development in fuel technology, oil shale technology development, petroleum refining technology development. Subspecialties: Chemical engineering; Oil shale. Home: 6 Mt Palomar Ct San Rafael CA 94903 Office: Chevron Research Co PO Box 1627 Richmond CA 94802

MOORE, ROBERT AVERY, electrical engineer, administrator; b. Cullman, Ala., Aug. 12, 1932; s. Robert Edwin and Dorothy Genevieve (Avery) M.; m. Shirley Dean Brunner, Dec. 19, 1956; children—Robert I., Phyllis L., Sharon E. B.S.E.E., U. Ala., 1954; M.S.E.E., Northwestern U., 1956, Ph.D. in Elec. Engring., 1960. Registered profl. engr., Md. Sr. engr. Westinghouse Def. and Electronic Ctr., Balt., 1958-62, supr., 1962-68, mgr., 1968—. Contbr. articles to profl. jours. Patentee in field. Active ch., PTA, Boy Scouts Am. Served to 2nd lt. Signal Corps, U.S. Army, 1958-59. Recipient IR-100 New Product awards Indsl. Research mag., Chgo. Mem. IEEE (sr.; adminstrv. com. on sonics and ultrasonics 1978—), Sigma Xi. Democrat. Presbyterian. Current work: Advancing technology in microwave and electromagnetic technology. Subspecialty: Electronics. Home: 1243 Balfour Dr Arnold MD 21012 Office: Westinghouse Defense and Electronic Ctr PO Box 746 MS 335 Baltimore MD 21203

MOORE, ROBERT BLAINE, biochemist, educator; b. Toronto, Ont., Can., July 27, 1949; came to U.S., 1978; s. Kenneth Wayne and Dorothy Mary (Camamile) M.; m. Elizabeth Gizella Koszegi, Aug. 4, 1973; 1 child, Nicole Elizabeth. B.S., U. Toronto, 1972, M.S., 1974, Ph.D., 1978. NIH trainee, Houston, 1980; asst. prof. biochemistry U. South Ala., Mobile, 1982—. Recipient new investigator award NIH, 1983; U. Toronto scholar, 1971; Muscular Dystrophy fellow, 1978. Mem. Am. Soc. Biol. Chemists, Soc. for Neurosci., Tissue Culture Assn., Can. Soc. Biochemistry. Current work: Erythocyte membranes, calcium, acetylcholinesterase, Ca2++Mg2+-ATPase, membrane peroxidation, polyphosphoinositide metabolism. Subspecialties: Biochemistry (medicine); Hematology. Home: 5704 Greentree Rd Mobile AL 36609 Office: Dept Pediatrics U South Ala 2451 Fillingim St Mobile AL 36617

MOORE, ROBERT YATES, neuroscientist, neurologist; b. Harvey, Ill., Dec. 5, 1931; s. Raymond Irwin and Marie Louise (Fisher) M.; m. Gertrude Colston Nauman, Sept. 12, 1959 (div. June 1968); children—Elizabeth, Matthew, Joshua, Thomas; m. Jean Ellen Kavanaugh, May 24, 1969. B.A., Lawrence Coll., 1953; M.D., U. Chgo., 1957, Ph.D., 1962; M.D. (hon.), U. Lund, Sweden, 1974. Diplomate Am. Bd. Psychiatry and Neurology. Intern U. Mich., 1958-59; resident in neurology U. Chgo., 1959-63, asst. prof. to prof., 1962-74; prof. U. Calif.-San Diego, 1974-79; prof. neurology SUNY-Stony Brook, 1979—, chmn. dept., 1979—. Contbr. articles to profl. jours. NIH grantee, 1962—. Fellow Am. Acad. Neurology; mem. Am. Neurol. Assn., Soc. for Neurosci. (councilor 1974-78), Am. Anat. Assn., Am. Soc. Neurochemistry. Current work: Neural basis of circadian rhythm generation and regulation. Subspecialties: Neurobiology; Neurology. Home: 15 Hill Crescent Rd Port Jefferson NY 11777 Office: Dept Neurology SUNY Stony Brook NY 11794

MOORE, RONALD LEE, solar physicist; b. Fort Wayne, Ind., Mar. 30, 1942; s. Akin E. and Vernice Marjorie (Bosserman) M.; m. Barbara Joyce Welenc, Apr. 22, 1972; children—Heather Grace, Shannon Jean, Megan Elliott. B.S., Purdue U., 1964; M.S., Stanford U., 1965, Ph.D., 1972. Aerospace engr. NASA Ames Research Ctr., Moffett Field, Calif., 1964; research asst. solar physics Stanford U., Palo Alto, Calif., 1968-72; research fellow solar physics Calif. Inst. Tech., Pasadena, 1972-75, sr. research fellow solar physics, 1975-81; astrophysicist (solar studies) NASA Marshall Space Flight Ctr., Huntsville, Ala., 1981—, co-chmn. advanced solar obs. study 1981—; assoc. prof. physics dept. U. Ala.-Huntsville, 1981—; mem. mgmt. ops. working group NASA Office Solar and Heliospheric Physics, NASA Hdqrs., Washington, 1984—. Contbr. articles, papers to profl. publs., chpt. to book. Mem. Am. Astron. Soc. (councilor solar physics div. 1981-85), Internat. Astron. Soc., Sigma Xi. Current work: Origin, properties and effects of solar magnetic fields, solar magnetic cycle, sunspots, flares, filament eruptions, spicules, energy balance of solar atmosphere. Subspecialty: Solar physics. Office: Marshall Space Flight Ctr Huntsville AL 35812

MOORE, THOMAS EARLE, physicist, educator; b. Portsmouth, N.H., Nov. 23, 1948; s. Eben Noel Moore and Gladys Arline Whitney; m. Marleen Mae Mehlhorn, Aug. 22, 1970 (div. Apr. 1982); m. Gwen Marie Fowler, Aug. 13, 1983. B.S., U. N.H., 1970, M.A.T., 1971; Ph.D., U. Colo., 1978. Tchr. secondary sch., Bradford, Vt., 1971-74; research asst. U. Colo., 1974-78; research U. N.H., Durham, 1979-81, sr. research scientist, 1981-83; research scientist NASA, Huntsville, Ala., 1983-84, chief magnetospheric physics br. solar-terrestrial div., Space Sci. Lab., NASA Marshall Space Flight Ctr., 1984—. Contbr. articles to profl. jours. Designer ion mass spectrometer, 1977—. Mem. Lee Mcpl. Budget Com., N.H., 1982-83; advisor Huntsville Explorer troop Boy Scouts Am., 1983-84. Grantee NASA, 1980-83, NSF, 1980-83. Mem. Am. Geophys. Union, Am. Phys. Soc., Phi Beta Kappa, Pi Mu Epsilon. Clubs: Spring City Cycle (Huntsville); Kaypro Users Group (Madison, Ala.). Current work: Physics of planetary and solar plasma atmospheres and their extension into space, magnetospheric physics; low energy plasma composition and distribution measurements. Subspecialties: Plasma physics; Planetary atmospheres. Home: 10105 Bluff Dr Huntsville AL 35803 Office: Space Sci Lab Marshall Space Flight Center ES53 NASA Huntsville AL 35812

MOORE-EDE, MARTIN CHRISTOPHER, physiologist, researcher; b. London, Nov. 22, 1945; s. Roderick and Margaret Hatton (Riggall) M.-E.; m. Donna Smith, May 27, 1977; 1 child, Andrew. B.Sc. in Physiology, U. London, 1967; M.B., B.S., Guy's Hosp. Med. Sch., U. London, 1970; Ph.D. in Physiology, Harvard U., 1974. Instr. physiology Guy's Hosp. Med. Sch., 1970; intern in medicine Toronto East Gen. Hosp., 1970-71; research fellow in surgery Peter Bent Brigham Hosp., 1971-74; assoc. in surgery and physiology Harvard Med. Sch., 1974-75, asst. prof. physiology, 1975-81, assoc. prof. physiology, 1981—; dir. research lab. investigating the circadian timing system, 1974—; physiologist dept. surgery Brigham and Women's Hosp., 1982—; chmn. commn. on circadian rhythms and sleep physiology Internat. Union Physiol. Scis. Author: The Price of Defense, 1978, The Clocks That Time Us, 1982, Mathematical Models of the Circadian Sleep-Wake Cycle, 1983; Assoc. editor: Am. Jour. Physiology, Regulatory, Integrative and Comparative Physiology; contbr. numerous articles on the circadian timing system to profl. jours. Mem. Boston Study Group, 1974—; mem. Internat. Physicians for Prevention of Nuclear War, 1981—. Frank Knox fellow Harvard Med. Sch., 1971; Sci. Research Council fellow, 1971; Warren fellow Harvard U., 1972; recipient Cate award for scholarship Peter Bent Brigham Hosp., 1973; Andrew W. Mellon faculty award Harvard Med. Sch., 1975; Career Devel. award NIH, 1977-82. Fellow Brit. Interplanetary Soc.; mem. AAAS, Am. Fedn. Clin. Research, Internat. Soc. Chronobiology, Am. Physiol. Soc., Am. Soc. for Photobiology, Aerospace Med. Assn., Fedn. Am. Scientists, Sleep Research Soc., Endocrine Soc., Soc. Neurosci. Current Work: Anatomy and physiology of the circadian timing system. Regulation of the biological clocks that control the sleep-wake cycle. Applications of circadian theory to clinical medicine, occupational shift work schedules and aerospace medicine. Subspecialties: Physiology (biology); Space medicine. Office: Dept Physiology and Biophysics Harvard Med Sch 25 Shattuck St Boston MA 02115

MOOS, HENRY WARREN, physicist, educator, cons.; b. N.Y.C., Mar. 26, 1936; s. Henry H. and Dorothy (Warren) M.; m. Doris Elaine McClure, July 13, 1957; children: Janet, Paul, Daniel, David. Sc.B., Brown U., 1957; M.A., U. Mich., 1959, Ph.D. in Physics, 1962. Research assoc. Stanford U., 1961-63, acting asst. prof. physics, 1963-64; asst. prof. physics Johns Hopkins U., Balt., 1964-68, assoc. prof., 1968-71, prof., 1971—; cons., mem. govt. coms. NASA, Dept. of Energy; co-investigator Apollo 17 Ultraviolet Spectrometer and Voyager Ultraviolet Spectrometer. Contbr. numerous articles profl. jours. Sloan fellow, 1965-69; vis. fellow Joint Inst. Lab. Astrophysics/Lab. Atmospheric and Space Physics, U. Colo., 1972-73, 81-82. Fellow Am. Phys. Soc.; mem. Am. Astron. Soc. Current Work: Ultraviolet spectroscopy of high temperature fusion plasmas, ultraviolet astronomy of the planets. Subspecialties: Plasma physics; Ultraviolet high energy astrophysics. Home: 804 Post Boy Ct Towson MD 21204 Office: Physics Dept Johns Hopkins University Baltimore MD 21218

MOOS, WALTER HAMILTON, medicinal chemist; b. Canton, N.Y., July 25, 1954; s. Gilbert Ellsworth and Ruth Carolyn (Feinthel) M.; m. Susan Mary Miller, Aug. 10, 1979. A.B., Harvard U., 1976; Ph.D., U. Calif.-Berkeley, 1982. Scientist Warner-Lambert/Parke-Davis Pharm. Research, Ann Arbor, Mich., 1982-84, sr. scientist, 1984, research assoc., 1984—. Contbr. articles to profl. jours. Patentee in field. Harvard U. scholar 1976; fellow E.C. Anthony Found., 1977, Standard Oil Calif. 1979, Miller Inst. Research 1978. Mem. Am. Chem. Soc., Assn. Harvard Chemists, Sigma Xi, Alpha Chi Sigma. Current work: Rational drug design and synthesis; synthetic organic chemistry; computer-assisted chemistry; quantitative structure activity relationships; neuro and cardiovascular sciences. Subspecialties: Medicinal chemistry; Organic chemistry. Home: 3760 Green Brier Blvd Apt 349B Ann Arbor MI 48105 Office: Warner-Lambert/Parke Davis Pharm Research 2800 Plymouth Rd Ann Arbor MI 48105

MOOZ, ELIZABETH DODD, biochemist; b. Middletown, Conn., Nov. 22, 1939; s. John Alfred and Lillian (Potter) Dodd; m. R. Peter Mooz, Aug. 29, 1964; children—Ralph Peter, Christopher Dodd. B.A., Hollins Coll., 1961; Ph.D., Tufts U., 1967. Instr. research U. Pa., Phila., 1967-69; postdoctoral fellow U. Del., Newark, 1969-71; asst. prof., 1971-73; research assoc. Bowdoin Coll., Brunswick, Maine, 1973-76; research assoc., asst. prof. Va. Commonwealth U., Richmond, 1977-79; research scientist Philip Morris USA, Richmond, 1979—. Contbr. articles to profl. jours. Active Leadership Met. Richmond, 1983—; mem. women's com. Richmond Symphony; active Jr. League, Richmond. Mem. Am. Chem. Soc. (women chemist com. 1981—), Va. Acad. Sci., Sigma Xi (pres. Va. Commonwealth U. chpt. 1982-83). Republican. Episcopalian. Club: Torch (bd. dirs. 1985—). Current work: Gene isolation; biotransformation of flavors; enzymology, especially enzyme relation to plants (tobacco in particular). Subspecialties: Biochemistry (biology); Genetics and genetic engineering (biology). Home: 100 Gun Club Rd Richmond VA 23221 Office: Philip Morris USA Research Ctr PO Box 26583 Richmond VA 23261

MORABITO, DAVID DOMINIC, engr.; b. Los Angeles, Jan. 27, 1952; s. Dominic Don and Mary (Matosian) M. B.S. in E.E, U. So. Calif., 1974, M.S. in E.E, 1976, Engr. in E.E., 1983. Lic. radio telephone operator FCC, 1971. Electronics test technician Hoffman Electronics, El Monte, Calif., 1973; engr. Jet Propulsion Lab., Pasadena, Calif., 1973—. Contbr. articles in field to profl. jours. Mem. IEEE, Am. Astron. Soc., Am. Geophys. Union. Current Work: Astronomy, geodesy; studing extragalactic radio sources using very long baseline interferometry. Subspecialties: Radio and microwave astronomy; Cosmology. Office: 4800 Oak Grove Dr Pasadena CA 91103

MORAN, EMILIO FEDERICO, tropical agriculture educator, consultant; b. Habana, Cuba, July 21, 1946; came to U.S. 1961, naturalized, 1968; s. Emilio Federico and Caridad Benita (Corrales) M.; m. Millicent Fleming, Dec. 15, 1972; 1 child, Emily Victoria. B.A., Spring Hill Coll., 1968; M.A., U. Fla., 1969, Ph.D., 1975. Asst. prof. Ind. U., Bloomington, 1975-79, assoc. prof., 1979-84, prof. anthropology and tropical agriculture, 1984—, chmn. dept., 1981—; vis. prof. soil sci. N.C. State U., Raleigh, 1984; cons. AID, Washington, 1978, 82, WHO/PAHO, Washington, 1980. Editor: Ecosystem Concept in Anthropology, 1984; Human Adaptability, 1982, Developing the Amazon, 1981. Editor: The Dilemma of Amazonian Development, 1983. Contbr. articles to profl. jours. Tinker Found. fellow, 1984; Fulbright grantee, 1977; NIMH grantee, 1974; Social Sci. Research Council fellow, 1973. Fellow AAAS, Am. Anthropol. Assn., Soc. for Applied Anthropology; mem. Internat. Soil Sci. Assn., Ecol. Soc. Am., Latin Am. Studies Assn., Sigma Xi. Democrat. Current work: Development of sustainable agricultural systems, with emphasis on soil management, vertically integrated production and marketing; humid tropics in Amazonia. Subspecialties: Agronomy; Integrated systems modelling and engineering. Home: 1022 E First St Bloomington IN 47401 Office: Rawles Hall 108 Indiana Univ Bloomington IN 47405

MORAN, THOMAS FRANCIS, chemistry educator; b. Manchester, N.H., Dec. 11, 1936; s. Francis Leo and Mamie Marie M.; m. Joan Elinor Belliveau, June 25, 1960; children: Dorothy, Michael, Linda, Mary. B.A., St. Anselm's Coll., 1958; Ph.D., Notre Dame U., 1962. AEC postdoctoral fellow Brookhaven Nat. Lab., Upton, L.I., N.Y., 1962-64, assoc. scientist, 1964-66; asst. prof. Ga. Inst. Tech., Atlanta, 1966-68, assoc. prof., 1968-72, prof., 1972—. Contbr. numerous articles on chemistry to profl. jours. Recipient Ferst research award, 1970; Danforth assoc., 1971—. Mem. Am. Chem. Soc., Am. Phys. Soc., Am. Soc. for Mass Spectrometry, AAAS, Sigma Xi. Current Work: Gaseous ionic collision phenomena, kinetics and mechanisms of gaseous ion-molecule reactions, electron impact phenomena, energy conversion processes in chemical reactions. Subspecialties: Physical chemistry; Kinetics. Home: 2324 Annapolis Ct NE Atlanta GA 30345 Office: Chemistry Dept Ga Inst Tech Atlanta GA 30332

MORAVEC, HANS PETER, research scientist; b. Kautzen, Austria, Nov. 30, 1948; came to Can., 1952, came to U.S., 1971. Student in Engring, Loyola Coll., Montreal, Can., 1967; B.S. in Math, Acadia U. N.S., Can., 1969; M.Sc. in Computer Sci, U. Western Ont., 1971; Ph.D., Stanford U., 1980. Research asst. Artificial Intelligence Lab., Stanford (Calif.) U., 1971-80; research scientist Robotics Inst. and dept. computer sci. Carnegie-Mellon U., Pitts., 1980-85, sr. research scientist, 1985—; cons. Contbr. articles to profl. jours., presentations and filmstrips to profl. confs.; developer pamphlets and programs in computer sci. Mem. AAAS, ACM, Brit. Interplanetary Soc., IEEE, Nat. Space Inst., Space Studies Inst. Current Work: Mobile robots, navigational computer vision and sonar, computational physics, robotics prognostication. Subspecialties: Artificial intelligence; Robotics. Office: Robotics Inst Carnegie-Mellon U Pittsburgh PA 15213

MORAWETZ, CATHLEEN SYNGE, mathematician; b. Toronto, Ont., Can., May 5, 1923; d. John Lighton and Elizabeth Eleanor Mabel (Allen) Synge; m. Herbert Morawetz, Oct. 28, 1945; children—Pegeen Ann, John Synge, Lida Joan, Nancy Babette. B.A., U. Toronto, 1945; S.M., MIT, 1946; Ph.D., NYU., 1951; D. Sc. (hon.), Eastern Mich. U., 1980, Smith Coll., 1982, Brown U., 1982. Research assoc. MIT, Cambridge, 1951-52; from research asst. to prof. NYU, N.Y.C., 1946—, assoc. dir. Courant Inst. Math Scis., 1978-81, chmn. dept. math., 1981-84, dep. dir., 1981-84, dir., head, 1984—; trustee Alfred P. Sloan Found., N.Y.C., 1980—; dir. NCR Corp., Dayton, Ohio, 1978—; mem. Mayor's Commn. Sci. and Tech., 1984—. Guggenheim fellow, 1966-67, 1978-79. Fellow AAAS, mem. Assn. Women in Math. (Emmy Noether lectr. 1983), Can. Math. Soc. (Jeffrey-Williams lectr. 1984), Math Assn. Am. (Lester R. Ford award 1980), Am. Math. Soc. (Gibbs lectr. 1981), Soc. Ind. and Applied Math. (invited addressee 1982). Subspecialty: Applied mathematics. Office: Courant Inst Math Scis 251 Mercer St New York NY 10012

MORDFIN, LEONARD, mechanical engineer, consultant; b. Bklyn., June 23, 1929; s. Samuel and Margaret (Flyer) M.; m. Norma Marcia Reich, Oct. 10, 1954; children: Stephen Jay, Theodore Gary, Robin Ilene. B.M.E., Cooper Union, 1946; M.S., U. Md., 1954, Ph.D., 1966. Engr. Nat. Bur. Standards, Washington, 1950-67, 69-77, dep. program mgr. for nondestructive eval., 1977—; phys. sci. adminstr. Office Aerospace Research, Arlington, Va., 1967-69; cons. in field. Contbr. numerous articles to profl. jours.; contbr. to ency.; editor: (with Fong and Dobbyn) Critical Issues in Materials and Mechanical Engineering, 1981. Recipient Bronze Medal U.S. Dept. Commerce. Mem. ASME, Am. Soc. Nondestructive Testing, ASTM, Soc. Exptl. Mechanics. Jewish. Current Work: Materials testing, both mechanical and nondestructive; program management for developing new and improved standards for nondestructive evaluation of material, structures. Subspecialties: Materials (engineering); Theoretical and applied mechanics. Home: 1609 Billman Ln Silver Spring MD 20902 Office: Nat Bur Standards B344 Materials Bldg Gaithersburg MD 20899

MORE, SYVER WAKEMAN, geologist; b. Washington, Jan. 27, 1950; s. John William and Virginia (Wakeman) M.; m. Judith Ann Bessler, May 25, 1974; 1 child, Kristin Elisabeth. B.S. in Geoscis., U. Ariz., 1972, M.S. in Geoscis., 1980. Asst. exploration geologist Continental Oil Co., Tucson, 1972-73, mine devel. geologist minerals dept., Florence, Ariz., 1973-75; exploration geologist Amax Exploration Inc., Tucson, 1979, Billiton Exploration U.S.A., Tucson, 1980—. DuVal Corp. fellow, 1977. Mem. Geol. Soc. Am., Soc. Mining Engrs. of AIME, AAAS, Soc. Econ. Geologists, Am. Inst. Profl. Geologists, Research or work interests: Exploration and development of base-and precious-metal deposits; exploration program design and management. Subspecialties: Geology; Mineral exploration and development. Office: Billiton Exploration USA Inc 4500 E Speedway Suite 26 Tucson AZ 85712

MORELLI, UGO, government official; b. Medford, Mass., Oct. 2, 1922; s. Michele and Genoveffa (Flammia) M.; m. Dorothy E. Madison, Dec. 20, 1983. A.B., Harvard U., 1945, M.A., 1948. Sr. intelligence specialist U.S. Air Force, Washington, 1948-57; long-range planner Martin-Marietta, Balt., 1957-68; div. dir. Logos, Ltd., Arlington, Va., 1968-71; policy analyst Fed. Emergency Mgmt. Agy., Washington, 1971—. Mem. Earthquake Engring. Research Inst. Current work: Application of science and technology to the solution of problems related to abating the risks to people, organizations and structures posed by natural hazards in the U.S. Home: 2501 Calvert St NW Apt 810 Washington DC 20008 Office: Fed Emergency Mgmt Agy Washington DC 20472

MOREST, DONALD KENT, neurobiologist, educator; b. Kansas City, Mo., Oct. 4, 1934; s. F. Stanley and Clara Josephine (Riley) M.; m. Rosemary R., June 13, 1963; children: Lydia R., D. Claude. B.A., U. Chgo., 1955; M.D., Yale U., 1960. Asst. prof. anatomy U. Chgo., 1963-65; asst. prof. Harvard Med. Sch., Boston, 1965-70, assoc. prof., 1970-77; prof. U. Conn., Farmington, 1977—. Mem. Internat. Soc. Developmental Neurosci., Am. Assn. Anatomists, Soc. Neurosci., Assn. Research Otolaryngology. Current Work: Teacher, researcher in the structure, function and development of the auditory system. Subspecialties: Neurobiology; Anatomy and embryology. Office: U Conn Health Ct Dept Anatomy Farmington CT 06032

MORETTI, PETER MARC ALLAN, mechanical engineering educator, mechanical engineering consultant; b. Zurich, Switzerland, Apr. 13, 1935; came to U.S., 1949; s. Allen D.E. and Irma (Kesselring) M.; m. D. Diane Darms, June 1, 1961 (div. 1977); children—Stephen, Susan, Lisa; m. Johanna Tate, Dec. 30, 1977; children—Martin, Adrienne. B.S., Calif. Inst. Tech., 1957, M.S., 1958; postgrad. T.H. Darmstadt, Fed. Republic Germany, 1958-59; Ph.D., Stanford U., 1964. Registered profl. engr., Okla. Project mgr. Interatom, Bensberg, Fed. Republic Germany, 1964-68; sr. engr. Westinghouse ARD, Waltz Mill, Pa., 1968-77; asst. prof. mech. engring. Okla. State U., Stillwater, 1970-76, prof., 1976—; faculty fellow Stanford and NASA, Palo Alto, Calif., 1972, 75, 76; program mgr. U.S. Dept. Energy, Washington, 1977-78; cons. for numerous firms, 1970—. Contbr. articles to profl. jours. Fulbright scholar, 1958-59. Mem. ASME Mensa. Current work: Consulting and research on flow-induced vibrations in heat exchangers; also alternative energy technology: wind power and stratified thermal storage. Subspecialties: Mechanical engineering; Wind power. Home: 2202 N Glenwood Dr Stillwater OK 74075 Office: MAE Dept Okla State U EN 218 Stillwater OK 74078

MOREY, ELSIE D., paleobotanist, laboratory executive; b. Cambridge, Mass., Nov. 25, 1940; d. William Culp and Helen Marie (Hilsman) Darrah; m. Philip R. Morey, June 10, 1967. B.A., W. Va. U., 1963; M.S., So. Ill. U., 1965. Research technician Tex. A&M Research Sta., U.S. Dept. Agr., 1973-74; owner Morey Paleobotany Lab., Lubbock, Tex., 1977-82, Morgantown, W. Va., 1982—; histology technician dept. pathology W.Va. U. Med. Center. Contbr. articles to profl. jours. Mem. Bot. Soc. Am., Paleontology Soc., Nat. Soc. Histotechnology, W. Va. Soc. Histotechnology, Sigma Xi. Current Work: Fossil woods, ferns, lepidodendrons. Subspecialties: Morphology; Paleobiology. Home and Office: 200 Wagner Rd Morgantown WV 26505

MOREY, PHILIP RICHARD, research microbiologist, educator; b. Cleve., July 3, 1940; s. Everett F. and Helen M. (Szabo) M.; m. Elsie Louise Darrah, June 10, 1967. B.S. in Biology, U. Dayton, 1962; M.S., Yale U., 1964, Ph.D., 1967. Cert. Am. Bd. Indsl. Hygiene. Lectr. Harvard U., Cambridge, Mass., 1967-70; mem. faculty Tex. Tech U., Lubbock, 1970-82, prof. biology, 1967-82; research indsl. hygienist environ. invesitations br. Nat. Inst. Occupational Safety and Health, Morgantown, W.Va., 1982—; instr. Mining Acad., Beckley, W.Va., 1982—; adj. prof. Wood Sci. Sch. Forestry, W.Va. U., Morgantown, 1982—. Author: How Trees Grow, 1973; contbr. articles to profl. publs. Chmn. United Way Drive for Biol. Scis., Tex. Tech. U., 1980. Recipient Faculty Research award Coll. Arts and Scis., Tex. Tech U., 1980. Mem. Am. Indsl. Hygiene Assn., Bot. Soc. Am. (Albert E. Diamond Fund award 1975), Panhellenic Assn. (Tex. Tech U. Teaching award 1972), Am. Conf Govtl. Indsl. Hygienists, Am. Acad. Indsl. Hygiene, ASHRAE (vice chmn. environ. health com.). Republican. Roman Catholic. Current Work: Industral hygiene aspects of indoor air pollution; quantification of airborne microbes in office ventilation systems. Subspecialties: Health services research; Environmental engineering. Home: 200 Wagner Rd Morgantown WV 26505 Office: 944 Chestnut Ridge Rd Morgantown WV 26505

MORGAN, BRIAN LESLIE GORDON, nutrition educator; b. Gillingham, Kent, Eng., Jan. 6, 1947; came to U.S., 1975; s. Sydney William Gordon and Grace Hanna (Milner) M.; m. Roberta Eddie, Apr. 8, 1973. B.Sc., London U., 1971, M.Sc., 1972, Ph.D., 1975. Post-doctoral fellow Inst. Human Nutrition, Columbia U., 1975-78, assoc., 1978-79, asst. prof., 1979—; cons. Self and Family Circle mags., New York, 1981—. Author: Diet and Nutrition Program for Your Heart, 1982; The Lifelong Nutrition Guide, 1983; The High Carbohydrate Weight Loss Program, 1983; The Drug Nutrient Interaction Guide, 1986; Brain Food, 1986. Mem. N.Y. Acad. Sci. (animal research com., conf. com.), N.Y. Acad. Medicine (nutrition edn. in med./dentral schs. com.), British Nutrition Soc., Am. Inst. Nutrition, Harvey Soc., Am. Assn. Dental Schs., N. Am. Assn. Study of Obesity. Current Work: Thermogenesis, brown adipose tissue, and its role in obesity, function of gangliosides and glycoproteins in neurotransmission, nutrition and brain development. Subspecialty: Nutrition (medicine). Office: Inst Human Nutrition Columbia U Coll Physicians & Surgeons 701 W 168th St New York NY 10011

MORGAN, ERIC LEE, aquatic ecologist; b. Hickory, N.C., Feb. 17, 1940; s. Karl Ziegler and Helen Lee (McCoy) M.; married July 13, 1965 (div. 1975); 1 child, Sean K. B.S., Middle Tenn. State U., 1964, M.S., 1969; Ph.D., Va. Polytech. Inst. & State U., 1973. Research asst. U. Ga. Savannah River Ecol. Lab., 1965-67; research assoc. Dept. Energy Comparative Animal Physiology Lab., 1967-68; asst. prof. U. Tenn., Chattanooga, 1969-70; asst. prof., dir. environ. biology research program Tenn. Tech. U., Cookeville, 1973-79; assoc. prof., dir. environ. biol. research program, 1979—, dir. upper Cumberland Biol. Sta., 1981-83; assoc. AWARE, Inc., Nashville, 1973—, ERM-Southeast, Inc., Brentwood, Tenn., 1980—; asst. Environ. Toxicology Cons., Inc., Little Rock, 1981—. Contbr. articles to sci. jours. Tenn. Acad. Sci. fellow; served as prin. investigator in charge of numerous research grants and contracts for indsl. and govtl. sources. Mem. Care Research Found., AAAS, Ecol. Soc. Am., Internat. Assn. Water Pollution Research. Soc. Internat. Limnologiae, Internat. Water Resources Assn., Soc. Environ. Toxicology and Chemistry, ASTM, Am. Soc. Limmology and Oceanography, Beta Beta Beta, Phi Sigma Xi. Democrat. Lutheran. Current work: Aquatic ecology and toxicology; biological monitoring; applications of automated computer assisted biological monitoring systems in ecological quality assessments. Subspecialties: Ecology (environmental science); Environmental toxicology. Home: 1570 Forrest Rd Cookeville TN 38501 Office: Tennessee Tech Univ Box 5187 Cookeville TN 38505

MORGAN, HOWARD EDWIN, physician, physiology educator; b. Bloomington, Ill., Oct. 8, 1927; s. Lyle Verdell and Ethel Emma (Bailey) M.; m. Helena Lawson, Sept. 12, 1947; children—Stephen Lyle, Patricia Lynn Morgan Wehler. M.D., Johns Hopkins U., 1949. Intern Vanderbilt U., Nashville, 1949-51, resident, 1949-53, research fellow, 1953-55; from asst. to prof. Physiology, 1957-67; prof. Pa. State U., Hershey, 1967—; adv. Nat. Heart, Lung and Blood Inst., Bethesda, Md., 1979-83, Howard Hughes Med. Inst., 1981—, Whitaker Found., 1980—. Contbr. articles to profl. jours. Served to capt. M.C., U.S. Army, 1955-57. Recipient Merit award Am. Heart Assn., 1979. Mem. Am. Physiol. Soc. (council, 1983—, chmn. com., 1980—), Am. Soc. Biol. Chemists. Current work: Regulation carbohydrate energy and protein metabolism in heart; cardiac hypertrophy; effects of insulin and diabetes. Subspecialties: Physiology (medicine); Biochemistry (medicine). Office: Dept Physiology Pa State U Hershey PA 17033

MORGAN, JOHN PAUL, physician, educator; b. Cin., Jan. 14, 1940; s. Bristo and Helen Louise (Neeley) M.; m. Claudia Garland Burghardt, Sept. 5, 1964; children—Jennifer Lyle, Zachary Ross. B.S., U. Cin., 1962, M.D., 1965. Diplomate Am. Bd. Internal Medicine. Intern, SUNY Upstate Med. Ctr., Syracuse, 1965-66, asst. resident, 1966-67; fellow medicine Johns Hopkins Sch. Medicine, Balt., 1969-70; asst. prof. medicine and pharmacology U. Rochester, N.Y., 1972-77; assoc. prof. Mt. Sinai Sch. Medicine, N.Y.C., 1977—; assoc. prof. medicine Sch. Biomed. Edn., CCNY, N.Y.C., 1977-81, prof. medicine, dir. pharmacology, 1981—; adj. scholar Ctr. Study Drug Devel., Rochester, 1979—. Author; editor: Abuse Misuse Amphetamine, 1980; Society and Medication, 1983; Adverse Reaction Phenylpropanolamine, 1984. Served to capt. USAF, 1967-69. Recipient Career Tch. award Nat. Inst. Drug Abuse, 1974-76, Characterizing Excessive Prescribing award Calif. Med. Soc., 1983, Generic Prescription Laws award Princeton Inst. Health Policy Research, 1982, Look Alike Drugs award Smith Kline French, 1979, Phenylpropanolamine Adverse Reactions award Thompson Med. Co., 1984. Fellow N.Y. Acad. Medicine; mem. Assn. Med. Sch. Pharmacology, Calif. Soc. Treatment of Alcoholism and Other Drug Dependencies, Am. Soc. Clin. Pharmacology and Therapeutics. Democrat. Subspecialty: Molecular pharmacology. Home: 251 W 89th St #10E New York NY 10024 Office: CUNY Med Sch CCNY Convent Ave at 138th St New York NY 10031

MORGAN, PAUL WINTHROP, chemist; b. West Chesterfield, N.H., Aug. 30, 1911; s. Herbert and Olive (Lermond) M.; m. Elsie Louise Bridges, Aug. 27, 1939; children—Dennis Lee, Patricia Morgan Harding. B.S. in Chemistry, U. Maine, 1937; Ph.D. in Organic Chemistry, Ohio State U., 1940. Postdoctoral fellow Ohio State U., Columbus, 1940-41; with E.I. duPont de Nemours & Co., Wilmington, Del., 1941-76, research fellow, 1957-73, sr. research fellow, 1973-76, chem. cons., West Chester, Pa., 1976—; cons., lectr. in field; chmn. Gordon Research Conf. on Polymers, 1974. Author: Condensation Polymers, 1965; contbr. articles to profl. jours. Asst. dist. commr. Minquas Trail dist. Chester County council Boy Scouts Am., 1956-61; asst. scoutmaster Chester County council, 1961-76, chmn. troop com., 1976—. Recipient Silver Beaver award Boy Scouts Am., 1967, Swinburne award Plastics and Rubber Inst., London, 1978, Engring. Materials Achievement award Am. Soc. Metals, 1978. Mem. Am. Chem. Soc. (Best Publ. of Yr. award Del. chpt. 1959, 78, nat. Polymer Chem. award 1976, Midgley award Detroit chpt. 1979), Nat. Acad. Engring., Franklin Inst. (Howard N. Potts medal 1976), Mineral. Soc. Pa., Sierra Club, Appalachian Trail Conf., Wilderness Soc., Audubon Soc., Nat. Wildlife Assn., Early Am. Industries Assn., Chester County (Pa.) Hist. Soc., Fiber Soc. (hon.). Research on low temperature polycondensation, heat resistant fibers, high-strength, high-modulus fibers Current Work: Consultant in polymer science and technology; specialist in condensation polymers, high tenacity fibers, liquid crystalline systems. Subspecialties: Polymer chemistry; Polymers (materials science). Home and Office: 822 Roslyn Ave West Chester PA 19382

MORGAN, STEPHEN LYLE, software engineer; b. Nashville, Oct. 20, 1949; s. Howard Edwin and Helena Mae (Lawson) M.; m. Renee Ellen Lautzenhiser, June 1, 1974; children: Jonathan, Geoffrey. B.A., Johns Hopkins U., 1971; M.S., Pa. State U., 1974. Grad. asst. Pa. State U., State College, 1971-74; cons., State College, 1974-77; engr. HRB-Singer, Inc., State College, 1977-79, advanced engr., 1979-81, sr. engr., 1981—; mayor's fellowship intern City of Balt., 1971. Mem. Nat. Computer Graphics Assn., Am. Assn. Geographers, Am. Congress on Surveying and Mapping, Am. Soc. Photogrammetry, Assn. Computing Machinery. Methodist. Clubs: Optimist (pres. 1981-82), Pa. Guild Craftsman, Nittany Valley Gem and Mineral. Current Work: Automated cartography, digital terrain analysis addressing problems of movement in space and locational analysis. Subspecialties: Graphics, image processing, and pattern recognition; Algorithms. Home: 335 Douglas Dr State College PA 16803 Office: HRB-Singer Inc Dept 123 Box 60 Science Park State College PA 16803

MORGAN, WILLIAM ANDREW, geologist, researcher; b. Madison, Wis., Jan. 24, 1953; s. James Robert and Evonne Marie (Kellerman) M. B.S. in Geology, U. Wis., 1975, M.S. in Geology, 1977. Assoc. geologist Conoco Inc., Casper, Wyo., 1977-78, geologist, Oklahoma City, petroleum geologist, staff geologist, project supr., 1978-83, sr. research scientist, research assoc., Ponca City, Okla., 1983—. Contbr. numerous articles to profl. and sci. jours. Mem. Am. Assn. Petroleum Geologists, Geol. Soc. Am., Oklahoma City Geol. Soc. (sec., v.p., Presdl. appointee 1982—), Soc. Economic Paleotologists and Mineralogists (v.p. mid-continent sect. 1984-85, mem. continuing edn. com. 1982—), Internat. Assn. Sedimentologists. Current work: Carbonate geology, petroleum geology. Subspecialties: Sedimentology; Fuels. Home: PO Box 20067 3329 Green Wing Ct Oklahoma City OK 73156 Office: Conoco Inc 1000 S Pine St Ponca City OK 74603

MORGAN, WILLIAM WILSON, astronomer, educator; b. Bethesda, Tenn., Jan. 3, 1906; s. William Thomas and Mary McCorkle (Wilson) M.; m. Helen Montgomery Barrett, June 2, 1928 (dec. 1963); children: Emily Wilson, William Barrett; m. Jean Doyle Eliot, 1966. Student, Washington and Lee U., 1923-26; B.S., U. Chgo., 1927, Ph.D., 1931; D.Honoris Causa, U. Cordoba, Argentina, 1971; D.Sc. (hon.), Yale U., 1978. Instr. Yerkes Obs., U. Chgo., Williams Bay, Wis., 1932-36, asst. prof., 1936-43, asso. prof., 1943-47, prof., 1947-66, Bernard E. and Ellen C. Sunny Distinguished prof. astronomy, 1966-74, prof. emeritus, 1974—, chmn. dept. astronomy, 1960-66; dir. Yerkes and McDonald Observatories, 1960-63; mng. editor Astrophys. Jour., 1947-52; Henry Norris Russell lectr. Am. Astron. Soc., 1961. Author: (with P.C. Keenan, Edith Kellman) An Atlas of Stellar Spectra, 1943, (with H.A. Abt and J.W. Tapscott) Revised MK Spectral Atlas for Stars Earlier than the Sun, 1978; contbr. research articles to profl. publs. Recipient Bruce gold medal Astron. Soc. Pacific, 1958, Henry Draper medal Nat. Acad. Scis., 1980. Mem. Am. Acad. Arts and Scis., Nat. Acad. Scis.; mem. Pontifical Acads. Scis.; Mem. Royal Danish Acad. Scis. and Letters, Royal Astron. Soc. (assoc. Herschel medal), Nat. Acad. Scis. Argentina, Soc. Royale des Sciences de Liege. Congregationalist. Current work: General System for classification of old stars of population II. Subspecialty: Optical astronomy. Office: Yerkes Observatory Box 258 Williams Bay WI 53191

MORGANROTH, JOEL, cardiologist; b. Detroit, Oct. 29, 1945; s. Benjamin and Grace (Greenfield) M.; m. Gail Morrison, June 25, 1982. B.S., U. Mich., 1968, M.D., 1970. Diplomate Am. Bd. Internal Medicine. Intern, Beth Israel Hosp., Boston, 1970-71, resident, 1971-72; resident Nat. Heart and Lung Inst., Bethesda, Md., 1972-74, Hosp. U. Pa., Philadelphia, 1974-75; asst. prof. medicine U. Pa., Phila., 1975-78; assoc. prof. Jefferson U., Phila., 1978-82, prof., 1982; prof. Hahnemann U., Phila., 1982—; dir. Nat. Cardiovascular Research Ctr., Haddonfield, N.J., 1982—; dir. sudden death prevention program Likoff Cardiovascular Inst., Phila., 1982—; cons. to numerous companies. Author 9 books on cardiology. Mem. editorial bd. circulation, 1981-83, Am. Jour. Cardiology, 1981—, Jour. Am. Coll. Cardiology 1982—, Jour. Clin. Ultrasound, 1982—. Contbr. articles to profl. jours. Pres. elect southeast Pa. chpt. Am. Heart Assn., 1985—; pres. Philadel Acad. Cardiology, 1985—. Served as surgeon USPHS, 1972-74. Fellow Am. Coll. Cardiology, ACP, Am. Coll. Chest Physicians, Am. Coll. Clin. Pharmacology, Councils of Clin. Cardiology and Atherosclerosis Am. Heart Assn. Current work: Clinical research in noninvasive technology, and study of new cardiac drugs and preventive atherosclerosis. Subspecialty: Cardiology. Home: 1344 Valley Rd Villanova PA 19085 Office: Hahemann U Broad and Vine Sts Philadelphia PA 19102

MORIARTY, JOHN ALAN, physicist, educator; b. Chgo., Jan. 17, 1944; s. Richard Joseph and Beverly (Bleeker) M.; m. Joyce Diane Harper, June 7, 1969; children—Kevin Neal, Joanne Gale. A.B., U. Calif.-Berkeley, 1965; Ph.D., Stanford U., 1971. Postdoctoral asst. Los Alamos Nat. Lab., 1971-73, U. Cambridge, Eng., 1973-74; research assoc. Coll. of William and Mary, Williamsburg, Va., 1974-79; asst. prof. U. Cin., 1979-82; physicist Lawrence Livermore Nat. Lab., Calif., 1982—. Contbr. articles to sci. jours. Recipient cert. of achievement NASA, 1979, grantee, 1974-83. Mem. Am. Phys. Soc. Current work: Theory of electronic structure and properties of solids and liquids, especially interatomic forces, structural phase stability and lattice dynamics. Subspecialty: Condensed matter physics. Home: 5427 Dudley Ct Pleasanton CA 94566 Office: Lawrence Livermore Nat Lab Mail Code L-299 Livermore CA 94550

MORIN, LAWRENCE PORTER, neuroscientist, researcher, educator; b. Portsmouth, N.H., Aug. 11, 1947; s. Lawrence J. and Barbara A. (Porter) M.; m. Margaret Burdick, Sept. 14, 1947; children: Abigail A., Jennifer B. A.B., Brown U., 1969; Ph.D., Rutgers U., 1974. NIMH postdoctoral fellow dept. psychology U. Calif., Berkeley, 1974-76; faculty dept. psychology Dartmouth Coll., 1976-81; research scientist L.I. Research Inst. Health Scis. Center; research asst.prof. psychiatry SUNY, Stony Brook, 1982—. Contbr. articles to profl. jours. Mem. Soc. Neurosci., AAAS, Internat. Soc. Chronobiology. Current Work: Reproductive system and biological rhythms. Circadian, Ultradian, rhythms, sex differences, hamsters, hormones, neural control, environmental influences. Subspecialties: Psychobiology; Chronobiology. Home: 34 Old Post Rd Setauket NY 11733 Office: Dept Psychiatry and Behavioral Science HSC 10T SUNY Stony Broo NY 11794

MORINO, LUIGI, aerospace and mechanical engineering educator, researcher; b. Rome, July 21, 1938; came to U.S., 1967; s. Renato and Maria (Corbo) M.; m. Arianna Fucini, Sept. 30, 1965 (div. 1976); children—Federica, Francesca; m. Nancy J. Roche, June 9, 1984. Dr. Mech. Engring., U. Rome, 1963, Dr. Aerospace Engring., 1966. Registered profl. engr., Mass. Asst. prof. aerospace engring. U. Rome, 1965-67; NATO fellow MIT, Cambridge, 1967-68, sr. research engr., 1968-69; adj. assoc. prof. Boston U., 1968-69, assoc. prof. aerospace and mech. engring., 1968-77, prof., 1977—, dir. computational continuum mechanics program, 1973-77, dir. Ctr. for Computational and Applied Dynamics, 1977—; cons. to govt. and industry; proposal reviewer NSF, Dept. Energy, Army Research Office. Reviewer Jour. Aircraft, AIAA Jour., IEEE Transaction on Automatic Control; contbr. articles and reports to profl. publs. Research grantee NASA, 1970—, NSF, 1975-80, Army Research Office, 1979—, Air Force Office of Sci. Research, 1983-84, Dept. Energy, 1975-78. Mem. AIAA, Am. Soc. Engring. Edn., AAAS, Nat. Assn. Profl. Engrs., Am. Helicopter Soc., ASME, Epsilon Nu Gamma, Tau Beta Pi.

Current work: Integral equation methods for solution of partial differential equations; applications to fluid dynamics and structural dynamics. Subspecialties: Aeronautical engineering; Analysis. Office: Boston Univ 110 Cummington St Boston MA 02215

MORLEY, BARBARA JANE, biochemist, researcher, educator; b. Cleve., Oct. 14, 1946; d. John James and Ruth Violet (Hockman) M. B.A., MacMurray Coll., 1968; Ph.D. U. Maine, 1973. Research assoc. U. Maine, Orono, 1972-73; asst. prof. biopsychology William Paterson Coll., Wayne, N.J., 1973-76; postdoctoral fellow U. Ala. Med. Sch., Birmingham, 1976-78, asst. prof., 1978-80; assoc. prof. biochemistry Creigton U. Med. Sch., Omaha, 1980—; staff scientist Boys Town Nat. Inst., Omaha, 1980—. Contbr. articles and abstracts to profl. jours., chpt. to books. Mem. Coalition for Sci. and Tech., Washington, 1983—. Grantee NSF, 1978, 79, 82, 84, Deafness Research Found., 1984, NIH, 1984. Mem. Soc. for Neurosci., N.Y. Acad. Scis., Sigma Xi, Phi Kappa Phi. Democrat. Methodist. Current work: Developmental aspects of brain organization; reorganization of brain following injury, using biochemical and immunocyto chemical procedures. Subspecialties: Neurochemistry; Neuropharmacology. Office: Boys Town Nat Inst 555 N 30th St Omaha NE 68131

MORLEY, HENRY BARCLAY, chemical company executive; b. Sydney, N.S., Can., Apr. 25, 1929; came to U.S., 1953, naturalized, 1962; s. Clarence Gregory and Jessie Bolby (Armstrong) Bohemian m. Annette Hauck, Dec. 16, 1972; children by previous marriage—Edward Bruce, Christopher Engen, Gary Stuart. B.Sc., St. Francis Xavier U., 1948; Ph.D., U. Toronto, 1953. Dir. Eastern Research Center, Stauffer Chem. Co., Dobbs Ferry, N.Y., 1962-67, asst. to pres., N.Y.C., 1967-68, v.p. tech., 1968-70, exec. v.p., 1970-72, pres., 1972-74, pres., chief exec. officer, Westport, Conn., 1974—, chmn. bd., 1977—; dir. Bank of N.Y., Champion Internat., Chesebrough-Pond's, Inc. Mem. Fairfield County council Boy Scouts Am.; trustee Greens Farms Acad., Nutrition Found., Inc. Mem. Soc. Chem. Industry. Clubs: Pequot Yacht, Board Room, Blind Brook, Fairfield Country, Econ. (N.Y.C.); Bohemian (San Francisco). Office: Stauffer Chem Co Westport CT 06881

MORRE, D. JAMES, biochemist; b. Owensville, Mo., Oct. 20, 1935; s. Harvey Henry and Donna Marie (Maurer) M.; m. Dorothy M. Wibberg, Aug. 25, 1956; children: Connie Marie, Jeffrey Thomas, Suzanne Anette. B.S., U. Mo., 1957; M.S., Purdue U., 1959; Ph.D., Calif. Inst. Tech., 1962; doctorate (hon.), U. Geneva, 1985. Asst. prof. Purdue U., 1963-66, asso. prof., 1966-71, prof., 1971—; dir. Purdue U. (Purdue Cancer Center), 1976—Current Work: Research in membrane biochemistry, membrane biogenesis, glycolipids and tumorigenesis. Subspecialties: Biochemistry (biology); Membrane biology. Office: Purdue Cancer Cente Pharmacy Bldg Purdue Uni West Lafayette IN 47907

MORRIS, CHARLES REGINALD, instrument and control engineer; b. Halifax, N.S., Can., July 29, 1953; came to U.S., 1978; s. George Reginald and Lise Ida (Brunet) M.; m. Pamela Jean Blissett, May 11, 1974. B.S. in Elec. Engring, McMaster U., 1975. Registered profl. engr., Ont. Jr. engr. in tng. Ont. Hydro, Rolphton, Ont., 1975-77, asst. tech. supr., Tiverton, 1978; jr. engr. Kans. Gas and Electric, Wichita, 1978-79, engr., 1979-80, engr. III, 1980-81, sr. engr., 1981-82, lead engr., 1982—. Mem. Am. Nuclear Soc., Assn. Profl. Engrs. Province Ont. Current Work: Design review for instrumentation and controls for the Wolf Creek Nuclear Plant. Responsible for all nuclear instrumentation and controls, radiation monitoring equipment and plant security. Subspecialties: Nuclear engineering; Electronics. Home: 1637 Timberline Dr Rose Hill KS 67133 Office: Kans Gas and Electric Co 201 N Market Wichita KS 67201

MORRIS, DON MELVIN, surgery educator, surgeon; b. Longview, Tex., Jan. 4, 1946; s. John Raymond and Martha (Walker) M.; m. Judy Ray Miller, Sept. 7, 1970 (div. 1979); 1 son, Curtis John Walker; m. Katherine Ruth Crowe, June 26, 1982. A.S., Kilgore Jr. Coll., 1966; B.A. in Biology, U. Tex.-Austin, 1968; M.D., U. Tex. Med. Br., 1972. Diplomate: Am. Bd. Surgery. Intern Bexar County Hosp., U. Tex. Med. Sch., San Antonio, 1972-73; resident U. Md. Hosp., Balt., 1973-75, 76-78, Balt. Cancer Research Ctr., 1975-76; instr. in surg. oncology U. Md. Hosp., Balt., 1978-80, asst. prof. surg. oncology, 1980-81; asst. prof. surgery La. State U. Med. Ctr., Shreveport, 1981-84, assoc. prof., 1984—, dir. breast cancer detection clinic, 1981—; prin. investigator La. State U. Med. Ctr. (Nat. Surg. Adjuvant Breast and Bowel Project), 1981—; chief surg. service VA Med. Ctr., Shreveport; cons. to hosps. Contbr. articles on breast, head and neck and colon cancer and other topics to profl. jours. Am. Cancer Soc. Jr. clin. faculty fellow, 1978-81. Fellow ACS; mem. AMA, Soc. Surg. Oncology, Am. Soc. Clin. Oncology, Alpha Omega Alpha. Republican. Mem. Christian Ch. (Disciples of Christ). Current Work: Breast cancer, head and neck cancer, colon cancer, surgical techniques and devices, electrical potentials of cancerous tissues, monolclonal antibodies. Subspecialties: Surgery; Chemotherapy. Home: 5210 Foxglove Dr Bossier City LA 71112 Office: La State U Med Ctr 1501 Kings Hw PO Box 33932 Shrevepor LA 71130

MORRIS, GEORGE VINCENT, chemist, educator; b. Providence, Nov. 18, 1930; s. Patrick J. and Mary A. (McKenna) M.; m. Mary Louise Morris, June 6, 1959; children: Susan E., Jennifer M. B.S., Providence Coll., 1952; M.S., U.R.I., 1957, Ph.D., 1962. Research chemist Eltex Chem. Co., 1957-60; Naval Underwater Systems Ctr., Newport, R.I., 1962-65; with Raytheon Co., Portsmouth, R.I., 1966—; now sr. chemist, prof. chemistry and physics Salve Regina Coll., Newport, 1963—; cons. in field. Mem. Republican City Com., Riverside, R.I., 1970-76. Served with U.S. Army, 1952-54. NSF fellow, 1968-69; grantee, 1968. Mem. Am. Chem. Soc. (chmn. R.I. sec 1982—). Patentee in field. Current Work: Kinetics of reactions in solution; thermochemistry; decomposition of inorganic solids, physical properties of composite materials, instrumentation. Subspecialties: Physical chemistry; Materials. Home: 41 Merritt Rd Riverside RI 02915 Office: Salve Regina Coll Newport RI 02840

MORRIS, J(OSEPH) ANTHONY, microbiologist, public interest organization official; b. Marboro, Md., Sept. 6, 1918; s. Charles Lafayette and Essie (Stokes) M.; m. Ruth Savoy, Nov. 1, 1942; children: Carol Ann, Marilyn T., Joseph A., Larry A. B.Sc., Cath. U. Am., 1940, M.Sc., 1942, Ph.D., 1947. Asst. scientist Josiah Macy Jr. Found., N.Y.C., 1943-44; virologist Depts. Agr., Interior, Laurel, Md., 1944-47; virologist, chief hepatitis virus research Walter Reed Army Inst. Research, Washington, 1947-56; virologist, asst. chief dept. virus and rickettsial diseases U.S. Army Med. Command, Japan, 1956-59; virologist chief sect. respiratory viruses, div. biologics standards NIH, Bethesda, Md., 1959—; dir. slow latent and temperate virus br. FDA, Bethesda, 1972-76; lectr. dept. microbiology U. Md., College Park, 1977-79; vice chmn., Bell of Atri, Inc., College Park, 1979-81, chmn., 1982; cons. Commn. on Influenza, Armed Forces Epidemiologic Bd., 1960—, Nat. inst. Neurol. Diseases and Blindness, 1962—. Mem. Soc. Tropical Medicine and Hygiene, Soc. Am. Microbiologists, Soc. Exptl. Biology and Medicine, Am. Assn., Immunologists, N.Y. Acad. Sci. Discoverer of respiratory sycytial virus. Current Work: Cause and prevention of infectious diseases; research on infectious hepatitis, respiratory disease of virus etiology and zoonosis. Subspecialties: Microbiology; Virology (biology). Home: 23-E Ridge Rd Greenbelt MD 20770 Office: PO Box 40 College Park MD 20740

MORRIS, NILS RONALD, pharmacology educator; b. N.Y.C., July 22, 1933; s. Walter B. and Mary M.; m. Patricia A. Flagg, Aug. 17, 1957; children—Joshua, Sarah. B.S., Yale U., 1955, M.D., 1959. Asst. prof. Yale U., New Haven, 1963-67; asst. prof. UMDNJ-Rutgers Med. Sch., Piscataway, 1967-68, assoc. prof., 1968-72, prof. pharmacology, 1972—. Contbr. articles to profl. jours. Mem. Genetic Soc. Am., Soc. Cell Biology. Current work: Molecular biology of mitosis; microtubules, mitosis, tubulin chromatin. Home: 1488 Main St Somerville NJ 08870 Office: UMDNJ-Rutgers Med Sch PO Box 1 Piscataway NJ 08854

MORRIS, RALPH WILLIAM, pharmacologist; b. Cleveland Heights, Ohio, July 30, 1928; s. Earl Douglas and Viola Minnie (Mau) M.; children: Christopher Lynn, Kirk Stephen, Timothy Allen and Todd Andrew (twins), Melissa Mary. B.A., Ohio U., Athens, 1950, M.S., 1953; Ph.D., U. Iowa, 1955; postgrad., Seabury-Western Theol. Sem., 1979-81. Research fellow in pharmacology, then teaching fellow U. Iowa, 1952-55; instr. dept. pharmacology Coll. Medicine, 1955-56; asst. prof. dept. pharmacognosy and pharmacology Coll. Pharmacy, 1956-62, assoc. prof., 1962-69; prof. pharmacology Med. Center, U. Ill., Chgo., 1969—; adj. prof. edn. Med. Center, U. Ill. (Circle campus), 1976-83; vis. scientist San Jose State U., Calif., 1982-83; mem. adv. com. 1st aid and safety Midwest chpt. ARC, 1972—; cons. in drug edn. to Dangerous Drug Commn., Ill. Dept. Public Aid, Chgo. and suburban sch. dists., profl. socs., social agys., trial attys., also others. Referee and contbr. articles to profl. and sci. jours., lay mags., radio and TV appearances. Trustee Palatine (Ill.) Public Library, 1967-72, pres., 1969-70; trustee N. Suburban Library System, 1968-72, pres., 1970-72, mem. long-range planning com., 1975-81; mem. Title XX Ill. Citizens' Adv. Council, 1981-83; bd. dirs. United Campus Ministry U. Ill. at Chgo., 1983—. Recipient Golden Apple Teaching award U. Ill. Coll. Pharmacy, 1966; cert. of merit Town of Palatine, 1972. Mem. AAAS, Am. Assn. Coll. Pharmacies, Am. Pharm. Assn., Ill. Pharm. Assn., Internat. Soc. Chronobiology, Am. Soc. Pharmacology and Exptl. Therapeutics, Drug Info. Assn., Am. Library Trustee Assn., Ill. Library Trustee Assn. (v.p. 1970-72, dir. 1969-72), Sigma Xi, Rho Chi, Gamma Alpha. Episcopalian. Current Work: Medical applications of biological rhythms to health, disease and drug therapy; positive drug education instead of drug abuse scare tactics, positive relationships amongst biological rhythms,drug responses and religious beliefs. Subspecialties: Chronobiology; Pharmacology. Home: 3302 W Golfview Rd McHenry IL 60050 Office: 833 S Wood St Chicago IL 60612

MORRIS, ROBERT HOWARD, mechanical and nuclear engineer; b. Roanoke, Va., Sept. 27, 1950; s. Warren L. and Margaret (Cummings) M.; m. Diana Humphreys, Apr. 22, 1978. B.S. with honors with honors in Mech. Engring., U. Hawaii, 1974; M.S. in Nuclear Engring., U. Wis., 1976. Registered profl engr., Tenn., Calif. Devel. assoc. III Oak Ridge Nat. Lab., Tenn., 1976-80; sr. engr. Burns and Roe, Inc., Oak Ridge, 1980-83, Nutech Engrs., San Jose, Calif., 1983-84; pres. RHM Engring., San Luis Obispo, Calif., 1984—. Contbr. articles on reactor safety and advanced reactor research. Mem. ASME, Am. Nuclear Soc., ASME, Am. Soc. Quality Control. Current work: Providing consulting services to the nuclear, defense and aerospace industry in the areas of quality assurance and quality control with special expertise in nuclear, mechanical and computer engineering for computer generating stations. Subspecialties: Mechanical engineering; Nuclear engineering. Home and Office: PO Box 3805 San Luis Obispo CA 93403

MORRIS, ROBERT SCOTT, chemist, research company executive; b. New Bedford, Mass., Mar. 8, 1947; s. Benson and Mary Lurenna (Durrigan) M.; m. Carole Ann Gardner, May 21, 1977; children—Julie Alixandra, Brian Scott Gardner. B.S. in Chemistry, Southeastern Mass. U., 1969; postgrad. U. Vt., 1969-70, Northeastern U., 1975-77. Staff scientist Giner, Inc., Waltham, Mass., 1976-79; sr. scientist ECO, Inc., Newton, Mass., 1979-83; v.p. Cape Cod Research, Buzzards Bay, Mass., 1983—. Bd. dirs. Opportunity Ctr., New Bedford, 1984. Current work: Use of novel magnetic polymeric materials in the separation of select chemicals from complex matrices. Subspecialties: Biomaterials; Separation science. Home: 32 Fort St Fairhaven MA 02719 Office: Cape Cod Research 228 Main St Buzzards Bay MA 02532

MORRISON, DAVID LEE, research institute administrator; b. Butler, Pa., Jan. 25, 1933; s. Charles R. and Mildred (McFadden) M.; m. Carole J. White, July 31, 1954; children—Scott, Karyn. B.S. in Math., Grove City Coll.; M.S. in Chemistry, Carnegie Inst. Tech., 1960, Ph.D. in Nuclear Chemistry, 1961; postgrad. Northwestern U., 1971, U. Calif., 1975. Chemist, Gallery Chem. Co., 1954-61; sr. chemist Battelle's Columbus Labs., Columbus, Ohio, 1961-64, project dir. nuclear reactor safety program, 1964-67, chief chem. physics div., 1967-70, mgr. environ. systems and processes dept., 1970-74, sr. program mgr., mgr. energy and environ. programs officer, 1974-75, assoc. dir., 1975-77; pres., trustee Ill. Inst. Tech. Research Inst., Chgo., 1977—; dir. AccuRay Corp., Columbus; adviser Golder, Thomas & Cressey Fund, Chgo., 1982—. Contbr. numerous articles to profl. jours. Mem. Utilities Commn., Western Springs, Ill., 1979-83; mem. Mayor Jane Byrne's Task Force on High Tech. Devel., Chgo., 1981-82; mem. Nat. Materials Adv. Bd., 1982—; bd. dirs. Chgo. High Tech. Assn., 1984—. Served with USAF, 1954-57. Mem. Grove City Coll. Alumni Assn. (Jack Kennedy achievement award 1981), Western Soc. Engrs. (chmn. awards com. 1982-84), Armed Forces Communications and Electronics Assn., AAAS, Am. Chem. Soc., Am. Nuclear Soc., Am. Def. Preparedness Assn., Chgo. Assn. Commerce and Industry, Sigma Xi. Clubs: Economic, Plaza (Chgo.); Cosmos (Washington). Current work: Development and management of technology for economic vitality and fulfillment of national missions; development and application of energy resources. Subspecialty: Energy research administration. Office: Ill Inst Tech Research Inst 10 W 35th St Chicago IL 60616

MORRISON, DOUGLAS WILDES, zoology educator, researcher; b. Schenectady, Nov. 8, 1947; s. Lincoln Wildes and Harriet (Drake) M.; m. Susan Hagen, July 31, 1976; children—Daniel, Julia. A.B., U. Rochester, 1969; Ph.D., Cornell U., 1975. Asst. prof. zoology Rutgers U., Newark, 1975-80, assoc. prof., 1980—. Contbr. articles to profl. jours. Grantee NSF, 1976-79, Nat. Geog. Soc., 1979. Mem. Animal Behavior Soc., Ecol. Soc. Am., Am. Soc. Mammalogists, Assn. Tropical Biology. Democrat. Current work: Social and foraging behavior of tropical fruit bats and birds, especially radio tracking studies. Subspecialties: Behavioral ecology; Sociobiology. Home: 31 Hanover Rd Mountain Lakes NJ 07046 Office: Dept Zoology Rutgers U Newark NJ 07102

MORRISON, FRANCIS SECREST, physician; b. Chgo., July 29, 1931; s. Clifton B. and Marie B. (LaPierre) M.; m. Dorothy Daniels, Nov. 29, 1957; children: Francis, Thomas, Kenneth. Student, U. Ill., Chgo., 1949-51; B.S. with honors, Miss. State U., 1954; M.D., U. Miss., 1959. Diplomate: Am. Bd. Internal Medicine. Intern Hosp. of U. Pa., Phila., 1959-60, resident in internal medicine, 1960-62; trainee in hematology Blood Research Lab., Tufts-New Eng. Med. Center, Boston, 1962-64, research fellow, 1964-65; vis. investigator St. Mary's Hosp., London, 1966; attending physician, dir. div. hematology and oncology Univ. Hosp., Jackson, Miss., 1969-80, dir. div. hematology, 1980—, dir. blood transfusion service, 1974—; cons. in hematology Miss. Meth. Rehab. Center, Jackson, 1976; asst. prof. medicine U. Miss., Jackson, 1969-70, dir. div. hematology, 1969—, assoc. prof., 1970-76, prof., 1976—; mem. faculty U. Miss. (Grad. Sch. Medicine), 1971—; profl. adv. Jackson Community Blood Bank, Inc., 1973-75; dir. regional cancer program, also regional blood program Miss. Regional Med. Program, 1971-75; exec. dir. Miss. Regional Blood Center, 1975-79; mem. adv. bd. Jackson-Hinds Comprehensive Health Center, 1973-78; research cons. Alcorn A. and M. Coll., 1973-74; guest lectr. various health orgns. and TV programs; mem., chmn. hemophilia adv. bd. Miss. Bd. Health, 1974—; chmn. task force on regionalization Am. Blood Commn., 1978-80; mem. Miss. Gov.'s Council on Aging, 1976—. Contbr. numerous articles on hematology and oncology to med. jours. Pres. parish council St. Peter's Cathedral, Jackson, 1972-74; chmn. Natchez-Jackson Diocesan Com. Community Services, 1972-76; bd. dirs. Miss. Opera Assn., 1973-78; pres. bd. St. Joseph High Sch., 1974-75. Served to comdr. M.C. USN. Fellow ACP; mem. Am. Assn. Blood Banks (sci. workshop com. 1975-78), Internat. Soc. Blood Transfusion, Am., Internat. socs. hematology, Jackson Acad. Medicine (pres. 1976), Am. Coll. Nuclear Medicine (alt. del. Miss. 1975), Am. Assn. Cancer Edn. (exec. com. 1978-81), Am. Assn. Cancer Research, N.Y. Acad. Scis., Miss. Acad. Scis., World Fedn. Hemophilia, Internat. Soc. Thrombosis and Haemostasis, Central Med. Soc., So. Med. Assn., Miss. Med Assn. (com. on blood transfusion 1976—), Am. Soc. Nuclear Medicine, Am. Soc. Clin. Oncology, S.W. Oncology Group (prin. investigator), Soc. Cryobiology, Am. Cancer Soc. (dir. 1971—, pres. Miss. div. 1977, chmn. exec. com. 1978, nat. del. 1981-82), South Central Assn. Blood Banks (program chmn. 1975, v.p. 1977-79), So. Blood Club (pres. 1977), Council Community Blood Centers (trustee 1975-79), Internat. Platform Assn., Sigma Xi, Phi Kappa Phi, Omicron Delta Kappa. Current Work: Research in acuteleukemia-treatment and supportive care, especially blood and blood cell transfusion support. Subspecialties: Hematology; Cancer research (medicine). Home: 1402 Hazel St Jackson MS 39202 Office: U Miss Sch Medicine 2500 N State St Jackson MS 39216

MORRISON, PHILIP, physics educator; b. Somerville, N.J., Nov. 7, 1915; m. Phyllis Singer; 1 son. B.S., Carnegie Inst. Tech., 1936; Ph.D., U. Calif.-Berkeley, 1940. Instr. physics San Francisco State Coll., U. Ill.-Urbana, 1941-42; physicist Metall. Lab., U. Chgo., 1943-44; physicist, group leader Los Alamos Sci. Lab., 1944-46; assoc. prof. to prof. physics Cornell U., Ithaca, N.Y., 1946-65; prof. physics MIT, Cambridge, 1965—, James R. Killian Jr. faculty achievement award lectr., 1984-85. Author: Powers of Ten; co-editor: The Search for Extra-terrestrial Intelligence; book reviewer Sci. Am.; contbr. articles in physics to profl. jours. Recipient Pregel prize, 1955, Babson prize, 1957; Westinghouse sci. writing prize AAAS; decorated Oersted medal, 1965. Fellow Am. Phys. Soc.; mem. Nat. Acad. Scis., Am. Astron. Soc. Subspecialty: High energy astrophysics. Office: Dept Physics MIT Cambridge MA 02139*

MORRISON, RODERICK GORDON, nuclear engineer, electronic production company executive; b. Alhambra, Calif., Apr. 16, 1924; s. Emery Alexander and Christine Katherine (McLean) M.; m. Bonnie Jean Parker, Dec. 28, 1943; children: Robert Emery, Allan Keith, James Ross. A.B., Fresno State U., 1948. Test engr. So. Calif. Edison, Big Creek, 1949-51; design engr. Kern County Land Co., Bakersfield, Calif., 1952-53, Los Alamos Nat. Lab., 1953-57, 60-67; test ops. mgr. EG & G, Las Vegas, Nev., 1957-60; devel. mgr. Phillips Petroleum, Idaho Falls, Idaho, 1967-71, GA Technologies, Inc., San Diego, 1978—. Mem. campaign com. Republican Nat. Conv., Carlsbad, Calif., 1980—. Served with USMC, 1941-46. Mem. Am. Nuclear Soc., IEEE. Republican. Patentee gamma compensated fission detection, 1971, isotopic precipitation gauge, 1974, low level snow precipitation gauge, 1976, flow measuring method and apparatus, 1977. Current Work: Improved microprocessor based measurement systems for nuclear source detector applications using semiconductor detectors; emphasis on miniaturization and low power consumption. Subspecialties: Microelectronics; Nuclear engineering. Home: 2022 Cima Ct Carlsbad CA 92008 Office: GA Technologies Inc PO Box 81608 San Diego CA 92138

MORRISON, ROGER BARRON, geologist, writer; b. Madison, Wis., Mar. 26, 1914; s. Frank Barron and Elise (Bullard) M.; m. Harriet Louise Williams, Apr. 7, 1941; children: John Christopher, Craig Brewster, Peter Hallock. B.A. in Geology, Chemistry, Cornell U., 1933, M.S. in Geology, 1934; Ph.D. in Geology, U. Nev.-Reno, 1964. Geologist U.S. Geol. Survey, Denver, 1939-76; vis./adj. prof. dept. geosciences U. Ariz., Tucson, 1976-80; consulting geologist Morrison and Assocs., Golden, Colo., 1978—, mng. ptnr., 1978—; adj. prof. MacKay Sch. Mines, U. Nev.-Reno, Lake Bonneville, 1983—. Author: Quartenary Stratigraphy of eastern Jordan Valley, 1965, (with J.C. Frye) Correlation of Middle and Late Quartenary Successions of Lake Lahontan, Lake Bonneville, 1965; also, U.S. Geol. Survey Profl. Papers; Editor: (with J.C. Frye) publs. of Internat. Assn. Quaternary Research; contbr. (with J.C. Frye) over 50 articles in field to profl. jours. NASA grantee Landsat and Skylab projects, 1972-75. Fellow Geol. Soc. Am.; mem. AAAS, Am. Soc. Photogrammetry, Soil Sci. Soc. Am., Internat. Soil Sci. Assn., Internat. Assn. Quaternary Research, Am. Quartenary Assn. Current Work: Environmental geology; quaternary geology and geomorphology; soil stratigraphy and pedology; remote sensing of earth resources; airphoto and image analysis/mapping of geologic terrains, soils, and minerals; quartenary stratigraphy and paleoclimatic history of NW Nev.; pliocene and quartenary stratigraphy and tectonics of Arizona. Subspecialties: Geology; Tectonics. Office: Morrison and Associates 13150 W 9th Ave Golden CO 80401

MORRISON, STANLEY ROY, chemical physics educator, administrator; b. Sask., Can., Sept. 24, 1926; s. Latto McKechnie and Lilian (Prowse) M.; m. Phyllis May Parkinson, Aug. 27, 1949; children—Catherine, Deborah, Barbara. B.A., U. B.C., M.A.; Ph.D., U. Pa., Research assoc. U. Ill.-Urbana, 1953-55; scientist, mgr. Honeywell, Hopkins, Minn., 1955-64; Stanford Research Inst., Menlo Park, Calif., 1964-82; prof., dir. Simon Fraser U., Burnaby, B.C., 1982—; vis. scientist U. Göttingen, W. Ger., 1971-72, U.S. Army Labs., Fort Monmouth, N.J., 1978. Author: Chemical Physics of Surfaces, 1977, Semiconductor Electro DES, 1981; co-author: Adsorption, 1972. Mem. Am. Phys. Soc., Can. Assn. Physicists, Can. Inst. Chemists. Current work: Physics and chemistry of semiconductor surfaces, coatings, gas sensors, semiconductors devices. Subspecialty: Surface chemistry. Office: Simon Fraser U Physics Dept Burnaby BC V5A 1S6 Canada

MORROW, GARY ROBERT, clinical psychology/research educator; b. Pitts., Mar. 4, 1944; s. J. Robert and Frances (Pertes) M.; m. Joan Marilyn Baumgartner, June 7, 1967; children: Andy, J.J., Jennifer. B.A., U. Notre Dame, 1966, B.S. in Mech. Engring, 1967; M.S., U. R.I., 1973, Ph.D., 1974. Lic. psychologist, N.Y. Intern U. Rochester, N.Y., 1975, post-doctoral fellow, 1975-77, asst. prof., 1977-83, assoc. prof. oncology in psychiatry, psychology, 1983—; ad hoc cons. Nat. Cancer inst., Washington, 1978—; mem. adv. com. Am. Cancer Soc., N.Y.C., 1981—, com. chmn., 1982—. Contbr. sci. articles, abstracts, procs. to profl. jours.; editorial bd.: Jour. Psychosocial Oncology, 1982. Com. mem. Cub Scouts Am., Pittsford, N.Y., 1976; div. dir./coach Pittsford Soccer League, 1978; asst. scoutmaster Boy Scouts Am., Pittsford, 1981. Served to lt. Submarine Service USN, 1967-71. Research grantee United Cancer Council, Rochester, 1979; Research grantee Nat. Cancer Inst., 1976, 79, 83; Research grantee Am. Cancer Soc., 1983. Mem. Am. Soc. Clin. Oncology, Am. Psychol. Assn., Acad. Behavioral Medicine Research. Repubican. Presbyterian. Current Work: Behavioral medicine, especially behavioral techniques for the control of the side effects of chemotherapy treatment for cancer. Subspecialties: Behavioral psychology; Cancer research (medicine). Home: 11 Sutherland St Pittsford NY 14534 Office: Dept Psychiatry/Psychology U Rochester Med Ctr 300 Crittenden Blvd Rochester NY 14642

MORROW, JODEAN, engineering educator, researcher, consultant; b. Woodbine, Iowa, Oct. 16, 1929; s. Wade Rankin and Lovina (Swackhammer) M.; m. Sally Coonrod, Dec. 23, 1950; children—JoDean, Jr., Daniel. L., Theodore A., Linda S. B.S. in Civil Engring., Rose Hulman Inst. Tech.; M.S. in Theoretical and Applied Mechanics, U. Ill., 1953, Ph.D., 1957. Asst. project engr. Ind. State Hwy. Commn., 1950-51; grad. asst. dept. theoretical and applied mechanics U. Ill., Urbana, 1953-57, prof., 1957—; mem. materials adv. commn. Assn. Am. R.R.s; cons. to various indsl., govt. agys. Contbr. articles to profl. jours. Served to cpl. C.E., U.S. Army, 1950-51. Fellow ASTM (Charles B. Dudley medal 1973, Merit award 1979); mem. Soc. Automotive Engrs. (cert. appreciation 1975), Japan Soc. Materials Sci., Sigma Xi. Current work: Research effort has been addressed to problems associated with failure due to fatigue in metals. Attempt to relate the cyclic stress-strain and life of laboratory samples to the life of actual parts in service. Subspecialties: Materials (engineering); Fracture mechanics. Office: 216 Talbot Labs 104 S Wright St U Ill Urbana IL 61801

MORROW, SCOTT IMLAY, chemist, microscopist; b. Oklahoma City, Sept. 11, 1920; s. Walter Alexander and Blanche (Teape) M.; m. Jean Young, Feb. 13, 1945 (div. 1970); children—Sarah Morrow Wallace, Paul, Charles. B.S., Case Western Res. U., 1946, M.S., 1948, Ph.D., 1951. Research chemist Monsanto, Miamisburg, Ohio, 1951-53, Everett, Mass., 1953-54; research chemist Mobil Research, Paulsboro, N.J., 1954-56, Thiokol, Denville, N.J., 1956-66, U.S. Army Munitions and Chem. Command, Picatinny Arsenal, Dover, N.J., 1966—. Contbr. articles to profl. jours. Patentee in field. Served with USNR, 1942-56, PTO. Mem. Am. Chem. Soc. Current work: Light and electron microscopy, explosives, propellants, phase studies, fluorine chemistry, failure analysis. Subspecialties: Inorganic chemistry; Physical chemistry. Home: 36 E Shore Rd Denville NJ 07834 Office: US Army Munitions and Chem Command Picatinny Arsenal B 3022 Dover NJ 07801-5001

MORROW, WALTER EDWIN, JR., elec. engr., univ. lab. adminstr.; b. Springfield, Mass., July 24, 1928; s. Walter Edwin and Mary Elizabeth (Ganley) M.; m. Janice Lila Lombard, Feb. 25, 1951; children—Clifford E., Gregory A., Carolyn F. S.B., M.I.T., 1949, S.M., 1951. Staff Lincoln Lab., M.I.T., Lexington, Mass., 1951-55, group leader, 1956-65; head div. communications M.I.T. Lincoln Lab., Lexington, Mass., 1966-68, asst. dir., 1968-71, asso. dir., 1972-77, dir., 1977—. Contbr. articles to profl. publs. Recipient award for outstanding achievement Pres. M.I.T., 1963, Edwin Howard Armstrong Achievement award IEEE Communications Soc., 1976. Fellow IEEE, Nat. Acad. Engring. Patentee synchronous satellite, electric power plant using electrolytic cell-fuel cell combination. Subspecialty: Electronics. Office: PO Box 73 Lexington MA 02173

MORSE, FREDERICK H., government energy administrator; b. N.Y.C., Feb. 20, 1936; s. Samuel and Mollie (Vikodetz) M.; m. Naomi S., June 14, 1959; children: Daniel, Joel. B.S., Rensselaer Poly. Inst., 1957; M.S., MIT, 1959; Ph.D., Stanford U., 1966. Instr. dept. mech. engring. Rensselaer Poly. Inst.; mem. faculty dept. mech. engring. U. Md., 1968-76; chief research and devel. br. Office Solar Applications ERDA, 1975-77; dir. Office Solar Applications, Dept. Energy, after 1977; now dir. Office Solar Heat Techs. Served to 1st lt. U.S. Army, 1957-62. Recipient Spl. Achievement award ERDA, Spl. Act of Service award Dept. Energy. Mem. Internat. Solar Energy Soc. (dir.). Current Work: Administration of National Solar Heat Technologies Program, including research and development of active solar heating and cooling, passive and hybrid solar, and solar thermal energy conversion; program planning; budget oversight. Subspecialty: Solar energy. Office: Dept Energy Office Solar Heat Techs 1000 Independence Ave Washington DC 20585

MORSE, PETER HODGES, ophthalmologist; b. Chgo., Mar. 1, 1935; s. Emerson Glover and Carol Elizabeth (Rolph) M. A.B., Harvard U., 1957; M.D., U. Chgo., 1963. Diplomate: Am. Bd. Ophthalmology. Intern U. Chgo. Hosp., 1963-64; resident Wilmer Inst. Johns Hopkins Hosp., Balt., 1966-69; fellow, retina service Mass. Eye and Ear Infirmary, Boston, 1969-70; asst. prof. ophthalmology, chief retina service U. Pa., 1971-75, asso. prof., 1975, U. Chgo., 1975-77, sec. dept. ophthalmology, 1976-77, chief retina service, prof., 1979—; prof. La. State U., 1978; chmn. dept. ophthalmology, chief retina service Ochsner Clinic and Found. Hosp., New Orleans, 1977-78; clin. prof. Tulane U., 1978. Author: Vitreoretinal Disease: A Manual for Diagnosis and Treatment, 1978; co-editor: Disorders of the Vitreous, Retina, and Choroid; Practical Management of Diabetic Retinopathy, 1985; bd. editors: Perspectives in Ophthalmology, 1976—, Retina, 1980—; contbr. articles to profl. jours. Served with USNR, 1964-66. Mem. AMA, New Orleans Acad. Ophthalmology, A.C.S., La., Miss. Ophthalmol. and Otolaryngol. Soc., Assn. Research Vision and Ophthalmology, Retina Soc., Soc. Heed Fellows, Ophthalmol. Soc. U.K., Pan Am. Assn. Ophthalmology, Orleans Parish, La. med. socs., Oxford Ophthalmol. Congress, All-India Ophthalmol. Soc., Soc. Eye Surgeons, Sigma Xi. Republican. Episcopalian. Current Work: Clinical research in diseases which affect vitreous, retina, and uvea. Subspecialty: Ophthalmology. Home: 5801 S Dorchester Ave Chicago IL 60637 Office: Dept Ophthalmology U Chgo 939 E 57th St Chicago IL 60637

MORSE, PHILIP DEXTER, II, biophysicist, consultant; b. Sacramento, Calif., Oct. 17, 1944; s. Philip Dexter and Constance Ruth (Brown) M.; m. Kiyo Ann Akaba, Sept. 3, 1966; children—Emiko, Keiko, Tami. A.A., Coll. San Mateo (Calif.), 1964; B.A., U. Calif.-Davis, 1967, Ph.D., 1971. Postdoctoral fellow U. Bern, Switzerland, 1971-73, Pa. State U., 1973-75; asst. prof. Wayne State U., 1975-81; research assoc. U. Ill., Urbana, 1982—; cons., tchr. Steppingstone Ctr. for the Potentially Gifted, Northville, Mich., 1981—; cons. URI-Therm-X, Champaign, Ill., 1984—. Contbr. articles to profl. jours. Grantee Office of Naval Research, 1976-78, Mich. Heart Assn., 1980-81. Mem. Biophys. Soc., AAAS. Democrat. Current work: Membrane dynamics; dynamics of intracullular environment; drug delivery systems; computer interfacing and laboratory programming. Subspecialties: Biophysics (biology); Membrane biology. Home: 42563 Five Mile Rd Plymouth MI 48170 Office: U Ill Coll Medicine 506 S Mathews St Urbana IL 61801

MORSE, RICHARD STETSON, corporate director, consultant, government official; b. Abington, Mass., Aug. 19, 1911; s. Kenneth Lee and Mary Celia (Skinner) M.; m. Marion Elsa Baitz, Nov. 27, 1935; children: Richard Stetson, Kenneth Paul. S.B., MIT, 1933; D.Sc. (hon.), Clark U., 1961; D.Eng. (hon.), Bklyn. Poly. Inst., 1960. Mem. sci. staff Eastman Kodak, 1935-40; pres. Nat. Research Corp., Cambridge, Mass., 1940-58; dir. research Asst. Sec. Army for Research and Devel., Washington, 1958-62; sr. lectr. Sloan Sch. Mgmt., MIT, 1962-77; now dir. Boston Five Bank, Dresser Industries Inc., Aerospace Corp, MIT Devel. Found., Tracer Tech. Inc., PMC/Beta Corp.; mem. gen adv. com. ERDA; chmn. Army Sci. Adv. Bd., Civilian Adv. Bd., Air Force Systems Command; mem. Commerce Tech. Adv. Bd.; founder Minute Maid Corp., 1948. Mem. corp. Woods Hole (Mass.) Oceanographic Inst., Boston Mus. Sci. Recipient Disting. Civilian Service medal U.S. Dept. Def., 1960. Mem. Am. Chem. Soc., World Affairs Council, Nat. Acad. Engring. Republican. Clubs: Quissett Yacht (Falmouth, Mass.); MIT Faculty (Cambridge, Mass.); St. Botolph, Merchants/Comml. (Boston); Braeburn Country (Newton, Mass.); St. Andrew's (Delray, Fla.). Patentee sound reprodn., vacuum dehydration, instrumentation, color reprodn., and other areas; commercialized lens coating, freeze drying. Current Work: Innovation and new enterprises; corporate director; consultant to government and new technical enterprises. Subspecialty: Batteries and industrial instruments; Management of new enterprises.

MORSE, STEPHEN SCOTT, microbiologist, educator; b. N.Y.C., Nov. 22, 1951; s. Murray H. and Phyllis M. Student, Harvard U., 1968, Balliol Coll., Oxford U., 1969; B.S., City Coll., CUNY, 1971; M.S., U. Wis.-Madison, 1974, Ph.D., 1977. Research fellow Med. Coll. Va., Richmond, 1977-80, asst. prof. dept. biology, 1980; asst. prof. dept. biochemistry and microbiology. Cook Coll., Rutgers U., New Brunswick, N.J., 1981-85, dir. Cell and Tissues Culture Lab., 1981-85; mem. faculty Rockefeller U., N.Y.C., 1985—; investigator, mem. Marine Biol. Lab., Woods Hole, Mass., 1981—. Nat. Cancer Inst. fellow, 1978-80; fellow Rutgers Coll. Mem. Am. Soc. Microbiology, Am. Assn. Pathologists, Biophys. Soc., AAAS, Sigma Xi. Current Work: Cell biology: phagocytic cells, macrophages; immunology of herpesviruses; cell culture; pathogenic microbiology; interferon and related compounds; mechanisms of host resistance to viruses and tumor cells; pathogenic mechanisms and host resistance in infectious diseases. Subspecialties: Infectious diseases; Immunology (medicine). Office: Rockefeller U Box 2 1230 York Ave New York NY 10021

MORTENSEN, EARL MILLER, chemistry educator; b. Salt Lake City, June 25, 1933; s. Earl Emanuel and Serena Mae (Miller) M.; m. Sharlene Wilcox Mortensen; children: Eric, Brian, Russell, Mark. B.A., U. Utah, 1955, Ph.D., 1959. Research assoc. U. Calif., 1960-62; asst. prof. chemistry U. Mass., 1962-69; assoc. prof. Cleve. State U., 1969—. NSF fellow, 1959-60. Mem. Am. Chem. Soc., Am. Phys. Soc., Sigma Xi. Mormon. Current Work: Determine reactive cross sections for atom-diatom reactions using quantum mechanical scattering theory. Subspecialties: Physical chemistry; Theoretical chemistry. Home: 24227 LeBern Dr North Olmsted OH 44070 Office: Cleveland State University Department of Chemistry Cleveland OH 44115

MORTILLARO, NICHOLAS A., physiologist, educator; b. Bklyn., Aug. 14, 1936; s. Nicolo and Pietrina (LaCorte) M.; m. Mildred Mary Detloff, July 30, 1962; children: Philip Michael, Susan Patricia. B.S. in Elec. Engring, Heald Engring. Coll., 1964; M.S. in Elec. Engring, Newark Coll. Engring., 1968; Ph.D., Coll. Medicine and Dentistry N.J., 1972. Project engr. Bendix Corp., Teterboro, N.J., 1964-68; research fellow U. Miss. Sch. Medicine, Jackson, 1972-74; instr. U. Miss., 1973-74; asst. prof. U. South Ala., Mobile, 1974-77, assoc. prof., 1977—; vis. assoc. prof. Tex. A&M U. Sch. Medicine, College Station, 1980. Author: Gastrointestinal Function, 1984; editor/contbr.: Physiology and Pharmacology of the Microcirculation Vols. I and II, 1983. Pres. Italian-Am. Cultural Soc. S. Ala., 1982-83. NIH research grantee, 1974—; Am. Heart Assn. research grantee, 1974-76. Mem. Am. Physiol. Soc., Microcirculatory Soc., Internat. Lymphology Soc., Am. Heart Assn., Splanchnic Circulation Group. Roman Catholic. Current Work: Local and nervous control of blood flow; capillary, interstitial and lymphatic fluid and solute exchange dynamics; properties of vascular smooth muscle. Subspecialties: Physiology (medicine); Gastroenterology. Home: 5700 Grandee Ct Mobile AL 36609 Office: U S Ala Dept Physiology College Medicine Mobile AL 36688

MORTIMER, JAMES ARTHUR, research director, neurophysiology educator; b. Boston, May 13, 1944; s. Carroll Joseph and Eileen Marie (Merrill) M.; m. Jeylan Martin Tekiner, Aug. 12, 1965; 1 child, Kent Douglas. B.S. magna cum laude, Tufts U., 1965; M.S., U. Mich., 1967, Ph.D., 1970. Research assoc. Logic of Computers Group, Ann Arbor, Mich., 1968-69; lectr. U. Mich., Ann Arbor, 1970; staff fellow NIH, Bethesda, Md., 1970-73; asst. prof. dept. neurosurgery U. Minn., Mpls., 1974-76, asst. prof. dept. neurology, 1976—; assoc. dir. Geriatric Research Edn. Clin. Ctr. VA Med. Ctr., Mpls., 1977—; cons. Waisman Ctr. U. Wis., Madison, 1981—; dir. Assn. for Alzheimer's Disease, Mpls., 1980-83; mem. study sect. NIH, Bethesda, Md., 1981-82, 85—. Editor: The Epidemiology of Dementia, 1981, The Aging Motor System, 1982, Some Mathematical Models in Biology, 1967; contbr. articles to profl. jours. Fellow Gerontological Soc. Am.; mem. Soc. for Neurosci. (charter), Internat. Neuropsychol. Soc., Soc. for Epidemiologic Research, AAAS, Phi Kappa Phi, Tau Beta Pi, Eta Kappa Nu. Current work: Neuropsychology of Parkinson's Disease; epidemiology of dementing illness; natural history of Alzheimer's and Parkinson's diseases; psychology of aging. Subspecialties: Neurophysiology; Epidemiology. Home: 5124 Emerson Ave S Minneapolis MN 55419 Office: VA Med Ctr GRECC 11G Minneapolis MN 55417

MORTIMER, ROBERT GEORGE, chemistry educator, researcher; b. Provo, Aug. 25, 1933; s. William Earl and Margaret Eastmond (Johnson) M.; m. Dorothy Jean Randall, June 23, 1960; children: Julia, Paul, Jeannine, John, David. B.S., Utah State U., 1958, M.S., 1959; Ph.D., Calif. Inst. Tech., 1963. Research chemist U. Calif., San Diego, 1962-64; asst. prof. chemistry Ind. U., 1964-70; asst. prof. Southwestern U. Memphis, 1970-72, assoc. prof., 1972-81, prof., 1981—. Author: Mathematics for Physical Chemistry, 1981. Served to 2d lt. USAR, 1959. Woodrow Wilson fellow, 1958-59; NSF fellow, 1959-62; grantee in field. Mormon. Current Work: Statistical mechanics, transport processes, chem. edn. instruction and research in phys. chemistry. Subspecialties: Physical chemistry; Statistical mechanics. Home: 2895 Falkirk Rd Memphis TN 38128 Office: 2000 N Parkway Memphis TN 38112

MORTON, RANDALL EUGENE, research and development executive, fiber optic and data acquisition researcher, consultant; b. Portland, Oreg., May 4, 1950; s. Eugene Randall and Kathryn Hazel (Myers) M.; m. Lori Kay Turner, Mar. 23, 1979. B.S. in Elec. Engring, U. Wash., Seattle, 1972; M.S. in Nuclear Engring, 1974, Ph.D., 1979. Registered nuclear engr., Wash. Exec. cons. Holloran & Assocs., Bellevue, Wash., 1977-81; corp. cons. AGA Cons., Bellevue, 1981-82; sr. mfg. systems analyst Eldec Corp., Lynnwood, Wash., 1982-83, sr. engr. research and devel. staff, 1983-85, engring. mgr. advanced product devel., 1985—. Contbr. articles to profl. jours. Mem. IEEE, Optical Soc. Am., Soc. Photo-Optical Instrumentation Engrs., Soc. Automotive Engrs. Current Work: Aerospace product development research and development. Subspecialties: Fiber optics; Aerospace engineering and technology. Home: 10320 181st St NW Redmond WA 98052 Office: Eldec Corp 16700 13th Ave W Po Box 100 Lynwood WA 98046

MOSCONA, ARON ARTHUR, scientist, educator; b. Israel, July 4, 1922; came to U.S., 1955, naturalized, 1965; s. David DeAstogne-Abarbanel and Lola (Krochmaal) M.; m. Malka Kempinsky, July 6, 1955; 1 dau., Anne. M.Sc., Hebrew U., Jerusalem, 1947, Ph.D., 1950; postgrad. fellow, Strangeways Research Lab., Cambridge U., Eng., 1950-52. Vis. investigator Rockefeller Inst., N.Y.C., 1955-57; prof. biology U. Chgo., 1958—, Louis Block prof. biol. scis., 1972—; chmn. Com. on Developmental Biology, 1970; vis. prof. Stanford U., 1959, U. Montreal, 1960, U. Palermo, Italy, 1966, Hebrew U., Jerusalem, 1972, Tel-Aviv (Israel) U., 1977, 79, Kyoto U., Japan, 1980. Chmn. bd. sci. counselors NICHD, 1983—. Editor: Current Topics in Developmental Biology, 1965, Mechanisms of Aging and Development, 1971, Cell Differentiation, 1975, Cancer Research, 1977, Devel. Neurosci, 1977, Experimental Cell Research, 1962-77; contbr. articles to profl. jours. Mem. Nat. Acad. Scis., Instituto Lombardo (Milan), N.Y. Acad. Scis., AAAS, Internat. Soc. Devel. Biology (pres. 1977-81), Soc. Devel. Biology, Internat. Soc. Cell Biology, Am. Soc. Zoology, Am. Soc. Anatomy, Sigma Xi. Subspecialty: Developmental biology.

MOSELEY, JOHN TRAVIS, research physicist, educator; b. New Orleans, Feb. 26, 1942; s. Fred Baker and Gay (Lord) M.; m. Belva McCall Hudson, Aug. 11, 1962 (div. 1978); children: Melanie Lord, John Mark; m. Susan Diane Callow, Aug. 5, 1979; children—Stephanie Marie, Shannon Eleanor. B.S., Ga. Inst. Tech., 1964, M.S., 1966, Ph.D., 1969. Asst. prof. U. West Fla., Pensacola, 1968-69; physicist SRI Internat., Menlo Park, Calif., 1969-74, sr. physicist, 1974-77, program mgr., 1977-79; assoc. prof. physics U. Oreg., Eugene, 1979-82, prof., 1982—, dir. Chem. Physics Inst. 1980-84, head dept. physics, 1984-85, v.p. research, 1985—. Contbr. articles to profl. jours. NSF fellow, 1964-68. Fellow Am. Phys. Soc.; mem. AAAS, AAUP, Sigma Xi (award for thesis research 1969), Phi Kappa Phi, Tau Beta Pi. Current Work: Processes involving molecular ions, in particular, photodissociation, spectroscopy, reactions and transport properties. Subspecialties: Atomic and molecular physics; Laser-induced chemistry. Home: 1925 Dogwood Dr Eugene OR 97405 Office: 110 Johnson Hall Dept Physics U Oreg Eugene OR 97403

MOSELEY, ROBERT DAVID, JR., radiologist, educator; b. Minden, La., Feb. 29, 1924; s. Robert David and Lettie E. (Looney) M.; m. Janet C. Watson, Mar. 15, 1947; children: Robert David III, Richard Havard, Marianne Lee. M.D., La. State U., 1947. Diplomate: Am. Bd. Radiology. Intern Highland Sanitarium and Clinic, Shreveport, La., 1947-48; asst. resident U. Chgo. Clinics, 1949-50; asst. resident Los Alamos spl. research project, dept. radiology U. Chgo., 1950-51; staff mem. U. Calif.-Los Alamos Sci. Lab., 1951-52, radiologist, asso. chief staff med. center, 1951-52; mem. staff dept. radiology U. Chgo., 1954-71, prof., chmn. dept., 1958-71; prof., asst. chmn., dir. div. diagnostic radiology U. N.Mex. Sch. Medicine, Albuquerque, 1971-78, prof., chmn. dept. radiology, 1978-85, emeritus prof. radiology, 1985—; chief of staff Bernalillo County Med. Center, 1971-72, 78, 79; Bd. dirs. Nat. Council Radiation Protection, 1973-80; mem. radiation study sect. USPHS, NIH, 1971-75; mem. radiology tng. com. NIH, 1966-70; chmn., 1969-70; U.S. rep. UN Sci. Com. on Effects Atomic Radiation, 1976—; chmn. adv. com. on biology and medicine U.S. AEC, 1967-73; chmn. U.S. delegation Internat. Congresses of Radiology, Rio de Janeiro, 1977, Brussels, 1981; pres. XVI Internat. Congress Radiology, Hawaii, 1985. Pres. bd. dirs. James Picker Found., 1972—. Served as lt. (s.g.) USNR, 1952-54. Fellow Chgo. Roentgen Soc. (past sec.-treas. bd. trustees, pres. 1966-67), Am. Coll. Radiology (pres. 1973-74, Gold medal 1980), Royal Coll. Radiologists (Eng.) (hon.), Swedish Soc. Med. Radiology (hon.); mem. Internat. Soc. Radiology (pres. 1985-89), N.Mex., Albuquerque, Bernalillo County med. socs., Assn. U. Radiologists (founding mem., past pres., Gold medal 1980), Am. Roentgen Ray Soc., Radiation Research Soc., Acad. Soc. Lund (Sweden) (corr.), Deutsche Röntgengesellshaft (corr.), Radiol. Soc. N.Am., Inter Am. Coll. Radiology, Royal Physiographic Soc. (fgn. mem., Lund, Sweden), N.Mex. Soc. Radiologists, Sigma Xi, Sigma Nu, Phi Chi. Clubs: Univ. (Chgo.); Four Hills Country (Albuquerque). Current Work: Imaging technology and evaluation; radiation protection. Subspecialties: Diagnostic radiology; Imaging technology. Home: 635 Running Water Circle SE Albuquerque NM 87123

MOSER, HUGO WOLFGANG, physician; b. Switzerland, Oct. 4, 1924; came to U.S., 1940, naturalized, 1943; s. Hugo L. and Maria (Werner) M.; m. Ann Boody, Dec. 28, 1963; children—Tracey, Peter, Karen, Lauren. M.D., Columbia U., 1948; A.M. in Med. Sci, Harvard U., 1956. Intern Columbia-Presbyn. Med. Center, N.Y.C., 1948-50; asst. in medicine Peter Bent Brigham Hosp., Boston, 1950-52; research fellow dept. biol. chemistry Harvard U., 1955-57; asst. resident, resident in neurology Mass. Gen. Hosp., 1957-59, asst. neurologist, 1960-67, asso. neurologist, 1967-69, neurologist, 1969-76; teaching fellow neuropathology Harvard Med. Sch., 1959-60, instr. neurology, 1960-64, asso. in neurology, 1964-67, asst. prof., 1967-69, asso. prof., 1969-72, prof., 1972-76; dir. research and tng. Walter E. Fernald State Sch., 1963-68, asst. supt., 1968-73, acting supt., 1973-74, supt., 1974-76; dir. Center for Research on Mental Retardation and Related Aspects of Human Devel., dir. univ. affiliated facilities for mentally retarded, 1965-74; co-dir. Eunice Kennedy Shriver Center for Mental Retardation, Inc., 1969-74; dir. John F. Kennedy Inst., Balt., 1976—; prof. neurology and pediatrics Johns Hopkins U., 1976—. Author: (with others) Mental Retardation: An Atlas of Diseases with Associated Physical Abnormalities, 1972; Contbr. (with others) articles to med. jours. Served with AUS, 1943-44; to capt. U.S. Army, 1952-54. Mem. Am. Acad. Neurology, Am. Assn. Mental Deficiency, Am. Assn. Neuropathologists, Am. Neurol. Assn., Internat. Soc. Neurochemistry, Am. Pediatrics Soc., Sigma Xi, Alpha Omega Alpha. . Home: 100 Beechdale Rd Baltimore MD 21210 Office: 707 N Broadway Baltimore MD 21205

MOSES, JOEL, computer scientist; b. Petach Tikvah, Israel, Nov. 25, 1941; came to U.S., 1954, naturalized, 1960; s. Bernhard and Golda (Losner) M.; m. Margaret A. Garvey, Dec. 27, 1970; children: Jesse, David. B.A., Columbia U., 1962, M.A., 1963; Ph.D., M.I.T., 1967. Asst. prof. dept. elec. engring. and computer sci. M.I.T., 1967-71, asso. prof., 1971-76, prof., 1976—, assoc. dir. Lab for Computer Sci., 1974-78, asso. head computer sci. and engring., dept. elec. engring. and computer sci., 1978-81, head dept., 1981—. Editor: The Computer Age: A Twenty Year View, 1979. Mem. Assn. Computing Machinery, IEEE. Subspecialties: Mathematical software; Artificial intelligence. Office: Mass Inst Tech 38-401 Cambridge MA 02139

MOSIER, BENJAMIN, analytical chemist, consultant, research company executive; b. Corsicanna, Tex., July 15, 1926; s. Phillip and Fannie (Zulauff) M.; m. Doreen N. Zidel, Aug. 22, 1954; children: Marc L., David M., Linda J., Adam J. B.S., Tex. A&M U., 1949, M.S., 1951; Ph.D., U. Ill., 1957. Cert. profl. chemist Nat. Certification Com. in Chemistry and Chem. Engring. Instr. chemistry Kilgore (Tex.) Coll., 1949-50; research scientist Gen. Dynamics, Ft. Worth, 1951-52; NSF fellow U. Ill., Urbana, 1954-57; research scientist Humble Oil & Refining Co., Houston, 1957-60; pres., dir. Inst. Research, Inc., Houston, 1960—, Inst. Research-Austin, Inc.; cons. Armour Indsl. Chem. Co., Chgo., 1961—, U. Tex., M.D. Anderson Tumor Inst. Dept. Exptl. Diagnostic Radiology, Dunn Found., 1973—; mem. adv. bd. analytical instrument program Houston Community Coll., 1980, Oilfield Service Corp. Am., Lafayette, La., 1980; assoc. research prof. Baylor Coll. Medicine, Houston; dir. Electronic Fin. Systems. Author articles. Served with USAF, 1944-46, 52-54. Recipient numerous awards NASA. Fellow Am. Inst. Chemists; mem. AAAS, Am. Council Ind. Labs., Am. Chem. Soc., Am. Petroleum Inst., Electrochem. Soc., Ill. Acad. Sci., Inst. Food Technologists, Nat. Assn. Corrosion Engrs., N.Y. Acad. Scis., Tex. Acad. Sci., Houston Soc. Clin. Pathologists, Sigma Xi, Phi Lambda Upsilon. Lodge: Rotary. Patentee in chem. field. Current Work: Corrosion, medical instrumentation, microencapsulation, phenolic foam, enhanced oil recovery. Subspecialties: Analytical chemistry; Polymer chemistry.

MOSKOWITZ, GERARD J., biochemist, research executive; b. Yonkers, N.Y., June 17, 1940; s. Hyman and Lillian (Miller) M.; m. Stephanie D. Spilton, Aug. 31, 1962; 1 child, Lisa D. B.A., U. Buffalo, 1962; Ph.D., SUNY-Buffalo, 1967. Research assoc. Baylor Med. Sch., Houston, 1967-69; lab. mgr. Wallerstein Co., N.Y.C., 1970-71, mgr. biochem. research, Chgo., 1971-76; sr. scientist Baxter Travenol, Chgo., 1976-77; tech. dir. Dairyland Food Labs, Waukesha, Wis., 1977—; advisor Walter V. Price Cheese Research Inst., Madison, Wis., 1984; advisor biology dept. Marquette U., Milw., 1983—. Author book chpts. Contbr. articles to sci. jours. Patentee in field. Publicity chmn. Congregation Beth Israel, Milw., 1978-82. NSF small bus. research grantee. Mem. Inst. Food Technologists, Am. Chem. Soc. (membership chmn. 1981-83), N.Y. Acad. Scis., Am. Dairy Sci. Assn. (editor 1982—), Sigma Xi. Current work: Enzymes, genetic engineering, flavor development in foods; application of biotechnology to food systems. Subspecialties: Biochemistry (biology); Enzyme technology. Home: 10411 W Bittersweet Ct Mequon WI 53092 Office: Dairyland Food Labs 620 Progress Ave Waukesha WI 53186

MOSKOWITZ, RONALD, technology company executive; b. N.Y.C., Feb.115, 1939; s. Morris and Nan M.; m. Phyllis Ann Lenes, June 29, 1957; children—Cindy Lynn, Barry David, Randy Scott, Jeffrey Alan. B.E.E., CUNY, 1961; M.S.E.E., Rutgers U., 1963, Ph.D. in Engring., 1966. With astroelectronics div. RCA Labs., 1961-67; instr. elec. engring. Rutgers U., 1965-67; prof. U. Miss., 1967; mgr. Avco Corp., 1967-68; mem. adj. faculty Lowell Tech. Inst., 1967-68; prin., pres. Ferrofluidics Corp., Nashua, N.H., 1968—. Contbr. articles to profl. jours. Patentee in field. AEC fellow, 1964, RCA fellow, 1963, NSF fellow, 1964-65. Registered profl. engr., Calif. Mem. IEEE, Am. Vacuum Soc., AAAS, Tech. Assn. of Graphic Arts, ASME, Am. Soc. Lubrication Engrs., Sigma Xi, Eta Kappa Nu. Subspecialty: Applied magnetics. Office: Ferrofluidics Corp 40 Simon St Nashua NH 03061

MOSMANN, TIMOTHY RICHARD, immunologist; b. Birkenhead, Cheshire, Eng., Mar. 7, 1949; came to U.S., 1982; s. Paul George and Joan Doris (Debbage) M.; m. Penella Eunice Farnham, Dec. 22, 1972. B.Sc., U. Natal, South Africa, 1968; B.Sc. with honors, Rhodes U., South Africa, 1969; Ph.D., U. B.C., 1973. Postdoctoral fellow Hosp. for Sick Children, Toronto, Ont., Can., 1973-75; postdoctoral fellow dept. biochemistry Glasgow (Scotland) U., 1975-77; asst. prof. dept. immunology U. Alta. (Can.), Edmonton, 1977-81; prin. scientist DNAX Research Inst., Palo Alto, Calif., 1982—. Contbr. articles to profl. jours. MRC of Can. grantee, 1977-81; Alta. Cancer Hosp. Bd. grantee, 1980-81; Alta. Heritage Fund grantee, 1981. Mem. Can. Soc. Immunology, Am. Assn. Immunologists. Current Work: analysis of antigen-specific molecules of lymphocytes and dection characterization and recombinant DNA cloning of immunoregulatory factors. Subspecialties: Immunobiology and immunology; Genetics and genetic engineering (biology). Home: 69 Lloyden Dr Atherton CA 94025 Office: DNAX Research Inst 901 California Ave Palo Alto CA 94304

MOSS, HERBERT IRWIN, materials scientist; b. Bklyn., Mar. 8, 1932; s. Jacob and Marcelle (Garblik) M.; m. Geraldine Georgia Germek, Sept. 10, 1960; children—Jennifer, David, Jessica. B.S., U. Louisville, 1953; Ph.D., Ind. U., 1960. Mem. tech. staff RCA Labs., Princeton, N.J., 1959—. Contbr. articles to profl. jours. Patentee in field. Mem. Am. Chem. Soc., Am. Ceramic soc., Electrochem. Soc., Am. Powder Metall. Inst., Metal Sci. Club, Sigma Xi. Current work: Development of materials for magnetic recording heads; pressure sintering; piezoelectric materials. Subspecialties: Electronic materials; Ceramics. Home: PO Box 569 Point Pleasant PA 18950 Office: RCA Labs Route 1 Princeton NJ 08540

MOSS, MARVIN, engineering physicist; b. N.Y.C., Dec. 8, 1929; m. Joan Carolyn Reinhold, Oct. 16, 1957; children—Janine, Diana. B.S., Queens Coll., 1951; Ph.D., Cornell U., 1963. Jr. engr. Sylvania Electric Co., N.Y.C., 1951-54; mem. tech. staff Sandia Nat. Labs., Albuquerque, 1963—. Contbr. articles to profl. jours. Patentee in field. Mem. Albuquerque Energy Conservation Council, 1977—, chmn. 1979—; mem. N.Mex. Democratic Central Com., 1977—, N.Mex. Dem. Rules Com., 1979—; pres., chmn. Albuquerque Montessori Soc., 1964-70. Mem. AAAS, Am. Phys. Soc., N.Mex. Acad. Sci. (sci. ctr. com. 1983—). Current work: Thermophysical properties. Subspecialty: Condensed matter physics. Office: Sandia Nat Labs PO Box 5800 Albuquerque NM 87185

MOSS, ROBERT LOUIS, physiology educator; b. Bklyn., Aug. 24, 1940; s. Robert C. and Susan (Tuccinardi) M.; m. Rita Mary Walsh, Sept. 22, 1962; children; Michele E., Robert C. B.S., Villanova U., 1962; M.S., Claremont Grad. Sch., 1967, Ph.D., 1969. Research asst. Behavioral Research Lab., Patton State Hosp., 1964-65; NIH postdoctoral fellow U. Bristol, Eng., 1969-71; asst. prof. physiology U. Tex. Health Sci. Ctr., Dallas, 1971-76, assoc. prof., 1976-80, prof., 1980-82, prof. physiology and neurology, 1983—, chmn. physiology grad. program, 1983—; co-dir. endocrinology/human reprodn. course Southwestern Med. Sch., 1977-83, co-dir. med. neurobiology course, 1977—. Recipient Research Career Devel. award. NIH., 1976-81; Young Scientist award Am. Psychol. Assn., 1969; Disting. Alumni award Villanova U., 1982; NIH grantee, 1972—; NSF grantee, 1974-76; Tex. Salk Inst. grantee, 1982—. Mem. AAAS, Am. Physiol. Soc., Endocrine Soc., Internat. Soc. Neuroendocrinology (charter mem.), Soc. for Neurosci. Republican. Roman Catholic. Lodge: K.C. Current Work: Neural and biochemical mechanisms involved in hypothalmic control over pituitary functions and reproductive behavior. Office: Dept Physiology U Tex Health Sci Ctr 5323 Harry Hines Blvd Dallas TX 75235

MOSSOBA, MAGDI MICHEL, chemist; b. Cairo, Oct. 12, 1948; came to U.S., 1974, naturalized, 1982; s. Michel Mossoba and Eugenie Farah; m. Nevin Yehia Fahmy, Dec. 31, 1975; children—Joseph T., Miriam E., Michael B. B.Sc, Am. U., Cairo, 1972; Ph.D., Georgetown U., 1980. Fogarty fellow NIH, Bethesda, Md., 1980-83; research chemist U. Md. Cancer Ctr., Balt., 1983, FDA, Washington, 1984—. Contbr. articles to profl. jours. Mem. Am. Chem. Soc., Sigma Xi. Current work: Detection of adulteration using chromatographic, spectroscopic and matrix isolation methods; characterization of food toxins. Subspecialty: Electron spin resonance. Home: 1822 Westmoreland St McLean VA 22101 Office: Food and Drug Admintrn 200 C St SW Washington DC 20204

MOSTELLER, FREDERICK, mathematical statistician, educator; b. Clarksburg, W.Va., Dec. 24, 1916; s. William Roy and Helen (Kelley) M.; m. Virginia Gilroy, May 17, 1941; children: William, Gale. B.S., Carnegie Inst. Tech. (now Carnegie-Mellon U.) 1938, M.S., 1939, D.Sc., 1974; A.M., Princeton U., 1942, Ph.D., 1946; D.Sc., U. Chgo., 1973, Wesleyan U., 1983; D.Social Scis., Yale U., 1981. Instr. math. Princeton U., 1942-44; research assoc. Office Pub. Opinion Research, 1942-44; spl. cons. research br. War Dept., 1942-43; research mathematician Statis. Research Group, Princeton, applied math. panel Nat. Devel. and Research Council, 1944-46; mem. faculty Harvard U., 1946—, prof. math. stats., 1951—, chmn. dept. stats., 1957-69, 75-77, chmn. dept. biostats., 1977-81, chmn. dept. health policy and mgmt., 1981—, Roger I. Lee prof., 1978—; vice chmn. Pres.'s Commn. on Fed. Stats., 1970-71; mem. Nat. Adv. Council Equality of Ednl. Opportunity, 1973-78, Nat. Sci. Bd. Commn. on Pre-coll. Edn. in Math., Sci. and Tech., 1982-83; Fund for Advancement of Edn. fellow, 1954-55; nat. tchr. NBC's Continental Class-room TV course in probability and stats., 1960-61; fellow Center Advanced Study Behavioral Sciences, 1962-63, bd. dirs., 1980—; Guggenheim fellow, 1969-70; Miller research prof. U. Calif. at Berkeley, 1974-75. Co-author: Gauging Public Opinion (editor Hadley Cantril), 1944, Sampling Inspection, 1948, The Pre-election Polls, 1948, 1949; author: Stochastic Models for Learning, 1955, Probability with Statistical Applications, 1961, Inference and Disputed Authorship, The Federalist, 1964, The National Halothane Study, 1969, Statistics: A Guide to the Unknown, 1972, On Equality of Educational Opportunity, 1972, Sturdy Statistics, 1973, Statistics By Example, 1973, Cost, Risks and Benefits of Surgery, 1977, Data Analysis and Regression, 1977, Statistics and Public Policy, 1977, Data for Decisions, 1982, Understanding Robust and Exploratory Data Analysis, 1983, Biostatistics in Clinical Medicine, 1983, Beginning Statistics with Data Analysis, 1983; Applied Bayesian and Classical Inference, 1984, Exploring Data Tables, Trends, and Shapes, 1985; also articles in field. Trustee Russell Sage Found.; mem. bd. Nat. Opinion Research Center, 1962-66. Recipient Outstanding Statistician award Chgo. chpt. Am. Statis. Assn., 1971; Myrdal prize Evaluation Research Soc.,

1978; Paul F. Lazarsfeld prize Council Applied Social Research, 1979. Fellow AAAS (chmn. sect. U 1973, dir. 1974-78, pres. 1980, chmn. bd. 1981), Inst. Math. Statistics (pres. 1974-75), Am. Statis. Assn. (v.p. 1962-64, pres. 1967), Social Sci. Research Council (chmn. bd. dirs. 1966-68), Math. Social Sci. Bd. (acad. governing bd. 1962-67), Am. Acad. Arts and Scis., Royal Statis. Soc. (hon.); mem. Am. Philos. Soc., Internat. Statis. Inst. (v.p. 1985—), Am. Math. Soc., Math. Assn. Am., Psychometric Soc. (pres. 1957-58), Inst. Medicine of Nat. Acad. Scis. (council 1978), Nat. Acad. Scis., Biometric Soc. Current Work: Health policy research, evaluation, robust methods. Subspecialty: Statistics. Office: 1 Oxford St Cambridge MA 02138

MOSTOW, GEORGE DANIEL, mathematics educator; b. Boston, July 4, 1923; s. Isaac J. and Ida (Rotman) M.; m. Evelyn Davidoff, Sept. 1, 1947; children: Mark Alan, David Jechiel, Carol Held, Jonathan Carl. B.A., Harvard U., 1943, M.A., 1946, Ph.D., 1948. Instr. math. Princeton U., 1947-48; mem. Inst. Advanced Study, 1947-49, 56-57, 75, trustee, 1982—; asst. prof. Syracuse U., 1949-52; asst. prof. math. Johns Hopkins U., 1952-53, asso. prof., 1954-56, prof., 1957-61; prof. math. Yale U., 1961-66, James E. English prof. math., 1966-81, Henry Ford II prof. math., 1981—, chmn., 1971-74; vis. prof. Conselho National des Pesquisas, Instituto de Matematica, Rio de Janiero, Brazil, 1953-54, U. Paris, 1966-67, Hebrew U., Jerusalem, 1967, Tata Inst. Fundamental Research, Bombay, 1970, Institut des Hautes Etudes Scientifiques, Bures-Sur-Yvette, 1966, 71, 75; Chmn. U.S. Nat. Com. for Math., 1971-73, 83-85; chmn. Office Math. Scis., NRC, 1975-78. Trustee Inst. Advanced Study, Princeton, 1982—. Asso. editor: Annals of Math, 1957-64, Trans. Am. Math. Soc, 1958-65, Am. Scientist, 1970-82; editor: Am. Jour. Math, 1965-69; asso. editor, 1969-79; author research articles. Fulbright research scholar, Utrecht U., Netherlands, also Guggenheim fellow, 1957-58. Mem. Nat. Acad. Sci. (chmn. sect. math 1982-84), Am. Acad. Arts and Scis., Am. Math. Soc. (v.p. 1979—, pres. elect 1985), Internat. Math. Union (chmn. U.S. del. to gen. assembly Warsaw 1982, mem. exec. com. 1983—), Phi Beta Kappa, Sigma Xi. Subspecialty: Group theory. Home: Beechwood Rd Woodbridge CT 06525 Office: Yale U New Haven CT 06520

MOSZKOWSKI, STEVEN ALEXANDER, theoretical nuclear physics educator; b. Berlin, Mar. 13, 1927; came to U.S., 1940, naturalized, 1945; s. Richard and Ruth H. (Bamberger) M.; m. Lena I. Iggers, Aug. 29, 1952 (div. Dec. 1977); children—Ben C., Richard D., Ronald B.; m. Esther Kleitman, Nov. 5, 1978. B.S., U. Chgo., 1946, M.S., 1950, Ph.D., 1952. Postdoctoral research asst. Columbia U., 1952-53; from asst. to prof. physics UCLA, 1953—, vice chmn. physics. dept., 1979-82; cons. Lawrence Livermore Lab, Calif., 1973—. Co-author: Beta Decay, 1966. Served with U.S. Army, 1945-46. Guggenheim fellow, 1961. Fellow Am. Phys. Soc. Current work: Nuclear forces, nuclear many body problem, shell model interacting boson medal. Subspecialties: Theoretical physics; Nuclear physics. Office: Dept Physics Univ Calif 405 Hilgard Ave Los Angeles CA 90024

MOTE, PETER ALLEN, engineering geologist; b. San Francisco, Dec. 27, 1941; s. Clayton Daniel and Eugenia (Isnardi) M.; m. Sharon Lee Prentice, Apr. 6, 1979; children—Peter Dewey, Jesse Daniel. B.A., U. Calif.-Berkeley, 1969. Asst. engring. geologist Bechtel Civil and Minerals Inc., San Francisco, 1969-70, engring. geologist, 1970-74, sr. engring. geologist, 1974-77, supervising engring. geologist, 1977—. Served with AUS, 1961-64. Mem. Assn. Engring. Geologists, Geol. Soc. Am., Soc. Mining Engrs. of AIME, Am. Soc. Engring. Mgmt., U.S. Com. on Large Dams. Republican. Club: Sausalito Yacht. Current work: Project mgr., hazardous chemical waste pojects; contaminant migration in ground water; geologic containment of hazardous materials; problem identification at existing hazardous waste sites. Subspecialties: Geology; Hazardous waste disposal. Home: 412 W Blithedale Ave Mill Valley CA 94941 Office: Bechtel Nat Inc PO Box 3965 San Francisco CA 94119

MOTICKA, EDWARD J., immunology educator; b. Oak Park, Ill., May 21, 1944; s. Edward and Vivian (Charvet) M.; m. Betty Horvath, June 21, 1969; children: Juli, Gabrielle, Danielle. B.A., Kalamazoo Coll., 1966; Ph.D., U. Ill. Med Ctr., Chgo., 1970. Postdoctoral fellow UCLA, 1970-71; vis. scientist Czechoslovak Acad. Scis., Prague, 1971-72; asst. prof. U. Tex. Health Sci. Ctr., Dallas, 1972-78; assoc. prof. So. Ill. U., Carbondale, 1978-80, Springfield, 1980. Contbr. articles to sci. jours. Mem. Am. Assn. Immunologists, Am. Soc. Zoologists. Current Work: Immunoregulatory mechanisms of autoantibody production and autoimmune disease. Subspecialty: Cellular engineering. Office: PO Box 3926 Springfield IL 62708

MOTTINGER, JOHN PHILIP, botany educator, researcher; b. Detroit, Nov. 28, 1938; s. Claude W. and Elizabeth E. M. B.A., Ohio Wesleyan U., 1961; Ph.D., Ind. U., 1968. Instr. botany U. R.I., Kingston, 1967-68, asst. prof., 1968-75, assoc. prof., 1975—; vis. research assoc. U. Calif., Berkeley, 1980. Served with U.S. Army, 1956-57. Mem. Genetics Soc. Am., AAAS, Sigma Xi. Current Work: Virus induced genetic instability and gene regulation in maize. Subspecialties: Genetics and genetic engineering (agriculture); Plant genetics. Home: 44 Wood Ave Narragansett RI 02882 Office: Department of Botany University of Rhode Island Kingston RI 02881

MOTULSKY, ARNO GUNTHER, geneticist, physician, educator; b. Fischhausen, Germany, July 5, 1923; s. Herman and Rena (Sass) Molton; m. Gretel C. Stern, Mar. 22, 1945; children: Judy, Harvey, Arlene. Student, Central YMCA Coll., Chgo., 1941-43, Yale U., 1943-44; B.S., U. Ill., 1945, M.D., 1947. Diplomate: Am. Bd. Internal Medicine. Intern, fellow, resident Michael Reese Hosp., Chgo., 1947-51; Staff mem. charge clin. investigation dept. hematology Army Med. Service Grad. Sch., Walter Reed Army Med. Center, Washington, 1952-53; research asso. internal medicine George Washington U. Sch. Medicine, 1952-53; from instr. to assoc. prof. dept. medicine U. Wash. Sch. Medicine, Seattle, 1953-61, prof. medicine, prof. genetics, 1961—; head div. med. genetics, dir. genetics clinic Univ. Hosp., 1959—, Children's Med. Center, 1966-72; dir. Center for Inherited Diseases, 1972—; attending physician Univ. Hosp., Seattle; cons. physician Children's Orthopedic Hosp. and Med. Center, Seattle; cons. various coms. NRC, NIH, WHO, others; mem. Am. Bd. Med. Genetics, 1979-82, Pres.'s Commn. for Study of Ethical Problems in Medicine and Biomed. and Behavioral Research, 1979-83. Editor: Am. Jour. Human Genetics, 1969-75, Human Genetics, 1969—, Progress in Med. Genetics, 1974—; editorial bd.: DM Disease a Month, Jour. AMA, and others. Spl. Commonwealth Fund fellow in human genetics Univ. Coll., London, Eng., 1957-58; John and Mary Markle scholar in med. sci., 1957-62; fellow Center Advanced Study in Behavioral Scis., Stanford U., 1976-77; Inst. Advanced Study Fellow, Berlin, 1984. Fellow A.C.P.; mem. Internat. Soc. Hematology, Am. Fedn. Clin. Research, AAAS, Genetics Soc. Am., Western Soc. Clin. Research, Am. Soc. Human Genetics, Am. Soc. Clin. Investigation, Am. Assn. Physicians, Inst. of Medicine, Nat. Acad. Sci., Am. Acad. Arts and Scis. Research and publs., including books, in field. Subspecialty: Genetics and genetic engineering (medicine). Office: U Wash Div Med Genetics Seattle WA 98195

MOTZ, LLOYD, astrophysics educator; b. Susquehanna, Pa., June 5, 1910; s. Solomon and Minnie (Seltzer) M.; m. Minne R. Rosenbaum, June 14, 1934; children—Robin Owen, Julie Ann. B.S. magna cum laude, CCNY, 1930; postgrad. U. Gottingen, Germany, 1928-29; Ph.D. in Physics, Columbia U., 1935. Instr. physics CCNY, N.Y.C., 1931-41; lectr. astronomy Columbia U., 1935-50, prof., 1950-78, prof. emeritus, 1958—. Author: This is Astronomy, 1955; This Is Outer Space, 1956; Essentials of Astronomy, 1967; World of the Atom, 1968; The Universe, 1975. Recipient Gravity Research award Gravity Research Found., 1960. Fellow Am. Phys. Soc., N.Y. Acad. Scis. (pres. 1970, award, 1972), Royal Astron. Soc. (Eng.), World Acad. Arts and Scis., Am. Astron. Soc., AAAS. Current work: Gravitational theory of the structure of elementary particles. Subspecialties: Cosmology; Relativity and gravitation. Office: Dept Astronomy Columbia U New York NY 10027

MOTZ, ROBIN OWEN, physician, cons. physicist and pharmacologist; b. Bronx, N.Y., Mar. 9, 1939; s. Lloyd and Minne (Rosenbaum) M.; m. Marcia Linda Motz, Aug. 29, 1959; children: Jeremy, Nicole, Benjamin. A.B. in Physics and Astronomy, Columbia U., 1959, Ph.D. in Physics, 1965, M.D., 1975. Diplomate: Dipolmate Am. Bd. Internal Medicine. Intern Columbia-Presbyn. Med. Ctr., N.Y.C., 1975-76, resident in internal medicine, 1976-78; asst. prof. physics Stevens Inst. Tech., 1965-71; lectr. Columbia U., 1971-78, asst. prof. clin. medicine, 1978—; med. dir. Thomas Ferguson Assocs.; cons. physicist Thexon Corp. Astronomy editor; asst. editor Am. Jour. Physics, 1969-72; editorial adv. bd. Drug Therapy, 1983—, Computer News for Physicians, 1983—; contbg. author: Columbia Ency, 1975; contbr. numerous articles to profl. jours. Fellow N.Y. Acad. Scis. (vice chmn. sect. physical scis. 1967-69) ACP; mem. AMA, Am. Phys. Soc., N.Y. Acad. Scis., Mensa, Sigma Xi. Current Work: Spray drying and ionic recombination, applied physics research for med. cures. Subspecialties: Internal medicine; Plasma physics. Office: 404 Tenafly Rd Tenafly NJ 07670

MOTZKIN, SHIRLEY MITTMAN, biology educator; b. N.Y.C., Jan. 12, 1927; d. Julius and Margit (Ullman) Mittman; m. Donald Jack Motzkin, June 22, 1952; children—Shelly, Beth, Glenn. B.S., Bklyn. Coll., 1947; M.A., Columbia U., 1949; Ph.D., NYU, 1958. Instr. Bklyn. Coll., 1947-52, adj. prof., 1952-69; instr. NYU Coll. Dentistry, N.Y.C., 1951-59, asst. prof., 1959-66; mem. faculty Poly. Inst. N.Y., Bklyn., 1966—, assoc. prof. biology, 1966-73, prof., 1973—, head life scis. program, 1973-81; vis. prof. Yale U. Coll. Medicine, 1976; guest lectr. Guggenheim Dental Clinic, 1968-69. Mem. Bioelectromagnetics Soc., Teratology Soc., European Teratology Soc., Bone and Tooth Soc. N.Y. Mechanisms and effects of low level millimeter waves on living systems with particular emphasis on cellular and subcellular systems. Subspecialties: Molecular biology; Developmental biology. Home: 171 Valley Rd New Rochelle NY 10804 Office: Poly Inst New York 333 Jay St Brooklyn NY

MOU, DUEN-GANG, biochemical engineer, educator; b. Nanking, China, Nov. 5, 1948; came to U.S., 1972; s. Jyh-Cherng and Jiing-Fang (Shy) M.; m. Florence Y. W. Pu, July 30, 1972; children—Sheau-Wha, Albert Lae. B.S. in Chem. Engring., Nat. Taiwan U., 1970; M.S. in Chem. Engring., U. R.I., 1974; Ph.D. in Biochem. Engring., MIT, 1979. Asst. research engr. Food Industry Research and Devel. Inst., Hsinchu, Taiwan, 1971-72; project supr. fermentation devel. Bristol-Myers Co., Syracuse, N.Y., 1979-80; sr. research scientist Research Labs., Eastman Kodak Co., Rochester, N.Y., 1980—; adj. prof. U. Rochester, 1984—. Contbr. articles to profl. jours. Pfizer fellow, 1974. Mem. Am. Chem. Soc., Am. Inst. Chem. Engring., AAAS, Sigma Xi, Phi Kappa Phi. Current work: Biotechnology commercial development; fermentation process development and scale-up; continuous steady-state process development and scale-up; on-line process computer application; strain improvement. Office: Kodak Research Labs B82 Kodak Park Rochester NY 14650

MOUDGIL, BRIJ MOHAN, materials engineering educator; b. Pataudi, Haryana, India, Aug. 4, 1945; s. Devki Nandan and Bhagwati Devi (Bhardwaj) M.; m. Sheela Moudgil, Oct. 1, 1973; children: Suniti, Sarika. B.S., DAV Coll., Jullundur, India, 1963-65; B.S. in Metall. Engring, Indian Inst. Sci., Bangalore, 1968; M.S., Columbia U., 1972, Sc.D., 1981. Research engr. Occidental Research Corp., Irvine, Calif., 1976-80; grad. research assoc. Columbia U., N.Y.C., 1978-81; assoc. prof. dept. material s. sci. and engring. U. Fla., Gainesville, 1981-85, prof., 1985—; dir. U. Fla. Ctr. for Research in Mining and Mineral Resources, 1982—. Contbr. articles to profl. jours. Mem. AIME (chmn. fundamentals), Am. Inst. Chem. Engrs., Am. Chem. Soc., Am. Ceramic Soc., Sigma Xi. Patentee in field. Current Work: Mineral beneficiation, applied surface chemistry; fine particle processing, mineral industry waste disposal. Subspecialties: Metallurgical engineering; Surface chemistry. Home: 2101 NW 20th St Gainesville FL 32605 Office: Dept Material Sci and Engring U Fla Gainesville FL 32611

MOULDEN, TREVOR HOLMES, aerospace engineering educator, researcher; b. Leicester, Eng., Oct. 13, 1939; came to U.S., 1966; s. George Harry and Olive May (Holmes) M. B.Sc. in Engring. with honors, Imperial Coll., London U., 1961; M.Phil., London U., 1968; Ph.D., U. Tenn., 1973. Sci. officer Nat. Phys. Lab., London, 1961-66; research engr. Lockheed-Ga. Co., Marietta, 1966-69; research fellow U. Tenn. Space Inst., Tullahoma, 1970-73, asst. prof. aerospace engring., 1973-78, assoc. prof., 1978—. Author: Fundamentals of Transonic Flow, 1984. Co-editor: Handbook of Turbulence, 1977. Mem. AIAA, Royal Aero. Soc., Soc. Indsl. and Applied Math. Subspecialties: Aeronautical engineering; Applied mathematics. Office: U Tenn Space Inst Tullahoma TN 37388

MOULTRIE, FRED, geneticist; b. Albertville, Ala., Apr. 18, 1923; s. Walter Louis and Minnie Alma (Bodine) M.; m. Frances Grace Aldridge, May 28, 1947; children—Marilyn R. Moultrie Phillips, Elizabeth A. Moultrie Becker, Janet C. Moultrie Gauger. B.S., Auburn U., 1948, M.S., 1949; Ph.D., Kans. State U., 1953. Assoc. prof. Auburn U., Ala., 1951-55, prof., 1955-56; geneticist Arbor Acres Farm, Inc., Glastonbury, Conn., 1956-59, research coordinator, 1959-62, v.p., dir. research, 1962-64, exec. v.p., 1964-72, pres. domestic div., 1972-73; pres. Corbett Breeders, Westover, Md., 1973-81; v.p., dir. research Kennebec Internat., Westover, 1981-84; geneticist Perdue Farms, Inc., Salisbury, Md., 1984—. Contbr. articles to profl. jours. Served with USCG, 1942-46. Mem. Am. Poultry Sci. Assn., Worlds Poultry Sci. Assn., Poultry Breeders Am. (pres. 1967-68), Am. Genetics Assn. Methodist. Current work: Poultry improvement through use of population genetics. Subspecialties: Genetics and genetic engineering (agriculture); Animal breeding and embryo transplants. Home: 1106 Coulbourne Mill Rd Salisbury MD 21801 Office: Perdue Farms Inc Salisbury MD 21801

MOUNTAINSPRING, STEPHEN, research biologist, educator; b. Cleve., Feb. 17, 1955; s. Steve Raymond and Mary Ann (Sefcik) Sabo; m. Susan Barbara Pritchard, Sept. 15, 1979; children—Orion, Naomi. B.S., John Carroll U., 1975; Ph.D., Cornell U., 1980. Teaching asst. Cornell U., Ithaca, N.Y., 1977-78, research asst., 1978-80; wildlife biologist U.S. Fish and Wildlife Service, Volcano, Hawaii, 1980-81, research biologist, 1983—; research assoc. Oreg. State U., Corvallis, 1981-83. Author: Forest Birds of the Hawaiian Islands, 1985; also articles. Planning commr. Adair Area Commn., Oreg., 1982-83. Recipient Chapman Meml. award Am. Mus. Natural History, 1981, 82; spl. achievement award U.S. Fish and Wildlife Service, 1983, 84. NSF fellow in ecology, 1975-79. Mem. Am. Ornithologists Union, Cooper Ornithol. Soc. (Painton award 1985), Ecol. Soc. Am., Wilson Ornithol. Soc., Wildlife Soc. Current work: Ecological relationships and conservation of native terrestrial Hawaiian ecosystems; ecology, behavior and evolution of land birds. Subspecialties: Ecology (environmental science); Resource management. Home: PO Box 88 Hawaii National Park HI 96718 Office: US Fish and Wildlife Service PO Box 44 Hawaii National Park HI 96718

MOUNTCASTLE, VERNON BENJAMIN, JR., neurophysiologist; b. Shelbyville, Ky., July 15, 1918; s. Vernon Mountcastle and Anne-Francis Marguerite (Waugh) M.; m. Nancy Clayton Pierpont, Sept. 6, 1945; children: Vernon Benjamin III, Anne Clayton, George Earle Pierpont. B.S. in Chemistry, Roanoke Coll., Salem, Va., 1938, D.Sc. (hon.), 1968; M.D., Johns Hopkins U., 1942; D.Sc. (hon.), U. Pa., 1976, Northwestern U., 1985; M.D. (hon.), U. Zurich, 1983, U. Siena, 1984. House officer surgery Johns Hopkins Hosp., 1942-43; mem. faculty Johns Hopkins Sch. Medicine, 1946—, prof. physiology, 1959, dir. dept., 1964-80, Univ. prof. neurosci., 1980—; dir. Bard Labs. Neurophysiology, 1981—, dir. neurosci. research program, 1981-84; pres. Neurosci. Research Found., 1981—; spl. univ. lectr. Univ. Coll., London, Eng., 1959; Penfield lectr. Am. U. Beirut, 1971; Sherrington lectr. U. Liverpool, Eng., 1974; Harmon lectr. Am. Assn. Anatomists, 1976; Kershman lectr. Eastern EEG Soc., 1976; Stevenson lectr. U. Western Ont., 1976; Mellon lectr. U. Pitts., 1977; Regents lectr. U. Helsinki, 1977; Hughlings Jackson lectr. McGill U., 1978; Harvey lectr., 1979; Bishop lectr. Washington U., 1979; Hines lectr. Emory U., 1979; Scott lectr. Wayne State U., 1981; vis. prof. Coll. de France, Paris, 1980; spl. research physiology brain. Chmn. physiology study sect.; mem. physiology tng. com. NIH, 1958-61; adv. council Nat. Eye Inst., 1971-74; mem. sci. adv. bd. USAF, 1969-71; vis. com. dept. psychology Mass. Inst. Tech., 1966-75; bd. biology and medicine NSF, 1970-73; mem. commn. on neurophysiology Internat. Union Physiol. Sci. Editor-in-chief: Jour. Neurophysiology, 1961-64; assoc. editor: Bull. Johns Hopkins Hosp, 1954-62; editorial bd.: Physiol. Revs, 1957-59, Jour. Neuropharm, 1966-71, Exptl. Brain Research, 1966—; editor, contbr.: Med. Physiology, 12th edit, 1968, 13th edit., 1974, 14th edit., 1980, (with G.M. Edelman) The Mindful Brain, 1978; author articles in field. Served to lt. (s.g.) M.C. USNR, 1943-46. Recipient Lashley prize Am. Philos. Soc., 1974, F.O. Schmitt prize and medal MIT, 1975, Sherrington prize and Gold medal Royal Acad. Medicine, London, 1977, Horowitz prize Columbia U., 1978, Fyssen Internat. prize Paris, 1983, Lasker award, 1983, Helmholtz prize, 1982. Mem. Am. Physiol. Soc., Am. Acad. Arts and Scis., Nat. Acad. Sci. (chmn. sect. physiology 1971-74), Harvey Cushing Soc., Am. Neurol. Assn. (Bennett lectr. 1978, hon. mem.), AAAS, Soc. Neurosci. (pres. 1970-72, Gerard Prize 1980), Am. Philos. Soc. (councillor 1979-82), Nat. Inst. Medicine, Phi Beta Kappa, Sigma Chi, Alpha Omega Alpha, Phi Chi. Club: 14 West Hamilton St. (Balt.). Current Work: Physiology of cerebral cortex and its relation to higher function of brain. Subspecialties: Neurobiology; Neurophysiology. Home: 31 Warrenton Road Baltimore MD 21210

MOUSTAKAS, THEODORE DEMETRI, physicist, researcher; b. Greece, Jan. 28, 1940, came to U.S., 1968, naturalized, 1982; s. Demetri and Elefteria M.; m. Elena M. Palumbo, July 6, 1974; children—Demetri, Christiana. B.S. in Physics, Aristotle U., Greece, 1964, M.S. in Electronics, 1967; M.Phil., Columbia U., 1974, Ph.D., 1974. Research asst. IBM, Yorktown Heights, N.Y., 1971-74; research fellow Harvard U., Cambridge, Mass., 1974-77; research assoc. Exxon Research and Engring. Co., Annandale, N.J., 1977—. Editor: Coatings, 1984. Contbr. articles to profl. jours. Inventor amorphous silicon devices, 1983. IBM fellow, 1974; Dept. Energy grantee, 1980-83. Mem. Am. Phys. Soc., Materials Research Soc., N.Y. Acad. Scis. Current work: Molecular beam epitaxy of III-V semiconductors, hydrogenated amorphous silicon, solar cells, metallic and semiconducting superlattices, sputtering, plasma enhanced chemical vapor deposition. Subspecialties: Semiconductors; Condensed matter physics. Home: 7 Cambridge Dr Annandale NJ 08801 Office: Exxon Research and Engring Co Route 22 E Annandale NJ 08801

MOVSHON, J(OSEPH) ANTHONY, neuroscientist, educator; b. N.Y.C., Dec. 10, 1950; s. George and Irene (Dann) M.; m. Margaret Elizabeth Beardsley, Aug. 30, 1975; 1 child, Nicholas Anthony, Clare Elizabeth. B.A. with honors, U. Cambridge, Eng., 1972, Ph.D., 1975. Asst. prof. dept. psychology NYU, N.Y.C., 1975-78, assoc. prof, 1978-84, prof., 1984—; mem. visual scis. B study sect. NIH, Bethesda, Md., 1982—. Editor Ann. Rev. of Neurosci., 1983-87. Author sci. papers. Recipient Research Career devel. award Nat. Eye Inst., NIH, 1980-85; Alfred P. Sloan Found. fellow in neurosci., 1977-81; research grantee NIH, 1977—, NSF, 1977-80, 83—. Mem. Assn. for Research in Vision and Ophthalmology (officer 1982-84), Soc. for Neurosci. Democrat. Current work: Neurophysiology and psychophysics of vision and visual development, applications of digital computing to vision. Subspecialties: Neurophysiology; Psychophysics. Home: 100 Bleecker St New York NY 10012 Office: Dept Psychology NYU 6 Washington Pl New York NY 10003

MOW, VAN C., biomedical engineering educator; b. Chengdu, China, Jan. 10, 1939; B.A.E., Rensselaer Poly. Inst., 1962, Ph.D., 1966. Vis. mem. staff Courant Inst. Math. Sci., NYU, 1967-68; mem. tech. staff Bell Labs., Whippany, N.J., 1968-69; assoc. prof. mechanics Rensselaer Poly. Inst., Troy, N.Y., 1969-76; prof. mechanics and biomed. engring., 1976-82, Clark and Crossan prof. engring., 1982—; vis. prof. Harvard U. Med. Sch., Boston, 1976-77; cons. in field; chmn. orthopedics and musculoskeltal study sect. NIH, Bethesda, Md., 1982-84. Contbr. articles to profl. jours. and books. NATO sr. fellow, 1978; recipient William H. Wiley Disting. Faculty award Rensselaer Poly. Inst., 1981; named hon. prof. Chengdu U., 1981, Shanghai U., 1983 (both People's Republic of China). Fellow ASME (chmn. biomechanics div. 1984-85, Melville award 1982); mem. Orthopaedic Research Soc. (pres. 1982-83), Am. Soc. Biomechanics (founding mem.), ASCE, Internat. Soc. Biorheology, Am. Acad. Orthopedic Surgeons (Kappa Delta award 1981). Current Work: Biomechanics; biorheology; articular cartilage; osteoarthritis; synovial joints; diarthrodial joints; synovial fluid rheology. Subspecialties: Biomedical engineering; Theoretical and applied mechanics. Office: Rensselaer Poly Inst Dept ME AE and M Troy NY 12180

MOWER, ROLAND DELOY, geography educator; b. Mount Pleasant, Utah, Dec. 25, 1928; s. Roland Grant and Viola (Hansen) M.; m. Nona I. Hall, Dec. 23, 1948; children—Carol, Connie, Christi, Roland, Richard. B.S., U. Utah, 1955; M.S., Okla. State U., 1959; Ph.D., U. Kans., 1971. Commd. 2d lt. U.S. Air Force, 1955; advanced through grades to lt. col., 1974; dep. chief. Avionics Lab., Wright Patterson AFB, Ohio; ret., 1974; prof. geography U. N.D., Grand Forks, 1974—, chmn. dept., 1984—, dir. Inst. for Remote Sensing, 1975—. Editor: Remote Sensing in Colombia, 1983. Fulbright-Hays fellow, 1978, 83; NASA-Am. Soc. Engring. Edn. fellow, 1979, 80. Mem. Assn. Am. Geographers, Am. Soc. Photogrammetry, Conf. Latin Am. Geographers, Sigma Xi. Republican. Mormon. Current work: Application of airborn video remote sensing techniques to environmental and resource problems. Subspecialty: Remote sensing (geoscience). Home: 3002 Clover Dr Grand Forks ND 58201 Office: Dept Geography Univ ND Grand Forks ND 58202

MOWERY, DWIGHT FAY, chemist, educator, researcher; b. Moorehead, Minn., May 1, 1915; s. Dwight Fay and Elizabeth King (McGiffert) M.; m. Suzanne Frame Lenderman, June 12, 1943. B.A. in Chemistry, Harvard U., 1937; Ph.D., M.I.T., 1940. Research chemist DuPont Co., Wilmington, Del., 1940-42, Hercules Powder Co., Wilmington, 1942-43; prof. chemistry Elms Coll., 1943-46; prof. Franklin Tech. Inst., 1946-49; instr. Trinity Coll., Hartford, Conn., 1949-53; prof. Ripon Coll., 1953-57; prof. Southeastern Mass. U., 1957-64, Commonwealth prof., 1964—; cons. in field. Contbr. numerous articles on organic chemistry, microanalytical chemistry, chromatography, and chem. edn. to profl. jours. L.F. Verges fellow, 1939; NSF research grantee, 1956. Mem. Am. Chem. Soc., AAUP, Sigma Xi, Sigma Pi Sigma. Republican. Unitarian. Current Work: Carbohydrate chemistry; organic analysis employing classical microchem. methods; gas, liquid and thin layer chromatography; mass, nuclear magnetic reasonance and infrared spectrophotometry; reaction mechanism and rate studies employing computer programming. Subspecialties: Organic chemistry; Mathematical software. Office: Southeastern Mass U North Dartmouth MA 02747

MOWRY, ROBERT WILBUR, physician, educator; b. Griffin, Ga., Jan. 10, 1923; s. Roy Burnell and Mary Frances (Swilling) M.; m. Margaret Neilson Black, June 11, 1949; children: Janet Lee, Robert Gordon, Barbara Ann. B.S., Birmingham So. Coll., 1944; M.D., Johns Hopkins U., 1946. Rotating intern U. Ala. Med. Coll., 1946-47, resident pathology, 1947-48; sr. asst. surgeon USPHS-NIH, Bethesda, Md., 1948-52; fellow pathology Boston City Hosp., 1949-50; asst. prof. pathology Washington U., St. Louis, 1952-53; asst. prof. pathology U. Ala. Med. Center, Birmingham, 1953-54, assoc. prof. pathology, 1954-57, prof., 1958—, prof. health services adminstrn., 1976—, dir. Anat. Pathology Lab., 1960-64; dir. grad. programs in pathology U. Ala. Med. Center (Anat. Pathology Lab.), 1964-72; sr. scientist U. Ala. Inst. Dental Research, 1967-72, dir. autopsy services, 1975-79; vis. scholar dept. pathology U. Cambridge, Eng., 1972-73; cons. FDA, 1975-81. Author: (with J.F.A. McManus) Staining Methods: Histologic and Histochemical, 1960; Editorial bd.: Jour. Histochemistry and Cytochemistry, 1960-75, Stain Tech, 1965—; editorial bd.: AMA Archives of Pathology, 1967-76. Served with USPHS, 1948-52. Mem. Am Assn. Pathologists, Histochem. Soc. (councillor 1974-78), Internat. Acad. Pathology, Biol. Stain Commn. (v.p. 1974—, pres. 1976-81, trustee 1966—), Am. Assn. U. Profs. Pathology, AMA, Phi Beta Kappa, Sigma Xi, Delta Sigma Phi, Alpha Kappa Kappa. Presbyn. Current Work: Cytochemistry of complex carbonohydrates and certain proteins, methods development and applications in diagnostic histopathology of human diseases. Subspecialties: Pathology (medicine); Cytology and histology. Home: 4165 Sharpsburg Dr Birmingham AL 35213

MOY, DAN, physicist, research engineer; b. Chgo., July 11, 1955; s. Sen Jing and Janice Oy (Yung) M.; m. Janice Lee Mantarian. B.S. in Physics, MIT, 1978; M.S. in Physics, U. Ill., 1980, Ph.D. in Physics, 1983. Teaching asst. U. Ill., Champaign-Urbana, 1978-79, research asst., 1979-82; sr. engr. Intel Corp., Santa Clara, Calif., 1983-84; research staff engr. IBM T.J. Watson Research Ctr., Yorktown Heights, N.Y., 1984—. Contbr. articles to profl. jours. Mem. Am. Phys. Soc., Am. Vacuum Soc. Current work: Research and development of thin films for interconnect or gate technology in VLSI applications. Subspecialties: Condensed matter physics; Low temperature physics. Home: 10 Diamond Ave Bethel CT 06801 Office: IBM TJ Watson Research Ctr PO Box 218 Yorktown Heights NY 10598

MOYER, JOHN RAYMOND, chemist; b. Buffalo, June 9, 1931; s. Percival and Catharine (Curtis) Moyer Teall; m. Elizabeth Ann Reber, Aug. 31, 1952; children—Ann Elizabeth, Jean Michele, Thomas John, Paul Frederick. A.B., Eastern Mich. U., 1952; M.S. in Chemistry, U. Mich., Ann Arbor, 1955, Ph.D., 1958. Assoc. research scientist Dow Chem. Co., Midland, Mich., 1968-76, research scientist, 1976—. Inventor in field. Mem. Am. Chem. Soc. Lutheran. Current work: Chlorination-phase, aq phase; synthesis of ceramic precursors. Subspecialties: Inorganic chemistry; Physical chemistry. Home: 2704 Swede Rd Midland MI 48640 Office: Dow Chem Co 1776 Building Midland MI 48640

MOYER, ROBERT FINDLEY, medical physicist; b. N.Y.C., May 12, 1937; s. James Herbert and Ina Ruth (Findley) M.; m. Cecelia Rita; 3 children. B.S., Pa. State U., 1959, M.S., 1961; Ph.D., UCLA, 1965. Cert. radiation equipment safety officer N.Y. State Dept. Health, 1974. Instr. SUNY Upstate Med. Center, Syracuse, 1965-70, asst. prof., 1970-81; chief physicist Reading (Pa.) Hosp. and Med. Ctr., 1981—; cons., researcher in field. Author: Personalized Instruction in Radiation Therapy, 1978, 79; contbr. articles to profl. publs.

Elder Presbyterian ch., 1968-85; cubmaster Hiawatha Council Boy Scouts Am., 1968-70. Recipient cert. of merit for exhibit Radiol. Soc. N.Am., 1977. Mem. Am. Assn. Physicists in Medicine, Am. Assn. Med. Dosimetrists (assoc.), Health Physics Soc., Am. Coll. Med. Physics. Republican. Current Work: Medical radiation physics and health physics. Subspecialties: Radiology; Medical physics. Home: 342 RD 2 Mertztown PA 19539 Office: Reading Hosp and Med Ctr Radiology Reading PA 19603

MOYSENKO, ANDREW EDWARD, electrical engineer; b. Haverhill, Mass., Apr. 25, 1950; s. Edward Frank and Rhoda Helen (Corthell) M.; m. Patricia Margaret Thomas, Aug. 21, 1971; 1 child, Kristen Michelle. S.B.E.E., MIT, 1974, S.M.E.E., 1974. Assoc. scientist Raytheon Research, Waltham, Mass., 1974-78; sr. materials engr. M/A-COM-GaAs Products, Burlington, Mass., 1978-82, engring. mgr., 1981-82; prin. engr. Sanders Assocs., Nashua, N.H., 1982-83, mgr. IC fabrication, 1983-85, mgr. gallium arsenide materials, 1985—; lectr. in field. Contbr. articles to profl. jours. Mem. Edn. Council MIT, Cambridge, Mass., 1977; mem. Central Catholic High Sch. Guild, Lawrence, Mass., 1982. Mem. Am. Mgmt. Assn., IEEE, Am. Vacuum Soc., Electrochem. Soc., Inst. Environ. Scis. (sr.), Assn. Old Crows. Club: MIT. Current work: Development of technology supporting Gallium Arsenide, Silicon and other semiconductor IC and discrete device fabrication; establish clean room facility. Subspecialties: Microchip technology (engineering); Condensed matter physics. Home: 16 Joyce Ave Lowell MA 01851 Office: Sanders Assoc NHQ 6-1517 DW Hwy S Nashua NH 03061

MREMA, JOHN E. K., veterinarian, pathologist, researcher, educator; b. Kilimanjaro, Tanzania, Sept. 30, 1944; came to U.S., 1971; s. Elisa Kileo and Anale Kelei (Mhache) M.; m. Catherine A. Worth, Mar. 29, 1975 (div. Sept. 1983); 1 child, Anale Elizabeth; m. Catherine W. Ndegwa, Sept. 31, 1984; 1 child, Tutu Geoffrey. B.V.M., U. Nairobi, Kenya, 1969; M.S. in Pathology, Colo. State U., 1973, Ph.D. in Pathology, 1976. Diplomate Veterinary Surgeons, Tanzania. Regional veterinary officer Tanzania Civil Service, Tanga, Kilimanjaro, 1969-71; research scientist dept. biology malaria program, U. N.Mex., 1977-78; asst. researcher Sch. Medicine, Albuquerque, 1977-83, research scientist Div. Tropical Medicine, Albuquerque, 1977-83; asst. research prof. Coll. Veterinary Medicine, U. Mo., Columbia 1983—; cons. pathologist Elars Bioresearch Labs., Fort Collins, Colo., 1976-77; mem. com. Electron Microscope Users, Albuquerque, 1981-83; reader, interviewer paraprofls. U. Mo., 1984. Contbr. articles to profl. jours. Rockefeller Found. fellow, 1974-76; prin. investigator incentive award U. Mo., Columbia, 1984-85. Mem. Am. Soc. Tropical Medicine and Hygiene, AVMA, Am. Soc. Primatologists, Am. Soc. Clin. Pathologists, Internat. Primate Soc., Veterinary Surgeons Tanzania, Am. Assn. Lab. Animal Sci. (Mo.). Current work: Involved in development of human malaria vaccine; clinical hematology and serum chemistries; effector cell surface markers and immunophenotyping of Aotus using Monoclonal antibodies; plasmodium flaciparum parasite immunity and immunization. Subspecialties: Immunocytochemistry; Hematology. Home: Box 18 Columbia MO 65205 Office: Coll Veterinary Medicine Dept Veterinary Pathology 1600 E Rollins W 213 U Mo Columbia MO 65211

MROZOWSKI, STANISLAW, physicist, educator; b. Warsaw, Poland, Feb. 9, 1902; U.S., 1939, naturalized, 1948; s. Josef and Amelia (Zlotnicka) M.; m. Irena M. Tarwacka, June 26, 1926 (dec. 1982). Ph.D., U. Warsaw, 1931; Dr. honoris causa, U. Bordeaux, France, 1964. Research fellow U. Warsaw, 1929-33, faculty, 1933-39; research fellow U. Calif. at Berkeley, 1939-40; research assoc. U. Chgo., 1940-45; asso. prof., chmn. physics dept. George Williams Coll., 1942-45; head physics dept. research and devel. div. Gt. Lakes Carbon Corp., 1945-49; prof. physics State U. N.Y. at Buffalo, 1949-72, prof. emeritus, 1972—, dir. carbon research lab., 1949-74, chmn. physics dept., 1959-64; Fulbright prof. Keio and Nagoya univs., Japan, 1963-64; vis. prof. U. Karlsruhe, Germany, summers, 1968, 72, U. Tokyo, fall 1970; adj. prof. Ball State U., Muncie, Ind., 1972—. Editor: Proc. Confs. on Carbon, 1955-62; editor-in-chief: Carbon, 1962-82; Contbr. articles to profl. jours. Trustee Kosciuszko Found., 1969—, vice chmn. bd., 1984—. Recipient M. Kernbaum prize in physics Warsaw Sci. Soc., 1932; 1st George Skakel Meml. award, 1969; Kosciuszko Found. medal, 1981; medal of merit City of Bordeaux, 1984. Fellow Am. Phys. Soc., Optical Soc. Am.; mem. Polish Phys. Soc. (chmn. Warsaw sect. 1938-39, hon. mem. 1967—), Soc. Rheology, Am. Assn. Physics Tchrs., Polish Inst. Arts and Scis. Am. (v.p. 1964-65, pres. 1965-74), Am. Carbon Soc. (chmn. 1957-63, exec. com. 1963-82), Sigma Xi (research plaque Buffalo 1969). Discoverer nuclear isotope effect in atomic and band spectra, 1931; (with Jenkins) interference effect in multipole radiation, 1940; research on atomic and molecular spectroscopy, electronic and other properties of chars, carbons and graphites. Office: Dept Physics and Astronomy Ball State U Muncie IN 47306

MUAN, ARNULF, university dean, geochemistry educator; b. Lökken Verk, Norway, Apr. 19, 1923; came to U.S., 1952, naturalized, 1962; s. Anders O. and Ingeborg (Engen) M.; m. Hildegard Hoss, Jan. 29, 1960; children: Michael, Ingrid. Diploma in chemistry, Tech. U. Norway, 1948; Ph.D. in Geochemistry, Pa. State U., 1955. Asst. prof. metallurgy Pa. State U., University Park, 1955-57, asso. prof., 1957-62, prof., 1962-66, prof. mineral scis., 1966—, head dept. geochemistry and mineralology, 1966-71, head dept. geoscis., 1971-73, assoc. dean research, 1976-85, acting dean, 1985—. Author: (with E.F. Osborn) Phase Equilibria Among Oxides in Steelmaking, 1965. Sr. NSF fellow, 1962; Fulbright-Hays lectr. USSR, 1973-74. Fellow Am. Ceramic Soc. (Ross Coffin Purdy award 1958, John Jeppson gold medal 1978), Mineral. Soc. Am. (v.p. 1973-74, pres. 1974-75), Geol. Soc. Am.; mem. Am. Inst. Metall. Engrs., AAAS, Geochem. Soc., Norwegian Chem. Soc., Royal Norwegian Acad. Sci. (fgn. mem.), Sigma Xi. Current Work: Chemistry and characterization of metal-, oxide- and carbide phases at high temperatures under various atmospheric conditions. Subspecialties: High-temperature materials; High temperature chemistry. Home: 400 Toftrees Ave Apt 107 State College PA 16803 Office: 416 Walker Bldg University Park PA 16802

MUCCINO, RICHARD ROBERT, chemist; b. West New York, N.J., May 19, 1946. B.A., Rutgers U., 1967, Ph.D., 1971. Predoctoral fellow NIH, Bethesda, Md., 1970-71, postdoctoral fellow, 1971-73; research fellow Hoffmann-LaRoche, Inc., Nutley, N.J., 1973—; chmn. internat. sci. com. 2d Internat. Symposium on Synthesis and Applications of Isotopically Labelled Compounds, 1982-85. Author: Organic Synthesis with Carbon-14, 1983. Editor: Proceedings of the Second International Symposium on the Synthesis and Applications of Isotopically Labelled Compounds, 1985. Subspecialty: Organic chemistry. Home: RD 3 Box 539 Ringoes NJ 08551 Office: Hoffmann-LaRoche Inc Nutley NJ 07110

MUCHMORE, HAROLD GORDON, physician, educator; b. Ponca City, Okla., Mar. 8, 1920; s. Clyde E. and Iola R. (Winner) M.; m. Donna M. Stevens, Feb. 23, 1954; children—Bruce, Nancy, Steven, Allan. B.A., Rice U., Houston, 1943; M.D., U. Okla., 1946. Intern U. Okla., 1946-47, resident internal medicine, 1954-56, infectious diseases, 1956-60; mem. faculty U. Okla. Coll. Medicine, 1947-62, 66—, prof. medicine, 1970—, Carl Puckett prof. pulmonary diseases, 1970—, adj. prof. microbiology and immunology, 1970—; mem. faculty U. Minn. Med. Sch., 1962-66. Served with AUS, 1943-45; Served with USAF, 1952-54. Fellow A.C.P., Infectious Diseases Soc. Am.; mem. Am. Thoracic Soc., Internat. Soc. Human and Animal Mycology, Explorers Club. Current Work: fungus diseases; immunity during isolation in the Antarctic. Subspecialties: Internal medicine; Infectious diseases. Home: 3005 Robin Ridge Rd Oklahoma City OK 73120 Office: PO Box 26901 Oklahoma City OK 73190

MUCKSTADT, JOHN A., operations research educator, consultant; b. Rochester, N.Y.; s. Paul and Eleanor R. (Offerman) M.; m. Linda J. Feary, Jan. 29, 1959; children—Paul, Steven, John, Andrew. A.B. in Math., U. Rochester, 1962; M.S. in Indsl. Adminstrn., U. Mich., 1964, M.A. in Math., 1965, Ph.D. in Indsl. Engring., 1966. Served to lt. col. U.S. Air Force, Dayton, Ohio, 1966-74; prof. ops. research, dir. Cornell U., Ithaca, N.Y., 1974—; cons. in field. Contbr. articles to profl. jours. Active Lutheran Ch., Ithaca, 1974—; coach Kawanis, Ithaca Youth Program, Wright-Patterson Youth Program, 1966-83. Grantee NSF, 1980-84, ONR, 1975-80. Mem. Ops. Research Soc. Am., Inst. Mgmt. Sci., Naval Research Logistics Quarterly (editor, assoc. editor). Republican. Current work: Design and analysis of multi stage production and distribution systems. Subspecialty: Operations research (engineering). Office: Upson Hall Cornell U Ithaca NY 14853

MUELLER, DENNIS, plasma physicist; b. Moline, Ill., Aug. 2, 1946; s. Warren Rudolph and Margie (Fitzpatrick) M.; m. Linda Klee, June 13, 1971; children—Luke Klee, Colby. B.A., MacMurray Coll., 1968; M.S., Mich. State U., 1974, Ph.D., 1976. Tchr., Lincoln High Sch., Ill., 1968-71, Seeger High Sch., West Lebanon, Ind., 1971-72; postdoctoral fellow Mich. State U., East Lansing, 1976; instr. Princeton U., N.J., 1976-78, staff physicist Princeton Plasma Physics Lab., 1978-82, research physicist, 1982—; cons. Middlesex Boro Council, N.J., 1978-79, Princeton Sci. Cons., 1982—. Contbr. articles to profl. jours. Mem. Am. Phys. Soc. (divs. plasma physics/nuclear physics). Current work: Research in controlled thermonuclear fusion, neutral beam heating in Tokamaks, ion beam optics. Subspecialties: Plasma physics; Nuclear physics. Home: 8 Hart Ave Hopewell NJ 08525 Office: Princeton Plasma Physics Laboratory PO Box 451 Princeton NJ 08545

MUELLER, GEORGE E., corporation executive; b. St. Louis, July 16, 1918; m. Maude Rosenbaum (div.); children: Karen, Jean; m. Darla Hix, 1978. B.S. in Elec. Engring, Mo. Sch. Mines, 1939; M.S. in Elec. Engring, Purdue U., 1940; Ph.D. in Physics, Ohio State U., 1951; hon. degrees, Wayne State U., N.M. State U., U. Mo., 1964, Purdue U., Ohio State U., 1965, Pepperdine U., 1979. Mem. tech. staff Bell Telephone Labs., 1940-46; prof. elec. engring. Ohio State U., 1946-56; cons. electronics Ramo-Wooldridge, Inc., 1955-57; from dir. electronic lab. to v.p. research and devel. Space Tech. Labs., 1958-62; asso. adminstr. for manned space flight NASA, 1963-69; corporate officer, sr. v.p. Gen. Dynamics Corp., N.Y.C., 1969-71; chmn., pres. System Devel. Corp., Santa Monica, Calif., 1971-80, chmn., chief exec. officer, 1981-83; sr. v.p. Burroughs Corp., 1982-83, cons., 1984—. Author: (with E.R. Spangler) Communications Satellites. Recipient 3 Distinguished Service medals NASA; Eugen Sanger award; Nat. Medal Sci., 1970; Nat. Transp. award, 1979; Medal of Paris, 1982; Fond Albert Enlekerem Space award, Hungary, 1983; Internat. Peace Cooperation award USSR, 1984; Herman Oberth medal, 1985. Fellow AAAS, IEEE, AIAA (Goddard medal 1983); Brit. Interplanetary Soc. (hon.), Am. Phys. Soc., Am. Astronautical Soc. (Space Flight award), Am. Geophys. Union, Brit. Interplanetary Soc.; mem. Nat. Acad. Engring., N.Y. Acad. Scis. Patentee in field. Subspecialty: Electrical engineering. Home: Santa Barbara CA Office: PO Box 5856 Santa Barbara CA 93108

MUELLER, HERBERT JOSEPH, dental research associate, consultant; b. Milw., Feb. 17, 1941; s. Herbert L. and Ann (Gemeiner) M. B.M.E., Marquette U., 1964; M.S., Northwestern U., 1966, Ph.D., 1969. Research fellow Northwestern U., 1964-69, postdoctoral fellow, 1977-80; asst. prof., chmn. dept. Loyola U., 1968-71; sec.-treas. Layton Park Pattern Works, 1971-77; research assoc. ADA, Chgo., from 1980. Contbr. articles to profl. jours., chpt. in book. Nat. Inst. Dental Research grantee, 1971. Mem. Am. Soc. Metals, Electrochem. Soc., Internat. Assn. Dental Research, Soc. Biomaterials, Sigma Xi, Pi Tau Sigma, Tau Beta Pi. Current Work: Interactions between dental biomaterials and saliva regarding electrochemistry of metals; binding of ions to protein, adsorption of proteins to surfaces. Currently using FT-IR, ESCA, SIMS. Development of improved dental materials to corrosion, fatigue, creep and wear as well as amalgams with new chemistries and dental instruments with implantation of specific ions. Subspecialties: Dental materials; Biomaterials. Home: 3533 W Lakefield Dr Milwaukee WI 53215 Office: Am Dental Assn Council Dental Materials Instruments and Equipment 211 E Chicago Ave Chicago IL 60611

MUELLER, MARVIN MARTIN, research physicist; b. Broken Arrow, Okla., Sept. 29, 1928; s. Martin John and Elsie Arlene (Peper) M.; m. Barbara Ann Holler, Oct. 22, 1966 (div. 1984). B.S. in Physics U. Okla., 1951, M.S. in physics, 1954, Ph.D. in Physics, 1959. Staff mem. Los Alamos Nat. Lab. 1959—. Contbr. articles to profl. jours. Mem. AAAS, Am. Phys. Soc., Am. Assn. Physics Tchrs., Phi Beta Kappa, Sigma Chi. Current work: Laser fusion, plasma physics, x-ray diagnostics, particle-plasma interaction. Subspecialties: Laser fusion; Plasma physics. Office: Los Alamos Nat Lab MS E554 Los Alamos NM 87545

MUELLER, PETER FRANCIS, optical scientist; b. Boston, Oct. 4, 1937; s. Victor Edward and Elizabeth (Homan) M.; m. Carol Ann Haley, Aug. 20, 1960; children—Peter, Andrea, Marie-Elaine, Eric, Gregory, Kristin. B.S. in Physics, Boston Coll., 1959; M.S. in Physics, Northeastern U., 1966. Engr., Northrop-Nontronics, Norwood, Mass., 1962-63; staff scientist Tech. Ops. Inc., Burlington, Mass., 1963-71, tech. dir., 1971-75; dir. optics Aerodyne Research Inc., Billerica, Mass., 1975-84; prin. engr. Electro-Optics div. Honeywell, Wilmington, Mass., 1984—; instr. optics Northeastern U., Boston, 1974-76. Inventor total optical color (TR 100 award 1972), 1969; patentee in field. Served to 1st lt. U.S. Army, 1960-62, Fed. Republic Germany. Mem. Optical Soc. Am., Soc. Photog. and Optical Scientists, Soc. Photo-Optical Instrumentation Engrs. Current work: Experimental Fourier optics applications; novel color image displays; information storage and retrieval systems; holographic techniques. Subspecialties: Optical image processing; Holography. Home: 210 Hunters Ridge Rd Concord MA 01742 Office: Electro-Optics div Honeywell 110 Fordham Rd Wilmington MA 01887

MUELLER-HEUBACH, EBERHARD AUGUST, medical educator, obstetrician-gynecologist; b. Berlin, Feb. 24, 1942; came to U.S., 1968; s. Heinrich G. and Elisabeth (Heubach) M.; m. Cornelia R. Uffmann, Feb. 6, 1968; 1 son, Oliver Maximilian. Abitur, Lichtenbergschule, Darmstadt, Ger., 1961; M.D., U. Cologne, W.Ger., 1966. Diplomate: Am. Bd. Ob-Gyn (maternal-fetal medicine, examiner). Intern U. Cologne, 1967-68; intern Middlesex Gen. Hosp., New Brunswick, N.J., 1968-69; research fellow Columbia U., N.Y.C., 1969-71; resident and chief resident Sloane Hosp. for Women, N.Y.C., 1971-75; asst. prof. U. Pitts. Sch. Medicine/Magee-Women's Hosp., 1975-81, assoc. prof., 1981—. Reviewer: Am. Jour. Ob-Gyn, 1978—, Obstetrics & Gynecology, 1979—; contbr. chpts. to books, articles to profl. jours. Fellow Am. Coll. Obstetricians and Gynecologists (Hoechst award 1972); mem. Tri-State Perinatal Orgn. (v.p. 1981), Pa. Perinatal Assn. (pres. 1984-86), Soc. Gynecologic Investigation, Soc. Perinatal Obstetricians, Am. Fedn. Clin. Research, Pitts. Ob-Gyn Soc. (pres.-elect 1985-86) Current Work: Animal studies in fetal and maternal physiology; diabetes mellitus in pregnancy, high risk obstetrics. Subspecialties: Maternal and fetal medicine; Reproductive biology (medicine). Office: Magee-Womens Hosp U Pitts Sch Medicine Pittsburgh PA 15213

MUGGERIDGE, DEREK BRIAN, engineer, educator; b. Godalmine, Surrey, Eng., Oct. 10, 1943; s. Donald William and Vera Elvina (Jackson) M.; m. Hanny Meta Buurman, Dec. 4, 1965; children—Karen Julie, Michael Brent. B.S., Calif. State Poly. U., 1965; M.A.Sc., U. Toronto, Ont., Can., 1966, Ph.D., 1970. Registered profl. engr. Nfld. Spl. lectr. U. Toronto, 1970-71; postdoctoral fellow Fleet Mfg. Co., Fort Erie, Ont., 1970-72; asst. prof. engring. Meml. U., St. John's, Nfld., 1972-76, assoc. prof., 1976-82, prof., 1982—; pres. Offshore Design Assocs., Ltd., St. John's, 1980—; sec., ptnr. Nfld. Ocean Cons. Ltd., St. John's, 1981—; ptnr. Frontier Ltd., Nfld., 1985—. Contbr. articles to profl. publs. Studentship, NRC, 1966-69; NRC fellow, 1970-72. Mem. Soc. Naval Architects and Marine Engrs., Marine Tech. Soc., Engring. Inst. Can. Progressive Conservative. Current work: Wave, wind and ice forces on offshore structures, hydrodynamic model studies. Subspecialty: Offshore technology. Home: Box 320 RR 1 Portugal Cove NF A0A 3K0 Canada Office: Faculty of Engring and Applied Sci Meml U Nfld Saint John's NF A1B 3X5 Canada

MUIRHEAD, VINCENT URIEL, aerospace engineer; b. Dresden, Kans., Feb. 6, 1919; s. John Hadsell and Lily Irene (McKinney) M.; m. Bobby Jo Thompson, Nov. 5, 1943; children: Rosalind, Jean, Juleigh. B.S., U.S. Naval Acad., 1941; B.S. in Aero. Engring, U.S. Naval Postgrad. Sch., 1948; Aero. Engr., Calif. Inst. Tech., 1949; postgrad., U. Ariz., 1962, 64, Okla. State U., 1963. Midshipman U.S. Navy, 1937, commd. ensign, 1941, advanced through grades to comdr., 1951; nav. officer U.S.S. White Plains, 1945-46; comdr. Fleet Aircraft Service Squad, 1951-52; with Bur. Aeros., Ft. Worth, 1953-54; comdr. Helicopter Utility Squadron I, Pacific Fleet, 1955-56; chief staff officer Comdr. Fleet Air, Philippines, 1956-58; exec. officer Naval Air Tng. Center, Memphis, 1958-61; ret., 1961; asst. prof. U. Kans., Lawrence, 1961-63, asso. prof. aerospace engring., 1964-76, prof., chmn. dept., 1976—; cons. Black & Veatch (cons. engrs.), Kansas City, Mo., 1964—. Author: Introduction to Aerospace, 1972, Thunderstorms, Tornadoes and Building Damage, 1975. Decorated Air medal. Assoc. fellow AIAA; mem. Am. Acad. Mechanics, Am. Soc. Engring. Edn., N.Y. Acad. Scis., Sigma Gamma Tau. Mem. Ch. of Christ (elder). Research on aircraft, tornado vortices, shock tubes and waves. Current Work: Dynamic ground effect on highly swept wings. Subspecialties: Aerospace engineering and technology; Fluid mechanics. Home: 503 Park Hill Terr Lawrence KS 66044

MUKHERJEE, ANIL BARAN, physician, medical researcher, emergency medical consultant; b. Suri, West Bengal, India, Jan. 20, 1942; came to U.S., 1962, naturalized, 1978; s. Shyama Pada and Sabasana M.; m. Diane Colleen Cunningham, May 25, 1956. B.Sc. with honors, U. Calcutta, India, 1962; M.S., U. Utah, 1964, Ph.D., 1966; M.D., SUNY-Buffalo, 1975. Postdoctoral fellow Columbia U., 1966-67; asst. prof. biology Queen's U., Kingston, Ont., Can., 1967-68; asst. research prof. pediatrics and human genetics SUNY-Buffalo, 1968-71; cons. in human genetics Children's Hosp., Buffalo, 1971-75; postgrad. in internal medicine Georgetown U. Med. Div., 1975-76; clin. assoc. NIH, Bethesda, Md., 1976-78, sr. investigator, 1978-80; chief sect. on devel. genetics, human genetics br. Nat. Inst. Child Helath and Human Devel., 1981 ; commd. capt., med. dir. USPHS, 1982. Contbr. numerous articles, chpts. to profl. publs. Recipient USPHS Clin. Soc. award, 1981, award for excellence in reprodn. research Brazilian Soc. Human Reprodn., 1981-82. Mem. Am. Soc. Human Genetics, Am. Soc. Cell Biology, AAAS, Am. Soc. Gynecologic Investigation, Sigma Xi. Club: Cosmos (Washington). Current Work: biochemistry of cellular development and differentiation, fetal alcohol syndrome, developmental genetics. Subspecialties: Internal medicine; Genetics and genetic engineering (medicine). Office: Nat Inst Child Health and Human Devel NIH Bethesda MD 20205

MUKHERJEE, SATYEN, electrical engineer; b. Calcutta, India, Dec. 16, 1954, came to U.S., 1981, naturalized, 1982; s. Phanindranath and Sagarika (Chakravarty) M. B.Tech., Indian Inst. Tech., Kharagpur, 1976; M.Tech., Philips Internat. Inst., Eindhoven, Netherlands, 1978; Ph.D., Carlton U., Ottawa, Ont., Can., 1981. Sr. research assoc. Indian Inst. Tech., New Delhi, 1976-77; sr. process engr. Intel Corp., Santa Clara, Calif., 1981-84; mgr. device characterization and modelling Exel Microelectronics, San Jose, Calif., 1984—. Contbr. articles to profl. jours. Inventor memory cell. Philips scholar, 1977; John Rupbash Meml. fellow, 1980, gold medallist, 1976. Mem. IEEE. Current work: Nonvolatile memories; high density CMOs technology; SOI technology. Subspecialty: Microchip technology (engineering). Home: 877 Willow St Apt 212 San Jose CA 95125 Office: Exel Microelectronics 2150 Commerce Dr San Jose CA 95131

MUKHTAR, HASAN, biochemist, educator; b. Lucknow, India, Jan. 1, 1947; came to U.S., 1974; s. Mukhtar and Samiunnisan (Begum) Husain; m. Ghizala Shakil, Nov. 10, 1973; children—Rahil Hasan, Kashif Hasan, Samira Hasan. B.S., Lucknow U.-India, 1965, M.S., 1967; Ph.D., Kanpur U., 1971. Vis. scientist Nat. Inst. Environ. Health Sci., Research Triangle Park, N.C., 1976-80; asst. prof. Case Western Res. U. and VA Med. Ctr., Cleve., 1980-84, assoc. prof., 1984—. Contbr. articles to profl. jours., chpts. to books. Mem. Am. Soc. Pharmacology and Exptl. Therapeutics, Am. Assn. Cancer Research, Soc. of Investigative Dermatology, Soc. Photobiology, AAAS. Current work: Cancer chemoprevention; drug metabolism and toxicology; role of skin enzymes in toxicology porphyrin phototoxicity. Subspecialties: Toxicology (medicine); Dermatology. Home: 3527 Woodridge Cleveland Heights OH 44121 Office: Dept Dematology Case Western Res Univ and VA Med Ctr Cleveland OH 44106

MULAY, LAXMAN N., materials science educator, researcher; b. Rahuri, India, Mar. 5, 1923; came to U.S., 1953, naturalized, 1976. B.S. in Phys. Chemistry with honors, Univ. Bombay, 1943, M.S. in Organic Chemistry, 1947, Ph.D. in Chem. Physics, 1953. Lectr. Univ. Bombay, Maharastra, 1939-53; research assoc. Northwestern U., Evanston, Ill., 1953-55, Harvard U., Cambridge, Mass., 1955-57; various teaching and research positions India, 1957-63; assoc. prof. solid state sci. Pa. State U., University Park, 1963-67, prof., 1967—; chmn. dept., 1967-72; cons. Cahn Instruments and Oil Industries, Calif., 1980—. Author: Magnetic Susceptibility, 1966. Editor: (with E.A. Boudreaux) Theory and Applications of Molecular Paramagnetism, 1976, Theory and Applications of Molecular Diamagnetism. 1976. Contbr. chpts. to books and 180 articles to profl. jours. Faculty adivsor Friends of India Assn., 1964-70. Fellow Royal Soc. Chemists; mem. IEEE (sr.), Am. Phys. Soc. Am. Chem. Soc. (vice chmn. 1964-65, chmn. central Pa. sect. 1965-66). Democrat. Hindu. Current work: Superparamagnetism of catalysts; Heisenberg exchange interactions, surface science, magnetism, electron paramagnetism. nuclear magnetic and Mossbauer spectroscopy. Subspecialties: Electronic materials; Magnetic physics. Home: 1011 Saxton Dr State College PA 16802 Office: Pa State Univ 136 MRL Bldg University Park PA 16802

MULCIHY, CASEY THOMAS, biomedical engineer, physician; b. Freeport, Tex., Jan. 30, 1955; s. Thomas William and Gloria Jean (Goodknight) M. B.E.E., U. Tex., 1977; M.D., U. Tex. Health Sci. Ctr., San Antonio, 1982. Computer design engr. Dow Chem., U.S.A., Freeport, Tex., 1974; biomed. engr. dept. biology U. Tex., Austin, 1977; reliability engr. Boeing Aerospace, Clear Lake, Tex., 1977-78; resident in pediatrics Central Tex. Med. Found., Austin, 1982-85. Fellow Am. Acad. Pediatrics (jr.); mem. IEEE, Tex. Med. Assn. Club: Bay Area Divers (Houston). Current work: Noninvasive cardiorespiratory monitoring for ventilation to perfusion ratios; diagnostic uses of radio frequency fields. Subspecialties: Pediatrics; Biomedical engineering. Home: 8408 Staunton Austin TX 78758

MULICK, JAMES ANTON, psychologist; b. Passaic, N.J., June 17, 1948; s. Andreus and Anna (Petruchkowich) M.; m. Nancy Elizabeth Witt, Aug. 8, 1970. A.B., Rutgers Coll., 1970; M.A., U. Vt., 1973, Ph.D., 1975. Lic. psychologist, R.I., N.C., Mass. Psychol. services dir. I SIB Program, Murdoch Ctr., Butner, N.C., 1976-77; chief psychologist Shriver Ctr., Waltham, Mass., 1977-78; dir. psychology and tng. Child Devel. Ctr., R.I. Hosp., Providence, 1978; vis. asst. prof. psychology Northeastern U., Boston, 1977-80; clin. asst. prof. pediatrics Brown U., Providence, 1978; adj. assoc. prof. psychology U. R.I., North Kingstown, 1979. Editor: Handbook of Mental Retardation, 1983, Parent Professional Partnership in Developmental Disability Services, 1983; mem. editorial bd.: Applied Research in MR, 1980; Contbr. articles to profl. jours. Mem. R.I. Gov.'s Com. on Mental Retardation, 1979-82. Fellow Behavior Therapy and Research Soc.; mem. Am. Psychol. Assn., Am. Assn. on Mental Deficiency (chmn. Region X 1983). Current work: Behavior analysis in mental retardation; learning and behavioral development, social policy analysis relating to children. Subspecialties: Behavioral psychology; Mental retardation. Home: 3 Harris Ave Johnston RI 02919 Office: Child Devel Ctr RI Hosp 593 Eddy St Providence RI 02902

MULKEY, JAMES ROBERT, JR., soil scientist, educator; b. Alamo, Tex., Oct. 30, 1935; s. James Robert and Ruby Myrl (Splawn) M.; m. Lillian Sylvia Schmidt, June 1, 1963; children—James Robert III, Steven Boyd, Jaroy Kent. B.S., Tex. A&I U., 1957; M.S., Okla. State U., 1960; Ph.D., Tex. A&M U., 1964. Asst. prof.-in-charge Tex. Agrl. Expt. Sta., Chillicothe, 1964-72, acting dir., Vernon, Tex., 1972-73, from asst. to assoc. prof., Uvalde, Tex., 1973-81, assoc. prof., acting dir., 1981-83, assoc. prof., 1983—. Contbr. articles to profl. jours. V.P. Little League Baseball, Uvalde, 1977-79; dir. Uvalde County Livestock Show, 1981-83. Served with U.S. Army, 1961-62, Mem. Soil Sci. Soc. Am., Am. Soc. Agronomy, Crop Sci. Soc. Am., Profl. Soil Sci. Assn. Tex., Alpha Zeta. Democrat. Methodist. Lodge: Lions (pres. 1969-70). Current work: Conduct research in irrigation, water management and conservation, soil fertility, new crops and crop culture. Subspecialties: Agronomy; Soil science. Home: 626 Dorothy Jo Circle Uvalde TX 78801 Office: Tex Agrl Expt Sta PO Drawer 1051 Uvalde TX 78802

MULLAN, JOHN FRANCIS, neurosurgeon, educator; b. Ireland, May 17, 1925; came to U.S., 1955, naturalized, 1962; s. John and Mary Catherine M.; m. Vivian C. Dunn, June 3, 1959; children—Joan, John, Brian. M.B., B.Ch., B.A.O., Queens U., Belfast, 1947, D.Sc. (hon.), 1976; postgrad., McGill U., 1953-55. Trained gen. surgery Royal Victoria Hosp., Belfast, No. Ireland, 1947-50, in neurosurgery, 1951-53; trained gen. surgery Guy's Hosp. and Middlesex Hosp., London, Eng., 1950-51, Montreal (Que., Can.) Neurosurg. Inst., 1953-55; asst. prof. neurosurgery U. Chgo., 1955-61, assoc. prof., 1961-63, prof., 1963—, John Harper Seeley prof., 1967—, chmn. neurosurgery, 1967—; dir. Brian Research Inst. Chgo. Contbr. articles in field to profl. publs. and textbooks. Recipient McClintock award, 1961. Fellow Royal Coll. Surgeons (Eng.), A.C.S.; mem. Soc. Neurol. Surgeons (pres. 1985—), Acad. Neurol. Surgery, Am. Assn. Neurol. Surgeons, Am. Neurosurg. Assn., Central Neurosurg. Soc., Chgo. Neurol. Soc., World Fedn. Neurol. Socs. (asst. sec.). Roman Catholic. Condr. research vascular diseases of the brain, pain, head injury. Current Work: Vascular diseases of brain; intractable pain; head injury; cerebral blood flow. Subspecialties: Neurosurgery; Microsurgery. Home: 5844 Stony Island Ave Chicago IL 60637 Office: 950 E 59th Chicago IL 60637

MULLANE, JOHN FRANCIS, pharmaceutical company executive; b. N.Y.C., Mar. 10, 1937; s. John G. and Rita A. (Hoben) M.; m. Ruth Ann Cecka, Nov. 17, 1962; children: Rosemarie, Michael, Kathleen, Therese, Thomas. M.D., SUNY-Downstate Med. Ctr., Bklyn., 1963, Ph.D., 1968; J.D., Fordham U., 1977. Assoc. dir. clin. research Ayerst Labs. div. Am. Home

Products Corp., N.Y.C., 1975, dir. clin. research, 1975-76, v.p. clin. research, 1977, v.p. sci. affairs, 1977-82, sr. v.p. sci. affairs, 1982, exec. v.p. sci. affairs worldwide, 1983—. Contbr. numerous articles to profl. jours. Recipient Achievement of Excellence in Medicine award Upjohn Co., 1970. Fellow Am. Coll. Clin. Pharmacology; mem. Am. Assn. Study Liver Disease, Am. Soc. Nephrology, Am. Fedn. Clin. Research. Roman Catholic. Current Work: Administer pre-clinical, clinical, and technical departments related to drug discovery and development. Subspecialty: Pharmacology. Office: Ayerst Labs Div Am Home Products Corp 685 3d Ave New York NY 10017

MULLANI, NIZAR ABDUL, medical educator, researcher; b. Daressalaam, Tanzania, Oct. 22, 1942; s. Abdulshamsh Husein and Noorbanu Jiwan-Hirjee M.; m. Linda Kay, June 21, 1975. B.S., Washington U., St. Louis, 1967. Research asst. biomed computer lab. Washington U., 1970-80; research assoc. div. radiation scis. Mallinkrodt Inst. Radiology, Sch. Medicine, 1976-80; asst. prof. medicine, tech. dir. positron diagnostic and research ctr., 1982—; U. Tex. Health Sci. Ctr., Houston, 1980—; asst. prof. gen. instrn. U. Tex. Grad. Sch. Biomed. Scis., Houston, 1981—; Mem. site visit rev. com. NIH and Dept. Energy; reviewer Jour. Nuclear Medicine, IEEE Transactions on Nuclear Sci., Jour. Computer Assisted Tomography. Contbr. articles to profl. jours. Grantee Am. Heart Assn. Mem. IEEE Nuclear Sci. Soc. (sr.), Soc. Nuclear Medicine, AAAS. Moslem. Current Work: Design, construction and application of positron emission tomographs to in vivo biochemical studies in man using radioactive tracers. Subspecialty: PET scan. Home: 15214 Beacham Houston TX 77070 Office: 6431 Fannin Houston TX 77025

MULLEN, ELLEN D., geology educator, researcher; b. N.Y.C., Oct. 17, 1948; d. William Russell and Laura Ellen (Hill) Domaratius; m. Richard Stow Mullen, June 13, 1970 (div. Dec. 1982); m. Robert Clarence Morris, June 30, 1984. B.S. in Geology, Dickinson Coll., 1970; M.S. in Geology, Oreg. State U., 1979, Ph.D. in Geology, 1983. Engring. geologist Peterson Engring., Salem, Oreg., 1972-76, Masson Engring., Escondido, Calif., 1978-79; teaching asst. Oreg. State U., Corvallis, 1980-82, instr., 1982; instr. U. Ark., Fayetteville, 1982-83, asst. prof., 1983—. Contbr. articles to profl. jours. Grantee NSF, 1984, Arco, 1984, Mem. Geol. Soc. Am. (research grants 1977-80), Am. Geophys. Union, Mineral. Soc. Am., Geochem. Soc., Sigma Xi (research grantee 1981). Current work: Basalt petrogenesis; island arc evolution; alkalic magmatism, geology of convergent margins. Subspecialties: Petrology; Geology. Office: Dept of Geology OH118 U Ark Fayetteville AR 72701

MULLER, JOHN PAUL, clinical psychologist; b. N.Y.C., Dec. 31, 1940; s. John and Magdolna (Jeromos) M. A.B., Fordham U., 1964, M.A., 1966; Ph.D. in Clin. Psychology, Harvard U., 1971. Diplomate in clin. psychology Am. Bd. Profl. Psychology. Instr. Harvard U., Cambridge, Mass., 1970-71; chmn. dept. human services Sinte Gleska Coll., Rosebud, S.D., 1971-74; coordinator psychol. services Convalescent Hosp. for Children, Cin., 1974-75; sr. researcher, mem. therapy staff Austen Riggs Ctr., Stockbridge, Mass., 1975—. Author: (with William J. Richardson) Lacan and Language: A Reader's Guide to Ecrits, 1982. Mem. Am. Psychol. Assn., N.Y. Acad. Scis. Current Work: Language in psychoanalysis; Jacques Lacan; ego as set of constraints. Subspecialties: Cognition; Psychoanalysis. Office: Austen Riggs Ctr Main St Stockbridge MA 01262

MULLER, LAWRENCE DEAN, animal science educator; b. Peoria, Ill., Nov. 26, 1941; s. Ralph A. and Corrine (Erford) M.; m. Delores Ann Lewin, Aug. 8, 1965; children—Michelle, Mark, Marcia. B.S., U. Ill., 1964, M.S., 1966; Ph.D., Purdue U., 1969. Asst. prof. Purdue U., West Lafayette, Ind., 1969-71; assoc. prof. S.D. State U., Brookings, 1971-76; prof. dairy sci. Pa. State U., University Park, 1976—. Recipient Outstanding Tchr. award, S.D. State U., 1976. Mem. Am. Dairy Sci. Assn. (Outstanding Advisor award 1983), Am. Soc. Animal Sci., Am. Inst. Nutrition, Am. Forage Grassland Council. Subspecialties: Animal nutrition; Animal physiology. Office: Dept Dairy and Animal Sci 213 Borland Lab Pa State U University Park PA 16802

MULLER, ROLF HUGO, research chemist; b. Aarau, Switzerland, Aug. 6, 1929; came to U.S., 1957; s. Wilhelm and Alice L. (Schmid) M.; m. Dorothy L. Donaldson, July 18, 1962; children—Wilhelm Karl, Alice Barbara. M.S., Swiss Fed. Inst. Tech., 1953, cert. higher teaching, 1955, Ph.D., 1957; postdoctoral U. Calif.-Berkeley, 1960-61. Research chemist E.I. du Pont deNemours & Co., Parkersburg, W.Va., 1957-60; research assoc. U. Calif.-Berkeley, 1961-62, staff sr. scientist Lawrence Berkeley Lab., 1962—, asst. div. head, 1970—, acting div. head, 1985, lectr. chem. engring. dept., 1966—. Contbr. chpts. to books, numerous articles to profl. jours. Editor 2 books in field. Mem. Electrochem. Soc. (chair San Francisco spct. 1971-72, sec.-treas. phys. electrochem. div. 1985—), Internat. Soc. Electrochemistry (Plenary lectr. 1976, co-chair div. 1973-77, sci. program chair 1984 meeting), Am. Chem. Soc., Swiss Chem. Soc., Optical Soc. Am., AAAS. Current work: Surface layers and thin films; electrochemical processes and mass transfer; optical methods for surface studies and chemical engineering research. Subspecialties: Chemical engineering; Thin film optical research. Home: 36 Highgate Rd Berkeley CA 94707 Office: Lawrence Berkeley Lab 62-203 Berkeley CA 94720

MULLINS, WILLIAM WILSON, physical metallurgist; b. Boonville, Ind., Mar. 5, 1927; s. Thomas Clinton and Ruth (Wilson) M.; m. June Bonner, June 26, 1948; children—William Wilson, Oliver Clinton, Timothy Bonner, Garrick Russell. Ph.B., U. Chgo., 1949, M.S. in Physics, 1951, Ph.D., 1955. Research physicist, then adv. physicist Westinghouse Research Labs., 1955-60; asso. prof. metall. engring. Carnegie Mellon U. Pitts., 1960-63, prof., head dept., 1963-66, dean engring. and sci., prof. applied sci., from 1970, now Inst. prof. applied sci., dir. ctr. for Joining of Materials. Chmn. phys. metallurgy Gordon Conf., 1966. Author articles in field. Served with USNR, 1944-46. Fulbright and Guggenheim fellowships U. Paris, France, 1961-62. Mem. Am. Inst. Metall. Engrs. (Mathewson gold medal 1963), Am. Inst. Mining, Metall. and Petroleum Engrs., Am. Phys. Soc., Am. Soc. Engring. Edn., N.Y. Acad. Scis., ACLU, Sigma Xi, Alpha Sigma Nu. Club: Unitarian. Special research surfaces, phase transformations, particulate rheology and thermodynamics. Subspecialty: Metallurgical engineering. Office: Carnegie-Mellon U Ctr for Joining of Materials Pittsburgh PA 15213

MULVEY, JOHN MICHAEL, engineering management educator and consultant; b. Chgo., Oct. 31, 1946; s. John J. and Mary M. (Steinberg) M.; m. Lauri D. Ervin, Sept. 28, 1982. B.S. in Engring, U. Ill.-Champaign, 1969, M.S. in Computer Sci, 1969; M.S. in Mgmt. Sci, UCLA, 1973, Ph.D. in Mgmt, 1975. Mem. tech. staff, mgr. TRW Systems Group, Redondo Beach, Calif., 1969-75; asst. prof. Harvard U., Cambridge, Mass, 1975-78; assoc. prof., dir. engring. mgmt. Princeton (N.J.) U., 1978—; co-founder Analysis Research and Computation Inc., Austin, Tex., 1973; cons. U.S. Congress, fed. govt. agys. Editor: Network Applications, 1981, Evaluating Math Programs, 1982; contbr. articles to profl. jours.; developer computer programs in network optimization. UCLA scholar, 1974; recipient dissertation award Inst. for Decision Scis., San Francisco, 1975; NSF grantee, 1978—. Mem. Math. Programming Soc. (exec. com.), Ops. Research Soc., Assn. Computing Machinery, Inst. Mgmt. Scis. Current Work: Design, test, and apply methods of mathematical programming, especially large-scale problems. Build algorithms for solving combinatorial and network optimization problems. Subspecialties: Operations research (engineering); Operations research (mathematics). Office: Sch Engring and Applied Sci Princeton U Olden Ave Princeton NJ 08544

MUMMERT, THOMAS ALLEN, manufacturing company executive; b. Toledo, Ohio, Dec. 24, 1946; s. James Allen and Betty Alice (Thomas) M.; m. Icia Linda Shearer, Dec. 17, 1966; children: Sherry Lynn, Robert Thomas, Michael Allen. Student, Toledo U., 1965-66. Pres. Mummert Electric & Mfg. Co. Inc., Toledo, 1969-70; research engr. Am. Lincoln Corp., Bowling Green, Ohio, 1970-73; test engr. Dura div. Dura Corp., Toledo, 1973-74; head research dept. Jobst Inst. Inc., Toledo, 1974-84, mgr. med. equipment design, 1984—. Served with U.S. Navy, 1968-69. Mem. Assn. for Advancement of Med. Instrumentation, Nat. Mgmt. Assn., Am. Soc. for Engring. Edn., Am. Soc. for Quality Control, AAAS, Ohio Acad. Sci., Laser Inst. Am., ASTM, N.Y. Acad. Scis., Biol. Engring. Soc. Patentee in field. Current Work: Therapeutic and rehabilitation devices for circulatory blood flow disorders; peripheral blood flow imaging technology. Subspecialties: Biomedical engineering; Bioinstrumentation. Home: 1448 Palmetto Ave Toledo OH 43606 Office: 653 Miami St Toledo OH 43694

MUNDA, RINO, physician, educator; b. Rome, Italy, Feb. 2, 1943; came to U.S., 1967; s. Salvador and Marina (Tabusso) M.; m. Margarita Landra, Nov. 11, 1968; children: Sergio, Franco. B.S., U.Nat. Mayor de San Marcos-Peru, 1960; M.D., Facultad De Medicina Cayetano Heredia-Peru, 1966. Cert., Am. Bd. Surgery, 1974. Instr. surgery N.Y. Med. Coll., N.Y.C., 1972-73; asst. prof. research surgery U. Cin. Coll Medicine, 1974-75, asst. prof., 1975-79, assoc. prof., 1979—; cons. in field. Mem. adv. com. Cin. Kidney Found., 1979—; mem. med. review bd. Ohio Valley Renal Network, 1981—. Am. Diabetes Assn. grantee, 1981-82. Mem. Surg. Soc. N.Y. Med. Coll., Assn. Acad. Surgery, Am. Soc. Transplant Surgeons, Transplantation Soc., Am. Coll. Surgeons, Surg. Infection Soc. (hon.), Soc. Peruana de Angiologia (Peru). Current Work: Academic surgeon. Subspecialties: Transplantation; Transplant surgery. Home: 315 Lafayette Ave Cincinnati OH 45220 Office: 234 Goodman St Cincinnati OH 65267

MUNDELL, BRIAN LEE, chemist; b. Moline, Ill., Aug. 11, 1950; s. James Nelson and Charlotte Elaine (Nesser) M.; m. Patricia Ann Burr, Aug. 27, 1983. B.A., Augustana Coll., 1972; Ph.D., U. Iowa, 1979. Research chemist Grain Processing Corp., Muscatine, Iowa, 1979—. Mem. Am. Chem. Soc. (pres. Ill.-Iowa chpt. 1985). Club: Toastmasters (v.p. 1984-85) (Muscatine). Current work: Starch modification, expanded roles for superabsorbents. Subspecialties: Organic chemistry; Polymer chemistry. Office: Grain Processing Corp Box 349 Muscatine IA 52761

MUNIAPPAN, RANGASWAMY NAICKER, entomologist; b. Coimbatore, Madras, India, June 1, 1941; emigrated to U.S., 1967, naturalized, 1976; s. Rangaswamy and Rangammal Naicker; m. Sheila Naidu, Feb. 25, 1972; 1 dau., Brindha. B.S., U. Madras, 1963, M.S., 1965; Ph.D., Okla. State U., 1969. Asst. lectr. Agrl. Coll., Coimbatore, 1965-67; research asst. Okla. State U., Stillwater, 1968-69, postdoctoral fellow, 1969-70; entomologist Dept. Agr., Mangilao, Guam, 1970-71, chief agr., 1971-75; assoc. prof. U. Guam, Mangilao, 1975-76, assoc. dean, 1976-81; assoc. dir. Agrl. Expt. Sta., 1982—. Fulbright research scholar, India, 1984-85. Mem. Pacific Sci. Assn. (entomology com.), Entomol. Soc. Am., Philippines Entomol. Soc., Hawaiian Entomol. Soc., Phi Sigma Phi. Current Work: Biological control of insects, weeds and snails, tropical agricultural research programs. Subspecialty: Biological control. Home: PO Box 8784 Yona 96914 Guam Office: Agrl Expt Sta U Guam Mangilao 96913 Guam

MUNK, WALTER HEINRICH, geophysicist; b. Vienna, Austria, Oct. 19, 1917; s. Hans and Rega (Brunner) M.; m. Judith Horton, June 20, 1953; children—Edith, Kendall. B.S., Calif. Inst. Tech., 1939, M.S., 1940; Ph.D., U. Calif., 1947; Ph.D. (hon.), U. Bergen, Norway, 1975. Asst. prof. geophysics U. Calif., 1947-49, asso. prof., 1949-54; prof. Inst. Geophysics and Planetary Physics and at the Scripps Inst., 1954—, Sec. of Navy Chair in Oceanography, 1985; assoc. dir. Inst. Geophysics and Planetary Physics systemwide, 1959-82. Guggenheim fellow Oslo U., 1948; Guggenheim fellow Cambridge, 1955, 62; Josiah Willard Gibbs lectr. Am. Math. Soc., 1970; Sr. Queen's fellow Australia, 1978; Arthur L. Day medal Geol. Soc. Am., 1965; Sverdrup Gold medal Am. Meteorol. Soc., 1966; Alumni Distinguished Service award Calif. Inst. Tech., 1966; gold medal Royal Astron. Soc., 1968; named Calif. Scientist of Year Calif. Mus. Sci. and Industry, 1969; 1st Maurice Ewing medal Am. Geophys. Union and USN, 1976; Capt. Robert Dexter Conrad award Dept. Navy, 1978; Nat. medal of Sci., 1985. Fellow Am. Meteorol. Soc., AAAS, Acoustical Soc. Am.; mem. Nat. Acad. Scis. (chmn. geophysics sect. 1975-78, Agassiz medal 1976), Am. Philos. Soc., Am. Geological Soc., Am. Acad. Arts and Scis., Deutsche Akademie der Naturforscher Leopoldina, Royal Soc. (fgn.). Current Work: Remote sensing of oceans by sound. Subspecialties: Geophysics; Oceanography. Home: 9530 LaJolla Shores Dr LaJolla CA 92037 Office: IGPP Mail Code A025 Univ Calif-San Diego La Jolla CA 92093

MUNNS, THEODORE W., biochemist, immunologist; b. Peoria, Ill., June 11, 1941; s. Charles Willard and Julia (Uppstrom) M. B.S. in Chemistry, Bradley U., 1963; Ph.D. in Biochemistry, St. Louis U., 1970. Asst. research prof. St. Louis U. Med. Sch., 1970-79; asst. prof. medicine Washington U. Med. Sch., St. Louis, 1979—. Contbr. articles to profl. jours., chpts. to books. Am. Chem. Soc. postdoctoral fellow St. Louis U., 1972, NASA predoctoral fellow St. Louis U., 1967; athletic scholar Bradley U., 1959; NIH grantee, 1982—. Mem. Am. Chem. Soc., Am. Soc. Biol. Chemists. Current work: Anti-nucleic acid antibodies, idiotypic peptides of anti-nucleic acid antibodies. Subspecialties: Biochemistry (medicine); Immunology (medicine). Office: Washington U Med Sch 660 S Euclid Ave Box 8045 Saint Louis MO 63110

MUNRO, HAMISH NISBET, biochemist, educator; b. Edinburgh, Scotland, July 3, 1915; came to U.S., 1966, naturalized, 1973; s. Donald and Margaret (Nisbet) M.; m. Edith E. Little, Apr. 5, 1946; children: Joan Bruce, Colin Scott, Andrew Fraser, John Michael. B.Sc., U. Glasgow, Scotland, 1936, M.B., 1939, D.Sc., 1956, M.D., 1983. Physician, pathologist Victoria Infirmary, Glasgow, 1939-45; lectr. physiology U. Glasgow, 1946-47, sr. lectr., reader biochemistry, 1948-63, prof. biochemistry, 1964-66; prof. physiol. chemistry Mass. Inst. Tech., Cambridge, from 1966; dir. USDA Human Nutrition Research Center on Aging, Tufts U., Boston, 1980-84, sr. scientist, 1984—. Editor: Mammalian Protein Metabolism, vols. 1-4, 1964-70; Contbr. articles in field of protein metabolism to profl. publs. Recipient Osborn Mendel award Am. Inst. Nutrition, 1968, Borden award, 1978; Bristol-Myers award for disting. achievement in nutrition research, 1981; Rank prize for significant advances in nutrition, 1982. Fellow Royal Soc. Edinburgh; mem. Nat. Acad. Sci., Am. Acad. Arts and Sci., Am. Soc. Biol. Chemists, Am. Inst. Nutrition (pres. 1978-79), Brit. Biochem. Soc. Presbyterian. Current Work: Bioregulatory studies on optimizing genome function throughout life, notably interaction of nutrition in expression of aging genome. Subspecialties: Cell and tissue culture; Nutrition (biology). Home: 159 Concord Ave Cambridge MA 02138 Office: Human Nutrition Center 711 Washington St Boston MA 02111 Also: Room 56-227 MIT Cambridge MA 02139

MUNROE, EUGENE GORDON, research entomologist, biogeographer, consultant; b. Detroit, Sept. 8, 1919; s. Donald Gordon and Helen Grace (Carroll) M.; m. Isobel Margaret Douglas; children—Janet Gordon Munroe Wilson, Donald Douglas (dec.), Susan Margaret, Elizabeth Anne. B.S., McGill U., 1940, M.S., 1941; Ph.D., Cornell U., 1947. Lectr. and research assoc. Inst. of Parasitology. Macdonald Coll., Ste. Anne de Bellevue, Que., Can., 1946-50; research scientist Can. Dept. Agr., 1950-65, 68-79; sci. adviser and prin. sci. adviser Sci. Secretariat, Privy Council Office, Ottawa, 1965-68; hon. research assoc. Lyman Entomol. Mus. and Research Lab., McGill U., Macdonald Campus, Ste. Anne de Bellevue, 1980—. Contbr. chpts. to books; author articles, monographs. Served with RCAF, 1942-45. Recipient Queen's Silver Jubilee medal, 1972. Fellow Entomol. Soc. Can. (editor 1958-61, pres. 1964, Gold Medal for Outstanding Achievement in Entomology 1982), Royal Soc. Can., Royal Entomol. Soc. London; mem. Entomol. Soc. Que., Entomol. Soc. Ont., Lepidopterists Soc. (hon. life mem., pres. 1959), Ottawa Field Naturalists Club (hon. life). Research or work interests: Systematics and evolution of lepidoptera, especially Pyralidae, biogeography. Subspecialties: Systematics; Ecology (biology). Office: Lyman Entomol Mus and Research Lab McGill U PO Box 800 Mcdonald Campus Sainte Anne de Bellevue PQ H9X 1C0 Canada

MUNSON, JOHN CHRISTIAN, acoustician; b. Clinton, Iowa, Oct. 9, 1926; s. Arthur J. and Frances (Christian) M.; m. Elaine Hendershot, Sept. 2, 1950; children: John Christian, Holly Elizabeth. B.S., Iowa State Coll., 1949; M.S., U. Md., 1952, Ph.D., 1962; Navy Dept. scholar, MIT, 1956. Electronic scientist Naval Ordnance Lab., Washington, 1949-66; tech. dir. navy portion Practice Nine, Naval Air Systems Command, 1967; supt. acoustics div. Naval Research Lab., 1968-85; asst. extension prof. elec. engring. U. Md., 1964-66; mem. Underwater Sound Adv. Group, 1969-75, U.S. Sonar Team, 1971-85, Mobile Sonar Tech. Com., 1972-85; cons., 1985—. Editor: Jour. Underwater Acoustics, 1983—. Mem. exec. bd. D.C. Bapt. Conv., 1973—, chmn. fin. com., 1973; trustee Midwestern Bapt. Theol. Sem., 1970-80; trustee D.C. Bapt. Home, 1976—, sec., 1978, v.p., 1979, treas., 1980-82, pres., 1982—. Served with USNR, 1944-46. Fellow IEEE, Acoustics, Speech and Signal Processing Soc. (adminstrv. com. 1974-76, chmn. underwater acoustics com. 1973-76), Acoustical Soc. Am.; mem. Sigma Xi. Patentee in field. Current Work: Developing technology base for future generation sonar systems (signal processing algorithms, systems concepts, modeling of temporal and spatial character of acoustic fields, performance prediction.). Subspecialties: Acoustics; Acoustical engineering. Home: 119 Marine Terr Silver Spring MD 20904 Office: Engring and Sci Assocs Inc 6110 Executive Blvd Suite 315 Rockville MD 20852

MUNSTER, ANDREW MICHAEL, surgeon, educator; b. Budapest, Hungary, Dec. 10, 1935; came to U.S., 1965, naturalized, 1969; s. Leopold Steven and Marianne (Barcza) M.; m. Joy O'Sullivan, Dec. 7, 1964; children: Andrea, Tara, Alexandra. M.D., U. Sydney, Australia, 1959. Diplomate: Am. Bd. Surgery. Resident in surgery Harvard Med. Sch., Boston, 1965-68; assoc. prof. Med. U. S.C., Charleston, 1971-76; assoc. prof. surgery Johns Hopkins U., Balt., 1976; dir. Regional Burn Ctr., Balt., 1976. Author: Burn Care for the House Officer, 1981, Surgical Anatomy, 1972; editor: Surgical Immunology, 1976. Pres. Chesapeake Research and Edn. Trust, Balt., 1980, Charleston Symphony Orch., 1973-74, Charleston Tricounty Arts Council, 1974-75; v.p. Chesapeake Physicians, Balt., 1979. Served to lt. col. U.S. Army, 1968-71. Recipient George Allan prize U. Sydney, 1959. Fellow Royal Coll. Surgeons (Eng.) (Edinburgh), So. Surg. Assn., Am. Assn. Surgery of Trauma; mem. Soc. Univ. Surgeons, Am. Burn Assn., others. Current Work: Burn and trauma care and research. Subspecialties: Surgery; Immunology (agriculture). Office: Johns Hopkins U Balt City Hosps 4940 Eastern Ave Baltimore MD 21224

MURAWSKI, WALTER TED, college observatory administrator; b. Jersey City, Sept. 20, 1945; s. Walter F. Murawski and Lucille H. (Jasinski) Karsanow; m. Anna Majda, Jan. 20, 1979; children—Thomas P., Catherine E. B.S., U. Ariz., 1967; M.S., Newark Coll. Engring., 1973; Ph.D., Jagiellonian U., Poland, 1980. X-ray physicist Machlet Labs., Stamford, Conn., 1967-69; instr. physics Coll. at Laurgarvatn, Iceland, 1972-75; sci. translator Polish Acad. Scis., Krakow, 1975-82; asst. prof. CUNY-New York, 1982-84; dir. astronomy obs. Lenoir-Rhyne Coll., Hickory, N.C., 1984—. Author: Catalog of Supernovae, 1980. Asst. editor Acta Physica Polonica, Krakow, 1975-82, Acta Cosmologica, Krakow, 1975-82. Inventor in field. Fellow Polish Inst. Arts and Scis. in Am.; mem. Am. Astron. Soc. Roman Catholic. Lodge: Kiwanis. Current work: Extragalactic astronomy, archeoastronomy, history of science, computing devices and techniques of ancient peoples. Office: Astron Obs Lenoir-Rhyne Coll Box 7210 Hickory NC 28603

MURAYAMA, MAKIO, biochemist; b. San Francisco, Aug. 10, 1912; s. Hakuyo and Namiye (Miyasaka) M.; children: Gibbs Soga, Alice Myra. B.A., U. Calif., Berkeley, 1938, M.A., 1940; Ph.D. (NIH fellow), U. Mich., 1953. Research biochemist Children's Hosp. of Mich., Detroit, 1943-48, Harper Hosp., Detroit, 1950-54; research fellow in chemistry Calif. Inst. Tech., Pasadena, 1954-56; research asso. in biochemistry Grad. Sch. Medicine, U. Pa., Phila., 1956-58; spl. research fellow Nat. Cancer Inst. at Cavendish Lab., Cambridge, Eng., 1958; research biochemist NIH, Bethesda, Md., 1958—. Author: (with Robert M. Nalbandian) Sickle Cell Hemoglobin, 1973. Fellow Am. Inst. Chemists; mem. Am. Chem. Soc., Am. Soc. Biol. Chemists, AAAS, Assn. Clin. Scientists, Internat. Platform Assn., W.African Soc. Pharmacology (hon.), Sigma Xi. Current Work: Discovered cause of acute mountain sickness and prevention of it; found a possible cause of cardiovascular diseases which appears to be also due to decompression platelet aggregation; decompression is the hydrodynamic Bernoulli effect; a pressure transducer in decompression induced aggregation of platelets appears to be the protein, calmodulin. Subspecialties: Biochemistry (medicine); Microscopy. Home: 5010 Benton Ave Bethesda MD 20814 Office: NIH Bldg 6 Room 139 Bethesda MD 20205

MURDOCH, BRUCE THOMAS, petroleum services company executive; b. Prague, Okla., Mar. 15, 1940; s. Thomas J. and Mary Ellen (Waller) M.; m. Carol Ann Heggblom, June 28, 1969; children—Vanessa Jean, Robert Waller. B.A., Carleton Coll., 1962; M.A., Rice U., 1966; Ph.D., Utah State U., 1975. Devel. engr. Goodyear Aerospace, Litchfield Park, Ariz., 1967-70; profl. assoc. U. Man., Winnipeg, Can., 1974-78; project devel. engr. Schlumberger Tech. Corp., Houston, 1978-82; sr. devel. engr. NL McCullough, Houston, 1982-83, mgr. nuclear systems devel., 1983—. Contbr. articles to profl. jours. Mem. Soc. Profl. Well Log Analysts, Soc. Petroleum Engrs., Am. Phys. Soc. Current work: Petroleum well measurement equipment for remote sensing using nuclear radiation sources and detectors. Subspecialties: Remote sensing (geoscience); Nuclear physics. Home: 3642 Fir Forest Spring TX 77388 Office: NL McCullough PO Box 60060 Houston TX 77205

MURDOCH-DOTY, LYNNE FRANCES, environmental scientist; b. Brockton, Mass., Feb. 28, 1958; d. Bruce Ogden and Virginia Charlotte (Clark) M.; m. David Scott Doty, May 29, 1981. B.S. in Biology, Westfield State Coll., 1980; M.S. in Environ. Sci., U. Okla., 1983. Registered profl. sanitarian, Okla. Lab. asst. dept. biology Westfield State Coll., 1977-80; grad. research asst. dept. botany and microbiology U. Okla., Norman, 1980-81, grad. research asst. dept. civil engring. and environ. sci., 1981-83; project coordinator Wilson E. Nolan Inc., Oklahoma City, 1983-84; environ. specialist Okla. State Dept. Health, Claremore, 1984—; instr. First Am. Tomorrow's Engrs. Program, Norman, 1982. Mem. Assn. Women in Sci., Ecol. Soc. Am., AAAS, Nat. Soc. Profl. Sanitarians, Okla. Soc. Profl. Sanitarians. Democrat. Roman Catholic. Current work: Environmental health protection and management; sewage sludge land application; hazardous waste management. Subspecialties: Ecology (environmental science); Environmental health protection. Home: 1640 N Lee St #B Claremore OK 74017 Office: Rogers County Health Dept 1415 N Florence St Claremore OK 74017

MURDOCK, WILBERT QUINC, research bioengineer; b. N.Y.C., July 3, 1958; s. William Quinc and Rosa (Washington) M. B.S.E.E., Poly. Inst. of N.Y., 1980, M.S. in Bioengring., 1983. Research fellow Poly. Inst. of N.Y., N.Y.C., 1980-82; adj. prof. elec. engring. N.Y.C. Tech. Coll., 1981-82; adj. prof. computer sci. Baruch Coll., N.Y.C., 1982-83; pres. Computers for Sports, Inc., N.Y.C., 1983—. Author: Voice Recognition System for Handicapped, 1983. Inventor knee alignment monitoring device, real-time motion analysis system. Mem. IEEE. Subspecialties: Biomedical engineering; Real-time video motion analysis.

MURPHREE, ALAN LINN, pediatric ophthalmologist, educator; b. Houston, Miss., June 6, 1945; s. John Alan and Maxine (Linn) M. B.S. in Biology and Chemistry, U. Miss., 1967; M.D., Baylor Coll. Medicine, 1972. Intern, resident in ophthalmology Baylor Coll. Medicine affiliated hosps., Houston, 1973-76, chief resident in ophthalmology, 1975-76; head fellow in ophthalmic genetics and pediatrics The Wilmer Inst., Johns Hopkins Hosp., Balt., 1976-77; asst. prof. dept. ophthalmology and pediatrics U. So. Calif., Los Angeles, 1978-83, assoc. prof., 1983—; dir. Clayton Found. Ctr. for Ocular Oncology Childrens Hosp. Los Angeles, 1978—, head div. ophthalmology, 1978—. Contbr. articles to profl. jours. Mem. profl. adv. com. Blind Children's Ctr., Los Angeles, 1980—. Fulbright scholar, 1967-68; Dolly Green scholar Research to Prevent Blindness Inc., 1984. Mem. Am. Acad. Ophthalmology (Honor award 1983), Am. Assn. Pediatric Ophthalmology and Strabismus, Assn. Research in Vision and Ophthalmology, Baylor Ophthalmology Residents Alumni Assn., Ophthalmic Genetics Study Club, Soc. Heed Fellows, Wilmer Residents Assn., Internat. Soc. Genetic Eye Disease. Current work: Retinoblastoma including gene cloning, determining function of gene, tumor chromosomal analysis, prenatal diagnosis of rb gene carriers, improved genetic counseling; genetic eye disease including description and definition; improved diagnosis and applying recombinant DNA technology to inherited eye diseases. Subspecialties: Ophthalmology; Genetics and genetic engineering (medicine). Office: Childrens Hosp Los Angeles 4650 Sunset Blvd Los Angeles CA 90027

MURPHY, BERNARD T., physicist; b. Hull, Eng., May 30, 1932; m. 1959; 2 children. B.Sc., U. Leeds, 1953, Ph.D. in Physics, 1959. Physicist-engr. Mullard Research Labs., Eng., 1956-59; supervisory engr. Westinghouse Elec. Co., Pa., 1959-62; dir. devel. Siliconix, Inc., Calif., 1962-63; dept head, then head microprocessor design dept. AT&T Bell Labs., Murray Hill, N.J., 1963—. Contbr. articles to profl. jours. Patentee in field of integrated circuits, microwave devices. Fellow IEEE; mem. Am. Phys. Soc. Subspecialties: Integrated circuits; Medical physics. Office: AT&T Bell Labs Murray Hill NJ 07974*

MURPHY, EUGENE FRANCIS, consultant, retired government official; b. Syracuse, N.Y., May 31, 1913; s. Eugene Francis and Mary Grace (Thompson) M.; m. Helene M. Murphy, Dec. 31, 1955; children: Anne Fitzpatrick, Thomas E. M.E., Cornell U., 1935; M.M.E., Syracuse U., 1937; Ph.D., Ill. Inst. Tech., 1948. Teaching asst. Syracuse U., 1935-36; engr. Ingersoll-Rand Co., Painted Post, N.Y., 1936-39; instr. Ill. Inst. Tech., 1939-41; from instr. to asst. prof. U. Calif., Berkeley, 1941-48; staff engr. Nat. Acad. Scis., Washington, 1945-48; adv. fellow Mellon Inst., Pitts., 1947-48; with VA, N.Y.C., 1948-83, now ret.; chief research and devel. div. Prosthetic and Sensory Aids Service, 1948-73; dir. Research Center for Prosthetics, 1973-78; dir. Office of Tech. Transfer, 1978-83, sci. advisor, 1983-85; Mem. council Alliance for Engring. in Medicine and Biology, 1969—; mem. adv. com. U. Wis., 1978-82, Case Western Res. U., 1981, Am. Found. for Blind, 1981-83. Contbg. author: Human Limbs and their Substitutes, 1954, Orthopaedic Appliances Atlas, vol. 1, 1952, vol. 2, 1960, Human Factors in Technology, 1963, Biomedical Engineering Systems, 1970, Critical Revs. in Bioengring, 1971, CRC Handbook of Materials, Vol. III, 1975,

Atlas of Orthotics, 1976, 2d edit., 1985, Therapeutic Medical Devices, Applications and Design, 1982, McGraw-Hill Encyclopedia of Science and Technology Yearbook, 1985; editor: Bull. Prosthetics Research, 1978-82; contbr. articles profl. jours. Recipient Silver medal Paris, France, 1961; Meritorious Service award VA, 1971; Disting. Career award VA, 1983; citation Outstanding Handicapped Fed. Employee, 1971; Profl. Achievement award Ill. Inst. Technology, 1983; Biomed. Engring. Leadership award Alliance for Engring. in Medicine and Biology, 1983; Fulbright lectr. Soc. and Home for Cripples, Denmark, 1957-58. Fellow AAAS, ASME, Internat. Soc. for Prosthetics and Orthotics, Rehab. Engring. Soc. N.Am.; assoc. fellow N.Y. Acad. Medicine; mem. Nat. Acad. Engring., N.Y. Acad. Sci., Acoustical Soc. Am., Optical Soc. Am., Sigma Xi, Tau Beta Pi, Phi Kappa Phi. Current Work: Biomedical engineering, broadly, especially rehabilitation research and development (prosthetics, orthotics, sensory aids, selected implants, biomaterials); writing, editing disseminating information. Subspecialty: Biomedical engineering. Home: 511 E 20th St New York NY 10010

MURPHY, GERALD PATRICK, medical institute administrator; b. Harve, Mont., July 16, 1934; s. Francis J. and Margaret H. (Dolan) M.; m. Mary Bridget Cunningham, June 20, 1959; children—Anne Marie, Margaret, George, Maureen, Bridget, Gerald. B.Sc. summa cum laude, Seattle U., 1955; M.D., U. Wash., 1959; D.Sc., St Thomas Inst., 1971, St John's U., Jamaica, N.Y., 1979; LL.D., Niagara U., 1973; Litt.D., St. Bonaventure U., 1977. Bushwell research fellow dept. urology U. Rochester, N.Y., 1959; intern in surgery Johns Hopkins Hosp., Balt., 1959-60; jr. asst. resident in urology Brady Urol. Inst., 1960-61, fellow in urology, 1964-65, sr. asst. resident in urology, 1964-65, chief resident, 1966-67, asst. prof. urology, 1968; asst. resident in surgery and urology Balt. City Hosp., 1961-62; research assoc., chief dept. surg. physiology Walter Reed Army Inst. Research, Washington, 1962-64; assoc. dir. clin. affairs Roswell Park Meml. Inst., Buffalo, 1968-70, chief dept urology, 1968-71, inst. dir., 1970—, chief dept. exptl. surgery, 1968—; assoc. prof. urology SUNY-Buffalo, 1968-70, prof., 1971—, research prof. exptl. pathology Grad. Sch., 1972—, 1st William J. Staubitz vis. prof. urology, 1982; prof. biology Niagara U., 1968—; trustee SUNY-Buffalo, 1971—; mem. adv. council N.Y. State Coll. Vet. Medicine, 1975-81, 82—; exec. dir. Health Research Council of N.Y. State, 1975—; sec.-gen. Internat. Union against Cancer, 1974—; mem. bd. sci. affairs Delta Regional Primate Research Ctr. (Tulane U.), 1979-81; also mem. (various other profl. adv. bds.), cons. in field; trustee Damon Runyon, Walter Winchell Cancer Fund, 1979—, v.p., bd. dirs., 1983; dir. nat. prostatic cancer project Nat. Cancer Inst., 1972—; vis. prof. surgery U. Stellenbosch, Bellville, Cape Province, South Africa, 1967-68; dir.-at-large Am. Cancer Soc., 1972—, pres., 1983, mem. exec. com. N.Y. State div., 1975-77, 78—, pres. N.Y. State div. 1974-75, bd. dirs. N.Y. State div., 1978—; mem. adv. council Gen. Motors Cancer Research Found., 1982—. Mem. editorial bd.: Yearbook of Cancer, 1968—, Jour. Medicine, Clin. and Exptl., 1970—, Urol. Surgery, 1972—, Internat. Jour. Cancer, 1975—, Cancer Bull. of M.D. Anderson Hosp., 1977—, Current Surgery, 1978—, Onkologie, 1978—, Oncology Times, 1980—, Anticancer Research, 1980—; editor-in-chief: Jour. Surg. Oncology, 1979—, Internat. Advances in Surg. Oncology, 1977—, The Prostate, 1979—; mem. editorial adv. bd.: Cancer, 1971—, Jour. Exptl. and Clin. Cancer Research, 1982—; cons. editor: Urology, 1972—; editor: Jour. Med. Primatology, 1973—, Oncology, 1975—; assoc. editor: N.Y. State Jour. Medicine, 1973—; corr. editor: African Jour. Medicine and Med. Sci., 1976; mem. internat. editorial rev. bd.: King Faisal Specialist Hosp. Med. Jour., 1981—; mem. internat. editorial adv. bd.: Arab Jour. Medicine, 1982—; mem. sci. rev. com.: Florence Jour. Surgery, 1983—. Served with M.C. U.S. Army, 1962-64. Recipient Schwentkeraward Johns Hopkins Hosp., 1962, Health Meml. award U. Tex. Cancer Ctr., M.D. Anderson Hosp. and Tumor Inst., 1978, cert. of appreciation for notable service in helping to save lives from cancer N.Y. State div. Am. Cancer Soc., 1982, Pro Pontifice et Ecclesia papal medal, 1982, silver medal Scientia Vincere Tenebras European Orgn. for Research and Treatment of Cancer, Brussels, 1982. Mem. ACS (sr. mem. Commn. on Cancer 1978—), Am. Urol. Assn. (registry genito-urinary pathology 1975—), Assn. Am. Cancer Insts. (pres. 1979-80, chmn. bd. dirs. 1980-81), N.Y. State Cancer Program Assn. (pres. 1982-83), Soc. Surg. Oncology (pres. 1982-83, chmn. exec. council 1983—), Johns Hopkins Med. and Surg. Assn., Am. Soc. Nephrology, Internat. Soc. Nephrology, Soc. Univ. Urologists, Buffalo Urol. Soc. (ann. award for outstanding contbns. to urology 1983), Soc. Univ. Surgeons, Am. Fedn. Clin. Research, N.Y. Acad. Scis., Buffalo Acad. Medicine, Am. Assn. Cancer Research, AMA, Assn. Genito-Urinary Surgeons, N.Y. State Soc. Surgeons, N.E. Soc. Clin. Oncology, Am. Surg. Assn., Am. Soc. Clin. Oncology, Am. Radium Soc. Subspecialties: Urology; Cancer research (medicine). Office: Roswell Park Meml Inst 666 Elm St Buffalo NY 14263

MURPHY, WILLIAM JAMES, steel company executive, metallurgical engineer; b. Lansing, Mich., Dec. 21, 1947; s. Leo Thomas and Kathryn (Wingeier) M.; m. Barbara Ann Byers, Oct. 16, 1976; children—Pamela M. Gargiulo, Cynthia D., Carl W. B.S. in Metall. Engring., Wayne State U., 1949, M.S., Lehigh U., 1951, Ph.D., 1955. Metallurgist Gen. Electric Co., Lynn, Mass., 1951-52; asst. prof. lehigh U., Bethlehem, Pa., 1952-57; div. chief U.S. Steel Research Lab., Monroeville, Pa., 1959-72, mgr. steel products, 1972-81, dir. corp. research, 1981—. Fellow Am. Soc. Metals; mem. AIME, Metals Soc., Am. Welding Soc., Sigma Xi. Home: 5353 Beeler St Pittsburgh PA 15217 Office: US Steel Tech Ctr One Tech Center Dr Monroeville PA 15146

MURRAY, ALLEN KETCIK, Biochemist, researcher; b. Santa Monica, Calif., Dec. 2, 1944; s. Allen Riddell and Josephine (Ketcik) M.; m. Jeanette Thaw Shelly, Feb. 16, 1980 (div. 1982). B.S., U. So. Calif., 1966; Ph.D., Mich. State U., 1971. USPHS postdoctoral fellow Wash. U. Sch. Med., St. Louis, 1971-74; asst. adj. prof. U. Calif.-Irvine, 1974-79; asst. dir. research devel. Muscular Dystrophy Assn., N.Y.C., 1979-81; pvt. cons., Irvine, 1981-82; pres. Glycozyme, Inc., Santa Ana, Calif., 1983—; Author book, 1981. Contbr. articles to profl. jours. Bd. dirs. Coll. Nat. Sci., Mich. State U., East Lansing, 1980-81; flotilla comdr. U.S. Coast Guard Aux., Tustin, Calif., 1984-85, div. ops. officer, 1983; v.p. Irvine Novaquatics, 1983—, mem. Irvine Sports Com. Recipient Someone Spl. award, City of Irvine, 1984. Mem. AAAS, N.Y. Acad. Sci., Am. Chem. Soc., Soc. for Inherited Metabolic Diseases, Sigma Xi. Current work: Glycosidases, glycoconjugates, glycoprotein structure, role of carbohydrate in glycoenzymes, and genetic modification of preceding. Subspecialties: Biochemistry (biology); Enzyme technology. Home: 5 Juniper Irvine CA 92715 Office: Glycozyme Inc 3873 S Main St Santa Ana CA 92707

MURRAY, JOHN FREDERIC, physician, educator; b. Mineola, N.Y., June 8, 1927; s. Frederic Seymour and Dorothy (Hanna) M.: m. Sarah Sherman, Sept. 15, 1949 (div. 1967); children—James R., Douglas S., Elizabeth; m. Diane Lain, Nov. 24, 1968. B.A., Stanford U., 1949, M.D., 1953; D.S.C. (hon.), U. Paris, 1982. Diplomate Am. Bd. Internal Medicine. Intern, asst. resident San Francisco Gen. Hosp., 1952-54; resident Kings County Hosp., Bklyn., 1954-56; instr. UCLA, 1957-59, asst. prof., 1959-64, assoc. prof., 1964-66; assoc. prof. medicine U. Calif.-San Francisco, 1966-69, prof., 1969—; vis. scientist Cardiothoracic Inst., London, Eng., 1972-73, Inst. Nat. de la Sante, Paris, 1979-80; mem. governing bd. Am. Bd. Internal Medicine, 1980—; mem., chmn. various coms. Nat. Heart, Lung and Blood Inst. Author: The Normal Lung, 1976; Diseases of the Chest, 1980. Cons. editor Cecil Textbook of Medicine, 1979. Contbr. chpt. to book. Served to lt. USMC, 1946-66. Recipient Calif. award Lung Assn. Calif., 1978; Josiah Macy Found. scholar, 1979-80; AAAS fellow, 1981. Mem. Am. Thorasic Soc. (pres. 1981-82), Assn. Am. Physicians, Am. Soc. Clin. Investigation (emeritus), Am. Physiol. Soc., Fleischner Soc. (pres. 1982-83). Democrat. Current work: Pulmonary pathophysiology; mechanisms, consequences and means of modifying acute lung injury. Subspecialties: Pulmonary medicine; Internal medicine. Home: 46 El Camino Real Berkeley CA 94705 Office: San Francisco Gen Hosp 1001 Potrero Ave San Francisco CA 94110

MURRAY, JOHN PATRICK, psychologist; b. Cleve., Sept. 14, 1943; s. John Augustine and Helen Marie (Lynch) M.; m. Ann Coke Dennison, Apr. 17, 1971; children—Jonathan Coke, Ian Patrick. B.A., John Carroll U., 1965; M.A., Cath. U. Am., 1968, Ph.D., 1970. Lic. psychologist, Nebr., D.C. Research dir. Office Surgeon Gen., Washington, 1969-72; asst. prof. Macquarie U., Sydney, Australia, 1973-77, assoc. prof., 1977-79; vis. assoc. prof. U. Mich., Ann Arbor, 1979-80; dir. youth and family policy Boys Town (Nebr.) Ctr., 1980-85; prof., head dept. family and child devel. Kans. State U., 1985—; mem. State Foster Care Rev. Bd., Lincoln, 1982-85, Advocacy Office for Children, Omaha, 1981—, Nat. Council for Children and TV, Princeton, N.J., 1982—; adj. prof. U. Nebr., 1982-85, U. Kans., 1983-85. Author: The Future of Children's Television, 1984, Status Offenders: A Sourcebook, 1983, Television and Youth: 25 Years of Research and Controversy, 1980, Small Screen, Big Business, 1979, Children and Families in Australia, 1979. NIMH fellow, 1972-73. Fellow Am. Psychol. Assn.; mem. Am. Sociol. Assn., AAAS, Soc. for Pediatric Psychology, Soc. for Research in Child Devel., Royal Commonwealth Soc. Current Work: Research and social policy formulation in area of children, youth and families; special interest in juvenile justice. Subspecialties: Developmental psychology; Social psychology. Office: Dept Family and Child Devel Kans State U Manhattan KS 66506

MURRAY, PETER, metallurgist, manufacturing company executive; b. Rotherham, Yorks, Eng., Mar. 13, 1920; came to U.S., 1967, naturalized, 1974; s. Michael and Ann (Hamstead) M.; m. Frances Josephine Glaisher, Sept. 8, 1947; children: Jane, Paul, Alexander. B.Sc. in Chemistry with honors, Sheffield (Eng.) U., 1941, postgrad., 1946-49; Ph.D. in Metallurgy, Brit. Iron and Steel Research Bursar, Sheffield, 1948. Research chemist Steetley Co., Ltd., Worksop, Notts, Eng., 1941-45; with Atomic Energy Research Establishment, Harwell, Eng., 1949-67, head div. metallurgy, 1960-64, asst. dir., 1964-67; tech. dir., mgr. fuels and materials, advanced reactors div. Westinghouse Electric Corp., Madison, Pa., 1967-74; dir. research Westinghouse Electric Europe (S.A.), Brussels, 1974-75; chief scientist advanced power systems divs. Westinghouse Electric Corp., Madison, Pa., 1975-81, dir. nuclear programs, Washington, 1981—; mem. divisional rev. coms. Argonne Nat. Lab., 1968-73; Mellor Meml. lectr. Inst. Ceramics, 1963. Contbr. numerous articles to profl. jours.; editorial adv. bd.: Jour. Less Common Metals, 1968—. Recipient Holland Meml. Research prize Sheffield U., 1949. Fellow Royal Inst. Chemistry (Newton Chambers Research prize 1954), Inst. Ceramics; mem. Brit. Ceramics Soc. (pres. 1965), Am. Ceramic Soc., Am. Nuclear Soc., Nat. Acad. Engring. Roman Catholic. Subspecialty: Nuclear energy research and development administration. Home: 20308 Canby Ct Gaithersburg MD 20879 Office: Westinghouse Electric Corp 1801 K St NW Washington DC 20006

MURRAY, RAYMOND HAROLD, physician; b. Cambridge, Mass., Aug. 17, 1925; s. Raymond Harold and Grace May (Dorr) M.; children—Maureen, Robert, Michael, Margaret, David, Elizabeth, Catherine, Anne. B.S., U. Notre Dame, 1946; M.D., Harvard U., 1948. Diplomate: Am. Bd. Internal Medicine, also Sub-bd. Cardiovascular Disease. Practice medicine, Grand Rapids, Mich., 1955-62; asst. prof. to prof. medicine Ind. U. Sch. Medicine, 1962-77; prof., chmn. dept. medicine Mich. State U. Coll. Human Medicine, 1977—; chmn. aeromed-bioscis panel Sci. Adv. Bd., USAF, 1977-81. Contbr. numerous articles to profl. publs. Served with USNR, 1942-45; Served with USPHS, 1950-53. Fellow A.C.P.; mem. Am. Heart Assn. (fellow council clin. cardiology), Am. Fedn. Clin. Research, Central Soc. Clin. Research, Am. Physiol. Soc. Subspecialty: Cardiology. Office: B220 Life Scis Bldg Mich State U East Lansing MI 48824

MURRAY, ROBERT FULTON, JR., physician; b. Newburgh, N.Y., Oct. 19, 1931; s. Robert Fulton and Henrietta Frances (Judd) M.; m. Isobel Ann Parks, Aug. 26, 1956; children—Colin Charles, Robert Fulton, III, Suzanne Frances, Dianne Akwe. B.S., Union Coll., Schenectady, 1953; M.D., U. Rochester, N.Y., 1958; M.S., U. Wash., Seattle, 1968. Diplomate: Am. Bd. Internal Medicine. Rotating intern Denver Gen. Hosp., 1958-59; resident in internal medicine U. Colo. Med. Center, 1959-62; staff investigator (service with USPHS) Nat. Inst. Arthritis and Metabolic Diseases, NIH, Bethesda, Md., 1962-65; NIH spl. fellow med. genetics U. Wash., 1965-67; mem. faculty Howard U. Coll. Medicine, Washington, 1967—, prof. pediatrics and medicine, 1974—, grad. prof., 1976, prof. oncology, 1976; mem. nat. adv. gen. med. scis. council NIH, 1971-75; sci. adv. bd. Nat. Sickle Cell Anemia Found.; mem. ethics adv. bd. to sec. HEW, 1978-80; chmn. Washington Mayor's Adv. Com. on Metabolic Disorders, 1980—; mem. Med. Com. Human Rights. Author: Genetic, Metabolic and Developmental Aspects of Mental Retardation, 1972; co-editor: Genetic Counseling: Facts, Values and Norms, 1979; asso. editor: Am. Jour. Clin. Genetics, 1977—; editorial adv. bd.: Ency. Bioethics, 1975-77. Trustee Union Coll., 1972-80. Rotary Found. fellow, 1955-56; research grantee NIH, 1969-75. Fellow A.C.P., AAAS, Inst. Medicine, Inst. Society, Ethics and Life Scis.; mem. Am. Soc. Human Genetics, Genetics Soc. Am., D.C. Med. Soc., Neighbors Inc. D.C., Sigma Xi. Unitarian. Current Work: Inherited susceptibility to disease; genetic screening and counseling; sickle cell disease and traits; bioethics. Subspecialties: Internal medicine; Genetics and genetic engineering (medicine). Home: 510 Aspen St NW Washington DC 20012 Office: Coll Medicine Box 75 Howard Univ Washington DC 20059

MURRAY, ROBERT GEORGE EVERITT, physician, scientist, educator; b. Ruislip, Middlesex, Eng., May 19, 1919; Everitt George Dunne and Harriet Winifred Hardwick (Woods) M.; m. Doris Marchand, Jan. 15, 1944; children—Alice Blair (Mrs. Norman Francis Rae), Peter Everitt, Thomas Everitt. Student, Lower Can. Coll., Montreal, 1931-36, McGill U., 1936-38; B.A., Cambridge U., 1941, M.A., 1945; M.D., C.M., McGill U., 1943, D.Sc. (h.c.), U. Western Ont., 1985. Lectr., Faculty Medicine U. Western Ont., London, 1945-46, asst. prof., 1946-48, asso. prof., 1948-49, acting head dept. bacteriology and immunology, 1948-49, prof., 1949—, head dept., 1949-74, acting dean sci., 1973-74, prof. dept. microbiology and immunology, 1974—; chief bacteriology service Victoria Hosp., London, 1948-64, hon. cons., 1966-70, St. Josephs Hosp., 1961—. Editor: Can. Jour. Microbiology, 1954-60, Bacteriol. Revs, 1969-79; Mem.: editorial bd. Jour. of Bacteriology, 1951-54, 80—, Bacteriological Revs., 1966-79, Internat. Jour. Systematic Bacteriology, 1982—; contbr. articles to profl. jours. Trustee Bergeys Manual, 1964—, vice chmn., 1967-68, chmn., 1976—; mem. governing bd. Biol. Council Can., 1966-73. Served as capt. M.C. Canadian Army, 1944-45. Recipient Coronation medal, 1953, Centennial medal, 1967, Queen's Jubilee medal, 1978. Fellow Royal Soc. Can. (Harrison prize 1957), Am. Acad. Microbiology; mem. Canadian Pub. Health Assn. (chmn. lab. sect. 1953), Canadian Soc. Microbiologists (chmn. founding com. 1950-51, founding pres. 1951-52, mem. council 1951-60, award 1963), Am. Soc. Microbiology (publs. bd. 1969-79, pres. 1972-73), Path. Soc. Gt. Britain and Ireland, Electron Microscope Soc. Am., Soc. for Gen. Microbiology, Internat. Union Microbiol. Socs. (mem. at large exec. bd. 1982-86). Am., Canadian socs. cell biology, Canadian Assn. Med. Microbiologists. Club: London Flying. Current work: Cellular ultra structure of bacteria; function of recognizable structures. Home: 872 Hellmuth Ave London ON N6A 3T8 Canada

MURRAY, ROYCE WILTON, chemistry educator; b. Birmingham, Ala., Jan. 9, 1937; s. Royce Leeroy and Justina Louisa (Herd) M.; m. Mirtha Umana, Dec. 11, 1982; children: Katherine, Stewart, Debra, Melissa, Marion. B.S. in Chemistry, Birmingham So. Coll., 1957; Ph.D., Northwestern U., 1960. Faculty U. N.C., Chapel Hill, 1960—, prof. chemistry, 1969-80, acting dept. chmn., 1970-71, vice chmn., 1972-75, chmn., 1980-85, Kenan prof., 1980—; On leave from U. N.C. in chemistry sect. NSF, Washington, 1971-72. Author two books, also articles in analytical chemistry and surface chemistry. Sloan research fellow, 1969-72; Guggenheim fellow, 1980-81. Mem. Am. Chem. Soc., Electrochem. Soc., Soc. Electroanalytical Chemists, Phi Beta Kappa, Sigma Xi, Omicron Delta Kappa, Phi Eta Sigma, Theta Sigma Lambda, Theta Chi Delta, Alpha Tau Omega, Alpha Chi Sigma. Subspecialty: Analytical chemistry. Office: Dept Chemistry U North Carolina Chapel Hill NC 27514

MURRAY, STEPHEN S., astrophysicist, consultant; b. N.Y.C., Aug. 28, 1944; s. Leon and Beatrice E. M.; m. Judith G. Gittlen, Aug. 31, 1965; children: Jeffrey J., Micah N. B.S., Columbia U., 1965; Ph.D., Calif. Inst. Tech., 1971. Staff scientist Am. Sci & Engring., Cambridge, Mass., 1971-72; physicist Smithsonian Astrophys. Obs., Cambridge, 1973-82, astrophysicist, 1982—; cons. Space Telescope Sci. Inst.; mem. Com. on Space Astronomy and Astrophysics; mem. x-ray astrophysics facility sci. working group; prin. investigator high resolution camera; chmn. Smithsonian Astrophys. Obs. telescope time allocation com.; lectr. Harvard Coll. Obs. Bd. dirs. Temple B'nai Abraham, Beverly, Mass. Mem. Am. Astron. Soc., Internat. Astron. Union, AAAS, Sigma Xi. Current Work: Extragalactic x-ray astronomy, high resolution imaging detectors; development of single photon imaging detectors for x-ray astronomy and low light level optical astronomy; research on x-ray background and extragalactic x-ray sources. Subspecialties: Optical astronomy; Satellite studies. Office: 60 Garden St B416 Cambridge MA 02138

MURRIN, LEONARD CHARLES, II, pharmacologist, educator, researcher; b. Iowa City, Oct. 9, 1943; s. Leonard Charles and Huberta Frances (Jones) J.; m. Kathryn Grace McDermott, Aug. 17, 1968; children: Leonard Charles III, Rose Colleen, Clare Rita. B.A., St. John's Coll., Camarillo, Calif., 1965; Ph.D., Yale U., 1975. Postdoctoral fellow Yale U., 1975, Johns Hopkins U., 1975-78; asst. prof. pharmacology U. Nebr. Med. Sch., Omaha, 1978-83, assoc. prof., 1983—. Contbr. numerous articles, abstracts to profl. jours. March of Dimes Birth Defects Found. grantee, 1979-84; NSF grantee, 1980-83. Mem. AAAS, Soc. Neurosci., Am. Soc. Pharmacology and Exptl. Therapeutics, Am. Soc. Neurochemistry, Internat. Soc. Neurochemistry. Current Work: Developmental neuropharmacology of central nervous system; experimental Parkinson's desease. Subspecialties: Neuropharmacology; Developmental biology. Home: 5204 N 86th St Omaha NE 68134 Office: Dept Pharmacology U Nebr Med Center Omaha NE 68105

MURTHY, VARANASI RAMA, geology educator; b. Visakapatnam, India, July 2, 1933; s. Varanasi Rama and Varanasi (Sodemma) Brahmam; m. Monique Danielle Bois, Aug. 21, 1959; children: V. Aanand, V. Katyayini. B.S., Andhra U., Waltair, India, 1951; A.I.S.M., Indian Sch. Mines, 1954; M.S., Yale, 1955, Ph.D., 1957. Research fellow Calif. Inst. Tech., 1957-59; asst. research geologist U. Calif., San Diego, 1959-62, asst. prof., 1962-65; asso. prof. U. Minn., Mpls., 1965-69, prof. geology and geophysics, 1969, head Sch. Earth Scis., 1971-83, acting dean Inst. Tech., 1983, v.p. for acad. affairs, provost, 1985—. Research grantee NASA and NSF; Tata Found. fellow, 1954-57. Mem. Am., Indian geophys. unions, Geochem. Soc., AAAS, Sigma Xi. Current Work: Geochemistry and chemical evolution of mantle and crust of earth; origin of igneous rocks. Subspecialties: Geochemistry; Petrology. Home: 906 Dartmouth Pl SE Minneapolis MN 55414

MURTHY, VISHNUBHAKTA SHRINIVAS, physician, pharmacologist, educator; b. Kanker, India, Jan. 1, 1942; s. V. M. and Veda Vati (Lanka) M.; m. Veda Vani Vishnubhakta, Aug. 11, 1978; children: Renuka, Kishori, Ashck, Vikrum. MBBS, M.G.M. Med. Coll., Indore, India, 1965; Ph.D., U. Man., Winnipeg, Can., 1972. Lectr. pharmacology M.G.M. Med. Coll., Indore, 1968-69; sr. scientist Warner Lambert Co., Ann Arbor, Mich., 1972-74; sr. research investigator Squibb Inst. for Med. Research, Princeton, N.J., 1974-78; asst. prof. dept. medicine, dir. cardiovascular research lab. Mt. Sinai Med. Center, Milw., 1981—. Contbr. articles to profl. jours. Mem. N.Y. Acad. Scis., Am. Soc. Clin. Pharmacology and Therapeutics, Am. Soc. Pharmacology and Exptl. Therapeutics. Hindu. Current Work: Research in hypertension and coronary artery disease, clin. pharmacology, patient care. Subspecialties: Internal medicine; Pharmacology. Home: 6655 Jean Nicolet Rd Glendale WI 53217 Office: 950 N. 12th St Milwaukee WI 53233

MUSACCHIA, X. J., university administrator; b. Bklyn., Feb. 11, 1923; s. Castrense and Orsolina (Mazzola) M.; m. Betty Cook, Nov. 23, 1950; children—Joseph, Mary, Thomas, Laura Ann. B.S., St. Francis Coll., 1943; M.S., Fordham U., 1947, Ph.D., 1949. Instr. biology Marymount Coll., N.Y., 1948-49; from instr. biology to prof. St. Louis U., 1949-65; prof. physiology U. Mo., Columbia, 1965-78; dean Grad. Sch. U. Louisville, 1978—. Co-author: Depressed Metabolism, 1969; Regulation of Depressed Metabolsim & Thermogenesis, 1976; Survival in Cold: Hibernation, 1981. Bd. govs. J. Graham Brown Regional Cancer Ctr., Louisville, 1979—. Grantee in field. Fellow AAAS; mem. Am. Physiol. Soc., Soc. Exptl. Biology and Medicine, Corp. Marine Biol. Lab., Sigma Xi (pres. St. Louis chpt. 1959-60). Current work: Environmental physiology; biochemistry of hibernation in reptiles and mammals; radiation biology and comparative physiology of intestinal absorption; physiology of depressed metabolism; hypothermia and hibernation; gravitational physiology. Subspecialties: Physiology (medicine); Radiation biology. Office: U Louisville Grad Sch 206 Jouett Hall Louisville KY 40292

MUSCHLITZ, EARLE EUGENE, JR., Chemist, educator; b. Palmerton, Pa., Apr. 23, 1921; s. Earle Eugene and Ferne Estelle (Altemose) M.; m. Barbara Pfahler, Sept. 17, 1953; children: Robert Earle, Karl William. B.S., Pa. State U., 1941, M.S., 1942, Ph.D., 1947. Instr. chemistry Cornell U., Ithaca, N.Y., 1947-51; from asst. prof. to assoc. prof. chemistry U. Fla., Gainesville, 1951-58, prof., 1958—, chmn. dept., 1973-77. Author articles. NSF sr. fellow, 1963-64; Alexander von Humboldt sr. U.S. scientist W.Ger., 1978; vis. fellow Joint Inst. for Lab. Astrophysics, 1968. Fellow Am. Inst. Chemists, Am. Phys. Soc.; mem. Am. Chem. Soc., Am. Soc. for Mass Spectrometry, Sigma Xi, Alpha Chi Sigma. Democrat. Current Work: The structure and properties of molecules in electronically excited states. Experimental investigations of inelastic collisions of electronically excited atoms and molecules using crossed molecular beam, mass spectrometric, and optical techniques. Subspecialties: Physical chemistry; Kinetics. Home: 4850 NW 20th Pl Gainesville FL 32605 Office: Dept Chemistry U Fla Gainesville FL 32611

MUSE, MARK DANA, psychologist; b. Pasadena, Calif., Mar. 1, 1952; s. Harry Lee and Nelda Hayward (Evans) M.; Gloria Frigola, Aug. 15, 1978; 1 dau., Dana Michele. B.S., No. Ariz. U., 1973, M.A., 1978, Ed.D., 1980; Licencido, U. Barcelona, 1983. Lic. psychologist, Md., Spain. Grad. asst. No. Ariz. U., 1978-80, adj. faculty, 1981; psychodiagnostician Inst. Human Devel., Flagstaff, Ariz., 1980-81; cons. psychologist Centro Psicologico, Ibiza, Spain, 1981—; dir. Pain Clinic, Sacred Heart Hosp., Cumberland, Md., 1982—. Author: Stress y Relax, 1983; Exercise for Chronic Pain, 1984. Contbr. articles to profl. jours. Mem. Am. Psychol. Assn., Phi Kappa Phi, Psi Chi. Democrat. Current Work: stress-related post traumatic chronic pain syndrome. Subspecialty: Cognition. Home: 937 Bishop Walsh St Cumberland MD 21502 Office: Sacred Heart Hosp 900 Seton Dr Cumberland MD 21502

MUSHINSKI, J. FREDERIC, research biochemist; b. Beaver Falls, Pa., May 18, 1938; s. Joseph Albert and Ruth Selina (Roberts) M.; m. Elizabeth Bridges, May 1, 1971. B.A., Yale U., 1959; M.D., Harvard U., 1963. Diplomate: Nat. Bd. Med. Examiners. Intern, fellow dept. medicine Duke U., 1963-65; research assoc. Nat. Cancer Inst., NIH, Bethesda, Md., 1965-69; sr. investigator Lab. Cell Biology, 1970-83; sr. investigator Lab. Genetics Nat. Cancer Inst., 1983—; vis. scientist Max Planck Inst. Exptl. Medicine, Goettingen, W. Ger., 1969-70. Contbr. numerous articles to profl. jours. Served with USPHS, 1965—. William O. Moseley Jr. travelling fellow Harvard U., 1969. Mem. Am. Soc. Biol. Chemists, Am. Assn. Immunolgists, Am. Assn. Cancer Research, AAAS. Current Work: Recombinant DNA studies of antibody and cancer genes. Subspecialties: Biochemistry (medicine); Immunogenetics. Office: Bldg 37 Room 2B26 NIH Bethesda MD 20205

MUSTAFA, SYED JAMAL, pharmacologist, educator, researcher; b. Lucknow, India, July 10, 1946; came to U.S., 1971, naturalized, 1978; s. Syed Mohd and Ahmad Jehan M.; m. Yasmeen Khan, June 11, 1973; children: Zishan, Farhan, Adnan. B.S., Lucknow U., 1962; M.S. in Biochemistry, 1965, Ph.D. in Biochemistry, 1969. NIH postdoctoral fellow dept. physiology U. Va. Med. Sch., Charlottesville, 1971-74; asst. prof. dept. pharmacology U. South Ala. Med. Sch., Mobile, 1974-77, assoc. prof., 1977-80; assoc. prof. dept. pharmacology East Carolina U. Med. Sch., Greenville, N.C., 1980-83, prof., 1983—. Contbr. articles to physiol. and pharm. jours., chpts. to books; referee editor several jours. NIH grantee, 1976—; Ala. Heart Assn. grantee, 1975-79. Mem. Am. Soc. Pharmacology and Exptl. Therapeutics, Am. Physiol. Soc., Soc. Exptl. Biology and Medicine, Internat. Soc. Heart Research, Am. Heart Assn., AAAS, N.Y. Acad. Scis., Islamic Med. Assn., Muslim Student Assn., Sigma Xi. Current Work: Cellular mechanism(s) of coronary flow regulation (metabolic) in normal and pathophysiological models; research in cardiovascular pharmacology. Subspecialties: Pharmacology; Cardiology. Office: Dept Pharmacology East Carolina U Med Sch Greenville NC 27834

MUSTARD, JAMES FRASER, research administrator, physician; b. Toronto, Ont., Can., Oct. 16, 1927; s. Alan Alexander and Jean Ann (Oldham) M.; m. Christine Elizabeth Sifton, 1952; children: Cameron, Anne, James, Duncan, John, Christine. M.D., U. Toronto, 1953; Ph.D., Cambridge (Eng.) U., 1956. Intern Toronto Gen. Hosp.; asst. prof. medicine U. Toronto, 1963; assoc. prof. McMaster U., Hamilton, Ont., Can., 1965, prof. pathology, chmn. dept. pathology, 1966-72, dean faculty health scis., 1972-80, prof. pathology, from 1982, v.p. health scis., 1980-82. Mem. editorial bd. Arteriosclerosis, Am. Jour. Pathology. Contbr. numerous articles to sci. jours. Recipient Internat. award for med. research Gairdner Found., 1967. Fellow Royal Soc., Royal Coll. Physicians, Can. Inst. Advanced Research (pres. 1982—). Current work: Study of platelet physiology and function in relation to vascular disease and thrombosis; causes of arteriosclerosis and clinical complications such as heart attacks and strokes. Subspecialty: Arteriosclerosis; Research administration. Office: Dept Pathology McMaster U Hamilton ON L8N 3Z5 Canada

MYER, JON H(AROLD), engineering physicist; b. Heilbronn, Germany, Sept. 29, 1922; came to U.S., 1948; s. Oscar N. and Greta C. (Wolf) M.; m. Gerda Rachel Simson, Apr. 20, 1948; children—Gary D., Eric J., Karen B., Kenneth B. B.E.E., Hebrew Tech. Coll., 1941. Instrument maker Anglo Iranian Oil Co., Abadan, Iran, 1942-44; instrument designer Hebrew Tech. Coll., Haifa, Israel, 1944-46; engring. cons., Haifa, Israel, 1946-47; instrumentologist dept. chemistry U. So. Calif., Los Angeles, 1947-53; with Hughes Aircraft Co.,

Malibu, Calif., 1953—, sub. lab. head, dept. mgr. semicondr. div., sr. mem. tech. staff optical circuits dept. Patentee 40 times in field of engring. physics. Mem. Optical Soc. Am., IEEE (chmn. student relations com. 1958), Am. Phys. Soc. Current work: Active and passive optical circuit components. Subspecialties: Fiber optics; Optical signal processing. Office: Hughes Research Labs Mail Sta RL68 3011 Malibu Canyon Rd Malibu CA 90265

MYEROWITZ, P. DAVID, cardiac surgeon. Assoc. prof., chief sect. cardiac transplantation U. Wis. Med. Sch., Madison. Subspecialties: Cardiac surgery; Transplant surgery. Office: U Wis Med Sch Cardio-Thoracic surgery Madison WI 53706

MYERS, HOWARD chemical physicist, system analyst, consultant; b. N.Y.C., Jan. 27, 1928; s. Howard Gould and Sally (Kline) M.; m. Lois Marie Lowe, July 19, 1948 (dec. Apr. 1968); m. Joan Cerwin Myers, May 29, 1976; children—Susanna, William, Sally. Ph.B., U. Chgo., 1950, B.S., 1952, M.S., 1953. Mem. tech. staff Hughes Research Lab., Culver City, Calif., 1954-57; research specialist Douglas Aircraft Co., Santa Monica, Calif., 1957-61; program mgr. Aerospace Corp., Los Angeles, 1961-66; mem. tech. staff TRW, Los Angeles, 1966-69; sr. research specialist McDonnell-Douglas Co., St. Louis, 1969-80; sr. system analyst Gen. Electric Co., Valley Forge, Pa., 1980—; pres. CPRL (Cons.), Paoli, Pa., 1968—. Patentee elastometer, 1956; contbr. numerous research and engring. articles to profl. jours. Principal collaborator on research resulting in Nobel Prize in chemistry awarded to Henry Taube, 1983. Mem. Am. Chem. Soc., Am. Geophys. Union, Research Soc. Am., AAAS, Am. Astron. Soc., N.Y. Acad. Sci. Current work: Systems definition and integration of communication satellites. Design of space-borne scientific instrumentation. Subspecialties: Physical chemistry; Systems engineering. Home: 599 Carroll Fox Rd Brick NJ 08723 Office: CPRL PO Box 983 Paoli PA 19301

MYERS, DONALD ARTHUR, geologist; b. Seattle, May 30, 1921; s. Arthur Raymond and Lydia Albertina (Lofgren) M.; m. Margaret Martin Pettus, Aug. 6, 1955; children: David, John, Alan. Student, U. Utah, 1938-40; B.A., Stanford U., 1943, postgrad., 1946-48; postgrad., Johns Hopkins U., 1948-50. Geologist U.S. Geol. Survey, Denver, 1948-84, guest scientist, 1984—. Author: Geology, Late Paleozoic Horseshoe Atoll, Tex., 1956. Served to 1st lt. USAF, 1943-46. N.Mex. Bur. Mines research assoc., 1978. Fellow Geol. Soc. Am.; mem. Paleontol. Soc., Soc. Econ. Paleontologists and Mineralogists, Am. Assn. Petroleum Geologists. Current Work: Fusulinid Forainnifera, research into specific and infraspecific variations in time as a tool to aid in regional and interregional stratigraphic correlation in Pennsylvanian and early Permian sedimentary rocks. Subspecialties: Biostratigraphy; Geology. Home: 1240 Cody St Lakewood CO 80215 Office: US Geol Survey Fed Ctr Box 25046 Mail Stop 918 Denver CO 80225

MYERS, EUGENE DOLAN, air force officer, computer communications analyst; b. Radford, Va., Aug. 30, 1952; s. Eugene Garnett and Helen Elizabeth (Webb) M.; m. Helene Wen-Hsin Young, May 1, 1975. B.S. in Computer Sci., Va. 1974; M.S. in Computer Sci, 1976; M.B.A., U. Okla., 1974. Commd. 2d lt. U.S. Army, 1974; officer U.S. Air Force, 1978, advanced through grades to capt., 1979, computer systems analyst, Offutt AFB, Nebr., 1978-79, computer communications analyst, 1979-82, Ft. Meade, Md., 1982—, also chief secure architectures br. Mem. Assn. Computing Machinery, IEEE. Current Work: Research in computer security, in network and computer architectures. Subspecialties: Distributed systems and networks; Cryptography and data security. Home: 4811-B Ninninger Ct Fort Meade MD 20755 Office: Dept Def Computer Security Center Fort Meade MD 20755

MYERS, JACK EDGAR, zoology and botany educator; b. Boyds Mills, Pa., July 10, 1913; s. Garry Cleveland and Caroline (Clark) M.; B.S., Juniata Coll., 1934, D.Sc., 1966; M.S., Mont. State Coll., 1935; Ph.D., U. Minn., 1939; m. Evelyn DeTurck, June 19, 1937; children—Shirley Ann, Jacquelyn, Linda Caroline, Kathleen. NRC fellow Smithsonian Inst., 1940-41; asst. prof. zoology U. Tex., Austin, 1941-45, assoc. prof., 1945-48, prof. zoology, 1948—, prof. botany, 1955—. Author: (with F.A. Matsen and N.H. Hackerman) Premedical Physical Chemistry, 1947. Sci. editor Highlights for Children, 1960—. Contbr. to publs. in field. Guggenheim fellow, 1959. Mem. Soc. Gen. Physiologists, Am. Soc. Plant Physiologists, Phycol. Soc., AAAS, Nat. Acad. Sci., Tex. Acad. Sci., Am. Soc. Photobiology (pres. 1975), Sigma Xi. Current work: Photosynthesis. Subspecialty: Plant physiology (biology). Office: U Tex Dept Zoology Austin TX 78712

MYERS, LYLE LESLIE, microbiologist, educator; b. Salem, Oreg., June 11, 1938; s. James Elton and Vesta Elizabeth (Carothers) M.; m. Patricia Ann Walter, Aug. 27, 1960; children: Diane Kay, Linda Ellen, Carolyn Sue. B.S. in Animal Sci, Oreg. State U., 1960; M.S., Mont. State U., 1962; Ph.D. in Agrl. Biochemistry, Purdue U., 1966. Asst. prof. dept. vet. sci. Mont. State U., Bozeman, 1966-71, assoc. prof., 1971-79, prof., 1979—, dir. enteric disease research program, 1980—. Contbr. articles to profl. jours. Mem. Conf. of Research Workers in Animal Diseases, Am. Soc. for Microbiology, Sigma Xi, Phi Lambda Upsilon. Republican. Current Work: Developed an E. coli vaccine now used commercially to prevent scours in calves caused by E. coli; now working to prevent other forms of scours in calves and lambs. Subspecialties: Microbiology (veterinary medicine); Preventive medicine (veterinary medicine). Home: 1490 Harper-Puckett Rd Bozeman MT 59715 Office: Dept Vet Sci Mont State U Bozeman MT 59717

MYERS, PHILIP CHERDAK, astrophysicist; b. Elizabeth, N.J., Nov. 18, 1944; s. Reney and Anne (Cherdak) M.; m. Anne Hoffman, July 21, 1972; children—David Hoffman, Joshua Ethan. B.A., Columbia U., 1966; Ph.D., MIT, 1972. Staff researcher MIT, 1972-75, asst. prof. physics, 1975-78, asso. prof. physics, 1978-82; staff Harvard-Smithsonian Ctr. Astrophysics, Cambridge, 1982—; sr. research asso. Nat. Acad. Scis., NRC, Goddard Inst. for Space Studies, N.Y.C., 1979-80, 82-84. Contbr. articles to books, refereed jours. Mem. Am. Astron. Soc., Internat. Union Radio Sci. Current Work: Dense star-forming interstellar clouds. Subspecialties: Radio and microwave astronomy; Biomedical engineering. Office: Harvard-Smithsonian Ctr Astrophysics D312 Cambridge MA 02138

MYERS, PHILLIP SAMUEL, mechanical engineering educator; b. Webber, Kans., May 8, 1916; s. Earl Rufus and Sarah Katharine (Breon) M.; m. Jean Frances Alford, May 26, 1943; children: Katharine Myers Muirhead, Elizabeth Myers Baird, Phyllis Myers Rathbone, John, Mark. B.S. in Math. and Commerce, McPherson Coll., 1940; B.S. in Mech. Engring, Kans. State Coll., 1942; Ph.D. in Engring, U. Wis., 1947. Registered profl. engr., Wis. Instr. Ind. Tech. Coll., Ft. Wayne, summer 1942; instr. U. Wis., Madison, 1942-47, asst. prof., 1947-50, assoc. prof., 1950-55, prof., 1955—, chmn. dept. mech. engring., 1979-83; cons. Diesel Engine Mfrs. Assn., U.S. Army, also various oil and ins. cos.; dir. Nelson Industries, Echlin Mfg. Corp. Contbr. articles to profl. jours. Chmn. Pine Lake com. W. Wis. Conf. Meth. Ch., 1955-60; Mem. Village Bd., Shorewood Hills, 1962-67. Recipient B.S. Reynolds Teaching award, 1964, McPherson Coll. Alumni citation of merit, 1971; Dugald Clerk award, 1971. Fellow ASME (Diesel Gas Power award 1971), Soc. Automotive Engrs. (Colwell award 1966, 79, Horning award 1968, nat. pres. 1969, hon. mem.); mem. Am. Soc. for Engring. Edn., AAAS, Nat. Acad. Engring., Blue Key, Sigma Xi, Phi Kappa Phi, Sigma Tau, Pi Tau Sigma (Gold medal 1949), Tau Beta Pi (Ragnar Onstad Service to Soc. award 1978). Mem. Ch. of the Brethren. Patentee in field. Current Work: Teaching; understanding the vagaries of internal combustion engines. Subspecialties: Combustion processes; Fuels. Home: Madison WI

MYERS, SAMUEL MAXWELL, physicist; b. Florence, S.C., Jan. 30, 1943; s. Samuel Maxwell and Juanita Beauford (Touchberry) M. B.S. in Physics, Duke U., 1965, Ph.D. in Physics, 1970. Postdoctoral assoc. Sandia Nat. Labs., Albuquerque, 1970-72, staff physicist, 1972-83, research supr., 1983—. Contbr. articles to profl. jours. Mem. Am. Phys. Soc., Metall. Soc., Materials Research Soc. Current work: Basic research in ion-solid interactions, solid state physics, metastable materials, hydrogen in materials. Subspecialties: Condensed matter physics; Materials.

MYERS, WADE HAMPTON, JR., engineering company executive; b. Durham, N.C., Nov. 2, 1941; s. Wade Hampton and Pauline Eugenia (Cross) M.; B.S. in Physics and Math, U. So. Miss., 1965. Sci. programmer Gen. Electric Co., Syracuse, N.Y., 1965, engr., 1966, systems engr., 1967; sr. systems engr. Honeywell Info. Systems, Phoenix, 1974-76; sr. engr. Courier Terminal Systems, Phoenix, 1977, Intel Corp., Santa Clara, Calif., 1977; sr. mem. sci. staff BNR, Inc., Mountain View, Calif., 1979; sr. engr. Signetics Corp., Sunnyvale, Calif., 1978, microsystems group software mgr., 1981-82; propr. Wade Myers Enterprises, 1982—; cons. in field. Mem. Assn. Computing Machinery, IEEE. Current Work: Operating systems, distributed processing, microprocessor development tools. Subspecialties: Computer architecture; Distributed systems and networks. Home: PO Box 640323 San Francisco CA 94164 Office: PO Box 880068 San Francisco CA 94188-0068

MYERS, WILLIAM GRAYDON, physician, scientist, educator; b. Toledo, Aug. 7, 1908; s. Leo J. and Anna C. (Johnson) M.; m. Florence R. Lenahan, Dec. 24, 1940. B.A., Ohio State U., 1933, M.Sc., 1937, Ph.D. in Physical Chemistry, 1939, M.D., 1941; D.Sc. (hon.), Bucknell U., 1977. Diplomate: Am. Bd. Nuclear Medicine. Grad. asst. chemistry Ohio State U., 1933-37, Comly asst. med. research, 1939-42; intern Univ. Hosp., 1941-42; research assoc. Ohio State U. Research Found., 1942-45; Julius F. Stone fellow med. Ohio State U., 1945-49, research assoc. prof., 1949-53, research prof. med. biophysics (depts. medicine, physiology and radiology), 1953-79, prof. emeritus radiology, 1979—; vis. prof. nuclear medicine U. Calif. at Berkeley, winters 1970—; vis. prof. Cornell Grad. Sch. Med. Scis., 1978—; investigator Meml. Sloan-Kettering Cancer Center, 1978—; cons. nuclear medicine to various labs. Monitor radiol. safety sect. atom bomb tests Operation Crossroads, Bikini, 1946; invited participant numerous nat. and internat. confs. on applications nuclear sci. in nuclear medicine. Author articles profl. jours. Exec. com. Columbus (Ohio) Civil Def., 1950—. Recipient Lucy Wortham James research award James Ewing Soc., 1966. Fellow Royal Soc. Arts (life), ACP; mem. Am. Chem. Soc., Am. Phys. Soc., Am. Physiol. Soc., Am. Assn. Cancer Research, Soc. Exptl. Biology and Medicine, AAAS, Ohio Acad. Sci., Am. Assn. Physicists in Medicine, Am. Radium Soc., Radiation Research Soc., Soc. Nuclear Medicine (1st Paul C. Aebersold award 1973, historian 1973—, Hevesy Nuclear Medicine Pioneer award 1981), Ohio State Med. Assn., Columbus Acad. Medicine, Phi Lambda Upsilon, Sigma Xi (chpt. pres. 1959-60), Alpha Omega Alpha. Clubs: Torch (Columbus); Explorers (N.Y.C.). Current Work: Applications of radioactive isotopes in med. diagnosis and therapy; presently serving about 25-35% of time at Memorial Sloan-Kettering Cancer Research Center in N.Y.C. doing research in applying radioisotopes in Dx & Tx. Subspecialties: Biophysical chemistry; Nuclear medicine. Home: 2724 Wexford Rd Columbus OH 43221-3218 Office: Ohio State Univ Hosp 410 W 10th Ave S-209 Rhodes Hall Columbus OH 43210-1228

MYHRE, BYRON ARNOLD, pathology educator; b. Fargo, N.D., Oct. 22, 1928; s. Ben Arnold and Amy Lillian (Gilbertson) M.; m. Eileen Marguerite Scherling, June 16, 1953; children—Patricia Ann, Bruce Allen. B.S., U. Ill., 1949; M.S., Northwestern U., 1953, M.D., 1953; Ph.D., U. Wis., 1962. Assoc. med. dir. Milw. Blood Ctr., 1962-65; asst. prof. pathology Marquette U., Milw., 1962-66; sci. dir. ARC, Los Angeles, 1966-72; prof. pathology UCLA, 1972—; sr. scientist Jet Propulsion Lab., Pasadena, Calif., 1978-81; cons. Wadsworth VA Hosp., Los Angeles, 1976—. Author: Quality Control in Blood Banks, 1974. Editor 9 books or monographs. Contbr. numerous articles to med. jours. Served to capt. USAF, 1954-56. Fellow NIH, 1960-62, Biol. Stains Commn., 1951-53. Fellow Am. Soc. Clin. Pathology (dep. commr. 1975-78); mem. Am. Assn. Blood Banks (pres. 1978-79), Los Angeles Acad. Medicine (sec. 1985—), Coll. Am. Pathologists (chmn. blood bank survey 1973-78), AMA. Club: Palos Verdes Breakfast (music chmn. 1984). Current work: Red cell survival, transfusion decision making. Home: 4004 Via Larga Vista Palos Verdes Estates CA 90274 Office: Dept Pathology Harbor-UCLA Med Ctr 1000 W Carson Torrance CA 90509

MYRICK, HENRY NUGENT, waste mgmt. cons.; b. Cisco, Tex., Apr. 30, 1935; s. Elbert Porter and Lila Faye (Hill) M.; m. Mary Frances Ross, June 15, 1968. B.S., Lamar State U., 1957; M.S., Rice U., 1959; Sc.D. in Environ. Sci. and Engring, Washington U., St. Louis, 1962. Fellow, instr. environ. engring. Rice U., Houston, 1962-63; fellow, instr. san. engring., 1963-65; assoc. prof. civil and environ. engring. U. Houston, 1965-74; pres. Process Co., Inc., Houston, 1970—. Pub.: Tex. Solid Waste Mgmt. News, 1972—; contbr. articles to profl. jours. Recipient H. P. Eddy award for noteworthy research Water Pollution Control Assn., 1961. Mem. Air Pollution Control Assn., Water Pollution Control Fedn., Nat. Solid Waste Mgmt. Assn., Govtl. Refuse Collection Disposal Assn., ASCE, Am. Inst. Chem. Engrs., Am. Inst. Chemistry. Presbyterian. Lodge: Rotary. Subspecialties: Water supply and wastewater treatment; Resource management. Office: 5704 Valverde Suite 2 Houston TX 77057

MYSLINSKI, NORBERT RAYMOND, neuroscientist; b. Buffalo, Apr. 14, 1947; s. Bernard and Amelia Joan M.; m. Patricia Ann Byrne, June 19, 1970 (dec. 1980). B.S. in Biology, Canisius Coll., Buffalo, 1969; Ph.D. in Pharmacology, U. Ill., 1973. Research assoc. dept. pharmacology and biochemistry Tufts U. Sch. Medicine, Boston, 1973-75; asst. prof. dept. pharmacology Sch. Dentistry U. Md., Balt., 1975-80, asso. prof. dept. physiology, 1980—, co-dir. neurosci. program, 1981—; research fellow U. Bristol, Eng., 1984-85; mem. faculty dept. dental aux. Community Coll. Balt., 1980-83; mem. dental com. Md. High Blood Pressure Coordinating Council, 1978-80. Editor: Md. Soc. Med. Research Newsletter, 1977-81; Contbr. articles to profl. jours. USPHS awardee, 1969-73. Mem. Md. Soc. Med. Research (dir. 1978—), Am. Soc. Pharmacology and Exptl. Therapeutics, Brit. Brain Research Assn. (hon. mem.), European Brain and Behavior Soc. (hon. mem.), N.Y. Acad. Scis., Soc. Neurosciences, Am. Assn. Dental Schs., Internat. Assn. Dental Research, Pharm. Mfrs. Assn., Internat. Union Pharmacology, Am. Assn. World Health (mem. U.S. com. for WHO 1979-81), Sigma Xi. Current Work: Neurophysiology of oral-facial function, brain research, pharmacology, neuroscience education. Subspecialties: Neuropharmacology; Neurophysiology. Home: 108 Rockrimmon Rd Reisterstown MD 21136 Office: 666 W Baltimore St Baltimore MD 21201

NA, GEORGE CHAO, research chemist; b. Liao-Ning, China, Mar. 23, 1947; came to U.S., 1970; naturalized, 1979; s. Yu Chun and Shu Fang Na; m. Grace T. Cheng, Oct. 7, 1973. B.S., Tunghai U., Taiwan, 1969; Ph.D., Boston U., 1975. Postdoctoral researcher Brandeis U., Waltham, Mass., 1975-81; research chemist U.S. Dept. Agr., Phila., 1981—. Author: Methods in Enzymology, 1982. Contbr. articles to profl. jours. NIH fellow, 1977-80. Mem. Am. Chem. Soc., Biophys. Soc., N.Y. Acad. Scis. Current work: Physical chemistry of biomacromolecular interaction, protein self associations and interactions with ligands. Subspecialties: Biochemistry (biology); Biophysical chemistry. Office: US Dept Agriculture 600 E Mermaid Ln Philadelphia PA 19118

NABHOLZ, JOSEPH VINCENT, ecologist, biologist; b. Memphis, Tenn., Nov. 3, 1945; s. Martin Peter and Helen Kathleen (Garbacz) N.; m. Sue Ann Winterburn, Aug. 12, 1972; children—Karen Stacey, Pamela Michele. B.S., Christian Bros. Coll., 1968; M.S., U. Ga., 1973, D.Phil., 1978. Sr. biologist EPA, Washington, 1979—; reviewer NSF, profl. jours., 1973—; evaluator Office of Experiential Learning U. Md., College Park, 1984—. Contbg. author, project officer: Methods of Ecological Toxicity, 1981, Testing for Effects of Chemicals on Ecosystems, 1981. Contbr. articles to profl. jours. Bd. dirs. 4th Sect. Community Assn. Rollingwood Village, Woodbridge, Va., 1981—, v.p., 1981-82, pres., 1983—. Served with U.S. Army, 1968-70, Vietnam. Decorated Army Commendation Medal with bronze oak leaf cluster; recipient Spl. Achievement award, Bronze Medal for Commendable Service, EPA. Mem. Ecol. Soc. Am., Internat. Assn. Ecology, AAAS, Assn. So. Biologists, Am. Inst. Biol. Studies, Phi Kappa Phi. Roman Catholic. Current work: Environmental risk assessment of industrial chemicals; development of aquatic and terrestrial microcosms as testing protocols; ecosystem ecology; mineral cycling in terrestrial watershed ecosystems. Subspecialties: Ecology (environmental science); Environmental toxicology. Home: 13627 Bentley Circle Woodbridge VA 22192 Office: EPA (TS-796) 401 M St SW Washington DC 20460

NACE, HAROLD RUSS, chemistry educator; b. Camden, N.J., July 5, 1921; s. Harold Harris and Ruth Lillian (Russ) N.; m. Mary Alice Griffith, June 24, 1944. B.S., Lehigh U., 1943; postgrad Inst. Paper Chemistry, Appleton, Wis., 1943-44; Ph.D., MIT, 1948; M.A. (hon.), Brown U., 1956. Research chemist Merck & Co., Inc., Rahway, N.J., 1944-45, Mayo Clinic, Rochester, Minn., 1949; research chemist DuPont Co., Deepwater, N.J., 1956-57, cons., 1957-60; vis. lectr. U. Wis., Madison, 1960; mem. faculty Brown U., 1948—, assoc. prof. chemistry, 1953-58, prof., 1959—; mem. bd. revision U.S. Pharacopeia, Rockville, Md., 1980—; cons. William S. Merrell Co., Cin., 1960-68, Wyeth Labs., West Chester, Pa., 1968-80. Contbr. articles to profl. jours. Patentee in field. Scoutmaster, Boy Scouts Am., 1952-59; dep. game warden R.I., 1964-69; constable Police Dept., Barrington, R.I., 1970-78. Grantee Research Corp., NSF, NIH, Hartford Found., 1951-75. Fellow Am. Inst. Chemists, N.Y. Acad. Scis.; mem. Am. Chem. Soc., AAAS, Explorers Club, Fedn. Fly Fishers. Congregationalist. Club: University (Providence). Current work: Steroid Chemistry; physical organic chemistry. Subspecialty: Organic chemistry. Home: 28 Chapin Rd Barrington RI 02806 Office: Dept Chemistry Brown U Providence RI 02912

NACHMAN, RONALD JAMES, research chemist; b. Takoma Park, Md., Feb. 1, 1954; s. Joseph Frank and Rosemary (Anderson) N.; m. Lita Rose Wilson, Dec. 18, 1976. B.S. in Chemistry, U. Calif.-San Diego, 1976; Ph.D. in Organic Chemistry, Stanford U., 1981. Research asst. Scripps Inst. Oceanography, La Jolla, Calif., 1974-76; research chemist Western Region Research Center USDA/ARS, Berkeley, Calif., 1981—; vis. scientist Labs. for Neuroendocrinology of Salk Inst., La Jolla, 1985. Contbr. articles to profl. jours. Nat. finalist Westinghouse Sci. Talent Search, 1972; recipient Bausch and Laumb award, 1972; Golden Scroll award Am. Acad. Acheivement, 1972; Western Regional Research Ctr. grantee, 1982. Fellow Jr. Sci. and Humanity Symposia; mem. N.Y. Acad. Sci., Am. Chem. Soc., AAAS, Entomol. Soc. Am., Am. Soc. Pharmacognosy, Am. Soc. Entomology. Current work: Insect neuropeptide synthesis and structure activity; nucleoside chemistry, natural products and synthesis, constituents of poisonous plants. Subspecialties: Organic chemistry; Neurochemistry. Home: 7 Peak Ct Hercules CA 94547 Office: 800 Buchanan St Berkeley CA 94710

NACHREINER, RAYMOND FRANCIS, veterinarian, endocrinologist, educator; b. Richland Center, Wis., Apr. 29, 1942; s. Sylvester Robert and Laura Marie (Reuschlein) N.; m. Mary Lou McMillan, Aug. 30, 1968; children—Sara Lynn, Rachel Jean, John Sebastian. D.V.M., Iowa State U., 1966; M.S., U. Wis., 1970, Ph.D., 1972. Research fellow U. Wis., Madison, 1968-72; asst. prof. Auburn U., Ala., 1972-77; prof. large animal surgery medicine Coll. Vet. Medicine, Mich. State U., East Lansing, 1977—. Served to capt. USAF, 1966-68. Mem. Am. Soc. Animal Sci., AVMA, Endocrine Soc. Republican. Roman Catholic. Current work: Veterinary diagnostic and therapeutic research which modifies and develops procedures valid for use in animals. Subspecialties: Endocrinology; Reproductive endocrinology. Home: 1874 Penobscot Dr Okemos MI 48864Office: Animal Health Diagnostic Lab Mich State U PO Box 30076 Lansing MI 48864

NACHT, SERGIO, biochemist, director biomedical research; b. Buenos Aires, Argentina, Apr. 13, 1934; came to U.S., 1965; s. Oscar and Carmen (Scheiner) N.; m. Beatriz Kahan, Dec. 21, 1958; children—Marcelo H., Gabriel A., Mariana S., Sandra M. B.A. in Chemistry, U. Buenos Aires, 1958, M.S. in Biol. Chemistry, 1960. Ph.D. in Biol. Chemistry, 1964. Asst. prof. biol. chemistry U. Buenos Aires, 1960-64; asst. prof. medicine U. Utah, Salt Lake City, 1965-70; research scientist Alza Corp., Palo Alto, Calif., 1970-73; sr. investigator Richardson-Vicks, Inc., Mt. Vernon, N.Y., 1973-76, asst. dir., dir. invest. research, 1976-83, dir. biomed. research, Shelton, Conn., 1983—; lectr. dermatology dept. SUNY Downstate Med. Ctr., Bklyn., 1977—. Contbr. chpt. to books, articles to sci. publs. (award Soc. Cosmetic Chemists 1981). Mem. Soc. for Investigative Dermatology, Soc. Cosmetic Chemists, Dermatology Found., Am. Physiol. Soc., Am. Acad. Dermatology (affiliate). Democrat. Jewish. Current work: Biochemistry and biophysics of human skin and hair. Subspecialties: Biophysics (biology); Cell biology. Office: Vicks Research Center Richardson-Vicks Inc One Far Mill Crossing Shelton CT 06484

NADEL, NORMAN ALLEN, civil engineering contracting company executive; b. N.Y.C., Apr. 10, 1927; s. Louis and Bertha (Julius) N.; m. Cynthia Jereski, July 6, 1952; children—Nancy Frank, Lawrence. B.S.C.E., CCNY, 1949; postgrad., Columbia U., 1949-50. Registered profl. engr., N.Y., Conn. Engr. Arthur A. Johnson Corp., N.Y.C., 1950-53; project engr. Slattery Contracting Co., N.Y.C., 1953-55; estimator Hartsdale Constrn. Corp., N.Y., 1955-59; mgr. MacLean Grove and Co., Inc., Greenwich, Conn., 1959-66, v.p., 1966-70, pres., 1970—; chmn. U.S. nat. com. tunneling Tech., Washington, 1980-81; U.S. del. Internat. Tunneling Assn., 1980; chmn. Gen. Contractors Assn., N.Y.C., 1974—. Mem. adv. council Pace U., N.Y.C.; trustee Welfare Fund, Tunnel Workers Union, N.Y.C. Served with USNR, 1945-46. Recipient Benjamin Wright award Conn. Soc. Civil Engrs., 1984; named Heavy Constrn. Man of Yr., United Jewish Appeal, 1984. Fellow ASCE; mem. Nat. Acad. Engring., Am. Arbitration Assn., The Moles (pres. 1982, Outstanding Achievement award 1985), Tau Beta Pi, Chi Epsilon. Subspecialty: Civil engineering. Office: MacLean Grove and Co Inc 1 E Putnam Ave Greenwich CT 06830

NADIN, MIHAI, semiotics and computer-aided design educator, consultant; b. Brasov, Romania, Feb. 2, 1938; came to U.S., 1980; s. Lowi and Ana (Catap) Nudelman; m. Elvira Palcsey, Sept. 14, 1971; children: Ari, Esther, Elisabeth. M.S., Poly. Inst., Bucharest, Romania, 1960; M.A., U. Bucharest, 1968, Ph.D., 1972; Dr. phil. habil., U. Munich, W.Ger., 1980. Editor Astra, Brasov, 1965-75; assoc. prof. U. Brasov, 1969-75; researcher Institut de Filosofie, Bucharest, 1976-79; prof. U. Munich, 1978-80, U. Essen, W.Ger., 1979-80; prof. semiotics and design R.I. Sch. Design, 1980-85; Eminent scholar in art and design tech. Advanced Computer Ctr., Ohio State U., 1985—; pres., cons. Nadin & Ockerse, Ltd., Providence, 1981-85. Author: Semiotics of the Energy Crisis, 1981, Zeichen und Wert, 1981; editor: New Elements of the Semiotics of Communication, 1982, Kodikas/Code, 1980. Recipient Richard Merton award U. Braunschweig, Germany, 1977, I. L. Caragiale award Nat. Acad. Romania, 1978. Mem. Assn. Computing Machinery, Semiotic Soc. Am., Deutsche Gesellschaft fur Semiotik. Current Work: New computer models based on fuzzy logic and parallel processing procedures; computer-related activities and artificial-intelligence methods as forms of semiotic practice; information provider systems; design-expert systems. Subspecialties: Semiotics of computer use and applied artificial intelligence; Information systems (Information science). Office: Advanced Computing Ctr 1501 Neil Ave Columbus OH 43201

NADLER, HENRY LOUIS, pediatrician, geneticist; b. N.Y.C., Apr. 15, 1936; s. Herbert and Mary (Kartiganer) N.; m. Benita Weinhard, June 16, 1957; children: Karen, Gary, Debra, Amy. A.B., Colgate U., 1957; M.D., Northwestern U., 1961; M.S., U. Wis., 1965. Diplomate: Am. Bd. Pediatrics, Am. Bd. Med. Genetics. Intern NYU Med. Ctr., 1961-62, sr. resident pediatrics, 1962-63, chief resident, 1963-64; teaching asst. NYU Sch. Medicine, 1962-63, clin. instr., 1963-64, U. Wis. Sch. Medicine, 1964-65; practice medicine specializing in pediatrics, Chgo., 1965—; fellow Children's Meml. Hosp. dept. pediatrics Northwestern U., 1964-65; assoc. in pediatrics Northwestern U. Med. Sch., 1965-66, asst. prof., 1967-68, assoc. prof., 1968-70, prof., 1970-81, chmn. dept. pediatrics, 1970-81; prof. Northwestern U. Med. Sch. (Grad. Sch.), 1971-80; mem. staff Children's Meml. Hosp., 1965-81, head div. genetics, 1969-81, chief of staff, 1970-81; dean, prof. pediatrics Wayne State U. Med. Sch., Detroit, 1981—, also prof. ob-gyn; mem. vis. staff, div. medicine Northwestern Meml. Hosp., 1972-81; staff Children's Hosp. of Mich., 1981—. Editorial bd.: Comprehensive Therapy, 1973-84, Am. Jour. Human Genetics, 1979-83, Pediatrics in Rev, 1980-83, Am. Jour. Diseases of Children, 1983—; contbr. articles to profl. jours. Recipient E. Mead Johnson award for pediatric research, 1973; Irene Heinz Given and John La Porte Given research prof. pediatrics, 1970-81. Fellow Am. Acad. Pediatrics; mem. Am. Soc. for Clin. Investigation, Am. Soc. Human Genetics, Am. Pediatric Soc., Soc. for Pediatric Research, Midwest Soc. for Pediatric Research, Pan Am. Med. Assn., Soc. for Exptl. Biology and Medicine, Alpha Omega Alpha. Subspecialty: Pediatrics. Home: 4669 Maura Ln West Bloomfield MI 48033 Office: Wayne State U Med Sch Scott Hall 540 E Canfield Detroit MI 48201

NAESER, CHARLES WILBUR, geologist, researcher; b. Washington, July 2, 1940; s. Charles R. and Elma (Meyer) N.; m. Barbara Sillcocks, July 13, 1963 (div. 1979); children—Christiana, Robert B.; m. Nancy Dearean Cozad, Feb. 6, 1982. A.B., Dartmouth Coll., 1962; M.A., 1964; Ph.D., So. Methodist U., 1967. Geologist, U.S. Geol. Survey, Menlo Park, Calif., 1967-71, Denver, 1971—. Scout leader Boy Scouts of Am., Denver, 1981, asst. scoutmaster, 1982—. Fellow Geol. Soc. Am.; mem. Am. Geol. Union, Colo. Sci. Soc. (councilor 1982-84). Current work: The use of geochronology (fission track dating) to solve geological problems in areas of tectonics, stratigraphy, mineral exploration and thermal history of sedimentary basins. Subspecialties: Geochronology; Tectonics. Office: US Geol Survey MS 424 Federal Ctr Denver CO 80225

NAESER, MARGARET ANN, neurology and neuroscience researcher; b. Washington, June 22, 1944; d. Charles Rudolph and Elma Mathilda (Meyer) N. B.A., Smith Coll., 1966; Ph.D., U. Wis., 1970; postgrad. UCLA, 1970-71, Calif. State U.-Long Beach, 1971-72; 2-yr. diploma New Eng. Sch. Acupunture, 1983. Cert. clin. competence in speech pathology, Mass.; registered acupuncturist, Mass. Chief speech pathology sect. Martinez VA Hosp., Calif., 1972-74, Palo Alto VA Hosp., Calif., 1974-77; research neurolinguist Boston VA Hosp., 1977—; assoc. research prof. neurology (psycholinguistics) Boston U. Sch. Medicine, 1978—; lectr. neurology Harvard U. Med. Sch., 1980—; clin. research assoc. dept. psychiatry Mass. Gen. Hosp., Boston, 1982—; affiliate asst. prof. psychology Clark U., Worcester, Mass., 1978—; sole practice speech pathology, Menlo Park, Calif., 1975-77; sole practice acupunture for neurol. disorders, Cambridge, Mass., 1983—; cons. in field. Contbr. articles to profl. jours., chpts. to books. Recipient Superior Performance award Martinez VA Hosp., 1973; NDEA Title VI fgn. lang. fellow, 1967; AAUW fellow, 1970-71. Mem. Acad. Aphasia, Linguistic Soc. Am., for Acoustical Soc. Am., Am. Speech, Lang. and Hearing Assn., Soc. for Neurosci., Internat. Neuropsychol. Soc. Club: Smith Coll. Current work: CT scan research in aphasia, Alzheimer's dementia, normal aging; CT scan research in laterality and cerebral dominance and recovery in aphasia; acupunture research in stroke patients with hemiplegia; research exchange with Shanghai First Med. Coll. Subspecialties: Acupuncture research for stroke cases with paralysis; CAT scan. Office: Psychology Research Dept 116-B Boston VA Med Ctr 150 S Huntington Ave Boston MA 02114

NAESER, NANCY DEARIEN, geologist, researcher; b. Morgantown, W.Va., Apr. 15, 1944; d. William Harold and Katherine Elizabeth (Dearien) Cozad; m. Charles Wilbur Naeser, Feb. 6, 1982. Student W.Va. U., 1963; B.S., U. Ariz., 1966; Ph.D., Victoria U., Wellington, N.Z., 1973. Geologic field asst. U.S. Geol. Survey, Flagstaff, Ariz., 1966, postdoctoral research assoc., Denver, 1979-81, geologist, 1980—; research asst. Victoria U., 1973-74; sci. editor N.Z. Dept. Sci. Indsl. Research, Wellington, 1974-76; postdoctoral research assoc. U. Toronto, Ont., Can., 1976-79; research assoc. Dartmouth Coll., Hanover, N.H., 1983—; adj. prof. U. Wyo., Laramie, 1984—. Contbr. articles to profl. jours., chpts. to books on fission track dating and ash flow tuffs, 1975—. Fulbright fellow, 1967-68. Fellow Geol. Soc. Am.; mem. Am. Assn. Petroleum Geologists, Soc. Econ. Paleontologists and Mineralogists, Am. Quaternary Assn., Colo. Sci. Soc. (treas. 1983-84). Republican. Methodist. Current work: Fission-track dating; use of fission-track dating to determine thermal history of sedimentary basins. Subspecialties: Geology; Geochronology. Home: 1000 S Foothill Dr Lakewood CO 80228 Office: US Geological Survey Mail Stop 424 Federal Ctr Denver CO 80225

NAFTOLIN, FREDERICK, physician, reproductive biologist educator; b. Bronx, N.Y., Apr. 7, 1936; s. Nathan and Jean (Pesacov) N.; m. Phyllis Barbara Kaptowsky, July 14, 1957; children: Michael Eugene, Joshua Joseph. A.A., UCLA, 1957; B.A. with honors, U. Calif., Berkeley, 1958; M.D. with honors, U. Calif., San Francisco, 1961; D.Phil., U. Oxford, 1970. Intern King County Hosp., Seattle, 1961-62; resident in ob-gyn UCLA, 1962-66; asst. chief gynecology, endocrine fellow USPHS, Seattle, 1966-68; NIH fellow Oxford (Eng.) U., 1968-70; asst. prof. ob-gyn U. Calif., San Diego Sch. Medicine, 1970-73; assoc. prof. ob-gyn Harvard Med. Sch., 1973-75; prof., chmn. ob-gyn dept. McGill Faculty Medicine, Montreal, 1975-78; prof., chmn. dept. ob-gyn Yale Med. Sch., New Haven, Conn., 1978—; vis. prof. U. Geneva, 1982-83. Author: Subcellular Mechanisms in Reproductive Neuroendocrinology, 1976, Abnormal Fetal Growth, 1978, Clinical Neuroendocrinology, 1979, Dilatation of the Uterine Cervix, 1980; 2-vol. series Basic Reproductive Medicine, Vol. I, Basis of Normal Reproduction, Vol. II, Male Reproduction; Metabolism of Hormonal Steroids in the Neuroendocrine Tissues; Mem. editorial bd.: Psychoneuroendocrinology; Contbr. articles to med. jours. Fogarty internat. fellow, 1982; John Simon Guggenheim fellow, 1983. Mem. Soc. Gynecological Investigation, Endocrine Soc., Internat. Soc. Neuroendocrinology, Internat. Soc. Psychoneuroendocrinology, New Haven Ob-Gyn Soc., Can. Fertility Soc., Am. Soc. Andrology. Subspecialty: Reproductive biology (medicine). Office: Dept Ob-Gyn Yale Med Sch 333 Cedar St New Haven CT 06510

NAG, SUBIR K., radiation oncologist; b. Calcutta, India, Dec. 10, 1951; came to U.S., 1977; s. Sunil K. and Bela R. (Dawn) N.; m. Sima Dutta, Mar. 9, 1982. M.B.B.S., All India Inst. Med. Sci., New Delhi, 1975. Diplomate: Am. Bd. Radiology. Resident in radiotherapy Montefiore Hosp., Bronx, N.Y., 1977-79, chief resident, 1978-79; fellow in radiotherapy Meml. Sloan Kettering Cancer Ctr., N.Y.C., 1980, spl. brachytherapy fellow, 1980-81; asst. prof. radiation oncology U. Tenn. Hosp., Memphis, 1981—, chief radiation oncology, 1983—; staff radiation oncologist City of Memphis Hosp., 1981—; cons. St. Judes Childrens Research Hosp., Memphis, 1982—, VA Med. Ctr., Memphis, 1981—. Contbr. articles to profl. jours. Mem. Am. Soc. Therapeutic Radiologists, Radiol. Soc. N.Am., AMA, Am. Coll. Radiology, Am. Soc. Clin. Oncologist, Radiation Research Soc., Am. Assn. Cancer Edn. Current Work: Enhancement of radiation response by hyperthermia, chemotherapy and radiation sensitisers, clinical brachytherapy. Subspecialties: Oncology; Cancer research (medicine). Home: 5111 Darlington Dr Memphis TN 38118 Office: Dept Radiation Oncology U Tenn Health Sci Ctr 800 Madison Ave Memphis TN 38163

NAGAMATSU, HENRY TAKESHI, aeronautical engineering educator; b. Garden Grove Calif. Dec. 13, 1916; s. Yachiro and Sumiko Nagamatsu; m. Apr. 9, 1942; children—Brian, Nancy. B.S. in Mech. Engring., Calif. Inst. Tech., 1938, B.S. in Aero. Engring., 1939, M.S., 1940, Ph.D., 1949. With Douglas Aircraft Co., Santa Monica, Calif., 1940-42; research engring. cons. Curtiss Wright Aircraft, Buffalo, 1942-44; research engr. Jet Propulsion Lab., Calif. Inst. Tech., Pasadena, 1946-49, sr. research fellow, dir. hypersonic tunnel, 1949-55; prof. aero. engring. Rensselaer Poly. Inst., Troy, N.Y., 1978—; cons. U.S. Naval Ordnance Test Sta., Inyokern, Calif., 1949-52, U.S. Army Watervliet Arsenal, N.Y., 1981—. Author: Aeroacoustics: Jet and Combustion Noise, 1975; Aeroacoustics: Fan, STOL and Boundary Layer Noise, 1975; Aeroacoustics: Jet Noise and Combustion Noise, 1976; Aeroacoustics: Fan Noise and Duct Acoustics, 1976; Aeroacoustics: STOL Noise; Airframe and Airfoil Noise, 1976. Recipient Recognition cert. NASA, 1984. Fellow Am. Phys. Soc., AIAA (aeroacoustics award 1980); mem. N.Y. Acad. Sci., AAAS, Sigma Xi. Current work: Transonic and gas dynamics; hypersonics; plasma, aeroacoustics; transonic airfoil drag reduction; high temperature heat transfer for gas turbines; arcs-in-flow and computational fluid mechanics; hypersonic flow in shock tunnel; aeroacoustics. Subspecialties: Combustion processes; Aerospace engineering and technology. Home: 1046 Cornelius Ave Schenectady NY 12309 Office: Dept Aerospace Engring Rensselaer Poly Inst Troy NY 12180

NAGAR, ARVIND KUMAR, mechanical engineer, researcher, educator; b. Achheja, Ghaziabad, India, July 4, 1939; came to U.S., 1960, naturalized, 1971; s. Kaley Singh and Risalo (Bhati) N.; m. Sampat Dhabhai, June 5, 1971; children: Anil, Sunil, Jayesh. B.S. in Mech. Engring, Okla. State U., 1969; M.M.E., Midwest Coll. Engring., Lombard, Ill., 1978; Ph.D. in Engring., Ohio State U., 1984. Registered profl. engr., Ohio, Ill. Assoc. mech. engr. Xerox Corp., Webster, N.Y., 1969-71; mech. engr. All Steel Inc., Aurora, Ill., 1973-79; research scientist fatigue and fracture projects Battelle Meml. Inst. Labs., Columbus, Ohio, 1979-81; lectr., grad. teaching assoc. engring. mechanics dept. Ohio State U., Columbus, 1980-84; sr. fracture mech. engr. B.F. Goodrich Aerospace & Def. Div., Troy, Ohio, 1985—. Served with U.S. Army, 1966-68. Recipient cert. of merit Toastmasters Internat., 1962. Mem. ASME (paper prize 1962), Pi Tau Sigma, Sigma Pi Sigma. Current Work: Fracture and crack growth of aerospace structures. linear/nonlinear elasticity. Subspecialties: Fracture mechanics; Solid mechanics.

NAGARAJAN, MADUKKARAI KRISHNARAO, physical chemist, industrial research scientist; b. Madras, India, Sept. 17, 1937; came to U.S., 1963; s. Madukkarai Narayanarao and Thangammal Krishnarao; m. Rao Kasturi, May 13, 1964; children—Vasanthi, Arvind. B.Sc., Madras U., 1956; M.Sc., Indian Inst. Sci., Bangalore, 1960; M.Sc., U. Man., Can., 1961, Ph.D., 1963. Postdoctoral fellow U. Pa., 1963-66; lectr. Indian Inst. Tech., Bombay, 1966-68; sr. research scientist Hindustan Lever Ltd., Bombay, 1968-81; postdoctoral fellow Clarkson U., 1981-82; research and devel. assoc. B.F. Goodrich Chem. Div., Avon Lake, Ohio, 1982—; vis. scientist Unilever Research, Port Sunlight, U.K., 1971-72, Vlaardingen, Netherlands, 1971-72; thesis examiner Indian Inst. Tech., Bombay, 1971-77. Contbr. articles to sci. jours. Patentee in field. Scoutmaster, Firelands Area council Black River Dist., Boy Scouts Am., 1984—. NRC of Can. Research grantee, 1962-63, AEC Research grantee, 1963-66. Mem. Am. Chem. Soc., Am. Oil Chemists' Soc. Current work: New raw materials development, product formulation, performance evaluation and definition of the role of hydrophilic polymers in soaps, detergents and specialty cleaning products; basic research in surface and colloid chemistry of hydrophilic polymers in detergent technology. Subspecialties: Surface chemistry; Polymer chemistry. Office: B F Goodrich Tech Ctr Walker & Moore Rds Avon Lake OH 44012

NAGASAWA, HERBERT TSUKASA, medicinal chemist, educator; b. Hilo, Hawaii, May 31, 1927; s. Yasuzo and Chie (Maeda) N.; m. Katherine Chizuko Imahiro, June 30, 1951; children: LLoyd Stuart, Scott Glenn. Student, U Hawaii, 1947-48; B.S., Western Res. U., 1950; Ph.D., U. Minn., 1955. Postdoctoral fellow in biochemistry U. Minn., Mpls., 1955-57, asst. prof. pharm. chemistry, 1959, assoc. prof. medicinal chemistry, 1963-72, prof., 1973—; sr. scientist VA Med. Center Lab. Cancer Research, Mpls., 1961-78; prin. scientist Gen. Med. Research Labs., VA Med. Center, Mpls., 1961—. Assoc. editor: Jour. Medicinal Chemistry, 1972-84, sr. editor, 1985—; contbr. articles to profl. jours. Served with Mil. Intelligence Corps U.S. Army, 1945-47. Mem. Am. Chem. Soc., Am. Soc. Pharmacology and Exptl. therapeutics, Soc. Toxicology, Research Soc. Alcoholism, Am. Assn. Cancer Research, AAAS, N.Y. Acad. Sci., Internat. Soc. Biomed. Research on Alcoholism. Current Work: Design and synthesis of trapping agts. for the detoxication of xenobiotic substances (including ethanol) that are activated to toxic metabolites in vivo and latentiated (prodrug) forms of biologically active substances. Subspecialties: Medicinal chemistry; Organic chemistry. Home: 6223 Harriet Ave S Richfield MN 55423 Office: 54th St and 48th Ave S Bldg 31 Minneapolis MN 55417

NAGEL, DAVID JOSEPH, physicist; b. Aurora, Ill., Feb. 20, 1938; s. Edgar Anthony and Loretta (Lies) N.; m. Carol Ann Koch, May 11, 1963; children: Ann, Paul. B.S., U. Notre Dame, 1960; M.S. in Physics, U. Md., 1969, Ph.D. in Materials Enging, 1977. Tech. liaison officer Naval Research Lab., 1962-64, physicist, 1964-72, sect. head, 1972-80, br. head condensed matter physics, 1980-85, supt. condensed matter and radiation scis. div., 1985—; cons. in field. Contbr. articles to profl. jours. Served with USN, 1960-64; served to capt. USNR, 1964—. Mem. Am. Phys. Soc., Optical Soc. Am., Tau Beta Pi. Current Work: X-ray physics with applications in x-ray lithography, fusion energy research and nuclear weapons effects simulation. Subspecialty: Condensed matter physics. Home: 3273 Rose Glen Ct Falls Church VA 22042 Office: Naval Research Lab Code 6600 Washington DC 20375

NAGEL, DONALD LEWIS, cancer research educator; b. Blue Island, Ill., May 24, 1941; s. Lewis A. and Annette G. (Jaedtke) N.; m. Maria M. Vissat, Aug. 24, 1963; 1 child, Keith Barrett. B.A., Knox Coll., 1967; Ph.D., U. Nebr., 1971. Instr. Eppley Cancer Inst., U. Nebr. Ctr., Omaha, 1971-74, asst. prof., 1974-79, assoc. prof., 1979—. Contbr. articles to profl. jours. Grantee Nat. Cancer Inst., NIH. Mem. Am. Assn. for Cancer Research, Am. Chem. Soc., Sigma Xi. Current work: Mechanisms of activations of chemical carcinogens and applications of nuclear magnetic resonance to biomedical problems. Subspecialties: Nuclear magnetic resonance; Organic chemistry. Home: 1323 S 93rd Ave Omaha NE 68124 Office: Epply Cancer Inst U Nebr Med Ctr Omaha NE 68105

NAGEL, SIDNEY ROBERT, physicist, educator; b. N.Y.C., Sept. 28, 1948; s. Ernest and Edith A. (Haggstrom) N. B.A., Columbia U., 1969; M.A., Princeton U., 1971, Ph.D., 1974. Research assoc. Brown U., Providence, R.I., 1974-76; asst. prof. U. Chgo., Ill., 1976-81, assoc. prof., 1981-84, prof. physics, 1984—. Contbr. articles to profl. jours. Mem. Am. Phys. Soc., AAAS. Current work: Disordered materials; glass transition; electronic and transport properties; molecular dynamics. Subspecialty: Condensed matter physics. Office: U Chgo Dept Physics 5640 S Ellis Ave Chicago IL 60637

NAGURNEY, ANNA BOBIAK, management educator; b. Windsor, Ont., Can.; s. Roman and Iwanna (Jarosz) B.; m. Ladimer Stadner Nagurney, June 18, 1977. A.B., Brown U., 1977, Sc.B., 1977, Sc.M., 1980, Ph.D., 1983. Systems analyst Systems Cons., Inc., Newport, R.I., 1977-79; sr. systems analyst Aquidneck Data Corp., Newport, 1979-80; asst. prof. Sch. Mgmt., U. Mass., Amherst, 1983—. Contbr. articles to profl. jours. Mem. Ops. Research Soc., Inst. Mgmt. Sci., Soc. Indsl. and Applied Math, Am. Math. Soc., Armed Forces and Communications Electronics Assn., Phi Beta Kappa, Sigma Xi. Current work: Competitive network equilibria with applications to economic equilibria, transportation, and communications. Subspecialties: Applied mathematics; Operations research (mathematics). Office: Sch Mgmt U Mass Amherst MA 01003

NAGY, BÉLA FERENC, biochemist; b. Nagybánhegyes, Hungary, May 15, 1926; came to U.S., 1957, naturalized, 1961; s. Béla and Julianna (Frühwirth) N.; m. Barbara Peyser, Jan. 16, 1958 (div. 1974); m. Henryka Urszula Bialkowska, Nov. 13, 1980; children—Andrew, Julianna. Chem. Dipls., Eötvös Loránd U., 1953; Ph.D., Brandeis U., 1964. Research assoc. Rockefeller Inst., N.Y.C., 1957-59, NYU, 1959-60, Inst. for Muscle Diseases, 1960-61; spl. research fellow Brandeis U., Waltham, Mass., 1961-64; research assoc. Retina Found., Boston, 1964-70; staff scientist Boston Biomed. Research Inst., 1970-78; prin. assoc. Harvard Med. Sch., Boston, 1970-78; assoc. prof. neurology, pharmacology and cell biophysics U. Cin., 1978—. Contbr. articles to profl. jours. Nat. Acad. Sci. fellow, 1957-59; NIH fellow, 1959-72; Nat. Research Found. grantee, 1973—. Mem. Am. Chem. Soc., Biochem. Soc. London, Biophys. Soc., Am. Soc. Biol. Chemists, N.Y. Acad. Sci., Soaring Seventh Flying Club (pres. 1984—). Current work: Chemistry and physiology of muscle contraction; chemistry and physical chemistry of proteins; research in molecular basis of muscle diseases. Subspecialties: Biophysics (biology); Biochemistry (medicine). Home: 3580 Epworth Ave Cincinnati OH 45211 Office: U Cin Dept Neurology 231 Bethesda Ave Cincinnati OH 45267

NAGY, DENES, consulting engineer, computer scientist; b. Budapest, Hungary, Oct. 19, 1929; came to U.S., 1957; s. Denes and Margit (Lukacs) N.; m. Margarita Penaherrera, Jan. 13, 1968. B.S.B.A., Hungarian Comml. Inst. Pest, Budapest, 1950; B.S.M.E., Tech. U. Budapest, 1954, M.S.M.E., 1954; postgrad. IBM Corp., Cleve., 1967; cert. GSA/Pub. Bldgs. Service, San Francisco, 1974, Fed. Energy Mgmt. Program., Chgo., 1982. Registered profl. engr., Ind., Ill., Wis., Wash., Calif., Mass., N.Y. Design engr. Gebr. Van Swaay, Mij., The Hague, The Netherlands, 1955-57; project engr. Walter Scholer & Assocs., Inc. Lafayette, Ind., 1957-65, Dalton-Dalton Assocs. Inc., Cleve., 1965-67; pres. Environ. Engring. Corp., Chgo., 1967-72, Marton, Nagy, Tonella & Assocs. Inc., Chgo., 1972-76, Denes Nagy Assocs., Ltd., Chgo., 1976—, MNT Internat., Quito, Ecuador, 1975—; pres. Hungarian Students in N.Am., Boston, 1957-58; lectr. 1st Internat. Congress Constructional Communication, Rotterdam, The Netherlands, 1972. Contbr. articles to Heating Ventilating Air Conditioning Mag. Served to res. capt. ROTC, 1950-54, Hungary. Mem. Am. Cons. Engrs. Council (com. 1972—), Cons. Engrs. Council Ill. (com. 1972—), Nat. Soc. Profl. Engrs., Ill. Soc. Profl. Engrs., Ill. Architect Engr. Council (pres., chmn. com. 1974-79, cert. 1983), Automated Procedures for Engring. Cons., Inc. (trustee, 1 chmn. com. 1967-78, cert. 1973), Assoc. Energy Engrs. (sr. charter, cert. 1984). Roman Catholic. Clubs: U.S. Power Squadron, U.S. Coast Guard Aux., Internat. Visitor Ctr., Council on Fgn. Relations (Chgo.). Current work: Design and construction of large medical, commercial, institutional and industrial projects; algorithms, information systems, storage, retrieval, database systems; distributed systems and networks. Subspecialty: Mechanical engineering. Home: 505 N Lake Shore Dr Apt 2604 Chicago IL 60611 Office: Denes Nagy Assocs Ltd 65 W Division St Chicago IL 60610

NAGY, KENNETH A., biology educator; b. Santa Monica, Calif., July 1, 1943; s. Alex J. and Phyllis F. Nagy; m. Patricia Vaughan, June 11, 1967; children—Mark S., Erik M. A.B. in Biology, U. Calif.-Riverside, 1967, Ph.D. in Biology, 1971. From asst. to prof. biology UCLA, 1971—. Contbr. articles to profl. jours. and chpts. to books. Com. mem. Crescent Bay council Boy Scouts Am., 1982—, merit badge counselor, 1982—. Served with USN, 1962-64. Grad. intern fellow, U. Calif., 1968-71; grantee NSF, 1979—, U.S. Dept. Energy, 1972—. Mem. AAAS, Ecol. Soc. Am., Am. Soc. Ichthyologists and Herpetologists. Current work: Physiological ecology of desert vertebrate animals. Subspecialties: Comparative physiology; Behavioral ecology. Home: 11833 Allaseba Dr Los Angeles CA 90066 Office: Lab Biomed Environ Scis Univ Calif 900 Veteran Ave Los Angeles CA 90024

NAHORY, ROBERT EDWARD, physicist, researcher; b. McKeesport, Pa., Mar. 1, 1938; s. Joseph and Elfrieda A. (Bostak) N.; m. Dawn G. Muse, June 10, 1960; children—Jill C., Douglas B., Robert S. B.S., Carnegie-Mellon U., 1960; M.S., Purdue U., 1962, Ph.D., 1967. Mem. tech. staff Bell Labs., Holmdel, N.J., 1967-82, supr., 1982-84, dist. mgr. Bell Communications Research, Murray Hill, N.J., 1984—; vis. scientist CNET, Paris, 1980. Contbr. articles to profl. jours. Patentee in field. Youth leader Lincroft Presbyterian Ch., (N.J.), 1971-76. Mem. Am. Phys. Soc., IEEE. Current work: Condensed matter physics; optical properties of semiconductors; growth of new epitaxial semiconductor materials and structures; design/fabrication of optoelectronic devices. Subspecialties: Condensed matter physics; Semiconductor lasers. Home: 30 Brae Burn Dr Lincroft NJ 07738 Office: Bell Communications Research 600 Mountain Murray Hill NJ 07974

NAHOUM, HENRY ISAAC, denistry educator, orthodontist; b. N.Y.C., Sept. 9, 1919; s. Isaac Joseph and Rebecca (Hasson) N.; m. Lillian deSoto, Mar. 28, 1948; 1 dau., Bonita. A.B., Bklyn. Coll., 1940; D.D.S., Columbia U., 1943. Diplomate: Am. Bd. Orthodontics.; cert. orthodontics, 1952. Research asst. Columbia U., N.Y.C., 1947-56, instr., 1957-60, asst. clin. prof., 1960-63, assoc. clin. prof., 1963-69, assoc. prof., 1969-75, prof. denistry, 1975—; attending dental surgeon Presbyn. Hosp., N.Y.C., 1969—. Bd. dirs. Sephardic Jewish Ctr., N.Y.C., 1965—. Served to capt. AUS, 1944-46, ETO. Named Alumnus of Yr. Columbia Orthodontic Alumni, 1980. Fellow Am. coll. Dentists (chmn. N.Y. sect. 1981), N.Y. Acad. Dentistry; mem. ADA, Am. Assn. Orthodontists, Sigma Xi, Omicron Kappa Upsilon. Inventor vacuum, forming dental appliances, 1959. Current Work: Research on open-bite malocclusion, appliance designs, practice orthodontics. Subspecialties: Orthodontics; Dental growth and development. Office: 785 Park Ave New York NY 10021

NAHRWOLD, DAVID LANGE, surgeon, educator; b. St. Louis, Dec. 21, 1935; s. Elmer William and Magdalen Louise (Lange) N.; m. Carolyn Louise Hoffman, June 14, 1958; children: Stephen Michael, Susan Alane, Thomas James, Anne Elizabeth. A.B., Ind. U., 1957, M.D., 1960. Diplomate: Am. Bd. Surgery, Am. Bd. Thoracic Surgery. Intern, then resident in surgery Ind. U. Med. Center, Indpls., 1960-65; postdoctoral scholar in gastrointestinal physiology VA Center, UCLA, 1965; asst. prof. surgery Ind. U. Med. Sch., 1968-70; assoc. prof. Pa. State U. Coll. Medicine, 1970-73, vice chmn. dept. surgery, 1971-82, assoc. provost, dean health affairs, 1981-82; prof. surgery, chief div. gen. surgery Milton S. Hershey Med. Center, 1974-82; Loyal and Edith Davis prof. surgery, chmn. dept. surgery Northwestern U. Med. Sch., Chgo., 1982—; surgeon-in-chief Northwestern Meml. Hosp., Chgo., 1982—. Author articles, abstracts in field, chpts. in books. Served with M.C. U.S. Army, 1966-68. Fellow ACS; mem. Am. Fedn. Clin. Research, Am. Gastroent. Assn., AMA, Am. Physiol. Soc. (asso.), Am. Surg. Assn., Assn. Acad. Surgery, Central Surg. Assn., Chgo. Med. Soc., Midwest Gut Club, Ill. State Med. Soc., Ill. Surg. Soc., Soc. Clin. Surgery, Soc. Surgery of Alimentary Tract, Soc. Univ. Surgeons, others. Current Work: Surgical educator and administratior. Gastrointestinal surgery and research. Subspecialty: Surgery. Office: Northwestern U Med Sch Dept Surgery 250 E Superior St Suite 201 Chicago IL 60611

NAIDES, STANLEY JAY, immunologist; b. Phila., Dec. 17, 1951; s. Abraham and Pauline (Fineman) N. A.B., Princeton U., 1974; M.D., Hahnemann U., 1978. Diplomate Am. Bd. Internal Medicine, Rheumatology. Intern, U. Miami, Fla., 1978-79; resident Temple U., Phila., 1979-81; fellow in rheumatology U. Calif.-San Diego, 1981-83; fellow in immunology Harvard U., Boston, 1983—. Mem. ACP, Am. Rheumatism Assn., Am. Assn. Immunology (assoc.), Phila. Rheumatism Assn. Current work: Autoimmune disease; immunoregulation research. Subspecialties: Rheumatology; Internal medicine. Office: Harvard Med Sch Dept Pathology 25 Shattuck St Boston MA 02115

NAIR, CHANDRA KUNJU, medical educator; b. Trichur, India, May 20, 1944; came to U.S., 1973; s. Kunju and Narayani (Pillai) N.; m. Nigar Sultana, June 19, 1976; children: Nisha, Reshma, Tanya. B.S., Bombay U., 1964, M.D., 1972; M.B.B.S., Armed Forces-India Med. Coll., 1968. Diplomate: , Am. Bd. Internal Medicine & Cardiology. Resident in internal medicine Bombay U. Hosp., 1969-70, registrar in cardiology, 1970-73; intern in internal medicine Med. Coll. of Ohio Hosp., Toledo, 1973-74, chief resident, 1975; cardiology fellow Creighton U. Hosp., Omaha, 1976-78, asst. prof. medicine, 1978-85, assoc. prof., 1985—. Contbr. articles in field to profl. jours. Fellow Am. Coll. Cardiology, ACP, Am. Heart Assn., Am. Coll. Chest Physicians; mem. Am. Fedn. Clin. Research, Midwest Clin. Soc., Cardiovascular Soc. Omaha, Met. Omaha Med. Soc., Am. Soc. Internal Medicine, Am. Inst. Ultrasound in Medicine. Current Work: Coronary heart disease; valvular heart disease. Subspecialty: Cardiology. Home: 9929 Devonshire Omaha NE 68132 Office: Creighton Cardiac Ctr 601 N 30th St Omaha NE 68132

NAIR, PANKAJAM K(ARUNAKARAN), biomedical engineering researcher, consultant; b. Changanachery, Kerala, India, Oct. 27, 1930; came to U.S., 1961, naturalized, 1980; d. Narayana and Devaki Pillai; m. Karunakaran A. Nair, Apr. 23, 1956; children—Meenakshikutty, Sankar. B.Sc., U. Madras, India, 1951, M.A., 1953; Ph.D., U. Iowa, 1964. Lectr., Skanda Varodaya Coll., Jaffna, Ceylon, 1955-57; teaching and research asst. U. Iowa, Iowa City, 1961-64, research assoc., 1964-67; research scientist St. Vincent Charity Hosp., Cleve., 1967-80; dir. cardiovascular research Cleve. Research Inst., 1980-83; sr. research scientist La. Tech., U., Ruston, 1983—; cons. to univs, 1980—; mem. peer rev. com. NIH, 1984. Contbr. chpt., articles to profl. publs., 1965—. NIH grantee, 1970—. Mem. Am. Physiol. Soc., Soc. Exptl. Biology and Medicine, Internat. Soc. Oxygen Transport to Tissue, Alumni Assn. U. Iowa (life), Sigma Xi. Subspecialties: Physiology (medicine); Neurophysiology. Home: PO Box 1115 Ruston LA 71273 Office: La Tech U Dept Biomed Engring PO Box 10348 Tech Sta Ruston LA 71272

NAITO, HERBERT K., clinical biochemist; b. Honolulu, Nov. 25, 1942; s. Yukio and Elsie T. (Sasamoto) N.; m. Jane Katherine Hershire, June 4, 1970 (div. 1974). B.A., U. No. Colo., 1963, M.A., 1965; Ph.D., Iowa State U., 1971. Cert. clin. chemist Am. Bd. Clin. Chemistry. Postdoctoral fellow Am. Heart Assn., Cleve. Clinic Found., 1971-73, head sect. lipids, nutrition and metabolic disease dept. biochemistry, div. lab. medicine, 1973—, sr. staff div. research, 1973-81; adj. asst. prof. dept. chemistry Cleve. State U., 1973-75, clin. asst. prof., 1975-77, clin. assoc. prof., 1977-80, clin. prof., 1980—; cons., lectr. in field. Editor: Detection and Treatment of Lipid and Lipoprotein Disorders and Childhood, 1985; Handbook of Electrophoresis, vol. IV, 1983; Nutritional Elements and Clinical Biochemistry, 1980; Nutrition and Heart Disease, 1982. Contbr. chpts. to books, articles to profl. jours. Mem. editorial bd.: Jour. Am. Coll. Nutrition; Atherogenesis; Clin. Physiology and Biochemistry; Trace Elements in Medicine; Selected Methods of Clinical Chemistry; Clinical Chemistry. Recipient Am. Assn. Clin. Chemistry Young Investigator award, 1977; George Grannis award Nat. Acad. Clin. Biochemistry, 1981. Fellow Assn. Clin. Scientists, Nat. Acad. Clin. Biochemistry (bd. dirs.), Am. Coll. Nutrition (council on nutrition and cardiovascular disease, bd. dirs.), Council on Atherosclerosis; mem. AAAS, Am. Heart Assn., Am. Chem. Soc., Am. Oil Chemists' Soc., Am. Assn. Clin. Chemistry (bd. dirs.), Am. Soc. Clin. Pathologists (assoc.), Soc. Exptl. Biology and Medicine, Am. Inst. Nutrition, Am. Assn. Exptl. Pathologists, Endocrine Soc., Sigma Xi, Lambda Sigma Tau, Phi Delta Kappa, Phi Kappa Phi. Current work: Cardiovascular and lipoprotein research. Subspecialties: Clinical chemistry; Health services research. Home: 3335 S Green Rd Beachwood OH 44122 Office: Dept Biochemistry Div Lab Medicine Cleve Clinic Found 9500 Euclid Ave Cleveland OH 44106

NAJARIAN, JOHN SARKIS, surgeon; educator; b. Oakland, Calif., Dec. 22, 1927; s. Garabed L. and Siranoush (Demirjian) N.; m. Arlys Viola Mignette Anderson, Apr. 27, 1952; children—Jon, David, Paul, Peter. A.B. with honors, U. Calif. Berkeley, 1948; M.D., U. Calif.-San Francisco, 1952; D.Sc. (hon.), Gustavus Adolphus Coll., 1981, L.H.D., Calif. Luth. Coll., 1983. Diplomate: Am. Bd. Surgery. Surg. intern U. Calif.-San Francisco, 1952-53, surg. resident, 1955-60, asst. prof. surgery, dir. surg. research labs., chief transplant service dept. surgery, 1963-66, prof., vice chmn., 1966-67; spl. research fellow in immunopathology U. Pitts. Med. Sch., 1960-61; NIH sr. fellow and asso. in tissue transplantation immunology Scripps Clinic and Research Found., La Jolla, Calif., 1961-63; prof., chmn. dept. surgery U. Minn. Hosp., Mpls., 1967—, chief hosp. staff, 1970; Spl. cons. USPHS, NIH Clin. Research Tng. Com., Inst. Gen. Med. Scis., 1965-69; cons. U.S. Bur. Budget, 1966-68; mem. sci. adv. bd. Nat. Kidney Found., 1968—; mem. surgery study sect. A div. research grants NIH, 1970—; chmn. renal transplant adv. group VA Hosps., 1971; mem. bd. sci. cons. Sloan-Kettering Inst. Cancer Research, 1971-78; mem. screening com. Dernham Postdoctoral Fellowships in Oncology, Calif. div. Am. Cancer Soc. Editor: (with Richard L. Simmons) Transplantation, 1971; editoral bd.; Jour. Surg. Research, 1968—, Minn. Medicine, 1968—, Jour. Surg. Oncology, 1968—, Am. Jour. Surgery, 1967-82; assoc. editor, 1982—; editoral bd.; Year Book of Surgery, 1970—, Transplantation, 1970, Transplantation Procs, 1970, Annals of Surgery, 1972—, World Jour. Surgery, 1976—; assoc. editor: Surgery, 1971. Bd. dirs., v.p. Variety Club Heart Hosp., U. Minn.; trustee, v.p. Minn. Med. Found. Served with USAF, 1953-55. Recipient award Calif. Trudeau Soc., 1962; named Alumnus of Yr. U. Calif.

Med. Sch. at San Francisco, 1977; recipient Ann. Brotherhood award NCCJ, 1978; Disting. Achievement award Modern Medicine, 1978; Disting. Achievement award Internat. Gt. Am. award B'nai B'rith Found., 1982; Markle scholar in acad. medicine, 1964-69. Fellow ACS; mem. Soc. Univ. Surgeons, Soc. Exptl. Biology and Medicine, AAAS, Am. Soc. Exptl. Pathology, Am. Surg. Assn., Am. Assn. Immunologists, AMA, Transplantation Soc., Am. Soc. Nephrology, Internat. Soc. Nephrology, Am. Assn. Lab. Animal Sci., Assn. Acad. Surgery (pres. 1969), Internat Soc. Surgery, Soc. Surg. Chairmen, Soc. Clin. Surgery, Central Surg. Assn., Minn., Hennepin County med. socs., Mpls., St. Paul, Minn., Howard C. Naffziger, Portland, Halsted surg. socs., Am. Heart Assn., Am. Soc. Transplant Surgeons (pres. 1977-78), Council on Kidney in Cardiovascular Disease, Hagfish Soc., Italian Research Soc., Minn. Acad. Medicine, Minn. Med. Assn., Minn. Med. Found., Surg. Biology Club, Sigma Xi, Alpha Omega Alpha, others. Subspecialty: Transplant surgery. Office: U Minn Health Sci Center Mayo Meml Bldg Box 195 Minneapolis MN 55455

NAJJAR, VICTOR ASSAD, physician, biochemist; b. Zalka, Lebanon, Apr. 15, 1914; came to U.S., 1938; s. Assad Maroun and Hala Assad (Ashkar) N.; children—Jennifer, Julie, Victor M. M.D., Am. U. of Beirut, Lebanon, 1935. Intern, Am. U. Beirut, Lebanon, 1936-38; resident Johns Hopkins U., Balt., 1938-44, asst. prof., dir. outpatient dept., 1944-46, assoc. prof., 1949-57; fellow NRC, Washington U., St. Louis, 1946-48, Cambridge U., Eng., 1948-49; prof., chmn. dept. microbiology Vanderbilt U. Sch. Medicine, 1957-68; chmn. protein chemistry, prof. molecular biology Am. Cancer Soc. and prof. pediatrics Tufts U. Med. Sch., Boston, 1968—. Editor: Molecular Cellular Biochemistry Jour., 1972-83; patentee Tuftsin, Tuftsinyltuftsin. Bd. govs. St. Jude Hosp., Mem. bd. govs. St. Jude Hosp., Memphis, 1968-84, bd. dirs. ALSAC, St. Jude Children's Research Hosp., Memphis, 1968-84, also mem. exec. com., 1970-84; mem. sci. group on Bilharziasis WHO, 1962. Recipient Meade Johnson award, 1951; Am. U. Beirut Gold medal award for Disting. Alumnus, 1956; Fulbright Hays award, 1976. Mem. Am. Pediatric Research, Am. Soc. Biol. Chemists, Am. Soc. Clin. Investigation, Alpha Omega Alpha. Christian. Current work: Mechanism of enzyme action and biologically active peptides. Subspecialties: Biochemistry (medicine); Pediatrics. Office: Tufts U Sch Medicine 136 Harrison Ave Boston MA 02111

NAKADA, YOSHINAO, physicist; b. Osaka, Japan, Apr. 5, 1934; came to U.S., 1950; s. Peter Nobunao and Masuko (Watanabe) N.; m. Anna Kazuko Kaku, June 14, 1959; children—Marian Tomoko, Peter Kazunao, Paul Takenao. A.B., Harvard U., 1958, M.S., 1959, Ph.D., 1963. Scientist, RCA Co., Needham, Mass., 1959-60; research fellow Harvard U., Cambridge, Mass., 1963-64; scientist U.S. Steel Co., Monroeville, Pa., 1964-68; mem. tech. staff Bell Labs., Allentown, Pa., 1968-82, supr., 1982—. Contbr. articles on materials sci. to profl. publs. Bd. dirs. Allentown YMCA, 1982-85. Mem. AAAS, Internat. Soc. Hybrid Microelectronics. Current work: Reliability of microchip devices; study of electronic materials; thick and thin film technologies. Subspecialties: Microchip technology (engineering); Electronic materials. Office: AT&T Bell Labs 555 Union Blvd Allentown PA 18103

NAKAJIMA, NOBUYUKI, polymer engineering educator; b. Tokyo, Nov. 3, 1923; came to U.S., 1951, naturalized, 1973; s. Kiyosh and Tomi (Tamura) N.; m. Ann McCollister, Sept. 13, 1958 (div. 1973); children—Charles, Leslie, Eric. B.S. in Chem. Engring., Tokyo U., Japan., 1945; student Goshen Coll., 1953; M.S., Poly. Inst. Bklyn., 1955; Ph.D., Case Inst. Tech., 1958. Research assoc. Case Inst. Tech., 1958-60, W.R. Grace Research Div., Clarksville, Md., 1960-62; sect. leader W.R. Grace Polymer Chem., Clifton, N.J., 1962-65; mgr. research Allied Chem. Plastics, Morristown, N.J., 1965-71; research and devel. fellow B.F. Goodrich Co., Avon Lake, Ohio, 1971-84; prof. polymer engring. U. Akron, Ohio, 1984—. Assoc. editor Rubber Chem. Tech. Jour., 1973—. Contbr. articles to profl. jours. Mem. Am. Chem. Soc., Am. Phys. Soc., Soc. of Rheology, Japanese Polymer Soc., Sigma Xi. Current work: Polymer processing; polymer structure-property relation; viscoelastic properties of polymeric substances. Subspecialties: Polymer engineering; Polymers (materials science). Office: Polymer Engring Ctr U Akron Akron OH 44325

NAKAMOTO, TETSUO, dentist, nutritionist; b. Kure, Hiroshima, Japan, Dec. 20, 1939; came to U.S., 1964; s. Takamori and Masae (Nakamuta) N.; m. Lynda G. Ward, May 14, 1980; children—Andrew Takamori, Christopher Ward Takamori. D.D.S., Nihon U., Tokyo, 1964; M.S., U. Mich., 1966, 71, U. N.D., 1968; Ph.D., MIT, 1978. Diplomate: Japanese Nat. Dental Bd. Research asst. U. N.D., 1968-69; asst. prof. physiology La. State U. Med. Ctr., New Orleans, 1978-84, assoc. prof., 1984—. NIH fellow, 1969-72, 72-78; U. N.D. fellow, 1967-68. Mem. Internat. Assn. Dental Research, Soc. Exptl. Biology and Medicine, Am. Inst. Nutrition, Am. Physiol. Soc., N.Y. Acad. Sci., Sigma Xi. Roman Catholic. Current Work: Bone and tooth growth and development in neonates. Infant nutrition and physiology. Subspecialties: Dental growth and development; Nutrition (medicine). Office: La State U Med Center 1100 Florida Ave New Orleans LA 70019

NAKANISHI, KOJI, chemistry educator, bioorganic institute executive; b. Hong Kong, May 11, 1925; came to U.S., 1969; s. Yuzo and Yoshiko (Sakata) N.; m. Yasuko Abe, Oct. 5, 1947; children: Kay, Jun. B.Sc., Nagoya U., 1947, Ph.D., 1954. Asst. prof. Nagoya U., 1955-58; prof. Tokyo Kyoiku U., 1958-63, Tohoku U., Sendai, Japan, 1963-69; Prof. Columbia U., N.Y.C., 1969-80, Centennial prof., 1980—; dir. research Internat. Ctr. Insect Physiology and Ecology, Nairobi, Kenya, 1969-80; dir. Suntory Inst. Bioorganic Research, Osaka, Japan, 1979—. Author: Infra-red Spectroscopy—Practical, 1962, Circular Dichroic Spectroscopy—Exciton Coupling in Organic Stereochemistry, 1983; author/editor: Natural Products Chemistry, vol. I, 1974, vol. II, 1975, vol. III, 1983; contbr. over 420 articles to profl. jours. Recipient Asahi Press Cultural award, 1968; E.E. Smissman medal U. Kans., 1979; H.C. Urey award Lambda Upsilon, Columbia U., 1980; Alcon award, 1985; Research award Am. Soc. Pharmacognosy, 1985. Mem. Japan Chem. Soc. (Pure Chemistry award 1954, Chemistry award 1979), Am. Chem. Soc. (E. Guenther award 1978, Remsen award 1981), Brit. Chem. Soc. (Centenary medal 1979), AAAS. Current Work: Isolation, structure determination and studies of biologically active naturally occurring compounds (bioactive natural products); bioorganic studies of visual pigments and bacteriorhodopsin; applications of spectroscopy in structure determinations at sub-mg levels. Subspecialty: Organic chemistry. Home: 560 Riverside Dr New York NY 10027 Office: Dept Chemistry Columbia U W 116th and Broadway New York NY 10027

NAKATANI, ROY EIJI, fisheries biologist; b. Seattle, June 8, 1918; s. Ushinosuke and Fuku (Matsuda) N.; m. Harue Okihara, May 28, 1955; children—Ronald L., Dale E., Scott M., Mika Lynn, Mark I. B.S. cum laude, U. Wash., 1947, Ph.D., 1960. Biol. scientist Fisheries Research Inst., U. Wash., Seattle, 1947-48, research assoc. Coll. Fisheries, 1954-59, asst. dir. Fisheries Research Inst., U. Wash., 1970-73, prof., assoc. dir., 1973—; mgr. aquatic biology Gen. Electric Co., Richland, Wash., 1959-66; mgr. ecology Battelle Northwest, Richland, 1966-70. Fishery cons. Westinghouse, 1970-71, Puget Power & Light, 1970-76, Cenralia City Light, Wash., 1976—. Served with AUS, 1941-46. Fellow AAAS; mem. Am. Inst. Fishery Research Biologists, Internat. Acad. Fishery Scientists, Am. Fisheries Soc., Sigma Xi. Water pollution biology, Pacific salmon biology, oil pollution. Subspecialties: Resource management; Environmental toxicology. Home: 6719 152d Ave NE Redmond VA 98052 Office: Fisheries Research Int U Wash Seattle WA 98195

NAKOS, JAMES THOMAS, mechanical engineer, researcher; b. Bridgeport, Conn., May 14, 1950; s. John and Florence (Lange) N.; m. Diane Griego, June 6, 1979. B.S. in Physics, N.Mex. Inst. Tech., 1973, M.S. in Mech. Engring., 1977. Registered profl. engr., N.Mex. Grad. asst. N.Mex. Inst. Tech., Socorro, 1971; draftsman Bridgers & Paxton, Cons. Engrs., Albuquerque, 1973-75; grad. asst. U. N.Mex., Albuquerque, 1975-77; staff mem. Sandia Nat. Labs., Albuquerque, 1978—. Contbr. articles to tech. jours. Mem. ASME, ASHRAE. Current work: High temperature high heat flux testing of various materials and of solar receiver designs. Testing of components in explosively driven shock tubes. Subspecialties: Mechanical engineering; Non-destructive testing. Office: Sandia Nat Lab Div 7533 PO Box 5800 Albuquerque NM 87185

NALAMWAR, ASHOK LAXMANRAO, semiconductor technologist; b. Wardha, India, July 24, 1946; came to U.S., 1969, naturalized, 1984; s. Laxmanrao M. and Parvatibai (Gangamwar) N.; m. Pushpa A. Duddalwar, Feb. 5, 1973; children—Omkar, Anagha. B.S., IIT, Bombay, 1969; M.S., Northwestern U., 1971, Ph.D., 1975. Prin. engr. Microswitch Honeywell, Freeport, Ill., 1976-78; mem. research staff Fairchild, Palo Alto, Calif., 1978-82; mgr. Gould AMI, Santa Clara, Calif., 1982—. Contbr. articles to profl. jours. Patentee in field. Mem. IEEE. Current work: Photolithography including dry etch technology for VLSI integrated circuits; process integration for CMOS devices. Subspecialties: Microchip technology (engineering); Integrated circuits. Home: 645 Singley Dr Milpitas CA 95035

NALCIOGLU, ORHAN, educator; b. Istanbul, Feb. 2, 1944; came to U.S., 1966, naturalized, 1974; s. Mustafa and Meliha N. B.S., Robert Coll., Istanbul, 1966; M.S., Case Western Res. U., 1968; Ph.D., U. Ore., 1970. Postdoctoral fellow dept. physics U. Calif.-Davis, 1970-71; Research assoc. dept. physics U. Rochester, N.Y., 1971-74; Research assocs. dept. physics U. Wis., Madison, 1974-76; sr. physicist EMI Med. Inc., Northbrook, Ill., 1976-77; assoc. prof. depts. radiol. scis., elec. engring. and medicine U. Calif.-Irvine, 1977—; cons. UN, 1980-81. Contbr. articles to profl. jours. Mobil scholar, 1961-66. Mem. Am. Phys. Soc., Am. Assn. Physicists in Medicine, IEEE. Democrat. Current Work: Digital radiography, nuclear magnetic resonance imaging; research in image science with applications in medical imaging. Subspecialty: Medical physics. Office: Dept Radiol Sci Univ Calif Irvine CA 92717

NAM, SANG BOO, physicist; b. Kyung-Nam, Korea, Jan. 30, 1936; came to U.S., 1959, naturalized, 1979; s. Sae Hi and Boon Hi (Kim) N.; m. Wonki Kim, June 1, 1969; children: Saewoo, Jean Ok. B.S., Seoul Nat. U., 1958; M.S., U. Ill.-Urbana, 1961, Ph.D., 1966. Vis. prof. Seoul Nat. U., 1970; asst. prof. U. Va., Charlottesville, 1968-71; vis. assoc. prof. Belfer Grad. Sch. Sci. Yeshiva U., N.Y.C., 1971-74; sr. fellow Nat. Acad. Scis.-NRC, 1974-76; research prof. U. Dayton (Ohio), 1976-80; sr. research physicist U. Research Center, Wright State U., Dayton, 1980—. Contbr. articles to profl. jours. Served with Korean Army, 1958-59. Ministry Edn. Korea nat. fellow, 1955-58; U. Ill. fellow, 1959-60. Fellow Am. Phys. Soc.; mem. AAAS, N.Y. Acad. Scis., Sigma Xi. Current Work: Low temperature physics, superconductivity, semiconductor physics, phase transition. Subspecialties: Condensed matter physics; Theoretical physics. Home: 7735 Peters Pike Dayton OH 45414

NAMKOONG, GENE, geneticist, researcher; b. N.Y.C., Jan. 25, 1934; s. David Yum and Joan (Wooh) N.; m. Carol Rosenkrance, Aug. 15, 1958; children—Barbara Jean, Gene David, Melanie Ann. B.S. in Forestry, SUNY-Syracuse, 1956, M.S. in Forestry, 1958; Ph.D. in Genetics, N.C. State U., 1963. Research forester U.S. Dept. Agr. Forest Service, Gulfport, Miss., 1958-60; geneticist U.S. Dept. Agr. Forest Service, Raleigh, N.C., 1963-72, pioneer research geneticist, 1972—; sci. policy advisor State of N.C., Raleigh, 1977-78; prof. biomath. faculty N.C. State U., Raleigh, 1984—, prof. genetics and forestry, 1972—; vis. prof. U. Chgo., 1969-70, Oxford U., Eng., 1979—; cons. in field. Author: Introduction to Quantitative Genetics in Forestry, 1978; (with others) A Philosophy of Breeding Strategy for Tropical Forest Trees, 1980; also articles. Editor Jour. Silvae Genetica. Pres., Rich Park Housing Corp., Raleigh, 1967-71; mem. Raleigh Community Relation Commn., 1973-75, N.C. gov.'s. Task Force on Small Woodlot Mgmt., Raleigh, 1978, N.C. Gov's. Planning Com. on Sch. for Sci. and Math., Raleigh, 1978. Recipient Disting. and Meritorious Service award Gov. of N.C., 1978; Disting. Service award U.S. Dept. Agr., 1979; sr. U.S. Sci. award von-Humboldt-Stiftung, 1983. NSF fellow. Mem. Internat. Union Forestry Research Orgns. (co-chmn. genetic working group 1967-71, leader genetics sect. 1977-82, sci. achievement 1972), Soc. Am. Foresters, Genetics Soc. Am., Sigma Xi (N.C. State U. exec. com. 1976-82). Population genetics of forest communities and quantitative genetics of forest tree breeding. Subspecialties: Plant genetics; Population biology. Home: 811 Beaver Dam Rd Raleigh NC 27607 Office: North Carolina State Univ Genetics Dept Box 7614 Raleigh NC 27695

NAMKUNG, WON, plasma physicist; b. Mokpo, Korea, Oct. 13, 1943; came to U.S., 1971; s. Hyung and Namchul (Kim) N.; m. Cookie Whang, Dec. 27, 1969; children—Ju, Young-Nan. B.S. in Physics, Seoul Nat. U. (Korea), 1965; Ph.D. in Physics, U. Tenn., 1977. Research assoc. U. Tenn.-Knoxville, 1978, U. Md., College Park, 1978-80, asst. prof., 1980-84; research physicist Naval Surface Weapons Ctr., White Oak, Md., 1984—. Contbr. articles to profl. jours. Dept. Energy grantee, 1982—; Air Force Office Sci. Research grantee, 1981-84. Mem. Am. Phys. Soc., IEEE. Roman Catholic. Current work: Microwave generation, particle beam physics, RF plasma heating, pulsed power engineering, accelerator physics. Subspecialties: Plasma physics; Electrical engineering. Home: 8601 Briarwood Ct Laurel MD 20708 Office: Code R43 Naval Surface Weapons Ctr White Oak MD 20910

NAMY, JEROME N., geologist; b. Cleve., Aug. 11, 1938; s. Nicholas and Della (Lynch) N.; m. Susan J. Milstead, July 6, 1963; children—David, Stephen, Catherine. B.A., Western Res. U., 1960; Ph.D., U. Tex., 1967. Petroleum geologist Pan Am. Petroleum, Fort Worth, 1967-70; asst. then assoc. prof. Baylor U., Waco, Tex., 1970-78; petroleum geologist Texland Petroleum, Fort Worth, 1978—; cons. Gen. Crude Oil, Houston, 1976-78, Tri Control, Houston, 1976, Texland, Fort Worth, 1974. Contbr. articles to profl. jours. Mem. Geol. Soc. Am., Am. Assn. Petroleum Geologists, Soc. Exploration Geophysicists, Soc. Econ. Paleontologists and Minerologists; Sigma Xi. Republican. Lutheran. Current work: Petrology; stratigraphy; hydrocarbon exploration. Subspecialty: Geology. Home: 8956 Random Rd Fort Worth TX 76179Office: 3402 Texas Am Bldg Fort Worth TX 76102

NANCE, RICHARD DAMIAN, geologist, educator; b. St. Ives, Cornwall, Eng., Oct. 25, 1951; came to U.S., 1980; s. Richard William Morton and Edith Eleanor (Leach) N.; m. Rita Felice Carpenter, Aug. 28, 1982; 1 son, Andre Bernard Carpenter. B.Sc. with honours, U. Leicester, Eng., 1972; Ph.D., U. Cambridge, Eng., 1978. Asst. prof. geology St. Francis Xavier U., Antigonish, N.S., Can., 1976-80; cons. geologist La. State U., Baton Rouge, 1978-81; assoc. prof. geology Ohio U., Athens, 1980—; sr. research geologist Exxon Prodn. Research Co., Houston, 1982—; cons. Radwaste Program, Dept. Energy, 1978-81. Contbr. articles to profl. jours. Natural Environment Research Council grantee, 1972-76; St. Francis Xavier U. Council for Research grantee, 1977-79; Natural Sci. and Engring. Research Council of Can. grantee, 1980; N.S. Geosci. Research Council grantee, 1981; Ohio U. Research Council grantee, 1981-82. Fellow Geol. Assn. Can.; mem. Geol. Soc. Am., Am. Geophys. Union, Sask. Geol. Soc., Ussher Soc. Eng., Royal Geol. Soc. Cornwall. Current Work: Episodicity in plate tectonics and its control of eustatic sea level; structural style and hydrocarbon traps in petroleum provinces; tectonic evolution of the Avalon zone of the Appalachians in southern New Brunswick. Subspecialties: Tectonics; Sea floor spreading. Home: 6555 Harbor Town Dr Apt 917 Houston TX 77036 Office: Exxon Production Research Co ST4112 PO Box 2189 Houston TX 77001

NANDI, JYOTIRMOY, biochemist, researcher; b. Howrah, West Bengal, India, May 12, 1949; came to U.S., 1979; s. Satya Charan and Gurupriya (Sett) N.; m. Bandana Pal, Aug. 10, 1978; 1 child, Arunima. B.Sc. in Chemistry, N.D. Coll., Howrah, India, 1967; M.Sc. in Biochemistry, Univ. Coll. Sci., Calcutta, 1969; Ph.D. in Biochemistry, Calcutta U., 1976. Chemistry lectr. West Bengal Bd. Tech. Edn., Howrah, 1970-75; research fellow Calcutta U., 1970-76; sr. research fellow Chittoranjan Nat. Cancer Research Ctr., Calcutta, 1977-78; assoc. biochemist Central Drugs Lab., Calcutta, 1978-79; postdoctoral fellow Washington U. Sch. Medicine, St. Louis, 1979-80; research assoc. SUNY Upstate Med. Ctr., Syracuse, 1980—. Author: Hydrogen Ion Transport, 1984. Council Sci. and Indsl. Research fellow, New Delhi, 1970. Mem. Biophys. Soc., Am. Physiol. Soc., AAAS, N.Y. Acad. Scis. Current work: Biochemical mechanisms involved in gastric hydrochloric acid secretion. Subspecialties: Biochemistry (biology); Membrane biology. Home: 25-3 Galloway Dr Liverpool NY 13088 Office: SUNY Upstate Med Ctr Dept Surgery 750 E Adams St Syracuse NY 13210

NANN, HERMANN, physics educator, researcher; b. Cologne, W. Ger., Oct. 8, 1940; came to U.S., 1973; s. Hermann Johannes Anton and Karoline (Wohlfarth) N.; m. Cornelia Ilse Stachowiack, Apr. 10, 1968; children—Daniela Annette, Barbara Angela, Hermann Andrew. Diploma in physics, U. Frankfurt, W. Ger., 1965, Ph.D., 1967, Habilitation, 1974. Vis. asst. prof. Mich. State U., 1974-76, vis. assoc. prof., 1976-77; sr. research assoc. Nortwestern U., Evanston, Ill., 1977-79; assoc. prof. Ind. U., Bloomington, 1979-1984, prof., 1984—. Contbr. articles to profl. jours. Mem. Am. Phys. Soc., Sigma Xi. Roman Catholic. Nuclear structure investigations with transfer reactions, mass measurements. Subspecialty: Nuclear physics. Home: 3624 Park Ln Bloomington IN 47401 Office: Dept of Physics Ind U Bloomington IN 47405

NANOS, GEORGE PETER, JR., naval officer, physicist; b. Torrington, Conn., Apr. 11, 1945; s. George Peter and Margaret Elizabeth (Kelleher) N.; m. Joanne Louise Knowles, July 5, 1969; 1 son, George P. B.S. in Engring, U.S. Naval Acad., 1967; M.A., Princeton U., Ph.D. in Physics, 1974. Commd. ensign U.S. Navy, 1967, advanced through grades to comdr., 1981; anti-submarine warfare officer USS Glennon, 1967-69; engr. officer USS Forrest Sherman, 1974-76; material officer Destroyer Squadron 10, 1976-78; mgr. tech. devel. Navy Directed Energy Weapons Program, Washington, 1978-82; combat systems officer Norfolk Naval Shipyard, Portsmouth, Va., 1982—; instr. physics No. Va. Community Coll. Trident scholar, 1966-67; Burke scholar, 1969-73. Mem. Am. Phys. Soc., Am. Assn. Physics Tchrs., Am. Astrophys. Soc., U.S. Naval Inst., Am. Soc. Naval Engrs., Soc. Naval Architects and Marine Engrs. Episcopalian. Current Work: Astrophysics, cosmology, laser physics; adaptive optics; shipboard combat systems; design, development, acquisition, repair and installation of naval weapons systems. Subspecialties: Cosmology; Laser physics. Home: Norfolk Naval Shipyard Quarters L Portsmouth VA 23709 Office: USS America CV66 Engring Dept FPO New York NY 09531-2790

NANZETTA, PHILIP NEWCOMB, mathematician, administrator; b. Wilmington, N.C., June 4, 1940; s. Leonard and Amy Virginia (Newcomb) N.; m. Virginia Elizabeth Griffith, June 3, 1962; children—Killi Phyllis, Margay Katherine. B.S., N.C. State U., 1962; M.S., U. Ill., 1963, Ph.D., 1966. Research assoc. Case Western Res. U., Cleve., 1966-67; asst. prof. math. U. Fla., Gainesville, 1967-70; assoc. prof. math. St. Mary's Coll., St. Mary's City, Md., 1970-74; dean sci. Stockton State Coll., Pomona, N.J., 1974-79, acad. v.p., 1979-82; project mgr. Nat. Bur. Standards, Gaithersburg, Md., 1982—. Author: Set Theory and Topology, 1971; editor: Calculus Concepts, 1973; also articles. Chmn. Galloway Municipal Utilities Authority, 1975-81; vice chmn. Galloway Planning Bd., 1977-82; active Galloway Council, 1978, N.J. Plinelands Commn., 1980-82. NSF grad. fellow, 1962-66. Mem. Am. Math. Soc., AAAS. Curent work: Computer integrated manufacturing; academic administration. Subspecialty: Applied mathematics. Home: 5612 Granby Rd Rockville MD 20855 Office: Nat Bur Standards B112 Metrology Bldg Gaithersburg MD 20899

NAPLES, VIRGINIA L., biology educator, functional morphology researcher; b. Worcester, Mass., June 24, 1950; d. Albert A. and Lenore A. (Miller) N.; m. Charles M. Kelecic Jr., Jan. 8, 1983. B.S., U. Mass., 1972, M.S., 1975, Ph.D. in Zoology, 1980. Teaching assoc. biology dept. U. Mass., Amherst, 1975-78; instr. biology Mt. Holyoke Coll., Mass., 1978-79; postdoctoral fellow, instr. U. Ill. Med. Ctr., Chgo., 1980-83; asst. prof. biology No. Ill. U., DeKalb, 1983—. Contbr. articles to profl. jours. Research grantee Sigma Xi, 1981, NSF, 1981-83. Mem. Am. Soc. Mammalogists (program com. 1984—), Soc. Study Evolution, Soc. Vertebrate Paleontology, Am. Soc. Zoologists, AAAS. Current work: Functional morphology, feeding mechanisms, xenarthrans. Subspecialties: Morphology; Paleobiology. Office: No Ill Univ Dept Biol Scis DeKalb IL 60115

NAPPI, CHIARA ROSANNA, physicist; b. Naples, Italy, Feb. 21, 1951; came to U.S., 1976, naturalized, 1979; s. Giovanni and Caterina (Iovino) N.; m. Edward Witten, June 17, 1979; children—Illana, Daniela. Laurea, U. Naples, 1972, Ph.D., 1976. Posdoctoral fellow Harvard U., Cambridge, Mass., 1977-80; mem. Inst. for Advanced Study, Princeton, N.J., 1980-83, research physicist Princeton U., 1983—. Contbr. articles to profl. jours. Mem. Am. Phys. Soc. Democrat. Current work: Work on supersymmetry and low energy effective lagrangians for quantumchromodynamics. Subspecialties: Theoretical physics; Particle physics. Home: 93 Maclean Circle Princeton NJ 08540Office: Dept Physics Princeton Univ Princeton NJ 08540

NAQVI, IQBAL MEHDI, electrical engineering educator, consultant; b. New Delhi, India, Jan. 6, 1939; came to U.S., 1958; s. Mehdi Hasan and Nazar Amna (Zaidi) N.; m. Alice L. Smith, Dec. 19, 1964 (div. May 1975); children—Javed Iqbal, Jasmin Noor. B.S., U. Panjab, Pakistan, 1958; B.E., Youngstown U., 1960; M.S., U. Pa., 1961; Ph.D., Cornell U., 1970. Sr. prin. engr. Honeywell Inc., Waltham, Mass., 1961-66; asst. prof. U. Hawaii, Honolulu, 1970-73; mem. research staff Fairchild Semiconductor, Palo Alto, Calif., 1973-75; mem. sr. tech. staff Rockwell Internat., Anaheim, Calif., 1975-78; head device engring. Hughes Aircraft Co., Newport Beach, Calif., 1978-82; vis. lectr. Calif. State U.+Fullerton, 1977, Calif. State Poly. U., 1978, U. Calif.-Irvine, 1981—; sr. cons. engr., head VLSI devel. MAI Basic Four, Tustin, Calif., 1982-85; cons. Western Digital Corp., Irvine, 1985—; lectr. tech. presentation Device Research Conf., 1968, 70; moderator panel discussion Engring. Workstations, 1984, Silicon compilers, 1985. Contbr. articles to tech. jours. Research scholar U. Pa., 1961; research fellow Cornell U., 1966-69; research grantee U. Hawaii, 1971-73. Mem. IEEE (sr.; program chmn. Orange County 1984-85, edn. chmn. 1984-85, chmn. circuits and systems/electron devices chpt. 1985—), Computer Soc., Circuits and Systems Soc., Electron Devices Soc. Clubs: Sierra (San Francisco). Current work: Directing microelectronic chip development activity for computer applications; responsible for computer-aided design; lecturer, organizer of profl. courses and workshops; device physics. Subspecialties: Electronics; Computer-aided design. Home: 14771 Doncaster Rd Irvine CA 92714 Office: Western Dittal Corp 2445 McCabe Way Irvine CA 92714

NARAHARA, HIROMICHI TSUDA, biochemistry educator, immunologist; b. Tokyo, Oct. 24, 1923; came to U.S., 1924, naturalized, 1934; s. Ushinosuke and Tama Mary (Miyanaga) N.; m. Ruth Kazuko Okada, Sept. 16, 1954; children—John A., Anne M., David K., Daniel M. B.A., Columbia U., 1943; M.D., 1947. Diplomate Am. Bd. Internal Medicine. Intern, Bellevue Hosp., N.Y.C., 1947-48, resident in medicine, 1949-50; fellow in pathology Beth Israel Hosp., Newark, 1948-49; resident in medicine Bronx VA Hosp., 1950-51; research fellow, instr. in medicine U. Wash., Seattle, 1953-58; research fellow in biochemistry Washington U., St. Louis, 1948-60, asst. prof. to assoc. prof. biochemistry, 1960-70; research physician N.Y. State Dept. Health, Albany, 1970—; assoc. prof. Albany Med. Coll., 1970—; mem. metabolic study sect. NIH, Bethesda, Md., 1970-73; mem. site visit team Med. Research Council Can., Winnipeg, Man., 1977, NIH, Phila., 1984. Contbr. articles to profl. jours., chpts. to books. Pres. bd. trustees First United Methodist Ch., Delmar, N.Y., 1977-82. NIH grantee, 1959-73, 1983—. Mem. Am. Diabetes Assn., Endocrine Soc., Am. Soc. Biol. Chemists. Current work: Regulation of sugar transport; muscle membrane proteins; antibodies to insulin. Subspecialties: Membrane biology; Immunology (medicine). Home: 3 Wisconsin Ave Delmar NY 12054 Office: Wadsworth Ctr for Labs and Research Empire State Plaza Albany NY 12201

NARAHASHI, TOSHIO, phamacologist, neuroscientist, educator; b. Fukuoka, Japan, Jan. 30, 1927; came to U.S., 1961; s. Asahachi Ishii and Itoko Yamasaki; m. Kyoko, Apr. 20, 1956; children: Keiko, Taro. B.S. in Vet. Medicine (equivalent D.V.M.), U. Tokyo, 1948, Ph.D. in Neurotoxicology (equivalent D.Sc.), 1960. Instr. lab. applied entomology U. Tokyo, 1951-60, 63-65; research asso. dept. physiology U. Chgo., 1961-62; asst. prof. dept. physiology and pharmacology Duke U. Med. Center, Durham, N.C., 1962-63, 65-67, asso. prof., 1967-69, prof., 1969-77, head pharmacology div., 1970-73, vice-chmn. dept., 1973-75; prof., chmn. dept. pharmacology Northwestern U. Med. and Dental Schs., Chgo., 1977—. Editor 5 books; specific field editor: Jour. Pharmacology and Exptl. Therapeutics; mem. editorial bd. 4 profl. jours.; contbr. sci. research articles to profl. jours. Recipient Japanese Soc. Applied Entomology and Zoology award, 1955; various NIH research and tng. grants. Fellow AAAS; mem. Am. Soc. Pharmacology and Exptl. Therapeutics, Am. Physiology Soc., Soc. Neurosci., Biophys. Soc. (Cole award 1981), Soc. Gen. Physiologists, Internat. Soc. Toxinology, Soc. Toxicology, Entomol. Soc. Am., Am. Chem. Soc. (div. agrochems.), N.Y. Acad. Scis., Sigma Xi. Current Work: Mechanism of action of toxins, therapeutic drugs and insecticides on ion channels of excitable membranes, as studied by electrophysiological methods. Subspecialties: Neuropharmacology; Neurophysiology. Home: 2130 Swainwood Dr Glenview IL 60025 Office: Dept Pharmacology Northwestern U Med Sch 303 E Chicago Ave Chicago IL 60611

NARANG, SARAN ADHAR, molecular genetics researcher; b. Agar, India, Sept. 9, 1930; came to U.S., 1962, naturalized Can. citizen, 1969; s. Sant Das and Kirpai Devi Narang; m. Sandhya Dheer, Oct. 10, 1959; 1 child, Monica Ajoo. B.Sc. with honors, Panjab U. (India), 1951, M.Sc. with honors, 1953; Ph.D., Calcutta U. (India), 1960. Postdoctoral fellow Johns Hopkins U., Balt., 1962-63; research assoc. Enzyme Research Unit, U. Wis., Madison, 1963-66; assoc. research officer Nat. Research Council, Ottawa, Can., 1966-73, sr. research officer, 1973-82, prin. research officer, 1982—; sci. advisor Internat. Centre Genetic Engring. and Biotech., Trieste, Italy and New Delhi, India, 1985—. Patentee synthetic gene, 1962; contbr. articles to profl. jours. Decorated officer Order of Can.; recipient Coachbihar Professorship Meml. award Indian Assn. Cultural Sci., 1973; Ottawa Biol. and Biochem. award Ottawa Soc., 1979; Johns Hopkins Scholar medal, 1979. Fellow Royal Soc. Can. Current work: Synthetic genes, cloning of lac-operator gene, linkers, proinsulin, synthetic Mu transposable element. Subspecialty: Genetics and genetic engineering (biology). Office: Nat Research Council Can 100 Sussex Dr Ottawa ON K1A 0R6 Canada

NARANG, SUDHIR KARL, geneticist, researcher; b. T. Nusrat, Panjab, India, Oct. 10, 1940; came to U.S., 1965, naturalized, 1985; s. Atma Ram and Laxmi (Gulati) N.; m. Neelam-Khera, Jan. 29, 1969; children—Anuj Steven, Deepa Carol, Aneesh Thomas. B.Sc. with honors, Panjab U., Chandigarh, India, 1964, M.Sc. with honors, 1965; M.S. in Zoology, U. Ill., 1968, Ph.D. in Zoology, 1970. Sr. scientist WHO/Indian Council Med. Research, Delhi, India, 1971; assoc. prof. genetics U. Brasilia, Brazil, 1972-79, chmn. biology dept., 1978; research scientist U. Fla., Gainesville, 1978—; cons. U.S.-Brazil Biomed. Program, Slavador, Brazil, 1973-77; supr. NRC Fellows, Brasilia, 1973-79; moderator Rockefeller Symposium, Bellagio, Italy, 1981. Editor: (with others) Recent Development in the Genetics of Insects Disease Vectors, 1982. Contbr. articles to profl. jours. Chmn. awards North Fla. council Boy Scouts Am., 1981-82; referee Youth Soccer Assn., Gainesville, Fla., 1982-83. Mem. Genetics Soc. Am., Am. Genetics Soc. (life), Fla. Entomol. Assn. Current work: Genetic engineering of insect disease vectors, gene cloning, gene transfer, genetic mapping, molecular population genetics. Subspecialties: Genetics and genetic engineering (biology); Genome organization. Home: 4406 NW 32d Ave Gainesville FL 32606 Office: USDA ARS PO Box 14565 Gainesville FL 32604

NARANJO, JENNINGS NEAL, marketing, management and research consultant; b. Lufkin, Tex., July 1, 1948; s. J. Neal and Stella Frances (Jennings) N.; m. Mary Ann Platz, Aug. 18, 1979. B.A., U. Tex., 1971; M.A., U. So. Calif., 1977, Ph.D., 1978. Mem. faculty psychology dept. Bklyn. Coll., 1971-74; mem. faculty dept. mgmt. U. So. Calif., Los Angeles, 1975-78, dept. mktg., 1978; asst. neuroanatomist McLean's Hosp., Belmont, Mass., 1979-81; fellow dept. anatomy Harvard Med. Sch., 1979, instr., 1980-81; teaching fellow dept. neurology Boston U. Sch. Medicine, 1980-81; dir. mktg. and mgmt., cons. Narjen Internat., Lufkin, Tex., 1981—. Author: Organizational Behavior, 1977; contbr. articles on neurosci. and physiol. psychology to various publs. Mem. sch. bd. St. Cyprian's Episcopal Sch., Lufkin, 1983—. Mem. Am. Psychol. Assn., Am. Mktg. Assn., SAR, Phi Beta Kappa, Sigma Xi, Psi Chi, Alpha Kappa Psi, Omicron Delta Pi. Clubs: Harvard (N.Y.C.); Jonathan (Los Angeles), Magic Castle (Los Angeles); Crown Colony Country. Lodges: Rotary (Lufkin); Masons; Shriners. Current work: Neuropsychology, marketing, stress, and aging. Subspecialty: Neuropsychology. Office: Narjen International PO Box 1745 Lufkin TX 75901

NARASIMHAN, THIRUPPUDAIMARUDHUR NARAYANAIYER, hydrogeologist, educator, researcher; b. Madras, India, Oct. 6, 1935; came to U.S., 1970, naturalized, 1985; s. Narayanaiyer T.S.L. and Lakshmi N.; m. Vijayalakshmi; 1 child, Lakshminarayanan Ravi. B.S. with honors in Geology, U. Madras, 1956; M.S. in Engring. Sci., U. Calif.-Berkeley, 1971, Ph.D. in Engring. Sci., 1975. Registered geologist, Calif. Geologist, Geol. Survey of India, 1956-70; staff scientist Lawrence Berkeley Lab., 1975-80, staff sr. scientist, 1980—; lectr. mineral engring. U. Calif.-Berkeley, 1977-82, prof. mineral engring. in residence, 1982—. Chmn., Gordon Research Conf., 1984; editor Spl. Paper 189, Geol. Soc. Am., 1982. Fellow Geol. Soc. India (life), Geol. Soc. Am.; mem. Am. Geophys. Union (life). Current work: Fluid flow in porous media; mathematical modeling. Subspecialties: Geology; Hydrology. Home: 1010 Richard Ln Danville CA 94526 Office: Lawrence Berkeley Lab Berkeley CA 94720

NARAYAN, JAGDISH, microelectronics educator, materials scientist; b. Kanpur, India, Oct. 15, 1945; came to U.S., 1969, naturalized, 1981; s. Sheo Nath and Radha Prasad; 1 son, Roger. B.S., IIT Kanpur (India), 1969; M.S., U. Calif.-Berkeley, 1970, Ph.D., 1971. Research metallurgist Lawrence Berkeley Lab., Calif., 1971-72; sr. mem. research staff, group leader Oak Ridge Nat. Lab., Tenn., 1972-84; prof. microelectronics, dir. N.C. State U., Raleigh, 1984—; dir. Microelectronics Ctr. N.C., 1984—. Author: Laser Processing of Materials 1984. Editor: Defects in Semiconductors, 1980; Laser Solid Interactions, 1982. Recipient Outstanding Research award U.S. Dept. Energy, 1982; IR-100 award Indsl. Research and Devel. Mag., 1979, 81, 82. Fellow Am. Phys. Soc., AAAS; mem. Materials Research Soc. (councillor 1984—). Current work: Defects and microstructures of electronic materials. Subspecialties: Electronic materials; Condensed matter physics. Home: 4917 Springwood Dr Raleigh NC 27612 Office: Microelectronics Ctr NC Research Triangle Park NC 27709

NARAYAN, KRISHNAMURTHI ANANTH, biochemist, researcher; b. Secunderabad, India, Oct. 1, 1930; came to U.S. 1954, naturalized 1970; s. A. Krishnamurthi and Rukmani K.; m. Suhasini Naik, Sept. 3, 1961; children—Krishnamurthi, Sheila. B.S. in Chemistry, Christian Coll., Madras, India, 1949; M.S. in Chem. Tech., Osmania U., Hyderabad, India, 1951; Ph.D. in Food Tech., U. Ill., 1957. Research assoc. Wash. State U., Pullman, 1957-61; asst. prof., U. Ill.-Urbana, 1962-71; research biochemist U.S. Army Natick Research and Devel. Ctr., Natick, Mass., 1971—. Contbr. chpts. to sci. books. Grantee NIH, 1966-70, Am. Cancer Soc., 1968-70, Am. Heart Assn., 1967-71; recipient research career devel. award NIH, 1966-70. Hindu. Home: 84 Indian Head Rd Framingham MA 01701 Office: Biochemistry Br Sci and Advanced Tech Lab Kansas St Natick MA 01760-5020

NARAYANA, ANAND DEO, mechanical engineer; b. Chapra, India, June 23, 1948; s. Brajendra Deo and Sharda (Bihari) N.; m. Pratima Narayana; children: Manu, Himanshu, Alok. B.S., Patna U., 1968; M.S., U. Cin., 1977, Ph.D., 1979. Lectr. mech. engring. Patna U., India, 1969-71; asst. exec. engr. Ministry Def. India, 1971-75; research asst. U. Cin., 1976-79; sr. mech. component design engr. Garett Turbine Engine Co., Phoenix, 1979-84; design engr. Gen. Electric Co., Aircraft Engine Bus. Group, Cin., 1984—. Indian Govt. Nat. scholar, 1963-68. Current Work: Design gas turbine disks and blades; solid mechanics including crack propagation and creep behavior in metals and alloys. Subspecialties: Mechanical engineering; Solid mechanics. Home: 9388 Kentonsrun Ct Loveland OH 45140 Office: 1 Newman Way Cincinnati OH 45215

NARAYANAMURTI, VENKATESH, physicist; b. Bangalore, India, Sept. 9, 1935; came to U.S., 1961; s. Duraiswami and Janaki N.; m. Jayalakshmi Krishnayya, Aug. 23, 1961; children—Arjun, Ranjini, Krishna. B.S. with honors, U. Delhi, India, 1958, M.Sc., 1960; Ph.D., Cornell U., 1965. Instr., research assoc. Cornell U., Ithaca, N.Y., 1967-68; mem. tech. staff AT&T Bell Labs, Murray Hill, N.J., 1968—, dept. head, 1976-81, dir., 1981—. Contbr. articles to profl. jours. Fellow AAAS, Am. Phys. Soc., India Nat. Sci. Acad.; mem. IEEE (sr. mem.), London Inst. Physics. Current work: Semiconductor physics and devices. Subspecialties: Condensed matter physics; Low temperature physics. Office: Room 1C426 AT&T Bell Labs 600 Mountain Ave Murray Hill NJ 07974

NARAYANAN, A. SAMPATH, biomedical educator, researcher; b. Tamilnadu, India, Jan. 14, 1941; came to U.S. 1969; s. Appathurai and Lakshmi; m. Lakshmi Raghavan, 1975; children—Nanda, Madhu. Ph.D., U. Madras, India, 1967. Asst. research prof. U. Wash., Seattle, 1975-78, assoc. prof., 1978—; chmn. Gordon Research Conf., New London, N.H., 1981. U.S. vis. fellow NIH, 1969-71. Mem. Am. Soc. Biol. Chemists, Internat. Assn. Dental Research, Can. Biochem. Soc. Hindu. Current work: Mechanisms of alterations in connective tissues such as skin, bone, heart disease and inflammatory diseases. Subspecialties: Biochemistry (medicine); Periodontics. Office: Dept Pathology U Wash Seattle WA 98195

NARAYANAN, C. S., radiation medical physicist, consultant; b. India, Sept. 29, 1944; s. C.R.S. Iyer and T.R. Janaki; m. Kamala, July 12, 1946; children: Anita, Anand. B.S. in Physics, Jain Coll, Madras, India, 1963; B.S. in Electronics, Madras Inst. Tech., 1968; M.E. in Radiation Physics, U. Va., 1976; M.S. in Bus. Adminstrn, St. Francis. Coll., Ft. Wayne, Ind., 1982. Sales engr. RCA, India, 1968-71; application engr. Capintec, N.Y., 1972-75; radiation physicist Highland Hosp., Rochester, N.Y., 1976-77; radiation physicist Luth. Hosp., Ft. Wayne, 1977—, tech. dir. radiation therapy, nuclear medicine and ultrasound, 1981—; mem. State Bd. Health, Radiation Emergency Response Com., Ind.; cons. Local hosps. and clinics. Contbr. sci. paper to profl. confs. Mem. Am. Assn. Physicists in Medicine, N.Y. Acad. Scis. Subspecialties: Radiology; Medical radiation physics. Home: 5926 Vance Ave Fort Wayne IN 46815 Office: Lutheran Hosp 3024 Fairfield Ave Fort Wayne IN 46807

NARAYANASWAMY, ONBATHIVELI SUBRAHMANYAN, mechanical engineer, researcher; b. Madras, India, May 13, 1936; came to U.S., 1962; s. Ramaswamy and Akilandam Subrahmanyan; m. Padmini Sreenivasan, Jan. 26, 1967. B.M.E., U. Madras, 1958; M.Sc., U. Sask., Can., 1962; Ph.D. in Engring. Mechanics, Case Western Res. U., 1965. Jr. sci. officer Atomic Energy Establishment, Bombay, India, 1959-60; lectr. Indian Inst. Tech., Madras, 1960-61; sr. research scientist Ford Motor Co., Dearborn, Mich., 1966-72, prin. research engr. assoc., 1972-81, staff scientist, 1981—. Fellow Am. Ceramic Soc. (Ross Coffin Purdy award 1973); mem. Soc. Exptl. Mechanics. Hindu. Current work: Computer simulation of processing of materials; annealing and tempering of glass, sheet metal forming, compression molding of fibre-reinforced plastic. Subspecialties: Solid mechanics; Materials processing. Office: Ford Motor Co 20000 Rotunda Dr Dearborn MI 48121

NARIBOLI, GUNDO ANNACHARYA, mechanics educator, researcher; b. Dharwar, India, Sept. 2, 1925; came to U.S., 1966; s. Annacharya N. and Ramabai A. (Savitri) N.; m. Usha G. Pramila, May 9, 1947 (div. July 1983); children—Manorama Vasundhara, Ashok, Anand, Anant; m. Pramoda G., Jan. 11, 1984. B.S. in Math. and Physics, Karnatak Coll. (Dharwar), 1947; M.S. in Pure Math., Ruia Coll., Bombay, India, 1952; M.S. in Applied Math., Indian Inst. Tech., Kharagpur, India, 1959. Tchr., V.H.S. Sch., Dharward, Karnatak, 1946-52; asst. lectr. math. B.V.B. Coll. Engring., Hubli, Karnatak, 1952-55, Indian Inst. Tech., Kharagpur, West Bengal, 1955-59; reader in math. dept. chem. tech. Bombay U., 1959-62, 64-66; prof. mechanics dept. engring. Iowa State U., Ames, 1962-64, 66—. Contbr. articles to sci. jours.; mem. editorial bd. Jour. Math. and Phys. Sci. (India). Mem. Soc. Indsl. and Applied Math., Am. Math. Soc., Math. Assn. Am., Am. Acad. Mechanics, Indian Soc. Theoretical and Applied Mechanics. Democrat. Hindu. Current work: Method of perturbation, wave propagation, group invariance, Backlund transformation. Subspecialties: Applied mathematics; Solid mechanics. Home: 209 N Wilmoth Ave Ames IA 50010 Office: Iowa State U Ames IA 50011

NASH, DONALD ROBERT, researcher; b. Pittsfield, Mass., Nov. 15, 1938; s. Joseph and Bernadette (Vallee) N.; m. Mary Campbell, June 23, 1963; 1 son, Brendon. B.A., Am. Internat. Coll., Springfield, Mass., 1961; M.S., Boston Coll., 1963; Ph.D., U. N.C., Chapel Hill, 1967; postgrad., U. Louvain, Belgium, 1968-69. Asso. prof. U. Hawaii, Honolulu, 1969-70; WHO fellow, Lausanne, Switzerland, 1970-72; research asso. prof. U. Tex. Health Center, Tyler, 1972—. Recipient Belgian Am. Ednl. Found. award, 1968-69; AMA Service Recognition award, 1970. Mem. Am. Assn. Immunologists, Am. Thoracic Soc., AAAS, Internat. Assn. Study of Lung Cancer, N.Y. Acad. Sci. Current Work: Lung cancer; immunochemistry; toxicology; infectious diseases. Subspecialties: Immunology (medicine); Microbiology (medicine). Office: Dept Microbiology U Tex Box 2003 Tyler TX 75710

NASH, JONATHON MICHAEL, engineering administrator, researcher; b. Little Rock, Aug. 10, 1942; s. Bertram B. and Nora B. (Shed) N.; m. Meta W. Smith, Aug. 12, 1972; children: Lillian Kendrick, Caroline Michael. B.S. in Mech. Engring, U. Miss., 1966, M.S. in Engring. Sci. 1970, Ph.D. in Engring. Sci, 1973. Registered profl. engr., Ala., Md., Miss. Jr. engr. IBM Fed. Systems Div., Huntsville, Ala., 1967-68, systems engr., mgr., 1973-78, advisory engr., Gaithersburg, Md., 1978-81, tech. planning mgr., 1981—; univ. fellow U. Miss., 1970-73; instr. U. Ala., Huntsville, 1977-78; adj. assoc. prof. mech. engring. dept. U. Miss., 1982—; research engring. res. officer U.S. Army Mobility Equipment Research and Devel. Command, Ft. Belvoir, Va., 1971—. Co- editor: Modeling, Simulation, Testing and Measurements for Solar Energy Systems, 1978; author book sect., invention disclosures. Vice pres. Arts Council of Frederick City and County, Md., 1982, dir., 1981-82; exec. com. Lafayette County Miss. Republicans, 1972-73. Served to 1st lt. U.S. Army, 1968-70. Recipient New Tech. award NASA, 1979, Apollo Achievement award, 1971. Assoc. fellow AIAA; mem. ASME (exec. com. solar energy div. 1981—, cert. appreciation 1982), Soc. Am. Mil. Engrs. (chpt. pres. 1976-77, engring. achievement award 1977, Tudor Medal 1978), Nat. Soc. Profl. Engrs. (chpt. dir. 1978, Ala. Young Engr. of Year 1978), Sigma Xi (chpt. pres. 1977-78), Alpha Tau Omega (pres. Huntsville alumni 1976-77). Current Work: Systems engineering technology and methodology as applied to data processing systems and energy conversion processes. Subspecialties: Systems engineering; Solar energy. Home: 300 Rockwell Terr Frederick MD 21701 Office: IBM Corp Fed Systems Div 18100 Frederick Pike Gaithersburg MD 20879

NASH, WILLIAM ARTHUR, structural engineer, educator, researcher; b. Chgo., Sept. 15, 1922; s. William and Rose (Keck) N.; m. Verna Lucile Baer, Aug. 8, 1953; children—Rebecca Anne, Phillip Arthur. B.S., Ill. Inst. Tech., 1944, M.S., 1946; Ph.D., U. Mich., 1949. Research engr. Armour Research Found., Chgo., 1944-46, David Taylor Model Basin, Washington, 1949-54; instr. U. Mich., Ann Arbor, 1947-49; prof. mechanics U. Fla., Gainesville, 1954-67; prof. civil engring. U. Mass., Amherst, 1967—; cons. Gen. Electric Co., King of Prussia, Pa., 1959-71, U.S. Air Force, Dayton, 1959—, Lockheed Corp., Sunnyvale, Calif., 1963-67. Author: Strength of Materials, 1957. Editor Non-Linear Mechanics Jour., 1966—. Recipient Curtis McGraw Research award Am. Soc. Engring. Educ., 1963. Fellow ASME; mem. Earthquake Engring. Assn., Internatl. Assn. Shell Structures, Laser Inst. Am., Am. Acad. Mechanics. Current work: Seismic behavior of structures, particularly liquid filled storage tanks, vibrational behavior of flight structures. Subspecialties: Solid mechanics; Theoretical and applied mechanics. Office: Dept Civil Engring Marston Hall Univ Mass Amherst MA 01003

NASSAU, KURT, chemist; b. Stockerau, Austria, Aug. 25, 1927; came to U.S., 1948; s. Julius and Frieda (Hauser) N.; m. Julia Wechsler, June 21, 1949. B.Sc. with honors, U. Bristol, Eng., 1948; Ph.D., U. Pitts., 1959. Research and devel. chemist Glyco Products Inc., Williamsport, Pa., 1948-54; research scientist Walter Reed Army Med. Ctr., Washington, 1954-56; research scientist AT&T Bell Labs., Murray Hill, N.J., 1959—; dir. GIA Gem Instruments Corp., Santa Monica, Calif. Author: Gems Made By Man, 1980; The Physics and Chemistry of Color, 1983; Gemstone Enhancement, 1984. Contbr. numerous articles to profl. jours. Patentee in field. Served with U.S. Army, 1954-56. Fellow Mineral. Soc. Am.; mem. Am. Crystallographic Assn., Am. Chem. Soc., Am. Ceramic Soc., Am. Optical Soc., Am. Assn. Crystal Growth (pres. Atlantic sect. 1975-77), Gemological Inst. Am. (bd. govs. 1975—), Sigma Xi, Phi Lambda Upsilon. Current work: Optical materials; crystal chemistry and growth; novel glasses; causes of color; gemstone synthesis and enhancement. Subspecialties: Solid state chemistry; Condensed matter physics. Office: AT&T Bell Labs Room 6D205 Murray Hill NJ 07974

NATALE, NICHOLAS ROBERT, chemistry educator, researcher, consultant; b. Phila., Oct. 30, 1953; s. Nicolo Rocco and Gloria Jean (Disciascio) N.; m. Hope C. Humphries, Dec. 28, 1974 (div. Oct. 1983). B.S., Drexel U., 1976, Ph.D., 1979. Lab. technician Campbell Soup, Camden, N.J., 1971; student trainee chemistry USDA, Phila., 1972-75; research asst. Drexel U., Phila., 1976-77, teaching asst., 1977-79; postdoctoral research assoc. Colo. State U., Ft. Collins, 1979-81; asst. prof. chemistry U. Idaho, Moscow, 1981—; cons. G.D. Searle, Skokie, Ill., 1984—. Contbr. articles to profl. jours. Mem. Idaho Acad. Sci., AAAS, Am. Chem. Soc. (Centennial Celebration award 1976), Sigma Xi, Phi Lambda Upsilon. Current work: Synthetic organic chemistry directed towards biologically significant molecules (anticancer agents, calcium entry antagonists); organo-lanthanide chemistry. Subspecialties: Organic chemistry; Organometallics. Office: U Idaho Dept Chemistry Moscow ID 83843

NATANSOHN, SAMUEL, research chemist; b. Rzeszow, Poland, June 18, 1929; came to U.S. 1949, naturalized, 1954; s. Saul and Rose (Teitelbaum) N.; m. Sidonia Schwimmer, June 20, 1951; children—Deborah, Rena, Sharon, Saul. Student U. Frankfort, Fed. Republic Germany, 1948-49; B.A. in Chemistry, Bklyn. Coll., 1955, M.A. in Chemistry, 1959. Sr. staff scientist GTE Labs., Inc., Waltham, Mass., 1955—. Contbr. articles to profl. jours. Patentee in field. Pres. Temple Israel, Sharon, Mass., 1980-81, v.p. 1977-80, trustee, 1973—. Mem. Am. Chem. Soc., Am. Ceramic Soc., Materials Research Soc., Sigma Xi (treas. GTE Labs. chpt. 1976, v.p. 1977-78, pres.-elect. 1978-79, pres. 1979-80). Current work: Synthesis and characterization of powders for structural ceramics; separation and recovery of strategic metals from secondary sources. Subspecialties: Synthetic chemistry; Materials processing. Office: GTE Labs Inc 40 Sylvan Rd Waltham MA 02254

NATELSON, SAMUEL, clinical chemist; b. Bklyn., Feb. 28, 1909; s. Max and Betty Ann N.; m. Ethel D. Nathan, Apr. 4, 1937; children: Stephen, Ethan, Elissa, Nina. B.S., CCNY, 1928; Sc.M., N.Y. U., 1930, Ph.D., 1931. Diplomate: Am. Bd. Clin. Chemistry. Teaching fellow N.Y. U., 1928-31; research chemist N.Y. Testing Labs., 1931-31, Jewish Hosp. of Bklyn., 1931-49; lectr. biochemistry and organic analysis Grad. Sch., Bklyn. Coll., 1939-49; head dept. biochemistry Rockford (Ill.) Meml. Hosp., 1949-58, St. Vincents Hosp., N.Y.C., 1958-59, Roosevelt Hosp., N.Y.C., 1959-65; Chmn. dept. biochemistry Michael Reese Hosp., Chgo., 1966-79; adj. prof. Vet. Sch. Medicine, U. Tenn., Knoxville, 1980—. Author textbooks in field.; Contbr. articles to profl. jours. Recipient Chgo. Sect. Sr. award Ill. State Soc. Bioanalysts Sci., 1971. Fellow Nat. Acad. Clin. Biochemistry, Am. Inst. Chemists; mem. Am. Assn. Clin. Chemistry (Ames award 1965, Van Slyke award 1961), Am. Chem. Soc. (50 Yr. mem.), Am. Microchem. Soc., Am. Soc. Applied Spectroscopy, AAAS, Sigma Xi. Patentee in field. Current Work: Epilepsy, intermediate nitrogen metabolism; research in guanidino compounds and their relationship to epilepsy. Subspecialties: Clinical chemistry; Biochemistry (biology). Home: 925 Southgate Rd Knoxville TN 37919 Office: Coll Vet Medicine U Tenn Knoxville TN 37901

NATH, RAVINDER, radiological physicist; b. Jullunda, India, Apr. 9, 1942; s. Kedar Nath and Rajrani (Katyal) N.; m. Rashmi Duggal, Nov. 20, 1971; children: Anjali, Sameer. B.Sc., Delhi U., 1963, M.Sc., 1965; Ph.D., Yale U., 1971. Cert. Am. Coll. Radiology. Asst. lectr. Delhi Coll, 1965-67; research staff physicist Yale U., 1971-73, research assoc. 1973-75, asst. prof., 1975-79, assoc. prof., 1979-85, prof., 1985—. Contbr. articles to profl. jours. Recipient Med. Physics award Am. Assn. Physicist in Medicine, 1975. Mem. Am. Assn. Physicists in Medicine, Am. Phys. Soc., Radiation Research Soc., Health Physics Soc., Am. Soc. Therapeutice Radiology. Current Work: Radiol. physics related to radiation therapy of cancer. Subspecialty: Radiological physics. Office: Yale Med Sch 333 Cedar St New Haven CT 06510

NATHANSON, LARRY, physician, educator; b. Boston, Dec. 23, 1928; s. Robert B. and Leah (Rabin) N.; m. Anna, May 17, 1963; children: Andrew, Aran, Nicholas. A.B., Harvard U., 1950; M.D., U. Chgo., 1955. Intern Los Angeles County Hosp., 1955-56; resident Stanford U. Hosp., 1958-60, chief resident, 1962-63; asst. in medicine Harvard U., 1965-66; jr. assoc. medicine Peter Bent Brigham Hosp., 1966-68; asst. physician New Eng. Med. Center Hosp., Boston, 1967-69, chief med. oncology services, 1969-79; prof. Tufts U, 1975-80; dir. oncology hematology div. Nassau Hosp., Mineola, N.Y., 1980—; prof. Sch. Medicine SUNY-Stony Brook, 1980—. Contbr. 100 articles in field to profl. jours. Served to capt. U.S. Army, 1957-59. Nat. Cancer Inst fellow, 1960-62; Straus Meml. lectr., 1973. Fellow ACP; mem. Sigma Xi. Clubs: Harvard of N.Y.C, Seawanhaka Corinthian Yacht. Current Work: Biology of malignant melanoma, experimental therapeutics of cancer. Subspecialties: Oncology; Chemotherapy. Office: Nassau Hosp 259 1st St Mineola NY 11501

NATHANSON, MORTON, neurologist, educator; b. N.Y.C., May 31, 1918; s. Nathan N. and Celia (Langbert) N.; m. Margret Regina Maier, Dec. 16, 1948; children: David, Madlyn, Laura. A.B., U. Mich., 1939; M.D., La. State U., New Orleans, 1943. Diplomate Am. Bd. Neurology. Resident NYU-Bellevue Hosp., 1946-49, dir. Multiple Sclerosis Research Program, 1950-54, instr. neurology Multiple Sclerosis Research Program, 1950-54; asst. prof. NYU Sch. Medicine, 1954-60, assoc. prof., 1960-67; clin. prof. neurology Mt. Sinai Sch. Medicine, N.Y.C., 1967-72, profl. lectr., 1973—; prof. neurology Sch. Medicine SUNY-Stony Brook, 1972—; adj. prof. neuropsychology Queens Coll., CUNY, 1978—, doctoral faculty, 1979—; emeritus chief neurology L.I. Jewish-Hillside Med. Center, New Hyde Park, N.Y., 1972—; resident in neuropathology Columbia Coll. Physicians and Surgeons, 1947. Contbr. chpts. to books and 57 articles to profl. jours. Served with M.C. U.S. Army, 1944-46. Recipient NIH contract award, 1978—. Fellow Am. Acad. Neurology; mem. Am. Neurol. Assn., Assn. Univ. Profs. Neurology, Am. Fedn. Clin. Research, Am. Assn. History Medicine, Soc. Neurosci., Brit. Brain Research Assn., European Brain and Behavior Soc., Internat. Soc. History of Medicine, Pan Am. Med. Assn. (neurol. council), N.Y. Acad. Sci., N.Y. Acad. Medicine, Sigma Xi. Current Work: Altered states of consciousness, brain stem function, perception (visual and somatic sensory), myoclonus of palate and related structures. Subspecialties: Neurology; Neurophysiology. Home: 1 Pebble Ln Roslyn Heights NY 11577 Office: Division of Neurology LI Jewish Hillside Medical Center New Hyde Park NY 11042

NATHANSON, S. DAVID, surgical oncologist; b. Johannesburg, South Africa, Dec. 12, 1943; s. Hymen Barnett and Freda Charlotte (Weinberg) N.; m. Maxine Elaine Zacks, Nov. 29, 1966 (div. 1978); children—Laurence Cecil, Joshua Russel; m. Jerrilyn Marie Burke, Feb. 18, 1979; children—Abigail Mary, Alison Megan. M.B.B.Ch., U. Witwatersrand, Johannesburg, 1966. Diplomate Am. Bd. Surgery. Intern, U. Pretoria, South Africa, 1967; lectr. anatomy U. Witwatersrand, Johannesburg, 1968, resident in surgery, 1969-74; postdoctoral fellow in immunology UCLA, 1975-77, postdoctoral fellow in surgery, 1977-80; resident in surgery U. Calif.-Davis, 1980-82; staff surgeon Henry Ford Hosp., Detroit, 1982—, dir. surg. research, 1982—; clin. assoc. prof. U. Mich., Ann Arbor, 1984—, endowed chair Interdisciplinary Cancer Research. Contbr. articles to profl. jours. Ford Found. grantee, 1982; Comprehensive Cancer Ctr. Detroit, grantee, 1983. Fellow A.C.S.; mem. Am. Soc. Clin. Oncology, Am. Assn. Cancer Research, Assn. Acad. Surgery, AAAS, AMA, Detroit Surg. Assn., Mich. State Med. Soc., Mich. Soc. Med. Research, Med. Assn. South Africa, N.Y. Acad. Scis., Royal Coll. Surgeons Edinburgh, Southwest Oncology Group, Wayne County Med. Soc. Republican. Jewish. Current work: Adoptive immunotherapy of solid tumors. Subspecialties: Oncology; Cellular engineering. Office: Henry Ford Hosp 2799 W Grand Blvd Detroit MI 48202

NATHENSON, STANLEY GAIL, research scientist, educator; b. Denver, Aug. 1, 1933; s. Abe and Esther (Kurl) N.; m. Susan Lawrence, Oct. 16, 1959; children: Matthew, John. M.D., Washington U., St. Louis, 1959. Postdoctoral fellow USPHS, Washington, 1960-62; Helen Hay Whitney fellow Blond Labs., East Grinstead, Sussex, Eng., 1964-67; asst. prof. dept. microbiology and immunology Einstein Coll. Medicine, Bronx, N.Y., 1967-69, assoc. prof., 1969-73, prof., 1973—. Contbr. articles to sci. jours. Served to asst. surgeon USPHS, 1962-64. USPHS grantee, 1966—. Mem. Am. Assn. Immunologists, AAAS, Phi Beta Kappa. Current Work: Research on molecular genetics and structural analysis of the major histocompatibility complex (MHC). Subspecialties: Immunogenetics; Transplantation.

NATION, JOHN ARTHUR, electrical engineering educator, director; b. Bridgwater Somerset, Eng., Aug. 8, 1935; came to U.S., 1965; s. Arthur John and Doris Edith (Rides) N.; m. Sally Gillian Leeds, May 31, 1961; children—Philip, Robert. B.Sc., Imperial Coll., London, 1957, Ph.D., 1960. Cons. CNEN, Frascati, Italy, 1960-62; staff scientist Central Electricity Generating Bd., Leatherhead, Eng., 1962-65; asst. prof., then prof. Cornell U., Ithaca, N.Y., 1965-84, prof., dir. sch. elec. engring., 1984—; cons. Schaeffer Assocs., Va., also others, 1982-83, Los Alamos Nat. Lab., N.Mex., 1983—. Contbr. articles to profl. jours. Fellow Am. Phys. Soc.; sr. mem. IEEE. Current work: Specialist in intense ion and electron beam physics and technology with special reference to collective processes in beams. Subspecialty: Plasma physics. Office: Cornell U 224 Phillips Hall Ithaca NY 14853

NAUGHTON, BRIAN ARTHUR, research hematologist, educator; b. N.Y.C., June 21, 1948; s. Patrick Joseph and Marie Gertrude (Hughes) N.; m. Gail Agnes Kolks, May 26, 1980; children—Eileen Marie, Meghan Elizabeth. B.S., Iona Coll., 1970, B.A., 1970; M.S., NYU, 1978, Ph.D., 1978. Teaching fellow NYU Coll. Dentistry, N.Y.C., 1975-77, research fellow A.S. Gordon Lab. Exptl. Hematology, 1976-78, sr. scientist 1977-78, research hematologist, 1978—; dir. med. lab. scis. Hunter Coll. Sch. Health Scis., N.Y.C., 1981—. Contbr. articles to profl. jours. Big brother Catholic Charities, Bronx, N.Y., 1967-77. Recipient Helen Flon Meml. award for excellence in histology NYU, 1978; named Outstanding Tchr., Westinghouse, 1971, 72. Mem. Internat. Soc. Hematology, Internat. Soc. Exptl. Hematology, Am. Soc. Hematology, Am. Physiol. Soc., Soc. Exptl. Biology and Medicine, Am. Assn. Anatomists, Harvey Soc. Republican. Roman Catholic. Subspecialties: Hematology; Immunology (medicine). Home: 277 Nassau Ave Brooklyn NY 11222 Office: Hunter Coll Sch Health Scis 425 E 25th St New York NY 10010

NAUGLE, JOHN EARL, space scientist, administrator; b. Belle Fourche, S.D., Feb. 2, 1923; s. John Earl and Delphia (Hall) N.; m. Ethel Hale, Dec. 7, 1945; children—Leleta Serafim, Merridy Pitts. B.S. in Physics, U. Minn., 1948, M.S., 1949, Ph.D., 1953. Assoc. adminstr. for space sci. NASA, Washington, 1967-74, dep. assoc. adminstr., 1974-75, assoc. adminstr., 1975-76, chief scientist, 1976-79; sr. div. advanced space systems Fairchild Space & Electronics Co., Germantown, Md., 1981-82; sr. dir. leasecraft Fairchild Space Co., Germantown, 1983—; chmn. bd., chief exec. officer Fairchild Space Ops. Co., 1983-85. Recipient Disting. Service medal NASA, 1969, 77; Outstanding Achievement award U. Minn., 1976. Mem. AIAA, Am. Phys. Soc., Am. Geophys. Soc., AAAS. Club: Cosmos. Subspecialty: Aerospace engineering and technology. Office: Fairchild Space Co 20301 Century Blvd Germantown MD 20874

NAUMAN, ROBERT VINCENT, chemistry educator; b. East Stroudsburg, Pa., Dec. 6, 1923; s. Carl Arnold and Bernice Irene (Zacharias) N.; m. Jean Marie Hodgeson, Aug. 29, 1955; children: Andrea Carol, Marcus Alan, Stephen Brian, Suzanne Marie. B.S., Duke U., 1944; Ph.D., U. Calif.-Berkeley, 1947. Research assoc. Cornell U., 1947-52; asst. prof. chemistry U. Ark., 1952-53; asst. prof. La. State U., 1953-56, assoc. prof., 1956-63, prof., 1963—, dir. chemistry grad. studies, 1981-84. Contbr. articles in field to profl. jours. Served with USMCR, 1943-44. Fulbright grantee, 1966-67, 85. recipient Standard Oil Ind. Outstanding Tchr. award, 1969. Mem. Am. Chem. Soc., Am. Phys. Soc., AAAS, Interamerican Photochemical Soc., Sigma Xi. Republican. Methodist. Current Work: Spectroscopy; photochemistry; photophysics; effect of geometry and conformation on electronic transitions. Subspecialties: Physical chemistry; Photochemistry. Office: Dept Chemistry La State Baton Rouge LA 70803

NAVANGUL, HIMANSHOO VISHNU, chemistry educator; b. Wai, Maharashtra, Inda., Dec. 22, 1941; s. Vishnu Narayan and Usha (Gokhale) N.; m. Neelarani B. Tilak, Sept. 18, 1964; children: Sangeeta, Bharat. B.Sc., U. Poona, India, 1961, B.Sc. with honors, 1962, M.Sc., 1963, Ph.D., 1967. Instr., vis. asst. prof. U. Mo., Kansas City, 1971-75; vis. asst. prof. N.E. Mo. State U., 1975-76; asso. prof. Al Fateh U., Tripoli, Libya, 1976-79; vis. faculty mem. Clemson (S.C.) U., 1979-80; asso. prof., chmn. dept. chemistry N.C. Weskeyan Coll., Rocky Mount, 1980—. Contbr. articles to profl. jours. Swiss Govt. scholar, 1967-69. Mem. Am. Chem. Soc., Am. Inst. Chemists, Sigma Xi. Hindu. Subspecialties: Physical chemistry; Use of computers in education.

NAYAK, DEBI PROSAD, virologist, educator, researcher; b. Eadpore, West Bengal, India, Apr. 1, 1937; came to U.S., 1961, naturalized, 1978; s. Sarat Chandra and Durga Rani (Mandal) N.; m. Abantika, June 18, 1965; children: Prasun, Dipak. B.V.Sc., U. Calcutta, India, 1957; M.S., U. Nebr., 1962, Ph.D., 1964. Instr. Bengal Vet. Coll., Calcutta, India, 1958-61; grad. research asst. dept. vet. medicine U. Nebr., 1961-64; acting asst. prof. UCLA, 1964-66, asst. researcher in virology, 1966-68, asst. prof. virology, 1968-71, assoc. prof., 1971-77, prof., 1977—. Am. Cancer Soc. Calif. Div. sr. Dernahm fellow, 1969-74; Grantee Am. Cancer Soc., 1970-74; Grantee Nat. Cancer Soc., 1972-77; Grantee Nat. Inst. Allergy and Infectious Disease, NIH, 1975—; Grantee NSF, 1975—. Mem. Am. Soc. Microbiology, AAAS, Am. Soc. Virology. Current Work: Influenza viruses; defective interfering viruses; nature of viral genes; expression of viral genes; recombinant DNA technology; gene expression; development of viral vaccine using recombinant DNA technology; genesis of defective interfering viruses. Subspecialties: Virology (biology); Molecular biology. Home: 1918 Granville Ave Los Angeles CA 90025

NAYLOR, ROBERT ERNEST, JR., See *Who's Who in America,* 43rd edition.

NEAGLE, LYLE H., grain company executive; b. Mutual, Oka., Nov. 6, 1931; m. Sandra D.; children—Deborah L., Mark B. B.S., Okla. State U., 1953; Ph.D., Iowa State U., 1960. Asst. dir. research Internat. Multifoods Co., Mpls., 1960-67; mgr. research Continental Grain Co., Libertyville, Ill., 1967-72, dir. research and devel., 1972-81, v.p. research and devel., 1981—. Mem. Am. Feed Mfrs. Assn. (chmn. nutriton council 1978). Subspecialty: Food science and technology. Office: Continental Grain Co PO Box 459 Libertyville IL 60048

NEARY, JOSEPH THOMAS, biochemist, researcher; b. Carbondale, Pa., Oct. 14, 1943; s. Joseph Francis and Mary Cecelia (McDonough) N.; m. Judith A. Clark, May 6, 1967; children: Robert, Suzanne. B.S., U. Scranton, 1965; Ph.D., U. Pitts., 1969. Postdoctoral fellow U. Ill, Urbana, 1969-71; assoc. in biochemistry and medicine Mass. Gen. Hosp. and Harvard U. Med. Sch., Boston, 1971-78; investigator Marine Biol. Lab., Woods Hole, Mass., 1978-85; research chemist, research asst. prof. VA Med. Ctr. and U. Miami Med. Sch., Fla., 1985—. Contbr. articles to sci. jours. NIH fellow, 1969-71; NSF scholar, 1964, 65. Mem. Am. Chem. Soc., AAAS, Soc. Neurosci., Am. Soc. Biol. Chemists. Democrat. Roman Catholic. Current Work: Biochemistry of behavior and learning; regulation of ion channels; calcium messenger systems, astrocyte cell cultures; protein phosphorylation. Subspecialties: Biochemistry (medicine); Neurobiology. Office: VA Med Ctr Research Services 1201 NW 16th St Miami FL 33125

NEBERT, DANIEL WALTER, molecular geneticist, pharmacologist, pediatrician; b. Portland, Oreg., Sept. 26, 1940; s. Walter and Marie (Schick) N.; m. Myrna E. Sisk, Mar. 12, 1960; children: Douglas Daniel, Dietrich Andrew; m. Kathleen Dixon, Aug. 15, 1981. B.A., Conn. Wesleyan U., 1961; M.S., U. Oreg. Sch. Medicine, Portland, 1964, M.D., 1964. Lic. physician, Calif. Pediatric intern and resident UCLA Hosps., 1964-66; postdoctoral fellow Nat. Cancer Inst., Bethesda, Md., 1966-68; sr. investigator Nat. Inst. Child Health and Human Devel., Bethesda, 1968-71, sect. head, 1971-74, acting chief neonatal and pediatric medicine br., 1974-75, chief lab. developmental pharmacology, 1975—; adj. prof. Uniformed Services U. Health Scis., Bethesda, 1980—; also lectr. Contbr. over 280 articles to sci. jours.; editorial bd.: Molecular Pharmacology, 1972-84, Biochem. Pharmacology, 1972—, Archives of Biochemistry and Biophysics, 1973-76, Archives Internationales de Pharmacodynamie et de Therapie, 1975-81, Jour. Environ. Scis. and Health, 1976-81, Chemico-Biol. Interactions, 1977-83, Developmental Pharmacology and Therapeutics, 1979—, Teratogenesis, Carcinogenesis, and Mutagenesis, 1980—, Anticancer Research, 1981-83. Served as med. officer USPHS, 1966—. Ann. Pfizer lectr., 1978, 79; recipient 1st prize Future Scientists Am., 1956; others. Mem. AAAS, Am. Soc. Pharmacology and Exptl. Therapeutics, Am. Soc. Biol. Chemists, Am. Soc. Clin. Investigation, Am. Soc. Pediatric Research, Sigma Xi. Republican. Unitarian. Current Work: Molecular genetics; pharmacology; enzyme regulation; chemical carcinogenesis; mutagenesis; teratogenesis; drug toxicity; environmental pollution; pediatric genetics. Subspecialty: Genetics and genetic engineering (medicine).

NECHAMKIN, HOWARD, chemistry educator; b. Bklyn., Aug. 18, 1918; s. Charles J. and Celia J. (Wiener) N.; m. Donna Rae Polensky, July 29, 1956 (div. June 1979); 1 dau., Emily Jean; m. Murielle Wolff, Dec. 22, 1979; 1 son, David A. Katz. B.A., Bklyn. Coll., 1939; M.S., Poly. Inst. Oklyn., 1949; Ed.D., N.Y.U., 1961. Analytical chemist R. H. Macy & Co., N.Y.C., 1939-42; research chemist Hazeltine Electronics, Little Neck, N.Y., 1942-45; assoc. prof. chemistry Pratt Inst., Bklyn., 1945-61; prof. chemistry Trenton (N.J.) State Coll., 1961—. Author: Organic Chemistry—Theory and Problems, 1978, others. Fellow Am. Inst. Chemists.; Mem. Phi Kappa Phi. Lodge: K.P. Current Work: Preparative procedures for reclamation of waste materials, consumer chemistry, reaction kinetics. Subspecialties: Inorganic chemistry; Organic chemistry. Home: 325 Glenn Ave Lawrenceville NJ 08648

NEE, TSU-WEI, physicist, educator; b. Kunming, China, May 3, 1940, came to U.S., 1963; naturalized, 1974; s. Chao and Ting-Wen (Lee) N.; m. Soe-Mie Foeng, Sept. 3, 1966; children—Phillip, Jocelyn. B.Sc., Nat. Taiwan U., 1961; M.Sc., U. Okla., 1965; Ph.D., U. Md., 1968. Research assoc. U. Md., 1968-69; asst. prof. U. Ariz., Tucson, 1970-77; prof. physics Nat. Taiwan U., Taipei, 1977; prof. Nat. Central U., Chungli, China, 1977-82; prof. Nat. Tsing Hua U., Hsindiu, China, 1982-83; research physicist Naval Weapons Ctr., China Lake, Calif., 1983—. Contbr. articles to profl. jours. Humboldt Research fellow, 1981. Mem. Am. Phys. Soc., Internat. Astronomy Union, Chinese Phys. Soc., Chinese Astronomy Soc., Sigma Xi. Current work: Transport and optical properties of semiconductor devices; non-linear and non-equilibrium properties of semiconductor devices. Subspecialties: Condensed matter physics; Infrared spectroscopy. Home: 509 Randall St Ridgecrest CA 93555Office: Naval Weapons Ctr China Lake CA 93555

NEEDLEMAN, ALAN, mech. engr., educator; b. Phila., Sept. 2, 1944; s. Herman and Hannah (Goodman) N.; m. Wanda Sapolsky, Apr. 12, 1970; children: Deborah, Daniel. B.S., U. Pa., 1966; M.S., Harvard U., 1967, Ph.D., 1971. Instr. applied math. M.I.T., 1970-72, asst. prof., 1972-75; asst. prof. engring. Brown U., Providence, 1975-78, assoc. prof., 1978-81, prof., 1981—. Guggenheim fellow, 1977. Mem. ASME, Am. Acad. Mechanics. Current Work: Plasticity of solids, ductile fracture mechanics, buckling of structures, finite element methods. Subspecialties: Solid mechanics; Fracture mechanics. Office: Div Engring Brown U Providence RI 02912

NEEL, JAMES VAN GUNDIA, geneticist, educator; b. Hamilton, Ohio, Mar. 22, 1915; s. Hiram Alexander and Elizabeth (Van Gundia) N.; m. Priscilla Baxter, May 6, 1943; children—Frances, James Van Gundia, Alexander Baxter. A.B., Coll. Wooster, 1935, D.Sc. (hon.), 1959; Ph.D., U. Rochester, 1939, M.D., 1944, D.Sc. (hon.), 1974; D.Sc. (hon.), Med. Coll. Ohio, 1981. Instr. zoology Dartmouth, 1939-41; fellow zoology NRC, 1941-42; intern, asst. resident medicine Strong Meml. Hosp., 1944-46; asso. geneticist lab. vertebrate biology, asst. prof. internal medicine U. Mich. Med. Sch., 1948-51, geneticist Inst. Human Biology, asso. prof. med. genetics, 1951-56, prof. human genetics, chmn. dept., 1956—, prof. internal medicine, 1957—, Lee R. Dice U. prof. human genetics, 1966—; Galton lectr. U. London, 1955; Cutter lectr. Harvard, 1956; Russel lectr. U. Mich., 1966; cons. USPHS, AEC, NRC, WHO.; Pres. 6th Internat. Congress Human Genetics. Author med. articles; mem. editorial bd.: Blood, 1950-62, Perspectives in Biology and Medicine, 1956—, Human Genetics Abstracts, 1962—, Mutation Research, 1964-75, Genetic Epidemiology, 1984—, Gene Geography, 1984—. Served to 1st lt. M.C. AUS, 1946-47; acting dir. field studies Atomic Bomb Casualty Commn., 1947-48. Recipient Albert Lasker award, 1960, Allan award Am. Soc. Human Genetics, 1965; Nat. Medal Sci., 1974. Mem. Am. Philos. Assn., Am. Acad. Arts and Scis., Inst. of Medicine, Nat. Acad. Scis. (mem. council 1970-72), Genetics Soc. Am., Am. Soc. Human Genetics (v.p. 1952-53, pres. 1953-54), Am. Fedn. Clin. Research, Am. Soc. Naturalists, Assn. Am. Physicians, Japanese, Brazilian socs. human genetics, Phi Beta Kappa, Sigma Xi, Alpha Omega Alpha. Club: Cosmos. Current Work: Population monitoring for genetic damage. Subspecialties: Genetics and genetic engineering (medicine); Environmental toxicology. Home: 2235 Belmont Rd Ann Arbor MI 48104

NEELY, DEAN PHILIP, veterinarian, reproductive physiologist and pathologist; b. Grove City, PA., Dec. 18, 1943; s. Lawrence Lester and Mildred Earla (Fisher) N.; m. Althea Fitz-Randolph Person, Dec. 18, 1965; children—Lori Denise, Jason Dean. B.S., Pa. State U., 1965; V.M.D., U. Pa.-Phila., 1969; Ph.D., U. Calif.-Davis, 1979. Diplomate Am. Coll. Theriogenologists. Resident in reprodn. U. Calif.-Davis, 1971-73, lectr., 1975-76, asst. prof., 1976-78; veterinarian Md. Equine Ctr., Cockeysville, 1978-80; assoc. prof. Mich. State U.-East Lansing, 1980-84; assoc., dir. Mid-Atlantic Equine Ctr., Ringoes, N.J., 1984—; mem. program devel. staff Mich. State U., East Lansing, 1980-84. Author: Genital Diseases of Stallion, 1980; Prevention of Equine Abortion, 1983; Equine Reproduction, 1983; performed 1st equine embryo transfer in Ea. U.S., 1981; produced 1st foal from frozen equine embryo, 1982. Mem. Am. Coll. Theriogenologists, AVMA, Am. Assn. Equine Practitioners, Soc. Theriogenology, Internat. Embryo Transfer Soc. Current work: Nonsurgical equine embryo transplantation; in-vitro fertilization of equine ova; research on freezing of equine semen; developed techniques for cryo-preservation of equine embryos; research on sex selection by treatment of equine semen. Subspecialties: Embryo transplants (veterinary medicine); Pathology (veterinary medicine). Home: PO Box 225 Solebury PA 18963

NEELY, HORACE HOLLIS, experimental physicist; b. Sabinal, Tex., Aug. 12, 1932; s. Hollis Hubert and Phylea Ann (Seabourn) N.; m. Norma Jean Warner, July 30, 1950; children—Karen Marie, Vic Allen, Rich Aaron. B.S., West Coast U., 1965. Mem. tech. staff Atomics Internat., Canoga Park, Calif., 1952-69; sr. cyclotron engr. UCLA, 1969-74; sr. staff engr. Rockwell Internat., Canoga Park, Calif., 1974—. Contbr. articles to profl. jours. Recipient ETEC Engr. of Yr. award, 1984. Mem. Am. Nuclear Soc., Am. Soc. for Nondestructive Testing, ASME, Am. Inst. Metall. Engrs., Sigma Xi. Club: Trail Dusters (Woodland Hills, Calif.) (pres. 1970-72). Current work: Study of LMFBR steam generator leak dynamics and inservice inspection; fusion reactor first wall liquid flow studies. Subspecialties: Nuclear fission; Heat transfer. Office: Rockwell Internat ETEC Div PO Box 1449 Canoga Park CA 91304

NEFF, WILLIAM DUWAYNE, research scientist, educator; b. Lomax, Ill., Oct. 27, 1912; s. Lyman M. and Emma (Jacobson) N.; m. Ernestine Anderson, Sept. 1937 (div. 1960); m. Florence Palmer Anderson, Sept. 23, 1961 (dec. May 1978); children—Carol Jean (Mrs. William Fritsch), Peter Lyman. A.B., U. Ill., 1936; Ph.D., U. Rochester, 1940. Research asso. Swarthmore (Pa.) Coll., 1940-42; research scientist Columbia, also U. Calif. divs. war research, New London, Conn., 1942-46; asst. prof., prof. U. Chgo., 1946-61; dir. lab. physiol. psychology Bolt, Beranek & Newman, Cambridge, Mass., 1961-63; research prof. Ind. U., Bloomington, 1963—; dir. Center For Neural Scis., 1964-78; Cons. NSF, NIH, NASA, EPA; staff adviser Nat. Acad. Scis.-NRC Com. on Hearing, Bioacoustics and Biomechanics. Editor: Contributions to Sensory Physiology, 1965; mem. editorial bd.: Handbook of Sensory Physiology; Contbr. articles profl. jours. Fellow Am. Acad. Arts and Scis.; mem. Nat. Acad. Scis., A.A.A.S., Am. Inst. Biol. Scis., Am. Physiol. Soc., Psychonomic Soc., Acoustical Soc. Am., Am. Acad. Arts and Scis., Soc. for Neurosci., Soc. Exptl. Psychology, Am. Otol. Soc., Otosclerosis Study Group, Am. Acad. Neurology, Brit. Royal Soc. Medicine (affiliate), N.Y. Acad. Scis., Internat. Soc. Audiology, Internat. Brain Research Orgn., Sigma Xi. Subspecialties: Neuropsychology; Sensory processes. Home: 3505 Bradley St Bloomington IN 47401

NEGELE, JOHN WILLIAM, physics educator, consultant; b. Cleve., Apr. 18, 1944; s. Charles Ferderick and Virgil Lea (Wettich) N.; m. Rose Anne Meeks, June 18, 1967; children—Janette Andrea, Julie Elizabeth. B.S., Purdue U., 1965; Ph.D., Cornell U., 1969. Research fellow Niels Bohr Inst., Copenhagen, 1969-70; vis. asst. prof. MIT, Cambridge, 1970-71, mem. faculty, 1971—, prof. physics, 1979; cons. Los Alamos Sci. Lab., 1972; mem. physics div. rev. com. Argonne Nat. Lab., Ill., 1977-83; mem. nuclear sci. div. rev. com. Lawrence Berkeley Lab., Calif., 1982—; mem. adv. bd., steering com. Inst. for Theoretical Physics, U. Calif.-Santa Barbara, 1982. Contbr. articles to profl. jours.; editor: Advances in Nuclear Physics, 1977. Grantee NSF, 1965-69, Danforth Found., 1965-69, Woodrow Wilson Found., 1965, Alfred P. Sloan Found., 1979, Japan Soc. for Promotion Sci., 1981, John Simon Guggenheim Found. Fellow Am. Phys. Soc. (exec. com. 1982—, editorial bd. Phys. Rev. 1980-82); mem. AAAS, Fedn. Am. Scientists. Subspecialties: Theoretical physics; Nuclear physics. Home: 45 Orchard St Belmont MA 02178 Office: Dept Physics 6-308 NL MIT 77 Massachusetts Ave Cambridge MA 02139

NEGOITA, CONSTANTIN VIRGIL, computer science educator; b. Bucharest, Romania, Feb. 3, 1936. Ph.D., Politech. Inst., Bucharest, 1970. Assoc. prof. Acad. Econ. Studies, U. Bucharest, 1970-82; head research lab. Inst. of Mgmt. and Computer Sci., Bucharest, 1972-82; prof. computer sci. CUNY, 1982—; expert Nat. Council for Sci. and Tech., Bucharest, 1967-72; organizer 3d Internat. Congress on Cybernetics and Systems, Bucharest, 1975; panelist Round Table on Fuzzy Systems, Universite Claude Bernard, Lyon, France, 1980; mem. com. for cybernetics, Acad. Scis., Bucharest, 1981; chmn. sect. on indsl. cybernetics 5th Internat. Congress on Cybernetics and Systems, Mexico City, 1981, vis. scholar Owen Grad. Sch. Mgmt., Vanderbilt U., Nashville, fall 1982; vis. prof. U. Mexico, Mexico City, summer 1982, Hunter Coll., spring 1983. Author: Applications of Fuzzy Sets, 1974; Management Applications of System Theory, 1979; Fuzzy Systems, 1981; Expert Systems, 1984. Editor: Fuzzy Systems, 1977. Mem. editorial bd. Human Systems Mgmt. Contbr. articles, book revs. to profl. jours. Recipient Sci. medal Council of Sci., 1972. Mem. IEEE (sr.), N.Y. Acad. Scis., N.Am. Fuzzy Info. Processing Soc. (bd. dirs. 1984). Current work: Approximate reasoning in artificial intelligence. Subspecialty: Artificial intelligence. Home: 34-38 75th St Jackson Heights NY 11372 Office: Hunter Coll CUNY 695 Park Ave New York NY 10021

NEIDHARDT, FREDERICK CARL, biology educator; b. Phila., May 12, 1931; s. Adam Fred and Carrie (Fry) N.; m. Elizabeth Robinson, June 9, 1956; children: Richard Frederick, Jane Elizabeth; m. Germaine Chipault, Dec. 3, 1977; 1 son, Marc Frederick. B.A., Kenyon Coll., 1952, D.Sc. (hon.), 1976; Ph.D., Harvard U., 1956. Research fellow Pasteur Inst., Paris, 1956-57; H.C. Ernst research fellow Harvard Med. Sch., 1957-58, instr., then assoc., 1958-61; mem. faculty Purdue U., 1961-70, assoc. prof, then prof., assoc. head dept. biol. scis., 1965-70; chmn., then prof. dept. microbiology and immunology U. Mich. Med. Sch., Ann Arbor, 1970—; Found. for Microbiology lectr. Am. Soc. Microbiology, 1966-67; cons. Dept. Agr., 1964-65; mem. grant study panel NIH, 1965-69; mem. commn. scholars Ill. Bd. Higher Edn., 1973-79; mem. test com. for microbiology Nat. Bd. Med. Examiners, 1975-83, chmn., 1979-83. Author papers in field. Mem. editorial bd. profl. jours. Recipient award bacteriology and immunology Eli Lilly and Co., 1966; Alexander von Humboldt Found. award for U.S. sr. scientist, 1979; NSF sr. fellow U. Copenhagen, 1968-69. Mem. Am. Soc. Microbiology (pres. 1981-82), Am. Soc. Biol. Chemists, Am. Inst. Biol. Scis., Soc. Gen. Physiology, Phi Beta Kappa, Sigma Xi. Current Work: Regulation of gene expression in bacteria; controls related to growth and macromolecule synthesis; heat shock and other stress responses of bacteria. Subspecialties: Microbiology; Molecular biology. Office: Dept Microbiology & Immunology U Mich Ann Arbor MI 48109

NEIDHART, JAMES ALLEN, physician; b. Steubenville, Ohio, Aug. 30, 1940; s. James Leonard and Mary Jane (Daniels) N.; m. Patricia Irene Harpkamp, Aug. 16, 1966 (div. 1985); children—James, Jeffrey, Jennifer. B.S., Union Coll., 1962; M.D., Ohio State U., 1966. Intern, Bronson Hosp.; resident, postdoctoral fellow Coll. of Medicine, Ohio State U., Columbus, 1972-74, asst. prof. medicine, 1974-78, assoc. prof., 1978-84, prof. interdisciplinary oncology unit Comprehensive Cancer Ctr., 1975-80, dep. dir., 1980-84; prof. medicine U. Tex. System Cancer Ctr., M.D. Anderson Hosp., Houston, 1984—, dep. head div. of medicine, chmn. dept of med. oncology, 1984—, Hubert L. and Olive Chair in Oncology, 1984. Contbr. chpts. to med. books. Bd. dirs. Am. Cancer Soc., Columbus; v.p. Ohio Cancer Research Assocs., Columbus. Mem. Am. Soc. Hematology, Am. Soc. Clin. Oncology, Am. Soc. Cancer Research, ACP, Southwest Oncology Group, Sierra Club, Wilderness Soc. Served to lt. USN (assigned to USMC), 1967-69, Vietnam. Subspecialty: Oncology. Home: 7827 Royan Dr Houston TX 77071 Office: U Tex System Cancer Ctr MD Anderson Hosp 6723 Bertner Ave Box 15 Houston TX 77030

NEIDLINGER, HERMANN HEINRICH, chemist; b. Bolanden, Germany, Feb. 13, 1944; came to U.S., 1975; s. Heinrich and Lieselotte (Korrell) N.; m. Kathleen Louise Darwin, Mar. 27, 1973; children—Petra, Karen, Erik. B.S., J. Gutenberg U., Mainz, Fed. Republic Germany, 1968, M.S., 1971, Ph.D., 1975. Research chemist BASF, Ludwigshafen, Fed. Republic Germany, 1970-71; NATO research fellow Stanford U., Calif., 1975-76; asst. prof. U. So. Miss., Hattiesburg, 1976-80, assoc. prof., 1980-82; sr. scientist Solar Energy Research Inst., Golden, Colo., 1982—. Contbr. articles to profl. jours. Fellow Deutscher Akademischer Austauschdienst, 1972, NATO, 1975-76; Dept. Energy grantee, 1977-83. Mem. Am. Chem. Soc., Miss. Acad. Scis. (chmn. 1979-81), Gesellschaft Deutscher Chemiker, Sigma Xi. Current work: Polymer structure-property relationships, solar applications of polymers, polymer degradation, permselective membranes, polymer morphology, elastic behavior, polymers for enhanced oil recovery. Subspecialties: Polymer chemistry; Solar energy. Office: Solar Energy Research Inst 1617 Cole Blvd Golden CO 80401

NEIHEISEL, JAMES, geologist, consultant; b. Cin., June 3, 1927; m. Betty W. Hilton, Apr. 4, 1952 (div. Dec. 1981); children—William J., Linda K. B.S., Ohio State U., 1950; M.S., U. S.C., 1958; Ph.D., Ga. Inst. Tech., 1973. Registered geologist, Ga. Chemist, V.C. Chem. Corp., Charleston, S.C., 1955-57; geologist U.S. Army C.E., Marietta, Ga., 1958-77, EPA, Washington, 1977—; spl. lectr. Ga. Inst. Tech., Atlanta, 1965-70; instr. geology Ga. State U., Atlanta, 1966-77; adj. prof. geology George Mason U., Fairfax, Va., 1981—. Contbr. articles to profl. jours., chpt. to book. Served with lt. USN, 1951-54; to comdr. Res. (ret.). Sec. of Army research fellow, 1964. Fellow Geol. Soc. Am.; mem. ASCE (assoc.; chmn. task com. 1977-83). Current work: Radioactive and hazardous waste disposal, concrete petrography, engineering geology, consultant, educator, sedimentology. Subspecialties: Geology; Hazardous waste disposal. Home: 2000 Huntington Ave 1112 Alexandria VA 22303 Office: EPA C M 2 ANR (461) Washington DC 20460

NEITZEL, G(EORGE) PAUL, JR., aerospace engineering educator, researcher; b. Atlanta, Nov. 28, 1947; s. George Paul Sr. and Bettymae Irene (Chapman) N.; m. E. Kathleen Heaps, Nov. 29, 1974; children—Erik P., Jason W., Michael B., Timothy J. B.S., Rollins Coll., 1969; M.S., Johns Hopkins U., 1974, Ph.D., 1979. Mathematician/aerospace engr. U.S. Army Ballistic Research Lab., Aberdeen Proving Ground, Md., 1969-79; asst. prof. mech. engring. Ariz. State U., Tempe, 1979-83, assoc. prof., 1983—; cons. Monsanto Corp., St. Louis, 1984—. Contbr. articles to profl. jours. Recipient Presdl. Young Investigator award NSF, 1984; Alexander Von Humboldt Research fellow, Fed. Republic Germany, 1984. Mem. Am. Phys. Soc., Am. Acad. Mechanics, AIAA, Soc. Indsl. and Applied Math., Sigma Xi. Democrat. Unitarian. Current work: Fluid mechanics-hydrodynamic stability of unsteady flows, computational fluid mechanics, crystal growth fluid mechanics. Subspecialties: Fluid mechanics; Applied mathematics. Home: 1035 E Wesleyan Dr Tempe AZ 85282 Office: Mech and Aerospace Engring Ariz State Univ Tempe AZ 85287

NELSON, ALAN CARIL, biophysics educator; b. Phoenix, Sept. 25, 1949; s. Caril Gayer and Zella Irene (Hill) N.; B.A. in Physics, U. So. Calif., 1972; M.S. in Geophysics, U. Berkeley, 1976, Ph.D. in Biophysics, 1980. Engring. physicist Xerox Corp., Pasadena, Calif., 1972-73; radiological physicist U. Calif., San Francisco, 1977-78; asst. prof. radiol. scis. MIT, Cambridge, 1980-85, assoc. prof., 1985—, dir. Lab. of Microscopy and Med. Imaging, 1981—; cons. Collaborative Research, Lexington, Mass., 1984—, Electro.-Scan, Andover, Mass., 1985—. Patentee image enhancement, surgical prosthetic junction, microtomography, environ. chamber. Recipient Teaching award MIT, 1984, Outstanding Prof. award Am. Nuclear Soc., 1984, endowed chair prof. W.M. Keck Found., 1983; Nat. Cancer Inst. grantee. Mem. N.Y. Acad. Sci., Radiation Research Assn., AAAS, Biophysical Soc., Sigma Xi. Current work: Direct programs and research in image science and technology emphasizing computer aided microscopy, medical imaging and true three dimensional data display. Subspecialties: Biomedical engineering; Magnetic resonance imaging. Office: MIT Dept Nuclear Engr/Health Sci Whitaker Coll E25-330 Cambridge MA 02139

NELSON, ALAN ROBERT, Quaternary geologist, researcher; b. Chgo., May 13, 1949; s. Robert E. and Margaret Ann (Southworth) N.; m. Barbara Gene Rankin, June 16, 1973; 1 child, Emily. B.S., U. Wis., 1971, M.S., 1973; Ph.D., U. Colo., 1978. Cert. profl. geologist, Ind. Geologist, Texaco, Inc., New Orleans, 1973-75, U.S. Bur. Reclamation, Denver, 1979-85, U.S. Geol. Survey, Golden, Colo., 1985—; postdoctoral fellow Dalhousie U., Halifax, N.S., 1978-79; research assoc. Inst. Arctic and Alpine Research, Boulder, Colo., 1980—. Contbr. articles to profl. jours. Recipient Performance award U.S. Bur. Reclamation, 1983, 84; fellow U. Colo., 1975-78, Killam fellow Dalhousie U., 1978. Mem. Geol. Soc. Am., Am. Quaternary Assn., Soc. Econ. Paleontologists and Mineralogists, Internat. Quaternary Assn., Soc. Archeol. Scis. Current work: Quaternary stratigraphy, sedimentology, and dating; geomorphology as applied to neotectonics. Subspecialties: Tectonics; Sedimentology. Home: 3375 19th St Boulder CO 80302 Office: US Geol Survey MS 966 PO Box 25046 Denver CO 80225

NELSON, ALFRED JOHN, See *Who's Who in America,* 43rd edition. .

NELSON, BERNARD WILLIAM, foundation executive; b. San Diego, Sept. 15; s. Arnold B. and Helene Christina (Falck) N.; m. Frances Davison, Aug. 9, 1958; children—Harry, Kate, Anne, Daniel. A.B., Stanford U., 1957, M.D., 1961. Asst. prof., asst. dean of medicine Stanford U., Palo Alto, Calif., 1965-67, assoc. dean, 1968-71; assoc. dean U. Wis.-Madison, 1974-77, acting vice chancellor, 1978-79; exec. v.p. Kaiser Family Found., Menlo Park, Calif., 1979—. Trustee, Morehouse Med. Sch., Atlanta, 1981-83. Fellow Inst. Medicine, Calif. Acad. Sci.; mem. Nat. Med. Fellowships (v.p., pres. 1968-77), Alpha Omega Alpha. Current work: Medical education; HMO's and medical schools; admissions policy; minority medical education. Subspecialty: Health services research.

NELSON, CHRISTIAN EMIL, engineer; b. Bergen, Norway, Dec. 28, 1923; s. Thron and Anny (Bergliot) H.; m. Phyllis Elaine Nelson, Oct. 14, 1970; children—Christian, Glen, Erik. B.S. in Engring., U.S. Mil. Acad., 1944; A.A., Cornell U., 1940; M.B.A., Fairleigh Dickinson U., 1955. Registered profl. engr., Fla. With Gulf Oil Corp., 1945-47, asst. marine supt., 1947-50; marine mgr. A.P. Green Co., 1950-56; pres. Thermal Refractories Corp., Kalon Engring., Inc., Tech. Specialites Corp., 1956-73; founder, pres., chmn. bd. Nat. Beryllia Corp., 1974; pres. Paulson Engring., Inc., Internat. Mar/plant Corp., Centerflex Technologies, Centerflex Internat. Corp., Hawthorne, N.J., 1974—; cons. engr., dir. Olympic Petroleum Corp.; dir. Poseidon Assocs., Inc. Served with USNR, 1942-45. Decorated Purple Heart; named Man of Yr., U.S. Mil. Acad., 1968. Mem. Soc. Naval Engrs., Soc. Naval Architects and Marine Engrs., ASME, Marine Tech. Soc., IEEE, Combustion Inst. Lutheran. Clubs: N.J. Country, Smokerise. Contbr. articles to profl. jours. Patentee in field. Home: 216 Brookvale Rd Kinnelon NJ 07405 Address: Centerflex Tech Corp 188 8th Ave Hawthorne NJ 07507 Office: 221 7th Ave Hawthorne NJ 07507

NELSON, CLIFFORD VINCENT, electrocardiology researcher; b. Boston, Sept. 23, 1915; s. Bengt Otto and Signe Amelia (Carlson) N.; m. Jane Veazie, Oct. 6, 1941; children—Susan, Lars. B.S., MIT, 1942; Ph.D., U. London, Eng., 1953. Engr., Sub Signal Co., Cambridge, Mass., 1942-47; research engr. Sanborn Co., Waltham, Mass., 1947-49; research asst. Mass. Gen. Hosp., Boston, 1949; asst. research prof. medicine U. Utah, Salt Lake City, 1954-56; research assoc. electrocardiology Maine Med. Ctr., Portland, 1956—. Mem. editorial bd. Am. Heart Jour., 1966-80, Jour. Electrocardiology, 1966-74. Co-editor: Theoretical Basis of Electrocardiology, 1976. Contbr. articles to profl. jours. Mem. research com. Maine Heart Assn., 1966-74. Fellow Am. Coll. Cardiology, AAAS; mem. Biophys. Soc., IEEE (sr.), Am. Physiol. Soc., Biomed. Engring Soc., Am. Radio Relay League. Current work: Theory and applications of electrocardiology. Subspecialties: Cardiology; Biomedical engineering. Home: Rural Route 5 Box 72 Gorham ME 04102 Office: Maine Med Ctr 22 Bramhall St Portland ME 04102

NELSON, DIANA FURST, radiation therapist; b. N.Y.C., Dec. 17, 1943; d. Joseph B. Furst and Helen Tunis Burrows; m. Fredric P. Nelson, Jan. 4, 1970; 1 son, Daniel Wolcott. B.A., Mount Holyoke Coll., 1965; M.D., Downstate Med. Ctr., 1969. Diplomate: Am. Bd. Radiology. Intern. U. Vt. Med. Ctr., Burlington, 1969-70; clin. fellow radiology Yale-New Haven Hosp., 1970-71; resident and clin. fellow radiation therapy Harvard Med. Sch., Boston, 1971-74; research fellow radiation biology Harvard Sch. Pub. Health, 1974-75; asst. prof. radiation oncology in radiology U. Rochester, 1975-78; asst. prof. radiation therapy Hosp. of U. Pa., Phila., 1979—; cons. radiation oncologist Pondville Hosp., Norfolk, Mass., 1974-75; assoc. radiation oncologist Strong Meml. Hosp., Rochester, N.Y., 1975-78; asst. attending radiation oncologist Genesee Hosp., Rochester, 1975-78; assoc. attending radiation oncologist Highland Hosp., Rochester, 1978-79; staff radiation therapist Hosp. of U. Pa., Phila., 1979—; staff Presbyn. U. Pa. Med. Ctr., VA Hosp., Phila., 1979—, Grad. Hosp., Phila., 1981—; mem., chmn. brain subcom. Radiation Therapy Oncology Group, 1982—, mem. protocol com., 1982—. Contbr. chpts. to books, articles to sci. jours. Mary Dole fellow, 1974; recipient Bernice MacLain Zoology prize Mount Holyoke Coll., 1963. Mem. Am. Soc. Therapeutic Radiologists, Am. Med. Women's Assn., Inc., Pa. Med. Soc., Phila. County Med. Soc., Am. Soc. Clin. Oncology, Am. Radium Soc. Current Work: Treatment of cancer patients with radiation therapy; clinical research on brain tumors and lymphoma. Subspecialty: Oncology. Home: 324 Llandrillo Rd Bala Cynwyd PA 19004 Office: Hosp U Pa 3400 Spruce St Philadelphia PA 19104

NELSON, DONALD FREDERICK, research physicist; b. East Grand Rapids, Mich., July 4, 1930; s. Paul Vine and Florence Dorothea (Atchison) N.; m. Margaret Ellen Fuerstenau, Dec. 18, 1954; children: Elizabeth Ellen, Julia Karen. B.S., U. Mich., 1952, M.S., 1953, Ph.D. in Physics (fellow), 1958. Postdoctoral fellow U. Mich., 1958-59; mem. tech. staff research area Bell Telephone Labs., Murray Hill, N.J., 1959-67, 68—; prof. physics U. So. Calif., 1967-68; vis. lectr. Princeton U., 1976. Author: Electric, Optic, and Acoustic Interactions in Dielectrics, 1979; contbr. numerous articles to profl. jours. Councilman City of Summit, N.J., 1981-84; mem. N.J. Gov.'s Sci. Adv. Com., 1982—; mem. N.J. Noise Control Council, 1983—; del. Union County Community Devel. Revenue Sharing Com., 1977—. Fellow Am. Phys. Soc.; mem. Optical Soc. Am., Acoustical Soc. Am. Patentee in field, including end pumping of lasers. Current Work: Nonlinear optics, nonlinear acoustics, mechanics, crystal physics; theory and experiment of high-field drift velocities of electrons and holes in semiconductors. Subspecialties: Condensed matter physics; Laser research.

NELSON, ERIC CHARLES, physician, medical educator, oncology researcher; b. Grinnell, Iowa, Oct. 22, 1946; s. Harry Alfred and Jean Buchanan (Bates) N.; m. Mary Lynn Bryant, Sept. 5, 1971; children: Mary Katherine, Bryant Buchanan. B.S., The Citadel, 1968; M.D., Wake Forest U., 1972. Diplomate: Am. Bd. Internal Medicine (medical oncology). Intern Wilford Hall USAF Med. Center, San Antonio, 1972-73, resident in internal medicine, fellow in hematology/oncology, 1973-77; chief hematology-oncology USAF Hosp., Keesler, Miss., 1977-79; asst. prof. internal medicine U. S.C., Columbia, 1979—, practice medicine specializing in hematology, oncology, Spartanburg, S.C., 1980—; prin. investigator S.W. Oncology Group, 1977-79, Piedmont Oncology Assn., 1978—. Bd. dirs. Am. Cancer Soc.; v.p. United Way. Served as maj. USAF, 1972-79. Mem. ACP, Am. Soc. Clin. Oncology, Am. Soc. Internal Medicine, AMA. Baptist. Current Work: Clinical trials cancer chemotherapeutic agents. Subspecialties: Chemotherapy; Hematology. Office: Spartanburg Hematology-Oncology Assocs 122 Dillon Dr Spartanburg SC 29302

NELSON, GORDON LEON, agricultural engineering educator; b. Chippewa County, Minn., Dec. 28, 1919; s. John Anton and Hilda (Weberg) N.; m. Florence Jeanne Wise, June 7, 1942; children: Gordon Leon, Carol (Mrs. James Earl), Linda (Mrs. Arthur Ochsner), Janet (dec.), David, Barbara. B.Agrl. Engring., U. Minn., 1942; certificate naval engring. design, U.S. Naval Acad. Postgrad. Sch., 1945; M.Sc., Okla. State U., 1951; Ph.D., Iowa State U., 1957. Sr. agrl. engr. Portland Cement Assn., Chgo., 1946-47; asso. prof. to prof. agrl. engring. Okla. State U., 1947-69; prof., chmn. dept. agrl. engring. Ohio State U., also Ohio Agrl. Research and Devel. Center, 1969—; dir. Ohio State U.-Ford Found. project Coll. Agrl. Engring., Punjab (India) Agr. Univ., 1969-72, cons. in field.; Mem. 7 engring. edn. and accreditation ad hoc visitation teams to evaluate agrl. engring. curricula Engrs. Council Profl. Devel. Contbr. articles to profl. jours. Chmn. bd. dirs. Stillwater (Okla.) Municipal Hosp., 1956-60; mem. grad. council Ohio State U., 1970-74; bd. dirs. Council for Agrl. Sci. and Tech., 1975-81. Served to comdr. USNR, 1942-68. NSF Sr. Postdoctoral fellow U. Calif., Berkeley and Davis, 1964, 65-66. Fellow Am. Soc. Agrl. Engrs. (dir. awards, bd. dirs., dir. edn. and research 1979, Metal Bldg. Mfg. award 1960, 8 outstanding Paper awards); mem. Am. Soc. Engring. Edn., Am. Assn. Engring. Socs. (chmn. continuing edn. com.), Sigma Xi, Tau Beta Pi, Sigma Tau, Alpha Epsilon, Phi Kappa Phi, Phi Tau Sigma, Gamma Sigma Delta. Republican. Baptist (chmn. deacons 1971). Current Work: Research interest include: cracking mechanics for crusted sorts, dynamic pressures in cylindrical grain storages, applications of similitude theory. Subspecialties: Agricultural engineering; Environmental engineering. Home: 6000 Sedgwick Rd Worthington OH 43085

NELSON, HAROLD STANLEY, physician, educator; b. New Britain, Conn., Jan 17, 1930; s. Harold Stanley and Ebba Arvida (Lawson) N.; m. Sarah Milledge, July 25, 1953; children: Erik, Mark, Stanley. A.B., Harvard U., 1951; M.S., U. Mich., 1969; M.D., Emory U., 1955. Diplomate: Am. Bd. Internal Medicine, Am. Bd. Allergy and Immunology. Commd. 2d lt. M.C. U.S. Army, 1956, advanced through grades to col., 1971, chief dept. medicine, Ft. Rucker, Ala., 1962-64, (5th Gen. Hosp.), Bad Cannstatt, W. Ger., 1964-67; chief allergy-immunology service (Fitzsimons Army Med. Center), Aurora, Colo., 1969—; clin. prof. medicine U. Colo. Center Health Scis., Denver, 1982—; cons. allergy-immunology Army Surgeon-Gen. Contbr. articles to profl. jours. Fellow Am. Acad. Allergy, ACP, Am. Coll. Allergists; mem. Am. Thoracic Soc., Am. Assn. Immunologists, Assn. Mil. Allergists. Current Work: Beta adrenergic agonists, subsensitivity, allergy immunotherapy, allergens and cross allergenicity; clinical practice, teaching and research. Subspecialties: Allergy; Internal medicine. Home: 4970 S Fulton St Englewood CO 80111 Office: Fitzsimons Army Med Center Aurora CO 80045

NELSON, JEREMIAH I., neurophysiologist; b. N.Y.C., June 2, 1943; s. Gilbert Isaac and Florence (Laikind) N.; m. Robin Hannay, June 13, 1967; 1 son, Lorrin H. B.A., Swarthmore Coll., 1965; Ph.D., SUNY Stony Brook, 1971. Asst. prof. SUNY Stony Brook, 1978-79, N.Y.U. Med. Center, N.Y.C., 1979-85; assoc. prof. Philipps U., Marburg, Fed. Republic Germany, 1985—. NSF fellow, 1971-72; Fulbright fellow Australia, 1972-74; grantee NIMH, Spencer Found., Fight for Sight, Dept. Def., Deutsche Forschungs Gemein schaft. Mem. Assn. Research in Vision and Ophthalmology, Soc. Neurosci. Current Work: Neurophysiological basis in brain of higher perceptual processes. Subspecialties: Neurophysiology; Sensory processes. Office: Working Group in Biophysics Philipps U Renthof 7 D-3500 Marburg Federal Republic Germany

NELSON, JOHN FRANKLIN, oral pathology educator, former military officer; b. Twin Falls, Idaho, Sept. 27, 1934; s. John Harold and Esther Louise (Ratcliffe) N.; m. Josephine Ellen Lillehei, Aug. 17, 1958; children; John Michael; Suzanne Ellen. B.S., U. Minn.-Mpls., 1957, D.D.S., 1959; M.Ed., George Washington U., 1971; Cert. oral medicine, U. Pa., Phila., 1968; cert. Oral pathology, Armed Forces Inst. Pathology, Washington, 1971. Diplomate: Am. Acad. Oral Pathology, Am. Acad. Oral Medicine. Commd. officer Dental Corps., U.S. Army, 1958, advanced through grades to col., 1977; mentor oral pathology residency Dental Corps. U.S. Army, Washington, 1978-79; chief div. pathology U.S. Army Inst. Dental Research, 1978-79; chief dental liaison officer U.S. Army Med Research and Devel. Command, Fort Detrick, Md., 1977-78; ret., 1980; prof. oral pathology U. Iowa, Iowa City, 1979-84; prof., chmn. dept. oral diagnosis and radiology Baylor Coll. Dentistry, Dallas, 1984—; mem. oral biology and medicine rev. com. NIH, Washington, 1978-79. Author U.S. Army tng. movie, 1980; contbr. articles, abstracts to profl. jours. County commr. Johnson City Broadband Telecommunications, Iowa City, 1980-84. Decorated Legion of Merit (2); Recipient instr. Yr. award U. Iowa Coll. Dentistry, 1981, 83. Fellow Am. Coll. Dentists, Internat. Coll. Dentists, Am. Acad. Oral Pathology; mem. ADA, Internat. Assn. Dental Research, AMA (affiliate), Beta Theta Pi, Psi Omega, Omicron Kappa Upsilon. Republican. Current Work: osteogenesis, epidemiology, dental education, radiology, oral disease, oral tumors. Subspecialties: Oral pathology; Oral medicine. Home: 11108 Sesame St Dallas TX 75238 Office: Baylor Coll Dentistry Dallas TX 75246

NELSON, LARRY DEAN, telecommunications and computer systems company executive, consultant; b. Newton, Kans., Aug. 5, 1937; s. Carl Aaron and Leta V. (Van Eaton) N.; m. Linda Hawkins, June 2, 1972. B.A., Phillips U., 1959; M.S., Kans. State U., 1962; Ph.D., Ohio State U., 1965. From research asst. to research assoc. Research Found., Ohio State U., Columbus, 1962-65; mathematician II, Batelle Meml. Inst., Columbus, 1962-65; from mem. tech. staff to supr. math. dept. and data systems devel. Bellcomm, Inc., washington, 1965-72; supr. mgmt. info. systems dept. Bell Telephone Labs., Murray Hill, N.J., 1972-77; supr. rate and tariff planning div. AT&T, N.Y.C., 1977-79; dep. adminstr. research and spl. programs adminstrn. U.S. Dept. Transp., Washington, 1979-81; pres. MCS, Inc., Washington, 1981—; cons. Contel Info. Systems, Denver, 1982—, Martin Marietta Corp., Denver, 1982—. Contbr. articles to profl. jours. Organizer, sponsor Odd Jobs Club, Washington, 1967-72; pres. Mountain County Condominiums Assn., Dillon, Colo., 1975-83; mem. Am. del. 5th Meeting of U.S.-USSR Joint Commn. on Cooperation in Field of Transp., Moscow, 1979; head Am. del. 5th Meeting of U.S.-USSR Working Group on Transport of Future, Moscow, 1979. Mem. IEEE (sec. D.C. sect. 1982, cert. appreciation 1968), Systems, Man and Cybernetics Soc. (sec. 1981, v.p. 1982-83), Math. Programming Soc., Am. Math. Soc., N.Y. Acad. Scis., Assn. Computing Machinery, Sigma Xi, Phi Kappa Phi, Pi Mu Epsilon. Democrat. Mem. Deciples of Christ. Current work: Analysis, design and development of computer and tele-communication systems, in particular, information systems, local area networks, data base systems. Subspecialties: Distributed systems and networks; Systems engineering. Home and Office: MCS Inc 440 New Jersey Ave SE Washington DC 20003

NELSON, NEIL DOUGLAS, biotechnology program leader, plant physiologist; b. Yankton, S.D., Sept. 22, 1944; s. Kermit Raymond and Kathryn Joanne (Jensen) N.; 1 child, Chad Matthew; m. Julie Ellen Berndt, June 27, 1981. B.S., in Forestry, Iowa State U., 1966; M.S. in Soil Sci., U. Wis.-Madison, 1968, Ph.D. in Plant Physiology, 1973. Research scientist Forest Service and Forest Products Lab., USDA, Madison, Wis., 1971-77, research plant physiologist, Rhinelander, Wis., 1977-81, project leader, 1982, program leader, 1983—; project mem. Internat. Energy Agy., 1985—. Fulbright Found. scholar, 1968-69; Fulbright Found. fellow, 1975-76. Mem. Am. Soc. Plant Physiologists, Soc. Am. Foresters, Internat. Soc. Plant Molecular Biology, Poplar Council of U.S., Fulbright Alumni Assn., Rhinelander Athletic Booster Club, Phi Kappa Phi, Sigma Xi. Baptist. Current work: Plant biotechnology and forest biotechnology; applying the new biotechnologies to genetic tree improvement. Yield physiology-photosynthesis and yield of forest trees. Subspecialties: Plant physiology (agriculture); Genetics and genetic engineering (agriculture). Office: Forestry Scis Lab Box 898 Rhinelander WI 54501

NELSON, OLIVER EVANS, JR., geneticist, educator; b. Seattle, Aug. 16, 1920; s. Oliver Evans and Mary Isabella (Grant) N.; m. Gerda Kjer Hansen, Mar. 28, 1963. A.B., Colgate U., 1941; M.S., Yale, 1943, Ph.D., 1947. Asst. prof. genetics Purdue U., 1947-49, assoc. prof., 1949-54, prof., 1954-69; prof. genetics U. Wis., Madison, 1969—; vis. investigator Biochem. Inst., U. Stockholm and Nat. Forest Research Inst., Stockholm, 1954-55; NSF, sr. postdoctoral fellow Calif. Inst. Tech., Pasadena, 1961-62. Recipient John Scott medal City of Phila., 1967; Hoblitzelle award Tex. Research Found., 1968; Browning award Am. Soc. Agronomy, 1974; Donald F. Jones medal Conn. Agrl. Exptl. Sta., 1976. Mem. Nat. Acad. Scis., Am. Acad. Arts and Scis., Genetics Soc. Am., Am. Genetics Assn., Am. Soc. Plant Physiologists, Crop Sci. Soc., AAAS, Sigma Xi. Current Work: Controlling elements; genes affecting starch synthesis. Subspecialties: Plant genetics; Gene actions. Home: 4197 Barlow Rd Cross Plains WI 53528 Office: Lab Genetics Univ Wis Madison WI 53706

NELSON, RICHARD D., technical entrepreneur, electrical engineer; b. Detroit; s. Richard Harold and Lorraine Nelson; m. Leigh Nelson; children—Brett, Sarah. B.S. in Physics and Math., U. W.Va., 1967; M.S. in Physics, Mich. State U., 1968, Ph.D. in Physics, 1972. Registered profl. engr., Calif. Physicist Rockwell Internat., Anaheim, Calif., 1972-73, supr., 1973-75, mgr., 1975-80; activity mgr. Ford Aerospace, Newport Beach, Calif., 1980—; tech. adv. bd. U. Calif.-Irvine, 1984—, Poly. U. N.Y., 1984—. Patentee (5); contbr. articles to profl. jours. Sr. mem. IEEE. Current work: Development of new insights and products in artificial intelligence, strategic systems, electro-optics devices and systems, semi-conductor devices, tactical weapons. Subspecialties: Artificial intelligence; Integrated circuits. Home: 12122 Red Hill Ave Santa Ana CA 92705 Office: Ford Aerospace Ford Rd Newport Beach CA 92660

NELSON, ROBERT M., astronomer; b. Los Angeles; s. Steve and Margaret (Yeager) N.; married; children: Tom, Chet. B.S. in Physics, CUNY, 1966; M.A. in Astronomy, Conn. Wesleyan U., 1969; Ph.D. in Earth and Planetary Sci., U. Pitts., 1977. Mem. faculty dept. geology Youngstown (Ohio) State U., 1977-78; NRC resident research assoc. Jet Propulsion Lab., Calif. Inst. Tech., Pasadena, 1978-80, sr. scientist, 1980—; co-chmn. So. Calif. Fedn. Scientists. Co-host: radio show about sci. The Wizards, KPFK-FM.; Contbr. articles to profl. jours. Mem. Internat. Astron. Union, Am. Inst. Physics, Am. Astron. Soc. (div. planetary scis.), AAAS, Am. Geophys. Union, Sigma Xi. Current Work: Research on the chemical and physical composition of the surfaces of solid surface bodies in the solar system. Subspecialties: Planetary science; Satellite studies.

NELSON, ROBERT NORTON, chemistry educator; b. Cin., Nov. 1, 1941; s. Norton A. and Rose S. (Cohen) N. Sc.B. in Chemistry, Brown U., 1963; Ph.D. in Phys. Chemistry, MIT, 1969. Asst. prof. chemistry Ga. So. Coll., 1970-76, 78-82, assoc. prof., 1982—; vis. asst. prof. chemistry Colgate U., 1977-78; vis. lectr. chemistry U. Ga., 1981. Scoutmaster, Boy Scouts Am., 1981—. Mem. Am. Chem. Soc., Am. Phys. Soc., Soc. Applied Spectroscopy, Sigma Xi. Current Work: Laser spectroscopy-CARS, molecular collisions. Subspecialties: Physical chemistry; Laser spectroscopy. Office: Georgia Southern College Chemistry 8064 Statesboro GA 30460 8064

NEMARICH, JOSEPH, physicist, researcher; b. New Orleans, Mar. 13, 1928; s. Peter and Jennie (Napolitano) N.; m. Patricia M. Rostella, Aug. 27, 1955; children—Christopher, Judith. B.S. in Physics, CCNY, 1949; M.S., U. Mich., 1950; Ph.D., U. Md., 1964. Research asst. U. Mich., 1950-53; adj. prof. physics Am. U., 1967-75; research physicist Harry Diamond Labs., Adelphi, Md., 1953—. Recipient Research and Devel. award U.S. Army, 1975, Significant Accomplishment award, 1984. Mem. Am. Phys. Soc., Sigma Pi Sigma. Current work: Over 60 technical publications and talks on microwave and optical properties of materials, tunable infrared lasers and millimeter wave propagation. Subspecialties: Condensed matter physics; Electrical engineering. Office: Harry Diamond Labs 2800 Powder Mill Rd Adelphi MD 20783-1197

NEMEROFF, CHARLES BARNET, psychiatrist, neurobiologist, educator; b. Bronx, N.Y., Sept. 7, 1949; s. Philip Peace and Sarah (Greenberg) N.; m. Melissa Ann Pilkington, May 24, 1980; 1 son, Matthew Pilkington N. B.S., CCNY, 1970; M.S., Northeastern U., 1973; Ph.D., U. N.C., 1976, M.D., 1981. Research assoc. Harvard U. Med. Sch., Boston, 1972-73; postdoctoral fellow U. N.C. Sch. Medicine, 1976-81; sr. research fellow Biol. Sci. Research Ctr., 1976-83; intern N.C. Meml. Hosp., Chapel Hill, 1981-82, resident in psychiatry, 1981-83; asst. prof. dept. pharmacology and psychiatry Duke U. Med. Ctr., Durham, N.C., resident in psychiatry, 1983-85, assoc. prof., 1985—. Contbr. numerous articles, chpts. to profl. publs. Recipient A.E. Bennett award Soc. Biol. Psychiatry, 1979; 2d prize Roche Lab. Award in Neurosci. and Mead Johnson Research Forum, 1979; new investigator award Am. Geriatrics Soc., 1985; Nat. Inst. Neurol. and Communicable Diseases and Stroke fellow, 1977; N.C. Alcoholism Research Authority co-grantee, 1980, 81. Mem. Soc. Neurosci., AMA, AAAS, Am. Psychiat. Assn., Endocrine Soc., Am. Soc. Neurochemistry, Am. Pain Soc., Internat. Soc. Psychoneuroendocrinology (Curt P. Richter award 1985). Current Work: Biological basis of major mental disorder; role of neuropeptides in central nervous system function. Subspecialties: Psychopharmacology; Neuropharmacology. Office: Box 3859 Duke U Med Ctr Durham NC 27710

NEMETH, EDWARD JOSEPH, chemical engineer; b. Glassport, Pa., Oct. 1, 1938; s. John M. and Ann (Breza) N.; m. Eleanor Zakrajsek, Aug. 3, 1968; children—Michael, John. B.S. in Chem. Engring., U. Pitts., 1960, Ph.D., 1967; M.S., U. Ill., 1962. Engr. textile fibers E.I. DuPont Co., Richmond, Va., 1963-64; sr. research engr. U.S. Steel, Monroeville, Pa., 1967-75, research supr., 1976-81, mgr. facility planning, Pitts., 1981-82, dir. research, Monroeville, 1982—. Contbr. articles to profl. jours. Patentee in field. Mem. Am. Inst. Chem. Engrs. Current work: Process and product research related to industrial and specialty chemicals and polymers. Subspecialty: Chemical engineering. Office: US Steel Chemicals Research One Tech Ctr Dr MS#30 Monroeville PA 15146

NEMPHOS, SPEROS PETER, chemist, researcher; b. N.Y.C., July 9, 1930; s. William S. and Philanthe (Exar) N.; m. Demitra Moralis, June 12, 1955; children—Phyllis, George, Steven. B.S., Ursinus Coll., 1952; M.S., U. Del., 1955, Ph.D., 1957. Sr. research chemist Monsanto Co., Springfield, Mass., 1956-62, research specialist, 1963-65, research group leader, 1965-74, mgr. research and devel., 1974-77, St. Louis and Research Triangle Park, N.C., 1978—. Patentee (8); contbr. articles to profl. jours. Bd. dirs., sec., treas. St. George Orthodox Ch., Springfield, 1960-70. Mem. Am. Chem. Soc. (sect. chmn. 1962-64, sec./treas. 1965-68, chmn. 1969), Am. Hellenic Progressive Assn. Current work: Polymer synthesis; kinetics and characterization of vinyl polymers; polymer degradations and stabilization; plastic foams; emulsion and suspension polymerizations; graft polymer systems; barrier resins; plastics fire safety; membrane science; separational technology. Subspecialty: Polymer chemistry. Office: Monsanto Co 800 N Lindbergh Ave Saint Louis MO 63167

NEPOMECHIE, RAFAEL I., physicist; b. Havana, Cuba, Mar. 8, 1958; came to U.S., 1965, naturalized, 1970; s. Nujim and Esther N. B.S. in Physics, U. Fla., 1978; M.S., U. Chgo., 1980, Ph.D. in Physics, 1982. Research assoc. Brandeis U., Waltham, Mass., 1982-84; research assoc. U. Wash., Seattle, 1984—. Contbr. articles to profl. jours. Recipient Telegdi prize U. Chgo., 1979; Nat. Merit scholar, 1976-78; NSF fellow, 1979-82. Mem. Am. Phys. Soc. Club: Mountaineers (Seattle). Current work: Classical and quantum field theory; quantum gravity. Subspecialties: Theoretical physics; Particle physics. Office: U Wash Physics Dept FM-15 Seattle WA 98195

NERY, EDMUNDO BARBIN, periodontist, dental researcher; b. Daet, Camarines Norte, Philippines, Apr. 6, 1930; came to U.S., 1953; naturalized, 1973; s. Jose Robel and Paula (Barbin) N.; m. Teresita Lacorte, July 2, 1966; children—Jose, Melissa. D.M.D., Nat. U., Manila, Philippines, 1951. Intern, then resident in oral surgery Balt. City Hosp., 1953-55; resident in gen. dentistry Albert Einstein Med. Ctr., Phila., 1956-57; postdoctoral fellow Temple U., Phila., 1957-58; research assoc. U. Pa., Phila., 1963-65, U. Pitts., 1965-68; assoc. clin. prof. Marquette U., Milw., 1974—; chief dental research VA Med. Ctr., Milw., 1973—; research cons. Elwyn Inst., Pa., 1969-71; chmn. VA Coop. Study Program, Milw., 1981—. Contbr. articles to profl. jours., books. Guggenheim Found. fellow, 1955-56; Am. Cancer Soc. fellow, 1964-65. Mem. ADA, Am. Acad. Periodontology, Internat. Assn. for Dental Research, Wis. Soc. Periodontists, Filipino-Am. Assn. Wis., Omicron Kappa Upsilon. Roman Catholic. Current work: Bone metabolism and ceramic implantology. Subspecialties: Periodontics; Implantology. Office: VA Med Ctr 5000 W National Ave Milwaukee WI 53193

NESS, GORDON EVERETT, geophysicist, geologist; b. San Francisco, May 17, 1940; s. Oscar and Marie (Schjerup) Fugelsnes; m. Loretta Ann Laubin, Dec. 23, 1964; 1 child, Kaare Konrad. B.S., Calif. State U., 1969; M.S., Oreg. State U., 1972, Ph.D., 1982. Registered profl. geologist, Oreg. Research asst. in marine geology Oreg. State U., Corvallis, 1969-72, geophysics, 1972-80, research assoc. in geophysics, 1980-82, sr. researcher, 1982—; cons. ptnr. NGA Geophysics, Corvallis, 1981—. Served with USCG, 1958-62. Grantee, Office Naval Research, NASA. Mem. Am. Geophys. Union, Geol. Soc. Am., Am. Assn. Petroleum Geologists, Am. Congress on Surveying and Mapping, Mexican Geophys. Union. Current work: Geophysical mapping and research on the origins, structures and evolution of continental margins. Subspecialties: Tectonics; Geophysics. Office: Coll Oceanography Oreg State U Corvallis OR 97331

NETTESHEIM, PAUL, pathologist; b. Cologne, Germany, Sept. 11, 1933; came to U.S., 1962, naturalized, 1971; s. Wilhelm and Antonie (Kaiser) N.; m. Barbara Louise Haegele; children—Ulrich, Klaus, Christoph. M.D., Med. Sch., Bonn, Fed. Republic Germany, 1959; P.M.S., Inst. Pharmacology, U. Bonn, 1959; M.S., U. Pa., 1964. Intern, U. Cologne, 1959-60; resident dept. pathology U. Freiburg, 1960-62, U. Pa., 1962-63; research biologist biology div. Oak Ridge Nat. Lab., 1963-69, group leader respiratory, carcinogenic div., 1969-77; chief Lab. Pulmonary Pathobiology, Nat. Inst. Environ. Health Sci., Research Triangle Park, N.C., 1977—; adj. prof. dept. pathology U. N.C., Chapel Hill, 1978—, Duke U., Durham, N.C., 1979—. Contbr. articles to profl. publs. Mem. Fedn. Am. Soc. Exptl. Biology and Medicine, Am. Soc. Exptl. Pathology, Am. Assn. Cancer Research, Am. Thoracic Soc., Internat. Assn. Study Lung Cancer (bd. dirs.). Current work: Cellular and molecular carcinogenesis, neoplastic development, progression and promotion, regulation of cellular differentation, pulmonary cell biology. Subspecialties: Cancer research (medicine); Pathology (medicine). Office: Lab Pulmonary Pathobiology Nat Inst Environ Health Sci Research Triangle Park NC 27709

NETZEL, JAMES PHILLIP, mech. engr.; b. Chgo., Nov. 16, 1940; s. Phillip and Ella (Freislinger) N.; m. Anita Francine Pahlke, June 5, 1965; children: Carol Ann, William James. B.S.M.E., U. Ill., Champaign, 1963. Mech. engr. Crane Packing, Morton Grove, Ill., 1963-67, sr. mech. engr., supr. mech. design group, 1967-79, asst. chief engr. product engring., 1979-81; chief engr. John Crane-Houdaille, Morton Grove, 1981—; instr. in engring. Oakton Community Coll., 1974-79. Contbr. articles on mech. seals and wear-related problems to profl. jours. Mem. ASME, Am. Soc. Lubrication Engrs. Current Work: Friction, wear, and lubrication as applied to mech. seals. Subspecialty: Mechanical engineering. Office: 6400 W Oakton St Morton Grove IL 60053

NETZEL, THOMAS LEONARD, chemist; b. Wausau, Wis., Dec. 5, 1946; s. Leonard and Carolyn (Frank) N.; m. Marla Schmerzler, June 16, 1968; children—Tirzah, Rivka, Adira. B.S., U. Wis., 1968; M.Phil., Yale U., 1970, Ph.D., 1972. Mem. tech. staff Bell Labs., Murray Hill, N.J., 1972-77; chemist Brookhaven Nat. Lab., Upton, N.Y., 1977-85; staff research chemist Amoco Corp., Naperville, Ill., 1985—. Contbr. articles to profl. jours. Research scholar NSF, 1970, NIH, 1971-72. Mem. Am. Chem. Soc. Current work: Identifying photo-chemical reaction intermediates and mechanisms in inoganic and organometallic complexes; laser spectroscopy, picosecond kinetics, catalysis, photon-based technologies and processes. Subspecialties: Inorganic chemistry; Laser photochemistry. Office: Amoco Corp Amoco Research Ctr Phys Tech Div PO Box 400 Naperville IL 60566

NETZER, CAROL, psychologist; b. N.Y.C., July 2, 1931; d. Jack and Pauline (Potofsky) Risika; m. Dick Netzer, Dec. 30, 1952; children: Jenny, Kate. B.A., U. Wis., 1949; M.A., Boston U., 1950. Psychologist S. Beach Psychiat. Ctr., Bklyn., 1973-83, supervising psychology, 1978-83, cons. in family therapy, 1979—, now pvt. practice psychotherapy. Contbr. articles to profl. jours. Mem. Am. Psychol. Assn., Soc. for Advancement Psychoanalytical Devel. Psychology. Current Work: Writer in psychoanalytic development psychology (theory) and in the theory of family therapy. Subspecialty: Developmental psychology. Address: 227 Clinton St Brooklyn NY 11201

NEUBERGER, JOHN WILLIAM, mathematics educator, mathematical and computational consultant; b. Ventura, Iowa, Aug. 14, 1934; s. John Mitchell and Pearl Lydia (Ax) N.; m. Barbara Ann Osher, July 6, 1959; children—John Michael, Sandra Ann. B.A., U. Tex., 1954, Ph.D., 1957. Instr. IIT, Chgo., 1957-59; asst. prof. U. Tenn., Knoxville, 1959-63; assoc. prof. Emory U., Atlanta, 1963-67, 1967-77; prof. North Tex. State U., Denton, 1977—; cons. Gaseous Diffusion Plant, Oak Ridge, 1959-65, Oak Ridge Nat. Lab., 1979—; mathematician Inst. Def. Analysis, Princeton, N.J., 1973. Editor Houston Jour. Math. Contbr. articles to profl. jours. Alfred P. Sloan Research Fellow, 1967-69. Mem. Am. Math. Soc., Soc. Indsl. and Applied Math., London Math. Soc., Edinburgh Math. Soc. Current work: Numerical and theoretical investigation of nonlinear systems of partial and functional differential equations. Subspecialties: Analysis; Numerical analysis (computer science). Home: 109 Ridgecrest Circle Denton TX 76105 Office: Dept Mathematics No Tex State Univ Denton TX 76205

NEUFFER, MYRON GERALD, geneticist; b. Preston, Idaho, Mar. 4, 1922; s. Myron and Camille (Cole) N.; m. Margaret McGregor, Mar. 18, 1943; children: David, John, Gregory, Dale, Barbara, Peggy, Linda. B.S., U. Idaho, 1947; M.S. in Genetics, U. Mo., 1949, Ph.D., 1952. Asst. prof. field crops U. Mo.-Columbia, 1951-56, assoc. prof., 1956-66, prof., 1966-67, prof. genetics, chmn. dept., 1967-70, prof. biol. scis., 1970-76, prof. agronomy, 1976—. Author: Mutants of Maize, 1968. Mem. AAAS, Genetic Soc. Am., Am. Genetics Assn., Crop Sci. Soc. Am., Sigma Xi. Mem. Ch. Jesus Christ of Latter-day Saints. Current Work: Maize genetics and mutation. Subspecialty: Plant genetics.

NEUGEBAUER, MARCIA, physicist, adminstrator; b. N.Y.C., Sept. 27, 1932; d. Howard Graeme MacDonald and Frances (Townsend) Marshall; m. Gerry Neugebauer, Aug. 25, 1956; children—Carol, Lee. B.S., Cornell U., 1954; M.S., U. Ill., 1956. Grad. asst. U. Ill., Urbana, 1954-56; vis. fellow Clare Hall Coll., Cambridge, Eng., 1975; sr. research scientist Jet Propulsion Lab., Calif. Inst. Tech., Pasadena, 1956—; mem. com. NASA, Washington, 1960—, Nat. Acad. Scis., 1981—. Contbr. numerous articles on physics to profl. jours. Named Calif. Women Scientist of Yr. Calif. Mus. Sci. and Industry, 1967; recipient Exceptional Sci. Achievement medal NASA, 1970. Mem. Am. Geophys. Union (sec., pres. solar planetary relationships sect. 1979-84). Democrat. Current work: Properties of the solar wind and comets. Home: 1720 Braeburn Rd Altadena CA 91001 Office: Jet Propulsion Lab Calif Inst Tech 4800 Oak Grove Dr Pasadena CA 91109

NEUHAUS, OTTO W., biochemist, educator; b. Germany, Nov. 18, 1922; came to U.S., 1927, naturalized 1932; s. Clemens and Johanna (Schnorr) N.; m. Dorothy E. Rehn, Aug. 30, 1947; children—Thomas W., Carol A., Joanne M. B.S., U. Wis., 1944; M.S., U. Mich., 1947, Ph.D., 1953. Biochemist Huron Milling Co., Harbor Beach, Mich., 1951-54; research assoc. Wayne State U., Detroit, 1954-58, asst. prof., 1958-64, assoc. prof., 1964-66; prof. biochemistry, chmn. dept. U. S.D., Vermillion, 1966—. Editor: Fish in Research, 1969. Author: Human Biochemistry, 10th edit., 1982. Pres. Friends W.H. Over State Mus., Vermillion, 1983-84. Mem. Am. Soc. Biol. Chemists, Am. Chem. Soc., AAAS, Sigma Xi. Lutheran. Current work: Studies on alpha 2u-globulin; sex-dependant protein adult male rats; control of renal reabsorption urinary proteins. Subspecialties: Biochemistry (medicine); Membrane biology. Office: Dept Biochemistry Univ SD Sch Medicine Vermillion SD 59069

NEUHAUSER, DUNCAN VON BRIESEN, community health educator; b. Phila., June 20, 1939; s. Edward B.D. and Gernda (von Briesen) N.; m. Elinor Toaz, Mar. 6, 1965; children: Steven, Ann. B.A., Harvard U., 1961; M.H.A., Mich. U., 1963; M.B.A., U. Chgo., 1966, Ph.D., 1971. Research assoc. Ctr. for Health Adminstrn. Studies, Grad. Sch. Bus., U. Chgo., 1965-70; asst. prof. health services adminstrn. Harvard Sch. Pub. Health, Cambridge, Mass., 1970-74, assoc. prof., 1974-79; cons. in medicine Mass. Gen. Hosp., 1975-80; prof. epidemiology and community health, Keck Found. sr. research scholar Case Western Res. U., Cleve., 1979—, prof. medicine, 1981—; adj. prof. orgnl. behavior Weatherhead Sch. Mgmt., 1979—; co-dir. Health Systems Mgmt. Ctr., Case Western Res. U., 1979—; cons. Cleve. Met. Gen. Hosp., 1981—; cons. in field; lectr. in field; chmn. Great Lakes VA Regional Health Services Research and Devel. Field Program adv. com., 1982-84, coordinating com. Cleve. Clin. Decision Analysis Group, 1982-85; adj. staff mem. Cleve. Clin. Found., 1984—; assoc. chmn. Program for Health Systems Mgmt., Harvard Bus. Sch. and Sch. Pub. Health, 1972-79; mem. Ctr. for Analysis of Health Practices, 1975-79; dir. Harvard Sch. Pub. Health/VA Region I Health Services Research & Devel. Unit, 1977-79. Adv. editor: Health Care Mgmt. Rev, 1975—editorial bd. New Eng. Jour. Human Services, 1980—, Internat. Jour. Tech. Assessment in Health, 1985—, Health Care Instrumentation, 1985—; editor: Medical Care, 1983—, Health Matrix, 1983—; contbr. articles to profl. jours.; author: (with Florence Wilson) Health Services in the U.S., 2nd edit, 1982, (with A. Kovner) Health Services Mgmt., 2nd edit, 1983, (with Milton Weinstein and others) Clinical Decision Analysis, 1980. First vice chmn. Vis. Nurse Assn. of Greater Cleve., 1982-84, chmn., 1984-85; bd. dirs. New Eng. Grenfell Assn., 1973—, Internat. Grenfell Assn., 1975-83, Braintree Hosp., 1975—, Mass. Eye and Ear Infirmary, 1977-79, Hospice Council of No. Ohio, 1980—, Blue Hill Hosp., Maine, 1983—, Cleve. Neighborhood Health Services, 1983—. Kellog fellow U. Chgo., 1963-65; Neuhauser lectr. Soc. Pediatric Radiology, 1982. Mem. Assn. Univ. Programs in Health Adminstrn., Am. Pub. Health Assn., Soc. for Clin. Decision Making, Forum of Health Services Adminstrs., Inst. Medicine of Nat. Acad. Scis., Beta Gamma Sigma. Club: St. Botolph. Current Work: Clinical decision analysis, evaluation of costs and quality of medical care, health services research, health services management and organization. Subspecialties: Epidemiology; Health services research. Home: 2655 N Park Blvd Cleveland Heights OH 44106 Office: Med Sch 2119 Abington Rd Cleveland OH 44106

NEUMANN, HERSCHEL, physicist, educator; b. San Bernardino, Calif., Feb. 3, 1930; s. Arthur and Dorothy (Greenhood) N.; m. Julia Black, June 15, 1951; children: Paul Alfred, Keith Edward. Student, San Bernardino Valley Coll., 1947-49; B.A. in Physics, U. Calif.-Berkeley, 1951; M.S. in Physics, U. Oreg.-Eugene, 1959; Ph.D. in Physics, U. Nebr.-Lincoln, 1965. Theoretical physicist Hanford Labs., Gen. Electric Co, Richland, Wash., 1951-57; instr. physics U. Nebr., 1964-65; asst. prof. physics U. Denver, 1965-71, assoc. prof., 1971-85, prof., 1985—, chmn. dept., 1985—; researcher. Contbr. articles to profl. jours. Mem. Am. Phys. Soc., Am. Assn. Physics Tchrs. Current Work: Theoretical studies of collisions between H/H+ and atmospheric gases, theoretical studies of collisions between ions and surfaces. Subspecialties: Atomic and molecular physics; Numerical analysis (computer science). Office: Dept Physics U Denver Denver CO 80208

NEUMEYER, JOHN LEOPOLD, medicinal chemist, educator; b. Munich, Germany, July 19, 1930; came to U.S., 1945, naturalized, 1950; s. Albert and Martha (Stern) N.; m. Evelyn, June 24, 1956; children: Ann, David, Elizabeth. B.S., Columbia U., 1952; Ph.D., U. Wis., 1961. Research chemist Ethicon Inc. div. Johnson and Johnson, Somerville, N.J., 1952-57; research chemist FMC Corp., Princeton, N.J., 1961-63; sr. staff scientist Arthur D. Little Inc., Cambridge, Mass., 1963-69; prof. medicinal chemistry Northeastern U., 1969—, prof. chemistry, 1976—, Disting. Univ. prof., 1980—; dir. Northeastern U. (Grad. Sch.), 1978-85; cons. in field; dir. Research Biochems. Inc. Assoc. editor: Jour. Medicinal Chemistry; Research, numerous publs. in field; contbr. chpts. to books. Served with U.S. Army, 1953-55. Recipient First prize Lundsford Richardson Award, 1961; Am. Found. Pharm. Edn. Gustavus N. Pfeiffer Meml. research fellow, 1975; Hayes-Fulbright sr. fellow, 1975. Fellow AAAS, Acad. Pharm. Scis. (Research Achievement award 1982); mem. Am. Chem. Soc. (chmn. div. med. chemistry 1982), Soc. Neurosci., Sigma Xi, Phi Kappa Phi, Rho Chi. Patentee in field. Current Work: Neuropharmacology-receptor interactions of dopamine agonists and antagonists, mechanism of action of CNS active agents, cancer chemotherapy, environmental effects of pesticides. Subspecialties: Medicinal chemistry; Organic chemistry.

NEURATH, ALEXANDER ROBERT, virologist, biochemist; b. Bratislava, Czechoslovakia, May 8, 1933; came to U.S., 1964, naturalized, 1970; s. Ernest and Lenka (Weinberger) N. Dipl. Ing., Inst. Tech., Bratislava, 1957; D.Sc., Inst. Tech. Vienna, Austria, 1968. Research scientist Inst. Biology, Slovak Acad. Scis., Bratislava, 1957-59; head biochem. control dept. Inst. for Sera and Vet. Vaccines (Bioveta), Nitra, Czechoslovakia, 1959-61; research scientist Inst. Virology, Czechoslovak Acad. Scis., Bratislava, 1961-64; vis. scientist Karolinska Inst., Stockholm, 1964; fellow Wistar Inst. Anatomy and Biology, Phila., 1964-65; research scientist Wyeth Labs., Inc., Phila., 1965-72; investigator Lindsley F. Kimball Research Inst., N.Y. Blood Center, N.Y.C., 1972—; cons. in field. Contbr. articles to profl. jours. Nat. Heart, Lung and Blood Inst. grantee, 1976-84; N.Y. State Health Research Council grantee, 1981. Mem. Am. Soc. Microbiology, AAAS, N.Y. Acad. Scis., Soc. Gen. Microbiology, Panam. Group for Rapid Viral Diagnosis, Am. Soc., Virology. Patentee in field. Current Work: Viruses transmitted by blood transfusion and products derived from blood; hepatitis B and nonA, nonB, antiviral vaccines, synthetic peptides as immunogens, diagnostic tests. Subspecialties: Virology (medicine); Infectious diseases. Home: 230 E 79th St Apt 5F New York NY 10021 Office: 310 E 67th St New York NY 10021

NEURINGER, JOSEPH LOUIS, mathematical physics educator, consultant; b. Bklyn., Jan. 16, 1922; s. Charles and Beckie (Kirsh) N. B.A., Bklyn Coll., 1943 M.A., Columbia U., 1948; Ph.D., NYU, 1951; cert. meteorology U. Chgo., 1944. Prin. staff engr. Republic Aviation Corp., Farmingdale, N.Y., 1951-62; sr. cons. scientist Avco Systems Div., Wilmington, Mass., 1962-70; prof. math. U. Lowell, Mass., 1970-85; cons. Avco Systems Div., Wilmington, Mass., 1977—. Contbr. articles to profl. jours. Served as 1st lt. USAF, 1943-46, ETO. Assoc. fellow AIAA (charter mem. plasma dynamics com. 1964); mem. Am. Phys. Soc., N.Y. Acad. Scis., Sigma Xi, Pi Mu Epsilon. Jewish. Lodge: Masons. Current work: Application of the fundamental principles of physics and mathematics to the solution of problems associated with space flight and aerospace industry in general. Subspecialties: Analysis; Aerospace engineering and technology.

NEVINS, JAMES LAWRENCE, JR., research laboratory administrator, electrical engineer; b. Boston, Dec. 31, 1927; s. James Lawrence and Muriel (Clayton) N.; m. Mabel Alice Rose, July 10, 1948; children—James Gary, Steven Michael, Paul Allen. B.S.E.E., Northeastern U., 1952; M.S., MIT, 1956. With Draper Lab (formerly MIT Instrumentation Lab), Cambridge, Mass., 1952—, leader robotics and assembly systems div.; invited lectr. and guest USSR Acad. Sci., 1971; past chmn. tech. com. for space Inst. Navigation; chmn. Japanese evaluation com. mechatronics panel Dept. Commerce. Contbr. articles to profl. publs. Co-patentee folded remote ctr. compliance device, servo-controlled mobility devices. Served with U.S. Army, 1946-47. Mem. IEEE (del. on Am. Automatic Control Council effects of automation com.), Am. Automatic Control Council (chmn. tech. com. on mfg. tech.), Internat. Fedn. Automatic Control (vice chmn. tech. com. on mfg. tech.), Robot Inst. Assn./Soc. Mfg. Engrs., AIAA. Current work: Applied research on advanced robotics, intelligent systems, and programmable automation/assembly systems. Subspecialty: Robotics. Office: Charles Stark Draper Lab Inc 555 Technology Sq Cambridge MA 02139

NEWELL, FRANK WILLIAM, ophthalmologist, educator; b. St. Paul, Jan 14, 1916; s. Frank John and Hilda (Turnquist) N.; m. Marian Glennon, Sept. 12, 1942; children: Frank William, Mary Susan Newell O'Connell, Elizabeth Glennon, David Andrew. M.D., Loyola U., Chgo., 1939; M.Sc., U. Minn., 1942. Diplomate: Am. Bd. Ophthalmology (chmn. bd. 1967-69, cons. 1971-74). Intern Ancker Hosp., St. Paul, 1939-40; teaching fellow U. Minn., 1940-42; research fellow, instr., asso. dept. ophthalmology Northwestern U. Med. Sch., 1946-53; now James and Anna Raymond prof. dept. ophthalmology U. Chgo. Med. Sch.; prof. extraordinario Autonomous U. Barcelona, Spain; sci. counselor Nat. Inst. Neurol. Diseases and Blindness, 1959-62, chmn., 1961-62; mem. nat. eye council NIH, 1972-75; mem. Internat. Council Ophthalmology, 1977-85. Author: Ophthalmology: Principles and Concepts, 6th edit, 1986; also articles.; Editor-in-chief, pub.: Am. Jour. Ophthalmology; editor: Hereditary Diseases of the Eye, 1980, Stedman's Med. Dictionary, 24th edit., 1982. Trustee Loyola U., Chgo., 1977-81. Served from 1st lt. to maj. M.C. AUS, 1942-46. Mem. Nat. Soc. Prevention Blindness (dir., chmn. research com. 1961-68, 70-81, v.p. 1970-81, pres. 1981-83, chmn. bd. 1983—), Am. Acad. Ophthalmology and Otolaryngology (pres. 1975), Inst. Barraquer (pres. 1970—), Assn. Research Ophthal. (chmn. bd. trustees 1967-68), Am. Ophthal. Soc. (pres.-elect 1985—; Howe medal 1979), Academia Ophthalmologica Internationalis (pres. 1980-84), Soc. Exptl. Biology and Medicine, Soc. Franc d'ophth., Sigma Xi, Alpha Omega Alpha. Roman Catholic. Clubs: Literary (Chgo.), Quadrangle (Chgo.). Current Work: Laser effects epithelial proliferation. Subspecialties: Ophthalmology; Laser medicine. Home: 4500 N Mozart St Chicago IL 60625 Office: 435 N Michigan Ave Chicago IL 60611

NEWELL, ROBERT TERRY, physicist; b. Whittier, Calif., Nov. 13, 1946; s. John Robert and Nan Marion (Bracken) N.; m. Elizabeth Carol Martin, Aug. 26, 1967; children: Darcy Lia, Jenna Michelle. B.S., N.Mex. Inst. Mining and Tech., 1968, Ph.D., 1981; M.S., U. West Fla., 1970. Asso. engr. Boeing Co., Albuquerque, 1967-68; research asst. N.Mex. Inst. Mining and Tech., 1977-79; jr. research asso. Nat. Radio Astronomy Obs., Socorro, N. Mex., 1979-81, research assoc., 1981-82; sr. scientist Scott Sci. and Tech., ALbuquerque, 1983—. Contbr. articles to profl. jours. Active pastor-parish relations com. Meth. Ch. Served with USN, 1968-76; Served with UNSR Ready Res., 1977—. Decorated Air medals.; Recipient Founders Award N.Mex.Inst. Mining and Tech., 1981. Mem. Am. Astron. Soc., AIAA, Naval Res. Assn. Republican. Current Work: Seismic instrumentation and data processing, stellar atmospheres, mass loss and evolution. Subspecialties: Radio and microwave astronomy; Theoretical astrophysics. Home: Rural Route 3 Box 1156 Los Lumas NM 87031 Office: Scott Sci and Tech 2601 Wyoming NE Suite C ALbuquerque NM 87112

NEWELL, STEVEN YOUNG, microbial ecologist; b. Cleve., Jan. 20, 1945; s. William H.B. and Elizabeth (Evans) N.; m. Becky McCranie, Apr. 9, 1966. B.Sc., U. Miami, Coral Gables, Fla., 1967; M.Sc., U. Miami Inst. Marine Sci., 1969, Ph.D., 1974. Research assoc. U. Miami Sch. Marine Atmospheric Sci., Fla., 1972-79; research assoc. U. Ga. Marine Inst., Sapelo Island, 1979-81, asst. research scientist, 1981-82, assoc. research scientist, 1982—. Contbr. articles to profl. jours. Mem. Am. Soc. Limnology and Oceanography, Am. Soc. Microbiology, Mycological Soc. Am., Brit. Mycological Soc., Estuarine and Brackish Water Scis. Assn. Democrat. Current work: Description of the functioning of fungi and other microbes in coastal marine ecosystems. Subspecialties: Ecology (biology); Microbiology. Office: U Ga Marine Inst Sapelo Island GA 31327

NEWKIRK, GORDON ALLEN, JR., astrophysicist; b. Orange, N.J., June 12, 1928; s. Gordon Allen and Mildred (Fleming) N.; m. Nancy Buck, Apr. 11, 1956; children—Sally, Linda, Jennifer. B.A., Harvard U., 1950; M.A., U. Mich., 1952, Ph.D., 1953. Research asst. Observatory, U. Mich., 1950-53; astrophysicist Upper Air Research Observatory, 1953; sr. research staff High Altitude Observatory, Boulder, Colo., 1955—; adj. prof. dept. astrogeophysics U. Colo., 1961-65, adj. prof. physics and astrophysics, 1965-76; dir. High Altitude Obs., 1968-79; cons. NASA, 1964—; mem. geophysics research bd. Nat. Acad. Sci., 1976-80. Contbr. articles on solar-interplanetary physics to profl. jours. Served with U.S. Army, 1953-55. Mem. AAAS, Am. Astron. Soc. (chmn. solar physics div. 1972-73), Internat. Astron. Union (pres. com. 10 1975-79), Research Soc. Am., Commn. V Union Radio Sci. Internat., Am. Geophysical Union, Sigma Xi. Current Work: Structure of solar corona and heliosphere, solar cycle modulation of galactic cosmic rays. Subspecialties: Optical astronomy; Solar physics. Home: 3797 Wonderland Hill Ave Boulder CO 80302 Office: High Altitude Observatory PO Box 3000 Boulder CO 80307

NEWMAN, ARNOLD LEWIS, engineer; b. N.Y.C., Mar. 3, 1951; s. Bernard and Erna May (Topper) N.; m. Lynnette Kaye Nieman, Oct. 30, 1976; 1 child, David J. B.A., Swarthmore Coll., 1973; postgrad. SUNY-Buffalo, 1973-76, B.S. in Elec. Engring., 1979. Researcher, Sloan-Kettering Inst. for Cancer Research, N.Y.C., 1976; elec. LTV-Sierra Research Div., Buffalo, 1979-82; program mgr. Johns Hopkins U. Applied Physics Lab., Laurel, Md., 1982—. Contbr. articles to profl. jours. Inventor in engring. field. Mem. IEEE, Tau Beta Pi. Current work: Technology transfer of space technology into medicine. Development of medical electronics devices; chemical and biological. Management of these programs. Subspecialties: Biomedical engineering; Electronics. Home: 4128 Warner St Kensington MD 20895 Office: Johns Hopkins U Applied Physics Lab Johns Hopkins Rd Laurel MD 20707

NEWMAN, DAVID JOHN, microbial biochemist, researcher; b. Grays, Essex, Eng., May 2, 1939; came to U.S., 1968, naturalized, 1976; s. Alfred Harrold and Clara Alma (King) N.; m. Peggy Lee Barnish, Aug. 2, 1969; 1 child, Alexander. M.S., U. Liverpool, Eng., 1963; D. Phil., U. Sussex, Eng., 1968; M.S.L.S., Drexel U., 1977. Research asst. J. Bibby & Sons Ltd., Neston, Cheshire, Eng., 1956-61; research organic chemist Ilford Ltd., Essex, 1963-64; asst. exptl. officer unit of nitrogen fixation ARC, U. Sussex, Brighton, Eng., 1964-68; sr. biochemist SK&F Labs, Phila., 1970-79, sr. investigator, Swedeland, Pa., 1979—. Contbr. articles to profl. jours. Patentee in field. Bd. dirs., sec. Roboda Civic Assn., Royersford, Pa., 1976-78; vice chmn. Ilford Young Conservatives, Eng., 1962-64. Fellow Royal Soc. Chemistry; mem. Inst. Biology, Am. Chem. Soc., Am. Soc. Microbiology. Current work: Enzymology; comparative biochemistry of lower eukaryotes; prokaryotes; cell-cell interactions at molecular level; metalloenzymes. Subspecialties: Biochemistry (biology); Microbiology. Home: 675 Crestwood Rd Wayne PA 19087 Office: SK&F Labs 709 Swedeland Rd Swedeland PA 19479

NEWMAN, DAVID WILLIAM, plant physiology, biochemistry educator; b. Pleasant Grove, Utah, Oct. 26, 1933; s. Frank Byrd and Edna (Holdaway) N.; m. JoAnne Marie Slighting, May 16, 1956; 1 child, Steven David. B.S., U. Utah, 1955, M.S., 1957, Ph.D., 1960; postdoctorate Oak Ridge Inst. Nuclear Studies, 1958. Select fellow U. Utah, Salt Lake City, 1955-59, research asst., 1959-60; asst. prof. plant physiology and biochemistry Miami U., Oxford, Ohio, 1960-66, assoc. prof., 1966-74, prof., 1974—. Editor: Instrumental Methods of Experimental Biology, 1964. Contbr. articles, photographs to profl. jours., mag. Contbr. essays to mags., jours. Served with U.S. Army, 1957. Recipient several NSF, indsl. grants. Fellow Ohio Acad. Sci.; mem. Am. Assn. Plant Physiologists, Am. Chem. Soc., Am. Oil Chemists Soc., Friends of Photography, AAAS, Internat. Platform Assn., Phi Beta Kappa, Sigma Xi, Phi Sigma, Phi Kappa Phi. Mormon. Current work: Physiology and biochemistry of plant membranes; physiological biochemistry of plant and plant cellular aging especially the latter stages of development, senescence. Subspecialties: Photosynthesis; Biochemistry (biology). Office: Miami U Dept Botany Oxford OH 45056

NEWMAN, JACK HUFF, biochemist, researcher; b. Roanoke, Va., Aug. 15, 1929; s. Carlis Raymond and Allene McCorkel (Chittum) N.; m. Jeanette Semones, July 25, 1956; children—Jack H., Jr., Jonathan R. Joel D. B.S. in Gen. Sci., Va. Poly. Inst. and State U., 1956, M.S. in Bacteriology, 1959. Research asst. Va. Poly. Inst. and Sci. U., Blacksburg, 1956-58; jr. biochemist Smith, Kline & French, Phila., 1958-62; group mgr. radioisotope group A.H. Robins Co., Richmond, Va., 1962—. Served to 2d lt. U.S. Army, 1952-53; Korea; Col. USAR. Mem. Am. Chem. Soc., Health Physics Soc. Current work: Drug metabolism using radioisotope tracer techniques. Subspecialties: Biochemistry (medicine); Health services research. Home: 8106 Diane Ln Richmond VA 23227 Office: A H Robins Co Inc 1211 Sherwood Ave Richmond VA 23220

NEWMAN, JAMES EDWARD, agrometerologist, climatologist, educator; b. Brown County, Ohio, Dec. 22, 1920; s. Roy Lee and Lola Rae (Schweickart) N.; m. L. Persis Haas, July 17, 1949; children—C. Shelley, Roy C., Arnold H. B.S., Ohio State U., 1947, M.S., 1949; postgrad Purdue U., 1950-53, U. Wis., 1957-58. Cert. prof. meteorologist, Asst. agronomist Ohio Agrl. Expt. Sta., 1947-49; asst. prof. agronomy, Purdue U., West Lafayette, Ind., 1950-59, assoc. prof., 1960-67, prof., 1968—; vis. prof. hort. sci. U. Calif.-Riverside, 1965-66; vis. scientist U. Alaska-Palmer, 1970; vis. prof. Wye Coll. U. London, 1977. Editor in chief Agrl. Meteorology jour., 1973-76. Contbr. articles to profl. jours. Served with USAAF, 1942-46. Fellow AAAS, Am. Soc. Agronomy (crops and soils award 1965), Ind. Acad. Sci.; mem. Am. Meteorol. Soc., Internat. Soc. Biometeorology (pres. elect. 1985-87, agrl. meteorol. award 1976). Subspecialties: Climatology; Agricultural meteorology. Office: Dept Agronomy Purdue U West Lafayette IN 47907

NEWMAN, JERRY OKEY, agricultural engineer, researcher; b. New Martinsville, W.Va., May 9, 1936; s. James Okey and Hazel Edna (Howell) N.; m. Patricia Grace Devericks, May 25, 1958; children: Tamrah M., Lucetta R., Symantha C., Onika M. B.S.Ag.E., W.Va. U., 1958, M.S.Ag.E., 1960; Ph.D. in Engring, U. Md., 1972. Registered profl. engr., W.Va. Grad. asst. W.Va. U., 1958-60; hosp. engr. VA, Clarksburg, W.Va., 1960-62; research engr. in rural housing U.S. Dept. Agr., Beltsville, Md., 1962-73; in rural housing and solar energy Agrl. Research Service, Clemson, S.C., 1973-85; cons. engring. services, 1985—; auctioneer; real estate broker. Author numerous Dept. Agr. publs.; contbr. numerous articles to profl. jours. Pres. Pickens County (S.C.) Retarded Citizens Assn., 1975-78. Recipient Superior Performance award VA, 1961; Danforth summer fellow, 1957. Mem. Am. Soc. Agrl. Engrs., Nat. Inst. Bldg. Sci., Internat. Solar Energy Soc., Sigma Xi, Tau Beta Pi. Democrat. Clubs: Red Necks (Clemson); 4H All Stars. Current Work: Energy conservation, housing, solar heating, house design, earth housing, insulation. Subspecialties: Agricultural engineering; Solar energy. Home: Route 1 Box 474 Central SC 29630 Office: PO Box 792 Clemson SC 29633

NEWMAN, JOHN DENNIS, neuroscientist; b. Newark, Sept. 28, 1940; s. Richard and Elsie (Brown) N.; m. Judith Osler Scaffidi, Aug. 18, 1962; children: Peter, Matthew. B.S., Cornell U., 1962; Ph.D., U. Rochester, 1969. Staff fellow Nat. Inst. Child Health and Human Devel., NIH, Bethesda, Md., 1969-74, research physiologist Lab. Devel. Neurobiology, 1982-84, Lab. Comparative Ethology, 1984—, reviewer Sci. Books and Films; vis. scientist Max Planck Inst. Psychiatry, Munich, W.Ger., 1974-75. Contbr. in field. Recipient Alexander von Humboldt Soc. award, 1974. Mem. AAAS, Soc. Neuroscience, Animal Behavior Soc., Am. Soc. Primatologist. Mem. United Ch. of Christ. Current Work: Brain mechanisms of primate communication; neurophysiology neuroethology; bioacoustics; evolution; communication; evolution of species-specific communication mechanisms, genetic programming of behavior. Subspecialties: Neurobiology; Ethology. Home: 10910 Stillwater Ave Kensington MD 20895 Office: Bldg T-18 NIHAC Bethesda MD 20205

NEWMAN, JOHN HUGHES, medical educator, researcher; b. Balt., Oct. 1, 1945; s. Elliot Voss and Ailsa (MacKay) N.; m. Rebecca Lyford, May 13, 1978; children—Katherine, Alexander. B.A., Harvard Coll., 1967; M.D., Columbia U., 1971. Diplomate Am. Bd. Internal Medicine, Am. Bd. Pulmonary Medicine. Intern Columbia-Presbyterian Hosp., N.Y.C., 1971-73; resident Johns Hopkins. U., Balt., 1973-74; fellow U. Colo., Denver, 1976-79; asst. prof. Vanderbilt U., Nashville, 1979-83, assoc. prof., 1983—, Elsa S. Hanigan Chair in Pulmonary Medicine; chief of pulmonary medicine St. Thomas Hosp., Nashville, 1984—. Contbr. articles to profl. jours. and books. Served to maj. U.S. Army, 1974-76; Korea. Recipient Clin. Investigator award NIH, 1981—. Mem. Am. Thoracic Soc., Am. Physiol. Soc. Episcopalian. Current work: Lung vascular physiology, inflammatory lung disease. Subspecialty: Pulmonary medicine. Home: 5710 Stoneway Trail Nashville TN 37209 Office: Vanderbilt U Med Ctr Nashville TN 37232

NEWMAN, LEONARD, chemist; b. N.Y.C., Jan. 15, 1931; s. Louis and Sarah (Pitlock) N.; m. Jacqueline Muller, June 14, 1953; children—Michael, Beverly. B.A., Poly. Inst. Bklyn., 1952; Ph.D., MIT, 1956. Chemist, Nat. Lead Co., Winchester, Mass., 1956-58, Brookhaven Nat. Lab., Upton, N.Y., 1958—. Mem. Am. Chem. Soc., AAAS, N.Y. Acad. Sci., Air Pollution Control Assn. Current work: Atmospheric chemistry as they relate to the impacts of air pollution. Subspecialties: Atmospheric chemistry; Environmental chemistry. Home: 23 Trent Ln Smithtown NY 11787 Office: Brookhaven Nat Lab Bldg 426 Upton NY 11973

NEWMAN, MELVIN SPENCER, chemist, educator; b. N.Y.C., Mar. 10, 1908; s. Jacob K. and Mae (Polack) N.; m. Beatrice N. Crystal, June 30, 1933; children: Kiefer, Susan, Beth, Robert. B.S., Yale U., 1929, Ph.D., 1932; D.Sc. (hon.), U. New Orleans, 1975, Bowling Green State U., 1978, Ohio State U., 1979. Instr. Ohio State U., 1936-39, Elizabeth Clay Howald scholar, 1939-40, asst. prof., 1940-44, prof. chemistry, 1944-78, prof. emeritus, 1978—, regents prof., 1966; Fulbright lectr. U. Glasgow, 1957, 67. Asso. editor: Jour. Organic Chemistry and Organic Syntheses. Guggenheim fellow, 1951; Recipient award, 1961, E.W. Morley medal, 1969, Columbus (Ohio) award, 1976, Roger Adams award, 1979; all Am. Chem. Soc.; W.L. Cross medal Yale U., 1970; Joseph Sullivant medal Ohio State U., 1976. Mem. Am., Brit. chem. socs., Nat. Acad. Sci., Sigma Xi. Current Work: Synthesis of new compounds of interest in theoretical chemistry and cancer related. Subspecialties: Organic chemistry; Synthetic chemistry. Home: 2239 Onandaga Dr Columbus OH 43221

NEWMAN, MORRIS, mathematics educator; b. N.Y.C., Feb. 25, 1924; s. Isaac and Sarah (Cohen) N.; m. Mary Aileen Lenk, Sept. 18, 1948; children: Sally Ann, Carl Lenk. A.B., NYU, 1945; M.A., Columbia U., 1946; Ph.D., U. Pa., 1952. Mathematician applied math. div. Nat. Bur. Standards, Washington, 1951-63, chief numerical analysis sect., 1963-70, sr. research mathematician, 1970-76; prof. math. U. Calif.-Santa Barbara, 1976—; dir. Inst. Interdisciplinary Applications of Algebra and Combinatorics, 1980—. Author: Matrix Representations of Groups, 1968, Integral Matrices, 1972; contbr. articles to math. jours. Recipient gold metal U.S. Dept. Commerce, 1966. Mem. Am. Math. Soc. (council 1980—), Math. Assn. Am., AAAS, London Math. Soc., Washington Acad. Scis., Sigma Xi. Jewish. Current Work: Applications of number theory to computation, matrix computations, exact computation. Subspecialties: Applied mathematics; Algorithms. Home: 1050 Las Alturas Rd Santa Barbara CA 93103 Office: Dept Math U Calif Santa Barbara CA 93106

NEWMARK, RICHARD ALAN, analytical chemist; b. Urbana, Ill., Nov. 11, 1940; s. Nathan M. and Anne (Cohen) N.; m. Joan Friedman, July 4, 1965; children—David, Merel. A.B., Harvard U., 1961; Ph.D., U. Calif.-Berkeley, 1964. Postgrad. fellow MIT, Cambridge, 1964-66; asst. prof. chemistry, U. Colo., Boulder, 1966-69; research chemist 3M, St. Paul, 1969-72, research specialist, 1972-76, sr. research specialist, 1976-81, staff scientist, 1981—. Pres. Dist. 1 council, St. Paul, 1984—. Mem. Am. Chem. Soc. (chmn. Minn. sect. 1983-84), Soc. Applied Spectroscopy, Phi Beta Kappa, Sigma Xi. Republican. Jewish. Current work: Nuclear magnetic resonance. Subspecialties: Nuclear magnetic resonance; Analytical chemistry. Home: 182 N Hazel St St Paul MN 55119 Office: 3M Bldg 201-BS-05 St Paul MN 55144

NEWNHAM, ROBERT EVEREST, physicist. Prof. solid state physics Pa. State U., University Park. Subspecialty: Crystallography. Office: Pa State U Dept Materials Sci University Park PA 16802

NEWSOM, GERALD HIGLEY, astronomer, educator; b. Albuquerque, Feb. 11, 1939; s. Carroll Vincent and Frances (Higley) N.; m. Ann Bricker, June 17, 1972; children: Christine, Elizabeth. B.A., U. Mich., 1961; Ph.D., Harvard U., 1968. Postdoctoral research asst. Imperial Coll. Sci. and Tech., London, 1968-69; asst. prof. Ohio State U., Columbus, 1969-73, assoc. prof. astronomy, 1973-82, prof. astronomy, 1982—; sr. postdoctoral research asst. Physikalisches Institut, U. Bonn, W.Ger., 1978. Author: (with W.M. Protheroe and E.R. Capriotti) Astronomy, 1976, Exploring the Universe, 1979; also articles. Mem. Internat. Astron. Union, Am. Astron. Soc. Current Work: Spectrum of SS 433; atomic absorption in ultraviolet wavelengths. Subspecialties: Optical astronomy; Atomic and molecular physics. Home: 46 W Weisheimer Rd Columbus OH 43214 Office: 174 W 18th Ave Columbus OH 43210

NEWTON, AMOS SYLVESTER, chemist, research scientist; b. Shingletown, Calif., July 26, 1916; s. James Albert and Mabel Kathryn (Fox) N.; m. Mary Elizabeth Powers, Apr. 25, 1942; children—Mabel Anne, Margaret. B.S. in Chemistry, U. Calif.-Berkeley, 1938; M.S., U. Mich., Ann Arbor, 1939, Ph.D. in Chemistry, 1941. Chemist, Eastman Kodak Co., Rochester, N.Y., 1941-42, Berkeley, Calif., 1946-62, Iowa State Coll. Manhattan Project, Ames, 1942-46; staff sr. scientist Lawrence Berkeley Lab., 1962—, also cons., 1946-62. Co-author: Radiation Effects on Organic Materials, 1963. Patentee in field (10). Author numerous sci. papers. Fellow AAAS; mem. Am. Chem. Soc., Am. Soc. Mass Spectrometry. Current work: Fundamental aspects of mass spectrometry and use of mass spectrometry in the study of environmental problems. Subspecialties: Physical chemistry; Environmental chemistry. Office: Lawrence Berkeley Lab 1 Cyclotron Rd Berkeley CA 94720

NEWTON, ROBERTA ANN, physical therapist, educator; b. Providence, May 8, 1947; d. Robert E. and Georgianna R. (La Croix) N. B.S. in Phys. Therapy, Med. Coll. Va., 1975, Physiology-Neurophysiology, 1973. Cert. phys. therapist, Va. Asst. prof. dept. phys. therapy Med. Coll. Va., Richmond, 1973-80, asso. prof., 1980—; manuscript reviewer. Author: (with Payton and Hirt) Scientific Bases for Neurophysiological Approaches to Therapeutic Exercies, 1977, (with Van Sant) Therapeutic Exercise Competencies for Entry Level Physical Therapists and Therapeutic Exercise Instructor, 1981, 85; contbr. (with Van Sant) numerous articles to sci. jours. Med. Coll. Va. grantee, 1973; HEW spl. improvement grantee, 1974-79. Mem. Soc. for Neurosci., AAAS, Am. Phys. Therapy Assn. (grant reviewer), Va. Acad. Sci., Sigma Xi. Methodist. Current Work: Neurophysiological bases of therapeutic exercise; physiological bases for high voltage galvanic electrotherapy. Subspecialty: Neurophysiology. Office: Dept Physical Therapy Med Coll Va Box 224 Richmond VA 23298

NEWTON, STEVEN ARTHUR, optical engineer, researcher; b. Teaneck, N.J., Feb. 6, 1954; s. Richard A. and Evelyn (Caruccio) N. B.S. in Physics summa cum laude, U. Mass., 1976; M.S. in Applied Physics, Stanford U., 1978, postgrad., 1978-83. Lab. asst. Hasbrouck Lab., U. Mass., Amherst, 1975-76; research asst. E.L. Ginzton Lab., Stanford U., Palo Alto, Calif., 1976-82, research assoc., 1982-83; summer intern Hewlett-Packard Labs., Palo Alto, 1978, mem. tech. staff, 1978—. Contbr. articles on laser light scattering, hollow cathode metal vapor lasers, single-mode fiber-optic components, fiber-optic gyros, fiber signal processing devices to profl. publs. Mem. Optical Soc. Am., Soc. Photo-Optical Instrumentation Engrs., IEEE, Phi Beta Kappa, Phi Kappa Phi. Current Work: High-speed optoelectronics. Subspecialties: Fiber optics; Optical signal processing. Home: 2044 Lyon Ave Belmont CA 94002 Office: 1651 Page Mill Rd Bldg 28C Palo Alto CA 94304

NEWTON, WILLIAM ALLEN, JR., pediatric pathologist, researcher; b. Traverse City Mich., May 19, 1923; s. William Allen and Florence Emma (Brown) N.; m. Helen Patricia Goodrich, Apr. 21, 1945; children—Katherine Germain, Elizabeth Gale, William Allen III, Nancy Anne. B.Sc. cum laude, Alma Coll., 1943; M.D., U. Mich., 1946. Diplomate Am. Bd. Pathology, Am. Bd. Pediatrics. Intern, Wayne County Gen. Hosp., Detroit, 1946; resident in pediatric pathology Children's Hosp. Mich., 1947-50, Children's Hosp., Phila., 1950; chief dept. lab. medicine Children's Hosp., Columbus, Ohio, 1952—; mem. faculty Coll. Medicine Ohio State U., 1952—, chief div. pediatric pathology; chmn. pathology com. Children's Cancer Study Group. Chmn. com. Ohio Cancer Coordinating Com.; chmn. sci. adv. com. Armed Forces Inst. Pathology. Served capt. U.S. Army, 1953-56; brig. gen. USAR. Contbr. articles (over 100) to profl. jours. Recipient numerous grants for childhood cancer and blood disorders. Mem. Midwest Soc. Pediatric Research (council 1960-63, pres. 1964-65), Soc. Pediatric Research, Am. Pediatric Soc., Am. Soc. Clin. Oncology, Internat. Soc. Pediatric Oncology, Ohio State Med. Assn. (chmn. com. on cancer), Pediatric Pathology Soc. (pres. 1968-69), Am. Cancer Soc. (Ohio div. bd. trustees, exec. com.), Nat. Am. Cancer Soc. (adv. com. childhood cancer), Sigma Xi, Phi Sigma Pi. Republican. Baptist (chmn., adv. com.). First to identify an enzyme deficiency as cause of chronic hemolytic anemia in man; pioneer in establishing principles of drug treatment of childhood cancer. Current work: Causes and types of childhood cancer; childhood cancer etiology, classification, epidemiology. Subspecialties: Cancer research (medicine); Pathology (medicine). Home: 2500 Harrison Rd Johnstown OH 43031 Office: 700 Childrens Dr Columbus OH 43205

NEY, EDWARD PURDY, physicist; b. Mpls., Oct. 28, 1920; s. Otto Frederick and Jessamine (Purdy) N.; m. June Felsing, June, 1942; children—Judy, John, Arthur, William. B.S., U. Minn., 1942; Ph.D., U. Va., 1947. Research asst., research asso. U. Va., 1940-46; cons. Naval Research Lab., 1943-44; asst. prof. U. Va., 1947; mem. faculty dept. physics and astronomy U. Minn., Mpls., 1947—, prof., 1955-74, U. Minn. regents prof., 1974—, chmn. dept. astronomy, 1974-78. Author: Electromagnetism and Relativity, 1962; contbr. articles to profl. jours. Recipient NASA Exceptional Sci. Achievement medal, 1975. Mem. Am. Phys. Soc., Am. Geophys. Union, Am. Astron. Soc., Nat. Acad. Sci., Am. Acad. Arts and Sci., Internat. Astron. Union, Sigma Xi. Subspecialties: Infrared astronomy; Geophysics. Home: 1925 Penn Ave S Minneapolis MN 55405 Office: Sch Physics and Astronomy 116 Church St SE Minneapolis MN 55455

NEY, ROBERT LEO, physician, educator, researcher; b. Brno, Czechoslovakia, May 22, 1933; came to U.S., 1941, naturalized, 1946; s. Paul E. and Katherine B. (Kroner) N.; m. Sally Sanford Burrage, June 24, 1956; children—Elizabeth, Sarah, Peter. B.A., Harvard U., 1954; M.D., Cornell U., 1958. Diplomate Am. Bd. Internal Medicine. Intern in medicine Vanderbilt U. Hosp., Nashville, 1958-59, asst. resident in medicine, 1960-61, fellow in endocrinology, 1961-63, asst. prof. medicine, 1965-67; investigator clin. endocrinology br. Nat. Heart Inst., NIH, Bethesda, Md., 1963-65; assoc. prof. U. N.C., Chapel Hill, 1967-70, prof., 1970-80, dir. endocrinology, 1967-72, chmn. dept. medicine, 1972-80, Eunice Bernhard disting. prof. medicine, 1977-80; prof. medicine, dir. div. endocrinology and metabolism Johns Hopkins U., Balt., 1981—, John Eager Howard prof. endocrinology and metabolism, 1984—. Assoc. editor Metabolism, 1970—. Contbr. numerous chpts., articles to profl. publs. Served to lt. comdr. USPHS, 1963-65. Recipient The Prof. award Sr. Class, U. N.C. Sch. Medicine, 1969. Fellow ACP; mem. Am. Soc. Clin. Investigation, Assn. Am. Physicians, Am. Fedn. Clin. Research, Endocrine Soc. (postgrad. com. 1972-75), Am. Clin. and Climatol. Assn., So. Soc. Clin. Investigation, AAAS, Am. Physiol. Soc. Interurban Clin. Club, Sigma Xi, Alpha Omega Alpha. Current work: Regulation of pituitary gland function; molecular biology of peptide hormones of the pituitary gland; neuroendocrinology. Subspecialty: Neuroendocrinology. Home: 4304 Wickford Rd Baltimore MD 21210 Office: Johns Hopkins Med Sch Dept Medicine 720 Rutland Ave Baltimore MD 21205

NEZU, ARTHUR MAGUTH, psychologist; b. N.Y.C., Nov. 24, 1952; s. Tetsuo and Mary (Yabutani) N.; m. Christine Maguth, June 12, 1983; stepchildren: Frank, Alice, Linda. B.A., SUNY Stony Brook, 1974, M.A., 1976, Ph.D., 1979. Lic. psychologist, N.Y., N.J. Clin. psychology intern Norwich Hosp., Conn., 1977-78; clin. asst. prof. dept. community dentistry Fairleigh Dickinson U., Hackensack, N.J., 1981—, dept. psychology, 1982-84, clin. assoc. prof., 1984-85, assoc. prof., 1985—, coordinator tng. div. psychol. services, asst. dir., 1978-85, co-dir Vets. Readjustment Program, 1982—, assoc. dir. Natural Setting Therapeutic Mgmt. Program, 1980-84; cons. Pilgrim State Hosp., L.I., 1977; adj. prof. psychology Ramapo Coll. N.J., 1980. Contbr. articles to profl. jours.; editor books. N.Y. State Regents scholar, 1970-74; recipient SUNY Stony Brook undergrad. psychology award, 1974. Mem. Am. Psychol. Assn., Assn. for Advancement Behavior Therapy, Assn. for Children with Down's Syndrome, Eastern Psychol. Assn., Am. Assn. Mental Deficiency, Soc. Behavioral Medicine, AAAS, Assn. Am. Dental Schs., Phi Beta Kappa. Current Work: Cognitive factors in psychopathology; problem-solving; clinical decision-making and judgement; behavioral problems of mentally retarded, depression, behavioral medicine/dentistry. Subspecialties: Behavioral psychology; Cognition. Office: Dept Psychology Fairleigh Dickinson U Teaneck NJ 07666

NG, LORENZ KENG YONG, physician, consultant, researcher; b. Singapore, Aug. 6, 1940; came to U.S., 1958, naturalized, 1969; s. Seak Khuan and Poh Hiang (Tan) N.; m. Roberta Melia, Dec. 7, 1981. A.B., Stanford U., 1961; M.D., Columbia U., 1965. Diplomate Am. Bd. Psychiatry and Neurology, Nat. Bd. Med. Examiners. Chief resident in neurology Hosp. of U. Pa., Phila., 1968-69; spl. research fellow NIMH, 1969-72, spl. asst. to dir. drug abuse, 1972-76; chief Intramural Research Lab., Nat. Inst. on Drug Abuse, Bethesda, Md., 1976-78, chief pain studies program, 1978-81; med. dir. Washington Pain Ctr., 1982—; asst. clin. prof. psychiatry Johns Hopkins U., 1978—, asst. clin. prof. neurosurgery, 1984; asst. clin. prof. neurology George Washington U., 1978—; med. dir. Consumers United Ins. Co., 1982—. Author: The Population Crisis: Implications and Plans for Action, 1964, Alternatives to Violence, 1968, Pain, Discomfort and Humanitarian Care, 1981, Strategies for Public Health, 1981, New Approaches to Treatment of Chronic Pain, 1981. Pres. World Man Fund. Served with USPHS, 1974-81. Recipient Young Investigators award for research in acupuncture Am. Soc. Chinese Medicine, 1975; Commendation medal USPHS, 1981. Mem. Am. Acad. Neurology (S. Weir Mitchell award 1971), Soc. for Neurosci., Soc. Biol. Psychiatry (A.E. Bennett award 1972), World Acad. Art and Sci. (pres. Am. div. 1982—); mem. Am. Inst. Stress (founding dir.). Club: Cosmos (Washington). Current Work: Treatment of pain and stress disorders; acupuncture; electro therapy; behavioral medicine and health enhancement. Subspecialties: Neurology; Preventive medicine. Office: 2026 R St NW Washington DC 20009

NG, PETER ANN-BENG, computer science educator; b. Young-Peng, Johore, Malaysia, Dec. 31, 1941; s. Peter Kim-Chong Ng and Swee-Huang (Chua); m. Ida Ah-Siew-Lim, May 25, 1969; children—Eric, Evan. B.Sc. in Math., St. Edwards U., 1969; Ph.D. in Computer Sci., U. Tex. at Austin, 1974. Asst. prof. computer sci. Hunter Coll., N.Y.C., 1974-76; asst. prof. U. Mo.-Columbia, 1976-81, assoc. prof., 1981-84, prof., chmn. dept. computer sci., 1984—; cons. U.S. Army, Huntsville, 1982—, Internat. Software Systems, Inc., Austin, Tex., 1982—. Editor: (with others) Procs. on Reliability in Distributed Software and Database Systems, 1983; Entity Relationship Approach to Database and Related Software, 1984; editor-in-chief: Entity Relationship Approach on Software Engineering, 1983; assoc. editor Jour. Data and Knowledge Engring., 1985—, IEEE Trans. on Software Engring., 1985—. Mem. Computer Soc. of IEEE, Assn. Computing Machinery, AAAS. Current work: Distributed systems and networks; protocols validation; database design and modeling. Subspecialties: Software engineering; Distributed systems and networks. Home: 4506 Georgetown Dr Columbia MO 65203

NG, THOMAS K., microbiologist; b. Macau, China, Sept. 30, 1954; s. Ming and Tsui Wah (Lee) N.; m. Theresa Puifun Chow, June 24, 1954. B.S., U. Wis.-Madison, 1975, M.S., 1977, Ph.D., 1981. Enzymologist Solar Energy Research Inst., Dept. of Energy, Golden, Colo., 1980-81; research scientist E.I. du Pont de Nemours & Co., Wilmington, Del., 1981—. Contbr. articles to profl. jours. Mem. Am. Soc. for Microbiology, Am. Chem. Soc., Sigma Xi. Current Work: Optimization and process control in fermentation; commodity and specialty chemicals production from biomaterials. Subspecialties: Microbiology; Enzyme technology. Office: E I du Pont de Nemours & Co Wilmington DE 19898

NG, YEE JACK, theoretical physicist; b. Kwangtung, China, Nov. 2, 1946; came to U.S., 1965, naturalized, 1978; s. Ying Kit and Tai (Lee) Ing; m. Yvonne Woonyu Lee, Sept. 5, 1971; children—Lenhard Lee, Jakun Willard. A.B., U. Calif.-Berkeley, 1968; A.M., Harvard U., 1969, Ph.D., 1974. Mem. Inst. for Advanced Study, Princeton, N.J., 1974-76; research assoc. Stanford Linear Accelerator Ctr., Calif., 1976-78; assoc. prof. U. N.C., Chapel Hill, 1978—. Contbr. articles to profl. jours. U.S. Dept. Energy Prin. Investigator Research grantee, 1979—; A.P. Sloan Found. fellow, 1980-84. Mem. Am. Phys. Soc., Mems. of the Inst. for Advanced Study Assn. Current work: Theoretical particle physics, gravitation and cosmology, statistical physics. Subspecialties: Particle physics; Relativity and gravitation. Home: 1107 Roosevelt Dr Chapel Hill NC 27514 Office: Dept Physics U NC Chapel Hill NC 27514

NGAI, KIA LING, physicist; b. Canton, China, May 20, 1940; came to U.S., 1962; s. Hei Ming and Hok Yee (Cheung) N.; m. Linsen Hsia, Dec. 23, 1967; children: Siann, Seagan, Serin. B.Sc., U. Hong Kong, 1962; M.S. in Math, U. So. Calif., 1964; Ph.D. in Physics, U. Chgo., 1969. Research assoc. James Franck Inst., U. Chgo., 1969; staff mem. Lincoln Lab., M.I.T., 1969-71; research physicist Naval Research Lab., Washington, 1971-80, cons., 1980—. Recipient Navy Civilian Superior Service award Dept. Def., 1976. Mem. Am. Phys. Soc., Am. Chem. Soc. Current Work: Unified model of universal relaxation properties of condensed matter. Subspecialties: Condensed matter physics; Polymer physics. Home: 6500 Bellamine Ct McLean VA 22101 Office: Naval Research Lab Washington DC 20375

NGO, PETER DINH-TUAN, communications, manager, researcher; b. Vinh, Socialist Rep. Vietnam, Aug. 30, 1936; came to U.S. 1954, naturalized 1974; m. Cecilia Thanh-Liem, Dec. 26, 1958; children—John, Paul, Theresa, Francis, Claire. B.S.E.E., U. Dayton, 1957; M.S.E.E., U. Notre Dame, 1958; Ph.D., Iowa State U., 1962. Mem. tech. staff Bell Labs., Holmdel, N.J., 1962-82, Am. Bell, Neptune, N.J., 1982-83, AT&T Bell Labs., Holmdel, 1983-84; dist. research mgr. Bell Communications Research, Inc., 1984—. Treas. Monmouth Friends of Vietnam Refugees, N.J., 1975-80; pub. chmn. Soc. for Info. Display Jour., Los Angeles, 1984—; program chmn. Mid-Atlantic chpt., for 1984-85; award chmn. 1984, Internat. Symposium, San Diego, 1983-84. Patentee in field. Contbr. articles to profl. jours. Soc. for Info. Display fellow, 1982, recipient Spl. Recognition award, 1979. Fellow Soc. for Info. Display; mem. IEEE (sr. mem., honor and award com. 1984), Tau Beta Pi. Current work: Conduct research and plasma, electroluminescent, liquid crystal display devices and data input/output devices. Research focus: large area display with full color gray scale for wide band video services made possible by high bandwidth optical communications. Subspecialty: Information systems, storage, and retrieval (computer science). Office: Bell Communications Research Inc 600 Mountain Ave 7C-207 Murray Hill NJ 07974

NGUYEN, CHINH TRUNG, electrical engineer, researcher; b. Hanoi, Vietnam, Nov. 19, 1946; emigrated to Can., 1971; s. Hau Van and Nga Thi (Vu) N.; m. Hallouma Khediri, Feb. 11, 1974; 1 child, Tien Gia. Diploma in Engring, Swiss Fed. Inst. Tech., Lausanne, 1970; M.S.E.E., Laval U., Que., 1972; Ph.D., U. Que., 1982. Research asst. Swiss Fed. Inst. Tech., Lausanne, 1970-71; computer analyst Hydro-Quebec, Varennes, Que., Can., 1972-76; sr. researcher IREQ, 1976—; invited prof. U. Que., Varennes, 1973-74. Contbr. articles to profl. publs. Mem. IEEE (sr., Paper award 1982, W.R.G. Baker award 1983), Order of Engrs. Que., Soc. Indsl. and Applied Math. Patentee frequency digital meter. Current Work: Numerical control systems, computer simulation of power systems, parallel processing, computer networking, digital measurement and instrumentation. Subspecialties: Computer engineering; Mathematical software. Office: Institute de Recherche d'Hydro-Quebec Varennes PQ J0L 2P0 Canada

NGUYEN, DUC THAI, civil engineering educator; b. Hanoi, Vietnam, July 19, 1952; s. Dac Khac and Thinh Thi (Thai) N. B.S., Northeastern U., 1975; M.S., U. Calif.-Berkeley, 1976; Ph.D., U.Iowa, 1982. Cons. engr. Gen. Electric Co., San Jose, Calif., 1976-77; research asst. U. Iowa, Iowa City, 1977-82; researcher NASA Langley Research Ctr., Hampton, Va., summers 1983, 84; asst. prof. civil engring. Northeastern U., Boston, 1982—. Contbr. articles to profl. jours. Adviser, Vietnamese Student Assn. Northeastern U., 1983—. NASA-Am. Soc. Engring. Edn. fellow, summers, 1983, 84. Mem. Am. Soc. Engring. Edn., Soc. Indsl. and Applied Math., Am. Acad. Mechanics. Current work: Computational structural mechanics; structural optimization. Subspecialties: Civil engineering; Computer-aided design. Home: 117 Park Dr #12A Boston MA 02215

NGUYEN, DUNG CHI, associate engineer, biomedical engineer; b. Hanoi, Vietnam, Sept. 26, 1953; came to U.S. 1979; s. Quyet Van and Mau Thi Nguyen; m. Ri Duong Nguyen, Mar. 15, 1984. B.S.E.E., Calif. State U.-Long Beach, 1980-82; M.D., U. Saigon, 1978. Pharmacy tech. T.M.C., Anderson Inst., Houston, 1980. Grantee Calif. State U.-Long Beach. Mem. IEEE, Tau Beta Pi, Eta Kappa Nu. Club: IBM (Boca Raton). Current work: computer design, pediatrics and oncology K research. Subspecialties: Computer engineering; Pediatrics. Home: 1580 NW 15th Ave A-7 Boca Raton FL 33432 Office: IBM 1000 NW 51st St Boca Raton FL 33432

NGUYEN, NHIEM YINH, electronics engineer; b. Saigon, Vietnam, Oct. 10, 1961; came to U.S. 1975; naturalized 1982; s. Manh Vinh Nguyen and Tram (Thi) Ngo. B.S.E.E., U. Ill.-Urbana, 1983; postgrad. U. Tex.-Austin, 1985 Design engr. GTE/Ill., Bloomington, 1982; device engr. Motorola, Austin, Tex., 1983—. Pres., Ch. of Christ Ill. Campus, Urbana, 1981-83; mem. Republican Nat. Com. Mem. IEEE, Electron Device Soc., Spl. Barbershop Singing and Harmonic Soc. Am., Elec. Engring. Alumni Assn. of Ill. Current work: Sub-micron, high density microprocessor process design and parametric testing methods. Subspecialties: Microchip technology (engineering); Semiconductors. Home: 11808 Tobler Trail Austin TX 78753 Office: Motorola Semiconductor Products Div 3501 Ed Bluestein Blvd Austin TX 78721

NGUYEN, VIETCHAU, research and development company executive; b. Hue City, Vietnam, Oct. 1, 1953; came to U.S., 1971, naturalized, 1981; s. Hai V. and Ha-Lanh (Ton-Nu) N.; m. Amy Catherine Hamlin, June 21, 1980; 1 son, Gabriel. B.S.C.E. with honors, U. Minn., 1974, M.S.C.E., 1976; M.A., Princeton U., 1977, Ph.D., 1979. Research staff St. Anthony Falls Hyd. Lab., U. Minn, Mpls., 1973-75; research lectr. Sch. Applied Sci. & Engring., Princeton (N.J.) U., 1979-82; prin. investigator, head Research Div. MKA Inc., Mpls., 1982—. Contbr. articles to profl. jours. Shell Found. fellow, 1977; NSF fellow, 1978; Wallace Meml. award Princeton Faculty, 1979. Mem. Am. Geophys. Union, Am. Inst. Chem. Engrs., ASCE, Internat. Assn. Math. and Computers in Simulation, Soc. Indsl. and Applied Math., Soc. Petroleum Engrs. of AIME. Current Work: Theoretical and exptl. studies of multiphase thermochem. flow in porous and fractured media. Subspecialties: Theoretical and applied mechanics; Numerical analysis (computer science). Office: 12800 Industrial Park Blvd Plymouth MN 55441

NIBHANUPUDY, JAGANNADHA RAO, medical physicist, consultant; b. Bapatla, India, June 19, 1940; came to U.S., 1968; s. Narasimha Rao and Tayaramma (Rachapudy) N.; m. Janaki Anuradha Poluri, Aug. 21, 1964; children: Narasimha Rao, Padmavathi. B.Sc., Andhra (India) U., 1959; M.S., Vikram (India) U., 1963; M.S.E., U. Wash., Seattle, 1970. Diplomate: Am. Bd. Radiology. Demonstrator Loyola Coll., Vijayawada, India, 1960-61; sci. officer Bhabha Atomic Research Center, Bombay, India, 1964-68; med. physicist Howard U. Hosp., Washington, 1971—; asst. prof. Howard U. Coll. Medicine, 1978—. Contbr. articles to profl. jours. Sec. Greater Washington Telugu Soc., 1976. Mem. Am. Assn. Physicists in Medicine. Current Work: Physics aspects of intra-operative radiotherapy, Brachy therapy, and hyperthermia in cancer treatment; teaching resident physicians, medical students and radiotherapy technology students. Subspecialties: Medical physics; Radiology. Home: 8509 Brae Brooke Dr Lanham MD 20706 Office: Dept Radiotherapy Howard Univ Hosp 2041 Georgia Ave NW Washington DC 20060

NICAISE, WALTER FERDINAND, nuclear physicist, educator; b. Nauvoo, Ill., Aug. 12, 1933; s. Ferdinand David and Winifred Mae (Truscott) N.; m. Virginia Ruth Gasper, Oct. 26, 1962; 1 dau., Caroline Laura. B.A., U. Chgo., 1955; M.S., U. Wis.-Milw., 1967; Ph.D., N.C. State U., 1972. Instr., Western Piedmont Community Coll., Morganton, N.C., 1973-74; asst. prof. N.C. State U., Raleigh, 1974-75; sr. scientist Nuclear Research Corp., Southampton, Pa., 1975-77; asst. prof. East Carolina U., Greenville, 1976-77; sr. scientist Radiation Mgmt. Corp., Phila., 1977-79, Rockwell Hanford Ops., Richland, Wash., 1979—. Contbr. articles to sci. jours. Local interviewer U. Chgo. Office of Admissions, Kennewick, Wash., 1982-84. Mem. Am. Phys. Soc., Am. Nuclear Soc., Health Physics Soc., Sigma Phi Sigma (v.p. N.C. State U. chpt. 1969-70). Episcopalian. Current work: Design and development of non-destructive assay and detection equipment and methods for analytical laboratories, environmental monitoring and nuclear fuels reprocessing. Subspecialties: Nuclear fission; Non-destructive testing. Home: 5705 W 25th Ave Kennewick WA 99337 Office: Rockwell Hanford Ops Richland WA 99352

NICASTRO, ANTHONY JOSEPH, physicist; b. Wilmington, Del., June 28, 1954; s. Anthony Joseph and Elvira (Novellino) N.; m. Michele Elizabeth Lang, June 7, 1980; 1 child, Anthony Joseph. B.S. in Physics, U. Del., 1976, B.S. in Math., 1980, M.S. in Astrophysics, 1980, Ph.D. in Physics, 1981. Research fellow, Bartol Found., Newark, Del., 1980-81; instr. physics U. Del., 1981; asst. prof. Bucknell U., Lewisburg, Pa., 1981—; cons. Small Bus. Devel. Ctr., Lewisburg, 1981—. Author newspaper column: The Skywalker, 1982—. Contbr. articles to profl. jours. Am. Philos. Soc. grantee, 1983, Research Corp. grantee, 1984. Mem. Am. Phys. Soc., Northeastern Assn. Microscopists, Am. Assn. Physics Tchrs., AAAS. Current work: Critical phenomena occurring at phase transitions in liquid crystals: nematic-isotropic transition at high electric fields; high pressure phase diagrams of lyotropic liquid crystals; structures of the blue phases. Subspecialty: Condensed matter physics. Home: 1303 Washington Ave Lewisburg PA 17837 Office: Dept Physics Bucknell U Lewisburg PA 17837

NICHIPORUK, WALTER, chemist, researcher; b. Zdolbunov, Poland, Sept. 5, 1919; came to U.S., 1946, naturalized, 1952; s. Alex Andrew and Anna Josephine (Radchuk) N.; m. Elizabeth Kellner, Aug. 14, 1958; 1 child, Brian. Student U. Warsaw, Poland, 1938-39, U. Munich, Germany, 1946; M.S., U. Chgo., 1950. Mem. staff Enrico Fermi Inst. U. Chgo., 1950-52; chemist Calif. Inst. Tech., Pasadena, 1952-68, U.S. Dept. Energy New Brunswick Lab., Argonne, Ill., 1977—; research assoc. Ariz. State U., Tempe, 1968-74; cons. chemistry, Tempe, 1974-77; mem. translations panel Plenum Publ. Corp., N.Y.C., 1967-77. Assoc. editor: Bibliography of Meteorites, 1953. Translator, reviser book by V.V. Cherdyntsev: Rasprostranennost' Khimicheskikh Elementov, 1961. Fellow Meteoritical Soc.; mem. Am. Chem. Soc., Geochem. Soc., Internat. Assn. Geochemistry and Cosmochemistry, Sigma Xi. Current work: Preparation and characterization of uranium assay reference materials, trace chemical characterization of high-purity uranium product materials. Subspecialties: Analytical chemistry; Space chemistry. Home: 107 W 65th Lake Dr Westmont IL 60559 Office: US Dept Energy 9800 S Cass Ave Argonne IL 90439

NICHOLAS, HAROLD JOSEPH, biochemist; b. St. Louis, Mar. 1, 1919; s. Joseph Lucas and Alma (Beger) N.; m. Dorothy Jean Reinhold, May 24, 1952; children—Mark, Christopher. B.S. in Chem. Engring., Mo. Sch. Mines and Metallurgy, 1941; Ph.D. in Biochemistry, St. Louis U., 1950. Asst. prof. dept. biochemistry U. Kans., Lawrence, 1950-53, asst. prof. dept. ob-gyn., Kansas City, 1956-61, assoc. prof., 1961-63; assoc. prof. dept. biochemistry St. Louis U., 1972, dir. exptl. medicine Inst. Medicine and Research, 1963, prof. biochemistry, 1973—. Contbr. articles to profl. jours. Patentee in field. Recipient Travel award Fedn. Am. Soc. Biol. Chemists, Tokyo, 1968. Mem. Am. Chem. Soc., Am. Inst. Chemists, Endocrine Soc., Am. Acad. Neurology, Am. Soc. Biol. Chemists, Am. Soc. Plant Physiology, Am. Soc. for Neurochemistry (charter mem.), Pan Am. Soc. Neurology, Am. Oil Chemists Soc., Am. Soc. Pharmacologists, Sigma Xi, Tau Beta Pi, Phi Chi. Current work: Neurochemistry, natural products including plant chemistry, plant biochemistry and liquid crystals. Subspecialties: Biochemistry (biology); Neurochemistry. Home: 12456 Merrick Dr Creve Coeur MO 63141 Office: Dept Biochemistry Inst Med Edn and Research 1605 S 14th St Saint Louis MO 63104

NICHOLAS, JAMES ROBBS, college dean; b. Jackson, Tenn., May 30, 1926; s. William Ed and Buela (Robbs) N.; m. Johnnie Jones; 1 child, Tina Jean Nicholas Benson. B.S., U. Tenn., 1949; M.S., U. Minn., 1955, Ph.D., 1957. Assoc. prof. dept. agrl. sci. Pa. State U., 1959-64; prof., head dept. agrl. sci. Va. Poly Inst. and Va. State U., Blacksburg, 1964-69, assoc. dean, dir. resident instrn., 1969-71, assoc. dean, dir. div. animal and vet. sci., 1973-75, dean coll. Agr. and Life Scis., 1975—, also dir.; exec. v.p., gen. mgr. Select Sires, Inc., Columbus, Ohio, 1971-73. Served to lt. USAAF, 1943-46. Named Man of Yr. in agr. in Va., Progressive Farmer Mag., 1975; recipient Spl. Citation, Va. Agribus. Council, 1983. Mem. Nat. Assn. State Univs. and Land-Grant Colls. (chmn. dir. agr. 1983-84, chmn. council adminstrv. heads of agr. 1982-83). Methodist. Lodges: Rotary, Lions. Current work: Agriculture and life sciences, agriculture policy; genetics, embryo transplants, breeding, biotechnology. Subspecialties: Animal breeding and embryo transplants; Animal genetics. Office: Coll Agr and Life Scis Va Poly Inst & State Univ 102 Hutcheson Hall Blacksburg VA 24061

NICHOLS, BUFORD LEE, JR., medical educator, physician, nutritionist, researcher; b. Ft. Worth, Dec. 21, 1931; married; 3 children. B.A., Baylor U., 1955, M.S., 1959; M.D., Yale U., 1960. Diplomate: Am. Bd. Pediatrics. Instr. in physiology Baylor U. Coll. Medicine, Houston, 1956-57, instr. in physiology and pediatrics, 1964-66, from asst. prof. to assoc. prof. pediatrics, 1966-67, instr. in physiology, 1966-74, prof. physiology and pediatrics, 1977—; sci. dir. Children's Nutrition Research Ctr.; instr. pediatrics Yale U., 1963-64. Mem. Am. Acad. Pediatrics, Am. Soc. Clin. Nutrition, Am. Coll. Nutrition (pres. 1975-76). Current Work: Environmental effects upon growth and development of the infant, especially alterations in body composition and muscle physiology in malnutrition; diarrhea and infectious deseases. Subspecialties: Nutrition (medicine); Pediatrics. Office: Dept Pediatrics Baylor Coll Medicine Tex Med Ctr Houston TX 77030

NICHOLS, DONALD RAY, geologist; b. Omaha, Mar. 26, 1927; s. Raymond Fred and Helen Iva (DeBord) N.; m. Louise Benson, June 11, 1948; children—Diane Louise Nichols Pope, Lawrence Scott, Gregory Alan, Sharon Jean. Student U. Va., 1944-45, 46-47; B.S., U. Nebr., 1950; postgrad. Yale U., 1950-51. Registered geologist, Calif. Geologist, U.S. Geol. Survey, Washington, 1951-65, staff geologist, 1965-67, research geologist, Menlo Park Calif., 1967-75, chief, earth scis. applications program, Reston, Va., 1975-79, chief br. engrng. geology, Denver, 1979-83, research geologist, Denver, 1983—; vice chmn. land use planning group Calif. Legis. Com. on Seismic Safety, 1970-74; mem. working group Office Sci. and Tech. Policy, Washington, 1977-78. Pres., James Monroe PTA, Arlington, Va., 1966 Editor: Environmental Planning and Geology, 1971. Recipient Superior Performance award U.S. Geol. Survey, 1960, 62, Outstanding Performance award, 1978. Fellow Geol. Soc. Am.; mem. Assn. Engrng. Geologists (sec. chmn. 1970-71), Internat. Assn. Engrng. Geology, Geol. Soc. Washington, Colo. Sci. Soc. Current work: Glacial and volcanic events in the Copper River Basin, Alaska; landslide information center to reduce landslide hazards nationally. Subspecialties: Arctic studies; Environmental geology. Home: 978 Coneflower Dr Golden CO 80401 Office: US Geol Survey MS 966 PO Box 25046 Denver CO 80225

NICHOLS, DUANE GUY, coal processing research executive, chemical research engineer; b. Blue, W.Va., July 18, 1937; s. Guy L. and G. June (Gorrell) N.; m. Louise Connell, Nov. 28, 1963; children—Tanya, Tracy; m. Susan DeWitt Allen, June 28, 1980; children—Paul Richer, Scott Ricker. B.S. in Chem. Engrng., W.Va. U., 1979; M.Chem. Engrng., U. Del., 1962, Ph.D., 1967. Technician, PPG Chem. Co. (Columbia-So. Co.), Natrium, W.Va., 1955-58; engr.-in-tng. Union Carbide Corp., Tonawanda, N.Y., 1959; asst. prof. W.Va. U., Morgantown, 1968-74, assoc. prof., 1974-77; supr. Research Triangle Inst., Durham, N.C., 1978-80; supr. coal processing research group Conoco Inc., Library, Pa., 1980—; cons. Systems Cons., Inc., Washington, 1975-77. NDEA fellow U. Del., Newark, 1959-62. Mem. Am. Inst. Chem. Engrs. (sec. Pitts. sect. 1984-85, award 1959, tech. editor procs. confs. on energy and environ. 1978, 80, 82). Current work: Laboratory and bench-scale research on the development of processing steps for the removal of sulfur and mineral matter from coals. Subspecialties: Chemical engineering; Coal. Office: Conoco Inc 4000 Brownsville Rd Library PA 15129

NICHOLS, GEORGE, oceanographer, researcher, educator; N.Y.C., May 15, 1922; s. George and Jane Norton (Morgan) N.; m. Nancy Taylor Pinks, July 1, 1944 (div. 1968, 74), children—George, Susan Leslie; m. Ann MacKay Ratcliff, Apr. 22, 1977; children—Pierce, Dominica. M.D., Columbia U., 1945. Diplomate Am. Bd. Internal Medicine. Resident in internal medicine Peter Bent Brigham Hosp., Boston, 1948-49; from teaching fellow to clin. prof. Harvard Med. Sch., Boston, 1948-73; pres. Ocean Research and Edn. Soc., Gloucester, Mass., 1975—, dir., 1975—; dir. Provincetown Ctr. Coastal Studies, Mass., 1984—; mem. Woods Hole Oceanographic Instn., Mass., 1973—. Editor: Cellular Mechanisms for Calcium Transfer and Homeostasis, 1972; contbr. articles to profl. jours. Served with USN, 1941-53. Grantee NIH, 1953-73, Hartford Found., NSF, Nat. Marine Fisheries. Mem. Am. Physiol. Soc., Assn. Am. Physicians, Am. Soc. Mammalogists, Am. Soc. Marine Mammology, Am. Soc. Cell Biology. Current work: Behavioral ecology of marine mammals especially whales. Subspecialties: Ecology (biology); Endocrinology. Office: Ocean Research and Edn Soc 19 Harbor Loop Gloucester MA 01930

NICHOLS, GRADY BARNEY, environmental engineer; b. Wilsonville, Ala., Mar. 18, 1933; s. William Barney and Lucille (Baker) N.; m. Suzanne Hackney, June 11, 1957; children—Pamela Nichols Cornutt, Patricia Nichols Campbell. S.B.E.E., MIT, 1957; Ph.D. E.E., U. Tokyo, 1982. Registered profl. engr., Ala. Project engr. Gen. Motors Proving Grounds, Milford, Mich., 1959-62; elec. engr. NASA, Greenbelt, Md., 1962-67; dir. research So. Research Inst., Birmingham, Ala., 1967—. Author: Electrostatic Precipitation, 1978. Contbr. chpts. to books. Patentee in field. Mem. Air Pollution Control Assn., Electrostatic Precipitation Assn. Republican. Presbyterian. Current work: Electrostatic precipitation, fabric filtration. Office: So Research Inst PO Box 55305 Birmingham AL 35255

NICHOLS, JAMES DALE, biologist, researcher; b. Waynesboro, Va., May 24, 1949; s. James Edward and Barbara (Irvin) N.; m. Lois Mayer, Aug. 29, 1970; children—Jonathan Michael, Christina Jean. B.S. in Biology, Wake Forest U., 1971; M.S. in Wildlife Mgmt., La. State U., 1973; Ph.D. in Wildlife Ecology, Mich. State U., 1976. Research biologist U.S. Fish and Wildlife Service, Patuxent Wildlife Research Ctr., Laurel, Md., 1976—. Contbr. articles to profl. jours. Coach youth athletic orgns., Bowie, Md., Crofton, Md., 1981—; active local PTA. Mem. Ecol. Soc. Am., Wildlife Soc. Presbyterian. Current work: Dynamics and management of natural animal populations; estimation of population parameters using capture-recapture, band recovery and nesting success models; estimation of extinction and speciation rates from fossil data. Subspecialties: Population biology; Ecology (biology). Home: 1722 Tedbury St Crofton MD 21114 Office: US Fish Wildlife Service Patuxent Wildlife Research Ctr Laurel MD 20708

NICHOLS, KATHRYN MARION, geologist, researcher; b. Santa Monica, Calif., Apr. 30, 1946; d. Myron Hiram and Gertrude Lenore (Foulkes) N.; m. Norman John Silberling, July 8, 1978. B.S., U. Calif.-Riverside, 1968; Ph.D., Stanford U., 1972. Research asst. Stanford U., Calif., 1970-72, postdoctoral fellow, 1972-76; post-doctoral fellow U.S. Geol. Survey, Menlo Park, Calif., 1976-77, geologist, Denver, 1977—. Contbr. articles to profl. jours. Mem. Geol. Soc. Am., Soc. Econ. Paleontologists and Mineralogists. Current work: Stratigraphy and depositional history of Paleozoic carbonate rocks in North America. Subspecialty: Petrology. Office: US Geol Survey Mail Stop 921 PO Box 25046 Fed Ctr Denver CO 80225

NICHOLS, KENNETH DAVID, retired army officer, civil engineer; b. Cleve., Nov. 13, 1907; s. Wilbur L. and M. May (Colbrunn) N.; m. Jacqueline Darrieulat, Dec. 15, 1932; children—Jacqueline Ann Nichols Thompson, Kenneth David. B.S., U.S. Mil. Acad., 1929; C.E., Cornell U., 1931, M.C.E., 1932; Ph.D., U. Iowa, 1937; Registered profl. engr., Md., Washington. Commd. 2d lt. U.S. Army C.E., 1929, advanced through grades to maj. gen. 1953, dist. engr. Manhattan Dist.-atomic bomb, 1942-46, chief Armed Forces Spl. Weapons Project, 1948-50, chief research and devel., Washington, 1952-53; gen. mgr. U.S. AEC, 1953-55; cons. engr., Dickerson, Md., 1955—. Decorated D.S.M. with oak leaf cluster; recipient Collinwood prize ASCE, 1937; Disting. Service medal U.S. AEC, 1955; Chiefs of Engr. award C.E., 1984. Fellow Am. Nuclear Soc.; mem. Nat. Acad. Engrng., ASME (hon.). Republican. Club: Army Navy (Washington). Current work: Nuclear energy. Subspecialty: Nuclear engineering.

NICHOLS, PAUL ARTHUR, nuclear engineer; b. Manchester, N.H., Feb. 6, 1956; s. Richard Arthur and Barbara Helen (Deans) N.; m. Gail Renee Lawyer, Feb. 2, 1980; children: Tracy, Kelly. B.Nuclear Engrng., Ga. Inst. Tech., 1978. Jr. engr. Cleve. Electric Illuminating Co., North Perry, Ohio, 1978-80, assoc. engr., 1980-82, lead NSSS engr., 1982—. Scoutmaster Greater Cleve. council Boy Scouts Am., 1979-83. Mem. Am. Nuclear Soc., ASME (assoc.). Republican. Fundamental Christian. Current Work: Design and installation engineering at nuclear plant. Subspecialties: Nuclear engineering; Mechanical engineering. Office: Perry Nuclear Power Plant 10 Center Rd North Perry OH 44081

NICHOLS, WALTER KIRT, surgeon, educator; b. Flint, Mich., Sept. 3, 1941; s. Walter H. and Hazel G. (Marshal) N.; m. C. Paula Cooper, June 19, 1965 (div. Dec. 1978); children: Krystin Jennifer, Kreg Kirt, Kecia Liane. A.S., Flint Jr. Coll., 1961; M.D., U. Mich., 1966. Diplomate: Am. Bd. Surgery. Intern. St. Joseph Mercy Hosp., Ann Arbor, Mich., 1966-67; resident U. Mo. Hosp., Columbia, 1967-68, 70-73, asst. prof. surgery, 1973-79, assoc. prof., 1979—; asst. chief surgery VA Hosp., Columbia, 1974—, acting chief, 1977-78. Contbr. articles to profl. jours. Served to capt. USAF, 1968-70. Fellow ACS; mem. Assn. Acad. Surgery, Internat. Cardiovascular Surg. Soc., Frederick A. Coller Surg. Soc., Midwestern Vascular Surg. Soc., Assn. Surg. Edn., Mo. State Surg. Soc. Current Work: Non-invasive vascular diagnosis: imaging; computer applications to medical care. Subspecialty: Surgery. Office: M580 Univ Med Center Columbia MO 65212

NICHOLS, WARREN DE FORREST, engineering company executive; b. Los Angeles, Sept. 9, 1926; s. Forrest Clifford and Gladys Harriet (Hunick) N.; m. Willene Dorothy Pegg, Sept. 3, 1949; children—Anne, Clifford, Charles, Carol. Student, UCLA, 1946-49. Registered profl. engr., Calif. with Hughes Aerospace Groups, Culver City, Calif., 1960-72; lab. mgr. Hughes Space and Communications Group, El Segundo, Calif., 1972-74, asst. mgr. mfg. div., 1974-77; asst. systems div. mgr. Hughes Missile Systems Group, Canoga Park, Calif., 1977-79; asst. co. mgr. Santa Barbara Research Ctr., Goleta, Calif., 1979-81, v.p. engrng., 1981—; mem. land remote sensing adv. com. Dept. Commerce, 1982-83. Served with USNR, 1944-46; PTO. Recipient Disting. Pub. Service medal NASA, 1983. Mem. Am. Astron. Soc. (W. Randolph Lovelace III award 1983). Republican. Methodist. Subspecialty: Electronics. Office: Hughes Aircraft Co Santa Barbara Research Ctr 75 Coromar Dr Goleta CA 93117

NICHOLS, WARREN WESLEY, research physician; b. Collingswood, N.J., May 16, 1929; s. David W. and Marie A. (Ringheiser) N.; m. June Helms, Aug. 28, 1953; children: Warren Wesley, Sean H., Lisa Karin. B.S., Rutgers U., 1950; M.D., Jefferson Med. Coll., 1954; Fil. Lic., U. Lund, Sweden, 1964, Ph.D., 1966. Diplomate: Am. Bd. Pediatrics. Chief med. staff Camden Mcpl. Hosp. Contagious Diseases, 1959-61; asst. physician Children's Hosp. Phila., 1959-65; assoc. Inst. Med. Research, Camden, N.J., 1959-65, mem., 1966—, asst. dir., 1963-81, Emlen Stokes prof. genetics, 1975—, v.p. research, 1981-84, also head dept. cytogenetics; sr. dir. genetic and cellular toxicology Merck Inst. Therapeutic Research, West Point, Pa., 1984—; adj. prof. human genetics U. Pa.; clin. prof. pediatrics N.J. Coll. Medicine and Dentistry. Contbr. articles to profl. jours and books. Served with USAF, 1957-59. Recipient Career Devel. award NIH, 1963-72, Alumni Achievement award Jefferson Med. Coll., 1980. Mem. AMA, Am. Acad. Pediatrics, Soc. Pediatric Research, Mendelian Soc., Genetics Soc. Am., Am. Soc. Human Genetics, John Morgan Soc., N.Y. Acad. Scis., Am. Soc. Clin. Investigation, Am. Assn. Cancer Research, Gerontol. Soc. Current Work: Research on spontaneous and induced gene and chromosome mutations and their role in carcinogenesis, aging and hereditary disease. Emphasis on virus induced cellular genetic changes and high risk cancer individuals and families. Subspecialties: Gene actions; Cancer research (medicine). Office: Merck Sharp & Dohme Research Labs West Point PA 19486

NICHOLSON, CHRISTOPHER, submersible vehicle designer. Founder Deep Sea Systems Internat., Inc., Falmouth, Mass. Subspecialty: Submersible vehicle design. Office: Deep Sea Systems Internat Inc Falmouth MA 02540

NICHOLSON, DWIGHT ROY, physicist; b. Racine, Wis., Oct. 3, 1947; s. Forrest Arlyn and Johanna Jacoba (Bergsma) N.; m. Jane Alice Mechling, June 14, 1969. B.S., U. Wis.-Madison, 1969; Ph.D., U. Calif.-Berkeley, 1975. Research assoc. U. Colo., Boulder, 1975-77; asst. prof., 1978, asst. prof. U. Iowa, Iowa City, 1978-81, assoc. prof., 1981—. Author: Introduction to Plasma Theory, 1983. Grantee NSF, NASA, Dept. Energy, 1978—. Mem. Am. Phys. Soc., AAAS, Union Radio Sci. Internat. Current work: Theoretical and computational plasma physics emphasizing turbulence. Subspecialties: Plasma physics; Statistical physics. Home: 402 Kimball Rd Iowa City IA 52240 Office: Physics and Astronomy Dept U Iowa Iowa City IA 52242

NICKAS, GEORGE DEMOSTHENES, physicist; b. Chg., Mar. 7, 1942; s. Andrew George and Delia N.; m. Mildred Anne McKee, Mar. 9, 1966; m. Jeanette Chelf, June 8, 1972; 1 son, George Demosthenes. B.S., Ill. Inst. Tech., 1964; M.S., U. Ill., 1967, Ph.D., 1972. Grad teaching and research asst. U. Ill., Urbana, 1965-72; postdoctoral research and teaching fellow U. B.C., Vancouver, 1972-74; writer book reviewer Vancouver (B.C.) Sun newspaper, 1974-78; research dir. McDonald Research Assocs. Ltd., Vancouver, 1978-80; instr. One-To-One Ednl. Services, Vancouver, 1980-81, Capilano Coll., North Vancouver, B.C., 1981-82; asst. prof. physics Trinity U., San Antonio, 1982-85, Ithaca Coll., N.Y., 1985—. Recipient Delta Star Scholarship award, 1961-64. Mem. Am. Astron. Soc., Capilano Coll. Faculty Assn., Sigma Pi Sigma. Greek Orthodox. Current Work: The dynamics of asymmetries in galaxies, theoretical astrophysics, theoretical physics. Subspecialties: Theoretical astrophysics; Theoretical physics. Home: 324 Hook Pl Ithaca NY 14850 Office: Ithaca Coll Ithaca NY

NICKELL, LOUIS G., plant physiologist, microbiologist; b. Little Rock, July 10, 1921; s. Louise G. and Idene (Brasher) N.; m. Natalie Wills, Sept. 30, 1942; children—Natalie, Louise Edward, Mary Barbara. B.S., Yale U., 1942, M.S., 1947, Ph.D., 1949. Research assoc. Bklyn. Botanic Garden, 1949-51; head phytochemistry lab. Pfizer, Inc., N.Y.C., 1951-61; dir. research Hawaiian Sugar Planters Assn., Honolulu, 1961-75; v.p. research div. W. R. Grace and Co., Columbia, Md., 1975-78; v.p. research and devel. Velsicol Chem. Corp., Chgo., 1978—; dir. Crop Genetics Internat., Columbia, Chem. Industry Inst. of Toxicology, Raleigh, N.C.; mem. com. on agrl. prodn. efficiency NRC, Washington, 1972-73; vice-chmn. adv. task force on energy policy, Honolulu, 1974-75; chmn. Gov.'s Adv. Com. Sci. and Tech. Honolulu, 1970-75; mem. bd. sci. and tech. for internat. devel. NRC, 1985—. Author: Plant Growth Regulators, 1982; (editor) Plant Growth Regulating Chemicals (2 vols.), 1983. Served to 1st. lt. USMC, 1942-45, PTO. Fellow Eaton, 1947, Sterling, 1948, Sheffield, 1949. Mem. Am. Soc. Plant Physiologists (treas. 1976-82, trustee 1984—), Plant Growth Regulator Soc. Am. (vice chmn. 1979, chmn. 1980), Am. Chem. Soc. (chmn. Hawaii sec. 1967-68, internat. activities com. 1984—). Clubs: Pacific (Honolulu); Carlton (Chgo.). Current work: Research administration, plant growth regulators, herbicides, plant cell and issue culture, biotechnology. Subspecialties: Plant physiology (agriculture); Plant cell and tissue culture. Home: 3730 N Lake Shore Dr Chicago IL 60613 Office: Velsicol Chem Corp 341 E Ohio St Chicago IL 60611

NICKERSON, KENNETH WARWICK, microbiologist; b. Attleboro, Mass., Nov. 19, 1942; s. Walter John and Helen (Kelsall) N.; m. Ann Weinkauff, July 1, 1972; children—David Warwick, Daniel Patrick. B.S., Rutgers U., 1964; Ph.D., U. Cin., 1969. Research assoc. Oreg. State U., Corvallis, 1969-71, USDA, Peoria, Ill., 1971-73; research assoc. U. Nebr., Lincoln, 1973-75, assoc. prof. biol. sci., 1975-85, prof., 1985—. Contbr. articles to profl. jours.; mem. editorial bd. Applied and Environ. Microbiology, 1982—. Mem. Am. Soc. Microbiology, Am. Soc. Biol. Chemists, Soc. Gen. Microbiology (U.K.), Entomol. Soc. Am., Soc. Invertebrate Pathology. Current work: Microbial Physiology: toxicity of bacteria to mosquito larvae; role of calmodulin in fungal dimorphism. Subspecialties: Microbiology; Biochemistry (biology). Home: 1241 N 41st St Lincoln NE 68503 Office: U Nebr Dept Biol Scis Lincoln NE 68588

NICKERSON, NORTON HART, biologist, ecologist, educator, consultant; b. Quincy, Mass., Apr. 14, 1926; s. Norton Hart and Mary Almina (Whitney) N.; m. Joan Young, Jan. 30, 1954; children: William, Susan, Jonathan. B.S., U. Mass., Amherst, 1949; M.A., U. Tex., Austin, 1951; Ph.D., Washington U., St. Louis, 1953. Instr. U. Mass., 1953-56; Cornell U., Ithaca, N.Y., 1956-58; asst. prof. botany Washington U., 1958-62, assoc. prof., 1962-63; assoc. prof. biology Tufts U., Medford, Mass., 1963-81, prof. environ. studies, 1981—; morphologist Mo. Bot. Garden, 1958-63; mem. commn. ecology Internat. Union Conservation of Nature; chmn. Mass. Hazardous Waste Facility Site Safety Council, 1980—; mem. Mass. Bd. Environ. Mgmt., 1977-82, Mass. Agrl. Lands Preservation Com., 1978—. Contbr. articles to tech. jours. Mem. Dennis (Mass.) Conservation Commn., 1964-82, health agt., Dennis, 1971-83. Served to cpl. USAF, 1944-45; 2d lt. Res., 1949-55. Fellow Linnean Soc. of London; mem. AAAS, Bot. Soc. Am., New Eng. Bot. Club (editor Rhodora 1982—), Ecol. Soc. Am., Explorers Club, Sigma Xi. Current Work: Functioning of coastal ecosystems (Mangroves, salt-marshes, barrier beaches); management of park resources. Subspecialties: Ecology (environmental science); Resource conservation. Office: Dept Biology Tufts U Medford MA 02155

NICKLAS, ROBERT BRUCE, cell biologist; b. Lakewood, Ohio, May 29, 1932; s. Ford Adelbert and Marthabelle (Beckett) N.; m. Sheila Jean Counce, Sept. 24, 1960. B.A., Bowling Green State U., 1954; M.A. (Eugene Higgins fellow), Columbia U., 1956, Ph.D., 1958. Instr. in zoology Yale U., 1958-61, asst. prof. zoology, 1961-64, asso. prof., 1964-65, Duke U., 1965-71, prof., 1971—, chairperson dept., 1983—; mem. NSF Postdoctoral Fellowship Panel, 1969-71, Am. Cancer Soc. Sci. Adv. Com. for Virology and Cell Biology, 1975-78. Contbr. numerous articles to profl. publs.; editorial bd.: Chromosoma, 1966-83, Jour. Exptl. Zoology, 1970-72, Jour Cell Biology, 1980-81, Jour. Cell Sci., 1984—. Recipient award for disting. teaching Duke Alumni, 1975; Yale fellow in scis., 1963-64; John Simon Guggenheim fellow, 1972-73; grantee Inst. Gen. Med. Scis. USPHS, 1960—. Fellow AAAS; mem. Am. Soc. Cell Biology (exec. com. 1976-78, council 1975-78), Am. Soc. Naturalists, Genetics Soc. Am., Soc. Gen. Physiologists, Sigma Xi. Subspecialty: Cell biology. Home: 3101 Camelot Ct Durham NC 27705 Office: Dept Zoology Duke U Durham NC 27706

NICKLAS, WILLIAM JOHN, biochemist, research, educator; b. Phila., Jan. 13, 1939; s. Julius and Ida (Perl) N.; m. Ruth Joan Horvay, Aug. 8, 1964; 1 son, John. B.A. in Chemistry (scholar), La Salle Coll., Phila., 1964; Ph.D. in Biochemistry (NASA fellow), Fordham U., 1969. Teaching asst. Fordham U., Bronx, N.Y., 1964-65; NIH postdoctoral fellow Johnson Research Found., U. Pa., Phila., 1968-70; research assoc. Columbia U. Coll. Physicians and Surgeons, N.Y.C., 1970-73; research asst. prof. Mt. Sinai Sch. Medicine, N.Y.C., 1973-77, research assoc. prof., 1977-80; assoc. prof. dept. neurology Univ. Medicine and Dentistry N.J.-Rutgers Med. Sch., Piscataway, 1980-85, prof., 1985—; adj. assoc. prof. dept. pharmacology, 1980—, mem. grad. faculty, 1980—, co-dir. Mollie and Jerome Levine Neurosci. Lab., 1980—. Contbr. numerous articles and abstracts to sci. publs., chpts. to books. Del. to local and county Democratic convs., 1980, 81, 82, active mem., officer local civic assns., 1974—. Served with U.S. Army Res., 1962-68. NIH grantee, 1973-80, 81—. Mem. Soc. for Neurosci., AAAS, Biochem. Soc. (editorial advisor Biochem. Jour. 1981-84). Am. Soc. for Neurochemistry (membership com. 1981—), Internat. Soc. Neurochemistry, Phi Beta Kappa, Sigma Xi, Phi Lambda Upsilon. Current Work: Research involves role of neuronal-glial interactions in regulation of transmitter amino acid metabolism and function. This involves classic biochemical techniques with newer aspects of cell biology. Subspecialties: Neurochemistry; Neurobiology. Office: Dept Neurology UMDNJ-Rutgers Med Sch Piscataway NJ 08854

NICOLAE, GHEORGHE, research chemist; b. Focsani, Romania, Oct. 2, 1943; came to U.S., 1979; s. Gheorghe Enache and Victoria (Vasiliu) N.; m. Mariana Lorisa Vasiliu, July 9, 1977; children: Ovidiu-Bogdan, Iulia-Cristina. M.S., U. Bucharest, 1966, Ph.D., 1974. Prof. asst. U. Bucharest, 1967-73, Poly. Inst., Bucharest, 1973-79; research chemist Wallace A. Erickson, Chgo., 1980; research mgr. Confi-Dental Co., Chgo., 1981—. Mem. Internat. Assn. Dental Research, Am. Assn. Dental Research; mem. Am. Chem. Soc.; Mem. Assn. Finishing Processes of Soc. Mfg. Engrs. (sr.). Club: Amoco Motor (Chgo.). Inventor in field. Current Work: Heterocyclic chemistry, phenoxathiins derivatives, octahydro-xanthylium compounds, octahydroacridinium compounds, pyrylium salts, acrylic monomers, urethanes derivatives. Subspecialties: Organic chemistry; Synthetic chemistry. Office: Confi-Dental Products Co 1900 N Clybourne Ave Chicago IL 60614

NICOLAU, GABRIELA, biochemist; b. Budapest, Hungary, June 11, 1928; came to U.S. 1971, naturalized 1977; m. Louis Edouard Nicolau, Apr. 17, 1951; children—Anca, Monica. B.S. in Chemistry, U. Bucharest, Romania, 1950, M.S. in Biochemistry, 1952, Ph.D. in Organic Chemistry, 1962. Asst. prof. biochemistry U. Bucharest, 1952-63, assoc. prof., 1963-70; research scientist Pub. Health Research Inst., N.Y.C., 1972-75; principal research scientist med. research div. Am. Cyanamid, Pearl River, N.Y., 1975-80, group leader Drug Metabolism, 1980—. Contbr. articles to profl. jours. Patentee in field. Recipient Nat. award for Organic Chemistry Research, Nat. Dept. Science, Ministry of Edn., Bucharest, 1968. Mem. Am. Chem. Soc., Internat. Soc. Study of Xenobiotics. Current work: Pharmacokinetics and drug metabolism, assay development for drugs in biological fluids, structure relationships for new drugs, stereo- chemistry of binding to biomolecules, metabolic reactions in the skin. Subspecialties: Biochemistry (biology); Pharmacokinetics. Office: Am Cyanamid Med Research Div Pearl River NY 10965

NICOLETTI, PAUL, veterinarian; b. Goodman, Mo., Oct. 26, 1932; s. Felix and Clarice (Campbell) N.; m. Earlene Blackburn, June 13, 1954; children—Diana, Julie, Nancy. B.S., U. Mo.-Columbia, 1956, D.V.M., 1956; M.S., U. Wis.-Madison, 1962. Diplomate Am. Coll. Veterinary Preventive Medicine. Epidemiologist, U.S. Dept. Agr., Springfield, Mo., 1956-60, Madison, Wis., 1960-62, Albany, N.Y., 1962-68, UN, Teheran, Iran, 1968-72, U.S. Dept. Agr., Jackson, Miss., also Gainesville, Fla., 1972-78; prof. veterinary medicine U. Fla.-Gainesville, 1978—, cons. Ecuador Project, 1983, Un-Fao Qatar, Kuwait, 1985. Contbr. chpts. to veterinary textbooks. Recipient Borden award Borden Co., 1979. Mem. Fla. Cattlemen's Assn., Fla. Dairymen's Assn., Fla. Veterinary Med. Assn., AVMA, Am. Assn. Bovine Practitioners, Alachua County Veterinary Soc. (pres. 1983-84). Current work: Brucellosis. Subspecialty: Microbiology (veterinary medicine). Home: 2552 SW 14th Dr Gainesville FL 32608 Office: U Fla J-137 Gainesville FL 32610

NICOLSON, GARTH L., cancer cell biologist, educator; b. Los Angeles, Oct. 1, 1943; s. Garth F. and Joan D. (Lamb) N. B.S. in Chemistry, UCLA, 1965; M.S. in Biophysics, U. Hawaii, 1967; Ph.D. in Cell Biology, U. Calif., San Diego, 1970. Research assoc. Salk Inst., La Jolla, Calif., 1971-74, head dept. cancer biology, 1974-76; prof. cell biology U. Calif.-Irvine, 1975-80; prof. physiology U. Calif. (Med. Sch.), 1977-80; Florence M. Thomas prof. cancer research, head dept. tumor biology U. Tex. Cancer Ctr., M.D. Anderson Hosp. and Tumor Inst., Houston, 1980—; adj. prof. vet. pathology Tex. A&M U., 1981—; prof. pathology U. Tex. Med. Sch., Houston, 1981—. Editor 12 books in field; contbr. numerous articles to profl. jours; editor: Cell Surface Revs, 1976—, Clin. and Exptl. Metastasis, 1981—; assoc. editor: Cancer Biology Revs, 1979—, Exptl. Cell Research, 1976—, Invasion and Metastasis, 1982—, Jour. Cellular Biochemistry, 1973—, Yearbook of Cancer, 1980—, Cancer Research, 1978—, Cancer Metastasis Revs, 1982—, Biochimica et Biophysica Acta, 1974-79, Gamate Research, 1978-83, Molecular Cell Biochemistry, 1982—. Recipient Presdl. award Electron Microscopy Soc. Am., 1971; Upjohn Biology Edn. award, 1976; Ann. award Japan Histochemical Soc., 1976; Guy Lipscomb Meml. award, 1979. Mem. Am. Soc. Cancer Research (bd. dirs.), Am. Soc. Biol. Chemists, Am. Soc. Cell Biology, Biophysical Soc., N.Y. Acad. Scis. Current Work: Mechanisms of cancer metastasis, cell surface properties of cancer, development of new procedures to treat metastatic cancer. Subspecialties: Cancer research (medicine); Cell biology. Office: Dept Tumor Biology U Tex Cancer Ctr MD Anderson Hosp and Tumor Inst Houston TX 77030

NIEBER, JOHN LITTLE, agricultural engineering professor; b. Hudson, N.Y., Mar. 3, 1950; s. Albert Henry and Hazel (Little) N.; m. Mary Elizabeth Egbertson, Aug. 5, 1972; children—Nathan, Benjamin, Kathryn, Christopher. B.S. in Engrng., Syracuse U., 1972; M.S. in Hydraulics and Hydrology, Cornell U., 1974, Ph.D. in Agrl. Engrng., 1979. Research technician Cornell U., Ithaca, N.Y., 1973-75; asst. prof. Tex. A&M U., College Station, 1979-85; assoc. prof. U. Minn.-St. Paul, 1985—. Mem. Am. Soc. Agrl. Engrs., Am. Geophys. Union, Am. Soc. Agronomy, Soil Conservation Soc. Am. Current work: Hydrologic modeling of surface and subsurface hydrology; experimental watershed research; agricultural, forest water management, groundwater quality management. Subspecialties: Agricultural engineering; Hydrology. Home: 28240 Olinda Trail Lindstrom MN 55045 Office: Dept Agrl Engrng U Minn 1390 Eckles Ave Saint Paul MN 55108

NIEDERHAUSER, WARREN DEXTER, chemist; b. Akron, Ohio, Jan. 2, 1918; s. Harold Warren and Edna Isabel (Dexter) N.; m. Floris Mae Eldredge, Dec. 31, 1949; 1 child, Sue Edmondson. A.B., Oberlin Coll., 1939, D.Sc. (hon.), 1984; Ph.D., U. Wis., 1943. Sr. chemist Rohm and Haas Co., Phila., 1943-55, sect. head, 1955-59, research supr., Phila. and Bristol, Pa., 1959-66, asst. dir. research, Bristol, 1966-73, dir. pioneer research, Spring House, Pa., 1973-83, cons., 1983—. Author: Legal Rights of Chemists and Engineers, 1977. Patentee in field. Mem. Am. Chem. Soc. (pres. 1984-85; Honor Scroll, Mems. and Fellows Lectr. award 1985), Council Sci. Soc. Pres. (chmn.-elect 1985—). Republican. Lutheran. Club: Lulu Country (North Hills, Pa.). Current work: Plastics, rocket propellants, surface-active agents, separation methods. Subspecialties: Organic chemistry; Polymer chemistry. Home: 1087 George Rd Meadowbrook PA 19046 Office: Rohm and Haas Co 727 Norristown Rd Spring House PA 19477

NIEDERJOHN, RUSSELL JAMES, electrical engineering educator; b. Schenectady, June 13, 1944; s. Russell K. and Jeanette O. (Burnison) N.; m.

Susan A. Swenson, June 7, 1969; children—Matthew Scott, Jeremy Michael. B.S.E.E., U. Mass., 1967, M.S., 1968, Ph.D., 1971. Registered profl. engr., Wis. Engr. asst. Gen. Electric Co., Syracuse, N.Y., summer 1966; asst. prof. Marquette U., Milw., 1971-75, assoc. prof., 1975-80, prof. elec. engring. and computer sci., 1980—. Contbr. numerous articles to profl. jours. Current work: Computer speech processing; computer applications for signal processing, control and man/machine interaction; hardware and software design. Subspecialties: Computer engineering; Automated language processing. Home: 2545 Brookside Pkwy New Berlin WI 53151 Office: Marquette U 1515 W Wisconsin Ave Milwaukee WI 53233

NIEDERKORN, IOAN STEFAN, research metallurgist; b. Oradea, Romania, June 14, 1930; s. Ioan Gavril and Adela Terezia Bekics (Dengyel) N.; m. Taisia Liapina, May 17, 1954; children: Emilia, Irena, Mihel. B.S., M.S., Urals Poly. Inst., Sverdlovsk, USSR, 1954; D.Sci., Inst. of Non-Ferrous Metals and Gold, Moscow, 1958. Researcher Mettall. Research Inst., Bucharet, Romania, 1958-59; sr. researcher Research Inst. Chemistry, Bucharest, 1959-66, head research lab., 1960-66; head research div. and labs. Research and Engring. Ctr. for Raioactive Metals, Bucharest, 1966-81; research metallurgist N.Mex. Inst. Mining and Tech., Socorro, 1982-83; dir. research and devel. Ultra Instrument Lab., Dallas, 1983—; postdoctoral fellow French Atomic Energy Commn., Paris, 1971; sr. research fellow, prof. Sci. and Devel. Com. Romania, Bucharest, 1976. Author 7 books in Romanian and Hungarian; Contbr. articles to profl. jours.; invited lectr. numerous confs. Mem. Am. Nuclear Soc., Metall. Soc. of AIME. Club: Scorro Tennis. Patentee in field. Current Work: Research on radioactive decay products removal from uranium mill tailings; Kinetics of catalitic oxidation of sphalerit concentrates. Subspecialties: Nuclear engineering; Metallurgical engineering. Office: Ultra Instrument Lab 10031 Monroe Dr Dallas TX 75229

NIEDERMEIER, WILLIAM, biochemist; b. Evansville, Ind., Apr. 1, 1923; s. Christian Henry and Emma (Sailer) N.; m. Jane Eleanor Bacon, July 30, 1945; children—Larry Wayne, Nancy Jane, Michael William, Craig William; m. Beverly Joan Ward, June 8, 1974; 1 child, Richard Edgar. B.S., Purdue U., 1946; M.S., U. Ala.-Birmingham, 1953, Ph.D., 1960. Chemist, Mead Johnson & Co., Evansville, Ind., 1946-49; biochemist U. Hosp., Birmingham, Ala., 1949-56; instr. Northwestern U., Evanston, Ill., 1956-60; asst. prof. U. Ala.-Birmingham, 1960-69, assoc. prof. biochemistry, 1969—, sr. scientist Cancer Ctr., 1975—, scientist Arthritis Ctr., 1979—. Contbr. articles to profl. jours. Chmn. exhibits com. SERMS, Am. Chem. Soc., 1972; mem. bd. sci. advisors Meml. Inst. Pathology, Birmingham, 1972-78. Served to comdr., USNR, 1941-45. Mem. Am. Chem. Soc. (alt. counselor, past chmn. Ala. sect.), Am. Soc. Biol. Chemists, Am. Assn. Immunologists, Soc. Complex Carbohydrates, AAAS, Sigma Xi. Current work: Elucidation of carbohydrate composition and characterization of immunglobulins and cell surface tumor antigens. Subspecialties: Biochemistry (medicine); Immunology (medicine). Home: 2016 Crest Ln Birmingham AL 35226 Office: Div Clin Immunology and Rheumatology U Ala Birmingham AL 35294

NIEGISCH, WALTER DIETRICH, chemist; b. Atlantic City, June 20, 1929; s. Walter Gustav and Kathe Elizabeth (Heidenreich) N.; m. Eleanor Dorothy Wendte, Dec. 4, 1955; children—Robert Walter, Karen Diane. B.S. in Chemistry, Columbia U., 1952; M.S. in Chemistry, Stevens Inst., 1959. Chemist, Union Carbide, Bound Brook, N.J., 1952-64, project scientist, 1964-68, research scientist, 1968—. Patentee in field. Contbr. articles to profl. jours. Capt., Watchung Rescue Squad, N.J., 1984. Served with U.S. Army, 1954-56. Indsl. Research award Indsl. Research Mag., 1973. Mem. Am. Chem. Soc., Am. Phys. Soc., Eastern Spectroscopy Soc. (pres. 1980), Material Analysis Soc., Electron Microscopy Soc. Am. Republican. Lutheran. Current work: Specialist in optical and electron microscopy; electron spectroscopy, thermal analysis; x ray fluorescence analysis; X ray diffraction. Subspecialties: Analytical chemistry; Polymers (materials science). Office: Union Carbide Corp S CD PO Box 670 Bound Brook NJ 08805

NIEH, BILL, computer scientist; b. Foochow, Fukien, China, July 1, 1947; came to U.S., 1970, naturalized, 1983; s. Yun-Tiao and Pi-Kung (Liu) N.; m. Wendy C. Nieh, Dec. 23, 1972; children: Rose, Audrey. B.S., Chung-Hsing U., 1969; M.S., West Coast U., 1973; Ph.D., UCLA, 1979. Research engr. UCLA, 1974-79; jr. specialist U. Calif., Berkeley, 1977-79; sr. tech. staff Logicon, San Pedro, Calif., 1979—; lectr. Sch. Bus. Adminstrn., Calif. State U., Long Beach, 1981-83. Mem. Ops. Research Soc. Am., Inst. Mgmt. Sci. Current Work: Software reliability studies, computer security and systems engineering of command, control and communication systems; software verification and validation. Subspecialties: Software engineering; Operations research (engineering). Office: 255 W 5th St San Pedro CA 90733

NIELSEN, DONALD WAYNE, otology educator; b. Cin., Oct. 26, 1941; s. Otto Emil and Sarah (Van Wagner) N.; b. Suzanne Edith Price, July 24, 1965; children—Aimee Beth, Bradley David. B.A., U. Cin., 1963; M.A., Wayne State U., 1967, Ph.D., 1968. Postdoctoral fellow U. Fla., Gainesville, 1968-70, asst. prof., 1970-74; Nat. Inst. Neurol., Communication and Stroke-NIH spl. fellow, 1971-73; adj. asst. prof. Wayne State U., Detroit, 1975-77, adj. assoc. prof. audiology and psychology, 1977-84, adj. prof. psychology, 1984—; dir. otol. research Henry Ford Hosp., Detroit, 1974—; nat. adv. bd. Inst. for Advanced Study Communication Scis., Gainesville, 1982-85; grant reviewer NSF, 1979—; ad hoc grant reviewer Nat. Inst. Occupational Safety and Health, USPHS, 1982. Author: Fundamentals of Hearing, 1977, 85. Contbr. chpts. to books, atricles and papers to profl. lit.; article reviewer 4 jours., 1977—. Mem. Centurion Club-Deafness Research Found., N.Y.C., 1975. Grantee Deafness Research Found., 1976, 77, Nat. Inst. Occupational Safety and Health, 1978, NIH Div. Animal Resources, 1978. Mem. Assn. for Research in Otolaryngology (sec.-treas. 1981-83, council mem. 1984—, pres. elect 1985-86), Sigma Xi., Psi Chi. Current work: Cochlear micromechanics, Cochlear prosthesis, effects of noise on hearing, animal psychoacoustics, research administration. Subspecialties: Otorhinolaryngology; Sensory processes. Home: 905 Robinhood Rd Bloomfield Hills MI 48013 Office: Dept Otology Henry Ford Hosp 2799 W Grand Blvd Detroit MI 48202

NIELSEN, HARALD CHRISTIAN, chemist; b. Chgo., Apr. 18, 1930; s. Svend Aage and Seena (Hansen) N.; m. Eloise Soule, Dec. 19, 1953; children—Brenda Mae, Paul Erick, Gloria Lynn. B.A. in Chemistry, St. Olaff Coll., 1952; Ph.D., Mich. State U., 1957. Biochemistry, No. Regional Research Ctr. U.S. Dept. Agr., Peoria, Ill., 1957—. Contbr. articles to profl. jours. Active Peoria Area Combined Fed. Campaign Coordinating Com., 1980—. Fellow AAAS; mem. Am. Chem. Soc., Am. Assn. Cereal Chemists, Am. Fedn. Govt. Employees (pres. local chpt. 1977—), Sigma Xi, Alpha Chi Sigma. Democrat. Lutheran. Current work: Molecular characterization of cereal grain proteins. Subspecialty: Biophysical chemistry. Home: 2318 N Gale Ave Peoria IL 61604 Office: Northern Regional Research Ctr US Dept Agr 1815 N University Ave Peoria IL 61604

NIELSEN, NIELS OLE, veterinary educator; b. Edmonton, Alta., Can., Mar. 3, 1930; s. Niels Ludvig and Maren Medom (Hansen) N.; m. Marilyn Anne Wilson, Mar. 5, 1955; children—Margo Lynn, John David, Gordon Ludvig. D.V.M., U. Toronto, 1951-56; Ph.D., U. Minn.-St. Paul, 1963. Diplomate Am. Coll. Veterinary Pathologists. Prof., Western Coll. Vet. Medicine U. Sask., 1964-84, dean, 1974-82; dir. Vet. Infectious Diseases Orgn. dean Ont. Vet. Coll., U. Guelph, 1985—; dir. Connaught Labs. Ltd., Toronto, Ont., 1980—, Assoc. Can. Univs. for No. Studies, 1981-85. Contbr. articles to profl. jours. Chmn., Sask. Environ. Adv. Com., 1978-82. Recipient Schofield medal Ont. Vet. Coll., 1982. Mem. AVMA, Am. Coll. Vet. Pathologists, Can. VMA (pres. 1968-69), Can. Assn. Vet. Pathologists. P Current work: Gastroenterology, comparative medicine. Subspecialty: Pathology (veterinary medicine). Office: Ontario Veterinary Coll U of Guelph Guelph ON NIG 2W1 Canada

NIENHUIS, ARTHUR WESLEY, physician, molecular biologist; b. Hudsonville, Mich., Aug. 9, 1941; s. Willard M. and Grace (Prince) N.; m. Sheryl Ann Kalmink, Sept. 20, 1968; children—Carol, Craig, Kevin, Heather. M.D., UCLA, 1968. Intern Mass. Gen. Hosp., Boston, 1968-68, asst. resident in med., 1969-70, clin. assoc. Nat. Heart Lung and Blood Inst., NIH, Bethesda, Md., 1970-72, chief clin. service molecular hematology br., 1973-77, dep. clin. dir., 1976-77, chief hematology br., 1977—; clin. fellow hematology Children's Hosp. Med. Ctr., Boston, 1972-73. Editor: Cellular and Molecular Regulation of Hemoglobin Switching, 1979; Organization and Expression of Globin Genes, 1981; Hemoglobins in Development and Differentiation, 1981; Globin Gene Expression and Hematopoietic Differentiation, 1983. Served with USPHS, 1970—. Regents' scholar UCLA, 1963-68; recipient Disting. Young Scientists award Md. Acad. Scis., 1975, Commendation medal NIH, 1980, Outstanding Service award NIH, 1984. Mem. Am. Fed. Clin. Research, Am. Soc. Clin. Investigation, Am. Soc. Hematology, Alpha Omega Alpha. Current work: Genetic mechanisms of acquired and congenital blood disorders. Home: 6320 Rockhurst Rd Bethesda MD 20814 Office: NIH NHLBI 9000 Rockville Pike Bldg 10 Room 7C103 Bethesda MD 20205

NIERENBERG, WILLIAM AARON, oceanography educator; b. N.Y.C., Feb. 13, 1919; s. Joseph and Minnie (Drucker) N.; m. Edith Meyerson, Nov. 21, 1941; children—Victoria Jean (Mrs. Tschinkel), Nicolas Clarke Eugene. Aaron Naumberg scholar, U. Paris, 1937-38; B.S., Coll. City N.Y., 1939; M.A., Columbia U., 1942, Ph.D. (NRC predoctoral fellow), 1947. Tutor Coll. City N.Y., 1939-42; sect. leader Manhattan Project, 1942-45; instr. physics Columbia, 1946-48; asst. prof. physics U. Mich., 1948-50; asso. prof. physics U. Calif. at Berkeley, 1950-53, prof., 1954-65; dir. Scripps Instn. Oceanography, 1965—; vice chancellor for marine scis. U. Calif. at San Diego, 1969—; dir. Hudson Labs., Columbia, 1953-54; assoc. prof. U. Paris, 1960-62; asst. sec. gen. NATO for sci. affairs, 1960-62; spl. cons. Exec. Office Pres., 1958-60; sr. cons. White House Office Sci. and Tech. Policy, 1976-78; chmn. White House Office Sci. and Tech. Policy acid rain peer rev. panel, 1982-84. Contbr. papers to profl. jours. E.O. Lawrence lectr. Nat. Acad. Sci., 1958, Miller Found. fellow, 1957-59, Sloan Found. fellow, 1958, Fulbright fellow, 1960-61; mem. U.S. Nat. Commn. UNESCO, 1964-68, Calif. Adv. Com. on Marine and Coastal Resources, 1967-71; adviser-at-large U.S. Dept. State, 1968—; mem. Nat. Sci. Bd., 1972-78, 82—; mem. Nat. Adv. Com. on Oceans and Atmosphere, 1971-77, chmn., 1971-75; mem. sci. and tech. adv. Council Calif. Assembly; mem. adv. council NASA, 1978-83, chmn. adv. council, 1978-82; mem. council Nat. Acad. Scis., 1979-82. NATO Sr. Sci. fellow, 1969; Decorated officer Nat. Order of Merit France; recipient Golden Dolphin award Assn. Artistico Letteraria Internazionale, Disting. Pub. Service medal NASA, 1982, Compass award Marine Tech. Soc., 1975; Procter prize Sigma Xi, 1977. Fellow Am. Phys. Soc. (council, sec. Pacific Coast sect. 1955-64); mem. Am. Acad. Arts and Scis., Nat. Acad. Engring., Nat. Acad. Scis., Am. Philos. Soc., Am. Assn. Naval Architects, Navy League, Fgn. Policy Assn. (mem. nat. council), Sigma Xi (pres. 1981-82). Club: Cosmos. Current Work: Expertise in a number of disparate fields. Original field was nuclear physics; that is continuing interest. Current in ocean science and ocean engineering with a secondary interest in civil aviation. Deeply concerned with defense matters in a variety of ways, including consultant to Defense Science Board and chairmanship of Jason group. Subspecialties: Nuclear physics; Oceanography. Home: 9581 La Jolla Farms Rd La Jolla CA 92037 Office: Scripps Instn Oceanography Dir's Office A-010 U Calif San Diego La Jolla CA 92093

NIESSE, JOHN EDGAR, materials engineer; b. Indpls., Nov. 30, 1927; s. John Leo and Jessie Louise (Pohlig) N.; m. Elaine Corrine Morin, Dec. 27, 1958; children—John A., Ann L. B.S., U.S. Naval Acad., 1950; S.M., Sc.D., MIT, 1958. Registered profl. engr., Mo. supervising engineer Crane Co., Chgo., 1959-60; various positions Carborundum Co., Niagara Falls, N.Y., 1960-67; leader metallurgics and ceramics Avco Corp., Lowell, Mass., 1967-72; sr. research group leader Monsanto Co., Research Triangle Park, N.C., 1972-75, specialist materials engr., St. Louis, 1975—. Contbr. articles to profl. jours. Patentee spl. ceramics, bond to steel. Served to lt. USN, 1950-55, capt. Res. ret. Crane Co. Fellow, 1957, 58. Mem. Nat. Assn. Corrosion Engrs. (chmn. T-5D com. 1981-83, chmn. planning com. 1985 plastics seminar 1984), Am. Ceramic Soc., Am. Soc. Metals. Current work: Internal consultant on materials selection, corrosion and failure analysis, chemical process equipment. Subspecialty: Corrosion. Home: 424 Glan Tai Dr Manchester MO 63011 Office: Monsanto Co 800 N Lindberg Blvd Saint Louis MO 63167

NIGAM, RAJENDRA C., systems analyst, computer scientist; b. Ghatampur, India, June 28, 1930; came to U.S., 1957, naturalized, 1968; s. Ram S. and Ram P. N.; m. Vimala Nigam, Mar. 5, 1953; children: Neeraj, Kamana, Alok, Arti. M.Sc. in Math, U. Lucknow, India, 1950; M.S. in Astronomy, U. Ill., 1958. Astronomer Smithsonian Astrophys. Obs., Cambridge, Mass., 1959-63; with IIT Intelcom Inc., Bellcom, Inc., Washington, 1963-67, MTS, Bedford, Mass., 1967-71; sr. fellow East-West Center, Honolulu, 1976; vis. prof. mgmt. B.H.U., Varanasi, India, 1979-80; systems analyst and designer MTS, Computer Scis. Corp., Silver Spring, Md., 1981-83; astronomer M/A-Com Sigma. Data Center, Nat. Space Sci. Data Ctr., Greenbelt, Md., 1983-85; research assoc. Health Systems Research Inst., Beltsville, Md., 1985—. Author: Happier Living, 1979; contbr. numerous articles to profl. jours. Mem. World Future Soc., Am. Astron. Soc. Hindu. Current Work: DBMS and computer software related to information storage and on-line retrieval. Subspecialties: Database systems; Astronautics. Home: 4813 Quimby Ave Beltsville MD 20705 Office: Health Systems Research Inst PO Box 163 Beltsville MD 20705

NIGHTINGALE, ELENA OTTOLENGHI, physician, scientist, educator, genetic counselor; b. Leghorn, Italy, Nov. 1, 1932; came to U.S., 1939, naturalized, 1948; d. Mario L. and Elisa V. (Levi) Ottolenghi; m. Stuart L. Nightingale, July 1, 1965; children: Elizabeth, Marisa. A.B. summa cum laude, Barnard Coll., 1954; postgrad., Columbia U., 1954-56; Ph.D. (fellow), Rockefeller U., 1961; M.D., NYU, 1964. Intern, Georgetown U. Hosp., 1973-74; resident instr. medicine NYU, 1964-65; asst. prof. microbiology Cornell U., 1965-70; asst. prof. Johns Hopkins U., 1970-73; sr. staff officer Nat. Acad. Scis./NRC, 1975-76; clin. instr. pediatrics Georgetown U., 1975-80, clin. asst. prof., 1980-82, adj. prof., 1982—; acting dir. div. health scis. policy Inst. Medicine Nat. Acad. Sci., 1979-80, dir. div. health promotion and disease prevention, 1977-80, sr. program officer, 1979-82, sr. scholar in residence, 1982-83; vis. assoc. prof. social medicine health policy Harvard U., 1980-84, lectr. in health policy, 1984—; genetics cons. Birth Defects Clinic, Georgetown U., 1975—; spl. adv. to pres. Carnegie Corp., 1983—. Contbr. articles to profl. jours. Nat. Acad. Sci./Sloan fellow, 1974-75. Fellow N.Y. Acad. Sci.; mem. The Harvey Soc., AAAS, Genetics Soc. Am., Am. Soc. Microbiology, Am. Soc. Human Genetics, Inst. of Medicine of Nat. Acad. Scis., Sigma Xi, Phi Beta Kappa. Current Work: Health and science policy; international health; maternal and child health; disease prevention; genetics molecular and clinical; medical education. Subspecialties: Genetics and genetic engineering (medicine); Neonatology.

NIIMURA, MASANOBU, physicist; b. Nagoya, Japan, June 3, 1939; came to U.S., 1968, naturalized, 1985; s. Koji and Chiyo (Mori) N.; m. Maria Neves Silva, Apr. 23, 1979; children—Friedia Monnamur, Joshua James Koji. B.S. in Physics, Waseda U., 1962, B.S. in Electronics, 1964, M.S., 1967; Ph.D., Colo. State U., 1973. Research assoc. Colo. State U., Fort Collins, 1973-74, Columbia U., N.Y.C., 1974-76; assoc. prof. U. Campinas, Brazil, 1976-82; research assoc. Hampton Inst., Va., 1982-83; grad. Faculty dept. elec. engring. Pa. State U., University Park, 1984—. Author: Fisica de Plasma, Vol. II, 1979; Fisica de Plasma, Vol. III, 1979. Mem. Am. Phys. Soc., Phys. Soc. Japan. Current work: Research on advanced fusion concepts via compact toroid formed by a reversed field configuration; magnetic reconnection; plasma physics and diagnostics, pulsed power technology. Subspecialties: Plasma physics; Fusion. Home: 801-A5 W Aaron Dr State College PA 16803 Office: Pa State U 202 Electrical Engring East University Park PA 16802

NIKLES, DAVID EUGENE, chemist; b. Akron, Ohio, July 3, 1954; s. Edward Eugene and Anna Lucile (Willis) N.; m. Jacqueline A. Werstler, June 16, 1979. B.S., U. Akron, 1977; Ph.D., Case Western Res. U., 1982. Lab. technician Firestone Synthetic Rubber and Latex Co., Akron, 1972-77; research chemist Celanese Research Co., Summit, N.J., 1982—. Contbr. articles to profl. jours. Mem. Am. Chem. Soc., Materials Research Soc., Electrochem. Soc., Soc. Photo-Optical Instrumentation Engrs. Current work: Materials science; polymeric materials for use in optical storage of information; optical characterization of materials. Subspecialties: Inorganic chemistry; Laser data storage and reproduction. Office: Celanese Research Co 86 Morris Ave Summit NJ 07901

NIKOLAI, ROBERT JOSEPH, university administrator, biomechanical engineer, consultant, educator; b. Rock Island, Ill., Apr. 6, 1937; s. Joseph Lawrence and Martha Marie (Holt) N.; m. Susan Eloise Shannon, June 10, 1961; children: Catherine, Teresa, Margaret, David, Philip. Student, Ill. Benedictine Coll., 1955-57; B.S. in Mech. Engring, U. Ill, Urbana, 1959, M.S. in Engring. Mechanics, 1961, Ph.D. in Engring. Mechanics, 1964. Registered profl. engr., Mo. Asst. prof. engring. and engring. mechanics St. Louis U., 1964-68, asso. prof. engring. mechanics, 1968-71, asso. prof. orthodontics, 1971-75, prof. biomechanics in orthodontics, 1975—; asst. dean St. Louis U. (Grad. Sch.), 1971-72, asso. dean, 1972—; adj. prof. civil and mech. engring. Washington U., St. Louis, 1980—; cons. in field. Author: Bioengineering Analysis of Orthodontic Mechanics, 1985. Research, publs. in field; editorial panel: Jour. Biomechanics, 1982—; manuscript cons. Am. Jour. Orthodontics, 1981—. Mem. University City (Mo.) Traffic Commn., 1972-79, chmn, 1975-77. Orthodontic Edn. and Research Found. grantee, 1981; Nat. Inst. Dental Research grantee, 1983-85. Mem. Am. Acad. Mechanics, Internat. Assn. Dental Research, Am. Assn. Dental Research, Orthodontic Edn. and Research Found. (hon.), Sigma Xi, Pi Tau Sigma. Current Work: Structural behavior of orthodontic appliances; graduate teaching and research in orthodontic bioengineering. Subspecialties: Solid mechanics; Orthodontics. Home: 7134 Stanford Ave University City MO 63130

NIKORA, ALLEN PETER, software systems designer and analyst; b. Stuttgart, W.Ger., July 17, 1955; s. Eugene S. and Lise L. (Kohler) N. B.S., Calif. Inst. Tech., 1977. With McDonnell-Douglas Astronautics Co., Huntington Beach, Calif., 1977-78; software systems designer, analyst Jet Propulsion Lab., Pasadena, Calif., 1978—. Mem. Assn. Computing Machinery, AIAA. Current Work: Design tests to validate the command and data susbystem flight software for Galileo Jupiter Orbiter. Develop spacecraft fault protection programs for Galileo Jupiter Orbiter. Task manager of effort to adapt Galileo command and data subsystem test software to Venus Radar Mapper CDS. Subspecialties: Distributed systems and networks; Software engineering. Office: 4800 Oak Grove Dr Pasadena CA 91109

NILAVER, GAJANAN, neurologist, immunocytochemist, educator; b. Bangalore, India, Aug. 30, 1946; came to U.S., 1971, naturalized, 1973; s. Shanker and Nalini (Katre) N. M.B., B.S., U. Madras, 1968. Resident in neurology St. Vincent's Hosp., N.Y.C., 1972-75; NIH Nat. Research Service postdoctoral fellow in neuroendocrinology Columbia U., N.Y.C., 1975-79, research assoc., asst. neurologist, 1979-81, asst. prof. neurology, 1982—. Contbr. articles to sci. jours. NIH grantee, 1979—. Mem. AMA, Soc. Neurosci., Am. Acad. Neurology, AAAS, N.Y. Soc. Electron Microscopists, N.Y. Acad. Scis. Current Work: Neuroendocrinology, immunocytochemistry, immunology. Subspecialties: Neuroendocrinology; Immunocytochemistry. Home: 151 Prospect Ave Apt 6E1 Hackensack NJ 07601 Office: Room 309 Black Bldg Columbia U 630 W 168th S New York NY 10032

NIRENBERG, MARSHALL WARREN, biochemist; b. N.Y.C., Apr. 10, 1927; s. Harry Edward and Minerva (Bykowsky) N.; m. Perola Zaltzman, July 14, 1961. B.S. in Zoology, U. Fla., 1948, M.S., 1952; Ph.D. in Biochemistry, U. Mich., 1957. Postdoctoral fellow Am. Cancer Soc. at NIH, 1957-59; postdoctoral fellow USPHS at NIH, 1959-60; mem. staff NIH, 1960—; research biochemist, chief lab. biochem. genetics Nat. Heart, Lung and Blood Inst., 1962—. Recipient Molecular Biology award Nat. Acad. Scis., 1962, award in biol. scis. Washington Acad. Scis., 1962, medal HEW, 1964, Modern Medicine award, 1963, Harrison Howe award Am. Chem. Soc., 1964, Nat. Medal Sci. Pres. Johnson, 1965, Hildebrand award Am. Chem. Soc., 1966, Research Corp. award, 1966, A.C.P. award, 1967, Gairdner Found. award merit Can., 1967, Prix Charles Leopold Meyer French Acad. Scis., 1967, Franklin medal Franklin Inst., 1968, Albert Lasker Med. Research award, 1968, Priestly award, 1968; co-recipient Louisa Gross Horowitz prize Columbia, 1968, Nobel prize in medicine and physiology, 1968. Fellow AAAS, N.Y. Acad. Scis.; mem. Am. Soc. Biol. Chemists, Am. Chem. Soc. (Paul Lewis award enzyme chemistry 1964), Am. Acad. Arts and Scis., Biophys. Soc., Nat. Acad. Scis., Washington Acad. Scis., Soc. for Study Devel. and Growth, Harvey Soc. (hon.), Leopoldina Deutsche Akademie der Naturforscher, Pontificial Acad. Scis. Spl. research mechanism protein synthesis, genetic code, nucleic acids, regulatory mechanisms in synthesis macromolecules, neurobiology. Subspecialty: Biochemistry (biology). Office: Nat Heart Inst NIH Lab Biochem Genetics Bethesda MD 20205*

NIRENBURG, SERGEI, computer scientist, artificial intelligence researcher. Mem. computer sci. dept. Colgate U., Hamilton, N.Y. Subspecialties: Artificial intelligence; Automated language processing. Office: Colgate U Dept Computer Sci Hamilton NY 13346

NISBET, PHILLIP CLARK, exploration geochemist, analytical geochemist; b. Ft. Benning, Ga., Mar. 29, 1956; s. Andrew and Haroldine May (Hart) N.; m. Marion Norton, Feb. 12, 1984. B.S. in Geology, U. Wash., 1980; M.S. in Geology, Ea. Wash. U., 1984. Research asst. U. Wash., Seattle, 1979-80; geochemist Savercool Mining Co., Kent, Wash., 1980, 82-83, Burlington No. R.R., Billings, Mont., 1981; exploration geochemist Nord Resources Corp., Albuquerque, N.Mex., 1984. Contbr. articles to profl. jours. Organizer Anderson for President, Olympic Penninsula, Wash., 1980; campaign mgr. Nisbet for rep., Clallam County, Wash., 1977-78; lobbyist mineral resources issues, Olympia, 1980-83. Served with U.S. Army, 1974-77. Mem. Soc. Mining Engrs., Geol. Soc. Am., Northwest Mining Assn., Spectroscopy Soc. Can., Tabbaco Roots Geol. Soc., Am. Legion. Republican. Current work: Trace element analysis of geological materials by atomic absorption spectroscopy and ICP emmision spectroscopy, application of trace element chemistry to mineral exploration, geochemical identification of ophiolite origins. Subspecialties: Geochemistry; Analytical chemistry. Home: 645 D Kitchen Dick Lane Rd Sequim WA 98382

NISONOFF, ALFRED, biochemist, educator; b. N.Y.C., Jan. 26, 1923; s. Hyman and Lillian (Klein) N.; m. Sarah Weiseman, July 17, 1946; children: Donald Michael, Linda Ann. B.S. (State scholar), Rutgers U., 1942; M.A., Johns Hopkins U., 1948, Ph.D. (AEC fellow), 1951. Postdoctoral fellow Johns Hopkins Med. Sch., 1951-52; research chemist U.S. Rubber Co., Naugatuck, Conn., 1952-54; sr. cancer research scientist Roswell Park Meml. Inst., Buffalo, 1954-57, assoc. cancer research scientist, 1957-60; assoc. prof. microbiology U. Ill., Urbana, 1960-62, prof., 1962-66; prof. microbiology U. Ill. Coll. Medicine, Chgo., 1966-69, head dept. biol. chemistry, 1969-75; prof. biology Rosenstiel Research Center, Brandeis U., Waltham, Mass., 1975—; Mem. grant rev. bds. allergy and immunology study sect. NIH, 1965-67, 71-74, 84—, Nat. Multiple Sclerosis Soc., 1972-75, 77-80. Author: The Antibody Molecule, 1975, Introduction to Molecular Immunology, 1982; Editorial bd.: Jour. Immunology, 1962-67, 69-74, sect. editor, 1971-74, sr. editor, 1975-79; editorial bd.: Immunochemistry, 1964-70, Bacteriological Revs, 1968-70, Jour. Exptl. Medicine, 1974-78, Critical Reviews in Immunology, 1980—; contbr. articles to profl. jours. Served to lt. (j.g.) USNR, 1943-46. Recipient Research Career award NIH, 1962-69; Pasteur Inst. medal, 1970. Fellow Am. Acad. Arts and Scis. Mem. Nat. Acad. Sci., Am. Assn. Immunologists (mem. council 1985—), Am. Soc. Biol. Chemists, Belgian Royal Acad. Medicine (fgn. corr.), Nat. Acad. Sci., Phi Beta Kappa, Phi Lambda Upsilon. Current Work: Studying genetic control of antibodies of defined specificity; also regulation of immune response. Subspecialty: Immunobiology and immunology. Home: 16 Winter St Waltham MA 02154 Office: Dept Biology Rosenstiel Research Center Brandeis U Waltham MA 02254

NITOWSKY, HAROLD MARTIN, physician, educator; b. Bklyn., Feb. 12, 1925; s. Max and Fannie (Gershowitz) N.; m. Myra Heller, Nov. 28, 1954; children—Fran Ellen, Daniel Howard. A.B., N.Y. U., 1944, M.D., 1947; M.S., U. Colo., 1952. Intern Mt. Sinai Hosp., N.Y.C., 1947-48; resident pediatrics U. Colo. Med. Center, 1948-50; USPHS postdoctoral fellow U. Colo., 1950-51; staff Sinai Hosp., Balt., 1953-67, dir. pediatric research, 1960-67; faculty Johns Hopkins Sch. Medicine, 1953-67, asso. prof. pediatrics, 1962-67; prof. pediatrics and genetics Albert Einstein Coll. Medicine, 1967—; cons. Nat. Inst. Child Health and Human Devel., 1966—; Sr. surgeon USPHS, 1951-53. Contbr. articles on nutrition, metabolism, genetics to profl. jours. Mem. Am. Pediatric Soc., Soc. Pediatric Research. Subspecialties: Genetics and genetic engineering (medicine); Pediatrics. Home: 25 Devonshire Rd New Rochelle NY 10804

NITZ, DAVID EDWIN, physics educator, researcher; b. Dallas, Feb. 19. 1951; s. Ralph A. and Thelma I. (Hanson) N.; m. Debra D. Ralstin, June 25, 1977. B.A., St. Olaf Coll., Northfield, Minn., 1973; M.A., Rice U., 1976, PH.D., 1978. Research assoc. Joint Inst. Lab. Astrophysics, Boulder, Colo., 1978-79; instr. physics St. Olaf Coll., 1979-80, asst. prof., 1980-85, assoc. prof., 1985—. Contbr. articles in field to profl. jours. Research Corp./Northwest Area Found. grantee, 1981-86. Mem. Am. Phys. Soc.; mem. Am. Assn. Physics Tchrs. Lutheran. Current Work: Interaction of radiation with atoms and molecules, molecular structure; undergraduate physics teaching. Subspecialties: Atomic and molecular physics. Office: Dept Physics Saint Olaf Coll Northfield MN 55057

NITZAN, DAVID, roboticist. Program dir. robotics SRI Internat., Menlo Park, Calif. Subspecialty: Robotics. Office: SRI Internat 333 Ravenswood Ave Menlo Park CA 94025

NOBE, KEN, chemical engineering educator; b. Berkeley, Calif., Aug. 26, 1925; s. Sidney and Kiyo (Uyeyama) N.; m. Mary Tagami, Aug. 31, 1957; children: Steven Andrew, Keven Gibbs, Brian Kelvin. B.S., U. Calif., Berkeley, 1951; Ph.D., UCLA, 1956. Jr. chem. engr. Air Reduction Co., Murray Hill, N.J., 1951-52; asst. prof. chem. engring. UCLA, 1957-62, asso. prof., 1962-68, prof., 1968—, chmn. dept. chem. engring., 1978-84. Div. editor: Jour. Electrochem. Soc, 1967—, Electrochimica Acta, 1977—. Served with U.S. Army, 1944-46. Mem. Electrochem. Soc., Am. Chem. Soc., Nat. Assn. Corrosion Engrs., Internat. Soc. Electrochemistry, Sigma Xi. Current Work: Electrode kinetics; photelectrochemistry and applied catalysis. Subspecialties: Chemical engineering; Corrosion. Office: UCLA 5405 Boelter Hall Los Angeles CA 90024

NOBEL, JOEL J., physician; b. Phila., Dec. 8, 1934; s. Bernard Davis Judovich and Golda Nobel; m. Bonnie Sue Goldberg, June 19, 1959 (div. 1973): children—Erika, Joshua; m. Loretta Schwart, Sept. 29, 1978. B.A. in English, Haverford Coll., 1956; M.A. in Internat. Relations, U. Pa., 1958; M.D., Jefferson Med. Coll., 1963. Diplomate Nat. Bd. Med. Examiners. Intern, Presby. Hosp., Phila., 1963-64; surg. resident U. Pa. Hosp., Phila., 1964-65, neurosurg. resident, 1965-66; pres. ECRI, Plymouth Meeting, Pa., 1968—; dir., chmn. tech. policy com. Consumers Union, Mt. Vernon, N.Y., 1980—. Inventor Mobile Intensive Care Unit, 1965. Contbr. articles to profl. jours. Served to lt. USN Submarine Force, 1966-68. Recipient Shain Practice of surgery award Jefferson Med. Coll., 1963, Shain Practice of Medicine award Jefferson Med. Coll., 1962; Smith Kline fgn. fellow to Nepal, 1962. Mem. AMA, Assn. for Advancement of Med. Instrumentation, Am. Def. Preparedness Assn., Am. Pub. Health Assn. Clubs: Union League, Sunday Breakfast (Phila.). Current work: Evaluation of medical equipment for safety, performance and cost effectiveness, technology assessment, safety and forensic engineering. Subspecialties: Biomedical engineering; Biomedical engineering. Home: 1434 Monk Rd Cladayne PA 19035 Office: ECRI 5200 Butler Pike Plymouth Meeting PA 19462

NOBEL, PARK S., biology educator, research plant physiological ecologist; b. Chgo., Nov. 4, 1938; s. James Dodman and Ruth Eleanor (Uetz) N.; m. Eiko Mizuguchi, Feb. 7, 1965; children: Catherine, Elizabeth. B. Engring. Physics, Cornell U., 1961; M.S., Calif. Inst. Tech., 1963; Ph.D., U. Calif., Berkeley, 1965. NSF postdoctoral fellow U. Tokyo, 1965-66, King's Coll., U. London, 1966-67; asst. prof. molecular biology UCLA, 1967-71, assoc. prof. biology, 1971-75, prof., 1975—; cons. in field. Contbr. numerous articles on biophysical plant physiology and ecology to profl. jours.; author 3 books on plant physiology, 1 book on cacti; editor 4 books on plant ecology. Guggenheim fellow Australian Nat. U., Canberra, 1973-74. Mem. Ecol. Soc. Am., Am. Soc. Plant Physiologists, Bot. Soc. Am. Current Work: Plant physiological ecology, especially desert plants; research, writing and teaching in plant physiology and ecology. Subspecialties: Plant physiology (biology); Ecology (biology). Office: Dept Biology U Calif Los Angeles CA 90024

NOBLE, MARK GREGORY, ecology educator, institute administrator; b. Mpls., Sept. 30, 1951; s. Earl J. and Julia Marie (Colianni) N. B.S., U. Minn., 1973, M.S., 1977; Ph.D., Australian Nat. U., 1982. Coordinator biology colloquium U. Minn., Mpls., 1974-75; vice chmn. bd. Springbrook Nature Ctr. Found., Fridley, Minn., 1974, chmn., 1975; research scholar Australian Nat. U., Canberra, 1978-82; research assoc. Inst. Arctic and Alpine Research, U. Colo., Boulder, 1982—, field dir., 1984—, dir. Mountain Research Sta., Nederland, Colo., 1984—. Contbr. numerous sci. articles to profl. jours. Active Minn. Pub. Interest Research Group, Mpls., 1974; organizer, mem. Fridley Beautification Assn., 1974. Research grantee NSF, 1975, 82, 83, Australian Nat. U., 1978, vis. fellow, 85, Nat. Park Service grantee, 1984, 85. Mem. Arctic Inst. N.Am. (research grantee 1974), Assn. Am. Geographers, Ecol. Soc. Am., Orgn. for Tropical Studies, N.W. Sci. Assn., Ecol. Soc. Australia, Nat. Audubon Soc. (bd. dirs. Mpls. chpt. 1975-76), Sigma Xi (research grantee 1974). Current work: Pedogenic and biotic processes in landscape ecology; historical and modern biogeography; dispersal of aquatic macroinvertebrates; intrageneric competition; theoretical aspects of plant succession. Subspecialties: Ecology (biology); Paleontology, paleoecology. Office: Mountain Research Station Univ Colo Nederland CO 80466

NOBLE, NANCY LEE, biochemist, University dean, researcher; b. Chattanooga, Mar. 1, 1922; d. Samuel Edward and Agnes Lee (Caulkins) N. B.S. in Chemistry, U. Chattanooga, 1943; M.S. in Biochemistry (Univ. fellow), Emory U., 1949, Ph.D. (USPHS predoctoral research fellow), 1953. Research asst. Organic Research Lab., Chattanooga Medicine Co., 1943-48; lab. asst. dept. biochemistry Emory U. Sch. Medicine, 1949-50; research asst. prof. dept. biochemistry U. Miami Sch. Medicine, 1953-57, asst. prof. biochemistry, 1957-63, assoc. prof. biochemistry and medicine, 1963—, assoc. dean for faculty affairs, 1981—; dir. Biochemistry Research Lab., Miami Heart Inst., 1953-56; investigator Labs. for Cardiovascular Research, Howard Hughes Med. Inst., Miami, Fla., 1956-70; bd. dirs., mem. com. sch. health and sci. careers Miami affiliate Am. Heart Assn., bd. dirs., mem. com. sch. health and sci. careers Fla. affiliate. Contbr. numerous articles abstracts, chpts. to profl. publs. Mem. Episcopal Cursillo Movement, Emory U. Grad. Council, 1980-84; vestryman, sr. warden Episcopal Ch., 1983-85. Co-recipient award for basic research relevant to problems of aging Ciba Found., 1957, 58, Outstanding Achievement in Research recogniztion Miami Profl. Women's Club, 1963, recognition for meritorious service in fight against heart disease Fla. Heart Assn., 1967, 69, 71, recognition for meritorious service in fight against heart disease Miami Heart Assn., 1968, 70; Spl. Service award Fla. affiliate Am. Heart Assn., 1980; recognition for 15 yrs. of dedicated service, 1981. Fellow Gerontol. Soc., Am. Inst. Chemists (cert.profl. chemist); mem. Am. Chem. Soc., AAAS, Am. Soc. Study Arteriosclerosis, N.Y. Acad. Scis., Soc. Exptl. Biology and Medicine (councilor Southeastern sect. 1974-79), Fla. Acad. Scis., Am. Heart Assn. Council on Basic Sci., Biochem. Soc., AAUP, Assn. Women in Sci., Am. Heart Assn. Council on Thrombosis, Am. Physiol. Soc., Emory Alumni Assn. (treas. Miami chpt. 1963-64, 79-81, v.p. chpt. 1964-65, pres. chpt. 1965-66), U. Tenn. Alumni Assn. (pres. S.E. Fla. chpt. 1976-78), Women's Panhellenic, Mortar Bd. (v.p. chpt. 1977-79), Mortar Bd. (v.p. chpt. 1984—), Sigma Xi (treas. chpt. 1974-78), Chi Omega. Current Work: Connective tissue, cardiovascular disease. Subspecialties: Biochemistry (medicine); Animal physiology.

NOCENTI, MERO RAYMOND, physiologist, editor; b. Masontown, Pa., Sept. 7, 1928; s. Silvio and Josephine (Pisani) N.; m. Louise I. Norante, Feb. 5, 1955; children: Mary, Ann, David. B.A., W.Va. U.-Morgantown, 1951, M.S., 1952; Ph.D., Rutgers U., 1955. Waksman-Merck postdoctoral fellow Rutgers U., New Brunswick, N.J., 1955-56; prof. physiology Columbia U., N.Y.C., 1956—. Recipient Tchr. of Year award Columbia Med. Students, 1973, 83, 84, Tchr. of Year award Columbia Dental Students, 1978, 83, Dean's Disting. Tchr. award Coll. Phys. and Surg., 1983. Mem. AAAS, Am. Physiol. Soc., Soc. Exptl. Biology and Medicine (exec. sec. 1974—, editor proceedings 1974—, Council Biology Editors), Sigma Xi. Roman Catholic. Current Work: Hormonal control of electrolyte and water balances. Subspecialties: Physiology (medicine); Endocrinology. Office: Columbia U 630 W 168th St New York NY 10032

NOCETI, RICHARD PAUL, chemist; b. Pitts., Jan. 16, 1947; s. Virgil Francis and Virginia Amelia (DeGasperi) N.; m. Christina Louise Moll, May, 1970; children—Stephanie Lyn, Pierina Marie, Chiara Ann. B.S., Duquesne U., 1968, M.S., 1974, Ph.D., 1979. Research chemist Calgon Corp., Pitts., 1968; teaching asst. Duquesne U., Pitts., 1971-75; research chemist U.S. Dept. Energy, Pitts., 1975—. Contbr. articles to profl. jours. Served with USN, 1969-71. Mem. Am. Chem. Soc., Soc. for Analytical Chemists of Pitts., Spectroscopy Soc. Pitts. (chmn. high sch. grants com. 1982-83), Naval Res. Assn. Republican. Roman Catholic. Current work: Chemistry of process water treatment; heterocyclic chemistry; synthetic organic chemistry; analytical chemistry; natural products. Subspecialties: Organic chemistry; Water supply and wastewater treatment. Home: 5530 Baptist Rd Pittsburgh PA 15236 Office: US Dept Energy PETC PO Box 10940 Pittsburgh PA 15236

NOGA, EDWARD JOSEPH, veterinarian, researcher; b. Chgo., Sept. 14, 1953; s. Edward Francis and Gwendolyn Honore N. B.S., Fla. Atlantic U., 1974, M.S., 1977; D.V.M., U. Fla., 1982. Teaching asst. Fla. Atlantic U., Boca Raton, 1975-76, research asst., 1976-77; fellow in aquatic medicine Cornell U., Ithaca, N.Y., 1978; fellow in comparative pathology Harvard U., Boston, 1980; research asst. U. Fla., Gainesville, 1980-82; asst. prof. aquatic animal medicine N.C. State U., Raleigh, 1982—. Contbr. articles to profl. publs. Patentee channel catfish virus vaccine. Faculty scholar Fla. Atlantic U., 1971-74, Univ. fellow, 1975; Lancaster scholar Fla. Farm Bur., 1978; grantee State of Fla., 1978, U.S. Dept. Agr., 1982, N.C. State U., 1982, Sea Grant, 1983-85. Mem. World Mariculture Soc., AVMA, Internat. Assn. Aquatic Animal Medicine, Tissue Culture Assn. (Wilton Earle award 1977), Am. Fisheries Soc. (fish health sect.), Sigma Xi, Phi Kappa Phi, Phi Zeta. Roman Catholic. Current work: Medical research, especially related to diseases of aquatic animals, particularly fin fishes. Subspecialties: Diseases of aquatic animals; Tissue culture. Office: Dept Companion Animal and Spl Species Medicine Sch Vet Medicine NC State Univ 4700 Hillsborough St Raleigh NC 27606

NOGAR, NICHOLAS STEPHEN, chemist, educator; b. Chgo., Jan. 19, 1950; s. Andrew R. and L. Catherine (Cremer) N.; m. Marcella M. Sanchez, Aug. 3, 1974; children—Anna Maria, Joshua N., Carmella L. B.S., U. N. Mex., 1971; Ph.D., U. Utah, 1976. Postdoctoral fellow U. Calif.-Berkeley, 1976-77; asst. prof., U. Nebr., Lincoln, 1977-80; staff Los Alamos Nat. Lab., 1980—. Contbr. articles to profl. jours. Fellow Stauffer Chem. Co., Phillips Petroleum Co. Mem. Am. Chem. Soc., AAAS, Sigma Xi, Current work: Resonance ionization mass spectrometry; intracavity absorption; optogalvanic. Subspecialties: Laser spectroscopy; Analytical chemistry. Home: 446 Connie Los Alamos NM 87544 Office: CHM-2 G378 Los Alamos Nat Lab Los Alamos NM 87545

NOGUEIRA, NADIA, medical researcher. With dept. med. and molecular parasitology, NYU. Subspecialty: Parasitology. Office: NYU Dept Med and Molecular Parasitology 341 E 25th St New York NY 10010

NOID, DONALD WILLIAM, research chemist, consultant; b. Marshalltown, Iowa, Feb. 6, 1949; s. William G. and Florence M. (Daman) N.; m. Barbara P. Joslin; children—William G., George A. B.S., Iowa State U., 1971; M.S., U. Ill., 1973, Ph.D., 1976. Chemist Oak Ridge Nat. Lab, 1977—; adj. assoc. prof. chemistry U. Tenn, Knoxville, 1983—; vis. assoc. prof. chemistry U. Wis.-Madison, 1983; vis. sr. scientist Inst. Def. Analysis, 1985. Contbr. articles to profl. jours. NSF fellow, 1976; Eugene P. Wigner fellow, 1977; Theoretical Chemistry Inst. fellow, 1983. Mem. Am. Phys. Soc. Current work: Molecular dynamics, laser chemistry. Subspecialties: Theoretical chemistry; Atomic and molecular physics. Home: 1802 Strathmore Rd Knoxville TN 37922 Office: Oak Ridge Nat Lab Oak Ridge TN 37830

NOLAN, PATRICK LEE, physicist, researcher; b. Colusa, Calif., Nov. 11, 1952; s. John Henry and Carol Lee (Harris) N. B.S., Calif. Inst. Tech., 1974; M.S., U. Calif.-San Diego, 1976, Ph.D., 1982. Teaching asst. U. Calif.-San Diego, La Jolla, 1974-75, research asst., 1975-81, postgrad. research physicist, 1982; research assoc. NRC/Naval Research Lab., Washington, 1982-84; research assoc. Stanford U., Calif., 1984—; NRC research assoc., 1982-84. Contbr. articles to physics jours. recipient NASA Group Achievement award, 1979; Marlar Found. fellow, 1981. Mem. Am. Astron. Soc., Am. Phys. Soc., AAAS. Democrat. Presbyterian. Current work: Developing space instruments for high-energy gamma ray observations, gamma ray bursts, X-rays from black hole candidates. Subspecialties: Gamma ray high energy astrophysics; X-ray high energy astrophysics. Office: WW Hansen Labs of Physics Stanford U Stanford CA 94305

NOLEN-HOEKSEMA, RICHARD CLARENCE, tectonophysicist, researcher; b. Washington, Mar. 17, 1956; s. Renze Lyle and Olive Marjorie (Coombes) Hoeksema; m. Susan Kay Nolen, May 10, 1981. B.A., Hope Coll., 1977; M.S., Yale U., 1979, M.Phil., 1980, Ph.D., 1983. Cartographic aide U.S. Geol. Survey, Reston, Va., 1978; research affiliate Yale U., New Haven, 1983, research assoc., 1983-84; research structural geologist Cities Service Oil & Gas Corp., Tulsa, 1984—; speaker in field. Author articles, abstracts and reports in field. Vol. Christian Community Action, New Haven, 1981-82, Jr. Achievement Greater Tulsa, 1985. Sigma Xi sr. research awardee, 1977; awardee U.S. Geol. Survey, 1978; NSF research grantee, 1980-83. Mem. Geol. Soc. Am., Am. Geophys. Union, Am. Assn. Petroleum Geologist, Geothermal Resources Council, Tulsa Geol. Soc. Current work: Structural geology and tectonics, basin analysis, terrestrial heat flow, naturally fractured systems. Subspecialties: Tectonics; Geophysics. Home: 4702 E 80th St Apt 13-N Tulsa OK 74136 Office: Structural Geol Research Cities Service Oil & Gas Corp 4500 S 129th East Ave PO Box 3908 Tulsa OK 74102

NOLL, CHARLES GORDON, physicist, researcher; b. Sunbury, Pa., Dec. 2, 1948; s. J. Herman and Helen E. (Gelnett) N.; m. Alice Marie Walters, Dec. 20, 1971; children—Carlton, Benjamin, Jennifer. B.A., Bloomsburg State Coll., 1970; M.S., Ohio State U., 1974; Ph.D., 1975. Lectr. dept. physics Ohio State U., Columbus, 1975-76; physicist United McGill Corp., Columbus, 1976-81, sr. physicist, 1981-83, mgr. corp. research and devel., 1983—. Contbr. articles to profl. jours. Mem. IEEE (sr.), Am. Phys. Soc., Electrostatics Soc. Am., Sigma Xi, Sigma Pi Sigma. Current work: Technical assessment of emerging technology, electromechanics of particulate matter with application to electrostatic precipitation, powder coating, fluidization, and pneumatic conveying. Subspecialties: Environmental engineering; Gas cleaning systems. Home: 121 Academy Ct Gahanna OH 43230 Office: United McGill Corp 1 Mission Pk Groveport OH 43125

NOLTIMIER, HALLAN COSTELLO, geology educator; b. Los Angeles, Mar. 19, 1937; s. Frederick Henry and Corinne Marie (Scheel) N.; m. Judith Walford Summers, July 14, 1961; children: Mark Andrew, Romy Ann. B.S., Calif. Inst. Tech., 1958; Ph.D. in Geophysics, U. Newcastle upon Tyne, Eng., 1965. Lectr. U. Newcastle upon Tyne, 1966-68; asst. prof. geology U. Okla., Norman, 1968-71, assoc. prof., 1971-72; assoc. prof. geology Ohio State U., Columbus, 1972-78, prof., 1978—; cons. in field. Contbr. chpts. to books. Fellow Royal Astron. Soc.; mem. Am. Geophys. Union, Geol. Soc. Am., AAAS, Ohio Acad. Sci., Sigma Xi (sec. Okla. 1969-71). Democrat. Current Work: Research in paleomagnetism of fossiliferous sediments using cryogenic magnetometry. Subspecialties: Geophysics; Low temperature physics. Office: Dept Geology and Mineralogy Ohio State U Columbus OH 43210

NOMURA, ABRAHAM MICHAEL YOZABURO, physician; b. Honolulu, July 23, 1939; s. George Giichi and Kaneyo N.; m. Susan Hitomi, Feb. 20, 1972; children: Liane Miyoko, Ryan Yoichi. B.S., John Carroll U., 1962; M.D., Loyola U., Chgo., 1966; M.P.H., Johns Hopkins U., 1972, Dr.P.H., 1974. Diplomate: Nat. Bd. Med. Examiners, Am. Bd. Preventive Medicine. Intern Michael Reese Med. Ctr., Chgo., 1966-67; resident in preventive medicine Johns Hopkins Hosp., Balt., 1971-74; asst. dir. Japan-Hawaii cancer study Kuakini Med. Ctr., Honolulu, 1974-76, dir., 1976—; epidemiologist Cancer Center Hawaii, U. Hawaii, Honolulu, 1974—; assoc. prof. Sch. Pub. Health, 1976-82, prof., 1982—; cons. NIH, 1983—. Assoc. editor: Am. Jour Epidemiology, 1982—; contbr. articles on research in gastrointestinal and breast cancer in profl. jours. Served to lt. USN, 1967-69. Nat. Cancer Inst. grantee, 1976—. Mem. Hawaii Med. Assn. Current Work: Activities devoted to identifying environmental causes of common cancers. Subspecialties: Epidemiology; Cancer research (medicine). Home: 486 Luakini St Honolulu HI 96817 Office: 347 N Kuakini St Honolulu HI 96817

NOMURA, MASAYASU, biochemist; b. Hyogo-Ken, Japan, Apr. 27, 1927; s. Hiromichi and Yaeko N.; m. Junko Hamashima, Feb. 10, 1957; children—Keiko, Toshiyasu. Ph.D., U. Tokyo, 1957. Asst. prof. inst. Protein Research, Osaka (Japan) U., 1960-63; asso. prof. genetics U. Wis., Madison, 1963-66, prof., 1966—, prof. genetics and biochemistry, 1970—, co-dir., 1970—. Recipient U.S. Steel award in molecular biology Nat. Acad. Scis., 1971; recipient Acad. award Japanese Acad. Arts and Scis., 1972. Mem. Am. Acad. Arts and Scis., Nat. Acad. Scis., Royal Danish Acad. Scis. and Letters. Subspecialty: Molecular biology. Office: Univ of Wis Inst for Enzyme Research 1710 University Ave Madison WI 53706

NOMURA, YASUMASA, engineering educator; b. Kumamoto, Japan, Sept. 25, 1921; s. Masaki and Aya N.; m. Kimi Higashi, Oct. 24, 1949; children: Kazuo, Etsuko. B.Eng., Tokyo Inst. Tech., 1945, D.Eng., 1962. Tchr. Yatsushiro (Japan) Jr. High Sch., 1946-47, Kumamoto (Japan) High Sch., 1948-52; asst. prof. Coll. of Coast Guard, Kure, Japan, 1952-57; asst. prof. Nat. Defence Acad., Yokosuka, Japan, 1957-62, prof. dept. aero. sci., 1962—, head aeor. sci. dept., 1971-73, 81—. Mem. AIAA, Japan Soc. Aero. and Space Sci. Current Work: Research of aerodynamics, especially three-dimensional boundary layer problems. Subspecialties: Aeronautical engineering; Aerospace engineering and technology. Home: Kotsubo 1-Chome 24-43 Zushi 239 Japan Office: National Defence Academy Hashirimizu 1-Chome Yokosuka 239 Japan

NOONAN, JAMES STEPHEN, mass spectroscopist; b. Sioux City, Iowa, Sept. 16, 1942; s. Martin James and Esther (Evers) N.; m. Mary Ellen Kubik, June 20, 1966. Student U. Iowa, 1960-62; B.A., Beloit Coll., 1964. Analytical chemist, Wis. Alumni Research Found., Madison, 1964-66; research assoc. II Ohio State U., Columbus, 1966—; expert witness Am. Show Horse Assn., N.Y.C., 1974. Contbr. articles to profl. jours. Recipient Achievement award U.S. Harness Writers Assn. 1970. Mem. Assn. Ofcl. Racing Chemists, Am. Chem. Soc. (analytical div.), Am. Soc. Mass. Spectrometry, Exptl. Aircraft Assn., Phi Beta Kappa, Phi Eta Sigma. Current work: Mass spectrometry and computers. Subspecialties: Mass spectrometry; Analytical chemistry. Office: Ohio State U 1935 Coffey Rd Columbus OH 43210

NOONAN, THOMAS WYATT, educator; b. Glendale, Calif., July 16, 1933; s. Gustave Vincent and Florence (Seely) N.; m. Annabel Smith, Aug. 24, 1966; children: Rachel, John, Matthew. B.S., Calif. Inst. Tech., 1955, Ph.D., 1961. Vis. asst. prof. physics dept. U. N.C., Chapel Hill, 1962-65, asst. prof., 1965-68; assoc. prof. physics Brockport State Coll., 1968-71, prof., 1971—. Author: Relativity and Cosmology, 1968. Mem. Royal Astron. Soc., Internat. Astron. Union, Internat. Soc. Gen. Relativity and Gravitation. Current Work: Astrophysics, gravitation, cosmology research, teaching. Subspecialties: Relativity and gravitation; Cosmology. Office: Physics Dept State Coll Brockport NY 14420

NOOR, AHMED KHAIRY, engineering educator; b. Cairo, Aug. 11, 1938; came to U.S., 1971, naturalized, 1976; s. Mohamed Sayed and Fatma Mohamed (El-Zeini) N.; m. Zakia Mahmoud Taha, Aug. 18, 1966; 1 son, Mohamed. B.S. with honors, Cairo U., 1958; M.S., U. Ill. Urbana, 1961, Ph.D., 1963. Asst. prof. aeros. and astronautics Stanford U., 1963-64; sr. lectr. structural mechanics Cairo U., 1964-67; vis. sr. lectr. structural mechanics U. Baghdad, Iraq, 1967-68; sr. lectr. structural mechanics U. New South Wales, Australia, 1968-71; prof. engring. and applied sci. George Washington U., NASA Langley Research Ctr., Hampton, Va., 1971—; mem. coms. computational mechanics and large space systems Nat. Acad. Engring., 1978 . Co editor: Trends in Computerized Structural Analysis and Synthesis, 1978, Computational Methods in Nonlinear Structural and Solid Mechanics, 1980, Advances and Trends in Structural and Solid Mechanics, 1982; State-of-the-Art Surveys on Finite Element Technology, 1983; Advances and Trends in Structures and Dynamics, 1985; contbr. articles in field to profl. jours. Mem. AIAA, ASME, ASCE, Am. Acad. Mechanics, Sigma Xi. Current Work: Computational mechanics, large space structures, fibrous composite structures. Subspecialties: Solid mechanics; Aerospace engineering and technology. Home: 31 Towler Dr Hampton VA 23666 Office: MS-246C GWU-NASA Langley Research Ctr Hampton VA 23665

NOORDERGRAAF, ABRAHAM, biophysicist, educator; b. Utrecht, Netherlands, Aug. 7, 1929; s. Leendert and Johanna (Kool) N.; m. Geertruida Alida Van Nee, Sept. 6, 1956; children: Annemiek,(Mrs. James A. Young), Gerrit Jan, Jeske Inette, Alexander Abraham. B.Sc., U. Utrecht, 1953, M.S., 1955, Ph.D., 1956; M.A. (hon.), U. Pa., 1971. Teaching asst. U. Utrecht, 1949-50, asst. dept. physics, 1951-53, research asst. dept. med. physics, 1953-55, research fellow dept. med. physics, 1956-58, sr. research fellow dept. med. physics, 1959-65; tchr. math. and physics Vereniging Nijverheidsonderwijs, Utrecht, 1951; research asst. U. Amsterdam, Netherlands, 1952; vis. fellow dept. therapeutic research U. Pa., Phila., 1957-58; asso. prof. biomed. engring. Moore Sch. Elec. Engring., 1964-70, acting head electromed. div., 1968-69, prof. biomed. engring., 1970—, prof. physiology Sch. Vet. Medicine, 1976—, prof. Dutch culture Sch. Arts and Scis., 1983—; assoc. dir. biomed. engring. tng. program Moore Sch. Elec. Engring., 1971-76, asso. dir. sch., 1972-74, chmn. grad. group in biomed. electronic engring., 1973-75, chmn. dept. bioengring., 1973-76, chmn. grad. group bioengring., 1975-76, dir. systems and integrative biology tng. program, 1979-84; vis. prof. biomed. engring. U. Miami, 1970-79, Erasmus U. Med. Sch., Rotterdam, Netherlands, 1970-71, Tech. U., Delft, 1970-71; mem. spl. study sect. NIH, 1966-68; cons. sci. affairs div. NATO, 1973—; participant numerous internat. confs. in field. Author: (with I. Starr) Ballistocardiography in Cardiovascular Research, 1967, Circulatory System Dynamics, 1978; contbg. author: Biological Engineering, 1969; Editor: (with G.N. Jager and N. Westerhof) Circulatory Analog Computers, 1963, (with G.H. Pollack) Ballistocardiography and Cardiac Performance, 1967, (with E. Kresch) The Venous System: Characteristics and Function, 1969, (with J. Baan and J. Raines) Cardiovascular System Dynamics, 1978, (with Reichenbach-Consten) Two Hundred Years of Netherlands-Am. Interaction, 1985; sci. editor Biophysics and Bioengring. Series, 1976—; contbr. numerous articles to profl. jours.; Referee: Biophys. Jour., 1968—, Physics in Medicine and Biology, 1969—, Bull. Math. Biophysics, 1972-84, Circulation Research, 1973—; mem. editorial adv. bd.: Jour. Biomechanics, 1969-84; assoc. editor: Bull. Math. Biology, 1973-84. Vice pres. Haverford Friends Sch. PTA, 1968-70. Recipient Herman C. Burger award, 1978. Fellow IEEE (mem. adminstrv. com. engring. in medicine and biology group 1967-70, mem. edn. com. group biomed. engring. 1968-70, sec. Phila. chpt. 1974-75, mem. regional council profl. group engring. in medicine and biology 1974-77), N.Y. Acad. Scis., AAAS, Explorers Club, Coll. Physicians Phila., Am. Coll. Cardiology; mem. Nederlandse Natuurkundige Vereniging, Ballistocardiograph Research Soc. U.S.A. (sec.-treas. 1965-67, pres. 1968-70), Biophys. Soc. (charter), European Soc. for Noninvasive Cardiovascular Research (co-founder 1960, sec.-treas. 1960-61, mem. com. on nomenclature 1960-61, officer 1961-62), Cardiovascular System Dynamics Soc. (co-founder 1976, pres. 1976-80), Franklin Inst., John Morgan Soc., Biomed. Engring. Soc. (founding mem., chmn. membership com. 1978-79, dir. 1972-75), Am. Heart Assn., Instrument Soc. Am. (sr. mem.), Soc. Math. Biology (charter mem.), Am. Physiol. Soc., Microcirculatory Soc., Am. Assn. Med. Systems and Informatics, Pa. Acad. Sci., Sigma Xi. Presbyterian. Current Work: Cardiovascular system dynamics. Subspecialties: Biophysics (physics); Cardiology. Home: 620 Haydock Ln Haverford PA 19041 Office: 553 Moore Bldg D2 Univ Pa Philadelphia PA 19104

NORA, JAMES JACKSON, physician, educator, researcher; b. Chgo., June 26, 1928; s. Joseph James and May Henrietta (Jackson) N.; m. Barbara June Fluhrer, Sept. 7, 1949 (div. 1963); children—Wendy, Penelope, Marianne; m. Audrey Faye Hart, Apr. 9, 1966; children—James J. Jr., Elizabeth H. A.B., Harvard U., 1950; M.D., Yale U., 1954; M.P.H., U. Calif.-Berkeley, 1978. Diplomate Am. Bd. Pediatrics, Am. Bd. Cardiology, Am. Bd. Med. Genetics. Intern Detroit Receiving Hosp., 1954-55; resident in pediatrics U. Wis. Hosps., Madison, 1959-61, fellow in cardiology, 1962-64; fellow in genetics McGill U., Montreal Children's Hosp., Que., Can., 1964-65; dir. pediatric cardiology U. Colo. Sch. Medicine, Denver, 1971-78, prof. pediatrics, 1974—, dir. preventive cardiology, 1978—, prof. genetics and preventive medicine, 1979—; dir. genetics Rose Med. Ctr., Denver, 1980—; cons., mem. task forces NIH, Bethesda, Md., 1973, 1975; editorial bds. Circulation, Birth Defects Compendium, others, 1973—; cons. in genetics and cardiology WHO, Geneva, Switzerland, 1983—. Author: (with others) Medical Genetics: Principles and Practice, 1981 (6 other textbooks); Editor: (with A. Takao) Congenital Heart Disease, 1984 (1 other textbook). Contbr. articles to profl. jours. Active coms. Nat. Found. March of Dimes., Am. Heart Assn., Boy Scouts Am. Served to lt. USAF, 1945-47, PTO. Recipient Virginia Apgar award Nat. Found., 1974; U.S.-USSR Exchange Program award, 1975; various research grants, 1965—. Fellow Am. Coll. Cardiology (various coms. 1968—), Am. Acad. Pediatrics; mem. Am. Pediatric Soc., Soc. Pediatric Research, Teratology Soc., Transplantation Soc., Am. Soc. Human Genetics, others. Democrat. Presbyterian. Current work: Genetics of cardiovascular diseases—causes and prevention of congenital heart disease and coronary heart disease. Subspecialties: Genetics and genetic engineering (medicine); Cardiology. Home: 6135 E 6th Ave Denver CO 80220 Office: U Colo Sch Medicine A-007 4200 E 9th Ave Denver CO 80262

NORCROSS, DAVID WARREN, research physicist; b. Cin., July 18, 1941; s. Gerald Warren and Alice Elizabeth N.; m. Mary Josephine Boudrias, Aug. 26, 1967; children: Joshua David, Sarah Elizabeth. A.B., Harvard U., 1963; M.Sc., U. Ill., 1965; Ph.D., Univ. Coll. London, 1970. Research physicist Sperry Rand Research Center, Sudbury, Mass., 1965-67; research assoc. Joint Inst. Lab. Astrophysics, Boulder, Colo., 1970-74; physicist Quantum Physics div. Nat. Bur. Standards, Boulder, 1974—; fellow Joint Inst. Lab. Astrophysics, 1974—; lectr. U. Colo., 1974—; vis. staff Los Alamos Nat. Lab., 1977—; cons. Lawrence Livermore Lab., 1978—; assoc. Harvard Coll. Obs., 1980-81; chmn. Joint Inst. Lab. Astrophysics, 1983-84. Contbr. articles to profl. jours. Recipient Sustained Superior Performance award Nat. Bur. Standards, 1979, Bronze medal Nat. Bur. Standards, 1982. Fellow Am. Phys. Soc.; mem. AAAS, Fedn. Am. Scientists. Current work: Interaction of radiation with structure and collisions of atoms and molecules. Subspecialties: Atomic and molecular physics; Theoretical physics. Office: U Colo Box 440 Boulder CO 80309

NORDGREN, RONALD PAUL, research engineer; b. Munising, Mich., Apr. 3, 1936; s. Paul A. and Martha B. N.; m. Joan McAfee, Sept. 12, 1959; children: Sonia, Paul. B.S.E., U. Mich., 1957, M.S.E., 1958; Ph.D., U. Calif.-Berkeley, 1962. Research asst. U. Calif.-Berkeley Inst. Engring. Research, 1959-62; with exploration and prodn. research Shell Devel. Co., Houston, 1963—, on spl. assignment, The Hague, Netherlands, 1970-71, sr. staff research engr., 1974-80, research assoc., 1980—; lectr. mech. engring. Rice U., 1965-68, U. Houston, 1980; mem. U.S. Nat. Commn. on Theoretical and Applied Mechanics, 1984—. Contbr. articles to profl. jours.; assoc. editor: Jour. Applied Mechanics, 1972-76, 81-85. Fellow ASME; mem. Soc. Indsl. and Applied Math., Sigma Xi, Tau Beta Pi. Patentee in field. Current Work: Applied mechanics-mechanics of solids, offshore engineering, petroleum engineering, Arctic engineering. Subspecialties: Solid mechanics; Petroleum engineering. Home: 14935 Broadgreen Dr Houston TX 77079 Office: Shell Devel Co PO Box 481 Houston TX 77001

NORDLIE, ROBERT CONRAD, biochemistry educator, researcher; b. Willmar, Minn., June 11, 1930; s. Peder Conrad and Myrtle (Spindler) N.; m. Sally Ann Christianson, Aug. 23, 1959; children: Margaret, Melissa, John. Student, Gustavus Adolphus Coll., 1948-49; B.S., St. Cloud State Coll., 1952; M.S., U. N.D.-Grand Forks, 1957, Ph.D., 1960. Postdoctoral research assoc. U. Wis.-Madison, 1960-62; Hill research prof. U. N.D., Grand Forks, 1962-74, Chester Friz disting. prof., 1974-76, prof. biochemistry, 1976—, chmn. dept., 1983—; cons. enzymology Oak Ridge Associated Univs., 1961-80. Editorial bd.: Biochem. Biophys. Acta, 1965—; contbr. articles to profl. jours. Served to cpl. U.S. Army, 1953-55. Recipient Golden Apple award U. N.D., 1968; Hon. Prof. San Marcos U., Lima, Peru, 1982; Disting. Alumnus St. Cloud State U., 1982; Edgar Dale award for Outstanding Teaching, 1983. Mem. Am. Soc. Biol. Chemists, Am. Inst. Nutrition, Am. Chem. Soc. (sec. local sect. 1970, organizer nat. symposium 1974), Sigma Xi (award 1969). Democrat. Lutheran. Lodge: Elks. Current Work: The enzymes of carbohydrate metabolism in mammals, blood glucose homeostatis, glucose-6-phosphate metabolism, glucose-6-phosphatase, mechanisms of hepatic glucose phosphorylation, non-hormonal and hormonal control of blood glucose. Subspecialties: Biochemistry (medicine); Nutrition (medicine). Home: 162 Columbia Ct Grand Forks ND 58201 Office: Dept Biochemistry U ND University Sta Grand Forks ND 58202

NORMAN, PHILIP SIDNEY, educator, physician; b. Pittsburg, Kans., Aug. 4, 1924; s. P. Sidney and Mildred Ada (Lawyer) N.; m. Marion Birmingham, Apr. 15, 1955; children: Margaret Reynolds, Meredith Andrew, Helen Elizabeth. A.B., Kans. State Coll., 1947; M.D., Washington U., St. Louis, 1951. Diplomate: Am. Bd. Internal Medicine and subplty. in allergy. Intern Barnes Hosp., St. Louis, 1951-52; asst. resident Vanderbilt U. Hosp., 1952-54; USPHS fellow Rockefeller Inst., N.Y.C., 1954-56; mem. faculty Johns Hopkins U., 1959—, prof. medicine, 1975—, head div. clin. immunology, 1970—. Contbr. articles to profl. jours. Served with USAF, 1943-46. Mem. Am. Fedn. Clin. Research, Am. Acad. Allergy, Am. Soc. Clin. Investigation, N.Y. Acad. Scis., Soc. Exptl. Biology and Medicine, Am. Clin. and Climatological Soc., Assn. Am. Physicians. Episcopalian. Current Work: Clinical trials in allergy and lung diseases. Subspecialties: Allergy; Immunopharmacology. Home: 13500 Manor Rd Baldwin MD 21013 Office: Good Samaritan Hosp 5601 Loch Raven Blvd Baltimore MD 21239

NORMANN, SIGURD JOHNS, pathologist; b. Cin., Oct. 24, 1935; s. Theodore Frederick and Bird (Krause) N.; married; children: Jennifer, Elizabeth. M.D., U. Wash., 1960, Ph.D., 1966. Intern U. Calif., San Francisco, 1960-61; resident in pathology U. Wash., 1960-66; prof. pathology U. Fla., 1968—. Contbr. articles to profl. jours. Served to capt. U.S. Army, 1966-68. Mem. Reticuloendothelial Soc., Am. Assn. Pathologists. Subspecialty: Pathology (medicine). Office: U Florida Box J-275 JHMHC Gainesville FL 32610

NORMENT, HILLYER GAVIN, research scientist, meteorologist, cons.; b. Washington, Jan. 13, 1928; s. Hillyer Gavin and Mary Thomas (Quisenberry) N.; m. Reva Lucille Shepherd, Mar. 28, 1953 (dec.); children: Eric Stuart, Jeffrey Leland, Philip Evan; m. Jean Eleanor Porter, July 21, 1973. B.S. in Chemistry, U. Md., 1951, Ph.D. in Phys. Chemistry, 1956. Group leader Callery Chem. Co., Pa., 1956-59; phys. chemist Naval Research Lab., Washington, 1959-62; ops. analyst Research Triangle Inst., Durham, N.C., 1962-63; sr. scientist Tech. Ops., Inc., Burlington, Mass., 1963-67, ARCON Corp., 1967-71; prin. scientist Mt. Auburn Research Assn., Newton, Mass., 1971-75; chief scientist propr. Atmospheric Sci. Assn., Bedford, Mass., 1975—, cons. Contbr. articles to profl. jours. Mem. Am. Meterol. Soc., Royal Meteorol. Soc. London, Am. Geophys. Union, Air Pollution Control Assn., AAAS, Am. Chem. Soc., Am. Crystallographic Soc., Sigma Xi. Current Work: Nuclear fallout modeling, aircraft icing, air pollution transport, aerosol physics boundary layer physics. Subspecialties: Meteorology; Fluid mechanics. Home: 186 Peter Spring Rd Concord MA 01742 Office: 363 Great Rd PO Box 307 Bedford MA 01730

NORTHUP, SHARON JOAN, toxicologist, researcher; b. Union, Mo., Dec. 26, 1942; d. Arthur Benneth and Elizabeth Gladys (Hickman) Carlson; m. William Carlton Northup, June 24, 1970; children: Richard Carlton, Karen Frances. B.S., Washington U., St. Louis, 1965; M.S., U. Mo.-Columbia, 1968, Ph.D., 1971; M.B.A., U. Chgo., 1985. Diplomate: Am. Bd. Toxicology. Research assoc. Cancer Research Center, Columbia, Mo., 1971-72; instr. U. Mo., Columbia, 1973; research chemist Vets. Hosp., Columbia, 1974-76; mgr. pharmacology Travenol Labs., Round Lake, Ill., 1976-77, asst. dir. pharmacology, 1977-78, assoc. dir. toxicology, 1978—; subcom. chmn. Pharm. Mgrs. Assn., Washington, 1980-82; mem. biocompatibility task force Health Industries Mfrs. Assn., Washington, 1980—; adv. Pan Am. Health Orgn., Sao Paulo, Brazil, 1980; cons. Chem. Mfrs. Assn., Washington, 1982-83. Trustee Bethel Baptist Ch., Columbia, Mo., 1976. Campus Chest scholar, 1961-62; Sarah Gentry Elston award, 1962-63; NSF scholar, 1967-70; Young Investigator's award Am. Cancer Soc., 1971. Mem. Am. Soc. Pharmacology and Exptl. Therapeutics, Soc. Toxicology, Am. Coll. Toxicology, Am. Chem. Soc., Soc. Biomaterials, Iota Sigma Pi (pres. chpt. 1985). Democrat. Baptist. Club: Student Wives (Columbia, Mo.) (pres. 1973-74). Current Work: Toxicology and biochemistry using in vitro models, hazard assessment, mathematical modeling, alternatives to animal testing, immunotoxicology, mutagenicity, carcinogenicity. Subspecialties: Toxicology (medicine); Immunotoxicology. Home: 24 Williamsburg Terrace Evanston IL 60203 Office: Travenol Labs Inc Route 120 and Wilson Rd Round Lake IL 60073

NORTON, JAMES MICHAEL, physiologist, educator; b. Bangor, Maine, July 22, 1946; s. Michael and Rita (O'Connor) N.; m. Lona Miriam Gove, Oct. 15, 1978; children—Graham Patrick, Gregory James. A.B., Coll. of Holy Cross, 1967; B.Med. Sci., Dartmouth Coll., 1969, Ph.D., 1979. USPHS fellow Dartmouth Coll. Med. Sch., Hanover, N.H., 1969-70; research asst. Maine Med. Ctr., Portland, 1971-74, research assoc., 1978-80; asst. prof. physiology U. New Eng., Biddeford, Maine, 1980-84, assoc. prof., 1984—; mem. adv. body York County Health Services, Saco, Maine, 1984—; mem. research com. Maine affiliate Am. Heart Assn., Augusta, 1984—. Contbr. articles to profl. jours. KROC Found. grantee, 1981-83. Mem. Am. Physiol. Soc., Internat. Soc. Oxygen Transport to Tissue, Am. Coll. Sports Medicine, AAAS, Sigma Xi. Democrat. Unitarian. Current work: Research involves membrane transport regulation in red cell precursors; also interested in determinants of erythrocyte deformability. Subspecialties: Physiology (medicine); Hematology. Office: U New Eng 11 Hill's Beach Rd Biddeford ME 04005

NORTON, JULIA ANNE, statistics educator; b. Birmingham, Ala., Oct. 19, 1948; d. Robert Louis and Betty Sue (Hawkins) N.; m. John Dewey Lovell, Dec. 25, 1978; children: Tanzy Lovell, Robert Norton. B.S. in Math, MIT, 1970; M.A. in Stats, Harvard U., 1974, Ph.D., 1977. Assoc. prof. stats. Calif. State U., Hayward, 1974—; ednl. cons. U. South Pacific, Suva, Fiji Islands, 1980-81. Author: Communication in the Eighties, 1981, Applied Time Series, 1982; reviewer, John Wiley Co., N.Y.C., 1982, Dellen Pub., San Francisco, 1982. Bookkeeper Univs. Nat. Anti-War Fund, Cambridge, 1970-73; cons. Hayward (Calif.) Area Recreational Dist., 1974, St. Christophers Episcopal Ch., San Lorenzo, Calif., 1982-83; treas. Starr King Unitarian Ch., Hayward, 1977-79. NSF trainee MIT, 1970. Mem. Am. Statis. Assn., Inst. Math. Stats., Internat. Time Series Assn. Current Work: Teaching statistics and data analysis; applied time series; statistics in psychology. Subspecialty: Statistics. Home: 27152 Grand View Ave Hayward CA 94542 Office: Calif State Dept Stats 25700 Carlos Bee Blvd Hayward CA 94542

NORTON, ROBERT ALAN, horticulturist, educator; b. Hazleton, Pa., Jan. 3, 1926; s. Leland Davis and Ester (Beck) N.; m. Elizabeth Mary Whelan, Oct. 14, 1950; children—Paul, David, John, Robert, Susan. B.S., Rutgers U., 1950, M.S., 1951; Ph.D., Mich. State U., 1954. From asst. prof. horticulture to assoc. prof. Utah State U., 1954-60; extension pomologist U. Calif.-Davis, 1960-62; supr., horticulturist Wash. State U., Mt. Vernon, 1962—; cons. Kenai Natives Assn., Alaska, 1975-77. Contbr. articles to profl. jours. Mem. Skagit County Boundary Rev. Bd., Mt. Vernon, 1984—; precinct committeeman Skagit County Republican Party, 1970—. Served with USN, 1944-46. Recipient W. Atlee Burpee award Burpee Seed Co., 1949. Mem. Am. Soc. Hort. Sci. (pres. western region 1966-67), Am. Pomological Soc. (advisor 1983—), Enological Soc. Pacific N.W. (bd. dirs. 1979-81, advisor 1983—), Western Wash. Hort. Assn. (bd. dirs. 1983—). Methodist. Club: Toastmasters (Davis). Lodge: Rotary (pres. 1970-71). Current work: Culture and selection of fruit plants for coastal climates; use of artificial lighting to enhance plant growth. Subspecialty: Horticulture. Home: 1571 McLean Rd Mount Vernon WA 98273 Office: Northwestern Wash Research Unit 1468 Memorial Hwy Mount Vernon WA 98273

NORTON, WILLIAM NICHOLSON, JR., biology educator; b. Nashville, May 6, 1945; s. William and Marge Ellen (Steven) N.; m. Betty Jo Jones, Jan. 20, 1968; children: Jennifer, Gregory, Brian. B.S., Troy State U., 1968; M.S., Miss. State U., 1969; Ph.D., Tex. A&M U., 1975. Instr. Troy (Ala.) State U., 1969-71; postdoctoral fellow Baylor Coll. Medicine, Houston, 1975-77; assoc. prof. biology Southeastern La. U., Hammond, 1977—; dir. Research Ctr. for Coll. of Sci. and Tech., 1982—. Contbr. articles to profl. jours. Fulbright research award Council Internat. Exchange of Scholars, Portugal, 1983; U.S. Air Force Office Sci. Research grantee, 1982; NSF grantee, 1978. Mem. La. Soc. Electron Microscopy, Electron Microscopy Soc. Am., AAAS, Sigma Xi, Phi Sigma. Democrat. Methodist. Current Work: Study of ultrastructural and cytochemical effects of aromatic hydrocarbons on specific animal model systems; study effects of riboflavin deficiency on internal organs of rats. Subspecialties: Microscopy; Cytology and histology. Home: 23 Cherry St Hammond LA 70402 Office: Southeastern La U PO Box 335 Hammond LA 70402

NORVELL, JOHN EDMONDSON, III, medical educator, neuroanatomist; b. Charleston, W.Va., Nov. 18, 1929; s. John Edmondson Jr. and Mathilde (Wood) N.; m. Rosemary Justice, June 2, 1962; children—John Edmondson IV, Scott Justice. B.S. cum laude, U. Charleston, 1953; M.S., W.Va. U., 1956; Ph.D., Ohio State U., 1966. Instr. anatomy U. Pitts., Johnstown, Pa., 1956-60; asst. prof. Otterbein Coll., Westerville, Ohio, 1960-62; asst. instr. Ohio State U., Columbus, 1962-65; asst. prof. Med. Coll. Va., Richmond, 1966-69, assoc. prof., 1969-76; prof., chmn. dept. anatomy Oral Roberts U., Tulsa, 1976—; anatomy cons. dept. surgery U.S. Naval Hosp., Portsmouth, Va., 1966-70; vis. lectr. U. Va., Charlottesville, 1972; chmn. Okla. Anat. Bd., Tulsa, 1978—; mem. Gov.'s Mini-Cabinet on Health and Human Resources, Oklahoma City, 1980—; vis. prof. U. Nairobi, Kenya, 1982. Author: Atlas of Cross Sections of Human Body, 1982; Human Anatomy, 1985. Contbr. articles to profl. jours. Named an Outstanding Tchr. of Yr., Med. Coll. Va., 1970, 71, 72, 75. Mem. Am. Assn. Anatomists, Assn. Anatomy Chmn., Soc. for Neurosci., Transplantation Soc., Sigma Xi. Methodist. Current work: Degeneration and regeneration of nerves in transplanted hearts and kidneys. Localization of biogenic amines and transmitters in the nervous system. Subspecialties: Anatomy and embryology; Regeneration. Home: 9909 S Kingston Ave Tulsa OK 74137 Office: Oral Roberts Univ 7777 S Lewis Ave Tulsa OK 74171

NORWOOD, FREDERICK REYES, theoretical and applied mechanics scientist; b. Mexico City, Mexico, May 13, 1939; came to U.S., 1954; s. Joseph and Elvira (Reyes) N.; m. Irene Gomez, July 2, 1966 (div. July 1982); children—Irene July, Frederick Adam. B.S., UCLA, 1962; M.S., Calif. Inst. Tech., 1963, Ph.D., 1967. Mem. tech. staff Sandia Nat. Labs, Albuquerque, 1966—; lectr. U. N.Mex., Albuquerque. Contbr. articles to profl. jours. Earl E. Anthony scholar Calif. Inst. Tech., 1962-63; NASA fellow, 1963-66. Mem. ASME, Soc. Indsl. and Applied Math., Am. Geophys. Union, Assn. Computing Machinery. Democrat. Roman Catholic. Current work: Analytic solution of transient problems in mechanics; numerical solution of problems in engineering design. Subspecialties: Theoretical and applied mechanics; Applied mathematics. Home: 1819 Ross Pl SE Albuquerque NM 87108 Office: Sandia Nat Labs PO Box 5800 Albuquerque NM 87185

NOSIL, JOSIP, medical physicist; b. Zagreb, Yugoslavia, June 16, 1944; s. Ivan and Durda (Matijevic) N.; m. Helena Bucar, May 2, 1969; children: Patrick, Cynthia. B. Sc., U. Zagreb, 1968, M.Sc. in Atomic and Nuclear Physics, 1971, D.Sci. in Physics, 1977. Cert. hosp. physicist IAEA. Physicist R. Boskovics Inst., Zagreb, 1968 75; med. physicist dept. nuclear medicine and oncology Dr. M. Stojanovic Hosp., Zagreb, 1975-78; vis. fellow Royal Post-Grad. Med. Sch., Hammersmith Hosp., Lond, 1974-75; cons. physicist Foothills Hosp., Calgary, Alta., Can., 1978—. Contbr. articles to profl. jours. Mem. Am. Assn. Physicists in Medicine, Soc. Nuclear Medicine, Can. Assn. Physicist. Mormon. Current Work: Mathematical organ modelling, nuclear cardiology, medical imaging technology, instrumentation. Subspecialty: Medical physics. Home: 120 Whitefield Close NE Calgary AB T1Y 4X7 Canada Office: 1403 29th St NW Calgary AB T2N 2T9 Canada

NOTTORF, ROBERT WILLIAM, photographic emulsion researcher; b. Dillon, Kans., Aug. 24, 1919; s. Henry William and Minnie (Kohman) N.; m. Lenore Myers, June 16, 1956; children—Kathryn Marie, Eric Walter. B.S. in Chemistry, Kans. State U., 1939; Ph.D. in Phys. Chemistry, Iowa State U., 1945. With Du Pont Co., Parlin, N.J., 1946-75, Brevard, N.C., 1975—, sr. research fellow photo systems and electronic products dept., 1982—. Patentee in field of photographic emulsion formulation. Served with U.S. Army, 1945-46. Recipient Jour. award Photog. Soc. Am., 1956. Mem. Am. Chem. Soc., Soc. Photog. Scientists and Engrs., Fedn. Am. Scientists, Union Concerned Scientists. Democrat. Presbyterian. Current work: Development of improved silver halide photographic emulsions and films. Subspecialties: Photochemistry; Physical chemistry. Home: 110 Hudson Dr Hendersonville NC 28739 Office: Photo and Electronic Products Dept Du Pont Co Brevard NC 28712

NOVACK, GARY DEAN, pharmacologist; b. Oakland, Calif., Nov. 21, 1953; s. Robert Lloyd and Dorothy Louise (Scheibner) N.; m. Dona Ann, Aug. 28, 1977; children—Rebecca Adrienne, Philip Willian. A.B. in Biology with honors, Kresge Coll., U. Calif., Santa Cruz, 1973; Ph.D. in Pharmacology and Environ. Toxicology (Anthony fellow), U. Calif., Davis, 1977. NIH postdoctoral scholar UCLA Mental Retardation Research Ctr., 1977-79; neuropharmacologist Merrell Dow Research Center, Cin., 1979-82; clin. coordinator Allergan Pharm., Irvine, Calif., 1982-84, mgr., 1985—; asst. research neurobiologist Ctr. Neurobiology, U. Calif., 1984—. Contbr. articles to profl. jours. Recipient Cum Laude award Assn. Ind. Secondary Schs., 1970. Mem. Soc. Neurosci., Assn. Psychophysiol. Study Sleep, Western Pharmacology Soc., Am. Soc. Clin. Pharm. Therapeutics. Neuropharmacology, Am. Soc. Clin. Pharm. Therapeutics. Subspecialty: Neuropharmacology. Office: Allergan Pharmaceuticals 2525 Dupont Dr Irvine CA 92715

NOVAK, JOHN ALLEN, zoology educator; b. Bedford, Ohio, Aug. 17, 1943; s. John George and Mildred Bertha (Olbreys) N.; m. Rose Mary Miller, Sept. 11, 1966; children: Pamela Jane, Emily Melissa. B.Ed., Kent State U., 1965, M.A., 1967; Ph.D., Wash. State U., 1972. Asst. prof. Colgate U., 1972-81, assoc. prof. zoology, 1982—. Free-lance photographer Animals, Animals-Earth Scenes, N.Y.C., 1981—, photographs appeared cover photos mags., books, advt.; contbr. articles to profl. jours. Sloan grantee, 1974; Carter-Wallce Fellowship awardee, 1975; Mellon Fund grantee, 1976-77; Colgate Research grantee, 1976, 79, 80. Mem. Entomol. Soc. Am., Wash. State Entomol. Soc., Sigma Xi. Episcopalian (vestryman, 1974-76, 78-80). Current Work: Systematics, behavior, biogeography and evolution of certain Diptera belonging to families Tephritidae and Syrphidae. Subspecialties: Systematics; Behaviorism. Home: Preston Hill Rd Hamilton NY 13346 Office: Dept Biology Colgate U Hamilton NY 13346

NOVICK, MELVIN ROBERT, statistian, educator, consultant; b. Chgo., Sept. 21, 1932; m. Naomi Spark, Sept. 15, 1957; children: Laura Renee, Raymond Lloyd. B.A., Roosevelt U., Chgo., 1957, B.S. and M.A. in Math. and Psychology, 1959; Ph.D. in Math. Stats, U. N.C.-Chapel Hill, 1963. Research asst. Assn. Am. Med. Colls., 1956-59; research asst. U. N.C.-Chapel Hill, 1959-62, research assoc., 1962-63; assoc. research statistician Ednl. Testing Service, Princeton, N.J., 1963-64, research statistician, 1964-68, sr. research statistician, 1968-70; dir. psychometric research Am. Coll. Testing Program, Iowa City, 1970-74; prof. measurement and stats. U. Iowa, Iowa City, 1970—; lectr. Univ. Coll. Wales, 1967-68; hon. lectr. Univ. Coll. London, 1967-73; vis. prof. edn. U. Pa., 1970; cons. U. London, 1968, Office of Edn., 1970, Am. Assn. Dental Schs., 1973, Nat. Inst. Edn., 1974, govt. agys. and corps.; participant profl. confs. Author: (with F.M. Lord) Statistical Theories of Mental Test Scores, 1968; (with P.H. Jackson) Statistical Methods for Educational and Psychological Research, 1974; contbr. chpts. to books, articles to profl. jours. Served in USAF, 1952-55, ETO. Grantee Office Naval Research; Grantee U.S. Office Edn.; Grantee NSF; Grantee NIH; Grantee Carnegie Corp.; Grantee others. Fellow Am. Psychol. Assn. (pres. div. 5 1980-81), Am. Statis. Assn.; mem. Am. Ednl. Research Assn. (award for disting. contbn.), Inst. Math. Stats., Nat. Council Measurement in Edn. (dir. 1980-82, award for disting. contbns.), Psychometric Soc. (trustee 1977-81, pres. 1979-80), Current Work: Behavioral statistics and computer-assisted data analysis; policy issues in testing. Subspecialties: Psychometrics; Statistics. Home: 306 Mullin Ave Iowa City IA 52240 Office: U Iowa 224B Lindquist Center Iowa City IA 52242

NOVICK, RICHARD PAUL, molecular biologist, research institute administrator, educator; b. N.Y.C., Aug. 10, 1932; s. Samuel John and Mollie (Forster) N.; m. Barbara Jane Zabin, June 1, 1958; children: Lynn, Dorothy. B.A., Yale U., 1954; M.D. with honors, NYU, 1959. Intern Yale Med. Ctr., New Haven, 1959-60; resident Vanderbilt U. Med. Ctr., Nashville, 1962-63; postdoctoral fellow Nat. Inst. Med. Research, London, 1960-62, Rockefeller U., N.Y.C., 1963-65; assoc. Pub. Health Research Inst., N.Y.C., 1968-71, assoc. mem., 1971-75, mem., chmn. dept. plasmid biology, 1976—, dir., 1980—; research prof. dept. microbiology NYU Med. Sch.; mem. Nat. Recombinant DNA Adv. Com., 1978—. Founder, editor-in-chief: Plasmid; contbr. articles to profl.jours. Grantee NIH, 1967—; Grantee NSF, 1972—; Grantee Am. Cancer Soc., 1978—. Mem. Am. Soc. Microbiology, Am. Genetics Soc., Harvey Soc. Current Work: Plasmids, transposons, antibiotic resistance, molecular cloning, gene expression, replication of DNA. Subspecialties: Molecular biology; Genetics and genetic engineering (biology). Office: Pub Health Research Inst 455 First Ave New York NY 10016

NOVICK, WILLIAM JOSEPH, JR., pharmacologist; b. Revoloc, Pa., Dec. 14, 1931; s. William J. and Rugh (Jones) N.; m. Joanne C. Imgrund, Sept. 17, 1955; children: William, Susan, Carol, Mary. B.S., St. Francis Coll., 1953; Ph.D., Duke U., 1961. Sect. head pharmacology Smith Kline & French, Phila., 1955-58, 61-67; mngr. pharmacology William H. Rorer, Fort. Washington, Pa., 1967-70; dir. biol. scis. Hoechst Roussel Pharms Inc., Somerville, N.J., 1970-83, sr. dir. internat. product devel., 1983—. Friends of St. Francis scholar, 1949-53; Walter Karr fellow, 1958-61. Mem. Am. Soc. Pharmacology and Exptl. Therapeutics, Am. Soc. Microbiology, N.Y. Acad. Sci. Republican. Roman Catholic. Subspecialties: Pharmacology; Microbiology (medicine). Office: Hoechst-Roussel Pharms Inc Route 202-206N Somerville NJ 08876

NOVOTNY, DONALD WAYNE, electrical engineering educator; b. Chgo., Dec. 15, 1934; s. Adolph and Margaret N.; m. Louise J. Eenigenburg, June 26, 1954; children: Donna Jo, Cynthia Jean. B.E.E., Ill. Inst. Tech., 1956, M.S., 1957; Ph.D., U. Wis., 1961. Registered profl. engr., Wis. Instr. Ill. Inst. Tech., 1957-58; mem. faculty U. Wis., Madison, 1958—, prof. elec. engring., 1969—, chmn. dept. elec. and computer engring., 1976—; vis. prof. Mont. State U., 1966, Eindhoven Tech. U., Netherlands, 1974; Fulbright lectr. Tech. U., Ghent, Belgium, 1981; dir. Wis. Electric Machines and Power Electronics Consortium, 1981—; cons. to industry. Author: Introductory Electromechanics, 1965; also research papers; assoc. editor: Electric Machines and Electromechanics, 1976—. Recipient Benjamin Smith Reynolds teaching award U. Wis.-Madison, 1984. Fellow Gen. Electric Co., 1956; Ford Found., 1960; recipient Kiekhofer Teaching award U. Wis., 1964; Outstanding Paper award Engring. Inst. Can., 1966; grantee numerous industries and govt. agys. Mem. IEEE (prize paper awards 1983, 84), Am. Soc. Engring. Edn., Sigma Xi, Tau Beta Pi, Eta Kappa Nu. Congregationalist. Subspecialty: Electrical engineering. Home: 1421 E Skyline Dr Madison WI 53705 Office: Dept Elec and Computer Engring 1415 Johnson Dr U Wis Madison WI 53706

NOVOTNY, JIRI, research biochemist; b. Kladno, Czechoslovakia, Dec. 15, 1943; came to U.S., 1979; s. Jaroslav and Eva (Foustkova) N.; m. Jarmila Novotna, Feb. 28, 1966; 1 dau., Paula. R.N.Dr., Charles U., 1970; Ph.D., Czechoslovak Acad. Sci., 1970. Scientist, Inst. of Organic Chemistry and Biochemistry Czechoslovak Acad. Sci., 1965-76; sr. scientist Czechoslovak Acad. Sci. (Inst. Molecular Genetics), 1976-79; vis. scientist, dept. molecular biophysics U. Oxford, Eng., 1979; research assoc. Harvard Med. Sch.-Mass. Gen. Hosp., 1980-81; asst. prof. biochemistry Harvard Med. Sch., 1981—. Recipient prize Czechoslovak Acad. Sci., 1979. Mem. Am. Assn. Immunologists; mem. Am. Chem. Soc.; Mem. N.Y. Acad. Sci. Club: Gull Point Yacht (Quincy, Mass.). Current Work: Study of protein structure and evolution, in particular antibody binding site by genetic engineering and computer modeling. Subspecialties: Genetics and genetic engineering (biology); Molecular biology. Home: 2 Howe St Quincy MA 02169 Office: Fruit St Boston MA 02114

NOWAK, WELVILLE BERENSON, mechanical engineering; b. Hartford, Conn., Oct. 6, 1921; s. Abraham and Ann (Segal) N.; m. Ruth Goldberg, Mar. 27, 1950; children: Ann Leslie, Michael David. B.S., M.I.T., 1942, Ph.D., 1949. Staff mem. Radiation Lab. M.I.T., Cambridge, 1942-45, Staff mem. metall. project, 1949-52; physicist Microwave Assocs., Boston, 1952-54; project mgr., dir. electronic research Nuclear Metals Co., Concord, Mass., 1954-62; prof. mech. engring. Northeastern U., Boston, 1962—, Donald W. Smith prof. mech. engring., 1980—, chmn. dept., 1975-81, cons. in field. Contbr. articles to profl. jours. Mem. Am. Phys. Soc., Am. Soc. for Metals, Am. Vacuum Soc., ASME, Am. Soc. for Engring. Edn. Patentee in field. Current Work: Electronic materials/processing (especially thin films); wear-resistant films; corrosion-resistant metal films; solar cells; teaching materials science. Subspecialties: Electronic materials; Corrosion. Home: 17 Furbush Ave West Newton MA 02165 Office: 360 Huntington Ave Boston MA 02115

NOWELL, PETER CAREY, pathologist, educator; b. Phila., Feb. 8, 1928; s. Foster and Margaret (Matlack) N.; m. Helen Worst, Sept. 9, 1950; children: Sharon, Timothy, Karen, Kristin, Michael. B.A., Wesleyan U., Middletown, Conn., 1948; M.D., U. Pa., 1952. Intern Phila. Gen. Hosp., 1952-53; resident pathology Presbyn. Hosp., Phila., 1953-54; med.-teaching, research specializing in exptl. pathology, Phila., 1956—; from instr. to prof. pathology Sch. Medicine U. Pa., 1956—, chmn. dept. pathology, 1967-73; dir. (Cancer Center), 1973-75. Served to lt., M.C. USNR, 1954-56. Recipient Research Career award USPHS, 1964-67, Parke-Davis award, 1965, Lindback Distinguished Teaching award, 1967, Passano award, 1984. Mem. Am. Soc. Exptl. Pathology (pres. 1970), Am. Assn. Cancer Research, Radiation Research Soc., Nat. Acad. Sci., Transplantation Soc., Am. Assn. Immunologists. Current Work: Tumor cytogenetics; lymphocyte biology. Subspecialties: Pathology (medicine); Immunology (medicine). Home: 345 Mt Alverno Rd Media PA 19063 Office: Dept Pathology Sch Medicine Univ of Pennsylvania Philadelphia PA 19104

NOWICKI, HENRY GEORGE, chemist; b. Granite City, Ill., July 6, 1940; s. Henry Stanley and Frances Ann (Knezevich) N.; m. Barbara Jean Sherman, Aug. 15, 1976; children—Henry George, III, Elizabeth Sherman. B.A. in Chemistry, So. Ill. U., 1964; Ph.D. in Biochemistry, St. Louis U., 1970; M.B.A., Robert Morris Coll., 1985. Research asst. Mallinkrodt Chem. Co., St. Louis, 1964-65; postdoctoral U. Calif.-Riverside, 1970-72; group leader U.S. Army Med. Lab., St. Louis, 1972-73; instr. Far East div. U. Md., Camp Zama, Japan, 1973-76; forensic chemist U.S. Army Crime Lab., Camp Zama, 1973-76; group leader advanced organic analysis Calgon Corp., Pitts., 1976—. Contbr. articles to profl. jours., chpts. to books. Mem. Am. Chem. Soc. (div. environ. scis.). Current work: Management science and theory; application of analytical chemistry to important problems. Subspecialties: Environmental chemistry; Analytical chemistry. Home: 409 Meade Dr Coraopolis PA 15108 Office: Calgon Corp Sub Merck PO Box 1346 Pittsburgh PA 15230

NOYCE, ROBERT NORTON, manufacturing company executive; b. Burlington, Iowa, Dec. 12, 1927; s. Ralph B. and Harriet (Norton) N.; m. Ann S. Bowers, Nov. 27, 1975; children: William B., Pendred, Priscilla, Margaret. B.A., Grinnell Coll., 1949; Ph.D., MIT, 1953. Research engr. Philco Corp., Phila., 1953-56; research engr. Shockley Semicondr. Lab., Mountain View, Calif., 1956-57; founder, dir. research Fairchild Semicondr., Mountain View, 1957-59, v.p., gen. mgr., 1959-65; group v.p. Fairchild Camera & Instrument, Mountain View, 1965-68; founder, pres. Intel Corp., Santa Clara, Calif., from 1968, chmn., 1968-75, vice chmn., 1979—; dir. Rolm Corp., Santa Clara, Calif., Diasonics Inc., Milpitas, Calif. Trustee Grinnell Coll., 1962—; regent U. Calif., 1982—. Recipient Stuart Ballentine award Franklin Inst., 1967, Harry Goode award AFIPS, 1978; Nat. Medal of Sci., Pres. of U.S., 1979; I.E.E. Gt. Britain Faraday medal, 1979; Harold Pender award U. Pa., 1980; named to Nat.

Inventors Hall of Fame. Fellow IEEE (Cledo Brunetti award 1978, medal of honor 1978); mem. Nat. Acad. Engring. Patentee in field (16). Subspecialty: Semiconductors. Home: Los Altos CA Office: IntelCorp 3065 Bowers Ave Santa Clara CA 95051

NOYES, RICHARD MACY, physical chemist, educator; b. Champaign, Ill., Apr. 6, 1919; s. William Albert and Katharine Haworth (Macy) N.; m. Winninette Arnold, July 12, 1946 (dec. Mar. 1972); m. Patricia Jean Harris, Jan. 26, 1973. A.B. summa cum laude, Harvard U., 1939; Ph.D., Calif. Inst. Tech., 1942. Research assoc. rocket propellants Calif. Inst. Tech., 1942-46; mem. faculty Columbia U., 1946-58, assoc. prof., 1954-58; Guggenheim fellow, vis. prof. U. Leeds, Eng., 1955-56; prof. chemistry U. Oreg., 1958—, head dept., 1963-68, 75-78. Editorial adv. com.: Chem. Revs, 1967-69; editorial adv. com.: Jour. Phys. Chemistry, 1973-80; assoc. editor: Internat. Jour. Chem. Kinetics, 1972-83, Jour. Phys. Chemistry, 1980-82; Contbr. to profl. jours. Fulbright fellow; Victoria U. Wellington, New Zealand, 1964; NSF sr. postdoctoral fellow Max Planck Inst. für Physikalische Chemie, Göttingen, Germany, 1965; sr. Am. scientist awardee Alexander von Humboldt Found., 1978-79. Fellow Am. Phys. Soc.; mem. Nat. Acad. Scis., Am. Chem. Soc. (chmn. div. phys. chemistry 1961-62, exec. com. div. 1960-75, mem. council 1960-75, chmn. Oreg. sect. 1967-68, com. on nominations and elections 1962-68, com. on publs. 1969-72), Chem. Soc. (London), Wilderness Soc., ACLU, Phi Beta Kappa, Sigma Xi. Club: Sierra (past chmn. Atlantic and Pacific N.W. chpts., N.W. regional v.p. 1973-75). Research mechanisms chem. reactions, developing gen. theories, intrepretation phys. properties chemicals. Current Work: Mechanisms of oscillating chemical reactions; unstable states of chemical systems. Subspecialty: Kinetics. Home: 2014 Elk Dr Eugene OR 97403

NUNAN, ADRIENNE NICHOLA, geophysicist, geologist; b. Cork, Ireland, Nov. 9, 1956; came to U.S., 1958, naturalized, 1963; d. Timothy Raymond and Bridget Carmel (Cotter) N. B.S. in Geology, U. Ala., 1979; M.S. in Geology, U. N.C., 1983. Research and teaching asst. geology dept. U. Ala., Birmingham, 1976-79, U. N.C., Chapel Hill, 1980-83; geologist Law Engring. and Testing Co., Atlanta, 1979-80, Miami, Fla., 1980; sr. geophysicist Exxon Co., U.S.A., Houston, 1983—. Contbr. abstracts to profl. jours. Martin fellow U. N.C., 1981. Mem. Geol. Soc. Am., Am. Assn. Petroleum Geologists, Soc. Exploration Geophysicists, Phi Kappa Phi. Current work: Geophysical and geological exploration for petroleum resources in Exxon's Alaska/Pacific division, currently focused on offshore California. Subspecialties: Geology; Geophysics. Home: 620-B Woodland Houston TX 77009 Office: Exxon Co USA A/P Div 440 Benmar St Houston TX 77060

NUNAN, CRAIG SPENCER, scientist; b. Medford, Oreg., Dec. 22, 1918; s. Charles J. and Mignon I. (Thompson) N.; m. Analee P. Freeman, Sept. 11, 1948; children: Lori, Shary, Kevin, Scott. Student engring. sci., Stanford U., 1968-69; B.S., U. Calif.-, Berkeley, 1940, M.S., 1949. Electronics engr. Bur. Ships, U.S. Navy, 1940-46; project engr. Lawrence Radiation Lab., U. Calif., 1946-53; dir. research Chromatic TV, 1953-55; gen. mgr. radiation div. Varian Assocs., Palo Alto, Calif., 1955-68, sr. scientist, 1968—. Patentee fields of color TV, electron linear accelerators, radiotherapy equipment, x-ray CT scanners, industrial x-ray equipment. Current Work: Invention of equipment for fields of diagnostic and therapeutic radiology and industrial x-ray. Subspecialty: Biomedical engineering. Home: 26665 St Francis Rd Los Altos Hills CA 94022 Office: Varian 611 Hansen Way Palo Alto CA 94303

NUNN, WALTER MELROSE, JR., electrical engineer, educator; b. New Orleans, Sept. 16, 1925; s. Walter Melrose and Leah Agnes (Hennessey) N.; m. Hortense Rosa Hillery, Aug. 14, 1949. B.S.E.E., Tulane U., 1950; M.S.E.E., Okla. State U., 1952; Ph.D. in Elec. Engring, U. Mich., 1961; M.S. in Physics, U. Ill., 1969. Registered profl. engr., Fla. Research engr. Hughes Aircraft Co., Los Angeles, 1954-56, now sr. staff engr.; research assoc. U. Mich., Ann Arbor, 1956-60; asst. prof. elec. engring. U. Minn. Mpls., 1960-63; prof. elec. engring. Tulane U., New Orleans, 1963-67; prof. elec. engring. Fla. Inst. Tech., Melbourne, 1969—; research scientist DBA Systems, Inc., Melbourne, Fla., 1983-85; cons. U.S. Army Missile Command, NASA, Harris Corp., U.S. Dept. Navy, Nat. Acad. Sci., Mpls. Honeywell Co. Contbr. articles to profl. jours. Served with USMC, 1943-46. Mem. Am. Phys. Soc., Tau Beta Pi, Sigma Pi Sigma. Current Work: Electromagnetic radiation, antennas, microwave measurements and techniques, electromagnetic radiation from highly-ionized plasmas, electron and atomic physics, lasers and quantum electronics. Subspecialties: Electrical engineering; Electronics. Office: Dept Elec Engring Fla Inst Tech Melbourne FL 32901

NUTTLI, OTTO WILLIAM, geophysicist; b. St. Louis, Dec. 11, 1926; s. Otto Peter and Marie Bertha (Wehinger) N. B.S., St. Louis U., 1948, M.S., 1950, Ph.D., 1953. Instr. geophysics St. Louis U., 1952-56, asst. prof., 1956-59, asso. prof., 1959-62, prof., 1962—; vis. research scientist U. Mich., summer 1962, U. Calif., Berkeley, summers 1964, 67; cons. to fed. govt. and industry; mem. U.S. Nat. Com. on Geology, 1975-79, Com. on Seismology, NRC, 1976-79, chmn. Com. on Safety Criteria for Dams, 1984; mem. adv. subcom. to U.S. Geol. Survey on Earthquake Studies, 1984—. Fellow Am. Geophys. Union (asso. editor Jour. Geophys. Research 1978-80), Royal Astron. Soc.; mem. Seismol. Soc. Am. (pres. 1976-77, editor Bull 1971-75), Soc. Exploration Geophysicists, Earthquake Engring. Research Inst. Current Work: Seismicity and earthquake hazard in Eastern U.S. earthquake source physics. Subspecialty: Geophysics. Home: 5422 Finkman St Saint Louis MO 63109 Office: 221 N Grand Blvd Saint Louis MO 63103

NUZZO, SALVATORE JOSEPH, electronics company executive; b. Norwalk, Conn., Aug. 6, 1931; s. Rocco and Angelina (Ranzulli) N.; m. Lucille Cocco, Oct. 3, 1953; children—James, David, Thomas, Dana. B.S. in Elec. Engring, Yale U., 1953; M.S. in Bus, Columbia U., 1974. With Hazeltine Corp., Greenlawn, N.Y., 1953—, v.p. govt. products and mktg., 1969-73, v.p. govt. products div., 1973-74, sr. v.p. ops., 1974-76, exec. v.p., chief operating officer, 1976, pres., chief operating officer, 1977—, chief exec. officer, 1980—. Mem. Armed Forces Communications and Electronics Assn., Am. Def. Preparedness Assn., Assn. U.S. Army, Electronic Industries Assn., Bus. Council N.Y. State (dir.), Nat. Security Indsl. Assn. (trustee), Am. Mgmt. Assn., NAM, Yale Sci. and Engring. Assn. (dir.). Subspecialty: Electronics company management. Home: 94 Holst Dr W Huntington NY 11743 Office: Hazeltine Corp Commack NY 11725

NWANGWU, PETER UCHENNA, clinical pharmacologist; b. Umuahia, Imo, Nigeria, June 13, 1949; came to U.S., 1972; s. Sidney Nwokeke and Phoebe (Akueke) N.; m. Patience Okaro, June 3, 1978; children: David, Daniel, Joy. B.A. in Chemistry, U. Nebr., 1974, M.S., 1976, Pharm.D., 1979, Ph.D. in Med. Scis, 1979. Registered pharmacist, Nebr. Proctor of physics U. Nebr., Lincoln, 1973-74; instr. biology U. Nebr. (Sch. Life Scis.), 1974; instr. chemistry SUNY-Syracuse, 1975; asst. prof. pharmacology and toxicology Sch. Pharmacy, Fla. A&M U., Tallahassee, 1979-81, dir. clin. research, 1979-81; assoc. prof. pharmacology and toxicology St. John's U., Jamaica, N.Y., 1981-83; mem. Pharm.D. program adv. bd.; clin. research monitor Ayerst Labs., N.Y.C., 1983—; internat. rep. Fine Future Co., Nigeria, 1976-77; v.p. ops. Finecoop, Nigeria, 1977-79; mem. vis. faculty Oak Ridge Associated Univs., Oak Ridge Nat. Labs. Author: Concepts and Strategies in New Drug Development, 1983, (with V.A. Skoutakis) Clinical Toxicology of Non Drugs, 1983; editorial adv. bd. (with V.A. Skoutakis), Clin. Toxicology Cons.; program dir. (with V.A. Skoutakis) NBC-TV series on new drug devel., 1977-81; Nat. Symposium on Concepts and Strategies in Clin. Research, N.Y.C., 1982; contbr. (with V.A. Skoutakis) book reviews, abstracts, manuscripts and articles to med. jours. Bd. dirs. Calvary Baptist Ch., Omaha. NIH grantee, 1981—. Fellow Am. Coll. Clin. Pharmacology, Am. Soc. Cons. Pharmacists, Am. Coll. Tropical Medicine; mem. Nat. Pharm. Alliance (tech. and drug regulatory com.), Am. Biog. Inst. (nat. bd. advs.), Am. Fedn. Clin. Research, Am. Pharm. Assn., Acad. Pharm. Scis., Am. Assn. Colls. Pharmacy, AAAS, N.Y. Acad. Scis., Smithsonian Instn., Drug. Info. Assn., Jaycees (charter), Fla. Pharm. Assn. (continuing edn. provider), Internat. Platform Assn., Union African Socs. Pharmacology, Phi Eta Sigma, Rho Chi, Sigma Xi. Developed rapid in vivo technique for screening antiarrhythmic agents in mice, 1977; rapid technique for identification of time of myocardial infarction employing Tc-99 pyrophosphate. Current Work: Clinical trials of new drugs; clinical toxicology; preventive medicine. Subspecialties: Pharmacology; Toxicology (medicine). Home: 157 Cocoanut St Brentwood NY 11717 Office: Ayerst Labs 685 3d Ave New York NY 11717

NYBERG, DENNIS, biologist; b. Oklahoma City, Feb. 11, 1944; s. Roy Carl and Veryl (Thornstrom) N.; m. Nancy Holmes, May 6, 1967; children: Carl, Ralph, Gustaf, Roy, Darwin. B.S., MIT, 1965; M.S., U. Ill., 1969, Ph.D., 1971; NSF fellow, U. Sussex, Brighton, Eng., 1971-72. Research assoc. Ind. U., Bloomington, 1972-73; asst. prof. U. Ill., Chgo., 1973-77, assoc. prof., 1977—. Contbr. articles to profl. jours. U. Ill. fellow, 1970-71; NSF fellow, 1967-70; NSF grantee, 1976-78; NIH grantee, 1979-82. Mem. AAAS, Genetics Soc. Am., Am. Genetic Assn., Soc. Study Evolution, Soc. Protozoologists. Current Work: Research in genetics of adaptation, evolution of sex, aging, recombination. Subspecialty: Evolutionary biology. Home: 323 S Humphrey St Oak Park IL 60302 Office: Dept Biol Sci U Ill Chicago IL 60680

NYLEN, MARIE USSING, government official; b. Copenhagen, Apr. 13, 1924; m. 1956; 3 children. D.D.S., Royal Dental Coll. Denmark, 1947, D.Odontologiae honoris causa, 1973. Individual practice dentistry, 1947-48; instr. ops. Royal Dental Coll., 1948-49, asst. prof. oral diagnosis, 1951-55; guest worker dental histology Nat. Inst. Dental Research, 1949-50, vis. assoc. biophysics, 1955-60, biologist, 1960-65, acting chief Lab. Histology and Pathology, 1965-69, chief Lab. Biol. Structure HEW, 1969-76, assoc. dir. intramural research, from 1976, now assoc. dir. extramural programs. Recipient Superior Service Honor award HEW, 1969, Fed. Womans award HEW, 1975. Fellow AAAS, Am. Coll. Dentists; mem. Electron Microscopy Soc., Am. Dental Assn., Internat. Assn. Dental Research (pres. Washington sect. 1971-72, mem. exhibits com. 1971—, mem. sr. fgn. dental scientist com. 1972—, chmn. local arrangements com. 1972-73), Internat. Assn. Dental Research (chmn. ad hoc com. consideration tooth designation 1972-73, research award 1970), Danish Dental Assn. Nordic Odontologic Assn., Fedn. Dentaire Internat., Washington Soc. Electron Microscopy (sec. treas. 1962-65), Am. Soc. Cell Biology, Am. Assn. Anatomists, Scandinavian Soc. Forensic Odontology, Am. Soc. Forensic Odontology, D.D. Ash Pathology Club (hon.). Subspecialty: Dental research institute administration. Office: Nat Inst Dental Research 9000 Rockville Pike Bethesda MD 20205

NYQUIST, GERALD WARREN, mechanical engineer; b. Detroit, Dec. 28, 1940; s. Paul Gustave and Lucille Phyllis (Reiter) N. B.S. in Civil Engring, Lawrence Inst. Tech., 1963; M.S. in Engring. Mechancis, Wayne State U., 1967; Ph.D., Mich. State U., 1970. Registered profl. engr., Mich. Product test engr. Ford Motor Co., Dearborn, Mich., 1963-65; research assoc. Biomechanics Research Ctr., Wayne State U., 1965-72; sr. research engr. Gen. Motors Research Lab., Gen. Motors Corp., 1972-76, sect. supr. environ. activities staff, 1976-80, staff analysis engr. engring. staff, 1980-82; pres. Gerald W. Nyquist, Inc., East Detroit, Mich., 1982—; research assoc. Bioengring. Ctr. Wayne State U., 1983—; cons. biomechanics and vehicle crash safety. Contbr. articles to tech. jours. Mem. Soc. Automotive Engrs., Sigma Xi. Current Work: Human impact tolerance, mechanical simulation of the human, automotive crash safety. Subspecialties: Biomedical engineering; Theoretical and applied mechanics. Address: 19059 Holbrook St East Detroit MI 48021

NYQUIST, WYMAN ELLSWORTH, biometry educator, researcher; b. Scobey, Mont., June 13, 1928; s. Rudolph Ephraim and Alyce Maria (Nordberg) N.; m. Ruth Malene, June 15, 1952; children: Elaine Annette, Craig Evan. B.S., Mont. State U., 1950; Ph.D., U. Calif., Davis, 1953. Instr. U. Calif., Davis, 1953-57, asst. prof., 1957-63; assoc. prof. Purdue U., West Lafayette, Ind., 1963-68, prof., 1968—. Served to 1st lt. USAF, 1954-56. NIH spl. research fellow, 1969-70. Mem. Am. Soc. Agronomy, Biometrics Soc., Council of Agr., Sci. and Tech., Crop Sci. Soc. Am., Genetics Soc. Am., Sigma Xi. Republican. Current Work: Research in biometry, experimental design, statistical genetics, quantitative genetics. Subspecialties: Statistics; Plant genetics. Home: 1600 Ravinia Rd West Lafayette IN 47906 Office: Dept Agronomy Purdue Univ West Lafayette IN 47907

NYSSEN, GERARD ALLAN, chemist, educator, researcher, translator; b. Hattiesburg, Miss., Nov. 9, 1942; s. Howard C. and Margreth Elizabeth (Faul) N.; m. Mary Jane, Aug. 21, 1965; children: John Mark, David, Amy. A.B., Olivet Nazarene Coll., 1965; Ph.D., Purdue U., 1970. Asst. prof. chemistry Trevecca Nazarene Coll., 1970-72, assoc. prof., 1972-76, prof., 1976—; vis. prof. Belmont Coll., 1970-83; postdoctoral researcher Okla. State U., summer 1971, Oak Ridge Nat. Lab., summer 1974, Vanderbilt U., 1976-77, and summer 1978, 84; translator Lang. Services, Nashville and Knoxville, Tenn., 1979-80; mem faculty Gov.'s Sch. of S.C. at Coll. Charleston, summer 1981; tchr. chemistry. Contbr. articles to profl. jours. Mem. PTA, Glenview Elem. Sch., Nashville; blood donor, CPR instr., lang. bank vol. Nashville sect. ARC. Mem. Am. Chem. Soc. (sec.-treas. Nashville sect. 1978-80). Subspecialty: Environmental chemistry. Home: 1902 Elanor Dr Nashville TN 37217 Office: 333 Murfreesboro Rd Nashville TN 37203

OAKES, LESTER CORNELIUS, electrical engineer, researcher; b. Knoxville, Oct. 11, 1923; s. Charles Vaughn and Maude (Harrison) O.; m. Kathleen Ann Clark; children—Michael, Richard, Cynthia, Melissa. B.S. in Elec. Engring., U. Tenn., 1949, M.S. in Elec. Engring., 1962. Registered profl. engr., Tenn. Devel. engr. Fairchild Engring. and Aircraft, Oak Ridge, 1949-51; devel. engr. Oak Ridge Nat. Lab., 1951-62, group leader, 1962-68, dept. head, 1968—, assoc. div. dir., 1973—. Patentee in field. Contbr. articles to profl. jours. Served with USAF, 1943-46. Fellow IEEE (chmn. awards com. 1976-80, adminstrn. com. 1977-80); mem. Am. Nuclear Soc. Presbyterian. Current work: Research and development toward improved instrumentation and control of nuclear fission reactors. Subspecialties: Nuclear fission; Electrical engineering. Home: 5016 Mountaincrest Dr Knoxville TN 37918 Office: Oak Ridge Nat Lab Oak Ridge TN 37831

OAKES, ROBERT J., physics educator; b. Mpls., Jan. 21, 1936. B.S., U. Minn., 1957, M.S., 1959, Ph.D., 1962. Asst. prof. Stanford U., Palo Alto, Calif., 1962-67; mem. staff Inst. for Advanced Study, Princeton, N.J., 1967-68; prof. Northwestern U., Evanston, Ill., 1968—; vis. staff mem. Los Alamos Lab., N.Mex., 1971—; vis. scientist Fermilab, Batavia, Ill., 1975—; faculty assoc. Argonne Labs., Ill., 1982—. A.P. Sloan Found fellow, 1965-68; AFSOR grantee, 1968-71; NSF grantee, 1971—; Fulbright Disting. prof., 1979-80. Fellow Am. Phys. Soc.; mem. AAAS, Ill. Acad. Sci. Current work: Theoretical high energy physics, elementary particles and their interactions. Subspecialties: Particle physics; Theoretical physics. Office: Dept Physics Northwestern U Evanston IL 60201

OAKS, ROBERT QUINCY, JR., geology educator; b. Houston, Aug. 29, 1938; s. Robert Quincy Sr. and Susie Elizabeth (Lawton) O.; children—Katherine Anne, John Robert Jordan. B.A. in Geology, Rice U., 1960; Ph.D. in Geology, Yale U., 1965. Field geologist Va. Div. Mineral Resources, Charlottesville, summer 1963; research geologist Exxon Prodn. Research, Houston, 1964-66; asst. prof. geology Utah State U., Logan, 1966-70, assoc. prof., 1970-79, prof., 1979—; cons. petroleum geologist Magellan Petroleum Australia, Ltd., Brisbane, 1979—. Author, editor: Post-Miocene Stratigraphy, Central and Southern Atlantic Coastal Plain, 1974. Contbr. articles, reports and abstracts to profl. publs. Fellow Geol. Soc. Am.; mem. Am. Assn. Petroleum Geologists, Soc. Econ. Paleontologists and Mineralogists, Internat. Assn. Sedimentologists, AAAS (life). Current work: Sedimentary provenance, petrology, petrography, and paragenesis/includes tectonics. Subspecialties: Sedimentology; Tectonics. Office: Utah State Univ Dept Geology Logan UT 84322

OATES, GORDON CEDRIC, aeronautical engineer, educator; b. Vancouver, B.C., Can., Feb. 28, 1932; came to U.S., 1959, naturalized, 1967; s. Arthur James Lawson and Kathleen Maude Alix (Binns) O.; m. Joan Buker, Aug. 23, 1961; children—Kenneth Marshall, Brian Cedric, Donald Lawson, Janine. B.A.Sc., U. B.C., 1954; M.Sc., U. Birmingham, Eng., 1956; Ph.D., Calif. Inst. Tech., 1959. Grad. apprentice Rolls Royce Co., Derby, Eng., 1954-55; asst. prof. dept. aeros. and astronautics M.I.T., 1959-64, asso. prof., 1964-67, U. Wash., 1967-70, prof., 1970—; guest prof. Royal Inst. Tech., Stockholm, 1970; disting. vis. prof. U.S. Air Force Acad., 1975-76; vis. prof. Air Force Office of Sci. Research, 1983; mem. propulsion and energetics panel Adv. Group for Aerospace Research and Devel.; cons. United Techs. Research Ctr., United Technologies Chem. Systems Div., Volvo Flygmotor. Contbr. articles and books in field. Recipient Disting. Teaching award U. Wash., 1982; John Leland Atwood award AIAA and Am. Soc. Engring. Edn., 1985. Athlone fellow, 1954-56; Asso. fellow AIAA. Mem. ASME, Sigma Xi. Patentee hydrodynamic focusing method and apparatus. Current work: Air breathing propulsion, fluid mechanics, energy conversion. Home: 4943 Stanford Ave NE Seattle WA 98105 Office: University of Washington Seattle WA 98195

OATLEY, DAVID HERBERT, health physicist, health physics consultant; b. St. John's, Mich., June 10, 1953; s. Herbert Lewis and Esther (Ferguson) O.; m. Eileen Doyle, Nov. 27, 1981. B.S., Central Mich. U., 1975; cert. secondary teaching, Mich. State U., 1976; M.S., U. Mich., 1980. Pharm. rep. Upjohn Co., Kalamazoo, Mich., 1977-78; research asst. U. Mich., 1978-80; radiol. engr. Portland Gen. Electric, Rainier, Oreg., 1979; health physicist Wash. Publ. Power Supply System, Elma, 1980-83, Pacific Gas and Electric Co., San Francisco, 1983—; pvt. practice health physics cons., Olympia, Wash., 1982—, Martinez, Calif., 1983—. Contbr. articles to profl. jours. Mem. Am. Nuclear Soc., Health Physics Soc. Congregationalist. Current Work: Radiation dosimetry, power reactor health physics and emergency preparedness for power reactors. Subspecialties: Nuclear fission; Physiology (biology). Home: 4929 Shadow Falls Martinez CA 94553 Office: Pacific Gas and Electric Co 77 Beale St San Francisco CA 94106

O'BEIRNE, ANDREW JON, virologist, administrator; b. Phila., Oct. 26, 1944; s. Carl Ellis and Gloria M. (Teti) O'B.; m. Patricia Ann O'Neill, June 22, 1968; children—Jonathan, Elizabeth. B.S., Phila. Coll. Pharmacy and Sci., 1966; M.P.H., U. Mich., 1972, Dr. P.H., 1973. Co-head, virus products Whittaker Bioproducts, Walkersville, Md., 1973-74, dir. research and devel., 1974-78, v.p. research and devel., 1978-80, v.p. ops. and research and devel., 1980-83, sr. v.p., 1983-84, gen. mgr. diagnostic div., 1984—; lectr. Hood Coll., Frederick, Md., 1983—, mem. sci. adv. council, 1983—. Editor Jour. Clin. Microbiology, 1983—; patentee in field. Served with USAF, 1970-71. Mem. Am. Soc. Microbiology, Am. Pub. Health Assn., Am. Assn. Pathologists, N.Y. Acad. Scis., Sigma Xi. Current work: Immunodiagnostics. Subspecialties: Animal virology; Immunology (agriculture). Home: 9403 Farmingdale Walkersville MD 21793 Office: Whittaker M A Bioproducts Biggs Ford Rd Walkersville MD 21793

OBENDORF, RALPH LOUIS, agronomist, educator; b. Milan, Ind., July 11, 1938; s. Louis Eugene and Miriam Clara (Stegemoller) O.; m. Sharon Kay Randel, Mar. 11, 1967; children: Michael Bradley, Kevin Andrew. B.S. in Agr, Purdue U., West Lafayette, Ind., 1960; M.S. in Agronomy, U. Calif.-Davis, 1962, Ph.D. in Plant Physiology, 1966. Asst. prof. crop sci. Cornell U., Ithaca, N.Y., 1966-71, assoc. prof., 1971-77, prof., 1977—; vis. scientist Inst. Cancer Research, Fox Chase, Phila., 1971-72; vis. plant physiologist Plant Growth Lab., U. Calif., Davis., 1983. Mem. Am. Soc. Plant Physiologists, Crop Sci. Soc. Am., Am. Soc. Agronomy, AAAS, Am. Assn. Cereal Chemists, Tissue Culture Assn. Current Work: In vitro soybean seed and pod cultures; plant tissue/organ culture; seed biology; seed formation; seed germination; seed physiology; plant physiology. Subspecialties: Plant cell and tissue culture; Plant physiology (agriculture). Home: 24 Dart Dr Ithaca NY 14850 Office: 619 Bradfield Hall Ithaca NY 14853

OBERLEY, TERRY DE WAYNE, physician, pathologist; b. Effingham, Ill., Jan. 23, 1946; s. James Donald and Ruby Eloise (Moore) O.; m. Edith Marjorie Toole, June 19, 1968; children: Mathew James, Alexander John. B.A., Northwestern U., 1968, Ph.D., 1973, M.D., 1974. Diplomate: Am. Bd. Pathology. Intern pathology U. Wis., Madison, 1974-75, USPHS pathology trainee, 1975-77, resident pathology, 1977-78, asst. prof. pathology, 1977-82, assoc. prof. pathology, 1983—; chief electron microscopy William S. Middleton VA Hosp., Madison, 1983—. Author: Understanding Your New Life with Dialysis, 1983; Contbr. articles to profl. jours. NIH postdoctoral fellow, 1975; research grantee, 1975; Am Cancer Soc. resident fellow, 1977; March of Dimes Basil O'Connor grantee, 1978; VA Rev. grantee, 1984—. Mem. Am. Assn. Pathologists, Am. Soc. Nephrology, Am. Soc. Microbiology, AMA, Nat. Kidney Found. Wis. (chmn. research com. 1983). Democrat. Unitarian. Current Work: Research on the regulation of cell growth, with emphasis on studies of regulation of growth of normal and cancerous kidney cells, studies of the role of oxygen metabolites in cell growth. Subspecialties: Cell and tissue culture; Tissue culture. Home: 5418 S Hill Dr Madison WI 53705 Office: Dept Pathology William S Middleton VA Hosp 2500 Overlook Terr Madison WI 53705

OBLAD, ALEXANDER GOLDEN, chemist, chemical engineer, educator; b. Salt Lake City, Nov. 26, 1909; s. Alexander H. and Louie May (Brewster) O.; m. Bessie Elizabeth Baker, Feb. 23, 1933; children: Alex Edward, Elizabeth (Mrs. D. Sonne), Virginia (Mrs. M. Christensen), John R.B., Hayward B., Jean Rio B.(Mrs. S. Calder). B.A. in Chemistry, U. Utah, 1933, M.A. in Phys. Chemistry, 1934, D.Sc. (hon.), 1980; Ph.D. in Phys. Chemistry, Purdue U., 1937, D.Sc. (hon.), 1959. Research chemist Standard Oil Co., Whiting, Ind., 1937-42; Research chemist Magnolia Petroleum Co., Dallas, 1942-43, sect. leader, 1943-46, chief chem. research, 1946; head indsl. research Tex. Research Found., Dallas, 1947; dir. chem. research Houdry Process Corp., Marcus Hook, Pa., 1947-52, asso. mgr. research and devel., 1952-55, mgr., 1955, v.p., dir., 1955-57; v.p. research and devel. M.W. Kellogg Co., N.Y.C., 1957-66, v.p. research and engring. devel., 1966-69; prof. metall. engring. and fuels engring. U. Utah, 1969-75, disting. prof. metallurgy and fuels engring., 1975—, prof. chemistry, 1975—; asso. dean U. Utah (Coll. of Mines), 1970-72, acting dean, 1972-75; co-founder, dir. Ireco Chems., Salt Lake City, 1958-72; mem. Sec. of Interior's Saline Water Conversion Adv. Com., Office of Saline Water, Washington, 1959-61; mem. fossil energy research working group Dept. Energy, 1980-82. Mem. editorial bd.: Catalysis Revs., Fuel Processing Tech, 1976; mem. internat. adv. bd.: Ency. of Chem. Processing and Design, 1973—; Contbr. numerous articles on phys. chemistry, catalysis, petroleum chemistry and chem. engring. to tech. and sci. jours. Mem. alumni research council Purdue Research Found., Lafayette, Ind., 1960-63; chmn. sustaining membership campaign Orange Mountain council Boy Scouts Am., 1966-67; mem. adv. council Brigham Young U., Provo, Utah, 1962-81; mem. nat. adv. council U. Utah, 1962-77; bd. dirs. Internat. Congress on Catalysis, 1956-65. Recipient First Purdue Chemist's award, 1959, Distinguished Alumni award U. Utah, 1962. Mem. Am. Chem. Soc. (mng. editor publs. div. petroleum chemistry 1857-69, sec. treas. div. petroleum chemistry 1952-54, chmn. 1956, E.V. Murphree award 1969), Am. Inst. Chem. Engrs., AAAS, Calif. Catalysis Soc., Rocky Mountain Fuel Soc., Nat. Acad. Engring., Am. Inst. Chemists (Chem. pioneer award 1972), Sigma Xi, Phi Lambda Upsilon, Sigma Pi Sigma, Phi Kappa Phi, Tau Beta Pi. Mem. Ch. of Jesus Christ of Latter-Day Saints. Club: Rotary. Patentee in field. Subspecialties: Chemical engineering; Physical chemistry. Home: 1415 Roxbury Rd Salt Lake City UT 84108 Office: 302 Browning Mineral Science Bldg Univ of Utah Salt Lake City UT

OBREMSKI, ROBERT JOHN, analytical chemist, researcher; b. Bklyn., Aug. 19, 1941; s. Thaddeus J. and Helen W. (Nowicka) O.; m. Arlene Joyce Bennett, Aug. 29, 1964; children—Christine Michelle, Robin Joyce. B.S., St. Johns U., 1962, M.S., 1964; Ph.D., U. Md., 1968. Research chemist Uniroyal Inc., Wayne, N.J., 1968-69; applications dept. Spectra-Physics, Mountain View, Calif., 1969-71; prin. chemist Beckman Instruments, Irvine, Calif., 1971-82, applications mgr., 1982—. Mem. Coblentz Soc. (bd. mgrs. 1981-85, treas. 1983—), Soc. Applied Spectroscopy, Am. Chem. Soc. Republican. Roman Catholic. Current work: Application of computer algorithms to enhance and provide final answers from spectroscopic data. Subspecialties: Analytical chemistry; Physical chemistry. Home: 19792 LaTierra Ln Yorba Linda CA 92686 Office: Beckman Instruments Inc PO Box C 19600 Irvine CA 92713

O'BRIEN, DAVID FRANK, chemist; b. Litchfield, Ill., Nov. 18, 1936; s. Maynard and Estelle (Gottrick) O'B.; m. Nancy Funkhouser, Aug. 23, 1959; children—James, Rebecca, Alice. A.B., Wabash Coll., 1958; Ph.D., U. Ill., 1962. Research chemist Eastman Kodak Research Labs., Rochester, N.Y., 1962-68, research assoc., 1968-73, 75—; vis. staff U. Calif.-Berkeley, 1973-74. Contbr. articles to profl. jours. Mem. Am. Chem. Soc., Biophys. Soc., Assn. for Research in Vision and Ophthalmology, Inter Am. Photochem. Soc., Sigma Xi. Current work: Reconstitution of visual chemistry in synthetic membranes, preparation and characterization of polymerized, membrane vesicles, incorporation of protein into synthetic membranes. Subspecialties: Biophysical chemistry; Biomaterials. Home: 398 Beresford Rd Rochester NY 14610 Office: Eastman Kodak Research Lab Rochester NY 14650

O'BRIEN, JAY PHILIP, organic chemist; b. Dayton, Ohio, Feb. 19, 1937; s. Philip Henry and Ella (Kubach) O'B. B.S., Rutgers U., 1960; M.S., Mich. State U., 1962. Scientist, Hoffmann-LaRoche, Nutley, N.J., 1963—. Contbr. articles to profl. jours. Patentee in field. Served with U.S. Army, 1962-66. Mem. Am. Chem. Soc. Current work: Alkaloids, isoquinolines and cardiovascular agents Subspecialty: Medicinal chemistry. Home: 71 Ridge Rd Cedar Grove NJ 07009 Office: Hoffmann LaRoche 740 Kingsland Rd Nutley NJ 07110

O'BRIEN, KENNETH STANLEY, mfg. co. ofcl.; b. Boston, Aug. 2, 1942; s. Stanley and Alice (Carroll) O'B.; m. Annette Marie, Jan. 16, 1966; children:

Michelle, Neal, Evan. B.S.M.E., Northeastern U., 1965, M.S. in Engring. Mgmt, 1972. Mech. devel. engr. Itek Corp., Lexington, Mass., 1965-68; mech. engr. Instron Corp., Canton, Mass., 1968-72; mgr. research and devel. A. W. Chesterton Co., Stoneham, Mass., 1972-76, corp. quality assurance mgr., 1976—. Mem. ASME, Am. Soc. Quality Control, Am. Mgmt. Assn., Pi Tau Sigma. Current Work: Application of computer tech. to quality assurance; devel. of quality assurance systems to multi-div., multi-nat. orgn. Subspecialties: Quality assurance; Mechanical engineering. Office: A W Chesterton Co Middlesex Indsl Park Route 93 Stoneham MA 02180

O'BRIEN, KERAN, physicist; b. Bklyn., Nov. 5, 1931; s. Raymond Keran and Mary Josephine (Marache) O'B.; m. Barbara Hope Zwickel, May 7, 1961; children—David Keran, Judith Nancy. B.S., Fordham U., 1953. Physicist Environ. Measurments Lab., N.Y.C., 1953—, dir. radiation physics div., 1981—. Contbr. articles to profl. jours., chpts. to book. Fellow Am. Nuclear Soc. (chmn. honors and awards com. 1976, Outstanding Div. Service award 1979-80, 84-85); mem. Am. Phys. Soc., Am. Geophys. Union, Am. Archeol. Inst., Radiation Research Soc. Current work: Generating and transport of neutrinos in the atmosphere by galactic cosmic rays; mathematical methods for neutron spectroscopy. Subspecialty: Nuclear physics. Home: 30 Dover Terr Monsey NY 10952 Office: Environ Measurment Lab 376 Hudson St New York NY 10014

O'BRIEN, MORROUGH PARKER, mechanical engineering educator; b. Hammond, Ind., Sept. 21, 1902; s. Morrough and Lulu (Parker) O'B.; m. Roberta Libbey, May 16, 1931 (div.); children—Sheila, Morrough; m. Mary Wallner Kremers, 1963. B.S., Mass. Inst. Tech., 1925; D.Sc., Northwestern U., 1959; Dr. Engring., Purdue U., 1961; LL.D., U. Calif., 1968. Registered profl. engr., N.Y., Calif. Engr. Hudson River Regulating Dist., 1925-27; research asst. Purdue U., 1925-27; Freeman scholar Am. Soc. C.E., 1927-28; asst. Royal Coll. Engring., Stockholm, Sweden, 1927-28; successively asst. prof., asso. prof., prof. U. Calif., 1928-59, prof. emeritus, 1959—, chmn. dept. mech. engring., 1937-43; dean U. Calif. (Coll. Engring.), 1943-59, dean emeritus, 1959—; adj. prof. coastal engring. U. Fla., 1983—; Dir. research and engring. Air Reduction, Inc., 1947-49; cons. engr. aerospace and def. group Gen. Electric Co., 1949—; mem. U.S. Beach Erosion Bd., 1936-61. U.S. Coastal Engring. Research Bd., 1961-78, Def. Sci. Bd., 1961-65, Army Sci. Adv. Panel, 1955-74; mem. nat. sci. bd. NSF, 1958-60. Author: Applied Fluid Mechanics, 1937. Mem. ASCE (hon.), ASME (hon.), Am. Soc. Engring. Edn. (Lamme medal), Am. Shore and Beach Preservation Assn. (past pres.), Nat. Acad. Engring., Sigma Xi, Tau Beta Pi, Delta Tau Delta. Clubs: Bohemian (San Francisco); Cosmos (Washington); Athenian-Nile (Oakland, Calif.); Faculty (Berkeley); Sleepy Hollow Country (Scarborough-on-Hudson., N.Y.). Current Work: Processes resulting from the interaction of an oceanic environment with sandy coasts. Subspecialty: Fluid mechanics. Home: PO Box 265 Cuernavaca Mexico 62000

O'BRIEN, PAUL JOSEPH, research biochemist; b. Haddonfield, N.J., Feb. 11, 1933; s. Joseph Aloysius and Irene Catherine (Conlin) O'B.; m. Barbara Marano, Apr. 22, 1961; children—Karen, John, Michael. B.S. in Biology, Mt. St. Mary's Coll., 1954; M.S. in Microbiology, St. John's U., 1956; Ph.D. in Biochemistry, U. Pa., 1960. Research chemist NIH and Nat. Inst. Arthritis and Metabolic Diseases, Bethesda, Md., 1960-64, Nat. Inst. Neurol. Disorders, Bethesda, 1964-70; research chemist Nat. Eye Inst., Bethesda, 1970-81, chief, sect. on cell biology, 1981—; trustee Assn. for Research in Vision and Ophthalmology, N.Y.C., 1978-81, pres., 1981. Editor: Exptl. Eye Research, N.Y.C., 1975—. Contbr. articles to profl. jours. Rep., City of Rockville Montgomery County Community Action Com., Md., 1969-72; mem. Human Relations Commn., Rockville, 1969-74, chmn., 1974. Mem. AAAS, Assn. Research Vision and Ophthalmology, Am. Soc. Biol. Chemists, Am. Soc. Cell Biology. Democrat. Roman Catholic. Current work: Photoreceptor metabolism and circadian rhythms, particularly as related to Rhododsin synthesis, modification and membrane shedding. Subspecialties: Biochemistry (biology); Cell biology. Home: 12 Duke St South Rockville MD 20850 Office: Bldg 6 Room BIA02 NEI-NIH Bethesda MD 20205

O'BRYAN, HENRY MILES, JR., ceramist, researcher; b. Cambridge, Mass., Aug. 20, 1934; s. Henry Miles and Eleanor Shea O'B.; m. Joan Kathleen Murray, Aug. 19, 1961; children—Joseph Henry, Jean Marie, Martin Murray, John Markward, Thomas More. B.S., U. Notre Dame, 1956; M.S. U. Mich., 1960, Ph.D., 1963. Mem. tech. staff AT&T Bell Labs., Murray Hill, N.J., 1963—. Contbr. articles to profl. jours. Patentee in field. Pres. United Way, Plainfield, N.J., 1981-83. Served to 1st. lt. U.S. Army, 1956-58. Recipient Disting. Mem. Tech. Staff award AT&T Bell Labs., 1984. Fellow Am. Ceramic Soc. (trustee 1984—, chmn. electronics div. 1979, Best Paper award 1980, chmn. program and meetings 1983). Roman Catholic. Current work: Relation of properties to processing, structure and composition for piezoelectric, electroptic and dielectrics, especially microwave materials. Subspecialties: Ceramics; Electronic materials. Home: 1600 Charlotte Rd Plainfield NJ 07060 Office: AT&T Bell Labs 6D-307 600 Mountain Ave Murray Hill NJ 07974

O'CALLAGHAN, DENNIS JOHN, virologist, biochemist; b. New Orleans, July 26, 1940; s. John J. and Odeal D (Fitzpatrick) O.; m. H. Frances Briscoe, June 24, 1967; 1 child, Brady. B.S. in Biology, Loyola U., New Orleans, 1962; Ph.D., U. Miss., 1968. Postdoctoral trainee U. Alta. Med. Ctr., Edmonton, Can., 1968-71; asst. prof. biochemistry, 1970-71; asst. prof. microbiology U. Miss. Med. Ctr., Jackson, 1971-74, assoc. prof., 1974-77, prof., 1977-84; prof., chmn. dept. microbiology and immunology La. State U. Med. Ctr., Shreveport, 1984—; mem. virology study sect. NIH, 1982—. Mem. editorial bd. Virology, 1985—, Virus Research, 1985—. Contbr. articles to profl. jours. Mem. Am. Assn. Cancer Research, Am. Soc. Biol. Chemists, Soc. Microbiology, Am. Soc. Microbiology, Am. Assn. Pathologists, Soc. Explt. Biology and Medicine, Soc. Gen. Microbiology, Sigma Xi. Current work: Herpesvirus tumorigenesis, molecular biology of herpesviruses. Subspecialty: Virology (medicine). Office: La State Univ Med Ctr Dept Microbiology and Immunology 1501 Kings Hwy Shreveport LA 71130

O'CALLAGHAN, JAMES PATRICK, research pharmacologist; b. West Palm Beach, Fla., Mar. 6, 1949; s. James Patrick and Paula Ann (Reinholtz) O'C. B.S. in Biology, Purdue U., 1971; Ph.D. in Pharmacology, Emory U., 1975. NIH postdoctoral fellow N.Y. State Div. Substance Abuse Services, Bklyn., 1975-78; pharmacology research assoc. Nat. Inst. Gen. Med. Scis., NIH, Bethesda, Md., 1978-80; research pharmacologist EPA, Research Triangle Park, N.C., 1980—. Contbr. chpts. to books, articles to profl. jours. NIH predoctoral trainee, 1971-75. Mem. AAAS, Soc. Neurosci., Am. Soc. Pharmacology and Exptl. Therapeutics, N.Y. Acad. Sci. Current Work: Nervous-system-specific proteins as biochemical indicators of neurotoxicity. Subspecialties: Neuropharmacology; Toxicology (medicine). Office: EPA Neurotoxicology Div (MD-74B) Research Triangle Park NC 27711

OCCOLOWITZ, JOHN LEWIS, pharmaceutical laboratories scientist; b. Melbourne, Victoria, Australia, July 30, 1931; came to U.S., 1967; s. John William and Bella Elizabeth (Thomas) O.; m. Airdrie Elizabeth MacNab, Mar. 10, 1962; children—Stacey Margaret, Peter John. Diploma in applied chemistry Footscray Tech. Coll., 1950; B.Sc., U. Melbourne, 1952, diploma edn., 1953, M.Sc., 1965. Instr., Victoria Edn. Dept., Melbourne, 1954-55; sci. officer Australian Govt. Dept. Supply, Melbourne, 1955-67; research assoc. Lilly Research Labs., Indpls., 1967—. Author: Analytical Chemistry of Phosphorous Compounds, 1972; Polyether Antibiotics-Naturally Occurring Acid Ionophores, vol. 2, 1983. Mem. Am. Soc. Mass Spectrometry. Current work: Determination of the structure of organic molecules using mass spectrometry; development of new mass spectrometric techniques. Subspecialties: Mass spectrometry; Organic chemistry. Home: 6840 Dover Rd Indianapolis IN 46220 Office: Lilly Research Labs Indianapolis IN 46285

OCHILLO, RICHARD FREDERICK, pharmacologist, toxicologist, educator, consultant, researcher; b. Yala, Kenya, Oct. 10, 1942; came to U.S., 1973; s. Yusuf O. and Klaris O. (Ragot) O.; m. Yvonne Hyacinth Richards, Aug. 30, 1969; children: Odera, Owino (dec.), Oremo, Fracella, Okelo. B.Sc., U. Victoria, B.C., Can., 1969; M.Sc., Dalhousie U., 1971; Ph.D., Vanderbilt U., 1977. Lectr. Siriba Coll., Maseno, Kenya, 1969, U. Nairobi, Kenya, 1971-73; asst. prof. pharmacology and toxicology Xavier U., New Orleans, 1977-80, assoc. prof., 1981—, chmn. div. basic pharm. scis., 1983—. Contbr. articles to profl. jours. NIH grantee, 1978—; Edward Schlieder grantee, 1978-82; NSF grantee, 1981-82. Mem. Am. Soc. Pharmacology and Exptl. Therapeutics, AAAS, S.E. Pharmacology Soc., Internat. Soc. Study Xenobiotics, Acad. Pharm. Scis., Am. Assn. Colls. Pharmacy, N.Y. Acad. Scis., Gerontol. Soc. Am., Soc. Toxicology, Am. Pharm. Assn. Current Work: Pharmacodynamics of cholinergic and cardiovascular agents with special interests on muscarine and its analogs; toxicology of natural toxins particularly African arrow poisons. Subspecialties: Pharmacology; Toxicology (medicine). Home: 6 Cocodrie Ct Kenner LA 70065 Office: 7325 Palmetto St New Orleans LA 70125

OCHOA, MANUEL, JR., physician, educator; b. N.Y.C., Apr. 22, 1930; s. Manuel and Maria (Diaz) O.; m. Suzanne Ellen Recca, Sept. 1, 1956; children—Elizabeth, Suzanne Elise. A.B., Columbia U., 1951, M.D., 1955. Diplomate Am. Bd. Internal Medicine. Intern in medicine N.Y. Hosp.-Cornell U. Med. Ctr., N.Y.C., 1955-56, research asst. dept. medicine, 1956; asst. resident in medicine Strong Meml. Hosp.-U. Rochester Sch. Medicine and Dentistry, N.Y., 1958-59, assoc. resident in medicine, 1959-60, trainee in medicine (hematology), 1960-61; chief resident in medicine, clin. fellow in oncology Francis Delafield Hosp.-Presbyn.-Columbia Med. Ctr., N.Y.C., 1961-62; NIH trainee in medicine (biochemistry and oncology) Inst. for Cancer Research, Presbyn.-Columbia Med. Ctr., 1962-64; vis. physician Delafield Cancer Inst., N.Y.C., 1963-68; asst. physician Presbyn. Hosp., 1964-68; asst. prof. medicine Columbia U., 1964-68; assoc. mem. Sloan Kettering Inst., 1968-84; attending physician Meml. Sloan-Kettering Cancer Ctr., N.Y.C., 1968—; assoc. prof. clin. medicine Cornell U., 1982—. Author: Alkylating Agents, 1968. Contbr. articles to profl. jours. Served to capt. USAF, 1956-58. Fellow ACP; mem. Am. Assn. Cancer Research, Am. Soc. Hematology, Am. Soc. Clin. Oncologists, Internat. Soc. Hematology. Roman Catholic. Current work: Cancer chemotherapy; pharmacology; oncology; cell studies; cancer biochemistry. Subspecialties: Oncology; Cancer research (medicine). Office: Meml Sloan-Kettering Cancer Ctr 1275 York Ave New York NY 10021

OCHOA, SEVERO, biochemist; b. Luarca, Spain, Sept. 24, 1905; came to U.S., 1940, naturalized, 1956; s. Severo and Carmen (Albornoz) O.; m. Carmen G. Cobian, July 8, 1931. A.B., Malaga (Spain) Coll., 1921; M.D., U. Madrid, Spain, 1929; D.Sc., Washington U., U. Brazil, 1957, U. Guadalajara, Mexico, 1959, Wesleyan U., U. Oxford, Eng., U. Salamanca, Spain, 1961, Gustavus Adolphus Coll., 1963, U. Pa., 1964, Brandeis U., 1965, U. Granada, Spain, U. Oviedo, Spain, 1967, U. Perugia, Italy, 1968, U. Mich., Weizman Inst., Israel, 1982; Dr. Med. Sci. (hon.), U. Santo Tomas, Manila, Philippines, 1963, U. Buenos Aires, 1968, U. Tucuman, Argentina, 1968; L.H.D., Yeshiva Univ., 1966; LL.D., U. Glasgow, Scotland, 1959. Lectr. physiology U. Madrid Med. Sch., 1931-35; head physiol. div. Inst. for Med. Research, 1935-36; guest research asst. in physiology Kaiser-Wilhelm Inst. for Med. Research, Heidelberg, Germany, 1936-37; Ray Lankester investigator Marine Biol. Lab., Plymouth, Eng., 1937; demonstrator Nuffield research asst. biochemistry Oxford (Eng.) U. Med. Sch., 1938-41; instr., research assoc. pharmacology Washington U. Sch. of Medicine, St. Louis, 1941-42; research assoc. medicine N.Y. U. Sch. Medicine, 1942-45, asst. prof. biochemistry, 1945-46, prof. pharmacology, chmn. dept., 1946-54, prof., chmn. dept. biochemistry, 1954-74, prof., 1974—; disting. mem. Roche Inst. Molecular Biology. Author publs. on biochem. of muscles, glycolysis in heart and brain, transphosphorylations in yeast fermentation, pyruvic acid oxidation in brain and role of vitamin B1; RNA and Protein biosynthesis; genetic code. Decorated Order Rising Sun Japan; recipient (with Arthur Kornberg) 1959 Nobel prize in medicine, Albert Gallatin medal N.Y. U., 1970, Nat. Medal of Sci., 1980. Fellow N.Y. Acad. Scis., N.Y. Acad. Medicine, Am. Acad. of Arts and Sci., A.A.A.S.; mem. Nat. Acad. Sci., Am. Philos. Soc., Soc. for Exptl. Biology and Medicine, Soc. of Biol. Chemists (pres. 1958, editor jour. 1950-60), Internat. Union Biochemistry (pres. 1961-67), Biochem. Soc. (Eng.), Harvey Soc. (pres. 1953-54), Alpha Omega Alpha (hon.); fgn. mem. German Acad. Nat. Scis., Royal Spanish, USSR, Polish, Pullian, Italian, Argentinian, Barcelona (Spain), Brazilian acads. sci., Royal Soc. (Eng.), Pontifical Acad. Sci., G.D.R. Acad. Scis., Argentinian Nat. Acad. Medicine. Subspecialty: Molecular biology. Office: Roche Inst Molecular Biology Nutley NJ 07110

OCHS, SIDNEY, neurophysiology educator; b. Fall River, Mass., June 30, 1924; s. Nathan and Rose (Kniaz) O.; m. Bess Ratner, Jan. 9, 1949; children—Rachel F., Raymond, S., Susan B. Ph.D., U. Chgo., 1952. Research assoc. Ill. Neuropsychiat. Inst., Chgo., 1953-54; research fellow Calif. Inst. Tech., Pasadena, 1954-56; asst. prof. medicine U. Tex.-Galveston, 1956-58; prof. physiology Ind. U.-Indpls., 1958—, dir. med. biophysics, 1968—; NSF sr. fellow biophysics U. London, Eng., 1963-64. Author: Elements of Neurophysiology, 1965; Axoplasmic Transport and Its Relation to Other Nerve Functions, 1982. Contbr. articles to profl. jours. Served with U.S. Army, 1943-45. Mem. Soc. Neurosci. (counselor 1970-74), Internat. Brain Research Orgn., Am. Soc. Neurochemistry, Am. Physiol. Soc. (neurophysiology com. 1978, commemorative com. 1979). Democrat. Jewish.Current work: Axoplasmic transport in nerve; studies in reflex mechanisms in the spinal cord; electrical activity of nerve; electrical responses in the cerebral cortex, direct cortical response; spreading depression in the cerebral cortex. Subspecialties: Neurophysiology; Neurobiology. Home: 912 Forest Blvd North Dr Indianapolis IN 46240 Office: Ind U Sch of Medicine 635 Barnhill Dr Indianapolis IN 46223

OCKERMAN, HERBERT WOOD, agricultural educator; b. Chaplin, Ky, Jan. 16, 1932; s. Herbert Newton and Addie Mae (Simpson) O.; m. Frances Ockerman. B.S., U. Ky., 1954, M.S., 1958; Ph.D., N.C. State U., 1962. Prof. meat sci. area dept. animal sci. Ohio State U., 1961—; cons. in field. Author: Source Book for Food Scientists, 1978; contbr. to books and profl. jours. Served to capt. USAF, 1955-58. Recipient Prof. award Pingtung U., Taiwan, 1978; commendation for internat. work in agr. Ohio Ho. of Reps., 1977; Badge of Merit for service to agr. Polish Govt., 1977; Plaque, Argentine Nat. Met Bd., 1981, U. Cordoba, Spain, 1982, Nat. Chung-Hsing U., Taiwan. Mem. Inst. Food Technology, Am. Meat Sci. Assn., Am. Soc. Animal Sci., Polish Vet. Soc. (hon.), Sigma Xi, Phi Tau Sigma, Gamma Sigma Delta. Current Work: Teaching and research in the meat and food areas, both domestically and internationally. Subspecialties: Food science and technology; Statistics. Office: 2029 Fyffe Rd Columbus OH 43210

O'CLOCK, GEORGE DANIEL, JR., electrical engineer, consultant, educator, researcher; b. Chgo., Sept. 25, 1939; s. George Daniel and Estelle June (Taylor) O'C.; m. Priscilla Marie, June 14, 1969; children: Michael Anthony, Kathleen Marie. B.S.E.E., S.D. Sch. Mines and Tech., 1962, M.S.E.E., 1967; Ph.D., 1979; M.B.A. in Fin, UCLA, 1977. Registered profl. engr., Calif., Minn. Sr. engr. RCA Advanced Tech. Labs., Van Nuys, Calif., 1970-73; research engr. Northrop Corp., Hawthorne, Calif., 1973-74; mem. tech. staff Rockwell Internat., Anaheim, Calif., 1974-76, mgr. research and engring., 1977-80; staff scientist Perkin-Elmer, Eden Prairie, Minn., 1979-82; prof. physics and engring. Mankato State U., 1982—; v.p. and gen. mgr. RCD & A Cons., Cypress, Calif., 1975 . Contbr. numerous articles to profl. jours. Served to 1st C.E. U.S. Army, 1962-64. Bush grantee, 1983, 85; NSF grantee, 1984. Mem. IEEE, Soc. Photo Optical Instrumentation Engrs., Sigma Xi, Eta Kappa Nu, Phi Kappa Phi, Theta Tau. Lodge: K.C. Patentee in field. Current Work: Communications systems, semiconductor materials and devices, electronics, communications, microwaves, optics, photovoltaics, spectroscopy. Subspecialties: Microelectronics; Semiconductors. Office: Dept Physics and Engring Mankato State U Mankato MN 56001

OCONE, LUKE RALPH, chemist, biotechnologist; b. Bridgeport, Conn., Mar. 10, 1925; s. Joseph and Catherine (Vuolo) O.; m. Ariadna Shugaevsky, Jan. 25, 1953; children—Daniel L., Anthony P., Steven L., Anne C. B.S. in Chemistry, N.Y. Poly. Inst., 1951; Ph.D. in Chemistry, Pa. State U., 1956. Chemist photoproducts dept. DuPont, Parlin, N.J., 1956-59; sr. chemist Pennwalt Corp., King of Prussia, Pa., 1959-61, group leader research, 1961-71, group leader comml. devel., 1971—. Contbr. articles to sci. jours. Patentee in field. Bd. dirs. Whitemarsh Village Assn., Montgomery County, Pa., 1960-62; bd. dirs. Coffee Concert Com., Phila., 1967-75. Served with USNR, 1943-46. Mem. Am. Chem. Soc. (chmn. Phila. sect. inorganic group 1963-64), Comml. Devel. Assn. (dir. 1984—, chmn. Phila. sect. 1978—), Tech. Transfer Soc., Licensing Exec. Soc. Current work: Chemical synthesis, especially involving catalysis, electrolysis, and extreme reaction conditions; product objectives include both organic and inorganic compounds and also specialty polymers. Subspecialties: Organic chemistry; Biophysical chemistry. Office: Pennwalt Corp 3 Parkway Philadelphia PA 19102

O'CONNELL, JAMES SHERIDAN, nuclear physicist; b. Chgo., Jan. 15, 1932; B.S., Beloit Coll., 1953; Ph.D., U. Ill.-Urbana, 1961. Research assoc. Yale U., New Haven, 1960-63; nuclear physicist Nat. Bur. Standards, Gaithersburg, Md., 1963—; vis. scientist Stanford U., Palo Alto, Calif., 1970-71; staff scientist Dept. Energy, Germantown, Md., 1975-76; vis. scientist MIT, Cambridge, 1979-80. Contbr. articles to profl. jours. Recipient Bronze medal Dept. Commerce, 1983. Fellow Am. Phys. Soc. Current work: Electromagnetic nuclear reactions. Subspecialty: Nuclear physics. Office: Ctr Radiation Research Nat Bur Standards Gaithersburg MD 20899

O'CONNELL, ROBERT FRANCIS, physicist, educator; b. Athlone, Ireland, Apr. 22, 1933; came to U.S., 1958, naturalized, 1969; s. William and Catherine (O'Reilly) O'C.; m. Josephine Mary Buckley, Aug. 3, 1963; children: Adrienne, Fiona, Eimear. B.Sc., Nat. U. Ireland, 1953; D.Sc., Nat. U. Reland, 1975; Ph.D., U. Notre Dame, 1962. Scholar Inst. Advanced Studies, Dublin, 1962-64; asst. prof., then assoc. prof. La. State U., Baton Rouge, 1964-69, prof. physics, 1969—. Contbr. articles on theoretical atomic, condensed-matter gravitation to profl. publs. Recipient Sir J.J. Larmor prize in physics, 1953; named Disting. Research Master La. State U., 1975. Fellow Am. Phys. Soc.; mem. Internat. Astron. Union, Am. Astron. Soc., Gen. Relativity and Gravitation Soc. Current Work: Two-dimensional systems; high Rydberg states; statistical mechanics. Subspecialty: Condensed matter physics. Home: 522 Bancroft Way Baton Rouge LA 70808 Office: Dept Physics La State U Baton Rouge LA 70803

O'CONNOR, DANIEL THOMAS, JR., physician; b. Chgo., Oct. 31, 1948; s. Daniel Thomas and Catherine Ann (Dougherty) O'C.; m. Kellie Elaina Evans, Nov. 7. 1981. B.S., Loyola U., Los Angeles, 1970; M.D., U. Calif.-Davis, 1974. Diplomate Am. Bd. Internal Medicine, Intern, U. Calif.-San Diego, 1974-75, resident in internal medicine, 1975, fellow in nephrology/hypertension, 1976-79, asst. prof. medicine 1979—; chief hypertension VA Med. Ctr., San Diego, 1979—. Contbr. articles or profl. jours. Established investigator Am. Heart Assn., 1983—. Fellow Am. Heart Assn. (Council for High Blood Pressure Research); mem. Am. Physiol. Soc., Am. Soc. Neprology, Western Soc. Clin. Investigation. Current work: Chromogranin A; hypertension. Subspecialties: Nephrology; Biochemistry (medicine). Office: Div Nephrology-Hypertension V-III-H Veterans Administration Medical Ctr San Diego CA 92161

O'CONNOR, G(EORGE) RICHARD, ophthalmologist; b. Cin., Oct. 8, 1928; s. George Leo and Sylvia Johanna (Voss) O'C. A.B., Harvard U., 1950; M.D., Columbia U., 1954. Resident in ophthalmology Columbia-Presbyn. Med. Center, N.Y.C., 1957-60; research fellow Inst. Biochemistry, U. Uppsala, Sweden, 1960-61, State Serum Inst., Copenhagen, 1961-62; asst. prof. ophthalmology U. Calif., San Francisco, 1962-68, prof., 1972—; dir. Francis I. Proctor Found. for Research in Ophthalmology, 1970-84; mem. Nat. Adv. Eye Council NIH, 1974-78. Author: (with G. Smolin) Ocular Immunology, 1981; assoc. editor: Am. Jour. Ophthalmology, 1976-84. Served with USPHS, 1955-57. Recipient Janeway prize Coll. of Physicians and Surgeons, Columbia U., 1954; NIH grantee, 1962-81; Doyne medal Oxford Ophthal. Congress, 1984. Mem. Am. Bd. Ophthalmology (examiner), Assn. for Research in Vision and Ophthalmology (trustee 1979-84), AMA, Am. Ophthal. Soc., Calif. Med. Assn., Frederic C. Cordes Eye Soc., Pan Am. Ophthal. Assn. Republican. Presbyterian. Club: Faculty. Subspecialties: Ophthalmology; Infectious diseases. Home: 22 Wray Ave Sausalito CA 94965

O'CONNOR, HOWARD GRANT, hydrogeologist, consultant; b. Kansas City, Kans., Mar. 14, 1923; s. Grant and Elizabeth (Poulsen) O.; m. Virginia Ruth Wollenberg, Sept. 10, 1945; children—Robert Milton, Peggy Elise. B.S. in Geology, Kans. State U., 1947; M.S. in Geology, U. Kans., 1959. Geologist, Kans. Geol. Survey, U. Kans., Lawrence, 1947-75, chief groundwater sect., 1975-77, sr. geologist groundwater sect., 1977—; hydrogeologist Applied Hydrogeology Assocs., Lawrence, 1984—. Contbr. articles to profl. jours. Served with U.S. Army, 1944-46, ETO. Mem. Geol. Soc. Am., Am. Assn. Petroleum Geologists, Assn. Engring. Geologists (editorial bd.), Nat. Water Well Assn. Republican. Current work: Groundwater, surface water, quality of water interactions; hydrogeology, groundwater pollution studies, well design. Subspecialties: Geology; Hydrology. Home: 1910 Melholland Rd Lawrence KS 66044 Office: Kans Geol Survey Univ Kans 1930 Constant Ave Lawrence KS 66044

O'CONNOR, TIMOTHY E., biomedical scientist; b. Cork, Ireland, Dec. 5, 1925; came to U.S., 1950; s. Edmond Francis and Josephine O. (Manning) O'C.; m. Elizabeth L. Clifford; children—Kevin, Kathleen, Clifford, Ruth, Eilleen, Carol. B.S., Nat. U. Ireland, 1947, M.S., 1948, Ph.D., 1951. Chemist, E.I. du Pont and Co., Wilmington, Del., 1952-61; spl. fellow Nat. Cancer Inst., Bethesda, Md., 1961-64, staff mem., 1964-75; sr. biologist Argonna Nat. Lab., Ill., 1975-81; prof. U. Chgo., 1976-81; assoc. dir. sci. affairs Roswell Park Meml. Inst., Buffalo, 1981—; research prof. biochemistry SUNY-Buffalo, 1983—; mem. nat. med. sci. bd. Leukemia Soc. Am., 1970-73. Author book chpt., research papers. Editor: Oncogenes and Retroviruses (Liss), 1983. Mem. Am. Assn. Cancer Research, AAAS, Am. Chem. Soc. Research or work interests: Administration of biomedical research; molecular biology and immunology; biotechnology. Subspecialties: Cancer research (medicine); Biochemistry (biology). Office: Roswell Park Meml Inst 666 Elm St Buffalo NY 14263

ODELL, ANDREW PAUL, astronomer; b. Galesburg, Ill., May 6, 1949; s. Athol F. and Mary Louise (Lagomarcino) O. B.A. in Physics and Astronomy, U. Iowa, 1970; Ph.D. in Astronomy, U. Wis., 1974. Asst. prof. U. No. Iowa, Cedar Falls, 1974-79; reaearch assoc. Lunar and Planetary Lab., Steward Obs., U. Ariz., Tucson, 1979-81; asst. prof. physics and astronomy No. Ariz. U., Flagstaff, 1981-85; assoc. prof. astronomy Universitäts-Sternwarte, U. Vienna, 1985—; researcher radiation transfer in planetary atmospheres, stellar evolution, pulsating stars. Mem. Am. Astron. Soc., AAAS., Internat. Astron. Union. Current Work: Physics and astronomy education, pulsating star research. Subspecialties: Theoretical astrophysics; Optical astronomy. Office: Universitäts-Sternwarte U Vienna Vienna Türkenschanzstrasse 17 Vienna A-1180 Australia

O'DELL, BOYD LEE, biochemistry educator; b. Hale, Mo., Oct. 14, 1916; s. Orvis Isaac and Flossie (Hoover) O'D.; m. Vera Louise Stone, Dec. 2, 1944; children—Ann Louise, David Lee. A.B., U. Mo.-Columbia, 1940, M.S., 1940, Ph.D., 1943. Sr. chemist Parke Davis & Co., Detroit, 1943-46; mem. faculty U. Mo.-Columbia, 1946—, assoc. prof. biochemistry, 1950-54, prof., 1955—. Mem. editorial bd. Jour. Nutrition, 1965-69, Physiol. Rev., 1979-84, Ann. Rev. Nutrition, 1981-85, Procs. Soc. Explt. Biol. Medicine, 1980—. Contbr. articles to profl. jours. Mem. Am. Soc. Biol. Chemistry, Am. Inst. Nutrition (pres. 1969, Borden award 1980), Soc. Exptl. Biology and Medicine, Sigma Xi. Current work: Roles of copper and zinc in nutrition and metabolism; bioavailability of trace elements. Subspecialties: Animal nutrition; Nutrition (medicine). Office: Dept Biochemistry U Mo Columbia MO 65211

ODEND'HAL, STEWART, veterinary medicine educator, researcher; b. San Diego, Mar. 25, 1937; s. Charles Joseph Odend'hal Jr. and Eloise (Stewart) Odend'hal Fulmer; m. Gail Sherlock, Sept. 22, 1960 (div. 1964); 1 child, Philip; m. Lin McNickle, June 25, 1977. Student U. of South, 1955-57; B.A., UCLA, 1960; D.V.M., U. Calif.-Davis, 1967; Ph.D., U. Mo., 1977. Lic. veterinarian, Calif. Asst. prof. Johns Hopkins U., Balt., 1967-71; research veterinarian Pfizer, Inc., Terra Haute, Ind., 1971-73; research assoc. U. Mo., Columbia, 1973-77; assoc. prof. Coll. Vet. Medicine, U. Ga., Athens, 1978—. Author: Geographic Distribution of Animal Viral Diseases, 1983; also articles. Pres. Central Mo. Humane Soc., 1976; treas. Unitarian-Universalist Ch., Athens, 1981; pres. Soc. Internat. Devel., Athens, 1982. Mem. Am. Assn. Vet. Anatomists, Soc. Internat. Devel. (citation 1983), Sigma Xi, Phi Zeta. Unitarian. Current work: Anatomy of the immune system and veterinary medicine in the developing countries. Subspecialties: Anatomy and embryology; Preventive medicine (veterinary medicine). Home: 1290 Colliers Creek Rd Watkinsville GA 30677 Office: Coll Vet Medicine U Ga Athens GA 30602

ODENWALD, STEN FELIX, JR., astronomer, researcher; b. Karlskoga, Sweden, Nov. 23, 1952; came to U.S., 1955, naturalized, 1973; s. Sten Felix and Rosa (Juhlin) O.; m. Susan Clermont, June 27, 1981. A.B., U. Calif.-Berkeley, 1975; A.M., Harvard U., 1976, Ph.D., 1982. Teaching fellow Harvard U., Cambridge, Mass., 1976-82, research fellow, 1976-81; astronomer Smithsonian Inst., Cambridge, 1981-82; research physicist Sachs/Freeman Assocs., Bowie, Md., 1982-84; astrophysicist Naval Research Lab., Washington, 1984—; sci. cons. Prentice-Hall Inc., Englewood Cliffs, N.J., 1978-84. Contbr. articles to profl. jours. Fellow Am. Astron. Soc.; mem. Planetary Soc. Democrat. Lutheran. Current work: Far infrared emission from star forming regions in our galaxy and in extragalactic objects; physics of early universe; history of modern physics; popularization of advanced science topics. Subspecialties: Infrared astronomy; Radio and microwave astronomy. Office: Naval Research Lab Code 4138-O Washington DC 20375

ODOM, JAMES VERNON, exptl. psychologist; b. Laurinburg, N.C., Aug. 26, 1948; s. James Calvin and Elizabeth Edna (Norton) O. Student, U. Montpellier, France, 1968-69, Goethe Institut, Radolfzell, W.Ger., summer 1969; A.B. in Psychology (Whitaker scholar 1966, Guttman scholar 1968, Dane scholar 1969), Davidson Coll, 1970; M.A. in Psychology, U. N.C., Greensboro, 1974, Ph.D. in Psychology, 1978. Adminstrv. asst., coordinator counselling services Consult Ed., Inc., Greensboro, 1970-71; research asst. U. N.C., Greensboro, 1971-75; instr. U. N.C. (Office Continuing Edn.), 1975-76, Guilford Coll., 1975; fellow Ctr. Creative Leadership, Greensboro, summer 1975, research asst., 1975-77; instr. N.C. Agrl. and Tech. State U., fall 1977; research assoc. Case Western Res. U., 1978-79; Nat. Research Service research fellow U. Calif., Berkeley, 1979-80; Nat. Research Service research fellow U. Fla., 1980-81, asst. research scientist, 1981-82; asst. prof. W. Va. U., Morgantown, 1982—; vis. fellow U. Calif., San Francisco, 1979-80. Contbr. chpt., articles to profl. publs.; author profl. papers. NIH grantee, 1981. Mem. Acad. Mgmt., AAAS, Am. Psychol. Assn., Assn. Research in Vision and Ophthalmology, N.Y. Acad. Scis., Soc. Neurosci., Soc. Research in Child Devel., Internat. Soc. Clin. Electrophysiology in Vision, Optical Soc. Am., Sigma Xi. Democrat. Current Work: Research on use of electrophysiological and psychophysiological methods to investigate normal and abnormal development of human visual functions, especially binocularity. Subspecialties: Psychophysiology; Sensory processes. Home: 416 Grant Ave Morgantown WV 26505 Office: Dept Ophthalmology W Va Med Ctr Morgantown WA 25606

O'DONNELL, TERENCE JOHN, chemist; b. Chgo., Nov. 13, 1951; s. Edward S. O'Donnell and Dolores (Haisler) O'Donnell Bakjian. B.S., U. Ill.-Chgo., 1973, M.S., 1976, Ph.D., 1980; postgrad. U. Marburg, Fed. Republic Germany, 1976. Postdoctoral fellow Nat. Resource Computation Chemistry, Berkeley, Calif., 1980-82; sr. theoretical chemist Abbott Labs., Ill., 1982—. Contbr. articles to profl. jours. Alfred P. Sloan Found. fellow, 1973, 74; German Acad. Exchange Service fellow, 1976. Mem. Am. Chem. Soc., AAAS, Sigma Xi. Current work: Application of computational chemistry to mechanism of drug action for drug design; uses of computer graphics in chemistry. Subspecialties: Drug design; Theoretical chemistry. Office: Abbott Labs D-47E Abbott Park IL 60064

O'DONOGHUE, JOHN (LIPOMI), pathologist, toxicologist, neuroscientist; b. Lowell, Mass., Apr. 12, 1947; s. James Gregory and Sarafina Frances (Lipomi) O'D.; m. Sandra G. Piekos, June 24, 1967; children: Shawn Michael, Bevin Ruth. Student, U. Mass.-Amherst, 1964-66; V.M.D., U. Pa., 1970, Ph.D., 1979. Cert. Am. Bd. Toxicology. Pathologist Eastman Kodak Co., Rochester, N.Y., 1974-79; pathology group leader Health and Environ. Lab., Eastman Kodak Co., 1979—; asst. prof lab. animal medicine U. Rochester, 1975—, asst. prof. toxicology, 1982—. Editor: Neurotoxicity of Industrial and Commercial Chemicals, 1985. Contbr. chpts. to books, articles to profl. publs. Leader Otetiana council Boy Scouts Am. Student research fellow, 1967; USPHS fellow, 1970; recipient Elks scholarship award, 1964, Phi Zeta award, 1970, Sigma Xi award, 1970. Mem. AVMA, AAAS, Am. Assn. Neuropathologists, Electron Microscopy Soc. Am. Roman Catholic. Current Work: Research on neurotoxicology and neuropathology of industrial chemicals. Subspecialties: Pathology (medicine); Toxicology (medicine). Home: 3915 Clover St Honeoye Falls NY 14472 Office: Eastman Kodak Co B320 Kodak Park Rochester NY 14650

O'DONOVAN, PATRICK ALEXANDER, research chemist, educator; b. Portland, Oreg., Nov. 19, 1927; s. John and Jean (Munro) O'D.; m. Elisa Castaneda, Nov. 18, 1961; children—John, Patrick, Michael, Colin, Terence, Bernard, Timothy, Brigette. B.S., U. Portland, 1950, M.S., 1951; postgrad U. Fla., 1952. Research chemist Am. Potash & Chem. Co., Whittier, Calif., 1952-53, Nutrilite Product Co., Buena Park, Calif., 1954-59; sr. chemistry specialist Aerojet Ordnance Co., Tustin, Calif., 1959—. Contbr. numerous articles to profl. jours. Served with U.S. Army, 1946-52. Mem. Am. Chem. Soc. Current work: Chemical phytotoxicity, chemical transport in soil, chemical energy conversion, analysis of high energy materials. Subspecialties: Physical chemistry; Analytical chemistry. Office: Aerojet Ordnance Co Route 4 Box 454 E Chino CA 91709

OECHEL, WALTER CLARENCE, biology educator; b. San Diego, Jan. 15, 1945; s. Walter C. and Gloria Dawn (Gordon) O.; m. Judith Lynne Riley, July 23, 1967. A.B., San Diego State U., 1966; Ph.D., U. Calif.-Riverside, 1970. Asst. prof. McGill U., Montreal, Que., Can., 1970-75, assoc. prof., 1975-79; research prof. San Diego State U., 1979-81, prof. biology, 1981—, also dir. systems ecology research group. Contbr. articles to profl. jours. Prin. investigator research NSF, 1981—, Dept. Energy, 1981—. Mem. AAAS, Ecol. Soc. Am. (chmn. physiol. ecol. sect. 1984), Sigma Xi. Current work: Effects of elevated atmospheric CO2 on functioning of natural ecosystems; research understanding Arctic and Mediterranean ecosystems. Subspecialties: Ecosystems analysis; Plant physiology (biology). Home: 6429 Gem Lake San Diego CA 92119 Office: Systems Ecology Research Group San Diego State Univ San Diego CA 92182

OEHME, REINHARD, physicist, educator; b. Wiesbaden, Germany, Jan. 26, 1928; came to U.S., 1956; s. Reinhold and Katharina (Kraus) O.; m. Mafalda Pisani, Nov. 5, 1952. Diploma Physiker, U. Frankfurt am Main, 1948; Dr. rer. nat., Goettingen, 1951. Asst., Max Planck Inst. fur Physik, Goettingen, 1949-53; research assoc. Fermi Inst. for Nuclear Studies, U. Chgo., 1953-56, asst. prof. dept. physics and Enrico Fermi Inst., 1958-60, assoc. prof., 1960-64, prof., 1964—; mem. Inst. for Advanced Studies, Princeton, N.J., 1956-58; vis. prof. U. Vienna, 1961, Imperial Coll., London, 1963-64, U. Karlsruhe, 1974, 75, 77, U. Tokyo, 1976, also others. Contbr. articles to physics jours., chpt. to books. Recipient Humboldt award, 1974; Guggenheim Found. fellow, 1963-64. Fellow Am. Phys. Soc. Current work: Quantum field theory, fundamental particles. Subspecialties: Particle physics; Theoretical physics. Office: Enrico Fermi Inst U Chicago 5630 Ellis Ave Chicago IL 60637

OELFKE, WILLIAM CLARENCE, physics educator, research physicist; b. Kansas City, Mo., May 28, 1941; s. Floyd Lester and Esther Marie (Horstman) O.; m. Sheila Marie Ryan, Oct. 3, 1964; children—Christina Marie, Steven William. B.S., Stanford U., 1963; Ph.D., Duke U., 1969. Research assoc. Duke U., Durham, N.C., 1968-69; prof. physics U. Central Fla., Orlando, 1969—, chmn. physics dept., 1984—, dir. optics inst., 1984—; vis. prof. Dartmouth Coll., Hanover, N.H., 1984. Served to 1st lt. U.S. Army, 1963-65. Recipient Joseph H. Defrees award Research Corp. 1980, Precision Measurement award Nat. Bur. Standards 1981. Named Researcher of Year U. Central Fla. 1982. Mem. Am. Phys. Soc., Am. Assn. Physics Tchrs., AAAS, Optical Soc. Am. Democrat. Presbyterian. Current work: Experimental gravitation, quantum non demolition measurements and squeezed states in lasers, quantum optics. Subspecialties: Laser spectroscopy; Relativity and gravitation. Home: 2319 Huron Trail Maitland FL 32751 Office: U Central Fla Physics Dept Orlando FL 32816

OELTMANN, THOMAS NAPIER, biochemist, educator; b. Covington, Ky., Dec. 28, 1941; s. Jerome Francis and Anna Mae (Napier) O.; m. Margaret Ann Turner, Aug. 26, 1965; children: Tim, John Ethan, Andrew Napier. Ph.D., U. Ga., 1967. Research asst. prof. U. Pitts., 1974-76; sr. research assoc. U. Iowa, Iowa City, 1976-79; asst. prof. medicine, research asst., prof. biochemistry Vanderbilt U. Med. Ctr., Nashville, 1979—. Contbr. articles to profl. jours. Served to capt., Chem, Corps U.S. Army, 1967-69. NIH grantee. Mem. AAAS, Am. Assn. for Cancer Research, Complex Carbohydrate Soc., Am. Chem. Soc., Am. Soc. Biol. Chemists, Am. Assn. Immunologists, N.Y. Acad. Scis., Cancer Center Task Force on Immunology. Roman Catholic. Current Work: Biochemistry of hybrid proteins and their applications to cell biology, tumor biology, and cancer research. Subspecialties: Biochemistry (biology); Molecular biology. Home: 158 Cottonwood Dr Franklin TN 37064 Office: Dept Medicine Div Oncolog Vanderbilt U Med Center Nashville TN 37232

OESTERWINTER, CLAUS, research astronomer; b. Hamburg, Germany, Jan. 18, 1928; s. Franz and Katharina (Boediger) O.; m. Ursula (Eckelmann); children: Angelica, Cary. M.S., Yale U., 1964, Ph.D., 1965. Research astronomer Naval Surface Weapons Ctr., Dahlgren, Va., 1959—. Mem. Am. Astron. Soc., Internat. Astron. Union. Current Work: Orbital motion of planets, natural and artificial satellites. Subspecialties: Celestial mechanics; Astronautics. Home: PO Box 431 Dahlgren VA 22448 Office: Naval Surface Weapons Ctr Code K10 Dahlgren VA 22448

OESWEIN, JAMES QUENTIN, pharmaceutical chemist; b. Louisville, Nov. 20, 1951; s. George Joseph and Evelyn Virginia (Thomas) O.; m. Rebecca Lane Reed, Sept. 10, 1977; children—Alyssa Lane, James Thomas. A.A., Jefferson Community Coll.; B.S., U. Ky.; Ph.D., U. Fla. Grad. teaching asst. U. Fla., Gainesville, 1977-82; sr. pharm. chemist Eli Lilly & Co., Indpls., 1982—. Contbr. articles to profl. jours. Served to sgt. U.S. Army, 1971-73. AAUP scholar, 1974. Mem. Am. Chem. Soc., AAAS. Current work: Effects of formulation components on physicochemical properties of human and pork insulins; analysis of protein self association and tertiary structural changes. Subspecialty: Biophysical chemistry. Home: 3919 N Mitthoeffer Rd Indianapolis IN 46236 Office: Lilly Research Labs 307 McCarty St Dept MC 741 Bldg 28/2 Indianapolis IN 46285

OETTGEN, HERBERT F., physician; b. Cologne, Germany, Nov. 22, 1923; came to U.S., 1958; s. Peter and Minna (Kaul) O.; m. Gertrud Hesberg, Feb. 16, 1957; children: Hans Christoph, Joerg Peter, Anne Barbara. M.D., U. Cologne, 1951. Intern U. Cologne, 1951, resident, 1952-54, 55-58, U. Marburg, Germany, 1954-55; mem. Sloan-Kettering Inst., 1958—; attending physician Meml. Hosp., N.Y.C., 1967—; prof. medicine and biology Cornell U., N.Y.C., 1966—. Contbr. articles to profl. jours. Served with German Navy, 1942-45. Recipient Wilhelm Warner award for cancer research, 1970; Lisec-Artz award for cancer research, 1982; NIH grantee; Am. Cancer Soc. grantee; other grants. Mem. Am. Assn. Cancer Research, Am. Soc. Clin. Oncology, Am. Soc. Hematology, Am. Assn. Immunologists, ACP, Harvey Soc., Internat. Soc. Hematology, Am. Fedn. Clin. Research. Presbyterian. Current Work: Cancer research, cancer immunology, cancer therapy, cancer medicine. Research in biological approaches to cancer therapy—vaccines, monoclonal antibodies, lymphokines, differentiating proteins. Subspecialties: Oncology; Cancer research (medicine). Home: 48 Overlook Dr New Canaan CT 06840 Office: 1275 York Ave New York NY 10021

OETTINGER, ANTHONY GERVIN, educator, mathematician; b. Nuremberg, Germany, Mar. 29, 1929; came to U.S., 1941, naturalized, 1947; s. Albert and Marguerite (Bing) O.; m. Marilyn Tanner, June 20, 1954; children: Douglas, Marjorie. A.B., Harvard U., 1951, Ph.D., 1954; Henry fellow, U. Cambridge, Eng., 1951-52; D.Litt. (hon.), U. Pitts., 1984. Mem. faculty Harvard, 1955—, asso. prof. applied math., 1960-63, prof. linguistics, 1963-75, Gordon McKay prof. applied math., 1963—, chmn. program on info. resources policy, 1972—, mem. faculty of govt., 1973—, prof. info. resources policy, 1975—; mem. command control communications and intelligence bd. Dept. Navy, 1978-83; mem. sci. adv. group Def. Communications Agy., 1979—; cons. Arthur D. Little, Inc., 1956-80, Office Sci. and Tech., Exec. Office of Pres., 1960-73, Bellcomm, Inc., 1963-68, Systems Devel. Corp., 1965-68, Nat. Security Council, Exec. Office of Pres., 1975-81, Pres.'s Fgn. Intelligence Adv. Bd., 1981—; chmn. Computer Sci. and Engring. Bd., Nat. Acad. Scis., 1968-73; commr. Mass. Community Antenna TV Commn., 1972-79, chmn., 1975-79; mem. research adv. bd. Com. for Econ. Devel., 1975-79. Author: A Study for the Design of an Automatic Dictionary, 1954, Automatic Language Translation: Lexical and Technical Aspects, 1960, Run Computer Run: The Mythology of Educational Innovation, 1969, High and Low Politics: Information Resources for the 80s, 1977; Editor: Proc. of a Symposium on Digital Computers and Their Applications, 1962. Fellow Am. Acad. Arts and Scis., AAAS, IEEE; mem. Assn. Computing Machinery (mem. council 1961-68, chmn. com. U.S. Govt. relations 1964-66, editor computational linguisitics sect. Communications 1964-66, pres. 1966-68), Soc. Indsl. and Applied Math. (mem. council 1963-67), Council on Fgn. Relations, Phi Beta Kappa, Sigma Xi. Clubs: Cosmos (Washington); Harvard (N.Y.C.). Subspecialties: Automated language processing; Information resources policy. Home: 65 Elizabeth Rd Belmont MA 02178 Office: 33 Oxford St Cambridge MA 02138

O'FARRELL, TIMOTHY JAMES, clinical psychologist, educator; b. Lancaster, Ohio, Apr. 22, 1946; s. Robert James and Helen Loretta (Tooill) O'F.; m. Jayne Sara Tlamage, May 19, 1973; 1 son, Colin. B.A., U. Notre Dame, 1968; M.A., Boston U., 1969, Ph.D., 1975. Diplomate: in clin. psychology Am. Bd. Profl. Psychology, Internat. Acad. Profl. Counseling & Psychotherapy. Mem. psychol. staff Boston City Hosp., 1974-75; mem. psychol. staff VA Med. Center, Brockton, Mass., 1975-77, chief alcoholism clinic, 1978-83, chief alcohol and family studies, 1981—; adj. assoc. prof. Boston State Coll., 1974-77; instr. psychology Harvard Med. Sch., Cambridge, Mass., 1977-82, asst. prof. psychology, 1982—. Contbr. chpts. to books and articles in field to profl. jours. Boston U. research grantee, 1974; VA med. research grantee, 1978, 81; Ayerest Labs. research grantee, 1981. Fellow Mass. Psychol. Assn., Behavior Therapy & Research Soc.; mem. Am. Psychol. Assn., Assn. Advancement Behavior Therapy, Eastern Psychol. Assn., AAAS, Am. Assn. Sex Educators, Counselors & Therapists. Current work: Development and evaluation of marital therapies for alcoholics; research on characteristics of marriages and families of alcoholics; alcoholism treatment outcome evaluation. Subspecialty: Behavioral psychology. Home: 260 High St Duxbury MA 02332 Office: VA Med Ctr 116B 940 Belmont St Brockton MA 02401

OFFENBACHER, STEVEN, periodontist, researcher; b. Dayton, Ohio, Dec. 26, 1950; s. George Earl and Shirley Ann (Campbell) O. B.A. in Chemistry, Boston U., 1972; D.D.S., Va. Commonwealth U., 1976, Ph.D. in Biochemistry, 1977; M.M.S. in Oral Biology, Harvard Med. Sch., 1980. Instr. dept. biochemistry Med. Coll. Va., 1976-77; research fellow in periodontology Harvard U. Sch. Dental Medicine, 1977-80; asst. prof. periodontology Emory U. Sch. Dentistry, 1980-81, asst. prof. biochemistry, 1980—, chmn. dept. periodontology, 1981—, dir. Periodental Research Ctr., 1981—; guest researcher Anaerobic Microbiology Lab., Ctrs. for Disease Control, 1984—. Contbr. numerous articles to profl. jours. Mem. Va. Acad. Sci., Am. Assn. Dental Research, Internat. Assn. Dental Research, Am. Acad. Periodontology, Ga. Soc. Periodontology, Delta Sigma Delta. Current work: Biochemistry of inflammation and bone destruction; prostaglandins. Subspecialties: Periodontics; Biochemistry (medicine). Office: Dept Periodontology Emory Dental Sch 1462 Clifton Rd NE Atlanta GA 30322

OFFICER, CHARLES B., geoscientist. Research prof. dept. earth scis. Dartmouth Coll., Hanover, N.H. Office: Dartmouth Coll Dept Earth Scis Hanover NH 03755

OFFNER, ABE, optical scientist; b. N.Y.C.; s. Harry David and Gussie (Arnovsky) O.; m. Rose Ornstein, 1935 (dec. 1940); m. Lillian Bachman, Nov. 19, 1941; children—Carl David, Bonnie Ann. A.B., Western Res. U., 1930, M.A., 1931, B.S.L.S., 1935. Library asst. Cleve. Pub. Library, 1931-37; physicist J.A. Maurer Inc., L.I., N.Y., 1937-47; sr. scientist Perkin-Elmer Corp., Wilton, Conn., 1947—. Author: (with others) Optical Shop Testing, 1978. Author numerous tech. and sci. papers. Patentee in field. Recipient Semmy award Semiconductor Equipment & Materials Inst. 1979, Achievement award Electronics Mag., 1980, Cledo Brunetti award IEEE 1983, Dennis Gabor award Soc. Photo-Optical Instrumentation Engr. 1984. Fellow Optical Soc. Am. (David Richardson medal 1981). Democrat. Jewish. Current work: Advanced optical systems for projection aligners used in the manufacture of very large sc integrated circuits. Home: 100 Leeuwarden Rd Darien CT 06820 Office: Perkin-Elmer Corp 50 Danbury Rd Wilton CT 06897

OGATA, KATSUHIKO, engineering educator; b. Tokyo, Jan. 6, 1925; came to U.S., 1952; s. Fukuhei and Teruko (Yasaki) O.; m. Asako Nakamura, Sept. 6, 1961; 1 child, Takahiko. B.S.M.E., U. Tokyo, 1947; M.S.M.E., U. Ill., 1953; Ph.D. in Engring. Sci., U. Calif.-Berkeley, 1956. Research asst. Sci. Research Inst., Tokyo, 1948-51; fuel engr. Nippon Steel Tube Co., Tokyo, 1951-52; asst. prof. U. Minn., Mpls., 1956-58, assoc. prof., 1958-60, prof., 1961—; prof. Yokohama Nat. U., Japan, 1960-61, 64-65, 68-69. Author: State Space Analysis of Control Systems, 1967; Modern Control Engineering, 1970; Dynamic Programming, 1973; System Dynamics, 1978. Recipient Outstanding Adv. award Inst. Tech., U. Minn., 1981. Mem. ASME, Sigma Xi, Pi Tau Sigma. Current work: Digital control systems; optimization techniques, robotics. Subspecialty: Robotics. Home: 1002 Kurone Bunkyo 2-23-12 Kasuga Bunkyo-ku Tokyo Japan Office: Dept Mech Engring U Minn Minneapolis MN 55455

OGAWA, JOSEPH MINORU, plant pathology, educator; b. Sanger, Calif., Apr. 24, 1925; s. Joseph Shosaku and Naomi (Yamaka) O.; m. Margie Hiroko Kawasaki, Nov. 7, 1954; children: Julie M., Martin K., Jo Ann. B.S., U. Calif.-Davis, 1950, Ph.D., 1954. Mem. faculty U. Calif.-Davis, 1953—, prof. plant pathology, 1968—, vice chmn., 1984—. Author: (with E.E. Wilson) Fungal Bacterial and Certain Nonparasitic Diseases of Fruit and Nut Crops in California, 1979; contbr. over 100 articles to profl. jours. Served with C.I.C. U.S. Army, 1945-46. Recipient plaques Calif. Freezer's Assn., 1962, San Joaquin Cherry Growers and Industries Found., 1972, Calif. Pistachio Commn., 1985. Mem. Am. Phytopathol. Soc. (pres., v.p. councilor Pacific div.), Calif. Aggie Alumni Assn (treas. 1953-68), Sigma Xi (sec., pres. U. Calif.-Davis chpt.). Democrat. Methodist. Club: Commonwealth (San Francisco). Current Work: Plant pathology, epidemiology and disease control, research on fruit and nut disease, postharvest diseases, fungicides, also tomato and hop diseases. Subspecialties: Plant pathology; Integrated pest management. Home: 806 Linden Ln Davis CA 95616 Office: Dept Plant Pathology U Calif Davis CA 95616

OGDEN, ROGER WAYNE, analytic chemist, researcher; b. Covington, Va., Apr. 9, 1946; s. Howard Raymond and Hazel Christine (Stinnett) O.; m. Dreama Carol Loudermilk, Sept. 3, 1976. Student N.C. State U., 1964-66; A.S. in Engring., Va. Western Coll., 1971; B.S. in Chemistry, Va. Poly. Inst. and State U., 1972, M.S. in Chemistry, 1974-75. Chemistry educator Covington City Schs., Va., 1972-74; sr. chemist research Westvaco Corp., Covington, 1974—. Com. mem. City Planning Commn., Covington, 1974-75. Served with U.S. Army, 1966-69, Vietnam. Pulp and Paper Found. scholar, 1964-66. Mem. Am. Chem. Soc., Am. Inst. Chemists (cert.), TAPPI (chem. methods, pulp testing coms.), Am. Forestry Assn. Republican. Associate Reformed Presbyterian. Club: Civitan (pres., v.p., sec.) (Covington). Subspecialties: Analytical chemistry; Pulp and paper engineering. Home: Route 5 Box 159 Intervale Covington VA 24426 Office: Westvaco Corp Research Ctr Covington VA 24426

OGILVIE, KELVIN K., chemistry educator; b. Windsor, N.S., Can., Nov. 6, 1942. B.Sc., Acadia U., N.S., 1963, B.Sc. in chemistry with honors, 1964; Ph.D., Northwestern U., 1968; Sc.D. (hon.), Acadia U., 1983. Asst. prof. chemistry U. Man., Winnipeg, 1968-72, assoc. prof., 1972-74; assoc. prof. McGill U., Montreal, Que., Can., 1974-78, prof., 1978—, Can. Pacific prof. biotechnology, 1984—, dir. office of biotechnology, 1984—. Contbr. articles to profl. jours. Patentee in field. Decorated Knight of Malta, Sovereign Order of St. John of Jerusalem, 1985; E.W.R. Steacie Meml. fellow, 1982-84; Upjohn fellow, 1974-76. Mem. AAAS, Ordre des Chimestes du Que., Chem. Inst. Can. (treas. 1971-72, chmn. 1973-74, fellow, 1977), Am. Chem. Soc. (Buck-Whitney medal 1983), Assn. Can.-francaise pour l'avancement des sciences. Current work: the chemical synthesis of a transfer RNA; the development of new methods for the synthesis, separation and identification of oligonucleotides; synthesis of analogues of necleic acids: a) antiviral compounds; b) anticancer agents; development of versatile protecting groups in organic syntheses. Subspecialty: Synthetic chemistry. Office: Office of biotechnology McGill U 853 Sherbrooke West Montreal PQ H2A 2T6 Canada

OGILVIE, RICHARD IAN, clinical pharmacologist; b. Sudbury, Ont., Can., Oct. 9, 1936; s. Patrick Ian and Gena Hilda (Olson) O.; m. Ernestine Tahedl, Oct. 9, 1965; children—Degen Elisabeth, Lars Ian. M.D., U. Toronto, 1960. Intern Toronto (Ont.) Gen. Hosp., 1960-61; resident Montreal Gen. and Univ. Alta. hosps., 1962-66; fellow in clin. pharmacology McGill U., Montreal, 1966-68, asst. prof. medicine, pharmacology and therapeutics, 1968-73, asso. prof., 1973-78, prof., 1978—, chmn. dept. pharmacology and therapeutics, 1978-83; clin. pharmacologist Montreal Gen. Hosp., 1968—, dir. div. clin. pharmacology, 1976-83; prof. medicine and pharmacology U. Toronto, 1983—; dir. div. cardiology and clin. pharmacology Toronto Western Hosp., 1983—. Grantee Med. Research Council Can. Quebec Heart Found.; Grantee Med. Research Council Can. Can. Kidney Found.; Grantee Med. Research Council Can. J.C. Edwards Found.; Grantee Med. Research Council Can. Can. Found. Advancement Therapeutics; Grantee Med. Research Council Can. Conseil de la recherche en santé du Québec. Fellow Royal Coll. Physicians of Can., A.C.P.; mem. Can. Soc. Clin. Investigation (council 1977-80), Can. Hypertension Soc. (dir. 1979—), Can. Found. Advancement Clin. Pharmacology (dir. 1978—), Canadian Soc. for Clin. Pharmacology (pres. 1979-82), Internat. Union Pharmacology (council mem. clin. pharmacology sect. 1981—), Que. Heart Found. (pres. med. adv. com. 1976-81), Pharm. Soc. Can., Can. Cardiovascular Soc., Am. Soc. Pharmacology and Exptl. Therapeutics, Am. Soc. Clin. Pharm., Am. Fedn. Clin. Research. Current Work: Clinical pharmacology of drugs affecting Cardiovascular system. Subspecialty: Pharmacology. Home: 79 Collard Dr Rural Route 1 King City ON L0G 1K0 Canada Office: 399 Bathurst St Toronto ON M5T 2S8 Canada

OGLE, DALE FRANCIS, chemist; b. Council, Idaho, Oct. 10, 1944; s. Thomas Effington and Margret Irene (Williams) O.; m. Shirley Kathleen Walters, July 13, 1974; children—Tina Marie, Robert Thomas; 1 stepchild, Carmon Kae Sullivan. B.S. in Agrl. Biochemistry, U. Idaho, 1966. Chemist U.S. Bur. Reclamation, Boise, Idaho, 1967-70; farmer, Indian Valley, Idaho, 1970-72; farm chem. salesman Edwall Chem., Wash., 1972-73; chemist Utah & Idaho Sugar Co., Moses Lake, Wash., 1973-74, Alta Lipids, Boise, 1975-77; lab. supr. North Shore San. Dist., Gurnee, Ill., 1977—. Mem. Am. Chem. Soc., Lake Mich. Water Analysts, Water Pollution Control Fedn., Water Pollution Control Assn., Assn. Ofcl. Analytical Chemists, Alpha Zeta, Phi Sigma. Congregationalist. Lodge: Eagles. Current work: Analytical on-line monitoring instrumentation in sewage; biological nitrification in waste activated sewage treatment. Subspecialty: Water supply and wastewater treatment. Home: 40460 Savage Rd Antioch IL 60002 Office: North Shore San Dist PO Box 750 Russell Rd Gurnee IL 60031

OGLESBY, RAY THURMOND, aquatic scientist, educator; b. Lynchburg, Va., Apr. 16, 1932; s. William Sterrett and Sadie (Thurmond) O.; m. Graciela Rocha Gaytan, July 4, 1955 (div. 1981); m. Janice Marie Ricardo, Aug. 4, 1981. B.S., U. Richmond, 1953; M.A., Coll. William and Mary, Williamsburg, Va., 1955; Ph.D., U. N.C., 1962. Fish research scientist U.S. Fish and Wildlife Svc., Beaufort, N.C., 1958-59; from asst. to assoc. prof. U. Wash., Seattle, 1962-68; from assoc. to prof. aquatics Cornell U., Ithaca, N.Y., 1968—, chmn. dept., 1982—; mem. governing bd. N.Y. Sea Grant, Albany, N.Y., 1983—; cons. in field. Co-editor: River Ecology and Man, 1972. Contbr. chpts. to books. Served to lt. USNR, 1955-62. Grantee U.S. EPA, 1982, Fockefeller Found., 1975, U.S. Office Water Research and Tech., 1977, Monsanto Chem. Co., 1980. Mem. Am. Soc. Limnology and Oceanography, Am. Fisheries Soc., Ecol. Soc. Am. Current work: Productivity of inland waters with emphasis on water quality, fish production and trophic level interactions. Subspecialties: Resource management; Resource conservation. Home: 1882 Danby Rd Ithaca NY 14850 Office: Dept Natural Resources Cornell U Ithaca NY 14853

OGUZ, SUHA, physicist; b. Istanbul, Turkey, Feb. 10, 1954; came to U.S., 1976; s. Haluk Eyyup and Sevim Bulent (Polat) O. B.S. in Elec. Engring., Bogazici U., 1976; M.S. in Applied Physics, Harvard U., 1978, Ph.D. in Applied Physics, 1981. Postdoctoral research fellow div. applied sci. Harvard U., Cambridge, Mass., 1981-84; sr. scientist Raytheon Research Div., Lexington, Mass., 1984—. Contbr. articles to physics jours. Mem. Am. Phys. Soc. Current work: Research on narrow bandgap seminconductors, infrared detector arrays based on mercury cadmium telluride. Subspecialties: Condensed matter physics; Semiconductors. Home: 20 Hamilton Rd Arlington MA 02174 Office: Raytheon Research Div 131 Spring St Lexington MA 02173

OH, JUNG HEE, transplantation immunologist, nephrologist, educator; b. Hamhung, Korea, Aug. 16, 1925; came to U.S., 1978; s. Yae Mook and Jee Sun (Kang) O.; m. Soon Ok Kim, Dec. 19, 1959; children: Helen, Frederick, Kenneth, Christopher. M.D., Seoul (Korea) Nat. U., 1951; Ph.D., McGill U., Montreal, Que., Can., 1969. Intern Mt. Sinai Hosp., Mpls., 1956-57; resident in medicine and nephrology Highland Park Hosp., Receiving Hosp., Detroit, 1957-63; research fellow in nephrology and transplantation Royal Victoria Hosp., Montreal, Que., Can., 1963-69; asst. prof. exptl. medicine and surgery McGill U., 1969-78; assoc. prof. medicine Emory U., 1978—; dir. Transplantation Lab. Grady Meml. Hosp., Atlanta. Served with M.C. Republic of Korea Army, 1950-56. Mem. Transplantation Soc., Am. Assn. Clin. Histocompatibility Testing, Am. Soc. Nephrology, Am. Soc. Transplant Physicians. Current Work: Histocompatibility testing; induction of immunological tolerance. Subspecialties: Transplantation; Nephrology. Office: 80 Butler St SE Atlanta GA 30303

OH, WHA TAK, veterinarian; b. Kwong Phung, Mekok, Korea, June 14, 1929; came to Can., 1965; s. Kap Sook and Ok Jung Oh; m. Bock Nim Nam, Jan. 17, 1949; children—Sang Hok, Tae Boem, Tae Ho, Tae Jong. D.V.M., Seoul City Coll., 1960; M.S., Kyungbook U., 1962. Sr. research scientist Nat. Vet. Research Labs., An Yang, Korea, 1965; mgr. research and devel. K-Vet Ltd., Hespeler, Ont., Can., 1965-71; dir. tissue culture Sterwing Labs., Millsboro, Del., 1971-73, dir. biol. prodn., Opelika, Ala., 1977-81; dir. biol. prodn.

Vineland Labs., N.J., 1973-77, dir. sci. affairs, 1985—; dir. tissue culture Maine Biol. Labs., Waterville, 1982-84. Served to 2d lt. Republic of Korea Army, 1951. Mem. Tissue Culture Assn., AVMA, Am. Soc. Microbiology Am. Soc. Cryobiology. Home: 1890 Lincoln Ave Apt 67 Vineland NJ 08360

OH, WILLIAM, pediatrician, perinatal medicine researcher; b. Cagayan de Oro, Philippines, May 22, 1931; s. Bun Kun and Chay Suat (Lim) O.; m. Mary Q. Ang, June 4, 1960. M.D., U. Santo Tomas, Manila, 1958; M.A. (hon.), Brown U., 1974. Intern, Deaconess Hosp., Milw., 1958-59; resident Michael Reese Hosp., Chgo., 1959-62; asst. prof. pediatrics Chgo. Med. Sch., 1966-69; assoc. prof. pediatrics UCLA Sch. Medicine, 1969-73; prof. med. sci. in pediatrics and obstetrics Brown U., Providence, R.I., 1974—; dir. neonatology Michael Reese Hosp., Chgo., 1966-69, Harbor Gen. Hosp. Torrance, Calif., 1968-74; pediatrician-in-chief Women and Infants Hosp., Providence, 1974—. Contbr. numerous articles to med. jours. Mem. Am. Pediatric Soc., Soc. for Pediatric Research, Perinatal Research Soc. (pres. 1980), Am. Thoracic Soc. Democrat. Roman Catholic. Club: Univ. (Providence). Current work: Research in Diabetes during pregnancy and perinatal biology. Subspecialties: Pediatrics; Neonatology. Home: 24 Robbins Dr Barrington RI 02806 Office: Women and Infants Hosp RI 50 Maude St Providence RI 02908

O'HALLORAN, THOMAS A., physicist, educator; b. Bklyn., Apr. 13, 1931; s. Alphonsus and Nora (Sheehan) O'H.; m. Barbara Joyce Hug, June 9, 1954; children—Theresa Joyce, Maureen Ann, Kevin Thomas, Patrick Joseph. B.S., Oreg. State Coll., 1953, M.S., 1954; Ph.D., U. Calif.-Berkeley, 1963. Postdoctoral fellow Lawrence Berkeley Lab., Calif., 1963-64; research fellow Harvard U., Cambridge, Mass., 1964-66; prof. U. Ill., Urbana, 1966—. Contbr. articles to profl. jours. Served to lt. USN, 1954-58. Guggenheim Found. fellow, 1979-80. Fellow Am. Phys. Soc. Current work: Experimental research in area of elementary particle physics. Subspecialty: Particle physics. Home: 706 W Iowa St Urbana IL 61801 Office: Physics Dept U Ill 1110 W Green St Urbana IL 61801

O'HANDLEY, ROBERT CHARLES, materials scientist, research and educator; b. Seattle, May 6, 1942; s. John Grenville and Marie Elizabeth (Schermerhorn) O'H; m. Carol Ann Delaney, Aug. 30, 1969; children—Kevin Dergin, Meghan Elizabeth, Kara Justine. B.A. in Physics, Marist Coll., 1965; M.S. in Physics, Poly. Inst. Bklyn., 1969, Ph.D. in Physics, 1971. NRC postdoctoral, research assoc. Michelson Lab., China Lake, Calif., 1971-74; staff physicist Allied Chem. Corp./Materials Research Ctr., Morristown, N.J., 1974-78; research staff mem. T.J. Watson Research Ctr. IBM, Yorktown Heights, N.Y., 1978-80; prin. research scientist MIT, Cambridge, 1980—; cons. Magnetic Materials. Author: Amorphus Magnetic Alloys, 1986. Contbr. articles (75) to profl. jours. Patentee in field. Mem. Am. Physi. Soc., IEEE, Materials Research Soc., Fed. Am. Scientists, Am. Assn. of Physics Tchrs. Roman Catholic. Current work: Electronic structure and magnetic properties of metals alloys and oxides; non-crystalline materials; magnetoelastic properties. Subspecialties: Electronic materials; Condensed matter physics. Home: 3 Glenn Cove Andover MA 01810 Office: RC O'Handley 4-051 MIT Cambridge MA 02139

O'HARA, PATRICK FRANCIS, geologist, researcher; b. Jamaica, N.Y., Apr. 4, 1948; s. Patrick and Gertrude Marie (Wulff) O. B.A., Queens Coll., 1971, M.A., 1976; Ph.D., Ariz. State U., 1980. Lectr., research assoc. Queens Coll., Flushing, N.Y., 1972-76, Ariz. State U., Tempe, 1977-80; lectr. Baruch Coll., N.Y.C., 1974-77; geologist Wyo. Minerals Inc., Miami, Ariz., 1978-79, CONOCO Inc., Prescott, Ariz., 1980-82; pres., geologist Kaaterskill Exploration, Prescott, 1982—. Contbr. articles to profl. jours. Mem. Central Ariz. Geol. Soc. (v.p. 1984.), Soc. Econ. Geologists, AIME, Geol. Soc. Am. (grantee 1978), Mineral. Soc. Am., Mineral. Soc. Can., Soc. Exploration Geochemists, N.Y. Acad. Sci. Current work: Statistical analysis of geochemical databases, phase equilibria of open and closed systems, geochemistry and petrology of igneous, metamorphic and hydrothermal processes, polyphase deformation, SEM-EDAX analysis of fine grained mineral assemblages. Subspecialties: Petrology; Geochemistry. Home: 691 Robinson Dr Prescott AZ 86301 Office: Kaaterskill Exploration 691 Robinson Dr Prescott AZ 86301

O'HARE, J. MICHAEL, physicist, educator; b. Des Moines, Oct. 2, 1938; s. J. Lawrence and Eleanor Ann (McGillicuddy) O'H.; m. Patricia Ann Cronin, June 21, 1964; children—Maureen, Colleen, Erin, Jennifer. B.S. in Phys, Loras Coll., Dubuque, Iowa, 1956-60; M.S. in Physics, Purdue U., 1962; Ph.D. in Physics, SUNY-Buffalo, 1962-66. Instr. physics SUNY-Buffalo, 1965-66; asst. prof. physics U. Dayton, Ohio, 1966-71, assoc. prof., 1971-77, prof., 1977—, chmn. dept. physics, 1983—; vis. scientist Materials Lab, Wright-Patterson AFB, Dayton, 1977-78; sr. research physicist U. Dayton Research Inst., 1979-80. Contbr. articles to profl. publs. Mem. Am. Physi. Soc., Optical Soc. Am., Sigma Pi Sigma, Delta Epsilon Sigma. Current work: Optical physics, optical properties of matter. Subspecialties: Theoretical physics; Condensed matter physics. Home: 6179 Laurelhurst Ln Centerville OH 45459 Office: Dept Physics U Dayton Dayton OH 45469

OHATA, CARL ANDREWS, physiologist; b. Pearl City, Hawaii, Sept. 22, 1947; s. Robert Osamu and Alice Hatsuyo (Osaki) O.; m. Sue Sachiko, Jan. 16, 1971; children: Heather Hatsuko, Brent Ryan. B.A., U. Hawaii, 1969, M.S., 1972; Ph.D., U. Alaska, 1976. Research asst. U. Hawaii, Honolulu, 1970-72, U. Alaska, Fairbanks, 1972-76; research asso. U. Tex. Med. Br., Galveston, 1976-77; NIH postdoctoral fellow U. Okla. Health Scis. Center, Oklahoma City, 1977-79; Commd. capt. U.S. Army, 1979; research physiologist U.S. Army Research Inst. Environ. Medicine, Natick, Mass., 1979-84, Walter Reed Army Med Ctr., Washington, 1985—. Contbr. articles on neural control of circulation, temperature regulation and physiology of marine mammals to sci. jours. Okla. affiliate Am. Heart Assn. grantee, 1978-79. Mem. Am. Physiol. Soc., Soc. for Neurosci., AAAS, Sigma Xi. Congregationalist. Current Work: Neural control of circulation, neuroanatomy of central autonomic regulation, temperature regulation, physiology of marine mammals. Subspecialties: Physiology (biology); Neurology. Home: 9307 Linden Ave Bethesda MD 20814 Office: US Army Inst Dental Research Washington DC 20307-5300

OHI, SEIGO, molecular biologist, researcher; b. Toyama-ken, Japan, Apr. 8, 1943; came to U.S. 1967, naturalized, 1975; s. Masazo and Eiko (Matsushita) O.; m. Norie Matsuda, Aug. 10, 1970; children—Ryoma, Keima, Yuki. B.S., Toyama U. Sch. Pharm. Scis., Japan, 1966; M.S., Princeton U., 1970, Ph.D., 1973. Lic. pharmacist Japan. Fellow Carnegie Inst. Washington, Balt., 1973-75; research assoc. U. Pitts., 1975-78, Johns Hopkins U., Balt., 1978-83; vis. scientist, NIH, Bethesda, Md., 1983—; vis. asst. prof. U. Conn., Farmington, 1980-82. Contbr. articles to profl. jours. Japan Scholarship Found. scholar, 1962-67; fellow Princeton U., 1968-73, Carnegie Inst. Washington, 1973-75. Mem. N.Y. Acad. Sci., Sci. Research Soc., AAAS, Am. Soc. Biol. Chemists, Am. Soc. Microbiology, Am. Soc. Cell Biology, Am. Chem. Soc., Biophys. Soc., Sigma Xi. Current work: Regulation and mechanism of DNA replication as studied in a viral system; gene cloning/genetherapy/in vitro DNA replication-transcription-translation. Subspecialties: Molecular biology; Virology (medicine). Home: 8 Darby Ct East Gaithersburg MD 20878 Office: Lab Biology of Viruses NIAID NIH Bldg 5 Room 304 Bethesda MD 20205

OHKAWA, TIHIRO, physicist, b. Kanazawa, Japan, Jan. 3, 1928; came to U.S., 1955; s. Ryoichi and Ryuko (Kitagawa) O.; m. Yoko Hitomi, June 2, 1959; children—Risa, Taro, Hana. B.S., U. Tokyo, 1950, Ph.D., 1955, D.Sc., 1958. Research assoc. Midwest U. Research Assn., Madison., Wis., 1955-57; prof. physics U. Tokyo, 1958; with European Orgn. Nuclear Research, Geneva, 1959-60; v.p. GA Tech. Inc., San Diego, 1960—; adj. prof. physics U. Calif.-San Diego, 1973—. Contbr. articles to profl. publs. Patentee in field. Fellow Am. Phys. Soc. (Maxwell award 1979), Am. Nuclear Soc. (bd. dirs. 1980-81; Nordheim award 1984). Current work: Magnetic fusion research including the Doublet III experiment of the U.S. Dept. Energy fusion program and the OHTE fusion confinement concept. Subspecialties: Plasma (energy science and technology); Plasma physics. Office: GA Tech Inc PO Box 85608 San Diego CA 92138

OHKI, KENNETH, plant physiologist; b. Livingston, Calif., June 13, 1922; s. Zenjiro and Yaye (Watanabe) O.; m. Kiyoki N., Apr. 15, 1945; children: Suzanne S. Hammond, Stephen K. B.S., U. Calif., Berkeley, 1949, M.S., 1951, Ph.D., 1963. Supr., specialist Internat. Minerals and Chem. Corp., Libertyville, Ill., 1964-70; asst. prof. agronomy U. Ga., Experiment, 1971-73, asso. prof., 1973-79, prof., 1979—. Served with U.S. Army, 1945-46. Mem. Am. Soc. Plant Physiology, Am. Soc. Agronomy, Crop Sci. Soc. Am., Soil Sci. Soc. Am., Gamma Sigma Delta. Current Work: Mineral nutrition related to plant growth, development and physiology, particularly with microelements; critical deficiency and toxicity levels related to plant growth and physiological processes. Subspecialties: Plant physiology (agriculture); Plant growth. Home: 206 Larcom Ln Griffin GA 30223 Office: Dept Agronomy U Ga Experiment GA 30212

OHLHORST, SHARON LEE, ecology educator; b. Sharon, Conn., Sept. 26, 1947; d. Warren and Vivian (Snow) Ohlhorst; m. W. David Liddell, Nov. 17, 1977. B.A., U. Wis.-Madison, 1969; Ph.D., Yale U., 1981. Instr. U. New Orleans, 1979-81; research asst. prof. Utah State U., Logan, 1981—. Author: (with others) Modern & Ancient Carbonate Environments of Jamaica, 1984. Contbr. articles to profl. jours. Summer lectr. for sr. citizens, Logan, 1983, 84. Mem. Am. Soc. for Limnology and Oceanography, Ecol. Soc. Am., Am. Fisheries Soc., Sigma Xi. Current work: Community ecology of coral reefs, including spatial competition; feeding biology and habitat partitioning among lacustrine fishes. Subspecialties: Marine biology; Limnology. Office: Fisheries and Wildlife Dept Utah State U Logan UT 84321

OHMINE, IWAO, molecular science educator; b. Nagano, Japan, Dec. 7, 1945; s. Seiji and Mieko (Shimamoto) O.; m. Haruko Hironaka, Jan. 28, 1949; children—Hideto, Makito. B.S., Tokyo U., 1968; M.S., Harvard U., 1970, Ph.D., 1976. Postdoctoral fellow MIT, Cambridge, 1976-77; postdoctoral fellow Inst. for Molecular Sci., Okazaki, Japan, 1977-80, assoc. prof., 1982—; research assoc. MIT, 1980-81, Keio U., Yokohama, Japan, 1981-82. Mem. Am. Phys. Soc. Current work: Theory of chemical reaction, excited state dynamics (photochemistry), chemical reaction in condensed phases, statistical mechanics of fluid, phase transition of Gel and Polymer solutions. Subspecialties: Theoretical chemistry; Statistical mechanics. Office: Inst for Molecular Sci Myodaiji Okazaki 444 Japan

OHNESORGE, WILLIAM EDWARD, chemistry educator; b. Acushnet, Mass., Sept. 11, 1931. Sc.B., Brown U., 1953; Ph.D., MIT, 1956. Prof. chemistry U. R.I., Kingston, 1956-65; Lehigh U., Bethlehem, Pa., 1965—, assoc. dean, 1982-84; vis. prof. U. Toronto, Ont., Can., 1974; program dir. NSF, Washington, 1980-81. Contbr. articles to profl. jours. Mem. Am. Chem. Soc. Current work: Luminescence of metal chelates; electrochemistry. Subspecialty: Analytical chemistry. Office: Lehigh U Bldg 6 Bethlehem PA 18015

OHNO, MIKIO, biochemist; b. Tokyo, Feb. 18, 1940; came to U.S., 1968; s. Tahei and Nobu O.; m. Nobuko Matsui, Jan. 7, 1974; 1 child, Mika. B.S. in Chemistry, Gakushuin U., Tokyo, 1962; M.S. in Organic Chemistry, 1964; M.S. in Pharmacology, Tufts U., 1970; Ph.D. in Biochemistry, Okla. State U., 1974. Research asst. Tufts U., Boston, 1968-70, Okla. State U., Stillwater, 1970-74; research fellow U. Calif.-San Diego, 1974-75; research assoc. U. Kans., Kansas City, 1975-77; sr. research assoc. U. Ariz., Tucson, 1977-80; sr. scientist Univ. City Sci. Ctr., Phila., 1980—; cons. Internat. Symposium on Basement Membrane, Tokyo, 1985. Contr. articles to profl. jours. Patentee in field. Bd. dirs. Japanese Assn. Phila., 1982—; pres. Japanese Culture Ctr., Phila., 1984—; instr. Main Line Sch., Harriton, Pa., 1984—. Mem. Am. Chem. Soc., AAAS, Sigma Xi. Current work: Structure and function of basement membranes and their components, especially laminin, the role of laminin in tumor development. Subspecialties: Biochemistry (medicine); Cancer research (medicine). Home: 6425 Malvern Ave Philadelphia PA 19151 Office: Univ City Sci Ctr 3624 Market St Philadelphia PA 19104

OHNO, SUSUMU, research geneticist; b. Seoul, Korea, Feb. 1, 1928; came to U.S., 1953; s. Kenichi and Satoshi (Saito) O.; m. Midori Aoyama, July 30, 1953; children—Azusa, Yukali, Takeshi. D.V.M., Tokyo U. Agr. and Tech., 1949; Ph.D., Hokkaido U., Sapporo, Japan, 1956, D.Sc., 1961; H.H.D. (hon.), Kansaigukuin U., Nishinomiya, Japan, 1983; D.Sc. (hon.), U. Pa., 1984. Research assoc. City of Hope Med. Ctr., Duarte, Calif., 1953-62, sr. research scientist, 1962-66, chmn. biology, 1966-81, Ben Horowitz Disting. Scientist, 1981—; vis. prof. Albert Einstein Med. Sch., Bronx, N.Y., 1973; mem. com. NRC, 1979-81. Author: Sex Chromosomes and Sex-liked Genes, 1968; Evolution by Gene Duplication, 1970; Major Sex Determining Genes, 1979. Recipient Kihara prize Japanese Sci. Genetics, Tokyo, 1983. Fellow Am. Acad. Arts and Scis. (Amory prize 1981); mem. Nat. Acad. Scis. Democrat. Current work: Evolution of genes and their construction characteristics. Subspecialties: Genetics and genetic engineering (biology); Evolutionary biology. Home: 7329 Oak Dr Glendora CA 91740 Office: Beckman Research Inst of City of Hope Med Ctr 1450 E Duarte Rd Duarte CA 91010

OHNUMA, TAKAO, oncologist, researcher; b. Sendai, Japan, May 16, 1932; came to U.S., 1958; s. Hachiji Inomata and Teruko Ohnuma; m. Yoko Nishikawa, July 24, 1967; children: Nancy, Mary, Kenneth. M.D., Tohoku U., Sendai, 1957; Ph.D. in Biochemistry, U. London, 1965. Cancer research clinician Roswell Park Meml. Inst., Buffalo, 1968-73; research asst. prof. medicine SUNY, Buffalo, 1970-73; assoc. prof. dept. neoplastic diseases Mt. Sinai Sch. Medicine, N.Y.C., 1973-79; assoc. attending staff Mt. Sinai Hosp., N.Y.C., 1973-79; prof. neoplastic diseases Mt. Sinai Sch. Medicine, 1980—; attending physician Mt. Sinai Hosp., 1980—. USPHS research grantee; recipient Nat. Cancer Inst. contracts; research grantee United Leukemia Fund, Inc. Mem. Am. Chem. Soc., Am. Assn. Cancer Research, Am. Soc. Clin. Oncology, Cancer and Leukemia Group B. Current Work: Experimental chemotherapy, clinical pharmacology, cellular pharmacology. Subspecialties: Cancer research (medicine); Chemotherapy. Home: 11 Paxford Ln Scarsdale NY 10583 Office: Mount Sinai Sch of Medicine Dept of Neoplastic Diseases One Gustave Levy Pl New York NY 10029

OHTA, ALAN TAKASHI, geneticist; b. Honolulu, Feb. 4, 1947; s. Kenneth Hiroshi and Umeyo Ann (Kanai) O.; m. Gayle Sanae Tabusa, July 3, 1971; children: Leigh, Aaron Takami. B.A., U. Hawaii, 1970, 5th yr. teaching diploma, 1972, Ph.D., 1977. Entomologist Dept. Primary Industries, Brisbane, Queensland, Australia, 1977-79; asst. researcher entomology U. Hawaii, 1980—. Served with Air NG, 1967-75. Mem. Soc. Study Evolution, Genetics Soc. Am., Am. Soc. Naturalists, Am. Genetic Assn., AAAS, Hawaii Acad. Sci., Sigma Xi. Current Work: Researcher in genetic basis of ovipositional behavior in Hawaii Drosophila. Subspecialties: Evolutionary biology; Gene actions. Office: Dept Entomology U Hawaii Honolulu HI 96822

OILER, LARRY WAYNE, educator, consultant; b. Bethany, Mo., Feb. 11, 1941; s. Harold Jay and Paula Rogene (Ballantyne) O.; m. Lila Mae White; children: Michael Scott, Kristin Renae, Bradley James. B.A., Graceland Coll., 1963; M.A., Drake U., 1967; Ph.D., Purdue U., 1974. Grad. instr. dept. biology Purdue U., 1967-71; asst. prof. biology Wabash Coll., Crawfordsville, Ind., 1974-78; sci. curriculum coordinator Villisca (Iowa) High Sch., 1978—, cons. sci. curriculum. Pres. Reorganized Latter Day Saints Social Services Corp., 1980—; Ordained priest, elder Reorganized Ch. of Jesus Christ of Latter Day Saints. Mem. Am. Soc. Microbiology. Republican. Club: Page County Amateur Radio. Mil. amateur radio service operator. Current Work: Autoassembly of bacterial flagellins. Subspecialties: Gene actions; Molecular biology. Home: PO Box 203 Stanton IA 51573 Office: 1000 Mustang Dr Shenandoah IA 51601

OISHI, NOBORU, cancer researcher, administrator; b. Kapaa, Kauai, Hawaii, Nov. 11, 1928; s. Masato and Shizuyo (Watada) O.; m. Violet Niimi, June 12, 1956; 1 child, Scott. A.B., Wash. U., 1949, M.D., 1953. Diplomate Am. Bd. Internal Medicine, Am. Bd. Oncology. Intern, Detroit Receiving Hosp., 1953-54, resident, 1956-58; fellow in hematology U. Rochester Sch. Medicine, 1958-59; dir. clin. sci. Cancer Research Ctr. Hawaii, Honolulu, 1974-84; mem. clin. cancer investigation research com. Nat. Cancer Inst. Current work: In vitro tumor biology, biologic markers; flow cytometry. Subspecialties: Hematology; Oncology. Home: 4399 Aukai Ave Honolulu HI 96816 Office: Hematology and Med Oncology Assn 1520 Liliha St Honolulu HI 96817

OJAKAAR, LEO, organic chemist; b. Valga, Estonia, Apr. 26, 1926; came to U.S., 1949, naturalized, 1955; s. Aleksander and Hilda (Telling) O.; m. Milvi R. Kaldvee, Aug. 15, 1959; children—Linda, Erik. B.S., Millikin U., 1953; Ph.D., Va. Poly. Inst. and State U., 1964. Sr. research chemist E.I. duPont de Nemours & Co., Wilmington, Del., 1964—. Contbr. articles to profl. jours. Patentee elastomeric polymers. Served with U.S. Army, 1954-56. Recipient J. Shelton Horsley Research award Va. Acad. Sci., 1966; fellow Allied Chem. Corp., 1963-64; grantee NIH. Mem. Am. Chem. Soc., Sigma Xi, Phi Lambda Upsilon. Republican. Lutheran. Club: Estonian Cultural Assn. (N.Y.C.). Current work: High molecule weight aromatic hydrocarbons; isocyanates and polyurethane polymers; synthetic hydrocarbon and flurocarbon elastomers research and rubber curing chemistry. Subspecialties: Organic chemistry; Polymer chemistry. Home: 8 Jacqueline Dr RD #1 Hockessin DE 19707 Office: E I duPont de Nemours & Co Exptl Sta Bldg 353 Wilmington DE 19898

OJEMANN, GEORGE ALVIN, neurological surgeon; b. Iowa City, Iowa, Dec. 25, 1935; s. Ralph Henry and Freda Elizabeth (Metzger) O.; m. Linda Moretti, May 20, 1967; children—Jeffrey, Steven, Ann-Elizabeth. B.A., U. Iowa, 1956, M.D., 1959. Diplomate Am. Bd. Neurol. Surgery. Intern, King County Hosp., Seattle, 1959-60; resident, U. Wash. Affiliated Hosps., Seattle, 1960-64; asst. prof. neurol. surgery U. Wash., Seattle, 1966-72, assoc. prof., 1972-79, prof. neurol. surgery, 1979—. Author: (with William Calvin) Inside the Brain, 1980. Assoc. editor Brain and Lang., 1982—; editorial bd. EEG Clin. Neurophysiol., Neurosurgery, Human Neurobiology, Applied Neurophysiology, Jour. Neurosurgery. Contbr. articles to profl. jours. Recipient Grass prize for neurosurg. research Soc. Neurol. Surgeons, 1984; Javits Neurosci. Investigator award NINCDS/NIH, 1984. Mem. Congress Neurol. Surgeons (exec. com. 1978-81), Am. Assn. Neurol. Surgeons (chmn. membership com. 1979-81), Am. Acad. Neurol. Surgeons, Soc. Neurol. Surgeons. Current work: Surgical treatment of epilepsy; brain organization for language and memory. Subspecialties: Neurosurgery; Neuropsychology. Office: Dept Neurol Surgery RI20 U Wash Seattle WA 98195

OJIMA, IWAO, chemistry educator; b. Yokohama, Kanagawa, Japan, June 5, 1945; s. Masaharu and Sumiko (Takatsuki) O.; m. Yoko Ogino, Apr. 24, 1971. B.S., U. Tokyo, 1968, M.S., 1970, Ph.D., 1973. Research fellow Sagami Chem. Research Ctr., Japan, 1970-76, sr. research fellow, 1976-83; assoc. prof. SUNY-Stony Brook, 1983-84, prof. chemistry, 1984—; mem. hydrocarbon com. Japan Soc. for Promotion of Sci., Tokyo, 1980-83. Contbr. articles to profl. jours. Patentee in field. Mem. Am. Chem. Soc., Chem. Soc. Japan (editorial bd. 1982-83, progress award 1976), N.Y. Acad. Sci., Soc. Synthetic Organic Chemistry Japan. Current work: Asymmetric synthesis, homogeneous catalysis of transition metal complexes, organic synthesis by means of organometallics, beta-Lactam Chemistry, peptide synthesis. Home: 6 Ivy League Ln Stony Brook NY 11790 Office: Dept Chemistry SUNY Stony Brook NY 11794

OKA, TAKESHI, physicist; b. Tokyo, June 10, 1932; came to Can., 1963, naturalized, 1973; s. Shumpei and Chiyoko O.; m. Keiko Nukui, Oct. 24, 1960; children: Ritsuko, Noriko, Kentaro, Yujiro. B.Sc., U. Tokyo, 1955, Ph.D., 1960. Research asso. U. Tokyo, 1960-63; fellow NRC Can., Ottawa, Ont., 1963-65, asst., 1965-68, asso., 1968-71, sr. research physicist, 1971—; prof. U. Chgo., 1981—. Mem. editorial bd.: Chem. Physics, 1972—, Jour. Molecular Spectroscopy, 1973—; Jour. Chem. Physics, 1975-77. Recipient Steacie prize, 1972; Earle K. Plyler prize, 1981. Fellow Royal Soc. Can., Am. Phys. Soc.; mem. Can. Assn. Physicists, Am. Astron. Soc. Current Work: Laser spectroscopy; double resonance; molecular ions; astrophysics; interstellar molecules; energy transfer. Subspecialties: Laser spectroscopy; Atomic and molecular physics. Home: 1463 E Park Pl Chicago IL 60637 Office: Dept Chemistry and Dept Astronomy and Astrophysics U Chgo Chicago IL 60637

OKABE, HIDEO, chemistry educator; researcher; b. Takato-machi, Nagano-ken, Japan, Dec. 13, 1923; came to U.S., 1952, naturalized, 1974; s. Tokujiro and Masu (Seto) O.; m. Tomoko Shoji, Mar. 15, 1959; children—Ken, Aya, Naomi. B.Engring. (applied chem.), U. Tokyo, 1947; Ph.D. in Phys. Chemistry, U. Rochester, 1957; postdoctorate NRC-Can., 1957-59. Research chemist Nat. Bureau Standards, Gaithersburg, Md., 1959-83, cons., 1983—; prof. chemistry Howard U., Washington, 1983—. Author: Photochemistry of Small Molecules, 1978, Patentee in field. Contbr. numerous articles to profl. jours. Recipient Gold Medal Dept. Commerce, 1973; Deutche Forshungs Gemeinschaft fellow U. Bonn., 1963-65, vis. fellow Tokyo Inst. Tech., 1978; sr. research grantee NASA, 1982-83. Fellow Washington Acad. Scis., Sigma Xi; mem. Am. Chem. Soc., Chem. Soc. Japan. Democrat. Buddhist. Current work: Photochemistry of small molecules, photodissociation dynamics, photochemistry of earth and planetary atmospheres. Subspecialties: Photochemistry; Kinetics. Home: 6700 Old Stage Rd Rockville MD 20852 Office: Dept Chemistry Howard U Washington DC 20059

OKADA, ROBERT DEAN, physician, educator; b. Seattle, Sept. 18, 1947; s. Yoshitaka Robert and Jane Reiko (Sugawara) O.; m. Carolyn Rose Casella, May 19, 1973; 1 son, David. B.A., U. Wash., 1969; M.D., U. Pa., 1973. Diplomate: Am. Bd. Internal Medicine. Intern U.Ariz. Health Scis. Center, Tucson, 1973-74, resident, 1974-76, cardiology fellow, 1976-78; clin. and research fellow in cardiology Mass. Gen. Hosp., Boston, 1978-79, sr. staff cardiology lab., 1979—, asst. in medicine, 1982—, cons. nuclear medicine, 1981—; instr. medicine Harvard U. Med. Sch., Boston, 1979-81, asst. prof. medicine, 1981—. Author: Noninvasive Cardiac Imaging, 1982; contbr. chpts. to books and articles in field to profl. jours. Fellow Am. Coll. Cardiology, Am. Heart Assn. (established investigator 1982—), ACP, Am. Coll. Chest Physicians; mem. Am. Fedn. Clin. Research. Current Work: Cardiac nuclear imaging; nuclear magnetic resonance. Subspecialties: Cardiology; Internal medicine. Home: 62 Oxford St Winchester MA 01890 Office: Cardiac Catherization Unit Mass Gen Hosp Fruit St Boston MA 02114

O'KELLEY, JOSEPH CHARLES, educator; b. Unadilla, Ga., May 9, 1922; s. Thomas Landrum and Maude (Hall) O'K.; m. Hallie LaVonne Held, June 16, 1951; children—Susan Elaine, Celia Anne, Thomas Burnell, Ellen Catherine. A.B., U. N.C., 1943, M.A., 1948; Ph.D., Iowa State U., 1950. Mem. faculty dept. biology U. Ala., University, 1951—, asso. prof., 1958-61, prof., 1961—, chmn. dept., 1969-74, research prof., 1977—. Served with USAAF, 1943-46. Decorated Air medal.; NSF postdoctoral fellow U. Wis., 1953-54; NIH spl. fellow Johns Hopkins, 1965-66. Fellow AAAS; mem. Am. Inst. Biol. Scis., Phi Beta Kappa. Current Work: History of science. Subspecialties: Sedimentology; Precambrian geology. Home: 2910 17th St E Tuscaloosa AL 35404 Office: PO Box 1927 University AL 35486

OKERHOLM, RICHARD ARTHUR, research company executive, researcher; b. Woburn, Mass., Nov. 10, 1941; s. Theodore and Elizabeth Anne (Johnston) O.; m. Rita V. Hutchinson, June 26, 1965; children—Heidi Ann, Erik Paul. B.S. in Chemistry, Lowell Tech., 1964; Ph.D. in Biochemistry, Boston U., 1970. Instr. Lowell Tech., Mass., 1962-65; sr. research biochemist Park-Davis & Co., Ann Arbor, Mich., 1970-77; dept. head Merrell Dow Research, Clin., 1977—. Contbr. articles to profl. jours. Treas., Fairfield Soccer Assn. of Youth, Ohio, 1979-80. Mem. Acad. Pharm. Scis., Am. Chem. Soc., Am. Soc. Pharmacology and Exptl. Therapeutics, Am. Soc. Clinical Pharmacology and Therapeutics, Soc. Exptl. Biology and Medicine, Am. Pharm. Assn., N.Y. Acad. Scis., Sigma Xi (recipient research award 1964). Clubs: Optimist Internat., Fairfield Optimist (mem. bd. dirs.). Current work: Pharmacokinetics and metabolism of drugs in animals and man. Subspecialties: Pharmacokinetics; Biochemistry (medicine). Home: 5664 Williamsburg Way Fairfield OH 45014 Office: Merrell Dow Research Inst 2110 E Galbraith Rd Cincinnati OH 45215

OKINAKA, YUTAKA, electrochemist; b. Osaka, Japan, Jan. 22, 1926; s. Tsuneyuki and Kiyono (Shoji) O.; m. Masayo Kitahara, May 18, 1950; children—Masato, Naomi. B.S., Tohoku U., Sendai, Japan, 1948; M.S., U. Minn., 1957; Ph.D., Tohoku U., Sendai, 1959. Research asst. Tohoku U., Sendai, Japan, 1948-55; research fellow U. Minn., Mpls., 1955-60; asst. prof. Tohoku U., Sendai, 1960-63; mem. tech. staff Bell Labs., Murray Hill, N.J., 1963-83; disting. mem. tech. staff Bell Communications Research, Murray Hill, 1984—. Contbr. articles to profl. jours. Patentee in field. Recipient Disting. Tech. Staff award Bell Labs., 1982. Mem. Electrochem. Soc. (life, div. editor 1977—, battery research award 1970, electrodeposition award 1981), Am. Electroplaters Soc. (vice chmn. research 1982—, silver medal awards 1980, 81, sci. achievement award 1984), Metal Finishing Soc. Japan, Electrochem. Soc. Japan (chmn. U.S. office 1980—). Current work: Research in fundamental aspects of electrodeposition and surface finishing technologies for electronics industry. Subspecialties: Analytical chemistry; Physical chemistry. Office: Bell Communications Research Inc 600 Mountain Ave Murray Hill NJ 07974

OKOBU, SUSUMU, high energy physicist, educator; b. Tokyo, Mar. 2, 1930; s. Yoshitaro and Yoshi (Sekiguchi) O.; m. Mary C. Catlin, June 30, 1965. B.Sc., U. Tokyo, 1952; Ph.D., U. Rochester, 1958. Vis. scientist U. Napoli, Italy, 1959-60, CERN, Geneva, 1960-61; sr. research assoc. U. Rochester, N.Y., 1962-64, prof. physics, 1964—. Contbr. articles to profl. jours. Recipient Nishina award, Japan, 1978; fellow Guggenheim Found., 1964, Nat. Found., Pakistan, 1967. Fellow Am. Phys. Soc. Current work: Particle physics.

Subspecialty: Particle physics. Office: Dept Physics U Rochester Rochester NY 14627

OKRENT, DAVID, educator; b. Passaic, N.J., Apr. 19, 1922; s. Abram and Gussie (Pearlman) O.; m. Rita Gilda Holtzman, Feb. 1, 1948; children—Neil, Nina, Jocelyne. M.E., Stevens Inst. Tech., 1943; M.A., Harvard, 1948, Ph.D. in Physics, 1951. Mech. engr. NACA, Cleve., 1943-46; sr. physicist Argonne (Ill.) Nat. Lab., 1951-71; regents lectr. U. Calif. at Los Angeles, 1968, prof. engring., 1971—; vis. prof. U. Wash., Seattle, 1963, U. Ariz., Tucson, 1970-71; Isaac Taylor chair Technion, 1977-78. Author: Fast Reactor Cross Sections, 1960, Computing Methods in Reactor Physics, 1968, Reactivity Coefficients in Large Fast Power Reactors, 1970, Nuclear Reactor Safety, 1981; contbr. articles to profl. jours. Mem. adv. com. on reactor safeguards AEC, 1963—, also chmn., 1966; sci. sec. to sec. gen. of Geneva Conf., 1958; mem. U.S. del. to all Geneva Atoms for Peace Confs. Guggenheim fellow, 1961-62, 77-78; recipient Distinguished Appointment award Argonne Univs. Assn., 1970. Fellow Am. Phys. Soc., Am. Nuclear Soc. (Tommy Thompson award 1980), Nat. Acad. Engring. Current Work: Nuclear reactor safety and technology; societal risks. Subspecialties: Nuclear fission; Nuclear engineering. Home: 439 Veteran Ave Los Angeles CA 90024

OKUN, DANIEL ALEXANDER, educator, consulting engineer; b. N.Y.C., June 19, 1917; s. William Howard and Leah (Seligman) O.; m. Elizabeth Griffin, Jan. 14, 1946; children—Michael Griffin, Tema Jon. B.S., Cooper Union, 1937; M.S., Calif. Inst. Tech., 1938; D.Sc., Harvard, 1948. Diplomate: Am. Acad. Environ. Engrs. (pres. 1969-70); registered profl. engr., N.C., N.Y. With USPHS, 1940-42; teaching fellow Harvard, 1946-48; with Malcolm Pirnie (cons. environ. engrs.), N.Y.C., 1948-52; asso. prof. dept. environ. scis. and engring. U. N.C. at Chapel Hill, 1952-55, prof., 1955-73, Kenan prof., 1973—, head dept. environ. scis. and engring., 1955-73; dir. Water Resources Research Inst., 1965—, chmn. faculty, 1970-73; Vis. prof. Technol. U. Delft, 1960-61, Univ. Coll., London, 1966-67, 73-75, Tianjin U., 1981; editor environ. scis. series Acad. Press, 1968-75; cons. to industry, cons. engrs., govtl. agys. World Bank, WHO. Author: (with Gordon M. Fair and John C. Geyer) Water and Wastewater Engineering, 2 vols, 1966, 68, Elements of Water Supply and Wastewater Disposal, 1971, (with George Ponghis) Community Wastewater Collection and Disposal, 1975, Regionalization of Water Management—A Revolution in England and Wales, 1977; (with C.R. Schulz) Surface Water Treatment for communities in Developing Countries, 1984. Contbr. to (with M.B. Pescod) publs. in field. Adv. bd. Ackland Meml. Art Mus., 1973-78; bd. dirs. Warren Regional Planning Corp., 1971-77, Inter-Ch. Council Housing Corp., 1975-83, N.C. Water Quality Council, 1975-77; adv. com. for med. research Pan Am. Health Orgn., 1976-79; chmn. Washington Met. Area Water Supply Study Com., 1976-80, Nat. Acad Scis.-NRC; bd. sci. and tech. for internat. devel. NRC, 1978-81, vice chmn. environ. studies bd., 1980-83. Served from lt. to maj. AUS, 1942-46. Recipient Harrison Prescott Eddy medal for research Water Pollution Control Fedn., 1950, Catedratico Honorario, Univ. Nacional de Ingenieria, Lima, Peru, 1957, Gordon Maskew Fair award Am. Acad. Environ. Engrs., 1973, Thomas Jefferson award U. N.C., Chapel Hill, 1973, Order Golden Fleece, 1982; Gordon Y. Billard award N.Y. Acad. Scis., 1975; Gordon Maskew Fair medal Water Pollution Control Fedn., 1978; N.C. Fuller award Am. Water Works Assn., 1983, Best Paper Award edn. div., 1985; Friendship medal Inst. Water Engrs. and Scientists, 1984. NSF fellow, 1960-61; Fed. Water Pollution Control Adminstrn. fellow, 1966-67; Fulbright-Hayes lectr., 1973-74. Fellow ASCE (chmn. environ. engring. div. 1967-68, Simon W. Freese award 1977); corp. fellow Inst. Water Pollution Control (Eng.), AAAS; mem. Nat. Acad. Engring., Inst. Medicine, AAUP (chpt. pres. 1963-64), Water Pollution Control Fedn. (hon. mem.; chmn. research com. 1961-66, dir.-at-large 1969-72), Sigma Xi (pres. chpt. 1968-69). Current Work: Water quality management; water reuse; regionalization of water management. Subspecialty: Water supply and wastewater treatment. Home: Linden Rd Route 7 Chapel Hill NC 27514

OLAH, GEORGE ANDREW, educator, chemist; b. Budapest, Hungary, May 22, 1927; came to U.S., 1964, naturalized, 1970; s. Julius and Magda (Rasznai) O.; m. Judith Agnes Lengyel, July 9, 1949; children: George John, Ronald Peter. Ph.D., Tech. U. Budapest, 1949. Mem. faculty Tech. U. Budapest, 1949-54; asso. dir. Central Chem. Research Inst., Hungarian Acad. Scis., 1954-56; research scientist Dow Chem. Can. Ltd., 1957-64, Dow Chem. Co., Framingham, Mass., 1964-65; prof. chemistry Case-Western Res. U., Cleve., 1965-69, C.F. Mabery prof. research, 1969-77; Donald P. and Katherine B. Loker disting. prof. chemistry, dir. Hydrocarbon Research Inst., U. So. Calif., Los Angeles, 1977—; vis. prof. chemistry Ohio State U., 1963, U. Heidelberg, Germany, 1965, U. Colo., 1969, Swiss Fed. Inst. Tech., 1972, U. Munich, 1973, U. London, 1973-79, L. Pasteur U., Strasbourg, 1974, U. Paris, 1981; hon. vis. lectr. U. London, 1981; cons. to industry. Author: Friedel-Crafts Reactions, Vols. I-IV, 1963-64, (with P. Schleyer) Carbonium Ions, Vols. I-V, 1969-76, Friedel-Crafts Chemistry, 1973, Carbocations and Electrophilic Reactions, 1973, Halonium Ions, 1975, (with G.K.S. Prakash and J. Somer) Superacids, 1984; also chpts. in books, numerous papers in field. Recipient Leo Hendrik Baekeland award N.J. sect. Am. Chem. Soc., 1966, Morley medal Cleve. sect., 1970; Alexander von Humboldt sr. U.S. scientist award, 1979; Guggenheim fellow, 1972. Fellow Chem. Inst. Can., AAAS; mem. Nat. Acad. Scis., Italian Nat. Acad. Scis., Am. Chem. Soc. (award petroleum chemistry 1964, award synthetic organic chemistry 1979), German Chem. Soc., Brit. Chem. Soc. (Centenary lectr. 1978), Swiss Chem. Soc., Sigma Xi. Patentee in field. Current Work: Mechanistic and synthetic organic chemistry; hydrocarbon chemistry; reactive intermediates; biological alkylating agents. Subspecialty: Organic chemistry. Office: Dept Chemistry Univ So Calif Los Angeles CA 90007

OLAJOS, EUGENE JULIUS, toxicologist; b. Steyr, Austria, July 13, 1945; came to U.S., 1950, naturalized, 1956; s. Eugene and Margaret (Huber) O.; m. Helen M. Bourgoin, Nov. 25, 1970; children—Elizabeth, Stephanie, Andrew, Allison. B.A., Wayne State U., 1969, M.S., 1972; Ph.D., U. Mich., 1976. Nat. Research Service fellow MIT, Cambridge, 1975-76; Nat. Research Service fellow Albany (N.Y.) Med. Coll., 1976-77, research asst. prof. toxicology, 1977-80; asst. prof. chemistry Old Dominion U., Norfolk, Va., 1980-82; pharmacologist Chem. Research and Devel. Ctr., U.S. Army, Aberdeen Proving Ground, Md., 1982—. Contbr. articles on toxicology to profl. jours., also chpts. to books. Mem. Am. Chem. Soc., Internat. Soc. Study Xenobiotics, Soc. Assn. Govt. Toxicologists, Toxicology, Soc. for Neurosci., Sigma Xi. Current Work: Researcher in biochemical mechanisms of neurotoxicity, enzymatic markers as correlates of neuropathology and toxicant-induced neurotransmitter alterations. Subspecialties: Toxicology (medicine); Neurochemistry. Home: 605 Webb Rd Newark DE 19711 Office: Chemical Research and Devel Ctr US Army Aberdeen Proving Ground MD 21010

OLD, LLOYD JOHN, cancer biologist; b. San Francisco, Sept. 23, 1933; s. John H. and Edna A. (Marks) O. B.A., U. Calif. at Berkeley, 1955; M.D. at, U. Calif. at Berkeley, San Francisco, 1958. Research fellow Sloan-Kettering Inst. Cancer Research, 1958-59, research asso., 1959-60, asso., 1960-64, asso. mem., 1964-67, mem., 1967—, chief div. immunology, 1967-72, William E. Snee chair of cancer immunology, 1983—; research asso. biology Sloan-Kettering div. Grad. Sch. Med. Scis., Cornell U. Med. Coll., 1960-62, asst. prof. biology, 1962-66, asso. prof. biology, 1966-69, prof. biology, 1969—; acting asso. dir. research planning Sloan-Kettering Inst. Cancer Research, 1972, v.p., asso. dir., 1973-76, v.p., asso. dir. for sci. devel., 1976—; asso. dir. for research Meml. Sloan-Kettering Cancer Center and Meml. Hosp., 1973—; cons. Nat. Cancer Inst., 1967-70, mem. developmental research working group, 1969, spl. virus cancer program, 1970, mem. virus cancer program adv. com., 1975-78, mem. bd. sci. counselors div. cancer cause and prevention, 1978-81; asso. med. dir. Cancer Research Inst., Inc., 1970, med. dir., 1971—. Adv. editor: Jour. Exptl. Medicine, 1971-75, Progress in Surface and Membrane Science, 1972-74; asso. editor: Virology, 1972-74.; Editorial adv. bd.: Cancer Research, 1967-70, Cancer, 1968-71, Recent Results in Cancer Research, 1972. Contbr. articles to profl. jours. Mem. med. and sci. adv. bd. Leukemia Soc. Am., Inc., 1970-73, trustee, 1970-73; mem. sci. adv. com. Ludwig Inst. Cancer Research, 1974—; mem. sci. adv. bd. Jane Coffin Childs Meml. Fund for Med. Research, 1970-75; mem. research council Public Health Research Inst. City N.Y., 1977-80, bd. dirs., 1979-81. Recipient Roche ward, 1957, Alfred P. Sloan award cancer research, 1962, Lucy Wortham James award James Ewing Soc., 1970, Louis Gross award, 1972, Cancer Research Inst. award for immunology research, 1975, Rabbi Shai Shacknai Meml. award, 1976; Research Recognition award Noble Found., 1978; N.Y. Acad. Medicine medal, 1985; G.H.A. Clowes Meml. lectr., 1980; Robert Roesler de Villiers award, 1981. Mem. N.Y. Acad. Scis., Reticuloendothelial Soc., Soc. Exptl. Biology and Medicine, Harvey Soc., Am. Acad. Arts and Scis., Am. Assn. Cancer Research (bd. dirs. 1980-83), AAAS, Am. Assn. Immunologists, Inst. Medicine of Nat. Acad. Scis., Phi Beta Kappa, Sigma Xi, Alpha Omega Alpha. Subspecialty: Cancer research (medicine). Office: Sloan-Kettering Inst Cancer Research 410 E 68th St New York NY 10021

OLDENBORG, RICHARD CHARLES, chemist; b. N.Y.C., Mar. 2, 1949; s. George Richard and Agnes (Kisac) O.; m. Carole Elizabeth Bretz, July 7, 1973; children—Jennifer Anne, Michael Richard. B.S., SUNY-Stony Brook, 1971; M.S., Columbia U., 1975, Ph.D., 1975. Staff, Los Alamos Nat. Lab., N.Mex., 1975-84, assoc. group leader, 1984—. Mem. Am. Chem. Soc. Current work: Laser based diagnostic techniques; chemical kinetics. Subspecialties: Kinetics; Laser photochemistry. Home: 456 Pruitt Ave Los Alamos NM 87544 Office: Los Alamos Nat Lab Group CHM4 MS J567 Los Alamos NM 87545

OLDHAM, JAMES WARREN, toxicologist, researcher; b. Helena, Ark., Jan. 1, 1950; s. Hershal B. and Agnes Bell (Wright) O.; m. Lesa Ann Cornelius, Nov. 29, 1975; children—Michael James, Rachel Ann, Gregory Warren. B.A. in Chemistry, U. Ark., 1972; B.S. in Med. Technology, 1974; Ph.D. in Toxicology, 1978. Diplomate Am. Bd. Toxicology. Research biologist Nat. Ctr. for Toxicological Research Jefferson, Ark., 1976-77; research asst. U. Ark. Med. Scis., Little Rock, 1977-78; research assoc. Ohio State U., Columbus, 1978-80; research scientist McNeil Pharm., Spring House, Pa., 1980-81, sr. scientist, 1981-82, prin. scientist, 1982—. Mem. Soc. Toxicology, Environ. Mutagen Soc., Am. Assn. Cancer Research, Genetic Toxicology Assn. Current work: Development and implementation of testing procedures to define the type and degree of toxicity induced by drugs and environmental chemicals on mammalian systems. Subspecialties: Toxicology (medicine); Cancer research (medicine). Office: McNeil Pharmaceutical Welsh and McKean Rds Spring House PA 19477

OLDROYD, L(AWRENCE) ANDREW, computer science educator, researcher; b. Urbana, Ill., Jan. 5, 1944; s. Carl Riley and Fortune (Willis) O.; m. Juanice Elaine Sims, July 14, 1979. B.S. with honors, U. Okla., Norman, 1967, M.A. in Math., 1972, M.S. in Info. and Computing Sci., 1976, Ph.D. in Math., 1977. Asst. prof. computer sci. U. Okla., 1976-79; supr. McDonnell Douglas Corp., St. Louis, 1979-81; asst. prof. Washington U., St. Louis, 1981—; phys. scientist Def. Mapping Agy. Aerospace Ctr., St. Louis, 1985—; cons. Ninetronix Inc., St. Louis, 1981-82; reviewer Holt, Rinehart, Winston, N.Y.C., 1981—, Benjamin/Cummings, Fort Collins, Colo., 1983—, Burgess Communications, Santa Rosa, Calif., 1984—. Co-author: MCL User Manual, 1981. Contbr. articles to profl. publs. Adviser Mus. Sci. and Natural History, St. Louis, 1984. NIH grantee, 1982. Mem. Am. Math. Soc., Assn. for Computing Machinery, Soc. Indsl. and Applied Math., Sigma Xi. Current work: Use of symbolic and semantic models in robot programming, computer vision, image analysis and computer-aided engineering, interactive use of human knowledge in artificial intelligence. Subspecialties: Robotics; Graphics, image processing, and pattern recognition. Home: 12947 Robandee Ln Saint Louis MO 63146 Office: Computer Sci Dept Washington U Campus Box 1045 Saint Louis MO 63130

OLDS, DURWARD, retired animal scientist, educator; b. Conneaut, Ohio, Apr. 12, 1921; s. Benjamin Harrison and Sada Hannah (Raudabaugh) O.; m. Gertrude M. Walk, Sept. 21, 1947; children: Beverly, John. D.V.M., Ohio State U., 1943; M.S., U. Ill., 1954, Ph.D. (AVMA research fellow), 1956. Lic. in vet. medicine, Ky. Artificial insemination technician Clark County (Wis.) Breeders Coop., 1944-46; researcher, prof. animal sci. U. Ky., Lexington, 1946-83, ret., 1983. Contbr. articles to profl. jours. Mem. Am. Dairy Sci. Assn., AVMA, Am. Soc. Animal Sci., Soc. Study of Reprodn. Lutheran. Holder copyright time of insemination dial for cattle; performed world's first non-surg. embryo transfer in cattle, 1964. Current Work: Artificial insemination and infertility of cattle, estrous behavior, management of breeding animals and embryo culture. Subspecialties: Animal breeding and embryo transplants; Animal physiology. Home: 1605 Elizabeth St Lexington KY 40503

O'LEARY, GERARD PAUL, JR., biology educator; b. Bridgeport, Conn., Oct. 16, 1940; s. Gerard Paul and Ethal (Shortell) O'L.; m. Janice E. Murray, Dec. 19, 1981. B.S., Mount St. Mary's Coll., 1962; M.S., N. Mex. State U., 1964; Ph.D., U. N.H., 1967. Mem. faculty Providence Coll., 1969 , prof. biology, 1982 ; Head Eastern Colls. Sci. Conf., Inc., Providence, 1981. Can. Research Council fellow McGill U., 1967-69. Mem. Am. Soc. Microbiologists, N.Am. Apiotherapy Soc., AAAS, Warren Meml. Arthritis Found. (research council 1981). Roman Catholic. Current Work: Arthritis; oncology; effects of heavy metals; muscle biochemistry; infection agents detection by isoelectric focusing; plasma emission spectroscopy. Subspecialties: Biochemistry (medicine); Cell biology (medicine). Office: Providence Coll Biology Dept 101 Hicke Research Bldg Providence RI 02918

OLEGO, DIEGO JOSE, physicist, researcher; b. San Nicolas, Argentina, Apr. 30, 1951; came to U.S., 1981; s. Jose and Amanda (Ruiz) O.; m. Magdalena Ruth Pauli, Dec. 27, 1974; children—Diego, Carolina, Valeria. M.Physics, U. Cordoba (Argentina), 1974; Ph.D. in Physics, U. Stuttgart, 1980. Teaching asst. U. Buenos Aires, 1974-76; research asst. Max-Planck Inst., Stuttgart, 1977-81; mem. staff Bell Labs., Holmdel, N.J., 1981-82; research physicist Stauffer Chem. Co., Elmsford, N.Y., 1982—. Contbr. articles to profl. jours. Mem. Am. Phys. Soc. Current work: Optical characterization of semiconductor materials; physical phenomena of solid state devices. Subspecialties: Condensed matter physics; Electronic materials. Office: Stauffer Chem Co Eastern Research Ctr Elmsford NY 10523

OLENCHOCK, STEPHEN ANTHONY, medical institute administrator, microbiology educator; b. Mt. Pleasant, Pa., Dec. 12, 1946; s. Steve and Virginia (Costabile) O.; m. Marcia Greene, May 31, 1969; children—Stephen Anthony Jr., Thomas, Benjamin. B.A. in Biology with honors, St. Vincent Coll., 1968; Ph.D. in Med. Microbiology, W.Va. U., 1975. Immunologist Nat. Inst. Occupational Safety and Health, Morgantown, W.Va., 1975-80, chief immunology sect., 1980—; instr. dept. microbiology W.Va. U., Morgantown, 1976-77, adj. asst. prof., 1977-82, adj. assoc. prof., 1982-85, adj. prof., 1985—; approved adviser research associateship program NRC, 1983; vis. scientist Forschungsinstitut fur Lungenkrankheiten und Tuberculose, Berlin-Buch, German Democratic Republic, 1983; cons. various orgns., 1975—. Contbr. articles and abstracts to profl. publs.; invited reviewer various jours. Asst. instr. educated childbirth classes childbirth and Parent Edn. Assn. of Morgantown, 1976-82; asst. coach Cheat Lake Youth Baseball, 1980, coach, 1981-83; coach Cheat Lake Youth Soccer, 1980-85; mem. sch. bd. St. Francis Central Grade Sch., 1981-83, sec., 1982-83; cubmaster Mountaineer Area council Boy Scouts Am., 1982—, unit commr., 1982—. Served to lt. USNR, 1969-72, comdr. USPHS, 1975—. Recipient commendation medal USPHS, 1980, cert. appreciation Ctrs. for Disease Control, 1981, Outstanding Service medal, 1985; named one of Outstanding Young Men Am., 1981, 83, Brotherhood mem. Order of Arrow, Boy Scouts Am. Mem. Am. Acad. Allergy and Immunology, Am. Assn. Immunologists, Am. Soc. Microbiology (industry and govt. agys. adv. council Allegheny br. 1980), Am. Thoracic Soc., Commd. Officers Assn. of USPHS (nat. and W.Va. br.), Nat. Eagle Scout Assn., Sigma Xi. Current work: Study of mechanisms of inflammation in the lung; immunotoxicity of agricultural dusts; study of complement interactions with inhaled dusts; gram-negative bacterial endotoxins. Subspecialties: Immunotoxicology; Microbiology (medicine). Office: Nat Inst Occupational Safety and Health 944 Chestnut Ridge Rd Morgantown WV 26505

OLESEN, DOUGLAS EUGENE, research institute executive; b. Tonasket, Wash., Jan. 12, 1939; s. Magnus and Esther Rae (Myers) O.; m. Michaele Ann Engdahl, Nov. 18, 1964; children: Douglas Eugene, Stephen Christian. B.S., U. Wash., 1962, M.S., 1963, postgrad., 1965-67, Ph.D., 1972. Research engr. space research div. Boeing Aircraft Co., Seattle, 1963-64; with Battelle Meml. Inst., Pacific NW Labs., Richland, Wash., 1967-84, mgr. water resources systems sect., water and land resources dept., 1970-71, mgr. dept., 1971-75, dep. dir. research labs., 1975, dir. research, 1975-79, v.p. inst., dir. NW div., 1979-84, exec. v.p., chief operating officer, Battelle Meml. Inst., Columbus, Ohio, 1984—; affiliate assoc. prof. U. Wash., 1973-84; mem. study adv. com. Joint Center for Grad. Study, 1979-84. Bd. dirs. United Way of Benton and Franklin Counties, 1978-84, chmn. 1983 campaign; Bd. dirs. Tri-City Nuclear Indsl. Council, 1979-84; bd. dirs., mem. exec. com. United Way of Wash., 1980-84, v.p., 1981-83, pres., 1983; gov.'s appointee Energy Fair '83 Commn., 1980-84; mem. Kadlec Hosp. Med. Center Found., 1980-84; mem. adv. bd. Sta. KCTS/9 Pub. TV, 1983-84; mem. Fed. Interagy. Task Force on Acid Precipitation, 1980-84; bd. dirs. Columbus Zoo, 1985—; chmn. Mid-Columbia U.S. Savs. Bond campaign, 1981. Mem. Water Pollution Control Fedn., Pacific NW Pollution Control Assn. (pres. 1977). Patentee process and system for treating waste water. Subspecialty: Water supply and wastewater treatment. Office: NW Div Lab Battelle Meml Inst 505 King Ave Columbus OH 43201

OLESON, NORMAN LEE, physicist, educator; b. Detroit, Aug. 19, 1912; s. Christian Gad and Mathilde Lorenzo (Halversen) O.; m. Gabrielle Dorothy Sauve, June 18, 1939; children: Karen A., Norman Lee, Richard P. B.S., U. Mich., 1935, M.S., 1937, Ph.D., 1940. Instr. U.S. Coast Guard Acad., 1940-46; physicist Gen. Electric Co., Cleve., 1946-48; assoc. prof. physics Naval Postgrad. Sch., 1948-49, prof., 1952-69; chmn. dept. physics U. South Fla., 1969-78, prof., 1978—; cons. physics Lawrence Livermore Lab., 1959-69; vis. prof. physics Queen's U., Belfast, 1955-56; vis. prof. nuclear engring. M.I.T., 1967-68. Contbr. articles to sci. jours. Served with USCGR, 1940-46. Fellow Am. Phys. Soc.; mem. AAAS, Sigma Xi, Sigma Pi Sigma. Current Work: Investigation of turbulent plasmas in magnetic fields, properties of ion acoustic waves. Subspecialty: Plasma physics. Home: 11003 Carrollwood Dr Tampa FL 33618 Office: Dept Physics U South Fla Tampa FL 33620

OLESZEK, GERALD MICHAEL, electrical engineering educator; b. Detroit, Sept. 29, 1940; s. Ignatius Lawrence and Helen (Lata) O.; m. Sharon Ann Green, Aug. 22, 1964; children—Kenneth, Kristine. B.S. in E.E., Wayne State U., 1964; M.S., Syracuse U., 1968, Ph.D., 1972. Pres., IC Assocs., Colorado Springs, Colo., 1978—; adv. engr. IBM Corp., Kingston, N.Y., 1964-78; assoc. prof. elec. engring. U. Colo., Colorado Springs, 1978—; sr. cons. UN, Geneva, 1975-82; dir. Microelectronics Research Lab., U. Colo., 1978-83; cons. in field. Contbr. articles to profl. jours. Patentee in field. Fulbright Found. Disting. scholar, 1984. Mem. IEEE, Electrochem. Soc. Current work: Microelectronics, integrated circuit fabrication processes and device physics, modeling and technologies. Subspecialties: Integrated circuits; Microchip technology (engineering). Home: 1510 Big Valley Dr Colorado Springs CO 80919 Office: Dept Elec Engring U Colo Colorado Springs CO 80919

OLHOEFT, GARY ROY, research geophysicist, photographer; b. Akron, Ohio, Feb. 15, 1949; s. Roy Carl and Helen Francis (Landefeld) O.; m. Jean Kane, Sept. 2, 1972. B.S.E.E., M.I.T., 1971, M.S.E.E., 1972; Ph.D., U. Toronto, 1975. Registered profl. engr., Ont. With Kennecott Copper Corp., Lexington, Mass., 1970-72, NASA Manned Spacecraft Ctr., Houston, 1971, M.I.T., Cambridge, 1971-72, Lockheed Electronics Co., Houston, 1972-73, U. Toronto, Ont., Can., 1973-75; research geophysicist U.S. Geol. Survey, Denver, 1975—; chief U.S. Geol. Survey (Br. Petrophysics and Remote Sensing), 1981-83; adj. prof. U. So. Calif., U. Colo.; mem. U.S. Com. for Rock Mechanics, 1983—; mem. sci. adv. com. Deep Observation and Sampling of Earth's Continental Crust, 1985—; advisor NASA, EPA, Bur. Mines, U.S. Dept. Energy, U.S. Navy, U.S. Army, Bur. Reclamation, Dept. Justice, U.S. Navy, U.S. Army, Def. Nuclear Agy. Assoc. editor: Geophysics; mem. editorial bd.: Internat. Jour. Thermophysics; assoc. editor Geophysics, 1985—; contbr. articles to profl. publs. in field. Vol. reader Recs. for the Blind; bd. dirs. Kipling Klub Townhouses, Amberwick Townhomes. Recipient Lunar Sci. Group achievement award, 1975. Mem. Am. Geophys. Union, ASTM (chmn. D-18.06), AAAS, Am. Astron. Soc. (div. planetary sci.), Soc. Exploration Geophysics (presentation award 1972), Soc. Photographic Scientists and Engrs., Soc. Profl. Well Log Analysts, Royal Soc. Chemists, IEEE (adv. com. geol. div., U.S. nat. com. rock mechanics). Current Work: Physical and chemical properties and processes of earth materials petrophysics, electrochemistry, induced polarization, complex resistivity, dielectrics, electrical properties, radar, geophysics, geotechnics, geothermal, minerals, permafrost, hazardous waste monitoring, lunar and planetary materials. Subspecialties: Geophysics; Electrochemistry. Office: PO Box 25046 DFC MS 964 Denver CO 80225

OLIEN, NEIL ARNOLD, government official; b. Lemmon, S.D., Mar. 3, 1935; s. Arthur and Lucile Eva (Williams) O.; m. Ronelle Leone Fort, Mar. 15, 1958; children—Howard Arthur, Allison Leslie. B.S. in Physics, S.D. Sch. Mines and Tech., 1960; M.A., Stanford U., 1961. Physicist, Nat. Bur. Standards, Boulder, Colo., 1961-65, project leader, 1965-72, sect. chief, 1972-80, div. chief, 1980-84, program analyst, Gaithersburg, Md., 1984-85, div. chief chem. engring. sci. div., Boulder, 1985—. Editor: Liquefied Natural Gas Data Book, 1980. Mem. editorial bd. Jour. Phys. and Chem. Reference Data, 1985—. Contbr. articles to profl. jours. Pres., Boulder Interfaith Housing, Inc., 1969-72. Served with U.S. Army, 1954-57. Recipient Centennial 100 award S.D. Sch. Mines and Tech., 1985; Silver medal Dept. Commerce, 1981. Mem. Am. Inst. Chem. Engrs., ASTM, AAAS. Lutheran. Current work: Critical evaluation of thermodynamic data; development of predictive models for thermophysical properties of fluid mixtures. Subspecialty: Chemical engineering. Office: Nat Bur Standards Thermophysics Div 325 Broadway Boulder CO 80303

OLIN, JACQUELINE SMITH, chemist, institution administrator; b. Lansford, Pa., Nov. 27, 1932; d. Walter Frantz and Anna Cornelia (Strickler) Smith; m. Charles Hilden Olin, Dec. 26, 1955; children—Deborah Ann, David Lind. B.S., Dickinson Coll., 1954; M.A., Harvard U., 1955; postgrad. U. Pa., 1955-56, NYU, 1961-62. Research asst. NIH, Bethesda, Md., 1956-57; instr. Dickinson Coll., Carlisle, Pa., 1959-60; research chemist Smithsonian Inst., Washington, 1963-83, adminstr., 1983—. Editor: Search for Ancient Tin, 1979, Archaeological Ceramics, 1982, Future Directions in Archaeometry, 1982. Cornell U. fellow, 1960-61; Nat. Endowment Humanities grantee, 1970. Fellow Am. Inst. Conservation of Historic and Artistic Works (sec. 1981-82), Internat. Inst. Conservation Historic and Artistic Works; mem. Phi Beta Kappa. Current work: Study of archaeological and historical artifacts using physical and chemical methods within well defined anthropological or art historical problems. Subspecialty: Archaeological chemistry. Home: 9506 Watts Rd Great Falls VA 22066 Office: Conservation Analytical Lab Smithsonian Inst Washington DC 20560

OLIVE, LINDSAY SHEPHERD, botanist, researcher; b. Florence, S.C., Apr. 30, 1917; s. Lindsay Shepherd and Sada (Williamson) O.; m. Anna Jean Grant, Aug. 28, 1942. A.B., U. N.C., 1938, M.A., 1940, Ph.D., 1942. Instr. U. N.C., Chapel Hill, 1942-44, prof., 1968-69, univ. disting. prof., 1969-82, univ. disting. prof. emeritus, 1982—; mycologist Dept. Agr., 1944-45; asst. prof. U. Ga., 1945-46; assoc. prof. La. State U., 1946-57, prof. Columbia U., 1957-67. Author: The Mycetozoans, 1975; contbr. 166 articles to profl. jours.; Ency. Americana; chpts. to books. Guggenheim fellow, 1956. Fellow AAAS; mem. Brit. Mycol. Soc. (hon.), Mycol. Soc. Am. (pres. 1966, Disting. Mycol. award 1982), Nat. Acad. Sci., Am. Bot. Soc., Soc. Protozoology, Nature Conservancy (hon.). Current Work: Fungi and mycetozoans. Subspecialties: Taxonomy; Morphology. Home: PO Box 391 Highlands NC 28741

OLIVER, CARL EDWARD, air force officer, mathematician; b. Anniston, Ala., Feb. 26, 1943; s. Joseph Carl and Evelyn Sybil (Wade) O.; m. Carole Elaine Harvard, Sept. 4, 1965; children—Keith Wade, Courtney Leigh. B.S., U. Ala., 1965, M.A., 1967, Ph.D., 1969. Asst. engr. Sperry Rand, Huntsville, Ala., 1965; NASA fellow U. Ala., 1965-69; commd. 1st lt., 1969, advanced through grades to lt col., 1984—; asst. prof. math. U.S. Air Force Inst. Tech., Dayton, Ohio, 1969-74; chief modeling and analysis sect. U.S. Air Force Weapons Lab., 1974-78; dep. dir. math., info. sci. Air Force Office Sci. Research, Washington, 1978-83; mgr. sr. sci. program U.S. Dept. Energy, 1983—; lectr. in field. Ireland Found. fellow Union Carbide, 1961; recipient mil. awards. Mem. Soc. Indsl. and Applied Math. (editor jour.), Am. Math. Soc., Math. Assn. Am., IEEE, Sigma Xi. Unitarian. Current work: Computational mathematics; research issues at interface of mathematics and computer science; computational science. Subspecialties: Numerical analysis (computer science); Algorithms. Home: 7305 Fathom Ct Burke VA 22015 Office: ER-7 GTN Dept Energy Washington DC 20545

OLIVER, CRAIG STANLEY, horticulturist, administrator; b. Brockton, Mass., Mar. 5, 1934; s. Stanley Thomas and Helen (Sabine) O.; m. Dorothy Mastalski, Apr. 13, 1955; children—Deborah R., Linda J. B.S., Pa. State U., 1957, M.Ed., 1960; Ph.D., Ohio State U., 1968. Tchr. Purchase Line High Sch., Pa., 1957-60, Hammonton High Sch., N.J., 1960-62; prof. Pa. State U., University Park, 1962-71, asst. dean, 1971-80; assoc. dean U. Ariz., Tucson, 1980-81; dir. U. Md., College Park, 1981—. Chmn. Harris Twp. Planning Commn. (Pa.); chmn. Harris Twp. Zoning Hearing Bd. Mem. Adult Edn. Assn., Am. Soc. Hort. Sci. Subspecialties: Plant genetics; Plant physiology (agriculture). Home: 12308 Mt Pleasant Dr Laurel MD 20708 Office: U Md Symons Hall College Park MD 20742

OLIVER, JACK ERTLE, geophysicist; b. Massillon, Ohio, Sept. 26, 1923; s. Chester L. and Marie (Ertle) O.; m. Gertrude van der Hoeven, Apr. 16, 1964; children—Cornelia Oliver, Amy Oliver. A.B., Columbia U., 1947, M.A., 1950,

Ph.D., 1953. Research asst., then research asso. Columbia, 1947-55, mem. faculty, 1955-73, prof. geology, 1961-71, chmn. dept., 1969-71, adj. prof., 1971-73; Irving Porter Church prof. engring. dept. geol. scis. Cornell U., 1971—, chmn. dept., 1971-81, dir. Inst. Study of Continents, 1983—; chmn. exec. com. COCORP; terrestrial physicist USAF Cambridge (Mass.) Research Labs., 1951; cons. AEC, 1969-72, ACDA, 1962-74, USAF Tech. Applications Center, 1959-65; mem. Polar Research Com., 1959-71, also nat. commn. uppermantle program, 1963-71; mem. panel solid earth problems Nat. Acad. Sci., 1962; mem. adv. com. U.S. Coast and Geodetic Survey, 1962-66, on seismology, 1960-72, chmn., 1966-70; mem. Geophysics Research Bd., 1969-70; U.S. coordinator 2d U.S.-Japan Earthquake Prediction Conf., Palisades, 1966; earth sci. panel NSF, 1962-65; mem. USAF Sci. Adv. Bd., 1960-63, 64-69; mem. geophysics adv. panel Office Sci. Research, USAF, 1961-74, chmn., 1966-68; U.S. del. Test Ban Conf., Geneva, Switzerland, 1958-59; intergovtl. meeting seismology and earthquake engring., mem. exec. com. IASPEI, 1968-71; mem. governing com. Internat. Seismol. Summary Commn., 1963-67, 75-76; mem. exec. com. UNESCO, Paris, France, 1964, U.S.-Japan Earthquake Prediction Conf., Tokyo, 1964; mem. UNESCO Joint Com. on Seismology and Earthquake Engring., 1965-71; chmn. exec. com. Office Earth Scis., NRC, 1976-79, Internat. Seismol. Centre, 1976-78; mem. U.S. Geodynamics Com., 1979—, chmn., 1984—; mem. Geol. Scis. Bd., Assembly of Math. and Phys. Scis., NRC, 1981-84; mem. adv. bd. Sch. Earth Scis., Stanford U., 1984-87; Cabot disting. vis. scholar U. Houston, 1985-86. Served with USNR, 1943-46. Fellow Am. Geophys. Union (pres. seismology sect. 1964-68, Walter H. Bucher medal 1981), Geol Soc. Am. (council 1970-73, mem. ad hoc com. for Decade of N.Am. Geology 1980—); mem. Nat. Acad. scis., Seismol. Soc. Am. (pres. 1964-65, bd. dirs. 1961-70, 72-76), Acoustical Soc. Am. (1954-69), Am. Phys. Soc. (1950-66), Soc. Exploration Geophysicists (Virgil Kauffman Gold medal 1983). AAAS, Sigma Xi. Current work: Multi-institutional COCORP project. Subspecialties: Geophysics; Tectonics. Home: 125 Cayuga Park Rd Ithaca NY 14850

OLIVER, JACK (WALLACE), veterinary pharmacology educator; b. Elletts-ville, Ind., Jan. 6, 1938; s. Levi Webster and Helen Marie (Stultz) O.; m. Martha Lou (Young); children: Jason B., Kevin M. B.S. in Agr, Purdue U., 1960, M.S. in Agr, 1963, D.V.M., 1966, Ph.D. in Vet. Physiology, 1969. Asst. prof. vet. pharmacology Purdue U., West Lafayette, Ind., 1969-70, Tex. A&M U., College Station, 1970-71, Ohio State U., Columbus, 1972-75; assoc. prof. vet. pharmacology U. Tenn., Knoxville, 1975-82, prof., 1982—, Lindsay Young Prof. vet. medicine, 1980; lab. dir. U. Tenn. (Clin. Endocrinology Service Lab., Coll. Vet. Medicine.). Fellow Am. Acad. Vet. Pharmacology and Therapeutics; mem. Am. Soc. Vet. Physiology and Pharmacology, Assn. Am. Vet. Med. Colls., Conf. Research Workers in Animal Disease, AVMA, Tenn. Vet. Med. Assn., Phi Zeta. Current Work: Thyroid physiology relationship to aberrant metabolism. Subspecialty: Veterinary pharmacology. Office: Dept Environmental Practice Coll Vet Medicine Univ Tenn Knoxville TN 37916

OLIVER, JAMES D., JR., electrical engineer, consultant; b. Abington, Pa., Jan. 5, 1954; s. James D. and Charlotte J. (Wetzel) O.; m. Joann Marie Kochera, May 28, 1977; 1 child, Paul J. B.S., Pa. State U., 1975; Ph.D., Cornell U., 1980. Research assoc. Cornell U., Ithaca, N.Y., 1979-80; cons. engr. Gen. Electric Co., Syracuse, N.Y., 1979-80; asst. prof. elec. engring. U. Va., Charlottesville, 1980-85; sr. engr. Microwave Semicondr. Corp., Somerset, N.J., 1985—; electronic engr. Nat. Bur. Standards, Washington, 1982—; elec. engr. U.S. Army Fgn. Sci. and Tech. Ctr., Charlottesville, 1982-85. Contbr. articles to profl. jours. Asst. scoutmaster Boy Scouts Am., Charlottesville, 1981-85; advancement chmn. Monticello Dist., Charlottesville. Recipient Most Outstanding Publ. award Jour. Electronic Materials, 1980; Rockwell Internat. fellow, 1976-80. Mem. IEEE (central Va. sect.; exec. com. 1982—, counselor U. Va. Student br., Outstanding Br. Counselor award Region 3 1985), Sigma Xi, Tau Beta Pi. Current work: Research on III-V semiconductor epitaxial materials, fabrication processes, and device design. Subspecialties: Semiconductors; Microelectronics. Office: Microwave Semicondr Corp 100 School House Rd Somerset NJ 08873

OLIVER, JOHN PARKER, astonomer; b. New Rochelle, N.Y., Nov. 24, 1939; s. James Parker and Evelyn Smithen (Grant) O.; m. Barbara McKenna, Nov. 2, 1963; children: Jennifer, Keith, Rebecca. B.S. in Physics, Rensselaer Poly. Inst., 1962; Ph.D. in Astronomy, UCLA, 1974. Asst. prof. astronomy U. Fla., 1970-77, assoc. prof. astronomy, 1977—; dir. U. Fla. (Rosemary Hill Obs.). Mem. Internat. Astron. Union. Current Work: Observation of binary stars; lunar occultation photometry; computer based instruments. Subspecialties: Optical astronomy; Astronomical instruments. Office: U Fla 211 SSRB Astronomy Gainesville FL 32611

OLIVER, KELLY HOYET, JR., biology educator, aquatic biology consultant; b. Rosboro, Ark., June 22, 1923; s. Kelly H. and Willye B. (Long) O.; m. Carley Dickey, Dec. 26, 1947; children: Carol A., Mark L., Rush H. B.S., So. Meth. U., 1952, M.S., 1953; Ph.D., Okla. State U., 1963. Assoc. prof. biology Ark. State U., Jonesboro, 1962-64; chief of biolab Vitro Services, Eglin AFB, Fla., 1964-68; prof. biology Henderson State U., Arkadelphia, Ark., 1968—; pres. Kocomoro, Inc., Arkadelphia, 1973—. Chmn. com. Boy Scouts Am., Ft. Walton Beach, Fla., 1964. Served with U.S. Army, 1943-46, ETO. Mem. Ark. Acad. Sci., Sigma Xi, Phi Delta Kappa. Democrat. Methodist. Club: Pullen's (Arkadelphia) (v.p. 1980-82). Lodges: Masons (De Queen, Ark.); Lions. Current Work: Effects of pesticides on fauna; bioassay of residues on fishes and selected invertebrates. Subspecialties: Ecology (environmental science); Environmental toxicology. Home: 204 N 27th St Arkadelphia AR 71923 Office: Henderson State U Henderson St Arkadelphia AR 71923

OLIVER, WILLIAM ALBERT, JR., paleontologist; b. Columbus, Ohio, June 26, 1926; s. William Albert and Mary Maud (Thompson) O.; m. Johanna Louise Kramer, Sept. 1, 1948; children—Robert Alan, James Andrew. B.S., U. Ill., 1948; M.A., Cornell U., 1950, Ph.D., 1952. From instr. to asst. prof. Brown U., Providence, 1952-57; research paleontologist U.S. Geol. Survey, Washington, 1957—; adj. prof. George Washington U., 1969-70. Editor: Animal Colonies, 1973; Advances in Paleobiology of Cnidaria, 1984. Contbr. articles (over 100) to profl. jours. Served with USN, 1943-45. Pres., Palontol. Research Inst., Ithaca, N.Y., 1983—, trustee, 1977—; pres. Am. Geol. Inst., Washington, 1976-77, bd. dirs., 1973-77. Grantee NSF, 1969-70, Smithsonian Research Found., 1968-79. Fellow Geol. Soc. Am.; mem. Paleontol. Soc. (pres. 1974-75, editor 1964-69). Current work: Biology, evolution and history of Silurian and Devonian rugose corals. Subspecialty: Paleobiology. Office: US Geol Survey E 305 Natural History Mus Washington DC 20560

OLLAPALLY, PHILIP JOSEPH, design engineer, entrepreneur; b. Kottayam, India, Dec. 21, 1949; came to U.S., 1973; s. Joseph Philip and Thankam (Joseph) O.; m. Elsie Phillipos, Mar. 26, 1977; children—Vineeta Maria, Priya Elizabeth. B.E., Birla Inst., Pilani, India, 1972; M.S.E.E., U. Tex.-El Paso, 1974; Ph.D., Carnegie-Mellon U., 1982. Digital design engr. Gus Mfg. Inc., El Paso, 1974-77; instr. SUNY-Buffalo, 1977-78; research assoc. Carnegie-Mellon U., Pitts., 1978-81; asst. prof. Tenn. State U., Nashville, 1981-83; pres. Intellimed, Inc., Madison, Tenn., 1984—. Mem. IEEE, Engring. in Medicine and Biology Soc., Eta Kappa Nu. Roman Catholic. Lodge: K.C. Current work: computer applications in medicine, computer graphics and artificial intelligence. Subspecialties: Biomedical engineering; Computer engineering. Home: 1285 Cheyenne Blvd Madison TN 27115 Office: Intellimed Inc 1285 Cheyenne Blvd Madison TN 37115

OLMSTEAD, WILLIAM EDWARD, mathematics educator, applied mathematician; b. San Antonio, June 2, 1936; s. William Harold and Gwendolyn (Littlefield) O.; m. Adele Cross, Aug. 14, 1957 (div. Sept. 1968); children—William Harold, Randell Edward. B.S., Rice U., 1959; M.S., Northwestern U., 1962, Ph.D., 1963. Mem. research staff Southwest Research Inc., San Antonio, 1959-60; Sloan fellow Johns Hopkins U., Balt., 1963-64; vis. mem. Courant Inst., NYU, 1967-68; vis. prof. Univ. Coll., London, 1973; prof. applied math. Northwestern U., Evanston, Ill., 1964—, dir. applied math., 1972-76, 78-80. Contbr. articles to math. jours. Recipient Teaching award Tech. Inst., Northwestern U., 1979; Sloan fellow, 1963. Mem. Am. Acad. Mechanics, Am. Phys. Soc., Soc. for Indsl. and Applied Math. (vis. lectr. 1972, 78), Sigma Xi, Tau Beta Pi, Sigma Tau. Episcopalian. Club: Am. Contract Bridge League (life master 1976—). Current work: Mathematical problems associated with reaction-diffusion phenomena, fluid dynamics, micropolar fluids and visco-elastic fluid stability. Subspecialties: Applied mathematics; Combustion processes. Office: Dept Engring Scis and Applied Math Northwestern U Evanston IL 60201

OLNESS, ROBERT JAMES, physicist; b. Milaca, Minn., Jan. 22, 1933; s. Fredrick F. and Esther Victoria (Johnson) O.; m. Sara Dolores Urquiza, June 17, 1957; children—James Manuel, Gwendolyn Esther, Michael Fredrick. B.S. in Physics, MIT, 1956; Ph.D., Duke U., 1962. Research assoc. dept. physics U. N.C., Chapel Hill, 1961-63; sr. physicist U. Calif. Lawrence Livermore Nat. Lab., 1963-68, sr. physicist, 1969—; assoc. prof. physics No. Mich. U., Marquette, 1968-69. Mem. Am. Phys. Soc., Calif. Acad. Scis. Democrat. Current work: Thermodynamics and statistical mechanics, atomic and molecular physics, plasma physics; theoretical development, computer simulation. Subspecialties: Statistical physics; Plasma physics. Home: 4345 Guilford Ave Livermore CA 94550 Office: U Calif Lawrence Livermore Nat Lab L-296 PO Box 808 Livermore CA 94550

OLSEN, DAVID KENNETH, chemist; b. Leadville, Colo., Oct. 9, 1949; s. Kenneth Raymond and Catherine (Bochatey) O.; m. Lois Jeanne Bungo, Aug. 19, 1978. B.S. in Chemistry, Colo. State U., 1971; M.S., Idaho State U., 1973; D.A., U., No. Colo., 1980. Prof. chemistry and petroleum Colo. N.W. Community Coll., Rangely, 1976-80; research assoc. Getty Oil Co., Houston, 1980-83; sr. research chemist Nat. Inst. Petroleum Research, Bartlesville, Okla., 1983-85; project leader in applied chemflood research, recovery process research, 1985—; cons. Ark. Mining, Leadville, Colo., 1967-80, Olsen Bungo Resources, Clearfield, Pa., 1976-80. Contbr. articles to profl. publs. Patentee in field. Boettcher fellow, 1975-76; Colo. Petroleum Producers Assn. fellow, 1979; State Colo. Higher Edn. fellow, 1976. Mem. Am. Chem. Soc., Am. Oil Chemists Assn., Soc. Petroleum Engrs. (sec. continuing edn. com. Houston chpt. 1983), Sigma Xi. Lodges: Elks, Lions (local sec. 1976-80). Current work: Enhanced oil recovery using surfactants, biosurfactants and polymers; reservoir engineering. Subspecialties: Fuels; Petroleum engineering. Office: Nat Inst Petroleum Research Box 2128 Bartlesville OK 74004

OLSEN, JOSEPH CARL, consultant engineer, lawyer; b. N.Y.C., Sept. 28, 1927; s. Henry and Rosetta Olsen; m. Dina Elizabeth Schotz, Oct. 26, 1954; children—Joseph Carl II, Paul Maurice. Tool/diemaking apprentice, 1948-53; B.S. in Mech. Engring., U. Wash., 1956, postgrad., 1958; postgrad. Stanford U., 1960-61; M.B.A., Santa Clara U., 1963, postgrad., 1964-65, J.D., 1973; D.Sc., Calif. Western U., 1982. Bar: Calif.; registered profl. engr., Calif. Pres., corp. counsel multi-disciplined cons. engring. firm, San Jose, Calif., 1963—; assoc. firm McCready, Doyle, Thompson & Olsen, San Jose and San Francisco. Contbr. articles to profl. jours. Patentee in field. Served with USNR, 1952-60. Mem. ASME, Nat. Soc. Profl. Engrs., Calif. Soc. Profl. Engrs., Cons. Engrs. Assn. Calif., Calif. Inventors Council (pres. 1971-73), State Bar Calif., Am. Trial Lawyers Assn., Calif. Trial Lawyers Assn. Club: San Jose Engineers. Subspecialty: Mechanical engineering. Office: Engring Cons Services PO Box 1809 8 S Montgomery St San Jose CA 95109

OLSEN, KATHIE LYNN, neurobiology educator; b. Portland, Oreg., Aug. 3, 1952; d. Roland Berg and Gladys Elizabeth (Eldreth) O. B.S., Chatham Coll., 1974; Ph.D., U. Calif.-Irvine, 1979; postdoctoral fellow Harvard U. Med. Sch., 1979-80. Research scientist L.I. Research Inst., Stony Brook, N.Y., 1980-83; research asst. prof. dept. psychiatry and behavioral sci. SUNY Med. Sch., Stony Brook, 1982-84, asst. prof., 1984—; assoc. program dir. NSF, Washington, 1984-86. Contbr. articles to profl. jours. Mem. Soc. Neurosci., Assn. Women in Sci., Internat. Acad. Sexual Research, AAAS, Animal Behavior Soc. Current work: Hormonal modulation of sex differences in brain and behavior. Subspecialties: Neurobiology; Neuroendocrinology. Office: Dept Psychiatry and Behavioral Sci HSC 10T SUNY Stony Brook NY 11794

OLSEN, KENNETH HARRY, manufacturing company executive; b. Bridgeport, Conn., Feb. 20, 1926; s. Oswald and Svea (Nordling) O.; m. Eeva-Liisa Aulikki Valve, Dec. 12, 1950. B.S. in Elec. Engring, MIT, 1950, M.S., 1952. Elec. engr. Lincoln Lab., MIT, 1950-57; founder, 1957, since pres. Digital Equipment Corp., Maynard, Mass.; dir. Polaroid Corp., Shawmut Assn., Ford Motor Co. Mem. Pres.'s Sci. Adv. Com., 1971-73; Mem. corp., v.p. Joslin Diabetes Found., Wentworth Inst., Boston, MIT, Cambridge; trustee Gordon Coll., Wenham, Mass. Served with USNR, 1944-46. Named Young Elec. Engr. of Year Eta Kappa Nu, 1960. Mem. Nat. Acad. Engring. (Founders medal 1982). Patentee magnetic devices. Subspecialty: Electrical engineering. Home: Weston Rd Lincoln MA 01773 Office: Digital Equipment Corp Maynard MA 01754

OLSEN, NORMAN HARRY, dentist, educator; b. Omaha, June 9, 1926; s. Carl and Johanna (Jorgensen) O.; m. Donna Roberts, Sept. 14, 1947; children—Karl Raymond, Heidi Roberts, Holly Roberts. Student, U. Idaho, 1945-46; D.D.S., Creighton U., 1951; M.S.D., Northwestern U., 1953. Diplomate: Am. Bd. Pedodontics (bd. examiners). Montgomery Ward fellow Northwestern U., 1951-53, prof. pedodontics, 1954—, chmn. dept., 1954-72, dean, 1972—; prof., chmn. dept. pedodontics U. Kansas City Sch. Dentistry, 1953-54; staff Meml. Mercy Hosp., Kansas City, 1953-54, Northwestern Meml. Hosp., 1974—; head dental service Children's Meml. Hosp., Chgo., 1954—; courtesy staff Evanston Hosp., St. Francis Hosp., Evanston; mem. Cleft Palate Inst., Northwestern U. and Childrens Meml. Hosp.; cons. Throat Culturing Research Program, Stickney Twp. Health Dept.; chmn. Am. Bd. Pedodontic Examiners, 1973-74; Commr. Joint Commn. on Accreditation Dental Labs. Co-editor: 4th edit. Current Therapy in Dentistry, 1970; editor pedodontic sect., 5th edit., 1974; Contbr.: chpt. Dental Clinics of N.Am, 1961; articles profl. jours. Sec. faculty com. intercollegiate athletics Northwestern U., 1962-68; chmn. profl. div. Evanston United Fund, 1967-68; Pres. First Ward Non-Partisan Civic Assn., Evanston; former trustee Roycemore Sch.; mem. exec. com. Dist. 65 Sch. Bd.; bd. dirs. Infant Welfare Soc., Chgo. Served with USNR, 1944-46. Recipient Service award Northwestern U., 1966; Merit award Am. Soc. Dentistry for Children, 1951; Alumni Merit award Creighton U., 1975. Fellow Am. Coll. Dentistry (vice chmn. Ill. sect. 1979-80, regent 1979, pres. 1985—), Internat. Coll. Dentists, Chgo. Inst. Medicine; mem. ADA (pedodontic adv. com. Joint Commn. Accreditation, past sect. chmn.), Ill. Dental Soc. (past program chmn.), Chgo. Dental Soc. (past program chmn.), Am. Acad. Pedodontics (pres. 1973-74), Am. Soc. Dentistry for Children (past pres. Ill., award of Excellence 1974, Man of Yr. award Ill. unit), Internat. Assn. Dental Research, Am. Assn. Cleft Palate Rehab., Am. Acad. Gold Foil Operators, Odontographic Soc. Chgo. (bd. govs., past program chmn.), Ill. Pedodontics (charter), Am. Dental Soc. of Europe (hon.), GV Black Soc. Northwestern U. (sec.), Northwestern U. Dental Alumni Assn. (past pres.), Am. Assn. Dental Schs. (past sect. chmn., chmn. council deans 1985-86), Sigma Alpha Epsilon, Delta Sigma Delta, Omicron Kappa Upsilon. Clubs: Evanston (Northwestern U.) (dir.), Rotary (Northwestern U.) (pres. Evanston chpt. 1980-81), John Evans (Northwestern U.) (dir.). Subspecialty: Pediatric dentistry. Home: 221 Winnetka Ave Winnetka IL 60093 Office: 311 E Chicago Ave Chicago IL 60611

OLSON, DAVID PETER, veterinarian, researcher; b. Mpls., Sept. 28, 1935; s. John W. and Gladys Regina (Hallstrom) L.; m. Jane Marie Nieters, June 20, 1959; children—Dree Ann, Steven William, Alane Marie. B.S., U. Minn., 1958, D.V.M., 1960; M.S., Mich. State U., 1972, Ph.D., 1975. Practice vet. medicine, Worthington, Minn., 1960-69; instr. Mich. State U., East Lansing, 1969-75; assoc. prof. vet. pathology U. Idaho, Moscow, 1975-81, prof., 1981—; mem. adj. grad. faculty Wash. State U., Pullman, 1980—; mem. affiliate faculty U. Wash. Sch. Medicine, Seattle, 1984; chmn. Coop. Western Regional Research Commn., 1983. Contbr. papers, book chpt. to profl. lit. Host student exchange program Am. Field Service, Moscow, 1981-82. Mem. AVMA, AAAS, N.Y. Acad. Scis., Sigma Xi, Gamma Sigma Delta. Current work: Morphologic and clinical pathology, pathophysiology, immunopathology, herd health management, principles and mechanisms of cell and tissue response to injury. Subspecialties: Pathology (veterinary medicine); Preventive medicine (veterinary medicine). Home: 1402 Borah Ave Moscow ID 83843 Office: Dept Vet Sci U Idaho Moscow ID 83843

OLSON, EDWARD COOPER, astronomer; b. Worcester, Mass., June 7, 1930; s. Nils and Marion (Cooper) O.; m. Margaret Jean Edmundson, May 31, 1959; children: Eric, Jeffrey. Ph.D., Ind. U., 1960. Faculty Smith Coll., 1960-64, Rensselaer Poly. Inst., Troy, N.Y., 1965-66; faculty U. Ill., Urbana, 1966—, now astronomer. Contbr. articles to profl. jours. Served with U.S. Army, 1953-55. NSF grantee, 1962—. Mem. Am. Astron. Soc., Internat. Astron. Union, Astron. Soc. Pacific, Internat. Amateur and Profl. Photoelectric Photometry. Current Work: Evolution of close binary systems. Subspecialties: Optical astronomy; Close binary stars. Office: Dept Astronomy U Ill 1011 W Springfield Urbana IL 61801

OLSON, ERIK JOSEPH, pharmacology educator; b. N.Y.C., Aug. 17, 1932; s. Joseph Olaf and Grace (Martin) O.; m. Baerbec Stober, Dec. 31, 1961 (div. July 1978); children—Christine, Maret, Lars. B.S., Cornell U., 1954; M.S., Purdue U., 1959, Ph.D., 1961. Instr., Vanderbilt U. Med. Sch., Nashville, 1961-63; research assoc. Western Res. U. Med. Sch., Cleve., 1963-64; asst. prof. Meharry Med. Coll., Nashville, 1964—. Contbr. articles to profl. jours. Active Friends of the Earth, Nashville, 1974. Served with AUS, 1957-58. Mem. Am. Physiol. Soc., N.Y. Acad. Scis. Democrat. Methodist. Club: Red Cell. Current work: Active calcium transport from erythrocytes, attachment of glyceraldehyde, phosphate dehydrgenase to red cells. Subspecialty: Membrane biology. Home: 246 White Bridge Rd Nashville TN 37209 Office: Dept Pharmacology Meharry Med Coll 1005 DB Todd Blvd Nashville TN 37209

OLSON, EVERETT CLAIRE, biology educator; b. Waupaca, Wis., Nov. 6, 1910; s. Claire Myron and Aimee (Hicks) O.; m. Lila Richardson, July 15, 1939; children Claire, George, Mary Ellen. B.S., U. Chgo., 1932, M.S., 1933, Ph.D., 1935. Instr. to prof. geology U. Chgo., 1935-69; prof. biology UCLA, 1969—, dept. chmn., 1970-72. Author: Evolution of Life, 1965, (with Agnes Whitmarsh) Foreign Maps, 1944, (with Robert Miller) Morphological Integration, 1958, Vertebrate Paleozoology, 1971, (with Jane Robinson) Concepts of Evolution, 1975; editor: (with Jane Robinson) jour. Geology, 1960-66, Evolution, 1952-58. NSF grantee. Mem. Soc. Vertebrate Paleontology, Soc. Study Evolution, Am. Soc. Zoologists, Geol. Soc. Am., Nat. Acad. Sci., Phi Beta Kappa, Sigma Xi. Current Work: Chronotaunal evolution; vertebrates. Subspecialty: Evolutionary biology. Home: 13760 Bayliss Rd Los Angeles CA 90049 Office: 405 Hilgarde St Los Angeles CA 90024

OLSON, FERRON ALLRED, metallurgy educator; b. Tooele, Utah, July 2, 1921; s. John Ernest and Harriet Cynthia (Allred) O.; m. Donna Lee Jefferies, Feb. 1, 1944; children—Kandace, Randall, Paul, Jeffery, Richard. B.S. in Chemistry, U. Utah, 1953, Ph.D. in Fuel Tech., 1956. Research chemist Shell Devel. Co., Emeryville, Calif., 1956-61, assoc. research prof. dept. metallurgy and metal. engring. U. Utah, Salt Lake City, 1961-63, assoc. prof., 1963-66, chmn. dept., 1966-74, prof., 1975—; dir. Utah Mining and Mineral Resources Resource Inst., Salt Lake City, 1980—; Fulbright instr. U. Belgrade, Yugoslavia, 1974-75; cons. in field. Contbr. articles to profl. jours. Bishop Mormon Ch., 1962-68, 1976-82. Named Disting. Prof. Fulbright Hayes Program, 1980. Mem. AIME (chmn. Utah sect. 1978-79), Soc. Mining Engrs., Am. Soc. Metallurgy, Fulbright Alumni Assn., Sigma Xi. Republican. Current work: Electrometallurgy, kinetics and mechanisms of decomposition metallurgical thermodynamics, energy utilization and surface chemistry. Subspecialties: Metallurgy; Metallurgical engineering. Home: 1862 Harbert Ave Salt Lake City UT 84108 Office: U Utah Dept Metallurgy & Metallurgical Engring Salt Lake City UT 84112

OLSON, GARY LEE, organic chemist; b. Ancon, C.Z., Mar. 15, 1945; s. Roy Edward and Eugenia Alberta (Grey) O.; m. Wilma Adeline King, June 28, 1969; 1 child, Andrew James. A.B., Columbia U., 1967; Ph.D., Stanford U., 1971. Sr. chemist Hoffmann-La Roche Inc., Nutley, N.J., 1971-80, asst. research group chief, 1980-83, research fellow, 1983-85, research investigator, 1985—; vis. exchange scientist F. Hoffman-La Roche & Co. Ltd., Basel, Switzerland, 1978-79; vis. lectr. Jilin U., Changchun, China, 1981. Contbr. articles to profl. jours. Patentee in field. Columbia U. scholar, 1963-67; Nichols fellow Stanford U., 1967. Mem. Am. Chem. Soc., Am. Acad. Arts and Scis., N.Y. Acad. Scis., Sigma Xi, Phi Lambda Upsilon. Current work: Design and synthesis of conformationally defined drugs as probes of receptor function and structure; drugs affecting the central nervous system; peptide mimetics. Subspecialties: Organic chemistry; Drug design. Home: 431 Everson Pl Westfield NJ 07090 Office: Hoffmann-LaRoche Inc 340 Kingsland St Nutley NJ 07110

OLSON, GAYLE AUGUSTINE, psychology educator, researcher; b. St. Louis, Jan. 9, 1945; d. George E. and Edith (Alpiser) Augustine; m. Richard D. Olson, Aug. 26, 1967. B.A., Butler U., 1966; M.S., St. Louis U., 1968, Ph.D., 1970. Asst. prof. St. Mary's Dominican Coll., New Orleans, 1970-71; asst. prof. U. New Orleans, 1971-74, assoc. prof., 1974-81, assoc. dean grad. sch., 1976-78, prof. dept. psychology, 1981—; psychologist DePaul Hosp., New Orleans, 1974-76. Author (with R. Olson and R. Smith); Learning in the classroom: Theory and Applications, 1971. Chmn. scholarship com. Seafarer's Internat. Union, Washington, 1977—. Mem. AAAS, Am. Psychol. Assn., Soc. Neuroscis., Psychonomic Soc., Sigma Xi, Psi Chi, Delta Gamma. Current work: Study of behavioral effects of neuropeptides including effects on learning, eating and drinking, activity, pain and tonic immobility, especially dealt with opiate neuropeptides and their antagonists. Home: 103 Doubloon Dr Slidell LA 70461 Office: Dept Psychology U New Orleans Lakefront New Orleans LA 70148

OLSON, GORDON LEE, physicist; b. Ortonville, Minn., Oct. 1, 1951; s. Gilbert E. and Zella Mae (Fetterly) O.; m. Linda Fay Madsen, Apr. 20, 1974; 1 son, Brian. B.Phys., U. Minn., 1973; M.S., U. Wis., 1975, Ph.D., 1977. Sci. collaborator Astrophys. Inst., Free U. Brussels, Belgium, 1977-79; research assoc. Joint Inst. for Lab. Astrophysics, U. Colo., Boulder, 1979-81; scientific staff Los Alamos Nat. Lab., 1981—. Contbr. articles to profl. jours. Mem. Am. Astron. Soc., AAAS. Current Work: Stellar winds in hot stars and radiative transfer. Subspecialties: Ultraviolet high energy astrophysics; Theoretical astrophysics. Home: 470 Aragon Ave White Rock NM 87544 Office: Los Alamos Nat Lab PO Box 1663 Los Alamos NM 87545

OLSON, KENNETH BARRIE, physician, educator; b. Seattle, Jan. 21, 1908; s. Donald Barrie and Hattie (Palmer) O.; m. Emma Naomi Tallman, Apr. 3, 1937; children—Karen Barrie Mason, Kenneth Barrie Jr. B.S., U. Wash., 1929; M.D., Harvard U., 1933. Resident in pathology Boston City Hosp., 1933-34; intern in surgery Presbyn. Hosp., N.Y.C., 1934-36, asst. resident and resident surgery, 1936-39; clin. asst. in surgery Columbia U. Sch. Medicine, N.Y., 1939-40, Trudeau Sanatorium, N.Y., 1941; asst. physician, acting pathologist Olive View Sanatorium, Calif., 1941-43; dir. Tb Control and dir. Firland Sanatorium, Seattle, 1943-45; asst. physician Glenridge Sanatorium, Schenectady, 1947-50; from instr. to assoc. prof. Albany Med. Coll., Union U., N.Y., from 1950, prof. medicine and head div. oncology, until 1972, prof. emeritus, 1972-73; chief diagnosis br. div. cancer biology and diagnosis Nat. Cancer Inst.; cons. Nat. Cancer Inst., Bethesda, Md., 1973—, Fla. Cancer Council, Tampa, 1974—, Halifax Hosp. Med. Ctr., Daytona Beach, Fla., 1974—; Contbr. articles to profl. jours., chpt. to book. Bd. dirs. Am. Cancer Soc., Daytona Beach, 1974—. Recipient Faculty Research award Albany Med. Sch., 1967, Golden Apple award for teaching, 1958, 66. Fellow ACP; mem. Am. Soc. Clin. Oncology (pres. 1971-72), Am. Assn. Cancer Edn. (chmn. 1958), Am. Assn. Cancer Research, Alpha Omega Alpha. Club: Smyrna Yacht. Current work: Chemotherapy of cancer; tumor markers. Subspecialties: Internal medicine; Chemotherapy. Address: 810 Oakview Dr New Smyrna Beach FL 32069

OLSON, MARK OBED JEROME, biochemist, educator; b. Boyd, Minn., Aug. 20, 1940; s. Gerhard O. and Ruth (Haakenson) O.; m. Joanne Kathleen Protheroe, Sept. 3, 1966; children—Peter, Matthew, Kristin. B.A., St. Olaf Coll., 1962; Ph.D., U. Minn., 1967. Postdoctoral fellow U. Alta, Edmonton, Can., 1967-69; asst. prof., Baylor Coll. Medicine, Houston, 1969-74, assoc. prof., 1974-79; assoc. prof. U. Miss. Med. Ctr., Jackson, 1979-83, prof., 1983—. Contbr. articles to profl. jours., chpts. to books. Active Common Cause. Nat. Cancer Inst. grantee, 1975-79; NIH grantee, 1981-86. Mem. Am. Soc. Biol. Chemistry, Am. Chem. Soc., AAAS, Am. Assn. Cancer Research, Am. Soc. Cell Biology. Lutheran. Current work: Protein chemistry, structure and function of proteins of the cell nucleus, organization of the nucleolus. Subspecialties: Biochemistry (biology); Cell biology. Home: 2247 Bellingrath Rd Jackson MS 39211 Office: Dept Biochemistry U Miss Med Ctr 2500 N State St Jackson MS 39216

OLSON, RICHARD EDWARD, research engineer; b. Downers Grove, Ill., Mar. 21, 1954; s. Richard V. and Josephine L. (Rathenau) O.; m. Vera Moy, June 26, 1982. B.S., U. Ill., 1976, M.S., 1978, Ph.D., 1983. Mem. tech. staff Sandia Labs., Albuquerque, 1983—. Contbr. articles to sci. jours. Mem. Am. Nuclear Soc., Am. Phys. Soc., IEEE, Sigma Xi. Current work: Pulsed power and particle beam research; current work involves design of the particle beam fusion target development facility. Subspecialties: Fusion; Laser fusion. Home: 1804 Gabaldon NW Albuquerque NM 87104 Office: Sandia Labs PO Box 5800 Albuquerque NM 87185

OLSSON, CARL ALFRED, urologist; b. Boston, Nov. 29, 1938; s. Charles Rudolph and Ruth Marion (Bostrom) O.; m. Mary DeVore, Nov. 4, 1962; children: Ingrid, Leif Eric. Grad., Bowdoin Coll., 1959; M.D., Boston U., 1963.

Diplomate: Am. Bd. Urology. Asst. prof. urology Boston U. Sch. Medicine, 1971-72, assoc. prof., 1972-74, prof., chmn. dept., 1974-80; dir. urology dept. Boston City Hosp., 1974-77; chief urology dept. Boston VA Med. Center, 1971-75; urologist-in-chief Univ. Hosp., Boston, 1971-80; John K. Lattimer prof., chmn. dept. urology Coll. Phys. and Surgs., Columbia U., N.Y.C., 1980—; dir. Squier Urol. Clinic, urology service Presbyn. Hosp., N.Y.C.; lectr. surgery Tufts U. Sch. Medicine. Boston Interhosp. Organ Bank, 1976-79; mem. working cadre Nat. Prostate Cancer Project, Nat. Cancer Inst., 1979—. Editorial bd. Jour. Microsurgery and Prostate; asst. editor Jour. Urology; contbr. chpts. to books, articles to med. jours. Recipient disting. alumnus award Boston U. Sch. Medicine, 1985. Fellow A.C.S.; mem. Am. Urol. Assn. (coordinator continuing med. edn. New Eng. sect. 1977-80, del. research com., Gold Cystoscope award 1979, Grayson-Carroll award 1971, 73), Boston Surg. Soc. (exec. com. 1976—), Am. Assn. Clin. Urologists, Am. Assn. Genitourinary Surgeons, Clin. Soc. Genitouninary Surgeons, Am. Fertility Soc., AMA, Assn. Acad. Surgery, Am. Soc. Artificial Internal Organs, Am. Soc. Transplant Surgeons, Assn. Med. Colls., Transplant Soc., Societe Internationale d'Urologie, Internat. Urodynamics Soc., Mass. Med. Soc., Soc. Govt. Urologists, New Eng. Handicapped Sportsmen's Assn. (exec. com. 1977—), Soc. Univ. Urologists, Alpha Omega Alpha. Episcopalian. Clubs: U.S. Yacht Racing Union, Yacht Racing Union L.I. Sound, Cottage Park Yacht, Larchmont Yacht. Current Work: Cancer research. Subspecialties: Urology; Oncology. Home: 18 Elm St Larchmont NY 10538 Office: 630 W 168th St New York NY 10032

OLSSON, RICHARD KEITH, geology educator, researcher, consultant; b. Newark, Mar. 23, 1931; s. Harold and Martha (Klenke) O.; m. Nancy Hunter, Apr. 27, 1957; children: Richard, Robert, Jeffrey. B.S., Rutgers U., 1953, M.S. in Geology, 1954; M.A., Princeton U., 1956, Ph.D. in Geology, 1958. Instr. geology Rutgers U., New Brunswick, N.J., 1957-60, asst. prof., 1960-63, assoc. prof., 1963-72, prof., 1972—, chmn. dept., 1977—; cons. Humble Oil Co., Md. Geol. Survey, ERT. Rutgers U. fellow, 1970-71; grantee Petroleum Research Fund-Am. Chem. Soc., Union Oil Calif. Found. Fellow Geol. Soc. Am.; mem. Am. Assn. Petroleum Geologists, Soc. Econ. Paleontologists and Mineralogists, Paleontol. Soc., Petroleum Exploration Soc. N.Y. (pres. 1979-80). Current Work: Biostratigraphy and paleoecology of planktonic and benthic foraminifer in the Mesozoic and Cenozoic eras of geologic time. Subspecialties: Paleontology, paleoecology; Biostratigraphy. Home: 115 Dodds Ln Princeton NJ 08540 Office: Rutgers U New Brunswick NJ 08903

OLSZEWSKI, JERZY ADAM, engineer, communication specialist; b. Nieswiez, Poland, Feb. 2, 1929; came to U.S., 1955, naturalized, 1960; s. Wincenty and Jadwiga (Malyszewicz) O.; 1 child, Renata Lidia. Diploma in Elec. Engring., Loughborough U. Tech., Eng., 1954, M.S., 1978. Engr., Joseph Lucas, Ltd., Birmingham, Eng., 1954-55; asst. dir. research Gen. Cable Co., Edison, N.J., 1955-80, tech. dir., 1981—; dir. engring. Okonite Co., Providence, 1980-81. Patentee in field. Contbr. articles to tech. jours. Mem. Rep. Presdl. Task Force, 1984. Mem. Optical Soc. Am., IEEE (sr.), N.Y. Acad. Scis. Roman Catholic. Current work: Telecommunications transmission lines phenomena. Subspecialties: Telecommunications; Optical engineering. Home: 327 Avenue E Apt 2 Bayonne NJ 07002 Office: Gen Cable Internat Inc 160 Fieldcrest Ave Edison NJ 08818

OLTON, DAVID STUART, neuropsychologist; b. Montclaire, N.J., Jan. 15, 1943; s. Robert Matthew and Minnie (Tiepel) O. B.A., Haverford Coll., 1964; M.A., U. Mich., 1968, Ph.D., 1969. Mem. faculty dept. psychology Johns Hopkins U., Balt., 1969—, prof., 1979—, chmn. dept., 1983—; mem. faculty dept. psychiatry and behavioral scis. Johns Hopkins U. Hosp., 1971—. Author: Biofeedback Clinical Applications in Behavioral Medicine, 1980. Treas. Jacksonville Vol. Fire Co., 1972—. Current Work: The neurochemical and neuroanatomical mechanisms of memory. Subspecialties: Neuropsychology; Physiological psychology. Home: 3704 Stansbury Mill Rd Phoenix MD 21131 Office: Dept Psychology Johns Hopkins U Baltimore MD 21218

O'MALLEY, JAMES J., researcher; polymer scientist; b. Phila., Sept. 17, 1940; s. Charles G. and Margaret (Coll) O.; m. Ann C. McNeill, June 6, 1964; children—Sharon, James, Melissa. B.S. in Chemistry, Villanova U., 1958-62; Ph.D. in Chemistry, SUNY-Syracuse, 1967. Scientist, Xerox Corp., Rochester, N.Y., 1967-74, research mgr., 1974-79; mgr. research dept. Exxon Chem. Co., Baytown, Tex., 1979—. Mem. editorial adv. bd. Macromolecular Synthesis, 1983—. Patentee in field. Contbr. articles to research publications. Mem. Am. Chem. Soc. (sec.-div. polymer chemistry 1980-82), Am. Phys. Soc. Current work: Synthesis and characterization of specialty polymers. Structure property and relations of block copolymers and polymer blends. Subspecialties: Polymer chemistry; Polymer physics. Office: Exxon Chem Co PO Box 5200 Baytown TX 77522

O'MALLEY, THOMAS FRANCIS, atomic and molecular physicist; b. N.Y.C., Nov. 13, 1928; s. Joseph and Kathryn (Kennedy) O'M.; m. Tanya M. Gardner, Feb. 14, 1962; 1 child, Deirdre Maureen. B.A., Bellarmine Coll., 1953; Ph.L., 1954; Ph.D., NYU, 1961. Research assoc. NYU, 1961-63; mem. staff Gen. Research Corp., Santa Barbara, Calif., 1964-70; assoc. prof. physics U. Conn., Storrs, 1970-72; research staff Dolphin Project, Miami, Fla., 1973-76; vis. fellow Queens U., Belfast, Ireland, Australian Nat. U., U. Western Ontario, 1976-80; specialist computations Gen. Electric Co., San Jose, Calif., 1980—. Contbg. author: Advances in Atomic and Molecular Physics 1971. Contbr. articles to profl. jours. Fellow Am. Phys. Soc. Current work: Electron transport in dense gases; dissociative electron attachment and recombination; electron collisions near thresholds; large scale computations. Subspecialty: Atomic and molecular physics. Office: Gen Electric Co MC-611 175 Curtner San Jose CA 95125

OMAN, CHARLES MCMASTER, scientist, educator, aeronautical engineer, consultant; b. Bklyn., Feb. 22, 1944; s. William Morse and Janet Lyle (McMaster) O.; m. Cherryl L. Huested, Oct. 26, 1974; children: Katherine, Peter. B.S.E. in Aerospace and Mech. Sci., Princeton U., 1966; S.M., MIT, 1968, Ph.D. in Instrumentation, Guidance and Control, 1972. Asst. prof. dept. aeros. and astronautics MIT, Cambridge, 1972-76, assoc. prof., 1976-78, prin. research scientist, 1979-80, sr. research engr., 1981, asso. dir. Man Vehicle Lab., 1982; cons. NASA, U.S. Air Force, Nat. Acad. Scis.; lectr. to govt. agys., univs., coll., hosps., confs., 1977—; Herman von Helmholtz assoc. prof. Harvard U.-MIT Program in Health Scis. and Tech., 1977-78. Contbr. articles to sci. jours. Grass fellow Marine Biol. Lab., Woods Hole, 1974. Mem. IEEE (sr.), Soc. Neurosci., Barany Soc., Aerospace Med. Assn., Assn. Research in Otology, Am. Soc. Space Bibliography. Current Work: Research on vestibular system, spatial orientation, motion sickness; investigator on space shuttle, Spacelab Missions 1, 4 and D-1 (vestibular experiments). Subspecialties: Aeronautical engineering; Biomedical engineering. Home: 5 Highland Terr Winchester MA 01890 Office: MIT Man Vehicle Lab Room 37-219 Cambridge MA 02139

OMAN, PAUL RICHARD, geologist; b. Manchester, N.H., Sept. 5, 1956; s. Ted and Mildred (Lindquist) O. B.S. in Geology and Oceanography, Calif. State U. Humboldt, 1977; M.B.A., U. Houston, 1984, postgrad., 1984—. Logging engr. Schlumberger, Houston, 1979; geologist J. Rose & Assoc., Houston, 1979-81, Total Petroleum, Houston, 1981-83; contract geologist, pres. Protec, Houston, 1983—. Contbr. articles to profl. jours. Mem. Houston Geol. Soc., Am. Assn. Petroleum Geologists. Current work: Statistical and economic geologic evaluations; remote sensing. Subspecialties: Petrology; Remote sensing (geoscience). Office: Protec PO Box 590011 Houston TX 77259-0011

OMAYE, STANLEY TERUO, biochem. nutritionist, toxicologist, pharmacologist; b. Detroit, Jan. 25, 1945; s. Shigeru and Teruye (Kanagaki) O. B.A. in Chemistry, Sacramento State Coll., 1968; M.S. in Pharmacology, U. Pacific, 1972; Ph.D. in Biochem. Nutrition, U. Calif., 1975. Postdoctoral fellow Calif. Primate Center, U. Calif., Davis, 1975-76; research chemist Letterman Army Inst. Research, San Francisco, 1976-80, cons. div. cutaneous hazards and toxicology group, 1980—; research nutritionist Western Regional Research Center, U.S. Dept. Agr., Berkeley, Calif., 1980-83, project leader, 1980-83; with Western Human Nutrition Research Ctr., Presidio of San Francisco, 1983—; adj. prof. dept. pharmacology U. of Pacific, 1976—. Contbr. articles on nutrition, pharmacology and toxicology to profl. jours. Mem. Am. Inst. Nutrition, Am. Soc. Pharmacology and Exptl. Therapeutics, Soc. Toxicology, Am. Coll. Toxicology, Sigma Xi, Rho Chi. Current Work: Nutrient and xenobiotic interactions, nutrient and nutrient interactions. Subspecialties: Nutrition (medicine); Pharmacology. Office: Western Human Nutrition Research Ctr PO Box 29997 Presidio of San Francisco CA 94129

OMURA, GEORGE ADOLF, medical oncologist; b. N.Y.C., Apr. 30, 1938; s. Bunji K. and Martha (Pilger) O.; m. Emily Fowler, Dec. 27, 1962; children—June Ellen, Susan, Ann, George F. B.A., Columbia U., 1958; M.D., Cornell U., 1962. Intern, Bellevue Hosp., N.Y.C., 1962-63, resident 1965-67; fellow Meml. Sloan Kettering Cancer Ctr., N.Y.C., 1967-70; asst. to assoc. prof. U. Ala.-Birmingham, 1970-78, prof. medicine, 1978—; cons. Nat. Cancer Inst., 1975—. Contbr. articles to profl. jours. Served to lt. USN, 1963-65. Fellow ACP; mem. Am. Soc. Clin. Oncology, Am. Assn. Cancer Research, Am. Soc. Hematology, Southeastern Cancer Study Group (chmn. 1983—), Gynec. Oncology Group, Phi Beta Kappa, Alpha Omega Alpha. Current work: Chemotherapy of acute leukemia, ovarian cancer, therapeutic trials in cancer. Subspecialties: Oncology; Hematology. Office: U Ala-Birmingham Birmingham AL 35294

ONDETTI, MIGUEL ANGEL, cardiopulmonary researcher, consultant; b. Buenos Aires, Argentina, May 14, 1930; came to U.S., 1960; s. Emilio Pablo and Sara Cecilia (Cerutti) O.; m. Josephine Elizabeth Garcia, June 6, 1958; children—Giselle C., Gabriel A. Dr. i Chemistry, U. Buenos Airesa, 1957. Research investigator Squibb Inst. for Med. Research, Buenos Aires, 1956-60, research investigator, New Brunswick, N.J., 1960-77, dept. dir., Princeton, N.J., 1977-80, assoc. dir., 1980-82, v.p. cardiopulmonary research, 1982-83, 84—; cons. NIH, NSF, Washington; mem. adv. com. dept. chemistry Princeton U., 1982—. Author: Peptide Synthesis, 1962, 2d edit., 1972. Contbr. articles to sci. jours. Patentee 110 times in field. Recipient A. Edison Patent award Council for Research and Devel. N.J., 1980; Ciba award Am. Heart Assn., 1983. Mem. Am. Chem. Soc. (A. Burger award 1981), Am. Soc. Biol. Chemists. Current work: Direct research on cardiovascular drugs. Subspecialties: Drug design; Medicinal chemistry. Office: E R Squibb & Sons PO Box 4000 Princeton NJ 08540

O'NEIL, JAMES RICHARD, research chemist, educator; b. Chgo., July 16, 1934; s. William J. and Mary V. (Murphy) O'N. B.S. with honors, Loyola U., 1956; M.S., Carnegie-Mellon U., 1959; Ph.D., U. Chgo., 1963. Research assoc. U. Chgo., 1963; research fellow Caltech, Pasadena, Calif., 1963-65; research chemist U.S. Geol. Survey, Menlo Park, Calif., 1965—; adj. prof., Stanford U., Calif., 1980—; cons. NSF, Washington, 1980-83. Editor: Geochimica et Cosmochimica, 1984. Loyola U. scholar, 1952; U.S.-U.S.S.R. Exchange fellow U.S. Govt., 1972; recipient Am. Inst. Chemist's medal, 1956. Fellow Geol. Soc. Am.; mem. Am. Geophys. Union, Geochem. Soc. Club: Palo Alto Bridge. Current work: Stable isotope geochemistry, geothermometry, structure of aqueous solutions, mantle processes, earthquake prediction. Subspecialties: Geochemistry; Physical chemistry. Home: 674 Webster St Palo Alto CA 94301 Office: US Geol Survey #937 345 Middlefield Rd Menlo CA 94025

O'NEIL, JOHN JAMES, pulmonary physiologist; b. Chgo., Feb. 9, 1935; s. Owen Rowe and Luella (Nadelhoffer) O'N.; m. Marilyn Joyce Streeter, Aug. 21, 1964; children—Lisa Marie, Sara Beth. B.S., Wheaton Coll., 1957; Ph.D., U. Calif.-San Francisco, 1974. Staff fellow Nat. Inst. Environ. Health Sci., Research Triangle Park, N.C., 1974-77; research physiologist, U.S. EPA, Research Triangle Park, 1977-79; chief, EPA Clin. Research Br., Chapel Hill, N.C., 1981—; sr. research fellow dept. physiology, Harvard Sch. Pub. Health, Boston, 1979-80; assoc. Harvard Mus. Comparative Zoology, Cambridge, Mass., 1980—; adj. assoc. prof. exptl. medicine, Duke U., Durham, N.C., 1978—; adj. asst. prof. of medicine, U. N.C., Chapel Hill, 1981—. Contbr. articles to profl. jours. Recipient EPA Innovative Research award, 1978; Bronze Medal, 1982. Mem. Am. Physio. Soc., Am. Thoracic Soc. (chmn. Sci. Assembly on Environ. and Occupational Health, 1980, bd. dirs., 1981-84, del. to China, 1982), Am. Lung Assn of N.C. (bd. dirs. Research Triangle br. 1983-86). Current work: Acute pulmonary response of humans to air pollutant exposure; comparative respiration of mammals of differing body mass. Subspecialty: Pulmonary medicine. Office: EPA Clin Research Br Univ NC Med Research Bldg C (224H) Chapel Hill NC 27514

O'NEIL, VERNON PATRICK, II, electrical engineer, semiconductor researcher; b. Pensacola, Fla., Oct. 1, 1942; s. Vernon Patrick and Mogi Thomas (Kinsey) O.; m. Edith Grace Marshment, Nov. 21, 1965 (div. Dec. 1977); children—Vernon Patrick III, Ian Alexander; m. Barbara Lee Johnson, Jan. 7, 1978; children—Brian Erick. B.S. in Physics, U. Wash., 1968; M.S. in Elec. Engring., Ariz. State U., 1973. Jr. physicist Motorola Semicondrs., Pheonix, 1968-73, semicondr. designer, 1977-83; semicondr. researcher Zenith Radio, Elk Grove Village, Ill., 1973-77; mem. tech. staff Motorola Govt. Electronics, Scottsdale, Ariz., 1983—; mem. sci. adv. bd. Motorola, 1980. Patentee in field. Contbr. articles to profl. jours. Served with USN, 1963-67, Vietnam. Mem. IEEE, Motorola Tech. Soc., Am. Legion, Motorola Exptl. Computer Club, David Webb Judo Acad. Current works: High speed electronics, gallium arsenide integrated circuits, fiber optics, communications, semiconductor processing. Subspecialties: Microelectronics; Integrated circuits. Home: 1155 E Malibu Dr Tempe AZ 85282 Office: Motorola Communications Research Facility 75 W Olive Ave Gilbert AZ 85234

O'NEILL, ROBERT VINCENT, system ecologist; b. Pitts., Apr. 13, 1940; s. Robert Vincent and Alice Catherine (McIlvane) O'N.; m. Elizabeth Gerry Goben, Jan. 21, 1967. B.A., Cathedral Coll., 1961; Ph.D., U. Ill., 1967. Research ecologist Oak Ridge Nat. Lab., 1967—. Author: Tarot Symbolism, 1985; (with others) Hierarchial Concept, 1985. Editor: Systems Ecology, 1979; Systems Analysis of Ecosystems, 1979. Fellow AAAS; mem. Ecological Soc. Am. Current work: Large scale ecological problems. Subspecialty: Ecosystems analysis. Home: 53 Outer Dr Oak Ridge TN 37830 Office: Oak Ridge Nat Lab Bldg 1505 Oak Ridge TN 37831

O'NEILL, RUSSELL RICHARD, engineering educator; b. Chgo., June 6, 1916; s. Dennis Alysious and Florence Agnes (Mathurin) O'N.; m. Margaret Bock, Dec. 15, 1939; children: Richard A., John R.; m. Sallie Boyd, June 30, 1967. B.S. in Mech. Engring. U. Calif. at Berkeley, M.S. in Mech. Engring, 1940; Ph.D., U. Calif. at Los Angeles, 1956. Registered profl. engr., Calif. Design engr. Dowell, Inc., Midland, Mich., 1940-41; design engr. Dow Chem. Co., Midland, 1941-44, Airesearch Mfg. Co., Los Angeles, 1944-46; lectr. engring. UCLA, 1946-56, prof. engring., 1956-84, prof. emeritus, 1984—, asst. dean engring., 1956-61, assoc. dean., 1961-73, acting dean, 1965-66, dean, 1974-83, dean emeritus, 1984—; staff engr. Nat. Acad. Sci.-NRC, 1954; dir. Data Design Labs., 1977—; Mem. engring. task force Space Era Edn. Study Fla. Bd. Control, 1963; mem. regional Export Expansion Council Dept. Commerce, 1960-66, Los Angeles Mayor's Space Adv. Com., 1964-69; mem. Maritime Transp. Research Bd., 1974-81; bd. adv. Naval Postgrad. Sch., 1976—. Trustee West Coast U., 1981—. Mem. Nat. Acad. Engring., Am. Soc. Engring. Edn., Soc. Naval Architects and Marine Engrs., Triangle, Sigma Xi, Tau Beta Pi. Subspecialty: Systems engineering. Home: 15430 Longbow Dr Sherman Oaks CA 91403 Office: 405 Hilgard Ave Los Angeles CA 90024

ONG, CHONG KOK, electrical engineer, consultant; b. Batu Pahat, Johor, Malaysia, Oct. 2, 1954; came to U.S., 1977; s. Chen Guan and Chin Ai (See) O.; m. Grace Loh Chi Shen, Jan. 6, 1979. B.Sc. with 1st class honors, Imperial Coll., U. London, 1977; M.S. in Elec. Engring., Columbia U., 1978; M.S. in Systems Sci., Washington U., St. Louis, 1979, D.Sc., 1982; associateship to City and Guilds Inst. of London, 1977. Lectr. Washington U., St. Louis, 1982; asst. prof. Clarkson Coll., Potsdam, N.Y., 1982-83; sr. engr. M/A-COM Research Ctr., Rockville, Md., 1983—; cons. in field. Mem. IEEE, Sigma Xi, Eta Kappa Nu. Current work: Satellite communications; land mobile communications; signal processing; perform analysis and evaluation of new communication systems; baseband signal processing. Subspecialties: Computer engineering; Telecommunications. Home: 7012 Needwood Rd Derwood MD 20855 Office: M/A-COM Devel Corp 1350 Piccard Dr Suite 400 Rockville MD 20850

ONG, HIAP LIEW, physicist; b. Singapore, Aug. 26, 1954; came to U.S., 1979; s. Eng Seng Ong and Ah Phang Tan. B.Sc., Nanyang U., Singapore, 1978; B.Sc. with honors, 1979; Ph.D., Brandeis U., 1984. Research assoc. Nanyang U., Singapore, 1979; teaching assoc. Brandeis U., Waltham, Mass., 1979-81, research assoc., 1982-84; mem. research staff IBM, Yorktown Heights, N.Y., 1984—. Contbr. articles to profl. jours. Served with Armed Forces, Singapore, 1972-75. Mem. Am. Phys. Soc., Optical Soc. Am. Current work: Interaction of liquid crystals with electromagnetic fields and with homogeneous and inhomogeneous surfaces, liquid crystal displays. Subspecialties: Materials; Optical engineering. Home: 16-5 Manville Ln Pleasantville NY 10570 Office: TJ Watson Research Ctr IBM Corp PO Box 218 Yorktown Heights NY 10598

ONG, RENE ASHWIN, physicist; b. Ann Arbor, Mich., Nov. 11, 1959; s. Rudi S. and Elizabeth (Schilling) Ong. B.S., U. Mich., 1981; M.S., Stanford U., 1982. Research asst. Space Physics Research Lab., Ann Arbor, Mich., 1979-80, Brookhaven Nat. Lab., Upton, N.Y., 1980; mem. research staff Randall Lab., U. Mich., Ann Arbor, 1980-81; physicist Stanford Linear Accelerator Ctr., Calif., 1981—. Contbr. articles to profl. jours. Mem. Phi Beta Kappa. Current work: Research in experimental particles physics; topics include design and study of high percision drift chambers and the measurement of lifetimes of very short lived particles. Subspecialty: Particle physics. Home: Escondido Village 2E Stanford CA 94305 Office: Stanford Linear Accelerator Ctr Exptl Group E Bin 61 PO Box 4349 Stanford CA 94305

ONGLEY, EDWIN DAVID, research scientist, research institute administrator, educator; b. Collingwood, Ont., Can., Aug. 2, 1941; s. Frederick George and Frances Lillian (Brittain) O.; m. Victoria Anne Weir, June 12, 1965; children—Christianna L., Michael W., Matthew G. B.A., U. Toronto, Ont., Can., 1965; Ph.D., U. Sydney, Australia, 1971. Prof. Queen's U., Kingston, Ont., Can., 1968-81; chief Nat. Water Research Inst. Environment Can., Winnipeg, 1982—; pres. Enviro-data Ltd., Winnipeg, 1981—; adj. full prof. U. Sask., Saskatoon, 1984—. Contbr. articles to profl. jours. Patentee in field. Commonwealth fellow Australian Govt., 1965-68, Can. Council fellow, 1977-78. Mem. Internat. Assn. for Great Lakes Research, Internat. Assn. for Sediment Water Sci. (sec.-treas. 1984-87). Mem. of Anglican Ch. Current work: Interaction between land use and toxic chemical pathways in aquatic systems. Major research directed to improvement of chemical and biological monitoring and effects sensing for toxic chemicals in fluvial and lake systems. . Office: Nat Water Research Inst Environment Can 501 University Crescent Winnipeg MB R3T 2N6 Canada

ONORATO, HOWARD LOUIS, nuclear engineer, consultant; b. Sea Isle City, N.J., Apr. 24, 1947; s. Frank Thomas and Kathryn (Everingham) O.; m. Nancy Carolyn Denty, Jan. 12, 1974; children: Rodney, Amy. Student, Southeastern Community Coll., Whiteville, N.C., 1977-79, Miss. Coll., 1980, Glouchester Community Coll., 1981-82. Cons. engr. Energy Inc., Idaho Falls, Idaho, 1981—; asst. engr. Pratt & Whitney Aircraft, West Palm Beach, Fla., 1971-75; reactor operator Carolina P & L, Southport, N.C., 1977-79; cons. engr. Quadrex, Campbell, Calif., 1979-81, Energy, Inc., Idaho Falls, 1981—. Served with USN, 1965-71, 75-77. Mem. Am. Nuclear Soc. Current Work: Provide operational support to run Salem nuclear support, update of procedures and equipment considering human factors. Subspecialties: Nuclear engineering; Human factors engineering. Home: 154 Edward Dr Swedesboro NJ 08085 Office: Energy Inc PO Box 736 Idaho Falls ID 83402

OPEL, WILLIAM, research institute executive; b. Pasadena, Calif., May 9, 1943; s. Arthur William and Lois Marie (Cohite) O.; m. Judy Louise Kopecky, Feb. 5, 1966; 1 child, Julianna Marie. B.A., Pepperdine Coll., 1968; postgrad. Harvard Sch. Pub. Health, 1977-78. Exec. dir. Pasadena Found. for Med. Research, Calif., 1961-81, Huntington Inst. Applied Med. Research, 1978-81, Huntington Med. Research Inst., 1982—. Contbr. articles to profl. jours. Mem., Univ. Club. of Pasadena, 1972—, dir., 1980-83, v.p., 1983. Recipient W. Alton James fellowship Cell Sci. Ctr., 1972. Mem. Tissue Culture Assn., Soc. Research Adminstrs., AAAS. Club: Rotary (Pasadena). Current work: Biomedical device development. Subspecialties: Cell and tissue culture; Biomedical engineering. Office: Huntington Med Research Inst 734 Fairmount Ave Pasadena CA 91105

OPGRANDE, JOHN DONALD, medical educator; b. Dickinson, N.D., Mar. 8, 1941; s. J. Lionel and Esther Caroline (Malkewick) O.; m. Carolyn Thea Holm, June 20, 1964; children: Heidi, Kristen, Julie, John. B.A., Concordia Coll.-Minn., 1963; B.S., U. N.D., 1963-65; M.D., U. Kans., 1967; Master's, U. Minn., 1979. Intern St. Luke's Hosp., Saginaw, Mich., 1967-68; resident Mayo Clinic, 1970-73, fellow, 1973-74; adj. prof. engring. N.D. State U., Fargo, 1976—; chmn. dept. orthopedic surgery N.D. State U. (Sch. Medicine), 1980—; hand surgeon Dakota Clinic Ltd., Fargo, 1974—, bd. dirs., 1980-82; bd. dirs. Dakota Med. Found., Fargo, 1981—. Contbr. articles in field to profl. jours. Mem. Lake Agassiz Arts Council, Fargo, 1979; mem. Arthritis Found., 1975—. Served to Capt. U.S. Army, 1968-70. Regional Med. Program grantee, 1977; Pfizer Pharm. grantee, 1983. Fellow Am. Acad. Orthopedic Surgeons (com. mem. 1979—, councilor 1983); mem. U.S. Army Assn. Flight Surgeons, AMA (del. 1980—), Orthopedic Research Soc., Am. Soc. Surgery of the Hand (com. mem. 1981—). Lutheran. Current Work: Biomechanical engineering; study of static and dynamic forces affecting function of the hand; pharmacology; investigation of a new drug to treat hand infections. Subspecialties: Orthopedics; Microsurgery. Home: 2485 Lilac Ln Fargo ND 58102 Office: U N D Dept Orthopedics Dakota Clinic Ltd PO Box 6001 1702 S University Fargo ND 58108-60001

OPIE, WILLIAM ROBERT, metallurgical engineer, consultant; b. Butte, Mont., Apr. 3, 1920; s. Ellison Stuart and Myrtle (Williams) O.; m. Constance E. Kickuth, Oct. 14, 1944; children: Lyle Margaret, Guy William. B.S., Mont. Sch. Mines, 1942, M.E. (hon.), 1965; Sc.D., MIT, 1949; student, Advanced Mgmt. Program, Harvard U., 1967; Sc.D. (hon.), Mont. Coll. Mineral Sci. and Tech., 1980. Foundry metallurgist Wright Aero Corp., Paterson, N.J., 1942-45; research asso. MIT, Cambridge, 1946-48; research metallurgist Am. Smelting and Refining, Perth Amboy, N.J., 1948-50; research supr. Nat. Lead Co., Sayreville, N.J., 1950-60; pres. Amax Base Metals Research & Devel., Inc., Carteret, N.J., 1960-85, cons., 1985—. Contbr. articles to profl. jours. Served with U.S. Navy, 1945-46. Fellow AIME, Am. Soc. Metals; mem. Can. Inst. Mining and Metallurgy, Nat. Acad. Engring. Club: Mining (N.Y.C.). Patentee in field. Subspecialty: Metallurgy. Home: 119 Crawfords Corner Rd Holmdel NJ 07733 Office: 400 Middlesex Ave Carteret NJ 07008

OPITZ, JOHN MARIUS, medical scientist; b. Hamburg, Germany, Aug. 15, 1935; came to U.S., 1950, naturalized, 1957; s. Friedrich and Erica Maria (Quadt) O.; children: Elisabeth, Gabriella, John, Chrisanthi, Felix. B.A., State U. Iowa, 1956, M.D., 1959; D.Sc. h.c., Mont. State U., 1983. Diplomate: Am. Bd. Pediatrics, Am. Bd. Med. Genetics. Intern State U. Iowa Hosp., 1959-60, resident in pediatrics, 1960-61; resident and chief resident in pediatrics U. Wis. Hosp., Madison, 1961-62; fellow in pediatrics and med. genetics U. Wis., 1962-64, asst. prof. med. genetics/pediatrics, 1964-69, assoc. prof., 1969-72, prof., 1972-79; dir. Wis. Clin. Genetics Ctr., 1974-79, Shodair Mont. Regional Genetics Program, Helena, 1979-83; clin. prof. med. genetics and pediatrics U. Wash., Seattle, 1979—; adj. prof. medicine, biology, history and philosophy of sci., vet. research and vet. sci. Mont. State U., Bozeman, 1979—; chmn. dept. med. genetics Shodair Children's Hosp., 1983—; adj. prof. med. genetics and pediatrics U. Wis.-Madison, 1982—; editor-in-chief, founder Am. Jour. Med. Genetics, 1977—; mng. editor European Jour. Pediatrics, 1977-85. Mem. Am. Soc. Human Genetics, Am. Pediatric Soc., Soc. Pediatric Research, Am. Bd. Med. Genetics, Birth Defects Clin. Genetic Soc., Am. Inst. Biol. Scis., Am. Soc. Zoologists, AAAS, Teratology Soc., Genetic Soc. Am., European Soc. Human Genetics, Soc. Study Social Biology, Am. Acad. Pediatric, German Pediatrics Soc., Western Soc. for Pediatrics Research, German Acad. Scis., Sigma Xi. Democrat. Roman Catholic. Current work: Human developmental genetics. Subspecialties: Developmental biology; Genetics and genetic engineering (medicine). Home: 579 2d St Helena MT 59601 Office: Shodair Children's Hospital PO Box 5539 840 Helena Ave Helena MT 59604

OPLER, PAUL ALEXANDER, biologist, editor; b. Ann Arbor, Mich., Aug. 3, 1938; s. Ascher Weinstein and Pauline Elizabeth (Schneirla) O.; m. Sandra Sue Segler, Oct. 21, 1961; children—Timothy, David Christian, Laura. B.S., U. Calif.-Berkeley, 1960, Ph.D., 1970; M.A., Calif. State U.-San Jose, 1965. Research assoc. Orgn. Tropical Studies, San Jose, Costa Rica, 1970-74; entomologist U.S. Fish and Wildlife Service, Washington, 1974-76; br. chief Office Endangered Species, 1976-82; chief editorial sect. Office Info. Transfer, Fort Collins, Colo., 1983—. Author: Oak Microlepidoptera, 1974; Butterflies East of the Plains, 1984 (Am. Assn. Book Pubs. award 1985). Contbr. articles to profl. jours. NSF fellow, 1969. Mem. Assn. Tropical Biology (exec. dir.), Am. Inst. Biol. Scis. (sec.-treas.), Entomol. Soc. Am. (bull. editor), Lepidopterist's Soc. (asst. editor 1965-70), Audubon Soc., Xerces Soc. (v.p.), Sigma Xi, Alpha Chi Rho. Current work: Lepidoptera systematics, community ecology and biogeography; tropical ecosystems: plant community phenology, dioecious plants, secondary succession, and plant-animal interactions. Subspecialties: Ecology (biology); Systematics. Home: 5100 Greenview Ct Fort Collins CO 80525Office: Editorial Sect Office Info Transfer Fish and Wildlife Aylesworth Hall CSU Fort Collins CO 80525

OPLER, STANLEY RONAL, pathologist, educator; b. Chgo., Sept. 3, 1923; s. Samuel Stephen and Ann Dorothy (Bremer) O.; m. Barbara Thrasher, Nov. 20, 1949; children—Stuart Thayer, Andrew Butler, A.B., Columbia U., 1944; M.D., N.Y. Med. Coll., 1947. Diplomate Am. Bd. Pathology, Am. Bd. Nuclear Medicine. Intern Albany Med. Coll. Hosp., 1947; asst. resident N.Y. Med. Coll., 1948-50; Columbia U. Med. Ctr.-Nat. Cancer Inst., 1950-51; fellow Columbia, U., 1953; from instr. to assoc. prof. N.Y. Med. Coll., 1953-55; asst. prof. Columbia U., N.Y.C., 1956-68; clin. assoc. prof. Stanford U., Calif., 1968-74, U. Calif.-San Francisco, 1974-82; clin. prof. pathology U. So. Calif., Los Angeles, 1979—. Contbr. articles to med. jours. Served to capt. USAF, 1953-55. Fellow Coll. Am. Pathologists; mem. Am. Soc. Pathologists, Am. Assn. Immunologists, Exptl. Biology and Medicine, Soc. Nuclear Medicine. Subspecialties: Cancer research (medicine); Nuclear medicine. Home: 485 Eleanor Dr Woodside CA 94062 Office: 222 W 39th St San Mateo CA 94401

OPPENHEIM, IRVING JEFFREY, engineering educator; b. N.Y.C., Mar. 20, 1948. B.E., Cooper Union Coll., 1968; M.S., Lehigh U., 1970; Ph.D., U. Cambridge (Eng.), 1972. Mem. faculty dept. civil engring. Carnegie-Mellon U., Pitts., 1972—. Mem. ASCE, Earthquake Engring. Research Inst. Current work: Construction robotics, structural systems. Subspecialties: Robotics; Structural engineering. Office: Carnegie-Mellon U Pittsburgh PA 15213

OPPENHEIM, JOOST J., cancer institute investigator, physician, educator; b. Venlo, Netherlands, Aug. 11, 1934, came to U.S., 1946, naturalized, 1952; Married; 4 children. A.B. with honors, Columbia Coll., 1956, M.D. cum laude, 1960. Diplomate Nat. Bd. Med. Examiners, Nat. Bd. Allergy and Immunology. Intern, King County Hosp., Seattle, 1961-62; clin. assoc. Nat. Cancer Inst., NIH, Bethesda, Md., 1962-65, sr. investigator cell biology sect. Lab. Biochemistry, Nat. Inst. Dental Research, 1966-69, tutor research assoc. seminar program, 1968-78, chief cellular immunology sect. Lab. Microbiology and Immunology, Nat. Inst. Dental Research, also instr. postgrad. program, 1970—, physician Allergy Clinic, Personnel Health Dept., 1975-82; med. dir. USPHS, 1975—; outpatient dept. physician Prince Georges County Six Towns Clinic for Sr. Citizens, 1975-77; sabbatical tng. Lab. Biochem. Immunology, Weizmann Inst., Rehovot, Israel, 1974-75; internist Mobile Med. Care, Montgomery County Free Clinics; 1977-81; immunology lectr. dept. zoology U. Md., 1977—, adj. prof. dept. zoology, 1979—; chief, biol. response modifiers program Lab. Molecular Immunoregulation, NIH, Frederick, Md., 1983—; organizer of 1st Internat Workshop on Lymphokine Research, 1976, co-organizer 3d workshop, 1982; mem. organizing com. Internat. Leukocyte Culture Confs., 1970—. Contbr. over 200 articles to profl. jours. Assoc. editor: Jour. Immunology, 1973-79; mem. editorial bd. Cellular Immunology, 1970—, Immunopharmacology, 1978, Lymphokine Reports, 1979, Lymphokine Research, 1982. NIH fellow, U. Birmingham, Eng., 1965; recipient Meritorious Service medal. USPHS, 1978, Ferdin and Von-Hebra prize for dermatological research, 1982. Mem. Am. Fedn. Clin. Research, Am. Assn. Immunologists, Am. Soc. Clin. Investigations, Reticuloendothelial Soc., Alpha Omega Alpha. Subspecialties: Immunology (medicine); Cancer research (medicine). Office: Nat Cancer Inst-NIH Biol Response Modifiers Program Lab Molecular Immunoregulation Bldg 560 Frederick MD 21701

ORCHIN, MILTON, educator, chemist; b. Barnesboro, Pa., June 4, 1914; s. Morris and Mary (Rivkin) O.; m. Ruth Wilner, June 4, 1941; children: Morton Lewis, Michael David. B.A., Ohio State U., 1936, M.A., 1937, Ph.D., 1939; D.Sc. (hon.), U. Cin., 1984. Chemist FDA, Cin., Chgo., 1939-42; chief organic chemistry sect. U.S. Bur. Mines, 1943-53; asso. prof. chemistry U. Cin., 1953-56, prof., head dept., 1956-62, prof. chemistry, dir. basic sci. lab., 1962-70; dir. Hoke S. Greene Lab. for Catalysis, 1970—, disting. service prof., 1981—. Co-author 7 books.; Contbr. numerous articles research publs. Bd. govs. Ben Gurion U. of Negev, Israel, 1974-80. Recipient E. J. Houdry award in applied catalysis N. Am. Catalysis Soc., 1983; Guggenheim fellow, 1947-48. Mem. AAAS (chmn. chemistry sect. 1963), Am. Chem. Soc. (chmn. Cin. sect. 1962, Eminent Chemist award Cin. sect. 1957, E.V. Murphree award in indsl. and engring. chemistry 1979, Morley medal Cleve. sect. 1980), Phi Beta Kappa, Sigma Xi. Patentee in field. Current Work: Homogeneous catalytic reactions with transition metal complexes. Subspecialty: Catalysis chemistry. Home: 3763 Middleton Ave Cincinnati OH 45220

ORDWAY, ELLEN, entomologist, biology educator, ecologist; b. N.Y.C., Nov. 8, 1927; d. Samuel Hanson and Anna (Wheatland) Ordway. B.A., Wheaton Coll., Norton, Mass., 1950; M.S., Cornell U., 1955; Ph.D., U. Kans., 1965. Field asst. N.Y. Zool. Soc., 1950-52; research asst. Am. Mus. Natural History, 1955-57; teaching and research asst. U. Kans., Lawrence, 1957-64; assoc. prof. biology U. Minn., Morris, 1965—; collaborator U.S. Dept. Agr., Tucson, 1971, 77, 83; vis. research scholar U. Ariz., Tucson, 1978. Contbr. articles to sci. jours. Active Nature Conservancy, Minn., 1978—. Grantee U. Minn., 1975-79, Nature Conservancy, 1975, U.S. Govt., 1970-75. Mem. Ecol. Soc. Am., Entomol. Soc. Am., Soc. Study Evolution, Soc. Systematic Zoology, Bee Research Assn., Internat. Union Study Social Insects, AAUP (chpt. sec.-treas. 1972-74), Ecol. Soc. Am. (chpt. v.p. 1971, councilman-at-large 1971-73). Current work: Research in behavioral ecology of native bees, pollination, ecology of prairies. Subspecialties: Species interaction; Behavioral ecology. Office: U Minn Div Sci and Math Morris MN 56267

OREL, ANN ELIZABETH, physicist; b. Lake Charles, La., Oct. 26, 1955; d. Bernard Anthony and Bernice Josephine (Toplikar) O. B.S. cum laude, Calif. Inst. Tech., 1977; Ph.D., U. Calif.-Berkeley, 1980. Staff scientist Lawrence Livermore Lab., Calif., 1980—. Contbr. articles to profl. jours. Mem. Am. Phys. Soc., Sigma Xi, Iota Sigma Pi (A.L. Hoffman award 1980). Democrat. Roman Catholic. Club: Vaqueros del Mar. Current Work: Low energy atomic and molecular physics; chemical physics. Subspecialty: Atomic and molecular physics. Office: Lawrence Livermore Nat Lab PO Box 808 L-486 Livermore CA 94550

ORLAND, FRANK JAY, oral microbiology educator, historiographer; b. Little Falls, N.Y., Jan. 23, 1917; s. Michael and Rose (Dorner) O.; m. Phyllis Therese Mrazek, May 8, 1943; children: Frank R., Carl, June, Ralph. A.B., U. Chgo., 1937, S.M., 1945, Ph.D., 1949; B.S., U. Ill.-Chgo., 1939, D.D.S., 1941. Diplomate: Am. Bd. Microbiology. Intern U. Chgo. Hosps. and Clinics, 1941-42; clin. fellow Zoller Meml. Dental Clinic, 1942-49, from instr. to prof. dental surgery and microbiology, 1949-58, dir., 1954-66; prof. Fishbein Ctr. for Study of History of Sci. and Medicine, 1976—, prof. oral microbiology and dental surgery, 1958—; mem. commn. on research Fedn. Dentaire Internationale, 1976-81. Author: The First Fifty Year History of the International Association for Dental Research, 1973; editor: Jour. Dental Research, 1958-69; editor, contbr.: Microbiology in Clinical Dentistry, 1982; chief advisor: Medical History of Dentistry, 1971-74; editor: Centennial Brochure, Loyola U. Sch. Dentistry, 1983. Chmn. Candidates Forum, Village Election, Forest Park, 1979, 83; pres. Hist. Soc. Forest Park, 1976—; chmn. exec. com. Forest Park Centenary Celebration, 1981-85; chmn. hist. com. Centennial Loyola U. Sch. Dentistry, 1982-83; chmn. heritage com. Bicentennial Commn., Forest Park, 1975-76; mem. adv. humanities council Triton Coll. Recipient numerous award including Hon. Alumnus award Loyola U. Sch. Dentistry, 1983. Fellow Inst. Medicine (chmn. com. pub. info.), AAAS (chmn. sect. Chgo.); mem. Internat. Assn. for Dental Research (pres. 1971-72), Am. Acad. History of Dentistry (pres. 1976-77, Hayden-Harris award 1980), Soc. Med. History (pres. Chgo. 1980-82, mem. council), Ill. State Dental Soc. (chmn. com. on history 1977—), Sigma Xi, Gamma Alpha (pres. Chgo. chpt. 1975—). Club: Chgo. Lit. Current Work: Historical writings of research in field of oral microbiology and dental sciences, conducting research seminars, providing lectures and demonstrations for graduate students in oral biology at different universities. Subspecialties: Microbiology; Oral biology. Home: 519 Jackson Blvd Forest Park IL 60130 Office: U Chgo 950 E 59th St Chicago IL 60637

ORLANSKI, ISIDORO, meteorologist; b. Rivera, Argentina, June 6, 1939; came to U.S., 1965; s. Samuel and Sara (Gezelevich) O.; m. Beatriz Gojchgileriut, Mar. 20, 1963; children—Diego, Guillerud, Elisa. Lic. Physics, U. Buenos Aires, 1964; Ph.D. in Geophysics, MIT, 1968. Meteorologist, Geophys. Fluid Dynamics Lab. NOAA, Princeton, N.J., 1968-75, sr. meteorologist, 1975—, dep. dir. Geophys. Fluid Dynamics Lab., 1980-83, acting dir., 1983-84. Mem. Am. Meteorol. Soc., Internat. Union of Geology and Geophysics (chmn. mesoscale working group 1979-85). Current work: Dynamic meteorology (mesoscale) and numerical weather prediction. Subspecialty: Mesoscale meteorology.

ORLOFF, JACK, physician, research physiologist; b. Bklyn., Dec. 22, 1921; s. Samuel and Rebecca (Kaplan) O.; m. Martha Vaughan, Aug. 4, 1951; children: Jonathan Michael, David Geoffrey, Gregory Joshua; 1 child by previous marriage, Lee Frances. Student, Columbia U., 1937-38, Harvard U., 1938-40; M.D., N.Y. U., 1943. Intern Mt. Sinai Hosp., N.Y.C., 1944; resident medicine Montefiore Hosp., N.Y.C., 1944-46; research fellow Yale Med. Sch., 1948-50; mem. sr. research staff Nat. Heart Inst., Bethesda, Md., 1950-57, dep. chief lab. kidney and electrolyte metabolism, 1957-62, chief lab., 1962-75; dir. intramural research Nat. Heart, Lung and Blood Inst., 1974—; professorial lectr. physiology, med. Georgetown U. Med. Sch., 1962—; disting. alumni lectr. N.Y. U. Sch. Medicine, 1966; Del.-at- large exec. council Fedn. Am. Sci., 1962-64, exec. com., treas., 1963-64. Contbg. author: Essays in Metabolism, 1957, Metabolic Disturbances in Clinical Medicine, 1958, The Metabolic Basis of Inherited Disease, 1972, Heart, Kidney and Electrolytes, 1962, Diseases of the Kidney, 1971, Cellular Function of Metabolic Transport, 1964, Hormones and the Kidney, 1964, Nobel Symposium on Prostaglandins, 1967, Physioli of Diuretic Agents, 1966, Ocytocin, Vasopressin and their Structural Analogues, 1964; Editorial bd.: Am. Jour. Physiology, sect. editor, 1964-68, Jour. Applied Physiology, 1964-68, Renal Physiology sect. 8, Handbook of Physiology, 1973; asso. editor: Kidney Internat; cons. editor: Life Scis, 1973-78. Trustee Greenacres Sch., Rockville, Md., 1960-64, v.p. bd. trustees, 1962-63; Mem. sci. adv. bd. Nat. Kidney Found., 1962-71; mem. Inst. Medicine Nat. Acad. Scis. Served to capt. M.C. AUS, 1946-48. Recipient Homer Smith award N.Y. Heart Assn., 1973, Meritorious Service award USPHS, 1974, Distinguished Alumni Achievement award in basic sci. N.Y. U. Sch. Medicine, 1976; Distinguished Service medal HEW, 1977. Mem. Am. Soc. Clin. Investigation, Am. Physiol. Soc., Fedn. Am. Scientists (vice-chmn. 1963-64), Assn. Am. Physicians, Am. Soc. Nephrology (sec.-treas. 1970-72, pres. 1973-74), Sigma Xi, Alpha Omega Alpha. Club: Cosmos. Current Work: Director intramural research. Subspecialties: Internal medicine; Nephrology. Office: Nat Heart Lung and Blood Inst Bethesda MD 20892

ORLOFF, NEIL, environmental research center administrator, lawyer; b. Chgo., May 9, 1943; s. Benjamin R. and Annette (Grabow) O.; m. Jan Krigbaum, Oct. 9, 1971 (div. June 1979). B.S., MIT, 1964; M.B.A., Harvard U., 1966; J.D., Columbia U., 1969. Ops. officer World Bank, Washington, 1969-71; dir. regional liaison staff OFA, EPA, Washington, 1971-73; legal counsel Pres. Council on Environ. Quality, Washington, 1973-75; prof. environ. law and policy Cornell U., 1975—, dir. Ctr. for Environ. Research, 1984—; vice chmn. bd. dirs. Southwest Research and Info. Ctr., Albuquerque, 1975-84. Author: The Environmental Impact Statement Process, 1978; Air Pollution Cases and Materials, 1980; The National Environmental Policy Act, 1980; mem. editorial bd. Natural Resource and Environment, 1984—. Vice chmn. City of Ithaca Environ. Commn., 1976-77; advisor Internat Joint Commn., Can., 1979-81; mem. governing bd. N.Y. Sea Grant Inst., 1984—; advisor N.Y. Dept. Environ. Conservation, 1984—. Mem. ABA (vice chmn. air quality com. 1983—). Current work: Regulation of toxic chemicals. Subspecialty: Environmental research management. Office: Cornell U Hollister Hall Ithaca NY 14853

ORLOWSKI, THOMAS EDWARD, chemical physicist; b. Amsterdam, N.Y., Aug. 6, 1950; s. Eugene Joseph and Sophie Anne (Adamkowski) O.; m. Diane Jean Jessop, Mar. 17, 1979; children—Melissa, Thomas, Amanda, Kevin. B.S., Rochester Inst. Tech., 1973; M.S., Calif. Inst. Tech., 1976, Ph.D., 1979. Sr. staff scientist Xerox Webster Research Ctr., Webster, N.Y., 1980—. Contbr. chpts. to books and articles to profl. jours. Robert R. McCormick fellow Enrico Fermi Inst. U. Chgo., 1978. Mem. Am. Phys. Soc., Am. Chem. Soc., Materials Research Soc., Sigma Xi. Current work: Electronic properties of amorphous semiconductors; picosecond dynamics. Subspecialties: Condensed matter physics; Laser spectroscopy. Office: Xerox Webster Research Ctr 800 Phillips Rd B-114 Webster NY 14580

ORMES, JONATHAN F., physicist, researcher; b. Colorado Springs, Colo., July 18, 1939; s. Robert Manly and Suzanne (Viertel) O.; m. Karen Lee Minnick; children: Laurie Kylee; m. Janet Carolyn Dahl, Sept. 12, 1964; children: Marina Elizabeth, Nicholas Stuart. B.S. in Physics, Stanford U., 1961; M.S. in Physics, U. Minn., 1966, Ph.D. in Physics, 1967. Teaching asst. U. Minn., 1961-62, research asst., 1962-67; postdoctoral research assoc. Nat. Acad. Sci., 1967-69; with NASA/Goddard Space Flight Center, 1969—; head high energy cosmic ray studies group NASA/Goddard Space Flight Center 1976—; head Cosmic Radiations br. NASA/Goddard Space Flight Center, 1982—; prin. investigator High Energy Astrophysics Obs., NASA, 1971, High Energy Cosmic Ray Spacelab Expt., 1979. Contbr. articles to profl. jours. Tchr. re-eval. counseling. Mem. Am. Geophys. Union, Am. Assn. Physics Tchrs., AAAS, Am. Phys. Soc., Am Astron. Soc. Unitarian. Current Work: Develop hypotheses and design and implement expts. to test them concerning sites and mechanisms for origin, acceleration and propagation of cosmic ray nuclei in the galaxy. Subspecialties: High energy astrophysics; Cosmic ray high energy astrophysics. Home: 4701 Cedar Ct Beltsville MD 20705 Office: NASA Goddard Space Flight Center Code 661 Greenbelt MD 20771

ORO, JUAN, biochemist, educator; b. Lerida, Spain, Oct. 26, 1923; came to U.S., 1952; s. Juan and Maria Florensa (Rue) Oro-Vallverdu; m. Francisca Forteza, May 19, 1948; children: Maria Elena, Juan, Jaime, David. Licenciate in Chem. Scis, U. Barcelona, Spain, 1947; Ph.D., Baylor U., 1956; Dr. honoris causa, U. Granada, Spain, 1972. Mem. faculty U. Houston, 1955—, asst. prof., 1956-58, asso. prof., 1958-63, prof., 1963—, chmn. dept. biophysical scis., 1967-69; research chemist Lawrence Radiation Lab., U. Cal. at Berkeley, summer 1962; Catedratico Universidad Autonoma de Barcelona, 1971; prin. investigator NASA Lunar Sample Analysis, 1967—; molecular analysis team mem. NASA Unmanned Mars Landing, 1970—; dir. Instituto de Biofisica y Neurobiologia, Barcelona, Spain, 1977; Founding mem., v.p. Spain and Tex. Soc., Inc., Houston, 1970—; mem. Parliament of Catalunya (Spain), 1980-81; pres. Sci. and Technol. Council Catalunya, 1980-81; pres. Sci. Council Inst. Fundamental Biology, Universidad Autonoma de Barcelona, 1981; mem. space sci. bd. NRC-Nat. Acad. Scis. U.S., 1980-83; mem. Jurado Premio Principe de Asturias de Investigacion Cientifica y Tecnica, Fundacion Principado de Asturias. Editor: Biogenesis sect. Jour. Molecular Evolution, 1972, (with others) Prebiotic and Biochemical Evolution, 1971, Viral Replication and Cancer, 1973, Cosmochemical Evolution and the Origins of Life, 1974, Reflections on Biochemistry, 1976, Avances de la Bioquimica, 1977, The Viking Mission and the Question of Life on Mars, 1979, Virus and Cancer, 1971, Energy Sources and Development, 1978, Catalunya Agricola, 1978, Planetes Comparats, 1980; contbr. (with others) articles to profl. publs. Recipient medal and hon. councilor Consejo Superior de Investigaciones Cientificas, 1969; Gran Cruz de la Orden Civil de Alfonso X el Sabio Madrid, 1974; Life Scientist award NASA, 1974-75; Gold medal City of Lerida, 1976; medal Narcis Monturiol al Merit Cientific y Tecnologic Catalunya, Spain, 1982; Gran Cruz de la Orden del Merito Aeronautico Madrid, 1983; named Important Scientist of Year Barcelona, 1970, Important Scientist of Year Madrid, 1977. Mem. Am. Soc. Biol. Chemists, Am. Chem. Soc., Nat. Assn. Chemists Spain, Spanish Soc. Biochemists, Royal Acad. Arts and Scis. of Barcelona, Inst. Hispanic Culture (founding mem.), Internat. Soc. for Study Origin of Life (exec. council 1974), Asociacion de Amigos de Gaspar de Portola (pres. 1981—), Spanish Soc. Biochemistry (hon.), Sigma Xi. Current Work: Synthesis of biochemical compounds under plausible primitive earth conditions; planetary exploration; studies on possibility of extra-terrestrial life. Subspecialties: Biochemistry (biology); Organic chemistry. Home: 11306 Endicott Ln Houston TX 77035 Office: Dept Biochem and Biophysical Scis SRI U Houston Houston TX 77004

O'ROURKE, THOMAS DENIS, civil engineering educator, researcher; b. Pitts., July 31, 1948; s. Lawrence Robert and Adel Mildred (Moloski) O.; m. Patricia Ann Lane, Aug. 12, 1978. B.S.C.E., Cornell U., 1970; M.S.C.E., U. Ill., 1973, Ph.D., 1975. Soils engr. Dames & Moore, N.Y.C., 1970; research asst. U. Ill., Urbana, 1970-75, asst. prof. civil engring., 1975-78; asst. prof. civil engring. Cornell U., Ithaca, N.Y., 1978-81, assoc. prof., 1981—. Mem. ASCE (pres. Ithaca sect. 1981-82, C.A. Hogentogler award 1976, Collingwood prize 1983), ASME, Earthquake Engring Research Inst., Internat. Soc. Rock Mechanics, Internat. Soc. Engring. Geology. Roman Catholic. Current work: Foundations, rock engineering, earthquake engineering, pipelines, tunneling, excavations. Subspecialties: Civil engineering; Geology. Home: 10 Woodcrest Ave Ithaca NY 14850 Office: 265 Hollister Hall Cornell Univ Ithaca NY 14853

ORR, WILLIAM HAROLD, engineering physicist; b. Buffalo, Nov. 3, 1930; s. William Joseph and Margaret Gertrude (Morrow) O.; m. Donola Yvonne Burcham, June 23, 1984; children by previous marriage—William Goehrig, Barron Joseph, Elise Morrow, Wade Frank. B.Engring. Physics, Cornell U., 1953, Ph.D., 1962; M.S., Cath. U., 1957. Research asst. Cornell U., Ithaca, N.Y., 1958-61; mem. tech. staff Bell Labs., Murray Hill, N.J., 1962-65, supr. IC devel. group, Allentown, Pa., 1966-70, head process capability dept., Indpls., 1970-73, head telephone tech. dept., 1974-83, head home mgmt. dept. Am. Tel. & Tel. Consumer Products, Indpsl., 1984—; mem. microelectronics com. Ind. Corp. for Sci. & Tech., Indpls., 1983—; indsl. adv. com. Ind. U./Purdue U., Ft. Wayne, 1982—; program com. Electronics Components Conf., 1976-82; trustee Fedn. Materials Socs., Washington, 1974-77, sec.-treas., 1977. Author: chpt.: Thin Film Technology, 1968, Physical Design of Electronic Systems, 1971. Contbr. articles to profl. jours. Patentee in field. Pres., Hamilton Centers Youth Service Bur., Noblesville, Ind., 1977-79, bd. dirs., 1973-79, 82-85, treas., 1983-85; mem. Carmel Clay Curriculum Adv. Com., Ind., 1979-82; vol. Marion County Juvenile Ct., Indpls., 1972-73; deacon Orchard Park Presbyn. Ch., Carmel, 1972-74, elder, 1975—, session, 1975-77, 84—, clk., 1977; mem. Dean's adv. com. Purdue U. Sch. Sci., Indpls., 1985—. Served with USN, 1953-57. NROTC fellow, 1949-53; John McMullen fellow, 1957-58. Mem. IEEE Consumer Electronics Soc., IEEE Communications Soc., IEEE Components, Hybrids and Mfg. Tech. Soc., Sigma Xi, Kappa Sigma, Phi Kappa Phi. Current work: Design and development of consumer electronics products including wireless emergency call systems. Subspecialties: Microelectronics; Materials (engineering). Home: 1114 Ridge Rd Carmel IN 46032 Office: Am Tel and Tel Consumer Products PO Box 1008 Indianapolis IN 46206

ORSI, JAMES JOHN, marine biologist; b. N.Y.C., Nov. 1, 1940; s. George Joseph and Mary Elizabeth (Varachi) O.; m. Yim Yuke Chan, May 15, 1971; children—Terry, Mark. B.S., Fordham U., 1962; M.S., U. Wash., 1965. Fishery biologist Calif. Dept. Fish and Game, Stockton, 1965-67, marine biologist, 1968—; advisor Oceanographic Inst. in Vietnam, AID, Washington, 1967-68. Contbr. articles to profl. jours. Mem. Pacific Estuarine Research Soc., San Francisco Bay and Estuarine Soc. Lodge: Lions. Current work: Biology and ecology of mysid shrimp and copepods, estuarine food webs. Subspecialties: Ecology (biology); Marine biology. Office: Calif Dept Fish and Game 4001 N Wilson Way Stockton CA 95205

ORSZAG, STEVEN ALAN, applied mathematician; b. N.Y.C., Feb. 27, 1943; s. Joseph and Rose (Siegel) O.; m. Reba Karp, June 21, 1964; children—J. Michael, Peter Richard, Jonathan Marc. B.S., M.I.T., 1962; postgrad. (Henry fellow), St. John's Coll., Cambridge (Eng.) U., 1962-63; Ph.D., Princeton U., 1966. Mem. Inst. Advanced Study, Princeton, N.J., 1966-67; asst. prof. math. M.I.T., 1967-70, asso. prof., 1970-75, prof. applied math., 1975-84; prof. applied math. Princeton U., 1984—; pres. CHI Inc., 1975—; chmn. Consortium for Sci. Computing, Inc., 1984—; cons. in field. Author: Studies in Applied Mathematics, 1976, Numerical Analysis of Spectral Methods, 1977, Advanced Mathematical Methods for Scientists and Engineers, 1978; editor: Springer Series in Computational Physics, 1977—, Springer Lecture Notes in Engineering, 1981—, Jour. Sci. Computation, 1985—; editorial bd.: Studies in Applied Math, 1975—, Computers & Mathematics, 1975—; research numerous publs. in field. A.P. Sloan Found. fellow, 1970-74. Fellow Am. Inst. Physics, AIAA, Soc. Indsl. and Applied Math. Subspecialties: Fluid mechanics; Numerical analysis (computer science). Office: 218 Fine Hall Princeton U Princeton NJ 08544

ORTHWEIN, WILLIAM COE, mech. engr.; b. Toledo, Ohio, Jan. 27, 1924; s. William Edward and Millie Minerva (Coe) O.; m. Helen Virginia Poindexter, Feb; children—Karla Frances, Adele Diana, Maria Theresa. B.S., M.I.T., 1946; M.S., U. Mich., 1957, Ph.D., 1959. Registered profl. engr., Ill., Ind., Ky. Aerophysicist Gen. Dynamics Co., Ft. Worth, 1951-52; research asso. U. Mich., 1952-59; adv. engr. IBM Corp., Owego, N.Y., 1959-61; dir. computer centers U. Okla., Norman, 1961-63; research scientist Ames Lab., NASA, Moffett Field, Calif., 1963-65; mem. faculty So. Ill. U., Carbondale, 1965—, prof. engring., 1967—; cons. in field. Author papers, revs. in field. Pres. Jackson County (Ill.) Taxpayers Assn., 1976. Served with AUS, 1943-46. Mem. ASME (Outstanding Service award 1972), Soc. Exptl. Stress Analysis, Tensor Soc., Soc. Mining Engrs., Am. Gear Mfrs. Assn., Am. Acad. Mechanics, Ill. Soc. Profl. Engrs. (chmn. salary and employment com. 1974, chmn. ad hoc com. continuing edn. 1975), Nat. Rifle Assn., Aircraft Owners and Pilots Assn., Sigma Xi. Mormon. Current Work: Machine design, theoretical stress analysis, computer-aided engineering and computer-aided product performance testing. Subspecialties: Mechanical engineering; Computer-aided design. Home: PO Box 3332 Carbondale IL 62901 Office: So Ill Univ Carbondale IL 62901

ORTIZ-SUAREZ, HUMBERTO JOSE, neurosurgeon; b. Santurce, P.R., Oct. 29, 1941; s. Humberto Ortiz and Antonia Suarez; m. Conchita Z. Ortiz, Dec. 21, 1964; children: Humberto, Elena. B.S., U. P.R., 1961, M.D., 1965; Ph.D., U. Minn., 1974. Intern Univ. Hosp. P.R. Med. Ctr., 1965-66; resident U. Tex., San Antonio, 1968-69; resident in neurosurgery U. Minn. Hosps., Mpls., 1969-74; asst. prof. neurosurgery U. P.R. Med. Sch., San Juan, 1974-77, assoc. prof., 1977-84, prof., 1984—; assoc. attending in neurol. surgery Univ. Dist. Hosp., 1977—, San Juan City Hosp., 1977—; attending in neurol. surgery VA Hosp., San Juan, 1982—. Contbr. articles to profl. jours. Bd. dirs. P.R. Soc. Epilepsy, 1975-78; mem. exec. com. Univ. Hosp., 1978-80. Served to capt. M.C. AUS, 1966-68, Vietnam. Decorated Air medal, Combat Med. badge, Bronze Star medal. Mem. AMA (Physicians Recognition award 1972, 76, 84), P.R. Assn. Neurol. Surgeons (sec. 1980-82), Am. Assn. Neurol. Surgeons, P.R. Med. Assn., Soc. Neuroscis., World Fedn. Neurol. Surgeons, Caribbean Assn. Neurol. Surgeons, ACS, Congress Neurol. Surgeons, Neurosurg. Soc. Am., So. Neurosurg. Soc., Alpha Omega Alpha. Roman Catholic. Current Work: Central nervous system trauma, vascular diseases of the nervous system, computerized tomography. Subspecialties: Neurosurgery; Enzyme technology. Office: Neurological Surgery Sect Med Scis Campus GPO Box 5067 San Juan PR 00936

ORTON, COLIN GEORGE, med. physicist; b. London, June 4, 1938; came to U.S., 1966, naturalized, 1981; s. Frederick G. and Audrey V. (Sewell) O.; m. Barbara Orton, July 25, 1964; children: Nigel, Susanne, Philip. B.Sc. with honors in physics, Bristol U., 1959; M.Sc., London U., 1961, Ph.D., 1965. Instr. St. Bart's Hosp. Med. Coll., London, 1961-66; chief physicist N.Y.U. Med. Center, 1966-75; R.I. Hosp., 1975-81; assoc. prof. Brown U., Providence, 1975-81; chief physicist Harper-Grace Hosps., Detroit, 1981—; prof. radiation oncology/radiology Wayne State U., Detroit, 1981—. Contbr. articles to profl. jours.; editor: Bull. Am. Assn. Physicists in Medicine, 1971-73, Radiological Physics Examination Review Book, Vol. 1, 1971, Vol II, 1978, Practical Aspects of Electron Beam Treatment Planning, 1978, Progress in Medical Radiation Physics, Vol. I, 1982, Vol. II, 1985. Inst. Physics London fellow, 1976—. Mem. Am. Assn. Physicists in Medicine (pres. 1981), Am. Inst. Physics, Brit. Inst. Radiology, Am. Soc. Therapeutic Radiology and Oncology, Am. Coll. Radiology, Radiation Research Soc., Am. Coll. Med. Physics (chmn. 1985), Health Physics Soc., Radiol. Soc. N.Am. Current Work: Research in radiotherapy, radiation biology, med. physics, radiation dosimetry. Subspecialties: Radiology; Medical physics.

ORWOLL, ROBERT ARVID, chemist, educator; b. Mpls., Aug. 28, 1940; s. Arvid L. and Agnes (Christiansen) O.; m. Betty M., Feb. 24, 1972; children: Katherine S., Karen E. B.A., St. Olaf Coll., 1962; Ph.D., Stanford U., 1966. Research instr. Dartmouth Coll, Hanover, N.H., 1966-68; research fellow U. Conn., Storrs, 1968-69; asst. prof. chemistry Coll. William and Mary, Williamsburg, 1969-72, assoc. prof., 1972-82, prof., 1982—. Mem. Am. Chem. Soc., AAAS, Va. Acad. Sci. Methodist. Current Work: Liquid crystal thermodynamics, polymer solution thermodynamics. Subspecialties: Physical chemistry; Polymer chemistry. Office: Dept Chemistry William and Mary Coll Williamsburg VA 23185

OSBORN, DANIEL CARGILL, III, nuclear radiation effects experimentor, field testing executive; b. Carbondale, Pa., Feb. 12, 1939; s. Daniel Cargill, Jr., and Marguerite (Henshaw) O.; m. Carolyn Joyce Wozniak, July 10, 1965; children—Susan, Mark, Theresa. B.S.E.E., Northeastern U., 1962; M.S.E.E., Syracuse U., 1964. Coop. student, staff mem. Gen. Electric Co., Syracuse and Utica, N.Y., 1958-68; mem. tech. staff Systems, Sci. & Software, San Diego, 1968-73, IRT Corp., San Diego, 1973-76; staff scientist Jaycor, San Diego, 1976-79; program mgr. Kaman Scis. Corp., Colorado Springs, Colo., 1979-85, dir. field testing, 1985—. Contbr. articles to profl. jours. Gen. Motors Co. scholar, 1958-62. Mem. IEEE, Tau Beta Pi. Current work: Radiation testing of electronics, materials and structures, to assess the nuclear hardness and survivability of space systems. Subspecialties: Aerospace engineering and technology; Nuclear engineering. Home: 615 Blackhawk Dr Colorado Springs CO 80919 Office: Kaman Scis Corp 1500 Garden of Gods Rd Colorado Springs CO 80907

OSBORN, ELBURT FRANKLIN, research scientist; b. Winnebago County, Ill., Aug. 13, 1911; s. William Franklin and Anna (Sherman) O.; m. Jean Thomson, Aug. 12, 1939; children: James Franklin, Ian Charles. B.A., DePauw U., 1932; M.S., Northwestern U., 1934; Ph.D., Calif. Inst. Tech., 1938. Teaching fellow geology Northwestern U., 1932-34, instr. geology, 1937; teaching fellow Calif. Inst. Tech., 1934-37; geologist Que-on-Gold Mines, Ltd., Que., 1936, Val d'Or, Que., 1938; petrologist geophys. lab. Carnegie Instn., Washington, 1938-42; phys. chemist div. I Nat. Def. Research Com., 1942-45; research chemist Eastman Kodak Co., Rochester, N.Y., 1945-46; prof. geochemistry Pa. State U., 1946-70; chmn. div. earth sci. Pa. State U. (Coll. Mineral Industries), 1946-52, asso. dean coll., 1952-53, dean, 1953-59, v.p. research, 1959-70, prof. emeritus geochemistry, v.p. research emeritus, 1971—; dir. U.S. Bur. Mines, 1970-73; distinguished prof. Carnegie Instn. Washington, 1973-77, emeritus, 1977—; sr. postdoctoral fellow Cambridge U., 1958; Com. adviser geophysics br. Office Naval Research, 1947-50; adviser panel mineral products div. Nat. Bur. Standards, 1958-62, chmn., 1958-59, adviser panel metallurgy div., 1958-64; adviser to com. basic research U.S. Army Research Office in Ceramics, 1960-63; mem. earth sci. panel NSF, 1953-55, div. com. math., phys. and engrng. scis., 1955-59, chmn., 1957-58, adv. panel phys. scis. facilities, 1960-64; exec. com. earth scis. div. Nat. Acad. Sci., 1969-72; mem. materials adv. com. Office Tech. Assessment, U.S. Congress, 1975-80; chmn. adv. com. on mining and mineral resources research U.S. Dept. Interior, 1978-83; mem. geoscis. adv. panel Los Alamos Sci. Lab., Dept. Energy, U. Calif., Berkeley, 1975-78. Mem. bd. Univ. Corp. Atmospheric Research, Pa. Health Research Inst., Geisinger Med. Center. Recipient Tech. Meeting award Am. Iron and Steel Inst., 1954. Fellow Geol. Soc. Am. (council 1959-62), Mineral. Soc. Am. (pres. 1960-61, asso. editor Am. Mineralogist 1953-55, Roebling medal 1972), Geochem. Soc. (pres. 1967-68), A.A.A.S. (council), Am. Ceramic Soc. (pres. 1964, chmn. basic scis. div. 1951-52, tech. adv. com. Nat. Bur. Standards 1954-58, chmn. 1957-58, chmn. publ. com. 1960-63, 70-71, Jeppson award 1973, Bleininger award 1976), Am. Geophys. Union; mem. Am. Chem. Soc., Geol. Soc. Washington, Am. Inst. Mining, Metall. and Petroleum Engrs. (Hardinge award 1974), Soc. Econ. Geologists (v.p. 1965, pres. 1972-73), Am. Geol. Inst. (dir. 1956-59), Nat. Acad. Engrng. (mem. engrng. aspects environ., quality com.), NRC (chmn. mineral sci. and tech. com. 1966-69, mem. materials adv. bd. 1965-69, chmn. bd. mineral resources 1974-77, mem. commn. natural resources 1974-77, geophysics research bd. 1974-77, chmn. workshop on continental drilling for sci. purposes 1978, chmn. com. geol. aspects of indsl. waste disposal 1980-82), Internat. Union Geol. Sci. (nat. com. 1961-64, 73-77, chmn. 1975-77), Can. Ceramic Soc. (hon.), Internat. Assn. Volcanologists, Nat. Assn. State Univs. and Land Grant Colls. (chmn. com. mineral resources 1969, mem. water resources com. 1965-71, council research policy adminstrn. 1965-71), Phi Beta Kappa, Sigma Xi (nat. exec. com. 1961-64, com. nat. lectureships 1969-71), Phi Lambda Upsilon, Delta Tau Delta, Phi Kappa Phi, Keramos. Current Work: Laborotory research on silicate systems at high temperatures and pressures; especially applicable to origins of volcanic magmas. Subspecialties: Geochemistry; Ceramics. Home: 330 E Irvin Ave State College PA 16801 Office: Deike Bldg Pa State U University Park PA 16802

OSBORN, WAYNE HENRY, astronomer, physicist, educator; b. Los Angeles, Oct. 8, 1942; s. Wyman Henry and Margaret Lois (Nash) O.; m. Marie-Therese Zehnder, Aug. 7, 1971; children: Nathalie, Christine, Wayne Henry. A.B., U. Calif.-Berkeley, 1964; postgrad., U. Md., 1964-65; M.A., Wesleyan U., Middletown, Conn., 1966; Ph.D., Yale U., 1971. With Universidad de Los Andes, Merida, Venezuela, 1971-76, Venezuelan Consejo de Investigaciones Cientificas y Tecnicas, 1972-76; assoc. prof. dept. physics Central Mich. U., Mt. Pleasant, 1976—, chmn. dept., 1979-85. Contbr. articles to profl. jours. Fellow Royal Astron. Soc.; mem. Internat. Astron. Union., Astron. Soc. Pacific (life), Am. Astron. Soc., Sigma Pi Sigma. Current Work: Variable stars, globular clusters, occultations. Subspecialty: Optical astronomy. Office: Dept Physics Central Mich U 220 Brooks Hall Mount Pleasant MI 48859

OSBORNE, ADAM, computer company executive; b. Bangkok, Thailand, Feb. 6, 1939; m. Cynthia Osborne (div.); children: Ian, Paul, Alexandra; m. Barbara Ann Burdick, Dec. 4, 1982. B.S., U. Birmingham, Eng., 1961; Ph.D. in Chemistry, U. Del. With M.W. Kellogg Co., 1961-64, Shell Devel. Corp., 1967-70; prin. Osborne & Assocs., 1970-81; founder, pres. Osborne Computer Corp., Hayward, Calif., 1981-83, chmn. bd., 1983—. Author computer guides and handbooks. Subspecialty: Computer engineering. Office: Paperback Software 2612-8th St Berkeley CA 94710

OSER, BERNARD LEVUSSOVE, food scientist, consultant; b. Phila., Feb. 2, 1899; s. Harris Elias and Frances (Levussove) O.; m. Clara deHirsch Kotkin, May 27, 1923; children—Zelda Zelinsky, Alan Stuart. B.S. in Chemistry, U. Pa., 1920, M.S., 1925; Ph.D., Fordham U., 1927. Pres., dir. Food & Drug Research Labs., Maspeth, N.Y., 1926-70, cons., chmn. bd., 1970-73; cons. Bernard L. Oser Assocs., N.Y.C., 1973—; asst. in physiol. chemistry Jefferson Med. Coll., 1920-21; biochemist Phila. Gen. Hosp., 1922-6; food protection com. Nat. Acad. Scis./NRC, 1964-71; joint expert com. on food additives FAO/WHO, 1961-68; mem. food sci. mission to European Common Market, U.S. Dept. Agr., 1963; adj. prof. pub. health nutrition Inst. Human Nutrition, Columbia U., 1959-71; bd. trustees Gordon Research Confs., 1954-57. Collaborator, co-author: Practical Physiological Chemistry, 9th, 10th and 11th edits. 1926-31, 37. Co-author, editor; Practical Physiological Chemistry, 12th and 13th edits. 1947, 54; Co-author, editor: Hawk's Physiological Chemistry, 14th edit. 1965. Contbr. articles to profl. jours. Editorial bd. Analytical Chemistry, 1946-49, Food Drug and Cosmetic Law Jour., 1957-80, Food Tech., 1947-51, Jour. Agrl. and Food Chemistry, 1955-58. Recipient Inst. Food Technologists Babcock Hart award, 1958, fellow, 1975; Soc. Toxicology Merit award, 1980; Am. Inst. Nutrition fellow, 1969; Toxicology Forum Disting. fellow, 1981. Fellow AAAS, Am. Assn. Clin. Chemists, Am. Inst. Chemists, N.Y. Acad. Sci., Inst. Food Technologists (pres. 1968-69); mem. Am. Chem. Soc., Am. Coll. Toxicology, Am. Indsl. Hygiene Assn., Am. Inst. Nutrition, Am. Soc. Pharmacology and Exptl. Therapeutics, Flavor Extracts Mfrs. Assn. (founder, chmn. 1960-85; expert panel), Assn. Vitamin Chemists, N.Y. Acad. Medicine (assoc.), Soc. Chem. Industry, Soc. Toxicology, Toxicology Forum, Sigma Xi, Phi Tau Sigma, Alpha Epsilon Pi. Club: The Chemists (N.Y.C.). Subspecialties: Nutrition (medicine); Toxicology (medicine). Address: Two Bay Club Dr Suite 20-Z4 Bayside NY 11360

O'SHAUGHNESSY, JAMES COLIN, environmental engineering educator; b. Cambridge, Mass., June 1, 1943; s. James Nicholas and Dorothy Ann (Dube) O'S.; m. Patricia L. Van Den Berghe, Sept. 21, 1963; children: Christine A., James P. B.S., U. N.H., 1965; M.S., Pa. State U., 1970, Ph.D, 1973. Registered profl. engr., Mass., N.H., Pa. Engr. Calif. Div. Water Resources, Los Angeles, 1965-66; engr. N.H. Dept. Hwys., Concord, 1966; instr. U.S. Army Engring. Sch., Ft. Belvoir, Va., 1966-68; research asst. Pa. State U., 1968-72; assoc. prof. dept. civil engring. Northeastern U., Boston, 1972—; dir. Environ. Engring. Labs., 1975—. Contbr. articles to profl. jours. Mem. ASCE, Water Pollution Control Fedn., Internat. Assn. Water Pollution Research, Boston Soc. Civil Engrs., Sigma Xi. Current Work: Industrial waste treatment, toxic materials treatment and impact on water quality. Subspecialties: Environmental engineering; Water supply and wastewater treatment. Home: 25 Sweetwater Ave Bedford MA 01730 Office: Dept Civil Engring Northeastern U Boston MA 02115

O'SHEA, DONALD CHARLES, physicist, educator, optical cons., author; b. Akron, Ohio, Nov. 14, 1938; s. Donald Joseph and Sarah (Walsh) O'S.; m. Helen Spustek, Oct. 20, 1962; children: Kathleen, Sean, Sheila, Patrick. B.S. in Physics, U. Akron, 1960; M.S. in Physics, Ohio State U., 1963; Ph.D. in Physics, Johns Hopkins U., 1968. Research fellow McKay Labs., Harvard U., 1968-70; asst. prof. physics Ga. Inst. Tech., Atlanta, 1970-75, assoc. prof., 1975—; Prin. lectr. laser system design U. Wis. Extension, 1979—. Author: (with Callen and Rhodes) Introduction to Lasers and Their Applications, 1976, Elements of Modern Optical Design, 1985. Fellow Internat. Soc. for Optical Engrs.; mem. Am. Phys. Soc., Optical Soc. Am., Am. Assn. Physics Tchrs., Sigma Xi. Current Work: Laser system design; optics education; optical design. Subspecialties: Laser spectroscopy; Optical design. Office: Sch Physics Ga Inst Tech Atlanta GA 30332

O'SHEA, PATRICK GERARD, physicist; b. Cork, Ireland, Apr. 30, 1957; came to U.S., 1980; s. Michael and Josephine Kathleen (Watkins) O'S. B.S., U. Coll. Cork, Ireland, 1979; M.S., U. Md., 1982, Ph.D., 1985. Instr. physics U. Coll. Cork, Ireland, 1977-79; lectr. physics Regional Tech. Coll., Cork, 1979-80; instr. physics U. Md., College Park, 1980-82, research assoc., 1982—; cons. U.S. Patent Office, Washington, 1984, EPCOM, Cork, 1982—. Contbr. articles to profl. jours. Sci. adjudicator Ann Arundel County Pub. Schs., Annapolis, Md., 1984. Cork City Council grantee, 1975. Mem. Am. Phys. Soc., IEEE, European Phys. Soc. Current work: Physics of intense electron and ion beams; beam plasma interactions; collective ion acceleration; use of intense beams for microwave generation; pulsed power accelerator technology. Subspecialty: Plasma physics. Office: U Md Energy Research Bldg College Park MD 20742

OSMOND, DENNIS GORDON, physician educator; b. N.Y.C., Jan. 31, 1930; s. Ernest Gordon and Marjorie Betha (Milton) O.; m. Anne Welsh, July 30, 1955; children—Roger Gordon, Martin Henry, David Richard. B.Sc. with first class honors, U. Bristol, Eng., 1951, M.B., Ch.B., 1954, D.Sc., 1975. House surgeon Royal Gwent Hosp., Newport, Eng., 1954-55; house physician Bristol Royal Infirmary, 1955; demonstrator, lectr. anatomy U. Bristol, 1957-60, 61-64; instr. anatomy U. Washington, Seattle, 1960-61; assoc. prof. anatomy McGill U., Montreal, Can., 1965-67, prof., 1967-74, Robert Reford prof. anatomy, 1974, chmn. dept. anatomy, 1985—; vis. scientist Walter and Eliza Hall Inst. Med. Research, Melbourne, Australia, 1972-73; hon. sr. research fellow U. Birmingham, Eng., 1979; vis. scientist Basel (Switzerland) Inst. Immunology, 1980. Contbr. numerous articles to profl. jours. Served with Royal Army Med. Corps, 1955-57. Fellow Royal Soc. Can.; mem. Am. Assn. Anatomists, Can. Assn. Anatomists (pres.), Anat. Soc. Gt. Britain and Ireland, Am., Can. assns. for immunology, Am. Assn. Immunology, Brit. Assn. Clin. Anatomists, Internat. Soc. for Exptl. Hematology, Brit. Soc. Hematology. Current work: Cells and tissues of the immune system; the contribution of the bone marrow to the lymphocyte populations and function of the immune system. Home: 116 rue de Touraine St Lambert PQ J4S 1H4 Canada Office: Dept Anatomy McGill Univ 3640 University St Montreal PQ H3A 2B2 Canada

OSTBY, FREDERICK PAUL, JR., meteorologist, government official; b. New Haven, Jan. 20, 1930; s. Frederick Paul and Edna Maria (Kruckenberg) O.; m. Joanne Bernice Sorvig, Jan. 1, 1955; children—Paul, Neil, Karen, Lynn. B.S. in Meteorology, NYU, 1951, M.S., 1960. Meteorologist TWA, N.Y.C., 1954-55, Kansas City, Mo., 1955-56, N.E. Weather Service, Lexington, Mass., 1955, Travelers Weather Service, Hartford, Conn., 1956-60; research scientist Travelers Research Center, Hartford, 1960-70; meteorologist Nat. Weather Service, Silver Spring, Md., 1970-72; dep. dir. Nat. Severe Storms Forecast Center, Dept. Commerce, Kansas City, Mo., 1972-80; dir. Nat. Severe Storms Forecast Center, 1980—. Contbr. papers to profl. lit. Served with USAF, 1951-53. Fellow Am. Meteorol. Soc. (council 1977-80, 84—). Subspecialty: Meteorology. Home: 11202 Cedar Dr Leawood KS 66211 Office: Nat Severe Storms Forecast Center 601 E 12th St Kansas City MO 64106

OSTER, GEORGE F., entomologist; b. N.Y.C., Apr. 20, 1940. B.S., U.S. Mcht. Marine Acad., 1961; M.S., Columbia U., 1963, Sc.D. in English, 1967. Instr., CCNY, 1964-67; NIH fellow biophysics Lawrence Radiation Lab., 1968-71; mem. faculty mech. engring. U. Calif.-Berkeley, 1971-72, mem. faculty entomology, 1972-74, assoc. prof. entomology, 1974-77, prof., 1978—. Guggenheim Found. fellow, 1975, MacArthur Found. fellow, 1985; recipient Louis E. Levy medal Franklin Inst., 1971, 74. Subspecialty: Developmental biology. Office: U Calif Dept Entomol Scis Berkeley CA 94720*

OSTER, GERALD, educator; b. Providence, Mar. 24, 1918; s. David and Sarah (Ark) O.; m. Selmaree Greene, May 11, 1973; children—Tatiana, Felix. B.Sc., Brown U., 1940; Ph.D., Cornell U., 1943. Research asso. M.I.T., 1943-44, Princeton U., 1944-45, Rockefeller Inst., 1945-49; asso. Birkbeck Coll., London, 1949-50; Rockefeller fellow Royal Instn., London, 1950-51; vis. scientist Sorbonne, Paris, 1951; prof. Poly Inst. Bklyn., 1951-69; prof. biophysics Mt. Sinai Sch. Medicine, N.Y.C., 1969—. Author: Physical Techniques in Biological Research, 1956, The Science of Moiré Patterns, 1964; contbr. numerous articles to profl. jours., art exhbts. moire constrns. Home: 241 W 11th St New York NY 10014 Office: Mount Sinai Sch Medicine Fifth Ave at 100th St New York NY 10014

OSTER, MARTIN WILLIAM, oncologist; b. N.Y.C., Apr. 9, 1947; s. Joseph A. and Bella (Lanzberg) O.; m. Karen Anita Oster, May 18, 1975; children: Bonnie Felice, Michelle Rae, Nancy Meredith. B.A., Columbia U., 1967, M.D., 1971. Diplomate: Am. Bd. Internal Medicine and Med. Oncology. Intern, resident in medicine Mass. Gen. Hosp., Boston, 1971-73; oncology fellow Nat. Cancer Inst., Bethesda, Md., 1973-76; asst. prof. clin. medicine Columbia U., 1976—; attending physician Columbia-Presbyn. Med. Center, 1976—. Contbr. articles med. jours. Served with USPHS, 1973-76. Recipient Asher Green award Columbia Coll., 1967, Mosby Med. award, 1970; jr. faculty clin. fellow Am. Cancer Soc., 1976-79; recipient Physician Recognition awards AMA, 1976-78, 78-81, 82-84. Fellow ACP; mem. Am. Soc. Clin. Oncology, Am. Assn. Cancer Research, N.Y. Cancer Soc., Phi Beta Kappa, Alpha Omega Alpha. Current Work: Mgmt. and treatment of cancer patients, med. oncologist, chemotherapist, med. sch. asst. prof., clin. oncology research. Subspecialties: Oncology; Chemotherapy. Home: 5 Birch Grove Dr Armonk NY 10504 Office: Columbia Presbyterian Medical Center 161 Fort Washington Ave New York NY 10032

OSTER, ZVI HERMAN, nuclear medicine physician; b. Burdwjeni, Rumania, Mar. 2, 1932; s. A. Edmond and Shifra (Sperber) O.; married, July 7, 1951; children: Michal, Ady, Shai. M.D., Hebrew U., 1962. Resident in medicine Hadassah U. Hosp., Jerusalem, 1962-67; assoc. dean Hebrew U. Med. Sch., Jerusalem, 1967-73; resident, fellow Johns Hopkins Instn., Balt., 1973-75; asst. prof. Johns Hopkins U., 1975-76, NYU, N.Y.C., 1976-77; dir. nuclear medicine Sheba Hosp., Israel, 1977-79; prof. radiology (nuclear medicine) SUNY-Stony Brook, 1979—, co-chief nuclear medicine, 1979—. Served to capt. M.C. Israeli Army, 1975. Mem. Soc. Nuclear Medicine, Assn. Univ. Radiologist, Radiol. Soc. N.Am. Current Work: Development and evaluation of new radiopharmaceuticals; tumor imaging. Subspecialty: Nuclear medicine. Home: 16 Stratton Ln Stony Brook NY 11790 Office: Health Scis Center SUNY Stony Brook NY 11794

OSTERBERG, ARNOLD CURTIS, pharmacologist; b. Rochester, Minn., Sept. 14, 1921; s. Arnold Erwin and Ann Elizabeth (Curtis) O.; m. Barbara Jane Towey, Apr. 6, 1946; children: Ann, Jane, Eric, John. B.S., U. Iowa, 1942; Ph.D., U. Minn., 1953. Lab. asst. U. Minn., Mpls., 1948-53; prin. research scientist Lederle Labs., Pearl River, N.Y., 1953-84. Contbr. articles on pharmacology to profl. jours. Served to lt. j.g. USN, 1942-46. Mem. Am. Soc. for Pharmacology and Exptl. Therapeutics, Internat. Narcotics Research Club. Roman Catholic. Current Work: Analgesics, antidepressants, anxiolytics, antipsychotics. Subspecialties: Neuropharmacology; Pharmacology. Home: Route 2 Box 2133 Spooner Lake WI 54801

OSTERBROCK, DONALD EDWARD, astronomy educator; s. William Carl and Elsie (Wettlin) O.; m. Irene L. Hansen, Sept. 19. 1952; children: Carol Ann, William Carl, Laura Jane. Ph.B., U. Chgo., 1948, B.S., 1948, M.S., 1949, Ph.D., 1952. Mem. faculty Princeton, 1952-53, Calif. Inst. Tech., 1953-58; faculty U. Wis.-Madison, 1958-73, prof. astronomy, 1961-73, chmn. dept. astronomy, 1966-67, 69-72; prof. astronomy U. Calif., Santa Cruz, 1972—; dir. Lick Obs., 1972-81; mem. staff Mt. Wilson Obs., Palomar Obs., 1953-58; vis. prof. U. Chgo., 1963-64, Ohio State U., 1980; Hill Family vis. prof. U. Minn., 1977-78. Author: Astrophysics of Gaseous Nebulae, 1974; James E. Keeler, Pioneer American Astrophysicist: And the Early Development of American Astrophysics, 1984. Editor: (with C.R. O'Dell) Planetary Nebulae, 1968; Letters editor: Astrophys. Jour., 1971-73. Served with USAAF, 1942-46. Recipient profl. achievement award U. Chgo. Alumni Assn., 1982; Guggenheim fellow Inst. Advanced Studies, Princeton, N.J., 1960-61, 82-83; NSF Sr. Postdoctoral Research fellow U. Coll., London, 1968-69. Mem. Nat. Acad. Scis. (chmn. astronomy sect. 1971-74, chmn. class phys. and math. scis. 1983-85; councilor 1985—), Am. Acad. Arts and Scis., Internat. Astron. Union (pres. commn. 34 1967-70), Royal Astron. Soc. (asso.), Am. Astron. Soc. (councilor 1970-73, v.p. 1975-77), Astron. Soc. Pacific. (chmn. history com. 1982—). Congregationalist. Current Work: Observational astronomy, astrophysics; astronomical spectroscopy. Subspecialties: Optical astronomy; High energy astrophysics. Home: 120 Woodside Ave Santa Cruz CA 95060

OSTERHOLM, JEWELL L., neurosurgeon. Chmn. neurosurgery Jefferson Med. coll. of Thomas Jefferson U., Phila. Subspecialty: Neurosurgery. Office: Jefferson Med Coll Dept Neurosurgery 1025 Walnut St Philadelphia PA 19107

OSTERHOUDT, HANS WALTER, physical chemist; b. Houston, Feb. 29, 1936; s. Walter Jabez and Gretchen Marie (Zierath) O.; m. Marjorie Scott, May 26, 1962; children—David Scott, Thomas Frederic. B.S., Colo. State U., 1958; Ph.D., U. Wis., 1964. Research chemist Armstrong World Industries, Lancaster, Pa., 1964-68; research assoc. Eastman Kodak, Rochester, N.Y., 1968—. Mem. Am. Chem. Soc., Electrochem. Soc., Soc. Plastics Engrs., Adhesion Soc. Republican. Episcopalian. Current work: Physical chemistry and materials science, physical and chemical properties of polymers, fabrication and performance of batteries. Subspecialties: Physical chemistry; Polymer chemistry. Home: 4090 Canal Rd Spencerport NY 14559 Office: Eastman Kodak Co Kodak Park Rochester NY 14650

OSTERMAN, LISA ELLEN, geologist; b. Cin., July 11, 1953; d. Clifford Paul Osterman and Norma Lee (Bledsoe) Osterman Gould; m. Mark Bykowsky, June 18, 1977; children—Marcus Burton, Spencer Paul. B.S., U. Dayton, 1975; M.S., U. Maine, 1977; Ph.D., U. Colo., 1982. Research assoc. Inst. Arctic and Alpine Research, U. Colo., Boulder, 1982—; presenter at nat. confs. Contbr. articles to profl. jours. NSF grantee 1981, 82, 84. Fellow Cushman Found. Foraminiferal Research; mem. Geol. Soc. Am. (J. Hoover Mackin award 1978, Penrose grant 1978), Am. Quaternary Assn., Soc. Econ. Paleontologists and Mineralogists (N.Am. micropaleontology sect.), AAAS. Current work: Foraminifera in glacial-marine sediments and reconstruction of Quaternary oceanography and glacial history of Arctic; glacial-marine sedimentation, ecology and paleoecology of polar, benthic, nearshore foraminifera. Subspecialties: Paleontology, paleoecology; Sedimentology. Office: Inst Arctic and Alpine Research Univ Colo Campus Box 450 Boulder CO 80309

OSTRACH, SIMON, engineering educator; b. Providence, Dec. 26, 1923; s. Samuel and Bella (Sackman) O.; m. Gloria Selma Ostrov., Dec. 31, 1944 (div. Jan. 1973); children: Stefan Alan, Louis Hayman, Naomi Ruth, David Jonathan, Judith Cele; m. Margaret E. Stern, Oct. 29, 1975. B.S. in Mech. Engring, U. R.I., 1944, M.E., 1949; Sc.M., Brown U., 1949, Ph.D. in Applied Math, 1950. Research scientist NACA, 1944-47; research assoc. Brown U., 1947-50; chief fluid physics br. Lewis Research Center NASA, 1950-60; prof. engring., head div. fluid, thermal and aerospace scis. Case Western Res. U., Cleve., 1960-70, Wilbert J. Austin Distinguished prof. engring., 1970—; Distinguished vis. prof. City Coll. CUNY, 1966-67; Lady Davis fellow, vis. prof. Technion-Israel Inst. Tech., 1983-84; cons. to industry, 1960—; Mem. research adv. com. fluid mechanics NASA, 1963-68. Contbr. papers to profl. lit. Recipient Conf. award for best paper Nat. Heat Transfer Conf., 1963; Richards Meml. award Pi Tau Sigma, 1964. Fellow Am. Acad. Mechanics, AIAA, ASME (Heat Transfer Meml. award 1975, Freeman scholar 1982, Max Jacob meml. award 1983); mem. Nat. Acad. Engring., Soc. Natural Philosophy, Sigma Xi (nat. lectr. 1978-79). Current Work: Natural convection; transport phenomena in industrial processes; physicochemical fluid dynamics. Subspecialties: Fluid mechanics; Applied mathematics. Home: 28176 Belcourt Rd Pepper Pike OH 44124 Office: Case Western Res U Cleveland OH 44106

OSTRIKER, JEREMIAH PAUL, astrophysicist, educator; b. N.Y.C., Apr. 13, 1937; s. Martin and Jeanne (Sumpf) O.; m. Alicia Suskin, Dec. 1, 1958; children—Rebecca, Eve, Gabriel. A.B., Harvard, 1959; Ph.D. (NSF fellow), U. Chgo., 1964; postgrad., U. Cambridge, Eng., 1964-65. Research assoc., lectr. astrophysics Princeton U. (N.J.), 1965-66, asst. prof., 1966-68, assoc. prof., 1968-71, prof., 1971—; chmn. dept. astronomy, dir. obs. Princeton (N.J.) U., 1979—; Charles A. Young prof. astronomy Princeton U. (N.J.), 1982—. Editorial bd., trustee Princeton U. Press; Contbr. articles to profl. jours. Alfred P. Sloan Found. fellow, 1970-72. Mem. Am. Astron. Soc. (councilor 1978-80, Warner prize 1972, Russell prize 1980), Internat. Astron. Union, Nat. Acad. Scis., Am. Acad. Arts and Scis. Current Work: Origin and evolution of galaxies. Subspecialties: Theoretical astrophysics; High energy astrophysics. Office: Princeton Univ Obs Peyton Hall Princeton NJ 08544

OSWALD, EDWARD THEODORE, plant ecologist, researcher; b. Kit Carson, Colo., Nov. 30, 1935; s. Theodore Winnifred and Catherine (Seaman) O.; m. Patricia Emma Pelton, May 27, 1961 (div. 1974); children—Theresa Marie, Vicky Sue, John Kenneth; m. 2d, Lorna Grace McCubbing, Apr. 27, 1979. B.A., Western State Coll., 1962, M.A., 1963; Ph.D., Mont. State U., 1966. Research officer Can. Forestry Service, Winnipeg, Man., Can., 1966-70, Victoria, B.C., 1970—. Contbr. articles to profl. jours. Served with USN, 1956-60. Mem. Ecol. Soc. Am., Can. Bot. Assn., Can. Com. Ecol. Land Classification (chmn. working group). Current work: Ecological land classification, forest productivity measurement, post-fire plant succession, and environmental impact assessment in Yukon Territory. Subspecialties: Ecology (environmental science); Ecosystems analysis. Home: 4551 Markham Rd Victoria BC V8Z 5N4 Canada Office; Pacific Forest Research Ctr 506 W Burnside Rd Victoria BC V8Z 1M5 Canada

OTHMER, DONALD FREDERICK, chemical engineer, educator; b. Omaha, May 11, 1904; s. Frederick George and Fredericka Darling (Snyder) O.; m. Mildred Jane Topp, Nov. 18, 1950. Student, Ill. Inst. Tech., Chgo., 1921-23; B.S., U. Nebr., 1924, D.Eng. (hon.), 1962; M.S., U. Mich., 1925, Ph.D., 1927; D.Eng. (hon.), Poly. Inst. N.Y., 1977, N.J. Inst. Tech., 1978. Registered profl. engr., N.Y., N.J., Ohio, Pa. Devel. engr. Eastman Kodak Co. and Tenn. Eastman Corp., 1927-31; prof. Poly. Inst. N.Y., Bklyn., 1933, Distinguished prof., 1961—, sec. grad. faculty, 1948-58, head dept. chem. engring., 1937-61; Hon. prof. U. Conception, Chile, 1951; cons. chem. engr., dir. various engring. and mfg. corps., licensor of process patents, 1931—, to numerous cos., govtl. depts., U.S., Can., Mexico, Cuba, P.R., Central and S.Am., Norway, Sweden, Finland, Denmark, Germany, France, Eng., Belgium, Switzerland, Italy, Spain, South Africa, India, Burma, Yugoslavia, Korea, Japan, Taiwan, Peoples Republic of China, P.I., Dominican Republic, United Arab Emirates, Poland; in field of chem. engring., cons. UN, UNIDO, WHO, Dept. Energy, Office Saline Water of U.S. Dept. Interior, Chem. Corps. and Ordnance Corps U.S. Army, U.S. Navy, WPB, Dept. State, HEW, Nat. Materials Advisory Bd., NRC sci. advisory bd., U.S. Army Munitions Command; mem. Panel Energy Advisers to Congress, other depts. U.S., fgn. govts.; Sr. gas officer Bklyn. Citizens Def. Corps.; lecture tours sci. and engring. fields, Swiss univs. for Am. Swiss Found. Sci. Relations, 1950; lecture tour Chem. Inst. Can., 1944, 50, Am. Chem. Soc., 1956, 58, 79, 80, Shri RAM Inst., India, 1980; Peoples Republic of China, 1983, hon. del. Engring. Congresses, Japan, 1983, Germany, Greece, Mexico, Czechoslovakia, Yugoslavia, Poland, P.R., France, Can., Argentina, India, Turkey, Spain, Rumania, Kuwait, Iran, Iraq, Algeria, China, United Arab Emirates; lectr. U.S. Army War Coll., 1964, Canadian Royal Mil. Coll., 1981. Contbr. over 350 articles on chem. engring., chem mfg., synthetic fuels, thermodynamics to tech. jours.; Co-founder, Co-editor: Kirk-Othmer Ency. Chem. Tech., 17 vols, 1947-60, 24 vols., 2d edit., 1963-71, 26 vols., 3d edit., 1976-84, Spanish edit., 16 vols., 1960-66; editor: Fluidization, 1956; Co-author: Fluidization and Fluid Particle Systems, 1960; Mem. adv. bd.: Perry's Chem. Engr.'s Handbook; tech. editor: UN Report, Technology of Water Desalination, 1964. Bd. regents L.I. Coll. Hosp., bd. dirs. numerous edn. and philanthropic instns., engring. and indsl. corps. Recipient Golden Jubilee award, 1975, Profl. Achievement award, 1978, also; named to Hall of Fame, 1981; (all Ill. Inst. Tech.). Fellow AAAS, Am. Inst. Cons. Engrs., Am. Inst. Chemists (Honor Scroll 1970, Chem. Pioneer award 1977), ASME (chmn. chem. processes div. 1948-49), N.Y. Acad. Scis. (hon. life fellow, chmn. engring. sect. 1972-73), Instn. Chem. Engrs. (London) ((hon. life)), Am. Inst. Chem. Engrs. (Tyler award 1958, chmn. N.Y. sect. 1944, dir. 1956-59); mem. Am. Chem. Soc. (council 1945-47, E.V. Murphree-Exxon award 1978, hon. life mem.), Soc. Chem. Industry (Perkin medal 1978), Am. Soc. Engring. Edn. (Barber Coleman award 1958), Engrs. Joint Council (dir. 1957-59), Societe de Chimie Industrielle (pres. 1973-74), Chemurgic Council (dir.), Japan Soc. Chem. Engrs., Assn. Cons. Chemists and Chem. Engrs. (award of Merit 1975), Newcomen Soc., Am. Arbitration Assn. (panel mem. or sole arbitrator numerous cases), Sigma Xi (citation disting. research 1983), Tau Beta Pi, Phi Lambda Upsilon, Iota Alpha, Alpha Chi Sigma, Lambda Chi Alpha; hon. life mem. Deutsche Gesellschaft für Cheme. Apparatewesen. Clubs: Norwegian (pres. 1974-75), Rembrandt (Bklyn.); Chemists (N.Y.C.). Designer chem. plants and processes for numerous corps., U.S., fgn. countries. Holder over 150 U.S. and fgn. patents on methods, processes and engring. equipment in mfg. of pharms., sugar, salt, acetic acid, acetylene, fuel-methanol, synthetic rubber, petro-chems., pigments, zinc, aluminum, titanium, also wood pulping, refrigeration, solar and other energy conversion, water desalination, sewage treatment, peat utilization, coal desulfurization, methanol production, pipeline heating, etc. Current Work: Production methods and fuel uses of methanol; waste water treatment systems. Subspecialty: Chemical engineering. Office: 333 Jay St Brooklyn NY 11201

OTT, EDGAR ALTON, animal nutritionist, educator; b. Ft. Wayne, Ind., Jan. 10, 1938; s. Earl S. and Luella Fay (Keister) O.; m. Judith Carlene Smith, June 9, 1963; children: Gregory Mark, Ronda Fay. B.S., Purdue U., 1959, M.S., 1963, Ph.D., 1965. Research assoc., mgr. product devel. for horses and sheep Ralston Purina Co., St. Louis, 1965-70; assoc. prof. animal nutrition U. Fla., Gainesville, 1970-79, prof., 1979—; prof.-in-charge U. Fla. (Horse Research Ctr.), 1970—. Contbr. articles to profl. jours. Leader 4-H Club, 1974-82. Served as 1st lt. U.S. Army, 1959-61. U.S. Brewers Assn. grantee, 1977-78; Fla. Canners Assn. grantee, 1974-75. Mem. AAAS, Am. Soc. Animal Sci., Equine Nutrition and Physiology Soc., Sigma Xi. Republican. Baptist. Current Work: Equine nutrition and physiology. Subspecialties: Animal nutrition; Animal physiology. Office: U Fla 210G Animal Sci Bldg Gainesville FL 32611

OVE, PETER, educator, biologist; b. Dellstedt, Germany, Aug. 31, 1930; came to U.S., 1957, naturalized, 1963; s. Paul and Thekla (Brockmann) O.; m. Maria Siert, July 20, 1956; children—Norman, Roger, Torsten. B.S., U. Pitts., 1963, Ph.D., 1967. Research technician Connaught Med. Research, Toronto, Ont., Can., 1953-57; research asst. dept. microbiology U. Pitts., 1957-63; asst. prof. U. Durham Med. Sch., 1967-69; asst. prof. dept. anatomy and cell biology U. Pitts. Med. Sch., 1969-73, asso. prof., 1973-78, prof., 1978—; Mem. study sect. NIH, 1976-79. Recipient NIH research grants, 1970-73, 74-75, 76-79. Mem. Am. Assn. Cancer Research, Am. Assn. Cell Biology. Current Work: Control of growth of normal and malignan cells; hormonal factors and regulation of DNA sylnthesis; mechanisms of hepatocarcinogenesis. Subspecialties: Cell biology (medicine); Cancer research (medicine). Home: 6225 Heberton St Verona PA 15147 Office: U Pitts Sch Medicine Pittsburgh PA 15213

OVED, YOEL, aeronautical engineering educator; b. Basra, Iraq, May 13, 1942; came to U.S., 1981; s. David and Nitza (Salomon) O.; m. Anny Hana Metoudi, Mar. 26, 1973; children: Gal, Iris. B.S., Technion, Israel Inst. Tech., 1968, M.Sc., 1973, D.Sc., 1976. Sr. research scientist Armament Devel. Authority, Haifa, Israel, 1968-77; research assoc. U. Victoria, B.C., Can., 1977-79, lectr. math., 1980-81; assoc. prof. aeronautical engring. Embry-Riddle Aeronautical U., Prescott, Ariz., 1981—. Contbr. articles to profl. jours. Mem. Israel Phys. Soc., Canadian Assn. Physicists, AIAA. Current Work: Teaching aerodynamics, fluid-mechanics, calculus, differential equations, research in aerodynamics and gasdynamics. Subspecialties: Fluid mechanics; Aeronautical engineering. Office: Embry-Riddle Aeronautical U 3200 N Willow Creek Rd Prescott AZ 86301

OVENS, STEPHEN ALEXANDER, geologist, petroleum consultant; b. Dunedin Otago, New Zealand, Oct. 29,. 1950; came to U.S., 1977; s. Ian James and Lorna Margaret (Walesby) O.; m. Jill Annette Blance, Jan. 12, 1974; children—Nicholas, Simon, Dustin. B.S., U. Auckland, New Zealand, 1973, M.S., 1976. Geologist Earth Scientists, New Zealand, 1975-77, sr. geologist, Coffeyville, Kans., 1977-82; pres. Stephen A. Ovens & Assocs., Inc., Coffeyville, 1982—; pres. Cherokee Basin Perforators, Coffeyville, 1982—; v.p. High Cotton Gas Pipeline, Coffeyville, 1984—. Mem. Am. Inst. Profl. Geologists, (sec. Kans. sect. 1985—), Am. Assn. Petroleum Geologists, Geol. Soc. Am., Kans. Geol. Soc. Anglican. Current work: Studying depositional environments and associated oil accumulation in selected areas in the mid-continental United States. Subspecialties: Geology; Petroleum exploration. Home: Route 1 2305 Timberlane Dr Coffeyville KS 67337 Office: Stephen A Ovens and Assoc Inc 3804 W 8th St Coffeyville KS 67337

OVENS, WILLIAM GEORGE, mechanical engineer, educator, consultant; b. Paterson, N.J., July 18, 1939; s. William George and Dora Jane (Mingle) O.; m. Jill Janet Whiton, Aug. 24, 1963; children: Bevan Jane, Janine Elise. B.S.E. in Mech. Engring, U. Mich., 1964; M.S., U. Conn., 1969, Ph.D., 1971. Registered engr.-in-tng., N.Y. State, 1976. Engr. Pratt & Whitney Aircraft, East Hartford, Conn., 1964-65; research specialist U. Conn., 1966-71; lectr. Papua New Guinea U. Tech., Lae, 1972-75; asst. prof. mech. and indsl. engring., area coordinator mfg. engring. Clarkson Coll. Techl., 1976-81; asso. prof. mech. engring. Rose-Hulman Inst. Techl., 1981; cons. Martin Marietta Aerospace Co., Tri Industries. Author profl. publs. Recipient Ralph R. Teetor award Soc. Automotive Engrs., 1976, Teaching Excellence award Pi Tau Sigma, 1977, Teaching Excellence award Tau Delta Kappa, 1980, Teaching Excellence award Tau Beta Pi, 1980; named Outstanding Adv. Clarkson Coll. Tech., 1980. Mem. U. Mich. Alumni Assn., ASME (chmn. materials div. 1982-83), Am. Soc. Metals. Current Work: Effect of processing on service life of advanced aerospace castings; research, development and teaching in mechanical properites of aerospace metals affected by various manufacturing processes; design of custom manufacturing machinery. Subspecialties: Mechanical engineering; Materials processing. Home: 4693 Woodshire Dr Terre Haute IN 47803 Office: 5500 Wabash Ave Terre Haute IN 47803

OVENSHINE, A(LEXANDER) THOMAS, geologist; b. N.Y.C., Mar. 25, 1936; s. Eugene Samuel and Ruth (Crago) O.; m. Elinor Hyle, June 7, 1959; children—Gordon, John, Sally. B.S., Yale U., 1958; M.S., Va. Poly. Inst., 1962; Ph.D., UCLA, 1965. Geologist, U.S. Geol. Survey, Menlo Park, Calif., 1965-70, asst. chief Alaskan Geology Br., 1970-72, chief Alaskan Geology Br., 1976-80, chief Office of Mineral Resources, Reston, Va., 1980-84, chief Office Internat. Geology, 1984—. Subspecialty: Geology. Office: US Geol Survey 917 National Center Reston VA 22092

OVERHAUSER, ALBERT WARNER, physicist; b. San Diego, Aug. 17, 1925; s. Clarence Albert and Gertrude Irene (Pehrson) O.; m. Margaret Mary Casey, Aug. 25, 1951; children—Teresa, Catherine, Joan, Paul, John, David, Susan, Steven. A.B., U. Calif. at Berkeley, 1948, Ph.D., 1951; D.Sc. (hon.), U. Chgo., 1979. Research asso. U. Ill., 1951-53; asst. prof. physics Cornell U., 1953-56, asso. prof., 1956-58; supr. solid state physics Ford Motor Co., Dearborn, Mich., 1958-62, mgr. theoret. scis., 1962-69, asst. dir. phys. scis., 1969-72, dir. phys. scis., 1972-73; prof. physics Purdue U., West Lafayette, Ind., 1973-74, Stuart prof. physics, 1974—. Served with USNR, 1944-46. Recipient Oliver E. Buckley Solid State Physics prize Am. Phys. Soc., 1975, Alexander von Humboldt sr. U.S. scientist award, 1979. Fellow Am. Phys. Soc., Am. Acad. Arts and Scis.; mem. Nat. Acad. Scis. Current Work: Theory of metals. Subspecialties: Theoretical physics; Condensed matter physics. Home: 236 Pawnee Dr West Lafayette IN 47906 Office: Dept Physics Purdue U West Lafayette IN 47907

OVERMAN, AMEGDA JACK, nematologist; b. Tampa, Fla., May 17, 1920; d. Nicholas George and Eloise Urquhart (Smith) Jack; m. Richard Douglas Overman, July 5, 1953. B.S., U. Tampa, 1942; M.S., U. Fla., 1951. Asst. soil chemistry U. Fla., Bradenton, 1951-56, asst. soil microbiologist, 1956-68, assoc. nematologist, 1968-73, nematologist, 1973—. Vice-chmn. Planning Commn., City of Bradenton, Fla., 1975—. Mem. Soc. Nematologists, European Soc. Nematologists, Orgn. Tropical Am. Nematologists, Fla. State Hort. Soc., Soil and Crop. Sci. Soc. Fla. Eastern Orthodox. Current Work: Biology and control of plant nematodes, vegetables, ornamentals, agronomic crops, soil fumigants, crop rotation, nematicides. Subspecialties: Plant pathology; Integrated pest management. Office: 5007 60th St E Bradenton FL 34203

OVERMAN, DENNIS ORTON, anatomy educator, researcher; b. Union City, Ind., Oct. 16, 1943; s. F. Orton and Marjorie J. (Mills) O.; m. Sue A. Sappenfield, June 4, 1966; children—Andrew, Michael, Amy. B.A. in Biology, Bowling Green State U., 1965; M.S. in Anatomy, U. Mich., 1967, Ph.D., 1970. Tchr. Community Sch., Tehran, 1967-68; research assoc. U. Colo., Boulder, 1970-71; instr. dept. anatomy W.V.A. U., Morgantown, 1971-72, asst. prof., 1972-76, assoc. prof., 1976—, adj. assoc. prof. dept. orthodontics, 1985—; vis. lectr. U. B.C., Vancouver, Can., 1979; vis. faculty Mayo Med. Sch., Rochester Minn., 1983, 84. Recipient Outstanding Tchr. award W.Va. Sch. Med., 1978, W.Va. Sch. Dentistry, 1978. Mem. Teratology Soc., Am. Assn. Anatomists, Soc. for Devel. Biology, Am. Assn. Dental Schs. Mennonite. Current work: Experimental teratology; in vitro teratology, cleft palate. Subspecialties: Anatomy and embryology; Teratology. Home: 461 Overhill St Morgantown WV 26505 Office: Dept Anatomy WV Univ Morgantown WV 26506

OVERMIER, JAMES BRUCE, psychology educator; b. Queens, N.Y., Aug. 2, 1938; s. James and Annette (Carleton) Wheelwright; m. Judith Ann Smith, Aug. 19, 1962; 1 dau., Larisa Nicole. A.B., Kenyon Coll., 1960; M.A., Bowling Green State U., 1962, U. Pa., 1964, Ph.D., U. Pa., 1965. Lic. cons. psychologist, Minn. Asst. prof. psychology U. Minn., Mpls., 1965-68, assoc. prof., 1968-71, prof., 1971—; exec. officer Ctr. for Research in Human Learning, Mpls., 1973-78, 81—; cons. Learning Strategies Corp., Mpls., 1981—; adv. panel psychobiology NSF, 1976-79. Editor: Learning & Motivation, 1973-76; assoc. editor: Physiol. Psychology, 1982—; regional editor: Behavioral Brain Research, 1980-84; author: (with others) Animal Learning: Survey and Analysis, 1979 (with F.R. Brush) Conditioning, Affect and Cognition; Essays on the Determinants of Behavior. Fulbright-Hays fellow Yugoslavia, 1980; Fogarty fellow, 1984; Sci. Exchange fellow Nat. Acad. Sci., Poland, 1972; NSF sr. postdoctoral fellow, 1971; USPHS predoctoral fellow, 1963-65. Fellow Am. Psychol. Assn.; mem. Psychonomic Soc. (governing bd. 1983—, sec.-treas. 1981-83), AAUP, Am. Acad. Behavioral Medicine, Delta Kappa Epsilon. Current Work: Mechanism of learning, motivation, behavior and the CNS substrates; emphasis on avoidance, punishment, stress. Subspecialties: Learning; Psychobiology. Home: 1965 E River Ter Minneapolis MN 55414 Office: Center for Research in Human Learning 75 E River Rd Minneapolis MN 55455

OVERSETH, OLIVER ENOCH, research physicist, educator; b. N.Y.C., May 11, 1928; s. Oliver Enoch and Jone (Johnson) O.; m. Anneke de Bruyn, Aug. 28, 1954 (div.); children—Alison, Tenley. B.S., U. Chgo., 1953; Ph.D., Brown U., 1958. Instr. Princeton U., N.J., 1957-61; asst. prof. physics U. Mich., Ann Arbor, 1961-65, assoc. prof., 1965-68, prof., 1968—; sci. assoc. European Ctr. for Nuclear Research, Geneva, 1974, 81—. Contbr. numerous research articles, papers to profl. publs. Fellow Am. Phys. Soc. Current work: Experiments on properties of elementary particles, high energy physics. Subspecialty: Particle physics. Office: Randall Lab U Mich Ann Arbor MI 48109

OVERWEG, NORBERT IDO ALBERT, physician, clinical pharmacologist; b. Enschede Netherlands; came to U.S., 1961; s. Ido and Bella Theresa (Lievenboom) O.; m. Angélique de Gorter, Oct. 27, 1959; children—Eleonore, Elizabeth, Harold. Med. Candidate, U. Amsterdam, Netherlands, 1954, M.D., 1957. Lic. Netherlands, N.Y. Intern, U. Amsterdam Hosps., 1958-60; resident Rochester Gen. Hosp., N.Y., 1961-62; postdoctoral fellow dept. pharmacology Coll. Physicians and Surgeons Columbia U., N.Y.C., 1962-65, research assoc. dept. surgery, 1967-71; instr. dept. pub. health Columbia U., 1965-66; research collaborator, asst. attending physician Brookhaven Nat. Lab., 1966-67; asst. prof. dept. physiology and pharmacology NYU, N.Y.C., 1971-78; practice medicine specializing in internal medicine, N.Y.C., 1967—; attending staff Cabrini Med. Ctr., St. Clare's Hosp. and Health Ctr., Med. Arts Ctr. Hosp.; cons. Lung Research Ctr. Yale U. Sch. Medicine, New Haven, 1972-73; investigator new drugs for pharm. cos., 1984—. Author articles in sci. jours. Vol. hosp. clinics, N.Y.C. Spl. fellow Nat. Inst. Child Health and Human Devel., NIH, 1964-65. Mem. N.Y. Acad. Scis., Am. Physiol. Soc., Am. Soc. Pharmacology and Exptl. Therapeutics, AAAS, Netherlands Am. Med. Soc., AAUP, Eastern Hypertension Soc., Med. Soc. State N.Y., N.Y. County Med. Soc., Harvey Soc., Royal Dutch Soc. for Advancement of Medicine, Sigma Xi. Club: Netherlands of N.Y. Current work: Action of drugs on gastrointestinal smooth muscle and secretion, vascular smooth muscle, hypertension, peptic ulcer, psychoactive drugs, regulation intestinal motility, nutrition, weight control, neuropeptides, prostaglandins, bronchial asthma. Subspecialties: Internal medicine; Pharmacology. Office: 133 E 73d St New York NY 10021

OVSHINSKY, STANFORD ROBERT, engring. co. exec.; b. Akron, Ohio, Nov. 24, 1922; s. Benjamin and Bertha T. (Munitz) O.; m. Iris L. Miroy, Nov. 24, 1959; children—Benjamin, Harvey, Dale, Robin Dibner, Steven Dibner. Student public schs., Akron; D.Sc. (hon.), Lawrence Inst. Tech., 1980; D.Engring. (hon.), Bowling Green State U., 1981. Pres. Stanford Roberts Mfg. Co., Akron, 1946-50; mgr. centre drive dept. New Britain Machine Co., Conn., 1950-52; dir. research Hupp Corp., Detroit, 1952-55; pres. Gen. Automation, Inc., Detroit, 1955-58, Ovitron Corp., Detroit, 1958-59; pres., chmn. bd. Energy Conversion Devices, Inc., Troy, Mich., 1960-78, pres., chief exec. officer, chief scientist, 1978—; adj. prof. engring. scis. Coll. Engring., Wayne State U.; adj. prof. physics U. Cin.; hon. advisor sci. and tech. Beijing Inst. Aeros. and Astronautics, Peoples Republic of China; chmn. Inst. Amorphous Studies. Contbr. articles on physics of amorphous materials, neurophysiology and neuropsychiatry to profl. jours. Recipient Diesel Gold medal German Inventors Assn., 1968; inducted into Mich. Chem. Engring. Hall of Fame, 1983. Fellow Am. Phys. Soc.; mem. IEEE (sr.), Cranbrook Inst. Sci. (bd. govs. 1981), Soc. Automotive Engrs., N.Y. Acad. Scis., Detroit Physiol. Soc., Electrochem. Soc., Engring. Soc. Detroit. Subspecialty: Solid state chemistry. Office: 1675 W Maple Rd Troy MI 48084

OWEN, DANIEL LEE, management consultant, educator; b. Flint, Mich., Mar. 12, 1947; s. Ben and Angeline (Tomczak) O. B.S., U. Mich., 1969; M.S., Carnegie-Mellon U., 1972; Ph.D., Stanford U., 1979. Registered profl. engr., Calif. Sr. engr. Westinghouse, Pitts., 1970-74; decision analyst SRI Internat., Menlo Park, CAlif., 1976-80; cons. Strategic Decision Group, Menlo Park, 1981—; cons. prof. Stanford U., 1980-82. Mem. Am. Nuclear Soc., Sigma Xi. Current Work: Structuring complex decision problems; development of corporate strategy; management of research and development. Subspecialty: Probability. Home: 660 Sunset Way Redwood City CA 94062 Office: Strategic Decision Group 3000 Sand Hill Rd Bldg 3 Suite 150 Menlo Park CA 94025

OWEN, DAVID GRAY, pediatric dentistry educator, researcher; b. Lowville, N.Y., Aug. 9, 1935; s. Allen Fulton and Ruth (Gray) O.; m. Patricia Ruth MacLeod, July 11, 1964; children: Sandra Elenora, Linda MacLeod. A.B., Syracuse U., 1960; D.D.S., McGill U., 1964; A.M., U. Chgo., 1969; certificate pedodontics, U. Ill., Chgo., 1970. Amanuensis and research asst. Royal Dental Coll., Copenhagen, 1964-66; instr., asst. prof. U. Chgo. Hosp. and Clinic, 1967-72; chief pediatric dentistry Wyler Children's Hosp., Chgo., 1970-72; asst. prof. pediatric dentistry U. Md. Dental Sch., Balt., 1972-75; assoc. prof. pediatric dentistry Balt. Coll. Dental Surgery, U. Md., 1975—; mem. Internat. Biol. Program, Chgo., 1970-72; cons. Kernan's cleft palate team, Balt., 1975—, John F. Kennedy Inst. Hosp., Balt., 1972—, Mercy Hosp., Balt., 1980—. Editor: McGill Dental Rev., 1964. Scoutmaster Boy Scouts Am., Troop 175, Balt., 1975-77; ruling elder Govans Presbyterian Ch., 1976-82; bd. mem. Cedarcroft Community Orgn., 1981-82. Served with U.S. Army, 1956-58. Zoller fellow U. Chgo., 1966-69. Mem. Internat. Assn. Dental Research, Am. Assn. Dental Schs., Md. Soc. Dentistry for Children (pres. 1981-82). Republican. Presbyterian. Current Work: Control mechanisms -craniofacial growth and development; and image enhancement determination of heavy metal dentin incorporation. Subspecialties: Dental growth and development; Environmental toxicology. Home: 402 Hollen Rd Baltimore MD 21212 Office: Balt Coll Dental Surgery U Md 666 Baltimore S Baltimore MD 21201

OWEN, ROBERT BARRY, research physicist; b. Chgo., Oct. 16, 1943; s. Jack Saunders and Dorothy Orleen (Riley) O.; m. Lyn Irvin, Oct. 31, 1970; children: Catherine Anne, Ruth Riley. B.S. in Physics, Va. Poly. Inst., 1966, Ph.D., 1972. Student trainee NASA Marshall Space Flight Center, Huntsville, Ala., 1962-66, aerospace technologist, 1966-72, research physicist, 1972—; grad. teaching asst. Va. Poly. Inst., Blacksburg, 1966-69; chief scientist Optical Research Inst.; cons. in optics. Contbr. articles to profl. jours. Recipient sect. prize IEEE, 1978; Service citation Soc. Photo-Optical Instrumentation Engrs., 1980; cert. of recognition NASA, 1979, 80, 81; others. Mem. Optical Soc. Am, Sigma Xi, Sigma Pi Sigma. Republican. Unitarian. Current Work: Original and novel application of advanced optical measurement techniques to space science, materials science, fluids, atmospheric science, oceanography, and medicine. Subspecialties: Optical measurement systems; Holography. Home: 1905 Orba Dr Huntsville AL 35801 Office: Marshall Space Flight Center ES 73 Huntsville AL 35812

OWEN, TOBIAS CHANT, astrophysicist, educator; b. Oshkosh, Wis., Mar 20, 1936; s. George Colville and Monica (Volkert) O.; m. Linda Lewis, Sept. 2, 1960; children: Jonathan, David. B.A., U. Chgo., 1955, B.S., 1959, M.A., 1960; postgrad., Goethe U., Frankfurt, Germany, 1956-57; Ph.D., U. Ariz., 1965. Asst. physicist to sci. advisor IIT Research Inst., Chgo., 1965-69; vis. assoc. prof. planetary sci. Calif Inst. Tech., Pasadena, 1970; faculty SUNY-Stony Brook, 1970—, prof. astronomy, 1972—; mem. NASA planetary missions: Viking to Mars, 1969-78, Voyager to Outer Planets, 1972, Galileo to Jupiter, 1977—; Vernadsky Inst lectr., USSR, 1982; cons. NASA, NAS, NRC. Contbr. articles to profl. jours.; author: (with Donald Goldsmith) The Search for Life in the Universe, 1980. Recipient NASA Medal for Exceptional Sci. Achievement, 1977, Group Achievement awards, 1971, 81; medal Aero Club of Cairo, 1977; AAS Group award of Newcomb Cleve. Prize, 1977; U. Chgo. Alumni Profl. Achievement award, 1983; NASA grantee, 1966—. Mem. AAAS, Am. Geophys. Union, Am. Astron. Soc., Astron. Soc. Pacific, Internat. Assn. Geochem. and Cosmochemistry, Internat. Astron. Union, Internat. Soc. Study Origin of Life, Royal Astron. Soc., N.Y. Acad. Scis., Com. for Space Research. Current Work: Composition, structure, origin of planetary atmospheres, comets, icy satellites. Subspecialties: Planetary science; Planetary atmospheres. Office: ESS SUNY Stony Brook NY 11794

OWENS, JAMES ARTHUR, JR., electrical engineer; b. St. Louis, Apr. 23, 1946; s. James Arthur and Dorothy Agnes (Weidinger) O. B.S., St. Louis U., 1968. Test engr. Emerson Electric Co., St. Louis, 1968-69, devel. engr., 1969-74; project engr. Byron Jackson Pump div. Borg Warner Co., Vernon, Calif., 1975-79, supr. motor design, Tulsa, 1980-82, mgr. project engring., 1982—. Mem. IEEE. Roman Catholic. Current work: Submersible motors-lamination design, heat transfer and bearing systems for use in submersible motor applications (irrigation, geothermal, petrochemical). Subspecialties: Applied magnetics; Mechanical engineering. Home: 7951 E 59th Pl S Tulsa OK 74145 Office: Byron Jackson Pump Div Borg Warner Co 4501 S 86th E Ave Tulsa OK 74101

OXENDER, DALE LAVERN, biochemist; b. Constantine, Mich., Aug. 30, 1932; m. 1955; 2 children. B.A., Manchester Coll., 1954; M.S., Purdue U., 1956, Ph.D., 1959. Research assoc. U. Mich., Ann Arbor, 1958-59, from instr. to assoc. prof., 1959-75, prof. biol. chemistry, 1975—. Subspecialty: Genetics and genetic engineering (biology). Office: U Mich Ann Arbor MI

OYAMA, JIRO, research scientist, gravitational biologist; b. Los Angeles, Aug. 2, 1925; s. Zengoro and Chiyo (Iwamoto) O.; m. Yasue Yukawa, Nov. 19, 1966; children—Sayuri Irene, Misa. B.S. in Chemistry, Northwestern U., 1949; M.S., George Washington U., 1956, Ph.D. in Biochemistry, 1960. Biochemist, NIH, Bethesda, Md., 1950-56; pharmacologist FDA, Washington, 1956-61; research scientist NASA Ames Research Ctr., Moffett Field, Calif., 1961—; lectr., cons. San Jose State U., 1969-74; lectr. Stanford U., 1970-79. Served with U.S. Army, 1944-46. Mem. Am. Chem. Soc., Am. Physiol. Soc., Am. Soc. Gravitational and Space Biology, Sigma Xi. Democrat. Buddhist. Current work: Gravitational biology research (mammalian animals), hypergravity (chronic centrifugation) exposure effects on animal growth and development; space station centrifuge design and use for artificial gravity studies on animals. Subspecialties: Gravitational biology; Physiology (biology). Office: Ames Research Ctr NASA Life Sci Div Moffett Field CA 94035

OYEKAN, SONI OLUFEMI, chemical engineer, research and development administrator; b. Aba, Nigeria, June 1, 1946; came to U.S., 1966; s. Theophildus Adebayo and Emilia Uduak (Inyang) O.; m. Priscilla Ann Parker, June 2, 1970; children—Oluranti, Ima, Olufemi. B.S., Yale U., 1970; M.S., Carnegie/Mellon U., 1972, Ph.D., 1977. Instr. phys. scis. U. Pitts., 1972-75, coordinator phys. scis., 1976-77; sr. research engr. Exxon Research and Engring Co., Baton Rouge, La., 1978-79; research sect. head petroleum processing dept. Engelhard, Newark, 1980-83, group leader, Edison, N.J., 1984, mgr. petroleum catalyst eval., 1985—; adj. prof. N.J. Inst. Tech., Newark, 1984—. Patentee in field. Recipient Black Achiever award Newark YWCA, 1984. Mem. Yale U. Manuscript Soc., Am. Chem. Soc., Am. Inst. Chem. Engrs., Nat. Orgn. Black Chemists and Chem. Engrs., Div. Petroleum Chemistry Inc. (area V Rep.), Sigma Xi, Phi Kappa Phi. Democrat. Current work: The use of catalysts in petroleum refining and management of catalyst evaluation activities for Engelhard speciality chemicals division; petroleum catalyst technologies such as fluid catalytic cracking, catalytic reforming, octafining, isomerization, etc. Subspecialties: Catalysis chemistry; Chemical engineering. Home: 6 Jeffrey Way Piscataway NJ 08854 Office: Engelhard Corp Specialty Chemicals Div Menlo Park CN28 Edison NJ 08818

OZDEMIR, LEVENT, mining educator, consultant; b. Diyarbakir, Turkey, Dec. 4, 1951; s. Kadri Umit and Bedriye O.; m. Kay Marie, May 19, 1973; children—Chad, Sean. B.S., Colo. Sch. Mines, 1973, M.S., 1975, Ph.D., 1977. Asst. research prof. Earth Mechanics Inst. Colo. Sch. Mines, Golden, 1977-80, assoc. research prof., 1980—, dir. Earth Mechanics Inst., 1980—; mem. U.S. nat. com. on tunneling tech. Nat. Acad. Scis., Washington, 1984—. Contbr. articles to profl. jours. Mem. Am. Inst. Mining Engrs., Inst. Shaft Drilling Tech. Moslem. Current work: High speed tunneling, undergroud construction, raise boring, shaft sinlize, water jet rock cutting and drilling, rock mechanics, machine instrumentation and automation, robotics application to mining machinery, tunnel cart modelling. Subspecialty: Mining engineering. Office: Earth Mechanics Inc Colo Sch Mines Golden CO 80401

OZER, HARVEY LEON, biochemist, educator; b. Boston, July 6, 1938; s. Samuel L. and Naomi (Smith) O.; m. Joy Hochstadt, Feb. 3, 1960; children: Juliane Hochstadt-Ozer. B.A., Harvard Coll., 1960; M.D., Stanford U., 1965. Intern Children's Hosp. Med. Ctr., Boston, 1965-66; research assoc. Nat. Inst. Allergy and Infectious Disease, NIH, Bethesda, Md., 1966-69; staff fellow Nat. Cancer Inst., NIH, Bethesda, Md., 1969-72; sr. scientist Worcester Found. Exptl. Biology, Shrewsbury, Mass., 1972-77; prof. biochemistry/biology Hunter Coll., CUNY, N.Y.C., 1977—, Thomas Hunter prof. sci. and math., 1983—; vis. scientist Inst. for Tumor Biology, Stockholm, 1964; vis. prof. Weizmann Inst. Sci., Israel, 1976; vis. prof. dept. molecular biology and genetics Johns Hopkins U. Med. Sch., Balt., 1983-84; cons., mem. virology study sect. NIH, 1978-82. Contbr. research publs. to profl. lit. Served with USPHS, 1966-68. NIH research grantee, 1972—; Am. Cancer Soc. scholar, 1983-84. Mem. Am. Soc. Genetics (nominating com. 1985), Am Soc. Microbiology, Am. Soc. Virology (charter), N.Y. Acad. Scis., AAAS, Sigma Xi. Current Work: Gene transfer, virus-cell interaction, DNA tumor viruses, cell mutants, DNA replication, carcinogenesis. Subspecialties: Genetics and genetic engineering (biology); Virology (biology). Home: 300 Central Park W Apt 14G New York NY 10024 Office: Hunter College 695 Park Ave New York NY 10021

OZIN, GEOFFREY A., chemist. Prof. dept. chemistry U. Toronto, Ont., Can. Subspecialty: Inorganic chemistry. Office: U Toronto Dept Chemistry Toronto ON M5S 1A1 Canada

PAAR, HANS PETER, physicist; b. Rotterdam, Netherlands, June 2, 1944; came to U.S., 1969; s. Pieter and Femia (Speek) P.; m. Jannette Adriana Lammertse, Nov. 29, 1967; children—Robin, Marie Suzanne. Student, Tech. U. Delft, Netherlands, 1968; M.A., Columbia U., 1971, M.Ph., 1974, Ph.D., 1974. Research assoc. Columbia U., N.Y.C., 1974-76; fellow CERN, Geneva, 1976-78; research assoc. Nationaal Instituut voor Kernfysica en Hoge-Energie Fysica, Amsterdam, Netherlands, 1978—; dep. spokesman TPC/Two Gamma expt. Stanford Linear Accelerator Ctr., 1984—. Contbr. articles to profl. publs. Served with Netherlands armed forces, 1968-69. Mem. Am. Phys. Soc. Current work: Electromagnetic and weak interactions, experiments on lepton production in hadron-hadron collisions, neutrino scattering, photon-photon scattering. Subspecialty: Particle physics. Home: 2240 Camino A Los Cerros Menlo Park CA 94025

PAARFUS, BARBARA LEIDHOLDT, psychologist; b. Hartford, Conn., Apr. 29, 1936; d. Louis Frederick and Helen Gladys Christine (Christenson) Leidholdt. B.A. in Psychology, Gettysburg Coll., 1957; M.A. in Clin. Psychology, Temple U., 1959. Lic. psychologist, Va.; cert. sch. psychologist. Tchr., Overbrook Sch. for Blind, Phila., 1958-60; guidance counselor Henrico County Schs., Va., 1960-61; psychologist, instr. dept. psychiatry Med. Coll. Va., Richmond, 1961-73; sch. psychologist, vocat. rehab. Richmond Pub. Schs., Va., 1973-78; psychology asst. Westbrook Psychiat. Hosp., Richmond, 1982-83; sch. psychologist Mecklenburg County Schs., Boydton, Va., 1984—; pvt. practice psychology, Va., 1967—; cons. spl. edn. dept. Richmond Pub. Schs., 1981, Fredericksburg Area Mental Hygiene Clinic, Va., 1966. Sec., Off Broad St. Players, Richmond, 1981; active Clarksville Community Players, Va., 1984—, also church and charity orgns. Mem. Am. Psychol. Assn., Va. Psychol. Assn., Va. Assn. Sch. Psychologists, Uni Club Singles Orgn. (sec. Richmond 1975), Parents Without Partners, Solo/Discovery Singles Orgn., Gettysburg Coll. Alumnae, Psi Chi, Alpha Psi Omega, Phi Delta Gamma, Chi Omega Alumnae. Current work: Use of videotapes as teaching tool, along with role playing and playbacks as means of psychotherapeutic intervention. Subspecialty: Educational psychology. Home: 803 West St Clarksville VA 23927 Office: Mecklenburg County Pub Schs PO Box 190 Boydton VA 23917

PABO, CARL OGREN, biochemist; b. Rochester, N.Y., Sept. 1, 1952; s. Waldemar and Shirley Ann (Ogren) P.; m. Laura Kahana, June 14, 1980; 1 child, Erika Ann. B.S. summa cum laude, Yale U., 1974; Ph.D., Harvard U., 1980. Postdoctoral fellow Harvard U., Cambridge, Mass., 1980-82; asst. prof. biophysics Johns Hopkins Med. Sch., Balt., 1982—. Contbr. papers and revs. to profl. publs. NSF fellow, 1974-77, Jane Coffin Childs fellow, 1980-82; recipient Am. Cancer Soc. jr. faculty research award, 1983—. Mem. AAAS, Am. Chem. Soc., Am. Crystallographic Assn., Phi Beta Kappa. Current work:

Crystallographic study of DNA-binding proteins, use of artificial intelligence programming methods to design novel peptides and proteins. Subspecialties: Biophysical chemistry; Molecular biology. Office: Dept Biophysics Johns Hopkins Med Sch 725 N Wolfe St Baltimore MD 21205

PACE, NELLO, physiologist, educator; b. Richmond, Calif., June 20, 1916; s. Colombo and Emilia (Sannazaro) P.; m. Barbara Dodge Bullis, Jan. 1, 1939 (div. 1957); children—Susan Joanne, Cynthia Jean; m. Mary Jo de Roulhac, June 28, 1959. B.S., U. Calif.-Berkeley, 1936, Ph.D., 1940. Research assoc. Med. Coll. Va., 1940-41; physiologist Naval Med. Research Inst., Bethesda, Md., 1941-46; research assoc. U. Calif.-Berkeley, 1946-48, prof. physiology, 1948-77, chmn. dept., 1964-67, prof. emeritus, 1977—; dir. White Mountain Research Sta., 1950-77; cons. ad hoc coms. NASA, U.S. Navy, 1958—. Contbr. numerous articles to sci. jours. Pres., Seadrift Property Owners Assn., 1977-79, 83—. Served to capt. USNR, 1941-46, 51-53. Fellow Aerospace Med. Assn., AAAS; mem. Am. Physiol. Soc., Internat. Acad. Astronautics, Internat. Union Physiol. Sci. (commn. on gravitational physiology 1974—), Biomed. Engring. Soc., Undersea Med. Soc. Republican. Clubs: Am. Alpine, Bohemian. Current work: Aerospace and gravitational physiology. Subspecialties: Physiology (biology); Physiology (medicine). Home: 1422 Scenic Ave Berkeley CA 94708 Office: Dept Physiology-Anatomy U Calif Berkeley CA 94720

PACER, JOHN CHARLES, nuclear scientist, researcher; b. Toledo, Apr. 23, 1947; s. Chester Anthony and Marie Felice (Matuszek) P.; m. Nora Lee Mary Kasmier, Aug. 21, 1970; children—Amy, John. B.S., U. Toledo, 1969; Ph.D., Purdue U., 1974. Postdoctoral fellow U.S. Dept. Energy, Ames, Iowa, 1974-76; sr. research scientist Bendix field Engring. Corp., Grand Junction, Colo., 1976-84; nuclear analyst Pa. Power and Light Co., Allentown, 1985—; tech. expert Internat. Atomic Energy Agy., Vienna, Austria, 1975—. Contbr. govt. reports and tech. jours. to profl. jours. Recipient Kreider Meml. Chemistry award U. Toledo, 1968, 69. Roman Catholic. Current work: Radiation field build up at commercial nuclear reactors; transport and deposition of isotopic species in reactor coolant systems; chemical decontamination; release of gaseous radio nuclides to the environment. Subspecialty: Nuclear chemistry. Home: 1139 Edward Ave Allentown PA 18103 Office: Pa Power and Light Co 2 N 9th St Allentown PA 18101

PACHECO-MALDONADO, ANGEL MANUEL, psychologist; b. San Juan, P.R., Aug. 10, 1946; s. Angel Manuel and Catalina (Pacheco) Maldonado; m. Blanca G. Silvestrini, July 25, 1968; children: Angel Jaime, Javier Francisco. B.A., U. P.R., 1968; Ph.D., SUNY-Albany, 1972; postdoctoral student, Harvard U., 1972-73. Dir. P.R. Research Inst., Rio Piedras, 1975-76; asst. prof. U. P.R., Rio Piedras, 1975-78, assoc. prof., 1978—; fellow Clark U., Worcester, Mass., 1980—; research fellow in edn. Harvard U., Cambridge, Mass., 1980—; adj. prof., cons. Cayey Sch. Medicine, San Juan, 1980-81; sci. adv. Drug Abuse Control Dept., San Juan, 1976-77; research cons. Govt. Venezuela, Caracas, 1976; tng. cons. Hilton Internat., San Juan, 1978. NRC sr. postdoctoral fellow, 1980; NIMH fellow, 1981-83; Nat. Inst. Drug Abuse grantee, 1978-80; Social Sci. Research Council fellow, 1973. Mem. Am. Psychol. Assn., InterAm. Soc. Psychology (nat. rep. 1981—), Phi Delta Kappa. Current Work: Critical person in environment transitions, such as migration; parental values and goals for self development across cultures. Subspecialties: Developmental psychology; Social psychology. Home: PO Box 22275 University Sta Rio Piedras PR 00931

PACHMAN, LAUREN MERLE, physician, pediatrician; b. Durham, N.C., Mar. 16, 1937; d. Daniel James and Vivian Allison (Futter) P.; m. Mark A. Satterthwaite; children: Emily Ann, Theodore Daniel. B.A., Wellesley Coll., 1957; M.D., U. Chgo., 1961. Diplomate: Am. Bd. Pediatrics, Am. Bd. Allergy and Clin. Immunology. Intern Phila. Gen. Hosp., 1961-62; resident Babies Hosp., N.Y.C., 1962-64; asst. prof. Hosp. of Rockefeller U., 1964-66; asst. dept. pediatrics Columbia U., 1964-66; instr. dept. pediatrics LaRabida-U. Chgo., 1966-69, asst. prof., 1969-71; assoc. prof. pediatrics Northwestern U., 1971-78, prof., 1978—; head div. immunology and rheumatology Children's Meml. Hosp., 1971—. Contbr. articles to profl. jours. Nat. Found. fellow, 1958; NIH fellow, 1964-66; William K. Ishmael vis. prof. and lectr. Oklahoma City, 1983. Fellow Am. Acad. Pediatrics; mem. Soc. Pediatric Research, Am. Assn. Immunologists, Am. Rheumatism Assn., AAAS. Current Work: Pediatric rheumatic diseases. Subspecialty: Pediatrics. Home: 1521 Brummel St Evanston IL 60202 Office: 2300 Children's Plaza Chicago IL 60614

PACHT, JORY ALLEN, research geologist, educator; b. Madison, Wis., Oct. 23, 1951; s. Asher Roger and Perle (Landau) P. B.S., Ohio U., 1973; M.S., U. Wyo., 1976; Ph.D., Ohio State U., 1980. Well-site geologist Sentry Engring. Co., Denver, 1973-74; teaching asst. U. Wyo., Laramie, 1975-76, Ohio State U., Columbus, 1976-78; asst. prof. Kent. State U., Ohio, 1979; lectr.-assoc. level U. Tex. at Dallas, 1982—; sr. research geologist Arco Oil and Gas Co., Dallas, 1980—. Contbr. articles to profl. jours. Hill fellow, 1974-75. Mem. Am. Assn. Petroleum Geologists, Internat. Assn. Sedimentologists, Soc. Econ. Paleontologists and Mineralogists (cert. service 1982, research conf. com. Houston 1982), Geol. Soc. Am. Phi Kappa Phi. Jewish. Current work: Seismic stratigraphy; basin analysis; sedimentology. Subspecialties: Sedimentology; Geophysics. Office: Arco Oil and Gas Co PO Box 2819 Dallas TX 75221

PACHUT, JOSEPH FRANCIS, JR., geology educator; b. Little Falls, N.Y., Mar. 6, 1950; s. Joseph F. and Marion E. (Steinberg) P.; m. Elizabeth A. Battisti, June 3, 1972; children: Jennifer, Melissa, Geoffrey. B.A., SUNY-Oneonta, 1972; Ph.D., Mich. State U., 1977. Grad. asst. Mich. State U., East Lansing, 1972-77, instr., 1975, 77, Albion (Mich.) Coll., 1975; asst. prof. geology Ind. U.-Purdue U., Indpls., 1977-83, assoc. prof., 1983—; speaker at invited seminars, 1977—. Contbr. articles in field to profl. jours. N.Y. State Regents scholar, 1968-72; NDEA fellow, 1975; recipient Sigma Xi research award, 1976; NSF grantee, 1982-85, 84-86. Mem. Paleontol. Soc., AAAS, Internat. Bryozoology Assn., Soc. Systematic Zoology, Soc. Econ. Paleontologists and Mineralogists, Sigma Xi. Democrat. Roman Catholic. Current Work: Influence of environmental conditions (inferred) on the genetic adaptive strategies and evolution of fossil bryozoans; biometrics, evolution and paleoecology of Paleozoic bryozoans. Subspecialties: Paleobiology; Paleontology, paleoecology. Home: 8924 Sunburst Circle Indianapolis IN 46227 Office: Dept Geology Ind U.-Purdue U 425 Agnes St Indianapolis IN 46202

PACIOREK, KAZIMIERA JOLA LILIANA, chemist; b. Krakow, Poland, Feb. 18, 1931; came to U.S., 1956, naturalized, 1964; d. Henryk Josef and Maria Ada (Haberfeld) Thieberg; m. Thaddeus Anthony Paciorek, Jan. 12, 1957; 1 child, Henryk Adam. B.Sc., U. Western Australia, Perth, 1952, B.Sc. (hon.), 1954, Ph.D., 1956; postgrad. Wayne State U., 1956-57. Research chemist Wyandotte Chem. Corp. (Mich.), 1957-61, U.S. Naval Ordnance Lab., Corona, Calif., 1961-64; sr. research scientist MHD Research Inc., Newport Beach, Calif., 1964-66; advanced tech. staff mem. Marquardt Corp., Newport Beach, 1966-70; sr. scientist Dynamic Sci., Irvine, Calif., 1970-72, Ultrasystems, Inc., 1972—. Contbr. articles to profl. publs. Patentee in field. Mem. Am. Chem. Soc. (mem. exec. com. fluorine div. 1982-84), Royal Australian Chem. Inst., N.Y. Acad. Scis. Current work: Synthesis of fluorinated heterocyclics, perfluorinated ethers, wear, oxidation and corrosion inhibitors for nonflammable fluids, high viscosity index fluids, fluid-seal interactions, flammability and combustion toxicology, boron-nitrogen polymers, acid drainage from coal mining and oil shale processing. Subspecialties: Organic chemistry; Polymer chemistry. Home: 1425 Seacrest Dr Corona del Mar CA 92625 Office: Ultrasystems Inc 16845 Von Karman Ave Irvine CA 92714

PACK, ALLAN IAN, medical educator, researcher; b. Gourock, Scotland, Nov. 28, 1943; came to U.S., 1976; s. Sidney Edward and Mary McDermaid (Clark) P.; m. Frances Bentley, May 17, 1967; children—Alison Mary, Angela Frances, Andrew Michael, Allan Ian. M.B. Ch.B., U. Glasgow, 1967, Ph.D., 1976. Registrar, Glasgow Royal Infirmary, 1970-73, sr. registrar, 1976, Wellcome research fellow, 1973-76; asst. prof. dept. medicine U. Pa., Phila., 1976—, dir. pulmonary diagnostic services, Hosp. of U. Pa., Phila., 1982—. Editor: Modelling the Respiratory System, 1985; author, co-author articles, chpts., revs. in field. Recipient Teaching Nursing Home award, NIA, 1982; participant NIH grant projects. Fellow Royal Coll. Physicians and Surgeons of Glasgow; mem. European Soc. Clin. Respiratory Physiology, Am. Fedn. Clin. Research, Am. Geriatrics Soc., Am. Physiol. Soc., Am. Thoracic Soc., Gerontol. Soc. Am. Current work: Investigation neural control of ventilation, transduction properties of airway receptors, central connections and central processing of afferent information, control of ventilation during sleep. Subspecialties: Pulmonary medicine; Neurophysiology. Home: 1513 Fairview Rd Havertown PA 19083 Office: Cardiovascular-Pulmonary Div 975 Maloney Bldg Hosp of Univ Pa 3600 Spruce St Philadelphia PA 19104

PACK, RUSSELL T., theoretical chemist; b. Grace, Idaho, Nov. 20, 1937; s. John Terrell and Mardean (Izatt) P.; m. Marion Myrth Hassell, Aug. 21, 1962; children—John R., Nathan H., Allen H., Miriam, Elizabeth, Quinn R., Howard H. B.S., Brigham Young U., 1962; Ph.D., U. Wis., 1967. Postdoctoral fellow U. Minn., Mpls., 1966-67; asst. prof. Brigham Young U., Provo, Utah, 1967-71, assoc. prof., 1971-75; staff scientist Los Alamos Nat. Lab., 1975-83, lab. fellow, 1983—, assoc. group leader, 1979-81; vis. prof. Max Planck Inst., Gottingen, W.Ger., 1981; adj. prof. Brigham Young U., 1975—; chmn. Gordon Research Conf., Wolfeboro, N.H., 1982. Contbr. articles to profl. jours. Humboldt Found. fellow, 1981. Fellow Am. Phys. Soc.; mem. Am. Chem. Soc., Sigma Xi. Mormon. Current work: Intermolecular potentials, molecular scattering theory; discoverer of angular momentum decoupling approximations. Subspecialties: Theoretical chemistry; Atomic and molecular physics. Home: 240 Kimberly Ln Los Alamos NM 87544 Office: Los Alamos Nat Lab T12 MsJ569 Los Alamos NM 87545

PACKARD, DAVID, manufacturing company executive, electrical engineer, former deputy secretary of defense; b. Pueblo, Colo., Sept. 7, 1912; s. Sperry Sidney and Ella Lorna (Graber) P.; m. Lucile Salter, Apr. 8, 1938; children: David Woodley, Nancy Ann Packard Burnett, Susan Packard Orr, Julie Elizabeth. A.B., Stanford U., 1934, E.E., 1939; LL.D. (hon.), U. Calif., Santa Cruz, 1966, Catholic U., 1970, Pepperdine U., 1972; D.Sc. (hon.), Colorado Coll., 1964; Litt.D. (hon.), So. Colo. State Coll., 1973; D.Eng. (hon.), U. Notre Dame, 1974. With vacuum tube engring. dept. Gen. Electric Co., Schenectady, 1936-38; co-founder, partner Hewlett-Packard Co., Palo Alto, Calif., 1939-46, pres., 1947-64, bd., 1964-68, 72—, chief exec. officer, 1964-68, dep. sec. defense, Washington, 1969-71; dir. Caterpillar Tractor Co., 1972-83, Standard Oil Co. of Calif., 1972-85, The Boeing Co., 1978—, Genentech, Inc., 1981—. Mem. Palo Alto Bd. Edn., 1947-56; mem. President's Commn. Personnel Interchange, 1972-74, Trilateral Commn., 1973-81; chmn. bd. regents Uniformed Services U. of Health Scis., 1975-82; mem. U.S.-USSR Trade and Econ. Council, 1975-82; bd. dirs. Santa Clara (Calif.) County Mfrs. Group, 1978—; mem. bd. overseers Hoover Instn., 1972—; bd. dirs. Nat. Merit Scholarship Corp., 1963-69, Found. for Study of Presidential and Congressional Terms, 1978—, Alliance to Save Energy, 1977—; bd. dirs. Atlantic Council, 1972—, vice chmn., 1972-83; bd. dirs. Am. Enterprise Inst. for Public Policy Research, 1978—; trustee Herbert Hoover Found., 1974—, Colo. Coll., 1966-69, U.S. Churchill Found., 1965-69; trustee Stanford U., 1954-69, pres. bd. trustees, 1958-60. Decorated Grand Cross of Merit Fed. Republic of Germany, 1972; recipient numerous awards including Medal of Honor Electronic Industries Assn., 1974, Silver Helmet Defense award AMVETS, 1973, Washington award Western Soc. Engrs., 1975, Hoover medal ASME, 1975, Gold Medal award Nat. Football Found. and Hall of Fame, 1975, Good Scout award Boy Scouts Am., 1975, Vermilye medal Franklin Inst., 1976, Internat. Achievement award World Trade Club of San Francisco, 1976, Merit award Am. Consulting Engrs. Council Fellows, 1977, Achievement in Life award Ency. Britannica, 1977, Engring. Award of Distinction San Jose State U., 1980, Thomas D. White Nat. Def. award U.S. Air Force Acad., 1981, Disting. Info. Scis. award Data Processing Mgmt. Assn., 1981, Sylvanus Thayer award U.S. Mil. Acad., 1982, Environ. Leadership award Natural Resources Def. Council, 1983. Fellow IEEE (Founders medal 1973); mem. Nat. Acad. Engring. (Founders award 1979), Instrument Soc. Am. (hon. mem.), Calif. C. of C. (dir. 1962-78), Am. Mgmt. Assn. (dir. 1956-59), Wilson Council, The Bus. Roundtable Advt. Council, Bus. Council, Am. Ordnance Assn. (Crozier Gold medal 1970), Sigma Xi, Phi Beta Kappa, Tau Beta Pi, Alpha Delta Phi (named Disting. Alumnus of Yr. 1970). Clubs: Bohemian (San Francisco), Commonwealth (San Francisco), Pacific Union (San Francisco), Engrs. (San Francisco); Exec. (Chgo.); The Links (N.Y.C.); Alfalfa (Washington), Capitol Hill (Washington); California (Los Angeles). Subspecialty: Electrical engineering. Office: 1501 Page Mill Rd Palo Alto CA 94304

PACKER, KATHERINE HELEN, librarian, educational administrator; b. Toronto, Ont., Can., Mar. 20, 1918; d. Cleve Alexander and Rosa Ruel (Dibblee) Smith; m. William A. Packer, Sept. 27, 1941; 1 dau., Marianne Katherine. B.A., U. Toronto, 1941; A.M.L.S., U. Mich., 1953; Ph.D., U. Md., 1975. Cataloguer William L Clements Library, U. Mich., 1953-55, U. Man. (Can.) Library, Winnipeg, 1956-59; cataloguer U. Toronto Library, 1959-63; asst. prof. Faculty Library Sci., 1967-75, asso. prof., 1975-78, prof., dean, 1979-84, prof. emeritus, 1984—; head cataloguer York U. Library, Toronto, 1963-64; chief librarian Ont. Coll. Edn., Toronto, 1964-67; rep. to Adv. Bd. on Sci. and Tech. Info., NRC Can., 1976-78. Author: Early American School Books, 1954. Recipient Disting. Alumnus award U. Mich., 1981. Mem. Am. Assn. Library Schs., ALA, Am. Soc. Info. Sci., Can. Library Assn. (Howard Phalin award 1972), Internat. Fedn. Library Assns., Phi Kappa Phi. Current Work: Research interests; education for library and information science; information science education in developing countries. Subspecialties: Information systems (Information science); Information systems, storage, and retrieval (computer science). Home: 53 Gormley Ave Toronto ON M4V 1Y9 Canada Office: Faculty Library and Info Sci U Toronto 140 Saint George St Toronto ON M5S 1A1 Canada

PACKER, LEO S., research director, engineer, diplomat; b. Roumania, Aug. 5, 1920, came to U.S., 1921, naturalized, 1929; s. Morris B. and Esther (Seidman) P.; m. Dorothy Slepian, Nov. 7, 1948; children—Janet Susan, Alex Jonathan, Michael Benjamin. B.M.E., CCNY, 1941; S.M., Harvard U., 1948; Ph.D., Cornell U., 1956. Registered profl. engr., N.Y. Gen. mgr. space and defense products div. Bausch and Lomb Optical Co., Rochester, N.Y., 1959-62; engring. mgr. info. systems div. Xerox Corp., Rochester, 1962-66; asst. postmaster gen. research and engring. U.S. Postal Service, Washington, 1966-69; v.p. corp. research Recognition Equipment, Inc., Dallas, 1969-73; dir. Office Tech. Policy, Washington, and sci. counselor U.S. Embassy Paris, U.S. Dept. State, 1973-78; resident dir. Egypt program, for applied sci. and tech. Nat. Acad. Sci. Washington, 1981-84; cons. agy. planning NASA hdqrs. Washington, 1969; cons. NSF, Office Tech. Assessment, Nat. Bur. Standards, 1979-80; cons. corp. research and devel. planning Kollmorgen Corp., Northampton, Mass., 1980-81; adj. prof. dynamics U. Buffalo Grad. Sch., 1950-51; lectr. in field. Contbr. articles to profl. jours. Served to capt. U.S. Army, 1943-47. Fellow AAAS; mem. ASME, IEEE. Clubs: Cosmos (Washington); American (Paris). Current work: Science and technology in international affairs; management of U.S. assistance in science and technology to developing countries; research and development management and planning for industry and governments. Home: 4 Ave Rodin 75116 Paris France

PACKER, LESTER, physiology educator, bioenergetics researcher; b. N.Y.C., Aug. 28, 1929; s. Samuel and Janette (Wilensky) P.; m. Mable Anne Graham, Dec. 6, 1956; children—David, Anna Beth, Michael. B.S., Bklyn. Coll., 1951; M.S., Yale U., 1952, Ph.D., 1956. Assoc. in Biophysics Johnson Research Found., Phila., 1957-59; assoc. in biochemistry Dartmouth Med. Sch., Hanover, N.J., 1959; asst. prof. U. Tex.-Dallas, 1960-61; assoc. prof. U. Calif.-Berkeley, 1961-68, prof., 1968—; chmn. comparative biochemistry, 1979—; dir. Membrane Bioenergetics Group, Lawrence Berkeley Lab., Berkeley, 1973—; faculty sr. scientist, 1980—. Author: Experiments in Cell Physiology, 1967; Editor: Methods in Enzymology Vols. 31, 32, 52, 53, 54, 55, 56, 1974—. Contbr. articles to profl. jours. Recipient Burroughs Wellcome Research award, 1981, U.S. Bioenergetics Group award, 1981; named Hon. Regional dir., Nat. Found. Cancer Research, 1982, Hon. Adj. Faculty, Jackson State U., 1983. Mem. Internat. Union Pure and Applied Physics Bioenergetics Group (chmn. 1974-76, symposium com. 1979—), Biophys. Soc., Am. Chem. Soc., Sigma Xi. Current work: Structure and function of bacteriorhodopsin; biological oxidation and bioenergetics; free radical generation and protection in membranes. Subspecialties: Membrane biology; Cancer research (medicine). Office: Dept Physiology Anatomy U Calif Berkeley CA 94720

PACKWOOD, DONALD LEE, electronics engineer; b. Golden City, Mo., Aug. 6, 1940; s. Eugene Smithson and Ella (Tibbot) P.; m. Lona Margaret Lewis, June 5, 1962; B.S. in Physics, Mo. Sch. Mines and Metall., 1963; M.S. in Physics, U. Mo.-Rolla, 1965; Ph.D. in Physics, U. Mo., 1971. Sr. engr. McDonnell Douglas Corp., St. Louis, 1971-74; staff engr. Nat. Semiconductor Corp., Santa Clara, Calif., 1974-77; process engr. Hewlett Packard, Palo Alto, Calif., 1977-78 process engr. mgr., 1978-80 mem. tech. staff, 1980-84. Contbr. articles to profl. jours. Mem. Am. Vacuum Soc. (bd. dirs. 1984—, No. Calif. chpt. chmn. 1983-84, conceived and organized surplus equipment exchange for schs. 1984), Thin Film Soc. of No. Calif. (chpt. vice chmn., chmn. 1981-83), Am. Phys. Soc., IEEE, Electro Chem. Soc., Materials Research Soc. Republican. Current work: Development of contact metallurgy to solve a beta degradation problem in bipolar microwave transistors - development of improved manufacturing processes. Subspecialties: Microchip technology (materials science); Microchip technology (engineering). Home: 2361 Camrose Ave San Jose CA 95130

PADDLEFORD, ROBERT RAY, veterinary anesthesiologist, educator; b. Long Beach, Calif., Mar. 27, 1946; s. Donald Edward and Pearl Crystal (Keiser) P.; m. Susan Christine Freese, June 20, 1970; 1 child, Julie Susan. D.V.M., U. Mo., 1970. Diplomate Am. Coll. Veterinary Anesthesiologists. Intern, Coll. Veterinary Medicine, Davis, Calif., 1970-71; resident Coll. Veterinary Medicine U. Mo., Columbia, 1971-73, asst. prof., 1973-76; asst. prof. Coll. Veterinary Medicine U. Tenn., Knoxville, 1976-79, assoc. prof., 1979—. Contbr. chpts. to books and articles to profl. jours. Recipient Norden Disting. Teaching award Student Body U. Mo., 1974. Mem. Am. Veterinary Med. Assn. (Educator of Yr. 1982), Am. Animal Hosp. Assn., Am. Soc. Anesthesiologists, Am. Assn. Veterinary Clinicians, Tenn. Soc. Anesthesiologists, Am. Coll. Veterinary Anesthesiologists (exec. sec. 1982—), Am. Soc. Veterinary Anesthesia (pres. 1975-76). Republican. Methodist. Current work: Pulminary dysfunction, shock syndrome, cardiovascular effects of anesthesia. Subspecialty: Veterinary anesthesiology. Office: Coll Veterinary Medicine Univ Tenn PO Box 1071 Knoxville TN 37901

PADDOCK, CAROLYN ALLISON, laser physicist; b. Endicott, N.Y., Sept. 2, 1957; d. Harold Edward and Caroline Sullinger (Pierce) P. A.B. Mt. Holyoke Coll., 1979; M.A. Princeton U., 1981, Ph.D., 1985; postdoctoral fellow physics dept. Gen. Motors Research Lab., Warren, Mich. Contbr. articles prof. jours. Reader monitor, Rec. for Blind, Princeton, N.J., 1983-84; patroller Nat. Ski P Patrol, Holyoke, Mass., 1976-79. IBM fellow, 1979-81. Mem. Am. Phys. Soc., Optical Soc. Am., Am. Women in Sci. Democrat. Current work: Picosecond surface spectroscopy, determination of thermal diffusivity of thin multi-layer metal films, ultra-fast phenomena. Subspecialty: Laser spectroscopy. Home: 4028 Three Oaks Blvd Apt 3B Troy MI 48098 Office: General Motors Research Labs Warren MI 48090-9055

PADIAN, KEVIN, evolutionary biologist, paleontologist; b. Morristown, N.J., Mar. 12, 1951; m. Nancy Schwartz, July 14, 1973; 1 child, Ann-Catherine. B.A., Colgate U., 1972, M.A.T., 1973; M.Phil., Yale U., 1978, Ph.D., 1980. Asst. prof. paleontology U. Calif.-Berkeley, 1980—; cons. Smithsonian Instn., Washington, 1979—, Calif. Acad. Scis., San Francisco, 1981—, NASA, Moffett Field, Calif., 1981-84. Author-editor: (with others) Evolution of Complex and Higher Organisms; NASA Workshop Report, 1985. Contbr. articles to profl. jours. Grantee NSF, 1978, Nat. Geog. Soc., 1981, 82, Am. Chem. Soc., 1981, 83. Fellow Calif. Acad. Sci.; mem. Soc. Vertebrate Paleontology, Soc. Study Evolution, Soc. Systematic Zoology, Sigma Xi. Current work: Vertebrate paleontology, evolution, and systematics, particularly Mesozoic archosaurs; macroevolution; evolution of flight; pterosaurs. Subspecialties: Evolutionary biology; Paleobiology. Office: Univ Calif Dept Paleontology Berkeley CA 94720

PAGALA, MURALI KRISHNA, muscle physiologist, researcher; b. Sri Kalahasti, Andhra, Chittoor, India, Oct. 2, 1942; came to U.S., 1970, naturalized, 1979; s. Lakshmaiah and Radhamma (Bhimavaram) P.; m. Vijaya Bhimavaram, Dec. 12, 1969; 1 child, Sobhana. Ph.D., Sri Venkateswara U., Tirupati, Andhra, India, 1969. Postdoctoral fellow Inst. Muscle Disease, N.Y.C., 1970-73, asst. mem., 1974; assoc. research scientist N.Y. U., N.Y.C., 1974-75; electrophysiologist Maimonides Med. Ctr., Bklyn., 1975—; vis. research scientist U. Saarland, Homburg, W.Ger., 1981, 82. Muscular Dystrophy Assn. postdoctoral fellow, 1970-73; Maimonides Research Fund grantee, 1983. Mem. Am. Physiol. Soc., Cell and Gen. Physiology Assn., N.Y. Acad. Scis. Democrat. Hindu. Current Work: Physiological studies on in vitro electromyography, neuromuscular transmission, neuromuscular fatigue, myasthenia gravis, human muscle electrophysiology, computer aided data and signal processing. Subspecialty: Neurophysiology. Office: Maimonides Med Center 4802 10th Ave Brooklyn NY 11219

PAGANO, FRANK PAUL, systems engineer; b. North Branford, Conn., June 29, 1957; s. Benjamin and Lillian Mary (Gianinni) P.; m. Janet Sue Paille, June 1, 1983. A.S., Quinnipiac Coll., 1979; B.S. in Mech. Engring., U. New Haven, 1980. Systems engr. Rockwell Internat., Kennedy Space Ctr., Capt Canaveral, Fla., 1980—. Mem. ASME, SHRAE. Democrat. Roman Catholic. Current work: Represent space shuttle prime contractor at all launch and landing sites; evaluate thermal performance of orbiter after each mission and support vehicle processing for launch. Subspecialty: Aerospace engineering and technology. Home: 19 South St Rockledge FL 32955 Office: Rockwell Internat Kennedy Space Center Cape Canaveral FL 32920

PAGANO, JOSEPH STEPHEN, physician; b. Rochester, N.Y., Dec. 29, 1931; s. Angelo and Marian (Vinci) P.; m. Nancy Louise Reynolds, June 8, 1957; children: Stephen and Christopher. A.B. with honors, U. Rochester, 1953; M.D., Yale U., 1957. Intern medicine Mass. Meml. Hosp., Boston, 1957-58; research asso. Wistar Inst., Phila., 1958-60; asst. resident Peter Bent Brigham Hosp., Boston, 1960-61; research asso. Karolinska Inst., Stockholm, Sweden, 1961-62; instr. pediatrics Children's Hosp., Phila., 1959-60; asso. medicine U. Pa., Phila., 1962-65; asst prof. medicine and bacteriology and immunology U. N.C. Sch. Medicine, Chapel Hill, 1965-68, co-dir. div. infectious diseases, 1969-72, asso. prof. medicine and bacteriology and immunology, 1973—; dir. U. N.C. Sch. Medicine (Cancer Research Center), 1974—; vis. prof. Swiss Inst. Cancer Research, Lausanne, 1970-71; dir. virology lab. N.C. Meml. Hosp., U. N.C. Sch. Medicine, Chapel Hill, 1969-74, attending physician medicine and infectious diseases, 1965—; dir. Nat. Research Service Award Tng. Grant, Cancer Research Center, 1975—; cons. Nat. Inst. Neurol. Diseases and Stroke, 1974—; ad hoc mem. Cancer Research Ctr. Rev. Com., 1975—, Cancer Spl. Program Adv. Com., 1975—. Mem. bd. assoc. editors: Cancer Research, 1976-80, Jour. Immunology, 1977-80; Contbr. articles to profl. jours. Bd. dirs. N.C. div. Am. Cancer Soc., 1980—. Served with USPHS, 1958-60. Recipient Research Career award USPHS, 1968-73, Sinsheimer Found award, 1966-71; Nat. Found. fellow, 1961-62. Mem. Infectious Diseases Soc. Am. (chmn. immunization com.), Am. Soc. Microbiology (chmn. div. DNA viruses 1982-83), Am. Fedn. Clin. Research, Elisah Mitchell Sci. Soc., Am. Assn. Immunologists, Soc. Gen. Microbiology, Am. Soc. Clin. Investigation, Am. Assn. Cancer Research, Am. Assn. Comparative Research Leukemia and Related Diseases, Assn. Am. Cancer Insts., So. Soc. Clin. Investigation, Sigam Xi. Current Work: Cancer and virus infections, tumor virology and molecular biology of herpes viruses, especially Epstein-Barr biruses. Subspecialties: Virology (medicine); Internal medicine. Home: 114 Laurel Hill Rd Chapel Hill NC 27514 Office: U NC Cancer Research Center Box 3 Swing Bldg Chapel Hill NC 27514

PAGE, MARY MICHAEL, organic geochemist, administrator; b. Tulsa, Mar. 8, 1946; d. Reavis Matthew and Patricia Ann (Thompson) Page. B.S. in Chemistry, UCLA, 1971; M.S. in Geology, U. So. Calif., Los Angeles, 1973; Ph.D. in Geochemistry, U. Tulsa, 1979. Geochemist, translator Amoco Prodn. Co., Tulsa, 1977-78; geochemist Williams Bros. Labs., Tulsa, 1978-79; geochemist Robertson Research (U.S.) Inc., Houston, 1979-82, research coordinator, 1982-83, sr. tech. rep., 1983-84, dir. project devel., 1984-85; internat. mgr., 1985—; tech. Russian translator, 1968—; mem. steering com. lab. technician program Houston Community Coll., 1982—. Contbr. articles to geol. jours. U. Tulsa grantee, 1974; Geol. Soc. Am. grantee, 1973. Mem. Geochem. Soc., Soc. Econ. Paleontologists and Mineralogists, Am. Assn. Petroleum Geologists, Houston Geol. Soc., Sigma Xi. Clubs: Tex. Running (Woodlands), Woodlands Toastmasters (cert. Toastmaster Internat. 1984). Current work: Technical-geochemistry of source rocks (mainly non-marine), developing and marketing regional studies. Subspecialties: Analytical chemistry; Fuels. Office: Robertson Research (US) Inc 16730 Hedgecroft Suite 306 Houston TX 77060

PAGE, MICHAEL GERALD, biomedical engineer; b. Chgo., Nov. 23, 1961; s. Gerald Rolland and Constance Rebecca (Ojek) P. B.S. in Biomed. Engring., Marquette U., 1983. Product engr. Tex. Instruments, Lewisville, Tex., 1983-84; design assurance engr. Medtronic, Fridley, Minn., 1984—. Coach Boy's Soccer League, Blaine, Minn., 1984. Mem. IEEE, Nat. Biomed. Honor Soc., Engring. in Medicine and Biology Soc., Tau Beta Pi. Roman Catholic. Club: Rabbits Athletic (Milw.). Current work: Reliability aspects of experimental, developmental and custom cardiac assist devices and pacing systems. Subspecialty: Biomedical engineering. Home: 479 Pleasure Creek Dr Blaine MN 55434 Office: Medtronic Inc Mail Sta T294 6951 Central Rd Fridley MN 55432

PAGE, MICHEL, biochemistry educator, researcher; b. Quebec, Que., Can., Feb. 18, 1940; s. Hector and Alma (Dussault) P.; m. Marthe Boudreau, Dec. 17, 1966; children—Brigitte, Marie, Charles, Madeleine. B.A., U. Laval, 1960; B.Sc., U. Ottawa, 1965, Ph.D., 1969. Registered profl. chemist. Postdoctoral fellow U. Colo., Boulder, 1968-70; cellular biochemist Mt. Sinai Sch. Medicine, N.Y.C., 1970-71; clin. chemist Hotel Dieu Hosp., Quebec, 1971-81; asst. prof. U. Laval, Quebec, 1974-78, assoc. prof., 1978-82, prof., 1982—. Author: La Cuisine sans Cholesterol, 1975; Le Cancer, maladie de la vie, 1984; contbr. articles to profl. jours. Mem. Am. Assn. Clin. Research, European Assn. Cancer Research, Am. Soc. Cell. Biology, AAAS, others. Current work: Cancer diagnosis and therapeutics. Subspecialties: Drug delivery systems; Immunopharmacology. Office: Cancer Lab Dept Biochemistry Faculty of Medicine Univ Laval Quebec PQ G1K 7P4 Canada

PAGE, ROBERT ALAN, JR., seismologist; b. N.Y.C., Nov. 28, 1938; s. Robert Alan and Louise Fulton (Gucker) P.; m. Martha Elizabeth Schrader; children—Benjamin Nicholas, Tovis Erika. A.B., Harvard U., 1960; Ph.D., Columbia U., 1967. Research assoc. Lamont-Doherty Geol. Obs., Palisades, N.Y., 1967-70; geophysicist U.S. Geol. Survey, Menlo Park, Calif., 1970-75, br. chief, 1975-78, program mgr., 1978-80, geophysicist, 1980—. Contbr. articles to profl. jours. Mem. Woodside Planning Commn. (Calif.), 1980-84. Recipient Meritorious Service award U.S. Dept. Interior, 1981. Fellow AAAS; mem. Seismological Soc. Am. (bd. dirs. 1974-80), Am. Geophys. Union, Geol. Soc. Am., Earthquake Engring. Research Inst. Current work: Seismicity and tectonics, particularly in southern Alaska; earthquake hazards evaluation and mitigation; earthquake prediction. Subspecialties: Seismology; Tectonics. Office: US Geol Survey 345 Middlefield Rd Menlo Park CA 94025

PAGE, ROY CHRISTOPHER, dentist, educator, periodontist, researcher; b. Campobello, S.C., Feb. 7, 1932; s. Milton and Annie Mae (Eubanks) P. A.B., Berea Coll., 1953; D.D.S., U. Md., 1957; cert. in periodontics, U. Wash., 1963, Ph.D., 1967; D.Sc. (hon.), Loyola U., Chgo., 1983. Asst. prof. dentistry U. Wash., Seattle, 1967-70, assoc. prof., 1970-73, prof., 1974—, dir. Ctr. Research Oral Biology, 1976—, dir. research Sch. Dentistry, 1976—; cons. Lever Research, Edgewater, N.J., 1984—, ADA, Chgo., 1984—, Fedn. Dental Internat., London, 1984—. Author: Periodontal Disease, 1977; (monograph) Periodontitis in Man and Other Animals, 1982. Served to comdr. USN, 1956-83. Recipient Career Devel. award NIH, 1961-67. Mem. Am. Assn. Dental Research (pres. 1981-82), Am. Acad. Periodontology (Geis award 1982), ADA, Internat. Assn. Dental Research (Basic Sci. Research award 1977). Club: Sand Point Golf and Country (Seattle). Current work: Research in inflammatory diseases, fibroblast physiology, collagen, mechanisms of tissue destruction, immune responses. Subspecialties: Periodontics; Pathology (medicine). Home: 8631 Inverness Dr NE Seattle WA 98115 Office: Dept Pathology SM-30 U Wash Med Sch Seattle WA 98195

PAGE, THOMAS LEE, applied ecology laboratory administrator, limnologist; b. Lima, Ohio, Mar. 5, 1941; s. Harold Alan and Chloe Hazel (Hudson) P.; m. Wilma Louise Pfister, Aug. 24, 1963; children—Alan Thomas, Stephanie Amber. B.A., Ohio No. U., 1963; M.A., Kent State U., 1966, Ph.D., 1971. Research fellow Washington U., St. Louis, 1970-71; sr. research scientist Battelle-Northwest Lab., Richland, Wash., 1942-77, assoc. mgr. freshwater scis., 1977-79, mgr. freshwater scis., 1979-82, mgr. applied ecology, 1982—. Contbr. articles to sci. jours., numerous tech. reports for Wash. Pub. Power Supply System, NRC, Pacific Northwest Lab., Northwest Energy Services Co.; author numerous symposium procs.; presentations to profl. socs. Mem. Am. Inst. Fisheries Research Biologists, AAAS, Ecol. Soc. Am., Ohio Acad. Sci., Am. Soc. Limnology and Oceanography, N.Am. Benthol. Soc., Am. Fisheries Soc., Northwest Sci. Assn., Alaska Acad. Engring. and Sci., Societas Internationalis Limnologie, Sigma Xi. Current work: Aquatic ecology and environmental fate and effects of trace constituents/metals. Subspecialties: Ecology (biology); Ecology (environmental science). Home: 1725 Birch St Richland WA 99352 Office: Battelle Northwest PO Box 999 Richland WA 99352

PAGE, THORNTON LEIGH, astrophysicist, space scientist; b. New Haven, Conn., Aug. 13, 1913; s. Leigh and Mary (Thornton) P.; m. Helen Ashbee, Aug. 28, 1938 (div. 1944); 1 child, Tanya; m. Lou Williams, Aug. 28, 1948; children—Mary Anne, Leigh Page II. B.S., Yale U., 1934; Ph.D., Oxford U., 1938; D.Sc. (hon.), Cordoba U., Argentina, 1969. Astronomy asst. Oxford U., Eng., 1937-38; instr. to asst. prof. U. Chgo., 1938-50; deputy dir. Ops. Research Office, Chevy Chase, Md., 1950-58; prof. astronomy Wesleyan U., Middletown, Conn., 1958-70; research astrophysicist NASA Johnson Space Ctr., Houston, 1970—; part-time prof. Yale U., New Haven, Conn., 1967-68, U. Houston, 1981—; research assoc. Smithsonian Astrophysical Observatory, Cambridge, Mass., 1964-66. Co-author and editor: Library of Astronomy, 9 vols., 1968-78; editor: Physical Sciences, 1947. Editor Ops. Research Jour. Served to Commr. USNR, 1942-46, PTO. Rhodes scholar Oxford U., 1934; recipient Pub. award Naval Research Lab., 1972, Exceptional Sci. Achievement award NASA, 1974. Fellow Royal Astron. Soc., AAAS (vice pres. 1969-72), Astron. Soc. of Pacific; mem. Am. Astron. Soc. (council 1964-67), Internat. Astronomical Union. Clubs: Cosmos (Washington); Explorers (N.Y.C.). Current work: Planetary nebulae, galaxy pairs and clusters, far ultraviolet sources, use of space telescope, astonomy from moon. Subspecialties: Optical astronomy; Satellite studies. Home: 18639 Point Lookout Dr Houston TX 77058 Office: NASA Johnson Space Ctr Code SN Houston TX 77058

PAGEL, DEBORAH JOANNE, health physicist; b. Chgo., Apr. 25, 1955; d. Raymond Frank and Amelia Emelda (Suchecki) Heppeler; m. Richard Arlin Pagel, Aug. 4, 1979. B.S. in Biology, Elmhurst Coll., 1981. Health physics sr. technician Argonne Nat. Lab., Ill., 1977-81; health physicist Commonwealth Edison, Dresden Sta., Morris, Ill., 1981—. Contbr. articles to profl. jours. Mem. Am. Nuclear Soc., Health Physics Soc., Assn. Women in Sci. Republican. Roman Catholic. Current Work: Radiation protection methods in the design and operation of a boiling water reactor. Subspecialties: Nuclear fission; Nuclear engineering. Home: 4035 Washington St Westmont IL 60559 Office: Commonwealth Edison Dresden Nuclear Power Station RR 1 Morris IL 60450

PAGELS, HEINZ RUDOLF, institute director, physicist, educator; b. N.Y.C., Feb. 19, 1939; m. Elaine L. Hiesey, June 7, 1969; children: Mark William. B.S. in Physics magna cum laude, Princeton U., 1960; Ph.D., Stanford U., 1965. Research assoc. Stanford Linear Accelerator Ctr., 1965, U. N.C., Chapel Hill, 1965-66; research assoc. Rockefeller U., N.Y.C., 1966-67, asst. prof., 1967-69, assoc. prof., 1969-82, adj. prof., 1982—; exec. dir., chief exec. officer N.Y. Acad. Scis., 1982—; vis. scientist/prof. Inst. Theoretical Physics, Serpukov, USSR, Oxford (Eng.) U., Cambridge (Eng.) U., CERN, Geneva, Fermi Nat. Accelerator Lab., Batavia, Ill., Los Alamos Sci. Lab., Lawrence Radiation Lab., Berkeley, Calif., Inst. Theoretical Physics, SUNY-Stony Brook; participant sci. confs., speaker; cons. Brookhaven Nat. Lab., 1967-74, White House Spl. Task Force to Sec. HEW, 1972, Los Alamos Sci. Lab., 1975, Inst. Advanced Study, Princeton, N.J., 1974-79, Dept. Energy, 1979. Author: The Cosmic Code: Quantum Physics as the Language of Nature, 1982, Perfect Symmetry: The Search for the Beginning of Time, 1985, over 70 sci. articles. Trustee Aspen Ctr. for Physics, 1972-78, treas., 1973-79, sec., 1972, mem. exec. com., 1977; trustee Internat. League Human Rights, 1978; mem. Com. Concerned Scientists. U.S. Steel Found. Sci. Writing award Am. Inst. Physics, 1982. Mem. N.Y. Acad. Scis. (bd. govs. 1976-82, v.p. 1976-80, pres.-elect 1980, pres., chief exec. officer 1981, chmn. Albert Einstein Lecture com. 1976, chmn. phys. scis. sect. 1973-76, chmn. human rights com. 1976-78, chmn. Einstein Centennial Com. 1976-79, chmn. affiliates com. 1979), Am. Phys. Soc., AAAS. Current Work: Relativistic quantum field theory; cosmology and the early universe. Subspecialties: Particle physics; Cosmology. Office: NY Acad Scis 2 E 63d St New York NY 10021

PAGNONCELLI, GIACOMO, neuropsychologist, researcher; b. Phila., June 6, 1906; s. Arturo and Rosalie (Hoenstauffen) P.; m. Martha Almira Davison, July 12, 1928; children—William Henry, Stuart, Melanie, Josie, Marin, James Jr. Ph.D., U. Utrecht (Germany), 1938; M.D., U. Heidelburg (Germany), 1951. Asst. prof. U. Heidelburg, 1951-55; dir. Inst. Sci. Research, Salt Lake City, 1955-68; dir. research and devel. Intergalactic Corp., Salt Lake City, 1963—. Author: Elektroneurologie, 1954; also articles. Served to lt. col. AUS, 1942-48. Mem. Am. Neurol. Soc., Am. Philos. Soc., Am. Soc. Psychology, AAAS, Soc. Med. Research, Am. Pathol. Soc. Current work: Neurological basis of paranormal activity. Subspecialty: Neuropsychology. Office: Intergalactic Corp Box 2025 Murray UT 84107

PAHWA, ASHOK, computer scientist; b. Ranikhet, India, Sept. 11, 1953; came to U.S., 1977; s. Jagdish Mitra and Sarla P.; m. Heman, Dec. 27, 1979. B.E. with honors, Birla Inst. Tech., Pilani, India, 1975; P.G. diploma, U. Roorkee, India, 1976; M.S., U. Kans., 1978; Ph.D., Ill. Inst. Tech., 1984. Specialist performance evaluation Gen. Electric Credit Co., Stamford, Conn., 1978-80; mem. tech. staff Bell Labs., Naperville, Ill., 1980-84. Mem. Assn. Computing Machinery, IEEE, Computer Measurement Group. Current Work: Computer database management system; computer performance evaluation. Subspecialties: Database systems; Computer architecture.

PAI, DAMODAR MANGALORE, research and development physicist; b. Mangalore, Mysore, India, Mar. 12, 1934; came to U.S., 1959; s. Venkatesh M. and Radha M. (Pai) P.; m. Malathi D. Prabhu, Sept. 2, 1965; children—Rekha, Venkatesh. B.S., U. Madras, Magalore, 1954; diploma Indian Inst. Sci., Bangalore, 1957; M.S. in E.E., U. Minn., 1961, Ph.D. in E.E., 1965. Sr. physicist, Xerox Corp., Rochester, N.Y., 1965-68, assoc. scientist, 1968-69, scientist, 1969-72, sr. scientist, 1972-80, prin. scientist, 1980—. Editor: Photoconductivity & Related Phenomena, 1975. Contbr. chpts. to books and articles to profl. jours. Patentee in field. Recipient Pres. award Xerox Corp., 1984. Fellow Am. Phys. Soc.; mem. Soc. Photog. Sci. and Engring. Current work: Electrophotography (copying machine), xerographic photoconductors both organic and inorganic, xerographic printers. Subspecialties: Materials (engineering); Semiconductors. Home: 72 Shagbark Way Fairport NY 14450 Office: Xerox Corp 800 Phillips Rd Webster NY 14580

PAI, SHIH I., research educator; b. Tatung, Anhwei, China, Sept. 30, 1913; came to U.S., 1947, naturalized, 1955; s. Hsi Chuan and Swe Lin (Cha) P.; m. Yu Feng Chi, Feb. 4, 1934 (dec. Feb. 1958); children: Stephen Ming, Sue Pai Yang, Robert Yang, Lou Lung; m. Alice Jen-lan Wang, July 2, 1960. B.S. in Elec. Engring, Nat. Central U., Nanking, China, 1935; M.S. in Aero. Engring, MIT, 1938; Ph.D. in Aero. Engring. and Math, Calif. Inst. Tech., Pasadena, 1940; Dr. Techn. (hon.), Tech. U. Vienna, Austria, 1968. Prof. aero. engring. Nat. Central U., Chunking, China, 1940-47; vis. prof. aero. engring. Cornell U., Ithaca, N.Y., 1947-49; research prof. Inst. Fluid Dynamics and Applied Math., U. Md., College Park, 1949-76; research prof. Inst. for Phys. Sci. and Tech., 1976-83, prof. emeritus, 1983—; vis. prof. Tokyo U., 1966-67, U. Karlsruhe, W.Ger., 1980-81, U. Paris, 1981; hon. prof. Northwestern Poly. U., Xian, China, 1980—. Author: Magnetodynamics, 1962, Radiation Gasdynamics, 1966, Two-Phase Flows, 1977, Modern Fluid Mechanics, 1981. Served to capt. Chinese Air Force, 1937-40. Guggenheim fellow, 1957; Academia Sinica (China) fellow, 1962; NSF sr. postdoctoral fellow, 1966; recipient Sr. U.S. Scientist award Alexander von Humboldt Found., W.Ger., 1980. Fellow AIAA (assoc.); mem. Internat. Acad. Astronautics (corr.), Am. Phys. Soc., Sigma Xi (Achievement award 1975). Republican. Episcopalian. Current Work: Jet flows, coherent structure of turbulent flow, magnetogasdynamics, radiation gasdynamics, two-phase flows, lunar ash flow. Subspecialties: Aeronautical engineering; Aerospace engineering and technology. Home: 4301 Sarasota Pl Beltsville MD 20705 Office: Inst for Phys Sci and Tech U Md College Park MD 20742

PAIK, HO JUNG, physics educator, researcher; b. Seoul, Korea, Mar. 25, 1944; came to U.S., 1968, naturalized, 1981; s. In Kee and Young Pal (Choi) P.; m. Minja Koh, Sept. 6, 1969; children—Ellen Trina, Terri Wren. B.S., Seoul Nat. U., 1966; M.S., Stanford U., 1970, Ph.D., 1974. Research assoc. Stanford U. (Calif.), 1974-78, vis. prof., 1984-85; asst. prof. physics U. Md., College Park, 1978-83, assoc. prof., 1983—. Patentee gravity gradiometer and accelerometer. Alfred Sloan fellow, 1981-83. Mem. Am. Phys. Soc., Am. Geophys. Union. Current work: Gravitational wave detection, test of gravitational inverse square law, development of DC Squids, development of superconducting accelerometers and gravity gradiometers. Subspecialties: Low temperature physics; Relativity and gravitation. Home: 1103 Cresthaven Dr Silver Spring MD 20903 Office: U Md Dept Physics and Astronomy College Park MD 20742

PAILLET, FREDERICK LAWRENCE, geophysicist; b. New Haven, Conn., Sept. 6, 1946; s. George Lawrence and Zenaide (Ferron) P.; m. M. Sandra Davies, Sept. 6, 1967 (div. Aug. 1985); children—Jennifer S., Aimee E. B.S. in Mech. Engring., U. Rochester, 1968, M.S., 1969, Ph.D. in Geophys. Fluid Mech., 1974. Civil engr. USAF, Mont., 1969-72; fluid dynamacist USAF Flight Dynamics Lab., Dayton, Ohio, 1974-76; asst. prof. dept. geology Wright State U., Dayton, 1976-78; geophysicist U.S. Geol. Survey, Denver, 1978—. Contbr. numerous articles to profl. jours. Mem. Soc. Exploration Geophysicists, Am. Geophys. Union, Geol. Soc. Am., Soc. Profl. Well Log Analysists (tech. com., 1983—, Best Paper award, 1980). Roman Catholic. Current work: Borehole geophysics especially the inversion of borehole data; fracture identification and characterization; acoustic properties of rocks; radiation of acoustic energy from fluid filled boreholes. Subspecialties: Geophysics; Hydrology. Home: 6549 S Allison Ct Littleton CO 80123 Office: US Geol Survey Denver Fed Ctr Denver CO 80225

PAINTER, GAYLE STANFORD, physicist, researcher; b. Columbia, S.C., Feb. 27, 1941; s. Garland Lee and Pearl Elizabeth (Marler) P.; m. June Elaine Griffin, June 22, 1962; children—Angela Gwyn, Jennifer Gayle. B.S., U. S.C., 1963, Ph.D., 1967. Research assoc. Quantum Theory Project, U. Fla., Gainesville, 1967-69; sr. research staff mem. metals and ceramics div. Oak Ridge Nat. Lab., 1969—; guest scientist U. Bristol, 1975, Institut fuer Festkoerperforschung der Kernsforschungsanlage, Juelich, Ger., 1974-75. Contbr. articles to profl. jours. Bd. dirs. United Ch. of Oak Ridge, 1980-83. Woodrow Wilson fellow, 1963. Fellow Am. Phys. Soc.; mem. Phi Beta Kappa. Democrat. Current work: Theoretical studies of electronic structure and bonding, properties of interfaces and atomic clusters; density functional theory; bonding of atoms and molecules at surfaces; impurity interactions with grain boundaries. Subspecialties: Condensed matter physics; Materials. Home: 19 Moore Ln Oak Ridge TN 37830 Office: Oak Ridge Nat Lab PO Box X Oak Ridge TN 37831

PAINTER, GENEVIEVE, clinical psychologist, consultant, author; b. Chgo., Sept. 5, 1919; d. Max and Amelia (Swartz) Berkowitz; m. David R. Schneidman, Aug., 1941 (div. 1956); children: Bruce, Terry; m. John Paul Painter, July 20, 1960 (dec. Dec. 1972). B.S., U. Ill.-Urbana, 1963, M.S., 1964, Ed.D., 1967; cert. psychotherapy, Alfred Adler Inst., Chgo., 1969. Music tchr. Lyon and Healy Sch. Music, Chgo., 1950-64; asst. prof. edn. U. Ill.-Urbana, 1967-68; pvt. practice psychology, Champaign, Ill., 1968-73; founder, dir. Family Edn. Ctrs., Champaign, 1968-73; instr. radio Hawaii Pacific Coll., Honolulu, 1975-84; instr. U. Hawaii, 1973-83; dir. Assocs. for Human Devel., Honolulu, 1973—, cons. schs. and agys., 1973—; Chmn. profl. standards com. Family Edn. Ctrs. Hawaii, Honolulu, 1974—; tchr., cons. Kapiolani/Children's Med. Ctr., Honolulu, 1982. Author: Teach Your Baby, 1971, 2d edit., 1982, The Practical Parent, 1975, 2d edit., 1984. Co-editor: Alfred Adler: As We Remember Him, 1977. Chmn. career women United Jewish Appeal, Honolulu, 1980-82. U.S. Office Edn. fellow, 1964; U.S. Office Vocat. Rehab. fellow, 1963. Mem. Am. Psychol. Assn., N.Am. Soc. Adlerian Psychology (del. assembly 1965-85), Soc. Advancement Psychology, Hawaii Psychol. Assn. (hon. life mem.). Current Work: Infant intellectual developmental acceleration, new psychological techniques for changing debilitating fixed beliefs of individuals, new psychological techniques for adolescents, relationship training, negotiations for world peace. Subspecialties: Behavioral psychology; Developmental psychology. Home: 2333 Kapiolani Blvd Apt 3214 Honolulu HI 96826 Office: Assocs for Human Devel PO Box 11206 Honolulu HI 96828

PAINTER, RICHARD GRANT, research scientist; b. Jacksonville, Fla., Dec. 10, 1945; s. George Latimer and Sarah Mae (Lancaster) P.; m. Rosemary Sodek, Dec. 23, 1967; children: Robert Aaron, Thomas Scott, Michele Marie. B.S., U. Fla., 1967; Ph.D. in Biochemistry, Duke U., 1971. Postdoctoral fellow U. Calif., San Diego, 1971-74; staff scientist Syntex Research, Palo Alto, Calif., 1974-77; assoc. mem. Scripps Clinic and Research Found., La Jolla, 1977—; cons. Nat. Inst. Heart and Lung Diseases. Contbr. articles to profl. jours. NASA fellow, 1967-70; NIH fellow, 1971-73; Am. Cancer Soc. sr. fellow, 1977; research career devel. award NIH, 1978-83. Mem. Am. Soc. Cell Biology, AM. Assn. Pathology, Am. Soc. Immunologists, AAAS. Democrat. Episcopalian. Current Work: Membrane structure-function relationships in leukocytes and platelets. Subspecialties: Cell biology; Membrane biology.

PAIS, ABRAHAM, educator, physicist; b. Amsterdam, Holland, May 19, 1918; s. Jesaja and Kaatje (van Kleeff) P.; m. Lila Atwill, Dec. 15, 1956 (div. 1962); 1 son, Joshua. B.Sc., U. Amsterdam, 1938; M.Sc., U. Utrecht, 1940, Ph.D., 1941. Research fellow Inst. Theoretical Physics, Copenhagen, Denmark, 1946; prof. Inst. Advanced Study, Princeton, N.J., 1950-63; prof. physics Rockefeller U., N.Y.C., 1963-81, Detlev W. Bronk prof., 1981—; Balfour prof. Weizmann Inst., Israel, 1977. Author: Subtle is the Lord (Am. Book award 1983). Recipient J.R. Oppenheimer Meml. prize, 1979; Guggenheim fellow, 1960, award Am. Inst. Physics-U.S. Steel Found., 1983. Fellow Am. Phys. Soc.; mem. Royal Acad. Scis. Holland (corr.), Am. Acad. Arts and Scis., Am. Philos. Soc., Nat. Acad. Scis., Council on Fgn. Relations. Current Work: Quantum field theory, relativity, history of science. Subspecialties: Particle physics; Theoretical physics. Home: 450 E 63d St New York NY 10021 Office: Rockefeller Univ New York NY 10021

PAISLEY, MARK ALAN, chemical engineer; b. Zanesville, Ohio, July 7, 1949; s. Donald Eugene and Donna Jean (Jewell) P.; m. Margaret Ann Hemmer, Jan. 13, 1973; children—Jewell Ann, Kirk Alan, Matthew Alan. B.S., U. Cin., 1972; postgrad. U. Akron, 1973-75. Registered profl. engr., Ohio, Pa. Co-op. engr. Armco Steel Co., Zanesville, 1968-71; research engr. Babcock & Wilcox, Alliance, Ohio, 1972-75; project engr. Bituminous Coal Research, Monroeville, Pa., 1975-80; prin. research engr. Battelle Columbus Lab., Ohio, 1980—. Contbr. articles to profl. jours. Sect. leader Worthington Civic Bank, Upper Arlington Band, 1980—. Served with N.G., 1972-78. Mem. Am. Inst. Chem. Engrs., Am. Chem. Soc. (assoc.), Kappa Kappa Psi. Republican. Lutheran. Current work: Deputy program manager wood gasification program, coal gasification and combustion research, air pollution control, materials for gasification environments, fluidized bed processing. Subspecialties: Biomass (energy science and technology); Coal. Home: 2720 Bristol Rd Columbus OH 43202 Office: Battelle Columbus Labs 505 King Ave Columbus OH 43201

PAISLEY, MELVYN R., See *Who's Who in America,* 43rd edition.

PAK, CHARLES Y.C., research physician, educator; b. Seoul, Korea, Nov. 27, 1935; s. You Pyung and Wechun (Kim) P.; m. Jane Ellen Riechers, June 15, 1963; children: Laura, Gregory, Marjorie. Student, Shimer Coll., 1953-55; B.S. with honors, U. Chgo., 1957, M.D., 1961. Intern U. Chgo. Clinics, 1962-63, sr. investigator, 1963-68; chief sect. mineral metabolism NIH, Bethesda, Md., 1968-72; asso. prof. medicine Southwestern Med. Sch., U. Tex., Dallas, 1972-75, prof., 1975—, program dir. gen. clin. research center, 1974—. Contbr. 270 articles to sci. jours.; author: Calcium Urolithiasis, 1978. Served to lt. comdr. USPHS, 1963-67. Mem. Endocrine Soc., Assn. Am. Physicians, Am. Soc. Clin. Investigation, Am. Soc. Nephrology. Current Work: Cause and management of renal stones, metabolic bone diseases and disorders of parathyroid function and vitamin D metabolism. Subspecialties: Endocrinology; Nephrology. Home: 7107 Churchill Way Dallas TX 75230 Office: 5323 Harry Hines Blvd Dallas TX 75235

PAKE, GEORGE EDWARD, research executive, physicist; b. Jeffersonville, Ohio, Apr. 1, 1924; s. Edward Howe and Mary Mabel (Fry) P.; m. Marjorie Elizabeth Semon, May 31, 1947; children—Warren E., Catherine E., Stephen G., Bruce E. B.S., M.S., Carnegie Inst. Tech., 1945; Ph.D., Harvard U., 1948. Physicist Westinghouse Research Labs., 1945-46; mem. faculty Washington U., St. Louis, 1948-56, 62-70, prof. physics, provost, 1962-69, exec. vice chancellor, 1965-69, Edward Mallinckrodt prof. physics, 1969-70; with Xerox Corp., 1970—, mgr. Xerox Palo Alto (Calif.) Research Center, 1970-78, v.p. corp. research, 1978-83, group v.p., 1983—; prof. physics Stanford U., 1956-62. Author: (with E. Feenberg) Quantum Theory of Angular Momentum, 1953, Paramagnetic Resonance, 1962, (with T. Estle) The Physical Principles of Electron Paramagnetic Resonance, 1973. Mem. gov. bd. Am. Inst. Physics, 1957-59; bd. dirs. St. Louis Research Council, 1964-70; mem. physics adv. panel NSF, 1958-60, 63- 66; chmn. physics survey com. Nat. Acad. Sci.-NRC, 1964-66; Mem. St. Louis County Bus. and Indl. Devel. Commn., 1963-66; chmn. bd. Regional Indsl. Devel. Corp., St. Louis, 1966-67, St. Louis Research Council, 1967-70; mem. President's Sci. Adv. Com., 1965-69; Bd. dirs. St. Louis Country Day Sch., 1964-70, Central Inst. for Deaf, 1965-70; trustee Washington U., from 1970, Danforth Found., from 1971. Fellow Am. Phys. Soc. (pres. 1977); mem. Am. Assn. Physics Tchrs., AAUP, AAAS, Am. Acad. Arts and Scis., Nat. Acad. Sci., Sigma Xi, Tau Beta Pi. Club: University (Palo Alto). Subspecialty: Research management. Office: Xerox Palo Alto Research Center 3333 Coyote Hill Rd Palo Alto CA 94306

PAKULIS, ELGA, research physicist; d. Janis Evalds and Zenta (Kumsare) Jekabsons; m. Ilmars Modris Pakulis, July 1, 1970; children—Nora, Zenta. Ph.D. in Physics, U. Calif.-Berkeley, 1982. Research staff mem. IBM T.J. Watson Research Ctr., Yorktown Heights, N.Y., 1982—. Contbr. articles to profl. jours. Mem. Am. Phys. Soc. Current work: Spin dependent properties of solids; studies of two dimensional electron systems. Subspecialty: Condensed matter physics. Office: IBM Watson Research Ctr PO Box 218 Yorktown Heights NY 10598

PAKVASA, SANDIP SIRISH, physicist, educator; b. Bombay, India, Dec. 24, 1935, came to U.S., 1961; s. Sirish Vijbhukhandas and Sumitra (Surati) P.; m. Heide Miller, Nov. 19, 1978. B.Sc., U. Baroda, India, 1954; M.Sc., 1957; Ph.D., Purdue U., 1965. Research assoc. Syracuse U., N.Y., 1965-67; assoc. physicist U. Hawaii, Honlulu, 1967-68, asst. prof. physics, 1968-70; assoc. prof., 1970-74, prof., 1974—; vis. mem. Inst. Adv. Study, Princeton, N.J., 1975; vis. prof. U. Wis., Madison, 1978, Tata Inst. Fund. Research, Bombay, India, 1983, KEK Nat. Lab., Japan, 1983; vis. assoc. CERN, Geneva, Switzerland, 1982. Author: (with others) Nonleptonic Weak Interactions, 1968; editor: (with others) Proceedings of Hawaii Topical Conference in Particle Physics, 1980; contbr. articles to profl. jours. Fellow Japan Soc. for Promotion Sci., 1981. Fellow Am. Soc. Physics. Current work: Unified theories of weak, electromagnetic and strong interactions and their confrontation with experimental data. Subspecialties: Theoretical physics; Particle physics. Office: U Hawaii Dept Physics and Astronomy 2505 Correa Rd Honolulu HI 96822

PALADE, GEORGE EMIL, cell biologist, educator; b. Jassy, Romania, Nov. 19, 1912; came to U.S., 1946, naturalized, 1952; s. Emil and Constanta (Cantemir) P.; m. Irina Malaxa, June 12, 1941 (dec. 1969); children—Georgia Teodora, Philip Theodore; m. Marilyn G. Farquhar, 1970. Bachelor, Hasdeu Lyceum, Buzau, Romania; M.D., U. Bucharest, Romania. Instr., asst. prof., then asso. prof. anatomy Sch. Medicine, U. Bucharest, 1935-45; vis. investigator, asst. assoc., prof. cell biology Rockefeller U., 1946-73; prof. cell biology Yale U., New Haven, now Sterling prof. emeritus, sr. research scientist, spl. advisor to dean Sch. Medicine. Author sci. papers. Recipient Albert Lasker Basic Research award, 1966, Gairdner Spl. award, 1967, Horwitz prize, 1970, Nobel prize, 1974. Fellow Am. Acad. Arts and Scis.; mem. Nat. Acad. Sci., Pontifical Acad. Sci. Subspecialty: Cell biology. Office: Cell Biology Dept Yale U Sch Medicine New Haven CT 06510

PALAFOX, ANASTACIO LAIDA, animal scientist, nutritionist, educator, researcher; b. Philippines, Apr. 24, 1914; came to U.S., 1931, naturalized, 1943; s. Emeterio Salvacion and Geronima Baisa (Laida) P.; m. Jesusa AVecilla, Mar. 16, 1950; children: Brian A., Neal A., Riley A., Edgar A. B.S., Wash. State U., 1940, M.S., 1941; Ph.D., Mich. State U., 1970. Asst. instr. U. Hawaii, 1946-47, instr., 1947-57, asst. prof. animal nutrition, 1957-70, assoc. prof., 1970-78, prof., 1978-80, prof. emeritus, 1980—; prof. animal scis. U. Guam, Mangilao, 1981—; cons. in field. Research numerous publs. in field. Chmn. ednl. com. United Filipino Council of Hawaii. Served with USN, 1942-46. Named Father of Yr. Filipino Community, Honolulu, 1978, Outstanding Filipino Overseas Pres. Marcos, Philippines, 1982; Research Council grantee; E. I. Dupont research grantee, 1948-51; Dept. Agr. grantee, 1982—. Mem. Poultry Sci. Assn., Worlds Poultry Sci. Assn., AAUP, AAAS, Inst Biol Scis., Sigma Xi, Gamma Sigma Delta. Roman Catholic. Club: Toastmasters (Honolulu) (pres. club 1968-70). Current Work: Nutrition, biochemistry, protein energy, metabolism, physiology, interrelationships, amino acids, carbohydrates energy, enzymes, mgmt. systems, growth, hormones. Subspecialties: Animal nutrition; Animal physiology. Home: 5276 Kimokeo St Honolulu HI 96821 Office: Coll Agr U Guam Mangilao 96913 Guam

PALAY, SANFORD LOUIS, educator, physician; b. Cleve., Sept. 23, 1918; s. Harry and Lena (Sugarman) P.; m. Victoria Chan Curtis, 1970; children: Victoria Li-Mei, Rebecca Li-Ming. A.B., Oberlin Coll., 1940; M.D. (Hoover prize scholar 1943), Western Res. U., 1943. Teaching fellow medicine, research assoc. anatomy Western Res. U., Cleve., 1945-46; NRC fellow med. scis. Rockefeller Inst., 1948, vis. investigator, 1953; from instr. anatomy to assoc. prof. anatomy Yale U., 1949-56; chief sect. neurocytology, lab. neuroanatomical scis. Nat. Inst. Neurol. Diseases and Blindness, NIH, Washington, 1956-61, chief lab. neuroanatomical scis., 1960-61; Bullard prof. neuroanatomy Harvard U., Boston, 1961—; Linnean Soc. lectr., London, 1959; vis. investigator Middlesex Hosp. (Bland-Sutton Inst.), London, Eng., 1961; Phillips lectr.

Haverford Coll., 1959; Ramsay Henderson Trust lectr. U. Edinburgh, Scotland, 1962; Disting. Scientist lectr. Tulane U. Sch. Medicine, 1969, 75; vis. prof. U. Wash., 1969; Rogowski Meml. lectr. Yale, 1973; Disting. lectr. biol. structure U. Miami, 1974; Disting. Scientist lectr. U. Ark., 1977; other Disting. lectureships; vis. prof. U. Osaka, Japan, 1978, Nat. U. Singapore, 1983; Mem. fellowship bd. NIH, 1958-61, cell biology study sect., 1959-65, adv. com. high voltage electron microscope resources, 1973-80, mem. rev. com. behavioral and neurol. scis. fellowships, 1979—, chmn. behavioral and neural scis. study sect., 1984-86; chmn. Gordon Research Conf. Cell Structure and Metabolism, 1960; assoc. Neuroscis. Research Program, 1962-67, cons. assoc., 1975—; mem. anat. scis. tng. com. Nat. Inst. Gen. Med. Scis., 1968-72; mem. sci. adv. com. Oreg. Regional Primate Research Center, 1971-76. Author: The Fine Structure of the Nervous System, 1970, 2d edit., 1976, Cerebellar Cortex, Cytology and Organization, 1973; Editor: Frontiers of Cytology, 1958, The Cerebellum, New Vistas, 1981; Mem.: sci. council Progress in Neuropharmacology and Jour. Neuropharmacology, 1961-66; editorial bd.: Exptl. Neurology, 1959-76, Jour. Cell Biology, 1962-67, Brain Research, 1965-71, Jour. Comparative Neurology, 1966—, Jour. Ultrastructure Research, 1966—, Jour. of Neurocytology, 1972—, Exptl. Brain Research, 1965-76, Neurosci, 1975—, Zeitschrift fur Anatomie und Entwicklungsgeschichte, 1968; co-mng. editor, 1978—; editor-in-chief: Jour. Comparative Neurology, 1981—; mem. adv. bd. editors: Jour. Neuropathology and Exptl. Neurology, 1963—, Internat. Jour. Neurosci, 1969-74, Tissue and Cell, 1969-85; contbr. articles to profl. jours. Served to capt. M.C. AUS, 1946-47. Recipient 50 Best Books of 1974 award Internat. Book Fair, Frankfurt, Germany, Best Book in Profl. Readership award Am. Med. Writers Assn., 1975; Guggenheim fellow, 1971-72; Fogarty scholar-in-residence NIH, Bethesda, 1980-81. Fellow Am. Acad. Arts and Scis.; mem. Nat. Acad. Scis., Am. Assn. Anatomists (chmn. nominating com. 1964, mem. exec. com. 1970-74, anat. nomenclature com. 1975-78, pres. 1980-81), Histochem. Soc., Electron Microscope Soc. Am., AAAS, Am. Soc. Cell Biology (program com. 1975), Internat. Soc. Cell Biology, Soc. for Neurosci., Washington Soc. Electron Microscopy (organizing com., sec.-treas. 1956-58), Soc. Francaise de Microscopie Electronique (hon.), Royal Microscopical Soc. (hon.), Golgi Soc. (hon.), Phi Beta Kappa, Sigma Xi, Alpha Omega Alpha. Club: Cajal (pres. 1973-74). Current Work: Fine structure of nerve cells and tissues, cytochemical localization of heuroactive substances in nerve cells of cerebellar cortex. Subspecialty: Anatomy and embryology. Home: 78 Temple Rd Concord MA 01742 Office: Dept Anatomy Harvard U Med Sch Boston MA 02115

PALAZZO, REGINALDO, JR., electrical engineer; b. Campinas, Sao Paulo, Brazil, Apr. 14, 1951; came to U.S., 1978; s. Reginaldo and Celia (Pery) P.; m. Cristina Guernelli, July 20, 1977. M.S.E.E., U. Campinas, 1977; engring. degree UCLA, 1981, Ph.D., 1984. Asst. research scientist U. Campinas, Sao Paulo, 1973-75, research scientist, 1975-77, asst. prof., 1984—; asst. scientist UCLA, 1981, post-grad. research scientist, 1982-83; cons. Hewlett Packard/Tech. Transfer Inst., Los Angeles, 1984, Quotron Systems, Los Angeles, 1984. Pantentee in field. Recipient Best Tchr. award U. Campinas, 1976; Grantee Fundacao de Amparo a Pesquisa do Estado de Sao Paulo State Agy., 1973-75, Capes Ministry Edn., Brazil, 1978-83. Mem. IEEE. Roman Catholic. Current work: Multi user information theory; coding theory; analysis of spread spectrum systems; computer communications. Subspecialties: Telecommunications; Cryptography and data security. Home: care John A Silvester 2634 Barry Ave Los Angeles CA 90064 Office: Dept Elec Engring Universidade Estadual de Campinas PO Box 6122 Cidade Universitaria Campinas SP 13100 Brazil

PALILLA, FRANK CHARLES, chemist; b. N.Y.C., Feb. 10, 1925; s. Calogero and Anna (Troisi) P.; m. Connie L. Sciortino, Sept. 9, 1945; children—Anita M., Francine M. B.S., Bklyn. Coll., 1948; M.S., Poly. Inst. Bklyn., 1952; Ph.D., Bklyn. Coll., 1975. Research and devel. chemist GTE Labs., Waltham, Mass., 1948—. Contbr. articles to profl. jours. Sec. to pres. Civic League of Middle Village, N.Y., 1958-62; pres. Property Owners Assn. of Lake Neepaulin, Sussex, N.J., 1964-66. Served with U.S. Army, 1943-45. Recipient Electronic Div. award Electrochem. Soc., 1971; Leslie Warner award, GTE Corp., 1978. Mem. Electrochem. Soc., Am. Chem. Soc., Am. Ceramic Soc., Materials Research Soc., Sigma Phi Phi Beta Kappa. Roman Catholic. Current work: Materials research w/emphasis on inorganic and rare earth chemicals with electronically interesting properties. Subspecialties: Electronic materials; Ceramics. Home: 13 Hickory Hill Ln Framingham MA 01701 Office: GTE Labs 40 Sylvan Rd Waltham MA 02254

PALKE, WILLIAM E., chemistry educator; b. Youngstown, Ohio, Feb. 5, 1941; s. Michael Petra and Rachel (England) P.; m. Nancy Jane Fantz, Dec. 16, 1940; children—Thomas, Amy. B.S., Calif. Inst. Tech., 1962; Ph.D. in Chem. Physics, Harvard U., 1966. Research fellow Calif. Inst. Tech., 1966-68; prof. chemistry U. Calif.-Santa Barbara, 1968—. Contbr. articles to profl. jours. Mem. Am. Phys. Soc. Current work: Electronic structure of atoms and molecules. Subspecialties: Theoretical chemistry; Physical chemistry.

PALL, AVTAR SINGH, consulting engineer; b. Manawala, India, Sept. 6, 1939; came to Can., 1975, naturalized, 1980; s. Shamsher Singh and Chanan Kaur (Ahluwalia) P.; m. Tripat Ahluwalia, May 14, 1967; children—Rashmi, Harpreet. Grad. in engring. Inst. Engrs., Calcutta, India, 1961; M. Eng., Concordia U., Montreal, Que., Can., 1976, Ph.D. in Engring., 1979. Exec. engr. Govt. of India, New Delhi, 1962-75; prin. engr. Deschenes & Assocs., Montreal, 1975-80; cons. The SNC Group, Montreal, 1980—; pres. Pall Dynamics Ltd., Pierrefonds, Que., Can., 1984—. Contbr. articles to profl. jours. Patentee anti-seismic devices for bldg. constrn. Mem. ASCE (Raymond C. Reese research prize 1983), Prestressed Concrete Inst., Instn. Engrs. India. Current work: Research and development of innovations for earthquake resistance of buildings; design of special structures and solutions for difficult structural problems. Subspecialties: Structural engineering; Earthquake engineering. Office: Pall Dynamics Ltd 12800 Berry St Montreal PQ H8Z 1N9 Canada

PALLADINO, NUNZIO JOSEPH, nuclear engineer; b. Allentown, Pa., Nov. 10, 1916; s. Joseph and Angelina (Trentalange) P.; m. Virginia Marchetto, June 16, 1945; children: Linda Susan, Lisa Anne, Cynthia Madaline. B.S., Lehigh U., 1938, M.S., 1939, D.Eng. (hon.), 1964. Registered profl. engr., Pa. Engr. Westinghouse Electric Co., Phila., 1939-42; nuclear reactor designer, Oak Ridge Nat. Lab., 1946-48; staff asst. to div. mgr. Argonne Nat. Lab., Lemont, Ill., 1948-50; mgr. PWR reactor design subdiv. Westinghouse Electric Corp., Pitts., 1950-59; head nuclear engring. dept. Pa. State U., University Park, 1959-66; dean Pa. State U. (Coll. Engring.), 1966-81; chmn. Nuclear Regulatory Commn., Washington, 1981—; past mem. Pa. Gov.'s Sci. Adv. Com., Gov.'s Energy Council; past mem. Pa.'s Commn. to Investigate TMI. Contbr. tech. articles to profl. jours. Served to capt. AUS, 1942-45. Recipient Order of Merit Westinghouse Electric Corp. Fellow ASME (Prime Movers award), Am. Nuclear Soc. (past pres.); mem. Am. Soc. Engring. Edn., Nat. Soc. Profl. Engrs., Nat. Acad. Engrs. Roman Catholic. Club: Rotary. Subspecialty: Nuclear engineering. Office: 1717 H St NW Washington DC 20555

PALLMANN, ALBERT JOSEF, earth and atmospheric scientist, science consultant, educator; b. Wiesbaden, Ger., Dec. 12, 1926; came to U.S., 1963, naturalized, 1978; s. Joseph Ferdin and Helene Maria (Schueller) P.; m. Margot Maria Simons, June 26, 1958; 1 son, Thomas R.S. Doctorand, U. Cologne, W. Ger, 1953, Dr.rer.nat., 1958. Research assoc. Geophys. Inst., U. Cologne, 1954-58; chief meteorologist Nat. Weather Analysis Center, El Salvador, 1959-62; indsl. cons. and prof. meteorology Escuela Nacional de Marina and Academia Nacional de la Fuerza Aerea, El Salvador, 1959-62; asst. prof. meteorology St. St. Louis U., 1962-65, assoc. prof., 1965-69, prof., 1969—; indsl. cons., El Salvador, 1959-62; sci. councilor Univ. Corp. for Atmospheric Research, Boulder, Colo., 1964-67, St. Louis U. sci. rep., 1967-80; cons. space div. McDonnell-Douglas Corp., 1966-67. Author: Basic Concepts of Radiative Transfer, 1983-86; contbr. articles sci. jours. Mem. St. Louis Council World Affairs, Inc., 1981—. Research grantee NASA; Research grantee NSF; Research grantee Nat. Environ. Satellite Service; Research grantee Dept. Energy. Mem. Am. Meteorol. Soc., Am. Geophys. Union, AAAS, Sigma Xi. Current Work: Radiative convection heating/cooling in Martian ground-atmosphere system, meteorol. radiometry, solar and terrestrial, satellite- and air-borne, ground-based, events of climatic extremes. Subspecialties: Meteorologic instrumentation; Planetary atmospheres. Office: PO Box 8099 Laclede Station St Louis MO 63156

PALMER, ALLISON RICHARD, zoology educator; b. Washington, Mar. 5, 1951; s. Allison Ralph and Patricia Ann (Richardson) P. B.S., SUNY-Stony Brook, 1973; Ph.D., U. Wash., 1980. Asst. prof. U. Alta., Edmonton, Can., 1980-85, assoc. prof., 1985—. Assoc. editor Paleobiology, 1982—; contbr. articles to profl. jours. Mem. AAAS, Am. Malacological Union, Am. Soc. Naturalists, Calif. Malacozoological Soc., Ecol. Soc. Am., Soc. Study Evolution. Current work: Ecology and evolution of marine gastropods: functional morphology, genetics of shell variation, geographic variation, speciation. Subspecialties: Evolutionary biology; Marine biology. Home: 1804-11027 87th Ave Edmonton AB T6G 2P9 Canada Office: U Alta Dept Zoology Edmonton AB T6G 2E9 Canada

PALMER, GUY HUGHES, research pathologist, educator; b. Denison, Tex., Sept. 30, 1955; s. Kenneth Lee and Norma June (Hutchison) P. B.S. in Biology, Kans. State U., 1977, D.V.M., 1980; Ph.D. in Pathology, Wash. State U., 1984. Diplomate Am. Coll. Vet. Pathologists. Intern Wash. Animal Disease Diagnostic Lab., U. Wash., Pullman, 1980, resident, 1980-83, NIH postdoctoral fellow, 1982-84, asst. prof. dept. vet. microbiology and pathology, 1984—. Contbr. articles to profl. jours. Recipient Diamond award for leadership Diamond Inc., 1980; award for devel. of subunit vaccine anaplasmosis U.S. Dept. Agr.-Wash. High Tech. Inst., 1983, 84; animal health research grantee Squibb Inc., 1983; J.J. Garbarino research grantee Animal Health Inst., Alexandria, Va., 1984. Mem. AAAS, Am. Assn. Vet. Immunologists, AVMA, Blue Key. Phi Kappa Phi. Democrat. Current work: Development of genetically engineered subunit vaccines for persistent infections of food animals primarily cattle (anaplasmosis, babesiosis, rickettsiosis.) Subspecialties: Genetics and genetic engineering (veterinary medicine); Pathology (veterinary medicine). Office: Dept Vet Microbiology and Pathology Coll Vet Medicine Wash State U Pullman WA 99164

PALUZZI, PETER RONALD, research geophysicist; b. Little Falls, N.Y., Jan. 4, 1951; s. Victor Joseph and Lucille Claire (Pepin) P., m. Susan Victoria Laigner, July 10, 1982. B.S. in Geology, SUNY-Albany, 1973; M.S. in Geology, U. So. Calif., 1979. Sr. scientist Jet Propulsion Lab., Pasadena, Calif., 1973-81; image processing dir. McQuest Marine, Burlington, Can., 1981-82; sr. research geophysicist Sohio Petroleum Co., Dallas, 1983—. Contbr. articles to profl. jours. N.Y. State Regents scholar, 1969. Mem. Am. Geophysical Union, Geol. Soc. Am., Assn. for Computing Machinery, Computer Soc. IEEE, Nat. Computer Graphics Assn. Current work: Computer graphics and computer image processing for geology and geophysics; systems analysis and design; hardward and software evaluation. Subspecialties: Graphics, image processing, and pattern recognition; Remote sensing (geoscience). Home: PO Box 791094 Dallas TX 75379 Office: Sohio Petroleum Co 5400 LBJ Suite 1200 Dallas TX 75240

PAN, HUO-PING, biochemist, researcher; b. Fuzhou, Fujian, China, Feb. 13, 1921; came to U.S., 1949; s. Bai-ming and Won-ching (Chen) P.; m. Chiou-Wen Sha, Feb. 26, 1955; 1 child, Peno. B.S. in Chemistry, Nat. Southwest Associated U., Kunming, China, 1946; Ph.D. in Food Sci., U. Ill., 1954. Teaching asst. dept. mining and metall. engring. Nat. Yunnan U., Kunming, 1946-49; research asst. dept. chemistry Kans. State Coll., Manhattan, 1949-50; staff mem. div. indsl. research MIT, Cambridge, 1954-55, staff mem. div. sponsored research, 1955-57, research assoc., 1957-58; asst. biochemist Agrl. Experiment Sta., U. Fla., Gainesville, 1958-63, asst. research prof. Coll. Engring., 1963-64; research biochemist Patuxent Wildlife Research Ctr., U.S. Fish and Wildlife Service, U.S. Dept. Interior, Gainesville, 1964-74, research chemist, 1974-77, research chemist Denver Wildlife Research Ctr., 1977—. Contbr. articles to profl. jours. Recipient Suggestion award U.S. Fish and Wildlife Service, 1971, award for Outstanding Publ., Denver Wildlife Research Ctr., 1981, Spl. Achievement award U.S. Fish and Wildlife Service, 1981. Mem. Am. Chem. Soc., Am. Inst. Biol. Scis., AAAS, Internat. Soc. Study Xenobiotics, Sigma Xi. Democrat. Current work: Exploring the species differences between birds and mammals in xenobiotic metabolism for selective animal depredation control. Subspecialties: Biochemistry (biology); Radiation chemistry. Home: 5295 S Jellison St Littleton CO 80123

PAN, IN-CHANG, immunopathologist, researcher; b. Tokyo, Mar. 28, 1929; came to U.S., 1963; s. Mu-tsu and Su-shia (Hsu) P.; m. Hwei-Chen Huang, June 6, 1954; children—Chun, Nen, Julie Chun-Lee. D.V.M., Nat Taiwan U., 1951; M.S., U. Calif.-Davis, 1960; Ph.D., Purdue U., 1966. Vet. med. officer Taiwan Inst. Animal Health, Tansui, 1951-54; instr. Nat. Taiwan U., Taipei, 1954-63; instr. Purdue U., West Lafayette, Ind., 1963-66; asst. prof. Ont. Vet. Coll., Guleph, Can., 1966-68; vet. med. officer Agrl. Research Service, U.S. Dept. Agr., Plum Island Animal Disease Ctr., Greenport, N.Y., 1968—. Contbr. articles to med. and sci. jours. Mem. Am. Assn. Pathologists, Am. Assn. Immunologists, N.Y. Acad. Scis., Conf. Research Workers in Animal Disease, Am. Assn. Vet. Immunologists, Sigma Xi. Current work: Elucidation of homeostatic mechanism in chronic African swine fever, virus infection and swine immune system, epitopes on surface of African swine fever, virus particles and epitope-mapping by monoclonal antibody. Subspecialties: Infectious diseases; Virology (veterinary medicine). Home: 319 N Bayview Rd Southold NY 11971 Office: Plum Island Animal Disease Ctr Agrl Research Service US Dept Agr PO Box 848 Greenport NY 11971

PAN, YUH KANG, chemistry educator, researcher; b. Guangzhou, China, Feb. 14, 1937; s. Shu Y. and Lie C. (Lian) P.; m. Su C. Wang, Jan. 3, 1938; children: Irene, Elsie. B.Sc., Nat. Taiwan U., 1959; Ph.D., Mich. State U., 1966. Postdoctoral fellow U. So. Calif., 1966, Harvard U., 1967; prof. chemistry Boston Coll., 1967—; vis. prof. Stuttgart (Ger.) U., 1974, Max-Planck Inst., Mülheim, Ger., 1975; hon. prof. Academia Sinica Jilin U., China; hon. prof. academia sinica Lanzhou U., China. Author: General Chemistry, 1956, Acids and Bases, 1959; editor: Jour. Molecular Sci, 1981—; contbr. book revs. and articles to profl. jours. Exec. dir. Nat. Assn. Chinese Ams. Mem. Am. Phys. Soc., Sci. and Edn. Soc. Current Work: Quantum chemistry, theortical chemistry. Subspecialty: Theoretical chemistry. Office: 140 Commonwealth Ave Newton MA 02167

PANDA, DURGA PRASAD, engineer, researcher; b. Berhampur, Orissa, India, Oct. 11, 1945; came to U.S., 1969; naturalized 1982; s. Maheswar and Sundarmani (Panda) P.; m. Fern Alane Lloyd, July 10, 1976; children—Robin Dev, Nina Anjali. B.S.E.E., Regional Engring. Coll., Rourkela, Orissa, India, 1968; M.S.E.E., Iowa State U., 1971; Ph.D. E.E., Purdue U., 1976. Elec. engr. Utkal Machinery Ltd. Kansbahal, Orissa, India, 1968-69; research engr. Purdue U., West Lafayette, Ind., 1971-72; faculty research assoc. U. Md., College Park, 1976-77; sr.-sr. prin. research scientist Honeywell Systems and Research Ctr., Mpls., 1977-81, staff research scientist, 1981-82, sect. chief, signal and image processing scis., 1982—. Contbr. articles to profl. jours. Bd. dirs. Internat. Ctr., West Lafayette, 1974-76; v.p. India Students Assn., West Lafayette, 1973. Govt. Coll. Merit Scholarship award, Govt. of India, 1963-68; recipient achievement awards (5) Honeywell, 1979-83. Mem. IEEE (reviewer), IEEE Computer Soc. (speaker 1984), Data Processing Mgmt. Assn. (speaker 1985), Advanced Target Recognizer Working Group (co-chmn. artificial intelligence com. 1984—), Soc. of Photo-Optical Instructing Engrs. (panelist application of artificial intelligence, 1985—), Am. Def. Preparedness Assn., Assn. for Unmanned Vehicle Systems, Soc. of Photo-Optical and Instrumentation Engrs., Orissa Soc. of Ams., Inc., Tau Beta Pi, Phi Kappa Phi. Current work: Research and development management in the areas of artificial intelligence, pattern recognition, machine vision, and high speed architecture leading to real time robot vision system for automated manufacturing, autonomous vehicle, and optical inspection systems. Subspecialties: Computer engineering; Graphics, image processing, and pattern recognition. Home: 1698 17th Ave NW New Brighton MN 55112 Office: Honeywell Systems & Research Ctr 2600 Ridgway Pkway Minneapolis MN 55413

PANDE, KRISHNA PRASAD, physicist; b. Uttar Pradesh, India, Jan. 3, 1946, came to U.S., 1977; s. Ram M. and Shitla (Devi) P.; m. Malti Shukla, June 6, 1973; children—Arunima, Parichay. B.S., U. Lucknow, India, 1967, M.S., 1969; Ph.D., Indian Inst. Tech., Madras, 1973. Scientist Nat. Phys. Lab., New Delhi, India, 1973-75; sr. research assoc. U. Durham, Eng., 1975-77; research assoc. Rensselaer Poly. Inst., Troy, N.Y., 1977-79; asst. prof. Rutgers U., New Brunswick, N.J., 1979-81; mgr. research, project leader, mem. tech. staff Bendix Aerospace Tech. Ctr./Allied Corp., Columbia Md., 1981—; cons. Universal Energy Systems/Air Force Avionics Lab., Dayton, Ohio, 1979-80. Contbr. numerous articles to profl. jours. Mem. IEEE (sr.), Am. Phys. Soc., Electrochem. Soc. Hindu. Current work: Ultra high speed integrated circuits based on InP-MISFETS and 3-5 HEMT device technology; epitaxy of 3-5 semiconductor materials by MO-CVD. Subspecialties: Electronics; Integrated circuits. Home: 5252 Candy Root Columbia MD 21045 Office: Bendix Aerospace Tech Ctr 9140 Old Annapolis Rd Columbia MD 21045

PANDEY, JANARDAN PRASAD, geneticist, educator; b. Gonda, U.P., India, May 4, 1946; s. Ram Chandra and Suryakala (Dubey) P. M.S., U. Wis., 1970, Ph.D., 1972. Postdoctoral fellow U.Wis., Madison, 1972-73, U. Conn., Storrs, 1973-74, U. Calif., San Francisco, 1974-75; instr. Med. U. S.C., Charleston, 1976-77, asst. prof. immunology, 1978-83, assoc. prof. immunology, 1983—. Contbr. articles to sci. jours. Mem. Genetics Soc. Am., Am Assn. Immunologists. Current Work: Genetics of human immunoglobulin allotypes and their role in immune response and diseases. Subspecialties: Gene actions; Immunogenetics. Home: 5 Lauden St Isle of Palms SC 29451 Office: Med U SC 171 Ashley Ave Charleston SC 29425

PANDYA, KRISHNAKANT HARIPRASAD, pharmacologist, educator, researcher; b. Mahemadavad, India, Oct. 19, 1935; came to U.S., 1970, naturalized, 1977; s. Hariprasad Jivanlal and Savitaben Chunilal P.; m. Ramaben Shankerlal Vyas, Sept 10, 1954; children: Prashant, Darshak. B.S. in Pharmacy, Gujarat U., 1958, M.S. in Pharmacy, 1961, Ph.D., 1968. Demonstrator L. M. Coll. Pharmacy, Gujarat U., 1958-61, tutor, 1961-63, jr. lectr. B.J. Med. Coll., 1963-69, asst. prof., 1969-70; instr. Kirksville (Mo.) Coll. Osteo. Medicine, 1971-72, asst. prof., 1972-77, assoc. prof., 1977—. Contbr. articles on pharmacology to profl. jours. Am. Osteo Assn. grantee, 1972,79,83; Warner Found. grantee, 1976; NIH grantee, 1978; Am. Lung Assn./Am. Thoracic Soc. grantee, 1979-83. Mem. Am. Soc. for Pharmacology and Exptl. Therapeutics. Current Work: Postnatal developmental changes in autonomic receptor function. Subspecialty: Pharmacology. Home: 1413 E Cottage Ln Kirksville MO 63501 Office: Kirksville Coll Osteo Medicine 800 W Jefferson Kirksville MO 65301

PANOFSKY, WOLFGANK KURT HERMANN, physics educator; b. Berlin, Apr. 24, 1919; s. Erwin and Dorothea (Mosse) P.; m. Adele Irene DuMond, July 24, 1942; children: Richard, Margaret, Edward, Carol, Steven. B.A., Princeton U., 1938; Ph.D., Calif. Inst. Tech., 1942; hon. degrees, Case Inst. Tech., 1963, U. Sask., 1964, Columbia U., 1977, Princeton U., 1983, U. Hamburg, 1984, Yale U., 1985. Dir. Office of Sci. Research and Devel. Calif. Inst. Tech., 1942-43; cons. Manhattan Project, Los Alamos, N.Mex., 1943-45; physicist U. Calif., Berkeley, 1945-46, asst. prof. to assoc. prof. physics, 1946-51; prof. physics Stanford U., 1951—, dir. high energy physics lab., 1953-61; dir. Stanford Linear Accelerator Ctr., 1961-84; cons. arms control and disarmament, high energy physics. Author: (with M. Phillips) Classical Electricity and Magnetism, 1955, 2d edit., 1962. Recipient Ernest Orlando Lawrence Meml. award, 1961; Disting. Alumni award Calif. Inst. Tech., 1966; Calif. Scientist of Yr. award, 1967; Nat. Medal of Sci., 1969; Franklin Inst. award, 1970; Public Service award Fedn. Am. Scientists, 1973; Enrico Fermi award, 1979; Leo Szilard award Am. Phys. Soc., 1982. Mem. Nat. Acad. Scis., Am. Acad. Scis., Am. Phys. Soc., Phi Beta Kappa, Sigma Xi. Current Work: High energy elementary particle physics and arms control and disarmament. Subspecialty: Particle physics. Home: 25671 Chapin Ave Los Altos Hills CA 94022 Office: PO Box 4349 Stanford CA 94305

PANZERA, CARL, ceramist, researcher; b. Acquaviava, Isernia, Italy, Aug. 11, 1945; came to U.S., 1954, naturalized, 1960; s. Paolino and Belinda (Petrocelli) P.; m. Connie Tummillo, June 15, 1968; children—Paul. B.S., Rutgers U., 1968, postgrad. 1981—; M.S., Rensselaer Poly. Inst., 1971; M.B.A., U. Conn., 1975. Registered profl. engr., N.J. Research asst. P&W Aircraft, Middletown, Conn., 1968-72; research assoc. Brunswick Corp., Milford, Conn., 1972-77; sr. engr. Xaloy, Inc., New Brunswick, N.J., 1977-79, Airco Research, Murray Hill, N.J., 1979-81; mgr. ceramic research and devel. J&J Dental, East Windsor, N.J., 1981—. Editor Trends and Techniques mag., 1984-85. Patentee in field. Contbr. articles to profl. jours. Bd. dirs. Little League, Hillsborogh, N.J., 1981-82, mgr., 1979-83. Mem. Am. Ceramics Soc., N.J. Ceramic Assn., Am. Soc. Metals, Cromwell Jayees (named Jaycee of Quarter, 1973), Keramos, Tau Beta Pi. Republican. Roman Catholic. Current work: Aesthetics of dental porcelain; advanced dental material. Subspecialties: Ceramics; Dental materials. Home: 7 Huntsman Ln Belle Mead NJ 08502 Office: J&J Dental Products Co 20 Lake Dr CN 7060 East Windsor NJ 08520

PAPAGIANNIS, MICHAEL D., astronomer; b. Athens, Greece, Sept. 3, 1932; s. Demetrios M. and Themitsa D. (Lucas) P.; m. Mary Hutton, May 29, 1961; children—Dimitrios, Christina. M.S., Nat. Poly. U. Athens, 1955, U. Va., 1960; Ph.D. in Physics and Astronomy, Harvard U., 1964. Lectr. astronomy Harvard U., 1964-66; asst. prof. astronomy Boston U., 1965-68, asso. prof., 1968-70, prof., 1970—, chmn. dept. astronomy, 1969-82; assoc. Harvard Obs., 1966-80; mem. exec. com. of corp. operating Haystack Radio Obs. Author: Space Physics and Space Astronomy, 1972; editor: 8th Texas Symposium on Relativistic Astrophysics, 1978, Strategies for the Search for Life in the Universe, 1980; contbr. articles to profl. publs. Trustee Hellenic Coll. and Holy Cross Sch. Theology, 1970—. Served with Greek Army, 1957-58. Fellow AAAS; mem. Am. Astron. Soc., Am. Geophys. Union, Internat. Astron. Union (Com. Sl-Search for Extraterrestrial Life 1982—), Internat. Union Radio Sci., Helicon (pres. 1968-69, 75-76), Acad. of Athens (corr.). Greek Orthodox. Club: Order Ahepa (sec. Ednl. Found. 1978-80, pres. Lexington Minuteman chpt. 1979-80, cert. of merit). Current Work: Active in new field of bioastronomy, which is the search for extraterrestrial life using astronomical techniques. President of new commission of International Astronomical Union on this subject. Subspecialties: Radio and microwave astronomy; Satellite studies. Home: 37 Coolidge Ave Lexington MA 02173 Office: Dept Astronomy Boston U Boston MA 02215

PAPAHADJOPOULOS, DEMETRIOS P., biochemistry educator, researcher; b. Patras, Greece, Aug. 24, 1934; s. George and Kiki (Berzeletos) P.; m. Agnese Udinotti, Apr. 24, 1984; m. Patricia Pifer, Dec. 20, 1959 (div. 1982). Diploma, Athens Coll., 1953; B.S., Nat. U., Athens, 1957; Ph.D., U. Wash., 1963. Research fellow Inst. Animal Physiology, Cambridge, Eng., 1964-67; prin. research scientist Roswell Park Meml. Inst., Buffalo, 1968-78; research assoc. prof. SUNY-Buffalo, 1971-74, research prof., 1974-78; prof. U. Calif.-San Francisco, 1978—; established investigator Am. Heart Assn., N.Y.C., 1967-72; chmn. sci. adv. bd. Liposome Tech., Inc., Menlo Park, Calif., 1981—; sci. advisor Internat. Genetic Sci., Jerusalem, 1982-84. Editor: Liposomes and Their Uses, 1978; contbr. articles to profl. jours.; patentee liposomes. Mem. Am. Soc. Biol. Chemists, Am. Soc. Cell Biology, Biophys. Soc. (K.C. Cole award 1980), Am. Chem. Assn. Current work: Cell membranes, liposomes, drug delivery, membrane fusion. Subspecialties: Biophysics (biology); Biomedical engineering. Home: 1515 Willard St San Francisco CA 94117 Office: U Calif Cancer Research Inst Dept Pharmacology Parnassus St San Francisco CA 94143

PAPAMARCOS, JOHN, editor; b. N.Y.C., Dec. 30, 1920; s. Demetri and Alma Cecelia (Nicolaysen) P.; m. Barbara Ann Johnson, Jan. 19, 1952; children—John S., Andrew A., Paula C., Mark S. B.E.E., Cooper Union Coll., 1941; M. in Mech. Engring., U. Del., 1951; M.E.E., Poly. Inst. Bklyn., 1953. Registered profl. engr., N.Y. Lectr. elec. engring. CCNY, 1948-52; instr. elect. engring. Poly. Inst. Bklyn., 1952-55; plant betterment engr. Ebasco Internat., N.Y.C., 1957-58; assoc. editor-mgr. editor Power Engring., Barrington, Ill., 1960-74, editor, 1974—. Contbr. articles to profl. jours. Com. mem. Barrington Area United Dr., 1974-75, v.p., 1975-76, pres., 1976-77. Mem. IEEE, ASME (exec. com. fuels div. 1974-78, chmn. exec. com. 1977-78, nat. nominating com. 1984-85), Am. Soc. Engring. Edn. Lodge: Kiwanis (pres. 1973-74). Current work: All 12000 categories (energy science and technology). Subspecialties: Coal; Fuels and sources. Home: 212 Coolidge Ave Barrington IL 60010

PAPASTAMATIOU, DIMITRI, earthquake engineering consultant, research consultant; b. Athens, Greece, Mar. 1, 1941; s. Yanni and Elli (Papanikolaou) P.; m. Caroline Ford-Dunn, July 24, 1976; children—Yanni, Alexi. M.Sc., Nat. Tech. U., Athens, 1964; Ph.D., Imperial Coll., London, 1971. Registered civil engr., Greece. Project engr. K & S Cons., Greece, 1967; research fellow Imperial Coll., 1970-74; sr. engr. Dames & Moore, London, 1974-80; dir. GeoGnosis Ltd., London, 1980-82, Delta Pi Assocs., London, 1982—; cons. UNESCO, 1977-82. Contbr. articles to profl. jours. Greek Scholarship Found. scholar, 1967. Mem. Tech. Chamber Greece, ASCE, Brit. Soc. Earthquake and Civil Engring. Dynamics (com. 1982). Current work: Definition of earthquake motion parameters for earthquake resistant design through seismotectonic investigations, post-earthquake field studies and strong motion recordings; rationalisation of criteria for earthquake resistant design. Subspecialties: Civil engineering; Seismology. Office: Delta Pi Assocs 9 Southfields Rd London SW18 1QW England

PAPE, HARRY RUDOLPH, JR., dental educator; b. Chgo., Mar. 31, 1937; s. Harry Rudolph and Vina Pearl (Derry) P.; m. Diana June Seagert, June 24,

1961; children: Nancy, Dale, Jerry, Yvonne. M.S., U. Mich., 1975, D.D.S., 1961. Pvt. practice dentistry, Quincy, Mich., 1963-71; instr. U. Mich., Ann Arbor, 1971-75, asst. prof., 1975-78, assoc. prof., 1978—; cons. Blissfield Migrant Workers Program, 1981—. Sec. Ridgeway Twp. Bd. Appeals; pres C. of C.; leader 4-H Garden Club. Served as lt. USNR, 1961-63. Recipient Outstanding Instr. award Jr. Class Sch. Dentistry, U. Mich., 1974, 75, 76, 78, 82. Mem. Am. Assn. Dental Schs. Republican. Lutheran. Clubs: Clark Lake Yacht (Jackson, Mich.); Western Square Dancing (Adrain, Mich.). Current Work: Caries and periodontal prevention in areas of flourides, nutrition, diet analysis, plaque control, patient education, TV projection of phase microscopy and bacteriology. Subspecialties: Cariology; Preventive dentistry. Home: 7241 Ridge Rd Ridgeway MI 49275 Office: U Mich Sch Dentistry Ann Arbor MI 48109

PAPKE, BRIAN LEE, chemist; b. Tucson, Mar. 20, 1955; s. Keith G. and Ruth Papke; m. Mary Ann Abbott, July 19, 1980; 1 child, Christina. B.S. in Chemistry, Oreg. State U., 1977; Ph.D. in Inorganic Chemistry, Northwestern U., 1982. Sr. chemist Texaco Inc., Beacon, N.Y., 1982—. Mem. Am. Chem. Soc. Republican. Baptist. Current work: Chemistry and physics of high temperature carbonaceous deposit formation on metal oxide surfaces. Subspecialties: Inorganic chemistry; Surface chemistry. Office: Texaco Inc Box 509 Beacon NY 12508

PAPPAS, JAMES JOHN, research chemist; b. Bridgeport, Conn., July 22, 1931; s. John D. and Irene J. (Krampovitis) P.; m. Sylvia J. Rahaniotis, Dec. 4, 1960; children—Maria, Irene, John. B.S. in Chemistry, MIT, 1952, B.S. in Chem. Engring., 1952, M.S. in Chemistry, 1954; Ph.D. in Chemistry, Columbia U., 1959. Sr. research chemist Esso Research and Engring. Co., Linden, N.J., 1959-62, 69-71; mgr. new products Inmont Corp., Clifton, N.J., 1962-69; mgr. applied research J.M. Huber Corp., Edison, N.J., 1971—. Contbr. articles to profl. jours. Patentee in field. Mem. Am. Chem. Soc., Tech. Assn. Graphic Arts. Greek Orthodox. Current work: Graphic arts, printing inks, toners, coatings, pigments, dyes, polymers, oils, sulfur and phosphorus chemistry. Subspecialties: Organic chemistry; Graphic arts chemistry. Home: 19 Trouville Dr Parsippany NJ 07054

PAPPAS, SOCRATES PETER, chemist, educator, cons.; b. Hartford, Conn., Feb. 3, 1936; s. Peter and Valentina (Apostolidou) P.; m. Betty C. Thompson, Sept. 30, 1961; children: Niki Thais, Paul Alexander. B.A in Chemistry, Dartmouth Coll., 1958; Ph.D. in Chemistry, U. Wis., 1962. Postdoctoral research asso. U. Wis., Madison, 1962-63, Brandeis U., 1963-64; asst. prof. Emory U., Atlanta, 1964-68; asst. prof. N.D. State U., Fargo, 1968-73, prof., 1973—; research assoc. DeSoto, Inc., 1973; vis. prof. U. Stuttgart, W. Ger., 1977, Royal Inst. Tech., Stockholm, 1982, Chem. Soc. Japan, Macromolecular Sci. Div., 1984, cons. coatings sci. Contbr. numerous articles on coatings sci. to profl. jours.; editor: UV Curing: Sci. and Tech, 1978, 85; co-editor: Photodegradation and Photostabilization of Coatings, 1981. NATO grantee, 1981-82; Dept. Interior grantee, 1978-80; Recipient Roon award, First Prize Fedn. Socs. of Coatings Tech., 1974,75,76,80; recipient DAAD award Ger. Acad. Exchange Service, 1977. Mem. Am. Chem. Soc., Inter-AM Photochem. Soc. Current Work: Photoinitiators, thermally activated latent catalysts and rectants, photostabilization of coatings. Subspecialties: Organic chemistry; Photochemistry. Office: Polymers and Coatings Dept N D State U Fargo ND 58105

PAPPENHEIMER, ALWIN M(AX), JR., biochemist, immunologist; b. Cedarhurst, N.Y., Nov. 25, 1908; s. Alwin Max and Beatrice (Leo) P.; m. Pauline Forbes, Sept. 10, 1938; children—Ruth Forbes, Sarah Ann, John Forbes. S.B., Harvard U., 1929, Ph.D., 1932. Instr., tutor biochem. sci. Harvard U., Cambridge, Mass., 1930-33, prof. biology, 1958-79, now with NRC fellow Nat. Inst. Med. Research, London, 1933-35; sr. chemist Antitoxin and Vaccine Lab., Jamaica Plain, Mass., 1936-39; asst. prof. biochemistry in bacteriology U. Pa., Phila., 1939-41; faculty NYU Coll. Medicine, N.Y.C., 1941-58, prof. microbiology, chmn. dept.; mem. regulatory biology panel NSF, Washington, 1953-55; master Dunster House, Harvard U., 1961-70. Contbr. sects. to books, sci. articles to profl. jours. Served to lt. col. AUS, 1942-45, PTO. Recipient Eli Lilly award in bacteriology Am. Assn. Microbiology, 1942; Louis L. Seaman award N.Y. Acad. Medicine, 1947. Fellow Am. Acad. Arts and Sci., Nat. Acad. Sci., AAAS; mem. Am. Assn. Immunologists (pres. 1954-55), other sci. socs., Phi Beta Kappa. Democrat. Club: Cambridge Boat. Current work: Biology and biochemistry of infectious disease. Subspecialty: Microbiology. Office: Biological Labs Harvard Univ 16 Divinity Ave Cambridge MA 02138

PAPSIDERO, LAWRENCE DEAN, cancer research scientist, immunologist; b. Buffalo, Sept. 2, 1949; s. Frank Peter and Marie Dolores (Pilla) P.; m. Barbara Jean Raiman, June 30, 1972; children—Sara Ann, Daniel Matthew. B.A., Buffalo State U., 1971; M.S., Ohio State U., 1973; Ph.D., SUNY-Buffalo, 1978. Postdoctoral fellow Roswell Park Meml. Inst., Buffalo, 1978-79, cancer research scientist, 1979—; sci. adv. bd. cons. Cellular Products Industry, Inc., Buffalo, 1984—. Contbr. articles to profl. jours. Recipient New Investigator Research award Nat. Cancer Inst., 1981; Nat. Cancer Inst. grantee, 1981—. Mem. Am. Assn. for Cancer Research, Am. Assn. Immunologists, Internat. Assn. for Breast Cancer Research, N.Y. Acad. Scis. Current work: Immunodiagnosis and therapy of cancer using monoclonal antibodies; tumor immunology. Subspecialties: Cancer research (medicine); Immunology (medicine). Home: 4155 Liberty Dr Orchard Park NY 14127 Office: Roswell Park Meml Inst 666 Elm St Buffalo NY

PAQUE, RONALD EDWARD, immunologist, educator; b. Green Bay, Wis., Apr. 29, 1938; s. E. A. and Lucille R. (Aerts) P. B.S. with honors, Wis. State U., Oshkosh, 1960; M.S., U. Wis.-Madison, 1963; Ph.D. (scholar), U. Ariz., Tucson, 1966. Assoc. dir. immunology div. Microbiol. Assocs., Bethseda, Md., 1966-68; USPHS fellow U. Ill. Med Ctr., Chgo., 1968-70, asst. prof., 1970-74; assoc. prof. U. Tex. Health Sci. Ctr., San Antonio, 1974—; cons. NIH, NSF, Nat. Cancer Inst.; pres. Outdoor Cons. Pub., San Antonio, 1981—; participant Internat. Symposium on RNA in Devel. and Differentiation, Peking, 1980. Contbr. articles, revs. to sci. jours. and books. Served to cpl. USMCR, 1956-62. Mem. Am. Assn. Immunologists, Am. Soc. Microbiology, N.Y. Acad. Scis., AAAS, Am. Assn. Cancer Research, North San Antonio C. of C. Republican. Club: Los Amigos Ski. Current Work: Nucleic acid programming of lymphoid cells; immunological cellular engineering; immunology of viral-induced myocarditis; immunology of infectious diseases, lymphokine technology; tumor immunotherapy. Subspecialties: Immunobiology and immunology; Cellular engineering. Office: 7703 Floyd Curl Dr San Antonio TX 78284

PARADISSIS, PANTELIS PETE, engineering executive; b. Chios, Greece, Jan. 1, 1938; came to U.S., 1957; s. Markos Pantelis and Efharis (Psaltakis) P.; m. Beverly Ann Hafer, June 1, 1960; children—Eftihea, Markos, Arthur, Katharine. B.S. in Elec. Engring., Ohio U., 1961; M.B.A., Baldwin Wallace Coll., 1984. Research and devel. engr. Lorain Products Co. (Ohio), 1961-78, research and devel. mgr., 1978-80, engring. mgr., 1980-83, dir. engring., 1983—. Contbr. articles to profl. jours.; patentee in field. Treas., St. Nicholas Greek Orthodox Ch., Lorain, 1974, pres., 1975. Mem. IEEE. Republican. Current work: Research on power conversion topologies. Home: 154 Rainbow Dr Amherst OH 44001 Office: 1122 F St Lorain OH 44052

PARANTO, JOSEPH NOLAN, laser system engineer, laser researcher; b. Deadwood, S.D., Sept. 12, 1958; s. Clayton Dennis and Mary Ann (Walenta) P. B.S. in Physics, Colo. State U., 1980. Mem. tech. staff Hughes Aircraft Co., Albuquerque, 1980—. Author: RF Waveguide Lasers, 1983. Contbr. articles to profl. jours. Patentee Mid-IR waveguide lasers, 1982, CW HF/DF radio frequency lasers, 1983. Mem. IEEE, Soc. Physics Students, Optical Soc. Am., Internat. Soc. Optical Engring. Current work: Development of laser radar systems and advanced sensors. Subspecialties: Optical engineering; Laser devices. Home: 506 Mesilla St NE Albuquerque NM 87108 Office: Hughes Aircraft Co 1600 Randolph Ct Albuquerque NM 87106

PARDEE, ARTHUR BECK, educator, biochemist; b. Chgo., July 13, 1921; s. Charles A. and Elizabeth B. (Beck) P.; m. Ruth Sager; children by previous marriage: Michael, Richard, Thomas, Elizabeth. B.S., U. Calif. at Berkeley, 1942; M.S., Calif. Inst. Tech., 1943, Ph.D., 1947. Merck postdoctoral fellow U. Wis., 1947-49; mem. faculty U. Calif. at Berkeley, 1949-61, asso. prof., 1957-61; NSF fellow Pasteur Inst., 1957-58; prof. biology, chmn. dept. biochem. scis. Princeton, 1961-67, prof. biochemistry, 1961-75, Donner prof. sci., 1966; prof. Sidney Farber Cancer Inst. and pharmacology dept. Harvard Med. Sch., Boston, 1975—; Mem. research adv. council Am. Cancer Soc., 1967-71. Co-author: Experiments in Biochemical Research Techniques, 1957; Editor: Biochemica et Biophysica Acta, 1962-68, 74—. Trustee Cold Spring Harbor Lab. Quantitative Biology, 1963-69. Recipient Young Biochemists travel award NSF, 1952, Krebs Medal Fedn. European Biochem. Socs., 1973, Rosenstiel award Brandeis U., 1975, 3M award Fedn. Am. Socs., Exptl. Biology, 1980. Mem. Nat. Acad. Sci. (editorial bd. proc. 1971-73, com. on scis. and pub. policy 1973-76), Am. Chem. Soc. (Paul Lewis award 1960), Am. Soc. Biol. Chemists (treas. 1964-70, pres. 1980-81), Am. Assn. Cancer Research (pres. 1985), Am. Acad. Arts and Scis., Am. Soc. Microbiologists, Japanese Biochem. Soc., Phi Beta Kappa, Sigma Xi. Current Work: Cancer research on growth control basic mechanisms, chemotherapy and carcinogenesis research. Subspecialties: Biochemistry (biology); Cell biology. Home: 30 Codman Rd Brookline MA 02146

PARDINI, STEVEN PETER, research chemist; b. San Francisco, Nov. 6, 1953; s. Peter and Gloria Marie (Pacini) P. B.S., San Jose State U., 1976; Ph.D., Iowa State U., 1981. Research chemist DuPont Textile Fibers, Camden, S.C., 1981—. Mem. Am. Chem. Soc., Bread for World. Democrat. Mennonite. Current work: Develop proprietary products and new enduses for synthetic textile fibers. Subspecialties: Physical chemistry; Polymer chemistry. Home: 101 Calloway Ct Columbia SC 29206 Office: DuPont Textile Fibers Drawer A Camden SC 29020

PARDUE, MARY LOU, biology educator; b. Lexington, Ky., Sept. 15, 1933; d. Louis A. and Mary A. (Marshall) P. B.S., Coll. William and Mary, 1955; M.S., U. Tenn.-Knoxville, 1959; Ph.D., Yale U., 1970; D.Sc. (hon.), Bard Coll., 1985. Am. Cancer Soc. postdoctoral fellow U. Edinburgh, 1970-72; assoc. prof. biology MIT, 1972-80, prof., 1980—; organizer Molecular Cytogenetics Course Cold Spring Harbor Lab., 1971-78; organizer Drosphila Course Cold Spring Harbor Lab. (course on Molecular Biology of Drosophila), 1979, 80; sci. adv. panel Wistar Inst., 1976; mem. cellular and moledular basis of disease rev. com. NIH, 1980-84. Editorial bd.: Genetics, 1973-83, Jour. Cell Biology, 1973-76, 84—, Cell, 1973-77, Chromosoma, 1976, Cell Biology Internat. Reports, 1982, Molecular and Cellular Biology, 1983, Biochemistry, 1986—, others. Contbr. articles to sci. jours. Recipient Ester Langer award for cancer research, 1977. Fellow AAAS, Am. Acad. Arts and Scis.; mem. Genetics Soc. Am. (pres. 1982-83), Nat. Acad. Scis., Am. Soc. Cell Biology, Am. Soc. Cell Biology (pres. elect 1984). Subspecialties: Cell biology; Molecular biology. Office: Biology 16 717 MIT Cambridge MA 02139

PARENT, DOUGLAS JOHN, environmental hygiene chemist; b. Waterbury, Conn., Dec. 20, 1957; s. Gordon Raymond and Irene (Duigou) P.; m. Karen Marie Viscosi, June 6, 1981. Student U. Conn., 1975-77; B.A. in Chemistry, Western Conn. State U., 1981; M.S. in Computer and Info. Scis., U. New Haven, 1985. Environ. hygiene chemist Olin Corp., New Haven, 1981—. Mem. Am. Chem. Soc. (div. computers in chemistry), Am. Indsl. Hygiene Assn. Roman Catholic. Current work: Development of new methods for sample analysis to ensure workers' safety and health; integration of computerization with laboratory data handling. Subspecialties: Analytical chemistry; Software engineering. Home: 57 Westbury Park Road Watertown CT 06795 Office: Olin Corp 91 Shelton Ave New Haven CT 06511

PARHAM, MARC ELLOUS, chemist, researcher; b. Quincy, Mass., Sept. 16, 1948; s. James Crowder and Mildred (Blackmon) P.; m. Kathleen Ann Quinlan, July 28, 1974; 1 child, Derek Michael. B.S. in Chemistry, Duke U., 1970; M.S. in Chemistry, U. Mich., 1972; Ph.D. in Bio-Organic Chemistry, Cornell U., 1977. Research asst. MIT, Cambridge, 1977-78; sr. chemist Ciba-Geigy Corp., Cranston, R.I., 1978-82; sr. scientist Baxter-Travenol Labs., Cambridge, 1982-83; sr. research scientist Amicon Corp., Lexington, Mass., 1983—; program mgr. W.R. Grace & Co., Lexington. Contbr. articles to profl. jours. Patentee in field. Mem. Am. Chem. Soc. Current work: Immobilization of biologicals on semipermeable, hollow-fiber membranes for use in enzymatic and immunochemical processes; also biomaterial devices and improved bio-compatibilty of polymers. Subspecialties: Organic chemistry; Biochemistry (medicine). Office: WR Grace Corp Tech Group Amicon Corp 25 Hartwell Ave Lexington MA 02173

PARHAM, PETER, research immunologist, educator; b. London, Eng., Aug. 15, 1950; s. Ronald James and Hilda (Walker) P.; B.A., Cambridge U., 1972, M.A., 1975; Ph.D., Harvard U., 1977. Jr. fellow Oxford U., Eng., 1977-78; jr. fellow Harvard U., Cambridge, Mass., 1978-80; asst. prof. immunology Stanford U., Calif., 1980—; cons. Becton Dickinson, Mountain View, Calif., 1982—; cons. NIH, Bethesda, Md., 1984—. Mem. Biochem. Soc., Am. Assn. Immunologists, Am. Soc. Histocompatibility and Immunogenetics. Current work: Structure and function of human histocompatability molecules; role of clathrin in intracellular transport of macromolecules. Subspecialties: Immunogenetics; Biochemistry (biology). Office: Dept Cell Biology Fairchild Bldg Stanford Med Ctr Stanford CA 94305

PARIS, STEVEN MARK, software engineer, educator; b. Boston, May 26, 1956; s. Julius Louis and Frances (Keleishik) P. B.S., Rensselaer Poly. Inst., 1978; M.S., Boston U., 1980, postgrad., 1980—. Sr. software engr. Prime Computer Inc., Framingham, Mass., 1978-82; sr. analyst Computervision Corp., Bedford, Mass., 1982-84, Lotus Devel. Corp., Cambridge, Mass., 1984—. Recipient Boston Sci. Fair 1st prize, 1973, 74; State of Mass. Sci. Fair 3d prize, 1973; 2d prize, 1974; nat. merit scholarship letter of Commendation. Mem. Assn. for Computing Machinery, IEEE, Boston Computer Soc., Planetary Soc. Jewish. Current Work: Research in massively parallel processing and functional programming. Subspecialties: Software engineering; Operating systems. Home: 27 Colwell Ave Brighton MA 02135 Office: 161 1st St Cambridge MA 02142

PARISER, RUDOLPH, chemist; b. Harbin, China, Dec. 8, 1923; came to U.S., 1941; s. Ludwig Jacob and Lia (Rubenstein) P.; m. Margaret Louise Marsh, July 31, 1972. B.S. in Chemistry, U. Calif.-Berkeley, 1944; Ph.D. in Phys. Chemistry, 1950. Research chemist E.I. du Pont de Nemours & Co., Wilmington, Del., 1950-54, research supr. organic chemicals dept., 1954-59, div. head elastomer chemicals Dept., 1959-63, asst. lab. dir. elastomer chemicals dept., 1963-67, lab. dir., 1967-70, dir. exploratory research, mgr. research and devel., 1970-72, mgr. market research and market devel., 1972-74, dir. pioneering research, 1974-79, research dir. polymer products dept., 1980-81, dir. polymer sci. central research and devel. dept., 1981—, liaison officer to Calif. Inst. Tech., 1976—. Assoc. editor Jour. Chem. Physics, 1966-69, Chem. Physics Letters, 1967-70, Du Pont Innovation, 1969-75. Mem. adv. bd. Jour. Polymer Sci., 1980—. Mem. NRC Com. on Chem. Scis., 1979-82; co-chmn. NRC Panel on Polymer Sci. and Engring., 1979-81; mem. Internat. Union Pure and Applied Chemistry, chem. Research Applied to World Needs, 1982—. Served with U.S. Army, 1944-46. Recipient Outstanding Achievement award U. Minn., 1976. Mem. Am. Chem. Soc. (Del. sect. award 1956), AAAS, N.Y. Acad. Scis., Am. Phys. Soc., NRC, Sigma Xi, Phi Lambda Upsilon. Clubs: Phila. Interlocutors (pres. 1972-76); DuPont Country. Subspecialty: Polymer chemistry. Home: RD #2 Box 106 Old Public Rd Hockessin DE 19707 Office: E I du Pont de Nemours & Co Central Research and Devel Exptl Sta E328/414 Wilmington DE 19898

PARISI, JOSEPH THOMAS, microbiologist, educator; b. Chgo., Apr. 28, 1934; s. Joseph A. and Josephine P.; m. Elaine Ann Smithbower, June 8, 1963; 1 dau., Melissa. B.S., Loyola U. Chgo., 1956; M.S., Ohio State U., 1958, Ph.D., 1962. With Duquesne U., Pitts., 1962-65; with U. Mo. Sch. Medicine, Columbia, 1965—, prof. microbiology, 1975. Contbr. articles to sci. jours. Mem. Am. Soc. Microbiology, Sigma Xi. Current Work: Genetics of antibiotic resistance, plasmid biology, epidemiology. Subspecialties: Microbiology (medicine); Genetics and genetic engineering (medicine). Home: 313 Defoe Dr Columbia MO 65203 Office: Dept Microbiology U Mo Sch Medicine Columbia MO 65212

PARK, CHAN HYUNG, cell biologist, physician; b. Seoul, Korea, Aug. 16, 1936; s. Chung Suh and Yoon Sook Yuh; m. Mary Hyungrok Kim, Apr. 16, 1966; 1 son, Christopher Myungwoo. M.D., Seoul Nat. U., 1962, M.S., 1964; Ph.D., U. Toronto, Ont., Can., 1972. Diplomate: Am. Bd. Internal Medicine with subplty. of med. oncology. Asst. prof. U. Kans. Med. Center, 1974-80, assoc. prof., 1980—. Transl. novel from German to Korean; contbr. articles to biomed. and sci. jours. Mem. editorial bd. Jour. Nutrition Growth and Cancer. Recipient research career devel. award USPHS, NIH, 1979—. Fellow ACP; mem. Am. Assn. Cancer Research, Am. Soc. Clin. Oncology, Am. Soc. Hematology, Internat. Soc. Exptl. Hematology, Cell Kinetics Soc., Am. Fedn. Clin. Research, Internat. Assn. for Vitamin and Nutritional Oncology. Current Work: Clinical application of in vitro chemotherapy, human growth modulation, and flow cytometry DNA analysis all for human tumors and leukemia. Subspecialties: Cell and tissue culture; Oncology. Home: 9137 Grandview Dr Overland Park KS 66212 Office: 39th and Rainbow Blvd Kansas City KS 66103

PARK, CHUL, aerospace engineer; b. Taegu, Korea, June 8, 1934; came to U.S., 1964; s. Hyung-jin and Ha-Woon (Ryang) P.; m. Chyon Sue Sohn, Sept. 29, 1962; children: Sora, Pora, Marie. B.S., Seoul (Korea) Nat. U., 1957, M.S., 1960; Ph.D., Imperial Coll. Sci. and Tech., U. London, 1964. Research assoc. NASA Ames Research Ctr., Moffett Field, Calif., 1964-67, aerospace engr., 1967—; vis. engr. M.I.T., 1971-72. Served to 1st lt. Korean Air Force, 1958-61. Mem. AIAA. Current Work: High temperature gas physics and fluid mechanics related to hypersonic flight and space travel. Subspecialty: Aerospace engineering and technology. Home: 21194 Bank Mill Rd Saratoga CA 95070 Office: Ames Research Center NASA Bldg 229-4 Moffett Field CA 94035

PARK, DONG HWA, neurobiologist, educator; b. Seoul, Mar. 3, 1937; came to U.S., 1963, naturalized, 1976; s. Chi Ho and Ok Nam (Shin) P.; m. Min Jung, Sept. 9, 1967; children: Henry, Bernard. B.S. in Chemistry, Seoul Nat. U., 1961; M.S. in Biochemistry, Brigham Young U., 1968, Ph.D. in Biochemistry, 1970. Nat. Vitamin Found. postdoctoral fellow Columbia U.-St. Luke's Hosp. Center, N.Y.C., 1970-72; asst. scientist N.Y.U., N.Y.C., 1972-75; instr. neurobiology Cornell U. Med. Coll., N.Y.C., 1975-78, asst. prof., 1978-84, assoc. research prof., 1984—. Contbr. articles to sci. jours. Mem. Am. Chem. Soc., Am. Soc. for Neurochemistry, N.Y. Acad. Scis., Soc. for Neurosci. Baptist. Current Work: Neurotransmitter synthesizing enzymes, purification, characterization, production of antibodies to the above enzymes and immunochemical studies. Subspecialties: Neurochemistry; Neurobiology. Home: 50-21 59th Pl Woodside NY 11377 Office: 411 E 69th St New York NY 10021

PARK, HEE KYUN, material scientist, microelectronics researcher; b. Pusan, Korea, Apr. 1, 1951; came to U.S. 1978, naturalized 1985; s. Sang Keun and Moon Young (Lee) P.; m. Ok-Shoon Shin, Apr. 20, 1978; children—Duke, David. B.S., Seoul Nat. U., Korea, 1977; M.S., N.C. State U., 1979, Ph.D., 1982. Process engr. Motorola, Seoul, 1977-78; research asst. N.C. State U., Raleigh, 1978-82; mem. research staff Tektronix, Inc., Beaverton, Oreg., 1982-84, project mgr., 1984—. Contbr. articles to profl. jours. Patentee in field. Mem. Am. Vacuum Soc., IEEE, Sigma Xi. Current work: High speed bipolar ICs with poly base and poly emitter, high performance bipolar and CMOS integration on a chip. Subspecialties: Integrated circuits; Microchip technology (materials science). Home: 12364 NW Barnes Rd #389 Portland OR 97229

PARK, JOHN THORNTON, physicist, educator; b. Phillipsburg, N.J., Jan. 3, 1935; s. Dawson J. and Margaret M. (Thornton) P.; m. Dorcas Marshall, June 1, 1956; children: Janet Ernst, Karen. B.A., Nebr. Wesleyan U., 1956; Ph.D., U. Nebr., 1963. Teaching asst. U. Nebr., 1956-58, research asst., 1958-62, research assoc., 1962-63; NSF postdoctoral fellow Univ. Coll., London, 1963-64; asst. prof. U. Mo.-Rolla, 1964-68, assoc. prof., 1968-71, prof. physics, 1971—, chmn. dept., 1977-83, vice chancellor acad. affairs, 1983-85, interim chancellor, 1985—; vis. assoc. prof. NYU, 1970-71; mem. NRC panel, 1975, 76; mem. gen. com. Internat. Conf. Physics of Acad. and Atomic Physics, 1975-79, Small Accelerator Conf., 1978—; honors lectr. Mid-Am. State Univ. Assn., 1973-77; mem. panel NSF-NATO postdoctoral fellowship, 1977, mem. program com. div. electron and atomic physics, 1974-75, mem. nominating com., 1978. Contbr. papers to profl. lit. Recipient Outstanding Tchr. award U. Mo.-Rolla, 1970; Young Alumni Service award Nebr. Wesleyan U., 1968; NSF research grantee, 1966—. Fellow Am. Phys. Soc. (div. electron and atomic physics); mem. Am. Assn. Physics Tchrs., Am. Vacuum Soc. Methodists. Lodge: Rotary. Current Work: Measurements of ion-atom collision cross sections with emphasis on proton-atomic hydrogen collisions. Subspecialty: Atomic and molecular physics. Office: 206 Parker Hall U Mo Rolla MO 65401

PARK, OK-CHOON, psychologist; b. Keumsan, Choongnam, Korea, Dec. 30, 1944; came to U.S., 1974; s. Dal-moon and Eon-yon (Yook) P.; m. Young-soon Yang, Sept. 10, 1974; children—Michael H., Christine J. M.A., U. Minn., 1976, Ph.D., 1978. Prin. researcher Control Data Corp., Mpls., 1979-85; asst. prof. SUNY-Albany, 1981-83; research psychologist U.S. Army Research Inst., Alexandria, Va., 1985—. Contbr. numerous articles to profl. jours. and books. Research fellow Health Service Research Center UMinn., 1977-78; SUNY Research found. fellow Albany, 1981. Mem. Am. Psychol. Assn., Am. Ednl. Research Assn., Assn. Devel. Computer-based Instructional Systems, Assn. Ednl. Communication and Technology, Phi Kappa Phi. Current Work: Combination of human cognitive info. processes and computers information processes into an artificial intelligence system; development computer-based instructional system. Subspecialties: Learning; Artificial intelligence. Home: 8926 Renshaw Ct Springfield VA 22153 Office: US Army Research Inst 5001 Eisenhower Ave Alexandria VA 22153

PARK, STEVEN LYNN, geologist; b. Denver, June 1, 1954; s. Edwin Herrick and Lynne (Neville) P. B.S., Principia Coll., 1976; M.S., Mackay Sch. Mines U. Nev.-Reno, 1983. Staff geologist Wold Nuclear Co., Casper, Wyo., 1976-79; project geologist Am. Nuclear Co., Casper, 1979-80, Gulf Mineral Resources Co., Reno, 1982-83, Barringer Resources Inc., Golden, Colo., 1983—. HEW Fellow 1980. Mem. Am. Assn. Petroleum Geologists, Geol. Soc. Am., Denver Region Exploration Geologists Soc. Current work: Precious metal exploration through western U.S. Subspecialty: Volcanology. Home: 838D S Vance St Lakewood CO 80226 Office: Barringer Resources Inc 1626 Cole Blvd #120 Golden CO 80401

PARK, U. YOUNG, nuclear engineer, mechanical engineer; b. Seoul, Korea, Oct. 12, 1940; s. M.W. amd and D.C. (Chang) P.; m. Linda L. Rugh; children: Tara, Thomas. B.S., Seoul Nat. U., 1963; M.S., U. Cin., 1970. Registered profl. engr., Calif. Power engr. State of Ohio, Columbus, 1975-78; nuclear engr. Battelle, Columbus, 1978-81; nuclear system engr. Bechtel Power Corp., San Francisco, 1981—. Contbr. articles to profl. jours. Mem. Am. Nuclear Soc. Current Work: Design of nuclear power plant. Subspecialties: Nuclear engineering; Mechanical engineering. Home: 2850 Madigan Ct Concord CA 94518

PARK, U-SUN, chemical engineer; b. Yong-Jung, Yun-Kil, Manchuria, China, Mar. 12, 1942; came to U.S., 1968; s. Yeun-Woo and Se-Jin (Kahng) P.; m. Haijoo Chung Park, June 29, 1968; children—Eugene Young-Joon, Catherine Yong-Eun. B.S., Seoul Nat. U., 1961, M.S., 1965; Ph.D. in Chem. Engring., U. Wash., 1974; postgrad. Colo. Sch. Mines, 1983-84. Registered profl. engr., Calif. Research engr. Inst. Fuel, Mining & Metallurgy, Seoul, Korea, 1963, Atomic Energy Research Inst., Seoul, 1963-65; patent engr. Cha Patent Office, Seoul, 1966-68; staff engr. Gen. Atomic Co., San Diego, 1974-80; dir. chem. engring. Sci. Applications, Inc., Golden, Colo., 1984—; dir. Techno-Search Internat., 1984—. Contbr. articles to profl. jours. Judge, sci. fair, San Diego, 1976-80. Scholarship Com. Korea scholar, 1963. Mem. Am. Inst. Chem. Engrs., Soc. Petroleum Engrs., Am. Nuclear Soc., Phi Lambda Upsilon. United Methodist. Current work: Oil shale retorting process devel. and plant design; fluidized bed combustion; enchanced oil recovery; nuclear fuel reprocessing especially the radioactive off-gas treatment; computer simulation, instrumentation and process control for one of a kind pilot plants; designer, operator first oil shale retorting plant using T3 process. Subspecialties: Oil shale; Nuclear fission. Home: 7421 Quail St Arvada CO 80005 Office: Sci Applications Internat Corp 1626 Cole Blvd Suite 270 Golden CO 80401

PARK, WILLIAM HAROLD, mechanical engineering educator, researcher, consultant; b. Carlisle, Pa., Mar. 2, 1929; s. Harold E. and Ruth E. (Green) P.; m. Ruth H. Dorsey, Jan. 30, 1954; children—Steven G., James A., Mary K., Carol A. Park Saunders. B.S., Pa. State U., 1952, M.S., 1959; Ph.D., Cornell U., 1966. Design engr. Sanders & Thomas, Pottstown, Pa., 1952-53; with Pa. State U., 1953—, assoc. prof. mech. engring., Univ. Park, 1966-79, prof., 1979—; cons. to various law firms and trucking cos. on accident reconstruction and portable scale weighing, 1966—. Contbr. numerous articles to profl. jours. NSF sci. faculty fellow, 1964-65; residence in engring. practice Ford Found., 1968-69; recipient Teaching award Pa. State U., 1982. Mem. Am. Soc. Mech. Engrs. (several sect. offices, chmn. 1962-68), Soc. Auto. Engrs. (nat. com. mem. 1974—), Instrument Soc. Am., Am. Soc. Engring. Edn. Methodist. Current work: Developing computer aided design and engineering methods for use in mechanical engineering curriculum; research in dynamics and vibrations as applied to engineering systems. Subspecialties: Mechanical engineering; Software engineering. Home: 537 Kemmerer Rd State College PA 16801 Office: PA State Univ 206 ME Bldg University Park PA 16802

PARK, YOON SOO, physicist; b. Raichun, Korea, July 4, 1929; came to U.S., 1955; s. Sai Hoon and Sung Hoon (Kang) P.; m. Dju Hyun, Nov. 26, 1960; children—Jeannie, Mimi, Lisa. B.S., Seoul Nat. U., Korea, 1952; M.S., U. Alta., Edmonton, Can., 1955; Ph.D., U. Cin., 1963. Research physicist D.H. Baldwin Co., Cin., 1956-62, Aerospace Research Lab., Dayton, Ohio, 1962-74; task mgr. Air Force Avionics Lab, Dayton, 1975-83; sr. scientist Air Force Office Sci. Research, Tokyo, 1983—; vis. scientist Korean Advanced Inst. Sci. and Tech., Seoul, 1980-84; adj. prof. physics Marquette U., Milw., 1981—; lectr. Pusan U., Korea, 1952, U. Dayton, 1968-69; cons. UN Indsl. Devel. Orgn., 1980-84. Patentee in field. Univ. fellow U. Alta., 1952-53; Laws fellow U. Cin., 1956-57; postdoctoral fellow Tech. U. Berlin, 1968-69; recipient Sci. Achievement award U.S. Air Force, 1971, 72, 77. Fellow Am. Phys. Soc., Korean Phys. Soc.; mem. IEEE (sr.), Japan Soc. Applied Physics, Korean Scientists and Engrs. Assn. (pres. Ohio chpt. 1973-74), Assn. Korean Physicists in Am. (pres. 1982-83), Sigma Xi. Current work: Ion implantation, crystal growth, solid state devices, materials characterization—electrical and optical properties. Subspecialties: Condensed matter physics; Semiconductors. Home: 2248 Brookpark Dr Dayton OH 45440 Office: Air Force Avionics Lab Wright-Patterson AFB OH 45433

PARKER, ALICE CLINE, electrical engineering educator, consultant; b. Birmingham, Ala., Apr. 10, 1948; d. Joseph Kalman and Elizabeth (Wenk) Cline; m. Donald Joseph Bebel, Aug. 9, 1980. B.S.E.E., N.C. State U., Raleigh, 1970; M.S.E.E., Stanford U., 1971; Ph.D., N.C. State U., 1975. Asst. prof. Carnegie-Mellon U., Pitts., 1975-80; asst. prof. elec. engring. U. So. Calif., Los Angeles, 1980-83, assoc. prof., 1983—; cons. Aerospace Corp., 1980—, Xerox Corp., 1981. NSF fellow, 1970-71. Mem. IEEE, Assn. Computing Machinery, Sigma Xi. Current Work: Automatic synthesis of integrated circuits from high-level behavioral specifications; includes optimization of cost-speed, testability requirements. Subspecialties: Computer-aided design; Artificial intelligence. Office: Elec Engring Systems Dep U So Cali Los Angeles CA 90089-0781

PARKER, CHARLES WARD, physician, researcher, educator; b. St. Louis, Mar. 23, 1930; s. William B. and Florence (Mershon) P.; m. Mary L. Langston, June 13, 1953; children: Keith, Charles, Kathy, Christy, Sandy. M.D., Washington U., St. Louis, 1953. Intern Barnes Hosp., St. Louis, 1953-54, resident, 1956-58, USPHS research fellow, 1961-62; head div. immunology Washington U., St. Louis, 1962—, prof. medicine, 1971—, prof. microbiology and immunology, 1975—; dir. Washington U. (Howard Hughes Lab. for Study Clin. Immunology and Allergy), 1977—. Served with USNR, 1954-56. Recipient Hixon award, Bausch & Lomb award, Mosby award; NIH grantee, 1962-72. Mem. Central Soc. Clin. Research, Am. Acad. Allergy, Am. Assn. Immunologists, Collegium Internationale Allergologicum, Am. Acad. Allergy (fellow), Sigma Xi, Alpha Omega Alpha, Phi Eta Sigma. Subspecialties: Allergy; Immunology (medicine).

PARKER, DONN BLANCHARD, computer security consultant; b. San Jose, Calif., Oct. 9, 1929; s. Donald Wiliam and Miriam Estelle (Blanchard) P.; m. Lorna Ruth Schroeder, Aug. 23, 1952; children—Diane Patricia, David Scott. B.A. in Math., U. Calif.-Berkeley, 1952, M.A., 1954. Computer mgr. Gen. Dynamics, San Diego, 1954-62; sr. research engr. Control Data Corp., Palo Alto, Calif., 1962-69; sr. mgmt. cons. SRI Internat., Menlo Park, Calif., 1969—. Author: Crime by Computer, 1977; Ethical Conflicts in Computer Technology, 1977; Manager's Guide to Computer Security, 1981; Fighting Computer Crime, 1983. NSF grantee, 1971-79; Dept. Justice grantee, 1979-84. Mem. Assn. for Computing Machinery (sec. 1970-75), Am. Soc. Indsl. Security. Republican. Lutheran. Lodge: Rotary. Current work: Computer crime. Subspecialty: Cryptography and data security. Home: 265 Vernal Ct Los Altos CA 94022 Office: SRI Internat 333 Ravenswood Ave Menlo Park CA 94025

PARKER, EARL RANDALL, educator; b. Denver, Nov. 22, 1912; s. Sam and Rebecca Rose (Presley) P.; m. Mary Mildred Larkin, June 2, 1935; children—Robert Earl (dec.), Margaret Mary, William John. Met.E., Colo. Sch. Mines, 1935. Research metallurgist Gen. Electric Research Lab., 1935-44; research metallurgist U. Calif. at Berkeley, 1944-45, asso. prof. metallurgy, 1945-49, prof., 1949—; chmn. div. mineral tech. U. Calif. at Berkeley (Coll. Engring.), 1953-57; dir. U. Calif. at Berkeley Inst. Engring. Research, 1958-64, Campbell Meml. lectr., 1957, Robert S. Williams lectr., 1957; Mem. Nat. Materials Bd., 1971. Author book, tech. papers in field. Recipient Distinguished Citizens award Denver, 1958, Vincent Bendix gold medal Am. Soc. Engring. Edn., 1969; Guggenheim fellow, 1960; named Calif. Scientist of Yr., 1970. Fellow Am. Inst. Mining, Metall. and Petroleum Engrs. (Mathewson gold medal 1956), Am. Phys. Soc.; mem. Am. Soc. Metals (pres. 1968, Sauveur Achievement award 1964, Gold medal 1972), Nat. Acad. Engring. (U.S. Pres.'s medal of sci. award 1980), Am. Soc. Engring. Edn. Subspecialty: Metallurgy. Office: U Calif Berkeley CA 94720

PARKER, EUGENE NEWMAN, physics educator; b. Houghton, Mich., June 10, 1927; s. Glenn H. and Helen D. (MacNair) P.; m. Niesje M. Parker, Nov. 24, 1954; children: Joyce M., Eric Glenn. B.S. in Physics, Mich. State U., 1948; Ph.D. in Physics, Calif. Inst. Tech., 1951; D.Sc. (hon.), Mich. State U., 1975. Instr. dept. math. U. Utah, 1951-53, asst. prof. dept. physics, 1953-55; with U. Chgo., 1955—, prof. physics, 1962—, prof astronomy and astrophysics, 1967—. Author: Interplanetary Dynamical Processes, 1963, Cosmical Magnetic Fields, 1979. Recipient Space Sci. award AIAA, 1962; Sydney Chapman medal Royal Astron. Soc., 1979; Disting. Alumnus award Calif. Inst. Tech., 1980. Mem. Nat. Acad. Sci. (Henryk Arctowski medal 1969), Am. Phys. Soc., Am. Astron. Soc. (Henry Norris Russel lecture 1969, George Ellery. Hale award 1978), Am. Geophys. Union (recipient John Fleming award 1968). Current Work: Theoretical researches into the nature and causes of the activity of the sun and other stars. Subspecialties: Theoretical astrophysics; Plasma physics. Office: Laboratory for Astrophysics and Space Research 933 E 56th St Chicago IL 60637

PARKER, FRANK(LIN) DOWNS, entomologist; b. Fallon, Nev., Aug. 17, 1936; s. Herbert George and Ethyl Sally (Downs) P.; children—Scott Franklin, Andrew Downs. B.S., U. Calif.-Davis, 1959, M.S., 1961, Ph.D., 1966. Survey entomologist Nev. State Dept. Agr., Reno, 1957-62; research asst. U. Calif.-Davis, 1959-66; entomologist U.S. Dept. Agr., Columbia, Mo., 1966-71, Logan, Utah, 1971—. Contbr. articles to profl. jours. Mem. Entomol. Soc. Am., Kans. Entomol. Soc., Pacific Coast Entomol. Soc., Internat. Bee Research Assn. Current work: Bee management for crop pollination, trap-nest studies behavior, nest architecture, description new species, biology, ecology. Subspecialty: Taxonomy. Office: USDA-ARS 261 NRB UMC 53 Utah State U Logan UT 84322

PARKER, GARALD GORDON, geologist; b. Leona, Oreg., July 2, 1905; s. Arta William and Bertha Mona (Smith) P.; m. Bernadette Elizabeth Spalding, Oct. 29, 1955 (div. 1955); children: Robert A., Elizabeth A., Carole L., Deborah E., Lisa E.; m. Martha Rosetta Harriger, July 3, 1925 (dec. Nov. 1954); children: Avonne A., Garald Gordon. A.B. magna cum laude, Central Wash. State Coll., Ellensburg, 1935; M.S. magna cum laude, U. Wash., Seattle, 1946. Cert. profl. geologist. Geologist, hydrologist U.S. Geol. Survey, Miami, Richland, Wash., Washington, Phila., Denver, Albany, N.Y., 1939-69; chief hydrologist and sr. scientist S.W. Fla. Water Mgmt. Dist., Brooksville, Fla., 1969-75; pres Garald G. Parker Sr. & Assocs., Tampa, 1978—; sr. hydrologist P.E. Lamoreaux & Assocs., Tampa, 1975-76; sr. scientist Geraghty & Miller, Tampa, 1976-78; pres., owner Garald G. Parker Sr. & Assocs., Tampa, 1978—; expert examiner geology U.S. CSC, 1950-59; mem. Water Resources Task Force Nat. Water Assessment, Washington, 1966-67; pres. N.Y. State Capitol dist. Fed. Exec. Council, 1967-68; teaching fellow U. Wash., Seattle, 1938-40; affiliate prof. hydrogeology Am. U., Washington, 1955-56; vis. lectr. Columbia U., N.Y.C., 1957-58; affiliate prof. hydrology Colo. State U., Ft. Collins., 1962-63; vis. prof. dept. agrl. engring. U. Fla., 1975-81. Author: Water Resources of Southeast Florida, 1955, Effect of Pleistocene Epoch on Geology and Water Resources of Florida, 1945 (Gold medal Fla. Acad. Scis.), Water Resources, Delaware River Basin, 1959 (Outstanding Achievement award Fla. Acad. Scis. Survey); assoc. editor: Am. Water Resources Assn. Jour, 1966-70 (pres.'s award 1970); contbr. over 100 articles to profl. jours. Bd. dirs. Fla. Canal Authority, Tallahassee, 1978-79, Chem. and Environ. Services Ctr., U. South Fla. Coll. Natural Scis., Tampa, 1980—; mem. Tampa Environ. Com., 1975-77. Recipient Outstanding Achievement awards S.W. Fla. Water Mgmt. Dist., 1975, Outstanding Achievement awards Fla. Audubon Soc., 1975, Outstanding Achievement awards S.E. Geol. Soc., 1976. Fellow Geol. Soc. Am., Am. Geophys. Union, Am. Water Resources Assn. (dir. Rocky Mountain dist. 1964-66, editorial bd. 1965-80, dir. 1965-68, pres. 1968-69); mem. Am. Inst. Profl. Geologists (pres. Fla. sect. 1967-68), Fla. Engring. Soc., Washington Geol. Soc. (sec., councilor 1953-54). Democrat. Club: Cosmos (Washington). Lodges: Kiwanis; Masons. Current Work: Geologic, water resources and environmental management consulting. Subspecialties: Hydrology; Resource management. Home: 3414 Reynoldswood Dr Tampa FL 33618 Office: PO Box 270089 Tampa FL 33688

PARKER, GEORGE RALPH, forestry educator; b. Tulsa, Sept. 16, 1942; s. Ralph B. and Gladys M. (Hellard) P.; m. Mary Lee Williams, Sept. 4, 1965; children—Ryan, Robin. B.S., Okla. State U., 1964, M.S., 1967; Ph.D., Mich. State U., 1970. Assoc. prof. forestry Purdue U., W. Lafayette, Ind., 1970—. Contbr. articles to profl. jours. Served with U.S. Army 1965. NSF grantee, 1974, 80. Mem. Ecol. Soc. Am., Ind. Acad. Sci., Nature Conservancy (bd. dirs. Ind. chpt. 1980-84), Sigma Xi, Phi Sigma Xi, Sigma Phi. Current work: Teaching forest ecology, ecological impact analysis, dendrology research, spatial and temporal dynamics of forest tree species. Subspecialties: Ecology (biology); Forestry. Office: Purdue U West Lafayette IN 47907

PARKER, JOHN CLARENCE, research company executive, microbiologist; b. Washington, Sept. 13, 1935; s. Marion W. and Katherine L. (Hagan) P.; m. Mary Ann Baker, June 10, 1957 (div. 1973); children: John C., Robert C.; m. Norma Leona Justmann, Jan. 9, 1975. B.S. in Zoology, U. Md., 1957, M.S. in Parasitology, 1961, Ph.D. in Parasitology, 1965. Project dir. Microbiol. Assocs., Bethesda, Md., 1961-78, dir. clin. diagnostic lab., 1973—, v.p. ops., 1976-79, pres., 1979-84; pres., chief exec. officer Daryl Labs. Inc./MAI, 1984—; cons. various sci. research orgns. and programs. Contbr. chpts. to research books; assoc. editor: Am. Assn. for Lab. Animal Sci, 1976—. Mem. AAAS, Am. Assn. Immunologists, Am. Assn. for Lab. Animal Sci. (Charles A. Griffin award 1979), Am. Soc. for Microbiology, Pan Am. Group for Rapid Viral Diagnosis, Soc. for Exptl. Biology and Medicine, Tissue Culture Assn. Republican. Episcopalian. Current Work: Virology: diseases of research animals useful as models of human diseases; biotechnology research for diagnosis of human diseases. Subspecialties: Microbiology (medicine); Infectious diseases. Home: 5023 Mussetter Rd Ijamsville MD 21754 Office: Microbiol Assocs Inc 5221 River Rd Bethesda MD 20816

PARKER, PETER DONALD MACDOUGALL, physics educator; b. N.Y.C., Dec. 14, 1936; s. Allan Elwood and Alice (Heywood) P.; m. Judith Curren, Dec. 27, 1958; children—Stephanie H., Gregory S. MacD., Gretchen R. B.A., Amherst Coll., 1958; Ph.D., Calif. Inst. Tech., 1963. Asst. physicist Brookhaven Nat. Lab., Upton, N.Y., 1963-66; prof. physics Yale U., New Haven, 1966—. Current work: Nuclear astrophysics. Subspecialty: Nuclear physics. Office: Dept Physics WNSL Yale U New Haven CT 06520

PARKER, ROBERT HALLETT, marine ecological consultant; b. Springfield, Mass., Feb. 14, 1922; married, 1945; 3 children. B.Sc., U. N.Mex., 1948, M.Sc., 1949; Mag. Sci. and Doctorand, Copenhagen U., 1962. Asst. in biology U. N.Mex., 1948-49; asst. in zoology Duke U., 1949-50; marine biologist State Game and Fish Commn., Tex., 1950-51; geophys. trainee Phillips Petroleum Co., 1951; research biologist Scripps Inst., U. Calif., 1951-58, jr. research ecologist, 1958-63; resident ecologist Systematics-Ecology Program, Marine Biol. Lab., Woods Hole, Mass., 1963-66; assoc. prof. biology and geology Tex. Christian U., 1966-70; pres., chmn. bd. Coastal Ecosystems Mgmt., Inc., Ft. Worth, 1970—; cons. Am. Mus. Natural History, 1957, Standard Oil Co. N.J., 1956-58, Pneumodyn Corp., 1960-61; research scientist Tex. Christian Research Found. Recipient awards Nat. Acad. Scis., 1959, 66, Acad. Scis. USSR, 1966. Fellow Geol. Soc. Am., Explorers Club Am.; mem. Soc. Systematic Zoology, Ecol. Soc. Am., Am. Soc. Limnology and Oceanography, Am. Assn. Petroleum Geology (assoc., award 1956). Subspecialties: Resource management; Sedimentology. Office: Coastal Ecosystems Management Inc 1031 N Henderson St Fort Worth TX 76107

PARKER, SHERWOOD I, physicist; b. Chgo., Mar. 31, 1932; s. Julius L. and Bertha S. (Sklovsky) P. B.S., U. Ill., 1953; M.A., U. Calif.-Berkeley, 1955, Ph.D., 1959. Asst. prof. U. Chgo., 1959-64, U. Calif., Berkeley, 1964-70; physicist Lawrence Berkeley Lab., 1971; U. Hawaii, Honolulu, 1972—. Contbr. articles to profl. jours. Mem. Am. Phys. Soc., IEEE, ACLU. Club: Commonwealth (San Francisco). Current work: Particle physics at the highest available energies, developing VLSI chips and new detectors for research at the Stanford Linear Accelerator Ctr., CERN (Geneva, Switzerland) and Fermilab. Subspecialty: Particle physics. Home: 520 Dwight Pl Berkeley CA 94704 Office: Lawrence Berkeley Lab Bldg 50A 6141 U Calif Berkeley CA 94720

PARKER, SIDNEY GLENN, research chemist; b. Cambell, Tex., Jan. 21, 1984; s. Sidney and Elizabeth (Ingle) P.; m. Betty Joyce Davis, Nov. 9, 1968; 1 child, Charles Covey. B.S., East Tex. State U., 1946; Ph.D., U. Tex., 1951. Research chemist Mobil Oil Co., Dallas, 1951-53, DuPont Co., Aiken, S.C., 1953-57; mem. tech. staff Tex. Instruments, Dallas, 1957—; cons. crystal growth NASA, Langley, Va., 1979-80, So. Meth. U., Dallas, 1981. Contbr. articles to profl. jours. and book. Patentee (7) in field. Mem. Am. Chem. Soc., Electrochem. Soc., Am. Assn. Crystal Growth. Republican. Baptist. Current work: Liquid phase epitaxial growth of HgCdTe on CdTe for infrared detectors. Subspecialties: Electronic materials; Solid state chemistry. Home: 6550 Highgate St Dallas TX 75214 Office: Texas Instruments PO Box 225936 MS147 Dallas TX 75265

PARKHURST, DAVID FRANK, mathematical ecologist; b. Pitts., Mar. 3, 1942; s. Howard Marion and Carrie Roberta (Frank) P.; m. Jennifer Ann Thompson, Dec. 28, 1965 (div. Jan. 1979); 1 child, Naomi Ann. B.S., U. Colo., 1965; M.S., U. Wis., 1968, Ph.D., 1970. Research asst. Inst. Arctic and Alpine Research, U. Colo., Boulder, 1962-66; lectr. U. Wis., Madison, 1967-70; research scientist Commonwealth Scientific & Indsl. Research Orgn., Aspendale, Victoria, Australia, 1970-73; assoc. prof. environ. sci. and biology Sch. Pub. and Environ. Affairs, Ind. U., Bloomington, 1973—; cons. Save Our Ind. Soils, Evansville, 1982-83, U.S. Forest Service, Washington, 1984; Electric Power Research Inst., Palo Alto, Calif., 1984—. Contbr. articles to profl. jours. commr., City of Bloomington Environ. Comm., 1974—, chmn., 1980-81. Fulbright-Hays grantee, Melbourne, Australia, 1966; Environ. Sci. and Engring. fellow AAAS and U.S. EPA, 1982. Mem. AAAS, Am. Soc. Plant Physiologists, Bot. Soc. Am., Ecol. Soc. Am., Soc. for Risk Analysis, Sigma Xi. Current work: Modelling CO2 diffusion and assimilation in relation to internal leaf structure, risk and decision analysis environmental toxicology. Subspecialties: Ecology (biology); Environmental risk and decision analysis. Office: Sch Public and Environmental Affairs Indiana Univ Bloomington IN 47405

PARKIN, JAMES LAMAR, surgeon, educator; b. Salt Lake City, June 2, 1939; s. E. Lamar and Mary Ilene (Soff) P.; m. Bonnie Dansie, July 1, 1963; children—Jeffrey L., Brett D., Matthew J., David S. B.S., U. Utah, 1963, M.D., 1966; M.S., U. Wash., 1970. Diplomate Am. Bd. Otolaryngology. Instr. dept. otolaryngology U. Wash., Seattle, 1971-72; asst. prof. dept. surgery U. Utah, Salt Lake City, 1972-76, assoc. prof., 1976-81, prof., 1981—, chmn. div. otolaryngology, 1974—, acting chmn. dept. surgery, 1982-84. Scoutmaster, dist. commr. Gt. Salt Lake council Boy Scouts Am., 1972-82; pres. Utah chpt. Am. Cancer Soc., Salt Lake City, 1984-86; bishop, stake pres. councilor Ch. of Jeses Christ of Latter Day Saints, Salt Lake City, 1978-85. Fellow Am. Acad. Otolaryngology, ACS, Am. Soc. Laser Medicine and Surgery, Am. Soc. Facial Plastic and Reconstructive Surgery; mem. Soc. Univ. Otolaryngology (pres. 1984-85), Assn. Acad. Depts. of Otolaryngology (sec. treas. 1982-84, pres.-elect 1984—). Republican. Club: Salt Lake Tennis. Current work: Cochlear implantation for the restoration of hearing; applications of laser technology in medicine and surgery. Subspecialties: Laser medicine; Otorhinolaryngology. Office: U Utah Sch Medicine 3C120 Univ Med Ctr Salt Lake City UT 84132

PARKINS, FREDERICK MILTON, pediatric dentistry educator; b. Princeton, N.J., Sept. 8, 1935; s. William Milton and Phyllis Virginia (Plyler) P.; m. Carolyn Rude; children—Bradford, Christopher, Eric. Student, Carleton Coll., 1956; D.D.S., U. Pa., 1960; M.S.D., U. N.C., 1965, Ph.D., 1969. Licensed dentist, Ky., Iowa, N.J., Pa. Asst. prof. U. Pa., Phila., 1967-68; chmn. dept. pediatric dentistry, 1968-69; chmn. dept. pedodontics U. Iowa, Iowa City, 1969-74, assoc. dean, 1974-79; dean dental sch. U. Louisville, Ky., 1979-84, prof., 1984—; cons. USPHS, Washington, 1969-74, VA, Phila., 1968-69. Contbr. articles to profl. publs., chpt. to book, presentations to profl. orgns. Vice pres. Youth Performing Arts Council, Louisville, 1981—; mem. exec. com. Falls City Sabanea Health Council, Louisville, 1981-83; campaign chmn. United Way-Dental Campaign, Louisville, 1983; v.p. St. Francis High Sch. Parents Assn., Louisville, 1982. Served to lt. USN, 1960-63. Fellow Am. Acad. Pediatric Dentistry, 1969, Inst. Medicine, 1977, AAAS, 1982, USPHS-NIH, 1964-69. Mem. Am. Dental Assn. (cons. 1973-81), Am. Assn. Dental Schs. (chmn. 1978-81), Internat. Assn. Dental research (mem. nat. affairs com. 1980—), Biophysical Soc., Sigma Xi. Unitarian. Lodge: Rotary. Current work: Fluoride therapy and body metabolism, vital tooth bleaching, health policy studies. Subspecialties: Cariology; Preventive dentistry. Home: 5401 Juniper Beach Prospect KY 40059 Office: U Louisville Sch Dentistry 501 S Preston Louisville KY 40292

PARKINSON, BRUCE ALAN, research chemist, photographer; b. Rochester, Minn., Mar. 1, 1951; s. George H. and Marion L. (Erickson) P. B.S. in Chemistry, Iowa State U., 1972; Ph.D. in Chemistry, Calif. Inst. Tech., 1977. Postdoctoral fellow Bell Labs., Murray Hill, N.J., 1978; staff scientist Ames Lab., Iowa, 1979-82; sr. scientist Solar Energy Research Lab., Golden, Colo., 1982-85; research chemist E.I. du Pont de Nemours, Wilmington, Del., 1985—. One-man show Meml. Union Iowa State U., 1979. Patentee in field. Mem. Am. Chem. Soc., Electrochem. Soc. Current work: Direct conversion of solar energy to fuels and chemicals. Subspecialties: Physical chemistry; Photochemistry. Home: 103 Topsfield Rd Hockess DE 19707 Office: DuPont Exptl Sta E328/105 Wilmington DE 19898

PARKS, ALLEN DANFORTH, astronomer, educator; b. Charleston, W.Va., Sept. 4, 1945; s. William Danforth and Pauline Elizabeth (Poff) P.; m. Firelei Dianne Midkiff, Sept. 6, 1969; children—Joshua Daniel, Nathan Allen, Tessa Anne. B.A. in Math., Marshall U., 1969; M.S. in Astronomy, Pa. State U., 1972, Ph.D. in Astronomy, 1975. Analyst Computer Scis. Corp., Silver Spring, Md., 1974-76; system engr. Gen. Electric Co., Springfield, Va., 1976-81; astronomer Naval Surface Weapons Ctr., Dept. Navy, Dahlgren, Va., 1981—; cons., Fredericksburg, Va., 1976-80. Contbr. articles to profl. publs. Prin. danseur Fredericksburg Ballet Co., 1982—. Recipient Outstanding Performance award Dept. Navy, 1982, 83, Research and Devel. award Def. Mapping Agy., 1983. Mem. Am. Astron. Soc. Current work: Satellite dynamics, orbit determination, mission analysis, planetary interiors, stellar structure and evolution, computational physics, computer simulation. Subspecialties: Satellite studies; Theoretical astrophysics. Home: 9 Norman Ct Fredericksburg VA 22401 Office: Space Flight Scis Br Naval Surface Weapons Ctr K-13 Dahlgren VA 22448

PARKS, CARL RAMSEY, retired research chemist; b. Alliance, Ohio, Mar. 20, 1918; s. Albert J. and Louesa W. (Smithberger) P.; m. Kathleen L. Hutson, Mar. 22, 1945; children—Linda L., Connie S. B.S., Mount Union Coll., 1939; M.S., Ohio U., 1941. Research chemist Goodyear Tire and Rubber Co., Akron, Ohio, 1941-46, sr. research chemist, 1947-66, research scientist, 1967-80, research assoc., 1981-84, ret., 1984. Contbr. articles to profl. jours. Patentee in field. Mem. Am. Chem. Soc. (rubber div.). Republican. Mem. Ch. of Brethren. Current work: Oxidation, ozonation and vulcanization of rubber. Subspecialties: Organic chemistry; Polymer chemistry. Home: 3025 Shade Rd Akron OH 44313

PARKS, LEO W., microbial physiology educator; b. Wetaug, Ill., Nov. 21, 1930; s. Marion and May Reola (Kearney) P.; m. Nancy Caroline Farrar, Aug. 17, 1957; children—Michael Douglas, Bruce William. B.S., U. Ill., 1952; A.M., Ind. U., 1953; Ph.D., U. Wash., 1956. Asst. prof. dept. microbiology Oreg. State U., Corvallis, 1958-64, assoc. prof., 1966-72, prof., 1973-83, 84—; vis. scientist U. Copenhagen, 1965-66; prof. conventionne U. Louis Pasteur, Strasbourg, France, 1972-73; sci. officer Office Naval Research, Arlington, Va., 1983-84. Contbr. articles to profl. jours. Fellow Am. Acad. Microbiology; mem. Am. Soc. Microbiology, Am. Soc. Biol. Chemists, Soc. Biol. Chemistry, Phi Kappa Phi. Lutheran. Lodge: Kiwanis (treas. Corvallis 1983—). Current work: Membrane physiology; structure function relationships of lipids; lipid synthesis. Subspecialties: Membrane biology; Microbiology. Home: 1105 NW Fernwood Circle Corvallis OR 97330 Office: Dept Microbiology Oreg State U Corvallis OR 97331

PARKS, OATTIS ELWYN, geologist; b. Atlanta, July 24, 1918; s. James Edward and Jennie M. (Oattis) P.; children—Oattis E., Jr., Henry B., Camilla F., Michele M. B.A., Emory U., 1947; M.A., Tex. Christian U., 1954; postgrad. Fla. State U., 1964-67. Guest lectr. U. Mass., Amherst, 1966, Fla. A&M U., Tallahassee, 1965; v.p. exploration and devel. Amax Coal, Indpls., 1967-72, v.p. Amax Internat. London, 1972-74; founder and pres. Newco Engring. & Coal Devel., Indpls., 1975—; pres. Newsel, Inc., Indpls., 1977—; bd. regents Wright State U., Dayton, Ohio, 1977—. Author geol. papers. Served to col. USAF, 1940-64, ETO. Decorated D.F.C., Commendation with oak leaf clusters, Silver Staf, Air Medal with four oak leaf clusters. Mem. Assn. Profl. Geological Scientists, Geol. Soc. Am., Soc. Econ. Geologists, Ind. Acad. Sci. Presbyterian. Lodge: Mason. Current work: Slinder holes in geophyis usage; depositional environments as related to coal deposits; model structuring, prediction of coal quality and roofing stability from models. Subspecialties: Sedimentology; Coal. Home: 109 C-4 Juniper St Freeport FL 32439 Office: Newco Engring & Coal Devel 6745 South Gray Rd Suite J Indianapolis IN 46237

PARLIMENT, THOMAS HOLDEN, chemist; b. Hackensack, N.J., Jan. 26, 1939; s. Clifford W. and Mildred (Holden) P.; m. Marjorie Wood, Oct. 3, 1964; children—Cynthia Lynne, Tammy Jeanne. B.S., Lehigh U., 1961; Ph.D., U. Mass., 1965. Research scientist, Gen. Foods, Tarrytown, N.Y., 1965—. Contbr. chpts. to books, articles to profl. jours. Patentee in field. Served to capt. U.S. Army, 1966-68. Recipient Chmn. award Gen. Foods Corp., 1971. Mem. Am. Chem. Soc. (chmn. flavor sub-div. 1984—), N.Y. Chromatography Soc. (chmn. 1981, bd. dirs., treas. 1979-80), Am. Chem. Soc., Sigma Xi. Current work: Isolation and identification of food aromas and other natural products; mechanisms of biological and thermal generation of aromas. Subspecialties: Food science and technology; Organic chemistry. Home: 11 Hereford Ln New City NY 10956 Office: Gen Foods Tech Center 555 S Broadway Tarrytown NY 10591

PARMENTER, ROBERT ROSS, biology, ecology educator; b. Boston, Oct. 15, 1951; s. William Kean and Rachel Ann (Ross) P.; m. Cheryl Ann Gast, Dec. 21, 1983; 1 child, Shane Michael. B.A., Colo. Coll., 1974; M.S., U. Ga., 1978; Ph.D., Utah State U., 1982. Biol. cons. Ga. Dept. Transp., Atlanta, 1978; postdoctoral research assoc. Utah State U. Ecology Ctr., Logan, 1982—. Contbr. articles to profl. jours. Mem. Ecol. Soc. Am., Am. Soc. Mammalogists, Am. Soc. Ichthyologists and Herpetologists. Current work: Plant and animal succession (re-colonization) on disturbed areas such as Mt. St. Helens volcano and surface coal mines. Subspecialties: Ecology (biology); Ecosystems analysis. Office: Dept Biology UMC-53 Utah State Univ Logan UT 84322

PARNELL, THOMAS ALFRED, physicist, educator; b. Lumberton, N.C., Nov. 24, 1931; s. Jonathan A. and Lula (Lashley) P.; m. Elizabeth Brite, June 4, 1955; children—Gina A., Marc T. B.S., U. N.C., 1954, M.S., 1962, Ph.D., 1965. Adj. researcher dept. physics, U. N.C., Chapel Hill, 1963-65; ops. analyst U.S. Air Force, Wiesbaden, Fed. Republic Germany, 1965-66; asst. prof. physics Marshall U., Huntington, W.Va., 1966-67; physicist NASA/Marshall Space Flight Ctr., Huntsville, Ala., 1967—; mem. grad. faculty U. Ala., Huntsville, 1977—. Contbr. articles to profl. jours. Served to lt. USN, 1954-58. Recipient Exceptional Sci. Achievement medal NASA, 1976, 80. Mem. Am. Phys. Soc., Sigma Xi. Club: Monte Sano (Huntsville). Current work: Cosmic ray physics, gamma ray astronomy, nuclear instrumentation techniques, astrophysics. Subspecialties: Cosmic ray high energy astrophysics; Gamma ray high energy astrophysics. Home: 907 Corinth Circle Huntsville AL 35801 Office: NASA Marshall Space Flight Ctr Mail Code E562 Huntsville AL 35812

PARR, ALBERT CLARENCE, research physicist; b. Tooele, Utah, June 22, 1942; s. Trafton C. and Esther L. (Schuldheisz) P.; m. Ruth E. Pieplow, June 27, 1965; children: Robin, Trafton. B.S. in Math, Oreg. State U., 1964; M.S. in Physics, U. Chgo., 1965, Ph.D. in Physics, 1971. Research assoc. U. Chgo., 1970; asst. prof. U. Ala.-Tuscaloosa, 1971-76, assoc. prof., 1976-80; research physicist far ultraviolet physics sect. Nat. Bur. Standards, Washington, 1980—. Contbr. articles to sci jours. Served with USNR, 1960-66. Recipient cert. of recognition Nat. Bur. Standards, 1979, 1981. Mem. Optical Soc. Am., Am. Phys. Soc. Lodge: Elks. Current Work: Photoelectron spectroscopy, synchrotron radiation. Subspecialty: Atomic and molecular physics.

PARR, GARY RAYMOND, biochemist, educator; b. Janesville, Wis., Nov. 22, 1942; s. Harold Lawrence and Thelma Irene (Quade) P.; m. Susan Dale Resneck, Sept. 27, 1968 (div. Feb. 1977); 1 dau., Alexandra Lynn. B.S., U. So. Calif.-Los Angeles, 1965; Ph.D., U. Wis.-Madison, 1973. Postdoctoral assoc. Cornell U., Ithaca, N.Y., 1973-75; research assoc. Ithaca Coll., 1975-76; staff fellow NIH, Bethesda, Md., 1976-78, sr. staff fellow, 1978-81; asst. prof.

Clemson (S.C.) Univ., 1982—. Served to 1st lt. U.S Army, 1966-68, Vietnam. Decorated Bronze Star. Mem. Am. Soc. Biol. Chemists, Am. Chem. Soc., N.Y. Acad. Scis., AAAS, Sigma Xi. Current Work: Mechanism of protein folding, fast kinetic techniques, differential scanning calorimetry. Subspecialties: Biophysical chemistry; Kinetics. Office: Clemson U Dept Biochemistry 132 Long Hall Clemson SC 29631

PARR, JAMES FLOYD, JR., soil microbiologist; b. Seattle, Feb. 20, 1929; s. James Floyd and Clara Georgian (Kestner) P.; m. Carol June Cunningham, Aug. 29, 1964; children: Lauren Melissa, James Floyd. B.S. in Agr, Wash. State U., 1952; M.S. in Soil Microbiology, Purdue U., 1957, Ph.D. in Soil Microbiology, 1961. Irrigation extension agt. Agrl. Extension Service, Wash. State U., Pullman, 1953-54; county extension agt. Agrl. Extension Service, Mont. State U., Bozeman, 1954-55; chemist Calif. Dept. Water Resources, Sacramento, 1957-58; instr. agronomy dept. Purdue U., West Lafeytte, Ind., 1958-61; research assoc. dept. botany U. Mich., Ann Arbor, 1961-63; research chemist, microbiologist TVA, Muscle Shoals, Ala., 1963-67; research leader Agrl. Research Service U.S. Dept. Agr., Baton Rouge, 1967-75, chief biol. waste mgmt. and organic resources Lab., Beltsville, Md., 1975-84; coordinator USDA/USAID Dryland Mgmt. Project, Beltsville, Md. and Washington, D.C., 1984—; cons. to developing countries on waste mgmt. and recycling of organic wastes. Contbr. numerous articles on soil microbiology to profl. jours. Served with USN, 1946-48. Recipient Dept. Agr. Superior Service award, 1977, Cert. of Merit, 1981. Fellow Am. Soc. Agronomy, Soil Sci. Soc. Am.; mem. Sigma Xi, Alpha Zeta, Phi Kappa Phi. Patentee in field. Current Work: Conduct research to develop methods for handling, processing, composting and utilizing, municipal, and industrial wastes on agricultural lands Subspecialties: Resource conservation; Soil science. Office: Nat Program Staff Agrl Research US Dept Agr Beltsville MD 20705

PARR, ROBERT GHORMLEY, chemistry educator; b. Chgo., Sept. 22, 1921; s. Leland Wilbur and Grace (Ghormley) P.; m. Jane Bolstad, May 28, 1944; children: Steven Robert, Jeanne Karen, Carol Jane. A.B. magna cum laude with high honors in Chemistry, Brown U., 1942; Ph.D. in Phys. Chemistry, U. Minn., 1947. Asst. prof. chemistry U. Minn., 1947-48; mem. faculty Carnegie Inst. Tech., 1948-62, prof. chemistry, 1957-62, Johns Hopkins U., 1962-74, chmn. dept., 1969-72; William R. Kenan, Jr. prof. theoretical chemistry U. N.C., Chapel Hill, 1974—; Vis. prof. chemistry, mem. Center Advanced Study U. Ill., 1962; distinguished vis. prof. State U. N.Y. at Buffalo, also Pa. State U., 1967; vis. prof. Japan Soc. Promotion Sci., 1968, 79, U. Haifa, 1977, Free U. Berlin, 1977; Firth prof. U. Sheffield, 1976; Chmn. com. postdoctoral fellowships in chemistry Nat. Acad. Sci.-NRC, 1961-63; chmn. panel theoretical chemistry Westheimer com. survey chemistry Nat. Acad. Sci., 1964; mem. council Gordon Research Conf., 1974-76; mem. Commn. on Human Resources, NRC, 1979-82. Author: Quantum Theory of Molecular Electronic Structure, 1963, also numerous articles.; Asso. editor: Jour. Chem. Physics, 1956-58, Chem. Revs, 1961-63, Jour. Phys. Chemistry, 1963-67, 77-79, Am. Chem. Soc. Monographs, 1966-71, Theoretica Chimica Acta, 1966-69; bd. editors: Jour. Am. Chem. Soc, 1969-77; adv. editorial bd.: Internat. Jour. Quantum Chemistry, 1967—, Chem. Physics Letters, 1967-79. Recipient Outstanding Achievement award U. Minn., 1968, N.C. Disting. Chemist award, 1982; fellow U. Chgo., 1949; research asso., 1957; Fulbright scholar U. Cambridge, Eng., 1953-54; Guggenheim fellow, 1953-54; NSF sr. postdoctoral fellow U. Oxford (Eng.) and Commonwealth Sci. and Indsl. Research Orgn., Melbourne, Australia, 1967-68; Sloan fellow, 1956-60. Fellow Am. Phys. Soc. (chmn. div. chem. physics 1963-64), AAAS; mem. Am. Chem. Soc. (chmn. div. phys. chemistry 1978), AAUP, Am. Acad. Arts and Sci., Nat. Acad. Scis., Internat. Acad. Quantum Molecular Sci. (v.p. 1973-79, hon. pres. 1979—), Phi Beta Kappa, Sigma Xi, Phi Lambda Upsilon, Pi Mu Epsilon. Subspecialty: Theoretical chemistry. Home: 701 Kenmore Rd Chapel Hill NC 27514 Office: Dept Chemistry U North Carolina Chapel Hill NC 27514

PARREIRA, HELIO CORREA, chemist; b. Rio de Janeiro, Brazil, July 12, 1926, came to U.S., 1960, s. Francisco Correa and Maria Faria Parreira; m. Dulcinea M. Moreira, Feb. 1, 1953; children—Rogerio M., Regina M. B.S. in Chemistry, U. Brazil, Rio de Janeiro, 1949, tchrs. diploma, 1950; Ph.D., U. Cambridge, 1958. Phys. chemist Brazilian Atomic Commn., 1958-67, research assoc. Columbia U., N.Y.C., 1960-62, dir. instrn. in chemistry Joint Program for Tech. Edn., 1960-64, asst. prof., 1963-65; group leader and prin. scientist Inmont Corp., Clifton, N.J., 1965-69; asst. dir. research Johnson & Johnson, Brazil, 1969-70, exec. dir. research, 1970-72, sr. research assoc., New Brunswick, N.J., 1972-84, sr. scientist, 1984—. Contbr. articles to profl. jours. Contbg. editor Chemistry A to Z, 1964. Brit. Council scholar Rio de Janeiro, 1954; Oliver Gatty Scholar U. Cambridge, 1956-58. Mem. Am. Chem. Soc., Sigma Xi. Current work: Electrokinetics; surface phenomena in general; transcutaneous drug delivery. Subspecialties: Surface chemistry; Physical chemistry. Office: Johnson & Johnson Products Research New Brunswick NJ 08903

PARRISH, JOHN WESLEY, JR., biologist, educator; b. Dennison, Ohio, Mar. 5, 1941; s. John Wesley and Dorothy Irene (Dickinson) P.; m. Paula Schmanke, July 9, 1966; children: Corinne Danelle, Wesley Allen. B.S., Denison U., 1963; M.A., Bowling Green State U., 1970, Ph.D. (Univ. fellow), 1974. Tchr. sci. Northside Jr. High Sch., Norfolk, Va., 1967; vis. instr. dept. biology Kenyon Coll., 1973-74; NIH postdoctoral fellow dept. zoology U. Tex., Austin, 1974-76; asst. prof. biology Emporia State U., 1976-82, assoc. prof., 1982—. Vice pres. Kanza Audubon Soc., Emporia, Kans., 1978, pres., 1979-80, bd. dirs., 1981—. Served to lt. USNR, 1964-67. Josselyn Van Tyne Fund grantee, 1968; Emporia State U. Faculty Research Com. grantee, 1977, 79-85; Kans. Fish and Game Commn. grantee, 1985; named Xi Phi Outstanding Univ. Faculty mem., 1985. Mem. Am. Ornithologist's Union (student award 1971), Am. Soc. Zoologists, Cooper Ornithol. Soc., Kans. Acad. Sci., Kans. Ornithol. Soc., Soc. Study Reprodn. Democrat. Methodist. Current Work: Photoreception, hematology, bioenergetics photoperiodism, pineal gland function, placental function, testicular function. Subspecialties: Comparative physiology; Reproductive biology. Office: Emporia State U Div Biol Sci Emporia KS 66801

PARRISH, MARK DAVID, entomologist; b. San Bernardino, Calif., June 21, 1956; s. Joseph Howard and Alma Jane (Resendez) P.; m. Patricia Clare Dooley, July 1, 1979. B.S. in Pest Mgmt., U. Calif.-Berkeley, 1978; M.S. in Entomology, Rutgers U., 1982, Ph.D. in Entomology, 1984. Intern, Inst. Biol. & Integrated Control, 1978-79; enomol. cons., N.J., 1982-84; tchr. Rutgers U., 1981-84; information specialist Rhone-Poulenc Inc., Agrochem. Div., Monmouth Junction, N.J., 1984—. Contbr. articles to profl. jours. N.J. Pest Control scholar, 1983-84; Compton Entomol. Trust award Rutgers U., 1983, 84. Mem. Entomol. Soc. Am., AAAS, Ecol. Soc. Am., Internat. Union Study of Social Insects, Sigma Xi. Roman Catholic. Current work: Aspects of foraging behavior in social insects; ecological modeling; statistical analysis; computer software engineering; agrochemical research and development. Subspecialties: Behavioral ecology; Software engineering. Home: 1701 S Crescent Blvd Yardley PA 19067 Office: Rhone-Poulenc Inc Agrochemical Div PO Box 125 BHL I Monmouth Junction NJ 08852

PARRISH, MILTON EARL, chemist; b. Richmond, Va., Apr. 22, 1946; s. Linwood Gibson and Jane Arrowsmith (Parsons) P.; m. Karla Jean Miller, Aug. 16, 1975; children—Lauren Gibson, Jessica Austin. B.Sc., U. Richmond, 1969. Research scientist Philip Morris Research and Devel., Richmond, Va., 1969—. Contbr. articles to profl. jours. Served with U.S. Army, 1969-71. Mem. Am. Chem. Soc., AAAS, Optical Soc. Am., Gamma Sigma Epsilon. Methodist. Current work: Use tunable diode laser infrared spectroscopy to quantitate gaseous components in complex and dynamic systems; use of computers and application of chemometrics to process data. Subspecialties: Laser spectroscopy; Analytical chemistry. Office: Philip Morris Research and Devel PO Box 26583 Richmond VA 23261

PARRISH, WILLIAM RUTLEDGE, chemical engineer; b. Indpls., Dec. 5, 1940; m. Joan S. Parrish, Sept. 16, 1967; children—Michael, Rachel, David. B.Chem. Engring., Ga. Inst. Tech., 1962; M.S., U. Calif.-Berkeley, 1966, Ph.D., 1970. Chem. engr. Nat. Bur. Standards, Boulder, Colo., 1971-78; sr. research engr. Phillips Petroleum Co., Bartlesville, Okla., 1978-80, research assoc., 1980—. Contbr. articles to profl. jours. Recipient Young Authors award Electrochem. Soc., 1970. Mem. Am. Inst. Chem. Engrs., Am. Chem. Soc., Am. Inst. Chem. Engring., Gas Processors Assn. (mem. enthalpy research com. 1982—), Sigma. Xi. Current work: Measurement and correlation of thermophysical properties of fluids, novel application of calorimetry, phase equilibria. Subspecialties: Chemical engineering; Thermodynamics.

PARROTT, ROBERT HAROLD, physician, educator; b. Jackson Heights, N.Y., Dec. 29, 1923; s. Harold Leslie and Ruth Mabel (Hargrove) P.; June 2, 1951; children: Timothy, Maureen, Daniel, Theresa, Christopher, Edward. Student, Fordham U.; M.D., Georgetown U., 1949. Intern Hosp. of St. Raphael, New Haven, Conn., 1949-50; resident Children's Hosp. of D.C., 1950-52; staff pediatrician, chief Pediatric Unit, Lab. of Clin. Investigation, Nat. Inst. Allergy and Infectious Diseases, NIH, Bethesda, Md., 1952-56; physician-in-chief, dir. Research Found., Children's Hosp. of D.C., Washington, 1956-62, dir., 1962-84, dir. emeritus, 1985—; prof. child health and devel. George Washington U. Mem. Am. Acad. Pediatrics, Am. Pediatric Soc., Am. Acad. Med. Dirs., Am. Coll. Physician Execs., D.C. Med. Soc., Infectious Diseases Soc. Subspecialty: Virology (medicine). Home: 9852 Singleton Dr Bethesda MD 20817 Office: 111 Michigan Ave NW Washington DC 20010

PARRY, JOHN O., health physicist, researcher; b. Oceanside, Calif., Apr. 16, 1952; s. John O. and Helen A. (Phetteplace) P.; m. Valorie D. Steller, June 9, 1979; children: Jennifer Lynn, Jason Charles. B.S. in Applied Physics, Mich. Technol. U., 1974; M.S. in Material Sci., Washington State U. Health physicist, unit 1 Dresden-Commonwealth Edison, Morris, Ill., 1974-76, lead health physicist, 1976-78, radiation protection/chem. supr., 1978-80; corp. health physicist Wash. Public Power System, Richland, 1980-82, sr. health physicist, 1982-83, prin. health physicist, 1983-85; radiation protection mgr. Indian-Point Consol. Edison, 1985—; pub. speaker on radiation protection, 1974-82. Served to capt. C.E. U.S. Army, 1974. Mem. Health Physics Soc. (chmn. public info. 1982-83, sec. 1983-84, nat. com. state and Fed. legislation 1983-86); mem. Am. Nuclear Soc. (assoc.). Club: Am. Bridge. Current Work: Radiation protection in nuclear power plants; radiation effects on materials. Subspecialties: Nuclear fission; Nuclear engineering. Office: Indian Point Nuclear Plant Broadway and Bleakley Aves Bucanan NY

PARS, HARRY GEORGE, chemist, pharmaceutical company executive, consultant; b. New Bedford, Mass., Feb. 7, 1928; s. George Peter and Areti (Courousi) P.; m. Joan Muriel Dunne, Aug. 17, 1952; children—Heather Ann Pars Campion, Dawn Elizabeth Pars McKenna. A.B., Harvard U., 1953; M.S. in Organic Chemistry, U. Mich., 1955, Ph.D. in Organic Chemistry, 1967. Mng. ptnr. Sharps Assocs., Cambridge, Mass., 1970—; chmn., chief exec. officer H.G. Pars Pharm. Labs., Inc., Cambridge, 1976—; chmn., chief exec. officer SISA Toxicol. Labs., Inc., Cambridge, 1983—. Editor: The Other Side of Marijuana Research, 1973; contbr. articles to profl. jours., chpts. to books. Chmn., founder Nat. Council Indsl. Innovation, Washington, 1979. Served with USN, 1945-47. Mem. Research Mgmt. Assn. Boston, Am. Chem. Soc., N.Y. Acad. Scis., Nat. Small Bus. Assn., AAAS. Current work: Drug research and development; nutrition and health. Subspecialty: Medicinal chemistry. Office: HG Pars Pharm Labs Inc 763 Concord Ave Cambridge MA 02138

PARSIGNAULT, DANIEL RAYMOND, physicist; b. Paris, Feb. 5, 1937; s. Roger and Carmen (Mora) P.; m. Helen M. Winter, Oct. 22, 1960 (div. 1979); children—Jennifer C., Daniel H., Cybele H. B.S. in Elec. Engring., U. Wis., 1960; M.S. in Physics, So. Ill. U., 1961; Docteur es Sciences, U. Paris, 1964. Research fellow Calif. Inst. Tech., Pasadena, 1964-66; asst. prof. Ohio State U., Columbus, 1966-68; sr. staff scientist AS & E, Cambridge, Mass., 1968-76; physicist Harvard/Smithsonian, Cambridge, 1976-78; sr. physicist Emmanuel Coll., Lexington, Mass., 1978-84; project dir. Ion Beam Tech., Beverly, Mass., 1984-85; sr. physicist Visidyde, Burlington, Mass., 1985—. Contbr. articles to profl. jours. Mem. Am. Phys. Soc. Current work: Upper atmospheric research. Subspecialty: X-ray high energy astrophysics. Office: Visidyne 5 Corporate Pl 5 Bedford St Burlington MA 01803

PARSONS, JAMES EUGENE, biology educator; b. Lima, Ohio, Nov. 10, 1939; s. Virgil Lorain and Dorothy Mae (Sandy) P. B.S., Ohio State U., 1961, M.S., 1963, Ph.D., 1977. Registered microbiologist, specialist microbiologist Am. Acad. Microbiology clin. lab. specialist Nat. Cert. Agy. for Med. Lab. Personnel. Clin. microbiologist Akron Gen. Med. Ctr., Akron, Ohio, 1977-81; adj. prof. biology U. Akron, 1979-81, adj. prof. Inst. Biomed. Engring. Research, 1979-81; asst. prof. clin. microbiology Northeastern Ohio U. Coll. Medicine, Rootstown, Ohio, 1978-81; asst. prof. biology Bloomsburg (Pa.) U., 1982—; chmn. bd. Animalcule, Ltd., Akron, 1978—; cons. Medina (Ohio) Community Hosp., 1978—. Bd. dirs. Canton (Ohio) Coll., 1978-81. Recipient Tchr of Yr. award Akron Gen. Med. Technologists, 1979. Mem. Am. Soc. Microbiology, Electron Microscopy Soc. Am., Med. Mycology Soc. Am., N.Y. Acad. Scis., Ohio Acad. Sci., South Central Assn. Clin. Microbiology, Sigma Xi, Phi Kappa Phi. Current work: Rapid identification of mycobacteria and pathogenic fungi; automated analysis in the clinical microbiology laboratory; clinical parasitology. Subspecialties: Microbiology (medicine); Epidemiology. Home: 3018 Olney Rd Kalamazoo MI 49007 Office: Bloomsburg State College 102 Harline Science Center Bloomsburg PA 17815

PARSONS, MICHAEL L., analytical chemist, consultant; b. Oklahoma City, Apr. 20, 1940; m. Karen O. Bridwell, Aug. 6, 1958 (div. 1970); children—Stephen M., David R.; m. Virginia E. Thomas, Mar. 23, 1972; children—Guinn E., L. Erin. Student Austin Coll., 1958-61; B.A., Kans. State Coll. (now Pittsburg State U.), 1962, M.S., 1963; Ph.D., U. Fla., 1966. Research chemist Phillips Petroleum Co., Bartlesville, Okla., 1966-67; asst. prof. chemistry Ariz. State U., Tempe, 1967-72, assoc. prof., 1972-78, prof., 1978-84; dep. group leader Los Alamos Nat. Lab., N.Mex., 1984—; cons. Goodyear Tire and Rubber Co., Akron, Ohio, 1983—, Motorola Co., Phoenix, 1976—. Author 4 books. Contbr. numerous articles to sci. jours. Mem. Soc. for Applied Spectroscopy (pres. 1979, William F. Meggers award 1967, 75), Am. Chem. Soc. (Outstanding chemist central Ariz. sect. 1981), Optical Soc. Am., Coblentz Soc., Sigma Xi. Republican. Unitarian. Current work: Analytical atomic spectroscopy, inductively coupled plasma excitation sources and multivariate statistical analysis of large chemical data bases. Subspecialty: Analytical chemistry. Home: 468 Aragon Los Alamos NM 87544Office: Los Alamos Nat Lab CHM-1 MS-G740 Los Alamos NM 87545

PARSONS, WILLIAM ANDREWS, environmental engineer; b. Cedar Rapids, Iowa, Nov. 11, 1923; s. Douglas Eugene and Olive Lyle (Chandler) P.; m. Amelia Skovenski, Jan. 12, 1953; children—Ted Richard, Nancy Ellen. B.S. in Sanitary Engring., U. Ill., 1949; Ph.D. in Environ. Sci., Rutgers U., 1954. Registered profl. engr., N.J., Va., N.C. Asst. research specialist Rutgers U., New Brunswick, N.J., 1953-56; prof. engring. Va. Poly. Inst., Blacksburg, 1956-67; assoc. Quirk Lawler Matusky Engrs., N.Y.C., 1967-70; exec. engr. Davy McKee Corp., Cleve., 1970-82; tech. dir. H.K. Ferguson Co., Cleve., 1983—. Author: Chemical Treatment of Wastes. Contbr. articles to profl. publs. Mem. ASCE, Am. Inst. Chem. Engrs., Water Pollution Control Fedn., Am. Water Works Assn., Sigma Xi. Subspecialties: Civil engineering; Hazardous waste disposal. Home: 3412 Ridge Park Dr Cleveland OH 44147 Office: HK Ferguson Co 1 Erieview Plaza Cleveland OH 44114

PARTHASARATHY, MANDAYAM VEERAMBHUDI, plant biologist, educator; b. Bangalore, India; m. Rama. B.S., U. Madras, India, 1953; M.S., U. Poona, India, 1957; Ph.D., Cornell U., 1966; Montgomery fellow, Technische Hochschule, Zurich, Switzerland, 1968-69. Asst. prof. plant biology Cornell U., Ithaca, N.Y., 1969-70, assoc. prof., 1977-80, assoc. prof. sect. plant biology, div. biol. scis., 1980-83, prof. plant biology, 1984—, chmn. dept., 1984—, also dir. electron microscopy facility. NSF grantee, 1976—. Mem. Bot. Soc. Am., Microbeam Analysis Soc., Electron Microscopy Soc. Current Work: Structure and function of the food conducting tissues in plant (phloem), cytoskeleton of higher plants cells. Subspecialties: Cell biology; Developmental biology. Office: Sect Plant Biology 204 Plant Sci Cornell U Ithaca NY 14853

PARTRIDGE, BRIAN LLOYD, researcher, biologist, educator; b. Berea, Ohio, May 16, 1953; s. Bruce James and Mary Janice (Smith) P.; m. Nancy Jane Meredith, May 11, 1974; children: Brett James, Justin Ross. Student, Stanford U., 1970-71; B.Sc. with honors (Govt. B.C. scholar, C.A. Banks Meml. fellow), U. B.C., 1974; D.Phil (NRC Can. fellow, NSF grad. fellow), Oxford (Eng.) U., 1978. NSF postdoctoral fellow Scripps Instn. Oceanography, 1978-79; lectr. U. Calif., San Diego, 1979; asst. prof. biology U. Miami, Coral Gables, Fla., 1979—; vis. research fellow Scripps Instn. Oceanography, 1980; cons. NSF, NIH. Reviewer numerous jours.; contbr. articles profl. jours. Grantee NIMH, 1982-83. Mem. Soc. Neurosci., Internat. Soc. Neuroethology (charter), Animal Behavior Soc., Assn. Study of Animal Behaviour, Sigma Xi. Current Work: Neuroethology, spatial sensing by teleost lateral lines, researcher in neuroethology. Subspecialties: Comparative neurobiology; Ethology. Home: 6221 SW 61st St South Miami FL 33143 Office: Dept of Biology University of Miami Coral Gables FL 33124

PARTRIDGE, LLOYD D(ONALD), physiology educator; b. Cortland, N.Y., Dec. 15, 1922; s. Bert James and L. Marian (Rice) P.; m. Jean Marie Rutledge, Aug. 6, 1944; children—L. Donald, Jr., David L., Gayle A. Partridge Spence. B.S. in Chemistry, U. Mich., 1948, M.S. in Physiology, 1949, Ph.D. in Physiology, 1953. Instr. Physiology U. Mich. Med. Sch., Ann Arbor, 1953-56; asst. prof. Yale U. Med. Sch., New Haven, Conn., 1956-62; assoc. prof. U. Tenn. Med. Sch., Memphis, 1962-70, prof., 1970—; vis. prof. U. Vt., Burlington, 1967-69, U. Western Ont., Can., 1980—, Med. Coll. Ohio, 1985. cons. UCLA, 1979—. Contbg. author: Handbook Bioengineering-Propriocepntive Measure, 1978; Handbook Physiology-Muscle The Motor, 1982. Contbr. articles to profl. jours., chpts. to books. Served with AUS, 1944-46. Mem. Bio-Engring. Soc. (exec. bd., publ. chmn.; sect. editor Annals Biomed. Engring.), Am. Phys. Soc. (chmn. totorial com.), IEEE (publ. bd., assoc. editor jours.), Neurosci. Soc., Am. Acad. Neurology. Current work: Biomedical engineering and computer analysis and modeling, information processing and neural control dynamics, muscle function as a controller; methods of measurement and analysis scientific communication and literature, sensory transduction and filtering. Subspecialties: Neurophysiology; Biomedical engineering. Office: U Tenn Med Sch Physiology Dept Memphis TN 38163

PARTRIDGE, ROBERT BRUCE, astronomy educator, university dean; b. Honolulu, May 16, 1940; s. Robert B. and Laura Lea (Johnson) P.; m. Jane C. Widseth, Aug. 28, 1976; 1 son, John. A.B., Princeton U., 1962; D.Phil., Oxford U., 1965. Inst. to asst. prof. Princeton (N.J.) U., 1965-70; asso. prof. to prof. astronomy Haverford (Pa.) Coll., 1970-82, dean, 1982—. Contbr. articles to profl. jours. Rhodes scholar, 1962; A.P. Sloan fellow, 1971-75; Fulbright fellow, 1979. Mem. Am. Phys. Soc., Internat. Astron. Union, Am. Astron. Soc., Sigma Xi. Current Work: Cosmology, microwave background radiation, galaxy formation, radio astronomy. Subspecialties: Cosmology; Radio and microwave astronomy. Home: 628 Overhill Rd Ardmore PA 19003 Office: Haveford Coll Haverford PA 19041

PARZEN, EMANUEL, statistical scientist, educator; b. N.Y.C., Apr. 21, 1929; s. Samuel and Sarah (Getzel) P.; m. Carol Tenowitz, July 12, 1959; children: Sara Leah, Michael Isaac. A.B. in Math, Harvard U., 1949; M.A., U. Calif.-Berkeley, 1951, Ph.D., 1953. Research scientist Columbia, 1953-56, asst. prof. math. stats., 1955-56; faculty Stanford, 1956-70, assoc. prof. stats., 1959-64, prof., 1964-70; prof. stats. SUNY-Buffalo, 1970-73, prof. statis. sci., 1973-78; disting. prof. stats. Tex. A and M U., College Station, 1978—; Guest prof. Imperial Coll., London, Eng., 1961-62; vis. prof. MIT, 1964-65, Harvard U., 1976. Author: Stochastic Processes, 1962, Modern Probability Theory and its Applications, 1960, Time Series Analysis Papers, 1967, also articles. Fellow Internat. Statis. Inst., Am. Statis. Assn., AAAS, Royal Statis. Soc., Inst. Math. Statistics; mem. Am. Math. Soc., Soc. Indsl. and Applied Math., Assn. Computing Machinery, Bernoulli Soc., Biometric Soc., N.Y. Acad. Scis., Phi Beta Kappa, Sigma Xi. Research in time series analysis, signal processing, forecasting, statistical computing, quantile function approach to statistical data analysis. Subspecialty: Statistics. Office: Dept Statistics Tex A & M U College Station TX 77843

PASK, JOSEPH ADAM, emeritus ceramic engineering educator; b. Chgo., Feb. 14, 1913; s. Adam Poskoczem and Catherine (Ramanauskas) P.; m. Margaret J. Gault, June 11, 1938; children: Thomas Joseph, Kathryn Edyth. B.S., U. Ill., 1934, Ph.D., 1941; M.S., U. Wash., 1935. Ceramic engr. Willamina Clay Products Co., Oreg., 1935-36; teaching asst. ceramic engring. U. Ill., 1938, instr., 1938-41; asst. ceramic engr. electrotech. lab. U.S. Bur. Mines, 1941; assoc. ceramic engr. N.W. Exptl. Sta., 1942-43; asst. prof. ceramic engring., head dept. Coll. of Mines, U. Wash., Seattle, 1941-43; research ceramist, lamp div. Westinghouse Electric Corp., N.J., 1943-46, research engr. ceramic sect., 1946-48; assoc. prof. ceramic engring., head ceramic group div. materials sci. and engring. U. Calif. at Berkeley, 1948-53, founder program ceramic engring. and sci., 1948, prof., 1953-80, prof. emeritus, 1980—, vice chmn. div., 1956-57, chmn. dept., 1957-61; asso. dean grad. student affairs U. Calif., Berkeley (Coll. Engring.), 1969-80; sr. faculty scientist materials and research scientist materials and molecular research div. Lawrence Berkeley Lab.; John Dorn Meml. lectr. Northwestern U., 1977; Mem. clay mineral com. NRC; mem. materials adv. bd., chmn. ad hoc com. ceramic processing, adv. commn. metallurgy div. U.S. Bur. Standards; chmn. NSF study objective criteria in ceramic engring. edn., U.S.-China Seminar on Basic Sci. of Ceramics, Shanghai, 1983. Recipient John F. Bergerson Meml. Service award Ceramic Engring. div. U. Wash., Seattle, 1969; gold medal for research and devel. French Soc. for Research and Devel., 1979; Berkeley citation U. Calif., 1980; Alumni honor award for disting. service in engring. U. Ill. Coll. Engring., 1982; Outstanding Achievement in Edn. award Com. of Confucius, 1982. Fellow Am. Ceramic Soc. (hon. life mem., v.p. 1953-54, pres. ednl. council 1954-55, trustee 1959-62, chmn. electronics div. 1959-60, John Jeppson award 1967, Ross Coffin Purdy award 1979), AAAS, Mineral. Soc. Am.; mem. Nat. Inst. Ceramic Engrs., Nat. Acad. Engring., Am. Soc. Metals, Brit. Ceramic Soc., Am. Soc. Engring. Edn. (chmn. materials com. 1961-63), Clay Minerals Soc., Keramos, Sigma Xi (Tau Beta Pi), Alpha Sigma Mu. Current Work: Bonding and joining of ceramics/metals at high temperatures; phase equililibria in the Al 203-Si02 0 2 systems. Subspecialties: Ceramics; Materials processing. Home: 994 Euclid Ave Berkeley CA 94708 Office: Dept Material Sci and Mineral Engring U Calif Berkeley CA 94720

PASS, FRANKLIN, biotechnology company executive. Chmn. Molecular Genetics, Inc., Minnetonka, Minn. Subspecialty: Biotechnology administration. Office: Molecular Genetics Inc 10320 Bren Rd E Minnetonka MN 55343

PASSWATER, RICHARD ALBERT, biochemist; b. Wilmington, Del., Oct. 13, 1937; s. Stanley Leroy and Mabel Rosetta (King) P.; m. Barbara Sarah Gayhart, June 1964; children—Richard Alan, Michael Eric. B.S. in Chemistry, U. Del., 1959; Ph.D. (hon.), Bernadean U., Las Vegas, 1976. Lab. supr. Allied Chem. Corp., Marcus Hook, Pa., 1959-64; product mgr. Baxter-Travenol Labs., Silver Spring, Md., 1964-77; research dir. Lifescience Labs., Rockville, Md., 1978-79; research dir. Solgar Nutritional Research Ctr., Berlin, Md., 1979—; sci. advisor Whole Foods, Meteuchen, N.J., 1984. Author: Guide to Fluorescence Literature, 3 vols., 1967-74; Supernutrition, 1976; Supernutrition for Healthy Hearts, 1978; Cancer, 1978; The Easy No-Flab Diet, 1979; Selenium as Food and Medicine, 1980; patentee feed supplement. Mem. editorial bd. Jour. Holistic Medicine, 1981—, Nutritional Perspectives, 1977—; Chief, Ocean Pines Vol. Fire Dept., Md., 1984; mem. adv. com. Worcester County Sch. Bd., Berlin, 1983. Recipient Outstanding Researcher award Com. for World Health, 1980; Top Book in Sci. Tech. Field in 1983 award Library Jours., 1984. Mem. Am. Chem. Soc. (legis. liaison com.), N.Y. Acad. Sci., Am. Aging Assn., AAAS, Ocean Pines C. of C. Methodist. Current work: Free-radical pathology; role of antioxidant nutrients, trace-elements and amino acids in cancer; isolation of unidentified growth factors. Subspecialties: Biochemistry (biology); Nutrition (biology). Home: 9015 Ocean Pines Berlin MD 21811 Office: Solgar Nutritional Research Ctr 4 Manklin Ct Berlin MD 21811

PASTOR, STEPHEN DANIEL, chemistry educator, researcher; b. New Brunswick, N.J., Feb. 15, 1947; s. Stephen and Irene (Bors) P.; m. Joan Ordemann, Apr. 3, 1971 (div. 1979); 1 child, Melanie; m. Joanne Behrens, July 13, 1985. B.A. in Chemistry, Rutgers U., 1969, M.S. in Chemistry, 1978, Ph.D. in Chemistry, 1983. Chemist Nat. Starch and Chem. Corp., Bridgewater, N.J., 1972-79; research group leader CIBA-Geigy Corp., Ardsley, N.Y., 1979—; asst. adj. prof. PACE U., Pleasantville, N.Y., 1984—. Contbr. articles to profl. jours. Patentee (10) in field. Served to 1st lt. U.S. Army, 1969-71, Vietnam. Mem. Am. Chem. Soc., Sigma Xi. Current work: Organophosphorus and organosulfur chemistry. Subspecialties: Organic chemistry; Organometallics. Home: 1080 Warburton Ave Apt 1C Yonkers NY 10701 Office: CIBA-Geigy Corp 444 Saw Mill River Rd Ardsley NY 10502

PASTORELLE, PETER JOHN, nuclear diagnostic laboratories executive; b. White Plains, N.Y., Jan. 23, 1933; s. Dominic John and Marguerite (Xavier) P.; m. Maria Rita Del Campo, Oct. 10, 1970. B.S., Fordham U., 1955; student, Juilliard Sch. Music, 1955-56; M.A., N.Y. U., 1961; B.D., Maryknoll (N.Y.) Sem., 1963. Producer/dir. UN-TV, N.Y.C., 1965-70; pres., founder NDL Orgn., Inc., Peekskill, N.Y., 1965—; Peter Pastorelle Prodns., Inc., Mount Kisco, N.Y., 1970—; panelist Nat. Acad. TV Arts and Scis., N.Y.C., 1981-83; lectr. Am. Chem. Soc., Health Physics Soc. Writer, producer, dir., music score: films Fung Seui, 1970 (N.Y. Internat. Film Festival Gold award), Face of Hunger, 1976 (N.Y. State Dept. Commerce award), Water, 1978 (N.Y. Internat. Film Festival Silver award), Samoa - Culture in Crisis, 1982 (CINE Gold medal). Served with AUS, 1956-58. Mem. Health Physics Soc., Am.

Nuclear Soc., Am. Pub. Health Assn., Soc. Motion Picture and TV Engrs., Am. Fedn. Musicians, Radiation Research Soc. Republican. Roman Catholic. Current Work: Radioactive waste disposal, radioactivity services and supplies. Subspecialties: Nuclear engineering; Radiology in nuclear medicine. Home: RFD 3 Armonk Rd Mount Kisco NY 10549 Office: NDL Orgn Inc PO Box 791 1000 Lower South St Peekskill NY 10566

PATE, FINDLAY MOYE, animal nutritionist; b. Davisboro, Ga., Jan. 24, 1941; s. William Wayne and Valeria (Moye) P.; m. Vicky Scruggs, Jan. 15, 1961; children—Julie, Celia, Joel, Craig. Student Abraham Baldwin Agrl. Coll., 1961-63; B.S. with honors, U. Ga., 1965, Ph.D., 1970; M.S., Oreg. State U., 1967. From asst. prof. to assoc. prof. animal nutrition Everglades Research and Edn. Ctr., Belle Glade, Fla., 1970-83; dir. Ona Agrl. Research and Edn. Ctr., Fla., 1983—; nutritionist Pantaleen, Guatemala, 1977—, Tecun, Guatemala, 1980—. Author: Molasses in Beef Nutrition, 1983. Mem. Am. Soc. Animal Scis. Methodist. Current work: Sugarcane product feeds utilization, beef cattle management, forage utilization, mineral u utilization. Subspecialty: Animal nutrition. Home: Route 1 Box 300A Wauchula FL 33873 Office: Univ Fla Agrl Research Ctr Ona FL 33865

PATÉ-CORNELL, MARIE-ELISABETH, industrial engineering educator; b. Dakar, Senegal, France, Aug. 17, 1948; came to U.S., 1971; d. Edouard Pierre Lucien and Madeleine (Tournissa) Paté; m. C. Allin Cornell, Jan. 3, 1981; children—Phillip, Ariane. B.S. in Math., Lyçee de Marseille, France, 1968; M.S. in Computer Sci., U. de Grenoble, France, 1970, in Operational Research, Stanford U., 1972; Engring. degree in Applied Math., Computer Sci., Inst. Polytech., Grenoble, France, 1971; Ph.D. in Engring. Econ. Systems, Stanford U., 1978. Asst. prof. dept. civil engring., MIT, Cambridge, Mass., 1978-81; asst. prof. indsl. engring. Stanford U., Calif., 1981-84, assoc. prof. indsl. engring., 1984—; mem. pub. adv. com. EPA, Santa Clara, Calif., 1984—; cons. Electric Power Research Inst., Palo Alto, Calif., 1984—. Contbr. articles to profl. jours. NSF grantee, 1981-82. Mem. Ops. Research Soc., Earthquake Engring. Research Inst., Soc. for Risk Analysis (council). Current work: Technological risk analysis and risk management, analysis and optimization of warning systems. Subspecialties: Probability; Industrial engineering. Home: 110 Coquito Way Portola Valley CA 94025 Office: Dept Indsl Engring Stanford U Stanford CA 94305

PATEL, ANIL S., biomedical engineer, researcher; b. Baroda, India, June 28, 1939; came to U.S. 1961; s. Shankerbhai S. and Gangaben (T.) P.; children—Ravi, Sunil. B.S., U. Baroda, India, 1960; M.S., Purdue U., 1963; Ph.D., Northwestern U., 1966. Sr. research scientist Baxter Travenol Labs. Inc., Morton Grove, Ill., 1968-74; chief scientist Cavitron Corp., N.Y.C., 1974-79; chief scientist and mgr. advanced products research Cooper Vision Systems div. Cooper Vision Inc. (formerly Cavitron Corp.), Irvine, Calif., 1979-83, Cooper Vision IOL div., Bellevue, Wash., 1983—. Contbr. articles to profl. jours. Patentee in field. Organizer Highland Park Chess Club, 1970-74, White Plains Chess Club, N.Y., 1974-77. NIH postdoctoral fellow Northwestern U., 1966-67; recipient free passage from India to U.S., Ministry Sci. and Cultural Affairs of Govt. India, 1961. Fellow Am. Soc. Laser Medicine and Surgery (founder); mem. Assn. Advancement Med. Instrumentation (chmn. infrared warmers and incubators standards com. 1978-80, pulmonary function devices-spirometer standards subcom. 1978-80), Assn. Research in Vision and Ophthalmology, Inc., Internat. Soc. Refractive Keratoplasty, AAAS, IEEE, Soc. Biomaterials, Sigma Xi. Subspecialties: Artificial organs and prostheses; Biomedical engineering. Office: Cooper Vision IOL 3190 160th Ave SE Bellevue WA 98008

PATEL, CHANDRA KUMAR NARANBHAI, research company executive; b. Baramati, India, July 2, 1938; came to U.S., 1958, naturalized, 1970; s. Naranbhai Chaturbhai and Maniben P.; m. Shela Dixit, Aug. 20, 1961; children: Neela, Meena. B.Engring., Poona U., 1958; M.S., Stanford U., 1959, Ph.D., 1961. Mem. tech. staff Bell Telephone Labs., Murray Hill, N.J., 1961—, head infrared physics and electronics research dept., 1967-70, dir. electronics research dept., 1970-76, dir. phys. research lab., 1976-81, exec. dir. research physics and acad. affairs div., 1981—; trustee Aerospace Corp., Los Angeles, 1979—. Contbr. articles to tech. jours. Recipient Adolph Lomb medal Optical Soc. Am., 1966; Ballantine medal Franklin Inst., 1968; Coblentz award Am. Chem. Soc., 1974; Honor award Assn. Indians in Am., 1975; Zworykin award Nat. Acad. Engring., 1976; Lamme medal IEEE, 1976; Founders prize Tex. Instruments Found., 1978; award N.Y. sect. Soc. Applied Spectroscopy, 1982; Schawhow medal Laser Inst. Am. Fellow Am. Acad. Arts and Scis., Am. Phys. Soc., IEEE, AAAS, Optical Soc. Am. (Townes medal 1982), Indian Nat. Sci. Acad. (fgn.), Inst. Telecommunications and Electronics Engring. India (fgn.), Third World Acad. Scis. (assoc.); mem. Nat. Acad. Scis., Nat. Acad. Engring., Am. Soc. for Laser Medicine and Surgery (hon.), Gynecologic Laser Surgery Soc. (hon.), Am. Soc. Laser Medicine and Surgery (hon.). Current Work: Atomic and molecular physics. Subspecialties: Laser spectroscopy; Atomic and molecular physics. Home: 77 Colt Rd Summit NJ 07901 Office: Bell Telephone Labs 600 Mountain Ave Murray Hill NJ 07974

PATEL, VIPINCHANDRA NATWARLAL, electrical engineer, researcher; b. Kampala, Uganda, Mar. 18, 1947; came to U.S., 1979, citizen U.K.; s. Natwarlal Gordhandas and Prabhavati (Javerbhai) P.; m. Jyotika Vipinchandra, Sept. 13, 1975; children—Hitaine Vipinchandra Patel. B.S. with honors, U. East Africa, 1970; M.S., Dundee U., Scotland, 1971, Ph.D., 1976. Lectr., Dundee Coll. Tech., 1971-76; prin. engr. Plessey Co., Towcester, Eng., 1977-79; assoc. prin. engr. Harris Corp., Melbourne, Fla., 1979-82; sr. engr. AT&T, Reading, Pa., 1982—. Contbr. articles to profl. jours. Dundee U. scholar, 1973-76. Mem. IEEE, Inst. Elec. Engrs. (assoc.), Inst. Physics. Hindu. Current work: High speed microchip technology, manufacture and research. Subspecialties: Integrated circuits; Microelectronics. Home: 707 Fritz Ave Shillington PA 19607 Office: 2525 N 12th St Reading PA 19610

PATERSON, PHILIP Y., physician, educator; b. Mpls., Feb. 6, 1925; s. Donald Gildersleeve and Margaret (Young) P.; m. Virginia Lee Bray, Mar. 22, 1947; children: Anne, Peter, Benjamin. B.S., U. Minn., 1946, M.B., 1947, M.D., 1948. Intern Mpls. Gen. Hosp., 1948-49; research fellow div. infectious diseases Tulane U. Sch. Medicine, 1949-50, instr. in medicine Am. Heart Assn. research fellow, 1950-51; Am. Heart Assn. research fellow dept. microbiology U. Va. Sch. Medicine, 1953, asst. resident and co-resident in medicine univ. hosp., 1953-55; asst. prof. microbiology, instr. in medicine, established investigator Am. Heart Assn., 1955-57; med. officer Lab. Immunology, Nat. Inst. Allergy and Infectious Diseases, NIH, Bethesda, Md., 1957-60; vis. asst. prof. microbiology N.Y. U., 1957-60, assoc. prof. medicine, 1960-65; assoc. prof. medicine, dir. Samuel J. Sackett Research Labs.; and chief sect. infectious diseases, dept. medicine Northwestern U., 1965-66; Samuel J. Sackett prof. medicine and chief infectious diseases, hypersensitivity sect., dept. medicine Northwestern U.-McGaw Med. Center, 1966-72, Samuel J. Sackett prof. medicine and microbiology, chief infectious diseases-hypersensitivity sect., 1972-75; prof. microbiology-immunology, chmn. dept. microbiology-immunology Northwestern U. Med. and Dental Schs., 1975—, Guy and Anne Youmans prof. microbiology/immunology, 1982—; prof. neurobiology and physiology Northwestern U., Evanston, Ill., 1983—; Christine Larsen lectr. Sch. Medicine, Albuquerque, 1973; Disting. lectr. Ann. Meeting Assn. Am. Physicians and Western Sect. Am. Fedn. Clin. Research, Carmel, Calif., 1974; Grace Faillace Meml. lectr. Leo Goodwin Inst. Cancer Research, Nova U., 1978; Ernest Witebsky Meml. lectr. 6th Internat. Convocation on Immunology, Niagara Falls, N.Y., 1978; Joseph E. Smadel Meml. lectr. Ann. Meeting, Infectious Diseases Soc. Am., Atlanta, 1978; mem. adv. com. on drug devel. Nat. Multiple Sclerosis Soc., 1973—; mem. research study com. Am. Heart Assn., 1978-81; mem. internat. med. adv. bd. Internat. Fedn. Multiple Sclerosis Socs., 1973—; participant Mid-West Immunol. Conf., sec.-treas., 1974-76, chmn., 1977-78; mem. adv. panel Am. Bd. Med. Lab. Immunology, 1978—. Editor and contbg. author: The Biological and Clinical Basis of Infectious Diseases, 1975, 2d edit., 1980, 3d edit., 1984; contbr. over 200 articles, chpts. and revs. on neuroimmunology, host-parasite interactions and infectious disease to books and profl. jours.; mem. editorial bd.: Procs. Soc. Exptl. Biology and Medicine, 1968-73, 1977—, Cellular Immunology, 1969—, Infection and Immunity, 1970-81, Clin. and Exptl. Immunology, 1970—, Clin. Immunology and Immunopathology, 1978—, Jour. Clin. and Lab. Immunology, 1979—; assoc. editor: Jour. Infectious Diseases, 1979-83. Served to capt., M.C. U.S. Army, 1951-53. Mem. Am. Fedn. Clin. Research, AAAS (council fellow), Am. Soc. Microbiology, Am. Assn. Immunologists, Harvey Soc., Am. Soc. Clin. Investigation, Infectious Diseases Soc. Am. (Gold medal 1978), Central Soc. Clin. Research, Am. Rheumatism Assn., Assn. Am. Physicians, Am. Clin. and Climatol. Assn., Sigma Xi, Alpha Omega Alpha. Current Work: Neuroimmunology. Subspecialties: Infectious diseases; Neuroimmunology. Home: 1025 Chestnut Ave Wilmette IL 60091 Office: 303 E Chicago Ave Chicago IL 60611

PATRICK, RICHARD MONTGOMERY, aeronautical engineer; b. Rockford, Ill., Sept. 24, 1928; s. Richard Montgomery and May Francis (O'Connor) P.; m. Mary Ann Raliegh, Oct. 20, 1958; children—Elizabeth, Susanne, Richard. Student, Iowa State Coll., 1946-48; B.S., Purdue U., 1950; M.S., 1951; Ph.D., Cornell U., 1956. Aero engr. NACA, Langley AFB, 1951, 53; aero. engr. Douglas Aircraft Co., Santa Monica, Calif., 1952; with Avco Everett Research Lab., Mass., 1956—, chmn. plasma physics com., 1965—, v.p. directed energy, 1970—. Contbr. articles to profl. jours. Fellow Am. Phys. Soc.; mem. Sigma Xi, Gamma Alpha Rho. Club: Winchester Boat. Patentee in field. Office: Avco Everett Research Laboratory Inc 2385 Revere Beach Pkwy Everett MA 02149

PATRICK, RUTH (MRS. CHARLES HODGE), limnologist, diatom taxonomist, educator; b. Topeka, Kans., d. Frank and Myrtle (Jetmore) Patrick; m. Charles Hodge, July 10, 1931; 1 child, Charles V. B.S., Coker Coll., 1929, LL.D., 1971; M.A., U. Va., 1931, Ph.D., 1934; D.Sc., Beaver Coll., 1970, PMS Colls., 1971, Phila. Coll. Pharmacy and Sci., 1973, Wilkes Coll., 1974, Cedar Crest Coll., 1974, U. New Haven, 1975, Hood Coll., 1975, Med. Coll. Pa., 1975, Drexel U., 1975, Swarthmore Coll., 1975, Bucknell U., 1976, Rensselaer Poly. Inst., 1976, St. Lawrence U., 1978; L.H.D., Chestnut Hill Coll., 1974. Assoc. curator microscopy dept. Acad. Natural Scis., Phila., 1939-47, sr. curator limnology dept., 1947—, chmn. dept., 1947-73, occupant Francis Boyer Research Chair, 1973—, chmn. bd. trustees, 1973-76, hon. chmn. bd. trustees, 1976—; curator Leidy Micros. Soc., 1937-47; lectr. botany U. Pa., 1950-70, adj. prof., 1970—; guest fellow of Saybrook Yale, 1975; participant Am. Philos. Soc. limnology expdn. to Mexico, 1947; leader Catherwood found. expdn. to Peru and Brazil, 1955; del. Gen. Assembly, Internat. Union Biol. Scis., Bergen, Norway, 1973; dir. E.I. duPont, Pa. Power and Light Co.; chmn. algae com. Smithsonian Oceanographic Sorting Ctr., 1963-68; mem. panel on water blooms Pres.'s Sci. Adv. Com., 1966; mem. panel on water resources and water pollution Gov.'s Sci. Adv. Com., 1966; mem. nat. tech. adv. com. on water quality requirments for fish and other aquatic life and wildlife Dept. Interior, 1967-78; mem. citizen's adv. council Pa. Dept. Environ. Resources, 1971-73; mem. hazardous materials adv. com. EPA, 1971-74, exec. adv. com., 1974-79, chmn. com.'s panel on ecology, 1974-76; mem. Pa. gov.'s Sci. Adv. Council, 1972-78; mem. exec. adv. com. nat power survey PFC, 1972-75; mem. council Smithsonian Instn., 1973—; mem. Phila. Adv. Council, 1973-76; mem. energy research and devel. adv. council Pres.'s Energy Policy Office, 1973-74; mem. adv. council Renewable Natural Resources Found., 1973-76, Electric Power Research Found., 1973-77; mem. adv. com. for research NSF, 1973-74; mem. gen. adv. com. ERDA, 1975-77; mem. com. on human resources NRC, 1975-76; mem. adv. council dept. biology Princeton, 1975—; mem com. on sci. and arts Franklin Inst., 1978—; mem. univ. council com. Yale Sch. Forestry and Environ. studies, 1978—; mem. sci. adv. council World Wildlife Fund, U.S., 1978—. Author: (with Dr. C.W. Reimer) Diatoms of the United States, Vol. 1, 1966, Vol. 22, Part 1, 1975. Mem. editorial bd. Science, 1974-76, American Naturalist, trustee Biological Abstracts, 1974-76. Contbr. articles to profl. jours. Trustee Aquarium Soc., Phila., 1951-58, Chestnut Hill Acad., Lacawac Sanctuary Found., Henry Found.; bd. dirs. Wissahickon Valley Watershed Assn.; mem. adv. council French and Pickering Creeks Conservation Trust; bd. govs Nature Conservancy; bd. mgrs. Wistar Inst. Anatomy and Biology. Recipient Disting. Dau. of Pa. award, 1952; Richard Hopper Day Meml. medal Acad. Natural Scis., 1969; Gimbel Phila. award, 1969; Gold medal YWCA, 1970; Lewis L. Dollinger Pure Environ. award Franklin Inst., 1970; Pa. award for excellence in sci. and tech., 1970; Eminent Ecologist award Ecol. Soc. Am., 1972; Phila. award, 1973; Gold medal Pa. State Fish and Game Protective Assn., 1974; Internat. John and Alice Tyler Ecology award, 1975; Gold medal Phila. Soc. for Promoting Agr., 1975; Pub. Service award Dept. Interior, 1975; Iben award Am. Water Resources Assn., 1976; Outstanding Alumni award Coker Coll., 1977; Francis K. Hutchinson medal Garden Club of Am., 1977; Golden medal Royal Zool. Soc., Antwerp, 1978. Fellow AAAS (com. environ. alterations 1973-74); mem. Nat. Acad. Scis. (chmn. panel com. on pollution 1966, mem. com. sci. and pub. policy 1973-77, mem. environ. measurements panel of com. on remote sensing programs for earth resource surveys 1973-74, mem. nominating co. 1973-75), Nat. Acad. Engring. (com. environ. engring.'s ad hoc study on explicit criteria for decisions in power plant siting 1973), Am. Philos. soc., Am. Acad. Arts and Scis., Bot. Soc. Am. (mem. Darbarker prize com. 1956, merit award 1971), Phycol. Soc. Am. (pres. 1954), Internat. Limnological Soc., Internat. Soc. Plant Taxonomists, Am. Soc. Plant Taxonomy, Am. Soc. Limnology and Oceanography, Pa. Zool. Soc., Water Pollution Control Fedn. (hon.), Colonial Dames Am., Soc. Study Evolution, Water Resources Assn., Del. River Basin, Am. Soc. Naturalists (pres. 1975-76), Ecol. Soc. Am., Am. Inst. Biol. Scis., Internat. Phycol. Soc. Sigma Xi. Presbyterian. Subspecialty: Limnology. Office: Acad Natural Scis Philadelphia PA 19103

PATSCH, JOSEF RUDOLF, med. educator, researcher; b. Vienna, Austria, Jan. 13, 1942; came to U.S., 1975; s. Josef Ferdin and Lydia (Wolf) P.; m. Brenda Sue Wittneben, Dec. 16, 1978; 1 dau., Katherin Michelle. M.D., U. Innsbruck, Austria, 1966. Diplomate: Am. Bd. Internal Medicine. Research fellow U. Vienna, 1967-68; resident in medicine U. Innsbruck, 1968-71, asst. prof., 1971-75; vis. scientist Baylor Coll., Houston, 1975-77, asst. prof., 1977-81, assoc. prof., 1981—; prin. investigator NIH, 1979-83, on 1975-77. Contbr. articles to med. jours. Recipient Irvine H. Page atherosclerosis research prize Am. Heart Assn., 1982. Fellow Am. Fedn. Clin. Research, Atherosclerosis Council. Roman Catholic. Current Work: Atherosclerosis, coronary heart disease, blood lipids, cholesterol, serum lipoproteins, preventive medicine, physical exercise. Subspecialties: Biochemistry (medicine); Internal medicine. Home: 4814 O'Meara Houston TX 77035 Office: Baylor Coll Medicine Tex Med Ctr Houston TX 77030

PATTABIRAMAN, NAGARAJAN, scientist; b. Madras, India, Nov. 24, 1951; came to U.S., 1981; s. Nagarajan Kollangottai and Jagadeeswari Nagarajan; m. Sitaraman Prabha, Feb. 7, 1980. M.Sc. in Physics, Presidency Coll., Madras, India, 1974; Ph.D. in Biophysics, Indian Inst. Sci., Bangalore, 1979. Research assoc. Indian Inst. Sci., Bangalore, 1979-81; postgrad. research chemist Sch. of Pharmacy, U. Calif.-San Francisco, 1981-83, asst. research chemist, 1984—. Contbr. articles on molecular biophysics and computer graphics to profl. jours. Recipient Young Scientists' award Indian Nat. Sci. Acad., New Delhi, 1980. Mem. Biophys. Soc. Current work: Conformations of nucleic acids and proteins, protein-nucleic acid interactions, drug design, computer graphics and protein engineering. Subspecialty: Biophysics (biology). Office: S-926 Sch Pharmacy U Calif San Francisco CA 94143

PATTEE, HAROLD EDWARD, research chemist; b. Phoenix, June 27, 1934; s. Earnest Harold and Ina Mae (Hamblin) P.; m. Phyllis Adams, June 8, 1956; children—Floyd, Phyllis, Linda, Deborah, Sherri, Sheila, Yvonne. B.S., Brigham Young U., 1958; M.S., Utah State U., 1960; Ph.D., Purdue U., 1962. Postdoctoral plant biochemist UCLA, 1962-63; research chemist U.S. Dept. Agr.-N.C. State U., Raleigh, 1963—. Editor: Peanut Science and Technology, 1982; Sensory Evaluation of Fruits and Vegetables, 1985. Editor Peanut Sci., 1976—, assoc. editor, 1974-76. Contbr. articles to sci. jours. Vice pres. program Occoneechee council Boy Scouts Am., 1984—. Served with U.S. Army, 1954-56; ETO. Recipient Golden Peanut Research award Nat. Peanut Council, 1977. Fellow Am. Peanut Research and Edn. Soc.; mem. Am. Chem. Soc. (alt. councilor 1979—, adv. bd. dirs. Jour. Agrl. and Food Chemistry 1984—), Inst. Food Technologists, Sigma Xi. Republican. Mormon. Current work: Physiology and biochemistry of seed maturation, after-ripening in peanuts and its relation to edible-quality, seed embryo-genesis and causes of embryo abortion in peanuts. Subspecialties: Plant physiology (biology); Biochemistry (biology). Home: 6201 Winthrop Dr Raleigh NC 27612 Office: USDA ARS SR-NC State U PO Box 7625 NC State U Raleigh NC 27695

PATTERSON, DAVID, geneticist, biologist; b. Medford, Mass., Aug. 24, 1944; s. David and Mildred (Hughes) P.; m. Norma Jean Riggs, June 3, 1967; children: Matthew, Jennifer. B.S., MIT, 1966; Ph.D., Brandeis U., 1971. With Eleanor Roosevelt Inst. Cancer Research, Denver, 1971—, sr. fellow, 1974-78, asst. prof. dept. biophysics/genetics, 1974-78, assoc. prof., 1978-83, assoc. dir., 1978—; assoc. prof. dept. medicine U. Colo. Health Scis. Ctr., Denver, 1982—, prof. biochemistry/biophysics/genetics, 1983—, prof. dept. medicine, 1984—; bd. dirs. Therapeutic Day Care Ctr., Denver, 1981-84; pres. Eleanor Roosevelt Inst. Cancer Research. Editor: Somatic Cell and Molecular Genetics, 1983, Trisomy 21, 1983. Mem. biotech. com. Colo. Commn. Higher Edn., Denver, 1983. Grantee Nat. Inst. Aging, 1975-86; Grantee March of Dimes, 1975-83; Grantee Kroc Found., 1982-84; Grantee Nat. Inst. Child Health and Human Devel., 1979—. Current Work: Gene regulation in mammalian cells related to aging, development, genetic disease, and cancer using molecular methods such as cloning of human genes, gene transfer, recombinant DNA, and nucleotide biochemistry. Subspecialties: Gene actions; Cancer research (medicine). Home: 4090 S Narcissus Way Denver CO 80220 Office: Eleanor Roosevelt Inst Cancer Research 4200 E 9th Ave B129 Denver CO 80262

PATTERSON, DONALD DUKE, polymer chemist. Prof. dept. chemistry McGill U. Recipient Dunlop Lecture award Chem. Inst. Can., 1985. Subspecialty: Polymer chemistry. Office: McGill U Dept Chemistry Montreal PA H3A 2T5

PATTERSON, MICHAEL MILTON, biomedical researcher, educator, university administrator; b. Muscatine, Iowa, Mar. 17, 1942; s. Harvey Milton and Vivienne Doris Ann (Bridgeman) P.; m. Janice Pauline Ficke, June 11, 1966; children: Michael Shane, Shad Milton. Student, Grinnell Coll., 1964, Ind. U., 1964-66; Ph.D., U. Iowa, 1969. NIH postdoctoral fellow U. Calif., Irvine, 1969-71; assoc. prof. Kirksville (Mo.) Coll. Osteo. Medicine, 1971-77; prof. psychology Coll. Osteo. Medicine, Ohio U., Athens, 1977—, prof. osteo. medicine, 1977—, dir. research affairs, 1977—, Louisa Burns Meml. lectr., 1980, cons. to research and ednl. groups; lectr. in field; grant reviewer. Cons. editor sci. jours.; contbr. numerous articles to sci. jours., chpts. to books. Scoutmaster, dist. chmn. Boy Scouts Am. NIH fellow, 1966-71; Am. Osteo. Assn. grantee, 1973—; NIH grantee, 1975—. Mem. Am. Psychol. Assn., Psychonomic Soc., Midwest Psychol. Assn., Soc. for Neurosci., Sigma Xi. Republican. Mem. Ch. of Christ Disciples. Tuesday. Lodge: Rotary Internat. Current Work: Spinal cord function including the effects of experience on spinal reflex patterns; brain-behavior relationships including alterations in brain activity during learning; effects of manipulative therapy on disease process. Subspecialties: Psychophysiology; Physiological psychology. Home: 88 Wonder Hills Dr Athens OH 45701 Office: Coll Osteo Medicine Ohio U Athens OH 45701

PATTERSON, ROBERT LOGAN, systems analyst; b. Pitts., Mar. 12, 1940; s. Walter Glenn and June (Logan) P.; m. Christine Borgmann, Feb. 6, 1965 (div. 1973); 1 dau., Caitlin Williams. B.A., U. Vt., 1962; M.A., San Jose State U., 1965; M.Ed., Boston State Coll., 1979; cert., Northeastern U., 1982; postgrad., Lesley Coll. Grad. Sch., 1982-83. Info. officer IBM U.K., London, 1966-68; systems analyst Info. Dynamics, Reading, Mass., 1968-70; automation librarian Boston Theol. Inst., Cambridge, Mass., 1971-73; systems analyst U. Mass., Boston, 1973—, psychology intern various mental health ctrs., 1978—; Active tng. program Boston Inst. Psychotherapists, 1981-82, Cambridge Hosp. Psychotherapy Ctr., 1982-83. Mem. Am. Psychol. Assn., Friends of Boston Psychoanalytic Soc. and Inst., Mass. Psychol. Assn., Mass. Tchrs. Assn., Northeastern Soc. Group Psychotherapy, SAR, Kappa Delta Pi. Psi Chi. Current Work: Research in marital separation. Subspecialties: Psychotherapy; Library systems automation. Home: 8 Winthrop Ave Bedford MA 01730 Office: U Mass Harbor Campus Boston MA 02125

PATTERSON, ROSALYN VICTORIA MITCHELL, cell biology educator; b. Madison, Ga., Mar. 25, 1939; d. Walter Melvin and Hazeltine (Jones) Mitchell; m. Joseph William Patterson, June 1, 1961; children: Hazelyn Mammette, Joseph William, Rosman Victor. B.A., Spelman Coll., 1958; M.S., Atlanta U., 1960; Ph.D., Emory U., 1967. Instr. biology Spelman Coll., Atlanta, 1960-66, asst. prof., 1966-68, assoc. prof., 1968-69, prof., 1969-70; postdoctoral research fellow Ga. Inst. Tech., Atlanta, 1969-70; staff specialist to commr. and cons. Bur. Reclamation, U.S. Dept. Interior, Washington, 1970-71; coordinator nat. environ. edn. devel. program Nat. Park Service, 1971-72; NIH postdoctoral fellow div. biologics standards Bur. Biologics, FDA, Bethesda, Md., 1972-73; assoc. prof. biology Ga. State U., Atlanta, 1974-76; assoc. prof., then prof. Atlanta U., 1977—, chairperson dept. biology, 1980—. Mem. adv. bd. Mays Acad., Atlanta, 1980—. Mem. AAAS, Am. Soc. Cell Biology, Soc. Developmental Biology. Baptist. Current Work: The role of free radical activity in the alteration of chromosome structure and mechanisms by which antioxidants (i.e. vitamin E) may reduce the free radical effects. Subspecialties: Cell and tissue culture; Genome organization. Home: 109 Burre Ln SW Atlanta GA 30331 Office: Atlanta U Dept Biology 223 Chestnut St Atlanta GA 30314

PATTERSON, TERENCE EDWARD, psychophysiological research scientist; b. Belfast, No. Ireland, Mar. 8, 1947; came to U.S., 1978, naturalized, 1982; s. Edward and Alice Elizabeth (Walsh) P.; m. Nancy Jean Crawford, 1983. B.A. with honors, Queens U., Belfast, 1969; Ph.D., Reading (Eng.) U., 1976. Clin. unit. dir. Ont. Hosp., Whitby, Ont., Can., 1969-71; postdoctoral fellow York (Eng.) U., 1974-77; pres. Patterson, Donnelly & Assocs., Toronto, Ont., 1977-78; prin. investigator dept. research Menninger Found., Topeka, 1978—; mem. faculty Menninger Sch. Psychiatry; cons. in field. Contbr. articles to profl. jours.; editorial cons. to jours. NIMH grantee, 1981. Mem. Soc. Psychophysiol. Research, AAAS, European Neurosci. Assn. Rifle designer/builder. Current Work: Three-dimensional representation of brain electrical activity during complex information processing in schizophrenics and normal human subjects. Subspecialties: Neuropsychology; Neurophysiology. Office: Menninger Found Box 829 Topeka KS 66601

PATTI, ROBERT DALE, electronic engr.; b. San Diego, Dec. 14, 1940; s. Angelo John and Frances Marie (Miosi) P.; m. Christine Cummings, June 17, 1967; children: Elaine T., Janel C., Robert Dale. B.S. in E.E, Calif. Poly. State U., 1963. Registered profl. engr., Calif. Reliability project engr. Gen. Precision, Inc., San Marcos, Calif., 1963-66; sr. reliability engr. Gen. Dynamics Corp., San Diego, 1966-68; supr. quality engring. Westinghouse Electric Corp., Mansfield, Ohio, 1968-76; mgr corporate reliability and quality engring. Baxter Travenol Labs., Inc., Round Lake, Ill., 1976-78; dir. quality assurance G.D. Searle Co., Skokie, Ill., 1978-82; dir. product assurance Medtronic, Inc., Mpls., 1982—. Contbr. articles to profl. jours. Mem. Am. Soc. Quality Control, Instrument Soc. Am., Am. Assn. Advancement Med. Instrumentation. Republican. Roman Catholic. Current Work: Assurance scis., reliability and quality engring. Subspecialties: Electronics; Bioinstrumentation. Home: 17020 32d Ave N Plymouth MN 55447 Office: PO Box 1453 Minneapolis MN 55440

PATTILLO, ROLAND A., physician, scientist; b. DeQuincy, La., June 12, 1933; s. James T. and Rhena F. P.; m. Marva Parks, June 20, 1959; children: Catherine, Michael, Patrick, Sheri, Mary E. B.S., Xavier U., 1955; M.D., St. Louis U., 1959. Diplomate: Am. Bd. Obstetrics and Gynecology. Intern, resident Milwaukee County Gen. Hosp., 1959-63; resident Boston Lying-in Hosp., Harvard U., 1963-64; fellow in reproductive oncology Johns Hopkins U., 1965-67; dir. Cancer Research and Reproductive Biology Labs., vice chmn. dept. ob-gyn Med. Coll. Wis., Milw., 1980-84. Contbr. articles to profl. jours. Bd. dirs. Milw div. Am. Cancer Soc., Jr. Acad. Medicine, Milw. Grantee NIH; Grantee Am. Cancer Soc.; Grantee DeRance Found.; Grantee Cudahy Found.; Grantee Stackner Found.; Grantee McBeath Found.; Grantee Steimke Found. Mem. AAAS, Am. Coll. Obstetricians and Gynecologists, Soc. Gynecologic Oncologists, Soc. Gynecologic Investigation, Internat. Soc. for Trophoblast Disease (founder, pres.). Roman Catholic. Current Work: Gynecologic oncology, reproductive biology, endocrinology, immunology and chemotherapy. Subspecialties: Gynecological oncology; Reproductive biology (medicine).

PATTIPATI, KRISHNA RAO, engineer, researcher, educator; b. Chayapuram, India, June 1, 1953; came to U.S., 1975; s. Chinna Venkatanna and Munemma P.; m. Aruna K. Mannaru, Dec. 6, 1981; 1 child Archana K. B.Tech. in Elec. Engring., Indian Inst. Tech., Kharaghpur, 1975; M.S. in Elec. Engring., U. Conn., 1977, Ph.D. in Elec. Engring., 1980. Registered profl. engr., Conn., Mass. Research asst. U. Conn., Storrs, 1975-80, lectr., 1984—; sr. engr. Alphatech, Inc., Burlington, Mass., 1980—. Contbr. articles to profl. jours. U. Conn. fellow, 1978. Mem. IEEE (Outstanding Young Engr. 1984), Ops. Research Soc. Hindu. Current work: Optimization, queueing networks, artificial intelligence applications to automated testing, management information systems. Subspecialties: Computer engineering; Operations research (mathematics). Office: Alphatech Inc 2 Burlington Exec Ctr Burlington MA 01803

PATTON, PETER CLYDE, computing research administrator; b. Wichita, Kans., June 11, 1935; s. Claude and Beryl Inez (Jones) Barney) P.; m. Naomi Julia Lawson, Aug. 21, 1957; children: Peter, Claudia, Theresa, Richard, Phillip. A.B. in Engring. and Applied Physics, Harvard U., 1957; M.A. in Math, Kans. U., 1959; Dr. in Aerospace Engring, Stuttgart (W. Ger.) U., 1966. Sci. cons. Sperry Internat., Lausanne, Switzerland, 1961-67; mgr. system design Sperry Univac, Roseville, Minn., 1967-69; gen. mgr. Analysts Internat., Mpls.,

1969-71; dir. U. Minn. Computer Center, Mpls., 1971-83; prin. scientist Micro-electronics and Computer Tech. Corp., Austin, Tex., 1983-85; dir. Minn. Supercomputer Inst., 1985—. Author: Data Structures & Computer Architecture, 1976; author, editor: Computing in the Humanities, 1981, Computer System Requirement, 1982. Fellow Inst. Math. & Its Applications; mem. IEEE (sr.), IEEE Computer Group, Assn. Computing Machinery. Current Work: Software automation, design and implementation of application generator software for super computers and parallel processors. Subspecialties: Computer architecture; Software engineering. Home: 7418 Borman Ave Inver Grove Heights MN 55075 Office: Minn Supercomputer Inst 100 Union St SE Minneapolis MN 55455

PATWARDHAN, BHALCHANDRA HARI, staff scientist; b. Amrroti, Maharashtra, India, Dec. 25, 1947; s. Hari Waman and Kamala H. P.; m. Rekha Swar, May 6, 1975; children—Vikram B. B.Sc., Inst. Sci., Nagpur, India, 1967; M.Sc., Nagpur U., 1969, Ph.D., 1973. Research assoc. Inst. for Organische Chemie, Bern, Switzerland, 1974; Heinemann postdoctoral fellow U. Catholique de Louvain, Belgium, 1975-76; research assoc. SUNY, Syracuse, 1979-81; research scientist Miles Labs., Elkhart, Ind., 1982-83, sr. research scientist, 1983-84, staff scientist, 1984—. Contbr. revs. and articles to profl. jours. Council of Sci. and Indsl. Research fellow, New Delhi, India, 1974. Mem. Royal Inst. Chemistry, Am. Chem. Soc., Sigma Xi. Current work: Bioseparations, solvent extraciton, high pressure liquid chromatography of proteins, process development. Subspecialty: Organic chemistry. Office: Miles Lab Inc 1127 Myrtle St Elkhart IN 46514

PAUDLER, WILLIAM WOLFGANG, chemistry educator, university dean; b. Varnsdorf, Czechoslovakia, Feb. 11, 1932; s. Fred and Johanna (Drabovsky) P.; m. Renee Eva West, Dec. 21, 1932; children: Gary, Leslie, David. B.S., U. Ill., 1954; Ph.D., Ind. U., 1958. Research chemist Proctor & Gamble Co., 1958-59; postdoctoral research assoc. Princeton U., 1960-61; asst. prof. chemistry Ohio U., Athens, 1961-65, assoc. prof., 1965-67, prof., 1967-70, disting. prof. chemistry, 1970-73; chmn., prof. U. Ala.-Tuscaloosa, 1973-81; dean Coll. Liberal Arts and Scis., prof. chemistry Portland (Oreg.) State U., 1981—. Author: Nuclear Magnetic Resonance, 1971, 74, (with George Newkome) Contemporary Heterocyclic Chemistry, 1982; contbr. (with George Newkome) articles to profl. jours. Fellow Am. Inst. Chemists; mem. Internat. Soc. Heterocyclic Chemists, Am. Chem. Soc. Jewish. Current Work: Heterocyclic chemistry, natural product, nuclear magnetic resonance, coal and wood chemistry. Subspecialties: Organic chemistry; Nuclear magnetic resonance. Home: 19521 Hidden Springs West Linn OR 97068 Office: Portland State U Portland OR 97207

PAUL, ARA GARO, university dean; b. New Castle, Pa., Mar. 1, 1929; s. John Hagop and Mary (Injejikian) P.; m. Shirley Elaine Waterman, Dec. 21, 1962; children: John Bartlett, Richard Goyan. B.S. in Pharmacy, Idaho State U., 1950; M.S., U. Conn., 1953, Ph.D. in Pharmacognosy, 1956. Cons. plant physiology Argonne (Ill.) Nat. Lab., 1955; asst. prof. pharmacognosy Butler U., Indpls., 1956-57; mem. faculty U. Mich., Ann Arbor, 1957—, prof. pharmacognosy, 1969—; dean U. Mich. (Coll. Pharmacy), 1975—; vis. prof. microbiology Tokyo U., 1965-66; mem. vis. chemistry faculty U. Calif., Berkeley, 1972-73. Contbr. articles to profl. jours. Del. U.S. Pharmacopeial Conv., 1980. G. Pfeiffer Meml. fellow Am. Found. Pharm. Edn., 1965-66; fellow Eli Lilly Found., 1951-53; fellow Am. Found. Pharm. Edn., 1954-56; fellow NIH, 1972-73; recipient Outstanding Tchr. award Coll. Pharmacy, U. Mich., 1969, Outstanding Alumnus award Idaho State U., 1976. Fellow AAAS; mem. Am., Mich. pharm. assns., Am. Soc. Pharmacognosy, Acad. Pharm. Scis., Am. Assn. Colls. Pharmacy, Washtenaw County Pharm. Soc., Am. Soc. Hosp. Pharmacists. Current Work: Biosynthesis of Alkaloids; phytochemistry of fungi; phytochemistry of cacti. Subspecialties: Pharmacognosy; Medicinal chemistry. Home: 1415 Brooklyn Ave Ann Arbor MI 48104 Office: Coll Pharmacy Univ Mich Ann Arbor MI 48109

PAUL, FRANK WATERS, mechanical engineer, consultant; b. Jersey Shore, Pa., Aug. 28, 1938; s. James D. and Elizabeth (Waters) P.; m. Gail Hart, Sept. 4, 1959; children—David H., Douglas J. B.S. in M.E., Pa. State U., 1960, M.S., 1964; Ph.D., Lehigh U., 1968. Instr. mech. engring. Lehigh U., Bethlehem, Pa., 1964-68; asst. prof., assoc. prof. Carnegie Mellon U., Pitts., 1968-77; assoc. prof. Clemson U., 1977-79, prof., 1979-83, McQueen Quattlebaum prof., 1983—, dir. Engring. Ctr. for Automated Mfg. Tech., 1981—; owner Paul Cons., Seneca, S.C., 1968—. Mem. ASME, Am. Soc. Engring. Edn., Robotics Internat./Soc. Mfg. Engrs. Current work: control, automated manufacturing, robotics Subspecialties: Robotics; Mechanical engineering. Office: Clemson U Mech Engring Riggs Hall Clemson SC 29634

PAUL, JOHN FRANCIS, physical oceanographer; b. Massillon, Ohio, July 6, 1947; s. John Francis and Irene Rose (Jenei) P.; m. Maureen Skelley, May 3, 1975; 1 son, Justin Morgan. B.S. in Engring. with high honors, Case Western Res. U., 1969, M.S., 1971, Ph.D., 1974. Teaching asst. dept. fluid and thermal scis. Case Western Res. U., Cleve., 1969-73, research assoc., 1973-75, sr. research assoc., 1975-77; environ. scientist EPA, Grosse Ile, Mich., 1977-81, research environ. scientist, Narragansett, R.I., 1981—; cons. and lectr. in field. Contbr. tech. reports and articles to profl. jours. NDEA fellow Case Western Res. U., 1969-72. Mem. N.E. Area Remote Sensing System Assn. (dir. 1982—), Am. Geophys. Union, Assn. for Computing Machinery, Internat. Assn. Gt. Lakes Research, AAAS. Roman Catholic. Current Work: Research interests include the development and application of quantitative assessment methodologies for predicting the impacts of waste disposal in the marine environment. Subspecialties: Oceanography; Fluid mechanics. Home: 1 Enterprise Terr Kingston RI 02881 Office: EPA S Ferry Rd Narragansett RI 02882

PAUL, PREM SAGAR, veterinary virologist, educator; b. Jullunder, India, Oct. 5, 1947; came to U.S. 1969, naturalized, 1977; s. Girdhari Lal and Leela (Rajput) P.; m. Melissa Jean Clemans, Aug. 24, 1973; children—Neena, Ryan. B.V.Sc. and A.H., Coll. Vet. Medicine (India), 1969; Ph.D., U. Minn., 1975. Diplomate Am. Coll. Vet. Microbiologists. Research asst. U. Minn., St. Paul, 1969-75, research assoc., 1975-78, assoc. grad. faculty, 1978; vet. med. officer Nat. Animal Disease Ctr., Ames, Iowa, 1978-85, research leader, 1982-85; assoc. prof. Vet. Med. Research Inst., Iowa State U., Ames, 1985—, prof./collaborator dept. vet. microbiology, 1985; chmn. vet. immune standards subcom. WHO. Patentee Monoclonal Antibodies to Porcine Immunoglobulins (Cash award 1984), 1984. Soccer coach Ames Parks and Recreation, 1982-84; active Prin.'s Adv. Com., Ames, 1983—. Recipient Merit scholarship Coll. Vet. Medicine, India, 1965-69; USDA research grantee, 1983. Mem. Am. Vet. Med. Assn., Am. Soc. Virology, Am. Assn. Vet. Immunologists (co-editor newsletter 1984—). Current work: Porcine Parvovirus research: gene mapping, genetic engineering of parvovirus subunit vaccine; reproductive immunology, research: monoclonal antibodies to porcine immunoglobulins, defense mechanisms. Transmissible gastroenteritis virus research: identification of immunogenic proteins, subunit vaccine, immune response, monoclonal antibodies; bovine virus diarrea virus research: immunogenic proteins identification, subunit vaccine, strain differentiation, monoclonal antibodies. Subspecialties: Virology (veterinary medicine); Microbiology (veterinary medicine). Office: Vet Med Research Inst Iowa State U Ames IA 50011

PAUL, RONALD STANLEY, research institute executive; b. Olympia, Wash., Jan. 19, 1923; s. Adolph and Olga (Klapstein) P.; m. Margery Jean Pengra, June 5, 1944; children—Kathleen (Mrs. Joel R. Crosby), Robert S., James N. B.S., U. Oreg., 1947, M.S., 1949, Ph.D., 1951. Dir., Battelle Pacific NW div., Richland, Wash., 1971-73; v.p. ops. Battelle Meml. Inst., Columbus, Ohio, 1973-76, sr. v.p., 1976-78, exec. v.p., chief operating officer, 1979-81, pres., chief operating officer, 1982-84, pres., chief exec. officer, 1984—; lectr. modern physics Ctr. for Grad. Studies, Richland, 1951-62. Contbr. to profl. publs. Served with USAAF, 1943-46. Named to Consultancy Internat. Atomic Energy Agy., Japan, 1962. Mem. Am. Phys. Soc., Am. Nuclear Soc., Sigma Xi, Sigma Pi Sigma, Pi Mu Epsilon. Republican. Baptist. Subspecialty: Nuclear physics. Office: Battelle Meml Inst 505 King Ave Columbus OH 43201

PAUL, WILLIAM ERWIN, immunologist; b. Bklyn., June 12, 1936; s. Jack and Sylvia (Gleicher) P.; m. Marilyn Heller, Dec. 25, 1958; children: Jonathan M., Matthew E. A.B., Bklyn. Coll., 1956; M.D., SUNY, Downstate Med. Ctr., 1960. Intern, asst. resident in medicine Univ. Hosp., Boston, 1960-62; clin. assoc. Nat. Cancer Inst., Bethesda, Md., 1962-64; fellow in pathology NYU Sch. Medicine, 1964-66, trainee to instr. in medicine, 1966-68; sr. investigator lab. immunology Nat. Inst. Allergy and Infectious Diseases, Bethesda, 1968-70, chief lab. immunology, 1970—; commd. med. officer USPHS, 1975—; mem. sci. rev. bd. Howard Hughes Med. Inst.; sci. adv. bd. Jane Coffin Childs Fund for Med. Research; bd. sci. visitors Okla. Med. Research Found.; mem. sci. adv. com. New Eng. Regional Primate Ctr. Contbr. numerous articles on immunology to profl. jours.; editor Ann. Rev. of Immunology, 1982—. Served with USPHS, 1962-64. Recipient Founders' prize Tex. Instruments Found., 1979; G. Burroughs Mider Lectureship award NIH, 1982. Mem. Am. Assn. Immunologists (councillor 1981-85, v.p. 1985-86), Am. Soc. for Clin. Investigation (Councillor 1976-79, pres. 1980-81), Nat. Acad. Scis., Assn Am. Physicians. Current Work: Mechanisms of lymphocyte activation, antigen regocnition, immune response gene function, and cellular interactions. Subspecialties: Immunobiology and immunology; Immunogenetics. Office: Bldg 10 Room 11N31 NIH Bethesda MD 20205

PAULE, MERLE GALE, pharmacologist, toxicologist; b. Sacramento, Calif., June 28, 1952; s. Loren Frenthrup Paule and Edith Anna (Coppin) Lewis; m. Candee Hope Teitel, Jan. 9, 1982; 1 child, Maxwell Teitel. A.A. in Fine Arts, Sacramento City Coll., 1974; B.S. in Biochemistry, U. Calif.-Davis, 1976, Ph.D. in Pharmacology and Toxicology, 1983; postdoctoral fellow, U. Ark., 1982-83. Staff fellow Nat. Ctr. Toxicological Research, Jefferson, Ark., 1983—. Contbr. numerous articles to profl. jours. Math. and Nat. Sci. scholar, 1974; Dreyfus Med. Research grantee, 1984. Mem. Soc. Neurosci., N.Y. Acad. Sci., Am. Soc. Primatologists, Nat. Med. Research Soc., Sigma Xi. Democrat. Current work: Behavioral pharmacology, toxicology with special emphasis on learning deficiencies as indicators of toxicity and aging; sites and mechanisms of action of psychotropic agents; developmental pharmacology/toxicology; behavioral effects of chronic marijuana use. Subspecialties: Neuropharmacology; Behavioral pharmacology/toxicology. Office: Nat Ctr Toxicological Research Div Reproductive and Devel Toxicology HFT132 Jefferson AR 72079

PAULING, LINUS CARL, chemistry educator; b. Portland, Oreg., Feb. 28, 1901; s. Herman Henry William and Lucy Isabelle (Darling) P.; m. Ava Helen Miller, June 17, 1923 (dec. Dec. 7, 1981); children: Linus Carl, Peter Jeffress, Linda Helen, Edward Crellin. B.S., Oreg. State Coll., Corvallis, 1922, Sc.D. (hon.), 1933; Ph.D., Calif. Inst. Tech., 1925; Sc.D. (hon.), U. Chgo., 1941, Princeton, 1946, U. Cambridge, U. London, Yale, 1947, Oxford, 1948, Bklyn. Poly. Inst., 1955, Humboldt U., 1959, U. Melbourne, 1964, U. Delhi, Adelphi U., 1967, Marquette U. Sch. Medicine, 1969; L.H.D., Tampa, 1950; U.J.D., U. N.B., 1950; LL.D., Reed Coll., 1959; Dr. h.c., Jagiellonian U., Montpellier (France), 1964; D.F.A., Chouinard Art Inst., 1958; also others. Teaching fellow Calif. Inst. Tech., 1922-25, research fellow, 1925-27, asst. prof., 1927-29, asso. prof., 1929-31, prof. chem., 1931-64; chmn. div. chem. and chem. engring., dir. Calif. Inst. Tech. (Gates and Crellin Labs. of Chemistry), 1936-58, mem. exec. com., bd. trustees, 1945-48; research prof. (Center for Study Dem. Instns.), 1963-67; prof. chemistry U. Calif. at San Diego, 1967-69, Stanford, 1969-74; pres. Linus Pauling Inst. Sci. and Medicine, 1973-75, 78-80, research prof., 1973—; George Eastman prof. Oxford U., 1948; lectr. chemistry several univs. Author several books, 1930—, including, Cancer and Vitamin C, 1979; Contbr. articles to profl. jours. Fellow Balliol Coll., 1948; Fellow NRC, 1925-26; Fellow John S. Guggenheim Meml. Found., 1926-27; Numerous awards in field of chemistry, including; U.S. Presdl. Medal for Merit, 1948; Nobel prize in chemistry, 1954; Nobel Peace prize, 1962; Internat. Lenin Peace prize, 1972; U.S. Nat. Medal of Sci., 1974; Fermat medal; Paul Sabatier medal; Pasteur medal; medal with laurel wreath of Internat. Grotius Found., 1957; Lomonosov medal, 1978; U.S. Nat. Acad. Sci. medal in Chem. Scis., 1979; Priestley medal Am. Chem. Soc., 1984; award for chemistry Arthur M. Sackler Found., 1984. Hon., corr., fgn. mem. numerous assns. and orgns. Subspecialties: Physical chemistry; Biophysical chemistry. Home: Salmon Creek Big Sur CA 93920 Office: Linus Pauling Inst Sci and Medicine 440 Page Mill Rd Palo Alto CA 94306

PAULK, CHARLES JASPER, JR., electrical engineer; b. Pensacola, Fla., Dec. 21, 1950; s. Charles Jasper and Ethel Mai (Harris) P.; m. Marilynn Jane Overton, Aug. 12, 1972; children: Charles Christopher, Monika Michelle. B.S., SUNY-Albany, 1980; A.S.E.E., Internat. Corr. Sch., 1981; B.A., N.C. Wesleyan Coll., 1982; M.B.A., Campbell U., 1985. Engr. Carolina Power & Light Co., New Hill, N.C., 1980-83, sr. engr., 1983—. Served with USN, 1971-80. Mem. Am. Nuclear Soc., IEEE. Baptist. Current Work: Shift technical adviser. Subspecialties: Electrical engineering; Nuclear physics. Home: 8513 Holly Springs Rd Apex NC 27502 Office: Carolina Power & Light Co PO Box 165 New Hill NC 27562

PAULL, CHARLES, marine geologist; b. Framingham, Mass., June 16, 1951; s. Richard and Lucia (Kerr) P. B.A. in Geology, Harvard U., 1974; M.S. in Marine Geology, U. Miami, 1976; Ph.D. in Oceanography, U. Calif.-San Diego, 1986. With U.S. Geol. Survey, Woods Hole, Mass., 1975-80; with Scripps Inst. Oceanography, San Diego, 1980—. Contbr. articles to profl. jours. Mem. Am. Assn. Petroleum Geologists, Am. Geophys. Union, Soc. Econ. Paleontologists and Mineralogists. Current work: Processes of initial formation and subsequent erosional modification of carbonate continental margins. Subspecialties: Marine biology; Oceanography. Office: Scripps Instn Oceanography A-008 LaJolla CA 92093

PAULS, JOHN FREDERICK, biostatistician; b. Washington, Iowa, Dec. 7, 1928; s. George A. and Hannah Esther (Jones) P.; m. Margaret M. Delashmutt, June 10, 1950; children: Debra J. O'Leary, Cathy Sue Aafjes, Douglas J. B.S., Iowa State U., 1952, M.S., 1954. Sr. Statistician Smith Kline Corp., Phila., 1956-58, group leader applied math. services, 1958-64, asst. sect. head stats., 1964-67; assoc. dir. Smith Kline Corp. (Lab. Stats.), 1967-75; asst. dir statis. services Carter-Wallace, Inc., Cranbury, N.J., 1975-82, dir. statis. services, 1982—; adj. assoc. prof. biometrics dept. Temple U., Phila., 1974-75. Chmn. Towamencin Mcpl. Swimming Club; mem. steering and operating com. Towamencin Twp., Montgomery County, Pa., 1967-75; treas. N. Pa. Sch. Dist. Authority, Lansdale, 1975-76. Served with USN, 1946-48. NSF fellow, 1952-53. Mem. Am. Statis. Assn., Biometrics Soc., Am. Soc. Quality Control, Soc. for Clin. Trials, Sigma Xi. Republican. Methodist. Current Work: Experimental design, statistical analysis, design and analysis clinical trials. Subspecialty: Statistics.

PAULY, JOHN EDWARD, anatomist; b. Elgin, Ill., Sept. 17, 1927; s. Edward John and Gladys (Myhre) P.; m. Margaret Mary Oberle, Sept. 3, 1949; children: Stephen John, Susan Elizabeth, Kathleen Ann, Mark Edward. B.S., Northwestern U., 1950; M.S., Loyola U., Chgo., 1952, Ph.D., 1955. Grad. asst. gross anatomy Stritch Sch. Medicine, Loyola U., Chgo., 1953-54; research asst. anatomy Chgo. Med. Sch., 1952-54, research instr., 1954-55, instr. in gross anatomy, 1955-57, asso. gross anatomy, 1957-59, asst. prof. anatomy, 1959-63, asst. to pres., 1960-62; asso. prof. anatomy Tulane U. Sch. Medicine, 1963-67; prof., head dept. anatomy U. Ark. for Med. Scis., Little Rock, 1967-83, prof., head dept. physiology and biophysics, 1978-80, vice chancellor acad. affairs and sponsored research, assoc. dean grad. sch., 1983—; tech. adviser Ency. Brit. Films, 1956; mem. safety and occupational health study sect. Nat. Inst. Occupational Safety and Health, Center for Disease Control, 1975-79. Author: (with Hans Elias) Human Microanatomy, 1960, 62, (with Elias and E. Robert Burns) Histology and Human Microanatomy, 1978; editor: (with Lawrence E. Scheving and Franz Halberg) Chronobiology, 1974, (with Heinz von Mayersbach and Lawrence E. Scheving) Biological Rhythms in Structure and Function, 1981, Am. Jour. Anatomy, 1980—; co-mng. editor Advances in Anatomy, Embryology and Cell Biology, 1980—; adv. editorial bd. Internat. Jour. Chronobiology, 1973-83; contbr. articles to profl. jours. Served with USNR, 1945-47. Recipient merit certificates AMA, 1953, 59; Bronze award Ill. Med. Soc., 1959; Lederle Med. Faculty award, 1966. Fellow AAAS; mem. Am. Assn. Anatomists (sec.-treas. 1972-80, pres. 1982-83), So. Soc. Anatomists (pres. 1971-72), Assn. Anatomy Chmn. (sec.-treas. 1969-71), Am. Physiol. Soc., Internat. Soc. Chronobiology, Pan-Am. Assn. Anatomy, Internat. Soc. Electrophysiol. Kinesiology, Internat. Soc. Steriology, Consejo Nacional de Profesores de Ciencias Morphológicas (hon.), Sigma Xi, Sigma Alpha Epsilon. Roman Catholic. Current Work: Chronopharmacology; chronotoxicology; chronochemotherapy of neoplasms; effect of various peptides on DNA synthesis. Subspecialties: Anatomy and embryology; Chronobiology. Home: 11 Hearthside Dr Little Rock AR 72207

PAUSTIAN, HAROLD HERMAN, nuclear engineer; b. Davenport, Iowa, July 13, 1951; s. Herbert Herman and Ruby Elanor (Poppe) P.; m. Mary Theresa Scott, Mar. 29, 1980. B.S. in Engring. Sci, Iowa State U., 1973, M.S. in Nuclear Engring, 1975. Registered profl. engr., Calif. Engr. Gen. Electric Co., San Jose, Calif., 1975-81, sr. engr., tech. leader, 1981—. Nat. Merit scholar, 1969. Mem. Am. Nuclear Soc. (assoc.). Republican. Lutheran. Current Work: Design of nuclear fuel for commercial fission power plants, with an emphasis on improving fuel cycle economics. Subspecialties: Nuclear engineering; Nuclear fission.

PAVELIC, ZLATKO PAUL, pathologist, researcher; b. Slavonski Brod, Yugoslavia, Aug. 14, 1943; came to U.S., 1975, naturalized, 1982; s. Mirko and Zlata (Godic) P.; m. Ljiljana Duic Pavelic, May 7, 1947. M.D., U. Zagreb, Croatia, Yugoslavia, 1969, M.S., 1971, Dr.S., 1974. Intern U. Zabreg Hosp., 1969-71, Gen. Hosp., Pakrac, Yugoslavia, 1969-71; resident in pathologic anatomy U. Zagreb, 1971-74, asst. prof. pathologic anatomy, 1970-75, assoc. prof., 1975; vis. scientist Roswell Park Meml. Inst., Buffalo, 1975-77, assoc. cancer research scientist, 1977—; clin. asst. prof. pathology SUNY, Buffalo, 1978-80, assoc. prof., 1980—, asst. research prof. dept. pharmacology, 1978—. Contbr. numerous articles in field to profl. jours. and books. Grantee in field. Mem. Med. Assn. Croatia, Yugoslavia Assn. Immunology, Yugoslavia Assn. Pathology, Am. Assn. Cancer Research, Am. Soc. Clin. Oncology, Am. Assn. Pathology, N.Y. Acad. Sci., AAAS, Sigma Xi. Current Work: Preclinical toxicological pathology; cloning and drug sensitivity of human solid tumors in soft agar. Subspecialties: Pathology (medicine); Pharmacology. Home: 136 Depew Ave Buffalo NY 14214 Office: 666 Elm St Buffalo NY 14263

PAVIA, EDGAR HUGO, environmental engineer; b. Elizabeth, N.J., Apr. 9, 1925; s. Renato and Nicolena (Arace) P.; m. Lillian Foster, Nov. 23, 1949. B.S. in Mech. Engring., La. Poly. Inst., 1950. Registered profl. engr., La., Miss., Ala., N.J., Tex.; diplomate Am. Acad. Environ. Engrs. Mech. engr. Bedell & Nelson, Engrs., New Orleans, 1952-55; assoc. G.A. Heft & Co., New Orleans, 1955-62; pres., chief engr. Pavia-Bryne Engring. Corp., New Orleans, 1963—; chmn. bd. Environ. Purification Systems, Inc., New Orleans, 1982—. Inventor in field of water pollution control and treatment. Served with USMC, 1943-47, 51-52. Recipient cert. of appreciation EPA, 1981. Mem. ASME (v.p. 1973-75), Water Pollution Control Fedn. (dir. 1976-79), Nat. Soc. Profl. Engrs., Pi Tau Sigma. Republican. Roman Catholic. Clubs: Internat. House (New Orleans); World Trade. Current work: Environmental control processes. Subspecialties: Environmental engineering; Mechanical engineering. Home: 7443 Onyx St New Orleans LA 70129 Office: Pavia-Byrne Engineering Corp 13152 Chef Menteur Hwy New Orleans LA 70129

PAVLIDIS, GEORGE THEOPHILOU, psychiatry educator, researcher; b. Thessaloniki, Greece, Apr. 16, 1949; came to arrived Eng., 1981; s. Theophilos and Parthena (Katseas) P.; m. Manolia Kalogridis, July 2, 1983; 1 son, Alexander Theophilos. B.A. with honors, Aristotelean U., Thessaloniki, Greece, 1972; Ph.D., U. Manchester, Eng., 1980. Lectr. U. Salford, Eng., 1972-75; tutor U. Manchester, Eng., 1973-80, research fellow, 1974-78, research fellow, 1978-80, sr. research fellow, 1981-83; vis. assoc. prof. psychiatry UMDNJ-Rutgers Med. Sch., Piscataway, N.J., 1981-83, vis. assoc. prof. pediatrics, 1981—; co-dir. Reading Disability Research Inst., 1982. Contbr. articles to profl. jours. Editor: Dyslexia Research and Its Applications to Education, 1981; Dyslexia: Neuropsychology and Treatment, 1986. Fellow Internat. Acad. Research in Learning Disabilities (v.p.); mem. Brain Research Assn., Exptl. Psychology Soc., Am. Psychol. Assn., Brit. Psychol. Soc., AAAS, N.Y. Acad. Sci. Patentee biodigitizer. Current Work: The relationship between eye movements and evoked potentials to: dyslexia, learning disabilities, schizophrenia, hyperactivity, alcoholism, higher cognitive processes and intelligence. Subspecialties: Neuropsychology; Developmental psychology. Office: UMDNJ-Rutgers Med Sch Dept Pediatrics Box 10 Piscataway NJ 08854

PAXSON, CHARLES L., JR., b. Columbus, Kans., Jan. 4, 1946; s. Charles L. Sr. and Freida (Derfelt) P.; m. Cathleen Joy Carlson, Oct. 13, 1974; children: Katherine Joy, Benjamin Charles. B.A., Pitts. Coll., 1968; M.D., U. Kans., 1971. Diplomate: Am. Bd. Pediatrics. Asst. prof. pediatrics U. Nebr., Omaha, 1976-79, asst. prof. physiology, 1976-79, dir. neontology research, 1977-79; dir. neonatology Central Plains Clinic, Sioux Falls, S.D., 1979-81; dir. newborn service St. Elizabeth Hosp., Youngstown, Ohio, 1981—; asst. prof. pediatrics Northeastern Ohio Univs. Coll. Medicine, Rootstown, 1982—. Editor: Van Leeuwen's New Medicine, 1979; contbr. articles to profl. jours. Am. Heart Assn. grantee, 1976-79. Fellow Am. Fedn. Clin. Research. Mem. Assemblies of God Ch. Current Work: Primary interest is in blood and volume expansion of hypotensive infants, and techniques to rapidly assess circulating blood volume. Subspecialty: Neonatology. Home: 209 Edna Poland Village OH 44514 Office: St Elizabeth Hosp Med Ctr 1044 Belmont Ave Youngstown OH 44501

PAXTON, HAROLD WILLIAM, steel company executive; b. Yorkshire, Eng., Feb. 6, 1927; came to U.S., 1953, naturalized, 1961; s. John Wilfrid and Hilda Annie (Vasey) P.; m. Ann Dorothy Davies, May 13, 1953; children: Jane Elizabeth, Sally Patricia, Anthony Charles, Nigel John. B.Sc. with 1st class honours, U. Man., 1947, M.Sc., 1948; Ph.D., U. Birmingham, Eng., 1952. Univ. fellow U. Birmingham, 1950-53; mem. faculty Carnegie-Mellon U., 1953-74, prof. metall. engring., 1962-74, Firth Sterling prof. metall. research, 1958-63; head dept. metallurgy and materials sci., dir. Metals Research Lab., 1966-71, dir. research, 1973-74; adj. sr. fellow Mellon Inst., 1965-67; dir. div. materials research NSF, 1971-73; v.p. research U.S. Steel Corp., 1974—; vis. prof. Mass. Inst. Tech., 1970; Campbell Meml. lectr., 1978; BCRA Carbonization Sci. Gold medal lectr., 1982; Australasian Inst. Mining and Metallurgy lectr., 1982; cons. to industry, 1953-74; Chmn. Internat. Conf. High Velocity Deformation, 1960, Internat. Conf. Fracture, 1962. Author: (with E. C. Bain), 3d edit.) Alloying Elements in Steel, 1966, also numerous articles. NSF sr. postdoctoral fellow Imperial Coll., London, Eng., 1962-63. Fellow Am. Soc. Metals (Bradley Stoughton Young Tchrs. award 1960, Zay Jeffries lectr. 1983, Gold medal for advancement of research 1983), Metall. Soc. of Am. Inst. M.E. (pres. 1976-77, v.p. inst. 1977-78), AAAS; mem. AIME (pres. 1982—), Am. Iron and Steel Inst., Nat. Acad. Engring., Iron and Steel Inst. of Japan (Yukawa Meml. lectr. 1985). Subspecialty: Metallurgy. Home: 115 Eton Dr Pittsburgh PA 15215 Office: Room 1365 600 Grant St Pittsburgh PA 15230

PAYNE, LAWRENCE EDWARD, mathematics educator; b. Enfield, Ill., Oct. 2, 1923; s. Robert Ulysses and Harriet (Lasher) P.; m. Ruth Marian Winterstein, Dec. 27, 1948; children—Steven L., John E., Marcia G., Christopher J., Michele T. Student, Miami U., Oxford, Ohio, 1943-44; B.S. in Mech. Engring., Iowa State U., 1946; M.S. in Applied Math, Iowa State U., 1948, Ph.D., 1950. Jr. engr. Linde Air Products, North Tonawanda, N.Y., 1946-47; asst. prof. math. U. Ariz., 1950-51; research asso. U. Md., 1951-52, asst. prof., 1952-55, asso. prof., 1955-60, prof., 1960-65, Cornell U., Ithaca, N.Y., 1965—, dir. Center for Applied Math., 1967-71, 76-77, 80-81; Lectr. in field; cons. Nat. Bur. Standards, 1958-65. Editorial bd.: Jour. of Elasticity, Applicable Analysis, Math. Methods in the Applied Sciences; Contbr. articles to profl. jours. Served with USNR, 1943-46. NSF sr. postdoctoral fellow, 1958-59; Recipient award sci. achievement math. Washington Acad. Scis., 1962. Mem. Am. Math. Soc. (Steele prize in math. 1972), Soc. Indsl. Applied Math., Math. Assn. Am., Am. Acad. Mechanics, Soc. Engring. Sci., Soc. Natural Philosophy, Sigma Xi. Current work: Partial differential equations and their applications in the physical and engineering sciences. Home: Ithaca NY

PAYNE, ROBERT WILLIAM, metallurgist, quality assurance executive; b. Indpls., Mar. 29, 1922; s. Francis William and Mary Louise (Hughel) P.; m. Eileen Ruth McCann; m. Maryan June Browning; children: Gregory Robert, Sheila Eileen, Linda Suzan. B.S. in Metallurgy, U. Calif.-Berkeley, 1947. Metallurgist and specifications examiner Columbia-Geneva div. U.S. Steel Corp., San Francisco, 1947-50, distbn. asst. wire and wire products, 1951-64; chief metallurgist, dir. quality assurance Western Forge & Flange Co., Santa Clara, Calif., 1964—; cons. in field. Served with USCG, 1942-43. Mem. ASME, Am. Soc. Metals, ASTM. Democrat. Mormon. Inventor in field. Current Work: Physical ferrous/non ferrous metallurgy; forgings, quality assurance. Subspecialties: Metallurgical engineering; Materials (engineering). Home: 5222 Colgate Ave Santa Clara CA 95051 Office: PO Box 327 Santa Clara CA 95052

PAZARGADI, SHAYAN, engineer; b. Tehran, Iran, Jan. 5, 1949; came to U.S., 1973, naturalized, 1980; s. Alaedin and Badri (Mossafa) P.; m. Fatemeh Moayeri, Aug. 21, 1979; 1 child, Leila. B.S., Arya-Mehr U. Tech., Tehran, 1971; M.S., U. Calif.-Berkeley, 1974, M.Engring., 1975; Ph.D., Stanford U., 1979. Research asst. Stanford U. (Calif.), 1978-79; sr. engr. Engring. Decision Analysis Co., Palo Alto, Calif., 1979-81; project mgr. NCT Engring., Lafayette, Calif., 1981-83; engring. research and practitioner Wyle Labs., Norco, Calif., 1983—; cons. to industry. Contbr. articles to profl. publs. Arya-Mehr U. Tech. fellow, 1973-78. Mem. IEEE, ASCE, Earthquake Engring. Research Inst., Soc. Automotive Engrs., AIAA. Current work: Structural dynamics, applied research, developing and applying computerized systems and methods in the field of structural dynamics. Subspecialties: Structural engineering; Systems engineering. Home: 19804 Grace Haven Yorba Linda CA 92686 Office: Wyle Labs Sci Services and Systems Group 1841 Hillside Ave Norco CA 91760

PAZDERNIK, THOMAS LOWELL, pharmacologist; b. Detroit Lakes, Minn., Jan. 3, 1943; s. Alvin Joseph and Irene Helen (Kersting) P.; m. Betty Catherine Platt, June 20, 1967; children: Lisa Ann, Nancy Lea. Student, Coll. St. Thomas, St. Paul, 1961-63; B.S. in Pharmacy, U. Minn., 1967; Ph.D. in Medicinal Chemistry, U. Kans., Lawrence, 1971. Postdoctoral fellow U. Kans. Med. Center, Kansas City, 1971-73, asst. prof., 1973-77, asso. prof. pharmacology, 1977-83, prof. pharmacology, toxicology and therapeutics, 1983—; vis. research scientist U. Helsinki, Finland, 1976—. Contbr. articles to profl. jours. NIH fellow, 1979-71, 71-73; research career devel. awardee, 1975-80. Mem. Am. Chem. Soc., Am. Soc. Pharmacology and Exptl. Therapeutics, Tissue Culture Assn., Sigma Xi, Rho Chi, Phi Lambda Upsilon. Roman Catholic. Current Work: Effects of drugs and chemicals on the immune system, autoradiographic localization of neurotransmitters in the brain. Subspecialties: Immunotoxicology; Neuropharmacology. Office: U Kans Med Center 39th and Rainbow Sts Kansas City KS 66103

PAZZAGLINI, MARIO PETER, psychologist; b. Endicott, N.Y., Mar. 9, 1940; s. Mario and Dina (Albertini) P. B.A., SUNY-Binghamton, 1961; M.A., U. Del., 1965, Ph.D., 1969. Lic. clin. psychologist, Del. Staff psychologist, co-dir. adolescent program Del. State Hosp., New Castle, 1968-77; psychologist-adminstr. Bur. Alcoholism and Drug Abuse, New Castle, 1970—; pvt. practice psychology, Newark, Del., 1973—; clin. instr. Jefferson Med. Sch., Phila., 1972—; clin. psychologist St. Francis Hosp., Wilmington, Del., 1977—; cons. Dept. Pub. Instrn., Dover, Del., 1972—, Dept. Health and Social Services, New Castle, 1972—, ct. system, Wilmington-Dover, 1972—, Dept. Corrections, Wilmington-Dover, 1972—. Co-author psychol. inventory, 1980; painter, illustrator, 1965—. Cons. community based free drug clinics, N.Y.C., 1968-75; cons. community based free drug clinics State of Del., 1968-74, community based emergency hot lines, 1968—, coms. for services to children and youth, 1971—. HEW grantee, 1971-72. Mem. AAAS, Am. Psychol. Assn., N.Y. Acad. Scis., N.Y. Gestalt Inst., Del. Psychol. Assn., Sigma Xi. Democrat. Roman Catholic. Current Work: Research in the field of imagery—crosscultural studies, historical-ancient studies, current therapeutic uses. Subspecialties: Behavioral psychology; Clinical psychology. Office: 523 Capitol Trail Newark DE 19711

PEAK, DAVID, physics educator; b. Bklyn., Nov. 28, 1941; s. William Henry and Blanche Ethel (Seckendorff) P.; m. Terry Handwerger, June 3, 1983. Ph.D., SUNY-Albany, 1969. Research assoc. SUNY-Albany, 1969-71, instr., 1971-75; asst. prof. Union Coll., Schenectady, 1975-79, assoc. prof. physics, 1979-85, prof. physics, 1985—; sr. fellow Inst. for Study of Defects in Solids, Albany, 1975—; vis. fellow Princeton U., N.J., 1978-79; vis. scientist Argonne Nat. Lab., Ill., 1983-84. Contbr. sci. articles to profl. jours. Recipient Outstanding Teaching award SUNY-Albany Faculty Senate, 1973, Profl. Devel. award NSF, 1978, Faculty Research award Argonne Nat. Lab., 1983. Mem. Am. Phys. Soc., Am. Assn. Physics Tchrs., Sigma Xi. Current work: Transport and reaction in condensed phases; radiation effects in solids; ion beam modification of materials. Subspecialties: Statistical physics; Condensed matter physics. Office: Physics Dept Union College Schenectady NY 12308

PEANASKY, ROBERT JOSEPH, biochemist, and medical educator, research scientist; b. Menominee, Mich., Oct. 18, 1927; s. Joseph John and Sophia E. (Simeth) P.; m. Elizabeth R. Bender, Sept. 12, 1953; children—Joseph F., Michael J., Paul J., Robert A., John S. B.S. cum laude, Marquette U., 1951, M.S., 1953; Ph.D., U. Wis., 1957. Trainee Marquette U., Milw., 1957, 58, 60, Dartmouth, Hanover, N.H., 1959; asst. prof. Marquette U. Med. Sch., Milw., 1960-65, assoc. prof., 1965-67; U. S.D. Med. Sch., Vermillion, 1967-70, prof. biochemistry, 1970—; vis. scientist U. Ky. Med. Ctr., Lexington, 1965, Facultie de Sciences U. Marseille-aix-en-Provence, 1966-67; vis. prof., Purdue U., West Lafayette, Ind., 1977; participant in various confs. Served to cpl. U.S. Army, 1946-47. Recipient Career Devel. award USPHS. USPHS sr. fellow, 1960-62; NIH grantee 1961—. Mem. Am. Chem. Soc. (sect. chmn.), Am. Soc. Biol. Chemists, Soc. Exptl. Biology and Medicine (council mem. 1976-79, referee editor Proceedings 1969-78), S.D. Acad. Scis. (exec. com. 1983—), Sigma Xi (chpt. pres. 1979-80). Democrat. Roman Catholic. Clubs: Coyote Coaches (Vermillion), Quarterback (Vermillion). Current work: Purification of proteins, characterization, structure and modification of proteins, role of protease inhibitors in Ascaris Lumbricoides, development of Ascaris. Subspecialties: Biochemistry (medicine); Parasitology. Home: 916 Jane St Vermillion SD 57069 Office: U SD Med Sch Dept Biochemistry Vermillion SD 57069

PEARCE, MALCOLM BULKELEY, JR., mech. engr.; b. West Haven, Conn., Nov. 12, 1929; s. Malcolm Bulkeley and Heneritta Louise (Bowyer) P.; m. Helen Christine Korn, Oct. 13, 1951; children: Malcolm Bulkeley III, April, Holly. B.S. in M.E, Ind. Inst. Tech., 1950; M.E., UCLA, 1953; M.D., U. N.H., 1968. Registered Engr., N.Y., Conn. Flight test NAA, Los Angeles, 1951-54; power plant engr. Pratt & Whitney Aircraft, East Hartford, Conn., 1954-57; aerospace engr. AVCO, Stratford, Conn., 1957-61; nuclear engr. Canel Pratt & Whitney Aircraft, Middletown, Conn., 1961-63; fuel controls CECO, West Hartford, Conn., 1963-66; spl. weapons E-B, Simsbury, Conn., 1966-68; dir. mgr. IBC Loctite, Newington, Conn., 1968-72; tech. market mgr. Rawl, N.Y.C., 1972-78; mgr. material engring. United Tech., Sikrosky, Conn., 1978—; mgr. spl. advance projects materials group Sikorsky Aircraft, Stratford, Conn., 1981—; cons. consumer preports. Dir. civil def., Durham, Conn., 1954—, dir. police services, 1970-82; mem. Republican Town Com., 1976—. Served with AUS, 1945-47. Mem. ASME, Soc. Automotive Engrs., Am. Nat. Standards Inst., Expansion Anchor Mfrs. Inst., Structural and Materials Process Engring. Assn. Republican. Mem. United Ch. (deacon, trustee). Lodges: Masons; Shriners. Patentee in field. Current Work: Aerospace investigation advanced projects management. 0H. Subspecialties: Composite materials; Aerospace engineering and technology. Home: 242 Bayberry Hill Durham CT 06422 Office: Sikorsky Aircraft N Main St Stratford CT 06602

PEARCE, WILLIAM JULIAN, physiology educator, researcher; b. Midland, Mich., July 30, 1952; s. Roscoe Lamont and Louise Elizabeth (Dye) P.; m. Querida Lee, June 28, 1981. B.S. in Zoology, U. Mich., 1974, Ph.D. in Physiology, 1979. Muscular Dystrophy fellow dept. physiology U. Mich., Ann Arbor, 1975-76; Am. Heart Assn. fellow dept. physiology UCLA, 1979-81, NIH postdoctoral trainee dept. pharmacology, 1981-82; owner, chief cons. Designer Software, Los Angeles, 1980—, dir. Macpherson Lab. White Meml. Med. Ctr., Los Angeles, 1982—; asst. prof. physiology Loma Linda U., Calif., 1982—. Contbr. articles to profl. jours. and book. Recipient Young Scientist award Internat. Soc. Cerebral Blood Flow, 1977, honorarium, 1981; honorarium Pittis VA Hosp., Loma Linda, Calif., 1984. Mem. Am. Physiol. Soc. (young scientist travel award 1979—), Western Pharmacol. Soc., Cyanotic Heart Assn. (founding mem., bd. dirs. 1983—), N.Y. Acad. Scis., AAAS. Current work: Computer-assisted continuous measurement of cerebral blood flow and its responses to chemical and neurogenic stimuli, in vitro study of excitation/concentration coupling in vascular smooth muscle. Subspecialties: Physiology (medicine); Software engineering. Home: 11011 Ayres Ave West Los Angeles CA 90064 Office: Macpherson Lab White Meml Med Ctr 1720 Brooklyn Ave Los Angeles CA 900³³

PEARL, WESLEY LLOYD, corrosion and water treatment consultant; b. Seattle, July 10, 1921; s. Louis and Lena (Stusser) P.; m. Alice August, Nov. 7, 1942; children—Glenn, Janice Pearl Azose, Dennis, Louise Pearl Droker. B.S., U. Wash., 1942; M.S., Lawrence U., 1948, Ph.D., 1951. Registered profl. engr., Calif. Project engr. Longview Fibre Co., Wash., 1951-52; project engr. Gen. Electric Co., Richland, Wash., 1952-55, mgr. chem. engring., San Jose, Calif., 1955-74; pres. NWT Corp., San Jose, 1974—. Contbr. articles to various sci. jours. Patentee in field of water treatment. Served to lt. col. AUS, 1942-46, PTO. Mem. Am. Nuclear Soc., Am. Inst. Chem. Engrs., ASME, Nat. Assn. Corrosion Engrs., Phi Lambda Upsilon, Tau Beta Pi, Zeta Mu Tau. Subspecialty: Corrosion. Office: NWT Corp 7015 Realm Dr San Jose CA 95119

PEARLMAN, ALAN LEE, neurobiologist; b. Des Moines, June 30, 1936. A.B., U. Iowa-Iowa City, 1958; M.D., Washington U., St. Louis, 1961. Diplomate Am. Bd. Psychiatry and Neurology. Intern, Barnes Hosp., St. Louis, 1961-62; resident in neurology Mass. Gen. Hosp., Boston, 1964-67; research fellow Harvard U. Med. Sch., Boston, 1967-69; asst. prof. neurology Washington U., St. Louis, 1969-73, assoc. prof., 1973-79, prof. neurology and physiology, 1979—. Editor: Neurological Pathophysiology, 1984. Served with USPHS, 1961-63. NIH grantee, 1969—. Mem. Soc. Neurosci., Am. Neurol. Assn., Am. Acad. Neurology, Am. Physiol. Soc. Current work: Development of the cerebal cortex. Subspecialties: Neurobiology; Neurology. Office: Dept Cell Biology Washington U Sch Medicine 4566 Scott Ave Saint Louis MO 63110

PEARSE, JAMES NEWBURG, engineer; b. LaCrosse, Wis., June 5, 1930; s. Richard Henry and Edith (Newburg) P.; m. Jeanette Kubiak, Dec. 27, 1951; children—James C., John P., Thomas G. Student Notre Dame U., 1948-51; B.S.E.E., U. Wis.-Madison, 1957. Registered profl. engr., Wis. Product engr. Allen-Bradley Co., Milw., 1957-97; v.p. research and devel. Appleton Electric Co., Chgo., 1967-75; group v.p., engring. Leviton Mfg. Co., N.Y.C., 1975—. Contbr. articles to profl. jours. Patentee in field. Served with U.S. Army, 1951-53. Mem. AAAS, ASTM, IEEE, Illuminating Engring. Soc., Nat. Fire Protection Assn., Newcomen Soc., Tau Beta Pi, Eta Kappa Nu. Subspecialties: Electrical engineering; Microelectronics. Home: 12 Buckingham Dr Dixhills NY 11746 Office: Leviton Mfg Co Inc 59-25 Little Neck Pkwy Little Neck Little Neck NY 11362

PEARSON, ANTHONY JOHN, chemist, educator; b. Birmingham, Eng., Sept. 20, 1944; came to U.S., 1982; s. Ralph Charles Dennis and Jessie Irene (Morris) P.; m. Philippa Joan Anne Heron, Sept. 13, 1975; children—Andrew, David, Matthew. B.Sc., Leeds U., 1971; Ph.D., Aston U. (Eng.), 1974. Postdoctoral fellow Australian Nat. U., Canberra, 1974-77; advanced fellow Cambridge U., Eng., 1977-82; fellow, tutor Girton Coll., Cambridge, 1978-81; assoc. prof. Case Western Res. U., Cleve., 1982-84, prof., 1984—. Author: Metallo-Organic Chemistry, 1985; also articles. Recipient Sir Gilbert Morgan medal Soc. Chem. Industry, 1973; Sigma Xi Research award Case Western Res. U., 1984. Mem. Am. Chem. Soc., Royal Soc. Chemistry. Current work: Organometallic chemistry, organic synthesis, natural products synthesis, catalysis, oxidation chemistry. Subspecialties: Organometallics; Synthetic chemistry. Office: Case Western Res U Dept Chemistry Cleveland OH 44106

PEARSON, DALE SHELDON, chemical engineer; b. Omaha, Oct. 4, 1942; s. Dwight Sheldon and Dorothy (Ellison) P.; m. Joan M. Wiechman, Dec. 5, 1964; children—James Dale, Steven Michael. B.S. in Chem. Engring., Iowa State U., 1964; M.S. in Chem. Engring., U. Akron, 1971; Ph.D. in Materials Sci., Northwestern U., 1978. Research engr. Firestone Tire and Rubber Co., Akron, Ohio, 1965-74; mem. tech. staff Bell Labs, Murray Hill, N.J., 1978-83; research assoc. Exxon, Annandale, N.J., 1983—. Contbr. articles to profl. jours. Mem. Am. Chem. Soc., Am. Phys. Soc., Soc. Rheology. Republican. Presbyterian. Current work: Relationship of molecular structure to the physical properties of polymers; polymer physics. Subspecialties: Chemical engineering; Polymers (materials science). Home: 165 Blackburn Rd Summit NJ 07901 Office: Exxon Research and Engring Co Route 22 E Annandale NJ 08801

PEARSON, JAMES EDWARD, electrical and laser optics engineer; b. Evanston, Ill., July 11, 1944; s. John Estel and Rubye Elias (Rose) P.; m. Nancy K. Youree, Sept. 11, 1965; children—Daniel James, Suzanne Marie. B.S. in E.E., Calif. Inst. Tech., 1967, M.S. in E.E., 1968, Ph.D. in E.E. and Physics, 1972. Mem. tech. staff Los Alamos Nat. Lab., N.Mex., 1972-73; sr. staff physicist Hughes Research Labs., Malibu, Calif., 1973-76; sr. scientist Pratt & Whitney, West Palm Beach, Fla., 1976-79; mgr. Optics and Tech. Lab., United Tech. Research Ctr., West Palm Beach, 1979-83, asst. dir. research, gen. mgr., 1984—; adj. prof. UCLA, 1974-76. Author: Parametric Processes, 1969; Adaptive Optics, 1979; contbr. articles to sci. jours.; patentee in field. Active Boy Scouts Am. Fellow Optical Soc. Am., Soc. Photo-Optical and Instrumentation Engrs.; mem. IEEE (sr.), Tau Beta Pi, Sigma Xi. Lutheran. Current work: Adaptive optics; high energy laser optical systems; electro-optics, space optics. Subspecialties: High energy lasers; Applied optics. Office: United Technologies Research Ctr Optics and Applied Tech Lab PO Drawer 4181 West Palm Beach FL 33402

PEARSON, JAMES MURRAY, industrial research chemist; b. Aberdeen, Scotland, Nov. 22, 1937; s. James Sellar and Jeannie Elizabeth (Hendry) P.; m. Hilary Lees Buckett, May 30, 1962; children—Dean, Jill. B.S. with honors, U. Aberdeen, 1949, Ph.D., 1962. Postdoctoral fellow N.Y. State Coll. Forestry, Syracuse, 1962-64, assoc. prof., 1966-68; lectr. U. Aberdeen, Scotland, 1964-66; research scientist Xerox Corp., Rochester, N.Y., 1968-79, Eastman Kodak Co., Rochester, 1979—. Author: Poly-Vinyl Carbazole, 1981. Contbr. articles to profl. jours. Mem. Am. Chem. Soc., N.Y. Acad. Sci. Presbyterian. Current work: Optical recording and microelectronic technologies. Subspecialties: Polymer chemistry; Electronic materials. Home: 944 Little Pond Way Webster NY 14580 Office: Eastman Kodak Co Research Labs B82 Rochester NY 14650

PEARSON, JEROME, aerospace engineer, consultant, researcher; b. Texarkana, Ark., Apr. 19, 1938; s. Elbert Sharp and Angela Lucille (Bond) P.; m. Jeannie Thompson, Aug. 22, 1965; children: Edmund B., Marcus A., Laura E. B.S. in Engring, Washington U., St. Louis, 1961; M.S. in Geology, Wright State U., 1977. Aerospace technologist NASA Langley Research Ctr., Hampton, Va., 1962-66; aerospace engr. NASA Ames Research Ctr., Mountain View, Calif., 1966-71, Air Force Wright Aero. Labs., Wright-Patterson AFB, Ohio, 1971—; tech. cons. to motion picture industry Disney EPCOT Ctr.; lectr. in field. Contbr. articles to profl. jours. Soccer coach Little League, Dayton, Ohio, 1976—. Served with USMCR, 1961-65. Recipient Apollo Achievement award NASA, 1969; Sci. Achievement award Air Force Systems Command, 1975; Eminent Engr. award Tau Beta Pi, 1979. Fellow Brit. Interplanetary Soc., AIAA (assoc.), Am. Astronautical Soc. (sr.), Soc. Automotive Engrs., Scientists' Inst. for Public Info., Mensa. Republican. Methodist. Conceived orbital tower, anchored lunar satellite, rotary rocket; inventor satellite sail; patentee zero-G massmeter; authored proposals to use rotating structures for spacecraft launching; developed Apollo lunar staff sensor, force-feedback control system. Current Work: Managing contracted and in-house research on vibration control of high-energy lasers and dynamics and control of large-space structures; independent space research. Subspecialties: Aerospace engineering and technology; Astronautics. Office: Air Force Wright Aero Labs AFWAL/FIB Wright-Patterson AFB OH 45433

PEARSON, JOHN STUART, research physicist; b. Ridgecrest, Calif., June 23, 1951; s. John and Ruth (Billhardt) P.; m. Sandra Frances Cedergren, June 22, 1974; children—Sarah Louise, Nicole Christine, Sean Edwin, Emily Ruth. B.S. in Physics, U. Calif.-Davis, 1973, M.A., 1975, Ph.D., 1981. Research specialist Rockwell Internat., Golden, Colo., 1981-82, critical mass lab. mgr., 1982—. Contbr. articles to profl. jours. Served to capt. USAR, 1973—. Mem. Am. Phys. Soc., Am. Nuclear Soc., Phi Beta Kappa, Sigma Xi, Phi Kappa Phi. Current work: Technical management and experimental research in critical mass physics to provide experimental and calculational data for nuclear safety. Subspecialties: Nuclear engineering; Particle physics. Home: 609 Glenwood Dr Lafayette CO 80026 Office: Rockwell Internat Bldg 886 PO Box 464 Golden CO 80401

PEARSON, MARK LANDELL, research director, molecular biologist; b. Toronto, Ont., Can., June 2, 1940; s. William Holmes and Marguerite Raechel (Landell) P.; m. Katharine Anne Brown, Aug. 2, 1962; children—Scott Wallace, Jennifer Anne. B.A.Sc., U. Toronto, Ont., Can., 1962, M.A., 1964, Ph.D., 1966. Asst. to assoc. prof. U. Toronto, 1969-79, adj. prof., 1979-81; sect. head devel. genetics Nat. Cancer Inst.-Frederick Cancer Research Facility, Md., 1979-83, dir. lab. molecular biology, 1982-83; adj. prof. U. Md., Baltimore County, 1982-83; assoc. dir.-dir. molecular biology central research and devel. dept. DuPont Exptl. Sta., Wilmington, Del., 1983—; sci. adv. bd. Genex Corp., Rockville, Md., 1978-83. Editor: Muscle Development: Molecular and Cellular Control, 1982; Gene Transfer and Cancer, 1984. Mem. editorial bd. Molecular and Cellular Biology, 1980—. Josiah Macy Found. fellow Stanford U., 1977-78, Helen Hay Whitney Found. postdoctoral fellow Stanford U., 1966-69. Mem. AAAS, Am. Soc. Biol. Chemists, Am. Soc. Cell Biology, Am. Soc. Microbiology. Current work: Regulation of transciption; muscle differentiation; creatine kinase isozyme switching; RNA polymerase II specificity; muscle gene expression; myoblast mutants; somatic cell genetics, gene structure and function. Subspecialties: Molecular biology; Genetics and genetic engineering (biology). Home: 914 Fairthorne Ave Greenville DE 19807 Office: EI duPont de Nemours & Co E328/241 Exptl Sta Wilmington DE 19898

PEARSON, PAUL G., university president, ecology educator; b. Lake Worth, Fla., Dec. 5, 1926; s. Eric Conrad and Dora Wilma (Capen) P.; m. Winifred Clowe, June 30, 1951; children—Thomas Conrad, Jean M. P. McCabe, P. Andrew. B.S., U. Fla., 1949, M.S., 1951, Ph.D., 1954; L.H.D. (hon.), Rutgers U., 1982; LL.D. (hon.), Juniata Coll., 1983. Asst. prof. U. Tulsa, Okla., 1954-55; asst. prof. zoology Rutgers U., New Brunswick, N.J., 1955-60, assoc. prof., 1960-64, prof., 1964-81, assoc. provost, 1972-77, exec. v.p., 1977-81; pres. Miami U., Oxford, Ohio, 1981—; dir. Sta. WFTD-TV, Dayton, 2d Nat. Bank, Hamilton, Ohio. Author: AIBS General Biology, 1967. Chmn. N.J. Noise Control Com., Trenton; mem. U.S. Army Sci. Bd., 1984-86. Served with USN, 1944-46. Fellow AAAS; mem. Am. Inst. Biol. Scis. (dir. 1976-79, pres. 1978), Ecol. Soc. Am. (sec. 1961-64, v.p. 1970, treas. 1974-77). Lodge: Rotary. Current work: Vertebrate populations, pesticide impact on ecosystems. Subspecialties: Ecology (biology); Behavioral ecology. Office: President's Office Miami Univ Oxford OH 45056

PEARSON, PHILLIP THEODORE, veterinarian, university dean; b. Ames, Iowa, Nov. 21, 1932; s. Theodore B. and Hazel C. (Christianson) P.; m. Mary Jane Barlow, Aug. 28, 1954; children: Jane Catherine, Bryan Theodore, Todd Wallace, Julie Ann. D.V.M., Iowa State U., 1956, Ph.D., 1962. Intern Angell Meml. Animal Hosp., Boston, 1956-57; instr. Coll. Vet. Medicine Iowa State U., 1957-59, asst. prof., 1959-63, assoc. prof., 1963-64, prof. vet. clin. scis. and bio-med. engring., 1965-72, dean, 1972—, dir. Vet. Med. Inst.; prof. Sch. Vet. Medicine, U. Mo., 1964-65. Bd. dirs. Iowa Sate Meml. Union, 1970—; v.p. Iowa State Meml. Union, 1975; chmn. council of deans Assn. Am. Vet. Medicine Colls., 1978-79. Recipient Riser award, 1956; distinguished Tchr. award Norden Labs., 1962; Gaines award Gen. Foods Corp., 1966; Outstanding Tchr. award Iowa State U., 1968; Faculty citation, 1974. Mem. Am., Iowa vet. med. assns., Am. Animal Hosp. Assn., Am. Assn. Vet. Clinicians, Am. Coll. Vet. Surgeons (bd. regents 1972, pres. 1977), Sigma Xi, Phi Kappa Phi, Phi Zeta, Alpha Zeta, Gamma Sigma Delta. Lodge: Kiwanis (dir., pres. Ames 1966—). Current Work: Research administration. Subspecialty: Surgery (veterinary medicine). Home: 1610 Maxwell Ave Ames IA 50010

PEARSON, RALPH GOTTFRID, educator; b. Chgo., Jan. 12, 1919; s. Gottfrid and Kerstin (Larson) P.; m. Lenore Olivia Johnson, June 15, 1941 (dec. June 1982); children—John Ralph, Barry Lee, Christie Ann. B.S., Lewis Inst., 1940; Ph.D., Northwestern U., 1943. Faculty Northwestern U., 1946-76, prof. chemistry, 1957-76, U. Calif., Santa Barbara, 1976—; Cons. to industry and govt., 1951—. Co-author 5 books. Served to 1st lt. USAAF, 1944-46. Guggenheim fellow, 1951. Mem. Am. Chem. Soc. (Midwest award 1966, Inorganic Chemistry award 1969), Nat. Acad. Sci., Phi Beta Kappa, Sigma Xi, Phi Lambda Upsilon (hon.). Lutheran. Originator prin. of hard and soft acids and bases. Current Work: Mechanisms of chemical reactions; nature of chemical bond. Subspecialties: Inorganic chemistry; Theoretical chemistry.

PEARSON, RONALD KORIN, electrical engineer; b. Kansas City, Kans., Nov. 4, 1952; s. Robert S. and Beatrice (Tompkins) P.; m. Annette R. King, May 20, 1972. B.S., U. Ark., 1973; M.S. in Elec. Engring, MIT, 1975, Ph.D., 1982. Design engr. Micro Sensors, Holliston, Mass., 1977; software design cons. Sullivan & Cogliano, Waltham, Mass., 1977-79; Draper fellow C.S. Draper Labs., Cambridge, Mass., 1979-82; research engr. E.I. duPont, Wilmington, Del., 1982—; adj. prof. U. Del., Newark, 1983. NSF fellow, 1973-76. Mem. IEEE, Soc. Indsl. and Applied Math, Sigma Xi. Current work: Applications of electronic instrumentation and mathematical signal processing to the monitoring and control of industrial chemical processes. Subspecialties: Electronics; Applied mathematics. Office: E I duPont de Nemours & Co Explt Sta Bldg 357 Wilmington DE 19898

PEARSON, SAMUEL DIBBLE, III, civil engineer; b. Augusta, Ga., Mar. 28, 1944; s. Samuel Dibble and Adelaide (DeBeaugrine) P.; m. Patricia Ann Johnson, Dec. 26, 1967 (dec. Dec. 1974); 1 son, Pierce DeBeaugrine; m. Deborah McGahee, Aug. 30, 1975; 1 dau., Elizabeth Allison. B.S., U. Ga., 1966; B.C.E., Auburn U., 1973. Registered profl. engr., Ga., S.C. Project engr. Babcock & Wilcox, Inc., Augusta, Ga., 1973-78; project mgr. Kimberly-Clark Corp., Waynesboro, Ga., 1978-80; engring. div. mgr. Chem-Nuclear Systems, Inc., Barnwell, S.C., 1980—. Served to capt. USAF, 1968-72. Mem. ASCE, Am. Nuclear Soc., Tau Beta Pi, Auburn U. Alumni Assn. (dir. 1976-78). Republican. Baptist. Current Work: Design and development of state of the art low level nuclear waste disposal sites, design and development of state of the art process equipment to handle low level nuclear waste generated by operating nuclear power plants. Subspecialties: Civil engineering; Nuclear engineering. Home: 4038 Indian Hills Dr Augusta GA 30906 Office: Chem-Nuclear Systems Inc Osborn Rd Snelling SC 29812

PEARSON, TERRY WILLIAM, immunologist, educator; b. Vernon, B.C., Can., Feb. 2, 1946; s. Francis Lawrence and Isobel Madeline Mae (Lovelace) P.; m. Elizabeth Anne Reed, Sept. 28, 1977; 1 child, Katie Malaika. B.Sc. with honors, U. B.C., Vancouver, 1967, Ph.D., 1973. Staff scientist MRC Molecular Biology, Cambridge, Eng., 1974-77, Internat. Lab. for Research on Animal Diseases, Nairobi, Kenya, 1977-79; asst. prof. biochemistry U. Victoria, B.C., 1979-83, assoc. prof., 1982—; dir. Sci. Council of B.C., Vancouver, 1981—; dir., trustee Terry Fox Med. Research Found., Vancouver, 1982—. Editor: Parasite Antigens: Towards New Strategies for Vaccines, 1985. Contbr. articles to profl. jours. Grantee Natural Scis. and Engring. Research Council Can., Internat. Devel. Research Ctr., WHO. Mem. Brit. Soc. Immunology, Can. Soc. Immunology. Current work: Immunology, disease diagnosis, nonoclonal antibodies, molecular parisitology. Subspecialty: Immunobiology and immunology. Office: U Victoria Biochemistry Dept PO Box 1700 Victoria BC V8W 2Y2 Canada

PEASE, DAVID NATHANIEL, environmental consulting firm executive; b. Concord, N.H., June 16, 1952; s. Nathaniel John and Helen Mabel (Edmark) P.; m. Donna-Marie Desautels, May 15, 1977. B.A. in Marine Biology, U. N.H., 1974; postgrad., U. B.C., Vancouver, 1974; M.S., U. N.H., 1983. Technician U. N.H., Durham, 1972-74; staff scientist Normandeau Assocs., Inc., Bedford, N.H., 1974-81; project mgr. offshore services Peck Environ. Lab., Inc., Hampton Falls, N.H., 1981-83; pres. Resource Analysts, Inc., 1983—. Mem. Estuarine Research Fedn., Marine Tech. Soc., Phi Beta Kappa, Phi Kappa Phi, Phi Sigma. Current Work: Management of environmental laboratory with specializations in organic contamination of soils, groundwater, and tissues. Manage projects related to environmental concerns in offshore petroleum exploration and development. Subspecialties: Resource management; Analytical chemistry. Home: PO Box 212 Hampton NH 03842 Office: Resource Analysts Inc 1 Lafayette Rd Hampton Falls NH 03844

PEASE, ROGER FABIAN WEDGWOOD, electrical engineering educator, consultant; b. Cambridge, Eng., Oct. 24, 1936; came to U.S. 1964; s. Michael Stewart and Helen Bowen (Wedgwood) P.; m. Caroline Ann Bowring, Sept. 17, 1960; children—Emma Ruth, Joseph Henry Bowring, James Edward. B.A., Cambridge U., 1960, M.A., 1964, Ph.D., 1964. Asst. prof. U. Calif., Berkeley, 1964-67; mem. tech. staff Bell Labs., Murray Hill, N.J., 1967-78; prof. Stanford U., Calif., 1978—; cons. Perkin Elmer Co., Hayward, Calif., 1979—, Xerox Corp., Palo Alto, Calif., 1978—, Lawrence Livermore Lab., Livermore, Calif., 1983—. Contbr. articles to profl. jours. Patentee in field. Served with RAF, 1955-57. Research fellow Trinity Coll., Cambridge, 1964. Mem. IEEE (sr., Rappaport award 1982). Church of England. Current work: Micropatterning technology, physical design of high performance systems. Subspecialties: Microchip technology (engineering); Microelectronics. Office: McCullough 204 Stanford U Stanford CA 94305

PEASLEE, DAVID CHASE, physicist; b. White Plains, N.Y., July 23, 1922; s. Arthur Frank and Anita Quigley (Clark) P.; m. Virginia Perry Close, Oct. 25, 1947 (dec. 1972); children—Anne C. (Mrs. R.J. Mroz), Frank D., Graham F. A.B., Princeton U., 1943; Ph.D., MIT, 1948. Research assoc. physics Columbia U., N.Y.C., 1951-54; prof. Physics Purdue U., Lafayette, Ind., 1954-59, Australian Nat. U., Canberra, 1959-76; vis. prof. Brown U., Providence, R.I., 1976-77; contract officer Dept. Energy, Germantown, Md., 1977-81; vis. prof. U. Md., College Park, 1981—. Author: (text) Elements of Atomic Physics, 1955. Fellow Am. Physical Soc. Republican. Current work: Hadron spectroscopy and structure. Subspecialties: Particle physics; Theoretical physics. Office: U Md Physics Dept College Park MD 20742

PEATMAN, JOHN GRAY, consulting firm executive, psychologist; b. Centerville, Iowa, Mar. 16, 1904; s. Clarence Albert and Binnie Oriel (Gray) P.; m. Lillie Burling; children: Alice Peatman Dettmers, John, William; m. Madeline Martin; 1 dau., Mary Peatman Fitzpatrick. B.A., Columbia U., 1927, M.A., 1928, Ph.D., 1931. Pres. Research Cons., Inc., Norwalk, 1950—; also dir.; ast. prof. psychometrics CCNY, 1929-42, assoc. prof., 1942-48, prof., 1948-70, Emeritus prof., 1970—; pres. Office of Research, Inc., N.Y.C., 1945-58, also dir.; cons. in field. Author: Descriptive and Sampling Statistics, 1947, Introduction to Applied Statistics, 1963; editor: (with Eugene Hartley) Festschrift to Gardner Murphy, 1960. Fellow Am. Psychol. Assn. (chmn. policy and planning bd. 1950-51); mem. Psychonomic Soc., Phi Beta Kappa,

Sigma Xi. Congregationalist. Club: University (N.Y.C.). Current Work: Research in applied mathematics and its applications. Subspecialties: Applied mathematics; Statistics. Home: Stonewood Comstock Hill Norwalk CT 06852 Office: Research Cons Inc 83 East Ave Norwalk CT 06851

PECHAR, HENRY WILLIAM, engineer; b. N.Y.C., Apr. 3, 1950; s. Henry William and Rose (Nemecek) P. B.S.E.E., N.Y. Tech., 1972. Engr. Sperry Gyro Corp., Great Neck, N.Y., 1972-74; prin. engr. Gen. Inst., Hicksville, N.Y., 1974-78; project engr. Am. Microsystems Inc., Santa Clara, Calif., 1978-79; engring. mgr. Standard Microsystems Corp., Hauppague, N.Y., 1979—. Patentee on integrated circuit design. Recipient Liss Meml. award, Liss Found., 1972, Landis Found. award, 1972. Mem. IEEE. Current work: Design of VISI circuits as standard products; CRT controller circuits and magnetic (disk) controllers. Subspecialty: Microchip technology (engineering). Office: 35 Marcus Blvd Hauppague NY 11788

PECHENICK, KAY RHODA, electrical equipment manufacturing company physicist; b. Phila., Mar. 30, 1950; d. William and Henrietta (Saver) P. B.A., U. Pa., 1973, M.S., 1973. Ph.D., 1983; postgrad. Harvard U., 1973-74. Systems engr. Gen. Electric Co., Valley Forge, Pa., 1981—. Contbr. articles to profl. jours. Fellow: Univ., 1978, Coll. Dean, 1979, Karcher Found., 1980. Mem. Am. Phys. Soc., Math. Assn. Am., Phi Beta Kappa, Mensa. Current work: Communication and earth resource satellite technology, including general relativistic effects, and physical geodesy. Subspecialties: Aerospace engineering and technology; General relativity. Home: 708 Cherrydale Dr Lafayette Hill PA 19444 OFfice: Valley Forge Space Systems Div General Electric Co PO Box 8555 Philadelphia PA 19101

PECK, DALLAS LYNN, geologist; b. Cheney, Wash., Mar. 28, 1929; s. Lynn Averill and Mary Hazel (Carlyle) P.; m. Tevis Sue Lewis, Mar. 28, 1951; children—Ann, Stephen, Gerritt. B.S., Calif. Inst. Tech., 1951, M.S., 1953; Ph.D., Harvard U., 1960. With U.S. Geol. Survey, 1954—, asst. chief geologist, office of geochemistry and geophysics, Washington, 1967-72, geologist, geologic div., 1972-77, chief geologist, 1977-81, dir., 1981—; mem. Lunar Sample Rev. Bd., 1970-71; chmn. earth scis. adv. com. NSF, 1970-72; vis. com. dept. geol. scis. Harvard U., 1972-78; mem. earth scis. adv. com. Stanford U., 1982—. Recipient Meritorious Service award Dept. Interior, 1971, Disting. Service award, 1979; Presdl. Meritorious Exec. award, 1980. Mem. Geol. Soc. Am., Soc. Econ. Geologists, Am. Geophys. Union (pres. sect. volcanology, geochemistry and petrology 1976-78). Subspecialty: Geology. Home: 2524 Heathcliff Ln Reston VA 22091 Office: US Geol Survey Reston VA 22092

PECK, JOHN HAZEN, geologist; b. Concord, Mass., July 20, 1937; s. William H. and Eleanor L. (Warren) P.; m. Nancy Jane Uljua, June 12, 1962; children—Susan, Sarah, Sharon. B.S., U. Mass., 1960; M.A., Dartmouth Coll., 1962. Geologist U.S. Geol. Survey, Flemingsburg, Ky., 1962-68, Boston, Mass., 1968-74; sr. geologist Stone & Webster Engring. Corp., Boston, 1974-76, cons. geologist, 1976-83, Amarillo, Tex., 1983—. Contbr. articles to profl. jours. Chmn. Conservation Com., Framingham, Mass., 1975-76; scoutmaster Flemingsburg council Boy Scouts Am., 1963-65. Fellow Geol. Soc. Am. Burwell award com., 1980-83); mem. Assn. Engring. Geologists (membership chmn., 1982-84, chmn. New Eng. sect., 1976-78, Legis. com., 1978, chmn. Waste Disposal Com., 1980-81). Republican. Lutheran. Lodge: Lions: (Flemingsburg, Ky.) (sec., treas., 1966-67). Current work: Geologic aspects of high level nuclear waste disposal; tectonics of continental United States. Subspecialties: Geology; Hazardous waste disposal. Home: 2108 Westcliff Pkwy Amarillo TX 79124 Office: Stone & Webster Engring Corp PO Box 829 Amarillo TX 79105

PECK, RALPH BRAZELTON, engineering educator; b. Winnipeg, Man., Can., June 23, 1912; s. Orwin K. and Ethel Indie (Huyck) P.; m. Marjorie Elizabeth Truby, June 14, 1937; children: Nancy Jeanne Peck Young, James Leroy. C.E., Rensselaer Poly. Inst., 1934, D.C.E., 1937, D.Eng., 1974; postdoctoral, Harvard U., 1938. Structural detailer Am. Bridge Co., Ambridge, Pa., 1937; asst. subway engr. soil investigations City of Chgo., 1939-43; chief engr. testing Holabird & Root, Scioto Ordnance Plant, Marion, Ohio, 1943; research asst. prof. soil mechanics U. Ill., Urbana, 1943, research prof. found. engring., 1948-57, prof. found. engring., 1957-74, emeritus, 1974—; cons. in field. Author: (with K. Terzaghi) Soil Mechanics in Engineering Practice, 1948, 2d edit., 1967; (with W.E. Hanson, T.H. Thornburn) Foundation Engineering, 1953, 2d edit., 1973; contbr. articles to profl. jours. Recipient Dept. Army Disting. Civilian Service award, 1973; Nat. medal of Sci., 1974; Washington award, 1976. Fellow Geol. Soc. Am., Am. Cons. Engrs. Council; mem. ASCE (hon., Norman medal 1944, Wellington prize 1965, Terzaghi award 1969), Nat. Soc. Profl. Engrs. (award 1972), Internat. Soc. Soil Mechanics and Found. Engring. (past pres.), Am. Ry. Engring. Assn., Nat. Acad. Engring., Sigma Xi, Tau Beta Pi, Chi Epsilon, Phi Kappa Phi. Current Work: Dams, tunnels. Subspecialty: Civil engineering. Home: 1101 Warm Sands Dr SE Albuquerque NM 87123

PECK, WILLIAM ARNO, physician, educator, researcher; b. New Britain, Conn., Sept. 28, 1933; s. Bernard Carl and Molla (Nair) P.; m. Patricia Ann Hearn. A.B., Harvard U., 1955; M.D., U. Rochester, 1960. Diplomate Am. Bd. Internal Medicine. Intern and resident in internal medicine and fellow in metabolism Barnes Hosp., St. Louis, 1960-63; chief resident Strong Meml. Hosp., Rochester, N.Y., 1965-66, sr. instr., 1966-67; asst. prof. U. Rochester, 1967-69, assoc. prof., 1969-73, prof., 1973-76; John E. and Adaline Simon prof. medicine Washington U., St. Louis, 1976—; physician in chief Jewish Hosp., St. Louis, 1976—; chmn. adv. com. FDA, 1976-78; chmn. study sect. NIH, 1979-81; chmn. Consensus Devel. Conf. on Osteoparosis, NIH, 1984. Editor Bone and Mineral Research Ann., 1982—. Contbr. articles to profl. jours. Active in Community Vols. of Rochester, 1970-73; bd. dirs. Jewish Ctr. for Aged, St. Louis, 1977—. Recipient Research Career Program award NIH 1971; named Clin. Tchr. of Yr., Washington U., 1984; Harvard U. scholar, 1954. Fellow ACP; mem. Endocrine Soc., Am. Soc. Clin. Investigation; Am. Soc. Bone and Mineral Research (pres. 1983-84), Assn. Am. Physicians. Current work: Metabolism of bone remodeling. Subspecialty: Endocrinology. Office: Jewish Hosp Dept Medicine 216 S Kingshighway St Louis MO 63110

PEDERSEN, CHARLES RUSSELL, engineering administrator, electrical engineer; b. Bklyn, Mar. 4, 1933; s. Charles Walter and Elvira Irma (Vilenius) P.; m. Althea Shalen, June 17, 1956; children—Jean Elizabeth, Sharon Louise, Robert Charles, John James Hurlburt. B.A., Columbia U., 1954, B.S.E.E., 1955, M.S.E.E., 1956, Ph.D., 1966. Tech. staff Aerospace Corp., Los Angeles, 1956-59; cons. Rand Corp., Santa Monica, Calif., 1960; research staff Riverside Research Inst., N.Y.C., 1961-67, mgr., 1967-81, asst. dir., 1981—. Mem. IEEE, Phi Beta Kappa, Sigma Xi, Tau Beta Pi, Eta Kappa Nu. Republican. Episcopalian. Current work: Radar systems, signal processing, data analysis and interpretation. Subspecialty: Electrical engineering. Office: Riverside Research Inst 330 W 42d St New York NY 10036

PEDERSON, DONALD OTIS, physicist; b. Waukegan, Ill., June 29, 1944; s. Otis A. and Dorothy Rose (Anderson) P.; m. Kathryn Elizabeth Werner, June 4, 1968; s. Julie Renee, Michael Andrew. B.S., Tex. Tech. U., 1966; Ph.D., Rice U., 1971. Asst. prof. in physics U. Ark., Fayetteville, 1972-78, assoc. prof., chmn. physics dept., 1978-83, prof., 1984—; assoc. dean Fulbright Coll. Arts and Scis., 1983—; instnl. rep. Oak Ridge Associated Univs., Tenn., 1984—. Contbr. articles to profl. jours. Robert A. Welch postdoctoral fellow Tex. Tech., 1971-72; grantee NSF, 1977, 80, 83-85, LTV Aerospace and Defense Co., 1984-85. Mem. Am. Physical Soc., Am. Assn. Physics Tchrs. (sect. rep. to nat. council 1975-79), Sigma Xi, Sigma Pi Sigma. Current work: Scattering of multiply charged low energy ions from surfaces, real time image processing in nonlinear optical solids, thermal properties of fluoride solid electrolytes. Subspecialties: Condensed matter physics; Optical image processing. Office: U Ark Fulbright Coll Arts and Scis Fayetteville AR 72701

PEDLOSKY, JOSEPH, oceanographer. Sr. scientist Doherty prof. oceanography Woods Hole Oceanographic Instn., Mass. Subspecialty: Oceanography. Office: Woods Hole Oceanographic Instn Woods Hole MA 02543

PEEBLES, PEYTON ZIMMERMAN, JR., engineering educator, consultant; b. Columbus, Ga., Sept. 10, 1934; s. Peyton Zimmerman Peebles and Maida Erlene (Denton) Dials; m. Barbara Ann Suydam, Sept. 6, 1969; children—Peyton, III, Edward. B.S. in Elec. Engring., Evansville Coll., Ind. 1957; M.S. in Elec. Engring., Drexel Inst., 1963; Ph.D., U. Pa., 1967. Systems engr. RCA, Moorestown, N.J., 1967-69; prof. elec. engring. U. Tenn., Knoxville, 1969-76, 77-81; vis. prof. elec. engring. U. Hawaii, Honolulu, 1976-77; prof. elec. engring. U. Fla., Gainesville, 1981-84, assoc. chmn., 1984—; past cons. RCA, ARO, BDM, Oak Ridge Nat. Lab. Author: Communication Systems Principles, 1976; Probability, Random Variables and Random Signal Principles, 1980; contbr. numerous articles to engring. jours. Patentee in field. Sarnoff (RCA) fellow, 1964-66. Mem. IEEE (sr.), Sigma Xi, Eta Kappa Nu, Tau Beta Pi, Sigma Pi Sigma, Phi Beta Chi. Democrat. Methodist. Current work: Radar and communication system theory. Subspecialties: Aerospace engineering and technology; Electrical engineering. Office: Dept Elec Engring U Fla Gainesville FL 32611

PEES, SAMUEL THOMAS, exploration geologist, consultant; b. Meadville, Pa., Nov. 16, 1926; s. H. Chester and Dorothy Marie (Cook) P. B.S., Allegheny Coll., 1950; M.S., Syracuse U., 1959; postgrad., Colo. Coll., 1949, Tulsa U., 1968. Cert. petroleum geologist cert. profl. geol. scientist. Exploration geologist Tex. Petroleum Co., Venezuela and Peru, 1953-61; fgn. exploration rep. Skelly Oil Co., S.Am. and Indonesia, 1962-68; exploration geologist Exploration Consortium, South Pacific, 1969-71; exploration cons. Patrick J. Delaney & Assocs., Rio de Janerio, Brazil, 1973-76; exploration project leader James A. Lewis Engrs., Tex. and, Argentina, 1976-78; sr. exploration geologist Samuel T. Pees & Assocs., Meadville, 1978—; sr. assoc. geologist Geoinformacao, Rio de Janeiro, 1976—; guest lectr. Allegheny Coll., 1971-76; cons. explorationist Pluspetrol S.A., Buenos Aires, Argentina, 1978; founder, donor S.T. Pees Caribbean Research Fund (Paleontol. Research Inst.), Ithaca, N.Y., 1977—. Contbr. articles to profl. jours. Collector Samuel T. Pees Art Collection, Allegheny Coll.; artists' sponsor Sanggar Ligar Sari, Bandung, Indonesia, 1969—; patron Meadville Arts Council, 1977. Served in U.S. Army, 1945-46, PTO, Korea. Fellow Geol. Soc. Am.; mem. Am. Assn. Petroleum Geologists, Am. Inst. Profl. Geologists, Pakontol. Research Am. Inst. (life), Am. Soc. Photogrammetry, AAAS, Malaysian Geol. Soc., Am. Legion, Sigma Alpha Epsilon, 749th Ry. Bn. Vets. Orgn., Crawford County Hist. Soc. Republican. Episcopalian. Current Work: Application of remote sensed morphotectonics in oil, gas and mineral exploration; basin mapping from satellite MSS imagery, return-beam vidicon and radar; determination of fractured zones via remote sensing; sub-surface mapping utilizing well data and remote sensed information, Appalachia Plateau (U.S.), Argentina and Brazil. Subspecialties: Geology; Remote sensing (geoscience). Home: 889 Porter St Meadville PA 16335 Office: Masonic Bldg #224 Meadville PA 16335

PEHLKE, ROBERT DONALD, materials and metallurgical engineering educator; b. Ferndale, Mich., Feb. 11, 1933; s. Robert William and Florence Jenny (McLaren) P.; m. Julie Anne Kehoe, June 2, 1956; children: Robert Donald, Elizabeth Anne, David Richard. B.S. in Engring, U. Mich., 1955; S.M., Mass. Inst. Tech., 1958, Sc.D., 1960; postgrad., Tech. Inst., Aachen, Ger., 1956-57. Registered profl. engr., Mich. Mem. faculty U. Mich., 1960—, prof. materials and metall. engring., 1968—, chmn. dept., 1973-84; cons. to metall. industries. Author: Unit Processes of Extractive Metallurgy, 1973; Editor, contbr. numerous articles to profl. jours. Pres. Ann Arbor Amateur Hockey Assn., 1977-79. NSF fellow, 1955-56; Fulbright fellow, 1956-57. Fellow Am. Soc. Metals (mem. tech. divs. bd. 1982-84, sec. metals acad. com. 1977), Metall. Soc. AIME (Gold medal sci. award extractive metallurgy div. 1976); mem. Am. Inst. Metall. Engrs., Iron and Steel Soc. of AIME (disting. life mem.; chmn. process tech. div. 1976-77, dir. 1976-79, Howe Meml. lectr. 1980), Germany, London, Japan socs. iron and steel, Am. Foundrymen's Soc., Am. Soc. Engring. Edn., Sigma Xi, Tau Beta Pi, Alpha Sigma Mu (pres. 1977-78). Current Work: Metallurgical engineering, iron and steelmaking, extractive metallurgy, computer applications. Subspecialties: Metallurgy; Materials. Home: 9 Regent Dr Ann Arbor MI 48104 Office: 2158 Dow Bldg North Campus Univ Mich Ann Arbor MI 48109

PEI, RICHARD YUSIEN, engineer; b. Soochow, China, July 24, 1927; came to U.S., 1955; s. Tseziang and Shihju (Char) P.; m. Paula C. Cheng, Dec. 3, 1951; children: Gabriel, Raphael, Michael. B.S., U. l'Aurore-China, 1947, M.S., 1948; Ph.D., Rensselaer Polytech. Inst., 1964. Supr. Gen. Electric, Schenectady, 1956-62; mem. staff Neptune Research Lab., Wallingford, Conn., 1962-64, Bellcomm Inc., Washington, 1964-67, Inst. Def. Analyses, Arlington, Va., 1967-69; sr. engr. TRW Systems Group, McLean, Va., 1969-71; dir. civil tech. program Rand Corp., Washington, 1971—; adj. faculty Cath. U. Am., Washington, 1964-67. Fellow AAAS; mem. ASME. Current Work: Operations research; energy science and technology. Subspecialties: Oil shale; Operations research (mathematics). Home: 1474 Waggaman Circle McLean VA 22101 Office: Rand Corp 2100 M St NW Washington DC 20037

PELI, ELIEZER, optometrist, biomedical engineer; b. Tel Aviv, June 2, 1951; came to U.S., 1979; s. Chaim and Yona (Eidelman) P.; m. Tamar Akselrod, Feb. 22, 1977; 1 child, Ben. B.Sc. in Elec. Engring., Technion I.I.T., Haifa, Israel, 1976, M.Sc. in Elec. Engring., 1979; O.D., New Eng. Coll. Optometry, 1983. Research asst. Technion I.I.T., 1976-78, adj. lectr., 1978-79, research engr., 1978-79; research assoc. New Eng. Coll. Optometry, Boston, 1979-83; staff assoc. Eye Research Inst., Boston, 1983—; asst. prof. sch. Medicine, Tufts U., Boston, 1983—; dir. low vision service Tufts U.-New Eng. Med. Ctr., Boston, 1983—. Contbr. articles to profl. jours. Served with Israel Def. Force, 1969-72. Mem. Am. Acad. Optometry, Assn. for Research in Vision and Ophthalmology, Soc. Photo-Optical Instrumentation Engrs., Am. Optometric Assn. Jewish. Current work: Control of eye movements, applications of technology to low-vision evaluation and aids. Subspecialties: Biomedical engineering; Computerized image enhancement. Office: Eye Research Inst 20 Staniford St Boston MA 02114

PELLA, PETER JOHN, physics educator; b. Meriden, Conn., Jan. 13, 1948; s. Juan B. and Evelyn (Millington) P.; m. Carol Krause, Jan. 8, 1977 (div. Sept. 1984). B.S. in Engring. U.S. Mil. Acad., 1970; M.S., Rensselaer Poly. Inst., 1977; Ph.D., Kent State U., 1983. Commd. 2d lt. U.S. Army, 1970, advanced to 1st lt., 1971; co. comdr. U.S. Army, El Paso, Tex., 1970-74, resigned, 1974; research asst. Rensselaer Poly. Inst., Troy, N.Y., 1974-77; dir. lab., physicist, dept. physics U.S. Mil. Acad., West Point, N.Y., 1977-80; research asst., dept. physics Kent State U., Ohio, 1980-83; asst. prof. dept. physics Hendrix Coll., Conway, Ark., 1983—. Regional coordinator Peace Acad., 1980—; bd. dirs. Faulkner County unit Am. Cancer Soc., 1984—. Disting. Grad. Student fellow Kent State U., 1981, 82. Mem. Am. Phys. Soc., Am. Assn. Physics Tchrs., AAAS, Fedn. Am. Scientists, ACLU. Democrat. Quaker. Current work: Neutron-deep-hole states using the P,N reaction; spin transfer coefficient measurement using the P,N reaction; missing Gamov-Teller strength in P,N reactions. Subspecialty: Nuclear physics. Home: 816 Center St Conway AR 72032 Office: Dept Physics Hendrix Coll Conway AR 72032

PELTIER, EUGENE JOSEPH, civil engineer, former naval officer, bus. exec.; b. Concordia, Kans., Mar. 29, 1910; s. Frederick and Emma Helen (Brasseau) P.; m. Lena Evelyn Gennette, June 28, 1932; children: Marion Joyce, Eugene Joseph, Carole Josephine, Kenneth Noel, Judith Ann. B.S. in Civil Engring., Kans. State U., 1933, LL.D., 1961. Registered profl. engr., Mo., N.Y., Kans., Fla., Va., Calif. Commd. lt. (j.g.) U.S. Navy, 1936, advanced through grades to rear adm., 1957, asst. public works officer, Great Lakes, Ill., 1940-42, sr. asst. supt. civil engr., Boston, 1942-44, officer-in-charge 137th Constrn. Bn., Okinawa, 1945, officer in charge 54th Constrn. Regt., 1945, officer various public works assignments, Pensacola, Fla., 1945-46, Memphis, 1946-49, Jacksonville, Fla., 1949-51; dist. public works officer (14th Naval Dist.), 1951-53, asst. chief maintenance and materials Bur. Docks, Washington, 1953-56, comdg. officer, Pt. Hueneme, 1956-57, chief Bur. Yards and Docks, Navy Dept., Washington, 1957-62, chief of civil engrs., 1957-62, ret., 1962; instrumentman, resident engr. Kans. Hwy. Commn., Norton, Topeka, Chanute, 1934-40; v.p. Sverdrup & Parcel & Assocs., Inc., St. Louis, 1962-64; sr. v.p. Sverdrup & Parcel & Assocs., Inc., 1964-66, exec. v.p., 1966-67, pres., dir., 1967-75, chief exec. officer, 1972-75, ptnr., 1966-75, cons., 1975-82; pres., dir. Sverdrup & Parcel & Assocs., N.Y., Inc., 1967-75; dir. Sverdrup & Parcel Internat., Inc., 1967-75; v.p., dir. ARO, Inc., Tullahoma, Tenn., 1966-75; cons. EPA, 1976-80; dir. Merc. Trust Co., St. Louis, 1971-81. Mem. emeritus Civic Progress, Inc.; bd. dirs. YMCA, St. Louis, 1972-76. Decorated Legion of Merit; recipient citation Am. Inst. Steel Constrn., 1973. Mem. ASCE (hon.), Am. Public Works Assn. (1 of Top Ten Public Works Men of Year 1960), Soc. Mil. Engrs. (pres. 1960-61), Am. Concrete Inst., Am. Road and Transp. Builders Assn. (pres. 1972-73), Nat. Soc. Profl. Engrs., Mo. Soc. Profl. Engrs., Public Works Hist. Soc. (pres. 1977-78, trustee 1975—), Nat. Acad. Engring., Cons. Engrs. Council (award of Merit 1962), Sigma Tau, Phi Kappa Phi. Clubs: Army-Navy Country (Washington); Old Warson Country (St. Louis). Current Work: Engineering consultant, primarily on construction project. Subspecialty: Civil engineering. 800 N 12th St Saint Louis MO 63101

PELUS, LOUIS MARTIN, cell biologist; b. Queens, N.Y., Oct. 18, 1951; s. Reno Louis and Mary (Sgarro) P.; m. Vivian Carol Defalco, Aug. 17, 1974; children—Jonathan Louis, Jeffrey Martin. B.A., Queens Coll., CUNY, 1973; M.S., Rutgers U., 1977, Ph.D., 1977; postdoctoral fellowship Sloan Kettering Inst., 1977-80. Assoc. researcher Sloan Kettering Inst., N.Y.C., 1977-80, research assoc., 1980-82, asst. mem., 1982—. Contbr. articles to sci. jours., chpts. to books. Leukemia Soc. Am. scholar, 1981; NCI grantee, 1981. Mem. Internat. Soc. Exptl. Hematology, Am. Soc. Hematology, Am. Assn. Immunologists, Sigma Xi. Democrat. Roman Catholic. Current work: Regulation of the differentiation and proliferation of hematopoietic stem cells. Subspecialties: Cell biology; Hematology. Home: 5 Westgate Rd Massapequa NY 11762 Office: Sloan Kettering Inst 1250 First Ave New York NY 10021

PELZER, CHARLES FRANCIS, geneticist, educator; b. Detroit, June 5, 1935; s. Francis J. and Edna Dorothy (Ladach) P.; m. Veronica A. Killeen, July 7, 1972; 1 child, Mary Elizabeth. B.S., U. Detroit, 1957; Ph.D., U. Mich., 1964. Kettering Found. fellow Wabash Coll., Crawfordsville, Ind., 1965-66; instr. U. Detroit, 1966-68; asst. prof., then asso. prof., then prof. biology Saginaw Valley State Coll. University Center, Mich., 1969—; research assoc. Mich. State U., East Lansing, 1976-77; research fellow Henry Ford Hosp., Detroit, 1982-83; vis. scientist Am. Inst. Biol. Scis., 1975-78; grant reviewer U.S. Dept. Edn., 1984-85. Referee Am. Jour. Phys. Anthropology, Human Biology. articles to profl. jours. Vice pres. Saginaw Valley Retinitis Pigmentosa Found., 1978-80. Recipient Alumni award Saginaw Valley State Coll., 1971; grantee NIH, 1961-64, Kellog Found., 1961, Saginaw Valley State Coll. Found., 1976-85, Mich. State U., 1977, Fund for Henry Ford Hosp., 1983. Mem. AAAS, Am. Soc. Human Genetics, N.Y. Acad. Scis., others. Current Work: Biochemical genetics, especially in humans and mammals. Gene action in health and disease. Analysis of genetic variant proteins by electrophoresis and isoelectric focusing. Subspecialties: Genetics and genetic engineering (medicine); Gene actions. Office: Biology Dept Saginaw Valley State Coll University Center MI 48710

PEMBLE, KIM RUSSELL, hospital systems executive; b. Milw., Mar. 31, 1955; s. Robert Russell and Bonnie Jean (Eitel) P. B.S., U. Wis.-LaCrosse, 1977; M.S., U. Minn., 1983. Programmer, analyst IBM Corp., Rochester, Minn., 1977-79, assoc. programmer, analyst, 1979-80; clin. systems analyst St. Luke's Hosp., Milw., 1982-84, mgr. med. systems, 1984—; instr. computer use-med. emphasis Coll. St. Francis, Ill., 1985—. CPR instr. Am. Heart Assn., Milw., 1982—, ARC, Minn., 1980-82; vol. Nat. Audubon Soc., Milw., 1983—, Wildlife Animal Rehab. Ctr., Milw., 1983—. Mem. Computer Soc. of IEEE, Am. Assn. Artificial Intelligence, Engring. in Medicine and Biology Soc. of IEEE, Soc. Clin. Data Mgmt. Systems (exec. bd. 1985), Nat. Eagle Scout Assn., Upsilon Pi Epsilon. Current work: Application of computer systems in intensive care, Ob/Gyn, emergency medicine, neurology and nuclear medical imaging; particular interest in the development and application of artificial intelligence and expert systems. Subspecialties: Theoretical computer science; Software engineering. Home: 8968 W Forest Home Ave Apt 4 Greenfield WI 53228 Office: Saint Luke's Samaritan Health Care Inc 2900 W Oklahoma Ave Milwaukee WI 53215

PENG, STEVEN TSU JIUNN, polymer rheologist; researcher; b. Taipei, Taiwan, Feb. 5, 1938; came to U.S., 1962; s. Tai-Kee and Swan-Mei (Fann) P.; m. Jannie D.J. Fan, May 7, 1966; children—Lynnus, Willard. B.S. in Civil Engring., Nat. Taiwan U., 1960; M.S. in Applied Mechanics, Kans. State U., 1964; Ph.D. in Engring. Mechanics, Iowa State U., 1968. Research fellow Calif. Inst. Tech., Pasadena, 1968-69, sr. scientist Jet Propulsion Lab., 1971-76, tech. staff, 1977—; resident research assoc. NRC, Washington, 1969-71; vis. prof. U. Iowa, Iowa City, 1976-77; adj. prof. U. Cin., 1978-83. Contbr. articles to profl. jours. Air Force Rocket Propulsion Lab. grantee, Edwards, Calif., 1982-84. Mem. Am. Acad. Mechanics, U.S. Soc. Rheology, Brit. Soc. Rheology, Am. Chem. Soc. (divs. rubber and polymer chemistry). Current work: Finite deformation of elastomer, non-Newtonian liquid, glassy polymer, composite materials. Subspecialties: Theoretical and applied mechanics; Polymer engineering. Home: 4814 Viro Rd La Canada CA 91011 Office: Jet Propulsion Lab Calif Inst Tech 4800 Oak Grove Dr Pasadena CA 91011

PENISTON, EUGENE G., clinical psychologist; b. Osceola, Iowa, June 23, 1931; s. James Milton and Delia B. (Young) P.; m. Helen M. Kerr, Oct. 16, 1959; children: Denise R., Eugene Lyle. A.B., Central State U., Wilberforce, Ohio, 1953; M.A., S.D. State U., 1962; Ed.D., Okla. State U., 1972. Lic. psychologist. Chief sch. psychologist Clarance (N.Y.) public schs., 1965-69; chief psychol. service and tng. center Va. State Hosp., Petersburg, 1972-75; assoc. prof. Va. State U., Petersburg, 1975-76; mental health cons. USPHS, Roosevelt, Utah, 1976-79, cons. clin. psychologist, Redfield, S.D., 1979-81; clin. psychologist VA Med. Center, Ft. Lyon, Colo., 1981—. Contbr. articles to profl. jours. Served to lt. U.S. Army, 1953-55. Mem. Am. Psychol. Assn., Am. Ednl. Research Assn., Phi Delta Kappa. Democrat. Lutheran. Current Work: Behavior therapy; memory; cerebral dysfunction; betaendorphins (neuropsychology; chronic pain; EMG biofeedback induced desensitization of combat Vietnam veterans with nightmares and flashbacks, clinical psychology); mental retardation (habilitation) deinstitutionalization; alcoholism, biofeedback training and relaxation training. Subspecialties: Behavioral psychology; Neuropsychology. Home: 1919 Cimarron Ave La Junta CO 81050 Office: VA Med Center Fort Lyon CO 81038

PENN, BENJAMIN GRANT, polymer scientist, researcher; b. Martinsville, Va., July 6, 1947; s. Thomas Henry and Mary Elizabeth (Hariston) P. B.S., Winston-Salem State U., 1969; M.S. in Chemistry, Rensselaer Poly. Inst., 1973; Ph.D. in Fiber and Polymer Sci., N.C. State U., 1978. Process chemist E.I. duPont de Nemours & Co., Kinston, N.C., 1977-78; postdoctoral research assoc. Va. Poly. Inst. and State U., Blacksburg, 1978-79; sr. research chemist Research Triangle Inst., Research Triangle Park, N.C., 1979-80; polymer scientist NASA/G.C. Marshall Space Flight Ctr., Huntsville, Ala., 1980—. Contbr. articles to profl. jours. Recipient NASA Suggestion award NASA/G.C. Marshall Space Flight Ctr., 1984. Mem. Am. Chem. Soc., Soc. Plastics Engrs., Soc. for Advancement of Material and Process Engring. (sec.-treas. 1982-83), Am. Ceramic Soc. Current work: Polymer synthesis and characterization; conductive polymers; composite materials, use of polymers as ceramic precursors; environmental effects on polymers and composites; polymer crystallization; materials processing in space. Subspecialties: Reproductive endocrinology; Polymers (materials science). Home: 1500 Sparkman Dr 32C Huntsville AL 35805 Office: Space Science Lab NASA/George C Marshall Space Flight Ctr ES73 Bldg 4481 Marshall Space Flight Center AL 35812

PENNEMAN, ROBERT ALLEN, See *Who's Who in America,* 43rd edition.

PENNER, STANFORD SOLOMON, educator; b. Unna, Germany, July 5, 1921; came to U.S., 1936, naturalized, 1943; s. Heinrich and Regina (Saal) P.; m. Beverly Preston, Dec. 28, 1942; children: Merilynn Jean, Robert Clark. B.S., Union Coll., 1942; M.S., U. Wis., 1943, Ph.D., 1946; Dr. rer. nat. (hon.), Technische Hochschule Aachen, W. Ger., 1981. Research asso. Allegany Ballistics Lab., Cumberland, Md., 1944-45; research scientist Standard Oil Devel. Co., Esso Labs., Linden, N.J., 1946; sr. research engr. (Jet Propulsion Lab.), Pasadena, Calif., 1947-50; mem. faculty Calif. Inst. Tech., 1950-63, prof. div. engring., jet propulsion, 1957-63; dir. research engring. div. Inst. Def. Analyses, Washington, 1962-64; prof. engring. physics, chmn. dept. aerospace and mech. engring. U. Calif. at San Diego, 1964-68, vice chancellor for acad. affairs, 1968-69; dir. U. Calif. at San Diego Inst. for Pure and Applied Phys. Scis., 1968-71, Energy Ctr., 1973—; U.S. mem. adv. group aero. research and devel. NATO, 1952-68, chmn. combustion and propulsion panel, 1958-60; mem. adv. com. engring. scis. USAF-Office Sci. Research, 1961-65; mem. subcom. combustion NACA, 1954-58; research adv. com. air-breathing engines NASA, 1962-64; mem. coms. on gas dynamics and edn. Internat. Acad. Astronautics, 1969-80; mem. coms. NRC; dir. Ogden Corp., 1985—; cons. to govt., univs. and industry, 1953—; chmn. NRC/U.S. com. Internat. Inst. Applied Systems Analysis, 1978-81; nat. Sigma Xi lectr., 1977-79; spl. guest Internat. Coal Sci. Confs., 1984, 85. Author: Chemical Reactions in Flow Systems, 1955, Chemistry Problems in Jet Propulsion, 1957, Quantitative Molecular Spectroscopy and Gas Emissivities, 1959, Chemical Rocket Propulsion and Combustion Research, 1962, Thermodynamics, 1968, Radiation and Reentry, 1968; sr. author: Energy, Vol. I (Demands, Resources, Impact, Technology and Policy), 1974, 81, Energy, Vol. II (Non-nuclear Energy Technologies), 1975, 77, 84, Energy, Vol. III (Nuclear Energy and Energy Policies), 1976; Editor: Chemistry of Propellants, 1960, Advanced Propulsion Techniques, 1961; Asso. editor: Jour. Chem. Physics, 1953-56; editor: Jour.

Quantitative Spectroscopy and Radiative Transfer, 1960—, Jour. Def. Research, 1963-67, Energy, The internat. Jour, 1975—. Recipient spl. awards People-to-People Program, spl. awards NATO, pub. service award U. Calif. San Diego; N. Manson medal Internat. Colloquia on Gasdynamics of Explosions and Reactive Systems.; Internat. Columbus award Internat. Inst. Communications, Genoa, Italy; Guggenheim fellow, 1971-72. Fellow Am. Phys. Soc., Optical Soc. Am., AAAS, N.Y. Acad. Scis., AIAA (dir. 1964-66, past chmn. com., G. Edward Pendray award 1975, Thermophysics award 1983, Energy Systems award 1983), Am. Acad. Arts and Scis.; mem. Nat. Acad. Engring., Internat. Acad. Astronautics, Am. Chem. Soc., Combustion Inst., Sigma Xi. Current Work: Aerospace engineering, synthetic fuels, propellants and combustion, laser spectroscopy,atomic and molecular physics. Subspecialties: Fuels and sources; Combustion processes. Home: 5912 Ave Chamnez La Jolla CA 92037 Office: U Calif San Diego CA 92093

PENNIMAN, W. DAVID, information scientist. Dir. Library and Info. Systems Ctr., AT&T Bell Labs., Murray Hill, N.J. Subspecialty: Information systems (Information science). Office: AT&T Bell Labs Library and Info Systems Ctr Murray Hill NJ 07974*

PENSE, ALAN WIGGINS, metallurgical engineer; b. Sharon, Conn., Feb. 3, 1934; s. Arthur Wilton and May Beatrice (Wiggins) P.; m. Muriel Drews Taylor, June 28, 1958; children—Daniel Alan, Steven Taylor, Christine Muriel. B.Metall. Engring., Cornell U., 1957; M.S., Lehigh U., 1959, Ph.D., 1962. Research asst. Lehigh U., Bethlehem, Pa., 1957-59, instr., 1960-62, asst. prof., 1962-65, asso. prof., 1965-71, prof., 1971—, chmn. dept. metallurgy and materials engring., 1977-83, assoc. dean Coll. Engring. and Phys. Scis.; cons. adv. com. on reactor safeguards NRC, 1965—. Author: (with R.M. Brick and R.B. Gordon) Structure and Properties of Engineering Materials, 4th edit, 1978; also articles. Recipient Robinson award Lehigh U., 1965, Stabler award, 1972; Danforth fellow, 1974—. Mem. Am. Soc. Metals, Internat. Inst. Welding, Am. Welding Soc. (William Spraragan award 1963, Adams membership award 1966, Jennings award 1970, William Hobart medal 1982, Adams lectr. 1980, William Hobart medal 1982), ASTM, Am. Soc. Engring. Edn. (Western Elec. award 1968). Republican. Evang. Congregationalist (pres. bd. trustees Evang. Sch. Theology). Current Work: Metallurgy and mechanical properties of high strength steels; fracture mechanics; cryogenic alloys; welding of metals. Subspecialties: Metallurgy; Nuclear fission. Home: 2227 West Blvd Bethlehem PA 18017 Office: Lehigh U 5 Bethlehem PA 18015

PENTO, J. THOMAS, pharmacologist, educator, cons.; b. Masontown, Pa., Sept. 1, 1943; s. Joseph and Pearl (Marchando) P.; m. Maureen Mae Daley, July 13, 1946; children: Kelly Lynn, Christopher Thomas. Student, Waynesburg Coll., 1961-62; B.A., W.Va. U., 1965, M.S., 1967; Ph.D., U. Mo., Columbia, 1970. Postdoctoral fellow Maimonides Med. Center, N.Y.C., 1970-71; from asst. prof. to prof. and sect. chief Coll. Pharmacy, U. Okla., Oklahoma City, 1971—; also cons. Contbr. articles to profl. jours. NDEA fellow, 1967-69; NSF grantee, 1974-78. Mem. Endocrine Soc., Am. Soc. Pharmacology and Exptl. Therapeutics, Am. Soc. Bone and Mineral Research, AAAS, Gideon Soc. Methodist. Current Work: Endocrine pharmacology; calcium metabolism; hormone secretion; antiestrogen mechanisms. Subspecialties: Pharmacology; Endocrinology. Home: 2217 Forister Ct Norman OK 73069 Office: 1110 N Stonewall Ave Oklahoma City OK 73190

PENZ, P. ANDREW, physicist; b. Detroit, July 19, 1939; s. Perry A. and Bernice C. (Sexton) P.; m. Sandra L. Newman; children—Daniel Eric, Mark Andrew. Sc.B. in Physics, Brown U., 1961; Ph.D. in Physics, Cornell U., 1967. Sr. scientist Ford Motor Co., Dearborn, Mich., 1966-72; sr. mem. tech. staff Tex. Instruments, Dallas, 1972—; ednl. cons. Advanced Display Concepts, Richardson, Tex., 1979—; lectr. UCLA, 1980—. Patentee Electronic timepiece, 1980; contbr. chpts. to books, articles to profl. jours. Regional dir. Brown U. Assoc. Alumni, Dallas-Ft. Worth, 1973-79, active devel. campaign, 1980-83. Fellow Am. Phys. Soc., Soc. Info. Display; sr. mem. IEEE; mem. AAAS, Sigma Xi. Clubs: North Tex. Brown U. (pres. 1977-82); Mich. Brown U. (pres. 1971-72). Current work: Research, development and manufacturing of liquid crystal displays; adaptation of brain-like models to solid state computational structures which are intra-active at the device level. Subspecialty: Condensed matter physics. Home: 2203 Eastwood Dr Richardson TX 75080 Office: Tex Instruments Inc Box 225936 MS154 Dallas TX 75265

PENZIAS, ARNO ALLAN, astrophysicist, research scientist; b. Munich, Germany, Apr. 26, 1933; came to U.S., 1940, naturalized, 1946; s. Karl and Justine (Eisenreich) P.; m. Anne Pearl Barras, Nov. 25, 1954; children: David Simon, Mindy Gail, Laurie Ruth. B.S., CCNY, 1954; M.A., Columbia U., 1958, Ph.D., 1962; Dr. honoris causa, Observatoire de Paris, 1976; Sc.D. (hon.), Rutgers U., 1979, others. Mem. tech. staff Bell Labs., Holmdel, N.J., 1961-72, head radiophysics research dept., 1972-76, dir. radio research lab., 1976-79, exec. dir. research, communications scis. div., 1979-81, v.p. research, 1981—; lectr. Princeton U., 1967-72, vis. prof., 1982-85; research asso. Harvard Coll. Obs., Cambridge, Mass., 1968-80; adj. prof. SUNY, Stony Brook, 1974-84; Edison lectr. U.S. Naval Research Lab., 1979; Kompfner lectr. Stanford U., 1979; Gamow lectr. U. Colo., 1980; mem. astronomy adv. panel NSF, 1978-79; trustee Trenton State Coll., 1977-79; mem. vis. com. Calif. Inst. Tech., 1977-79, Max Planck Inst., 1978—; mem. Fachbeirat, 1978-80, chmn., 1981-83. Mem. editorial bd.: Ann. Rev. Astronomy and Astrophysics, 1974-78; asso. editor: Astrophys. Jour, 1978-82; contbr. numerous articles to profl. jours. Served to lt. Signal Corps U.S. Army, 1954-56. Recipient Henry Draper medal Nat. Acad. Sci., 1977; Herschel medal Royal Astronom. Soc., 1977; Nobel prize in physics, 1978. Mem. Nat. Acad. Scis., Am. Astron. Soc., Am. Acad. Arts and Scis., Am. Phys. Soc., Internat. Astron. Union, Com. Concerned Scientists (vice chmn.). Republican. Jewish. Research on cosmology, interstellar molecules, astrophysics, communication techniques. Current Work: Information technology, its potential applications and impacts. Subspecialties: Cosmology; Planetary science. Office: Murray Hill NJ 07924

PENZIEN, JOSEPH, structural engineering educator; b. Philip, S.D., Nov. 27, 1924; s. John Chris and Ella (Stebbins) P.; m. Jeanne Ellen Hunson, Apr. 29, 1950 (dec. Feb. 18, 1985); children—Robert Joseph, Karen Estelle, Donna Marie, Charlene May. Student, Coll. Idaho, 1942-43; B.S., U. Wash., 1945; Sc.D., Mass. Inst. Tech., 1950. Mem. staff Sandia Corp., 1950-51; sr. structures engr. Consol. Vultee Aircraft Corp., Fort Worth, 1951-53; asst. prof. U. Calif. at Berkeley, 1953-57, assoc. prof., 1957-62, prof. structual engring., 1962—; dir. Earthquake Engring. Research Center, 1968-73, 77—; Cons. engring. firms; chief tech. adv. Internat. Inst. of Seismology and Earthquake Engring., Tokyo, Japan, 1964-65. NATO Sr. Sci. fellow., 1969. Fellow Am. Acad. Mechanics; mem. ASCE (Walter Huber Research award), Am. Concrete Inst., Structural Engrs. Assn. Calif., Seismol. Soc. Am., Nat. Acad. Engring. Current Work: Research in earthquake engineering with emphasis on seismic performance of civil engineering structures. Subspecialty: Civil engineering. Home: 800 Solana Dr Lafayette CA 94549 Office: Davis Hall Univ Calif Berkeley CA 94720

PEOPLES, JOHN, JR., physicist; b. S.I., N.Y., Jan. 22, 1933; s. John and Annie Alice (Wall) P.; m. Brooke Detweiler, Dec. 16, 1955; children—Jennet, Vanessa. B.S.E.E., Carnegie Inst. Tech., 1955; M.A., Columbia U., 1961, Ph.D., 1966. Engr. Martin Co., Middle River, Md., 1955-60; asst. prof. Columbia U., N.Y.C., 1966-69; asst., then assoc. prof. Cornell U., Ithaca, N.Y., 1969-72; scientist Fermilab, Batavia, Ill., 1972—; mem. adv. panel high energy physics, 1975-80, 84—. Alfred P. Sloan fellow, 1972. Fellow Am. Phys. Soc. (chmn. div. particles and fields, 1984, div. exec. com. 1983—). Current work: Experimental particle physics, project manager of the Tevatron I Project (colliding beams) 1981—. Subspecialties: Particle physics; Particle accelerator design. Office: Fermilab PO Box 500 Mail Stop 341 Batavia IL 60510

PEPARATA, FRANCO PAOLO, electrical engineering and computer science educator, consultant, researcher; b. Reggio, Italy, Dec. 29, 1935; came to U.S., 1965; s. Vincenzo and Stefania (Bergomi) P.; m. Rosamaria Cupi, Apr. 30, 1964; children—Paola, Claudia. Dr. Engring., U. Rome, 1959; Libera Docenza, Italian Univ. System, 1969. Tech. mgr. Univac, Rome, 1960-63; sr. system designer Selenia (Raytheon), Rome, 1963-65; asst. prof. elec. engring. and computer sci. U. Ill.-Urbana, 1966-68, assoc. prof., 1968-70, prof., 1970—; cons. Telettra, Milan, Italy, 1972-76, Olivetti, Ivrea, Italy, 1974, IBM, Yorktown Heights, 1981-83. Co-author: Introduction to Discrete Structures, 1973; Introduction to Computer Engineering, 1984; contbr. numerous articles to profl. jours. Fellow IEEE; mem. Assn. Computing Machinery, European Assn. Theoret. Computer Sci. Current work: Design and analysis of algorithms, computational aspects of VLSI, VLSI architectures, computational geometry. Subspecialties: Theoretical computer science; Computer architecture. Home: 2012 Silver Ct E Urbana IL 61801

PEPINE, CARL JOHN, physician, educator; b. Pitts., June 8, 1941; s. Charles John and Elizabeth (Hovan) P.; m. Lynn Divers, Aug. 3, 1963; children: Mary Lynn, Anne, Elizabeth. B.S., U. Pitts., 1962; M.D., N.J. Coll. Medicine, 1966. Intern Allegheny Gen. Hosp., U. Pitts., 1966-67; resident in internal medicine Jefferson Med. Coll. Hosp., Phila., 1967-68, fellow in physiology and cardiovascular disease, 1969-71; asst. prof. medicine Jefferson Med. Coll., Phila., 1973-74; asst. prof. medicine U. Fla., Gainesville, 1974-75, assoc. prof., 1975-79, prof., 1979—, dir. cardiovascular research, 1974—, assoc. dir. div. cardiovascular medicine, 1982—; dir. cardiology catheterization lab. Shands Hosp., U. Fla., Gainesville, 1974—; dir., chief cardiology VA Regional Med. Ctr., Gainesville, 1978—. Mem. editorial bd.: Circulation; Am. Jour. Cardiology, Jour. Am. Coll. Cardiology, Cardiac Catherization, Cardiovascular Diagnosis; contbr. articles to profl. jours.; developer catheters to measure blood flow and heart circulation. Served to comdr. USN, 1968-74. VA grantee, 1975—; Am. Heart Assn. grantee, 1977—; NIH grantee, 1985—. Fellow Am. Coll. Cardiology, Am. Heart Assn. (council on clin. cardiology and on circulation), Assn. Univ. Cardiologists, Am. Fedn. Clin. Research, Soc. Cardiac Angiography, Am. Soc. Clin. Investigation; mem. N.Y. Acad. Scis., AAAS, Pi Kappa Alpha. Democrat. Roman Catholic. Current Work: Dynamics of the coronary circulation; coronary artery spasm and stenosis; effects of lasers on blood vessels; silent ischemia. Subspecialties: Cardiology; Laser medicine. Office: U Fla 1400 SW Archer Rd Box J-277 Gainesville FL 32610

PERCIVAL, STEPHEN FRANCIS, JR., micropaleontologist; b. Camden, N.J., Aug. 27, 1932; s. Stephen Francis and Clara (Caskey) P., m. Jeannette Kennedy, June 15, 1957; children—George Donald, Linda Percival Staab. B.A. in Geology, U. Pa., 1956; M.S. in Geology, Pa. State U., 1959; Ph.D. in Geology, Princeton U., 1972. Micropaleontologist Mobil Oil de Venezuela, Anaco, 1958-60, Mobil Oil Can., Tripoli, Libya, 1960-61, Mobil Field Research Lab., Dallas, 1962-72, Mobil Oil, Dallas, 1972—. Author: (with others) Joides Leg 3 Deep Sea Drilling, 1970, Joides Leg 42B Deep Sea Drilling, 1978, Joides Leg 73 Deep Sea Drilling, 1984. Served to cpl. U.S. Army, 1952-54. Mem. Am. Assn. Petroleum Geologists, Geol. Soc. Am., AAAS. Republican. Current works: Stratigraphic micropaleontology using calcareous nannofossils. Subspecialties: Paleontology; Geology. Home: 326 Suddith Ln Midlothian TX 76065 Office: Mobil Oil Corp PO Box 900 Dallas TX 75221

PERCY, JOHN REES, astronomer, educator; b. Windsor, Eng., July 10, 1941; s. George Francis and Christine (Holland) P.; m. Maire Ede Robertson, June 16, 1962; children: Carol Elaine. B.Sc., U. Toronto, 1962, M.A., 1963, Ph.D., 1968. Tchr. Bloor Collegiate Sch., Toronto, 1964-65; mem. faculty U. Toronto, 1967—, assoc. prof. astronomy, 1973-78, prof., 1978—. Contbr. articles to profl. jours. Leverhulme fellow Cambridge (Eng.) U., 1972-73; Recipient Royal Jubilee medal Govt. of Can., 1977. Mem. Internat. Astronom. Union. Current Work: Structure, evolution, and stability of stars. Subspecialty: Optical astronomy. Office: U Toronto 60 St George St Toronto ON M5S 1A7 Canada

PERDEW, JOHN PAUL, physics educator; b. Cumberland, Md., Aug. 30, 1943; s. Paul Raymond and Elma Lillian (Carr) P. A.B. Gettysburg Coll., 1965; Ph.D., Cornell U., 1971. Postdoctoral fellow U. Toronto, 1971-74, Rutgers U., New Brunswick, N.J., 1974-77; asst. prof. phsics Tulane U., New Orleans, 1977-79, assoc. prof., 1979-82, prof., 1982—. Contbr. articles to profl. jours. Grantee: NSF, 1978—. Mem. Am. Phys. Soc., Phi Beta Kappa, Sigma Xi. Current work: Fundamentals of the density functional theory of many-particle systems; density functional approximations and their applications to atoms and crystals. Subspecialties: Condensed matter physics; Statistical physics. Office: Dept Physics Tulane U New Orleans LA 70118

PERDUE, PHILIP TAW, research health physicist; b. Salem, Va., June 11, 1917; s. Peter Taw and Willie Mae (Doss) P.; m. Ione C. Sisson, Nov. 15, 1937 (div. 1953); children: Julia, Patricia Ann; m. Stella Wilson, Sept. 20, 1959; 1 dau.: Karen Rae. Student, Roanoke Coll., Salem, 1935-37. Registered radiation protection technologist radio telephone lic. FCC. Health physicist Oak Ridge Nat. Lab., 1954—. Contbr. articles to profl. jours. Bd. dirs. Oak Ridge Community Playhouse, 1964-66, 73-75. Mem. Health Physics Soc. (treas. East Tenn. chpt. 1982-84, Disting. Service award 1980), Am. Nuclear Soc. (Appreciation cert. 1982), N.Y. Acad. Scis., AAAS. Unitarian. Patentee determine radon in air, fast-neuron solid-state dosemeter. Current Work: Quantitative dtermination of radioisotopes in homes and soil, particularly daughters of the radon isotopes. Subspecialties: Geochemistry; Environmental engineering. Home: 103 Oak Ln Oak Ridge TN 37830 Office: Oak Ridge Nat Lab PO Box X Oak Ridge TN 37830

PEREIRA, MICHAEL ALAN, pharmacologist, toxicologist, cancer researcher; b. Bronx, N.Y., May 3, 1944; s. Frank F. and Eleanor (Minowitz) P.; m. Bette Ann Weinstein, Sept. 17, 1967; children: Arlene, Steve. B.S. in Microbiology, Ohio State U., 1967, Ph.D. in Pharmacology, 1971. Postdoctoral fellow NIH, Bethesda, Md., 1971-73; research asso. N.Y. Blood Center, N.Y.C., 1973-74; research scientist NYU Med. Ctr., Tuxedo, N.Y., 1974-78; br. chief, pharmacologist EPA, Cin., 1978—; adj. asst. prof. Ohio State U. Coll. Medicine, Columbus, 1979—. Contbr. articles to profl. jours. Damon Runyon fellow, 1971-73. Mem. Soc. Toxicology, Am. Assn. for Cancer Research, Environ. Mutagen Soc., Am. Coll. Toxicology. Jewish. Current Work: Research in cause and prevention of cancer; mechanism of chemical carcinogenesis; tumor promotion; chemical mutagenesis; environ. carcinogenesis and toxicology; biochem. toxicology. Subspecialties: Toxicology (medicine); Cancer research (medicine). Home: 12165 Brookston Dr Cincinnati OH 45240 Office: EPA 26 W St Clair St Cincinnati OH 45268

PEREL, JAMES MAURICE, pharmacologist, educator, cons.; b. Argentina, Mar. 30, 1933; came to U.S., 1947, naturalized, 1954; s. Adolph and Bella (Silverberg) P.; m. Audrey Feldman, Apr. 19, 1972; children: Allan B., Alissa A., Stephen M. B.S., CCNY, 1956; M.S., N.Y.U., 1961, Ph.D. (NSF fellow), 1964. Nuclear chemist N.Y. Naval Shipyard, 1956-58; asso. research scientist N.Y.U. Med. Sch., 1963-67; asst. prof. medicine and chemistry Emory U., Atlanta, 1967-70; asst. prof. psychiatry Coll. Physicians and Surgeons, Columbia U., 1970-76, asso. prof. clin. pharmacology and psychiatry, 1976-80; chief psychiat. research N.Y. State Psychiat. Inst., 1976-80; prof. psychiatry and pharmacology U. Pitts. Sch. Medicine, 1980—; dir. clin. pharmacology program Western Psychiat. Inst. and Clinic, 1979—; cons. in clin. pharmacology VA Med. Center, Pitts., Found. for Research in Mania and Depression, N.Y.C., FDA, N.Y. State Dept. Mental Health and Mental Retardation, Obstetric Anesthesiology Found., N.Y.C. Contbr. chpts. to books, articles to profl. jours. Recipient Founder's Day award N.Y.U., 1964; USPHS fellow, 1963-65; grantee, 1967, 70, 73, 76, 79-80, 80—. Fellow Am. Inst. Chemists; mem. Am. Soc. Pharmacology and Exptl. Therapeutics, Am. Fedn. Clin. Research, Soc. Biol. Psychiatry, Am. Soc. Clin. Pharmacology and Therapeutics, N.Y. Acad Scis., Harvey Soc. Current Work: Mechanisms of drug actions in humans, psychopharmacology of antidepressants and neuroleptics, drug metabolism and pharmacokinetics. Subspecialties: Pharmacology; Pharmacokinetics. Office: 3811 O'Hara St Pittsburgh PA 15213

PEREZ, FRANCISCO IGNACIO, clinical psychologist, behavioral researcher; b. Havana, Cuba, May 21, 1947; came to U.S., 1960, naturalized, 1969; s. Francisco Jose and Maria F. (Villa) P.; m. Georgina M. Montero, Aug. 21, 1971; children: Francisco A., Teresa M. B.A., U. Fla.-Gainesville, 1969, M.A., 1970, Ph.D., 1972. Lic. psychologist, Tex. Pvt. practice clin. psychology, Houston, 1972—; asst. prof. psychology U. Houston, 1975—, dir. clin. edn. lab., 1972-75; clin. asst. prof. neurology and physical medicine Baylor Coll. Medicine, 1980—, dir. Neuropsychology Lab., 1975-80. Contbr. in field. Bd. dirs. Houston Youth Community Council. NIH grantee, 1975-80, 78-80; Marion Labs. grantee, 1978-80. Mem. Am. Psychol. Assn., Internat. Neuropsychology Soc., Tex. Psychol. Assn., Biofeedback Soc. Am. Roman Catholic. Current Work: Behavioral research in dementia and the elderly; biofeedback applications; computerized cognitive retaining in the brain injured. Subspecialties: Behavioral psychology; Neuropsychology. Home: 3407 Fawn Creek Dr Kingswood TX 77339 Office: PGO and Associates PC 6560 Fannin St Suite 1224 Houston TX 77030

PEREZ, RICARDO, electrical engineer, consultant; b. Mexico City, Jan. 12, 1959; came to U.S. June 3, 1959, naturalized 1980; s. Esperanza (Perez) Gascon; m. Sandra Sophia Deak, Sept. 19, 1981; children—Lorenzo, Antonio. B.S.E.E., Ill. Inst. Tech., 1981, M.S.E.E., 1983. Cert. profl. engr. Component engr. Zenith Elec. Corp., Glenview, Ill., 1981-83; sr. engr. Teledyne Co., Lewisburg, Tenn., 1983—; cons. Am. Devel. Co., Nashville, 1984—. Ill. Inst. Tech. scholar, 1978, Latins of United Latin American Citizens scholar, 1979, Latins Involved in Further Edn. scholar, 1980. Mem. IEEE, Am. Entreprenuers Assn. Republican. Roman Catholic. Current work: Reliability improvements in integrated circuit technology fabrication. The utilization of computer network design to increase the services of telecommunications. Subspecialties: Microelectronics; Integrated circuits. Home: 106 8th Ave Columbia TN 38401 Office: Teledyne Bldg III PO Box 51 Industrial Park Lewisburg TN 37091

PERI, BARBARA ANN immunologist, educator; b. Richmond, Calif., May 15, 1925; d. Walter George Miller and Dorothy Gertrude Webster; m. John Baynard Peri, July 21, 1946; children—Pamela Peri Pazoles, Phyllis Peri Johnson, Janet Peri Gillies. B.S., U. Calif.-Berkeley, 1946; M.S., U. Wis., 1948; Ph.D., U. Notre Dame, 1970. Asst. then assoc. prof. Valparaiso U., Ind., 1958-66; research assoc., asst. prof., U. Chgo., 1974-83, assoc. prof., 1983—. Contbr. articles to profl. jours. Grantee NIH, 1976, 81. Mem. Am. Assn. Immunologists, Am. Assn. Microbiology, N.Y. Acad. Sci., Chgo. Assn. Immunologists. Current work: Mucosal immunity; maternal fetal immune interactions; neonatal immune reaction. Subspecialties: Immunology (medicine); Infectious diseases. Office: Box 133 U Chgo 5841 Maryland Ave Chicago IL 60637

PERI, JOHN BAYARD, physical chemist; b. Stockton, Calif., May 5, 1923; s. John Joseph and Alta Josephine (Scheffer) P.; m. Barbara Anne Miller, July 21, 1946; children—Pamela Elizabeth, Phyllis Irene, Janet Ellen. B.S., U. Calif., 1943; M.S., U. Wis., Madison, 1948, Ph.D., 1949. Research chemist Calif. Research Corp., Richmond, 1949-57; project chemist Standard Oil Co., Whiting, Ind., 1957-58; sr. project chemist Am. Oil Co., 1958-60; sr. research scientist Amoco Oil Co., 1960-62, research assoc., 1962-79, sr. research assoc., Naperville, Ill., 1979—; chmn. Gordon Research Conf. on Catalysis, 1965. Mem. editorial adv. bd. Jour. Phys. Chemistry, 1978-82. Contbr. articles to profl. jours. and chpts. to books. Patentee in field. Served to lt. (j.g.) USNR, 1943-46. Mem. Am. Chem. Soc., Catalysis Soc. (dir. 1980-84), Sigma Xi. Club: Chgo. Catalysis (pres. 1963, past dir.). Current work: Infrared study of fundamental surface properties of catalysts; general surface chemistry and colloidal properties of dispersed systems. Subspecialties: Surface chemistry; Catalysis chemistry. Home: 221 Ravine Rd Hinsdale IL 60521 Office: Amoco Oil Co Research & Devel Amoco Research Ctr PO Box 400 Naperville IL 60566

PERIASAMY, RAVINDRAN, chemical engineer, researcher; b. Vellore, Tamil Nadu, India, Oct. 8, 1954; came to U.S., 1976; s. Balakrishnan and Mohana Bai (Sundaresan) P. B.E. with distinction, Annamalai U., India, 1976; M.S., Clarkson U., 1978; Ph.D., U. N.Mex, 1982. Ptnr., M/S Periasamy & Sons, Vellore, India, 1970-76; research asst., tchr. Clarkson U., 1976-78, U. N.Mex., 1978-80; research asst. Inst. Paper Chemistry, Appleton, Wis., 1980-82, research assoc., 1983; research assoc. U. Wash., Seattle, 1983—. Contbr. articles to profl. jours. Recipient honararium Elsevier Sci. Pub. Co., Amsterdam, Netherlands, 1981. Mem. Am. Inst. Chem. Engrs. (mem. jour. rev. bd. 1980—), Am. Chem. Soc., Dec Computer Users Soc., Sigma Xi. Hindu. Current work: Chemical engineering, light scattering, chemical physics and transport processes or aerosol particles, numerical simulation, optimization techniques, adsorption phenomena. Subspecialties: Chemical engineering; Particle physics. Office: Univ Wash Dept Chem Engring Mail Stop BF-10 Seattle WA 98195

PERKINS, COURTLAND DAVIS, aeronautical engineer, educator; b. Phila., Dec. 27, 1912; s. Harry Norman and Emily Cramp (Taylor) P.; m. Jean Elizabeth Enfield, Sept. 27, 1941 (dec. Oct. 1980); children: William Enfield, Anne Taylor. B.S., Swarthmore Coll., 1935, D.Eng. (hon.), 1977; M.S., Mass. Inst. Tech., 1941; D.Eng. (hon.), Lehigh U., 1977, Rensselear Poly. Inst., 1977. Br. engr. Am. Radiator Co., Phila., 1935-39; prof. aero. engring. Princeton U., 1945—, chmn. dept., 1951-63, chmn. dept. aerospace and mech. scis., sch. engring. and applied sci., 1963-74, assoc. dean Sch. Engring., 1974-75; dir. Fairchild-Industries Corp., 1962-75, Am. Airlines, 1967-75; Keuffel & Esser Corp., 1969-75; trustee Mitre Corp., C. Stark Draper Labs.; Aero engr. USAF, Air Materiel Command, Dayton, Ohio, 1941-45; chief scientist USAF, 1956-57; asst. sec. Research and Devel., 1960-61; mem. sci. adv. bd. USAF, chmn., 1969-73, 77-78; mem. def. sci. bd. Def. Dept., 1969-73, 77-78; chmn. adv. group for aero. research and devel. NATO, 1963-67; chmn. space systems com. NASA, 1973-77. Author: (with Robert E. Hage) Airplane Performance Stability and Control, 1949. Decorated Legion of Honor France). Fellow AIAA (hon., pres. 1964), Am. Acad. Arts and Scis., Royal Aero. Soc.; mem. Nat. Acad. Engring. (pres. from 1975), Nat. Acad. Sci. (mem. space sci. bd. 1964-70), Sigma Xi, Tau Beta Pi. Subspecialty: Aeronautical engineering. Office: Princeton Univ Dept Aero Engring Princeton NJ

PERKINS, DAVID D(EXTER), geneticist; b. Watertown, N.Y., May 2, 1919; s. Dexter M. and Loretta F. (Gardiner) P.; m. Dorothy L. Newmeyer, Aug. 1, 1952; 1 dau., Susan J. A.B. in Biology, U. Rochester, 1941; Ph.D. in Zoology, Columbia U., 1949. Mem. faculty Stanford U., 1949—, prof. biology, 1961—; research fellow U. Glasgow, Scotland, 1954-55, Columbia U., 1962-63, Australian Nat. U., Canberra, 1968-69; vis. scholar univs. Wash., Hawaii and Calif., San Diego, 1975-76; participant India-U.S. Exchange Scientists Program, 1974; mem. genetics tng. com. USPHS, 1961-65. Editor Genetics, 1963-67. Served with USAAF, 1943-45. Recipient Research Career award USPHS, 1964—. Mem. Internat. Genetics Fedn. (exec. bd. 1978-83), Genetics Soc. Am. (pres. 1977), Nat. Acad. Scis. Subspecialty: Genetics and genetic engineering (biology). Office: Dept Biol Scis Stanford U Stanford CA 94305

PERKINS, FRANK OVERTON, institute administrator, college dean; b. Fork Union, Va., Feb. 14, 1938; s. Frank Otie and Mary Ella (Hughes) P.; m. Alma Vivian Smith, June 15, 1961. B.A., U. Va., 1960; M.S., Fla. State U., 1962, Ph.D., 1966. Marine scientist Va. Inst. Marine Sci., Coll. William and Mary, Gloucester Point, Va., 1966-69, sr. marine scientist, 1969-77, asst. dir., 1977-81, dean, dir., 1981—. Editor: Haplosporidian and Haplospridian-like Diseases of Shellfish, 1979. Baptist. Current work: Diseases of commercially signifiant marine organisms, identification and role of ultraplankton in Chesapeake Bay, and cell biology of fungi and protozoa. Subspecialty: Marine biology. Office: Sch Marine Sci Va Inst Marine Sci The Coll William and Mary Gloucester Point VA 23062

PERKINS, GLENN RICHARD, nuclear engineering cons.; b. Portsmouth, N.H., Nov. 3, 1947; s. Milo Orman and Rosamond (Thorner) P.; m. Linda Soley Swalm, May 23, 1970; 1 child, Dain Eyrikur. A.S., Wentworth Inst., 1969; B.S., Northeastern U., 1972. Asst. test engr. Newport News Shipbldg. and Drydock Co., Va., 1972-73; devel. engr. Combustion Engring. Co., Windsor, Conn., 1973-78, prin. devel. engr., 1978-79, supr. inservice inspection group, 1979-81; pres. NDE Engring. Cons., Storrs, Conn., 1981—; cons. NUSCO, Hartford, Conn., 1982, Yankee Atomic Electric Co., Framingham, Mass., 1981-82, Fla. Power & Light Co., Miami, 1981-82, NES, Danbury, Conn., 1981. Cubmaster Boy Scouts Am., 1982. Mem. Am. Nuclear Soc., Am. Soc. NonDestructive Testing. Current Work: Development and implementation of Non Destructive Examination programs to meet NRC and industry codes and standards for commercial nuclear power plants. Subspecialties: Non-destructive testing; Data management. Home: 241 Woodland Rd Storrs CT 06268 Office: NDE Engring Cons PO Box 535 Storrs CT 06268

PERKINS, RONALD DEE, geologist, educator; b. Covington, Ky., May 18, 1935; s. Stanley E. and Pauline L. (Greene) P.; m. Beverly L. Hughes, June 8, 1957; children—Lisa, Debra. B.S., U. Cin., 1957; M.S., U. N.Mex., 1959; Ph.D. in Geology, Ind. U., 1962. Research geologist Shell Devel. Co., Houston, 1962-63, project leader, Coral Gables, Fla., 1963-68; mem. faculty Duke U., Durham, N.C., 1968—, prof. geology, 1975—, chmn. dept., 1978—; cons. to industry. Author numerous papers in field. NSF grantee, 1969—. Mem. Internat. Assn. Sedimentologists, Soc. Econ. Paleontologists and Mineralogists (sec.-treas. 1978-82), Geol. Soc. Am., Am. Assn. Petroleum Geologists, Sigma Xi. Current work: Carbonate petrology, modern and ancient depositional facies. Office: Duke U Old Chemistry Bldg Rm 211 Durham NC 27706

PERL, MARTIN LEWIS, physicist, educator; b. N.Y.C., June 24, 1927; s. Oscar and Fay (Rosenthal) P.; m. Teri Hoch, June 19, 1948; children: Jed, Anne, Matthew, Joseph. B.Chem. Engring., Poly. Inst. Bklyn., 1948; Ph.D., Columbia U., 1955. Chem. engr. Gen. Electric Co., 1948-50; asst. prof. physics U. Mich., 1955-58, asso. prof., 1958-63; prof. Stanford, 1963—. Author: High

Energy Hadron Physics, 1975; contbr. articles on high energy physics and on relation of sci. to soc. to profl. jours. Served with U.S. Mcht. Marine, 1944-45; Served with AUS, 1945-46. Recipient Wolf prize in physics, 1982. Fellow Am. Phys. Soc.; mem. Nat. Acad. Scis., AAAS. Current Work: Experimental particle physics. Subspecialty: Particle physics. Home: 525 Lincoln Ave Palo Alto CA 94301 Office: Stanford Linear Accelerator Center Stanford U Stanford CA 94305

PERLIS, ALAN J., educator, computer scientist; b. Pitts., Apr. 1, 1922; s. Louis Phillip and Zelda Anne (Gilfond) P.; m. Sydelle Gordon, Oct. 28, 1951; children—Mark Lawrence, Robert Gordon, Andrea Lynn. B.S. in Chemistry, Carnegie Inst. Tech., 1943; postgrad., Calif. Inst. Tech., 1946-47; M.S., Mass. Inst. Tech., 1950, Ph.D. in Math, 1950; D.Sc. (hon.), Davis and Elkins Coll., 1968, Purdue U., 1973, Waterloo U., 1974; D.Sc. hon. doctorate, Sacred Heart U., 1979. Asst. prof. math., dir. computer center Purdue U., 1952-56; mem. faculty Carnegie Inst. Tech., 1956-71, prof. math., dir. computer center, 1960-71, head dept. math., 1961-64, head dept. computer sci., 1965-71; Eugene Higgins prof. computer sci. Yale U., 1971—, chmn. dept., 1976—; Gordon and Betty Moore vis. prof. engring. Calif. Inst. Tech., 1977; mem. NSF computer com. Nat. Joint Computer Com., 1954-56, Gov. Pa. Council Sci. and Tech., 1963—; com. computers research NIH, 1963—; mem. computer sci. and engring. research bd. Nat. Acad. Sci., 1968—; mem. Assembly of Engring., NRC, 1978—. Served to 1st lt. USAAF, 1942-45, ETO. Mem. Assn. Computing Machinery (pres. 1962-64, editor-in-chief jour. Communications 1958-62), Soc. Indsl. and Applied Math., Am. Math. Soc., Math. Assn., Am. Acad. Arts. and Scis., Conn. Acad. Sci. Engring., Nat. Acad. Engring. Am. Subspecialties: Programming languages; Software engineering. Home: 19 Tumblebrook Rd Woodbridge CT 06525 Office: Yale Univ New Haven CT 06520

PERLMUTTER, DANIEL D., educator; b. Bklyn., May 24, 1931; s. Samuel and Fannie (Kristal) P.; m. Felice Davidson, Oct. 23, 1954; children—Shira, Saul, Tova. B.S. in Chem. Engring, N.Y. U., 1952; D.Eng., Yale, 1956. Prof. U. Pa., Phila., 1965—. Author: Introduction to Chemical Process Control, 1965, Stability of Chemical Reactors, 1972. Guggenheim fellow, 1964; Fulbright fellow, 1968, 72. Mem. Am. Inst. Chem. Engrs., AAAS. Subspecialty: Chemical engineering. Office: 311 Towne U Pa Philadelphia PA 19119

PERLOVSKY, LEONID ISAACOVICH, nuclear magnetic, resonance research and development company scientist; b. Odessa, Ukrain, USSR, Nov. 11, 1948; came to U.S., 1978; s. Isaac E. and Riva B. (Bormashenko) P.; m. Diana Vinkovetsky, Feb., 1985; children: Ilya, Boris, Daniel. M.S. with honors, Novosibirsk U., 1971; Ph.D., Joint Inst. Nuclear Research, Dubna, 1975. Asst. prof. Siberia Civil Engring. Inst., Novosibirsk, U.S.S.R., 1975-77; assoc. prof., 1977-78; research prof. NYU, N.Y.C., 1979-80; sr. research physicist Exxon Prodn. Research, Houston, 1980-81, research specialist, 1981-83, sr. research specialist, 1983-84; prin. research scientist Advanced NMR Systems, Boston, 1985—; cons. Sibera Agrl. Inst., Novosibirsk, USSR, 1975-78, Software Devel., Inc., N.Y.C., 1979-80. Contbr. articles in field to profl. jours. Mem. Soc. Exploration Geologists, Soc. Profl. Well Log Analysts, Soc. Indsl. and Applied Math., Am. Statis. Assn. Current Work: Nuclear magnetic resonance imaging, new techniques for fast-imaging data collection, radio frequency pulse applications; new algorithms for magnetic field in homogeneity corrections, corrections for gradient field and RF-pulse imperfectnesses artificial intelligence techniques, pattern recognition, signal processing, filtering, deconvolution, estimation of parameters, imaging and inverse problem solutions, wave propagation. Subspecialties: Geophysics; Applied mathematics. Home: 30 Griggs Rd Brookline MA 02146 Office: Advanced NMR Systems Inc 30 Sonar Dr Woburn MA 01801

PERLOW, MARK JACOB, neurologist, neurobiologist; b. Chgo., Feb. 26, 1942; s. Samuel and Bertha (Shapiro) P. M.D., Northwestern U., 1967. Intern Cook County Hosp., Chgo., 1967-68; resident, fellow Albert Einstein Coll. Medicine, Bronx, N.Y., 1968-72; staff physician NIH, Bethesda, Md., 1974-80; assoc. prof. neurology Mt. Sinai Sch. Medicine, N.Y.C., 1980-81; practice medicine specializing in neurology, Chgo., 1981—; chief neurology service West Side VA Hosp., Chgo., 1981—; assoc. prof. neurology U. Ill. Med. Sch. Contbr. articles on neurology to profl. jours.; prin. author paper demonstrating for first time brain tissue transplanted between Mammals can function appropriately in host. Served as maj. U.S. Army, 1972-74. Recipient George Cotzias prize Am. Parkinson's Disease Found., 1980. Mem. Am. Acad. Neurology, Endocrine Soc. Current Work: Nervous tissue transplantation, growth and regeneration, biological rhythms, neuroendocrinology. Subspecialties: Neurobiology; Chronobiology.

PERNICK, BENJAMIN, research scientist; b. N.Y.C., June 9, 1931; s. Abraham and Rose (Federbush) P.; m. Nancy R. Horn, June 10, 1956; children: Jonathan, Gary, Alice. B.S., CCNY, 1954; M.S., Stevens Inst. Tech., 1958, Ph.D., 1965. Sr. staff scientist Grumman Aerospace Corp., Bethpage, N.Y., 1965—; adj. asst. prof. physics CUNY, 1964-77, adj. assoc. prof. math., 1978—. Contbr. articles to profl. jours.; patentee. Mem. Optical Soc. Am., Am. Phys. Soc., Sigma Pi Sigma. Current Work: Research and development in laser technology and applications, signal processing, guided waves, electro-optics, acousto-optics, photoconductivity. Subspecialties: Laser research; Optical signal processing. Home: 110-11 Queens Blvd Apt 23E Forest Hills NY 11375 Office: Research Dept Grumman Aerospace Bethpage NY 11714

PERRELLA, ANTHONY JOSEPH, electronics engineer; b. Boulder, Colo., Sept. 16, 1942; s. Anthony Vincent and Mary Domenica (Forte) P.; m. Pamela Smith, July 19, 1980; 1 child, Kathleen. B.S., U. Wyo., 1964, postgrad., 1965; postgrad. U. Calif.-San Diego, 1966-67, U. Calif.-Irvine, 1968-70. Flight engr. U.S. Naval Tng. Devices Ctr., San Diego, 1965-67; research engr. Collins div. Rockwell Internat. (formerly Collins Radio Co.), Newport Beach, Calif., 1967-69, electromagnetic interference and TEMPEST group head, 1969-74, supr. 1974-75, mgr., 1975-77, mgr. systems integration, 1977, mgr. space communication systems, 1977-78; sr. mem. tech staff ARGOSystems Inc., Sunnyvale, Calif., 1978, program mgr., 1978-84, dept. mgr., 1984—; v.p. research and devel. Things Unlimited, Inc., Laramie, Wyo., 1965-72, pres., 1972-75. Mem. Am. Mgmt. Assn., IEEE, AAAS, N.Y. Acad. Scis., Assn. Old Crows, Tau Kappa Epsilon. Roman Catholic. Current work: Detection of weak continuous and pulsed radio signals especially as related to automated reception and signal processing systems which cross correlate such signals with known patterns to yield useful and concise information. Subspecialties: Electronics; Telecommunications. Home: 931 Brookgrove Ln Cupertino CA 95014 Office: ArgoSystems Inc 884 Hermosa Ct Sunnyvale CA 94086

PERRIN, EDWARD BURTON, statistician, public health educator; b. Greensboro, Vt., Sept. 19, 1931; s. Justus N. and Dorothy E. (Willey) P.; m. Carol Anne Hendricks, Aug. 18, 1956; children—Jenifer, Scott. B.A., Middlebury Coll., 1953; postgrad. (Fulbright scholar) in stats, Edinburgh (Scotland) U., 1953-54; M.A. in Math. Stats, Columbia U., 1956; Ph.D., Stanford U., 1960. Asst. prof. dept. biostats. U. Pitts., 1959-62; asst. prof. dept. preventive medicine U. Wash., Seattle, 1962-65, assoc. prof., 1965-69, prof., 1969-70, chmn. dept. biostats., 1970-72, prof. dept. health services, 1975—, chmn. dept. health services, 1982—; clin. prof. dept. community medicine and internat. health Sch. Medicine, Georgetown U., Washington, 1972-75; dep. dir. Nat. Center for Health Stats., HEW, 1972-73, dir., 1973-75; research scientist Health Care Study Center, Battelle Human Affairs Research Centers, Seattle, 1975-76, dir., 1976-78; dir. Health and Population Study Cent er, Battelle Human Affairs Research Centers, Seattle, 1978-82; sr. cons. biostats. Wash./Alaska regional med. programs, 1967 -72; biometrician VA Co-op Study on Treatment of Esophageal Varices, 1961-73; mem. panel on health services research NRC, 1981. Contbr. articles on biostats., health services and population studies to profl. publs.; mem. editorial bd.: Jour. Family Practice, 1978—. Mem. tech. bd. Milbank Meml. Fund, 1974-76. Recipient Outstanding Service citation HEW, 1975. Fellow AAAS, Am. Public Health Assn. (Spiegelman Health Stats. award 1970, program devel. bd. 1971, chmn. stats. sect. 1978-80), Am. Statis. Assn. (mem. adv. com. to div. statis. policy 1975-77); mem. Inst. Medicine of Nat. Acad. Sci., Population Assn. Am., Biometrics Soc. (pres. N.Am. region 1971), Internat. Union for Sci. Study of Population, Inst. Math. Stats., Internat. Epidemiologic Assn., Sigma Xi, Phi Beta Kappa. Subspecialties: Statistics; Health services research. Home: 4900 NE 39th St Seattle WA 98105 Office: Dept Health Services U Wash SC-37 Seattle WA 98195

PERRINE, RICHARD LEROY, environmental engineering educator; b. Mountain View, Calif., May 15, 1924; s. George Alexander and Marie (Axelson) P.; m. Barbara Jean Gale, Apr. 12, 1945; children: Cynthia Gale, Jeffrey Richard. A.B., San Jose State Coll., 1949; M.S., Stanford U., 1950, Ph.D. in Chemistry, 1953. Research chemist Calif. Research Corp., La Habra, 1953-59; asso. prof. U. Calif. at Los Angeles, 1959-63, prof. engring. and applied sci., 1963—, chmn. environ. sci. and engring., 1971-82; cons. environ. sci. and engring., energy resources, flow in porous media; mem. Los Angeles County Energy Commn., 1973-81; mem. adv. council South Coast Air Quality Mgmt. Dist., 1977-82; mem. air conservation com. Los Angeles County Lung Assn., 1970—. Editor-in-chief The Environ. Profl., 1985—. Served with AUS, 1943-46. Recipient Outstanding Engr. Merit award in environ. engring. Inst. Advancement Engring., 1975. Mem. Am. Chem. Soc., Soc. Petroleum Engrs., Am. Inst. Chem. Engrs., Can. Inst. Mining and Metallurgy, N. Am. Assn. Environ. Edn., Nat. Assn. Environ. Profls., Air Pollution Control Assn., Am. Water Resources Assn., AAAS, N.Y. Acad. Scis., Western Regional Sci. Assn., Internat. Assn. Gt. Lakes Research, Soc. Environ. Toxicology and Chemistry, Sierra Club, Wilderness Soc., Audubon Soc., Sigma Xi, Tau Beta Pi, Phi Lambda Upsilon. Subspecialty: Environmental engineering. Home: 22611 Kittridge St Canoga Park CA 91307 Office: Engring I Room 2066 U Calif Los Angeles CA 90024

PERRY, DAVID R., engineering geologist, geophysicist, consultant; b. Pitts., Apr. 14, 1960; s. Joseph J. and Theresa A. (Attkisson) P. Student, James Madison U., 1982; B.S. in Geology, U. Pitts., 1982, M.S. in Geophysics, 1985. Engring. geologist, geophysicist GeoMechanics Inc., Belle Vernon, Pa., 1982-85; geophysicist/geologist NVS Corp., Pitts., 1985—; cons. geophysicist RCP Inc., Elizabeth, Pa., 1983—. Mem. Nat. Water Well Assn., Soc. Exploration Geophysicists, Assn. Engring. Geologists, Geol. Soc. Am. Republican. Current work: Use of geophysical methods for the detection of and analysis of geological hazards; mine subsidence abatment research; use of geophysical methods for the solution of engineering problems; hydrogeology and geology at active and inactive hazardous waste sites. Subspecialty: Remote sensing (geoscience). Home: 4407 Old William Penn Hwy Murrysville PA 15668 (412) 327-3676 Office: NVS Corp Park West Two Cliff Mine Rd Pittsburgh PA 15275

PERRY, DENNIS GORDON, computer scientist; b. Bakersfield, Calif., July 8, 1942; s. Cleo Hoot and Amanda Katherine (Johnson) P.; m. Linda Ellen Jones, June 27, 1964; children—Lynellen, Elizabeth. B.A., Westmont Coll., 1964; Ph.D., U. Washington, 1970; M.B.A., U. N.Mex., 1982. Research assoc. Brookhaven Nat. Lab., Upton, N.Y., 1970-72; staff mem. Los Alamos Nat. Lab., N.Mex., 1972-78, asst. then assoc. group leader, 1978-80, dep. group leader, 1980-81, leader, 1981—; cons. in field. Contbr. articles to profl. jours. Leader Evang. Ch., Los Alamos, Mem. IEEE, AAAS, Assn. Computing Machinery, Am Chem. Soc. Current work: Development of super computer networks; high speed communications; computer security; distributed computer networks. Subspecialties: Distributed systems and networks; Software engineering. Home: 2738 A Walnut Los Alamos NM 87544 Office: Los Alamos Nat Lab C5 MS B255 Los Alamos NM 87545

PERRY, DWIGHT, computer consultant company executive; b. Newark, Apr. 11, 1951; s. Obbie and Bertha Lee (Clark) P. A.B., Cornell U., 1973; M.S. in Physics, Ariz. State U., 1976; M.S. in Computer Sci., Rutgers U., 1983. Assoc. mem. tech. staff Bell Labs., Murray Hill, N.J., 1977-80; programmer, designer AT&T Communications, Piscataway, N.J., 1980-84; v.p. R&D Computer Cons., Inc., Martinsville, N.J., 1984—. Author: The Perry Notes on Physics, 1973. Mem. Am. Phys. Soc., Ind. Computer Cons. Assn. Current work: Involved in the design of various application systems for businesses, professionals and corporate users. Subspecialties: Software engineering; Distributed systems and networks. Home: 831 Central Ave Plainfield NJ 07060 Office: R&D Computer Cons Inc 1832 Middle Rd Martinsville NJ 08836

PERRY, NELSON ALLEN, radiological physicist, cons.; b. Louisville, Mar. 26, 1937; s. Leslie I. and Sue H. (Harris) P.; m. Sarita S. Cornn, July 1, 1938; children: Melody S., Kimberly D. A.A., Campbellsville Jr. Coll., 1956; B.A., U. Louisville, 1962; M.S., U. Okla., 1966. Cert. hazard control exec., health care safety profl. Radiation safety officer Michael Reese Hosp., Chgo., 1966-67; instr., radiol. physicist St. Francis Hosp., Beech Grove, Ind., 1968-70; asst. prof., radiation safety officer U. Ind. Med. Center, Indpls., 1970-73; assoc. prof., radiation cons. Perry Radiol. Cons., Inc., Indpls., 1973-76; asst. prof., radiation safety officer U. South Ala., Mobile, 1976—. Contbr. articles to profl. jours. Active CD, Indpls., 1969-76, Mobile, 1978—. USPHS trainee, 1965-66; Named hon. Ky. Col. Mem. Health Physics Soc., Am. Assn. Physicists in Medicine, Jaycees (state dir. 1968-73, also v.p., conv. club pres.). Current Work: Radiation safety; radiological instrument calibration and shielding design; teaching radiation physics and radiation biology. Subspecialties: Nuclear engineering; Radiology. Home: 1150 Byronell Dr Mobile AL 36609 Office: 370 Cancer Center Mobile AL 36688

PERRY, THEODORE SONNE, physicist; b. Salt Lake City, Apr. 8, 1952; s. Theodore Sonne and Jean James (Pearce) P.; m. Kathleen Cannon, Mar. 17, 1976; children—Kristine, Karen, Nathan. B.S. in Math., Utah State U., 1974, B.S. in Physics, 1975, M.S. in Math., 1976; M.A. in Physics, Princeton U., 1978, Ph.D. in Physics, 1983. Physicist, Lawrence Livermore Nat. Lab. (Calif.), 1981—. Originator sci. instrument fiber optics active crystal spectrometer, 1983; discoverer low temperature magnetic boundary resistance, 1981. NSF fellow, 1976. Mem. Am. Phys. Soc., Phi Kappa Phi (R.C. Gibbs award 1976). Mormon. Current work: New X-ray diagnostics for investigating nuclear weapon explosions. Subspecialties: Plasma physics; Low temperature physics. Home: 765 Curlew Rd Livermore CA 94550 Office: Lawrence Livermore Nat Lab MS L-379 PO Box 808 Livermore CA 94550

PERRYMAN, LANCE EDWARD, veterinary pathologist; b. Tacoma, Wash., Apr. 7, 1946; s. Edward L. and Pauline J. (Krutilla) P.; m. Shirley J. Armstrong, June 29, 1968; children—Kristin L., Lyssa J. D.V.M., Wash. State U., 1970; M.S., Ohio State U., 1973; Ph.D., Wash. State U., 1975. Faculty Wash. State U., Pullman, 1975—, prof. vet. and comparative pathology, 1984—. Contbr. articles to profl. jours. Mem. Am. Coll. Vet. Pathologists, Am. Coll. Vet. Immunologists (v.p. 1985—), Am. Assn. Immunologists, Am. Assn. Pathologists. Current work: Investigation and correction of genetically-determined immunodeficiency disorders; biotechnological approaches to prevention of infectious diseases. Subspecialties: Immunobiology and immunology; Pathology (veterinary medicine). Office: Wash State U Dept Vet Microbiology and Pathology Pullman WA 99164

PERSEK, STEPHEN CHARLES, management science educator, nonlinear differential equations researcher; b. Long Island City, N.Y., May 4, 1945; s. Stephen George and Zora Jane (Duzbaba) P. B.S. in Applied Math, MIT, 1966; M.S. in Applied Math, Courant Inst., 1968, Ph.D. in Applied Math, 1976. Instr. in bus. stats. N.Y. Inst. Tech., 1968-76; asst. prof. math. Marist Coll., 1977-79; asso. prof. mgmt. sci. St. John's U., Jamaica, N.Y., 1979—; staff cons. GSP Cons., N.Y.C., 1981—; stats. cons. Purchasing Mgmt. Assn. N.Y., N.Y.C., 1981—. Contbr. articles to math. jours. Mem. Soc. Indsl. and Applied Math., Am. Math. Soc., Math. Assn. Am., Inst. Mgmt. Sci. Roman Catholic. Current Work: Applied mathematics: Nonlinear ODE's, nonlinear PDE's, stability theory, uniform approximations, bifurcation theory, nonlinear oscillations and wave motions. Subspecialties: Applied mathematics; Operations research (mathematics). Home: 160 Banbury Rd Mineola NY 11501 Office: CBA-Mgmt St John's U Grand Central and Utopia Pkwys Jamaica NY 11439

PERSON, DONALD AMES, pediatrician, rheumatologist; b. Fargo, N.D., July 17, 1938; s. Ingwald Haldor and Elma Wilhelmina (Karlstrom) P.; m. Blanche Durand, Apr. 28, 1962; children: Donald Ames, David Wesley. Student, Gustavus Adolphus Coll., 1956-58, U. Minn., 1958-59; B.S., U. N.D., 1961; M.D., U. Minn., 1963. Intern Mpls.-Hennepin County Gen. Hosp., 1963-64; resident neurol. surgery Mayo Clinic and Mayo Grad. Sch. Medicine, Rochester, Minn., 1967, fellow in microbiology, 1968-70; research asso. Baylor Coll. Medicine, Houston, 1971, Arthritis Found. fellow, 1972-74, mem. faculty, 1971—, asst. prof. pediatrics, 1980—, resident in pediatrics, 1978-80; asst. attending pediatrics Harris County Hosp. Dist., 1980—; rheumatologist Tex. Children's Hosp., 1980—, attending pediatrician, 1982—; cons. Kelsey Seybold Clinic, 1980—. Contbr. articles to profl. jours. Served with AUS, 1964-66. Arthritis Found. sr. investigator, 1975-77. Fellow Am. Acad. Pediatrics; mem. AAAS, Am. Fedn. Clin. Research, AMA, Am. Rheumatism Assn., Am. Soc. Microbiology, Soc. Pediatric Research, Am. Soc. Tropical Medicine and Hygiene, Arthritis Found. (dir., med. adv. bd.), Assn. Mil. Surgeons U.S., Harris County Med. Soc., Houston Acad. Medicine, Houston Pediatric Soc., Internat. Orgn. Mycoplasmologists, N.Y. Acad. Sci., N.D. Acad. Sci., Soc. Exptl. Biology and Medicine, So. Soc. Pediatric Research, S.W. Sci. Forum, Tex. Med. Assn., Tex. Pediatric Soc., Tex. Rheumatism Assn., Tissue Culture Assn., U.S. Fedn. Culture Collections. Subspecialties: Pediatrics; Virology (biology). Office: Texas Children's Hosp Dept Rheumatology Box 20269 Houston TX 77030

PERSON, WILLIS BAGLEY, chemistry educator; b. Salem, Oreg., Apr. 23, 1928; s. Carl Waldo and Grace Cassity (Bagley) P.; m. Krystyna Szczepaniak, 1985. B.S., Willamette U., 1947; M.S., Oreg. State Coll.-Corvallis, 1949; Ph.D., U. Calif.-Berkeley, 1953. Research fellow U. Minn., 1952-54; inst. Harvard U., 1954-55; asst. prof. U. Iowa, 1955-61, assoc. prof., 1961-66; NSF postdoctoral fellow, vis. assoc. prof. U. Chgo., 1965-66; prof. chemistry U. Fla., Gainesville, 1966—; vis. staff mem. Los Alamos Nat. Lab., 1975—; UNESCO cons. State U. Campinas, Brazil, 1980; vis. prof. Inst. for Molecular Sci., Okazaki, Japan, 1984, Universite Pierre et Marie Curie, Paris, 1985; assoc. mem. commn. on molecular spectroscopy IUPAC, 1982—. Author: (with R. S. Mulliken) Molecular Complexes, 1969; editor: (with G. Zerbi) Vibrational Intensities in Infrared and Raman Spectroscopy, 1982; contbr. over 140 articles in field to profl. jours. Guggenheim fellow U. Chgo., 1960-61; Chem. Soc. sr. postdoctoral fellow, 1978. Mem. Am. Chem. Soc., Optical Soc. Am., Chem. Soc. (London), AAAS, Coblentz Soc. Current Work: Molecular spectroscopy, particularly vibrational intensities and laser spectroscopy, with applications to molecular structure, photochemistry and biophysics. Subspecialties: Physical chemistry; Laser spectroscopy. Office: Dept Chemistry U Fla Gainesville FL 32611

PERTSCHUK, LOUIS PHILIP, pathologist; b. London, July 4, 1925; s. Isaac M. and Rose P.; m. Andrea Roberts, June 28, 1985; children: Eric, Shawn, Brandy. A.B., NYU, 1946; D.O., Phila. Coll. Osteo. Medicine, 1950. Diplomate: Am. Bd. Pathology. Instr. Downstate Med. Ctr., SUNY-Bklyn., 1974-75, asst. prof., 1975-79, assoc. prof., 1979—; cons. Corning (N.Y.) Glass Works, 1982—, Zeus Sci. Co., 1982—, Abbott Labs., 1982—. Editor: Localization of Putative Steroid Receptors, 1985. Served with U.S. Army, 1943-46. NCI/NIH grantee, 1979, 82, 85. Fellow Coll. Am. Pathologists, Am. Soc. Clin. Pathologists; mem. Am. Assn. Pathologists, AAAS, Internat. Acad. Pathology, N.Y. Acad. Sci. Current Work: Identification of steroid hormone binding sites in human neoplasms by histochemical and immunohistological techniques. Subspecialty: Pathology (medicine). Home: Bridlepath House New Hempstead NY 10977 Office: Box 25 Downstate Med Center 450 Clarkson Ave Brooklyn NY 11203

PESCH, WILLIAM ALLAN, systems engineer, photographic company executive; b. Buffalo, Jan. 18, 1948; s. William Adam and Anna Martha (Hinz) P.; m. Cheryle Lynn Ryer, Oct. 3, 1969; children: Pamela Ann, William Allan, Jennifer Lynn. B.S.I.E., SUNY-Buffalo, 1970; M.S.I.E., Purdue U., 1971, postgrad., 1972. Instr. Purdue U., West Lafayette, Ind., 1970-72; engr. Eastman Kodak Co., Rochester, N.Y., 1972-74, mgr. domestic shipping, 1974-76, mgr. adminstrn., 1976-78, systems supr., 1978-81, mgr. tech., planning and research, 1981-85; mgr. Productivity Devel. Ctr., 1985—; mgmt. cons. Western N.Y. Hosp. Assn., Buffalo, 1970; computer cons. Gates Pub. Library, Rochester, 1982-83; Chpt. reviewer Handbook of Industrial Engineering, 1983. Committeeman Monroe County Dem. Com., Rochester, 1975-80; budget dir. Washington Irving Sch. PTA, 1981. Named Student Engr. of Yr. N.Y. State Soc. Profl. Engrs., Erie County, 1970; Engring. Student of Yr. Sch. Engring., SUNY-Buffalo, 1970. Mem. Inst. Mgmt. Sci., Ops. Research Soc., Am. Inst. Indsl. Engrs. Current Work: Working to provide operations research-based decision support tools for company management; automating information and control systems and office automation systems. Subspecialties: Artificial intelligence; Information systems, storage, and retrieval (computer science). Home: 23 Pine Knoll Dr Rochester NY 14624 Office: Eastman Kodak Co/Distbn Div 343 State St B-205 Rochester NY 14650

PESHKIN, MURRAY, physicist; b. Bklyn., May 17, 1925; s. Jacob and Bella Ruth (Zuckerman) P.; m. Frances Julie Ehrlich, June 15, 1955; children—Michael, Sharon, Joel. B.A., Cornell U., 1947, Ph.D., 1951. Instr., asst. prof. Northwestern U., Evanston, Ill., 1951-59; physicist, sr. physicist, assoc. dir. physics div. Argonne Nat. Lab. (Ill.), 1959—; fellow Weizmann Inst. Sci., Rehovot, Israel, 1959-60, 68-69, 84. Contbr. articles to sci. jours. Fellow Am. Phys. Soc. (regional sec. 1969-72); mem. AAAS. Current work: Fundamental Issues in quantum mechanics. Subspecialty: Theoretical physics. Office: Argonne Nat Lab ANL-203 Argonne IL 60439

PESTAK, MARK WILLIAM, physicist; b. Cleve., Nov. 21, 1955; s. Thomas Charles and Mary Elizabeth (McGee) P. B.S., Heidelberg Coll., Tiffin, Ohio, 1977; M.S., U. Toledo, 1979; Ph.D., Pa. State U., 1983. Sr. physicist Sohio Petroleum Co., Cleve., 1983—. Contbr. articles to profl. jours. Recipient Teaching award dept. physics Pa. State U., 1982. Mem. Am. Phys. Soc., Pax Christi, Sigma Xi, Sigma Pi Sigma. Roman Catholic. Current work: Enhanced oil recovery by miscible fluid injection, phase behavior of hydrocarbon mixtures. Subspecialties: Condensed matter physics; Petroleum engineering. Office: Standard Oil Co 4440 Warrensville Center Rd Cleveland OH 44128

PESTKA, SIDNEY, biochemist; b. Drobnin, Poland, May 29, 1936; came to U.S., 1937, naturalized, 1957; s. Harry and Bernice (Gerlitz) P.; m. Joan Sparacin, June 19, 1960; children—Robert Kenneth, Sharon Dianna, Steven Benjamin. B.A. in Chemistry, Princeton U., 1957; M.D., U. Pa., 1961. Research asst. Princeton U., N.J., 1955-57; intern Balt. City Hosp., 1961-62; med. officer Nat. Heart Inst., NIH, Bethesda, Md., 1961-66, Nat. Cancer Inst., 1966-69; assoc. mem. Roche Inst. Molecular Biology, Nutley, N.J., 1969-74, mem., 1975-79, lab head, 1980—; adj. prof. pathology Columbia U., N.Y.C., 1972—. Patentee; editor: Interferons, Methods in Enzymology, 1981. Pres. North Caldwell Bd. Health, N.J., 1977-79, 85. Recipient Selman A. Waksman award Microbiology, 1977. Mem. Am. Soc. Biol. Chemists, Am. Soc. Microbiology, N.Y. Acad. Scis., AAAS, Harvey Soc., Internat. Soc. Interferon Research, Phi Beta Kappa, Sigma Xi. Current work: Interferon: biosynthesis; structure; cloning and expression in bacterial recombinants; receptors. Anti-RNA and Anti-mRNA. Regulation of gene expression. Differentiation and development; carcinogenesis; control of cell growth. Subspecialties: Genetics and genetic engineering (medicine); Molecular biology. Office: Roche Inst Molecular Biology 340 Kingsland St Nutley NJ 07110

PETERLE, TONY JOHN, zoologist, educator; b. Cleve., July 7, 1925; s. Anton and Anna (Katic) P.; m. Thelma Josephine Coleman, July 30, 1949; children—Ann Faulkner, Tony Scott. B.S., Utah State U., 1949; M.S., U. Mich., 1950, Ph.D. (Univ. scholar), 1954; Fulbright scholar, U. Aberdeen, Scotland, 1954-55; postgrad., Oak Ridge Inst. Nuclear Studies, 1961. With Niederhauser Lumber Co., 1947-49, Macfarland Tree Service, 1949-51; research biologist Mich. Dept. Conservation, 1951-54; asst. dir. Rose Lake Expt. Sta., 1955-59; leader Ohio Coop. Wildlife Research unit U.S. Fish and Wildlife Service, Dept. Interior, 1959-63; asso. prof., then prof. zoology Ohio State U., Columbus, 1959—, chmn. faculty population and environmental biology, 1968-69, chmn. dept. zoology, 1969-81, dir. program in environ. biology, 1970-71; co-organizer XIII Internat. Congress Game Biology, chmn. internat. affairs com., mem. com. ecotoxicology, 1979-80; mem. com. rev. EPA pesticide decision making Nat. Acad. Scis.-NRC; mem. vis. scientists program Am. Inst. Biol. Scis.-ERDA, 1971-77; mem. com. pesticides Nat. Acad. Scis., com. on emerging trends in agr. and effects on fish and wildlife; mem. ecology com. of sci. adv. council EPA, 1979—; co-organizer NSF Symposium U.S./Czechoslovakia Toxic Substance Effects on Wildlife, 1983; mem. research units coordinating com. Ohio Coop. Wildlife and Fisheries, 1963—. Editor: Jour. of Wildlife Management, 1969-70, 84-85. Served with AUS, 1943-46. Fellow AAAS, Am. Inst. Biol. Scis., Ohio Acad. Sci.; mem. Wildlife Disease Assn., Wildlife Soc. (regional rep. 1962-67, v.p. 1968, pres. 1972), Ecol. Soc., Nat. Audubon Soc. (bd. dirs.), INTECOL-NSF panel U.S.-Japan Program, Xi Sigma Pi, Phi Kappa Phi. Current Work: Professor of zoology, research on transport, fate, effects of toxic substances in environment; editor-in-chief Journal of Wildlife Management, 1984-85. Subspecialties: Environmental toxicology; Ecology (environmental science). Office: Dept Zoology Ohio State U 1735 Neil Ave Columbus OH 43210

PETERS, CHARLES WILLIAM, corporate executive; nuclear physicist; b. Pierceton, Ind., Dec. 9, 1927; s. Charles Frederick and Zelda May (Line) P.; m. Katharine Louise Schuman, May 29, 1953; children: Susan K., m. Patricia Ann Miles, Jan. 2, 1981; children—Bruce Merkle, Leslie Sanaie, Philip Merkle, William Merkle. B.A., Ind. U., 1950; postgrad., U. Md., 1952-58. Supervisory research physicist Naval Research Lab., 1950-71; physicist EPA, 1971-76; mgr. advanced systems Consol. Controls Corp., Springfield, Va., 1976—. Contbr. numerous articles to profl. jours. Served to cpl. AUS, 1945-47. Mem. IEEE, Am. Phys. Soc., AAAS. Current Work: Radiation measurement systems, radiation detectors, robotic applications, applications of inelastic-gamma ray spectrography, fast-neutron radiography. Subspecialties: Nuclear physics; Operations research (mathematics). Home: 12303 Mulberry Ct Woodbridge VA 22192 Office: PO Box 726 Springfield VA 22150

PETERSDORF, ROBERT GEORGE, internist, medical educator, university chancellor and dean; b. Berlin, Feb. 14, 1926; s. Hans H. and Sonja P.; m. Patricia Horton Qua, June 2, 1951; children: Stephen Hans, John Eric. B.A. cum laude, Brown U., 1948; M.D., Yale U., 1952; D.Sc. (hon.), Albany Med. Coll., 1979, Bethel Coll. Pa., 1982; A.M. (hon.), Harvard U., 1980. Diplomate: Am. Bd. Internal Medicine, 1959, past chmn. Intern Yale U., 1952-53, resident, 1953-54, chief resident, 1957-58; researcher Johns Hopkins U., 1955-57, asst. prof. medicine, 1958-60; assoc. prof. U. Wash., 1960-62, prof., 1962-79, chmn. dept. medicine, 1964-79; prof. Harvard U., 1969-81; pres. Brigham and Women's Hosp., 1979-81; prof. U. Calif.-San Diego, 1981—; now vice chancellor for health scis., dean U. Calif.-San Diego (Sch. Medicine); dir. Am. Hosp. Supply Corp. Contbr. numerous articles to profl. publs.; editor numerous books. Served with USAAF, 1944-46. Recipient Lederle Med. Faculty award, Wiggers award Albany Med. Coll., 1979, Keen Disting. Alumni award Bonn U., 1980. Mem. ACP (pres. 1975-76, Alfred E. Stengler Meml. award 1980), Am. Soc. Clin. Investigation (counselor 1969-72), Assn. Am. Physicians (pres. 1977), Western Assn. Physicians, Western Soc. Clin. Investigation (pres. 1971-72), Am. Acad. Arts and Scis., Inst. Medicine. Club: Cosmos (Washington). Current Work: Pathogenesis of bacterial infections; biomedical administration; clinical medicine and teaching. Subspecialties: Internal medicine; Infectious diseases. Office: U Calif-San Diego Sch Med La Jolla CA 92093

PETERSEN, LAWRENCE JOHN, electron microscopist; b. Clinton, Iowa, Mar. 26, 1927; s. Holger Hedegaard and Irma Viola (Heldt) P.; m. Merna Arlene Hall, Sept. 26, 1948; children: Carol Ann Petersen McCarthy, Nancy Sue Petersen McClish. Student, Denver U., 1951-52; B.Sc., Colo. State U., 1955, M.S., 1958; postgrad., U. Calif.-Davis., 1958-62. Plant pathologist Experiment Sta., Colo. State U., Fort Collins, 1955-58; prin. lab. technician U. Calif.-Davis, 1958-65, staff research asso. dept. plant pathology, 1965—. Contbr. articles in field to profl. jours. Served with USN, 1945-46; 1st lt. U.S. Army, 1955-58. Research award Colo. Wyo. Acad. Sci., 1958. Mem. Am. Phytopath. Soc., Sigma Xi, Xi Sigma Pi, Phi Kappa Phi. Current Work: Researcher in plant virology, scanning and transmission electron microscopy. Subspecialties: Plant pathology; Plant virology.

PETERSEN, ROBERT V., pharmacy educator; b. S. Jordan, Utah, Apr. 21, 1926; s. Edgar Ray and Martha (Smith) P.; m. Betty Jayne Bigler, Oct. 23, 1950; children: Robyn, Kent Earl, Susan, Marilyn. B.S., U. Utah, 1950; Ph.D., U. Minn., 1955. Teaching asst. U. Minn., 1951-54; asst. prof. pharm. chemistry Oreg. State Coll., 1955-57; asst. prof. pharmacy U. Utah, 1957-61, asso. prof., 1961-67, chmn. dept. applied pharm. scis., 1965-78, chmn. dept. pharms., 1978-82, prof., 1967—; exec. com. Am. Assn. Colls. Pharmacy, 1968-74, v.p., 1971-72, pres., 1972-73. Contbr. articles sci., scholastic jours. Served with AUS, 1944-46. Mem. Am. Chem. Soc., Am., Utah pharm. assns., Acad. Pharm. Sci., Am. Inst. History Pharmacy, Sigma Xi, Rho Chi (exec. council 1970-72, 74-76), Phi Lambda Upsilon. Research field nonaqueous emulsions, plastics composition and toxicology, biodegradable polymers as drug delivery devices, skin permeation of cosmetics. Current Work: Nonaqeous emulsions, plastics composition and toxicology, biodegradable polymers as drug delivery devices; cosmetics. Home: 4639 Meadow Rd Murray UT 84107 Office: Coll Pharmacy U Utah Salt Lake City UT 84112

PETERSON, ALAN HERBERT, research chemist; b. Moline, Ill., Aug. 27, 1932; s. Rolland and Grace Marie (Lundberg) P.; m. Dolores DeWolfe, June 1955; children—Bradley, Mark. B.A., Augustana Coll., 1955; Ph.D., U. Ill., 1960; Chemist trainee Rock Island Arsenal, Ill., 1953-55; teaching asst. U. Ill., Urbana, 1955-56, research asst., 1956-59; research chemist Marathon Oil Co., Littleton, Colo., 1959—. Patentee in field. Mem. Am. Chem. Soc., Soc. Automotive Engrs., Am. Soc. Testing Materials, Coordinating Research Council, Sigma Xi. Republican. Lutheran. Club: Cherry Creek Gun (Denver) (pres. 1983, 84). Current work: Research and technical service in catalytic petroleum refining processes including reforming hydrotreating and catalytic cracking. Subspecialty: Catalysis chemistry. Home: 4217 E Davies Pl Littleton CO 80122 Office: Marathon Oil Co PO Box 269 Littleton CO 80160

PETERSON, BRADLEY MICHAEL, astronomer; b. Mpls., Nov. 26, 1951; s. Harry C. and Dona M. (Erickson) P.; m. Janet Rae, Oct. 19, 1978; children—Evan, Erika. B. Physics, U. Minn., 1974; Ph.D., U. Ariz., 1978. Research asso. U. Minn., 1979; postdoctoral fellow Ohio State U., 1979-80, asst. prof. astronomy, 1980-84, assoc. prof., 1984—. Contbr. numerous articles to sci. jours. NSF grantee, 1981-85. Mem. Am. Astron. Soc., Astron. Soc. Pacific, Internat. Astron. Union. Roman Catholic. Current Work: Spectra of Seyfert galaxies and quasars. Subspecialty: Optical astronomy. Office: Dept Astronomy Ohio State U 174 W 18th Ave Columbus OH 43210

PETERSON, CHARLES, agricultural engineering educator. Mem. dept. agrl. engring. U. Idaho, Moscow. Subspecialty: Agricultural engineering. Office: U Idaho Dept Agrl Engring Moscow ID 83843

PETERSON, DONALD WILLIAM, geologist; b. San Francisco; Mar. 3, 1925; s. Herman William and Alice M. (Korslund) P.; m. Betty Ann Leitch, Mar. 21, 1948; children—Karen Lee, Kristine Ann, Susan Lynn. B.S., Calif. Inst. Tech., 1949; M.S., Wash. State U., 1951; Ph.D., Stanford U., 1961. Geologist U.S. geol. Survey, 1952—; scientistin charge Hawaiian Volcano Obs., Hawaii Nat. Pk., 1970-75, Cascades volcano Obs., Vancouver, Wash., 1980—. Served with USN, 1944-46, 1951-52, PTO. Recipient Meritorious Service award U.S. Dept. Interior, 1983. Fellow Geol. soc. Am.; mem. Am. Geophys. Union, Soc. Econ. Geologists, AAAS. Current work: Direct and participate in monitoring and research on volcanoes, including Mount St. Helens. Subspecialties: Volcanology; Petrology. Office: US Geol Survey 5400 MacArthur Blvd Vancouver WA 98661

PETERSON, JAMES ROBERT, engineering psychologist; b. St. Paul, Minn., Apr. 16, 1932; s. Palmer Elliot and Helen Evelyn (Carlson) P.; m. Marianna J. Stockvig, June 26, 1954; 1 dau., Anne Christine. B.A. in Psychology cum laude, U. Minn., 1954, M.A. in Exptl. Psychology, 1958; Ph.D. in Engring. Psychology, U. Mich., 1965. Engring. aide Honeywell, Inc., Mpls., 1958-59, devel. engr., 1961-65, sr. devel. engr., 1965-67, staff engr., Clearwater, Fla., 1967—; sponsor student insect flight expt. on space shuttle, Mar. 1982. Contbr. numerous articles and papers to profl. jours. Recipient Founder's medal Tampa Bay sect. AIAA, 1982. Fellow AIAA (assoc.); mem. Human Factors Soc., Am. Psychol. Assn., Soc. Engring. Psychologists. Lodge: Masons. Current Work: Analysis, design and development of man-machine systems; development of manned spaceflight systems. Subspecialties: Aerospace engineering and technology; Human factors engineering. Home: 3303 San Gabriel St Clearwater FL 33519 Office: Space and Strategic Avionics Div Honeywell Inc 13350 US Hwy 19 Clearwater FL 33546

PETERSON, MARK EARL, clinical veterinary endocrinologist, researcher; b. Olivia, Minn., Apr. 19, 1952; s. Earl H. and Lois J. (Buboltz) P. B.S., U. Minn., 1974; D.V.M., 1976. Diplomate Am. Coll. Vet. Internal Medicine. Intern in medicine and surgery Animal Med. Ctr., N.Y.C., 1976-77, resident in medicine, 1977-79, postdoctoral NIH fellow in endocrinology, 1979-81, staff endocrinologist dept. medicine, 1981—; dir. clin. medicine Ctr. for Research Animal Resources, Cornell U. Med. Coll., N.Y.C., 1981—. Mem. editorial bd. Domestic Animal Endocrinology Jour., 1984—; Seminars in Small Animal Medicine and Surgery Jour., 1984—. Contbr. articles to profl. jours. Fellow NIH, 1979-81; grantee Am. Diabetes Assn., 1982, Cornell U. Med. Coll., 1984, NIH, 1984. Mem. AAAS, Am. Diabetes Assn., Am. Fedn. Clin. Research, AVMA, Endocrine Soc., N.Y. Acad. Scis. Current work: Development of spontaneous animal endocrine disorders as model for the corresponding human disorders. Subspecialties: Internal medicine (veterinary medicine); Laboratory animal medicine. Home: 333 E 79th St Apt 8M New York NY 10021 Office: Animal Med Ctr 510 E 62nd St New York NY 10021

PETERSON, MELVIN NORMAN ADOLPH, marine geologist, oceanographer, academic administrator; b. Evanston, Ill., May 27, 1929; s. Fredrick Gothard Walter and Norma Alberta (Johnson) P.; m. Margaret Stewart Forbes, June 14, 1958; children—Katrina E., John F.F., Bruce N.S., Valerie A. B.S., Northwestern U., 1951, M.S., 1956; Ph.D., Harvard U., 1960. Registered geologist, Calif. Asst. research geologist Scripps Inst. Oceanography, La Jolla, Calif., 1960-62, asst. prof. oceanography, 1963-66, assoc. prof. oceanography, 1967-72, acad. adminstr. U Calif.-San Diego, 1972—, chief scientist Deep Sea Drilling Project, 1967-72, project dir., 1972—; pres. Pacific Research Found., La Jolla, 1984—. Dir., mgr. Initial Reports of the Deep Sea Drilling Project (Blue Pencil award 1970), 1969-85. Pres. Del Mar Union Elem. Sch. Bd., 1973, 74. Recipient Spl. citation for Outstanding Achievement for Deep Sea Drilling Project, Marine Tech. Soc., 1970. Fellow Geol. Soc. Am.; mem. N.Y. Acad. Scis. Republican. Presbyterian. Current work: Marine: sediments, geochemistry, tectonics; deep ocean drilling; science administration; international scientific organization. Subspecialty: Offshore technology. Office: Deep Sea Drilling Project U Calif-San Diego LaJolla CA 92093

PETERSON, NORMAN LEE, metallurgist; b. Aurora, Ill., Jan. 16, 1935; s. Conrad Arnold and Mildred Sarah (Umbreit) P.; m. Mary Irene Lee, Oct. 12, 1963. B.S., MIT, 1957, M.S., 1959, Ph.D. in Metallurgy, 1961. Asst. metallurgist Argonne Nat. Lab. (Ill.), 1961-64, assoc. metallurgist, 1964-70, sr. metallurgist, 1970—, group leader, 1977—, assoc. dir., 1968-77; mem. rev. com. Material Research Lab., U. Ill., 1981-85. Editor: Radiation Damage in Metals, 1976; Atomic Defects in Metals, 1978; contbr. articles to profl. jours. NSF fellow, 1964-65; Humboldt Found. sr. scientist awardee, 1973. Fellow Am. Soc. Metals (chmn. awards com.), Am. Phys. Soc., Am. Ceramics Soc. (editorial com.); mem. Metall. Soc. of AIME (chmn. awards com.), Current work: Basic research on point defects and diffusion mechanisms in metals, oxides, glasses and grain boundaries; mechanisms of high temperature oxidation of metals. Subspecialties: Ceramics; Materials. Home: 10 S 512 Glenn Dr Hinsdale IL 60521 Office: Argonne Nat Lab 9700 S Cass Ave Argonne IL 60439

PETERSON, ROBERT MICHAEL, geologist, consultant; b. Ames, Iowa, Sept. 28, 1949; s. Howard Carl and Margery (Starrett) P.; m. Kathleen Kay Stevens, May 9, 1981; children—Samuel Michael, Sarah Elizabeth. B.S. in Geology, Marietta Coll. (Ohio), 1971; M.S., Bowling Green State U. (Ohio), 1973; Ph.D., U. Kans., 1978. Carbonate sedimentologist Phillips Petroleum Co., Bartlesville, Okla., 1977-80; geologist Keplinger & Assocs., Keplinger Labs., Tulsa, 1980-82, staff geologist, 1982-84, sr. geologist, 1984—. Mem. Am. Assn. Petroleum Geologists (chmn. com. on preservation of samples and cores 1982—), Soc. Econ. Paleontologists and Mineralogists, Geol. Soc. Am., N.Y. Acad. Scis., Sigma Xi. Current work: Study of hydrocarbon reservoirs to better understand influence of sedimentologic and petrographic aspects on production efficiency, origin and diagenesis of hydrocarbon bearing stratigraphic intervals. Subspecialties: Sedimentology; Paleontology, paleoecology. Office: Keplinger and Assocs Inc 6849 E 13th St Tulsa OK 74112

PETERSON, RUDOLPH NICHOLAS, pharmacologist, educator; b. N.Y.C., June 6, 1932; s. Peter and Christina Mary (Kavanagh) Pantalakis. B.S., St. John's U., 1957; M.A., Bklyn. Coll., 1962; Ph.D., U. Fla., 1965. Mem. faculty dept. pharmacology N.Y. Med. Coll., Valhalla, 1966-76, assoc. prof., 1973-76; prof. pharmacology dept. physiology-pharmacology Sch. Medicine, So. Ill. U., Carbondale, 1976—. Contbr. chpts. to books, articles to profl. jours. Served with USAF, 1951-55. Mem. Am. Soc. Pharmacology and Exptl. Therapeutics, Am. Soc. Cell Biology. Current Work: Cell surface of mammalian gametes. Subspecialties: Gynecological oncology; Biochemistry (medicine). Office: Sch Medicine So Ill Univ Carbondale IL 62901

PETERSON, THOMAS MARK, orthodontist; b. Norfolk, Va., Mar. 3, 1954; s. Thomas W. and Margaret (Hogard) P. B.S., Va. Poly. Inst. and State U., 1975; D.D.S., Med. Coll. Va., 1979, ortho-certificate, 1981. Asst. prof. orthodontics Med. Coll. Va., Richmond, 1981—; cons. Craniofacial Deformities Clinic, Richmond, 1981-83. Med. Coll. Va. Orthodontic Found. grantee, 1982-82; So. Soc. Orthodontics grantee, 1981-82. Mem. Internat. Assn. Dental Researchers, Am. Dental Assn., Am. Assn. Orthodontics, Va. Dental Assn., Med. Coll. Va. Orthodontic Found., Am. Assn. Dental Schs., So. Soc. Orthodontics. Current Work: Electromyography, craniofacial morphology, orthographic surgery, dento-facial orthopedics. Subspecialties: Orthodontics; Dental growth and development. Home: 1505 Largo St T-2 Richmond VA 23229 Office: Med Coll Va 566 Med Coll Va Sta Richmond VA 23226

PETERSON, VERN LEROY, research scientist; b. Gothenburg, Nebr., Nov. 8, 1934; s. Elmer Robert and Vera Theresa (Maline) P.; m. Roberta Vye Elsey, June 3, 1961; children: Susan, Stephen, Scott. B.S. in Engring. Physics, U. Colo., 1956; M.A. in Astronomy, Ind. U., 1961, Ph.D. in Astrophysics, 1963. Research physicist-atmosphere NOAA, Boulder, Colo., 1963-69; assoc. prof. physics Utah State U., Logan, 1969-74; prof. adj. in meteorology U. Sao Paulo, Brazil, 1974-77; sr. scientist Research Analysis and Devel., Colorado Springs, Colo., 1977-78; pres., chief scientist Centennial Sciences, Inc., Colorado Springs, 1978-80; sr. tech. dir. ODSI Def. Systems, Inc., Monterey, Calif., 1980—. Author articles. Served with U.S. Army, 1957-59. Named Outstanding Prof. Physics, Utah State U., 1973. Mem. Am. Geophys. Union, Am. Meteorol. Soc., Am. Astron. Soc. Current Work: Atmospheric and oceanographic studies, distributed computer systems and networks, satellite image processing. Subspecialties: Meteorology; Satellite studies. Home: 22610 Murietta Rd Salinas CA 93908 Office: 2600 Garden Rd Suite 202 Monterey CA 93940

PETERSON, WILLIAM ROBERT, JR., organosilicon manufacturing company executive, organic chemist; b. Phila., Oct. 2, 1940; s. William Robert and Evelyn Katherine (Boone) P.; m. Sandra Rita Hoffman, Mar. 25, 1961; children—Kimberly Ann, William Robert III. B.S. in Chemistry, Muhlenberg Coll., 1963; M.A. in Chemistry, Temple U., 1972, Ph.D. in Chemistry, 1974. Chemist Livingston Elec. Co., Montgomeryville, Pa., 1963-64; research scientist U.S. Army, Phila., 1964-76; pres. Petrarch Systems, Inc., Bristol, Pa., 1976—; dir. Concern, Fleetword, Pa. Patentee in field. Recipient Outstanding Achievement award U.S. Army Sci. Conf., 1964, sci. commendation U.S. Army Research, 1966, 68, 70, 71, 72. Mem. Am. Chem. Soc., Research Soc. Am. (award for excellence 1964), Am. Chem. Soc. (Phila. sect.), Franklin Inst. Pa., Soc. Photo-Optical Instrumentation Engrs., Sigma Xi. Republican. Current work: Synthetic chemistry, electronics, microelectronics, microchip technology, electronic materials. Subspecialties: Organometallics; Organic chemistry. Home: 10 Nottingham Dr Fallsington PA 19054 Office: Petrarch Systems Inc Bartram Rd Bristol PA 19007

PETIT, PARKER HOLMES, health care corporation executive; b. Decatur, Ga., Aug. 4, 1939; s. James Percival and Ethel (Holmes) P.; m. Jo Ann Armour, June 26, 1960; children—William Wright, Patricia Monique. B.A.M.E., Ga. Inst. Tech., 1962, M.S.M.E., 1964; M.B.A., Ga. State U., 1973. Engr. Gen. Dynamics Corp., Fort Worth, 1966-67; engring. project mgr. Lockheed-Ga. Co., Marietta, 1967-71; founder, pres., chmn. Healthdyne, Inc., Marietta, 1971—; dir. Atlantic Southeast Airlines, Atlanta, Hybridoma Scis., Atlanta; chmn. SIDS Inst., Atlanta. Author: Primer on Composite Materials, 1968. Inventor in field. Bd. dirs. chmn. Sudden Infant Death Syndrome Inst., Atlanta, 1983—. Served to 1st lt. U.S. Army, 1964-66. Recipient Humanitarian award La Soc. Francaise de Bienfaisance, 1981. Mem. Health Industry Mfrs. Assn. Republican. Presbyterian. Current work: Biotechnology. Subspecialty: Biomedical engineering. Office: Healthdyne Inc 2253 Northwest Pkwy Marietta GA 30067

PETRAKIS-PAWSON, STELLA, oncology clinical nurse specialist; b. San Juan, P.R., Mar. 5, 1948. B.A., Cornell U., 1970; B.S., Sch. Nursing, U. Calif.-San Francisco, 1973, M.S., 1978. R.N., Calif. Clin. oncology nurse Surg. Oncology Clinic, UCLA, 1973-74; research nurse U. Calif.-San Francisco-G.W. Hooper Found., San Francisco, 1974-77, research assoc., 1977—; oncology/-hospice nurse specialist Vis. Nurse Assn., Oakland, Calif., 1977-84; adult oncology clin. nurse specialist Pacific Presbyterian Med. Ctr., San Francisco, 1984—; asst. prof. physiol. nursing Sch. Nursing, U. Calif.-San Francisco, 1983—; "When You Care" project dir. Calif. div. Am. Cancer Soc., Oakland, 1982-83. Primary developer: Caring for the Person with Cancer at Home: A Family Care Givers Manual, 1985. Contbr. articles to profl. jours. Recipient Spl. Achievement Vol. award San Francisco unit Am. Cancer Soc., 1977. Calif. div. Am. Cancer Soc. grantee, 1982-83. Mem. Oncology Nursing Soc., Bay Area Oncology Nursing Soc. (pres. 1978-79), East Bay Oncology Nurse Interest Group (founder, chmn. East Bay Cancer Program 1980-83). Current work: Consultant to nursing staff, patients, and physicians in care of cancer patients; management of pain, symptoms, chemotherapy and side effects, and terminal care. Subspecialties: Oncology; Chemotherapy. Home: 387 Los Palmos Dr San Francisco CA 94127 Office: Pacific Presbyn Med Ctr Room P6819 Clay at Buchanan Sts San Francisco CA 94115

PETRARCA, BRUCE FREDERICK, electrical engineer, educator; b. Denver, Apr. 8, 1949; s. Frederick Anthony and Adela (Ryman) P.; m. Linda Lee Anderson, July 21, 1979. B.E.E., Calif. State Poly. U., 1970; M.E.E., U. Calif.-Santa Barbara, 1974. Project engr. Applied Magnetics Corp., Goleta, Calif., 1970-73; chief engr. Western Magnetics Corp., Glendale, Calif., 1973-74; staff engr. Storage Tech., Louisville, Colo., 1974-78; engring. mgr. AMPEX, Colorado Springs, Colo., 1978-79; mfg. engr. supr. Digital Equipment Corp., Natick, Mass., 1979-81, prin. engr., Colorado Springs, 1981—; assoc. instr. Calif. State Poly. U., San Luis Obispo, 1970; prof. U. Colo., Colorado Springs, 1982-83. Emergency coordinator Amateur Radio Relay League, Colorado Springs, 1983-84. Mem. IEEE, Eta Kappa Nu. Current work: High performance digital tape and disk head design, education, research and manufacturing. Subspecialties: Applied magnetics; Magnetic physics. Home: 2898 Keystone Circle Colorado Springs CO 80918 Office: Digital Equipment Corp 301 Rockrimmon Blvd S Colorado Springs CO 80919

PETRAS, CHARLES EDWARD, electronics consultant, electronics/software design engineer; b. Toledo, Mar. 4, 1956; s. Martin Cuthbert and Katherina (Hunger) P. B.E.E., Clev. State U., 1980. Cons. Firestone Tire and Rubber Co., Cleve., 1978-80; sr. design engr. Boeing Co., Seattle, 1980-84; sr. cons. Booz-Allen & Hamilton, Bethesda, Md., 1984—. Mem. IEEE, Am. Assn. Artificial Intelligence, Am. Def. Preparedness Assn. Current work: Developing methods for the engineering development of ground support systems for the military; microprocessor based automatic test equipment; research in the development of cryptographic/cryptoanalysis systems for small scale computer systems. Subspecialties: Systems engineering; Software engineering. Office: Booz-Allen & Hamilton 509 W Ward St Suite B Ridgecrest CA 93555

PETRI, WILLIAM HENRY, III, oral and maxillofacial surgeon, researcher, consultant; b. Hopkinsville, Ky., Nov. 8, 1938; s. William Henry and Edna Alice (Walker) P. B.A., U. Louisville, 1961, D.M.D., 1965. Diplomate: Am. Bd. Oral and Maxillofacial Surgery. Intern U. Louisville and VA Hosp., Louisville, 1965-66; commd. ensign U.S. Navy, 1966, advanced through grades to capt., 1981; resident Naval Regional Med. Ctr., Portsmouth, Va., 1972-75, staff oral and maxillofacial surgeon, 1975-76, 80-81, head oral and maxillofacial surgery, Subic Bay, Philippines, 1976-77, Naval Regioal Dental Ctr., Little Creek, Va., 1977-79; head dental dept. USS Nimitz, Norfolk, Va., 1979-80; prin. investigator Naval Med. Research Inst., Bethesda, Md., 1981—; cons. in field Nat. Naval Med. Ctr., Bethesda, 1981—; cons. instrumentation Walter Lorenz Inc., Jacksonville, Fla., 1981—; lectr., temporomandibular joint diseases Nat. Naval Grad. Dental Sch., Bethesda, 1981—. Author: One Year, 1970; contbr. monogram, articles to profl. jours. Pres. Merrifields Civic League, Portsmouth, 1976, Hatton Point Civic Assn., 1977; mem. administrv. bd. Centenary Methodist Ch., 1979; tchr. adult Sunday Sch., 1977-80. Fellow Am. Assn. Oral and Maxillofacial Surgeons; mem. ADA, Tidewater Soc. Oral Surgeons (pres. 1980), Psi Chi. Republican. Inventor surg. instruments. Current Work: Wound healing oral and maxillofacial injuries, bone physiology; researcher in skin wound closures, microvascular anastamosis of vascularized, freeze-dried, free bone allografts. Osteogenesis in anti-biotic supplemented allograft. Subspecialties: Oral and maxillofacial surgery; Physiology (medicine). Office: US Naval Med Research Inst Mail Stop 18 Bethesda MD 20814

PETRI, WILLIAM HUGH, developmental geneticist, apiculturist, consultant; b. San Francisco, Dec. 30, 1944; s. Marino and Aida Clair P.; m. Arlene Ruth Wyman, July 30, 1976; children: Jonah Wyman, Sonya Ruth,. B.A., U. Calif.-Berkeley, 1966, Ph.D. in Genetics, 1972. Research fellow Harvard U., 1972-76; asst. prof. biology Boston Coll., 1976-81, assoc. prof., 1981—. Mem. Genetics Soc. Am., Soc. Developmental Biology. Current Work: Teaching and research in developmental genetics. Subspecialties: Gene actions; Developmental biology. Office: Dept Biology Boston College Chestnut Hill MA 02167

PETROFSKY, JERROLD SCOTT, physiologist, biomedical research institute administrator; b. St. Louis, May 5, 1948; married, 1974; 1 child. A.B., Washington U., St. Louis, 1970; Ph.D. in Physiology, St. Louis U., 1974. With dept. physiology St. Louis U., 1968-69, fellow, 1974-76, asst. prof. physiology, 1976-79; asst. prof. to prof. physiology and biomed. engring. Wright State U., Dayton, Ohio, 1978—; exec. dir. Nat. Ctr. for Rehab. Engring., Wright State U. Mem. Am. Physiol. Soc., IEEE, Biomed. Engring. Soc., Am. Coll. Sports Medicine, Sigma Xi. Subspecialties: Biomedical engineering; Physiology (biology). Office: Nat Ctr Rehab Engring Wright State U Rike Hall Dayton OH 45435*

PETRONE, ROCCO A., aerospace manufacturing executive; b. Amsterdam, N.Y., Mar. 31, 1926; s. Anthony and Theresa (DeLuca) P.; m. Ruth Holley, Oct. 29, 1955; children—Teresa, Nancy, Kathryn, Michael. B.S., U.S. Mil. Acad., 1946; degree Mech. Engring, Mass. Inst. Tech., 1952; D.Sc. (hon.), Rollins Coll., 1969. Devel. officer Redstone Missile Devel., Huntsville, Ala., 1952-55; mem. army gen. staff Dept. Army, Washington, 1956-60; mgr. Apollo program Kennedy Space Center, 1960-66, dir. launch ops., 1966-69; Apollo program dir. NASA, Washington, 1969-73; dir. Marshall Space Flight Center, Huntsville, Ala., 1973-74; asso. adminstr. NASA, Washington, 1974-75; pres., chief exec. officer Nat. Center for Resource Recovery, Washington, 1975-81; exec. v.p. Space Transp. and Systems Group, Rockwell Internat., Downey, Calif., 1981-82, pres., 1982—. Decorated D.S.M. with 2 clusters NASA; Commendatore Ordine al Merito, Italy). Fellow Am. Inst. Aeros. and Astronautics; mem. Nat. Acad. Engring., Sigma Xi. Subspecialty: Aerospace engineering and technology. Home: 1329 Granvia Altamira Palos Verdes Estates CA 90274

PETSCHEK, ALBERT GEORGE, physicist; b. Prague, Czechoslovakia, Jan. 31, 1928; s. Hans and Eva (Epler) P.; m. Marilyn Adiene Poth, June 25, 1949; children: Evelyn A., Rolfe G., Elaine L., Mark A. B.S., MIT, 1947; M.S., U. Mich., 1948; Ph.D., U. Rochester, 1952. Jr. research physicist Carter Oil Co., Tulsa, 1948-49; staff mem., group leader Los Alamos (N.Mex.) Sci. Lab., 1952-66; prof. physics N.Mex. Inst. Mining and Tech., Socorro, 1966-68, 71—; sr. research scientist Systems Sci. and Software, La Jolla, Calif., 1968-71; also dir.; fellow Los Alamos Nat. Lab., 1980—; cons. Los Alamos Sci. Lab., Sandia Corp., Systems Sci. and Software, Mission Research Corp.; dir. Interhealth, Inc., 1970-71. Contbr. sci. papers to profl. publs. Mem. Am. Phys. Soc., Am. Astron. Soc., AAAS. Current Work: Inertial confinement fusion, thunderstorm modeling, supernovae, quasars, gamma bursts. Subspecialties: Applied physics; Theoretical astrophysics. Home: 122 Piedra Loop Los Alamos NM 87544 Office: MS 434 Los Alamos Nat Lab Los Alamos NM 87545 Office: Dept Physics New Mexico Tech Socorro NM 87801

PETTENGILL, GORDON H(EMENWAY), physicist; b. Providence, Feb. 10, 1926; s. Rodney Gordon and Frances (Hemenway) P.; m. Pamela Anne Wolfenden, Oct. 28, 1967; children—Mark Robert, Rebecca Jane. B.S., M.I.T., 1948; Ph.D., U. Calif., Berkeley, 1955. Staff mem. Lincoln Lab., M.I.T., Lexington, 1954-63, 65-68; asso. dir. Arecibo (P.R.) Obs., 1963-65, dir., 1968-71; prof. planetary physics, dept. earth and planetary scis. MIT, Cambridge, 1971—, dir. Ctr. for Space Research, 1984—. Served with inf., Signal Corps AUS, 1944-46. Mem. Am. Phys. Soc., Am. Astron. Soc., AAAS, Internat. Astron. Union, Internat. Radio Sci. Union, Nat. Acad. Sci., Am. Acad. Arts and Sci. Pioneer several techniques in radar astronomy for describing properties of planets and satellites; discovered 59-day rotational period of planet Mercury. Current Work: Study of planetary surfaces using radio/radar techniques. Subspecialties: Planetary science; Remote sensing (geoscience). Office: Room 37-241 Mass Inst Tech Cambridge MA 02139

PETTEY, DIX HAYES, mathematics educator; b. Salt Lake City, Mar. 16, 1941; s. Leo Melvin and Kathleen (Hayes) P. B.S., U. Utah, 1965, Ph.D., 1968. Asst. prof. to prof. U. Mo., Columbia, 1968—; vis. prof. U.S. Mil. Acad., 1984; sr. scientist Presearch, Inc., summer 1985. Contbr. articles to profl. jours. Mem. Math. Assn. Am., Soc. Indsl. and Applied Math., Ops. Research Soc. Am., Mormon. Current Work: Reliability of communications networks; military applications; computer memory systems; P-minimal and P-closed topological spaces. Subspecialty: Operations research (mathematics). Office: U Mo 208 Math Science Bldg Columbia MO 65211

PETTIJOHN, FRANCIS JOHN, geologist, educator; b. Waterford, Wis., June 20, 1904; s. John J. and Elizabeth (Shenkenberg) P.; m. Dorothy M. Bracken, Aug. 9, 1930; children—Norma, Clare, Loren. A.B., U. Minn., 1924, M.A., 1925, Ph.D., 1930; D.H.L., Johns Hopkins U., 1978; Instr. geology Oberlin Coll., Ohio, 1925-29; from instr. to prof. geology U. Chgo., 1929-52; part-time geologist U.S. Geol. Survey, Washington, 1943-53; prof. Johns Hopkins U., Balt., 1952-73, prof. emeritus, 1973—; cons. Shell Devel. Co. Bellaire, Tex., 1953-63. Author: Sedimentary Rocks, 1975; Memoirs of an Unrepentant Field Geologist, 1984; (with others) Sand and Sandstone, 1972.

Contbr. various other books and articles to profl. jours. Fellow Geol. Soc. Am. (Penrose medal 1975); mem. Soc. Econ. Paleontology and Mineralogy (pres. 1955, Twenhofel medal 1974), Geol. Soc. London (Wollaston medal 1974), Internat. Assn. Sedimentologists (Sorby medal 1982), Nat. Acad. Scis., Am. Acad. Arts and Scis., Am. Assn. Petroleum Geologists. Democrat. Unitarian. Club: Explorers (N.Y.). Current work: History of geological sciences. Subspecialties: Sedimentology; Precambrian geology. Office: Johns Hopkins U Dept Earth and Planetary Scis Baltimore MD 21218

PETTINATI, HELEN MARIE, psychologist; b. Washington, Mar. 31, 1951; d. John Charles and Mary Josephine (Bearly) Rimkus; m. Joseph Vincent Pettinati, June 23, 1973; children—Lisa Marie, Anne Theresa, Joseph Charles. B.S., Drexel U., 1973; Ph.D., Med. Coll. Pa., 1979. Research asst. Med. Coll. Pa., Phila., 1974, E. Pa. Psychiat. Inst., 1975; research asst/assoc. Inst. of Pa. Hosp., Phila., 1975-79; coordinator research activities Carrier Found., Belle Mead, N.J., 1979-81, asst. dir. research, 1981—; adj. asst. prof. Rutgers Med. Sch., 1981—; referencing asst. Internat. Jour. Clin. & Exptl. Hypnosis, 1975-80. Contbr. articles to profl. jours.; guest interviewee various radio broadcasts. Med. Coll. Pa. fellow, 1974-75; recipient J. Peterson Ryder award for Women Drexel U., 1973. Mem. AAAS, Am. Psychol. Assn., Am. Soc. Clin. Hypnosis, Internat. Soc. Hypnosis (co-chmn. film program 1976), Soc. Clin. and Exptl. Hypnosis (co-chmn. sci. program 1983-84), Eastern Psychol. Assn., Am. Geriatric Assn., Gerontol. Soc. Am., Soc. Biol. Psychiatry, Gerontol. Soc. N.J. Roman Catholic. Current Work: Clinical psychiatric research in etiology of and current treatment for problems in aging, alcoholism, anorexia nervosa, bulimia, depression, cognition and memory disturbance; investigation of nature of hypnosis and its usefulness in medicine, especially psychiatry. Subspecialties: Psychiatry; Cognition. Home: 568 Fernwood Ln Fairless Hills PA 19030 Office: Carrier Found Research Div Belle Mead NJ 08502

PETTINGER, WILLIAM A., physician, researcher, educator; b. Cumberland, Iowa, May 26, 1932; s. Adolph P. and Virginia E. (Lauhoff) P.; m. Margaret C. Carney, Aug. 12, 1961; children: Maria, Tom, Elise, Will. B.S. in Math, Creighton U., 1954, M.S. in Physiology, 1957, M.D., 1959. Intern, asst. resident in medicine Jersey City Hosp., 1959-61; clin. investigator exptl. therapeutics Nat. Heart and Lung Inst., NIH, Bethesda, Md., 1961-63; sr. resident in medicine Yale-Grace New Haven Hosp., New Haven, 1963-64; postdoctoral fellow, asst. prof. pharmacology and internal medicine Vanderbilt U., Nashville, 1964-67; dir. cardiovascular renal research Hoffman-LaRoche, Nutley, N.J., 1967-71; asso. prof. medicine N.J. Coll. Medicine, 1967-71; assoc. prof. pharmacology and internal medicine U. Tex. Health Sci. Ctr., Dallas, 1971-74, prof., 1974—, dir. clin. pharmacology, 1971—; cons. pharm. industries; William N. Creasy vis. prof. in clin. pharmacology, 1977, 81; mem. pharmacology test com. Nat. Bd. Med. Examiners; mem. study sect. Nat. Heart, Lung and Blood Inst., 1985—. Contbr. numerous articles to sci. jours.; editor-in-chief: Jour. Cardiovascular Pharmacology, 1978-80; mem. editorial bd.: Annals of Internal Medicine; mem. editorial adv. bd.: Jour. Pharmacology and Exptl. Therapeutics. Burroughs-Wellcome scholar awardee in clin. pharmacology, 1974-79; recipient Rawls-Palmer award Am. Soc. Clin. Pharmacology and Exptl. Therapeutics, 1982. Fellow ACP, Am. Coll. Cardiology; mem. So. Soc. Clin. Investigation, Am. Soc. Clin. Investigation, Soc. Exptl. Biology and Medicine, Am. Soc. Clin. Pharmacology and Therapeutics (dir.), Am. Heart Assn. (med. adv. bd.). Current Work: Hypertension, antihypertensive drugs, cardiovascular and renal regulation, alpha adrenergic receptors. Subspecialties: Internal medicine; Pharmacology. Home: 3548 University Blvd Dallas TX 75205 Office: 5323 Harry Hines Blvd Dallas TX 75235

PETTIT, FLORA HUNTER, biochemist, educator; b. Bellvue, Pa., Sept. 17, 1928; d. Thomas P. and Nancy Ellen (Pryor) Hunter; m. Rowland Pettit, July 21, 1959 (dec. Dec. 10, 1981); children: George Hunter, Nancy Selina. B.A., U. Houston, 1952; Ph.D., U. Tex., 1961. Research assoc. U. Tex., Austin, 1961-63, lectr. in nutrition, 1966-71; research scientist assoc. Clayton Found., 1963-74, research scientist, 1974—. Mem. AAAS, Fedn. Am. Soc. Exptl. Biology, Sigma Xi. Current Work: purification, characterization and regulation of the alpha-Keto acid dehydrogenase complexes from mammalian tissue. Subspecialties: Biochemistry (biology); Enzyme technology. Home: 3833 Ben Creek Court Aledo TX 76008 Office: Clayton Found Biochemical Research U Tex Austin TX 78712

PETTIT, GEORGE ROBERT, chemist, educator; b. Long Branch, N.J., June 8, 1929. B.S. in Chemistry, Wash. State U., 1952; M.S., Wayne State U., 1954, Ph.D., 1956. Teaching asst. Wash. State U., 1950-52, lecture demonstrator, 1952; research chemist E.I. dupPont de Nemours & Co., 1953; grad. teaching asst. Wayne State U., 1952-53, research fellow, 1954-56; sr. research chemist Morton Norwich Co., 1956-57; asst. prof. chemistry U. Maine, 1957-61, assoc. prof., 1961-65, prof., 1965; prof. chemistry Ariz. State U., 1965—, chmn. organic div., 1966-68; dir. Cancer Research Ariz. State U. 1974-75, dir. Cancer Research Inst. Lab., 1975—, Dalton prof. chemistry, 1982-85; vis. prof. Stanford U., 1965; mem. cancer treatment adv. bd. div. cancer treatment Nat. Cancer Inst., 1971-74, adv. div., 1965-76; vis. prof. So. African Univs., 1978; lectr. in field. Mem. editorial bd.: Synthetic Communications, 1970—; contbr. numerous articles to profl. jours. Fellow Am. Inst. Chemists; mem. Am. Chem. Soc., Chem. Soc. London, Pharmacognosy Soc., Am. Assn. Cancer Research, Sigma Xi, Phi Lambda Upsilon. Subspecialties: Organic chemistry; Cancer research (medicine). Office: Cancer Research Inst Dept Chemistry Arizona State University Tempe AZ 85281

PÉWÉ , TROY LEWIS, geologist, educator; b. Rock Island, Ill., June 28, 1918; s. Richard E. and Olga (Pomrank) P.; m. Mary Jean Hill, Dec. 21, 1944; children—David Lee, Richard Hill, Elizabeth Anne. A.B. in Geology, Augustana Coll., 1940; M.S., State U. Iowa, 1942; Ph.D., Stanford, 1952. Head dept. geology Augustana Coll., 1942-46; civilian instr. USAAC, 1943-44; instr. geomorphology Stanford, 1946; geologist Alaskan br. U.S. Geol. Survey, 1946—; chief glacial geologist U.S. Nat. Com. Internat. Geophys. Year, Antarctica, 1958; prof. geology, head dept. U. Alaska, 1958-65; prof. geology Ariz. State U., 1965—, chmn. dept., 1965-76; dir. Mus. Geology, 1976—; lectr. in field, 1942—; Mem. organizing com. 1st Internat. Permafrost Conf. Nat. Acad. Sci., 1962-63, chmn. U.S. planning com. 2d Internat. Permafrost Conf., 1972-74, chmn. U.S. del. 3d Internat. Permafrost Conf., 1978, chmn. U.S. organizing com. 4th Internat. Permafrost Conf., 1979-83; com. to study Good Friday Alaska Earthquake Nat. Acad. Scis., 1964-70, mem. glaciological com. polar research bd. Good Friday Alaska Earthquake, 1971-73, chmn. permafrost com., mem. polar research bd. Good Friday Alaska Earthquake, 1975-81; organizing chmn. Internat. Assn. Quarternary Research Symposium and Internat. Field Trip Alaska, 1965; mem. Internat. Commn. Periglacial Morophology, 1964-71, 80—; mem. polar research bd. NRC, 1975-78, late Cenozoic study group, sci. com. Antarctic research, 1977-80. Contbr. numerous papers to profl. lit. Recipient U.S. Antarctic Service medal, 1966; Outstanding Achievement award Augustana Coll., 1969; Internat. Geophysics medal USSR Nat. Acad. Sci., 1985; 1st hon. internat. fellow Soc. Glaciology and Geocryology Academica Sinica, People's Republic China, 1985. Fellow AAAS (pres. Alaska div. 1956, com. on arid lands 1972-79), Geol. Soc. Am. (editorial bd. 1975-82, chmn. cordilleran sect. 1979-80, chmn. geomorphology div. 1981-82), Arctic Inst. N.Am. (bd. govs. 1969-74, exec. bd. 1972-73), Iowa Acad. Sci., Ariz. Acad. Sci. (pres. 1982-83); mem. Assn. Geology Tchrs., Glaciological Soc., N.Z. Antarctic Soc., Am. Soc. Engring. Geologists, Am. Quaternary Assn. (pres. 1984—), Internat. Geog. Union. Current Work: Arctic and desert environmental geology; geology for land use planning. Subspecialty: Geology. Home: 538 E Fairmont Dr Tempe AZ 85282

PEZZUTO, JOHN MICHAEL, biochemist, consultant, researcher, educator; b. Hammonton, N.J., Aug. 29, 1950; s. Michael Louis and Elizabeth (Brown) P.; m. Arlene Angela, May 2, 1969 (div. Aug. 1984); 1 dau., Jennifer Anne. A.B., Rutgers U., 1973; Ph.D., Coll. Medicine and Dentistry N.J., 1977. NIH fellow M.I.T., 1977-79; instr. chemistry, NIH fellow U. Va., 1979-80; asst. prof. U. Ill.-Chgo., 1980-84, assoc. prof., 1985—. NIH Research Career Devel. awardee, 1985—. Mem. Am. Chem. Soc., AAAS, Am. Soc. Pharmacognosy, Am. Assn. Cancer Research, Am. Soc. Biol. Chemists. Current Work: Mechanisms of mutagenesis and carcinogenesis, inhibition of tumorigenesis, bioassay specific evaluation of cancer chemotherapeutic agts. Subspecialties: Biochemistry (medicine); Cancer research (medicine). Home: 97 S Park Blvd Glen Ellyn IL 60137 Office: Coll Pharmacy U Ill Health Scis Center Chicago IL 60612

PFAHLER, PAUL LEIGHTON, geneticist, educator; b. Essex County, Ont., Can., Nov. 3, 1930; s. Charles and Vivian (Gawley) P.; m. Mary Lucile Neely, Aug. 25, 1967; children: Diane, Beth. B.S., U. Mich., 1952; M.S., Mich. State U., 1954; Ph.D., Purdue U., 1957. Research assoc. Stanford (Calif.) U., 1955; postdoctoral fellow Purdue U., West Lafayette, Ind., 1957-58; asst. prof. U. Fla., Gainesville, 1958-65, assoc. prof., 1965-71, prof., 1971—; vis. scientist Czechoslovak Acad. Sci., 1973, 85; vis. prof. Nijmegen U., The Netherlands, 1977. Contbr. articles to profl. jours. AEC grantee, 1963-67; U. Fla. Faculty Devel. awardee, 1969, 77. Mem. Genetic Soc. Am., Am. Genetics Assn., Crop Sci. Soc. Am., AAAS. Presbyterian. Current Work: Population and quantitative genetics with maize, oats, rye. Subspecialties: Plant genetics; Population biology. Home: 2609 NW 12th Ave Gainesville FL 32605 Office: Univ Fla Dept Agronomy 304 Newell Hall Gainesville FL 32611

PFAU, CHARLES JULIUS, biologist; b. Troy, N.Y., Sept. 29, 1935; s. Charles and Blanche (Finn) P.; children—Dianne, David, Lise. B.S., Rensselaer Poly. Inst., 1956; M.S., Ind. U., 1958, Ph.D., 1960. Postdoctoral fellow Yale U., New Haven, 1960-62, State Serum Inst., Copenhagen, Denmark, 1962-64; asst. prof. U. Mass., Amherst, 1964-71; assoc. prof. Rensselaer Poly. Inst., Troy, N.Y., 1971-75, prof., 1975—, chmn. dept. biology, 1982—. NIH Career Devel. awardee, 1965. Mem. AAUP, Am. Assn. Immunologists, Am. Soc. Microbiology, Am. Soc. Virology. Current work: Immunopathology; virus-cell interactions. Subspecialties: Infectious diseases; Virology (medicine). Home: 27 Langmore Ln RD 3 Troy NY 12180 Office: Rensselaer Poly Inst Dept Biology Troy NY 12180

PFEFFER, LAWRENCE MARC, cell biologist, researcher; b. Bronx, N.Y., Nov. 28, 1951; s. Paul and Bess (Wilkens) P.; m. Susan Ritterstein Pfeffer, Sept. 19, 1976. B.S., SUNY-Albany, 1972; Ph.D., Cornell U., 1977. Grad. fellow Sloan Kettering Inst., 1972-77; postdoctoral fellow Rockefeller U., 1977-80, research assoc., 1980-81, asst. prof. virology, 1981—. Contbr. articles to profl. jours. Recipient Jr. Faculty Research award Am. Cancer Soc., 1982. Mem. N.Y. Acad. Sci., Am. Soc. Microbiology, Am. Soc. Virology, Cell Cycle Soc., Sigma Xi. Democrat. Jewish. Current Work: Animal virus host cell interactions, interferon; biologic regulatory molecules, interferon, membrane biology. Office: 1230 York Ave New York NY 10021

PFEFFER, PHILIP ELLIOT, research chemist; b. N.Y.C., Apr. 8, 1941; s. Charles and Della (Smith) P.; m. Judith Stadlen, Sept. 28, 1942; children—Charles, Ari, Shira. B.S., Hunter Coll., City Univ. N.Y., 1962; M.S., Rutgers Univ., 1964, Ph.D., 1966. Research assoc. Univ. Chgo., 1968; research leader U.S. Dept. Agr., Phila., 1968—. Recipient Bond award Am. Oil Chem. Soc., 1976; Sci. and Edn. award U.S. Sci. and Edn., 1982; ERRC award Dept. Agr., 1983; named Fed. Scientist of Yr., Phila. Fed. Bus. Assn., 1978. Mem. Am. Chem. Soc. (Phila. sect. award 1982), Soc. for Applied Spectroscopy, AAAS, Internat. Soc. Magnetic Resonance Editor: Carbohydrate Chemistry. Contbr., chpts. in books, articles to profl. jours. Patentee in field. Current work: Solid state 13C NMR spectroscopy and applications to agr. polymers, carbohydrate chemistry; in vivo-NMR studies of plant and animal tissues; biochemistry and plant physiology studies. Subspecialties: Nuclear magnetic resonance; Biophysical chemistry. Home: 812 Lorraine Dr Warrington PA 18976 Office: USDA Eastern Regional Research Ctr 600 E Mermaid Ln Philadelphia PA 19118

PFEFFER, RICHARD LAWRENCE, educator; b. Bklyn., Nov. 26, 1930; s. Lester Robert and Anna (Newman) P.; m. Roslyn Ziegler, Aug. 30, 1953; children—Bruce, Lloyd, Scott, Glenn. B.S. cum laude, CCNY, 1952; M.S., Mass. Inst. Tech., 1954, Ph.D., 1957. Research asst. Mass. Inst. Tech., 1952-55, guest lectr., 1956; atmospheric physicist Air Force Cambridge Research Center, Boston, 1955-59; sr. research scientist Columbia U., 1959-61, lectr., 1961-62, asst. prof. geophysics, 1962-64; asso. prof. meteorology Fla. State U., Tallahassee, 1964-67; prof., dir. Geophys. Fluid Dynamics Inst., 1967—; cons. NASA, 1961-64, N.W. Ayer & Son, Inc., 1962, Ednl. Testing Service, Princeton, N.J., 1963, Voice of Am., 1963, Grolier, Inc., 1963, Naval Research Labs., 1971-76; Mem. Internat. Commn. for Dynamical Meteorology, 1972-76. Editor: Dynamics of Climate, 1960; Contbr. articles to profl. jours. Bd. dirs. B'nai B'rith Anti-Defamation League; chmn. religious concern and social action com. Temple Israel, Tallahassee, 1971-72. Mem. Am. Meteorol. Soc. (program chmn. ann. meeting 1963), Am. Geophys. Union, N.Y. Acad. Scis. (chmn. planetary scis. sect. 1961-63), Sigma Xi, Chi Epsilon Pi, Sigma Alpha. Current Work: Global atmospheric circulation; hurricane formation; atmospheric dynamics, laboratory and computer modeling. Subspecialty: Meteorology. Home: 926 Waverly Rd Tallahassee FL 32312

PFEFFERKORN, ELMER ROY, microbiologist, educator; b. Manitowoc, Wis., Dec. 13, 1931; s. Elmer R. and Mollie (Meyer) P.; m. Lorraine M. Cassidy, Apr. 4, 1964. B.A., Lawrence College., 1954; B.A. (Rhodes scholar), Oxford (Eng.) U., 1956, M.A., 1959; Ph.D., Harvard Med. Sch., Boston, 1960. Instr. Harvard Med. Sch., 1960-64, asst. prof., 1964-67; assoc. prof. microbiology Dartmouth Med. Sch., 1967-70, prof., 1970—, chmn. dept. microbiology, 1981-84; mem. virology study sect. NIH, 1970-74, tropical medicine parasitology study sect., 1981—. NIH grantee, 1960—. Fellow AAAS; mem. Am. Soc. Biol. Chemists, Am. Soc. Tropical Medicine and Hygiene, Am. Soc. Parasitologists. Current Work: Biochemistry and genetics of intracellular protozoan parasites. Subspecialties: Parasitology; Biochemistry (medicine). Home: 24 Rope Ferry Rd Hanover NH 03755 Office: Dept Microbiology Dartmouth Med Sch Hanover NH 03756

PFEIFER, ROBERT FREDERICK, engineer; b. Chgo., Nov. 29, 1937; s. George Toland and Florence Esther (Lutz) P.; m. Bessie Bonita Cooper, Dec. 12, 1957 (div. 1969); children—Lisa Suzanne, Karl Vincent; m. Barbara Jean Watts, Dec. 18, 1970. B.S.E.E., U. Ill., 1964, M.S.E.E., 1966, Ph.D.E.E., 1971. Sr. Engr. Westinghouse Research and Devel., Churchill Boro, Pa., 1970-73; cons. engr. NCR Corp., Miamisburg, Ohio, 1973-84; sr. scientist Universal Energy Systems, Dayton, Ohio, 1985—. Contr. articles to profl. jours. Patentee in field. Served with USAF, 1956-60. Mem. IEEE, Electrochemical Soc., Audio Engring. Soc. (assoc.), Sigma Tau, Eta Kappa Nu. Current work: Integrated circuit device characterization and modeling, integrated circuit process characterization and modeling, device failure analysis, ion implantation technology. Subspecialties: Microchip technology (engineering); Semiconductors. Home: 280 Devay Ave Centerville OH 45459 Office: Universal Energy Systems 4401 Dayton-Xenia Rd Dayton OH 45432

PFEIFFER, RAYMOND JOHN, astrophysics educator; b. Trenton, N.J., Apr. 29, 1937; s. John Joseph and Mary Constance (Bumbera) P.; m. Cecelia Dolores Cumesty, June 22, 1974 (dec. Dec. 1978); 1 child, Katherine. B.S. in Edn., U. Mich., 1961; M.A., Trenton State Coll., 1964; M.S., Temple U., 1968; Ph.D., U. Pa., 1975. Instr. sci. Trenton State Coll., 1964-67, asst. prof. physics, 1967-77, assoc. prof. physics, 1977-80, prof., 1980—; research asst. U. Pa., Phila., 1969-70. Contbr. articles to astronomy jours. Zaccheus Daniel fellow, 1972; grantee: NASA, 1980, NSF, 1977. Mem. Internat. Astron. Union, Am. Astron. Soc., Astron. Soc. of Pacific, Am. Assn. Physics Tchrs. (N.J. chpt.). Current work: Photopolarimetry and spectrophotometry of close binary stars using both satellite and ground-based data, computer modeling of circumstellar scattering. Subspecialties: Optical astronomy; Atomic and molecular physics. Home: 8 Barbara Ln Titusville NJ 08560 Office: Dept Physics Trenton State Coll Trenton NJ 08625

PFENDER, EMIL, mechanical engineering, consulting company executive; b. Stuttgart, Fed. Republic Germany, May 25, 1925; came to U.S., 1964; s. Vinzenz and Anna Maria (Dreher) P.; m. Maria Katharina Staiger, Oct. 22, 1954; children—Roland, Norbert, Corinne. Student U. Tuebingen, Fed. Republic Germany, 1947-49; diploma in physics, U. Stuttgart, 1953, Dr. Engring. in E.E., 1959. Research assoc. U. Stuttgart, 1953-55, asst., 1955-61, first asst., 1962-64; vis. scientist Aerospace Research Labs., Wright Patterson AFB, Ohio, 1961-62; assoc. prof. mech. engring. U. Minn., 1964-67, prof. 1967—. Contbr. numerous articles in field to profl. jours. Patentee in field. Recipient Adams Meml. Membership award Am. Welding Soc., 1966; U.S. Sr. Scientist award Fed. Republic Germany, 1978. Fellow ASME; mem. Am. Phys. Soc., IEEE (assoc.). Current work: Electric arc technology; plasma heat transfer; thermal plasma processing. Subspecialties: Plasma (energy science and technology); High temperature chemistry. Home: 1947 Bidwell St West Saint Paul MN 55118 Office: Univ Minn 111 Church St SE Minneapolis MN 55455

PFENNINGER, KARL HANS, cell biologist; b. Stafa, Switzerland, Dec. 17, 1944; came to U.S., 1971; s. Hans R. and Delie M. (Zahn) P.; m. Marie-France Maylié , July 12, 1974; children: Jan Patrick, Alexandra Christina. M.D., U. Zurich, Switzerland, 1971. Predoctoral researcher Brain Research Inst., U. Zurich, 1966-71; postdoctoral researcher dept. anatomy Washington U., St. Louis, 1971-73, sect. cell biology Yale U., 1973-76; assoc. prof. Columbia U., 1976-81, prof. anatomy and cell biology, 1982—. Contbr numerous articles to profl. jours. Served to 1st lt. Swiss Army, 1965-71. Recipient C. J. Herrick award in comparative neurology Am. Assn. Anatomists, 1977; I. T. Hirschl Career Scientist award, 1977. Mem. AAAS, Am. Soc. Cell Biology, Soc. Neurosci., N.Y. Acad. Sci., Harvey Soc. Current Work: Cellular and developmental neurobiology; molecular mechanisms of neuronal sprouting and synaptogenesis. Subspecialties: Cell biology; Neurobiology. Office: Dept Anatomy and Cell Biology Coll Physicians and Surgeons Columbia U 630 W 168th St New York NY 10032

PFORZHEIMER, HARRY, JR., oil consultant; b. Manila, Philippines, Nov. 19, 1915; s. Harry and Mary Ann (Horan) P.; m. Jean L. Barnard, June 2, 1945; children: Harry, Thomas. B.S. in Chem. Engring, Purdue U., 1938; postgrad., Case Western Res. U., 1939-41; postgrad. in law, George Washington U., 1942-43. With Standard Oil Co. Ohio, various locations, 1938-80, v.p. oil shale and tar sands, 1971-80; pres. White River Shale Oil Corp., 1974-76; program dir. Paraho Oil Shale Demonstration, Grand Junction, Colo., 1974-80; pres. chmn. bd., chief exec. officer Paraho Devel. Corp., Grand Junction, Colo., 1980-82, sr. mgmt. advisor, dir., 1982-85; pres. Harry Pforzheimer Jr. and Assocs., 1983—; adj. prof. chem. engring. Cleve. State U.; dir. IntraWest Bank of Grand Junction, Colo. Contbr. articles to profl. jours. Chmn. Wayne Aspinall Found.; Mem. adv. bd. St. Mary's Hosp.; mem. Petroleum Administrn. for War in Washington, 1942-45; bd. dirs. Colo. Sch. Mines Research Inst. Recipient Disting. Student award Purdue U., 1938. Mem. Am. Inst. Chem. Engrs., Am. Mining Congress, Colo. Mining Assn., Grand Junction-Mesa County C. of C., Sigma Alpha Epsilon, others. Republican. Roman Catholic. Clubs: Denver Petroleum, Army and Navy, Bookcliff Country. Current Work: Consulting. Subspecialty: Oil shale. Home: 2700 G Rd Apt 1C Grand Junction CO 81506 Office: 2754 Compass Dr Grand Junction CO 81506

PFRANG, EDWARD OSCAR, association executive; b. New Haven, Aug. 9, 1929; s. Luitpold and Anna P.; m. Jacquelyn Marcia Montefalco, June 7, 1958; children: Lori Ann, Leslie Jean, Philip Edward. B.S., U. Conn., 1951; M.E., Yale U., 1952; Ph.D., U. Ill., 1961. Registered profl. engr., Md., N.Y., Calif. Sect. chief structures sect., bldg. research div. Nat. Bur. Standards, Washington, 1966-83, mgr. housing tech. program, 1970-73, chief structures materials safety div., 1973-83; exec. dir. ASCE, Washington, 1983—. Contbr. articles to profl. jours. Served with USNR, 1953-56. Fellow ASCE, Am. Concrete Inst. (pres.); mem. Earthquake Engring. Inst., Sigma Xi, Tau Beta Phi, Chi Epsilon, Sigma Tau. Subspecialty: Civil engineering. Office: Amer Soc Civil Engineers 345 E 47th St New York NY 10017

PHATAK, ARUN, theriogenologist, consultant fertility domestic animals; b. Poona, India, June 23, 1938; came to U.S., 1975, naturalized, 1984; s. Purushottam B. and Manorana Phatak; m. Nalini S. Lele, June 6, 1964; children—Sanjay, Vaishali. D.V.M., U. Bombay (India), 1962, M.V.Sc., 1965; M.S., U. Minn., 1978, Ph.D., 1982. Diplomate Am. Coll. Theriogenologists. Sr. scientist BAIF, Uruli, Kamchan, India, 1966-75; research fellow U. Minn., St. Paul, 1976-82; tech. dir. Golden State Breeders, Escalan, Calif., 1982-84; dir. research Genetics Dynamics, Salt Lake City, 1984-85; advisor Fresno State U., Calif., 1983-84. Mem. Am. Dairy Sci. Assn., Am. Vet. Med. Assn., Soc. Theriogenology Assn. Democrat. Hindu. Current work: Preservation of male and female gametes; causes of infertility in domestic animals; cryo preservation. Subspecialties: Animal nutrition; Embryo transplants (veterinary medicine). Home: 249 Laramie Ct Oakdale CA 95361 Office: Golden State Breeders 18907 E Lone Tree Escalan CA 95361

PHELPS, CAROL JO, neuroendocrinologist, anatomy educator; b. Sendai, Honshu, Japan, Apr. 20, 1948 (parents Am. citizens); d. Harry Joe and Helen Iva (Davies) P.; m. James Baxter Turpen, June 13, 1969 (div. Apr. 1982); children—James Matthew, John Alan; m. David Lowell Hurley, Oct. 12, 1985. B.S., U. Denver, 1969; Ph.D., La. State U. Med. Ctr., 1974. NIH postdoctoral fellow U. Rochester Med. Ctr., N.Y., 1974-76, asst. prof., 1982—; research asst. Pa. State U., University Park, 1976-77, 80-81, instr. biology, 1977-80, postdoctoral scholar, 1981-82. Contbr. articles to profl. jours. Mem. Otetiana council Cub. Scouts Am., 1983—; con. mem. PTA, Honeoye Falls, N.Y., 1983—. Recipient New Investigator Research award NIH, 1983; named an Outstanding Young Woman Am., 1983. Mem. Soc. for Neurosci., Endocrine Soc., Am. Assn. Anatomists, NOW, Cajal Club, Phi Sigma (pres. 1968-69), Kappa Delta (membership chmn. 1968-69). Current work: Regulation of prolactin secretion, catecholaminergic control of pituitary function, regeneration in catecholaminergic pathways, characterization of pituitary tumors. Subspecialties: Neuroendocrinology; Regeneration. Home: 192 East St Honeoye Falls NY 14472 Office: Univ Rochester Med Ctr Dept Neurobiology and Anatomy 601 Elmwood Ave Rochester NY 14642

PHELPS, RICHARD ARTHUR, research and development scientist; b. Pittsfield, Mass., Aug. 5, 1928; s. Harley Proctor and Beatrice (Nichols) P.; m. Carolyn Acola, May 19, 1961; 1 child, Gary Richard. B.S., Purdue U., 1951; M.S., Mich. State U., 1955, M.S., 1956, Ph.D., 1959. Asst. dir. research and edn. Nat. Cottonseed Products Assn., Memphis, 1958-65, chmn. research com., 1975-76; dir. tech. info. services Anderson Clayton Co., Houston, 1965-78, dir. research and devel. services, 1979—; chmn. research com. Soybean Research Council, Washington, 1977-78; speaker to various profl. groups. Contbr. reviews to Poultry Sci. jour. Served to 1st lt. U.S. Army, 1951-53. Mem. Am. Chem. Soc., Am. Oil Chemists' Soc., Poultry Sci. Assn., Am. Dairy Sci. Assn., Am. Soc. Animal Sci. Current work: Nutrition, biochemistry, remote sensing, meteorology, immunology, mycology. Subspecialties: Animal nutrition; Food science and technology. Office: Anderson Clayton Co PO Box 2538 Houston TX 77252

PHEMISTER, ROBERT DAVID, university dean; b. Framingham, Mass., July 15, 1936; s. Robert Irving and Georgia Nora (Savignac) P.; m. Ann Christine Lyon, June 14, 1960; children: Katherine, David, Susan. D.V.M., Cornell U., 1960; Ph.D., Colo. State U., Ft. Collins, 1967. Diplomate: Am. Coll. Vet. Pathologists. Research assoc. U. Calif., Davis, 1960-61; staff scientist Armed Forces Inst. Pathology, Washington, 1962-64; sect. leader to dir. collaborative radiol. health lab. Colo. State U., 1964-77; mem. faculty Coll. Vet. Medicine and Biomed. Scis., 1968-85, prof. vet. pathology, 1973-85, assoc. dean, 1976-77, assoc. dir. expt. sta., 1977-85, dean, 1977-85, acad. v.p., 1982, interim pres., 1983-84, spl. counselor to pres., 1984-85; dean Coll. Vet. Medicine, Cornell U., 1985—, prof., 1985—; vis. research pathologist U. Calif., Davis, 1974-75; cons. Miss. State U., 1977-81; commr. Colo. Advanced Tech. Inst., 1983-84. Author papers in field. Served to comdr. USPHS, 1960-68. Recipient Charles A. Lory award Colo. State U., 1984; Disting. Service award Colo. Vet. Med. Assn., 1985. Mem. AAAS, AVMA, Assn. Am. Vet. Med. Colls. (pres. 1982-83), Internat. Acad. Pathology, Radiation Research Soc., Colo. Vet Med. Assn., Sigma Xi, Phi Zeta, Phi Kappa Phi. Current Work: Pathology of development; pathology of low-level irradiation; reproductive physiology of the dog; canine renal pathology. Subspecialties: Pathology (veterinary medicine); Reproductive biology. Home: 1253 Ellis Hollow Rd Ithaca NY 14850 Office: Coll Vet Medicine Cornell U Ithaca NY 14853

PHILBIN, DANIEL MICHAEL, anesthesiologist, researcher; b. Dunmore, Pa., June 2, 1935; s. Leo Patrick and Josephine Theresa (Barrett) P.; m. Patricia Carol Flynn, Nov. 28, 1964; children—Daniel Michael Jr., Patrick Francis. B.S., Duquesne U., 1957; M.D., St. Louis U., 1961. Diplomate Am. Bd. Anesthesiology. Intern, St. Mary's Group of Hosp., St. Louis, 1961-62; resident Col. Pres. Med. Ctr., N.Y., 1965-68; asst. anesthetist Mass. Gen. Hosp., Boston, 1973-76, assoc. anesthetist, 1977-82, anesthetist, 1983—, dir. cardiac anesthesiology, 1983—; asst. prof. Harvard Med. Sch., Boston, 1971-79, assoc. prof., 1980-85, prof., 1985—; fellow Magdalen Coll., Oxford U., 1982-83; research prof. Nuffield Dept. Anesthetics, Oxford, 1982-83. Editor: Anesthetic Management of Patients with Cardiovascular Disease, 1979; jour. Anesthesia and Analgesia, 1980—. Contbr. articles to profl. jours. Served to lt. USNR, 1962-64. Recipient Rank Vic. Prof. Faculty of Anesthetists, Great Britain, 1983; NIH fellow, 1967-68; Fogarty Sr. Internat. fellow, Oxford, 1982-83. Fellow Am. Coll. Cardiologists; mem. Assn. Cardiac Anesthesiologists (pres. 1978-79), Am. Physiol. Soc., Am. Soc. Anesthesiologists (1st prize research 1969), Assn. Univ. Anesthetists. Republican. Roman Catholic. Current work: Neuro-endocrine response to anesthesia and surgery; effects of anesthesia on cardiac function; effects of anesthesia and open cardiac surgery on renal and hormonal function. Subspecialties: Anesthesiology; Cardiovascular physiology. Office: Mass Gen Hosp 32 Fruit St Boston MA 02114

PHILBRICK, DAVID ALAN, researcher and state official; b. Ross, Calif., Apr. 20, 1948; s. Shirley Seavey, Jr. and Emily King (Browning) P.; m. Cathey Lee McPhaden, July 15, 1972; children: Kenneth Alan, John Lee. A.B. magna cum laude, Brown U., 1970; Ph.D. in Biophysics, U. Calif.-Berkeley, 1976. Researcher Donner Lab., Berkeley, Calif., 1972-76; environ. specialist Oreg. Dept. Energy., Salem, 1976-78; adminstr. renewable resources div. Oreg. Dept. Energy, 1978-83; program leader Oreg. Energy Extension Service, 1983—. Mem. Internat. Solar Energy Soc. Current Work: Energy policy development and evaluation of energy technologies. Subspecialties: Solar energy; Geothermal power. Office: Oreg State Extension Service Oreg State U Corvallis OR 97331

PHILIP, A.G. DAVIS, astronomer, educator, editor; b. N.Y.C., Jan. 9, 1929; s. Van Ness and Lilian (Davis) P.; m. Kristina Drobavicius, Apr. 25, 1964; 1 dau., Kristina Elizabeth Elanor. B.S., Union Coll., Schenectady, 1951; M.S., N.Mex. State U., 1959; Ph.D., Case Inst. Tech., 1964. Tchr. Brooks Sch., 1954-59; instr. Case Inst. Tech., 1962-64; asst. prof. astronomy U. N.Mex., 1964-66; asst. prof. astronomy SUNY, Albany, 1966-67, assoc. prof., 1967-76; prof. astronomy Union College., 1976—; astronomer Dudley Obs., 1967-81, Van Vleck Obs., 1982—; Frank L. Fullam chair astronomy, 1980-81; vis. prof. Yale U., 1972, 73, vis. fellow, 1976; vis. prof. La. State U., 1973, 76, Acad. Scis. Lithuania, 1973, 76, 79, Stellar Data Center, Strasbourg, France, 1978, 79, 80, 82, 85; Harlow Shapley lectr. Am. Astron. Soc., 1973-85; dir., sec.-treas. N.Y. Astron. Corp.; lst U.S. observer Soviet Union's 6-meter reflector telescope, 1979 -82; exhibited 2d Ann. Photog. Regional, Albany, 1980; pres., treas. L Davis Press, Inc. Exec. com. Arts. and Scis. Council, 1975-76. Author: (with M. Cullen and R.E. White) UBV Color—Magnitude Diagrams of Galactic Globular Clusters; editor: (with M.F. McCarthy) Galactic Structure in the Directon of the Galactic Polar Caps, (with M.F. McCarthy and G.V. Coyne) Spectral Classification of the Future, In Memory of Henry Norris Russel, (with D. DeVorkin) The HR Diagram: The One-Hundredth Anniversary of Henry Norris Russel, (with D.S. Hayes) Problems of Calibration of Multicolor Photometric Systems, IAU Colloquium No. 68, Astrophysical Parameters for Globular Clusters, (with A.R. Upgren) The Nearby Stars and the Stellar Luminosity Function, (with Hoyes, Pasinetti) Calibration of Fundamental Stellar Quantities, Dudley Obs. Reports, 1977-81, ASNY News Letter, 1976—, Contbns. of Van Vleck Obs., 1983—; contbr. articles profl. jours., chpts. in books. Served with AUS, 1951-53. Fellow Royal Astron. Soc., AAAS; mem. Am. Phys. Soc., Am. Astron. Soc., Internat. Astron. Union (sec. commn galactic structure 1973-76, v.p. commn. radial velocity 1979-82, pres. 1982—, chmn working group spectroscope and photometric data 1982—, mem. working group standard stars), N.Y. Acad. Scis., Astron. Soc. Pacific, Astron. Soc. N.Y. (sec.-treas.), Sigma Xi. Current work: Population II Stars. Home: 1125 Oxford Pl Schenectady NY 12380 Office: Van Vleck Obs Middletown CT

PHILIPP, DAVID PORTER, biochemical geneticist, researcher; b. Paterson, N.J., July 11, 1948; s. William Francis and Margery Ann (Porter) P.; m. Wendie Ann Farrington, Aug. 7, 1970 (div. Nov. 1979); 1 child, David Balfour Farrington. B.S. in Chemistry, Lafayette Coll., 1970; M.S. in Biochemistry, U. Mass., 1973, Ph.D. in Biochemistry, 1976. Research assoc. U. Ill., Urbana, 1975-77; research geneticist Ill. Natural History Survey, Champaign, 1977-80, asst. prof. scientist, 1980-83, assoc. fisheries geneticist, 1983—; pres., research dir. Aquagentex, Urbana, 1983—. Editor, author: Biochemical Genetics of Large-mouth Bass, 1982. Served to capt. U.S. Army, 1974-75. Grantee NSF, 1981-84, U.S. Fish and Wildlife Service 1981-86, Ill. Dept. Energy and Natural Resources, 1982-85, Ill. Dept. Conservation, 1983-86. Mem. Ill. Am. Fisheries Soc. (sec., v.p., pres. 1982—), Am. Genetics Assn., AAAS, Am. Fisheries Soc. (pres. com. on fish genetics 1984—), Internat. Soc. for Differentiation. Club: Illini Bassmasters (Champaign) (bd. dirs. 1984—). Current work: Genetic conservation of fish and wildlife species; evolution of gene regulatory mechanisms; evolution of alternative reproductive strategies in fish. Subspecialties: Gene actions; Evolutionary biology. Home: 4 Buena Vista Ct Urbana IL 61801 Office: Ill Natural History Survey 607 E Peabody Dr Champaign IL 61820

PHILIPPART, MICHEL, pediatrics, neurology and psychiatry educator; b. Ixelles, Belgium, Aug. 1, 1935; came to U.S., 1962; s. E-Paul and Denise A. (Wodon) Philippart DeFoy; m. Corinne B. Dratz, Oct. 14, 1958; children—Henry, Claire Aimee. M.D., Free U. Brussels, 1960. Intern, St. Pierre Hosp., Brussels, 1959-60; resident Bunge Inst. Antwerp, Belgium, 1960-61, Hosp. for Sick Children, Paris, 1961-62, Johns Hopkins U., Balt., 1962-64; head neurochemistry lab. Inst. Bunge, Antwerp, 1965; head developmental neurology lab. Born-Bunge Found. for Research, Antwerp, 1966-67; asst. prof. UCLA, 1967-69, assoc. prof., 1969-75, prof., 1975—. Contbr. articles to profl. jours. Recipient Travel award Laureate of Belgian Govt., 1963, Neurochem. Studies award Instituto Pediatrico Giannina Gaslini, Genoa, Italy, 1977; Belgium Am. Edn. Found. fellow, 1962-63, Parkinson Disease Found. fellow, 1965-66. Mem. Brain Research Inst., Internat. Child Neurology Assn., Am. Acad. Neurology, Soc. Neurosci., Internat. Soc. Neurochemistry, Belgian Soc. Neurology. Current work: Neurochemistry, lysosomal storage diseases and inherited neurological disorders. Subspecialties: Neurology; Neurochemistry. Office: UCLA Neuropsychiat Inst 760 Westwood Plaza Los Angeles CA 90024

PHILLIP, MICHAEL J., educator; b. Trinidad, W.I., May 27, 1929; came to U.S., 1962; s. Maxwell William and Iris (Simon) P.; m. Germaine Joan Phillip, Sept. 9, 1956; children—Roger Maxwell Joseph, Brian Matthew. B.Sc., U. Toronto, 1960, M.Sc., 1962; Ph.D., Mich. State U., 1964. Asst. prof. biology John Carroll U., Univ. Hts., Ohio, 1964-69, assoc. prof., 1969-72; assoc. prof. microbiology U. Detroit Dental Sch., 1972-77, prof., 1977—, dir. genetics, 1982—. Contbr. articles to profl. jours. Pres., Trinidad and Tobago Assn., Detroit, 1975-84; chmn. bd. trustees, 1984—; sec. Polit. Action Com. of Civic Citizens, Southfield, Mich., 1984; vice chmn. bd. dirs. Alexandria House, Detroit, 1979-84. Willoughby Oncol. Soc. grantee, 1971, 72; Disting. Faculty award U. Detroit Black Alumni, 1983; Outstanding Fgn. Student, Mich. State U., 1963. Current work: Effect of chemilluminescence on growth and devel. of transplanted tumors in mice. Subspecialties: Animal genetics; Microbiology. Home: 23739 Rutland Ave Southfield MI 48075 Office: Univ Detroit Dental Sch 2985 E Jefferson Detroit MI 48207

PHILLIPS, ALFRED, JR., electronics manufacturing corporation physicist; b. Chgo., Apr. 16, 1936; s. Alfred Perry and Doesrous Lanolia (Thurman) P.; m. Serena Teresa Williams, Jan. 13, 1967 (div. Apr. 1978); children—Joseph Perry, Malcolm Martin, Douglass Dubois, Raphael Imhotep. B.S., Loyola U., Chgo., 1961; M.S., Howard U., 1964, Ph.D., 1969. Research assoc. NASA, Greenbelt, Md., 1967-68; physicist IBM Corp., East Fishkill, N.Y., 1968—. Contbr. articles to profl. jours. Patentee in field. Mem. Am. Phys. Soc., IEEE (sr. Centennial medal 1984, chmn. sect. 1980, chmn. area 1984), Sigma Xi. Democrat. Club: Howard University Alumni Assn. (pres. Mid-Hudson area 1971-73). Current work: Fabricating integrated circuit transistors for computers; mathematical modeling of transistors and effects in and properties of semiconductors. Subspecialties: Microchip technology (engineering); Condensed matter physics. Home: 37 Alpert Dr Wappingers Falls NY 12590 Office: IBM Corp East Fishkill 48A Hopewell Junction NY 12533

PHILLIPS, DONALD DAVID, chemical company executive; b. Los Angeles, Apr. 12, 1926; s. Charles Henry and Beatrice Grace (Johnson) P.; m. Joan T. Cockeram, Jan. 26, 1950; children—Catherine, Janet, David, Barbara. B.Sc. with honors, U. Alta., 1949; Ph.D. in Organic Chemistry, U. Calif., Berkeley, 1952. Asst. prof. chemistry Cornell U., Ithaca, N.Y., 1952-58; supr. Shell Devel. Co., Modesto, Calif., 1958-63; lab. mgr. Mobil Chem. Co., Metuchen, N.J., 1963-67, mgr. comml. devel., central research, N.Y.C., 1967-78, gen. mgr. research and devel., Edison, N.J., 1978—. U.S. Rubber fellow, 1951-52; Lalor Found. fellow, 1955; Sloan fellow, 1955-58. Fellow Am. Inst. Chemists; mem. Plastics Inst. Am. (trustee 1973—), Am. Chem. Soc., Am. Mgmt. Assn., Soc. Chemistry Industry (London), Sigma Xi. Clubs: Plainfield (N.J.) Country; Westfield (N.J.); Glee, Westfield Coll. Men's. Patentee in field. Current work: Management of research and development activities in thermoplastic polymers and organic synthesis. . Home: 294 Seneca Pl Westfield NJ 07090 Office: PO Box 240 Edison NJ 08818

PHILLIPS, DONALD LUNDAHL, biostatistician, ecologist; b. Wilmington, Del., July 15, 1952; s. Donald Delaney and Mary Evelyn (Lundahl) P.; m. Margaret Cornelia Arentz, Aug. 5, 1978; children—Kevin, Paul. B.S. in Zoology with honors, Mich. State U., 1974; M.S. in Biology, Utah State U., 1977, Ph.D. in Biology, 1978. Asst. prof. Emory U., Atlanta 1978-83; biostatistician Ctr. Environ. Health, Ctrs. Disease Control, Atlanta, 1983—; adj. prof. Emory U., 1983—; cons. Haday, Inc., Salt Lake City, 1980, Oak Ridge Nat. Lab., 1982. Contbr. articles to profl. jours. Nat. Merit scholar Mich. State U., 1970-74; NSF fellow, 1970; Utah State U. fellow, 1974-75, 75, 76; grantee NSF, USDA Forest Service, Highland Biol. Found. Mem. Ecol. Soc. Am. (cert. sr. ecologist), AAAS, Brit. Ecol. Soc., Highlands Biol. Found. (trustee 1980—), Sigma Xi. Current work: Disturbance ecology; succession; exposure of populations to environmental toxins; use of statistics in environmental health and ecology. Subspecialties: Ecology (biology); Statistics. Home: 3130 Belingham Dr Atlanta GA 30345 Office: Ctr Environ Health 1600 Clifton Rd Atlanta GA 30333

PHILLIPS, GEORGE NEAL, JR., biophysicist, educator; b. Dallas, Aug. 6, 1952; s. George Neal and Mary Jo (Mayfield) P.; m. Jeana Carol Ruland, June 10, 1981; B.A., Rice U., 1974, Ph.D., 1977. Postdoctoral fellow Brandeis U., Waltham, Mass., 1977-80, sr. research assoc., 1980-82; asst. prof. U. Ill., Urbana, 1982—. Contbr. articles to profl. jours. Recipient Established investigatorship Am. Heart Assn., 1983—; Pub. Health Service, Med. Found. Inc. fellow. Mem. Biophysical Soc., Am. Crystallographic Assn., Sigma Xi, Phi Lambda Upsilon. Current work: X-ray crystallography of protein molecules; mechanisms of regulation of muscle contraction; relationship of structure to function of proteins. Subspecialties: Biophysics (biology); Biochemistry (biology). Home: 311 S David St PO Box 382 Sidney IL 61877 Office: U Ill Dept Physiology and Biophysics 524 Burrill Hall 407 S Goodwin Ave Urbana IL 61801

PHILLIPS, JULIA MAE, physicist; b. Freeport, Ill., Aug. 17, 1954; d. Spencer Kleckner and Marjorie Ann (Figi) Phillips. B.S., Coll. of William and Mary, 1976; Ph.D., Yale U., 1981. Mem. tech. staff ATT Bell Labs., Murray Hill, N.J., 1981—. Contbr. papers to profl. jours. Mem. Am. Physical Soc., Materials Research Soc., AIME (electronic materials com. of Metall. Soc.), Sigma Xi, Phi Beta Kappa. Current work: THe growth and characterization of expitaxial metals and insulators on semiconductors. Subspecialties: Condensed matter physics; Materials. Office: ATT Bell Labs Room 1E-431 600 Mountain Ave Murray Hill NJ 07016

PHILLIPS, LAWRENCE RICHARD, research chemist; b. Ann Arbor, Mich., Mar. 2, 1952; s. Richard Beattie and Lillian Angeline (Ficek) P.; m. Diane DiMarchi, Nov. 26, 1977; 1 child, Lawrence Richard Jr. B.S. in Chemistry, U. Ill., 1974; M.S. in Organic Chemistry, Ind. U., 1977. Mass spectroscopist Ind. U., Bloomington, 1977-78; engring. mgr. Mich. State U. Mass Spectrometry Facility, East Lansing, 1979; vis. scientist Walter Reed Army Inst. Research, Washington, 1984—; research chemist Office of Biologics, FDA, Bethesda, Md., 1980—. Contbr. articles to profl. jours. Mem. Am. Chem. Soc., Am. Soc. Mass Spectrometry, Soc. Complex Carbohydrates. Current work: Synthesis-structure-function relationships of biomolecules to cell-surface phenomena; biochemical applications of mass spectrometry. Subspecialties: Organic chemistry; Biochemistry (biology). Office: Div Biochemistry and Biophysics Office of Biologics Research and Review FDA 8800 Rockville Pike Bethesda MD 20205

PHILLIPS, MICHAEL IAN, physiologist, educator; b. London, Eng., July 30, 1938. B.Sc., U. Exeter, U.K., 1962; M.Sc., U. Birmingham, U.K., 1965, Ph.D., 1967. Postdoctoral fellow Brain Research Labs., U. Mich., 1967-80, vis. asst. prof., 1968-69; research fellow Calif. Inst. Tech., 1969-70; asst., then asso. prof. physiology U. Iowa, 1970-76, acting chmn. dept., 1976-77, prof., 1977; prof., chmn. dept. physiology U. Fla., Gainesville, 1980—; vis. scientist U. Zurich, 1975, NIH, 1979-80; Humboldt scholar U. Heidelberg, 1976-77; mem. NIH Exptl. Cardiovascular Research Rev. Bd., 1980-85, NSF Neurobiology Rev. Bd., 1977-80. Author numerous articles in field.; Editor: Brain Unit Activity During Behavior, 1973, IBRO News, 1982—, (with others) The Renin Angiotens in System in the Brain, 1982. Named Tchr of Yr. U. Iowa, 1976, 79; recipient NIMH research career devel. award, 1974-80; grantee NIH; grantee NSF. Mem. Am Physiol. Soc., Neurosci. Soc., Internat. Brain Research Orgn. (exec. com.), Assn. Chmn. Depts. Physiology (councillor). Current Work: Research on peptides, brain, hypertension and thirst. Subspecialties: Neuroendocrinology; Neurophysiology. Office: U Fla Dept Physiology Box J-274 Gainesville FL 32610

PHILLIPS, RAYMOND BRUCE, botanist, educator; b. Urbana, Ill., May 31, 1949; s. James Alfred and Marilyn Virginia (Hopkins) P. B.A., Pomona Coll., 1973; Ph.D. (NSF grantee, Inst. Profl. Edn., scholar), U. Calif., Berkeley, 1982. Asst. prof. dept. botany and microbiology U. Okla., Norman, 1980—. Fellow Linnean Soc. London; mem. Am. Soc Plant Taxonomist, Internat. Assn. Plant Taxonomy, Bot. Soc. Am., Soc. Systematic Zoology, Classification Soc., AAAS, Sigma Xi. Current Work: Plant systematics: application of computer-assisted methods in biological classification, especially cladistic (phylogenetic) approaches; classificatory bases in evolutionary history; evolutionary relationships of Parnassia, Saxifragaceae, Scrophulariaceae; information storage and retrieval for herbarium specimens; flora of Okla. Subspecialties: Systematics; Taxonomy. Home: 1915 Oakhollow Dr Norman OK 730071 Office: Dept Botany and Microbiology U Okla Norman OK 73019

PHILLIPS, RICHARD DEAN, physiologist, administrator; b. Sacramento, Sept. 17, 1929; s. Sidney Edwin Phillips and Hazel D. (Jones) Phillips Hallow; m. Elizabeth A. Evans, Aug. 26, 1950. B.A., U. Calif.-Berkeley, 1958, Ph.D., 1966. Research physiologist U.S. Naval Radiol. Def. Lab., San Francisco, 1958-69; sr. staff scientist Battelle Pacific Northwest Lab., Richland, Wash., 1969-84; div. dir. EPA, Research Triangle Park, N.C., 1984—. Editor: Biological Effects of Non Ionizing Radiation, 1978; editor-in-chief Bioelectromagnetics, 1983—. Contbr. articles to profl. jours. Served to airman 1st class USAF, 1952-56. Ednl. fellow US Naval Radiol. Defense Lab., San Francisco, 1966. Mem. Physiol. Soc., Bioelectromagraphics (bd. dirs. 1981-82), IEEE (COMAR chmn. 1984—), Soc. Exptl. Biology and Medicine (sec. treas. 1978-79). Club: Prairie Shufflers (treas. 1972-75). Current work: Original research on hazardous wastes, toxic chemicals and the biological effects of non-ionizing radiation, including D.C. and ELF electromagnetic fields and microwave radiation. Subspecialties: Physiology (biology); Environmental toxicology. Office: EPA Research Triangle Park Mail Stop MD-71 Research Triangle Park NC 27711

PHILLIPS, SIDNEY LEON, chemistry thermodynamics researcher; b. Salem, Mass., Nov. 24, 1929; s. David and Bessie (Sieff) P.; m. Lucia Sutton, June 4, 1955; children—Michael, David, Daniel. A.B., Boston Univ., 1953; A.M., Dartmouth Coll., 1958; Ph.D., Univ. Wis.-Madison, 1964. Chemist, Shell Oil Refinery, Deer Park, Tex., 1953-56; analytical chemist IBM Research, Poughkeepsie, N.Y., 1958-60, advisor engr. IBM Corp., Poughkeepsie, San Jose, Calif., 1964-72; asst. prof. chemistry Vassar Coll., Poughkeepsie, 1967-68; research assoc. NBS, Gaithersburg, Md., 1968-69; staff scientist Lawrence Berkeley Lab., Berkeley, Calif., 1972—. Contbr. articles to profl. publs. Patentee (co-inventor) in electrodeposition field. Served to cpl. U.S. Army, 1947-49, Korea. Recipient Creative Devel. award IBM Corp., 1965, Patent award, 1968; Mem. Am. Chem. Soc. (chmn. Mid-Hudson sect. 1966-67). Current work: Thermodynamic properties to high temperature, high ionic strength; electroanalytical kinetics. Subspecialties: Thermodynamics; Analytical chemistry. Home: 171 El Toyonal Orinda CA 94720 Office: Lawrence Berkeley Lab One Cyclotron Rd Berkeley CA 94720

PHILLIPS, THOMAS L., engineering and electronics corporation executive; b. May 2, 1924. B.S.E.E., Va. Poly. Inst., 1947, M.S.E.E., 1948; hon. doctorates, Stonehill Coll., 1968, Northeastern U., 1968, Lowell Technol. Inst., 1970, Gordon Coll., 1970, Boston Coll., 1974, Babson Coll., 1981. With Raytheon Co., Lexington, Mass., 1948—, exec. v.p., 1961-64, pres., chief operating officer, 1964-68, chief exec. officer, 1968—, chmn. bd., 1975—, dir., 1962—; dir. John Hancock Life Ins. Co., State St. Investment Corp. Trustee Gordon Coll., Northeastern U.; mem. corp. Joslin Diabetes Found., Mus. Sci., Boston. Recipient Meritorious Pub. Service award for work in Sparrow III missile system, U.S. Navy, 1958. Mem. Nat. Acad. Engring., SRI Internat. Council, Bus. Council, Bus. Roundtable. Clubs: Pilgrims U.S. (Boston), Algonquin (Boston), Comml. (Boston); Weston Golf. Current Work: Engineering company management. Office: Raytheon Co 141 Spring St Lexington MA 02173

PHILLIPS, WILLIAM EVANS, mechanical engineer; b. Pascagoula, Miss., May 25, 1944; s. Jack Oliver and Emma Josephine (Evans) P.; m. Sherril Ann Poche, Sept. 28, 1968; 1 dau., Julie Anne. B.S., Miss. State U., 1966; M.B.A., U. Houston, 1973. Registered profl. engr., Wis. Prodn. technician Union Carbide Corp., Taft, La., 1966-68; project group asst., Houston, 1968-70; vessel engr. M.W. Kellog Co., Houston, 1970-73; vessel engr. Foster Wheeler Energy Corp., Houston, 1973-77, lead vessel engr., 1977-81, sr. lead vessel engr., 1981—; cons. high temperature tech. Author corp. design manuals. Mem. ASME. Democrat. Methodist. Inventor valves, vessels, insulating and erosion resistant material systems, high temperature fluid solids systems apparatus. Current Work: High temperature and erosion resistant refractory and other materials, high temperature solids transfer systems. Subspecialties: Mechanical engineering; High-temperature materials. Office: PO Box 22395 Houston TX 77227

PHILLIPS, WINFRED MARSHALL, university administrator, mechanical engineering educator; b. Richmond, Va., Oct. 7, 1940; s. Claude Marshall and Gladys Marian (Barden) P.; children: Stephen, Sean. B.S.M.E., Va. Poly. Inst., 1963; M.A.E., U. Va., 1966, D.Sc., 1968. Asst. prof. aerospace engring. Pa. State U., 1968-74, assoc. prof., 1974-76, prof., 1976-80; assoc. dean Pa. State U. (Research Coll.), 1979-80; prof., head Sch. Mech. Engring., Purdue U., 1980—; vis. prof. Institut de Pathologie Cellulaire, U. Paris, 1976-77; mem. Ind. Boiler and Pressure Vessel Bd., Indpls., 1981—; mem. com. quality of engring. edn. Nat. Assn. State Univ. and Land-Grant Colls., 1982. Contbr. numerous articles, abstracts on biofluid dynamics, cardiovascular devices, fluid mechanics, rheology to profl. jours.; assoc. editor: Jour. Biomech. Engring, 1977—. Recipient Outstanding Young Faculty Mem. award Am. Soc. Engring. Edn. and Dow Chem. Co., 1971, Research Career Devel. award USPHS, 1975-80; named Eminent Engr. Tau Bet Pi, 1981; NSF trainee, 1965-67. Assoc. fellow AIAA; fellow AAAS ASME; mem. Am. Soc. Engring. Edn., am. Soc. Artificial Internal Organs (trustee 1982—, councilman-at-large 1982-83). Lodge: Rotary (bd. dirs., v.p.). Current Work: Fluid mechanics, cardiovascular fluid dynamics, biofluid dynamics, biorheology, gas dynamics. Subspecialties: Mechanical engineering; Fluid mechanics. Home: 300 Valley St West Lafayette IN 47905 Office: Sch Mech Engring 211 Mech Engring Bldg Purdue U West Lafayette IN 47907

PHILLIS, JOHN WHITFIELD, physiologist; b. Port of Spain, Trinidad, April 1, 1936; came to U.S., 1982; s. Ernest and Sarah Anne (Glover) P.; m. Beverly Shane Wright, Jan. 24, 1969; children: David, Simon, Susan. B.V.Sc., Sydney (Australia) U., 1958, D.V.Sc., 1976; Ph.D., Australian Nat. U., Canberra, 1961; D.Sc., Monash U., Melbourne, 1970. Cert. veterinarian. Sr. lectr. Monash U., 1963-69; vis. prof. Ind. U., 1969; prof. and assoc. dean U. Man., Winnipeg, 1970-73; prof., chmn. U. Sask., Saskatoon, 1973-81; prof., chmn. Wayne State U., Detroit, 1982—; mem. scholarship, grants coms. Med. Research Council, Ottawa, Can., 1973-79. Author: Pharmacology of Synapses, 1970; editor: Veterinary Physiology, 1976, Physiology and Pharmacology of Adenosine Derivatives, 1983; editor Progress in Neurobiology, 1973—; Mem. sci. bd. Muscular Dystonia Found., Beverley Hills, Calif., 1980-84; mem. sci. adv. panel World Soc. for Protection of Animals, 1982—. Mem. Can. Physiol. Soc. (pres. 1978-79), Brit. Pharmacol. Soc., Am. Physiol. Soc., The Physiol. Soc., Soc. Neuroscience. Anglican. Current Work: Identification of synaptic transmitters in the central nervous system; development of psychoactive agents. Subspecialties: Neuropharmacology; Neurophysiology. Home: 25501 Circle Dr Southfield MI 48075 Office: Dept Physiol Wayne State U 540 E Canfield Ave Detroit MI 48201

PHINNEY, BERNARD ORRIN, botanist. Prof. dept. biology UCLA. Elected mem. Nat. Acad. Scis., 1985. Subspecialty: Plant growth. Office: UCLA Dept Biology 90024*

PIANKA, ERIC RODGER, population biologist; b. Hilt, Calif., Jan. 23, 1939; s. Walter Henry and Virginia Lincoln (High) P.; m. Helen Louise Dunlap, Dec. 20, 1965 (div. Dec. 1980); children—Karen Elizabeth, Gretchen Anna; m. Elizabeth Ann Winger, Sept. 23, 1983; B.A., Carleton Coll., 1960; Ph.D. (NIH fellow), U. Wash., 1965. NIH postdoctoral fellow Princeton U., 1965-68, U. Western Australia, Nedlands, 1966-67; asst. prof. zoology U. Tex., Austin, 1968-72, asso. prof., 1972-77, prof., 1977—; vis. prof. U. Kans., 1978, U. P.R., 1981. Author: Evolutionary Ecology, 3d edit, 1983, also, Japanese, Spanish, Polish and Russian transl.; Ecology and Natural History of Desert Lizards, 1986; co-editor: Lizard Ecology: Studies of a Model Organism, 1983; mng. editor: The Am. Naturalist, 1971-74; mem. editorial bd., 1975-77, BioSci, 1975-80, Nat. Geog. Research, 1985—; contbr. articles to profl. publs. Guggenheim fellow, 1978-79; NSF grantee, 1966-82; Nat. Geog. Soc. grantee, 1975-79. Fellow AAAS; mem. Am. Soc. Naturalists, Ecol. Soc. Am., Am. Soc. Ichthyologists and Herpetologists, Soc. for Study Evolution, Herpetologists League, Western Australian Naturalists. Research on ecology and diversity of desert lizards. Current Work: Natural history and ecology of desert lizards; life historical phenomena; community structure and resource partitioning. Subspecialties: Population biology; Evolutionary biology. Office: Dept Zoology U Tex Austin TX 78712

PICKARD, DAVID KENNETH, statistical educator; b. Summerside, Can., July 8, 1945; came to U.S., 1977; s. George Campbell and Molly Patricia (Joyce) P.; m. Dale E. Dixon, May 24, 1968; children: Damon Lee, Darcy Christine. B.S., Mount Allison U., Can., 1967; M.S., Stanford U., 1970; Ph.D., Australian Nat. U., 1977. Lectr. dept. math. Mount Allison U., Sackville, Can., 1967-68, 71-73; math. master Jaima (Sierra Leone) Secondary Sch., 1968-69; research scholar Australian Nat. U., Canberra, 1974-77; asst. prof. dept. stats. Harvard U., Cambridge, Mass., 1977-80, assoc. prof., 1980-85; assoc. prof. dept. math. and stats. Queen's U., Kingston, Ont., Can., 1985—; research assoc. Nat. Sci. and Engring Research Council Can., 1967, 68, 71, 74, 78-81. Contbr. articles to profl. jours. NSF grantee, 1981—. Mem. Am. Statis. Assn., Math. Assn. Am., Am. Math. Soc., Inst. Math. Stats. Current Work: Stochastic sedimentation; random packing; statistical inference for Markov fields; spatial processes; stock/option price modelling; feline leukemia; biomedical modelling; pharmacokinetics and anesthetic uptake. Subspecialties: Probability; Chemical engineering. Office: Dept Math and Statistics Queen's U Kingston ON K7L 3N6 Canada

PICKERING, HOWARD WILLIAM, metallurgy educator; b. Cleve., Dec. 15, 1935; s. Howard William and Marian Amelia (Vittes) P.; m. Judith Ann Burch, Apr. 20, 1963; children: John, Kim Anne, Scott, Carolyn. B.S. in Metallurgy Engring, U. Cin., 1958, M.S., 1959; Ph.D., Ohio State U., 1961. Scientist, sr. scientist U.S. Steel Corp., Monroeville, Pa., 1962-72; from assoc. prof. to prof. metallurgy Pa. State U., University Park, 1972—; vis. scientist Max Planck Inst. for Phys. Chemistry, Gottingen, W. Ger., 1964-65; vis. research prof. physics U. Tokyo, Japan, 1982. Editor: Jour. Corrosion Science, 1975—; contbr. articles to profl. jours. Grantee NSF, Office of Naval Research, others; Nat. Steel fellow; Bethlehem Steel fellow. Mem. AIME, Sigma Xi, Tau Beta Pi. Current Work: Thin film analysis by atom probe film and electrochemical studies of metals; educator and research director in the metal-environmental reaction area. Subspecialties: Metallurgy; Corrosion.

PICKERING, WILLIAM HAYWARD, physics educator, scientist; b. Wellington, N.Z., Dec. 24, 1910; s. Albert William and Elizabeth (Hayward) P.; m. Muriel Bowler, Dec. 30, 1932; children—William B., Anne E. B.S., Calif. Inst. Tech., 1932, M.S., 1933, Ph.D. in Physics, 1936; hon. degrees, Clark U., 1966, Occidental Coll., 1966, U. Bologna, 1974. Mem. Cosmic Ray Expdn. to, India, 1939, Mexico 1941; faculty Calif. Inst. Tech., 1940—, prof. elec. engring., 1946-80, prof. emeritus, 1980—, dir. jet propulsion lab., 1954-76; Mem. sci. adv. bd. USAF, 1945-48; chmn. panel on test range instrumentation (Research and Devel. Bd.), 1948-49; mem. U.S. nat. com. tech. panel Earth Satellite Program, 1955-60; mem. Army Sci. Adv. Panel, 1960-64. Decorated Order of Merit Italy; knight comdr. Order Brit. Empire; recipient James Wyld Meml. award Am. Rocket Soc., 1957; Columbus medal Genoa, 1964; Prix Galabert for Astronautics; Goddard award Nat. Space Club, 1965; NASA Distinguished Service medal, 1965; Army Distinguished Civilian Service award, 1959; Spirit of St. Louis medal, 1965; Crozier medal Am. Ordnance Assn., 1965; Man of Year award Indsl. Research Inst., 1968; Interprofl. Coop. award Soc. Mfg. Engrs., 1970; Marconi medal Marconi Found., 1974; Nat. Medal of Sci., 1976; Fahrney medal Franklin Inst., 1976; award of merit Am. Cons. Engrs. Council, 1976. Fellow Am. Inst. Aeros. and Astronautics (pres. 1963, Louis W. Hill Transp. award 1968), Am. Acad. Arts and Sci., IEEE (Edison medal 1972); mem. AAAS, Nat. Acad. Scis., Am. Geophys. Union, Internat. Astronautical Fedn. (pres. 1965-66), Royal Soc. N.Z., Nat. Acad. Engring., AAUP. Current Work: Unmanned spacecraft systems. Subspecialty: Aerospace engineering and technology. Home: 292 St Katherine Dr Flintridge CA 91011

PICKETT, JACKSON BRITTAIN ELBRIDGE, neurologist, researcher; b. San Antonio, Apr. 30, 1943; s. Jackson B. E. and Mary Ruth (Brittain) P. B.A., Occidenta Coll., 1964; M.D., Yale U., 1968. Diplomate: Am. Bd. Psychiatry and Neurology. Intern Grady Meml. Hosp., Atlanta, 1968-69; resident U. Calif.-San Francisco, 1969-72; asst. prof. neurology U. Calif., San Francisco, 1975-81; assoc. prof. Med. U. S.C., 1981—; staff neurologist VA Med. Ctr., Charleston, S.C., 1981—. Served to maj. USAF, 1971-74. Mem. Am. Acad.

Neurology. Subspecialty: Neurology. Office: Neurology Service VA Med Ctr Bldg 127 Charleston SC 29403

PIEL, GERARD, editor, publisher; b. N.Y.C., Mar. 1, 1915; s. William Ferdinand Joseph and Loretto (Scott) P.; m. Mary Tapp Bird, Feb. 4, 1938; children—Jonathan, Samuel (dec.); m. Eleanor Virden Jackson, June 23, 1955; 1 child, Eleanor Jackson, Jr. A.B., Harvard U., 1937; Sc.D., Brandeis U.; L.H.D. (hon.), Rutgers U., Columbia U.; LL.D., Carnegie-Mellon U. Sci. editor Life Mag., N.Y.C., 1938-45; asst. to pres. Henry J. Kaiser Co., Oakland, Calif., 1945-46; pres., pub. Scientific American, N.Y.C., 1947-84, chmn. bd., 1984—; overseer Harvard Coll., 1966-68, 72-78. Author: Science in the Cause of Man, 1962; The Acceleration of History, 1972. Trustee Henry Kaiser Family Found., N.Y. Bot. Garden, Am. Mus. Natural History, Philipps Acad.; trustee Mayo Clinic, 1970-82; lay mem. Am. Bd. Med. Specialties, Chgo., 1980—. Recipient Rosenberger medal U. Chgo., 1970; George Polk award L.I. U.; Mo. medal U. Mo. Fellow Am. Acad. Arts and Scis., AAAS (pres.); mem. Inst. of Medicine, Am. Philos. Soc. Clubs: Century, Cosmos, Somerset. Home: 320 Central Park W New York NY 10075 Office: Scientific American Inc New York NY 10017

PIEPER, DAVID ROBERT, physiologist, educator; b. Highland, Ill., Nov. 27, 1948; s. Ralph Howard and Margaret Alice (McMains) P.; m. Barbara Ann Datres, Feb. 26, 1971; children—Mark Ernest, Anne Marie. B.A., Asbury Coll., 1970; Ph.D., Wayne State U., 1978. Research asst. U.S. Army, Natick, Mass., 1972-74; grad. asst. Wayne State U., Detroit, 1970-71, 74-78; postdoctoral fellow U. Mich., Ann Arbor, 1978-80; asst. prof. U. Detroit, 1980-84, assoc., 1984—. Contbr. articles to profl. jours. Mem. AAAS, Endocrine Soc., Soc. Neurosci., Am. Physiol. Soc., Soc. Study Reproduction. Current work: Research interrelationship between reproductive system, olfactory system and photoperiodism in rats and golden hamsters. Subspecialty: Reproductive biology. Home: 20231 Warrington Detroit MI 48221 Office: U Detroit Dept Biology 4001 W McNichols Detroit MI 48221

PIEPER, GEORGE F(RANCIS), aerospace center administrator; b. Boston, Jan. 1, 1926; s. George Francis and Katherine Gertrude (Cross) P.; m. Barbara Ferguson, Dec. 27, 1950; children: Pamela, Lynell Pieper Smillie. B.A., Williams Coll., 1946; M.S. in Engring, Cornell U., 1949; Ph.D., Yale U., 1952. Staff mem. Radiation Lab. M.I.T., 1944-45; instr. physics Yale U., 1952-55, asst. prof., 1955-60; head exptl. satellites project Applied Physics Lab. Johns Hopkins U., 1960-64; dep. asst. dir. advanced research NASA Goddard Space Flight Ctr., Greenbelt, Md., 1964-65, dir. scis., 1965-83, asst. ctr. dir. for policy planning and devel., 1983-84, assoc. ctr. dir., 1984—. Contbr. in field. Recipient NASA medal for exceptional sci. achievement, 1969, medal for outstanding leadership, 1977. Fellow Am. Phys. Soc., Am. Astronautical Soc.; mem. Am. Astron. Soc.; mem. Am. Geophys. Union, AAAS. Current Work: Senior staff in overall direction of Goddard Space Flight Center. Subspecialties: Satellite studies; Nuclear physics. Office: NASA Goddard Space Flight Center Code 100 Greenbelt MD 20771

PIERCE, CALVIN JUDSON, dentist, educator, behavioral science researcher; b. Weymouth, Mass., Mar. 16, 1949; s. Lewis Judson Pierce, Jr. and Marguerite (Goodrich) P. B.A. in Zoology magna cum laude, U. N.H., 1971; D.M.D., Tufts U., 1975; postgrad in clin. psychology SUNY-Buffalo, 1980—. Licensed gen. dentist, N.Y., Mass., N.H. U.S. Army dental intern William Beaumont Army Med. Ctr., El Paso, Tex., 1975-76; gen. dentist U.S. Army Dental Corps., Dexhiem, W. Ger., 1976-79, Ft. Ord, Calif., 1979-80, Erie County Health Dept., Buffalo, N.Y., 1980-81; gen. practice dentistry, Buffalo, 1981—; clin. instr. SUNY-Buffalo, 1984—. Mem. Physicians for Social Responsibility, chtr. mem. Buffalo chpt., 1982—. Served to major U.S. Army, 1975-80. U.S. Armed Forces Health Profs. scholar, 1973-75; NIH research fellow NIH-Nat. Inst. Dental Research. Mem. AAAS, ADA, Am. Assn. Dental Schs., Internatl. Assn. Dental Research, Am. Soc. Clin. Hypnosis, Am. Psychol. Assn. Phi Beta Kappa, Phi Sigma, Alpha Epsilon Delta. Current work: Behavioral medicine and dentistry, bruxism, temporomandibular disorders, biofeedback, pain and phobias; psychotherapy and behavioral medical intervention. Subspecialties: Behavioral dentistry/medicine; Clinical psychology. Home: 58 Raintree Island Apt 9 Tonawanda NY 14150 Office: 141 Goodyear Farber Hall Buffalo NY 14214

PIERCE, DANIEL THORNTON, research physicist; b. Los Angeles, July 16, 1940; s. Daniel Gordon and Celia Francis (Thornton) P.; divorced; children: Jed, Maia. B.S. in Physics, Stanford U., 1962, Ph.D. in Applied Physics, 1970; M.A., Conn. Wesleyan U., 1966. Research assoc. Stanford Electronics Lab., 1970-71; research physicist Swiss Fed. Inst. Tech., 1971-75; research physicist radiation physics div. Nat. Bur. Standards, Washington, 1975—. Contbr. chpts. to books, articles to profl. jours. Recipient Dept. Commerce Silver medal, 1978; Washington Acad. Sci. Achievement award, 1981. Mem. Am. Phys. Soc., Am. Vacuum Soc., Swiss Phys. Soc. Current Work: Experimental surface physics, spin polarized electron scattering and emission, surface magnetism. Subspecialty: Condensed matter physics. Home: 1353 Carlsbad Dr Gaithersburg MD 20879 Office: Nat Bur Standards Gaithersburg MD 20899

PIERCE, ELLIOT STEARNS, chemistry and physics research administrator; b. Attleboro, Mass., Apr. 30, 1922; s. Clifford Ernest and Mary Evelyn (Pratt) P.; m. Vivianne Edith Wuilleumier, Dec. 26, 1946; children—Elliot Stearns, Cheryl Diana, Roxanne Taillard. B.S., Yale Coll., 1943; M.S., Yale U., 1948, Ph.D., 1951. Instr. chemistry U. Mass., Amherst, 1950-51; research chemist, group leader, Am. Cyanamid Co., Bound Brook, N.J., 1951-55, sci. recruiter, N.Y.C., 1955-56, govt. research and devel. liaison, Washington, 1956-59; chemist Air Force Office Sci. Research, Washington, 1959-61; chemist Atomic Energy Commn., Washington, 1961-67, dep. then dir. nuclear edn. and tng., 1967-73, dir. chem. scis. (name changed to Energy Research Devel. Adminstrn. then Dept. Energy), 1973—, dir. engring., math., geosci., 1973-79. Contbr. articles to profl. jours. Patentee in field. Treas. Congl. election campaign N.J. 6th dist., 1953, 54; founder, various offices PTA, Kensington, Md., 1958-61; exec. sec., v.p., dir. Montgomery County Scholarship Fund, Rockville, Md., 1960-70, chmn. Conf. Edn., 1961, dir. Home Study, Inc., Kensington, Md., 1962-70, Chmn., dir. Com. for Pub. Schs., 1965-67; chmn. Ad Hoc Com. to Review Certification of Teachers in State of Md., Balt., 1965-68; mem. Profl. Standards Bd., Balt., 1969-71. Served to lt. (j.g.) USNR, 1944-46, PTO. Recipient Hornbook Award Montgomery County Edn. Assn., 1964. Fellow AAAS; mem. Md. Congress Parents and Tchrs. (life), Ken-Gar Civic Assn. (life), Am. Chem. Soc. (councilor 1968, mem. various coms. 1968—), Am. Phys. Soc., Sigma Xi. Current work: Directing national program of energy-related basic research in chemistry and some areas of physics. Subspecialties: Nuclear chemistry; Atomic and molecular physics. Home: 10705 Brunswick Ave Kensington MD 20895 Office: Div Chemical Sciences ER-14 MS G-226 Dept Energy Washington DC 20545

PIERCE, JOHN ROBINSON, educator, researcher; b. Des Moines, Mar. 27, 1910; s. John Starr and Harriet Ann (Robinson) P.; m. Martha Peacock, Nov. 5, 1938 (div. 1964); children—John Jeremy, Elizabeth Ann; m. Ellen Richter, Apr. 1, 1964. B.S., Calif. Inst. Tech., 1933, M.S., 1934, Ph.D., 1936; hon. degrees Yale U., Columbia U., Northwestern U. Mem. tech. staff Bell Telephone Labs., Murray Hill, N.J., 1936-71, exec. dir. research, to 1971; prof. engring. Calif. Inst. Tech., Pasadena, 1971-80; chief technologist Jet Propulsion Lab., Pasadena, 1980-83; prof. music emeritus Stanford U., Calif., 1983—; Author: Symbols, Signals and Noise, 1961; Science, Art and Communication, 1968; The Science of Musical Sound, 1983; Information Technology and Civilization, 1984. Recipient Nat. medal Sci., Pres. U.S., 1963; Founders award Nat. Acad. Engring., 1977, Marconi Internat. fellow, 1979, Japan prize Sci. and Tech. Found. Japan, 1985. Fellow Acoustical Soc. Am., IEEE; mem. Am. Philos. Assn., Nat. Acad. Scis., Nat. Acad. Engring. Republican. Current work: Invented Pierce gun, used in microwave vacuum tubes, proponent of satellite communication, through which echo and telstar satellites came into being, much research in microwaves and communication, present interests in computer-generated sound and musical acoustics. Subspecialties: Acoustical engineering; Electrical engineering. Office: Ctr Computer Research Music and Acoustics Stanford U Stanford CA 94305

PIERCE, ROBERT RAYMOND, materials engineer, consultant; b. Helena, Mont., Feb. 17, 1914; s. Raymond Everett and Daisy Mae (Brown) P.; m. Stella Florence Kankos, June 12, 1938; children—Keith R., Patricia L., Diana L. B.S. in Chem. Engring., Oreg. State U., 1937. Process supr. Pennwalt Corp., Portland, Oreg., 1941-45, asst. tech. service mgr., Tacoma, 1945-47, gen. mgr., Phila., 1947-58, Natrona, Pa., 1958-65, tech. mgr., Phila., 1965-78, sr. tech. cons., Phila., 1978-80; self-employed cons., also Ohio State U., 1980—. Contbr. articles to prof. jours. Patentee in field. Vice chmn. Phila. Air Pollution Control Bd., Phila., 1969-79, chmn. Ad Hoc #1, 1974-79; Ky. Colonel, Louisville 1975—. Recipient Phila. award City of Phila., 1973, Resolution award, City of Phila., 1979. Mem. Am. Inst. of Chem. Engrs., Nat. Assn. of Corrosion Engr., Internat. Com. for Industrial Chimneys (recipient best paper award Dusseldorf, Germany 1970), Am. Ceramic Soc., Nat. Inst. of Ceramic Engrs. Lutheran. Current work: Engineering of coatings; engineering of brickwork; stress analyses of coatings; stress analyses of brickwork; corrosion of non-metallic materials; design of polymeric concrete; design of chimney linings. Subspecialties: Corrosion; Materials. Home: 412 Robin Rd Waverly OH 45690 Office: Ohio State Univ-Refractory Research Ctr 176 Watts Hall 2041 College Rd Columbus OH 43210

PIERCE, WILLIAM SCHULER, cardiac surgeon; b. Wilkes Barre, Pa., Jan. 12, 1937; s. William Harold and Doris Louise (Schuler) P.; m. Peggy Jayne Stone, June 12, 1965; children: William Stone, Jonathan Drew. B.S., Lehigh U., 1958; M.D., U. Pa., 1962. Resident in surgery Hosp. U. of Pa., 1962-70; asst. prof. M.S. Hershey Med. Ctr., Pa. State Coll. Medicine, Hershey, 1970-73, assoc. prof., 1973-77, prof. surgery, 1977—. Contbr. numerous articles on cardiac surgery to profl. jours. Served with USPHS, 1965-67. Fellow ACS; mem. AMA, Pa. Med. Soc., Am. Soc. Artificial Internal Organs, Internat. Cardiovascular Soc., Soc. Vascular Surgery, Soc. Univ. Surgeons, Am. Surg. Assn., Soc. Clin. Surgery. Inventor cardiac valve, blood pump. Current Work: Mechanical ventricular assistance, artificial heart, pneumatic blood pump development, implantable, motor driven blood pumps, long-term circulatory support in animals, polyurethanes for flexible blood contacting. surfaces. Subspecialties: Cardiac surgery; Artificial organs and prostheses. Office: Dept Surgery MS Hershey Med Ctr Hershey PA 17033

PIERRE, DONALD ARTHUR, electrical engineering educator; b. Bloomington, Wis., July 2, 1936; s. Joseph J. and Odile M. (LeGrave) P.; m. Mary Louise Pierre, Nov. 21, 1959; children: Michael, Louise, John. B.S.E.E. with honors, U. Ill., 1958; M.S.E.E., U. So. Calif., 1960; Ph.D., U. Wis., 1962. Registered profl. engr., Mont. Part-time instr. U. So. Calif., Los Angeles, 1959-60; mem. tech. staff Hughes Aircraft Co., Los Angeles, 1958-62; asst. prof. elec. engring. Mont. State U., Bozeman, 1962-65; assoc. prof. elec. engring., mem. staff Mont. State U. (Electronics Research Lab.), 1965-69, prof. elec. engring., group leader systems group, 1969—, head elec. engring. and computer sci. dept., 1979-84. Author: Optimization Theory with Applications, 1969, Mathematical Programming Via Augmented Lagrangians, 1975; contbr. articles to profl. jours.; mem. editorial adv. bd.: Jour. Computers and Electrical Engring, 1971—. Francis Rogers Bacon fellow, 1958-59; FIER-GE fellow, 1959-60; recipient Wiley award for meritorious research Mont. State U., 1982. Mem. Am. Soc. Engring. Edn., IEEE, Instrument Soc. Am., Sigma Xi, Tau Beta Pi, Eta Kappa Nu, Pi Mu Epsilon. Roman Catholic. Current Work: Control systems, computer control, power systems. Subspecialty: Electrical engineering. Home: 6343 Aajker Creek Rd Bozeman MT 59715 Office: Elec Engring Dept Mont State U Bozeman MT 59717

PIERRE, HARVEY HAROLD, chemist; b. Spirit Lake, Iowa, May 14, 1958; s. Robert Dea and June Marjorie (Vanderhoff) P. A.A. in Sci., Fresno City Coll., 1978; B.S. in Chemistry, Calif. State U.-Fresno, 1981. Chemist, Petroleum Testing Service, Inc., Santa Fe Springs, Calif., 1981—, opened new lab., Anchorage, 1985; research chemist off-shore and land based Chevron oil rigs, Santa Barbara, Calif., 1984. Fundraiser City of Hope, Upland, Calif., 1984. Mem. Am. Chem. Soc. (cert. chemist). Republican. Mem. Christian Ch. Current work: testing waters and brines; core handling, on site sampling, in house casting, slabbing, plugging, preserving and photography; geo-chemical research. Subspecialties: Analytical chemistry; Geochemistry. Home: 890 N Euclid Ave Upland CA 91786 Also: 2900 Concord Ln Anchorage AK 99502 Office: Petroleum Testing Service Inc 12051 Rivera Rd Sante Fe Springs CA 90670 Also: 4450 W 50th Ave Anchorage AK 99502

PIERRET, ROBERT FRANCIS, educator; b. East Cleve., Aug. 20, 1940; s. Frank S. and Elsie (Svoboda) P.; m. Linda J. Pierz, Aug. 22, 1965; children—Ross, Suzanne, John. B.S., Case Inst. Tech., 1962; M.S., U. Ill.-Urbana, 1963, Ph.D., 1966. Asst. prof. U. Ill.-Urbana, 1966-70; assoc. prof. Purdue U., West Lafayette, Ind., 1970-77, prof. dept. elec. engring., 1977—; con. editor Addison-Wesley Pub. Co., Reading, Mass., 1985—. Author: Semiconductor Fundamentals, Field Effect Devices, 1983; also articles; patentee Separate comb transducer, 1984. Recipient D.D. Ewing Teaching award Purdue U., 1976. Sr. mem. IEEE. Current work: Metal-insulator-semiconductor devices, electrical characterization techniques, molecular beam epitaxy of III-V materials. Subspecialties: Semiconductors; Electronic materials. Home: 2563 Nottingham Pl West Lafayette IN 47906 Office: Purdue U Sch Elec Engring West Lafayette IN 47907

PIERSON, RICHARD NORRIS, JR., physician, educator; b. N.Y.C., Sept. 22, 1929; s. Richard Norris and Dorothy (Stewart) P.; m. Anne Bingham, July 10, 1954 (div. 1974); children: Richard, Olivia, Alexandra, Cordelia; m. Alice Roberts, Aug. 26, 1974. B.A., Princeton U., 1951; M.D., Columbia U., 1955. Diplomate: Am. Bd. Internal Medicine, Am. Bd. Nuclear Medicine. Intern St. Luke's Hosp., N.Y.C., 1955-56, resident, 1958-61; dir. nuclear medicine div. St. Luke's-Roosevelt Hosp. Ctr., N.Y.C., 1965 ; dir. medicine Hackensack (N.J.) Hosp., 1973-74; prof. clin. medicine Columbia U., N.Y.C., 1980 ; cons. CAPINTEC, Montvale, N.J., 1979-82. Editor: Quantitative Nuclear Cardiography, 1975; contbr. med. articles to profl. jours. Pres. Englewood (N.J.) Bd. Health, 1966-73. Served as lt. USN, 1956-58. Fellow ACP, N.Y. Acad. Medicine (chmn. bioengring. com. 1980); mem. N.Y. County Health Services Rev. Orgn. (chmn. 1980-82), N.Y. County Med. Soc. (pres. 1977-78), N.Y. State Med. Soc. (chmn. med. sch. relations 1980), AMA (del. 1978), Am. Med. Peer Rev. Assn. (speaker 1984), Am. Bur. Med. Advancement in China (pres. N.Y.C. 1980). Episcopalian. Club: Century (N.Y.C.). Current Work: Nuclear cardiology, body composition research. Subspecialties: Nuclear medicine; Biomedical engineering. Home: 94 Beech Rd Englewood NJ 07631 Office: Nuclear Medicine Div Saint Luke's Hosp Ctr Amsterdam Ave at 114th St New York NY 10025

PIETRUSKI, JOHN M., JR., pharmaceutical company executive. Chmn., Sterling Drug Inc., N.Y.C. . Office: Sterling Drug Inc 90 Park Ave New York NY 10016*

PIETRZYK, ZBIGNIEW ADAM, nuclear engineer educator; b. Warsaw, Poland, Aug. 12, 1935; came to U.S., 1973; s. Czeslaw and Jadwiga (Poremrska) P.; m. Maria Elzbieta Budeck, Oct. 19, 1963. M.S. in Aero. Engring., Warsaw Tech. U., 1960; Ph.D. in Applied Physics, Polish Acad. Sci., Warsaw, 1966. Asst prof. Inst. Fundamental Tech. Research, Warsaw, 1960-68, head gas dynome group, 1970-72; from research assoc. prof. to research prof. nuclear engring. Univ. Wash., Seattle, 1974—; cons. in field. Tech. editor: Laser-Induced Discharge, Phonomena, 1976. Contbr. articles to profl. jours. Mem. Am. Phys. Soc. Current work: Plasma physics; thermonuclear fusion; laser plasma ineractions; nonlinear processes in plasma; electron acceleration by plasma waves; CO2 lasers. Subspecialties: Plasma physics; Nuclear fusion. Office: Univ Washington Seattle WA 98195

PIETSCH, PAUL ANDREW, neuroanatomy educator; b. N.Y.C., Aug. 8, 1929; s. Elwood Paul and Bridget Elizabeth (McDonnell) P.; m. Myrtle Evelyn Miller, Dec. 8, 1950; children—Samuel, Benjamin, Mary Pietsch Randall, Abigail. A.B., Syracuse U., 1954; Ph.D., U. Pa., 1960. Asst. instr. Ohio State U., Columbus, 1954-56; asst. instr., instr. U. Pa., Phila., 1956-60; instr. Bowman Gray Sch. Medicine, Winston-Salem, N.C., 1960-61; asst. prof. SUNY-Buffalo, 1961-64; sr. researcher Dow Chem. Co., Midland, Mich., 1964-70; assoc. prof. Ind. U., Bloomington, 1970-78, prof. anatomy, 1978—; treas. Local 2254, Am. Fedn. Tchrs., Bloomington, 1971-74, pres., 1974-75. Author: Shufflebrain, 1981. Candidate for county clk., Midland, 1968; mem. exec. com. Midland County Democratic party, 1968-70. Served with AUS, 1946-49, PTO. Named Tchr. of Yr., Ind. U. Student Optometric Assn., 1972, 74, 77, 79, 85, Outstanding Tchr., Ind. U. Sr. Class Council, 1972; recipient Med. Journalism award AMA, 1973, Disting. Service award Nat. Optometric Student Assn., 1974. Mem. Am. Assn. Anatomists, AAAS. Current work: Regeneration and memory. Subspecialty: Developmental biology. Office: Dept Anatomy Ind U 800 E Atwater St Bloomington IN 47405

PIETTE, LAWRENCE HECTOR, educator, biophysicist; b. Chgo., Jan. 4, 1932; s. Gerald John and Lillian (Bumgardner) P.; m. Mary Irene Harris, Aug. 15, 1957; children—Jeffrey, Martin. B.S., Northwestern U., 1953, M.S., 1954; Ph.D., Stanford, 1957. Mgr. research biochemistry and biophysics Varian Assos., 1956-65; prof. biophysics U. Hawaii, 1965—, chmn. dept., 1968—; dir. U. Hawaii (Cancer Research Lab.), 1970—; exec. dir. Cancer Center Hawaii, 1974; Chmn. cancer adv. com., regional med. program, research com. Hawaii div. Am. Cancer Soc. Contbr. articles to profl. jours.; Asso. editor: Jour. Organic Magnetic Resonance. Mem. Am. Chem. Soc., Biophys. Soc., A.A.U.P. Current Work: Mechanism of carcinogenesis, electron spin resonance of free radicals. Subspecialties: Biophysics (biology); Cancer research (medicine). Home: 4954 Kolohala Ave Honolulu HI 96816

PIETZ, RICHARD IRWIN, soil scientist; b. Tracy, Minn., Sept. 3, 1942; s. Kenneth Irwin and Lois Bernetta (Scrivner) P.; m. Sharron Kay Keiffer, Dec. 19, 1964; 1 dau., Barbara. B.S., U. Minn., 1965, M.S., 1967, Ph.D., 1971. Sci. sec. Nat. Acad. Sci., Washington, 1971-72; research assoc. Purdue U., West Lafayette, Ind., 1972-73; soil scientist Met. San. Dist. Greater Chgo., Canton, Ill., 1973—. Contbr. articles to profl. jours. Pres. YMCA Parents Swim Team Assn., Canton, 1983; chmn. personnel com. Trinity Lutheran Ch., Canton, 1980-82, council mem., 1981-82. Mem. Soil Sci. Soc. Am., Am. Chem. Soc., Soc. Environ. Geochemistry & Helath, Council Agrl. Sci. and Tech. Current work: Sewage sludge and organic wastes, micronutrients, heavy metals, organic priority pollutants, water quality, land reclamation, and soil and crop relationships. Subspecialties: Soil science; Environmental chemistry. Home: 1435 E Locust St Canton IL 61520 Office: Met Sanitary Dist Greater Chgo Research and Devel Lab PO Box 368 Canton IL 61520

PIGEAUD, ADOLPH, materials scientist, electrochemist; b. Bandung, Indonesia, Nov. 5, 1927; came to U.S., 1946; s. Frans Derk and Henriette Françoise (vanWely) P.; m. Mary Marjorie Quinlan, Dec. 30, 1961; children—Danielle Mary, François Philippe, Grace Martine. B.S., Roanoke Coll., 1949; M.S., Cornell U., 1954; Ph.D., U. Cin., 1974. Teaching and research asst. Cornell U., Ithaca, N.Y., 1951-54; electrochemist Imperial Oil Ltd., Sarnia, Ont., Can., 1955-65; WPAFB research mgr. U. Dayton (Ohio), 1965-67; instr. U. Cin., 1970-74; project engr. Inst. Gas Tech., Chgo., 1976-78; program mgr. MCFC tech. Energy Research Corp., Danbury, Conn., 1978—. Contbrg. editor Handbook of Materials Science, 1975. Contbr. articles to tech. jours. Patentee in field Dist. commr. Boy Scouts Can., 1960-65. Mem. Chem. Inst. Can., Am. Chem. Soc., Electrochem. Soc., AAAS, Fed. Am. Scientists, Internat. Assn. for Hydrogen Energy. Current work: Development of the second generation direct reforming Molten Carbonate Fuel Cell for large scale, fuel-to-electric power conversion. Subspecialty: High-temperature materials. Office: Energy Research Corp 3 Great Pasture Rd Danbury CT 06810

PIGFORD, THOMAS HARRINGTON, nuclear engineering educator; b. Meridian, Miss., Apr. 21, 1922; s. Lamar and Zula Vivian (Harrington) P.; m. Catherine Kennedy Cathey, Dec. 31, 1948; children: Cynthia Pigford Naylor, Julie Pigford Earnest. B.S. in Chem. Engring, Ga. Inst. Tech., 1943; S.M. in Chem. Engring, M.I.T., 1948, Sc.D. in Chem. Engring, 1952. Asst. prof. chem. engring., dir. Sch. Engring. Practice, M.I.T., 1950-52, asst. prof. nuclear and chem. engring., 1952-55, asso. prof., 1955-57; head engring., dir. nuclear reactor projects and asst. dir. research lab. Gen. Atomic Co., La Jolla, Calif., 1957-59; prof. nuclear engring., chmn. dept. nuclear engring. U. Calif., Berkeley, 1959—; mem. Pres.'s Commn. on Accident at 3-Mile Island, 1979; mem. bd. radioactive waste mgmt. NRC; chmn. waste isolation systems panel, mem. waste isolation pilot plant panel; chmn. adv. council Inst. Nuclear Power Op.; cons. in field. Author: (with Manson Benedict) Nuclear Chemical Engineering, 1958, 2d edit., 1981; contbr. numerous articles to profl. jours. Served with USNR, 1944-46. Recipient John Wesley Powell award U.S. Geol. Survey, 1981; named Outstanding Young Man of Greater Boston Boston Jaycees, 1955; E. I. DuPont DeNemours research fellow, 1948-50; Japan Soc. for Promotion Sci. fellow, 1974-75; NSF grantee, 1960-75; EPA grantee, 1973-78; Dept. Energy grantee, 1979—; Ford Found. grantee, 1974-75; Electric Power Research Inst. grantee, 1974-75. Fellow Am. Nuclear Soc. (Arthur H. Compton award 1971); mem. Nat. Acad. Engring., Am. Chem. Soc., Am. Inst. Chem. Engrs. (Robert E. Wilson award 1980, award for Service to Soc. 1985), Atomic Indsl. Forum (dir.), AIME, Sigma Xi, Phi Kappa Phi, Tau Beta Pi. Patentee in field. Subspecialty: Nuclear engineering. Home: 1 Garden Dr Kensington CA 94708 Office: Dept Nuclear Engring U Calif Berkeley CA 94720

PIGOTT, JOHN DOWLING, geology educator; b. Gorman, Tex., Feb. 2, 1951; s. Edwin and Emma Jane (Poe) P.; m. Patricia Karen Bettis, June 17, 1978. B.A. in Zoology, U. Tex.-Austin, 1974, B.S. in Geology, 1974, M.A., 1977; Ph.D., Northwestern U., 1981. Geologist Amoco Internat. Oil Co., Chgo., 1978-79; sr. petroleum geologist Amoco Prodn. Co., Houston, 1979-81; asst. prof. geology U. Okla., Norman, 1981—. Penrose research grantee Geol. Soc. Am., 1977; Mobil scholar, 1979; U. Okla. jr. faculty research fellow, 1983. Mem. Am. Assn., Petroleum Geologists, Geol. Soc. Am., Soc. Exploration Geophysicists, Sigma Xi. Democrat. Current Work: Investigation of secular trends in the geochemistry of the earth's surface environment; interactions between tectonics and sedimentary geochemistry. Subspecialties: Geochemistry; Sedimentology. Home: 1511 Barwick St Norman OK 73069 Office: Univ Okla Sch Geology and Geophysics 830 Van Vleet Oval Norman OK 73019

PILBEAM, DAVID ROGER, paleontologist, educator; b. Brighton, Eng., Nov. 21, 1940. B.A., Cambridge (Eng.) U., 1962; Ph.D. in Biology, Geology and Anthropology, Yale U., 1967. Demonstrator in phys. anthropology Cambridge U., 1965-68; from asst. prof. to assoc. prof. Yale U., New Haven, 1968-74, prof. anthropology, geology and geophysics, chmn. dept. anthropology, 1974-81; prof. anthropology Harvard U., Cambridge, Mass., 1981—. Author: The Evolution of Man, 1970, The Ascent of Man, 1972. Wenner-Gren Found. fellow, 1968. Mem. Am. Anthrop. Assn., Am. Assn. Phys. Anthropology, Brit. Soc. Study Human Biology. Discoverer of Sivapithecus indicus, Pakistan, 1980. Current Work: paleontology. Subspecialty: Paleontology. Office: Dept Anthropology Peabody Museum Harvard U 11 Divinity Ave Cambridge MA 02138*

PILGERAM, LAURENCE OSCAR, research biochemist; b. Great Falls, Mont., June 23, 1924; s. John R. and Bertha R. (Phillips) P.; m. Cynthia Ann Moore, Feb. 11, 1951; children: Karl E., Kurt J. A.A., U. Calif.-Berkeley, 1948, B.A., 1949, Ph.D., 1953. Postdoctoral fellow U. Calif.-Berkeley, 1953-54; instr. physiology U. Ill. Sch. Medicine, Chgo., 1954-55; asst. prof. biochemistry Stanford (Calif.) U. Sch. Medicine, 1955-57; dir. arteriosclerosis research lab. U. Minn. Sch. Medicine, Mpls., 1957-71; dir. coagulation lab. Baylor U. Coll. Medicine, Houston, 1971-75; dir. Cell Culture Lab., Santa Barbara, Calif., 1975—; cons. NIH, 1973-75. Contbr. over 70 articles to research jours.; guest editor: Nat. Dairy Council Jour, 1974, Biomedicine and Pharmacotherapy, 1982. Recipient award CIBA, London, 1959; Karl Thomae award, Germany, 1973; grantee NIH; grantee Am. Heart Assn. Fellow Am. Heart Assn. Council on Stroke and Council on Thrombosis; mem. Am. Soc. Biol. Chemists (nat. corr. office pub. affairs 1969-75). Patentee detecting and measuring intravascular blood clotting. Current Work: Research on thrombosis and cell biology. Subspecialties: Biochemistry (medicine); Cell biology (medicine). Office: PO Box 1583 Goleta Sta Santa Barbara CA 93116

PILKEY, ORRIN H., geologist; b. N.Y.C., Sept. 19, 1934; s. Orrin H. and Elizabeth (Street) P.; m. Sharlene M. Greenaa, Dec. 29, 1956; children—Charles, Linda, Diane, Keith, Kerry. B.S., Wash. State U., 1957; M.S., Mont. State U., 1959; Ph.D. Fla. State U., 1962. Research asso. U. Ga. Marine Inst., Sapelo Island, 1962-65; asso. prof. geology Duke U., 1965-72, prof., 1972—, James B. Duke prof. geology, 1983—; vis. prof. U. P.R. at Mayaguez, 1972-73; sr. marine scientist U.S. Geol. Survey, Woods Hole, Mass., 1975-76. Editor: (with D.J. Swift and D.B. Duane) Shelf Sediment Transport, 1972; author: (with O.H. Pilkey Sr.) How to Live with an Island, 1975, (with O.H. Pilkey Sr. and William Neal) Currituck to Calabash, 1978, (with Wallace Kaufman) The Beaches are Moving, 1979; editor: (with S. Fritz) Marine Atlas of Puerto Rico, 1976, Jour. Sedimentary Petrology, 1977-83, (with Larry J. Doyle) Geology of Continental Slopes, 1979, (with O.H. Pilkey Sr., W.D. Pikley and William Neal) Coastal Design, 1983; contbr. articles to profl. jours. Active shoreline conservation. Mem. N.C. Acad. Sci. (pres. 1981-82). Research on geol. oceanography and coastal geology. Subspecialties: Coastal zones; Geology. Office: Dept Geology Duke Univ Durham NC 27708

PILSON, MICHAEL EDWARD QUINTON, oceanographer, educator; b. Ottawa, Ont., Can., Oct. 25, 1933; s. Edward Charles and Frances A. (Ferguson) P.; m. Joan E. Johnstone, July 4, 1977; children: Diana, John. B.S., Bishops U., 1954; M.S., McGill U., 1959; Ph.D., U. Calif.-San Diego, 1964. Chemist Windsor Mills (Que.)Paper Co., 1954-55; research asst. McGill U., U. Calif.-San Diego, 1956-63; asst. research biologist San Diego Zool. Soc., 1963-66; asst. to assoc. prof. U.R.I., Narragansett, 1966-78; prof. oceanography, 1978—; dir. Marine Ecosystems Research Lab., 1976—; cons. in field. Author numerous articles in profl. publs. Scripps Inst. Oceanography Sverdrup fellow, 1959. Mem. AAAS, Am. Geophys. Union, Am. Soc. Limnology and Oceanography, Am. Soc. Mammalogists, Sigma Xi. Club: Saunderstown Yacht (treas.). Current Work: Experimental analysis of marine ecosystems. Structure and function of marine mesocosms; fates and effects of chemicals. Subspecialties: Marine ecosystems; Environmental toxicology. Home: Box 27 Saunderstown RI 02874 Office: URI Grad Sch Oceanography Narragansett RI 02882

PIMENTEL, GEORGE CLAUDE, chemist; b. Rolinda, Calif., May 2, 1922; s. Emile J. and Lorraine Alice (Reid) P.; children: Anne Christine, Tess Loren, Janice Amy. A.B., UCLA, 1943; Ph.D. in Chemistry, U. Calif. - Berkeley, 1949. From instr. to asso. prof. chemistry U. Calif., Berkeley, 1949-59, prof., 1959—; dep. dir. Nat. Sci. Found., Washington, 1977-80; dir. Lab. Chem. Biodynamics, U. Calif., Berkeley, 1981—; participant U.S.-Japan Eminent Scientists Exchange Program, 1973-74. Editor: Chemistry—An Experimental Science, 1963; co-author: Understanding Chemistry, 1971, Introductory Quantitative Chemistry, 1956; editor: Chem. Study, 1960; contbr. papers to profl. jours. Served with USNR, 1944-46. Recipient Campus Teaching award U. Calif., Berkeley, 1968, Coll. Chemistry Teaching award Mfg. Chemists Assn., 1971, Joseph Priestley Meml. award Dickinson Coll., 1972, Joseph Priestley Meml. award Spectroscopy Soc. Pitts., 1974, Alexander von Humboldt Sr. Scientist award, 1974, Pauling medal, 1982, Wolf prize, 1982, Debye award, 1983, Madison Marshall award, 1983; Nat. Medal of Sci., 1985; Franklin medal Franklin Inst., Phila., 1985; Guggenheim fellow, 1955. Fellow Am. Acad. Arts and Sci.; mem. Nat. Acad. Scis., Am. Chem. Soc. (Precision Sci. award 1959, award Calif. sect. 1957, pres.-elect 1984—), Am. Phys. Soc. (Earle K. Plyer prize 1979, Lippencott medal 1980), Optical Soc. Am., Phi Beta Kappa, Sigma Xi, Phi Eta Sigma, Phi Lambda Epsilon, Alpha Chi Sigma. Subspecialty: Biophysical chemistry. Home: 754 Coventry Rd Kensington CA 94707 Office: Lab Chem Biodynamics U Calif Berkeley CA

PINCUS, ALEXIS GEORGE, ceramist; b. Newark, Aug. 11, 1911; s. Joseph William and Elizabeth Florence (Lipman) P.; m. Thelma Hillson, Sept. 2, 1938 (div. 1967); children—Richard E., Judy, Betty; m. Carmen Cira Cabrera, May 4, 1983. B.Sc. in Ceramics, Rutgers U., 1932, M.Sc. in Ceramics, 1934; Ph.D. in Ceramics, Pa. State U., 1940, Ceramist Am. Optical Co., Southbridge, Mass., 1932-48, Horizons, Inc., Cleve., 1948-49, Gen. Electric Co., Schenectady, 1949-66; sr. ceramist Ill. Inst. Tech. Research Inst., Chgo., 1966-70; glass technologist Am. Cystoscope Makers, N.Y.C., 1970-71; vis. prof. Rutgers U., New Brunswick, N.J., 1971-83; researcher, tchr. U. Calif.-Berkeley, 1962-63; adj. prof. Rensselaer Poly. Inst., Troy, N.Y., 1963-64; cons. in field, 1971—. Author: (with others) Uses of Ceramics in Microelectronics, 1971. Editor: Processing in the Glass Industry (15 vols.), 1976-84; Jour. Glass Industry, 1971-83. Contbr. articles to profl. jours. Patentee in field. Fellow Am. Ceramic Soc. (emeritus). Democrat. Jewish. Current work: Joining ceramics or glasses to metals; fiber optics. Subspecialties: Ceramics; Fiber optics. Home: 20 Redcliff Ave Highland Park NJ 08904

PINDERA, JERZY TADEUSZ, mechanical engineer; b. Czchow, Poland, Dec. 4, 1914; emigrated to Can., 1965, naturalized, 1975; s. Jan Stanislaw and Natalia Lucia (Knapik) P.; m. Aleksandra-Anna Szal, Oct. 29, 1949; children: Marek Jerzy, Maciej Zenon. B.S. (equivalent) in Mech. Engring, Tech. U., Warsaw, 1936; M.S. in Aero. Engring, Tech. U., Warsaw and Lodz, 1947; D.Applied Scis., Polish Acad. Scis., 1959; D.Habil. (D.Sc.) in Applied Mechanics, Tech. U., Cracow, 1962. Registered profl. engr., Ont. Asst. Lot Polish Airlines, Warsaw, 1947; head lab. Aero. Inst., Warsaw, 1947-52, Inst. Metallography, Warsaw, 1952-54; dep. prof., head lab. Polish Acad. Scis., 1954-59; head lab. Bldg. Research Inst., Warsaw, 1959-62; vis. prof. mechanics Mich. State U., E. Lansing, 1963-65; prof. mechanics U. Waterloo, Ont., Can., 1965-83, adj. prof., 1983—, dir. Inst. for Exptl. Mechanics, 1983—; pres. J.T. Pindera & Sons Engring. Services, Inc., Waterloo; chmn. Internat. Symposium Exptl. Mechanics at univ., 1972, 10th Can. Fracture Conf., 1983; vis. prof. in, France and W. Ger., cons. in field. Author tech. books, also articles, chpts. in books.; Editorial adv. bd. Mechanics Research Communications, 1974—; mem. bd. editors Theoretical and Applied Fracture Mechanics—Mechanics and Physics of Fracture, 1984—. Served with Polish Army, 1939. Mem. Canadian Soc. Mech. Engring. (chmn. exptl. group research and devel. div.), Gesellschaft angewandte Mathematik und Mechanik, N.Y. Acad. Scis., Soc. Engring. Sci., Soc. Exptl. Stress Analysis (N.M. Frocht award 1978), ASME, Soc. Française des Mécaniciens, Assn. Profl. Engrs. Ont. Current Work: Experimental mechanics; theory of modelling, observations and measurements, reliability of analytical and experimental evaluations, viscoelasticity of polymers; flow of energy in deformed bodies; photoelasticity; fracture mechanics; composite structures. Subspecialties: Theoretical and applied mechanics; Fracture mechanics. Home: 310 Grant Crescent Waterloo ON N2K 2A2 Canada Office: Institute for Experimental Mechanics Univ of Waterloo 200 University Ave Waterloo ON N2L 3G1 Canada

PINE, CHARLES JOSEPH, clinical psychologist, health services administrator; b. Excelsior Springs, Mo., July 13, 1951; s. Charles Edison and LaVern (Upton) P.; m. Mary Day, Dec. 30, 1979; 1 son, Charles Andrew. B.A., U. Redlands, 1973; M.A., Calif. State U.-Los Angeles, 1975; Ph.D., U. Wash., 1979. Lic. psychologist, Calif. Teaching asst. U. Wash., 1976-78; intern in psychology VA Outpatient Clinic, Los Angeles, 1978-79; asst. prof. Okla. State U., 1979-80; postdoctoral scholar UCLA, 1980-81; asst. prof. Wash. State U., 1981-82; clin. psychologist, dir. behavioral health services Riverside/San Bernardino County (Calif.) Indian Health Inc., 1982—. Editorial cons.: White Cloud Jour, 1982—. Recipient stipend Inst. Indian Studies, U. Wash., 1975-76; UCLA Inst. Am. Cultures grantee, 1981-82. Mem. Am. Psychol. Assn. (mem. minority edn. tng. task force 1982), Nat. Indian Cousnelros Assn., Soc. Indian Psychologists (pres. 1981-83), Western Psychol. Assn., Internat. Council Psychologists, Sigma Alpha Epsilon. Republican. Baptist. Club: Calif. Paso-Fino Assn. (Saugus). Current Work: Studying psychological factors related to such health problems as obesity, hypertension and diabetes from a cross-cultural perspective, especially as they relate to American Indians. Subspecialties: Health psychology; Clinical psychology. Home: 365 W Grove Rialto CA 92376 Office: Riverside/San Bernardino County Indian Health Inc 11555-1/2 Petrero Rd Banning CA 92220

PINEDA, MAURICIO HERNAN, reproductive physiologist; b. Santiago, Chile, Oct. 17, 1930; came to U.S., 1970, naturalized, 1982; s. Teofilo Pineda-Garcia and Bertila Pinto-Bouvret; m. Rosa A. Gomez, July 26, 1956; children: Anamaria, George H., Monserrat. D.V.M., U. Chile, 1955; M.S., Colo. State U., 1965, Ph.D., 1968. Prof. Coll. Vet. Medicine, Austral U. Chile, Valdivia, 1958-63, prof., head animal reprodn. lab., 1968-70; postdoctoral trainee U. Wis., Madison, 1970-72; postdoctoral fellow Colo. State U., Ft. Collins, 1972-74, research assoc., 1972-78; assoc. prof. physiology, dept. physiology and pharmacology Coll. Vet. Medicine, Iowa State U., Ames, 1979-84, prof., 1984—. Contbr. chpts. to books, articles to profl. jours. Recipient Best Student award U. Chile Coll. Vet. Medicine, 1954; Rockefeller Found. scholar, 1963; Morris Animal Found. fellow, 1974. Mem. Chilean Vet. Med. Assn., Soc. for Study of Reprodn., Soc. for Study of Fertility (Eng.), Sigma Xi, Beta Beta Beta, Phi Kappa Phi. Current Work: Development of contraceptives to control pet population; research on male and female gametes as related to the development of methods to detect mammalian embryonic viability; microinjection and manipulation of embryos. Subspecialties: Reproductive biology; Animal contraception. Office: Dept Physiology and Pharmacology Vet Med Iowa State U Ames IA 50011

PINES, DAVID, physicist; b. Kansas City, Mo., June 8, 1924; s. Sidney and Edith (Adelman) P.; m. Aronelle Siegerman, June 15, 1948; children: Catherine Deirdre, Jonathan David. A.B., U. Calif. at Berkeley, 1944; M.A., Princeton, 1948, Ph.D., 1950. Instr. U. Pa., 1950-52; research asst. prof. U. Ill. at Urbana, 1952-55; asst. prof. Princeton U., 1955-58; mem. Inst. Advanced Study, Princeton, 1958-59; prof. physics and elec. engring. U. Ill., 1959—; dir. U. Ill. (Center Advanced Study), 1967-70, assoc., 1972-73, prof., 1978—; prof. assoc. Faculty des Scis., U. Paris, France, 1962-63; vis. prof. NORDITA, Copenhagen, 1970; Lorentz prof. U. Leiden, Netherlands, 1971; Fritz London Meml. lectr. Duke, 1972; Guilio Racah Meml. lectr. Hebrew U., Jerusalem, 1974; Marchon lectr. Newcastle-Upon-Tyne U., 1976; Sherman Fairchild disting. scholar Calif. Inst. Tech., 1977-78; exchange prof. U. Paris, 1978; Eugene Feenberg meml. lectr. Washington U., 1982; disting. lectr. U. Rochester, 1983; Gordon Godfrey prof. U. New South Wales, 1985; Emil Warburg lectr. U. Bayreuth, 1985; dir. W.A. Benjamin, Inc., N.Y.C., 1963-71; mem. physics survey com. Nat. Acad. Scis., 1963-65; v.p. Aspen Center for Physics, 1968-76, chmn. exec. com. bd. trustees, 1976-77; mem. council for biology and human affairs Salk Inst., 1969-73; co-chmn. Joint Soviet-U.S. Symposia on Theory of Condensed Matter, 1968, 70, 71, 73, 74, 76; mem. NRC Commn. Internat. Relations, 1974-79, Com. Scholarly Communication with People's Republic of China, 1974-78; mem. bd. advisors Inst. Theoretical Physics, U. Calif., Santa Barbara, 1979-81; mem. theoretical div. adv. com. Los Alamos Nat. Lab., 1977-85, chmn., 1980-85; chmn. Nat. Acad. Scis.-NRC Bd. Internat. Sci. Exchange, 1974-77; chmn. Working Group on Physics US-USSR Joint Commn. on Sci. and Tech. Coop., 1974-82, NRC Commn. US-USSR Coop. Physics, 1978-82; mem. space sci. bd. NRC, 1978-81; trustee Assn. Univ. Research Astronomy, 1975-78, 79—, exec. com., 1981-82; v.p. Santa Fe Inst., 1985—. Author: The Many Body Problem, 1961, Elementary Excitations in Solids, 1963, (with P. Nozières) Theory of Quantum Liquids, 1966; Editor: Frontiers of Physics, 1961—, Lecture Notes and Supplements in Physics, 1962—, Revs. of Modern Physics, 1973—; Mem. editorial adv. bd.: Jour. of Non-Metals. Recipient Frieman prize in condensed matter physics, 1983; Dirac medal, 1984; Feenberg medal, 1985; NSF sr. postdoctoral fellow, 1957-58; Guggenheim fellow, 1962-63, 70. Fellow AAAS, Am. Phys. Soc., Am. Astron. Soc.; mem. Nat. Acad. Scis., Am. Acad. Arts and Scis., Internat. Astron. Union, Phi Beta Kappa, Sigma Xi. Club: Cosmos. Subspecialties: Theoretical astrophysics; Condensed matter physics. Home: 403 W Michigan St Urbana IL 61801

PINIZZOTTO, RUSSELL FELIX, materials scientist; b. Vineland, N.J., Dec. 13, 1950; s. Russell Felix and Rosalie Marie (Scache) P.; m. Dana Whitney Smith, Sept. 9, 1972; children—Wendy Matia, John Russell. B.S., Calif. Inst. Tech., 1972; Engr., UCLA, 1977, Ph.D., 1978. Registered profl. engr., Tex. Engr. Structural Composites Industries, Inc., Azusa, Calif., 1972-73; research assoc. IBM, Yorktown Heights, N.Y., 1978; sr. mem. tech. staff Tex. Instruments, Dallas, 1978-84; pres. Ultrastructure, Inc., 1984—. Contbr. articles to profl. jours., chpts. to books. Patentee in field. Percussionist Richardson Community Band, Tex., 1980-83, Plano Community Band, Tex., 1981—. Mem. Electronic Materials Com., N. Tex. Materials Characterization Soc. (v.p. 1984, pres. 1985), Electrochem. Soc., Am. Vacuum Soc., Materials Research Soc., Electron Microscopy Soc. Am., Am. Phys. Soc., Tex. Soc. Electron Microscopy, AAAS. Current work: All aspects of transmission electron microscopy, automation of TEM, quantification of TEM images via computer processing, new and unique TEM applications. Subspecialties: Materials; Microchip technology (materials science). Home: 1902 Clover Trail Richardson TX 75081 Office: Ultrastructure Inc 1850N Greenville Ave 140 Richardson TX 75081

PINKHAM, CLARKSON WILFRED, structural engineer; b. Los Angeles, Nov. 25, 1919; s. Walter Hampden and Dorothy (Burdorf) P.; m. Emmalu Hull, May 8, 1942; children—Nancy Pinkham Ballance, Timothy Hull, Anthony Hull. B.A.S., U. Calif.-Berkeley, 1943, B.S., 1947. Registered profl. engr. Ariz., Calif., Ga., Fla., Iowa, Ill., Ind., Wash., Wis., Tex. Structural designer S.B. Barnes and Assocs., Los Angeles, 1947-54, assoc., 1954-68, pres., 1968—. Author: Natural Hazards Evaluation of Existing Buildings, 1975; A Methodology for Seismic Evaluation of Multi-story Residential Buildings, 1978. Served with USNR, 1941-46, PTO. Fellow Am. Concrete Inst. (bd. dirs. 1975-78), Inst. Advancement Engring., ASCE; mem. Structural Engrs. Assn. So. Calif. (bd. dirs. 1968-73, pres. 1970-71, hon. mem. 1984, S.B. Barnes award 1985), Structural Engrs. Assn. Calif. (bd. dirs. 1972-76, pres. 1974-75), ASTM (com. mem. 1976—, Am. Nat. Standards Inst. (com. mem. 1976-82), Am. Inst. Steel Constrn. (specification com. 1970—), Earthquake Engring. Research Inst. (com. mem. 1973—), Am. Welding Soc., (com. mem. 1976—), Internat. Assn. Bridge and Structural Engrs., Internat. Conf. Bldg. Ofcls., Nat. Inst. Bldg. Scis. (cons. council), Cons. Engrs. Assn. Calif., Am. Iron and Steel Inst. (adv. com. cold formed steel 1973—), Masonry Soc., Am. Nat. Metric Council, Ret. Officers Assn., Town Hall. Subspecialty: Structural engineering. Home: 3276 Granville Ave Los Angeles CA 90066 Office: SB Barnes and Assocs 2236 Beverly Blvd Los Angeles CA 90057

PINNAS, JACOB LOUIS, physician, allergist-immunologist; b. Newark, Jan. 31, 1940; m. Ellen Susan Reiff. M.D., M.S. in Pathology, U. Chgo., 1965. Resident Upstate Med. Center, Syracuse, N.Y., 1965-66, 68-70; med. epidemiologist Center Disease Control, Atlanta, 1966-68; research and clin. fellow in allergy and immunology Scripps Clinic and Research Found., La Jolla, Calif., 1970-73; assoc. prof. internal medicine, attending staff U. Ariz., 1973—; attending staff, dir. allergy service Univ. Hosp., 1973—, VA Hosp., Tucson, 1973—. Contbr. articles to profl. jours. Served with USPHS, 1966-68. Robert Wood Johnson Found. scholar, 1961-65. Fellow Am. Acad. Allergy, ACP; mem. Am. Assn. Immunologists, Western Soc. Allergy and Immunology (pres. 1984). Current Work: Hypersentivity reactions, antiallergic drugs, asthma. Subspecialties: Internal medicine; Immunology (medicine). Office: 1501 N Campbell Tucson AZ 85724

PINNEY, FRANK BATCHELDER, jet engine company executive; b. Montpelier, Vt., May 12, 1933; s. Perry Batchelder and Eva Jane (Littlefield) P.; m. Alice Marie Garrity, Nov. 26, 1960; children: Joyce Marie, Anne Marie, Thomas Batchelder. B.S.M.E., U. N.H., 1955; M. Engring. Sci. in Mettal. Engring, Renssaeler Poly. U., 1973. Engr. Bethlehem Steel, Sparrows Point, Md., 1955-56, Quincy, Mass., 1958-63, Hamilton Standard, Windsor Locks, Conn., 1963-64; with Pratt & Whitney Aircraft, East Hartford, Conn., 1968—, supr., 1973-81, gen. supr. exptl. process planning, 1981-83, mgr. tool engring. and devel., 1983—. Bd. dirs. Metacomet Homes, Inc., East Granby, Conn., 1973—, pres., 1983—; pres. Parish Council, St. Bernard's Ch., Tariffville, Conn., 1975-78, East Granby (Conn.) Soccer Club, 1978-81. Served with U.S. Army, 1956-58. Mem. ASME, Hartford Engrs. Club. Republican. Patentee, inventor fiber reinforced composites, 1968-70. Current Work: Mgmt. activities in computer-aided mfg. and computer process planning, particularly related to computer graphics. Subspecialties: Materials processing; Computer-aided manufacturing. Home: 59 Wynding Hills Rd East Granby CT 06026

PINTSOV, LEON ARON, computer scientist, researcher; b. Leningrad, USSR, Aug. 5, 1948; came to U.S., 1980, naturalized, 1985; s. Aron Moses and Maya (Ronkin) P.; m. Emiliya Gurevich, May 30, 1969; 1 child, Anna. M.S. in Math. magna cum laude, Leningrad State U., 1970; Ph.D. in Applied Math., Inst. Telecommunication Engring., Leningrad, 1978. Research engr. Inst. TV Equipment, Leningrad, 1970-78, cons. engr., 1978-79; sr. engr. Scan Optics Inc., East Hartford, Conn., 1981-82, project mgr., 1982-83; sr. engr. Pitney Bowes, Danbury, Conn., 1983-85, mgr. systems and software, 1985—; adj. prof. U. Hartford, West Hartford, Conn., 1982-83. Co-author: Sensors in Television Systems, 1978; also articles, 1973-83. Patentee in field. Mem. IEEE (sr.), Pattern Recognition Soc. Current work: Optical character recognition; image processing; robotics and artificial intelligence. Subspecialties: Graphics, image processing, and pattern recognition; Telecommunications. Home: 365 Mountain Rd West Hartford CT 06107 Office: Pitney Bowes 37 Commerce Park Danbury CT 06107

PIORE, EMANUEL RUBEN, physicist; b. Wilno, Russia, July 19, 1908; came to U.S., 1917, naturalized, 1924; s. Ruben and Olga (Gegusin) P.; m. E. Nora Kahn, Aug. 26, 1931; children—Michael Joseph, Margot Deborah, Jane Ann. A.B., U. Wis., 1930, Ph.D., 1935, D.Sc. (hon.), 1966; D.Sc. (hon.), Union U., 1962. Asst. instr. U. Wis., 1930-35; research physicist RCA, 1935-38; engr. in charge TV lab. CBS, 1938-42; head spl. weapons group, bur. ships U.S. Navy, 1942-44; head electronics br. Office Naval Research, 1946-47, dir. phys. sci., 1947-48, dep. for natural sci., 1949-51, chief sci., 1951-55; v.p., dir. Avco Mfg. Corp., 1955-56; dir. research IBM Corp., 1956-61, v.p. research and engring., 1961-63, v.p., group exec., 1963-65, v.p., chief scientist, 1965—; also dir.; physicist research lab. electronics Mass. Inst. Tech., 1948-49; Dir. Sci. Research Assos., Inc., Health Advancement, Inc., Paul Revere Investors, Guardian Mut. Fund. Mem. Pres.'s Sci. Adv. Com., 1959-62; mem. Nat. Sci. Bd., 1961—; bd. dirs. N.Y. State Found. for Sci.; past bd. dirs. NSF; chmn. vis. com. Nat. Bur. Standards; chmn. bd. Hall of Science, N.Y.C.; mem. corp. Woods Hole Oceanographic Instn.; mem. exec. com. Resources for Future; bd. dirs. Stark Draper Lab., Nat. Info. Bur.; mem. vis. com. to elec. engring. dept. Mass. Inst. Tech., 1956-57; vis. com. Harvard Coll., 1958-70; trustee Sloan-Kettering Inst. Cancer Research; mem. N.Y.C. Bd. Higher Edn., 1976—. Served to lt. comdr. USNR, 1944-46. Recipient Indsl. Research Inst. award, 1967; Distinguished Civilian medal Dept. Navy; Kaplun award Hebrew U., 1975. Fellow AAAS, Royal Soc. Arts (London, Eng.), Am. Phys. Soc., IEEE, Am. Acad. Arts Scis.; mem. Sci. Research Soc. Am., Sci. Research Assn. (dir.), Nat. Acad. Sci., Nat. Acad. Engring., Am. Inst. Physics (dir.), Am. Philos. Soc., Sigma Xi. Clubs: University (N.Y.C.); Cosmos (Washington). Subspecialties: Atomic and molecular physics; Superconductors. Home: 115 Central Park W New York City NY 10023 Office: Armonk NY 10504

PIPES, ROBERT BYRON, university administrator, mechanical and aerospace engineer, educator, consultant; b. Shreveport, La., Aug. 14, 1941; s. Walter H. and Mattye Mae (Wilson) P.; m. Ruth Ellen, June 27, 1964; children: Christopher Franz, Mark Robert. B.S., La. Poly. Inst., 1964, M.S., 1965; M.S.E., Princeton U., 1969; Ph.D., U. Tex., 1972. Sr. structures engr. Gen. Dynamics Corp., Ft. Worth, 1969-72; asst. prof. mech. engring. Drexel U., 1972-74; assoc. prof. mech. and aerospace engring. U. Del., 1974-80, prof., 1980-85, dean Coll. Engring., 1985—, dir. Ctr. Composites Mfg. Sci. and Engring., 1985—; cons. in field; mem. nat. materials adv. bd. NRC. Author: Experimental Mechanics of Fiber-Reinforced Composite Materials, 1982; contbr. numerous articles to profl. jours. Active Boy Scouts Am. Mem. ASME (Gustus Larson award 1983), Soc. Exptl. Stress Analysis, ASTM, Tau Beta Pi, Pi Tau Sigma, Omicron Delta Kappa. Methodist. Current Work: Composite materials. Subspecialty: Composite materials. Home: 100 Mason Dr Newark DE 19711 Office: Office of Dean Univ Del Newark DE 19716

PIROFSKY, BERNARD, physican, educator; b. N.Y.C., Mar. 27, 1926; s. Hyman and Yetta (Herman) P.; m. Elaine Friedwald, June 19, 1953; children: Daniel Niles, Tandy Ellen, Jillann Yetta. A.B., NYU, 1946, M.D., 1950. Intern, Bellevue Hosp., N.Y.C., 1950-51, resident medicine, 1951-52, 54-55; research fellow U. Oreg., 1955-56; dir. Pacific N.W. Regional Blood Center, 1956-58; instr. medicine U. Oreg., 1956-59, asst. prof., 1959-63, asso. prof., 1963-66, prof., 1966—, prof. microbiology, 1973—, head div. immunology, allergy and rheumatology, 1965-85, dean research, 1985—; cons. immunohematologist Portland VA Hosp., Pacific N.W. Regional Blood Center; mem. med. adv. bd. Leukemia Soc., 1965-69; vis. prof. Nat. Inst. Nutrition, Mexico, 1966-67, Med. Research Council, South Africa, 1977; vis. scientist Nat. Acad. Sci., RERF, Japan, 1978-79. Author: Autoimmunization and the Autoimmune Hemolytic Anemias, 1969, Blood Banking Principles, 1973; contbr. articles to profl. jours. Served as capt. USAF, 1952-54. Commonwealth Fund fellow, 1966-67; recipient Gov.'s N.W. Sci. award, 1968; Emily Cooley award Am. Assn. Blood Banks, 1972. Fellow ACP; mem. Internat. Soc. Hematology, Internat. Soc. Blood Transfusions, Am. Soc. Hematology, Mexican Soc. Hematology (hon. mem.), Transplantation Soc., Am. Assn. Immunologists. Research on immunology and hematology. Subspecialties: Immunology (medicine); Hematology. Home: 10370 SW Ridgeview Ln Portland OR 97219

PIRTLE, EUGENE CLAUDE, microbiologist; b. Wichita Falls, Tex., Nov. 17, 1921; s. Claude Howell and Jettie Alma P.; m. Julianne Pirtle, Nov. 29, 1944; children: Edith, Victor, Margaret, David, James. B.S., U. Colo., 1948; M.S., U. Iowa, 1950, Ph.D., 1952. Asst. prof. microbiology U. S.D., 1952-56, assoc. prof., 1956-60; dir. Virus Lab. Dept. Health, State of Hawaii, 1960-61; microbiologist Agrl. Research Service, Nat. Animal Disease Ctr., Ames, Iowa, 1961—. Contbr. numerous articles to profl. jours. Served with U.S. Army, 1942-44. Recipient Cert. of Appreciation U.S. Dept. Agr., 1978. Mem. Tissue Culture Assn., Sigma Xi, Phi Zeta. Current Work: Pathogenesis of viral diseases; DNA fingerprinting. Subspecialties: Microbiology (medicine); Animal virology. Office: PO Box 70 Ames IA 50010

PISTER, KARL STARK, university dean; b. Stockton, Calif., June 27, 1925; s. Edwin LeRoy and Mary Kimball (Smith) P.; m. Rita Olsen, Nov. 18, 1950; children: Francis, Therese, Anita, Jacinta, Claire, Kristofer. B.S. with honors, U. Calif., Berkeley, 1945, M.S., 1948; Ph.D., U. Ill., Urbana, 1952. Instr. theoretical and applied mechanics U. Ill., 1949-52; mem. faculty U. Calif., Berkeley, 1952—, prof. engring. scis., 1962-85, Roy W. Carlson prof. engring., 1985—, dean Coll. Engring., 1981—; Richard Merton guest prof. U. Stuttgart, W. Ger., 1978; cons. to govt. and industry. Author research papers in field; assoc. editor: Computer Methods in Applied Mechanics and Engring, 1972, Jour. Optimization Theory and Applications, 1982; editorial bd.: Res Mechanica, 1978. Served with USNR, World War II. Recipient Wason Research medal Am. Concrete Inst., 1960; Fulbright scholar Ireland, 1965; Fulbright scholar W. Ger., 1973. Fellow Am. Acad. Mechanics; mem. Nat. Acad. Engring., ASCE, ASME, Earthquake Engring. Research Inst., Soc. Engring. Sci. Current Work: Mechanics of solids and structures, particularly finite deformation problems with inelastic material behavior; constitutive modeling of inelastic materials. Computer-aided design of structures, with emphasis on optimization-based design of dynamically loaded structures and applications to earthquake resistant design. Subspecialties: Computer-aided design; Theoretical and applied mechanics. Home: 828 Solana Dr Lafayette CA 94549 Office: Coll Engring Univ Calif Berkeley CA 94720

PISTOLE, THOMAS GORDON, microbiology educator; b. Detroit, Sept. 17, 1942; s. Leotis Merton Pistole and Lillian Nell (Bosley) Besser; m. Donna Dulcie Straw, Sept. 11, 1965; children—James Alexander, Jennifer Katharine. Ph.B., Wayne State U., Detroit, 1964, M.S. in Biology, 1966; Ph.D. in Microbiology, U. Utah, 1969. Postdoctoral fellow U.S. Army, Frederick, Md., 1969-70; research assoc. U. Minn., Mpls., 1970-71; asst. prof. microbiology U. N.H., Durham, 1971-77, assoc. prof., 1977-83, prof., chmn. dept. microbiology, 1983—; vis. scientist Weizmann Inst. Sci., Rehovot, Israel, 1979. Co-editor: Biomedical Applications of the Horseshoe Crab, 1979. NRC fellow, 1969; grantee NIH, 1975, NSF, 1981. Mem. Am. Soc. Microbiology, Am. Assn. Immunologists, AAAS, Internat. Soc. Devel. and Comparative Immunology, Sigma Xi (sec. local chpt. 1974-76) Unitarian/Universalist. Current work: Defense mechanisms in marine invertebrates, biological activity of lectins from invertebrates, mechanisms of pathogen recognition by host defense cells, microbial adherence and pathogenesis. Subspecialties: Microbiology; Immunobiology and immunology. Office: U NH Dept Microbiology Spaulding Life Sci Bldg Durham NH 03824

PITCHER, GEORGIA ANN, psychology educator, psychologist; b. Indpls., Feb. 22, 1927; d. Arling Edgar and Lyda Lucille (Doty) P.; m. Donald Aubrey Baker, Aug. 21, 1948 (div. Apr. 1968); children: Catherine Lucille Baker Black, Martha Ann Baker, Susan Jane Baker Oakley, Daniel Pitcher Baker. B.S., Butler U., 1948, M.S., 1951; Ph.D., Purdue U., 1969. Lic. Psychologist, Nat. Register of Health Service Providers in Psychology. Asst. prof. Butler U., 1964-68; asst. prof. Purdue U.-West Lafayette, Ind., 1969-74; dir. psychol. services St. Elizabeth Hosp., Lafayette, Ind., 1974-81; instr. Butler U., 1981-83; pvt. practice psychology, Indpls., 1980—; assoc. faculty Ind. U.-Purdue U. at Indpls., 1985—; psychologist Cary Home Diagnostic Center, Lafayette, Ind., 1980-81; cons. Lafayette Head Start, 1976-81; cons. psychologist Comprehensive Devel. Centers, Monticello, Ind., 1975-76; evaluator Pre-Sch. Project Title III, Mishawaka, Ind., 1971-72. Contbr. articles to profl. jours. Mem. Nat. Govtl. Activities Com., United Cerebral Palsy Assns. Inc., N.Y.C., 1976-77; v.p. United Cerebral Palsy Ind., Indpls., 1976—; mem. Protective Services Task Force Com., State of Ind., 1976-77. Mem. Am. Psychol. Assn., Am. Ednl. Research Assn., Nat. Acad. Neuropsychology, Com. for Found. of Internat. Orgn. Psychophysiology. Democrat. Current Work: Development and traumatic causes of learning disorders, particularly brain behavior relationships; cognitive and affective Subspecialties: Developmental psychology; Neuropsychology. Home: 3725 E Thompson Rd Indianapolis IN 46237

PITCHER, WAYNE HAROLD, JR., enzyme manufacturing company executive; b. St. Louis, Jan. 5, 1944; s. Wayne Harold and Ethel Pauline (Gehrke) P.; m. Julia Frances Liberace, Aug. 22, 1970; children—Wayne Harold III, Maria Beatrice. B.S., Calif. Inst. Tech., 1966; S.M., MIT, 1968, Sc.D., 1972. Sr. chem. engr. Corning Glass Works, N.Y., 1972-74, sr. research chem. engr., 1974-76, engring. supr., 1976-81, mgr. biotech. portfolio, 1981-83; v.p. devel. Genencor, South San Francisco, Calif., 1983—. Editor: Immobilized Enzymes for Food Processing, 1980. Contbr. chpts. to books, articles to profl. jours. Patentee in field. Mem. Am. Inst. Chem. Engrs., Am. Chem. Soc., AAAS, N.Y. Acad. Sci., Sigma Xi. Subspecialty: Biotechnology research and development. Office: Genencor 180 Kimball Way South San Francisco CA 94080

PITCHUMONI, CAPECOMORIN S., medical educator, gastroenterologist; b. Madura, India, Jan. 20, 1938; came to U.S., 1967; s. Sankar Harihar and Jaya Lekshmi P.; m. Prema Iyer, Nov. 11, 1964; children: Sheila, Shoba, Suresh. M.B.B.S., Med. Coll., Trivandrum, Kerala, India, 1960, M.D., 1965. Intern Med. Coll. Hosp., Trivandrum, Kerala, India, 1960-61; resident Norwalk (Conn.) Hosp., 1967-68; asst. prof. N.Y. Med. Coll., Valhalla, 1972-75, assoc. prof., 1975-80, prof. clin. medicine, 1980—; dir. div. gastroenterology Misericordia Hosp. Med. Ctr., Bronx, N.Y., 1980—, prof. medicine, 1983—, acting dir. medicine, 1983-85, assoc. dir., 1984—. Co-author: Progress in Gastroenterology, Vol. III, 1978, Hand Book of Infectious Diseases, 1982; Pancreas Biology and Pathobiology, 1984; Clinics in Gastroenterology, 1984; Pancreatitis Concepts and Classification, 1984. Trustee Hindu Temple N. Am., 1978. Recipient Hechst Omprakash award Indian Soc. Gastroenterology, 1976.

Fellow Royal Coll. Physicians and Surgeons Can., ACP, Am. Coll. Gastroenterology; mem. Am. Gastroenterological Assn. Current Work: Pancreatic calculi intestinal gas. Subspecialties: Gastroenterology; Nutrition (medicine). Home: 178 Fairmount Ave Glenrock NJ 07452 Office: Misericordia Hosp Med Ctr 600 E 233d St Bronx NY 10466

PITELKA, LOUIS FRANK, biology educator, researcher, administrator; b. Berkeley, Calif., Mar. 28, 1947; s. Frank Alois and Dorothy Gretchen (Riggs) P.; m. Sandra Lea Sanders, Sept. 20, 1969; children: Erik Loren, Jessica Kristine. Researcher, adminstr. B.S., U. Calif.-Davis, 1969; Ph.D. in Biol. Scis., Stanford U., 1974. Asst. prof. biology Bates Coll., Lewiston, Maine, 1974-81, assoc. prof., 1981-84, chmn. biology dept., 1982-84, program dir. population biology and physiol. ecology; program NSF, Washington, 1983-84; project mgr. Electric Power Research Inst., Palo Alto, Calif., 1984—. Contbr. articles on biol. scis. to profl. jours. NSF grantee, 1980-82, 1982-84; Research Corp. grantee, 1979-81. Mem. Ecol. Soc. Am., Bot. Soc. Am. (chmn. ecol. sect. 1982-83), Am. Inst. Biol. Scis., Internat. Soc. Plant Population Biologists, Torrey Bot. Club, AAAS. Current Work: Plant ecology, ecology and population biology of clonal plants, responses of plants to environmental pollutants, forest ecology. Subspecialties: Ecology (environmental science); Population biology. Home: 838 Richardson Ct Palo Alto CA 94303 Office: Electric Power Research Inst PO Box 10412 Palo Alto CA 94303

PITOT, HENRY CLEMENT, physician, educator; b. N.Y.C., May 12, 1930; s. Henry Clement and Bertha (Lowe) P.; m. Julie S. Schutten, July 29, 1954; children: Bertha, Anita, Jeanne, Catherine, Henry, Michelle, Lisa, Patrice. B.S. in Chemistry, Va. Mil. Inst., 1951; M.D., Tulane U., 1955, Ph.D. in Biochemistry, 1959. Instr. pathology Tulane U. Med. Sch., 1955-59; postdoctoral fellow McArdle Lab., U. Wis.-Madison, 1959-60; mem. faculty U. Wis. Med. Sch.-Madison, 1960—, prof. pathology and oncology, 1966—, chmn. dept. pathology, 1968-71; acting dean Sch. Medicine, 1971-73; dir. McArdle Lab., 1973—. Mem. Nat. Cancer Adv. Bd., 1976-82, chmn., 1979-82. Recipient Borden undergrad. research award, 1955; Lederle Faculty award, 1962; Career Devel. award, 1965; Parke-Davis award in exptl. pathology, 1968 Noble Found. Research Recognition award, 1983, 1983; Langer award in cancer research U. Chgo., 1984. Fellow N.Y. Acad. Scis.; mem. AAAS, Am. Soc. Cell. Biology, Am. Assn. Cancer Research, Am. Soc. Biol. Chemists, Am. Chem. Soc., Am. Assn. Pathologists (pres. 1976-77), Soc. Exptl. Biology and Medicine, Soc. Developmental Biology, Soc. Surg. Oncology (Lucy J. Wortham award 1981), Am. Soc. Preventive Oncology. Roman Catholic. Subspecialties: Oncology; Pathology (medicine). Home: 1812 Van Hise Ave Madison WI 53705

PITT, BERTRAM, cardiologist; b. Kew Gardens, N.Y., Apr. 27, 1932; s. David and Shirley (Blum) P.; m. Elaine Liberstein, Aug. 10, 1962; children: Geoffrey S., Jessica M., Jillian A. B.A., Cornell U., 1953; M.D., U. Basel, Switzerland, 1959. Diplomate: Am. Bd. Internal Medicine. Intern Beth Israel Hosp., N.Y.C., 1959-60, resident in medicine, Boston, 1960-63; fellow in cardiology Johns Hopkins Hosp., 1966-67; instr. to prof. medicine Johns Hopkins U., 1967-77; prof. medicine, dir. div. cardiology U. Mich., 1977—; pres. Cardiovascular Research Cons., Inc. Served to capt. U.S. Army, 1963-65. Mem. Am. Physiol. Soc., Am. Heart Assn., Am. Soc. Clin. Investigation, Am. Assn. Physicians, ACP, Am. Coll. Cardiology. Jewish. Current Work: Therapeutic approaches to heart failure, nuclear cardiology; central nervous system control of coronary circulation; myocardial infarction and ischemia; reperfusion in acute myocardial infarction; role of prostaglandins in ischemic heart disease. Subspecialty: Cardiology. Home: 24 E Ridgeway Ann Arbor MI 48104 Office: University Hospital Ann Arbor MI 48109

PITTS, DAVID EUGENE, meteorologist, researcher; b. Oklahoma City, July 29, 1939; s. Sidney Albert and Alma Imogene (Ross) P.; m. Paula Ann Plosila, Sept. 10, 1963; children—Donald Andrew, Susan Elizabeth. B.S. U. Okla., 1961, M.S., 1964, D.Engring., 1971. Registered profl. engr., Tex. Aerospace technologist NASA Johnson Space Ctr., Houston, 1963—; prin. Pitts Engring., Houston, 1981—. Author: Home Energy Applications, 1983; author various symposia presentations and tech. reports. Contbr. articles to profl. jours. Patentee in field. Asst. scoutmaster Sam Houston Area council Boy Scouts Am., 1976-82. Recipient Lyndon B. Johnson Space Ctr. cert. of commendation, 1984. Mem. Am. Meteorol. Soc., AAAS, IEEE, Soc. Exploration Geophysicists, Am. Soc. Photogrammetry, Pi Tau Pi, Chi Epsilon Pi, Sigma Tau. Methodist. Current Work: Remote sensing of atmospheric and vegetation biophysical properties using optical and microwave sensors aboard aircraft and spacecraft. Subspecialties: Remote sensing (atmospheric science); Meteorology. Home: 16011 Stonehaven Dr Houston TX 77059 Office: NASA Johnson Space Ctr SN3 Houston TX 77059

PITTS, GROVER CLEVELAND, physiology educator, researcher; b. Richmond, Va., Apr. 4, 1918; s. Grover Cleveland and Ruby Louise (Richardson) P.; m. Cora Minta Ledbetter, Apr. 5, 1947; children—Geoffrey R., John F., James C. B.A., U. Richmond, 1939; A.M., Harvard U., 1940, Ph.D., 1943. Tutor biochem. scis. Harvard Coll., Cambridge, Mass., 1942-44; research asst. Harvard Fatigue Lab., Cambridge, 1942-44; physiologist Naval Med. Research Inst., Bethesda, Md., 1944-50; from asst. prof. to assoc. prof. physiology U. Va. Sch. Medicine, Charlottesville, 1950-79, prof., 1979—; co-investigator Soviet Cosmos 1129 Mission, Moscow, 1979-80; investigator U. Wis. expedition to S.Am., 1959, Biosatellite Project, 1965-70. Served to lt. (s.g.) USNR, 1944-47. Recipient Laudatory Cert., Inst. Biomed. Problems, Moscow, 1979; Cosmos Achievement award, 1981. Fellow AAAS; mem. Am. Phys. Soc., AAUP, Internat. Union Physiol. Scis., Va. Acad. Sci. Clubs: Colonnade (bd. govs. 1977-79), Greencroft (Charlottesville). Current work: Physiological regulation of body composition, body composition response to gravity, exercise, obesity, growth. Subspecialties: Physiology (medicine); Gravitational biology. Home: 110 Woodstock Dr Charlottesville VA 22901 Office: U Va Dept Physiology Sch Medicine Charlottesville VA 22908

PITTS, NATHANIEL GILBERT, neurophysiologist; b. Macon, Ga., Apr. 2, 1947; s. Raymond J. and Kathleen Lenora (Cook) P. B.A., Whittier Coll., 1969; Ph.D., U. Calif., Davis, 1974. Sci. fellow Rockefeller U., 1974-77; asst. program dir. in neurobiology NSF, Washington, 1977-79, assoc. program dir. in neurobiology, 1979-83, program dir. in integrative neural systems, 1983—. Contbr.: numerous articles to Exptl. Brain Research. Recipient Sustained Superior Performance award NSF, 1979; Porter Devel. Found. fellow, 1972-74; NIH postdoctoral fellow, 1975-77. Mem. AAAS, Soc. Neurosci. Soc., European Neurosci. Soc., N.Y. Acad. Scis., Internat. Brain Research Orgn. Current Work: Neurophysiology of motor and sensory systems. Subspecialties: Neurophysiology; Neurobiology. Office: 1800 G St NW Washington DC 20550

PITZER, KENNETH S., chemist, educator; b. Pomona, Calif., Jan. 6, 1914; s. Russell K. and Flora (Sanborn) P.; m. Jean Mosher, July 1935; children—Ann, Russell, John. B.S., Calif. Inst. Tech., 1935; Ph.D., U. Calif., 1937; D.Sc., Wesleyan U., 1962; LL.D., U. Calif. at Berkeley, 1963, Mills Coll., 1969. Instr. chemistry U. Calif., 1937-39, asst. prof., 1939-42, assoc. prof., 1942-45, prof., 1945-61, asst. dean letters and sci., 1947-48, dean coll. chemistry, 1951-60; pres., prof. chemistry Rice U., Houston, 1961-68, Stanford, Calif., 1968-70; prof. chemistry U. Calif. at Berkeley, 1971—; tech. dir. Md. Research Lab. for OSRD, 1943-44; dir. research U.S. AEC, 1949-51, mem. gen. adv. com., 1958-65, chmn., 1960-62; Centenary lectr. Chem. Soc. Gt. Britain, 1978; mem. adv. bd. U.S. Naval Ordnance Test Sta., 1956-59, chmn., 1958-59; mem. commn. chem. thermo-dynamics Internat. Union Pure and Applied Chemistry, 1953-61; dir. Owens-Ill., Inc.; mem. Pres.'s Sci. Adv. Com., 1965-68. Author: (with others) Selected Values of Properties of Hydrocarbons, 1947, Quantum Chemistry, 1953, (with L. Brewer) Thermodynamics, rev, 1961; Editor: Prentice-Hall Chemistry series, 1955-61; Contbr. articles to profl. jours. Trustee Pitzer Coll., 1966—; Mem. program com. for phys. scis. Sloan Found., 1955-60. Recipient Robert A. Welch award, 1984. Guggenheim fellow, 1951; Precision Sci. Co. award in petroleum chemistry, 1950; 1 of 10 Outstanding Young Men U.S. Jr. C. of C., 1950; Clayton prize Instn. Mech. Engrs., London, 1958; Priestley Memorial award Dickinson Coll., 1963; Priestley medal Am. Chem. Soc., 1969; Nat. medal for sci., 1975. Fellow Am. Nuclear Soc., Am. Inst. Chemists (Gold medal award 1976), Am. Acad. Arts and Scis., Am. Phys. Soc.; mem. Am. Chem. Soc. (award pure chemistry 1943, Gilbert N. Lewis medal 1965, Williard Gibbs medal 1976), Faraday Soc., AAAS, Nat. Acad. Scis. (councilor 1964-67, 73-76), Am. Philos. Soc., Chem. Soc. (London), Am. Council Edn. Clubs: Chemists (hon.), Bohemian; Cosmos (Washington). Subspecialties: Physical chemistry; Theoretical chemistry. Office: Dept Chemistry U Calif Berkeley CA 94720

PIVIK, RUDOLPH TERRY, psychologist, educator, researcher; b. Rock Springs, Wyo., Jan. 11, 1943; emigrated to Can., 1975; s. Rudolph Lewis and Flossie Mae (Sturgeon) P.; m. Margaret McGarvey, Sept. 8, 1962; children: Jane, Lisa, Suzanne, Christopher. Student, So. Methodist U., 1961-62, Western Wyo. Jr. Coll., 1962; B.A., U. Wyo., 1965, M.A. in Exptl. Psychology, 1966; Ph.D. in Physiol. Psychology, Stanford U., 1970. Biosci. trainee Stanford U., 1966-70; NIMH research fellow in psychiatry Harvard U. Med. Sch., 1970-72; asst. prof., research assoc. depts. psychiatry and psychology U. Chgo., 1972-75; asst. prof. psychiatry U. Ottawa, Ont., Can., 1975-79, asst. prof. psychology, 1976-79, assoc. prof. psychiatry and psychology, 1979-84, prof. psychiatry, psychology and physiology, 1984—; research assoc. psychology Carleton U., Ottawa, 1978—; dir. Clin. Psychophysiology Lab., Ottawa Gen. Hosp., 1975—. Contbr. chpts., articles, numerous abstracts to profl. publs.; mem. editorial bd.: Psychiat. Jour, U. Ottawa, 1976—. Ont. mental health research scholar, 1977-82; Ont Mental health research assoc., 1982-86; U. Ottawa Rector's Fund grantee, 1976-78; Med. Research Council Can. grantee, 1977-81; Sunnybrook Med. Centre and Sunnybrook Hosp.-U. Toronto Centre Funds grantee, 1977-78; Physicians' Services Incorporate Found. grantee, 1978-79; U. Ottawa Faculty Social Sci. grantee, 1979, 81-83; Ont. Mental Health Found. grantee, 1981-82, 83-85; U. Ottawa Dean's Funds grantee, 1981-82; Hosp. for Sick Children Found. grantee, 1982-84, 84-86. Fellow Internat. Orgn. Psychophysiology; mem. Sleep Research Soc., Soc. Neurosci., Ottawa Neuroscis Soc. (treas. 1981-82, co-organizer ann. symposium for 1982), Can. Psychiat. Assn., Cans. for Health Research, Can. Coll. Neuropsychopharmacology (interim sec. 1979-80), Group-Without-A-Name Internat. Psychiat. Research Soc., Can. Psychol. Assn., Phi Beta Kappa, Sigma Xi. Democrat. Roman Catholic. Current Work: Biological psychiatry; psychophysiology and neurophysiology of sleep; neurophysiology and psychophysiology of mental illness and sleep. Subspecialties: Psychophysiology; Neurophysiology. Office: Ottawa Gen Hosp 501 Smyth Rd Ottawa ON K1H 8L6 Canada

PIZZO, SALVATORE VINCENT, pathology researcher, physician; b. Phila., June 22, 1944; s. George J. and Aida R. (Alcaro) P. B.S., St. Joseph's Coll., 1966; Ph.D., Duke U., 1972, M.D., 1973. Diplomate: Am. Bd. Pathology. Asst. prof. Duke U., Durham, N.C., 1976-80, assoc. prof. dept. pathology and biochemistry, 1980-85, prof., 1985—; intern Duke U. Med. Ctr., 1973-74, resident, 1974-76; cons. Huntleigh Group, London, 1980—, Kaki Co., Stockholm, 1981—, Mitsubishi Co., Tokyo, 1981—, Dade Corp., Miami, 1980—, Burroughs Wellcome Research Park, N.C., Wellcome Biotech. Ltd., Kent, Eng., 1984—. Contbr. articles to profl. jours. NIH med. scientist tng. program fellow, 1966-73; named Best Basic Sci. Tchr. Duke Med. Sch., 1980. Mem. Am. Chem. Soc., AAAS, Am. Heart Assn., Am. Assn. Pathologists, Am. Soc. Biol. Chemists, Am. Soc. Coagulationists, Sigma Xi, Alpha Sigma Nu, Phi Beta Kappa, Alpha Omega Alpha. Current Work: Study of blood coagulation and clinical diseases, host tumor interactions, regulation of proteases. Subspecialties: Biochemistry (medicine); Pathology (medicine). Office: Duke U Med Center Box 3712 Durham NC 27710

PLAKOSH, PAUL, JR., psychologist, clinic administrator, researcher; b. Pitts., May 17, 1949; s. Paul and Leonora (Durso) P. Student, Case Western Res. U., 1967-70; B.S. summa cum laude, U. Pitts., 1973; M.A., U. Iowa, 1976; Ph.D., Palo Alto Sch. Profl. Psychology, 1979. Research psychologist U. Calif.-SanFrancisco Med. Ctr.-Langley Porter Inst., 1978-81; exec. dir. Franklin Clinic, San Francisco, 1980—. Contbr. articles to profl. jours. Mem. Internat. Neuropsychol. Soc., Am. Psychol. Assn., AAAS. Subspecialties: Behavioral psychology; Neuropsychology. Home: 291 Broderick St San Francisco CA 94117 Office: Franklin Clinic 2509 Bush St San Francisco CA 94115

PLATSOUCAS, CHRIS DIMITRIOS, immunology educator and researcher; b. Athens, Greece, Apr. 17, 1951; came to U.S., 1973; s. Dimitrios and Maria (Tsonidis) P. B.S., U. Patras, Greece, 1973; postgrad., Purdue U., 1974-75; Ph.D., MIT, 1978. Research asst. MIT, 1975-78; research fellow Meml. Sloan-Kettering Cancer Ctr., N.Y.C., 1978-79, research assoc., 1979-80, asst. mem., 1980-85, asst. prof., 1981-85, head lab. biol. response modifiers, 1981-85; assoc. prof., assoc. immunologist M.D. Anderson Hosp. and Tumor Inst., Houston, 1985—; spl. rev. study sect. NIH, Bethesda, Md., 1982. Contbr. articles to profl. jours. Nat. Research Service awardee NIH, 1978-79; Am. Cancer Soc. grantee, 1980—; NIH grantee, 1982—; NSF grantee, 1982—. Mem. Am. Assn. Immunologists, Am. Assn. Cancer Research, Am. Soc. Hematology, Biophys. Soc., N.Y. Acad. Scis., Sigma Xi. Current Work: Human immunology, cytotoxic T cells, monoclonal antibodies, lymphoproliferative disorders, T-T cell hybrids. Subspecialty: Immunobiology and immunology. Office: MD Anderson Hosp and Tumor Inst Dept Immunology HMB 178 6723 Bertner Ave Houston TX 77030

PLAUT, ANDREW GEORGE, physician, researcher; b. Leipzig, Ger., Feb. 19, 1937; s. Otto L. and Johanna (Lowenstein) P.; m. Linda Fields, June 23, 1965; children: Julie, John. B.S., Ohio State U., 1958; M.D., Tufts U., 1962. Diplomate: Am. Bd. Internal Medicine. Intern Bellevue Hosp. Cornell U. and Meml. Hosp. for Cancer, N.Y.C., 1962-63, resident, 1963-64, fellow, 1964-65; asst. prof. SUNY, Buffalo, 1968-73; physician, prof. medicine Tufts U.-New Eng. Med. Ctr. Hosp., 1973—; cons. NIH. Contbr. articles to profl. jours. Served to capt. U.S. Army, 1966-68. Mem. Am. Soc. Clin. Investigation, Am. Soc. Microbiology, Infectious Disease Soc. Am., Am. Gastroent. Assn., ACLU, Union Concerned Scientists. Current Work: Immunity of bacterial infection, subversion of immunity by bacteria, enzymology. Subspecialties: Infectious diseases; Gastroenterology. Office: 171 Harrison Ave Boston MA 02111

PLAVEC, MIREK JOSEF, astronomer; b. Sedlcany, Bohemia, Czechoslovakia, Oct. 7, 1925; came to U.S., 1970, naturalized, 1981; s. Antonin and Anezka (Beranova) P.; m. Zdenka Bazikova, Mar. 15, 1930; children: Helena Kirkpatrick, Jirka G. B.Sc., Charles U., Prague, 1949, Ph.D., 1955, D.Sc., 1968. Prin. sci. officer Astron. Inst. Ondrejov, Czechoslovak Acad. Scis., 1965-69; prof. astronomy UCLA, 1970—, chmn. dept., 1975-77. Author: Komety a Meteory, 1957, Clovek a Hvezdy, 1960, (with Popper and Ulrich) Close Binary Stars: Observations and Interpretation, 1980. Mem. Internat. Astron. Union (pres. commn. 42 1970-73), Am. Astron. Soc., Astron. Soc. Pacific. Current Work: Studies of interacting binary stars; their evolution, structure, spectra in ultraviolet and optical regions; observations and theoretical modeling. Subspecialties: Ultraviolet high energy astrophysics; Theoretical astrophysics. Home: 767 Jacon Way Pacific Palisades CA 90272 Office: UCLA 8907 MS Bldg Los Angeles CA 90024

PLONSEY, ROBERT, electrical and biomedical engineer, educator; b. N.Y.C., July 17, 1924; s. Louis B. and Betty (Vinograd) P.; m. Vivian V. Vucker, Oct. 1, 1948; 1 son, Daniel. B.E.E., Cooper Union, 1943; M.S. in Elec. Engring, NYU, 1948; Ph.D., U. Calif. at Berkeley, 1955; postgrad., Med. Sch., Case Western Res. U., 1969-71. Registered profl. engr., Ohio. Asst. prof. elec. engring. U. Calif. at Berkeley, 1955-57; asst. prof. elec. engring. Case Inst. Tech., Cleve., 1957-60, asso. prof., 1960-66, prof., 1966-68, dir. bioengring. group, 1962-68; prof. biomed. engring. Sch. Engring. and Sch. of Medicine, Case Western Res. U., 1968-83, chmn. dept., 1976-80; vis. prof. biomed. engring. Duke U., 1980-81, prof. biomed. engring., 1983—, prof. physiology, 1984—; mem. biomed. fellowships rev. com. NIH, 1966-70; mem. tng. com. Engr. in Medicine and Biology, 1972-73, cons., 1974—; cons. NSF, 1973; mem. com. on electrocardiography Am. Heart Assn., 1976-82; mem. bioengring. panel Engring. Research Bd., NRC, 1984-85. Author: (with R. Collin) Principles and Applications of Electromagnetic Fields, 1961, Bioelectric Phenomena, 1969; with J. Liebman and P. Gillette Pediatric Electrocardiography, 1982; with T. Pilkington Engineering Contributions to Biophysical Electrocardiography, 1982; Mem. editorial bd.: Trans. IEEE Biomed. Engring, 1965-70, asso. editor, 1977-79; editorial bd.: T.I.T. Jour, 1971-81, Electrocardiology Jour, 1974—; proc. editor: Engring. in Medicine and Biology, 17th Ann. Conf, 1964. Vice pres. Your Schs., Cleveland Heights, Ohio, 1968-69, 73-75; provisional trustee Am. Bd. Clin. Engrs., 1973-74, pres., 1975, trustee, 1976-84. Served with AUS, 1944-46. NIH sr. postdoctoral award, 1980-81. Fellow IEEE (chmn. Cleve. chpt. group on biomed. electronics 1962-63, chmn. publs. com. group on engring. in medicine and biology 1968-70, 83-85, v.p. adminstrv. com. 1970-72, pres. 1973-74, chmn. fellows com. 1977-79, mem. fellow com. 1983-85, William S. Morlock award 1979); mem. Alliance for Engring. in Medicine and Biology (treas. 1976-78), Biophys. Soc., Biomed. Engring. Soc. (dir. 1975-78, 79-83, pres. 1981-82), AAUP, Am. Physiol. Soc., Am. Soc. Engring. Edn. (dir. biomed. engring. div. 1978-83, chmn. 1982-83), AAAS. Current Work: Biomedical engineering educator; research on bioelectricity including cardiac electrophysiology and electrocardiography and mathematical modelling. Subspecialties: Biomedical engineering; Cardiac electrophysiology. Office: Dept Biomed Engring 276 Engineering Annex Duke U Durham NC 27706

PLOTSKY, PAUL MITCHELL, biomedical researcher and educator; b. Kansas City, Mo., Feb. 1, 1952; s. Herbert and Frances (Kern) P.; m. Andrea Gayle, Aug., 1971; children: Melissa Michelle, Alyson Rose. B.A., U. Kans., 1974; Ph.D., Emory U., 1980. Teaching fellow Brown U., Providence, 1980-82; research assoc. R.I. Hosp., Providence, 1980-82; asst. prof. Salk Inst., San Diego, 1982—; cons. biomed., instrument and pharm. mfrs. Editorial bd. Endocrinology. Contbr. articles to sci. jours. Mellon Found. grantee, 1982—. Mem. AAAS, Endocrine Soc., Soc. Neurosci. Current Work: Neural control of hypophysiotrophic factors regulating anterior pituitary gland hormone secretions. Subspecialties: Neuroendocrinology; Neurophysiology. Office: PO Box 85800 San Diego CA 92138

PLOTZ, PAUL HUNTER, physician, researcher, educator; b. N.Y.C, Oct. 19, 1937; s. Milton B. and Helen D. (Ratnoff) P.; m. Judith A. Plotz, Sept. 1, 1963; children: John, David. A.B., Harvard U., 1958, M.D., 1963. Intern and resident in medicine Beth Israel Hosp., Boston, 1963-65; clin. assoc. NIH, Bethesda, Md., 1965-68; Helen Hay Whitney Found./Nat. Inst. Med. Research fellow, London, 1968-70; sr. investigator arthritis and rheumatism br. Nat. Inst. Arthritis, Diabetes, Digestive and Kidney Diseases, NIH, Bethesda, 1970—, chief connective tissue diseases sect., 1984—; clin. prof. medicine U.S. Univ. Health Scis., Bethesda, 1980—. Recipient prize French Soc. Rheumatology, 1981; Philip Hench award, 1984. Mem. Am. Soc. Clin. Investigation, ACP, Am. Assn. Immunology, Arthritis and Rheumatism Assn. Subspecialties: Immunology (medicine); Internal medicine. Home: 3221 Livingston St NW Washington DC 20015 Office: 10/9N244 NIH Bethesd MD 20205

PLUNKETT, JOSEPH CHARLES, electrical engineering educator; b. Centerville, Tenn., Dec. 3, 1933; s. Harold and Lorraine (Lewis) P. B.S. Math. and Physics, Middle Tenn. State U., 1964; B.S.E.E., U. Tenn., 1966; M.S.E.E., Ga. Inst. Tech., 1973; Ph.D., Tex. A&M U., 1978. Registered profl. engr., Mass. Devel. engr. Martin-Marietta Corp., Orlando, Fla., 1966-69, Raytheon Co., Wayland, Mass., 1969-71; research engr. IIT Research Inst., Annapolis, Md., 1971-72; prof. Calif. State U., Fresno, 1977—, chmn. dept. elec. engring. 1980-84. Mem. editorial bd. Am. Acad. Higher Edn., 1984—. Contbr. articles to profl. jours. Fellow Internat. Biog. Inst.; mem. N.Y. Acad. Sci., IEEE, Sigma Xi, Eta Kappa Nu. Mem. Ch. of Christ. Current work: Research interests in integrated circuit and device processing; photovoltaic technology; microwave communications. Subspecialties: Computer engineering; Integrated circuits. Home: 83 W San Jose St Clovis CA 93612 Office: Calif State U Dept Elec Engring Cedar and Shaw Ave Fresno CA 93740

PLUNKETT, ROBERT, mech. engr., educator; b. N.Y.C., Mar. 15, 1919; s. Charles Robert and Helen Rebecca (Edwards) P.; m. Helen Catharine Bair, May 11, 1946; children—Christopher Robert, Brian Charles, Margaret Louise. B.C.E., Mass. Inst. Tech., 1939, Sc.D. in Mech. Engring, 1948; Docteur (hon.), U. Nantes, France, 1966. Research asst. in elec. engring. Mass. Inst. Tech., Cambridge, 1939-41, instr. mech. engring., 1941, asst. prof., 1946-48; asst. prof. mech. engring. Rice U., Houston, 1948-51; cons. engr. acoustics and mechanics Gen. Electric Co., Schenectady, 1951-60; prof. applied mechanics U. Minn., Mpls., 1960—; cons. engr. Hughes Tool Co., Hamilton Standard Co., Ford Co., USN, U.S. Army, USAF, Honeywell Corp., Control Data Corp., Worthington Corp., Westinghouse Co. Served to maj. C.E. AUS, 1942-46. Fulbright scholar Nantes, 1964; Fulbright scholar Technion, Israel, 1971. Fellow ASME, AAAS, Acoustical Soc. Am., Am. Inst. Aeros. and Astronautics (asso.); mem. Nat. Acad. Engring. Current Work: Viscoelastic behavior and damage in composite materials, wave propagation in solids, solid-fluid interaction. Subspecialties: Materials; Theoretical and applied mechanics. Home: 1920 1st St S #1401 Minneapolis MN 55454 Office: 107 Akerman Hall U Minn 110 Union St SE Minneapolis MN 55455

PLYMATE, STEPHEN REX, b. Omaha, Aug. 7, 1943; s. Oliver and Lenore Marie (Monahan) P.; m. Lisa Catherine Goldiamono, Dec. 2, 1978; children: Stephanie, Duncan, Sarah, Corinne. M.S., M.D., U. Nebr., 1968. Diplomate: Am. Bd. Internal Medicine, 1972. Commd. lt. col. U.S. Army, 1968; sr. fellow endocrinology Madigan Army Med. Ctr., Tacoma, 1971-73; chief endocrine clinic William Beaumont Army Med. Ctr., El Paso, Tex., 1973-75, Fitzsimons Army Med. Ctr., Denver, 1975-76; active staff Lovelace Bataan Med. Ctr., Albuquerque, 1976-78; asst. dir. endocrinology U. N. Mex., Albuquerque, 1976-78; chief clin. studies service Madigan Army Med. Ctr., Tacoma, 1978—; assoc. dir. endocrine fellowship program, clin. asst. prof. medicine U. Wash. Sch. Medicine, Seattle; asst. prof. medicine U. N. Mex., Albuquerque, 1973-77. Reviewer: Jour. AMA; contbr. numerous articles to sci. publs. Adv. Am. Youth Diabetes Assn., 1978, Blue Cross-Blue Shield Med. Adv. com. mem., 1976-77; Adv. Am. Heart Assn. grant review com., 1976-78, Albuquerque. Recipient U. Nebr. Dr. David Richardson Ob-Gyn Senior Student award, 1968. Mem. Endocrine Soc., Pacific Coast Fertility Soc., Am. Fertility Soc., ACP (assoc.), Am. Fedn. Clin. Research, Alpha Delta Omicron, Alpha Omega Alpha. Current Work: research in reproductive endocrinology; regulation of sex hormone binding globulin and testicular steroidogenesis. Subspecialties: Endocrinology; Internal medicine. Home: 2820 N Warner Tacoma WA 98407 Office: Dept Clinical Investigation Madigan Army Med Center Box 99 Tacoma WA 98431

PODBROS, LINDA ZOE, neuropsychologist; b. Albany, N.Y., June 25, 1947; d. Robert Selig and Sara (Grodson) P.; m. James Marshall Waters, Sept. 11, 1977. 1 child, David Podbros Waters. B.A., U. Mass., 1973; M.A., SUNY-Stony Brook, 1978, Ph.D. in Psychology, 1981. Lic. psychologist, Mass. Research asst. VA Med. Ctr., Boston, 1973-74; attached clin. worker Nat. Hosp. Nervous Diseases, Maida Vale, London, Eng., 1976-77; part-time staff neuropsychologist Assn. Help Retarded Children, Infants' Services, Suffolk County, N.Y., 1979-81; staff neuropsychologist Braintree Hosp., Mass., 1981-84, dept. rehab. medicine New Eng. Med. Ctr., 1984—; instr. dept. psychology SUNY-Stony Brook, 1978, SUNY Coll.-Old Westbury, 1979; lectr. U. Mass., Boston, fall 1983; clin. instr. pediatric neurology Tufts U. Sch. Medicine, Boston, 1981—, asst. prof. rehab. medicine, 1984—; also cons., lectr. Contbr. articles to profl. publs. Biomed. research fellow, 1978, 80; grantee Sigma Xi, 1978, 80, SUNY-Stony Brook, 1978. Mem. Am. Psychol. Assn., Am. Congress Rehab. Medicine, Assn. Advancement Behavior Therapy (behavioral neuropsychol. group), Internat. Neuropsychol. Soc., Nat. Head Injury Found., Soc. Neurosci., Women in Neuroscis. Democrat. Jewish. Current work: Research on brain-behavior relationships, most especially frontal and basal ganglia functions; research on memory remediation. Subspecialty: Neuropsychology. Home: 1140 Washington St Canton MA 02021 Office: Tufts-New Eng Med Ctr Dept Rehab Medicine 171 Harrison Ave Box 150 Boston MA 02111

PODOWSKI, MICHAEL ZBIGNIEW, nuclear engineering educator, researcher; b. Warsaw, Poland, May 15, 1940; came to U.S., 1979; s. Roman Damazy and Halina Eugenia (Paprocka) P.; m. Irene Gryszko, Mar. 26, 1966; children: Raphael M., Martin L. M.S. in Nuclear Engring, Warsaw Tech. U., 1965, Ph.D. in Nucelar Engring, 1972, Habilitation in Nuclear Engring, 1975; M.S. in Math, U. Warsaw, 1970. Teaching asst. to assoc. prof. Warsaw Tech. U., 1965-79; vis. assoc. prof. nuclear engring. Oreg. State U., 1979-80; vis. assoc. prof. Rensselaer Poly. Inst., Troy, N.Y., 1980-82, assoc. prof., 1982—; cons. Westinghouse Electric Corp., Yankee Atomic Electric Corp. Author: Nuclear Radiation Detection, 1973, Reactor Thermal-Hydraulics, 1977, Nuclear Reactor Safety, 1979; contbr. numerous articles to profl. jours. Mem. Am. Nuclear Soc., Soc. Engring. Sci. Current Work: Reactor systems modeling under transient and accident conditions, degraded core thermal-hydraulics, stability analysis for multidimensional BWR models, stability methods for nonlinear reactor systems. Subspecialties: Nuclear engineering; Applied mathematics. Office: Dept Nuclear Engineering Rensselaer Poly Inst Tibbits Ave Troy NY 12181

POETTMANN, FRED HEINZ, petroleum engineering educator; b. Germany, Dec. 20, 1919; s. Fritz and Kate (Hussen) P.; m. Anna Bell Hall, May 29, 1952; children—Susan Trudy, Phillip Mark. B.S., Case Western Res. U., 1942; M.S., U. Mich., 1944, Sc.D., 1946; grad., Advanced Mgmt. Program, Harvard U., 1966. Registered profl. engr., Colo., Okla. Research chemist Lubrizol Corp., Wickliffe, Ohio, 1942-43; mgr. production research Phillips Petroleum Co., Bartlesville, Okla., 1946-55, asso. research dir., 1955-72; mgr. comml. devel. Marathon Oil Co., Littleton, Colo., 1972-83; prof. petroleum engring. Colo. Sch. Mines, 1983—. Contbr. articles to numerous publs.; Co-author, editor 9 books in field. Chmn. S. Suburban Met. Recreation and Park Dist., 1966-71; chmn. Littleton Press Council, 1967-71; bd. dirs. Hancock

Recreation Center, Findlay, Ohio, 1973-77. Mem. Nat. Acad. Engring., Soc. Petroleum Engrs., Am. Inst. Chem. Engring., Am. Chem. Soc., Am. Petroleum Inst., Sigma Xi, Tau Beta Pi, Alpha Chi Sigma, Phi Kappa Phi. Republican. Holder 45 patents. Current Work: Research in enhanced oil recovery, natural gas engineering, hydocarbon phase behavior and oil production operations. Subspecialties: Chemical engineering; Petroleum engineering. Home: 47 Eagle Dr Littleton CO 80123 Office: PO Box 269 Littleton CO 80160

POHL, JENS GERHARD, architect, educator; b. Wetzlar, W.Ger., Sept. 18, 1940; s. Ernst Richard and Hildegard Wilhelmine (Gorschlueter) P.; m. Barbara Moyra Penrose, June 30, 1962; children: Sonya Karen, Kym Jason. B.Arch., U. Melbourne, Australia, 1965; M.Bldg. Sci., U. Sydney, Australia, 1967, Ph.D. in Archtl. Sci, 1970. Registered architect, Victoria and N.S.W., Australia. Architect Victoria Dept. Pub. Works., 1965-68; sr. lectr. Sch. Bldg., U. New South Wales, Sydney, 1969-72; ptnr. Archtl. Design and Research Group, Sydney, 1969-72; prof. architecture Calif. Poly. State U.-San Luis Obispo, 1973—; pres. Educol. Inc., San Luis Obispo, 1981—. Author 8 books on computer applications, bldg. lighting, acoustics, bldg. sci.; contbr. articles to profl. jours. Life bd. govs. Sports Union, U. Sydney. Recipient Recognition award NASA, 1977. Fellow Royal Australian Inst. Architects; mem. Am. Inst. Constructors, Australian Inst. Bldg. Patentee lightweight concentrating solar collectors (2). Current Work: Solar energy in architecture and agriculture, microcomputer applications in architecture and construction, lightweight systems in building construction. Subspecialties: Solar energy; Software engineering. Home: 650 Highlands Hill Rd Nipomo CA 93444 Office: Calif Poly State U San Luis Obispo CA 93407

POIESZ, BERNARD JOSEPH, physician; b. Phila., Sept. 4, 1948; s. Theodore Joseph and Patricia Mary (Corson) P.; m. Elvira Celia Poiesz, Nov. 9, 1974; children—Michael, Erica. A.B., LaSalle Coll., 1970; M.D., U. Pa., 1974. Diplomate Am. Bd. Internal Medicine. Research asst. Albert Einstein Hosp., Phila., 1966-70, Fox Chase Cancer Ctr., Phila., 1970-74; resident in Medicine SUNY-Upstate Med. Ctr., Syracuse, 1974-77; clin. assoc. NIH, Bethesda, 1977-78, research assoc. tumor cell lab., 1978-80; assoc. prof. SUNY-Upstate Med. Ctr., 1980—; research investigator Barbara Kopp Research Ctr., Auburn, N.Y., 1980-84. Served to lt. comdr. USPHS, 1977-80. Recipient Med. Research award Bausch and Lomb, 1974; Am. Cancer Soc. Jr. Clin. fellow, 1981-84; VA clin. Investigator award, 1984-87. Mem. Am. Soc. Clin. Oncology, Am. Soc. Microbiology, AAAS, Am. Assn. Cancer Research, Am. Soc. Hematology, N.Y. Acad. Scis. Democrat. Roman Catholic. Current work: Clinical oncology research and basic research on human retroviruses. Subspecialty: Oncology. Office: SUNY-Upstate Med Ctr 750 E Adams St Syracuse NY 13210

POINAR, GEORGE ORLO, JR., biologist, educator; b. Spokane, Wash., Apr. 25, 1936; s. George Orlo and Helen Louise (Ladd) P.; married; children: Hendrik, Maya, Gregory. B.S., Cornell U., 1958, M.S., 1960, Ph.D., 1962. Research asst. Cornell U., Ithaca Coll., 1958-62; postdoctoral fellow U. Calif.-Riverside, Hilo, Hawaii, 1962-63, Rothamsted Exptl. Sta., Eng., 1963-64; invertebrate pathologist U. Calif.-Berkeley, 1964—, also mem. faculty. Author: The Natural History of Nematodes, 1983, Nematodes for the Biological Control of Insects, 1979, Entomogenous Nematodes, 1975, Diagonostic Manual for Identification of Insect Diseases, 1978; Laboratory Guide to Insect Pathogens and Parasites, 1984; mem. editorial bds. profl. jours. Fulbright scholar, 1962-63; NIH fellow, 1963-64; Nat. Acad. Scis. award, 1969. Mem. Soc. Invertebrate Pathology, Nematologists Socs. (U.S. and Europe). Current Work: Entomogenous nematodes, amber. Subspecialties: Parasitology; Integrated pest management. Office: 336 Hilgard Hall Dept Entomology U Calif Berkeley CA 94720

POLAND, ARTHUR IRA, astrophysicist; b. Asbury Park, N.J., Mar. 30, 1943; s. Harris David and Dorothy (Epstein) P.; m. Helen Mantell, June 14, 1964. B.S., U. Mass., 1964; Ph.D., Ind. U., 1969. Scientist Nat. Ctr. for Atmospheric Research, 1969-80; astrophysicist NASA/Goddard Space Flight Ctr., Greenbelt, Md., 1980—. Recipient tech. advancement award Nat. Ctr. for Atmospheric Research, 1974. Mem. Am. Astron. Soc., Internat. Astron. Union, Sigma Xi. Current Work: Solar chromosphere, corona, ultraviolet spectroscopy computer modeling, image processing, data handling. Subspecialties: Optical astronomy; Solar physics. Home: PO Box 1107 Warrenton VA 22186 Office: NASA/Goddard Code 682 Greenbelt MD 20771

POLATNICK, JEROME, research biochemist; b. N.Y.C., Oct. 4, 1922; s. Jack and Gussie (Seiden) P.; m. Selma Amster, Aug. 21, 1948; children: Lois, Judith, Barbara. Research chemist Schenley Research Inst., Ind. and N.Y., 1943-47; research chemist N.Y. Bot. Gardens, N.Y.C., 1948-50; biochemist Columbia U., 1950-54; prin. investigator Manhattan Eye and Ear Hosp., N.Y.C., 1954-57; research chemist Plum Island Animal Disease Center, U.S. Dept. Agr., Greenport, N.Y., 1957-80, 1980—, acting lab. chief, 1980. Contbr. numerous articles to profl. jours. Mem. biochem. and biophys. investigations unit receiving Presdl. citation, 1965. Mem. Am. Soc. Microbiology, Am. Chem. Soc., N.Y. Acad. Sci., Sigma Xi. Patentee in field. Current Work: Viral protein and ribonucleic acid synthesis; viral-induced enzymes; intracellular transport of viral components. Subspecialties: Molecular biology; Virology (biology). Home: 1310 Crittens Ln Southold NY 11971 Office: PO Box 848 Greenport NY 11944

POLAY, JANET SKINNER, mfg. co. exec.; b. Newark, Apr. 4, 1945; d. Lester Albert and Ruth (Jacobsen) Skinner; m. Michael S. Polay, Jan. 8, 1977; children: John Bryce, Robert Michael, Andrew Evan. R.N., B.S., Wagner Coll., 1967. Clin. coordinator for clin. research Columbia U., 1972-77; clin. researcher Organon, Inc., West Orange, N.J., 1977-82; mgr. product devel. market research The West Co., Phoenixville, Pa., 1982—; cons. Procter & Gamble, Cin., 1972-77. Contbr. articles to profl. jours. Served with USNR, 1967-69. Mem. AAAS, N.Y. Acad. Scis., Am. Fedn. Clin. Research, Am. Soc. Bone and Mineral Research, Am. Soc. Parenteral and Enteral Nutrition. Republican. Episcopalian. Current Work: Product development for medical device and pharmaceutical components. Subspecialty: Biomaterials. Home: PO Box 295 Chester Springs PA 19425 Office: The West Co W Bridge St Phoenixville PA 19460

POLEFKA, THOMAS GREGORY, biochemist; b. Passaic, N.J., Mar. 12, 1952; s. Emil and Stephanie P.; m. Maryann Brigida, Aug. 29, 1981. B.S., Upsala Coll., 1974; Ph.D., N.J. Med. Sch., 1979. Research fellow Boston Biomed./Harvard, Boston, 1979-80; sr. research chemist Colgate-Palmolive, Piscataway, N.J., 1980—. Contbr. articles to profl. jours. Mem. Am. Chem. Soc., AAAS. Current work: Investigation of mechanisms and the means of preventing peridontal disease. Subspecialties: Biophysical chemistry; Biochemistry (medicine). Home: 79 Ellison Rd RD#3 Somerset NJ 08873 Office: Colgate-Palmolive 909 River Rd Piscataway NJ 08854

POLESTAK, WALTER JOHN STEPHEN, chemist; b. N.Y.C., Oct. 27, 1926; s. Stephen and Eva (Piatek) P.; m. Mary Ann Carsten, Aug. 22, 1959; children—Andrea Ellen, Elizabeth Carsten, Stephen Walter. B.S., Manhattan Coll., 1950; M.S., Tex. A&M Univ., 1955; Ph.D. in Phys. Chemistry, Univ. Pa., 1960. Asst. instr. Univ. Pa., Phila., 1955-59; research chemist duPont, Seaford, Del., 1959-62; Celanese Research Co., Summit, N.J., 1962-68; sect. leader basic group ITT Rayonier, Whippany, N.J., 1968-71; lab. mgr. Diamond Shamrock Co., Morristown, N.J., 1971-80; group leader Ga. Kaolin Research Co., Springfield, N.J., 1980—. Patentee in fields of polymer stabilization and modification, fiber formation and thermoplastic extrusion processes. Fellow Am. Inst. Chemists; mem. Am. Chem. Soc., N.Y. Acad. Scis., Soc. Plastics Engrs., N.Y. Soc. Coating Tech., ASTM, Sigma Xi. Roman Catholic. Current work: Technical focus on kaolins, silicas and related minerals-processes and products. Subspecialties: Polymer chemistry; Physical chemistry. Home: 36 Beekman Rd Summit NJ 07901 Office: Georgia Kaolin Research 25 Route 22 E Springfield NJ 07081

POLGAR, GEORGE, pediatrics educator, pulmonary consultant; b. Gyongyos, Hungary, Apr. 5, 1919; came to U.S., 1957, naturalized, 1962; s. Istvan and Borbala (Szilard) P.; m. Katherine David, Feb. 21, 1945 (div. May 1971); children—Steven, Barbar Polgar Massey, George; m. Tulu Imre, Oct. 1, 1971. M.D., U. Szeged, 1943; M.A. (hon.), U. Pa., 1971. Diplomate Hungarian Bd. Pediatrics, 1950. Adj. in pediatric pulmonology State Sanitarium for Children, Budapest, Hungary, 1950-56; research fellow U. Pa., Phila., 1957-61, asst., prof., 1961-67, assoc. prof. pediatrics, physiology, 1967-74; prof. pediatrics, assoc. physiology Wayne State U., Detroit, 1974-85; adj. prof. pediatrics U. Phila., Phila., 1985—; vis. assoc. prof. U. Geneva, 1970-71; dir. respirator disease sect. Children's Hosp. Phila., 1971-74; dir. pediatric pulmonary ctr. Coop. Multiuniv., Phila., 1972-74; dir. pulmonary disease div., cystic fibrosis ctr. network Children's Hosp. Mich., Detroit, 1974-85; vis. prof. U. Graz, Austria, 1982. Author: Pulmonary Function Testing in Children, 1971. Editor: Pediatric Pulmonology, 1983. Contbr. articles to profl. jours. Research grantee: USPHS-Nat. Heart and Lung Inst., 1962-72, USPHS-Nat. Inst. Childhood Disease, 1965-68. Mem. Am. Physiol. Soc., Am. Thoracic Soc., Soc. for Pediatrics, Acad. Pediatrics. Current work: Pulmonary physiology in infants and children; pediatric pulmonary diseases, cystic fibrosis. Subspecialties: Pediatrics; Pulmonary medicine.

POLGAR, LESLIE GEORGE, technical venture executive, physicist; b. Budapest, Hungary, July 26, 1943; came to U.S. 1953, naturalized 1957; s. Laszlo and Antonia (Szilard) P.; m. Susan Elisabeth Cook, May 8, 1965; children—David Szilard, Sara Elisabeth. B.S. in Physics, U. Mich., 1965; M.S. in Physics, Carnegie-Mellon U., 1967, Ph.D. in Physics, 1971; M.B.A., U. Conn., 1977. Sr. research scientist TRC Environ. Cons., Wethersfield, Conn., 1972-77; sr. assoc. Am. Petroleum Inst., Washington, 1977-79; mgr. long range planning Stauffer Chem. Co., Westport, Conn., 1979-81, mgr. elec. chem. project, 1981-83, dir. corp. projects, 1983—; assoc. prof., lectr. mgmt., George Washington U., Washington, 1978-79. Contbr. articles to profl. jours. Fund raiser Carnegie Mellon U., Pitts., 1973—. NASA fellow, 1965-68; U. Mich. scholar, 1964-65, McGraw scholar U. Mich., 1964-65. Mem. IEEE, Am. Physical Soc., North Am. Soc. Corp. Planning, Sigma Xi, Phi Kappa Phi, Beta Gamma Sigma. Clubs: MGT Register (Oneonta, N.Y.); Winterset Ski (Newtown, Conn.). Current work: New ventures in semiconductor electronics. Subspecialties: Condensed matter physics; Semiconductors. Home: 41 West St Newtown CT 06470 Office: Stauffer Chem Co Nyala Farm Rd Westport CT 06881

POLINSKY, MURRAY ARTHUR, engineer; b. Newark, N.J., Feb. 24, 1973; s. Rubin and Betty (Murar) P.; m. Paula Rudnick, Aug. 23, 1959; children—Michael, Gary, Susan. B.S.E.E., Newark Coll. of Engring., 1958, M.S.E.E., 1960. Asst. instr. of math. Newark Coll. of Engring., N.J., 1958-60; engr. RCA Corp., Somerville, N.J., 1960-80; adv. engr. Westinghouse DEC, Balt., 1980—. Patentee in field. Mem. IEEE, Eta Kappa Nu, Tau Beta Pi. Subspecialties: Integrated circuits; Semiconductors. Home: 10473 Sternwheel Pl Columbia MD 21044 Office: Westinghouse DEC Baltimore MD 21203

POLITIS, DEMETRIOS JOHN, plant pathologist, researcher, consultant; b. Athens, Greece, Oct. 10, 1935; came to U.S., 1969; s. John Demetrios and Violetta (Koutsoyannis). B.S., Coll. Agr., U. Athens, 1960; M.S., McGill U., 1965; Ph.D. (dissertation fellow), U. Ky., 1974. Research asst. Benaki Research Inst., Kifissia, Greece, 1960-63; research assoc. McGill U., Montreal, Que., Can., 1967-69; research specialist U. Ky., Lexington, 1969-72, postdoctoral fellow, 1974-75; research microbiologist U. Mo.-Columbia, 1975-79; team leader Dynamac Corp., Rockville, Md., 1979-81; research assoc., project assoc. Pa. State U., Frederick, Md., 1982—, cons. in agrl. scis., 1982—. Contbr. articles to sci. jours. Calif. Dept. Food and Agr. grantee, 1981-85. Mem. Am. Phytopath. Soc., Hellenic Phytopath. Soc. Current Work: Biological control of noxious weeds using exotic (imported) pathogens such as rust fungi from Eurasia. Subspecialties: Plant pathology; Cell biology. Home: 18638 Grosbeak Terr Gaithersburg MD 20879 Office: Bldg 1301 Fort Detrick Frederick MD 21701

POLITZER, PETER ALEXANDER, research physicist; b. Reigate, Surrey, Eng., Feb. 23, 1943; came to U.S., 1946, naturalized, 1952; s. Alan A. and Valerie T. (Diamant) P.; m. Lisa Nan Izenberg, June 19, 1966; children—Benjamin, Rebecca. B.S., MIT, 1964; Ph.D., Princeton U., 1969. Mem. research staff research lab. of electronics MIT, Cambridge, 1969-73, asst. prof. nuclear engring., 1973-78, assoc. prof., 1978-80, prin. research scientist plasma fusion ctr., 1980-84; sr. staff scientist GA Techs., Inc., San Diego, 1984—. Contbr. articles to profl. jours. Mem. Am. Phys. Soc., AAAS, Sigma Xi. Current work: Development of advanced magnetic fusion concepts. Subspecialties: Nuclear fusion; Plasma physics.

POLKINGHORN, ROBERT WILLIAM, electronics engineer; b. Glen Ridge, N.J., Apr. 5, 1936; s. Frank Allan and Priscilla Alden (Douglas) P.; m. Marilyn Fasone, Apr. 7, 1973. B.S.E.E., U. Mich., 1959. Electronics engr. Nat. Security Agy., Ft. Meade, Md., 1959-61; research engr. Rockwell Autovetics div., Anaheim, Calif., 1961-70, mgr. Microelectronics div., 1970-80; prin. engr. Rockwell Semiconductor, Newport Beach, Calif., 1980-83; design engr. Holt, Inc., Irvine, Calif., 1983-85; mem. tech. staff Rockwell Microelectronics Research and Devel. Ctr., Anaheim, 1985—, instr., 1970-76; lectr. Calif. State U.-Long Beach, 1977-81. Patentee MOS circuits and systems. Served to 1st lt. U.S. Army, 1959-61. Mem. IEEE, IEEE Computer Soc. (chpt. chmn. 1969-70), Electron Devices Soc. Current work: Design and development of CMOS analog and digital integrated circuits. Special emphasis on microcomputers and switched capacitor techniques. Subspecialty: Integrated circuits. Home: 19151 Glen Arran Ln Orange CA 92669 Office: Rockwell Internat 3370 Mira Loma Ave BD24 Anaheim CA 92803

POLLACK, GERALD HARVEY, physiologist, educator, researcher; b. Bklyn., May 20, 1940; s. Max and Helen (Solomon) P.; m. Sylvia Ann Byrne, Aug. 12, 1966 (div. Mar. 1982); children—Seth, Ethan; m. Marilyn Lee Senuty-Gearheart, June 18, 1983; 1 child, Peregrin. B.S.E.E., Poly. Inst. Bklyn., 1961; Ph.D. in Biomed. Engring., U. Penn., 1968. Research trainee med. physics U. Utrecht, The Netherlands, 1962; research trainee physiology and biophysics U. Wash. Sch. Medicine, Seattle, 1963; asst. prof. anesthesiology, div. bioengring., 1968-73, assoc. prof., 1973-77, prof., 1977—; mem. selection com. for Katz award, 1977-78; mem. cardiovascular-pulmonary study sect., 1979-80. Editor: (with others) Ballistocardiography and Cardiac Performance, 1967; Cross-bridge Mechanism in Muscle Contraction, 1979; Contractile Mechanisms in Muscle, 1984. Mem. editorial bd. Jour. Molecular and Cellular Cardiology, 1975-80, Am. Jour. Physiology (Heart and Circulatory Physiology), 1975-80, Circulation Research, 1982—. Contbr. articles to profl. jours. Named established investigator Am. Heart Assn., 1974-79. Mem. Am. Physiol. Soc., IEEE, Profl. Group on Biomed. Engring., Washington State Heart Assn., Biomed. Engring. Soc., Biophys. Soc., Cardiac Muscle Soc., Internat. Soc. for Heart Research, Am. Heart Assn. (basic sci. council, exec. com.), Bioengring. Soc. (bd. dirs. 1977-79), Tau Beta Pi (Kulka award 1961), Eta Kappa Nu (Kulka award 1961). Current work: Molecular mechanism of muscular contraction. Subspecialties: Physiology (medicine); Biomedical engineering. Home: 3714 48th Ave NE Seattle WA 98105 Office: Univ Wash Div Bioengring WD-12 Seattle WA 98195

POLLACK, R. STUART, radiology administrator; b. N.Y.C., Apr. 20, 1946; s. David and Ruth (Vrouble) P.; m. Joanne M. Cobb, Sept. 24, 1972; children: Deborah, Aaron. B.A., L.I. U., 1968, M.S., 1970. Cert. technologist Nuclear Medicine Tech. Cert. Bd. Adminstrv. dir. depts. nuclear medicine, ultrasound CAT scan SLS Diagnostics, Huntington, N.Y., 1977—; ednl. dir. Sch. Nuclear Medicine Tech., 1973—; adj. instr. radiologic tech. Middlesex County Coll., Edison, 1970—; cons. physicist Somerset West Essex Gen. and South Bergen hosps., 1974—; chmn. hosp.-wide coms. on tech. assessment and data processing.; also cons. pvt. corps.; cons. N.J. Commn. on Radiation Protection, vice chmn. N.J. adv. com. on nuclear medicine. Author manuals and tng. programs. Active Jewish Community Ctr. of No. Middlesex County. Recipient commendation Waldemar Cancer Research Found.; USPHS grantee. Mem. AAAS, Soc. Nuclear Medicine (computer council, pres. Greater N.Y. chpt. technologists sect. 1974—, chmn. program com. nat. technologist sect. 1975—), Am. Assn. Physicists in Medicine, Am. Registry Radiologic Technologists, Am. Inst. Ultrasound in Medicine, Am. Hosp. Radiology Adminstrs. Jewish. Current Work: Nuclear magnetic resonance, information systems, radiology, imaging technology. Subspecialties: Nuclear medicine; CAT scan. Home: 4 Glendale Dr Huntington Station NY 11746 Office: SLS Diagnostics Huntington Station NY 11746

POLLACK, SYLVIA BYRNE, tumor immunologist, educator; b. Ithaca, N.Y., Oct. 18, 1940; d. Raymond Tandy and Elsie Frances (Snell) Byrne; children: Seth Benjamin, Ethan David. B.A., Syracuse U., 1962; Ph.D., U. Pa., 1967. Instr. dept. anatomy Woman's Med. Coll. Pa., 1967-68; research assoc. microbiology U. Wash., 1968-73, research asst. prof. microbiology and immunology, 1973-77, research assoc. prof., 1977-81, research assoc. prof. biol. structure, 1981-85, research prof., 1985—; asst. mem. Fred Hutchinson Cancer Research Center, 1975-79, assoc. mem., 1979-81; mem. exptl. immunology study sect. NIH, 1983-85. Assoc. editor: The Journal of Immunology, 1977-79, the Journal of the Reticuloendothelial Society, 1982-84, Natural Immunity and Cell Growth Regulation, 1984—; contbr. articles in field. NIH fellow, 1967-67; Nat. Cancer Inst. grantee, 1973—; Am. Cancer Soc. grantee, 1973-79. Mem. Am. Assn. Immunologists, Soc. Developmental Biology, Am. Assn. Cancer Research, Reticuloendothelial Soc., Phi Beta Kappa. Current Work: Tumor immunology, natural killer cells, antibody-dependent cellular cytotoxicity, cell-cell interactions, immune regulation, immunogenetics. Subspecialties: Immunobiology and immunology; Cancer research (medicine). Home: 4838 36th Ave NE Seattle WA 98105 Office: Biological Structure SM-20 University of Washington Seattle WA 98195

POLLAK, GREGORY DANIEL, physicist, researcher; b. Augusta, Ga., Sept. 2, 1951; s. Cyril Desmoines and Nadine Jeanette (Fenstermacher) P. B.S., Pa. State U., 1971; postgrad. U. Calif.-Berkeley, 1971-72; Ph.D., Harvard U., 1977. Research physicist Analytic Scis. Corp., Reading, Mass., 1977-78, Lawrence Livermore Nat. Lab. (Calif.), 1978-85, Los Alamos Nat. Lab., N.Mex., 1985—. Contbr. articles to physics jours. Recipient Evan Pugh silver and gold medals Pa. State U., 1971. Mem. Am. Phys. Soc. Democrat. Current work: X-ray laser physics, high precision theoretical atomic calculations; line transport plasma physics; supergravity, supersymmetry theories. Subspecialties: Particle physics; Atomic and molecular physics. Office: MSE 538 Los Alamos Nat Lab Los Alamos NM 87545

POLLAK, HENRY LEWIS, geophysicist, researcher; b. Ostrava, Moravia, Czechoslovakia, Oct. 18, 1923; came to U.S. 1964; naturalized 1983; s. Leo and Else (Winterstein) P.; B.S. in Geology, U. London, 1956; Ph.D. in Theoretical Geophysics, U. Pitts., 1971. Geologist, Geol. Survey, Ottawa, Ont., Can., 1963; scientific officer Dominion Obs., Ottawa, 1964; research project devel. U. Pitts., 1972-73; staff geologist and geophysicist Dames & More, Cranford, N.J., 1973-74; project scientist U. Wis., Madison, 1976-77; research scientist U. Calif., Santa Barbara, 1978—. Recipient U.S. Antarctic Service medal NSF, 1979. Mem. IEEE, Assn. of Geoscientists for Internat. Devel., Sierra Club, Nat. Audubon Soc., Am. Mus. of Nat. History. Current work: Integrability of systems of (partial) differential equations of elasticity; incompatiblities and their geometrical interpretation (fractures and non-geometrical dissipators); spontaneous energy releases under deformation. Subspecialties: Solid mechanics; Applied mathematics. Home: PO Box 13950 UCSB Santa Barbara CA 93107 Office: Math Dept U Calif Santa Barbara CA 93106

POLLAK, HENRY OTTO, utility research executive; b. Vienna, Austria, Dec. 13, 1927; came to U.S., 1940, naturalized, 1945; s. Ludwig and Olga (Weil) P.; m. Ida Jeanne Tobias, May 7, 1949; children—Katherine, James. B.A., Yale, 1947; M.A., Harvard U., 1948, Ph.D., 1951; D.Sc., Rose Poly, Inst., 1964, Monmouth Coll., 1975, Bowdoin Coll., 1977, Technol. U., Eindhoven, 1981, Montclair State Coll., 1984. With Bell Telephone Labs., Murray Hill, N.J., 1951-83, mem. tech. staff, 1951-59, head dept. communications fundamentals II, 1959-61, acting dir. math. and mechanics research center, 1961-62, dir. math. and statistics research center, 1962-83; asst. v.p. Math., Communications, and Computer Scis. Research Lab., Bell Communications Research 1984—. Mem. sch. math. study group, com. on undergrad. program in math. Internat. Commn. on Math. Instrn., 1970-74, 82—; mem. adv. bd. Unified Sci. and Maths. for Elementary Schs., 1969-77; mem. adv. com. for sci. edn. NSF, 1977-80, chmn., 1978-80; program chmn. 4th Internat. Congress Math. Edn., 1980. Mem. Am. Math. Soc., Math. Assn. Am. (pres. 1975-76), Nat. Council Tchrs. Math., AAAS, Elizabethan Club, Austria Philatelic Soc. N.Y., Austrian Stamp Club of Gt. Brit., Phi Beta Kappa, Sigma Xi. Mem. Christ Ch. Current work: Applied mathematics; mathematics education. Subspecialties: Applied mathematics; Analysis. Home: 40 Edgewood Rd Summit NJ 07901 Office: Bell Communications Research Morris Research and Engring Ctr 435 South St Morristown NJ 07960

POLLARD, ARTHUR JOSEPH, II, biology educator, botanical researcher; b. San Francisco, Aug. 14, 1956; s. Arthur Joseph and Edythe (Keever) P.; m. Lesley Christina Helliwell, June 13, 1981. B.S., Duke U., 1977; Ph.D., U. Cambridge, Eng., 1981. Asst. prof. Okla. State U., Stillwater, 1981—; steering com. mem. Flora Okla. Project, 1983—. Contbr. articles to profl. jours. Churchill scholar Winston Churchill Found. U.S., 1977. Mem. Botanical Soc. Am., Ecol. Soc. Am., Brit. Ecol. Soc., Southwestern Assn. Naturalists, Phi Beta Kappa, Sigma Xi. Current work: Ecological genetics, plant-herbivore interactions, intraspecific variation in plant defense mechanisms. Subspecialties: Evolutionary biology; Population biology. Home: 2006 W Fifth Ave Stillwater OK 74074 Office: Dept Botany and Microbiology Oklahoma State Univ Stillwater OK 74078

POLLARD, GERALD TILMAN, research pharmacologist; b. Dunn, N.C. Ph.D., N.C. State U., 1981. Research pharmacologist Wellcome Research Labs., Research Triangle Park, N.C., 1974—. Mem. AAAS, N.Y. Acad. Scis., Am. Psychol. Assn., Soc. for Stimulus Properties Drugs, Soc. for Neurosci., Behavioral Pharmacology Soc., Southeastern Pharmacology Soc., MLA. Current Work: Researcher in animal models of psychopathology, animal behavioral methods for identification of psychoactive drugs. Subspecialties: Behavioral psychology; Psychopharmacology. Office: Wellcome Research Labs Dept Pharmacology 3030 Cornwallis Rd Research Triangle Park NC 27709

POLLARD, HARVEY BRUCE, biochemist; b. San Antonio, May 26, 1943. B.A., Rice U., 1964; M.D., U. Chgo., 1969, Ph.D., 1973. Research assoc. Nat. Inst. Arthritis, Diabetes Digestive and Kidney Diseases, NIH, Bethesda, Md., 1969-71, sr. investigator, 1975-79, sect. chief, 1979-81, lab. chief, 1981—; sr. investigator Nat. Inst. Child Health and Devel., 1971-75. Recipient Commendation medal USPHS, 1982. Current Work: Biochemistry and cell biology of hormone secretion. Subspecialty: Cell and tissue culture. Office: Nat Inst Arthritis Diabetes Digestive and Kidney Diseases NIH Lab Cell Biology and Genetics Bldg 4 Room 310 Bethesda MD 20205

POLLARD, MORRIS, microbiologist, educator; b. Hartford, Conn., May 24, 1916; s. Harry and Sarah (Hoffman) P.; m. Mildred Klein, Dec. 29, 1938; children: Harvey, Carol, Jonathan. D.V.M., Ohio State U., 1938; M.S., Va. Poly. Inst., 1939; Ph.D. (Nat. Found. Infantile Paralysis fellow), U. Calif.-Berkeley, 1950; D.Sc. (hon.) Miami U., Ohio, 1981. Mem. staff Animal Disease Sta., Nat. Agrl. Research Center, Beltsville, Md., 1939-42; asst. prof. preventive medicine Med. br. U. Tex., Galveston, 1946-48, asso. prof., 1948-50, prof., 1950-61; prof. biology U. Notre Dame, Ind., 1961-66, prof., chmn. microbiology, 1966-81, prof. emeritus, 1981-85, Coleman prof. life scis., 1985—; dir. (Lobund Lab.), 1961—; vis. prof. Fed. U. Rio de Janeiro, Brazil, 1977; mem. tng. grant com. NIH, 1965-70; mem. adv. bd. (Inst. Lab. Animal Resources), 1965-68; mem. adv. com. microbiology (Office Naval Research), 1966-68, chmn., 1968-70; mem. sci. adv. com. (United Health Found.), 1966-70; cons. U. Tex., M.D. Anderson Hosp. and Tumor Inst., 1958-66; mem. project rev. com. United Cancer Council, 1966-70, 74—; mem. colon cancer com. Nat. Cancer Inst., 1972-76, chmn. tumor immunology com., 1976-79; mem. com. cancer cause and prevention NIH, 1979-81; program rev. com. Argonne Nat. Lab, 1979—, chmn., 1983-85; lectr. Found. Microbiology, 1978. Editor: Perspectives in Virology Vol. I to XI, 1959-80; contbr. articles to profl. jours. Served from 1st lt. to lt. col. Vet. Corps, AUS, 1942-46. McLaughlin Faculty fellow Cambridge U., 1956; Raine Found. prof. U. Western Australia, 1975; vis. scientist Chinese Acad. Med. Scis., 1979, 81; hon. prof. Chinese Acad. Med. Scis., 1982—; Disting. Alumnus Ohio State U., 1979; decorated Army Commendation medal. Mem. Am. Acad. Microbiology (charter), Brazilian Acad. Scis., Soc. Exptl. Biology and Medicine, Am. Soc. Microbiology, Am. Assn. Pathologists, Am. Soc. Lab. Animal Sci., Assn. Gnotobiotics (pres.), Internat. Commn. Lab. Animal Sci., AAAS, Sigma Xi. Subspecialty: Microbiology. Home: 3540 Hanover Ct South Bend IN 46614 Office: Lobund Lab Notre Dame IN 46556

POLLARD, THOMAS DEAN, cell biology, anatomy educator; b. Pasadena, Calif., July 7, 1942; s. Dean Randall and Florence (Dierker) P.; m. Patricia Snowden, Feb. 7, 1964; children—Katherine, Daniel. B.A. cum laude, Pomona Coll., 1964; M.D. cum laude, Harvard, 1968. Intern Mass. Gen. Hosp., Boston, 1968-69; staff assoc. NIH, Bethesda, Md., 1969-72; from asst. prof. anatomy to assoc. prof. Harvard Med. Sch., Boston, 1972-78; prof., dir. cell biology and anatomy Johns Hopkins Med. Sch., Balt., 1977—; overseas fellow Churchill Coll., Cambridge, Eng., 1984; mem. NIH study sects., 1975-80, 1984—; cons. Markey Charitable Trust, Miami, Fla., 1984—. Editorial bd. Jour. Cell Biology, 1977-82; assoc. editor, 1984—. Contbr. articles to profl. jours. Pres. Kernewood Improvement Assn., Balt., 1981—. Recipient Research Career Devel. award NIH, 1973-78; research grantee Muscular Dystrophy Assn., 1982—; Guggenheim fellow, 1984. Mem. Am. Soc. Cell Biology (council 1976-79), Am. Soc. Biol. Chemists, Biophysical Soc. (council 1977-80). Current work: Contractile proteins; molecular basis of cellular motility. Subspecialties: Cell biology (medicine); Biochemistry (medicine). Office: Johns Hopkins U Dir Dept Cell Biology Anatomy 725 N Wolfe St Baltimore MD 21205

POLLETT, FREDERICK C., Canadian government forestry official; b. Buchans, Nfld., Can., May 22, 1942; s. Gordon and Violet (Thorne) P.; m. Sandra Elizabeth Hunt, June 6, 1968; children—Aaron, Jonathon, Amber. B.A., B.Sc., Meml. U., 1964, M.Sc., 1967; Ph.D., Durham U., 1972. Biologist, Can. Forestry Service, Nfld., 1967-72, research scientist, 1972-75, program mgr., 1975-83, exec. dir. Petawana Nat. Forestry Inst., Chalk River, Ont., 1983—. Author: Peat Resources of Newfoundland, 1968. Editor: Wetland Classification, 1981. Contbr. chpt. to book, articles to profl. jours. Chmn. wetlands working group Can. Commn. Land Classification, 1977-80; chmn. Can. Nat. Commn. Internat. Peat Soc., 1980-81, chmn. commn. I, 1983. Mem. United Ch. of Can. Current work: Management of research programs including plant biotechnology, micropropagation, molecular genetics, forest management systems. Office: Petawana Nat Forestry Inst Canadian Forestry Service Chalk River ON K0J 1J0 Canada

POLLMAN, CURTIS DEVIN, aquatic chemist; b. Lewes, Del., Aug. 2, 1951; s. Ralph Calvin and Shirlee June (Lengerich) P.; m. Kathleen Doughty, Sept. 19, 1981. B.A., U. Del., 1973; M.S., U. Fla., 1977, Ph.D., 1983. Staff scientist Environ. Sci. & Engring., Inc., Gainesville, Fla., 1979—. Contbr. articles to profl. jours. Mem. Am. Soc. Limnology and Oceanography, Am. Geophys. Union, Internat. Soc. Ecol. Modeling, Internat. Assn. Water Pollution Research and Control, AAAS, Geochem. Soc., Sigma Xi. Current work: Chem. and phys. dynamics of lake sediments; ecol. effects of acidic deposition; model devel. of aquatic chem. processes. Subspecialties: Limnology; Environmental chemistry. Home: 3910 SW 21st St Gainesville FL 32608 Office: Environ Sci & Engring Inc PO Box ESE Gainesville FL 32602

POLLOCK, E. KEARS, chemical company executive; b. Marion Center, Pa., July 18, 1940; s. Frank M. and Clara Ann (Barr) P.; m. Karen L. Pifer, June 9, 1962; children—Steven, Sean, David, Ann Marie. B.S. in Chem. Engring., Carnegie Inst. Tech., 1962, M.S. in Chem. Engring., 1964; J.D., Duquesne U., 1970. Registered profl. engr., Pa. Engr. Esso (Exxon), Linden, N.J., 1963-66; engr. PPG Industries, Pitts., 1966-70, patent atty., counsel, 1970-81, dir. research and devel., 1982—. Patentee (4); contbr. articles to profl. jours. Pres. Sch. Bd. Hampton Pa. Pub. Schs., Allison Park; bd. dirs. Pitts. Regional Ctr. Sci. Tchrs., 1983—; com. mem. Pa. State C. of C. Edn. Com., Harrisburg, 1985. Served to 1st lt. U.S. Army, 1963-65. Mem. Am. Inst. Chem. Engrs., Am. Ceramic Soc. Club: Pitts. Field. Current work: Research and development relating to glasses, ceramics, and related inorganic materials, coatings, and other modification and processing of basic materials. Subspecialty: Ceramics. Office: PPG Industries Glass Research and Devel Ctr PO Box 11472 Pittsburgh PA 15232

POLLOCK, R. DONALD, aerospace technology company executive. Pres. Spar Aerospace Ltd., Toronto, Ont., Can., 1984—. Subspecialty: Aerospace engineering and technology. Office: Spar Aerospace Ltd Royal Bank Plaza South Tower Toronto ON M5J 2J2 Canada*

POLLOCK, ROY VAN HORN, veterinarian, educator; b. Detroit, Dec. 23, 1949; s. Alexander Samuel and Doris Louise (Van Horn) P.; m. Barbara Kathleen James, Aug. 22, 1970; children—Roy Alexander, Irene Eva. B.A., Williams Coll., 1972; D.V.M., Cornell U., 1978, Ph.D., 1981. Lectr. anatomy N.Y. State Coll. Veterinary Medicine, Ithaca, 1978-81, asst. prof. microbiology, 1981-85, asst. dean curriculum, 1981-85, asst. prof., dir. ctr. med. informatics, 1985—. Author: Provides, computer-assisted diagnosis system, 1982; contbr. articles to profl. jours. Mem. Am. Veterinary Med. Assn., Am. Animal Hosp. Assn. (mem. long-term planning com. 1982—), Am. Veterinary Computer Soc., Phi Beta Kappa, Phi Zeta. Current work: Development of computer-based veterinary medical information system. Subspecialties: Information systems, storage, and retrieval (computer science); Virology (veterinary medicine). Office: NY State Coll Veterinary Medicine Cornell U Ithaca NY 14853

POLLS, IRWIN, aquatic biologist, water quality specialist; b. Thunder Bay, Ont., Can., Oct. 30, 1944; came to U.S., 1954, naturalized, 1964; s. Joseph and Fanny (Segal) P.; m. Jill Lawrence, Apr. 11, 1981; 1 child, Elissa Sara. B.S., U. Ill., Chgo., 1967; M.S., Oreg. State U., 1970. Aquatic biologist Met. San. Dist. of Greater Chgo., 1971—. Contbr. numerous articles on water quality to profl. jours. Served as sgt. U.S. Army, 1970-71, Vietnam. Mem. Internat. Assn. Water Research, Soc. Internat. Limnology, Water Pollution Control Fedn., Am. Water Resources Assn., N. Am. Benthological Soc., Sigma Xi. Democrat. Jewish. Current work: Design of water and sediment quality monitoring studies for point and nonpoint sources of pollution; the effects of domestic and industrial waste discharges on urban rivers and lakes; use of benthic invertebrates for assessing water quality. Subspecialties: Ecology (environmental science); Limnology. Office: Met San Dist of Chgo 550 S Meacham Rd Schaumburg IL 60193

POLONIS, DOUGLAS HUGH, engineering educator; b. North Vancouver, B.C., Can., Sept. 2, 1928; came to U.S., 1955, naturalized, 1963; s. William and Ada (Burrows) P.; m. Vera Christine Brown, Jan. 30, 1953; children: Steven Philip, Malcolm Eric, Douglas Hugh, Christine Virginia. B.A.Sc., U. B.C., 1951, Ph.D., 1955; M.A.Sc., U. Toronto, 1953. Metall. engr. Steel Co. Can., Hamilton, Ont., 1951-52; mem. faculty U. Wash., Seattle, 1955—, prof. metall. enging., 1962—, chmn. dept. mining, metall. and ceramic engring., 1969-71, 73-82; metall. cons., 1955—. Contbr. articles to profl. jours. Fellow Am. Soc. Metals, AIME, Am. Soc. Engring. Edn., Tau Beta Pi, Alpha Sigma Mu, Sigma Phi Delta. Mem. Christian Ref. Ch. Current Work: Structure and properties of alloys, mechanical behavior of materials phase transformations in solids microstructure-property relationships. Subspecialties: Materials (engineering); Metallurgy. Home: 19227 46th Ave NE Seattle WA 98155

POLTORAK, ALEXANDER (ISRAEL), physicist, computer scientist; b. Krasnodar, USSR, Oct. 4, 1957; came to U.S. 1982; s. Abraham and Raisa (Poltorak) Kleinerman; m. Valeria Leah Farber, June 24, 1978; children—Ilya, Ruth, David. Ph.D., State U. Kuban, Krasnodar, USSR, 1980. Asst. prof. biomath. Cornell U. Med. Coll., N.Y.C., 1982-85; pres. Rapitech. Systems, Inc., N.Y.C., 1983—. Contbr. articles to profl. jours. Mem. Am. Phys. Soc., N.Y. Acad. Scis., Assn. Computing Machinery, IEEE. Jewish. Current work: Study of energy problem in general/relativity; development of covariant theory of gravitation; research and development in language translation and compilers; software and hardware development. Subspecialties: Relativity and gravitation; Graphics, image processing, and pattern recognition. Home: 18 Calvert Dr Monsey NY 10952 Office: Rapitech Systems Inc 565 Fifth Ave New York NY 10017

POLZ-SCHAERFFENBERG, ERIKA, research chemist; b. Cologne, Germany; came to U.S., 1979; d. Bruno and Marta (Mertens) Schaerffenberg. Ph.D., U. Graz, Austria, 1973. Asst. prof. U. Graz Sch. Medicine, 1973-79; research scientist U. So. Calif. Sch. Medicine, Los Angeles, 1979-81; chief research and devel. Healthkeepers Med. Labs., San Francisco, 1983—; cons. to clin. labs. Contbr. articles to profl. jours. HEW fellow, 1975. Mem. Am. Assn. Clin. Chemistry, Am. Assn. Clin. Pathologists, AAAS, N.Y. Acad. Scis. Current work: Characterization, structure and metabolic studies of serum apolipoproteins and glycoproteins related to atherosclerosis, development of novel test methodologies in clinical chemistry. Subspecialties: Biochemistry (medicine); Clinical chemistry. Home: 416 Sherwood Dr Sausalito CA 94965 Office: Healthkeepers Med Labs 950 Illinois St San Francisco CA 94107

POMALAZA RAEZ, CARLOS ARTURO, engineering educator; b. Chaupimarca, Pasco, Peru, May 12, 1952; came to U.S., 1983; s. Gines Cesareo Pomalaza Cosme and Haydee Raez Malpartida; m. Barbara Ann Lloyd, Feb. 4, 1982; 1 child, Raoul Daniel. B.S.E.E. and B.S.M.E., U. Naci Ingenieria, Lima, Peru, 1974; M.S. in Elec. Engring., Purdue U., 1977, Ph.D., 1980. Registered profl. engr., Peru. Engr., Ins. Geophys. Peru, Ancon, 1975-76; research assoc. Purdue U., West Lafayette, Ind., 1980-81; lectr. Nat. Inst. Higher Edn., Limerick, Ireland, 1981-83; asst. prof. engring. Clarkson U., Potsdam, N.Y., 1983—; cons. Argo Communication, New Rochelle, N.Y., 1984—, Jet Propulsion Lab., Pasadena, Calif., 1984—. Contbr. articles to profl. jours. Recipient Research in Robotics award, Westinghouse, 1983. Mem. IEEE. Current work: Statistical analysis of coherent communication systems; algorithms for multispectral signal processing; scheduling problems in TDMA satellite communication systems. Subspecialties: Telecommunications; Graphics, image processing, and pattern recognition. Office: ECE Dept Clarkson U Potsdam NY 13676

POMERANTZ, MARTIN, chemistry educator; b. N.Y.C., May 3, 1939; s. Harry and Pauline (Sietz) P.; m. Maxine Miller, June 4, 1961; children: Lee Allan, Wendy Jane, Heidi Lauren. B.S., CCNY, 1959; M.S., Yale U., 1961, Ph.D. (NSF, Woodrow Wilson, hon. Sterling and Leeds and Northrup fellow), 1964. NSF postdoctoral fellow U. Wis., 1963-64; asst. prof. Case Western Res. U., Cleve., 1964-69; assoc. prof. Belfer Grad. Sch. Sci., Yeshiva U., N.Y.C., 1969-74, prof., 1974-76, acting chmn. dept., 1971-72, chmn. chemistry dept., 1973-76; vis. assoc. prof. U. Wis., 1972; vis. prof. Columbia U., N.Y.C., part-time, 1970-75; Alfred P. Sloan Found. fellow, 1971-76; vis. prof. Ben-Gurion U. Negev, Israel, summer, 1981, 85; prof. chemistry U. Tex.-Arlington, 1976—; cons. in field. Contbr. numerous articles on chemistry to profl. jours. Robert A. Welch Found. grantee, 1977—; Petroleum Research Fund grantee, 1964-71; NSF grantee, 1967-69, 80-84. Mem. Am. Chem. Soc., Royal Soc. Chemistry, Phi Beta Kappa, Sigma Xi. Current Work: Organic chemical reaction mechanisms, synthesis and study of phosphorus-nitrogen compounds, reactive intermediates, strained molecules, coal chemistry. Subspecialty: Organic chemistry. Home: 5521 Williamstown Dallas TX 75230 Office: Dept Chemistry U Tex at Arlington PO Box 19065 Arlington TX 76019

POMERANTZ, MARTIN ARTHUR, physics educator, researcher; b. Bklyn., Dec. 17, 1916; s. Joseph and Henrietta (Moses) P.; m. Molly Bernstein, Aug. 10, 1941; children—Jane, Martin Arthur Jr. A.B., Syuracuse U., 1937; M.S., U. Pa., 1939; Ph.D., Temple U., 1951; ScD., Swarthmore Coll., 1973; Fil.Dr. honoris causa (hon.), U. Uppsala, Sweden, 1967. Research asst. Bartol Research Found. of the Franklin Inst., 1939-41, research fellow 1941-43, physicist, 1943-59, dir. 1959—, v.p., 1967; Fulbright scholar and vis. prof. Muslim U., Aligarh, United Provinces, India, 1952-53; prof. physics Thomas Jefferson U., 1968-77, U. Del., 1977—; leader of a number of Nat. Geographic Soc. Expeditions; v.p. com. for internat. yrs. of quiet sun Internat. Council Sci. Unions, Comite International de Geophysique; mem. com. polar research Nat. Acad. Scis., 1959-71, space bd., 1963-70, Geophysics Research Bd. 1959-73; vis. prof. astronomy Swarthmore Coll., 1961, 64, 67; nat. lectr. Sigma Xi Scientific Research Soc. Am., 1968; vis. prof. Organ. Am. States, 1973. Author: Cosmic Rays, 1971. Editor of Jour. of the Franklin Inst.; editorial bd. Antartic Research Series, 1967-76, Space Sci. Reviews, 1963—; contbr. numerous articles to profl. jours. Recipient Centennial Gold medal Syracuse U., 1970. Fellow Am. Phys. Soc., AAAS, Am. Geophys. Union; mem. Sigma Xi (hon.). Club: Explorer's (Phila. explorers award 1980); Cosmos. Current work: Cosmic rays; solid state; radiation effects; geophysics; solar terrestrial physics; astrophysics, astronomy. Subspecialties: Solar physics; Cosmic ray high energy astrophysics. Home: 46 Bridle Brook Ln Covered Bridge Farms Newark DE 19711 Office: Bartol Research Found Univ Del Newark DE 19716

POMERANTZ, MELVIN, physicist; b. Bklyn., May 10, 1932; s. Isidore and Evelyn (Salland) P. B.S., Poly. Inst., 1953; M.A., U. Calif.-Berkeley, 1955, Ph.D., 1959. Postdoctoral research Centre d'Etudes Nucleaires Saclay, France, 1958-59; mem. staff IBM Research Ctr., Yorktown Heights, N.Y., 1960-68, 69—; vis. lectr. U. Calif.-Berkeley, 1968-69. Contbr. articles to profl. jours. Patentee in field. Co-chmn. Com. Concerned Scientist, N.Y., 1973, bd. dirs., 1974—. Fulbright fellow, 1968; recipient Invention Achievement award IBM, 1980, Outstanding Innovation award IBM, 1982. Fellow Am. Phys. Soc.; mem. N.Y. Acad. Scis., Research Soc. Am. Current work: Two-dimensional magnets; granular superconductors; magnetic multilayers. Subspecialties: Condensed matter physics; Magnetic physics. Office: IBM Research Ctr Box 218 Yorktown Heights NY 10598

POMERANZ, YESHAJAHU, cereal chemist, food analyst; b. Tlumacz, Poland, Nov. 28, 1922; came to U.S., 1959, naturalized, 1967; s. David and Rysia (Bildner) P.; m. Ada Waisberg, Oct. 27, 1948; children: Shlomo, David. B.Sc., Israeli Inst. Tech., 1945; Ph.D., Kans. State U., 1962. Dir. Central Food Testing Lab., Govt. Israel, Haifa, 1948-59; research chemist U.S. Dept. Agr., Manhattan, Kans., 1962-69; dir. U.S. Dept. Agr. Grain Mktg. Research Ctr., Agrl. Research Service, 1973—; dir. Barley and Malt Lab., prof. U. Wis., Madison, 1969-73, dir. short courses on cereal sci. and tech. and vis. prof. throughout world, 1975—. Author: (with Meloan) Food Analysis, 1971, Food Analysis-Experimental, 1976, (with Shellenberger) Bread, 1971; editor, co-author 11 books; contbr. over 350 articles to sci. and tech. publs. Recipient Disting. Service award U.S. Dept. Agr., 1983; M.P. Neuman medal W. Ger., 1978; Von Humboldt award sr. U.S. scientist W. Ger., 1981. Fellow Inst. Food Technologists, AAAS; mem. Internat. Assn. Cereal Chemists (exec. com.), Am. Assn. Cereal Chemists (sci. editor Advances in Cereal Sci. and Tech., T.B. Osborne medal 1980, W.F. Geddes medal 1982), Am. Chem. Soc., Assn. Ofcl. Analytical Chemistry (H. Wiley award 1980), Nat. Assn. Chem. Engring. Mex. (hon.), Gamma Sigma Delta. Patentee in field. Current Work: Director of research on the relation between the structure, chemical composition, and end use properties of cereal grains, and on the biochemistry of breadmaking. Subspecialties: Food science and technology; Biochemistry (biology). Office: USDA Grain Mktg Research Lab 1515 College Ave Manhattan KS 66502

POMPHREY, RICHARD BRYAN, science engineering liaison, space scientist; b. St. Louis, May 11, 1946; s. Martin Michael Sr. and Marcella J. P. B.S., Washington U., 1969; M.S., U. Fla., 1975, Ph.D., 1977. Research asst. The Aerospace Corp., El Segundo, Calif., 1973-76; sr. computer analyst Bionetics Corp., Pasadena, Calif., 1976-77; sr. scientist Jet Propulsion Lab., Pasadena, 1977-79, Voyager experiment rep., 1980-82, mem. tech. staff, 1983—; mgr. advanced studies NASA Hdqrs., Washington, 1982-83. Editor World Space Found. newsletter, 1979. Adviser St. Bede's Youth Orgn., La Canada, Calif., 1979—. Mem. Am. Astron. Soc., Astron. Soc. of Pacific. Current work: Conceptual design of scientific data systems; planetary exploration; space station planning. Subspecialties: Aerospace engineering and technology; Planetary science. Home: PO Box 1425 La Canada CA 91011 Office: Jet Propulsion Lab 4800 Oak Grove Dr Pasadena CA 91109

PONDER, HERMAN, geologist; b. Light, Ark., Jan. 31, 1928; s. Herman Cook and Sylvia Adell (Cameron) P.; m. Barbara Elaine Sands, May 10, 1947; children: Teresa Elaine, David Mark. B.A., U. Mo., 1955, Ph.D., 1959. Registered profl. engr., Colo. Research engr. A.P. Green Refractories Co., Mexico, Mo. 1959-61, lab. mgr., 1961-63; project engr., then mgr. mining div. Colo. Sch. Mines Research Inst., Golden, 1963-67, dir. research, 1967-70; pres. Research Inst. Colo. Sch. Mines, prof. geology, 1970-85; pres. ATI Exploration, Inc., 1985—; v.p. tech. Northern Copper Corp., 1985—; chmn. bd. Colo. Nat. Bank, Golden. Served with USN, 1946-47. Mem. AIME, Rocky Mountain Assn. Geologists, Colo. Mining Assn. Current Work: Mineral occurrences and mineral recovery processes. Subspecialties: Geology; Materials processing. Home: 1919 Mt Zion Dr Golden CO 80401 Office: PO Box 112 Golden CO 80401

PONG, RAYMOND S., urological surgeon, cancer researcher; s. David C. and Saufong (Wong) P. A.B., Dartmouth Coll., 1960; M.S., M.I.T., 1966, Ph.D., 1970; M.D., Case Western Res. U., 1975. Diplomate: Am. Bd. Med. Examiners, Am. Bd. Urology. Research asso. M.I.T., 1970-71; research fellow Case Western Res. U., 1971-73, surg. resident, 1975-77, fellow, 1976-77; urology resident Mass. Gen. Hosp., 1977-80, chief resident, 1980; fellow in surgery Harvard Med. Sch., 1979-80; sr. surgeon urology City of Hope Med. Center, Duarte, Calif., 1980-83; pvt. practice, Downey, Calif., 1983—; asst. clin. prof. U. So. Calif., 1980—; assoc. clin. prof. U. Calif., Irvine, 1982—. Contbr. articles to profl. jours. NIH grantee, 1968, 71. Mem. N.Y. Acad. Sci., Am. Soc. Cell Biology, AAAS, Los Angeles Urol. Soc., Sigma Xi. Current Work: Surgical oncology and carcinogenesis. Subspecialties: Cancer research (medicine); Urology. Office: 11411 Brookshire Ave Suite 402 Downey CA 90241

PONNAMPERUMA, CYRIL ANDREW, chemist, educator; b. Galle, Sri Lanka, Oct. 16, 1923; came to U.S., 1959, naturalized, 1967; s. Andrew and Grace (Siriwardene) P.; m. Valli Pal, Mar. 19, 1955; 1 dau., Roshini. B.A., U. Madras, 1948; B.Sc., U. London, 1959; Ph.D., U. Calif., Berkeley, 1962. Research assoc. Lawrence Radiation Lab., U. Calif., 1960-62; research scientist, then chief chem. evolution br. Ames Research Center, NASA, 1962-70; prof. chemistry U. Md., College Park, 1971—; dir. Lab. Chem. Evolution, 1971—. Author books, articles in field; editor-in-chief: Origins of Life, 1973-83. Recipient A.I. Oparin Gold medal Internat. Soc. for Study Origin of Life, 1980. Fellow Royal Inst. Chemistry, Indian Nat. Sci. Acad. (fgn. fellow); mem. Am. Chem. Soc. (chmn. internat. activities com. 1981), Astron. Assn., Am. Soc. Biol. Chemists, Explorers Club. Club: Cosmos (Washington). Current Work: Chemical studies on the origin of life—search for extraterrestrial life. Subspecialties: Biochemistry (biology); Space chemistry. Office: Lab Chem Evolution U Md College Park MD 20742

PONPIPOM, MITREE MICHAEL, organic chemist, researcher; b. Bangkok, Thailand, Dec. 1, 1939; came to U.S. 1971, naturalized 1980; s. Charoen and Seal-Lai (Lau) P.; m. Amelia Mo Yi Cheng, Oct. 1, 1969; children—Ada, Matthew, Amy. B.S. with honors, 1st class, Mount Allison U., 1964; Ph.D., U. Alberta, Edmonton, Can., 1968. Postdoctoral fellow U. London, Eng., 1968-69, U. Montreal, Can., 1969-70; research assoc. U. Manitoba, Winnipeg, Can., 1970-71; sr. research chemist Merck & Co., Inc., Rahway, N.J., 1971-77, research fellow, 1977-82, sr. research fellow, 1982—. Author: A Chapter in Liposomes Technology, 1984. Mem. Am. Chem. Soc., N.Y. Acad. Sci. Current work: Synthetic organic chemistry; carbohydrate chemistry. Subspecialties: Organic chemistry; Synthetic chemistry. Office: Merck & Co Inc PO Box 2000 Rahway NJ 07065

POOL, JAMES CHRISTOPHER THOMAS, scientific software company executive; b. Wellsville, Kans., Feb. 27, 1937; s. James Lester and Gwendolyn (Manners) P.; m,. Madlyn Kay Skilling, July 1, 1956 (div. 1983); children—Arlan Lamont, Danielle Christine; m. Doris M. Pahis, Aug. 9, 1985. B.A., U. Kans., 1959; Ph.D., U. Iowa, 1963. Sr. scientist sci. lab. Ford Motor Co., Dearborn, Mich., 1963-64, 65-66; asst. mathematician applied math. div., Argonne Nat. Lab., Ill., 1966, 67-68, asst. div. dir., 1969-71, assoc. div. dir., 1971; research fellow physics U. Hamburg, Fed. Republic Germany, 1966-67, U. Geneva, Switzerland, 1967; asst. prof. math. U. Mass., 1968-69; dir. applied math. scis. Dept. Energy, Washington, 1977-80; dir. math. and computer scis. div. Office of Naval Research, 1980-82; exec. v.p. Numerical Algorithms Group, Downers Grove, Ill., 1982—. NSF fellow, 1964-65. Fellow Inst. Math. and Applications; mem. Soc. Indsl. and Applied Math. (v.p. 1977-80) bd. trustees 1978-83). Current work: Numerical algorithms and software for scientific and engineering computations; computer architecture; science policy. Subspecialty: Mathematical software. Home: 5935 Oakwood Dr Lisle IL 60532 Office: Numerical Algorithms Group 1101 31st St Suite 100 Downers Grove IL 60515

POP, EMIL, research chemist; b. Tirgu Mures, Romania, Aug. 12, 1939; came to U.S., 1983; s. Victor and Rosalia (Graf) P.; m. Elena Petrina Petri, Apr. 28, 1964; 1 child, Andreea Christina. B.S., Babes-Bolyai U., (Romania), 1961; Ph.D., Inst. Chemistry (Romania), 1973. Chemist Chem. Pharm. Research Inst., Cluj-Napoca, Romania, 1962-65, researcher, 1965-78, sr. researcher, 1978—; researcher Rugjer Boskovic Inst., Zagreb, Yugoslavia, 1971-72; postdoctoral research assoc. U. Fla., Gainesville, 1983—. Contbr. articles to profl. jours. Recipient Romanian Acad. award for chemistry. Mem. Am. Chem. Soc. Roman Catholic. Club: Universitatea Cluj-Napoca. Current work: Design and synthesis of pharmaceutical compounds in particular chemical drug delivery systems and applications of quantum chemistry to natural products. Subspecialties: Organic chemistry; Medicinal chemistry. Home: 6519 Newberry Rd Apt 708 Gainesville FL 32605 Office: U Fla Gainesville FL 32605

POPE, HARRISON GRAHAM, JR., psychiatrist, researcher; b. Lynn, Mass., Dec. 26, 1947; s. Harrison Graham and Alice (Rider) P.; m. Mary Quinn, June 7, 1974; children—Kimberly, Hilary. A.B., Harvard U., 1969, M.P.H., 1972, M.D., 1974. Resident McLean Hosp., Harvard Med. Sch., Belmont, Mass., 1974-77, asst. psychiatrist, 1977-85, assoc. psychiatrist, 1985—; instr. psychiatry Harvard Med. Sch., Boston, 1977-82, asst. prof., 1982—; staff psychiatrist Hampstead Hosp., N.H., 1976-80; vis. fellow Maudsley Hosp., London, 1977, l'Hôpital Ste. Anne, Paris, 1977. Author: Voices From the Drug Culture, 1971; The Road East, 1974; New Hope for Binge Eaters: Advances in the Understanding and Treatment of Bulimia, 1984. Contbr. articles to profl. jours. Recipient James Tolbert Shipley prize Harvard Med. Sch., 1974; Harvey Shein award McLean Hosp., 1977; Dupont-Warren fellow Harvard Med. Sch., 1976-77; Scottish Rite fellow, 1977-81; Charles A. King Trust fellow, 1977-79. Mem. Am. Psychiat. Assn., Phi Beta Kappa. Current work: Pharmacological treatment of anorexia nervosa and bulimia, diagnosis and classification of psychiatric disorders, drug abuse, psychopharmacology. Subspecialties: Psychiatry; Psychopharmacology. Office: McLean Hosp 115 Mill St Belmont MA 01742

POPE, THEODORE CAMPBELL, JR., mechanical engineer; utility executive; b. Sanford, Fla., Oct. 28, 1932; s. Theodore Campbell and Mary (Cook) P.; m. Edith L. Carlton (div. 1972); m. Jeris Julia Dawson, Nov. 21, 1973; children—Theodore C., III, Jeffrey A., Laura L. B.S. in Mech. Engring., U. Fla., 1954, M.B.A., 1959. Registered profl. engr., Fla. Results engr. Orlando Utilities Commn., Fla., 1959-64, plant supt., 1964-67, dir. generation, 1967-70, asst. mgr. electric dept., 1970-72, mgr. water dept., 1972-84, asst. gen. mgr., 1984-85, gen. mgr., 1985—. Patentee in field. Bd. dirs. Central Fla. Fair Bd., Orlando, 1984—, United Fund, Brevard County, Fla., 1965-66. Fellow Fla. Engring. Soc.; mem. Am. Acad. Environ. Engrs., ASME (Engr. of Yr., Fla. chpt. 1972), Am. Water Works Assn. (hon. mem., bd. dirs. 1981-83, past chmn. bd. trustees nat. research found. 1979-83, George Warren Fuller award 1981), Nat. Assn. Corrosion Engrs., Nat. Soc. Profl. Engrs., Fla. Mcpl. Utilities Assn. (bd. dirs. 1985—). Democrat. Clubs: University; Smyrna Yacht. Lodges: Elks; Rotary. Subspecialties: Water supply and wastewater treatment; Mechanical engineering. Home: 723 Baxter Ave Orlando FL 32806

POPESCU, NICOLAE CONSTANTIN, microbiologist; b. Bucharest, Romania, Mar. 4, 1940; came to U.S. 1971, naturalized, 1980; s. Constanin-Atanasie and Florance Sofia (Oancea) P.; m. Susan Eleanor Armiger, May 27, 1977; 1 child, Julie. B.S., U. Bucharest, 1964, Ph.D., 1971. Head cellular biology dept. Oncological Inst., Bucharest, Romania, 1967-71; vis. scientist Somatic Cell Genetics Nat. Cancer Inst., 1977-81; staff fellow Lab. Biology Nat. Cancer Inst. NIH, Bethesda, Md., 1981-84, microbiologist, 1984—. Contbr. articles to profl. jours. and book; mem. editorial bd. Cancer Genetics and Cytogenetics, 1984. Cancer research fellow Internat. Agy. Cancer Research, 1971. Mem. Am. Assn. Cancer Research, European Cancer Soc. Eastern Orthodox. Current work: Chemical and physical carcinogenesis with in vitro cell model, genetic alterations in carcinogenesis, human and animal cytogenetics, gene mapping, oncogenes localization and transposition. Subspecialties: Cancer research (medicine); Genetics and genetic engineering (medicine). Home: 7608 Marbury Rd Bethesda MD 20817 Office: Nat Cancer Inst 9000 Rockville Pike Bethesda MD 20205

POPOV, DAN, clinical psychologist; b. Butte, Mont., Sept. 27, 1945; s. Frederick Michael and Patricia (Tauson) P.; m. Carol Lark, Mar. 6, 1973 (div. 1980); m. Linda Kavelin, July 20, 1981. B.S., U.S. Mil. Acad., 1968; M.A., U. Colo.-Boulder, 1971, Ph.D., 1973. Lic. psychologist. Commd. 2d lt. U.S. Army, 1968, advanced through grades to capt., 1970; chief behavior sci. cons. service (Letterman Army Med. Ctr.), San Francisco, 1974-76; psychologist (U.S. Army Orgn. Effectiveness Tng. Ctr.), Ft. Ord, Calif., 1976-78; ret., 1978; v.p. research and devel. Systems Effectiveness Assn., Monterey, Calif., 1977—, Info. Access Systems, Boulder, Colo., 1981—; developer Mgmt. Support Tech., Inc., Denver, 1981—, dir., 1981—; v.p. research and devel. Advanced Info. Design, Portland, Oreg., 1982—, chmn. bd., 1982—; exec. dir. LRI Assocs., Inc., Boulder, 1980-82; dir. Linguistic Research Inst., 1985—; v.p. research and devel. Devel. Specialists Internat., Inc. 1985—. Co-author: Person, Place, World, 1982. Author: Paradigm, 1984; Corporate Advantage, 1985; Snugli Companion, 1985. Mem. Am. Psychol. Assn., Am. Soc. Tng. and Devel., AAAS, Mid-Coast Psychol Assn. (pres. 1976-77), Monterey Peninsula Psychol. Assn. (pres. 1977-78). Current Work: Application of artificial intelligence on micrcomputers to problems in management; organizational, and behavioral sciences using a descriptive psychological approach. Subspecialties: Organizational/Clinical Psychology; Artificial intelligence. Home: 1777 Larimer St Suite 1901 Denver CO 80202 Office: Mgmt Support Tech Inc 1560 Broadway Suite 755 Denver CO 80202

POPOV, EGOR PAUL, emeritus civil engineering educator; b. Kiev, Russia, Feb. 19, 1913; s. Paul T. and Zoe (Derabin) P.; m. Irene Zofia Jozefowski, Feb. 18, 1939; children—Katherine, Alexander. B.S., U. Calif., 1933; M.S., Mass. Inst. Tech., 1934; Ph.D., Stanford, 1946. Registered civil, structural and mech. engr., Calif. Structural engr., bldg. designer, Los Angeles, 1935-39; asst. prodn. engr. Southwestern Portland Cement Co., Los Angeles, 1939-42; machine designer Goodyear Tire & Rubber Co., Los Angeles, 1942-43; design engr. Aerojet Corp., Calif., 1943-45; asst. prof. civil engring. U. Calif. at Berkeley, 1946-48, assoc. prof., 1948-53, prof., 1953-83, prof. emeritus, 1983—, chmn. structural engring. and structural mechanics div., dir. structural engring. lab., 1956-60; Miller research prof. Miller Inst. Basic Research in Sci., 1968-69.

Author: Mechanics of Materials, 1952, 2d edit., 1976, Introduction to Mechanics of Solids, 1968; Contbr. articles profl. jours. Recipient Disting. Tchr. award U. Calif.-Berkeley, 1976-77, Berkeley citation U. Calif.-Berkeley, 1983. Mem. Am. Soc. Metals, Internat. Assn. Shell Structures (hon. mem.), ASCE (Ernst E. Howard award 1976, J. James R. Croes medal 1979, 82, Nathan M. Newmark medal 1981), Soc. Exptl. Stress Analysis (Hetenyi award 1967), Am. Soc. Engring. Edn. (Western Electric Fund award 1976-77, Disting. Educator award 1979), AAAS, Am. Concrete Inst., Nat. Acad. Engring., Soc. Engring. Sci., Internat. Assn. Bridge and Structural Engring., Am. Inst. Steel Constrn. (adv. com. specifications), Sigma Xi, Chi Epsilon, Tau Beta Pi. Current Work: Seismic behavior of steel and reinforced concrete strctures. Hysteretic material behavior. Subspecialties: Civil engineering; Solid mechanics. Home: 2600 Virginia St Berkeley CA 94709

POPOWICZ, ANTHONY MICHAEL, research chemist, educator; b. Bklyn., July 31, 1952; s. Michael and Maria (Bober) P. B.S., Bklyn. Coll., 1974; M. Philosophy, CUNY, 1979, Ph.D., 1981. Research assoc. SUNY-Stony Brook, 1981—. Contbr. articles to profl. jours. Patentee liquid nitrogen level controller. Mem. Am. Chem. Soc., N.Y. Acad. Scis., Am. Phys. Soc., AAAS, Sigma Xi. Roman Catholic. Use of stable isotopes in the elucidation of molecular forces and structure through thermodynamic and kinetic means; novel methods for practical isotope separation. Subspecialty: Physical chemistry. Office: SUNY Dept Chemistry Stony Brook NY 11794

POPP, JOHN THOMAS, geologist; b. Altenburg, Mo., Nov. 9, 1950; s. Richard Paul and Rose Elda (Mahnke) P. B.S. in Geology, Eastern Ill. U., 1972; M.S., So. Ill. U., 1974. Registered geologist Ind., Va. Geologist U.S. Bur. Mines, Pitts., 1975-77, Ill. State Geol. Survey, Champaign, 1977-79, Dames & Moore, Cin., 1979-84, Nerco Coal Co., Cin., 1984—. Contbr. articles to profl. jours. Mem. Geol. Soc. Am., Soc. Econ. Paleontologists & Mineralogists, Soc. Mining Engrs., Ill. Mining Inst. Lutheran. Current work: Coal geology; mining and exploration geology; reserve evaluation and property acquisition. Subspecialties: Geology; Sedimentology. Office: Nerco Coal Co 4225 Malsbary Rd Cincinnati OH 45242

POPPERS, PAUL JULES, anesthesiologist, educator; b. Enschedé, Netherlands, June 30, 1929; came to U.S., 1958; naturalized, 1963; s. Meyer and Minca (Ginsburg) P.; m. Ann Feinberg, June 3, 1969; children—David M., Jeremy S. M.D., U. Amsterdam, Netherlands, 1955. Diplomate Am. Bd. Anesthesiology. Intern in medicine and surgery Univ. Hosp., Amsterdam, 1956-58; resident in medicine Beth El Hosp., Bklyn., 1958-59; resident in anesthesiology Columbia U., N.Y.C., 1959-61, NIH research fellow, 1961-62, asst. prof. anesthesiology, 1962-70, assoc. prof., 1970-74; prof., vice chmn. anesthesiology NYU, N.Y.C., 1974-79; prof., chmn. anesthesiology SUNY-Stony Brook, 1979—; cons. in field. Author: (with B. van Dijk) Advances in Regional Anesthesia, 1977. Editor: Beta Blockade and Anaesthesia, 1980. Contbr. articles to profl. jours. Mem. Assn. Univ. Anesthetists, Fedn. Am. Socs. Exptl. Biology, Soc. Acad. Anesthesia (chmn. com.), Am. Soc. Anesthesiologists, Royal Soc. Medicine, Assn. Anaesthetists Gt. Britain and Ireland, Internat. Anesthesia Research Soc., Soc. Obstetric Anesthesia and Perinatology. Current work: Directing clinical research and teaching activities of medical school staff; directing development of critical care monitoring and information science in a university hospital setting. Office: State U New York Health Sci Ctr Stony Brook NY 11794-8480

PORIES, WALTER J., surgeon; b. Munich, Ger., Jan. 18, 1930; came to U.S., 1940, naturalized, 1945; s. Theodore F. and Frances (Lowen) P.; m. Mary Ann Rose, June 4, 1977; children: Susan, Mary Jane, Carolyn, Kathy, Lisa, Michael. B.A., Conn. Wesleyan U., 1952; M.D. with honors, U. Rochester, 1955. Intern in surgery and obstetrics Strong Meml. Hosp., U. Rochester, N.Y., 1955-56; fellow in head and neck cancer Center du Cancer, U. Nancy, France, 1956-58; grad. research fellow AEC, U. Rochester, 1958-59; resident in gen. and thoracic surgery, 1958-62; with East Carolina U., 1977—, prof., chmn. dept. surgery, 1977—; chief surgery Pitt County Meml. Hosp., Greenville, N.C., 1977—. Mem. Acad. Medicine Cleve. (dir.), AAAS, Am. Assn. Cancer Edn., Am. Assn. Cancer Research, Am. Burn Assn., Am. Coll. Cardiology, Am. Coll. Nutrition, Am. Coll. Surgeons, Am. Fedn. Clin. Research, Am. Nuclear Soc., Am. Soc. Clin. Oncology, Am. Surg. Assn., Am. Trauma Soc., Assn. Acad. Surgery, Assn. Mil. Surgeons of U.S., Central Surg. Assn., Cleve. Surg. Soc., Cleve. Vascular Soc., Internat. Assn. Bioinorganic Scientists, Internat. Cardiovascular Soc., Ohio State Med. Assn., Pan-Am. Med. Assn., Royal Soc. Health, Soc. U. Surgeons, Soc. Vascular Surgery, Soc. Surg. Oncology, So. Assn. Vascular Surgery, Soc. Surg. Chmn., Soc. Environ. Geochemistry and Health (pres.-elect), Surg. Biology Club. Subspecialties: Surgery; Biochemistry (medicine). Office: East Carolina U Sch Medicine Greenville NC 27834

PORSKIEVIES, THOMAS ANTHONY, electronic engineer; b. Red Bank, N.J., Feb. 10, 1960; s. Robert and Mary (Glass) P. B.S., Monmouth Coll., N.J., 1982. Tech. coordinator Marebob Corp., Keansburg, N.J., 1979-80; communications engr. Planning Research Corp., Eatontown, N.J., 1982—; engr. U.S. Army CECOM, Fort Monmouth, 1981. Monmouth Trustees scholar, 1978. Mem. IEEE (chmn. student activities N.J. coast sect. 1984-85), Armed Forces Communications Assn., Assn. Computing Machinery. Democrat. Roman Catholic. Current work: Simulation and modeling of communications with emphasis on traffic flow and optimization. Subspecialties: Computer engineering; Systems engineering. Office: Planning Research Corp 142 State Hwy 35 Eatontown NJ 07724

PORTARE, ANTHONY FRANK, nuclear physicist, operations researcher; b. Phila., Jan. 8, 1954; s. Frank Michael and Priscilla Mildred (Caruso) P.; m. Patricia Mary Biehl, June 19, 1976; 1 son, Anthony Frank, Jr. B.A. in Physics, West Chester State U., 1975; M.S. in Systems Mgmt., U. So. Calif., 1979. Teaching asst. Drexel U., Phila., 1975, tchr. Archdiocese of Phila., 1975-76; phys. scientist U.S. Army Nuclear and Chem. Agy., Fort Belvoir, Va., 1976-80; research scientist Kaman Scis. Corp., Arlington, Va., 1980—. Author: Nuclear Survivability Methodology Tradeoff, 1980; Base Surge Phenomenology, 1982; Army Thermal Transmissivity Calculations, 1984; Unit Effectiveness on the Integrated Battlefield, 1982. Leader, Explorer Troop, Boy Scouts Am., 1977. Served with U.S. Army, 1976-80. Mem. Am. Phys. Soc., Ops. Research Soc. of Am. Roman Catholic. Current work: Calculational procedures for nuclear weapons effects, in particular radiation transport; devel. methodology for determining system vulnerability to nuclear weapons and analysis and design of directed energy weapons. Subspecialties: Nuclear physics; Operations research (mathematics). Office: Kaman Scis Corp 1911 Jefferson Davis Hwy Suite 1200 Arlington VA 22202

PORTER, FREDERICK CHARLES, aerospace company executive, consultant; b. New Orleans, Jan. 10, 1937; s. Frederick Charles and Jane (Currens) Fitz-Randolph; m. Gayle Mae Johnson, June 7, 1959; children: Steve, Linda. B.S. in M.E, U. Colo., 1959; mgmt. cert., Alexander Hamilton Inst., N.Y.C., 1965. Registered profl. engr., Calif. Research asst. U. Colo., 1957-59; structures engr. Rockwell Internat., Los Angeles, 1959-60; sr. project engr. Gen. Dynamics/Convair, San Diego, Calif., 1960—; Contbr. in field. Mem. nat. adv. bd. Am. Security Council; mem. Republican Nat. Com. Fellow AIAA (assoc.; treas. San Diego sect. 1970-71), Nat. Mgmt. Assn. Republican. Club: Hacienda Recreation Assn. (pres. 1974-76). Current Work: Develop new aerospace programs in fields of advanced missile weapon systems, space transportation and advanced space applications. Subspecialty: Aerospace engineering and technology. Home: 1950 WoodGlen Way El Cajon CA 92020 Office: General Dynamics Convair PO Box 85357 San Diego CA 92138

PORTER, JOHN ROBERT, JR., consulting company executive; b. Oklahoma City, Feb. 27, 1935; s. John Robert and Margaret Florence (Nicholson) P.; m. Amelie Wallace, June 2, 1962; children: Jennifer, Amy. A.B., Dartmouth Coll., 1957; M.S., Okla. U., 1964. Sci. project officer govt. agy., Washington, 1962-66; chief earth resources program NASA, Washington, 1966-69; pres. Earth Satellite Corp. (EarthSat), cons. specializing in remote sensing applied to oil and mineral exploration, crop forecasting and image enhancement software, Chevy Chase, Md., 1969—; dir. Stauffer Communications, Inc., 1962—; mem. Remote Sensing Adv. Com. Dept. Commerce.; mem. Space Applications Com. NRC. Contbr. articles on clay mineralogy, remote sensing to profl. jours. Trustee Washington Gallery Modern Art, 1964-65. Served to 1st lt. Signal Corps U.S. Army, 1960-62. Mem. Am. Assn. Petroleum Geologists (cert. petroleum geologist). Clubs: University (Washington), Chevy Chase (Washington). Subspecialties: Remote sensing (geoscience); Satellite studies. Office: 7222 47th St Chevy Chase MD 20815

PORTER, JOHNNY R., physiology educator; b. Bernice, La., Sept. 18, 1944; s. John Tilman and Betty (Roach) P.; m. Terry Cambell, July 27, 1967; children—Tricia, Julie, John. B.S., Western Ky. U., 1966; M.S., Northeast La. U., 1968; Ph.D., La. State U., 1973. Grad. asst. Northeast La. U., Monroe, 1966-68, La. State U. Med. Ctr., New Orleans, 1968-73, instr., 1973-77, asst. prof., 1977-82, assoc. prof. physiology, 1982—, dir. physiology course, 1977-80, endocrinology course, 1973—, grad. student Coordinator physiology, 1980—. Contbr. articles to med. jours. Lay Bible tchr. Metairie Baptist Ch., New Orleans, 1979—, deacon, 1981—. Grantee: Edward G. Schlieder Found., 1975, Am. Heart Assn., 1977, 82, 84, NIH, 1982—, Diabetes Assn., 1984. Mem. Am. Physiol. Soc., ADA, AAAS, Am. Men and Women in Sci., Sigma Xi. Democrat. Current work: Research interests are in the regulation of pituitary-adrenal system, particular emphasis on the study of the regulation in disease states such as hypertension, obesity and diabetes. Subspecialties: Physiology (medicine); Neuroendocrinology. Home: 5209 Fairfield St Metairie LA 70006 Office: Dept Physiology La State U Med Ctr 1100 Florida Ave New Orleans LA 70119

PORTER, KAREN GLAUS, zoology educator, ecologist; b. Perth Amboy, N.J., Feb. 8, 1947; d. Sam and Mary (Christensen) Glaus; m. James W. Porter, Jan. 1, 1972; 1 child, Delene. B.A., Vassar Coll., 1968; M.S., Ph.D. Yale U. Teaching asst. Yale U., 1970-71; asst. prof. U. Mich., 1973-78; mem. staff Marine Biol. Lab., Woods Hole, Mass., 1977-78; mem. faculty Discovery Bay Marine Lab., Jamaica, 1978; assoc. prof. zoology U. Ga., Athens, 1977—; assoc. v.p. research U. Ga. Research Found., Athens, 1984—. Contbr. articles to profl. jour. NSF grantee. Mem. Am. Soc. Limnology and Oceanography, Ecol. Soc. Am. Subspecialties: Ecology (biology); Limnology. Office: Zoology Dept U Ga Athens GA 30602

PORTER, MAX LEE, structural engineering educator; b. Hamburg, Iowa, Oct. 25, 1942; s. Harry Ellis and Mary Olive (Stafford) P.; m. Monica Gaye Munyer, Aug. 2, 1969; 1 child, Nathan Allen. B.S., Iowa State U., 1965, M.S., 1968, Ph.D., 1974. Registered profl. engr., Iowa. Asst. engr. County of Los Angeles, 1965, Am. Bridge U.S. Steel, Chgo., 1966; instr. to asst. prof. Iowa State U., Ames, 1966-77, assoc. prof., 1977-81, prof. structural engring., 1981—; cons. numerous engring. firms, 1974—; Patentee (with others) prestressed metal and concrete composite structures. Contbr. over 60 articles to profl. jours. and presentations. Vice-chmn. Neighborhood Assn., City of Ames, 1981-84; com. mem. Ames Rental Housing Code, 1981-84. Grantee Am. Iron and Steel Inst., 1967-78, Iowa State U. Engring. Research Inst., 1968, Iowa Dept. Transp., 1974-75, Metal Crafters of Cedar Rapids, Inc., 1976-77, Iowa Civil Def., 1974-81, NSF, 1976-86, ASCE, 1981-84, U.S. Nuclear Regulatory Commn., 1982-84, Nucor Steel Corp., 1982-86, Wheeling-Pitts. Steel Corp., 1982-86, Iowa High Tech. Devel. Commn., others. Mem. ASCE (chmn. composite constrn. com. 1979-83), Am. Concrete Inst., Earthquake Engring. Research Inst., Nat. Soc. Profl. Engrs. (chmn. constn. and bylaws commn. 1981-82 parliamentarian 1982-83, Young Engr. of Yr. award 1978), Iowa Engring Soc. (pres. Anson Marston Chpt. 1977-78, chmn. profl. devel. com. 1975-77, chmn. chpt. activities com. 1978-80, pres. 1983-84, John Dunlap-Sherman Woodward award 1977), Structural Engr. Assn. Central Iowa, Masonry Soc., Can. Soc. Civil Engrs., Soc. Exptl. Stress Analysis, Internat. Assn. Bridge and Structural Engring., Sigma Xi, Phi Kappa Phi, Tau Beta Pi, Chi Epsilon, Phi Eta Sigma, Scabbard & Blade. Republican. Presbyterian. Current work: Experimental evaluation of structures; structural damage investigations; diaphragm floor slabs; composite masonry; sandwich walls; steel deck-reinforced slabs. Subspecialty: Structural engineering. Home: 3224 Kingman Ames IA 50010 Office: Iowa State U Civil Engring Dept Ames IA 50011

PORTER, STEPHEN CUMMINGS, geological sciences educator; b. Santa Barbara, Calif., Apr. 18, 1934; s. Lawrence J. and Frances C. (Cummings) Seger P.; m. Anne M. Higgins, Apr. 2, 1959; children: John, Maria, Susannah. B.S., Yale U., 1955, M.S., 1958, Ph.D., 1962. Asst. prof. geol. scis. U. Wash., Seattle, 1962-66, assoc, . prof., 1966-69, prof., 1969—; dir. Quaternary Research Ctr., 1981—; v.p. Cambria Corp., Seattle, 1981—. Editor: Late Quaternary Environments of the United States, Vol. 1, 1982; editor: Quaternary Research, 1977—; assoc. editor: Radiocarbon; editorial bd.: Quaternary Scis. Revs.; bd. earth scis.: Nat. Acad. Scis./NRC, 1983-85. Served to lt. USNR, 1955-57. Recipient Benjamin Silliman prize Yale U., 1962; Fulbright fellow, N.Z., 1973-74; vis. fellow Cambridge U., 1980-81. Fellow Arctic Inst. N.Am. (gov. 1972-77), Geol. Soc. Am.; mem. AAAS, Internat. Glaciological Soc. Club: Am. Alpine (N.Y.). Current Work: Quaternary glaciation of alpine regions, especially Alps, Himalayas, Andes, North American Cordillera, Hawaii; volcanology and tephrochronology; Quaternary stratigraphy and chronology. Subspecialty: Geology. Home: 18034 15th Ave NW Seattle WA 98177 Office: Quaternary Research Ctr U Wash Seattle WA 98195

PORTER, WALTER JAMES, JR., chemical engineer; b. Washington, Apr. 10, 1930; s. Walter James and Elizabeth (Schaaff) P.; m. Bernice Diana Fritz, June 21, 1952; children—Dianne Lynn, Judith Anne, Bethany Jeanne. B.S. in Chem. Engring, Lehigh U., 1952; M.S., La. State U., 1957. Vice pres. Asia Pacific, Exxon Chem. Co., Hong Kong, 1970-73, plastics tech. mgr., Baytown, Tex., 1973-75, v.p. specialties, Darien, Conn., 1975-77, v.p. plastics, 1977-80, v.p. tech., 1980—. Patentee in field. Served to 1st lt. U.S. Army, 1952-54. Mem. Am. Inst. Chem. Engrs, AAAS, N.Y. Acad. Sci., Council for Chem. Research (chmn. 1983-84). Republican. Lutheran. Current work: Science and technology management. Home: 31 Codfish Ln Weston CT 06883 Office: Exxon Chem Co 9 Old Kings Hwy S Darien CT 06820

PORTERFIELD, WILLIAM WENDELL, educator; b. Winchester, Va., Aug. 24, 1936; s. Donald Kennedy and Adelyn (Miller) P.; m. Dorothy Elizabeth Dail, Aug. 24, 1957; children—Allan Kennedy, Douglas Hunter. B.S., U. N.C., 1957, Ph.D., 1962; M.S., Calif. Inst. Tech., 1960. Sr. research chemist Hercules, Inc., Cumberland, Md., 1962-64; asst. prof. chemistry Hampden-Sydney (Va.) Coll., 1964-65, assoc. prof., 1965-68, prof. chemistry, 1968—, chmn. natural sci. div., 1973-77, chmn. dept. chemistry, 1982-85. Author: Concepts of Chemistry, 1972, Inorganic Chemistry, 1984; Contbr. articles to profl. jours. Mem. Am. Chem. Soc., Royal Chem. Soc. (London, Eng.), Phi Beta Kappa. Current Work: Theory of cluster bonding; spectroscopic properties of low temperature molten salts. Subspecialty: Inorganic chemistry. Home: Box 697 Hampden Sydney VA 23943

PORTOGHESE, PHILIP SALVATORE, medicinal chemist, educator; b. N.Y.C., June 4, 1931; s. Philip A. and Constance (Antonelli) P.; m. Christine L. Phillips, June 11, 1960; children—Stephen, Stuart, Philip. B.S., Columbia, 1953, M.S., 1958; PH.D., U. Wis., 1961. Asst. prof. Coll. Pharmacy, U. Minn., Mpls., 1961-64, asso. prof., 1964-69, prof. medicinal chemistry, 1969—, dir. grad. study in medicinal chemistry, 1974—; cons. NIMH., 1971-72; mem. med. chemistry B sec. NIH, 1972-76; mem. pharmacology, substance abuse and environ. toxicology interdisciplinary cluster President's Biomed. Research Panel, 1975. Mem. editorial adv. bd. jour.: Med. Chemistry, 1969-71; editor, 1972—; editorial adv. bd.: Med. Chem. series, 1972—. Served with U.S. Army, 1954-56. Recipient Research Achievement award in med. chemistry Am. Pharm. Assn. Found./Acad. Pharm. Sci., 1980; Volwiler award outstanding research achievement in phar. scis., 1984. Fellow Acad. Pharm. Scis.; mem. Am. Pharm. Assn., Am. Chem. Soc., Am. Soc. Pharm. Exptl. Therapeutics, Internat. Union Pure and Applied Chemistry (commn. on medicinal chemistry 1978-82, internat. com. med. chemistry 1982—), AAAS, Sigma Xi, Rho Chi, Phi Lambda Upsilon. Current work: Opioids and narcotic antagonists; development of new concepts in drug design. Home: 2165 W Hoyt Ave Saint Paul MN 55108 Office: Coll Pharmacy U Minn Minneapolis MN 55455

POST, JOSEPH, physician, researcher; b. N.Y.C., Mar. 6, 1913; s. Charles and Mollie P.; m. Anne Bretzfelder, Mar. 1, 1942; children—David Louis, Thomas Charles. B.S., CUNY, 1932; M.D., U. Chgo., 1937; D. in Med. Sci., Columbia U., 1941. Diplomate Am. Bd. Internal Medicine. Intern Michael Reese Hosp., Chgo., 1937-38; resident Columbia U. Research Div., N.Y.C., 1938-42; attending physician Goldwater Meml. Hosp., N.Y.C., 1946—, Lenox Hill Hosp., N.Y.C., 1947—, Univ. Hosp., N.Y.C., 1971—; prof. clin. medicine NYU, 1971—; cons. internist VA Hosp., Bronx, N.Y.C., 1946-54; cons. gastroenterologist U.S. Navy, N.Y.C., 1950-58; vis. prof. medicine Sch. Medicine U. Hawaii, Honolulu, 1970, Hawaii Cancer Ctr., Honolulu, 1974. Contbr. articles to profl. jours. Served to maj. AUS, 1942-46, PTO, Okinawa. Fellow N.Y. Acad. Medicine (pres. 1979-80 Plaque for Service 1982), ACP; mem. Am. Gastroent. Soc., Am. Assn. Cancer Research, Am. Soc. Cell Biology, Am. Soc. Clin. Investigation. Current work: Tumor cell biology; cell cycle kinetics, human cancer. Subspecialties: Internal medicine; Gastroenterology. Home: 29 Washington Sq W New York NY 10011 Office: 20 E 68th St New York NY 10021

POST, MADISON JOHN, physicist; b. Detroit, Oct. 4, 1946; s. Madison and Clara Agnus (Krause) P.; m. Donna Darlene Horky, Oct. 25, 1953. B.S. in Elec. Engring; B.S. in Math, U. Ill., 1969; M.S. in Astro-geophysics, U. Colo., 1975; M.S. in Optical Scis., U. Ariz., 1983, Ph.D. in Optical Scis., 1985. Asst. sta. sci. leader ESSA, Byrd Sta., Antarctica, 1969-70; engr. NOAA, Boulder, 1970-75, physicist, 1975—, Wave Propagation Lab., 1975—. Contbr. numerous articles in optics and atmospheric research to profl. jours. Mem. Optical Soc. Am., Sigma Xi. Clubs: Colo. Mountain (Boulder). Current Work: Design, analysis of coherent Doppler lidar for atmospheric science; remote wind sensing by coherent laser radar. Subspecialties: Remote sensing (atmospheric science); Optical engineering. Office: 325 Broadway R E WP2 Boulder CO 80303

POSTLETHWAIT, SAMUEL NOEL, biology educator, researcher, consultant; b. willeysville, W.Va., Apr. 16, 1918; s. Albert Franklin and Marietta (Mason) Postlehwait; m. Sara Cover, Mar. 22, 1942; children: John Harvey, Robert Neil. A.B. in Biology, Fairmont State Coll., 1940; M.S. in Botany, W.Va. State U., 1947; Ph.D. in Plant Anatomy, State U. Iowa, 1949; Dr. Pedagogy (hon.), Doan Coll., 1982. Tchr., W.Va. Pub. Schs., 1940-41; instr. botany and biology State U. Iowa, Iowa City, 1948-49; asst. prof. biology Purdue U., West Lafayette, Ind., 1949-56, assoc. prof. biology, 1956-63, prof., 1963—; adv. bd. Community Coll. Forum. Author: (with J. Novak, H.T. Murray) An Integrated Experience Approach to Learning - With Emphasis on Independent Study, 1969, 72; author: Exploring Teaching Alternatives, 1979; editor: Minicourses in Biology, 1978; contbr. articles on biol. scis. to profl. jours. NSF fellow Manchester U., 1957-58; Fulbright grantee Macquarie U., Australia, 1968; recipient Purdue Student Govt. Best Tchr. award, 1965, Best Tchr. award Sigma Delta Chi, 1965, Helping Students Learn award, 1983; Ind. Acad. Sci. Speaker of Yr. award, 1978; Internat. Congress Individualized Instrn., Postlethwait award, 1980. Fellow Ind. Acad. Sci., AAAS; mem. Bot. Soc. Am., Nat. Assn. Biology Tchrs., Internat. Soc. Plant Morphology, Am. Inst. Biol. Scis., Internat. Soc. Sterology, Am. Genetic Assn., NEA, Ind. Sci. Tchrs. Assn., Internat. Platform Assn., Nat. Assn. Resources in Sci. Teaching, Torrey Bot. Club, Sigma Xi, Omicron Delta Kappa, Kappa Delta Kappa, Phi Eta Sigma. Current Work: Plant morphology and science education, audio-tutorial instruction, instructional design, developmental morphology of maize, gene control of form, three-dimension of structure and its interpretation. Subspecialties: Plant growth; Developmental biology. Home: 3180 Soldiers Home Rd West Lafayette IN 47906 Office: 221 Chemistry Bldg Purdue West Lafayette IN 47907

POSTMA, HERMAN, research instn. exec.; b. Wilmington, N.C., Mar. 29, 1933; s. Gilbert and Sophie Hadrian (Verzaal) P.; m. Patricia Dunigan, Nov. 25, 1960; children: Peter, Pamela. B.S. summa cum laude, Duke U., 1955; M.S., Harvard U., 1957, Ph.D., 1959. Registered profl. engr., Calif. Summer staff Oak Ridge Nat. Lab., 1954-57, physicist thermonuclear div., 1959-62; co-leader Oak Ridge Nat. Lab. (DCX-1 Group), 1962-66, asst. dir. thermonuclear div., 1966, asso. dir. div., 1967, dir. div., 1967-73, dir. nat. lab., 1974—; v.p. Martin Marietta Energy Systems, 1984—; vis. scientist FOM-Instituut voor Plasma-Fysica, The Netherlands, 1963; cons. Lab. Laser Energetics, U. Rochester.; mem. energy research adv. bd. spl. panel Dept. Energy. Editorial bd.: Nuclear Fusion, 1968-74. Bd. dirs. The Nucleus; chmn. bd. trustees Hosp. of Meth. Ch.; mem. adv. bd. Coll. Bus. Adminstrn., U. Tenn., 1976-84, Energy Inst., State of N.C.; bd. dirs., exec. com. Tenn. Tech. Found., 1982—; commr. Tenn. Higher Edn. Commn., 1984—. Fellow Am. Phys. Soc. (exec. com. div. plasma physics), AAAS, Am. Nuclear Soc. (dir.); mem. C. of C. (exec. com., v.p. 1981—), Phi Beta Kappa, Beta Gamma Sigma, Sigma Pi Sigma, Omicron Delta Kappa, Sigma Xi, Pi Mu Epsilon, Phi Eta Sigma. Current Work: Technical management of research and development, particularly large interdisciplinary teams. Subspecialties: Plasma physics; Atomic and molecular physics. Office: Oak Ridge Nat Lab PO Box X Oak Ridge TN 37830

POTASH, LOUIS, virologist; b. Boston, Sept. 14, 1924; s. Morris and Ethel (Gerstein) P.; m. Carole Ina Appleberg, Dec. 25, 1951; children: Moira Elayne, Stuart Alan, Neil Bradley. Student, Northeastern U., 1942-43; B.A., Boston U., 1947; M.Sc. in Hygiene, Harvard Sch. Pub. Health, 1951; Ph.D. in Microbiology, Tulane U., 1958. Lab. technician Harvard Med. Sch., 1947-48, Sch. Pub. Health, 1948-49; bacteriologist Chem. Warfare Labs., Ft. Detrick, Md., 1951-52; research assoc. microbiology Tulane U., 1952-53, grad. asst., 1953-54, research assoc. in epidemiology, 1954-58, instr., 1958-59; research assoc. Merck Inst. Therapeutic Research, West Point, Pa., 1959-64; sr. scientist, program mgr., supr. Flow Labs., Inc., McLean, Va., 1964—. Served with U.S. Army, 1943-44. USPHS fellow, 1956-58. Mem. Am. Soc. Microbiology, N.Y. Acad. Scis., Union Concerned Scientists, Fedn. Am. Scientists, Sigma Xi. Democrat. Jewish. Current Work: Virology, respiratory disease agents, influenza, parainfluenza and respiratory syncytial viruses; non-bacterial gastroenteritis agents; rotavirus, Norwalk agent. Subspecialties: Virology (biology); Virology (medicine). Home: 5337 Pooks Hill Rd Bethesda MD 20814 Office: 7655 Old Springhouse Rd McLean VA 22102

POTCHEN, EDWARD JAMES, radiologist, educator; b. Queens County, N.Y., Dec. 2, 1932; s. Joseph Anton and Eleanore (Joyce) P.; m. Geraldine J. Jeplawy, Sept. 1, 1956; children: Michelle M., Kathleen A., Michael J., Joseph E. B.S., Mich. State U., 1954; M.D., Wayne State U., 1958; postgrad. (fellow), Harvard U., 1964-66; M.S. in Mgmt. (Sloan fellow), MIT, 1972. Intern Butterworth Hosp., Grand Rapids, Mich., 1958-59; pvt. practice gen. medicine, Grand Rapids, Mich., 1959-61; resident in radiology Peter Bent Brigham Hosp., Boston, 1961-64, chief resident radiologist, 1964; dir. div. nuclear medicine Harvard Med. Sch. dept. radiology, 1965; assoc. radiologist Barnes Hosp., St. Louis, 1966; dir. nuclear medicine div. Edward Mallinckrodt Inst. Radiology, Washington U. Sch. Medicine, St. Louis, 1967; chief diagnostic radiology Edward Mallinckrodt Inst., 1971-73; prof. radiology, dean mgmt. resources Johns Hopkins U. Sch. Medicine, 1973-75; prof. radiology and health systems mgmt. Mich. State U., East Lansing, 1975—, chmn. dept. radiology, 1973—; prof. radiology Washington U. Sch. Medicine, 1969-73; cons. Nat. Heart Inst., Nat. Inst. Gen. Med. Scis., div. biology and medicine U.S. AEC; mem. liaison com. on med. edn. Assn. Am. Med. Colls./AMA, 1980—, chmn. liaison com. on med. edn., 1982—; mem. Med. Radiation Adv. Bd. FDA, 1982—; examiner Am. Bd. Radiology. Editor: Endocrine Radiology, 1966, Frontiers of Pulmonary Radiology, 1969, Diagnostic Radiology, 1971, Fundamentals of Tracer Method, 1972, Neuro-Nuclear Medicine, 1972, Current Concepts in Radiology, 1972, 3d edit., 1977; also contbr. to jours. Recipient John J. Larkin award for basic med. research, 1963; James Picker Found. fellow in acad. radiology Nat. Acad. Scis.-NRC, 1965-66; Sloan fellow Mass. Inst. Tech., 1972-73. Mem. AMA (mem. ho. of dels., sect. on nuclear medicine 1976—, council on med. edn. 1979), Am. Fedn. Clin. Research, Central Soc. Clin. Research, Am. Soc. Clin. Investigation, Soc. Nuclear Med. (trustee, nat. pres. 1975-76), Am. Physiol. Soc., Am. Radium Soc., Assn. of Univ. Radiologists, Liaison Com. on Med. Edn., Alpha Omega Alpha. Home: 4810 Arapaho Dr Okemos MI 48864 Office: Dept Radiology Mich State U B220 Clinic Center East Lansing MI 48824

POTEL, MICHAEL JOHN, computing and biophysics educator; consultant; b. Champaign, Ill., June 22, 1948; s. John Joseph and Patricia Delores (Domack) P. B.S., U. Mich., 1970; M.S., U. Chgo., 1971, Ph.D., 1977. Research assoc. U. Chgo., 1977-79, research assoc., asst. prof., 1979-84, research assoc., assoc. prof., 1984—; cons. Hoffmann-LaRoche Inc., Nutley, N.J., 1982—, Apple Computer Inc., Cupertino, Calif., 1982—, Siemens Gammasonics Inc., Des Plaines, Ill., 1982—, NBC News, Chgo., 1982. Contbr. articles to profl. jours. Chgo. Heart Assn. grantee, 1982-84; NIH Research grantee, 1983—. Mem. Assn. Computing Machinery, IEEE, EMSA. Current work: Image processing in electron microscopy of macromolecular structures; image enhancement, reconstructions, molecular graphics; design of computer image analysis systems; medical image acquisition, display, and quantitation. Subspecialties: Graphics, image processing, and pattern recognition; Molecular biology. Home: 5716 S Kenwood Ave Chicago IL 60637 Office: U Chgo 920 E 58th St Chicago IL 60637

POTTASH, A.L.C., physician, psychopharmacologist, researcher; b. Phila., Nov. 30, 1948; s. R.R. and M.E. P. B.S., Trinity Coll., Hartford, Conn., 1970; M.D., Yale U., 1974. Intern Baystate Med. Ctr., Springfield, Mass., 1974-75; resident, fellow Yale U. Sch. Medicine, 1975-78, lectr. dept. psychiatry, 1978-81, cons., 1981—; clin. dir. Whiting Forensic Inst., Middletown, Conn., 1976-78; exec. med. dir. Fair Oaks Hosp., Delray Beach, Fla., 1984—, Lake Hosp. of the Palm Beaches, Lake Worth, Fla., 1984—; med. dir. Regent Hosp., N.Y.C., 1981—, PANJ, Fair Oaks Hosp., Summit, N.J., 1978—; psychiatrist-in-chief Falkirk Hosp., Central Valley, N.Y., 1982—; co-dir. 800-Cocaine, toll-free helpline; numerous appearances radio and TV. Contbr. numerous articles to profl. jours. Fellow Nat. Acad. Clin. Biochemistry, Am. Coll. Clin. Pharmacology; mem. Soc. Neurosci., Am. Psychiat. Assn., AMA, Am. Acad. Clin. Psychiatrists, N.J. Med. Soc., Phi Beta Kappa. Clubs: N.Y. Athletic; Canoe Brook Country (Summit), Beacon Hill (Summit). Current Work: Psychopharmacology; neuroendocrinology and depression; drug abuse; clinical laboratory testing in psychiatry. Subspecialties: Psychopharmacology; Neuropharmacology. Home: PO Box 184 Summit NJ 07901

POTTER, MICHAEL, cancer researcher. Head genetics lab. Cancer Biology and Diagnosis Div., Nat. Cancer Inst. Recipient Lasker award in basic med. research, 1984. Subspecialty: Cancer research (medicine). Office: Nat Cancer Inst Cancer Biology and Diagnosis 9000 Rockville Pike Bethesda MD 20205

POTTER, MILES BUTTLES, sci. cons.; b. Old Forge, Pa., June 5, 1909; s. Lewis M and Ruth (Buttles) P.; m. Helen Rose Bocci, Dec. 31, 1937 (div.); children: Patsy Carol, Barbara Ann, Donna Helen, Miles Milton. Student, Gettysburg (Pa.) Coll., 1927-29; B.S., Bloomsburg (Pa.) State Coll., 1933; postgrad., U. Del.; D.Sc. (hon.), U. London, 1972. Registered profl. engr., N.J., Fla., Maine, Pa., N.Y. Mem. faculty The Citadel, 1943-44, U. North Ga., 1944-45, Va. Mil. Inst., 1945-47, Washington and Lee U., 1946-47; Mem. faculty Villanova U., 1947-57, assoc. dir. research, 1950-56; pres. Harris, Henry & Potter, Inc., Buckingham, Pa., 1956-72; with Mcpl. Environ. Assocs., Inc., Spring House, Pa., 1972—; chmn. exec. com. MDD Inc., 1980—; dir. East Coast Chem. Disposal Inc., Pa.; treas. Pa. Cons. Engrs. Council, 1960-69; sci. cons. Mem. PTA, 1947-55, 74-78. Served with Va. Militia, 1945-47. Republican. Methodist. Current Work: Providing a transition of scientific (engineering) information to an engineering basis in order to enable technical planning and engineering design. Subspecialties: Civil engineering; Water supply and wastewater treatment. Office: 908 Bethlehem Pike Spring House PA 19477

POTTER, ROBERT GENE, chemical company executive; b. Terre Haute, Ind., Apr. 16, 1939; s. Thomas Benjamin and Violet Eve (King) P.; m. Patricia Anne Smolik, Sept. 10, 1966; children—Brian, Michael, Timothy. B.S. in Indsl. Econs., Purdue U., 1961; M.B.A., Ind. U., 1962; postgrad., U. Calif.-Berkeley, 1978. Bus. dir. function products Monsanto Indsl. Chem. Co., St. Louis, 1975-77, gen. mgr. detergent and phosphate div., 1977-79; gen. mgr. comml. div. Monsanto Chem. Intermed. Co., St. Louis, 1979-82, v.p., mng. dir., 1982-83; group v.p., mng. dir. Monsanto Indsl. Chem. Co., St. Louis, 1983-84; group v.p., mng. dir. Monsanto Polymer Products Co., 1984—. Bd. dirs. Monsanto Fund, 1981—; chmn. Monsanto United Way campaign, 1976; mem. devel. bd. St. Louis Children's Hosp., 1979-81; bd. dirs. YMCA of Greater St. Louis, 1978—. Served to lt. USN, 1962-65. Mem. Soap and Detergents Assn. (dir.). Republican. Mem. Christian Ch. Club: Bellerive Country. . Home: 37 Muirfield Ln Saint Louis MO 63141 Office: 800 N Lindbergh Blvd Saint Louis MO 63167

POTTS, DONALD CAMERON, ecology and evolutionary biology educator, researcher; b. Edinburgh, Scotland, Apr. 4, 1942; came to U.S. 1965; s. Edward Dickinson and Jean Julia Mairi (Cameron) P.; m. Laurel Ruth Fox, Dec. 20, 1970; children—Stephen Edward, Shaina Sophie. B.Sc., U. Queensland, Brisbane, Australia, 1963, B.Sc. (hon.), 1965; Ph.D., U. Calif.-Santa Barbara, 1972. Lectr. Bishops U., Quebec, Can., 1971-72, Flinders U., South Australia, 1972-73; research fellow Australian Nat. U., Canberra, 1974-78; asst. prof. U. Calif-Santa Cruz, 1978-85, assoc. prof., 1985—. Contbr. articles to profl. jours. Ford Found. fellow, 1968-71. Mem. Ecol. Soc. Am., Brit. Ecol. Soc., Australian Marine Scis. Assn. (councilor 1974-77), Australian Coral Reef Soc. (councillor 1973-77) Soc. Study Evolution, Sigma Xi. Current work: Ecology, evolution, paleoecology of reef corals, biology of clonal organisms. Subspecialties: Ecology (biology); Evolutionary biology. Office: Ctr Marine Studies U Calif Santa Cruz CA 95064

POTTS, HOWARD CALVIN, agronomy educator, seed technologist, plant breeder; b. Stillwater, Okla., Oct. 18, 1928; s. Henry Clay and Gladys (Sneary) P.; m. Wanda Lee Rounds, Aug. 26, 1950; children—Steven Clay, Ken Wilson, Nancy Sue. B.S., Okla. State U., 1950; M.S., Miss. State U., 1956; Ph.D., Tex. A&M U., 1966. Technician, Found. Seed Sta., College Station, Tex., 1952-54; prodn. mgr. Harpool Seeds, Inc., Denton, Tex., 1955-59; assoc. extension agronomist Va. Poly. Inst., Blacksburg, 1959-63; agronomist, prof. Miss. State U., 1966—; cons. UN Devel. Program, AID, N.Y.C., 1971. Contbr. chpts. to books, numerous articles to tech. jours. Served as 1st lt. U.S. Army, 1950-52, Korea. Mem. Am. Soc. Agronomy (chmn. C-4 1975-76), Am. Genetics Assn., Sigma Xi, Gamma Sigma Delta. Baptist. Current work: Seed factors influencing germination, emergence and stand establishment, pre-harvest preservation of seed quality, breeding creeping bentgrass. Subspecialties: Agronomy; Plant genetics. Office: Seed Technology Lab Box 5267 Mississippi State MS 39762

POULARIKAS, ALEXANDER DEMITRIOS, engineering educator, researcher, consultant; b. Desylla, Greece, Sept. 1, 1933; came to U.S., 1957, naturalized, 1968; s. Demitri A. and Ageliki G. (Mpalta) P.; m. Barbara H. Heinen, Dec. 30, 1962; children—Demitri, Natasha. B.S., U. Ark., 1960, M.S., 1963, Ph.D., 1966. Instr. U. Ark., Fayetteville, 1964-65; asst. prof. U. R.I., Kingston, 1965-69, assoc. prof., 1969-76, prof., 1976-83; prof. engring., chmn. dept. engring. U. Denver, 1984-85; prof., chmn. dept. elec. and computer engring. U. Ala. in Huntsville, 1985—; cons. Underwater Systems Ctr., New London, Conn., 1983—; vis. scientist dept. elec. engring. MIT, 1971-72. Author: Electromagnetics, 1979; Electrical Engineering, 1982; Workbook on Electrical Engineering, 1982; Introduction to Signals and Systems, 1985; also numerous articles. Active Hellenic Cultural Soc., Providence, 1976-83; mem. R.I. Heritage Com., Providence, 1979-83. Fulbright scholar U. Ark., 1956; NSF fellow Stanford U., summer 1966; NASA faculty fellow Goddard Space Flight Ctr., summers 1968, 71. Mem. IEEE (sr.) (info. theory group, pattern analysis and machine intelligence group, edn. group, systems, man and cybernetics group, communications group, antennas and propagation group), Soc. Photo-Optical Instrumentation Engrs., Optical Soc. Am., Am. Assn. Engring. Edn., Ark. Acad. Elec. Engring. (charter), Sigma Xi, Tau Beta Pi. Current work: Optical signal processing and optical communications; signal processing and pattern recognition. Subspecialties: Electrical engineering; Optical signal processing. Office: U Ala in Huntsville Dept Elec and Computer Engring Huntsville AL 35899

POULTNEY, SHERMAN KING, physicist; b. Leonminster, Mass., Mar. 18, 1937; s. George S. and Ruth (King) P.; m. Joan McGuire, Aug. 6, 1966; 1 child, Christopher. B.S., Worcester Poly. Inst., 1958; M.A., Princeton U., 1960, Ph.D., 1962. Asst prof. physics U. Md., College Park, 1964-73; research assoc. prof. Old Dominion U., Norfolk, Va., 1973-75; sr. staff scientist Perkin-Elmer Corp., Wilton, Conn., 1975-80, mgr. spectrometric systems, Danbury, Conn., 1980-83, sr. scientist, 1983—; cons. U.S. Navy, Indian Head, 1970-73; McMillan Press, N.Y.C., 1982—. Author chpt. in book: Single Photon Detection and Timing: Experiments, 1974. Contbr. articles to profl. publs. Patentee in field. Served to 1st lt. U.S. Army, 1962-64. Recipient Apollo Achievement award NASA, 1969, Sci. Paper award Perkin-Elmer, 1983, 84. Mem. Optical Soc. Am. (Newport fellowship com.), Am. Phys. Soc. (vis. physicist 1978—), Am. Geophys. Union. Soc. Photo-Optical Instrumentation Engrs. Current work: Electro-optic and spectrometric sensing of earth, planetary space atmospheres and natural resources. Subspecialties: Remote sensing (atmospheric science); Planetary atmospheres. Home: 279 Cheese Spring Rd Wilton CT 06897 Office: Perkin-Elmer Corp 100 Wooster Heights Rd Danbury CT 06810

POUNDER, ELTON ROY, physicist, educator; b. Montreal, Que., Can., Jan. 10, 1916; s. Roy M. and Norval (McLeese) P.; m. Marion Crane Wry, Feb. 15, 1941; children—David Crane, Norval Gillian. B.Sc., McGill U., Montreal, 1934, Ph.D., 1937. Field engr. Bell Telphone Co. Can., Ottawa, Ont., Montreal, 1937-39; faculty McGill U., 1945—, prof. physics, 1959—. Author: (with J.S. Marshall and R.W. Stewart) Physics, 2d edit, 1967, The Physics of Ice, 1965, also numerous articles. Fellow Royal Soc. Can.; mem. Canadian Assn. Physicists (past pres.), Am. Phys. Soc., Am. Geophys. Union. Research on constrn. cyclotron, neutron prodn., doppler radar used mid-Can. line, geophysics of sea ice. Current Work: Analysis of oceanographic data collected in the Arctic. Subspecialties: Geophysics; Oceanography. Office: Physics Dept McGill U 3600 University St Montreal PQ H3A 2T8 Canada

POUR, PARVIZ M., pathologist; b. Tehran, Iran, Jan. 4, 1933; came to U.S., 1971, naturalized, 1979; s. Timour and Nasimeh (Omid) P.; m. Adelheid Guldimann, July 25, 1951; children: Schahrzad, Schahrameh, Farid. M.D., Duesseldorf (Ger.) Med. Sch., 1963. Diplomate: Am. Bd. Anatomic Pathology. Asst. prof. Hannover (Ger.) Med. Sch., 1968-71; assoc. prof. U. Nebr. Med. Center, Omaha, 1971-72; prof. U. Nebr. Med. Center (Eppley Inst. and dept. pathology and lab. medicine), 1972—; cons. in toxicology. Contbr. articles to profl. jours. Nat. Cancer Inst./NIH grantee, 1972—. Mem. Am. Assn. for Cancer Research, Soc. Toxicologic Pathologists, Am. Pancreatic Assn., Internat. Assn. on Prevention and Detection of Cancer. Moslem. Current Work: Pancreas cancer: prevention, diagnosis, therapy. Subspecialties: Pathology (medicine); Cancer research (medicine). Home: 9727 Spring St Omaha NE 68124 Office: 42d and Dewey Omaha NE 68105

POUTSMA, MARVIN LLOYD, chemistry research administrator; b. Grand Rapids, Mich., Aug. 7, 1937; s. John and Johanna (Dykstra) P.; m. Yolanda A. Arco., July 20, 1968; children—John, Julie. A.B., Calvin Coll., 1958; Ph.D., U. Ill., 1962. From staff mem. to sr. group leader Corp. Research Lab., Union Carbide Corp., Tarrytown, N.Y., 1961-78; from group leader to div. dir. chemistry Oak Ridge Nat. Lab., 1978—; Chmn. Gordon Research Conf. on Hydrocarbon chemistry, 1977, Gordon Research Conf. Free Radical Chemistry, 1983. Contbr. articles to profl. jours. Fellow N.Y. Acad. Sci. (chmn. chem. sci. sect. 1973-74); mem. Am. Chem. Soc., AAAS. Presbyterian. Current work: Organic chemistry; free-radical reactions; coal chemistry; heterogenous catalysis; research adminstration. Subspecialties: Organic chemistry; Catalysis chemistry. Home: 143 Newport Dr Oak Ridge TN 37830 Office: Oak Ridge Nat Lab PO Box X Oak Ridge TN 37831

POWE, RALPH ELWARD, university administrator; b. Tylertown, Miss., July 27, 1944; s. Roy Elward and Virginia Alyne (Bradley) P.; m. Sharon Eve Sandifer, May 20, 1962; children: Deborah, Ryan, Melanie. B.S.M.E., Miss. State U., 1967, M.S.M.E., 1968; Ph.D. in Mech. Engring, Mont. State U., 1970. Student trainee NASA, 1962-65; research asst., lab. instr. Miss. State U., 1968, instr. in mech. engring., 1968, assoc. prof. mech. engring., 1974-78, prof., 1978-79, assoc. dean engring., dir. engring. and indsl. research sta., 1979-80, assoc. v.p. for research, 1980—; research asst. Mont. State U., 1968-69, teaching asst., 1969-70, asst. prof., 1970-74; cons. energy conservation programs, coal fired power plants, torsional vibration, accident analysis. Contbr. numerous articles to profl. jours., procs. Mem. ASME (Miss. sect. Outstanding Service award 1980), Soc. Automotive Engrs. (Ralph E. Teetor award 1971), Am. Soc. Engring. Edn., Internat. Centre Heat and Mass Transfer, Miss. Acad. Scis., Miss. Engring. Soc., Blue Key, Sigma Xi (Miss. State U. chpt. Research award 1976), Tau Beta Pi (Outstanding Engring. Faculty Mem. 1978), Pi Tau Sigma, Phi Kappa Phi, Omicron Delta Kappa, Kappa Mu Epsilon. Current Work: Energy systems, magnetohydrodynamics, heat transfer, energy conservation. Subspecialties: Mechanical engineering; Fluid mechanics. Home: 110 Pinewood Dr Starkville MS 39759 Office: Drawer G Mississippi State U Mississippi State MS 39762

POWELL, BENJAMIN NEFF, research geologist; b. Montclair, N.J., Oct. 28, 1941; s. George Neff and Elsie Miriam (Davies) P.; m. Susan Elizabeth Wolfe, Aug. 29, 1964; 1 child, Amy Elizabeth. B.A., Amherst Coll., 1964; M.A., Columbia U., 1966, Ph.D., 1969. Research assoc. Harvard-Smithsonian Ctr. for Astrophysics, Cambridge, Mass., 1969-70; asst. prof. Rice U., Houston, 1970-75, lectr., 1976-80; sr. research geologist Phillips Petroleum Co., Bartlesville, Okla., 1980—. Contbr. numerous articles to profl. jours. Instr. Bartlesville Assn. for Gifted and Talented, 1983—. Grantee NASA, 1971-76, NSF, 1976-79. Fellow Meteoritical Soc.; mem. Geol. Soc. Am., Mineral. Soc. Am., Sigma Xi. Republican. Episcopalian. Clubs: Model A Ford Am. (officer Houston chpt. 1979-80). Current work: Petrology and diagenesis of sandstones; petrology of igneous and metamorphic rocks; electron microprobe and scanning electron microscope analysis of geological materials; mineralogy and geochemistry of geothermal systems. Subspecialties: Petrology; Mineralogy. Home: 2390 Mountain Dr Bartlesville OK 74003 Office: Phillips Petroleum Co 237 GB Bartlesville OK 74004

POWELL, EDWARD GORDON, research physicist; b. Washington, Apr. 5, 1946; s. Edward Carter and Hilda Rae (Blanchard) P.; m. Lona Noel Carlson, Oct. 1, 1977; children: Mary, Soren, Piri, Lynnis. B.S., U. Md., 1968, M.S., 1972, postgrad. in astrophysics, 1972-73. Research physicist U.S. Naval Ordnance Sta., Indian Head, Md., 1968-73, U.S. Naval Ordnance Lab., White Oak, Md., 1973-74, U.S. Surface Weapons Center, White Oak, 1973-83, Mitre Corp., McLean, Va., 1983—. Contbr. articles to profl. jours. Mem. Am. Astron. Soc., Assn Computational Linguistics., Assn. Computing Machinery, Am. Assn. Artificial Intelligence. Current Work: Artificial intelligence for planning, signal understanding. Subspecialty: Artificial intelligence. Office: Code W-93 Mitre Corp Mitre Corp 1820 Dolley Madison Blvd McLean VA 22102

POWELL, GEORGE LOUIS, research chemist; b. Wallace, N.C., Oct. 17, 1940; s. George Oliver and Katie (Rich) P.; m. Sylvia Chestnutt, Sept. 6, 1964; 1 child, Kimberly Renee. B.S. in Chemistry, Presbyn. Coll., 1963; Ph.D. in Chemistry, U. N.C., 1967. Devel. chemist Martin Marietta Energy Systems Inc., Oak Ridge Y-12 Plant, 1967—. Patentee in field of ceramic articles, uranium processing. Recipient IR100 award Indsl. Research Mag., 1984. Mem. Am. Chem. Soc., AAAS, Sigma Xi. Presbyterian. Current work: Hydrogen transport in metals; surface analysis of lithium compounds; optical and infrared kinetic spectroscopy. Subspecialties: Physical chemistry; Surface chemistry. Home: 298 East Dr Oak Ridge TN 37830 Office: Martin Marietta Energy Systems Inc PO Box Y Oak Ridge TN 37831

POWELL, HENRY CALEB, pathology educator, physician; b. Dublin, Ireland, Sept. 1, 1946; came to U.S., 1970; s. Antony G. and Mary Celine (Delaney) P.; m. Geraldine M. Tierney, July 29, 1970 (div. 1975); m. Mary Lucille Johnson, Sept. 24, 1981. M.B., B.Ch., Univ. Coll., Nat. U. Ireland, 1970. Diplomate Am. Bd. Anat. and Clin. Pathology, Neuropathology. Intern, Phila. Gen. Hosp., 1970-71; resident in pathology U. Calif.-La Jolla., 1971-75; fellow Harvard Med. Ctr., Boston, 1975-76; asst. prof. U. Calif.-San Diego, La Jolla, 1976-81, assoc. prof. pathology, 1981—; cons. VA Hosp., U. Med. Ctr., San Diego, 1976—, Mercy Hosp., San Diego, 1981—; instr. U. Calif.-San Diego Extension, 1980-84. Contbr. chpts. to books. Mem. San Diego County Pathology Soc. (pres. 1981—). Democrat. Current work: Peripheral neuropathy; neurotoxicology; diabetic neuropathy; nerve edema; electron microscopy. Subspecialty: Pathology (medicine). Home: 940 Runnymead Ln Point Loma San Diego CA 92106 Office: M-012 Dept Pathology U Calif-San Diego La Jolla CA 92093

POWELL, JAMES CHARLES, educator, consultant; b. Edmonton, Alta., Can., Nov. 18, 1931; s. Edgar Ernest Charles and Hazel Fern (Alcorn) P.; m. Frances Adelaide Cochrane, May 7, 1954. B.Ed., U. Alta., 1956, B.A., 1957, Ph.D., 1970; M.Ed., U. Toronto, 1962; diploma in bus. adminstrn, U. Western Ont., 1973. Tchr. various locations, 1957-65; lectr. edn. U. Alta., Edmonton, 1965-69; tchr. Roman Cath. Schs., Edmonton, 1969-70; sch. psychologist County of Lac Ste. Anne, Sangudo, Alta., 1970-71; asst. prof. edn. U. Sask., Saskatoon, 1971-72; assoc. prof. edn. U. Windsor, Ont., 1973—; cons. Ball, Powell Agy., Windsor, 1980—, T.D. Wearne & Assocs., Windsor, 1976-80. Author: The Exploratory Loop, 1981, Loading Learning, 1985, Achievement Information from Wrong Answers, 1970. IBM fellow, 1979. Mem. AAAS, Am. Ednl. Research Assn., Am. Psychol. Assn., Nat. Council Measurement in Edn., Psychometric Soc. Current Work: Exploring instructional and measurement implications that current achievement measurement practices are invalid when applied to cognition higher than retrieval. Subspecialties: Cognition; Information systems (Information science). Home: 408 Moy Ave Windsor ON N9A 2N4 Canada Office: Faculty of Edn U Windsor 600 3d Concession Rd Windsor ON N9E 1A5 Canada

POWELL, JOHN EDWARD, geologist, hydrologist; b. Galesville, Wis., Dec. 2, 1918; s. John Justin and Gertrude (Vickerman) P.; m. Margaret Jane Owens, Apr. 2, 1943; children: Diane Kay, John Everett. Ph.B., Marquette U., 1940; B.S.C.E., U. N.D., 1950, B.S. in Geology, 1951; postgrad., U. Wis., 1940-41. Registered profl. engr., N.D., S.D. Geologist U.S. Geol. Survey, Grand Forks, N.D., 1946-51, hydraulic engr., 1951-58, dist. engr., Huron, S.D., 1958-66, dist. chief, 1966-78, cons. hydrologist/geologist, Huron, 1978—. Contbr. articles to profl. jours. Mem. Mcpl. Water Bd., Huron, 1979—. Served to lt. col. USAF, 1941-46, ETO. Fellow Geol. Soc. Am.; mem. Nat. Soc. Profl. Engrs., Nat. Water Well Assn., S.D. Soc. Profl. Engrs., Res. Officers Assn. (life), Am. Legion, VFW. Roman Catholic. Lodges: Masons; Shriners. Current Work: Design of monitoring systems for ground water pollution; availability of ground water in vicinity of igneous intrusives. Subspecialty: Hydrology. Home: 1831 McClellan Dr Huron SD 57350

POWELL, MICHAEL ROBERT, biophysicist; b. Detroit, Nov. 23, 1941; s. Herschel Homer and Julia (Dickun) P.; m. Mary Grace Power, Aug. 8, 1964; children—Andrew, Christie, Kevin, Eric. B.S., Mich. State U., 1963, M.S., 1967, Ph.D., 1969. Research biophysicist Union Carbide, Tarrytown, N.Y., 1968-75; dir. Hyperbaric Lab. Inst. Applied Physiology and Medicine, Seattle, 1975-77; physiologist Inst. Aerospace Medicine, Bonn, W. Germany, 1977-80, dir. dept. hyperbaric physiol. and biophysics Inst. Applied Physiology and Medicine, Seattle, 1980—. Mem. Am. Chem. Soc., Am. Physiol. Soc., Aerospace Med. Soc., Undersea Med. Soc., Biophys. Soc. Evangelical. Current work: Hyperbaric physiology and medicine; decompression sickness; biomagnetics, charge transport phenomena. Subspecialties: Biophysics (biology); Physiology (medicine). Home: 3604 84th St Mercer Island WA 98040 Office: 701 16th Ave Seattle WA 98122

POWELL, RICHARD GRANT, research chemist; b. Avon, Ill., Oct. 29, 1938; s. Glenn E. and Marcia E. (Mummey) P.; m. Betty A. Remer, Aug. 7, 1960 (div. 1975); children—Rodney, Glenn; m. Rosemary J. Holzinger, June 2, 1979. B.S., Western Ill. U., 1961, M.S. Ed., 1963; postgrad. Iowa State U., 1962-63, U. St. Andrews, Scotland, 1966-67. Research chemist USDA, Peoria, Ill., 1963—. Patentee in field (7). Contbr. articles to profl. jours. Recipient Disting. Alumni award Western Ill. U., 1981. Mem. Am. Chem. Soc. (alt. councilor 1984), Am. Soc. Pharmacognosy, Phytochem. Soc. N.Am., Soc. Econ. Botany. Current work: Natural products, alkaloids, antitumor agents, plant growth regulators. Subspecialties: Organic chemistry; Pharmacognosy. Home: 4724 N Laurel Dr Peoria IL 61614 Office: 1815 N University Peoria IL 61604

POWELL, THOMAS EDWARD, III, biological supply company executive, physician; b. Elon College, N.C., Aug. 1, 1936; s. Thomas Edward, Jr., and Sophia Maude (Sharpe) P.; m. Betty Durham Yeager, June 19, 1965; children—Frances Elizabeth, Thomas Edward IV, Caroline Yeager. A.B. in Biology, Va. Mil. Inst., 1957; M.D., Duke U., 1961; M.A., Harvard U., 1966. Surgeon USPHS, 1966-68; co-founder Biomed. Reference Labs., Inc., Burlington, N.C., 1969, exec. v.p., 1969-75, chmn. exec. com., 1979-82, also dir.; exec. v.p. Carolina Biol. Supply Co., Burlington, N.C., 1968-80, chmn., 1977-80, pres., 1980—; pres. Wolfe Sales Corp., Burlington, 1980-84, Waubun Labs. Inc., Schriever, La., 1980—, Bobbitt Labs., Inc., Burlington, 1983—; bd. mgrs. Wachovia Bank and Trust Co. N.A., Burlington. Contbr. articles to profl. jours. Bd. dirs. United Way Alamance County, Burlington, 1968—; bd. dirs. Elon Coll., N.C., 1968—, sec., 1975—; bd. dirs. Am. Cancer Soc., Burlington, 1971—; bd. dirs. Burlington Day Sch., 1973—, pres., 1974-78, 80-84; bd. dirs. N.C. Citizens for Bus. and Industry, Raleigh, 1983—, Nat. Found. for Study of Religion and Econs., Greensboro, 1984—, Blue Ridge Sch., Dyke, Va., 1985—. Served to capt. USAR, 1957-66. Recipient Citizens Service award Elon Coll. Alumni Assn., 1980. Mem. Assn. Biology Lab. Edn., N.C. Acad. Sci., Alamance-Caswell Med. Soc., N.C. Med. Soc., Assn. Venture Founders, Newcomen Soc. Democrat. Mem. Ch. of Christ. Clubs: Alamance Country (Burlington); Capital City (Raleigh, N.C.); Congl. Country (Washington); Country of N.C. (Pinehurst); Hope Valley Country (Durham, N.C.); Greensboro City. Subspecialty: Biological supplies company management. Office: Carolina Biol Supply Co 2700 York Rd Burlington NC 27215

POWER, DANIEL JOSEPH, management and decision sciences educator, researcher; b. Waterloo, Iowa, Feb. 9, 1950; s. LaVern Joseph and Maxine May (Jindrich) P.; m. Carol Esther Pokodner, Jan. 12, 1985. B.S. in Gen. Sci., U. Iowa, 1974, M.A. in Bus. Adminstrn., 1977; M.B.A. in Mgmt., U. Wis.-Madison, 1981, Ph.D. in Bus. Adminstrn., 1982. Lectr. U. Wis.-Madison, 1978-82; asst. prof. U. Md., College Park, 1982—. Patentee in field. Contbr. articles to profl. jours. Chairperson County Democratic Party, Iowa City, 1974-76. Kohler fellow U. Wis., 1981. Mem. Acad. Mgmt., AAAI, Inst. Mgmt. Scis., Am. Inst. Decision Scis. Subspecialties: Information systems (Information science); Artificial intelligence. Home: 4313 Knox Rd Apt 217 College Park MD 20740 Office: Coll Bus U Md College Park MD 20742

POWERS, DENNIS ALPHA, biochemist, educator; b. Detroit, May 4, 1938; s. Earl Wilson and Helen Virginia (Williams) P.; m. Dianne Williamson, Nov. 22, 1963; children—Kathy, Wendy, Julie. B.A., Ottawa U., 1963; Ph.D., U. Kans., 1970. Postdoctoral fellow AEC, Argonne, Ill., 1970-71, NSF, Stonybrook, N.Y., 1972, Marine Biology Lab., Woods Hole, Mass., 1972; asst. prof. Johns Hopkins U., Balt., 1972-78, assoc. prof., 1978-82, prof., 1982—; chmn., 1983—; dir. McCollum Pratt Inst., Balt., Chesapeake Bay Inst., Balt.; cons. UN, FAO, Rome, Cousteau Soc., Brazil, Electric Power Research Inst, Palado, Calif.; grant reviewer NSF, NIH, Sea Grant, NOAA, Hudson River Found; numerous sci. expeditions NSF, Cousteau Soc. Editorial bd. profl. jours. Biol. Oceanography, Physiol. Zoology, Molecular Biology and Evolution. Revs. numerous jours. Contbr. articles to profl. jours. Served to cpl. USMC, 1957-59. Recipient Mathematic Honors award; NSF fellow; grantee NSF, NIH, NOAA, Cousteau Soc., Tex. Instruments, Nat. Geographic Soc., Md. Sea Grant. Mem. Assn. Biol. Chemistry, AAAS, Soc. Study Evolution, Biophys. Soc., Genetics Soc. Am., Am. Chem. Soc., N.Y. Acad. Sci., Md. Acad. Sci., Am. Soc. Zoologists, Sigma Xi. Current work: Molecular evolution of fishes; biotechnology and genetic engineering of marine organisms; biochemistry of metallothioneins; moleculartecology of fish hemoglobins. Subspecialties: Biochemistry (biology); Genome organization. Office: Johns Hopkins U Dept Biology 3400 N Charles St Baltimore MD 21218

POWERS, EDWARD LAWRENCE, biologist, educator; b. Columbia, S.C., Dec. 30, 1915; s. Edward Lawrence and Emilie (Devereux) P.; m. Mary Eleanor Fogarty, Dec. 27, 1939; children: Mary Eugenia Powers Anderson, Emilie Devereux Powers Dacunto, Judith Ann, Catherine Powers Schourek, Patricia Powers Swanney, Christina Powers Barnett, Barbara Clare Powers Crockett. Student, U. Notre Dame, 1933-34; B.S., Coll. of Charleston, S.C., 1938; Litt.D., 1974; Ph.D., Johns Hopkins, 1941. Teaching asst. Coll. Charleston, 1936-38; asst. zoology Johns Hopkins, 1938-41; vis. lectr. genetics Fordham U., 1941, vis. lectr. biology, 1943; instr., then asst. prof. U. Notre Dame, 1941-45; assoc. biologist Argonne Nat. Lab., 1946-49, sr. biologist, 1949-65, assoc. dir. div. biol. and med. research, 1950-59; prof. zoology, dir. Lab. Radiation Biology, U. Tex., Austin, 1965—, T.S. Painter Centennial prof., 1985—, dir. Center for Fast Kinetics Research, 1965—. Editor Oxygen and Oxy-radicals in Chemistry and Biology, 1982; contbr. articles to profl. jours. Mem. Park Forest (Ill.) Planning and Zoning Commn., 1949-52, chmn., 1950-52; mem. Park Forest Zoning Bd. Appeals, 1951-52, Park Forest Bldg. Code Bd. Appeals, 1951-52; Bd. dirs. Park Forest Family Counseling Services, 1951-52. Tomlinson fellow Coll. Charleston, 1937; Guggenheim fellow, 1958; Douglas Lea Meml. lectr. U. Leeds, Eng., 1961; vis. prof. Christie Hosp., Holt Radium Inst., Manchester, Eng., 1972. Fellow A.A.A.S.; mem. Am. Soc. Human Genetics, Am. Soc. Microbiologists, Am. Soc. Naturalists, Am. Soc. Zoologists, Brit. Assn. Radiation Research, Genetic Assn. Am., Genetics Soc., Radiation Research Soc. (sec.-treas. 1958-64, pres. 1964-65), Phi Beta Kappa, Sigma Xi. Spl. research expt. and theory radiation damage biol. systems. Current Work: Basic physical and chemical mechanisms in radiation-induced changes in cells. Subspecialties: Cell biology; Radiation biology.

POWERS, JEFFRY EARL, electronics engineer, consultant; b. Santa Monica, Calif., Aug. 22, 1950; s. Charles Leslie and Adelaide Blanche (Clough) P.; m. Betty Jane Dominy, Aug. 5, 1978. B.S. in Physics, U. Calif.-San Diego, 1972, M.S. in Engring., 1974; Ph.D. in Elec. Engring., U. Wash., 1980. Engr. U. Wash., Seattle, 1978-80; postdoctural fellow Kantonsspital, Basel, Switzerland, 1980-81; prin. engr. Advanced Tech. Labs., Bellevue, Wash., 1982—; cons. Ultrasonic Arrays, Inc., Woodinville, Calif., 1978—. Contbr. articles to profl. jours. Patentee in field. Mem. IEEE. Methodist. Current work: Ultrasound imaging systems, phased array signal processing, doppler flow imaging systems, complex digital signal processing. Subspecialties: Ultrasound; Electronics. Home: 3639 Pleasant Beach Dr NE Bainbridge Island WA 98110 Office: Advanced Tech Labs 13208-Northup Way PO Box 6639 Bellevue WA 98007

POWERS, JOSEPH, chemist, materials engineer; b. Fall River, Mass., June 4, 1931; s. Joseph Patrick and Julia (Healy) P.; m. Mary Griffin, Jan. 19, 1957; children—Deborah, Janet. B.S., U. Mass., 1953, M.S., 1959, Ph.D., 1961. Project leader Nat. Bur. Standards, Washington, 1961-65; project leader Am. Cyanamid Co., Stamford, Conn., 1965-69, group leader, 1969-72; asst. prof. U. Bridgeport, Conn., 1972-73; materials engr. United Techs., South Windsor, Conn., 1973-84; sr. materials engr. Sikorsky Aircraft Co., Stratford, Conn., 1982—. Contbr. articles to profl. jours. Patentee in field. Served to lst lt. U.S. Army, 1953-55. NRC/Nat. Acad. Sci. postdoctoral fellow Nat. Bur. Standards, Washington, 1961. Mem. Am. Chem. Soc., Am. Phys. Soc., N.Y. Acad. Scis., Sigma Xi. Roman Catholic. Subspecialties: Composite materials; Polymer physics. Home: 26 Spring St Riverside CT 06878 Office: Sikorsky Aircraft N Main St Stratford CT 06601

POWERS, LINDA SUE, research biophysicist; b. Pitts., Feb. 8, 1948; d. Luther Thurston and Helen Grace (Currence) P. B.S. in Physics and Chemistry, Va. Poly. Inst. and State U., 1970; M.S. in Physics, Harvard U., 1972, Ph.D. in Biophysics, 1976. Mem. tech. staff AT & T Bell Labs., Murray Hill, N.J., 1976—; adj. asst. prof. biochemistry and biophysics dept., U. Pa. Med. Sch., Phila., 1977-80, adj. assoc. prof., 1980—; vis. fellow chemistry dept., Princeton U., N.J., 1981-82. Contbr. articles to profl. jours. Fellow Am. Phys. Soc. (biologphysics div. exec. com. 1979-83, chmn.-elect 1984—); mem. Biophys. Soc., Am. Assn. Biol. Chemists, Am. Chem. Soc., N.Y. Acad. Scis., Sigma Pi Sigma, Phi Lambda Upsilon. Current work: Investigation of structure-function-energy relationship of electron transfer proteins and metalloenzymes using x-ray absorption spectroscopy, scattering, and optical methods. Subspecialties: Biophysics (physics); Biophysics (biology). Home: 398 Charnwood Rd New Providence NJ 07974 Office: AT & T Bell Labs Rm 1D467 600 Mountain Ave Murray Hill NJ 07974

POWERS, RICHARD WALLACE, geologist, consultant; b. Boise, Idaho, Jan. 20, 1926; s. Wallace Henry and Rosa Elisabeth (Ulmer) P.; m. Marte Marie Ledahl, Jan. 20, 1951; children—Cydnie Christin, Dirk Frederick. B.A., U. So. Calif., 1946; M.S., Yale U., 1960, Ph.D., 1961. Geologist, sr. geologist Arabian Am. Oil Co., Dhahran, Saudi Arabia, 1947-61, chief geologist, mgr. exploration, 1961-70, v.p. govt. affairs, 1970-71, sr. v.p. finance, relations, 1971-73, pres., vice chmn., 1973-80; cons. geology, Austin, Tex., 1980—; pres., chief exec. officer Trans-Arabian Pipeline Co. (Tapline), Beirut, Lebanon, 1971-73. Author: USGS Professional Paper, Geology of Saudi Arabia, 1966; International Lexicon of Stratigraphy for Saudi Arabia, 1968. Author articles on classification of carbonate rocks. Served to 1st lt. USMC, 1943-46, PTO, 1951-52. Mem. AAAS, Geol. Soc. Am. Soc. Petroleum Engrs., Am. Assn. Petroleum Geologists, Sigma Xi. Republican. Unitarian. Current work: Advisor to several major concerns on energy acquistion and oil-search activities. Subspecialties: Geology; Petroleum engineering. Home and Office: 11101 Champions Lane Austin TX 78747

POWERS, ROBERT WILLIAM, physical chemist; b. Peoria, Ill., Feb. 3, 1922; s. William Frederick and Edna Catherine (Davis) P.; m. Mary Agnes Pohl, June 27, 1950; 1 child, David Eric. B.S., Bradley U., 1943; Ph.D., U. Ill., 1946. Research chemist E.I. duPont Expt. Sta., Wilmington, Del., 1946-47; research assoc. Ohio State U., Columbus, 1947-51; phys. chemist Gen. Electric Corp. Research and Devel., Schenectady, 1951—. Patentee in field of batteries. Mem. Am. Chem. Soc., Am. Phys. Soc., Electrochem. Soc., Am. Ceramic Soc. Republican. Current work: Electrochemical machining; fabrication, characterization, degradation studies of beta-alumina solid electrolyte. Subspecialties: Physical chemistry; Materials. Home: 1507 Kingston Ave Schenectady NY 12308 Office: Gen Electric Corp Research and Devel PO Box 8 Schenectady NY 12301

POWERS, SCOTT KLINE, physiologist, educator, researcher; b. Richlands, Va., May 28, 1950; s. Kline Reed and Negntha (Gourley) P.; m. Lou Dunson, Aug. 27, 1977. B.S., Carson Newman Coll., 1972; M.Ed., U. Ga., 1973; Ed.D., U. Tenn., 1980. Asst. prof. physiology, dir. applied physiology lab. La. State U., Baton Rouge, 1980—; cons. William C. Brown Pub., Dubuque, Iowa, 1982—. Author: Experiences in Work Physiology, 1981. Contbr. articles to profl. jours. Grantee NSF, La. State U. Fellow Am. Coll. Sports Medicine; mem. Am. Physiol. Soc., Fedn. Am. Socs. for Exptl. Biology, AAAS. Baptist. Club: South (Baton Rouge). Current work: Exercise physiology with special reference to pulmonary adaptations to work; gas exchange kinetics during work; ventilatory control. Subspecialty: Physiology (medicine). Office: Louisiana State U Baton Rouge LA 70803

POWERS, WILLIAM FRANCIS, engineering manager, researcher; b. Phila., Dec. 11, 1940; s. Francis Simpson and Kathryn (Thoroughgood) P.; m. Linda Nell Shelton, Sept. 7, 1963; children—Stephen, Leigh. B.S. in Aerospace Engring., U. Fla., 1963; M.S. in Aerospace Engring., U. Tex., 1966, Ph.D. in Engring. Mechanics, 1968. Aerospace engr. NASA Marshall Space Flight Ctr., Huntsville, Ala., 1960-64; prof. U. Mich., Ann Arbor, 1968-80; mgr. Ford Motor Co. Research, Dearborn, Mich., 1979—; cons. NASA Johnson Space Ctr., Houston, 1970-79, various corps., 1968-79. Editor: Astrodynamics, 1975; author tech. articles, videotape series. Named Best Tchr., Coll. Engring. U. Mich., 1974; participant U.S.-USSR research exchange, Nat. Acad. Scis., 1976. Assoc. fellow AIAA; mem. IEEE, ASME, Soc. Automotive Engrs. Current work: Microprocessor-based control systems for automobiles, computer-aided design of control systems. Subspecialties: Systems engineering; Aerospace engineering and technology. Home: 2032 Greenview Ann Arbor MI 48103 Office: Ford Motor Co Research PO Box 2053 Dearborn MI 48121

POWNALL, THOMAS GILMORE, corporate executive. Chmn., Martin Marietta Corp., Bethesda, Md. Subspecialty: Aerospace engineering and technology. Office: Martin Marietta Corp 6801 Rockledge Dr Bethesda MD 20034*

POYDOCK, MARY EYMARD, cancer researcher, educator, nun; b. Sykesville, Pa., Dec. 3, 1910; d. John Andrew and Anna Mary (Dryna) P. A.B., Mercyhurst Coll., 1943; M.A., U. Pitts., 1946; Ph.D., St. Thomas Inst., 1965. Joined Sisters of Mercy, 1932, tchr. elem. sch., Erie, Pa., 1935-41, tchr. high sch., 1941-47; faculty biology St. Justin Sch., 1960-75; now dir. cancer research Mercyhurst Coll., Erie, Pa. Contbr. articles to profl. jours; author lab. guides. Mem. Am. Cancer Soc. (sec. bd. dirs., chmn. cancer prevention study II), Pa. Acad. Sci., AAAS, Sigma Xi, Tri Beta. Club: Zonta. Current Work: Cancer research using Vitamins C and B 12. Subspecialties: Cancer research (medicine); Nutrition (medicine). Address: 501 E 38th St Erie PA 16546

POZUELO, JOSE, psychiatrist; b. Fuentesclaras, Spain, Mar. 19, 1933; s. Leonardo and Felisa (Utanda) P.; m. Lola Claros Halcon, Sept. 20, 1936; children: Leopoldo, Fatima, Marcarena. Bachiller, Instituto Afonso VIII, 1952; M.D., U. Madrid, 1959, Dr. Sci., 1960. Sec. Coll. Antonio de Nebrija, U. Madrid, 1960; resident in internal medicine U. Madrid, 1959-62; resident in psychiatry Mayo Clinic, Rochester, Minn., 1966-68, staff psychiatrist, 1969-73, Cleve. Clinic Found., 1974—. Contbr. articles to profl. jours. Mem. AMA, Am. Psychiat. Assn., Internat. Council on Alcohol and Addictions, Internat. Narcotic Research Conf. Roman Catholic. Patentee treatment of narcotic addiction, alcoholism and schizophrenia. Current Work: Research in substance abuse and depression. Subspecialties: Psychopharmacology; Neurochemistry. Office: Cleveland Clinic Found 9500 Euclid Ave Cleveland OH 44106

PRABHU, VENKATRAY G., pharmacologist, educator, researcher; b. Shirali, India, Mar. 15, 1930; came to U.S.,, naturalized, 1979; s. Govind N. and Radhabai G. P.; m. Nalini V., May 19, 1957; children: Nirmala, Satish. Ph.D., Loyola U., 1962. Sr. research pharmacologist Arnar Stone Lab., Inc., Mt. Prospect, Ill., 1962-63; assoc. dir., dept. head Sarabhai Chems. Research Inst., Ahmedabad, India, 1963-67; instr. Chgo. Coll. Osteo. Medicine, 1967-68, asst. prof., 1968-71, assoc. prof., acting chmn., 1971-75, prof., chmn., 1975—; researcher in pathophysiology of neuromuscular system. Contbr. articles on pharmacology to profl. jours. Mem. Am. Soc. Pharmacology and Exptl. Therapeutics, AAAS. Subspecialties: Pharmacology; Neuropharmacology. Office: Chicago Coll Osteo Medicine Dept Pharmacology 1122 E 53d St Chicago IL 60615

PRABHU, VILAS ANANDRAO, medicinal chemistry educator, researcher; b. Bombay, India, Oct. 11, 1948; came to U.S., 1971; s. Anandrao Baburao and Lalita A. (Kini) P.; m. Sneha Vilas, Aug. 15, 1975; children: Shilpa, Ajay, Smita. B.S., U. Bombay, 1970; M.S., Idaho State U., 1973; Ph.D., U. Tex., 1977. Teaching asst. Idaho State U., Pocatello, 1971-73, U. Tex., Austin, 1973-77; asst. prof. Wash. State U., Pullman, 1977-80; asst. prof. medicinal chemistry Sch. Pharmacy, Southwestern Okla. State U., Weatherford, 1980—. Participant: revision U.S. Pharmacopeia XIX, 1975; contbr. articles to profl. jour. Mem. Am. Pharm. Assn., Acad. Pharm. Scis., Am. Assn. Colls. Pharmacy, Okla. Acad. Scis., Sigma Xi, Rho Chi, Phi Kappa Phi, Phi Delta Chi (sponsor 1982—). Hindu. Current Work: Synthesis and structure-activity relationship of potentially active medicinal agents; synthesis of novel psychotropic agents and adrenergic blockers. Subspecialty: Medicinal chemistry. Home: 1304 Lee St Weatherford OK 73096 Office: Sch Pharmacy Southwestern Okla State U Weatherford OK 73096

PRADA, KENNETH EDWIN, electronics engineer; b. Boston, Dec. 10, 1937; s. Herman Edwin and Emma Anice (Legere) P.; m. Judith Dorothea Kaun, Dec. 10, 1960; children—Anthony Paul, Beth Ann. Student U. Mass., 1956-58. Service mgr. Hudson TV, Gardena, Calif., 1963-65; research assoc. Woods Hole Oceanographic, Mass., 1966-73, research specialist, 1973-81; sr. research specialist, 1981-82, mgr. applied engr. lab., 1982—; sr. engr. cons. Yes Computer Sci., New Bedford, Mass., 1974—; owner, engr. cons. Upper Cape Systems, Falmouth, Mass., 1973—. Contbr. articles to profl. jours.; patentee digital correlation rec. Served to sgt. USMC, 1959-63. Mem. IEEE, IEEE Computer Soc., IEEE Geosci. and Remote Sensing Soc., IEEE Oceanic Engring. Soc. Lutheran. Current work: Computer and instrument systems for Oceanographic data aquisition and analysis; data rec. methods; Arctic acoustics research methods; oceanographic sensors. Subspecialties: Ocean engineering; Computer engineering. Home: 29 Prince Henry Dr East Falmouth MA 02536 Office: Woods Hole Oceanographic Inst Water St Woods Hole MA 02543

PRADHAN, ANIL KUMAR, atomic physics educator; b. Fategarh, India, July 26, 1951; came to Can., 1968, U.S., 1983; s. Mahesh Chandra and Sarojini (Saxena) P.; m. Indira, Aug. 20, 1975; 1 child, Alka. B.Sc., U. Windsor, 1972, M.Sc., 1973; Ph.D., U. London, 1977. Research fellow Univ. Coll. London, 1974-78; research assoc. Joint Inst. Lab. Astrophysics, Boulder, Colo., 1978-80, mem., 1983—. Contbr. articles to profl. jours. Natural Scis. and Engring. Research Council fellow dept. physics U. Windsor, Ont., Can., 1980-83. Mem. Am. Phys. Soc. Current Work: Atomic processes in lab. and astrophys. plasmas; teaching. Subspecialties: Atomic and molecular physics; X-ray high energy astrophysics. Office: Joint Inst Lab Astrophysics U Colo Boulder CO 80309

PRAGER, GERALD DAVID, geologist, petroleum researcher; b. Norfolk, Va., Oct. 25, 1940; s. Omar Raymond and Evelyn Juanita (Melville) P.; m. Brenda Gayle Stamm, Apr. 15, 1973. B.S., U. Kans., 1962; Ph.D., U. Cin., 1971; C.A.G.S., Northeastern U., 1978. Geologist, Valley Geoservices, Cin., 1971-73; asst. prof. Northeastern U., Boston, 1973-78; assoc. prof. Ohio U., Athens, 1978-80; chief geologist Howard-Donley Assoc., Redwood City, Calif., 1980-81; exploration stratigrapher Texaco USA, New Orleans, 1981—; cons. Boston Edison, 1976, N.Y. State Electric and Gas, N.Y.C., 1977, Pitts. Plate Glass, Charleston, W.Va., 1980. Contbr. articles to profl. jours. Served to lt. USN, 1962-66. Recipient Haworth award U. Kans., 1962, W.A. Tarr award Sigma Gamma Epsilon, 1962; NDEA fellow U. Cin., 1966. Mem. Geol. Soc. of Am., Am. Assn. Petroleum Geologists, History of Earth Scis. Soc., New Orleans Geol. Soc., Sigma Xi. Current work: Structural analysis field techniques in complex terrances; migration and entrapment of hydrocarbons; applications of remote sensing to tectonics and resources exploration. Subspecialties: Tectonics; Petroleum geology. Home: 2027 Saint Nick Dr New Orleans LA 70114 Office: Texaco USA PO Box 60252 New Orleans LA 70160

PRAGER, MORTON DAVID, biochemistry educator; b. Dallas, Dec. 12, 1927; s. William and Elizabeth (Levy) P.; m. Lois Lurie, Nov. 22, 1951; children—Karen, David, Neal, Brian. B.A., U. Tex., 1947; M.S., Purdue U., 1949, Ph.D., 1951. Research chemist B.F. Goodrich Co., Brecksville, Ohio, 1951-53; sr. investigator, asst. dir. research Wadley Research Inst., Dallas, 1954-67; faculty mem. Baylor U. Grad. Research Inst., Dallas, 1954-68; prof. surgery, biochemistry U. Tex. Health Sci. Ctr., Dallas, 1967—; cons. VA Ctr., Temple, Tex., 1960-68; vis. prof. Tex. Christian U., Fort Worth, 1967. Contbr. chpts. to books, articles to profl. jours. Com. mem. Goals for Dallas. Grantee: NIH, 1956—, Am. Cancer Soc., 1978-80, Leukemia Soc. Am., 1960-61. Mem. Am. Chem. Soc. (v.p. Dallas-Fort Worth sect. 1969—, pres. 1970—), Am. Assn. for Cancer Research (assoc. editor Jour. 1980—), Am. Assn. Immunologists, Am. Soc. Hematology, Internat. Soc. Hematology, AAAS. Jewish. Club: Dallas Town and Gown (pres. 1969-70). Lodge: B'nai B'rith (exec. com.). Current work: Cancer research-immunology of tumors, immunotherapy, effect of differentiation inducing agents on selected enzymes of cancer cells. Subspecialties: Cancer research (medicine); Biochemistry (medicine). Home: 3830 Pallos Verdas Dallas TX 75229 Office: U Tex Health Sci Ctr 3523 Harry Hines Ave Dallas TX 75235

PRAKASH, SHAMSHER, civil engineering educator, researcher; b. Mansa, Panjab, India, Jan. 3, 1933; s. Rishiran and Kalavati P. B.E., U. Roorkee, 1954, postgrad. diploma, 1959; M.S., U. Ill., 1961, Ph.D., 1962. Lectr. Roorkee U., India, 1957-62, reader in civil engring., 1962-66, prof. soil dynamics, 1966-70, prof. civil engring., 1970-78, prof. and head civil engring. U. Roorkee, 1982-83, dir. Central Bldg. Research Inst., Roorkee, 1983-84; prof. civil engring. U. Mo.-Rolla, 1978—; mem., chmn. coms. Indian Standards Instn., 1983-84; mem. program adv. com. dept. sci. and tech. Govt. of India, 1983-84; lectr. Nat. Bur. Standards, Washington, 1984, GSA, Washington, 1984, U. New South Wales, Sydney, 1975, 77, U. Wallongong, New South Wales, 1975, 77, U. Singapore, Chulalongkorn U., Bangkok, 1975, Sydney U., 1975, U. Hiroshima, Kyushu U., 1977, U. Ill., U. Mo., Ohio State U., Calif. Inst. Tech., Detroit Inst. Tech., U. Calif.-Berkeley, U. Calif.-Sacramento, SUNY-Stony Brook, 1976, U. Tokyo, Calif. State U.-Long Beach, U. B.C., Va. Poly. Inst. and State U., U. Ill., Chgo., Purdue U., Northwestern U., 1979, Washington U., St. Louis, U. Wales, Swansea, Kings Coll., London, Bldg. Research Sta., Watford, U.K., Manchester U., Laboratorie Central Des Ponts and Chaussess, Ecole Polytechnique Federale de Lausanne, 1980, Netherlands Soc. Siol Mechanics Lab., Delft, 1980, Sherbrook U., Can., Syracuse U., 1981, Indian Inst. Tech., Delhi, Bombay, Osmania U., Jadavpur U., Roorkee U., various engring. colls., Instn. of Engrs. India.; chmn. internat. confs., 1983, 84, 81, chmn. splty. sessions Moscow conf. 1973, co-reporter Tokyo conf. 1977, panel reporter Stockholm conf. 1981, discussion leader San Francisco conf., 1985; leader Indian dels. internat. conf., 1975, 77; del. research conf. 1971. Author; Soil Dynamics, 1981; co-author; Analysis and Design of Foundations and Retaining Structures, 1979; Laboratory Geotechnical Testing, 1978; Problems in Soil Engineering, 1976; Soil Mechanics and Foundation, 1984; author numerous papers and progress reports. Speaker All India Radio, 1978, Australian Broadcasting Commn., Sydney, 1975, Lima, Peru, 1979; lectr. on Yoga, Australia, India, Japan, U.S., Singapore, Can., Sweden, Norway. Recipient Ministry of Irrigation prize, Govt. India, 1980, Khosla Research Gold Medal and prize, 1978, 74, 67; Fedn. Indian Chamber Commerce and Industry grantee, 1985. Fellow Instn. of Engrs. India (council 1973-77), Inst. Civil Engrs. London, ASCE; mem. ASTM, Earthquake Engring. Research Inst., Internat. Soc. Soil Mechanics and Foundation Engring., Indian Geotech. Soc. (instrumentation prize 1980, pres. 1971-73, 73-75), Indian Soc. Earthquake Tech. (sec. 1970, pres. 1985-87), Indian Soc. Tech. Edn., Indian Soc. Engring. Geology, Indian Road Congress, Indian Soc. Desert Tech., Sigma Xi, Phi Kappa Phi. Current work: Soil dynamics, piles and machine foundations, liquefaction of soils, geotechnical engineering, mass housing, indigenous materials, standardization. Subspecialty: Civil engineering. Office: 308 Civil Engring Dept U Mo-Rolla Rolla MO 65401

PRANGE, ROBERT KEITH, educator plant science, researcher; b. Pembroke, Ont. Can., Oct. 11, 1951; s. Willard Earl and Rosanna May (Edwards) P.; m. Lydia MacKenzie Nelson, Apr. 1, 1972. B.Sc., Acadia U., 1973; M.Sc., U. B.C., Can., 1976; Ph.D., U. Guelph, Can., 1981. Lectr. N.S. Agrl. Coll., Truro, N.S., 1976-81, asst. prof., 1981-83, assoc. prof., 1983—, head dept. plant sci., 1984—; bd. dirs. Atlantic Inst. Biotechnology, 1985—. Contbr. articles to profl. jours. Bd. dirs. Agrl. Credit Union, Truro, 1984—. Mem. Am. Soc. Plant Physiology, Am. Soc. Horticultural Sci., Can. Soc. Plant Physiology, Can. Soc. Horticultural Sci., Assn. Faculties Agr. Can. (sec.-treas., bd. dirs. 1982—). Current work: Effect of environmental stresses on plant growth and development; environmental control of potato production and storage. Subspecialties: Plant physiology (agriculture); Photosynthesis. Office: Dept Plant Sci Nova Scotia Agrl Coll PO Box 550 Truro NS B2N 5E3 Canada

PRASAD, ANANDA SHIVA, medical educator; b. Buxar, Bihar, India, Jan. 1, 1928; came to U.S., 1952, naturalized, 1968; s. Radha Krishna and Mahesha (Kaur) Lall; m. Aryabala Ray, Jan. 6, 1952; children: Rita, Sheila, Ashok, Audrey. B.Sc. with honors, Patna (India) Sci. Coll., 1946, M.B. B.S., 1951; Ph.D., U. Minn., 1957. Diplomate: Am. Bd. Nutrition. Intern Patna Med. Coll. Hosp., 1951-52; resident St. Paul's Hosp., Dallas, 1952-53, U. Minn., 1953-56, VA Hosp., Mpls., 1956; instr. dept. medicine Univ. Hosp., U. Minn., Mpls., 1957-58; vis. asso. prof. medicine Shiraz Med. Faculty, Nemazee Hosp., Shiraz, Iran, 1960; asst. prof. medicine and nutrition Vanderbilt U., 1961-63; mem. faculty, dir. div. hematology dept. medicine Wayne State U., Detroit, 1963—, asso. prof., 1964-68, prof., 1968—; mem. staff Harper-Grace Hosp., VA Hosp., Allen Park, Mich.; Mem. trace elements subcom. Food and Nutrition Bd., NRC-Nat. Acad. Scis., 1965-68; chmn. trace elements com. Internat. Union Nutritional Scis.; reviewer several profl. jours. Author: Zinc Metabolism, 1966, Trace Elements in Human Health and Disease, 1976, Trace Elements and Iron in Human Metabolism, 1978, Zinc in Human Nutrition, 1979; editor: Clinical, Biochemical and Nutritional Aspects of Trace Elements, Am. Jour. Hematology; co-editor: Zinc Metabolism, Current Aspects in Health and Disease, 1977, Clinical Applications of Recent Advances in Zinc Metabolism; mem. editorial bd.: Nutrition Research; contbr. articles to profl. jours. Trustee Detroit Internat. Inst., Detroit Gen. Hosp. Research Corp., 1969-72. Pfizer scholar, 1955-56; Recipient research recognition award Wayne State U., 1964, award Am. Coll. Nutrition, 1976. Fellow ACP, AAAS, Internat. Soc. Hematology; mem. Am. Soc. Clin. Nutrition (awards com. 1969-70, Robert H. Herman award 1984), Am. Fedn. Clin. Research (pres. Mich. 1969-70), Am. Inst. Nutrition (trace elements panel), Am. Physiol. Soc., Am. Soc. Clin. Investigation, Am. Soc. Hematology, Assn. Am. Physicians, Central Soc. Clin. Research, Soc. Exptl. Biology and Medicine (councillor Mich. 1967-71), Wayne County Med. Soc., AMA (Goldberger award 1975), Internat. Soc. Internal Medicine, Sigma Xi. Club: Cosmos (Washington). Subspecialties: Hematology; Nutrition (medicine). Home: 4710 Cove Rd Orchard Lake MI 48033 Office: 540 E Canfield Ave Detroit MI 48201

PRASAD, SATISH CHANDRA, radiologic physicist; b. Chapra, Bihar, India, Apr. 1, 1944; s. Shib Chandra and Sitapati Devi P.; m. Jayshri Prasad, July 1, 1954; children: Monica, Anita, Sunita. B.S., Patna (India) U., 1963; M.S. in Physics, U. Mass., 1968, Ph.D. in Physics, 1972; M.S. in Radiol. Physics, U. Colo. Med. Ctr., 1976. Cert. in diagnostic and therapeutic radiol. physics Am. Bd. Radiology, 1978. Research asst. physics U. Mass., Amherst, 1967-72; research assoc. physics U. Rochester, N.Y., 1972-74; research asst. radiation physics U. Colo. Med. Ctr., Denver, 1974-76; asst. prof. radiation physics Washington U. Med. Ctr., St. Louis, 1976-81; asst. prof. Upstate Med. Ctr., SUNY, Syracuse, 1981-84, assoc. prof., 1984—. Contbr. articles to profl. jours. Mem. Am. Assn. Physicists in Medicine, Am. Phys. Soc., AAAS, Am. Coll. Radiology, Phi Kappa Phi. Current Work: Radiation therapy and diagnostic radiological physics; computed tomography, radiation dose to tissues from x-rays, gamma rays and electron beams. Office: 750 E. Adams St Syracuse NY 13210

PRATHER, LAWRENCE ALBERT, data acquisition integrated circuit design engineer; b. Bremerton, Wash., Aug. 2, 1955; s. Bert E. and Katherine (Lindquist) P.; m. Katherine F. Hawk, Aug. 2, 1976. B.S. E.E., Oreg. Inst. Tech., 1978. Analog test engr. Intersil, Inc., Cupertino, Calif., 1978-80, digital integrated circuit design engr., 1980-83, Siliconix, Inc., Santa Clara, Calif., 1983—. Mem. IEEE, Alpha Chi. Current work: Curvature corrected bandgap voltage reference implemented in CMOS; dual slope a/d converters and switched capacitor a/d converters; CMOS d/a converters using thin film resistor technology; thin film resistor evaluation especially laser trimming effects on matching drift and stability. Subspecialty: Integrated circuits. Home: 774 Lakehaven Dr Sunnyvale CA 94089 Office: Siliconix Inc 2201 Laurelwood R Santa Clara CA 95054

PRATT, ALLAN DANIEL, library systems specialist, educator; b. Traverse City, Mich., Sept. 26, 1933; s. Gilbert Sheldon and Mary Marie (Buhro) P.; m. Nancy Gordon, Oct. 18, 1959 (div. 1972); children—Sheldon, Nelson, Grodon, Madelon, Kendall; m. 2d, Ellen Altman, Oct. 27, 1984. B.A., U. Mich., 1955; M.L.S., Western Res. U., 1959; Ph.D., U. Pitts., 1974. Librarian, Corvair, San Diego, 1959-61; librarian, systems designer IBM, San Jose, Calif., 1961-67, library cons., Milford, Conn., 1984—; prof. library sci. Ind. U., Bloomington, 1967-80, U. Ariz., Tucson, 1980-84. Author: Information of the Image, 1981. Contbr. articles to profl. jours. Served to lt. U.S. Army, 1955-57. Fulbright prof., 1976. Mem. ALA, Am. Soc. Info. Sci. Subspecialty: Information systems (Information science). Office: IBM Corp 472 Wheelers Farms Rd Milford CT 06460

PRATT, ARNOLD W., govt. ofcl., physician; b. Binghamton, N.Y., Nov. 24, 1920; s. Donald Patrick and Agnes Kate (Smith) P.; m. Mary Durfee, June 17, 1945; children: Mary Pratt Grant, Susan Broomfield, Janet Pratt Oliver. Sc.D., Hobart Coll., 1973; M.D., U. Rochester, 1946. Mem. house staff N.Y. Hosp. (Cornell U. Med. Center), N.Y.C., 1946-47; research asso. Cornell U. Med. Sch., 1947-48; head sect. energy metabolism lab. physiology Nat. Cancer Inst., NIH, Bethesda, Md., 1948-66, dir. div. computer research and tech., 1966—. Editorial bd.: Computers and Biomed. Research, 1967—, Methods of Info. in Medicine, 1970—, Computer Programs in Biomedicine, 1972—. Recipient Superior Service award HEW, 1968, Meritorious Exec. award Sr. Exec. Service, 1980. Subspecialties: Information systems, storage, and retrieval (computer science); Computers in medicine. Office: 9000 Rockville Pike Bldg 12A Bethesda MD 20205

PRATT, BENJAMIN CABELL, civil engineer, consultant; b. Battle Creek, Mich., May 29, 1930; s. Percy Paul and Frances Isabel (Cabell) P.; m. Jacquelyn Blanche Lusby, Aug. 31, 1957; children—Dennis, Timothy, Kerry Mayo. B.S. in Civil Engring., Va. Mil. Inst., 1951; M.S. in Environ. and Urban Systems, Fla. Internat. U., 1980. Diplomate Am. Acad. Environ. Engrs.; registered profl. engr., Fla., Ga., N.C., Va., Md., N.Y., Mass., Maine, La., Tex.; registered land surveyor, Fla., La. Jr. engr. RF & P R.R., Alexandria, Va., 1953-54; sr. regional engr. Shell Oil Co., Scarsdale, N.Y., 1954-69; gen. mgr. Southland Prestressed Concrete, Ft. Myers, Fla., 1969-70; dir. pub. works Lee County, Fla., Ft. Myers, 1970-83; v.p., prin. Wilson, Miller, Barton, Soll & Peek, Ft. Myers, 1983—; cons. engring., land use, zoning, pub. works. Nat. bd. mem. Boy Scouts Am., 1976-78, council commr. SW Fla. council, 1976-78, mem. exec. bd. SW Fla. council, 1974—. Served with USMC, 1947-53, Korea; to col. USMCR, 1953-76. Research fellow in water resources Glazer Research, 1980; recipient Local Govt. award Fla. Shore and Beach Preservation Assn., 1978. Fellow Fla. Engring. Soc. (chpt. treas., sec., v.p., pres. 1981-85, Engr. of Yr. Calusa chpt. 1980); mem. Am. Pub. Works Assn. (exec. bd. 1981—, Mem. of Yr. Fla. chpt. 1984, Top Ten Pub. Works Leaders U.S. and Can. 1982), ASCE (Meritorious Pub. Service award 1982), Fla. Soc. Profl. Land Surveyors. Republican. Roman Catholic. Lodges: Masons, Shriners, Rotary. Research or work interests: Water resources, civil engineering and public works. Subspecialty: Civil engineering. Home: 2431 Jasper Ave Fort Myers FL 33907 Office: Wilson Miller Barton Soll & Peek Inc 1625 Hendry St Fort Myers FL 33901

PRATT, GEORGE L., agrl. engr., educator; b. Fargo, N.D., Jan. 31, 1926; s. Robert W. and Anne S. (Mangach) P.; m. Patricia Jones, Nov. 23, 1955; children: Thomas, Nancy Pratt Coash. B.S. in Agr, N.D. State U., 1950; M.S. in Agrl. Engring, Kans. State U., 1951; Ph.D., Okla. State U., 1967. Registered profl. engr., N.D. Sales Clay Equipment Corp., Cedar Falls, Iowa, 1952-53; instr. dept. agrl. engring. N.D. State U., Fargo, 1951-52, asst. prof., 1953-57, assoc. prof., 1957-67, prof., 1967—, chmn. dept., 1976—. Contbr. articles to profl. jours. Served with USMC, 1944-46. Mem. Am. Soc. Agrl. Engrs. (Metal Bldgs. Mfrs. award 1978), Sigma Xi., Phi Kappa Phi. Congregationalist. Lodges: Kiwanis; Elks; Masons. Current Work: Energy demonstration farm involving solar collectors, methane digesters, and minimum tillage crop production. Processing and use of vegetable oil as fuel for diesel engines. Subspecialties: Agricultural engineering; Biomass (agriculture). Home: 2519 Willow Rd Fargo ND 58102 Office: Dept Agrl Engring ND State U Fargo ND 58105

PRATT, JEREMY, ecologist, energy scientist, consultant; b. Winslow, Wash., June 10, 1954; s. Drusilla Adele Pratt. B.A., The Evergreen State Coll., 1976; M.S., Washington State U., 1979. Assoc. in research Wash. State U, Pullman, 1977-79; ecologist, project mgr. Seattle City Light, 1979-80; energy analyst Wash. State Legis., Olympia, 1979-81; tech. editor, sr. writer Wm. Nesbit & Assocs., Santa Rosa, Calif., 1982-83; prin. BioSystems Analysis, Inc., Sausalito, Calif., 1981—; dir., founder Inst. Human Ecology, Sausalito, 1982—; energy chmn., dir. Seattle Audubon Soc., 1980-81; dir. Wash. Bald Eagle Symposium, Seattle, 1980, The Evergreen State Coll. Ecology Symposium, Olympia, 1973. Contbr. articles to profl. jours. Chmn. ways and means com., bd. dirs. Western Wash. Solar Energy Assn., Seattle, 1980-81; comnr., chmn. Pullman Envir. Quality Commn., 1977-79; docent, v.p. Bouverie Audubon Preserve, Sonoma, Calif., 1983-84; mem. Pullman State Environmental Policy Act Review Bd., 1978-79, Skagit River Bald Eagle Adv. Com., Seattle, 1979-80. Mem. Soc. Human Ecology, Calif. Acad. Scis., Ecol. Soc. Am., Raptor Research Found., Somona Bird Rescue Ctr., Phi Kappa Phi. Current work: Ecology; applied human ecology; energy. Subspecialties: Ecology (biology); Energy and society. Office: Inst for Human Ecology Bldg 1055 Ft Cronkhite Sausalito CA 94965

PRATT, RICHARD HOUGHTON, physics educator; b. N.Y.C., May 5, 1934; s. Karl Chapman and Gertrude (Gennis) P.; m. Elizabeth Ann Glass, Nov. 1, 1958; children—Jonathan, Kathryn, Caroline, Paul. A.B., U. Chgo., 1952, S.M., 1955, Ph.D., 1959. Research assoc. Stanford U., Calif., 1959-61, asst. prof., 1961-64; assoc. prof. U. Pitts., 1964-69, prof., 1969—, acad. dean semester at sea, 1984; cons. Lawrence Livermore Nat. Lab., Calif., 1960—; mem. Govs. Sci. Adv. Com., Harrisburg, Pa., 1978, advisor Govs. Energy Council, Harrisburg, 1979. Grantee NSF, 1981—, NSF, 1983—, Lawrence Livermore Nat. Lab., Fellow Am. Phys. Soc.; mem. AAAS, European Phys Soc., Sierra Club (regional v.p. 1982-83, nat. com. 1980-82). Current work: Electron-photon interactions in atomic and nuclear fields; bremsstrahlung; photoeffect; photon and electron scattering; quantum electrodynamics; atomic processes at high temperature and pressure. Subspecialties: Theoretical physics; Atomic and molecular physics. Home: 1131 Shady Ave Pittsburgh PA 15232 Office: Dept Physics and Astronomy U Pitts Pittsburgh PA 15260

PRAVDA, MILTON FRANK, nuclear engineering company executive; b. N.Y.C., Dec. 25, 1923; s. Frank and Nellie (Preplata) P. B.S. in Elec. Engring, Newark Coll. Engring., 1947. Project engr. Gen. Electric Co., Phila., 1947-50, resident engr., Schenectady, 1950-54, mgr. reactor design, 1954-60; mgr. reactor systems Martin Marietta Corp., Balt., 1960-64, dir. engring. and research, 1964-68; chmn. bd., pres. Dynatherm Corp., Cockeysville, Md., 1968—; chmn. bd. Bossalina Machine Co., Inc., Cockeysville, 1968—. Editor: Heat Pipe Design Handbook, 1972; Contbr. articles to profl. jours. Mem. IEEE (sr.), Am. Nuclear Soc. (sr.), AAAS, Tau Beta Pi. Patentee in fields of nuclear reactors, isotopic generators, heat pipes, heat exchangers, and absorption systems. Current Work: Research on a very thin films generated on tapered surfaces rotating at high rotational velocities. This is the basis of a new absorption heat pump for use on automobiles and in industry to save energy. Subspecialties: Nuclear engineering; Electrical engineering. Home: 7708 Greenview Terr Towson MD 21204 Office: Dynatherm Corp One Industry Ln Cockeysville MD 21030

PRAY, LLOYD CHARLES, geology educator; b. Chgo., June 25, 1919; s. Allan Theron and Helen (Palmer) P.; m. Carrel Myers, Sept. 14, 1946; children—Lawrence, John Allan, Kenneth, Douglas. B.A., Carleton Coll., 1941; M.S., Calif. Inst. Tech., 1943, Ph.D., 1952. With U.S. Geol. Survey Geologist Mineral Deposits, Calif., S.D., Southeastern states, 1943-44, 46-56; instr. to assoc. prof. Calif. Inst. Tech., Pasadena, 1949-56; research geologist to research assoc. Denver Research Ctr., Marathon Oil Com, Littleton, Colo., 1956-68; prof. geology U. Wis., Madison, 1968—; visiting prof. or scientist (short term) U. Colo., Tex., Alberta, Can., Imperial Coll. of Sci. and Tech.-London, 1966—; short course lectr. Am. Assn. Petroleum Geologists, Colo. Sch. Mines, various U.S. locations. Author, editor, symposium and field trip organizer and leader, 1963-84. Author numerous articles and abstracts. Pres. Colo. Diabetes Assn., Denver, 1966. Served to lt. (j.g.) USNR, 1944-46, PTO. Fellow Geol. Soc. Am.; mem. Am. Assn. Petroleum Geologists (recipient Matson and Levorsen awards, best paper, 1966-67), Soc. Economic Paleontologists and Mineralogists (treas., v.p., pres. 1969-70, hon. mem. Permian Basin sect. 1977, 82), Internat. Assn. Sedimentologists, Phi Beta Kappa. Named Layman of Yr. Am. Diabetes Assn., 1968. Current work: Sedimentary geology particularly that of ancient carbonate sedimentary environments associated with reef and bank-to-basin facies complexes, their deposition and diagenesis including porosity evolution; regional geology, particularly of southern N.M. and West Tex. and field excursions therein. Subspecialties: Sedimentology; Geology. Home: 7664 Tumbledown Trail Verona WI 53593 Office: U Wis Dept Geology and Geophysics 1215 Dayton St Madison WI 53706

PREFFER, FREDERIC IRA, immunologist, research scientist; b. N.Y.C., July 23, 1953; s Samuel J. and Shirley (Blatt) P.; m. Trisha Jenkyns, Oct. 9, 1983; 1 child, Frances Jonina. B.A., SUNY-Buffalo, 1975, M.S., 1977, Ph.D., 1981. Research assoc. Roswell Park Meml. Hosp., Buffalo, 1975-77; research fellow Cancer Research Inst., N.Y.C., 1981-82; Mass. Gen. Hosp. Harvard Med. Sch., Boston, 1982—; instr. pathology, Harvard Med. Sch., 1985; asst. immunology, dir. flow cytometry Mass. Gen. Hosp., 1985; cons. Author: Monoclonal Antibodies in Pathology, 1985. Contbr. articles to profl. jours. N.Y. State Regent scholar, 1971-75. Mem. Assn. Gnotobiology, Soc. Analytical Cytology. Current work: Flow cytometric analysis of lymphocytes from heart/renal/liver transplantation patients. modulation of Class I and II antigens on human tumor cells with substances derived from activated lymphocytes. Subspecialties: Cancer research (medicine); Transplantation. Office: Dept Pathology Cox-5 Mass Gen Hosp Blossom St Boston MA 02144

PREISS, IVOR LOUIS, educator; b. N.Y.C., Mar. 24, 1933; s. Louis H. and Carolyn P.; m. Jane M. Rose, Jan. 28, 1956; children: Susan Lai, Sharon, Sandra; m. Lorraine M. Dixson, June 7, 1970; children—Bradley, Michelle. B.S., Rensselaer Poly. Inst., 1955; M.S., U. Ark., 1957; Ph.D., 1960. Research fellow U. Ark., 1957-60; research assoc. physics Yale U., 1960-66; asst. dir. Heavy Ion Lab., Yale U., 1961-66, lectr. chemistry, 1961-66; prof. chemistry Rensselaer Poly. Inst., Troy, N.Y., 1966—; adj. prof. physics SUNY Albany, 1967—; bd. dirs. Found Analytical Research in Art, 1979-82. Contbr. articles to profl. jours. Bd. dirs. N.Y. State PTA, 1971-78. Mem. Am. Chem. Soc., Am. Phys. Soc., Soc. Applied Spectroscopy, Zeta Psi. Roman Catholic. Current Work: Analysis of trace elements, nuclear scattering, radioisotope utilization, production and application, radiation detection, x-ray fluorescence. Subspecialties: Analytical chemistry; Nuclear physics. Home: 6 County View Rd Latham NY 12110 Office: Cogswell Lab Rensselaer Poly Inst Troy NY 12110

PRELAS, MARK ANTHONY, nuclear engineer, educator; b. Pueblo, Colo., July 7, 1953; s. George B. and Katheryn (Beck) P.; m. Rosemary Roberts, May 21, 1979. B.S., Colo. State U.-Ft. Collins, 1975; M.S., U. Ill.-Urbana, 1976, Ph.D., 1979. Asst. prof. nuclear engring. U. Mo.-Columbia, 1979-85, assoc. prof., 1985—, dir. Mo. Mirror Project, 1982 , research scientist, 1980 ; v.p. Nuclear Pumped Laser Corp., Kingston, N.J., 1980 . Contbr. chpts. to books, articles to profl. publs. NSF grantee, 1980, 82-85; McDonnell Douglas Corp. grantee, 1981; Gas Research Inst. fellow, 1981; NSF Presdl. Young Investigator awardee, 1984. Mem. AAAS, Am. Nuclear Soc., Am. Phys. Soc., IEEE, Sigma Xi. Current Work: Superconducting magnet design and operation; charged particle transport in various media; plasma chemistry; laser design; gaseous electronics; energy conversion; plasma engineering. Subspecialties: Nuclear engineering; Plasma physics. Home: 1904 Love Joy Ln Columbia MO 65202 Office: U Mo Engring Dept Columbia MO 65211

PREM, KONALD ARTHUR, physician, educator; b. St. Cloud, Minn., Nov. 6, 1920; s. Joseph E. and Theresa M. (Willing) P.; m. Phyllis Edelbrock, June 14, 1947; children: Mary Kristen, Stephanie, Timothy. B.S., U. Minn., 1947; M.B., 1950, M.D., 1951. Diplomate: Am. Bd. Ob-Gyn (with spl. competence in gynecologic oncology). Intern Mpls. gen. Hosp., 1950-51; fellow dept. obstetrics and gynecology U. Minn., Mpls., 1951-54, instr., 1955-58, asst. prof., 1958-60, assoc. prof., 1960-69, prof., 1969—, dir. div. gynecologic oncology, 1969-83, head dept. obstetrics and gynecology, 1976-84. Served to capt. USAR, 1941-46; brig. gen. M.C. USAR (Ret.). Decorated Legion of Merit. Mem. Am. Coll. Ob-Gyn, Am. Gynec. and Obstet. Soc., Central Assn. Ob-Gyn, Hennepin County Med. Soc., Soc. Pelvic Surgeons, Minn. Ob-Gyn Soc., Soc. Gynecologic Oncologists, Soc. Gynecologic Surgery, Minn. Acad. Medicine, Am. Radium Soc., Gynecologic Urology Soc., Mpls. Surg. Soc., Soc. Med. Cons. to Armed Forces. Roman Catholic. Club: Decathlon. Subspecialty: Gynecological oncology. Home: 4806 Sunnyside Rd Edina MN 55424 Office: PO Box 395 Mayo Bldg 420 Delaware St SE Minneapolis MN 55455

PRENTKY, ROBERT ALAN, psychology educator; b. L.I.C., Aug. 21, 1947; s. Peter Isaac and Janet (Weinberger) P. Ph.D., Northwestern U., 1975. Dir. Research Mass. Treatment Ctr., Bridgewater, 1980—; research assoc. Brandeis U., Waltham, Mass., 1981—; asst. prof. Boston U., 1981—. Author: Creativity and Psychopathology, 1980; editor: Biological Aspects of Normal Personality, 1979. NIMH postdoctoral fellow U. Mass., 1975-77; NIMH postdoctoral fellow U. York, Eng., 1977-78; NIMH postdoctoral fellow U. Rochester Med. Ctr., 1978-80. Mem. Union of Concerned Scientists, Physicians for Social Responsibility, Am. Psychol. Assn., Soc. for Psychophysiol. Research, N.Y. Acad. Sci., Soc. for Life History Research in Psychopathology, AAAS. Current Work: Bio-social antecedents of human sexual and nonsexual aggression; psychopathy; episodic dyscontrol; impulsivity; taxonomic analysis of criminal conduct. Subspecialties: Psychobiology; Neurochemistry. Home: 35 Howland Ln Hingham MA 02043 Office: Mass Treatment Ctr PO Box 554 Bridgewater MA 02324

PRESANT, CARY A., med. oncologist; b. Buffalo, Dec. 16, 1942; s. Allen N. and R. (Reeta) (Coplon) P.; m. Sheila Lassman, June 11, 1966; children: Seth, Sean, Jaron, Jaclyn. M.D., SUNY, Buffalo, 1966. Diplomate: Am. Bd. Internal Medicine, 1970. Staff assoc. Nat. Cancer Inst., 1967-69; asst. prof. medicine and radiology Washington U., St. Louis, 1973-79; dir. med. oncology City of Hope Med. Ctr., Duarte, Calif., 1979-82; med. oncologist Wilshire Oncology Med. Group, West Covina, Calif., 1982—; chmn. melanoma-sarcoma com. S.E. Cancer Study Group, 1975-82; prof. medicine U. So. Calif.; cons. Scott Labs. and Oncology Labs., Providence; bd. sci. advs. Vestar Research Corp., Pasadena, Calif. Contbr. articles to profl. jours., chapts. to books. Served with USPHS, 1967-69. Roswell Park Meml. Inst. fellow, 1963; USPHS grantee, 1972-86; Louis Sklarow Meml. lectr. Maimonides Med. Soc., Buffalo, 1982. Fellow ACP; mem. Am. Soc. Hematology, Am. Soc. Clin. Oncology, Am. Assn. Cancer Research, Phi Beta Kappa, Alpha Omega Alpha. Jewish. Current Work: Leukemia and solid tumor treatment; diagnosis and treatment with liposomes. Subspecialties: Chemotherapy; Cancer research (medicine). Office: 935 S Sunset West Covina CA 91790

PRESCHUTTI, JOSEPH PAUL, electronics engineer; b. Jessup, Pa., Nov. 4, 1948; s. Ethello Paul and Anne Marie (Masko) P.; m. Melanie Maliniak, Jan. 4, 1980; children—Stanley, Eliot, Jesse. B.S.E.E., Pa. State U., 1970, M.S.E.E., 1972; student U. Scranton, 1966-68. Engr., C-Cor Electronics, State College, Pa., 1972-83, v.p. engring., 1983-84; pres. E-com. div. AM Cable TV Ind., Quakertown, Pa., 1984—. Contbr. articles to profl. jours. Mem. IEEE, Soc. Cable TV Engrs. Subspecialties: Electronics; Telecommunications. Home: 655 Belmont Circle State College PA 16803 Office: AM Cable TV Industries Inc PO Box 505 Quakertown PA 18951

PRESLEY, JOE ANDREW, JR., engineer; b. Little Rock, Feb. 26, 1953; s. Joe Andrew and Arralee (Matthews) P.; m. Farzaneh Mahtafar, Dec. 13, 1975; children—Joe Andrew, III, Mary Roya. B.S. in Oceanography, Fla. Inst. Tech., 1975; M.S. in Applied Ocean Sci., U. Calif.-San Diego, 1978. Research assoc. Marine Phys. Lab., La Jolla, Calif., 1975-81; program mgr., sr. prin. engr. ORINCON, La Jolla, 1981—. Patentee in field. Contbr. articles to profl. jours. NSF fellow, 1975-76, Fannie and John Hertz Found. fellow, 1976-81. Mem. IEEE, Acoustic Soc. Am. Current work: Sonar and radar signal processing. Subspecialties: Electrical engineering; Oceanography.

PRESS, FRANK, educator, geophysicist; b. Bklyn., Dec. 4, 1924; s. Solomon and Dora (Steinholz) P.; m. Billie Kallick, June 9, 1946; children: William Henry, Paula Evelyn. B.S., CCNY, 1944, LL.D. (hon.), 1972; M.A., Columbia U., 1946, Ph.D., 1949; D.Sc. (hon.), Notre Dame U., 1973, U. R.I., U. Ariz., Rutgers U., CUNY, 1979. Research assoc. Columbia, 1946-49, instr. geology, 1949-51, asst. prof. geology, 1951-52, assoc. prof., 1952-55; prof. geophysics Cal. Inst. Tech., 1955-65, dir. seismol. lab., 1957-65; prof. geophysics, chmn. dept. earth and planetary scis. MIT, 1965-77; sci. advisor to Pres., dir. Office Sci. and Tech. Policy, Washington, 1977-80; Inst. prof. M.I.T., 1981; pres. Nat. Acad. Scis., 1981—; cons. USAF, 1958, U.S. Geol. Survey, 1957, USN, 1957—, Office Spl. Asst. for Sci. and Tech., 1961-64, Office Sci. and Tech., 1964—, ACDA, 1961-68, AID, 1961-64; dir. United Electro Dynamics; expert UNESCO Tech. Assistance Adminstrn., 1953; seismology and glaciology panel U.S. nat. com. IGY, 1955; chmn. U.S. del. Nuclear Test Ban Conf., 1960; mem. Pres.'s Sci. Adv. Com. and Internat. Geophysics Com., 1961-64, Lunar and Planetary Mission Bd., 1965-70; chmn. adv. bd. Nat. Center Earthquake Research, 1966—; mem. Nat. Sci. Bd., 1970—. Author: (with M. Ewing, W.S. Jardetzky) Propagation of Elastic Waves in Layered Media, 1956, (with R. Siever) Earth, 1974; Co-editor: (with R. Siever) Physics and Chemistry of the Earth, 1957—. Recipient Columbia medal for excellence, 1960, pub. service award U.S. Dept. Interior, 1972, gold medal Royal Astron. Soc., 1972, pub. service medal NASA, 1973. Mem. Am. Acad. Arts and Scis., Geol. Soc. Am. (councilor), Am. Geophys. Union (pres. 1973), Soc. Exploration Geophysicists, Seismol. Soc. Am. (pres. 1963), AAUP, Nat. Acad. Scis. (councilor), Phi Beta Kappa. Subspecialty: Geophysics. Office: Nat Acad Scis 2101 Constitution Ave Washington DC 20418*

PRESS, JEFFERY BRUCE, pharmaceutical company executive; b. Rochester, N.Y., May 24, 1947; s. James Herbert and Mildred (Hau) P.; m. Linda Helen Seghers, Dec. 20, 1976. B.S. in Chemistry, Bucknell U., 1969; Ph.D. in Organic Chemistry, Ohio State U., 1973. Postdoctoral Harvard U., Cambridge, Mass., 1973-75; research scientist Lederle Lab., Pearl River, N.Y., 1975-81, group leader, 1981-83; research mgr. Ortho Pharm., Raritan, N.J., 1983—. Co-sec. Organic Reactions Editorial Bd., 1983—. Contbr. articles to profl. jours. Patentee in field. Mem. Am. Chem. Soc., Internat. Soc. Heterocyclic Chemistry, Sigma Xi, Alpha Chi Sigma. Current work: Cardiovascular drugs: sulfur containing molecules, heterocycles, synthetic methods; drug design and molecular design. Subspecialties: Organic chemistry; Medicinal chemistry. Office: Ortho Pharm Corp Route 202 Raritan NJ 08869

PRESS, MICHAEL FREDRICK, pathologist, educator; b. St. Louis, May 11, 1948; s. Oliver Herbert and Martha Elfriede (Weidenbach) P.; m. Sarah Elizabeth Pizzo, Nov. 26, 1977; children—Oliver A., Lara C., Eric W., David J. B.A., Wash. U.-St. Louis, 1970; Ph.D., U. Chgo., 1975, M.D., 1977. Diplomate Am. Bd. Pathology. Resident U. Chgo., 1977-81, asst. prof., 1981—. Mem. Internat. Acad. Pathology, Am. Assn. Pathologists, Internat. Soc. Gynecol. Pathologists. Current work: Gynecologic cancer; estrogen receptor biology. Subspecialties: Pathology (medicine); Cancer research (medicine). Office: Dept Pathology U Chicago Hosps Clinics 5841 S Maryland Ave Chicago IL 60637

PRESS, WILLIAM HENRY, astrophysicist; b. N.Y.C., May 23, 1948; s. Frank and Billie (Kallick) P.; m. Margaret Ann Lauritsen, Sept. 9, 1969 (div. 1982); 1 dau., Sara Linda. A.B., Harvard Coll., 1969; M.S., Calif. Inst. Tech., 1971, Ph.D., 1972. Asst. prof. theoretical physics Calif. Inst. Tech., 1973-74; asst. prof. physics Princeton (N.J.) U., 1974-76; prof. astronomy and physics Harvard U., Cambridge, Mass., 1976—, chmn. dept. astronomy, 1982-85; mem. adv. coms. and panels NSF, NASA, Nat. Acad. Scis., NRC; vis. mem. Inst. Advanced Study, spring 1983; mem. Def. Sci. Bd., 1985—; mem. program com. Sloan Found., 1985—. Contbr. articles to profl. jours. Sloan Found. research fellow, 1974-78. Mem. Am. Astron. Soc. (Helen B. Warner Prize 1981), Am. Phys. Soc., Internat. Astron. Union, Internat. Soc. Relativity and Gravitation. Current Work: Galaxy and cluster of galaxy formation, astrophysical fluid dynamics; computational methods; relativistic astrophysics. Subspecialties: Cosmology; Theoretical astrophysics. Office: 60 Garden St Cambridge MA 02138

PREST, WILLIAM MARCHANT, JR., scientist, physics executive; b. Boston, Nov. 4, 1941; s. William Marchant, Sr. and Margaretta (Traver) P.; m. Edith Goodhue, July 12, 1969; children—Peggy-Jean, Catherine. B.S. in Physics, Union Coll., 1963; M.S. in Physics, U. Pa., 1965; M.S. in Polymer Sci., Engring., U. Mass., 1969, Ph.D. in Polymer Sci., Engring., 1972. With research tech. program Gen. Electric R&D Center, Schenectady, N.Y., 1965-68; assoc. scientist polymer scis. area Xerox Webster Research Ctr., 1971, scientist, 1972-77, sr. scientist, 1977-79, project leader polymer physics, 1979-81, prin. scientist materials sci. lab., 1981—, mgr. physics of materials area, 1983-85, mgr. polymer sci., 1985—; chmn. Gordon Research Conf. on Polymers (West), 1984. Assoc. editor Polymer Physics section Jour. of Applied Physics, 1983—. Author numerous papers. Patentee (4) in field. Herman Mark fellow Plastics Inst. Am., 1970; NSF research grantee, 1984. Fellow Am. Physical Soc. div. of High Polymer Physics (vice chmn. 1985—); mem. North Am. Thermal Analysis Soc. (awards chmn. 1983-84), Am. Chemical Soc., Soc. of Rheology, Soc. of Plastics Engrs. (Best Paper of Yr. award, 1977). Current work: Compatability of polymer blends; thermodynamic and spectroscopic properties of glasses; orientation processes in polymers; rheological properties of polymer melts; structure and optical properties of polymer films; polymorphism of PVF2, FTIR. Subspecialties: Polymer physics; Polymers (materials science). Home: 616 Lake Rd Webster NY 14580 Office: Xerox Corp 800 Phillips Rd 0114/39D Webster NY 14580

PRESTON, CHARLES RICHARD, biology educator, researcher; b. Ft. Smith, Ark., Oct. 9, 1952; s. Charles Meyers and Mary Ellen (Breedlove) P.; m. Penny Sue Hatcher, Mar. 25, 1983. B.S., Ark. Tech. U., 1974; M.S., U. Ark., 1978, Ph.D., 1982. Asst. curator sci Mus. Sci. and History, Little Rock, 1975-76; grad. research asst. U. Ark., Fayetteville, 1976-77, research assoc., 1977-82, asst. prof. biology, 1982—; cons. Comprehensive Planning Inst., Dallas, 1981-82, Ark. Game and Fish Commn., Little Rock, 1982—. Referee for various jours. Contbr. numerous articles to profl. jours. Recipient J.A. Scholtz Meml. award U. Ark. Mus., 1980. Mem. Am. Ornithologists Union, Ecol. Soc. Am., Animal Behavior Soc., Raptor Research Found., Sigma Xi. (Aubrey E. Harvey award 1982). Current work: Habitat selection and utilization by birds; the effects of habitat alteration on vertebrate community organization; raptor foraging ecology. Subspecialty: Behavioral ecology. Office: Dept Biology U Ark 33d and University Sts Little Rock AR 72204

PRESTON, FREDERICK WILLARD, surgeon, educator, researcher; b. Chgo., June 27, 1912; s. Frederick Augustus and Margaret (Atwater) P.; m. Gertrude Eldred, June 23, 1942 (div. 1960); children—Frederick Willard Jr., David Eldred, William Blackmore; m. Barbara Hess, July 30, 1961. B.A., Yale U., 1935; M.D., Northwestern U.-Chgo., 1940, M.S., 1944; M.S., U. Minn., 1947. Diplomate Am. Bd. Surgery. Intern Presbyn. Hosp., Chgo., 1939-41; fellow in surgery Mayo Clinic, Rochester, Minn., 1941-42, 46-48; assoc. to prof. surgery Northwestern U. Med. Sch., Chgo., 1949-75; chief surg. service VA Research Hosp., Chgo., 1954-69; dir. surg. edn. Santa Barbara Cottage Hosp., Calif., 1975-83; chmn. dept surgery Santa Barbara Gen. Hosp., 1976-78; bd. dirs. Love Med. Research, Inc., Santa Barbara, 1984—. Author, editor: Loose Leaf Practice of Surgery, 1964-73; Basic Surgical Physiology, 1969; Manual of Ambulatory Surgery, 1982; also articles. Bd. dirs. Schweppe Found., Chgo., 1958—; governing mem. Shedd Aquarium, Chgo., 1967-75; mem. Hepatitis Commn., Chgo., 1969-72. Served to maj. U.S. Army, 1942-46. NIH grantee, 1959-60; Abbott Labs. and Upjohn Co. grantee, 1960-65. Fellow ACS; mem. Western Surg. Assn. (recorder, mem. council 1961-67), Chgo Surg. Soc. (sec. 1961-63, pres. 1968-69), Am. Surg. Assn., Chgo. Acad. Scis. (sec. 1961-67); Pacific Coast Surg. Assn., Central Surg. Assn., Pan Pacific Surg. Assn., Soc. Surgery Alimentary Tract. Republican. Episcopalian. Clubs: La Cumbre Golf and Country, Santa Barbara (Santa Barbara); Univ. (Chgo.). Current Work: Tumor immunology, effect of hormones on breast cancer, surgical treatment of portal hypertension, transplantation of the intestine, surgical treatment of obesity. Subspecialties: Surgery; Oncology. Home: 755 Via Airosa Santa Barbara CA 93110 Office: Santa Barbara Cottage Hosp Bath at Pueblo Sts Santa Barbara CA 93105

PRESTON, JACK, chemist, consultant; b. Birmingham, Ala., Aug. 7, 1931; s. Earl Walter and Ada Idella (Aldridge) P.; children—John Brock, Joan Catherine; m. Sue Waterman, Aug. 4, 1974 (div. 1984). B.S., Howard Coll., 1952; M.S., U. Ala., 1954; Ph.D., 1957. Research chemist Chemstrand Corp., Decatur, Ala., 1957-60, Chemstrand Research Ctr., Durham, N.C., 1960-65; fellow, 1965-74, sr. fellow, 1974-81; sr. fellow Monsanto Fibers Co., Pensacola, Fla., 1981—; sr. research assoc. Dept. Chemistry, Duke U., Durham, 1977—. Editor (with others) 5 books. Contbr. articles to profl. jours. Patentee in field. Mem. Am. Chem. Soc., Fiber Soc. Democrat. Current work: Heat and flame resistant fibers; high strength and high modulus fibers; acrylic and nylon fibers. Subspecialty: Polymers (materials science). Home: 11409 High Springs Rd Pensacola FL 32514 Office: Monsanto Fiber Co PO Box 12830 Pensacola FL 32575

PRESTON, RICHARD SWAIN, physics educator; b. Natick, Mass., Feb. 4, 1925; s. Arthur Charles and Esther (Swain) P.; m. Angela Camurati, July 25, 1954; children—Claire, Mark. B.A., Wesleyan U., 1949, M.A., 1950; Ph.D., Yale U., 1954. Assoc. dir. Yale U. Geochronometric Lab., New Haven, 1954-55; physicist Argonne Nat. Lab., Ill., 1955-72; prof. physics No. Ill. U., DeKalb, 1970—. Contbr. articles to profl. jours. Served with USN, 1942-46, 50. Mem. Am. Phys. Soc., Am. Assn. Physics Tchrs., Fedn. Am. Scientists. Current work: Applications of Mössbauer spectroscopy to study of amorphous metals; surfaces; precipitation in alloys and diffusion in solids. Subspecialty: Condensed matter physics. Home: 1025 S 1st St DeKalb IL 60115 Office: Physics Dept No Ill U DeKalb IL 60115

PREUS, MARTIN WILLIAM, chemist; b. Chgo., Feb. 26, 1954; s. Fred Albert and Evelynne Ruth (Wendt) P.; m. Susan Rader, June 26, 1976; 1 child, Kevin David. B.S., Calif. State Poly. U., 1975; M.S., U. Calif.-San Diego, 1978, Ph.D., 1979. Research chemist Rohm and Haas, Co., Bristol, Pa., 1980-81, Magna Corp., Santa Fe Springs, Calif., 1981-84, Union Oil Sci. and Tech. Div., Brea, Calif., 1984—. Contbr. articles to sci. jours. Mem. Am. Chem. Soc., Nat. Assn. Corrosion Engrs. Current work: Synthesis of emulsion polymers for coatings and adhesive applications, synthesis of natural products, chemical treatment of oil production facilities. Subspecialties: Polymer chemistry; Organic chemistry. Office: Union Oil Sci and Tech Div 376 S Valencia Ave Brea CA 92621

PREUSS, ROBERT DAVID, engineering educator, researcher; b. Teaneck, N.J., Dec. 29, 1953; s. Harold Paul and Phyllis (Burnap) Brooks. A.B., Boston U., 1975, M.S. in Applied Mech., 1977; Ph.D. in E.E., Okla. State U.-Stillwater, 1983. Cons., Aerospace Systems Inc., Burlington, Mass., 1977-78; project leader The Mitre Corp., Bedford, Mass., 1978-84; Fulbright prof. Tampere U. Tech., Finland, 1984-85; guest research scientist Ecole Nationale Supérieure des Télécommunications, Paris, 1985—. Contbr. articles to tech. jours. Recipient NASA Certificate of Recognition, 1982; Fulbright grantee, U.S. Ednl. Found. in Finland, 1984. Mem. IEEE, Phi Kappa Phi, Eta Kappa Nu. Bahá'í. Current work: Digital signal processing; estimation and information theory; finite element methods and wave mechanics applied to modeling and analysis of time series including speech and electroencephalograms. Subspecialties: Applied mathematics; Electrical engineering. Address: Care 70 Bethel Rd Centerville OH 45459

PREVITE, JOSEPH JAMES, educator, researcher; b. Lawrence, Mass., Jan. 25, 1936; s. Albert and Sarah (Amante) P.; m. Rachel Dorothy Damphousse, Sept. 9, 1936; children—Christopher J., Lisa M., Stephen J., Matthew J., Joseph J. A.B. in Biology, Merrimack Coll., 1956; M.S. in Physiology, Boston Coll., 1959; Ph.D., in Physiology, Bryn Mawr Coll., 1962. Instr., Villanova U., Pa., 1958-62; asst. prof. Smith Coll., Northampton, Mass., 1962-63; research microbiologist U.S. Army Natick Labs., Mass., 1963-68; research physiologist U.S. Army Research Inst., Environ. Medicine, Natick, 1968-70; prof. Framingham State Coll., Mass., 1970—; cons. in field. Author: Human Physiology, 1983; (with others) Topic guidelines in Microbiology, 1980. Cons. Framingham Sch. Com., 1975, State Senate Ad Hoc Com. to Reorganize Pub. Higher Edn., 1977. Fellow Am. Acad. Microbiology; mem. Am. Physiol. Soc., Soc. Exptl. Biology and Medicine, AAAS, Am. Soc. Microbiology. Roman Catholic. Current work: Stress physiology; physiology of disease; rapid methods of microbial detection. Subspecialties: Immunobiology and immunology; Physiology (biology). Office: Dept Biology HA519 State St Framingham MA 01701

PREWITT, RUSSELL LAWRENCE, cardiovascular physiologist; b. St. Louis, June 19, 1943; s. Russell L. and Cornelia J. (Maloney) P.; m. Diana Monahan, Feb. 3, 1967 (div. 1980); 1 son, Phillip S.; m. Lee Ammerman, May 24, 1980. A.B., St. Louis U., 1965; Ph.D., U. Mo., 1971. Research assoc. U. Ariz., Tucson, 1971-74; asst. prof. U. Tenn., Memphis, 1974-81; assoc. prof. dept. physiology and biophysics La. State U. Med. Ctr., Shreveport, 1981-85; assoc. prof. physiology Eastern Va. Med. Sch., 1985—. Contbr. articles to profl. jours. NIH fellow, 1968-71; NIH grantee, 1974—. Fellow Council for High Blood Pressure Research of Am. Heart Assn.; mem. Am. Physiol. Soc., Microcirculatory Soc., Internat. Soc. Hypertensions. Club: Shreveport Yacht. Current work: Role of the microcirculation in long term control of blood flow in hypertension. Subspecialties: Physiology (medicine); Microscopy. Office: Dept Physiology Eastern Va Med Sch 700 Olney Rd Norfolk VA 23501

PREWITT-DIAZ, JOSEPH ORLANDO, teacher educator, school psychologist; b. San Juan, P.R., Nov. 23, 1943; s. Joe Crawford and Leonor (Diaz) Prewitt-D.; m. Maria Dolores Rodriguez, Nov. 3, 1969; children: Joseph Orlando, Maria J., Ana J., Victoria J. B.A., U. P.R., 1967, B.Ed., 1970, M.Ed., 1972, Ph.D., 1979. Tchr. head tchr., prin. Dept. Instrn., Cayey, P.R., 1968-70; instr. U. P.R., Cayey, 1970-72; counseling specialist Sch. Allied Health Professions, U. Conn., Storrs, 1973-74; project dir. Hartford (Conn.) Public Schs., 1974-75; vice prin. Buckeley High Sch., Hartford, Conn., 1975-79; asst. prof. edn. and sch. psychology Pa. State U., University Park, 1979—. Contbr. articles to profl. jours. Commr. Human Relations Commn., Hartford, 1976-79; trustee Community Coll. System, 1976-79, Hartford; bd. dirs. World Edn. Fellowship, Storrs, 1977-79; chmn. Pa. Assn. Bilingual Edn., 1979—. World Edn. fellow, 1976; Gestalt Inst. Cleve. fellow, 1982; Kellogg fellow, 1982—. Mem. Am. Psychol. Assn., Nat. Assn. Bilingual/Bicultural Edn., Am. Ednl. Research Assn. Lodge: Masons. Current Work: Cross cultural research methodology; personality test translation and validation. Subspecialty: Social psychology. Home: 119 Cedar Ln State College PA 16801 Office: Sch Edn Pa State U University Park PA 16801

PRIBOR, HUGO CASIMER, physician; b. Detroit, June 12, 1928; s. Benjamin Harrison and Wanda Frances (Mioskowski) Priborsky; m. Judith Eleanor Smith, Dec. 22, 1955; children: Jeffrey D., Elizabeth F., Kathryn A. B.S., St. Mary's Coll., 1949; M.S., St. Louis U., 1951, Ph.D., 1954, M.D., 1955. Diplomate: Am. Bd. Pathology. Intern Providence Hosp., Detroit, 1955-56; resident pathologic anatomy and clin. pathology NIH, Bethesda, Md., 1956-59; field investigator gastric cytology research project Nat. Cancer Inst., Bowman-Gray Sch. Medicine, Winston-Salem, N.C., 1959-60; assoc. pathologist, dir. clin. lab. Bon Secours Hosp., Grosse Pointe, Mich., 1960-63; pathologist, dir. labs. Samaritan Hosp. Assn., East Side Gen. Hosp., Detroit, 1963-64, Anderson Meml. Hosp., Mt. Clemens, Mich., 1963-64; cons. pathologist Middlesex County Med. Examiners Office, New Brunswick, N.J., 1964-73; dir. dept. labs., chief pathologist, sr. attending physician Perth Amboy (N.J.) Gen. Hosp., 1964-73; chmn., chief exec. officer Ctr. Lab. Medicine, Inc., Metuchen, N.J., 1968-77; v.p. med. affairs Damon Corp., Med. Services Group, 1977-78; exec. med. dir. MDS Health Group, Inc., Red Bank, N.J., 1978-80; med. dir. Internat. Clin. Labs., Inc., Nashville; physician Assoc. Pathologists (P.C.), Nashville, 1981—; research assoc. dept. pathology St. Louis U. Sch. Medicine, 1954-55; instr. pathology Bowman-Gray Sch. Medicine, Winston-Salem, N.C., 1959-60; asst. prof. chemistry U. Detroit, 1961-64; instr. pathology Wayne State U. Sch. Medicine, Detroit, 1962-64; clin. assoc. prof. dept. pathology Rutgers Med. Sch., Rutgers, The State U., New Brunswick, N.J., 1966-68; cons. Health Facilities Planning and Constrn. Service, USPHS, HEW, Rockville, Md., 1970-71; prof. biomed. engring. Coll. Engring., Rutgers, The State U., New Brunswick, N.J., 1971-75, 80—; chmn. bd. trustees St. Mary's Coll., Winona, Minn., 1972-74, chmn. fin. com., 1971-72; clin. prof. pathology Vanderbilt U. Sch. Medicine, Nashville, 1981—. Author: (with G. Morrell and G. H. Scherr) Drug Monitoring and Pharmacokinetic Data, 1980; contbr. articles in field to profl. jours. Fellow Am. Soc. Clin. Pathologists (Silver award 1968); mem. AMA (physicians recognition award 1969, 74), Am. Assn. Exptl. Pathology, Coll. Am. Pathologists (chmn. subcom. 1974-78), Internat. Acad. Pathology, Pan Am. Med. Assn. (life), Assn. Advancement Med. Instrumentation, N.J. State Med. Soc., Acad. Medicine N.J. (chmn. clin. pathology sect. 1965-67), N.J. Soc. Pathologists (exec. com. 1965-67), Sigma Xi. Republican. Roman Catholic. Current Work: Application of computer technology to the practice of medicine, laboratory automation, and laboratory management. Subspecialties: Pathology (medicine); Information systems, storage, and retrieval (computer science). Home: 200 Olive Br Rd Nashville TN 37205

PRICE, ALAN ROGER, biochemistry educator, university executive; b. Pontiac., Mich., Jan. 15, 1942; s. Ralph Eugene and Helen Grace (Van Atta) P.; m. Katherine Jean Ralph, July 14, 1962; children: Anita Marie, Michael Ned, Mark Alan, Audra Katherine. B.S. in Chemistry, Fla. State U., 1964; Ph.D. in Biochemistry, U. Minn., 1968; post-grad., Mich. State U., 1968-69. Asst. prof. biol. chemistry Med. Sch. U. Mich., 1970-75, asst. dean research and devel., 1979-81, assoc. prof., 1975—, asst. v.p. research, 1980-83, assoc. v.p. research, 1983—; researcher Univ. Inst. Biol. Chemistry, Copenhagen, Denmark, 1976-77. Contbr. articles in field to profl. jours. Am. Council on Edn. fellow, 1980; U.S. Dept. Energy grantee, 1970-82; recipient Rumsey Meml. research award Fla. State U., 1968; Disting. Service award U. Mich., 1973. Mem. AAAS, Am. Soc. Microbiology, Am. Soc. Biol. Chemists, Sigma Xi. Current Work: Enzymology of nucleotide and nucleic acid biosynthesis; biochemistry of viral infections, biosynthesis and function of unusual nucleosides in deoxyribonucleic acids. Subspecialties: Biochemistry (biology); Virology (biology). Home: 1450 Covington St Ann Arbor MI 48103 Office: U Mich 4070 Administration Bldg Ann Arbor MI 48109

PRICE, BOBBY EARL, civil engineer, educator, consultant; b. Henderson, Tex., Nov. 21, 1937; s. Earl and Mary Maurine (Grigsby) P.; m. Patsy Ruth Patrick, Mar. 8, 1958; children: Barry Earl, Kami Kay. B.S. in Civil Engring, Arlington State Coll. (now U. Tex.-Arlington), 1962; M.S. in Civil Engring, Okla. State U., 1963; Ph.D. in Civil Engring, U. Tex.-Austin, 1967. Registered profl. engr., La., Tex. Civil engr. City of Dallas, 1960-62; grad. asst. Okla. State U., 1962-64; civil engr. City of Austin, Tex., 1964; USPHS trainee U. Tex.-Austin, 1964-66, research engr., 1966-67; assoc. prof. civil engring., div. engring. research La. Tech U., 1967-76, prof., 1976—; dir. La. Tech U. (Water Resources Ctr.), 1967—, dir. engring. grad. studies, 1978-82, dir. engring. undergrad. studies, 1982—. Contbr. articles to profl. jours., procs.; editor, dir. confs., Sch. Engring., La. Poly. Inst., 1969, La. Tech. U., 1970. Pres. Cedar Creek Sch. Bd. Dirs., Ruston, La., 1980-83. Recipient Ednl. Achievement award La. Tech. Engring. Found., 1969, 74, 76, 77. Fellow ASCE (La. Tech. U. Student chpt. Outstanding Tchr. award 1970-71, 72-73, 76-77, 81-82, Faculty Adv. award 1977, 78); mem. Am. Soc. Engring. Edn., Am. Water Works Assn., La. Engring. Soc., Tau Beta Pi (Excellence in Teaching award 1972-73, 74-75), Chi Epsilon, Omicron Delta Kappa, Epsilon Nu Gamma. Republican. Baptist. Current Work: Channel and pipe hydraulics; computer applications to hydraulics. Subspecialties: Civil engineering; Hydrology. Home: 1610 Hodges Rd Ruston LA 71270 Office: PO Box 10348 T S Ruston LA 71272

PRICE, CARL ARTHUR, biochemistry educator; b. Long Beach, Calif., Feb. 16, 1927; s. Lauren A. and Helen (Seiler) P.; m. Elizabeth Turner, Apr. 14, 1951; children—Daria A., A. Turner, Philip C., Christopher W. Sc.B., Calif. Inst. Tech., 1949; M.Sc., Harvard U., 1951, Ph.D., 1952. Assoc. prof. plant physiology Rutgers U., New Brunswick, N.J., 1959-63, prof. plant physiology, 1963-64, prof. plant biochemistry, 1964—. Author: Molecular Approaches to Plant Physiology, 1970; Centrifugation in Density Gradients, 1982. Served with USN, 1945-46. AEC fellow, 1950-52; NSF fellow, 1952-54; USPHS fellow, Geneva, 1967-68. Mem. AAAS, Am. Soc. Plant Physiologists, Internat. Soc. Plant Molecular Biology. Democrat. Current work: Gene expression in plastids; translation in plastids. Subspecialties: Molecular biology; Plant physiology (biology). Office: Waksman Inst Rutgers U PO Box 759 Piscataway NJ 08854

PRICE, CHARLES RONALD, chemical engineer; b. Wolfe, W.Va., Sept. 17, 1932; s. Tanner Hale and Mary Lucille (Walk) P.; m. Yetta Patricia Samacovlis, Feb. 3, 1961; children—Charles Ronald, Jr., Victoria Lynn. B.S., Va. Poly. Inst. and State U., Blacksburg, 1953, M.S., 1956, Ph.D., 1958. Asst. plant mgr. So. Cotton Oil Co., Savannah, Ga., 1953; research engr. E.I. DuPont, Wilmington, Del., 1958-63; sr. research engr. Carbon div. J.M. Huber Corp., Borger, Tex., 1963-71, tech. dir. Clay div., Macon, Ga., 1971—. Contbr. articles to profl. jours. Patentee in field. Advisor Eagle Scouts Boy Scouts Am., Borger, Tex., 1966-70. Recipient Am. Oil Co. scholarship, 1957-58. Mem. Am. Chem. Soc., TAPPI (Appreciation award 1979), AAAS, Clay Minerals Soc., Am. Ceramic Soc. Methodist. Lodge: Elks. Current work: Major areas of activity include fine particle technology, minerals processing, surface chemistry and paper coating technology. Subspecialty: Chemical engineering. Home: 4655 Savage Hills Dr Macon GA 31210 Office: JM Huber Corp Route 4 Macon GA 31298

PRICE, DAVID ALAN, research scientist; b. N.Y.C., July 16, 1948; s. Marvin and Helen Jane (Douglass) P.; m. Rebecca Kyle Bouton, June 22, 1974; children—Franklin Douglass, Anne MacRae. B.S., The Cooper Union, N.Y.C., 1970; Ph.D., Fla. State U., 1977. Research assoc. Fla. State U., 1977-81; asst. research scientist C.V. Whitney Lab. U. Fla., St. Augustine, 1981—. Mem. Soc. Neurosci. Current work: Neuropeptides: structure and function, evolution; molluscan cardio-regulatory neuropeptides; peptide purification and sequencing. Subspecialties: Comparative neurobiology; Neurochemistry. Home: Rt 5 Box 66H Saint Augustine FL 32084 Office: Whitney Marine Lab Rt 1 Box 121 Saint Augustine FL 32086

PRICE, DAVID CECIL LONG, physicist; b. London, Jan. 17, 1940; came to U.S., 1966; s. Cecil Long and Freda (Salusbury) P.; m. Theodora Hadzisteliou, Dec. 26, 1966; children—Morgan, Alkes. B.A., Cambridge U., 1961, Ph.D., 1966. Research assoc., Brookhaven Nat. Lab., Upton, N.Y., 1966-68; asst. physicist Argonne Nat. Lab., Ill., 1968-71, physicist, 1971-74, dir. Solid State Sci. div., 1974-79, dir. Intense Pulsed Neutron Source, 1979-81, sr. physicist Materials Sci. div., 1981—; mem. panel on neutron facilities Nat. Acad. Scis., Washington, 1976-77; vis. fellow Japan Soc. Promotion of Sci., 1977. Editor: Applications of Neutron Scattering in Condensed Matter Science, 1985. Contbr. articles to profl. jours. Mem. Am. Phys. Soc., AAAS. Current work: Investigation of structure and dynamics of condensed matter with neutron scattering and other microscopic probes. Subspecialty: Condensed matter physics. Home: 7S 621 Donwood Dr Naperville IL 60540 Office: Materials Sci Div Argonne Nat Lab Argonne IL 60439

PRICE, HAROLD JAMES, genetics educator, researcher; b. Bremerton, Wash., Oct. 7, 1943; s. Bud M. and Jeanette (Gray) P.; m. Patricia Gail Krisher, Sept. 3, 1966; children—Ginger Rosanne, Susan Nichol. B.A., Western Wash. State Coll., 1965; M.S., Brigham Young U., 1967; Ph.D., U. Calif.-Davis, 1970. Research assoc. Brookhaven Nat. Lab., Upton, N.Y., 1970-72; asst. prof. genetics Fla. Tech. U., Orlando, 1972-74; asst. prof. Tex. A&M U., College Station, 1975-78, assoc. prof., 1978-84, prof., 1984—. Contbr. articles to profl. jours. Research grantee NSF, 1978, 80. Mem. Genetics Soc. Am., Botanical Soc. Am., Soc. Study Evolution. Current work: Roles of variation of genome size on wild and crop plant adaptation and development. Subspecialties: Genome organization; Plant genetics. Home: 1021 Rose Circle College Station TX 77840 Office: Tex A&M Univ Dept Soil and Crop Scis College Station TX 77843

PRICE, HOWARD CHARLES, chemist; b. South Gibson, Pa., Feb. 26, 1942; s. Howard Thomas and Rachael Emma (Michael) P.; m. Delores Ann Wilson, July 1, 1967; children—Susanne, Thomas. B.S., Dickinson Coll., 1963, Brown U., 1964; Ph.D., SUNY-Binghamton, 1971. NIH fellow Albert Einstein Coll. Medicine, Bronx, N.Y., 1970-71; asst. prof. chemistry Marshall U., Huntington, W.Va., 1971-77, assoc., 1978-80; sr. research chemist research and devel. div. Zimmer Inc., Warsaw, Ind., 1981-83, mgr. polymers and chems., 1984—; vis. prof. Ohio U., Ironton, 1973-74. Patentee in field. Contbr. articles to profl. jours. Active Kosciusko County United Way, 1984. Served to 1st lt. U.S. Army, 1964-66. Grantee Sprctroscopy Soc. Pitts., Marshall U., 1980, NSF, Marshall U., 1975, Sigma Xi, 1975. Mem. Am. Chem. Soc. (advisor student affiliates 1974-75, treas. 1975-76), Soc. Plastic Engrs. Am., AAAS, Soc. Advancement Material and Process Engring.; Chi Beta Phi (hon.). Current work: Basic applied research and development on biomaterial including composites, thermoplastic and thermoset polymers for use in orthopaedic and related medical devices. Subspecialties: Polymers (materials science); Artificial organs and prostheses. Home: Route 2 Box 84 Warsaw IN 46580 Office: Zimmer Inc PO Box 708 Warsaw IN 46580

PRICE, PAUL BUFORD, physicist, educator; b. Memphis, Nov. 8, 1932; s. Paul Buford and Eva (Dupuy) P.; m. JoAnn Margaret Baum, June 28, 1958; children—Paul Buford III, Heather Alynn, Pamela Margaret, Alison Gaynor. B.S. summa cum laude, Davidson Coll., 1954, D.Sc., 1973; M.S., U. Va., 1956, Ph.D., 1958. Fulbright scholar U. (Eng.) Bristol, 1958-59; NSF postdoctoral fellow Cambridge (Eng.) U., 1959-60; physicist Gen. Elec. Research & Devel. Center, Schenectady, 1960-69; vis. prof. Tata Inst. Fundamental Research, Bombay, India, 1965-66; adj. prof. physics Rensselaer Poly. Inst., 1967-68; prof. physics U. Calif. at Berkeley, 1969—; dir. U. Calif. at Berkeley (Space Scis. Lab.), 1979-85; dir. Terradex Corp., Walnut Creek, Calif.; cons. for NASA (on Lunar Sample Analysis Planning Team); mem. space sci. bd. Nat. Acad. Scis. Author: (with others) Nuclear Tracks in Solids; Contbr. (with others) articles to profl. jours. Recipient Distinguished Service award Am. Nuclear Soc., 1964, Indsl. Research awards, 1964, 65, E.O. Lawrence Meml. award AEC, 1971, medal exceptional sci. achievement NASA, 1973; John Simon Guggenheim fellow, 1976-77. Fellow Am. Phys. Soc., Am. Geophys. Union; mem. Nat. Acad. Scis. (chmn. geophysics sect.), Am. Astron. Soc. Research on space and astrophysics, nuclear physics, particularly devel. solid state track detectors and their applications to geophysics, space and nuclear physics problems Current Work: Cosmic ray origin, relativistic nucleus-nucleus collisions, particle physics. Subspecialties: Cosmic ray high energy astrophysics; Nuclear physics.

PRICE, PETER J., theoretical physicist; b. London, July 29, 1924. B.A., Oxford U., Eng., 1948; Ph.D., Cambridge U., Eng., 1951. With Royal Naval Sci. Service, 1944-46; with Inst. for Advanced Study, Princeton, N.J., 1952-53; theoretical physicist IBM, N.Y.C., then IBM T.J. Watson Research Ctr., Yorktown Heights, N.Y., 1953—. Fellow Am. Phys. Soc. Current work: Physics of electrons in solids; current interest: electron transport; semiconductor heterostructures. Subspecialties: Condensed matter physics; Statistical physics. Office: IBM Watson Research Ctr Yorktown Heights NY 10598

PRICE, R(ICHARD) MARCUS, educational administrator; b. Colorado Springs, Colo., Jan. 18, 1940; m. Elaine Haley, Sept. 13, 1968; 2 children. B.S., Colo. State U., 1961; Ph.D., Australian Nat. U., 1966. Cert. sr. exec. service Office Personnel Mgmt., U.S. Govt, 1979. Asst. prof. physics M.I.T., 1968-74, assoc. prof., 1974-75; spectrum mgr., head astronomy research sect. NSF, Washington, 1975-79; prof., chmn. dept. physics and astronomy U. N.Mex., Albuquerque, 1979-85, assoc. v.p. acad. affairs, 1985—; cons. in field. Contbr. articles to profl. jours. Committeeman Monmouth council Boy Scouts Am. Served to capt., Signal Corps U.S. Army, 1965-67; mem. USAR, 1961-71. Fulbright fellow Australia, 1961-62; M.I.T. Research Lab. Electronics fellow, 1971; NSF grantee. Mem. Internat. Astron. Union, Am. Astron. Soc., Optical Soc. Am., Am. Assn. Phys. Tchrs. Current Work: Studies of nuclear regions of spiral galaxies, methods of science education, use of the radio spectrum for scientific research. Subspecialties: Radio and microwave astronomy; Infrared astronomy. Office: Acad Affairs Office U NMex Albuquerque NM 87131

PRICE, WILLIAM CHARLES, geologist, geophysics researcher; b. Fort Worth, Aug. 26, 1930; s. Jesse B. and Eula Kathrine (Weems) P.; m. Helen JoAnn, Nov. 30, 1952; children—Darrell Dean, Dwayne Douglas. B.S. in Geology, U. Tex., 1958. Electro/mech. engr. Martin-Marietta Corp., Denver, 1960-64; systems engr., geologist Lockheed Aircraft Co., Marietta, Ga., 1964-70; engring. geologist Dept. Main Rds., Sydney, Australia, 1970-74; geologist Geotechnics, Austin, Tex., 1974-78; geologist Bur. Solid Waste Mgmt. Tex. Dept. Health, Austin, 1978-80, program chief hydrology and geotech. Bur. Radiation Control, 1980—. Author tech. guide Use of Earth Resistivity in Solid Waste Mgmt. 1980; patentee in field; developer simplified technique for performing earth sensitivity sounding Named Price array, 1985. Served with USAF, 1950-54. Mem. Austin Geol. Soc., Am. Inst. Profl. Geologists (cert.), Geol. Soc. Am., Assn. Engring. Geology. Republican. Current work: Promoting use of earth resistivity since 1964, to evaluate subsoils for locating faults, sand, clay, monitoring moisture migration in vadose zone at waste burial and construction sites. Subspecialties: Geology; Geophysics. Home: 8909 Briardale Dr Austin TX 78758 Office: Tex Dept of Health Bur Radiation Control 1100 W 49th St Austin TX 78756

PRIEN, SAMUEL DAVID, electron microscopist, plant physiologist; b. Amarillo, Tex., May 30, 1956; s. Lester Joseph and Joyce Ann (Chesney) P.; m. Cynthia Kay, Dec. 28, 1982. B.S. in Botany, Tex. Tech. U., 1978, M.S. in Botany, 1980. Student asst. Tex. Tech. U., 1977-79, research asst., 1979, teaching asst., 1979-80; electron microscope technician II Tex. Tech. U. (Health Scis. Center), 1980-82; coordinator Tex. Tech. U. (Electron Microscope Lab., Health Scis. Center), 1982—. Contbr. papers to profl. meetings. Mem. AAAS, Sigma Xi (assoc.). Current Work: Structure-function relationships in biol. organisms; biol. ultra-structural exam, using the techniques of electron microscopy, freeze fracture, and micro-elemental analysis. Subspecialties: Microscopy; Plant physiology (biology). Home: 2210 20th Lubbock TX 79411 Office: Dept Anatomy Tex Tech U Health Scis Center Lubbock TX 79430

PRIGGE, EDWARD CHRISTIAN, JR., ruminant nutrition researcher, animal sci. educator; b. Bklyn.; s. Edward Christian and Annette (Melamendorf) P.; m. Domenica Prigge, Aug. 6, 1966; children: Christopher, Jonathan, Michelle. B.S., Delaware Valley Coll., 1964; M.S., U. Tenn., 1966; Ph.D., U. Maine, 1973. Fellow Okla. State U., 1973-75; farm advisor Coop. Extension U. Calif., 1975-77; asst. prof. dept. animal sci. W.Va. U., 1977—. Editorial bd.: Jour. Animal Sci, 1982—; contbr. articles to profl. jours. Mem. Am. Soc. Animal Sci. Lutheran. Current Work: Carbohydrate and protein and fatty acid metabolism in ruminants; examining methods to increase production for ruminants by altering intermediate metabolism of carbohydrate fatty acids and protein. Subspecialties: Animal nutrition; Biochemistry (biology). Home: Route 7 Cedarhurst Morgantown WV 26505 Office: Division of Animal and Veterinary Science W Va U Morgantown WV 26506

PRIGOGINE, ILYA, physics educator; b. Moscow, Jan. 25, 1917; s. Roman and Julie (Wichmann) P.; m. Marina Prokopowicz, Feb. 25, 1961; children: Yves, Pascal. Ph.D., Free U. Brussels, 1942; hon. degrees, U. Newcastle (Eng.), U. Poitiers (France), U. Chgo., U. Bordeaux (France), numerous others. Prof., U. Brussels, 1947—; dir. Internat. Insts. Physics and Chemistry, Solvay, Belgium, 1962—; dir. Ilya Prigogine center statis. mechanics and thermodynamics U. Tex., Austin, 1967—. Author: (with R. Defay) Traite de Thermodynamique, conformement aux methodes de Gibbs et de de Donder, 1944, 50, Etude Thermodynamique des Phenomenes Irreversibles, 1947, Introduction to Thermodynamics of Irreversible Processes, 1962, (with A. Bellemans, V. Mathot) The Molecular Theory of Solutions, 1957, Statistical Mechanics of Irreversible Processes, 1962, (with others) Non Equilibrium Thermodynamics, Variational Techniques and Stability, 1966, (with R. Herman) Kinetic Theory of Vehicular Traffic, 1971, (with R. Glansdorff) Thermodynamic Theory of Structure, Stability and Fluctuations, 1971, (with G. Nicolis) Self-Organization in Nonequilibrium Systems, 1977, From Being to Becoming-Time and Complexity in Physical Sciences, 1979, Order Out of Chaos, 1979, La Nouvelle Alliance, Les Métamorphoses de la Science, 1979. Recipient Prix Francqui, 1955; Prix Solvay, 1965; Nobel prize in chemistry, 1977; Honda prize, 1983; medal Assn. Advancement of Sci., France, 1975; Rumford gold medal Royal Soc. London, 1976; Descartes medal U. Paris, 1979. Mem. Royal Acad. Belgium, Am. Acad. Sci., Royal Soc. Scis. Uppsala (Sweden), Nat. Acad. Scis. U.S.A. (fgn. assoc.), Soc. Royale des Scis. Liege Belgium (corr.), Soviet Acad. Scis. (fgn. mem.), Acad. Gottingen Ger., Deutscher Akademie der Naturforscher Leopoldine (medaille Cothenius 1975), Osterreichische Akademie der Wissenschaften (corr.), Chem. Soc. Poland (hon.), others. Subspecialties: Statistical mechanics; Thermodynamics. Address: Ilya Prigogine Ctr Statis Mechanics U Tex Austin TX 78712

PRIKRYL, IVAN, physicist; b. Olomouc, Czechoslovakia, Apr. 5, 1946; came to U.S., 1980, naturalized, 1985; s. Josef and Jindriska (Smolan) P.; m. Jarmila Polak, Mar. 5, 1970; children—Helena, Jana. M.S., Palacky U., Olomouc, Czechoslovakia, 1969, Rer. Nat. Dr., 1973, C.Sc., 1978. Asst. research scientist Meopta Optics and Precision Mechanics Works, Prerov, Czechoslovakia, 1969-72; assoc. research scientist Palacky U., Olomouc, Czechoslovakia, 1972-80; vis. assoc. research scientist U. Mich., Ann Arbor, Mich., 1981-83; sr. physicist Goodyear Tire and Rubber Co., 1983—. Contbr. articles to profl. applied optics jours. Patentee hologram synthesis, 1984. Mem. Optical Soc. Am. Current work: Computer aided optical measurement techniques, holographic interferometry and related techniques, photoelesticity, optical information processing. Subspecialties: Holography; Optical information processing. Home: 2528 Call Rd Stow OH 44224 Office: Goodyear Tire and Rubber Co 142 Goodyear Blvd Akron OH 44316

PRIMAK, WILLIAM L., scientist, consultant; b. N.Y.C., June 4, 1917; s. Nathan and Elizabeth (Kaimowitz) P.; m. Dorothy M. Newfang, Oct. 24, 1953 (dec. May 1973); children—John Jefferson, Margaret Kay, Robert Carl. B.S., CCNY, 1937; M.S., Poly. Inst. Bklyn., 1943, Ph.D., 1946. Sr. chemist Argonne Nat. Lab., Ill., 1946-84; cons. Wolfe Loeb & Co., Hinsdale, Ill., 1984—. Contbr. articles to profl. jours. Patentee ski overboot, 1968, automatic photoelastimeter, 1972. Mem. Am. Chem. Soc., Am. Phys. Soc., Sigma Xi, Phi Lambda Upsilon. Mem. United Ch. of Christ. Clubs: Chgo. Mountaineering; Alpine of Can. Current work: Physical property changes of materials (ceramics, glasses, graphite) in radiation environments; studies of small dimensional changes in materials; optical and other applications. Office: Wolfe Loeb & Co 735 S Quincy St Hinsdale IL 60521

PRINCE, HELEN DODSON, astronomy educator, solar cons.; b. Balt., Dec. 31, 1905; d. Henry Clay and Helen Falls (Walter) Dodson; m. Edmond Lafayette Prince, Oct. 24, 1956 (dec.). A.B., Goucher Coll., 1927, Sc.D. (hon.), 1952; M.A., U. Mich., 1932, Ph.D., 1933. Asst. prof. Wellesley Coll., 1933-45; mem. staff radiation lab. M.I.T., 1943-45; prof. astronomy Goucher Coll., 1945-50; mem. faculty U. Mich., 1947-76, prof. astronomy, 1957-76, prof. emeritus, 1976—; assoc. dir. McMath-Hulbert Obs., 1962-76; solar cons. Applied Physics Lab. Johns Hopkins U., 1979-85. Contbr. articles to profl. jours. Recipient Disting. Faculty Achievement award U. Mich., 1975. Mem. Am. Astron. Soc. (Annie Jump Cannon prize 1954), Internat. Astron. Union, Am. Geophys. Union, Phi Beta Kappa. Episcopalian. Current Work: Study of solar activity, especially solar flares with consideration of geophysical effects. Subspecialties: Optical astronomy; Solar physics. Home: 4800 Fillmore Ave Apt 820 Alexandria VA 22311

PRINCE, JOHN LUTHER, III, engineering educator, consultant; b. Austin, Tex., Nov. 13, 1941; s. John Luther and Glynda Norma (Chollett) P.; m. Martha Ann Hight, Mar. 4, 1960; children—Cynthia Kay, John IV, Alan Douglas, David William. B.S.E.E., So. Methodist U., 1965; M.S.E.E., N.C. State U., 1968, Ph.D., 1969. Mem. tech. staff Tex. Instruments, Dallas, 1970-75; prof. Clemson U., S.C., 1975-80; dir., reliability assurance Intermedics Inc., Freeport, Tex., 1980-83; prof. U. Ariz., Tucson, 1983—; analyst, cons. U.S. Navy, 1976—; cons. Palisades Inst., N.Y.C., 1980—. Author: (with others) Very Large Scale Integration, 1979. Contbr. articles to profl. jours. Bd. dirs. YMCA, Clemson, 1977-80, Youth Sports Orgn., Plano, Tex., 1973-75. NSF fellow, 1965-68. Mem. IEEE (sr. mem.), Am. Soc. Quality Control, Am. Philatelic Soc., Latin Am. Philatelic Soc., Sigma Xi, Eta Kappa Nu, Phi Eta Sigma. Lutheran. Lodge: Demolay (master 1958-59). Current work: Director electronic packaging research program U. Ariz.; active in electronic packaging research and microelectronic reliability research, with several funded grants and contracts. Subspecialties: Microelectronics; Electronics. Home: 7542 N San Lorenzo Tucson AZ 85704 Office: ECE Dept U Ariz Tucson AZ 85721

PRINCE, MARTIN IRWIN, chemist, consultant; b. N.Y.C., Sept. 19, 1937; s. Max and Sadie P.; m. Fay Rubin, July 10, 1960; children—Mitchel, Lara, Adam. B.S., NYU, 1958, M.S., 1960, Ph.D., 1962. Sr. research scientist NYU, N.Y.C., 1960-67; pres. Synthatron Corp., Parsippany, N.J., 1967—; cons. Batelle Research, Columbus, Ohio, 1984—, Linde, AG, Munich, Fed. Republic Germany, 1984—; dir. Synthatron Corp. Mem. N.Y. Acad. Sci., Am. Chem. Soc., AAAS, Optical Soc., Sigma Xi. Current work: Preparation of high purity gases and liquids for use by the semi-conductor and fiber optic industries. Subspecialties: Organic chemistry; Organometallics. Home: 58 Darlington Dr Wayne NJ 07470 Office: Synthatron Corp 50 Intervale Rd Parsippany NJ 07054

PRINCE, MORTON BRONENBERG, physicist, technical administrator; b. Phila., Apr. 1, 1924; s. David H. and Jennie (Bronenberg) P.; m. Blanche E. Stern, June 15, 1947; 1 child, Judith Ann. A.B., Temple U., 1947; Ph.D., MIT, 1951. Mem. tech. staff Bell Telephone Labs., Murray Hill, N.J., 1951-56; v.p., gen. mgr. Hoffman Electronics Corp., El Monte, Calif., 1956-61; div. mgr. E.O.S. of Xerox Corp., Pasadena, Calif., 1961-69; pres. SSR Instruments Co., Santa Monica, 1970-74; Meret, Inc., Santa Monica, Calif., 1974-75; branch chief U.S. Dept. Energy, Washington, 1975—. Contbr. articles to numerous profl. jours. and books. Served to Tech. Sgt., U.S. Army, 1943-46, Asia. Recipient Marconi premium British Inst. Radio Engrs., 1959. Fellow IEEE; mem. Am. Physical Soc., Internatl. Solar Energy Soc. Club: Cosmos (Washington) Subspecialties: Solar energy; Condensed matter physics. Home: 2700 Virginia Ave NW Washington DC 20037 Office: US Dept Energy 1000 Independence Ave SW Washington DC 20585

PRINCEN, LAMBERTUS H(ENRICUS), chemist, government science administrator; b. Eindhoven, Netherlands, Aug. 31, 1930; came to U.S., 1955, naturalized, 1966; s. Hermanus H. A. and Engelina A. (Verhoeckx) P.; m. Gertrudis E. Wiesen, July 14, 1955; 1 son, Norman H. B.S., State U. Utrecht, Netherlands, 1952, Ph.D., 1955, D.Sc., 1959. Research assoc. U. So. Calif., Los Angeles, 1955-58; research scientist Nat. Def. Research Council-TNO, Delft, Netherlands, 1958-60; research scientist No. Regional Research Ctr., Agrl. Research Service, Dept. Agr., Peoria, Ill., 1960-74, lab. chief, 1974-82, assoc. ctr. dir., 1982-84, acting ctr. dir., 1984—. Editor: Scanning Electron Microscopy of Polymers and Coatings I, 1971, II, 1974; Co-editor: New Sources of Fats and Oils, 1981. Contbr. numerous articles to profl. jours. Patentee in field. Served to lt. Royal Dutch Army, 1959-60. Recipient Superior Service award Dept. Agr., 1969. Fellow Ill. State Acad. Sci. (pres. 1982, mem. council 1976—;

mem. Am. Chem. Soc. (councilor 1972-84, div. chmn. 1973), Am. Oil Chemists Soc. (editorial bd. jour. 1982—), Soc. Econ. botany (councilor 1981), Sigma Xi. Current work: Farm product utilization; nutrition and food safety; biotechnology; chemicals and energy from agriculture; new crops; fermentation. Subspecialties: Science administration; Science administration. Home: 677 E High Point Terr Peoria IL 61614 Office: Dept Agr Agrl Research Service No Regional Research Ctr 1815 N University St Peoria IL 61604

PRIOR, FRED WILLIAM, biomedical engineer, engineering manager; b. Warren, Ohio, Jan. 4, 1952; s. Frank William and Mabel Luella (McCracken) P.; m. Amanda Jane Davis, Jan. 20, 1972 (div. 1977); children—Tara Monique, Isis Casandra; m. 2d, Linda Jean Larson, Oct. 25, 1980. B.A. in Chemistry, Case Western Res. U., 1974, M.A. in Anthropology, 1976, M.S. in Biomed. Engring., 1984. Supr. reconstrn. software Technicare Corp., Solon, Ohio, 1980-84; mgr. reconstrn. software Imatron Inc., So. San Francisco, 1984—; v.p. Structured Design, Inc., Stow, Ohio, 1982-84. Mem. IEEE. Democrat. Current work: Design of large scale software systems, computed tomography reconstruction algorithms, parallel processor systems for high speed image processing. Subspecialties: CAT scan; Mathematical software. Home: 2286 Nina St Hayward CA 94541 Office: Imatron Inc 389 Oyster Point Blvd S San Francisco CA 94080

PRITCHARD, LOIS BREUR, process engineer, researcher, consultant; b. Paterson, N.J., Mar. 26, 1946; d. George Leonard and Ruth Margaret (Farquhar) Breur; m. Bruce N. Pritchard, Aug. 10, 1968 (div. May 1982); children—John Douglas, Tiffany Anne. B.S. cum laude in Chemistry/Physics, Fairleigh Dickinson U., 1980. Sr. analyst Lever Bros. Research and Devel., Edgewater, N.J., 1976-80; mem. photomask engring. staff Bell Labs., Murray Hill, N.J., 1980-84; mem. tech. staff RCA, Somerville, N.J., 1984—; cons. in field. Patentee package design field. Troop leader, trainer, cons., Bergen County council Girl Scouts U.S.A., 1969-80; troop leader Morris Area council Girl Scouts U.S.A., 1980-83; township com. head Mt. Olive Township council Girl Scouts U.S.A., 1980-81. Mem. Electronic Components Conf. (program com. 1981—), Am. Chem. Soc., Assn. Women in Sci., AAUW, MENSA. Republican. Episcopalian. Current work: Manufacture of photomasks by electronbeam tech.; leading edge of sub-micron tech. research. Subspecialties: Microchip technology (materials science); Information systems, storage, and retrieval (computer science). Home: 80 Lozier Rd Budd Lake NJ 07828 Office: RCA Solid State Tech Ctr Route 202 Somerville NJ 08876

PRITCHETT, PHILIP LENTNER, physicist, educator; b. Chgo., Jan. 29, 1944; s. Charles Herman and Marguerite Almira (Lentner) P. A.B., Oberlin Coll., 1965; M.S., Stanford U., 1966, Ph.D., 1970. NATO postdoctoral fellow DESY, Hamburg, Fed. Republic Germany, 1970-71; research assoc. Northwestern U., Evanston, Ill., 1971-73, vis. asst. prof., 1973-75; NSF energy fellow UCLA, 1975-76, asst. research physicist, 1976-81, assoc. research physicist 1981—. Contbr. articles to research jours. NSF fellow, 1965-69, 75; Woodrow Wilson Found. fellow, 1965; Mem. Am. Phys. Soc., Am. Geophys. Union, Sigma Xi. Current work: computational plasma physics with applications to kinetic and fluid processes in magnetospheric and fusion plasma physics. Subspecialties: Plasma physics; Magnetospheric physics. Office: Physics Dept UCLA 405 Hilgard Ave Los Angeles CA 90024

PRIVETT, ORVILLE SAMUEL, biochemistry educator, researcher; b. London, Ont., Can., June 6, 1919; came to U.S., 1949; s. Harry and Ruby (Essary) P. B.S., U. Toronto, 1942; M.S., McGill U., 1944, Ph.D., 1947. Research fellow Purdue U., West Lafayette, Ind., 1946-48; postdoctoral fellow Hormel Inst., U. Minn., Austin, 1949-52, asst. prof., 1952-55, assoc. prof., 1955-60, prof., 1960—. Contbr. numerous articles to profl. jours; lectr. Tohoku U. Med. Sch., Japan 1972. Recipient Stefano Fachini medal Italian Oil Chemists Soc., 1968. Mem. Am. Oil Chemists Soc. (Alton E. Bailey award 1980, Merit award 1982), Am. Chem. Soc., Am. Biol. Chemists. Lodge: Elks. Current work: Lipid chemistry, nutrition, biochemistry, lipid analysis. Subspecialties: Biochemistry (biology); Analytical chemistry. Home: 1300 2d St NW Austin MN 55912 Office: 801 16th Ave NE Austin MN 55912

PROAKIS, ANTHONY GEORGE, pharmacologist; b. Chios, Greece, May 26, 1940; came to U.S., 1946, naturalized, 1953; s. George John and Fotine (Parikakis) P.; m. Nancy Lee Pietranton, Feb. 23, 1963; children: Lisa, Andrea, Steven. B.S. in Pharmacy, W.Va. U., 1962; Ph.D. in Pharmacology (NIH fellow), Purdue U., 1972. Registered pharmacist, W.Va., Va., Calif. Pharmacist Medco Pharmacies Inc., Los Angeles, 1962-63, mgr., 1963-66, v.p., 1966-67; sr. research biologist A.H. Robins Research Labs., Richmond, Va., 1972-77, research asso., 1977-80, mgr. cardiovascular pharmacology, 1980—. Contbr. articles to profl. jours. Mem. Soc. Exptl. Biology and Medicine, Am. Soc. Pharmacology and Exptl. Therapeutics, Sigma Xi, Phi Kappa Phi, Rho Chi. Club: AHEPA. Patentee method of increasing coronary blood flow in mammals. Current Work: Mechanism of action of antihypertensive, antiarrhythmic and antianginal agts.; direct research in discovery and devel. of drugs for therapeutic utility in cardiovascular diseases. Subspecialties: Pharmacology; Cardiology. Home: 1811 Carbon Hill Dr Midlothian VA 23113 Office: 1211 Sherwood Ave Richmond VA 23220

PROBST, CURTIS WARE, veterinary surgery educator; b. Frankfurt, W.Ger., Aug. 7, 1954; s. Kurt Robert and Mary (Ware) P.; m. Maralyn Ridgeway, Aug. 29, 1976; 1 child, Caleb Ware. D.V.M., U. Ga., 1978. Intern, Western Coll. Vet. Medicine, Saskatoon, Sask., Can., 1978-79; surg. resident U. Fla., Gainesville, 1979-82; asst. prof. surgery Mich. State U., East Lansing, 1982—, cons. Vet. Clin. Ctr., 1982—. Contbr. chpts. to textbooks, articles to profl. jours. Vet. advisor Explorer post Chief Okemos council Boy Scouts Am., 1983. Mem. AVMA, Mich. Vet. Med. Assn., Am. Assn. Vet. Clinicians, Am. Animal Hosp. Assn., Omega Tau Sigma. Current work: Supine hypotension in pregnant bitches, pulmonary function in pregnant bitches, split-thickness skin grafting in dogs, pneumoperitoneum in dogs. Subspecialty: Surgery (veterinary medicine). Home: 4568 Keweenaw Dr Okemos MI 48864 Office: Coll of Veterinary Medicine Mich State U East Lansing MI 48824

PROBSTEIN, RONALD FILMORE, engineering educator; b. N.Y.C., Mar. 11, 1928; s. Sidney and Sally (Rosenstein) P.; m. Irene Weindling, July 30, 1950; 1 son, Sidney. B.M.E., N.Y. U., 1948; M.S.E., Princeton U., 1950, A.M., 1951, Ph.D., 1952; A.M. (hon.), Brown U., 1957. Research asst. physics N.Y. U., 1946-48, instr. engring. mechanics, 1947-48; research asst. dept. aero. engring. Princeton U., 1948-52, research assoc., 1952-53, asst. prof., 1953-54; asst. prof. divs. engring., applied math. Brown U., 1954-55, assoc. prof., 1955-59, prof., 1959-62; prof. mech. engring. M.I.T., 1962—; disting. prof. engring. U. Utah, 1973; sr. partner Water Purification Assos., Cambridge, 1974-82; chmn. bd. Water Gen. Corp., Cambridge, 1982-83; sr. corp. tech. adv. Foster-Miller Inc., Waltham, Mass., 1983—. Author: Hypersonic Flow Theory, 1959, Hypersonic Flow, Inviscid Flows, 1966, Water in Synthetic Fuel Production, 1978, Synthetic Fuels, 1982; editor: Introduction to Hypersonic Flow, 1961, Physics of Shock Waves, 1966; contbr. articles to profl. jours. Guggenheim fellow, 1960-61. Fellow Am. Acad. Arts and Scis. (councilor 1975-79), Am. Phys. Soc., AIAA, AAAS; mem. Internat. Acad. Astronautics, Nat. Acad. Engring., ASME (Freeman award 1971), Am. Inst. Chem. Engrs., Water Pollution Control Fedn. Jewish. Patentee in field. Current Work: Fluid mechanics and its application to water treatment technologies. Subspecialties: Fluid mechanics; Water supply and wastewater treatment. Office: 77 Massachusetts Ave Cambridge MA 02139

PROCTOR, CHARLES LAFAYETTE, II, mechanical engineering educator; b. Crawfordsville, Ind., Nov. 21, 1954; s. Charles Lafayette and Marjorie E. (Purdue) P.; m. Dixie Lee Huffer, May 22, 1976. B.S.M.E., Purdue U., 1976, M.S.M.E., 1979, Ph.D., 1981. Asst. prof. and dir. Combustion Lab., U. Fla., Gainesville, 1981—; owner Proctor Engring. Research and Cons.; cons. Gainesville Regional Utilities, 1982—, MUVA, Gainesville, 1982—. Mem. Combustion Inst., Am. Soc. Engring. Edn., ASME, Air Pollution Control Assn., ASTM, AIAA. Current Work: Combustion research investigating the interaction of fluid mechanics and chemistry using advanced optical diagnostic techniques; emphasis on soot formation and turbulence. Subspecialties: Combustion processes; Fluid mechanics. Home: 6051 NW 19th Pl Gainesville FL 32605 Office: Univ Fla Dept Mech Engring Gainesville FL 32611

PROCUNIER, JAMES DOUGLAS, biology educator; b. Demerrara River, Guyana, Dec. 7, 1944; came to U.S., 1979; s. James Albert and Kay Rose (Brady) P.; married; children: Mark, Michael. M.Sc., U. B.C., 1968; Ph.D., U. Calgary, 1973. Fellow Inst. for Cancer Research, Phila., 1973-76, U. B.C., Vancouver, Can., 1976-79; asst. prof. dept. biology Rice U., Houston, 1979-85. NRC scholar, 1971-73; fellow, 1973-75; NIH research grantee, 1980-86. Mem. Genetics Soc. Am. Current Work: Genetics, cloning, Drosophila melanogaster. Subspecialties: Gene actions; Molecular biology. Home: Apt 335 1580 Adelaide St London ON Canada Office: Zoology Dept U Western Ont London ON N6A 3K7 Canada

PROEBSTING, EDWARD LOUIS, agrl. researcher; b. Woodland, Calif., Mar. 2, 1926; s. Edward Louis and Dorothy (Critzer) P.; m. Patricia Connolly, Aug. 3, 1925; children: William Martin, Patricia Louise, Thomas Alan. B.S. in Pomology, U. Calif., Davis, 1948; Ph.D. in Horticulture, Mich. State U., 1951. Horticulturist Irrigated Agr. Research and Extension Ctr., Wash. State U., Prosser, 1951—. Contbr. numerous articles to profl. jours. Served to lt. USNR, 1943-46, 52-54. Fellow Am. Soc. Hort. Sci. (pres. 1983-84 Gourley award 1955, Woodbury award 1958, Nat. Food Processors award 1979, Stark award 1984, 85), Japan Soc. Promotion of Sci. (fellow 1978). Methodist. Current Work: Supercooling and ice nucleation in low temperature resistance of Prunus flower buds and fruit. Fruit tree response to controlled plant water deficits. Subspecialties: Pomology; Plant physiology (agriculture). Home: 1929 Miller Ave Prosser WA 99350 Office: Irrigated Agr Research and Extension Center PO Box 30 Prosser WA 99350

PROMISEL, NATHAN E., materials scientist, metallurgical engineer; b. Malden, Mass., June 20, 1908; s. Solomon and Lyna (Samwick) P.; m. Evelyn Sarah Davidoff, May 17, 1931; children: David Mark, Larry Jay. B.S., M.I.T., 1929, M.S., 1930; postgrad., Yale U., 1932-33; D.Engring. (hon.), Mich. Tech. U., 1978. Asst. dir. lab. Internat. Silver Co. Meriden, Conn., 1930-40; chief materials scientist and engr. Navy Dept., Washington, 1940-66; exec. dir. nat. materials adv. bd. Nat. Acad. Scis., Washington, 1966-74, cons. on materials and policy, internationally, 1974—; mem., chmn. NATO Aerospace Panel, 1959-71; U.S. rep. (materials) OECD, 1967-70; U.S. chmn. U.S./USSR Sci. Exchange Program (materials), 1973-77; hon. guest USSR Acad. Scis.; permanent hon. pres. Internat. Conf. on Materials Behavior; dir. Value Engring. Co.; mem. Nat. Materials Adv. Bd.; adv. com. Oak Ridge Nat. Lab., Lehigh U., U. Pa., U.S. Navy Dept. Labs, U.S. Congress Office Tech. Assessment. Contbr. 65 articles to profl. publs.; contbr., editor: Advances in Materials Research, 1963, Science and Technology of Refractory Metals, 1964, Science, Technology and Application of Titanium, 1970; other books. Named Nat. Capitol Engr. of Yr. Council Engring. and Archtl. Socs., 1974; recipient Outstanding Accomplishment awards Navy Dept., 1955-64; annual hon. lectr. Electrochem. Soc., 1970. Fellow Am. Soc. Metals (pres. 1972, hon. mem., Carnegie lectr. 1959, Burgess award 1961, lectr. 1967, nat. disting. lectr. 1984), Brit. Inst. Metals, AIME (hon. mem., nat. disting. lectr.), Soc. Advanced Materials and Process Engring.; mem. Nat. Acad. Engring., Fedn. Materials Socs. (pres. 1972-73, Decennial award), Soc. Automotive Engrs. (chmn. aerospace materials div. 1959-74), Brit. Metals Soc., ASTM (hon.; ann. disting. lectr. 1964), Alpha Sigma Mu (hon.). Inventor in electroplating, 1930-40; metall. devels., 1941-66. Current Work: Consultant internationally and to US government and industry on transfer of technology, advanced processes for productivity, high temperature and high strengtn materials, national policy on research and resources. Subspecialties: Corrosion; Materials (engineering). Home and Office: 12519 Davan Dr Silver Spring MD 20904

PROTHERO, DONALD ROSS, geology educator; b. Glendale, Calif., Feb. 21, 1954; s. Clifford Ross and Shirley Mae (McDonald) P. B.A., U. Calif.-Riverside, 1976; M.A., Columbia U., 1978, M.Phil., 1979, Ph.D., 1982. Instr., Vassar Coll., Poughkeepsie, N.Y., 1979-81; asst. prof. geology Knox Coll., Galesburg, Ill., 1982-85; asst. prof. geology Occidental Coll., Los Angeles, 1985—; downstate Ill. liaison, Coms. of Correspondence, 1982-85. Author: Stratigraphy and Geochronology. Contbr. articles to profl. jours. NSF fellow, 1976-79; Petroleum Research Fund grantee, 1983—. Mem. Soc. Vertebrate Paleontology, Paleontol. Soc. Am., Geol. Soc. Am., Soc. Systematic Zoology, Am. Geophys. Union, Sigma Xi (grant-in-aid for research 1981). Current work: Biostratigraphic and paleomagnetic correlation of faunal and climatic events during Late Eocene/Oligocene; fossil rhinos, camels and horses, chert artifacts. Subspecialties: Paleobiology; Systematics. Home: 4634 York Blvd #1 Los Angeles CA 90041 Office: Dept Geology Occidental Coll Los Angeles CA 90041

PROUT, GEORGE RUSSELL, JR., med. educator; b. Boston, July 23, 1924; s. George Russell and Marion (Snow) P.; m. Loa Katherine Wheatley, Oct. 17, 1950; children—George Russell III, Elizabeth Louise. Student, Union Coll., 1943; M.D., Albany Med. Coll., 1947; M.A. (hon.), Harvard. Resident N.Y. Hosp., 1952-56; asst. attending Meml. Center for Cancer and Allied Disease, N.Y.C., 1956-57; asst. clinician surgery James Ewing Hosp., N.Y.C., 1956-57; asso. prof., chmn. div. urology U. Miami, 1957-60; prof., chmn. div. urology Med. Coll. Va., 1960-69; chief urol. service Mass. Gen. Hosp., Boston; also prof. surgery Harvard Med. Sch., 1969—; Chmn. Adjuvants in Surg. Treatment of Bladder Cancer; mem. advisory task force to Nat. Cancer Inst., 1968—; chmn. Nat. Bladder Coop. Group, 1973—. Bd. editors of: Contemporary Medicine. Served with USNR, 1950-52. Fellow A.C.S., Acad. Medicine Toronto (corr.); mem. Am., Canadian urol. assns., Am. Cancer Soc., Soc. Pelvic Surgeons, Soc. Surg. Oncology, Soc. Univ. Urologists, AAUP, AMA, Dallas So. Clin. Soc. (hon.), Am. Assn. Genitourinary Surgeons, Soc. Pediatric Urology, Alpha Omega Alpha. Current Work: Urological oncology. Subspecialties: Surgery; Urology. Home: 174 Puritan Rd Swampscott MA 01907 Office: Fruit St Boston MA 02114

PROVASOLI, LUIGI, biologist; b. Busto Arsizio, Italy, Feb. 13, 1908; naturalized U.S. citizen; married. B.S., U. Milan, 1931, Ph.D. in Zoology, 1939. Asst. prof. entomology U. Milan, 1933-42; prof. U. Camerino, 1943-46; instr. biology St. Francis Coll., N.Y., 1947, prof., chmn. dept., 1948-51; mem. staff Haskins Labs., 1951-81, sec., 1969-81; sr. research biologist Yale U., 1976—. Editor: Jour. Phycol. Soc. Am., 1965-75. Recipient G.M. Smith medal Nat. Acad. Scis., 1982. Subspecialty: Marine biology. Office: Yale U Biology Dept New Haven CT 06520*

PROVINE, ROBERT RAYMOND, psychologist, educator; b. Tulsa, May 11, 1943; s. Robert William and Thelma Fern (Morgan) P.; m. Helene Vona; children: Kimberly, Robert. B.S., Okla. State U., 1965; Ph.D., Washington U., St. Louis, 1971. Research asso., research asst. prof. Washington U., St. Louis, 1971-74; asst. prof. psychology U. Md.-Baltimore County, Catonsville, 1974-76, assoc. prof., 1976-83, prof., 1983—. Cons. editor Devel. Psychobiology. Contbr. articles to profl. jours. Mem. Soc. for Neurosci. Psychonomic Soc., Animal Behavior Soc., Sigma Xi. Current Work: Behavioral neuroembryology, neuroethology, comparative neuroscience. Subspecialties: Psychobiology; Neurobiology. Office: Dept Psychology U Md Balt County Catonsville MD 21228

PRUITT, BASIL ARTHUR, surgeon, army officer; b. Nyack, N.Y., Aug. 21, 1930; s. Basil Arthur and Myrtle Flo (Knowles) P.; m. Mary Sessions Gibson, Sept. 4, 1954; children: Scott Knowles, Laura Sessions, Jeffrey Hamilton. A.B., Harvard U., 1952, postgrad., 1952-53; M.D., Tufts U., 1957. Diplomate: Am. Bd. Surgery. Intern Boston City Hosp., 1957-58, resident in surgery, 1958-59, 61-62; commd. capt., M.C. U.S. Army, 1959, advanced through grades to col., 1972; resident (Brooke Gen. Hosp.), Ft. Sam Houston, Tex., 1962-64; chief clin. div. (Inst. Surg. Research), Ft. Sam Houston, 1965-67; chief profl. services, Vietnam, 1967-68; comdr., dir. U.S. Army Inst. Surg. Research, Brooke Army Med. Center, Ft. Sam Houston, 1968—; clin. prof. surgery U. Tex. Med. Sch., San Antonio, 1975—; prof. surgery Uniformed Sers. U. Health Scis., Bethesda, Md., 1978—; mem. burns adv. bd. Shriners Hosps. for Crippled Children, 1985—; mem. surgery, anaesthesiology and trauma study sect. NIH, 1978-82; mem. Am. Bd. Surgery, 1982—, dir., 1985—. Author med. books; contbr. chpts. to textbooks, articles to profl. jours.; asso. editor: Jour. Trauma; mem. editorial bd.: Archives Surgery, Consultations in Surgery, Clin. Shock. Decorated Bronze Star. Fellow A.C.S. (gov. 1973-79, pre- and postoperative care com. 1969-79 com. on trauma 1974-84, internat. relations com. 1983—); mem. Am. Burn Assn. (pres. 1975-76), Internat. Soc. Burn Injuries (co-chmn. disaster planning com.), Smoke Burn and Fire Assn. (adv. council), Am. Trauma Soc. (dir., pres. Tex. div. 1974-75), Soc. Univ. Surgeons, Am. Surg. Assn. (2d v.p. 1980-81), Tex. Surg. Assn., Western Surg. Assn., So. Surg. Assn., Halsted Soc. (pres. 1984-85), Am. Assn. Surgery of Trauma (recorder 1976-80, pres. 1982-83), Surg. Biol. Club, Internat. Soc. Surgeons, Assn. Acad. Surgery, Surg. Infection Soc. (recorder 1980-83, pres. 1985-86), Internat. Surg. Group. Current Work: Burn and trauma care and research in shock, infection, alteration of host resistance, metabolic response to injury, surgical nutrition, and the pathophysiology of injury. Subspecialty: Surgery. Office: US Army Inst Surgical Research Fort Sam Houston TX 78234

PRYOR, ROGER WELTON, physicist; b. Worcester, Mass., May 21, 1939; s. Walter Eugene and Opal Margaret (Lukey) P.; m. Beverly Ellen Clark, June 10, 1967; 1 child, James. B.S. in Physics, Worcester Poly. Inst., 1968; M.S. in Physics, Pa. State U., 1971, Ph.D. in Physics, 1972. Mem. tech. staff Bell Labs., Whippany, N.J., 1972-76; project mgr. Pitney Bowes, Norwalk, Conn., 1976-79, project group mgr., 1979-81, mgr. phys. scis., 1981-82, sr. mem. tech. staff, 1982-84; mgr. info. prodn. Energy Conversion Devices, Troy, Mich., 1984—; vis. assoc. prof. U. Conn.-Storrs, 1979-84. Contbr. articles to profl. jours. Patentee in field. Served with USN, 1958-62. Mem. N.Y. Acad. Scis., IEEE (chmn. 1982—), Am. Inst. Physics, Am. Vacuum Soc., Sigma Xi. Republican. Methodist. Current work: Application of amorphous technology to microelectronics. Subspecialties: Condensed matter physics; Theoretical physics. Office: Energy Conversion Devices 1675 W Maple Rd Troy MI 48084

PRYSTOWSKY, HARRY, physician, educator; b. Charleston, S.C., May 18, 1925; s. Moses Manning and Raye (Karesh) P.; m. Rhalda Betsy Bressler, Mar. 8, 1951; children: Michael Wayne, Ray Ellen, Jay Bressler. B.S., The Citadel, 1944, D.Sc., 1974; M.D., Med. Coll. S.C., 1948, L.H.D., 1975. Diplomate: Am. Bd. Obstetrics and Gynecology (dir., asso. examiner). Intern Johns Hopkins Hosp. and Med. Sch., 1948-49, resident, 1950-51, 53-55, instr., 1955-56, asst. prof., 1956-58; research fellow U. Cin. Sch. Medicine, 1949; research fellow physiology Yale Med. Sch., 1955-56; prof., chmn. obstetrics and gynecology U. Fla. Coll. Medicine, 1958-73; provost Milton S. Hershey Med. Center, Pa. State U., 1973-84, sr. v.p. health affairs, 1984—; dean Coll. Medicine, 1973—; Cons. surgeon general USAF; dir. STV Engrs., Inc., Key Pharms., Inc. Contbr. articles to med. jours. Bd. visitors U. Pitts. Sch. Medicine. Served as capt., M.C. U.S. Army, 1951-53. Named 1 of 10 outstanding young men U.S. Jr. C. of C. Fellow A.C.S. (gov.); mem. AMA, Council of Deans, Assn. Am. Med. Colls., Assn. Acad. Health Centers, AAAS, A.M.A., Soc. Gynecol. Investigation, Am. Coll. Obstetrics and Gynecology, Am. Assn. Obstetricians and Gynecologists, Am. Fedn. Clin. Research, Pa. Med. Soc., Am. Gynecol. Soc., S. Atlantic Assn. Obstetricians and Gynecologists, N.Y. Acad. Scis., Assn. Profs. Gynecology and Obstetrics (pres.), U. Fla. Alumni Assn. (hon.), Alpha Omega Alpha. Subspecialties: Medical administration; Obstetrics and gynecology. Home: 1141 Cocoa Ave Hershey PA 17033

PSAROS, GEORGE EMANUEL, project engineer; b. Weirton, W.Va., Oct. 24, 1939; s. Emanuel and Catherine (Kladakis) P.; m. Adamantia E. Karamiha, Nov. 25, 1977; children: Emanuel, Steven. B.S. in Aerospace Engring, W.Va. U.-Morgantown, 1961; M.S., U. Wash.-Seattle, 1965; postgrad., U. Mich.-Ann Arbor, 1965-71, Eastern Mich. U., Ypsilanti, 1968-73. Registered profl. engr., Mich. Assoc. research engr. Boeing Co., Seattle., 1961-65; sr. engr. Bendix Corp., Ann Arbor, 1965-73; sr. project engr. Chrysler Corp., Detroit, 1973-82, Gen. Dynamics, Center Line, Mich., 1982—. Mem. AIAA (sec. 1971-72, vice chmn. 1972-73, chmn. 1973-75), Engring. Soc. Detroit, Nat. Soc. Profl. Engrs., Mich. Soc. Profl. Engrs. (vice chmn. 1973-75). Greek Orthodox. Current Work: Spacecraft thermal control; environmental control; engine and transmission design (Cooling); engine air filtration (turbine and Diesel) Air flow through screen, grills and ducts. Subspecialties: Aerospace engineering and technology; Mechanical engineering. Home: 14370 Four Lakes Sterling Heights MI 48078Office: General Dynamics 25999 Lawrence St Center Line MI 48015

PSCHIGODA, LORAINE MAE, molecular mechanics, computer graphics operator; b. St. Joseph, Mich., May 20, 1937; d. Daniel and Mildred Johanna (Quade) P. B.A., Hope Coll., 1959. Spectroscopist Upjohn, Kalamazoo, Mich., 1959-82, molecular mechanics asst., research chemist, 1982—. Mem. Am. Chem. Soc., Computers in Chemistry. Baptist. Current work: Computer graphics as aid in drug design. Subspecialties: Graphics, image processing, and pattern recognition; Drug design. Home: 429 Amos Kalamazoo MI 49008 Office: Upjohn 301 Henrietta Kalamazoo MI 49001

PSUTY, NORBERT PHILLIP, geomorphologist, university administrator; b. Hamtramck, Mich., June 13, 1937; s. Phillip and Jessie (Proszykowski) P.; m. Sylvia Helen Zurinsky, June 13, 1959; children: Eric, Scott, Ross. B.S., Wayne State U., 1959; M.S., Miami U., Oxford, Ohio, 1960; Ph.D., La. State U., 1966. Instr. depts. geography and geology U. Miami, 1964-65; asst. prof. dept. geography U. Wis.-Madison, 1965-69; assoc. prof. depts. geography and geology Rutgers U., New Brunswick, N.J., 1969-73, prof. depts. geography and geology, 1973—; dir. Rutgers U. (Marine Scis. Ctr.), 1972-76, Rutgers U. (Ctr. for Coastal and Environ. Studies), 1976—; cons. Nat. Park Service, State of N.J.; vis. scientist U. Liverpool, Eng., 1983. Mem. East Brunswick Twp. (N.J.) Water Policy Adv. Bd., 1981—. Grantee Nat. Park Service, 1975, 76, 77, 81, 82; Grantee NSF, 1970; Grantee State of N.J., 1975, 77, 78, 81, 82; Grantee Minerals Mgmt. Service, 1982. Mem. AAAS, Assn. Am. Geographers, Coastal Soc. (pres. 1980), N.J. Acad. Sci. (pres. 1981-82). Current Work: Coastal geomorphologic process-response studies, coastal natural resource management, public policy in the coastal zone, coastal ecology. Subspecialties: Resource management; Sedimentology.

PTASHNE, MARK STEPHEN, molecular biologist; b. Chgo., June 5, 1940; s. Fred and Mildred P. B.A. in Chemistry, Reed Coll., Portland, Oreg., 1961; Ph.D. in Molecular Biology, Harvard U., 1968. Lectr. dept. biochemistry and molecular biology Harvard U., 1968-71, prof., 1971—, chmn. dept. biochemistry and molecular biology, 1980-83; Harvey lectr., 1975. Contbr. articles profl. jours. Jr. fellow Harvard Soc. Fellows, 1965-68; recipient Ledlie award Harvard U., 1968; Guggenheim fellow, 1973-74; recipient Eli Lilly award in biol. chemistry, 1975; NATO sr. scientist awardee, 1977-78; recipient le Prix Charles-Leopold Mayer, 1977; award in molecular biology U.S. Steel Found., 1979; Louisa Gross Horwitz prize, 1985; Gairdner Found. internat. award, 1985. Fellow Am. Acad. Arts and Scis., N.Y. Acad. Scis.; mem. Nat. Acad. Scis., AAAS. Subspecialties: Molecular biology; Biochemistry (biology).

PUCHTLER, HOLDE, histochemistry educator; b. Kleinlosnitz, Germany, Jan. 1, 1920; came to U.S., 1955; d. Gottfried and Gunda (Thoma) P. Candidate in Medicine, U. Würzburg, Germany, 1944; M.D., U. Köln, Germany, 1949, Dr. med., 1951. Research assoc. U. Cologne, 1949-51, resident in pathology, 1951-55; research fellow Damon Runyon Found., McGill U., Montreal, Que., Can., 1955-58; research assoc. to assoc. research prof. Med. Coll. Ga., Augusta, 1959-68, prof. pathology, 1968—. Mem. editorial bd.: Histochemistry, 1977—, Jour. Histotech, 1982—; contbr. articles to sci. jours. honoree Symposium on Connective Tissues in Arterial and Pulmonary Diseases, 1980. Fellow Royal Microscopical Soc., Am. Inst. Chemists; mem. Gesellschaft für Histochemie, Histochem. Soc., Royal Soc. Chemistry (Gt. Britain), Am. Assn. Anatomists, Anatomishe Gesellschaft, Am. Soc. for Cell Biology, Internat. Acad. Pathologists, Am. Assn. Pathologists, Am. Soc. Zoologists, Biol. Stain Commn., So. Soc. Anatomists, N.Y Acad. Scis. Current Work: Histochemistry of collagen, elastin, myosin, amyloid. Development of new technics for light, polarization, visible and infrared fluorescence microscopy based on chemistry of textile and leather dyeing, theoretical chemistry and x-ray diffraction data. Subspecialties: Histochemistry; Pathology (medicine). Office: Dept Pathology Med Coll Georgia Augusta GA 30912

PUCK, THEODORE THOMAS, educator, geneticist, biophysicist; b. Chgo., Sept. 24, 1916; s. Joseph and Bessie (Shapiro) Puckowitz; m. Mary Hill, Apr. 17, 1946; children: Stirling, Jennifer, Laurel. B.S., U. Chgo., 1937, Ph.D., 1940. Mem. commn. airborne infections Office Surgeon Gen., Army Epidemiol. Bd., 1944-46; asst. prof. depts. medicine and biochemistry U. Chgo., 1945-47; sr. fellow Am. Cancer Soc., Calif. Inst. Tech., Pasadena, 1947-48; prof. biophysics U. Colo. Med. Sch., 1948—, chmn. dept., 1948-67; dir. Eleanor Roosevelt Inst. Cancer Research, 1962—; Disting. research prof. Am. Cancer Soc., 1966—; nat. lectr. Sigma Xi, 1975-76. Author: The Mammalian Cell as a Microorganism: Genetic and Biochemical Studies in Vitro, 1972. Mem. Commn. on Physicians for the Future. Recipient Albert Lasker award, 1958; Borden award med. research, 1959; Louisa Gross Horwitz prize, 1973; Gordon Wilson medal Am. Clin. and Climatol. Assn., 1977; award Environ. Mutagen Soc., 1981. Fellow Am. Acad. Arts and Scis.; mem. Am. Chem. Soc., Soc. Exptl. Biology and Medicine, AAAS (Phi Beta Kappa award and lectr. 1983), Am. Assn. Immunologists, Radiation Research Soc., Biophys. Soc., Genetics Soc. Am., Am. Assn. Cancer Research, Am. Soc. Cell Biology (E. B. Wilson medal 1984), Nat. Acad. Sci., Inst. Medicine, Phi Beta Kappa, Sigma Xi. Current Work: The genetic-biochemical nature of cancer; human gene mapping; reversal of cancer; somatic cell genetics and its application to medicine. Subspecialties: Genetics and genetic engineering (biology); Cancer research (medicine). Address: 10 S Albion St Denver CO 80222

PUCKETT, ALLEN EMERSON, aeronautical engineer; b. Springfield, Ohio, July 25, 1919; s. Roswell C. and Catherine C. (Morrill) P.; m. Betty J. Howlett;

children—Allen W., Nancy L., Susan E.; m. Marilyn I. McFarland; children—Margaret A., James R. B.S., Harvard, 1939, M.S., 1941; Ph.D., Calif. Inst. Tech., 1949. Lectr. aeros., chief wind tunnel sect. Jet Propulsion Lab., Calif. Inst. Tech., 1945-49; tech. cons. U.S. Army Ordnance, Aberdeen Proving Ground, Md., 1945-60; mem. sci. adv. com. Ballistic Research Labs., 1958-65; with Hughes Aircraft Co., Culver City, Calif., 1949—, exec. v.p., 1965-77, pres., 1977-78, chmn. bd., chief exec. officer, 1978—; dir. Am. Mut. Fund, Lone Star Industries; mem. steering group OASD adv. panel on aeros.; cons. Pres.'s Sci. Adv. Com.; chmn. research adv. com. control, guidance and navigation NASA, 1959-64; vice chmn. Def. Sci. Bd., 1962-66; mem. Army Sci. Adv. Panel, 1965-69, NASA tech. and research adv. com., 1968-72, space program adv. council, 1974-78; Wilbur and Orville Meml. lectr. Royal Aero. Soc., London, 1981. Author: (with Hans W. Liepmann) Introduction to Aerodynamics of a Compressible Fluid, 1947; editor: (with Simon Ramo) Guided Missile Engineering, 1959; contbr. tech. papers on high-speed aerodynamics. Trustee U. So. Calif. Recipient Lawrence Sperry award Inst. Aero. Scis., 1949, Lloyd V. Berkner award Am. Astronautical Soc., 1974; named Calif. Mfr. of Yr., 1980. Fellow AIAA (pres. 1972); mem. Aerospace Industries Assn. (chmn. 1979), Los Angeles World Affairs Council (pres.), Nat. Acad. Scis., Nat. Acad. Engring., A.A.A.S., Sigma Xi, Phi Beta Kappa. Subspecialty: Aeronautical engineering. Office: Hughes Aircraft Co PO Box 1042 El Segundo CA 90245

PUDDEPHATT, RICHARD JOHN, chemistry educator; b. Aylesbury, Buckinghamshire, Eng., Oct. 12, 1943; s. Harry and Ena May (Bowler) P.; m. Alice Ruth Poulton, June 14, 1969; children—Susan Clare, Antony James. B.Sc., Univ. Coll., London, 1965, Ph.D., 1968. Teaching postdoctoral fellow U. Western Ont., London, 1968-70, faculty, 1978—, prof. chemistry, 1978—; lectr. U. Liverpool, Eng., 1970-77, sr. lectr., 1977-78. Author: The Periodic Table of the Elements, 1972; The Chemistry of Gold, 1978. Fellow Chem. Inst. Can. (Alcan award 1985). Current work: Chemistry of the noble metals; reaction mechanisms in homogeneous catalysis. Subspecialties: Organometallics; Inorganic chemistry. Office: Dept Chemistry U Western Ontario London ON N6A 5B7 Canada

PUDZIANOWSKI, ANDREW THADDEUS, research chemist; b. Ludwigsburg, West Germany, Dec. 2, 1947; came to U.S., 1951, naturalized, 1963; s. Casimir and Zdzislawa Maria (Kapusta) P.; m. Anna Marie Kucharski, Jan. 2, 1982. B.S. with honors, U. Ill.-Chgo., 1970, M.S., 1973, Ph.D., 1979. Research asst. Evanston Hosp., Ill., 1970-71; grad. asst. U. Ill., Chgo., 1971-78; postdoctoral fellow SRI Internat., Menlo Park, Calif., 1979-81, staff scientist, 1981-82; research investigator Squibb Inst., New Brunswick, N.J., 1982-85, Princeton, N.J., 1985—. Contbr. articles to profl. jours. Founding participant Squibb/North Brunswick Twp. High Sch. Industry Edn. project, New Brunswick, 1982—. Mem. Am. Chem. Soc., AAAS, N.Y. Acad. Scis., Common Cause, League of Conservation Voters, Phi Kappa Phi. Current work: Applications of physical and theoretical chemistry to enzymatic and nonenzymatic reaction mechanisms; theoretical and computational methods in pharmaceutical research. Subspecialties: Physical chemistry; Theoretical chemistry. Office: Squibb Inst for Med Research PO Box 4000 Princeton NJ 08540

PUENTE, ANTONIO ENRIQUE, psychologist, educator; b. Havana, Cuba, Feb. 14, 1952; s. Antonio A. and Silvia (Llanso) P.; m. Linda Newman, June 11, 1977; children—Krista L., Antonio N. B.A., U. Fla., 1973; Ph.D., U. Ga., 1978. Lic. psychologist, N.C. Asst. prof. neuroanatomy St. George's (Grenada) U., 1978-79; clin. psychologist Northeast Fla. State Hosp., Maclenny, 1979-81; asst. prof. psychology U. N.C., Wilmington, 1981—; cons. Author, editor, translator various sci. books and articles. Fulbright scholar to Argentina, 1982. Mem. Am. Psychol. Assn., Southeastern Psychol. Assn., Soc. Neurosci., Soc. Psychophysiol. Research, Nat. Acad. Neuropsychologists, N.C. Psychol. Assn., Sociedad Interamericana de Psicologia, So. Soc. Philosophy and Psychology, Psi Chi, Phi Theta Kappa. Roman Catholic. Current Work: Assessment of brain damage and schizophrenia using neuropsychological and psychophysiological techniques. Translation and dissemination of research into Spanish. Behavioral medicine. Subspecialties: Neuropsychology; Neurophysiology. Home: 103 Parmele Blvd Wrightsville Beach NC 28480 Office: Dept Psychology U NC Wilmington NC 28403

PULLIAM, H. RONALD, zoology educator; b. Miami Beach, Fla., Sept. 7, 1945; s. Joe and Rachel (Miller) P.; m. Janice Crowder, June 21, 1969; 1 child, Juliet Rachel Crowder. B.S., U. Ga., 1967; Ph.D., Duke U., 1970. Postdoctoral fellow U. Chgo., 1970-71; prof. U. Ariz., Tucson, 1971-78; research biologist H.S. Colton Ctr., Flagstaff, Ariz., 1978-80; prof. SUNY-Albany, 1980-84, U. Ga., Athens, 1984—; bd. dirs. Appleton-Whittell Research Ranch, Elgin, Ariz. Author: Programmed to Learn, 1980. Editor: Ecology and Ecological Monographs, 1980-84. Contbr. articles to profl. jours. Recipient numerous grants NSF. Mem. Ecol. Soc. Am. (council mem. 1981-83), Animal Behavior Soc. Quaker. Current work: Feeding ecology and social behavior of birds; optimal foraging theory; evolution of vertebrate social behavior. Subspecialties: Ecology (biology); Behavioral ecology. Office: Dept Zoology U Ga Athens GA 30602

PULLING, NATHANIEL H(OSLER), mechanical engineer, researcher; b. Boston, Jan. 10, 1920; s. Howard Edward and Mildred (Hosler) P.; m. Lillian E. Donnelly, Sept. 9, 1955. A.B., Brown U., 1942; Ph.D., Harvard U., 1951. Registered profl. engr., Mass. Chief optics subsection U.S. Naval Bur. Ordnance, Washington, 1945-46; research fellow Harvard U., 1950-52; devel. engr. Gen. Electric Co. Lynn, Mass., 1953-61, product and bus. planner, 1962-66; project dir. automotive safety Liberty Mut. Ins. Co., Hopkinton, Mass., 1967—. Adj. prof. mech. engring. Worcester Poly. Inst., 1973—. Contbr. articles to profl. jours. Patentee in field. Served to lt. comdr. USNR, 1942-46. Editorial bd. Accident Analysis and Prevention, 1968—. Mem. ASME, Soc. Auto Engrs., Transp. Research Bd., Am. Assn. Auto Medicine, Profl. Photographers Am., Photographic Soc. Am., Provincetown Art Assn., Photog. Resource Center Boston, Creative Arts Ctr. Chatham. Current work: Human factors in highway driving performance; crashworthiness and repairability of highway vehicles. Club: Boston Camera. Lodge: Rotary. Subspecialty: Human factors engineering. Home: Manito Rd PO Box 335 East Orleans MA 02643 Office: Liberty Mut Research Ctr 71 Frankland Rd Hopkinton MA 01748

PULLMAN, MAYNARD EDWARD, biochemist, researcher; b. Chgo., Oct. 26, 1927; s. Harry and Gertrude (Atlas) P.; m. E. Phyllis Light, Sept. 12, 1948; children—H. Cydney, B. Valerie, Jacky Leigh. B.S., U. Ill., Urbana, 1948; M.S., U. Ill.-Chgo., 1950; Ph.D., Johns Hopkins U., 1953. Fellow in pediatrics Johns Hopkins U., Balt., 1953-54; from asst. to mem. Pub. Health Research Inst., N.Y.C., 1954-65, assoc. dir., 1983—; research assoc. prof. NYU Med. Sch., 1966-76, research prof., 1976—; vis. prof. U. Sao Paulo, Brazil, 1963-64; mem. biochemistry adv. group NIH, 1969-73. Co-editor: Methods in Enzymology, 1967; editor: An Era in New York Biochemistry; A Festschrift for Sarah Ratner, 1983; mem. editorial bd. Jour. Biol. Chemistry, 1967-71, 78-80. Fellow N.Y. Acad. Scis. (vice chmn. biochem. sect. 1978-80); mem. Am. Soc. Biol. Chemists, Am. Chem. Soc. Current work: Research activities are focused on the control of the production and utilization of energy in the mitochondria of living cells. Subspecialties: Biochemistry (biology); Membrane biology. Home: 338 Archer St Freeport NY 11520 Office: Pub Health Research Inst 455 1st Ave New York NY 10016

PUN, PATTLE PAK TOE, microbiologist, educator; b. Hong Kong, Sept. 30, 1946; s. Sak-Chi and Ngan-Chu (Kwan) P.; m. Gwen Yam Qun, Aug. 22, 1970; children: Patrick Hank, Benjamin Tim. B.S. in Chemistry with high honors and distinction, San Diego State U., 1969; M.A. in Biology, SUNY-Buffalo, 1972, Ph.D., 1974. Resident assoc. div. biol. and med. research Argonne Nat. Lab., Ill., 1974-76; vis. microbiologist U. Ill. Med. Ctr., Chgo., 1980-81, No. Ill. U., DeKalb, 1985; prof. biology Wheaton Ill. Coll., 1973—. Author: Evolution: Nature and Scripture in Conflict?1982, Chinese edit., 1984. Contbr. articles to profl. jours. Research Corp. grantee, 1975, 76, 79, 80, 82, 83; NSF Subcontractor, 1985. Mem. Am. Soc. Microbiology, N.Y. Acad. Scis., Am. Sci. Affiliation. Mem. Chinese Bible Ch. Current Work: Cloning of the conditional asporogenous and rifampicin resistant gene of bacillus subtilis and its genetic and biochemical analysis. Subspecialties: Microbiology; Genetics and genetic engineering (biology). Office: Dept Biology Wheaton Coll Wheaton IL 60187

PURCELL, EDWARD MILLS, physics educator; b. Taylorville, Ill., Aug. 30, 1912; s. Edward A. and Mary Elizabeth (Mills) P.; m. Beth C. Busser, Jan. 22, 1937; children: Dennis W., Frank B. B.S. in Elec. Engring, Purdue U., 1933, D. Engring. (hon.), 1953; Internat. Exchange student, Technische Hochschule, Karlsruhe, Germany, 1933-34; A.M., Harvard U., 1935, Ph.D., 1938. Instr. physics Harvard U., 1938-40, asso. prof., 1946-49, prof. physics, 1949-58, Donner prof. sci., 1958-60, Gerhard Gade Univ. prof., 1960-80, emeritus, 1980—; sr. fellow Soc. of Fellows, 1949-71; group leader Radiation Lab., MIT, 1941-45. Contbg. author: Radiation Lab. series, 1949, Berkeley Physics Course, 1965; contbr. sci. papers on nuclear magnetism, radio astronomy, astrophysics, biophysics. Mem. Pres.'s Sci. Advisory Com., 1957-60, 62-65. Co-winner Nobel prize in Physics, 1952; recipient Oersted medal Am. Assn. Physics Tchrs., 1968; Nat. Medal of Sci., 1980. Mem. Am. Philos. Soc., Nat. Acad. Sci., Phys. Soc., Am. Acad. Arts and Scis. Subspecialties: Theoretical astrophysics; Biophysics (biology).*

PURCHASE, HARVEY GRAHAM, research veterinarian, administrator; b. Zambia, Africa, Aug. 8, 1936; came to U.S., 1961, naturalized, 1966; s. Harvey Spurgeon and Vera Margaret (Cooper) P.; m. Nancy Ruth Schneider, July 6, 1963; children: Deborah Ruth, Kenneth Graham. B.Sc., U. Witwatersrand, 1955; B.V.Sc., U. Pretoria, 1959; M.R.C.V.S., U. London, 1961; M.S., Mich. State U., 1965, Ph.D., 1970. Gen. practice vet. medicine, South Africa and Eng., 1960-61; research veterinarian U.S. Dept. Agr., East Lansing, Mich., 1961-74, staff scientist poultry, Beltsville, Md., 1974-78, chief livestock and vet. scis. staff, 1978-82, nat. program leader for bioregulation, 1982-84, spl. sci. advisor to area dir., 1984—; assoc. prof. Mich. State U., 1972-74. Mem. editorial bd.: Avian Diseases, 1974—, Poultry Sci, 1978—; contbr. numerous articles in field. Leader Nat. Capital Area Council Boy Scouts Am., 1979—. Recipient Sir Arnold Theiler medal, 1959, Arthur S. Fleming award, 1971, Tom Newman Meml. award of Gt. Britain, 1973. Mem. AVMA, Am. Assn. Avian Pathologists, Brit. Vet. Assn., U.S. Animal Health Assn., D.C. Vet. Med. Assn., Poultry Sci. Assn., Soc. Virology. Presbyterian (elder). Patentee vaccine for immunizing poultry against Marek's disease. Current Work: Major research was on avian tumor viruses, work interests are administration of research and research on problems of animal agriculture. Subspecialties: Cancer research (veterinary medicine); Virology (veterinary medicine). Home: 8905 Eastbourne Ln Laurel MD 20708 Office: US Department Agriculture BARC West Beltsville MD 20705

PURDOM, PAUL WALTON, JR., computer scientist, educator; b. Atlanta, Apr. 5, 1940; s. Paul Walton and Bettie (Miller) P.; m. Donna Lee Armstong, Aug. 16, 1965; children: Barbara, Linda, Paul. B.S., Calif. Inst. Tech., 1961, M.S., 1962, Ph.D., 1966. Asst. prof. computer sci U. Wis.-Madison, 1965-70, assoc. prof., 1970-71; mem. tech. staff Bell Labs., Naperville, Ill., 1970-71; assoc. prof. computer sci. Ind. U., Bloomington, 1971-82, prof., 1983—, chmn., 1978-82. Mem. Assn. Computing Machinery, Soc. Indsl. and Applied Math. Methodist. Current Work: Analysis of search algorithms, game playing, and compiler design. Subspecialties: Theoretical computer science; Compiler design. Home: 2212 Belhaven St Bloomington IN 47401 Office: Ind U Bloomington IN 47405

PURDY, WILLIAM CROSSLEY, educator, chemist; b. Bklyn., Sept. 14, 1930; s. John Earl and Virginia (Clark) P.; m. Myrna Mae Moman, June 17, 1953; children—Robert Bruce (dec.), Richard Scott, Lisa Patrice, Diana Lori. B.A., Amherst Coll., 1951; Ph.D., MIT, 1955. Instr. U. Conn., Storrs, 1955-58; faculty U. Md., College Park, 1958-76, prof. chemistry, 1964-76, head div. analytical chemistry, 1968-76; prof. chemistry, asso. in medicine McGill U., 1976—; vis. prof. Institut für Ernahrungswissenschaft, Justus Liebig-Universitat, Giessen, Germany, 1965-66; Nat. lectr. Am. Assn. Clin. Chemistry, 1971; Fisher Sci. Lecture award Chem. Inst. Can., 1982; cons. Surg. Gen., U.S. Army, 1959-75; sci. adviser Balt. dist. FDA. Author: Electro-analytical Methods in Biochemistry, 1965, also numerous articles.; Bd. editors: Clin. Chemistry, 1971-80, Anal. Letters, 1979—, Anal. Chim. Acta, 1979—, Clin. Biochemistry, 1983—; adv. bd. editors: Analytical Chemistry, 1971-73. Fellow Nat. Acad. Clin. Biochemistry, Royal Soc. Chemistry (London), Assn. Clin. Scientists, Chem. Inst. Can., mem. Am. Chem. Soc., Am. Assn. Clin. Chemistry (award 1984), Soc. Electroanalytic Chemistry, Can. Soc. Clin. Chemists, Sigma Xi. Research on application of modern analytical methods to biochem. and clin. systems, separation sci., trace metal analysis. Subspecialties: Analytical chemistry; Clinical chemistry. Home: 1321 Sherbrooke St W C-40 Montreal PQ H3G 1J4 Canada Office: McGill U 801 Sherbrooke St W Montreal PQ H3A 2K6 Canada

PURI, PRATAP, mathematics educator; b. Lahore, Pakistan, Mar. 15, 1938; s. Kidar Nath and Shakuntala Devi (Trehan) P.; m. Irene Maria Gulowska, Aug. 31, 1968; children—Amrita Monica, Salil Kumar. B.A., P.U. Camp Coll., 1957; M.A., St. Stephen's Coll., U. Delhi, 1959; M.Tech., I.I.T. Kharagpur, West Bengal, 1960, Ph.D., Indian Inst. Tech., Kharagpur, 1965. Assoc. lectr. Indian Inst. Tech., Bombay, 1962-63; postdoctoral fellow Polish Acd. Scis., Warsaw, 1966; lectr. Indian Inst. Tech., Bombay, 1963-68; asst. prof. math U. New Orleans, 1968-71, assoc. prof., 1971-76, prof., 1976—. Contbr. articles to profl. jours. Council Sci. Research India fellow, 1960-61. Mem. Am. Math. Soc., Soc. Indsl. and Applied Math, Calcutta Math. Soc., Am. Acad. Mechanics. Current work: Boundary value problems and wave propagation in fluid mechanics; theory of elasticity. Subspecialty: Applied mathematics. Home: 5112 St Bernard Ave New Orleans LA 70122Office: Dept Math U New Orleans New Orleans LA 70148

PURPURA, DOMINICK PAUL, university dean, medical scientist; b. N.Y.C., Apr. 2, 1927; s. John R. and Rose (Ruffino) P.; m. Florence M. Williams, May 31, 1948; children—Craig, Kent, Keith, Allyson. A.B., Columbia U., 1949; M.D., Harvard U., 1953. Intern Columbia-Presbyn. Med. Center, N.Y.C., 1953-54; resident Neurol. Inst., N.Y.C., 1954-55; assoc. prof. neurosurgery, neurology and anatomy Columbia Coll. Physicians and Surgeons, 1958-66; prof., chmn. dept. anatomy Albert Einstein Coll. Medicine, Bronx, N.Y., 1967-74, chmn. dept. neurosci., 1974-81; dean, assoc. v.p. med. affairs Stanford (Calif.) U., 1981-84; dean Albert Einstein Coll. Medicine, N.Y.C., 1984—; sci. dir. Rose F. Kennedy Center for Research in Mental Retardation, N.Y.C., 1969-72, dir., 1972—; NIH adv. com. on epilepsies USPHS; councillor Soc. Neuroscis. Chief editor: Brain Research. Served with USAAF, 1945-47. Mem. Am. Physiol. Soc., Am. Neurol. Assn., Am. Epilepsy Assn., AAAS. Research on structure and function of mature and immature brain; origin of brain waves; developmental neurobiology; mechanisms of epilepsy. Subspecialties: Neurobiology; Medical education and research administration. Office: Albert Einstein Coll Medicine 1300 Morris Park Ave Bronx NY 10461

PURSER, PAUL EMIL, systems engineer, consultant; b. Amite, La., Dec. 9, 1918; s. Brittain Birdsong and Ethel Elizabeth (Hungate) P.; m. Carlotta Mary King, Aug. 5, 1939; children: Mary Elizabeth Beeman, Margaret King. B.Sc. in Aero. Engring, La. State U., 1939; postgrad., U. Va. Extension, 1942-44. Registered profl. engr., La., Tex. Research engr. Nat. Adv. Com. for Aeronautics, Hampton, Va., 1939-58; research engr. NASA, Hampton, 1958-62; spl. asst. to dir. Manned Spacecraft Ctr., Houston, 1962-70; cons. Paul E. Purser, P.E., Houston, Humble, Tex., 1970—; sr. systems engr. GURC, Bellaire, Tex., 1974-84; cons. Nat. Acad. Engring.-Marine Bd., Washington, 1972-82, Stanford U. Sch. Medicine, Palo Alto, Calif., 1971-76; spl. asst. to pres. U. Houston, 1968-69. Sr. editor: Manned Spacecraft: Engineering Design and Operation, 1964. Bd. dirs. ARC, Houston chpt., 1965-71; dir. Houston Mus. Natural Sci., 1965—. Recipient Cert. of Commendation NASA-Manned Spacecraft Ctr., 1965, Group Achievement awards, 1964, 67. Assoc. fellow AIAA (mem. local council 1962-67); mem. Marine Tech. Soc. (mem. local council 1976-79, meritorious service award and cert. of appreciation 1978), Am. Soc. Engring. Edn., Systems Safety Soc., Soc. Petroleum Engrs., C. of C., mem. sci. and tech. com. (1970-77, cert. of appreciation 1974), Tau Beta Pi, Omicron Delta Kappa, Sigma Gamma Tau. Republican. Presbyterian. Current Work: Application of systems engineering and aerospace technology to cardiovascular medicine, petroleum and geothermal energy, offshore and marine engineering, diving, marine salvage, explosive ordnance disposal, oil spill prevention. Subspecialties: Systems engineering; Aerospace engineering and technology. Home and Office: 8950 Shoreview Ln Humble TX 77346

PURVIS, GEORGE ALLEN, research administrator, nutritionist; b. Las Animas, Colo., Mar. 30, 1933; s. Francis C. and Delma F. (Gillespie) P.; m. Norma Henerberg, Sept. 12, 1959; children—Amy, Beth, Thomas, Margaret. B.S., Colo. State U., 1954, M.S., 1962; Ph.D., Mich. State U., 1968. Assoc. Colo. Expt. Sta., Ft. Collins, 1960-62, Ohio Expt. Sta., Columbus, 1962-63; lab. mgr. Gerber Products Co., Fremont, Mich., 1963-69, research mgr., 1969-77, dir. nutrition, 1977-80, v.p. nutrition scis., 1980—. Author: Technology Iron Fortification, 1984. Served with U.S. Army, 1954-56. Recipient Outstanding Alumni award Mich State U., 1984. Mem. Am. Inst. Nutrition, Inst. Food Techs., Am. Coll. Nutrition, Sigma Xi. Republican. Congregationalist. Lodge: Rotary. Current work: Infant nutrition, food consumption, research administration. Subspecialties: Nutrition (medicine); Food science and technology. Office: Gerber Products Co 445 State St Fremont MI 49412

PUSKAS, ELEK, parachute company executive; b. Kassa, Hungary, Nov. 29, 1942; came to U.S., 1961; s. Elek and Olga (Derfinyak) P.; m. Lona Lee Zimmerman, Dec. 30, 1969 (dec. 1977); m. Holly Ann LeClair, Aug. 25, 1982. Auto mechanic Keystone Motors, Berwyn, Pa., 1961-64; engring. technician S. Snyder Enterprises Inc., Cherry Hill, N.J., 1964-69; dir. ops. Para-Flite, Inc., Pennsauken, N.J., 1969-77, pres., 1977—; pres. Ripcord Para Ctr., Inc., Medford, N.J., 1967-76. Contbr. articles to publs. Mem. Parachute Equipment Industry Assn. (chmn. 1981—), AIAA (sr., tech. com.), Am. Mgmt. Assn., U.S. Parachute Assn., AAAS. Democrat. Patentee. Current Work: Lifting aerodynamic decelerators. Subspecialties: Aeronautical engineering; Aerospace engineering and technology. Home: Conestoga Ln Mount Holly NJ 08060 Office: Para-Flite Inc 5800 Magnolia Ave Pennsauken NJ 08109

PUSKAS, WILLIAM LOUIS, electrical engineering company executive, electrical engineer; b. Bridgeport, Conn., June 25, 1943; s. Louis William and Helen Margret (Beres) P. B.E.E., Rensselaer Polytech. Inst., 1965; M.S. in Math., U. Bridgeport, 1970, M.E.E., 1971. Assoc. engr. IBM, East Fishkill, N.Y., 1965-67; project engr. Avco/Lycoming Co., Stratford, Conn., 1967-70; dir. research and devel. Branson Ultrasonics Corp., Shelton, Conn., 1970-84; chmn. bd. Electronic Power Components, inc., New London, N.H., 1984—; instr. lab physics Rensselaer Polytech. Inst., Troy, N.Y., 1964-65; instr. electronics U. Bridgeport, Conn., 1979-81. Patentee in field (7). Mem. IEEE. Roman Catholic. Current work: Ultrasonic frequency power electronics. Office: Electronic Power Components Inc PO Box 1676 N Pleasant St New London NH 03257

PUTNAM, ALAN R., horticulture educator; b. Keene, N.H., Apr. 3, 1939; married; 3 children. B.S., U. N.H., 1961; M.S., Mich. State U., 1963, Ph.D., 1966. Asst. prof. Mich. State U., East Lansing, 1966-70, assoc. prof., 1970-74, prof., 1974—. Vis. prof. agronomy Cornell U., 1973, botany U. Calif., Davis, 1981-82. Contbr. articles to profl. jours. Mem. AAAS, Internat. Soc. Chem. Ecologists, Weed Sci. Soc. Am., North Central Weed Control Conf., Council Agrl. Sci. and Technology, Intersociety Consortium Plant Protection, Sigma Xi, Phi Kappa Phi, Alpha Zeta. Current work: Mechanisms for interactions of plants and associated microbes; natural product herbicides; weed biology and control. Subspecialty: Plant physiology (agriculture). Office: 105 Pesticide Reseasrch Ctr Mich State U East Lansing MI 48824

PUTNAM, HUGH DYER, aquatic microbiology company executive; b. Carrington, N.D., Feb. 12, 1928; s. Hugh Rodney and Blanche (Ebbert) P.; m. Natalie Joy Knott, Dec. 23, 1950; children—Mark, Lynn, Hugh Charles. B.A., U. Minn., 1953, M.S., 1956, Ph.D., 1963. With engring. faculty U. Fla., Gainesville, 1963-73; founder, v.p. Environ. Sci. and Engring., Gainesville, 1965-74; v.p. Water and Air Research, Inc., Gainesville, 1974—. Contbr. articles to profl. jours. Served with U.S. Army, 1946-48, 1950-53, Korea. Mem. Water Pollution Control Fedn., Am. Soc. Limnology and Oceanography, Am. Soc. Microbiology, ASTM, Ecol. Soc. Am. Democrat. Presbyterian. Subspecialty: Environmental engineering. Office: Water and Air Research Inc PO Box 1121 Gainesville FL 32602

PYE, EARL LOUIS, chemical company executive, university dean; b. Merino, Colo., Aug. 18, 1926; s. Guy William and Gladys (Cooper) P.; m. Shirley M. Adicks, Mar. 10, 1949 (div.); children: Deborah, Deanna, Douglas, Cynthia, Mark, Michael. A.B., Chico State U., 1958; M.S., U. Calif.-Davis, 1961; Ph.D., La. State U., 1966. Registered profl. engr., Calif. Pres. CCS Control Systems, San Dimas, Calif., 1976—, Alpha Research Co., San Dimas, 1976—; dean grad. studies and research, prof. chemistry Calif. State Poly. U., Pomona, 1961—. Served with USNR, 1944-46. Recipient Pomona City Civic award, 1972. Mem. Am. Chem. Soc., Nat. Assn. Corrosion Engrs., Sigma Xi, Phi Kappa Phi. Republican. Lodge: Elks. Patentee in field. Current Work: Instantaneous and instrumental methods of corrosion rate measurements. Subspecialties: Corrosion; Physical chemistry. Office: Calif Poly U Pomona CA 91768 Also: CCS Control Systems 415 W Foothill Blvd Suite 221 Claremont CA 91711

PYKETT, IAN LEWIS, physicist; b. Nottingham, Eng., Jan. 11, 1953; came to U.S., 1980; s. William L. and Margaret (Grieves) P.; m. Gwen A. Brown, July 16, 1977. B.Sc. with honors in Physics, London U., 1974; M.Sc. in Radiobiology, Birmingham U., 1975; Ph.D. in Physics, Nottingham U., 1978. Exptl. officer dept. physics U. Nottingham, Eng., 1975-76, postdoctoral research fellow, 1978-80; prin. physicist Technicare Corp., Solon, Ohio, 1980-83; research fellow in physics Mass. Gen. Hosp., Boston, 1980-82, dir. NMR research, 1983; pres. Advanced NMR Systems, Inc., Woburn, Mass., 1983—. Contbr. articles to profl. jours. Mem. Hosp. Physicists Assn. U.K., Am. Assn. Physicists in Medicine, Soc. Magnetic Resonance Imaging, Internat. Soc. Magnetic Resonance, Inst. Physics (U.K.), Soc. Magnetic Resonance in Medicine. Methodist. Current Work: Development and clinical applications of nuclear magnetic resonance imaging technology. Subspecialties: Magnetic resonance imaging; Bioinstrumentation.

PYLE, GERALD FREDRIC, medical geographer, educator; b. Akron, Ohio, Dec. 22, 1937; s. Russell Roy and Ruth (Martin) P.; m. Carole Wood, Aug. 29, 1959; children—Eric, Frances. B.A., Kent State U., 1963; M.A., U. Chgo., 1968, Ph.D., 1970. Cartographer, Rand McNally, Chgo., 1962-64; research geographer Ency. Britannica, Chgo., 1964-65; cartographer U. Chgo., 1965-70; asst. to full prof. U. Akron, Ohio, 1970-80; prof. geography and earth sci. U. N.C., Charlotte, 1980—; research dir. Center for Urban Studies, Akron, 1973-80; tech. dir. Akron Area Census File, 1974-80. Author: Heart Disease, Cancer and Stroke in Chicago, 1971; Spatial Dynamics of Crime, 1974; Applied Medical Geography, 1979; Diffusion of Influenza: Patterns and Paradigms, 1986. Sr. editor Med. Geography, Social Sci. and Medicine, 1977-84. Ill. Regional Med. grantee, 1969; Law Enforcement Adminstrn. Agy. grantee, 1972, 74; NSF grantee, 1979, 82. Fellow Ohio Acad. Sci.; mem. Assn. Am. Geographers, Nat. Council Geog. Edn. Democrat. Anglican. Lodge: Lions (treas.). Current work: Continued research in spatial diffusion of infectious diseases and the location of health care delivery facilities. Subspecialty: Urban geography. Address: Dept Geography and Earth Sci Univ NC UNCC Station Charlotte NC 28223

QUATE, CALVIN FORREST, engineering educator; b. Baker, Nev., Dec. 7, 1923; s. Graham Shepard and Margie (Lake) Q.; m. Dorothy Marshall, June 28, 1945; children: Robin, Claudia, Holly, Rhodalee. B.S. in Elec. Engring, U. Utah, 1944; Ph.D., Stanford U., 1950. Mem. tech. staff Bell Telephone Labs., Murray Hill, N.J., 1949-58; dir. research Sandia Corp., Albuquerque, 1959-60, v.p. research, 1960-61; prof. dept. applied physics and elec. engring. Stanford (Calif.) U., 1961—, chmn. applied physics, 1969-72, 78-81; assoc. dean Sch. Humanities and Scis., 1972-74, 82-83; sr. research fellow Xerox Palo Alto Research Ctr., 1984—. Served as lt. (j.g.) USNR, 1944-46. Fellow IEEE (Morris N. Liebmann award 1981), Am. Acad. Arts and Scis., Acoustical Soc., Royal Microscopical Soc. (hon.); mem. Nat. Acad. Engring., Nat. Acad. Scis., Am. Phys. Soc., Sigma Xi, Tau Beta Pi. Subspecialty: Electrical engineering. Office: Dept Applied Physics Stanford Stanford CA 94305*

QUEBBEMANN, ALOYSIUS JOHN, pharmacology educator; b. Chgo., Jan. 19, 1933. B.S., U. Alaska, 1960; Ph.D., SUNY at Buffalo, 1968. Asso. prof. pharmacology U. Minn., 1975—. Served with U.S. Army, 1951-54. Mem. Am. Soc. Pharmacology and Exptl. Therapeutics, Am. Soc. Nephrology, Internat. Soc. Nephrology. Current Work: Renal pharmacology and toxicology. Subspecialty: Pharmacology. Home: 1564 Fulman St Saint Paul MN 55108 Office: Med Sch U Minn 3-260 Millard Hall Minneapolis MN 55455

QUEK, SWEE-MENG, elec. engr.; b. Republic of Singapore, Dec. 15, 1955; came to U.S., 1972; s. Soo-Tong and Soo-Kiang Q.; m. Yee-Chin Lee, Jan 7, 1981; 1 son: Joo-Kwang Justin. B.S.E.E., Stanford U., 1977; M.S.E.E., 1977. Teaching asst. Stanford U., 1975-76; design engr. Data Gen. Corp., Westboro, Mass., 1977-78; sr. mem. tech. staff, project leader Four Phase Systems, Cupertino, Calif., 1978-81; engring. mgr. Storage Tech. Corp., Santa Clara, Calif., 1981—. Mem. IEEE, Assn. for Computing Machinery, SIGARCH, SIGMICRO. Current Work: High speed processors and algorithms. Engineering management and technical design of main-frame computers using VLSI CMOS. Subspecialties: Computer engineering; Computer architecture. Home: 2874 Grafton Way San Jose CA 95148 Office: 3450 Central Expressway Santa Clara CA 95051

QUIMBY, FRED WILLIAM, pathologist, educator, consultant; b. Providence, Sept. 19, 1945; s. Edward Harold and Isabelle Bella (Barber) Q.; m. Cynthia Claire Connelly, Aug. 21, 1965; children: Kelly Ann, Cynthia Jane. V.M.D., U. Pa., 1970; Ph.D., 1974. Diplomate: Am. Coll. Lab. Animal Medicine, 1980; Accredited U.S. Dept. Agr., 1970. Fellow Tufts-New Eng. Med. Center, Boston, 1974-75, research assoc. in hematology, instr. surgery, 1975-76; asst. prof. pathology and surgery Tufts Med. Sch., Boston, 1976-79; assoc. prof. pathology Cornell U. Med. Coll., N.Y.C., 1979—, N.Y. State Coll. Vet. Medicine, Ithaca, N.Y., 1979—; dir. Ctr. for Research Animal Resources, Cornell U., Ithaca, 1979—; cons. Harvard U., 1977-79, Sidney Farber Cancer Inst., Boston, 1978-79, St. Elizabeth's Hosp., Boston, 1975-79. Contbr. chpts. to books, articles to profl. jours. Mem. AVMA, Am. Assn. Lab. Animal Sci. (Bernard F. Trum award New Eng. br. 1979), Am. Soc. Primatology, N.Y. Acad. Scis. Current Work: Genetic control of the immunologic abnormalities associated with autoimmune disease. Subspecialties: Animal pathology; Immunology (agriculture). Home: 700 Warren Rd 19-1F Ithaca NY 14850 Office: NY State Coll Veterinary Medicine 221 VRT Ithaca NY 14853

QUINN, JAMES ALLEN, research plant pathologist; b. Gary, Ind., Mar. 29, 1954; s. Gerald N. and Helen L. (Sparks) Q.; m. Mildred A. Creager, Sept. 11, 1976; children—John N., Sarah E. B.S. cum laude, Ohio U., 1975, M.S., 1978; Ph.D., Ohio State U., 1980. Research plant pathologist Rohm and Haas Co., Springhouse, Pa., 1980—. Mem. Council of Southside Orgns., Columbus, Ohio, 1979-80; trustee Livingston Park Neighborhood, 1979-80. Mem. Am. Phytopath. Soc., Mycol. Soc. Am., Can. Phytopath. Soc., AAAS. Current Work: Fungicides, insecticides, herbicides, computer modelling. Subspecialty: Plant pathology. Home: 216 Lower Valley Rd North Wales PA 19454 Office: Research Lab Rohm & Haas Co Springhouse PA 19477

QUINN, JAMES AMOS, JR., biology educator, ecologist, researcher; b. Chickasha, Okla., Aug. 12, 1939; s. James Amos and Esther Ann (Roth) Q. B.S., Panhandle State U., 1961; M.S., Colo. State U., 1963, Ph.D. (NSF fellow), 1966. Asst. prof. botany Rutgers U., New Brunswick, N.J., 1966-71, assoc. prof., 1971-77, prof. biol. scis., 1977—, dir. grad.program botany and plant physiology, 1983-86, assoc. chmn. for personnel dept. biol. scis., 1981-82, mem. exec. council Grad. Sch., 1983-86; sec. Rutgers Coll. Biol. Scientists, 1969-71, 1973-75; instr. N.J. Conservation Commn., 1970; research fellow U. New Eng., N.S.W., Australia, 1981; cons. Ont. (Can.) Council Grad. Studies, 1982. Contbr. articles on botany and ecology to profl. jours.; editoral bd.: Am. Jour. Botany, 1980-82; editoral bd.: Bull. Torrey Bot. Club, 1983-85. NSF grantee, 1968-70; Rockefeller grantee, 1970; Rutgers Research Council faculty fellow Australia, 1972-73. Mem. Am. Forage and Grassland Council, Am. Inst. Biol. Scis., Bot. Soc. Am. (vice-chmn. 1977, chmn. 1978, ecol. sect.), Ecol. Soc. Am., N.J. Acad. Sci. (council 1972-76, treas. and exec. com. 1976-79, 1979-81), Soc. Range Mgmt., Torrey Bot. Club (council 1970-82, pres. 1982-83), Sigma Xi. Current Work: Adaptive differences among populations of a species along environmental gradients, evolution of pollution-tolerant populations, reproductive biology of amphicarpic species, life-histories and sex ratios in populations of dioecious species. Subspecialties: Ecology (environmental science); Population biology. Office: Dept Biol Scis Rutgers U Piscataway NJ 08854

QUINN, JOHN ALBERT, chemical engineering educator, consultant; b. Springfield, Ill., Sept. 3, 1932; s. Edward Joseph and Marie Regina (Von de Bur) Q.; m. Frances W. Daly, June 22, 1957; children: Sarah D., Rebecca V., John E. B.S., U. Ill., 1954; Ph.D., Princeton U., 1959. Asst. prof. dept. chem. engrng. U. Ill., Urbana, 1958-64, assoc. prof., 1964-66, prof., 1966-70; prof. dept. chem. engrng. U. Pa., Phila., 1971—, chmn. dept., 1980-85, Robert D. Bent prof., 1978—; adj. prof. U. Technologie de Compiegne, 1974—; 6th Mason lectr. Stanford U., 1981; OAS lectr., Argentina, 1981; Katz lectr. U. Mich., 1985; Sherman Fairchild disting. scholar Calif. Inst. Tech., 1985. Editorial bd.: Jour. Membrane Sci, 1976—, Rev. Chem. Engring, 1982—; contbr. articles to profl. jours.; patentee in field. NSF sr. postdoctoral fellow, 1965; recipient S. Reid Warren award U. Pa., 1974; Fairchild scholar Calif. Inst. Tech., 1985. Mem. Am. Inst. Chem. Engrs. (Allan P. Colburn award 1966), Nat. Acad. Engring., Am. Chem. Soc., Nat. Acad. Engrs., AAAS, Internat. Soc. on Oxygen Transfer to Tissue, Alpha Chi Sigma. Current Work: Synthetic membranes and the application of membranes in chemical processes, bioseparations, biochemical engineering. Subspecialties: Chemical engineering; Enzyme technology. Office: U Pa Dept Chem Engring 311A Towne Bldg D3 Philadelphia PA 19104

QUINNAN, GERALD VINCENT, food and drug adminstration official, virologist, internist, researcher; b. Boston, Sept. 7, 1947; s. Gerald and Mary (Lally) Q.; m. Mary Lou Woodward, Aug. 23, 1969; children—Kevin, Kylie, Kathleen. A.B. in Chemistry, Coll. Holy Cross, 1969; M.D. cum laude, St. Louis U., 1973. Diplomate Am. Bd. Internal Medicine. Intern Univ. Hosp., Boston, 1973-74; resident, then fellow Boston U. Med. Ctr., 1974-77; med. officer Bur. Biologics, Bethesda, Md., 1977-80; dir. herpes virus br. Bur. Biologics, Bethesda., 1980-81; dir. div. virology Ctr. for Drugs and Biologics, Office Biologics Research and Rev., FDA, Bethesda, 1981—. Contbr. chpts. to profl. books. Served with USPHS, 1977—. Mem. Am. Assn. Immunology, Infectious Diseases Soc. Am., Am. Soc. Clin. Investigation, Am. Fedn. Clin. Research, Alpha Omega Alpha. Current work: Virology, immunology, viral vaccines, infectious diseases. Subspecialties: Infectious diseases; Virology (biology). Office: FDA 8800 Rockville Pike Bethesda MD 20205

QUINTANILHA, ALEXANDRE TIEDTKE, biophysicist, educator; b. Maputo, Mozambique, Aug. 9, 1945; came to U.S., 1974; s. Aurelio Pereira da Silva and Ludowicka Ana Maria (Tiedtke) Q. B.Sc., U. Witwatersrand, Johannesburg, South Africa, 1967, B.Sc. Hons., 1976, Ph.D., 1972; Agregation, U. do Porto, Portugal, 1981, D.Sc. (hon.), 1977. Lectr., U. Witwatersrand, Johannesburg, 1971-74; vis. prof. Inst. Biomedico, Porto, Portugal, 1976—; staff scientist Lawrence Berkeley Lab. U. Calif.-Berkeley, 1974—, asst. head div., 1983—, adj. prof. physiology U. Calif.-Berkeley, 1982—; dir. summer sch. UNESCO, Porto, Portugal, 1984; dir. advanced study inst. NATO, Braga, Portugal, 1985. Author: Environmental Monitoring: Water, Vol. II, 1985; editor: Environmental Monitoring: Radiation, Vol. I, 1983; mem. editorial bd. Ciencia Biologica, 1980—, Archives of Biochemistry and Biophysics, 1981—. Gulbenkian fellow U. Paris, France, 1969-71; Nat. Acad. Sci.-NRC grantee, 1978. Mem. Am. Assn. Biol. Chemists, Biophys. Soc., Am. Soc. Photobiology, Internat. Soc. Magnetic Resonance. Current work: Oxygen toxicity and protection during physical exercise; membrane biophysics; oxidative damage to lipids and proteins, and protective mechanisms. Subspecialties: Biophysics (biology); Physiology (biology). Office: Lawrence Berkeley Laboratory U Calif Berkeley CA 94720

QUIRION, REMI, pharmacologist; b. Lac-Drolet, Que., Can., Jan. 9, 1955; s. Joseph and Fernande (Lessard) Q.; m. Pierrette Gaudreau, July 26, 1980; 1 son: Sylvain. B.Sc., U. Sherbrooke, 1976, M.Sc., 1977, Ph.D., 1980. Med. Research Council of Can. fellow NIMH-NIH, Bethesda, Md., 1980-82, pharmacologist, 1982—; vis. lectr. U. Calgary, Can., 1981. Conseil de la Recherche Ensante du Quebec scholar, 1978-80. Mem. AAAS, Am. Soc. Neurosci., Internat. Narcotics Conf. Current Work: Neuropeptides pharmacology, brain receptors, autoradiography, bioassay; drug abuse. Subspecialties: Neuropharmacology; Pharmacology. Home: Apt 101 13214 Twinbrook Pkwy Rockville MD 20851 Office: Neurosci Branch NIMH NIH Bethesda MD 20205

QUIVERS, WILLIAM WYATT, JR., physics educator; b. McDonough, Ga., Feb. 3, 1948; s. William Wyatt and Evelyn Cecilia (Seace) Q. B.S. Morehouse Coll., 1969; M.S. MIT, 1972; Ph.D., 1982. Teaching asst. MIT, Cambridge, Mass., 1969-71, research asst., 1977-81, post-doctoral assoc., 1982-83; asst. prof. Wellesley Coll., Mass., 1984—; vis. scientist MIT Spectroscopy Lab., Cambridge, 1983—. Contbr. articles to prof jours. Mem. Mass. Pub. Interest, Boston, 1984. Grad. fellow IBM, Xerox; NSF trainee in physics, 1971. Mem. Am. Phys. Soc., AAAS, N.Y. Acad. Sci., Sigma Xi. Methodist. Current work: Theoretical modeling of laser optical pumping of atoms as applied to laser-induced nuclear orientation of excited nuclei for nuclear physics studies. Subspecialties: Theoretical physics; Laser spectroscopy. Home: 270 Highland Ave Apt 14 Somerville MA 02143Office: Wellesley College Wellesley MA 02181

RAAB, G. KIRK, biotechnology company executive; b. N.Y.C., Sept. 27, 1935; s. George Rufus and Ann Maria (Wood) R.; m. Astrid Lois Lindberg, Apr. 30, 1960; children—Kristina Elizabeth, Alyson Ann, Michael George. B.A. with honors, Colgate U., 1959. With Pfizer Inc., 1959-65; sales mgr. Pfizer Chile, 1965; gen. mgr. A.H. Robins Co., Mex., 1965-68; v.p. Latin Am. Beecham Group Ltd., 1968-75; v.p. Latin Am., then exec. v.p. internat. Abbott Labs., North Chicago, Ill., 1975-79, corp. group v.p., 1980-81, pres., chief operating officer, dir., 1981-85; pres. Genentech, Inc., South San Francisco, Calif., 1985—; dir. Amyen Inc. Mem. Barrington Hills (Ill.) Plan Commn., 1977; mem. sch. and devel. coms. Chgo. Art Inst., 1980; trustee Evanston Hosp. Served with AUS, 1954-55. Mem. Am. Mgmt. Assn., Pharm. Mfrs. Assn., Council Americas. Clubs: Barrington Hills Country, Lake Zurich (Ill.) Golf, Economic., Commonwealth. Subspecialty: Biotechnology administration. Office: Genentech Inc 460 Point San Bruno Blvd South San Francisco CA 94080

RAAM, SHANTHI, cancer researcher, immunochemist, consultant; b. Madras, India, Nov. 26, 1941; came to U.S., 1964, naturalized, 1976. B.S., Madras U., 1960, M.S., 1962; Ph.D., U. Ga., Athens, 1973. Research asst. in parasitology U. Tenn., 1964-65; teaching asst. dept. microbiology Med. Coll. Ga., Augusta, 1968-70, U. Ga., 1970-73; postdoctoral fellow Cancer Research Center, Tufts U., Boston, 1973-75; chief oncology lab. Tufts U. Med. Cancer unit Lemuel Shattuck Hosp., Boston, 1975-77, dir. oncology lab., 1977—; research assoc. dept. medicine Tufts U.; cons. NIH, New Eng. Nuclear, Leary Labs. Contbr. articles to profl. jours. Mem. LWV. Grantee Am. Cancer Soc., N.Y., 1979-83; Nat. Cancer Inst. research awardee, 1984—; Aid to Cancer research awards, 1983-85. Mem. Endocrine Soc. Am., Am. Assn. Immunology, Am. Assn. Cancer Research, Am. Assn. Clin. Oncology, Am. Assn. Microbiology. Current Work: Molecular mechanism of steroid hormone action and significance of steroid hormone receptors in cancers of the human breast, uterus and the brain (immunology of estrogen receptors of human breast carcinoma). Subspecialties: Oncology; Receptors. Office: Tufts University Medical Center Unit Lemuel Shattuck Hosp 170 Morton St Boston MA 02130

RABENSTEIN, DALLAS LEROY, chemistry educator; b. Portland, Oreg., June 13, 1942; s. Melvin Leroy and Rose Marie (Nelson) R.; m. Gloria Carolyn Duncan, Aug. 28, 1964; children—Mark David, Lisa Heather Diane. B.S., U. Wash., 1964; Ph.D., U. Wis., 1968. Research chemist Chevron Research Co., Richmond, Calif., 1968-69; prof. chemistry U. Alta., Edmonton, Can., 1969-85, U. Calif.-Riverside, 1985—. Fellow Chem. Inst. Can. (Fisher Sci. Lecture award 1984); mem. Am. Chem. Soc. Current work: Development and application of nuclear magnetic resonance techniques for bioanalytical chemistry. Subspecialties: Analytical chemistry; Nuclear magnetic resonance. Office: Dept Chemistry U Calif Riverside CA 92521

RABI, ISIDOR ISAAC, emeritus physics educator; b. Austria, July 29, 1898; came to U.S. in infancy,; s. David and Jennie (Teig) R.; m. Helen Newark, 1926; children: Nancy Elizabeth, Margaret Joella. B.Chem., Cornell U., 1919; Ph.D., Columbia U., 1927, Sc.D., 1968; grad. study in, Munich, Copenhagen, Hamburg, Leipzig, Zurich, 1927-29; D. Sc. (hon.), Princeton U., 1947, Harvard, 1955, Williams Coll., 1958, U. Birmingham, 1960, Clark U., 1962, Adelphi Coll., 1962, Technion, 1963, Franklin Marshall Coll., 1964, Brandeis U., 1965, U. Coimbra, Portugal, 1966, Hebrew U., Jerusalem, 1972, Coll. City N.Y., 1977, Bates Coll., 1977, LIU, 1977; L.H.D., Hebrew Union Coll., Cin., 1958, Oklahoma City U., 1960; LL.D., Dropsie Coll., 1956; D.H.L., Yeshiva U., 1964; Litt. D., Jewish Theol. Sem., 1966. Tutor in physics Coll. City N.Y., 1924-27; lectr. Columbia U., 1929-30, asst. prof., 1930-35, assoc. prof., 1935-37, prof., 1937-64, Higgins prof., 1950-64, U. prof., 1964-67, Univ. prof. emeritus, 1967—, also exec. officer, dept. physics, 1945-49, Karl Taylor Compton vis. prof. physics, 1968-71; lectr. U. Mich., summer 1936; Stanford U., summer 1938; cons. sci. adv. com. Ballistic Research Lab., Aberdeen, 1939-65; mem. sci. bd. Itek Corp.; Staff mem. and assoc. dir. Radiation Lab., M.I.T., 1940-45; mem. gen. adv. com. AEC, 1946—, chmn., 1952-56, cons., 1956—; chmn. sci. adv. Com. ODM, 1953-57; cons. Dept. State, 1958—; mem. Naval Research Adv. Com., 1952—; cons., sci. adv. com., v.p. Internat. Conf. on Peaceful Uses Atomic Energy, Geneva, 1955, 58, 64; v.p. UN Conf. on Peaceful Uses Atomic Energy, 1971—; U.S. rep. adv. com. to sec. gen. UN, 1955—; mem. President's Sci. Adv. Com., 1957-68, chmn., 1957; cons. Los Alamos Sci. Lab., 1943-45, 56—; mem. NATO Sci. Com., 1958—; cons. Research and Devel. Bd., 1946-49; U.S. del. UNESCO Conf., Florence, Italy, 1950; mem. U.S. Nat. Commn. UNESCO, 1950-53, 58, UN Sci. Com., 1954—, IAEA Sci. Com., 1958-72; vis. prof. Rockefeller U. (formerly Inst.), 1957-79; Shreve fellow Princeton, 1961-62; Karl Taylor Compton lectr. Mass. Inst. Tech., 1962; gen. adv. com. ACDA, 1962—. Author: My Life and Times as a Physicist, 1960, Science: The Center of Culture, 1970; Assoc. editor: Physical Review, 1935-38, 1941-44; Contbr. to sci. jours. in field. Trustee Assoc. Univs., Inc., 1946—, pres., 1961-62, chmn. bd., 1962-63; bd. govs. Weizmann Inst. Sci., Rehovoth, Israel, 1949—; trustee Mt. Sinai Hosp., 1960—. Served in S.A.T.C., 1918. Decorated Officer French Legion of Honor, 1956; comdr., 1968; Barnard fellow, 1927-28; Internat. Ednl. Bd. fellow, 1928-29; Ernest Kempton Adams fellow, 1935; Sigma Xi Semicentennial prize for physical scis., 1936; Henrietta Szold award, 1956; 1,000 prize from AAAS, for study of radio frequency spectra of atoms and molecules, 1939; Elliot Cresson medal of Franklin Inst., 1942; Nobel Prize in Physics, 1944; Barnard medal, 1960; U.S. Medal for Merit, 1948; King's Medal British, 1948; Comdr., Order So. Cross Brazil, 1952; Priestley Meml. award Dickenson Coll., 1964; Niels Bohr Internat. Gold Medal, 1967; co-recipient Atoms for Peace award, 1967; Tribute of Appreciation State Dept., 1978; Pupin Gold medal Columbia U. Sch. Engring., 1981. Fellow Am. Phys. Soc. (pres. 1950-51); mem. Council on Fgn. Relations, Am. Philos. Soc., Japan Acad. Sci. (fgn. mem.), Nat. Acad. Scis. (Pub. Welfare medal 1985), N.Y. Acad. Scis., Sigma Xi. Clubs: Cosmos (Washington); Faculty (Columbia U.); Athenaeum (London). Subspecialty: Nuclear physics. Office: Columbia U Dept Physics New York NY 10027

RABII, SOHRAB, electrical engineering educator; b. Ahwaz, Iran, Dec. 30, 1937, came to U.S., 1958, naturalized, 1970; s. Mohammad Hossain and Mohtaram (Khosrovi) R.; m. Patricia A. Berg, Nov. 29, 1966; children—Susan M., Elizabeth L. B.S., U. So. Calif., 1961; M.S., MIT, 1962, Ph.D., 1966; M.A. (hon.), U. Pa., 1973. Research fellow MIT, Cambridge, 1966-67; sr. research physicist Monsanto Co., St. Louis, 1967-69; asst. prof. U. Pa., Phila., 1969-73, assoc. prof., 1973-78, chmn. elec. engring., sci., 1977-82, prof. elec. engring., 1978—; cons. MacMillan Pub. Co., N.Y.C., 1984—. Editor: Physics of IV-VI Compounds and Alloys, 1974. Contbr. articles to profl. jours. Fellow Max Planck Soc. Advancement Sci. Fed. Republic Germany; mem. IEEE (sr.), Am. Phys. Soc. Current work: Theoretical investigation of electronic structure of molecules and solids. Subspecialties: Semiconductors; Condensed matter physics. Home: 358 Prussian Ln Wayne PA 19087 Office: U Pa Dept Elec Engring Philadelphia PA 19104

RABIN, BRUCE S., clinical immunopathologist, educator; b. Buffalo, Jan. 25, 1941; s. Eli and Dorothy Rabin; children—Andrew, Alison. B.A., Western Res. U., 1962; M.D., SUNY-Buffalo, 1969, Ph.D., 1969. Diplomate Am. Bd. Med. Lab. Immunology. Resident in pathology Med. Coll. of Va., Richmond, 1969, E. J. Meyer Meml. Hosp., Buffalo, 1970; asst. prof. pathology SUNY-Buffalo, 1970-72; faculty Ctr. Immunology, Buffalo, 1970-72; asst. prof. pathology U. Pitts., 1972-74, assoc. prof. pathology, 1974—; dir. clin. immunopathology U. Health Ctr., Pitts., 1972—. Contbr. articles to profl. jours. Fellow Am. Soc. Microbiology; mem. Am. Assn. Pathologists, Am. Assn. Immunologists, Internat. Soc. Heart Transplantation, Am. Soc. Transplant Physicians. Current work: Immunology of transplantation rejection, immunologic monitoring of transplant patients, role of nutrition in immunologic ageing and development of autoimmune disease. Subspecialties: Immunology (medicine); Transplantation. Home: 1235 Malvern Ave Pittsburgh PA 15217 Office: U Pitts 406 Scaife Hall Pittsburgh PA 15261

RABIN, HERBERT, university administrator; b. Milw., Nov. 14, 1928 s. Irving and Ida (Holland) R.; m. Annie Rosenvey, Apr. 15, 1962; children—Elise, Marc. B.S. in Physics, U. Wis.-Madison, 1950; M.S. in Physics, U. Ill., 1951; Ph.D., in Physics, U. Md., 1959. Various tech. and mgmt. positions Naval Research Lab., Washington 1952-71; assoc. dir. research, 1971-79; dept. asst. Sec. of Navy, Navy Dept., Washington, 1979-83; dir. engring. research ctr., prof. elec. engring., assoc. dean coll. engring. U. Md., College Park, 1983—; mem. naval studies bd. space panel Nat. Acad. Scis., Washington, 1978—; mem. space and earth scis. adv. bd. NASA, Washington, 1982—; trustee Nat. Technol. U., Fort Collins, Colo., 1984—; mem. panel on engring. and sci. edn. DOD-Univ. Forum, 1984—. Editor: Quantum Electronics, 1975. Contbr. articles to profl. jours. Patentee in field. Recipient Meritorious Civilian Service award U.S. Navy, 1969; E.O. Hulburt Sci. award U.S. Navy, 1970; Disting. Civilian Service award U.S. Navy, 1976, 83; Disting. Civilian Service award Dept. Defense, 1979. Fellow Am. Phys. Soc., Optical Soc. Am., AAAS, AIAA; mem. Brazilian Acad. Sci. (corresponding), Inst. Elec. Electronics Engrs. (sr.). Current work: University-industry collaborative programs, as through technology extension program; "incubator" for startup technology based companies; and research partnerships. Subspecialties: Satellite studies; Condensed matter physics. Home: 7109 Radnor Rd Bethesda MD 20817 Office: Engring Research Ctr U Md College Park MD 20742

RABIN, MICHAEL O., computer science and mathematics educator; b. Breslau, Ger., Sept. 1, 1931; s. Israel A. and Else (Hess) R.; m. Ruth Scherzer, May 31, 1954; children: Tal, Sharon. M.S. in Math, Hebrew U. of Jerusalem, 1953; Ph.D. in Math, Princeton U., 1956. Instr. Princeton U., 1956-57; mem. Princeton U. (Inst. for Advanced Study), Princeton, N.J., 1957-58; vis. prof. U. Calif.-Berkeley, 1962, MIT, 1963, 72-78; U. Paris, 1965, Yale U., 1967, N.Y.U., 1970; Albert Einstein prof. Hebrew Univ. of Jerusalem, 1965—; prof. Harvard U., 1981—; cons. computer industry. Recipient Rothschild prize in Math. Rothschild Found., 1974; A. M. Turing Award in Computer Sci., 1976; Harvey prize Sci. and Tech. Technion Soc., 1980. Mem. Nat. Acad. Scis. Current Work: Theory of algorithms, randomizing algorithms, computer security. Subspecialties: Algorithms; Cryptography and data security.

RABIN, MONROE STEPHEN ZANE, physics educator; b. Bklyn., Dec. 19, 1939; s. Louis and Helen (Haspel) R.; m. Joan Greenblatt, Feb. 27, 1965; children—Elaine Judith, Carolyn Sandra. A.B. in Math., Columbia U., 1961; M.S. in Physics, Rutgers U., 1964, Ph.D. in Physics, 1967. Physicist, Lawrence Berkeley Lab., Calif., 1967-72; assoc. prof. physics U. Mass., Amherst, 1972-81, prof., 1981—. Pulitzer scholar, 1957; NSF co-prin. investigator, 1978—. Mem. Am. Phys. Soc., Sigma Xi. Current work: Experimental elementary particle physics, searches for rare events buried in large cross section processes. Subspecialties: Particle physics; Graphics, image processing, and pattern recognition. Home: 21 Atwater Circle Amherst MA 01002 Office: Dept Physics U Mass Amherst MA 01003

RABINER, LAWRENCE RICHARD, electrical engineer; b. Bklyn., Sept. 28, 1943; s. Nathan Marcus and Gloria Hannah (Bodinger) R.; m. Suzanne Login, June 23, 1968; children: Sheri, Wendi, Joni. B.S., M.I.T., 1964, M.S., 1964, Ph.D., 1967. With Bell Labs., Murray Hill, N.J., 1962—, supr. human-machine voice communication group, 1970-85, head speech research dept., 1985—; cons. U.S. govt. Author: Theory and Application of Digital Signal Processing, 1975, Digital Processing of Speech Signals, 1979, Multirate Digital Signal Processing, 1983; contbr. articles to profl. jours. Mem. IEEE (award for paper 1971, Piori award 1979), Acoustical Soc. Am. (Biennial award 1974). Jewish. Patentee. Current Work: Speech recognition by machine. Subspecialty: Computer engineering. Home: 58 Sherbrook Dr Berkeley Heights NJ 07922 Office: Bell Laboratories Room 2D533 Murray Hill NJ 07974

RABINOVICH, ELIEZER M., glass and ceramic scientist; b. Moscow, Apr. 4, 1937, came to U.S., 1980; s. Meir and Brakha (Medalje) R.; m. Gesya M. Asinovsky, Apr. 25, 1967; 1 child, Asya; 1 child by previous marriage, Irina. M.Sc. in Ceramic Engring. Moscow Mendeleev Inst. Chem. Tech., 1959, Candidate of Scis. (Ph.D.), 1964. Cert. chem. engr., Israel. Research engr. Research Inst. Glass for Vacuum Electronics, Moscow, 1959-63, sr. researcher, 1964-67, group supr., 1967-73; sr. researcher Israel Ceramic and Silicate Inst., Haifa, 1974-79, prin. researcher, 1979-80; mem. staff AT&T Bell Labs., Murray Hill, N.J., 1981—; adj. asst. prof. Technion (Israel Inst. Tech.), Haifa, 1975-80. Contbr. articles to profl. jours. Patentee in field. Mem. Am. Ceramic Soc., Materials Research Soc. Current work: Glass-ceramics, phase separation in glasses, sintering of glass; currently, sol-gel methods of glass preparation. Subspecialties: Ceramics; Inorganic chemistry. Home: 52 Evergreen Dr Berkeley Heights NJ 07922 Office: AT&T Bell Labs Room 7A-313 600 Mountain Ave Murray Hill NJ 07974

RABINOVITCH, BENTON SEYMOUR, chemist, educator; b. Montreal, Que., Can., Feb. 19, 1919; came to U.S., 1946; s. Samuel and Rachel (Schachter) R.; m. Marilyn Werby, Sept. 18, 1949; children—Peter Samuel, Ruth Anne, Judith Nancy, Frank Benjamin; m. Flora Reitman, 1980. B.Sc., McGill U., 1939, Ph.D., 1942. Postdoctoral fellow Harvard, 1946-48; mem. faculty U. Wash., 1948—, prof. chemistry, 1957—; Cons. and/or mem. sci. adv. panels, coms. NSF, Nat. Acad. Scis.-NRC; adv. com. phys. chemistry Nat. Bur. Standards. Editor: Ann. Rev. Phys. Chemistry; editorial bd.: Internat. Jour. Chem. Kinetics; mem. editorial bd.: Rev. of Chem. Intermediates, Jour. Am. Chem. Soc., Jour. Phys. Chemistry. Served to capt. Canadian Army, 1942-46; ETO. Recipient Michael Polanyi medal Royal Soc. Chemistry, Peter Debye award in phys. chemistry. Nat. Research Council Can. fellow, 1940-42; Royal Soc. Can. Research fellow, 1946-47; Milton Research fellow Harvard, 1948; Guggenheim fellow, 1961; vis. fellow Trinity Coll., Oxford, 1971, Sigma Xi award for original research. Fellow Am. Phys. Soc., Am. Acad. Arts and Scis.; mem. Am. Chem. Soc. (past chmn. Puget Sound sect., past chmn. phys. chemistry div., editor jour.), Faraday Soc., AAUP. Spl. research Unimolecular gas phase reaction. Home: 12530-42 Ave NE Seattle WA 98125

RABINOW, JACOB, electrical engineer; b. Kharkov, Russia, Jan. 8, 1910; came to U.S., 1921, naturalized, 1930; s. Aaron and Helen (Fleisher) Rabinovich; m. Gladys Lieder, Sept. 26, 1943; children: Jean Ellen, Clare Lynn. B.S. in Elec. Engring., CCNY, 1933, E.E., 1934; D.H.L. (hon.), Towson State U., 1983. Radio serviceman, N.Y.C., 1934-38; mech. engr. Nat. Bur. Standards, Washington, 1938-54; pres. Rabinow Engring. Co., Washington, 1954-64; v.p. Control Data Corp., Washington, 1964-72; research engr. Nat. Bur. Standards, 1972—; Regent's lectr. U. Calif.-Berkeley, 1972; lectr., cons. in field. Author. Recipient Pres.'s Cert. of Merit, 1948; cert. appreciation War Dept., 1949; Exceptional Service award Dept. Commerce, 1949; Edward Longstreth medal Franklin Inst., 1959; Jefferson medal N.J. Patent Law Assn., 1973; named Scientist of Yr. Indsl. R&D mag., 1980. Fellow IEEE (Harry Diamond award 1977), AAAS; mem. Nat. Acad. Engring., Philos. Soc. Washington, Audio Engring. Soc., Sigma Xi. Club: Cosmos (Washington). Patentee in field. Current Work: Study of invention;patents; innovation and productivity; research and develeopment in robotics; sound reproduction; post office automation. Subspecialties: Electrical engineering; Mechanical engineering. Home: 6920 Selkirk Dr Bethesda MD 20817 Office: Nat Bur Standards Washington DC 20899

RABINOWITZ, DEBORAH, biologist, educator; b. Windham, Conn., Sept. 9, 1947; d. Louis and Margaret Henry (Camp) R.; m. Peter Thurston Ewell, Dec. 20, 1983. A.B., New Coll., 1970; Ph.D., U. Chgo., 1975. Asst. prof. biology U. Mich.-Ann Arbor, 1975-81, assoc. prof., 1981-82; assoc. prof. Cornell U., Ithaca, N.Y., 1982—. Current work: Rarity, ecology of grasses and grasslands, introgression, gene flow, Solanum, agroecology, crop evolution, potatoes. Subspecialties: Ecology (biology); Population biology. Home: 104 Devon Rd Ithaca NY 14850 Office: Cornell U Sect Ecology and Systematics Corson Hall Ithaca NY 14853

RABINOWITZ, ISRAEL NATHAN, biochemist; b. N.Y.C., Jan. 24, 1935; s. Hyman and Lena (Rosep) R.; m. Lynn S. Schneiderman, Dec. 20, 1959; children—Mirle D., Josua P. B.S., CCNY, 1956; M.S., U. Washington, 1962; Ph.D., Rutgers U., 1965. Research fellow Kings Coll., London, 1965-67; research assoc. Stanford U., 1968-74; research chemist Palo Alto VA Hosp., Calif., 1975-77; dir. biol. research Sci. Spectrum, Santa Barbara, Calif., 1977-79; dir. research and devel. Biodyne Co., 1979-82, M&T Labs., Chico, Calif., 1982—. Contbr. articles to profl. jours. Inventor in field. Mem. AAAS, Am. Crystallographic Assn., Am. Chem. Soc., N.Y. Acad. Scis., Inst. Food Technologists. Current work: Molecular biology; natural products; animal nutrition; microbiology; plant physiology; biochemical engineering. Subspecialties: Food science and technology; Biochemistry (biology). Home: 2534 Foothill Rd Santa Barbara CA 93105

RABINS, MICHAEL JEROME, mechanical engineering educator; b. N.Y.C., Feb. 24, 1932; s. Herman and Ida Rabins; m. Joan Wrynn, Apr. 6, 1956; children—Andrew, Evan, Alexandra. B.S.M.E., MIT, 1953; M.S.M.E., Carnegie Inst. Tech., Pitts., 1954; Ph.D. in Mech. Engring., U. Wis.-Madison, 1959. Registered mech. engr., Calif. Asst. prof. U. Wis., 1959-60; from asst. to assoc. prof. NYU, 1960-70; prof., dir. Poly. Inst. Bklyn., 1970-75; dir. univ. research U.S. Dept. Transp., Washington, 1975-77; prof. mech. engring., chmn., assoc. dean research and grad. programs Wayne State U., Detroit, 1977—; cons. in field. Author: Control and Dynamic Systems Response, 1970, Introduction Systems and Controls, 1974; contbr. numerous articles to profl. jours. Patentee (2) self-energized friction clutches. Chmn. 3 Ctr. Transp. Com., Detroit, 1978-82. Recipient Sec. and Superior Performance award U.S. Dept. Transp., 1976-77, Silver medal U.S. Dept. Transp., 1977; Cert. of Appreciation, Mayor of Detroit, 1980. Fellow ASME and Engring. Soc. of Detroit (v.p. ASME 1960-84, visit USSR 1978); mem. Am. Soc. Engring. Edn., Am.

Automatic Control Council (pres. 1984-85). Current work: Automatic control system design; mechanical engineering component and system design; research adminstrn. Subspecialties: Mechanical engineering; Systems engineering. Home: 29988 Fernhill Dr Farmington Hills MI 48018 Office: Grad Programs Coll Engrng Wayne State Univ Detroit MI 48202

RABKIN, MITCHELL THORNTON, physician, hospital administrator, educator; b. Boston, Nov. 27, 1930; s. Morris Aaron and Esther (Quint) R.; m. Adrienne M. Najarian, June 24, 1956; children: Julia Margaret, David Gregory. A.B. magna cum laude, Harvard U., 1951, M.D. cum laude, 1955; D.Sc. (hon.), Brandeis U., 1983; D.Pharm. (hon.), Mass. Coll. Pharmacy, 1983. Intern Mass. Gen. Hosp., Boston, 1955-56, resident in internal medicine, 1956-57, 59-60, chief resident, 1962, mem. staff, 1963-72, bd. consultation, 1972-80, hon. physician, 1981—; clin. fellow NIH, Bethesda, Md., 1957-59; gen. dir. Beth Israel Hosp., Boston, 1966-80, pres., 1980—; asst. prof. medicine Harvard U., 1969-70, assoc. prof., 1971-83, prof., 1983—; vis. lectr. Harvard Sch. Public Health, 1977—. Chmn. bd. dirs. Corp. for Boston. Served with USPHS, 1957-59. Fellow A.C.P.; mem. AAAS, Am. Fedn. Clin. Research, Mass. Med. Soc., Soc. Med. Adminstrs., Hastings Inst. Soc., Ethics and Life Scis., Assn. Am. Med. Colls. (past chmn. Council Teaching Hosps.), Conf. Boston Teaching Hosps. (past chmn.), Inst. Medicine, Nat. Acad. Scis. Jewish. Clubs: Century Assn. (N.Y.C.); Harvard (Boston). Subspecialty: Medical administration. Office: Beth Israel Hospital Boston MA 02215

RABKIN, RALPH, researcher; b. Cape Town, South Africa, June 12, 1935; came to U.S. 1978, naturalized 1984; s. Judel and Fanny (Baker) R.; m. Melanie Carolle Schravesande, Oct. 21, 1964; children—Gary M., Brian A., Steven M. M.B. Ch.B. U. Cape Town, South Africa, 1960; M.D., U. Witwatersrand, South Africa, 1977. Intern King Edward VIII and Groote Schuur Hosp., South Africa, 1961; resident U. Natal, U. Witwatersrand, 1962-66; renal fellow Northwestern U., Chgo., 1966-68; sr. chief research officer U. Cape Town Med. Research Council, 1968-69; specialist physician and lectr. Groote Schuur Hosp. and Univ., Cape Town, 1969-70, sr. specialist physician and lectr., 1970-72; prin. renal physician, head renal div. U. Witwatersrand/Johannesburg Gen. Hosp., 1972-75; assoc. prof. med. U. Tenn., Memphis, 1975-78, Stanford U., 1978—; chief nephrology Santa Clara Valley Med. Ctr., Calif., 1978-82, V.A. Med. Ctr., Palo Alto, 1984—; mem. sci. adv. council Kidney Found. North Calif., San Mateo, 1979—; mem. research Council Santa Clara county Am. Heart Assn., San Jose, Calif., 1979—. Contbr. articles to profl. jours. and books. Research awardee Glaxo-Allenbury, 1969, Charlotte Roberts Trust Found., 1974; research grantee NIH, 1976—, VA, 1983—. Fellow Royal Coll. Physicians; mem. Am. Soc. Clin. Invest, Am. Soc. Nephrology, Internatl. Soc. Nephrology, Am. Diabetes Assn. Jewish. Current work: Renal metabolism of polypeptide hormones. Subspecialties: Nephrology; Physiology (medicine). Office: VA Med Ctr 111R 3801 Miranda Ave Palo Alto CA 94304

RABOVSKY, JEAN, biochemist; b. Balt., Aug. 18, 1937. B.S., U. Md., 1959; Ph.D., Brandeis U., 1964. Postdoctoral fellow Brandeis U., Waltham, Mass., 1964-65; postgrad. research biochemist U. Calif.-Riverside, 1965-66, research chemist, 1968-70, asst. research biologist, Irvine, 1972-76; postdoctoral assoc. U. Fla., Gainesville, 1976-78; research chemist NIOSH, Morgantown, W.Va., 1978—. Contbr. articles to profl. jours. Mem. AAAS, N.Y. Acad. Sci., Biophys. Soc., Am. Chem. Soc., Internat. Soc. for Study of Xenobiotics, Sigma Xi. Current work: Detoxication and bioactivation mechanisms; cytochrome P450; glutathione; environmental/occupational health. Subspecialties: Biochemistry (biology); Environmental toxicology. Office: Nat Inst Occupational Safety and Health Div Respiratory Disease Studies 944 Chestnut Ridge Rd Morgantown WV 26505

RABOW, GERALD, systems engineer; b. Berlin, July 6, 1928, came to U.S., 1940, naturalized, 1946; s. Arthur and Margaret (Dannenberg) R.; m. Sylvia Schlachter, May 15, 1960; children—Lois Ellen, Alfred Arthur. B.E.E. summa cum laude, City Coll. N.Y., 1951; S.M., MIT, 1952; Sc.D. in engring., Columbia U., 1963. With ITT, Nutley, N.J., 1952-74, sr. sci., 1961-74; sr. research engr. Otis Elevator Corp. Research Ctr., Parsippany, N.J., 1974-77; with ATT Bell Labs., Whippany, N.J., 1978—, mem. tech. staff, 1979—. Author: The Era of the System: How the Systems Approach Can Help Solve Society's Problems, 1969. Co-editor: IEEE Tech. and Soc. mag., 1984. Contbr. articles jours. Mem. IEEE (Centennial medal, 1984), IEEE Soc. on Social Implications of Tech. (publ. chmn., adminstrv. com., 1982—). Current work: Research on application of systems engineering techniques to societal problems such as achievement of peace. Subspecialties: Systems engineering; Electrical engineering. Home: 21 Berkeley Terr Livingston NJ 07039 Office: ATT Bell Labs Whippany Rd Whippany NJ 07981

RABSON, THOMAS AVELYN, electrical engineering educator; b. Houston, July 21, 1932; s. Charles Avelyn and Sara Kathleen (Drake) R.; m. Sylvia Mary Jenny, Aug. 22, 1957; children—William, Tamara, Robert. B.A., Rice Inst., 1954, B.S., 1955, M.A., 1957, Ph.D., 1959. Registered profl. engr., Tex. Asst. prof. Rice U., Houston, 1959-63, assoc. prof., 1963-70, prof. elec. engring., 1970—. Contbr. articles to profl. jours. Patentee in field. NSF sr. faculty fellow, 1965. Mem. IEEE (sr.), Am. Phys. Soc., Soc. Photo and Instrumental Engrs., Optical Soc. Am. Republican. Methodist. Current work: Semiconductor and opto electronic memories. Subspecialties: Semiconductors; Optical signal processing. Home: 4521 Ivanhoe Houston TX 77027 Office: Dept Electrical Engring Rice U PO Box 1892 Houston TX 77251

RACE, GEORGE JUSTICE, physician, educator; b. Everman, Tex., Mar. 2, 1926; s. Claude Ernest and Lila Eunice (Bunch) R.; m. Annette Isabelle Rinker, Dec. 21, 1946; children: George William Daryl, Jonathan Clark, Mark Christopher, Jennifer Anne (dec.), Elizabeth Margaret Rinker. M.D., U. Tex., Southwestern Med. Sch., 1947; M.S. in Pub. Health, U. N.C., 1953; Ph.D. in Ultrastructural Anatomy and Microbiology, Baylor U., 1969. Intern Duke Hosp., 1947-48, asst. resident pathology, 1951-53; intern Boston City Hosp., 1948-49; asst. pathologist Peter Bent Brigham Hosp., Boston, 1953-54; pathologist St. Anthony's Hosp., St. Petersburg, Fla., 1954-55; staff pathologist Children's Med. Center, Dallas, 1955-59; dir. labs. Baylor U. Med. Center, Dallas, 1959—, chief dept. pathology, 1959—, vice chmn. exec. com. med. bd., 1970-73; cons. pathologist VA Hosp., Dallas, 1955-73; adj. prof. anthropology and biology So. Meth. U., Dallas, 1969; instr. pathology Duke, 1951-53, Harvard Med. Sch., 1953-54; asst. prof. pathology U. Tex. Southwestern Med. Sch., 1955-58, clin. asso. prof., 1958-64, clin. prof., 1964-72, prof., 1973—, dir. Cancer Center, 1973-76, asso. dean for continuing edn., 1973—; pathologist-in-chief Baylor U. Med. Center, 1959—; prof. microbiology Baylor Coll. Dentistry, 1962-68, prof. pathology, 1964-68, prof., chmn. dept. pathology, 1969-73; dean A. Webb Roberts Continuing Edn. Center, 1973—; spl. adv. on human and animal diseases Gov. Tex., 1979-83. Editor: Laboratory Medicine (4 vols.), 1973, 11th edit., 1985; Contbr. articles to profl. jours., chpts. to textbooks. Pres., Tex. div. Am. Cancer Soc., 1970; chmn. Gov.'s Task Force on Higher Edn., 1981. Served with AUS, 1944-46; from 1st lt. to maj. USAF, 1948-51. Decorated Air medal. Fellow Coll. Am. Pathologists, Am. Soc. Clin. Pathologists, A.A.A.S., Am. Coll. Legal Medicine; mem. A.M.A. (chmn. multiple discipline research forum 1969), Am. Assn. Pathologists, Internat. Acad. Pathology, Am. Assn. Med. Colls., Am. Assn. Cancer Research, Am. Assn. Phys. Anthropologists, Sigma Xi. Current Work: Immunopathology due to animal parasites; Hypertension and adrenal diseases; surgical pathology and oncology. Subspecialties: Pathology (medicine); Parasitology. Home: 3429 Beverly Dr Dallas TX 75205

RADCLIFF, ROGER DALE, electrical engineering educator; b. Huntington, W.Va., May 23, 1956; s. Ralph William and Mary Ruth (MacPherson) R.; m. Buffie White, Apr. 3, 1982; children—Pamela, Elizabeth. B.S.E.E., W.Va. U., 1978, M.S.E.E., 1979, Ph.D. in E.E., 1982. Assoc. prof. Ohio U., Athens, 1982—. Contbr. articles to profl. jours. W.Va. Found. fellow, 1979; NSF grantee, 1984. Mem. IEEE, Geosci. and Remote Sensing Soc. of IEEE, Antennas and Propagation Soc. of IEEE, Sigma Xi, Pi Mu Epsilon, Eta Kappa Nu, Tau Beta Pi. Republican. Methodist. Current work: Geophysical tomography; wave propagation; antenna analysis and design; avionics (navigational aids) research. Subspecialties: Electromagnetic theory; Remote sensing (geoscience). Home: 33 Ball Dr Athens OH 45701 Office: ECE Dept Ohio U Clippinger Labs Athens OH 45701

RADCLIFFE, JOHN DAVID, nutrition educator; b. Ramsey, Gt. Britain, Feb. 1, 1951, came to U.S., 1978; s. William Frederick and Catherine Margaret (Quirk) R.; m. Dawn P. Parris, Jan. 8, 1978. B.Sc. in Human Nutrition, U. London, 1972; M.Sc. Animal Nutrition, U. Aberdeen, Scotland, 1973, Ph.D. Nutrition, 1977. Research fellow Wageningen U., Netherlands, 1977-78, Nat. Cancer Inst., Bethesda, Md., 1978-80; research nutritionist IIT Research Inst., Chgo., 1980-82; asst. prof. Tex. Woman's U., Houston, 1979—; mem. exec. adv. com. grad. studies in nutrition U. Tex., Houston, 1984. Contbr. articles to profl. jours. Recipient Commonwealth prize U. Aberdeen, 1973; Von Humbolt Found. fellow, 1980. Mem. British Nutrition Soc., Am. Oil Chemists Soc., Am. Inst. Nutrition, Soc. for Exptl. Biology and Medicine, Inst. Food Technologists. Current work: Use of Japanese Quail for a model to study atherosclerosis; genesis of cancer anorexia and cachexia in cancerous rats. Subspecialties: Nutrition (medicine); Atherosclerosis. Home: 7575 Cambridge #404 Houston TX 77054 Office: Tex Women's U Dept Nutrition and Food Sci 1130 M.D. Anderson Blvd Houston TX 77030

RADFORD, ALBERT ERNEST, botany educator, plant taxonomist; b. Augusta, Ga., Jan. 25, 1918; s. Albert Furman and Eloise Harriet (Moseley) R.; m. Laurie Marguerite Stewart, Oct. 10, 1941; children: David Eugene, John Stewart, Linda Katherine Radford Vinson. B.S., Furman U., 1939; Ph.D. in Botany, U. N.C.-Chapel Hill, 1948. Lab. asst. Furman U., 1938-39; teaching asst. botany U. N.C., Chapel Hill, 1946-49, instr., 1949-53, asst. prof., 1953-58, assoc. prof., 1958—, prof., 1960—, former dir. herbarium, sr. prof. Author: Manual of the Vascular Flora of the Carolinas, 1968, Vascular Plant Systematics, 1974, Potential Ecological Natural Landmarks, 1975, Natural Heritage, 1981. Chmn. bd. Highlands Biol. Sta.; trustee N.C. Nature Conservancy. Served to capt. U.S. Army, 1941-46. Decorated Croix de Guerre avec Palme; Order of Leopold Belgium; Croix de Guerre avec Etoile d'Argent France; recipient Tanner award U. N.C., 1956; Conservation award-Oak Leaf award Nature Conservancy, 1978. Mem. N.C. Acad. Scis., Assn. Southeastern Biologists (Meritorious Teaching award 1978), Am. Soc. Plant Taxonomists, Internat. Assn. Plant Taxonomists, AAAS. Republican. Presbyterian. Current Work: Plant systematics. Subspecialties: Systematics; Taxonomy. Home: 111 Purefoy Rd Chapel Hill NC 27514 Office: U N C 402 Coker Hall Chapel Hill NC 27514

RADFORD, KENNETH CHARLES, metallurgical engineer, researcher; b. Manchester, Eng., July 1, 1941; came to U.S., 1968, naturalized, 1982; s. Frederick Owen and Evelyn Vivian (James) R.; children—Amanda, Joanna, Celia. B.Sc., Imperial Coll., London, 1963, Ph.D., 1967. Assoc. Royal Sch. Mines, London U., 1963; mem. research staff Imperial Coll., London, 1966-68; sr. engr. Westinghouse Research & Devel. Ctr., Pitts., 1968-78, fellow engr., 1978-84, adv. engr., 1984, mgr. fuel cycle and ceramic tech., 1984—. Contbr. articles to profl. publs. Patentee in field. Mem. Instn. Metallurgists, Am. Ceramic Soc. Current work: Nuclear materials; ceramics; composites; electrical ceramics; sensors; nuclear fuels. Subspecialties: Nuclear engineering; Ceramics. Office: Westinghouse Research & Devel Ctr 1310 Beulah Rd Pittsburgh PA 15235

RADFORD, STANLEY FRITZ, theoretical physicist, physics educator; b. Detroit, Sept. 23, 1952; s. Fritz L. and Robie (Lawrence) R.; m. Pamela T. Cameron, Aug. 22, 1976; children—Diane Katherine, Laura Elise. B.S., Mich. State U., 1976, Ph.D., Wayne State U., 1980. Postdoctoral research assoc. physics and astronomy Wayne State U., Detroit, 1980—; adj. prof. physics U. Detroit, 1984. Contbr. articles to profl. jours. Mem. Am. Phys. Soc., Sigma Xi. Current work: Quantum field theory; color confinement in quantum chromodynamics; quark-antiquark potentials and spectroscopy; quantum electrodynamics. Subspecialties: Particle physics; Theoretical physics. Office: Dept Physics and Astronomy Wayne State U Detroit MI 48202

RADHAKRISHNAMURTHY, BHANDARU, biochemistry educator; b. Vemulapalli, India, July 1, 1928; came to U.S., 1961, naturalized, 1984; s. Rajeswararao and Sathyavathi (Banda) Bhandaru; m. Sulochana Yallapragada, Feb. 20, 1983; m. Sakuntala Kandukuri, Sept. 3, 1953 (dec. Nov. 1980); children—Rajeswararao, Uma, Hema, Srinivas. B.S., Nizam Coll., 1951; M.S., Osmania U., 1953, Ph.D., 1958. Lectr., Osmania U., Hyderabad, India, 1953-61; asst. prof. La. State U. Sch. Medicine, New Orleans, 1963-68, assoc. prof., 1968-74, prof. biochemistry, 1974—; mem. research grants rev. com. Am. Heart Assn. La., New Orleans, 1971-79, mem. med. student research com., 1979—. Contbr. numerous sci. articles to profl. jours. Pres., Hindu Temple Soc. New Orleans, 1979-83, trustee, 1979—. Mem. Am. Soc. Bio. Chemistry, Am. Chem. Soc., AAAS, Am. Soc. Exptl. Biol. Sci., Soc. Complex Carbohydrates. Current work: Biochemistry of cardiovascular diseases. Subspecialties: Biochemistry (medicine); Biochemistry (biology). Home: 6568 Milne Blvd New Orleans LA 70124 Office: Dept Medicine La State U Sch Medicine 1542 Tulane Ave New Orleans LA 70112

RADOSKI, HENRY ROBERT, physicist, govt. phys. sci. adminstr.; b. Jersey City, Aug. 18, 1936; s. Henry Thomas and Stephanie Agatha (Gasior) Radozycki; m. Elizabeth Ann Patton, June 27, 1959; children: Raymond Regis, Henry Zachary, Derek Peter. B.S. in Physics, Holy Cross Coll., 1958; Ph.D. in Physics, M.I.T., 1963. Research assoc. prof. geophysics Boston Coll., Weston, Mass., 1963-68; research physicist Air Force Cambridge (Mass.) Research Labs., 1968-76; program mgr. Air Force Office Sci. Research, Washington, 1976—. Contbr. articles to profl. jours.; Co-editor: Physics of the Magnetosphere, 1968. Mem. Am. Phys. Soc., Am. Geophys. Union, Am. Astron. Soc., Sigma Xi. Current Work: Plans, develops and manages a program in astronomy and astrophysics, including solar, interplanetary, magnetospheric, ionospheric physics and aeronomy relevant to USAF. Subspecialties: Plasma physics; Satellite studies. Office: Air Force Office Sci Research/NP Bldg 410 Bolling AFB Washington DC 20332

RADTKE, SCHRADE FRED, metallurgist, metals company executive; b. Mpls., Aug. 21, 1919; s. Schrade Fred and Adelheid R.; m. Genevieve N., Apr. 18, 1942; children—Schrade F., Mark L. B.S. in Organic Chemistry and Engring Adminstrn., MIT, 1940, Ph.D. in Metallurgy and Inorganic Chemistry, 1949. Chemistry instr. MIT, Cambridge, Mass., 1946-49; research supr. E.I. DuPont, Newport, Del., 1949-53; dir. metall. research labs. Reynolds Metals Co., Richmond, Va., 1953-58; pres., chief exec. officer Internat. Lead Zinc Research Orgn., N.Y.C., 1958-84; pres. Cosmos Engring, Inc., New Canaan, Conn., 1984—. Contbr. articles to profl. jours. Numerous patents in field. Trustee R.I. Sch. Design, Transp. Mus. Served to lt. col., U.S. Army, 1942-45. Recipient Wendel Wilkie award Freedom House, 1949; Ordnance award; MIT scholar; U.S. Rubber fellow, 1948-49. Mem. AIME, Assn. Iron and Steel Engrs., Am. Chem. Soc., Am. Soc. for Metals. Republican. Club: Dorclan. Current work: Consultant, chemist, metallurgist, inventor of several patents, Am. Mgmt. Assn. book on Cooperative Research and Development, 1984. Subspecialties: Inorganic chemistry; Corrosion. Home: 76 Soundview Ln New Canaan CT 06840 Office: Cosmos Engring Inc 76 Soundview Ln New Canaan CT 06840

RADZIEMSKI, LEON JOSEPH, physicist; b. Worcester, Mass., June 18, 1937; s. Leon Joseph and Josephine Elizabeth (Janczukowicz) R.; married; children: Michael Leon, Timothy Joseph. B.S., Coll. Holy Cross, Worcester, Mass., 1958; M.S., Purdue U., 1961, Ph.D., 1964. Staff physicist Los Alamos Nat. Lab., 1967-83; head dept. physics N. Mex. State U, 1983—; vis. scientist Laboratoire Aime Cotton, Orsay, Frances, 1974-75; vis. assoc. prof. dept. nuclear engring. U. Fla., Gainesville, 1978-79. Book editor. Contbr. articles to profl. jours. Served with USAF, 1964-67. Mem. Am. Phys. Soc., Optical Soc. Am., Soc. Applied Spectroscopy, Laser Inst. Am. Patentee in field. Current Work: Applications of lasers and spectroscopy, laser spectrochemistry, laser-induced breakdown spectroscopy, plasma spectroscopy. Subspecialties: Atomic and molecular physics; Laser spectroscopy. Home: 4709 Falcon Dr Las Cruces NM 88001 Office: Dept Physics Box 3D N Mex State U Las Cruces NM 88003

RADZIKOWSKI, PAWEL, computer information science educator, researcher; b. Gluszyca, Poland, Oct. 17, 1948; came to U.S., 1977; s. Wladyslaw and Danuta (Kielkiewicz) R. M.S. in Chemistry, Warsaw U., Poland, 1972, M.S. in Math. and Computer Sci., 1974; M.B.A., Fordham U., 1979; Ph.D., Wroclaw Econ. Acad., Poland, 1980. Programmer analyst Inst. Electrotechnics, Warsaw, 1972-77; system analyst Coopers & Lybrand, N.Y.C., 1977-79; div. mgr. Inst. Chem. Econs., Warsaw, 1979-81; asst. prof. computer info. sci. Seton Hall U., South Orange, N.J., 1981—; contract researcher Warsaw U. Inst. Informatics, 1974-77; cons. Inst. Teleadiotechnics, Warsaw, 1975-77. Contbr. numerous papers to profl. publs. Author discriminative optimization method, decision support expert system: KOMIS; co-author fin. forecasting system: AutoPak; also designer various software. Mem. Assn. Computing Machinery, Am. Math. Soc., Assn. Automated Reasoning, Ops. Research Soc. Am. (coordinator SIG artificial intelligence), Soc. Indsl. and Applied Math. Current work: Decision support expert systems; discriminative optimization. Subspecialties: Operations research (mathematics); Artificial intelligence. Office: Seton Hall U Sch Bus South Orange NJ 07079

RAE, WILLIAM HOWARD, JR., aeronautical engineer, educator; b. Tacoma, Nov. 16, 1927; s. William Howard and Evelyn Mae (Goddard) R.; m. Roberta Lee Fairless, July 11, 1953; 1 child, Richard. B.S., U. Wash., 1953, M.S., 1959. Supr. aero. lab. U. Wash., Seattle, 1956-66, assoc. dir. aero. lab., 1966—, assoc. prof. aero. and astronautics, 1966—; cons. USAF, Tullahoma, Tenn., 1979-80. Author: Low Speed Wind T, 1984. Contbr. articles to profl. publs. Served as sgt. USAF, 1946-49. Grantee NASA-Langley Lab., 1964-78, U.S. Army, 1974-77. Mem. AIAA, Subsonic Aerodynamic Testing Assn. (founding mem., vice-chmn. 1984-85), Wildlife Commn. Wash. (pres. 1967-69). Current work: Low speed aerodynamics and wind tunnel testing. Subspecialties: Aeronautical engineering; Non-destructive testing. Office: Aero Lab U Wash FS 10 Seattle WA 98195

RAEDEKE, KENNETH JOHN, biologist; b. Evanston, Ill., May 6, 1948; s. Gerhard Raedeke and Eloise Loraine (Meyer) Scheffel. B.S., U. Mont., 1970; Ph.D., U. Wash., 1979. Research assoc. U. Mont., Missoula, 1967-70; regional biologist Corp., Nacional Forestal, Punta Arenas, Chile, 1972-75; research assoc. U. Wash., Seattle, 1971, grad. research assoc., 1975-79, research asst., prof. biology, 1979—. Pres., owner Raedeke Assocs., Seattle, 1981—. Contbr. articles to profl. jours., chpts. to books. Vol. Peace Corps, Chile, 1972-75. Fellow Pres.'s, 1967-68, Anderson, 1976, Merrill, 1979. Mem. Am. Soc. Mammalogists, Pacific NW Bird Mammalogists Soc. (v.p. 1984), Ecol. Soc. Am. (cert.), Wildlife Soc., NW Sci. Assn. Current work: Population dynamics of large mammals; modelling population response to habitat change; wildlife conservation; wetlands succession and management. Subspecialties: Ecology (biology); Ecosystems analysis. Home: 118 N 41st St Seattle WA 98103 Office: Coll Forest Resources U Wash Seattle WA 98195

RAEDEKE, LINDA DISMORE, research geologist; b. Great Falls, Mont., Aug. 20, 1950; d. Albert Browning and Madge (Hogan) Dismore; m. Kenneth John Raedeke, Dec. 26, 1971 (div. 1982). B.A. in History, U. Wash., 1971, M.Sc. in Geology, 1979, Ph.d., 1982. Geomorphologist, park planner Corporacion Nacional Forestal, Punta Arenas, Chile, 1972-74; glacial geologist Empresa Nacional del Petroleo, Punta Areanas, 1972-75; geologist Food and Agr. Orgn. UN, Punta Areanas, 1974; geologist Lamont-Doherty geol. obs. Columbia U., Tierra del Fuego, Chile, 1974-75; wetlands evaluation project coordinator Wash. Dept. Agr. U. Wash., Seattle, 1975-76; geomorphology cons. Okanogan County Planning, Oceanographic Inst. Wash., Seattle, 1976; curator remote sensing applications lab. U. Wash., 1976-77; geol. cons. Amoco, Denver, 1978; petrologist Lamont-Doherty geol. obs., 1979; geol. cons. Empresa Minera de Mantos Blancos, Tierra del Fuego, 1980; geol. research asst. U. Wash., Seattle, 1977-81; exploration geologist Chevron Resouces Co., Denver, 1982-84; research geologist Chevron Oil Field Research Co., LaHabra, Calif., 1984—. Contbr. articles to profl. jours. Mem. Am. Geophys. Union, Geol. Soc. Am., Mineral Soc. Am., Denver Region E Exploration Geologists Soc. Current work: Organic geochemist working on petroleum exploration and development. Subspecialty: Geochemistry. Office: Chevron Oil Field Research Co PO Box 446 LaHabra CA 90631

RAFF, HERSHEL, physiologist, educator, endocrinologist researcher; b. Paterson, N.J., May 23, 1953; s. Emanuel and Ruth (Novack) R.; m. Judy Lynn Kornfeld, June 27, 1976; 1 child, Jonathan Louis. B.A., Union Coll., Schenectady, 1975; Ph.D., Johns Hopkins U., 1981. Fellow U. Calif.-San Francisco, 1980-83; asst. prof. medicine and physiology Med. Coll. Wis., Milw., 1983—; dir. endocrine research St. Luke's Hosp., Milw., 1983—. Contbr. numerous articles to profl. jours., 1981—. NIH Nat. Research Service award, 1980-83; Am. Heart Assn. grantee-in-aid, 1984. Mem. Am. Physiol. Soc., Endocrine Soc., Sigma Xi, Delta Omega. Current work: Hypoxia-lung disease; pituitary-adrenal studies; renin-angio-aldosterone. Subspecialties: Physiology (medicine); Neuroendocrinology. Office: St Luke's Hosp 2900 W Oklahoma Ave Milwaukee WI 53215

RAFFE, MARC ROYE, veterinarian, educator, anesthesiologist; b. Chgo., Nov. 5, 1950; s. Philip and Mildred (Bain) R.; m. Mayda Janis Kantor, Jan. 5, 1975; children—Jennifer, Daniel. B.S., U. Ill.-Urbana, 1973, D.V.M., 1975; M.S., Purdue U., 1978. Diplomate Am. Coll. Veterinary Anesthesiologists. Intern, Auburn U., 1975-76; surgical resident Purdue U., 1976-78; resident in anesthesia U. Minn., St. Paul, 1978-80, asst. prof., 1980-84, assoc. prof. veterinary medicine, anesthesiology, 1984—; mem. staff Infant Pulmonary Research Ctr., Children's Hosp., St. Paul, 1981—; cons. anesthesia St. Paul-Ramsey Hosp., St. Paul, 1980—. Assoc. editor: Handbook of Veterinary Procedures and Emergency Treatment, 4th edit., 1985; contbr. articles to sci. jours., chpts. to books. Mem. Am. Veterinary Med. Assn., Am. Soc. Anesthesiologists, Internat. Anesthesia Research Soc., Phi Zeta. Jewish. Current work: Pain research; parenteral nutrition; ventilation support of critical illness. Subspecialty: Surgery (veterinary medicine). Office: Small Animal Clin Scis Univ Minn 1352 Boyd Ave Saint Paul MN 55108

RAGAVAN, VANAJA VIJAYA, internist; b. Madras, India, Mar. 7, 1949; came to U.S., 1970, naturalized, 1975; d. M. D. Vijaya and Vimala (Vasudevan) R.; m. Robert Jim Berrier, June 2, 1979; 1 son, Justin Vikram. A.B., Harvard U., 1972; M.D., N.Y. U., 1976. Diplomate: Am. Bd. Internal Medicine. Intern Kings County Hosp., Bklyn., 1976-77; resident in medicine, 1977-79; fellow in endocrinology Columbia U.-Presby N. Med. Centers, N.Y.C., 1976-81, U. Pa. Sch. Medicine, Phila., 1981-82; staff physician Coatesville (Pa.) VA Med. Center, 1982—; mem. staff dept. medicine Wilmington (Del.) Med. Center, 1982—. USPHS tng. grantee, 1979-81, 81-82. Mem. Am. Fedn. Clin. Research. Current Work: Clinical and basic investigation in neuroendocrinology and reproductive endocrinology; medical practice limited to general endocrinology and metabolism. Subspecialty: Neuroendocrinology. Home: 51 Chapel Hill Rd Media PA 19063 Office: Coatesville VA Med Center Coatesville PA 19320 Heritage Profl Plaza Suite 8 Wilmington DE 19808

RAGHAVENDRA, KRISHNAMURTHY, science researcher; b. Bangalore, Karnataka, India, Feb. 18, 1947; came to U.S., 1980; s. S. Krishnamurthy and K. Gokilam; m. Saraswathi Ramachandran, June 18, 1972; children—Sangeetha, Srilatha. B.S., Bangalore U., India, 1965, M.S., 1968; Ph.D., Indian Inst. Sci., Bangalore, 1978. Instr. physics U. Agrl. Scis., Bangalore, 1969-74; research assoc. Indian Inst. Sci., Bangalore, 1978-79; postdoctoral fellow I.R.B.M., C.N.R.S. U., Paris, 1979-80, SUNY, Albany, 1980-81, U. Conn., Storrs, 1981—. Indian Inst. Sci. fellow, 1974-78. Mem. Biophysical Soc. Current work: Structure, function and assembly of biopolymers and research in biophysical studies of Tobacco Mosaic Virus assembly. Subspecialties: Plant virology; Biophysical chemistry. Home: 61 Cheney Dr Storrs CT 06268 Office: U Conn U-125 Biochemistry Biophysics Storrs CT 06268

RAGHEB, MAGDI, nuclear engineering researcher and educator; b. Nov. 25, 1946; m. Barbara Rose Wesolek, Feb. 16, 1980. M.Sc., U. Wis., 1974, Ph.D., 1978. Research asst. dept. nuclear engring. U. Wis.-Madison, 1973-78, post-doctoral project assoc. dept. nuclear engring., 1978-79, cons., 1979-80; asst. prof. dept. nuclear engring. U. Ill., Urbana-Champaign, 1979—; vis. research scientist Brookhaven Nat. Lab., Upton, N.Y., 1975, cons., 1981—; research assoc. Oak Ridge Nat. Lab., 1978. Contbr. articles, reports, revs. to profl. jours. Mem. Am. Nuclear Soc. (program com. 1979—), AAAS, AAUP, N.Y. Acad. Scis., Sigma Xi. Current Work: Advanced energy systems; fusion, fission reactor design; advanced fusion fuel cycles; transport theory; monte carlo theory; neutronics and shielding design of fusion reactors; numerical computations in energy research. Subspecialties: Nuclear engineering; Nuclear fusion. Home: 401 Edgebrook Dr Champaign IL 61802 Office: U Ill Nuclear Engring Lab 103 S Goodwin Ave Urbana IL 61801

RAGHUNATHAN, RENGACHARI, biochemist, educator, researcher; b. Amoor, India, Mar. 22, 1943; s. Rengachari and Sakunthala R.; m. Kamala Raghunathan, Dec. 1, 1972; children: Anand, Adithya. B.S. in Agr., Mysore U., 1962; M.S. in Microbiology, Annamalai U., 1965; Ph.D. in Biochemistry, U. Bombay, 1974, D.I.M. in Mgmt., 1973; H.M.B. in Homeopathic Medicine, U. Bangalore, 1960; D.H.M.S. in Homeopathic Medicine, U. Madras, 1963. Research asst. Tb Chemotherapy Centre, Madras, India, 1965-68; jr. sci. officer Bhabha Atomic Research Centre, Bombay, India, 1968-72, sr. sci. officer, biochemistry, 1972-75; instr. ob-gyn Meharry Med. Coll., Nashville, 1976-78, asst. prof. ob-gyn, 1979—, asst. prof., dir. div. research dept. ob-gyn, 1985—. Contbr. articles to nat., internat. profl. jours. and popular papers and mags. Bd. dirs. March of Dimes, Nashville, 1976-78; trustee Hindu Cultural Ctr. Tenn., 1981—. Fellow Phytopath. Soc.; mem. Internat. Soc. Preventive

Oncology, Microbiol. Soc., Soc. Biol. Chemists. Current Work: Plant disease resistance mechanism; prenatal diagnosis of inborn errors; carbohydrate metabolism and regulation; enzymology, proteins, clinical chemistry. Subspecialties: Plant pathology; Developmental biology. Home: 822 Kendall Dr Nashville TN 37209 Office: Dept Ob Gy Meharry Med Coll Nashville TN 37208

RAGOTZKIE, ROBERT AUSTIN, oceanography educator; b. Albany, N.Y., Sept. 13, 1924; s. Robert W. and Edith N. (Van Wormer) R.; m. Elizabeth M. Post, Aug. 1, 1925; children: Peter D., Kim E., Susan J. B.S. in Biology, Rutgers U., 1948, M.S. in Sanitation, 1950; Ph.D. in Zoology-Meteorology, U. Wis.-Madison, 1953. Asst. prof., then assoc. prof. biology, dir. Marine Inst., U. Ga., Athens, 1954-59; from asst. prof. to prof. meteorology U. Wis.-Madison, 1959—; dir. Sea Grant Inst., 1968—. Author 1 book, numerous sci. articles. Served to 2d lt. USAF, 1943-45. Decorated Air medal. Fellow AAAS; mem. Am. Meteorol. Soc., Am. Geophys. Union, Am. Soc. Limnology and Oceanography, Internat. Soc. Limnology, Internat. Assn. Great Lakes Research (past pres.). Current Work: Great Lakes limnology, heat budgets of lakes. Subspecialties: Oceanography; Aquatic ecology. Home: 2334 Tanager Trail Madison WI 53711 Office: 1800 University Ave Madison WI 53705

RAGSDALE, CHARLES WILLIAM, electronics engineer, consultant; b. St. Petersberg, Fla., July 24, 1943; s. William Edward and Ida Marie (Chamberlain) R.; m. Barbara Louise Cannard, Nov. 2, 1969; 1 child, Melody. B.E.E., U. Fla., 1966; M.S. in Bioengring., U. Wyo., 1972. Design engr. Harry Diamond Labs, Washington, 1966-71; engr. specialist Bourns Life Systems, Riverside, Calif., 1972-75; program mgr. Gulton Electro Optics, Santa Barbara, Calif., 1975-77; mgr. biotronics Engring. Cavitron/Syntel, Irvine, Calif., 1977-79; sr. research specialist, dir. electronics engring. Cordis Dow/Seratronics, Concord, Calif., 1979-83; mgr. electronics engring. Mistogen Equipment Co., Oakland, Calif., 1983-84; v.p. engring., quality analystist Seratronics Ins., Concord, 1984—; free-lance cons. for various firms. Contbr. articles to prof. jours. Church organist in various chs. Bay area. Mem. IEEE. Current works: Development of medical systems in the areas of cardiac monitoring surgical monitoring, respiratory therapy, ophthalmology, dialysis. Subspecialties: Biomedical engineering; Electronics. Office: Seratronics Inc 4090 Pike Ln Concord CA 94520

RAHM, DAVID CHARLES, physicist; b. Ironwood, Mich., Dec. 1, 1927; s. David W. and Stella M. (Brown) R.; m. Laura Winchester, 1951 (div. 1980); children—Elizabeth Rahm Moog, Kent D.; m. Corinne Levrat, Jan. 2, 1981. Ph.B., U. Chgo., 1948, S.B., 1949; M.S., U. Mich., 1951, Ph.D., 1956. Asst. physicist to sr. physicist Brookhaven Nat. Lab., Upton, N.Y., 1954—; vis. scientist Saclay, France, 1960-61, CERN, Geneva, 1968-69, 75-76. Contbr. articles to sci. jours. Served with USN, 1945-46. Fellow Am. Phys. Soc. Current work: Particle physics, detector development, superconducting magnets, particle accelerators. Subspecialties: Particle physics; Cryogenics. Home: 6 Hawkins Ln Brookhaven NY 11719 Office: Brookhaven Nat Lab Dept Physics Upton NY 11973

RAHMAN, IFTEKHAR, engineering educator, researcher; b. Dhaka, Bangladesh, Feb. 1, 1952; came to U.S., 1971; s. Latifar and Jahanara (Begum) R.; m. Erika Marsilio, July 15, 1983. B.S.E.E., Northeastern U., Boston, 1975, M.S.E.E., 1976, Ph.D., Elec. Engring., in 1981. Instr. elec. engring. Northeastern U., Boston, 1976-81, asst. prof., 1982-85; mem. tech. staff A.T.&T. Bell Labs., 1985—; engring. specialist CNR, Inc., Needham, Mass., 1981-82; cons. Milcom, Needham, 1983-85. Mem. IEEE. Current work: Application of communication theory in coding and modulation, signal processing, detection and estimation, communication systems analysis. Subspecialty: Electrical engineering. Home: 72 Crimson Rd Billerica MA 01866 Office: AT&T Bell Labs 1600 Osgood St North Andover MA 01845

RAHMAT-SAMII, YAHYA, research scientist, consultant, lecturer; b. Tehran, Iran, Aug. 20, 1948; came to U.S., 1971, naturalized, 1984; s. Kareem and Derakhshi (Ameri) R-S. B.S. E.E. with highest honors, U. Tehran, 1970; M.S. E.E., U. Ill., 1972, Ph.D. in E.E., 1975; postgrad. short courses, Boston U., 1977, George Washington U., 1980, Calif. Inst. Tech., 1980-85. research asst. electromagnetics lab. U. Ill., Urbana, 1971-75, vis. postdoctoral research assoc., 1975-76, vis. prof., 1976-77; cons. NASA-Jet Propulsion Lab. satellite antenna project, 1977-78; research engr., mem. tech. staff NASA-Jet Propulsion Lab., Calif. Inst. Tech., Pasadena, 1978—; nat., internat. lectr. confs., univs., industry; apptd. research council rep. by Nat. Acad. Scis. to confs. Internat. Union Radio Sci., 1981, 84, U.S. del., 1978-84, session chmn., 1980; invited lectr. NATO Advanced Inst., 1979. Guest editor spl. issue Radio Sci., 1984; nat. guest jour. reviewer for antenna papers, 1981-84; assoc. editor newsletter Soc. Antennas and Propagation IEEE, 1976-80; reviewer various tech. jours.; contbr. chpts. to 4 books in field; author over 100 sci. papers, tech. reports. U. Tehran scholar, 1967-70; Henry George Booker fellow, Nat. Acad. Scis., 1984 conf.; recipient NASA cert. recognition, 1981-85. Fellow IEEE (nat. disting. lectr. 1982—, mem. AP-S Ad com., 1981—, assoc. editor Antennas and Propagation Transactions 1980-83, mem. prize papers awards com. 1980, mem., chmn. coms. various symposia), Soc. Microwave Theory and Techniques, Soc. Antennas and Propagation, Electromagnetics Soc. (dir. 1980-84), Union Radio Union, AIAA, Sigma Xi, Eta Kappa Nu. Research or work interests: Advanced antenna technology for space and satellite communication programs and ground stations, large space systems and space station technology, microwave near-field and holography techniques for measuring large antennas and mathematical, analytical and computer modeling in electromagnetics. . Office: NASA/Jet Propulsion Lab 4800 Oak Grove Dr Pasadena CA 91109

RAHN, HERMANN, physiologist; b. East Lansing, Mich., July 5, 1912; s. Otto and Bell S. (Farrand) R.; m. Katharine F. Wilson, Aug. 29, 1939; children: Robert F., Katharine B. A.B., Cornell U., 1933; student, U. Kiel, 1933-34; Ph.D., U. Rochester, 1938, D.Sc. (hon.), 1973; Docteur Honoris Causa, U. Paris, 1964; LL.D. (hon.), Yonsei U., Korea, 1965; Titulo de Profesor Honorario U. Peruana Cayetano Heredia, Peru, 1980; Dr. Medicinae h.c., U. Bern, Switzerland, 1981. NRC fellow Harvard U., 1938-39; instr. physiology U. Wyo., 1939-41; asst. physiology Sch. Medicine, U. Rochester, 1941-42, instr., 1942-46, asst. prof., 1946-50, asso. prof., vice chmn. dept., 1950-56; Lawrence D. Bell prof. physiology, chmn. dept. Sch. Medicine, U. Buffalo (now SUNY-Buffalo), 1956-73, distinguished prof. physiology, 1973—; vis. prof. Med. Faculty San Marcos U., Lima, Peru, 1955, Dartmouth Med. Sch., 1962, Lab. de Physiologie Respiratoire, CNRS, Strasbourg, France, 1971, Max-Planck-Inst. für experimentelle Medizin, Göttingen, W.Ger., 1977; mem. adv. com. biol. sci. Air Force Office Sci. Research and Devel., 1958-64; mem. physiol. study sect. NIH, 1958-62; mem. working committee space sci. bd. Nat. Acad. Sci.-NRC, 1962-65; mem. gen. med. research program project com. NIH, 1964-67; mem. research career award com. Nat. Inst. Gen. Med. Scis., 1968-72; cardiopulmonary adv. com. Nat. Heart Inst., 1968-71; mem. nat. adv. bd. R/V Alpha Helix, 1968-71; chmn. com. on underwater physiology and medicine NRC, 1972-74. Author: (with W.O. Fenn) A Graphical Analysis of the Respiratory Gas Exchange, 1955, (with others) Blood Gases: Hemoglobin, Base Excess and Maldistribution, 1973; editorial bd.: Am. Jour. Physiology, Jour. Applied Physiology, 1953-62, sect. editor for respiration, 1962, bd. publ. trustees, 1959-62; editor: (with W.O. Fenn) Handbook of Physiology-Respiration, Vols. I, II, 1964-65, Physiology of Breath-Hold Diving and the Ama of Japan, 1965; (with G.C. Whittow) Seabird Energetics; (with O. Prakash) Acid-base Regulation and Body Temperature. Recipient Sr. U.S. Scientist award Alexander von Humboldt Found., 1976. Mem. Am. Inst. Biol. Sci. (adv. com. physiol. 1957-64, adv. panel 1967-71), Am. Physiol. Soc. (council 1960-65, pres. 1963-64), Nat. Acad. Sci., Inst. Medicine, Nat. Acad. Sci., Harvey Soc. (hon.), Soc. Exptl. Biology and Medicine, Internat. Union Physiol. Scis. (council 1965-74, U.S. nat. com. 1966-74, v.p. 1971-74, exec. com. 1971-74), Am. Soc. Zoologists, Am. Acad. Arts and Sci., Sigma Xi. Research in pulmonary, comparative and environmental physiology. Current Work: Problems of gas exchange. Subspecialties: Animal physiology; Comparative physiology. Home: 75 Windsor Ave Buffalo NY 14209

RAICHEL, DANIEL RICHTER, engineering educator; b. Paterson, N.J., Aug. 22, 1935; s. Israel and Regina Pearl (Richter) R.; m. Geri Wahrman, Mar. 23, 1967; children—Adam Mark, Dina Karen. B.S. in Mech. Engring., Rensselaer Poly. Inst., 1957; S.M. in Nuclear Engring., MIT, 1958; M.E., Columbia U., 1962; D. Engring. Sci., NYU, 1970. Registered profl. engr., N.J., N.Y., Mo., Ill. Asst. project engr. Curtiss Wright Corp., Wood-Ridge, N.J., 1960-62; instr. Case-Western Res., Cleve., 1962-63; instr. mech. engring., adj. prof. N.J. Inst. Tech., Newark, 1965-67, 78-81; prof. engring., Pratt Inst., Bklyn., 1983—; prin. Raichel Tech. Group, Midland Park, N.J., 1980—; prin. mech. engr. Lord & Grayson Inc., Fair Lawn, N.J., 1982—; cons., 1964—. Author, translator: (with others) Applied Kinetics, 1967; contbr. articles to profl. jours. Patentee wide dispersion speaker system. Tech. advisor. Gifted Child Soc., Glen Rock, N.J., 1981—. Fellow Cornell U., AEC at MIT. Mem. ASME, Am. Phys. Soc., Acoustical Soc. Am., Audio Engring. Soc., Sigma Xi, Tau Beta Pi, Pi Tau Sigma. Current work: Research in acoustics; robotics; non-newtonian fluid mechanics; theoretical physics. Subspecialties: Fluid mechanics; Acoustics. Home: 532 Spencer Dr Wyckoff NJ 07481 Office: Pratt Inst Sch Engring 200 Willoughby Ave Brooklyn NY 11205

RAINNIE, WILLIAM OGG, JR., ocean engineer; b. Ashtabula, Ohio, Apr. 27, 1924; s. William Ogg and Beryl Naomi (McBride) R.; m. Sara Ann Cross, July 25, 1925; children: William Ward, Michael Curtis. B.S., U.S. Naval Acad., 1946. Commd. ensign U.S. Navy, 1946, advanced through grades to lt., 1952, resigned, 1954; project engr. Fairbanks Morse & Co., Beloit, Wis., 1954-57, tech. rep., Washington, 1957-60; tech. asst. Nat. Acad. Sci., Washington, 1960-61; ocean engr. Woods Hole (Mass.) Oceanographic Inst., 1961-77; chief engring. div. Data Buoy Office NOAA, NASA Space Tech. Labs. station, Miss., 1977—; Program mgr. deep research vehicle Alvin, 1964. Vestryman Trinity Episcopal Ch., Pass Christian, Miss., 1977—. Recipient civilian service award USN, 1966, 73. Mem. Am. Soc. Naval Engrs., Marine Tech. Soc. Club: Pass Christian Yacht (commodore 1982, dir. 1979—). Lodge: Rotary (sec. Falmouth, Mass. 1973). Current Work: Engineering activity to develop, test and operate environmental monitoring systems for marine uses. Subspecialty: Ocean engineering. Home: 104 Hursey Ave Pass Christian MS 39571 Office: NOAA Data Buoy Ctr NSTL Station MS 39529

RAJA, SRINIVASA N., anesthesiologist, researcher; b. Madras, India, Nov. 5, 1950; s. Venkataraman and Sarada S.; m. Geetha Rajam, Feb. 7, 1979. M.B.B.S., Patna U., India, 1974. Diplomate: Am. Bd. Anesthesiology. Resident in anesthesiology U. Wash., Seattle, 1977-79; research fellow U. Va., 1979-81; asst. prof. Johns Hopkins U. Sch. Medicine, Balt., 1981—. Contbr. articles to profl. jours. Recipient award Nat. Inst. Gen. Med. Scis., 1979-81, New Investigator research award, 1984-86. Mem. Am. Soc. Aneshtesiologists, Internat. Assn. Study Pain, Soc. Neurosci., Am. Soc. Regional Anesthesiology, Internat. Anesthesia Research Soc. Current Work: Mechanism of action of drugs of abuse; interactions of drugs of abuse and anesthetics; psychophysical and neurophysiological aspects of peripheral neural mechanism of pain; effects of anesthetics on response properties of primary afferents. Subspecialties: Neuropharmacology; Neurophysiology. Office: John Hopkins Hosp 600 N Wolfe St Meyer 8-134 Baltimore MD 21205

RAJAN, KANNAN RAMALINGAM, physician, researcher; b. Bangalore, India, July 16, 1931; came to U.S., 1963, naturalized, 1981; s. Ramalingam and Amarthammal (Amartham) R.; m. Kalanidhi Doraisawmy, Oct. 15, 1960. B.Sc., St. Joseph's Coll., Bangalore, 1951; M.B., B.S., Mysore Med. Coll., 1958. Resident med. officer Misericordia Gen. Hosp., Winnipeg, Man., Can., 1969-72; staff physician Vets. Hosp., Batavia, N.Y., 1972-73; practice medicine St. Joseph's Hosp., Toronto, Ont., Can., 1973-74; staff physician VA Med. Ctr., Long Beach, Calif., 1974—. Contbr. articles to profl. jours. Recipient cert. Am. Vets. World War II, Korea and Vietnam, 1976, cert. Jewish War Vets. U.S.A., 1976, 78, 79; named Physician of Year Jewish War Vets. U.S.A., 1982. Fellow Royal Coll. Physicians and Surgeons Can., Am. Coll. Gastroenterology; mem. ACP, Am. Fedn. Clin. Research, AMA, N.Y. Acad. Scis. Democrat. Hindu. Current Work: Colonic function in spinal cord injury patients. Subspecialties: Gastroenterology; Internal medicine. Home: 14021 Montgomery Dr Westminster CA 92683 Office: VA Med Center 5901 E 7th St Long Beach CA 90822

RAJANBABU, T. V., chemical researcher; b. Kottayam, Kerala, India, Feb. 5, 1950; came to U.S., 1972; s. N.V. Kurup and K. Thankamma; m. Latha, Nov. 26, 1978; 1 child, Arun. B.Sc., Kerala U., Trivandrum, India, 1969; M.Sc., Indian Inst. Tech., Madras, 1971; Ph.D., Ohio State U., 1977. Research fellow, Harvard U., 1978-79; mem. research staff Central Research and Devel. Dept., E.I. duPont, Wilmington, Del., 1980—. Contbr. articles to profl. jours. Co-discoverer of group transfer polymerization. Eastman Kodak fellow, 1975-76. Mem. Am. Chem. Soc. Current work: Organic synthesis, new methodology for synthesis; organometallic applications, carbohydrate chemistry. Subspecialties: Organic chemistry; Organometallics. Office: Central Research and Devel Dept E I duPont Co E328/208 Exptl Sta Wilmington DE 19898

RAJEEVAKUMAR, T. V., physicist; b. Pandanad, India, Oct. 3, 1952; came to U.S., 1974; s. Velayudhad Pillai Rajeevakumar and Sarojini (Devi) Nair; m. Smita Rajeev Kumar, Jan. 13, 1981. B.S. in Physics, Kerala U., India, 1972; M.S. in Physics, Calicut U., India, 1974; Ph.D. in Physics, Wayne State U., 1979. Research staff mem. IBM Corp., Yorktown Heights, N.Y., 1979—. Contbr. articles to profl. publs. Patentee in field. Recipient Invention Achievement award IBM Corp., 1983, 85. Mem. Am. Phys. Soc., IEEE, Sigma Xi (Outstanding Research Grad. award 1979). Current work: VLSI engineering, design of VSLI logic and memory components, device physics, computer simulation of circuits, device phenomena. Subspecialties: Condensed matter physics; Integrated circuits. Home: 107 Lakeview Ave Scarsdale NY 10583 Office: IBM Watson Research Ctr PO Box 218 Yorktown Heights NY 10598

RAJHATHY, TIBOR, See *Who's Who in America,* 43rd edition.

RAJU, NAMBOORI BHASKARA, biologist, researcher; b. Pothumarru, Andhra Pradesh, India, Jan. 1, 1943; came to U.S., 1974; s. Venkatrama and Suramma (Chintalapati) R.; m. Swarajya Rudraraju, Aug. 20, 1950; children: Geeta, Suja, Meena. M.Sc. in Agr, Banaras Hindu U., 1967; Ph.D., U. Guelph, 1972. Research asso. in biol. scis. Stanford U., 1974—. Contbr. numerous articles to biol. jours. Mem. Mycol. Soc. Am. Current Work: Cytogenetics of fungi, especially Neurospora and the mushroom fungus Coprinus. Subspecialties: Plant genetics; Microbiology. Office: Biol Scis Dept Stanford U Stanford CA 94305

RAKOFF, VIVIAN MORRIS, psychiatrist, educator; b. Capetown, South Africa, Apr. 28, 1928; married, 1959; 3 children. B.A., U. Capetown, 1947, M.A., 1949; M.B., B.S., U. London, 1957; D. Psych., McGill U., Montreal, Que., Can., 1963. Psychologist Tavistock Clinic, 1950-511; house officer in surgery St. Charles Hosp., 1957; house officer in medicine Victoria Hosp., 1958; registrar Groote Schuur Hosp., 1958-61; resident in psychiatry McGill U., 1961-63; assoc. dir. research Jewish Gen. Hosp., 1963-67, asst. prof. and dir. research, 1967-68; from assoc. prof. to prof. psychiatry U. Toronto, Ont., Can., 1968-74, dir. postgrad. edn., 1968-71, prof. psychiat. edn., 1974—, prof. psychiatry, chmn. dept. psychiatry, 1980; now also psychiatrist in chief dept. psychiatry; dir. and psychiatrist in chief Clarke Inst. Psychiatry. Fellow Royal Coll. Physicians (Can.); mem. Am. Psychiat. Assn., Can. Psychiat. Assn., Am. Coll. Psychiatrists. Subspecialty: Psychiatry. Address: 250 College St Toronto ON M5T 1R8 Canada*

RAKOWSKI, ROBERT FRANK, research scientist, physiology educator; b. Rahway, N.J., Oct. 8, 1941; s. Frank Stanley and Helen (Mackowicki) R.; m. Linda Hall Eakin, July 25, 1964; children—Emily, Jennifer, Cara. B. in Chem. Engring., Cornell U., 1964, M. in Engring., 1966; Ph.D., U. Rochester, 1972. Fellow, Yale U., New Haven, Conn., 1972-74, Cambridge U., Eng. 1974-75; asst. prof. Washington U., St. Louis, Mo., 1975-84; assoc. prof. physiology Chgo. Med. Sch., North Chicago, Ill., 1984—; cons. Chgo. Heart Assn., Chgo., 1985—. Contbr. articles to prof. jours. Served to capt., USAF, 1964-68. Research grantee NIH, 1979—, 1983—, Muscular Dystrophy Assn., 1975—. Mem. Marine Biol. Lab. (corp. mem.), Biophys. Soc., Soc. Gen. Physiologists, Am. Soc. Zoologists, AAAS. Current works: Regulation of calcium release in skeletal muscle, voltage dependence of ionic channels and active transport in cells. Subspecialties: Biophysics (biology); Membrane biology. Office: Chgo Med Sch 3333 Green Bay Rd North Chicago IL 60064

RALL, DAVID PLATT, pharmacologist, physician; b. Aurora, Ill., Aug. 3, 1926; s. Edward Everett and Nell (Platt) R.; m. Edith Levy, July 17, 1954; children: Jonathan D., Catharyn E. B.S., North Central Coll., Naperville, Ill., 1946; M.S., Northwestern U., 1948, M.D., Ph.D., 1951. Intern Bellevue Hosp., N.Y.C., 1952-53; commd. officer USPHS, 1953—, asst. surgeon gen., 1971—; sr. investigator Lab. Chem. Pharmacology, Nat. Cancer Inst., NIH, Bethesda, Md., 1953-55, Clin. Pharmacology and Exptl. Therapeutics Service, 1956-58, head service, 1958-63; chief Clin. Pharmacology and Exptl. Therapeutics Service gen. medicine br., 1963-69; assoc. sci. dir. for exptl. therapeutics Nat. Cancer Inst., 1966-71; dir. Nat. Inst. Environ. Health Scis., 1971—, dir. Nat. Toxicology Program, 1978—; adj. prof. pharmacology U. N.C., Chapel Hill, 1972—. Mem. AAAS, Am. Assn. Cancer Research, Am. Pub. Health Assn., Soc. Risk Analysis, Am. Coll. Preventive Medicine, Am. Soc. Clin. Investigation, Am. Soc. Pharmacology and Exptl. Therapeutics, Inst. Medicine, Soc. Occupational and Environ. Health, Soc. Toxicology. Subspecialty: Toxicology (medicine). Office: Nat Inst of Environ Health Scis NIH Research Triangle Park NC 27709

RALL, ELIZABETH PRETZER, geologist; b. Cleve., Apr. 10, 1922; d. Clarence A. and Hannah Elizabeth (Ruetenik) Pretzer; m. Raymond Wallace, June 11, 1949; children—Mary E. Sorrell, Robert D., Lucile A. Uhlig, Virginia E. B.A., Brown U., 1943; M.A., Columbia U., 1945; Ph.D., U. Ill., 1956. Assoc. geologist Cities Service Oil and Gas Corp., Denver, 1983-85; pvt. practice cons., Denver, 1985—. Mem. Geology Soc. Am., Rocky Mountain Geology Soc., Sigma Xi. Unitarian. Subspecialties: Petrology; Stratigraphy. Home: 4808 E Mineral Circle Littleton CO 80122 Office: Cities Service Oil and Gas Corp 1600 Broadway Denver CO 80202

RALL, JOSEPH EDWARD, physician; b. Naperville, Ill., Feb. 3, 1920; s. Edward Everett and Nell (Platt) R.; m. Caroline Domm, Sept. 28, 1944 (dec. Apr. 1976); children—Priscilla, Edward Christian; m. Nancy Lamontagne, Apr. 15, 1978. B.A., North Central Coll., 1940; M.S., Northwestern U., 1944, M.D., 1945; Ph.D., U. Minn., 1952; D.Sc. (hon.), N. Central Coll., 1966; Dr.h.c., Faculty of Medicine, Free U. Brussels, Belgium, 1975. Asso. mem. Sloan Kettering Inst., N.Y.C., 1950-55; chief clin. endocrinology br. Nat. Inst. Arthritis, Metabolism and Digestive Diseases, NIH, 1955-62, dir. intramural research, 1962-83; dep. dir. intramural research NIH, 1983—; Mem. NRC, 1960-65. Author numerous articles, chpts. in books on thyroid gland and radiation. Served to capt. M.C. AUS, 1946-48. Recipient Van Meter prize Am. Goiter Assn., 1950, Fleming award, 1959, Outstanding Achievement award Mayo Clinic and U. Minn., 1964; Disting. Service award Am. Thyroid Assn., 1967; Disting. Service award HEW, 1968; named Outstanding Alumnus N. Central Coll., 1966. Mem. AAAS, Am. Soc. Clin. Investigation, Am. Phys. Soc., Endocrine Soc., Assn. Am. Physicians, Societe de Biologie (France), Royal Acad. Medicine (Brussels), Nat. Acad. Scis. Current Work: Endocrinology and biochemistry, including work on mechanism of action of thyroid hormones and effects of radiation on thyroid gland. Subspecialties: Biochemistry (medicine); Endocrinology. Office: National Institutes Health Bldg 1 Bethesda MD 20205

RALLS, KATHERINE, biologist; b. Oakland, Calif., Mar. 21, 1939; d. Alvin Wallingsford and Ruth (McQueen) Smith; m. Kenneth M. Ralls, June 1958 (div. Sept. 1968); children—Robin, Tamsen, Kristin. A.B., Stanford, 1960; M.A., Radcliffe Coll., 1962; Ph.D., Harvard, 1965. Guest investigator Rockefeller U., N.Y.C., 1968-70, adj. asst. prof., 1970-76; asst. prof. biology Sarah Lawrence Coll., Bronxville, N.Y., 1970-73; research zoologist Inst. for Research in Animal Behavior, N.Y. Zool. Soc., 1970-73; research zoologist Nat. Zool. Park, Smithsonian Instn., 1976—; fellow Radcliffe Inst., 1973-74, Smithsonian Instn., 1973-76, AAUW, 1975-76. Contbr. articles to profl. jours. Office: Nat Zoo Smithsonian Instn Washington DC 20008

RAMAN, JAY, biochemist, consultant; b. Tanjore, Madras, India, Aug. 12, 1937; came to U.S., 1966; s. Anantha and Seetha Laxmi (Subramanian) R.; m. Kamakshi Krishnamurthi, Oct. 21, 1974; children—Laxmi, Priya. B.S., U. Madras, India, 1958; M.S., U. N.H., 1968; Ph.D., Cornell U., 1973. Tutor Madras U., India, 1958-60; sr. scientist Central Food Research Inst., Mysore, India, 1960-66; mgr. Specialty Foods Corp., Johnson City, N.Y., 1973-75; dir. Loblaws, Inc., Buffalo, 1975-77; asst. dir. Pennwalt Corp., Newark, 1977-81; prin. scientist Schering Corp., Union, N.J., 1981—; cons. FAO, Washington, 1981—, World Bank, Washington, 1981. Inventor antimicrobial agts. Mem. Inst. Food Technologists (internat. indsl. achievement award 1973), AAAS, Am. Chem. Soc., N.Y. Acad. Scis., Sigma Xi. Hindu. Current work: Isolation purification and characterization of biologically active proteins from recombinant bacteria. Subspecialties: Enzyme technology; Food science and technology. Home: 2 Hastings Ave Nutley NJ 07110 Office: Schering Corp 1011 Morris Ave Union NJ 07083

RAMANUJA, TERALANDUR KRISHNASWAMY, structural engineer; b. Mysore, Mysore, India, June 23, 1941; came to U.S., 1967, naturalized, 1979; s. Teralandur and Padmammal Krishnaswamy; m. Jayalakshmi Ramanuja, Jan. 18, 1971; children: Srinivasan, Rekha. B.S. in Civil Engring, U. Mysore, 1962; M.S. in Civil Engring, U. Notre Dame, 1969. Registered profl. engr., Ill., Ind., Mich. Design engr. Mil. Engring. Service, Bangalore, India, 1962-67; structural engr. Clyde E. Williams, Inc., South Bend, Ind., 1969-73; head structural dept. Ayres, Lewis, Norris & May, Ann Arbor, Mich., 1973-76; sr. project mgr. Johnson & Anderson Inc., Pontiac, Mich., 1978-84; engr. L.I. Lighting Co., N.Y., 1985—; mem. engring. supr. Bechtel Power Corp., Ann Arbor, Mich., 1985—. Fellow ASCE; mem. Concrete Inst., Chi Epsilon. Current Work: Structural and foundation design of nuclear and fossil power plants, industrial, petrochemical plants, water and waste treatment facilities. Subspecialty: Civil engineering. Office: LI Lighting Co Shoreham Power Plant Shoreham NY 11784

RAMEY, DAVID WILLIAM, veterinarian; b. Louisville, Sept. 21, 1956; s. William Millard Ramey and Joan (Gilliam) Ramey-Ford. B.S., Colo. State U., 1979, D.V.M., 1983. Intern in equine medicine and surgery Iowa State U., Ames, 1983-84; pvt. practice equine vet. medicine, Los Angeles, 1984—. Contbr. articles to profl. jours. Mem. Am. Assn. Equine Practitioners, AVMA, Phi Beta Kappa, Phi Kappa Phi, Gamma Sigma Delta. Current work: Intestinal healing, tendon injuries and healing, orthopedics. Subspecialty: Surgery (veterinary medicine). Office: PO Box 295 Sun Valley CA 91353

RAMEY, ROY RICHARD, refractories executive, research scientist, ceramic engineer; b. Kansas City, Mo., July 11, 1947; s. Richard Basil and Sarah Elise (Atkins) R.; m. Nancy Irene Wiggins, Jan. 24, 1970; children—Jennifer Lea, Michael Richard Thomas. Student U. Mo.-Columbia, 1965-67; B.S., U. Mo.-Rolla, 1970, M.S., 1972, Ph.D., 1974. Research engr. Inland Steel Co., East Chicago, Ind., 1974-79; sr. research mgr. A.P. Green Refractories Co., Mexico, Mo., 1979—. Mem. Am. Ceramic Soc., Ceramic Ednl. Council, Nat. Inst. Ceramic Engrs., ASTM. Mem. Christian Ch. Current work: Technical ceramics; sintering of oxide materials. Subspecialties: Ceramic engineering; Ceramics. Home: 1909 Osage St Mexico MO 65265 Office: AP Green Refractories Co Green Blvd Mexico MO 65265

RAMO, SIMON, engineering executive; b. Salt Lake City, May 7, 1913; s. Benjamin and Clara (Trestman) R.; m. Virginia Smith, July 25, 1937; children: James Brian, Alan Martin. B.S., U. Utah, 1933, D.Sc. (hon.), 1961; Ph.D., Calif. Inst. Tech., 1936; D.Eng. (hon.), Case Inst. Tech., 1960, U. Mich., 1966, Poly. Inst. N.Y., 1971; D.Sc. (hon.), Union Coll., 1963, Worcester Poly. Inst., 1968, U. Akron, 1969, Cleve. State U., 1976; LL.D. (hon.), Carnegie-Mellon U., 1970, U. So. Calif., 1972, Gonzaga U., 1983, Occidental Coll., 1984. With Gen. Electric Co., 1936-46; v.p. ops. Hughes Aircraft Co., 1946-53; with Ramo-Woolridge Corp., 1953-58; sci. dir. U.S. intercontinental guided missile program, 1954-58; dir. TRW Inc., 1954—, vice chmn. bd., 1961-78, chmn. exec. com., 1969-78; chmn. bd. TRW-Fujitsu Co., 1980-83; pres. The Bunker-Ramo Corp., 1964-66; vis. prof. mgmt. sci. Calif. Inst. Tech., 1978—; Regents lectr. UCLA, 1981-82, U. Calif. at Santa Cruz, 1978-79; chmn. Center for Study Am. Experience, U. So. Calif., 1978-80; Faculty fellow John F. Kennedy Sch. Govt., Harvard U., 1980—; dir. Union Bank, Atlantic Richfield Co.; past dir. Times Mirror Co.; Mem. White House Energy Research and Devel. Adv. Council, 1973-75; mem. adv. com. on sci. and fgn. affairs U.S. State Dept., 1973-75; chmn. Pres.'s Com. on Sci. and Tech., 1976-77; mem. adv. council to Sec. Commerce, 1976-77; co-chmn. Transitition Task Force on Sci. and Tech. for Pres.-elect Reagan; mem. roster consultants to adminstr. ERDA, 1976-77; bd. advisors for sci. and tech. Republic of China, 1981—. Author sci., engring. and mgmt. books; also Tennis by Machiavelli, 1985. Bd. dirs. Los Angeles World Affairs Council; bd. dirs. Music Center Found., Los Angeles, Los Angeles Philharm. Assn.; trustee Calif. Inst. Tech., Nat. Symphony Orch. Assn., 1973-83; trustee emeritus Calif. State Univs.; bd. visitors UCLA Sch. Medicine, 1980—; bd. dirs. W. M. Keck Found., 1983—; bd. govs. Performing Arts Council of Music Ctr. Los Angeles, pres., 1976-77. Recipient award IAS, 1956; award Am. Inst. Elec. Engrs., 1959; award Arnold Air Soc., 1960; Am. Acad. Achievement award, 1964; award Am. Iron and Steel Inst., 1968; Distinguished Service medal Armed Forces Communication and Electronics Assn., 1970; medal of achievement WEMA, 1970; awards U. So. Calif., 1971, 79; Kayan medal Columbia U., 1972; award Am. Cons. Engrs. Council, 1974; medal Franklin Inst., 1978; award Harvard Bus. Sch. Assn., 1979; award Nat. Medal

Sci., 1979; Disting. Alumnus award U. Utah, 1981; UCLA medal, 1982; Presdl. Medal of Freedom, 1983; Jr. Achievement Bus. Hall of Fame award, 1984; others. Fellow IEEE (Electronic Achievement award 1953, Golden Omega award 1975, Founders medal 1980), Am. Acad. Arts and Scis.; mem. Nat. Acad. Engrng. (founder, council mem., Bueche award), Nat. Acad. Scis., Am. Phys. Soc., Am. Philos. Soc., Inst. Advancement Engrng., Internat. Acad. Astronautics, Eta Kappa Nu (eminent mem. award 1966). Subspecialty: Engineering management. Office: One Space Park Redondo Beach CA 90278

RAMON, CEON, bioengineering researcher, educator; b. Lucknow, India, Dec. 2, 1945; came to U.S., 1966; s. Ram A. and Ram K. (Devi) Srivastava; m. Sneh K. Varma, Aug. 15, 1972 (div. May 1981). B.S., Agra U. (India), 1963; B.E. with honors, Indian Inst. Sci., Bangalore, 1966; Ph.D., U. Utah, 1973. Asst. prof. SUNY-Stony Brook, 1978-79; research bioengr. Children's Orthopeadic Hosp., Seattle, 1979-80; sr. scientist Inst. Applied Physics & Medicine, Seattle, 1980—; asst. prof. Seattle U., 1981-82. Contbr. articles to profl. jours. Mem. IEEE, Bioelectromagnetic Soc., Sigma Xi, Eta Kappa Nu. Budhist. Current work: Computer models of electro and magnetocardiograms, biological effects of electro magnetic fields. Subspecialties: Biomedical engineering; Electrical engineering. Office: Inst Applied Physiology and Medicine 701 16th Ave Seattle WA 98122

RAMOS, JUAN IGNACIO, engineering educator, consultant; b. Bernardos, Spain, Jan. 28, 1953; came to U.S., 1977; s. Florentino Ramos and Maria Sobrados. B.A. in Engrng., Madrid Polit. U., 1975, Dr. Engrng., 1983; M.A., Princeton U., 1979, Ph.D., 1980. Design engr. Aero. Constrns. Ltd., 1976-77; Guggenheim fellow Princeton U., N.J., 1977-80; lectr. Carnegie-Mellon U., Pitts., 1980, asst. prof. mech. engrng., 1980-85, assoc. prof., 1985—; cons. PPG Industries, Inc., Pitts., 1982-84, Forensic Cons. and Engrs., Pitts., 1984. Contbr. articles to profl. jours. Served as 2d lt. Spanish Air Force, 1975-77. Recipient Ralph R. Teetor award Soc. Automotive Engrs., 1981; Aero. Engrng. medal, 1977; Nat. award in Aero. Engrng., 1977; fellow Van Ness Lothrop, 1979-80, Guggenheim Found. fellow, 1977, 78. Mem. Soc. Indsl. and Applied Math., AIAA, Sigma Xi. Roman Catholic. Current work: Applied mathematics, combustion, perturbation methods, internal combustion engines, fluid mechanics. Subspecialties: Fluid mechanics; Applied mathematics. Office: Carnegie-Mellon U Schenley Park Pittsburgh PA 15213

RAMOS-LORENZI, JORGE RAMON, psychiatrist; b. Fajardo, Puerto Rico, Nov. 28, 1939; s. Ramon and Celina (Lorenzi) R.; 1 child, Lisette Denise. B.S. in Elec. Engrng., U. Puerto Rico, San Juan, 1960, M.D., 1969. Diplomate Am. Bd. Psychiatry and Neurology. Registered profl. engr., P.R. Elec. engr. P.R. Cement Co., San Juan, 1960-62; elec. engr. Coloso Sugar Co., P.R. 1962-64; psychiat. resident L.I. Jewish Hillside Med. Ctr., Glen Oaks, N.Y., 1972-74; research psychiatrist, 1974—, asst. dir. aftercare services, 1976-77, dir. aftercare services, 1977—. Contbr. articles to profl. jours. Mem. IEEE, AAAS, N.Y. Acad. Sci., Am. Psychiat. Assn., Puerto Rico Coll. Engrs. and Surveyors. Current work: Research in clinical psychopharmacology; schizophrenia and affective disorders. Subspecialties: Psychopharmacology; Electrical engineering. Office: Long Island Jewish Hillside Med Ctr 75-59 263rd St Glen Oaks NY 11004

RAMPINO, MICHAEL ROBERT, research scientist, educator; b. N.Y.C., Feb. 8, 1948; s. Michael A. and Annette (Cohen) R. B.A., City U. of N.Y., 1968; Ph.D., Columbia U., 1978. Instr., adj. lectr. CUNY, 1972-77; adj. asst. prof. Barnard Coll., N.Y.C., 1982-83; vis. asst. prof. Dartmouth Coll., Hanover, N.H., 1982; assoc. research scientist Lamont-Doherty Geol. Obs. of Columbia U. and NASA Goddard Inst. for Space Studies, N.Y.C., 1980—; asst. prof. NYU, 1985—. Editor book, 1986. Nat. Acad. Scis. resident research assoc., 1978-80. Mem. Geol. Soc. Am., Am. Geophys. Union, N.Y. Acad. Scis., AAAS, Nat. Assn. Geology Tchrs., Phi Beta Kappa. Subspecialty: Climatology. Office: NASA Goddard Inst for Space Studies 2880 Broadway New York NY 10025

RAMSEY, FRANK ALLEN, army officer, veterinarian; b. Rocksprings, Tex., May 1, 1929; s. Reynolds Allen and June (Burdette) R.; m. Lucette C. Reboul, Jan. 1958; children—Randal R., Ramsay A. D.V.M., Tex. A & M U., 1954; grad., U.S. Army Command and Gen. Staff Coll., 1965, U.S. Army War Coll., 1972. Commd. 1st lt. U.S. Army Vet. Corps, 1955, advanced through grades to brig. gen., 1980; chief vet. service, Ft. Leonard Wood, Mo., 1958-61; acad. vet. U.S. Mil. Acad., West Point, N.Y., 1962-64; vet. staff officer U.S. Army Combat Devel. Command Med. Service, Ft. Sam Houston, Tex., 1965-67; asst. chief profl. programming and planning br. Office Surgeon Gen., Washington, 1967-68, chief profl. programming and planning br., 1968-71, chief food inspection policy office, 1972-73, sr. vet. staff officer, 1973-77; asst. chief of staff Vet. Service, 7th Med. Command, Army Europe and 7th Army, Heidelberg, W. Ger., 1977-80; asst. for vet. services to surgeon gen., chief U.S. Army Vet. Corps and dep. comdg. gen. U.S. Army Med. Research and Devel. Command, Hdqrs. Dept. Army, Washington, 1980-85. Decorated D.S.M., Legion of Merit, Army Commendation medal, Legion of Merit with oak leaf cluster. Mem. AVMA, Assn. Fed. Veterinarians, Assn. Mil. Surgeons U.S., Assn. Equine Practitioners, Am. Assn. Food Hygiene Veterinarians, Conf. Pub. Health Veterinarians, Tex. Vet. Med. Assn. Presbyterian. Lodge: Masons (32 degree). Home and Office: 423 Larkwood Dr San Antonio TX 78209

RAMSEY, NORMAN, physicist; b. Washington, Aug. 27, 1915; s. Norman F. and Minna (Bauer) R.; m. Elinor Jameson, June 3, 1940; children: Margaret, Patricia, Janet, Winifred. A.B., Columbia U., 1935; B.A., Cambridge (Eng.) U., 1937, M.A., 1941, D.Sc., 1954; Ph.D., Columbia U., 1940; M.A. (hon.), Harvard U., 1947; D.Sc. (hon.), Case Western Res. U., 1968, Middlebury Coll., 1969, Oxford (Eng.) U., 1973. Kellett fellow Columbia U., 1935-37, Tyndall fellow, 1938-39; Carnegie fellow Carnegie Inst. Washington, 1939-40; asso. U. Ill., 1940-42; asst. prof. Columbia U., 1942-46; assoc. MIT Radiation Lab., 1940-43; cons. Nat. Def. Research Com., 1940-45; expert cons. sec. of war, 1942-45; group leader, assoc. div. head Los Alamos Lab., 1943-45; assoc. prof. Columbia U., 1945-47; head physics dept. Brookhaven Nat. Lab. of AEC, 1946-47; assoc. prof. physics Harvard U., 1947-50, prof. physics, 1950-66, Higgins prof. physics, 1966—; sr. fellow Harvard Soc. of Fellows, 1970—; Eastman prof. Oxford U., 1973-74; Luce prof. cosmology Mt. Holyoke Coll., 1982-83; prof. U. Va., 1983-84; dir. Harvard Nuclear Lab., 1948-50, 52-53, Varlan Assocs., 1963-66; mem. Air Forces Sci. Adv. Com., 1947-54; sci. adviser NATO, 1958-59; mem. Dept. Def. Panel Atomic Energy; exec. com. Cambridge Electron Accelerator and gen. adv. com. AEC. Author: Nuclear Moments and Statistics, 1953, Nuclear Two Body Problems, 1953, Molecular Beams, 1956, Quick Calculus, 1965; contbr.: articles Phys. Rev.; other sci. jours. on nuclear physics, molecular beam experiments, radar, nuclear magnetic moments, radiofrequency spectroscopy, masers, nucleon scattering. Trustee Asso. Univs., Inc., Brookhaven Nat. Lab., Carnegie Endowment Internat. Peace, 1962—, Rockefeller U., 1977—; pres. Univs. Research Assocs., Inc., 1966-72, 73-81, pres. emeritus, 1981—. Recipient Presdl. Order of Merit for radar devel. work, 1947, E.O. Lawrence award AEC, 1960; Columbia award for excellence in sci., 1980; Medal of Honor, IEEE, 1984; Guggenheim fellow Oxford U., 1954-55. Fellow Am. Acad. Sci., Am. Phys. Soc. (council 1956-60, pres. 1978-79, Davisson-Germer prize 1974); mem. N.Y., Nat. acads. sci., Am. Philos. Assn., AAAS (chmn. physics sect. 1977), Am. Inst. Physics (chmn. bd. govs. 1980—), Phi Beta Kappa (senator 1979—, v.p. 1982—), Sigma Xi. Current Work: Experiments on time reversal symmetry and parity; molecular beams,neutron beams. Subspecialties: Atomic and molecular physics; Particle physics. Home: 55 Scott Rd Belmont MA 02178 Office: Lyman Lab Harvard Univ Cambridge MA 02138

RAMSEY, ROBERT BRUCE, plans and development executive; b. Moline, Ill., Jan. 4, 1944; s. Ralph Samuel and Florence Isabelle (Adams) R.; m. Penny Tina Germain, June 10, 1967; children: Anne M., Sarah E. A.B. in Chemistry, Augustana Coll., Rock Island, Ill., 1966; Ph.D. in Biochemistry, St. Louis U., 1971, postdoctoral, 1971, M.B.A., 1984. Postdoctoral work Inst. Neurology, U. London, 1971-73; asst. prof. neurology St. Louis U. Sch. Medicine, 1972-79, assoc. prof., 1979-80, assoc. clin. prof., 1980—; mgr. plans and devel. McDonnell-Douglas Health Systems Co., St. Louis, 1985—; product mgr. Lancer div. Sherwood Med., St. Louis, 1980-85. Contbr. articles to profl. jours. Mem. Am. Soc. Biol. Chemists, Am. Chem. Soc., Biochem. Soc. (U.K.), Am. Assn. Clin. Chemists. Republican. Presbyterian. Subspecialty: Immunobiology and immunology. Home: 1133 Ridgelynn Dr Ladue MO 63124 Office: 600 McDonnell Blvd Saint Louis MO 63042

RAMSHAW, JOHN DAVID, physicist; b. Salt Lake City, Mar. 20, 1944; s. William Edwin and Margaret Louise (Park) R.; m. Jean Tomer, Sept. 7, 1968; children—Michael John, David Scott. B.S., Coll. Idaho, 1965; Ph.D., MIT, 1970. Air Force Office of Sci. Research/NRC postdoctoral fellow U. Md., College Park, 1970-71; research assoc., instr. U. Utah, Salt Lake City, 1971-72; sci. staff Applied Theory, Inc., Los Angeles, 1972-73; assoc. scientist Aerojet Nuclear Co., Idaho Falls, Idaho, 1973-75; staff Los Alamos Nat. Lab., 1975—. Contbr. articles, tech. reports and conf. presentations. Mem. Am. Phys. Soc. Current work: Equilibrium and nonequilibrium statistical physics, analytical and numerical fluid dynamics, theory of dielectrics, theory of liquids, physics of fluids, stochastic processes. Subspecialty: Statistical physics. Home: 533 Ridgecrest Ave Los Alamos NM 87544 Office: Los Alamos Nat Lab PO Box 1663 Los Alamos NM 87545

RAND, STEPHEN COLBY, physicist; b. Seattle, Nov. 20, 1949; s. Charles Gordon and Margaret (Colby) R.; m. Paula Dian Fraser, Sept. 6, 1976; children—Kevin Colby, Spencer Fraser. B.Sc., McMaster U., 1972; M.Sc., U. Toronto, Ont., Can., 1974, Ph.D., 1978. World Trade postdoctoral fellow IBM Research, San Jose, Calif., 1978-80; research assoc. dept. physics Stanford (Calif.) U., 1980-82; scientist Hughes Research, Malibu, Calif., 1982—; referee Phys. Rev. Letters and Optics Letters. Mem. Optical Soc. Am., Am. Phys. Soc. Current Work: Research in nonlinear pair interactions in solids, four-wave mixing in color centers and non-linear optics in fibers; inventor of tunable diamond laser. Subspecialty: Laser spectroscopy. Office: 3011 Malibu Canyon Rd Malibu CA 90265

RANDA, JAMES PAUL, theoretical physicist, electrical engineer; b. Chgo., Jan. 26, 1947; s. John Joseph and Catherine Anna (Baier) R.; m. Susan Bulmann, June 12, 1970; 1 child, David John. B.Sc., Ill. Benedictine Coll., 1969; M.Sc., U. Ill., 1970, Ph.D., 1974. Vis. asst. prof. Tex. A&M U., 1974-75; postdoctoral fellow U. Manchester, Eng., 1975-78; asst. prof. U. Colo., Boulder, 1978-83, lectr., 1985—; physicist Nat. Bur. Standards, Boulder, 1983—. Co-editor: Quantum Chromodynamics, Quantum Flavordynamics and Unified Field Theories, 1980; contbr. articles to profl. jours. Mem. Am. Phys. Soc., IEEE. Current work: Characterization of complex electromagnetic environments, nonionizing radiation hazards; theory and phenomenology of elementary particles. Subspecialties: Electrical engineering; Particle physics. Office: Nat Bur Standards 723 03 325 Broadway Boulder CO 80303

RANDALL, DAVID CLARK, medical educator, research physiologist; b. St. Louis, Apr. 23, 1945; s. Walter Clark and Gwendolyn Ruth (Niebel) R.; m. Pamela Kaye Reynolds, June 14, 1968 (div. 1984); children: Christopher Clark, Matthew Faubion; m. Lea Carol Wylder, Sept. 1, 1985. B.A., Taylor U., 1967; Ph.D., U. Wash., 1971. Asst. prof. Johns Hopkins U., Balt., 1972-75; asst. prof. U. Ky. Coll. Medicine, Lexington, 1975-78, assoc. prof. dept. physiology and biophysics, 1978-85, prof. dept. physiology and biophysics, 1985—. Contbr. article to profl. jour. Mem. Am. Physiol. Soc., Soc. Neurosci., Pavlovian Soc. (pres. 1983). Current Work: Autonomic neural control of cardiovascular function in intact, unanesthetized animals; bio-behavioral bases of cardiovascular disease; brainstem control of heart rate. Subspecialties: Physiology (medicine); Psychophysiology. Office: Univ Ky Coll Medicine Lexington KY 40536-0084

RANDALL, JOHN DEL, nuclear engineer; b. Whittier, Calif., Nov. 19, 1932; m. 1953; 4 children. B.S., U. Calif., 1955, M.S., 1956; Ph.D. in Nuclear Engrng., Tex. A&M U., 1965. Physicist, Lawrence Radiation Lab., Calif., 1955-56; nuclear engr. Nucleonics Div., Aerojet Gen. Corp., Gen. Tire and Rubber Co., 1956-58; asst. prof. nuclear engrng. Tex. A&M U., College Station, 1958-63, assoc. head Nuclear Sci. Ctr. 1963-65; prof. nuclear engrng and dir. Nuclear Sci. Ctr., 1965—. Subspecialty: Nuclear engineering. Office: Tex A&M U Nuclear Sci Ctr College Station TX 77843*

RANDALL, JOHN DOUGLAS, modeling analyst; b. Corning, N.Y., July 23, 1942; s. Alfred Griffin and Elsie Jane (Manning) R.; m. Catherine Louise Frisch, June 28, 1969; children—Ian Douglas, Trevor Jonathan. B.M.E., Cornell U., 1965, Ph.D., 1972; M.S., Clarkson Coll., 1967. Teaching asst. Clarkson Coll., Potsdam, N.Y., 1965-66; instr., 1965-67; teaching fellow Cornell U., Ithaca, N.Y., 1967-68, 71-72; sr. engr. Johns Hopkins U. Applied Physics Lab., Laurel, Md., 1973-80; program mgr. U.S. Nuclear Regulatory Commn., Washington, 1980—. Contbr. articles to profl. jours. Recipient Voyager citation U.S. Dept. Energy, 1977. Mem. Am. Geophys. Union, AAAS, ASME, Soc. Indsl. and Applied Math., Cornell Soc. Engrs. Democrat. Club: East Coast Aikido (ikkyu 1985) (Columbia, Md.). Current work: Program management of research projects related to radioactive waste disposal; mathematical models of hydrological, geochemical, corrosion, and leaching phenomena. Subspecialties: Fluid mechanics; Applied mathematics. Home: 6329 Tamar Dr Columbia MD 21045 Office: US Nuclear Regulatory Commn MS1130SS Washington DC 20555

RANDALL, RUSSEL R., well log specialist; b. Tulsa, Mar. 9, 1948; s. Russel R. and Shirley L. (Light) R.; m. Bonnie Jean Carpenter, May 1970; children: Brent E., Regina Kay. B.A., Kans. State Tchrs. Coll., 1970; M.S., Kans. State U., 1972, Ph.D., 1975. With Dresser Atlas Industries Inc., Houston, 1975—, sr. project physicist, 1977-81, mgr. pulsed neutron devices, 1981—. Mem. Am. Phys. Soc., Soc. Profl. Well Log Analysis, Soc. Petroleum Engrs. Republican. Patentee in field. Current Work: Research and development of sealed Deuterium-Tritium neutron sources for pulsed neutron oil well logging; research and development of nuclear oil well logging systems. Subspecialties: Nuclear physics; Atomic and molecular physics. Office: PO Box 1407 Houston TX 77001

RANDALL, WALTER C(LARK), physiology educator, researcher; b. Akeley, Pa., Dec. 12, 1916; s. Harry Warren and Ruth Nancy (Wiggins) R.; m. Gwendolyn Ruth Niebel, Aug. 1, 1943; children—David Clark, Marilyn Ruth, Douglas Warren, Craig Mathias. A.B., Taylor U., 1938; M.S., Purdue U., 1940, Ph.D., 1942; postgrad. Western Res. U., 1942-43. From instr. to assoc. prof. physiology St. Louis U., 1943-53; prof., chmn. dept. physiology Loyola U., Chgo., 1954-75, prof. physiology, 1975—; mem. heart program, project com. Nat. Heart Inst., Bethesda, Md., 1963-67, 68-72; mem. Nat. Bd. Med. Examiners, Phila., 1964-68. Contbr. numerous articles to physiol. jours. Editor: Nervous Control of Heart, 1965; Neural Regulation Heart, 1977; Nervous Control of Cardiovascular Function, 1984. Trustee Taylor U., Upland, Ind., 1970—, ofcl. bd. dirs. Park Ridge United Meth. Ch., Ill., 1977-83; Suburban Aid to Retarded, Park Ridge, 1977—; Northwest mem. com. Boy Scouts Am., Post 101, Park Ridge, 1960-75. Mem. Am. Physiol. Soc. (pres. 1982-83, council, Wiggers award 1979). Am. Heart Assn. (sci. council 1972-75), Chgo. Heart Assn. (research council 1976-78), Soc. Exptl. Biology and Medicine (pres. Ill. chpt. 1959-60), Am. Inst. Biol. Scis. (bd. govs. 1976-79), Sigma Xi (pres. Loyola chpt. 1959-60). Current work: Neural control of heart, autonomic regulation of cardiovascular system, temperature regulation in mammals, graduate education in physiology. Subspecialties: Physiology (medicine); Neurophysiology. Home: 624 N Hamlin Ave Park Ridge IL 60068 Office: Loyola U Med Ctr 2160 S 1st Ave Maywood IL 60153

RANDERATH, KURT, pharmacology educator, researcher; b. Dusseldorf, Ger., Aug. 2, 1929; came to U.S., 1963, naturalized, 1972; s. Edmund M. and Mathilde A. (Sachs) R.; m. Erika Randerath, Dec. 19, 1962. M. D., Heidelberg U., 1955; M.S. in Chemistry, 1959. Intern Stuttgart (Ger.) City Hosp.; asst. prof. biol. chemistry Harvard U., 1968-71; assoc. prof. pharmacology Baylor Coll., 1971-74, prof., 1974—. Author: Thin-Layer Chromatography, 1966; editorial bd.: Jour. Chromatographic Sci, 1969; contbr. in field. Recipient NIH Career Devel. award, 1968; Am. Cancer Soc. Faculty Research award. Mem. Am. Chem. Soc., Am. Soc. Biol. Chemists, Am. Assn. Cancer Research, AAAS. Current Work: Actions of anticancer drugs and carcinogens at the molecular level; nucleic acid structure; development of ultrasensitive analytical methods. Subspecialties: Cancer research (medicine); Molecular pharmacology. Office: Depart Pharmacology Baylor College Medicine Houston TX 77030

RANDOLPH, JAMES EUGENE, aerospace mission designer; b. Los Angeles, Jan. 19, 1940; s. Wallace L. and Katherine L. R.; m. Marilyn Miller, May 19, 1968; 1 son, John James. B.S., Calif. State U.-Los Angeles, 1964; M.S., U. So. Calif., Los Angeles, 1967. Systems engr. advanced s/c studies to Venus and Mars Jet Propulsion Lab., Pasadena, Calif., 1968-70; mission engr. Mariner, Voyager, Shuttle Radar, 1970-77; sci. integration team chief Voyager, 1978, Starprobe study mgr., 1977—, advanced mission engring. group supr., mission design sect., 1980—. Fellow AIAA (assoc.); mem. Am. Astron. Soc. Current Work: Advanced spacecraft mission and system design management, aerospace engineering and technology, astronautics, systems engineering. Subspecialties: Aerospace engineering and technology; Astronautics. Office: 4800 Oak Grove Dr 156-220 Pasadena CA 91109

RANDOLPH, LYNWOOD PARKER, physicist, educator; b. Richmond, Va., May 21, 1938; s. Samuel Lynwood and Ora Estelle (Harris) R.; m. Judith Howard, Aug. 27, 1960; children—Leslie Patrice, Lynwood Parker II, Leonard Patrick, Lemuel Preston. B.S., Va. State U., 1959; M.S., Howard U., 1964, Ph.D., 1972; postgrad. U. Md., 1975-77, Harvard U. Sch. Bus., 1982. Research physicist Harry Diamond Labs., Adelphi, Md., 1964-75; mgr. aeros. and space tech. NASA, Washington, 1975-82, dep. dir. productivity, 1982—; adj. prof. U. D.C., 1972—, Howard U., 1980-81. Contbr. articles to profl. jours. Pres., PTA, Suitland, Md., 1970. Served to 1st lt. Ordnance Corps, AUS, 1959-61. Recipient Superior Performance award NASA, 1976. Mem. AIAA, Am. Phys. Soc., AAAS, Sigma Pi Sigma, Beta Kappa Chi, Alpha Phi Alpha. Democrat. Baptist. Current work: Productivity management and measurement, organizational development. Subspecialties: Aerospace engineering and technology; Programming languages. Home: 3000 Fairhill Ct Suitland MD 20746 Office: NASA 400 Maryland Ave SW Washington DC 20546

RANGASWAMY, SUBRAMANIAM, materials scientist, researcher; b. Palghat, Kerala, India, Oct. 20, 1949; came to U.S. 1978; s. Subramaniam Rangaswamy and Seethalakshmi Subramaniam; m. Janaki Ramaswami, Sept. 14, 1973; children—Priya, Sowmya. B. Tech. with honors, India Inst. Tech., Kharagpur, 1972; M.S., SUNY-Stonybrook, 1980, postgrad., 1980—. Chief supr. H.A.L., Bangalore, India, 1972-78; grad. asst. SUNY-Stonybrook, 1978-80; engr. Metco, Westbury, N.Y., 1980-84, sr. engr., 1984—. Patentee in field. Mem. Am. Soc. Metals, Am. Ceramic Soc., Materials Research Soc., Nat. Inst. Ceramic Engrs. Current work: Advanced thermal spray coating materials research, including ceramics, carbides, high temperature super alloys and amorphous alloys. Subspecialties: High-temperature materials; Composite materials. Home: 488 North Bicycle Path Port Jefferson Station NY 11776 Office: Metco Inc 1101 Prospect Ave Westbury NY 11590

RANKEN, PAUL FREDERICK, research chemist; b. Norfolk, Va., Sept. 3, 1944; s. William Paul and Florence Bertha (Spinken) R.; m. Jenelle Elizabeth Cross, Aug. 29, 1970; children—John William, Catherine Marie, Michael Paul. B.S., Va. Poly. Inst., 1966; Ph.D., U. Fla., 1971. Postdoctoral research assoc. dept. chemistry U. Utah, Salt Lake City, 1972-73; research chemist Ethyl Corp., Baton Rouge, 1973-78, sr. research chemist, 1978-83, research assoc., 1983—. Contbr. articles to profl. jours. Co-patentee in field. Mem. Am. Chem. Soc. Roman Catholic. Current work: Organic chemistry research in area of organosulfur compounds and aluminum-catalyzed reactions of aromatic compounds. Subspecialty: Organic chemistry. Home: 10345 Westwood Ave Baton Rouge LA 70809 Office: Ethyl Corp PO Box 341 Baton Rouge LA 70821

RANKIN, DAVID THOMAS, ceramist, researcher; b. Pitts., May 24, 1941; s. David Harrison and Margaret Catherine (Broker) R.; m. Mary Anne Sudder, June 5, 1965, children—Anne Marie, Alison Beth. B.S. in Ceramics, Rutgers U., 1963, Ph.D. in Ceramics, 1967. Research asst. Rutgers U., New Brunswick, N.J., 1963-67; research ceramist E.I. Dupont-Savannah River Lab., Aiken, S.C., 1967-68, 1970-76, staff ceramist, 1976-81, research staff ceramist, 1981-84, research assoc., 1984—; Contbr. numerous tech. papers to profl. jours. Official U.S. Swimming Team, St. of Georgia, 1983—; v.p. Central Savannah River Swim League, Augusta, Ga., and Aiken, 1984, pres., 1985, vice chmn. Augusta Swim League, 1984-85 Served to capt. U.S. Army, 1968-70. Recipient research assistenceship Rutgers U., 1963-67; Rutgers U. Alumni scholar, 1959-63. Mem. Am. Ceramic Soc. (program chmn. 1982-83, sec. 1983-84, chmn. 1985-86), Keramos, Sigma Xi. Roman Catholic. Clubs: Fermata (Aiken) (chmn. bd. dirs.), Aiken Toastmasters (v.p. 1980-81), Hounds Lake Country. Current work: Processing and characterization of nuclear ceramic materials, especially effects of phase diagrams on processing conditions and properties. Subspecialties: Ceramics; Materials processing. Home: 1438 Moultrie Dr Aiken SC 29801 Office: E I Dupont de Nemours and Co Savannah River Lab Aiken SC 29809

RANNEY, WAYNE DONALD, geologist, educator; b. Riverside, Calif., July 1, 1954; s. Donald Lester and Prudence (Ricca) R. B.S. in Recreation Resource Mgmt., No. Ariz. U., 1980, B.S. in Earth Sci., 1980, M.S. in Geology, 1986. Interpretation leader Nat. Park Service, Grand Canyon, Ariz., 1975-78; teaching asst. No. Ariz. U., Flagstaff, 1979-80, 82-84; white water guide Grand Canyon, 1980-83; research geologist Mus. No. Ariz., Flagstaff, 1979-80; edn. camp coordinator Student Cons. Assn., Zion Park, Utah, 1984, Capitol Reef Park, Utah, 1985; instr. No. Ariz. U., Flagstaff, 1984-85. Vol. Big Bros. No. Ariz., Flagstaff, 1984-85. E. Blois du Bois scholar, 1982—. Mem. Geol. Soc. Am., Ariz. Hist. Soc., Utah Hist. Soc., Phi Kappa Phi, Sigma Gamma Epsilon. Democrat. Roman Catholic. Club: No. Ariz. U. Geology (treas., 1983-84, pres., 1984-85). Current work: Reconstruct geologic history of Verde Valley, Ariz.; evolution of Colorado River through Grand Canyon and sequence of events which formed Grand Canyon, Arizona. Subspecialty: Geology. Home: 823 1/2 W Aspen #5 Flagstaff AZ 86001 Office: No Ariz U Dept Geology PO Box 6030 Flagstaff AZ 86011

RANSOM, CRAIG MITCHELL, computer corporation research scientist; b. Buffalo, Oct. 13, 1946; s. Chester Theodore and Rita Mary (Hollands) R. B.A., SUNY-Buffalo, 1968; M.S., Syracuse U., 1975, Ph.D., 1979. Jr. scientist IBM Corp., Fishkill, N.Y., 1968-70, assoc. engr., 1970-75, sr. assoc. engr., 1975-79, staff engr., 1979-81, research staff mem., Yorktown Heights, N.Y., 1981—. Served with AUS, 1970-72. Mem. Am. Phys. Soc., Electrochem. Soc. Current work: Semiconductor processing induced damage; point defects in semiconductors; device physics as related to processing damage. Subspecialties: Microchip technology (materials science); Semiconductors. Office: Thomas J Watson Research Ctr IBM Corp PO Box 218 Yorktown Heights NY 10598

RAO, DABEERU CHANDRASEKHARA, educator, administrator; b. Santabommali, India, Apr. 6, 1946; came to U.S., 1972; s. Rama and Venkataratnam R.; m. Sarada Patnaik, July 31, 1974; children: Ravi, RLakshmi. B.Stat., Indian Stats. Inst., 1967, M.Stat., 1968, Ph.D., 1971. Postdoctoral fellow dept. probability and stats. U. Sheffield, Eng., 1971-72; asst. geneticist pop. genetics lab. U. Hawaii, Honolulu, 1972-78, assoc. geneticist pop. genetics lab., 1978-80; assoc. prof., dir. biostatis., assoc. prof. psychiatry and genetics, adj. prof. math. Wash. U., St. Louis, 1980-82, prof., dir. biostatistics, prof. psychiatry and genetics, adj. prof. math., 1982—. Author: A Source Book for Linkage in Man, 1979, Methods in Genetic Epidemiology, 1983; Genetic Epidemiology of Coronary Heart Disease, 1984. Editor-in-chief Genetic Epidemiology, 1984—. NIMH grantee, 1981; Nat. Inst. Gen. Med. Scis. grantee, 1981. Mem. Am. Soc. Human Genetics, Am. Assn. Phys. Anthropologists, AAAS, Biometric Soc., Soc. Epidemiological Research. Current Work: Familial transmission of diseases and risk factors; statistical methods in human genetics; genetic epidemiology; genetics of common diseases. Home: 6316 Pershing St Louis MO Office: Div Biostatistics Dept Preventive Medicine Wash U Sch Medicine Box 8067 4566 Scott Ave St Louis MO 63110

RAO, DANDAMUDI VISHNUVARDHANA, nuclear physicist, educator; b. Maredumaka, India, Apr. 5, 1944; came to U.S., 1968, naturalized, 1979; s. Veeraraghaviah and Sarojini D. (Koneru) R.; m. Sujata L. Rao, Feb. 27, 1967; children: Saroja, Neeraja. M.S., U. Mass., 1970, Ph.D., 1972. Instr. radiology Albert Einstein Coll. Medicine, Bronx, N.Y., 1972-74; asst. prof. radiology U. Medicine and Dentistry, Newark, 1974-78, assoc. prof. radiology, 1978—, dir. health physics, 1974-78; tech. expert IAEA. Contbr. articles to profl. jours.; Author: Physics of Nuclear Medicine, 1977. Editor: Physics of Nuclear Medicine; Recent Advances, 1984. Am. Cancer Soc. grantee, 1975-77; Biomed. Research grantee, 1977-78; Nat. Cancer Inst., NIH grantee, 1982—. Mem. Am. Assn. Physicists in Medicine (program dir. summer sch. 1983), Soc. Nuclear Medicine, Soc. Magnetic Resonance Imaging, Am. Coll. Med. Physics. Patentee radioactive erbium complexes. Current Work: In vivo study of radiation effects in Spermatoponial cells from low energy electrons emitted by nuclear medicine radiopharmaceuticals. Subspecialties: Nuclear medicine; Imaging technology. Office: U Medicine and Dentistry of NJ 100 Bergen St Newark NJ 07103

RAO, GOPAL SUBBA, pharmacologist, researcher; b. Mangalore, India, Aug. 12, 1938; came to U. S., 1961, naturalized, 1980; s. Subba Gopal and Sharada Bai (Bhat) R.; m. Harsha Purushottam Udeshi, May 29, 1972; 1 son, Raveen. B.Sc., Madras U., India, 1958; M.S., Howard U., 1965; Ph.D., U. Mich., 1969. Chemist Pub. Health Inst., Bangalore, India, 1958-61; research asst. Howard U. Coll. Pharmacy, Washington, 1961-65, instr., 1962-65; research asst. U. Mich. Coll. Pharmacy, Ann Arbor, 1965-69; internat. fellow Nat. Heart and Lung Inst., NIH, Bethesda, Md., 1969-72, spl. fellow, 1972-74,

NIH grantee, 1974-82; dir., chief research scientist div. biochemistry Research Inst., Am. Dental Assn. Health Found., Chgo., 1978-85, head pharmacology lab., 1974-85; clin. prof. biochemistry Loyola U. Dental Sch., Maywood, Ill., 1985—. Contbr. numerous articles on pharmacology to profl. jours.; abstractor: Dental Abstracts, 1975—. Am. Fund for Dental Health grantee, 1978-80; NIH grantee, 1984; Smokeless Tobacco Research Council grantee, 1985. Mem. Assn. Scientists of Indian Origin (councillor 1980-82, chmn. membership com. 1982), Am. Soc. Pharmacology and Exptl. Therapeutics, Am. Coll. Toxicology, Soc. Toxicology, AAAS, Am. Chem. Soc., Am. Pharm. Assn., Acad. Pharm. Sci., Internat. Assn. Dental Research, Am. Assn. Dental Research, Am. Soc. Pharmacognosy, Sigma Xi (lectr. U. Miss. Med. Center 1982), Rho Chi. Current Work: Biochemical etiology of periodontal diseases, development of new diagnositc methods and novel drugs and procedures, useful in the treatment of oral diseases, salivary nitrite and carcinogenic nitrosamine formation, occupational hazards in dental practice. practice; metabolism and pathology of smokeless tobacco constituents in oral cavity. Subspecialties: Pharmacology; Oral biology. Office: Dept Biochemistry Loyola U Dental Sch Maywood IL 60153

RAO, GOPALAKRISHNA M., chemist, educator, consultant; b. Udupi, India, Mar. 17, 1944; came to U.S., 1978; s. Lakshminarayana Shanbouge and Krishnaveni (Saraswathi) Rao; m. Kavitha Gopalakrishna Rao, Oct. 19, 1975. B.S., M.G.M. Coll., Udupi, India, 1964; M.S., Mysore U., India 1966; Ph.D., Meml. U., Nfld., Can., 1973. Lectr. A.P.S. Coll., Bangalore, India, 1966-67; demonstrator Meml. U., Nfld., Can., 1968-74; postdoctoral research assoc. U. Alta., Can., 1974-77; postdoctoral fellow, Queen's U., Ont., Can., 1977-78; research assoc. Stanford U., Calif., 1978-81; research specialist Dow Chem. U.S.A., Freeport, Tex., 1981—; cons., Alta., 1974-77, Stanford, Calif., 1978-81, Lake Jackson, Tex., 1981—. Author writings in field. Active polit. orgns., India, 1955-64, ethnic clubs, 1964—; advisor Explorer, Brazosport, 1982—. Recipient various prizes and awards, assns. and instns. India, 1956-66, scholarships and fellowships, Can., 1968-78. Mem. Electrochem. Soc., Chem. Inst. Can., Am. Assn. Crystal Growth, Am. Chem. Soc., Am. Soc. Metals, Metallurg. Soc. of AIME. Hindu. Club: Dow Career (Freeport). Current work: Electrodeposition of metals and semiconductors, molten salt technology, electroanalytical applications, chemistry of minerals and antibiotics, batteries, fuel cells and gas evolution reactions. Subspecialties: Physical chemistry; Solar energy. Home: 312 Huckleberry Lake Jackson TX 77566 Office: Dow Chemical USA Freeport TX 77541

RAO, KAMESWARA KOLLA, design engineer, researcher; b. Kasimkota, India, July 28, 1944; came to U.S., 1970, naturalized, 1981; s. Subba Kolla and Ammaji Kolla (Paluri) R.; m. Vasavi Kolla Namburi, Nov. 17, 1972; children—Swathi, Sandhya, Preethi. B.Sc. hons., Andhra U., Waltair, Andhra, India, 1963, M.Sc., 1964, Ph.D., 1968; Ph.D., U. of Wis., 1975. Asst. prof. physics Western Mich. U., Kalamazoo, 1975-79; staff engr. Nat. Semiconductor, Santa Clara, Calif., 1979-81; sect. head signetics, Sunnyvale, Calif., 1981-83; project mgr. Intel., Santa Clara, 1983—. Contbr., articles to prof. jours. Undergrad. scholar Atomic Energy Commn. of India, 1959-63, postgrad. scholar, 1963-64. Mem. Am. Phys. Soc., IEEE. Current work: Design of VLSI non-volatile memories. EPROMS and EEPROMS. Subspecialties: Microelectronics; Condensed matter physics. Home: 1172 Arlington Ln San Jose CA 95129 Office: Intel MS SC9-1-11 3601 Juliete Ln Santa Clara CA 95051

RAO, SERIN RANGENENI, environmental engineer, environmental health consultant, educator; b. Hyderabad, India, Jan. 28, 1946; came to U.S. 1969, naturalized 1983; s. Saraswathi R.; m. Aban Jokhy, Aug. 26, 1977; children—Nadia, Shawn, Justin. B.S., Osmania U., Hyderabad, 1968; M.S., So. Ill. U., 1971; M.B.A., U. Ill., 1981. Registered profl. engr., Ill. Project engr. Kakathiya Industries, Hyderabad, 1968-69; environ. engr. Ill. Dept. Pub. Health, Peoria, 1971-73, supervising environ. engr., 1973-76, asst. regional environ. engr., 1976—; environ. cons. Am. Environ. Cons., Inc., Chgo., 1970; part-time faculty Ill. Central Coll., East Peoria, 1981—; cons. Internat. Inst. Environment and Devel., Contbr. articles to profl. jours. Mem. Am. Acad. Environ. Engrs. (diplomate), Am. Pub. Health Assn., Nat. Environ. Health Assn., Ill. Environ. Health Assn., Am. Water Works Assn., Am. Air Pollution Control Assn., Ill. Pub. Health Assn. Current work: Environmental toxicology and epidemiology, toxic chemicals and wastes, chemical audit, indoor air quality, water supply and waste water, recreational waters, public health management. Subspecialties: Environmental toxicology; Water supply and wastewater treatment. Home: 6706 N Foxpoint Ct Peoria IL 61614 Office: Ill Dept Pub Health 5415 N University Ave Peoria IL 61614

RAO, SURENDAR PURUSHOTHAY, nuclear engineer; b. Bombay, India, Jan. 5, 1946; s. Purushotham and Indira R.; m. Alka Surendar, Jan. 23, 1976; children—Avinash, Ansali. B.Sc., U. Bombay, 1968, M.Sc., 1974; M.E., U. Va., 1976. Vice prin. Teaching Inst., Bombay, 1970-73; research asst. U. Va., Charlottesville, 1974-76; nuclear engr. Combustion Enging. Inc., Windsor, Conn., 1976-80; lead engr. EDS Nuclear Inc., Melville, N.Y., 1980; tech. specialist Birchwood, Warrington, Eng., 1981—. Mem. Am. Nuclear Soc. Current Work: Nuclear safety kinetics, nuclear systems safety, probabilistic risk assesments for the U.K. pressurized water reactor, systems interactions for U.K. pressurized water reactor. Subspecialties: Nuclear fission; Nuclear engineering. Office: EDS Nuclear Inc Genesis Centre Garretfield Birchwood Warrington WA3 7BH England

RAPAPORT, FELIX THEODOSIUS, surgeon, educator; b. Munich, Ger., Sept. 27, 1929; s. Max W. and Adelaide (Rathaus) R.; m. Margaret Birsner, Dec. 14, 1969; children: Max, Benjamin, Simon, Michel, Adelaide. A.B., NYU, 1951, M.D., 1954. Diplomate: Am. Bd. Surgery, 1963. Intern Mt. Sinai Hosp., N.Y.C., 1955-56; resident, chief resident NYU Surg. Services, 1958-62, USPHS postdoctoral fellow in pathology, 1956; trainee in allergy and infectious diseases N.Y. U., 1958-61; head, transplantation and immunology div. N.Y. U. Surg. Services, 1965-77; dir. research Inst. Reconstrn. and Plastic Surgery, N.Y. U., 1965-77; assoc. prof. surgery Inst. Reconstrn. and Plastic Surgery, NYU Med. Center, 1965-70, prof., 1970-77; prof., dep. chmn. dept. surgery, prof. pathology, dir. transplantation service SUNY, Stony Brook, 1977—; attending SUNY (Univ. Hosp.), 1980—; cons. VA Hosp., N.Y.C., 1963-77, Northport, N.Y., 1977—. Editor-in-chief: Transplantation Proc, 1968—; assoc. editor: Am. Jour. Kidney Diseases, 1981—, Am. Jour. Craniofacial Genetics and Developmental Biology, 1980—; contbr. over 300 articles to profl. jours.; author/editor 9 books on transplantation. Served to lt. comdr. M.C. USNR, 1956-58. Decorated comdr. Order Sci. Merit, chevalier Ordre National du Merite, France, 1970; recipient Gold medal Societe d'Encouragement au Bien, 1979; grand croix Ordre des Palmes Academiques, 1981. Mem. Soc. Univ. Surgeons, N.Y. Surg. Soc., Am. Surg. Assn., ACS, Am. Assn. Immunologists, Soc. Exptl. Biology and Medicine, Harvey Soc., Am. Assn. Transplant Surgeons, Am. Assn. Clin. Histocompatibility Testing, Internat. Soc. Exptl. Hematology, Transplantation Soc. (founding sec., v.p., pres.), Alpha Omega Alpha. Democrat. Jewish. Current Work: Induction of permanent tolerance to major transplantable organs in man; research concerned with effects of total body irradiation and bone marrow transplantation in the production of host unresponsiveness to tissue allografts. Subspecialties: Transplant surgery; Transplantation. Office: Dept Surgery Health Scis Ctr SUNY Stony Brook Stony Brook NY 11794

RAPKIN, MARWIN JOEL, physicist; b. Jersey City, Dec. 25, 1951; s. Morris and Ethel Rapkin. B.S., St. Peter's Coll., 1974; M.S. in Radiation Sci., Rutgers U., 1981. Instr. physics St. Peter's Coll., Jersey City, 1981-82; research assoc. Lawrence Berkeley Lab., Calif., 1982-84; health physicist Brookhaven Nat. Lab., Upton, N.Y., 1984-85; cons. physicist/programmer Singer Corp., Wayne, N.J., 1985—. Contbr. articles to profl. jours. Mem. Am. Assn. Physics Tchrs., Am. Phys. Soc. Jewish. Current work: Designing calibration software for inertial navigation systems. Subspecialty: Nuclear physics. Office: Singer/Kearfott MS 12B38 150 Totowa Rd Wayne NJ 07470

RAPMUND, GARRISON, army officer, physician; b. Buenos Aries, Argentina, Aug. 11, 1927; s. Joseph L. and Kathleen (Henry) R.; m. Janet Campbell, May 10, 1957; children—Neil Bruce, Elizabeth Campbell. A.B., Harvard U., 1949; M.D., Columbia U., 1953. Intern Bellevue Hosp., N.Y.C., 1953-54; resident Babies Hosp., N.Y.C., 1954-57; commd. M.C. U.S. Army, 1957, advanced through grades to maj. gen., 1981; mem. staff Walter Reed Army Inst. Research, Washington, 1957-58, 61-64, 74-76, dep. dir., 1975, dir., 1976-79; mem. staff Inst. Med. Research, Kuala Lumpur, Malaysia, 1958-60, 64-69; mem. staff hdqrs. U.S. Army Med. Research and Devel. command, 1969-71; dep. comdr. U.S. Army Med. Research and Devel. Command, 1971; asst. surgeon gen. research and devel. U.S. Army, Washington; also comdr. U.S. Army Med. Research and Devel. Command, Ft. Detrick, Md., 1979—. Contbr. articles to profl. jours. Decorated Legion of Merit with oak leaf cluster and others. Fellow Royal Soc. Tropical Medicine and Hygiene; mem. Am. Soc. Tropical Medicine and Hygiene, Malaysian Soc. Parasitology and Tropical Medicine (past pres.). Subspecialty: Parasitology. Office: Asst Surgeon Gen R&D Dept Army Washington DC 20310

RAPP, DONALD, research scientist, author; b. Bklyn., Sept. 27, 1934; s. Jacob and Irene (Levenson) R.; m. Zolita Sue Sverdlove, May 30, 1956; children: Erica, Melissa. B.Chem. Engring., Cooper Union, 1955; M.S., Princeton U., 1956; Ph.D., U. Calif.-Berkeley, 1960. Staff scientist Lockheed Co., Palo Alto, Calif., 1959-65; assoc. prof. Poly. Inst. Bklyn., 1965-69; prof. U. Tex., Dallas, 1969-79; div. technologist Jet Propulsion Lab., Calif. Tech., Pasadena, 1979—, sr. research scientist, 1980—. Author: Quantum Mechanics, 1971, Statistical Mechanics, 1972, Solar Energy, 1981; also articles. Fellow Am. Phys. Soc. Current Work: Energy systems, concurrent processing computers, micromechanical devices. Subspecialties: Atomic and molecular physics; Solar energy. Home: 1445 Indiana Ave South Pasadena CA 91030 Office: Jet Propulsion Lab Calif Inst Tech MS 157-316 4800 Oak Grove Dr Pasadena CA 91109

RAPP, PAUL ERNEST, neurophysiologist; b. Chgo., Sept. 2, 1949; s. John Henry and Mary Katherine (Hendershot) R.; m. Dorrie Louise Tholke, June 11, 1970 (div. 1982). B.S. in Physiology, U. Ill.-Urbana, 1972, B.S. in Engring., 1972; Ph.D. in Math., Cambridge U., 1975. Fellow Caius Coll., Cambridge U., 1975-79; asst. prof. Med. Coll. Pa., Phila., 1979-81, assoc. prof. neurophysiology, 1982—; vis. faculty Rutgers U., New Brunswick, N.J., 1978. Editor: Biological Oscillators, 1979. Winston Churchill Found. scholar, 1972; NIH prin. investigator grantee, 1982—. Fellow Cambridge Philos. Soc.; mem. Soc. Math. Biology (bd. dirs. 1982—), Am. Math. Soc. Current work: Application of dynamical systems theory and nonlinear control theory to the study of the human central nervous system, with specific reference to convulsive disorders. Subspecialties: Neurophysiology; Systems engineering. Home: B621 Presidential Commons Philadelphia PA 19131 Office: Med Coll Pa 3300 Henry Ave Philadelphia PA 19129

RAPP, ULF RUEDIGER, cancer scientist, researcher; b. Wernigerode/Harz, Germany, Dec. 22, 1943; came to U.S., 1970, naturalized, 1981; s. Albert C. and Martha J. (Weindel) R.; m. Marieluise Gertrud, Dec. 21, 1970. Teaching asst. in anatomy U. Freiburg, 1965-66, in biochemistry, 1967-69, intern univ. clinics, 1970; postdoctoral fellow McArdle Lab. Cancer Research, U. Wis.-Madison Grad. Sch. 1970-75; vis. scientist Nat. Cancer Inst. NIH, Frederick, Md., 1975—; chief viral pathology sect. Nat. Cancer Inst. NIH (Lab. Viral Carcinogenesis), 1979—. Contbr. articles to profl. jours. Current Work: Tumor genes; retroviruses; chem. transformed cells; devel. biology; membrane receptors. Subspecialties: Cell study oncology; Virology (biology). Office: Nat Cancer Inst Bldg 560 Room 21-77 Frederick MD 21701

RAPPORT, DAVID JOSEPH, ecologist, educator; b. Omaha, Nebr., Feb. 16, 1939; s. Arthur and Ruth (Herbster) R.; m. Ellen Larsen, May 2, 1965 (div.); 1 child, Joshua; m. Agneta Birgitta Oden; 1 child, Nils Benjamin. B.B.A., U. Mich., 1960, M.A. in Econs., 1966, Ph.D. in Econs., 1967. Research assoc. in Econs. U. Mich., Ann Arbor, 1967-68; postdoctoral fellow in zoology U. Toronto, Ont., Can., 1969-70; asst. prof. biology Simon Fraser U., Burnaby, B.C., Can., 1970-74; ecologist Stats. Can., Ottawa, 1974-81, sci. adviser, 1981—; prof. zoology U. Toronto, 1977-82; del. Orgn. Econ. Coop. Devel., Paris, 1977, Econ. Commn. Europe, Geneva, 1981-84; cons. Commns. Research Insts., 1978—. Author: Towards a Comprehensive Environmental Data System for Canada, 1979. Contbr. articles to sci. jours. Killam Sr. Research scholar, 1970-74; grantee Nat. Sci. Engr. Council, 1979-81, Can. Internat. Devel. Agy., 1982. Mem. Am. Soc. Naturalists, Data for Devel., Ecol. Soc. Am. Current work: Ecosystem behavior under stress, stress ecology, environmental indicators, ecosystem pathology, integration of economics and ecology. Subspecialties: Ecosystems analysis; Ecology (environmental science). Home: Box 4622 Ottawa ON K1S 5H8 Canada Office: Statistics Can Ottawa ON K1A 0T6 Canada

RAPPORT, ROBERT, diagnostic radiologist; b. Havana, Cuba, Sept. 23, 1953; came to U.S., 1961; s. Morris and Suzy (Pearl) R. B.S., U. Fla., 1974; M.D., U. Miami, 1978. Diplomate: Nat. Bd. Med. Examiners. Clin. assoc. U. So. Fla. Coll. Medicine, Tampa, 1978-82, chief resident in diagnostic radiology, 1981-82. Mem. Radiol. Soc. N.Am., Fla. West Coast Radiol. Soc., N.Y. Acad. Scis., AAAS, Fla. Med. Assn., Hillsborough County Med. Assn. Jewish. Current Work: Ophthalmoplegia due to spontaneous thrombosis in a patient with bilateral cavernous carotid aneurysms. Subspecialty: Diagnostic radiology. Home: 3132 W Lambright Ave Unit 906 Tampa FL 33614 Office: Dept Radiology Centro Espanol Hosp Tampa FL 33614

RASCHKE, CURT ROBERT, electronic device development scientist, electronic materials researcher; b. N.Y.C., Sept. 11, 1944; s. Charles Frederick and Grace Evelyn (van Nostr) R.; m. Susan Michele Hourigan, Oct. 14, 1972; 1 dau., Kimberly Darcy. B.A., Whitman Coll., Walla Walla, Wash., 1966; M.S., Cornell U., 1968, Ph.D., 1971. Sr. physicist A.M. Internat., Warrensville, Ohio, 1972-74; sr. chemist Union Carbide Corp., Bound Brook, N.J., 1974-78; mem. tech. staff Xerox Corp., Dallas, 1978-82, Tex. Instruments, Dallas, 1982—. Referee: Jour. Applied Physics, 1976—. Mem. Am. Phys. Soc., Sigma Xi, Phi Beta Kappa. Republican. Episcopalian. Clubs: Cornell Tex. (Dallas), Brookhaven Country (Dallas). Patentee in field. Current Work: Electroacoustic devices; research and engineering into materials development and processing for microwave surface acoustic wave, ink jet printing and polymer electret devices. Subspecialties: Microelectronics; Electronic materials. Home: 10140 Bettywood Ln Dallas TX 75243 Office: Texas Instruments MS 255 13500 N Central Espressway Dallas TX 75222

RASENICK, MARK MITCHELL, biomedical educator; b. Chgo., Sept. 5, 1949; s. Maurice M. and Eleanore Ruth (Fox) R.; m. Helene J. Shambelan, Sept. 1, 1974; children—Elliot S., Matthew M. B.A., Case Western Res. U., 1971; Ph.D., Wesleyan U., 1977. Postdoctoral fellow Yale U. Med Sch., 1980; assoc. research Scientist Yale U. Med. Sch., 1981-83; asst. prof. U. Ill. Coll. Medicine-Chgo., 1983—. Contbr. articles to profl. jours. Mem. U.S. Peace Council, 1981—. Recipient nat. research service award NIH, 1978-81; research grantee Air Force Office Sci. Research, 1982—, NIMH, 1984—; Chgo. Community Trust fellow, 1984—. Mem. Soc. for Neurosci., Am. Soc. Biol. Chemists, Fedn. Am. Scientists, AAAS, N.Y. Acad. Scis. Current work: Regulation of neurotransmitter activated adenylate cyclase by membrane and cytoskeletal components in brain and cultured neural cells. Subspecialties: Membrane biology; Neuropharmacology. Home: 1113 Juniper Terr Glenview IL 60025 Office: Dept Physiology and Biophysics U Ill Coll Medicine PO Box 6998 Chicago IL 60680

RASLEAR, THOMAS GREGORY, research psychologist; b. N.Y.C., Nov. 25, 1947; s. John William and Catherine (Turchin) R.; m. Lois T. Keck, Aug. 7, 1971. B.S. with honors, CCNY, 1969; Sc.M., Brown U., 1972, Ph.D., 1974. Vis. asst. prof. Boston U., 1974-75; asst. prof. Wilkes Coll., Wilkes-Barre, Pa., 1975-79; research psychologist Walter Reed Inst. Research, Washington, 1979—; vis. asst. prof. (research) Brown U., Providence, 1976. Contbr. numerous articles to profl. jours. N.Y. State Regents scholar, 1965-69; USPHS research fellow, 1970-72. Mem. Acoustical Soc. Am., Am. Psychol. Assn., Eastern Psychol. Assn., Phi Beta Kappa, Sigma Xi. Current Work: Use behavior analytic methods to study sensory and perceptual processes in animals, including auditory perception and time perception. Subspecialties: Psychophysics; Behavioral psychology. Office: Dept Med Neuroscis Walter Reed Army Inst Research Washington DC 20307-5100

RASMUSSEN, JOHN OSCAR, JR., See *Who's Who in America,* 43rd edition.

RASSIGA, ANNE LOUISE, hematology and oncology educator; b. Oceanside, N.Y., June 19, 1942; d. William August and Edna (Chickray) R.; m. George Bernard Pidot, Jr., Sept. 5, 1962 (div. 1972); m. Charles H. Pimlott, Jr., July 5, 1974; children: Andrew William, Christopher Thomas. A.B., Bryn Mawr Coll., 1962; M.D., Harvard U., 1966. Diplomate: Am. Bd. Hematology, Am. Bd. Oncology, Am. Bd. Internal Medicine. Intern Mary Hitchcock Meml. Hosp., Hanover, N.H., 1966-67; resident in internal medicine Dartmouth Affiliated Hosps., Hanover, 1967-69; assoc. dir. div. hematology and oncology St. Luke's Hosp., Cleve., 1979-85; mem. Eucid Clinic Found., 1985—; asst. prof. medicine Case Western Res. U., 1972—; asst. chief hematology and oncology Cleve. VA Med. Ctr., 1972-79; instr. Dartmouth Coll., 1971-72; med. adv. com. Am. Cancer Soc., Cleve., 1981—. Alumnae dist. counselor Bryn Mawr Coll., 1983—, alumnae recruiting coordinator No. Ohio, 1977-83; patroller central div. Nat. Ski Patrol System, Inc., 1974—. NIH spl. postdoctoral research fellow in hematology, 1969-71. Fellow ACP; mem. Am. Women's Med. Assn., Hospice Council No. Ohio, Am. Fedn. Clin. Research, Am. Soc. Hematology, Am. Soc. Clin. Oncology (clin. practice com. 1982—), Acad. Medicine Cleve. (pres. 1985—), Women's Med. Soc. Cleve. (sec.-treas. 1981-83). Club: Cleve. Skating. Current Work: Clinical and therapeutic trials of cancer treatment; undergraduate and postgraduate medical education. Subspecialties: Hematology; Oncology. Office: Euclid Clinic Found 18599 Lake Shore Blvd Euclid OH 44119

RASSIN, DAVID KEITH, biochemist; b. Liverpool, Eng., Dec. 1, 1942; came to U.S., 1953; s. Meyer and Ella Rosetta Laura (House) R.; m. Glennda McConnell, Feb. 5, 1965; children: Meya Glynne, Keith David, Heather. A.B., Columbia U., 1965; Ph.D., Mt. Sinai Grad. Sch., CUNY, 1974. Research asst. Columbia U., 1966-67; asst. research scientist N.Y. State Inst. Basic Research Mental Retardation, 1967-70, research scientist, 1970-77, asso. research scientist, 1977-80; asso. prof. pediatrics, human biol. chemistry and genetics U. Tex. Med. Br., Galveston, 1980-85, prof., 1985—. Contbr. articles to profl. jours. Bd. dirs. East End Hist. Dist. Assn., Galveston, 1981-82. Mem. Soc. Pediatric Research, Internat. Soc. Neurochemistry, Am. Soc. Clin. Nutrition, Am. Soc. Neurochemistry, Am. Inst. Nutrition, Am. Soc. Pharmacology and Exptl. Therapeutics, Am. Soc. Neursci. Current Work: Amino acid metabolism, especially sulfur containing compounds in neurochemistry, nutrition and inherited metabolic diseases. Subspecialties: Neurochemistry; Nutrition (medicine). Home: 1318 Sealy Galveston TX 77550 Office: Dept Pediatrics U Tex Med Br Galveston TX 77550

RAST, HOWARD EUGENE, JR., physicist; b. Mexia, Tex., June 8, 1934; s. Howard Eugene and Mary Louise (Cleveland) R.; m. Yoko Watanabe, Apr. 10, 1958; children—Dieter, David, B.A., U. Tex., Austin, 1956; M.S., U. So. Calif., 1977; Ph.D., U. Oreg., 1964. Research chemist Calif. Ink Co., Berkeley, 1958-59; research fellow U. Oreg., 1959-64; phys. chemist Naval Weapons Center, Corona, Calif., 1964-70; research physicist Naval Electronics Ctr., San Diego, 1970-78; supervisory scientist Naval Ocean Systems Ctr., San Diego, 1978—. Patentee fiber optics, optics communications; contbr. articles to profl. jours. Served to 1st lt. USMC, 1956-58. Fellow, Crown Zellerbach, 1960, NIH, 1962; recipient Best Sci. Paper of Yr. award Sigma Xi, 1969. Mem. Am Phys. Soc., Western Spectroscopy Assn., N.Y. Acad. Scis. Current work: Optical properties of gases, liquids, solids, optical spectra; fiber optics technology; optical communications, countermeasures. Subspecialties: Fiber optics; Laser spectroscopy. Office: Naval Ocean Systems Ctr Code 562 San Diego CA 92152

RAST, WALTER, JR., limnologist, hydrologist; b. San Antonio, Jan. 14, 1944; s. Walter Sr. and Jane Irene (Tudyk) R.; m. Claudia Leigh Jones, July 16, 1970; children—Margaret Amanda, Elizabeth Miranda. B.A., U. Tex., 1969; M.S., U.Tex.-Dallas, 1974, M.S., 1976, Ph.D., 1978. Hydrologic field asst. U.S. Geol. Survey, San Antonio, Tex., 1969-70, research hydrologist, Sacramento, 1982-85, Austin, Tex., 1985—; research asst. U. Tex.-Richardson, 1972-75, teaching asst., 1975-77; limnologist Internat. Joint Commn., Windsor, Ont., Can., 1977-79, sr. environ. advisor, Washington, 1979-82; cons. EnviroQual Inc., Plano, Tex., 1975-77. Contbr. articles to profl. jours. Chmn. U. Tex.-Dallas, Recycling Com., Richardson, Tex., 1975-77. Served to SP4 Army N.G., 1966-72. Sommers Drug Co. Inc. scholar, 1962, Richardson Environ. Action League scholar, 1975, 76. Mem. AAAS, Am. Soc. Limnology and Oceanography, Internat. Soc. Applied and Theoretical Limnology, North Am. Lake Mgmt. Soc., Water Pollution Control Fedn., Sierra, Nat. Wildlife Fedn. Roman Catholic. Current work: Aquatic chemistry; chemical limnology; eutrophication; environmental modeling; water quality management; chemical and biological aspects of water pollution. Subspecialties: Environmental chemistry; Hydrology. Office: 300 E 8th St Austin TX 78701

RATAJCZAK, HELEN VOSSKUHLER, immunologist, educator, researcher; b. Tucson, Apr. 9, 1938; d. Max P. and Marion H. (Messer) Vosskuhler; m. Edward F. Ratajczak, June 1, 1959 (div. 1968); children: Lorraine, Eric, Peter, Eileen. B.S., U. Ariz., 1959, M.S., 1970, Ph.D., 1976. Asst. research scientist U. Iowa Coll. medicine, Iowa City, 1976-78; instr. immunology U. Pitts., 1978-80, research assoc., 1980-81; asst. prof. Loyola U., Maywood, Ill., 1981—. Am. Thoracic Soc. fellow, 1974-76; NIH fellow, 1978; Loyola U. grantee, 1981. Mem. Am. Thoracic Soc., Assn. Research in Vision and Ophthalmology, Am. Assn. Immunologists, Sigma Xi, Phi Lambda Upsilon. Republican. Roman Catholic. Current Work: Cell mediated immunity of hypersensitivity diseases of the lung, eye; tumor immunology; chemotaxis. Subspecialties: Immunology (medicine); Cancer research (medicine). Office: Department of Pathology Stritch School Medicine Loyola University 2160 S 1st Ave Maywood IL 60153

RATHBUN, EDWIN ROY, consulting engineer, physicist; b. Kansas City, Mo., Apr. 6, 1922; s. Edwin Roy and Jennie Viola (Thompson) R.; m. Frances Evelyn Merritt, May 14, 1949; children—Roy Alan, Gloria Sue, Ellen May, Kenneth Roger, Keith Raymond. B.S. in Elec. Engring., Iowa State U., 1948, M.S. in Physics, 1950. Asst. electronic engr. Argonne Nat. Lab., Lamont, Ill., 1954-56; staff engr. nuclear sci. Cook Electric Co., Morton Grove, Ill., 1956-64; cons. engr. Gen. Electric Co., Phila., 1965-68, engr. nucleonics specialist, Syracuse, N.Y., 1968-69; electronics engr., physicist Naval Surface Weapons Ctr., White Oak, Md., 1969-84; ind. cons. engr., physicist, Colesville, Md., 1984—; cons. engr. Astron Corp., Springfield, Va., 1981—. Dir. Radiol. Def.-Civil Def., Des Plaines, Ill., 1962-64. Served with USMC, 1943-46. Mem. IRE (profl. group nuclear sci., vice chmn. nat. meeting), IEEE. Methodist. Current work: Electromagnetics, antennas, E-M coupling, electromagnetic pulse, nuclear vulnerability and hardening, nuclear weapons phenomena and effects, nuclear radiation phenomena and effects, computer models. Subspecialties: Nuclear physics; Electronics. Home: 212 Mowbray Rd Colesville MD 20904 Office: Four Star Ventures 212 Mowbray Rd Colesville MD 20904

RATHJENS, GEORGE WILLIAM, scientist, educator; b. Fairbanks, Alaska, June 28, 1925; s. George William and Jennie (Hansen) R.; m. Lucy van Buttingha Wichers, Apr. 5, 1950; children: Jacqueline, Leslie, Peter. B.S., Yale U., 1946; Ph.D., U. Calif., Berkeley, 1951. Instr. chemistry Columbia U., 1950-53; staff weapons systems evaluation group Dept. Def., 1953-58; research fellow Harvard U., 1958-59; staff spl. asst. to Pres. U.S. for sci. and tech., 1959-60; chief scientist Advanced Research Projects Agy., Dept. Def., 1961, dep. dir., 1961-62; dep. asst. dir. U.S. ACDA, 1962-64, spl. asst. to dir., 1964-65; dir. weapons systems evaluation div. Inst. Def. Analyses, 1965-68; prof. dept. polit. sci. MIT, 1968—. Fellow Am. Acad. Arts and Scis.; mem. AAAS, Council for a Livable World (chmn.), Fedn. Am. Scientists, Council Fgn. Relations, Inst. Strategic Studies, Sigma Xi. Current Work: Arms control and defense policy; energy and environmental policy; science and public policy; technology assessment. Subspecialty: Systems engineering. Office: Mass Inst Tech Cambridge MA 02139

RATHKE, JEROME WILLIAM, research chemist; b. Humboldt, Iowa, July 10, 1947; s. Albert William and Josephine Elizabeth (Speltz) R.; m. Barbara JoAnn Andrews, Aug. 31, 1968; children—Benjamin, Joseph. B.S., Iowa State U., 1969; Ph.D., Ind. U., 1973. Postdoctoral fellow Cornell U., 1973-75; asst. chemist Argonne Nat. Lab., Ill., 1975-80, chemist, 1980-81, group leader, 1981—. Mem. Am. Chem. Soc., AAAS, Sigma Xi. Current work: Fuel related catalysis research. Subspecialties: Catalysis chemistry; Organometallics. Home: 581 Buckingham Way Bolingbrook IL 60439 Office: Argonne Nat Lab CMT-205 9700 S Cass Ave Argonne IL 60439

RATHOD, MULCHAND SHAMJIBHAI, mechanical engineering educator, consultant; b. Pathri, Gujarat, India, Mar. 3, 1945; came to U.S., 1970, naturalized, 1981; s. Shamjibhai Laljibhai and Ramaben (Rathod) R.; m. Damayanti Thakor, Aug. 15, 1970; children—Prerana, Falgun, Sejal. B.Engring., Sardar Patel U., 1970; M.S., Miss. State U., 1972, Ph.D., 1975. Registered profl. engr., Ala., Miss., Mo., N.C., N.Y., Tenn. Research, grad. asst. Miss. State U., 1970-75; cons. engr. Bowron & Butler, Jackson, Miss., 1975-76; asst. prof. Tuskegee Inst., Ala., 1976-78; assoc. prof. mech. engring. SUNY, Binghamton, 1979—; tech. staff mem. Jet Propulsion Lab., Pasadena, Calif., summers 1980, 81; mem. summer faculty IBM, Endicott, N.Y., 1982-85; cons., 1982—; cons. Interpine, Hattiesburg, Miss., 1977-79, Jet Propulsion Lab., Pasadena, 1980-83. Patentee in field. Pres., India Assn. of Miss. State U., 1972-73; den leader Webelos, Boy Scouts Am., Vestal, N.Y., 1983-84. Grantee: SUNY Found., 1984, IBM, U.S. Dept. Energy, 1978; recipient Tech. Innovation award NASA, 1982. Mem. Am. Soc. for Enging. Edn. (reviewer

1975—), ASME (Appreciation certs. 1982, 83, 84, 85, faculty advisor 1981-85), ASHRAE, N.Y. State Engring. Tech. Soc., Pi Tau Sigma. Democrat. Hindu. Current work: Research and development in artificial heart, heat transfer, thermo-dynamics, electronic packaging, energy management, fluid and solid mechanics areas. Subspecialties: Mechanical engineering; Biomedical engineering. Home: 216 Warren St Vestal NY 13850 Office: Dept Engring Tech Watson Sch SUNY Binghamton NY 13901

RATLIFF, FLOYD, scientist, educator; b. La Junta, Colo., May 1, 1919; s. Charles Frederick and Alice (Hubbard) R.; m. Orma Vernon Priddy, June 10, 1942; 1 dau., Merry Alice. B.A.; magna cum laude, Colo. Coll., 1947, D.Sc. honoris causa, 1975; M.Sc., Brown U., 1949, Ph.D., 1950; NRC postdoctoral fellow, Johns Hopkins, 1950-51. Head Lab. Biophysics, 1974—; Instr., then asst. prof. Harvard, 1951-54; assoc. Rockefeller Inst., 1954-58; mem. faculty Rockefeller U., 1958—, prof. biophysics and physiol. psychology, 1966—; pres. Harry Frank Guggenheim Found., 1983—; cons. to govt., 1957—. Author: Mach Bands: Quantitative Studies on Neural Networks in the Retina, 1965, also articles.; Editor: Studies on Excitation and Inhibition in the Retina, 1974; editorial bd.: Jour. Gen. Physiology, 1969—. Served to 1st lt. AUS, 1941-45, ETO. Decorated Bronze Star; recipient Howard Crosby Warren medal Soc. Exptl. Psychologists, 1966; Edgar D. Tillyer medal Optical Soc. Am., 1976; medal for disting. service Brown U., 1980; Pisart vision award N.Y. Assn. for Blind, 1983. Fellow Am. Acad. Arts and Scis.; mem. Nat. Acad. Scis., Am. Inst. Physics, AAAS, Am. Psychol. Assn. (Disting. Sci. Contbn. award 1984), Manhattan Philos. Soc., Internat. Brain Research Orgn., Am. Philos. Soc., China Inst. Am., Oriental Ceramic Soc. (London), Oriental Ceramic Soc. (Hong Kong), Asia Soc., Japan Soc., Phi Beta Kappa, Sigma Xi. Subspecialties: Neurophysiology; Physiological psychology. Home: 500 E 63d St New York NY 10021 Office: Rockefeller U 1230 York Ave New York NY 10021 Office: Harry Frank Guggenheim Found Woolworth Bldg 233 Broadway New York NY 10279

RATNAM, BHARATI ASOKA, physicist, educator; b. Shahajahanpur, India, Oct. 23, 1944, came to U.S., 1979; s. Perala and Kamala (Thapan) R.; m. Mridula Rattanchand Sharma, Sept. 6, 1973; children—Urvasi, Malavika. B.Sc. with honors, Delhi U., India, 1964; diploma in Russian, M.Sc., Moscow State U., 1968; M.S., Ph.D., U. Ill., 1972. Fellow Tata Inst., Bombay, India, 1972-79; vis. asst. prof. Clemson U., S.C., 1979-81; asst. prof. Tufts U., Medford, Mass., 1981—; cons. GTE, Waltham, Mass., 1982. Contbr. articles to profl. jours. India Merit scholar Delhi U, 1961-64; India Research scholar Moscow State U., 1968; Tufts U. fellow, 1982. Fellow Indian Cryogenic Council; mem. Indian Phys. Soc., Am. Phys. Soc. Hindu. Current work: Experimental condensed matter physics; semiconductor and superconductor tunneling under pressure. Subspecialties: Condensed matter physics; Low temperature physics. Home: 96 Packard Ave Somerville MA 02144 Office: Tufts U Physics Dept Medford MA 02155

RATNATUNGA, KAVAN UPAJIVA, astrophysicist; b. Colombo, Sri Lanka, Oct. 4, 1952; s. Percival Upajiva and Irene (Jayakody) R.; m. Ransirinie Anoma Senanayake, May 30, 1979. B.S., U. Ceylon, 1976; M.S., U. Pitts., 1979; Ph.D., Australian Nat. U., 1983. Lectr. dept. physics U. Sri Lanka, Colombo, 1976-78; mem. Inst. Advanced Study, Princeton, N.J., 1984—. Contbr. articles to profl. jours. Fellow Royal Astron. Soc.; mem. Indian Astron. Soc. (life), Am. Astron. Soc., Astron. Soc. of Pacific. Current work: Study of the kinematics and chemical abundances of in-situ samples of K giants in the outer region of our galactic halo. Subspecialties: Optical astronomy; Graphics, image processing, and pattern recognition. Office: Inst Advanced Study Princeton NJ 08540

RATNER, MICHAEL IRA, astronomer; b. N.Y.C., June 30, 1949; s. Henry and Ruth (Novak) R.; m. Mary L. Bezjak, June 28, 1975; children—Andrew, Paul. B.S. in Physics, Yale Coll., 1971; Ph.D. in Astro-Geophysics, U. Colo., 1976. Research assoc. MIT dept. earth planetary sci., Cambridge, 1976-82, Harvard Obs., Cambridge, 1983—. Mem. Am. Astron. Soc. Democrat. Current work: Astrometry of radio sources, fluctuations in the cosmic microwave background. Subspecialty: Radio and microwave astronomy. Office: Room B-221 Harvard Obs 60 Garden St Cambridge MA 02138

RATNOFF, OSCAR DAVIS, physician, educator; b. N.Y.C., Aug. 23, 1916; s. Hyman L. and Ethel (Davis) R.; m. Marian Foreman, Mar. 31, 1945; children: William Davis, Martha. A.B., Columbia U., 1936, M.D., 1939; LL.D. (hon.), U. Aberdeen, 1981. Intern Johns Hopkins Hosp., Balt., 1939-40; Austin fellow in physiology Harvard Med. Sch., Boston, 1940-41; asst. resident Montefiore Hosp., N.Y.C., 1942; resident Goldwater Meml. Hosp., N.Y.C., 1942-43; asst. in medicine Columbia Coll. Physicians and Surgeons, N.Y.C., 1942-46; fellow in medicine Johns Hopkins, 1946-48, instr. medicine, 1948-50, instr. bacteriology, 1949-50; asst. prof. medicine Case Western Res. U., Cleve., 1950-56, asso. prof., 1956-61, prof., 1961—; asst. physician (Univ. Hosp.), Cleve., 1952-56, asso. physician, 1956-67, physician, 1967—. Author: Bleeding Syndromes, 1960; editor: Treatment of Hemorrhagic Disorders, 1968, (with C. D. Forbes) Disorders of Hemostasis, 1984; Mem. editorial bd.: Jour. Lab. Clin. Medicine, 1956-62; Circulation, 1961-65, Blood, 1963-69, 78-83, Am. Jour. Physiology, 1966-72, Jour. Applied Physiology, 1966-72, Jour. Lipid Research, 1967-69, Jour. Clin. Investigation, 1969-71, Circulation Research, 1970-75, Annals Internal Medicine, 1973-76, Perspectives in Biology and Medicine, 1974—, Thrombosis Research, 1981-84, Jour. Urology, 1981—; Contbr. articles to med. jours. Career investigator Am. Heart Assn., 1960—. Served to maj. M.C., 1943-46, Ind. Recipient Henry Moses award Montefiore Hosp., 1949; Disting. Achievement award Modern Medicine, 1967; James F. Mitchell award, 1971; Murray Thelin award Nat. Hemophilia Found., 1971; H.P. Smith award Am. Soc. Clin. Pathology, 1975; Joseph Mather Smith prize Columbia Coll. Physicians and Surgeons, 1976. Mem. A.C.P. (John Phillips award 1974, master 1983), A.M.A., Am. Fedn. Clin. Research (emeritus), Nat. Acad. Scis. (Kovalenko award 1985), Soc. Scholars of Johns Hopkins U., Am. Soc. Clin. Investigation (emeritus), Central Soc. Clin. Research, Assn. Am. Physicians (Kober lectr. 1985), Am. Soc. Hematology (Dameshek award 1972), Internat. Soc. Hematology, Internat. Soc. Thrombosis (Grant award 1981), Am. Physiol. Soc., Am. Soc. Biol. Chemists, Royal Coll. Physicians and Surgeons Glasgow (hon.), Sigma Xi, Alpha Omega Alpha. Current Work: Hemostasis and thrombosis. Subspecialty: Hematology. Home: 2916 Sedgewick Rd Shaker Heights OH 44120 Office: University Hospitals of Cleve Cleveland OH 44106

RAUCH, HERBERT EMIL, electrical engineer, researcher; b. St. Louis, Oct. 6, 1935; s. Herbert Leopold and Vera Hilda (Sieloff) R.; m. Marjorie Ann Beyer, June 18, 1961; children—Marta Andrea, Erik Herbert, Evan Christopher, Loren Curtis. B.S., Calif. Inst. Tech., 1957; M.S., Stanford U., 1958, Ph.D., 1962. Mem. tech. staff Hughes Aircraft, Culver City, Calif., 1958-62; sr. staff scientist Lockheed Co., Palo Alto, Calif., 1962—; cons. Stanford U., 1972-73; asst. prof. San Jose State U. (Calif.), 1968-70. Editor: (with others) Astrodynamics, 1975; Control Applications of Nonlinear Programming, 1980, Applications of Nonlinear Programming to Optimization and Control, 1983; editor-in-chief Jour. Astronautical Scis., 1980—; editor IEEE Control Systems mag., 1985—. Mem. Peninsula Sch. Bd., Menlo Park, Calif., 1973-82, Selective Service Bd., Santa Clara County, Calif., 1972-75; chmn. People for Los Altos Now (Calif.), 1974-75; trustee Los Altos Sch. Dist., 1974-75. Fellow Am. Astronautical Soc. (v.p. 1980-84, Outstanding Service award 1984), AIAA (assoc.; mem. publs. com. 1975—, Space Shuttle Flag award 1984); mem. IEEE (sr. mem., Community Service award 1977, Centennial medal 1984), Control Systems Soc. of IEEE (bd. govs. 1984—), AAAS (del. engring. sect. 1981—), Internat. Fedn. Automatic Control (chmn. math. of control com. 1984—). Current work: Signal processing, control systems, astrodynamics, probability for computer-based expert systems. Subspecialties: Electrical engineering; Astronautics. Office: Lockheed 92-20/205 3251 Hanover St Palo Alto CA 94304

RAUDKIVI, UNO, programmer, analyst, researcher; b. Karu, Estonia, Nov. 26, 1925; came to U.S. 1951, naturalized 1958; s. Joosep and Anna (Wendt) R. B.E.E., SUNY-Buffalo, 1965; M.E.E., Cleve., State U., 1979; postgrad., 1981-82. Sr. design and devel. engr. Picker Corp., Cleve., 1969-75; project engr. Case Western Res. U., Cleve.., 1975-77; programmer, analyst Cleve. Clinic Found., 1977—. Contbr. articles to profl. jours. Mem. IEEE, Soc. Magnetic Resonance Imaging. Republican. Lutheran. Current work: Statistical tissue-type classifier, operating in vector space of measured and computed MR parameters, interactive computer-graphics simulation of responses to sequence of rf-pulses and periods of relaxation. Subspecialties: Magnetic resonance imaging; Graphics, image processing, and pattern recognition. Home: 200 Chatham Way Apt 865 Mayfield Heights OH 44124 Office: Cleveland Clinic Found 9500 Euclid Ave Cleveland OH 44106

RAUP, DAVID MALCOLM, paleontologist, educator; b. Boston, Apr. 24, 1933; s. Hugh Miller and Lucy (Gibson) R.; m. Susan Creer Shepard, Aug. 25, 1956; 1 son, Mitchell D. B.S., U. Chgo., 1953; M.A., Harvard U., 1955, Ph.D., 1957. Instr. Calif. Inst. Tech., 1956-57; faculty Johns Hopkins, 1957-65, asso. prof., 1963-65; mem. faculty U. Rochester, 1965-78, prof. geology, 1966-78, chmn. dept. geol. scis., 1968-71; dir. U. Rochester (Center for Evolution and Paleobiology), 1977-78; curator geology, chmn. dept. geology Field Mus. Natural History, Chgo., 1978—, dean of sci., 1980-82; prof. geophys. sci. U. Chgo., 1980—, chmn. dept., 1982—, now Sewell Avery disting. service prof. geophysics; geologist U.S. Geol. Survey, part-time, 1959-77; vis. prof. U. Tubingen, Germany, 1965, 72. Author: (with S. Stanley) Principles of Paleontology, 1971, 78; editor: (with B. Kummel) Handbook of Paleontological Techniques, 1965; Contbr. articles to profl. jours. Recipient Best Paper award Jour. Paleontology, 1966; Schuchert award Paleontol. Soc., 1973; Calif. Research Corp. grantee, 1955-56; Am. Assn. Petroleum Geologists grantee, 1957; Am. Philos. Soc. grantee, 1957; NSF grantee, 1960-66, 75—; Chem. Soc. grantee, 1965-71; NASA grantee, 1983—. Fellow Geol. Soc. Am.; mem. Nat. Acad. Sci., Paleontol. Soc. (pres. 1976-77), Am. Soc. Naturalists (v.p. 1983), Soc. Econ. Paleontology and Mineralogy, Soc. for Systematic Zoology, Soc. for Study Evolution, AAAS, Sigma Xi. Subspecialty: Paleontology. Home: 5801 S Dorchester Ave Chicago IL 60637 Office: Dept Geophys Scis U Chgo Chicago IL 60637

RAUSEN, AARON REUBEN, pediatric oncologist-hematologist; b. Jersey City, June 30, 1930; s. David and Ruth (Schwartz) R.; m. Emalou Watkins Rausen, Apr. 7, 1968; children: David Jacob, Susan Dinah, Elisabeth Ann. Student, Dartmouth Coll., 1947-50; M.D., SUNY Downstate Med. Center, N.Y.C., 1954. Cert. Am. Bd. Pediatrics (subbd. pediatric hematology-oncology). Intern. in pediatrics Bellevue Hosp., N.Y.C., 1954-55; resident in pediatrics, 1955-56; chief resident in pediatrics Mt. Sinai Hosp., N.Y.C., 1958-59; fellow in pediatric hematology Children's Hosp. Med. Center, Boston, 1959-61; chief pediatrics Greenpoint Hosp., Bklyn., 1962-64, City Hosp. Center, Elmhurst, N.Y., 1964-73; dir. pediatrics Beth Israel Hosp., N.Y.C., 1973-81; prof. pediatrics Mt. Sinai Sch. Medicine, N.Y.C., 1972-81, N.Y.U. Sch. Medicine, 1981—; chief pediatric oncology N.Y.U. Sch. Medicine (Med. Ctr.), 1981—; adj. prof. Rockefeller U., 1980—; chief sect. pediatric hematology Lenox Hill Hosp., N.Y.C., 1981—. Contbr. chpts. to books and articles to profl. jours. Served to capt., M.C. U.S. Army, 1956-58. Mem. Am. Pediatrics Soc., Am. Soc. Hematology, Am. Assn. Cancer Research, Am. Soc. Clin. Oncology, Am. Acad. Pediatrics, N.Y. Acad. Medicine, Phi Beta Kappa, Alpha Omega Alpha. Club: Dartmouth (N.Y.C.). Current Work: Pediatric oncology-hematology, childhood leukemia, Hodgkin's disease, cell differentiation, edn. and clin. care. Subspecialties: Oncology; Hematology. Office: 530 1st Ave Suite 6A New York NY 10016

RAVEN, PETER HAMILTON, botanical garden executive; b. Shanghai, China, June 13, 1936; s. Walter Francis and Isabelle Marion (Breen) R.; m. Tamra Engelhorn, Nov. 29, 1968; children—Alice Catherine, Elizabeth Marie, Francis Clark, Kathryn Amelia. A.B., U. Calif., Berkeley, 1957; Ph.D., UCLA 1960. Taxonomist Rancho Santa Ana Bot. Garden, Claremont, Calif., 1961-62; asst. prof., asso. prof. biol. scis. Stanford, 1962-71; dir. Mo. Bot. Garden, Engelmann prof. biology Washington U., St. Louis, 1971—; mem. Nat. Mus. Services Bd., 1977—, chmn., 1984—; mem. governing bd. NRC, 1983-86. Author: Biology of Plants, 1971, 4th edit., 1985; Principles of Tzeltal Folk Taxonomy, 1974, Biology, 1985, others.; Contbr. articles to profl. jours. Mem. Bd. Commrs., Tower Grove Park, 1971—; Vice-pres. XIII Internat. Bot. Congress, Sydney, 1981; bd. dirs. World Wildlife Fund-U.S., 1983—. Recipient Disting. Service award Am. Inst. Biol. Scis., 1981; John and Catherine T. MacArthur Found. fellow, 1985—. Fellow Am. Acad. Arts and Scis., Calif. Acad. Scis., AAAS; mem. Nat. Acad. Scis., Bot. Soc. Am. (past pres.), Soc. for Study Evolution (past pres.), Am. Soc. Plant Taxonomists (past pres.), Am. Assn. Bot. Gardens and Arboreta, Assn. Systematics Collections (past pres.), Orgn. Tropical Studies (dir.) (pres. 1985-86), Japan Am. Soc. (past pres. St. Louis), Phi Beta Kappa, Sigma Xi. Clubs: University (St. Louis), Noonday (St. Louis). Current Work: Evolution and systematics of higher plants; biogeography of the southern hemisphere. Subspecialties: Evolutionary biology; Systematics. Home: 2361 Tower Grove Ave Saint Louis MO 63110 Office: PO Box 299 Saint Louis MO 63166

RAW, CECIL JOHN GOUGH, chemistry educator; b. Ixopo, Natal, South Africa, Oct. 20, 1929; s. Cecil H. and Beryl Natalie (Gough) R.; m. Gillian Carole Galt, Jan. 7, 1956; children: Jeremy, Timothy, Matthew, Rebecca. B.S. with honors, U. Natal, 1951, M.S., 1952, Ph.D., 1956. Lectr., sr. lectr. in chemistry U. Natal, 1954-59, African Explosives and Chem. Industries Research fellow, 1957-59; research fellow U Minn., Mpls., 1959-60; vis. prof. molecular physics U. Md., 1962; asst. prof. phys. chemistry St. Louis U., 1960-62, assoc. prof., 1962-66, prof., 1966—. Contbr. articles to profl. jours. Mem. Am. Chem. Soc., AAUP, Sigma Xi. Current Work: Oscillatory chemical reactions, molecular reaction dynamics, thermodynamics of systems far from equilibrium, microcomputers in physical chemistry. Subspecialties: Physical chemistry; Kinetics. Office: Dept Chemistry St Louis U Saint Louis MO 63103

RAWAL, BHARAT SINGH, materials company executive; b. New Delhi, India, Dec. 4, 1948; came to U.S., 1970; s. Ram Singh and Shakuntla (Dhingra) R.; m. Reeta Pawa, Jan. 18, 1975; 1 child, Ekta. B. Tech., Indian Inst. of Tech., Kanpur Uttar Pradesh, India, 1970; M.S., N.C. State U., 1971; M.S., Case Western Res. U., 1973; Ph.D., Rensselaer Poly. Inst., 1976. Research assoc. N.C. State U., Raleigh, 1977-78; materials scientist AVX Corp., Myrtle Beach, S.C., 1978-79, sect. mgr., 1979-80, group mgr., 1980-83, ops. mgr., 1983-84, v.p., 1984—, dir. ops., 1984. Patentee in field. Contbr. articles to prof. jours. Mem. Am. Ceramic Soc., IEEE. Current work: Electronic properties of ceramics, microstructure and related phenomena, reliability and failure analysis. Subspecialty: Ceramics. Home: 531 Forestbrook Dr Myrtle Beach SC 29577 Office: Integrated Capacitor Div PO Box 867 Myrtle Beach SC 29577

RAWAT, ARUN KUMAR, biochemist, researcher, educator, consultant; b. Agra, U.P., India, Sept. 19, 1945; came to U.S., 1969, naturalized, 1973; s. Pyre L. and Shyama L. Rawat; m. Anu R. Sharma, July 26, 1976; children: Atul, Angeli. B.S., U.Lucknow, 1962, M.S., 1964; D.Sc., U. Copenhagen, 1969. Asst. prof. SUNY-Bklyn., 1971-72; assoc. prof. Med. Coll. Ohio, Toledo, 1973-78; prof. U. Toledo, 1979—; exec. dir. Midwest Inst. for Treatment and Study of Alcoholism, Toledo, 1973—. Contbr. articles on biol. chemistry to profl. jours. Mem. Am. Soc. Neurochemistry, Fedn. Am. Soc. Biol. Chemists, Am. Coll. Toxicologists. Current Work: Neurobehavioral toxicology, brain development, alcohol metabolism, fetal alcohol syndrome enzymology. Subspecialties: Biochemistry (medicine); Neuropharmacology. Office: Midwest Inst PO Box 5888 Toledo OH 43613

RAY, CHARLES DEAN, neurosurgeon; b. Americus, Ga., Aug. 1, 1927; s. Oliver Tinsley and Katherine (Broadfield) R.; m. Christie Ross, Dec. 24, 1952 (dec. 1972); children—Bruce, Kathy, C. Marlene, Thomas; m. Roberta Mann Brenden, Dec. 17, 1978; children—John, Blythe. A.B., Emory U., 1950; M.S., U. Miami, 1952; M.D., Med. Coll. Ga., 1956; Ph.D., Mayo Found., 1962. Diplomate Am. Bd. Neurologsurgery, Am. Bd. Electroencephalography. Fellow, research asst. Mayo Clinic and Found., Rochester, Minn., 1962-64; asst. prof. neurosurgery Johns Hopkins U. Sch. Medicine, Balt., 1964-68; chief dept. med. engring. Hoffman-LaRoche, Basel, Switzerland, 1968-72; v.p. med. research Medtronic, Inc., Mpls., 1972-79; assoc. dir., chief of neuroaugmentive surgery Inst. for Low Back Care, Mpls., 1979—; sr. cons. Sister Kenny Inst., Mpls., 1974—; pres. Charles Ray, Ltd., Wayzata, Minn., 1981—; cons. designer Herman Miller, Inc., Zeeland, Mich., 1984—; adv. panel on chemonucleolysis, Smith Labs., Inc., Northbrook, Ill., 1984—; industry rep. Panel Neurol. Devices, Washington, 1974-78; dir. Herman Miller, Inc., Zeeland, Mich., Newart Elect. Sci., Inc., Mpls., Assn. Advanced Med. Instrumentation Found., Washington, 1973—; cons. New Med. Sch., St. Gall, Switzerland, 1969-72; lectr. Burgerspital, Basil, 1968-72. Author: Principles of Engineering Applied to Medicine, 1964; Medical Engineering, 1974. Editor-in-chief Med. Program Through Tech., 1970-80; co-editor: Lumbar Spine Surgery, 1985. Contbr. articles to profl. jours. Patentee med. devices. Served with USNR, 1945-49. Fellow A.C.S., Royal Soc. of Health; mem. Pan Am Med. Assn., AMA, Am. Assn. Neurol. Surgeons, Sigma Xi, Alpha Omega Alpha. Republican. Episcopalian. Clubs: Mpls., Lafayette (Mpls.), Cosmos (Washington). Current work: Design, development and production of medical and surgical devices and systems, development and documentation of neurosurgical techniques, low back surgery. Home: 19550 Cedarhurst Wayzata MN 55391 Office: Inst for Low Back Care 2737 Chicago Ave Minneapolis MN 55407

RAY, PRASANTA KUMAR, tumor immunologist, researcher; b. Calcutta, W. Bengal, India, Sept. 29, 1941; came to U.S., 1969; s. Benode Behari and Labanya Prava (Das) R.; m. Khana Basu, Aug. 7, 1969; children: Partha, Amartya. B.S. with honors, U. Calcutta, 1962, M.S., 1964, Ph.D., 1968, D.Sc., 1974. Research specialist, instr. dept. surgery U. Minn., 1969-73; sr. sci. officer, head cancer immunobiology Bhabba Atomic Research, Bombay, India, 1973-76; dir. Chittaranjan Nat. Cancer Research Ctr., Calcutta, 1976-77; research dir. Bengal Immunity Research Ctr., Calcutta, 1977-78; dir. Alma Dea Morani Lab. Medical Coll. Pa., Phila., 1978—; Mem. editorial bd. Jour. Plasma Therapy, Boston, 1981—; chief com. immunology and nutrition Internat. Federation Human Health, 1980—. Editor: Immunobiology of Transplantation, Cancer and Pregnancy, 1983. Recipient cancer research award Indian Council Medical Research, 1977; fellow Indian Coll. Allergy and Applied Immunology, 1974-78; grantee cancer research W.W. Smith Charitable Trust, 1980-83, R.J. Reynolds Industries, Inc., 1981-83; grantee biomedical research NIH, 1980. Mem. Indian Immunology Soc., Am. Assn. Immunologists, N.Y. Acad. Scis., Am. Assn. Apheresis. Current Work: Teaching, guiding and directing research on tumor immunology and immunotherapy and chemo-immunotherapy. Subspecialties: Cancer research (medicine); Immunobiology and immunology. Office: Alma Dea Morani Lab Surg Immunobiology Medical Coll Pa 3300 Henry Ave Philadelphia PA 19129

RAY, RICHARD HALLETT, neurophysiologist; b. Charlotte, N.C., May 31, 1951; s. George Irving and Katherine Knight (Hallett) R.; m. Elizabeth Cadieu, Aug. 6, 1971; children: Richard Hallett, Scott Howell. Student, Bucknell U., 1969-70; B.A. in psychology, U. N.C., Charlotte, 1972; Ph.D. in Physiology, Med. Coll. Ga., 1980. Grad. teaching asst. dept. physiology Med. Coll. Ga., 1974-80; Ahmanson fellow Brain Research Inst., dept. anatomy UCLA, 1980-82; asst. prof. physiology East Carolina U., Greenville, N.C., 1982—, mem. grad. faculty, 1983—. Contbr. in field. Mem. Soc. Neuroscience, Am. Physiol. Soc., AAAS, Sigma Xi. Democrat. Current Work: Coding in sensory systemsof vertebrates; cerebral cortical devel. and plasticity; characterization of myocardial afferents in renal hypertension and heart failure. Subspecialties: Neurophysiology; Sensory processes. Home: 230 Chippendale Dr Greenville NC 27834 Office: Dept Physiolog Sch Medicine East Carolina Greenville NC 27834

RAY, RICHARD SCHELL, veterinarian, educator; b. Antwerp, Ohio, May 21, 1928; s. Alton D. and Dorothy Fransis (Schell) R.; m. Diane Maxine Foster, June 12, 1954; children: Kathleen F., David A., Elizabeth A. B.A., Ohio State U., 1950, D.V.M., 1955, M.S., 1958, Ph.D., 1963. Lic. Ohio Bd. Vet. Examiners; accredited U.S. Dept. Agr. Practice vet. medicine, Toledo, 1955. Instr. vet. clin. scis. and Grad. Sch. Ohio State U., Columbus, 1955-63, asst. prof., 1963-67, assoc. prof., 1967-73, prof., 1973-84, prof. emeritus, 1984—, teaching team leader, 1969-74, 77-84; cons. forensic pharmacology and metabolic disease; dir. Pre- and Post-Race Drug Detection Lab., Ohio State U., 1969-84. Contbr. articles to profl. jours. Grantee Harness Racing Inst., 1965-68; Grantee N.Y. Racing Asn., 1965-68; Grantee Jockey Club, 1965-68; Grantee U.S. Trotting Assn., 1969, 71; Grantee Horseman's Benevolent Protective Assn., 1971; Grantee Nat. Assn. State Racing Commrs., 1976; Grantee Snyder Mfg. Co., 1970; Grantee USPHS, 1967-71; Grantee HEW, NIH, 1973; Grantee Ohio Thoroughbred Fund, 1967-84. Fellow Am. Coll. Vet. Pharmacology and Therapeutics; mem. Am. Soc. Vet. Physiologists and Pharmacologists, World Assn. Vet. Physiologists, Pharmacologists and Biochemists, Assn. Ofcl. Racing Chemists, Assn. Drug Detection Labs., Am. Chem. Soc. (div. medicinal chemistry), Am. Assn. Vet Clinicians, Am. Assn. Equine Practitioners, Phi Zeta, Omega Tau Sigma, Alpha Sigma Phi. Republican. Methodist. Lodge: Masons. Current Work: Development of new methods for the detection and identification of unauthorized drugs, using gas chromatography, high performance thin layer and liquid chromatography and computer enhanced gaschromatography-mass spectrography. Subspecialties: Pharmacology; Biochemistry (medicine). Home: 2752 Folkstone Rd Columbus OH 43220 Office: 1935 Coffey Rd Columbus OH 43210

RAY, TUSHAR KANTI, membrane biologist, biochemist, educator; b. Calcutta, West Bengal, India, Oct. 31, 1939; came to U.S., 1967; s. Kamalakshya and Dhumabati R.; m. Mukta Mala Ghose, July 14, 1966; children: Amit, Asim. B.Sc. with honors, U. Calcutta, 1960, M.Sc., 1962, Ph.D., 1966. Research fellow U. Pitts., 1967-68; research assoc. U. Rochester, 1968-70; asst. research physiologist U. Calif., Berkeley, 1970-75; sr. research scientist U. Tex., Houston, 1975-78; assoc. prof. surgery and physiology SUNY-Upstate Med. Ctr., Syracuse, 1978—, now prof., dir. surg. research labs., 1978—. NIH grantee, 1977; NIH award, 1977. Mem. Am. Physiol. Soc., Am. Soc. Biol. Chemists, Biophys. Soc., N.Y. Acad. Sci., AAAS. Democrat. Hindu. Current Work: Studying the molecular mechanism and control of gastric acid secretion and trying to use the knowledge for anti-ulcer drug development. Subspecialty: Membrane biology. Home: 302 Greenwood Rd Dewitt NY 13214 Office: SUNY Upstate Med Ctr 750 E Adams St Syracuse NY 13210

RAY, WESLEY CARL, chemistry researcher; b. Asheboro, N.C., Mar. 20, 1946; s. John Frank and Mary Carter (Jones) R.; m. Janet Hancock, Sept. 13, 1969; children—Andrew Morgan, Emily Marie. B.S., U. N.C., 1967; Ph.D., U. Ga., 1972. Sr. chemist Borg Wagner Chemicals, Washington, W.Va., 1972-74, group leader, 1974-79, sect. mgr., 1979-84, assoc. tech. dir., 1984—. Contbr. articles to profl. jours. Patentee in field. Baseball, soccer coach Vienna Recreation Dept., W.Va., 1984—. Served to capt. U.S. Army. Mem. Am. Chem. Soc. (sec. mid Ohio Valley sect. 1978-79), Soc. of Plastics Engrs. Democrat. Methodist. Current works: Chemistry and structures and mechanisms of polymer stabilization; synthesis of phosphorus chemicals as polymer additives. Subspecialties: Organic chemistry; Polymer chemistry. Home: 5403 10th Ave Vienna WV 26105Office: Borg-Warner Chem PO Box 68 Washington WV 26181

RAYMOND, DELMAR RICHARD, paper manufacturing company executive; b. Maine, Mar. 12, 1943. B.S. in Chem. Engring., U. Maine, 1965, M.S., 1966, Ph.D., 1969. Sr. devel. engr. research and devel. St. Regis, West Nyack, N.Y., 1970-72, mgr. research and devel., 1972-74, mgr. environ. tech., 1974-75, dir. chems. and energy, 1975-77; mgr. energy dept. research and devel. Weyerhaeuser, Tacoma, 1977-81, dir. energy sci. and tech., 1981—; chmn. research com., dir. U. Maine-Orono Pulp and Paper Found. Recipient Edward R. Gay award St. Regis Paper Co., 1973; U. Maine-Orono Found. Honor award, 1981. Mem. TAPPI, Am. Inst. Chem. Engrs. (past chmn. forest products div.; award 1982), Am. Paper Inst. (chmn. research and devel. subcom.). Office: Weyerhaeuser Co WTC 2B19 Tacoma WA 98477

RAYNAL, DUDLEY JONES, botany educator; b. Greenville, S.C., Jan. 1, 1947; s. Charles E. and Laetita (Jones) R.; m. Georgia Pender, June 12, 1971; children—Ann E., George D. B.S., Clemson U., 1969; Ph.D., U. Ill., 1974. Vis. lectr. U. Ill., Urbana, 1974; from asst. prof. to assoc. prof. botany SUNY-Syracuse, 1974-84, prof., 1984—; chmn.-elect Nat. Atmospheric Deposition Program, 1984—. Contbr. articles to profl. jours. Mem. Ecol. Soc. Am., Bot. Soc. Am., Brit. Ecol. Soc., AAAS. Democrat. Presbyterian. Current work: Plant ecology, environmental biology. Subspecialty: Ecology (biology). Home: 152 Tejah Ave Sycaruse NY 13210 Office: SUNY Coll Environ Sci and Foresty Syracuse NY 13210

RE, GERALD JAMES, dental educator; b. Oak Park, Ill., July 22, 1943; s. Donald Charles and Ruth (Fishback) Swenson; m. Judy Carol Colvin, Jan. 9, 1965; children: Craig Allen, Christine Angela. B.S., U. Ill., 1966; D.M.D., U. Ky., 1972. Pvt. practice dentistry, Berea, Ky., 1973-77; restorative instr. U. Ky., Lexington, 1973-77; assoc. prof. operative dentistry U. Tex., San Antonio, 1977—. Mem. Am. Assn. Dental Research, Am. Assn. Dental Schs. Current Work: Causes and prevention of vertical tooth fracture, clinical caries detection and removal, methods which facilitate performance of operative dental restorations. Office: Restorative Dentistry Dept 7703 Floyd Curl Dr San Antonio TX 78284

READ, GEORGE WESLEY, pharmacologist, educator; b. Los Angeles, June 24, 1934; s. Earl George and Gertrude Louise (Mason) R.; m. Dorothy Davis, Aug. 22, 1954 (div. Nov. 1981); children: Gregory Cecil, Lani Louise (dec.), Bonnie Alice. A.A., Menlo Coll., 1957; B.A. in Biology, Stanford U., 1959, M.S. in Physiology (Rosenberg scholar), 1962; Ph.D. in Pharmacology, U. Hawaii, 1969. Cert. tchr., Calif. Instr. U. Hilo, Hawaii, 1963-64; asst. prof. U. Hawaii, Honolulu, 1968-74, assoc. prof., 1974—; vis. scientist U. Tex., 1975, 84, U. Wash., 1975, NIH, 1978, Northeast London Poly., 1982, St. Louis U., 1983. Contbr. articles to profl. jours., chpts. to books. Mem. Am. Soc.

Pharmacology and Exptl. Therapeutics, Western Pharmacology Soc. Current Work: Research on histamine secretion, drug-receptor interactions. Subspecialties: Molecular pharmacology; Receptors. Office: Pharmacology Dept John A Burns Sch Medicine U Hawaii Honolulu HI 96822

READ, RALSTON BAKER, microbiologist; b. Rehoboth, Mass., Mar. 31, 1926; s. Ralston Baker and Ida (Horton) R.; m. Helen Elizabeth Murdoch, June 11, 1949; children—Judith Elizabeth, Ralston Baker III, Steven Edward. A.B., Brown U., 1946; M.S., U. N.H., 1949; Ph.D., U. Mass., 1956. Asst. prof. U. Mass., Amherst, 1956-60; microbiologist USPHS, Cin., 1960-70; dep. dir. FDA, Washington, 1971-76, dir. div. microbiology, 1976—; chmn. food hygiene com. WHO, 1981—. Contbr. articles to sci. jours. Patentee method of preparation of viral vaccines. Served with USN, 1944-46. Recipient award of merit FDA, 1972, 83. Mem. Am. Soc. Microbiology, Internat. Assn. Sanitarians. Microbiological problems of foodborne origin that pertain to acute and chronic human disease. Subspecialty: Microbiology (medicine). Office: Div Microbiology Food and Drug Adminstrn 200 C St SW Washington DC 20204

READEY, DENNIS WILLIAM, ceramic engineering educator, consultant; b. Aurora, Ill., Aug. 6, 1937; s. William George and Lenoa Katherine (Kopp) R.; m. Suzann Dalton, May 21, 1958; children—Michael, Kevin. B.S. in Metallurgy, U. Notre Dame, 1959; Sc.D. in Ceramics, MIT, 1962. Group leader Argonne Nat. Labs., Ill., 1964-67; lab. mgr. Raytheon Co., Waltham, Mass., 1967-74; program mgr. U.S. ERDA, Washington, 1974-77; assoc. prof. ceramic engrng. Ohio State U., 1977-82, prof., chmn. dept., 1982—; mem. Nat. Materials Adv. Bd., Washington, 1983—. Contbr. articles to profl. jours. Served to capt. U.S. Army, 1962-64. Fellow Am. Ceramic Soc.; mem. AAAS. Current work: Ceramic processing, corrosion, dielectic properties, microwave properties, properties and characterization of provous materials. Subspecialty: Ceramic engineering. Home: 2315 Severhill Dr Dublin OH 43017 Office: Ohio State U 2041 College Rd Columbus OH 43210

READING, JOHN FRANK, physicist, educator; b. West Bromwich, Eng., Oct. 19, 1939; s. Frank Leslie and Winnifred Gertrude (Mason) R.; m. Anne Elizabeth Reading, Aug. 24, 1963; children: Daniel, Emma, Louise, Patience. B.A., Christ Church, Oxford (Eng.) U., 1960; M.A., Oxon, 1963; Ph.D., Birmingham (Eng.) U., 1964. Instr. physics MIT, 1964-66; sr. research assoc. U. Wash., Seattle, 1966-68; assoc. prof. physics Northeastern U., Boston, 1969-71; assoc. prof. Tex. A&M U., 1971-80, prof., 1980—; cons. Oak Ridge Nat. Lab. Contbr. articles to profl. jours. Hoff fellow, 1968-69. Fellow Am. Phys. Soc. Current Work: Scattering theory in atomic, nuclear and solid state physics; ab initio calculator of ion-atom cross sections for fusion. Subspecialties: Atomic and molecular physics; Nuclear physics. Home: 1223 Merry Oaks College Station TX 77840 Office: Dept Physics Texas A&M U College Station TX 77843

REAGAN, WILLIAM JOSEPH, chemist; b. Salem, Mass., Nov. 16, 1943; s. Joseph F. and Mary L. (Dionne) R.; m. Claudette A. Marcheterre, Aug. 28, 1965; children—Lisa, Kelly, Amy. B.S., Boston Coll., 1965; Ph.D., Mich. State U., 1969. Research chemist Mobil Research and Devel. Corp., Princeton, N.J., 1970-78; group leader, research assoc. Engelhard Corp., Menlo Park, Edison, N.J., 1978—. Patentee in field. Mem. Am. Chem. Soc., N.Am. Catalysis Soc. Subspecialties: Catalysis chemistry; Inorganic chemistry. Home: 10 Manor Dr Englishtown NJ 07726 Office: Engelhard Corp Menlo Park Edison NJ 08818

REAM, GREGORY LAWRENCE, electrical engineer; b. Sioux Falls, S.D., Aug. 28, 1949; s. Philip Henry and Eleanor Theresa (Utley) R.; m. Sieglinde Margaretha Kopp, Apr. 3, 1971; children—Jeffrey David, Jennifer Katherine, Amber Diana. B.S. in Elec. Engrng., MIT, 1971; M.S. in Elec. Engrng., U. Colo., 1972. Project engr. Unirad Corp., Denver, 1974-77; adv. engr. IBM Corp., Boulder, 1977—. Patentee ultrasonic scanner, 1980; compensation ink jet aero, 1981; breakoff uniformity maintenance, 1983; contbr. articles to profl. jours. NSF fellow, 1971; Outstanding Tech. Achievement award IBM Corp., 1984, Best Tech. Report award, 1984. Mem. IEEE, Eta Kappa Nu. Methodist. Current work: Development and modeling of ink jet printing technologies; ultrasonic imaging technology. Subspecialties: Electrical engineering; Acoustics. Home: 1124 E 5th Ave Longmont CO 80501 Office: IBM Corp 54E/025-2 6300 Diagonal Hwy Boulder CO 80302

REARDEN, CAROLE ANN, clinical pathologist, educator; b. Belleville, Ont. Can., June 11, 1946, came to U.S., 1971; d. Joseph Brady and Honora Patricia (O'Halloran) R. B.Sc., McGill U., Montreal, Can., 1969, M.Sc., 1971, M.D.C.M., 1971. Diplomate Am. Bd. Pathology, Am. Bd. Immunohematology and Blood Banking. Resident and fellow Children's Meml. Hosp., Chgo., 1971-73; resident pediatric U. Calif., San Diego, 1974, resident, fellow 1975-79; dir. histocompatability and clin. immunology lab., asst. prof. pathology U. Calif. San Diego Med. Ctr., 1979—. Contbr. articles to profl. jours. Prin. investigator devel. monoclonal antibodies to erythroid antigens. Mem. Mayor's Task Force on Acquired Immunodeficiency Syndrome, San Diego, 1983. Recipient Young Investigator Research award NIH, 1979; grantee U. Calif. Cancer Research Coordinating Com., 1982, NIH, 1983. Mem. Am. Assn. Pathologists, Am. Fed. Clin. Research, Am. Soc. Hematology, Am. Assn. Blood Banks (com. organ transplantation and tissue typing 1982—), Am. Assn. Clin. Histocompatibility Testing, Am. Soc. Transplant Physicians. Current work: Production of monoclonal and polyclonal antibodies to native erythroid antigens and to synthetic peptides corresponding to amino acid sequences of erythroid-specific proteins; application of monoclonal antibodies and molecular biology techniques in clinical laboratory practice. Subspecialty: Transplantation. Office: U Calif San Diego Med Ctr Dept Pathology H-720 225 Dickinson St San Diego CA 92103

REASOR, MARK J., toxicologist, educator; b. Evansville, Ind., Nov. 3, 1945; s. Chester T. and Catherine (Drury) R.; m. Mary Louise Comer, Aug. 19, 1967; children—Michael Andrew, Meredith Kathleen. B.S., Purdue U., 1967; M.A., Duke U., 1969; Ph.D., Johns Hopkins U., 1975. Diplomate Am. Bd. Toxicology. Asst. prof. W.Va. U.-Morgantown, 1976-80, assoc. prof., 1980-84, prof. toxicology, 1984—; cons. Procter & Gamble, Cin., 1983-84, Ctr. Environ. Health and Human Toxicology, Washington, 1985. Co-editor: Toxicology and the Newborn, 1984; mem. editorial bds. Toxicology, 1980—; Toxicology and Environmental Health, 1984; contbr. numerous articles to sci. jours. Served with AUS, 1969-71. Pharm. Mfrs. Assn. Found. Research Starter grantee, 1976-78, NIH grantee, 1979-82, Ctr. Alternatives to Animal Testing Research grantee, 1984. Mem. Soc. Toxicology, Am. Soc. Pharmacology and Exptl. Therapeutics. Club: Mountaineer Swim (past pres.). Current work: Drug toxicity; pulmonary toxicology; drug-induced phospholipidosis as it relates to health. Subspecialties: Toxicology (medicine); Cellular pharmacology. Home: 1153 Cambridge Ave Morgantown WV 26505 Office: Dept Pharmacology and Toxicology W Va U Med Ctr Morgantown WV 26506

REAVES, TROY ALBERT, JR., physiologist; b. Fort Worth, Aug. 7, 1945; s. Troy Albert and Emalyn (Sumner) R.; m. Antha Ruth May, June 2, 1984; children—Kenneth Raymond, Jack Melton, Kelly Renee. B.S., West Tex. State U., 1969; M.S., North Tex. State U., 1971; Ph.D., U. Ill., 1976. Asst. dept. zoology, U. Fla., Gainesville, 1974-75; vis. asst. prof. U. Ill., Urbana, 1975-76; postdoctoral fellow U. N.C., Chapel Hill, 1976-79, asst. prof., 1979-82; clin. research assoc. Alcon Labs., Fort Worth, 1982—. Contbr. articles to profl. jours. Fellow, grantee Nat. Inst. Neurological Communicative Disease & Stroke, Bethesda, Md., 1977-82; grantee N.C. Heart Assn., 1978. Mem. Soc. Neurosci., Am. Physiol. Soc. Current work: Development of ophthalmic products to treat external diseases of eye and glaucoma; neuroophthalmology; neuropeptide regulation visual function; neuroendocrinology. Subspecialties: Neurophysiology; Ophthalmology. Home: 1908 Jamestown Ct Arlington TX 76013 Office: Alcon Labs 6201 S Freeway Fort Worth TX 76134

REAZIN, GEORGE HARVEY, JR., chemist; b. Chgo., Feb. 3, 1928; s. George Harvey and Katherine Maria (Cole) R.; m. Ruth, June 3, 1950; children: Diane Reazin Clinton, David, Elizabeth. B.S., Northwestern U., 1949; M.S., U. Mich., 1951, Ph.D. (Univ. fellow), 1954. Research assoc. Brookhaven Nat. Lab., Upton, N.Y., 1954-56; with Joseph E. Seagram & Sons, Louisville, 1956—, head chemistry sect., 1971-81, mgr. chemistry research and services, 1982—; J. Guymon Meml. lectr. Am. Soc. Enologists, 1981. Contbr. articles to profl. jours. Mem. Bot. Soc. Am., Am. Chem. Soc., Am. Soc. Plant Physiology, Sigma Xi. Episcopalian. Current work: Chemistry of flavors and biochemistry of their formation; research into ways to measure organoleptic impact of different flavors. Subspecialties: Plant physiology (biology); Biochemistry (biology). Home: 25 Brantwood Ln Stamford CT 06903 Office: JE Seagram & Sons Tech Ctr 3 S Corporate Park Dr White Plains NY 10604

REBBERT, RICHARD EDWARD, chemist; b. Balt., Oct. 1, 1927; s. Richard and Anna Regina (Kaltenbach) R.; m. Alicia Contreras, Aug. 13, 1952; children—Maria Ann, Richard Fernando, Alicia Claire, Carolyn Rose. B.S., Loyola Coll., 1948; Ph.D., Cath. U. Am., 1952. Fellow, Can. Nat. Research Council, Ottawa, 1951-53; research chemist Ethyl Corp., Detroit, 1953-55; asst. prof. chemistry Georgetown U., Washington, 1955-61; research chemist Nat. Bur. Standards, Washington, 1961—. Contbr. articles to profl. jours. Current work: Use of chromatography in the analysis of various chemicals of environmental interest; preparation and analysis of various standard reference materials. Subspecialties: Analytical chemistry; Physical chemistry. Home: 5153 Sherrier Place NW Washington DC 20016 Office: Nat Bur Standards Gaithersburg MD 20899

REBBI, CLAUDIO, physicist; b. Trieste, Italy, Mar. 1, 1943; came to U.S., 1974; s. Piero and Arnalda (Montagnari) R.; m. Carla Casalini, Dec. 2, 1967; children—Ariella, Parvina. D.Physics, U. Torino, Italy, 1965, Specialist in Nuclear Physics, 1967. Postdoctoral fellow Calif. Inst. Tech., Pasadena, 1968-69; professore incaricato U. Trieste, 1970-72; research assoc. European Orgn. for Nuclear Research, Geneva, 1972-74; vis. assoc. prof. MIT, Cambridge, 1974-77; scientist Brookhaven Nat. Lab., Upton, N.Y., 1977-83, sr. scientist, 1983—. Editor: Lattice Gauge Theories and Monte Carlo Simulations, 1983; Solitons and Particles, 1984. Contbr. research articles and revs. to profl. publs. Mem. Am. Phys. Soc., N.Y. Acad. Scis. Roman Catholic. Current work: Field theory, theory of strong interactions, numerical simulation of quantum field theories. Subspecialties: Particle physics; Theoretical physics. Home: 10 Lubber St Stony Brook NY 11790 Office: Physics Dept 510A Brookhaven Nat Lab Upton NY 11973

REBEC, GEORGE VINCENT, neuroscientist, cons.; b. Harrisburg, Pa., Apr. 6, 1949; s. George Martin and Nadine (Bosko) R. A.B., Villanova U., 1971; M.A., U. Colo., 1974, Ph.D., 1975. Postdoctoral research fellow dept. psychiatry U. Calif., San Diego, 1975-77; asst. prof. psychology Ind. U., Bloomington, 1977-81, assoc. prof., 1981-85, prof., 1985—, acting dir. program in neurol. sci., 1984—; cons. NIMH. Contbr. articles to profl. jours. NIMH fellow, 1975-77; recipient Eli Lilly award Ind. U., 1979-80; NSF grantee, 1979-82, 85—; Nat. Inst. Drug Abuse grantee, 1979—. Mem. AAAS, Soc. Neurosci. (chpt. chmn.). Current Work: Mechanisms of action of psychotropic drugs, including hallucinogens, neuroleptics, and stimulants; drug-induced changes in neuronal activity and electrochemical signals are recorded simultaneously. Subspecialties: Neuropharmacology; Neurochemistry. Office: Dept Psychology Ind U Bloomington IN 47405

REBEIZ, CONSTANTIN ANIS, plant physiology educator; b. Beirut, July 11, 1936; came to U.S., 1969, naturalized, 1975; s. Anis C. and Valentine A. (Choueyri) R.; m. Carole Louise Conness, Aug. 18, 1962; children: Paul A., Natalie, Mark J. B.S., Am. U., Beirut, 1959; M.S., U. Calif. - Davis, 1960, Ph.D., 1965. Dir. dept. biol. scis. Agrl. Research Inst., Beirut, 1965-69; research assoc. biology U. Calif. - Davis, 1969-71; assoc. prof. plant physiology U. Ill., Urbana-Champaign, 1972-76, prof., 1976—. Contbr. articles to sci. publs. plant physiology and biochemistry. Recipient Funk award, 1985; named Outstanding Innovator, Sci. Digest, 1984-85. Fellow Explorers Club; mem. Am. Soc. Plant Physiologists, Comite Internat. de Photobiologie, Am. Soc. Photobiology, AAAS, Lebanese Assn. Advancement Scis. (exec. com. 1967-69), Sigma Xi. Greek Orthodox. Research on pathway of chlorophyll biosynthesis, chloroplast devel., bioengring. of photosynthetic reactors; pioneered biosynthesis of chlorophyll in vitro; duplication of greening process of plants in test tube, demonstration of operation of multibranched chlorophyll biosynthetic pathway in nature; formulation and design of laser herbicides. Current Work: Bioengineering of photosynthetic reactors of photosynthetic membranes; chloraphyll chemistry and biochemistry. Subspecialties: Nitrogen fixation; Biochemistry (biology). Home: 301 W Pennsylvania Ave Urbana IL 61801 Office: Vegetable Crops Bldg U Ill Urbana IL 61801

REBELLO, TESSIO ESTEVAM, biochemistry educator; b. Nakuru, Kenya, Oct. 15, 1941; came to U.S., 1980; s. Antonio and Maria R.; m. Gail Ann Vlcek, Feb. 17, 1984. B.Sc. with honors, U. Liverpool, Eng., 1970; Ph.D., U. London, 1974. Postdoctoral research Guys Hosp. Med. Sch., London, 1974-80; fellow U. Calif., Davis, 1980-81; research assoc. U. Nebr., Omaha, 1981-82, instr., 1982-83; asst. adj. prof. U. Calif., Irvine, 1983—. Contbg. chpt. to ency. 1977. Mem. Biochem. Soc., Am. Fedn. Clin. Research, AAAS, N.Y. Acad. Scis. Current work: Studies on etiology of hypertension; vitamin A and relationship to cancer. Subspecialties: Nutrition (biology); Biochemistry (biology). Home: 2007A S Circle View Dr Irvine CA 92715 Office: U Calif Irvine Med Ctr 101 City Dr S Orange CA 92668

REBER, ELWOOD F., nutrition educator, food science educator; b. Reading, Pa., June 24, 1919; s. Aquilla Peter and Irene Phoebe R.; m. Alta Mae Davis, Dec. 18, 1942; children—Ruth, Margaret, Rebecca. B.S., Berea Coll., 1944; M.S., Cornell U., 1948; M.S., Ph.D., Okla. State U., 1951. Prof. veterinary physiology and pharmacology U. Ill., Urbana, 1952-64; prof., head dept. food and nutrition U. Mass., Amherst, 1964-68; prof., head dept. food and nutrition Purdue U., 1968-73; dean coll. nutrition, textiles and human devel. Tex. Woman's U., 1974-78, prof. nutrition, 1978—. Contbr. numerous articles to sci. jours. Mem. Am. Inst. Nutrition, Inst. Food Technologists, Am. Chem. Soc. Current work: Protein, amino acids, zinc, aluminum, nutritional value in plant proteins, e.g., cottonseed; food safety of cottonseed. Subspecialties: Nutrition (biology); Biomass (agriculture). Home: 1824 Concord St Denton TX 76205 Office: Tex Woman's U PO Box 24134 Denton TX 76204

REBER, JERRY DONALD, physics educator; b. Lebanon, Pa., May 25, 1939; s. Hylton H. and Ruth E. (Ake) R.; m. Dixie E. Hill, July 13, 1963; children—Ellen M., Matthew H. B.A. in Physics, Franklin and Marshall Coll., 1961; Ph.D. in Physics, U. Ky., 1967. Research assoc. U. Va., Charlottesville, Va., 1967-68, asst. prof. physics, 1968-69; asst. prof. physics SUNY-Geneseo, 1969-72, assoc. prof., 1972-80, prof., 1980—, chmn. dept., 1980—; cons. Westinghouse Corp., Pitts., 1980—. Contbr. articles to atomic and nuclear physics to profl. publs. Mem. Geneseo Central Sch. Bd., 1977-82; coach Fingers Lake Youth Hockey, Geneseo, 1978—; lay leader Methodist Ch., Geneseo, 1983—. Grantee NSF, 1970-80, Suny Research Found., 1972-74; faculty research fellow NASA/ASEE, 1982-84. Mem. Am. Phys. Soc., Sigma Pi. Current work: Trace element analysis using PIXE techniques, 2 Mev Van de Graaff experiments, computers and computer interfacing. Subspecialties: Nuclear physics; Atomic and molecular physics. Home: 31 Stuyvesant Manor Geneseo NY 14454 Office: Dept Physics SUNY Geneseo NY 14454

RECHE, JOHN JOSEPH, electrical engineer; b. Saint Germain-en-laye, France, Feb. 18, 1939; came to U.S.; s. Michel Andre and Renee (Bezardin) R.; m. Yvette Suzanne Bellayer; children—Elizabeth, Anna. B.Applied Sci., U.B.C., 1971, M.Applied Sci., 1973. Registered profl. engr., B.C., Can. Research engr. Glenayre, Vancouver, B.C., Can., 1973; thin film research engr. GTE Lenkurt, 1974-78; mgr. materials tech. Memorex, Santa Clara, Calif., 1978-80; chief engr. P/M Industries, Portland, Oreg., 1980-82; mgr. thin film materials Censtor, San Jose, Calif., 1982-83; pres., cons. Optomag, Los Gatos, Calif., 1984—. Contbr. articles to profl. jours. Served with French Marines, 1959-61. Mem. Internat. Soc. Hybrid Microelectronics, IEEE, Optical Soc. Am., Am. Vacuum Soc., Internat. Soc. Optical Engring. Current work: Thin film devices and materials; microelectronics device fabrication; magnetic thin film heads and sputtered media; laser micromachining and magneto optic instruments. Subspecialties: Microelectronics; Laser data storage and reproduction. Home: 212 Lester Lane Los Gatos CA 95030 Office: Optomag 212 Lester Lane Los Gatos CA 95030

RECHNITZER, ANDREAS BUCHWALD, marine science and technology consultant; b. Escondido, Calif., Nov. 30, 1924; s. Ferdinand Martin and Dagmar (Buchwald) R.; m. Martha Jean Mitchell, Aug. 18, 1946; children: David Franklin, Andrea Jeanne, Martin Allan, Michael Jon. B.S., Mich. State U., 1947; M.A., UCLA, 1951; Ph.D., U. Calif.-San Diego, 1956. Coordinator deep submergence program Naval Electronics Lab., San Diego, 1956-61; chief scientist deep submergence N.Am. Aviation, Anaheim, Calif., 1961-70; tech. advisor Office Chief Naval Ops., Washington, 1970-85; pres. Sci. Diving Cons., San Diego, Cedam Internat., Dallas, 1968-77. Exec. producer: films Treasure of Scorpion Reef, 1968 (gold medal), Five Fathoms to a Lost Ship's Grave, 1968 (gold medal). Served to capt. USNR. Recipient gold medal Chgo. Geography Soc., 1960, Richard Hopper Day Phila. Acad. Sci, 1960, Underwater Photog. Soc. Am. award, 1961. Fellow Marine Tech. Soc. (sect. pres.); mem. Am. Oceanic Orgn., Explorers Club, Nat. Geog. Soc. (hon. life). Club: Cosmos. Scientist in charge record dive 35,800 feet, 1960 (disting. civilian service award). Current Work: Advanced concepts in ocean engineering and deep ocean technology. Subspecialties: Ocean engineering; Robotics. Home: 1345 Lomita Dr El Cajon CA 92020 Office: Science Applications Internat Corp 1345 Lomita Dr El Cajon CA 92020

RECHTIN, EBERHARDT, aerospace systems company executive; b. East Orange, N.J., Jan. 16, 1926; s. Eberhardt Carl and Ida H. (Pfarrer) R.; m. Dorothy Diane Denebrink, June 10, 1951; children: Andrea C., Nina, Julie Anne, Erica, Mark. B.S., Calif. Inst. Tech., 1946, Ph.D. cum laude, 1950. Asst. dir., dir. Deep Space Network, Calif. Inst. Tech. Jet Propulsion Lab., 1949-67; dir. Advanced Research Projects Agy., Dept. Def., 1967-70, prin. dep. dir. def. research and engring., 1970-71, asst. sec. def. for telecommunications, 1972-73; chief engr. Hewlett-Packard Co., Palo Alto, Calif., 1973-77; pres. Aerospace Corp., El Segundo, Calif., 1977—. Served to lt. USNR, 1943-56. Recipient major awards NASA, Dept. Def. Fellow AIAA (major awards), IEEE (major awards); mem. Nat. Acad. Engring., Tau Beta Pi. Subspecialty: Electrical engineering. Home: 1665 Cataluna Pl Palos Verdes Estates CA 90274 Office: 2350 E El Segundo Blvd El Segundo CA 90245*

RECKEL, RUDOLPH PETER, immunologist; b. N.Y.C., Feb. 14, 1934; s. Peter Rudolph and Christine Theresa (Stepp) R.; m. Phyllis Vincenza Bozzo, Sept. 8, 1957; children—Rudolph Peter, Steven Philip, Matthew Anthony. B.S. in Chemistry, Bklyn. Coll., 1956; M.S. in Chemistry, Georgetown U., 1962; Ph.D. in Biochemistry, Rutgers U., 1968. Biochemist U.S. Dept. Agr., Beltsville, Md., 1958-62; immunologist Ortho Research Found., Raritan, N.J., 1963-73; clin. immunologist Ortho Diagnostics Inc., Raritan, 1974-80; dir. clin. immunology Ortho Diagnostic Systems Inc., Raritan, 1980-85; dir. immunology Immunomedics, Newark, 1985—; mem. com. on reagent standards WHO. Contbr. articles to profl. jours. Patentee in field. Mem. rescue squad, Martinsville, N.J., 1970-74; scoutmaster Watchung council Boy Scouts Am., Bridgewater, N.J., 1978-76; vestryman St. Martins Episcopal Ch., Martinsville, 1969-80. Mem. Am. Assn. Blood Banks, Nat. Com. Clin. Lab. Standards, N.Y. Acad. Scis. Republican. Episcopalian. Current work: In-vitro and in-vivo diagnostic reagent development, auto immune diseases, rheumatological diseases, cancer diagnostics, isotopic-non isotopic immunoassays and imaging reagents. Subspecialties: Infectious diseases; Cellular engineering. Home: 1359 Roger Ave Bridgewater NJ 08869 Office: Ortho Diagnostic Systems Inc Hwy 202 Raritan NJ 08869

RECKTENWALD, DIETHER JOSEPH, biophysicist, research scientist; b. Voelklingen, Saar, Fed. Republic Germany, June 7, 1950; s. Alois and Rita Maria (Singer) R.; m. Jutta Maria Jaehnert, Sept. 5, 1975; 1 child, Benedict Arthur. B.S. in Phys. Chemistry, U. Saarlandes, Fed. Republic Germany, 1972, M.S. in Chemistry, 1974; Ph.D. in Biochemistry, Ruhr U., Bochum, Fed. Republic Germany, 1978. Research scientist Max Planck Inst., Dortmund, Fed. Republic Germany, 1976-79; vis. scientist Med. Sch., Stanford U., Calif., 1979-80, vis. scientist chem. dept., 1980-81; sr. scientist Becton Dickinson Monoclonal Ctr., Mountain View, Calif., 1981—; sci. advisor Sci. Logics, Inc., Cupertino, Calif., 1984—, Govt. of Pakistan, 1984—. Contbr. articles on bioenergetics, enzyme mechanisms, material properties to profl. jours. Patentee in field. Recipient award for outstanding creativity Internat. Expn. Inventions, 1970. Mem. Am. Chem. Soc., AAAS, Soc. for Analytical Cytology. Roman Catholic. Current work: Instrument and reagent systems for automated cell analysis, computer-based data acquisition, data reduction, algorithms and software, fluorescent dyes, image analysis. Subspecialty: Biophysics (biology). Office: Becton Dickinson Immunocytometry 2375 Garcia Ave Mountain View CA 94043

RECORDS, RAYMOND EDWIN, ophthalmology educator, physician; b. Ft. Morgan, Colo., May 30, 1930; s. George Harvey and Sara Barbara (Louden) R.; 1 dau., Lisa Rae. B.S., U. Denver, 1956; M.D., St. Louis, 1961. Diplomate: Am. Bd. Ophthalmology. Intern St. Louis U. Hosp. Group, 1961-62; resident in ophthalmology U. Colo. Med. Ctr., 1962-65; asst. prof. surgery U. Colo., Denver, 1965-70; prof. ophthalmology U. Nebr. Coll. Medicine, Omaha, 1970—, chmn. dept. ophthalmology, 1970—; cons. VA, Omaha, 1970—. Author: Physiology of Human Eye, 1979, Biomedical Foundations of Ophthalmology, 1982. Fellow Am. Acad. Ophthalmology; mem. Nebr. Med. Assn., Omaha Ophthal. Soc. (pres. 1980-81), Nebr. Acad. Ophthalmology. Current Work: Bacterial endophthalmitis, ocular physiology. Subspecialty: Ophthalmology. Home: 9916 Devonshire Dr Omaha NE 68114 Office: U Nebr Med Ctr 42d St and Dewey Ave Omaha NE 68105

REDDELL, DONALD LEE, agricultural engineer, educator; b. Tulia, Tex., Sept. 28, 1937; s. Kimball Tuscola and Winonah (Claiborne) R.; m. Minnie Ellen Cox, Jan. 27, 1957; children—Revis Diane, Cheryl Renee, Stephen Patrick. B.S., Tex. Tech. U., 1960; M.S., Colo. State U., 1967, Ph.D., 1969. Engr. High Plains Underground Water Conservation Dist., Lubbock, Tex., 1960-65; prof. agrl. engring. Tex. A&M U., College Station, 1969—; sec., treas. RES Engring. Inc., Bryan, Tex., 1981—. Contbr. articles to profl. jours. Mgr. Little League Baseball, Bryan, 1979-81. Recipient Disting. Performance award Tex. Agrl. Expt. Sta., 1980. Fellow Am. Soc. Agrl. Engrs. (Agrl. Engr. of Yr. award 1975, Disting. Young Agrl. Engr. award 1977, Best Paper award 1977, 83). Baptist. Club: River Oaks Racquet (Bryan). Current work: Development of numerical models describing air, water and solute movement in aquifers; storage of solar energy by injecting hot and cold water into aquifers; injection of air to decrease specific retention of water table aquifers. Subspecialties: Agricultural engineering; Hydrology. Home: 3808 Courtney Circle Bryan TX 77802 Office: Agrl Engring Dept Tex A&M U College Station TX 77843

REDDI, A(KEPATI) HARI, research biologist; b. Madras, India, Oct. 20, 1942; came to U.S., 1968, naturalized, 1978; s. Ramakrishna and Kausalya (Reddi) R.; m. Anu, June 4, 1972; children—Ajoy, Amit, Anand. B.Sc., Annamalai U., India, 1961, M.Sc., 1962; Ph.D., U. Delhi, India, 1966. Research assoc. Johns Hopkins U., Balt., 1968-69; research assoc. U. Chgo., 1969-71, asst. prof., 1972-77; vis. scientist NIH, Bethesda, Md., 1977-78, research biologist, 1978—, chief bone cell biology sect. Nat. Inst. Dental Research, 1980—. Editor: Biochemistry of Collagen, 1976; Extracellular Matrix Biochemistry, 1984. Mem. Am. Physiol. Soc., Am. Soc. Cell Biology, Endocrine Soc. Current work: Role of extracellular matrix in development, mineralization, local and systemic factors in bone formation. Subspecialties: Cell biology; Developmental biology. Home: 3525 Raymoor Rd Kensington MD 20895 Office: NIH 9000 Rockville Pike Bethesda MD 20205

REDDY, CHINTHAMANI CHANNA, biochemistry educator; b. Anantapur, India, Sept. 8, 1947; came to U.S., 1975, naturalized, 1978; s. Chinthamani Venkata Rami Reddy and Chinthamani (Obulamma) R.; m. Chinthamani Santha Reddy, Aug. 27, 1972; children; Chinthamani Deepika, Chinthamani Radhika. B.Sc., Regional Coll. Edn., India, 1968, B. Ed., 1969; M.Sc., Mysore U., 1971; Ph.D., Indian Inst. Sci., 1975. Postdoctoral fellow dept. chemistry Pa. State U., University Park, 1975-77, sr. research technologist, 1977-79, research assoc. Ctr. for Air Environ. Studies, 1979-81, asst. prof. vet. sci. dept., 1981-85, assoc. prof., 1985—. Recipient Gold medal Mysore U., 1971; Research Career Devel. award NIH, 1983—; Nat. Sci. Talent Research scholar, 1966-75. Mem. Am. Soc. Biol. Chemists, N.Y. Acad. Scis., AAAS. Current Work: Lipid peroxidation; biochemical interaction of vitamin E and selenium; prostaglandins; prostacyclins; thromboxanes and leukotrienes; pulmonary toxicity; glutathione S-transferases. Subspecialties: Biochemistry (biology); Environmental toxicology. Home: 229 Canterbury Dr State College PA 16803 Office: 226 Fenske Lab University Park PA 76802

REDDY, CHITRANJAN, electrical engineer; b. Hydreabad, India, Feb. 8, 1956; came to U.S., 1977, naturalized, 1980; s. Buchi N. and Ramulama Reddy; m. Elsa A. Reddy, Oct. 17, 1982. B. Tech., Jawaharial Nehru U., India, 1977; M.S. in Engring., Utah State U., 1978. Design engr. Nat. Semiconductor, Salt Lake City, 1978-80; sect. mgr. Tex. Instruments Inc., Houston, 1980-82, br. mgr., 1982-83; design mgr. Cypress Semiconductor, Santa Clara, Calif., 1983-84; dir. memories Modular Semiconductor, Santa Clara, 1984-85; v.p. engring. Alliance Semiconductor Inc., Santa Clara, 1985—. Patentee Dynamic ram. Nat. Merit scholar Govt. India, 1972-77. Mem. IEEE. Current work: Work involves the design of the most advanced semiconductor integrated circuits called DYNAMIC RAMs using sub-micron complementary metal oxide; designed a 64K and 256K dynamic at Tex. Instruments and currently working on megabit and beyond RAMs. Subspecialties: Microchip technology (engineering); Integrated circuits. Home: 1848 Country Club Dr Milpitas CA 95035 Office: Alliance Semiconductor Corp 1930 Zanker Rd San Jose CA 95112

REDDY, D. RAJ, computer science educator, institute administrator, consultant; b. Katoor, Chittoor, India, June 13, 1937; came to U.S., 1963; m. Anuradha; children—Shyamala, Geetha. Student Loyola U., Madras, India, 1952-54; B.E., Coll. Engring. U., Madras, 1958; M.Tech., U. New South Wales, Sydney, Australia, 1960; M.S., Stanford U., 1964, Ph.D., 1966. Applied sci. rep. IBM, Sydney, Australia, 1960-64; asst. prof. computer sci. Stanford U., 1966-69; assoc. prof. computer sci. Carnegie-Mellon U., Pitts., 1969-73, prof., 1973-85, Univ. prof., 1985—, dir. Robotics Inst., 1980—; cons. Westinghouse Electric, Pitts., Siemens, Munchen, W. Ger., Data Gen., Boston; mem. NASA Space Sci. and Tech. Adv. Com. Decorated Cross of Legion of Honor (France); Guggenheim fellow, 1976. Fellow IEEE, Acoustical Soc. Am.; mem. Nat. Acad. Engring., Am. Assn. Artificial Intelligence. Current work: Computer science, artificial intelligence, man-machine communication, machine architecture, robotics, speech, vision. Subspecialties: Robotics; Artificial intelligence. Office: Carnegie Mellon Univ Robotics Inst Pittsburgh PA 15213

REDDY, NARANDER PABBATHI, biomedical engineering educator; b. Karimnagar, India, May 5, 1947; came to U.S., 1969; s. Pabbathi Kakshma and Rathnamma (Annam) R.; m. Swarna Latha Vedire, Feb. 20, 1976; children—Haricharan, Vishnu-krupa. B.E., Osmania U., Hyderabad, India, 1969; M.S., U. Miss., 1971; Ph.D., Tex. A&M U., 1974. Research asst. Tex. A&M U., College Station, 1971-74, research assoc., 1974-75; research assoc. Baylor Coll. Medicine, Houston, 1975-76; postgrad. research physiologist U. Calif.-San Francisco, 1977-78; sr. research scientist Helen Hayes Hosp., West Haverstraw, N.Y., 1978-81; assoc. prof. biomed. engring. U. Akron (Ohio), 1981—; adj. assoc. prof. Rensselaer Poly. Inst., Troy, N.Y., 1979-80; adj. sci. staff mem. Edwin Shaw Hosp., Akron, 1984—. Contbr. 110 articles to profl. jours. Mem. Biomed. Engring. Soc. (sr.), ASME, Am. Soc. Engring. Edn., Rehab. Engr. Soc. N.Am., Sigma Xi. Current work: Application of biomechanics and computer modeling to problems in various clinical disciplines including orthopaedics, rehabilitation and cardiopulmonary medicine. Subspecialties: Biomedical engineering; Mechanical engineering. Home: 1231 Millhaven Akron OH 44321 Office: U Akron Biomed Engring Dept Akron OH 44325

REDDY, THOMAS BRADLEY, chemist; b. Amesbury, Mass., Sept. 11, 1933; s. Anthony William and Loretta Clare (Hanley) R.; m. Josina Maria van der Maas, Dec. 29, 1956 (div. Apr. 1977); children—David P., Peter J., Josina C. B.S., Yale U., 1955; Ph.D., U. Minn., 1960. Research assoc. U. Ill., Urbana, 1959-61; mem. tech. staff Bell Labs, Murray Hill, N.J., 1961-65; prin. research chemist Am. Cyanamid Co., Stamford, Conn., 1965-79; dir. battery tech. Stonehart Assocs., Madison, Conn., 1979-80; dir. tech. Power Conversion Inc., Elmwood Park, N.J., 1980—. Contbr. articles to profl. jours. Patentee in field. Mem. Water Control Commn., Town of Pound Ridge, N.Y., 1977-79, 80-81, chmn., 1981-82, mem. Planning Bd., 1982—. Edwin Rice fellow Gen. Electric Ednl. Found., 1958-59. Mem. Electrochem. Soc. (bd. dirs. 1969-71, chmn. electro-organic div. 1969-71), Am. Chem. Soc. Current work: Research and development work related to primary and secondary lithium batteries. Subspecialties: Physical chemistry; Analytical chemistry. Home: David's Ln Pound Ridge NY 10576 Office: Power Conversion Inc 495 Boulevard Elmwood Park NJ 07407

REDDY, VANGALA VENKATARAMI, biochemist; b. R.J. Dinne, India, June 3, 1939; came to U.S., 1969; s. Vangala Narayana and Ramakka Vangala (Onteddu) R.; m. Mary Vangala Mareddy, June 22, 1967; children—Suresh, Ramesh, Rajesh, Madhuri. B.S. in Chemistry, Sri Venkateswara U., Thirupati, India, 1959; M.S., Maharaja Sayagirao U., Baroda, India, 1964, Ph.D., 1968; M.D., St. Lucia Health Sci. U., St. Lucia, W.I., 1983. Postdoctoral fellow Drexel U., 1969-70; Rockefeller fellow U. Calif.-San Diego, 1970-73; research assoc. Worcester Found., Shrewsbury, Mass., 1973-76; instr. medicine Hahnemann Med. Sch., Phila., 1976-77; research asst. prof. ob-gyn Temple U., Phila., 1977-81, research assoc. prof., 1983—, chief Ob-Gyn Research Lab., 1977—. Contbr. numerous articles to sci. jours. Pres., Delaware Valley Telugu Assn., Phila., 1983. Council for Sci. Indsl. Research fellow, India, 1964-67. Mem. Am. Chem. Soc., Am. Soc. Neurochemistry, Endocrine Soc., Soc. Gynecol. Investigation, N.Y. Acad. Scis. Roman Catholic. Current work: Steroid metabolism in brain and other tissues; control mechanisms of neuroendocrine function and catacholestrogens in female reproduction and physiology. Subspecialties: Neuroendocrinology; Reproductive endocrinology. Home: 15-S Birchwood Park Dr Cherry Hill NJ 08003 Office: Temple Univ Med Sch 3400 N Broad St Philadelphia PA 19140

REDFIELD, ALFRED GUILLOU, biophysicist; b. Boston, Mar. 11, 1929; s. Alfred Clarence and Martha (Putnam) R.; m. Sarah Cossum, July 15, 1970; children—Rebecca, Samuel Duthie, Wendy. B.A., Harvard U., 1950; Ph.D., U. Ill., 1953. Fellow Harvard U., 1953-55; prof. physics IBM Watson Lab., Columbia U., 1955-70; research assoc. biochemistry U. Calif.-Berkeley, 1970-72; prof. physics and biochemistry Brandeis U., 1972—. Mem. Nat. Acad. Sci., Am. Acad. Arts and Scis. Subspecialty: Biophysics (physics). Office: Brandeis Univ Dept Physics Waltham MA 02154

REDGRAVE, TREVOR GORDON, biophysics educator; b. Perth, Australia, Jan. 26, 1940; came to U.S., 1981; s. Lindsay Gordon and Freda Vivien (Riegert) R.; m. Wendy Anne Lenton, June 17, 1960; children—Nicholas, Amanda, Leo. M.B., B.S., U. Western Australia, 1963, Ph.D., 1967. Research fellow Australian Nat. U., Canberra, 1969-71; reader in physiology U. Melbourne, Australia, 1972-80; assoc. prof. physiology and biophysics Boston U., 1981—. Contbr. articles to profl. jours.; mem. editorial bd. Jour. Lipid Research, 1981—. USPHS fellow, 1978. Mem. Am. Physiol. Soc., Am. Oil Chemists Soc., Am. Heart Assn. Current work: Metabolism of dietary fats and cholesterol and interactions of chylomicrons and remnant lipoproteins with plasma lipoproteins, cells and blood vessel walls. Subspecialties: Physiology (medicine); Biophysics (biology). Office: Boston U Med Ctr Biophysics Inst 80 E Concord St Boston MA 02118

REDISH, EDWARD FREDERICK, physicist, educator; b. N.Y.C., Apr. 1, 1942; s. Jules and Sylvia (Coslow) R.; m. Janice Copen, June 18, 1967; children: Aaron D., Deborah M. A.B. magna cum laude, Princeton U., 1963; Ph.D., M.I.T., 1968. Postdoctoral fellow Ctr. for Theoretical Physics, U. Md., College Park, 1968-70, asst. prof., 1970-74, assoc. prof., 1974-79, prof. physics, 1979—, chmn. dept., 1982-85; sabbatical visitor Ind. U. Cyclotron Facility, 1985-86; vis. fgn. collaborator C.E.N., Saclay, France, 1973-74; resident sr. research assoc. Goddard Space Flight Center, Greenbelt, Md., 1977-78. Recipient Kusaka Meml. prize in physics, 1963; Inst. Sci. medal Central Research Inst. Physics, Budapest, 1979; hon. Woodrow Wilson fellow; NSF predoctoral fellow. Fellow Am. Phys. Soc.; Mem. AAAS. Current Work: Research in theoretical nuclear physics and many particle scattering theory. Subspecialties: Nuclear physics; Theoretical physics. Office: Dept Physics and Astronomy U Md College Park MD 20742

REDMOND, ROBERT FRANCIS, nuclear engineering educator; b. Indpls., July 15, 1927; s. John Felix and Marguerite Catherine (Breinig) R.; m. Mary Catherine Cangany, Oct. 18, 1952; children: Catherine, Robert, Kevin, Thomas, John. B.S. in Chem. Engring, Purdue U., 1950; M.S. in Math, U. Tenn., 1955; Ph.D. in Physics, Ohio State U., 1961. Engr. Oak Ridge Nat. Lab., 1950-53; scientist, adviser-cons. Battelle Meml. Inst., Columbus, Ohio, 1953-70; prof. nuclear engring. Ohio State U., Columbus, 1970—, asso. dean Coll. Engring., dir. Engring. Experiment Sta., 1977—. Contbr. articles to profl. jours. V.p. Argonne Univs. Assn., 1976-77, trustee, 1972-80; mem. Ohio Power Siting Commn., 1978-82. Served with AUS, 1945-46. Mem. Am. Nuclear Soc. (chmn. Southwestern Ohio sect.), AAAS, Am. Soc. Engring. Edn., Sigma Xi, Tau Beta Pi. Current Work: University research administration. Subspecialties: Nuclear engineering; Nuclear fission. Home: 3112 Brandon Rd Columbus OH 43221

REED, ADAM VICTOR, engineering psychologist, workstation engineer; b. Torun, Poland, Jan. 11, 1946; came to U.S., 1959; s. Henry Kenneth and Eva (Tenenbaum) R.; m. Barbara Irene Birnbaum, Dec. 24, 1982. B.S.E.E., MIT, 1967, M.S.E.E., M.S. in Biology, 1970; Ph.D. in Math. Psychology, U. Oreg., 1974. Assoc. engr. Hewlett Packard Co., Palo Alto, Calif., 1966-67; mem. research staff Riverside Research Inst., N.Y.C., 1970-71; postdoctoral fellow, adj. asst. prof. Rockefelller U., N.Y.C., 1974-78; asst. prof. New Sch. Grad. Faculty, N.Y.C., 1977-81; mem. tech. staff Bell Labs. AT&T Info. Systems, Holmdel/Lincroft/Neptune, N.J., 1981—. Contbr. articles to profl. jours. Fellow NDEA Title IV, 1967, NSF, 1970, NIMH, 1975; NIH trainee, 1974. Mem. Assn. Computing Machinery, IEEE, Am. Psychol. Assn., Am. Soc. Cybernetics, Soc. Math. Psychology. Libertarian. Jewish Humanist. Current work: Biological and cognitive human factors in the design of user interface peripherals for computer systems. Subspecialties: Human factors engineering; Cognition. Home: 6 Gander Ln Manalapan NJ 07726 Office: AT&T Info Systems Route 66 Neptune NJ 07753

REED, CHARLES ALLEN, anthropologist, educator, zoologist; b. Portland, Oreg., June 6, 1912; s. Charles Allen and Gladys Ann (Donohoe) R.; m. Lois Ruth Wells, Aug. 15, 1951; children—Allen, Robert, Brian. Student Whitman Coll., 1929-30; B.S. in History and Geography, U. Oreg., 1937; Ph.D. in Zoology, U. Calif.-Berkeley, 1943. Instr. various schs., Oreg., Calif., Ariz., 1936-49; asst. prof. Coll. of Pharmacy U. Ill. Med. Ctr., Chgo., 1949-54, 55-57, assoc. prof., 1957-61; research assoc. dept. anthropology U. Chgo., 1954-55; assoc. prof. dept. biology, curator Peabody Mus. Natural History Yale U., New Haven, Conn., 1961-66; prof. depts. biology, sociology U. Ill.-Chgo., 1966-67, prof. dept. anthropology, 1967-80, acting head, 1967-70, prof. emeritus, 1980—; research assoc. Mus. No. Ariz., Flagstaff, 1949-51, div. of zoology Field Mus. Natural History, Chgo., 1966—; fossil collector stratigraphic div. U.S. Geol. Survey, summer 1950; mem. Iraq-Jarmo Project Oriental Inst. U.Chgo., 1954-55, Iranian Archeol. Project 1960, U.S. Nat. Com. of Internat. Union for Quaternary Research Nat. Acad. Sci., Washington, 1966-72, The U. of Istanbul's and U. Chgo.'s Joint Project for Prehistoric Research in Southeastern Anatolia, autumn 1970; dir. Yale U. prehistoric expedition to Nubia, 1962-65; pres. Kennicott Natural History Soc., Chgo., 1978-79; trustee Link Unlimited, Chgo., 1978-82; mem. bd. sci. govs. Chgo. Acad. Scis., 1978—. Editor: Origins of Agriculture, 1977. Contbr. numerous articles to sci. jours, abstracts. Mem. Am. Assn. Anthropologists (life), AAAS (life); mem. Am. Assn. Phys. Anthropologists, Current Anthropology (assoc.), Chgo. Anthrop. Soc., Chgo. Archeol. Soc. Am. Soc. for Mammalogists, Soc. Ichthyologists and Herpetologists (life), Soc. for Study of Evolution, Soc. of Vertebrate Paleontology, Am. Assn. Anatomists, Am. Soc. Zoologists, Am. Quaternary Assn., Internat. Soc. Cryptozoology, Explorers Club, Sigma Xi (life), Phi Beta Kappa (pres. chpt. 1985—), Kappa Sigma. Current work: Osteo-archaeology, origins of domestication, energy traps and tools in the animal kingdom. . Home: 423 N Cuyler Ave Oak Park IL 60302 Office: Dept of Anthropology U Ill at Chgo Chicago IL 60680

REED, HELEN LOUISE, mechanical engineering educator; b. Havre De Grace, Md., Oct. 3, 1956; d. Harry Leroy and Helen Catherine (Fuenfgeld) Reed. A.B., Goucher Coll., 1977; M.S., Va. Tech. Inst., 1980, Ph.D., 1981. Math. aid NASA Langley, Hampton, Va., 1976, aerospace tech., 1977-81; research asst. Va. Tech. Inst., Blacksburg, 1979-81, assoc., 1981, asst. prof. Stanford U., Calif., 1982-85; assoc. prof. mech. engring. Ariz. State U., Tempe, 1985—; cons. Internat. Cons. Sci. Tech., Blacksburg, 1981; vis. prof. Sandia Nat. Labs., Albuquerque, 1983. Contbr. articles to profl. jours. Merit scholar State Md., 1974; NASA fellow, 1976; Cunningham fellow Va. Tech. Inst., 1981; recipient Oustanding Achievement award NASA, 1978; Presdl. Young Investigator award NSF, 1984. Mem. Am. Phys. Soc., AIAA, Soc. Indsl. and Applied Math., Am. Soc. Engring. Edn., Internat. Assn. Computational Mechanics, ASME, Math. Assn. Am., Sigma Xi. Republican. Lutheran. Current work: Hydrodynamic stability; laminar flow control; computational fluid mechanics; transonic aerodynamics; perturbation methods; separated and transitional flows. Subspecialties: Fluid mechanics; Mechanical engineering. Office: Dept Mech and Aero Engring Ariz State U Tempe AZ 85287

REED, LESTER JAMES, educator, biochemist; b. New Orleans, Jan. 3, 1925; s. John T. and Sophie (Pastor) R.; m. Janet Louise Gruschow, Aug. 7, 1948; children—Pamela, Sharon, Richard, Robert. B.S., Tulane U., 1943; D.Sc. (hon.), 1977; Ph.D., U. Ill., 1946. Research asst. NDRC, Urbana, Ill., 1944-46; research asso. biochemistry Cornell U. Med. Coll., 1946-48; faculty U. Tex., Austin, 1948—, prof. chemistry, 1958—, Ashbel Smith prof., 1984—; research scientist Clayton Found. Biochem. Inst., 1949—, asso. dir., 1962-63, dir., 1963—. Contbr. articles profl. jours. Mem. Nat. Acad. Scis., U.S., Am. Acad. Arts and Scis., Am. Soc. Biol. Chemists, Am. Chem. Soc. (Eli Lilly & Co. award in biol. chemistry 1958), Phi Beta Kappa, Sigma Xi. Current work: Structure, function and regulation of multienzyme complexes; enzyme chemistry. Subspecialties: Biochemistry (biology); Molecular biology. Home: 3502 Balcones Dr Austin TX 78731

REED, MICHAEL CHARLES, mathematics educator; b. Kalamazoo, May 7, 1942; s. Gerald and Helen (Freund) R.; m. Marianne Szalkowski, Aug. 24, 1963 (div. Dec. 1971); 1 child, David; m. Jacqueline Ann Ariail, May 26, 1973; children—Isaac, Jacob. B.S., Yale U., 1963; M.S., Stanford U., 1966, Ph.D., 1969. Asst. prof. math Princeton U. (N.J.), 1968-74; prof. math Duke U., Durham, N.C., 1974—, chmn. dept. math., 1982-85. Author: (with Barry Simon) Methods of Modern Mathematical Physics, vol. 1, 1972, vol. 2, 1975, vol. 3, 1978, vol. 4, 1979. Mem. Am. Math. Soc. Current work: Problems of singularities in nonlinear waves; applications of mathematics to physiology and medicine. Office: Dept Math Duke U Durham NC 27706

REED, NORMAN DUANE, microbiologist, educator; b. Lyons, Kans., July 6, 1935; s. Francis L. and Helen J. (Rankin) R.; m. Sharon Lynn Mertel, Apr. 8, 1961; children—Kendall, Robin, Mary, Kimberly. B.S. in Microbiology, Kans. State U., 1959, M.S., 1962; Ph.D., Mont. State U., 1966. Asst. prof. U. Nebr.-Lincoln, 1966-70, asst. then assoc. prof. Mont. State U., Bozeman, 1970-76, prof., 1976-77, chmn. dept. microbiology, 1977—; affiliate prof. U. Wash.-Seattle, 1984—; Mem. editorial bd. Microbiol. Revs., 1981—, Exptl. Cell Biology, 1979—, Jour. Reticuloendothelial Soc., 1974-82. Served to cpl. U.S. Army, 1955-57. Recipient Research Career Devel. award NIH, 1972-77. Mem. Am. Assn. Immunologists, Am. Assn. Pathologists, Am. Soc. Parasitologists, Am. Soc. Microbiology (chmn. div. immunology 1983), Soc. Exptl. Biology and Medicine. Current work: Immune response to infectious agents; host parasite relationships; thymus gland. Subspecialties: Immunobiology and immunology; Microbiology (medicine). Office: Mont State U Dept Microbiology Bozeman MT 59717

REED, STEVEN GREGORY, research immunologist, consultant tropical medicine; b. Walla Walla, Wash., July 13, 1950; s. Delward L. and Mary J. (Juliano) R. B.A., Whitman Coll., 1973; M.S. in Microbiology, U. Mont., 1977, Ph.D., 1979. Scientist, Nat. Research Inst. of the Amazon, Manaus, Amazonas, Brazil, 1979-80; research assoc. Cornell Med. Coll., 1980-81, asst. prof., 1981—; prin. investigator Issaquah Health Research, Issaquah, Wash., 1984—; cons. Cornell-Bahia Project, 1984—. Contbr. articles to sci. jours. Mem. Am. Assn. Immunologists, Am. Soc. Tropical Medicine and Hygiene, AAAS. Current work: Using molecular biology to define specific antigens for immunization and diagnosis of parasitic diseases. Subspecialties: Immunobiology and immunology; Molecular biology. Office: Issaquah Health Research Inst 1595 NW Gilman Blvd Issaquah WA 98027

REEG, CLOYD PRITCHARD, oil company executive, researcher; b. Blissfield, Mich., Apr. 23, 1922; s. Cloyd Martin and Marguerite (Pritchard) R.; m. Bea Cheely, Dec. 12, 1970; 1 child, Cloyd P. B. Chem. Engring. cum laude, Ohio State U. Registered profl. engr., Calif. Devel. engr. research dept. Union Oil Co., Brea, Calif., 1948-53, sect. leader process engring. and design, 1953-59, group leader process research and devel., 1959-64, supr. tech. sales, 1964-68, mgr. refining research, refining and products research div., 1968-73, assoc. dir. research dept., 1973-78, head refining and products div., 1973-80, v.p. sci. and tech. div., 1978-80, pres. sci. and tech. div., corp. v.p., 1980—. Patentee in field. Mem. Orange County World Affairs Council, Calif., 1981—. Served to capt. USAAF, 1942-46. Recipient Benjamin G. Lamme medal Coll. Engring., Ohio State U., 1982. Mem. Am. Petroleum Inst., Nat. Petroleum Refiners Assn., Am. Inst. Chem. Engrs., Soc. Petroleum Engrs., Indsl. Research Inst. Republican. . Home: 2040 Skyline Dr Fullerton CA 92631 Office: Sci and Tech Div Unocal Corp 376 S Brea Blvd Brea CA 92621

REEL, JERRY ROYCE, research director, educator; b. Washington, Ind., May 4, 1938; s. Royce Howard and Anna Belle (Valin) R.; m. Joan Kay Wedberg, Aug. 14, 1965; 1 dau., Justine Jeanette. B.A., Ind. State U., 1960; M.S., U. Ill., 1963, Ph.D., 1966. Diplomate: Am. Bd. Toxicology. Am. Cancer Soc. postdoctoral fellow Oak Ridge Nat. Lab., 1966-68; sect. dir. endocrinology Warner-Lambert/Parke-Davis Research Labs., Warner Lambert Pharm. Co., Ann Arbor, Mich., 1968-78; dir. life scis. and toxicology div. Research Triangle Inst., Research Triangle Park, N.C., 1978-85; dir. endocrinology Sterling-Winthrop Research Inst., Rensselaer, N.Y., 1985—; adj. assoc. prof. Wayne State U., Detroit, 1973-78; Mem. adv. bd. Kildaire Homeowners Assn., Cary, N.C., 1979-82. Editor: Hypothalamic Hormones, 1973, Steroid Hormones and Cancer, 1975. Rev. panel mem. WHO, 1979; grant reviewer NSF, 1975, 78; mem. contract rev. panel NIH, 1979. Mem. Endocrine Soc., Am. Physiol. Soc., Am. Chem. Soc., Soc. Toxicology. Current Work: Research in reproductive and general endocrinology/toxicology; computer applications in research and development/biotechnology. Subspecialties: Reproductive biology; Endocrinology. Home: 3606 Coventry Ln East Greenbush NY 12061 Office: Sterling-Winthrop Research Inst 81 Columbia Turnpike Rensselaer NY 12144

REEMTSMA, KEITH, physician; b. Madera, Calif., Dec. 5, 1925; children—Lance Brewster, Dirk Van Horn. B.S., Idaho State Coll.; M.D., U. Pa., 1949; Med.Sci.D., Columbia U., 1958. Asst. surgery Columbia Coll. Phys. and Surg., 1957; faculty Tulane U. Sch. Medicine, 1957-66, prof. surgery, 1966; prof., head dept. surgery U. Utah Coll. Medicine, Salt Lake City, 1966-71; chmn. dept. surgery Valentine Mott prof. surgery; Johnson and Johnson distinguished prof. surgery Columbia U., N.Y.C., 1971—. Contbr. articles to profl. jours. Mem. Soc. Clin. Surgery, Am. Surg. Assn., Soc. U. Surgeons, A.C.S., So. Soc. for Clin. Research, Am. Fedn. for Clin. Research, Am. Assn. for Thoracic Surgery, Soc. for Vascular Surgery, Internat. Cardiovascular Soc., So. Thoracic Surg. Assn., New Orleans Surg. Soc., Surg. Assn. La., AMA, La. State, Orleans Parish med. socs., Alpha Omega Alpha. Subspecialty: Surgery. Office: Dept Surgery Columbia U 622 W 168th St New York NY 10032

REES, LAWRENCE BRENT, physicist; b. Tremonton, Utah, Sept. 21, 1953; s. Max Eugene and Ilene (Lawrence) R.; m. Loralee Kotter, July 21, 1978; children—Adam Brent, Nathan Kotter, Ellen. B.S., Brigham Young U., 1976; M.S., U. Md., 1979, Ph.D., 1983. Instr. U. Md.-Catonsville, 1980; research assoc. U. Md., College Park, 1983; physicist Los Alamos Nat. Lab., 1983—. Contbr. articles to profl. jours. Joseph Fielding Smith scholar Brigham Young U., 1971. Mem. Am. Phys. Soc., Am. Assn. Physics Techs. Mem. Ch. of Jesus Christ of Latter-day Saints. Current work: Nucleon and cluster knockout with polarized beam, pion elastic scattering, pion induced knockout, polarization transfer reactions. Subspecialty: Nuclear physics. Home: 78 Isleta Dr Los Alamos NM 87544 Office: P-2 Los Alamos Nat Lab MS D-456 Los Alamos NM 87545

REGELMAN, DALE FRANCIS, research chemist; b. Williamsport, Pa., Oct. 8, 1949; s. Augustus Thompson and Francis Martha (Andrews). B.A. in Chemistry, Cornell U., 1971; Ph.D. in Chemistry, U. Ariz., 1977. Postdoctoral fellow U. Ariz., 1977-79; instr. Pima Community Coll., 1977-79; research scientist Upjohn Co., North Haven, Conn., 1979—. Contbr. chpts. to books. Book reviewer Polymer News, London, 1983—. Patentee. Judge, Conn. State Sci. Fair, U. Conn., 1980—; grant reviewer NSF, 1982—. Mem. Am. Chem. Soc., N.Y. Acad. Scis., Am. Chem. Soc. (polymer sect), Aircraft Owners and Pilots Assn. Club: Cornell. Current work: Use of new Isocyanate chemistry to prepare new, high performance polymeric materials. Subspecialties: Organic chemistry; Polymer chemistry. Home: 42 Hope Hill Rd Wallingford CT 06492 Office: Upjohn Co 410 Sackett Point Rd North Haven CT 06473

REICHEN, JUERG, medical educator; b. Aarau, Aargau, Switzerland, Jan. 23, 1946; came to U.S., 1976; s. Hans A. and Susi K. (Aeberhard) R.; m. Suzi Graden, May 29, 1970; children: Hansjakob, Annemarie, Katharina. B.A., B.S., Staedt. Gymnasium Burgdorf, 1964; M.D., U. Berne, Switzerland, 1971. Fellow in pharmacology Hoffmann-LaRoche, Basel, Switzerland, 1972; fellow in clin. pharmacology U. Berne (dept. clin. pharmacology), 1973-76; guest scientist NIH, Bethesda, Md., 1976-78; resident VA Med. Ctr., Georgetown U., Washington, 1978-79; fellow in gastroenterology U. Colo. Hosp., Denver, 1979-80, asst. prof. medicine, 1980—. Swiss Nat. Fedn. Sci. Research fellow, 1976; Pharm. Mfrs. Assn. Found. grantee, 1981; NIH grantee, 1981. Mem. Swiss Med. Soc., Am. Fedn. Clin. Research, Western Soc. Clin. Investigation, Am. Gastroent. Assn., Am. Assn. Study Liver Disease. Current Work: Physiology of bile secretion and pathophysiology of cholestasis, quantitation of para and transcellular fluid movement, microcirculation of the liver, quantitation of liver function, pharmacological manipulation of portal hypertension. Subspecialties: Gastroenterology; Pharmacology. Home: 13104 E Exposition Ave Aurora CO 80012 Office: U Colo Med Sch 4200 E 9th Ave PO Box B-158 Denver CO 80262

REICHGOTT, MICHAEL J., physician, educator; b. Newark, July 26, 1940; s. Leo and Gertrude (Millman) R.; m. Lynn G. Haar, Dec. 22, 1962; children: Jay, Seth, Douglas. A.B., Gettysburg Coll., 1961; M.D., Albert Einstein Coll. Medicine, 1965; Ph.D. in Pharmacology, U. Calif., San Francisco, 1972. Diplomate: Am. Bd. Internal Medicine. Resident in internal medicine U. Calif., San Francisco, 1965-67, fellow in clin. pharmacology, 1969-72; asst. prof. medicine and pharmacology U. Pa., 1972-81, assoc. prof., 1981-84, dir. clin. practice dept. medicine, 1978-80; assoc. chief of staff for ambulatory care VA Hosp., Phila., 1980-81, chief sect. gen. medicine, 1981-84; assoc. prof. medicine Albert Einstein Coll. Medicine, 1984—, asst. dean, 1984—; med. dir. Bronx Mcpl. Hosp. Ctr., 1984—; chmn. South Eastern Pa. High Blood Pressure Control Program, 1980-84; cons. Teaching Nursing Home Program, Robert Wood Johnson Found., 1981—. Contbr. articles, revs. to profl. lit. Vice pres. Beth David Reform Congregation, Phila.; cubmaster, also mem. troop com. Boy Scouts Am. Served to maj. M.C. U.S. Army. Decorated Army Commendation medal. Fellow Phila. Coll. Physicians, ACP; mem. Am. Fedn. Clin. Research, Soc. Research and Edn. in Primary Care Internal Medicine, Am. Soc. Pharmacology and Exptl. Therapeutics, Alpha Omega Alpha. Democrat. Jewish. Current Work: Hospital administration, student education, non-physician health care provision, clinical research, trainee education. Subspecialties: Health services research; Pharmacology. Office: Bronx Mcpl Hosp Ctr Pelham Pkwy Bronx NY 10461

REICHLE, DAVID EDWARD, ecologist; b. Cin., Oct. 19, 1938; married; 3 children. B.S., Muskingum Coll., 1960; M.S., Northwestern U., 1961, Ph.D. in Biol. Sci., 1964. AEC fellow Oak Ridge Nat. Lab., 1964-66, research ecologist, 1966-75, assoc. dir. environ. sci. div., 1975—. Subspecialties: Ecology (biology); Ecosystems analysis. Office: Environmental Sciences Oak Ridge National Lab Oak Ridge TN 37831

REICHLE, FREDERICK ADOLPH, surgeon, educator; b. Neshaminy, Pa., Apr. 20, 1935; s. Albert and Ernestine R. B.A. summa cum laude, Temple U., 1957, M.D., 1961, M.S. in Biochemistry, 1961, M.S. in Surgery, 1966. Diplomate: Am. Bd. Surgery. Intern Abington Meml. Hosp., 1962; resident Temple U. Hosp., Phila., 1966, surgeon, 1966—, practice medicine specializing in surgery, Phila., 1966—; assoc. attending surgeon Epis. Hosp., St. Mary's Hosp., St. Christopher's Hosp. for Children, Phoenixville Hosp.; cons. VA Hosp., Wilkes Barre, Pa., Germantown Dispensary and Hosp.; chmn. dept. surgery Presbyn.-U. Pa. Med. Center, 1980—; prof. surgery U. Pa., 1980—. Contbr. articles to profl. jours. Recipient Surg. Residents Research Paper award Phila. Acad. Surgery, 1964, 66, Gross Essay prize, 1976; Am. Heart Assn. grantee, 1973. Fellow A.C.S., Coll. Physicians Phila.; mem. Am. Surg. Assn., Soc. Univ. Surgeons, AMA, Pa. Med. Soc., Assn. Acad. Surgery, N.Y. Acad. Sci., AAAS, Am. Fedn. Clin. Research, Nat. Assn. Professions, Am. Gastroent. Assn., Am. Assn. Cancer Research, Am. Heart Assn., Phila. Acad. Surgery, Heart Assn. Southeastern Pa., Internat. Soc. Thombosis and Haemostasis, Nat. Kidney Found., Soc. for Surgery Alimentary Tract, Soc. Vascular Surgery, Colleguim Internationale Chirurgie Digestivae, Am. Soc. Pharmacology and Exptl. Therapeutics, Am. Inst. Ultrasound in Medicine, Am. Physiol. Soc., Soc. Internationale de Chirurgie, Am. Soc. Abdominal Surgeons, Surg. Hist. Soc., Am. Aging Assn., Am. Geriatrics Soc., Gerontol. Soc., Am. Diabetes Assn., Surg. Biology Club, Omega Alpha, Sigma Xi, Phi Rho Sigma. Current Work: Lipid metabolism, blood vessel research, portal hypertension. Subspecialties: Surgery; Biochemistry (medicine). Home: 771 Easton Rd Warrington PA 18976 Office: 51 N 39th St Philadelphia PA 19104

REICHMANIS, ELSA, chemist, researcher; b. Melbourne, Victoria, Australia, Dec. 9, 1953; came to U.S., 1962, naturalized, 1972; d. Peteris and Nina (Meiers) R.; m. Francis J. Purcell, June 2, 1979. B.S., Syracuse U., 1972, Ph.D., 1975. Postdoctoral fellow Syracuse U., N.Y., 1975-78; mem. tech. staff AT&T Bell Labs., Murray Hill, N.J., 1978-84, supr., 1984—. Contbr. articles to profl. jours. Patentee in field. Chaim Weismann fellow, 1976-78. Mem. Am. Chem. Soc., AAAS, SPIE. Current work: Chemistry related to development of radiation sensitive materials for lithographic applications. Subspecialties: Organic chemistry; Polymers (materials science). Office: AT&T Bell Labs 600 Mountain Ave 1A261 Murray Hill NJ 07974

REID, ALLEN FRANCIS, biophysicist, educator, research and devel. consultant; b. Deer River, Minn., July 31, 1917; s. Allen Roy and Rose Cordelia; m. Dorothy Mary Cullen, May 31, 1943; children: Sally Anne, David Mark. B.Chemistry, U. Minn., 1940; A.M., Columbia U., 1942, Ph.D., 1943; M.D., U. Tex., Dallas, 1959. Clin. chemist Nat. Registry Clin. Chemists, 1968;

Dir. radioactivity labs. Columbia U., N.Y.C., 1942-45; indsl. cons., Phila. and N.Y.C., 1945-47; prof., chmn. dept. biophysics and phys. chemistry Grad. Research Inst., Baylor U., Dallas, 1947-50; assoc. prof. Southwestern Med. Sch., U. Tex., Dallas, 1947-51, prof., 1951-60, chmn. dept. biophysics, 1947-60; prof., chmn dept. biology U. Dallas, 1960-68, head sci. div., 1961-68; clin. prof. pathology Downstate Med. Ctr., SUNY, N.Y.C., 1968-74; dir. clin. biochemistry Bklyn.-Cumberland Med. Ctr., 1968-74; dir. pathology Cumberland Hosp., Bklyn., 1970-74; prof., chmn. dept. biology SUNY, Geneseo, 1974—; ptnr. Halff & Reid, Dallas, 1961—, profl. cons., 1947—. Contbr. articles to profl. jours. Fellow AAAS, Am. Inst. Chemists; mem. Am. Chem. Soc., Am. Phys. Soc., Am. Physiol. Soc., AMA, N.Y. Acad. Sci., Am. Assn. for Cancer Research, Sigma Xi, Phi Lambda Upsilon. Republican. Roman Catholic. Patentee in field. Current Work: Methodology of improving thermal energy conversion efficiency by increasing the temperature of heat supplied to a turbine working fluid above the warm sea water temperature. Subspecialties: Ocean energy conversion; Chemical engineering. Office: 4736 Reservoir Rd Geneseo NY 14454

REID, JOSEPH LEE, physical oceanographer, educator; b. Franklin, Tex., Feb. 7, 1923; s. Joseph Lee and Ruby (Cranford) R.; m. Freda Mary Hunt, Apr. 7, 1953; children—Ian Joseph, Julian Richard. B.A. in Math., U. Tex., 1942; M.S. in Phys. Oceanography, Scripps Inst. Oceanography, 1950. Asst. research oceanographer, Scripps Inst. Oceanography, La Jolla, Calif., 1957-61, assoc. research oceanographer, 1961-66, research oceanographer, 1966-74, assoc. dir. Inst. Marine Resources, 1975-82, prof. oceanography, 1974—, dir. Marine Life Research Group, 1974—; cons. Sandia Nat. Labs., Albuquerque, 1980-85. Author: Intermediate Waters of the Pacific Ocean, 1965. Contbr. articles to profl. jours. Mem. editorial adv. bd. Deep Sea Research, Oxford, Eng., 1980—, Ciencias Marinas, Ensenada, Mex., 1982—. Served to lt. USNR, 1942-46; ATO, PTO, MTO. Fellow Am. Geophys. Union (pres. oceanography sect. 1972-74, 84-86), AAAS. Current work: World ocean circulation, patterns of tracers, formation of subsurface layers. Subspecialty: Oceanography. Office: Scripps Inst Oceanography MLR Group A-030 La Jolla CA 92093

REID, MICHAEL BARON, respiratory physiologist; b. Ft. Worth, Aug. 28, 1952; s. Walter Floyd and Dorothy Jean (Thames) R.; m. Laurel Colleen Anderson, Apr. 14, 1984. B.S., U. Tex.-Arlington, 1974; Ph.D., U. Tex. Health Sci. Ctr., Dallas, 1980. Research fellow U. Tex. Health Sci. Ctr., Dallas, 1980-81; research fellow Harvard U., Boston, 1981-83, research assoc., 1983—; spl. lectr. Simmons Coll., Boston, 1981-83; speaker Grad. Student Research Forum, Galveston, Tex., 1979. Reviewer: Jour. Clin. Investigation, Procs. Exptl. Biology and Medicine, 1980—. Fellow: St. Paul Fund, 1976, NIH, 1976-83. Mem. Am. Physiol. Soc., AAAS, N.Y. Acad. Scis. Current work: Respiratory muscle physiology and pathophysiology, chest wall mechanics, proprioceptive control of breathing, control of skeletal muscle blood flow. Subspecialties: Physiology (medicine); Physiology (biology). Home: 38 Crowninshield Rd Brookline MA 02146 Office: Bldg 1 Room 307 Harvard U Sch Pub Health 665 Huntington Ave Boston MA 02115

REID, ROBERT LELON, mech. engr., educator, researcher, cons.; b. Detroit, May 20, 1942; s. Lelon and Verna Beulah (Custer) R.; m. Judy Nestell, July 21, 1962; children: Robert, Bonnie, Matthew. B.S.E. in Chem. Engring, U. Mich., 1963; M.S.E., So. Methodist U., 1966, Ph.D., 1969. Registered profl. engr., Tenn., Tex. Research engr. ARCO Prodn. Research, Dallas, 1964-65; staff engr. Linde div. Union Carbide, Tonawanda, N.Y., 1966-68; asst. prof. mech. engring. U. Tenn., Knoxville, 1969-75, assoc. prof., then prof., 1977-82; then asst. dir. Energy, Environment, and Resources Ctr., 1979-82; asso. prof. Cleve. State U., 1975-77; prof. mech. and indsl. engring., chmn. dept. mech. and indsl. engring. U. Tex., El Paso, 1982—; cons. Oak Ridge Nat. Lab. Contbr. numerous articles on heat transfer, solar energy, energy conservation to profl. jours.; assoc. editor: Jour. Solar Energy Engring, 1981—. Mem. ASME (Centennial medallion 1980, vice chmn. div. solar energy 1983—), ASHRAE, Am. Solar Energy Soc., Am. Soc. Engring. Edn. Lutheran. Current Work: Solar energy, energy conservation. Subspecialties: Mechanical engineering; Chemical engineering. Office: Dept Mech and Indsl Engring U Tex El Paso TX 79968

REID, TOY FRANKLIN, See *Who's Who in America,* 43rd edition.

REIDENBERG, MARCUS MILTON, clinical pharmacologist, educator; b. Phila. M.D., Temple U., 1958. Diplomate: Am. Bd. Internal Medicine. Intern Community Gen. Hosp., Reading, Pa., 1958-59; resident Temple U. Hosp., Phila., 1962-65; practice medicine specializing in pharmacology; mem. staff N.Y. Hosp.; vis. phys. Rockefeller U. Hosp.; mem. faculty Cornell U. Med. Coll., N.Y.C., 1975—, prof. pharmacology and medicine, 1980—, acting assoc. dean, 1981-82. Served with USN, 1960-62. Current Work: Research and teaching in clinical pharmacology, especially drug problems in the elderly; care of patients with problems of drug therapy. Subspecialties: Pharmacology; Internal medicine. Office: Cornell University Medical College Dept Pharmacology 1300 York Ave New York NY 10021

REIDER, BRUCE, surgeon, educator; b. N.Y.C., Feb. 9, 1949; s. Edward and Blanche (Goodman) R. A.B., Yale U., 1971; M.D., Harvard U., 1975. Diplomate: Am. Bd. Orthopaedic Surgery. Intern, vis. clin. fellow dept. surgery Columbia U. Hosp., N.Y.C., 1975-76; resident, fellow in surgery Cornell U. Hosp., N.Y.C., 1976-80, resident, instr. surgery, 1978-80; fellow sports medicine U. Wis., Madison, 1980-81; asst. prof. surgery/orthopedics Pritzker Sch. Medicine, U. Chgo., 1981—, dir. sports medicine, 1981—, head team physician, 1981—. Contbr. articles to profl. jours. Yale U. Alumni Fund rep., 1971—. Yale Nat. scholar, 1967-71. Mem. Am. Coll. Sports Medicine, Am. Orthopedic Soc. for Sports Medicine, Phi Beta Kappa. Club: Quadrangle. Current Work: Athletic injuries of knee and shoulder, biomechanics of knee ligament injuries, disorders of the patella. Subspecialty: Orthopedics.

REIF, ARNOLD EUGENE, cancer researcher; b. Vienna, Austria, July 15, 1924; came to U.S., 1947, naturalized, 1956; s. Henry and Margaret (Gestetner) R.; m. Jane C. Chess; m. Katherine E. Hume, July 7, 1979; children: Betrand Paul, John Henry, Joseph Peter. B.A., Cambridge (Eng.) U., 1945, M.A., 1949; B.Sc., London U., 1946; M.S., Carnegie-Mellon U., 1949, D.Sc., 1950; grad. course in basic physics and med. applications of radioisotopes, New Eng. Roentgen Ray Soc. and M.G.H., 1962. Postdoctoral fellow McArdle Lab. Cancer Research, U. Wis. Med. Sch., 1950-53, research assoc. dept. physiol. chemistry, 1953; research assoc. dept. biochemistry Lovelace Found. Med. Edn. and Research, Albuquerque, 1953-57; asst. prof. surgery Tufts U. Sch. Medicine, 1957-69, assoc. prof., 1969-75, lectr. in surgery, 1975—; Am. Cancer Soc. faculty research assoc. Sch. Medicine, 1967-68; research pathologist Mallory Inst. Pathology, Boston City Hosp., 1973—; chief Exptl. Cancer Immunotherapy Lab., 1979—; research prof. pathology Boston U. Sch. Medicine, 1975—; exec. v.p. Vols. for Health Awareness, 1970—; vice chmn. Boston Cancer Research Assn., 1976-77; vis. prof. U. Conn., summer 1979. Contbr. numerous articles, abstracts, letters to profl. jours.; editor: Immunity and Cancer in Man: an Introduction, 1975; co-editor: Immunity to Cancer, 1985. Mem. Am. Assn. Immunologists, Transplantation Soc., Am. Assn. Cancer Research (session chmn. immunology and genetics 1971, 72, 74, 77), N.Y. Acad. Scis., Health Physics Soc. (dir. New Eng. chpt. 1976-77), AAAS, Sigma xi. Current Work: Immunotherapy of cancer in mouse model systems; differences in susceptibility to cancer. Subspecialties: Cancer research (medicine); Immunology (medicine). Office: Boston City Hosp Boston MA 02118

REIFSNYDER, WILLIAM EDWARD, meteorologist; b. Ridgway, Pa., Mar. 29, 1924; s. Howard William and Madolin (Boyer) R.; m. Marylou Bishop, Dec. 19, 1954; children—Rita, Cheryl, Gawain. B.S. in Meteorology, NYU, 1944; M.F., U. Calif., Berkeley, 1949; Ph.D., Yale U., 1954. Cert. cons. meteorologist Pacific S.W. Forest and Range Expt. Sta., 1952-55; mem. faculty Yale U., 1965—, prof. forest meteorology and biometeorology, 1967—; cons. World Meteorol. Orgn. Author: Hut Hopping in the Austrian Alps, Footloose in the Swiss Alps, The High Huts of the White Mountains, Radiant Energy in Relation to Forests, Weathering the Wilderness; regional editor: Agrl. Meteorology, 1977—. Bd. dirs. Am. Youth Hostels. Service with USAAF, 1943-47. Fellow AAAS; mem. Am. Meteorol. Soc. (Bioclimatology award 1981), Soc. Am. Foresters, Internat. Soc. Biometeorology. Subspecialties: Meteorology; Climatology. Office: Yale U Sch Forestry and Environmental Studies New Haven CT 06520

REILLY, PETER JOHN, chemical engineer, educator, consultant; b. Newark, Dec. 26, 1938; s. Edward Thomas and Anita (Galdieri) R.; m. Rae Messer, July 3, 1976; children: Diane, Karen. A.B. in Chemistry, Princeton U., 1960; Ph.D. in Chem. Engring, U. Pa., Phila., 1964. Research engr. E. I. du Pont de Nemours & Co., Deepwater, N.J., 1964-68; asst. prof. chem. engring. U. Nebr., Lincoln, 1968-74; assoc. prof. chem. engring. Iowa State U., Ames, 1974-79, prof., 1979—. Mem. Am. Chem. Soc., Am. Inst. Chem. Engrs., AAUP, Sigma Xi, Phi Kappa Phi. Current Work: Kinetics of soluble and immobilized enzymes, enzymatic hydrolysis of polysaccharides, utilization of agrl. residues. Subspecialties: Chemical engineering; Enzyme technology. Home: 1807 Wilson Ave Ames IA 50010 Office: Dept of Chem Engring Iowa State U Ames IA 50011

REINECKE, THOMAS LEONARD, physicist, research laboratory administrator; b. Park Falls, Wis., Sept. 14, 1945; s. Leonard Herbert and Eleanor Dorthea (Stauber) R. B.A., Ripon Coll., 1968; Ph.D., Oxford U., 1972. Research assoc. dept. physics Brown U., Providence, 1972-74; research assoc. Naval Research Lab., Washington, 1974-76, research physicist, 1976-80, supervisory research physicist, 1980—; vis. scientist Max Planck Inst., Stuttgart, Fed. Republic Germany, 1979; mem. artificially structured materials com. Nat. Acad. Scis., 1984, steering com. Greater Washington Solid State Physics Colloquium, 1978—. Contbr. articles to profl. jours. Rhodes scholar, 1968-72. Fellow Am. Phys. Soc.; mem. Assn. Rhodes Scholars, Sigma Xi. (Outstanding Research in Pure Sci. award 1982). Current work: Research in theoretical solid state physics with emphasis on semiconductors, surfaces and phase transitions. Subspecialties: Condensed matter physics; Theoretical physics. Home: 7115 Vantage Dr Alexandria VA 22306 Office: Code 6877 Naval Research Lab Washington DC 20375

REINEMUND, JOHN ADAM, geologist, consultant; b. Muscatine, Iowa, Jan. 14, 1919; s. Julius Adam and Eva Elizabeth (Nelson) R.; m. Ruth Ramona Rees, Nov. 29, 1943. B.A., Augustana Coll., 1940, D.H.L., 1968; postgrad. U. Chgo., 1940-42, 50-51. Geologist, U.S. Geol. Survey, Washington, 1942-53, chief midcontinent region fuels br., Denver, 1953-56, sr. geologic cons., Quetta, Pakistan, 1956-64, chief Office of Internat. Geology, Washington and Reston, Va., 1964-84; exec. dir. Circum-Pacific Council for Energy and Mineral Resources, Leesburg, Va. and Houston, 1984—. Contbr. articles to profl. jours. Recipient Meritorious Service award U.S. Geol. Survey, 1976, Disting. Service award, 1980; Spl. Service medal Circum-Pacific Council for Energy and Mineral Resources, 1982. Fellow Geol. Soc. Am.; mem. Am. Assn. Petroleum Geologists, Am. Geophys. Union, Geol. Soc. of Washington, Internat. Unio Geol. Scis. (treas., 1979—). Republican. Lutheran. Club: Cosmos (Washington). Current work: Research on mineral and energy resources in relation to tectonic development, especially in the Pacific region. Subspecialties: Geology; Coal. Home: PO Box 890 Leesburg VA 22075 Office: Circum-Pacific Council for Energy and Mineral Resources PO Box 890 Leesburg VA 22075

REINES, FREDERICK, physicist, educator; b. Paterson, N.J., Mar. 16, 1918; s. Israel and Gussie (Cohen) R.; m. Sylvia Samuels, Aug. 30, 1940; children: Robert G., Alisa K. M.E., Stevens Inst. Tech., 1939, M.S., 1941; Ph.D., NYU, 1944; D.Sc. (hon.), U. Witwatersrand, 1966, D. Engring. (hon.), 1984. Mem. staff Los Alamos Sci. Lab., 1944-59; group leader Los Alamos Sci. Lab. (Theoretical div.), 1945-59; dir. (AEC expts. on Eniwetok Atoll), 1951; prof. physics, head dept. Case Inst. Tech., 1959-66; prof. physics U. Calif.-Irvine, 1966—, dean phys. scis., 1966-74. Contbr. numerous articles to profl. jours.; Contbg. author: Effects of Atomic Weapons, 1950. Mem. Cleve. Symphony Chorus, 1959-62. Recipient J. Robert Oppenheimer meml. prize, 1981; Nat. Medal of Sci., 1983; Guggenheim fellow, 1958-59; Sloan fellow, 1959-63. Fellow Am. Phys. Soc., AAAS; mem. Am. Assn. Physics Tchrs., Argonne U. Assn. (trustee 1965-66), Am. Acad. Arts and Scis., Nat. Acad. Sci., Phi Beta Kappa, Sigma Xi, Tau Beta Pi. Co-discoverer elementary nuclear particle, free antineutrino, 1956. Current Work: Stability of proton; neutrino physics. Subspecialty: Particle physics. Office: U Calif at Irvine Irvine CA 92717

REINHARDT, CHARLES FRANCIS, See *Who's Who in America,* 43rd edition.

REINHOLD, RICHARD CLARKE, electro-optical engineer; b. Redding, Calif., Apr. 21, 1940; s. Richard Samuel and Doris Mary (Clarke) R. B.S., U. Wash., 1962, M.S. in Elec. Engring., 1980; M.S., Ohio State U., 1964. Sr. engr. Boeing Co., Seattle, 1972-81, Itek Applied Tech., Sunnyvale, Calif., 1981-82; sr. staff engr. Teledyne Electronics, Newbury Park, Calif., 1982-85; sr. staff engr. Eaton/AIL, Melville, N.Y., 1985—. Mem. Am. Phys. Soc., Optical Soc. Am., Internat. Soc. Optical Engring., IEEE, Soc. Indsl. and Applied Math., Assn. Old Crows, Soc. Actuaries. Current work: Developed optical correlator and instantaneous frequency measurement receivers for ELINT. Subspecialties: Optical signal processing; Systems engineering. Office: Eaton/AIL Advanced Systems Dept Old Walt Whitman Rd Melville NY 11747

REINKE, LESTER ALLEN, pharmacologist, educator, researcher; b. Davenport, Nebr., Sept. 29, 1946; s. Herman Dick and Alma Ida (Grosshans) R.; m. Carol Sue Paulsen, Sept. 1, 1968; children: Jonathan Paul, Lisa Sue. B.S. in Pharmacy, U. Nebr., 1969, M.S. in Medicinal Chemistry, 1975, Ph.D. in Medicinal Chemistry, 1977. Registered pharmacist, Nebr. Research asst. prof. U. N.C. Sch. Medicine, Chapel Hill, 1980; asst. prof. pharmacology U. Okla. Health Scis. Center, Oklahoma City, 1980-86. Contbr. articles to sci. jours. Served with U.S. Army, 1969-73. Nat. Cancer Inst. fellow, 1977-80; research award, 1980-86. Mem. Am. Soc. Pharmacology and Exptl. Therapeutics, Internat. Soc. for Study Xenobiotics, Sigma Xi, Rho Chi. Lutheran. Current Work: Drug metabolism; alcohol; chemical carcinogenesis; intermediary metabolism. Subspecialty: Pharmacology. Home: 1302 NW 21st St Oklahoma City OK 73106 Office: Pharmacology Dept U Okla PO Box 26901 Oklahoma City OK 73190

REINMAN, ROBERT ANDREW, air force officer, telecommunications engineering executive; b. Newark, Oct. 26, 1939; s. Fred Anthony and Mildred Anna (Miller) R.; m. Jean Agnes Hornung, Nov. 26, 1966; children—Paul Conrad, Erica Ann. B.S. in Elec. Engring., Newark Coll., Engring., 1961; M.S. in Elec. Engring., Air Force Inst. Tech., 1965; M.S. Math., U. Ill., 1971, Ph.D. in Elec. Engring., 1975. Commd 2d lt. U.S. Air Force, 1962, advanced through grades to col.; assoc. prof. elec. engring. Air Force Inst. Tech. Dayton, Ohio, 1972-76; chief engring. div. Def. Commn. Agy., Stuttgart, Ger., 1976-78; comdr. 1836 Engring. Installation Group, Wiesbaden, Fed. Republic Germany, 1978-81; sr. research fellow Nat. Def. U., Washington, 1981-82; dir. Def. Communications Engring. Ctr., Reston, Va., 1982-84, Command and Control Systems Orgn., Arlington, Va., 1984-85; comdr. Engring. Installation Div., Tinker AFB, Okla, 1985—. Contbr. articles to profl. jours. Excalibur award nominee U.S. Congress, Washington, 1979; decorated Def. Superior Service medal, Legion of Merit. Mem. IEEE, Armed Forces Communications Electronics Assn. Roman Catholic. Current work: Engineering and installation of all Air Force Communications, radar and navigational aids worldwide. Subspecialties: Electrical engineering; Probability. Home: 5310 Spaatz Dr Tinker AFB OK 73145

REIS, DONALD JEFFERY, neurologist, neurobiologist, educator; b. N.Y.C., Sept. 9, 1931; s. Samuel H. and Alice (Kiesler) R. A.B., Cornell U., 1953, M.D., 1956. Intern N.Y. Hosp., N.Y.C., 1956; resident in neurology Boston City Hosp.-Harvard Med. Sch., 1957-59; Fulbright fellow, United Cerebral Palsy Found. fellow, London and Stockholm, 1959-60; research asso. NIMH, Bethesda, Md., 1960-62; spl. fellow NIH, Nobel Neurophysiology Inst., Stockholm, 1962-63; asst. prof. neurology Cornell U. Med. Sch., N.Y.C., 1963-67, asso. prof. neurology and psychiatry, 1967-71, prof., 1971—, First George C. Cotzias Disting. prof. neurology, 1982—; Mem. U.S.-Soviet Exchange Program; adv. councils NIH; bd. sci. advisers Merck, Sharpe and Dohm; cons. biomed. cos. Contbr. articles to profl. jours.; mem. editorial bd. various profl. jours. Mem. Am. Physiol. Soc., Am. Neurol. Assn., Am. Pharmacol. Soc., Am. Assn. Physicians, Telluride Assn., Am. Soc. Clin. Investigation, Phi Beta Kappa, Sigma Xi, Alpha Omega Alpha. Current Work: Neurochemical, and molecular biological substrates of emotional behavior, brain and autonomic nervous system, brain control of the circulation. Subspecialties: Neurochemistry; Neurophysiology. Home: 190 E 72d St New York NY 10021 Office: 1300 York Ave New York NY 10021

REISER, MORTON FRANCIS, educator, psychiatrist; b. Cin., Aug. 22, 1919; s. Sigmund and Mary (Roth) R.; m. Lynn Whisnant, Dec. 19, 1976; children: David E., Barbara, Linda. B.S., U. Cin., 1940, M.D., 1943; grad., N.Y. Psychoanalytic Inst., 1960. Diplomate: Am. Bd. Psychiatry and Neurology. Intern King's County Hosp., Bklyn., 1944; resident Cin. Gen. Hosp., 1944-49, practice medicine, specializing in psychiatry, Cin., 1947-52, Washington, 1954-55, N.Y.C., 1955-69; mem. faculty Cin. Gen. Hosp., also U. Cin. Coll. Medicine, 1949-52, Washington Sch. Psychiatry, 1953-55; faculty Albert Einstein Coll. Medicine, Yeshiva U., N.Y.C., 1955-69, prof. psychiatry, 1958-69, dir. research dept. psychiatry, 1958-65; chief div. psychiatry Montefiore Hosp. and Med. Center, N.Y.C., 1965-69; chmn. dept. psychiatry Yale Med. Sch., 1969—, prof., 1969-78, Charles B.G. Murphy prof., 1978—; cons. Walter Reed Army Inst. Research, 1957-58, High Point Hosp., Port Chester, N.Y., 1957-69; com. WHO, 1963; mem. profl. adv. com. Jerusalem Mental Health Center, 1972—; mem. clin. program projects rev. com. NIMH, 1970—, chmn., 1973-74; also lectr.; mem. Josiah Macy, Jr. Found. Commn. on Present Condition and Future Acad. Psychiatry, 1977. Author: (with H. Leigh) The Patient: Biological, Psychological, and Social Dimensions of Medical Practice, 1980; Mind, Brain, Body: Toward a Convergence of Psychoanalysis and Neurobiology, 1984; editor: American Handbook of Psychiatry, vol. IV, 1975; editor-in-chief: Psychosomatic Medicine, 1962-72; editorial bd.: AMA Archive of Gen. Psychiatry, 1961-71, (with H. Leigh) Psychiatry Medicine and Primary Care, 1978; contbr. articles to profl. jours. and books. Recipient Stella Fels Hoffheimer Meml. prize U. Cin. Coll. Medicine, 1943. Fellow Am. Coll. Psychiatrists, Am. Psychiat. Assn.; mem. Am. Soc. Clin. Investigation, Am. Psychosomatic Soc. (pres. 1960-61), Am. Fedn. Clin. Research, Am. Assn. Chairmen Depts. Psychiatry (exec. com. 1971—, pres. 1975-76), Acad. Behavioral Medicine Research (exec. council 1978), Am. Psychoanalytic Assn. (pres.-elect 1980-82, pres. 1982-84), Internat. Psycho-Analytical Assn., Assn. Psychophysiol. Study of Sleep, Internat. Coll. Psychosomatic Medicine (pres. 1975), Psychiat. Research Soc., A. Graeme Mitchell Undergrad. Pediatric Soc., World Psychiat. Assn. (organizing com. sect. psychosomatic medicine 1967), Benjamin Rush Soc., Rapaport-Klein Study Group, Sigma Xi, Phi Eta Sigma, Pi Kappa Epsilon, Alpha Omega Alpha. Current Work: Neurobiology and psychoanalysis; neurobiology of major psychiatric disorders. Subspecialties: Psychopharmacology; Psychobiology. Home: 99 Blake Rd Hamden CT 06517 Office: 25 Park St New Haven CT 06519

REISMAN, SCOTT, psychologist; b. N.Y.C., Oct. 9, 1951; s. Emanuel and Myra (Deutch) R.; m. Susan A. Greenberg, Apr. 3, 1982. B.G.S., Ohio U., Athens, 1974; M.S. in Counseling, Nova U., Ft. Lauderdale, 1978, M.S. in Psychology, 1981. Mental health technician Dade County (Fla.), Miami, 1974-77; program evaluator Nova Clinics, Inc., Ft. Lauderdale, 1979-82; clin. psychology intern VA Med. Ctr., Miami, Fla., 1984-85; clin. assoc. Alan A. Jaffe & Assocs., P.A., Lauderhill, Fla., 1985—; adj. faculty Nova Coll., 1981. Mem. Am. Psychol. Assn., Assn. for Advancement of Behavior Therapy, Biofeedback Soc. Am., Fla. Psychol. Assn. Current Work: Research on physiological and psychological effects of several methods of stress management training for professionals. Subspecialty: Behavioral psychology. Office: Nova U 3301 College Ave Fort Lauderdale FL 33314

REISNER, RONALD MORTON, physician; b. Buffalo, May 2, 1929; s. Daniel and Helen (Rapport) R.; m. Ellen Mosko, Jan. 29, 1972; children—David Alan, Andrew Evan. B.A., UCLA, 1952; M.D., UCLA, 1956. Intern, Harbor Gen. Hosp., 1956-57; resident in dermatology UCLA Sch. Medicine, 1957-59, chief resident, 1959-60, research trainee in dermatology, 1960; chief Div. Dermatology, Harbor Gen. Hosp., Campus of UCLA Sch. Medicine, Torrance, 1962-72; asst. prof. medicine/dermatology UCLA Sch. Medicine, 1962-68, assoc. prof., 1968-72, prof. medicine/dermatology, 1972—, chief div. dermatology, 1973—; coordinator dermatology UCLA Complex of Affiliated Hosps., 1973-77; dir. dermatology resident tng. Wadsworth VA Hosp., Los Angeles, 1976-77, chief dermatology service, 1977—, dir. dermatology resident tng., combined UCLA-Wadsworth VA Hosp. program, 1977—; lectr. in field; cons. in field; conductor seminars in field. Contbr. articles to profl. jours. Served to lt. comdr., USN, 1960-62. Fellow Am. Acad. Dermatology, Pan Am. Med. Assn.; mem. Soc. Investigative Dermatology, Am. Dermatol. Assn., Western Soc. Clin. Investigation, Pacific Dermatol. Assn., Los Angeles Dermatol. Soc., AAAS. Soc. Tropical Dermatology, Assn. Mil. Surgeons of U.S., Am. Sch. Health Assn., Am. Dermatol. Assn., Am. Geriatric Soc., Am. Fedn. Clin. Research, Assn. Profs. of Dermatology, Soc. for Pediatric Dermatology, Am. Soc. Dermatol. Surgery, Am. Venereal Diseases Assn., Am. Assn. Med. Systems and Informatics, Phi Beta Kappa, Alpha Omega Alpha, Pi Gamma Mu, Phi Eta Sigma, Alpha Mu Gamma. Subspecialty: Dermatology. Home: Los Angeles CA 90064 Office: UCLA Sch Medicine 10833 Le Conte Ave Los Angeles CA 90024

REISS, ERROL, microbial immunochemist; b. N.Y.C., Jan. 16, 1942; s. Jack and Claire (Litman) R.; m. Cheryl Linda Aaronson, Jan. 20, 1968; children: Brendan K., Merryl D. B.Sc. (N.Y. State Regents scholar), CCNY, 1963; Ph.D., Rutgers U.-New Brunswick, N.J., 1972. Bacteriologist VA Hosp., Washington, 1966-67; postdoctoral fellow NIH, Bethesda, Md., 1972-74; research microbiologist Centers for Disease Control, Atlanta, 1974—, head Immunochemistry Lab. div. mycotic diseases, 1980—; adj. prof. U. N.C.; lectr. Morehouse Coll. Medicine; adj. prof. Ga. State U. Contbr. articles to profl. jours.; mem. editorial bd.: Jour. Clin. Microbiology, 1982—. Served to 1st lt. U.S. Army, 1963-65. Recipient Service award USPHS, 1980. Mem. Am. Chem. Soc., Am. Assn. Immunologists; mem. Am. Acad. Microbiology; Mem. Am. Soc. Microbiology (cert. recognition 1982). Current Work: Molecular immunology and molecular biology of microbial infections, especially mycotic infections; immunochemistry; carbohydrate biochemistry; enzymology; cellular immunology; preceptor for graduate students. Subspecialties: Microbiology; Immunocytochemistry. Home: 3642 Castaway Ct Chamblee GA 30341 Office: 1600 Clifton Rd NE 5-B-36 Atlanta GA 30333

REITAN, DANIEL KINSETH, electrical engineering educator; b. Duluth, Minn., Aug. 13, 1921; s. Conrad Ulfred and Joy Elizabeth R.; m. Marian Anne Stemme, July 18, 1946; children: Debra Leah, Danielle Karen. B.S.E.E., N.D. State U., 1946; M.S.E.E., U. Wis., 1949, Ph.D., 1952. Registered profl. engr., Wis. Engr., Gen. Electric Co., Schenectady, N.Y., 1946-48; transmission line engr. Gen. Telephone Co., Madison, Wis., 1949-50; mem. faculty Coll. Engring. U. Wis., Madison, 1952—, prof. elec. and computer engring., 1962—, dir. power systems simulation lab., 1968—, also dir. wind power research Energy Ctr.; cons. in field. Contbr. articles to profl. jours. Served with U.S. Army, World War II. Recipient Outstanding Tchr. award Polygon Engring. Council., Gov.'s citation for service to State of Wis. Fellow IEEE (Centennial medal and cert. for outstanding achievement 1984), IEEE Power Engring., Computer, Control, Indsl. Applications, and Edn. Socs., Conf. Internat. des Grands Reseaux Electriques a Haute Tension, Am. Soc. Engring. Edn., Wis. Acad. Scis., Sigma Xi, Tau Delta Pi, Tau Beta Pi, Eta Kappa Nu, Kappa Eta Kappa. Lutheran. Patentee in field. Current Work: Computer solutions of EHV-AC/DC electric power network; analysis of co-generation and other small power producers interfaces with large electric utility grids. Subspecialties: Electrical engineering; Wind power. Office: Elec and Computer Engring Dept 1425 Johnson Dr Madison WI 53706

REITAN, RALPH MELDAHL, psychologist; b. Beresford, S.D., Aug. 29, 1922; s. John O. and Anna (Meldahl) R.; m. Ann Kirsch, Feb. 15, 1952 (div. 1978); children: Ellen, Jon, Ann, Richard, Erik. B.A., Central YMCA Coll., Chgo., 1944; Ph.D., U. Chgo., 1950. Asst. prof. to prof. psychology Ind. U. Med. Ctr., Indpls., 1951-70; prof. U. Wash., Seattle, 1970-77; prof. psychology U. Ariz., Tucson, 1977—; cons. NASA, Washington, 1964-65; NIH, 1959-70. Author: Clinical Neuropsychology, 1974; Aphasia and Sensory-Perceptual Deficits in Adults, 1984; Aphasia and Sensory-Perceptual Deficits in Children, 1985; co-author: The Halstead-Reitan Neuropsychological Test Battery: Theory and Clinical Interpretation, 1985; Neuroanatomy and Neuropathology: A Clinical Guide for Neuropsychologists, 1985; contbr. articles to profl. jours. Served with AUS, 1943. Recipient Barrows award Ind. Psychol. Assn., 1968; Research award Ariz. Psychol. Assn., 1982. Fellow Am. Psychol. Assn.; mem. Am. Neurol. Assn., Am. Acad. Neurology. Current Work: Human brain-behavior relationships. Subspecialties: Neuropsychology; Physiological psychology. Home: 1338 E Edison St Tucson AZ 85719 Office: Dept Psychology U Ariz Tucson AZ 85721

REITEMEIER, RICHARD JOSEPH, physician; b. Pueblo, Colo., Jan. 2, 1923; s. Paul John and Ethel Regina (McCarthy) R.; m. Patricia Claire Mulligan, July 21, 1951; children: Mary Louise, Paul, Joseph, Susan, Robert, Patrick, Daniel. A.B., U. Denver, 1944; M.D., U. Colo., 1946; M.S. in Internal Medicine, U. Minn., 1954. Diplomate: Am. Bd. Internal Medicine (gov. 1971-79, chmn. 1978-79, rep. to Federated Council Internal Medicine 1977-80, 83—, accreditation council grad. med. edn. 1979—, chmn. 1982-83). Intern Corwin Hosp., Pueblo, 1946-47; resident Henry Ford Hosp., Detroit, 1949-50, Mayo Found., Rochester, Minn., 1950-53; cons. internal medicine and gastroenterology Mayo Clinic, Rochester, 1954—; chmn. dept. internal medicine Mayo Clinic (Mayo Clinic and Mayo Med. Sch.), 19.67-74, prof., 1971—; bd. govs. Mayo Clinic, 1970-74. Author: (with C. G. Moertel)

Advanced Gastrointestinal Cancer, Clinical Management and Chemotherapy, 1969; contbr. (with C. G. Moertel) numerous articles to med. jours. Trustee Mayo Found., 1970-74; trustee St. Mary's Hosp., Rochester, 1976-82. Served with U.S. Army, 1947-49. Recipient Alumni award U. Colo. Sch. Medicine. Fellow A.C.P. (regent 1979-82, gov. for Minn. 1975-79, pres. 1983-84), Am. Gastroenterol. Assn., AMA, Am. Clin. and Climatol. Assn., Am. Fedn. Clin. Research, Am. Soc. Clin. Oncology, Council Med. Splty. Socs., Inst. Medicine, Am. Assn. Cancer Research, Am. Assn. Study Liver Disease, Alpha Omega Alpha. Republican. Roman Catholic. Current Work: Medical education; healthcare delivery. Subspecialties: Gastroenterology; Chemotherapy. Home: 707 12th Ave SW Rochester MN 55901 Office: 200 1st Ave SW Rochester MN 55901

REITER, LEON, seismologist, regulator; b. N.Y.C., Dec. 10, 1931; s. Bernard and Musia (Abramovsky) R.; m. Harriet Buchweitz, Dec. 2, 1959; children—Ehud, Dan, David. B.A., Bklyn. Coll., 1958; M.A., U. Mich., 1970, M.S., 1968, Ph.D., 1971. Postdoctoral fellow Inst. Geophysics and Planetary Physics, LaJolla, Calif., 1971-72; asst. prof. U. Okla., Norman, 1972-76; geophysicist U.S. Nuclear Regulatory Commn., Washington, 1976-79, leader seismology sect., 1979—; lectr. Internat. Atomic Energy Agy., San Francisco, 1982; cons. State of Calif., 1983, Israel, Egypt, 1984. Author: Seismic Hazard Review for Systematic Evaluation Program, A Use of Probability in Decision Making, 1983. Contbr. articles to profl. jours. Served with U.S. Army, 1956-58. Recipient High Quality Performance award U.S. Nuclear Regulatory Commn., 1981. Mem. Seismol. Soc. Am., Am. Geophys. Union, Soc. Exploration Geophysicists, Earthquake Engring. Research Inst. Current work: Seismic hazard estimation, probabilistic risk assessment, earthquake engineering, earthquake ground motion estimation, decision making. Subspecialties: Seismology; Geophysics. Home: 1960 Dundee Rd Rockville MD 20850 Office: US Nuclear Regulatory Commn P-514 Washington DC 20555

REITZ, BRUCE ARNOLD, cardiac surgeon, educator; b. Seattle, Sept. 14, 1944; s. Arnold and Ruth (Stillings) R.; m. Nan Norton; children: Megan, Jay. B.S., Stanford U., 1966; M.D., Yale U., 1970. Diplomate: Am. Bd. Surgery, 1980, Am. Bd. Thoracic Surgery, 1981. Intern Johns Hopkins U., Balt., 1970-71; resident Stanford (Calif.) Med. Ctr., 1971-72, 74-77; asst. prof. cardiovascular surgery Stanford U. Sch. Medicine, 1977-81, assoc. prof., 1982; prof. surgery Johns Hopkins U. Sch. Medicine, Balt., 1982—; also cardiac surgeon-in-charge Univ. Hosp. Served with USPHS, 1972-74. Mem. AMA, Soc. Univ. Surgeons, Samson Thoracic Soc., Transplantation Soc., Assn. Clin. Cardiac Surgeons. Current Work: Heart and Heart-lung transplantation; developing techniques for combined heart and lung transplants. Subspecialty: Cardiac surgery. Office: Johns Hopkins U Sch Medicine 720 Rutland Ave Baltimore MD 21205

REITZ, RICHARD ELMER, physician, laboratory administrator; b. Buffalo, Sept. 18, 1938; s. Elmer Valentine and Edna Anna (Guenther) R.; m. Gail Ida Pounds, Aug. 20, 1960; children: Richard Allen, Mark David. B.S., Heidelberg Coll., 1960; M.D., SUNY-Buffalo, 1964. Intern Hartford (Conn.) Hosp., 1964-65, resident in medicine, 1966-67; asst. resident in medicine Yale U., 1965-66; research fellow in medicine Harvard Med. Sch., Mass. Gen. Hosp., Boston, 1967-69; vis. research assoc. NIH, Bethesda, Md., 1967-68; dir. Endocrine Metabolic Center, Oakland, Calif., 1973—; asst. prof. medicine U. Calif.-San Francisco, 1971-76; assoc. clin. prof. medicine U. Calif.-Davis, 1976—; chief endocrinology Providence Hosp., Oakland, Calif., 1972—. Contbr. articles to profl. jours., chpt. to book. Mem. Scholarship Com., Bank of Am., San Francisco, 1983. Served to lt. comdr. USNR, 1969-71. Mem. Endocrine Soc., Am. Soc. Bone and Mineral Research, Am. Fedn. Clin. Research, Am. Fertility Soc., Am. Soc. Internal Medicine, Am. Fedn. Clin. Research. Democrat. Lodge: Rotary. Current Work: Cytoreceptor assay for 1, 25 dihydroxy Vitamin D.; parathyroid hormone and calcitonin radioimmunoassay; role of calcium regulating hormones in metabolic bone disease of renal failure; bone GLA protein assay. Subspecialties: Critical care; Receptors. Home: 867 Stonehaven Dr Walnut Creek CA 94598 Office: Endocrine Metabolic Center 3100 Summit St Oakland CA 94623

REITZ, RONALD CHARLES, biochemist, educator; b. Dallas, Feb. 27, 1939; s. Percy A. and Hazel A. (Thomison) R.; m. Jeanne M. Geiger, Jan. 23, 1965; children: Erica Anne, Pieter Brett. B.S., Tex. A&M U, 1961; Ph.D., Tulane U., 1966. NIH postdoctoral fellow U. Mich., Ann Arbor, 1966-69; vis. scientist Unilever Ltd., Welwyn, Hertfordshire, Eng., 1968; asst. prof. dept. biochemistry U. N.C., Chapel Hill, 1969-75; assoc. prof. U. Nev., Reno, 1979-80, prof., 1980—; vis. scientist I.E. DuPont de Nemours & Co., Wilmington, Del., 1984. Contbr. articles on biochemistry to profl. jours. Coach soccer YMCA, 1982. Mem. Am. Soc. Biol. Chemists, Am. Soc. Pharmacology and Exptl. Therapeutics, Research Soc. on Alcoholism, AAAS. Methodist. Lodge: Elks. Current Work: Biochemistry of alcohol tolerance and dependence. Subspecialties: Biochemistry (medicine); Neuropharmacology. Home: 3237 Susileen Dr Reno NV 89509 Office: Dept Biochemistry 153 Howard Med Sci Bldg U Nev Reno NV 89557

REKLAITIS, GINTARAS VICTOR, chemical engineering educator; b. Posnan, Poland, Oct. 20, 1942; came to U.S., 1952; s. Mechislav Martin and Halina (Lorenz) R.; m. Janine Konauka, Aug. 20, 1966; children—Victor, George. B.S. in Chem. Engring., Ill. Inst. Tech., 1965; M.S., Ph.D. in Chem. Engring., Stanford U., 1969. Research asst. Stanford U., 1965-69; postdoctoral fellow Inst. for Ops. Research, Zurich, Switzerland, 1969-70; asst. to assoc. prof. Purdue U., West Lafayette, Ind., 1970-80, prof. chem. engring., 1980—; sr. Fulbright lectr. Lithuania Acad. Sci., Vilnius, 1980. Author: Introduction to Material and Energy Balances, 1983; Engineering Optimization, 1983; co-editor: Selected Topics on Computer Aided Proc. Design and Analysis, 1982; Computer Applications to Chemical Engineering, 1980. NSF fellow, 1969; grantee NSF, Dept. of Energy, pvt. founds; mem. Computing in Chem. Engring. award Am. Inst. Chem. Engring., 1984. Roman Catholic. Current work: Computer aided process design and analysis, applications to batch processes, process modeling and analysis, process simulation and optimization. Subspecialties: Chemical engineering; Systems engineering. Home: 3220 Soldiers Home Rd West Lafayette IN 47906 Office: Purdue Univ Sch Chem Engring West Lafayette IN 47907

RELMAN, ARNOLD SEYMOUR, physician, educator; b. N.Y.C., June 17, 1923; s. Simon and Rose (Mallach) R.; m. Harriet Morse Vitkin, June 26, 1953; children: David Arnold, John Peter, Margaret Rose. A.B., Cornell U., 1943; M.D., Columbia U., 1946; M.A. (hon.), U. Pa.; Sc.D. (hon.), Med. Coll. Wis.; Sc. D. (hon.), Union U.; D.M.Sc. (hon.), Brown U.; D.L.H. (hon.), SUNY. Diplomate: Am. Bd. Internal Medicine. House officer New Haven Hosp., Yale, 1946-49; NRC fellow Evans Meml., Mass. Meml. hosps., 1949-50, practice medicine, specializing in internal medicine, Boston, 1950-68, Phila., 1968-77; asst. prof., prof. medicine Boston U. Sch. Medicine, 1950-68; dir. Boston U. Med. Services, Boston City Hosp., 1967-68; prof. medicine, chmn. dept. medicine U. Pa., chief med. services Hosp. of U. Pa., 1968-77; editor New Eng. Jour. Medicine, Boston, 1977—; sr. physician Brigham and Women's Hosp., Boston, 1977—; prof. medicine Harvard Med. Sch., 1977—; Cons. NIH, USPHS. Editor: Jour. Clin. Investigation, 1962-67, (with F.J. Ingelfinger and M. Finland) Controversy in Internal Medicine, Vol. 1, 1966, Vol. 2, 1974; Contbr. articles profl. jours. Recipient Columbia Alumni Gold medal, 1980. Fellow Am. Acad. Arts and Scis., A.C.P. (master); mem. Assn. Am. Physicians (council, pres. 1983-84), Am. Physiol. Soc., AMA, Mass. Med. Soc., Inst. Medicine of Nat. Acad. Scis. (council 1979-82), Am. Soc. Clin. Investigation (past pres.), Am. Fedn. Clin. Research (past pres.), Phi Beta Kappa, Alpha Omega Alpha. Subspecialty: Internal medicine. Office: New Eng Jour Medicine 10 Shattuck St Boston MA 02115

REMBERT, DAVID HOPKINS, JR., biologist, educator; b. Columbia, SC., Jan. 14, 1937; s. David Hopkins and Mary Aldrich (Wyman) R.; m. Margaret Rose Rainey, Apr. 23, 1960; children: Rainey, Augusta, Llewellyn, David. B.S., U. S.C., 1959, M.S. Biology, 1964; Ph.D., U. Ky., 1967. Asst. prof. biology U. S.C., Columbia, 1967-72, assoc. prof., 1972-81, prof., 1981—; asst. dean Coll. Sci. and Math., 1972-76, acting dean, 1975. Mem. Central Midlands Planning Council, 1973-77, Hist. Columbia Found., 1980—. Served to lt. USAF, 1961-62; with S.C. Air N.G., 1957-61. Belser fellow, 1959; Haggin fellow, 1966. Fellow Linnean Soc. London; Mem. Bot. Soc. Am., Assn. Southeastern Biologists, Internat. Soc. Plant Morphology, Soc. Bibliography of Natural History, Appalachian Bot. Club, So. Garden Hist. Soc., S.C. Acad. Sci., Sigma Xi. Episcopalian. Current Work: Ovule development in legumes with special reference to phylogeny; floristics of Southeastern U.S.; botanical history. Subspecialties: Morphology; Botanical history. Office: U SC Dept Biology Columbia SC 29208

REMER, DONALD SHERWOOD, engineering educator, consultant; b. Detroit, Feb. 16, 1943. B.S.E., U. Mich., 1965; M.S., Calif. Inst. Tech., 1966, Ph.D., 1970. Registered profl. engr., Calif., Mich., La. Process engr. Exxon Co., Baton Rouge, 1970-72, div. coordinator, 1973, econ. analyst, 1974, task force leader, 1975; assoc. prof. engring. Harvey Mudd Coll., Claremont, Calif., 1975-80, prof., 1980—, dir. Energy Inst., 1981-83; cofounder, ptnr. Claremont Cons. Group, 1978—. Contbr. research articles to profl. jours. Case study editor Engring. Economist Jour., 1976—; editorial bd. Engring. Costs and Prodn. Econs. Jour., 1983—. Shelter mgr. ARC, Baton Rouge, 1972-75. Recipient Alumni Fund award Calif. Inst. Tech., 1975, Meritorious Tech. award NASA, 1983; named Outstanding Seminar Speaker, Occidental Research, LaVerne, Calif., 1976. Mem. Am. Inst. Chem. Engrs. (nat. pub. relations award 1976), Nat. Energy Found. (adv. bd. 1981—). Club: Claremont Toastmasters (pres. 1976-77). Current work: Economic evaluation of technical projects in energy, space communications, biotechnology, chemical processes, and medical applications. Subspecialties: Engineering economics; Chemical engineering.

REMO, JOHN LUCIEN, physicist; b. Bklyn., Dec. 13, 1941; s. John G. and Mary (DiVitis) R.; m. Claudia J. Kyser, Aug. 28, 1977; children: John Christopher, Allison Mary. B.S., Manhattan Coll., 1963; M.S. in Earth and Space Sci, SUNY-Stony Brook, 1971; M.S. in Physics, Poly. Inst. N.Y., 1973, Ph.D., 1979. Research assoc. Inst. for Space Studies, NASA, N.Y.C., 1967-69; Amanuensis Copenhagen (Denmark) U. Obs., 1969-70; faculty Wash. U., Pullman, 1973-75; adj. assoc. prof. physics and geology Hofstra U., Hempstead, N.Y., 1975-84; prof. engring. SUNY-Stony Brook, 1983-84; prof. engy mgmt. and mech. engring. N.Y. Inst. Tech., 1983—; research assoc. Poly. Inst. N.Y. Farmingdale, 1978-81; pres., chief scientist ERG Cons., St. James, N.Y., 1981—. Contbr. articles in geophysics, laser optics and solar energy to profl. jours. Recipient Nininger Meteorite award, 1972-73, chancellor's award for excellence in teaching SUNY, 1976; NASA fellow, 1978, 79. Mem. Am. Phys. Soc., Am. Geophys. Union, Optical Soc. Am., IEEE, Meteoritical Soc., Met. Solar Energy Soc., N.Y. Acad. Scis., Sigma Xi, Sigma Pi Sigma. Current Work: Research in math. theory of laser resonators, solar energy systems, planetary geophysics and computer based expert systems. Subspecialties: Lasers/resonator theory; Solar energy. Home: Brackenwood Path Head of the Harbor NY 11780

REMPEL, WILLIAM EWERT, animal science educator; b. Lowe Farm, Man., Can., July 6, 1921; came to U.S., 1948, naturalized, 1955; s. Peter K. and Margaretha (Ewert) R.; m. Leola I. Seip, Dec. 23, 1948; children: R. Barrie, Bonnie Gail. B.S., U. Man., 1944, M.Sc., 1946; Ph.D., U. Minn., St. Paul, 1952. Lectr. U. Man., 1946-47; agr. rep. Man. Dept. Agr., Swan River, 1947-48; research asst. U. Minn., 1948-49, research fellow, 1949-50, instr., 1950-52, asst. prof., 1952-54, assoc. prof., 1954-64, prof. animal sci., 1964—; tchr. genetics Summer Inst., U. Wis., River Falls, 1962, 65; dir. Genetics Center, U. Minn., 1965-68; tchr. animal breeding Beijing Agr. U., 1981. Mem. Am. Soc. Animal Sci., Genetics Soc. Am., Am. Genetics Soc., NOW, Amnesty Internat., War Resisters League. Democrat. Current Work: Swine and sheep breeding, teaching principles of animal breeding; research in swine breeding related to porcine stress system and efficiency of lean tissue growth. Subspecialties: Animal breeding and embryo transplants; Animal genetics. Home: 1424 Belmont Ln W Saint Paul MN 55113 Office: 125 Peters Hall U Minn Saint Paul MN 55108

RENARD, KENNETH GEORGE, hydraulic engineer; b. Sturgeon Bay, Wis., May 5, 1934; s. Harry H. and Margaret (Buechner) R.; m. Virginia R. Heibel, Sept. 6, 1956; children: Kenlynn, Craig, Andrew. B.S., U. Wis., 1957, M.S., 1959; Ph.D. in Civil Engring, U. Ariz., 1972. Registered profl. engr., Ariz. With Agrl. Research Service, Dept. Agr., 1957—; resident engr. Walnut Gulch Expt. Watershed, Tombstone, Ariz., 1959-64; hydraulic engr. Southwest Watershed Research Ctr., Tucson, 1964-71; dir. S.W. Watershed Research Ctr., 1972—. Contbr. to publs. in field. Recipient Outstanding Performance award Dept. Agr., 1969. Mem. ASCE (past pres. Ariz. sect., editor Jour. Drainage Engring. 1982-85), Am. Soc. Agrl. Engrs., Soil Conservation Soc. Am., Am. Geophys. Union, Sigma Xi. Current Work: Modeling of natural resources, especially semiarid water resources, erosion and sedimentation. Subspecialties: Hydrology; Water resource management.

RENARDY, MICHAEL, mathematician; b. Stuttgart, Germany, Apr. 9, 1955; s. Heinz and Eva-Maria (George) R.; m. Yuriko Yamamuro, Apr. 9, 1981. Dipl. Math, U. Stuttgart, 1977, Dipl. Phys., 1978, Dr. rer. nat., 1980. Research assoc. U. Stuttgart, 1978-80; postdoctoral fellow Deutsche Forschungsgemeinschaft U. Wis.-Madison, 1980-81, asst. prof., 1982-85, assoc. prof., 1985—. Fellow U. Minn., Mpls., 1981-82; recipient Presdl. Young Investigator award, 1985. Mem. Soc. Indsl. and Applied Math., Soc. Rheology, Am. Math. Soc., Soc. Natural Philosophy, Internat. Soc. for Interaction of Math. and Mechanics. Roman Catholic. Current Work: Nonlinear partial differential equations, viscoelastic liquids, bifurcation theory. Subspecialties: Analysis; Applied mathematics. Home: 310 Glenway St Madison WI 53705 Office: Math Research Ctr U Wis Madison WI 53705

RENARDY, YURIKO, mathematician; b. Sapporo, Hokkaido, Japan, Jan. 15, 1955; came to U.S., 1980; d. Sadayuki and Akiko (Maeda) Yamamuro; m. Michael Renardy, Apr. 9, 1981. B.Sc., Australian Nat. U., 1976; Ph.D., U. Western Australia, 1980. Research assoc. Math. Research Ctr., U. Wis.-Madison, 1980-81, 82—, program coordinator, project assoc., 1983—; lectr. U. Minn., Mpls., 1981-82. Mem. Soc. Indsl. and Applied Math, Am. Phys. Soc. Current Work: Applied mathematics. Subspecialty: Applied mathematics. Office: Math Research Ctr 610 Walnut St Madison WI 53705

RENNELS, MARSHALL LEIGH, neuroanatomist; b. Marshall, Mo., Sept. 2, 1939; s. Ivory Paul and Alfrieda (Schuetz) R.; m. Margaret Baker, Dec. 28, 1971. B.S., Eastern Ill. U., 1961; M.A., U. Tex.-Galveston, 1964, Ph.D., 1966. Asst. prof. anatomy and neurology U. Md. Med. Sch., Balt., 1966-71, assoc. prof., 1971-79, prof. anatomy, assoc. prof. neurology, 1979—. Contbr. articles to profl. jours. Mem. Am. Assn. Anatomists, Soc. Neuroscience, Internat. Soc. Cerebral Blood Flow and Metabolism, AAAS, Cajal Club, Sigma Xi. Current Work: Brain capillaries; central innervation of cerebral vasculature; cerebral extracellular space; tracer studies of nerve cells. Subspecialties: Neurobiology; Morphology. Office: U Md Med Sch 655 W Baltimore St Baltimore MD 21201

RENNER, WENDEL DEAN, medical physicist; b. Indpls., Aug. 28, 1948; s. Donald Wayne and Thelma Lydia (Slaybaugh) R.; m. Constance Witter Beaman, May 15, 1976; children: Elizabeth Witter, Samuel Oak, Peter Eli. B.S. in Physics, U. Cin., 1970, M.S. in Radiol. Sci, 1973; M.S. in Applied Math, Purdue U., 1980. Cert. therapeutic radiol. physics Am. Bd. Radiology, 1977. Asst. prof. radiology W.Va. U. Med. Center, Morgantown, 1973-75; radiation physicist Community Hosp. of Indpls., 1975—. Contbr. writings to profl. publs. in field. Served with U.S. Army, 1971-73. Recipient hon. mention, Talbert Abrams award Am. Soc. Photogrammetry, 1977. Mem. Am. Assn. Physicists in Medicine (exhibit award 1977). Presbyterian. Current Work: Radiation therapy, imaging, improvement in technology for delivering radiation therapy treatments. Subspecialties: Medical physics; Imaging technology.

RENNIE, IAN DRUMMOND, nephrologist; b. Leeds, Yorkshire, Eng., Jan. 31, 1936; came to U.S., 1967; s. John King and Isabel Brownlee (Wiese) R.; m. Silvia Gabriella Nussio, July 3, 1958; children: Caroline, Nicholas. M.B., B.Chir., U. Cambridge, Eng., 1960, M.A., M.D., 1969. Assoc. prof. medicine Rush-Presbyn.-St. Luke's Med. Sch., Chgo., 1967-77; assoc. prof. medicine Harvard Med. Sch., 1977-81; prof. medicine Rush U., Chgo., 1982—; chmn. medicine West Suburban Hosp., Oak Park, Ill., 1981—; cons. Pan Am. Health Orgn., 1975—, Rand Corp., 1981—. Dep. editor: New Eng. Jour. Medicine, 1977-81; contbg. editor: Jour. AMA, 1983—; contbr. articles to profl. jours. Recipient Gold medal in medicine Guy's Hosp., London, 1958, Gold medal in ophthalmology, 1959. Fellow Royal Coll. Physicians, ACP; mem. AMA, Council Biology Editors, AAAS. Club: Alpine (London). Current Work: High altitude physiology; societal and economic aspects of high technology treatment. Subspecialty: Physiology (medicine). Home: 40 E Delaware Pl Chicago IL 60611 Office: West Suburban Hosp 518 N Austin Blvd Oak Park IL 60302

RENTZEPIS, PETER M., chemist; b. Kalamata, Greece, Dec. 11, 1934; s. Michael T. and Levki G. R.; m. Alma Elizabeth Keenan, Dec. 30, 1960; children—Michael John, John Peter. B.S., Dennison U.; M.S., Syracuse U.; Ph.D., Cambridge U., Eng. Mem. tech. staff Research Labs. Gen. Electric Co., Schenectady; mem. tech. staff Bell Labs., Murray Hill, N.J.; later head phys. and inorganic chemistry research, adj. vis. prof. Yale U., U. Tel-Aviv, Mass. Inst. Tech. Asso. editor: Jour. Lasers and Chemistry; mem. editorial bd.: Biophys. Jour; Contbr. articles to profl. jours. Recipient I. Langmuir prize in chem. physics, 1973, Scientist of Yr. award, 1977, A. Crosby Morrison award in natural scis., 1978, ISCO award Am. Chem. Soc., 1979. Fellow N.Y. Acad. Scis., Am. Phys. Soc.; mem. Nat. Acad. Scis. Patentee in field. Subspecialty: Physical chemistry. Home: 1682 Valley Rd Millington NJ 07946 Office: Bell Labs 600 Mountain Ave Murray Hill NJ 07974

REPENNING, CHARLES ALBERT, mammalian paleontologist, researcher; b. Oak Park, Ill., Aug. 4, 1922; s. Albert Ellsworth and Estelle Lorraine (Vallincourt) R.; m. Derryberry, Sept. 17, 1939 (div.); children: Jean, John, Patricia, William. B.S., U. N.Mex., 1949; M.A., U. Calif.-Berkeley, 1964. Mammalian paleontologist U.S. Geol. Survey, Reston, Va., 1949—; research assoc. Smithsonian Instn., Washington, 1970—. Contbr. over 80 sci. articles to profl. publs. Served with AUS, 1942-45. Decorated Bronze Star, Purple Heart; recipient Meritorious Service Honor award U.S. Dept. Interior, 1982, Superior Performance award U.S. Geol. Survey, 1981. Mem. Am. Soc. Mammalogists, Soc. Systematic Zoology, Paleontology Soc., Soc. Vertebrate Paleontologists, Am. Quaternary Assn. Republican. Current Work: Mammalian biochronology; evolution; biogeography; Neogene; biochronology of rodents, primarily cricetid. Subspecialties: Paleobiology; Chronobiology. Office: US Geol Survey Mail Stop 919 Federal Ctr Box 25046 Denver CO 80225

REPPERT, STEVEN MARION, pediatrician, educator; b. Sioux City, Iowa, Sept. 4, 1946; s. Ray Fred and Norma Grace (Coppock) R.; m. Mary Alice Herman, Dec. 28, 1968; children—Jason Steven, Katherine Mary, Christina Marie. B.S., U. Nebr., 1973; M.D. with distinction, U. Nebr.-Omaha, 1973. Diplomate Am. Bd. Med. Examiners. Pediatric intern, then resident Mass. Gen. Hosp., Boston, 1973-76; clin. assoc. NIH, Bethesda, Md., 1976-79; instr. Harvard U. Med. Sch., Boston, 1979-81, asst. prof. pediatrics, 1981-85, assoc. prof., 1985—; established investigator Am. Heart Assn., 1985—. Contbr. articles to profl. jours., chpts. to books. Regents scholar; Pfizer Lab. Med. scholar; Charles King Trust Research fellow; grantee NIH. Mem. Endocrine Soc., Soc. for Pediatric Research, Soc. for Neurosci., Physicians for Social Responsibility, Alpha Omega Alpha. Democrat. Current work: Research in areas of circadian rythms, developmental neurobiology, pineal physiology and peptide physiology. Subspecialties: Pediatrics; Neurobiology. Office: Mass Gen Hosp 32 Fruit St Boston MA 02114

RESCH, JOSEPH ANTHONY, neurologist; b. Milw., Apr. 29, 1914; s. Frank and Elizabeth (Zetsch) R.; m. Rose Catherine Ritz, May 25, 1939; children—Rose, Frank, Catherine. Student, Milw. State Tchrs. Coll., 1931-34; B.S., U. Wis., Madison, 1936, M.D., 1938. Intern St. Francisco Hosp., LaCrosse, Wis., 1938-39; gen. practice medicine, Holmen, Wis., 1939-40; med. fellow in neurology U. Minn., 1946-48, clin. instr. neurology, 1948-51, clin. asst. prof., 1951-55, clin. asso. prof., 1955-62, assos. prof., 1962-65, prof., 1965-84, prof. emeritus, 1984—, head dept. neurology, 1976-82, asst. v.p. health sci., 1970-79, prof. lab. medicine and pathology, 1979-84; Practice medicine specializing in neurology, Mpls., 1948-62. Contbr. articles and abstracts to profl. jours., chpts. in books. Served to lt. col. M.C. U.S. Army, 1940-46; col. Med. Res. 1946-53. Mem. Hennepin County Med. Soc., Minn. Med. Assn., AMA, Minn. Soc. Neurol. Scis., Central Assn. Electroencephalographers, Am. Acad. Neurology, Am. Neurol. Assn., Am. Assn. Neuropathologists, Am. EEG Soc., Am. Heart Assn., Sonoma County Med. Assn., Am. Epilepsy Soc., Current Work: Neuroimmunology, Alzheimer's disease. Subspecialties: Neurology; Neuroimmunology. Home: 900 River Beach Rd The Sea Ranch CA 95497

RESCORLA, ROBERT ARTHUR, psychology educator; b. Pitts., May 9, 1940; s. Arthur Renbeck and Mildred (Jenkins) R.; m. Marged Lindner, June 18, 1962 (dec. 1969); m. Leslie Altman, Feb. 22, 1970; children—Eric, Michael. B.A., Swarthmore Coll., 1962; Ph.D., U. Pa., 1966; M.A. (hon.) Yale U., 1975. Asst. prof. psychology Yale U., after 1966, prof., to 1980; prof. U. Pa., Phila., 1980—. Author: Pavlovian Second-Order Conditioning, 1980. Contbr. articles to profl. jours. NSF grantee, 1966—. Fellow Am. Psychol. Assn. (pres. div. 3 1985—), AAAS; mem. Eastern Psychol. Assn. (bd. dirs. 1983—), Psychonomic Soc. (gov. bd. 1980—, pub. bd. 1982—), Soc. Exptl. Psychologists, Nat. Acad. Scis. Current work: Elementary learning processes, associative learning, Pavlovian conditioning. Subspecialties: Learning; Psychobiology. Office: Dept Psychology U Pa 3815 Walnut St Philadelphia PA 19104

RESHOTKO, ELI, aerospace engineer, educator; b. N.Y.C., Nov. 18, 1930; s. Max and Sarah (Kalisky) R.; m. Adina Venit, June 7, 1953; children: Deborah, Naomi, Miriam Ruth. B.S., Cooper Union, 1950; M.S., Cornell U., 1951; Ph.D., Calif. Inst. Tech., 1960. Aero. research engr. NASA-Lewis Flight Propulsion Lab., Cleve., 1951-56, head fluid mechanics sect., 1956-57; head high temperature plasma sect. NASA-Lewis Research Center, 1960-61, chief plasma physics br., 1961-64; asso. prof. engring. Case Western Res. U., Cleve., 1964-66, prof. engring., 1966—, chmn. dept. fluid thermal and aerospace scis., 1970-76, chmn. dept. mech. and aerospace engring., 1976-79; Susman vis. prof. dept. aero. engring. Technion-Israel Inst. Tech., Haifa, Israel, 1969-70; cons. United Technologies Research Ctr., Gould Corp., United Research Corp., Scott-Fetzer Co., Dynamics Tech. Inc., Arvin/Calspan Inc., Rockwell Internat.; Mem. adv. com. fluid dynamics NASA, 1961-64; mem. aeros. adv. com. NASA, 1980—, chmn. adv. subcom. on aerodynamics, 1983—; chmn. U.S. Boundary Layer Transition Study Group, NASA/USAF, 1970—; U.S. mem. fluid dynamics panel AGARD-NATO, 1981—; chmn. steering com. Symposium on Engring. Aspects Magneto-hydro-dynamics, 1966. Contbr. articles to tech. jours. Chmn. bd. govs. Cleve. Coll. Jewish Studies, 1981-84. Guggenheim fellow Calif. Inst. Tech., 1957-59. Fellow Am. Phys. Soc., Nat. Acad. Engring., AAAS, Am. Acad. Mechanics (pres.-elect 1985), AIAA (Fluid and Plasma Dynamics award) (1980), ASME; mem. AAUP, Sigma Xi, Tau Beta Pi, Pi Tau Sigma. Current Work: Fluid mechanics; propulsion, power generation; studies in boundary layer stability and transition as related to drag reduction. Subspecialties: Fluid mechanics; Aeronautical engineering. Office: Case Western Res Univ University Circle Cleveland OH 44106

RESLER, STEVEN CHARLES, environmental analyst, field researcher; b. Ft. Worth, Jan. 20, 1953; s. Louis C. and Augusta R. (Salers) R. Cert., SUNY-Cornell Coop. Extension Scope Marine Sci. Inst., 1976; cert., Adelphi U. Inst. Suburban Studies, 1977, Va. Inst. Marine Sci., 1977; postgrad., SUNY-Stonybrook, Empire State Coll., 1979. Environ. analyst Town of Smithtown (N.Y.) Conservation Commn., 1973-81; founder, pres. Sub-Sea Diving Systems, Inc., Smithtown, 1973—; co-investigator Octopus dofleini research team Ministry Fisheries and Oceans, Vancouver Island, B.C., Can., 1981-81; research coordinator octopus joubini research team Brandeis U., St. Joseph Bay, Fla., 1979-80; diving officer in charge SUNY Lab. Undersea Lab., Smithtown Bay, L.I., N.Y., 1977—; exec. dir. Marine Research Found., Inc., St. James, N.Y., 1981—; mem. estuarine sanctuaries steering com. U.S. Dept. Commerce, NOAA, Washington, Hauppauge, N.Y., 1979-81; mem. N.Y. State Shellfish Adv. Com., Stony Brook, 1978—; mem. regional marine resources council Dredging Adv. Commn., Houppauge, N.Y., 1975-77; adv. ocean engring. program SUNY-Stony Brook, 1976—. Author: Nissequogwe River - A Screening Study, 1978. Mem. Suffolk County Solar Energy Commn., Hauppaugue, N.Y., 1978; mem. L.I. Assn. Town Environ. Ofcls., 1979. Recipient 1st place awards N.Y. State Assn. Conservation Commn., 1978, 79, 80; Ford Found. grantee, 1973. Mem. Marine Tech. Soc., Internat. Oceanographic Found., Earthwatch, N.Y. Acad. Scis., N.Y. State Divers Assn. Club: Grumman Scuba (Bethpage, N.Y.). Current Work: Marine field research and scientific diving procedures, current interests in sonic tracking of marine vertebrates and invertebrates (octopuses) and behavior of same. Subspecialties: Resource management; Marine environmental sciences. Home: 37 Baylor Dr Smithtown NY 11787 Office: Marine Research Found 115 Long Beach Rd St James NY 11780

RESNICK, OSCAR, neuroscientist; b. Bayonne, N.J., Apr. 27, 1924; s. Samuel and Rebecca (Rubinstein) R.; m. Janice Zelda Ravitz, July 13, 1949; children: Sandra, Scott. A.B., Clark U., 1944; M.A., Harvard U., 1945; Ph.D., Boston U., 1955. Research fellow U. Iowa Med. Sch., 1945-46; instr. St. Petersburg Jr. Coll., 1946-47; research fellow U. Kans., 1947-49; instr. U. Minn., 1949-50; editorial asst. Biol. Abstracts, U. Pa., 1950-51; scientist Nat. Drug Co., Phila., 1951-53, Worcester Found. Exptl. Biology, Shrewsbury, Mass., 1953—; now sr. scientist; lectr. Boston U., 1961—, Clark U., 1965—; dir. research Worcester County Rehab. and Detention Ctr., West Boylston, Mass., 1965-76; cons. Medfield (Mass.) State Hosp., 1958-68, Norwich (Conn.) State Hosp., 1964-68;

mem. mental retardation research com. NIH, 1975-78. Contbr. articles to profl. jours. NIH grantee, 1957—. Fellow Am. Coll. Neuopsychopharmacology; mem. AAAS, Soc. Biol. Psychiatry, Am. Psychopatho. Soc., N.Y. Acad. Sci., Soc. Neurosci., Sigma Xi. Current Work: Prenatal nutrition in role of developing central nervous system; transgenerational effects. Subspecialties: Neurochemistry; Nutrition (medicine). Home: 5 Meadow Ln Worcester MA 01602 Office: 222 Maple Ave Shrewsbury MA 01545

RESNICK, SOL DONALD, hydrologist; b. Milw., June 15, 1918; s. Samual and Esther (Schneiderman) R.; m. Susan Kay Golden, June 21, 1981; children—Harry, Rachel. B.S. in Agrl. Engring., U. Wis., 1941, B.S. in Civil Engring., 1942, M.S. in Civil Engring., 1949. Registered profl. engr., Ariz., Colo. Asst. hydraulic engr. TVA, Knoxville, 1942-43; asst. prof. civil engring. Colo. State U., Ft. Collins, 1949-52; irrigation engr. AID, Nagpur, India, 1951-57, water resources engr., Bicol, Philippines, 1969; dir. Water Ctr., U. Ariz., Tucson, 1957-83, dir. emeritus, 1983—; prof. hydrology Asian Inst. Tech., Bangkok, Thailand, 1959; prof. agrl. engring. U. Ceara, Fortaleza, Brazil, 1964-66; mem. adv. com. Water Dept., City of Tucson, 1978-80. Author: (with others) Brackish Water, 1968; Arid Lands in Perspective, 1969; More Water for Arid Lands, 1974. Mem. adv. com. Planning and Zoning, City of Tucson, 1968-78, Pima County Health Dept., Tucson, 1979-83; mem. Ariz. Gov.'s Environ. Com., 1976-83. Served to 1st lt. M.I., U.S. Army, 1943-47. Grantee Dept Interior, 1965-83, U.S. Corps Engrs., 1978-82, Defenders of Wildlife, 1979-83. Mem. ASCE, Am. Soc. Agrl. Engrs., U.S. Com. on Irrigation and Drainage. Jewish. Current work: Part-time teaching and consulting regarding water resources management and urban hydrology. Subspecialties: Hydrology; Civil engineering. Office: U Ariz Tucson AZ 85721

RESS, RUDYARD JOSEPH, cardiovascular physiologist; b. Bronx, N.Y., Oct. 7, 1950; s. Joseph John and Kathrina (Fasser) R.; m. Kathleen McCarthy, Aug. 1, 1981. B.S. in Pharmacy, U. Fla., 1974, Ph.D., 1981. Registered pharmacist, Fla. Pharmacist ind. pharmacies, Gainesville, Fla., 1974-81; NIH research fellow Pa. State U., 1981-83; sr. research pharmacologist Am. Hoechst Corp., Somerville, N.J., 1983—. Contbr. articles to profl. jours. Mem. Am. Physiol. Soc. Current work: Cardiovascular physiology and pharmacology; calcium ion fluxs and vascular smooth muscle contraction. Subspecialties: Physiology (medicine); Pharmacology. Home: PO Box 2182 Flemington NJ 08822 Office: Am Hoechst Corp Dept Pharmacology Route 202-206 N Somerville NJ 08876

RESTAINO, ALFRED JOSEPH, research director; b. Bklyn., Feb. 18, 1931; s. Clement and Celia (Orlando) R.; m. Raffaela B. Sessa, June 27, 1954; children: Stephen, Alfred, Peter, Mario, Lisa. B.S. in Chemistry magna cum laude, St. Francis Coll., 1952; M.S. in Phys. and Polymer Chemistry, Poly. Inst. Bklyn., 1954, Ph.D., 1956. Unit supr. Martin Aircraft Corp., 1956-58; supr. radiation research ICI Americas (formerly Atlas Chem. Co.), Wilmington, Del., 1958-63, mgr. radiation research, 1963-68, mgr. radiation and plymer research, 1968-70, asst. dir. dept. chem. research, 1970-75, dir. dept. corp. research, 1975—; mem. faculty U. Del.; mem. tech. exchange with USSR, 1972; sci. advisor to gov. State of Del.; mem. adv. council U.S. AEC. Author: Encyclopedia of Materials Science and Engineering; contbr. articles to profl. jours. Mem. Soc. Chem. Industry, Am. Chem. Soc., N.Y. Acad. Scis., Assn. Research Dirs., Indsl. Research Inst., Sigma Xi. Patentee in fields of organic and polymer chemistry. Current Work: Specialty chemicals; high performance plymers; research administration. Subspecialties: Polymer chemistry; Materials (engineering). Office: ICI Americas Wilmington DE 19897

RESWICK, JAMES BIGELOW, rehabilitation engineer, educator; b. Ellwood City, Pa., Apr. 16, 1922; s. Maurice and Katherine (Parker) R.; m. Irmtraud Orthlies Hoelzerkopf, Dec. 27, 1973; children by previous marriage: James Bigelow, David Parker (dec.), Pamela Patchin. S.B. in Mech. Engring, Mass. Inst. Tech., 1943, S.M., 1948, Sc.D., 1952; D.Eng. (hon.), Rose Poly. Inst., 1968. Asst. prof., then assoc. prof., head machine design and graphics div. Mass. Inst. Tech., 1948-59; Leonard Case prof. engring., dir. Engring. Design Center, Case Western Res. U., 1959-70; dir. Rehab. Engring. Center, Rancho Los Amigos Hosp.; prof. biomed. engring. and orthopaedics U. So. Calif., also dir. of research dept. orthopaedics, 1970-80; assoc. dir. tech. Nat. Inst. Handicapped Research, U.S. Dept. Edn.; now dir. VA Rehab. Research and Devel. Evaluation Unit VA Med. Ctr., Washington; engring. cons. on automatic control, product devel., automation and bio-med. engring. Mem. com. prosthetics research and devel. Nat. Acad. Scis., 1962—; chmn. design and devel. com.; mem. bd. rev. Army Research and Devel. Office, 1965-68; mem. applied physiology and biomed. engring. study sect. NIH, 1972-78; mem. com. on trauma research Commn. on Life Scis., NRC and Inst. Medicine, 1984-85; mem. conf. com. Engring. Found., 1985—. Author: (with C.K. Taft) Introduction to Dynamic Systems, 1967; also articles.; Editor: (with F.T. Hambrecht) Functional Electrical Stimulation, 1977; series on engring. design, 1963—. Chmn. Mayor's Commn. for Urban Transp., Cleve., 1969. Served to lt. (j.g.) USNR, 1943-46, PTO. NSF sr. postdoctoral fellow Imperial Coll., London, Eng., 1957; Recipient Product Engring. Master Designer award, 1969; Isabelle and Leonard H. Goldenson award United Cerebral Palsy Assn., 1973. Fellow IEEE; mem. ASME (honor award for best paper 1956, sr. mem.), Am. Soc. Engring. Edn., Instrument Soc. Am., Biomed. Engring. Soc. (sr. mem., pres. 1973, dir.), Am. Acad. Orthopedic Surgeons (asso.), Inst. Medicine of Nat. Acad. Scis., Nat. Acad. Engring., Internat. Soc. Orthotics and Prosthetics, Orthopaedics Research Soc., Rehab. Engring. Soc. N.Am. (founding pres.), Sigma XI. Patentee in field. Current Work: Technology for handicapped persons; functional electrical stimulations; design, development, evaluation production and distribution of technology for the handicapped. Subspecialties: Biomedical engineering; Mechanical engineering. Home: 1003 Dead Run Dr McLean VA 22101 Office: VARR & D Evaluation Unit (153) VA Med Ctr 50 Irving St NW Washington DC 20422

RETTNER, CHARLES THOMAS, research chemist; b. London, Dec. 8, 1953; came to U.S., 1979; s. Charles William and Bella (Anastasio) R.; m. Elizabeth Jane Wakelin, June 26, 1976; 1 dau., Emily Jane. B.S., Birmingham (Eng.) U., 1975, Ph.D., 1978. Postdoctoral asst. MIT, Cambridge, 1979; Postdoctoral asst. Stanford U., 1980, research assoc. dept. chemistry, 1981—. Contbr. articles on chemistry to profl. jours. Hills Meml. fellow, 1977-79. Mem. AAAS, Planetary Soc. Current Work: Studies of the dynamics of elementary chemical reactions using lasers both to prepare reagents and to probe reaction products. Subspecialties: Laser photochemistry; Laser-induced chemistry. Office: Stanford University Dept Chemistry Stanford CA 94305

REUTHER, JAMES JOSEPH, combustion research scientist; b. Passaic, N.J., Jan. 29, 1950; s. Frederick William and Virginia (McBride) R.; m. Theresa Mary, Aug. 27, 1972; children: Adam James, Laura Ann. B.A., SUNY-Oneonta, 1973; M.A., SUNY-Binghamton, 1976; Ph.D., Pa. State U., 1979. Prin. research scientist Battelle Columbus Labs., Ohio Contbr. articles to profl. jours. Mem. Am. Chem. Soc., Am. Phys. Soc., Sigma Xi, Phi Kappa Phi, Phi Lamda Upsilon. Current Work: Directing basic and applied combustion research. Subspecialty: Fire suppression. Home: 1961 Samada Ave Worthington OH 43085 Office: Battelle Columbus Labs 50 S King Ave Columbus OH 43201

REVELLE, ROGER RANDALL DOUGAN, scientist educator; b. Seattle, Mar. 7, 1909; s. William Roger and Ella Robena (Dougan) R.; m. Ellen Virginia Clark, June 22, 1931; children—Anne Shumway, Mary Ellen Paci, Carolyn Hufbauer, William Roger. B.A., Pomona Coll., 1929; Ph.D., U. Calif.-Berkeley, 1936; Sc.D. (hon.), Pomona Coll., Carlton Coll., Colby Coll., Dartmouth Coll, Bucknell U., U. Mass., Utah State U., U. Miami, Old Dominion U.; L.H.D. (hon.), Williams Coll.; LL.D. (hon.) Carnegie Mellon U.; M.A. (hon.), Harvard U. Research asst., from instr. to prof. and dir. Scripps Inst. Oceanography, U. Calif.-San Diego, LaJolla, 1931-64, prof. sci. and pub. policy, 1976—; sci. adviser to Sec. of Interior, Washington, 1961-63; univ. dean of research U. Calif., 1963-64; Richard Saltonstall prof. population policy and dir. Harvard U. Ctr. of Population Studies, Cambridge, Mass., 1964-78; bd. fellow Claremont U. Ctr., 1978—; chmn. bd. sci. and tech. in devel. NRC, Washington, 1961-65; U.S. del. Gen. Conf., UNESCO, Paris and Belgrade, 1963, 79, mem., vice chmn. U.S. Nat. Commn., 1958-64, 70-76, chmn. U.S. del. Intergovt. Oceanographic Commn., Paris, 1962, 63; U.S. del. UN Conf. on Sci. and Tech., Vienna, 1978. Author: Land and Water Development in the Indus Plain, 1964, others. Editor: Consequences of Rapid Population Growth, 1972; (with Hans Landsberg) America's Changing Environment, 1969. Hon. bd. dirs. La Jolla Chamber Music Soc., 1978—; trustee Theater and Arts Found. of San Diego County, 1958—. Served to comdr., USNR, 1941-48. Revelle Coll. named in his honor, 1965. Recipient Sittary y Imtiaz, Govt. Pakiston, 1964; Tyler prize for environment, 1984; Vannevar Bush award Nat. Sci. Bd., 1984; New Eng. Aquarium medal, 1981, others. Fellow AAAS, Am. Acad. Arts and Scis., Am. Geophys. Union; mem. Nat. Acad. Sci., Am. Philos. Soc., Council on Fgn. Relations. Democrat. Clubs: Cosmos (Washington); Century Assn. (N.Y.C.); Bohemian (San Francisco); Tavern, Saturday (Boston). Current work: CO2 in the atmosphere, oceans and biota; earth's carrying capacity for human beings. Subspecialty: Oceanography. Home: 7348 Vista Del Mar La Jolla CA 92037 Office: U Calif San Diego Q 060 La Jolla CA 92093

REVESZ, GEORGE, radiologic physicist, educator, consultant; b. Budapest, Hungary, July 29, 1923; s. Nicholas and Elizabeth (Wallerstein) R.; m. Gabrielle Sophia Stern, Dec. 23, 1948; children: Julie Ann, Barbara Eva. M.S., Swiss Fed. Inst. Tech., Zurich, 1948; Ph.D., U. Pa., 1964. Staff engr. Gen. Electric Co. of Eng., 1949-54; sr. engr., tech. dir. Robertshaw Controls Co., 1954-61; research sect. mgr., mgr. instrumentation Philco-Ford Co., 1961-68; assoc. prof. Sch. Medicine Temple U., Phila., 1966-76, prof. radiology, 1976—; cons. v.p. Info/Consult; dir. Accu-Sort Systems Co. Contbr. articles to profl. publs. Recipient Bowen award Brit. Inst. Physics, 1954. Mem. Assn. Univ. Radiologists (Stauffer award 1982), Am. Assn. Physicists in Medicine, Optical Soc. Am., Am. Thermographic Soc., Sigma Xi. Current Work: Optical and computer processing of radiologic images; medical decision analysis. Subspecialties: Imaging technology; Optical image processing.

REYES, EDWARD, pharmacologist, educator, researcher; b. Albuquerque, May 5, 1944; s. Salvador and Faustina (Gabaldon) R.; m. Shirley Ann Trott, Aug. 15, 1970; children—David Joshua, Elizabeth Ann, Steven Mark. B.S. in Pharmacy, U. N.Mex., 1968; M.S. in Pharmacology, U. Colo., 1970, Ph.D. in Pharmacology, 1974. Registered pharmacist, Colo., N.Mex. Asst. prof. Sch. Pharmacy, U. Wyo., Laramie, 1974-75; asst. prof. Sch. Medicine, U. N.Mex., Albuquerque, 1975-85, assoc. prof., 1985—; cons. NIH-Minority Biomed. Research Support, 1973—. Author: Pharmacology Labbook, 1973; contbr. articles to profl. jours. Preacher, Rio Grande Baptist Ch., Albuquerque, 1980—. Grantee NSF, NIMH, NIH-Minority Biomed. Research Support, N.Mex. Child Health, 1983. Mem. Soc. for Neurosci., Western Pharmacology Soc., Soc. for Alcohol Research. Club: Sentry (Albuquerque) (leader 1980—). Current work: The effects of maternal alcohol consumption on brain and glutamyl transpeptidase and on behavioral characteristics in adult offspring. Subspecialties: Pharmacology; Neuropharmacology. Office: U NMex Sch Medicine Dept Pharmacology Albuquerque NM 87131

REYNAFARJE, BALTAZAR DAVILA, physiology and biochemistry educator, researcher; b. Chachapoyas, Amazonas, Peru, Sept. 21, 1925; s. Baltazar and Rosa Victoria (Davila) R.; m. Victoria Salome, Mar. 11, 1956; children: Jaime Baltazar, Patricia Orfelia, Lourdes Victoria, Alberto, Mariela Asunta. B.S. in Medicine, Universidad San Marcos, Peru, 1953, M.D., 1953, Ph.D., 1971. Instr. Faculty of Medicine, U. San Marcos, 1953-55, head dept. enzymology, 1957-65, assoc. prof., 1965-71, prof., 1971-75; research scientist Johns Hopkins U., Balt., 1975-79, research assoc., 1979—. Mem. AAAS, Am. Soc. Biol. Chemists, Peruvian Chem. Soc. (pres. biochem. br. 1974-75), Sociedad Peruana de Ciencias Fisologicas (founding), Sociedad Latino Americana de Ciencias Fisologicas, Sociedad Peruana de Bioquimica, Sociedad Peruana de Patologia, Sigma Xi. Catholic. Club: Regatas (Lima). Current Work: Mechanisms of energy transformation in mitochondria and its efficiency in organisms exposed to hypoxia and/or high altitudes. Subspecialties: Cell biology; Molecular biology. Home: 9 Haymarket Ct Baltimore MD 21236 Office: Johns Hopkins U 725 N Wolfe St Baltimore MD 21205

REYNOLDS, GEORGE OWEN, physicist, educator; b. Haverhill, Mass., July 5, 1937; s. William I. and Marjorie E. (Walker) R.; m. Anne Learnard, June 17, 1961; children: William, Gordon, Andrew. B.S., U. N.H., 1959, M.S. in Physics, 1961. Cons. A.S. Thomas Inc., Westwood, Mass., 1961-63; dir. applied scis. Tech. Ops. Inc., Burlington, Mass., 1963-75; dir. optical scis. Aerodyne Research Inc., Bedford, Mass., 1975-76; sr. staff scientist Arthur D. Little Inc., Cambridge, Mass., 1976-81; sr. staff engr. Electro-optics div. Honeywell Electro Optics Ops., Wilmington, Mass., 1981—; lectr. Northeastern U., Boston, 1966—; vis. indsl. prof. Tufts U., Medford, Mass., 1984—. Co-author: Theory and Applications of Holography, 1967; contbr. to: Handbook of Optical Holography, 1979; contbr. articles to profl. jours. Fellow Optical Soc. Am., Photo-Optical Instrumentation Engrs. (dir. 1982-83, sec. 1984—); mem. IEEE (sr. mem.), Am. Phys. Soc., New Eng. Optical Soc. (exec. council 1975—, rep. to Mass. Engring. Council 1979-81, dir. 1981—), Sigma Xi (sr. mem.). Patentee in field. Current Work: Holography, image processing, phase conjugation, atmospheric effects on light propagation, imaging systems, Fourier optics. Subspecialties: Holography; Optical image processing. Office: 2 Forbes Rd Lexington MA 02173 Office: 110 Fordham Rd Wilmington MA 01887

REYNOLDS, HAROLD GENE, design engineer; b. Winfield, Kans., Dec. 9, 1952; s. Donald Maurice and Leona (Saltz) R.; m. Donna Glenn Groom, Dec. 9, 1972; children—Sara Beth, Aaron Patrick. B.S. in Mech. Engring., Wichita State U., 1978. Registered profl. engr., Fla. Design engr. Pratt & Whitney Aircraft, West Palm Beach, Fla., 1978-81, sr. design engr., 1981—. Served with USNR, 1972-74. Mem. ASME. Republican. Methodist. Club: Fla. Gold Coast Classics (bd. dirs.). Current work: Design, procurement and test of gas turbine hardware; department representative on a committee to direct application of computer-aided design. Subspecialties: Mechanical engineering; Computer-aided design. Home: 5180 El Claro Dr S West Palm Beach FL 33415 Office: Pratt & Whitney Aircraft PO Box 2691 West Palm Beach FL 33402

REYNOLDS, JOHN GORDON, research chemist, chemical engineer; b. Oakland, Calif., Nov. 10, 1949; s. Oliver Clyde and Elizabeth Mary (Lorang) R. A.A. in Chem. Tech., Merritt Coll., Oakland, 1972; B.S. in Chemistry, U. Calif.-Berkeley, 1976; Ph.D. in Inorganic Chemistry, Stanford U., 1980. Research asst. Lawrence Berkeley Lab., Calif., 1974-76; research asst. Stanford Magnetic Research Lab., Calif., 1976-79; postdoctoral assoc. Calif. Inst. Tech., Pasadena, 1980-81; research engr. Chevron Research Co., Richmond, Calif., 1981—; enologist, owner Bay Cellars Winery, Emeryville, Calif., 1982—. Contbr. articles to sci. jours. Mem. Am. Chem. Soc. (petroleum, fuel and bus. sect.). Current work: Determination of metal non-porphyrins in heavy crudes and residua; inorganic modeling of non-porphyrins reactive centers. Subspecialties: Synthetic chemistry; Petroleum engineering. Home: 529 Dimm St Richmond CA 94805 Office: Chevron Research Co Richmond CA 94802

REYNOLDS, LARRY OWEN, electrical engineer, biomedical engineer; b. Norfolk, VA., Dec. 11, 1940; s. Herman Jewell and Kathryn (Key) R.; m. Laurel Lee Cutts, June 6, 1966 (div. 1971). B.S.E.E., U. Wash., 1969, M.S.E.E., 1970, Ph.D., 1975. NIH sr. fellow Ctr. for Bioengring., U. Wash., Seattle, 1975-76, research asst. prof., 1981-82, research assoc. prof., 1982—, research assoc. dept. elec. engring., 1976-79, research asst. prof. dept. nuclear engring., 1979-82, research assoc. prof., 1982—; cons. scientist Puget Sound Blood Ctr., 1976-77, Math. Scis. N.W., Bellevue, Wash., 1978—, Physio Control, Redmond, Wash., 1982, Abbott Labs., Chgo., 1982-83, Am. Hosp., Irvine, 1983—, Sorenson Research, Salt Lake, 1984—. Contbr. articles to profl. jours. NSF grantee, 1978; NIH grantee, 1980, 84. Mem. Optical Soc. Am., Soc. for Biomaterials, Soc. for Indsl. and Apllied Math., AAAS, Sigma Xi, Tau Beta Pi. Inventor blood plasma optical pH measurement system, particle size analyser for multiple scattering media. Current Work: Theoretical and experimental investigations of inverse and direct electromagnetic wave propagation and radiative transport techniques for characterizing dense scattering media. Subspecialties: Applied magnetics; Biomedical engineering. Office: U Washington Seattle WA 98195

REYNOLDS, MITCHELL WILLIAM, geologist; b. Denver, Dec. 6, 1937; s. Lewis Alfred Lovett and Marjorie Madelyn (Todd) R.; m. Sandra Anita Pettinga, Oct. 26, 1963; children—Elizabeth Johanna, Lenora Marjorie, Eliot Francis Todd. A.B., Harvard U., 1959; Ph.D., U. Calif.-Berkeley, 1969. Geologist, U.S. Geol. Survey, Denver, 1963-69, 73-79, program mgr., acting asst. chief geologist for program, Reston, Va., 1979-82, research geologist, Denver, 1982—; asst. prof. geology U. Calif.-Berkeley, 1969-72. Editor: Mesozoic Paleogeography of the West-Central U.S., 1983. Contbr. articles and maps to profl. publs. Mem. Evergreen Chorale (Colo.), 1977—, bd. dirs., 1983—; bd. dirs. Jeffco Action Ctr., Lakewood, Colo., 1983. NSF grantee, 1970-72. Fellow Geol. Soc. Am. (assoc. editor jour. 1972-75); mem. Soc. Econ. Paleontologists and Minerologists, Colo. Sci. Soc. (sec. 1975-78, councilor 1978-79, v.p. 1984—), Rocky Mountain Assn. Geologists, Sigma Xi. Current work: Tectonics and regional structure of Cordilleran overthrust belt, Montana, relation between tectonics and seidmentation, Mesozoic and Cenozoic rocks, western U.S. Subspecialties: Tectonics; Geology. Home: 11780 Swadley Dr Lakewood CO 80215 Office: US Geol Survey MS 905 Box 25046 Denver CO 80225

REYNOLDS, PETER JAMES, physicist, educator; b. N.Y.C., Nov. 19, 1949; s. Rudolph and Lydia Mary (Schanzer) R.; m. Louise E. Perini, Aug. 7, 1982. A.B., U. Calif.-Berkeley, 1971; Ph.D., MIT, 1979. Lectr. dept. physics Boston U., 1979, research assoc. Boston U. Ctr. Polymer Studies, 1979, asst. research prof., 1979—; staff sci. Lawrence Berkeley Lab., U. Calif., 1980—. Contbr. articles to profl. jours., chpts. to books. Fellow NSF, 1971-74, IBM, 1975; Lawrence Berkeley Lab. grantee, 1982 Mem. Am. Phys. Soc., N.Y. Acad. Scis., Phi Beta Kappa, Sigma Xi. Lutheran. Current work: Monte Carlo methods in molecular physics; stochastic solution of the Schrödinger equation; phase transitions and critical phenomena in disordered materials such as polymers and gels. Subspecialties: Condensed matter physics; Theoretical chemistry. Office: Lawrence Berkeley Lab Mail Stop 50D U Calif Berkeley CA 94720

REYNOLDS, ROBERT DONALD, pharmacologist; b. Butler, Pa., Dec. 11, 1944; s. Frank Edward and Betty Jean (Orner) R.; m. Mary C. Gruenwald, Aug. 17, 1974; children: Ty Douglas, Bret David, Alysia Marie, Scott Edward, Steven Joseph. B.A., Clarion State Coll., 1970; Ph.D., U. Cin., 1974. Research asso. dept. pharmacology Med. Coll. Pa., 1974-76; research investigator Am. Critical Care, McGaw Park, Ill., 1976-78, sr. research investigator, 1978-81, group leader, 1981-83, sr. research fellow, 1983-84, project mgr. (clin.), 1984-85, asst. dir. (clin.), 1985—; adj. asst. prof. Med. Coll. Wis., Milw., 1982—. Served with USMC, 1966-68. Am. Heart Assn. fellow, 1975-76. Mem. Am. Soc. Pharmacology and Exptl. Therapeutics, Am. Heart Assn., Phila. Physiol. Soc. Current Work: Clinical monitor cardiovascular physiology and pharmacology, arrhythmia, myocardial infarction, angina, antiarrhythmic drugs; beta-adrenergic blockers, calcium entry blockers. Subspecialties: Pharmacology; Physiology (medicine). Home: 971 Dunbar Mundelein IL 60060 Office: Am Critical Care McGaw Park IL 60085

REYNOLDS, WILLIAM CRAIG, mechanical engineer; b. Berkeley, Calif., Mar. 16, 1933; s. Merrill and Patricia Pope (Galt) R.; m. Janice Erma, Sept. 18, 1953; children—Russell, Peter, Margery. B.S. in Mech. Engring, Stanford U., 1954, M.S. in Mech. Engring, 1955, Ph.D. in Mech. Engring, 1957. Faculty mech. engring. Stanford U., 1957—, chmn. dept. mech. engring., 1972-82; chmn. Stanford U. (Inst. for Energy Studies), 1974-81. Author: books, including Engineering Thermodynamics, 2d edit, 1976; contbr. numerous articles to profl. jours. NSF sr. scientist fellow Eng., 1964. Fellow ASME; fellow Am. Phys. Soc.; mem. AAUP, AIAA, Nat. Acad. Engring., Sigma Xi, Tau Beta Pi. Research in fluid mechanics and applied thermodynamics. Subspecialties: Mechanical engineering; Fluid mechanics. Office: Stanford U Dept Mech Engring Stanford CA 94305

REZEK, EDWARD ANTHONY, electrical engineer; b. Omaha, July 19, 1954; s. Edward George and Elizabeth Helen (Kuckta) R.; m. Gloria Elia Lopez-Sauer, Nov. 14, 1981. B.S. in Elec. Engring., Washington U., St. Louis, 1976; A.B. in Physics, 1976; M.S. in Elec. Engring., U. Ill., Urbana, 1977, Ph.D., 1980. Mem. tech. staff TRW Tech. Research Ctr., El Segundo, Calif., 1980-84; sect. head TRW Electro-Optics Research Ctr., Redondo Beach, Calif., 1984—. Contbr. articles to profl. jours. Patentee crystal growth technique. Mem. IEEE, Electrochem. Soc., Am. Phys. Soc., AAAS, Tau Beta Pi, Eta Kappa Nu, Omicron Delta Kappa, Phi Kappa Phi. Republican. Roman Catholic. Current work: Semiconductor material growth and characterization; development of InGaAsP/InP Injection laser diodes; light emitting diodes; PIN and avalanche photodetector diodes; fiber optic communications. Subspecialties: Semiconductors; Fiber optics. Home: 1908 Carnegie Ln #D Redondo Beach CA 90278 Office: TRW-EORC m/s 147-1393G 1 Space Pk Redondo Beach CA 90278

RHEE, CHOONG HEE, civil engineer; b. Seoul, Korea, Aug. 21, 1931; came to U.S., 1964, naturalized, 1972; s. Sang Bong and Shin Soon (Shir) R. B.S. in Fiber Engring., Seoul Nat. U., 1957; B.S. in Maths., Calif. State U., 1969; M.S., U. So. Calif., 1973, Ph.D., 1977. Registered profl. engr., Calif. Exec. tech. dir. Daewon Paper Mills Co., Seoul, 1957-68; project engr. Flintkote Co., Vernon, Calif., 1969-73; sr. engr. Sanitation Dist. of Los Angeles County, 1973—; lectr. Los Angeles Tech. Coll., 1971—. Contbr. articles to profl. jours. Mem. Am. Acad. Environ. Engrs., Water Pollution Control Fedn. Current work: In-depth analyses of complex existing and proposed indsl. wastewater systems and establishment of future trends based on comprehensive research activities. Home: PO Box 1041 Huntington Beach CA 92647 Office: Sanitation Dist of Los Angeles County 1955 Workman Mill Rd Whittier CA 90607

RHEIN, ROBERT ALDEN, research chemist; b. San Francisco; s. Reginald Walter and Gaynelle Kathleen (Brunner) R.; m. Ellen Jane Emerson, June 9, 1956; children—Robert A., Jr., Mark E., Kathleen E., Dirck N., Jane M. B.S. in Engring. Physics, U. Calif.-Berkeley, 1955; M.S. in Mech. Engring., U. Pitts., 1958; Ph.D. in Chem., U. Wash., 1962. Sr. scientist Jet Propulsion Lab., Pasadena, Calif., 1962-79; research chemist Naval Weapons Ctr., China Lake, Calif., 1979—. Mem. Am. Chem. Soc. Democrat. Roman Catholic. Current work: Thermally stable elastomers; energetic polymers and plasticizers; combustion chemistry; silicon chemistry; computer chemistry thermodynamics. Subspecialties: Polymer chemistry; Synthetic chemistry. Home: 424 E Kendall Ave Ridgecrest CA 93555 Office: Naval Weapons Center China Lake CA 93555-6001

RHEINBOLDT, WERNER CARL, mathematics educator; b. Berlin, Sept. 18, 1927; came to U.S., 1956, naturalized, 1963; s. Karl Leo and Gertrud Anna (Hartwig) R.; m. Cornelie J. Hogewind, 1959; children—Bernd Michael, Matthew Cornelius. Dipl. Math, U. Heidelberg, Ger., 1952; Dr.rer.nat., U. Freiburg, Ger., 1955. Mathematician Computer Lab., Nat. Bur. Standards, Washington, 1957-59; dir. Computer Center, asst. prof. math. Syracuse (N.Y.) U., 1959-62; dir. Computer Sci. Center, U. Md., 1962-65, prof. math. and computer sci., 1965-78, dir. interdisciplinary applied math. program, 1974-78; A.W. Mellon prof. math. U. Pitts., 1978—; vis. prof. Gesellschaft für Mathematik und Datenverarbeitung, Bonn, W. Ger., 1969; adv. panel computer sci. NSF, 1972-75; adv. com. Army Research Office, 1974-78; chmn. applied math. com. NRC, 1979-85, mem. bd. math. scis., 1984—; cons. editor Acad. Press, N.Y.C., 1967—; cons. in field. Author: (with J. Ortega) Iterative Solution of Nonlinear Equations in Several Variables, 1970, Methods of Solving Systems of Nonlinear Equations, 1974; also articles. Served with German Army, 1943-45. Grantee NSF, 1960-62, 65—; Grantee NASA, 1963-73; Grantee Office Naval Research, 1972—. Mem. Soc. Indsl. and Applied Math. (editor 1964—, v.p. publs. 1976, pres. 1977-78, council 1979-80, trustee 1982—, chmn. bd. trustees 1985—), Math. Assn. Am., Am. Math. Soc., AAAS. Lutheran. Current Work: Numerical problems for nonlinear problems; finite element methods; adaptive strategies for numerical computations; numerical approaches to problems in continuum mechanics; parallel numerical computations; numerical data structures. Subspecialties: Numerical analysis (computer science); Applied mathematics. Office: Dept Math and Statistics U Pitts Pittsburgh PA 15260

RHEINSTEIN, PETER HOWARD, government official, physician, lawyer; b. Cleve., Sept. 7, 1943; s. Franz Joseph Rheinstein and Hede Henrietta (Neheimer) Lerner; m. Miriam Ruth Weissman, Feb. 22, 1969; 1 child, Jason Edward. B.A. with high honors, Mich. State U., 1963, M.S., 1964; M.D., Johns Hopkins U., 1967; J.D., U. Md.-Balt., 1973. Diplomate Am. Bd. Family Practice; bar: Md. 1973, D.C. 1980. Intern, USPHS Hosp., San Francisco, 1967-68; resident in internal medicine USPHS Hosp., Balt., 1968-70; instr. medicine U. Md. Med. Sch., Balt., 1970-73; practice medicine specializing in family practice, Balt., 1970—; med. dir. extended care facilities CHC Corp., Balt., 1972-74; adj. prof. forensic medicine George Washington U., Washington, 1974-76; dir. div. drug advt. and labeling FDA, Rockville, Md., 1974-81, acting dep. dir. Office of Drugs, 1981-82, acting dir., 1982-83, dir., 1983—, del. U.S. Pharmacopeial Conv., 1985—; cons. drug regulation Nat. Inst. for Control Pharm. and Biol. Products, Beijing, Peoples Republic of China, 1981—. Spl. editorial advisor Good Housekeeping Guide to Medicines and Drugs, 1977—; mem. editorial bd. (newsletter) Legal Aspects of Med. Practice, 1981—, Drug Info. Jour., 1982—. Served as surgeon USPHS, 1967-70. Recipient Commendable Service award FDA, 1981. Fellow Am. Coll. Legal Medicine (bd. govs. 1983—, chmn. model statutes and bioethical issues com. 1983-85, treas., chmn. fin. com. 1985—), Am. Acad. Family Physicians; mem. Drug Info. Assn. (pres. 1984-85, bd. dirs. 1981—), AMA, ABA, Fed. Bar Assn. (chmn. food and drug com. 1976-79, Disting. Service award 1977), Mich. State U. Alumni Assn. (life), U. Md. Alumni Assn. (life), Johns Hopkins U. Alumni Assn., U.S. Power

Squadron, Mensa (life), Delta Theta Phi. Clubs: Chartwell Golf and Country (Severna Park, Md.); Johns Hopkins (Balt.). Current work: Diffusion of new technologies into the clinical practice of medicine; integrating drug information into the drug regulatory system. Subspecialties: Pharmacology; Legal medicine. Home: 621 Holly Ridge Rd Severna Park MD 21146 Office: Office Drug Standards FDA 5600 Fishers Ln Rockville MD 20857

RHIM, JOHNG SIK, physician, researcher; b. Korea, July 24, 1930; came to U.S., 1958, naturalized, 1968; s. Hac Woon and Moo Duc (Choi) R.; m. Mary Margaret Lytle, Aug. 25, 1962; children: Jonathan, Christopher, Peter, Andrew, Michael, Kathleen. M.D., Seoul (korea) Nat. U., 1957. Intern Seoul Nat. U. Hosp., 1957-58; research fellow Children's Hosp. Research Found., Cin., 1958-60, Baylor U., 1961; Grad. Sch. Public Health, U. Pitts., 1962; research assoc. La. State U. Sch. Medicine, New Orleans, 1962-64; vis. scientist Nat. Inst. Arthritis and Infectious Diseases, NIH, Bethesda, Md., 1964-76; project dir. cancer research Microbiol. Assocs. Inc., Bethesda, 1976-78; sr. research scientist Nat. Cancer Inst., NIH, Bethesda, 1978—. Research, publs. on cancer and viral diseases. Bd. dirs. Winchester Sch., Silver Spring, Md. Mem. AAAS, Am. Assn. Cancer Research, Am. Assn. Immunologists, AMA, Am. Soc. Microbiologts, Soc. Exptl. Biology and Medicine, N.Y. Acad. Sci., Internat. Assn. Comparative Leukemia Research, Internat. Soc. Preventive Oncology. Democrat. Current Work: Viral carcinogenesis, chem. carcinogenesis, factors regulating cellular transformation, mechanism of carcinogenesis, identification and characterization of oncogenes. Subspecialties: Cancer research (medicine); Virology (medicine). Home: 8309 Mebdy Ct Bethesda MD 20817 Office: 9000 Rockville Pike Bethesda MD 20205

RHINESMITH, ROBERT J., research chemist; b. East Orange, N.J.; s. James F. and Helen (Geney) R. A.B., Rutgers U.-Newark, 1962, Ph.D., 1982; M.S., Rutgers U.-New Brunswick, 1965. Instr. physics Drew U., Madison, N.J., 1973-75; instr. physics Rutgers U., Newark, 1975-78, instr. chemistry, 1979-82; postdoctoral scientist Smith Kline Beckman, Phila., 1982-84; research chemist Colgate-Palmolive Co., Pascataway, N.J., 1984—. NSF summer fellow, 1963. Am. Inst. Chem. Engrs., Am. Chem. Soc., Phi Beta Kappa, Sigma Xi, Sigma Pi Sigma. Current work: Rheology of dense dispersions; laboratory automation. Subspecialties: Physical chemistry; Kinetics. Office: Colgate-Palmolive Co E-202 909 River Rd Piscataway NJ 08854

RHOADES, RODNEY ALLEN, physiology educator; b. Greenville, Ohio, Jan. 5, 1939; s. John Hiram and Floris (Warner) R.; m. Judith Ann Brown, Aug. 6, 1961; children—Annelisa, Kirsten. B.S., Miami U., Oxford, Ohio, 1961, M.S., 1963; Ph.D., Ohio State U., 1966. Asst. prof. physiology Pa. State U., State College, 1966-74, assoc. prof., 1974-75; research scientist NIH, Bethesda, Md., 1975-76; assoc. prof. physiology Ind. U. Med. Sch., Indpls., 1976-79, prof., 1979-81, chmn. dept., 1981—. Author: Physiology, 1983. Contbr. articles to profl. jours. NASA fellow, 1962; NIH career research devel. award, 1976. Mem. Am. Physiol. Soc., Am. Heart Assn., Am. Thoracic Soc., Sigma Xi. Current work: Pulmonary physiology; lung injury; lung lipid metabolism; lung vasoactive hormones. Subspecialties: Physiology (medicine); Pulmonary medicine. Home: 7525 N Audubon St Indianapolis IN 46250 Office: Med Sch Ind U 635 Barnhill Dr Indianapolis IN 46223

RHODES, CHARLES KIRKHAM, physics educator, researcher; b. Mineola, N.Y., June 30, 1939; s. Walter Cortlyn and Evelyn (Kirkham) R.; m. Barbara Dowe, Aug. 28, 1964 (div.); children—Lisa Porterfield, Gregory Cortlyn; m. Mary Cannon, Oct. 23, 1976; children—Edward Kirkham, Elizabeth Mayhew. B.E.E., Cornell U., 1963; M.E.E., MIT, 1965, Ph.D. in Physics, 1969. Physicist, head gas laser group Lawrence Livermore Lab., U. Calif., 1970-75, lectr. dept. applied sci. Livermore extension U. Calif.-Davis, 1971-75; program mgr. molecular physics lab. SRI Internat., Menlo Park, Calif., 1975-78; cons. prof. Stanford U., Calif., 1975-78; prof. physics U. Ill.-Chgo., 1978-82, research prof. physics, 1982—. Sr. mem. com. recommendations for U.S. Army sci. research NRC, 1979-82. Contbr. articles to profl. jours. Patentee in field of lasers. Fellow Honors Coll., U. Ill.-Chgo., 1983—. Fellow Am. Phys. Soc., Optical Soc. Am.; mem. IEEE (sr. mem.), Quantum Electronics and Applications Soc. (sr. mem.), European Physical Soc. Subspecialties: X-ray lasers; Pharmacognosy. Office: Dept of Physics U Ill at Chicago PO Box 4348 Chicago IL 60680

RHODES, DALLAS D., geology educator; b. El Dorado, Kans., Aug. 8, 1947; s. Earl Rhodes and Peggy Lee (White) Smith; m. Lisa Ann Rossbacher, Aug. 4, 1979. B.S. with honors, U. Mo., 1969; M.S., Syracuse U., 1973, Ph.D., 1973. Instr. Syracuse U., N.Y., 1972-73; asst. prof. U. Vt., Burlington, 1973-77; asst. prof. geology Whittier Coll., Calif., 1977-81, assoc. prof., 1981—; cons. geologist N.Y. State Geol. Survey, Albany, 1975-76; cons. geologist Jet Propulsion Lab., Pasadena, Calif., 1981—; resident dir. Danish Internat. Student Com. Study Program, Copenhagen, 1983-84. Editor: (with Garnet P. Williams) Adjustments of the Fluvial System, 1979. NASA fellow, 1980-81. Mem. Geol. Soc. Am., Am. Geophys. Union, Sigma Xi. Club: University (Whittier). Current work: Hydraulic geometry of river channels; paleogeomorphology of Mars. Subspecialties: Geomorphology; Hydrology. Home: 13803 Walnut St Whittier CA 90602 Office: Dept Geology Whittier Coll Whittier CA 90608

RHODES, DONALD FREDERICK, research physicist, educator; b. Johnstown, Pa., July 1, 1932; s. Frederick D. and Irene M. (Ankney) R.; m. Patricia J. Beaumariage, Dec. 22, 1956. B.S., U. Pitts., 1954, M.Litt., 1956; Ph.D., Pacific Western U., 1982. Instr. physics U. Pitts., 1954-55; engr. Westinghouse Electric Pitts., 1956-57; research physicist Gulf Research & Devel., Pitts., 1958—, educator aviation tech., 1975—. Recipient IR 100 award Indsl. Research, 1968. Mem. Am. Nuclear Soc., Health Physics Soc. Club: Aero of Pitts. Patentee nuclear instrumentation. Current Work: Research in nuclear applications, instrumentation and ultrasonics. Subspecialties: Nuclear physics; Electronics. Home: 439 Trestle Rd Pittsburgh PA 15239 Office: Gulf Research & Devel Co PO Drawer 2038 Pittsburgh PA 15230

RHODES, EDWARD JOSEPH, JR., astronomer, educator; b. San Diego, June 1, 1946; s. Edward Joseph, Sr. and Flora Bernice (Mosser) R.; m. Beverly Ann Zahka, June 24, 1972; 1 child, Edward Joseph III. B.S., UCLA, 1968, M.A., 1971, Ph.D., 1977. Scientist Jet Propulsion Lab., Pasadena, Calif., 1970-77, mem. tech. staff., 1978—; research fellow dept. physics Calif. Inst. Tech., Pasadena, 1977-78; asst. in research astronomy dept. UCLA, 1978-79, adj. asst. prof., 1978-79, asst. prof., 1979—; co-chmn. solar oscillations sci. working group NASA, 1983-84. Contbr. articles to profl. jours. Percussionist, Caltech Symphonic Wind Ensemble, Pasadena, 1974. Recipient cert. of recognition NASA, 1983; Teaching Excellence award Mortar Bd., 1983; NASA research grantee, 1979-85; NSF internat. research grantee, 1984-85. Mem. Internat. Astron. Union, Am. Astron. Soc., Am. Geophys. Union, Phi Beta Kappa, Sigma Xi. Democrat. Current work: Observational and theoretical studies of solar internal structure and dynamics; helioseismology; spacecraft instrument development for future missions. Subspecialties: Solar physics; Optical astronomy. Home: 11801 Killimore Ave Northridge CA 91326Office: Dept Astronomy Univ So Calif SHS 360 Los Angeles CA 90089

RHODIN, THOR NATHANIEL, applied physicist, educator, industrial consultant; b. Buenos Aires, Argentina, Dec. 9, 1920; s. Thor N. and Pearl R. R.; m. Elspeth Lindsay, Sept. 21, 1949; children: Robert, Ann, Lindsay, Jeffrey. B.S., Haverford Coll., 1942; A.M., Princeton U., 1945, Ph.D., 1946. Research asst. Manhattan Project, Princeton, N.J., 1944-46; research assoc. Inst. for Study Metals; instr. chemistry U. Chgo., 1946-51; research asso. Engring. Research Lab., E.I. Du Pont de Nemours & Co., Inc., Wilmington, Del., 1951-58; asso. prof. applied and engring. physics Cornell U., Ithaca, N.Y., 1958-65, prof., 1965—. Editor, contbr. 6 books.; editorial advisor 5 current sci. jours.; contbr. over 200 articles to sci. jours. Mem. Am. Phys. Soc., Am. Vacuum Soc., Am. Chem. Soc., AAUP. Quaker. Current Work: Physics and chemistry of surfaces and solid interfaces; solid state chemical physics; condensed matter; semiconductor surfaces and interfaces; synchrontron radiation; electron spectroscopy; physical chemistry. Subspecialties: Condensed matter physics; Surface chemistry. Home: 222 Miller St Ithaca NY 14850 Office: 217 Clark Hal Cornell Ithaca NY 14853

RIAHI, NOUROLLAH, physicist, educator, researcher; b. Shahrekord, Iran, Oct. 30, 1943; came to U.S., 1968; s. Ali Mohammed and Gohartaj (Ale-Ebrahim) R.; m. Eglantini Perez, May 26, 1984. B.S., Tehran U. (Iran), 1966; M.S., Fla. State U., 1970, Ph.D., 1974. Research asst. Fla. State U., Tallahassee, 1970-74, research assoc., 1974-77; math. faculty Winthrop Coll., Rock Hill, S.C., 1977-78; fluid mechanics researcher UCLA, 1978-80; vis. asst. prof. U. Ill.-Urbana, 1980-82, asst. prof., 1982—; cons. social work Fla. State U., 1970-71. Reviewer books; contbr. articles to profl. jours. Served to lt. Iranian Army, 1967-68. Recipient Postdoctoral Research award Fla. State U., 1974-77; Travel award NSF, 1983. Mem. Soc. Indsl. and Applied Math., Am. Inst. Physics, Am. Phys. Soc. (internat. physics group), Sigma Xi. Current work: Thermal convection and heat-transfer, instability and transition to turbulence, rotating fluid, megnetohydrodynamics, boundary layers, nonlinear problems, waves. Subspecialties: Fluid mechanics; Applied mathematics. Office: 216 Talbot Lab U Ill 104 S Wright St Urbana IL 61801

RIBAK, CHARLES ERIC, neuroscientist, educator; b. Albany, N.Y., July 19, 1950; s. Marcus and Adele (Blank) R.; m. Julia Marianne Wendruck, Jan. 2, 1977; children—Marc Aaron, William Michael. B.S., SUNY-Albany, 1971; Ph.D., Boston U., 1975. Mem. faculty Newbury Jr. Coll., Boston, 1972-74; Lab instr. Boston U., 1973-75; assoc. research scientist City of Hope Med. Ctr., Duarte, Calif., 1975-78; asst. prof. anatomy U. Calif.-Irvine, 1978-83, assoc. prof., 1983—; ad hoc reviewer NIH and NSF, Washington, 1979—. Assoc. editor Jour. Neurocytology, 1984—. Contbr. articles to profl. jours., chpts. to books. Klingenstein fellow, 1983-86. Mem. AAAS, Am. Assn. Anatomists, Soc. for Neurosci., N.Y. Acad. Scis., Internat. Brain Research Orgn. Current work: Study of neuronal circuitry in the hippocampus and the analysis of the role of GABAergic, inhibitory neurons in animal nodels of genetic and focal epilepsy. Subspecialties: Neurobiology; Cell biology. Office: Dept Anatomy U Calif Irvine CA 92717

RIBE, FRED LINDEN, nuclear engineering educator; b. Laredo, Tex., Aug. 14, 1924; s. Otto Emil and Viola (Crowell) R.; m. Mally Graham Kemp, Mar. 23, 1946; children—James K., Frederick C., Robert G., Thomas E. B.S.E.E., U. Tex., 1944; Ph.D., U. Chgo., 1951. Div. leader Los Alamos Nat. Lab., 1951-77; prof. nuclear engring. U. Wash., Seattle, 1977—; mem. adv. com. on magnetic fusion U.S. Dept. Energy, Washington, 1985—. Editor Physics of Fluids, 1982—. Contbr. chpts. on nuclear and plasma physics to books. Served to lt. (j.g.) USN, 1944-46. Guggenheim Meml. Found. fellow, 1963. Fellow Am. Phys. Soc. (chmn. div. plasma physics 1975); mem. Am. Nuclear Soc., Sierra Club. Subspecialties: Nuclear fusion; Plasma physics. Home: 6003 Princeton Ave NE Seattle WA 98115 Office: U Wash MS BF-10 Seattle WA 98115

RIBIERO, LAIR G(ERALDO) T(HEODORO), clinical research director, educator; b. Juiz De Fora, Minas, Brazil, July 6, 1945; came to U.S., 1976; s. Francisco and Ruth (Reis) Ribeiro; m. Edna May Ottoni Porto, Jan. 1, 1968 (div. 1978); children: Frederico, Claudia; m. Mary Miller, May 22, 1979; 1 dau., Christine. B.S., Fundação Machado Sobrinho, 1967; M.D., Juiz De Fora Med. Sch., 1972. Teaching asst. in anatomy Med. Sch. of Fed. U., Juiz de Fora, 1969-71, teaching asst. in cardiology, 1971-72; resident in cardiology Pontificia Universidade Catolica do Rio de Jeneiro, Brazil, 1973, instr. cardiology, 1974; cardiologist Cantral Army Hosp., Rio de Jeneiro, 1974; asst. prof. cardiology Med. Sch., Barbacena, Brazil, 1975-76; research fellow in medicine Peter Bent Prigham Hosp. and Harvard Med. Sch., Boston, 1976-78; fellow in cardiology Meth. Hosp.-Baylor Coll. Medicine, Houston, 1978-80; asst. dir. Deborah Cardiovascular Research Inst., Browns Mills, N.J., 1980-82; dir. clin. research-domestic Merck Sharp & Dohme Research Labs., West Point, Pa., 1982—; adj. asst. prof. physiology Thomas Jefferson Coll. Medicine, Phila., 1981—. Author: Coronary Spasm, 1983; co-author: Myocardial Ischemia, 1978, Platelets and Prostaglandins, 1981; contbr. articles to profl. jours. Served with Brazilian Army, 1964. Recipient 1st place in cardiology postgrad. tng. Cath. U., 1973. Fellow Am. Coll. Cardiology; mem. Brazilian Cardiology Soc., Am. Fedn. Clin. Research, N.Y. Acad. Scis. Current Work: Protection of ischemic mycardium and reduction of myocardial infarct size; prostaglandins; sudden death. Subspecialties: Cardiology; Pharmacology. Home: 14 Robbins Way Vincentown NJ 08088 Office: Merck Sharp & Dohme Research Labs West Point PA 19486

RICE, BART FRANCIS, engineer; b. Miami Beach, Fla., Mar. 12, 1943. B.A., Rice U., 1965; Ph.D., La. State U., 1969; M.S. in Computer Sci., Johns Hopkins U., 1976, M.S.E.E., 1982. Instr. math. La. State U., 1967-69; asst. prof. math. Naval Postgrad. Sch., Monterey, Calif., 1971-72; mathematician Nat. Security Agy., Fort Meade, Md., 1972-84; sr. staff engr. Lockheed Missiles and Space Co., Sunnyvale, Calif., 1984—; treas. Crypto-Math Inst., Fort Meade, 1978-80; Served to lt. USNR, 1969-72; comdr. Res. Mem. IEEE (sr. mem.), Armed Forces Communications and Electronics Assn. Subspecialties: Electrical engineering; Applied mathematics. Office: Lockheed Missiles and Space Co 1111 Lockheed Way Sunnyvale CA 94086

RICE, DONALD BLESSING, research institute executive; b. Frederick, Md., June 4, 1939; s. Donald Blessing and Mary Celia (Santangelo) R.; m. Susan Fitzgerald, Aug. 25, 1962; children—Donald Blessing III, Joseph John, Matthew Fitzgerald. B.S. in Chem. Engring., U. Notre Dame, 1961, D.Engring. (hon.), 1975; M.S. in Indsl. Adminstrn., Purdue U., 1962, Ph.D. in Econs., 1965, D.Mgmt. (h.c.), 1985. Dir. cost analysis Office Sec. Def., Washington, 1967-69, dep. asst. sec. def. resource analysis, 1969-70; asst. dir. Office Mgmt. and Budget, Exec. Office Pres., 1970-72; pres., chief exec. officer Rand Corp., Santa Monica, Calif., 1972—; dir. Wells Fargo Bank, Pacific Lighting Corp., Wells Fargo & Co., Uniform Software Systems; mem. Nat. Sci. Bd., 1974—; chmn. Nat. Commn. Supplies and Shortages, 1975-77; mem. Nat. Commn. on U.S.-China Relations; mem. nat. adv. com. oceans and atmosphere Dept. Commerce, 1972-75; mem. adv. panel Office Tech. Assessment, 1976-79; adv. council Coll. Engring., U. Notre Dame, 1974—; mem. Def. Sci. Bd., 1977-83, sr. cons., 1984—; dir. for sec. def. and Pres. Def. Resource Mgmt. Study, 1977-79. Author articles. Bd. dirs. Los Angeles World Affairs Council. Served to capt. AUS, 1965-67. Recipient Sec. Def. Meritorious Civilian Service medal, 1970; Ford Found. fellow, 1962-65. Fellow AAAS; mem. Am. Econ. Assn., Council Fgn. Relations, Inst. Mgmt. Scis. (past pres.), Los Angeles Area C. of C. (bd. dirs.), Tau Beta Pi. Home: 518 Georgina Ave Santa Monica CA 90402 Office: The Rand Corporation 1700 Main St Santa Monica CA 90406

RICE, DONALD LESTER, geochemistry educator, researcher; b. Chamblee, Ga., Sept. 10, 1949; s. Lester C. and Clara M. (Warbington) R. B.S., Ga. Inst. Tech., 1970, M.S., 1974, Ph.D., 1979. Research asst. Skidaway Inst. Oceanography, Savannah, Ga., 1977-79; asst. prof. marine sci. U. S.C., Conway, 1979-80; asst. prof. geology sci. SUNY-Binghamton, 1980-84; assoc. prof. Chesapeake Biol. Lab., U. Md., 1984—; editorial cons. Merrill Pub. Co., Columbus, Ohio, 1981—. Served with U.S. Army, 1970-72. Recipient award for best dissertation in sci. Sigma Xi, 1979. Mem. Geochem. Soc., Am. Soc. Limnology and Oceanography, AAAS, Estuarine Research Fedn. Episcopalian. Current Work: Nutrient and trace element biogeochemistry in marine environments. Subspecialties: Geochemistry; Oceanography. Home: Box 546 Solomons MD 20688 Office: Chesapeake Biol Lab Solomons MD 20688

RICE, GARY WAYNE, chemist; b. Fort Smith, Ark., Feb. 7, 1948; s. Gerald Wayne and Betty Jean (Ramay) R.; m. Catherine Ellen Owens, Mar. 2, 1973; 1 child, Amanda Jean. B.S., Ouachita Bapt. U., 1970; Ph.D., Purdue U., 1975. Postdoctoral fellow Tex. A&M U., College Station, 1976-78; chemist Exxon Research & Engring., Clinton, N.J., 1978—. Contbr. articles to profl. jours. Mem. Am. Chem. Soc., Am. Ceramic Soc. Democrat. Current work: High temperature synthesis, catalysts and ceramics. Subspecialties: Inorganic chemistry; Laser-induced chemistry. Office: Exxon Research & Engring Route 22 E Annandale NJ 08801

RICE, JAMES ALLEN, research physicist; b. Houston, Apr. 15, 1958; s. Allen Gene Rice and Joyce Marcella (Baldridge) Mason; m. Paula Hughes, Jan. 25, 1979; children—Bobbie Marcella, Adam Baldridge Hughes. B.A., Rice U., 1979, Ph.M., 1981, M.A., 1982, Ph.D., 1983. Engr., Amax Petroleum Co., Houston, 1976-77; physicist Argonne Nat. Lab., Ill., 1978; contract physicist Exxon Prodn. Research Co., Houston, 1979-83, sr. research physicist, 1983—; v.p. Inded Corp., Baytown, Tex., 1982—. Contbr. articles to profl. jours. Patentee acoustic quadrupole log, 1984. Nat. Merit scholar, 1976; NSF fellow, 1979. Mem. Am. Phys. Soc., AAAS, Soc. Exploration Geophysicists, Sigma Xi, Sigma Pi Sigma. Republican. Baptist. Current work: Study of nature of wave phenomena in the seismic frequency band in order to develop a more accurate seismic wave equation. Subspecialties: Seismology; Particle physics. Home: 15827 Maple Manor Houston TX 77095 Office: Exxon Prodn Research Co N225 3120 Buffalo Speedway Houston TX 77005

RICE, JAMES ROBERT, engineering scientist, geophysicist; b. Frederick, Md., Dec. 3, 1940; s. Donald Blessing and Mary Celia (Santangelo) R.; m. Renata Dmowska, Feb. 28, 1981; children by previous marriage: Douglas, Jonathan. B.S., Lehigh U., 1962, Sc.M., 1963, Ph.D., 1964. Postdoctoral fellow Brown U., Providence, 1964-65, asst. prof. engring., 1965-68, asso. prof., 1968-70, prof., 1970-81, Ballou prof. theoretical and applied mechanics, 1973-81; McKay prof. engring. sci. and geophysics Harvard U., Cambridge, Mass., 1981—. Recipient awards for sci. publs. ASME, awards for sci. publs. ASTM, awards for sci. publs. U.S. Nat. Com. Rock Mechanics. Fellow ASME, AAAS; mem. Nat. Acad. Engring., Nat. Acad. Sci., ASCE, Am. Geophys. Union, Soc. Rheology. Research contbns. to solid mechanics, materials sci. and geophysics. Subspecialties: Solid mechanics; Geophysics. Office: Dept Engring Sci Harvard U Cambridge MA 02138*

RICE, MICHAEL JOHN, theoretical physicist, cons.; b. Cowes, Isle of Wight, Eng., Dec. 25, 1940; came to U.S., 1968; s. Thomas John and Elizabeth Emma (Keeping) R.; m. Annegret Thekla Richter, Sept. 17, 1965; children: Juliet, Jeremy, Jennifer. B.S. with spl. honors, Queen Mary Coll., U. London, 1961, Ph.D., 1965. Research fellow Imperial Coll., U. London, 1965-68; mem. sci. staff Gen. Electric Research and Devel. Ctr., Schenectady, 1968-71; theoretical physicist Brown Boveri Research Ctr., Baden, Switzerland, 1971-74; sr. scientist Xerox Webster Research Ctr., Webster, N.Y., 1974-79, prin. scientist, 1979—; sr. vis. research scholar Corpus Christi Coll., Cambridge, Eng., 1984-85; cons. govt. research labs.; lectr. in field. Contbr. numerous articles on physics to profl. jours. Nordita prof. of physics U. Copenhagen, 1979-80. Fellow Am. Phys. Soc. Current Work: Frontier problems in theoretical condensed matter physics, conducting polymers, molecular metals and superconductors, fractionally charged particles. Subspecialties: Condensed matter physics; Theoretical physics. Office: 800 Phillips Rd Bldg 114 Webster NY 14580

RICE, STEPHEN LANDON, mechanical engineer, educator; b. Oakland, Calif., Nov. 23, 1941; s. Landon Frederick and Elda Genevieve (Hunt) R.; m. Penny Baum, Dec. 29, 1965; children: Andrew Landon, Katherine Grace. B.S., U. Calif., Berkeley, 1964, M. Eng., 1969, Ph.D., 1972. Registered profl. engr., Fla. Design engr. U. Calif. Lawrence Berkeley Lab., 1982-83; asst. prof. mech. engring. U. Conn., Storrs, 1972-77, asso. prof., 1977-82, prof. mech. engring, elec. engring. and computer sci., also dir. Automation, Robotics and Mfg. Lab., 1982-83; prof. engring. U. Central Fla., Orlando, 1983—, chmn. dept. mech. engring. and aerospace scis., 1983—. Contbr. articles to profl. jours. Recipient Teetor Edn. award Soc. Automotive Engrs., 1975; Fulbright-Hays sr. research awardee, 1978-79. Mem. ASME, Am. Soc. for Engring. Edn. (Outstanding Young Faculty award New Eng. sect. 1975), Am. Soc. Lubrication Engrs., Soc. Mfg. Engrs. Current Work: Fundamental research in wear of materials, including novel techniques using laser speckle metrology; applied research in robotics, computer-aided-design and manufacturing (CAD/CAM); devel. of computer-based educational materials; ednl. evaluation. Subspecialties: Wear of materials; CAD/CAM. Office: Dept Mech Engring and Aerospace Scis Central Fla Orlando FL 32816

RICE, STUART ALAN, chemist, educator; b. N.Y.C., Jan. 6, 1932; s. Harry L. and Helen (Rayfield) R.; m. Marian Ruth Coopersmith, June 1, 1952; children—Barbara, Janet. B.S., Bklyn. Coll., 1952; M.A., Harvard, 1954, Ph.D., 1955. Jr. fellow Harvard, 1955-57; faculty U. Chgo., 1957—, prof. chemistry, 1960-69, Louis Block prof. phys. scis., 1969—, chmn. dept. chemistry, 1971-76, Frank P. Hixon disting. service prof., 1977—, dean phys. scis. div., 1981; dir. U. Chgo. (Inst. Study Metals), 1962-68; Mem. Nat. Sci. Bd., 1980. Author: Polyelectrolyte Solutions, 1961, Statistical Mechanics of Simple Liquids, 1965, Physical Chemistry, 1980; bd. dirs.: also numerous articles. Bull. Atomic Scientists. Guggenheim fellow, 1960-61; Falk-Plautt lectr. Columbia, 1964; Riley lectr. Notre Dame U., 1964; NSF sr. postdoctoral fellow, 1965-66; USPHS spl. postdoctoral fellow U. Copenhagen, 1970-71; Univ. lectr. chemistry U. Western Ont., 1970; Seaver lectr. U. So. Calif., 1972; Noyes lectr. U. Tex., Austin, 1975; Foster lectr. SUNY, Buffalo, 1976; Frank T. Gucker lectr. Ind. U., 1976; Fairchild lectr. Calif. Inst. Tech., 1979. Mem. Am. Chem. Soc. (award Pure Chemistry 1963, Leo Hendrik Backeland award 1971, Debye award 1984), Nat. Acad. Scis., Am. Acad. Scis., Am. Phys. Soc., AAAS, Faraday Soc. (Marlowe medal 1963), N.Y. Acad. Scis. (A. Cressy Morrison prize 1955), Danish Acad. Sci. and Letters (fgn.). Current Work: Theory of liquids; photophysical and photochemical processes; statistical mechanics; energy transfer; molecular dynamics. Subspecialties: Physical chemistry; Theoretical chemistry.

RICH, CLAYTON, university administrator; b. N.Y.C., May 21, 1924; s. Clayton Eugene and Leonore (Elliot) R.; m. Mary Bell Hodgkinson, Dec. 19, 1953 (div. May 2, 1974); 1 son, Clayton Greig.; m. Carolyn Sue Miller, Apr. 8, 1982. Grad., Putney Sch., 1942; student, Swarthmore Coll., 1942-44; M.D., Cornell U., 1948. Diplomate Am. Bd. Internal Medicine. Intern Albany (N.Y.) Hosp., 1948-49, asst. resident, 1950-51; research asst. Cornell U. Med. Coll., 1949-50; asst. Rockefeller U., 1953-58, asst. prof., 1958-60; asst. prof. medicine U. Wash. Sch. Medicine, 1960-62, assoc. prof., 1962-67, prof., 1967-71, assoc. dean, 1968-71; chief radioisotope service VA Hosp., Seattle, 1960-70, assoc. chief staff, 1962-71, chief staff, 1968-70, v.p. med. affairs, dean Sch. Medicine; prof. medicine Stanford U., 1971-79, Carl and Elizabeth Naumann prof., 1977-79; chief staff Stanford U. Hosp., 1971-77, chief exec. officer, 1977-79; sr. scholar Inst. Medicine, Nat. Acad. Sci., Washington, 1979-80; Mem. gen. medicine B study sect. NIH, 1969-73, chmn., 1972-73; mem. spl. med. adv. group VA, 1977-81; provost U. Okla., Oklahoma City, 1980—, v.p. for health scis., 1983—; also exec. dean, prof. U. Okla. (Coll. Medicine), 1980-83. Editorial bd.: Calcified Tissue Research, 1966-72, Clin. Orthopedics, 1967-72, Jour. Clin. Endocrinology and Metabolism, 1971-72; Contbr. numerous articles to med. jours. Bd. dirs. Children's Hosp. at Stanford, Stanford U. Hosp., 1974-79; chmn. Gordon Research Conf. Chemistry, Physiology and Structure of Bones and Teeth, 1967; bd. dirs. Leadership Oklahoma City, 1981—, v.p., 1985—; bd. dirs., exec. Com. Okla. Med. Research Found. Served to lt. USNR, 1951-53. Fellow ACP; mem. Assn. Am. Physicians, Western Assn. Physicians, Am. Soc. Mineral and Bone Research (adv. bd. 1977-80), Am. Soc. Clin. Investigation, Assn. Am. Med. Colls. (exec. council 1975-79), Inst. of Medicine, Assn. Acad. Health Ctrs. (bd. dirs. 1984—), Western Soc. Clin. Research (v.p. 1967-68), Endocrine Soc., Sigma Xi, Alpha Omega Alpha. Subspecialties: Endocrinology; Health services research. Home: 143 Lake Aluma Dr Oklahoma City OK 73121 Office: Provost Office U Okla Oklahoma City OK 73190

RICH, JIMMY RAY, nematologist; b. Collins, Ga., Oct. 29, 1950; s. Bernease and Carolyn Murtle (Outen) R. Student, Abraham Baldwin Agrl. Coll., 1968-70; B.S.A., U. Ga., 1972, M.S., 1973; Ph.D., U. Calif., Riverside, 1976. Asst. prof. nematology U. Fla., Live Oak, 1976-81, assoc. prof., 1981—; also acting dir. Agrl. Research Center; chmn. Tobacco Disease Council, 1978, Fla. Nematology Forum, 1980. Assoc. editor: Nemtropica, 1977-82; author articles. Bd. dirs. Fla. Kiwanis Found., 1982-84. Mem. Soc. Nematologists, Am. Phytopathol. Soc., Orgn. Tropical Am. Nematologists, Sigma Xi, Phi Kappa Phi, Gamma Sigma Delta, Omicron Delta Kappa, Alpha Zeta, Blue Key. Clubs: Suwannee Ind. Football League, Kiwanis. Current Work: Nematode management systems and nematode-plant host-parasite physiology. Subspecialties: Plant pathology; Nematology. Office: AREC Route 2 Box 2181 Live Oak FL 32060

RICHARD, MICHAEL ALAN, chemist; b. Hartford, Conn., Oct. 30, 1951; s. Edward Joseph and Fleur-Ange (Jean) R.; m. Patricia Susan Yitts, May 25, 1974; children—Allison, Kieth, Jennifer. B.A., U. Conn., 1973; Ph.D., MIT, 1977. Research chemist, Shell Devel. Co., Houston, 1977-80, Exxon Research & Engring. Co., Clinton, N.J., 1980—. Patentee in field. Mem. Am. Chem. Soc., N. Am. Thermal Analysis Soc., N.Y. Catalysis Soc., Phi Beta Kappa, Sigma Xi, Phi Kappa Phi, Phi Lambda Upsilon. Republican. Roman Catholic. Club: Toastmasters (Florham Park, N.J.). Current work: Catalysis, kinetics and mechanisms of catalytic reactions, thermal analysis, catalytic materials, surface science, reaction engineering. Subspecialties: Catalysis chemistry; Physical chemistry. Home: 30 Paterson Rd Fanwood NJ 07023 Office: Exxon Research and Engring Co Route 22 E Annandale NJ 08801

RICHARDS, KENNETH JULIAN, metallurgical engineer; b. Long Beach, Calif., Nov. 29, 1932; s. Julian D. and Charlotte M. (Parker) R.; m. Shirlene Milne, July 12, 1958; children—Brian David, Kevin Mark, Steven Vance. B.S. in Chem. Engring., U. Utah, 1956, Ph.D., in Metall. Engring., 1963. Sr. scientist Kennecott Copper, Salt Lake City, 1967-69, sect. head, refining research, 1969-72, mgr. process metallurgy, 1972-74, dir. research and devel., 1974-79, v.p. process tech., 1979-84; v.p. tech. div. Kerr-McGee Corp., Oklahoma City, 1984—; mem. com. NRC, Washington, 1983—; adv. council mem. Coll. Mines and Mineral Industries, U. Utah, Salt Lake City, 1977—; mem. adv. council generic ctr. communication U.S. Bur. Mines, 1983—.

Contbr. articles to profl. jours. Served to capt. USAF, 1957-67. Organizer Internat. Symposium on Sulfied Smelting, San Francisco, 1983, (with others) First Internatl. Symposium on Automatic Control in Mineral Processing and Process Metallurgy, Los Angeles, 1984. Mem. Am. Inst. Chem. Engrs., Am. Chem. Soc., Metall. Soc. of AIME, Soc. Mining Engrs. (disting. mem. class of '85), Licensing Execs. Soc. Current work: manage research, development and process engineering functions of technology division in support of existing business operations and in support of invention and application of new technologies. Office: Kerr-McGee Corp 123 Robert S Kerr Ave Oklahoma City OK 73102

RICHARDS, PAUL LINFORD, educator, physicist; b. Ithaca, N.Y., June 4, 1934; s. Lorenzo A. and Zilla (Linford) R.; m. Audrey Jarratt, Aug. 24, 1965; children—Elizabeth Anne, Mary Ann. A.B., Harvard, 1956; Ph.D., U. Calif. at Berkeley, 1960. Research fellow Cambridge U. (Eng.), 1959-60; mem. tech. staff Bell Telephone Labs., 1960-66; prof. physics U. Calif. at Berkeley, 1966—; Cons., U.S. govt. agys., bus. corps. Contbr. articles to tech. jours. Guggenheim Found. fellow Cambridge (Eng.) U., 1973-74; recipient Calif. Scientist of Yr. award, 1981; Alexander von Humboldt sr. scientist award Stuttgart, Germany, 1982. Fellow Am. Phys. Soc., Am. Acad. Arts and Scis., Nat. Acad. Scis.; mem. Phi Beta Kappa, Sigma Xi. Subspecialty: Low temperature physics. Home: 900 Euclid Ave Berkeley CA 94708

RICHARDS, ROGER THOMAS, acoustical scientist; b. Akron, Ohio, June 19, 1942; s. Clyde Irvin and Thelma Jo (Whitaker) R. B.S., Westminster Coll., 1964; M.S., Ohio U., 1968; Ph.D., Pa. State U.-State College, 1980. Research asst. Ohio U., Athens, 1966-68; engr. Gen. Dynamics, Rochester, N.Y., 1968-71; grad. asst. Pa. State U., State College, 1974-80; staff assoc. Applied Research Lab., State College, 1977-80; mem. tech. staff Rockwell Internat., Groton, Conn., 1980—; dir. U.S. Othello Assn., Falls Church, Va., 1979—. Mem. Pa. State U. Alumni Exec. Bd., State College, 1973-74, mem. grad. faculty council, 1974-76, edn. policy com. bd. trustees, 1973-74. NASA fellow, 1971-74. Mem. Acoustical Soc. Am., AIAA, Nat. Speleological Soc. (vice-chmn. Nittany Grotto 1977-78, life), Am. Cryptogram Assn. (editorial bd. 1982—), Sigma Xi, Sigma Pi Sigma. Current Work: Structural vibration and underwater sound propagation. Subspecialties: Acoustics; Cryptography and data security. Home: Edgemere Manor RD 1 Stonington CT 06378 Office: Rockwell Internat 1028 Poquonnock Rd PO Box L Groton CT 06340

RICHARDSON, CARL REED, animal scientist, educator, cons.; b. Monticello, Ky., Dec. 20, 1947; s. Ervin Rossevelt and Cretia Marie (Dodson) R.; m. Nora Jean Fletcher, Dec. 18, 1971; 1 son, Kevin Reed. B.S., U. Ky., 1971, M.S., 1973; Ph.D., U. Ill., 1976. Research assoc. U. Ill., Urbana, 1976; asst. prof. animal sci. Tex. Tech. U., Lubbock, 1976-81, assoc. prof., 1981—, cons. beef cattle nutrition. Contbr. numerous articles to profl. jours. Served as lt. U.S. Army, 1971-76. Named Outstanding Researcher in Coll. AGrl. Scis. Tex. Tech. U., 1982; grantee in field of beef cattle nutrition research. Mem. Am. Inst. Nutrition, Am. Soc. Animal Sci., Am. Dairy Sci. Assn., Plains Nutrition Council, Sigma Xi, Alpha Zeta, Gamma Sigma Delta. Republican. Baptist. Current Work: Improvement in grain and roughage feedstuffs through chemical, biological and mechanical processing. Subspecialty: Animal nutrition. Home: 8010 Raleigh Lubbock TX 79424 Office: Dept Animal Sc Tex Tech U Lubbock TX 79409

RICHARDSON, CAROL LYNN, microbiologist, biochemist; b. Little Rock, Oct. 18, 1948; d. Gerald H. Pannell and Violet Jane Fields. B.S., Purdue U., 1969, Ph.D., 1976; M.A., Cornell U., 1970. Clin. microbiologist Riley Meml. Hosp., Meridian, Miss., 1970-72; asst. supr. microbiology Med. Center Hosps., Norfolk, Va., 1972-73; microbiologist Purdue U. Cancer Center, West Lafayette, Ind., 1976; scientist sr., scientist, prin. scientist Meloy Labs., Springfield, Va., 1977-81; dir. mktg. Gibco Labs., Chagrin Falls, Ohio, 1981-84; v.p. DNA STAR Inc., Madison, Wis., 1984—. Contbr. articles to profl. jours. Treas. Scholarship Com. for Grad. Women in Sci. Recipient award for support of cancer research Phi Beta Psi, 1972. Mem. Am. Assn. for Cancer Research, N.Y. Acad. Scis., AAAS, Sigma Delta Epsilon, Iota Sigma Pi. Patentee in field. Current Work: Vice president of sales and marketing and general manager of biotechnology software company. Subspecialties: Biochemistry (medicine); Microbiology (medicine). Office: 1801 University Ave Madison WI 53705

RICHARDSON, CHARLES CLIFTON, biochemist, educator; b. Wilson, N.C., May 7, 1935; s. Barney Clifton and Florence Elizabeth (Barefoot) R.; m. Ute Ingrid Hanssum, July 29, 1961; children—Thomas Clifton, Matthew Wilfrid. B.S.M., Duke U., 1959, M.D., 1960; A.M. (hon.), Harvard U., 1967. Intern dept. medicine Duke U., Durham, N.C., 1960-61; postdoctoral fellow dept. biochemistry Stanford U. Med. Sch., Calif., 1961-63; asst. prof. biol. chemistry Harvard Med. Sch., Boston, 1964-67, assoc. prof., 1967-69, prof. biol. chemistry, 1969—, chmn. dept. biol. chemistry, 1978—, Edward S. Wood prof., 1979—; mem. physiol. chemistry study sect. NIH, 1970-74; mem. nucleic acids and protein adv. com. Am. Cancer Soc., 1975-78; mem. Nat. Bd. Med Examiners, 1973-76; mem Fachbeirat of the Max-Planck Inst. fur Moleculare Genetik, Berlin, Fed. Republic Germany, 1980—; assoc. Helicon Found., San Diego, 1983—. Assoc. editor Ann. rev. Biochemistry, 1972-83, editor, 1983—; mem. editorial bd.: Jour. Biol. Chemistry, 1968-73, 84—, Jour. Molecular Biology, 1976-79. Recipient Career Devel. award NIH, 1967-76. Fellow Am. Acad. Arts and Scis; mem. Nat. Acad. Scis., Am. Chem. Soc. (Eli Lilly Co. biol. chem. award 1968), Am. Soc. Biol. Chemists (mem. nominationg com. 1974-75, 83-84). Subspecialties: Biochemistry (medicine); Genetics and genetic engineering (medicine). Office: Harvard Med Sch 25 Shattuck St Boston MA 02115

RICHARDSON, DAVID WALTHALL, cardiologic educator, consultant; b. Nankning, China, Mar. 22, 1925; s. Donald William and Virginia (McIlwaine) R.; m. Frances Lee Wingfield, June 12, 1948; children—Donald, Sarah, David. B.S., Davidson Coll., 1947; M.D., Harvard U., 1951. Diplomate Am. Bd. Internal Medicine, Am. Bd. Cardiology. Intern, resident Yale New Haven Hosp., Conn., 1951-53; resident, fellow Med. Coll. Va., Richmond, 1953-56, assoc. prof. to prof. medicine, 1962—, chmn. div. cardiology, 1972—; chief cardiology, assoc. chief staff for research VA Hosp., Richmond, 1956-61; vis. scientist Oxford U., Eng., 1961-62; vis. prof. U. Milan, Italy, 1972-73. Contbr. articles to profl. jours. Moderator Hanover Presbytery, Presbyterian Ch. U.S., Richmond, 1970. Served with USN, 1944-46. Fellow. Am. Coll. Cardiology (gov. VA. 1970-72), Am. Heart Assn. (council clin. cardiology); mem. Am. Soc. Clin. Investigation, Am. Clin. and Climatol. Assn. Current work: Cardiac arthythmias, hypertension, clinical trials. Subspecialties: Cardiology; Internal medicine. Home: 5501 Queensbury Rd Richmond VA 23226 Office: Va Commonwealth U Box 105 MCV Station Richmond VA 23298

RICHARDSON, JAMES WYMAN, chemistry educator; b. Sioux Falls, S.D., Aug. 8, 1930; s. Lewis Gerhard and Maurine Katherine (Withey) R.; m. Eileen Mae Johnson, Dec. 24, 1952; children: Janilyn, James, Barbara, Gregory. B.S., S.D. Sch. Mines and Tech., 1952; Ph.D., Iowa State U., 1956. Research assoc. U. Chgo., 1956-57; with Purdue U., 1957—, prof. chemistry, 1973—; vis. scientist Philips Research Labs., Eindhoven, Netherlands, 1967-68. Contbr. articles to profl. jours. NSF grantee. Mem. Am. Chem. Soc., Am. Phys. Soc. Current Work: Quantum-mechanical theory of bonding, spectra, magnetic and electrical properties of transition-metal compounds. Subspecialties: Theoretical chemistry; Atomic and molecular physics. Office: Dept Chemistry Purdue U West Lafayette IN 47907

RICHARDSON, JOSEPH HILL, physician; b. Rensselaer, Ind., June 16, 1928; s. William Clark and Vera (Hill) R.; m. Joan Grace Meininger, July 7, 1950; children: Lois N., Ellen M., James K. B.S. in Medicine, Northwestern U., 1950, M.D., 1953. Diplomate: Am. Bd. Internal Medicine. Intern U.S. Naval Hosp., Great Lakes, Ill., 1953-54; resident, fellow in internal medicine Cleve. Clinic, 1956-59; med. staff Marion (Ind.) Gen. Hosp., 1957-67, Parkview Hosp., Ft. Wayne, Ind., 1967—; med. cons. Marion Gen. Hosp., 1977—. Contbr. articles to profl. jours. Served with USN, 1953-56. Fellow ACP, AAAS; mem. Am. Assn. Clin. Research, Am. Assn. Med. Writers. Subspecialty: Internal medicine. Home: 8726 Fortuna Way Fort Wayne IN 46815 Office: 3010 E State Blvd Fort Wayne IN 46805

RICHARDSON, PETER DAMIAN, mechanical engineer; b. West Wickham, Eng., Aug. 22, 1935; came to U.S., 1958; s. Reginald W. and Marie S. R. B.Sc. in Engring, Imperial Coll., U. London, 1955, A.C.G.I., 1955, Ph.D. (Unwin scholar), 1958, D.I.C., 1958; D.Sc. in Engring., U. London, 1974. Demonstrator dept. mech. engring. Imperial Coll., U. London, 1955-58; vis. lectr. Brown U., 1958-59, research asso., 1959-60, asst. prof. engring., 1960-65, asso. prof., 1965-68, prof., 1968—; chmn. exec. com. Center Biomed. Engring., 1972—; cons. to industry, U.S. govt. agys.; on leave at U. London, 1967, U. Paris, 1968, Orta Dogu Teknik Universitesi, Ankara, Turkey, 1969, Medizinischen Fakultat, RWTH, Aachen, Germany, 1976. Contbr. numerous articles on engring., physics, geology, biology and medicine to profl. publs.; asso. editor asaio: Jour. Recipient Sr. Scientist award Alexander Von Humboldt Found., 1976. Mem. ASME, Am. Soc. Engring. Edn., Am. Soc. Artificial Internal Organs. European Soc. Artificial Organs. Subspecialty: Biomedical engineering. Office: Box D Brown U Providence RI 02912

RICHARDSON, ROBERT COLEMAN, physics educator; b. Washington, June 26, 1937; s. Robert Franklin and Lois (Price) R.; m. Betty Marilyn McCarthy, Sept. 27, 1962; children—Jennifer Joan, Pamela Ann. B.S., Va. Poly. Inst., 1958, M.S., 1959; Ph.D., Duke U., 1966. Research assoc. Cornell U., Ithaca, N.Y., 1966-67, asst. prof., 1967-71, assoc. prof., 1971-74, prof., 1974—. Recipient Simon prize Brit. Phys. Soc., 1976; Guggenheim fellow 1975, 82. Fellow Am. Phys. Soc. (Buckley prize 1981), AAAS, Internat. Union Pure and Applied Physics (chmn. commn. on Low Temp. Phys. 1981-84). Current work: Studies of matter at very low temperatures, nuclear magnetic resonance, preoperties of superfluid 3He. Subspecialties: Low temperature physics; Condensed matter physics. Home: 4 Hunters Ln Ithaca NY 14850 Office: Dept Physics Cornell Univ Ithaca NY 14853

RICHART, FRANK EDWIN, JR., civil engineer; educator; b. Urbana, Ill., Dec. 6, 1918; s. Frank Erwin and Fern (Johnson) R.; m. Elizabeth Goldthorp, Feb. 21, 1945; children—John Douglas, Betsy, Willard Clark. B.S., U. Ill., 1940, M.S., 1946, Ph.D., 1948; postgrad. U. Mich., 1940-41; D.Sc., U. Fla., 1972. Research asst., then asso. dept. civil engring. U. Ill., 1946-48; asst. prof. mech. engring. Harvard, 1948-52; asso. prof. dept. civil engring. U. Fla., 1952-54, prof., 1954-62; prof. civil engring U. Mich., 1962-77, W. J. Emmons Distinguished prof., 1977—, chmn. dept., 1962-69; cons. Moran, Proctor, Mueser, Rutledge, N.Y.C., summers 1953-55, 57, also Office Engrs., U.S. Army, NASA. Contbr. tech. papers to profl. jours. Served to lt. comdr. USNR, 1941-46. Fellow ASCE (T.A. Middlebrooks award 1956, 59, 60, 67, Wellington prize 1963, Terzaghi lectr. 1974, Terzaghi award 1980); mem. Nat. Acad. Engring. Current Work: Soil dynamics, vibrations of soils and foundations, dynamic soil behavior, machine vibrations. Subspecialty: Civil engineering. Home: 2210 Hill St Ann Arbor MI 48104

RICHERSON, PETER J., ecologist, educator; b. San Mateo, Calif., Oct. 11, 1943; s. Orlando Chester and Catherine (Haughawout) R.; m. Lois A Callaghan, Feb. 18, 1978; children—Scott, Kate. B.S., U. Calif.-Davis, 1965, Ph.D., 1969. Asst. prof. ecology U. Calif.-Davis, 1971-77, assoc. prof., 1977-83, prof., 1983—, dir. Inst. Ecology, 1983—. Author: Culture and the Evolutionary Process, 1985. Mem. editorial bd. Human Ecology, 1980—, Jour. Social Biol. Structures, 1980—. Guggenheim Found. fellow, 1984; NSF grantee, 1975-84. Mem. Ecol. Soc. Am., Am. Soc. Limnology Oceanography, AAAS, Sigma Xi. Current work: Limnology, including phytoplankton competition and tropical lakes; theory of cultural evolution. Subspecialties: Theoretical ecology; Evolutionary biology. Office: Inst Ecology U Calif Davis CA 95616

RICHMAN, JACK WILLIAM, physicist; b. Gillingham, England, Feb. 20, 1941; s. Henry George and Ellen Rebecca (Williams) R.; m. Sylvia Helen Brennish; children: Oliver Page, Melanie Blair. B.Sc., U. Wales, 1963; M.Sc., U. Man., Can., 1968, Ph.D., 1972; diploma, Von Karman Inst., Brussels, 1969. Physicist Bristol Aerospace Co., Winnipeg, Man., 1966-68; cons. engr. Dilworth Secord, Toronto, Ont., Can., 1972-74; group leader, Bechtel Corp., Toronto, 1974-77; design engr. specialist Ont. Hydro, Toronto, 1977-78, supr. design engr., 1978-79, nuclear equipment and processes engr., 1979-81, tech. mgr. fusion fuel tech. project, 1981—. Contbr. articles to profl. jours. Served as officer RCAF, 1964-67. NRC scholar, 1966-74; postdoctoral fellow, 1972-74. Mem. Am. Nuclear Soc., Can. Nuclear Soc., Canadian Nuclear Assn., Assn. Profl. Engrs. Ont. (chmn. 1980-82), Royal Can. Mil. Inst. Current Work: Fusion energy and fusion fuels. Subspecialties: Nuclear fission; Nuclear fusion. Office: Canadian Fusion Fuel Technology Project 620 University Ave Toronto ON M5G 1X6 Canada

RICHMAN, JOSEPH BEN, biochemist, researcher; b. Pasadena, Calif., July 2, 1952; s. Benjamin and Mary Elizabeth (Glidden) R.; m. Kristin Coleman, Oct. 27, 1984; children—Yona Anne, Joanna Elizabeth. B.S., Oreg. State U., 1972; M.A., Calif. State U., 1976. Research asst. dept. anatomy UCLA, 1976-77; tech. assoc., profl. Allergan, Irvine, Calif., 1979-83, profl. drug metabolism and pharmacokinetics dept., 1983-85, sr. profl., 1985—. Mem. Am. Chem. Soc. Methodist. Current work: Measuring ocular penetration of drugs in vitro, including effects of vehicle on permeability and studying metabolism of drugs and prodrugs by the cornea. Subspecialties: Biochemistry (biology); Pharmacokinetics. Home: 392 S Olive St Orange CA 92666 Office: Allergan Pharmaceuticals Drug Metabolism and Pharmacokinet Dept 2525 DuPont Ave Irvine CA 92715

RICHMOND, JULIUS BENJAMIN, physician, educator; b. Chgo., Sept. 26, 1916; s. Jacob and Anna (Dayno) R.; m. Rhee Chidekel, June 3, 1937; children: Barry J., Charles Allen, Dale Keith (dec.). B.S., U. Ill., 1937, M.S., M.D., 1939; D.Sc. (hon.), Ind. U., 1978, Rush-Presbyn.-St. Luke Med. Center, 1978, U. Ill., 1979, Georgetown U., 1980; D.Med. Sci. (hon.), Med. Coll. Pa., 1980; D. Public Service, Nat. Coll. Edn., Evanston, Ill., 1980. Intern Cook County Hosp., Chgo., 1939-41, resident, 1941-42, 46, Municipal Contagious Disease Hosp., Chgo., 1941; mem. faculty U. Ill. Med. Sch., Chgo., 1946-52, prof. pediatrics, 1950-53, dir. Inst. Juvenile Research, 1952-53; prof., chmn. dept. pediatrics Coll. Medicine, State U. N.Y. at Syracuse, 1953-65, dean med. faculty, chmn. dept. pediatrics, 1965-70; prof. child psychiatry and human devel., prof., chmn. dept. preventive and social medicine Harvard Med. Sch., 1971-77, prof. health policy, 1981—; also faculty Harvard Sch. Public Health; psychiatrist-in-chief Children's Hosp. Med. Center, Boston, 1971-77, adv. on child health policy, 1981—; dir. Judge Baker Guidance Center, Boston, 1971-77; asst. sec. health and surgeon gen. HHS, 1977-81; mem. Pres.'s Commn. on Mental Health, 1977. Author: Pediatric Diagnosis, 1962, Currents in American Medicine, 1969. Nat. dir. Project Head Start; dir. Office Health Affairs OEO, 1965-66. Served as flight surgeon USAAF, 1942-46. Recipient Agnes Bruce Greig Sch. award, 1966; C. Anderson Aldrich award Am. Acad. Pediatrics, 1966; Myrdal Prize, 1977; ann. award Sect. on Community Pediatrics, 1977; outstanding contbn. award Section Community Pediatrics, 1978; Parents Mag. award, 1966; Disting. Service award Office Econ. Opportunity, 1967; Martha May Eliot award Am. Public Health Assn., 1970; Family Health Mag. award, 1977; award for disting. sci. contbn. Soc. for Research in Child Devel., 1979; Dolly Madison award Inst. on Clin. Infants Programs, 1979; Public Health Disting. Service award HEW, 1980. Fellow Am. Orthopsychiat. Assn.; distinguished fellow Am. Psychiat. Assn.; hon. mem. Am. Acad. Child Psychiatry; mem. Inst. Medicine of Nat. Acad. Scis., AMA, Am. Pediatric Soc., Am. Acad. Pediatrics, Soc. Pediatric Research, Am. Psychosomatic Soc., Am. Public Health Assn., Sigma Xi, Alpha Omega Alpha, Phi Eta Sigma. Current Work: Child development, maternal and child health; public policy and health. Subspecialties: Pediatrics; Psychiatry. Office: Harvard Univ Div of Health Policy Research and Education 641 Huntington Ave Boston MA 02115

RICHNAFSKY, ALBERT MICHAEL, geologist, energy and environmental consultant, educator; b. Clairton, Pa., July 22, 1953; s. Albert George and Margaret Magdelena (Dzuricsko) R.; m. Patricia Louise Pomorski, Apr. 4, 1981; 2 children—Jennifer Patricia, Albert Anthony. B.S. in Geology, Edinboro U. of Pa., 1975; M.S. in Geology, W.Va. U., 1977. Geologist U.S. Steel Corp., Pitts., 1978-81, Charleston, W.Va., 1982-83, supr., 1980-81, mgr., 1982-83; geologist, mgr., cons., founder Erie Geol. Contractors, Pa., 1983—; mem. geology faculty Mercyhurst Coll., Erie, 1984—. Author: Coal Selection, Considerations and Methods for Producing Coke, 1982. Mem. Geol. Soc. Am., Am. Inst. Profl. Geologists, Am. Assn. Petroleum Geologists (jr.), Pitts. Geol. Soc., Pa. Oil and Gas Assn. Democrat. Roman Catholic. Current work: Development of personally generated oil and gas prospects; consulting for hydrological and environmental projects; minerals exploration. Subspecialties: Sedimentology; Hydrology. Home and Office: 2824 Pennsylvania Ave Erie PA 16504

RICHTER, BURTON, physicist, educator; b. N.Y.C., Mar. 22, 1931; s. Abraham and Fanny (Pollack) R.; m. Laurose Becker, July 1, 1960; children: Elizabeth, Matthew. B.S., MIT, 1952, Ph.D., 1956. Research assoc. Stanford U., 1956-60, asst. prof. physics, 1960-63, assoc. prof., 1963-67, prof., 1967—, Paul Pigott prof. phys. sci., 1980—, tech. dir. Linear Accelerator Ctr., 1982-84, dir. Linear Accelerator Ctr., 1984—; cons. NSF, Dept. Energy. Contbr. articles to profl. publs. Recipient E.O. Lawrence medal ERDA, 1975; Nobel prize in physics, 1976. Fellow Am. Phys. Soc., N.Y. Acad. Sci.; mem. Nat. Acad. Sci. Research elementary particle physics. Subspecialty: Particle physics. Office: Stanford U Linear Accelerator Ctr Stanford CA 94305

RICHTER, CURT PAUL, psychobiologist; b. Denver, Feb. 20, 1894; s. Paul Ernst and Martha (Dressler) R.; m. Phyllis Greenacre, Sept. 30, 1920 (div. 1930); children—Ann (Mrs. William A. Roy), Peter; m. Leslie Prince Bidwell, Apr. 11, 1936; 1 child, Martha. B.S., Harvard U., 1917; Ph.D., Johns Hopkins U., 1921, LL.D. (hon.), 1970; Sc.D. (hon.), U. Chgo., 1968. Dir. psychobiology lab Johns Hopkins Hosp., Balt., 1923—, prof. emeritus psychobiology, 1957—; mem. NRC coms. neurology, food-habits, stress, rodent and insect control, World War II. Author: Biological Clocks in Medicine and Psychiatry, 1965. Served to 1st lt. U.S. Army, 1917-19. Recipient Passano award, 1977, Lashley award, 1980, Warren medal, 1950. Mem. Am. Philos. Soc., Nat. Acad. Scis., Am. Acad. Arts and Scis., Halsted Soc., Phi Beta Kappa (hon.). Republican. Clubs: Elkridge (Balt.); Sakonnet (R.I.). Current work: Human and animal behavior; sympathetic and cortical neurology. Subspecialty: Psychobiology. Office: Adolf Meyer Bldg Phipps Psychiatric Clinic Johns Hopkins Hosp Baltimore MD 21205

RICHTER, GEORGE BROWNELL, technical educator; b. St. Cloud, Minn., Feb. 21, 1927; s. Charles Herman and Mazie Katherine (Brownell) R.; m. Patricia Grain, Mar. 31, 1951; children: Mary Baker, Elisabeth Gibson, Mark Richter, Melodie Hart, Joseph. B.Phys., U. Minn., 1950, M.A., 1968, Ph.D., 1972; B.A., St. Johns U., 1951. Registered profl. engr., Minn. Lectr. graphics St. Thomas Coll., St. Paul, 1966—; tech. div. mgr. St. Paul Tech. Vocat. Inst., 1959—. Served with USNR, 1945-46. Mem. Soc. Mfg. Engrs., John Henry Newman Hon. Soc. Democrat. Roman Catholic. Current Work: Maintaining technician programs at current technology levels to meet industrial demands. Subspecialties: Mechanical engineering; Statistics. Home: 2016 Merriam Ln Saint Paul MN 55104 Office: Saint Paul Tech Vocat Inst 235 Marshall Ave Saint Paul MN 55102

RICHTER, JUDITH ANNE, pharmacologist, educator; b. Wilmington, Del., Mar. 4, 1942; d. Henry John and Dorothy Madeline (Schroeder) R. B.A., U. Colo., 1964; Ph.D., Stanford U., 1969. Postdoctoral fellow Cambridge (Eng.) U., 1969-70, Inst. Psychiatry, U. London, 1970-71; asst. prof. pharmacology Ind. U. Sch. Medicine, Indpls., 1971-78, assoc. prof. pharmacology and neurobiology, 1978-84, prof., 1984—; mem. biomed. research rev. com. Nat. Inst. Drug Abuse, 1981-85. Mem. editorial bd.: Jour. Neurochemistry; contbr. numerous articles to sci. jours. Mem. Am. Soc. Pharmacology and Exptl. Therapeutics, Am. Soc. Neurochemistry, Internat. Soc. Neurochemistry, Soc. Neurosci., AAAS, Sigma Xi. Current Work: Effects of barbiturates on cholinergic and other neurons; scientific research, teaching. Subspecialty: Neuropharmacology. Office: Inst Psychiatric Research Ind U Med Sch 791 Union Dr Indianapolis IN 46223

RICK, CHARLES MADEIRA, JR., geneticist, educator; b. Reading, Pa., Apr. 30, 1915; s. Charles Madeira and Miriam Charlotte (Yeager) R.; m. Martha Elizabeth Overholts, Sept. 3, 1938 (dec. Apr. 1983); children: Susan Charlotte Rick Baldi, John Winfield. B.S., Pa. State U., 1937; A.M., Harvard U., 1939, Ph.D., 1940. Asst. plant breeder W. Atlee Burpee Co., Lompoc, Calif., 1936, 37; instr., jr. geneticist U. Calif., Davis, 1940-44, asst. prof., asst. geneticist, 1944-49, asso. prof., asso. geneticist, 1949-55, prof., geneticist, 1955—; chmn. coordinating com. Tomato Genetics Coop., 1950-82; mem. genetics study sect. NIH, 1958-62; mem. Galapagos Internat. Sci. Project, 1964; mem. genetic biology panel NSF, 1971-72; mem. nat. plant genetics resources bd. Dept. Agr., 1975-82; Carnegie vis. prof. U. Hawaii, 1963; vis. prof. Universidade São Paulo, Brazil, 1965, U. Rosario, Argentina, 1980; vis. scientist U. P.R., 1968; centennial lectr. Ont. Agr. Coll. U. Guelph, Ont., Can., 1974. Contbr. articles in field to books and sci. jours. Fellow Calif. Acad. Sci., AAAS (Campbell award 1959); mem. Nat. Acad. Scis., Bot. Soc. Am. (Merit award 1976), Am. Soc. Hort. Sci. (M.A. Blake award 1974, Vaughan Research award 1946), Am. Genetics Assn. (Frank N. Meyer medal 1982), Mass. Hort. Soc. (Thomas Roland medal 1983). Current Work: Genetics and cytogentics of the tomato (Lycopersicon) species; crossability; F1 features; controlled introgression; genetic distance based on allozyme context. Subspecialties: Plant genetics; Genetics and genetic engineering (biology). Office: U Calif Davis CA 95616

RIDDLE, DONALD LEE, geneticist; b. Vancouver, Wash., July 26, 1945; s. Joseph Gerald and Marjory Helen (Shelley) R.; m. Beverly Dianne Riddle, July 5, 1969; children: Brian Patrick, David Joseph. B.S., U. Calif.-Davis, 1968; Ph.D., Berkeley, 1971. Research assoc. U. Calif.-Santa Barbara, 1971-72; Jane Coffin Childs Meml. Fund fellow MRC Lab. Molecular Biology, Cambridge, Eng., 1973-75; asst. prof. biol. scis. U. Mo.-Columbia, 1975-81, assoc. prof., 1981-85, prof., 1985—; dir. Caenorhabditis Genetics Ctr., 1979—. Contbr. articles to profl. jours. NIH grantee, 1977—; career devel. awardee, 1981—. Mem. Genetics Soc. Am., Soc. Devel. Biology, Soc. Nematologists. Current Work: Research in developmental genetics, neurobiology. Subspecialties: Developmental biology; Gene actions. Office: Dept Biol Scis U Mo Columbia MO 65211

RIDE, SALLY KRISTEN, astronaut; b. Los Angeles, May 26, 1951; d. Dale Burdell and Carol Joyce (Anderson) R.; m. Steven Alan Hawley, July 24, 1982. B.A. in English, Stanford U., 1973, B.S. in Physics, 1973, Ph.D., 1978. Teaching asst. Stanford U., Palo Alto, Calif., researcher dept. physics; astronaut candidate, trainee NASA, 1978-79, astronaut, 1979—, on-orbit capsule communicator STS-2 mission Johnson Space Ctr., Houston, on-orbit capsule communicator STS-3 mission, mission specialist STS-7, 1983. Subspecialty: Astronautics. Office: NASA Johnson Space Ctr Houston TX 77058

RIEBMAN, LEON, electronics company executive. Pres., Am. Electronic Labs., Inc., Montgomeryville, Pa. Subspecialty: Electronics. Office: Am Electronic Labs Inc 306 Richardson Rd Montgomeryville PA 18936*

RIECKEN, HENRY WILLIAM, psychologist; b. Bklyn., Nov. 11, 1917; s. Henry William and Lilian Antoinette (Nieber) R.; m. Frances Ruth Manson, Aug. 7, 1955; children—Mary Susan, Gilson, Anne. A.B., Harvard, 1939, Ph.D., 1950; M.A., U. Conn., 1941. Social sci. analyst Dept. Agr., 1941-46; teaching fellow Harvard, 1947-49, lectr. social psychology, research asso. clin. psychology, 1949-54; asso. prof., then prof. sociology and sr. mem. Lab. Research Social Relations, U. Minn., 1954-58; program dir. social sci. research NSF, 1958-59; head Office Social Sci., 1959-60, asst. dir. social scis., 1960-64, assoc. dir. sci. edn., 1964-66; v.p. Social Sci. Research Council, 1966-69; pres., 1969-71; prof. behavioral scis. Sch. Medicine U. Pa., 1972-85; assoc. dir. planning and evaluation Nat. Library Medicine, 1985—; fellow Center for Advanced Study in Behavioral Scis., Stanford, Calif., 1971-72; Paterson Meml. lectr. U. Minn., 1970; Jensen lectr. Duke U., 1973; charter mem. inst. medicine Nat. Acad. Scis.; adv. com. to dir. NIH, 1966-70, chmn. internat. centers com., 1970-73; pres. Am. Psychol. Found., 1971-73; vice chmn., chmn. com. on nat. needs for biomed. and behavioral research personnel NRC, 1975-80; mem. commn. on sociotech. systems Nat. Acad. Scis., 1976-79. Author: The Volunteer Work Camp, 1952, When Prophecy Fails, 1956, Social Experimentation, 1974, Experimental Testing of Public Policy, 1976, also articles.; Contbr. profl. jours. Bd. dirs. Found. for Child Devel. (formerly Assn. Aid Crippled Children), N.Y.; trustee William T. Grant Found.; chmn. bd. trustees Bur. Social Sci. Research. Served with USAAC, 1943-45. Recipient Harold M. Hildreth award Am. Psychol. Assn., 1971. Fellow Am. Psychol. Assn., Am. Acad. Arts and Scis.; mem. Am. Sociol. Assn., Am. Assn. Pub. Opinion Research, Sociol. Research Assn. (pres. 1966). Clubs: Harvard (N.Y.C.); Cosmos (Washington). Office: Nat Library Medicine Bethesda MD

RIEGLER, GEROLD ERNST, research scientist, project manager; b. Enns, Austria, June 8, 1956; s. Ernst Ignaz and Gertrude Rosina (Roitinger) R. Diploma, Tech. U. Vienna, 1979; Ph.D., Tech. U. Graz, 1982. Engr. FAG, Schweinfurt, F.R. Germany, 1975-76; scientist Patent Agy., Vienna, 1979; research scientist, project mgr. wind energy Research Ctr. Graz, Austria, 1979—. Author: Windturbines for Tethered Systems, 1983. Mem. AIAA. Roman Catholic. Patentee a wind power plant, 1982. Current Work: Investigations of innovative wind energy concepts like tethered wind systems; principles of the energy extraction from a free stream, wind tunnel tests. Subspecialties: Wind power; Fluid mechanics. Home: Raiffeisenstrasse 50b Graz A-8010 Austria Office: Research Ctr Graz Inffeldgasse 12 Graz A-8010 Austria

RIES, STANLEY K., horticulture educator; b. Kenton, Ohio, Sept. 6, 1927. B.S., Mich. State U., 1950; M.S., Cornell U., 1951, Ph.D., 1954. Asst. prof. horticulture Mich. State U., East Lansing, 1953-58, assoc. prof., 1958-65, prof., 1965—, acting dir. Pesticide Research Ctr., 1976-77; vis. prof. CSIRO, Australia, 1979-80, Peolpe's Republic China, 1982; adviser IAEA, Vienna, 1972-75, 76-82. Contbr. articles to profl. jours. Grantee Ford Found., Mich. State U., AID; recipient Disting. Faculty award Mich. State U., 1978, Hall of Fame Pickle Packers Internat., 1967. Fellow AAAS; mem. Am. Soc. Plant Physiologists, Am. Soc. Hort. Sci., Weed Sci. Soc. Am., Plant Growth Regulation Soc. Am., Sigma Xi, Phi Kappa Phi, Alpha Zeta. Current work: Plant growth regulation. Subspecialty: Plant physiology (agriculture). Office: Dept Horticulture Mich State U East Lansing MI 48824

RIESE, WALTER CHARLES, geologist, geochemist; b. Newport, R.I., June 8, 1951; s. Walter H. and Katherine E. (Moore) R.; m. Beverly D. Reece, Jan. 6, 1973 (div. Aug. 1984); m. Trisha Leigh Laura, Nov. 23, 1984; 1 son, Clay Jonathan. B.S., N.Mex. Tech., 1973; M.S., U. N.Mex., 1977, Ph.D., 1980. Cert. profl. geologist. Asst. geologist Vanguard Exptl., Spokane, Wash., 1971, N.Mex. Bur. Mines, Socorro, 1972-73; geologist Tech. Application Ctr., Albuquerque, 1973-74; project geologist Gulf Minerals, Albuquerque, 1974-81; project geochemist Anaconda Minerals Co., Denver, 1981-83; adminstrv. coordinator Anaconda Minerals, 1983-84; sr. geologist ARCO Exploration, Houston, 1984—; affiliate faculty Colo. State U., 1983—; instr. Arapahoe Community Coll., 1983, U. Houston, 1985—. Contbr. articles to profl. jours. Mem. Am. Assn. Petroleum Geologists, Am. Inst. Profl. Geologists (state sec., v.p., 1979-81), Geol. Soc. Am., Assn. Exploration Geochemists, Soc. Econ. Geologists, Sigma Xi, Sigma Gamma Epsilon. Republican. Roman Catholic. Current work: Research in biogeochemistry in exploration; work interests petroleum geology. Subspecialties: Geology; Geochemistry. Home: 722 Fernglade Dr Richmond TX 77469 Office: ARCO Exploration Co 1900 St James Pl Houston TX 77251

RIFKIN, BARRY RICHARD, experimental pathologist, dental educator; b. Trenton, Mar. 30, 1940; s. Samuel and Ida (Rosenthal) R.; married; children: Avery, Carl. B.S., Ohio State U., 1961; M.S., U. Ill.-Champaign, 1964; D.D.S., Temple U., 1968; Ph.D., U. Rochester, 1974. NIH trainee U. Rochester, 1968-73, asst. prof. pathology, 1973-80; assoc. pathologist Strong Meml. Hosp., Rochester, N.Y., 1974-80; assoc. prof. dept. oral medicine chmn. dept. oral medicine NYU, 1980—. Contbr. numerous articles on bone resorption and pathogenesis of periodontal disease to profl. jours., 1976—. NIH grantee, 1976-80. Mem. Internat. Assn. Dental Research, AAAS, Internat. Acad. Pathology, Am. Assn. Dental Schs., Am. Soc. Bone and Mineral Research, Sigma Xi. Democrat. Jewish. Current Work: Pathogenesis of bone loss in periodontal disease; mechanisms of bone resorption origin, structure and function of osteoclast. Subspecialties: Oral biology; Pathology (medicine). Office: NYU Dental Ctr 421 First Ave New York NY 10010

RIFKIND, ARLEEN B., pharmacologist, educator; b. N.Y.C., June 29, 1938; d. Michael C. and Regina (Gottlieb) Brenner; m. Robert S. Rifkind; children: Amy, Nina. B.A., Bryn Mawr Coll., 1960; M.D., NYU, 1964. Diplomate: Nat. Bd. Med. Examiners. Intern, then resident NYU-Bellevue Hosp., N.Y.C., 1964-65; clin. assoc. NIH, Bethesda, Md., 1965-68; research asso. Rockefeller U., N.Y.C., 1968-71, adj. asst. prof., 1971-74; asst. prof. pediatrics Cornell U. Med. Coll., N.Y.C., 1971-75, asst. prof. medicine, 1971-83, asso. prof., 1983—, asst. prof. pharmacology, 1973-78, asso. prof. pharmacology, 1978-83, prof., 1983—; asst. resident physician Rockefeller U. Hosp., 1968-71; physician outpatient dept. N.Y. Hosp., 1968-71, asst. attending physician, 1971-77, clin. affiliate in medicine, 1977—. Contbr. numerous articles and chpts. to sci. lit. Mem. environ. health scis. revue com. Nat. Inst. Environ. Health Scis.; mem. ad hoc study sects. NIH. Recipient Andrew W. Mellon Tchr.-Scientist award Cornell U. Med. Coll., 1976-78; Nat. Inst. Child Health and Human Devel. staff fellow, 1965-68; USPHS spl. fellow, 1968-70, 71-72. Mem. Am. Soc. Clin. Investigation, Am. Soc. Pharmacology and Exptl. Therapeutics, Am. Soc. Clin. Pharmacology, Endocrine Soc., AAAS, N.Y. Acad. Scis. Current Work: Research in heme synthesis and P-450 function, mechanisms of polyhalogenated hydrocarbon toxicity and developmental pharmacology and toxicology. Subspecialties: Pharmacology; Toxicology (medicine). Office: Cornell U Med Coll 1300 York Ave New York NY 10021

RIGANATI, JOHN PHILIP, electrical engineer, computer scientist; b. Mount Vernon, N.Y., Apr. 11, 1944; s. Philip Anthony and Grace Ann (Fiorentino) R.; m. Jo Ann Marie DeMaso, July 23, 1966; children—Michelle Ann, John Philip, Robert James. B.E.E. cum laude, Rensselaer Poly. Inst., 1965, M.Eng., 1966, Ph.D., 1969. Coop. engr. IBM, Poughkeepsie, Yorktown Heights, N.Y., 1961-65; engr. Gen. Electric, Schenectady, N.Y., 1966; mem. tech. staff Electronics Research Ctr., Rockwell Internat., Anaheim, Calif., 1969-76; chief scientist Collins Communication Switching Systems Div., Anaheim, 1977-79; chief computer system components div. Nat. Bur. Standards, Gaithersburg, Md., 1979-85, mem. research adv. com., 1982—; dir. systems research Supercomputing Research Ctr. Inst. Def. Analyses, Lanham, Md., 1979—. Contbg. editor jour. Computers and Standards, Patentee in field. Co-organizer Sr. Citizens Group, Placentia, Yorba Linda, Calif., 1973; leader Christian Family Movement Yorba Linda, Gaithersburg, 1970—; adult edn. coordinator St. Rose of Lima Parish, Gaithersburg, 1980-82, mem. council, 1985—. Recipient Dept. Commerce Bronze medal, 1981; Wynant James Williams prize in elec. engring.; named Engr. of Yr., Rockwell Internat., 1978; Xerox fellow, NSF fellow. Mem. IEEE (bd. standards 1981—, various coms., Orange County service awards), Computer Soc., Assn. Computing Machinery, AAAS, Sigma Xi, Tau Beta Pi, Tau Kappa Epsilon. Roman Catholic. Current work: Concurrent architectures and systems, high performance numerical and symbollic processing, supercomputers, systems and peripherals. Subspecialties: Computer engineering; Computer architecture. Home: 13013 Brandon Way Gaithersburg MD 20878 Office: Supercomputing Research Ctr Inst Def Analyses 4380 Forbes Blvd Lanham MD 20706

RIGBY, PERRY GARDNER, educator, physician; b. E. Liverpool, Ohio, July 1, 1932; s. Perry Lawrence and Lucille Ellen (Orin) R.; m. Joan E. Worthington, June 16, 1957; children—Martha, Peter, Thomas, Matthew. B.S., Mt. Union Coll., 1953; M.D., Case Western Res. U., 1957; D.Sc., Mt. Union Coll., 1976. Diplomate Nat. Bd. Med. Examiners, Am. Bd. Internal Medicine, Am. Bd. Hematology, Ohio Med. Bd. Exam. Intern, U. Va. Hosp., Charlottesville, Va., 1957-58, asst. resident in medicine, 1958-60; prof. internal medicine U. Nebr., Omaha, 1964-66, prof. anatomy, 1964-66, dean, 1974-78; prof. internal medicine La. State U., Shreveport, 1978—, dean Med. Ctr., 1982-85, chancellor, Med. Ctr., 1985—; chmn. dean's com. Shreveport VA Hosp., 1978—; bd. dirs. Health Planning Council of the Midlands, Omaha, 1976-78; cons. WHO, Kabul, Afganistan, 1976. Contbr. articles to profl. jours. Bd. dirs. Fontenelle Forest, Omaha, 1976-78, River Cities High Tech. Group, Shreveport, 1982—. Markle Found. scholar, 1965. Mem. Am. Fedn. Clin. Research (councillor 1971), AMA, Am. Soc. Hematology, N.Y. Acad. Sci., Am. Assn. Med. Colls., Shreveport C. of C. (dir.), Phi Rho Sigma, Alpha Omega Alpha. Presbyterian. Subspecialties: Internal medicine; Hematology. Office: La State U Med Center 1501 Kings Hwy Shreveport LA 71130-3932

RIGGS, BYRON LAWRENCE, JR., physician; b. Hot Springs, Ark., Mar. 24, 1931; s. Byron Lawrence and Elizabeth Ann (Patching) R.; m. Janet Templeton Brewer, June 24, 1955; children: Byron Kent, Ann Templeton. B.S., U. Ark., 1953, B.S. in Medicine, 1955, M.D., 1955; M.S. in Medicine, U. Minn., 1962. Diplomate: Am. Bd. Internal Medicine. Intern Letterman Army Hosp., San Francisco, 1958-59; resident in internal medicine Mayo Grad. Sch. Medicine Hosp., Rochester, Minn., 1958-61; asst. to staff Mayo Clinic, 1961; mem. staff internal medicine and metabolism Mayo Clinic and Found., 1962—; mem. faculty U. Minn. Med. Sch., 1962—, asso. prof., 1970—; prof. medicine Mayo Med. Sch., 1974—; chmn. div. endocrinology and metabolism Mayo Clinic and Med. Sch., 1974—; mem. gen. medicine B study sect. NIH, 1979-82. Contbr. articles to med. jours. Served with M.C. AUS, 1956-58. Recipient Mayo Found. postgrad. travel award, 1961; Kappa Delta award Am. Acad. Orthopedic Surgery, 1972; traveling fellow Royal Soc. Medicine, 1973. Fellow A.C.P.; mem. Am. Diabetes Assn., AMA, Am. Soc. Clin. Investigation, Endocrine Soc., Am. Fedn. Clin. Research (councillor Midwest sect. 1979-81), Am. Soc. for Bone and Mineral Research (pres.-elect), Central Soc. Clin. Research (councillor), AAAS. Current Work: Calcium and bone metabolism; osteoporosis. Subspecialty: Endocrinology. Home: 432 SW 10th Ave Rochester MN 55901 Office: 200 SW 1st St Rochester MN 55902

RIGGS, DENNIS MICHAEL, materials engineer; b. Troy, N.Y., Apr. 26, 1951; s. Charles William and Ruth Eva (Mero) R.; m. Jo-Ann Smi, June 3, 1972 (div.); children—Monica Ruth, Nancy Elizabeth, Sarah Ann. B.S., Rensselaer Polytech. Inst., 1973, M.S., 1975, Ph.D., 1976. Research and devel. officer U.S. Army Materials and Mechanics Research Ctr., Watertown, Mass., 1977-80; mgr. research and devel. Exxon Enterprises, Fountain Inn, S.C., 1980-84, sr. research assoc. E.I. DuPont de Nemours div., 1984—; adj. prof. chem. engring. Clemson U., S.C., 1981—; panel mem. NRC, Washington, 1983-84, Office Naval Research, Boston, 1978. Contbr. articles to profl. jours. and books; patentee in field. Served to capt. U.S. Army, 1976-80. Recipient Spl. Merit award Exxon Enterprises, 1980-83. Mem. AAAS, Am. Chem. Soc., Am. Carbon Soc., Alpha Sigma Mu. Republican. Roman Catholic. Current work: Processing carbon fiber from liquid crystalline pitch, pitch chemistry. Subspecialties: Composite materials; High-temperature materials. Home: 1615 Rustic Homes Ln Signal Mountain TN 37377 Office: DuPont Co Chattanooga TN 37415

RIGGS, KARL A., JR., geologic cons., educator; b. Thomasville, Ga., Aug. 12, 1929; s. Karl. A. and Marjorie Elizabeth (Urquhart) R.; m. Patricia Ann Hartrick, June 28, 1952; children: George, Kathryn Ann Riggs Keen, Linda Kay. B.S. with honors in Geology, Mich. State U., 1951; M.S., 1952; Ph.D. in Geology, Iowa State U., 1956. Cert. profl. geologist., Am. Inst. Profl. Geologists. Research assoc. Iowa State U., 1953-56, instr., 1952-56; sr. research technologist Mobil Research and Devel. Lab., Dallas, 1956-59; asst. prof. Western Mich. U., Kalamazoo, 1966-68; mem. faculty dept. geology Miss. State U., 1968—, assoc. prof., 1973—. Author: Principles of Rock Classification, 1975; contbr. articles to profl. jours. Fellow Geol. Soc. Am.; mem. Am. Assn. Petroleum Geologists, Mineral. Soc. Am., Assn. Engring., Geologists. Republican. Methodist. Current Work: Petroleum, mining and engineering geology. Subspecialty: Geology. Home: 109 Grandridge Dr Starkville MS 39759 Office: Box KR Mississippi State MS 39762

RIGGS, LORRIN ANDREWS, psychologist; b. Harput, Turkey, June 11, 1912; s. Ernest Wilson and Alice (Shepard) R.; m. Doris Robinson, 1937; 2 children. Ed., Dartmouth Coll., Clark U. NRC fellow biol. scis. U. Pa., 1936-37; instr. U. Vt., 1937-38, 39-41; faculty Brown U., 1938-39, 41—, asst. prof. psychology, assoc. prof., to 1951, prof., 1951—, L. Herbert Ballou Found. prof., 1960-68, Edgar J. Marston U. prof., 1968-77, prof. emeritus, 1977—. Contbr. articles to profl. jours. Guggenheim fellow, 1971-72; recipient Charles F. Prentice award Am. Acad. Optometry, 1973, Disting. Sci. Contbn. award Am. Psychol. Assn., 1974, Kenneth Craik award Cambridge U., 1979. Mem. Am. Psychol. Assn. (div. pres. 1962-63), Eastern Psychol. Assn. (pres. 1975-76), AAAS, Optical Soc. Am. (recipient Edgar D. Tillyer award 1969, Frederic Ives medal 1982), Nat. Acad. Scis., Am. Physiol. Soc., Internat. Brain Research Orgn. Soc. Neurosci., Internat. Soc. Clin. Electrophysiology of Vision, Soc. Exptl. Psychologists (recipient Howard Crosby Warren medal 1957), Am. Acad. Arts and Scis., Assn. for Research in Vision and Ophthalmology (pres. 1977, recipient Jonas S. Friedenwald award 1966). Current Work: Research in human vision. Subspecialties: Sensory processes; Psychophysics. Office: Hunter Lab Psychology Brown U Providence RI 02912

RIKER, DONALD KAY, biomedical scientist, consultant; b. N.Y.C., Oct. 22, 1945; s. Walter F., Jr. and Virginia H. (Jaeger) R.; m. Leigh Bartley, Oct. 30, 1965; children: Scott B., Hal S. Student, Hamilton Coll., 1963-65; B.A., U. Kans., 1969; postgrad. fellow Rockefeller U., 1969-70; Ph.D., Cornell U., Ithaca, N.Y., 1977. Postdoctoral fellow in pharmacology Yale U. Sch. Medicine, New Haven, 1976-79, research staff scientist, 1979-80, research assoc., 1980-82, research affiliate, 1982—; research health scientist West Haven (Conn.) VA, 1980-81; sr. research investigator Vicks Research Center, Richardson-Vicks, Inc., Shelton, Conn., 1982-84, prin. research investigator, 1984—; cons. Nat. Football League, N.Y.C., 1980—; scientist U.S. Antarctic Research Program, NSF, 1968. Contbr. articles, abstracts to profl. lit. Recipient U.S. Antarctic Service medal U.S. Congress, 1969; Frank M. Chapman award Am. Mus. Natural History, 1971, 72; NIH nat. research service fellow, 1977-78. Mem. AAAS, Soc. Neurosci., Am. Soc. Pharmacology and Exptl. Therapeutics, Internat. Soc. Neurochemistry, Am. Soc. Neurochemistry, Sigma Xi. Club: Yale (N.Y.C.). Current Work: Basic and clinical research and development of drugs, research management, over-the-counter drugs. Subspecialties: Neuropharmacology; Neurochemistry. Home: 166 Mather St Hamden CT 06517 Office: One Far Mill Crossing Shelton CT 06484

RILEY, JOHN THOMAS, chemist, educator; b. Bardstown, Ky., Apr. 2, 1942; s. John N. and Mary F. (Jury) R.; m. Rita Caroll, Dec. 23, 1963; children: Sheila, John Paul. B.S., Western Ky. U., 1964; Ph.D., U. Ky., 1968. Asst. prof. Western Ky. U., Bowling Green, 1968-76, assoc. prof., 1976-81, prof. chemistry, 1981—, also dir. Western Ky. U. Ctr. for Coal Sci.; cons. to local industry. Contbr. articles to profl. jours. Bd. dirs. Eastland Park Pool, 1974-80, pres., 1979, v.p., 1978. Grantee Inst. Mining and Minerals Research, 1979-81, DOT, 1983-85, NSF, 1985-87, DOE, 1985-87, various pvt. corps., 1981-85. Mem. Am. Chem. Soc., Ky. Acad. Scis., Sigma Xi. Democrat. Roman Catholic. Current Work: Development of new methods of analysis of components in coal and coal-derived products; anodic stripping Voltammetric analysis of trace materials. Subspecialties: Coal chemistry; Analytical chemistry. Home: 1511 Woodhurst Dr Bowling Green KY 42101 Office: Dept Chemistry Western Ky U Bowling Green KY 42101

RILEY, MONICA, biochemist; b. New Orleans, Oct. 4, 1926; d. Chauncey and Maude R.; m. Vincent J. Lusby, Jan. 1, 1949 (div.); children: Adam, Christine, Katherine. A.B., Smith Coll., 1947; Ph.D., U. Calif.-Berkeley, 1960. Asst. prof. bacteriology U. Calif. Davis, 1960-66; asso. prof. biochemistry SUNY-Stony Brook, 1966-75, prof., 1975—, provost biol. scis., 1975-78. Contbr. articles to profl. jours. and chpts. to sci. books. Grantee NSF; Grantee NIH; Grantee Am. Cancer Soc. Mem. Am. Soc. Biol. Chemists, Am. Soc. Microbiologists, Am. Soc. Microbiology (chmn. com. on molecular and genetic microbiology, pub. and sci. affairs bd.), Genetics Soc. Am. Current Work: Researcher in molecular mechanisms of evolution of DNA and genome organization in bacteria. Subspecialties: Genetics and genetic engineering (biology); Evolutionary biology. Office: Dept Biochemistry SUNY Stony Brook NY 11794

RILEY, PATRICK PAUL, geologist; b. Weston, W.Va., Aug. 9, 1951; s. Thomas Francis and Frances Louise (Esposito) R.; m. Vicky Lee Troy, Aug. 1975; children—Tara Ann, Vanessa Jo, Patrick Ian. B.S. in Geology, Marshall U., 1976. Field insp. Huntington Urban Renewal Authority, W.Va., 1969-75; hwy. insp. in trng. W.Va. Dept. Hwys., Barboursville, 1975-76; geologist Gaddy Engring. Co., Huntington, 1976-79, Geol. Services Inc., Huntington, 1979-80; pres. Riley, Mannon & Sturgeon, Ltd., Huntington, 1980—. Mem. Geol. Soc. Am., Ky. Geol. Soc., Soc. Petroleum. Engrs. (assoc.). Current work: Coal bed paleoenvironments research; wireline well logging services for coal, hydrocarbon and water exploration. Subspecialties: Geophysics; Geology. Office: Riley Mannon & Sturgeon Ltd West Virgina Bldg Huntington WV 25701

RIMEL, REBECCA WEBSTER, neurosurgery educator, researcher; b. Charlottesville, Va., Apr. 10, 1951; d. John Malangathon IV and Gladys Yvonne (Winebarger) R. B.S. in Nursing, U. Va., 1973; M.B.A., James Madison U., 1982. Head nurse U. Va., Charlottesville, 1973-74, coordinator med. out-patient facilities, 1974-75, nurse practitioner, 1975-77, instr. neurosurgery, 1977-80, asst. prof. neurosurgery, 1981—; dir. NIH Head Injury Study, Charlottesville, 1979—; prin. investigator Robert Wood Johnson Found., Princeton, N.J., 1981—, Pew Meml. Trust, Phila., 1982—. Co-author: Clinical Neurosurgery, 1982; contbr. articles to profl. jours. Bd. Dirs. Nat. Head Injury Found., Boston, 1982—; sec. Neurol. Reserach Inst., Culpeper, Va., 1981—; bd. dirs. Airport Commn., Charlottesville, 1983—. Kellogg Found. fellow, 1982-85. Mem. Am. Assn. Automotive Med. (membership com. 1983), Am. Assn. Neurol. Nurses, Am. Nurses Assn., Am. Pub. Health Assn., Va. State Nurses Assn. Methodist. Current Work: Clinical research in neurosurgery, specifically in head injury; restoring social competence after injury; minor head injury and athletic head injuries. Subspecialty: Neurology. Home: 1703 Galloway Dr Charlottesville VA 22901 Office: Dept Neurosurgery U Va Box 180 Charlottesville VA 22908

RIMOIN, DAVID LAWRENCE, physician, medical geneticist, educator; b. Montreal, Que., Can., Nov. 9, 1936; came to U.S., 1963; s. Michael and Fay (Lecker) R.; m. Maryann Singleton, Sept. 1, 1962 (div. 1979); 1 dau., Ann Walsh; m. Ann Piilani Garber, July 27, 1980; children—Michael Keone Garber, Lauren Piilani. B.S., McGill U., 1957, M.S., 1961, M.D., C.M., 1961; Ph.D., Johns Hopkins U., 1967. Diplomate Am. Bd. Internal Medicine, Am. Bd. Med. Genetics. Asst. prof. pediatrics and medicine, Washington U., St. Louis, 1967-70; assoc. prof. pediatrics and medicine, UCLA, 1970-73, prof., 1973—; chief div. med. genetics Harbor-UCLA Med. Ctr., Torrance, Calif., 1970—. Co-editor: Genetic Disorders of Endocrine Glands, 1971; Principles and Practice Medical Genetics, 1983; author writings in book chpts., sci. publs. Research career devel. awardee NIH, 1967; recipient E. Mead Johnson award for research in pediatrics Am. Acad. Pediatrics, 1976; Ross Outstanding Young Investigator award Western Soc. Pediatric Research, 1976. Mem. Am. Soc. Human Genetics (pres. 1984, bd. dirs. 1977-79), Western Soc. Clin. Research (pres. 1978), Am. Fedn. Clin. Research (sec.-treas. 1973-76), Am. Bd. Med. Genetics (pres. 1980-83). Current work: Medical genetics and genetic disease, specialty related to dwarfism, collagen, genetics disorders of the endocrine glands, diabetes mellitus and birth defects. Subspecialties: Genetics and genetic engineering (medicine); Internal medicine. Home: 595 36th St Manhattan Beach CA 90266 Office: Harbor-UCLA Med Ctr 1000 W Carson Torrance CA 90509

RINEHART, DAVID ALAN, environmental engineer, consultant; b. Akron, Ohio, July 7, 1944; s. Lewis Arnold and Lois Arlene (Kimes) R.; m. Melinda Marie Lewis, July 31, 1968. B.S., Heidelberg Coll., 1967. Chemist, Goodyear Tire and Rubber Co., Akron, 1966-78; project leader Republic Steel Co., Independence, Ohio, 1978-80; environ. engr. Diebold, Inc., Canton, Ohio, 1980—; pres. Whetherill Cons. Co., Akron, 1982—. Mem. Am. Genetic Assn., Am. Pub. Health Assn., Am. Pigeon Fanciers Council, Bd. Hazard Control Mgmt., AAAS. Republican. Lodge: Masons (master). Current work: Asbestos containment and disposal, hazardous waste and solid waste disposal, research of electromegnetic effects on animal orientation and homing abilities. Subspecialties: Environmental engineering; Hazardous waste disposal. Home: 559 Alandale Dr Tallmadge OH 44278 Office: Diebold Inc 818 Mulberry Rd SE Canton OH 44711

RINEHART, JOHN SARGENT, physicist, cons.; b. Kirksville, Mo., Feb. 8, 1915; s. Rupert Lloyd and Gertrude Jane (Upright) R.; m. Marion Sladky, Aug. 10, 1940; children: Margot, Eric. B.S., N.E. Mo. State Tchrs. Coll., 1934, A.B. in Physics, 1935; M.S. in Physics, Calif. Inst. Tech., 1937; Ph.D. in Physics, State U. Iowa, 1940. Tech. aide Nat. Def. Research Com., 1942-46; sr. physicist N.Mex. Sch. Mines, 1946-49; research scientist Naval Ordnance Test Sta., China Lake, Calif., 1950-55; asst. dir. Smithsonian Astro-phys. Obs., Cambridge, Mass., 1955-58; prof. mining engring. Golo. Sch. Mines, Golden, 1958-64; dir. research and devel. Coast and Geodetic Survey, Washington, 1964-66; sr. research fellow NOAA, Boulder, Colo., 1966-73, cons. in field. Author 3 books on explosives and their effects, 2 books on geysers and geothermal energy; contbr. articles to profl. jours. Mem. AAAS, Am. Phys. Soc., Am. Geophys. Union, Explorers Club, Sigma Xi. Club: Cosmos (Washington). Current Work: Mechanical effects of explosives; geothermal and related geophysical phenomena. Subspecialties: Geothermal power; Solid mechanics. Home: PO Box 392 Santa Fe NM 87051

RINES, HOWARD WAYNE, geneticist; b. Portland, Ind., Feb. 19, 1942; s. Ray G. and N. Norene (Redford) R.; m. Donna R. Olsen, Aug. 22, 1965; children: David, Deborah, Kenneth. B.S. in Agrl. Sci, Purdue U., 1964, M.S. in Genetics, 1965; Ph.D., Yale U., 1969. Asst. prof. dept. botany U. Ga., Athens, 1971-76; research geneticist Agrl. Research Service, U.S. Dept. Agr., 1976—; adj. assoc. prof. dept. agronomy and plant genetics U. Minn., St. Paul, 1976—. Served to capt. U.S. Army, 1969-71. Nat. Merit scholar, 1960-64; Louis G. Ware fellow, 1964-67; NIH fellow, 1967-69. Mem. Am. Soc. Agronomy, Genetics Soc. Am., Internat. Soc. Plant Tissue Culture. Current Work: Genetics of oats, anther culture, tissue culture, plant breeding, mutagenesis. Subspecialties: Plant genetics; Plant cell and tissue culture. Home: 4292 Nancy Pl Saint Paul MN 55112 Office: Dept Agronomy Univ of Minn Saint Paul MN 55108

RINGLER, IRA, pharmaceutical company executive; b. Bklyn., Feb. 11, 1928; s. Louis and Bessie (Diamond) R.; m. Nancy Moss, June 6, 1954; children—Susan, Julie, Ralph; m. Edgra Kessel, Nov. 29, 1969. B.S., Ohio State U., 1951; M.Nutritional Scis., Cornell U., 1953, Ph.D. in Biochemistry, 1955. With Lederle Labs., Pearl River, N.Y., 1957-75, dir. research, 1969-75; v.p. research mgmt. and corp. devel. Abbott Labs., N. Chicago, Ill., 1975-76, v.p. pharm. products research and devel., 1976-83; pres. TAP Pharms., 1983—. Served with U.S. Army, 1946-48. Mem. Am. Soc. Pharmacology and Exptl. Therapeutics, Endocrine Soc., Am. Soc. Biol. Chemists, Am. Chem. Soc., Internat. Soc. Biochem. Pharmacology, Sigma Xi, Phi Kappa Phi. Home: Plum Tree Rd Barrington Hills IL 60010 Office: TAP Pharmaceuticals 1400 Sheridan Rd North Chicago IL 60064

RIORDAN, JAMES MICHAEL, chemist; b. Tampa, Fla., Aug. 26, 1946; s. James Jerimah and Rosa Marie (Brinkman) R.; m. Rebecca Schwartz, June 3, 1972; children—Amy Rebecca, Kristen Nicole, Jonathan James. B.S., Ga. Inst. Tech., 1968; Ph.D., U. Ga., 1975. Research assoc. U. Ala., Birmingham, 1976-78, research scientist, 1978-84; sr. chemist So. Research Inst., Birmingham, 1984—. Mem. Am. Chem. Soc., Sigma Xi. Current work: Molecular spectroscopy, NMR spectroscopist. Subspecialties: Organic chemistry; Cancer research (medicine). Home: 535 Danton Ln Birmingham AL 35210Office: So Research Inst 2000 9th Ave S PO Box 55305 Birmingham AL 35255

RIPPIE, EDWARD GRANT, pharmacy educator; b. Beloit, Wis., May 29, 1931; s. Edward George and Esther Audella (Stevens) R.; m. Dorothy Ruth Tegtmeyer, Sept. 24, 1955; 1 child, E. Glenn. B.S., U. Wis., 1953, M.S., 1956, Ph.D., 1959. Asst. prof. pharm. tech. Coll. Pharmacy, U. Minn., Mpls., 1959-62, assoc. prof. pharmaceutics, 1962-66, prof. pharmaceutics, 1966—, head. pharmaceutics dept., 1966-74; mem. revision com. U.S. Pharmacopeia, 1970-80. Mem. editorial adv. bd.: Jour. Pharm. Scis, Washington, 1978—; contbr. numerous articles to sci. publs. Served with U.S. Army, 1956-58. Fellow Acad. Pharm. Scis. (chmn. indsl. pharm. sect. 1984-88), Am. Pharm. Assn. (Ebert prize 1982); mem. Am. Chem. Soc., AAAS. Current Work: Particulate solids mass transport within powder beds; thermodynamics of protein binding; hydrodynamics of drug dissolution; the study of pharmaceutical tablet internal structure via stress/strain viscoelastic analysis. Home: 2 N Mallard Rd North Oaks Saint Paul MN 55110 Office: Univ Minn Coll Pharmacy Minneapolis MN 55455

RIS, HANS, zoologist, educator; b. Bern, Switzerland, June 15, 1914; came to U.S., 1938, naturalized, 1945; s. August and Martha (Egger) R.; m. Hania Wislicka, Dec. 26, 1947 (div. 1971); children: Christopher Robert, Annette Margo; m. Theron Caldwell, July 14, 1980. Diploma high sch. teaching, U. Bern, 1936; Ph.D., Columbia, 1942. Lectr. zoology Columbia U., 1942; Seessel fellow in zoology Yale U., 1942; instr. zoology Johns Hopkins U., 1942-44; asst. Rockefeller Inst., N.Y.C., 1944-46, asso., 1946-49; asso. prof. zoology U. Wis., Madison, 1949-53, prof., 1953-84, prof. emeritus, 1984—. Mem. Am. Acad. Arts Scis., Nat. Acad. Scis., AAAS. Researcher mechanisms of nuclear div., chromosome structure, cell ultrastructure, electron microscopy. Current Work: Cell biology. Subspecialty: Cell biology. Office: Zoology Research U Wis Madison WI 53706

RISER, MARY ELIZABETH, geneticist, cell biology educator; b. Richland, Wash., Aug. 1, 1945; s. Manning Walker and Mary Virginia (Dillard) R.; m. Robert D. Colligan, Sept. 1, 1978. B.S., Tulane U., 1967; M.S., U. Tex.-Houston, 1970, Ph.D., 1973. Postdoctoral fellow Baylor Coll. Medicine, Houston, 1974-77, asst. prof. dept. cell biology, 1977—. Contbr. articles in field to profl. jours. Named Outstanding Trainee M.D. Anderson Hosp. and Tumor Inst., 1982. Mem. Am. Soc. Cell Biology, Tissue Culture Assn. (mem. council 1979-81, pres. Tex. br. 1980-81), Tex. Genetics Soc., Sigma Xi. Methodist. Current Work: Genetic research into the controls of endocrine system using somatic cell hybrids and recombinant DNA technologies. Subspecialties: Genetics and genetic engineering (biology); Cell and tissue culture. Home: 5623 Dumfries St Houston TX 77096 Office: Baylor Coll Medicine 1200 Moursund St Houston TX 77030

RISLOVE, DAVID JOEL, educator; b. Rushford, Minn., Nov. 16, 1940; s. Elmer S. and Beatrice H. (Otis) R.; m. Susan M. Schacht, June 15, 1963; children: Kaye E., Lori J. B.A., Winona State U., 1962; Ph.D., N.D. State U., 1968. Chemist Mayo Clinic, Rochester, Minn., 1962; research and teaching asst. Iowa State U., Ames, 1963; Am. Petroleum Inst. research asst. N.D. State U., Fargo, 1964-68; prof. chemistry Winona (Minn.) State U., 1968—. Recipient Merit awards Winona State U., 1977-81. Mem. Am. Chem. Soc., No. Intercollegiate Conf. Episcopalian. Club: Barbershoppers. Lodge: Elks (Winona). Current Work: Synthesis and characterization of pyrroles, porphyrins and metalloporphyrins and polyporphyrins; kinetics of acid-base reactions in hydrocarbon solvents. Subspecialties: Organic chemistry; Synthetic chemistry.

Home: 745 47th Ave Winona MN 55987 Office: Pasteur Hall Winona State U Winona MN 55987

RITCHIE, ALEXANDER WEBB, geology educator, researcher; b. Durham, N.C., Apr. 8, 1944; s. Howard Raymond and Dorothy (Webb) R.; m. Kathleen Adams Hill, Nov. 23, 1969. B.S. in Geology, U. N.C., 1966; M.A., U. Tex., 1969, Ph.D., 1975. Asst. prof. geology Furman U., Greenville, S.C., 1974-78, U. South Fla., Tampa, 1978-82; assoc. prof. geology Coll. of Charleston (S.C.), 1982—; cons. in field of metals and petroleum exploration in Central and South Am., 1978—. Author: Laboratory Manual for Physical Geology, 1977; Physical Geology Lab Manual, 1984; contbr. articles to profl. jours. Served to capt. U.S. Army, 1969-71. NDEA Title IV fellow, 1966-69; U. South Fla. Research Council and Dept. Geology and Instituto Geografico Nacional, Guatemala grantee, 1980; Belmac Corp. contract grantee, 1980-81; World Bank-Sunmark Honduras Project and Republic of Honduras grantee, 1984. Mem. Geol. Soc. Am., Carolina Geol. Soc., Southeastern Geol. Soc., Phi Kappa Phi, Sigma Xi, Sigma Gamma Epsilon. Current work: Research in neogene tectonics of Central Am.; consulting in metals and petroleum exploration. Subspecialty: Tectonics. Home: 2413 Sylvan Shores Dr Charleston SC 29407 Office: Dept Geology Coll of Charleston Charleston SC 29424

RITCHIE, DENNIS M., computer scientist. With AT&T Bell Labs., Murray Hill, N.J. Recipient Turing award Assn. for Computing Machinery, 1983. . Office: AT&T Bell Labs Murray Hill NJ 07974

RITCHIE, JERRY CARLYLE, ecologist, soil scientist; b. Richfield, N.C., Dec. 13, 1937; s. Clarence Lee and Bernice Laura (Ballard) R.; m. Carole Jean Atanasoff, Sept. 17, 1966; children—Jarryl Brooke, Karen Lynn. B.A., Pfeiffer Coll., 1960; M.S., U. Tenn., 1962; Ph.D., U. Ga., 1967. Ecologist, U. Ga., Tifton, 1967-69; soil scientist U.S. Dept. Agr. Sedimentation Lab., Oxford, Miss., 1969-78, program scientist nat. program Agrl. Research Service, Beltsville, Md., 1978-83, ecologist, soil scientist Agrl. Research Service Hydrology Lab., Beltsville, 1983—. Served with U.S. Army, 1962-64. Lutheran. Current work: Application of remote sensing technology to natural resource models, expert systems. Subspecialties: Ecology (environmental science); Soil science. Home: 12224 Shadetree Ln Laurel MD 20708 Office: US Dept Agr Hydrology Lab BARC West Bldg 007 Beltsville MD 20705

RITT, PAUL EDWARD, electronics company executive; b. Balt., Mar. 3, 1928; s. Paul Edward and Mary (Knight) R.; m. Dorothy Ann Wintz, Dec. 30, 1950; children: Paul Edward, Peter M., John W., James T., Mary Carol, Matthew J. B.S. in Chemistry, Loyola U., Balt., 1950, M.S. in Chemistry, 1952; Ph.D. in Chemistry, Georgetown U., 1954. Research asso. Harris Research Lab., Washington, 1950-52; aerospace research chemist Melpar, Inc., Falls Church, Va., 1952-60, research dir., 1960-62, v.p. research, 1962-65, v.p. research and engring., 1965-67; v.p., gen. mgr. Tng. Corp. Am., 1965-67; pres. applied sci. div., applied tech. div. Litton Industries, Bethesda, Md., 1967-68; v.p., dir. research GTE Labs., Waltham, Mass., 1968—; instr. U. Va., 1956-58, Am. U., 1959—. Contbr. articles to profl. jours. Mem. dean's adv. council U. Mass. Sch. Engring.; mgmt. bd. advs. Worcester Poly. Inst.; adv. council Stanford U. CIS; mem. adv. bd. Coll. Engring., Wash. State U.; mem. Mass. High Tech. Council. Fellow Am. Inst. Chemists, AAAS; mem. Am. Phys. Soc., Royal Soc. Chemistry, IEEE, Am. Inst. Physics, Electrochem. Soc., Am. Vacuum Soc., Am. Ceramic Soc., Am. Chem. Soc., Washington Acad. Sci., N.Y. Acad. Sci., Sigma Xi. Patentee in field. Current Work: Direction of research in materials; electronic devices, telecommunication systems and services. Subspecialties: Materials; Information systems (Information science). Home: 36 Sylvan Ln Weston MA 02193 Office: 40 Sylvan Rd Waltham MA 02254

RITTER, CARL ALAN, pharmacologist, educator; b. Confluence, Pa., Jan. 23, 1932; s. John M. and Louise (Frantz) R.; m. Jeanette Lois Smart, Jan. 18, 1936; 1 son, Alan B. Student, Gettysburg Coll., 1950-52, Syracuse U., 1952-55; Ph.D., SUNY, 1964. Postdoctoral fellow, Johnson Research Found. U. Pa., 1963-66, asst. prof., Sch. Vet. Medicine, 1966-71, head, Lab. Pharmacology, 1968-71, asso. prof., 1972—. Contbr. numerous articles to profl. jours. Mem. AAAS, Am. Soc. Microbiology, Am. Soc. Pharmacology and Exptl. Therapeutics, N.Y. Acad. Scis., Am. Coll. Vet. Toxicologists, Am. Coll. Vet. Pharmacology and Therapeutics, Phi Zeta. Current Work: Altering permeability and responses of cells to drugs and metabolites using vesicles made of normal phospholipids. Subspecialties: Membrane biology; Cellular pharmacology. Office: 3800 Spruce St Philadelphia PA 19174

RITTER, GERHARD X., mathematics, computer science educator, educator; b. Bochum, Westphalia, Ger., Oct. 27, 1936; came to U.S., 1955, naturalized, 1966; s. Karl Friedrich and Luzie (Golla) R.; m. Cheri Ann Reiche, June 1, 1963; children: Andrea Ann, Erika Renee. B.A., U. Wis., 1966, Ph.D., 1971. Instr. U. Wis. Ext. Ctr., Madison, 1967-70; prof. dept. math. U. Fla., Gainesville, 1971—, prof. dept. computer sci., 1985—; joint appointments dept. math, computer sci. and U. Fla. (Ctr. Info. Research), 1980-82; research cons. NASA, 1979, Ctr. Info. Research, 1979—, co-dir., 1980-81; research geophysicist Texaco, Inc., Bellaire, Tex., 1981; research contact Det. Advanced Research Project Agy., 1984—. Contbr. articles to profl. jours.; referee various tech. jours. Served with USAF, 1958-62. NASA fellow, 1979; USAF fellow, 1982; NSF grantee, 1982; Air Force Office Scientific Research grantee, 1983. Mem. Am. Math. Soc., Math. Assn. Am., IEEE, Soc. Indsl. and Applied Math., N.Y. Acad. Sci. Democrat. Roman Catholic. Current Work: Parallel image processing and pattern recognition techniques as applied to guided weapons systems. Subspecialties: Applied mathematics; Graphics, image processing, and pattern recognition. Home: 4107 NW 33 Pl Gainesville FL 32601 Office: Dept Math Fla Gainesville FL 32611

RITZ-GOLD, CAROLINE JOYCE, biophysicist; b. Cleve., Oct. 23, 1943; d. George Henry and Katherine (Baerg) R.; m. Clifford Martin Gold, Mar. 31, 1978. B.S. in Chemistry, Long Beach State U., 1966, M.S. in Chemistry, 1969; Ph.D. in Biochemistry, U. So. Calif., 1978. Cancer Ctr. predoctoral fellow U. So. Calif., Los Angeles, 1974-77; Cardiovascular Research Inst. postdoctoral fellow U. Calif.-San Francisco, 1978-82, Am. Heart Assn. advanced research fellow, 1980-81; NSF vis. prof. San Francisco State U., 1983, vis. prof., dept. chemistry, 1984—. Contbr. articles to profl. jours. Mem. Biophys. Soc., Am. Phys. Soc., N.Y. Acad. Scis., Sigma Xi. Current work: Theory and modeling of biological signal and energy transducing systems; application of condensed matter theory to structural transitions and dynamics of biopolymers and macromolecular assemblies. Subspecialties: Biophysics (physics); Condensed matter physics. Home: 38451 Timpanogas Fremont CA 94536

RIVIER, NICOLAS YVES, physics educator, researcher; b. Lausanne, Vaud, Switzerland, Aug. 5, 1941; m. Lynn A. McElroy; children: Andre, Catherine. Dipl. Physics, U. Lausanne, 1964; Ph.D., Cambridge (Eng.) U., 1968. Asst. prof. UCLA, 1968-69; lectr. U. Calif.-Riverside, 1969-70; lectr. physics Imperial Coll., U. London, 1970—. Contbr. numerous articles to profl. jours. Mem. Am. Phys. Soc., Inst. Physics, European Phys. Soc. Current Work: Glasses, structure and topology of disordered materials; gauge aspects of condensed matter. Subspecialties: Low temperature physics; Statistical physics. Home: 15 Coalecroft Rd London SW15 6LW England Office: Dept Physics Imperial Coll Prince Consort Rd London SW7 2BZ England

RIVIERE, GEORGE ROBERT, dental immunologist; b. Decatur, Ill., Feb. 26, 1943; s. Robert Frank and Mary Frances (Cowan) R.; m. Holliston Lee Brown, Aug. 14, 1971; children: Michael Andrew, Kathryn Holliston. B.A., Drake U., 1966; B.S.D., U. Ill., 1966, D.D.S., 1968, M.S., 1970; Ph.D., UCLA, 1973. Practice pediatric dentistry, Chgo., 1968-70; USPHS postdoctoral trainee UCLA Schs (Dentistry and Medicine), 1970-73, asst. prof., 1975-76, assoc. prof., 1977-82, prof., 1982—. Contbr. articles to profl. jours. Served to lt. comdr. USN, 1973-75. NIH awardee, 1976-81. Mem. AAAS, Am. Assn. Immunologists, Am. Assn. Dental Research, Internat. Assn. Dental Research. Current Work: Immunopathology of Soft tissue disease in man. Subspecialties: Immunology (medicine); Pediatric dentistry. Office: UCLA Sch Dentistry Los Angeles CA 90024

RIVKIN, MAXCY CALVIN, indsl. research mgr.; b. Columbia, S.C., Mar. 31, 1937; s. Lewis Stanley and Jennie (Winter) R.; m. Judith Frances Hirschman, June 7, 1959; children: Victor Jay, Jan Winter. B.S. in Mech. Engring, U. S.C., 1959. Tech. service engr. Kraft div. Westvaco Corp., 1963, group leader tech. service, 1963-70; group leader process systems Covington Research Center, 1970-78; dir. research Laurel Research Center, Md., 1978—; mem. indsl. steering com. Dept. Energy/Nat. Bur. Standards. Served to lt. (j.g.) USN, 1959-62. Mem. AAAS, TAPPI, Instrument Soc. Am., N.Y. Acad. Sci., Soc. Rheology, History of Sci. Soc., Soc. History of Tech., Am. Mgmt. Assn. Current Work: Process dynamics, control and implementation of computer-based process control systems in the pulp and paper industry; directing research in paper product and process devel. Subspecialties: Materials processing; Applied mathematics. Office: Westvaco Corp 11101 Johns Hopkins Rd Laurel MD 20707

RIVLIN, RONALD SAMUEL, mathematics educator emeritus; b. London, Eng., May 6, 1915; came to U.S., 1952, naturalized, 1955; s. Raoul and Bertha (Aronsohn) R.; m. Violet Larusso, June 16, 1948; 1 son, John Michael. B.A., St. John's Coll., Cambridge U., 1937, M.A., 1939, Sc.D., 1952; D.Sc. h.c., Nat. U. Ireland, 1980, Nottingham U., 1980, Tulane U., 1982; Doctor L.C., Thessaloniki U. Research physicist Gen. Electric Co., Eng., 1937-42; sci. officer Telecommunications Research Establishment, Ministry Aircraft Prodn., Eng., 1942-44; research physicist, head phys. research, supt. research British Rubber Producers Research Assn., 1944-52; head research group Davy-Faraday Lab., Royal Instn., London, 1948-52; cons. Naval Research Lab., Washington, 1952-53; prof. applied math. Brown U., 1953-63; L. Herbert Ballou U. prof., 1963-67, prof. applied math. and engring. sci., 1963-67, chmn. div. applied math., 1958-63; prof. associé U. Paris, 1966-67; Centennial Univ. prof., dir. Center for Application of Math., Lehigh U., Bethlehem, Pa., 1967-80, prof. emeritus, adj. Univ. prof., 1980—; co-chmn. Internat. Congress Rheology, 1963; Russell Severance Springer vis. prof. U. Calif., Berkeley, 1977. Contbr. articles profl. jours.; Editorial com.: Jour. Rational Mechanics and Analysis, 1952-57, Archive for Rational Mechanics and Analysis, 1957-72, Jour. Math. Physics, 1960, Jour. Applied Physics, 1960-63, Acta Rheologica, 1963—, Internat. Jour. Biorheology, 1972-74, Mechanics Research Communications, 1974—, Jour. Non-Newtonian Fluid Mechanics, 1975—, Meccanica, 1975—. Recipient Panetti prize, 1975; von Humboldt Sr. award, 1981; Guggenheim fellow, 1961-62, Inst. for Advanced Studies (Berlin) fellow, 1984-85. Fellow Acad. Mechanics, ASME (mem. exec. com. applied mechanics div. 1975-80, vice-chmn. and sec. 1978-79, chmn. 1979-80); Fellow Am. Phys. Soc.; mem. Soc. Natural Philosophy (chmn. 1963-64), Am. Acad. Arts and Scis., Washington Acad. Scis., Inst. Physics (gov. 1974-76), Soc. Rheology (exec. com. 1957-59, 71-77, Bingham medal 1958, v.p. 1971-73, pres. 1973-75, nat. com. theoretical and applied mechanics 1973—, chmn. 1976-78, vice chmn. 1978-80), Internat. Union Theoretical and Applied Mechanics (gen. assembly 1975—, chmn. U.S. del. 1978), Nat. Acad. Engring., Council Sci. Soc. Pres. (sec.-treas. 1975, exec. bd. 1975-77), Mexico Soc. Rheology (hon.), Accademia dei Lincei (fgn.). Subspecialties: Solid mechanics; Fluid mechanics. Office: Center for Application Math Lehigh U 203 E Packer Ave Bethlehem PA 18015

RIZACK, MARTIN ARTHUR, biochemist, pharmacologist, physician, educator; b. N.Y.C., Nov. 19, 1926; s. Pincus and Lillie (Finerman) R.; m. Lea van Leeuwen, Mar. 26, 1964; children: Jonathan, Lillie, Joshua, Michele, Tina. A.B., Columbia U., 1946, M.D., 1950; Ph.D., Rockefeller U., 1960. Diplomate: Am. Bd. Internal Medicine. Intern, then asst. resident Bellevue Hosp.-Cornell U., 1950-51; asst., then chief resident St. Luke's Hosp., N.Y.C., 1953-56; fellow Rockefeller U., N.Y.C., 1957-60, asst. prof., 1960-65, asso. prof. biochemistry and pharmacology, also physician, 1965—; head Lab. Cellular Biochemistry and Pharmacology, 1967—. Contbr. articles to biochem. and pharmacol. jours.; Cons. editor: Med. Letter on Drugs and Therapeutics. Served to capt. M.C. USNR, 1951-53. Fellow ACP; mem. Am. Soc. Biol. Chemists, Am. Soc. Pharmacology and Exptl. Therapeutics. Current Work: Biochemistry and pharmacology of peptide hormones and their cellular mechanisms of action. Subspecialties: Biochemistry (biology); Cellular pharmacology. Office: Rockefeller U 1230 York Ave New York City NY 10021

RIZVI, SYED QALAB ABBAS, industrial scientist, researcher; b. Rawalpindi, Panjab, Pakistan, Aug. 27, 1945; came to U.S., 1974; s. Ali Asghar and Kaneez (Fatima) R.; m. Ada Luz Santiago, Mar. 4, 1978; children—Syed Ali Abbas, Sophia Tabassum. B.Sc, Panjab U., Lahore, 1963; M.Sc., Peshawar U. (Pakistan), 1966; Ph.D., Flinders U., Australia, 1973. Analyst, Burrough's Wellcome, Karachi, Pakistan, 1967-68; asst. prof. chemistry Edwardes Coll., Peshawar, 1968-69; sr. research assoc. U. East Anglia, Norwich, Eng., 1973-74; research assoc. Ohio State U., Columbus, 1974-76, Temple U., Phila., 1976-78; instr., postdoctoral assoc. Drexel U., Phila., 1978-79; research scientist Lubrizol Corp., Wickliffe, Ohio, 1979—. Contbr. articles to profl. jours. Sci. Research Council fellow, 1973-74; NSF fellow, 1974-76; NIH fellow, 1976-78. Mem. Am. Chem. Soc. Muslim. Current work: Related to specialty chemicals with emphasis on lubricant and fuel additives. Subspecialties: Organic chemistry; Synthetic chemistry. Home: 7910 Viewmount Dr Painesville OH 44077 Office: Lubrizol Corp 29400 Lakeland Blvd Wickliffe OH 44092

ROACHE, PATRICK JOHN, research scientist; b. Detroit, Sept. 15, 1938; s. Emmet Joseph and Amelia (Schmiehowski) R.; m. Catharine Stewart, June 1, 1963; children—Amelia, Anne, James, Elizabeth, Emmet. B.S., U. Notre Dame, 1960, M.S., 1963, Ph.D., 1967. Instr. U. Detroit, 1962-64; asst. prof. U. N.D. Grand Forks, 1964-65; research aerodynamicist Sandia Labs., Albuquerque, 1967-73; sr. scientist Sci. Applications, Inc., Albuquerque, 1973-75; pres. Ecodynamics, Albuquerque, 1975—; cons. Sci. Applications, Inc., La Jolla, Calif., 1983—, Sandia Labs., Albuquerque, 1974-80, Los Alamos Labs., 1974-75, Kozo Keikaku, Inc., Tokoyo, 1978. Author: Computational Fluid Dynamics, 1972. Ward sec. Albuquerque Republican Com., 1972-73, ward chmn., 1973-74; mem. N.Mex. Gov.'s Commn. on Mcpl. Funding, 1977; mem. central com. John Anderson for Pres., Albuquerque, 1978. Mem. AIAA, Am. Phys. Soc., Am. Soc. Engring. for Edn., Soc. Indsl. and Applied Math., Internat. Solar Energy Soc. Roman Catholic. Current work: Algorithm development for computation fluid dynamics, heat transfer and electric field calculations for lasers using finite difference methods and symbolic manipulation. Subspecialties: Aeronautical engineering; Applied mathematics. Home: 748 Valverde SE Albuquerque NM 87108Office: Ecodynamics Research Assos Inc PO Box 8172 Albuquerque NM 87198

ROANE, PHILIP RANSOM, JR., virologist; b. Balt., Nov. 20, 1927; s. Philip Ransom and Mattie (Brown) R.; m. Vernice Reed, Roane, Aug. 1, 1981. B.Sc., Morgan State Coll., 1952; Sc.M., Johns Hopkins U., 1960; Ph.D., U. Md., 1965-70. Cert. dir. clin. labs., Md., 1973. Virologist, dir. quality control Microbiol. Assocs., Inc., Bethesda, Md., 1964-72; asst. prof. virology Howard U., 1972-77, assoc. prof., 1977—; cons. HEM Research Inc., Rockville; mem. virology study sect. NIH, 1976-80; mem. rev. com. viral and rickettsial diseases U.S. Army, 1979-82. Contbr. articles in field. Served with USAAF, 1946-47. NIH grantee, 1973-74, 72-80; recipient Kaiser-Permanente award for Excellence in Teaching, 1979; Med. Student Council award for Inspirational Leadership, 1982; arad. Student Council Merit Award, 1982. Mem. Am. Assn. Immunologists, Am. Soc. Microbiology, N.Y. Acad. Sci. Current Work: Molecular virology, viral immunology; current research involves studies of the molecular interaction beteen herpes simplex virus and hepatitis B virus. Subspecialties: Virology (biology); Virology (medicine). Home: 7503 Harpers Dr Fort Washington MD 20744 Office: Howard U Coll Medicine 520 W St NW Washington DC 20059

ROBAKIS, NIKOLAOS KONSTANTINOU, molecular biologist; b. Finikounda, Messinia, Greece, Dec. 4, 1945; came to U.S., 1974; s. Konstantinos Georgiou and Efstathia Antoniou (Koutris) R.; m. Davida Scharf, June 4, 1974; children—Thalia, Daphne. Diploma, Aristotelian U., Greece, 1971; M.S., NYU, 1976, Ph.D., 1979. Teaching fellow NYU, 1974-77, research assoc., 1977-79; postdoctoral fellow Roche Inst. Molecular Biology, Nutley, N.J., 1979-82; research assoc. Hoffmann-LaRoche Research Ctr., Nutley, 1982-83; sr. research scientist N.Y. State Inst. for Basic Research in Devel. Disabilities, S.I., 1983—. Contbr. articles to profl. jours. NIH grantee, 1984. Mem. Am. Chem. Soc., Am. Soc. Microbiology, AAAS, Orgn. Greek Scientists U.S. (pres. 1984). Current work: Genetic code of slow viruses affecting the central nervous system (scrapie); elucidation of mechanisms of formation of pair helical filaments in Alzheimers patients; regulation of gene expressions. Subspecialties: Biochemistry (biology); Molecular biology. Home: 515 W 110th St Apt 4G New York NY 10025 Office: NY State Inst for Basic Research in Developmental Disabilities 1050 Forest Hill Rd Staten Island NY 10314

ROBB, WALTER LEE, manufacturing company executive; b. Harrisburg, Pa., Apr. 25, 1928; s. George A. and Ruth (Scantlin) R.; m. Anne Gruver, Feb. 27, 1954; children: Richard, Steven, Lindsey. B.S., Pa. State U., 1948; M.S., U. Ill., 1950, Ph.D., 1951. With Gen. Electric Co., 1951—; mgr. research/devel. Silicone Products Dept., Waterford, N.Y., 1966-68; venture mgr. Med. Devel. Ops., Schenectady, 1968-71; sr. v.p., group exec. Med. Systems Group, Milw., 1973—; industry rep. OTA Health Care Adv. Council. Recipient IR-100 awards. Mem. Nat. Acad. Engring., Health Industry Mfg. Assn. (exec. com., bd. dirs.). Patentee in field of membranes and gas separation. Subspecialty: Chemical engineering. Home: 3665 Mary Cliff Ln Brookfield WI 53005 Office: PO Box 414 Milwaukee WI 53201

ROBBERSON, DONALD L., molecular geneticist, educator; b. Shawnee, Okla., Sept. 10, 1941; s. Lewis Bert and Lela Merle (Attebery) R.; m. Barbara Lois Maxey, Dec. 28, 1963 (div.); children—Kirsten Dawn, Erik Lee, Amy Leigh. B.S., Okla. Bapt. U., 1963; Ph.D., Calif. Inst. Tech., 1971. Faculty assoc. M.D. Anderson Hosp., U. Tex. System Cancer Ctr., Houston, 1972-73, asst. prof. biology, 1973-74, assoc. prof. biology, 1979-84, prof. genetics, 1984—, chief sect. molecular genetics, 1983—. Author, co-editor: Perspectives on Genes and the Molecular Biology of Cancer, 1982. Mem. Am. Soc. Biol. Chemists, Am. Soc. Cell Biology. Current work: Mitochondrial DNA structure and replication in normal and malignant cells; repair of chemical damage to DNA; electron microscopy. Subspecialties: Cell study oncology; Genetics and genetic engineering (biology). Office: Dept Genetics MD Anderson Hosp 6723 Bertner Ave Houston TX 77030

ROBBINS, CHANDLER SEYMOUR, wildlife research biologist; b. Belmont, Mass, July 17, 1918; s. Samuel Dowse and Rosa Margaret (Seymour) R.; m. Eleanor Graham Cooley, Apr. 16, 1948; children—Jane Seymour, Stuart Bradley, George Chandler, Nancy Ellen. A.B., Harvard U., 1940; M.S., George Washington U., 1950. Wildlife biologist U.S. Fish and Wildlife Service, Laurel Md., 1945—; dir. Bleitz Wildlife Found., Los Angeles, 1967, Cornell Lab. Ornithology, Ithaca, N.Y., 1981, Nature Conservancy, Md., 1982. Author: Birds of North America, 1966; co-author: Birds of Maryland and the District of Columbia, 1958. Recipient Arthur A. Allen award Cornell Lab. Ornithology, 1979; Paul Bartsch award Audubon Naturalist Soc., 1979; Service award U.S. Dept. Interior, 1979; Ludlow Griscom award Am. Birding Assn., 1984. Fellow Am. Ornithologists Union; mem. Am. Meteorol. Soc., Brit. Trust for Ornithology, Internat. Bird Ringing Com., Wilson Ornithol. Soc. Democrat. Methodist. Current work: Habitat requirements, census methods and population trends of migratory birds. Subspecialties: Ecosystems analysis; Species interaction. Home: 7900 Brooklyn Bridge Rd Laurel MD 20707 Office: Patuxent Wildlife Research Ctr Laurel MD 20708

ROBBINS, FREDERICK CHAPMAN, physician; b. Auburn, Ala., Aug. 25, 1916; s. William J. and Christine (Chapman) R.; m. Alice Havemeyer Northrop, June 19, 1948; children—Alice, Louise. A.B., U. Mo., 1936, B.S., 1938; M.D., Harvard, 1940; D.Sc. (hon.), John Carroll U., 1955, U. Mo., 1958; D.Sci. (hon.), U. N.C., 1979, Tufts U., 1983, Med. Coll. Ohio, 1983; LL.D., U. N.Mex., 1968. Diplomate: Am. Bd. Pediatrics. Sr. fellow virus disease NRC, 1948-50; staff research div. infectious diseases Children's Hosp., Boston, 1948-50, assoc. physician, assoc. dir. isolation service, asso. research div. infectious diseases, 1950-52; instr., assoc. in pediatrics Harvard Med. Sch., 1950-52; dir. dept. pediatrics and contagious diseases Cleve. Met. Gen. Hosp., 1952-66; prof. pediatrics Case-Western Res. U., 1952-80; dean Case-Western Res. U. (Sch. Medicine), 1966-80, dean emeritus, 1980—; pres. Inst. Medicine, Nat. Acad. Scis., 1980—; vis. scientist Donner Lab., U. Calif., 1963-64. Served as maj. AUS, 1942-46; chief virus and rickettsial disease sect. 15th Med. Gen. Lab. investigations infectious hepatitis, typhus fever and Q fever. Decorated Bronze Star, 1945; recipient 1st Mead Johnson prize application tissue culture methods to study of viral infections, 1953; co-recipient Nobel prize in physiology and medicine, 1954; Med. Mut. Honor Award for, 1969; Ohio Gov.'s award, 1971. Mem. Am. Epidemiol. Soc., Am. Acad. Arts and Scis., Am. Soc. Clin. Investigation (emeritus mem.), Am. Acad. Pediatrics, Soc. Pediatric Research (pres. 1961-62, emeritus mem.), Am. Assn. Immunologists, Am. Pediatric Soc., Am. Philos. Soc., Phi Beta Kappa, Sigma Xi, Phi Gamma Delta. Subspecialty: Pediatrics. Home: 7021 Oak Forest Ln Bethesda MD 20817 Office: 2101 Constitution Ave NW Washington DC 20418

ROBBINS, HERBERT ELLIS, mathematics educator; b. New Castle, Pa., Jan. 12, 1915; s. Mark Louis and Celia (Klebansky) R.; m. Mary Dimock, 1943 (div. 1955); children: Mary Susannah, Marcia (Mrs. Weston T. Borden); m. Carol Hallett, 1966; children—Mark Hallett, David Herbert, Emily Carol. A.B., Harvard, 1935, Ph.D., 1938; Sc.D., Purdue U., 1974. Instr. math. N.Y. U., 1939-42; asso. prof. math. statistics U. N.C., 1946-50, prof., 1950-52; prof. math. statistics Columbia, 1953-66, 68-74, Higgins prof., 1974-85; prof. math. U. Mich., Ann Arbor, 1966-68; mem. Inst. Advanced Study, 1938-39, 52-53. Author: (with R. Courant) What is Mathematics?, 1941, (with Y.S. Chow and D. Siegmund) Great Expectations: The Theory of Optimal Stopping, 1971, (with J. Van Ryzin) Introduction to Statistics, 1975; Selected Papers, 1985. Contbr. articles to profl. jours. Served with USNR, 1942-46. Guggenheim fellow, 1952, 75. Mem. Inst. Math. Statistics (pres. 1966), Internat. Statis. Inst., Nat. Acad. Scis., Am. Acad. Arts and Scis. Current Work: Theory of sequental experimentation; empirical Bayes methods; stochastic approximation, applications of statistics in the law. Subspecialties: Probability; Statistics. Office: Dept of Statistics Columbia U New York NY 10027

ROBBINS, JACKIE WAYNE DARMON, agricultural engineering educator; b. Spartanburg, S.C., Feb. 6, 1940; s. Jack Dennis and Laura Christina (Champion) R.; m. Betty Jo Wright, June 17, 1963; children—Jackie Wayne, Robin Craig. B.S. in Agrl. Engring., Clemson U., 1961, M.S., 1965; Ph.D. in Agrl. Engring., N.C. State U., 1970. Registered profl. engr., La., Tex. Constrn. engr. Bur. Reclamation, Page, Ariz., 1961; asst. prof. La. State U., Baton Rouge, 1963-65; research asst. N.C. State U., Raleigh, 1968-69, research assoc., 1969-70; assoc. prof. U. Mo., Columbia, 1970-71; prof., head agrl. engring. La. Tech. U., Ruston, 1971—; vis. prof. U. Hawaii, 1977-78; cons. Dept. Agrl. Tech. Services, Republic South Africa, 1979, cons. on livestock Water Research Commn., 1981, Contbr. articles to tech. jours. Patentee drip irrigation hose. Bd. dirs. St. Peter Water Dist., Ruston, 1978; mem. Wastewater Adv. Com., Ruston, 1982. Served with AUS, 1961-62. NSF profl. devel. grantee, 1977. Mem. Am. Soc. Agrl. Engr. (Disting. Agrl. Engr. award La. sect. 1984), Nat. Soc. Profl. Engrs., Irrigation Assn., Am. Soc. Engring. Edn., La. Engring. Soc., Tau Beta Pi (Eminent Engr. 1978). Republican. Baptist. Current work: Salt gradient solar ponds; solar energy; biomass energy; agricultural wate management, irrigation, drip/trickle irrigation. Subspecialties: Agricultural engineering; Biomass (agriculture). Home: Route 3 Box 1241 Ruston LA 71270 Office: Dept Agrl Engring La Tech Univ Ruston LA 71272

ROBBINS, LEONARD G(ILBERT), geneticist; b. Bklyn., Aug. 10, 1945; s. William Henry and Bertha (Elkind) R.; m. Ellen Swanson; 1 son, Daniel Chaim. B.A., CUNY, 1965; Ph.D., U. Wash., 1970. Postdoctoral trainee U. Tex., Austin, 1970-72; vis. scientist U. Wash., Seattle, summer 1976; asst. prof. Mich. State U., East Lansing, 1972-77, assoc. prof. dept. zoology, 1977-83, prof. dept. zoology, 1983—; vis. scientist U. Calif., San Diego, summer 1978; NIH sr. internat. fellow Centro de Biologia Molecular Universidad Autónoma de Madrid, 1980-81. Contbr. articles to sci. jours. NSF grantee, 1975-79, 79-81, 82—. Mem. Fedn. Am. Scientists, AAAS, Genetics Soc. Am. Jewish. Club: Metropolitan Flying (Lansing). Current Work: Organization of chromosomes with particular attention to analysis of ribosomal gene clusters and recombination among them. Role of maternal gene information during development and the transition to zygotic gene activity. Subspecialties: Genome organization; Genetics and genetic engineering (medicine). Office: Mich State U East Lansing MI 48824

ROBBINS, ROBERT RAYMOND, botany educator; b. Des Moines, May 28, 1946; s. Harold Raymond and Marjorie Eunice (Brown) R.; m. Susan Ann Lohr, May 11, 1985. B.S., Iowa State U., 1968; M.S., U. Ill., 1973, Ph.D., 1977. Undergrad. teaching asst. Iowa State U., Ames, 1966-68; grad. teaching asst. U. Ill., Urbana, 1971-75; instr. Ctr. Electron Microscopy, 1973, 75, lectr. botany, 1976, postdoctoral research assoc., 1977; asst. prof. botany U. Wis.-Milw., 1977-84; asst. prof. biology Colo. Coll., Colorado Springs, 1984-85; asst. prof. biol. scis. Idaho State U., Pocatello, 1985—. Contbr. articles to profl. jours. Vol., Sta. WUWM. Served with U.S. Army, 1969-71. Mem. Bot. Soc. Am., Am. Inst. Biol. Scis., AAAS, Am. Bryological and Lichenological Soc., Nature Conservancy, Am. Fern Soc., ACLU, Bot. Club Wis., Wis. Acad. Scis., Arts, and Letters, Sigma Xi. Current Work: Research in cell biology and cell development of various reproductive structures of plants, including pollen, flagellated sperms of lower land plants, and mechanisms of fertilization in plants. Subspecialties: Cell biology; Reproductive biology. Office: Dept Biol Scis Idaho State U Pocatello ID 83209

ROBEL, ROBERT JOSEPH, biology educator; b. Lansing, Mich., May 21, 1933; s. Joseph John and Loretta Rose (Pung) R.; m. Anice Marie Blanc, Mar. 27, 1960. B.S., Mich. State U., 1956; M.S., U. Idaho, 1958; Ph.D., Utah State

U., 1961. Cert. wildlife biologist. Biologist aide Idaho Dept. Fish and Game, Boise, 1957-58; Univ. fellow Utah State U., Logan, 1958-61; asst. prof. biology Kans. State U., Manhattan, 1961-66, assoc. prof., 1966-71, prof., 1971—; Fulbright scholar, Aberdeen, Scotland, 1967-68; project mgr. Office Tech. Assessment, Washington, 1976-77; chmn. Mid-Am. Solar Energy Complex, Mpls., 1978-80; mem. research adv. council Dept. Interior, 1980-83. Author: Enhanced Oil Recovery, 1978. Contbr. articles to profl. jours. Fellow AAAS; mem. Kans. Acad. Sci. (past sec., pres.), Sigma Xi. Lodge: Elks. Current work: Wildlife ecology, technology transfer, environmental biology, population dynamics, natural resources management, environmental assessments, scientific technology applied to societal needs, energy and environmental considerations. Subspecialties: Ecology (environmental science); Population biology. Home: 211 Cedar Dr Manhattan KS 66502 Office: Kansas State U Ackert Hall Manhattan KS 66506

ROBERDS, RICHARD MACK, nuclear engineer; b. Lawrence, Kans., June 22, 1934; s. Wesley M. and Dorothy (McBroom) R.; m. Marian Marchena, June 29, 1936; children: Michael R., Catherine M., Wendy M. Student, UCLA, 1952-54; A.B., Kans. U., 1956, M.A., 1963; Ph.D., Air Force Inst. Tech., 1975. Commd. 2d lt. U.S. Air Force, 1956, advanced through grades to col., 1978; dep. chief tech. div. (Air Force Weapons Lab.), Kirtland AFB, N.Mex., 1973-77; chief reconnaissance and weapon delivery div. (Avionics Lab.), Wright Patterson AFB, Ohio, 1977-80; ret., 1980; head engring. tech. dept. Coll. Engring. Clemson (S.C.) U., 1980-84; dean Sch. Engring. Tech. and Engring., U. Tenn., Martin, 1984—. Decorated Legion of Merit, D.F.C. (2), Air medal (8). Mem. Am. Nuclear Soc., Am. Phys. Soc., Am. Soc. Engring. Edn., Air Force Assn. Baptist. Lodge: Rotary. Current Work: Dean of engineering school. Subspecialties: Nuclear engineering; Nuclear physics. Home: 104 Brundige St Martin TN 38237 Office: 113 EPS Bldg Univ Tenn Martin TN 38238

ROBERS, JONATHAN DAVID, geological engineer; b. Covina, Calif., May 16, 1954; s. Dallas Kennedy and Betty Mae (McCartney) R.; m. Katrinka Ruth Guy, June 12, 1982; children—Rebecca Marie, Christianna Ruth. B.Sc. in Geology, Calif. State Poly. U., 1976; M.Sc. in Civil Engring., U. Calif.-Berkeley, 1978, M.E., 1980, Ph.D. in Civil Engring., 1982. Registered professional engr., Calif. Staff geologist Dames & Moore, Inc., Los Angeles, 1974-76; field geologist U.S. Borax & Chem. Corp., Los Angeles, 1976; research engr. U. Calif.-Berkeley, 1977-79; geol engr. J. David Rogers & Assocs., Berkeley, 1979-82, Alan Kropp & Assocs., Berkeley, 1982-84; geol. engr. in charge Profl. Engring. Cons., Lafayette, Calif., 1984—; dir. Robert Martin Constrn. Co.; v.p. Pacific State Devel. Co., Inc., 1981-82; cons. in field; mem. U.S. com. Internat. Commn. on Large Dams, 1980. Author: Groundwater Geomorphology, 1984; Guide to Western Grand Canyon, 1984. Served to lt. USNR, 1982—. Recipient AIME Best Presentation medal, 1976, Hon. Mention award Cons. Engrs. Council, 1980. Mem. ASCE (disting. lectr. award 1977), Geol. Soc. Am., Assn. Engring. Geologists, Soil and Found. Engrs. Assn., Assn. Soil and Found. Engrs., Internat. Plastic Modelers, Nat. Eagle Scout Assn. Chi Epsilon (pres. Calif. chpt. 1979-80). Republican. Baptist. Current work: Geomorphology of hillslopes, landslides; expansive soil behavior; development of govermental policy concerning gradding ordinances and professional registration. Subspecialties: Marrow transplant; Civil engineering. Office: Profl Engring Cons 340 Mt Diablo Blvd Lafayette CA 94549

ROBERT, ANDRE, biologist, researcher; b. Montreal, Que., Can., Oct. 6, 1926; came to U.S., 1955; s. Aristide and Eva (Paiement) R.; m. Therese Desjardins, June 23, 1951 (div. 1972); children—Danielle, Jean-Baptiste, Pierre-Louis, Marie; m. Rose Wechter, Dec. 8, 1984. B.A., Stanislas Coll., Montreal, 1944; M.D., U. Montreal, 1950, Ph.D., Inst. Exptl. Med. Surgery, 1957. Intern, Hotel-Dieu Hosp., Montreal, 1950-51; asst. prof. endocrinology U. Montreal Med. Sch., 1952-55; sr. scientist Upjohn Co., Kalamazoo, 1955—. Contbr. aticles to profl. jours., chpts. to books. Mem. Am. Physiol. Soc., Am. Gastroent. Assn., AMA, Corp. Physicians and Surgeons Que., Soc. Exptl. Biology and Medicine. Current work: Gastric secretion; peptic ulcer; prostaglandins. Subspecialties: Gastroenterology; Pathology (medicine). Home: 2820 Taliesin Dr Kalamazoo MI 49008 Office: Upjohn Co Kalamazoo MI 49001

ROBERTS, BRADLEY LEE, physicist, educator; b. Bristol, Va., Aug. 11, 1946; s. Bradley and Irene (Wood) R.; m. Lynn M. Walter, Jan. 7, 1984. B.S. in Physics, U. Va., 1968; M.S., Coll. William and Mary, 1970, Ph.D., 1974. Research assoc. Rutherford Lab., Oxford, Eng., 1974-76; research assoc. MIT Lab. for Nuclear Sci., Cambridge, 1976-77, research affiliate, 1977—; asst. prof. physics Boston U., 1977-83, assoc. prof., 1983—; guest assoc. physicist Brookhaven Nat. Lab., Upton, N.Y., 1977—; sec. users group Bates Linear Accelerator, Middleton, Mass., 1978-79. Contbr. articles to profl. jours. NSF grantee. Mem. Am. Phys. Soc., Harvard Musical Assn., Sigma Xi. Current work: Intermediate energy particle and nuclear physics, hyperon physics, weak interactions and Muon physics, exotic atoms and medium energy photo nuclear physics. Subspecialties: Particle physics; Nuclear physics. Home: 3 Kenilworth Rd Winchester MA 01890 Office: Physics Dept Boston U 590 Commonwealth St Boston MA 02215

ROBERTS, BRUCE ROGER, plant physiologist; b. Leonia, N.J., May 19, 1933; s. Clarence Roger and Florence (Kingsbury) R.; divorced; children: Amy V., Mark K. A.B., Gettysburg (Pa.) Coll., 1956; M.F., Duke U., 1960, Ph.D., 1963. Reseach plant physiologist Agrl. Research Service, U.S. Dept. Agr., Delaware, Ohio, 1963—. Contbr. chpts. to books, articles to profl. jours. Mem. Am. Soc. Plant Physiologists, Internat. Soc. Arboriculture (research award 1975, author's citation award 1981, bd. dirs. 1985, hon. life mem.), Am. Soc. Hort. Sci., Sigma Xi. Current Work: Physiological response of plants to environmental stress. Subspecialty: Plant physiology (agriculture). Home: 72 W Winter St Delaware OH 43015 Office: 359 Main Rd Delaware OH 43015

ROBERTS, CORNELIUS SHELDON, materials scientist, consultant; b. Rupert, Vt., Oct. 27, 1926; s. Cornelius Vivian and Lola Jones (Sheldon) R.; m. Patricia Rose Wiseman, Oct. 21, 1950; children—David M., Steven H., Wayne E. B.Met.E., Rensselaer Poly. Inst., 1948; S.M., MIT, 1949, Sc.D., 1951. Lic. profl. engr., Calif. Research metallurgist Dow chem. Co., Midland, Mich., 1951-56; sr. staff mem. Shockley Labs., Palo Alto, Calif., 1956-57; co-founder, head materials Fairchild Semicondr. Corp., Palo Alto, 1957-61; co-founder, head spl. devices Amelco Semicondr. div. Teledyne Inc., Mountain View, Calif., 1961-63; cons. materials and processes, Los Altos, Calif., 1963-78, San Jose, Calif., 1978-84, Sunriver, Oreg., 1984. Author: Magnesium and Its Alloys, 1958; also numerous articles. Trustee Rensselaer Poly. Inst., 1972—, San Francisco Conservatory Music, 1983—. Served with USNR, 1944-46. Recipient Alfred Noble award Combined Engring. Socs., 1954. Mem. Am. Soc. Metals (trustee 1984-87), IEEE, AIME, Soc. Air Safety Investigators, Sigma Xi, Tau Beta Pi. Republican. Methodist. Club: University (N.Y.C.). Lodge: Elks. Current work: Electronic microchip technology; failure analysis, materials and aircraft. Subspecialties: Electronic materials; Materials processing. Home: 4 Grouse Ln Sunriver OR 97707 Office: PO Box 4576 Sunriver OR 97707

ROBERTS, EDWARD BAER, technology management educator; b. Chelsea, Mass., Nov. 18, 1935; s. Nathan and Edna (Podradchik) R.; m. Nancy Helen Rosenthal, June 14, 1959; children: Valerie Jo, Mitchell Jonathan, Andrea Lynne. B.S., MIT, 1958, M.S., 1958, M.S. in Mgmt, 1960, Ph.D., 1962. Founding mem. systems dynamics program MIT, 1958—, instr., 1959-61, asst. prof., 1961-65, assoc. prof., 1965-70, prof., 1970—, David Sarnoff prof. mgmt. of tech., 1974—, assoc. dir. research program on mgmt. sci. and tech., 1963-73, chmn. tech. and health mgmt. group, 1973—; co-founder, pres. Pugh-Roberts Assocs., Inc., Cambridge, Mass., 1963—; also dir.; dir. MIT-Boston VA Joint Center on Health Care Mgmt., 1976-80; dir. MIT Joint Program on Mgmt. of Tech., 1980—, Med. Info. Tech. Inc., Cambridge, Advanced Magnetics, Inc., Zero Stage Capital Equity Fund, Univ. Bank & Trust Co.; cons. Assn. Am. Med. Colls., also numerous corps.; mem. Task Force on Nuclear Medicine, ERDA, 1975-76, Nat. Research Council Com. on Ionizing Radiation Effects. Author: The Dynamics of Research and Development, 1964, (with others) Systems Simulation for Regional Analysis, 1969, The Persistent Poppy, 1975, The Dynamics of Human Service Delivery, 1976; prin. author, editor: (with others) Managerial Applications of System Dynamics, 1978; editor: (with others) Biomedical Innovation, 1981; editorial bd.: IEEE Trans. on Engring. Mgmt, 1968—, Indsl. Mktg. Mgmt, 1975—, Health Care Mgmt. Rev, 1976-78, Technol. Forecasting and Social Change, 1980—; Jour. Product Innovation Mgmt, 1984—; contbr. articles to profl. jours. Mem. IEEE, Inst. Mgmt. Sci. (pres. Boston chpt. 1962-63), Sigma Xi, Tau Beta Pi, Eta Kappa Nu, Tau Kappa Alpha. Current Work: Management of technical innovation; technical entrepreneurship. Subspecialties: Management of technology; Systems engineering. Home: 17 Fellsmere Rd Newton MA 02159 Office: 50 Memorial Dr Cambridge MA 02139

ROBERTS, FRED STEPHEN, mathematics educator, author; b. N.Y.C., June 19, 1943; s. Louis and Frances (Lindner) R.; m. Helen Miriam Marcus, June 22, 1972; children—Sarah, David. A.B., Dartmouth Coll., 1964; M.S., Stanford U., 1967, Ph.D., 1968. Postdoctoral fellow U. Pa., Phila., 1968; profl. staff Rand Corp., Santa Monica, Calif., 1968-71; postdoctoral fellow Inst. Advanced Study, Princeton, N.J., 1971-72; assoc. prof. math. Rutgers U., New Brunswick, N.J., 1972-76, prof. math., 1976—; vis. prof. Cornell U., Ithaca, N.Y., 1979-80. Author: Discrete Mathematical Models, 1976; Graph Theory and its Applications to Problems of Society, 1978; Measurement Theory with Applications to Decisionmaking, Utility, and the Social Sciences, 1979; Applied Combinatorics, 1984. Fellow Woodrow Wilson Found. 1967-68, Alexander von Humboldt Found. (declined) 1984; NSF grantee. Daniel Webster scholar 1963-64. Named Outstanding Math. Lectr., U. New Haven, 1984. Mem. Soc. Indsl. and Applied Math. (v.p. 1984—, sec. 1976-80). SIAM Inst. Math. and Soc. (bd. dirs. 1983—), Math. Assn. Am., Am. Math. Soc., Consortium Math. and Applications (council mem. 1982—), Ops. Research Soc. Am., Soc. Math. Psychology. Current work: Discrete mathematics, mathematical modeling of social, biological and environmental problems, graph theory, combinatorics, theory of measurement, operations research. Subspecialties: Discrete mathematics; Operations research (mathematics). Office: Rutgers U Dept Mathematics New Brunswick NJ 08903

ROBERTS, GEORGE PHILIP, polymer chemist; b. Barton, Vt., Dec. 25, 1937; s. Vernon E. and Sylvia M. (Perry) R.; m. Barbara DeMar., Sept. 6, 1959; children—Kent, Deirdre, Dawn, Thomas. B.S. in Chemistry, U. Vt., 1959; Ph.D. in Phys. Chemistry, Northwestern U., 1964. Group leader Uniroyal Chem., Naugatuck, Conn., 1969-74; mgr. polymer research Uniroyal, Inc., Middlebury, Conn., 1974-85, dir. new tech., 1985—. Bd. dirs. Child Guidance Clin., Inc., Waterbury, Conn.; founder Woodbury Scholarship Fund. Mem. Soc. Plastics Engrs. (chmn. div. 1975-76), Am. Chem. Soc. Current work: Structure property relationships in high polymers. Subspecialties: Polymer chemistry; Physical chemistry. Home: 42 School St Woodbury CT 06798 Office: Uniroyal Inc R-1-36 Benson Rd Middlebury CT 06749

ROBERTS, JOHN D., chemist, educator; b. Los Angeles, June 8, 1918; s. Allen Andrew and Flora (Dombrowski) R.; m. Edith Mary Johnson, July 11, 1942; children: Anne Christine, Donald William, John Paul, Allen Walter. A.B., UCLA, 1941, Ph.D., 1944; Dr. rer. nat. h.c., U. Munich, 1962; D.Sc., Temple U., 1964. Instr. chemistry U. Calif. at Los Angeles, 1944-45; NRC fellow chemistry Harvard, 1945-46, instr. chemistry, 1946, Mass. Inst. Tech., 1946, asst. prof., 1947-50, asso. prof., 1950-52; vis. prof. Ohio State U., 1952, Stanford U., 1973-74; prof. organic chemistry Calif. Inst. Tech., 1953-72, Inst. prof. chemistry, 1972—, dean of faculty, v.p., provost, 1980-83, chmn. div. chemistry and chem. engring., 1963-68, acting chmn., 1972-73; Foster lectr. U. Buffalo, 1956; Mack Meml. lectr. Ohio State U., 1957; Falk-Plaut lectr. Columbia U., 1957; Reynaud Found. lectr. Mich. State U., 1958; Bachmann Meml. lectr. U. Mich., 1958; vis. prof. Harvard, 1958-59, M. Tishler lectr., 1965; Reilly lectr. Notre Dame U., 1960; Am.-Swiss Found. lectr., 1960; O.M. Smith lectr. Okla. State U., 1962; M.S. Kharasch Meml. lectr. U. Chgo., 1962; K. Folkers lectr. U. Ill., 1962; Phillips lectr. Haverford Coll., 1963; vis. prof. U. Munich, 1962; Sloan lectr. U. Alaska, 1967; Disting. vis. prof. U. Iowa, 1967; Sprague lectr. U. Wis., 1967; Kilpatrick lectr. Ill. Inst. Tech., 1969; Pacific Northwest lectr., 1969; E.F. Smith lectr. U. Pa., 1970; vis. prof. chemistry Stanford U., 1973-74; S.C. Lind lectr. U. Tenn.; Arapahoe lectr. U. Colo., 1976; Mary E. Kapp lectr. Va. Commonwealth U., 1976; R.T. Major lectr. U. Conn., 1977; Nebr. lectr. Am. Chem. Soc., 1977; Leermakers lectr. Wesleyan U., 1980; Iddles Meml. lectr. U. N.H., 1981; Arapahoe lectr. Colo. State U., 1981; Winstein lectr. UCLA, 1981; Gilman lectr. Iowa State U., 1982; Marvel lectr. U. Ill., 1982; King lectr. Kans. State U., 1984; vis. lectr. Inst. Photog. Chemistry, Beijing, Peoples Republic China, 1983, Lanzhow U., Peoples Republic China, 1985; dir., cons. editor W.A. Benjamin, Inc., 1961-67; cons. E.I. du Pont Co., 1950—; mem. adv. panel chemistry NSF, 1958-60, chmn., 1959-60, chmn. divisional com. math., phys. engring. scis., 1962-64, mem. math. and phys. sci. div. com., 1964-66; chemistry adv. panel Air Force Office Sci. Research, 1959-61; chmn. chemistry sect. Nat. Acad. Scis., 1968-71; chmn. Nat. Acad. Scis. (Class I), 1976-78, councillor, 1980-83; dir. Organic Syntheses, Inc. Author: Basic Organic Chemistry, Part I, 1955, Nuclear Magnetic Resonance, 1958, Spin-Spin Splitting in High-Resolution Nuclear Magnetic Resonance Spectra, 1961, Molecular Orbital Calculations, 1961, (with M.C. Caserio) Basic Principles of Organic Chemistry, 1964, 2d edit., 1977, Modern Organic Chemistry, 1967, (with R. Stewart and M.C. Caserio) Organic Chemistry-Methane To Macromolecules, 1971; cons. editor: McGraw-Hill Series in Advanced Chemistry, 1957-60; editor-in-chief: Organic Syntheses, vol. 41; editorial bd.: Tetrahedron, Nouveau Chimie, Spectroscopy, Magnetic Resonance in Chemistry, Spectroscopy. Trustee L.S.B. Leakey Found.; bd. dirs. Huntington Med. Research Insts. Recipient Alumni Profl. Achievement award UCLA, 1967; Guggenheim fellow, 1952-53, 55-56; recipient Am. Chem. Soc. award pure chemistry, 1954; Harrison Howe award, 1957; Roger Adams award in organic chemistry, 1967; Alumni Achievement award UCLA, 1967; Nichols medal, 1972; Tolman medal, 1975; Michelson-Morley award, 1976; Norris award, 1978; Pauling award, 1980; Theodore Wm. Richards medal, 1982; Willard Gibbs Gold medal, 1983. Mem. Am. Chem. Soc. (chmn. organic chemistry div. 1956-57, exec. com. organic div. 1953-57), Nat. Acad. Scis., Am. Philos. Soc. (council), Internat. Soc. Magnetic Resonance (council), Am. Acad. Arts and Scis. (exec. com. Western sect.), Sigma Xi, Phi Lambda Upsilon, Alpha Chi Sigma. Current Work: Applications of nuclear magnetic resonance spectroscopy to organic chemistry; biology and medicine; computers and chemistry; theoretical organic chemistry. Subspecialties: Organic chemistry; Biochemistry (biology). Office: Calif Inst Tech Pasadena CA 91125

ROBERTS, JOHN LAWSON, chemist; b. Auckland, N.Z., July 3, 1947; came to U.S., 1975; s. William and Norma (Johnston) R.; m. Jennifer Beth Palmer, Feb. 21, 1970; children—Jan Molony, Sara Joanne, Amy Amanda, Melanie Alane, Stephen Parry, Michael Lawson. B.Sc., U. Auckland, 1967, M.Sc. with 1st honors, 1971, Ph.D., 1973. Lectr. Auckland Tech. Inst., 1972-73; postdoctoral fellow U. Alta., Edmonton, Can., 1974; research assoc. U. Utah, Salt Lake City, 1975-78; sr. research scientist Hoffmann La Roche, Nutley, N.J., 1978—. Contbr. articles to sci. jours. Postgrad. fellow Univ. Grants Com. N.Z., Auckland, 1971; postdoctoral fellow Univ. Grants Com. N.Z., Alta., 1974. Mem. Am. Chem. Soc. (divs. organic chemistry and medicinal chemistry). Mem. Ch. of Jesus Christ of Latter-day Saints. Current work: Synthetic organic chemistry, total synthesis of antibiotics, drug design in area of antibiotics, B-lactams, medicinal chemistry, enzyme inhibitors. Subspecialties: Synthetic chemistry; Medicinal chemistry. Home: 9 Glenside Dr Budd Lake NJ 07828 Office: Hoffmann LaRoche Chem Research Nutley NJ 07110

ROBERTS, JOSEPH, biochemist, researcher, educator; b. Bardejov, Czechoslovakia, May 24, 1936; came to U.S., 1963; s. Alexander and Anna (Stern) R.; m. Julie Roberts, Nov. 8, 1964; children: Lori Jennifer, Jeffrey Andrew. B.Sc., U. Toronto, 1959; M.S., U. Wis., 1961; Ph.D., McGill U., 1963. Research assoc. Johns Hopkins U., 1963-64; asst. prof. Baylor U., 1964-69, U. Wash., Seattle, 1969-73; assoc. prof. Cornell U., 1973-84; prof. U.S.C., 1984—; assoc. mem. lab. head Sloan-Kettering inst. Cancer Research, Rye, N.Y., 1973-84. Editor: Enzymes As Drugs, 1981. Leukemia Soc. Am. scholar, 1965-70; recipient Research Career Devel. award USPHS, 1971-73. Mem. Am. Assn. Cancer Research, Am. Chem. Soc. Current Work: Devel. of novel enzymes for use as therapeutic agents; enzyme engring.; devel. of new methods for targeting drugs to tumors. Subspecialties: Chemotherapy; Enzyme technology. Home: 6 Sunturf Circle Columbia SC 29223 Office: Coll Pharmacy USC Columbia SC 29208

ROBERTS, LIONA RUSSELL, JR., engineer, consultant; b. Sheffield, Ala., Apr. 9, 1928; s. Liona Russell and Julia Phillipia (Harrison) R.; m. Norma Jean Walker, Mar. 15, 1952 (div. 1972); children—Laura Lee, Boyd Harrison, John King, Jenna Lynne; m. Carole Jeanne Hedges, Dec. 29, 1973. B.S. in Physics, U. Miss., 1958; M.S. in Electronics Engr., U.S. Navy Grad. Sch., Monterey, Calif., 1961; Ph.D. in Mech. Engring., Catholic U. Am., 1977. Commd. ensign U.S. Navy, 1948, advanced through grades to capt., 1970; chief scientist Interstate Electronics, Anaheim, Calif., 1970-83; v.p. Enigmatics, Inc., La Habra, Calif., 1983—; vis. lectr. U. Calif.-Irvine, 1981—. Author: Signal Processing Techniques, 1977. Inventor drilling mud-gas detector, 1980. Mem. Service Acad. Selection Bd., Fullerton, 1982—. Mem. IEEE, Sigma Xi. Current work: Anti-submarine warfare, underwater acoustics, detection and estimated theory, signal processing. Subspecialty: Systems engineering. Home and office: 1885 Kashlan Rd La Habra CA 90631

ROBERTS, MICHAEL FOSTER, physiology educator; b. Guatemala, Aug. 8, 1943; came to U.S., 1945; s. Ralph Jackson and Arleda (Allen) R.; m. Mary Sherill Noe, Dec. 27, 1966; 1 child, Rosemary. B.A., U. Calif.-Berkeley, 1966; M.A., U. Wis.-Madison, 1968, Ph.D., 1972. Postdoctoral fellow in epidemiology Yale U., New Haven, Conn., 1972-76, asst. prof., 1976-81; asst. prof. biology Linfield Coll., McMinnville, Oreg., 1981-84, assoc. prof., 1984—; mem. peer rev. com. Oreg. affiliate of Am. Heart Assn., Portland, 1982—. Contbr. articles to profl. jours. NIH, Am. Heart Assn. grantee. Mem. Am. Physiol. Soc., Sigma Xi. Subspecialty: Physiology (biology). Office: Dept Biology Linfield Coll McMinnville OR 97128

ROBERTS, MORTON SPITZ, astronomer; b. N.Y.C., Nov. 5, 1926; m. Josephine Taylor, Aug. 2, 1951; 1 dau., Elizabeth Mason. B.A., Pomona Coll., 1948; Sc.D. (hon.), 1979; M.Sc., Calif. Inst. Tech., 1950; Ph.D. (Lick Obs. fellow), U. Calif., Berkeley, 1958. Asst. prof. physics Occidental Coll., 1949-52; lectr. astronomy dept. U. Calif., Berkeley, 1959-60; lectr., research asso. Harvard Coll. Obs., Harvard U., 1960-64; scientist Nat. Radio Astronomy Obs., Charlottesville, Va., 1964-68, sr. scientist, dir., 1978—; Sigma Xi nat. lectr., 1970-71; vis. educator SUNY, Stony Brook, 1968, Cambridge U., 1972, U. Groningen, 1972. Bd. editors: Astronomy and Astrophysics, 1971-80; asso. editor: Astron. Jour, 1977-79. NSF postdoctoral fellow, 1958-59. Mem. Am. Astron. Soc. (vis. prof. program 1965-73, v.p. 1971-72, mem. council 1983—, publs. bd. 1979-80), AAAS (council mem. 1973-79), Internat. Astron. Union, Internat. Sci. Radio Union., Nat. Acad. Sci. Current Work: Spectroscopy of extra galactic systems; scientific administration. Subspecialty: Radio and microwave astronomy. Home: 1826 Wayside Pl Charlottesville VA 22903 Office: Nat Radio Astronomy Obs Charlottesville VA 22901

ROBERTS, RALPH JACKSON, geologist, consultant; b. Rosalia, Wash., Jan. 31, 1911; s. Halcot Everett and Rhoda Eva (Boozer) R.; m. Arleda Hope Allen Roberts; children—Michael, Steven, Kim. Student Washington State U., 1930-32; B.S., U. Wash., 1935, M.S., 1937; Ph.D., Yale U., 1949. Registered geologist, Calif. Geologist, U.S. Geol. Survey, Washington, Salt Lake City, Menlo Park, Calif., 1939-80; vis. prof. Northwestern U., Evanston, Ill., spring, 1968. Contbr. articles to profl. jours. Recipient Distinguished Service award Dept. of Interior, 1983. Fellow Geol. Soc. Am.; mem. Soc. Econ. Geologists, Am. Inst. Mining Engrs., Sigma Xi. Current work: Studied controls of mineral deposits in western states and Saudi Arabia, leading to discovery of Carlin and Mahd adh Dhahab gold deposits. Exploration for gold deposits in northcentral Nevada. Subspecialty: Geology. Home: Box 136 Lilliwaup WA 98555 Office: 2000 Melarkey Winnemucca NV 89445

ROBERTS, RICHARD JOHN, molecular biologist, researcher; b. Derby, Eng., Sept. 6, 1943; came to U.S., 1969; s. John Walter and Edna Wilhelmina (Alsopp) R.; m. Elizabeth Dyson, Aug. 17, 1965 (dec.); children—Alison, Andrew. B.Sc., Sheffield U., Eng., 1965, Ph.D., 1968. Postdoctoral fellow Harvard U., Cambridge, Mass., 1969-70, research assoc., 1970-72; staff investigator Cold Spring Harbor Lab., 1972—; N.Y., cons. New Eng. Biolabs., Beverly, Mass., 1975—, Genex Corp., Rockville, Md., 1978—; mem. nat. adv. com. GENBANK, 1982, BIONET, 1984—. Contbr. numerous articles to sci. jours. Guggenheim Found. fellow, 1979. Mem. AAAS, Fedn. Am. Socs. for Exptl. Biology, Am. Soc. Microbiology. Current work: Restriction endonucleases and their applications for DNA sequence analysis and genetic engineering, molecular biology of adenovirus-2. Subspecialty: Molecular biology. Home: 1 Glen Ln Laurel Hollow NY 11724 Office: Cold Spring Harbor Lab Cold Spring Harbor NY 11724

ROBERTS, ROBERT RUSSELL, microbiologist; b. Fitchburg, Mass., Mar. 4, 1931; s. Mede Ira and Lillian Mae (Vogel) R.; m. Midori Komatsu, Dec. 24, 1953; children—Linda K., Lillian T., Ira G. B.S., Brigham Young U., 1970, M.S., 1972, Ph.D., 1975. Enlisted U.S. Army, 1948, advanced to sgt. maj., 1964; fixed communications sta. chief U.S. Army, 1948-68; microbiologist Hawaiian Sugar Planters Assn., Aiea, 1976—. Mem. Am. Soc. Microbiology, Soc. Indsl. Microbiology, Am. Chem. Soc., AAAS, N.Y. Acad. Sci., Sigma Xi. Mormon. Current work: Microbial fermentations; applications of microbiology to agriculture, immunological techniques for chemical analysis. Subspecialties: Microbiology; Immunobiology and immunology. Home: 92-737 Nenelea St Ewa Beach HI 96707 Office: Hawaiian Sugar Planters Assn 99-193 Aiea Heights Dr Aiea HI 96701

ROBERTS, THOMAS GEORGE, retired physicist; b. Ft. Smith, Ark., Apr. 27, 1929; s. Thomas Lawrence and Emma Lee (Stanley) R.; m. Alica Ann Harbin, Nov. 14, 1958; children—Lawrence Dewey, Regina Ann; foster child, Marcia Yvette Barber. A.A., Armstrong Coll., 1953; B.S., U. Ga., 1956, M.S., 1957; Ph.D., N.C. State U., 1967. Research physicist U.S. Army Missile Command, Huntsville, Ala., 1958-85; cons. industry and govt. agys., 1970—. Contbr. articles to profl. jours. Patentee in field. Served to sgt. USAF, 1948-52. Fellow Am. Optical Soc.; mem. Am. Phys. Soc., IEEE, Huntsville Optical Soc. Am. (pres. 1980). Episcopalian. Club: Toastmaster Internat. (pres. 1963). Current work: Laser physics, optics, particle beams and instrumentation; diagnostic devices and techniques development. Subspecialties: Laser physics; Plasma physics. Home: 2815 Bentley St SE Huntsville AL 35801 Office: Technoco PO Box 4723 Huntsville AL 35815

ROBERTS, WALTER ORR, solar astronomer; b. West Bridgewater, Mass., Aug. 20, 1915; s. Ernest Marion Roberts and Alice Elliot Orr; m. Janet Naomi Smock, June 8, 1940; children—David Stuart, Alan Arthur, Jennifer, Jonathan Orr. A.B., Amherst Coll., 1938, D.Sc. (hon.); M.A., Harvard U., 1940, Ph.D., 1943; D.Sc. (hon.), Ripon Coll., Colo. Coll., C.W. Post Coll. of L.I. U, Carleon Coll., Southwestern at Memphis Coll., U. Colo., U. Denver, U. Alaska; D.Eng. (hon.), Colo. Sch. Mines. Founder, dir. solar coronagraph sta. Harvard Coll. Obs., Climax, Colo., 1940-46; dir. High Altitude Obs., Boulder, Colo., 1946-60, Nat. Ctr. Atmospheric Research, Boulder, 1960-68; pres. Univ. Corp. for Atmospheric Research, Boulder, 1960-73, pres. emeritus, 1980—; dir. program in food, climate and the world's future Aspen Inst. Humanistic Studies, 1973-82. Author: A View of Century 21, 1970; (with H. Lansford) Climate Mandate, 1980; The Cold and the Dark, 1984. Recipient Hodgkins medal Smithsonian Instn., 1972; Mitchell prize Woodlands Conf., 1979, Internat. Environ. Leadership medal UN 1982. Mem. Am. Astron. Soc., AAAS, Internat. Astron. Union, Am. Geophys. Union, Am. Meteorol. Soc., Royal Astron. Soc., AIAA, Am. Acad. Arts and Scis., Internat. Acad. Astronautics, Air Pollution Control Assn., Quadrato della Radio, Colo.-Wyo. Acad. Sci., Fedn. Am. Scientists, Acad. Ind. Scholars, World Future Soc., Explorers Club, Council on Fgn. Relations, Phi Beta Kappa, Sigma Xi, Sigma Pi Sigma. Club: Century Assn. Current work: Climate and food relationships; sun-weather research. Subspecialties: Solar physics; Climatology. Home: 1829 Bluebell Ave Boulder CO 80302 Office: Univ Corp for Atmospheric Research PO Box 3000 Boulder CO 80307

ROBERTSON, ANDREW, scientific program administrator, aquatic ecology researcher; b. Port Huron, Mich., Sept. 15, 1936; s. Andrew and Agnes M. (Atkins) R.; m. Mary Steele Johnson, Dec. 19, 1965; children—Andrew, Ian Charles. B.S., U. Toledo, 1958; M.A., U. Mich., 1961, Ph.D., 1964. Research assoc. U. Mich., Ann Arbor, 1964-68; assoc. prof. U. Okla., Norman, 1968-71; fishery biologist Internat. Field Yr. for Gt. Lakes Project Office, NOAA, Rockville, Md., 1971-74, group head biology-chemistry Gt. Lakes Environ. Research Lab., Ann Arbor, 1974-81, dep. dir. Office Marine Pollution, Rockville, 1981-82, dir. Nat. Marine Pollution Program Office, 1982—; cons. Commonwealth Edison, Chgo., 1969-73; dir. U. Okla. Fishery Lab., Noble, 1970-71. Editor: Lake Ecosystem Modeling, 1979. Contbr. articles to profl. jours. Mem. Ecol. Soc. Am., Am. Soc. Limnology and Oceanography, Crustacean Soc., Internat. Assn. for Gt. Lakes Research (pres. 1966-67, assoc. editor 1982—). Subspecialties: Environmental chemistry; Ecology (environmental science). Home: 9336 Orchard Brook Potomac MD 20854 Office: NMPPO/NOAA N/MPP Room 610 Rockwall Bldg 11400 Rockville Pike Rockville MD 20852

ROBERTSON, BRIAN MAX, psychiatrist, psychoanalyst; b. Christchurch, Canterbury, N.Z., July 23, 1940; came to Can., 1967; s. Malcolm and Dorothy Elisabeth (Rogers) R.; m. Suzanne Shirley Corbett, Aug. 19, 1961 (div. 1974); children—Johanna Ruth, Malcolm; m. Erica Judith Hall, May 24, 1974; children—Colin Brian, Catherine Erica. M.B., Ch.B., Otago U., Dunedin, N.Z., 1964; Diploma in Psychiatry, McGill U., Montreal, Que., Can., 1971. Intern,

Christchurch Hosp. 1965-66; resident Douglas Hosp., Verdun, Que., Can., 1967-68, Jewish Gen. Hosp., Montreal, 1968-69, Royal Victoria Hosp., Montreal, 1969-71; staff psychiatrist Douglas Hosp., Montreal, 1971-80, dir. psychotherapy, 1975-76, dir. med. edn., 1977-80; dir. Sloan Meml. Inst., Royal Victoria Hosp., Montreal, 1981—, psychiatrist-in-chief, 1981—; cons. psychiatrist Maimonides Hosp., Montreal, 1981—; lectr. dept. psychiatry McGill U., 1971-76, asst. prof., 1976-80, assoc. prof., 1981—. Contbr. articles to profl. publs. Mem. Commn. de Sante Mentale de Conseil Regional, Montreal, 1983—, Commn. Executif de Sante Mentale, Montreal, 1985. Mem. Que. Psychiat. Assn., Can. Psychiat. Assn., Royal Coll. Physicians Surgeons Can., Can., Internat. Psychoanalytic Soc., Can. Psychoanalytic Inst. (pres. Que. English br. 1981), Nat. Inst. Psychoanalysis Can. (sec.-treas. 1983—). Current work: Hospital administration, teaching psychotherapy, psychoanalysis, application of psychoanalytic theory to organizations, technique of psychoanalysis. Subspecialty: Psychiatry. Office: Allan Meml Inst 1025 Pine Ave W Montreal PQ H3A 1A1 Canada

ROBERTSON, GENE DIXON, electronics engineer, electronics manufacturing company executive; b. Overland, Mo., July 22, 1924; s. Watson Nimrod and Lucile (Vance) R.; m. Jean Ellen Ryan, May 21, 1946; children—Thomas, Diane, Wendy, Bruce, Katherine, Amy. B.S., U. Tex., 1945; S.B., MIT, 1948; D.Engring. (hon.), Tri-State U., 1985. Registered prof. engr., D.C. Sr. v.p. research and devel. Magnavox Govt. & Indsl. Elec. Co., Ft. Wayne, Ind., 1953—, also dir.; mem. tech. staff Bell Telephone Labs., Whippany, N.J., 1965-66. Bd. dirs. Anthony Wayne Rehab. Ctr., Ft. Wayne, 1978—, Ft. Wayne Mental Health Ctr., 1982—. Summit Tech. Ind. Com. for Humanities, 1984—. Served from ensign to lt. USN, 1945-53. Decorated Merit medal. Mem. IEEE sr., AAAS. Club: Quest (Ft. Wayne) (gov.). Current work: Underwater acoustics, information theory, computer science, communications systems. Office: Magnavox Govt and Indsl Elec Co 1313 Production Rd Fort Wayne IN 46808

ROBERTSON, JAMES BRAGG, educator; b. Plainfield, N.J., Mar. 7, 1943; s. James Bragg and Lee (Pace) R.; married; children: James, Andrea, George, Denise. B.Sc., Miami U., Oxford, Ohio, 1969; M.S., Harvard U., 1974, Sc.D., 1976. Diplomate: Am. Bd. Toxicology. Research scientist Los Alamos (N.Mex.) Sci. Lab., 1976-77; research assoc. Harvard U., Sch. Pub. Health, Cambridge, Mass., 1977-80; asst. prof. Clarkson Coll. Tech., Potsdam, N.Y., 1980-85; assoc. prof. East Carolina U., Greenville, N.C., 1985—; cons. Harvard U., 1980—, Canadian U. Ins. Co., Boston, 1983. Contbr. articles to profl. jours. Served to 1st lt. USMC, 1961-72. Recipient Culler prize Miami U., Ohio, 1968; AEC spl. fellow, 1972-74. Mem. Radiation Research Soc., Am. Forestry Assn., Sigma Xi. Current Work: Med. application of laser activated flow microfluorometry; detection of environmental mutagens/carcinogens; late health effects of nuclear power; space travel. Subspecialties: Toxicology (medicine); Cancer research (medicine). Home: Route 2 Box 383 Chocowinty NC 27817 Office: Dept Environ Health East Carolina U Greenville NC 27834

ROBERTSON, JAMES CRAIG, nuclear engineering educator, researcher; b. Kinlichleven, Scotland, Mar. 29, 1936; came to U.S., 1976, naturalized, 1982; s. Charles Alexander and Isabel Blyth (Craig) R.; m. Moira Malcolm Campbell, Aug. 18, 1961; children—Alan, David. B.S. with honors, Glasgow U., 1957, Ph.D., 1961. Lic. sr. reactor operator. Sci. sr. officer Nat. Phys. Lab., Teddington, Eng., 1961-72; lectr., radiation safety officer Dundee Coll. Tech., Scotland, 1972-76; assoc. prof. U. Mich., Ann Arbor, 1976-78; assoc. prof. U. N.Mex., Albuquerque, 1978-80, prof., 1980—; cons. B.D.M. Corp., Albuquerque, 1982-83, City of Albuquerque, 1982, Scotoil Inspection, Scotland, 1975. Author: A Guide to Radiation Protection, 1976. Author sci. articles. Varsity coach U. N.Mex. Soccer Team, 1983—. Mem. Am. Nuclear Soc., IEEE. Presbyterian. Current work: nuclear instrumentation, nuclear data acquisition and measurement, nuclear physics, health physics. Subspecialties: Nuclear fusion; Nuclear engineering. Home: 3509 Haines Ave Albuquerque NM 87106 Office: U NMex Dept Chem and Nuclear Engring Albuquerque NM 87131

ROBERTSON, JAMES RICHARD, JR., polymer chemist, industrial researcher; b. Atlanta; s. James Richard Robertson and Betty Anne (Perkins) Archer; m. Janice Duncan, Dec. 15, 1973. B.S., North Ga. Coll., Dahlonega, 1973; B.S., Ga. Inst. Tech., 1975, M.S., 1978, Ph.D., 1981. Grad. research asst., Ga. Inst. Tech., Atlanta, 1975-80; sr. research chemist Am. Enka Co., N.C., 1980-82; sr. organic chemist Ciba Vision Care, Atlanta, 1982-84, research scientist, 1984—. Active Simpsonwood United Methodist Ch., Norcross, Ga., 1983—. Recipient Honors award Textile Vets. Assn., 1975; Gulf Oil fellow, 1976, Tenn. Eastman fellow, 1978. Mem. Am. Chem. Soc., N.Y. Acad. Scis., S.W. Contact Lens Soc. (speaker). Current work: Polymer chemistry and engineering for opthalmic products including contact lenses, eye care solutions, biomaterial replacement surgical materials. Subspecialties: Polymer chemistry; Biomaterials. Home: 3415 Aubusson Trace Alpharetta GA 30201 Office: Ciba Vision Care 2910 Amwiler Ct Atlanta GA 30360

ROBERTSON, LARRY DEE, plant breeder; b. Gooding, Idaho, May 15, 1939; s. Alma Alexander and Phyllis Sarah (Larsen) R.; m. Joe Anne Severance, May 22, 1959 (div. July 1978); children—Andrew Lane, David Allen, Janice Elaine, Dana Rae; m. Lanaia Aleen Sims, Mar. 9, 1979; children—Benjamin LaMar, Lyle Douglas. B.S., West Tex. State U., 1963; M.S., Colo. State U., 1965, Ph.D., 1966. Mgr. wheat research Funk Seeds Internat., Bloomington, Ill., 1966-73; sr. wheat breeder N.Am. Plant Breeders, Berthoud, Colo., 1973-78; owner, operator Plants-n-Things Garden, Loveland, Colo., 1978-79; head Colby Experiment Sta., Kans. State U., Colby, 1979—. NDEA fellow, 1963. Mem. Am. Soc. Agronomy, Crop Sci. Soc. Am., Sigma Xi. Republican. Mormon. Current work: Plant breeding, conservation tillage, crop production systems, alternative crops, horticultural crops. Subspecialties: Plant genetics; Agronomy. Office: Colby Experiment Station Rural Route 2 Box 830 Colby KS 67701

ROBERTSON, LAWRENCE MARSHALL, electrical engineering consultant; b. Denver, Jan. 20, 1900; s. Hugh Lawrence and Grace (Worden) R.; m. Nov. 15, 1924 (dec. July 29, 1971); 1 child, Lawrence M., Jr. B.E.E., U. Colo., 1922, E.E., 1927, M.E.E., 1938; LL.B., Westminster Law Sch., 1930; J.D., U. Denver, 1979; Dr. Engring. (hon.), U. Colo., 1955. Registered profl. engr. Colo., Wyo., Wash., Calif., Ill., N.Y. Engr. Pub. Service Co. Colo., Denver, 1922-25, engr. in charge, 1925-48, supr., 1948-53, mng. engr., 1953-66, v.p. engring., 1966-68, ret.; cons. Power Authority, Buenos Aires, Argentina, 1969, Pub. Service Dist. Wenatchee, Washington, 1976-79, Pub. Service Co. Santo Domingo, Dominican Republic, 1981; tech. adv. Fed. Power Commn. Gen. Power Survey, 1962-67. Author: U.S. Safety Ski Lifts U.S. Standard Electrical, 1975. Chmn. com. waste Denver Regional Council, 1971; mem., chmn. State Bd. Registration-Engring., Denver, 1969-69; adv. Denver Pub. Library, 1943-60. Served with U.S. Army, 1918. Named Disting. Alumnus, U. Colo., 1968; recipient Attwood award Conf. Internat., Paris, 1982. Fellow IEEE (v.p. 1945-47, chmn. sect. 1941, bd. dirs. 1956-69, centennial medal, 1984, Habersham award 1963), mem. Colo. Engring. Council (pres. 1950—, Gold medal 1954), Colo. Soc. Engrs. (pres. 1948, Ryan award 1969), Sigma Xi. Republican. Methodist. Lodge: Masons. Current work: Power generation and transmission electric. Subspecialties: Electrical engineering; Systems engineering. Home: 320 Ash St Denver CO 80220

ROBERTSON, LESLIE EARL, structural engineer; b. Los Angeles, Feb. 12, 1928; s. Garnet Roy and Tina (Grantham) R.; m. Saw-Teen See, Aug. 11, 1982; children: Jeanne, Christopher Alan, Sharon Miyuki, Karla Mei. B.S., U. Calif., Berkeley, 1952. Structural engr. Kaiser Engrs., Oakland, Calif., 1952-54, John A. Blume, San Francisco, 1954-57, Raymond Internat. Co., N.Y.C., 1957-58; mng. ptnr. Skilling, Helle, Christiansen, Robertson, N.Y.C., Seattle and Anchorage, 1958-82; chmn. Robertson, Fowler & Assocs., P.C., N.Y.C., 1982—; vice chmn. Council on Tall Bldgs. and Urban Habitat; commr. NRC, vice chmn. Com. Earthquake Engring, Facilities and Instrumentation, also mem. com. on natural disasters; dir. Wind Engring. Research Council; Vollmer W. Fries lectr. Rensselaer Poly. Inst., 1984; Richard J. Carroll Meml. lectr. Johns Hopkins U., 1985. Author papers in field. Mem. Engring. Coll. Council Cornell U. Served with USNR, 1944-46. Fellow ASCE (Raymond C. Reese Research prize 1974); mem. Nat. Acad. Engring. Subspecialty: Structural engineering. Home: PO Box 8284 New Fairfield CT 06812 Office: 211 E 46th St New York NY 10017

ROBERTSON, RICHARD EARL, chemist, physicist; b. Long Beach, Calif., Nov. 12, 1933; s. Earl Austin and Alice Isobel (Roberts) R.; m. Joyce W. Conger, Sept. 4, 1955 (div. 1972); children—Christopher E., Jill K.; m. Patricia L. Richmond, Apr. 20, 1974. B.A., Occidental Coll. 1955; postgrad. UCLA; Ph.D., Calif. Inst. Tech., 1960. Postdoctoral fellow Washington. U., St. Louis, Mo., 1959-60; phys. chemist Gen. Elec. Research and Devel. Ctr., Schenectady, 1960-70; staff sci. Ford Motor Co., Dearborn, Mich., 1970—. Contbr. numerous articles to profl. jours. Fellow Am. Phys. Soc.; mem. Am. Chem. Soc., Sigma Xi. Current work: Polymer structure and mechanical properties, theory; fibre composites; properties fatigue and failure. Subspecialties: Polymer physics; Composite materials. Office: Ford Motor Co Research Staff PO Box 2053 Dearborn MI 48121-2053

ROBIN, MITCHELL WOLFE, psychology educator; b. Bklyn., Apr. 30, 1944; s. Ben and Lee (White) R.; m. Regina Catherine Spires, Mar. 26, 1972; children: Elaine Dara, Abigail Alice. B.B.A., Baruch Sch. CCNY, 1965; M.A., New Sch. Social Research, 1969; Ph.D., NYU, 1983. Teaching fellow Baruch Sch. CCNY, 1965-67; lectr. N.Y.C. T.C., CUNY, 1968-70, asst. prof., 1970—; mem. faculty New Sch. for Social Research, 1970—; cons. in field. Contbr. articles to profl. jours.; co-author/contbr.: Cross Cultural Psychology at Issue, 1982; media cons.: jour. Psychology, 1971-72; contbr. articles to profl. jours. Mem. Am. Psychol. Assn., Internat. Orgn. for Study of Group Tensions (exec. sec.), Internat. Council Psychologists, Psi Chi. Democrat. Jewish. Current Work: Cross cultural approaches to child rearing and handling of deviance in childhood; psychological impact of video games. Subspecialty: Developmental psychology. Office: Social Sci Dept CUNY 300 Jay St Brooklyn NY 11201

ROBINS, E. CLAIBORNE, JR., See *Who's Who in America,* 43rd edition.

ROBINS, LEE NELKEN, sociology educator; b. New Orleans, Aug. 29, 1922; d. Abe and Leona (Reiman) Nelken; m. Eli Robins, Feb. 22, 1946; children: Paul, James, Thomas, Nicholas. Student, Newcomb Coll., 1938-40; B.A., Radcliffe Coll., 1942, M.A., 1943, Ph.D., 1951. Mem. faculty Washington U., St. Louis, 1954—, prof. sociology in psychiatry, 1968—, prof. sociology, 1969—; former mem. Nat. Adv. Council on Drug Abuse, Pres.'s Commn. on Mental Health task panels; expert adv. panel mental health WHO.; Salmon lectr. N.Y. Acad. Medicine, 1983. Author 3 monographs; editor 7 books; contbr. articles to profl. jours. Recipient Research Scientist award USPHS, 1970—; Pacesetter Research award Nat. Inst. Drug Abuse, 1978; Radcliffe Coll. Grad. Soc. medal, 1979; Research grantee NIMH; Research grantee Nat. Inst. on Drug Abuse; Research grantee Nat. Inst. on Alcohol Abuse and Alcoholism. Fellow Am. Coll. Epidemiology; Mem. Am. Sociol. Assn., Internat. Sociol. Assn., Inst. of Medicine, Internat. Epidemiological Assn., Soc. Epidemiol. Research, Am. Psychopathol. Assn. (Paul Hoch award 1978, v.p. 1985), Am. Public Health Assn. (Rema Lapouse award 1979), Soc. Life History Research in Psychopathology, Am. Coll. Neuropsychopharmacology. Current Work: Risk and protective factors in major mental disorders. Subspecialties: Epidemiology; Psychiatry. Office: Dept Psychiatry Med Sch Washington U Saint Louis MO 63110

ROBINS, MORRIS JOSEPH, organic chemist, educator; b. Nephi, Utah, Sept. 28, 1939; s. Waldo George and Mary Erda (Anderson) R.; m. Jerri Johnson, June 11, 1960 (div. 1972); children—Dayne M., Diane, Douglas W., Debra, Dale C.; m. Jackie Alene Robinson, Aug. 24, 1973; children: Mark K., Janetta A. B.A., U. Utah, 1961; Ph.D., Ariz. State U., 1965. Cancer research scientist Roswell Park Meml. Inst., Buffalo, 1965-66; research assoc. U. Utah, Salt Lake City, 1966-69; asst. prof. dept. chemistry U. Alta. (Can.), Edmonton, 1969-71, asso. prof., 1971-78, prof., 1978—; cons. in organic biochemistry. Mem. editorial bd.: Nucleic Acids Research, 1980-83; contbr. articles to profl. jours. NSF fellow, 1963-64. Mem. Am. Chem. Soc., Am. Assn. for Cancer Research, Chem. Inst. Can., Phi Beta Kappa, Sigma Xi, Phi Eta Sigma, Phi Kappa Phi. Mormon. Patentee in field. Current Work: Organic chemistry and biol. effects of nucleic acid related compounds, nucleoside and nucleotide chemistry; biol. effects of nucleosides and analogues; organic and bioorganic chemistry edn. Subspecialties: Organic chemistry; Medicinal chemistry. Office: Dept Chemistry U Alberta Edmonton AB T6G 2G2 Canada

ROBINS, NORMAN ALAN, steel company executive; b. Chgo., Nov. 19, 1934; s. Irving and Sylvia (Robbin) R.; m. Sandra Ross, June 10, 1956; children: Lawrence Richard, Sherry Lynn. S.B. in Chem. Engring, MIT, 1955, S.M., 1956; Ph.D. in Math, Ill. Inst. Tech., 1972. Metallurgist Inland Steel Co., Chgo., 1956-60, research metallurgist, 1960-62, asst. mgr., 1962-67, assoc. mgr., 1967-72, dir. process research, 1972-77, v.p. research, 1977-84, v.p. technol. assessment, 1984—. Mem. Am. Iron and Steel Inst. (Regional Tech. Meeting award 1967, 72), AIME (Nat. Open Hearth Conf. award 1972), Am. Inst. Chem. Engrs., Indsl. Research Inst., Mathematics Assn. Am. Patentee: (with F.H. Bugajski) control of coating thickness of hot-dip metal coating. Current Work: Process modelling and computer control. Subspecialties: Chemical engineering; Metallurgical engineering. Office: 3210 Watling St East Chicago IN 46312

ROBINSON, CLARK, mathematics educator, researcher; b. Seattle, Dec. 29, 1943; s. Rex J. and Ruth E. (Clark) R.; m. Margaret Susan Crose, Aug. 20, 1966. B.S., U. Wash., 1966; Ph.D., U. Calif.-Berkeley, 1969. Asst. prof. math. Northwestern U., Evanston, Ill., 1969-73, assoc. prof., 1973-78, prof., 1978—, chmn. math. dept., 1984—. Contbr. articles to math. jours. NSF grantee, 1969—. Mem. Am. Math. Soc., Math. Assn. Am., Soc. Indsl. and Applied Math. Presbyterian. Current work: Structural stability questions in dynamical systems, questions of resonance of nonlinear oscillators. Subspecialty: Analysis. Office: Northwestern U 2033 Sheridan Rd Evanston IL 60201

ROBINSON, DEAN WENTWORTH, chemist, educator; b. Boston, July 22, 1929; s. Lawrence Dean and Doris Elizabeth (Prowse) R.; children: Dean W., Amy E., Jonas W. B.S., U. N.H., 1951, M.S., 1952; Ph.D., M.I.T., 1955. Mem. faculty Johns Hopkins, 1955—, prof. chemistry, chmn. dept., 1976-83. Author research papers. Guggenheim fellow, 1966; Fulbright fellow, 1966. Mem. Am. Chem. Soc., AAAS. Current Work: Polyatomic chemical lasers; gas-phase kinetics and energy transfer; laser induced physical chemistry. Subspecialties: Laser photochemistry; Laser-induced chemistry. Home: 10 Sonachan Ct Baltimore MD 21204 Office: Chemistry Dept Johns Hopkins U Baltimore MD 21218

ROBINSON, EARL JAMES, information systems educator; b. Wilmington, Del., Apr. 15, 1949; s. Harry and Minerva Ruth (James) R.; m. Karen Frances Smith, July 5, 1980; children—Ruth Frances, Sarah Rebecca. A.B., Davidson Coll., 1971; M.S., Bucknell U., 1973; Ph.D., U. Ga., 1977. Registered psychologist, N.S. Testing services asst. dir. Central Susquehanna Intermediate Unit, Lewisburg, Pa., 1972-73; asst. dir. Instr. Evaluation Services, Athens, Ga., 1973-77; asst prof. U. Ga., Athens, 1977-78; asst prof. St. Mary's U., Halifax, N.S., 1978-81, assoc. prof. mgmt. sci., 1981-84, chmn. dept., 1981-84; assoc. prof. info. systems St. Joseph's U., Phila., 1984—, chmn. dept., 1984—; cons. in field; bd. dirs. Internat. Assn. Students of Econs. and Commerce, Halifax, 1982-84. Contbr. articles to profl. jours. Recipient Golden 'M' award St. Mary's U., 1981; NSF grantee, 1978; FAA grantee, 1978; Ashland Oil Corp. grantee, 1978. Mem. Am. Inst. Decision Scis., Am. Psychol. Assn., Can. Psychol. Assn., Am. Statis. Assn., Ops. Research Soc. Am., Inst. Mgmt. Sci., Psychometric Soc., Sigma Xi, Sigma Phi Epsilon. Current Work: Active in in-roads into applied computer tech. and edn., specifically in social scis., tech. in higher levels of statis. analysis. Subspecialty: Information systems (Information science). Home: 150 Union Ave Bala Cynwyd PA 19004 Office: Mgmt and Info Systems Dept Saint Joseph's U 5600 City Ave Philadelphia PA 19004

ROBINSON, EDWARD J., physicist, educator; b. N.Y.C., June 16, 1936; s. Irving L. and Fannie (Freeman); m. Toni Sandler, Dec. 26, 1959; children: Ian S., Gregory J. B.S., Queens Coll., 1957; Ph.D., NYU, 1964. Research assoc. Joint Inst. Lab. Astrophysics, Boulder, Colo., 1964-65; mem. faculty NYU, N.Y.C., 1965—, prof. physics, 1982—. Contbr. articles to profl. jours. Mem. Am. Phys. Soc. Current Work: Atomic and molecular physics, including laser-related problems and scattering theory. Subspecialties: Atomic and molecular physics; Theoretical physics. Office: 4 Washington Pl New York NY 10003

ROBINSON, FARREL RICHARD, pathologist, toxicologist; b. Wellington, Kans., Mar. 23, 1927; s. Farrel Otis and Norine (Sloan) R.; m. Mimi Agatha Hathaway, June 5, 1949; children—Farrel Richard, Kelly S., E. Scott, Brian A. B.S., Kans. State U., 1950, D.V.M., M.S., 1958; Ph.D., Tex. A&M U., 1965. Diplomate: Am. Coll. Vet. Pathologists, Am. Bd. Vet. Toxicology (v.p. 1971-74, pres. 1976-79). Served with USN, 1945-46; commd. 2d lt. USAF, 1951, advanced through grades to lt. col., 1971; vet. pathologist Aerospace Med. Research Labs., Wright-Patterson AFB, Ohio, 1958-68; chief Vet. Pathology div. Armed Forces Inst. Pathology, Washington, 1968-74; ret., 1974; scientist asso. Univs. Asso. for Research and Edn. in Pathology, Inc., 1972-74; asst. clin. prof. pathology George Washington U. Sch. Medicine, 1972-74; instr. NIH Grad. Program, 1973-74; prof. toxicology-pathology Sch. Vet. Medicine, Purdue U., 1974—; dir. Animal Disease Diagnostic Lab., 1978-85, head dept. vet. sci., 1978-85, cons. vet. pathology USAF surg. gen. and asst. surg. gen. for vet. services, 1970-74. Mem. editorial bd.: Human and Vet. Toxicology, 1976—; Contbr. sci. articles to profl. jours. Decorated USAF Commendation medal, Meritorious Service medal; recipient Aerospace Med. Research Labs. Scientist of Year award, 1967. Mem. AVMA, Am. Coll. Vet. Toxicologists, Am. Assn. Vet. Lab. Diagnosticians (gov.), Wildlife Disease Assn., Conf. Research Workers in Animal Disease, Soc. Toxicology, Am. Animal Health Assn., Sigma Xi, Phi Kappa Phi, Alpha Zeta, Phi Zeta. Democrat. Methodist. Current Work: Pathologic changes caused by chemicals. Subspecialties: Pathology (veterinary medicine); Toxicology (medicine). Home: 201 W 600 N West Lafayette IN 47906 Office: Animal Disease Diagnostic Lab Purdue U West Lafayette IN 47907

ROBINSON, HARRY JOHN, med. adminstr.; b. Elizabeth, N.J., July 30, 1913; s. Harry and Ann (McCourt) R.; m. Marion Neunert, Sept. 9, 1939; children: Linda Miele, Harry John, Raymond P. B.A. in Biology, N.Y. U., 1940; Ph.D. in Microbiology, Rutgers U., 1943; M.D., Columbia U., 1948; D.Sc. (hon.), Bucknell U., 1974. Asst. dir. research Merck Inst., Rahway, N.J., 1943-48, assoc. dir., 1948-56, dir., 1956-65; pres. Quinton Co. div. Merck & Co., Inc., Rahway, 1965-68; sr. v.p. Merck Sharp & Dohme Research Labs., 1968-70, v.p. sci. affairs, 1971-76; v.p. med. affairs Allied Corp., Morristown, N.J., 1976—; acting chmn. dept. bacteriology Coll. Medicine and Dentistry N.J., 1960-62, now clin. prof. medicine.; Mem. N.J. State Sci. Adv. Com., 1981—, N.J. Pub. Health Council, 1953-77. Contbr. numerous articles to sci. jours. Office Sci. Research and Devel. grantee, 1945. Mem. Am. Soc. Clin. Investigation, Am. Soc. Clin. Pharmacology and Therapeutics, Am. Soc. Microbiology, Am. Soc. Pharmacology and Exptl. Therapeutics, Infectious Diseases Soc., Genetic Toxicology Assn., Royal Soc. Medicine, Soc. Exptl. Biology and Medicine. Congregationalist. Clubs: Princeton (N.Y.C.); Baltusrol Country (Springfield, N.J.). Current Work: Diagnostic medicine, preventive medicine, therapeutics, toxicology, clinical chemistry, biotechnology, immunology, immunoassays applied to diagnosis and treatment of disease. Subspecialties: Microbiology (medicine); Molecular pharmacology.

ROBINSON, JAMES LAWRENCE, biochemist, educator; b. Boston, Feb. 23, 1942; s. Lawrence Hanny and C. Ruth (Conklin) R.; m. Janet Lynn Thorpe, Feb. 23, 1963; children—Mark L., Marjorie L., J. Glen. B.S. in Chemistry, U. Redlands, 1964; Ph.D. in Biochemistry, UCLA, 1968. Postdoctoral researcher Inst. Cancer Research, Phila., 1968-70; asst. prof. U. Ill., Urbana, 1970-76, assoc. prof. biochemistry, 1976-85, prof., 1985—; vis. scientist Centre de Nutrition, Meudon, France, 1978-79. Contbr. articles to profl. jours. Named Excellent Tchr., U. Ill., 1978, 1980; grantee Nat. Dairy Council, 1974-83, Holstein Assn., 1984-87. Mem. Am. Soc. Biol. Chemists, Am. Dairy Sci. Assn., Am. Inst. Nutrition. Democratic. Methodist. Current work: Metabolic regulation; inherited enzyme deficiency in dairy cattle; consequences of orotic acid consumption in man and other species. Subspecialties: Biochemistry (biology); Nutrition (biology). Home: 902 Mumford Dr Urbana IL 61801 Office: U Ill Dept Animal Sci 1207 W Gregory Dr Urbana IL 61801

ROBINSON, JAMES ROBERT, engineering administrator, educator; b. Pitts., Apr. 18, 1927; s. Roger Robert and Marie (McDermott) R. B.S.M.E., U. Pitts., 1952; postgrad., San Diego State U., 1979. Supr. Devel. Lab., Reaction Motors Inc., Denville, N.J., 1952-54; flight test engr., asst. site mgr. Gen. Dynamics, Convair, San Diego, 1954-60, sr. project engr., 1960-69, site mgr., Quincy, Mass., 1969-75; lectr. in elec./computer engring. San Diego State U., 1976—; engring. mgr. Sci. Applications, Ft. Irwin Facility, La Jolla, Calif., 1982—, lectr. energy conversion systems; researcher, report co-author Satellite Receiver Sta., 1981. Editor-in-chief: Skyscraper Engr, 1950-51. Mem. Republican Presdl. Task Force, Washington. Mem. IEEE (exec. com. at large), IEEE Computer Soc. (chmn. San Diego chpt. 1982—), Soc. Photooptical Instrumentation Engrs., Air Force Assn., Amateur Radio Relay League, Pi Tau Sigma, Sigma Beta Sigma. Republican. Presbyterian. Current work: Distributed systems and networks: local area networks, assisting in establishing 1800 Port Packet switching network for USAF; fiber optics: development of fibre optic local area network in conjunction with distributed systems and networks: satellite studies. Subspecialties: Distributed systems and networks; Robotics. Office: Science Applications Inc 1200 Prospect La Jolla CA 92038 Office: San Diego State U San Diego CA 92182

ROBINSON, RUSSELL LEE, scientific administrator, researcher; b. Louisville, July 30, 1931; s. Russell Bates and Margaret Lee Robinson; m. Velda June Flener, Aug. 1, 1953; children—Jannelle, Julie, Rachel. B.S., U. Louisville, 1953, M.S., Ind. U., 1955, Ph.D., 1958. Research scientist Oak Ridge Nat. Lab., Tenn., 1958-74, group leader, 1974-83, sci. dir. Holifield Heavy Ion Research Facility, 1983—. Editor: Nuclear Spin Parity Assignment, 1956; Reactions between Complex Nuclei, 1974. Contbr. articles to prof. jours. Fellow Am. Phys. Soc.; mem. Am. Phys. Soc. Baptist. Current work: Scientific director of the Holifield Heavy Ion Research Facility. Research in gamma-ray-spectroscopy and in reaction mechanisms of nuclei. Subspecialty: Nuclear physics. Home: 134 Newell Ln Oak Ridge TN 37830 Office: Oak Ridge Nat Lab Oak Ridge TN 37831

ROBISON, G(EORGE) ALAN, pharmacology educator; b. Lethbridge, Alta., Can., Nov. 4, 1934; s. Douglas Charles and Margaret Elizabeth (Barr) R.; m. Jill Jeanine Seaman, Mar. 12, 1956; children: James Darcy, Amelia N'Orlean. B.Sc., U. Alta., 1957; M.S., Tulane U., 1960, Ph.D., 1962. Postdoctoral research fellow Western Res. U., Cleve., 1962-63; research assoc. Vanderbilt U., Nashville, 1963-64, instr. dept. pharmacology, 1964-66, asst. prof., 1966-70, assoc. prof. physiology and pharmacology, 1970-72; prof., chmn. dept. pharmacology U. Tex. Med. Sch.-Houston, 1972—; mem. research council Nelson Research and Devel. Co., Irvine, Calif., 1971—. Author: (with R.W. Butcher and E.W. Sutherland) Cyclic AMP, 1971; editor: (with P. Greengard) Advances in Cyclic Nucleotide Research, 1972—; contbr. articles to profl. jours. Recipient J. Murray Luck award Nat. Acad. Scis., 1979. Mem. Am. Chem. Soc., Am. Soc. Pharmacology and Exptl. Therapeutics, Endocrine Soc., Soc. Neurosci., Am. Humanist Assn. Current Work: Mechanism of drug action; cyclic nucleotide research. Subspecialties: Molecular pharmacology; Cellular pharmacology. Home: 250 Stoney Creek Houston TX 77024 Office: PO Box 20708 Houston TX 77025

ROBKIN, MAURICE ABRAHAM, nuclear engineer; b. N.Y.C., Apr. 25, 1931; s. Simon and Sylvia (Grauer) R.; m. Anne Lou Hawkins, Dec. 30, 1962; children—Matthew Holmes, Jeremy Alexander, Susan Ruth. B.S., Calif. Inst. Tech., 1953; cert., Oak Ridge Reactor Tech. Sch., 1954; Ph.D., M.I.T., 1961. Registered profl. engr., Wash. Scientist Bettis Atomic Power Lab., Pitts., 1954-56; sr. scientist Vallecitos Atomic Lab., Pleasanton, Calif., 1961-67; mem. faculty U. Wash., Seattle, 1967—, prof. nuclear engring., 1979—, prof. environ. health, 1981—, dir. Nuclear Reactor Lab., 1983—. Author papers in field. Mem. Am. Nuclear Soc., AAAS, Radiation Research Soc., Health Physics Soc., N.Y. Acad. Scis., Sigma Xi. Developed service for invitro culture of rodent embryos. Current work: Teaching and research in nuclear engineering and health physics. Office: BF10 U Wash Seattle WA 98195

ROCCA, JEFFREY JOHN, biomedical engineer, computer scientist; b. Jersey City, Apr. 18, 1956; s. Theodore and Martha (Onuschak) R. B.S., Rutgers U., 1978, M.S., 1980. Project engr. Electro-Biology, Inc., Fairfield, N.J., 1980-81; software engr. New Brunswick Sci. Co., Edison, N.J., 1981-83; computer scientist Siemens Med. Systems, Inc., Iselin, N.J., 1983—. Mem. IEEE, ACM, Tau Beta Pi, Eta Kappa Nu, Upsilon Pi Epsilon. Current work: Research and development activities in the area of computer systems and software for magnetic resonance imaging. Subspecialties: Magnetic resonance imaging; Software engineering. Home: 34 Raven Dr Colonia NJ 07067 Office: Siemens Med Systems Inc 186 Wood Ave S Iselin NJ 08830

ROCCO, VINCENT ANTHONY, environmental consultant; b. Hoboken, N.J., Mar. 13, 1945; s. Bernard James and Margaret (Gloria) R.; m. Mary Elizabeth Bathe, Oct. 11, 1969. B.S. in Mech. Engring., Stevens Inst. Tech., 1967; M.S., U. Tenn.-Tullahoma, 1970; M.B.A., U. Tenn., 1973. Registered profl. engr., Ill., N.J., Mo., Tenn., Tex., Wis. Dir. environ. planning Ryckman, Edgerly, Tomlinson and Assocs., St. Louis, 1972-73, Wis. Electric Power Co., Milw., 1973-74; v.p. Environ. Research & Tech., Inc., Concord, Mass., 1975-79; pres., chief exec. officer, dir. TRC Cos., Inc., East Hartford, Conn., 1979—; dir. TRC Advanced Analytics, Inc., Toronto, Ont., Can. Contbr.

articles on air pollution and environ. planning to profl. jours. Patentee pressure-temperature sensors. Bd. dirs. Xavier High Sch., N.Y.C., 1983—. Served to capt. USAF, 1968-72. Recipient USAF award for sci. achievement Dept. Def., 1972; Gen. Motors scholar, 1963-67. Mem. Air Pollution Control Assn., Nat. Soc. Profl. Engrs., ASME, Young. Pres.'s Orgn. Roman Catholic. Club: Hartford Canoe (East Hartford). Current work: IR remote sensing instrumentation; mobile applications of triple quadruple mass spectrometry for toxic substance characterization. Subspecialties: Mechanical engineering; Environmental toxicology. Office: TRC Environmental Consultants Inc 800 Connecticut Blvd East Hartford CT 06108

ROCHESTER, EUGENE WALLACE, JR., research and engineering educator; b. Greenville, S.C., July 15, 1943; s. Eugene Wallace, Sr. and Mary Usona (Hughey) R.; m. Phyllis Parker, June 2, 1968; children—Paul Wallace, Alan Parker. B.S., Clemson U., 1965; M.S., N.C. State U., 1968, Ph.D., 1970. Registered profl. engr., Ala. Prof., Auburn U., Ala., 1970—; cons., Auburn, 1975—. Contbr. articles to profl. jours. Scout master Chattahoochee council Boy Scouts Am., 1984. Named Young Engr. of Yr., Ala. Soc. Profl. Engrs., 1977; W.H. Smith faculty fellow Ala. Agrl. Expt. Sta., 1977. Mem. Am. Soc. Agrl. Engrs., Irrigation Assn. Baptist. Lodge: Kiwanis. Current work: Irrigation systems for agricultural crops; water and energy utilization for irrigation systems; computer simulations. Subspecialty: Agricultural engineering. Home: 625 Jennifer Dr Auburn AL 36830 Office: Dept Agrl Engring Auburn U Auburn AL 36849

ROCHET, JEAN PAUL, geologist, explorationist; b. Chambery, France, June 12, 1924, came to U.S., 1979; m. Couchet Genevieve, June 15, 1958; children—Paule, Martine, Francois. Master Ensic, Nancy, France, 1948; Master/Ph.D., Enspm, Rveil, France, 1950. Regional geologist Serept, Tunisia, 1950-57; exploration mgr. Ifp, France, 1957-68, Beicip, France, 1968-78; sr. explorationist World Bank, Washington, 1979—. Mem. Am. Assn. Petroleum Geologists, Soc. Geol. de France. Current work: Petroleum exploration; regional studies; technical assistance. Subspecialties: Geology; Geophysics. Home: 3853 Oliver St NW Washington DC 20015 Office: World Bank 1818 H St NW Washington DC 20433

ROCHOW, JOHN JOSEPH, plant ecologist, environmental scientist; b. Bay City, Mich., May 10, 1939; s. Clarence Charles and Marquerite Mary (Walraven) R.; m. Ellen Joyce Walker, Aug. 17, 1968; children—Garrick, Gretchen. A.A., Bay City Jr. Coll., 1959; B.S., Central Mich. U., 1968; M.S., U. Mo., 1969, Ph.D., 1972. Environ. technician Oak Ridge Nat. Lab., 1971; grad. teaching asst. U. Mo., Columbia, 1970-72; sr. environ. planner Consumers Power Co., Jackson, Mich., 1972-78, supr. environ. services, 1978-81, staff environ. sci., 1981—. Contbr. articles to profl. jours., chpt. to book. Served with U.S. Army, 1962-65. NSF trainee, 1969. Mem. Ecol. Soc. Am., AAAS, Sigma Xi. Roman Catholic. Lodge: Lions. Subspecialties: Ecology (environmental science); Ecosystems analysis. Home: 6150 Bowerman Rd Horton MI 49246 Office: Consumers Power Co 1945 Parnall Rd Jackson MI 49201

ROCKENSIES, KENNETH JULES, physics educator; b. N.Y.C., June 10, 1938; s. John William and Wilma (Mercz) R.; m. Eileen Regina Dros, June 6, 1970; children—Kevin John, Patricia Ann, Regina Marie. B.S., Poly. Inst. Bklyn., 1960, M.S., 1962; postgrad. NYU, 1965-67, Adelphi U., 1969-75. Physicist, Western Union Telegraph, N.Y.C., 1962-63; prof. physics N.Y.C. Tech. Coll., CUNY, Bklyn., 1963—. Mem. Optical Soc. Am., Am. Assn. Physics Tchrs., Soc. Coll. Sci. Tchrs., Nat. Sci. Tchrs. Assn. Subspecialty: Physical optics. Office: Dept Physics NYC Tech Coll CUNY 300 Jay St Brooklyn NY 11201

ROCKLAND, KATHLEEN SKIBA, neuroanatomist; b. Stamford, Conn., Oct. 10, 1947; d. Charles and Sophie (Markisz) Skiba; m. Charles Rockland, Aug. 2, 1970. B.A., Wellesley Coll., 1969; M.A., Princeton U., 1972; Ph.D., Boston U., 1979. Research fellow div. biology Calif. Inst. Tech., Pasadena, Calif., 1978-79; research fellow in neurology Children's Hosp. Med. Center, Boston, 1979-80; research assoc. dept. ophthalmology Med. U. S.C., Charleston, 1980-82; sr. research fellow E. K. Shriver Ctr., Waltham, Mass., 1982—; adj. asst. prof. dept. anatomy Boston U., 1983—. Contbr. articles to profl. jours. Woodrow Wilson fellow, 1969; Princeton Nat. fellow, 1969-72; NDEA fellow, 1969-72; NIH trainee, 1974-78; recipient Nat. Research Service award NIH, 1978-80. Mem. Assn. Research in Vision and Ophthalmology, Soc. Neurosci. Current Work: Neuroanatomy; cerebral cortex, visual system primates. Subspecialties: Neurobiology; Neurophysiology.

ROCKWELL, NED MILES, chemical research engineer, chemist; b. Valparaiso, Ind., Nov. 29, 1956; s. Richard Vernon and Marcia Anne (Taylor) R.; m. Amy Lucinda Hartzell, June 25, 1983. B.S. in Chemistry, Purdue U., 1979; postgrad. Ill. Inst. Tech., 1979—. Research engr. Stepan Co., Northfield, Ill., 1979—. Mem. Am. Chem. Soc., Am. Oil Chemists Soc. Current work: Chemical process design; esterification processes; synthetic lubricant development. Subspecialties: Chemical engineering; Organic chemistry. Home: 634 Chip Ct Gurnee IL 60031Office: Stepan Co 22 W Frontage Rd Northfield IL 60093

ROCKWOOD, DONALD LEE, forestry educator, consultant; b. Rockford, Ill., Oct. 28, 1944; s. Claude Leslie and Agnes Anna (Krueger) R.; m. Virginia Joanne, Aug. 18, 1968; children: Kimberly, Brian. B.S., U. Ill., 1966, M.S., 1968; Ph.D., N.C. State U., 1972. Research assoc. U. Fla., Gainesville, 1972-73, asst. prof. forestry, 1973-80, assoc. prof., 1980—. Contbr. articles to profl. jours. Mem. AAAS, Soc. Am. Foresters, Sigma Xi, Gamma Sigma Delta. Current Work: Research in tree improvement, woody biomass production and forest measurement. Subspecialties: Plant genetics; Biomass (energy science and technology). Office: University of Florida School of Forest Resources and Conservation Gainesville FL 32611

RODBELL, MARTIN, biochemist; b. Balt., Dec. 1, 1925; s. Milton William and Shirley Helen (Abrams) R.; m. Barbara Charlotte Ledermann, Sept. 6, 1950; children—Paul, Suzanne, Andrew, Phillip. B.A., Johns Hopkins U., 1949; Ph.D., U. Wash., 1954. Nutrition and endocrinology chemist NIH, Bethesda, Md., 1956-70, chief sect. membrane regulation, 1970-85, chief lab. nutrition and endocrinology, 1972-84, sci. dir. Nat. Inst. Environ. Health Scis., Research Triangle Park, N.C., 1985—; Jacobeus lectr. Scandinavian Endocrine Soc., Norway, 1973. Recipient Superior Service award HEW, 1973; award of merit NIH, 1984; Gairdner Internat. award, Can., 1984. Mem. Am. Soc. Biol. Chemists. Current work: Mechanism of hormone action; transduction of signal transfer across biological membranes; structure/function relation of peptide hormones. Subspecialties: Receptors; Membrane biology. Office: Nat Inst Environ Health Scis Research Triangle Park NC

RODDIS, LOUIS HARRY, JR., retired naval officer, consulting engineer; b. Charleston, S.C., Sept. 9, 1918; s. Louis Harry and Winifred Emily (Stiles) R. B.S., U.S. Naval Acad., 1939; M.S., MIT, 1944. Registered profl. engr., Pa., D.C., N.Y., N.J., S.C. chartered engr., U.K. Commd. ensign U.S. Navy, 1939, advanced through grades to capt., 1957, various assignments, sea duty, 1939-41, Pearl Harbor, 1941, assigned Phila. Naval Shipyard, 1944, staff of comdr. Joint Task Force I, atomic weapons tests, Bikini, 1946, assigned Clinton Labs., Manhattan Engring. Dist. (now Oak Ridge Nat. Lab.), 1946, staff bur. ships Dept. Navy, Washington; staff bur. ships, nuclear ship propulsion program AEC, assisted nuclear reactor design U.S.S. Nautilus Dept. Navy, 1947-55; dep. dir. div. reactor devel. AEC, 1955-58; pres., dir. Pa. Electric Co., Johnstown, 1958-67, chmn., 1967-69; dir. nuclear power activities Gen. Pub. Utilities Corp., N.Y.C., 1967-69; vice chmn. Consol. Edison Co. N.Y., 1969, 73-74, pres., 1969-73, also trustee; pres., chief exec. officer John J. McMullen Assos., Inc., N.Y.C., 1975-76; asso. co. Panero-Tizian Assos., Inc., 1975-76, cons. engr., 1976—; dir. Hammermill Paper Co., Detroit Edison Co., Inc., Gould Inc., Research-Cottrell, Inc.; mem. Pres.'s Adv. Council on Energy Research and Devel., 1973-75; cons. U.S. Dept. State, Disarmament Commn., 1960-61, U.S. Maritime Adminstrn., 1959-62; chmn. maritime research adv. com. Nat. Acad. Scis.-NRC, 1958-60; mem. Gov.'s Com. of 100 for Better Edn., 1962-64, Gov.'s Council Sci. and Tech., 1963-65, Pa. Indsl. Devel. Authority, 1961-68; pres. Atomic Indsl. Forum, 1962-64; mem. adv. com. Rockefeller U., 1972—; mem. energy research adv. bd. Dept. Energy, 1978-85, chmn., 1981-84. Author tech. articles on nuclear power and energy subjects. Bd. dirs. Mercy Hosp., Johnstown, 1959-67, Metal Properties Council, 1970-74. Recipient Outstanding Service award AEC, 1957; Arthur S. Flemming career award Washington C. of C., 1958; Outstanding Citizen award Johnstown Inter-Service Club Council, 1963. Fellow Royal Instn. Naval Architects; mem. ASME (Fellowship award), IEEE, Am. Nuclear Soc. (pres. 1969-70, Fellowship award 1970), Soc. Naval Engrs., Am. Soc. Naval Architects and Marine Engrs., Nat. Acad. Engring., Nat. Soc. Profl. Engrs., ASHRAE, N.Y. C. of C., Edison Electric Assn. (dir. 1969-73), Human Factor Soc., Am. Gas Assn. (dir. 1973-74), Commerce and Industry Assn. N.Y. (dir. 1969-74), Sigma Xi, Tau Beta Pi. Clubs: Army Navy (Washington); Rotary (Charleston); Chemists (N.Y.). Current Work: Energy policy and especially research and development of all energy forms. Subspecialty: Energy research and development. Home and Office: PO Box 1513 Charleston SC 29402

RODE, ANDRIS, Canadian government science advisor, physiologist; b. Riga, Latvia, Nov. 22, 1940; came to Can., 1951; s. Paulis and Valija (Boks) Mernieks; m. Doris Floding, Dec. 15, 1973; children—Jason, Jessie. B.P.H.E., B.A., M.Sc., Ph.D., U. Toronto. Dir. Eastern Arctic Sci. Resource Ctr., Igloolik, N.W.T., Can., 1975-84; sci. advisor Govt. of Yukon, Whitehorse, Can., 1985—. Contbr. articles to profl. jours. Served with Can. Navy, 1961-62. Research fellow NRC, 1968-70, Med. Research Council, 1970-72. Mem. Can. Soc. for Circumpolar Health. Current work: Research in exercise and work physiology; research management. Subspecialties: Preventive medicine; Physiology (medicine). Office: Exec Council Offices Govt of Yukon PO Box 2703 Whitehorse YK Y1A 2C6 Canada

RODGERS, JOHN, educator, geologist; b. Albany, N.Y., July 11 1914; s. Henry D. and Louise W. (Allen) R. B.A., Cornell U., 1936, M.S., 1937; Ph.D., Yale U., 1944. Geologist, U.S. Geol. Survey, 1938-46, intermittently, 1946—; sci. cons. U.S. Army Engrs., 1944-46; instr. geology Yale U., 1946-47, asst. prof., 1947-52, asso. prof., 1952-59, prof., 1959-62, Silliman prof., 1962—; vis. lectr. Coll. de France, Paris, 1960; sec.-gen. commn. on stratigraphy Internat. Geol. Congress, 1952-60; commr. Conn. Geol. and Natural History Survey, 1961-71. Author: (with C.O. Dunbar) Principles of Stratigraphy, 1957, The Tectonics of the Appalachians, 1970; also articles in field.; editor: Symposium on the Cambrian System, 3 vols., 1956, 61; asst. editor: Am. Jour. Sci., 1948-54, editor, 1954—. NSF Sr. postdoctoral fellow France, 1959-60; exchange visitor Geol. Inst., Acad. Scis. USSR, 1967; Guggenheim fellow Australia, 1973-74; recipient medal of freedom U.S. Army, 1947. Fellow Geol. Soc. Am. (councillor 1962-65, pres. 1970, Penrose medal 1981), AAAS; mem. Am. Acad. Arts and Scis., Am. Assn. Petroleum Geologists, Conn. Acad. Sci. and Engring. (charter), Conn. Acad. Arts and Scis. (pres. 1969), Am. Geophys. Union, Nat. Acad. Scis., Geol. Soc. London (hon.), Société géologique de France (asso. mem., v.p. 1960), Acad. Scis. USSR (hon. fgn. mem.), Academia Real de Ciencias y Artes Barcelona (fgn. corr. mem.), Sigma Xi. Club: Elizabethan (New Haven). Subspecialties: Geology; Tectonics. Address: Dept Geology Yale U PO Box 6666 New Haven CT 06511

RODIN, ERVIN YECHIEL-LASZLO, applied mathematician, consultant, editor; b. Budapest, Hungary, Jan. 17, 1932; came to U.S., 1957, naturalized, 1967; s. Mor Rothmann and Rose (Deutsch) Rothmann Kaufmann; m. Sarah Leibovitz, Apr. 15, 1956; children—Daphna Cynthia, Eytan Murray, Allon Kenneth. B.A., U. Tex., 1960, Ph.D., 1964. Spl. instr. U. Tex., Austin, 1960-64; sr. mathematician Wyle Labs., Huntsville, Ala., 1964-66; prof. Washington U., St. Louis, 1966—; cons. unsteady aerodynamics br. NASA, 1968-74; mem. com. anti-ballistic missile def. Nat. Research Council, 1970-73, Grad. Fellowship Programs, NSF, 1973-76. Co-editor: Energy Methods in Finite Element Analysis, 1979; Mathematical Modelling in Science and Technology, 1984; editor-in-chief Internat. Jour. Computers and Math. with Applications, 1973—, Internat. Jour. Math. Modelling, 1979—. Mem. Soc. Engring. Sci. (pres. 1978-80), Internat. Assn. Math. Modelling (v.p. 1982—), Am. Math. Soc., ACM, IEEE. Jewish. Current work: Applications of mathematics to diverse fields of human endeavor, and the integration of computerized approaches therein. . Home: 31 Nantucket Ln Saint Louis MO 63132 Office: Washington U Box 1040 Saint Louis MO 63130

RODIN, JUDITH, psychology and psychiatry educator; b. Phila., Sept. 9, 1944; d. Morris and Sally (Winson) Seitz; m. Bruce Rodin, June 12, 1966 (div. 1972); m. Nicholas Niejelow, Feb. 12, 1978; 1 child, Alexander. A.B., U. Pa., 1966; Ph.D., Columbia U., 1970. Asst. prof. psychology NYU, 1970-72; NSF postdoctoral fellow U. Calif.-Irvine, 1971; asst. prof. psychology Yale U., New Haven, 1972-75, assoc. prof., 1975-79, prof., 1979-83, Philip R. Allen prof. psychology, 1984—, prof. psychiatry, 1980—, dir. grad. studies, 1978-83; chmn. John D. and Catherine T. MacArthur Found. for Research Network on Health-Promoting and Health-Damaging Behavior, 1984—. Mem. editorial bd. Internat. Jour. Obesity, 1977—, Health Psychology, 1981—, Behavioral Medicine, 1978-84; assoc. editor Personality and Social Psychology Bull., 1976-79; chief editor Appetite, 1979—. Fellow AAAS; mem. Am. Psychol. Assn. (Disting. Sci. award 1977, Outstanding Health Psychology Contbn. award, div. 38 1980, pres. 1982-83), Eastern Psychol. Assn. (pres. 1982-83), Inst. Medicine. Current work: Health psychology and behavioral medicine; cognitive and physiological determinants of motivational states, especially eating behavior and the development of obesity; effects of perceived control on behavior; stress and coping; adult development and aging. Subspecialty: Behavioral psychology.

RODRIGUE, CHRISTINE M., geography educator, researcher, consultant; b. Los Angeles, Oct. 27, 1952; d. John-Paul and Josephine Genevieve (Gorsky) R. A.A. Pierce Coll., 1972; B.A. summa cum laude, Calif. State U.-Northridge, 1973, M.A., 1976; C.Phil., Clark U., 1979, postgrad., 1980—. Instr. in geography Calif. State U.-Northridge, 1974-75, instr. geography and urban studies, 1980—; remote sensing computer analyst Jet Propulsion Labs., Pasadena, Calif., 1977; teaching asst. Clark U., Worcester, Mass., 1976-79, research asst., 1977; instr. earth scis., Pierce Coll., Woodland Hills, Calif., 1981—; cons. Area Location Systems, Northridge, 1984—, Equinart, Reseda, Calif., 1984—; lectr. in field. Contbr. articles to profl. jours. Mem. AAAS, Assn. Am. Geographers (chmn. Specialty group), Los Angeles Geog. Soc. (editor 1981-84), Planetary Soc., Sierra Club, Union of Concerned Scientists, NOW, Internat. Arabian Horse Assn. Democrat. Current work: Economic archaeology of Near East 20,000-5000 B.P.; economic development, mainly of Califoria; biogeography, succession in Mediterraean assemblages; computer, remote sensing applications. Subspecialties: Economic Geography; Remote sensing (geoscience). Office: Dept Geography Calif State U Northridge CA 91330

RODRIGUEZ, ELOY, biologist, phytochemist, educator, consultant; b. Edinburg, Tex., Jan. 7, 1947; s. Everardo and Hilaria (Calvillo) R. B.S. in Zoology, U. Tex., Austin, 1969, Ph.D., 1975. Postdoctoral scientist U. B.C. (Can.), Vancouver, 1976; asst. prof. U. Calif.-Irvine, 1976-78, assoc. prof.-/research scientist, 1978-83, prof., research scientist, 1983—. Contbr. articles to sci. jours. Ford Found. Mexican-Am. fellow, 1972-74; Nat. Chicano Council fellow, 1978; Fulbright sr. scholar, 1978; NIH Research Career Devel. award, 1982-87; Rosser-Rivera Lectureship award, 1985; Outstanding Hispanac Prof. award, 1984. Mem. Am. Chem. Soc., Phytochem. Soc., Am. Bot. Soc., Internat. Soc. Chem. Ecology, Soc. Advancement of Chicanos and Native Ams. Current Work: Phytochemistry, plant allergens, medicinal plant chemistry, chemical ecology. Subspecialties: Pharmacognosy; Medicinal chemistry. Office: Phytochem Lab Dept Ecology and Biology U Calif Irvine CA 92717

RODRIGUEZ, LUIS FELIPE, radio astronomer; b. Merida, Yucatan, Mexico, May 29, 1948; s. Vicente and Edith (Jorge) R.; m. Rosa Maria Ezquerro, Dec. 17, 1973. M.A., Harvard U., 1975, Ph.D. in Astronomy, 1978, diploma, 1979. Researcher Nat. U. Mexico, Mexico City, 1979—; dir. Nat. U. Mexico (Inst. Astronomy), 1980—, also mem. tech. council. Contbr. articles to profl. jours. Recipient Robert J. Trumpler award Astron. Soc. Pacific, 1980. Mem. Internat. Astron. Union, Am. Astron. Soc., Mex. Soc. Physics. Current Work: Radio astronomical studies of interstellar medium. Microwave and milimiter spectroscopy, radio interferometry, very long baseline interferometry. Contributions to understanding of nature of nucleus of Milky Way and of phenomena related to star formation. Subspecialty: Radio and microwave astronomy. Home: Villa Olimpica 11-102 Mexico 14020 Mexico Office: Instituto de Astronomia Universidad Nacional de Mexico Alvaro Obregon Mexico Mexico

RODRIGUEZ, SERGIO, physicist; b. Lautaro, Chile, Dec. 12, 1930; s. Gregorio and Berta Elena (Fontannaz) R.; m. Caridad Rebecca Floro, May 22, 1959; children—Cecilia, Katrin. B.A., U. Calif.-Berkeley, 1955, M.A., 1956, Ph.D., 1958. Asst. prof. physics U. Wash., Seattle, 1958-59; research asst. prof. U. Ill., Urbana, 1959-60; mem. faculty Purdue U., West Lafayette, Ind., 1960-61, 62—, assoc. prof. physics, 1962-64, prof., 1964—; asst. prof. elec. engring. Princeton U., 1961-62; cons. Argonne Nat. Lab. Ill., 1960-70, Ford Motor Co., Dearborn, Mich., 1959, 65. Contbr. articles to profl. jours. Recipient Alexander von Humboldt sr. scientist award, Bonn, 1974; Guggenheim fellow, 1967. Fellow Am. Phys. Soc. Current work: Condensed matter theory. Subspecialties: Condensed matter physics; Theoretical physics. Office: Dept Physics Purdue U West Lafayette IN 47907

ROE, KENNETH KEITH, engineering and construction company executive; b. Phila., Oct. 17, 1945; s. Kenneth Andrew and Hazel (Thropp) R.; m. Elizabeth Eaton, June 28, 1975; children: Kenneth Andrew Roe II, Whitney Elizabeth, Edward Scott, Graham Bradford. B.S.N.E., Princeton U., 1968; M.E. in Nuclear Engring, MIT, 1974, M.S. in Nuclear Engring, 1974; postgrad., Harvard U., 1980. Lic. profl. engr., Calif., N.J., N.Y., Wash., P.R. Engr. Burns & Roe Inc., Hempstead, N.Y., 1971-75, asst. project mgr., 1975-77, project engr., resident project engr., Woodbury, N.Y., 1977-78, project engring. mgr., Oradell, 1978-79, asst. v.p., 1979-80, v.p., 1980-82, exec. v.p., 1982-84, pres., 1984—, dir., 1971—, dir. indsl. services, Paramus, N.J., 1974—; dir. Burns and Roe Synthetic Fuels, 1980—, Fegles Power Service Corp., Mpls., Gen. Physics Corp., Columbia, Md. Mem. adv. council dept. mech. engring. Columbia U., N.Y.C., 1982—; chmn. pastor-parish relations com. First Ch. Round Hill, Greenwich, Conn., 1981-84, trustee, 1984—. Served to lt. USN, 1969-71. Sloan Found. fellow MIT, 1971. Mem. Am. Nuclear Soc., ASME (exec. com. net. sect. 1981—), Am. Inst. Chem. Engrs., AAAS, Water Pollution Control Assn., Colegio de Ingenieros. Republican. Clubs: Princeton of N.Y. (Greenwich), Stanwich (Greenwich); Coral Beach (Paget, Bermuda); Sankaty Head (Siasconset, Mass). Current Work: Development of improved plant designs for both conventional fossil and nuclear fueled power plants and introduction of advanced power technologies, such as breeder reactors, fusion, synthetic fuels, and others. Subspecialties: Mechanical engineering; Nuclear engineering. Office: Burns and Roe Inc 800 Kinderkamack Rd Oradell NJ 07649

ROE, SHELDON FORD, JR., chemical engineer, bioengineer, market researcher; b. Elmira, N.Y., May 16, 1932; s. Sheldon Ford and Florence Gertude (Knapp) R.; m. Shirley Ann Shaffer, Nov. 1, 1959. B.S. in Chem. Engring., Bucknell U., 1954; postgrad. U. Miami, 1956. Registered profl. engr., Fla.; cert. energy mgr., cert. hazardous waste mgr. Research dir., asst. prof. Thatcher Glass, Elmira, 1953-62; mgr. material research Owens Illinois, Inc., Toledo, 1962-69; dir. field services Applied Research Labs, Miami, Fla., 1970-75; cons. The Munters Corp., Ft. Meyers, Fla., 1975—. Contbr. articles to profl. jours., chpts. to books. Served with U.S. Army, 1956-58. Patentee in field. Mem. Am. Chem. Soc., Am. Inst. Chem. Engrs., Am. Soc. Metals, ASTM, Am. Water Works Assn., Assn. Energy Engrs., Fla. Engring. Soc., Fla. Pollution Control Assn., Soc. Plastics Engrs., Water Pollution Control Fedn., World Future Soc., Engrs. Club. Republican. Presbyterian. Club: Sailing. Current work: Packed bed reactor internals for anaerobic and aerobic digestion, solids handling, bioengineering, VOC strippers, S02 scrubbing. Subspecialties: Water supply and wastewater treatment; Hazardous waste disposal. Home: 5375 Coral Ave Cape Coral FL 33904

ROEDERER, JUAN GUALTERIO, physics educator; b. Trieste, Italy, Sept. 2, 1929; came to U.S., 1967, naturalized, 1972; s. Ludwig Alexander and Anna Rafaela (Lohr) R.; m. Beatriz S. Cougnet, Dec. 20, 1952; children: Ernesto, Irene, Silvia, Mario. Ph.D., U. Buenos Aires, 1952. Research scientist Max Planck Inst., Gottingen, Germany, 1952-55; group leader Argentine AEC, 1953-59; prof. physics U. Buenos Aires, 1959-66, U. Denver, 1966-77; dir. Geophys. Inst., U. Alaska, Fairbanks, 1977—, dean coll. environ. scis., 1978-82; vis. staff Los Alamos Nat. Lab., 1969-81. Author: Dynamics of Geomagnetically Trapped Radiation, 1970, Physics and Psychophysics of Music, 1973, 3rd edit. 1979; contbr. articles to profl. jours. Mem. U.S. Arctic research com. Bd. Atmospheric Scis. and Climate. NAS/NASA Sr. research fellow, 1964-66. Fellow AAAS, Am. Geophys. Union; mem. Asociación Argentina de Geodestas y Geofísicos, Internat. Council Sci. Unions (sci. com. on solar-terrestrial physics). Current Work: Study of plasma and energetic particles in the earth's magnetosphere; sci. policy issues for the Arctic; study of perception of music. Subspecialties: Space physics; Psychophysics. Home: 105 Concordia Dr Fairbanks AK 99701 Office: Geophys Inst Univ Alaska Fairbanks AK 99775-0800

ROEL, LAWRENCE EDMUND, neurochemist; b. Bklyn., Aug. 19, 1949; s. Edmund Lawrence and Leslie Adele (Gonzales) R. A.B., Princeton U., 1971; Ph.D., M.I.T., 1976; Muscular Dystrophy Assn. postdoctoral fellow, U. Calif., San Diego, 1976-78; postgrad, U. Pa., 1981—. Asst. prof. anatomy Northwestern U. Med. Sch., Chgo., 1978-81; research assoc. U. Pa., Phila., 1981—; cons. Sunmark Research Co., Arlington, Va., Newsource Publs., Huntington, N.Y. Contbr. articles to profl. jours. Am. Cancer Soc. grantee, 1980. Mem. Soc. Neurosci., N.Y. Acad. Scis., AAAS, Am. Chem. Soc., Sigma Xi. Club: Princeton of Phila. Current Work: Neurochemistry of monoamine, protein synthesis interacions. Subspecialties: Neurochemistry; Neurology. Home: 4310 Spruce St Philadelphia PA 19104

ROELFS, ALAN PAUL, plant pathologist; b. Stockton, Kans., Nov. 18, 1936; s. Paul Martin and Florence Lorene (Lewin) R.; m. Anita Faye Clark, Sept. 3, 1956 (div. 1981); children: David Alan, Judith Lynne, Lorene Mary.; m. LuAnne Beatrice Martell, June 11, 1983. B.S., Kans. State U., 1959, M.S., 1964; Ph.D., U. Minn., 1970. Technician Agrl. Research Service, U.S. Dept. Agr., Manhattan, Kans., 1959-64, plant pathologist, St. Paul, 1965-70, Animal and Plant Health Inspection Service, St. Paul, 1971-75, Agrl. Research Service, St. Paul, 1975—; cons. Interam. Inst. for Agrl. Research, Interam. Inst. Coop. on Agr., 1980, 82. Contbr. articles to profl. jours. Served with U.S. Army, 1959-61. Dept. Agr. grantee, 1980, 82-84, 85-87. Mem. Am. Phytopathol. Soc., AAAS, Internat. Assn. for Aerobiology, U.S. Fedn. for Culture Collections, Internat. Soc. Plant Pathology, Sigma Xi, Gamma Sigma Delta. Current Work: Epidemiology of the rusts of cereals; effects of the environment, pathogen genotype and host genotype on disease devel. and losses in the U.S. and Mexico; rust epidemiology worldwide. Subspecialty: Plant pathology. Home: 132 DeMont St Apt 238 Saint Paul MN 55117 Office: Cereal Rust Lab U Minn Saint Paul MN 55108

ROELOFS, WENDELL LEE, biochemistry educator, consultant; b. Orange City, Iowa, July 26, 1938; s. Edward and Edith (Beyers) R.; m. Marilyn Joyce Kuiken, Sept. 3, 1960; children: Brenda Jo, Caryn Jean, Jeffrey Lee, Kevin Jon. B.A., Central Coll., Pella, Iowa, 1960, D.Sc. (hon.), 1985; Ph.D., Ind. U., 1964; postdoctoral fellow, MIT, 1965; Asst. prof. N.Y. State Agrl. Expt. Sta., Geneva, 1965-69, assoc. prof., 1969-76, prof., 1976—, Liberty Hyde Bailey prof. insect biochemistry, 1976—; cons. Albany Internat. Co. Contbr. over 200 articles to sci. jours. Recipient Alexander von Humboldt award in Agr., 1977; recipient Outstanding Alumni award Central Coll., 1978, Wolf prize for Agr., 1982; Disting. Alumnus award Ind. U., 1983. Fellow AAAS; mem. Entomol. Soc. Am. (J. Everett Bussart Meml. award 1973, Founder's Meml. award 1980), Am. Chem. Soc., Nat. Acad. Sci., Sigma Xi. Republican. Presbyterian. Patentee in field (10). Current Work: Insect sex pheromones research: biosynthesis, behavior, genetics, identification of active components. Subspecialties: Physiology (biology); Biochemistry (biology). Home: 4 Crescence Dr Geneva NY 14456 Office: NY State Agrl Expt Sta Geneva NY 14456

ROESSLER, DAVID MARTYN, physicist; b. London, Apr. 29, 1940; came to U.S., 1966; s. Alfred Ernest and Elizabeth Minnie (Cornish) R.; m. Linda Jean Beare, May 19, 1983; children—Elizabeth Ruth, Sarah Lindsay. B.Sc. in Math. and Physics, King's Coll., U. London, 1961, Ph.D. in Ultraviolet Spectroscopy-Physics, 1966. Asso. King's Coll., 1961; postdoctoral research fellow physics dept. U. Calif., Santa Barbara, 1966-68; temporary mem. tech. staff Bell Labs., Murray Hill, N.J., 1968-70; staff research scientist physics dept. Gen. Motors Research Labs., Warren, Mich., 1970—. Contbr. articles on spectroscopy to profl. jours. Mem. Optical Soc. Am., Internat. Solar Energy Soc., Inst. Physics (U.K.), Sigma Xi. Patentee photoacoustic spectroscopy field. Current Work: Interaction of light and matter; spectroscopy, including optical properties of solids and aerosols, luminescence, photoacoustic spectroscopy, laser processing of materials. Subspecialties: Condensed matter physics; Laser spectroscopy. Home: 22610 Oak Ct Hazel Park MI 48030 Office: Physics Dept Gen Motors Research Labs Warren MI 48090

ROFFMAN, MARK, clinical pharmacologist, educator; b. Boston, July 8, 1945; s. William and Florence A. Tobias (Ableman) R.; m. Ina Ellen Marritt, July 13, 1968; children: Gary William, Jeremy Michael. A.B., Boston U., 1967; M.S., U. R.I., 1971, Ph.D. in Behavioral Pharmacology, 1972. NIMH postdoctoral trainee dept. psychiatry N.Y. U., 1972-73; assoc. in psychiatry Harvard Med. Sch., Boston, 1973-75, asst. prof. dept. psychiatry, 1975-76;

lectr. in psychology Emmanuel Coll., Boston, 1975-76; sr. scientist II dept. pharmacology, pharms. div. CIBA-GEIGY Corp., Summit, N.J., 1976-78, sr. assoc. clin. pharmacology, 1978-80, asst. dir. clin. pharmacology, 1980-81, assoc. dir. clin. pharmacology, 1981—, dir. clin. pharmacology, 1982, exec. dir. clin. research, 1983—; instr. Bloomfield (N.J.) Coll., 1977—; adj. asso. prof. psychiatry Coll. Medicine and Dentistry N.J.-Rutgers Med. Sch., Piscataway, 1977—; adj. asso. prof. grad. faculty Rutgers U., 1979—. Contbr. articles to profl. jours. Fellow Am. Coll. Clin. Pharmacology; mem. AAAS, Am. Soc. Pharmacology and Exptl. Therapeutics, Soc. Neuroscience, Soc. Stimulus Properties of Drugs, Am. Soc. Clin. Pharmacology and Therapeutics, N.Y. Acad. Sci., Soc. Clin. Trials, Sigma Xi, Rho Chi, Phi Sigma. Current Work: Preclinical and clinical pharmacology. Subspecialties: Neuropharmacology; Psychopharmacology. Office: CIBA-GEIGY Corp 556 Morris Ave Summit NJ 07901

ROGERS, DONALD PHILIP, botanist, educator; b. Toledo, Ohio, Feb. 5, 1908; s. Philip John and Ella Leona (Johnston) R.; m. Alpha Mae Looney, Dec. 25, 1934; 1 child, Helen Patricia Keyt. Student, Toledo U., 1925-26; B.A., Oberlin Coll., 1929; postgrad., U. Nebr., 1929-30; Ph.D., U. Iowa, 1935. Instr. botany Oreg. State Coll., 1936-40, Brown U., 1941-42; assoc. prof. biology Am. Internat. Coll., Springfield, Mass., 1942-45; asst. prof. botany U. Hawaii, Honolulu, 1945-47; curator N.Y. Bot. Garden, N.Y.C., 1947-57; prof. botany U. Ill., Urbana, 1957-76, prof. emeritus, 1976—. Mem. Mycological Soc. Am. Democrat. Episcopalian. Current Work: Basidial morphology and fungal taxonomy; interpretation of basidial septation, history of mycology. Subspecialties: Morphology; Taxonomy. Home: 1809 20th St NE Auburn WA 98002

ROGERS, EDWIN HENRY, computer scientist, mathematician; b. Newton, Mass., Nov. 5, 1936; s. Eliot Francis and Lila Edith (Knight) R.; m. Joan Barclay Grant, May 28, 1960; children—Andrew Kelvin, Anne Knight, Margo Elizabeth. B.S. in Physics, Carnegie Inst. Tech., 1958, M.S. in Math., 1960, Ph.D. in Math., 1962. Research asst. Woods Hole Oceanographic Inst., Mass., 1955-58; prof. computer sci. Rensselaer Poly. Inst., Troy, N.Y., 1965—; vis. research prof. U. Waterloo, Ont., Can., 1976-77; vis. research scientist Gen. Elec. Research and Devel. Lab., Schenectady, N.Y., 1983; cons. N.Y. State Edn. Dept., Albany, 1975—, Educom, Princeton, N.J., 1985. Served to 1st lt. U.S. Army, 1963-64. Leverhulme fellow, 1962-63. Mem. Soc. Indsl. and Applied Math. (mng. editor 1975-81), IEEE Computer Soc., Assn. Computing Machinery, AAAS. Current work: Wafer scale integration of data base and logical inference architectures, VLSI wafer yield analysis, technology in science education. Subspecialty: Foundations of computer science. Home: 10 Eastwood Dr Ballston Lake NY 12019 Office: Computer Sci Dept Rensselaer Poly Inst Troy NY 12180

ROGERS, JACK DAVID, plant pathologist, educator; b. Point Pleasant, W.Va., Sept. 3, 1937; s. Jack and Thelma Grace (Coon) R.; m. Belle Clay Spencer, June 7, 1958; children: Rebecca Ann, Barbara Lee. B.S., Davis & Elkins Coll., 1960; M.F., Duke U., 1960; Ph.D., U. Wis., 1963. Mem. faculty Wash. State U.-Pullman, 1963—. Mem. Mycol. Soc. Am., Bot. Soc. Am., Am. Phytopath. Soc. Current Work: Diseases of forest trees, genetics of fungi, cytology of fungi. Subspecialties: Plant pathology; Evolutionary biology. Home: NW 1435 Kenny Dr Pullman WA 99163 Office: Dept Plant Pathology Wash State U Pullman WA 99164

ROGERS, KENNETH CANNICOTT, college president; b. Teaneck, N.J., Mar. 21, 1929; s. Ralph Waldo and Ruth (Geltner) R.; m. Katharine Munzer, Aug. 4, 1956; children—Margaret, Christopher, Thomas. B.S., St. Lawrence U., 1950, D.H.L. (hon.), 1983; M.A. in Physics, Columbia U., 1952, Ph.D., 1956; M.Engring. (hon.), Stevens Inst. Tech., 1964. Research assoc. Lab. Nuclear Studies Cornell U., Ithaca, N.Y., 1956-57; asst. prof. physics Stevens Inst. Tech., Hoboken, N.J., 1957-60, assoc. prof., 1960-64, prof., 1964-68, head physics dept., 1968-72, acting provost, dean of faculty, 1972, pres., 1972—; dir. First Jersey Nat. Corp., Pub. Service Electric & Gas Co. Trustee Christ Hosp. Found.; mem. N.J. com. Regional Plan Assn.; mem. N.J. Gov.'s Com. Sci. and Tech., chmn. sub-task force telecommunications. Fellow AAAS; mem. Am. Phys. Soc., Royal Soc. Arts, IEEE, N.Y. Acad. Scis., Am. Assn. Physics Tchrs., Newcomen Soc., N.J. Research and Devel. Council (adv. bd.), Sigma Xi. Club: Cosmos. Patentee in field. . Home: Hoxie House Castle Point Station Hoboken NJ 07030 Office: Stevens Institute Technology Castle Point Station Hoboken NJ 07030

ROGERS, MARY F., college dean, sociology educator. B.A., in Chemistry, Marycrest Coll., 1966; M.A. in Sociology U. Mass., 1969, Ph.D. in Sociology, 1972. Instr. sociology Marycrest Coll., Davenport, Iowa, 1967-68, U. Mass., Amherst, summer 1971; asst. prof. Providence Coll., R.I., 1971-75; spl. lectr. Bryant Coll., Smithfield, R.I., 1975-76; assoc. prof. U. West Fla., Pensacola, 1976—, chmn. dept. sociology, anthropology, and geography, 1980-82, interim dean Coll. Arts and Scis., 1984—. Author: Sociology, Ethnomethodology, and Experience: A Phenomenological Critique, 1983; The Literary Vocation: Toward a Phenomenological Sociology of Literature, (in press). Referee Am. Jour. Sociology, 1972-77, Sociol. Symposium, 1975, Soc. Forces, 1978, Rural Sociology, 1980, 84; reviewer U. Chgo. Press, 1981, 82, 84. Contbr. articles, chpts. and book revs. to profl. publs. Grantee NEH, 1977, 78, 80. Mem. Am. Sociol. Assn., So. Sociol. Soc., Southwestern Soc. Sci. Assn., MLA, Semiotic Soc. Am. Office: Univ West Florida Coll Arts and Scis Pensacola FL

ROGERS, QUINTON RAY, nutritional biochemist; b. Palco, Kans., Nov. 24, 1936; s. Irwin Tollie and Margret Helen (Baldwin) R.; m. Deana Joyce Dykstra, Dec. 28, 1956; children: Katrina Lynn, Terrill Dean, Tamara Gayle, Kevin Andrew. B.S., U. Idaho, 1958; M.S., U. Wis., 1960, Ph.D., 1963. Asst. prof. dept. nutrition and food sci. M.I.T., 1964-66; from asst. prof. to assoc. prof. physiol. chemistry dept. phys., sci. Sch. Vet. Medicine, U. Calif.-Davis, 1966-69, prof., 1976—. Contbr. articles to profl. jours. Mem. Am. Inst. Nutrition, Am. Physiol. Soc., AAAS. Current Work: Amino acid nutrition and metabolism, control of food intake, feline and canine nutrition. Subspecialties: Nutrition (biology); Nutrition (medicine). Home: 1918 Alpine Pl Davis CA 95616 Office: Dept Physiol Sci Veterinary Medicine U Calif Davis CA 95616

ROGERS, SAM, research chemist; b. London, June 6, 1907; came to U.S., 1908; s. Harry and Mary Rogover; 1 child, Sandra. Student Crane Coll., 1923-29; B.S., Kansas City Coll., Mo., 1930, M.S., 1938, Ph.D., 1939. Chief chemist Dental Research Labs, Chgo., 1946, Ill. Research Labs, Chgo., 1948; chief chemist Vitaliner Co., Chgo., 1948—; pres. Rogers Anti Stats, Chgo., 1948—; cons. in field. Patentee in field. Developed heavy density smoke screen used in World War II, also involved in developing atomic bomb; developer anti-static chems., plastic wood. Mem. Am. Chem. Soc. (emeritus). Mem. Royal Soc. of London (hon.), Royal Soc. of Health (hon.). Democrat. Current work: Germicides. Subspecialties: Dental materials; Biochemistry (biology). Office: Rogers Anti-Stats 18 S Michigan Ave Room 920 Chicago IL 60603

ROGERS, STEVEN RAY, physicist; b. Tachikawa, Japan, Dec. 6, 1952; came to U.S. 1954; s. Harold Edward, Jr. and Mary Lu (Bowles) R.; m. Robina Rae Behel, Dec. 27, 1975; children—Miranda Rae, Kellina Gail. B.A. in Math. and Physics, U. No. Colo., 1975; M.S. in Physics, Kans. State U., 1977. Instr. Kans. State U., Manhattan, 1978-79; mem. tech. staff ElectroMagnetic Applications, Lakewood, Colo., 1979-82, MITRE Corp., Colorado Springs, Colo., 1982—. Mem. IEEE, Sigma Pi Sigma, Lambda Sigma Tau. Current work: Interests in the impacts of natural and manmade threats to command, control, communications, and intelligence systems for the design, specification, and testing of survivable C3I systems. Subspecialty: Information systems (Information science). Office: MITRE Corp 1257 Lake Plaza Dr Colorado Spings CO 80906

ROGOLSKY, MARVIN, microbiology educator; b. Passaic, N.J., Apr. 17, 1939; s. Reuben and Ruth R. B.A., Rutgers U.-Newark, 1960; M.S., Northwestern U., 1962; Ph.D., Syracuse U., 1965. Postdoctoral fellow Scripps Clinic and Research Found., 1965-67; asst. prof. microbiology U. Utah Coll. Medicine, Salt Lake City, 1967-76; assoc. prof. biology and medicine U. Mo.-Kansas City, 1976-81, prof. biology and medicine, 1981—; researcher. Contbr. articles to sci. jours. NIH grantee, 1968-71, 72-75, 76-79. Mem. Am. Soc. Microbiology. Current Work: Research on mechanism of action of genetic transfer and genetic regulation of toxin synthesis in Staphylococcus aureus. Subspecialties: Microbiology; Gene actions. Home: 10109 W 93rd Overland Park KS 66212 Office: Biol Scis Bldg Univ Mo Kansas City MO 64110

ROHLES, FREDERICK HENRY, JR., univ. research adminstr., psychologist, researcher, educator; b. Chgo., Dec. 23, 1920; s. Frederick Henry and Anna (Kiefer) R.; m. Mertyce Bliss, Nov. 9, 1943; children: Nancy Rohles Denning, Frederick Henry, Susan Rohles Grapengater. B.S., Roosevelt U., 1942; M.S., U. Tex., Austin, 1950, Ph.D., 1956. Enlisted in U.S. Air Force, 1942, advanced through grades to lt. col., 1961; research psychologist (USAF Aviation Psychology Program), 1942-49; chief psychol. br. (Arctic Aeromed. Lab.), Fairbanks, Alaska, 1950-53; research psychologist (USAF Sch. Aviation Medicine), Randolph AFB, Tex., 1954-56; chief sect. unusual environments (USAF Aeromed. Research Lab.), Wright-Patterson AFB, Ohio, 1956-58; dir. research, chief comparative psychology (USAF Aeromed Research Lab.), Holloman AFB, N.Mex., 1958-63; ret., 1963; dir. Inst. Environ. Research, Kans. State U., Manhattan, 1963—; cons. in field. Contbr. numerous articles to profl. jours. Chmn. aviation com. C. of C. Manhattan, 1975-80; mem. Manhattan Aviation Com., 1978-80. Fellow Am. Psychol. Assn., Aerospace Medicine Assn. (assoc.), Human Factors Soc., ASHRAE; mem. Psychonomic Soc. Presbyterian. Current Work: Human thermal comfort; environmental ergonomics. Subspecialties: Human factors engineering; Physiological psychology. Home: 700 Harris Ave Manhattan KS 66502 Office: Inst Environ Research Kans State U Manhattan KS 66506

ROHSENOW, WARREN MAX, mechanical engineer, educator; b. Chgo., Feb. 12, 1921; s. Fred and Selma (Gorss) R.; m. Katharine Towneley Smith, Sept. 20, 1946; children—John, Brian, Damaris, Sandra, Anne. B.S., Northwestern U., 1941; M.Eng., Yale, 1943, D.Eng., 1944. Teaching asst., instr. mech. engring. Yale, 1941-44; mem. faculty Mass. Inst. Tech., 1946—, prof. mech. engring., 1955—, dir. heat transfer lab., 1954—; Chmn. bd. dirs. Dynatech Corp. Author: (with Choi) Heat Mass and Momentum Transfer, 1961; Editor: Developments in Heat Transfer, 1964, (with Hartnett) Handbook of Heat Transfer, 1973. Served as lt. (j.g.) USNR, 1944-46; mech. engr. gas turbine div. Engring. Expt. Sta. Annapolis, Md. Recipient Pi Tau Sigma gold medal Am. Soc. M.E., 1951; award for advancement sci. Yale Engring. Assn., 1952; merit award Northwestern Alumni, 1955. Fellow Am. Acad. Arts and Scis., Nat. Acad. Engring., Am. Soc. M.E. (Heat Transfer Meml. award 1967, Max Jakob Meml. award 1970); mem. Sigma Xi, Tau Beta Pi, Pi Tau Sigma. Current Work: Application of heat transfer; boiling condensation and heat exchanger's. Subspecialty: Mechanical engineering. Home: 47 Windsor Rd Waban MA 02168 Office: Massachusetts Institute of Technology Cambridge MA 02138

ROIZMAN, BERNARD, educator, microbiologist; b. Chisinau, Rumania, Apr. 17, 1929; came to U.S., 1947, naturalized, 1954; s. Abram and Liudmilla (Seinberg) R.; m. Betty Cohen, Aug. 26, 1950; children: Arthur, Niels. B.A., Temple U., 1952, M.S., 1954; Sc.D. in Microbiology, Johns Hopkins, 1956; D.Litt. (hon.), Gov.'s State U., 1984. From instr. microbiology to asst. prof. Johns Hopkins Med. Sch., 1956-65; mem. faculty div. biol. scis. U. Chgo., 1965—, prof. microbiology, 1969-85, prof. biophysics, 1970-85, chmn. com. virology, 1969—, Joseph Regenstein prof., 1981—, Joseph Regenstein disting. service prof., 1984—, prof., chmn. dept. molecular genetics and cell biology, 1985—; convener herpesvirus workshop, Cold Spring Harbor, N.Y., 1972—; lectr. Am. Found. for Microbiology, 1974-75; Mem. spl. virus cancer program, devel. research working group Nat. Cancer Inst., 1967-71, cons. inst., 1967-73; mem. steering com. human cell biology program NSF, 1971-74, cons. found., 1972-74; mem. adv. com. cell biology and virology Am. Cancer Soc., 1970-74; chmn. herpesvirus study group for Internat. Commn. Taxonomy of Viruses, 1971—; mem. Internat. Microbiol. Genetics Commn., Internat. Assn. Microbiol. Scis., 1974—; sci. adv. council N.Y. Cancer Inst., 1971—; med. adv. bd. Leukemia Research Found., 1972-77; mem. herpesvirus working team WHO/FOA, 1972-81; mem. bd. sci. consultants Sloan Kettering Inst., N.Y.C., 1975-81; mem. study sect. on exptl. virology NIH, 1976-80; mem. task force on virology Nat. Inst. Allergy and Infectious Disease, 1976-77; mem. external adv. com. Emory U. Cancer Center, 1973—, Northwestern U. Cancer Center, 1979—; cons. Institut Merieux, Lyon, France.; mem. sci. adv. com. Internat. Assn. for Study and Prevention Virus Assoc. Cancers, 1983—; mem. com. to establish vaccine priorities Nat. Inst. Medicine, 1983—; chmn. sci. adv. bd. Showa U. Inst. Biol. Scis., 1983—. Author sci. papers, chpts. in books.; Mem. editorial bd.: Jour. Hygiene, 1958-61; editor: Herpes viruses, 4 vols., 1982-85. Mem. editorial bd.: Infectious Diseases, 1965-69, Jour. Virology, 1970—, Jour. Intervirology, 1972—, Archives of Virology, 1975—, Virology, 1976-78, 83—, Microbiologica, 1978—, Cell, 1979-80. Trustee Goodwin Inst. for Cancer Research, 1977—. Recipient Lederle Med. Faculty award, 1960-61, Career Devel. award USPHS, 1963-65, Pasteur award Ill. Soc. Microbiology, 1972, Esther Langer award for achievement in cancer research, 1974, Outstanding Alumnus in Pub. Health award Johns Hopkins U., 1984; Am. Cancer Soc. scholar cancer research at Pasteur Inst. Paris, 1961-62; faculty research asso., 1966-71; traveling fellow Internat. Agy. Research Against Cancer, Karolinska Inst., Stockholm, Sweden, 1970; grantee USPHS/NIH, 1958—; grantee Am. Cancer Soc., 1962—; grantee NSF, 1962-79; grantee Whitehall Found., 1966-74. Hon. fellow Pan Am. Cancer Soc.; mem. Nat. Acad. Scis., Am. Assn. Immunologists, Soc. Exptl. Biology and Medicine, Am. Soc. Microbiology, A.A.A.S., Am. Soc. Biol. Chemists, Brit. Soc. Gen. Microbiology. Club: Quadrangle (Chgo.). Subspecialty: Virology (medicine). Home: 5555 S Everett Ave Chicago IL 60637

ROLFE, STANLEY THEODORE, civil engineer, educator; b. Chgo., July 7, 1934; s. Stanley T. and Eunice (Fike) R.; m. Phyllis Williams, Aug. 11, 1956; children: David Stanley, Pamela Kay, Kathleen Ann. B.S., U. Ill., 1956, M.S., 1958, Ph.D., 1962. Registered profl. engr., Pa., Kans. Supr. structural-evaluation sect. ordnance products div. U.S. Steel Corp., 1962-69, div. chief mech. behavior of metals div., 1969; Ross H. Forney prof. civil engring. U. Kans., 1969—, chmn. civil engring. dept., 1975—; Chmn. metall. studies panel ship research com. Nat. Acad. Scis., 1967-70. Author: Fracture and Fatigue Control in Structures—Applications of Fracture Mechanics; co-author: textbook Strength of Materials; Contbr.: numerous articles to profl. jours. T.R. Higgins lectr., 1980; Recipient Sam Tour award Am. Soc. Testing Materials, 1971, H.E. Gould Distinguished Teaching award U. Kans., 1972, 75, AWS Adams Meml. Educator award, 1974. Mem. Nat. Acad. Engring., ASTM, ASCE (chmn. task force on fracture), ASME, Soc. Exptl. Stress Analysis, Am. Soc. Engring. Edn., Nat. Acad. Engring., Chi Psi. Conglist. Club: Elk. Current Work: Application of fracture mechanics to fracture and fatigue control in structures. Subspecialties: Fracture mechanics; Civil engineering. Home: 2001 Camelback Dr Lawrence KS 66046

ROLLINO, JOHN, chemistry, physics educator; b. Bklyn., Oct. 11, 1944; s. John Anthony and Edith Ann (Patti) R.; m. Florence Alice Fink, Jan. 10, 1970; children—John Anton, Daniel Joseph. B.S., St. Francis Coll., 1966; Ph.D., MIT, 1969. Prof. chemistry and physics St. Francis Coll., Bklyn., 1969-83; computer specialist Walden Sch., N.Y.C., 1983-84; prof. chemistry and physics Upsala Coll., East Orange, N.J., 1984—; adj. prof. Baruch Coll., N.Y.C., 1984—, Manhattan Coll., N.Y.C., 1984. Sec. Ridgewood Glendale Middle Village Little League, Glendale, N.Y. Union Carbide fellow, 1968; NSF fellow 1970, 71. Mem. Am. Chem. Soc., Am. Phys. Soc., Chi Beta Phi, Alpha Phi Delta. Republican. Roman Catholic. Current work: Thermo-electric properties of electrochemical solid-state cells. Subspecialty: Physical chemistry. Home: 45 Wells Ct Bloomfield NJ 07003 Office: Upsala Coll Prospect St East Orange NJ 07019

ROLLINS, REED CLARK, emeritus botany educator; b. Lyman, Wyo., Dec. 7, 1911; s. William (Clarence) and Clara Rachel (Slade) R.; m. Alberta Fitz-Gerald, Sept. 23, 1939 (div. 1976); children: Linda Lee White, Richard Clark; m. Kathryn W. Roby, Apr. 2, 1978. A.B., U. Wyo., 1933; S.M., Wash. State Coll., 1936; Ph.D. (fellow Soc. of Fellows), Harvard U., 1941. Teaching fellow Wash. State Coll., 1934-36; teaching asst. summer sch. U. Wyo., 1935; teaching asst. biology Harvard U., 1936-37; instr. biology, asst. curator Dudley Herbarium, Stanford U., 1940-41, asst. prof., curator, 1941-47, assoc. prof., curator, 1947-48; asso. geneticist Guayule Research Project, Dept. Agr., 1943-45; prin. geneticist Stanford Research Inst., 1946-47; geneticist div. rubber plant investigations Dept. Agr., 1947-48; assoc. prof. botany Harvard U., 1948-54, Asa Gray prof. systematic botany, 1954-82, emeritus, 1982—; dir. Harvard U. (Gray Herbarium), 1948-78; chmn. Inst. Research Gen. Plant Morphology, 1955-65, Inst. of Plant Scis., 1965-69; supr. Bussey Instn., Harvard U., 1968-78; chmn. adminstrv. com. Farlow Library and Herbarium, 1974-78; v.p. nat. com. XI Internat. Bot. Congress, Seattle, 1969; v.p. XII, Leningrad, USSR, 1975; pres. sect. nomenclature XIII, Sydney, Australia, 1981. Author: (with E. Shaw) The Genus Lesquerella (Cruciferae) in North America; Past editor-in-chief: Rhodora; editor: Contributions from the Gray Herbarium, 1948-78; occasional papers Farlow Herbarium, 1974-78; Contbr. articles and tech. papers to profl. jours. Recipient Centenary medal French Bot. Soc., 1954; cert. of merit Bot. Soc. Am., 1960; Congress medal XI Internat. Bot. Congress, 1969, XII, 1975. Fellow AAAS, Linnean Soc. (London); mem. Orgn. Tropical Studies (pres., chmn. bd. 1964-65), Am. Soc. Naturalists (pres. 1966), Am. Acad. Arts and Scis., Am. Inst. Biol. Scis. (governing bd. 1961-63), Am. Soc. Plant Taxonomists (pres. 1951), Bot. Soc. Am. (v.p. 1961), Calif. Bot. Soc. (treas. 1945-48), Genetics Soc. Am., Internat. Assn. Plant Taxonomy (past pres., 25th Anniversary medal 1975), Nat. Acad. Scis., N.E. Bot. Club (past pres.), Soc. Study Evolution., Phi Beta Kappa, Sigma Xi, Sigma Chi, Phi Kappa Phi. Current Work: The role of interspecific hybridization in plant evolution; the evolution of seed-dispensing mechanisms, monographic studies of the Cruciferae of North America. Subspecialties: Systematics; Evolutionary biology. Home: 19 Chauncy St Cambridge MA 02138 Office: Gray Herbarium 22 Divinity Ave Cambridge MA 02138

ROLLO, F. DAVID, med. affairs exec., co. exec., educator; b. Endicott, N.Y., Apr. 15, 1939; s. Frank C. and Augustine R.; m. Deane M. Rollo, June 8, 1967; children—Mindanao, Alexander. A. in Chem. Tech, Broome Tech. Community Coll., Binghamton, N.Y., 1957; diploma indsl. engring, Internat. Corr. Schs., Scranton, Pa., 1958; B.A., Harpur Coll., Binghamton, 1959; M.S. in Radiol. Physics, U. Miami, 1965; Ph.D. in Physics, Johns Hopkins U., 1968; M.D., SUNY-Upstate Med. Center, Syracuse, N.Y., 1972. Diplomate: Am. Bd. Nuclear Medicine; med. lic. Calif., Tenn., Ky. Devel. research physicist IBM Glendale Lab., Endicott, 1959-60; asso. prof. math., physics Broome Tech. Community Coll., 1960-64; cons. physicist Sinai Hosp., Balt., 1965-68, Md. Gen. Hosp., Balt., 1965-68, Greater Balt. Med. Center, 1965-68; research asst. Johns Hopkins Med. Instn., 1968, research cons., 1969—; research cons. dept. nuclear medicine Duke U., 1969-72; Intern U. Calif.-San Francisco, 1972-73, resident in radiology, 1972-76, resident nuclear medicine sect., 1973-74, hosp. radiation physicist, 1973-76, asst. prof. medicine, 1974-77, asst. prof. radiology, 1974-77; asst. chief nuclear medicine service VA Hosp., San Francisco, 1974-77, dir. radiol. services, 1977-81, acting dir. radiol. sci. div., 1977-78, asso. prof. radiology and radiol. scis., 1977-79, prof., 1979—, dir. med. services, 1979-81, asst. to dean hosp. affairs, 1979-81; chief nuclear medicine VA Hosp., Nashville, 1977-79, asst. chief, 1979-81; v.p. advanced med. tech. and med. affairs Humana, Inc., Louisville, 1980-84, sr. v.p. med. affairs, 1984—; cons. Capintec, Hewlett Packard, New England Nuclear, Mediphysics/Hoffman La Roche. Editorial bd.: Computerized Tomography Jour, 1980—; editorial rev. bd.: Picker Jour. Nuclear Med. Instrumentation, 1980—; manuscript reviewer: Jour. Physics in Medicine and Biology, 1975—, Jour. Nuclear Medicine, 1975—, Am. Jour. Radiology, 1976—; contbr. numerous articles in field to profl. jours. Grantee in field. Fellow Am. Coll. Nuclear Physicians; mem. Soc. Nuclear Medicine (Calif. chpt. chmn. Ednl. com. 1975-77, chmn. quality assurance com. 1976-77, mem. exec. com. 1975-77, chmn. membership com. 1976-77, chmn. quality control com. instrumentation 1977—, pres. 1978-79, trustee 1979-82, chmn. info. subcom. 1980—), Am. Math. Soc., Assn. Physicists in Medicine and Biology, Health Physics Soc., Nat. Assn. Residents and Interns, Assn. Univ. Radiologists, Am. Coll. Radiologists, Radiol. Soc. N. Am., AMA, Jefferson County Med. Assn., Ky. Med. Assn., Louisville Radiol. Soc., Phi Theta Kappa. Current Work: To assess and implement appropriate technologies and methodologies to improve quality of health care. Subspecialties: Imaging technology; Radiology. Home: 3717 Hillsdale Rd Louisville KY 40222 Office: PO Box 1438 500 W Main St Louisville KY 40201

ROLLWAGEN, JOHN A., computer company executive. Chmn., pres., chief exec. officer Cray Research, Inc., Mpls. Subspecialty: Computer company management. Office: Cray Research Inc 608 2d Ave S Minneapolis MN 55402

ROMAGNANO, MARY ANN ANTOINETTE, neurology researcher; b. N.Y.C., Nov. 28, 1951; d. Anthony and Mary Rose (Bonanno) R.; m. William John Kingston, Nov. 27, 1976; 1 child, William Anthony. B.S. summa cum laude, CCNY, 1973; Ph.D., Albert Einstein Coll. Medicine, 1978. Postdoctoral fellow U. Rochester, N.Y., 1978-80; instr. neuroscis. 1979-85, asst. prof. anatomy, 1980-82, asst. prof. neurology, 1982—, co-dir. neorosci. course, 1982-83. Editor: Jour. Brain Research, Anns. Neurology. Contbr. articles to profl. jours. Fellow Albert Einstein Coll. Medicine, 1973-77, U. Rochester, 1978-80. Mem. Soc. for Neurosci., AAAS, Phi Beta Kappa. Current work: Peptidergic sympathetic neuroanatomy. Office: Dept Neurology Monroe Community Hosp 435 E Henrietta Rd Rochester NY 14603

ROMÁN, GUSTAVO CAMPOS, neurologist, educator; b. Bogotá, Colombia, Sept. 7, 1946; came to U.S., 1975; s. Gustavo B. and Helena (Campos) R.; m. Lydia Isabel Navarro, July 14, 1972; children—Gustavo, Natalia Isabel, Andrés Santiago. B.A., Emmanuel D'Alzon U., Bogotá, 1964; M.D., Nat. U. Colombia, Bogotá, 1971. Diplomate Am. Bd. Neurology. Intern, S.J.D.D. Univ. Hosp. Bogotá, 1971, Hôpital de la Salpêtriére, Paris, 1973-75; resident U. Vt., Burlington, 1975-78, fellow, 1978-79; instr. then asst. prof. Nat. U. Colombia, Bogotá, 1972-81, El Rosario U., Bogotá, 1982-83, Tex. Tech. U., Lubbock, 1983-84, assoc. prof., 1985—; cons. Ministry Health, Bogotá, 1982-83. Author: (textbook) Neurología Práctica, 1980, (with others) Neurología Tropical, 1983. Editor: Avances en Neurobiología, 1981, Bases Moleculares de la Vida, 1980. Contbr. articles to profl. jours. Am. Paralysis Assn. grantee, 1982, 85. Fellow ACP; mem. Am. Acad. Neurology, World Fedn. Neurology, Am. Assn. Electromyography and Electrodiagnosis, Columbian Nat. Acad. Medicine (C Esguerra medal 1971, Colombian nat. med. award 1980). Current work: Tropical neurology and neuroepidemiology; nerve regeneration; use of low-amplitude DC currents in neural regeneration; diagnostic use of biomagnetism. Subspecialties: Neurobiology; Regeneration. Office: Dept Neurology Tex Tech Lubbock TX 79430

ROMAN, HERSCHEL LEWIS, geneticist; b. Szumsk, Poland, Sept. 29, 1914; came to U.S., 1921, naturalized, 1927; s. Isadore and Anna R.; m. Caryl Kahn, Aug. 11, 1938; children—Linda, Ann. A.B., U. Mo., 1936, Ph.D., 1942. Instr. U. Wash., 1942-46, asst. prof., 1946-47, asso. prof., 1947-52, prof., 1952—, chmn. dept. genetics, 1959-80; vis. investigator Carlsberg Lab., Copenhagen, 1960; vis. prof. Australian Nat. U., Canberra, 1966; cons. in field. Editor: Ann. Rev. Genetics, 1965-84. Served with AC U.S. Army, 1943-46. Guggenheim fellow, 1952; Fulbright fellow, 1956; recipient Gold medal Emil Christian Hansen Found., Copenhagen, 1980. Mem. Am. Acad. Arts and Scis., Nat. Acad. Scis., Genetics Soc. Am. (pres. 1968; Thomas Hunt Morgan medal 1985), Research, publs. on maize genetics, yeast genetics. Current Work: Studies of recombination in the yeast Saccharomyces cerevisiae. Subspecialty: Genetics and genetic engineering (biology). Home: 5619 NE 77th St Seattle WA 98115 Office: Dept Genetics U Wash Seattle WA 98195

ROMAN, IAN CHARLES, chemical and research engineer; b. Brisbane, Australia, July 26, 1953; came to U.S., 1979; s. Walter and Eugenia (Mendia) R.; m. Valeria Iaccarino, Feb. 1, 1979; 1 child, Peter. M.S. cum laude in Chem. Engring., U. Naples, Italy, 1979. Research engr. Bend Research, Inc., Oreg., 1979-81, sr. research engr., 1981-83; research engr. DuPont, Wilmington, Del., 1983—. Patentee in field. Recipient I-R 100 award Research and Devel. Mag., 1984. Mem. Am. Inst. Chem. Engring., European Soc. Membrane Sci. and Tech., Am. Chem. Soc. Current work: Gas separation with membranes, reverse osmosis, microfiltration and ultrafiltration. Subspecialty: Water supply and wastewater treatment. Home: Wilmington DE 19803 Office: Dupont Exptl Station E-323 Wilmington DE 19898

ROMANISHIN, WILLIAM, astronomer, educator; b. Pa., Dec. 1, 1952; s. William and Kathy (Beltram) R.; m. Janet E. Davidson, Jan. 2, 1982. A.B., Harvard U., 1974; Ph.D., U. Ariz., 1980. Postdoctoral scholar UCLA, 1980, adj. asst. prof., 1980-82; research assoc. NASA/Goddard Space Flight Ctr., Greenbelt, Md., 1982-84; faculty research assoc. dept. physics Ariz. State U., Tempe, 1984—. Contbr. articles to profl. jours. Mem. Am. Astron. Soc., Astron. Soc. of Pacific, Royal Astron. Soc. (London). Current work: Study of star formation in spiral galaxies. Subspecialty: Optical astronomy. Office: Dept Physics Ariz State U Tempe AZ 85287

ROMME, WILLIAM HOWARD, biology and ecology educator, research plant ecologist; b. Denver, Mar. 20, 1948; s. Howard A. and Maurine (Trumble) R.; m. Janet C. Johnston, June 19, 1971; 1 child, Matthew E. B.A., U. N.Mex., 1970; M.S., U. Wyo., 1977, Ph.D., 1979. Asst. prof. biology and ecology Eastern Ky. U., Richmond, 1979-82, Fort Lewis Coll., Durango, Colo., 1982—; cons. Nature Conservancy, Boulder, Colo., 1984—. Contbr. articles to sci. jours. Grantee NSF, 1984, U. Wyo.-Nat. Park Service, 1977, 82. Mem. Ecol. Soc. Am. (Cooper award 1985), AAAS, Internat. Assn. for Vegetation Sci., Colo-Wyo. Acad. Sci. Democrat. Current work: Community structure, function and diversity; disturbance theory; fire ecology; landscape ecology; forest insect/plant interactions. Subspecialties: Ecology (biology); Theoretical ecology. Home: 604 Hocker Dr Durango CO 81301 Office: Dept Biology Fort Lewis Coll Durango CO 81301

ROMMEL, FREDERICK ALLEN, microbiologist/immunologist, immunochemist; b. Carlisle, Pa., Feb. 27, 1935; s. Norman Connelly and Myra Nancy (Allen) R.; m. Constance Ann Esposito, Aug. 30, 1957; 1 child, Frederick Allen II. B.S., U. Miami, 1957; Ph.D., U. Miami and Howard Hughes Med. Inst., 1967. Chief microbiology and immunology Kansas City Gen. Hosp., Mo., 1975-76; research chemist Plum Island Animal Disease Ctr., Dept. Agr., Greenport, N.Y., 1976-81; v.p. research and devel. ImmunoGenetics, Dover, N.H., 1981-83; cons. BioMed Con, Camp Hill, Pa., 1983-84; lab. dir. Dermatology, Allergy and Clin. Immunology Reference Lab., Johns Hopkins U. Med. Sch., Balt., 1984—. Contbr. articles to profl. jours., 1958-82. Served with USAF, 1958-62. Grantee NIH, 1971 (3), Non Smokers Club, 1973. Mem. Am. Assn. Immunologists, Am. Soc. Microbiologists, Am. Assn. Vet. Immunologists, World Mariculture Soc., N.Y. Acad. Scis. Current work: Immunity; immunodiagnostics; phagocytosis; venoms and toxins; tissue regeneration; aquaculture; diseases of aquatic invertebrates; allergy. Subspecialties: Immunology (medicine); Microbiology (medicine). Home: 3815 Market St Camp Hill PA 17011 Office: Johns Hopkins Med Instns GSH 5601 Loch Raven Blvd Baltimore MD 21239

ROMNEY, CARL F., seismologist; b. Salt Lake City, June 5, 1924; m. Barbara Doughty; children: Carolyn Ann, Kim. B.S. in Meteorology, Calif. Inst. Tech.; Ph.D., U. Calif. Seismologist U.S. Dept. Air Force, 1955-58; asst. tech. dir. Air Force Tech. Applications Center, 1958-73; dep. dir. Nuclear Monitoring Research Office, Def. Advanced Research Projects Agy., 1973-75, dir., 1975-79; dep. dir. Def. Advanced Research Projects Agy., 1979-83; dir. Ctr. for Sersmic Studies, 1983—; tech. adviser U.S. reps. in negotiations Test Ban Treaty; mem. U.S. del. Geneva Conf. Experts, 1958, Conf. on Discontinuance Nuclear Weapons Tests, 1959, 60; negotiations on threshold Test Ban Treaty, Moscow, 1974; mem. U.S. del. Peaceful Nuclear Explosions Treaty, Moscow, 1974-75. Contbr. articles to tech. jours. Recipient Exceptional Civilian Service awards Air Force, 1959, Exceptional Civilian Service awards Dept. Def., 1964, 79; Pres.'s award for Distinguished Fed. Civilian Service, for outstanding contbns. to devel. of control system for underground nuclear tests, 1967; Presdl. Rank of Meritorious Exec., 1980. Research on earthquake mechanism, seismic noise; generation, propagation, detection seismic waves from underground explosions. Current Work: Generation, propagation; detection of Seismic Waves from underground nuclear explosives; discrimination between explosions and earthquakes; yield estimation. Subspecialty: Geophysics. Home: 4105 Sulgrave Dr Alexandria VA 22309 Office: 1300 N 17th St Suite 1450 Arlington VA 22209

ROMNEY, SEYMOUR LEONARD, physician; b. N.Y.C., June 8, 1917; s. Benjamin and Anna (Senter) R.; m. Shirley Gordon, Nov. 4, 1945; children—Benjamin, Mary Clark, Dana, Anne. B.A., Johns Hopkins U., 1938; M.D., NYU, 1942. Diplomate Am. Bd. Obstetrics and Gynecology. Resident in obstetrics and gynecology Boston Lying-In Hosp., Free Hosp. for Women, 1946-48, fellow Harvard Med. Coll., Boston, 1946-48, from instr. to assoc. prof., 1948-57; prof., chmn. Albert Einstein Med. Coll., Bronx, N.Y., 1957-72, prof., 1972—, dir. gynec. cancer research, 1976—. Co-editor: The Health Care of Women, 1980. Served to lt. USN, 1943-45. Josiah Macy Jr. Found. Research fellow, 1954-56. Mem. Am. Gynecol. and Obstet. Soc., Soc. Gynecol. Investigation, Am. Assn. Cancer Research, Alpha Omega Alpha. Jewish. Current work: Nutritional influences in cervix cancer with special emphasis upon role of vitamins A and C and the cyclic nucleotides in cancer prevention. Subspecialties: Cancer research (medicine); Nutrition (biology). Office: Albert Einstein Coll Medicine 1300 Morris Park Ave Bronx NY 10461

RONA, PETER ARNOLD, geophysicist, educator; b. Trenton, Aug. 17, 1934; s. Gustav G. and Elizabeth (Herzog) R.; m. Donna Cook, Aug. 16, 1974; 1 child, Jessica. A.B., Brown U., 1956; M.S., Yale U., 1957, Ph.D., 1967. Exploration geologist Standard Oil Co., Durango, Colo., 1957-59; research assoc. Columbia U. Hudson Labs., Dobbs Ferry, N.Y., 1960-69; sr. research geophysicist NOAA, Miami, Fla., 1969—; adj. prof. marine geology and geophysics U. Miami, 1974—; cons. UN, N.Y.C., 1970—; chmn. NATO Advanced Research Inst., 1982. Editor: Mid-Atlantic Ridge, 1976; NOAA Atlas of North Atlantic, 1980; Seafloor Spreading Centers: Hydrothermal Systems, 1981; Hydrothermal Processes at Seafloor Spreading Center, 1983. Contbr. over 150 articles to profl. jours. Chmn. Mus. of Sci., Inc., 1979-80, v.p., 1977—; trustee Internat. Oceanographic Found., 1981—; officer Dade County Council for Arts and Scis., 1979-84; counselor Boy Scouts Am., 1981—. Brown U. scholar, 1952-56; Dana fellow, 1956-57; Gibbs fellow, 1956-57; Sheffield fellow, 1963-67. Fellow Geol. Soc. Am. (assoc. editor 1975-82), AAAS; mem. Acoustical Soc. Am., Am. Assn. Petroleum Geologists, Am. Geophys. Union, Am. Mgmt. Assn., Marine Tech. Soc., Miami Geol. Soc., Soc. Exploration Geophysicists, Soc. Vertebrate Paleontologists, Soc. Econ. Geologists, Soc. Econ. Paleontologists and Mineralologists, Yale U. Sci. and Engring. Assn., Explorers Club, Sigma Xi. Clubs: Brown U., Yale U. (Miami); President's (U. Miami). Current work: Marine geological and geophysical research on structure and development of continental margins and ocean basins with emphasis on seafloor mineral and energy resources. Office: NOAA 4301 Rickenbacker Causeway Miami FL 33149

RONDESTVEDT, CHRISTIAN S(CRIVER), chemist; b. Mpls., July 13, 1923; s. Christian and Stella (Robertson) R.; m. Estelle Sloman, Sept. 10, 1944; children—Karen Anne, Nancy Carol. B.Chemistry, U. Minn., 1943; Ph.D., Northwestern U., 1947. Mem. faculty U. Mich., Ann Arbor, 1947-56; Guggenheim fellow U. Munich, 1956-57; research assoc. E.I. DuPont de Nemours & Co., Inc., Wilmington, Del., 1957—. Contbr. articles to profl. jours. Patentee in field. Com. chmn. 1st Unitarian Ch., 1960—. Mem. Am. Chem. Soc. Republican. Current work: Organofluorine compounds, monomers and polymers, textile treatments; processes for aromatic amines; crosslinking polysaccharides; organic titarium compounds. Subspecialties: Organic chemistry; Polymer chemistry. Home: 2547 Deepwood Dr Wilmington DE 19810 Office: EI DuPont de Nemour & Co Inc Jackson Lab Wilmington DE 19898

RONSHEIM, PAUL ANDREW, materials scientist; b. Columbus, Ohio, Jan. 18, 1950; s. Samuel Burns and Marian Gail (Riebe) R.; m. Joyce Karen Ringham, Mar. 18, 1978; 1 child, Jennifer. B.S. in Physics, U. Minn., 1978; Ph.D. in Materials sci., 1981. Postdoctoral fellow U. Minn., Mpls., 1981; mem. tech. staff AT&T Bell Labs, Indpls., 1981-83; staff engr. IBM, East Fishkill, N.Y., 1983—. Contbr. articles to profl. jours. Mem. Am. Phys. Soc. Current work: Analytic or physical characterization of materials used in electronic devices— relating their properties to the processing. Subspecialties: Electronic materials; Materials processing. Office: IBM East Fishkill Z48A Route 52 Hopewell Junction NY 12533

ROOKS, WENDELL HOFMA, II, biologist, administrator; b. Ann Arbor, Mich., Oct. 2, 1931; s. Wendell Hofma and Geesje (Uitslager) R.; m. Nancy Marjorie Wiersma, Jan. 12, 1955; children—Cynthia N., David P., Lynelle G., Cheryl J., Phillip J. A.B., Calvin Coll., 1953; M.S., U. Mich., 1954. Staff scientist Worcester Found. Exptl. Biology, Shrewsbury, Mass., 1956-64; asst. dept. head Bioassay Inst. Hormone Biology, Syntex Corp., Palo Alto, Calif., 1964-65, head dept. bioassay, 1965-80; asst. dir. Inst. Biol. Sci., Syntex Research, Palo Alto, 1973—. Contbr. articles to profl. jours. Patentee in field. Served with U.S. Army, 1954-56. Mem. Am. Soc. Pharmacology and Exptl. Therapeutics. Mem. Christian Reformed. Ch. Current work: Steroid, anti-inflammatory, analgesic, prostaglandin, inflammatory mediator and reproductive pharmacology. Subspecialty: Endocrinology. Home: 686 Teresi Ln Los Altos CA 94022 Office: Syntex USA Inc R7-101 3401 Hillview Ave Palo Alto CA 94304

ROOP, ROBERT DICKINSON, environmental scientist; b. Plainfield, N.J., Sept. 23, 1949; s. Robert Wendell and Katherine (Booth) R.; m. Edna Southerland Wieland, Jan. 25, 1981; 1 child, Jay Lee. B.A. magna cum laude, Hiram Coll., 1971; M.A., SUNY-Stony Brook, 1975. Research asst. SUNY-Stony Brook, 1971-74, staff ecologist Inst. Ecology, Washington, 1974-76; research assoc. Oak Ridge Nat. Lab., 1976—. Author: Biomass Energy Systems and the Environment, 1981. Contbr. articles to profl. jours. Mem. Water Pollution Control Fed. (vice chmn. ecology com. 1984), Ecol. Soc. Am., Am. Inst. Biol. Scis., Phi Beta Kappa. Current work: Low-level radioactive waste disposal, biomonitoring in water pollution control, biomass energy systems, human food systems. Subspecialties: Ecology (environmental science); Water supply and wastewater treatment. Office: Oak Ridge Nat Lab PO Box X Bldg 2001 Oak Ridge TN 37831

ROOT, JOHN WALTER, research scientist, microcomputer consultant; b. Kansas City, Mo., Oct. 5, 1935; s. Floyd Walter and Alice Elizabeth (Duff) R.; m. Jessie Ann Cramer, Aug. 20, 1960; children—Cheryl Ann, Laura Lynn. B.A. in Chem., U. Kans., 1957, Ph.D., in Chem., 1964; postgrad. UCLA, 1966. Asst. prof. chemistry U. Calif.-Davis, 1966-70, assoc. prof., 1970-75, prof., 1975-85; mem. research staff Los Alamos Nat. Lab., 1985—; cons. MicroComputing, Los Alamos, 1984—. Editor: Fluorine Containing Free Radicals: Kinetics and Dynamics of Reactions, 1978; co-editor Short-lived Radionuclides in Chemistry and Biology, 1981. Contbr. numerous articles to profl. jours. Guggenheim fellow Brookhaven Nat. Lab., 1972-73, Assoc. Western Univs. fellow Los Alamos Nat. Lab., 1985; NSF fellow, 1960-63. Mem. Am. Chem. Soc., Am. Phys. Soc., Radiation Research Soc., Sigma Xi. Current work: Use of short-lived radioisotopes in chemistry and biology, radiotracer and laser probes of kinetic phenomena, nuclear magnetic resonance studies of angular momentum relaxation in gases and liquids, kinetic collision theories of chemical reaction rates and of physical transport processes, use of microcomputers in science, education and business, scientific text editing and electronic communications, distributed computing. Subspecialties: Physical chemistry; Kinetics. Office: C-10 MS-B296 Los Alamos Nat Lab Los Alamos NM 87545

ROOT, RICHARD BRUCE, ecologist, educator; b. Dearborn, Mich., Sept. 7, 1936; s. Charles Augustus and Doris Mabel (Jewell) R.; m. Elizabeth Eichstedt, June 15, 1953 (div. 1980); children—Jennifer Susan, Bryan Thomas. B.S., U. Mich., 1958; Ph.D., U. Calif.-Berkeley, 1964. Asst. prof. Cornell U., Ithaca, N.Y., 1964-71, assoc. prof., 1971-78, prof. ecology, 1978—; mem. field staff Rockefeller Found., Cali, Colombia, 1970-71; dir. Orgn. for Tropical Studies, San Jose, Costa Rica, 1976—; counselor Assn. for Tropical Biology, Washington, 1983—. Editor Ecology Ecol. Monographs Jour., 1970-73. Contbr. articles to profl. jours. Recipient A. Brazier Howell award Cooper Ornithol. Soc., 1962; NSF research grantee, 1967—. Fellow Royal Entomological Soc. London; mem. Ecol. Soc. Am. (pres. 1984—, v.p. 1979-80), Am. Ornithologists Union (elected), Am. Soc. Naturalists. Democrat. Buddhist. Current work: Impact of herbivores on plants, evolution of plant-arthropod associations, influence of resource dispersion on population dynamics, agricultural ecology. Subspecialty: Ecology (biology). Office: Cornell U Sect Ecology and Systematics Ithaca NY 14853

ROOT, SAMUEL I., geology educator, consultant; b. Winnipeg, Man., Can., Mar. 1, 1930; came to U.S., 1963, naturalized, 1969; s. Shep and Rose (Olasker) R.; m. Esther Root, Nov. 16, 1952; children—Sharon, Malcolm, Joel. B.Sc. with honors, U. Man., 1952, MSc., 1956; Ph.D., Ohio State U., 1958. Petroleum geologist Exxon, Colombia and Peru, 1957-63, Brazil, 1978-82; geologist Pa. Geol. Survey, Harrisburg, 1963-78; Shoolroy prof. geology Coll. of Wooster (Ohio), 1983—; cons. World Bank, Washington, 1983—. Contbr. articles to profl. publs. Am. Assn. Petroleum Geologists grantee, 1956. Fellow Geol. Soc. Am.; mem. Am. Assn. Petroleum Geologists, Soc. Econ. Geologists. Current work: Structure Triassic basins, structure basement Ohio, Pa. Subspecialties: Sedimentology; Tectonics. Home: 816 College Ave Wooster OH 44691 Office: Dept Geology Coll of Wooster Wooster OH 44691

ROOT, THOMAS MICHAEL, biologist, educator, researcher; b. Detroit, Mar. 6, 1952; s. Robert Leonard and Margaret Ludwina (Reese) R.; m. Lorraine Zack, May 22, 1976. B.S. in Biology, U. Detroit, 1974; M.S. in Zoology and Physiology, U. Wyo., 1976, Ph.D. in Zoology and Physiology, 1979. Vis. lectr. U. Wyo., Laramie, 1979; asst. prof. biology Middlebury (Vt.) Coll., 1979—. Contbr. articles to sci. jours., chpt. to book. Mem. Soc. for Neurosci., AAAS, Am. Soc. Zoologists. Current work: Neural control of behavior; behavior of scorpions. Subspecialties: Comparative neurobiology; Ethology. Office: Biology Dept Middlebury College Middlebury VT 05753

ROPER, LEON DAVID, physics educator, researcher; b. Shattuck, Okla., Dec. 13, 1935; s. Fred Loyd and Eva Lucille (Franklin) R.; m. Thelma Lee Rowland, May 29, 1955; children—Tamra Dawn Roper Oliver, Truda Gaye Roper Demirbulak. A.B. with honors, Okla. Baptist U., 1958; Ph.D., MIT, 1963. With Lawrence Livermore Lab., Livermore, Calif., 1963-65; asst. prof. Ky. So. Coll., Louisville, 1965-67; from asst. prof. to prof. physics Va. Poly. Inst. and State U., Blacksburg, 1967—, assoc. dir. for acad. computing Computing Ctr., 1985—; research physicist CERN, Switzerland, ICTP, Italy, U. Glasgow, Scotland, 1973-74, Nat. Lab. for High Energy Physics, Japan, 1980-81; sr. lectr. U. Papua New Guinea, Port Moresby, 1983. Author: The Dirac Delta Function in Physics, 1971; Simple Membrane Electrodiffusion Theory, 1972; The Metals and Mineral Fuels Crisis, 1976. Fellow Am. Phys. Soc., Biophys. Soc., World Future Soc. (pres. S.W. Va. chpt. 1984-85). Democrat. Subspecialties: Particle physics; Biophysics (physics). Office: Dept Physics Va Poly Inst and State Univ Blacksburg VA 24061

ROPES, JOHN WARREN, fishery biologist; b. Salem, Mass., May 17, 1927; s. Harold Earle and Lucille (Lane) R.; m. Mary Wimmer, Apr. 30, 1965. B.A., Alfred U., 1953; M.S., U. Del., 1978. Fishery aide Bur. Comml. Fisheries, Newburyport, Mass., 1954-55; fishery biologist, Kingston, R.I., 1955-70, NOAA, Nat. Marine Fisheries Service, Dept. Commerce, Oxford, Md. and Woods Hole, Mass., 1970—. Contbr. articles to profl. jours. Served with USN, 1945-47. Fellow Am. Inst. Fishery Research Biologists; mem. Am. Fishery Soc. (cert. fishery biologist), Am. Malacologists Assn., Am. Soc. Limnology and Oceanography, Nat. Shellfish Assn. Lodge: Rotary (pres. St. Michaels, Md.). Current work: Biological research related to management of bivalve shellfish resources. Subspecialties: Marine biology; Population biology. Home: 21 Pattee Rd East Falmouth MA 02536 Office: NOAA Nat Marine Fisheries Service Dept Commerce Water St Woods Hole MA 02541

ROPP, WALTER SHADE, chemist; b. Lakeland, Fla., Oct. 15, 1922; s. Walter Omer and Julia A. (Walker) R.; children—James B., Patricia A., Donald C. B.S., Fla. So. Coll., 1943; M.S., Pa. State U., 1944, Ph.D., 1948. Research chemist Hercules Inc., Wilmington, Del., 1947-52, supr., 1952-56, tech. rep., 1956-58, sr. research chemist, 1958-68, research assoc., 1968-79, sr. research assoc. 1979—. Contbr. articles to profl. jours. Patentee in field. Current work: Isolation, properties and modification of natural products. Subspecialties: Surface chemistry; Polymer chemistry. Home: RD 5 Box 151 Hockessin DE 19707 Office: Hercules Inc Research Ctr Wilmington DE 19894

ROSARIO-GARCÍA, EFRAÍN, physics educator, researcher; b. Ciales, P.R., Oct. 6, 1938; s. Benedicto Rosario and María García; m. Ana Delia Rodríguez, Nov. 28, 1963; children—Ana María, Efraín, Jr. B.S. in Physics, U. P.R., 1961, M.S. in Nuclear Sci., 1965; Ph.D. in Physics, SUNY-Albany, 1976. Asst. researcher P.R. Nuclear Ctr., Mayaguez, 1961-63; instr. physics, U. P.R., Mayaguez, 1963-68, asst. prof., 1968-76, assoc. prof., 1976-81, prof., 1981—, researcher in nuclear physics, 1976-81, researcher in acoustics, 1981-84; lectr. in field. Mem. Consejo Consultive Editorial Revista Atenea, Mayaguez, 1981—. Contbr. articles to profl. jours. Army Research Office grantee, 1981. Mem. Am. Phys. Soc., Am. Assn. Physics Tchrs., Sigma Pi Sigma. Roman Catholic. Current work: Nuclear physics (photonuclear reactions, neutron charge particle reaction) Acoustics (resonance theory). Subspecialties: Nuclear physics; Acoustics. Home: Box 5279 College Station Mayaguez PR 00709 Office: U PR Mayaguez Campus Mayaguez PR 00708

ROSE, ALBERT, consulting physicist; b. N.Y.C., Mar. 30, 1910; s. Simon and Sarah (Cohen) Rosenblum; m. Lillian Loebel, Aug. 25, 1940; children: Mark Loebel, Jane Susan. A.B., Cornell U., 1931, Ph.D., 1935. Research RCA Labs., Princeton, N.J., 1935-75; dir. research Labs. RCA Ltd., Zurich, Switzerland, 1955-58; vis. scientist Exxon Labs., 1979—; mem. planning com. Internat. Confs. on Semiconductors, Internat. Conf. on Photoconductivity, Internat. Conf. on Electrophotography; vis. prof. Stanford U., 1976, Hebrew U., Jerusalem, 1976-77, Boston U., 1977, 78, Poly. Inst., Mexico City, 1978, U. Del., 1979. Author: Concepts in Photoconductivity, 1963, Vision: Human and Electronic, 1974; editorial bd.: Phys. Rev, 1956-58, Advances in Electronics, 1948-75, Jour. Physics and Chemistry of Solids, 1958-75; contbr. articles to profl. jours. Recipient certificate of merit USN, 1946, TV Broadcasters award, 1945, David Sarnoff Gold medal Soc. Motion Picture and TV Engrs., 1958; Mary Shephard Upson distinguished prof. Cornell U., 1967; Fairchild distinguished scholar Calif. Inst. Tech., 1975; recipient Leo Friend award in chem. tech., 1982. Fellow Am. Phys. Soc., IEEE (Morris Liebman award 1945, Edison medal 1979); mem. Nat. Acad. Engring., Société Suisse de Physique., Soc. Photog. Scientists and Engrs. (hon.). Patentee in field. Subspecialty: Electronics. Home: 292 Stockton Rd Princeton NJ 08540

ROSE, ARTHUR WILLIAM, geochemistry educator; b. Bellefonte, Pa., Aug. 8, 1931; s. Arthur and Elizabeth (Gates) R.; m. Marjorie M. Wright, 1971; children—Theresa M., Bruce A., Edith A. B.S., Antioch Coll., 1953; M.S., Calif. Inst. Tech., 1955, Ph.D., 1958. Geologist, sr. geologist Bear Creek Mining Co., Salt Lake City, 1957-64; mining geologist State of Alaska, Anchorage, 1964-67; asst. prof., assoc. prof. geochemistry Pa. State U., University Park, 1967-75, prof., 1975—; mem. Nat. Commn. for Geochemistry, 1978-81; mem. bd. energy and mineral resources NRC, 1983—; cons. Brookhaven Nat. Labs., Upton, N.Y., 1983—. Author: Geochemistry in Mineral Exploration, 1979. Contbr. articles to profl. jours. Fellow Mineral. Soc. Am.; mem. Assn. Exploration Geochemists (pres. 1980-81), Soc. Mining Engrs. (chmn. geochemistry com. 1976), Geochem. Soc., Soc. Econ. Geologists. Current work: Geochemistry and geology of metallic and non-metallic ore deposits, geochemical exploration for ore, and environmental geochemistry. Subspecialties: Geochemistry; Environmental chemistry. Home: 726 Edgewood Circle State College PA 16801 Office: Pa State U 332 Deike Bldg University Park PA 16802

ROSE, DAVID JOHN, nuclear engineering educator, researcher; b. Victoria, B.C., Can., May 8, 1922; came to U.S., 1947, naturalized, 1958; s. David Angus and Nora (Birkett) R.; m. Constance Vivienne Fox, Feb. 6, 1948 (div. 1972); children—Elizabeth Constance, Victoria Ann (dec.), Hugh Alexander, Andrew David; m. Renate Stella Papke, July 20, 1973. Student Victoria Coll., 1939-40; B.A.Sc., U. B.C., Vancouver, 1947; Ph.D., MIT, 1950. Registered profl. engr., Mass. Scientist, B.C. Research Council, Vancouver, 1950-51; mem. tech. staff Bell Telephone Labs., Murray Hill, N.J., 1951-58; assoc. prof. MIT, Cambridge, 1958-60, prof., 1960-85, prof. emeritus, 1985—; vis. staff U.K. Atomic Energy Authority, Culham, 1968; scientist Oak Ridge Nat. Lab., Tenn., 1967-68, dir. long range planning, 1969-71; faculty Salzburg Seminar in Am. Studies, Austria, 1973; mem. ABA-AAAS Joint Conf. Lawyers and Scientists, 1975-85; cons. Govt. of Brazil, 1975, Govt. of W. Ger., 1977; trustee Scientists Inst. Pub. Info., N.Y.C., 1980—; vis. research fellow East-West Ctr., Honolulu, 1981-84; mem. energy engring. bd. NRC, Washington, 1982—; con. in field various indsl. firms and U.S. Govt. Author: (with M. Clark Jr.) Plasmas and Controlled Fusion, 1961. Editor: Nuclear-Electric Power in the Asia-Pacific Region, 1984. Contbr. articles to profl. jours. Mem. com. Ch. and Soc., World Council of Chs., Geneva, 1975-83. Served to capt. Canadian Army, 1942-45. Recipient James R. Killian Jr. Faculty Achievement award MIT, 1979-80. Fellow Am. Acad. Arts Scis., AAAS, Am. Phys. Soc. (chmn. div. plasma physics 1965-66); mem. Am. Nuclear Soc., Nat. Acad. Scis. (com. nuclear and alt. energy systems 1975-79). Episcopalian. Current work: Nuclear power technology, policy and environmental effects; assessment of technology and impacts of energy use and provision. Subspecialties: Energy policy and technology assessment; Nuclear fission. Office: MIT Cambridge MA 02139

ROSE, GLENN ROBERT, computer system consultant; b. Phila., Oct. 20, 1946; s. Victor Lamar and Edith Marion (Deakin) Rose Takatsuka; m. Barbara Siegel, June 1, 1969; children: Peter Aarron, Laura Yvonne. B.S.E.E., Drexel U., 1969; M.S.E.E., Stanford U., 1970. Mem. tech. staff Bell Telephone Labs., Holmdel, N.J., 1969-79, GTE Auto. Elec. Labs., Phoenix, 1979-80; pres. Computereze, Inc., Neshanic Station, N.J., 1980-82, Polymorphic Systems, Holmdel, 1982—. Mem. Assn. Computing Machinery, Tau Beta Pi, Phi Kappa Phi, Eta Kappa Nu. Republican. Current Work: Database systems and distributed systems. Subspecialty: Database systems. Home: 501 Sheppard Ct Neshanic Station NJ 08853 Office: Polymorphic Systems Inc PO Box 237 Holmdel NJ 07733

ROSE, GREGORY MANCEL, psychobiologist, behavioral pharmacologist; b. Eugene, Oreg., Feb. 3, 1953; s. Mancel Lee and Ilione (Schenk) R.; m. Kathleen Ann Frye, June 30, 1979; 1 child, Julian Mancel. B.S., U. Calif.-Irvine, 1975, Ph.D., 1980. Research fellow MPI for Psychiatry, Munich, W. Ger., 1976. research assoc. Miescher Lab., MPI, Tuebingen, W. Ger., 1980-81; fellow dept. pharmacology U. Colo. Health Sci. Ctr., 1981-84, asst. prof., 1984—; research biologist VA Med. Ctr., Denver, 1981—. Contbr. articles to profl. jours. VA Research Service grantee, 1981—. Mem. Soc. Neurosci. Democrat. Current work: Elucidation of physiological substrates of learning and memory, and the role of hippocampal formation in these processes; indentification of CNS alterations responsible for memory defects with aging. Subspecialties: Neuropsychology; Neuropharmacology. Office: VA Med Ctr Research Service 1055 Clermont St Denver CO 80220

ROSE, KENNETH DAVID, science educator; b. Newark, N.J., June 21, 1949; s. Victor William and Odette Adele (Messler) R.; m. Jennie Jerome Neumann, Apr. 25, 1981. B.S., Yale U., 1972; M.A., Harvard U., 1974; Ph.D., U. Mich-Ann Arbor, 1979. Post-doctoral fellow dept. paleobiology Smithsonian Instn., 1979-80; asst. prof. cell biology and anatomy Johns Hopkins U., Balt., 1980—; research collaborator dept. paleobiology Nat. Mus. Natural History Smithsonian Instn. Contbr. articles to profl. jours. Nat. Geographic Soc. grantee, 1981-82; Am. Philos. Soc. grantee, 1982-83; NSF grantee, 1983—. Mem. Soc. Vertebrate Paleontology, Paleontol. Soc., Am. Soc. Mammalogists (Shadle fellow 1978), Soc. Systematic Zoology, Sigma Xi. Current Work: Systematics, evolution and comparative and functional anatomy of early Cenozoic mammals, chiefly North American. Subspecialties: Paleobiology; Anatomy and embryology. Home: 1101 Argonne Dr Baltimore MD 21218 Office: Johns Hopkins U Med Sch 107 Hunterian Baltimore MD 21218

ROSE, RONALD PALMER, nuclear reactor mfg. company executive; b. Boston, Sept. 20, 1930; s. Arthur Burnham Hatch and Ann Margaret (Palmer) R.; m. Marjorie Joann Staples, Aug. 6, 1955; children: Linda, Randolph, Pamela, Bryan. A.B., Dartmouth Coll., 1952, M.S., 1953; Ph.D., U. Pitts., 1960. Fellow engr. Bettis Atomic Power Lab., Pitts., 1954-64; sect. chief analysis Phillips Petroleum Co., Idaho Falls, 1964-67; mgr. systems analysis Westinghouse Astronuclear Lab., Pitts., 1967-71; mgr. systems analyst Westinghouse Astronuclear Lab. (PWR div.), 1971-73; mgr. fusion projects Nuclear Energy Systems, 1975—; vis. fellow Princeton Plasma Physics Lab., 1973-75, mem. lithium blanket module adv. group, 1980-81; mem. joint US/USSR group on fusion-fission Electric Power Research Inst./Kurchatov Inst., 1976-79. Mem. Peters Twp. Sch. Dist. Long-Range Planning Group, McMurray, Pa., 1977; mem. Peters Twp. Planning Commn., 1979-81. AEC fellow, 1955. Mem. Am. Nuclear Soc., ASME, Sigma Xi. Club: Sports Car Club Am. Lodge: Elks. Patentee inertial confinement fusion concept to produce a line source of neutrons. Current Work: Fusion energy, fusion-fission hybrids, aerospace nuclear power, breeder reactors, nuclear reactor safety, energy systems analysis and forecasts. Subspecialties: Nuclear fission; Nuclear fusion. Home: 200 Grouse Dr Apt 1 Elizabeth PA 15037 Office: Westinghouse Advanced Reactors Div Madison PA 15663

ROSE, WILLIAM KENNETH, astronomy educator; b. Ossining, N.Y., Aug. 10, 1935; s. Kenneth and Shirley Hazel (Near) R.; m. Sheila L. Tuchman, Apr. 3, 1961; children: Kenneth, Edward, Cindy. A.B., Columbia U., 1957, Ph.D., 1963. Research Staff Princeton (N.J.) U., 1963-67; asst. prof. M.I.T., Cambridge, 1967-71, assoc. prof., 1971; assoc. prof. astronomy U. Md., College Park, 1971-76, prof., 1976—. Contbr. articles to profl. jours. Recipient Washington Acad. Sci. ann. award for achievement in phys. sci., 1975. Mem. AAUP, AAAS, Washington Acad. Sci. (fellow), Internat. Astron. Union, Am. Astron. Soc. Club: Cosmos. Current Work: Theoretical astrophysics, high energy astrophysics, stellar evolution. Subspecialties: Theoretical astrophysics; High energy astrophysics. Home: 10916 Picasso Ln Potomac MD 20854 Office: Astronomy Program U Md College Park MD 20742

ROSEMAN, SAUL, biochemist, educator; b. Bklyn., Mar. 9, 1921; s. Emil and Rose (Markowitz) R.; m. Martha Ozrowitz, Sept. 9, 1941; children: Mark Alan, Dorinda Ann, Cynthia Bernice. B.S., CCNY, 1941; M.S., U. Wis., 1944, Ph.D., 1947; (hon.) M.D., U. Lund, Sweden, 1984. From instr. to asst. prof. U. Chgo., 1948-53; from asst. prof. to prof. biol. chemistry, also Rackham Arthritis Research Unit, U. Mich., 1953-65; Ralph S. O'Connor prof. biology Johns Hopkins, 1965—, chmn. dept., 1969-73; dir. McCollum-Pratt Inst., 1969-73; cons. NIH, NSF, Am. Cancer Soc., Hosp. for Sick Children, Toronto; sci. counselor Nat. Cancer Inst. Author articles on metabolism of complex molecules containing carbohydrates and on solute transport.; former mem. editorial bd.: Biochemistry; mem. editorial bd.: Jour. Biol. Chemistry. Served with AUS, 1944-46. Recipient Sesquicentennial award U. Mich., 1967; T. Duckett Jones Meml. award Helen Hay Whitney Found., 1973; Rosenstiehl award Brandeis U., 1974; Internat. award Gairdner Found., 1981. Mem. Am. Soc. Biol. Chemists, Am. Soc. Cell Biology, Am. Acad. Arts and Scis., Nat. Acad. Scis., Am. Chem. Soc., Am. Soc. Microbiologists. Current Work: Membrane transport; cell-cell recognition, adhesion. Subspecialties: Membrane biology; Cell biology. Home: 8206 Cranwood Ct Baltimore MD 21208

ROSEN, ARTHUR D., neurologist, neurophysiologist; b. Bklyn., Sept. 19, 1935; s. Elihu and Gertrude (Simonson) R.; m. Deborah Mandelberg, June 29, 1958; children: Jody Lynn, Matthew Scot. B.A., Columbia U., 1956; M.D.,

SUNY, Bklyn., 1960. Diplomate Am. Bd. Psychiatry and Neurology. Intern Bklyn. Jewish Hosp., 1960-61; instr. physiology SUNY Downstate Med. Center, Bklyn., 1961-64, asst. prof. neurology, 1966-73, dir. Sci. Computing Center, 1970-73, USPHS fellow in neurophysiology, 1961-62; resident Kings County Hosp., Bklyn., 1962-64; asso. prof. neurology SUNY, Stony Brook, 1973-80, prof., 1980—, dir. div., 1973-80; mem. adv. bd. Nat. Amyotrophic Lateral Sclerosis Found. Contbr. numerous articles on neurology and neurophysiology to sci. jours. Served to lt. comdr., M.C. USNR, 1964-66. Fellow Am. Acad. Neurology; mem. Soc. for Neurosci., Am. Epilepsy Soc. Current Work: Neurophysiology of epilepsy, epilepsy, neurophysiology of multiple sclerosis. Subspecialties: Neurology; Neurophysiology. Office: Dept Neurology SUNY Stony Brook NY 11794

ROSEN, C(HARLES) A., artificial intelligence researcher; b. Toronto, Ont., Can., Dec. 7, 1917; naturalized U.S. citizen; married; 4 children. B.E.E., Cooper Union, 1940; M.Engring., McGill U., 1950; Ph.D. in Elec. Engring., Syracuse U., 1956. Sr. examiner British Air comn., N.Y.C., 1940-43; project engr. Fairchild Aircraft, Ltd., Can., 1943-47; co-owner Electrollabs Regist, 1947-50; cons. engr. Gen. Elec. Co., 1950-57; mgr. applied physics lab. SRI Internat., Sunnyvale, Calif., 1957-70, mgr. artificial intelligence group, info. sci. lab., 1970—; chief scientist Machine Intelligence Corp., Sunnyvale. Recipient Taylor award IEEE, 1975. Subspecialty: Artificial intelligence. Office: Machine Intelligence Corp 330 Potrero Ave Sunnyvale CA 94086*

ROSEN, JUDAH BEN, computer scientist; b. Phila., May 5, 1922; s. Benjamin and Susan (Hurwich) R.; children—Susan Beth, Lynn Ruth. B.S. in Elec. Engring, Johns Hopkins U., 1943; Ph.D. in Applied Math, Columbia U., 1952. Research asso. Princeton (N.J.) U., 1952-54; head applied math. dept. Shell Devel. Co., 1954-62; vis. prof. computer sci. dept. Stanford (Calif.) U., 1962-64; prof. computer sci. dept. and math. research center U. Wis., Madison, 1964-71; prof., head computer sci. dept. Inst. Tech., U. Minn., Mpls., 1971—; Fulbright prof. Technion, Israel, 1968-69; Lady Davis vis. prof., 1980; invited lectr. Chinese Acad. Sci., Peking, 1980; lectr.; cons. Argonne (Ill.) Nat. Lab.; mem. Nat. Computer Sci. Bd. Editor: Nonlinear Programming, 1970; asso. editor: Soc. Indsl. and Applied Math. Jour. on Control and Orgn, 1965-77, Jour. Computer System Scis, 1966—; contbr. articles to profl. jours. NSF grantee, 1969—. Mem. Assn. Computing Machinery, Soc. Indsl. and Applied Math., Math. Programming Soc. Current Work: Research on algorithms and computational methods for large-scale optimization problems. Subspecialties: Numerical analysis (computer science); Algorithms. Home: 1904 W 49th St Minneapolis MN 55409 Office: Dept Computer Sci U Minn 207 Church St SE Minneapolis MN 55455

ROSEN, LOUIS, physicist; b. N.Y.C., June 10, 1918; s. Jacob and Rose (Lipionski) R.; m. Mary Terry, Sept. 4, 1941; 1 son, Terry Leon. B.A., U. Ala., 1939, M.S., 1941; Ph.D., Pa. State U., 1944; D.Sc. (hon.), U. N.Mex., 1980. Instr. physics U. Ala., 1940-41, Pa. State U., 1943-44; mem. staff Los Alamos Sci. Lab., 1944—, group leader nuclear plate lab., 1949-65, alt. div. leader exptl. physics div., 1962-65, dir. meson physics facility, also div. leader medium energy physics div., 1965—; Sesquicentennial hon. prof. U. Ala., 1981. Author papers in nuclear sci. and applications of particle accelerators.; bd. editors: Applications of Nuclear Physics. Mem. Los Alamos Town Planning Bd., 1962-64; mem. Gov.'s Com. on Tech. Excellence in N.Mex.; mem. Nat. Acad. Panel on Nuclear Sci., chmn. sub-panel on accelerators; mem. N.Mex. Cancer Control Bd., 1976-80, v.p., 1979-80; mem. panel on future of nuclear sci. Nat. Research Council of Nat. Acad. Scis., 1976; mem. panel on instl. arrangements for orbiting space telescope NRC-Nat. Acad. Scis., 1976; mem. U.S.A.-USSR Joint Coordinating Com. on Fundamental Properties of Matter, 1976—; Co-chmn. Los Alamos Vols. for Stevenson, 1956; Democratic candidate for county commr., 1962; bd. dirs. Los Alamos Med. Center, 1977-83, chmn., 1983. Recipient E.O. Lawrence award AEC, 1963; Golden Plate award Am. Acad. Achievement, 1964; N.Mex. Disting. Public Service award, 1978; named Citizen of Year, N.Mex. Realtors Assn., 1973; Guggenheim fellow, 1959-60; alumni fellow Pa. State U., 1978. Fellow Am. Phys. Soc. (mem. council 1975-78, chmn. panel on public affairs 1980, chmn.-elect div. nuclear physics 1984), AAAS. Louis Rosen prize established in his honor by bd. dirs. Meson Faculty Users Group, 1984. Current Work: Energy options; national security. Subspecialties: Nuclear physics; Particle physics. Home: 1170 41st St Los Alamos NM 87544 Office: PO Box 1663 Los Alamos NM 87545

ROSEN, MARTIN HOWARD, biochemistry, educator; b. Bklyn., July 29, 1942; s. Edward Morris and Gussie (Klar) R.; m. Beth Dee Werfel, June 9, 1967. B.S., Bklyn. Coll., 1964; M.A., CUNY, 1967; Ph.D., NYU, 1974; postgrad. MIT, 1977. Teaching asst. Bklyn. Coll., 1964-67, teaching fellow, 1966-67; lectr. N.Y.C. Community Coll., Bklyn., 1966-67, Queensborough Community Coll., Queens, N.Y., 1968, Kingsborough Community Coll., Bklyn., 1968; instr. Manhattan Community Coll., N.Y.C., 1969, 70; assoc. prof. Coll. Staten Island, CUNY, 1968—, dep. chmn., evening session supr. biology dept., 1978—; research asst. Beth Israel Hosp., N.Y.C., 1965-67; research assoc. N.Y.U., Washington Square, 1974-78, N.Y.U. Med. Center, dept. dermatology, N.Y.C., 1978-82. Contbr. articles in field to profl. jours. Bd. dirs. Met. Assn. Coll. and Univ. Biologists, 1977-79, Found. Research Against Disease, 1979-83; trustee S.I. Zoo, 1981—. Recipient numerous awards and grants in field. Mem. AAAS, Am. Inst. Biol. Scis., N.Y. Acad. Sci., Sigma Xi, others. Current Work: Biochemical research in enzymatic analysis of skin cells. Subspecialties: Biochemistry (biology); Physiology (biology). Office: Dept Biology Coll Staten Island CUNY 715 Ocean Terrace Staten Island NY 07748

ROSEN, MICHAEL ROBERT, electrophysiologist, pharmacology educator; b. N.Y.C., Oct. 8, 1938; s. Jacob Selig and Gertrude Harriet (Laibson) R.; m. Tove Smulovitz, June 14, 1964; children: Nadine Miriam, Jennifer Naomi, Rachel Susannah. B.A., Wesleyan U., Conn., 1960; M.D., SUNY, Bklyn., 1964. Diplomate: Am. Bd. Internal Medicine. Intern Montefiore Hosp., N.Y.C., 1964-65, resident, 1965-66, 68-70; fellow Columbia U., N.Y.C., 1970-72, asst. prof. pharmacology, 1973-75, asst. prof. pharmacology and pediatrics, 1975-76, assoc. prof., 1976-81, prof., 1981—; sr. investigator N.Y. Heart Assn., 1972-75; mem. cardiovascular-pulmonary study sect. NIH, 1977-81. Asso. editor: Circulation Research, 1975-81; mem. editorial bd.: Circulation, 1983—; contbr. over 150 articles, revs. and abstracts to profl. jours. Served to capt., M.C. USAF, 1966-68. Irma T. Hirschl Trust fellow, 1975-79; Nat. Heart, Lung and Blood Inst. grantee, 1975—. Mem. Am. Coll. Clin. Pharmacology (pres. 1982-84), Cardiac Electrophysiologic Soc. (pres. 1981-82), Am. Heart Assn., ACP, Am. Coll. Cardiology, Am. Soc. Pharmacology and Exptl. Therapeutics, Alpha Omega Alpha, others. Current Work: Research on mechanisms responsible for cardiac arrhythmias, on interactions of heart with autonomic nervous system, developmental changes in cardiac function. Subspecialties: Pharmacology; Physiology (medicine). Office: Dept Pharmacology Columbia U 630 W 168th St New York NY 10032

ROSEN, RICHARD DAVID, research meteorologist; lecturer; b. Bklyn., Feb. 23, 1948; s. Leonard and Lucille (Poss) R.; m. Michele D. Litvin, May 20, 1973. S.B., MIT, 1970, S.M., 1970, Ph.D., 1974. Staff scientist ERT, Inc., Concord, Mass., 1974-82; sr. staff scientist Atmospheric and Environ. Research Inc., Cambridge, Mass., 1982—; sr. lectr. dept. earth, atmospheric and planetary scis. MIT, Cambridge, 1974—; mem. com. earth scis. Nat. Acad. Scis., Washington, 1982-84; mem. spl. study group Internat. Assn. Geodesy, Paris, 1983—. Contbr. articles to profl. jours. Mem. Am. Meteorol. Soc. (asso. editor Monthly Weather Rev. 1984—), Am. Geophys. Union. Current work: dynamics of the general circulation of the atmosphere; atmospheric excitation of earth rotation and polar motion; interannual variability of large-scale circulation; diagnostic studies of quality of modern data assimilation techniques. Subspecialty: Meteorology. Office: Atmospheric and Environ Research Inc 840 Memorial Dr Cambridge MA 02139

ROSENBERG, ERIC RONALD, physician, radiology educator; b. Morristown, N.J., Feb. 18, 1949; s. Alvin Abe and Evelyn Claire (Thaler) R.; m. Jean Lynn Defanti, May 21, 1977; 1 dau., Caroline. A.B., Rutgers U., 1971; M.D., N.Y. Med. Coll., 1975. Diplomate: Am. Bd. Radiology. Resident in radiology Duke U. Med. Ctr., 1975-79, fellow in radiology, 1979-80, asst. prof. radiology, 1980—. Mem. Am. Inst. Ultrasound in Medicine, Am. Coll. Radiology, Radiol. Soc. N.Am. Current Work: Diagnostic ultrasound. Subspecialties: Diagnostic radiology; Ultrasound. Office: Dept of Radiology Duke U Med Ctr Durham NC 27710

ROSENBERG, HOWARD CHARLES, pharmacology educator; b. Atlantic City, Apr. 17, 1947; s. Leroy A. and Henrietta (Tenenbaum) R.; m. Ann R., June 22, 1969; children: Martin J., Lewis A. B.A., Ithaca Coll., 1969; Ph.D., Cornell U., 1975, M.D., 1976. Fellow in pharmacology Cornell U. Med. Coll., N.Y.C., 1976-77; asst. prof. Med. Coll. of Ohio, Toledo, 1977-82, assoc. prof., 1982—; cons. Chem. Dependency Ctr. Flower Hosp. Contbr. articles to profl. jours. Nat. Inst. on Drug Abuse grantee, 1979—. Mem. Am. Soc. Pharmacology and Exptl. Therapeutics, AAAS, Soc. for Neurosci., Sigma Xi. Current Work: Research on tolerance to and dependence on sedative and tranquilizer drugs. Subspecialties: Pharmacology; Neuropharmacology. Office: Medical College of Ohio CS #10008 Toledo OH 43699

ROSENBERG, LEON EMANUEL, medical school dean; b. Madison, Wis., Mar. 3, 1933; s. Abraham Joseph and Celia (Mazursky) R.; m. Elaine Lewis, Aug. 29, 1954 (div. Nov. 1971); children—Robert, Diana, David; m. Diane Drobnis, July 4, 1979; 1 child, Alexa. B.A., U. Wis., 1954, M.D., 1957. Intern, Columbia-Presbyn. Hosp., N.Y.C., 1957-58; resident, 1958-59; resident Yale-New Haven Hosp., 1962-63; asst. prof. medicine Sch. Medicine, Yale U., New Haven, 1965-68, assoc. prof. pediatrics and medicine, 1968-72, chmn., prof. human genetics, 1972-84, C.N.H. Long prof. human genetics, 1980—, dean Sch. Medicine, 1984—. Author: Amino Acid Metabolism and Its Disorders, 1974. Editor: Metabolic Control and Disease, 1981. Served to sr. surgeon USPHS, 1959-65. Recipient Disting. Alumni citation U. Wis., 1982. Fellow AAAS, Am. Acad. Arts and Scis.; mem. Nat. Acad. Scis. Inst. of Medicine, Am. Soc. for Clin. Investigation (v.p. 1978-79), Am. Soc. for Human Genetics (pres. 1980-81), Assn. Am. Physicians, Am. Pediatric Soc., Am. Soc. Biol. Chemists. Democrat. Jewish. Current work: Amino acid metabolism; biogenesis of mitochondrial enzymes; inherited disorders. Subspecialties: Internal medicine; Genetics and genetic engineering (medicine). Office: Sch Medicine Yale U 333 Cedar St New Haven CT 06510

ROSENBERG, NORMAN JACK, agricultural meteorologist; b. Bklyn., Feb. 22, 1930; s. Jacob and Rae (Dombrowitz) R.; m. Sarah Zacher, Dec. 30, 1950; children: Daniel Jonathon, Alyssa Yael. B.S., Mich. State U., 1951; M.S., Okla. State U., 1958; Ph.D., Rutgers U., 1961. Soil scientist Israel Soil Conservation Service, Haifa, 1953-55, Israel Water Authority, Haifa, 1955-57; research asst. Okla. State U., 1957-58; research fellow Rutgers U., 1958-61; asst. prof. agrl. meteorology U. Nebr., Lincoln, 1961-64, asso. prof., 1964-67, prof., 1968—, prof. agrl. engring., 1975—, prof. agronomy, 1976—, George Holmes prof. agrl. meteorology, 1981—, leader sect. agrl. meteorology, 1974; dir. Center for Agrl. Meteorology and Climatology, 1979; cons. Dept. State AID, NOAA, Am. Public Health Assn.; mem. numerous ad hoc coms., and mem. standing com. for internat. geosphere-biosphere program Nat. Acad. Scis./NRC, 1975-78, mem. bd. on atmospheric sci. and climate; vis. prof. agrl. meteorology Israel Inst. Tech., Haifa, 1968; Lady Davis fellow Hebrew U., Jerusalem, 1977. Author: Microclimate: The Biological Environment, 1974, 2d edit., 1983, Chinese transl., 1983, Russian transl., 1986; also numerous articles in profl. jours.; editor: North American Droughts, 1978, Drought in the Great Plains: Research on Impacts and Strategies, 1980; tech. editor: Agronomy Jour, 1974-79; cons. editor: Irrigation Sci., Agrl. and Forest Meteorology, Climatic Change, Jour. Climate and Applied Meteorology. NATO sr. fellow in sci., 1968; recipient Centennial medal Nat. Weather Service, 1970. Fellow AAAS, Am. Soc. Agronomy, Am. Meteorol. Soc. (outstanding achievement in bioclimatology award 1978, councillor 1981-84); mem. Arid Zone Soc. India, Sigma Xi, Alpha Zeta, Gamma Sigma Rho. Jewish. Clubs: Malib Poker Soc. of Lincoln; Cosmos (Washington). Current Work: Effects of increasing global carbon dioxide on climate and agriculture; drought management strategy. Subspecialties: Micrometeorology; Climatology. Home: 3145 S 31st St Lincoln NE 68502 Office: 243 LW Chase Hall U of Nebr Lincoln NE 68583

ROSENBERG, PAUL, physicist, consultant; b. N.Y.C., Mar. 31, 1910; s. Samuel and Evelyn (Abbey) R.; m. Marjorie S. Hillson, June 12, 1943; 1 dau., Gale B.E. A.B., Columbia U., 1930, M.A., 1933, postgrad., 1933-40. Chemist Hawthorne Paint & Varnish Corp., N.J., 1930-33; grad. asst. physics Columbia, 1934-39, lectr., 1939-41; instr. Hunter Coll., N.Y.C., 1939-41; research asso. elec. engring. Mass. Inst. Tech., Cambridge, 1941; staff mem. Radiation Lab., Nat. Def. Research Com., 1941-45; pres. Paul Rosenberg Assocs. (cons. physicists), Larchmont, N.Y., 1945—, Inst. Nav., 1950-51; Mem. war com. radio Am. Standards Assn., 1942-44; gen. chmn. joint meeting Radio Tech. Commn. for Aeros., Radio Tech. Commn. for Marine Services and Inst. of Nav., 1950; co-chmn. Nat. Tech. Devel. Com. for upper atmostphere and interplanetary nav., 1947-50; mem. maritime research Adv. com. Nat. Acad. Scis.-NRC, 1959-60; chmn. cartography panel space programs Earth resources survey NRC, 1973-76; chmn. panel on nav. and traffic control space applications study Nat. Acad. Scis., 1968. Bd. dirs. Center for Environment and Man, 1976-85. Contbr. sci., tech. articles to prof. jours.; Editorial com.: Jour. Aerospace Scis, 1952-60. Fellow AAAS (council 1961-73, v.p. 1966-69), IEEE, Am. Inst. Chemists, Explorers Club, AIAA (asso.); mem. Am. Phys. Soc., Am. Chem. Soc., Nat. Acad. Engring., Acoustical Soc. Am., Armed Forces Communication Assn., Optical Soc. Am., N.Y. Acad. Scis., Am. Soc. Photogrammetry (Talbert Abrams award 1955), Am. Assn. Physics Tchrs., Sigma Xi, Zeta Beta Tau. Clubs: Beach Point Yacht (Mamaroneck, N.Y.); Columbia U. Patentee in field. Current Work: Navigation, photogrammetry, lasers, robotics, ultrasonics, electrooptics, semiconductors. Subspecialties: Remote sensing (geoscience); Solar energy. Home: 53 Fernwood Rd Larchmont NY 10538 Office: PO Box 729 Larchmont NY 10538

ROSENBERG, PHILIP, pharmacologist, educator, editor, researcher; b. Phila., July 28, 1931; s. Morris and Rose (Schwartz) R.; m. Sybil Edith Stepman, Oct. 21, 1956; children: Stuart Owen, Rachelle, Gail Linda. B.S., Temple U., 1953; M.S., U. Kans., 1955; Ph.D., Thomas Jefferson U., 1957. Registered pharmacist, Pa. Asst. prof. Jefferson U., Phila., 1957-58; research fellow, asst. prof. Columbia U. Coll. Physicians and Surgeons, N.Y.C., 1958-68; prof. pharmacology Pharmacy Sch., U. Conn., Storrs, 1968—, chmn. sect. pharmacology and toxicology, 1968—; cons. in field; Meyerhoff sr. fellow Weizmann Inst. Sci., Rehovoth, Israel, 1982-83. Editor: Toxins: Animal, Plant and Microbial, 1978; contbr. chpts. to books, articles to profl. jours. USPHS spl. postdoctoral fellow, 1960-62; USPHS career devel. award, 1964-68; NIH grantee, 1978—; U.S. Army Med. Research and Devel. Command grantee, 1982—. Fellow Acad. Pharm. Scis. (Redi award 1982); mem. AAAS, Am. Assn. Colls. Pharmacy, Am. Chem. Soc., Am. Pharm. Assn., Am. Profs. for Peace in Middle East (co-chmn. U. Conn. chpt.), Am. Soc. Neurochemistry, Am. Soc. Pharmacology and Exptl. Therapeutics, Corp. Marine Biol. Lab. (Woods Hole, Mass.), Council Biology Editors, Harvey Soc., Internat. Soc. on Toxinology, N.Y. Acad. Scis., Sigma Xi, Phi Kappa Phi, Rho Chi, Rho Pi Phi. Jewish. Current Work: Cholinergic system and action of anticholinesterases; phospholipid function and action of phospholipases on nerve, muscle and synapse; use of toxins as tools in studying bioelectrical phenomenon. Subspecialties: Pharmacology; Neurochemistry. Home: 40 Middle Rd Ellington CT 06029 Office: Sch Pharmacy U Conn Storrs CT 06268

ROSENBERG, ROBERT BRINKMANN, research organization executive; b. Chgo., Mar. 19, 1937; s. Sidney and Gertrude (Brinkmann) R.; m. Patricia Margaret Kane, Aug. 1, 1959; children: John Richard, Debra Ann. B.S. in Chem. Engring. with distinction, Ill. Inst. Tech., 1958, M.S. in Gas Tech, 1961, Ph.D. in Gas Tech, 1964. Registered profl. engr., Ill. Adj. asst. prof. Ill. Inst. Tech., 1965-69; mem. staff Inst. Gas Tech., Chgo., 1962-77, v.p. engring. research, 1973-77; v.p. research and devel. Gas Research Inst., Chgo., 1977-78, exec. v.p., 1978-83, sr. v.p., 1983—. Author. Mem. Hinsdale (Ill.) Home Rule Ad Hoc Com., 1975-77; emeritus bd. dirs. Hinsdale Cultural Arts Soc., 1977—; pres. Triangle Frat. Edn. Found., 1974—; mem. vis. com. dept. chemistry U. Tex. Mem. Am. Inst. Chem. Engrs., Am. Gas Assn. (ex officio mem. mng. com. of operating sect.), Inst. Gas. Engrs., Combustion Inst. (past treas. bd. central states sect.), Atlantic Gas Research Exchange (chmn. mng. bd. 1980—), Internat. Gas Union (U.S. mem. subcom. F-2 1974-83), Gas Appliance Engrs. Soc. (past trustee), Air Pollution Control Assn. (past sect. com. residential pollution sources). Patentee in field. Current Work: Research on production; distribution and utilization of natural gas and substitute gaseous fuels. Subspecialties: Fuels; Combustion processes. Office: 8600 W Bryn Mawr Ave Chicago IL 60631

ROSENBERG, SAUL ALLEN, oncologist, educator; b. Cleve., Aug. 2, 1927. B.S., Western Res. U., 1948, M.D., 1953. Diplomate: Am. Bd. Internal Medicine. Intern Univ. Hosp., Cleve., 1953-54; resident in internal medicine Peter Bent Brigham Hosp., Boston, 1954-61; research asst. toxicology AEC Med. Research Project, Western Res. U., 1948-53; asst. prof. medicine and radiology Stanford (Calif.) U., 1961-65, asso. prof., 1965-79, chief div. oncology, 1965—, prof. medicine and radiology, 1970—, Am. Cancer Soc. prof.; chmn. bd. No. Calif. Cancer Program, 1974-80. Contbr. numerous articles to profl. jours., chpts. to textbooks. Served to lt. M.C. USNR, 1954-56. Recipient Eleanor Roosevelt Internat. Fellows award Am. Cancer Soc., 1971-72. Fellow ACP; mem. Am. Assn. Cancer Research, Inst. Medicine of Nat. Acad. Sci., Am. Assn. Cancer Edn., Am. Fedn. Clin. Research, Am. Soc. Clin. Oncology (pres. 1982-83), Assn. Am. Physicians, Calif. Acad. Medicine, Radiation Research Soc., Western Soc. Clin. Research, Western Assn. Physicians. . Office: Div Oncology Stanford U Sch Medicine Stanford CA 94305

ROSENBLATT, MURRAY, mathematics educator; b. N.Y.C., Sept. 7, 1926; m. Adylin, July 1949; children—Karin, Daniel. B.S., CCNY, 1946; M.S., Cornell U., 1947, Ph.D. in Math., 1949. Asst. prof. U. Chgo., 1950-55; assoc. prof. math. Ind. U., 1956-59; prof. probability and stats. Brown U., 1959-64; prof. U. Calif.-San Diego, 1964—; vis. asst. prof. Columbia U., 1955; guest scientist Brookhaven Nat. Lab., 1959; vis. fellow U. Stockholm, 1953, Univ. Coll. London, 1965-66, Imperial Coll. and Univ. Coll. London, 1972-73, Australian Nat. U., 1976, 79; vis. scholar Stanford U., 1982. Author: (with U. Grenander) Statistical Analysis of Stationary Time Series, 1957, Random Processes, 1962, Edited Time Series Analysis, 1963, Markov Processes, Structure and Asympototic Behavior, 1971; editor: The North Holland Series in Probability and Statistics, 1981—, The Birkhauser Boston Inc. Progress in Probability and Stats. Series, 1982; mem. editorial bd.: Jour. Multivariate Analysis, 1970—, Ind. Jour. Math., 1957—, Jour. Time Series Analysis, 1981—; contbr. articles to profl. jours. Office Naval Research grantee, 1949-50; Guggenheim fellow, 1965-66, 71-72; overseas fellow Churchill Coll., Cambridge U., 1979; recipient Bronze medal U. Helsinki, 1978. Fellow Inst. Math. Stats., AAAS, Internat. Statis. Inst.; mem. Am. Math. Soc., Nat. Acad. Scis., Sigma Xi, Phi Beta Kappa. Current Work: Probability theory; stochastic processes; time series analysis; turbulence. Subspecialty: Statistics. Office: Dept Math U Calif-San Diego La Jolla CA 92093

ROSENBLUTH, MARSHALL NICHOLAS, physicist, educator; b. Albany, N.Y., Feb. 5, 1927; s. Robert and Margaret (Sondhein) R.; m. Sara Unger, Feb. 6, 1979; children by previous marriage—Alan Edward, Robin Ann, Mary Louise, Jean Pamela. B.A., Harvard, 1945; M.S., U. Chgo., 1947, Ph.D., 1949. Inst. Stanford, 1949-50; staff mem. Los Alamos Sci. Lab., 1950-56; sr. research adviser Gen. Atomic Corp., San Diego, 1956-67; prof. U. Calif., San Diego, 1960-67, Inst. for Advanced Study, Princeton, N.J., 1967-80; lectr. with rank prof. in astrophys. scis. Princeton U.; also vis. sr. research physicist Princeton U. (Plasma Physics Lab.), 1967-80; dir. Inst. for Fusion Studies, U. Tex., 1980—; Andrew D. White vis. prof. Cornell U., 1976; cons. AEC, NASA, Inst. Def. Analysis. Served with USNR, 1944-46. Recipient E.O. Lawrence award, 1964, Albert Einstein award, 1967, Maxwell prize, 1976. Mem. Am. Phys. Soc., Nat. Acad. Sci., Am. Acad. Arts and Scis. Subspecialty: Plasma physics. Office: Dept Physics U Tex Austin TX 78712

ROSENBROOK, WILLIAM, JR., chemist; b. Omaha, Mar. 28, 1938; s. William and Dorothy (Johnson) R.; m. Edith Jean Lawrence, June, 1960 (div. Sept. 1966); children—William Warren, Edward; m. Jeannette Marie Miller, Feb. 22, 1969. Student Carleton Coll., Northfield, Minn., 1956-59; B.A., U. Omaha, 1960; Ph.D., Mont. State U., 1964. Postdoctoral fellow U. Calif.-Berkeley, 1964-65; sr. research chemist Abbott Labs., North Chicago, Ill., 1965—. Contbr. articles to profl jours. Patentee in field. Mem. Am. Chem. Soc., Sigma Xi. Current work: Modification of and synthesis of antibiotics. Subspecialties: Organic chemistry; Synthetic chemistry. Home: 15440 W Fair Ln Libertyville IL 60048 Office: Abbott Labs Abbott Park North Chicago IL 60064

ROSENFELD, AZRIEL, computer science educator, administrator, consultant; b. N.Y.C., Feb. 19, 1931; s. Abraham Hirsh and Ida B. (Chadaby) R.; m. Eve Hertzberg, Mar. 1, 1959; children—Elie, David, Tova. B.A., Yeshiva U., 1950, M.S., 1954, M.L.H., 1953, D.L.H., 1955; M.A., Columbia U., 1951, Ph.D., 1957; D.Tech. (hon.), Linkoping U., Sweden, 1980. Ordained rabbi, 1952. Physicist Fairchild Controls Corp., N.Y.C., 1954-56; engr. Ford Instrument Co., Long Island City, N.Y., 1956-59; mgr. research electronics div. Budd Co., Long Island City, McLean, Va., 1959-64; prof. computer sci., dir. U. Md., College Park, 1964—; vis. asst. prof. Yeshiva U., N.Y.C., 1957-63; pres. ImTech, Inc., Silver Spring, Md., 1975—. Current work: Computer vision, image processing, pattern recognition, artificial intelligence, theoretical computer science. Subspecialties: Graphics, image processing, and pattern recognition; Artificial intelligence.

ROSENFELD, ISADORE, medical educator, cardiologist, lecturer; b. Montreal, Que., Can., Sept. 7, 1926; came to U.S., 1958; s. Morris and Vera (Friedman) R.; m. Camilla Master, Aug. 19, 1956; children: Arthur, Stephen, Hildi, Herbert. B.S., McGill U., 1947, M.D.C.M., 1951, diploma internal medicine, 1956. Intern Royal Victoria Hosp., Montreal; also resident Balt. City Hosp.; clin. asst. prof. medicine Cornell Med. Coll., N.Y.C., 1964-71, clin. assoc. prof., 1971-79, clin. prof., 1979—; attending N.Y. Hosp., N.Y.C., 1964—; pres. Rosenfeld Heart Found., N.Y.C., 1974—; juror Lasker Sci. Awards, 1972; pres. Found. Bio-Med. Research, N.Y.C., 1982, lectr., TV commentator.; vis. prof. Baylor U. Coll. Medicine, 1982. Author: ECG and X-Ray in Diseases of the Heart, 1963, The Complete Medical Exam, 1978, Second Opinion, 1981. Bd. dirs. N.Y. Heart Assn., 1979-82; mem. NTL adv. com. Harriman Inst. Advanced Study of Soviet Union, 1982; bd. overseers Cornell U. Med. Coll., 1980—. Recipient Vera award The Voice Found., 1981. Fellow ACP, Am. Coll. Chest Physicians, Am. Coll. Cardiology, Royal Coll. Physicians Can., N.Y. County Med. Soc. (bd. censors 1979-83, v.p. 1983-84, pres. 1985-86), Cornell U. Med. Coll. Alumni (hon.). Jewish. Current Work: Hypertension, angina pectoris, sudden cardiac death, arteriosclerosis. Subspecialty: Cardiology. Office: 125 E 72d St New York NY 10021

ROSENFELD, JOHN LANG, geology educator; b. Portland, Oreg., July 14, 1920; s. James Wendel and Gladys (Lang) R.; m. Juanita Jeanette Baker, Oct. 23, 1943; children—Susan Jane, John L., Jr. A.B., Dartmouth Coll., 1942; A.M., Harvard U., 1949, Ph.D., 1954. Teaching fellow Harvard U., 1946-49, research fellow, 1963-64, hon. research assoc., 1971-72; asst. prof. Mo. Sch. Mines and Metallurgy, 1949-55; vis. asst. prof. Wesleyan U., 1955-57; from asst. prof. to prof. geology UCLA, 1957—. Author: Rotated Garnets in Metamorphic Rocks, 1970; also articles. Advisor on geology to govtl., community, and environ. orgns.; commr. Geol. and Natural History Survey, State of Conn., 1955-57. Served to 1st lt. USAAF, 1942-45. Guggenheim fellow, 1963-64. Fellow Mineralogical Soc. Am., Geol. Soc. Am.; mem. AAUP (pres.-elect Calif. Conf. 1985), New Eng. Intercollegiate Geol. Conf. (participant), Am. Geophys. Union, AAAS, Oreg. Hist. Soc., Nature Conservancy Soc., Sigma Xi. Democrat. Jewish. Club: Faculty. Current work: Back-folding; theory of schistosity; solid inclusion piezothermometry; geology of southeast Vermont, eastern Connecticut, and central Alps; use of microstructures and phase assemblages in understanding tectonics and mechanisms of metamorphic recrystallization. Subspecialties: Geology; Petrology. Office: Dept Earth and Space Scis UCLA Los Angeles CA 90024

ROSENHEIM, DONALD EDWIN, electrical engineer; b. N.Y.C., Mar. 23, 1926; s. Seymour Lawrence and Leah Rebecca (Rosenberg) R.; m. Judith Comfort Hyman, June 22, 1958; children—Micah Robert, Jay Aaron. B.S. in Elec. Engring. magna cum laude, Poly. Inst. Bklyn., 1949; M.S., Columbia U., 1957. Devel. engr. Servo Corp. Am., 1949-51; mem. research staff IBM Corp., 1951—, dir. San Jose (Calif.) Research Lab., 1973-83; dir. tech. coordination, 1983-84, asst. dir., 1984—; lectr. CCNY, 1956, Columbia U., 1958. Sr. mem. IEEE; mem. Sigma Xi. Tau Beta Pi, Eta Kappa Nu. Fields: Electrical, computer engineering. Home: 128 Smith Creek Dr Los Gatos CA 95030 Office: IBM Research Lab K01/282 5600 Cottle Rd San Jose CA 95193

ROSENKILDE, CARL EDWARD, physicist; b. Yakima, Wash., Mar. 16, 1937; s. Elmer Edward and Doris Edith (Fitzgerald) R.; m. Bernadine Doris Blumenstine, June 22, 1963; children: Karen Louise, Paul Eric. B.S. in Physics, Wash. State Coll., 1959; M.S. in Physics, U. Chgo., 1960, Ph.D. in Physics, 1966. Postdoctoral fellow Argonne (Ill.) Nat. Lab., 1966-68; asst. prof. math. NYU, 1968-70; asst. prof. physics Kans. State U., Manhattan, 1970-76, assoc. prof., 1976-79; physicist Lawrence Livermore (Calif.) Nat. Lab., 1979—, cons., 1974-79. Contbr. articles on physics to profl. jours. Woodrow Wilson fellow, 1959, 60. Mem. Am. Phys. Soc., Am. Astron. Soc., Soc. for Indsl. and Applied Math., Am. Geophys. Union, Acoustical Soc. Am., Phi Beta Kappa, Phi Kappa Phi, Phi Eta Sigma, Sigma Xi. Republican. Presbyterian. Club: Tubists Universal Brotherhood Assn. (TUBA). Current Work: Nonlinear wave propagation, in complex media. Subspecialties: Theoretical physics; Fluid dynamics. Office: Lawrence Livermore Nat Lab PO Box 808 Livermore CA 94550

ROSENKRANTZ, HARRIS, biochemical pharmacologist, educator, consultant; b. Bklyn., Mar. 23, 1922; s. Abraham and Miriam (Heller) E.; m. Natalee Faye Rosenkrantz, May 19, 1951; children: Elliot Dale, Mark Steven. A.B., Bklyn. Coll., 1943; M.S., N.Y. U., 1946, Cornell U. Med. Sch., 1948; Ph.D., Tufts U. Med. Sch., 1952. Research fellow Worcester Found. Exptl. Biology, Shrewsbury, Mass., 1951-52, staff scientist, 1952-59; spl. lectr. in biochemistry Clark U., Worcester, Mass., 1955-58, asso. prof. biology, 1959-62, prof. biochemistry, 1963—; adj. prof. toxicology dept. comparative medicine Tufts U. Sch. Vet. Medicine, 1981—; dir. biochemistry, dir. biochem. pharmacology EG&G Mason Research Inst., Worcester, 1959-85, v.p., 1961-85; cons. in life scis. Contbr. articles to sci. publs., chpts. to books. Recipient Admiral Earle award Worcester Engring. Soc., 1956, sci. achievement award, 1984. Mem. Am. Soc. Biol. Chemists, AAAS, Am. Chem. Soc., Am. Inst. Chemists, Am. Soc. Pharmacology and Exptl. Therapeutics, Coblentz Soc., Endocrine Soc., N.Y. Acad. Scis., Soc. Toxicology, Am. Physiol. Soc., Sigma Xi. Democrat. Jewish. Current Work: Drugs of abuse; drugs to treat iron overload; contraceptive and fertility drugs. Subspecialties: Biochemistry (medicine); Toxicology (medicine). Home: 136 S Flagg St Worcester MA 01602

ROSENKRANZ, HERBERT S., microbiologist; b. Vienna, Austria, Sept. 27, 1933; came to U.S., 1948, naturalized, 1954; s. Samuel and Lea Rose (Marilles) R.; m. Deanna Eloise Green, Jan. 27, 1959; children: Pnina Gail, Eli Joshua, Marguerite E., Dara V., Jeremy Emil, Sara C., Naomi, Cynthia. B.S., CCNY., 1954; Ph.D., Cornell U., 1959. Predoctoral fellow Sloan-Kettering Inst. Cancer Research, N.Y.C., 1954-59, postdoctoral research fellow, 1959-60, research assoc., 1960; research assoc. dept. biochemistry Sch. Medicine, U. Pa., Phila., 1960-61; asst. prof. dept. microbiology Columbia U., N.Y.C., 1961-65, assoc. prof., 1965-69, prof., 1969-76; prof., chmn. dept. microbiology, prof. pediatrics N.Y. Med. Coll., Valhalla, 1976-81; cons. pathology Westchester County Med. Ctr., Valhalla, 1976-81; prof. epidemiology and community health, biochemistry and radiology, dir. Ctr. Environ. Health Scis., Case Western Res. U. Sch. Medicine, Cleve., 1981-84, prof., chmn. dept. environ. health scis., prof. biochemistry, pediatrics and radiology, 1985—; vis. prof. microbiology Hebrew U.-Hadassah Med. Sch., 1971-72; mem. panel on carcinogenicity and mutagenicity Nat. Cancer Inst., 1976—; cons. U.S. EPA, 1977—; mem. Internat. Commn. Protection Against Environ. Mutagens and Carcinogens, 1978—; mem. sci. rev. panel health research U.S. EPA, 1980—; cons. Internat. Agy. Research on Cancer WHO, 1980—. Mem. editorial bd.: Mutation Research, 1976—, Mutation Research Letters, 1980—, Environmental Mutagenesis, 1981—. Recipient Faculty Summer Research award Lalor Found., 1963, Career Devel. award USPHS, 1965-75, Spl. Corp. Recognition award Xerox Corp., 1980; named Aaron Bendich Meml. lectr. Cornell U. Med. Coll., 1980; Ochs-Adler scholar, 1954-56; Alfred P. Sloan Found. predoctoral fellow, 1956-59; Nat. Cancer Inst. postdoctoral fellow, 1959-60. Mem. AAAS, Am. Assn. Cancer Research, Am. Chem. Soc., Am. Soc. Biol. Chemists, Am. Soc. Microbiology, Corp. Marine Biol. Lab., Enzyme Club, Harvey Soc., Soc. Gen. Physiologists, Environ. Mutagen Soc., Am. Soc. Photobiology, Infectious Diseases Soc. Am., Genetic Soc. Am., Sigma Xi. Current Work: Causes and prevention of cancer. Subspecialties: Cancer research (medicine); Molecular biology. Office: Case Western Res U Sch Medicine 2119 Abington Rd Cleveland OH 44106

ROSENKRANZ, ROBERTO PEDRO, pharmacologist; b. Mexico City, Mar. 30, 1950; s. George and Edith Rosenkranz; m. Heather Blum, Aug. 21, 1983. A.B. in Psychology, Stanford U., 1971; Ph.D. in Comparative Pharmacology/-Toxicology, U. Calif.-Davis, 1980. Neurobiologic researcher Instituto Nacional de Neruologia, Mex., 1971-72; Mexican del. Internat. Group on Drug Legis. and Programs, Geneva, 1971-73; dir. research Centro Mexicano de Estudios en Farmacodependencia, 1972-73; research fellow dept. medicine Stanford (Calif.) U., 1980-82; staff research II, Syntex Research, Palo Alto, Calif., 1982—; cons.; pres. Lic. Luis Echeverria Alvarez. Contbr. articles on pharmacology to profl. jours. Mex. del. Joint U.S.-Mex. Exec. Conf. on Drug Abuse Planning, 1972; Mex. del. UN Social Def. Research Inst., Rome, 1971-72. Mem. AAAS, N.Y. Acad. Scis., Soc. Neurosci., Am. Soc. Pharmacology and Exptl. Therapeutics, Western Pharmacology Soc., Internat. Soc. Study of Xenobiotics. Current work: Dopaminergic mechanisms, renovascular pharmacology, pharmacology of vasoactive amines, calcium antagonists. Subspecialties: Pharmacology; Neuropharmacology. Office: Syntex Research 3401 Hillview Palo Alto CA 94305

ROSENSHEIN, JOSEPH SAMUEL, hydrologist, geologist; b. Kimball, W.Va, Apr. 19, 1929; s. Samuel and Ida Sarah (Sattar) R.; m. Helene Silverman; children—Leonard, Richard, Susan. B.A., U. Conn., 1952; M.A., Johns Hopkins U., 1953; Ph.D., U. Ill., 1967. Ground-water geologist U.S. Geol. Survey, Indpls., 1953-64, chief R.I. subdist., Providence, 1964-67, chief Tampa subdist., Fla., 1967-75, dist. chief Kans., Lawrence, 1975—; mem. U.S. del. 7th session UN Commn. on Natural Resources, Econ. and Social Commn. for Asia and the Pacific, Bankok, Thailand, 1980; mem. nat. research council U.S. Nat. Commn. for Internat. Assn. Hydrologists, 1981-84. Editor: (with others) Ground-water Hydraulics, 1984. Contbr. articles to profl. jours., reports to books. Served to sgt. U.S. Army, 1946-48. Recipient Best Paper award Jour. Ground Water, 1978, Meritorious Service award Dept. Interior, 1983. Fellow Geol. Soc. Am.; mem. Am. Geophys. Union (chmn. ground-water com. 1978-80), Internat. Assn. Hydrogeologists, Am. Water Resources Assn., Am. Inst. Hydrology (cert., bd. registration Mpls. chpt. 1984). Current work: Management and direction of scientifically diverse programs in hydrology; hydrologic and water-resources investigations. Subspecialties: Hydrology; Geology. Office: US Geol Survey 1950 Constant Ave Campus West Univ Kans Lawrence KS 66046

ROSENSWEIG, RONALD ELLIS, chemical engineer, researcher; b. Hamilton, Ohio, Nov. 8, 1932; s. Herman and Deana (Meisel) R.; m. Ruth E. Cohen, Sept. 5, 1954; children—Scott E., Beth E., Perry E. S.M., MIT, 1956, Sc.D., 1959; Ch.E., U. Cin., 1955. Asst. prof. MIT, Cambridge, Mass., 1959-62; prin. scientist Avco Corp., Lowell, Mass. 1962-69; founding pres., tech. dir. Ferrofluidics Corp, Burlington, Mass., 1969-72, chmn. bd., 1973, dir., 1969-83; sr. research assoc. Exxon Research and Engring. Co., Annandale, N.J., 1973—; vis. prof. U. Minn., Mpls., 1980; cons. Union Carbide, Dynatech, NRC, others, 1959-62. Author: Ferrohydrodynamics, 1985. Contbr. articles to profl. jours. Patentee in field. Chmn. MIT Regional Alumni fund, Lexington, Mass., 1965; chief YMCA Indian Guides, Summit, N.J., 1975. NSF fellow; grantee NASA, USAF, Avco Corp., 1965-69; recipient 4 IR-100 awards Ind. Research mag., 1965-72; named Young Engr. of Yr., Avco Space Systems div., 1966. Mem. Nat. Acad. Engring., Am. Inst. Chem. Engrs., IEEE (magnetics affiliate). Jewish. Club: Motley (N.J.). Current work: Ferrohydrodynamic stability studies and application to fluidization, chemical reactors, separation processes, and rheological measurement, magnetic fluid research, self-organizing systems. Subspecialties: Fluid mechanics; Magnetic physics. Home: 34 Gloucester Rd Summit NJ 07901 Office: Exxon Research and Engring Co Route 22 East Annandale NJ 08801

ROSENTHAL, MYRON MARTIN, electronics engineer, educator, author; b. Bklyn., Nov. 5, 1930; s. Murray Morris and Selma Locke (Belsky) R.; m. Dolores Elaine Winard, June 21, 1953; children—Lynn, Debbie, Richard. B.E.E., CCNY, 1953; M.S., Adelphi U., 1957. Registered profl. engr., N.J.; lic. public acct., N.J. Sr. engr. Republic Aviation Corp., Farmingdale, L.I., 1955-61; pres. Myron M. Rosenthal & Staff, 1957-61; program mgr. Loral Electronics, Bronx, N.Y., 1962-64; engring. mgr. Singer-Kearfott div. The Singer Co., Wayne, N.J., 1964—; prof. Poly. Inst. N.Y., Bklyn., 1954—; bd. dirs. Electronics and Aerospace Conv., 1971-82, treas., 1972-82, chmn. bd., 1974; bd. dirs. Nat. Aerospace and Electronics Conf., 1972-75; notary pub. N.J. Founder Randal Carter PTA cultural workshop, Wayne, 1965; lighting commr. Wayne, 1956. Patentee inflatable antenna, cylindrical flat plate 35 GHz antenna, rotating lens antenna seeker-head. Amateur radio operator. Recipient Picatinny Arsenal U.S. Army Engring. and Leadership commendations, 1969, 71, 73; Poly. Inst. N.Y. faculty award, 1975, Disting. Faculty award, 1982, Nat. Aerospace and Electronics Conf. award, 1968, 75, 76; Electronics and Aerospace Conv. award, 1974, 80, 82. Mem. IEEE (sr., award 1972, 74, Centennial medal 1984, Faculty Advisor award 1985), Nat. Soc. Profl. Engrs., AIAA, ASME, ASCE, Illuminating Engring. Soc., Am. Assn. Clin. Chemistry, Am. Inst. Indsl. Engrs., Assn. U.S. Army Navy League, U.S. Naval Inst., Marine Corps. Assn., Am. Def. Preparedness Assn., Air Force Assn., ASTM, Aerospace Electronics and Systems Soc. (bd. govs. 1968-82, v.p., 1972, chmn. N.Y.-N.J. Met. chpt. 1972-82, Disting. Service award 1972-74, 79, 82), Armed Forces Communications and Electronics Assn., AAUP, N.Y. Acad. Scis., Am. Soc. Indsl. Security, Am. Chem. Soc., Am. Assn. Physics Tchrs., Am. Physics Soc., Am. Soc. Safety Engrs. (profl.), Am. Vocat. Assn. (life), Am. Soc. Nondestructive Testing, Constrn. Specifications Inst., Am. Soc. Public Adminstrn., Am. Public Works Assn., Am. Assn. Cost Engrs., Am. Ceramic Soc., Nat. Mgmt. Assn. (cert.), Nat. Council Tchrs. of Math., Nat. Council Tchrs. of English, Adult Edn. Assn., Am. Radio Relay League, Nat. Assn. Accts., Nat. Soc. Public Accts., ALA, Soc. Automotive Engrs., Am. Craft Council, Nat. Soc. Architects, Am. Soc. Interior Design, Nat. Sci. Tchrs. Assn., Soc. Plastics Engrs., Audio Engring. Soc., Internat. Assn. Assessing Officers, Am. Hist. Assn., Am. Philos. Assn., MLA, Inst. of Nav. (program com. 1978), Am. Judicature Soc., Aircraft Owners and Pilots Assn., Refrigeration Service Engrs. Soc., Am. Motorcycle Assn., AAAS, Boat Owners Assn., Am. Assn. Higher Edn., Nat. Aeros. Assn., Nat. Assn. Social Workers, Nat. Council Young Israel, Am. Rose Soc., Nat. Audubon Soc., Nat. Assn. of Deaf, Nat. Eye Research Found., Am. Council for Blind, Am. Diabetes Assn., Nat. Rehab. Assn., Am. Jewish Congress, Workmen's Circle, Sigma Xi, Eta Kappa Nu. Republican. Jewish. Clubs: B'nai B'rith (trustee 1976-77), Toastmasters (pres. 1969, area gov. 1970, best speaker of the year 1967, 68, 69, 75, 77). Home: 48 Tall Oaks Dr Wayne NJ 07470 Office: 333 Jay St Brooklyn NY 11201

ROSNOW, RALPH L(EON), psychology educator, researcher; b. Balt., Jan. 10, 1936; s. Irvin and Rebecca (Faber) R.; m. Marion Audrey Quin, Aug. 12, 1963. B.S., U. Md., 1957; M.A., George Washington U., 1958; Ph.D., Am. U., 1962. Asst. prof. Boston U., 1963-67; assoc. prof. Temple U., Phila., 1967-70, prof., 1970-82, Thaddeus L. Bolton prof., 1982—, dir. Social Psychology div., 1985—; Gen. series editor Oxford Univ. Press, N.Y.C., 1975-82; vis. prof. London Sch. Econs., 1973, Harvard U., 1974. Author: (with K. Craik et al) New Directions in Psychology IV, 1970, (with Robert E. Lana) Introduction to Contemporary Psychology, 1972, (with Robert Rosenthal) The Volunteer Subject, 1975, Primer of Methods for the Behavioral Sciences, 1975, Japanese edit., 1976, (with Gary Alan Fine) Rumor and Gossip: The Social Psychology of Hearsay, 1976, Japanese edit., 1982, Paradigms in Transition: The Methodology of Social Inquiry, 1981, (with Robert Rosenthal) Essentials of Behavioral Research: Methods and Data Analysis, 1984, Understanding Behavioral Science: Research Methods for Research Consumers, 1984, Contrast Analysis: Focused Comparisons in the Analysis of Variance, 1985; editor: (with Edward J. Robinson) Experiments in Persuasion, 1967, (with Robert Rosenthal) Artifact in Behavioral Research, 1969, (with Robert E. Lana) Readings in Contemporary Psychology, 1972, Reconstruction of Society Series, 4 vols, 1975-77. Grantee NSF, 1966-73; Grantee NIH, 1964-66. Fellow AAAS, Am. Psychol. Assn.; mem. Soc. Exptl. Social Psychology, Eastern Psychol. Assn. Current Work: Conceptual and empirical work on the social psychology of research and the scientific method; social psychology of rumor and gossip; benevolent and malevolent pretenses of everyday life. Subspecialty: Social psychology. Home: 177 Biddulph Rd Radnor PA 19087 Office: Temple U Philadelphia PA 19122

ROSS, DIANA LYNN, pediatric neurologist, researcher; b. Cleve., Sept. 8, 1947; d. James Edward and Mary Elizabeth (Dormish) R.; m. Thomas Edward Goad, Dec. 16, 1983. B.S., Purdue U., 1968; M.D., Case-Western Res. U., 1972. Diplomate Am. Bd. Psychiatry and Neurology, Am. Bd. Pediatrics. Pediatric resident St. Louis Children's Hosp., 1972-74; neurology resident Barnes Hosp., St. Louis, 1974-76; child neurology fellow U. Minn., Mpls., 1976-77, child neurology faculty mem., 1977-79; asst. prof. child neurology, U. Cin., 1979-82; child neurologist Cin. Neurologic Assocs., 1982—. Contbr. articles to profl. jours., chpts. to books. Mem. pub. relations com. Cin. Acad. Medicine, 1984—; mem. exec. bd. Cin. Classical Guitar Soc. Fellow Am. Acad. Pediatrics, Am. Acad. Neurology; mem. Child Neurology Soc. (mem. membership com. 1980-81, tng. com., 1981-82, bylaws com. 1982-83, nominating com., 1983—), Soc. Neurosci. Current work: Neuroendocrinology, neuropeptide roles in neurologic and psychiatric disorders, including infantile autism, anorexia nervosa, infantile spasms. Subspecialties: Neurology; Pediatrics. Home: 3379 Aultview Ave Cincinnati OH 45208 Office: Cincinnati Neurologic Assn 111 Wellington Pl Cincinnati OH 45219

ROSS, DOUGLAS TAYLOR, software company executive, educator; b. Canton, China, Dec. 21, 1929; s. Robert Malcolm and Margaret (Taylor) R.; m. Patricia Mott, Jan. 24, 1951; children: Jane Louise, Kathryn Ross Chow, Margaret Ross Thrasher. A.B., Oberlin Coll., 1951; S.M., MIT, 1954; postgrad., 1954-58. Head computer applications group Electronic Systems Lab., MIT, Cambridge, 1952-69, lectr. elec. engring., 1960-69, lectr. elec. engring. and computer sci., 1983—; pres. SofTech, Inc., Waltham, Mass., 1969-75, chmn. bd., 1975—; dir. Cognition, Inc., Burlington, Mass., 1985—; chmn. evaluation panel for Inst. Computer Scis. and Tech. of Nat. Bur. Standards, 1978-83, chmn., 1981-83; mem. exec. com. MIT Enterprise Forum, 1984—; trustee Charles Babbage Inst., 1984—. Mem. editorial bd. Software: Practice and Experience, 1971—, IEEE Transactions on Software Engring, 1975-79; mem. editorial adv. bd.: Computers in Industry, 1978—; contbr. articles to profl. jours. Mem. Lexington (Mass.) Town Meeting, 1960-70; mem. exec. com. MIT Enterprise Forum, 1984—; trustee, bd. dirs. Charles Babbage Inst., 1984—. Recipient Joseph Marie Jacquard award Numerical Control Soc., 1975; Disting. Contbn. award Soc. Mfg. Engrs., 1980; named Outstanding Young Man of Yr. Greater Boston Jaycees, 1959; Hon. Engr. of Yr. San Fernando Valley Engrs. Council, 1981. Mem. Assn. Computing Machinery, AAAS, Internat. Fedn. Info. Processing, Sigma Xi. Mem. United Ch. of Christ. Current Work: PLEX philosophy of structure, structured analysis, user-oriented systems design and engineering. Subspecialties: Systems analysis; Software engineering. Home: 33 Dawes Rd Lexington MA 02173 Office: 460 Totten Pond Rd Waltham MA 02154

ROSS, HUGH COURTNEY, consulting electrical engineer; b. Turlock, Calif., Dec. 31, 1923; s. Clare W. and Jeanne (Pierson) R.; m. Sarah Gordon, Dec. 16, 1950 (dec.); children: John, James, Robert; m. Patricia A. Malloy, Apr. 1, 1984. Student, Calif. Inst. Tech., 1942; student, San Jose State Coll., 1946-47; B.S.E.E., Stanford U., 1950, postgrad. in high voltage, 1951. Registered profl. engr., Calif. Instr. San Benito High Sch. and Jr. Coll., 1950-51; chief engr. Jennings Radio Mfg. Corp., San Jose, Calif., 1951-62, ITT Jennings, San Jose, 1962-64; chief engr., owner Ross Engring. HV (high voltage) Corp., San Jose Calif., 1964—; pres., chief engr. Ross Engring. Corp., Campbell, Calif., 1964—. Served with USAAF, 1943-46. Fellow IEEE; mem. Am. Soc. Metals, Am. Vacuum Soc. Patentee in field. Current Work: Energy sources and generation; consulting, design, development and production of high voltage devices, fiberoptics systems and energy sources. Subspecialties: Electrical engineering; Electronics. Home: 1854 Ashmeade Ct San Jose CA 95125 Office: 540 Westchester Dr Campbell CA 95008

ROSS, IAN MUNRO, electrical engineer; b. Southport, Eng., Aug. 15, 1927; came to U.S., 1952, naturalized, 1960; m. Christina Leinberg Ross, Aug. 24, 1955; children: Timothy Ian, Nancy Lynn, Stina Marguerite. B.A., Gonville and Caius Coll., Cambridge (Eng.) U., 1948; M.A. in Elec. Engring, Cambridge U., 1952, Ph.D., 1952; D.Sc. (hon.), N.J. Inst. Tech., 1983; D.Engring. (hon.), Stevens Inst. Tech., 1983. With Bell Telephone Labs., Inc. (now AT&T Bell Labs.), 1952—, exec. dir. network planning div., 1971-73, v.p. network planning and customer services, 1973-76, exec. v.p. systems engring. and devel., Murray Hill, N.J., 1976-79, pres., 1979—; dir. Gulton Industries, Inc., Thomas & Betts Corp., B.F. Goodrich Co. Author. Recipient Liebmann Meml. prize IEEE, 1963; Pub. Service award NASA, 1969. Fellow IEEE, Am. Acad. Arts and Scis.; mem. Nat. Acad. Engring. Patentee in field. Subspecialties: Systems engineering; Electrical engineering. Office: AT&T Bell Labs Crawfords Corner Rd Holmdel NJ 07733

ROSS, JOHN, chemistry educator; b. Vienna, Oct. 2, 1926; came to U.S., 1940; s. Mark and Anne (Kremer) R.; m. Eva Madarasz, Aug. 15, 1982; m. Virginia Ross, (div.); children—Elizabeth, Robert K. B.S., Queens Coll., N.Y.C., 1948; Ph.D., MIT, 1951. Ph.D. (hon.), Weizmann Inst. Sci., 1984. Prof. chemistry Brown U., Providence, 1962-66; prof. chemistry MIT, Cambridge, 1966-80, chmn. dept., 1966-71, F.G. Keye prof., 1971-80; prof. chemistry Stanford U., Calif., 1980—, Camille and Henry Dreyfus prof., 1984—, chmn. dept., 1983—; pres. Ross Cons., Inc., Stanford, 1982—. Author: Molecular Beams, 1966; Physical Chemistry, 1980. Contbr. articles to profl. jours. Bd. govs. Weizmann Inst. Sci., Rehovot, Israel, 1971—. Served to 2d lt. AUS, 1944-46. Fellow Am. Acad. Arts and Scis., Am. Phys. Soc., AAAS; mem. Am. Chem. Soc., Nat. Acad Scis. Current work: Chemical instabilities; periodic reactions, spatial structures. Subspecialties: Physical chemistry; Kinetics. Office: Dept Chemistry Stanford U Stanford CA 94305

ROSS, JOHN MUNDER, psychologist; b. N.Y.C., June 20, 1945; s. Nathaniel and Barbara (Munder) R.; m. Katherine Wren Ball, Aug. 17, 1974; 1 son, Matthew Munder Ball. B.A. magna cum laude, Harvard U., 1967; M.A., NYU, 1973, Ph.D., 1974; postgrad., London Sch. Econs., 1969-70. Asst. prof. Ferkauf Grad. Sch., N.Y.C., 1976-78; vis. asst. prof. Albert Einstein Coll. Medicine, Bronx, 1977-78; clin. asst. prof. Downstate Med. Ctr., Bklyn., 1978-80; clin. instr. Cornell Med. Coll., N.Y.C., 1978-80, adj. asst. prof., 1980—; clin. assoc. prof. psychiatry Downstate Med. Ctr., 1980—; cons. Child Devel. Research, Port Washington, N.Y., 1977-79; mem. adv. bd. Bank St. Fatherhood Project, N.Y.C., 1981—; bd. dirs. Primary Prevention, Detroit, 1981—; pvt. practice psychotherapy, N.Y.C., 1974—. Contbr. articles to profl. jours.; co-editor: Father and Child Developmental and Clinical Perspectives, 1982. Recipient Detur prize, John Harvard and Harvard Coll. scholarships, 1963-67; NIMH fellow, 1967-68, 69-71; Leverhulme fellow Lond Sch. Econs., 1968-69; Disting. Tchr. award Downstate Med. Sch., 1979, 80; award for outstanding book in behavioral scis. Am. Assn. Pubs., 1982. Mem. Am. Psychol. Assn., Am. Psychoanalytic Assn., N.Y. Psychol. Assn., World Assn. for Infant Psychiatry. Democrat. Clubs: Harvard (N.Y.C.); Signet Soc. (Cambridge, Mass.). Current Work: Research in parenthood and father's role in child development; sexuality in Eastern and Western literature. Subspecialty: Developmental psychology. Home: 277 West End Ave New York NY 10023 Office: 243 West End Ave New York NY 10023

ROSS, LINDA ANNE, veterinarian, researcher; b. Chgo., Jan. 22, 1951; d. Warren Robert and Ruth Bernice (Luebke) R. B.S., U. Ill.-Urbana, 1972, D.V.M., 1974; M.S., U. Ga., 1980. Diplomate Am. Coll. Veterinary Internal Medicine. Intern, South Shore Veterinary Assn., South Weymouth, Mass., 1974-75; research asst. Purdue U., 1975-76; practice vet. medicine Decatur Vet. Hosp., Atlanta, 1976-77; clin. resident U. Ga.-Athens, 1977-80; practice vet. medicine Andover Animal Hosp. Mass., 1980-81; asst. prof. vet. medicine Tufts U., 1981—. Contbr. articles to profl. jours., chpts. to books. Morris Animal Found. grantee, 1984-86. Mem. AVMA, Am. Animal Hosp. Assn., Am. Soc. Nephrology, Am. Assn. Veterinary Clinicians, Am. Coll. Veterinary Internal Medicine, NOW. Current work: Clinical small animal internal medicine; characterization of the pathophysiology of chronic renal failure, especially the role of hypertension. Subspecialty: Internal medicine (veterinary medicine). Home: 727 Heath St Chestnut Hill MA 02167 Office: Dept Medicine Tufts U 200 Westboro Rd N Grafton MA 01536

ROSS, RUSSELL, pathologist, educator; b. St. Augustine, Fla., May 25, 1929; s. Samuel and Minnie (DuBoff) R.; m. Jean Long Teller, Feb. 22, 1956; children: Valerie Regina, Douglas Teller. A.B., Cornell U., 1951; D.D.S., Columbia U., 1955; Ph.D., U. Wash., 1962. Intern Columbia-Presbyn. Med. Center, 1955-56, USPHS Hosp., Seattle, 1956-58; spl. research fellow pathology U. Wash. Sch. Medicine, 1958-62; asst. prof. pathology and oral biology U. Wash. Sch. Medicine and Dentistry, 1962-65, asso. prof. pathology, 1965-69, prof., 1969—, adj. prof. biochemistry, 1978—; asso. dean for sci. affairs Sch. Medicine, 1971-78, chmn. dept. pathology, 1982—; vis. scientist Strangeways Research Lab., Cambridge, Eng.; mem. research com. Am. Heart Assn.; mem. adv. bd. Found. Cardiologique Princess Liliane, Brussels, Belgium; vis. fellow Clare Hall, Cambridge U.; Guggenheim fellow, 1966-67; mem. adv. council Nat. Heart, Lung and Blood Inst., NIH, 1978-81. Mem. editorial bd.: Proceedings Exptl. Biology and Medicine, 1971—, Jour. Cell Biology, 1972-74; assoc. editor: Arteriosclerosis, Jour. Cellular Physiology; contbr. articles in arteriosclerosis research growth factors, and wound healing to profl. jours. Recipient Birnberg Research award Columbia U., 1975, Gordon Wilson medal Am. Clin. and Climatol. Assn., 1981; fellow Japan Soc. Promotion of Sci., 1985. Mem. Am. Soc. Cell Biology, Tissue Culture Assn., Gerontol. Soc., Am. Assn. Pathologists, Internat. Soc. Cell Biology, Electron Microscope Soc. Am., Am. Heart Assn. (fellow Council on Arteriosclerosis), Royal Micros. Soc., AAAS, Am. Soc. Biol. Chemists, Belgian Acad. Medicine (fgn. corr. mem.), Sigma Xi. Current Work: Cell and molecular biology, experimental pathology, atherscierosis, growth control of cells, connective tissue metabolism, inflammation, and cell proliferation. Subspecialties: Cell biology (medicine); Pathology (medicine). Home: 4811 NE 42d St Seattle WA 98105 Office: U of Wash Sch Medicine SM-30 Seattle WA 98195

ROSSA, ROBERT FRANK, mathematics educator, researcher; b. Kankakee, Ill., Aug. 17, 1942; s. Frank Louis and Launa Elizabeth (Lovejoy) R.; m. Dean Shelton, May 31, 1969; 1 child, Jennifer. B.A., U. Okla., 1963, M.A., 1966, Ph.D., 1971. Asst prof. Ark. State U., State University, 1969-73, assoc. prof., 1973-84, prof., 1984—. Mem. Am. Math. Soc., Math. Assn. of Am., Assn. for Computing Machinery, IEEE, Phi Beta Kappa, Sigma Xi. Mem. Christian Ch. (Disciples of Christ). Current Work: Radical theory in nonassociative rings. Home: 1901 Starling Dr Jonesboro AR 72401 Office: PO Box 151 State University AR 72467

ROSSI, BRUNO, physicist, emeritus educator; b. Venice, Italy, Apr. 13, 1905; s. Rino and Lina (Minerbi) R.; m. Nora Lombroso, Apr. 10, 1938; children—Florence S., Frank R., Linda L. Student, U. Padua, 1923-25, U. Bologna, 1925-27; hon. doctorate, U. Palermo, 1964, U. Durham, Eng., 1974, U. Chgo., 1977. Asst. physics dept. U. Florence, 1928-32; prof. physics U. Padua, 1932-38; research assoc. U. Manchester, Eng., 1939; research assoc. in cosmic rays U. Chgo., 1939-40; assoc. prof. physics Cornell U., 1940-43; prof. physics Mass. Inst. Tech., 1946—, Inst. prof., 1966-70, Inst. prof. emeritus, 1970—; Mem. staff Los Alamos Lab.; 1943-46, hon. fellow Tata Inst. Fundamental Research, Bombay, India, 1971; mem. physics com. NASA; hon. prof. U. Mayor, San Andres, La Paz, Bolivia. Author: Rayons Cosmiques, 1935, (with L. Pincherle) Lezioni di Fisca Sperimentale Elettrologia, 1936, Lezioni di Fisica Sperimentale Ottica, 1937, (with Staub) Ionization Chambers and Counters, 1949, High Energy Particles, 1952, Optics, 1957, Cosmic Rays, 1964, (with S. Olbert) Introduction to the Physics of Space, 1970. Recipient Nat. Medal of Sci., 1955; Cresson medal Franklin Inst., 1974; decorated Order of Merit Republic of Italy). Mem. Am. Acad. Arts and Scis. (Rumford prize 1976), Nat. Acad. Sci. (space sci. bd., astronomy survey com.), Deutsche Akademieder Naturforscher Leopoldina, Am. Phys. Soc., Am. Inst. Physics, Accademia dei Lincel (Internat. Feltrinelli award 1971), Internat. Astron. Union, Am., Royal astron. socs., Accademia Patavina di Scienze, Letteree Arti, Accademia Ligure di Scienze e Lettere, Bolivian Acad. Scis. (corr.), A.A.A.S., Am. Philos. Soc., Italian Phys. Soc. (Gold medal 1970), Sigma Xi. Subspecialty: Cosmic ray high energy astrophysics. Address: 221 Mt Auburn St Cambridge MA 02138

ROSSI, RONALD CHARLES, research scientist, chemical company executive; b. North Tonawanda, N.Y., June 17, 1934; s. Charles B. and Mary (Cavalleri) R.; m. Geraldine Marie Albert, Aug. 16, 1958; children—Christopher, Regina. B.S., Alfred U., 1960; M.S., U. Calif.-Berkeley, 1962, Ph.D., 1964. Sr. engr. Aeronutronics, Newport Beach, Calif., 1964-65; dept. head Aerospace Corp., El Segundo, Calif., 1965-77; dir. Tylan Corp., Carson, Calif., 1977—. Contbr. articles to profl. jours. Patentee in field. Chmn. Ad Hoc Com. for Freeway Study, Torrance, Calif., 1969. Served with U.S. Army, 1954-56. Mem. Am. Ceramics Soc. Democrat. Roman Catholic. Current work: Develop chemical vapor deposition process for thin film deposition on silicon for very large scale integration devices. Subspecialties: Ceramics; Microchip technology (materials science). Home: 23217 Robert Rd Torrance CA 90505 Office: Tylan Corp 23301 S Wilmington Ave Carson CA 90745

ROSSING, ROBERT GRANGAARD, internist, educator; b. Denver, June 6, 1925; s. Torstein Harald and Luella Enanda (Grangaard) R.; m. Dolores Christenson, June 7, 1947 (dec. Dec. 1952); children—David, Thomas; m. Lynette Hjerpe, Feb. 25, 1955 (dec. Apr. 15, 1985); 1 child, John. Student Luther Coll., 1943; M.D., U. Minn., 1949, Ph.D., 1961. Diplomate Am. Bd. Internal Medicine. Instr., U. Minn., Mpls., 1955-61; research physician USAF Sch. Aerospace Medicine, Brooks AFB, Tex., 1961-71; assoc. chief staff VA Ctr. Temple, Tex., 1971—; prof. internal medicine Tex. A&M Coll., Temple, 1980—. Contbr. articles to profl. jours. Served to 1st lt. U.S. Army, 1951-53; Korea. Mem. Sigma Xi, Alpha Omega Alpha. Lutheran. Club: Torch (pres. 1973-74, 81-82) (Temple). Current work: Medical education, computer applications to biology and medicine; statistical research and teaching. Subspecialties: Pulmonary medicine; Statistics. Home: 4000 Hickory Rd 9 Temple TX 76502 Office: VA Ctr 14A 1901 S 1st St Temple TX 76501

ROSSINGTON, DAVID RALPH, engring. educator; b. London, July 13, 1932; s. George Leonard and Clara Fanny (Simmons) R.; m. Angela Mae Reynolds, Sept. 3, 1955; children: Andrew, Carolyn, Nicholas, Philip. B.Sc. with honors in Chemistry, U. Bristol, Eng., 1953, Ph.D. in Phys. Chemistry, 1956. Research fellow N.Y. State Coll. Ceramics, 1956-58; tech. officer Imperial Chem. Industries Ltd., Eng., 1958-60; asst. prof. N.Y. State Coll. Ceramics, 1960-63, assoc. prof., 1963-69, prof., 1969—, head div. engring. sci., 1982-84, dean Sch. Engring., 1984—. Contbr. articles to profl. jours. Justice Town of Alfred, N.Y., 1976-84. Recipient SUNY Chancellors award for Excellence in

Teaching, 1976. Fellow Am. Ceramic Soc.; mem. Nat. Inst. Ceramic Engrs., Am. Chem. Soc. Current Work: Surface reactions; adsorption of gases on solids; catalysis; nuclear waste disposal. Subspecialties: Ceramic engineering; Physical chemistry. Home: 14 High St Alfred NY 14802 Office: NY State College of Ceramics Alfred U Alfred NY 14802

ROSSINI, FREDERICK DOMINIC, scientist, educator, consultant; b. Monongahela, Pa., July 18, 1899; s. Martino and Costanza (Carrara) R.; m. Anne K. Landgraff, 1932 (dec. 1981); 1 child, Frederick Anthony; m. Dorothy T. Purcell, 1983. B.S., Carnegie Inst. Tech. (now Carnegie Mellon U.), 1925, M.S., 1926, D.Sc. (hon.), 1948; Ph.D., U. Calif.-Berkeley, 1928; Ph.D. hon. degrees; D.Engr. Sci., Duquesne U., 1955; D.Sc., U. Notre Dame, 1959, Loyola U., Chgo., 1960, U. Portland, 1965; Litt.D., St. Francis Coll., Loretto, Pa., 1962; Ph.D., U. Lund, Sweden, 1974. Lab. asst. in physics Carnegie Inst. Tech., 1923-24, teaching asst. math., 1924-26, Silliman prof., head dept. chemistry, dir. chem. and petroleum research lab., 1950-60; teaching fellow chemistry U. Calif.-Berkeley, 1926-28; phys. chemist Nat. Bur. Standards, 1928-36, chief sect. on thermochemistry and hydrocarbons, 1936-50; prof. chemistry U. Notre Dame, 1960-71, dean Coll. Sci., 1960-67, v.p. research, 1967-71, prof. emeritus, 1971—; prof. chemistry Rice U., 1971-75, prof. emeritus in residence, 1975-78, prof. emeritus, 1978—; mem. panel on research materials and info. U.S.-Japan Coop. Sci. program, 1965; mem. adv. panel for chemistry NSF, 1951-54; mem. policy adv. bd. Argonne Nat. Lab., 1958-66; trustee State Ind. Ednl. Service Found., 1968-71; mem. tech. adv. com. State Ill. Bd. Higher Edn., 1970-71; chmn. environ. measurements adv. com. EPA, 1976-78, mem. sci. adv. bd. exec. com., 1976-78, cons., 1978-79; lectr. and cons. in field; pres. World Petroleum Congresses, 1967-75. Author: 11 books Including Thermochemistry of Chemical Substances, 1936, Hydrocarbons from Petroleum, 1953, Thermodynamics and Physics of Matter, 1955, Experimental Thermochemistry, 1956, Fundamental Measures and Constants for Science and Tehnology, 1974; contbr. numerous articles to profl. jours. Recipient Gold Medal exceptional Service award U.S. Dept. Commerce, 1950; award in chemistry Pitts. Jr. C. of C., 1957; Laetare medal U. Notre Dame, 1965; John Price Wetherill medal Franklin Inst., 1965; Redwood medal Inst. Petroleum, London, 1972; Carl Engler medal Deutsche Gesellschaft fur mineralolwissenschaft und Kohlechemie, Germany, 1976; Nat. Medal Sci. U.S.A., 1977. Fellow AAAS, Am. Inst. Chemists (life), Am. Phys. Soc., Washington Acad. Sci. (editor jour. 1937-40, sec. 1940-43, bd. mgrs. 1943-46, pres. 1948); mem. Nat. Acad. Sci., Am. Acad. Arts and Scis., Am. Chem. Soc. (mem. editorial bd. jour. 1946-56, chmn. com. constitution and bylaws 1949-50, mem. adv. bd. petroleum research fund 1954, 57-59, Nichols medal N.Y. sect. 1966, Priestley medal 1971), Am. Inst. Chem. Engrs., Am. Petroleum Inst. (bd. dirs.), Am. Soc. Engring. Edn., Chem. Soc. London, Geochem. Soc., Philos. Soc. Washington, Albertus Magnus Guild, Cath. Assn. Internat Peace, Sigma Xi, Phi Kappa Theta (found. bd. trustees 1963-66, 73-76), Phi Lambda Upsilon, Tau Beta Pi. Republican. Roman Catholic. Club: Cosmos (Washington). Current Work: Thermochemistry and thermodynamics; data for science and technology; physical chemistry of hydrocarbons and petroleum.

ROSSMAN, ELMER CHRIS, agronomist, plant breeder, educator; b. Rawlins, Wyo., Nov. 17, 1919; s. Chris and Margreth (Knudsen) R.; m. Elizabeth Jean Schell, Aug. 8, 1942; children—Chris, Janet, David. B.S., Oreg. State U., 1941; M.S., Mich. State U., 1943; Ph.D., Iowa State U., 1948. Asst. prof. crop sci. Mich. State U., East Lansing, 1948-53, assoc. prof., 1953-57, prof., 1957—. Contbr. articles to profl. jours. Fellow AAAS; mem. Am. Soc. Agronomy, Am. Soc. Plant Physiologists, Genetics Soc. Am., Genetics Soc. Can., Am. Genetics Assn., Sigma Xi, Phi Kappa Phi, Sigma Gamma Delta, Phi Kappa Psi (bd. dirs. 1953—, faculty advisor 1953—). Republican. Current work: Corn breeding and production; developed numerous inbred parents and hybrids for improved corn cultivars and production. Subspecialties: Plant genetics; Agronomy. Home: 943 Lantern Hill Dr East Lansing MI 48823 Office: Dept Crop Soil Scis Mich State U East Lansing MI 48824

ROSSMANN, MICHAEL GEORGE, biochemist, educator; b. Frankfurt, Germany, July 30, 1930; s. Alexander and Nelly (Schwabacher) R.; m. Audrey Pearson, July 24, 1954; children—Martin, Alice, Heather. B.Sc. with honors, Polytechnic, London, 1951, M.Sc. in Physics, 1953; Ph.D. in Chemistry, U. Glasgow, 1956. Fulbright scholar U. Minn., 1956-58; research scientist MRC Lab. Molecular Biology, Cambridge, Eng., 1958-64; asso. prof. biol. scis. Purdue U., West Lafayette, Ind., 1964-67, prof., 1967-78, Hanley Disting. prof. biol. scis., 1978—, prof. biochemistry, 1975—. Editor: The Molecular Replacement Method, 1972; editorial bd.: Jour. Biol. Chemistry, 1975-80; contbr. articles to profl. jours. NIH grantee; NSF grantee; recipient Herbert Newby McCoy award for sci achievement Purdue U., 1974; Sigma Xi research award Purdue U., 1980. Mem. Am. Soc. Biol. Chemists, Am. Chem. Soc., Biophys. Soc., Am. Crystallographic Assn., Brit. Biophys. Soc., Inst. Physics, Chem. Soc. (U.K.), Am. Acad. Arts and Scis., Nat. Acad. Scis. Democrat. Club: Lafayette Sailing. Current work: X-ray crystallography, virus and enzyme structure and evolution. Home: 1208 Wiley Dr West Lafayette IN 47906 Office: Dept Biol Scis Purdue Univ West Lafayette IN 47907

ROST, THOMAS LOWELL, botany educator; b. St. Paul, Dec. 28, 1941; s. Lowell Henry Rost and Agnes Marie (Wojtowicz) Rost Jurek; m. Ann Marie Ruhland, Aug. 31, 1963; children: Christopher, Timothy, Jacquelyn. B.S., St. John's U., Collegeville, Minn., 1963; M.A., Mankato State U., 1965; Ph.D., Iowa State U., 1970. Postdoctoral fellow Brookhaven Nat. Lab., Upton, N.Y., 1970-72; asst. prof. botany U. Calif., Davis, 1979-80, faculty asst. to chancellor, 1982—, prof. botany, 1977-82; vis. fellow Research Sch. Biol. Scis., Australian Nat. U., Canberra, 1979-80; FAO cons. Faculty Agronomy, U. Uruguay, Montevideo, summer 1979. Co-author: Botany, A Brief Introduction to Plant Biology, 1979, Botany, An Introduction to Plant Biology, 1981, Laboratory Studies in Botany, 1982; contbr. articles to profl. jours.; co-editor: Mechanisms and Control of Cell Division, 1977. Served to capt. USAR, 1965-67. NSF grantee, 1978. Fellow Royal Micros. Soc.; mem. Bot. Soc. Am., Am. Inst. Biol. Sci., Sigma Xi, Gamma Sigma Delta. Current Work: Effects of stress on cell division in plant root meristems, aspects of morphogenesis in plants especially root growth and development, seed anatomy and histochemistry. Subspecialties: Cell and tissue culture; Plant growth. Office: Dept Botany U Calif Davis CA 95616

ROSTHAUSER, JAMES WILLIAM, industrial research chemist; b. Erie, Pa., Sept. 19, 1951; s. Kenneth H. and Gloria E. (Gallagher) R.; m. Jacqueline Kay Laboda, Sept. 22, 1979. B.S. in Chemistry/Engring., Gannon U., 1975; Ph.D. in Organic Chemistry, W.Va. U., 1979. Sr. chemist coatings applications devel. Mobay Chem. Corp., Pitts., 1979-80, sr. research chemist, 1980-84, project leader coatings research, 1984-85, group leader coatings research, 1985—. Contbr. articles to profl. jours. Patentee in field. Mem. Am. Chem. Soc., (polymer chemistry div., polymeric materials sci. and engring. div.). Subspecialties: Polymer chemistry; Polymers (materials science). Office: Mobay Chem Corp Mobay Rd Pittsburgh PA 15205

ROTA, GIAN-CARLO, educator, mathematician; b. Vigevano, Italy, Apr. 27, 1932; came to U.S., 1950, naturalized, 1961; s. Giovanni and Gina (Facoetti) R.; m. Teresa Rondón-Tarchetti, June 23, 1956 (div. 1979). B.A. summa cum laude, Princeton U., 1953; M.A., Yale U., 1954; Ph.D., Yale, 1956. Vis. fellow Courant Inst. Math. Scis., N.Y.U., 1956-57; B. Pierce instr. Harvard, 1957-59; asst. prof., then asso. prof. math. M.I.T., 1959-65, prof. math., 1967-74, prof. applied math. and philosophy, 1975—; prof. math. Rockefeller U., 1965-67; vis. prof. U. Calif. at Berkeley, 1961, Courant Inst. Math. Scis., 1964, U. Ill., 1965, Ind. U., 1964, U. Paris, 1972, U. Mex., 1973, Scuola Normale Superiore, 1975, U. Buenos Aires, 1975, U. Strasbourg, 1976, 78; Taft lectr. U. Cin., 1971; spl. vis. prof. U. Colo., 1969-82; Andre' Aisenstadt vis. prof. U. Montreal, 1971; Hardy lectr. London Math. Soc., 1973; professore linceo, Rome, 1979; cons. Rand Corp., 1965-71; Sigma Xi nat. lectr., 1980-81; fellow Los Alamos Sci. Lab., from 1966; cons. Brookhaven Nat. Lab., 1969-71. Author: (with G. Birkhoff) Ordinary Differential Equations, 1962, (with H. Crapo) Combinational Geometries, 1970, Finite Operator Calculus, 1975, MAA Survey in Combinatorics, 1978; also articles combinatorial theory, differential equations, probability, philosophy.; Editor: Jour. Combinatorial Theory, 1966—, Jour. Math. and Mechanics, 1965-71, Jour. Math. Analysis, 1966—, Utilitas Mathematica, 1973—; asso. editor: Am. Math. Monthly, 1966-73; (with H. Crapo) Procs. Royal Soc. Edinburgh, 1976—, Advances in Mathematics, 1967—; editor in chief: Advances in Applied Math, 1980—; editor: Bull. Am. Math. Soc, 1967-73, 79-84, (with H. Crapo) Ency. of Math, 1974—. Sloan fellow, 1962-64. Fellow Am. Acad. Arts and Scis., Academia Argentina de Ciencias, Inst. Math. Statistics, Nat. Acad. Scis., AAAS; mem. Am. Math. Assn. (Hedrick lectr. 1967), Am. Math Soc. (council 1967-72), London Math. Soc., Heidegger Circle, Soc. Indsl. and Applied Math. (v.p. 1975), Am. Philos. Assn., Soc. Phenomenology and Existential Philosophy, AAUP, Unione Mathematica Italiana, Phi Beta Kappa (pres. chpt. 1978-80). Roman Catholic. Current Work: Combinatorics, probability, logic. phenomenology, especially Husserl. Subspecialties: Parasitology; Probability. Address: 2-351 Mass Inst Tech Cambridge MA 02139

ROTELLA, FRANK J., crystallographer, research chemist, computer operator and programmer; b. Chgo., June 2, 1949; s. Frank M. and Rose M. (Eulo) R.; m. Mary Ellen Kaminski, Sept. 23, 1984. Student U. Ill.-Chgo., 1967-68, M.S. in Chemistry, 1974; student Wilbur Wright Coll., Chgo., 1968-69; B.S. in Chemistry, Loyola U., Chgo., 1972; Ph.D., SUNY-Buffalo, 1979. Postdoctoral appointee solid state sci. div. Argonne Nat. Lab., Ill., 1979-81, asst. chemist intense pulsed neutron source program, 1981—. Contbr. articles to profl. jours. Mem. Am. Chem. Soc., Am. Crystallographic Assn., AAAS, N.Y. Acad. Scis., Sigma Xi. Roman Catholic. Subspecialties: Crystallography; Inorganic chemistry. Office: Argonne Nat Lab IPNS Program Bldg 360 9700 S Cass Ave Argonne IL 60439

ROTENBERG, DON HARRIS, optical company executive; b. Portland, Oreg., Mar. 31, 1934; s. Morris Hyman and Helen (Harris) R.; m. Barbara Ress, June 29, 1958; children—Laura, Debra. B.A., U. Oreg., 1955; A.M., Harvard U., 1956; Ph.D., Cornell U., 1960. Research chemist Exxon Research and Engring Co., Enjay Chem. Lab., Linden, N.J., 1960-67, sr. research chemist Enjay Polymer Lab., 1967-71; mgr. polymer sci. and engring. Am. Optical Corp., Southbridge, Mass., 1971-75, dir. Materials and Process Lab., 1975-80, v.p. research and devel., 1980—. Contbr. articles to profl. jours. Patentee in field. Todd Research fellow. Mem. Am. Chem. Soc., AAAS, Phi Beta Kappa, Sigma Xi. Current work: Development of photochromic and abrasion resistant coated plastic ophthalmic lenses and precision optics and contact lenses. Subspecialties: Polymer chemistry; Materials. Office: Am Optical Corp 14 Mechanic St Southbridge MA 01550

ROTENBERG, KEITH SAUL, pharmacokineticist; b. San Francisco, Oct. 10, 1950; s. Harry and Helen (Tenenbaum) R.; m. Rochelle Marilyn Rubin, Sept. 14, 1976; children—Beth Jessica, Markus Ross. B.A., U. Calif.-Berkeley, 1972; Ph.D., U. Md., 1978. Teaching asst. U. Md., Balt., 1973-77; pharmacologist Bur. Drugs, FDA, Rockville, Md., 1977-81, tech. supr., 1981-82; sec. head biopharmaceutics Pennwalt Corp., Rochester, N.Y., 1982-83, assoc. dir. clin. pharmacology, 1984—. Contbr. articles to profl. jours., chpts. to books. Recipient award of merit FDA, 1981. Mem. Pharm. Mfrs. Assn. (steering com. drug metabolism subsect, 1984—), Am. Pharm. Assn., N.Y. Acad. Scis., Am. Soc. Clin. Pharmacology and Therapeutics, Am. Chem. Soc., Soc. Clin. Trials, Acad. Pharm. Sci., AAAS. Current work: Directing Phase I clinical research including dose tolerance studies, clinical pharmacology, clinical pharmacokinetics, and participate in the development of drug delivery systems. Subspecialties: Pharmacokinetics; Health services research. Home: 15 Sturbridge Ln Pittsford NY 14534 Office: Pennwalt Pharm Div Pennwalt Corp 755 Jefferson Rd Rochester NY 14623

ROTH, HAROLD P., physician; b. Cleve., Aug. 2, 1915; s. Abraham J. and Ida (Harris) R.; m. Kelly Cecile Rabinovitch, Dec. 9, 1952; children—Anita Alix, Edward Harris. B.A., Western Res. U., Cleve., 1936, M.D., 1939; M.S. in Hygiene, Harvard U., 1967. Diplomate: Am. Bd. Internal Medicine. Intern Cin. Gen. Hosp., 1939-40; house officer Boston City Hosp., 1940-42; asst. resident in medicine Barnes Hosp., St. Louis, 1942-43; clin. instr. Western Res. U., Cleve., 1949-52, sr. clin. instr., 1953-55, asst. prof., 1955-63, asso. prof., 1963—; asso. prof. dept. community health Case Western Res. U., 1971—; chief gastroenterology service VA Hosp., Cleve., 1947—; dir. gastroenterology tng. program Univ. Hosps. and VA Hosp., 1963—; asso. physician Univ. Hosps. of Cleve., 1969-74; cons., asst. physician Highland View Hosp.; vis. physician in gastroenterology dept. medicine Cleve. Met. Gen. Hosp.; dir. div. digestive diseases and nutrition, assoc. dir. for digestive diseases and nutrition Nat. Inst. Arthritis, Diabetes and Digestive and Kidney Diseases, NIH, Bethesda, Md., 1974—; mem. Nat. Commn. on Digestive Diseases, Nat. Digestive Diseases Adv. Bd.; vice chmn, Digestive Diseases Interagy. Coordinating Com. Contbr. articles to med. jours. Served with AUS, 1943-46. USPHS fellow, 1966-67. Mem. Am. Gastroenterol. Assn., Am. Assn. Study of Liver Disease, Midwest Gut Club, Central Soc. Clin. Research, ACP, Soc. Clin. Trials (pres. 1978-80), Phi Beta Kappa. Current work: Clinical epidemiology and data systems; development of a national liver transplantation data base and a program using visual aids and voice recognition for recording the findings on endoscopic procedures. Subspecialties: Internal medicine; Gastroenterology. Home: 10319 Gary Rd Potomac MD 20854 Office: 9000 Rockville Pike Bldg 31 Bethesda MD 20205

ROTH, JAMES LUTHER AUMONT, physician, educator; b. Milw., Mar. 8, 1917; s. Paul Wagner and Rose Marie (Schulzke) R.; m. Marion S. Main, June 7, 1938 (div.); children—Stephen Andrew, Kristina Marie, Lisa Kathryn; m. Mary Alice Burns, Dec. 30, 1983. B.A., Carthage Coll., 1938, D.Sc. (hon.), 1957; M.A., U. Ill., 1939; M.D., Northwestern U., 1944, Ph.D., 1945. Intern Mass. Gen. Hosp., Boston, 1944-45; resident (Grad. Hosp.), 1945-46, 49-50, Hosp. U. Pa., Phila., 1948-49; practice medicine specializing in gastroenterology, Phila., 1950—; instr. physiology Northwestern U., 1942-44; instr. div. gastroenterology Grad. Sch. Medicine, U. Pa., 1950-52, asso., 1952-54, asst. prof., 1954-56, asso. prof., 1956-59, clin. prof. gastroenterology, 1959-68, dir. div., 1961-69, prof. clin. medicine, 1968—, chief gastroenterology clinic Grad. Hosp., 1953-67, chief gastroenterology service, 1961-69; dir. Inst. Gastroenterology, Presbyn. U. Pa. Med. Center, 1965—; cons. USN, Bethesda, Md., 1967—, USAF, 1946-48. Editorial bd.: Gastroenterology, 1960-67, Am. Jour. Gastroenterology, 1976-79, Current Therapy, 1972—, Current Concepts in Gastroenterology, 1976-81; editor: Bockus' 4th edit. Gastroenterology; Contbr. articles to med. jours. Recipient Bronze medal AMA, 1944; certificates of merit Am. Roentgen Ray Soc.; Disting. Alumni award Carthage Coll., 1979. Fellow A.C.P.; mem. AMA, Pan Am. Med. Assn., N.Y. Acad. Sci., Am. Physiol. Soc., Am. Fedn. Clin. Research, Am. Gastroent. Assn. (chmn. admissions com.), Am. Coll. Gastroenterology (trustee 1977-82, chmn. grad. edn. com. 1978-81, v.p. 1981), Bockus Internat. Soc. Gastroenterology (pres. 1973-75), Digestive Disease Fedn. (dir.), Union League Phila., Sigma Xi, Alpha Omega Alpha; hon. mem. Fla., Colombian, Venezuelan, Dominican Republic socs. gastroenterology. Republican. Lutheran. Subspecialty: Gastroenterology. Office: 51 N 39th St Philadelphia PA 19104

ROTH, JESSE, endocrinologist; b. N.Y.C., Aug. 5, 1934. B.A., Columbia U., 1955; M.D., Albert Einstein Coll. Medicine, Yeshiva U., 1959; hon. degree, U. Uppsala, Sweden, 1980. Intern Barnes Hosp., Washington U., St. Louis, 1959-60, resident, 1960-61; Am. Diabetes Assn. research fellow radioisotope service Bronx (N.Y.) VA Hosp., 1961-63, clin. assoc., 1963-65, sr. investigator, 1965-66, chief diabetes sect., clin. endocrinology br., 1966-74; chief diabetes br. Nat. Inst. Arthritis, Diabetes, Digestive and Kidney Diseases, Bethesda, Md., 1974-83, dir. div. intramural research, 1983—; regents' lectr. U. Calif., 1977; G. Burroughs Mider lectr. NIH, 1978. Recipient Eli Lilly award Am. Diabetes Assn., 1974; Ernst Oppenheimer Meml. award Endocrine Soc., 1974; Spl. Achievement award HEW, 1974; David Rumbough Meml. award Juvenile Diabetes Found., 1977; Lita Annenberg Hazen award Mt. Sinai Sch. Medicine; Diaz Cristobal Found. prize Internat. Diabetes Found., 1979; Annual award Gairdner Found., 1980; Disting. Service medal Public Health Service, 1980. Current Work: Receptors; hormones, neurotransmitters, insulin, human disease, evolution. Subspecialties: Endocrinology; Evolutionary biology. Office: Bldg 10 Room 9N222 Nat Inst Arthritis, Diabetes, Digestive and Kidney Diseases 9000 Rockville Pike Bethesda MD 20205

ROTH, J(OHN) REECE, engineering educator; b. Washington, Pa., Sept. 19, 1937; s. John Meyer and Ruth E. (Iams) R.; m. Helen Marie De Crane, Jan. 14, 1972; children: Nancy Ann, John Alexander. S.B. in Physics, Mass. Inst. Tech., 1959; Ph.D. in Engring. Physics, Cornell U., 1963. Aerospace research scientist NASA Lewis Research Center, Cleve., 1963-78; prin. investigator NASA Lewis Research Center (Lewis Bumpy Torus project), 1967-78; vis. prof. elec. engring. U. Tenn., Knoxville, 1978-82, prof. physics, 1982—, prof. elec. engring., 1983—; cons. Westinghouse Corp., Pitts., 1980, TVA, Chattanooga, 1982 . Assoc. editor: IEEE Transactions on Plasma Sci, 1973 ; contbr. numerous sci. articles to profl. publs. Recipient Awareness award NASA, 1976; Sloan scholar MIT, 1955-59; Ford fellow Cornell U., 1961-62. Fellow IEEE (mem. exec. com. East Tenn. chpt. 1982-84, chmn. 1984-85); mem. IEEE Nuclear and Plasma Scis. Soc. (adminstrv. com. 1974-77, sec. 1975), Am. Nuclear Soc., AIAA, Am. Phys. Soc., AAAS (life), Archaeol. Inst. Am., Am. Soc. Engring. Edn., Sigma Xi (life). Current Work: Electric field dominated plasmas; alternate magnetic confinement concepts; advanced fusion reactions; public policy issues of fusion energy; plasma-wall interactions. Subspecialties: Plasma physics; Nuclear fusion. Home: 4301 Hiawatha Dr Knoxville TN 37919 Office: U Tenn 409 Ferris Hall Knoxville TN 37996-2100

ROTH, ROBERT ANDREW, JR., toxicologist, educator, cons.; b. McKeesport, Pa., Aug. 15, 1946; s. Robert and Jane (Cox) R.; m. Kathleen Johnson, June 12, 1970; children: Evan, Kelly. B.A., Duke U., 1968; Ph.D., Johns Hopkins U., 1975. Diplomate: Am. Bd. Toxicology. Research fellow Yale U. Sch. Medicine, New Haven, 1975-77; asso. prof. dept. pharmacology and toxicology Mich. State U., East Lansing, 1972-76, prof., 1976—; cons. Contbr. articles to profl. jours. Served in U.S. Army, 1969-71. NIH grantee, 1977—. Mem. Am. Soc. Pharmacology and Exptl. Therapeutics, Soc. Toxicology. Current Work: Pulmonary and hepatic toxicology; mechanism of action of toxicants; monocrotaline induced cardiopulmonary injury; lung's role in metabolism of chemicals; carbon monoxide effects on pharmacokinetics. Subspecialties: Toxicology (medicine); Environmental toxicology. Home: 1465 Birchwood Dr Okemos MI 48864 Office: Mich State U East Lansing MI 48864

ROTH, SANFORD IRWIN, pathologist, educator, researcher; b. McAlester, Okla., Oct. 14, 1932; s. Herman Moe and Blanche (Brown) R.; m. Kathryn Ann Corliss, Sept. 3, 1961; children—Jeffrey Franklin, Elisabeth Francyne, Gregory James, Suzannah Joan. Student Vanderbilt U., 1949-52; M.D., Harvard U., 1956. Diplomate Nat. Bd. Med. Examiners, Am. Bd. Pathology. Intern Mass. Gen. Hosp., Boston, 1956-57, resident, 1957-60, pathologist, 1962-75; from assoc. to assoc. prof. Med. Sch., Harvard U., Boston, 1962-75; prof., chmn. dept. pathology U. Ark., Little Rock, 1975-81; prof. pathology Northwestern U., Chgo., 1981—; chief lab. VA Lakeside Med. Ctr., Chgo., 1981—; attending pathologist Northwestern Meml. Hosp., Chgo., 1981—. Served as capt. M.C., U.S. Army, 1960-62. Am. Cancer Soc. faculty research assoc., 1965-70. Fellow Coll. Am. Pathologists; mem. Am. Assn. Pathologists, Internat. Acad. Pathology, Am. Soc. Cell Biology. Subspecialty: Pathology (medicine). Office: Northwestern U Med Sch 303 E Chicago Ave Chicago IL 60611

ROTHBART, HERBERT L., government official, research chemist; b. Bklyn., Feb. 5, 1937; s. Abraham David and Doris (Mogulevsky) R.; m. Marian Block, Mar. 12, 1961; 1 child, Bradley Ethan. B.S., Bklyn. Coll., CUNY, 1958; Ph.D., Rutgers U., 1963. Playground tchr. N.Y. Bd. Edn., Bklyn., part-time 1955-58; researcher, mem. faculty Rutgers U., New Brunswick, N.J., part-time 1958-66; researcher, adminstr. U.S. Dept. Agr.-ARS-ERRC, Phila., 1966-83, Agrl. Research Service, U.S. Dept. Agr., North Atlantic Area, Phila., 1983—; mem. adv. com. dept. food sci. Rutgers U., 1981—, U. Del.-Newark, 1983—, Bd. City Trusts, Phila., 1982—. Contbr. articles to profl. jours., chpts. to books. Patentee in field. Recipient Fed. Service award Fed. Bus. Assn., 1976; cert. of merit Dept. Agr., 1967, 68, 73, 78. Mem. Am. Chem. Soc., AAAS, Inst. Food Technologists. Current work: Direction of federal research in the agricultural and food sciences (soils, plants, animals, postharvest technology, human nutrition) in the North Atlantic States of the U.S. Subspecialties: Analytical chemistry; Food science and technology. Home: 411 Norfolk Rd Flourtown PA 19031 Office: North Atlantic Area Agrl Research Service US Dept Agr 600 E Mermaid Ln Philadelphia PA 19118

ROTHBERG, RICHARD MARTIN, medical educator, researcher; b. N.Y.C., July 15, 1933; s. Morris and Beatrice (Jacobs) R.; m. Laura Gail Clayman, June 26, 1955; children: Benjamin, Miriam, Jonathan. B.A., U. Rochester, 1955; M.D., U. Chgo., 1958. Diplomate: Am. Bd. Pediatrics, 1966. Resident in pediatrics U. Pitts., 1958-62; research fellow in immunology Scripps Clinic and Research Found., La Jolla, Calif., 1964-66; mem. faculty U. Chgo. Med. Sch., 1966—, prof. pediatrics and pathology, 1974—. Contbr. articles to sci. jours. Mem. Cystic Fibrosis Ctr. Com., 1982-85, vice chmn., 1985. Served to lt. comdr., M.C. USN, 1962-64. USPHS grantee, 1967-85. Mem. Ill. Soc. Allergy and Clin. Immunology (pres. 1981-82), Am. Assn. Immunologists, Am. Pediatric Soc., Soc. Pediatric Research. Democrat. Jewish. Current Work: Immune response of newborn (effects of maternal environmental antigens on infant responses); immunologic reconstitution of patients with immunologic deficiency diseases. Subspecialties: Immunology (medicine); Pulmonary medicine. Office: Box 133 950 E 59th St Chicago IL 60637

ROTHE, CARL FREDERICK, physiologist, educator; b. Lima, Ohio, Feb. 6, 1929; s. Calvin H. and Katharine (Boegel) R.; m. Mary Louise Hawk, Aug. 16, 1952; children—Sarah Katharine Rothe Lee, Thomas Herbert. B.S., Ohio State U., 1951, M.S., 1952, Ph.D., 1955. Sr. asst. scientist USPHS, Savannah, Ga., 1955-58; instr. physiology Ind. U., Indpls., 1958-59, asst., then assoc. prof., 1960-70, prof., 1970—; mem. sect. cardiovascular study NIH, 1971-75. Contbr. articles to profl. jours., chpts. to books. Recipient Prin. Investigator award NIH, 1962—. Mem. Biomed. Engring. Soc. (charter mem.; bd. dirs. 1982—), Am. Physiol. Soc., Am. Heart Assn. (established investigator award 1963-68). Mem. United Ch. Christ. Current work: Role of vascular capacitance in maintenance of cardiovascular function; biomedical instrumentation; computer simulation of physiological systems. Subspecialties: Biomedical engineering; Physiology (medicine). Office: Dept Physiology and Biophysics Ind U 635 Barnhill Dr Indianapolis IN 46223

ROTHE, ERHARD WILLIAM, chemical engineering educator, researcher in chemical physics; b. Breslau, Germany, Apr. 15, 1931; came to U.S., 1937, naturalized, 1944; s. Erich Hans and Hildegard (Ille) R.; m. Daria Alexandra Reshetylo, Aug. 29, 1959; children—Lisa Catherine, Margaret Louise. B.S. in Chemistry, U. Mich., 1952, M.S., 1954, Ph.D., 1959. Staff scientist Gen. Dynamics Co., San Diego, 1959-69; adj. prof. chemistry San Diego State U., 1967-69; prof. chem. engring. Wayne State U., Detroit, 1969—; cons. Phys. Dynamics, Inc., San Diego, 1975—; guest researcher Max-Planck Inst. für Stromungs Forschung, Gottingen, Fed. Republic Germany, 1979—. Contbr. articles to profl. jours. Fellow Am. Phys. Soc.; mem. Am. Chem. Soc., Sigma Xi. Current work: Study of chemical dynamics by use of molecular-beam and laser techniques. Subspecialties: Laser-induced chemistry; Chemical engineering. Office: Coll Engring Wayne State U Detroit MI 48202

ROTHENBERG, SHELDON PHILIP, physician, educator, researcher, hematologist, oncologist; b. N.Y.C., May 28, 1929; s. Louis and Gussie (Elstein) R.; m. Rosalie Weisenhoff, June 3, 1957; children—Pamela, Diane. A.B., NYU, 1950; M.D., Chgo. Med. Sch., 1955. Diplomate Am. Bd. Internal Medicine. Intern Maimonides Hosp., Bklyn., 1955-56, resident in medicine, 1956-57; resident in medicine Bronx VA Hosp., N.Y., 1959-60; fellow in hematology L.I. Jewish Hosp., Queens, N.Y., 1960-61; with N.Y. Med. Coll., N.Y.C., 1961-80; prof. medicine SUNY Downstate Med. Ctr., Bklyn., 1980—; chief hematology/oncology Bklyn. VA Hosp., 1980—. Contbr. chpts. to books, articles to profl. jours. Served to capt. USMC, 1957-59. NIH grantee, 1961-85. Fellow ACP; mem. Am. Soc. Clin. Investigation, Am. Assn. Physicians, Am. Soc. Hematology, Am. Assn. Cancer Research. Current work: Metabolism of vitamin B12; metabolism of folate cofactors and antifolate drugs. Subspecialties: Hematology; Cancer research (medicine). Home: 114 Monterey Dr Manhasset Hills NY 11040 Office: Bklyn VA Hosp 800 Poly Pl Brooklyn NY 11204

ROTHFUS, JOHN ARDEN, chemist; b. Des Moines, Dec. 25, 1932; s. Truman Clinton and Beatrice Adele (Kennedy) R.; m. Paula Kay Harris, Sept. 26, 1959; children—Lee Ellen, David Merrill. B.A., Drake U., 1955; Ph.D., U. Ill., 1960. Asst. U. Ill., Urbana, 1955-59; instr. U. Utah, Salt Lake City, 1961-63; asst. prof. UCLA, 1963-65; prin. research chemist U.S. Dept. Agr., Peoria, Ill., 1965-70, investigation head, 1970-74, research leader, 1974—. Contbr. articles to profl. jours. Fellow Procter and Gamble Co., 1957-58, USPHS, 1959-61. Mem. AAAS, Am. Assn. Cereal Chemists, Am. Chem. Soc., Am. Oil Chemists Soc., Am. Soc. Plant Physiologists, N.Y. Acad. Scis., Jojoba Soc. Current work: Leading groups investigating lipid polymorphism, membrane fluidity, plant cell and tissue culture, secondary metabolism, modulator proteins, botanical resources, photomorphogenesis and photosynthetic regulation. Subspecialties: Biochemistry (biology); Biophysical chemistry. Home: 5615 N Sherwood Peoria IL 61614 Office: US Dept Agr Northern Region Research Ctr 1815 N University Peoria IL 61604

ROTHMAN, STEVEN JOHN, materials scientist, researcher; b. Giessen, Germany, Dec. 18, 1927; came to U.S., 1938; s. Stephen and Irene E. (Mannheim) R.; m. Barbara A. Kirkpatrick, Oct. 14, 1951; children—Ann, Nick. Ph.B., U. Chgo., 1947; B.S., Stanford U., 1951, M.S., 1953, Ph.D., 1955. Asst. metallurgist Argonne Nat. Lab., Ill., 1954-60, assoc. metallurgist, 1960-70, metallurgist, 1970—; disting. prof. Tuskegee Inst., Ala., 1966; vis. assoc. prof. Northwestern U., Evanston, Ill., 1968; vis. prof. Tech. U., Tampere,

Finland, 1973; Fulbright sr. lectr., 1973. Editor: Nuclear Methods: Solid State, 1984. Contbr. numerous articles to profl. jours. Precinct committeeman Milton Twp. Democratic Com., 1960-76, 84. NSF postdoctoral fellow, 1962-63. Mem. AIME, Am. Phys. Soc. Current work: Research in mass transport in solids. Subspecialties: Metallurgy; Ceramics. Home: 902 N Stoddard St Wheaton IL 60187 Office: Argonne Nat Lab 212-C211 Argonne IL 60439

ROTHROCK, RAY ALAN, marketing executive; b. Ft. Worth, Dec. 1, 1954; s. Nate Paul and Wanda Sue (Brewer) R. B.S., Tex. A&M U., 1977; S.M., MIT, 1978. Assoc. engr. Yankee Atomic Elec. Co., Westboro, Mass., 1978-80; staff engr. Exxon Minerals, Houston, 1980-82; product mgr. Sagus Corp., Campbell, Calif., 1982-83; sales and mktg. staff Impell Corp., 1983-84; CAD/CAM market devel. mgr. Sun Microsystems, Mountain View, Calif., 1985—; mem. subcom. Atomic Indsl. Forum, Washington, 1978-80; cons. Sagus Corp., 1982—. Vol. Am. Cancer Soc., Westboro, Mass., 1980; mem. Westboro Community Chorus, 1980; asst. scoutmaster Boy Scouts Am. Mem. Am. Nuclear Soc., Nat. Soc. Profl. Engrs. Club: Am. Radio Relay League. Current Work: Utilization of microprocessor based systems for large scale, integrated engineering applications. Subspecialties: Software engineering; Nuclear engineering. Home: 807 Runningwood Circle Mountain View CA 94040

ROTHSCHILD, HENRY, acad. physician, molecular biologist; b. Horstein, Germany, June 5, 1932; came to U.S., 1939, naturalized, 1945; s. William Wolf and Fanny (Hahn) R.; married; children: Shoshana Tamar, Jamin Kahlil. B.A., Cornell U., 1954; M.D., U. Chgo., 1958; Ph.D., Johns Hopkins U., 1968. Intern U. Chgo. Clinics, 1958-59; resident in internal medicine Univ. Hosp., Balt., 1959-62; instr. medicine Mass. Gen. Hosp., Boston, 1970-71; assoc. prof. medicine La. State U. Med. Center, New Orleans, 1971-75, assoc. prof. anatomy and research, 1972-75; assoc. La. State U. Med. Center (Grad. Faculty), 1973—, prof. medicine and anatomy, 1975—; med. dir. New Orleans Home and Rehab. Center, St. Margaret's Daus. Home; vis. prof. Universidad Autonoma de Nuevo Leon, Mex., 1981. Fellow ACP; mem. Am. Soc. Exptl. Pathology, Am. Fedn. Clin. Research, So. Soc. Clin. Investigation, Soc. Exptl. Biology and Medicine. Current Work: Molecular biology, genetics of lung cancer, gerontology. Subspecialties: Genetics and genetic engineering (medicine); Gerontology. Home: 705 Pine St New Orleans LA 70118 Office: 1542 Tulane Ave New Orleans LA 70112

ROTHSCHILD, KENNETH JOSEPH, biophysicist, educator; b. N.Y.C., Feb. 9, 1948; s. Samuel and Marjorie (Schwebel) R.; m. Loan Thi Duong, May 24, 1974; children—Brian, David. B.S., Rensselaer Polytech. Inst., 1969; Ph.D., MIT, 1974. Research fellow Harvard U.-MIT, Cambridge, 1974-76; asst. prof. physics Boston U., 1976-81, asst. prof. physiology, 1976-82, assoc. prof. physics and physiology, 1982—, dir. cellular biophysics, 1984—. Contbr. articles to profl. jours. Patentee in field. Recipient Whitaker Found. award MIT, 1980 grantee NIH, Am. Heart Assn., NSF; established investigator Am. Heart Assn., 1979—. Mem. Biophys. Soc., AAAS. Current work: Biophysical studies of biomembranes using vibrational spectroscopy, proton transport, energy transduction, development of new biomaterials, molecular electronics. Subspecialties: Biophysics (physics); Biomaterials. Office: Boston Univ 590 Commonwealth Ave Boston MA 02215

ROTHWELL, HAROLD LEROY, JR., physicist; b. Salem, Ohio, Feb. 28, 1948; s. Harold L. and Leona (Myers) R.; m. Cathy Barnes, June 6, 1971; 1 child, Elizabeth. Ph.D., U. Denver, 1975. Engring. specialist GTE Sylvania, Salem, Mass., 1978—. Contbr. articles in field of plasma physics to profl. jours. Inventor devices related to arc lamps. Mem. Am. Phys. Soc. Current work: High pressure gas discharges; development of models to describe the operation of a mixed metal vapor-mercury arc. Subspecialty: Plasma physics. Home: 3 Waldingfield Rd Georgetown MA 01833

ROTRUCK, JOHN TRUMAN, research scientist; b. Cumberland, Md.; s. Truman Maxwell and Evelyn Lucille (Secrist) R.; m. Jane Ann Yost, Aug. 12, 1967; children—Robert, Jennifer. B.S., W.Va. U., 1966; M.S., U. Wis., 1968, Ph.D., 1971. Research scientist, mgr. Procter & Gamble Co., Cin., 1971—. Contbr. articles to profl. jours. Vice pres. Acad. Excellence Orgn., Oxford, Ohio, 1984-85; coach Oxford City Little League Baseball, 1982-83. Mem. Am. Inst. Nutrition, Sigma Xi, Gamma Sigma Delta. Mem. Brethren Ch. Club: Country (bd. dirs. 1984-86) (Oxford). Current work: Drug development, research and management. Subspecialties: Nutrition (biology); Biochemistry (biology). Office: Procter & Gamble Co PO Box 39175 Cincinnati OH 45247

ROTTENBERG, DAVID ALLAN, neurologist, researcher; b. Detroit, Jan. 8, 1942; s. Leon and Adeline (Sax) R.; m. Rochelle E. Rottenberg, June 16, 1963; children: Elizabeth Grace, Catherine Anne. B.A., U. Mich., 1963; M.Sc., Cambridge (Eng.) U., 1967; M.D., Harvard Med. Sch., 1969. Diplomate: Am. Bd. Psychiatry and Neurology, (examiner, 1980). Intern in surgery Mass. Gen. Hosp., 1969-70; research asso. NIH, 1970-72; resident in neurology N.Y. Hosp., 1972-74, chief resident, 1974-75, asst. attending neurologist, 1975—; asst. prof. neurology Cornell U. Med. Coll., 1975-79, assoc. prof., 1979—; asst. attending neurologist Meml. Hosp., 1975-79, assoc. attending neurologist, 1979—; assoc. mem. Meml. Sloan-Kettering Cancer Ctr., 1985—; cons. NIH, also site reviewer. Reviewer med. and sci. jours.; Contbr. articles to profl. jours. Served to lt. comdr. USPHS, 1970-72. Grantee NINCDS. Mem. Am. Acad. Neurology, AAAS, Am. Neurol. Assn., Harvey Soc., Soc. Computerized Tomography and Neuro-Imaging, Soc. Neurosci., Phi Beta Kappa. Current Work: Positron emission tomography of the central nervous system, quantitative aspects of CT. Subspecialties: Physiology (medicine); Imaging technology. Office: 1275 York Ave New York NY 10021

ROTTER, ANDREJ, neurobiologist, educator; b. Beijing People's Republic of China, Nov. 19, 1952; came to U.S., 1978; s. Konrad and Ching-Yu (Chang) R. B.Sc., Univ. Coll. London, 1974; Ph.D., Nat. Inst. Med. Research, London, 1978. Vis. fellow NIH, Bethesda, Md., 1978-80, NIMH, Bethesda, 1980; asst. prof. pharmacology U. Calif.-Irvine, 1981—. Contbr. articles to profl. jours. NIH grantee, 1982. Mem. AAAS, Soc. for Neurosci., Am. Soc. Pharmacology and Exptl. Therapeutics. Club: University. Current work: Chemistry of neuronal development. Subspecialties: Neurobiology; Neuropharmacology. Office: Dept Pharmacology Univ Calif Irvine CA 92717

ROUHANI, SAYD ZIA, thermal-hydraulics researcher; b. Nahavand, Iran, Dec. 23, 1930; came to U.S., 1979; s. Sayd-Abdel-Hossein and Maassoomeh (Zarrab) R.; m. Hosnieh Khoskebarchi, July 12, 1961; children: Anita-Helena, Viola-Goli. Electro-mech. engring. diploma, U. Tehran, 1955; cert., Internat. Sch. Nuclear Sci. and Engring., Pa. State U. and Argonne Nat. Lab., 1959; M.Sc., U. Calif.-Berkeley, 1959; Dr. Tech., Royal Inst. Tech., Stockholm, 1979. Research engr. AB Atomenergi, Studsvik, Sweden, 1960-67, group leader, Stockholm, 1967-70; project mgr. Joint Scandinavian Research, Riso, Denmark, 1970-73; cons. engr. AB Atomenergi, Studsvik, Sweden, 1973-76; project engr. Studsvik Energiteknik AB, 1976-80; sr. engring. specialist E G & G Idaho, Inc., Idaho Falls, 1980—. Co-author: Two-Phase Flow and its Application to Nuclear Reactors, 1978. Mem. Am. Nuclear Soc., ASME. Patentee in field. Current Work: Theoretical and experimental aspects of two-phase, cyrogenics, magneto hydrodynamics and fusion power systems. Subspecialties: Fluid mechanics; Nuclear engineering. Home: 3028 Hartert Dr Idaho Falls ID 83401 Office: EG&G Idaho Inc PO Box 1625 Idaho Falls ID 83415

ROUNDS, FRED GRAFTON, tribologist; b. Pullman, Wash., June 4, 1925; s. Fred G. and Ruth (Wikoff) R.; m. Muriel Frances Waltz, June 6, 1959; children—Richard, David. B.S. in Chem. Engring. Wash. State Univ., 1949; postgrad. Wayne State U., 1950-52. Sr. Staff research engr. Gen. Motors Research Labs., Warren, Mich., 1949—. Contbr. articles to profl. jours. Patentee in lubricants and combustion fields. Served with U.S. Army, 1943-45, ETO. Fellow Am. Soc. Lubrication Engrs. (dir. 1973-79); mem. Am. Chem. Soc. Presbyterian. Current work: Effects of lubricant composition on friction, wear and fatigue, oil additive mechanisms, additive interactions, diesel soot effects on wear, engine combustion. Subspecialty: Surface chemistry. Home: 6332 Canmoor St Troy MI 48098 Office: Gen Motors Research Labs Twelve Mile and Mounds Rds Warren MI 48090

ROUSCH, PATRICIA MARIE BARRY, chemist; b. Richwood, Va., May 29, 1952; d. Thomas Byrnes and Marie (Sauerwald) Barry; m. David Michael Roush, June 23, 1973 (div. 1981); 1 child, Jennifer. B.S., Coll. William and Mary, 1973; Ph.D., U. Calif.-Davis, 1977. Research staff Western Electric, Princeton, N.J., 1977-81; research chemist Internat. Minerals and Chem. Corp., Terre Haute, Ind., 1981-83; sr. applications chemist Perkin Elmer Corp., Ridgefield, Conn., 1983—. Contbr. articles to profl. jours. Mem. Am. Chem. Soc., N.Y. Acad. Scis., Soc. Applied Spectroscopy (chmn. publicity 1982, pres. 1986), ASTM (sec. 1982—), Fedn. Analytical Chemistry and Applied Spectroscopy (chmn. program 1984), AAAS. Current work: Fourier transform infrared spectroscopy; developing new applications for FT IR including hyphenated techniques; software development. Subspecialty: Analytical chemistry. Home: 93 Great Plain Rd Danbury CT 06811 Office: Perkin Elmer Corp 761 Main Ave Norwalk CT 06859-0903

ROUSE, ROY DENNIS, educational administrator; b. Andersonville, Ga., Sept. 20, 1920; s. Joseph B. and Janie (Wicker) R.; m. Madge Mathis, Mar. 6, 1946; children—David Benjamin, Sharon. Student, Ga. Southwestern Coll., 1937-39; B.S. in Agr, U. Ga., 1942, M.S., 1947; Ph.D., Purdue U., 1949. Asst. prof. agronomy and soils Auburn (Ala.) U., 1949-50, asso. prof., 1950-56, prof., 1956-66; asso. dir., asst. dean Auburn (Ala.) U. (Sch. Agr. and Agrl. Expt. Sta.), 1966-72, dean, dir., 1972-81, emeritus, 1981—; mem. Com. of Nine, Dept. Agr., 1970-74. Contbr. articles to profl. jours. Served to capt. USNR, 1942-67, PTO. Recipient Leadership award Farm-City Com. Ala., 1975; Disting. Service award Catfish Farmers Am., 1976; Disting. Service award Ala. Vocat.-Agrl. Tchrs. Assn., 1976; Man of Yr. in Agr. award Progressive Farmer, 1977; named Hon. State Farmer Future Farmers Am., 1976, Man of Yr. Crop Improvement Assn., 1981, Hon. County Agt., 1981; named to Ala. Agrl. Hall of Fame, 1985. Fellow Am. Soc. Agronomy, Soil Sci. Soc. Am.; mem. So. Assn. Agrl. Scientists (pres. 1976), Assn. So. Agrl. Expt. Sta. Dirs. (chmn. 1974), Assn. Univs. and Land-Grant Colls. (chmn. expt. sta. com. on orgn. and policy 1977), Sigma Xi, Alpha Zeta, Phi Kappa Phi, Xi Phi Xi, Gamma Sigma Delta. Presbyterian. Clubs: Lions (Auburn), Men's Camellia (Auburn), Outing (Auburn). Current Work: Calibrating chemical analyses with crop response to addition of plant nutrients and to liming of soil. Subspecialties: Soil science; Plant physiology (agriculture). Home: 827 Salmon Dr Auburn AL 36830

ROUSH, MARVIN LEROY, nuclear engineering educator; b. Topeka, Kans., Dec. 26, 1934; s. Leroy Mulvane and Clara Margaret (Roglitz) R.; m. Joanne Rae Witham, May 29, 1955; children—Paul, Brenda, Mark. B.Sc., Ottawa U., 1956; Ph.D., U. Md., 1964. Asst. prof. Baker U., Baldwin, Kans., 1959-61; asst. prof. Tex. A&M U., College Station, Tex., 1965-66; prof. dept. chem. and nuclear engring./physics U. Md., College Park, 1966—; cons. Univ. Research Found, Greenbelt, Md., 1982—, Trident Engring., Annapolis, Md., 1984—. Author: Energy in Perspective, 1982. Contbr. articles to profl. jours. Trustee, Ottawa U., Kans., 1984—, Midwestern Bapt. Theol. Sem., 1980—. Mem. Am. Nuclear Soc., Am. Phys. Soc., Am. Vacuum Soc., Am. Assn. Physics Tchrs. Baptist. Current work: Reliability engring., probabilistic risk assessment. Subspecialties: Nuclear engineering; Nuclear fission. Home: 7613 16th Ave Takoma Park MD 20912 Office: Chem and Nuclear Enging Univ MD College Park MD 20742

ROWE, DAVID JOHN, physicist, educator; b. Totnes, Devon, Eng., Feb. 4, 1936; came to Can., 1968; s. Herbert Tyack and Marguerite (Whitehead) R.; m. Una Mary Dawson, Sept. 8, 1958; children—Mark J.D., J. Amanda. B.A., Cambridge U., 1959; B.A., Oxford U., 1959, M.A., 1962, D.Phil., 1962. Research assoc. U. Rochester, N.Y., 1966-68; assoc. prof. U. Toronto, Ont., 1968-76, prof., 1974—, assoc. chmn. dept. physics, 1978-83, assoc. dean Sch. Grad. Studies, 1984—. Author: Nuclear Collective Motion, 1970. Editor: Dynamic Structure of Nuclear States, 1972; mem. editorial bd. Phys. Rev., 1983-86. Contbr. articles to profl. jours. Ford Found. fellow, 1962-63; U.K. Atmoic Energy Authority fellow, 1963-66; Alfred P. Sloan fellow, 1970-72; Erskine fellow, 1984; recipient Rutherford Meml. medal and prize Royal Soc. Can., 1983. Mem. Can. Assn. Physicists (chmn. theoretical physics div. 1971-72), Am. Phys. Soc. Current work: Theoretical nuclear physics, mathematical physics. Subspecialty: Theoretical physics. Home: 5 Scarth Rd Toronto ON M4W 2S5 Canada Office: Dept Physics U Toronto Toronto ON M5S 1A7 Canada

ROWE, JOSEPH EVERETT, electrical engineer; b. Highland Park, Mich., June 4, 1927; s. Joseph and Lillian May (Osbourne) R.; m. Margaret Anne Prine, Sept. 1, 1950; children: Jonathan Dale, Carol Kay. B.S. in Engring, U. Mich., 1951, B.S. Engring. in Math, 1951, M.S. in Engring, 1952, Ph.D., 1955. Mem. faculty U. Mich., Ann Arbor, 1953-74, prof. elec. engring., 1960-74, dir. electron physics lab., 1958-68, chmn. dept. elec. and computer engring., 1968-74; vice provost, dean engring. Case Western Res. U., Cleve., 1974-76; provost Case Inst. Tech., 1976-78; v.p. tech. Harris Corp., Melbourne, Fla., 1978-81; v.p., gen. mgr. Harris Corp. (Controls div.), 1981-82; exec. v.p. research and def. Gould Inc., 1982, vice chmn., chief tech. officer, 1983—; cons. to industry. Mem. adv. group electron devices Dept. Def., 1966-78, U.S. Army Sci. Bd. Author: Nonlinear Electron-Wave Interaction Phenomena, 1965, also articles. Recipient Distinguished Faculty Achievement award U. Mich., 1970. Fellow IEEE (chmn. adminstrv. com. group electron devices 1968-69, editor proc. 1971-73), AAAS; mem. Am. Phys. Soc., Am. Soc. Engring. Edn. (Curtis McGraw research award 1964), Nat. Acad. Engring., Sigma Xi, Phi Kappa Phi, Tau Beta Pi, Eta Kappa Nu. Subspecialty: Electrical engineering. Address: Gould Inc 10 Gould Center Rolling Meadows IL 60008

ROWLAND, LEWIS PHILLIP, neurologist, educator; b. Bklyn., Aug. 3, 1925; s. Henry Alexander and Cecile (Coles) R.; m. Esther Edelman, Aug. 31, 1952; children: Andrew Simon, Steven Samuel, Judith Mora. B.S., Yale U., 1945, M.D., 1948. Diplomate: Am. Bd. Psychiatry and Neurology. Intern New Haven Hosp., 1949-50; asst. resident N.Y. Neurol. Inst., 1950-52, fellow, 1953; clin. asso. NIH, Bethesda, Md., 1953-54, practice research medicine, specializing in neurology, N.Y.C., 1954-67, Phila., 1967-73, N.Y.C., 1973—; asst. neurologist Montefiore Hosp., N.Y.C., 1954-57; vis. fellow Nat. Inst. Med. Research, London, Eng., 1956; from asst. prof. to prof. neurology Columbia Coll. Phys. and Surg., 1957-67; prof., chmn. dept. neurology U. Pa., Med. Sch., 1967-73, Columbia Coll. Phys. and Surg., 1973—; from asst. neurologist to attending neurologist Presbyn. Hosp., 1957-67; co-dir. Neurol. Clin. Research Center, 1961-67, dir. neurology service, 1973—; Mem. med. adv. bd. Myasthenia Gravis Found., pres., 1971-73; med. adv. bd. Muscular Dystrophy Assos., Nat. Multiple Sclerosis Soc., Com. to Combat Huntington's Disease; pres. Parkinson's Disease Found., 1979—; mem. tng. grants com. Nat. Inst. Neurol. Communicable Diseases and Stroke, NIH, 1971-73, bd. sci. counselors, 1978-82, chmn., 1980-82. Editorial bd.: Archives of Neurology, 1968-76, Advances in Neurology, 1969—, Italian Jour. Neurol. Sci., 1979—, Handbook of Clin. Neurology, 1982—; editor-in-chief: Neurology, 1977—. Served with USNR, 1942-44; with USPHS, 1953-54. Mem. Am. Neurol. Assn. (pres. 1980), Am. Acad. Neurology, Phila. Neurol. Soc. (pres. 1972), Assn. Research Nervous Mental Disease (pres. 1969, trustee 1976—, v.p. 1980), Assn. U. Profs. Neurology (sec. 1971-74, pres. 1978), Eastern Pa. Multiple Sclerosis Soc. (chmn. med. adv. bd. 1969-73), N.Y.C. Multiple Sclerosis Soc. (chmn. med. adv. bd. 1977—). Subspecialty: Neurology. Home: 404 Riverside Dr New York NY 10025 Office: Neurological Inst 710 W 168th St New York NY 10032

ROWLANDS, DAVID THOMAS, pathology educator; b. Wilkes-Barre, Pa., Mar. 22, 1930; s. David Thomas and Anna Jule (Morgan) R.; m. Gwendolyn Marie York, Mar. 1, 1958; children: Julie Marie, Carolyn Jane. M.D., U. Pa., 1955. Diplomate: Am. Bd. Pathology, Am. Bd. Allergy and Immunology. Intern Pa. Hosp., Phila., 1955-56; resident Cin. Gen. Hosp., 1956-60; asst. prof. U. Colo., 1962-64, Rockefeller U., 1964-66; assoc. prof. Duke U., Durham, N.C., 1966-70; prof. pathology U. Pa., Phila., 1970-82, chmn. dept. pathology, 1973-78, prof. medicine, 1979-82; prof., chmn. dept. pathology U. So. Fla., Tampa, 1982—, assoc. dean, 1983-84. Mem. editorial bd.: Am. Jour. Pathology, 1971—, Developmental and Comparative Immunology, 1977-79. Served with USNR, 1960-62. Recipient Lederle Med. Faculty award U. Colo., 1964, Jacob Ehrenzeller award Pa. Hosp., 1976. Mem. Am. Assn. Pathologists, Internat. Acad. Pathology, Am. Soc. Clin. Pathology, Am. Assn. Immunologists. Presbyterian. Subspecialty: Pathology (medicine). Home: 13804 Cypress Village Circle Tampa FL 33624 Office: Dept Pathology Coll Medicine U South Fla Tampa FL 33612

ROWLANDS, ROBERT EDWARD, engring. educator, cons.; b. Trail, C., Can., July 7, 1936; came to U.S., 1960; s. Edward Howell and Eda May (Randell) R.; m. Mary Roma Ranaghan, Nov. 14, 1959; children: Robert Philip, Edward Hugh. B.A.Sc., U. B.C., Vancouver, 1959; M.S., U. Ill., Urbana, 1964, Ph.D., 1967. Registered profl. engr., Wis. Mech. engr. MacMillan & Bloedel, Powell River, B.C., 1959-60; research engr. Ill. Inst. Tech. Research Inst., Chgo., 1967-71, sr. research engr., 1971-74; asst. prof. engring. U. Wis., 1974-76, assoc. prof., 1976-79, prof., 1979—; lectr. and cons. in field; Am. rep. to USSR-U.S.A. Advanced Composite Materials meeting, Riga, Latvia, 1978; mem. U.S.A. organizational com. U.S.A.-USSR Composite Materials Meeting, 1980. Contbr. articles profl. jours., chpts. in books. Active boys program YMCA, Park Forest, Ill., 1970-74; youth racing program Madison Ski Club, 1978—; mem. com. Boy Scouts Am., Madison, 1975—, Guardian mem. Mohawk dist. council, 1976—. Fellow Soc. Exptl. Stress Analysis (Hetenyi award 1971, 77); mem. ASME, N.Am. Photonics Assn., Am. Acad. Mechanics. Current Work: Stress analysis and materials, exptl. mechanics. Subspecialties: Mechanical engineering; Solid mechanics. Home: 5401 Russett Rd Madison WI 53711 Office: Mechanics Dept U Wis 1415 Johnson Dr Madison WI 53706

ROWLEY, JANET DAVISON, physician; b. N.Y.C., Apr. 5, 1925; d. Hurford Henry and Ethel Mary (Ballantyne) Davison; m. Donald A. Rowley, Dec. 18, 1948; children: Donald, David, Robert, Roger. B.S., U. Chgo., 1946, M.D., 1948. Research fellow Levinson Found., Cook County Hosp., 1955-61; intern Marine Hosp., USPHS, Chgo., 1950-51; research fellow Levinson Found., Cook County Hosp., Chgo., 1955-61; clin. instr. neurology U. Ill., 1957-61; research assoc. dept medicine U. Chgo., 1962-71, assoc. prof., 1971-78, prof., 1978—, research cytogenetic analysis of human hematologic malignant diseases; mem. Nat. Cancer Adv. Bd., 1979-84. Contbr. chpts. to books, articles to profl. jours. Trustee Adler Planetarium, 1978—. Served with USPHS, 1950-51. Recipient First Kuwait Cancer prize, 1984. Mem. Nat. Acad. Scis., Inst. of Medicine, Am. Soc. Human Genetics, Am. Soc. Hematology, Am. Assn. Cancer Research. Episcopalian. Current Work: Identification of chromosome abnormalities in human leukemia and lymphoma. Subspecialties: Cancer research (medicine); Hematology. Home: 5310 University Ave Chicago IL 60615 Office: Box 420 5841 Maryland Ave Chicago IL 60637

ROWND, ROBERT HARVEY, biochemistry and molecular biology educator; b. Chgo., July 4, 1937; s. Walter Lemuel and Marie Francis (Joyce) R.; m. Rosalie Anne Lowery, June 13, 1959; children: Jennifer Rose, Robert Harvey, David Matthew. B.S. in Chemistry, St. Louis U., 1959; M.A. in Med. Scis, Harvard U., 1961, Ph.D. in Biophysics, 1963. Postdoctoral fellow Med. Research Council, NIH, Cambridge, Eng., 1963-65; postdoctoral fellow Nat. Acad. Scis.-NRC, Institut Pasteur, Paris, 1965-66; prof., chmn. molecular biology and biochemistry U. Wis., Madison, 1966-81; John G. Searle prof., chmn. molecular biology and biochemistry Med. and Dental Schs., Northwestern U., Chgo., 1981—, dir. combined M.D./Ph.D. degree program, 1982—; cons. NIH, NSF, Nat. Acad. Scis.-NRC. Contbr. numerous articles to sci. jours., books.; Mem. editorial bd.: Jour. of Bacteriology, 1975-81; editor, 1981—, assoc. editor Plasmid, 1977—; series editor Advances in Plasmid Molecular Biology, 1984—. Mem. troop com., treas. Four Lakes council Boy Scouts Am., Madison, 1973-77, mem. People to People Program del. of microbiologists to China, 1983. Fellow NSF; Fellow NIH, 1959-66; research grantee, 1966—; tng. grantee, 1970-79; USPHS Research Career Devel. awardee, 1968-73; recipient Alumni Merit award and vis. prof. St. Louis U., 1984. Mem. Am. Soc. Microbiology, Assn. Harvard Chemists, Am. Soc. Biol. Chemists, Am. Acad. Microbiology, N.Y. Acad. Scis. Subspecialty: Molecular biology. Home: 506 Lake Ave Wilmette IL 60091 Office: Northwestern U Med and Dental Schs 303 E Chicago Ave Chicago IL 60611

ROY, DENIS L., research physicist; b. Cap Chat, Que., Can., Nov. 21, 1946; s. Charles and Marguerite R.; m. Anne Marie Masson, July 6, 1968. B.Sc., Laval. U., 1970, M.Sc., 1971, D.Sc., 1974. Assoc. prof. Laval U., 1974-80, Nat. Sci. Engring. Research Council Can. research attache, 1980—. Contbr. articles to profl. jours. Mem. Assn. Canadienne-Francaise pour L'Avancement des Sciences, Can. Assn. Physicists, Am. Phys. Soc., Royal Astron. Soc. Can., Can. Nature Fedn. Current Work: Research atomic and molecular physics, electron scattering spectroscopy. Subspecialty: Atomic and molecular physics. Office: Dept Physics Pav Vachon Laval U Quebec PQ G1K 7P4 Canada

ROY, RUSTUM, materials science educator; b. Ranchi, India, July 3. 1924; came to U.S., 1945, naturalized, 1961; s. Narendra Kumar and Rajkumari (Mukherjee) R.; m. Della M. Martin, June 8, 1948; children: Neill, Ronnen, Jeremy. B.Sc., Patna (India) U., 1942, M.Sc., 1944; Ph.D., Pa. State U., 1948. Research asst. Pa. State U., 1948-49, mem. faculty, 1950—, prof. geochemistry, 1957—, prof. solid state, 1968—, chmn. solid state tech. program, 1960-67, dir. sci. tech. and soc. program, 1977—, dir. materials research lab., 1962-85, Evan Pugh prof., 1981—; sr. sci. officer Nat. Ceramic Lab., India, 1950; mem. com. mineral sci. tech. Nat. Acad. Scis., 1967-69, com. survey materials sci. tech., 1970-74; exec. com. chem. div. NRC, 1967-70, nat. materials adv. bd., 1970-77, mem. com. radioactive waste mgmt., 1974-80, chmn. panel waste solidification, 1976—, chmn. com., USSR and Eastern Europe, 1976—; sci. policy fellow Brookings Instn., 1982-83; mem. Pa. Gov.'s Sci. Adv. Com.; chmn. materials adv. panel, 1965—; mem. adv. com. engring. NSF, 1968-72, adv. com. to ethical and human value implications sci. and tech., 1974-76, adv. com. div. materials research, 1974-77; Hibbert lectr. U. London, 1979; dir. Kirkridge, Inc., Bangor, Pa.; cons. to industry. Author: Crystal Chemistry of Non-metallic Materials, 1974; Radioactive Waste Disposal, Vol. 1, the Waste Package, 1983; Lost at the Frontier, U.S. Sci. and Tech. Policy Audit, 1985; also articles.; Editor-in-chief: Materials Research Bull, 1966—, Bull. Sci. Tech. and Soc, 1981—; prin. editor Jour. Materials Research, 1985—. Chmn. bd. Dag Hammarskjold Coll., 1973-75; mem. ad hoc com. sci., tech. and ch. Nat. Council Chs., 1966-68. Mem. Nat. Acad. Engring., Mineral. Soc. Am. (award 1957), Am. Chem. Soc. (Petroleum Research Fund award 1960), Royal Swedish Acad. Engring. Scis. (fgn. mem.), Indian Nat. Acad. Sci. Current Work: Science policy; novel materials preparation and synthesis; especially those involing solution-made ceramics via DMS and sol-gel techniques for zero expansion, high energy shortage, and radioactive waste solidification. Subspecialties: Ceramics; High-temperature materials. Home: 528 S Pugh St State College PA 16801 Office: 102 Materials Research Lab University Park PA 16802

ROY-BURMAN, PRADIP, molecular biologist, biochemist, educator; b. Comilla, India, Nov. 12, 1938; came to U.S., 1963, naturalized, 1976; s. Prafulla Nath and Mrinalini (Barman) Roy-B.; m. Sumitra Ghosh, Nov. 26, 1963; children: Arup, Paula. B.Sc. in Chemistry with honors, Calcutta U., 1956, M.Sc., 1958, Ph.D., 1963. Asst. prof. biochemistry U. So. Calif., 1970, asst. prof. biochemistry and pathology, 1970-71, assoc. prof., 1972-78, prof., 1978—, chmn. grad. com. exptl. pathology, 1974—, chmn. biomed. research support grant com., 1984—; prin. investigator viral oncology research Nat. Cancer Inst. and Am. Cancer Soc. Contbr. articles to profl. jours. Dernham Sr. Research fellow in oncology, 1966-71; Am. Cancer Soc. grantee, 1966-70; Nat. Cancer Inst. grantee, 1970—; So. Calif. Edison Co. grantee, 1979-82. Mem. Am. Soc. Biol. Chemists, Am. Soc. Microbiology, AAUP, Internat. Assn. Comparative Research on Leukemia and Related Diseases. Democrat. Current Work: Viral and cellular oncogenes, molecular oncology, molecular genetics of cancer, oncodevelopmental genes, feline leukemia virus, leukemogenesis, oncogenes and regulation of their expression in normal and leukemic hematopoietic cells, recombinant DNA technology. Subspecialties: Cancer research (medicine); Virology (medicine). Office: U So Calif Sch Medicine Dept Pathology Los Angeles CA 90033

ROYDS, ROBERT B., clinical pharmacologist, physician; b. Harrogate, Yorks., Eng., Oct. 3, 1944; came to U.S., 1974; s. John Edmund and Ailsa Dorothea (Williams) R.; m. Marilyn Maria Valerio, Apr. 23, 1977; children: Elizabeth Caroline, Leslie Alexandra. M.B.B.S., St. Bartholomew's Hosp., London, 1967; M.R.C.S., L.R.C.P., 1967. Research fellow St. Bartholomew's Hosp., London, Eng., 1970-72, chief asst., 1972-74; assoc. dir. Merck, Sharp & Dohme Labs., Rahway, N.J., 1975-76; sr. research physician Hoffmann-La Roche Inc., Nutley, N.J., 1976-79; v.p. Besselaar Assocs., Princeton, N.J., 1979-82; chmn. Theradex Systems, Inc., Princeton, N.J., 1982—; adj. asst. prof. pharmacology U. Pa.-Phila., 1981—. Fellow Royal Soc. Medicine; mem. Royal Coll. Physicians of London, Am. Soc. Clin. Pharmacology and Therapeutics, Am. Fedn. Clin. Research. Current Work: Computer assisted clinical study monitoring. Subspecialties: Pharmacology; Bioinstrumentation. Office: Theradex Systems Inc CN 5257 Princeton NJ 08540

ROYER, GARFIELD PAUL, biochemist; b. Waynesboro, Pa., Dec. 2, 1942; s. Paul Franklin and Dolores (Schnurr) R.; m. Alvilda Ann Hopcraft, Aug. 13, 1966; children: Thaddeus, Corynn, Paul. B.S., Juniata Coll., 1964; Ph.D., W.Va., U., 1968; postgrad., Northwestern U., 1968-70. Prof. biochemistry Ohio State U., Columbus, 1970-82; dir. biotech. div. Amoco Corp., Naperville, Ill., 1983—; cons. to various corps. Author: Fundamentals of Enzymology, 1982; mem. editorial bd.: Jour. Molecular Catalysis, 1977—; contbr. articles to profl. jours. NIH Research Career Devel. awardee, 1975. Mem. Am. Chem. Soc., Am. Soc. Biol. Chemists, AAAS. Lutheran. Patentee. Current Work: Research in areas of enzyme engineering, synthetic enzyme models, and genetic engineering. Subspecialties: Enzyme technology; Genetics and genetic engineering (agriculture). Office: Amoco Research Center PO Box 400 Naperville IL 60566

ROZEN, JEROME GEORGE, JR., research entomologist, mus. curator and adminstr.; b. Evanston, Ill., Mar. 19, 1928; s. Jerome George and Della (Kretchmar) R.; m. Barbara L. Lindner, Dec. 18, 1948; children—Steven George, Kenneth Charles, James Robert. Student, U. Pa., 1946-48; B.A., U. Kans., 1950; Ph.D., U. Calif. at Berkeley, 1955. Entomologist (taxonomy) U.S. Dept. Agr., 1956-58; asst. prof. entomology Ohio State U., 1958-60; asso. curator Hymenoptera, dept. entomology Am. Mus. Natural History, N.Y.C., 1960-65, curator of Hymenoptera, 1965—, chmn. dept., 1960-71, dep. dir. for research, 1972—; field expdns., U.S., Europe, Trinidad, Chile, Brazil, Morocco, So. Africa, Pakistan, Venezuela. Fellow AAAS; mem. Entomol. Soc. Am. (editor misc. publs. 1959-60), Soc. Study Evolution, Soc. Systematic Zoology, N.Y. Entomol. Soc. (pres. 1964-65), Washington Entomol. Soc. Club: Cosmos. Research in evolutionary biology, especially systematics of bees and beetles. Current Work: Evolutionary and systematic relationships of insects; especially bees. Subspecialties: Evolutionary biology; Systematics. Home: 55 Haring St Closter NJ 07624 Office: Am Museum Natural History Central Park W at 79th St New York NY 10024

RUBEN, ZADOK, pathologist, veterinarian, researcher; b. Baghdad, Iraq, Mar. 9, 1942; resident Israel, 1951; came to U.S. 1965; s. Salman Menashe and Violet (Ezra) R. B.S. in Zoology, Iowa State U., 1969, D.V.M., 1972, M.S. in Vet. Pathology, 1973; A.M. in Exptl. Pathology, Harvard U., 1975; Ph.D. in Pathobiology, U. Conn., 1980. Research asst. vet. pathology Iowa State U., Ames, 1972-73; research fellow in pathology Harvard Med. Sch., Boston, 1973-75; research assoc. div. tumor immunology Sidney Farber Cancer Ctr., Boston, 1974-75; research assoc. I. dept. pathobiology U. conn., Storrs, 1975-79; gen. practice vet. medicine specializing in small animals, Somers, Conn., 1978-79, Belmont, Mass., 1979; pathologist G.D. Searle & Co., Skokie, Ill., 1979—; cons. dept. biochemistry Chgo. Med. Sch., North Chgo., Ill., 1983—; special adv. to exec. directorship bd. Sch. Vet. Med. The Hebrew U. Jerusalem, 1984—; asst. prof. dept. pathology Rush Med. Coll., Chgo., 1984—. Research sect. editor and gen. co-editor of The Iowa State U. Veterinarian, 1970-72; contbr. numerous articles to profl. jours. Foreign student scholar Iowa State U., 1967-71, Leob Found. scholar 1966-73, Salsbury Labs scholar for grad. students Iowa State U., 1972-73, div. med. sci. grad. scholar Harvard U., 1975; postdoctoral fellow Cancer Research Inst., 1973-74, grad. fellow U. Conn., 1976. Served to corp. Israeli Def. Forces, 1959-62, Israel. Mem. AVMA, Internat. Acad. Pathology, Soc. Toxicol. Pathologists, Am. Coll. Vet. Pathologists (cert.), Am. Assn. Pathologists, Am. Assn. Lab. Animal Sci., Soc. Exptl. Biology and Medicine, many other regional and local toxicology, pathology, drug-safety and alumni organs., Phi Eta Sigma, Phi Kappa Phi, Gamma Sigma Delta. Jewish. Current work: Experimental pathology, toxicology. Subspecialties: Pathology (veterinary medicine); Toxicology (medicine). Home: 2514 Prairie Ave Evanston IL 60201 Office: G D Searle & Co 4901 Searle Pkwy Skokie IL 60077

RUBENSTEIN, ARTHUR HAROLD, physician, educator; b. Johannesburg, South Africa, Dec. 28, 1937; came to U.S., 1967; s. Montague and Isabel (Nathanson) R.; m. Denise Hack, Aug. 19, 1962; children: Jeffrey Lawrence, Errol Charles. M.B., B.Ch., U. Witwatersrand, 1960. Fellow in endocrinology Postgrad. Med. Sch., London, 1965-66; fellow in medicine U. Chgo., 1967-68, asst. prof., 1968-70, asso. prof., 1970-74, prof., 1974—, Lowell T. Coggeshall prof. med. sci., 1981—, asso. chmn. dept. medicine, 1975-81, chmn., 1981—; attending physician Billings Hosp., U. Chgo., 1968—; mem. study sect. NIH, 1973-77; mem. adv. council Nat. Inst. Arthritis, Metabolism and Digestive Diseases, 1978-80; chmn. Nat. Diabetes Adv. Bd., 1982, mem., 1983—. Editorial bd.: Diabetes, 1973-77, Endocrinology, 1973-77, Jour. Clin. Investigation, 1976-81, Am. Jour. Medicine, 1978-81; contbr. articles to profl. jours. Recipient David Rumbough Meml. award Juvenile Diabetes Found., 1978. Fellow ACP, Coll. Physicians (S. Africa), Royal Coll. Physicians (London); mem. Am. Soc. for Clin. Investigation, Am. Diabetes Assn. (Eli Lilly award 1973, Banting medal award 1983), Endocrine Soc., Am. Fedn. for Clin. Research, Central Soc. for Clin. Research, Assn. Am. Physicians. (exec. com., treas. 1984—), Am. Acad. Arts and Scis. Current Work: Etiology and pathogenesis of diabetes; mutant insulins improved therapy of diabetes with insulin, C-peptide and proinsulin. Subspecialties: Endocrinology; Internal medicine. Home: 5517 S Kimbark Ave Chicago IL 60637 Office: 5841 S Maryland Ave Chicago IL 60637

RUBENSTEIN, EDWARD, physician, educator; b. Cin., Dec. 5, 1924; s. Louis and Nettie R.; m. Nancy Ellen Millman, June 20, 1954; children: John, William, James. M.D., U. Cin., 1947. Intern, jr. asst. resident, sr. asst. resident internal medicine Cin. Gen. Hosp., 1947-50; fellow May Inst., Cin., 1950; sr. asst. resident Ward Med. Service, Barnes Hosp., St. Louis, 1953-54; chief of medicine San Mateo County Hosp., Calif., 1960-70; asso. dean postgrad. med. edn., prof. clin. medicine Stanford U. Sch. Medicine, 1971—. Author: textbook Intensive Medical Care; editor-in-chief: textbook Sci. Am. Medicine, 1978—. Served with USAF, 1950-52. Fellow ACP; mem. Inst. Medicine, Nat. Acad. Scis., Calif. Acad. Medicine, Western Assn. Physicians, Soc. Photo-Optical Engrs., Alpha Omega Alpha. Research on synchrotron radiation. Current Work: Non-invasive coronary angiography. Origin of chiral molecules. Subspecialties: Imaging technology; Internal medicine. Office: TC 129 Stanford Med Center Stanford CA 94305

RUBERG, ROBERT LIONEL, physician, educator; b. Phila., July 22, 1941; s. Norman and Yetta (Wolfman) R.; m. Cynthia Lief, June 26, 1966; children: Frederick, Mark, Joshua. B.A., Haverford Coll., 1963; M.D., Harvard Med. Sch., 1967. Diplomate: Am. Bd. Surgery, Am. Bd. Plastic Surgery. Intern Hosp. U. Pa., 1967-68, resident, 1968-75; asst. instr. surgery U. Pa., 1967-72, instr. surgery, 1972-75; asst. prof. surgery Ohio State U., Columbus, 1975-81, assoc. prof. surgery, 1981—, dir. div. plastic surgery, 1985—; dir. Nutrition Support Service, Ohio State U. Hosps., 1976-84, co-dir. Burn Unit, 1975, dir., 1984; bd. dirs. Am. Soc. for Parenteral and Enteral Nutrition, 1983-85. Trustee Columbus Hebrew Sch., 1982. Research grantee Plastic Surgery Ednl. Found., 1976, 78; basic sci. prize, 1977. Fellow ACS; mem. Am. Assn. Plastic Surgeons, Central Surg. Assn., Plastic Surgery Research Council, Am. Soc. Plastic and Reconstructive Surgeons. Club: Aesculapian (Boston). Current Work: Nutrition and drug effects on skin grafts and skin flaps, solutions and techniques for parenteral feeding. Subspecialties: Surgery; Nutrition (biology). Home: 6243 Peach Tree Rd Columbus OH 43213 Office: Ohio State Univ Hosp Room N-809 410 W Tenth Ave Columbus OH 43213

RUBERT, MARY LOU, psychologist; b. San Juan, Oct. 5, 1951; d. Guillermo and Francisca (del Valle) R.; div.; 1 son, Guillermo Morales Rubert. B.A., U. P.R., 1972; M.S., Caribbean Center for Advanced Studies, 1976; Ph.D., Calif. Sch. Profl Psychology, 1980. Prof. psychology and clin. supr. Caribbean Center for Advanced Studies, Santurce, P.R., 1980—; v.p. Bd. Examiners in Psychology, P.R., 1984—. Ford Found. fellow, 1978-80. Mem. Am. Psychol. Assn., AAAS, Internat. Soc. Polit. Psychology. Current Work: Laboratory design for research on info. processing and developmental difference in individuals; behavioral dimension and decision-making models related to biomed. ethics. Subspecialties: Clinical psychology; Developmental psychology. Home: Cond Parque San Patricio 2 Apt 306 Caparra Heights PR 00922 Office: Suite 201-A Plaza Las Americas Hato Rey PR 00918

RUBIN, A(LBERT) ROBERT, agricultural engineering educator; b. Loma Linda, Calif., Feb. 16, 1945; s. Edward H. and Irene (Goldsmith) R.; m. Linda Peterson, Apr. 24, 1974; children—Joshua, Eric, Brent. Student Riverside City Coll., 1962-65; B.S., U. Calif.-Irvine, 1967; Ed.D., N.C. State U., 1980. Research asst. N.C. State U., Raleigh, 1978-79, asst. prof. agrl. engring., 1979—. Author: Land Treatment Considerations, 1978; Sub-Surface Treatment of Wastewater, 1983; Operations and Maintenance Considerations in Land Treatment of Wastewater and Sludge, 1983. Served to capt. USAF, 1967-74. Mem. Am. Soc. Agrl. Engrs. (chmn. waste mgmt. com. 1982-83), co-chmn. symposium on on-site wate treatment 1983-84, chmn. SW 262). Jewish. Current work: Land treatment of municipal, industrial and agricultural wastewater and sludge. Subspecialties: Agricultural engineering; Water supply and wastewater treatment. Home: 34 Avdley Chapel Hill NC 27514 Office: NC State U BAE 210A Weaver Box 7625 Raleigh NC 27695

RUBIN, BERNARD, pharmacologist, researcher; b. N.Y.C., Feb. 15, 1919; s. Charles and Anna (Slutskin) R.; m. Betty Rose Schindler, June 17, 1945; children: Stefi Gail, Robert Henry. Ph.D. in Pharmacology, Yale U., 1951. Bacteriologist Bur. Labs., N.Y.C. Dept Health, 1940-43; med. lab. technician U.S. Marine Hosp., S.I., N.Y., 1944; health insp. Bur. Foods and Drugs, N.Y.C. Dept. Health, 1945; research biologist Nepera Chem. Co., Yonkers, N.Y., 1945-48; pharmacologist, sr. research group leader Squibb Inst. Med. Research, Princeton, N.J., 1950-84. Contbr. articles to profl. jours. Served with AUS, 1942-43. AEC fellow, 1949-50; CIBA fellow, 1948. Mem. Am. Soc. Pharmacology and Exptl. Therapeutics, Internat. Soc. Hypertension, Soc. Exptl. Biology and Medicine, Am. Pharm. Assn., Am. Heart Assn. (council for high blood pressure research). Current Work: Consultant; cardiopulmonary research; information service, licensing. Subspecialty: Pharmacology. Office: PO Box 4000 Princeton NJ 08540

RUBIN, CAROL ANN, mechanical engineering educator; b. N.Y.C., Apr. 2, 1945; d. Herman and Mollie (Cooper) Shames; m. Abba Rubin, June 9, 1963; children—Aviel, Rachel, Tova, Yaacov. B.S. in Mech. Engring., Columbia U., 1966; M.S., Kans. State U., 1969, Ph.D., 1971. Registered profl. engr., Ala. Asst. machine design engr. Gibbs & Cox, Inc., N.Y.C., 1967; lectr. Technion, Haifa, Israel, 1971-76; asst. prof., then assoc. prof. U. Ala.-Birmingham, 1976-80; assoc. prof. mech. engring. Vanderbilt U., Nashville, 1980—. Contbr articles to profl. jours. Bd. dirs. Akiva Sch., Nashville, 1983—. Grantee, Office Naval Research, 1980—, NSF, 1981—. Mem. ASME, Sigma Xi. Current work: Finite element modeling, fracture mechanics, vibration of musical instruments. Subspecialties: Theoretical and applied mechanics; Mechanical engineering. Office: Vanderbilt U PO Box 1670 Station B Nashville TN 37235

RUBIN, GERALD M., molecular biologist, educator; b. Boston, Mar. 31, 1950; s. Benjamin H. and Edith R.; m. Lynn Suzanne Mastalir, May 7, 1978; 1 son, Alan F. B.S., M.I.T., 1971; Ph.D., Cambridge (Eng.) U., 1974. Helen Hay Whitney Found fellow dept. biochemistry Stanford U. Sch. Medicine, 1974-76; asst. prof. biol. chemistry Sidney Farber Cancer Inst./Harvard Med. Sch., Boston, 1977-80; staff mem. dept. embryology Carnegie Instn. of Washington, Balt., 1980-83; faculty dept. biochemistry U. Calif.-Berkeley, 1983—. Contbr. articles to profl. publs. NSF fellow, 1971-73; U.S. Churchill Found. fellow, 1974-76; U.S. Steel Found. award in molecular biology, 1985. Mem. Phi Beta Kappa, Phi Lambda Epsilon. Current Work: Transposable elements in drosophila. Subspecialties: Genome organization; Molecular biology. Office: Univ Calif Dept Biochemistry Berkeley CA 94720

RUBIN, LAWRENCE G(ILBERT), physicist, laboratory manager; b. Bklyn., Sept. 17, 1925; s. Harry E. and Ruth R. (Feirberg) R.; m. Florence Ruth Kagan, Feb. 11, 1951; children—Michael G., Richard D., Jeffrey N. B.S. in Physics, U. Chgo., 1949; M.A., Columbia U., 1950. Mem. staff research div. Raytheon Co., Waltham, Mass., 1950-64; group leader Nat. Magnet Lab.-M.I.T., Cambridge, 1964-78, div. head, 1978—; mem. adv. panel Nat. Acad. Scis. to Nat. Bur. Standards, 1976-82, 1985—; bd. dirs. Lake Shore Cryotronics, Columbus, Ohio, 1982—; gen. chmn. 6th Internat. Temperature Symposium, Washington, 1982. Mem. editorial bd. Rev. of Sci. Instruments, 1968-70, 1979-81. Editor: Temperature, its Measurement and Control in Science and Industry, 1972 (vol. 4). Contbr. articles to profl. jours. Served to sgt. U.S. Army, 1943-46; ETO. Fellow Am. Phys. Soc. (1st chmn. Instrument and Measurement Sci. group 1985—), IEEE (various coms.); Instrument Soc. Am., Am. Vacuum Soc. Jewish. Current work: Operation of National High Magnetic Field Facility and the instrumentation required for experiments conducted. Subspecialties: Instrument and measurement science; Cryogenic thermometry. Home: 1504 Centre St Newton Centre MA 02159 Office: Nat Magnet Lab MIT Bldg NW 14 170 Albany St Cambridge MA 02139

RUBIN, ROBERT HOWARD, astrophysicist, educator; b. Phila., Mar. 26, 1941; s. Abraham D. and Betty B. (Farber) R. B.S., Case Inst. Tech., 1963, Ph.D. in Astrophysics, 1967. Research assoc. Nat. Radio Astronomy Obs., Charlottesville, Va., 1967-69; research assoc. asst. prof. U. Ill., Urbana, 1969-72; assoc. prof. Calif. State U., Fullerton, 1972-81; sr. nat. research council assoc. NASA Ames Research Ctr., Moffett Field, Calif., 1981-83, research assoc., 1983—; vis. prof. research astronomer UCLA, 1983—. Contbr. writings to profl. publs. Stanford/NASA Ames faculty fellow, summers 1980, 81; Santa Clara U./NASA faculty fellow, summer 1979; NSF grantee, 1970-72. Mem. Am. Astron. Soc., Internat. Astron. Union, Union Radio Sci. Internat. Club: Pacific Wing and Rotor Flying. Current Work: Studies of interstellar medium, theoretical modeling of gaseous nebulae with emphasis on predicting infrared line intensities. Subspecialties: Theoretical astrophysics; Radio and microwave astronomy. Home: 436 Sierra Vista Mountain View CA 94043 Office: NASA Ames Research Center Mail Stop 245-6 Moffett Field CA 94035

RUBIN, ROBERT JOSHUA, physicist; b. N.Y.C., Aug. 17, 1926; s. Benjamen and Bessie (Stambler) R.; m. Vera Cooper, June 25, 1948; children—David Michael, Judith Sharn, Karl Cooper, Allan Mattathias. B.S., Cornell U., 1948, Ph.D., 1951. Mem. staff Johns Hopkins U. Applied Physics Lab., Silver Spring, Md., 1951-55; vis. asst. prof. dept. chemistry U. Ill., Champaign-Urbana, 1955-57; physicist Nat. Bur. Standards, Gaithersburg, Md., 1957—; vis. prof. Inst. Theoretical Physics U. Kyoto, Japan, summer, 1968, dept. chem. engring. U. Calif.-Berkeley, winter, 1981. Contbr. articles to profl. jours. Mem. theoretical biology group NIH, 1976-77. NSF sr. postdoctoral fellow, 1963-64. Fellow Am. Phys. Soc.; mem. Am. Chem. Soc., Soc. Indsl. and Applied Math. Current work: Statistical physics of disordered systems; theory of random walks; Brownian motion; configurational statistics of polymer chains. Subspecialties: Statistical physics; Physical chemistry. Office: Nat Bur Standards Gaithersburg MD 20899

RUBIN, STANLEY GERALD, aerospace engineering educator, researcher; b. N.Y.C., May 11, 1938; s. Harry Jack and Cele (Sake) R.; m. Carol Ruth Kalvin, Sept. 29, 1963; children—Stephany Irene, Elizabeth Faith, Barbara Joy. B.S. in Aerospace Engring., Poly. Inst. Bklyn., 1959; Ph.D., Cornell U., 1963. Asst. prof. Poly. Inst. Bklyn., Farmingdale, N.Y., 1964-67, assoc. prof., 1967-73, prof., 1973-79, assoc. dir. aerodynamics lab., 1977-79; prof., head aerospace engring. and applied mechanics U. Cin., 1979—; vis. scientist Inst. Computer Applied Sci. and Engring., Hampton, Va., 1973; vis. prof. Old Dominion U., Norfolk, Va., 1973-74; cons. in field. Contbr. articles to profl. jours. Assoc. fellow AIAA (student honors award 1959, 60); mem. ASME, Soc. Indsl. and Applied Math., Am. Soc. Engring. Edn., Sigma Xi, Tau Beta Pi, Sigma Gamma Tau. Current work: Computational methods for solution of fluid dynamic problems involving strong viscous/inviscid interactions; algorithm development for reduced navier-stokes equations, transonic flow, separated flow, three-dimensional flow. Subspecialties: Aeronautical engineering; Aerospace engineering and technology. Home: 10695 Deershadow Ln Cincinnati OH 45242 Office: Dept Aerospace Engring and Engring Mechanics ML 70 U Cin Cincinnati OH 45221

RUBIN, VERA COOPER, research astonomer; b. Phila., July 23, 1928; d. Philip and Rose (Applebaum) Cooper; m. Robert J. Rubin, June 25, 1948; children—David M., Judith S., Karl C., Allan M. B.A., Vassar Coll., 1948; M.A., Cornell U., 1951; Ph.D., Georgetown U., 1954; D.Sc. hon., Creighton U., 1978. Research assoc. to asst. prof. Georgetown U., Washington, 1955-65; physicist U. Calif.-LaJolla, 1963-64; astronomer Carnegie Instns., Washington, 1965—; Chancellor's Disting. prof. U. Calif.-Berkeley, 1981; vis. com. Harvard Coll. Obs., Cambridge, Mass., 1976-82. Assoc. editor: Astrophys. Jour. Letters, 1977-82; editorial bd.; Sci. Mag., 1979—; contbr. numerous articles sci. jours.; assoc. editor: Astron. Jour., 1972-77. Mem. Smithsonian Instn. Council, 1979—; Phi Beta Kappa scholar, 1982-83. Mem. Am. Astron. Soc. (council 1977-80), Internat. Astron. Union (pres. Commn. on Galaxies 1982-85), Assn. Univs. Research in Astronomy (dir. 1973-76), Nat. Acad. Scis. (Space Sci. Bd. 1974-77), Am. Acad. Arts and Scis., Phi Beta Kappa. Democrat. Jewish. .

RUBINOFF, IRA, biologist, research administrator, conservationist; b. N.Y.C., Dec. 21, 1938; s. Jacob and Bessie (Rose) R.; m. Roberta Wolff, Mar. 19, 1961; 1 son, Jason; m. Anabella Guardia, Feb. 10, 1978; children: Andres, Ana. B.S., Queens Coll., 1959; A.M., Harvard U., 1960, Ph.D., 1963. Biologist, asst. dir. marine biology Smithsonian Tropical Research Inst., Balboa, Republic of Panama, 1964-70, asst. dir. sci., 1970-73, dir., 1973—; asso. in ichthyology Harvard U., 1965—; courtesy prof. Fla. State U., Tallahassee, 1976—; mem. sci. adv. bd. Gorgas Meml. Inst., 1964—; trustee Rare Animal Relief Effort, 1976—; bd. dirs. Charles Darwin Found. for Galapagos Islands, 1977—; chmn. bd. fellowships and grants Smithsonian Instn., 1978-79; vis. fellow Wolfson Coll., Oxford (Eng.) U., 1980-81. Author Strategy for Preservation of Moist Tropical Forests; Contbr. articles to profl. jours. Bd. dirs. Internat. Sch., Panama, 1983—. Fellow Linnean Soc. (London); mem. Am. Soc. Naturalists, Soc. Study of Evolution, N.Y. Acad. Scis., Orgn. Tropical Studies. Club: Cosmos (Washington). Current Work: Analysis of diving behavior and physiology of sea snakes using radiotelemtry; conservation strategy for tropical forests. Subspecialties: Evolutionary biology; Behavioral ecology. Home: Box 2281 Balboa Republic of Panama Office: Smithsonian Tropical Research Inst APO Miami FL 34002

RUBINSTEIN, MICHAEL, theoretical physicist; b. Odessa, USSR, Dec. 20, 1956, came to U.S., 1977, naturalized, 1982; s. George and Rose (Koifman) R.; m. Helen Mandel, Oct. 21, 1983. B.S., Calif. Inst. Tech., 1979; M.A., Harvard U., 1980, Ph.D. in theoretical physics, 1983. Research asst. Fermi Nat. Lab., Batavia, Ill., 1978; research asst. Calif. Inst. Tech., Pasadena, 1977-79; teaching fellow Harvard U., Cambridge, Mass., 1980-82, research asst., 1981-83; research asst. IBM Research Ctr., Yorktown Heights, N.Y., 1982; postdoctoral fellow AT&T Bell Labs., Murray Hill, N.J., 1983-85; research scientist Kodak Research Labs., Rochester, N.Y., 1985—. Contbr. articles to profl. jours. Recipient Carnation and Caltech Prizes Calif. Inst. Tech., 1978. Mem. Am. Phys. Soc., N.Y. Acad. Scis., Tau Beta Pi. Current work: Glass transition; polymer rheology; viscoelasticity and entanglements; phase transitions; in disordered systems; diffusion controlled reactions; fractals. Subspecialties: Condensed matter physics; Polymer physics. Home: 89-D Greenleaf Meadows Rochester NY 14612 Office: Research Labs Eastman Kodak Co Rochester NY 14650

RUBIS, DAVID D., plant geneticist, educator; b. Jackson, Minn., May 30, 1924; s. Steve Rubis; divorced; children—Daniel, Ann, Karl. B.S., U. Minn., 1948; M.S., Iowa State U., 1950, Ph.D., 1954. Research asst. Iowa State U., Ames, 1948-52; agronomist U.S. Dept. Agr., Mesa, Ariz., 1952-56; asst. then assoc. prof. U. Ariz., Tucson, 1956-64, prof., 1964—. Mem. Am. Soc. Agronomy, Crop Sci. Soc. Am., Guayule Rubber Soc. (pres. 1980-82). Current work: Domestication and development of new crops; developed safflower, plantago, lesquereulla, guar and guayule as new crops; developer new plant breeding materials. Subspecialties: Agronomy; Plant genetics. Home: 5755 Calle Del Ciervo Tucson AZ 85715 Office: Dept Plant Sci U Ariz Tucson AZ 85721

RUBY, DOUGLAS EARLY, biologist, educator; b. Balt., Oct. 4, 1946; s. Herbert Edgar Jr. and Helen Marie (Early) R.; m. Sara Wilson, June 19, 1971; children—Daniel Ellis, Rebecca Sue. B.A., Gettysburg Coll., 1968; M.S., U. Mich., 1970, Ph.D., 1976. Teaching intern Purdue U., West Lafayette, Ind., 1976-77; asst. prof. Xavier U., New Orleans, 1977-82; adj. assoc. prof. biol. sci. Drexel U., Phila., 1982-84, vis. assoc. prof., 1984—; dir. birdwatcher weekends Camp Swatara, Bethel, Pa., 1982—. Contbr. chpt. to book, articles to profl. publs. Recipient LOCI Program award NSF, 1979-81; grantee NSF, 1973-74, Nat. Geog. Soc., 1984. Mem. AAAS, Ecol. Soc. Am., Animal Behavior Soc., Am. Soc. Ichthyologists and Herpetologists. Republican. Mem. Ch. of the Brethren. Current work: Reptile behavior; mating systems; territoriality. Subspecialties: Behavioral ecology; Ethology. Home: 1804 S Broad St Lansdale PA 19446 Office: Drexel U Dept Biol Sci Philadelphia PA 19104

RUCH, RICHARD JULIUS, chemistry educator; b. Perryville, Mo., Jun 9, 1932; s. Julius Maurus and Zita Elizabeth (Boxdorfer) R.; m. Leola Sander, June 20, 1954; children: Stephen, David, Susan, Daniel. B.S., S.E. Mo. State U., 1954; M.S., Iowa State U., 1956, Ph.D., 1959. Asst. prof. chemistry State U. S.D., 1959-62; So. Ill. U., Carbondale, 1962-66; assoc. prof. chemistry Kent (Ohio) State U., 1966—. Author: (with T. Sato) Stabilization of Colloidal Dispersions by Polymer Adsorption, 1980; contbr. (with T. Sato) articles to profl. jours. Mem. Am. Chem Soc., Fedn. Socs. for Coatings Tech. Republican. Lutheran. Current Work: Properties of colloidal dispersions and film coatings, using dielectric, wetting, and rheological techniques. Subspecialties: Physical chemistry; Surface chemistry. Home: 1955 Pineview Dr Kent OH 44240 Office: Dept Chemistry Kent State U 214B WMH Kent OH 44242

RUCKMICK, JOHN CHRISTIAN, geologist; b. Iowa City, Iowa, Nov. 26, 1926; s. Christian Alban and Katherine T. R.; m. Jane E. Douglas, Sept. 10, 1955; children: Stephen C., Melissa K. B.A., Amherst Coll., 1952; M.S., Calif. Inst. Tech., 1954, Ph.D., 1957. Chief geologist Orinoco Mining Co., Ciudad Piar, Venezuela, 1957-67; exploration mgr. Homestake Mining Co., Kalgoorlie, Western Australia, 1967-70, Tucson, 1970-74, Texasgulf, Inc., Golden, Colo., 1974-82; exec. v.p. Exploration Ventures Co., 1982. Contbr. articles to profl. jours. Served with USNR, 1944-46. Fellow Geol. Soc. Am.; mem. Soc. Econ. Geologists, AIME, Am. Assn. Petroleum Geologists, Northwest Mining Assn. Republican. Subspecialties: Geology; Geochemistry. Home: 2266 Pebble Beach Ct Evergreen CO 80439 Office: Exploration Ventures Co Inc 2266 Pebble Beach Ct Evergreen CO 80439

RUDAVSKY, ALEXANDER BOHDAN, civil engr., educator; b. Poland, Jan. 17, 1925; s. Leo and Zenovia (Orlov) R.; m. Juanita Jean Enga, Nov. 5, 1955; 1 dau., Natica. Sc.D. (Dr.Ing.), Franzius Inst., Ger., 1966; B.S. and M.S., U. Minn., 1956. Civil engr. Justin & Courtney, Phila., 1956-57, Iran 1957-58; mem. faculty San Jose (Calif.) State U., 1960—, prof., 1975—; dir., owner, pres. Hydro Research Sci., Santa Clara, Calif., 1964—; cons. Contbr. numerous articles to profl. jours. ASCE Freeman scholar Europe, 1958. Mem. U.S. Com. Large Dams, Internat. Assn. Hydraulic Research, ASCE. Current Work: Hydraulic research through model studies of engineering problems related to hydraulic structures, ports and harbors, coastal protection and thermal pollution. Subspecialties: Fluid mechanics; Hydrology. Office: 3334 Victor Ct Santa Clara CA 95050

RUDDAT, MANFRED, biology educator; b. Insterburg, Ger., Aug. 21, 1932; came to U.S., 1961; s. Otto and Helene (Naujoks) R.; m. Helga Kuntzel, Nov. 3, 1962; children: Michael, Monica. Ph.D., U. Tübingen, Ger., 1960. Sci. asst. botany U. Tübingen, 1960-61; NSF fellow Calif. Inst. Tech., Pasadena, 1961-64; asst. prof. botany U. Chgo., 1964-68, asst. prof. biology, 1968-70, assoc. prof. biology, 1970—, assoc. prof. molecular genetics and cell biology, 1984—. Editor: Bot. Gazette, 1974. Recipient Quantrell award, 1969. Mem. Am. Soc. Plant Physiologists, Bot. Soc. Am., Japanese Soc. Plant Physiologists, AAAS, Internat. Plant Growth Substances Assn. Current Work: Developmental biology and biochemistry of plants and fungi, physiology and biochemistry of plant growth regulators. Subspecialties: Plant physiology (biology); Plant growth. Office: Dept Biology U Chgo Barnes Lab 5630 S Ingleside Ave Chicago IL 60637

RUDDLE, FRANCIS HUGH, genetics educator; b. West New York, N.J., Aug. 19, 1929; s. Thomas Hugh and Mary Henley (Rodda) R.; m. Nancy Marion Hartman, Aug. 1, 1964; children: Kathlyn Gabrielle, Amy Elizabeth. B.A., Wayne State U., Detroit, 1953, M.S., 1956; Ph.D., U. Calif.-Berkeley, 1960; hon. degree, Lawrence U., 1982, Weizmann Inst., Israel, 1983. Asst. prof. Yale U., New Haven, 1961-67, assoc. prof., 1967-72, prof. biology and human genetics, 1972—, Ross Granville Harrison prof. biology, 1983—, chmn. dept. biology, 1977-83; adv. com. Am. Type Culture Collection, 1963-71; planning com. 1st Internat. Congress on Cell Biology, 1975; mem. cell study sect. NIH, 1965-70, chmn. mutant cell lines com., 1972-77; R.E. Dyer lectr., 1978; Merck lectr. Montreal Cancer Inst., 1979; Condon lectr. U. Oreg., 1981. Editorial bd.: Exptl. Cell Research, 1975—, Genetics, 1973—, In Vitro, 1970—, Somatic Cell Genetics, 1975—, Am. Jour. Cell Biology, Biochemistry. Served with USAAF, 1946-49. Recipient Dickson prize in medicine U. Pitts., 1981, Disting. Alumni award Wayne State U., 1981, Herman Beerman award Soc. for Investigative Dermatology, 1982; NIH postdoctoral fellow U. Glasgow, Scotland, 1960-61. Fellow N.Y. Acad. Scis.; Mem. Nat. Acad. Scis., Am. Acad. Arts and Scis., Conn. Acad. Sci. and Engring., Harvey Soc., Soc. Devel. Biology (pres. 1971-72, trustee 1970-73), AAAS, Am. Soc. Cell Biology, Am. Soc. Human Genetics (dir. 1972-75, pres. 1984-85, Allan award 1983), Am. Soc. Naturalists, Am. Soc. Zoologists, Genetics Soc. Am., Am. Soc. Biochemistry, Pattern Recognition Soc., Tissue Culture Assn. (dir.), Am. Cancer Soc., Sigma Xi. Subspecialty: Cell biology. Office: Kline Biology Tower Yale U New Haven CT 06520

RUDIS, VICTOR AUGUSTINE, research forester, resource analyst; b. Boston, Aug. 27, 1950; s. Hans Heinrich and Stella (Okuniewski) R.; m. Mary Rita DeRonde, Aug. 14, 1976; 1 son, Jeffrey DeRonde. B.S., Boston Coll., 1972; M.S. in Ecology, Rutgers U., 1975; M.S. in Forestry, U. Wis.-Madison, 1978. Instr., Rutgers Prep. Sch., Somerset, N.J., 1972-73; teaching and research asst. Rutgers U., New Brunswick, N.J., 1973-74; research asst. U. Wis.-Madison, 1976-78; planning asst. Wis. Dept. Natural Resources, Madison, Wis., 1979; research forester U.S. Dept. Agr. Forest Service, New Orleans, 1980-83, Starkville, Miss., 1983—. Contbr. articles to tech. jours. Mem. Ecol. Soc. Am., Soc. Am. Foresters. Current work: Forest inventory methods; dispersed recreation resources supply and use in forested areas; forest resources assessments; nontimber resources on timberland. Subspecialty: Resource conservation. Office: U S Dept Agr Forest Service So Forest Expt Sta PO Box 906 Starkville MS 39759

RUDNEY, HARRY, biochemist, educator, researcher; b. Toronto, Ont., Can., Apr. 14, 1918; came to U.S., 1948, naturalized, 1956; s. Joshua and Dina (Gorback) R.; m. Bernice Diana Snider, June 25, 1946; children—Joel D., P. Robert. B.A., U. Toronto, 1947, M.A., 1948; Ph.D., Western Res. U., 1952. Instr., Case Western Res. U., Cleve., 1952-53, asst. prof., 1953-57, assoc. prof., 1957-65, prof., 1965-67; prof. biochemistry, dir. dept. biochemistry Coll. Medicine, U. Cin., 1967—; cons. in field. Editorial bd. Jour. Biol. Chemists, 1975-80, Archives Biochemistry and Biophysics, 1967—. Contbr. articles to profl. jours. Recipient Research Career Devel. award NIH, 1958-63; Research Career award NIH, 1963-67; Rieveschel award U. Cin., 1977. Mem. Am. Soc. Biol. Chemists, Assn. Med. Sch. Depts. Biochemistry (pres. 1981-82). Current work: Regulation of cholesterol biosynthesis. Subspecialties: Biochemistry (biology); Cell biology. Home: 4040 Winding Way Cincinnati OH 45229 Office: U Cin Coll Medicine Dept Biochemistry and Molecular Biology 231 Bethesda Ave Cincinnati OH 45267

RUDNICK, ISADORE, physicist; b. N.Y.C., May 8, 1917; s. Joseph A. and Jennie (Siedlecki) R.; m. Mildred Karasik, Sept. 16, 1939; children—Joseph Alan, Charles Franklin, Deborah Ann, Michael Ira, Daniel Lars. B.A., UCLA, 1938, M.A., 1940, Ph.D., 1944. Researcher Duke U., 1942-45; asst. prof. physics Pa. State U., 1945-48; mem. faculty U. Calif., Los Angeles, 1948—, prof. physics, 1958—, Faculty research lectr., 1975-76; vis. prof. U. Paris, 1972-73, Technion, Haifa, Israel, 1973, U. Tokyo, fall 1977, U. Nanjing, China, fall 1979. Fulbright fellow to Denmark, Royal Inst. Tech., Copenhagen, 1957-58; Fulbright fellow Israel Inst. Tech., Haifa, 1965; Guggenheim fellow, 1957-58; Recipient Fritz London Meml. award Commn. for Very Low Temperature Physics, Internat. Union Pure and Applied Physics, 1981. Fellow Am. Phys. Soc.; Mem. Acoustical Soc. Am. (Biennial award 1948, pres. 1969-70, Silver medal 1975, Gold medal 1982), Am. Inst. Physics (governing bd. 1967-69), Nat. Acad. Scis. Subspecialties: Acoustics; Low temperature physics. Office: Physics Dept University of California Los Angeles CA 90024

RUDY, YORAM, biomedical engineering educator; b. Tel-Aviv, Israel, Feb. 12, 1946; came to U.S., 1973, naturalized, 1981; s. Nahum and Yafa (Krinkin) R. B.Sc. in Physics, Technion, Israel Inst. Tech., 1971, M.Sc. in Physics, 1973; Ph.D. in Biomed. Engring, Case Western Res. U., 1978. Research assoc. in biomed. engring. Case Western Res. U., Cleve., 1978-79, vis. asst. prof. biomed. engring., 1979-81, asst. prof. biomed. engring., 1981—; vis. prof. biomed. engring. Technion, Haifa, Israel, 1982-83; mem. cardiovascular and pulmonary study sect. NIH, 1984—. Guest editor: Annals of Biomed. Engring, 1983; contbr. sci. articles to profl. jours. NIH research grantee, 1978—. Mem. Biomed. Engring. Soc. (sr.), Am. Physiol. Soc., IEEE Group on Engring. in Medicine and Biology, Am. Heart Assn. (basic sci. council), AAAS, Sigma Xi. Current Work: Bioelectric phenomena, cardiac electrophysiology, biophysical basis of electrocardiography, electrocardiographic body surface potential mapping. Subspecialties: Biomedical engineering; Biophysics (physics). Office: Case Western Reserve University University Circle Cleveland OH 44106

RUDYS, STASYS KESTUTIS, molecular spectroscopist, researcher; b. Sveksna, Lithuania, May 8, 1940; came to U.S., 1949; s. Stasys and Akvile (Jakubenas) R.; m. Zivile Maria Pauliukonis, Jan. 6, 1973; children—Audra, Raminta, Rimas, Algis, Dana. B.S., U. Chgo., 1961; postgrad. U. Ill.-Urbana, 1961-63; M.S., U. Iowa, 1965, Ph.D., 1974. Research assoc. U. Fla.-Gainesville, 1966-68; research chemist E. I. DuPont de Nemours, Old Hickory, Tenn., 1968-74, sr. research chemist, Wilmington, Del., 1974-84, Richmond, Va., 1985—. Contbr. articles to sci. jours. Patentee in field. Tchr., prin. Lithuanian Saturday Sch., Phila., 1978-79; den leader Cub Scouts Am., 1984. Mem. Am. Chem. Soc., TAPPI, ASTM (chmn. task group 1984—), Sigma Xi. Roman Catholic. Current work: New uses for properties of nonwovens; nonwoven fundamentals, new products. Subspecialty: Infrared spectroscopy. Office: E I DuPont Textile Fibers Dept Spruance Research and Devel Lab Richmond VA 23261

RUDZIK, ALLAN D., pharmacology executive; b. Mundare, Alta., Can., Nov. 30, 1934; came to U.S., 1963; s. Harry G. and Francis (Medynski) R.; m. Jill L. Rudolph, Apr. 18, 1960; children—Michael, Francine. B.S. in Pharmacy, U. Alta., 1956, M.S. in Biochemistry, 1958; Ph.D. in Pharmacology, U. Wis., 1962. Pharmacologist, Ayerst Labs., Montreal, Que., Can., 1962-63; sr. pharmacologist Dow Chem. Co., Zionsville, Ind., 1963-66; group mgr. Upjohn Co., Kalamazoo, 1966-82; exec. v.p. Berlex Labs., Cedar Knolls, N.J., 1982—; vis. prof. U. Wis.-Madison, 1972. Editor: Hypnotics, 1975; contbg. author: Minor Tranquilizers, 1978; patentee in field. Mem. County Mental Health Bd., Kalamazoo, 1977; rep. Democratic Party, Mich., 1964-68. Recipient M.J. Warner award U. Alta., 1955, Gold medal, 1956, Honor prize, 1956; Upjohn award, 1974. Mem. Pharmacology Soc., AAAS, Can. Pharm. Assn., N.Y. Acad. Scis. Roman Catholic. Current work: Cardiovascular and neuropharmacology, study of drug-receptor interactions. Subspecialties: Pharmacology; Neuropharmacology. Home: 17 Blackbirch Dr Randolph NJ 07869

RUEGSEGGER, DONALD RAY, JR., radiol. physicist; b. Detroit, May 29, 1942; s. Donald Ray and Margaret Arlene (Elliot) R.; m. Judith Ann, Aug. 20, 1965; children: Steven, Susan, Mark, Ann. B.S., Wheaton Coll., 1964; M.S., Ariz. State U., Tempe, 1966, Ph.D., 1969. Diplomate: Am. Bd. Radiology. Radiol. physicist cons. VA Hosp., Dayton, Ohio, 1970-77; adj. asst. prof. physics Wright State U., Fairborn, Ohio, 1973—, clin. asst. prof. radiology, 1976-81, clin. assoc. prof. radiology, 1981—; radiol. physicist, chief med. physics sect. Miami Valley Hosp., Dayton, Ohio, 1969—; civilian cons. Wright Patterson AFB Med. Center, Fairborn, Ohio, 1982—. NDEA fellow, 1966-69. Mem. Am. Assn. Physicists in Medicine (chpt. pres. 1982-83), Am. Coll. Radiology, Am. Phys. Soc., Health Physics Soc., AAAS. Republican. Baptist. Current Work: Applying physical principals and techniques in radiation therapy and nuclear medicine to develop better ways to treat cancer patients with radiation. Subspecialties: Radiation therapy; Radiology in nuclear medicine. Home: 2018 Washington Creek Ln Centerville OH 45459 Office: 1 Wyoming St Dayton OH 45409

RUEGSEGGER, PAUL MELCHIOR, physician, researcher; b. Berne, Switzerland, June 27, 1921; came to U.S., 1948, naturalized, 1954; s. Paul and Frieda Beatrice (Schmocker) R.; m. Freya Bundi Wipf, Sept. 6, 1948; children: Theodore Bernard, Christine Monica, Carole Suzanne. M.D., U. Zurich, Switzerland, 1946. Diplomate: Am. Bd. Internal Medicine. Intern Bellevue Hosp., N.Y.C., 1948-51, resident, 1951-52; resident in cardiology Meml. Sloan Kettering Cancer Center, N.Y.C., 1952-53, 55-56; asst. prof. clin. medicine Cornell U. Med. Sch., N.Y.C., 1959; research assoc. Sloan Kettering Inst., N.Y.C., 1959-67; attending physician Meml. Center for Cancer, N.Y.C., 1959-69, N.Y. Hosp., 1956-69; research dir. Med. Imaging Lab. (name now Biotronics Inst.), N.Y.C., 1970—; aero-med. cons. Swissair Lines, N.Y.C., 1956—; thermography cons. Trial Lawyers Assn., N.Y.C., 1982—; cons. med. imaging Hoffmann-LaRoche Corp., Nutley, N.J., 1969—. Author: Transaminase Tests, 1956, Coronary Thrombolysis, 1959, Walking EKG Stress Test, 1963, Thermography of Pain, 1969, 81. Served to capt. USAF, 1953-55, Japan. Mem. N.Y. Acad. Scis., Am. Fedn. Clin. Research, Harvey Soc. N.Y., N.Y. County Med. Soc., Am. Acad. Thermology, European Thermology Soc., Am. Soc. Internat. Medicine, Zool. Soc. N.Y., N.Y. Bot. Garden, Swiss Soc. N.Y. Current Work: Cybernetics of chronicity, recurrence in chronic pain, other disorders; infrared television imaging of altered physiological states. Subspecialties: Thermography of diseases; Neuropsychology. Office: Biotronics Inst 115 E 61st St New York NY 10021

RUESINK, ALBERT WILLIAM, biologist, educator; b. Adrian, Mich., Apr. 16, 1940; s. Lloyd William and Alberta May (Foltz) R.; m. Kathleen Joy Cramer, June 8, 1963; children: Jennifer Li, Adriana Eleanor. B.A., U. Mich., 1962; M.A., Harvard U., 1965, Ph.D., 1966. Postdoctoral Swiss Fed. Inst. Tech., Zurich, 1966-67; mem. faculty Ind. U., Bloomington, 1967—, prof. plant scis., 1980—. Contbr. articles to sci. jours. Recipient Disting. Teaching award Amoco, 1980. Mem. Am. Soc. Plant Physiology, Bot. Soc. Am., Am. Inst. Biol. Scis., Ind. Acad. Sci., Sigma Xi. Democrat. Mem. United Ch. Christ. Current Work: Plant physiology, especially cell wall-plasma membrane interactions; education. Subspecialties: Plant physiology (biology); Plant cell and tissue culture. Home: 2605 E 5th St Bloomington IN 47401 Office: Ind U Dept Biology Bloomington IN 47405

RUFF, ROBERT LOUIS, physiologist, neurologist, educator; b. N.Y.C., Dec. 16, 1950; s. John Joseph and Rhoda (Alpert) R.; m. Louise Seymour Acheson, Apr. 26, 1980. B.S., Cooper Union U., 1971; M.D., U. Wash.-Seattle, 1976, Ph.D., 1976. Diplomate: Am. Bd. Neurology and Psychiatry. Intern U. Wash., Seattle, 1976-77; neurology resident Cornell Med. Coll., N.Y.C., 1977-79, neurology chief resident, 1979-80; asst. prof. dept. physiology, biophysics, neurology U. Wash., Seattle, 1980—. Recipient Tchr.-Investigator award NIH, 1980. Mem. Biophys. Soc., Am. Acad. Nuerology, Soc. Neurosci., Stroke Counsel, AAAS, N.Y. Acad. Scis., Alpha Omega Alpha, Sigma Pi Sigma. Current Work: Endocrine myopathy, electrical studies of human muscle, animal models of stroke. Subspecialties: Physiology (medicine); Neurology. Office: U Wash Dept Physiology and Biophysics SJ-40 Seattle WA 98195

RUFFOLO, ROBERT RICHARD, JR., pharmacologist; b. Yonkers, N.Y., Apr. 14, 1950; s. Robert Richard and Lorraine Regina (Varipapa) R.; m. Christine Bernice Nettleship, July 1, 1972. Ph.D., Ohio State U., 1976. Postdoctoral fellow Ohio State U., Columbus, 1976-77; staff fellow NIH, Bethesda, Md., 1977-78; sr. pharmacologist Lilly Research Labs., Indpls., 1978-82, research scientist, 1982—. Contbr. numerous articles to sci. publs. Mem. Am. Soc. Pharmacology and Exptl. Therapeutics. Current Work: Adrenergic pharmacology and adrenergic receptors; hypertension, cardiovascular research. Subspecialty: Pharmacology. Home: 9903 Carefree Dr Indianapolis IN 46256 Office: Lilly Research Labs (MC-304) Indianapolis IN 46285

RUGGERO, MARIO ALFREDO, neurophysiologist, educator; b. Resistencia, Argentina, Nov. 7, 1943; came to U.S., 1961; s. Juan Mario Ruggero and Carolina Felicia Volpe; m. Elsa Luisa Statzner, Apr. 2, 1973. B.A. in Biology, Cath. U. Am., 1965; Ph.D. in Physiology, U. Chgo., 1972. Postdoctoral fellow dept. neurophysiology U. Wis.-Madison, 1972-75; asst. prof. dept. otolaryngology U. Minn., Mpls., 1975—. Contbr. articles to sci. publs. Research grantee NIH, NSF and Deafness Research Found. Mem. Acoustical Soc. Am., Soc. Neurosci., AAUP, AAAS. Current work: Structure and function of peripheral auditory system, especially mechanisms whereby inner ear vibrations are signaled by impulses in cochlear nerve. Subspecialties: Neurophysiology; Neurobiology. Home: 315 1/2 8th St SE Minneapolis MN 55414 Office: Dept Otolaryngology U Minn 2630 University Ave SE Minneapolis MN 55414

RUGGLES, KENNETH WARREN, meteorologist, weather services company executive; b. San Francisco, May 18, 1932; s. Charles F. Ruggles and Helen Elizabeth (Anderson) Ruggles Morrelli; m. Gilda Ide, June 26, 1958; children—Anne Catherine, Kenneth William. B.S., Naval Acad., 1954; M.S., Naval Postgrad. Sch., 1960; Ph.D., MIT, 1969. Cert. cons. meteorologist. Commd. ensign U.S. Navy, 1954, advanced through grades to capt., 1972; dir. project FAMOS, Suitland, Md., 1969-72; ops. officer Fleet Numerical Weather Ctr., Monterey, Calif., 1972-75; asst. for environ. scis. Dept. Def., Washington, 1975-78, ret., 1978; v.p. Global Weather Dynamics, Inc., Monterey, Calif., 1978-82, pres., 1982—; mem. Sec. Commerce's Adv. Bd. for Satellite Systems, 1982—; pres. Nat. Aviation Computer Sevices Council, 1984—. Pres. Rancho Tierra Grande Assn., Monterey, 1980. Recipient Sec. Navy award, 1960; Sec. Def. award, 1975; Carl Gustav Rossby award MIT, 1969. Mem. Am. Meteorol. Soc. (regional pres.), AAAS, Sigma Xi. Current work: Satellite imagery data processing Subspecialty: Meteorology. Office: Global Weather Dynamics Inc 2400 Garden Rd Monterey CA 93940

RUGH, JOHN DOUGLAS, dental psychology educator; b. Corvallis, Oreg., Feb. 20, 1941; s. Harold Kelly and Vida Esther (Toney) R.; m. Annie Louise Taylor, Dec. 30, 1960. A.A., Coll. San Mateo, 1965; B.A., U. Calif.-Santa Barbara, 1968, Ph.D., 1975. Dir. Psycho-tech. Lab., Claremont Grad. Sch., 1974-77; asst. prof. dept. psychiatry and dept. oral and maxillofacial surgery U. Tex. Health Sci. Ctr., San Antonio, 1977-80, assoc. prof., 1980-84, prof., 1984—; dir. U. Tex. Health Sci. Ctr. Temporomandibular Joint Clinic, 1977-81; mem. Oral Biology and Medicine Study Sect., Nat. Inst. Dental Research, NIH, Bethesda, Md., 1982-86. Author: books, including Biofeedback in Dentistry, 1977, Oral Motor Behavior, 1979; contbr. numerous chpts., articles, abstracts to profl. publs. Served with USN, 1959-63. Mem. Biofeedback Soc. Am. (dir. 1980-82, pres. 1983-84), Am. assn. Dental Research (pres. San Antonio chpt. 1982-83), Soc. Behavioral Medicine, Am. Assn. Advancement Med. Instrumentation, Omicron Kappa Upsilon (hon.). Inventor, patentee bio-alarm security system, 1978. Current Work: Investigations into etiology, diagnosis and treatment of stres-related oral disorders (bruxism, temporo-mandibular joint disorders and soft-tissue lesions); also biomedical instrumentation development and application. Subspecialties: Physiological psychology; Bioinstrumentation. Office: U Tex Health Sci Ctr Dept Oral and Maxillofacial Surgery 7703 Floyd Curl Dr San Antonio TX 78284

RUGH, WILSON JOHN, II, electrical engineering educator; b. Tarentum, Pa., Jan. 16, 1944; s. Wilson John and Florence May (Saul) R.; m. Theresa Marie Winter, June 26, 1976; children—David, Karen. B.S.E.E., Pa. State U., 1965; M.S., Northwestern U., 1967, Ph.D., 1969. Mem. faculty Johns Hopkins U., Balt., 1969—, chmn. dept. elec. engring., 1980-83. Author: Mathematical Description of Linear Systems, 1975; Nonlinear System Theory, 1981. Mem. IEEE, Soc. Indsl. Applied Math., Math. Assn. Am. Current work: Nonlinear systems and control theory. Subspecialties: Electrical engineering; Systems engineering. Office: EECS Dept Johns Hopkins U Charles and 34th Sts Baltimore MD 21218

RUIBAL, RODOLFO, biologist; b. Cuba, Oct. 27, 1927; s. Rodolfo and Antonia R.; m. Irene Shamu, Oct. 25, 1948; 1 son, Claude. B.A., Harvard U., 1950; Ph.D., Columbia U., 1955. Prof. biology U. Calif., Riverside, 1967—, chmn. dept. biology, 1979-82; chmn. nongame wildlife adv. com. Calif. Fish and Game Dept. Served with U.S. Army, 1946-48. Guggenheim fellow, 1967-68. Current Work: Ecology of desert anurans; structure of amphibian skin. Subspecialties: Evolutionary biology; Ecology (environmental science). Office: Dept Biology U Calif Riverside CA 92521

RUIZ, LEONARD PERCY, JR., food company research administrator; b. Napoleonville, La., Aug. 4, 1944; s. Percy Leonard and Marie (Triche) R.; m. DeLinda Jane Sanders, Aug. 3, 1968; children—Trevor Daniel, Christopher Michael. B.S., La. State U., 1969, Ph.D., 1973. Research assoc. La. State U., 1973-74; research mgr. nutrition World Bank Project, Kuala Lumpur, Malaysia, 1978-79; research mgr. Land O Lakes, Inc., Mpls., 1979-84, assoc. dir. food research, 1984—. Served with U.S. Army, 1963-66. N.Z. Nat. Adv. Council fellow, 1974-77. Mem. Am. Chem. Soc., Am. Dairy Sci. Assn., Inst. Food Technologists, Mensa. Current work: New protein food ingredients, infant formula ingredients; high performance animal feed ingredients. Subspecialties: Food science and technology; Immunology (agriculture). Home: 299 Cottage Pl Shoreview MN 55112 Office: Land O Lakes Inc PO Box 116 Minneapolis MN 55440

RUMENNIK, VLADIMIR, physicist, consultant; b. Moscow, Jan. 28, 1946; came to U.S., 1977, naturalized, 1984; s. Ilya and Anna Rumennik; m. Galina Khavitch, Aug. 31, 1982. M.S., Inst. Alloys, Moscow, 1969; Ph.D., Inst. Physics and Engring., Moscow, 1974. Engr. Internat. Rectifier, El Segundo, Calif., 1977-79; cons. SEMICS, Playa Del Rey, Calif., 1982-83; mem. tech. staff XEROX, El Segundo, 1979-83; lab. mgr. microelectronics Philips Labs., Briarcliff Manor, N.Y., 1983—. Contbr. numerous articles to tech. jours. Patentee in field. Mem. IEEE. Current work: Research on power and high voltage integrated circuits and devices. VLSI and submicron technology development. Subspecialties: Semiconductors; Microelectronics. Office: Philips Labs 345 Scarborough Rd Briarcliff Manor NY 10510

RUMSEY, VICTOR HENRY, electrical engineering educator; b. Devizes, Eng., Nov. 22, 1919; s. Albert Victor and Susan Mary (Norman) R.; m. Doris Herring, Apr. 2, 1942; children: John David, Peter Alan, Catherine Anne. B.A., Cambridge U., 1941, D.Sc. in Physics, 1972; D.Eng., Tohoku U., Japan, 1962. With U.K. Sci. Civil Service, 1941-48; asst. to asso. prof. Ohio State U., 1948-54; prof. U. Ill., 1954-57; prof. U. Calif., Berkeley, 1957-66, prof. elec. engring. and computer scis., San Diego, 1966—, dept. chmn., 1977-81. Author 1 book in field; contbr. articles to profl. jours. Guggenheim fellow.; recipient George Sinclair award Ohio State U., 1982. Fellow IEEE (Morris Liebman prize), Union Radio Scientifique Internationale, Internat. Astron. Union; mem. Nat. Acad. Engring. Patentee in field. Subspecialty: Electrical engineering. Home: 465 Hidden Pines Ln Del Mar CA 92014 Office: U Calif San Diego CA 92093

RUMSFELD, DONALD H., business executive. Chmn., G.D. Searle & Co., Skokie, Ill., The Rand Corp., Santa Monica, Calif. . Office: GD Searle & Co 4901 Searle Pkwy Skokie IL 60077*

RUNDLE, JOHN BELTING, geophysicist; b. Somerville, N.J., Aug. 31, 1950; s. David Bradford and Dorothy (Belting) R.; m. Marie Cardoza, July 27, 1974; 1 child, Paul Belting. B.S.E. magna cum laude, Princeton U., 1972; M.S., UCLA, 1973, Ph.D., 1976. Postdoctoral fellow dept. earth and space sci. Calif. Inst. Tech., Los Angeles, 1976-77, vis. faculty, 1981-84; mem. tech. staff Sandia Nat. Labs., Albuquerque, 1977—. Contbr. articles to profl. jours. Mem. Am. Geophys. Union, Seismological Soc. Am., Sigma Xi, Phi Beta Kappa, Tau Beta Pi, Phi Eta Sigma. Republican. Clubs: Princeton (v.p.) Current work: Theoretical models of crustal deformation; physical processes of active volcanic systems; earthquake prediction; physics of near surface planetary processes. Subspecialties: Geophysics; Seismology. Office: Div 1541 Sandia Nat Labs PO Box 5800 Albuquerque NM 87185

RUPPEL, EARL GEORGE, research plant pathologist; b. Milw., Nov. 10, 1932; s. George Albert and Ida Elizabeth (Ptaschinski) R.; m. Joyce Ruth Port, Sept. 6, 1958; children: Susan T., Julia R., Michael R. B.S., U. Wis.-Milw., 1958; Ph.D., U. Wis.-Madison, 1962. Plant pathologist Agrl. Research Service, U.S. Dept. Agr., Mayagues, P.R., 1963-65, Mesa, Ariz., 1965-69, Ft. Collins, Colo., 1969—; faculty affiliate plant pathology and weed sci. dept. Colo. State U., 1969—, mem. grad. faculty, 1971—. Contbr. numerous articles to sci. jours. Served with AUS, 1953-55. Am. Cancer Found. grantee, 1960, 62. Mem. Am. Phytopath. Soc., Internat. Soc. Plant Pathology, Mycol. Soc. Am., Am. Soc. Sugar Beet Technologists, Rocky Mountain Plant Protection Group, Sigma Xi, Gamma Sigma Delta. Democrat. Roman Catholic. Club: Fort Collins Camera. Current Work: Epidemiology of sugarbeet diseases; nature of resistance to plant pathogens; breeding for resistance to plant pathogens. Subspecialties: Plant pathology; Plant virology. Office: USDA Crops Research Lab Colo State U Fort Collins CO 80523

RUPPEL, EDWARD THOMPSON, geologist; b. Fort Morgan, Colo., Oct. 26, 1925; s. Henry George and Gladys Myrtle (Thompson) R.; m. Phyllis Beale Tanner, June 17, 1956; children—Lisa, David, Douglas, Kristin. B.A., U. Mont., 1948; M.A., U. Wyo., 1950; Ph.D., Yale U., 1958. Geologist, U.S. Geol. Survey, Washington and Denver, 1947—, sr. geologist, Denver, 1976—. Author tech. reports and maps on geology of No. Rocky Mountains. Fellow Geol. Soc. Am.; mem. Soc. Econ. Geologists, Geol. Soc. Washington, Colo. Sci. Soc., Tobacco Root Geol. Soc., Am. Inst. Profl. geologists. Democrat. Lutheran. Subspecialties: Geology; Tectonics. Office: US Geol Survey Br of Central Regional Geology Box 25046 MS 913 Fed Ctr Denver CO 80225

RUSCH, PETER F., information systems specialist. Dir. chem. info. services Dialog Info. Services, Inc., Palo Alto, Calif. Subspecialty: Information systems (Information science). Office: Dialog Info Services Inc 3460 Hillview Ave Palo Alto CA 94304

RUSH, RICHARD MARION, environmental analyst, chemistry researcher; b. Bristol, Va., Dec. 5, 1928; s. Richard Irwin and Marion (Fillinger) R.; m. Patricia Paynter, June 25, 1955; children—Helen Lewis, John Woodward. A.B., Princeton U., 1949; M.S., U. Va., 1952, Ph.D., 1954. Research asst. MIT, Cambridge, 1953-54; asst. prof. Haverford Coll., Pa., 1954-56; research staff mem. Oak Ridge Nat. Lab., 1956—. Mem. Oak Ridge Bd. Edn., 1969-73, United Fund Anderson County, Oak Ridge, 1964-69. Mem. AAAS, Am. Chem. Soc., Am. Nuclear Soc., N.Y. Acad. Scis., Sigma Xi. Presbyterian. Subspecialty: Physical chemistry. Home: 102 Dana Dr Oak Ridge TN 37830 Office: Oak Ridge Nat Lab PO Box X Oak Ridge TN 37831

RUSH, RICHARD WILLIAM, consulting geologist; b. Austin, Minn., July 14, 1921; s. James Francis and Irene (Peterson) R.; m. Florence Allison Rayman, Sept. 1945 (div. 1972); children: Richard William, Lucy E., Frederick J., Cynthia I. B.A., U. Iowa, 1945; M.A., Columbia U., 1948, Ph.D., 1954; diploma, Nat. Tech. Schs., Los Angeles, 1976. Registered profl. geologist, Calif. Instr. Colby Coll., Waterville, Maine, 1949-51; asst. prof. U. Tex.-Austin, 1952-57; assoc. prof. No. Ariz. U., Flagstaff, 1963-69; cons. Plateau Corp. River Products, Colo., Iowa, 1961-64, pvt. cons. geologist, Phoenix, 1969—; pres. ULC Opr., Los Angeles, 1974-75, WESGOE, Denver, 1982; cons. FMC Corp., White & Co., Austin, Tex., 1954-57, U.S. Steel Co., Que., 1960, and others. Mem. adv. bd. Republican Nat. Com., 1980—; supt. Episcopal Ch. Schs., Flagstaff, Ariz., 1965-67. Fellow Geol. Soc. Am., AAAS; mem. Am. Inst. Profl. Geologists (charter), N.Y. Acad. Sci., Am. Assn. Petroleum Geologists, Am. Geophys. Union, Sigma Gamma Epsilon. Current Work: Application of computer electronics to regional geologic tectonics. Subspecialties: Tectonics; Information systems, storage, and retrieval (computer science).

RUSHTON, BRIAN MANDEL, chemical company executive; b. Sale, Cheshire, Eng., Nov. 16, 1933; came to U.S., 1957; s. Ronald Henry and Edith (Slater) Riley; m. Jean Wrigley, Apr. 1, 1958; children—Jacqueline, Lisa, Amy. A.I.R.C. in Chemistry, U. Salford, Eng., 1957; M.S. in Phys. Organic Chemistry, U. Minn., 1959, Ph.D., U. Leicester, Eng., 1963; postgrad., St. Exec. Program, MIT, 1972. Prodn. mgr. trainee 3M Co. U.K., 1959-60; sr. research chemist Petrolite Corp., 1963-65, group leader, 1965-66; sect. mgr. Ashland Chem. Co., 1966-69; corp. research mgr. Hooker Chem. Corp. subs. Occidental Petroleum, 1969-72, dir. polymer and plastics research and devel., 1972-74, v.p. research and devel. chem. and plastics div., 1974-75; pres. Celanese Research Corp., 1975-80; corp. v.p. tech. Celanese Corp.; also pres. Celanes Research Corp., 1980-81; v.p. research and devel. Air Products & Chem., Inc., Allentown, Pa., 1981—; nat. materials bd. NRC, 1980—; dir. Indsl. Research Inst., 1980-83. Contbr. articles to profl. jours.; patentee in field. Mem. life scis. vis. com. Lehigh U.; trustee Summit YMCA, N.J., 1976-79. Mem. Council Chem. Research (dir., treas.), Am. Chem. Soc., Soc. Chem. Industry, Am. Mgmt. Assn., N.Y. Acad. Scis. Episcopalian. Clubs: Canoe Brook Country (N.J.); Saucon Valley Country (Bethlehem, Pa.). Current work: Research and development administration. Home: RD 4 Bingen Rd Bethlehem PA 18015

RUSOFF, IRVING I(SADORE), food scientist; b. Newark, Jan. 29, 1915; s. Max and Rachel (Dodin) R.; m. Perle Greenspan, Sept. 12, 1941; children—Susan, Arnold. B.S., U. Fla., 1937, M.S., 1939; Ph.D., U. Minn., 1943. Head nutrition research Standard Brands, Inc., N.Y.C., 1946-47; head nutrition, fats and oils Gen. Foods Corp., Hoboken, N.J. and Tarrytown, N.Y., 1947-62; mgr. research DCA Food Industries, N.Y.C., 1962-63; dir. nutritional biochemistry Beech Nut Life Savers, N.Y.C., 1963-66; dir. basic studies Nabisco, Inc., Fair Lawn, N.J., 1966-76, sr. scientist, Parsippany, N.J., 1976-85. Contbr. articles to profl. jours. Patentee in field. Liaison chmn. Nat. Inventors Hall of Fame, Washington, 1980—. Fellow Inst. Food Technologists; mem. Am. Oil Chemists Soc., Am. Inst. Nutrition, Am. Assn. Cereal Chemists, N.Y. Acad. Scis., Sigma Xi, Phi Tau Sigma. Hebrew. Lodge: Elks. Current work: Nutritional quality of foods, dental caries prevention, textured vegetable proteins, chocolate flavor. Subspecialties: Food science and technology; Nutrition (biology). Home: 15 Zeeland Dr Toms River NJ 08757

RUSS, FRITZ JUNIOR, See *Who's Who in America,* 43rd edition.

RUSS, WESLEY DALE, biochemist, researcher; b. New Orleans, Aug. 27, 1957; s. Alton Earl and Margret Genelle (Brooks) R.; m. Rhonda Lorene Cooper, May 22, 1983. B.S. in Chemistry, Central Mo. State U., 1982. Research chemist VA Med. Ctr., Omaha, 1983-84; research biochemist Coulter Immunology, Hialeah, Fla., 1984—. Contbr. articles to profl. jours. Mem. Am. Chem. Soc. Democrat. Current work: Development of techniques to purify monoclonal antibodies; conjugation of monoclonal antibodies to organic dyes and their purification. Subspecialties: Biochemistry (medicine); Pulmonary medicine. Home: 5450 NW 159th St Apt 404 Hialeah FL 33014 Office: Coulter Immunology 440 W 20th St Hialeah FL 33010

RUSSELL, ALLEN STEVENSON, retired aluminum company executive; b. Bedford, Pa., May 27, 1915; s. Arthur Stainton and Ruth (Stevenson) R.; m. Judith Pauline Sexauer, Apr. 5, 1941. B.S., Pa. State U., 1936, M.S., 1937, Ph.D., 1941. With Aluminum Co. Am., 1940—, asso. dir. research, 1973-74; v.p. Alcoa Labs., Alcoa Center, Pa., 1974-78, v.p. sci. and tech., Pitts., 1978-81, v.p., chief scientist, 1981-82; adj. prof. U. Pitts., 1981. Contbr. articles to profl. jours. Named IR-100 Scientist of Yr., 1979; Pa. State U. alumni fellow, 1980; K.J. Bayer medalist, 1981; recipient chem. Pioneer award Am. Inst. Chemists, 1983. Fellow Am. Soc. Metals (Gold medal 1982), AIME; mem. Am. Chem.

Soc., Dirs. Indsl. Research, Nat. Acad. Engring. (council 1978-84), Sigma Xi. Republican. Presbyterian. Patentee in field. Subspecialties: Physical chemistry; Metallurgy. Home: 929 Field Club Rd Pittsburgh PA 15238

RUSSELL, B. DON, engr., educator; b. Denison, Tex., May 25, 1948; s. Bill D. and Mickye R.; m. Rebecca Joan Crawford, Jan. 6, 1973; children: Christyn Joan, Jennifer Rebecca, John Paul. B.S. in Elec. Engring, Tex. A&M U., 1970, M.E., 1971; Ph.D., U. Okla., 1975. Registered profl. engr., Tex. Engr. asst. Tex. Instruments, Dallas, 1967-70; mem. faculty Abilene Christian Coll., 1971-73, U. Okla., 1973-74; design engr. Okla. Gas & Electric Co., Oklahoma City, 1974; cons. Electric Power Research Inst., Palo Alto, Calif., 1975-81; mem. faculty Tex. A&M U., College Station, 1976—; assoc. prof., research prin. investigator Tex. Engring. Experiment Sta., 1976—; pres. MICON Engring., Inc., 1978—. Editor: Power System Control and Protection, 1978; assoc. editor: Electric Power System Research, 1975—; contbr. articles to profl. jours. Recipient Outstanding patent submission award Electric Power Research Inst., 1975; Outstanding Young Engr. Brazos chpt. Tex. Soc. Profl. Engrs., 1978; Outstanding Engring. Achievement award Nat. Soc. Profl. Engrs. Mem. IEEE, Nat. Soc. Profl. Engrs., Tex. Soc. Profl. Engrs., Tex. Soc. Energy Auditors, Instrument Soc. Am., Power Engring. Soc. Republican. Mem. Ch. of Christ. Current Work: Microcomputer applications to the automation, control and protection of process industry and power systems, electromagnetic interference in power systems. Subspecialties: Electrical engineering; Power and energy transmission. Home: Box 2 Route 218 College Station TX 77840 Office: Dept Elec Engring Tex A&M U College Station TX 77843

RUSSELL, DAVID ALLISON, aeronautical engineering educator; b. Saint John, N.B., Can., Apr. 25, 1935; came to U.S., 1954, naturalized, 1967; s. James Vener and Helen Ringen (Allison) R.; m. Hazel Anne Garnett, Mar. 22, 1957; children: Karen, Kristen, Kathryn. Student, U. N.B., Fredericton, 1950-54; B.Mech.Engring., U. So. Calif., 1956; M.Sc. in Aeros, Calif. Inst. Tech., 1957, Ph.D. in Aeros. and Physics, 1961. Sr. scientist Jet Propulsion Lab., Pasadena, Calif., 1961-67; research asso. prof. aeros. and astronautics U. Wash., 1967-70, asso. prof., 1970-74, prof., 1974—, chmn. dept. aeros. and astronautics, 1977—; cons. in field. Contbr. articles on fluid mechanics and gas physics to profl. jours., especially on shock processes and laser fluid dynamics. Mem. Kirkland (Wash.) Planning Commn., 1971-79, chmn., 1977-79; chmn. Kirkland Land Use Policy Plan, 1977-79; mem. Kirkland City Council, 1980-84. NASA grantee, 1969-78, 84-86; Dept. Def. grantee, 1969-71, 73-81. Assoc. fellow AIAA, (Pacific N.W. Council, Pacific N.W. sect. award for contbns. to aerospace tech. 1972); fellow Am. Phys. Soc. (exec. council div. fluid dynamics 1977-78); mem. Sierra Club, Sigma Xi, Tau Beta Pi, Pi Tau Sigma. Subspecialty: Aeronautical engineering. Home: 4507 105th St NE Kirkland WA 98033 Office: 206 Guggenheim Hall U Wash FS-10 Seattle WA 98195

RUSSELL, EUGENE A., mechanical engineer, corp. energy cons.; b. Centerville, Tenn., July 13, 1914; s. P.R. and Bessie I. (Mallory) R.; m. Jean C. Russell, July 13, 1952; children: David, Mark, Eric, Betsy, Cynthia. M.E., Columbia U., 1949; M.B.A., U. Calif.-Berkeley, 1950. Dir. research Electronic Devel. of Fla., 1954-58; dir research Automated Equipment Corp., Nashville; now dir. research Corp. Cons. (name changed to Corp. Energy Cons. 1980), Hermitage, Tenn. Served with USMC, 1945. Mem. Internat. Solar Energy Soc., ASHRAE. Lodges: Masons; Shriners. Patentee in field. Current Work: Research in field of energy alternates geothermal and solar. Subspecialties: Solar energy; Geothermal power. Home: 6000 Panama Dr Hermitage TN 37076 Office: PO Box 332 Hermitage TN 37076

RUSSELL, RAY WILLIAM, astronomer, astrophysicist; b. Burlington, Vt., May 17, 1950; s. Edwin and Gloria Isabel (MaGill) R.; m. Andrea Marie, Jan. 8, 1972; 1 son, Brian James. B.S., SUNY, Stony Brook, 1972; M.S., U. Calif., La Jolla, 1974, Ph.D., 1978. Research physicist Cornell U., Ithaca, N.Y., 1978-81; mem. tech. staff Aerospace Corp., Los Angeles, 1981—. Contbr. articles to profl. jours. Mem. Am. Astron. Soc. Republican. Quaker. Current Work: Astrophysical researcher in airborne infrared spectroscopy; development of far infrared photoconductive detectors, space-based detection systems. Subspecialty: Infrared astronomy. Office: Aerospace Corp M2-266 PO Box 92957 Los Angeles CA 90009

RUSSELL, ROBERT LEE, pharmacologist, educator; b. Independence, Mo., June 27, 1927; s. James Elijah and Kathryn Dorothea (Hiller) R.; m. Mary Frances Stewart, Nov. 25, 1950; children: Brett Vernon, Mark Stewart. A.B., U. Mo., 1950, M.A., 1952, Ph.D., 1954. Asst. in physiology and pharmacology U. Mo., Columbia, 1950-54, mem. faculty, 1954—, assoc. prof. pharmacology, 1957-65, prof., 1966—. Served with U.S. Army, 1945-46. Fellow AAAS; mem. Soc. for Exptl. Biology and Medicine, Am. Soc. for Pharmacology and Exptl. Therapeutics. Current Work: Drugs affecting lipid metabolism. Subspecialties: Pharmacology; Cellular pharmacology. Home: Rural Route 4 Box 149 Columbia MO 65201 Office: U Mo M515 Med Center Columbia MO 65212

RUSSELL, VIRGINIA WILLIS, foundation administrator, researcher; b. Buffalo, Feb. 13, 1913; d. Jay Burroughs and Faith Lillian (Wright) Willis; m. James Washington Russell; children—James Willis, Brian Jay, Robert Alan, Gary Lloyd. B.A., SUNY-Buffalo, 1934, postgrad., 1934-47. Mem. staff Erie County Emergency Walfare Services, 1941-45; research assoc. physics SUNY-Buffalo, 1959-65; tree farmer, Buffalo, 1952—; founder, dir. Universal Field Found., Buffalo, 1958—. Contbr. articles to profl. jours.; editor Audubon Outlook. Mem. Erie County Bd. Suprs.; N.Y. State chmn. conservation Fedn. Women's Clubs' chmn. Women's Day 125th Anniversary Buffalo; dirs. Erie County LWV. Recipient Civil Def. award, Republican woman of Yr. award. Mem. N.Y. Acad. Sci., AAAS, Am. Chem. Soc., Planetary Soc., History of Sci. U. Buffalo Alumni Assn. (treas, v.p.), Tesla Soc. (dir.), AAUW, Buffalo Soc. Natural Sci. Republican. Presbyterian. Club: Sierra. Current work: Writing patents on control of Radiation emissions; researching Universal Field equations. Subspecialties: Hazardous waste disposal; Theoretical physics. Home: 435 Crescent Ave Buffalo NY 12414 Office: Universal Field Found 435 Crescent Ave Buffalo NY 14214

RUSSELL-HUNTER, W(ILLIAM) D(EVIGNE), zoology educator, research biologist, writer; b. Rutherglen, Scotland, May 3, 1926; came to U.S., 1963, naturalized, 1968; s. Robert R. and Gwladys (Dew) R.-H.; m. Myra Porter Chapman, Mar. 22, 1951; 1 son, Peregrine D. B.Sc. with honors, U. Glasgow, 1946, Ph.D., 1953, D.Sc., 1961. Sci. officer Bisra/Brit. Admiralty, Millport, Scotland, 1946-48; asst. lectr. U. Glasgow, 1948-51, univ. lectr. zoology, 1951-63; examiner in biology Pharm. Soc. Gt. Britain, Edinburgh, 1957-63; chmn. dept. invertebrate zoology Marine Biol. Lab., Woods Hole, Mass., 1964-68; trustee, 1967-75, 77—; prof. zoology Syracuse (N.Y.) U., 1963—; cons. editor McGraw-Hill Encys., 1977—; dir. Upstate Freshwater Inst., Syracuse, 1981—. Author: Biology of Lower Invertebrates, 1967, Biology of Higher Invertebrates, 1968, Aquatic Productivity, 1970, A Life of Invertebrates, 1979; mng. editor: Biol. Bull, Woods Hole, Mass., 1968-70; contbr. more than 110 articles to profl. jours. Carnegie and Browne fellow, 1954; research grantee NIH, 1964-70; research grantee NSF, 1971-81. Fellow Linnean Soc. London, Royal Soc. Edinburgh, Inst. Biology U.K., AAAS; mem. Ecol. Soc. Am. Current Work: Writing and editing of books and articles on biology; research on ecology and physiology of marine and freshwater invertebrates, actuarial bioenergetics, prevention of fouling and boring organisms. Subspecialties: Behaviorism; Physiology (biology). Home: 23 Hurd St Cazenovia NY 13035 Office: Syracuse University 027 Lyman Hall Syracuse NY 13210

RUSSO, IRMA HAYDEE ALVAREZ, physician, pathologist; b. San Rafael, Mendoza, Argentina, Feb. 28, 1942; d. Jose Maria and Maria Carmen (Martinez) Alvarez; m. Jose Russo, Feb. 8, 1969; 1 dau., Patricia Alexandra. B.A. in Edn, Escuela Normal M.T.S.M. de Balcarce, 1959; M.D., U. Nat. of Cuyo, Mendoza, Argentina, 1970. Diplomate: Am. Bd. Pathology, 1980. Intern Sch. of Medicine Hosps., Mendoza, 1969-70; resident in pathology Wayne State U. Sch. Medicine, Detroit, 1976-80; guest lectr. Sch. Medicine, U. Nat. of Cuyo, Mendoza, 1965-71, research asst., instr., 1963-71, assoc. prof. histology, 1970-72; research assoc. Inst. for Molecular and Cellular Evolution, U. Miami, Fla., 1972-73; research assoc. Exptl. Pathology Lab., Mich. Cancer Found., Detroit, 1973-75, research scientist, 1975-76, vis. research scientist, 1976-80; pathologist, dept. pathology, 1982—, asst. mem., 1982—; co-dir. Pathology Reference Lab., 1982—; resident physician Wayne State U. Sch. Medicine, Detroit, 1976-78, chief resident physician, 1978-80, asst. prof. pathology, 1980—; mem. med. staff in pathology Harper-Grace Hosps., Detroit, 1980-82. Contbr. numerous sci. articles and abstracts to profl. pubs. Rockefeller Found. grantee, 1972-73; Nat. Cancer Inst. grantee, 1978-81, 84—. Mem. Am. Soc. Clin. Pathologists, Am. Assn. Cancer Research, Mich. Soc. Pathologists, AMA, Electron Microscopy Soc. Am., Mich. Electron Microscopy Forum, Sigma Xi. Roman Catholic. Current Work: Studies on the pathogenesis and prevention of chemically induced breast carcinoma in experimental animals and pathogenesis and prevention of human breast cancer. Subspecialties: Cancer research (medicine); Pathology (medicine). Office: 110 E Warren Ave Detroit MI 48201

RUST, JOHN HOWARD, pharmacologist, pathologist, radiobiologist, educator; b. Many, La., Sept. 29, 1909; s. Milbern James and Lucile (Osborn) R.; m. Mary Jo Cortelyou, Sept. 29, 1932; children—Mary V. Rust Townsend, M. James, John Henry, Joan H. Rust Johnson. D.V.M., Kans. State U., 1932, D.Sc., 1963; Ph.D., U. Chgo., 1956. Diplomate Am. Coll. Vet. Pathology. Gen. practice vet. medicine, Concord, N.H., Wellesley, Mass., 1932-35; commd. 2d lt. U.S. Army, 1935, advanced through grades to col., 1958; various med. dept. assignments; prof. U. Chgo., 1958-75, prof. emeritus, 1975—. Editor and co-author books in field. Contbr. articles to profl. jours. Current work: Nature of injury from physical and chemical agent used in medicine. Subspecialties: Pharmacology; Pathology (medicine). Home: 5715 Kenwood Ave Chicago IL 60637

RUTAN, BURT, aircraft designer; b. 1943. Student, Calif. Poly. Inst. Civilian stability and control specialist Edwards AFB, 1972-75; aircraft designer J. Bede, Kans., 1975; founder Rutan Aircraft Factory, Mojave, Calif., 1975—. Designer more than 90 aircraft, including Variviggen and other kits, Solitaire sailplane, Starship I; designer Voyager aircraft for nonstop around-the-world record attempt. Subspecialty: Aeronautical engineering. Office: Rutan Aircraft Factory Mojave CA 93501*

RUTERBUSCH, PAUL HUGO, optical engineer; b. Bay City, Mich., Oct. 25, 1953; s. Eldon Lorey and Rosemary Helen (Gollin) R. A.S., Delta Coll., 1975; B.S., Saginaw Valley State Coll., 1979; M.S., Pa. State U., 1981. Lab. asst. Saginaw Valley State Coll., University Center, Mich., 1978-79; research asst. Wayne State U., Detroit, 1979-80; research asst. Pa. State U., University Park, 1980-82; ptnr. Applied Optical Tech., Bay City, Mich., 1982-83; optical engr. Gen. Electric Co., Syracuse, N.Y., 1983—. Contbr. articles to profl. jours. Mem. Optical Soc. Am. Lutheran. Current work: Holography, holographic interferometry, optical image processing, solar energy collection systems, photography, opto-mechanical design. Subspecialties: Holography; Optical engineering. Home: 8 Town Garden Dr #8 Liverpool NY 13088 Office: Gen Electric Co Electronics Park 6-337 Syracuse NY 13221

RUTFORD, ROBERT HOXIE, university administrator; b. Duluth, Minn., Jan. 26, 1933; s. Skuli and Ruth (Hoxie) R.; m. Marjorie Ann, June 19, 1954; children: Gregory, Kristian, Barbara. B.A., U. Minn., 1954, M.A., 1963, Ph.D., 1969. Football and track coach Hamline U., 1958-62; research fellow U. Minn., 1963-66; asst. prof. geology U. S.D., 1967-70, asso. prof., 1970-72, chmn. dept. geology, 1968-72, chmn. dept. physics, 1971-72; dir. Ross Ice Shelf Project U. Nebr., Lincoln, 1972-75, vice chancellor for research and grad. studies, prof. geology, 1977-82, interim chancellor, 1980-81; pres. U. Tex., Dallas, 1982; dir. div. Polar Programs, NSF, Washington, 1975-77. Served to 1st lt. U.S. Army, 1954-56. Recipient Antarctic Service medal, 1964, Distinguished Service award NSF, 1977, Ernie Gunderson award for service to amateur athletics S.D. AAU, 1972. Fellow Geol. Soc. Am.; mem. Antarctican Soc., Arctic Inst. N.Am., Explorers Club, Am. Polar Soc., Nat. Council Univ. Research Adminstrs., Sigma Xi. Lutheran. Club: Cosmos. Current Work: Antarctic mineral resources and glacial history of antarctica. Subspecialties: Geomorphology; Geology. Home: 6809 Briar Cove Dr. Dallas TX 75240 Office: Univ. of Texas at Dallas PO Box 830688 Richardson TX 75083-0688

RUTLEDGE, JAMES LUTHER, physicist, administrator; b. Woodward, Okla., Oct. 1, 1937; s. Thomas Henry and Tena Bertha (Croissant) R.; m. Barbara Ann Johns, Aug. 10, 1963; children—Matthew Ben, Kathleen Marie. B.S., Okla. State U., 1963, M.S., 1966, Ph.D., 1968. Sr. physicist Motorola, Phoenix, 1967-72, dir., 1974-83, v.p., 1982—; project mgr. Fairchild Co., Mountain View, Calif., 1972-74. Served with USN, 1955-60. Mem. Am. Phys. Soc., IEEE, Sigma Pi Sigma. Republican. Lutheran. Current work: Mos and bipolar integrated technology and device physics. Subspecialties: Microchip technology (engineering); Microelectronics. Home: 4007 S River Dr Tempe AZ 85282 Office: Motorola Inc 2200 W Broadway Mesa AZ 85202

RUTMAN, ROBERT J., biochemist, educator; b. N.Y.C.; s. Leon and Anne (Porringer) R.; married; children: Rose, Randy Rutman Allen, Stephen Johnson, Ellen Johnson, David Johnson. B.S., Pa. State U., 1940, M.S., 1975; Ph.D., U. Calif., Berkeley, 1950. Asst. prof. Jefferson Med. Coll., Phila., 1950-53; research assoc. in biology U. Pa., 1954-56, research assoc. in chemistry, 1956-61, assoc. prof. chemistry, 1961-68; prof. biochemistry U. Pa. Sch. Vet. Medicine, 1968—, chair biochemistry, 1971-72, 80-81; vis. prof. U. Ibadan, Nigeria, 1973-74, external examiner, 1977—, coordinator exchangeprogram, 1980—. Contbr. over 150 articles to profl. jours. Pres. Phila. Peace Council, 1968-70. Served to capt. AUS, 1946-50. Mem. Am. Assn. Sci. Workers (nat. sec.), Am. Soc. Biol. Chemistry, Am. Assn. Cancer Research, AAAS, AAUP, Am. Soc. Vet. Oncology (chmn. sci. com. on chem.-biol. warfare). Patentee in field. Current Work: Mechanism of anti-cancer DNA reactive drugs, monoclonal antibodies to modified DNA; biological response modifiers, membrane biochemistry. Subspecialties: Biochemistry (biology); Chemotherapy. Home: Park Plaza Apt PH-P Philadelphia PA 19131 Office: Sch Vet Medicine U Pa Philadelphia PA 19104

RUTTER, WILLIAM J., biochemist, educator; b. Malad City, Idaho, Aug. 28, 1928; s. William H. and Cecelia (Dredge) R.; m. Jacqueline Waddoups, Aug. 31, 1950 (div. Nov. 1969); children—William Henry II, Cynthia Susan; m. Virginia Alice Bourke, Oct. 3, 1971 (div. 1978). B.A., Harvard, 1949; M.A., U. Utah, 1950; Ph.D., U. Ill., 1952. USPHS postdoctoral fellow U. Wis., 1952-54, Nobel Inst., 1954-55; from asst. prof. to prof. biochemistry, dept. chemistry U. Ill., 1955-65; prof. biochemistry U. Wash., 1965-69; Hertzstein Prof. biochemistry U. Calif.-San Francisco, 1969—, chmn. dept. biochemistry and biophysics, 1969-82; mem. USPHS Biochemistry and Nutrition Fellowship Panel, 1963-66; Cons. physiol. chemistry study sect. NIH, 1967-71; mem. basic sci. adv. exec. com. Nat. Cystic Fibrosis Research Found., 1969-74, chmn., 1972-74, pres.'s adv. council, 1974-75; exec. com. div. biology and agr. NRC, 1969-72; mem. developmental biology panel NSF, 1971-73; mem. biomed. adv. com. Los Alamos Sci. Lab., 1972-75; pres. Pacific Slope Biochem. Conf., 1972-73; mem. bd. sci. counselors Nat. Inst. Environ. Health Scis., 1976—; mem. adv. com. biology div. Oak Ridge Nat. Lab., 1976-80; basic research adv. com. Nat. Found., 1976—; bd. dirs. Keystone Life Sci. Study Center, 1976—. Asso. editor: Jour. Exptl. Zoology, 1968-72; editor: PAABS Revista, 1971-76, Jour. Cell Biology, 1976-78, Archives Biochemistry and Biophysics, 1978—, Developmental Genetics, 1979—; editorial bd. various jours. Served with USNR, 1945. Guggenheim fellow, 1962-63. Mem. Nat. Acad. Scis., Am. Soc. Biol. Chemists (treas. 1970-76, mem. editorial bd. jour. 1970-75), Am. Soc. Cell Biology, Am. Chem. Soc. (Pfizer award enzyme chemistry 1967), Am. Soc. Developmental Biology (pres. 1975-76). Subspecialty: Biochemistry (biology). Office: U Calif San Francisco Dept Biochemistry Third Ave and Parnassus San Francisco CA 94143

RUUD, CLAYTON OLAF, materials research scientist; b. Glasgow, Mont., July 31, 1934; s. Asle and Myrtle (Bleken) R.; m. Eithne Brigit McLoughlin, Sept. 1, 1965; children—Kelley Astrid, Kirsten Anne. B.S. in Phys. Metallurgy, Wash. State U., 1957; M.S. in Materials Sci., San Jose State U., 1967; Ph.D. in Materials Sci., U. Denver, 1970. Registered profl. engr., Calif., Colo. Metallurgist, Boeing Airplane Co., Seattle, 1958-61; research engr. Lockheed M and S, Sunnyvale, Calif., 1962-64, FMC Corp., San Jose, Calif., 1964-67; sr. research scientist U. Denver, 1970-79; sr. research assoc., dir. nondestructive testing and evaluation programs Pa. State U., University Park, 1979—; pres. Denver X-Ray Instruments, Inc., Englewood, Colo., 1979—; cons. to various firms; chmn. particle subcom., safe drinking Nat. Acad. Sci., 1976-77; chmn. edn. subcom. Joint Com. on Powder Diffraction, 1980—. Editor numerous books in field. Contbr. articles to profl. jours. Inventor X-ray stress devices. Mem. Soc. Exptl. Stress Analysis, Am. Soc. Matell. Engrs., Materials Research Soc. Republican. Lutheran. Current work: Materials and engineering science, including materials characterization, residual stresses, materials processing, nondestructive materials characterization, X-ray diffraction. Subspecialties: Materials (engineering); Metallurgy. Office: Pa State U 159 MRL University Park PA 16802

RUWE, WILLIAM DAVID, medical neuroscientist; b. Lafayette, Ind., Feb. 18, 1953; s. Alfred Carl and Marcelline Emma (Warbelton) R. B.A., Wabash Coll., 1975; M.S., Purdue U., 1977; postgrad., U. N.C.-Chapel Hill, 1979-80; Ph.D., Purdue U., 1980. NIMH fellow Purdue U., West Lafayette, Ind., 1975-76, research asst., 1976-78, teaching asst., 1978-79; research fellow U. N.C., Chapel Hill, 1979-80; Alta. Heritage Found. Med. Research fellow U. Calgary, Alta., Can., 1981—. Lay tchr. Christian and Missionary Alliance Ch., Calgary, Alta., 1981—; lay leader Presbyn. Ch., West Lafayette, Ind., 1977-80; youth coordinator Babe Ruth Baseball Assn., 1971-75. NIMH predoctoral fellow Purdue U., 1975; Alta. Heritage Found. Med. Research research fellow U. Calgary, 1981—. Mem. Am. Physiol. Soc., Soc. Neurosci., Phi Beta Kappa, Sigma Xi, Psi Chi. Republican. Mem. Christian and Missionary Alliance Ch. Current Work: Neuropharmacological basis of basic physiological functions including thermoregulation, alcohol addiction, febrile convulsions. Subspecialties: Physiology (medicine); Neuropharmacology. Home: Apt H206 1919 University Dr NW Calgary AB T2N 4L1 Canada Office: U Calgary 3330 Hospital Dr NW Calgary AB T2N 1N4 Canada

RUZO, LUIS OCTAVIO, chemist, consultant; b. Lima, Peru, Aug. 15, 1949; came to U.S., 1966; s. Daniel and Olga (Mosselli) R.; m. Jacquelyn Evans, Jan. 13, 1983. B.A. in Chemistry, Boston U., 1970; Ph.D. in Chemistry, Mich. State U., 1974. Research asst. Mich. State U., East Lansing, 1970-74; postdoctoral fellow U. Guelph, Ont., 1974-75; vis. scholar U. Amsterdam, 1975-76; specialist U. Calif.-Berkeley, 1976-78; asst. prof. research chemist U. Calif.-Berkeley, 1978-81, assoc., 1981—; mem., advisor NRC Can., 1981-82; advisor Office for Evaluation of Natural Resources, Peru, 1982—; mem. adv. bd. Jour. Agrl. Food Chemistry, 1984—. Contbr. articles to profl. jours. Patentee in field. Mem. Am. Chem. Soc., Inter-Am. Photochem. Soc., AAAS. Roman Catholic. Current work: Chemical, photochemical and metabolic degradation processes of organic toxicants, pesticides and pollutants, especially with regard to possible activation mechanisms, characterization of resulting products with emphasis on mass spectrometric techniques. Subspecialties: Photochemistry; Environmental toxicology. Home: 2037 Francisco St Berkeley CA 94709 Office: Dept Entomology U Calif Berkeley 101 Wellman Hall Berkeley CA 94720

RYACIOTAKI-BOUSSALIS, HELEN ALEXANDRA, electrical engineer educator; b. Katerini, Greece, Oct. 10, 1951, came to U.S., 1974, naturalized, 1980; d. Basilios and Angela (Sakellariou) R.; m. Dhemetrios Boussalis, Dec. 26, 1976; children—Constantine, Basil. B.S., N.Y. Inst. Tech., 1974; M.S., N.Mex. State U., 1975, Ph.D., 1979. Grad. asst. N.Mex. State U., Las Cruces, 1975-79, asst. prof., 1980; sr. engr. Jet Propulsion Lab., Pasadena, Calif., 1980-82; assoc. prof. Calif. State U.-Northridge, 1982—. Contbr. articles to profl. jours. Mem. IEEE (sr.), Tau Beta Pi. Club: Hellenic U. (Los Angeles). Current work: Research in control systems; large scale systems and stability. Subspecialty: Electrical engineering. Home: 2710 Piedmont Ave #19 Montrose CA 91020 Office: Calif State U Northridge CA 91330

RYAN, DANIEL JOSEPH, electrical engineer; b. Columbus, Ohio, Apr. 5, 1954; s. Donald Joseph and Elizabeth Delores (Kiefer) R.; m. Jodell Sue Newman, Oct. 3, 1980. B.E.E., Ohio State U., 1976, M.E.E., 1977, Ph.D. in Elec. Engring., 1982. Research assoc. Ohio State U., Columbus, 1981-82, sr. research assoc., 1982-83; lead elec. engr. Tex. Instruments, Dallas, 1983—; cons. Visioneering Inc., Columbus. Mem. Optical Soc. Am., IEEE, Soc. Photo-Optical Instrumentation Engrs., AAAS, N.Y. Acad. Scis. Current work: Image processing as related to infra-red imaging; signal processing for state of the art infra-red systems. Subspecialties: Electrical engineering; Semiconductor lasers. Home: 944 Cherokee Trail Plano TX 75023 Office: Tex Instruments PO Box 660246 M/S 3196 Dallas TX 75266

RYAN, JAMES BERNARD, agricultural chemical researcher; b. Greenville, S.C., Aug. 4, 1945; s. Edward Henry and Marjorie (Gowen) R.; m. Evelyn T. Nemeth, Nov. 22, 1969; children: Michael James, Macqueline E., Daniel E. B.S. in Plant Sci, Rutgers U., 1967, M.S. in Soils and Crops, 1969, Ph.D. in Weed Sci, 1975. Grad. research asst. aquatic weed control Rutgers U., 1967-69; field research rep. agrl. chems. Rohm & Haas Co., Phila., 1969-71, field research rep. Western US, Fresno, Calif., 1971-72, field research mgr. agrl. chems., Spring House, Pa., 1973-75, N.Am. regional mgr. research and product devel. agrl. chems., Phila., 1975—. Republican committeeman, 1982—. Mem. Weed Sci. Soc. Am., Council Agrl. Sci. and Tech., Am. Phytopath. Soc., So. Weed Sci. Soc., Plant Growth Regulators Soc. Am., Alpha Zeta. Roman Catholic. Club: Central Bucks Gymnastics. Current Work: Research, development and registration of products for improvement of yield and quality of agronomic and horticultural crops. Subspecialty: Weed science; Agriculture chemicals development. Home: 439 Pine Run Rd Doylestown PA 19801 Office: Rohm and Haas Co Independence Mall W Philadelphia PA 19105

RYAN, STEWART RICHARD, physicist, educator; b. Schenectady, Jan. 26, 1942; s. August R. and Frances A. (Ruth) R.; m. Rita M. Sandman, July 9, 1966; children: Kathleen, Colleen, Ellen Mary. B.S. in Physics, U. Notre Dame, 1964; M.S., U. Mich., 1965, Ph.D., 1971. Research staff physicist, then instr. Yale U., New Haven, 1971-74; staff physicist U. Ariz., Tucson, 1974-77; asst. prof. physics U. Okla., Norman, 1977-82, asso. prof., 1982—; mem. engring. physics com. U. Okla. (Coll. Engring.). Contbr. numerous articles to profl. pubs. Mem. Am. Phys. Soc., Am. Assn. Physics Tchrs., Am. Soc. Engring. Edn., Okla. Acad. Sci., Sigma Xi. Current Work: Experimental atomic and molecular physics, applied physics and instrumentation, energy conservation, experimental low temperature physics. Subspecialties: Atomic and molecular physics; Applied physics. Home: 2711 Willow Creek Dr Norman OK 73071 Office: Dept Physics and Astronomy U Okla Norman OK 73019

RYAN, UNA SCULLY, med. researcher, cons.; b. Kuala Lumpur, Malaysia, Dec. 18, 1941; came to U.S., 1964; d. Henry and Amy (Yee) Scully; m. David Spencer Smith, July 18, 1964; 1 dau., Tamsin Spencer; m. James Walter Ryan, June 17, 1973; 1 dau., Amy Jean Susan. B.S., Bristol U., Eng., 1963; Ph.D., U. Cambridge, Eng., 1966. Fellow dept. biology U. Va., Charlottesville, 1964-66; fellow dept. medicine U. Miami, 1966-67, instr. medicine, 1967-72, adj. asst. prof. biology, 1968-71, asst. prof. medicine, 1972-77, assoc. prof., 1977-80, research prof., 1980—; vis. investigator Labs. Cardiovascular Research, Howard Hughes Med. Inst., Miami, 1967-71; dir. Labs. Cardiovascular Research, Howard Hughes Med. Inst. (Lab. Ultrastructure Studies), 1970-71; sr. scientist Papanicolaou Cancer Research Inst., Miami, 1972-77; chairperson heart lung and blood research rev. com. NIH, 1980-81. Editor: Tissue & Cell, 1981—; contbr. numerous articles to profl. jours. Mem. vestry St. Stephen's Ch., Miami; trustee Sch. Dept. Sci. and Indsl. Research, fellow, 1963. Ethel Sargant Research fellow, 1964, 65; Sci. Research Council fellow, 1966. Mem. Am. Soc. Cell Biology, Soc. Neurosci., Tissue Culture Assn., Am. Heart Assn., European Soc. Microcirculation, Am. Microcirculatory Soc., Am. Thoracic Soc., N.Y. Acad. Scis. Episcopalian. Current Work: Cell biology of pulmonary endothelium. Subspecialties: Cell biology (medicine); Pulmonary medicine. Home: 3420 Poinciana Ave Miami FL 33133 Office: 1399 NW 17th Ave Miami FL 33125

RYKER, NORMAN JENKINS, JR., aerospace engineering and technology company executive; b. Seattle, Dec. 25, 1927; s. Norman Jenkins and Adelia Gustine (Macombee) R.; m. Kathleen Marie Crawford (div.); children: Jeanne Ryker Flores, Christina, Vickie Ryker Risley, Norman Jenkins, III, Cathy. B.S., U. Calif., 1949, M.S., 1951; M.S., Harvard U., 1973. Registered profl. engr., Calif. With North Am. Aviation (now Rockwell Internat.), El Segundo, Calif., 1951—, Apollo asst. chief engr., 1961-64, 67-68; v.p. research and test engring. North Am. Aviation (Space div.), 1968-70; v.p. research engring. and test newspaper press group, v.p. ops. newspaper press, 1973; v.p., gen. mgr. (Comml. Web div.), 1974, (Transp. Equipment div.), 1974-76; pres. (Rocketdyne div.), 1976-83; sr. v.p. aerospace ops. (Pneumo Corp.), Boston, 1983—; mem. NASA Manned Spacecraft Ctr. team which evaluated and recommended the lunar orbit rendezvous concept for landing men on the moon; dir. Warner Ctr. Bank. Recipient award of merit NASA, 1969, Disting. Pub. Service medal, 1981; Silver Knight award Nat. Mgmt. Assn., 1979; Indsl. Tech. Mgmt. award Calif. Soc. Profl. Engrs., 1979; Companion Instn. Prodn. Engrs., London, 1981; Engr. of Yr. award Inst. Advancement Engring. and Orange County Engring. Council, 1982. Fellow AIAA, Inst. Advancement Engring.; mem. ASCE, Am. Astron. Soc., Nat. Mgmt. Assn., Sigma Xi, Phi Epsilon. Current Work: Responsible for companies of Cleveland Pneumatic, National Water Lift. Subspecialty: Aerospace engineering and technology. Office: 6633 Canoga Ave Canoga Park CA 91304

RYU, JAI HYUN, bioengineer, neurophysiologist, otolaryngology educator, researcher; b. Ham-Nam, Korea, Oct. 27, 1940; s. Chang Yul and Byung Sun (Park) R.; m. Jacqueline Ellen Brisbin, June 16, 1973; children—Juliette Jaie, Jessica Jaie, Jennifer Jaie. B.S.E., U. Mich., 1966; M.S.E., U. Iowa, 1972, Ph.D., 1979. Research asst. dept. otorhinolaryngology U. Mich., Ann Arbor, 1961-66; assoc. research scientist dept. Otolaryngology U. Iowa, Iowa City, 1966-74, research scientist, dir. research, 1974-80, assoc. prof. biomed. engring. Coll. Engring. and assoc. prof., otolaryngology, dir. research Coll. Medicine, 1980-84; prof., dir. research Bowman Gray Sch. Medicine, Wake Forest U., Winston-Salem, N.C., 1984—. Author: The Vestibular System, 1975; Vestibular Physiology in Understanding the Dizzy Patient, 1980; also articles. Mem. Barany Soc., AIAA, Am. Acad. Otoloryngology, Head-Neck Surgery, N.Y. Acad. Scis., Aerospace Med. Assn., Soc. Neurosci., Bioengring. Soc., Sigma Xi. Roman Catholic. Current work: Neurophysiology; vestibular physiology; biological control system. Subspecialties: Neurophysiology; Biomedical engineering. Home: 1007 Kendale Dr Winston-Salem NC 27104 Office: Wake Forest U Bowman Gray Sch Medicine 300 S Hawthorne Rd Winston-Salem NC 27103

SAADA, ADEL SELIM, civil engineer, educator; b. Heliopolis, Egypt, Oct. 24, 1934; came to U.S., 1959, naturalized, 1965; s. Selim N. and Marie (Chahyne) S.; m. Nancy Helen Hernan, June 5, 1960; children: Christiane Mona, Richard Adel. Ingénieur des Arts et Manufactures, École Centrale, Paris, France, 1958; M.S., U. Grenoble, France, 1959; Ph.D. in Civil Engring, Princeton U., 1961. Registered profl. engr., Ohio. Engr. Société Dumez, Paris, 1959; research asso. dept. civil engring. Princeton (N.J.) U., 1961-62; asst. prof. civil engring. Case Western Reserve U., Cleve., 1962-67, asso. prof., 1967-72, prof., 1973—, chmn. dept. civil engring., 1978—; cons., lectr. soil testing and properties Waterways Expt. Sta. (C.E.), Vicksburg, Miss., 1974-79; cons. to various firms, 1962—. Author: Elasticity Theory and Applications, 1974; contbr. numerous articles on soil mechanics and foundation engring. to profl. jours. Fellow ASCE; Mem. Internat. Soc. Soil Mechanics, ASTM. Club: Executive. Inventor pneumatic analog computer and loading frame. Current Work: Soil mechanics, foundations, mechanical behavior of particulate media; mechanics of solids and fracture. Subspecialties: Civil engineering; Fracture mechanics. Home: 3342 Braemar Rd Shaker Heights OH 44120 Office: Dept Civil Engring Case Inst Tech Case Western Reserve Univ Bingham Bldg Cleveland OH 44106

SAALFELD, FRED ERIC, chemist, research adminstr.; b. Joplin, Mo., Apr. 9, 1935; s. Eric A. and Milla E. (Kessler) S.; m. Elizabeth Renner, Nov. 22, 1958; 1 child, Fred E. B.S., S.E. Mo. State U., 1957; M.S., Iowa State U., 1959, Ph.D., 1961. Chemist Naval Research Lab., Washington, 1962, head mass spectrometry sect., 1963-73, head phys. chemistry br., 1974-75, supt. chemistry div., 1976-82; chief scientist and sci. dir. Officer Naval Research br. office, London, 1980; dir. research program Office Naval Research, Arlington, Va., 1982—. Contbr. numerous articles on chemistry to profl. jours. Sec. Lake Braddock High Sch. PTA, 1976. Farmers and Mchts. Bank scholar, 1956; recipient Navy Meritorious Civilian Service award, 1981. Mem. Am. Chem. Soc., Am. Soc. Mass Spectrometry, Soc. for Applied Spectroscopy, AAAS, Sigma Xi. Current Work: Life support, contaminant ident, combustion, solid state chemistry. Subspecialties: Physical chemistry; Analytical chemistry. Office: Office of Naval Research 800 N Quincy St Arlington VA 22217

SAAM, JOHN CARLTON, chemist; b. St. Paul, July 17, 1929; s. Clement Martin and Louise Catherine (Morton) S.; m. Lou Ella Halbur, Aug. 14, 1954; children—Thomas, Paul, Mary, John, Mark. B.S., St. Thomas Coll., 1951; M.S., U. Iowa, 1954, Ph.D., 1956. Research chemist Dow Corning Corp., Midland, Mich., 1956-60, group leader, 1960-64, research supr., 1964-74, research scientist, 1974-82, sr. research scientist, 1982—; vis. prof. U. Minn., Mpls., 1983-84. Contbr. articles to profl. publs. Patentee in field. Served with U.S. Army, 1951-52. Named Outstanding Inventor of Yr., 1984. Mem. Am. Chem. Soc. (polymer div., rubber div.), AAAS, Sigma Xi. Current work: Organosilicone chemistry, organosilicone polymers, elastomers, colloids, coating. Subspecialties: Polymer chemistry; Organic chemistry. Office: Dow Corning Corp Midland MI 48640

SABATINI, DAVID DOMINGO, biochemist. Frederick L. Ehrman prof., chmn. dept. cell biology NYU Sch. Medicine. Elected mem. Nat. Acad. Scis., 1985. Subspecialty: Cell biology. Office: NYU Sch Medicine 550 1st Ave New York NY 10016

SABBAGH, HAROLD ABRAHAM, engineering analyst, company executive; b. West Lafayette, Ind., Jan. 9, 1937; s. Elias Morshed and Waded Katherine (Corey) S.; m. Sandra Claire Abookire, June 18, 1966; children—Elias Harold, Kahlil George, Amira Ann. B.S., M.S. in Elec. Engring., Purdue U., Ph.D., 1964. Prof. elec. engring. and physics Rose-Hulman Inst. Tech., Terre Haute, Ind., 1964-72; research engr. Naval Weapons Support Ctr., Crane, Ind., 1972-80; pres. Sabbagh Assocs., Bloomington, Ind., 1980—. Served to lt. j.g. USN, 1958-61. Sr. mem. IEEE (Centennial medal 1984); mem. Sigma Xi. Current work: Computer modelling in electromagnetics, static and dynamic structural analysis, acoustics, quantitative nondestructive evaluation. Subspecialties: Electrical engineering; Non-destructive testing. Home: 2634 Round Hill Ln Bloomington IN 47401

SABBAGHA, RUDY E., obstetrician, gynecologist, educator; b. Tel Aviv, Israel, Oct. 29, 1931; s. Elias C. and Sonia B. S.; m. Asma E. Sahyouny, Oct. 5, 1957; children: Elias, Randa. B.A., M.D., Am. U., Beirut, Lebanon. Sr. physician Tapline, Saudi Arabia, 1958-64, ob-gyn specialist, 1969-70; teaching fellow U. Pitts., 1965-68; asst. prof. ob-gyn, 1970-75; prof. Northwestern U., 1975—; obstetrician, gynecologist Prentice Women's Hosp., Chgo. Author: Ultrasound-High Risk Obstetrics, 1979; editor: Ultrasound Applied to Obstetrics and Gynecology, 1980; contbr. articles to profl. jours. Fellow Am. Coll. Obstetricians and Gynecologists; mem. Soc. Gynecologic Investigation, Central Assn. Obstetricians and Gynecologists, Assn. Profs. Ob-Gyn, Am. Inst. Ultrasound in Medicine. Current Work: Research in diagnostic ultrasound, obstetrics and gynecology. Subspecialty: Ultrasound. Home: 2415 Meadow Dr Wilmette IL 60091 Office: Prentice Women's Hosp Chicago IL 60611

SABBAH, HANI NAIEF, cardiovascular researcher; b. Nazareth, Israel, Apr. 18, 1949; came to U.S. 1967; s. Naief Jacob and Rose Marcell (Farran) S.; m. Carole Ruth Ezell, Feb. 16, 1973; 1 child, Jon-Paul Bernard. B.S., U. Okla., 1972. Research asst. U. Okla., Norman, 1972-74, research assoc., 1974-76; assoc. investigator Henry Ford Hosp., Detroit, 1976-81, research coordinator, 1981-84, asst. staff investigator, 1984—. Contbr. articles to profl. jours. Lectr. in field. Mem. Am. Fedn. Clin. Research, Am. Physiol. Soc., ASME, Biomed. Engring. Soc., Republican. Roman Catholic. Current work: Application of principles of engineering particularly fluid dynamics to diagnosis and treatment of cardiovascular diseases. Subspecialties: Cardiology; Biomedical engineering. Office: Henry Ford Hosp 2799 W Grand Blvd Detroit MI 48202

SABBAN, ESTHER LOUISE, biochemist, educator; b. Detroit, July 21, 1948; d. Ephraim and Jean (Abrams) Ralph; m. Yitzchak Sabban, Mar. 17, 1968; children—Deborah, Behir, Ronald. B.Sc., Hebrew U., Jerusalem, 1971, M.Sc., 1972; Ph.D., NYU, 1977. Asst. research scientist NYU Med. Ctr., N.Y.C., 1977-80, research asst. prof., 1980-83; asst. prof. biochemistry N.Y. Med. Coll., Valhalla, 1983—. Contbr. articles to profl. jours. Mem. Am. Soc. Biol. Chemists, Am. Soc. Cell Biology, Soc. for Neurosci., N.Y. Acad. Sci., AAAS. Current work: Regulation of catecholamine biosynthetic enzymes. Subspecialty: Biochemistry (biology). Office: NY Med Coll Dept Biochemistry Valhalla NY 10595

SABEL, JOSEPH MORRIS, geologist; b. Newark, Dec. 22, 1953; s. Nathan and Freda (Samilson) S.; m. Mary J. Sommerfeldt, July 13, 1975. B.S., Iowa State U., 1975; M.S., S.D. Sch. Mines and Tech., 1981. Research asst. S.D. Sch. Mines and Tech., Rapid City, 1979-80, fellow, 1980-81; geologist Chevron USA, Casper, Wyo., 1981—. Contbr. articles to profl. jours. Vice pres. Casper Renaissance Assn., 1982. Served to lt. USN, 1975-79. Mem. Am. Assn. Petroleum Geologists, Geol. Soc. Am., Soc. Econ. Paleontologists and Mineralogists, Wyo. Geol. Assn. (field conf. com., activity chmn. 1984), NOW, Casper Chamber Music Soc. (charter). Current work: Evaporite formation and deposition; character and age of permo-traissic boundary in North America; basement tectonic control on subsequent sedimentation in the Northern Rocky Mountain region. Subspecialties: Sedimentology; Geophysics. Home: 945 S Beech St Casper WY 82601 Office: Chevron USA PO Box 2619 Casper WY 82602

SABIN, CULLEN MILO, mechanical engineer, research and development company executive; b. Los Angeles, Oct. 1, 1930; s. Milo Rudd and Lucille (Ankeny) S.; m. Katherine Roberta Kerr, Dec. 20, 1953; children—Scott Cullen, Martin Willard, Leslie Lynn. B.S., Stanford U., 1953, M.S., 1954, Ph.D., 1964. Research engr. NACA, Sunnyvale, Calif., 1954; aero. engr. Convair div. Gen. Dynamics Corp., San Diego, 1957-60; research asst. Stanford U., Calif., 1960-63; prin. scientist Geoscience, Ltd., Solana Beach, Calif., 1963—, v.p., dir., 1966—; dir. Thermonetics Corp., San Diego. Author: Technology of Forced Flow Boiling, 1975. Patentee flow measurements. Trustee Solana Beach Elem. Sch. Dist., 1967-75, pres., 1974-75; elder Presbyn. Ch. Served with U.S. Army, 1954-56. Mem. Sigma Xi. Republican. Club: San Diego Yacht. Current work: Boiling heat transfer; forced convection enhanced heat transfer; fluid mechanics; onset of turbulence; heat exchange instrumentation. Subspecialties: Mechanical engineering; Fluid mechanics. Office: Geoscience Ltd 410 S Cedros Ave Solana Beach CA 92075

SABISTON, DAVID COSTON, JR., surgeon, educator; b. Onslow County, N.C., Oct. 4, 1924; s. David Coston and Marie (Jackson) S.; m. Agnes Barden, Sept. 24, 1955; children—Anne Barden Leggett, Agnes Foy Butler, Sarah Coston. B.S., U. N.C., 1943; M.D., Johns Hopkins U., 1947. Diplomate: Am. Bd. Surgery (chmn. 1971-72). Successively intern, asst. resident, chief resident surgery Johns Hopkins Hosp., 1947-53; successively asst. prof., assoc. prof., prof. surgery Johns Hopkins Med. Sch., 1955-64, Howard Hughes investigator, 1955-61; Fulbright research scholar U. Oxford, Eng., 1960; research assoc. Hosp. Sick Children, U. London, Eng., 1961; James B. Duke prof. surgery, chmn. dept. Duke Med. Sch., 1964—; Hunterian lectr. Editor: David-Christopher Testbook of Surgery; editor: Gibbon's Surgery of the Chest; chmn. editorial bd.: Annals of Surgery; mem. editorial bd.: Jour. Thoracic and Cardiovascular Surgery, Circulation, Annals Clin. Research, Archives of Surgery, Surgery, Gynecology and Obstetrics. Served to capt., M.C. AUS, 1953-55. Recipient Career Research award NIH, 1962-64; N.C. award in Sci., 1978; Disting. Achievement award Am. Heart Assn. Sci. Council, 1983. Mem. A.C.S. (chmn. bd. govs. 1974-75, regent 1975—, chmn. bd. regents 1982—), Am. Surg. Assn. (pres. 1977-78), So. Surg. Assn. (sec. 1969-73, pres. 1973-74), Am. Assn. Thoracic Surgery (pres. 1984-85), Soc. Clin. Surgery, Internat. Soc. Cardiovascular Surgery, Soc. Vascular Surgery (v.p. 1967-68), Soc. Univ. Surgeons (pres. 1968-69), Halsted Soc., Inst. of Medicine, Surg. Biology Club II, Soc. Thoracic Surgery, Soc. Surgery Alimentary Tract, Soc. Surg. Chairmen (pres. 1974-76), Soc. Thoracic Surgeons Great Britain and Ireland, Royal Coll. Surgeons Edinburgh (hon.), Royal Coll. Surgeons Eng. (hon.), Asociación de Cirugia del Litoral (Argentina) (hon.), Phi Beta Kappa, Alpha Omega Alpha. Subspecialty: Surgery. Office: Duke U Med Ctr Dept Surgery Durham NC 27710

SABLIK, MARTIN JOHN, research physicist; b. Bklyn., Oct. 21, 1939; s. Martin C. and Elsie M. (Fuzia) S.; m. Beverly A. Shively, Nov. 26, 1965; children—Jeanne, Karen, Marjorie, Lawrence. B.A., Cornell U., 1960; M.S., U. Ky., 1965; Ph.D., Fordham U., 1972. Jr. engr. Martin Co., Orlando, Fla., 1962-63; instr. U. Ky., Lexington, 1963-65; research assoc. Fairleigh Dickinson U., Teaneck, N.J., 1965-67, instr. physics, 1967-72, prof., 1972-80; sr. research scientist Southwest Research Inst., San Antonio, 1980—. Contbr. articles to profl. jours. Mem. Am. Phys. Soc., Am. Assn. Physics Tchrs., IEEE, Am. Soc. Nondestructive Testing, Acoustical Soc. Am. Roman Catholic. Current work: Theory-magnetic properties of rare earth materials; application of electro-magnetic theory to nondestructive evaluation; use of statistical energy analysis for structure borne sound; computer simulation of space science instrumentation. Subspecialties: Magnetic physics; Acoustics. Office: Southwest Research Inst 6220 Culebra Rd San Antonio TX 78284

SABOL, STEVEN LAYNE, biochemistry researcher; b. Phoenix, Sept. 21, 1944; s. Frank P. and Lois A. (Beaty) S.; m. Margaret Choa, Sept. 20, 1980; 1 child, Mark Lewis. B.S., Yale Coll., 1966; M.D., NYU, 1973, Ph.D., 1973. Diplomate Am. Bd. Med. Examiners. Sr. staff fellow NHLBI Lab. Biochem. Genetics, Bethesda, Md., 1974-79, med. officer research, 1979—. Mem. Am. Soc. Biol. Chemists, Soc. for Neurosci. Current work: Molecular neurobiology, opioid peptides, neuropeptide biosynthesis. Subspecialties: Biochemistry (biology); Molecular biology. Office: NIH Bldg 36 Room 1C-06 Bethesda MD 20205

SACHAN, DILEEP S., nutrition educator, researcher; b. Makhauli, India, Dec. 18, 1938; came to U.S., 1964, naturalized 1974; s. Jagdeo P. and Parag Sachan; m. Cheryl Lyn Hill, Nov. 2, 1968; children—Rashmi D., Ravi C., Vinay K. B.V.Sc., Vet. Coll., Jabalpur, India, 1961, M.V.Sc., 1963; M.S., U. Ill., 1966, Ph.D., 1968. Asst. prof. pharmacology MeHarry Med. Coll., Nashville, 1971-75; research chemist VA Hosp., Cleve., 1976-78; fellow in nutrition and gastroenterology Vanderbilt U. Med. Ctr., Nashville, 1978-79; assoc. prof. nutrition U. Tenn., Knoxville, 1979—, assoc. prof. pediatrics, 1984—, adj. prof. vet. medicine, 1984—. Contbr. articles to profl. jours. Active Knoxville Assn. for Talented and Gifted. Mem. Am. Inst. Nutrition, N.Y. Acad. Scis., Internat. Soc. Biochemistry and Pharmacology. Club: Torch. Current work: Nutritional aspects of alcoholism, cancer and environmental toxicology. Subspecialties: Nutrition (medicine); Biochemistry (biology). Office: Dept Nutrition and Food Sci U Tenn Knoxville TN 37996 1900

SACHS, BENJAMIN DAVID, biopsychologist; b. Madrid, Spain, Mar. 4, 1936; s. Georg Eduard and Leonie Bernardine (Feiler) S.; m. Jacqueline Sachs, June 12, 1965; 1 dau.; Naomi. B.A., CCNY, 1957; M.S. Ed., 1961; Ph.D., U. Calif., Berkeley, 1966. Nat. Inst. Child Health and Human Devel. postdoctoral fellow Inst. Animal Behavior, Rutgers U., Newark, 1966-68; asst. prof. U. Conn., Storrs, 1968-72, assoc. prof., 1972-76, prof., 1976—; Vis. scholar Stanford Med. Sch., 1975-76. Editor: (with McGill and Dewsbury) Sex and Behavior, 1978; editorial adv. bd.: Current Contents/Life Scis, 1968—; contbr. articles to profl. jours. Served with AUS, 1958-60. USPHS grantee, 1969—. Fellow Am. Psychol. Assn.; mem. Eastern Psychol. Assn., Animal Behavior Soc., Internat. Soc. Psychoneuroendocrinology, Internat. Soc. Devel. Psychobiology, Soc. Neurosci., Sigma Xi, Psi Chi. Current Work: Hormone-brain-behavior relations, especially regarding reproductive behavior. Subspecialties: Neuropsychology; Psychobiology. Office: Dept Psychology U Conn Storrs CT 06268

SACHS, LESTER MARVIN, computer systems analyst, physicist; b. Chgo., May 16, 1927; s. Maurice Arthur and Leona Cecille (Goodman) S.; m. Blanche Cohen, Jan. 27, 1958; 1 dau., Deborah. B.S. in Physics, Ill. Inst. Tech., 1950, M.S. in Physics, 1954, Ph.D. in Physics, 1961. Sr. scientist Martin Marietta Corp., Relay, Md., 1965-69; pres., tech. dir. Computer Program Assocs., Inc., Columbia, Md., 1969-71; cons., Balt., 1972; computer systems analyst Bur. Labor Stats., Washington, 1972-75; system devel. specialist Social Security Adminstrn., Woodlawn, Md., 1975-79, tech. advisor, 1979—; cons., 1972-74. Contbr. articles to physics jours. Served with AUS, 1945-46. Argonne Nat. Lab. resident student assoc., 1958-60; Wayne State U. Faculty fellow, summer 1962. Mem. Am. Phys. Soc., Assn. Computing Machinery, Brit. Computer Soc. (assoc.). Jewish. Subspecialties: Information systems, storage, and retrieval (computer science); Atomic and molecular physics. Home: 8823 Stonehaven Rd Randallstown MD 21133

SACHS, ROBERT GREEN, physicist, educator, laboratory administrator; b. Hagerstown, Md., May 4, 1916; s. Harry Maurice and Anna (Green) S.; m. Selma Solomon, Aug. 28, 1941; m. Jean K. Woolf, Dec. 17, 1950; children: Rebecca, Jennifer, Jeffrey, Judith, Joel; m. Carolyn L. Wolf, Aug. 21, 1968; stepchildren: Thomas Wolf, Jacqueline Wolf, Katherine Wolf. Ph.D., Johns Hopkins U., 1939; D.Sc. (hon.), Purdue U., 1967, U. Ill., 1977. Research fellow George Washington U., 1939-41; instr. physics Purdue U., 1941-43; on leave as lectr., research fellow U. Calif. at Berkeley, 1941; sect. chief Ballistic Research Lab., Aberdeen (Md.) Proving Ground, 1943-46; dir. theoretical physics div. Argonne Nat. Lab., Ill., 1945-47; asso. prof. physics U. Wis., 1947-48, prof., 1948-64; assoc. dir. Argonne Nat. Lab., 1964-68, dir., 1973-79; prof. physics U. Chgo., 1964—; dir. Enrico Fermi Inst., 1968-73, 83—; Higgins vis. prof. Princeton U., 1955-56; vis. prof. U. Paris, 1959-60, Tohoku U., Japan, 1974; cons. Ballistic Research Labs., 1945-59, Argonne Nat. Lab., 1947-50, 60-64; cons. radiation lab. U. Calif. at Berkeley, 1955-59; adv. panel physics NSF, 1958-61; mem. physics survey com., chmn. elem. particle physics panel Nat. Acad. Scis., 1969-72; high energy physics adv. panel div. research AEC, 1966-69; mem. steering com. Sci. and Tech., A Five Year Outlook, 1979. Author: Nuclear Theory, 1953; Chief editor: High Energy Nuclear Physics, 1957; editor: National Energy Issues: How Do We Decide?, 1979, The Nuclear Chain Reaction-Forty Years Later, 1984. Guggenheim fellow, 1959-60. Fellow Am. Acad. Arts and Scis. v.p.; chmn. Midwest Center 1980-83); mem. Nat. Acad. Scis. (chmn. physics sect. 1977-80, chmn. Class I, Math. and Phys. Scis. 1980-83), Am. Phys. Soc. (council 1968-71, regional sec. Central States 1964-69), AAAS (v.p., chmn. physics sect. 1970-71), Am. Inst. Physics (mem. governing bd. 1969-71), Phi Beta Kappa, Sigma Xi. Research in theoretical nuclear and atomic physics, terminal ballistics, nuclear power reactors, theoretical particle physics. Current Work: Theory of weak and electro magnetic interactions of fundamental particles, violation of time-reversal and CP invariances. Subspecialties: Particle physics; Theoretical physics. Home: 5490 South Shore Dr Chicago IL 60615 Office: Enrico Fermi Inst 5630 Ellis Ave U Chgo Chicago IL 60637

SACHTLER, WOLFGANG MAX HUGO, chemistry and chemical engineering educator; b. Delitzsch, Germany, Nov. 8, 1924; came to U.S., 1983; s. Gottfried Hugo and Johanna Elisabeth (Bollmann) S.; m. Luise Annelore Adrian, Dec. 14, 1953; children—Johann Wolfgang Adriaan, Heike Kathleen Julia, Yvonne Rhea Valeska. Diplom-Chemiker, Tech. Hochschule, Braunschweig, W.Ger., 1949, Dr. rer. nat., 1952. Research chemist Kon/Shell Laboratorium Amsterdam, Netherlands, 1952-60, group leader, 1961-71, dir. research dept., 1962-83; research chemist Shell Devel. Co., Emeryville, Calif., 1960-61; dir. Catalysis Ctr., Ipatieff prof. Northwestern U., Evanston, Ill., 1983—; prof. part-time U. Leiden (Netherlands), 1963-84. Contbr. articles to profl. jours. Mem. Royal Netherlands Acad. Sci., Nederlandse Chemische Vereniging, Am. Chem. Soc., N.Am. Catalysis Soc. (Burwell lectr.), Gordon Research Conf. Catalysis (chmn. 1985), Internat. Congress Catalysis (v.p.). Current work: Fundamental research in heterogeneous catalysis. Subspecialties: Catalysis chemistry; Surface chemistry. Home: 2141 Ridge Ave Evanston IL 60201 Office: Dept Chemistry Northwestern U Evanston IL 60201

SACK, EDGAR ALBERT, JR., microcircuits and microcomputers manufacturing company executive; b. Pitts., Jan. 31, 1930; s. Edgar Albert and Margaret (Engelmohr) S.; m. Eugenia Ferris, June 7, 1952; children—Elaine Kimberly, Richard Warren. B.E.E., Carnegie Mellon Inst., 1951, M.E.E., 1952, Ph.D., 1954. Mgr. engring. Westinghouse Electric Corp., Elkridge, Md., 1961-66, gen. mgr., 1966-69; v.p. Gen. Instrument Co., Hicksville, N.Y., 1969-76, sr. v.p., 1976-84; pres., chief exec. officer Zilog, Campbell, Calif., 1984—. Contbr. articles to sci. and tech. jours. Patentee in field. Poly. Inst. N.Y. fellow, 1981. Fellow IEEE; mem. Semicondr. Industry Assn., Tau Beta Pi, Eta Kappa Nu. Current work: Management of development in VLSI components and minicomputers. Subspecialties: Microelectronics; Microchip technology (engineering). Home: 21412 Sarahills Ct Saratoga CA 95070 Office: Zilog 1315 Dell Ave Campbell CA 95008

SACKS, WILLIAM, neurochemist; b. Phila, Feb. 17, 1924; s. Harry F. and Bessie (Schechter) S.; m. Shirley Sacks, Apr. 4, 1954; children: Harriet Sacks Cook, Roberta Sacks Malone, Stuart Barry. B.S., Pa. State U., 1947, M.S., 1948, Ph.D., 1951. Dir. chemistry lab. Einstein Med. Ctr. So. Div., Phila., 1951-58; prin. research scientist Rockland Research Inst. Kline Inst. Psychiat. Research, Orangeburg, N.Y., 1958—; also dir. Cerebral Metabolism Lab., research assoc. prof. psychiatry N.Y. U. Sch. Medicine, N.Y.C., 1979—. Contrb. articles to profl. jours. Served with U.S. Army, 1944-46, PTO. Mem. Internat. Soc. Neurochemistry, Am. Soc. Neurochemistry, Am. Chem. Soc., AAAS, Soc. Biol. Chemists, Soc. Neurosci., Soc. Biol. Psychiatry, Sigma Xi, Phi Eta Sigma, Phi Lambda Upsilon, Gamma Sigma Delta. Current Work: Cerebral metabolism in humans in vivo using an original arteriovenous technique. Have demonstrated a difference in brain metabolism of chronic mental patients. Subspecialties: Neurochemistry; Biochemistry (medicine).

SADHAL, SATWINDAR SINGH, mechanical engineering educator; b. Nairobi, Kenya, Nov. 14, 1951; came to U.S., 1976; s. Jaswant Singh and Bir Kaur (Dhanjal) S.; m. Manjit Kaur Matharu, Oct. 27, 1980. B.A.Sc., U. Toronto, Ont., Can., 1975, M.A.Sc., 1976; Ph.D., Calif. Inst. Tech., 1978. Asst. prof. U. Pa., Phila., 1978-81; asst. prof. mech. engring. U. So. Calif., Los Angeles, 1982-84, assoc. prof., 1984—. NSF grantee, 1981; Presdl. Young Investigator awardee NSF, 1984-89. Mem. ASME, Am. Inst. Chem. Engrs., Am. Acad. Mechanics. Current work: Fluid mechanics, heat transfer, engring. math.; research in change of phase heat transfer and fluid mechanics, multiphase compound drops and bubles, sprays. Subspecialty: Fluid mechanics. Home: 4977 Avenida de las Estrellas Yorba Linda CA 92686 Office: U So Calif University Park OHE 430 Los Angeles CA 90089-1453

SADJADI, FIROOZ AHMADI, electrical engineer, research scientist, consultant; b. Tehran, Mar. 18, 1949; came to U.S., 1968; s. Ali Akbar Ahmadi and Fakhri (Mohsen) S.; m. Carolyn Joann Elkins, 1981; 1 child, Farzad Ali. B.S. in Elec. Engring., Purdue U., 1972, M.S. in Elec. Engring., Engr. degree in Elec. 1974; Engring., U. So. Calif., 1976; postgrad. in elec. engring., U. Tenn., 1983. Research asst. Image Processing Inst. U. So. Calif., Los Angeles, 1974-76; cons. Oak Ridge Nat. Lab., 1980; research asst., researcher dept. elec. engring. U. Tenn., 1977-83; research scientist Honeywell Inc., Mpls., 1983—. Contbr. articles to profl. jours. Mem. IEEE, Soc. Photo-Optical Instrumentation Engrs., Am. Assn. for Artificial Intelligence, Sigma Xi. Current work: Three dimensional signal processing, sensor fusion and multisensor processing, artificial intelligence, image processing. Subspecialties: Electrical engineering; Graphics, image processing, and pattern recognition. Office: Honeywell Systems & Research Ctr 2600 Ridgway Pkwy Minneapolis MN 55440

SADJADI, MORTEZA, research geneticist; b. Brodjerd, Iran, Feb. 12, 1954; came to U.S., 1977; s. Naghi and Fatemeh Sadjadi. B.S., Rezaiyeh U. (Iran), 1976; M.S., Wash. State U., 1979; Ph.D., Oreg. State U., 1982. Research geneticist Peterson Industries, Decatur, Ark., 1982—. Contbr. articles to profl. jours. Spl. Grad. scholar Ferdowsi U., Iran, 1977; Oreg. State U., grad. scholar, 1980, 81. Mem. Poultry Sci. Assn., World Poultry Sci. Assn., Am. Genetics Assn., Sigma Xi, Phi Kappa Phi, Alpha Zeta, Gamma Sigma Delta. Current work: Reproduction and genetic selection of gene pool lines in the primary poultry breeding program. Subspecialties: Animal genetics; Animal physiology. Home: PO Box 304 Decatur AR 72722 Office: Peterson Industries PO Box 248 Decatur AR 72722

SADLER, STANLEY GENE, research engineer; b. Spring Lake, Utah, Mar. 6, 1938; s. Hector Baden-Powel and Maida Ann (Butler) S.; m. Suzanne Rich, Aug. 23, 1963; children—Nathan, Rebecca, Jennifer, Jared, Rachelle. B.S. in Mech. Engring., U. Utah, 1963; M.S. in Mech. Engring., U. Rochester, 1964, Ph.D. in Mech. and Aerospace Sci., 1967. Research asst. U. Utah, Salt Lake City, 1962-63; research tng. asst. U. Rochester, N.Y., 1964-67; research engr., group head aeromechanics Rochester Applied Sci. Assocs., 1967-72; sr. research engr. Homelite div. Textron, Charlotte, N.C., 1972-78; chief rotor dynamics bell helicopter Textron, Fort Worth, 1978—; cons. Teledyne, Mobile, Ala., 1976. NDEA fellow U. Rochester, 1963-67. Mem. Am. Helicopter Soc., AIAA, ASME. Republican. Mormon. Current work: Rotor dynamics: aeroelasticity, rotor and rotor-induced vibrations and loads, ground and air resonance, flight simulation, full and scale model testing. Subspecialties: Aerospace engineering and technology; Computer-aided design. Home: 1002 Curtis Ct Arlington TX 76012 Office: Bell Helicopter Textron Inc PO Box 482 Fort Worth TX 76101

SADOWSKY, JOHN, mathematician; b. Worcester, Mass., Aug. 27, 1949; s. Samuel and Edith (Miller) S.; m. Emilie Arlene Hoffman, June 18, 1972; children—Rebecca Anne, Joshua William. B.A., Johns Hopkins U., 1971; M.A., U. Md., 1973, Ph.D., 1980. Mathematician, U.S. Bur. of Census, Washington, 1977-79; sr. software engr. Hadron, Inc., McLean, Va., 1979-81; prin. mathematician System Engring & Devel. Corp., Columbia, Md., 1981—; mem. adj. grad. faculty in computer sci. Johns Hopkins U., 1981—. Author: Asymptotic Diophantine Approximation, 1980. Mem. Am. Math. Soc., Math. Assn. Am., Soc. Indsl. and Applied Math., AAAS. Current work: Computational complexity; analysis of algorithms; applications of number theory to signal processing; design of signal processing algorithms for highly concurrent architectures. Subspecialties: Algorithms; Algebra and number theory. Home: 9006 Scotch Pine Ct Columbia MD 21045 Office: System Engring & Devel Corp 9150 Rumsey Rd B-12 Columbia MD 21045

SADUN, ALBERTO CARLO, astrophysicist; b. Atlanta, Apr. 28, 1955; s. Elvio Herbert and Lina (Ottolenghi) S. B.S., MIT, 1977, Ph.D., 1984, postdoctoral 1984; M.S., U. Md., 1979. Dir. Bradley Obs., Agnes Scott Coll., Decatur, Ga., 1984—, asst. prof. astronomy, 1984—. Contbr. articles to profl. jours. Mem. Am. Astronomical Soc., Astronomical Soc. Pacific, Sigma Xi. Democrat. Jewish. Current work: Theoretical and observational studies of active galactic nuclei; quasar jets; high energy extragalactic phenomena.

Subspecialties: Theoretical astrophysics; Optical astronomy. Home: 206 E Davis St Decatur GA 30030 Office: Agnes Scott Coll Decatur GA 30030

SADUN, ALFREDO ARRIGO UMBERTO, neuro-ophthalmologist; b. New Orleans, Oct. 23, 1950; s. Elvio H. and Lina (Ottolenghi) S.; m. Debra Rice, Mar. 18, 1978; children—Rebecca Eli, Elvio Aaron. S.B., M.I.T., 1972; Ph.D., Albert Einstein Med. Sch., 1976, M.D., 1978. Intern Huntington Meml. Hosp., Pasadena, Calif., 1978-79; resident in ophthalmology Harvard U. Med. Sch., Cambridge, Mass., 1979-82, Heed Found. fellow in neuro-ophthalmology, 1982-83, instr., 1983, asst. prof. ophthalmology, 1984. asst. prof. ophthalmology and neurol. surgery U. So. Calif., 1984—; NIH prin. investigator Howe Labs. and Doheny Found., 1982-85. Contbr. articles to profl. jours. Mem. Am. Assn. Anatomists, Soc. for Neurosci., Assn. for Research in Vision and Ophthalmology, Mass. Soc. Eye Physicians and Surgeons. Current Work: Researcher in tracing fiber pathways in the human visual system; neuropathology of human optic nerve. Subspecialties: Ophthalmology; Neuroanatomy. Home: 2070 Robin Rd San Marino CA 91108 Office: Estelle Doheny Eye Found/U So Calif 1355 Sam Pablo St Los Angeles CA 90033

SAEGEBARTH, KLAUS ARTHUR, organic chemist; b. Berlin, Jan. 5, 1929; came to U.S., 1932; s. Eric Otto and Elly Margarete (Hübner) S.; m. Mary Ann Douglass, June 27, 1953; children—Eric Weston, Katherine Ann, Margaret Mary. B.S. in Chemistry, U. Calif.-Berkeley, 1953; Ph.D. in Organic chemistry, U. Wash., 1957. Research chemist E.I. DuPont, Wilmington, Del., 1957-64, devel. supr., Beaumont, Tex., 1964-67, research mgr., lab. dir., Wilmington, 1967-72, dir. sales/mktg., 1972-78, dir. research and devel. div., 1978—. Contbr. articles to profl. jours. Patentee in field. Served with U.S. Army, 1950-52. Mem. Am. Chem. Soc., Sigma Xi, Phi Lambda Upsilon. Republican. Current work: Research and development senior adminstration, agricultural chemicals. Subspecialty: Organic chemistry. Home: 604 Haverhill Rd Wilmington DE 19803 Office: EI DuPont Agrl Chem Dept Barley Mill Plaza WM-1-272 Wilmington DE 19898

SAEVA, FRANKLIN D., chemist, researcher; b. Rochester, N.Y., Nov. 28, 1938; s. John P. and Jean R. (Giuffre) S.; m. Irene M. Masters Apr. 20, 1963; children—Sandra A., Maureen A., Rebecca L. B.S. in Chemistry, Bucknell U., 1960; Ph.D. in Organic Chemistry, SUNY-Buffalo, 1968. Mem. research staff Xerox Corp., Rochester, 1968-79; research assoc. Eastman Kodak Co., Rochester, 1979—; adj. asst. prof., lectr. chemistry U. Rochester, 1973-81. Editor: Liquid Crystals, 1979. Mem. Am. Chem. Soc., Inter-Am. Photochem. Soc. (sec. 1984-86). Subspecialties: Organic chemistry; Photochemistry. Home: 1219 Gerrads Cross Webster NY 14580

SAFARJAN, WILLIAM ROBERT, psychologist; b. Visalia, Calif., Feb. 17, 1943; s. Robert and Alice Joy (Sharp) S.; m. Paula Ann Tinder, May 26, 1978. B.A. in Internat. Relations, U. Calif-Berkeley, 1966; A.B. in Psychology, San Diego State U., 1971, M.A., 1976; Ph.D. in Psychology, Rutgers U., 1980; cert. in clin. psychology Calif. Sch. Profl. Psychology, 1985. Lic. psychologist, Calif. Research asst. San Diego State U., 1971-72, Naval Personnel Research and Devel. Ctr., San Diego, 1972-73, Bell Telephone Lab., Holmdel, N.J., 1977; teaching asst., instr. Rutgers U., New Brunswick, N.J., 1974-78, research intern, 1978-80; exptl. psychologist Porterville (Calif.) State Hosp., 1980-84; clin. psychologist, fellow Atascadero State Hosp., Calif., 1984—. Contbr. articles to sci. publs., also chpts. to books. Served to lt. USN, 1966-69. Mem. Assn. for Advancement of Psychology, Am. Psychol. Assn., Western Psychol. Assn., San Luis Obispo County Psychol. Assn., Delta Sigma Phi. Subspecialties: Developmental psychology; Learning. Office: Atascadero State Hosp PO Box A Atascadero CA 93423

SAFE, STEPHEN HARVEY, environmental science educator, researcher; b. Belleville, Ont., Can., May 14, 1940; s. Benjamin and Doris (Samuels) S.; m. Lorna Margaret Craig, June 2, 1962; children—Sara, Carol. B.Sc., Queen's U., Kingston, Ont., Can., 1962, M.Sc., 1963; D.Phil., Oxford U., 1965. Research assoc. Harvard U., Boston, 1967-68; research officer NRC, Halifax, N.S., Can., 1968-73; to prof. U. Guelph, Ont., Can., 1973—; prof. environ. sci., Tex. A&M U., College Station, 1981-84, disting. prof., 1984—; cons. EPA, NIEHS, Dept. Justice. Author 3 books; contbr. articles to profl. jours. Recipient Queens Jubilee award, 1978; named Queen's Quest Lectr., 1980; commonwealth scholar, 1963. Mem. Soc. Toxicology, Can. Soc. Toxicology, Am. Chem. Soc., Am. Coll. Toxicology, Chem. Inst. Can., Sigma Xi. Current work: Toxicology, environmental sciences, biochemistry. Subspecialties: Environmental toxicology; Toxicology (agriculture). Home: 1207 Charles Ct College Station TX 77840 Office: Vet Physiology and Pharmacology College Station TX 77843

SAFFIOTTI, UMBERTO, pathologist; b. Milan, Italy, Jan. 22, 1928; came to U.S., 1960, naturalized, 1966; s. Francesco Umberto and Maddalena (Valenzano) S.; m. Paola Amman, June 21, 1958; children—Luisa M., Maria Francesca P. M.D. cum laude, U. Milan, 1951, splty. diploma occupational medicine cum laude, 1957. Intern Inst. Pathol. Anatomy, U. Milan, 1951-52; research asst. oncology Chgo. Med. Sch., 1952-54, research asso., 1954-55; asst. to chmn. occupational medicine, chief lab. pathology Inst. Occupational Medicine, U. Milan, 1956-60; fellow Inst. Gen. Pathology, 1957-60; from asst. prof. to prof. oncology Chgo. Med. Sch., 1960-68; mem. staff Nat. Cancer Inst., NIH, Bethesda, Md., 1968—, assoc. dir. carcinogenesis, 1968-76, chief lab. exptl. pathology, 1974—; mem. pathology B study sect. NIH, 1964-68; mem. numerous other cons., govt. agy. advisory coms.; mem. Internat. Union Against Cancer cancer prevention com., 1959-66, panel on carcinogenicity, 1963-66; chmn. ad hoc com. evaluation of low levels of environ. carcinogens HEW, 1969-70. Author, co-author sci. articles, reports; co-editor books. Bd. dirs. Rachel Carson Trust, 1976-79. Recipient Career Devel. award NIH, 1965-68; Superior Service Honor award HEW, 1971; Pub. Interest Sci. award Environ. Def. Fund, 1977; Spl. Recognition award USPHS, 1980. Mem. AAAS, Am. Assn. Cancer Research (pres. Chgo. 1966-67), Am. Assn. Pathologists, European Assn. Cancer Research, N.Y. Acad. Scis., Internat. Commn. Occupational Health, Soc. Occupational and Environ. Health (councillor 1972-76, v.p. 1976-78, pres. 1978-82), Soc. Toxicology, Washington Soc. Pathologists, Sigma Xi. Democrat. Current work: Chemical carcinogenesis; pathology of respiratory tract; environmental and occupational cancer; neoplastic cell transformation. Subspecialties: Cancer research (medicine); Pathology (medicine). Home: 5114 Wissioming Rd Bethesda MD 20816 Office: Lab Exptl Pathology Nat Cancer Inst NIH Bldg 560 Frederick MD 21701

SAFFITZ, JEFFREY ERNEST, pathologist, educator; b. Washington, Mar. 19, 1949; s. Abraham Alan Saffitz and Dorothy Irene (Horowitz) Adler; m. Sharon Epstein, June 13, 1971; children—Emily Lauren, Jane Leslie. B.A., Case Western Reserve, 1971, M.S., 1971, Ph.D., 1977, M.D., 1978. Intern pathology Barnes Hosp., St. Louis, 1978-79, resident in pathology, 1979-82; research fellow in cardiology Washington U., St. Louis, 1979-82; vis. fellow path. br. Nat. Heart, Lung and Blood Inst., NIH, Bethesda, Md., 1982-83; asst. prof. pathology and medicine, Washington U., 1983—. Contbr. articles to profl. publs. Mem. Am. Fedn. Clin. Research, Am. Assn. Pathology. Current work: Experimental cardiovascular pathology. Subspecialties: Pathology (medicine); Cardiology. Office: Washington U 660 S Euclid Ave Saint Louis MO 63110

SAFKO, JOHN LOREN, physics and astronomy educator; b. San Diego, Oct. 29, 1938; s. Loren Edmund and Lillian Mae (Spitzer) Carvaneau; m. Peggy Jean Ferrell, Aug. 21, 1964; children—Tanya, John. B.S., Case Inst. Tech., 1960; Ph.D., U. N.C., 1965. Asst. prof. physics and astronomy U. S.C., Columbia, 1964-70, assoc. prof., 1970-75, prof., 1975—. Author instrs. manual, 1978—; lab. manual, 1978, 82, 85. Mem. Richland County Election Commn., 1978—. Mem. AAAS Am. Astron. Soc., Am. Phys. Soc., Am. Assn. Physics Tchrs., Sigma Xi (pres. 1972-73). Republican. Methodist. Current work: Exact solutions in gravity, observational radio astronomy. Subspecialties: Relativity and gravitation; Radio and microwave astronomy. Home: 3010 Amherst St Columbia SC 29205 Office: Dept Physics and Astronomy Univ SC Columbia SC 29208

SAFLEY, JOHN MARCUS, JR., ecological scientist; b. Milan, Tenn., Jan. 4, 1947; s. John Marcus and Gladys (Williams) S.; m. Mary Kendrick Riley, June 13, 1970; children—Rachel Anne, James Marcus. B.A., Vanderbilt U., 1968; M.S., U. Tenn., 1970, Ph.D., 1974. Biologist U.S. Army C.E., Nashville, 1969-70; resource conservationist Soil Conservation Service, U.S. Dept. Agr., Nashville, 1974-78, program analyst, Washington, 1978-79, environ. specialist, 1979-83, environ. data specialist, 1983-84, asst. dir. ecol. scis. div., 1984—. Contbr. articles to profl. jours. Recipient cert. of merit Soil Conservation Service, 1982. Mem. Ecol. Soc. Am. (sr. ecologist), Am. Inst. Biol. Scis., Soil Conservation Soc. Am., Assn. Southeastern Biologists. Methodist. Current work: Plant community analysis; environmental impact evaluation and analysis; resource conservation and planning. Subspecialties: Resource conservation; Ecosystems analysis. Office: Soil Conservation Service PO Box 2890 Washington DC 20013

SAFRAN, SAMUEL ABRAHAM, physicist; b. N.Y.C., Nov. 22, 1951; s. Joseph and Frida (Stern) S.; m. Marilyn Stern, Aug. 25, 1975; children—Moshe, Hannah. B.A., Yeshiva U., 1973; Ph.D., MIT, 1978. Postdoctoral mem. tech. staff Bell Labs., Murray Hill, N.J., 1978-80; sr. staff physicist Exxon Research & Engring. Co., Clinton, N.J., 1980—; chmn. Internat. Symposium on Complex and Supermolecular Fluids, Annandale, N.J., 1985. Contbr. articles to profl. jours. Mem. Am. Phys. Soc., Am. Chem. Soc. Current work: Condensed matter physics theory; statistical mechanics; microemulsions; micelles; intercalated graphite; kinetics of phase transitions. Subspecialties: Condensed matter physics; Statistical physics. Office: Exxon Research & Engring Co Clinton Township Route 22 E Annadale NJ 08801

SAFRON, SANFORD ALAN, chemistry educator; b. Chgo., July 24, 1941; s. Sol and Helen (Treitman) S.; m. Penny Jane Gilmer, Sept. 9, 1980; children—Helena Marjorie, Nathaniel Steven. B.S., U. Calif.-Berkeley, 1963; M.A., Harvard U., 1965, Ph.D., 1969. Asst. prof. chemistry Fla. State U., Tallahassee, 1970-76, assoc. prof., 1976—. Contbr. articles to chemistry jours. Mem. Am. Chem. Soc. (sec. chpt. 1977), Am. Phys. Soc., AAAS. Current work: Ion/molecule reactions, reactive scattering in crossed molecular beams, models of chemical reaction, atom surface scattering. Subspecialties: Physical chemistry; Atomic and molecular physics. Office: Fla State U Dept Chemistry Tallahassee FL 32306

SAGALYN, PAUL LEON, physicist, researcher; b. N.Y.C., Mar. 21, 1921; s. Ernest Sagalyn and Fanny (Schwartzman) Sagalyn Ress; m. Rita Catherine Callahan, May 20, 1952; children—Michael E., Roger R. B.S., Harvard U., 1942; Ph.D., MIT, 1952. Staff mem. radiation lab. MIT, Cambridge, 1943-45, postdoctoral mem. physics dept., 1952-56; scientist Army Materials and Mechanics Research Ctr., Watertown, Mass., 1956—. Contbr. articles to profl. jours. Patentee in field. Mem. Am. Phys. Soc. (sec., treas. New Eng. sect. 1978-82), Materials Research Soc. Current work: Materials properties modification by ion implantation; characterization of organic and inorganic materials by high resolution liquid and solid state nuclear magnetic resonance. Subspecialties: Materials; Condensed matter physics. Office: Army Materials and Mechanics Research Ctr Watertown MA 02172

SAGAN, CARL EDWARD, astronomer, educator, author; b. N.Y.C., Nov. 9, 1934; s. Samuel and Rachel (Gruber) S.; m. Ann Druyan; children by previous marriages: Dorion Solomon, Jeremy Ethan, Nicholas; 1 dau., Alexandra. A.B. with gen. and spl. honors, U. Chgo., 1954, B.S., 1955, M.S., 1956, Ph.D., 1960; Sc.D. (hon.), Rensselaer Poly. Inst., 1975, Denison U., 1976, Clarkson Coll. Tech., 1977, Whittier Coll., 1978, Clark U., 1978, Am. U., 1980; D.H.L. (hon.), Skidmore Coll., 1976, Lewis and Clark Coll., 1980, Bklyn. Coll., CUNY, 1982; LL.D. (hon.), U. Wyo., 1978. Miller research fellow U. Calif.-Berkeley, 1960-62; vis. asst. prof. genetics Stanford Med. Sch., 1962-63; astrophysicist Smithsonian Astrophys. Obs., Cambridge, Mass., 1962-68; asst. prof. Harvard U., 1962-67; mem. faculty Cornell U., 1968—, prof. astronomy and space scis., 1970—, David Duncan prof., 1976—, dir. Lab. Planetary Studies, 1968—, asso. dir. Center for Radiophysics and Space Research, 1972-81; pres. Carl Sagan Prodns. (Cosmos TV series), from 1977; nonresident fellow Robotics Inst., Carnegie-Mellon U., from 1982; NSF-Am. Astron. Soc. vis. prof. various colls., 1963-67, Condon lectr., Oreg., 1967-68; Holiday lectr. AAAS, 1970; Vanuxem lectr. Princeton U., 1973; Smith lectr. Dartmouth Coll., 1974, 77; Wagner lectr. U. Pa., 1975; Bronowski lectr. U. Toronto, 1975; Philips lectr. Haverford Coll., 1975; Disting. scholar Am. U., 1976; Danz lectr. U. Wash., 1976; Clark Meml. lectr. U. Tex., 1976; Stahl lectr. Bowdoin Coll., 1977; Christmas lectr. Royal Instn., London, 1977; Menninger Meml. lectr. Am. Psychiat. Assn., 1978; Carver Meml. lectr. Tuskegee Inst., 1981; Feinstone lectr. U.S. Mil. Acad., 1981; Pal lectr. Motion Picture Acad. Arts and Scis., 1982; Dodge lectr. U. Ariz., 1982; other hon. lectureships. Author: Atmospheres of Mars and Venus, 1961, Planets, 1966, Intelligent Life in the Universe, 1966, Planetary Exploration, 1970, Mars and the Mind of Man, 1973, The Cosmic Connection, 1973, Other Worlds, 1975, The Dragons of Eden, 1977, Murmurs of Earth: The Voyager Interstellar Record, 1978, Broca's Brain, 1979, Cosmos, 1980; also numerous articles; editor: Icarus: Internat. Jour. Solar System Studies, 1968-79, Planetary Atmospheres, 1971, Space Research, 1971, UFO's: A Scientific Debate, 1972, Communication with Extraterrestrial Intelligence, 1973; editorial bd.: Origins of Life, from 1974, Icarus, from 1962, Climatic Change, from 1976, Science 80, 1979-82. Mem. various adv. groups NASA and Nat. Acad. Scis., 1959—; mem. council Smithsonian Instn., from 1975; vice chmn. working group moon and planets, space orgn. Internat. Council Sci. Unions, 1968-74; lectr. Apollo flight crews NASA, 1969-72; chmn. U.S. del. joint conf. U.S. Nat. and Soviet Acads. Sci. on Communication with Extraterrestrial Intelligence, 1971; responsible for Pioneer 10 and 11 and Voyager 1 and 2 interstellar messages; judge Nat. Book Awards, 1975; mem. fellowship panel Guggenheim Found., from 1976. Recipient Smith prize Harvard U., 1964; NASA medal for exceptional sci. achievement, 1972; Prix Galabert, 1973; John W. Campbell Meml. award, 1974; Klumpke-Roberts prize, 1974; Priestley award, 1975; NASA medal for disting. public service, 1977, 81; Pulitzer prize for lit., 1978; Washburn medal, 1978; Rittenhouse medal, 1980; Peabody award, 1981; Hugo award, 1981; Seaborg prize, 1981; Roe medal, 1981; NSF fellow, 1955-60; Sloan research fellow, 1963-67. Fellow AAAS (chmn. astronomy sect. 1975), Am. Acad. Arts and Scis., AIAA, Am. Geophys. Union (pres. planetology sect. 1980-82), Am. Astronautical Soc. (council 1976-81, Kennedy Astronautics award 1984), Brit. Interplanetary Soc., Explorers Club (75th Anniversary award 1980); mem. Am. Phys. Soc., Am. Astron. Soc. (councillor, chmn. div. for planetary scis. 1975-76), Fedn. Am. Scientists (council 1977-81), Am. Com. on East-West Accord, Soc. Study of Evolution, Genetics Soc. Am., Internat. Astron. Union, Internat. Acad. Astronautics, Internat. Soc. Study Origin of Life (council from 1980), Planetary Soc. (pres. from 1979), Authors Guild, Phi Beta Kappa, Sigma Xi. Current Work: Research on physics and chemistry of planetary atmospheres and surfaces, origin of life, exobiology, spacecraft observations of planets. Subspecialties: Cosmology; Planetary science. Address: Space Sci Bldg Cornell Univ Ithaca NY 14853

SAGE, ANDREW PATRICK, JR., engineering educator; b. Charleston, S.C., Aug. 27, 1933; s. Andrew Patrick and Pearl Louise (Britt) S.; m. LaVerne Galhouse, Mar. 3, 1962; children: Theresa Annette, Karen Margaret, Philip Andrew. B.S. in Elec. Engring, The Citadel, 1955; S.M., MIT, 1956; Ph.D., Purdue U., 1960. Registered profl. engr., Tex. Instr. elec. engring. Purdue U., 1956-60; asso. prof. U. Ariz., 1960-63; mem. tech. staff Aerospace Corp., Los Angeles, 1963-64; prof. elec. engring. and nuclear engring. scis. U. Fla., 1964-67; prof., dir. Info. and Control Scis. Center, So. Methodist U., Dallas, 1967-74, head elec. engring. dept., 1973-74; Quarles prof. engring. sci. and systems U. Va., Charlottesville, 1974-84, chmn. dept. chem. engring., 1974-75, chmn. dept. engring. sci. and systems, 1977-84, assoc. dean, 1974-80; First Am. Bank prof. info. tech. George Mason U., Fairfax, Va., 1984—, assoc. v.p. acad. affairs, 1984-85, dean Sch. Info. Tech. and Engring., 1985—; cons. Martin Marietta, Collins Radio, Atlantic Richfield, Tex. Instruments, LTV Aerospace, Battelle Meml. Inst., TRW Systems, NSF, Analytic Scis. Corp., Engring. Research Assocs., Inst. Def. Analyses; gen. chmn. Internat. Conf. on Systems, Man and Cybernetics, 1974; mem. spl. program panel on system sci. NATO, 1981-82. Author: Optimum Systems Control, 1968, 2d edit., 1977, Estimation Theory with Applications to Communications and Control, 1971, System Identification, 1971, An Introduction to Probability and Stochastic Processes, 1973, Methodology for Large Scale Systems, 1977, Systems Engineering: Methodology and Applications, 1977, Linear Systems Control, 1978, Economic Systems Analysis, 1983; asso. editor: IEEE Transactions on Systems Sci. and Cybernetics, 1968-72; editor: IEEE Transactions on Systems, Man and Cybernetics, 1972—; assoc. editor: Automatica, 1968-81; editor, 1981—; editorial bd.: Systems Engring, 1968-72, IEEE Spectrum, 1972-73, Computers and Electrical Engineering, 1972—, Jour. Interdisciplinary Modeling and Simulation, 1976-80; Control Theory and Advanced Technology, 1984—, Jour. Intelligent Machines, 1985—; editor Elsevier North Holland textbook series in system sci. and engring., Matrix Press textbook series on circuits and systems, 1976—; co-editor-in-chief: Jour. Large Scale Systems: Theory and Applications, 1978—; contbr. articles on mgmt. sci. and systems engring. to profl. jours. Recipient Frederick Emmonds Terman award Am. Soc. for Engring. Edn., 1970; M. Barry Carlton award IEEE, 1970; also Norbert Wiener award; Case Centennial scholar, 1980. Fellow IEEE, AAAS; mem. IEEE Systems Man and Cybernetics Soc. (pres. 1984-85), Inst. Mgmt. Scis., Am. Soc. for Engring. Edn., Am. Inst. Decision Sci., Internat. Inst. Forecasting, Ops. Research Soc. Am., Sigma Xi, Eta Kappa Nu, Tau Beta Pi. Current Work: Design of decision support systems; expert system and intelligent data base research; management science. Subspecialties: Systems engineering; Artificial intelligence. Home: 8011 Woodland Hills Ln Fairfax Station VA 22039

SAGE, GLORIA WELT, research environmental chemist; b. Bklyn., Mar. 7, 1936; d. Harold L. and Syd (Colin) W.; m. Martin L. Sage, June 15, 1958; 1 child, Daniel. A.B., Cornell U., 1957; A.M., Radcliffe Coll., 1958; Ph.D., Harvard U., 1963. Instr., research assoc. U. Oreg., Eugene, 1961-67; research assoc. Syracuse U., N.Y., 1967-70; research assoc. SUNY-Upstate Med. Ctr., Syracuse, 1970-72, 76-77, asst. prof., 1972-76; research assoc. Tel Aviv U., Israel, 1977-78; cons. Radiation Tech. Inc., Rockaway, N.J., 1978-80; research assoc. Syracuse Research Corp., 1980—. Contbr. articles to profl. jours. Mem. Am. Chem. Soc., AAAS, Assn. Harvard Chemists. Current work: Data base development, assessment of environmental fate of chemicals. Subspecialties: Environmental chemistry; Physical chemistry. Home: 1217 Jamesville Ave Syracuse NY 13210

SAGGIOMO, ANDREW JOSEPH, chemist, administrator; b. Phila., Mar. 20, 1931; s. Angelo and Ernestine Agatha (Iannelli) S.; m. Dolores Durelli, June 27, 1953; children—Andrew Joseph, Michael, David. B.A., LaSalle Coll., 1952; M.A., Temple U., 1954, postgrad., 1954-56. Research fellow Research Inst. (now Germantown Labs.), Temple U., Phila., 1953-56, sr. research chemist, 1956-61, project dir. 1961-80, v.p., 1972-80; adminstrv. mgr. Franklin Research Ctr., Phila., 1980—, mgr. quality assurance, 1982—; dir. Germantown Labs., Inc. Contbr. articles on organic and medicinal chemistry to profl. jours. Patentee in field. Mem. Am. Chem. Soc., Am. Soc. Quality Control. Roman Catholic. Current work: Psychopharmacological agents, antimalarial drugs; research in fluorine chemistry, medicinals, organometallics, dyes, PCB removal. Subspecialties: Organic chemistry; Medicinal chemistry. Home: 1817 Schley St Philadelphia PA 19145 Office: Franklin Research Ctr 20th and Race Sts Philadelphia PA 19103

SAH, CHIH-TANG, engineering and physics educator; b. Peking, China, Nov. 10, 1932; came to U.S., 1949, naturalized, 1962; s. Pan-tung and Sushen (Huang) S.; m. Linda Chang; children—Dinah, Robert. B.S. in Engring. Physics, U. Ill., 1953, M.S.E.E., 1953; M.S.E.E., Stanford U., 1954, Ph.D., 1956; D. honoris causa, U. Leuven, Belgium, 1975. Sr. mem. tech. staff Shockley Transistor Corp., Palo Alto, Calif., 1956-59; head, mgr. physics dept. Fairchild Semicondr. Lab., Palo Alto, 1959-64; prof. physics, prof. elec. engring., dir. Solid State Electronics Lab., U. Ill., Urbana, 1963—; sr. ptnr. C.T. Sah Assocs., Urbana, 1973—; cons., researcher in field. Patentee in field. NSF grantee, 1980, 83; named to 1000 Most Cited Scientists, Sci. Info. Survey, 1981. Fellow Am. Phys. Soc., IEEE; mem. Nat. Research Council. Current work: Reliability physics, chemistry and metallurgy of silicon VLSI transistors and VLSI conductors, semiconductors deep level physics, solar cells and applications. Subspecialties: Semiconductors; Integrated circuits. Office: Elec Engring Dept U Ill 1406 W Green St Urbana IL 61801

SAHA, BIDHAN CHANDRA, physicist, researcher; b. Rangunia, Bangladesh, Sept. 29, 1946; came to U.S., 1981, naturalized, 1985; s. Chinta Haran and Charu Bala Saha; m. Krishna Saha, June 29, 1979; 1 child, Paban. B.Sc., Dacca U., Bangladesh, 1966; M.Sc., Rajshahi U., Bangladesh, 1969; Ph.D., Calcutta U., India, 1976. Postdoctoral fellow I.A.C.A., Jadavpur, Calcutta, 1976-78; research scientist Flinders U. South Australia, Adelaide, 1979-80; research assoc. Yale U., New Haven, 1981, U. Okla., Norman, 1982—. Contbr. articles to profl. jours. Mem. Am. Phys. Soc. Current work: Quantum collision theory of electrons, atoms and molecules; three-body rearrangement processes; Rydberg states. Subspecialties: Atomic and molecular physics; Theoretical physics. Office: Dept Physics and Astronomy U Okla 440 W Brooks Norman OK 73019

SAHA, SUBRATA, bioengineering educator; b. Kushtia, India, Nov. 2, 1942; came to U.S., 1968, naturalized, 1976; s. Jaladhar K. and Sushama S.; m. Pamela Sunday, Oct. 30, 1972; children: Sunil, Supriya. B.S., Calcutta U., 1963; M.S., Tenn. Tech. U., 1969; Ph.D., Stanford U., 1973. Engr. cons. firms, 1963-67; research and teaching asst. Tenn. Tech. U., Cookeville, 1968-69, Stanford U., 1969-74; asst. prof. Yale U., 1974-79; assoc. prof., coordinator bioengring. La. State U. Med. Ctr., Shreveport, 1979-84, prof., coordinator bioengring. dept. orthopedic surgery, 1984—; conf. chmn. So. Biomed. Engring. Conf. 1982, 86. Contbr. numerous articles to nat. and internat. jours.; also abstracts. Recipient Research Career Devel. award NIH, 1978-83, U.S.-India Exchange Scientist award, 1978; Fulbright award, 1982; Engring. Achievement of year award, 1985. Mem. ASME, Soc. Exptl. Stress Analysis, Soc. Biomaterials, Orthopaedic Research Soc., Biomed. Engring. Soc., Am. Soc. Biomechanics, ASCE, Am. Acad. Mechanics, IEEE, AAAS, Am. Inst. Ultrasound in Medicine, Sigma Xi. Current Work: Biomedical engineering, ultrasound in medicine, bioelectrical stimulation. Subspecialties: Biomedical engineering; Biomedical engineering. Home: 7601 Old Spanish Trail Shreveport LA 71105 Office: Dept Orthopaedic Surgery La State U Med Ctr PO Box 33932 Shreveport LA 71130

SAHELY, CAMILLE, computer company executive; b. El-Kefeir, Lebanon, Mar. 5, 1931; came to U.S., 1962; s. Albert and Zahia (El-Hage) S.; m. Venice C. Cahaly, Oct. 24, 1964; children—Alexander, Nadia, Colette, Stephanie. B.S. in Indsl. Chemistry, Ecole Superieure des Arts et Metiers, 1953; postgrad. in chem. engring. Latrobe U., 1955-57, Cin. U., 1963-64, Babson Coll., 1978-79, MIT-Sloan Sch. Mgmt., 1982. Research and devel. chemist Dubois Chem. Co., Cin., 1962-64, P.A. Hunt Chem. Co., Lincoln, R.I., 1964-66, Shipely Co., Newton, Mass., 1966-68; sr. prin. engr. Honeywell Info. Systems, Billerica, Mass., 1968-74; tech. dir. Astro Circuit Co., Tewksbury, Mass., 1974-76; prin. engr. Data Gen., Southboro, Mass., 1976-77; mgr. external tech. tracking Digital Equipment Corp., Maynard, Mass., 1977—. Patentee in field. Mem. IEEE Computer Soc. (tech. com. on packaging 1979—), Internat. Soc. for Hybrid Microelectronics, IEEE Elec. Computer Conf. (packaging com. 1984—), Internat. Elec. Packaging Soc. (chmn. 1982), Am. Chem. Soc., Royal Australian Chem. Inst. Greek Orthodox. Current work: Computer technology-technology trends, technology tracking and application, long range planning 2-10 years, packaging/interconnect technologies for supercomputers, mainframes, medium and low-end systems. Subspecialties: Computer engineering; Materials (engineering). Home: 61 Ivy Rd Wellesley MA 02181

SAHNI, OMESH, research scientist; b. Lahore, Jan. 15, 1940; came to U.S., 1969; s. Chaman and Vimla (Rathore) S.; m. Tiia Taks, June 17, 1970; 1 dau., Sarita Lea. M.S., Banaras Hindu U., Varanasi, India, 1960; M.E.E., Indian Inst. Tech., Bombay, 1962; Ph.D., Rennselaer Poly. Inst., 1972. Lectr. Indian Inst. Tech., Bombay, 1963-67; research assoc. Ctr. Nuclear Studies, AEC, Saclay, France, 1967-68; Lab. Plasma Physics, U. Paris, Orsay, 1968-69; research and teaching asst. electrophysics div. Rensnselaer Poly. Inst., Troy, N.Y., 1969-72; mem. research staff IBM, Watson Research Ctr., Yorktown Heights, N.Y., 1972—. Contbr. articles to sci. jours. Mem. IEEE, Am. Phys. Soc., Soc. Info. Disply, Sigma Xi (treas. 1978-79, v.p. 1979-80, pres. chpt. 1980-81). Patentee I/O technologies. Current Work: Physics and technology of information display and non-impact printing devices. Subspecialties: Information systems, storage, and retrieval (computer science); Electron devices. Home: Box 47 RFD Hanover St Yorktown Heights NY 10598 Office: IBM Watson Research Center Yorktown Heights NY 10598

SAHU, SAURA CHANDRA, biochemist, researcher, cons., educator; b. Cuttack, India, June 29, 1944; came to U.S., 1966, naturalized, 1978; s. Gopinath and Ichhamoni S.; m. Jharana Sahu, May 29, 1966; children: Meghamala, Sudhir, Subir. M.S. (faculty fellow), Columbia U., 1967; Ph.D., U. Pitts., 1971. Research asso. Mich. State U., East Lansing, 1971-72, C.F. Kettering Research Lab., Yellow Springs, Ohio, 1972-74; asst. research prof. Duke U. Med. Center, Durham, N.C., 1974-79; research biochemist Health Scis. Labs., Consumer Product Safety Commn., Washington, 1979—, cons., in field. Contbr. articles on lung biochemistry to sci. jours. Govt of India Atomic Energy fellow, 1964-66; India Found. Scholar, 1966. Mem. Am. Soc. Biol. Chemists, Am. Soc. Pharmacology and Exptl. Therapeutics, Soc. Complex Carbohydrates, Soc. Toxicology, N.Y. Acad. Scis. Current Work: Lung biochemistry; inhalation toxicology; structure, function and metabolic activity of the lung. Subspecialty: Biochemistry (medicine). Home: 13321 Kurtz Rd Woodbridge VA 22193 Office: Health Scis Labs Consumer Product Safety Commn 200 C St SW Washington DC 20204

SAHYUN, MELVILLE RICHARD VALDE, physical chemist; b. Santa Barbara, Calif., Feb. 11, 1940; s. Melville and Geraldine (Valde) S.; m. Irene

Marie Nordquist; children—Steven C., Michael N. A.B., U. Calif.-Santa Barbara, 1959; Ph.D. UCLA, 1963. Sr. asst. scientist USPHS, Bethesda, Md., 1962-65; research assoc. Calif. Inst. Tech., Pasadena, 1965-66; sr. chemist 3M Imaging Research, St. Paul, 1966-70, research specialist, 1970-74, sr. research specialist, 1974-81; staff scientist 3M Central Research, St. Paul, 1981—. Mem. editorial bd. Jour. Imaging Tech., 1974—; contbr. articles to profl. jours. Patentee in field. Active Indianhead council Boy Scouts Am., 1978—. Fellow Soc. Photog. Scientists and Engrs.; mem. Am. Chem. Soc., Royal Soc. Chemistry. Current work: Photophysics, imaging processes, photoassisted catalysis. Subspecialties: Photochemistry; Kinetics. Office: 3M Central Research 3M Center 201-2E-04 Saint Paul MN 55144

SAI-HALASZ, GEORGE ANTHONY, physicist; b. Budapest, Hungary, Dec. 7, 1943; came to U.S., 1967, naturalized, 1973; s. Anthony F. and Margit T. (Tabar) S.; m. Martha Judith Magy, Jan. 9, 1971; 1 child, Christine. Diploma in Physics, Roland Eotvos U., Budapest, 1966; Ph.D. in Physics, Case Western Res. U., 1972. Research assoc. Case Western Res. U., Cleve., 1968-72; postdoctoral fellow U. Pa., Phila., 1972-74; mem. research staff IBM T.J. Watson Research Ctr., Yorktown Heights, N.Y., 1974-84, research mgr., 1984—. Contbr. articles to profl. publs. Patentee semicondr. tech. Mem. Am. Phys. Soc., IEEE (sr.). Current work: Physics and technology of microchip miniaturization. Subspecialties: Condensed matter physics; Microchip technology (engineering). Home: 26 Timber Ridge Mount Kisco NY 10549 Office: IBM TJ Watson Research Ctr Yorktown Heights NY 10598

SAIIDI, MEHDI, civil engineering educator and researcher, structural engineering consultant; b. Tehran, Iran; came to U.S., 1975; s. Ramazan Saiidi and Mansoureh (Karimbeck) Karimbeck; m. Sohila Bemanian, Aug. 12, 1977; 1 child, Dustin. M.S., Tehran U., 1973; M.S., U. Ill., 1977, Ph.D., 1979. Registered profl. engr., Nev., Calif. Structural engr. Nisaia Cons. Engrs., Tehran, 1972-75; research asst. U. Ill.-Urbana, 1977-79; asst. prof. U. Nev.-Reno, 1979-83, assoc. prof., 1983—; cons. various firms, 1979—. Contbr. articles to profl. jours. Mem. ASCE, Am. Concrete Inst., Earthquake Engrs. Research Inst. Current work: Earthquake engineering of buildings and bridges; computer aided design; reinforced concrete structures. Subspecialties: Civil engineering; Computer-aided design. Home: 3780 Tannenbaum Way Reno NV 89509 Office: Civil Engr Dept U Nev Reno NV 89557

SAILER, REECE IVAN, entomology educator, researcher; b. Roseville, Ill., Nov. 8, 1915; s. Ethan Calvin and Ruth Millicent (Coghill) S.; m. Jessie Marie Bradbury, Sept. 7, 1939; children—Sigrid Eileen, Enid Louise. B.A., Kans. U., 1938, Ph.D., 1942. Diplomate Am. Registry Profl. Entomologists. Assoc. entomologist Bur. Entomology and Plant Quarantine, USDA, Washington, 1942-48, entomologist, 1948-53; entomologist Entomol. Research div. Agrl. Research div. USDA, Washington, 1953-57; asst. dir. Insect Identification Parasite Introduction Research br. Agrl. Research Service, Beltsville, Md., 1957-60, chief, 1967-76, chmn., 1972-73; research entomologist in charge European Parasite Lab USDA, Nanterre, France, 1960-66; grad. research prof. U. Fla., Gainesville, 1973—; lectr. U. Md., College Park, 1952-60; adj. prof. N.C. State U., Raleigh, 1968-73. Contbr. articles to profl. jours. Recipient Sr. Faculty award Merit Gamma Sigma Delta, 1981. Fellow AAAS; mem. Am. Inst. Biol. Sci., Entomol. Soc. Am. (pres. 1977), Entomol. Soc. Washington (pres. 1958), Ecol. Soc. Am. Democrat. Current work: Biological control of insect pests important in Florida; inbreeding depression as a measure of genetic load. Subspecialty: Taxonomy. Home: 3847 SW 6th Pl Gainesville FL 32607 Office: Dept Entomology and Nematology U Fla Gainesville FL 32611

SAINATI, STEPHEN MITCHELL, physician, neuroscientist; b. Chgo., Nov. 28, 1952; s. Bruno and Margaret Arlene (Cook) S.; m. Deanna Dawn Olson, Jan. 2, 1982; children—Tatiana Elizabeth. B.A., Vanderbilt U., 1974; Ph.D., Loyola U., 1983, M.D., 1985. Research asst. Loyola U., Chgo., 1982-84; fellow Mayo Clinic, Rochester, Minn., 1985—; reviewer Pharmacology Biochemistry and Behavior, Fayetteville, N.Y., 1980-83. Arthur J. Schmitt Found. fellow, 1982; pre-clinical research fellow Loyola U., 1981. Mem. AMA, N.Y. Acad. Scis., AAAS, Soc. Neurosci., Am. Numis. Assn., Can. Numis. Assn., Alpha Omega Alpha. Current work: Behavioral correlates of activity of central nervous system GABA, benzodiazepine and monoaminergic neurotransmitter systems. Subspecialties: Neurology; Neurophysiology. Home: 625 19th St NW Apt 204 Rochester MN 55901 Office: Mayo Grad Sch Medicine Mayo Clinic Rochester MN 55905

ST. CLAIR, ANNE KING, chemist, researcher; b. Bluefield, W.Va., May 31, 1947; d. Otis Gardner and Mayble Isabel (Lawrence) King; m. Terry Lee St. Clair, Dec. 28, 1971; 1 child, Tyler Lawrence. B.A. in Chemistry, Queens Coll., 1969; grad. student honors program Argonne Nat. Lab., 1969; M.S. in Chemistry, Va. Poly. Inst. and State U., 1972. Research assoc. Va. Poly. Inst. and State U./NASA, Hampton, 1972-77; aerospace technologist NASA-Langley Research Ctr., Hampton, 1977-82, sr. research scientist, 1982—. Contbr. articles to profl. jours., chpts. to books. Patentee in field. Recipient IR-100 award Indsl. Research and Devel., Chgo., 1981; Outstanding Research Paper award, 1982; named Inventor of Yr., NASA-Langley Research Ctr., 1981. Mem. Assn. Women in Sci., Am. Chem. Soc., Soc. for Advancement of Materials, Process and Engring. (editorial rev. bd. jour. 1981—, speakers bur., 1981—), Phi Lambda Upsilon. Republican. Presbyterian. Current work: High performance polymers for applications on advanced aircraft and spacecraft-includes synthesis and development of polymers for structural composites, adhesives, films and coatings. Subspecialties: Polymer chemistry; Polymers (materials science). Home: 17 Roberts Landing Dr Poquoson VA 23662 Office: NASA-Langley Research Ctr Mail Stop 226C Hampton VA 23665

ST. CLAIR, RICHARD WILLIAM, pathology educator, atherosclerosis researcher; b. Sioux Falls, S.D., Oct. 10, 1940; s. Ralph and Dorothy Jane (Niendorf) St. C.; m. F. Jeanne Peterson, May 21, 1940; children—David William, Daniel James. B.S. in Animal Nutrition, Colo. State U., 1962, Ph.D., 1965. NIH fellow Bowman Gray Sch. Med., Wake Forest U., Winston-Salem, N.C., 1965-67, asst. prof. pathology, 1967-71, assoc. prof., 1971-76, prof., 1976—; mem. program com. V Internat. Symposium on Atherosclerosis, 1979—; mem. council on Arteriosclerosis Am. Heart Assn., 1969, program com., 1975-77, assembly del., 1980—, mem. program com., 1981-84, mem. pathology research study com. 1972-74, chmn. program com. council on arteriosclerosis, 1985—; mem. research com. N.C. Heart Assn., 1969-72, chmn. research com. 1971-72, mem. med. and community programs com., 1970-71, bd. dirs., 1976-79; bd. dirs. Forsyth County Heart Assn., 1970-77, chmn. med. and community programs com., 1973-75; mem. ad hoc com. for Non-Divisible Restricted Gifts for research devel. N.C. Affiliate Am. Heart Assn., 1981-82, mem. research com., 1983—; mem. research rev. com. B, NIH, 1978-82, chmn., 1981-82. Contbr. articles to profl. jours., chpts. to books. Bd. dirs. Central YMCA, Winston-Salem, 1974—; trustee Nature Sci. Ctr. Forsyth County, N.C., 1978-81; chmn. program com. Met. YMCA, Winston-Salem, 1981-85. Named established investigator Am. Heart Assn., Dallas, 1970-75; recipient Gold Service Recognition medal N.C. Heart Assn., 1977. Mem. AAAS, Am. Soc. Exptl. Biology and Med., Tissue Culture Assn., Sigma Xi, Phi Kappa Phi, Beta Beta Beta. Republican. Episcopalian. Current work: Pathobiology of atherosclerosis; studies with animal models (nonhuman primates and pigeons); lipoprotein cell interactions. Subspecialties: Pathology (medicine); Cell biology (medicine). Office: Bowman Gray Sch Med Wake Forest U 300 S Hawthorne Rd Winston-Salem NC 27103

ST. GEORGE, GEORGE MICHAEL, research chemist; b. Evanston, Ill., Mar. 20, 1956; s. George Quirico and Alice Catherine (Beaton) St. G. S.B., MIT, 1976; Ph.D., U. Ill., 1982. Research asst. MIT, Cambridge, Mass., 1976; research fellow and asst. U. Ill., Urbana, 1976-82, teaching asst., 1976-81; sr. research chemist Dow Chem. Co., Freeport, Tex., 1981—. Contbr. articles to profl. jours. Composer marches, polkas. Fellowship leader The Way Internat., Champaign, Ill., Lake Jackson, Tex., 1979-84. Nat. Merit scholar, 1973; named Outstanding Young Man Am., 1984. Mem. Am. Chem. Soc. Club: Community Band (Lake Jackson). Current work: Organometallic/inorganic chemistry, cluster chemistry; Friedel-Crafts catalysis and polymer chemistry. Subspecialties: Inorganic chemistry; Organic chemistry. Home: 312 Redwood St Lake Jackson TX 77566 Office: Dow Chem USA B-1214 Bldg Freeport TX 77541

ST. JOHN, BILL, geologist, business executive; b. Wink, Tex., July 27, 1932; s. Mackie Doyle and Anne Elizabeth (Ker) St. J.; children—Michael E., Tad S., Kevin G., W. Doyle. B.S. in Geology, U. Tex., 1958, M.A., 1960, Ph.D., 1965. Survey field worker Tex. Bur. Econ. Geology, 1960; regional subsurface and field studies geologist Am. Overseas Petroleum, Ltd., Libya, Mauritania, 1960-63; field mapper Underground Atomic Explosion Detection Agy., 1963; prodn. geologist Humble Oil Co., Andrews, Tex., and offshore New Orleans, 1965-66; mem. North Sea Study Group, Esso Exploration Co., 1966, 68-69, mem. Global Studies Group, 1971-73; well-site geologist Esso Exploration Norway, offshore Norway and Morocco, 1966-68; mem. staff offshore geology div. Esso Prodn. Research Co., Houston, 1969-71; chief frontier geologist, mgr. internat. ops. LVO Corp., 1973-74, v.p., mgr. exploration, 1974-78; exec. v.p., chief operating officer Agri-Petco Internat., Inc., Tulsa, 1978-80, pres., chief exec. officer, 1980-81; pres., chief exec. officer Primary Fuels, Inc., Houston, 1981—, also dir. Author profl. publs. Served with USMC, 1951-54, Korea. Mem. Am. Assn. Petroleum Geologists (program chmn. Wallace E. Pratt Meml. Conf. 1984), Am. Geophys. Union, Am. Petroleum Inst., Am. Gas Assn., Geol. Soc. Am., Houston Geol. Soc., Ind. Petroleum Assn. Am., Tex. Ind. Producers and Royalty Owners Assn. Current work: Sedimentary basins of the world; giant oil and gas fields of the world; plate tectonics as related to basin formation and occurences of oil and gas. Subspecialties: Geology; Tectonics. Office: Primary Fuels Inc PO Box 569 Houston TX 77001

ST. LOUIS, ROBERT VINCENT, chemistry educator, researcher; b. Los Angeles, Dec. 13, 1932; s. Vincent Theodore and Eileen Alena (Mattson) St. L.; m. Nadine Margaret Small, July 30, 1960; 1 child, Paula Leigh. B.S., UCLA, 1954; Ph.D., U. Minn., 1962. Research assoc. Johns Hopkins U., Balt., 1962-63; research chemist U.S. Borax Research Corp., Anaheim, Calif., 1963-66; research assoc. U. So. Calif., Los Angeles, 1966-68; prof. chemistry U. Wis.-Eau Claire, 1968—. Patentee in field. Served with U.S. Army, 1954-56. Dow Chem. fellow, 1957. Mem. Am. Chem. Soc., Am. Phys. Soc., Soc. Applied Spectroscopy. Club: Indianhead Track (Eau Claire) (pres. 1975-76). Current work: Applications of microcomputers in physical chemistry and in science education; spectroscopy of dispersed systems; instrumentation; solvent effects. Subspecialties: Physical chemistry; Surface chemistry. Office: Dept Chemistry U Wis Eau Claire WI 54701

ST. OMER, VINCENT EDMUND VICTOR, vet. pharmacologist, educator; b. Castries, St. Lucia, W.I., Nov. 16, 1934; s. Victor and Josephine M. (Laurent) St. O.; m. Margaret Moran Muir, May 5, 1962; children: Ingrid, Denise, Jeffrey, Raymond. D.V.M., U. Toronto, Ont., Can., 1962; M.Sc., U. Man., Winnipeg, Can., 1965; Ph.D., U. Guelph, Ont., 1969. Pvt. vet. practice, 1962-63; research assoc. Bur. Child Research. U. Kans., 1968-71; asst. prof. vet. pharmacology Kans. State U., 1972-74; assoc. prof. Coll. Vet. Medicine, U. Mo., Columbia, 1974-84, prof., 1984—; assoc. prof. Sch. Medicine, U. Mo., Columbia, 1974—; adj. prof. physiology and cell biology U. Kans., 1970-83; cons., researcher neurotoxicology, devel. toxicology, behavioral teratology. Contbr. articles to profl. jours., chpts. in books. Recipient numerous research grants, 1970—. Fellow Am. Acad. Vet. Pharmacology and Therapeutics; mem. Soc. Neurosci., Research Workers in Animal Disease, N.Y. Acad. Sci., Am. Animal Hosp. Assn. Roman Catholic. Club: Optimist. Current Work: Devel., neurobehavioral and neurochem. toxicology, devel. toxicology, behavioral toxicology, vet. pharmacology, neurotoxicology, neurochemistry, environ. toxicology, neuropharmacology. Subspecialty: Neurochemistry. Home: 2504 Mallard Ct Columbia MO 65201 Office: Dept Vet Biomed Scis U Mo Columbia MO 65211

SAINT-AMAND, PIERRE, earth scientist, educator; b. Tacoma, Feb. 4, 1920; s. Cyrias Zephyr and Mable (Berg) S.; m. Marie Poss, Dec. 9, 1945; children—Gene Pierre, Barbara Michelle, Denali Marie, David C.H. B.S., U. Alaska, 1949; M.S., Calif. Inst. Tech., 1951, Ph.D. in Geophysics, Geology, 1953. Geophys. observer Carnegie Inst. Wash., Coll. Alaska, 1939-41; mem. U. Alaska Geophysical Obs., College, 1945-49; research assoc. Seismological Lab. Calif. Inst. Tech., Pasadena, 1951-53; physicist Naval Ordnance Test Station, Pasadena and China Lake, Calif., 1954-57; prof. geology U. Chile with U.S. Embassy, Santiago, 1957-61; fed. exec. Naval Weapons Ctr., China Lake, Calif., 1961-84; adj. prof. geology U. Nev., Reno, 1978—; adj. prof. atmospheric sci. U. N.D., 1984; cons. UN, Argentina, Chile, Mex., Orgn. Am. States, World Bank, Phillipine, Rhodesian and Italian agencies and numerous others. Contbr. articles to profl. jours.; editor books. Dir. Am. Field Service, 1962-63, Maturango Mus. 1963-64, Desert Counselling Clinic, 1965-67; pres. Coll. Community Assn., Alaska, 1947; bd. dirs. Ridgecrest Community Hosp., Indian Wells Valley Airport Dist. Served with U.S. Army, 1941-46. Recipient Disting. Service award USN, 1967, Disting. Pub. Service award Fed. Exec. Bd., 1976, L.T.E. Thompson award Naval Weapons Ctr., 1973, Thunderbird award Weather Modification Assn., 1972, Spl. award Phillipine Air Force, Ridgecrest Community Hosp., Recognition in Congl. Record, 1984; Fulbright scholar to France, 1954. Fellow Geol. Soc. Am., AAAS, Earthquake Engring. Research Assn.; mem. Seismol. Soc. Am., Weather Modification Assn., Gt. Basin Found. (hon. life), Sigma Xi. Clubs: Sister Cities Assn., Footprints Internat. (dir. 1984). Lodge: Rotary (pres. 1978). Current work: Cons. in geology, geophysics, weather modification and disaster investigation, especially earthquakes. Subspecialties: Weather modification; Geology. Home: 1800 Blueridge Rd Ridgecrest CA 93555 Office: Office Tech Dir Code 013 Naval Weapons Ctr China Lake CA 93555

SAIRAM, MALUR RAMASWAMY, institute administrator, medical educator; b. Bangalore, India, Jan. 10, 1943; came to Can., 1974; s. M. L. Ramaswamy Iyengar and Yadugiri R. Sairam; m. Jayashree G.N., Apr. 9, 1969; children—Ashwin M., Charith M. B.Sc., Central Coll., Bangalore, 1961, M.Sc., 1963; Ph.D., Indian Inst. Sci., Bangalore, 1969. Research fellow Indian Inst. Sci., Bangalore, 1963-69; postgrad. research biochemist U. Calif.-San Francisco, 1969-71, asst. research biochemist, 1971-74; dir. Reprodn. Research Lab., Clin. Research Inst. of Montreal, Que., Can., 1974—; assoc. mem. physiology dept. McGill U., Montreal, 1979—, research dir. exptl. medicine 1979—; assoc. prof. dept. Medicine U. Montreal, 1979-85, prof., 1985—; mem. task forces Human Reproduction Research WHO, Geneva, 1979-83. Contbr. articles to profl. jours. Mem. Endocrine Soc. U.S., Soc. for Study of Reprodn. U.S., AAAS, Am. Soc. Biol. Chemists U.S., N.Y. Acad. Scis., Can. Biochem. Soc. Hindu. Current work: Gonadotropic hormones, pituitary, placenta, biochemistry, physiology, mechanism of action, reproductive biology, contraception. Subspecialties: Reproductive biology (medicine); Reproductive endocrinology. Office: Reproduction Research Lab Clin Research Inst of Montreal 110 Pine Ave W Montreal PQ H2W 1R7 Canada

SAJDEL-SULKOWSKA, ELIZABETH MARIA, biochemist, educator, researcher; b. Warsaw, Poland, May 2, 1944; came to U.S., 1962; d. Adolf and Jozefa (Klepa) Sajdel; m. Adam Sulkowski, Oct. 28, 1972; children—Adam Jozef, Gregory Michael, Victor Amadeusz. B.S., MIT, 1967, M.S., 1969, D.Sc., 1972. NIH trainee MIT, 1969-72, teaching asst., 1971; research fellow in surgery Harvard U. Med. Sch. and Mass. Gen. Hosp., Boston, 1976-78; asst. in biochemistry Shriner Burns Inst. and Mass. Gen. Hosp., 1978-79; vis. fellow McLean Hosp., Belmont, Mass., 1980-82, asst. biochemist, 1982—; lectr. psychobiology Harvard U. Med. Sch., Boston, 1980-83, instr., 1983—; acting prin. investigator Shriners Burns Inst., Boston, 1977; thesis advisor Harvard Coll., Boston, 1978. Leader, Boy Scouts Am., Sudbury, Mass., 1982-84; tchr. Our Lady of Fatima Ch., Sudbury, 1982—. Mem. Am. Soc. for Cell Biology, Soc. for Neurosci., AAAS. Roman Catholic. Current work: Regulation of RNA and protein metabolism in brain during normal aging and in Alzheimer's disease. Subspecialties: Cell biology (medicine); Neurochemistry. Office: McLean Hosp Mailman Research Ctr 115 Mill St Belmont MA 02178

SAKAGUCHI, RONALD LOUIS, dental researcher; b. Los Angeles, Aug. 3, 1955; s. Louis and Hatsy S. B.S., UCLA, 1976; D.D.S., Northwestern U. Chgo., 1980; M.S. in Prosthodontics, U. Minn., 1984. Research asst. biol. chemistry UCLA, 1973-76; researcher Am. Dental Assn., Chgo., 1977—; staff dentist Chgo. Osteo. Med. Ctr., 1980-82; instr. prosthodontics U. Minn., 1982—, research assoc., 1984—; cons. Research Triangle Inst., 1981, Pediatric and Adolescent Comprehensive Care Program, Chgo., 1981-82; dental examiner, coordinator Little Village Health Fair, Chgo., 1980-82, Kosminski Sch., Chgo., 1982, Chgo. Dental Soc., 1981. Research grantee Northwestern U., 1979. Mem. Am. Assn. Dental Research, Internat. Assn. Dental Research, Am. Coll. Prosthodontists, Minn. Assn. Prosthodontists, Xi Psi Phi. Current Work: Relationship of practice characteristics to urinary mercury levels in dentists, acoustic transmission and systems analysis of joint function; simulation and modelling of occlusion, friction and wear of natural and prosthetic dental materials. Subspecialties: Prosthodontics; Biomedical engineering. Office: School of Dentistry University of Minnesota 515 Delaware St SE Minneapolis MN 55455

SAKITA, BUNJI, physics educator, theoretical physicist; b. Inami, Japan, June 6, 1930; came to U.S., 1956; s. Eiichi and Fumi (Morimatsu) S.; children—Mariko, Taro. B.S., Kanazawa U. (Japan), 1953; M.S., Nagoya U. (Japan), 1956; Ph.D., U. Rochester (N.Y.), 1959. Postdoctoral assoc. U. Wis., Madison, 1959-62, asst. prof., 1962-64, prof., 1966-70; assoc. physicist Argonne Nat. Lab. (Ill.), 1964-66, cons., 1966-70; disting. prof. dept. physics CCNY, 1970—; vis. prof. IHES, Bures-sur-Yvette, France, 1970-71, Ecole Normale Superieur, Paris, 1979-80. Fellow Guggenheim Found., 1970-71, Japan Soc. for Promotion of Sci., 1975, 80; recipient Nishina Meml. Found. prize, 1974. Fellow Am. Phys. Soc. Current work: Quantum field theory, application of quantum field theory to particle physics and statistical physics. Subspecialties: Theoretical physics; Particle physics. Home: 7002 Blvd East Apt 34E Guttenberg NJ 07093 Office: Dept Physics CCNY 138 St and Convent Ave New York NY 10031

SAKOVER, RAYMOND PAUL, radiologist; b. Chgo., Oct. 8, 1944; s. Max and Maria Adele (Berardi) S.; m. Patricia Ellyn Taylor, June 7, 1969; children: Shelley, Michael, David, Raymond. M.D., U. Ill.-Chgo., 1969. Diplomate: Am. Bd. Radiology, Nat. Bd. Med Examiners. Intern St. Francis Hosp., Evanston, Ill., 1969-70, resident in radiology, 1970-73; radiologist Riverside Radiology Med. Group, Calif., 1975—; pres. Computerized Diagnostic Med. Group, Riverside, 1979-82. Bd. dirs. Riverside Humane Soc., 1981-83. Served to lt. comdr. USNR, 1973-75. Mem. Am. Coll. Radiology, Soc. Nuclear Medicine, AMA, Calif. Med. Assn., Riverside County Med. Assn. (mediation com. 1982—), Am. Lung Assn. (dir. Riverside County chpt. 1976-83). Republican. Roman Catholic. Club: Rotary (Magnolia Center, Calif.). Subspecialties: Radiology; Radiology in nuclear medicine. Office: 6941 Brockton Ave Riverside CA 92506

SALADINI, JOHN LOUIS, research biologist; b. Detroit, Feb. 13, 1946; s. John and Elaine (Bogardus) S. B.A. with high honors, W.Va. U., Morgantown, 1968; M.S., U. Fla., Gainesville, 1971; Ph.D., Ohio State U., Columbus, 1976. Research biologist E. I. duPont de Nemours & Co. (Expt. Sta.), Wilmington, Del., 1976-78, research and devel. rep., Denver, 1979-83. Served to capt. Chem. Corps. USAR, 1971. Mem. Am. Phytopath. Soc., Entomol. Soc. Am., Weed Sci. Soc. Am., Phi Beta Kappa, Phi Kappa Phi. Republican. Presbyterian. Current Work: Product development for cereal and fallow herbicides. Subspecialty: Agrichemicals. Home: 2612 Stephenson Dr Wilmington DE 19808 Office: DuPont Co Agrichems Dept BRML 38/3-186 Wilmington DE 19898

SALAFSKY, BERNARD P., pharmacology educator, administrator, researcher; b. Chgo., Dec. 27, 1935; s. M.B. Salafsky and Jeanette (Pritikin) B.; m. Marilyn Ritchie, June 18, 1961; children—Joshua, Daniel, David. B.S. in Pharmacy, Phila. Coll. Pharmacy and Sci., 1958; M.S. in Pharmacology, U. Wash., 1961, Ph.D., 1962. Instr., U. Wash. Sch. Medicine, Seattle, 1962-64; from asst. to assoc. prof. U. Ill. Coll. Medicine, Chgo., 1964-70; adj. assoc. prof. U. Pa., Phila., 1970-72; prof. WHO, Geneva, 1973-75; prof. pharmacology U. Ill.-Rockford, 1977—. Mem. Local Devel. Corp., Rockford, 1983—, Community Hosp. Council, Rockford, 1983—. Fulbright fellow, 1968; spl. fellow Muscular Dystrophy Assn., 1973. Fellow Royal Soc. Tropical Medicine and Hygiene; mem. Am. Soc. Pharmacology and Exptl. Therapy, Am. Soc. Tropical Medicine and Hygiene, AAAS. Current work: Pharmacology, schistosomiasis. Subspecialties: Pharmacology; Tropical medicine. Office: Univ Ill Coll of Medicine-Rockford 1601 Parkview Ave Rockford IL 61101

SALAMA, KAMEL, mechanical engineering educator; b. Sohag, Egypt, Apr. 1, 1932; came to U.S., 1966, naturalized, 1973; s. Salama Mishriky and Faiza (Salama) Bibawy; m. Gwendolyn Doucet, July 17, 1971; children—Emilie, Joseph. B.Sc. with honors, Cairo U., 1951, M.Sc., 1955, Ph.D., 1959. Research assoc. Uppsala U., Sweden, 1962-64; lectr. Cairo U., 1960-65; research cons. Ford Sci. Lab., Dearborn, Mich., 1966-68; sr. research scientist Rice U., Houston, 1968-73; assoc. prof. mech. engring. U. Houston, 1973-78, prof., 1978—, dir. materials engring. Coll. Engring., 1979—. Contbr. articles to profl. jours. Recipient Acad. Engring. Wallenberg Found. research award, Sweden, 1983; grantee NSF, Office Naval Research, Air Force Office Sci. Research, Electric Power Research Inst., 1974—. Mem. Am. Phys. Soc., Am. Soc. for Metals, Metall. Soc. of AIME. Current work: Materials science and engineering-nondestructive evaluation. Subspecialties: Materials; Metallurgy. Home: 13818 Kimberley Houston TX 77079 Office: Dept Mech Engring Coll Engring Univ Houston Houston TX 77004

SALAMA, MAMDOUH M., mechanical engineer, researcher; b. Cairo, Feb. 11, 1945; s. Mohamed I. and Soria B. (Samour) S.; m. Nadia El-Khosht; children: Yasmine, Kareem, Mohammed. B.Sc., Ain shams U., Cairo, 1966, M.Sc., 1969; S.M., MIT, 1971, Mech.E., 1972, Sc.D., 1976. Research asst. MIT, 1970; with Stone & Webster Engring., Boston, 1972-77; dir. marine and materials sect. petroleum research and devel. dept. Conoco, Inc., Ponca City, Okla., 1977—. Contbr. articles to profl. jours. Mem. ASME, Am. Welding Soc., ASTM, Soc. Petroleum Engrs. Republican. Moslem. Current Work: Research activities related to oil production and offshore developments. Subspecialties: Fracture mechanics; Metallurgy. Home: 400 Wren Dr Ponca City OK 74601 Office: Conoco Inc Ponca City OK 74603

SALAME, MORRIS, physical chemist; b. Jacksonville, Fla., June 18, 1932; s. Theodore and Rebecca (Saban) S.; m. Marjorie Anne Innes, June 30, 1957; children—Karen, Laurie. S.B. in Chem. Engring., MIT, 1960. Research asst. Cryovac Corp., Cambridge, 1957-60; chemist Monsanto Co., Bloomfield, Conn., 1960-62, group leader, 1963-70, mgr., 1970-81, Monsanto sr. fellow, 1981—. Contbr. articles to sci. jours. Patentee in field. Inventor Permachor, method of permeability prediction, 1967. Mem. Am. Chem. Soc. (chmn. polymer chemistry com. on intersoc. relationships, 1980-83), AAAS. Republican. Unitarian. Club: Exchange (pres. 1982) (Windsor, Conn.). Current work: Permeability and diffusion through polymers, new polymer developments, food packaging, food/polymer interactions, high barrier polymers, polymer physics. Subspecialties: Polymer chemistry; Polymers (materials science). Office: Monsanto Co 101 Granby St Bloomfield CT 06002

SALAMON, MYRON BEN, physicist; b. Pitts., June 4, 1939; s. Victor William and Helen (Sanders) S; m. Sonya M. Blank, June 12, 1960; children—David. Aaron. B.S., Carnegie Mellon U., 1961; Ph.D., U. Calif.-Berkeley, 1966. NSF postdoctoral fellow Inst. Solid State Physics, Tokyo, 1966, vis. prof., 1972; asst. prof., assoc. prof., then prof. physics U. Ill., Urbana, 1967—; dir. NSF Materials Research Lab., 1984—; vis. prof. Tech. U. Munich, Fed. Republic Germany, 1974-75, U. Grenoble/CNRS, France, 1982-83. Co-editor: Modulated structures, 1975; editor: Physics of Superionic Conditions, 1979. Contbr. articles to profl. publs. Recipient U.S. Sr. Scientist award A. von Humboldt Found., 1974-75; A.P. Sloan fellow, 1971-73. Fellow Am. Phys. Soc.; mem. AAAS. Current work: Phase transitions and critical phenomena in solid state materials, disorder and randomness in materials, charge density wave phenomena. Subspecialties: Condensed matter physics; Magnetic physics. Office: Dept Physics U Ill 1110 W Green Urbana IL 61801

SALAMONE, JOSEPH CHARLES, polymer chemist, consultant, educator; b. Bklyn., Dec. 27, 1939; s. Joseph John and Angela S. B.S. in Chemistry, Hofstra U., 1961; Ph.D. in Chemistry, Poly. Inst. Bklyn., 1966. NIH postdoctoral fellow U. Liverpool, Eng., 1966-67; research assoc. U. Mich., 1967-70; asst. prof. dept. chemistry Lowell (Mass.) Technol. Inst., 1970-73, assoc. prof., 1973-76; assoc. prof. dept. chemistry U. Lowell, 1973-76, prof., 1976—, chmn. dept., 1975-78; dean U. Lowell (Coll. Pure and Applied Sci.), 1978-84. Mem. editorial bd. Polymer, Jour. Macromolecular Science and Chemistry; adv. bd. Jour. Polymer Sci.; Contbr. numerous articles on polymer chemistry to sci. jours. Mem. Am. Chem. Soc. (divs. polymer chemistry, polymoric materials sci. and engring., chmn. div. polymer chemistry 1982). Current Work: Synthesis of new monomers and polymers, particularly ionic systems; properties of polyelectrolytes. Subspecialty: Biomaterials. Home: Dept Chemistry U Lowell North Campus Lowell MA 01854

SALAMUN, PETER J(OSEPH), botanist, educator, consultant; b. La Crosse, Wis., June 12, 1919; s. Peter and Melana (Hardi) S.; m. Lorraine Anne Saurman, June 6, 1946; children: Mary Salamun Conrad, Elizabeth Alice, Charles Peter, William Mark, Edward Joseph, David Robert, Lawrence George, Katherine Anne. B.S., Wis. State Tchrs. Coll., 1941; M.S., U. Wis., Madison, 1947, Ph.D., 1950. Instr. biology Wis. State Coll. (now U. Wis.), Milw., 1948-51, assoc. prof., 1951-56, prof. botany, 1957-85, prof. emeritus, 1985—, chmn dept., 1957-61, dir. herbarium, 1966-84, cons. Contbr. articles to sci. jours. Served in USAF, 1941-45, CBI. Recipient AMOCO Teaching award, 1976. Mem. AAAS, Am. Inst. Biol. Scis., Am. Meteorol. Soc., Am. Soc. Plant Taxonomists, Bot. Soc. Am., Ecol. Soc. Am., Internat. Assn. Plant Taxonomy, Nature Conservancy, Soc. Study of Evolution, Wis. Acad. Sci., Sigma Xi. Roman Catholic. Current work: Floristics of vascular plants of Wisconsin; vegetational analysis of the Lake Michigan shoreline. Subspecialties: Taxonomy; Ecology (environmental science). Home: 5013 N Elkhart Ave Whitefish Bay WI 53217 Office: U Wis-Milw LAP 450 Milwaukee WI 53201

SALANE, DOUGLAS EDWARD, research mathematician; b. Bklyn., July 10, 1952; s. Edward Peter and Helen Ann (Serravalle) S. B.A. in Math., CUNY-Queens Coll., 1976; M.S. in Applied Math., SUNY-Stony Brook, 1978, Ph.D. in Applied Math., 1981. Research mathematician Exxon Research and Engring. Co., Linden, N.J., 1981-83, Sandia Nat. Labs., Albuquerque, 1983—. Mem. Am. Math. Assn., Soc. Indsl. and Applied Math., Computer Soc. IEEE, Assn. for Computing Machinery. Current work: Computational mathematics; computer modelling and simulation. Subspecialties: Numerical analysis (mathematics); Mathematical software.

SALANS, LESTER BARRY, physician, educator; b. Chicago Heights, Ill., Jan. 25, 1936; s. Leon K. and Jean (Rudnick) S.; m. Lois Audrey Kapp, Dec. 21, 1958; children—Laurence Eliot, Andrea Eileen. B.A., U. Mich., 1957; M.D. with honors, U. Ill., 1961. Internal medicine intern Stanford U. Med. Center, 1961, resident, 1962-64; USPHS postdoctoral and spl. fellow Rockefeller U., 1964-67, asst. prof., 1967-68; asst. prof. medicine Dartmouth Coll., 1968-70, assoc. prof., 1970-77, adj. prof., 1977-84; assoc. dir. diabetes, endocrinology, metabolism, also chief lab. cellular metabolism and obesity Nat. Inst. Arthritis, Metabolism and Digestive Diseases, NIH, Bethesda, from 1976; dir. Nat. Inst. Arthritis, Diabetes, Digestive and Kidney Diseases, NIH, 1982-84; mem. dept. medicine Mt. Sinai Sch. Medicine, N.Y.C., 1984—; v.p. preclinical research Sandoz Research Inst.; vis. prof. U. Geneva, Switzerland, 1974-75. Contbr. articles on insulin, diabetes mellitus, obesity to profl. jours., textbooks. Recipient NIH Research Career Devel. award, 1972-76, NIH Dirs. award, 1980, Juvenile Diabetes Fedn. Pub. Service award, 1979. Fellow ACP; Mem. Am. Soc. Clin. Investigation, Am. Fed. Clin. Research, Am. Diabetes Soc., Endocrine Soc., Assn. Am. Physicians, AAAS, Harvey Soc., Am. Soc. Clin. Nutrition. Subspecialty: Endocrinology. Office: Sandoz Research Inst Route 10 East Hanover NJ 07936

SALANT, ABNER SAMUEL, laboratory director; b. Cin., Mar. 18, 1930; s. Jacob and Ida (Levine) S.; m. Priscilla F. Erlichman, Sept. 14, 1952; children—David, Harold, Sharon. B.A., N.Y.U., 1950; Ph.D., Rutgers U., 1953. Assoc. technologist Gen. Foods Corp., Hoboken, N.J., 1953-56; project leader Tenco div. Coco-Cola, Linden, N.J., 1956-62; project mgr. Monsanto Co., St. Louis, 1962-68, v.p. Flavor/Essence div., N.Y.C., 1968-75; dir. food engring. lab. U.S. Army Natick Research and Devel. Ctr., Natick, Mass., 1976—. Fellow N.Y. Acad. Scis., Am. Inst. Chemists; mem. Am. Chem. Soc., AAAS, Inst. Food Technologists, Sigma Xi, Phi Lambda Upsilon. Current work: Food, packaging, process, food service equipment, food service systems, market/business development, venture management. Subspecialties: Food science and technology; Systems engineering. Home: 35 Norwich Rd Wellesley Hills MA 02181 Office: US Army Natick Research and Devel Ctr Kansas St Natick MA 01761

SALARI, EZZATOLLAH, computer and electrical engineering educator; b. Shahi, Mazandran, Iran, Mar. 28, 1952; came to U.S., 1976; s. Shaban and Norjis (Ahmadi) Salarieh; m. Diane Kathleen Monaco, June 18, 1978; 1 child, Rustam. B.S.E.E., Iran Coll. Sci. and Tech., 1974; M.S. in Elec. and Computer Engring., Wayne State U., 1978, Ph.D. in Elec. and Computer Engring., 1982. Elec. engr. Iranian Nat. Steel Corp., Isfahan, 1974-76; grad. asst. Wayne State U., Detroit, 1979-82; asst. prof. dept. computer and info. sci. Cleve. State U., 1982-85; asst. prof. dept. elec. engring. U. Toledo, 1985—. Served to 2nd lt. Iranian Army, 1974-76. Mem. IEEE, Am. Assn. Artificial Intelligence. Current work: Shape analysis and representation including skeletonization, symmetry, and shape decomposition. Subspecialty: Graphics, image processing, and pattern recognition. Home: 4654 Tamworth Sylvania OH 43560 Office: Dept Elec Engring U Toledo Toledo OH 43606

SALCMAN, MICHAEL, neurol. surgeon, educator, researcher; b. Pilsen, Czechoslovakia, Nov. 4, 1946; s. Arthur and Edith (Atlas) S.; m. Ilene, July 27, 1969; children: Joshua, Dara. B.A., M.D., Boston U., 1969. Diplomate: Am. Bd. Neurol. Surgeons, 1978, Nat. Bd. Med. Examiners, 1970. Intern in surgery Boston U. Med. Center, 1969-70; research assoc. Nat. Inst. Neurol. Diseases, NIH, Bethesda, Md., 1970-72; resident in neurosurgery Neurol. Inst. N.Y., Columbia U., N.Y.C., 1972-76; asst. prof. neurol. surgery U. Md. Sch. Medicine, Balt., 1976-79, assoc. prof., 1979-84, chief neurooncology, 1978—, prof., chmn. neurosurgery, 1984—; dir. Neurotrauma Ctr., Md. Inst. Emergency Med. Services, 1984—. Author: Neurologic Emergencies; assoc. editor: Neurosurgery, 1982; Contbr. articles to sci. jours. Served with USPHS, 1970-72. Recipient award Lange Med. Pub., 1966; Nat. Eye Inst. grantee, 1972-78; Am. Cancer Soc. grantee, 1978-80; Nat. Inst. Neurol. and Communicative Disorders and Stroke grantee, 1980-82, 82-84. Mem. Washington Print Club, Friends of Modern Art (pres. 1984-86), Balt. Mus. Art, Print and Drawing Soc. Balt. Mus. Art.; Fellow ACS; mem. Am. Assn. Neurol. Surgeons, AMA, Assn. Acad. Surgeons, Research Soc. Neurol. Surgery, Soc. Univ. Neurosurgeons, AAAS, Am. Physiol. Soc., ASME, Assn. Advancement Med. Instrumentation, IEEE, N.Y. Acad. Sci., Soc. Neurosci., Congress Neurol. Surgeons (sec. 1983-86), Begg Soc., Phi Beta Kappa, Alpha Omega Alpha. Jewish. Patentee chronic microelectrode; co-developer microwave hyperthermia for brain; DMSO. Current Work: Multimodality attack on malignant brain tumors using computer-controlled microwave hyperthermia, computer-guided radiation sources, polychemotherapy facilitated by drug opening of the blood-brain barrier, development of model brain tumors in animals and monoclonal antibodies to same; analysis of cat visual cortex neuron firing patterns; interaction of biomedical engineering and clinical neurosurgery. Subspecialties: Oncology; Neurobiology. Home: 5501 St Alban's Way Baltimore MD 21212 Office: 22 S Greene St Baltimore MD 21201

SALEH, BAHAA E. A., electrical engineering educator, consultant; b. Cairo, Sept. 30, 1944; B.S., Cairo U., 1966; Ph.D., Johns Hopkins U., 1971. Asst. prof. U. Santa Catarina, Brazil, 1971-74; research asst. Max Planck Inst., Göttingen, Fed. Republic Germany, 1974-76; mem. faculty U. Wis., Madison, 1977—, prof. elec. engring., 1981—. Author: Photoelectron Statistics, 1978. Topical editor Jour. Optical Soc. Am., 1983—. Contbr. articles to profl. jours. Guggenheim fellow, 1984-85. Fellow Optical Soc. Am.; mem. IEEE. Subspecialties: Optical engineering; Optical image processing. Home: 2909 Brandon Rd Madison WI 53719 Office: Dept Elec and Computer Engring Univ Wis 1415 Johnson Dr Madison WI 53706

SALENSKY, GEORGE, chemical engineer; b. N.Y.C., July 2, 1925; s. Isaac and Anna S.; m. Rita Velten, Sept. 22, 1953; children—Marianne, Kathryn. B.Chem. Engring., Poly. Inst. N.Y., 1945, M.Chem. Engring., 1947. Chem. engr. Keystone Varnish Co., Bklyn., 1945-48, Philip A. Hunt Co., Palisades Park, N.J., 1948-54; tech. dir., v.p. Gusmer Coatings, Inc., Woodbridge, N.J., 1954-63; sr. devel. scientist Union Carbide Corp., Bound Brook, N.J., 1963—; mem. Ph.D. examiners com. Lehigh U., Bethlehem, Pa., 1980-84. Patentee in field. Mem. Am. Chem. Soc., Nat. Assn. Corrosion Engrs., Sigma Xi, Tau Beta Pi, Phi Lambda Upsilon. Current work: Corrosion control, epoxy resins for electronics, surface studies, interface modifiers for adhesion enhancement, liquid and powder coatings, reactive polymer systems. Subspecialties: Materials; Corrosion. Home: RD 3 Scrabbletown Rd Whitehouse Station NJ 08889 Office: Union Carbide Corp PO Box 670 Bound Brook NJ 08805

SALERNO, JACK PETER, electronic materials scientist; b. Bklyn., Dec. 25, 1954; s. Gaspare and Mary Winifred (Gallo) S.; m. Mary Elizabeth Cross, Dec. 29, 1981. B.A., Ohio Wesleyan U., 1976; M.S., Vanderbilt U., 1978; Ph.D., MIT, 1983. Sr. mem. tech. staff GTE Labs. Inc., Waltham, Mass., 1982-85; tech. mgr. Kopin Corp., Taunton, Mass., 1985—; lectr. continuing edn. Northeastern U., Boston, 1983—. Patentee compensating semiconductor materials; contbr. articles to profl. jours. Mem. IEEE, Electrochem. Soc., Am. Assn. Crystal Growth, Sigma Xi, Pi Mu Epsilon. Current work: Preparation and characterization of electronic materials and devices, current emphasis on molecular beam epitaxy of semiconductor heterostructures. Subspecialties: Electronic materials; Microchip technology (materials science). Office: Kopin Corp 695 Myles Standish Blvd Taunton MA 02780

SALES, BRIAN CRAIG, physicist; b. Durham, N.C., Dec. 19, 1947; s. Reames Hawthorne and Elenore C. (Catlip) S.; m. Kathleen Alice Cleveland, Dec. 8, 1974; children—Mark Allen, David Hawthorne. B.S. in Physics, Carnegie Mellon U., Pitts., 1969; Ph.D., U. Calif.-San Diego, 1974. Research staff mem. Solid State div. Oak Ridge Nat. Lab., 1981—; research physicist U. Cologne, W.Ger., 1975-76; postgrad. research physicist U. Calif.-San Diego, 1976-78, asst. research physicist, 1978-81. Contbr. articles to profl. jours. Recipient award for significant implication for energy tech. in solid state physics Dept. Energy, 1984; IR-100 award, 1985; named Inventor of Yr., Martin-Marietta Energy Systems, 1985. Mem. Am. Phys. Soc., Materials Research Soc., Phi Kappa Phi. Current work: Properties and structure of phosphate and silicate glasses, oscillatory chemical reactions, low temperature properties of rare earch compounds, the coupling of bulk phase transitions to surface reactions, superconducting materials, fractals. Subspecialties: Condensed matter physics; Materials. Home: 869 W Outer Dr Oak Ridge TN 37830 Office: Oak Ridge Nat Lab Bldg 2000 Solid State Div Oak Ridge TN 37831

SALGANICOFF, LEON, pharmacologist, educator, cons.; b. Buenos Aires, Argentina, Sept. 11, 1924; came to U.S., 1964, naturalized, 1977; s. Marcos and Ana (Zelicson) S.; m. Matilde Saffier, Apr. 12, 1957; children: Alina, Marcos. D.Sc., U. Buenos Aires, 1955. Cert. Argentine Bd. Clin. Biochemistry. Vis. prof. Johnson Found., U. Pa., Phila., 1964-68; assoc. prof. dept. pharmacology Temple U. Sch. Medicine, Phila., 1968-76; pharmacology sect. leader Temple U. Sch. Medicine (Thrombosis Research Ctr.), 1972-82, prof. pharmacology, 1976—; vis. prof. dept. gen. pathology U. Rome, 1977—, NATO vis. prof., 1982. Contbr. articles to profl. jours. Mem. Am. Soc. Pharmacology and Exptl. Therapeutics, AAAS. Current Work: Physiology and pharmacology of activated platelets; cyclic adenosin monophosphate and calcium control of contractile function. Subspecialties: Cellular pharmacology; Molecular pharmacology. Home: 6409 N 11th St Philadelphia PA 19126 Office: 3F Pharmacology Temple U 3400 N Broad St Philadelphia PA 19140

SALINGAROS, NIKOS ANGELOS, mathematical physicist; b. Perth, Australia, Jan. 1, 1952; came to U.S. 1967, naturalized, 1982; s. Stelios Salingaros and Chryssoula Pierson. B.Sc. cum laude U. Miami, Coral Gables, Fla., 1971; M.A., SUNY-Stony Brook, 1974, Ph.D., 1978. Asst. prof. physics U. Mass., Boston, 1979-80, U. Crete, Iraklion, Greece, 1980-81; asst. prof. math. U. Iowa, Iowa City, 1981-83, U. Tex., San Antonio, 1983—. Editor: Hadronic Jour.; referee: Jour. Math. Physics, Foundations of Physics, Phys. Rev. Letters; reviewer Zentralblatt fur Mathematik. Contbr. articles to profl. jours. Mem. Am. Phys. Soc., Am. Math. Soc., Internat. Assn. Math. Physics, Math. Assn. Am. Greek Orthodox. Current work: Algebraic descriptions of nature, field theory, motion of charged particles, symmetries of elementary particles. Subspecialty: Theoretical physics. Home: 611 Mason St San Antonio TX 78208 Office: Div Math Computer Sci Systems Design U Tex San Antonio TX 78285

SALISBURY, JOHN WILLIAM, geoscientist; b. Palm Beach, Fla., Feb. 6, 1933; s. John William Salisbury and Mary Francis (Bates) Massey; m. Lynne Marie Trowbridge, June 7, 1957; children—John William, Matthew Trowbridge. B.A., Amherst Coll., 1955; M.S., Yale U., 1957, Ph.D., 1959. Research scientist Air Force Cambridge Research Labs., Bedford, Mass., 1959-61, br. chief remote sensing, 1961-76; br. chief geothermal energy U.S. Dept. Energy, Washington, 1976-78, dep. div. dir., 1978-80, div. dir., 1980-81; dir. Eros program U.S. Geol. Survey, Reston, Va., 1981-83, research scientist remote sensing, 1983—; vis. prof. Purdue U., Lafayette, Ind., 1964-66; guest lectr. Am. Mus.-Hayden Planetarium, N.Y.C., 1966-76; cons. CBS, N.Y.C., 1969-71, NASA, Washington, 1964—. Editor: The Lunar Surface Layer, 1964. Contbr. articles to profl. jours. Served to 1st lt. USAF, 1959-61. Fellow Geol. Soc. Am.; mem. Am. Geophys. Union, AAAS, Phi Beta Kappa, Sigma Xi. Current work: Research on visible near infrared and mid infrared spectral behavior of minerals and rocks with emphasis on development of remote sensing techniques for determination of rock type and location of mineral deposits. Subspecialties: Remote sensing (geoscience); Geothermal power. Home: 5529 Coltsfoot Ct Columbia MD 21045 Office: US Geol Survey MS 927 Reston VA 22092

SALISBURY, TAMARA PAULA, foundation research administrator, chemist; b. N.Y.C., Dec. 14, 1927; d. Paul Terrance and Nadine (Korolkoff) Voloshin; m. Franklin C. Salisbury; children—Franklin, John, Elizabeth, Elaine, Claire. B.A., Coll. Notre Dame, Balt., 1948. Technician, Army Inst. Pathology, Washington, 1942-46; research asst. Nat. Cancer Inst., Bethesda, Md., 1948-52; project officer Office Naval Research, Washington, 1952-55; dep. dir., co-founder Nat. Found. for Cancer Research, Bethesda, Md., 1974—. Past bd. dirs. Washington chpt. ARC. Decorated Order of Leopold II (Belgium); recipient award Internat. Soc. Quantum Biology, 1983. Mem. Am. Chem. Soc. Republican. Episcopalian. Current work: Research administration. Home: 10811 Alloway Dr Potomac MD 20854 Office: Nat Found for Cancer Research 7315 Wisconsin Ave Bethesda MD 20814

SALK, JONAS EDWARD, physician, scientist; b. N.Y.C., Oct. 28, 1914; s. Daniel B. and Dora (Press) S.; m. Donna Lindsay, June 8, 1939; children: Peter Lindsay, Darrell John, Jonathan Daniel; m. Francoise Gilot, June 29, 1970. B.S., CCNY, 1934, LL.D. (hon.), 1955; M.D., NYU, 1939, Sc.D. (hon.), 1955; LL.D. (hon.), U. Pitts., 1955; Ph.D. (hon.), Hebrew U., 1959; LL.D. (hon.), Roosevelt U., 1955; Sc.D. (hon.), Turin U., 1957, U. Leeds, 1959, Hahnemann Med. Coll., 1959, Franklin and Marshall U., 1960; D.H.L. (hon.), Yeshiva U., 1959; LL.D. (hon.), Tuskegee Inst., 1964. Fellow in chemistry NYU, 1935-37, fellow in exptl. surgery, 1937-38, fellow in bacteriology, 1939-40; Intern Mt. Sinai Hosp., N.Y.C., 1940-42; NRC fellow Sch. Pub. Health, U. Mich., 1942-43, research fellow epidemiology, 1943-44, research asso., 1944-46, asst. prof. epidemiology, 1946-47; asso. research prof. bacteriology Sch. Medicine, U. Pitts., 1947-49, dir. virus research lab., 1947-63, research prof. bacteriology, 1949-55, Commonwealth prof. preventive medicine, 1955-57, Commonwealth prof. exptl. medicine, 1957-63; dir. Salk Inst. Biol. Studies, 1963-75, resident fellow, 1963-84, disting. prof. in internat. health scis., 1984—, founding dir., 1975—; developed vaccine, preventive of poliomyelitis, 1955, cons. epidemic diseases sec. war, 1944-47, sec. army, 1947-54; mem. commn. on influenza Army Epidemiol. Bd., 1944-54, acting dir. commn. on influenza, 1944; mem. expert adv. panel on virus diseases WHO; adj. prof. health scis., depts. psychiatry, community medicine and medicine U. Calif., San Diego, 1970—. Author: Man Unfolding, 1972, The Survival of the Wisest, 1973, (with Jonathan Salk) World Population and Human Values: A New Reality, 1981, Anatomy of Reality, 1983; Contbr. sci. articles to jours. Decorated chevalier Legion of Honor France, 1955, officer, 1976; recipient Criss award, 1955, Lasker award, 1956, Gold medal of Congress and presdl. citation, 1955, Howard Ricketts award, 1957, Robert Koch medal, 1963, Mellon Inst. award, 1969; Presdl. medal of Freedom, 1977; Jawaharlal Nehru award for internat. understanding, 1976. Fellow A.A.A.S., Am. Pub. Health Assn.; asso. fellow Am. Acad. Pediatrics (hon.); mem. Am. Coll. Preventive Medicine, Am. Acad. Neurology, Assn. Am. Physicians., Soc. Exptl. Biology and Medicine, Am. Soc. Clin. Investigation, Am. Assn. Immunologists, Am. Epidemiol. Soc., Phi Beta Kappa, Alpha Omega Alpha, Delta Omega. Office: Salk Inst Biol Studies PO Box 85800 San Diego CA 92138

SALMOIRAGHI, GIAN CARLO, scientist; b. Gorea, Minore, Italy, Sept, 19, 1924; came to U.S., 1952, naturalized, 1958; s. Giuseppe Carlo and Dina (Rinetti) s.; m. Eva Tchoukourlieva, Dec. 5, 1970; 1 child, George Charles. M.D., U. Rome, 1948; Ph.D., McGill U., 1959. Sr. med. officer Internat. refugee Orgn., Naples, Italy, 1949-52; research fellow Cleve. Clinic Found., 1952-55; lectr. dept. physiology McGill U., Montreal, Que., Can., 1956-58; from neurophysiologist to dir., div. spl. mental health research NIMH, Washington, 1959-73; assoc. commr. research N.Y. State Dept. Mental Hygiene, Albany, 1973-77; assoc. dir. research Nat. Inst. Alcohol Abuse and Alcoholism, HHS, Bethesda, Md., 1977-84; prof. neurology and physiology Hahnemann U., Phila., 1984—, vice provost research affairs, 1984—; clin. prof. psychiatry George Washington U., 1966-73. Contbr. articles to profl. jours. Recipient Superior Service award HEW, 1970. Fellow Am. Coll. Neuropsychopharmacology; mem. AAAS, Am. Physiol. Soc., Am. Soc. Pharmacology and Exptl. Therapeutics, Internat. Brain Research Orgn., Internat. Soc. Psychoneuroendocrinology, Soc. for Neurosci., Royal Soc. Medicine, Soc. Biol. Psychiatry, Assn. Research Neurol. and Mental Diseases. Club: Cosmos (Washington). Current work: Neuroregulation—overseeing of research in a health sciences university. Subspecialties: Comparative neurobiology; Research management. Home: 212 W Gravers Ln Philadelphia PA 19118 Office: Hahnemann U Broad and Vine Sts Philadelphia PA 19102

SALOMAN, EDWARD BARRY, physicist; b. N.Y.C., May 30, 1940; s. Joseph Jonah and Ida E. (Feinberg) S.; m. Ora Rachel Frishberg, July 1, 1968. A.B., Columbia U., 1961, M.A., 1962, Ph.D., 1965. Research asst. Columbia Radiation Lab., Columbia U., N.Y.C., 1959-65, teaching asst. in physics, 1961-62, lectr. physics, 1962-63, research physicist Radiation Lab., 1965-66; asst. prof. physics, Brown U., Providence, 1966-72, cons. materials scis. program, 1972; physicist Nat. Bur. Standards, Gaithersburg, Md., 1972—. Contbr. articles to profl. jours. Mem. Am. Phys. Soc., Optical Soc. Am., AAAS. Current work: Electric field effects on autoionizing states, atomic spectroscopy utilizing synchrotron radiation, laser spectroscopy, far ultraviolet spectroscopy and radiometry. Subspecialties: Atomic and molecular physics; Radiometry. Home: 600 Rollins Ave Rockville MD 20852 Office: Nat Bur Standards A-251 Physics Bldg Gaithersburg MD 20899

SALOMONE, WILLIAM GERALD, civil engineer, consultant; b. Flushing, N.Y., Apr. 14, 1948; s. Harry and Mary (Tartaro) S.; m. Mary Jo Piano, July 22, 1978; 1 child, Jennifer Ann. B.C.E., Manhattan Coll., 1970; M.C.E., UCLA, 1971; Ph.D. in Civil Engring., Purdue U., 1978. Registered profl. engr., N.Y., N.J., Fla., Ill., Md., Ga., Ala. Research fellow UCLA, 1970-71; project engr. Dames & Moore, Cranford, N.J., 1971-75; research asst. Purdue U., West Lafayette, Ind., 1975-78; project mgr. Woodward-Clyde Cons., Chgo., 1978-80; prin. geotech. engr. Fluor Power Services, Chgo., 1980-81; v.p. geotech. engr. Bromwell Engring., Lakeland, Fla., 1981-82; cons. William G. Salomone, Lakeland, Fla., 1982—. Contbr. articles to profl. jours. Judge, Lakeland Regional Sci. Fair, Polk County Dept. Edn., 1983. Recipient letters of commendation Mayor of Lakeland. Sheriff of Bartow, Fla. Mem. ASCE (letter of commendation, Young Civil Engr. of Yr. award 1982), Earthquake Engring. Research Inst., Fla. Engring. Soc. (recording sec. 1982-83, practice sect. rep. 1983-84, Young Engr. of Yr. award 1983), Internat. Soc. Soil Mechanics and Found. Engrs., Nat. Soc. Profl. Engrs. (coll. scholarship com. 1983), ASTM (soil and geotextile coms. 1982), Chi Epsilon (v.p. 1969-70), Tau Beta Pi. Current work: Geotextiles in earth structures, modification of statute regarding sinkhole loss coverage for homeowners, government liability under federal tort claim act regarding water well contamination, environmental law, land use control law. Subspecialty: Civil engineering. Office: 3520 Cleveland Heights Blvd Suite 111 Lakeland FL 33803

SALPETER, EDWIN ERNEST, educator; b. Vienna, Austria, Dec. 3, 1924; came to U.S., 1949, naturalized, 1953; s. Jakob L. and Frieder (Horn) S.; m. Miriam Mark, June 11, 1950; children—Judy Gail, Shelley Ruth. M.S., Sydney U., 1946; Ph.D., Birmingham (Eng.) U., 1948; D.Sc., U. Chgo., 1969, Case-Western Reserve U., 1970. Research fellow Birmingham U., 1948-49; faculty Cornell U., Ithaca, N.Y., 1949—; now J.G. White prof. phys. scis.; mem. U.S. Nat. Sci. Bd., 1978-84. Author: Quantum Mechanics, 1957, 77; Editorial bd.: Astrophys. Jour, 1966-69; asso. editor: Rev. Modern Physics, 1971—; Contbr. articles to profl. jours. Mem. AURA bd., 1970-72. Recipient gold medal Royal Astron. Soc., 1973; J.R. Oppenheimer Meml. prize, 1974. Mem. Am. Astron. Soc. (v.p. 1971-73), Am. Philos. Soc., Nat. Acad. Scis., Am. Acad. Arts and Scis., Deutsche Akademie Leopoldina. Subspecialties: Theoretical astrophysics; Radio and microwave astronomy. Home: 116 Westbourne Ln Ithaca NY 14850

SALSBURY, JASON MELVIN, management consultant; b. Richmond, Va., June 12, 1920; s. John and Tillie Inez (Berman) S.; m. Miriam Heller, June 23, 1946; children—David Lewis, Michael Heller. B.S., U. Richmond, 1940; M.S., U. Va., 1943, Ph.D., 1945. Dir. chem. research div. Am. Cyanamid, Stamford, Conn., 1946-81; cons. Saljas Mgmt. & Cons., Boca Raton, Fla., 1981—; dir. indsl. opportunities ctr. Ga. Inst. Tech., Atlanta, 1982—; pres. Indsl. Research Inst., N.Y.C., 1979-80, chmn. emeriti com., 1984—; mem. nat. materials adv. bd. NRC, 1977-79; cons. Societe Nationale Elf Aquitaine, Paris, 1982—. Mem. Indsl. Research Inst. (pres. 1979-80, bd. dirs. 1973-76, 77-81), Am. Chem. Soc., Dirs. Indsl. Research. Current work: Organic chemistry, university-industry relations; management of research. Subspecialties: Organic chemistry; Polymer chemistry. Home: 3530 Piedmont Rd Apt 11L The Barclay Atlanta GA 30305 Office: Ga Inst Tech 400 10th St NW Centennial Research Bldg Room 286 Atlanta GA 30332

SALTER, ROBERT B., orthopedic surgeon. Sr. orthopedic surgeon Hosp. for Sick Children, Toronto, project dir. The Research Inst. Prof. U. Toronto Faculty of Medicine. Subspecialty: Orthopedics. Office: Suite M299 Hosp for Sick Children 555 University Ave Toronto ON M5G 1X8 Canada

SALTERS, GRACE HEYWARD, botany educator; b. Florence, S.C., May 25, 1933; d. John Wayne and Wilhelmena (Wright) Heyward; m. Walter Leon Salters, Dec. 21, 1963; 1 dau., Damita Renee. B.S., Bennett Coll., Greensboro, N.C., 1955; M.S., Atlanta U., 1962, Ph.D., 1977. Tchr. sci. Alexander County (N.C.) Sch., 1956-59, Bonds-Wilson High Sch., North Charleston, S.C., 1960-68; instr. biology S.C. State Coll., 1968-72, asst. prof., 1972-81, assoc. prof., 1981—; assoc. dir. Minority Access to Research Careers/Honors Undergrad.; Research Tng. program, 1980—. Vice pres. bd. dirs. Boylan-Haven-Mather Acad., Camden, S.C., 1979-83. NSF fellow, summers 1964-66; NSF COSIP fellow, 1973-74; NIH MARC fellow, 1974-77; NSF grantee, summer 1958, 59-60. Mem. S.C. State Employees Assn. (bd. dirs. 1980—), Assn. Southeastern Biologists, NAACP, Bennett Coll. Alumnae (pres. chpt. 1970—), Phi Delta Kappa, Delta Sigma Theta (treas. chpt. 1983-85, pres. 1985—), Beta Kappa Chi. Democrat. Methodist. Clubs: Shamrock Social (Orangeburg, S.C.) (pres. 1979-81); Alpha Wives (v.p. 1979-81, pres. 1983-85). Subspecialties: Plant growth; Plant cell and tissue culture. Home: 2111 Chestnut St NE Orangeburg SC 29115 Office: SC State Coll PO Box 2013 Orangeburg SC 29117

SALTON, GERARD, computer science educator; b. Nuremberg, Germany, Mar. 8, 1927; s. Rudolf and Elisabeth (Tuchmann) S.; m. Mary Birnbaum, Aug. 31, 1950; children—Mariann, Peter. B.A magna cum laude, Bklyn. Coll., 1950, M.A., 1952; Ph.D., Harvard U., 1958. Mem. staff computation lab. Harvard U., 1952-58, instr., then asst. prof. applied math., 1958-65; prof. computer sci. Cornell U., 1965—, chmn. dept., 1971-77; cons. to industry. Author: Automatic Information Organization and Retrieval, 1968, The Smart System-Experiments in Automatic Document Processing, 1971, Dynamic Information and Library Processing, 1975, Introduction to Modern Information Retrieval, 1983; editor-in-chief: Assn. Computing Machinery Communications, 1966-68; Editor-in-chief: Assn. Computing Machinery Jour., 1969-72; editor: Info. Systems, 1974—, ACM Computing Surveys, ACM Transactions on Data Base Systems. Guggenheim fellow, 1963. Fellow AAAS; mem. Assn. Computing Machinery (council 1972-78, Outstanding Contbn. award 1983), Phi Beta Kappa. Current work: Automatic text processing; content analysis of texts; automatic storage and retrieval. . Home: 221 Valley Rd Ithaca NY 14850 Office: Upson Hall Cornell U Ithaca NY 14853

SALUJA, JAGDISH KUMAR, high technology energy company executive; b. Jhelum, West Punjab, Pakistan, Jan. 14, 1934; came to U.S., 1956, naturalized, 1967; s. Kirpa Ram and Raksha Devi (Ajmani) S.; m. Subhashini Guddie Bhalla, June 9, 1967; children: Sunil, Samir. B.S.E. in Elec. Engring, U. Mich., 1957, B.S.E. in Math, 1958, M.S.E., 1959; Ph.D., U. Fla., 1966. Nuclear engr. Argonne Nat. Lab., Ill., 1959-62; sr. nuclear engr. Westinghouse Electric Co., Pitts., 1967-77; pres. Viking Energy Corp., Pitts., 1978—. Editor: Instrumentation and Controls Analysis Status Report for the 1137400 E Nerva Engine, 1972. Mem. Republican Presdl. Task Force, 1982. Mem. Am. Nuclear Soc. Democrat. Current Work: Nuclear power plant safety, development of alternate energy technologies including conservation and development of mobile robots for work in hazardous environments. Subspecialties: Nuclear fission; Solar energy. Office: Viking Energy Corp 121 N Highland Ave Suite 203 Pittsburgh PA 15215

SALVAGGIO, JOHN EDMOND, physician, educator; b. New Orleans, May 19, 1933; s. Louis and Z.A. (Engman-Riley) S.; m. Anne M. Poillon, Apr. 17, 1958; children—John, Garry, Wayne, Peggy. B.S., Loyola U., 1954; M.D., La. State U., 1957. Diplomate Am. Bd. Allergy and Immunology, Am. Bd. Internal Medicine. Intern Charity Hosp., New Orleans, 1957-58; resident in medicine, 1958-60; NIH fellow Harvard U. Med. Sch., 1960-63; prof. La. State U. Med. Sch., New Orleans, 1964-73; NIH fellow, prof. U. Colo. Med. Sch., Denver, 1963-74; Henderson prof., chmn. dept. medicine Tulane U. Med. Sch., New Orleans, 1975—; bd. dirs. Am. Bd. Internal Medicine, 1975-81. pres. Am. Bd. Allergy and Immunology, 1975-78; mem. pulmonary disease adv. council NIH, 1974-79. Contbr. articles to profl. jours. Bd. govs. Asthma and Allergy Found. Am., 1981—. Recipient Hall of Distinction award La. State U., 1980; career investigator, NIH, 1974, Davison Meml. award So. Allergy Assn., 1976, William Peck Sci. research, Nat. Med. Assn., 1975. Fellow ACP, Am. Acad. Allergy and Immunology (pres.); mem. Am. Thoracic Soc. (council), Am. Assn. Immunologists, Am. Soc. Clin. Investigation, Assn. Am. Physicians Club: So. Yacht. Current work: The immune response of man, lung immunology. Subspecialties: Internal medicine; Immunology (medicine). Home: 5726 St Charles Ave New Orleans LA 70115 Office: Dept Medicine Tulane U Med Sch 1430 Tulane Ave New Orleans LA 70112

SALVATORELLI, JOSEPH J., engineer, consultant; b. Phila., Oct. 22, 1924; s. Luigi and Agnes (D'Amario) S.; m. Dolores A. Biello, Aug. 11, 1946; 1 son, Joel Girard. Diploma in Civil Engring., Drexel U., 1954, B.S.C.E., 1956. Registered profl. engr. N.J., Pa., Md., Va., Del., N.Y., Nebr.; lic. sewage/water treatment plant operator; diplomate Am. Acad. Environ. Engrs.; With Albright & Friel, Inc., Phila., 1946-71, ptnr., 1959-71, v.p., 1962-71, also dir.; sr. assoc. Taylor Wiseman Taylor, Mt. Laurel, N.J., 1971-75, v.p., ptnr., 1975—. Contbr. to profl. publs. Pres. Assn. Island House Unit Owners, 1974-76, 79-84; pres. Island House Condominium Assn., Margate, N.J., 1976-77. Served as sgt. U.S. Army, 1943-46, PTO. Recipient Alumni Achievement award Drexel U., 1959, named Alumnus of Yr., 1976. Mem. Nat. Soc. Profl. Engrs., Franklin Inst., Water Pollution Control Assn. Pa. (pres. 1971-72; High Hat award 1975, Hazeltine award 1980), Water Pollution Control Fedn. (dir. 1973-76; Arthur Sidney Bedell award 1973, Service award 76), Eastern Pa. Water Pollution Control Operators Assn. (Service award 1973, Bolenius-Wiest Clean Streams award 1983), ASCE (dir. Phila. sect., chmn. san. engring. div. 1968-69), Am. Water Works Assn., N.J. Water Pollution Control Assn., Pa. Mcpl. Authorities Assn., Authorities Assn. of N.J. (dir. 1972-74), Alpha Sigma Lambda. Republican. Roman Catholic. Lodge: Yeadon Kiwanis (sec. 1968-70, pres. 1972, dir.) (Pa.). Current work: Consultant in environmental engineering, engineering management, forensic engineering. Subspecialties: Civil engineering; Environmental engineering. Home: 8014 Lagoon Dr Margate City NJ 08402 Office: Taylor Wiseman & Taylor 306 Fellowship Rd Mount Laurel NJ 08054

SALVATORI, VINCENT LOUIS, research and consulting company executive; b. Phila., Apr. 22, 1932; s. Louis and Lydia (Tofani) S.; m. Enid Joan Dodd, Oct. 4, 1952; children: Leslie Ann, Robert Louis, Sandra Ann. B.S.E.E., Pa. State U., 1958. Electronic insp. automation systems Automation Timing & Control Corp., King of Prussia, Pa., 1952-54; head spl. detection group HRB-Singer, Inc., State College, Pa., 1959-60, head microwave techniques sect. and antennae lab., 1960-63, mgr. passive ECCM systems and DF technique programs, 1963-67; mgr. reconnaissance systems dept. Radiation Systems, Inc., McLean, Va., 1967-69, v.p. engring., 1969-73; v.p. tech. Quest Research Corp., McLean, 1973-81; now dir.; exec. v.p. tech. and planning, dir. QuesTech, Inc., McLean, 1981—; dir. DHR, Inc., Dynamic Engring., Inc., Engring. Resources, Inc. Contbr. articles to profl. jours. Served to sgt. USAF, 1948-52. Recipient 115-pound Championship Golden Gloves award, 1945. Mem. IEEE, Am. Optical Assn., Assn. Old Crows. Club: Annapolis (Md.) Yacht. Patentee cubic function generation. Current Work: Application of corporate resources to technology exploitation. Subspecialties: Systems engineering; Electronics. Office: 6858 Old Dominion Dr McLean VA 22101

SALVO, RINO ANTHONY, biochemist; b. N.Y.C., Dec. 31, 1938; s. Anthony Augustus and Zina (Modica) S.; m. Jane Louise Trentin, June 29, 1974; children—Randall, Michael. B.S., New England Coll., 1963; M.S., L.I.U., 1968; Ph.D., U. Houston, 1972. Technician clin. medicine Albert Einstein Coll. Medicine, N.Y.C., 1963-69, research assoc., 1972-76; research scientist Ga. Inst. Tech., Atlanta, 1976-79; instr., research assoc. Atlanta U., 1980; research scientist Emory U. Sch. Medicine, Atlanta, 1980—. Contbr. articles to profl. jours. Served to 1st lt. Army N.G., 1963-69. Robert A. Welch Found. chemistry fellow, 1971-72; N.Y. Heart Assn. fellow, 1972-75. Mem. N.Y. Acad. Scis., Biophys. Soc., Am. Chem. Soc., Sigma Xi. Republican. Roman Catholic. Current work: Genetic inborn errors of metabolism; nucleic acid structure and function. Subspecialties: Biochemistry (medicine); Genetics and genetic engineering (medicine). Home: 2588 Sunset Dr Atlanta GA 30345 Office: Emory U Sch Medicine Div Med Genetics 2040 Ridgewood Dr Atlanta GA 30322

SALWASSER, HAL JAMES, wildlife ecologist; b. Fresno, Calif., Aug. 4, 1945; s. Mervin James and Elizabeth Jean (Thonen) S.; m. Susan Louise Fite, July 12, 1969; 1 child, James Barrett. B.A., Calif. State. U.-Fresno, 1971; Ph.D., U. Calif.-Berkeley, 1979. Cert. wildlife biologist. Research assoc. U. Calif.-Berkeley, 1976-78; regional wildlife ecologist U.S. Dept. Agr. Forest Service, San Francisco, 1978-82; nat. wildlife ecologist, Washington, 1982-85; dir. wildlife and fisheries, Washington, 1985—. Contbr. articles to profl. jours. Lay youth leader United Ch. of Christ, 1977-82. Served with U.S. Army, 1965-68. Recipient cert. of merit U.S. Forest Service, 1979, 83. Mem. Wildlife Soc. (pres. 1980), Soc. Am. Foresters, Soc. Range Mgmt., Sigma Xi. Republican. Current work: Wildlife-forest relationships integrated resource management planning; habitat management to maintain faunal diversity; endangered species planning; population viability of vertebrates. Subspecialties: Resource management; Ecosystems analysis. Home: 1621 N Kent St Arlington VA 22204 Office: PO Box 2417 Washington DC 20013

SALWEN, HAROLD, physicist; b. N.Y.C., Jan. 30, 1928; s. Nathan and Minnie (Levin) S.; m. Marie Kopman, June 11, 1950; children—Julie, Sharon, Cynthia, Nathan, Deborah, Fay. S.B., MIT, 1949; Ph.D., Columbia U., 1955. Research asst. IBM Watson Labs., N.Y.C., 1953-55; research assoc. Syracuse U., N.Y., 1955-57; research fellow Harvard U., Cambridge, Mass., 1957-59; asst. prof. physics Stevens Inst. Tech., Hoboken, N.J., 1959-64, assoc. prof., 1964-81, prof., 1981—; vis. scientist Imperial Coll. Sci. and Tech., London, 1980, Nat. Maritime Inst., Teddington, Eng., 1982; vis. prof. math. Rensselaer Poly. Inst., Troy, N.Y., 1982; adj. prof. oceanography Old Dominion U., Norfolk, Va., 1981—. Contbr. articles to sci. publs. Mem. Am. Phys. Soc., AAAS, Sigma Xi. Current work: Linear stability of fluid flows and transition to turbulence, effects of stagnat. Subspecialties: Fluid mechanics; Theoretical physics. Home: 703 Riverview Ave Teaneck NJ 07666 Office: Stevens Inst Tech Hoboken NJ 07030

SALZBERG, BRIAN MATTHEW, neurobiologist, biophysicist, educator; b. N.Y.C., Sept. 4, 1942; s. Saul and Betty Bernice (Jacobs) S. B.S., Yale U., 1963; A.M. (Woodrow Wilson fellow), Harvard U., 1965, Ph.D., 1971; A.M. (hon.), U. Pa., 1982. Research asst. physics dept. Harvard U., 1964-71; research assoc. dept. physiology Yale U. Med. Sch., New Haven, 1971-75; asst. prof. physiology U. Pa., Phila., 1975-80, assoc. prof., 1980-82, prof., 1982—; Steps fellow Marine Biol. Lab., 1977, 78, trustee, 1980-84. Contbr. numerous articles on biophysics and neurobiology to sci. publs. Mem. editorial bd. Jour. Gen. Physiology, 1984—, Cellular and Molecular Neurobiology, 1980—. Recipient MBL prize Marine Biol. Lab., 1981. Mem. Biophys. Soc., Soc. Gen. Physiologists, Am. Phys. Soc., AAAS, Phi Beta Kappa, Sigma Xi. Co-discoverer merocyanine probes of membrane potential. Current Work: Optical measurement of membrane potential; neurophysiology, optical probes, membrane biophysics, potential dependent absorption and fluorescence changes; tissue culture of identified neurons. Subspecialties: Neurobiology; Biophysics (biology). Office: 4010 Locust St Philadelphia PA 19104

SALZMAN, GARY CLYDE, physicist, microbiology researcher; b. Palo Alto, Calif., May 25, 1942; s. Harvey Austin and Amy Alfreda (Davis) S.; m. Joan Carolyn Hoyer, Jan. 30, 1965; children—Sonja, Eric. A.B., U. Calif., 1965; M.S., U. Oreg., 1968, Ph.D., 1972. Tchr. sci. U.S. Peace Corps., Asankranqwa, Ghana, 1965-67; postdoctoral fellow Los Alamos Nat. Lab., 1972-73, staff mem., 1973—; cons. NIH, Bethesda, Md., 1974—. Contbr. articles to profl. jours. Patentee in field. Mem. editorial Bd. Cytometry, Cell Biophysics, 1983. ROI Research grantee NIH, 1979-83, 83-86. Mem. AAAS, Am. Soc. Microbiology, Soc. Analytical Cytology, Biophys. Soc. Republican. Current work: Optical properties of biological cells, flow cytometry, microbiology instrumentation, molecular structure. Subspecialties: Microbiology; Biophysics (biology). Home: 108 Sierra Vista Dr Los Alamos NM 87544 Office: Los Alamos Nat Lab MSM888 PO Box 1663 Los Alamos NM 87545

SALZMAN, STEVEN KERRY, physiologist, pharmacologist, cons., researcher; b. N.Y.C., Feb. 19, 1952; s. Martin and Rose (Lakner) S.; m. Barbara Elaine Boutwell, June 24, 1974; children: Katherine Milann, Elana Rose. B.S. (scholar), U. Fla., Gainesville, 1974; Ph.D. in Pharmacology (NIMH fellow), U. Conn., 1979. Technician U. Fla., 1975, technologist, 1976; research asst. dept. biobehavioral sci. U. Conn., 1976-79; postdoctoral fellow Alfred I. DuPont Inst., Wilmington, Del., 1979-82; research scientist A.I. DuPont Inst. of Nemours Found., Wilmington, 1982—; guest lectr. U. Del.; cons. drug therapy and usage. Contbr. articles and abstracts to profl. jours. Recipient Outstanding Achievement award Miami Optimist Club, 1970. Mem. Soc. Neurosci. (treas. Del. chpt.). Current Work: CNS and hemostatic pathophysiology of spinal trauma, neurotransmitter mechanisms of drug addiction. Subspecialties: Molecular biology; Neurophysiology. Home: 105 Wentworth Dr Claymont DE 19703 Office: PO Box 269 Wilmington DE 19899

SAMAAN, NAGUIB ABDELMALIK, endocrinologist; b. Girga, Egypt, Apr. 2, 1925; s. Abdelmalik and Amasil Hanna S.; m. Jean Moffatt, Nov. 18, 1961; children—Sarah Ann, Mary Elizabeth, Jane Susan, Catherine Thia, Michael James. M.B., Ch.B., Alexandria (Egypt) U., 1951; D.M. in Internal Medicine, 1953; Ph.D. in Medicine, U. London, 1964. Rotating intern Alexandria U. Hosp., 1951-52, resident, 1952-54, sr. med. resident, instr., 1954-55; sr. research fellow Chest Inst., Brompton Hosp., London, 1955-56, Neurology Inst., Queen Sq., London, 1956; clin. fellow Postgrad. Med. Sch., London, 1957; clin. asst. prof. dept. endocrinology and therapeutics, asst. physician Royal Infirmary, Edinburgh, Scotland, 1957; sr. med. resident North Cambridge (Eng.) Hosps., 1958-60; staff physician, asst. prof., sr. research fellow Royal Postgrad. Med. Sch., London, 1960-64; research asso., asst. physician and endocrinologist Case Western Res. U., Cleve., 1964-66; staff physician, asst. prof. dept. internal medicine U. Iowa Hosps., Iowa City, 1966-69; med. staff physician, chief endocrinology VA Hosp., Iowa City, 1966-69; chief sect. endocrinology U. Tex. M.D. Anderson Hosp. and Tumor Inst., Houston, 1969—, asso. internist, asso. prof. medicine, 1969-72, internist, prof. medicine, 1972—; prof. medicine and physiology U. Tex. Grad. Sch. Biomed. Scis., Houston, 1969-72, prof., 1972—; prof. internal medicine U. Tex. M.D. Anderson Hosp. and Tumor Inst. and U. Tex. Med. Sch., Houston, 1973—; cons., attending physician dept. internal medicine Hermann Hosp., Houston, 1970—. Contbr. numerous articles to med. jours. Brit. Med. Research Council grantee, 1962-64; NIH grantee, 1969—; Am. Cancer Soc. grantee, 1971—. Fellow Royal Coll. Physicians (Scotland) Royal Coll. Physicians (Eng.); mem. Brit. Med. Assn., AMA, Am. Endocrine Soc., Am. Fedn. Clin. Research, Am. Physiol. Soc., Fedn. Am. Socs. Exptl. Biology, Central Soc. Clin. Research, Soc. Gynecologic Investigation, N.Y. Acad. Sci., Harris County Med. Soc., Houston Soc. Internal Medicine, Am. Thyroid Assn., Am. Diabetes Assn. Club: Nottingham Forest (Houston). Current Work: Investigations of the mechanism of production of pituitary tumors, diagnosis and management; early diagnosis of thyroid and parathyroid tumors and managnment; investigations of possible mechanism of production of diabetes mellitus. Subspecialties: Neuroendocrinology; Cancer research (medicine). Home: 14315 Heatherfield St Houston TX 77024 Office: MD Anderson Hosp and Tumor Inst 6723 Bertner Ave Houston TX 77030

SAMARAS, GEORGE MICHAEL, bioengr., physiologist, educator, cons.; b. Ottawa, Ont., Can., Jan. 6, 1948; came to U.S., 1949, naturalized, 1954; s. Demetrios George and Margaret (O'Connor) S.; m. Harrie Renee Stein, May 30, 1977. B.S.E.E., U. Md., 1972, M.S. in Physiology, 1974, Ph.D. in Neurophysiology/Neuropharmacology, 1976; postgrad. in engring. adminstrn, George Washington U., 1981—. Registered profl. engr., Md. Biochemistry lab. technician Bur. Radiol. Health, HEW, 1968-70, computer technician, 1970-71; biomed. engr. EPA, 1971-72; grad. teaching asst. dept. zoology U. Md., College Park, 1974-76; asst. prof. dept. radiation therapy U. Md. (Sch. Medicine), 1976-80, research asso. prof., 1980-82, assoc. prof., 1982—; dir. Neuro Oncology Research Labs., 1978-82; external reviewer NSF, 1978—, VA, 1981—; bioengring. cons. G.M.S. Engring. Corp. Contbr. articles to sci. jours., chpt. to book. Huntington's Chorea Found. grantee, 1973-77; Am. Cancer Soc. grantee, 1978-80; Whitaker Found. grantee, 1978-81; Nat. Inst. Neurol. Communicative Disease and Stroke grantee, 1979-83; U. Md. faculty research award, 1976-78. Mem. AAAS, Assn. for Advancement Med. Instrumentation (high frequency therapeutic device nat. standards com. 1977—), IEEE (sr.), Soc. for Neurosci., Nat. Soc. Profl. Engrs., N.Y. Acad. Scis. Current Work: Microwave hyperthermia for brain tumor treatments; automated prostheses for the autonomic nervous system. Subspecialties: Biomedical engineering; Physiology (biology). Address: 8940-D Route 108 Columbia MD 21045 Also: 10 S Pine St MSTF 6-34 Baltimore MD 21201

SAMIOS, NICHOLAS PETER, physicist; b. N.Y.C., Mar. 15, 1932; s. Peter and Niki (Vatick) S.; m. Mary Linakis, Jan. 12, 1958; children: Peter, Gregory, Alexandra. A.B., Columbia U., 1953, Ph.D., 1957. Instr. physics Columbia U., N.Y.C., 1956-59; asst. physicist Brookhaven Nat. Lab., Upton, N.Y., 1959-62, asso. physicist, 1962-64, physicist, 1964-68, sr. physicist, 1968—, group leader, 1965-75, chmn. dept. physics, 1975-81, dep. dir. for high energy and nuclear physics, 1981, dir., 1982—; adj. prof. Stevens Inst. Tech., 1969-75, Columbia U., 1970—. Contbr. articles in field to profl. jours. Recipient E.O. Lawrence Meml. award, 1980; award in phys. and math. scis. N.Y. Acad. Scis., 1980. Fellow Am. Phys. Soc., Am. Acad. Arts and Scis.; mem. Nat. Acad. Scis., Sigma Xi. Expert field of particle spectroscopy and weak interactions. Subspecialty: Particle physics. Office: Office of Director Brookhaven Nat Lab Upton NY 11973

SAMMET, JEAN E., computer scientist; b. N.Y.C.; d. Harry and Ruth S. B.A., Mount Holyoke Coll., Sc.D. (hon.), 1978; M.A., U. Ill. Group leader programming Sperry Gryoscope, Great Neck, N.Y., 1955-58; sect. head, staff cons. programming Sylvania Electric Products, Needham, Mass., 1958-61; with IBM, 1961—, Boston adv. program mgr., 1961-65, program lang. tech. mgr., 1965-68; programming tech. planning mgr. Fed. Systems div., 1968-74, programming lang. tech. mgr., 1974-79, software tech. mgr., 1979-81, div. software tech. mgr., 1981-82, programming lang. tech. mgr., 1983—; chmn. history of computing com. Am. Fedn. Info. Processing Socs., 1977-79. Author: Programming Languages: History and Fundamentals, 1969; editor-in-chief: Assn. Computing Machinery Computing Revs, 1979—; contbr. articles to profl. jours. Mem. Assn. Computing Machinery (pres. 1974-76), Math. Assn. Am., Nat. Acad. Engring., Upsilon Pi Epsilon. Subspecialties: Programming languages; Software engineering. Office: IBM Fed Systems Div 6600 Rockledge Dr Bethesda MD 20817

SAMMON, PETER, reservoir simulation scientist; b. Penticton, B.C., Can., Aug. 26, 1951; s. Andrew and Kathleen D. (Auton) S.; m. Christine E. Hellwig, Dec. 23, 1978. Sc.B., U. B.C., 1973, M.Sc., 1975; Ph.D., Cornell U., 1978. Asst. scientist Math Research Ctr., Madison, Wis., 1978-79; Dickson instr. U. Chgo., 1979-81; simulation scientist Computer Modelling Group, Calgary, Alta., Can., 1981-83, sr. simulation scientist, 1983-85; v.p. Dynamic Reservoir Systems, Ltd., 1985—. Contbr. articles to profl. jours. NRC Can. postdoctoral scholar, 1976-79. Mem. Soc. Indsl. and Applied Math.; assoc. mem. Soc. Petroleum Engrs. Current Work: Efficient numerical techniques for petroleum reservoir simulation. Subspecialties: Applied mathematics; Petroleum engineering. Office: Dynamic Reservoir Systems Ltd 505 3d St SW #1630 Calgary AB T2P 3E6 Canada

SAMN, SHERWOOD, mathematician, researcher; b. Los Angeles, Apr. 20, 1941; s. Calvin and Tze (Lam) S.; m. Maria Claudette Wong, July 27, 1968; children—Valerie, Jonathan. A.B., U. Calif.-Berkeley, 1963, Ph.D., 1968. Asst. prof. Ind.-Purdue U., Indpls., 1968-74; mathematician U.S. Air Force Sch. Aerospace Medicine, San Antonio, 1974—. Contbr. articles to profl. publs. Mem. Am. Math. Soc., Soc. Indsl. and Applied Math. Current work: Mathematical modeling and simulation of biomedical phenomena. Subspecialties: Applied mathematics; Algorithms. Home: 8807 Cattail Creek San Antonio TX 78239 Office: USAF Sch Aerospace Medicine Brooks AFB San Antonio TX 78235

SAMOILOV, SERGEY MICHAEL, chemist, researcher; b. Baku, Russia, Dec. 17, 1925; came to U.S., 1977; s. Michael Jacob and Lydia Jacob (Kaplan) S.; m. Elena Alexander Krasnostchekova, Dec. 9, 1961 (div. Apr. 1976); 1 child, Michael. M.S., Moscow Inst. Fine Chem. Tech., 1949; Ph.D., USSR Acad. Scis., 1958. Engr. Nat. Inst. Synthetic Fuels, Moscow, 1949-51, Combine 16, Angarsk, USSR, 1951-55; research assoc. USSR Acad. Scis., Irkutsk., 1958-61; sr. research assoc. Nat. Inst. Petrochemistry, Moscow, 1962-76; research assoc. Columbia U., N.Y.C., 1977-78, Celanese Research Co., Summit, N.J., 1978-81; sr. research chemist Allied Corp., Morristown, N.J., 1981—. Abstractor USSR Chem. Abstracts Jour., 1955-76. Contbr. articles to sci. jours. Patentee in field. Mem. Am. Chem. Soc. Current work: Synthesis, studies and applications of polymers, particularly polyolefins; modification of polymers with organometallic compounds, Ziegler catalysts. Subspecialties: Polymer chemistry; Catalysis chemistry. Home: 501 Lindsley Dr Apt 2-F Morristown NJ 07960

SAMSON, JAMES ALEXANDER ROSS, physics educator; b. Kilmarnock, Scotland, Sept. 9, 1928; came to U.S., 1953, naturalized, 1958; s. James and Agnes (Ferguson Ross) S.; m. Mary Simpson Richardson, Apr. 17, 1954; children—Ross, Scott. B.Sc., Glasgow U., Scotland, 1952, D.Sc (hon.), 1970; M.S., U. So. Calif., 1955, Ph.D., 1959. Research physicist Harvard U., Cambridge, Mass., 1960-61; dir. exptl. physics GCA Corp., Bedford, Mass., 1961-70; prof. physics U. Nebr., Lincoln, 1970—, Regents prof. physics, 1980—; mem. adv. screening com. in physics Council for Internat. Exchange of Scholars, 1978-81; mem. internat. program com. 7th Internat. Conf. on Vacuum Ultraviolet Radiation Physics, 1983; mem. com. on line spectra of elements-atomic spectroscopy NRC, 1981-84. Author: Techniques of Vacuum Ultraviolet Spectroscopy, 1967; contbr. chpts. to World Book Ency., numerous articles to profl. jours.; reviewer sci. books, papers, and govt. contract proposals; patentee in field. Served with RAF, 1946-48. Fulbright-Hayes sr. fellow, 1976-77. Fellow Am. Phys. Soc. (div. electron and atomic physics, div. chem. physics), Optical Soc. Am. (medal com. 1983, chmn. 1985); mem. Sigma Xi. Current work: Vacuum ultraviolet radiation research; photoelectron spectroscopy. Subspecialty: Atomic and molecular physics. Office: U Nebr Physics Dept Lincoln NE 68588

SAMUEL, ARYEH HERMANN ALBERT, research scientist; b. Hildesheim, West Germany, Feb. 19, 1924; came to U.S., 1941, naturalized, 1957; s. Rudolf and Erna (Ballheimer) S.; m. Betty Roth, Mar. 28, 1954 (dec. Nov. 1983); 1 son, Joshua Reuven. B.S., U. Ill.-Urbana, 1943; M.S., Northwestern U., 1946; Ph.D., U. Notre Dame, 1953. Research scientist Broadview Research, Burlingame, Calif., 1956-60, Stanford Research Inst., Menlo Park, Calif., 1960-65, 67-72; research mgr. Gen Precision Research Lab., Little Falls, N.J., 1965-67; ops. analyst Vector Research, Inc., Ann Arbor, Mich., 1974-77; prin. research scientist Battelle Meml. Inst., Washington, 1977—. Served with Israel Army, 1948-49. Mem. Ops. Research Soc. Am. (Lanchester prize 1962). Current Work: Analysis of public sector systems (especially military, postal); radiation chemistry, mass spectrometry. Subspecialties: Operations research (engineering); Physical chemistry. Home: 10861 Bucknell Dr Wheaton MD 20902 Office: Battelle Memorial Institute 2030 M St NW Washington DC 20036

SAMUEL, CHARLES E., biochemistry and molecular biology educator; b. Portland, Oreg., Nov. 28, 1945; married, 1968; 2 children. B.S., Mont. State U., 1968; Ph.D., U. Calif.-Berkeley, 1972. Damon Runyon scholar Duke U. Med. Ctr., 1972-74; asst. prof. U. Calif.-Santa Barbara, 1974-79, assoc. prof. biochemistry and molecular biology, 1979-83, prof., 1983—. Mem. editorial bd. Virology, 1980—, Jour. Interferon Research, 1980—, Jour. Virology, 1984—; contbr. articles to numerous publs. in field. Recipient Research Career Devel. award NIH, 1979-84; Am. Cancer Soc. grantee, 1975-84; NIH grantee, 1975—. Mem. Am. Soc. Biol. Chemists, Am. Soc. Virology, Am. Soc. Microbiology. Current Work: Molecular virology, biochemistry of animal virus-cell interactions, mechanism of interferon action. Subspecialties: Virology (biology); Molecular biology. Office: Dept Biol Scis U Calif Santa Barbara CA 93106

SAMUEL, MARK AARON, physicist, educator; b. Montreal, Que., Can., Jan. 26, 1944; s. Michael and Molly (Ofter) S.; m. Carol Anne, Dec. 23, 1965; children: Kenneth Brian, Tamara Sue. B.S., McGill U., 1964, M.S., 1966; Ph.D., U. Rochester, 1969. Asst. prof. physics Okla. State U., Stillwater, 1969-75, assoc. prof., 1975-81, prof. physics, 1981—; vis. scientist Aspen Ctr. for Physics, 1981, 85, Niels Bohr Inst., 1977, Stanford Linear Accelerator Ctr., 1973, 75, Am. Physics Soc., 1982. Author: Group Theory Made Easy for Scientists and Engineers, 1979; contbr. articles to publs. Dept. Energy/ERDA research grantee, 1976—. Mem. Am. Phys. Soc., Am. Assn. Physics Tchrs., Can. Assn. Physicists. Current Work: Perturbative QED and QCD, properties of weak bosons, large order perturbation theory. Subspecialties: Theoretical physics; Particle physics. Office: Physics Dept Okla State U Stillwater OK 74078

SAMUEL, PAUL, physician; b. Janoshaza, Hungary, Feb. 17, 1927; came to U.S., 1954, naturalized, 1960; s. Adolf and Magda (Zollner) S.; m. Gabriella R. Zeichner, Mar. 27, 1954; children: Robert Mark, Adrianne Jill. Baccalaureat, Kemeny Zsigmond Gymnasium, Budapest, 1945; M.D., U. Paris, 1953. Intern Queens Hosp. Ctr., N.Y.C., 1954-55; resident L.I. Jewish Med. Ctr., New Hyde Park, N.Y., 1959-61; adj. prof. chemistry Queens Coll., N.Y.C., 1969—; adj. prof. Rockefeller U., N.Y.C., 1971-81; adj. prof. medicine Cornell U., N.Y.C., 1979—; clin. prof. medicine Albert Einstein Coll. Medicine, Bronx, 1981—; dir. Arteriosclerosis Research Lab., L.I. Jewish-Hillside Med. Ctr., New Hyde Park, 1962—; chmn. N.Y. Lipid Research Club, Rockefeller U., 1977-78. Contbr. articles to profl. jours. Pres. Am. Heart Assn., Nassau County, 1980. Fellow Am. Coll. Cardiology; mem. Am. Heart Assn. (fellow council on arteriosclerosis, Disting. Achievement award 1975), Am. Fedn. Clin. Research, Harvey Soc., ACP. Current Work: Cholesterol metabolism and kinetics; bile acid metabolism; arteriosclerosis and coronary heart disease. Subspecialties: Cardiology; Biochemistry (medicine). Home: 25 Nassau Dr Great Neck NY 11021

SAMUELS, GEORGE JOSEPH, chemist; b. Des Moines, Aug. 23, 1952; s. George Joseph and JoAnn Donice (Townsend) S.; m. Joan Ellen Holland, Sept. 2, 1978. B.S., U. Ill., 1974; Ph.D., Iowa State U., 1979. Postdoctoral assoc. U. N.C., Chapel Hill, 1978-80; research chemist Allied Corp., Syracuse, N.Y., 1980-82, sr. research chemist, 1983—. Contbr. articles to profl. jours. Patentee in field. Mem. Am. Chem. Soc., Inst. for Interconnection and Packaging of Electronic Circuitry (lab. rep.), Am. Electroplaters Soc., Sigma Xi. Current work: Development of new materials and processes for use in the electronics industry, particularly the connector circuit board and chip carrier businesses within Allied Corp. Subspecialties: Inorganic chemistry; Materials. Office: Allied Corp PO Box 1021R Morristown NJ 07960

SAMUELSON, DON ARTHUR, morphologist, mycologist, educator; b. Boston, Aug. 30, 1948; s. John Arthur and Laura Kotrina (Ornstedt) S.; m. Leslie Joyce Gilbert, Feb. 14, 1977; 1 son, Peter Andrew. B.A., Boston U., 1971; M.S., U. Fla., 1975, Ph.D., 1977, M.S., 1982. EPA researcher U. Fla., Gainesville, 1978-79; NIH research div. comparative ophthalmology U. Fla. (Coll. Vet. Medicine), 1980-82, asst. prof. dept. comparative ophthalmology, 1982—. Contbr. articles to profl. jours. Mem. Assn. Southeastern Biologists, Mycological Soc. Am., Assn. Research in Vision and Ophthalmology. Congregationalist. Lodge: Lions. Current Work: Biochemical, physiologic and morphologic development of inherited cataract in a colony of dogs; biochemical, physiologic and morphologic progression of primary open angle glaucoma in a colony of dogs. Subspecialties: Ophthalmology; Microbiology. Office: Coll Vet Medicine U Fla Box J-115 JHMHC Gainesville FL 32610

SAMUELSON, DOUGLAS ALAN, operations research analyst, consultant; b. Reno, July 27, 1948; s. Norman Harold and Shirley (Leder) S.; m. Francine Ruth Kimel, Jan. 7, 1979; children—Diane Stephanie, Andrew Neil. B.A., U. Calif.-Berkeley, 1969; M.S., George Washington U., 1981, postgrad., 1981—. Computer systems analyst Bank of Am., San Francisco, 1972-73; cons. computer systems, San Rafael, Calif., 1973-75; econ. statistician Dept. Interior, Washington, 1975-77; mathematician Fed. Preparedness Agy., 1977-78; ops. research analyst Dept. Energy, Washington, 1978-80, FAA, Washington, 1980-82, Evaluation Research Corp., Vienna, Va., 1982-83; cons. ops. research analyst, Falls Church, Va., 1983—; pres. Micro-Zeit, Inc., 1985—; staff analyst White House Task Force on Inland Energy Impacts, Washington, 1977. Presdl. scholar, 1965. Mem. Washington Ops. Research Mgmt. Sci. Council (treas. 1982-83, trustee 1984-85), Washington Statis. Soc. (membership chmn. 1981-83, natural resources program chmn. 1980-81), Am. Statis. Assn. (com. on sci. freedom 1980—, chmn. 1985—), Ops. Research Soc. Am., Inst. Mgmt. Scis., Washington Acad. Scis. Current Work: Probability modeling, reliability and risk analysis, statistical and operations research software for microcomputers, statistical pattern recognition, optimization modeling, forecasting, telecommunications and computer systems performance analysis, educational measurement. Subspecialties: Operations research (mathematics); Probability. Home: 3443 Skyview Terr Falls Church VA 22042

SAMY, ANANTHA T. S., biochemist, researcher, educator; b. Hungenahally, Karnataka, India, Sept. 8, 1936; s. Suryanarayana T. and Rukminiamma Gundappa Iyer; m. Mangala Nuggehally, Nov. 3, 1965; children: Sanjay, Sharad. B.Sc. in Agr., U. Mysore, India, 1958; M.S. in Agr. Chemistry, U. Poona, India, 1960; Ph.D. in Biochemistry, Indian Inst. Sci., Bangalore, 1966. Postdoctoral research assoc. hormone research lab. U. Calif. Med. Ctr., San Francisco, 1966-69; Ford Found. fellow Indian Inst. Sci., Bangalore, 1969-72; research assoc. Sidney Farber Cancer Inst., Boston, 1972-82; assoc. prof. dept. oncology U. Miami, Fla., 1982—. NIH grantee, 1974-82; Am. Cancer Soc. grantee, 1982—. Mem. Biochem. Soc. (London), Am. Assn. Cancer Research, Am. Soc. Biol. Chemists, AAAS, N.Y. Acad. Scis. Current Work: Structure of antitumor proteins, mechanism of action of antitumor antibiotics on DNA; pharmacology and pharmacokinetics of antitumor drugs in experimental animals; understanding mechanism of drug resistance in cancer cells; targeting of drugs and efficient utilization of drugs in cancer chemotherapy. Subspecialties: Biochemistry (biology); Chemotherapy. Office: Dept Oncology PO Box 016960 (R 71) Miami FL 33101

SANADI, D. RAO, research institute administrator, biochemistry educator, researcher; b. India, July 8, 1920; married, 1950; 2 children. Ph.D. in Biochemistry, U. Calif., 1949. Fellow Nat. Cancer Inst., 1949-52, research assoc., 1952-53; asst. prof. biochemistry U. Wis., 1953-55; asst. prof., U. Calif., 1955-58; chief sect. comparative biochemistry NIH, 1958-66; dir. dept. cell physiology Boston Biomed. Research Inst., 1966—, exec. dir., 1969-71, 75-77; assoc. prof. dep. biol. chemistry Harvard U. Med. Sch., Boston, 1975—; chmn. Gordon Research Conf. on Energy Coupling Mechanisms, 1969, 74, Gordon Research Conf. on Biology of Aging, 1974; mem. adult devel. and aging research and tng. com. Nat. Inst. Child Health and Human Devel., 1970-73; mem. adv. panel metabolic biology NSF, 1971-74. Chief editor: Jour. Bioenergetics Biomembrane, 1975—. Established investigator Am. Heart Assn., 1954-58. Fellow Gerontol. Soc.; mem. AAAS, Am. Chem. Soc., Am. Soc. Biol. Chemistry. Subspecialty: Cell biology. Office: Dept Cell Physiology Boston Biomed Research Inst 20 Staniford St Boston MA 02114

SANBERG, PAUL RONALD, neuroscientist; b. Coral Gables, Fla., Jan. 4, 1955; s. Bernard and Molly (Spector) S. B.Sc. with honors, York U., Can., 1976; M.Sc., U. B.C. (Can.), 1978; Ph.D., Australian Nat. U., 1981. Research asst. York U., Toronto, Ont., 1974-75; grad. research asst. U. B.C., Vancouver, 1976-78; postdoctoral research asst. Australian Nat. U., Canberra, 1981; postdoctoral fellow depts. neurosci. and psychiatry Johns Hopkins U., Balt., 1981-83-; asst. prof. psychology and biomed. scis. Ohio U., Athens, 1983—. Contbr. articles to profl. jours.; editor: Bird Behaviour. Recipient Maurice Klugman Meml. award Tourette Syndrome Assn., 1982, Sir. J.G. Crawford prize Australian Nat. U., 1981; NIH grantee; travel awardee Am. Coll. Neuropsycho-pharmacology, 1984—. Mem. Soc. Neurosci., Internat. Brain Research Orgn., Psychonomic Soc., Am. Psychol. Assn. Current Work: Research into elucidating the role of the basal ganglia and specific neurotransmitter systems in motor and complex behavior. In addition, animal models of human movement disorders and diseases of dementia are being developed; development of brain tissue transplantation techniques. Subspecialties: Psychopharmacology; Psychobiology. Office: Dept Psychology Ohio U Athens OH 45701

SANCAKTAR, EROL, mech. engr., educator; b. Ankara, Turkey, July 13, 1952; came to U.S., 1974; s. Mehmet Ali and Ulker Mualla (Elveren) S.; m. Teresa Sue Davis, Feb. 16, 1979; 1 son, Orhan Ali. B.S. in Mech. Engring. with honors (Coll. scholar), Robert Coll. (now Bosphorus U.), Istanbul, Turkey, 1974; M.S. in Mech. Engring, Va. Poly. Inst. and State U., 1975, Ph.D. in Engring. Mechanics, 1979. Teaching asst. dept. physics Robert Coll., 1971-74, dept. mech. engring., 1973-74; trainee engr. Chrysler Corp., Istanbul, summers 1972-73; research asst. dept. mech. engring. Va. Poly. Inst. and State U., 1974-75, dept. engring. sci. and mechanics, 1975-76, 77, research assoc., 1976-77, instr., 1977-78; research assoc. NASA Langley Research Ctr., Hampton, Va., 1976; instr. Clarkson Coll. Tech., 1978-79, asst. prof. mech. engring., 1979—; invited lectr./cons. NASA Langley Research Ctr. Contbr. articles to profl. jours., confs. Olin Corp. Trust grantee, 1979-80; Clarkson Coll. Tech. Research Award grantee, 1980, 81; NSF grantee, 1980-82; Gen. Electric Co. grantee, 1982; NASA Langley Research Ctr. grantee, 1982-83. Current Work: viscoelasticity, adhesives, material characterization, rate and time dependence, stress analysis, experimental solid mechanics, plastics, creep, cure, fracture. Subspecialties: Solid mechanics; Polymers (materials science). Home: 65 Lawrence Ave Potsdam NY 13676 Office: Dept Mech and Indsl Engring Clarkson Coll Potsdam NY 13676

SANCAR, AZIZ, biochemistry educator; b. Savur, Turkey, Sept. 8, 1946; came to U.S., 1973; s. Gani and Meryem (Suleyman) S.; m. Gwendolyn Esta Boles, Aug. 16, 1978. M.D., Istanbul Med. Sch. (Turkey), 1969; Ph.D., U. Tex. at Dallas, 1977. Physician Turkish Ministry of Health, Savur, 1970-71; research asst. U. Tex.-Dallas, 1974-77; postdoctoral assoc. Yale U., New Haven, 1977-82; assoc. prof. biochemistry U. N.C., Chapel Hill, 1982—. Inventor Maxicells, 1979; discoverer excinuclease, 1983. Fellow Pfizer Inc., 1964, NATO, 1965; NATO scholar, 1971; NSF Presdl. Young investigator, 1984. Mem. Am. Soc. Biol. Chemists, Am. Soc. Microbiology. Current work: Isolation of DNA repair enzymes, DNA repair and cancer, photoreactivation, chemical carcinogens. Subspecialties: Molecular biology; Biochemistry (medicine). Home: 418 Chateau Apts Carrboro NC 27510 Office: U NC Dept Biochemistry 231H Chapel Hill NC 27514

SANCETTA, CONSTANCE ANTONINA, geological oceanographer, researcher; b. Richmond, Va., Apr. 17, 1949; d. Anthony Louis and Joyce Louise (Kellogg) S. A.B., Brown U., 1971, M.Sc., 1973; Ph.D., Oreg. State U., 1976. Research assoc. Stanford U., 1976-78; assoc. research scientist Lamont-Doherty Geol. Obs., Columbia U., Palisades, N.Y., 1978-84, research scientist, 1984—. Editor Catalogue of Diatoms book series, 1985—; assoc. editor Marine Micropaleontology jour., 1983—; contbr. articles to sci., profl. jours. NSF grad. trainee, 1972. Fellow Geol. Soc. Am.; mem. Am. Geophys. Union (chmn. com. 1984—), AAAS, N.Y. Acad. Scis. (chmn. geology sect. 1983-84), Assn. Women Geoscientists (treas. 1977, del. 1982), Phi Beta Kappa. Current work: Use of marine microfossils (diatoms) to interpret modern and ancient depositional and oceanographic environment; paleoceanography. Subspecialties: Oceanography; Paleontology. Office: Lamont-Doherty Geol Obs Palisades NY 10964

SANCHEZ, ISAAC CORNELIUS, chemical physicist; b. San Antonio, Aug. 11, 1941; s. Isaac, Jr. and Mercedes (Aguilar) S.; m. Karen Patricia Horton, Aug. 7, 1976; children—Matthew Bryce, Timothy Garrett. B.Sc. magna cum laude, St. Mary's U., San Antonio, 1963; Ph.D., U. Del., 1969. NRC/Nat. Acad. Sci. postdoctoral fellow Nat. Bur. Standards, Washington, 1969-71, research chemist polymers div., 1977-81, supervising research chemist, 1981—; assoc. scientist Xerox Corp., Webster, N.Y., 1971-72; asst. prof. U. Mass., Amherst, 1972-77, adj. prof., 1977—. Contbr. chpts. to books, articles to profl. jours. Served as lt. USN, 1963-67. Recipient Bronze medal Dept. Commerce, 1980, Silver medal, 1983; Edward U. Condon award Nat. Bur. Standards, 1983. Fellow Am. Phys. Soc. (chmn. div. high polymer physics 1983-84, mem. exec. bd. div. high polymer physics 1981-85); mem. Am. Chem. Soc. (sec. Connecticut Valley sect. 1976-77). Current work: Theoretical studies on polymer blends, equations of state, polymer solutions, interfacial phenomena, critical point phenomena, diffusion. Subspecialties: Polymer physics; Polymers (materials science). Office: Polymers Div Nat Bur of Standards Gaithersburg MD 20899

SANDAGE, ALLAN REX, astronomer; b. Iowa City, June 18, 1926; s. Charles Harold and Dorothy (Briggs) S.; m. Mary Lois Connelley, June 8, 1959; children—David Allan, John Howard. A.B., U. Ill., 1948, D.Sc., 1967; Ph.D., Calif. Inst. Tech., 1953; D.Sc., Yale, 1966, U. Chgo., 1967, Miami U., Oxford, Ohio, 1974; LL.D., U. So. Calif., 1971, Graceland Coll., 1985. Astronomer Mt. Wilson Obs., Palomar Obs., Carnegie Instn., Washington, 1952—; Peyton postdoctoral fellow Princeton U., 1952; asst. astronomer Hale Obs., Pasadena, Calif., 1952-56, astronomer, 1956—; vis. lectr. Harvard, 1957; cons. NSF, 1961-64; Sigma Xi nat. lectr., 1966; vis. prof. Mt. Stromlo Obs., Australian Nat. U., 1968-69. Mem. astron. expdn. to South Africa, 1958; Mem. permanent organizing com. Solvay Conf. in Physics. Served with USNR, 1944-45. Recipient gold medal Royal Astron. Soc., 1967, Pope Pius XI gold medal Pontifical Acad. Sci., 1966, Rittenhouse medal, 1968, Rittenhouse medal Nat. Medal Sci., 1971; Fulbright-Hayes scholar, 1972. Mem. Am. Astron. Soc. (Helen Warner prize 1960, Russell prize 1973), Royal Astron. Soc. (Eddington medal 1963, Gold medal 1967), Astron. Soc. Pacific (Gold medal 1975), Franklin Inst. (Elliott Cresson medal 1973), Phi Beta Kappa, Sigma Xi. Current Work: Research in observational cosmology and stellar evolution. Age dating of stars and star clusters. The size and age of the universe. Subspecialties: Cosmology; Optical astronomy. Home: 8319 Josard Rd San Gabriel CA 91775 Office: 813 Santa Barbara St Pasadena CA 91101

SANDBERG, CHARLES ALBERT, conodont biostratigrapher, petroleum geologist; b. Boston, June 12, 1929; s. Allan A. and Frances (Beres) S.; m. Dorothy Ann Taylor, Sept. 22, 1956; children: Susan Ann, Janet Lynn, William Allan. Geologist U.S. Geol. Survey, Denver, 1950—. Contbr. over 110 geol. articles to profl. publs. Served with U.S. Army, 1952-54, Korea. Fellow Geol. Soc. Am.; mem. Paleontol. Soc., Pander Soc., Am. Assn. Petroleum Geologists. Current Work: Devonian and Mississippian conodont biostratigraphy, paleoecology, zonation, and taxonomy of North America and Europe. Subspecialty: Paleontology, paleoecology. Home: 395 S Lee St Lakewood CO 80226 Office: US Geol Survey Box 25046 Mail Stop 940 Fed Center Denver CO 80225

SANDBERG, IRWIN WALTER, research mathematician; b. N.Y.C., Jan. 23, 1934; s. Ben and Estelle (Hornick) S.; m. Barbara A. Zimmerman, June 15, 1958; 1 child, Heidi L. Student, CCNY, 1951-53; B.E.E., Poly. Inst. Bklyn., 1955, M.E.E. (Westinghouse fellow), 1956, D.E.E. (Bell Telephone Labs. fellow), 1958. Tech. aid Bell Telephone Labs. Inc., Murray Hill, N.J., 1954, mem. tech. staff, 1958-67, head systems theory research dept., 1967-72, mem. math. and statis. research ctr., 1972—; engr. Wheeler Labs., Great Neck, N.Y., 1955; vis. prof. U. Calif.-Berkeley, 1965; lectr. study insts. NATO, Knokke, Belgium, 1966, Copenhagen, Denmark, 1970; disting. lectr. Asilomar Conf., 1973, 74; lectr. European Conf. Circuit Theory and Design, 1981. Del. Union Radio Scientifique Internationale, Munich, 1966; U.S. rep. NATO conf., 1972. Recipient disting. staff award Bell Labs., 1983. Fellow IEEE (vice chmn. group circuit theory 1971-72; centennial medal 1984); mem. Nat. Acad. Engring., AAAS, Eta Kappa Nu, Sigma Xi, Tau Beta Pi. Patentee in elec. engring. field. Current Work: Research mathematician. Subspecialties: Electrical engineering; Applied mathematics. Home: 100 Lenape Ln Berkeley Heights NJ 07922 Office: 600 Mountain Ave Murray Hill NJ 07974

SANDEL, BILL ROY, physicist; b. Brady, Tex., Nov. 19, 1945; s. Roy and Mary Lucretia (Collins) S.; m. Karen Kay DeLay, July 26, 1980; children: Aaron Francis Archer, Brody Steven Sandel. B.A. in Physics, Rice U., 1968, M.S. in Space Sci., 1971, Ph.D. in Space Sci., 1972. Sr. research assoc. Kitt Peak Nat. Obs., Tucson, 1973-78; research assoc. Lunar and Planetary Lab., U. Ariz., 1978-79; research scientist Ctr. for Space Scis., U. So. Calif., 1979-83; assoc, research scientist Lunar and Planetary Lab., U. Ariz., 1983—; co-investigator Voyager Ultraviolet Spectrometer Expt., 1978-. Contbr. articles on planetary sci., ultraviolet spectroscopy to profl. jours. Served to capt. USAR. Recipient Exceptional Sci. Achievement award NASA, 1981, Group Achievement award, 1981, 81. Mem. Am. Geophys. Union, Am. Astron. Soc., AAAS. Current Work: Investigation of bound and extended atmospheres of giant planets and their satellites; development of imaging detectors for ultraviolet rays. Subspecialties: Planetary science; Planetary atmospheres. Home: 4442 E 6th St Tucson AZ 85711 Office: 3625 E Ajo Way Tucson AZ 85713

SANDER, LEONARD MICHAEL, physics educator; b. St. Louis, Aug. 17, 1941; s. Earl Arthur and Sarah (Gutenberg) S.; m. Mae Ellen Feldman, Mar. 1, 1964; 1 child, Evelyn. B.S., Washington U., St. Louis, 1963; Ph.D., U. Calif.-Berkeley, 1968. Postdoctoral fellow U. Calif.-San Diego, La Jolla, 1968-69; asst. prof. physics U. Mich., Ann Arbor, 1969-75, assoc. prof., 1975-81, prof., 1981—. Contbr. articles to profl. jours. Mem. Am. Phys. Soc. Current work: Theory of condensed matter, particularly application of density functional methods and growth of many-particle systems far from equilibrium. Subspecialties: Condensed matter physics; Statistical physics. Home: 1616 Brooklyn St Ann Arbor MI 48104 Office: Physics Dept U Mich Randall Lab Ann Arbor MI 48109

SANDERS, CHARLES ADDISON, pharmaceutical company executive, physician; b. Dallas, Feb. 10, 1932; s. Harold Barefoot and May Elizabeth (Forrester) S.; m. Elizabeth Ann Chipman, Mar. 6, 1956; children: Elizabeth, Charles Addison, Carlyn, Christopher. M.D., U. Tex., 1955. Intern, asst. resident Boston City Hosp., 1955-57, chief resident, 1957-58; clin. and research fellow in medicine Mass. Gen. Hosp., Boston, 1958-60, chief cardiac catheterization lab., 1962-72, gen. dir., 1972-81, physician, 1973-81, program dir. myocardial infarction research unit, 1967-72, program dir. MEDLAB systems, 1969-72; exec. v.p. E.R. Squibb and Sons, 1981—84, Squibb Corp., 1984—; assoc. prof. medicine Harvard U. Med. Sch., 1969-80, prof., 1980-83; lectr. MIT, 1973-81; dir. Bank of Boston Corp., New Eng. Life Ins. Co.; mem. Inst. Medicine, Nat. Acad. Scis.; chmn. Nat. Council Health Care Tech., 1980-81. Mem. editorial bd.: New Eng. Jour. Medicine, 1969-72. Past trustee Mass. Hosp. Assn. Served to capt. M.C. USAF, 1960-62. Mem. Am. Fedn. for Clin. Research, Am., Mass. heart assns., Mass. Med. Soc., A.C.P., Am. Physiol. Soc., Am. Clin. and Climatol. Soc., Am. Coll. Cardiology, Am. Soc. for Clin. Investigation, Soc. Hosp. Adminstrs., Greater Boston C. of C. (dir. 1977-81). Unitarian. Club: Harvard. Subspecialty: Cardiology. Home: 70 Independence Dr Princeton NJ 08540 Office: Squibb Corp P O Box 4000 Princeton NJ 08540

SANDERS, DONALD BENJAMIN, neurologist, neurophysiologist, educator; b. Sumter, S.C., Aug. 3, 1938; s. Colclough Eugene and Frances Ann (Humphries) S.; m. Polly Sandridge, Nov. 28, 1965; 1 dau., Colclough Allison; m. Lynda Frank, July 17, 1975; 1 dau., Kathleen Chatterton. B.S., U. of South, 1959; M.D., Harvard U., 1964. Diplomate: Am. Bd. Psychiatry and Neurology, 1972. From asst. prof. to asso. prof. neurology U. Va. Sch. Medicine, Charlottesville, 1972-80; prof. medicine Duke U. Med. Center, Durham, N.C., 1980—, also dir. electromyography lab. Contbr. numerous articles to sci. jours. Served to maj. USAF, 1969-72. USPHS fellow, 1961-62; Nat. Inst. Neurol. and Communicative Disorders and Stroke grantee, 1976-79; Muscular Dystrophy Assn. grantee, 1977-80, 82. Mem. Am. Acad. Neurology, Am. Neurol. Assn., Am. Assn. Electromyography and Electrodiagnosis, Soc. Neurosci., Myasthenia Gravis Found. Current Work: Diagnosis and treatment of nerve, muscle and neuromuscular diseases. Subspecialties: Neurology; Neurophysiology. Office: Duke U Med Center Box 3403 Durham NC 27710

SANDERS, FRED JOSEPH, See *Who's Who in America*, 43rd edition.

SANDERS, GILBERT OTIS, research psychologist, consultant, educator; b. Oklahoma City, Aug. 7, 1945; s. Richard Allen and Evelyn Wilmoth (Barker) S.; m. Marline Marie Lairmore, Nov. 1, 1969 (div. Oct. 1982); 1 dau., Lisa Dawn. A.S., Murray State Coll, 1965; B.A., Okla. State U., 1967; M.S., Troy State U., 1970; Ed.D., U. Tulsa, 1974. Research psychologist U.S. Army Research Inst., Ft. Hood, Tex., 1978-79; engring. psychologist U.S. Army Tng. and Doctrine Command Systems Analysis Activity, White Sands Missile Range, N. Mex., 1979-80; project dir./research psychologist Applied Sci. Assocs., Ft. Sill, Okla., 1980-81; research psychologist Res. Components Personnel and Adminstrn. Ctr., St. Louis, 1981—; cons. behavioral sci., St. Louis, 1981—; adj. prof. bus. and psychology Columbia Coll.-Buder Campus, St. Louis, 1982—; chmn. dept. computer sci., dir. computer services Calumet Coll., Whiting, Ind., 1975-78; dir. edn. Am. Humane Edn. Soc., Boston, 1975. Prin. editor: TRADOC Training Effectiveness Analysis Handbook, 1980; author research reports. Hon. col. Okla. Gov.'s Staff, Oklahoma City, 1972; hon. ambassador Gov. Okla., 1974. Recipient Kavanough Found. Community Builder award, 1967. Mem. Am. Psychol. Assn., Human Factors Soc., Am. Personnel and Guidance Assn., Assn. Ednl. Communications Tech., Tex. Psychol. Assn., Okla. Psychol. Assn., Mo. Psychol. Assn., Okla. Hist. Soc., Res. Officers Assn. Lodge: Masons. Current Work: Research in area of human-machine interface of developing military weapon systems and the development of cognitive skill test to predict training success; weapon systems include new battlefield computers (TACFIRE) and the Pershing II. Subspecialty: Learning. Home: 184 Rue Grand Lake Saint Louis MO 63367 Office: Res Components Personnel and Adminstrn Ctr 9700 Page Blvd Saint Louis MO 63132

SANDERS, GLORIA TOLSON, physical therapy educator, researcher; b. Jacksonville, N.C., Nov. 17, 1944; d. William Mattocks and Zeta (Tolson) S. Student, N.C. Wesleyan Coll., 1962-65; B.S., Med. Coll. Va., 1967; M.S., East Carolina U., 1976. Cert. phys. therapist. Staff therapist Grady Meml. Hosp., Atlanta, 1967-69, Kennestone Hosp., Marietta, Ga., 1969-70; instr. East Carolina U., Greenville, N.C., 1970-71, assoc. prof. dept. phys. therapy, 1974—; dir. phys. therapy Univ. Hosp. of Jacksonville, Fla., 1971-74; mem. N.C. Bd. Phys. Therapy Examiners, 1982-83; mem., cons. State Arthritis Adv. Com., 1979-82; reviewer Profl. Exam. Service, N.J., 1980-83. Author Lower Limb Amputations: A Guide to Rehabilitation; manual, articles in field. 1983. Grantee N.C. Dept. Human Resources, 1980, 81, 82; Grantee East Carolina U., 1977, 78. Mem. Am. Phys. Therapy Assn., N.C. Phys. Therapy Assn. (peer reviewer 1975-83), Delta Kappa Gamma, Alpha Omicron Pi (chpt. advisor 1976-79). Democrat. Methodist. Current Work: Study of barriers of handicapped information; research: nausea control during chemotherapy, pelvic tilt measurement, sacro-iliac joint mobility. Subspecialty: Physical medicine and rehabilitation. Home: 1205 E Fifth St Greenville NC 27834 Office: East Carolina Univ Greenville NC 27834

SANDERS, ROBERT BURNETT, biochemist, educator; b. Augusta, Ga., Dec. 9, 1938; s. Robert and Lois Mabel (Jones) S.; m. Gladys Nealous, Dec. 23, 1961; children: Sylvia, William. B.S., Paine Coll., Augusta, 1959; M.S., U. Mich., 1961, Ph.D., 1964. Teaching fellow, trainee U. Mich., 1959-64; postdoctoral fellow U. Wis., Madison, 1964-66; asst., then assoc. prof. biochemistry U. Kans., Lawrence, 1966—; vis. scientist Battelle Northwest, Richland, Wash., 1970-71; vis. asso. prof. U. Tex. Med. Sch., Houston, 1974-75; program dir. NSF, 1978-79; now cons.; cons. NIH, NSF. Contbr. articles to profl. jours. Bd. dirs. United Child Devel. Center, 1968—. Served with USAR, 1955-62. Paine Coll. Alumni Scholar, 1958-59; USPHS trainee, 1959-64; Am. Cancer Soc. postdoctoral fellow, 1964-66; Battelle Meml. Inst. fellow, 1970-71; NIH fellow, 1974-75; also research grantee. Mem. Am. Soc. Biol. Chemists, Am. Soc. Pharmacology and Exptl. Therapeutics, Sigma Xi, Alpha Kappa Mu. Methodist. Current Work: Biochemistry of reproduction; biochemistry of the rat uterus. Subspecialties: Biochemistry (biology); Biochemistry (medicine). Office: Dept Biochemistry U Kans Lawrence KS 66045

SANDERS, WILTON TURNER, III, physicist; b. Greenwood, Miss., Sept. 4, 1947; s. Wilton Turner Jr. and Virginia (Jones) S. B.A., Johns Hopkins U., 1969; M.S., U. Wis., 1972, Ph.D., 1976. Lectr., research assoc. dept. physics U., Wis.-Madison, 1976-77, asst. scientist, 1977-81, assoc. scientist, 1981—. Contbr. articles to profl. jours. Marie Christine Kohler fellow, 1972-74. Mem. AAAS, Am. Phys. Soc., Am. Astron. Soc., Internat. Astron. Union, Phi Beta Kappa, Sigma Xi. Current Work: Study of the low energy x-ray (0.1-2 kev) diffuse background, its spatial and spectral characteristics and the local interstellar medium which is thought to be origin of these x-rays; also stellar x-ray emission. Subspecialty: X-ray high energy astrophysics. Home: 2433 Fox Ave Madison WI 53711 Office: Dept Physics U Wis 1150 University Ave Madison WI 53706

SANDERSON, GLEN CHARLES, research administrator, research biologist; b. Wayne County, Mo., Jan. 21, 1923; s. Albert Charles and Lillie Bell (Nelson) S.; m. Beverley Carrick, Nov. 26, 1947; children—James William, Laurie Jean. B.S. in Agr., U. Mo., 1947, M.A. in Zoology, 1949; Ph.D. in Animal Scis., U. Ill., 1961. Game biologist Iowa Conservation Commn., Marion, 1949-55; research biologist, Ill. Natural History Survey, Champaign, 1955-63, head sect. wildlife research, 1963—; prof. zoology U. Ill., Urbana, 1965-76, prof. ecology, ethology and evolution, 1976—; adj. prof. So. Ill. U., Carbondale, 1964—. Editor: Wild Turkey Management, 1970; Ducks, Geese & Swans of North America, 1975; Management of Migratory Birds in North America, 1977; Midwest Furbearer Management, 1981. Chmn. adv. com. Champaign County Forest Preserve Dist., Ill., 1975-76; chmn., bd. dirs. Champaign County Devel. Council Found., Ill., 1977—; bd. dirs. Ill. chpt. Nature Conservancy, Chgo., 1980—. Served to 1st lt. U.S. Army, 1943-46, Okinawa. Named Conservationist of Yr., Am. Motors, 1972; recipient Oak Leaf award The Nature Conservancy, Chgo., 1975. Mem. Wildlife Soc. (Appreciation award 1982), AAAS, Am. Inst. Biol. Scis., Am. Soc. Mammalogists (chmn. com.), Council Biology Editors. Methodist. Current work: Reproductive physiology of wild animals, lead poisoning in waterfowl. Subspecialties: Wildlife biology; Reproductive biology. Office: Ill Natural History Survey 607 East Peabody Champaign IL 61820

SANDERSON, H. REED, wildlife biologist, range scientist; b. Huston, Idaho, July 8, 1932; s. Roland and Hazel Leanore (Stinson) Frost; m. Georgiana Weisgerber, Feb. 11, 1961; children: Christine Marie, Allen Reed. B.S., Humboldt State U., 1957; M.S., Colo. State U., 1959. Cert. wildlife biologist. With Forest Service Research, U.S. Dept. Agr., 1960—, involved in browse propagation, 1960-63, mountain meadow ecology and annual grass mgmt., Calif., 1963-66, eastern gray squirrel habitat mgmt., W.Va., 1966-76, integrated resource mgmt. research, La Grande, Oreg., 1976—. Contbr. articles to profl. jours. Served with U.S. Navy, 1950-54. Memm. Soc. Range Mgmt., Wildlife Soc. Current Work: Evaluation of the effects of range management activities on the other natural resources. Subspecialties: Ecology (environmental science); Range and wildlife habitat. Home: Route 4 Box 4377 La Grande OR 97850 Office: Route 2 Box 2315 La Grande OR 97850

SANDHU, TALJIT SINGH, physicist; b. Kot, India, June 25, 1949; came to U.S., 1970, naturalized, 1977; s. Jogindar Singh and Pritam Kaur (Jhaz) S.; m. Laurie A. Sandhu, Apr. 20, 1982. B.Sc. in Physics with honors, U. Delhi, India, 1968, M.Sc. in Physics, 1970; Ph.D., SUNY-Buffalo, 1975. Cert. therapeutic radiol. physics Am. Bd. Radiology. Cancer research scientist Roswell Park Meml. Inst., Buffalo, 1975-77, med. physicist, 1977-78; sr. med. physicist Henry Ford Hosp., Detroit, 1978-81; adj. asst. prof. Wayne State U., 1979-81; asst. prof. radiology U. Utah, Salt Lake City, 1981—. Contbr. articles to profl. jours. Mem. Am. Assn. Physicists in Medicine, Radiation Research Soc., Bioelectromagnetics Soc., IEEE. Current Work: Interaction of ionizing and non-ionizing radiation with tissues; radiation, x-rays, gamma-rays, charged particles, microwaves, rf fields, hyperthermia, effects of ionizing and non-ionizing radiation on tumors and normal tissues, electromagnetic properties of tissues. Subspecialties: Biophysics (physics); Biomedical engineering. Office: Dept Radiology U Utah Medical Center Salt Lake City UT 84132

SANDORFY, CAMILLE, chemistry educator; b. Budapest, Hungary, Dec. 9, 1920; emigrated to Can., 1951, naturalized, 1957; s. Kamill and Paula (Fenyes) S.; m. Rolande Cayla, Aug. 24, 1971. B.Sc., U. Szeged, Hungary, 1943, Ph.D., 1946; D.Sc., Sorbonne, U. Paris, 1949. Attache de recherches Centre Nationale de la Recherche Scientifique, Paris, France, 1947-51; postdoctoral fellow Nat. Research Council of Can., 1951-53; asst. prof. chemistry U. Montreal, Que., Can., 1954-56, asso. prof., 1956-59, prof., 1959—; vis. prof. U. Paris, 1968, 74. Author: Les Spectres Electroniques en Chimie Theorique, 1959, Electronic Spectra and Quantum Chemistry, 1964, (with R. Daudel) Semi-empirical Wave-Mechanical Calculations on Polyatomic Molecules, 1971. Recipient Prix Marie-Victorin Quebec, 1982; Recipient medal Chem. Inst. Can., 1983; Killam Meml. scholar, 1978. Fellow Royal Soc. Can. Research, numerous publs. in chemistry. Subspecialty: Theoretical chemistry. Office: U Montreal Dept Chemistry Montreal PQ H3C 3J7 Canada

SANDSTEAD, HAROLD HILTON, physician, laboratory administrator; b. Omaha, May 25, 1932; s. Harold Russel and Florence (Hilton) S.; m. Kathryn Brownlee, June 6, 1959; children: Eleanor, James, William. B.A., Ohio Wesleyan U., 1954; M.D., Vanderbilt U., 1958. Diplomate: Am. Bd. Internal Medicine, Am. Bd. Clin. Nutrition, 1967. Intern Barnes Hosp., Washington U., St. Louis, 1958-59; asst. resident in medicine 1959-60; asst. resident in pathology Vanderbilt U. Hosp., Nashville, 1960-61, chief resident medicine, 1964-65, instr. medicine, 1965-68, asst. prof. medicine, 1968-71, asst. prof. biochemistry, 1965-70, assoc. prof. nutrition, 1970-71; dir. U.S. Dept. Agr.-Agrl. Research Service, Human Nutrition Research Ctr., Grand Forks, N.D., 1971-84, dir. Human Nutrition Research Ctr. on Aging, Boston, 1984—; adj. prof. biochemistry U. N.D. Sch. Medicine, from 1971, clin. prof. internal medicine, from 1976; cons. WHO. Contbr. numerous articles to sci. publs. Served as asst. surgeon USPHS, 1961-63, Egypt. Named Nutrition Found. Future Leader 1968-70; recipient Am. Inst. Nutrition Mead Johnson award, 1971. Fellow ACP; mem. Am. Soc. Clin. Nutrition (pres. 1982-83), Am. Inst. Nutrition, Central Soc. Clin. Research, So. Soc. Clin. Investion. Current Work: Nutritional biochemistry; essential trace elements and toxic elements in nutrition and physiologic function; nutrition and fetal development; nutrition and brain function and development; clinical nutrition, human requirements. Subspecialties: Nutrition (medicine); Internal medicine. Office: USDA-ARS Human Nutrition Research Ctr 711 Washington St Boston MA 02111

SANDUSKY, JR. GEORGE EARL, pathologist; b. Columbus, Ohio, May 18, 1945; s. George Earl and Jane Elizabeth (Herbert) S.; m. Susan L. Boley, Feb. 14, 1976; children—Kristen, Shea, Stacey. B.S., Ohio U., 1967; D.V.M., Ohio State U., 1971, M.S., 1978; Ph.D., La. State U., 1980. Diplomate Am. Coll. Vet. Pathology. Instr. La. State U., Baton Rouge, 1978-80; pathologist Eli Lilly & Co., Indpls., 1980—. Contbr. articles to profl. jours. Bd. dirs. Ind. Heart Assn., Greenfield, 1982—; negotiator Am. Heart Assn., Indpls., 1984—. Mem. Am. Coll. Vet. Pathology, AVMA, Phi Zeta. Current work: Immunocytochemistry. Subspecialties: Pathology (medicine); Immunotoxicology. Home: RR 1 Box SW 206 New Balestine IN 46163

SANETO, RUSSELL PATRICK, neurobiologist; b. Burbank, Calif., Oct. 10, 1950; s. Frank Saneto and Mitzi (Akino) Seddon. B.S., San Diego State U., 1972, M.S., 1975; Ph.D., U. Tex. Med. Br., 1981. Teaching asst. San Diego State U., 1974-76; predoctoral fellow U. Tex., Galveston, 1976-81, Jeanne B. Kempner postdoctoral fellow, 1981; postdoctoral fellow UCLA, 1982-84, biochemist, 1984—; vis. scholar in ethics So. Bapt. Theol. Sem., 1981. Author Cell Culture in the Neurosciences, 1985, Handbook of Nervous System and Muscle Factors, 1985. Contbr. articles to profl. jours. Organizer Run for World Hunger, Galveston, 1980, Charity Med. Care for Mex., Juarez, 1980-83. Neuropsychiat. Inst. grantee UCLA, 1985. Mem. N.Y. Acad. Scis., Am. Soc. Neurochemistry, Soc. Neurosci., AAAS, Sierra Club, Bread for the World, Sigma Xi. Democrat. Mem. Evangelical Free Ch. Current work: Use of primary tissue culture to study of factors responsible for the proliferation and maturation of oligodendrocytes. Subspecialties: Neurobiology; Developmental biology. Office: UCLA 760 Westwood Plaza Los Angeles CA 90024

SANFORD, BARBARA HENDRICK, geneticist; b. Brockton, Mass., Oct. 17, 1927; d. Arthur A. and Grace E. (Brennan) Hendrick; divorced (div.); children: Arthur, Jane, Brian, Paul. Ph.D., Brown U., 1963. Dir. Jackson Lab., Bar Harbor, Maine, 1981—. Mem. Genetics Soc. Am., Am. Assn. Immunologists, Am. Assn. Cancer Research. Current Work: Mammalian genetics; administration. Subspecialty: Animal genetics. Office: Jackson Lab Bar Harbor ME 04609

SANFORD, JAY PHILIP, physician, government official; b. Madison, Wis., May 27, 1928; s. Joseph Arthur and Arlyn (Carlson) S.; m. Lorraine Burklund, Apr. 7, 1950; children—Jeb, Nancy, Sarah, Philip, Catherine. M.D., U. Mich., 1952. Intern Peter Bent Brigham Hosp., Boston, 1952-53; research fellow Harvard Med. Sch., Boston, 1953-54; resident Duke U. Hosp., Durham, N.C., 1956-57; practice medicine specializing in internal medicine, Dallas, 1957-75; mem. faculty U. Tex. Southwestern Med. Sch. at Dallas, 1957-75; prof. internal medicine, 1965-75; dean Sch. Medicine, Uniformed Services U. Health Scis., Bethesda, Md., 1975—, pres., 1981—; chief microbiology lab. Parkland Meml. Hosp., Dallas, 1957-75, pres. med. staff, 1968-69; form mem. staff St. Paul Hosp., Dallas, Presbyn. Hosp., Dallas, John Peter Smith Hosp., Ft. Worth; cons. Dallas VA Hosp., Wilford Hall USAF Hosp., Brooke Gen. Hosp., Ft. Sam Houston; mem. adv. council Dallas Health and Sci. Mus., 1968-75; chmn. Am. Bd. Internal Medicine, 1978-79; mem. Gov.'s Commn. Phys. Fitness, 1971-75. Contbr. articles to profl. jours. Served with M.C. U.S. Army, 1954-56. Recipient Cert. of award Div. Health Moblzn. USPHS, 1963, 64; Pfizer award for CD, 1965; Presdl. citation for Health Moblzn. Planning, 1970; Bristol award Infectious Disease Soc. Am., 1981; Dept. of Def. Pub. Service Medal, 1982. Fellow Am. Acad. Microbiology, A.C.P. (master); mem. Assn. Am. Physicians, Nat. Inst. Allergy and Infectious Diseases (chmn. tng. grant com. 1971), Am. Fedn. Clin. Research (pres. 1968-69), Am. Soc. Microbiology, Central Soc. Clin. Research, Soc. Exptl. Biology and Medicine, Am. Soc. Clin. Investigation, Soc. Med. Consultants to Armed Forces (pres. 1976-77), Am. Thoracic Soc., Infectious Disease Soc. Am. (pres. 1978-79), Inst. of Medicine of Nat. Acad. Scis., Sigma Xi. Current Work: Pharmacology of antimcrobial agents. Subspecialties: Internal medicine; Infectious diseases. Home: 10409 Windsor View Dr Potomac MD 20854 Office: Uniformed Services Univ of the Health Scis 4301 Jones Bridge Rd Bethesda MD 20814

SANGER, GARY EDWARD, geophysicist; b. Rochester, N.Y., Aug. 9, 1950; s. Bernard Frank and Betty Rosemary (Boehmer) S. B.S., SUNY-Brockport, 1977; M.S., U. Akron, 1980. Analyst, U.S. Govt., Washington, 1981—. Editor, Frontiers, 1980. Served with USAF, 1968-72. Fellow Brit. Interplanetary Soc.; mem. Am. Astronautical Soc., Am. Geophys. Union, AIAA, Space Studies Inst. (sr. assoc.). Roman Catholic. Club: Upstate Space Alliance (bd. dirs. 1980-81). Current work: Analysis of circular surface features near New Baltimore, Ohio, using remotely sensed data. Subspecialties: Remote sensing (geoscience); Planetology. Home: 11691 Charter Oak Ct #T1 Reston VA 22090

SANI, BRAHMA P., biochemist; b. Trichur, India, Sept. 13, 1937; s. Brahma L. and T. V. (Annam) Porinchu; m. Alice C. Sani, Nov. 27, 1967; children: Anita, Renju. B.S., St. Thomas Coll., Kerala, India, 1960; M.S., Holkar Coll., Indore, India, 1962; Ph.D., Indian Inst. Sci., 1967. Sr. research fellow Indian Inst. Sci., Bangalore, 1962-68; staff fellow Boston Biomed. Research Inst., 1968-71; research cons. Retina Found., Boston, 1970-71; research assoc. Inst. for Cancer Research, Fox Chase, Phila., 1971-74; sr. biochemist So. Research Inst., Birmingham, Ala., 1974-78, head protein biochem. sect., 1979—. NIH grantee, 1977—. Mem. Am. Assn. Cancer Research, Am. Soc. Biol. Chemists. Current Work: Molecular basis of carcinogenesis and anti carcinogensis; mechanism of action of retinoids and trace elements in growth and in chemoprevention of cancer. Subspecialty: Biochemistry (biology). Office: 2000 9th Ave S Birmingham AL 35255

SANNELLA, JOSEPH LEE, industrial company executive; b. Boston, July 27, 1933; s. Theodore and Anna (Barone) S.; m. Nancy Marshall, June 6, 1959; children: Joseph A., Sueanne E., Stephen J. A.B., Harvard U., 1955; M.S., U. Mass., 1958; Ph.D., Purdue U., 1963; M.B.A., U. Del., 1969. Product evaluation and tech. service supr. FMC Corp., Marcus Hook, Pa., 1962-67; with Ball Corp., Muncie, Ind., 1967—, supr. chem. research, 1971-74, dir. research, 1974-85; dir. corporate lab. services, 1985—. Contbr. articles to profl. pubs. Bd. dirs. Big Bros./Big Sisters, Delaware County, Ind., 1969-78, Isanogel Center, Delaware County, 1979, Ball Corp. Employees Credit Union, 1981—, Ball Corp. Polit. Action Com., 1978—. Mem. Am. Chem. Soc., Soc. Plastic Engrs., Nat. Metal Decorating Assn. Lodge: Kiwanis. Patentee in field. Current Work: Evaluation of new technologies related to plastic, metals and glass. Subspecialties: Polymers (materials science); Materials. Home: 2803 W Woodbridge St Muncie IN 47304 Office: 1509 S Macedonia St Muncie IN 47302

SANNER, JOHN HARPER, pharmacologist; b. Anamosa, Iowa, Apr. 29, 1931; s. Lee Michael and Helen Grace (Smyth) S.; m. Marilyn Joan Eichorst, Dec. 28, 1958; children: Linda, Steven. B.S., U. Iowa, 1954, M.S., 1961, Ph.D., 1964. Lic. pharmacist, Iowa. Research investigator G. D. Searle & Co., Chgo., 1963-69, sr. research investigator, 1969-75, research fellow, 1975—. Contbr. articles to profl. jours. and books. Served to 1st lt. USAF, 1955-57. Mem. Am. Soc. Pharmacology and Exptl. Therapeutics, AAAS. Republican. Current Work: Pharmacological antagonism of prostaglandins and related compounds. Subspecialty: Pharmacology. Home: 959 Apple Tree Ln Deerfield IL 60015 Office: 4901 Searle Pkwy Skokie IL 60077

SANSLONE, WILLIAM ROBERT, research executive, educator; b. Vineland, N.J., Feb. 16, 1931; s. Fortunato and Rose (Pelli) S.; m. Alice Elizabeth Koury, June 25, 1960; 1 child, Catherine M. B.S., Rutgers U., 1953, Ph.D., 1961; M.S., U. N.H., 1955. Biochemistry research asst. U. Conn., Storrs, 1955-56; instr. biochemistry SUNY-Downstate Med. Ctr., Bklyn., 1961-64, asst. prof., 1964-70, assoc. prof., 1970-71; project scientist NIH, Bethesda, Md., 1971-72, sr. project scientist, 1972-73, exec. sec. biochemistry study sect., 1973-74, program dir. for rev. activities Nat. Cancer Inst., 1974-83, assoc. dir. sci. program ops. Div. Lung Diseases, Nat. Heart, Lung and Blood Inst., 1983—; vis. assoc. prof. physiology and biophysics Med. Coll. Pa., Phila., 1970; cons. Greiner Chem. Co., N.Y.C., 1968-70. Contbr. articles to sci. jours. Served to 1st lt. USAF, 1956-58; ETO. Recipient U. N.H. Research award, 1955; Spl. Achievement award Nat. Cancer Inst., NIH, 1977, Quality Step Increase, 1978. Mem. Fedn. Am. Soc. for Exptl. Biology, Am. Inst. Nutrition, Soc. for Exptl. Biology and Medicine, Harvey Soc., Sigma Xi. Roman Catholic. Current work: Basic and clinical pulmonary diseases research program planning and evaluation. Subspecialties: Biochemistry (medicine); Nutrition (medicine). Home: 6835 Old Stage Rd Rockville MD 20852 Office: Div Lung Diseases Nat Heart Lung & Blood Inst NIH Bethesda MD 20205

SANTI, GINO P., aerospace engineer; b. Bklyn., Feb. 5, 1916; s. Joseph and Emma (Grandi) S.; m. Dorothy Edna Hardy, May 23, 1948; children: Janice, Martha, Victor, Linda, Laura. B.C.E., CCNY, 1936, M.C.E., 1937; postgrad., Ohio State U., 1948-52, U. Dayton, 1956-60. Registered profl. engr., Ohio. Civil engr. Nat. Excavation Corp., N.Y.C., 1937-38, Johnson, Drake & Piper, Inc., Freeport, N.Y., 1938-39; naval architect Dept. Navy, Mare Island, Calif., 1939-40, NASA, Langley Field, Va., 1940-44; aerospace engr. Dept. Air Force, Wright-Patterson AFB, Ohio, 1947-80. Served to capt. USAAF, 1944-47; Served to capt. USAF, 1951-53. Recipient Meritorious Civilian Service award Dept. Air Force, 1977. Mem. AIAA, Survival and Flight Equipment Assn., Sigma Xi. Republican. Roman Catholic. Inventor automatic escape system release; designer 1st aircraft high-speed crew escape ejection seat. Current Work: Conception, analysis, research, development and test of U.S. Air Force aircraft escape systems and the determination of research and development programs in all technical elements necessary to achieve performance requirements for advanced aircraft. Subspecialty: Aerospace engineering and technology. Home: 201 Enfield Rd Dayton OH 45459

SANTILLI, JOHN, JR., pediatrician, allergist, immunologist; b. Waterbury, Conn., Mar. 29, 1942; s. John and Caroline (Pranaiss) S.; m. Beverly M. McKee, July 2, 1966; children: Susan, Michael, Sandra. B.S., Villanova U., 1964; M.D., Georgetown U., 1968. Diplomate: Am. Bd. Pediatrics, Am. Bd. Allergy and Clin. Immunology. Intern in pediatrics Georgetown U. Hosp., Washington, 1968-69, resident in pediatrics, 1969-71, individual practice medicine specializing in clin. immunology and allergy, Bridgeport, Conn., 1975—; chief Allergy Clinic, Bridgeport Hosp., 19—. Contbr. numerous sci. articles to profl. publs. Served to maj. USAF, 1973-75. Mem. AMA, Am. Acad. Allergy. Roman Catholic. Current Work: Molds as allergens and immunogentics in allergy; clinical allergist and researcher. Subspecialty: Allergy. Office: 4675 Main St Bridgeport CT 06606

SANTORO, ROBERT JOHN, physicist, chemical engineer; b. Somerville, Mass., Oct. 21, 1946; s. Arthur Joseph and Mary Grace (Liberatore) S.; m. Phyllis Ann McLellan, Nov. 3, 1973; children—Andrea Lee, Elizabeth Marie. B.S. in Physics, Boston Coll., 1968, M.S. in Physics, 1974, Ph.D. in Physics, 1975. Electrical engr. IBM, Fishkill, N.Y., 1968-69; research asst. Boston Coll., Chestnut Hill, Mass., 1969-74, lectr., 1974-75; research staff mem. Princeton U., N.J., 1975-78; physicist Nat. Bur. Standard, Gaithersburg, Md., 1978—. Contbr. articles to profl. jours. Recipient Presdl. Bicentennial award Boston Coll., 1974. Mem. Am. Phys. Soc., Am. Chem. Soc., The Combustion Inst., Sigma Xi, Sigma Pi Sigma. Roman Catholic. Current work: The study of particulate formation and growth in chemically reacting flows using laser diagnostics; particle property measurements using laser based techniques; flame and combustion chemistry. Subspecialties: Combustion processes; Chemical engineering. Home: 1506 Bradley Ave Rockville MD 20851 Office: Nat Bur Standards Bldg 221 Room B252 Gaithersburg MD 20851

SANTOS, EUGENIO MIGUEL, molecular biologist, researcher; b. Salamanca, Spain, May 5, 1953; came to U.S., 1979; s. Julian Santos and Angela De Dios; m. Isabel Santos, Jan. 3, 1982; child, Miguel. B.Sc., U. Salamanca, Spain, 1975, M.Sc., 1975, Ph.D., 1978. Postdoctoral fellow Roche Inst. Molecular Biology, Nutley, N.J., 1979-81; vis. fellow Nat. Cancer Inst., Bethesda, Md., 1981-84; prof. microbiology Salamanca U., Spain, 1984; staff scientist Nat. Cancer Inst., Frederick, Md., 1984-85; vis. scientist lab molecular microbiology NIH, Nat. Cancer Inst., Bethesda, 1985—. Contbr. articles to profl. jours. and books. Spanish-N. Am. Com. Sci. Coop. fellow, 1981; Fundacion Juan March, fellow, 1982; recipient medal U. Salamanca, 1983; Annual Monographic award Spanish Assn. against Cancer, 1984. Mem. Am. Soc. Microbiology, Spanish Biochem. Soc., Spanish Soc. Microbiology, Royal Acad. Medicine (Salamanca, Spain). Roman Catholic. Current work: Study of human oncogenes; molecular mechanisms involved in malignant transformation and human cancer; initiation and progression of tumor development. Subspecialties: Molecular biology; Cell biology. Office: Lab Molecular Microbiology NIH Bldg 5 Room B1-26 Bethesda MD 20205

SANTOS, GEORGE WESLEY, physician, educator, researcher, consultant; b. Oak Park, Ill., Feb. 3, 1928; s. George and Emma Adelaide (Corrigan) S.; m. Joanne Agnes Corrigan, 1952; children—Susan Elizabeth, George Wesley II, Kelly Anne, Amy Coburn. B.S., MIT, 1951, M.S., 1951; M.D., Johns Hopkins U., 1955. Diplomate Am. Bd. Internal Medicine. Asst. resident Osler med. service Johns Hopkins Hosp., Balt., 1958-60, asst. physician, 1960-63, physician, 1962-74, physician outpatient dept., 1965—, mem. active staff dept. oncology and medicine, 1974—; instr. medicine, 1962-63, asst. prof., 1963-68, assoc. prof., 1968-73, prof. oncology and medicine, 1973—; asst. physician-in-chief med. service (oncology) Balt. City Hosps., 1963-77, vis. physician, 1960-77; cons in field. Contbr. numerous articles to profl. jours. Mem. editorial bds. Internat. Soc. for Exptl. Hematology, 1977-81, Transplantation, 1973—; mem. editorial adv. bd. Cancer Research; Editor-in-chief: Contemporary Topics in Immunobiology, 1970—; editor Blood. Served to lt. USN, 1956-58. Leukemia Soc. Am. scholar, 1961-66. Mem. Am. Soc. Hematology (immunohematology subcom. 1973), Transplantation Soc., Am. Assn. Immunologists, Johns Hopkins Med. Soc., Am. Assn. Cancer Research, Inc., Internat. Soc. Exptl. Hematology (bd. dirs. 1972-76, Councillor 1973, pres. 1981), Am. Cancer Soc. (bd. dirs. Baltimore County unit 1973-76), Am. Assn. Clin. Oncology, Am. Soc. Clin. Investigation, Am. Clin. and Climatological Assn., Kappa Sigma. Democrat. Episcopalian. Current work: Hematology, marrow transplant, immunology, cellular engineering, oncology. Subspecialties: Marrow transplant; Cellular engineering. Home: 13523 Bardon Rd Phoenix MD 21131 Office: Johns Hopkins Oncology Ctr 3-127 600 N Wolfe St Baltimore MD 21205

SAPERSTEIN, ALVIN MARTIN, physics, educator; b. Bronx, N.Y., June 3, 1930; s. Morris and Eva (Finkelstein) S.; m. Harriet Eve Brown, June 10, 1956; children: Shira, Rina. B.A., NYU, 1951; M.S., Yale U., 1952, Ph.D., 1956. Research assoc. Woods Hole Oceanographic Instn., U. Mich., Brown U., 1957-59; asst. prof. U. Buffalo, 1959-62; assoc. prof. Wayne State U., Detroit, 1963-67, prof., 1967—, dir. program in environ. studies, 1977-80; mem. exec. bd. Ctr. Peace and Conflict Studies Wayne State U., 1979—, chmn. exec. bd., dir research, 1985; vis. prof. Univ. Coll. London, 1969-70, Open U., Eng., 1976-77, 84. Research fellow Argonne Nat. Lab., 1962-63, Peace Research Inst., Stockholm, 1983, Internat. Inst. Strategic Studies, 1984. Author: Energy: Physics in the Environment, 1975; contbr. articles to profl. jours. Mem. exec. bd. Met. Detroit chpt. ACLU. NSF fellow, 1976; NSF grantee. Fellow Am. Phys. Soc., AAAS; mem. Am. Assn. Physics Tchrs., Fedn. Am. Scientists, Union Concerned Scientists, United Campuses to Prevent Nuclear War, Phi Beta Kappa, Sigma Xi. Jewish. Current Work: Theoretical physics, relations between science and society, impact of science and technology on environment, war and peace questions. Subspecialties: Theoretical physics; Nuclear physics. Home: 1500 Chateaufort Pl Detroit MI 48207 Office: Dept Physics Wayne State U Detroit MI 48202

SAPERSTEIN, LEE WALDO, mining engineering educator; b. N.Y.C., July 14, 1943; s. Charles Levy and Freda Phyllis (Dornbush) S.; m. Priscilla Frances Hickson, Sept. 16, 1967; children: Adam Geoffrey, Clare Freda. B.S. in Mining Engring, Mont. Sch. Mines, 1964; D.Phil. in Engring. Sci. (Rhodes scholar), Oxford U., 1967. Registered profl. engr., Pa. Laborer, miner, engr. The Anaconda Co., Butte, Mont., and; N.Y.C., 1963-64; asst. prof. mining engring. Pa. State U., University Park, 1967-71, asso. prof., 1971-78, prof., 1978—, sect. chmn., 1974—; mem. exec. com. of engring. accreditation commn. Accreditation Bd. for Engring. and Tech.; cons. Contbr.: articles refereed jours. Mem. Soc. Mining Engrs., AIME, Am. Assn. Rhodes Scholars. Current Work: Mining engineering education; surface mine design; reclamation and land use planning; mine subsidence; training developments for miners. Subspecialty: Mining engineering. Home: 337 Ridge Ave State College PA 16803 Office: 118 Mineral Sciences Bldg University Park PA 16802

SAPP, DANNY LEE, chemist, microbiologist, researcher; b. Macon, Ga., July 16, 1960; s. Chester Leroy and Eleanor Christine (Smallwood) S. B.S., Ga. Coll., 1981. Chief chemist, microbiologist Nord Kaolin Co., Jeffersonville, Ga., 1981—. Mem. Am. Chem. Soc., BBB Biol. Honor Soc. Republican. Baptist. Current work: Identification and control of microorganisms in clay slurry. Subspecialties: Microbiology; Inorganic chemistry. Home: 107 Forest Pointe Dr Macon GA 31210 Office: PO Box 297 Jeffersonville GA 31044

SAPPINGTON, JOHN OLIVER, electro-optics engineer; b. Spartanburg, S.C., Sept. 23, 1948; s. John Weston Jr. and Annie Louise (Smith) S.; m. Lynda Louisa Burton, July 17, 1971; children—Jennifer Louisa, David John. B.S. in Engring., U. S.C., 1970; M.S., U. Dayton, 1979. Electronics engr. Naval Ship Research and Devel. Ctr., Bethesda, Md., 1970-73, fgn. tech. div. U.S. Air Force, Wright Patterson AFB, Ohio, 1973-79; sr. staff mem. Quest Research Corp., Dayton, Ohio, 1979-81; sr. engr. IIT Research Inst., Dayton, 1981-84; sr. supervisory scientist Sci. Applications Internat. Corp., Dayton, 1984—. Author tech. reports and papers on application of infrared and electro-optical tech. to nat. def. Ford Found. grantee, 1969. Recipient Bausch & Lomb Hon. Sci. award, 1967; Outstanding Sr. award IEEE, 1970. Mem. Assn. Old Crows, Optical Soc. Am. Republican. Baptist. Current work: Analysis of state-of-the-art infrared and electro-optical systems through development of computer models and mathematical algorithms. Subspecialties: Algorithms; Optical engineering. Home: 1928 N Sulphur Springs Rd West Alexandria OH 45381 Office: Sci Applications Internat Corp 1010 Woodman Dr Dayton OH 45432

SARACHEK, ALVIN, geneticist; b. Pitts., July 29, 1927; s. Harry E. and Bertha (Balter) S.; m. Rosa Lee Ireland, Apr. 22, 1977. B.A., U. Mo., Kansas City, 1948, M.A., 1950; Ph.D., Kans. State U., 1957; postdoctorate, Inst. Microbiology, Rutgers U., 1957-58. Research microbiologist Am. Research Kitchens, Kansas City, Mo., 1948-50; research assoc., biol. research lab. So. Ill. U., 1951-54; asst. prof. biol. scis. Wichita State U., Kans., 1958-59, assoc. prof., 1959-61, prof., 1961—; program mgr. molecular genetics AEC, 1965-66; sr. profl. assoc. sci. edn. directorate NSF, Washington, 1977-78; Endowment Assn. disting. prof. natural scis. Wichita State U., 1974—; cons., mem. adv. com., panelist AEC, Dept. Energy, NSF, Am. Cancer Soc. Contbr. articles to profl. jours. Served with AUS, 1954-55. Office Naval Research grantee, 1958-65; Am. Cancer Soc. grantee, 1958-74; AEC grantee, 1968-73; recipient Teaching Excellence award Wichita State Regents, 1969. Fellow Am. Acad. Microbiology; mem. Am. Soc. Microbiology, Genetics Soc. Am., Environ. Mutagen Soc., Internat. Soc. Animal and Human Mycology, AAAS, Sigma Xi, Phi Kappa Phi. Current Work: Researcher in devel. of artificial parasexual systems for genetic analysis of asexual pathogenic or industrially significant yeasts. Subspecialties: Genetics and genetic engineering (biology); Microbiology. Office: Dept Biol Scis Wichita State U Wichita KS 67208

SARACHIK, MYRIAM PAULA, physics educator; b. Antwerp, Belgium, Aug. 8, 1933, came to U.S., 1947, naturalized, 1953; d. Solomon and Sarah (Segal) Morgenstein; m. Philip E. Sarachik, Sept. 6, 1954; 1 child, Karen. B.A., Barnard Coll., 1954; M.S., Columbia U., 1957, Ph.D., 1960. Research asst. IBM Watson Labs., N.Y.C., 1954-60; research assoc., 1960-61; mem. tech. staff Bell Telephone Labs., Murray Hill, N.J., 1962-64; asst. prof. CCNY, 1964-67, assoc. prof., 1967-70, prof. physics, 1970—. Contbr. articles to profl. jours. Grantee Dept. of Energy, Air Force Office of Sci. Research, CUNY Profl. Staff Congress-Bd. Higher Edn. Fellow Am. Phys. Soc. Subspecialties: Condensed matter physics; Magnetic physics. Home: 201 W 86th St New York City NY 10024 Office: Physics Dept CCNY Convent Ave and 138th St New York NY 10031

SARACHMAN, THEODORE NICHOLAS, physics educator; b. W. Warwick, R.I., Feb. 26, 1932; s. Theodore and Tekla (Krawchuk) S.; m. Joann Marilyn McCulloch, July 24, 1965; children: Elisabeth Ann, Suzanne Alix. A.B., B.S., M.S., U. Chgo., 1954; Ph.D., Harvard U., 1961. NBS/NRC research assoc., 1961-63; asst. prof. physics SUNY, Buffalo, 1963-70; assoc. prof. physics, chmn. dept. Whittier (Calif.) Coll., 1970—; chmn. bd. dirs. Western Obs., 1979-82. Contbr. articles to profl. jours. Mem. AAAS, Western Observatorium, Am. Phys. Soc., Am. Assn. Physics Tchrs. Current Work: Laser spectroscopy, biophysics. Subspecialty: Atomic and molecular physics. Office: Dept Physics Whittier Coll Whittier CA 90608

SARADA, THYAGARAJA, research scientist; b. Ambur, Madras, India, Apr. 19, 1929; came to U.S., 1967, naturalized, 1984; s. Thyagaraja M. Iyer and Ranganayaki Srinivasa Thyagaraja. B.Sc. with honors, Annamalai U., Chidambaram, India, 1951, M.A., 1955; M.S., Am. U., 1970, Ph.D., 1972. Research asst. Am. U., Washington, 1975-78, asst. prof., 1978-79; sr. chemist Celanese Research, Summit, N.J., 1979-82, Pitney Bowes, Norwalk, Conn., 1982—. Contbr. articles to profl. jours. Fulbright grantee, 1966, Epworth study grantee, 1967-72; NSF grantee, 1972. Mem. Am. Chem. Soc., TAPPI. Democrat. Hindu. Current work: Adhesives, membranes, batteries, fuel cells, ink jets, ink-paper interactions, inks, coating, surface characterization, materials. Subspecialties: Physical chemistry; Surface chemistry. Home: 230 Sunrise Hill Rd Norwalk CT 06851 Office: Pitney Bowes 276 Main Ave Norwalk CT 06851

SARAVIS, CALVIN ALBERT, immunochemist; b. Englewood, N.J., Feb. 27, 1930; s. Max and Eve Rachele (Adler) S.; m. Judith Alice Bloch, Sept. 12, 1954; children: Susan, Peter, Ellen, Joanne. A.B., Syracuse U., 1951; M.S., W.Va. U., 1955; Ph.D., Rutgers U., 1958. Head antiserum product and devel. Blood Grouping Lab., Boston, 1958-59; dir. immunochem. lab. Blood Research Inst., Boston, 1959-72; chief immunology div. Harvard Surg. Unit, Boston City Hosp., 1966-72; sr. research assoc. G.I. Research Lab., Mallory Inst. Pathology, Boston, 1971—; prin. assoc. in surgery Harvard Med. Sch., 1971—; sr. research assoc., dept. pathology Boston U. Med. Sch., 1974—; sr. research assoc. Cancer Research Inst., New Eng. Deaconess Hosp., 1979—, mem., 1982—. Contbr. articles to profl. jours. Mem. AAAS, Transplantation Soc., Am. Assn. Immunologists, Electrophoresis Soc. Patentee in field. Current Work: Development of immunoaassays systems to detect and characterize clinically important molecules; tumor markers; biomedical instrument development. Subspecialties: Cancer research (medicine); Immunology (agriculture). Home: 110 Evelyn Rd Waban MA 02168 Office: 784 Massachusetts Ave Boston MA 02118

SARDAR, DHIRAJ KUMAR, physics educator, researcher; b. Calcutta, West Bengal, India, Oct. 10, 1948; came to U.S., 1975; s. Harekrishna and Dasibala Sardar; m. Ratna Sardar; July 2, 1978; 1 child, Satrajit. B.S., U. Calcutta, 1968, M.S., 1970; Ph.D., Okla. State U., 1980. Lectr. U. Calcutta, India, 1971-75; postdoctoral assoc. Okla. State U., Stillwater, 1980-82, lectr., 1982-83; asst. prof. Ind.-Purdue U., Ft. Wayne, 1983-84; asst. prof. U. Tex., San Antonio, 1984—. Contbr. articles to profl. jours. Mem. Am. Phys. Soc., Optical Soc. Am. Current work: Investigation of optical properties of potential laser materials. Subspecialties: Materials (engineering); Laser spectroscopy. Home: 6034 John Chapman San Antonio TX 78285 Office: Physics Univ of Tex San Antonio TX 78285

SARDELLA, DENNIS JOSEPH, chemistry educator; b. Lawrence, Mass., July 3, 1941; s. Joseph Nasisp and Lucianna (Charron) S.; m. Marjorie Sheipe, Aug. 28, 1966; children—Marjorie Phyllis, Elizabeth Sarah, Dennis Joseph Christopher, David Samuel Matthew. B.S. in Chemistry, Boston Coll., 1962; Ph.D., Ill. Inst. Tech., 1967. Postdoctoral fellow U. Western Ont., London, 1966-67; asst. prof. chemistry Boston Coll., 1967-71, assoc. prof., 1971-81, prof. chemistry, 1981—. Contbr. articles to profl. jours. Mem. Am. Chem. Soc. Roman Catholic. Current work: Electronic structure and reactivity of organic molecules; NMR spectroscopy; molecular orbital studies. Subspecialties: Organic chemistry; Nuclear magnetic resonance. Home: 597 Maple St Franklin MA 02038 Office: Dept Chemistry Boston Coll Chestnut Hill MA 02167

SARGENT, ANNEILA ISABEL, astronomer; b. Kirkcaldy, Fife, Scotland, June 30; d. Richard Anthony and Annie (Blaney) Cassells; m. Wallace Leslie William Sargent, Aug. 5, 1964; children: Lindsay Eleanor, Alison Clare. B.Sc. with honors in Physics, U. Edinburgh, 1963; M.S. in Astronomy, Calif. Inst. Tech., 1967, Ph.D., 1977. Research asst. Royal Greenwich Obs., 1963-64; sr. research asst. Calif. Inst. Tech., 1967-71, 72-74, postdoctoral research fellow, 1977-80; scientist, mem. profl. staff, 1980-84, sr. scientist, 1984—. Mem. Royal Astron. Soc., Am. Astron. Soc. Current Work: Millimeter/submillimeter wave astrophysics infrared astronomy. Subspecialties: Infrared astronomy; Millimeter/submillimeter wave astrophysics. Home: 400 S Berkeley Ave Pasadena CA 91107 Office: Downs Lab Physics Calif Inst Tech Pasadena CA 91125

SARGENT, ERNEST DOUGLAS, aerospace company executive; b. New Berlin, N.Y., Dec. 17, 1931; s. Jess Howard and Edna Ester (Strain) S.; m. Genevieve June Pettee, Feb. 13, 1982; children: Theresa, Mark, Doug. B.S.E.E., Heald Engring. Sch., 1957; M.S., U. So. Calif., 1975. Registered profl. engr., Calif. cert. community coll. instr., Calif. Research engr. Lockheed Corp., Sunnyvale, Calif., 1964-66, supr. engring., 1966-68, mgr. systems engring., 1968-72, program mgr., 1972-76, dir. product assurnce, 1976-80, dir. engring. and tech., 1980-83, v.p. engring., 1983-85; pres. Lockheed Space Ops. Co., 1985—; instr. Foothill Coll., 1976—; dir. Reliability and Maintanability Symposium, Orlando, Fla., 1979—. Chmn. div. fund raiser Jr. Achievement, Sunnyvale, Calif., 1979. Served with USN, 1950-55. Mem. Am. Soc. Quality Control (recipient Ben Lubelsky award 1979), AIAA, ASME, Am. Def. Preparedness Assn., Am. Secrit Indsl. Assn. Current Work: General systems approach to implementing innovative concepts. Subspecialties: Systems engineering; Aerospace engineering and technology. Home: Box 1269 Cocoa Beach FL 32931 Office: Lockheed Space Ops Co 1100 Lockheed Way Titusville FL 32780

SARI, SEPPO OLIVER, laser and information scientist; b. Helsinki, Finland, Mar. 13, 1945; came to U.S., 1950, naturalized, 1955; s. Ole and Rita (Quarnstrom) S.; m. Elizabeth Mary Robinson, July 1, 1967; children—Jonathan Paavo, Britta Ann. B.S., U. Wash., 1967; Ph.D., Princeton U., 1971. Research assoc., instr. MIT, Cambridge, Mass., 1971-75; asst. prof. U. Ariz., Tucson, 1975-79; assoc. prof. Oreg. State U., Corvallis, 1979-80; mem. tech. staff Rockwell Sci. Ctr., Thousand Oaks, Calif., 1980—. Contbr. articles to profl. jours. Princeton U. fellow 1968; Research Corp. grantee, 1976. Mem. Soc. Photographic and Instrumentation Engring., Optical Soc. Am., Am. Phys. Soc., Phi Beta Kappa. Current work: Phase-conjugate image reconstruction, laser optical materials development. Subspecialties: Laser data storage and reproduction; Materials. Home: 175 Tarkio St Thousand Oaks CA 91360 Office: Rockwell Internat Sci Ctr 1049 Camino Dos Rios Thousand Oaks CA 91360

SARICH, VINCENT M., anthropologist, educator; b. Chgo., Dec. 13, 1934; s. Matt and Manda S.; m. Jorjan Snyder; children: Kevin, Tamsin. B.S., Ill.

Inst. Tech., 1955; Ph.D., U. Calif.-Berkeley, 1967. Instr. anthropology Stanford (Calif.) U., 1965; asst. prof. anthropology U. Calif.-Berkeley, 1967-80, assoc. prof., 1970-81, prof., 1981—. Mem. AAAS, Am. Assn. Phys. Anthropology, Am. Soc. Mammals. Current Work: Research on application of biochemistry to problems in evolution. Subspecialties: Biochemistry (biology); Evolutionary biology. Office: Dept Anthropology U Calif Berkeley CA 94720*

SARJEANT, WALTER JAMES, electrical engineer; b. Strathroy, Ont., Can., Apr. 7, 1944; came to U.S., 1978; s. Walter Burns and Margaret (Laurie) S.; m. Ann Richards, June 22, 1977; children—Eric William, Cheryl Elizabeth. B.Sc., U. Western Ont., 1966, M.Sc., 1967, Ph.D., 1971. Profl. engr., Ont. Asst. dir. research/devel. Gen. Tech., Inc., Quebec City, 1971-73; staff Lumonics Research Ltd., Ottawa, Ont., 1973-75, Nat. Research Council Can., Ottawa, 1975-79; mem. staff Los Alamos Sci. Lab., 1979-81; prof. elec. engring. SUNY-Buffalo, 1981—; cons. W.J. Schafer and Assocs., Washington, 1981—. Contbr. articles to profl. jours. Grantee in field. Sr. mem. IEEE. Current work: High field material research; lasers. Subspecialties: Polymer engineering; Electronic materials. Office: Dept Elec Engring SUNY-Buffalo Bonner Hall Room 312 Buffalo NY 14260

SARKAR, NITIS, physical chemist, industrial research scientist; b. Gauhati, India, Dec. 1, 1938; came to U.S., 1962, naturalized, 1976; s. Srish Chandra and Nalini Prova (Bose) Sircar; m. Chandana Sen, Jan. 18, 1970; children—Richik, Prateek. B.S. with honors, Gauhati U., India, 1957; M.S., Calcutta U., India, 1960; Sc.D., MIT, 1965. Research asst. MIT, Cambridge, Mass., 1962-65; research chemist Dow Chem. Co., Midland, Mich., 1965-70, sr. research chemist, 1970-77, research specialist, 1977, research assoc., 1979-84, assoc. scientist, Freeport, Tex., 1984—. Contbr. articles to profl. jours. Mem. Am. Chem. Soc. Current work: Surface and colloid chemistry, flocculation, water soluble polymer, rheology of polymer and dispersed systems, polymer characterization, engineering plastics. Subspecialties: Surface chemistry; Polymer chemistry. Home: 202 Arrow Wood Lake Jackson TX 77566 Office: Dow Chem Co B 3817 Bldg Freeport TX 77541

SARKAR, NURUL HAQUE, molecular virologist educator; b. Noroshinga Pur, West Bengal, India, Aug. 5, 1937; came to U.S., 1967, naturalized, 1982; s. Patana Uddin and Aleya (Mondal) S.; m. Rabeya Choudbury, Mar. 9, 1965; children: Atom, Tina. B.Sc. with honors (merit scholar), U. Calcutta, 1957, M.Sc., 1960, Ph.D., 1966. Lectr. Hooghly Moshin Coll., West Bengal, 1961-67; hon. research scholar biophysics div. Saha Inst. Nuclear Physics, Calcutta, India, 1961-67; research fellow Inst. for Med. Research, Camden, N.J., 1967-68, research assoc., 1968-69, assoc., 1969-71, assoc. mem., 1971-73, head div. electron microscopy, 1972-73; asst. prof. research pediatrics U. Pa. Sch. Medicine, Phila., 1972-75; assoc. prof. biology Sloan-Kettering div. Cornell U., N.Y.C., 1975-80, assoc. prof. genetics and molecular biology, 1981—; assoc. mem., head Lab. Molecular Virology, Sloan-Kettering Inst. for Cancer Research, N.Y.C., 1973—; mem. breast cancer task force exptl. biology com. NIH, 1976-79. Contbr. numerous articles on modification of low energy electron scattering theory for carbon and its application to electron microscopy, detection of virus-like particles assoc. with human breast cancer to sci. jours. Mem. Electron Microscopy Soc. Am. (bd. cert.), Am. Soc. for Microbiology, Am. Soc. for Virology, N.Y. Acad. Sics. Current Work: To understand the mechanism by which virus causes breast cancer in mice and to extend such studies in discovering the etiology of human breast cancer. Subspecialties: Molecular biology; Cancer research (medicine). Home: 1161 York Ave Apt 5-L New York NY 10021 Office: 1275 York Ave Room 915-K New York NY 10021

SARMA, ABUL CHANDRA, research and development and production executive, educator; b. Mangaldoi, Assam, India, Feb. 1, 1939; came to U.S., 1965, naturalized, 1977; m. Delora J. Polk, Aug. 22, 1970 (dec. Aug. 1976); 1 son, Aryan; m. Eva Gohaun, Feb. 10, 1979; 1 son, Gaurab. B.Sc. with honors, Gauhati U., India, 1961; M.Sc., 1963; M.S., U. Minn., 1968; Ph.D., U. Louisville, 1971. Lectr. chemistry Cotton Coll., Gauhati, 1963-65; research assoc. U. Louisville, 1971-73, adj. assoc. prof., 1976—; exec. asst. to v.p. research and devel. Whip-Mix Corp., Louisville, 1973—. Contbr. articles to profl. jours. Pres. Assam Found. N. Am., 1981. Govt. India scholar, 1960-63; U. Minn. scholar, 1966; U. Louisville fellow, 1968-70. Mem. Am. Chem. Soc., Internat. Assn. Dental Research, Am. Nat. Standard Inst./ADA, Sigma Xi. Democrat. Hindu. Patentee in field. Current Work: In mechanism of using investments in foundry, dentistry, precision casting, high technology. Duplicating materials. Industrial waces, colloidal sclica, silica, and phosphate chemistry. Use of precious, semi-precious and non-precious metals and alloys. Studies in special cements with phosphate and silicate binding systems; Pyrolitic reactions. Subspecialties: Solid state chemistry; High-temperature materials. Home: 2105 Merriwood Ct Louisville KY 40299 Office: Whip-Mix Corp 361 Farmington Ave Louisville KY 40217

SARMA, P.S. BALA, medical educator, psychiatrist; b. India, Aug. 8, 1941; came to U.S., 1964, naturalized, 1976. M.B., B.S., Stanley Med. Coll., 1963. Asst. prof. Univ. of Health Sci., Chgo. Med. Sch., North Chicago, Ill., 1972-80, assoc. prof., dir. child psychiatry, 1980—. Fellow Am. Acad. Child Psychiatry; mem. AMA, Am. Psychiat. Assn. Current Work: Minor neurological signs in children; psychiatric evaluation of the elementary school child. Subspecialty: Psychiatry. Office: Department of Psychiatry University of Health Sciences Chicago Medical School 3333 Greenbay Rd North Chicago IL 60064

SARNO, MARIA ERLINDA CO, chemist; b. Manila, Philippines, July 26, 1944; came to U.S., 1968, naturalized, 1976; d. Miguel and Elena (Marcelo) Co Seng; m. Felicisimo Sarreal Sarno; children—Lynnette, Michael, Albert. B.S. in Chemistry, U. Santo Tomas, Manila, 1967; M.S. in Chemistry with top honors, Calif. State U., 1975. Sr. chemist Rachelle Labs, Los Angeles, 1968-74; head radioisotope lab. Curtis Nuclear, Los Angeles, 1974; research assoc., asst. to dir. quality control Nichols Inst., San Pedro, Calif., 1975; devel. mgr. Hyland Labs., Duarte, Calif., 1975—. Contbr. articles to tech. publs. Recipient Tech. award Baxter Travenol, 1978, 80. Mem. Am. Chem. Soc., Am. Assn. Clin. Chemistry, Internat. Soc. Pharm. Engrs., Clin. Ligand Soc., N.Y. Acad. Sci., Am. Mgmt. Assn. Current work: Purification of proteins and analytical research. Subspecialties: Biochemistry (medicine); Organic chemistry. Office: Hyland Therapeutic Research and Devel 1710 Flower Ave Duarte CA 91010

SARTIANO, GEORGE P., oncologist, hematologist, educator; b. Bklyn., Nov. 16, 1934; s. George A. and Josephine (Tramantano) S.; m. Dianne M. E. Connolly, May 17, 1970; 3 children. B.A. magna cum laude, Blkyn. Coll., 1956; M.D., N.Y.U., 1960. Intern Bklyn. Jewish Hosp., 1960-61; resident in medicine N.Y. VA Hosp., 1961-63; clin. research trainee in hematology Meml. Hosp., 1963-64; fellow N.Y. Hosp. Cornell Med. Center, 1968-69, NIH fellow in hematology, 1969-70, asst. physician, 1968-70; chief hematology Meth. Hosp., Bklyn., 1964-66; asst. to dir. oncology Western Pa. Regional Med. Program, 1970-73; asst. prof. medicine U. Pitts., 1970-76; assoc. prof., dir. div. hematology and oncology U. S.C., 1976—, prof., 1979—; mem. staff VA Hosp., Columbia, S.C., 1976—, Richland Meml. Hosp., Columbia, S.C., 1976—. Contbr. numerous articles in field to profl. jours. Served with MC U.S. Army, 1966-68. Recipient E. Lipson Siegel award, 1956; Sloan-Kettering Inst. fellow, 1963-64. Mem. Am. Assn. Blood Banks, AAAS, Am. Cancer Soc., Am. Fedn. Clin. Research, Am. Soc. Hematology, N.Y. Acad. Scis., Piedmont Oncology Assn., S.C. Oncology Assn., So. Soc. Clin. Investigation. Roman Catholic. Current Work: Mechanisms of action of chemotherapeutic agents; clin. cancer chemotherapy. Subspecialties: Chemotherapy; Cancer research (medicine). Office: U SC Sch Medicine VA Enclave Columbia SC 29201

SARTIN, JAMES LEWIS, JR., physiologist, researcher; b. Jacksonville, N.C., Feb. 15, 1952; s. James L. and Exa (Halford) S.; m. Eva Ann Martin, Dec. 29, 1976; 1 child, Matthew. B.A., Auburn U., 1973, M.S., 1976; Ph.D., Okla. State U., 1978. Teaching assoc. Okla. State U., Stillwater, 1978-79; postdoctoral trainee Temple U., Phila., 1979-81, staff biologist, 1981-82; asst. prof. physiology Auburn U., Ala., 1982—. Editor, Domestic Animal Endocrinology; contbr. chpts. to books, articles to profl. jours. Mem. Am. Physiol. Soc., Am. Soc. Animal Sci., Soc. Study Reprodn., N.Y. Acad. Scis., Sigma Xi. Democrat. Baptist. Current work: Metabolic hormone secretion. Subspecialties: Animal physiology; Neuroendocrinology. Office: Auburn U Sch Vet Medicine Dept Physiology and Pharmacology Auburn AL 36849

SARTORELLI, ALAN CLAYTON, pharmacology educator; b. Chelsea, Mass., Dec. 18, 1931; m. Alice C. Anderson, July 7, 1969. B.S., New Eng. Coll. Pharmacy Northeastern U., 1953; M.S., Middlebury (Vt.) Coll., 1955; Ph.D., U. Wis., 1958; M.A. (hon.), Yale U., 1967. Research chemist Samuel Roberts Noble Found., Ardmore, Okla., 1958-60, sr. research chemist, 1960-61; mem. faculty dept. pharmacology Yale Sch. Medicine, 1961—, prof., 1967—, head devel. therapeutics program Comprehensive Cancer Center, 1974—, chmn. dept. pharmacology 1977-84, dep. dir. Comprehensive Cancer Ctr., 1982-84, dir. Comprehensive Cancer Ctr., 1984—; Charles B. Smith vis. research prof. Meml. Sloan-Kettering Cancer Center, 1979; William N. Creasy vis. prof. clin. pharmacology Wayne State U., 1983; Mayo Found. vis. prof. oncology Mayo Clinic, 1983; sci. adv. bd. ImmunoGen, Inc., 1981—; Mem. cancer clin. investigation rev. com. Nat. Cancer Inst., 1968-72, chmn. com. to establish nat. coop. drug discovery groups, 1982-83; cons. in biochemistry U. Tex. M.D. Anderson Hosp. and Tumor Clinic, Houston, 1970-76; mem. exptl. therapeutics study sect. NIH, 1973-77, mem. working cadre nat. large bowel cancer project, 1973-76; mem. council analysis and projection Am. Cancer Soc., 1978-79; mem. bd. sci. counselors, div. cancer treatment Nat. Cancer Inst., 1978-81; mem. adv. com. Cancer Research Center, Washington U. Sch. Medicine, 1971-75; mem. external adv. com. Wis. Clin. Cancer Center, 1978-79, Duke Comprehensive Cancer Ctr., 1983—; mem. sci. adv. com. U. Iowa Cancer Center, 1979-83; mem. external adv. bd. U. Ariz. Cancer Ctr., 1982—, U. So. Calif. Cancer Ctr., 1983—; mem. nat. program com. 13th Internat. Cancer Congress, 1979-81; mem. selection com. Bristol-Myers prize in cancer research, 1977-85, chmn., 1979-81; mem. adv. bd. Drug and Vaccine Devel. Corp. (Center for Public Resources), 1980-81; mem. external adv. bd. Clin. Cancer Research Center, Brown U., 1980—; adv. bd. Specialized Cancer Center, Mt. Sinai Med. Center, 1981—; cons. Bristol-Myers Co., 1982; mem. med. and sci. adv. com. grants rev. subcom. Leukemia Soc. Am., 1984—; mem. steering com. Metastasis Research Soc., 1984—. Regional editor: Am. Continent Biochem. Pharmacology, 1968—; mem. editorial adv. bd.: Cancer Research, 1970-71; asso. editor, 1971-78; editorial bd.: Internat. Ency. Pharmacology and Therapeutics, 1972—; editor: Handbuch der experimentellen Pharmakologie vols. on antineoplastic and immunosuppressive agts, 1974-75; exec. editor: Pharmacology and Therapeutics, 1975—; editorial bd.: Seminars in Oncology, 1973-83, Chemico-Biol. Interactions, 1975-78, Jour. Medicinal Chemistry, 1977-82, Cancer Drug Delivery, 1982—, Jour. Enzyme Inhibition, 1984—, Anti-cancer Drug Design, 1984—; adv. bd. Advances in Chemistry Series, ACS Symposium Series, 1977-80; editor: series on cancer chemotherapy Am. Chem. Soc. Symposium, 1976; editorial cons. Biol. Abstracts, 1984—; Current Awareness in Biological Scis., 1983—; contbr. articles to profl. jours. Fellow N.Y. Acad. Scis.; mem. AAAS, Am. Assn. Cancer Research (dir. 1975-78, 84—, v.p. 1985, fin. com. 1985—), Am. Chem. Soc., Am. Soc. Microbiology, Am. Soc. Biol. Chemists, Am. Soc. Cell Biology, Am. Soc. Pharmacology and Exptl. Therapeutics. Current Work: Mechanism of chemotherapeutic drug action; development of new chemotherapeutic agents; study of differentiation; study of metastatic process; resistance mechanisms. Subspecialties: Cancer research (medicine); Pharmacology. Home: 4 Perkins Rd Woodbridge CT 06525 Office 333 Cedar St New Haven CT 06510

SARWER-FONER, GERALD JACOB, physician, educator; b. Volkovsk, Grodno, Poland, Dec. 6, 1924; emigrated to Can., 1932, naturalized, 1935; s. Michael and Ronia (Caplan) Sarwer-F.; m. Ethel Sheinfeld, May 28, 1950; children—Michael, Gladys, Janice, Henry, Brian. B.A., Loyola Coll. U., Montreal, 1945, M.D., 1951; D.Psychiatry, McGill U., 1955; cert. psychoanalyst, Can. Inst. Psychoanalysis, Montreal, 1963. Diplomate: Am. Bd. Psychiatry and Neurology. Intern Univ. Hosps. U. Montreal Sch. Medicine, 1950-51; resident Butler Hosp., Providence, 1951-52, Hosps. Western Res. U., Cleve., 1952-53, Queen Mary Vets. Hosp., Montreal, 1953-55; lectr., psychiatry U. Montreal 1953-55; lectr., assoc. prof. McGill U., 1955-70; prof., chmn. psychiatry U. Ottawa, Ont., 1971—; dir. dept. psychiatry Ottawa Gen. Hosp., 1971—; cons. in psychiatry Ottawa Civic Hosp., Royal Ottawa Hosp., Nat. Def. Med. Ctr., Children's Hosp. of Eastern Ont., Ottawa Pierre Janet Hosp., Hull, Que., Ottawa Sch. Bd. Editor: Dynamics of Psychiatric Drug Therapy, 1960, Research Conference on the Depressive Group of Illnesses, 1966, Psychiatric Crossroads-the Seventies, Research Aspects, 1972; editor in chief: Psychiat. Jour. U. Ottawa, 1976—; editor numerous audio-video tapes; contbr. numerous articles to profl. jours. Bd. govs. Queen Elizabeth Hosp., Montreal, 1966-71; cons. Protestant Sch. Bd., Westmount, Que., 1966-71; advisor Com. on Health, City of Westmount, 1969-71. Served to lt. col. Royal Can. Med. Corps, 1949-62. Decorated Knight of Malta. Recipient Sigmund Freud award Am. Assn. Psycholanalytic Physicians, 1982; Simon Bolivar lectr. Am. Psychiat. Assn., New Orleans, 1981. Fellow Royal Coll. Physicians; mem. Am. Acad. Psychiatry and the Law (pres. 1977, recipient Silver Apple award 1978), Soc. Biol. Psychiatry (pres. 1983—), Am. Coll. Psycholanalysts (pres. elect 1983), Am. Coll. Psychiatrists, Can. Psychoanalytic Soc. (pres. 1977-81), Can. Assn. Profs. of Psychiatry (pres. 1976-77, 82-83). Clubs: Cosmos (Washington); Cercle Universitaire (Ottawa). Current work: Ego defences, psychopharmacology, schizophrenia, depressive illness. . Home: 152 Kamloops Ave Ottawa ON K1V 7C9 Canada Office: Dept Psychiatry U Ottawa Sch Medicine 501 Smyth Rd Ottawa ON K1H 8L6 Canada

SARYAN, LEON ARAM, biochemical toxicologist; b. Wilmington, Del., July 18, 1948; s. Sarkis Saro and Armine (Manougian) S.; m. Shirley Ann Kalajian, Nov. 21, 1981; children—Ani Lucine, Armen Levon. B.A. in Natural Sci., Johns Hopkins U., 1970, Ph.D. in Biol. Chemistry, 1975. Engr. petroleum lab. E.I. DuPont Co., Deepwater, N.J., 1968-69; NSF fellow Roswell Park Meml. Inst., Buffalo, 1970; NIH postdoctoral fellow dept. chemistry U. Wis., Milw. 1975-78; research assoc., 1979-81; adj. asst. prof. chemistry, 1981-82; tech. dir. indsl. toxicology lab. West Allis Meml. Hosp., Wis., 1982—. Contbr. articles on trace elements, cancer biochemistry, and cancer magnetic resonances to profl. jours. Pub. relations dir. Armenian Youth Fedn. Am., Watertown, Mass., 1975-76; trustee St. Hagop Armenian Apostolic Ch., Racine, Wis., 1981-82. Recipient Johns Hopkins U. Delmarva Alumni award, 1968, Ralston Purina Bright Idea award, 1979. Mem. Am. Chem. Soc. Current work: Biol. trace elements analysis and metabolism. Blood lead and protoporphyrin testing for industrial exposure. Biochemical analysis of cancer cells, tissues, and novel antineoplastic agents. Subspecialties: Toxicology (medicine); Biochemistry (medicine). Office: Indsl Toxicology Lab West Allis Meml Hosp 8901 W Lincoln Ave West Allis WI 53227

SASHIN, DONALD, medical physicist, radiology educator; b. N.Y.C., Dec. 11, 1937; s. David and Pearl (Taub) S.; m. Kathleen Flaherty, July 24, 1967; children—Deirdre Moira, Courtenay Aileen. B.S., MIT, 1960; M.S., Carnegie Inst. Tech., 1962; Ph.D., Carnegie-Mellon U., 1968. Instr. radiology U. Pitts., 1967-70, asst. prof., 1970-74, assoc. prof., 1974—. Contbr. articles to profl. jours. Patentee in field. Grantee NIH, Philips Med. Systems, Lions Club. Mem. Am. Assn. Physicists in Medicine, Health Physics Soc., Sigma Xi. Democrat. Roman Catholic. Lodge: Lions. Current work: Research and development of improved techniques of radiological imaging at lower radiation exposure. Subspecialty: Medical physics. Home: 4360 Centre Ave Pittsburgh PA 15213 Office: U Pitts RC 406 Scaife Hall Pittsburgh PA 15261

SASLAW, LEONARD DAVID, chemist, toxicologist; b. Bklyn., Aug. 27, 1927; s. Issay and Sara (Singer) S. B.S., CCNY, 1949; M.S. in Biochemistry, George Washington U., 1954; Ph.D. in Chemistry, Georgetown U., 1963. Lic. clin. lab. dir. N.Y.C. Chemist Nat. Cancer Inst., NIH, 1951-57, div. biophysics Sloan-Kettering Inst., 1957-58, biochem. br. Armed Forces Inst. Pathology, 1958-65; dir. div. biochem. pharmacology of cancer chemotherapy dept. Microbiol Assos., Inc., 1965-68; sr. biochemist Nat. Drug Co., 1968-69; chief Lab. Cellular Biochemistry, Albert Einstein Med. Center, 1969-70; clin. lab. dir. Med. Diagnostic Centers, Inc., 1970-71; lab. dir., research asso. Renal Lab., N.Y. Med. Coll., 1971-73; mgr. biochem. investigations Bio/dynamics Inc., N.J., 1973-74; profl. assoc. Smithsonian Sci. Info. Exchange, 1975-77; cons. Burton Parsons Co. Inc., Seat Pleasant, Md., 1977-78; physiologist div. toxicology Bur. Vet. Medicine, FDA, Washington, 1978—. Contbr. articles to sci. jours. Pres. Balt.-Washington Area chpt. B'nai B'rith Young Men, 1954. Served with USN, 1945-46. Recipient Meritorious Achievement award Armed Forces Inst. Pathology, 1964. Mem. Am. Chem. Soc., Am. Soc. Pharmacology and Exptl. Therapeutics, Clin. Ligand Assay Soc., Am. Assn. Cancer Research, Am. Coll. Toxicology, Soc. Toxicology, Beethoven Soc., Washington Print Club, Sigma Xi. Democrat. Jewish. Current Work: Metabolism and mode of action of drugs, analytical biochemistry and clinical chemistry. I am directly involved in regulatory area of the scientific assessment of safety of additives and drugs in animal feeds. Subspecialties: Toxicology (medicine); Cancer research (medicine). Home: 425 G St SW Washington DC 20024 Office: HFV-156 Parklawn Bldg 5600 Fishers Ln Rockville MD 20857

SASSE, RONALD ANTHONY, research chemist; b. N.Y.C., Feb. 7, 1933; s. Harold Winfield and Hazel Margaret (Martin) S.; m. Lethem Leila Verlander, Aug. 23, 1953 (div. 1980); 1 child, Christine Ann; m. Lois Marie Krisser, Aug. 21, 1982; children—Cindy, Kimberly, David. B.A. in Chemistry, Hofstra U., 1955; postgrad. Johns Hopkins U., 1966-70. Radiation chemist Nuclear Effects Lab, Edgewood, Md., 1958-73; researcher liquid propellants Ballistic Research Lab, Aberdeen Proving Ground, Md., 1973-79, researcher solid propellants, 1979—; cons. to govt. agys. on black powder research; mem. internat. exchange panels. Author numerous govt. research reports, open lit. publs., book chpt. Mem. Am. Chem. Soc., Sigma Xi. Current work: Expert in black powder combustion and the effect of physical properties on both ignition and combustion. Subspecialty: Radiation chemistry; Propellant chemistry. Office: US Army Ballistic Research Lab Aberdeen Proving Ground MD 21005

SATCHLER, GEORGE RAYMOND, physicist; b. London, Eng., June 14, 1926; U.S., 1959; s. George Cecil and Georgina Lily (Strange) S.; m. Margaret Patricia Gibson, Mar. 27, 1948; children—Patricia Ann, Jacqueline Helen. B.A., Oxford U., 1951, M.A., 1951, Ph.D., 1955. Research fellow Clarendon Lab., Oxford U., 1954-59, 71; research assoc. physics dept. U. Mich., 1956-57; physicist Oak Ridge Nat. Lab., 1959—, assoc. dir. physics div., 1967-74, theoretical physics dir., 1974-76, disting. research staff mem., 1976—. Author: (with D.M. Brink) Angular Momentum, 1962; Introduction to Nuclear Reactions, 1980; Direct Nuclear Reactions, 1983. Contbr. articles to profl. jours. Served with RAF, 1944-48. Union Carbide Corp. research fellow, 1976—. Fellow Am. Phys. Soc. (mem. exec. com. nuclear physics div. 1974-75, T.W. Bonner prize 1977). Subspecialties: Nuclear physics; Theoretical physics. Office: Oak Ridge Nat Lab PO Box X Oak Ridge TN 37830

SATHER, JOHN HENRY, ecologist, wetland ecosystem consultant; b. Presho, S.D., July 12, 1921; s. Anton and Anna (Imster) S.; m. Shirley Mae Johnson, Aug. 21, 1948; children—Kristi, Signe, Ingrid. B.S., U. Nebr. 1943, Ph.D., 1953; M.A., U. Mo., 1948. Research biologist State of Nebr., Lincoln, 1948-55; prof., grad. dean Western Ill. U., Macomb, Ill., 1955-79, adj. prof., 1979—; gen. biologist U.S. Fish and Wildlife Service, Washington, 1984—; wetland ecologist Creative Cons. Corp. Internat., Ft. Collins, Colo., 1982-83. Author: Muskrat Life History, 1958; Proceedings Wetland Value Assessment Workshop, 1984; co-author: Coyote Food Habits, 1955; Overview of Wetland Functions, 1984. Served with USAAF, 1942-45, ETO. Edward K. Love fellow U. Mo., 1946-48. Mem. AAAS, Ecol. Soc. Am., Am. Inst. Biol. Scis., Ill. Acad Scis., Sigma Xi. Republican. Lutheran. Current work: Assessment of functional values of wetlands. Subspecialties: Ecology (biology); Resource management. Home and Office: 103 Oakland Ln Macomb IL 61455

SATO, HIROSHI, materials engineering educator, researcher; b. Matsuzaka, Mie Prefecture, Japan, Aug. 31, 1918; came to U.S., 1954, naturalized, 1977; s. Masayoshi and Fusae (Ohara) S.; m. Kyoko A., Sept. 8, 1922; children: Norie M. Sato Berry, Nobuyuki Albert, Erika Michiko. B.S., Hokkaido (Japan) U., 1938, M.S., 1941; D.Sc., Tokyo U., 1951. Research asso. Hokkaido U., 1941-42, asst. prof., 1942-43; research physicist Inst. Phys. Chem. Research, Tokyo, 1943-47; prof. Tohoku U., Sendai, Japan, 1945-58; research physicist Westinghouse Research Labs., Pitts., 1954-56; prin. research scientist sci. lab. Ford Motor Co., Dearborn, Mich., 1956-74; prof. materials engring. Purdue U., 1974—, Ross Disting. prof. engring., 1984—; cons. in field. Contbr. numerous articles, chpts. to profl. publs.; editor: Single Crystal Films, 1964. Recipient prize of Merit in metal physics Japan Inst. Metals, 1951; Humboldt U.S. Sr. Scientist award, 1980; Guggenheim fellow, 1966; Japan Soc. for Promotion of Sci. Disting. fellow for sci. exchange with Japan, 1979. Fellow Am. Phys. Soc.; mem. Japan Phys. Soc., Japan Inst. Metals (hon.), Am. Ceramic Soc., AIME, N.Y. Acad. Sci., Sigma Xi. Congregationalist. Patentee in field. Current Work: Theoretical and exptl. study of solid state reactions and phase transitions; specific interest in irreversible stat. mechanics of transport phenomena, diffusion, superionic condrs., magnetism, transmission electron microscopy. Subspecialties: Condensed matter physics; Solid state chemistry. Home: 1601 Woodland Ave West Lafayette IN 47906 Office: Sch Materials Engring Purdue U West Lafayette IN 47907

SATTERTHWAITE, CAMERON B., physics educator; b. Salem, Ohio, July 26, 1920; s. William David and Mabel (Cameron) S.; m. Helen Foster, Dec. 23, 1950 (div. 1979); children—Mark Cameron, Tod Foster, Tracy Lynn, Keith Alan. B.A., Coll. Wooster, 1942; postgrad. Ohio State U., 1942-44; Ph.D., U. Pitts., 1951. Research chemist Monsanto, Dayton, Ohio, 1942-47, duPont, Wilmington, Del., 1950-53; research physicist Westinghouse, Pitts., 1953-61; prof. U. Ill., Urbana, 1961-79; prof., chmn. dept. physics Va. Commonwealth U., Richmond, 1979—; exec. sec. SURA, Arlington, Va., 1984. Patentee (6). Editor: Electronic Properties, 1983; contbr. articles to profl. jours. Dir. Monroeville Sch. Bd., Pa., 1959-61; Congl. cand. Democratic Party, Ill., 1966; pres. Fedn. Am. Scientists, 1969, Ill. Democratic Coalition, 1968. NSF grantee, 1970-84. Fellow Am. Phys. Soc.; mem. AAAS. Democrat. Mem. Soc. of Friends. Current work: Superconductivity, hydrogen in metals. Subspecialties: Low temperature physics; Condensed matter physics. Home: 3311 Kensington Ave Richmond VA 23221 Office: Va Commonwealth U Dept Physics Richmond VA 23284

SATZER, WILLIAM JOSEPH, JR., applied mathematician, systems engineer; b. Mpls., July 29, 1949; s. William Joseph and Eleanor Marie (Saevig) S.; m. Joyce Amy Mitchell, Jan. 31, 1982; 1 child, Michael B. B.A., Coll. St. Thomas, 1970; Ph.D., U. Minn., 1976. Instr., Colgate U., Hamilton, N.Y., 1976-77; systems analyst Logicon, Inc., San Diego, 1977-81; sr. engr. Bolt Beranek and Newman, Inc., San Diego, 1981—. Contbr. articles to profl. jours. Woodrow Wilson Nat. Found. fellow, 1972; NSF trainee, 1973-74. Mem. Math. Assn. Am., Soc. Ind. and Applied Math. Current work: Numerical linear algebra, computer network design, simulation and Monte Carlo methods. Subspecialties: Applied mathematics; Systems engineering. Home: 4041 Haines St San Diego CA 92109 Office: Bolt Beranek and Newman Inc 4015 Hancock St 101 San Diego CA 92109

SAU, ARJUN CHANDRA, chemist, researcher; b. Patahesal, West Bengal, India, July 17, 1948; came to U.S., 1976; s. Jagatpal and Gouri Sau; m. Jyotsna Singh, Feb. 24, 1978; 1 child, Navanjali Jagatpal. B.S. with honors, U. Burdwan, West Bengal, 1969, M.S., 1971; Ph.D., Indian Inst. Sci., 1976. Research assoc. U. Mass., Amherst, 1976-81; research chemist Hercules Inc., Wilmington, Del., 1982—. Author: Advances in Inorganic and Radiochemistry, 1978. Contbr. articles to profl. jours. Patentee in field. Indian Nat. Merit scholar, 1969. Current work: Water soluble polymers, systhesis and characterization of main group elements, inorganic heterocycles and biomedical polymers. Subspecialties: Synthetic chemistry; Polymer chemistry. Office: Hercules Inc Research Ctr Wilimngton DE 19894

SAUER, ROBERT JAY, chemist; b. Joliet, Ill., Sept. 1, 1936; s. Willard Meier and Wilma May (Weyrick) S.; m. Sue Emily Koehler, June 19, 1960; 1 child, Carl Frederick. B.A., N. Central Coll., 1958; Ph.D., U. Ill., 1962. Research chemist E.I. duPont & Co., Wilmington, Del., 1964-72; sr. scientist Owens Corning Fiberglas, Granville, Ohio, 1973-76, research supr., 1976-79, research assoc., 1979-84, sr. research assoc., 1984—. NIH fellow, 1962-64. Mem. Am. Chem. Soc., AAAS, Combustion Inst., Sigma Xi. Presbyterian. Current work: Product and process research on glass fibers; flammability of plastics and composites. Subspecialties: Organic chemistry; Composite materials. Office: Owens Corning Fiberglas Corp PO Box 415 Granville OH 43023

SAUNBY, JOHN BRIAN, petrochemical company executive; b. Hull, Eng., Mar. 7, 1933; came to U.S., 1959; s. Clive Henry and Frances Evelyn (Smith) S.; m. Eileen Mary Hillman, Sept. 1, 1956; children—Carole, Linda. B.S. in Chem. Engring., Birmingham U., Eng., 1954, Ph.D., 1957. Postdoctoral fellow NRC, Ottawa, Can., 1957-59; chem. engr. Union Carbide Corp., South Charleston, W.Va., 1959-65, group leader, 1965-73, assoc. dir., 1973-80, dir. licensing, 1978-80, dir. research and devel., 1980-84. Chmn. NSF Exptl. Program for Stimulation of Competitive Research, W.Va., 1980—. Patentee in field. Bd. dirs. Kanawha Valley Youth Orch., Charleston, 1972-78, pres., Charleston, 1972-78; bd. dirs. W.Va. Opera Theater, Charleston, 1978-79. Fellow Trinidad Leaseholds Ltd., 1954-56, Shell Petroleum Co., 1956-57. Mem. Am. Inst. Chem. Engrs. Club: Les Amis du Vin (Charleston). Current work: Management of research and development on polymers and petrochemicals with specific interest in C-1 chemistry. . Office: Union Carbide Corp PO Box 8361 Bldg 770 South Charleston WV 25303

SAUNDERS, GEORGE CHERDRON, pathology educator; veterinarian; b. Flushing, N.Y., Jan. 4, 1940; s. George Carmichael and Margaret Ruth (Cherdron) S.; m. Elizabeth Grace Hinckley, Apr. 22, 1967; children—Mark, Gregory, Maria. V.M.D., U. Pa., 1964; student Colo. Sch. Mines, 1957-58, Pa. State U., 1958-60. Postdoctoral fellow U. Colo. Med. Ctr., Denver, 1964-66, instr. pathology, 1966-67, asst. prof. pathology, 1967-72; sr. staff mem. Los

Alamos Nat. Lab., N.Mex., 1972—; adj. asst. prof. pathology U. N. Mex., 1972-77, adj. assoc. prof. pathology, 1977—. Contbr. articles to profl. jours., chpts. to books. Patentee in field. Treas., E. Park Pool Assn., Los Alamos, 1981-83. Recipient Inventors award, Los Alamos Nat. Lab., 1982. Mem. Am. Assn. Pathologists, Soc. Analytical Cytology. Current work: Immunoassay development, monoclonal antibody development, methods development for ultrasensitive analysis. Subspecialties: Pathology (medicine); Immunology (medicine). Home: Route 1 Box 4328 Espanola NM 87532 Office: Exptl Pathology Group Los Alamos Nat Lab Mail Stop M888 Los Alamos NM 87545

SAUNDERS, PAUL RICHARD, wildland and dispersed recreation management educator, researcher; b. Indpls., Nov. 12, 1950; s. Robert Iles and Mary Josephine (Jaenich) S. B.S., Purdue U., 1972, M.S., 1972; Ph.D., Duke U., 1979. Teaching and research asst. Purdue U., West Lafayette, Ind., 1971-72; lectr. Ind. U., Kokomo and Richmond, 1973; research asst., lectr. Duke U., Durham, N.C., 1974-77; vis. instr. Clemson U., S.C., 1977-79, asst. prof., 1979-81; assoc. prof. Wash. State U., Pullman, 1981—; outdoor recreation planner Arapaho and Roosevelt Nat. Forest, Ft. Collins, Colo., 1980; dir. recreation course Forest Service, Clemson U., 1979-81; editor extension and research papers Dept. Recreation and Park Adminstrn., Clemson, 1977-81. Contbr. articles to sci. jours. Codirector, instr. interpretation tng. for Mt. St. Helens Nat. Volcanic Monument, 1981-83. Asst. dir. North-South Ski Patrol, Nat. Ski Patrol System, North-South Ski Bowl, Idaho, 1984-86, treas., 1983-85; interpreter, guide Great Smoky Mountains Spring Wildflower Pilgrimage, Gatlinburg, Tenn., 1979-81. Mem. Nat. Soc. Park Resources (bd. dirs. 1981—), Ecological Soc. Am., Soc. Am. Foresters, Assn. Interpretive Naturalists (profl.), Sigma Xi, Xi Sigma Pi, Delta Sigma Rho-Tau Kappa Alpha, CERES. Club: Wash. State U. Ski Patrol (faculty advisor 1984-85). Current work: Effect of human and natural disturbances on subalpine spruce-fir ecosystems in inland empire, Northern Rocky Mountains, and Southern Appalachian Mountains. Subspecialties: Ecosystems analysis; Resource conservation. Home: SW 400 State St Pullman WA 99163 Office: Dept Forestry and Range Mgmt Wash State U Pullman WA 99164-6410

SAUNDERS, ROBERT NORMAN, pharmacologist; b. Fairbury, Ill., Sept. 25, 1938. B.S., Purdue U., 1961, M.S., 1966, Ph.D., 1968. Research investigator Searle Labs., Skokie, Ill., 1968-74, group leader, 1974-79; sect. head Sandoz, Inc., E. Hanover, N.J., 1980-84, dept. head, 1984-85, dir. dept., 1985—. Current work: Platelets, thrombosis, platelet-activating factor, platelet-derived growth factor, atherosclerosis. Subspecialties: Cell biology (medicine); Pharmacology. Address: Sandoz Research Inst Route 10 East Hanover NJ 07936

SAUTER, FRANZ FABIAN, structural engineer; b. San Jose, Costa Rica, Feb. 7, 1933; s. Federico Schmid and Hilda (Fabian) S.; m. Maria Angeles Ortiz, June 30, 1957; children—Arnold, Hans Peter, Krista Maria, Manfred, Helmuth. C.E., U. Costa Rica, 1956; postgrad. Internat. Inst. Seismology and Earthquake Engring., Tokyo, 1963-64. Structural engr. Leonhardt & Andraä, Stuttgart, W.Ger., 1957-58; chief engr., then v.p. Productos Concreto, San Jose, 1958-63; ptnr., pres. Franz Sauter & Assocs., S.A., San Jose, 1964—; prof. structural engring. U. Costa Rica, San Jose, 1958-70; dir. Productos Concreto S.A., Atlas Electrica S.A., Ricalit S.A. (all San Jose). Pres., Institucion Cultural Germano-Costarricense, San Jose, 1969-73. Decorated German Cross of Merit, 1972. Mem. Colegio Federado Ingenieros y Arquitectos, Asociacion Centroamericana de Cemento y Concreto (hon.), Asociacion Costarricense Ingenieria Estructural (pres. 1985), ASCE, Am. Concrete Inst. Roman Catholic. Lodge: Rotary (San Jose). Current work: Earthquake engineering; seismic risk; earthquake insurance. Subspecialty: Civil engineering. Home: Apartado 6260 San Jose Costa Rica

SAVAGE, BLAIR DEWILLIS, astronomer; b. Mt. Vernon, N.Y., June 7, 1941; s. Rufus Llewellyn and Christine (Burney) S.; m. Linda Jean Wilber, June 25, 1966; children—Reid Hamilton, Keith Wesley. B.Engring. Physics, Cornell U., 1964; M.S., Princeton U., 1966, Ph.D., 1967. Research assoc. Princeton U., 1967-68; asst. prof. U. Wis., Madision, 1968-73, assoc. prof., 1973-78, prof. astronomy, 1978—, chmn. dept., 1982—; vis. fellow Joint Inst. Lab Astrophysics, Boulder, Colo., 1974-75; co-investigator space astronomy projects NASA, 1968-83. Contbr. articles to profl. jours. Peyton fellow Princeton U., 1964-66; NASA fellow Princeton U., 1966-67; research grantee NASA, NSF, 1968-83. Mem. Am. Astron. Soc., Internat. Astron. Union, Tau Beta Pi. Current work: Ultraviolet space astronomy, observational studies of interstellar gas and dust. Home: 4015 Hiawatha Dr Madison WI 53711 Office: Dept Astronomy U Wis 475 N Charter St Madison WI 53706

SAVAGE, JAY MATHERS, biologist, educator; b. Santa Monica, Calif., Aug. 26, 1928; m. Rebbeca E. Papendick, Ichthologists 30, 1981; children—Nancy Diane, Charles Richard. A.B., Stanford U., 1950, M.A., 1954, Ph.D., 1955. Asst. prof. Pomona Coll. Claremont, Calif., 1954-56; instr. U. So. Calif., Los Angeles, 1956-57, asst. prof., 1957-59, assoc. prof., 1959-64, prof., 1964-82; prof., chmn. biology dept. U. Miami, Coral Gables, Fla., 1982—; assoc. dir. Allan Hancock Found., U. So. Calif., Los Angeles, 1964-82; research dir. Evolution Ecology Biol. Sect., 1977-82; chmn. Nat. Acad. Scis. Comn. Biol. Humid Tropics, Washington, 1980-82. Author: Evolution, 1977, 3d edit., Ecological Aspects of Development in the Humid Tropics, 1982. Guggenheim fellow, 1963-64. Fellow Explorers Club; mem. Am. Soc. Ichthologists and Herpetologists (pres. 1982), Orgn. Tropical Studies (dir. 1963—, pres. 1974-80), So. Calif. Acad. Scis. (pres. 1966-68), Univ. Nat. Oceanographic Lab. System (vice chmn. 1971-73), Internatl. Comn. on Zoology (commr. 1982—). Subspecialties: Evolutionary biology; Systematics. Office: U Miami Dept Biology PO Box 249118 Coral Gables FL 33124

SAVAGE, WILLIAM FREDERICK, aeronautical engineer; b. Anchorage, May 23, 1923; s. Gordon Prescott and Josephine Isabelle S.; m. Mary Helen Carter, June 25, 1949; children: Kathleen C., William S. B.S. in Aero. Engring, Rensselaer Poly. Inst., 1943; M.S. in Aero. Engring, Purdue U., 1949; student, Oak Ridge Sch. Reactor Tech., 1957-58. Registered profl. engr., Ohio. Aerodynamicist Convair, Ft. Worth, 1944-46; asst. prof. U. Ky., Lexington, 1946-52; chief engr. Kett Corp., Cin., 1952-55; mgr. tech. analysis Gen. Electric Co., Cin., 1956-60; dir. nuclear products Martin Co., Balt., 1960-67; asst. dir. Office of Saline Water, Dept of Interior, Washington, 1967-74; chief advanced systems Dept. Energy, Washington, 1974-82, dir. instnl. and regulatory systems, 1982-85, dep. dir. nuclear plant performance, 1985—. Contbr. articles to tech. jours. Served to capt. USAR and USAFR, 1948-58. Recipient Outstanding Performance award Dept. Interior, 1968, spl. achievement award ERDA, 1976, performance awards Dept. Energy, 1982-84. Mem. Am. Nuclear Soc., ASME. Methodist. Current Work: Analysis of nuclear plant technical and economic performance. Subspecialties: Nuclear engineering; Aeronautical engineering. Home: 8025 Garlot Dr Annandale VA 22003

SAVAGEAU, MICHAEL ANTONIO, microbiology educator, researcher, cons.; b. Fargo, N.D., Dec. 3, 1940; s. Antonio D. and Jennie E. (Kaushagen) S.; m. Ann E., June 22, 1967; children: Mark E., Patrick D., Elisa M. B.S., U. Minn., 1962; M.S., U. Iowa, 1963; Ph.D. (Santa Clara Med. Soc. fellow, NIH fellow), Stanford U., 1967. NIH fellow UCLA, 1967-68; NIH fellow Stanford U., 1968-70, lectr., 1968; asst. prof. microbiology U. Mich., Ann Arbor, 1970-74, assoc. prof., 1974-78, prof., 1978—, acting chmn. dept. microbiology and immunology, 1979-80, 82-85; Fulbright sr. research fellow Max Planck Inst. Biophys. Chemistry, Gottingen, W.Ger., 1976-77; vis. scientist, CSIRO div. computing research, fellow dept. biochemistry John Curtin Sch. Med. Research, Australian Nat. U., Canberra, 1983-84; mem. spl. study sect. NIH; ad hoc reviewer NSF, Research Corp. and numerous sci. jours. Author: Biochemical Systems Analysis: A Study of Function and Design in Molecular Biology, 1976; contbr. numerous articles, chpts. to profl. publs.; mem. editorial bd.: Math. Bioscis, 1976—. Guggenheim fellow, 1976-77; NSF grantee, 1970-82; NIH grantee, 1982—; Australian Nat. U. fellow, 1983-84. Mem. AAAS, Am. Chem. Soc., Am. Soc. Microbiology, Biophys. Soc., IEEE, N.Y. Acad. Sci., Soc. Gen. Physiologists, Soc. Indsl. and Applied Math., Soc. Math. Biology, Sigma Xi. Current Work: Function, design and evolution of biochemical and genetic regulatory systems; development and application of mathematical methods in biology; mathematical modeling in biochemical engineering. Subspecialties: Microbiology; Applied mathematics. Home: 813 Berkshire Ann Arbor MI 48104 Office: Dept Microbiology U Mich Ann Arbor MI 48109

SAVILLE, THORNDIKE, JR., coastal engineer, consultant; b. Balt., Aug. 1, 1925; s. Thorndike and Edith Stedman (Wilson) S.; m. Janet Foster, Aug. 28, 1950; children: Sarah, Jennifer, Gordon. A.B., Harvard Coll., 1947; M.S., U. Calif.-Berkeley, 1949. Research asst. U. Calif., Berkeley, 1947-49; hydraulic engr. Beach Erosion Bd. and Coastal Engring. Research Center, Ft. Belvoir, Va., 1949-81, chief research div., 1964-71, tech. dir., 1971-81. Author numerous papers in engring. and sci. lit. Served with USAAF, 1943-46. Recipient Meritorious Civilian Service award Dept. Army, 1981. Fellow AAAS, Wash. Acad. Scis., ASCE (Moffatt-Nichol award 1979); mem. Am. Geophys. Union, Internat. Assn. for Hydraulic Research, Nat. Acad. Engring., Permanent Internat. Assn. Navigation Congresses (hon. mem. 1985). Current Work: Sediment transport on coasts. Subspecialties: Coastal, port, harbor engineering; Nearshore oceanography. Home and Office: 5601 Albia Rd Bethesda MD 20816

SAVIN, SAMUEL MARVIN, geologist; b. Boston, Aug. 31, 1940; s. George and Sarah (Lewiton) S.; m. Norma Goulder, Nov. 4, 1978; children: Robert Goulder, Lisa Rebecca. B.A., Colgate U., 1961; Ph.D., Calif. Inst. Tech., 1967. Asst. prof. geol. scis. Case Western Res. U., Cleve., 1967-73, assoc. prof., 1973-76, prof., 1976—, dept. chmn., 1977-82; industry fellow Marathon Oil Co., Denver, 1976; mem. adv. panel earth scis. NSF, 1978-81, 85. Asso. editor: Geochimica et Cosmochimica Acta, 1976-79, Marine Micropaleontology, 1979—; contbr articles to sci. jours.; producer ednl. video documentaries. Fellow AAAS; mem. Geol. Soc. Am., Am. Assn. Petroleum Geologists, Am. Geophys. Union, Geochem. Soc., Clay Minerals Soc. (councillor 1978-81), Nat. Assn. Geology Tchrs., No. Ohio Geol. Soc. Subspecialties: Geochemistry; Oceanography. Home: 2236 Demington Dr Cleveland Heights OH 44106 Office: Dept Geol Scis Case Western Res U Cleveland OH 44106

SAVITT, SIDNEY ALLAN, chemical engineer, consultant; b. N.Y.C., Apr. 14, 1920; s. Joseph and Rose (Smerin) S.; m. Malvina Meister, Sept. 15, 1946; children—Jill, Brad, Hope, Wade. B.S. in Chemistry, CCNY, 1940; M.Ch.E., Poly. Inst.. N.Y., 1945, D.Ch.E., 1948. Registered profl. engr., N.J. Research engr. M.W. Kellogg, N.Y.C., 1947-49; tech. dir. Consol. Products, N.Y.C., 1949-53; pres. S.A. Savitt Assocs., Inc., Clark, N.J., 1953—, Process Plants Service, Inc., Clark, 1953—; cons., div. hazardous wastes N.J. Dept. Environ. Protection; tech. expert Citizen's Adv. Com., Gowanus Canal, 1983-84. Reviewer for chem. and sci. jours. Contbr. articles to profl. jours. Recipient Disting. Alumnus award Poly. Inst. N.Y., 1985. Fellow N.Y. Acad. Scis. (bd. govs. 1971-73, conf. orgn. com. 1971-73, fin. com. 1972-73, sect. activities com. 1982-83, chmn. engring. sect. 1968, 70, 81-82, 82-83, 85, vice-chmn. engring. sect. 1967-68, 84, chmn. ednl. adv. com. 1969-72), Am. Inst. Chemists; mem. Am. Inst. Chem. Engrs., ASME, Nat. Soc. Profl. Engrs., N.J. Soc. Profl. Engrs., Am. Soc. Engring. Edn., Am. Inst. City N.Y. (trustee 1977—), N.J. Acad. Scis., Am. Inst. Sci. and Tech. (pres. 1985, chmn. sci. fair com. 1984-85), Sigma Xi, Tau Beta Pi (eminent engr. 1983), Phi Lambda Upsilon. Current work: Design and process layout in development of commercial plants, environmental and pollution control; design of biotechnical plants; extractive metallurgy-strategic alloys. Home: 1050 George St New Brunswick NJ 08901 Office: SA Savitt Assocs 287 Central Ave Clark NJ 07066

SAW, CHENG-KIONG, physicist, educator; b. Malaysia, June 13, 1950; came to U.S., 1970; s. Hai Gan and Neoh Onn Saw; m. Chian Horng Ling, Dec. 16, 1979; 1 dau., Christine H.T. B.A., Berea Coll. Ky., 1974; Ph.D., U. R.I., 1980. Research assoc. Ames Lab., Iowa, 1980-82, Argonne Nat. Lab., (Ill.), 1982—. Contbr. articles to profl. jours. Mem. Am. Phys. Soc., Sigma Pi Sigma. Current work: Atomic and magnetic structures of amorphous alloys, dense random packed computer simulations of amorphous systems, x-ray and neutron scattering studies on condensed matter. Subspecialties: Condensed matter physics; Metallurgy. Office: MST Div Argonne Nat Lab Argonne IL 60439

SAWYER, CHARLES HENRY, anatomist, educator; b. Ludlow, Vt., Jan. 24, 1915; s. John Guy and Edith Mabel (Morgan) S.; m. Ruth Eleanor Schaeffer, Aug. 23, 1941; 1 dau., Joan Eleanor. B.A., Middlebury Coll., 1937, D.Sc. (h.c.), 1975; student, Cambridge U., Eng., 1937-38; Ph.D., Yale, 1941. Instr. anatomy Stanford, 1941-44; asso., asst. prof., asso. prof., prof. anatomy Duke U., 1944-51; prof. anatomy U. Calif., Los Angeles, 1951—, chmn. dept., 1955-63, acting chmn., 1968-69, faculty research lectr., 1966-67. Editorial bd.: Endocrinology, 1955-59, Proc. Soc. Exptl. Biology and Medicine, 1959-63, Am. Jour. Physiology, 1972-75; Author papers on neuroendocrinology. Mem. Internat. Brain Research Orgn. (council 1964-68), AAAS, Am. Assn. Anatomists (v.p. 1969-70, Henry Gray award 1984), Am. Physiol. Soc., Am. Zool. Soc., Neurosci. Soc., Endocrine Soc. (council 1968-70, Koch award 1973), Am. Acad. Arts and Scis., Nat. Acad. Scis., Soc. Exptl. Biology and Medicine, Soc. Study Reprodn. (dir. 1969-71, Hartman award 1977), Internat. Neuroendocrine Soc. (council 1972-76), Hungarian Soc. Endocrinology and Metabolism (hon.), Nat. Acad. Scis., Japan Endocrin Soc. (hon.), Phi Beta Kappa, Sigma Xi. Current Work: Mechanisms by which the brain controls endocrine secretions, especially the pituitary gonadotropins and ovarian steroids. Technics include stereotaxic surgery electrophysiology, neuropharmacology and radioimmunoassay. Subspecialties: Neuroendocrinology; Anatomy and embryology. Home: 466 Tuallitan Rd Los Angeles CA 90049 Office: U Calif Sch Medicine Los Angeles CA 90024

SAWYER, CONSTANCE BRAGDON, solar physicist, oceanographer; b. Lewiston, Maine, June 3, 1926; d. William Hayes, Jr. and Beatrice Goulding (Burr) S.; m. James Walter Warwick, Sept. 6, 1947; children: Sarah, David, Rachel Warwick, Joel McCulloch. A.B., Smith Coll., 1947; M.A., Radcliffe Coll., 1948, Ph.D., 1952. With Sacramento Peak Obs., Sunspot, N.Mex., 1952-55; with High Altitude Obs., Nat. Ctr. for Atmospheric Research, Boulder, Colo., 1955-58, staff scientist, 1979-82; research assoc. dept. astrophys., planetary, and atmospheric scis. U. Colo., 1984-85. with Space Environ. Lab., NOAA, Boulder, 1958-74, Atlantic Oceanic and Meteorol. Lab., Miami, Fla., 1975-76, Pacific Marine Environ. Lab., Seattle, 1976-79. Author: Solar Flare Prediction. Contbr. research papers to profl. jours. Mem. Am. Astron. Soc. (sec. solar physics div. 1982-85), Am. Geophys. Union, AAAS, Internat. Astron. Union, Internat. Union Geology and Geophysics, Sigma Xi. Current Work: Solar activity, solar corona, spacecraft observations of sun, corona, planets. Subspecialties: Solar physics; Remote sensing (atmospheric science). Home: 850 20th St Apt 705 Boulder CO 80302 Office: Radiophysics 5475 Western Ave Boulder CO 80301

SAWYER, STANLEY ARTHUR, mathematics and genetics, educator; b. Juneau, Alaska, Mar. 19, 1940; s. Selwyn K. and Marie H.S. B.S., Calif. Inst. Tech., 1960, Ph.D., 1964; M.A. (hon.), Brown U., 1969. Instr., Courant Inst., NYU, 1965-67; asst. prof. math. Brown U., Providence, 1967-69; with Yeshiva U., N.Y.C., 1969-78; prof. Purdue U., West Lafayette, Ind., 1978-84; prof. Washington U., St. Louis, 1984—. Mem. Am. Math. Soc., Inst. Math. Stats. (assoc. editor Jour. Annals of Probability 1979-85), Genetics Soc. Am. Current work: Research in mathematics, population genetics, probability theory. Subspecialty: Probability. Office: Dept Math Washington U Saint Louis MO 63130

SAXENA, SURENDRA KUMAR, geotechnical engineering educator, consultant, researcher; m. Sandra L. Pruitt; 1 child, Anil. B.S. Aligarh U., India, 1955; M.S., Duke U., 1965, Ph.D., 1971. Registered profl. engr., N.Y., N.J., Ill., Fla. Dist. engr. Pub. Works Dept., State Govt. Rajasthan, Jaipur, India, 1955-62; soils engr. Port Authority of N.Y., N.J., 1969-74; sr. engr. Dames & Moore, Cranford, N.J., 1974-76; assoc. prof. Ill. Inst. Tech., Chgo., 1976-81, prof., chmn. dept. civil engring., 1981—. Contbr. articles to profl. jours. and confs. Editor geotech. books. Fellow Am. Soc. Civil Engrs. (publs. com. of Geotech. Jour., com. numerical methods of geotechnical div., chmn. geotech. div. Ill. sect. 1982); mem. ASTM (marine geotechnics com., past chmn. subcom. properties of soils), Transp. Res. Bd. (rigid pavement com. 1978—), Earthquake Engring. Research Inst. (pres. Great Lakes chpt. 1983-84), Internat. Soc. Soil Mechanics and Found. Engring., Assn. Asian Indians in Am. (pres. 1982-83, 84-85), Sigma Xi. Current work: Earthquake engineering, soil-structure interaction, static and dynamic soil properties, ballast-soil geotextile behavior, unsaturated soils, thermal properties of soils. Subspecialty: Civil engineering. Home: 1 South 130 Pine Ln Lombard IL 60148 Office: Dept Civil Engring Ill Inst Tech 3201 S Dearborn Chicago IL 60616

SAXENA, VINOD KUMAR, meteorology educator, consultant atmospheric sciences; b. Agra, India, May 23, 1944; came to U.S., 1968, naturalized, 1977; s. Kishori L. and Uma S.; m. Indra Nigam, Aug. 19, 1973; 1 dau.: Rita. Lectr. physics Agra Coll., 1963-64; asst. prof. U. Saugar, Sagar, India, 1967-68; fellow U. Mo.-Rolla, 1968-71; cloud physicist U. Denver, 1971-77; research assoc. prof. U. Utah, 1977-79; assoc. prof. meteorology N.C. State U., Raleigh, 1979—; invitational cons. State of N.C., Raleigh, 1980—, WRAL-TV, Raleigh, 1982—. Contbr. articles in field to profl. jours. Research grantee NSF, 1971—; Research grantee U.S. Navy, 1972-75; Research grantee Dept. Energy, 1977—; recipient Meteorol. award U. Utah, 1979. Mem. Am. Meteorol. Soc., Am. Geophys. Union, Am. Water Research Assn., Himalayan Internat. Inst., Brit. Royal Meteorol. Soc., Am. Platform Assn., Sigma Xi. Hindu. Developer cloud condensation nucleus spectrometer. Current Work: Cloud, aerosol and precipitation physics; particulate pollution; mechanisms involving the generation and scavenging of natural aerosols, development of instrumentation for cloud-active aerosols. Subspecialties: Meteorologic instrumentation; Atmospheric chemistry. Home: 3616 Greywood Dr Raleigh NC 27604 Office: Dept Marine Earth and Atmospheric Scis N C State U Box 5068 Raleigh NC 27650

SAXER, RICHARD KARL, government official. Dir., Def. Nuclear Agy., Alexandria, Va. . Office: Def Nuclear Agy 6801 Telegraph Rd Alexandria VA 22310*

SAXON, DAVID STEPHEN, university administrator, physicist; b. St. Paul, Feb. 8, 1920; s. Ivan and Rebecca (Moss) S.; m. Shirley Goodman, Jan. 6, 1940. B.S., MIT, 1941, Ph.D., 1944. Prof. physics UCLA, 1958-83, dean phy. scis., 1966-68, vice chancellor, 1968-75; provost U. Calif., 1974-75, pres., 1975-83; corp. chmn. MIT, Cambridge, Mass., 1983—; dir. Eastman Kodak Co., Houghton Mifflin Co. Author: Elementary Quantum Mechanics, 1968; (with William B. Fretter) Physics for the Liberal Arts Student, 1971. Contbr. articles to profl. jours. Recipient Disting. Teaching award UCLA, 1967; named to Royal Order of No. Star, 1979, Hon. Citizen Georg-August U., Gottingen, 1982. Fellow AAAS, Am. Phys. Soc.; mem. Am. Assn. Physics Tchrs., Am. Inst. Physics, Phi Beta Kappa, Sigma Pi Sigma, Sigma Xi. Current work: University administration. Subspecialties: Nuclear physics; Theoretical physics. Office: MIT 77 Massachusetts Ave Cambrige MA 02139

SAYEGH, SOHEIL I(SKANDAR), electrical engineer, educator; b. Alexandria, Egypt, Dec. 13, 1952; came to U.S., 1975, s. Iskandar and Violette (Zeitoun) S. B.Sc, U. Alexandria, 1974; M.S., U. Wis.-Madison, 1977, Ph.D., 1982. Asst. prof. elec. engring. Mich. State U., East Lansing, 1982—. Contbr. articles to profl. jours. NSF grantee, 1983. Mem. IEEE, Optical Soc. Am. Current work: Communication theory; communication networks; digital signal processing. Subspecialty: Telecommunications. Home: 4465 Kenneth Apt D 211 Okemos MI 48864 Office: Mich State U Dept Elec Engring East Lansing MI 48824

SAYLOR, WILLIAM WARDELL, nuclear engineer; b. Phila., Aug. 18, 1950; s. Wardell Hicks and Eleanor Carie (Wright) S.; m. Cathleen Gail Crowley, Feb. 24, 1973 (div.); children—Daniel Wardell, Cathleen Gail; m. Mary Katherine Devoti, Nov. 9, 1981. B.S. in Nuclear Engring., U.S. Mil. Acad., 1972; M.S. in Nuclear Engring., MIT, 1977. Registered profl. engr., Pa. Commd. 2d lt. U.S. Army, 1972, advanced through grades to capt., 1976; mem. C.E., Fed. Republic Germany, Va., Saudi Arabia, 1972-81, ret., 1981; analytical nuclear engr. Gilbert-Commonwealth, Reading, Pa., 1981-83; mem. staff Los Alamos Nat. Lab., N.Mex., 1983—. Mem. Am. Nuclear Soc., Am. Phys. Soc. Republican. Current work: Conceptual design, systems engineering, and engineering analysis of inertial confinement fusion concepts and advanced defense-related concepts and technologies. Subspecialties: Nuclear fusion; Systems engineering. Home: 119 Rover Blvd Los Alamos NM 87544 Office: Los Alamos Nat Lab PO Box 1663 MS F611 Los Alamos NM 87545

SBORDONE, ROBERT JOSEPH, neuropsychologist, educator; b. Boston, May 6, 1940; s. Saverio and Phylliss (Dellaria) Vella; m. Melinda Welles, June 30, 1972 (div. 1977). A.B., U. So. Calif., 1967; M.A., Calif. State U.-Los Angeles, 1969; Ph.D., UCLA, 1976, postdoctoral, 1977. Cert. psychologist Calif. Mem. staff psychology UCLA, 1977-78; sole practice psychology, Los Angeles, 1978-80; asst. prof. psychology U. Calif.-Irvine, 1980-82, asst. clin. prof., 1983—; pres. Robert Sbordone Inc., Garden Grove, Calif., 1982—. Contbr. chpt. to book and articles to profl. jours.; editor: Clinical Neoropsychology jour, 1979—. Mem. bd. dirs. So. Calif. Head Injury Found., 1982—; mem. adv. bd. Mardan Sch., Costa Mesa, Calif., 1982—. Served with USAF, 1962-66. NIMH grantee, 1973-77. Mem. Am. Psychol. Assn., Internat. Neuropsychol. Soc., Nat. Head Injury Found., Internat. Soc. Research in Aggression, N.Y. Acad. Scis. Developer of computer software, 1982. Current Work: Neuropsychological assessment of brain injured; development of computer software for assessment and rehabilitation of brain injured patients. Subspecialties: Neuropsychology; Cognition. Home: 13412 Donegal Dr Garden Grove CA 92644 Office: Robert J Sbordone Inc 13412 Donegal Dr Garden Grove CA 92644

SCAIANO, JUAN CESAR, chemist; b. Buenos Aires, Jan. 4, 1945; came to Can., 1975; s. Domingo and Elida (Gargallo) S.; m. Elda Ester Prakapavicius, Dec. 28, 1967; children—Gus, Veronica, Adriana, Martin. Ph.D., U. Chile, 1970; Licencee in chemistry, U. Buenos Aires, 1967. Assoc. prof. U. Rio Cuarto, Argentina, 1973-74; vis. scientist Nat. Research Council Can., Ottawa, Ont., 1975-76, research officer, 1979-84, sect. head reaction intermediates, 1984—; profl. specialist U. Notre Dame, Ind., 1976-79. Contbr. articles to profl. jours., chpts. to books. Rutherford Meml. medal, Royal Soc. Can., 1983. Fellow Royal Soc. Can.; mem. Chem. Inst. Can., Royal Soc. Chemistry, Interam. Photochem. Soc., European Photochemistry Assn. Current work: Study of short-lived reaction intermediates, photochemistry, laser techniques. Subspecialties: Kinetics; Photochemistry. Home: 2196 Emard Crescent Gloucester ON K1J 6K6 Canada Office: Nat Research Council Can 100 Sussex Dr Ottawa ON K1A 0R6 Canada

SCANDALIOS, JOHN GEORGE, geneticist; b. Nisyros Isle, Greece, Nov. 1, 1934; s. George John and Calliope (Broujos) S.; m. Penelope Anne Lawrence, Jan. 18, 1961; children: Artemis Christina, Melissa Joan, Nikki Eleni. B.A., U. Va., 1957; M.S., Adelphi U., 1962; Ph.D., U. Hawaii, 1965. Asso. in bacterial genetics Cold Spring Harbor Labs., 1960-62; NIH postdoctoral fellow U. Hawaii Med. Sch., 1965; asst. prof. Mich. State U., East Lansing, 1965-70, asso. prof., 1970-72; prof., head dept. biology U. S.C., Columbia, 1973-75; prof., head dept. genetics N.C. State U., Raleigh, 1975-85, Disting. Univ. prof., 1985—; vis. prof. genetics U. Calif., Davis, 1969; vis. prof. OAS, Argentina, Chile and Brazil, 1972; mem. recombinant DNA adv. com. NIH. Author: Physiological Genetics, 1979; Editor: Developmental Genetics, Advances in Genetics, Current Topics in Med. Biol. Research; co-editor: Isozymes, 4 vols., 1975, Monographs in Developmental Biology, 1968—. Served with USAF, 1957. Alexander von Humboldt travel fellow, 1976; mem. exchange program NAS, US/USSR. Mem. Genetics Soc. Am. (bd. dirs.), Am. Soc. Human Genetics, Am. Genetic Assn. (pres.), AAAS, Soc. Devel. Biology (dir.), Am. Inst. Biol. Scis., Am. Soc. Plant Physiologists, Sigma Xi. Current Work: Studing regulation of gene expression in eukaryotes (maize) during development at the molecular level; developmental-molecular genetics, use of recombinant-DNA to study gene expression in plants. Subspecialties: Genetics and genetic engineering (biology); Gene actions. Office: Dept Genetics NC State U PO Box 7614 Raleigh NC 27695

SCANDELLA, CARL JOHN, biochemist; b. Price, Utah, Apr. 4, 1944; s. Ben and Pauline (Quilico) S.; m. Dorothea Hostettler, Jan. 3, 1968 (div. 1982); 1 child, Nathan; m. Nancy Logan Haigwood, Sept. 24, 1983. B.S. in Chemistry, Calif. Inst. Tech., 1966; Ph.D. in Biochemistry, Stanford U., 1971. Postdoctoral fellow Stanford U., Palo Alto, Calif., 1971-72; postdoctoral fellow Biocenter, U. Basel, Switzerland, 1972-74; asst. prof. biochemistry SUNY, Stony Brook, 1975-81; prin. research sci. Genex Corp., Gaithersburg, Md., 1981-83; sr. sci. Chiron Corp., Emeryville, Calif., 1983—. Contbr. articles to profl. jours. NIH grantee. Mem. Biophys. Soc. Democrat. Current work: Large scale purification of human proteins from recombinant organisms; cell membrane biochemistry and biophysics. Subspecialties: Enzyme technology; Biochemistry (medicine). Office: Chiron Corp 4560 Horton St Emeryville CA 94608

SCANES, COLIN GUY, animal physiology educator; b. London, July 11, 1947; s. Herbert Alfred and Marjorie Amy (Barltrop) S.; m. Carla Joy Turk; children—Rosalind Amanda, Jacqueline Diana. B.S., U. Hull, Eng., 1969; Ph.D., U. Wales, 1972. Lectr., U. Leeds, Eng., 1972-78; assoc. prof. physiology Rutgers U., New Brunswick, N.J., 1978-82, chmn. dept., 1981—, prof., 1982—; cons. Monsanto Co., St. Louis, 1984, Hoffman LaRoche, Nutley, N.J., 1983, Upjohn Co., Kalamazoo, 1979-82. Editor 2 books on avian endocrinology, 1982, 84. Contbr. numerous articles to profl. jours., chpt. to books. NSF grantee, 1981—. Mem. Am. Physiol. Soc., Poultry Sci. Assn., Endocrine Soc., Am. Soc. for Animal Sci., Am. Soc. Zoology. Lutheran. Current work: Hormonal control of growth and metabolism. Subspecialties: Animal nutrition; Animal pathology. Home: 1430 Seneca Rd North Brunswick NJ 08902 Office: Dept Animal Sci Rutgers U New Brunswick NJ 08903

SCARF, HERBERT ELI, economics educator; b. Phila., July 25, 1930; s. Louis H. and Lena (Elkman) S.; m. Margaret Klein, June 28, 1953; children—Martha Samuelson, Elizabeth Stone, Susan Johnson. A.B., Temple U., 1951; M.A., Princeton U., 1952, Ph.D., 1954; L.H.D. (hon.), U. Chgo., 1978. With Rand Corp., Santa Monica, Calif., 1954-57; asst. prof. stats. Stanford U., Calif., 1957-62; vis. assoc. prof. Yale U., New Haven, 1959-60, prof. econs., 1963-70, Stanley Resor prof. econs., 1970-78, Sterling prof. econs., 1979—, dir. div. social scis., 1971-72, 73-74, dir. Cowles Found. for Research in Econs., 1967-71, 81-84; fellow Ctr. for Advanced Study, Stanford, 1962-63. Author: Mathematical Theory of Inventory, 1958; Computation of Economic Equilibria, 1973. Editor: Applied General Equilibrium Analysis, 1984. Recipient Lanchester prize Operations Research Soc. Am., 1974, Von Neumann medal, 1983. Fellow Econometric Soc., Am. Acad. Arts and Scis.; mem. Econometric Soc. (pres. 1983), Nat. Acad. Scis. Club: New Haven Lawn. Current work: general equilibrium theory; game theory; mathematical methods. Subspecialties: Operations research (mathematics); Applied mathematics. Office: 1 Cowles Foundation Yale University Box 2125 Yale Station New Haven CT 06520

SCARL, DONALD, physicist, educator; b. Easton, Pa., Sept. 17, 1935; m. Barbara S. Cohen, Nov. 24, 1979; 1 dau., Judith Cohen. B.A., Lehigh U., 1957; Ph.D., Princeton U., 1962. Assoc. prof. physics Poly. Inst. N.Y., Farmingdale, 1966—. Contbr. articles to profl. jours. Mem. Am. Phys. Soc., Optical Soc. Am., AAAS, Phi Beta Kappa. Patentee in field. Current Work: Quantum optics, atomic state dynamics. Subspecialties: Atomic and molecular physics; Semiconductor lasers. Home: 8 Woodland Rd Glen Cove NY 11542 Office: Polytechnic Institute of NY Farmingdale NY 11735

SCARRATT, WILLIAM KENT, veterinarian, educator; b. Winnipeg, Man., Can., July 19, 1951; came to U.S., 1975; s. William Nevil and Doris Fern (Cooney) S.; m. Anne Lorraine Kristian, Feb. 25, 1977; children—Jamie, Bryan, Kristen. B.S., U. Calgary, 1971; D.V.M., U. Sask., Can., 1975. Diplomate Am. Coll. Vet. Internal Medicine. Intern, Okla. State U.-Stillwater, 1975-76; resident, Cornell Univ., 1976-78; asst. state veterinarian Tioga Park, Nichols, N.Y., 1976-78; asst. prof. vet. medicine U. Fla.-Gainesville, 1978-82, Va. Inst. Tech., 1982—; mem. credentials com. Am. Coll. Vet. Internal Medicine, 1984—. Contbr. articles to profl. jours., chpts. to books. Province of Alta. Scholarship award, U. Calgary, 1971. Mem. Am. Coll. Vet. Internal Medicine, AVMA, B.C. Vet. Med. Assn., Can. Vet. Med. Assn. Current work: Response to vaccination with Brucella Strain 19 in the horse. Subspecialty: Internal medicine (veterinary medicine). Home: 2010 Christopher Dr Blacksburg VA 24060 Office: Va-Md Regional Coll Vet Medicine Southgate Dr Va Inst Tech Blacksburg VA 24061

SCATTERGOOD, THOMAS W., planetologist, analytical chemist; b. Mt. Holly, N.J., Oct. 3, 1946; s. William E. and Grace (Paulin) S. B.S. in Chemistry, U. Del., Newark, 1968; M.S., SUNY-Stony Brook, 1972, Ph.D. in Chemistry, 1975. Teaching asst. SUNY-Stony Brook, 1970-72, research asst., 1972-75, research assoc., 1975-76, sr. research assoc., 1979—, adj. asst. prof., 1984—; research assoc. NRC, Nat. Acad. Scis., NASA Ames Research Ctr., 1977-78, Titan Probe Sci. Study Group, NASA Ames Research Ctr., Moffett Field, Calif., 1979-81, Mars Exobiology Research Consortium, NASA, 1984. Contbr. articles to profl. publs. Pres. Cypress Point Lakes Homeowners Assn., Central Coast Counties Camera Club Council. Mem. AAAS, Am. Geophys. Union, Am. Astron. Soc. (div. planetary scis.), Planetary Soc., Photog. Soc. Am. Quaker. Club: Cameraderie Camera (Mountain View, Calif.). Current Work: Study of photochemistry and energetic particle initiated chemistry in atmospheres of outer planets; determination of identity (composition) and optical properties of clouds of Titan. Subspecialties: Planetary atmospheres; Space chemistry. MS 239-12 NASA Ames Research Center Moffett Field CA 94035

SCAWTHORN, CHARLES, engineering researcher, consultant; b. Bklyn., Dec. 27, 1944; s. Charles and Lillian (Beer) S.; m. Nini Jensen, Dec. 31, 1981; 1 child, Charles Tobias. B.E., Cooper Union, 1966; M.S.C.E., Lehigh U., 1968; Ph.D., Kyoto U., Japan, 1981. Registered profl. engr., N.Y., Calif. Engr., Consol. Edison Co., N.Y.C., 1968-71; sr. engr. Bechtel Corp., San Francisco, 1974-76; cons. engr. Dame & Moore, San Francisco, 1981—; sec. com. on urban earthquake hazards Earthquake Engrng. Research Inst. Editor: The Anticipated Tokai Earthquake, 1984; Urban Earthquake Hazards Reduction, 1984. Contbr. articles to profl. jours. Recipient internat. bridge design award U.S. Steel Corp., 1966. Mem. ASCE (safety bldgs. com.), Seismol. Soc. Am., Soc. Risk Analysis. Democrat. Current work: Seismic damage estimation and mitigation, including economic effects and effects of fire following earthquake. Subspecialties: Structural engineering; Seismology. Home: PO Box 3326 San Francisco CA 94119 Office: Dames & Moore 500 Sansome St San Francisco CA 94111

SCHACHMAN, HOWARD KAPNEK, molecular biologist, educator; b. Phila., Dec. 5, 1918; s. Morris H. and Rose (Kapnek) S.; m. Ethel H. Lazarus, Oct. 20, 1945; children—Marc, David. B.S. in Chem. Engrng, Mass. Inst. Tech., 1939; Ph.D. in Phys. Chemistry, Princeton, 1948; D.Sc. (hon.), Northwestern U., 1974. Fellow NIH, 1946-48; instr., asst. prof. U. Calif. at Berkeley, 1948-54, asso. prof. biochemistry, 1954-59, prof. biochemistry and molecular biology, 1959—, chmn. dept. molecular biology, dir. virus lab., 1969-76. Author: Ultracentrifugation in Biochemistry, 1959. Served from ensign to lt. USNR, 1945-47. Guggenheim Meml. fellow, 1956; Recipient John Scott award, 1964, Warren Triennial prize Mass. Gen. Hosp., 1965. Mem. Nat. Acad. Sci., Am. Chem. Soc. (recipient award in Chem. Instrumentation 1962, Calif. sec. award 1958), AAAS, Am. Soc. Biol. Chemists, Am. Acad. Arts and Scis., Sigma Xi. Current Work: Proteins, enzymes, nucleic acids. Macromolecular interactions. Subspecialties: Biochemistry; Biophysical chemistry. Office: Molecular Biology and Virus Lab U Calif Berkeley CA 94720

SCHACHT, JOCHEN HEINRICH, biochemistry educator; b. Konigsberg, Germany, July 2, 1939, came to U.S., 1969; s. Heinz and Else (Sprenger) S.; m. Helga Seidel, Jan. 27, 1967; children—Miriam, Daniel. M.S., U. Heidelberg, Fed. Republic Germany, 1965, Ph.D., 1968. Asst. prof. U. Mich., Ann Arbor, 1973-78, assoc. prof., 1978-84, prof. biol. chemistry, 1984—; chmn. program on physiol. acoustics U. Mich., Ann Arbor, 1981—. Contbr. articles to profl. jours. Chercheur Etranger, France, 1984, Javits Neurosci. investigator NIH, 1984; Fogarty Sr. Internat. fellow NIH, 1979. Mem. German Assn. Biol. Chemistry, Am. Soc. Neurochemistry, Soc. Neuroscis., Assn. Research Otolaryngology, Am. Soc. Biol. Chemists. Subspecialties: Biochemistry (biology); Otorhinolaryngology. Office: U Mich Kresge Hearing Research Inst Ann Arbor MI 48109

SCHAD, THEODORE MACNEEVE, research administrator, consultant; b. Balt., Aug. 25, 1918; s. William Henry and Emma Margaret (Scheldt) S.; m. Mary Kathleen White, Nov. 5, 1944; children—Mary Jane, Rebecca Christina. B.E., Johns Hopkins U., 1939. With U.S. Govt., various locations, 1939-58; dep. dir. Congressional Research Service, Washington, 1958-68; exec. dir. Nat. Water Commn., Washington, 1968-73; exec. sec. Environ. Studies Bd. Nat. Acad. Sci., Washington, 1973-77, dep. exec. dir. Commn. on Natural Resources, 1977-83; exec. dir. Nat. Ground Water Policy Forum The Conservation Found., Washington, 1984—; staff dir. select Com. on water resources U.S. Senate, 1959-61; cons. Chesapeake Research Consortium, Shadyside, Md., 1984. Contbr. articles to profl. jours. Bd. dirs., v.p. Veterans Coop. Housing Assn., Washington, 1958-81. Recipient Meritorious Service award U.S. Dept. Interior, 1950; Iben award Am. Water Resources Assn., 1978. Fellow ASCE (pres. Nat. Capital sect. 1967-68); mem. Am. Acad. Environ. Engrs., Am. Geophys. Union, Am. Inst. Hydrology, Nat. Acad. Pub. Adminstrn., Am. Water Works Assn. (hon.). Christian. Clubs: Cosmos, Potomac Appalachian Trail (chmn. mountaineering sect. 1954-55); Colo. Mountain; Seattle Mountaineers. Current work: Water resources policy, environmental policy, science policy, public administration Subspecialties: Civil engineering; Hydrology. Office: Conservation Found 1717 Massachusetts Ave NW Washington DC 20036

SCHADE, ROBERT RICHARD, medical educator, researcher; b. Rockville Centre, N.Y., Jan. 5, 1948; s. Robert Richard and Loretta K. (McGovern) S.; m. Rosann Foster, Oct. 14, 1972; children: Danielle Nicole, Kimberly Anne, Allison Janine. A.B., Colgate U., 1969; M.D., George Washington U., 1973. Diplomate: Am. Bd. Internal Medicine, Nat. Bd. Med. Examiners. Intern Rush-Presbyn. Med. Ctr., Chgo., 1973-74, resident in internal medicine, 1974-76; fellow liver disease unit Yale U., New Haven, 1976-78, fellow in gastroenterology, 1978-80; assoc. prof. medicine U. Pitts. Med. Sch., 1980—; dir. Clin. Gastrointestinal lab. Presbyn. U. Hosp., Pitts., 1982—; attending VA Hosp. of Oakland, Pitts., Children's Hosp. Pitts. Contbr. articles to profl. jours. Mem. sci. adv. bd. Pitts. chpt. Nat. Found. Ileitis and Colitis, 1981—. Mem. Am. Gastroent. Assn., N.Y. Acad. Sci., ACP, Am. Soc. Internal Medicine, Am. Coll. Gastroenterology, Am. Soc. Gastrointestinal Endoscopy, AAAS, Am. Fedn. for Clin. Research, Am. Assn. Study Liver Diseases. Republican. Roman Catholic. Current Work: Liver disease and liver transplantation; effects of alcohol on pituitary hormone secretion; studies in gastrointestinal motility. Subspecialties: Gastroenterology; Internal medicine. Office: U Pitts Pittsburgh PA 15261

SCHADLER, DANIEL LEO, biologist, educator; b. Dayton, Ky., Apr. 5, 1948; s. Alvin Peter and Irma Catherinne (Schack) S. A.B., Thomas More Coll., 1970; M.S., Cornell U., 1972, Ph.D., 1974. NSF grad. trainee Cornell U., Ithaca, N.Y., 1970-74; postdoctoral research assoc. U. Wis., Madison, 1974-75; asst. prof. biology Oglethorpe U., Atlanta, 1975-79, assoc. prof., 1979-84, prof., 1984—. Mem. Am. Chem. Soc., Am. Phytopath. Soc., Internat. Soc. Plant Pathology, Ga. Chrysanthemum Soc. Roman Catholic. Current Work: Phytotoxins; teaching introductory microbiology courses. Subspecialties: Plant pathology; Microbiology. Home: 4218 Admiral Dr Chamblee GA 30341 Office: 4484 Peachtree Rd NE Atlanta GA 30319

SCHAECHTER, MOSELIO, microbiologist, academic administrator; b. Milan, Italy, Apr. 26, 1928; s. Abraham Isaac and Victoria C. (Waksmann) S.; m. Barbara Ruth Thompson, Dec. 13, 1953; children: Judith A., John N. M.A., U. Kans., 1951; Ph.D., U. Pa., 1954. Postdoctoral State Serum Inst., Copenhagen, Denmark, 1956-58; instr. to assoc. prof. U. Fla., 1958-62; assoc. prof., prof. Tufts U., Boston, 1962—, chmn. dept. molecular biology, 1970—; chmn. NIH study sect. on bacteriology and mycology, 1978-79, mem., 1975-79; grant reviewer NSF. Contbr. chpts. to books, articles to profl. publs. Served with U.S. Army, 1954-56. NIH research career devel. awardee, 1959-68. Mem. Am. Soc. Microbiology (chmn. com. on genetics, molecular and systematic microbiology 1979—, pres. 1985-86), Soc. Genetic Microbiology, Boston Mycol. Club, Assn. Med. Sch. Microbiology Chmn. (pres. 1984-85), Sigma Xi. Current Work: DNA replication in bacteria. Subspecialties: Microbiology; Molecular biology. Home: 855 Commonwealth Newton MA 02159 Office: 136 Harrison Ave Boston MA 02111

SCHAEFER, ALBERT RUSSELL, physicist, educator; b. Oklahoma City, Oct. 13, 1944; s. Albert R. and Marcella (Russell) S.; m. Judith Ann Bracewell, Jan. 19, 1968; children: Amy, Brandon. B.S. in Physics with spl. distinction, U. Okla., 1966, Ph.D. in Atomic Physics, 1970. Physicist Nat. Bur. Standards, Washington, 1970—; adj. prof. physics Montgomery Coll., 1974—. Contbr. articles to profl. jours. Co-organizer, past bd. dirs. Greater Laytonville Area Citizens Assn. Recipient Outstanding Performance awards Nat. Bur. Standards, 1978, 80; Bronze medal Dept. Commerce, 1981; NSF fellow, 1966. Mem. Am. Phys. Soc., Optical Soc. Am., Soc. Photo-optical Instrumentation Engrs., Sigma Xi, Phi Beta Kappa. Current Work: Radiometric physics, optical detectors, spectroscopy, silicon photodiodes, electro-optics, photometry, atomic lifetimes, astronomy. Subspecialties: Photo-optical instrumentation; Atomic and molecular physics. Office: Nat Bur Standards B-306-MET Gaithersburg MD 20899

SCHAEFER, JACOB WERNLI, research laboratory executive, consultant; b. Paullina, Iowa, June 27, 1919; s. Louis B. and Minnie (Wernli) S.; m. Mary Snow Carter, July 26, 1941; children: Joanna, James, Scott. B.M.E., Ohio State U., 1941, D.Sc. (hon.), 1976. Mem. staff Bell Labs., 1941-84; dir. Kwajalein (Marshall Islands) Field Sta., 1963-65, exec. dir., Holmdel, N.J., 1968-80, Murray Hill, N.J., 1980-81, Mil. Systems Div., 1981-84; cons. mil. systems. Author articles in field. Pres. Watchung (N.J.) Sch. Bd., 1954-63; pres. Bancroft Sch., Haddonfield, N.J., 1978-82, trustee, 1973—; chmn. Watchung Planning Bd., 1967—; mem. Watchung Area council Boy Scouts Am., 1966-69. Served to capt. Ordnance Corps AUS, 1942-46. Decorated Commendation medal; recipient Disting. Alumnus award Ohio State U., 1966, 84, Outstanding Civilian Service medal. Fellow IEEE; mem. Nat. Acad. Engring., ASME, Army Ordnance Assn. Republican. Patentee command guidance for anti-aircraft missiles, optical tracking systems for anti-aircraft fire control. Current Work: Military systems: guided missile defense systems, underwater surveillance systems, and computer applications. Subspecialty: Systems engineering. Home: 115 Century Ln Watchung NJ 07060

SCHAEFFER, NORMAN M., physicist, cons.; b. Camden, Ark., Nov. 1, 1927; s. Sam and Lena (Sabludowski) S.; m. Cecille Marion Levinson, Aug. 14, 1949; children: Marc A., Jeanette A., Susan R. B.S., La. State U., 1947, M.S., 1949; Ph.D., U. Tex., 1953. With Gen. Dynamics, Ft. Worth, 1953-62, mgr. nuclear research, 1956-62; pres. Radiation Research Assocs., Ft. Worth, 1962—. Author: Reactor Shielding for Nuclear Engineers, 1973. Fellow Am. Nuclear Soc.; mem. Am. Phys. Soc. Current Work: Reactor shielding, radiation transport; manage research co. specializing in radiation shielding and atmospheric optics. Subspecialties: Nuclear fission; Nuclear engineering. Office: 3550 Hulen Fort Worth TX 76107

SCHAEFFER, ROBERT L., JR., biology educator; b. Allentown, Pa., Oct. 31, 1917; s. Robert L. and Millie Louisa (Ochs) S. B.S., Haverford Coll., 1940; Ph.D., U. Pa., 1948. Instr. botany U. Pa., Phila., 1946-47; asst. prof. biology Upsala Coll., East Orange, N.J., 1948-54; asst. prof. biology Muhlenberg Coll., Allentown, Pa., 1954-59, prof., 1960—. Author: Vascular Flora of Northampton County, Pa, 1948. Elder St. John's United Ch. of Christ, Allentown; active Lehigh County Hist. Soc. Served with USN, 1944-46. Recipient Lindbach Teaching award, 1963. Mem. Am. Fern Soc., Phila. Bot. Club, Torrey Bot., Am. Soc. Plant Taxonomists, Sigma Xi., Phi Beta Kappa. Current Work: Vascular flora of the Lehigh Valley. Subspecialties: Taxonomy; Systematics. Home: 32 N 8th St Allentown PA 18101 Office: Muhlenberg Coll Allentown PA 18104

SCHAFER, JOHN FRANCIS, plant pathologist; b. Pullman, Wash., Feb. 17, 1921; s. Edwin George and Ella Frances (Miles) S.; m. Joyce A. Marcks, Aug. 16, 1947; children: Patricia, Janice, James. B.S., Wash. State U., 1942; Ph.D., U. Wis.-Madison, 1950. Mem. faculty dept. plant pathology Purdue U., 1949-68, prof., 1958-68; prof., head dept. plant pathology Kans. State U., 1968-72; prof., chmn. dept. plant pathology Wash. State U., 1972-80; integrated pest mgmt. coordinator sci. and edn. U.S. Dept. Agr., Beltsville, Md., 1980-81; acting nat. research program leader plant pathology and nematology Agrl. Research Service, 1981-82, dir. Cereal Rust Lab., St. Paul, 1982—; vis. research prof. Duquesne U., 1965-66; adj. prof. plant pathology U. Minn. Served with AUS, 1942-46. Fellow AAAS, Ind. Acad. Sci.; mem. Am. Phytopath. Soc. (past pres.), Am. Soc. Agronomy, Crop Sci. Soc. Am. Co-breeder of 30 cultivars of cereal crops including Arthur wheat. Current Work: Durability of plant disease resistance. Subspecialty: Plant pathology. Home: 1753 Lindig St St Paul MN 55113 Office: 1551 Lindig St St Paul MN 55108

SCHAFFER, MARTIN HARRY, psychiatry educator; b. Houston, June 6, 1947; s. Elliot Nathan and Della (Shapiro) S.; m. Barbara Noyes; children—Sarah, Nathaniel. A.B in Chemistry, Washington U., St. Louis, 1969; M.D., Stanford U., 1975. Diplomate Am. Bd. Psychiatry and Neurology. Intern, UCLA Harbor Gen. Hosp., Los Angeles; resident dept. psychiatry U. Chgo., chief resident dept. psychiatry 1978-79, research fellow, 1979-81, asst. prof., 1981—. Contbr. articles to profl. jours. Mem. Soc. Neurosci. Current work: Molecular biology of neuropeptides. Office: Dept Psychiatry Univ Chgo Student Mental Health Clinic 5743 Drexel Ave Chicago IL 60637

SCHAIRER, GEORGE SWIFT, aerodynamic engineer; b. Pitts., May 19, 1913; s. Otto Sorg and Elizabeth Blanche (Swift) S.; m. Mary Pauline Tarbox, June 20, 1935; children: Mary Elizabeth, George Edward, Sally Helen, John Otto. B.S., Swarthmore (Pa.) Coll., 1934, D.Eng. (hon.), 1958; M.S., MIT, 1935. With Bendix Aviation Corp., South Bend, Ind., 1935-37; cons. Vultee Aircraft Corp., San Diego, 1937-39; with Boeing Airplane Co., Seattle, 1939—, mem. aerodynamic staff, 1948-51, chief tech. staff, 1951-56, asst. chief engr., 1956-57, dir. research, 1957-59, v.p. research and devel., 1959-73, v.p. research, 1973-78; cons. in field; mem. aero. and space engrng. bd. NRC, 1977-80. Contbr. articles to profl. jours. Trustee, contemporary Theatre Cornish Sch. Recipient Spirit of St. Louis medal ASME, 1959; Guggenheim medal, 1967. Fellow AIAA (hon.; Sylvanus Albert Reed award 1950, Wright Brothers lectr. 1964); mem. Nat. Acad. Engring., Nat. Acad. Scis., Internat. Acad. Aeronautics, Sigma Xi, Sigma Tau. Current Work: Consultant aerospace industry. Subspecialties: Aerospace engineering and technology; Astronautics. Home: 4242 Hunts Point Rd Bellevue WA 98004 Office: Boeing Co Box 3707 Seattle WA 98124

SCHALLY, ANDREW VICTOR, medical research scientist; b. Poland, Nov. 30, 1926; came to U.S., 1957; s. Casimir Peter and Maria (Lacka) S.; married; children: Karen, Gordon; m. Ana Maria Comaru, Aug. 1976. B.Sc., McGill U., Can., 1955, Ph.D. in Biochemistry, 1957; 10 hon. doctorates. Research asst. biochemistry Nat. Inst. Med. Research, London, 1949-52; dept. psychiatry McGill U., Montreal, Que., 1952-57; research assoc., asst. prof. physiology and biochemistry Coll. Medicine, Baylor U., Houston, 1957-62; chief endocrine and polypeptide labs. VA Hosp., New Orleans, 1962—; asso. prof. Sch. Medicine, Tulane U., New Orleans, 1962-67, prof., 1967—; sr. med. investigator VA, 1973—. Author several books; contbr. articles to profl. jours. Recipient Dir.'s award for outstanding med. research VA Hosp., New Orleans, 1968; Van Meter prize Am. Thyroid Assn., 1969; Ayerst-Squibb award Endocrine Soc., 1970; William S. Middletown award VA, 1970; Ch. Mickle award U. Toronto, 1974; Gairdner Internat. award, 1974; Borden award Assn. Am. Med. Colls. and Borden Co. Found., 1975; Lasker Basic Research award, 1975; co-recipient Nobel prize for medicine, 1977; USPHS sr. research fellow, 1961-62. Mem. Endocrine Soc., Am. Physiol. Soc., Soc. Biol. Chemists, AAAS, Soc. Exptl. Biol. Medicine, Internat. Soc. Research Biology Reprodn., Soc. Study Reprodn., Soc. Internat. Brain Research Orgn., Mexican Acad. Medicine, Am. Soc. Animal Sci., Nat. Acad. Sci., Nat. Acad. Medicine Brazil, others. Current Work: Hypothalamic hormones, endocrine dependent cancer. Subspecialties: Neuroendocrinology; Oncology. Home: 5025 Kawanee Ave Metairie LA 70002 Office: 1601 Perdido St New Orleans LA 70146

SCHANFIELD, MOSES SAMUEL, geneticist, research director; b. Mpls., Sept. 7, 1944; s. Abraham and Fannie (Schwartz) S.; m. Nancy Bergren; 2 daus., Sara Abigail, Amanda Phylisa. B.A., U. Minn., 1966; M.A., Harvard U., 1969; Ph.D., U. Mich., 1971. Postdoctoral fellow dept. medicine U. Calif., San Francisco, 1971-74; asst. research geneticist dept. medicine, 1974-75; dir. reference lab. and transfusion service Milw. Blood Ctr., 1975-78; asst. dir. blood services, head immunohematology lab. ARC Blood Services, Bethesda, Md., 1978-83; dir. immunogenetics Serologicals, Inc., Atlanta, 1983—. Contbr. articles to profl. jours. NIH fellow, 1972-74; recipient gold medal 1st Latin Am. Congress Hemotherapy and Immunohematology, 1979. Mem. Am. Assn. Blood Banks, Am. Soc. Human Genetics, Am. Assn. Phys. Anthropologists, Soc. Study Human Biology, Human Biology Council, Am. Assn. Immunology, AAAS, Sigma Xi. Current Work: Biological properties of genetic markers of antibodies. Subspecialties: Immunogenetics; Evolutionary biology. Office: Serologicals of Atlanta 401 W Peactree St NW Suite 1660 Atlanta GA 30308

SCHARDEIN, JAMES LOREN, toxicologist; b. Mt. Ayr, Iowa, Apr. 27, 1934; s. Glenn William and Margaret Louise (McCandless) S.; m. Mary Lorayne Miller, Nov. 26, 1954; children—Laura, Carolyn, Barbara. M.S., State U. Iowa, 1958, B.A., 1956. Sect. head Parke, Davis & Co., Ann Arbor, Mich., 1958-77; sect. dir. Warner-Lambert, 1977-81; dept. dir. Internat. Research & Devel. Corp., Mattawan, Mich., 1981-82, asst. div. dir., 1982—. Author: Drugs as Teratogens, 1976; Chemically-Induced Birth Defects, 1985. Contbr. articles to profl. jours. Bd. dirs. Chelsea Library Bd., 1972-74; mem. Chelsea Planning Commn., Mich., 1974-76; trustee Chelsea Village Council, 1976-80. Mem. Soc. Toxicology (sect. pres. 1984-85), Teratology Soc., Midwest Teratology Assn. (pres. 1983-84), Am. Coll. Toxicology, Am. Soc. Andrology, European and Japanese Teratology Soc. Republican. Current work: Laboratory and clinical congenital malformations induced by drugs and chemicals. Subspecialties: Teratology; Toxicology (medicine). Home: 4179 N 6th St Kalamazoo MI 49009 Office: Internat Research & Devel Corp 500 N Main St Mattawan MI 49071

SCHARFF, MATTHEW DANIEL, immunologist, cell biologist, educator; b. N.Y.C., Aug. 28, 1932; s. Harry and Constance S.; m. Carol Held, Dec. 19, 1954; children—Karen, Thomas, David. A.B., Brown U., 1954; M.D., N.Y. U., 1959. House officer II and IV med. service Boston City Hosp., 1959-61; research assoc. NIH, 1961-63; asst. prof. Albert Einstein Coll. Medicine, Yeshiva U., Bronx, N.Y., 1963-67, asso. prof., 1967-71, prof. dept. cell biology, 1971—, chmn. dept., 1972-83, dir. div. biol. scis., 1975-81; assoc. dir. Cancer Center, 1975—. Served with USPHS, 1961-63. Recipient Alumni Achievement award N.Y. U. Sch. Medicine, 1980. Mem. Am. Assn. Immunologists, Am. Soc. Clin. Investigation, Nat. Acad. Scis., Am. Acad. Arts and Scis., Phi Beta Kappa, Sigma Xi, Alpha Omega Alpha. Current Work: Studies on the genetic control of antibody production and diversity in cultured cells including hybridomas. Subspecialties: Immunobiology and immunology; Cell biology. Office: Dept Cell Biology Albert Einstein Coll Medicine 1300 Morris Park Ave Bronx NY 10461

SCHARRER, BERTA VOGEL, emeritus anatomy educator; b. Munich, Germany, Dec. 1, 1906; came to U.S., 1937, naturalized, 1944; d. Karl Phillip and Johanna (Greis) Vogel; m. Ernst Albert Scharrer, Mar 1, 1934 (dec. 1965). Ph.D., U. Munich, 1930; M.D. honoris causa, U. Giessen, W.Ger., 1976; Sc.D. (hon.), Northwestern U., 1977, U. N.C., 1978, Smith Coll., 1980, Harvard U., 1982, Yeshiva U., 1983, Mt. Holyoke Coll., 1984, SUNY, 1985; LL.D. (hon.), U. Calgary, Alta., Can., 1982. Research assoc. Research Inst. Psychiatry, Munich, 1931-34, Neurol. Inst., Frankfurt-am-Main, Germany, 1934-37; dept. anatomy U. Chgo., 1937-38, Rockefeller Inst. Med. Research, N.Y.C., 1938-40; sr. instr., fellow dept. anatomy Western Res U., Cleve., 1940-46; Guggenheim fellow dept. anatomy U. Colo. Sch. Medicine, Denver, 1947-48, USPHS spl. research fellow, 1948-50, asst. prof. research, 1950-55; prof. anatomy Albert Einstein Coll. Medicine, N.Y.C., from 1955, now prof. anatomy and neurosci. emeritus, acting chmn., 1965-66, 74-77. Co-editor: Cell and Tissue Research, 1957; editorial bd.: Jour. Gen. Comparative Endocrinology, 1968—, Biol. Bull. Recipient Kraepelin Gold medal, 1978, Koch medal, 1980, Henry Gray award Am. Assn. Anatomists, 1982; Nat. Medal of Sci., 1985. Fellow AAAS; mem. Am. Assn. Anatomists (pres. 1978-79), Nat. Acad. Scis., Am. Acad. Arts and Scis., Deutsche Akademie der Naturforscher Leopoldina, Royal Netherlands Acad. Arts and Scis. (fgn.), Internat. Soc. Neuroendocrinology, Internat. Brain Research Orgn., NRC (com. brain scis.), Endocrine Soc. Researcher comparative neuroendocrinology, neurosecretion, fine structure neuroglandular elements, neurotrophic factors in tumor growth. Current Work: Neuropeptides and neuropetide receptors in invertebrates. Subspecialties: Neuroendocrinology; Comparative neurobiology. Home: 1240 Neill Ave Bronx NY 10461 Office: 1300 Morris Park Ave Bronx NY 10461

SCHAUFELE, ROGER DONALD, aircraft manufacturing company executive; b. Woodbridge, N.J., Mar. 30, 1928; s. Franklin A. and Josephine (Schmidt) S.; m. Barbara Powell Harkness, Oct. 8, 1949; children—Margaret Jo, Roger Donald. B.S. in Aero. Engrng., Rensselaer Poly. Inst., 1949; M.S. in Aeros., Calif. Inst. Tech., 1952. Mem. aerodynamics research group, McDonnell Douglas Corp., 1949-51; aerodynamicist DC-8 project Douglas Aircraft Co., Long Beach, Calif., 1955-59, supr. stability and control, 1959-62, aerodynamicist DC-9 project, 1962-67, asst. chief aerodynamics DC-10 comml. program, 1967-71, dir. techs., 1971-76, dir. advanced engrng., 1976-79, dir. aircraft design, 1979-81, v.p. engrng., 1981—; mem. aeros. and space engrng. bd. NRC, Washington, 1982—, aeros. adv. com. NASA, Washington, 1981—, engrng. adv. and devel. council Calif. State U.-Long Beach, 1983—, aero. engrng. tech. indsl. adv. bd. Ariz. State U., Tempe, 1983—, com. on sci. and tech., congl. adv. com. on aeros. U.S. Ho. of Reps., Washington, 1984—. Contbr. articles to profl. jours. Patentee in field. Served as lt. USN, 1953-55. Fellow AIAA; mem. Inst. for Advancement Engring., ASME, Soc. Automotive Engrs., Inc. (tech. bd. dirs. 1983—, aerospace council 1981—), Aero Club of So. Calif., Tau Beta Pi, Gamma Alpha Rho. Subspecialties: Aeronautical engineering; Fluid mechanics. Home: 13112 Wheeler Pl Santa Ana CA 92705 Office: Douglas Aircraft Co 3855 Lakewood Blvd Long Beach CA 90846

SCHAWLOW, ARTHUR LEONARD, physicist, educator; b. Mt. Vernon, N.Y., May 5, 1921; s. Arthur and Helen (Mason) S.; m. Aurelia Keith Townes, May 19, 1951; children: Arthur Keith, Helen Aurelia, Edith Ellen. B.A., U. Toronto, 1941, M.A., 1942, Ph.D., 1949, LL.D. (hon.), 1970; D.Sc. (hon.), U. Ghent, Belgium, 1968, U. Bradford, Eng., 1970. Postdoctoral fellow, research assoc. Columbia, 1949-51; vis. assoc. prof. Columbia U., 1960; research physicist Bell Telephone Labs., 1951-61, cons., 1961-62; prof. physics Stanford U., 1961—, now J.G. Jackson-C.J. Wood prof. physics, exec. head dept., 1966-70, acting chmn. dept., 1973-74. Author: (with C.H. Townes) Microwave Spectroscopy, 1955; Co-inventor (with C.H. Townes), optical maser 1958. Recipient Ballantine medal Franklin Inst., 1962, Thomas Young medal and prize Inst. Physics and Phys. Soc., London, 1963; Nobel prize in physics, 1981; named Calif. Scientist of Year, 1973, Marconi Internat. fellow, 1977. Fellow Am. Acad. Arts and Scis., Am. Phys. Soc. (council 1966-70, chmn. div.

electron and atomic physics 1974, pres. 1981), Optical Soc. Am. (dir.-at-large 1966-68, pres. 1975, Frederick Ives medal 1976); mem. Nat. Acad. Scis., IEEE (Liebmann prize 1964), AAAS (chmn. physics sect. 1979). Current Work: Radio frequency, optical and microwave spectroscopy, lasers and quantaum electronics. Subspecialties: Atomic and molecular physics; Laser spectroscopy. Office: Stanford Univ Dept Physics Stanford CA 94305

SCHECHTER, DANIEL, physics educator; b. Bklyn., Sept. 18, 1931; s. Irving and Sophie (Levy) S.; m. Roslyn Miriam Schwartz, Jan. 17, 1962; children—Evan Joseph, Jonathan Stewart. A.B., UCLA, 1953; M.S., Carnegie Tech. Inst., 1955, Ph.D., 1958. Sr. engr. Gen. Telephone Labs., Bayside, N.Y., 1958-62; prof. electrophysics Bklyn. Poly. Inst., Farmingdale, N.Y., 1962-65; mem. tech. staff TRW Systems, Redondo Beach, Calif., 1965-69; prof. physics Calif. State U.-Long Beach, 1969—; cons. Aerojet Electrosystems, Azusa, Calif., 1984—, Hughes Aircraft Co., Carlsbad, Calif., 1980-83, Rockwell Internat., Anaheim, Calif., 1974-79. Contbr. articles to physics jours. Mem. Am. Phys. Soc. Current work: Optical and infrared properties of semiconductors, impurities and electronic structure of semiconductors. Subspecialties: Condensed matter physics; Semiconductors. Home: 3541 Carnation Circle Long Beach CA 90740 Office: Dept Physics Calif State U-Long Beach 1250 Bellflower Blvd Long Beach CA 90840

SCHECHTER, MARTIN DAVID, pharmacologist; b. Bklyn., Feb. 28, 1945; s. Harry P. and Frances E. (Maybloom) S.; m. Audrey Ellen Freeman, June 27, 1968; 1 child, Jason Ben. B.S., Bklyn. Coll., 1965; Ph.D., SUNY Sch. Medicine, Buffalo, 1970. Research asso. Med. Coll. Va., Richmond, 1970-72; sr. research fellow U. Melbourne, Australia, 1972-74; asst. prof. Eastern Va. Med. Sch., 1974-76, assoc. prof., 1976-78; assoc. prof. Northeastern Ohio U. Coll. Medicine, 1978-82, prof., chmn. 1982—; coordinator clin. psychopharmacology courses Fallsview Psychiat. Clinic, Akron (Ohio) Gen. Hosp., 1979—. Served with USAF, 1965-67. NIMH grantee, 1980—; Nat. Inst. Environ. Health Inst. grantee, 1982-84. Mem. Am. Soc. Pharmacology and Exptl. Therapeutics, Soc. Exptl. Biol. Medicine, Soc. Stimulus Prop. Drugs, AAAS, Sigma Xi. Current Work: Psychopharmacology, behavioral toxicology, drug discrimination, hyperkinesis. Subspecialties: Psychopharmacology; Toxicology (medicine). Office: 4209 SR 44 Roostown OH 44272

SCHEFFER, ROBERT PAUL, plant science educator and researcher; b. Newton, N.C., Jan. 26, 1920; s. Paul and Mary Alice (Shuford) S.; m. Beulah Jennie Spoolman, June 12, 1951; children: Thomas Jay, Mary Karen. B.S., N.C. State U., 1947, M.S., 1949; Ph.D., U. Wis., 1952. Research asst. N.C. State U., Raleigh, 1947-49; research asst. U. Wis., 1949-52; research assoc., 1952-53; asst. prof. Mich. State U., 1953-58, prof. botany and plant pathology, 1963—, disting. prof., 1985—; vis. researcher Rockefeller U., N.Y.C., 1960-61; cons. panel regulatory biology NSF, 1965-68. Contbr. numerous articles to profl. jours., chpts. to books. Served with USAAF, 1941-45. NSF grantee, 1958—. Fellow Am. Phytopath. Soc., Am. Soc. Plant Physiologists, AAUP. Current Work: Research on the physiology and biochemistry of disease development in plants and in disease resistance. Research on host-selective determinants of disease. Subspecialties: Plant pathology; Plant physiology (biology). Home: 912 Gainsborough Dr East Lansing MI 48823 Office: Dept Botany and Plant Pathology Mich State U East Lansing MI 48824

SCHEIBEL, LEONARD WILLIAM, pharmacologist, educator; b. Hays, Kans., Jan. 18, 1938; s. Raymond P. and Thelma (Bane) S.; m. Melania Parada Valdes, May 1, 1976; 1 child, William Scheibel, Jr. B.S., Creighton U., 1960, M.S. in Chemistry, 1962; D.Sc., Johns Hopkins U., 1967; M.D., U. Fla., 1973. Diplomate: Am. Bd. Preventive Medicine, Nat. Bd. Med. Examiners. Rotating intern Gorgas Hosp., Balboa Heights, C.Z., 1973-74, resident in internal medicine, 1974-77; asst. prof. Lab. Parasitology, staff physician Rockefeller U. and Hosp., N.Y.C., 1977-81; assoc. prof. dept. preventive medicine and biometrics Sch. Medicine, Uniformed Services U. Health Scis., Bethesda, Md., 1981-82, assoc. prof., 1982—; assoc. dept. pathobiology Sch. Hygiene and Pub. Health, Johns Hopkins U., Balt., 1982—; adj. assoc. prof. U. Md. Sch. Medicine, Balt., 1982; diving medicine cons. Panama Canal Co., 1973-77; cons. Med. Service Cons., Inc., Arlington, Va., 1978—; guest prof. Gorgas Meml. Lab., Panama City, Panama, 1973-77; vis. asst. prof. tropical medicine Cornell U. Med. Coll., 1977-81; mem. U.S. Army Med. Research and Devel. Adv. Com., 1982—, U.S. Army Source Selection Bd. for Testing Antileishmanial Compounds, 1982—; anti-infective drugs adv. com. FDA, 1982—. Mem. editorial bd.: Jour. Parasitology, 1981—; ad hoc reviewer: Molecular and Biochem. Parasitology; contbr. articles to sci. jours. Served to capt. U.S Army, 1967-70. Recipient Igor I. Sikorsky Helicopter Rescue award, 1973; Physician's Recognition award AMA, 1979—; NIH fellow, 1962-67. Fellow ACP, Am. Coll. Preventive Medicine; mem. Fedn. Am. Sos. Exptl. Biology, Am. Soc. Pharmacology and Exptl. Therapeutics (div. clin. pharmacology and drug metabolism), Am. Soc. Tropical Medicine, N.Y. Soc. Tropical Medicine, Am. Soc. Parasitologists, Isthmian Med. Assn., Microbiol. Soc. Panama, Tropical Medicine Assn. Washington, Undersea Med. Soc., Inter-Am. Assn. San. Engring. Current Work: Research and teaching in tropical medicine with emphasis on metabolism and chemotherapy of protozoal and helminthic disease; rational design of new pharmacologic agents, their testing and employment in the field, especially in areas where drug resistant parasites have emerged. Subspecialties: Molecular pharmacology; Preventive medicine. Office: 4301 Jones Bridge Rd Bethesda MD 20814

SCHEID, VERNON EDWARD, mineral resources educator; b. Balt., Sept. 5, 1906; s. Charles Christian and Blanche McLenny (Donaldson) S.; m. Martha Frances Helm, Aug. 17, 1934; children: Donald Edward, Margaret Kathryn. A.B. in Geology, Johns Hopkins U., 1928, Ph.D. in Econ. Geology, 1946; M.S. in Geol. Engring, U. Idaho, 1940. Registered profl. engr., Nev.; registered geologist, Calif. Instr. dept. geology Johns Hopkins U., Balt., 1931-34; prof. dept. geology U. Idaho, Moscow, 1934-42, 47-51; geologist U.S. Geol. Survey, Idaho, Mont., Wash., 1942-47; dean Mackay Sch. Mines, Reno, Nev., 1951-72, prof., 1972—; dir. Nev. Bur. Mines & Geology, Reno, 1951-72; cons. UN, 1973—. Author reports in field. Chmn., dir. Nev. Adv. Councils Mining, Maps, Water and Energy, 1953-72; chmn., dir. Nev. Oil & Gas Conservation Commn., 1953-72; mem. Nat. Adv. Com. Oceans & Atmosphere. Mem. Soc. Mining Engrs., AIME (McConnell award 1980), Soc. Econ. Geologists (leader del. to China 1982, to South Africa 1983), Geol. Soc. Am., Assn. Am. State Geologists, Assn. Geoscientists Internat. Devel. Lodge: Rotary. Current Work: Mineral resources and economics; economic and engineering geology; national mineral policy. Subspecialty: Economic geology. Home: 33 Rancho Manor Dr Reno NV 89509 Office: Mackay Sch Mines U Nev Reno NV 89557

SCHELBERT, HEINRICH RUEDIGER, radiological sciences educator; b. Wuerzburg, Germany, Nov. 5, 1939; came to U.S., 1966; s. Heinrich Johannes and Hedwig (Fahnemann) S.; m. Barbara Wilde, Nov. 28, 1969; children: Kristina, Mark. M.D., U. Wuerzburg, 1964, Ph.D., 1965. Lic. physician, W.Ger., Calif. Intern Mercy Med. Ctr., Darby, Pa., 1966-67, resident in medicine, 1967-68, 70-71; resident in cardiology U. Duesseldorf, W. Ger., 1971-72; resident in physiology U. Calif., San Diego, 1968-69; assoc. prof. radiol. sci. UCLA Sch. Medicine, 1977-80, prof., 1980—; mem. VA merit rev. bd., Washington, 1982-84, NIH cardiovascular study sect., Bethesda, Md., 1983—. Recipient Georg Von Hevesy Found. prize, 1978, 82. Fellow Am. Coll. Cardiology, Am. Heart Assn. (council circulation.); mem. Soc. Nuclear Medicine (silver medal 1977), Los Angeles Heart Assn. (vice-chmn. research com. 1982-84). Current Work: Noninvasive study of myocardial metabolism in health and disease with positron emission computed tomgraphy and metabolic tracers. Subspecialties: Nuclear medicine; Cardiology. Home: 412 Mount Holyoke Ave Pacific Palisades CA 90272 Office: Div Nuclear Medicine UCLA Sch Medicine Los Angeles CA 90024

SCHELLMAN, JOHN ANTHONY, chemistry educator; b. Phila., Oct. 24, 1924; s. John A. and Margaret Mary (Mason) S.; m. F. Charlotte, Mar. 14, 1922; children: Heidi, Lise. A.B., Temple U., 1948; M.S., Princeton U., 1949, Ph.D., 1951; hon. doctorate Chalmers U., Sweden. NIH fellow U. Utah, 1951-53, Carlsberglab, Denmark, 1953-55; DuPont fellow U. Minn., Mpls., 1955, asst. prof. chemistry, 1956-58; prof. chemistry, research assoc. Inst. Molecular Biology, U. Oreg., Eugene, 1958—. Served with U.S. Army. Guggenheim fellow, 1969-70. Fellow Am. Phys. Soc.; mem. Am. Chem. Soc., Am. Acad. Arts and Scis., Biophys. Soc., Am. Soc. Biol. Chemistry, Nat. Acad. Scis., Sigma Xi. Current Work: Biophysical chemistry. Subspecialty: Physical chemistry. Office: Chemistry Dept U Oreg Eugene OR 97403

SCHELSKE, CLAIRE L., limnologist; b. Fayetteville, Ark., Apr. 1, 1932; s. Theodore J. and Ida S. S.; m. Betty Breukelman, June 2, 1957; children—Cynthia, John, Steven. A.B., Kans. State Tchrs. Coll., Emporia, 1955, M.S., 1956; Ph.D., U. Mich., 1961. Teaching and research asst. dept. biology Kans. State Tchrs. Coll., 1952-55, vis. instr., summer 1960; teaching fellow dept. zoology U. Mich., 1955-57, asst. prof. radiol. health dept. environ. health; asst. research limnologist Gt. Lakes Research Div., Inst. Sci. and Tech., 1967-68, asso. research limnologist, 1969-71, research limnologist, 1971—, asst. dir., 1970-72, acting dir., 1973-76, asso. prof. limnology, dept. atmospheric and oceanic sci., 1976—; asso. prof. natural resources Sch. Natural Resources, 1976—; research fellow Inst. Fisheries Research, Mich. Dept. Conversation, 1957-60; research asso. U. Ga. Marine Inst., 1960-62; fishery biologist, supervisory fishery biologist, chief Estuarine Ecology Program, Bur. Comml. Fisheries, Radiobiol. Lab., Beaufort, N.C., 1962-66; adj. asst. prof. dept. zoology N.C. State U., Raleigh, 1964-66; tech. asst. Office Sci. and Tech., Exec. Office of Pres., Washington, 1966-67; mem. NRC ocean scis. bd. site rev. team for Gt. Lakes Environ. Research Lab., NOAA, 1976; cons. Ill. Atty. Gen., 1977-79. Author: (with J.C. Roth) Limnological Survey of Lakes Michigan, Superior, Huron and Erie, 1973. UNESCO. NSF travel grantee to 18th Limnol. Congress, Leningrad, 1971; research grantee NSF, 1976-79, 83—, EPA, 1973-82, Dept. Energy, 1969—. Fellow AAAS, Am. Inst. Fishery Research Biologists (regional and dist. dir. South-Central Gt. Lakes Dist. 1977-80); mem. Am. Soc. Limnology and Oceanography (sec. 1976-85), Ecol. Soc. Am. (asso. editor 1972-75), Internat. Assn. Gt. Lakes Research (editorial bd. 1970-73, chmn. 20th Conf. 1977, assoc. editor 1984—), Am. Fisheries Soc., Phycological Soc. Am., Societas Internationalis Limnologiae. Current work: Using paleontological record in the Great Lakes to study ecological and chemical changes caused by nutrient enrichment. . Home: 1439 Glastonbury Rd Ann Arbor MI 48103 Office: Gt Lakes Research Div U Mich Ann Arbor MI 48109

SCHEMNITZ, SANFORD DAVID, wildlife scientist, educator, researcher; b. Cleve., Mar. 10, 1930; s. David A. and Evelyn (Farber) S.; m. Mary Newby, July 8, 1958; children—Ellen Kay, Steven David, Stuart Carl. B.S. in Forestry, U. Mich., 1952; M.S. in Forestry, U. Fla., 1953; Ph.D. in Wildlife, Okla. State U., 1958. Cons., aide Mich. Dept. Conservation, 1951-52; research asst. N.Y. State Coll. Forestry, Newcomb, 1952; with waterfowl project Wis. Conservation Dept., Horicon, 1953; unit fellow Okla. Coop. Wildlife Research Unit, Stillwater, 1954-57; game research biologist Minn. Dept. Conservation, St. Paul, 1958-59; asst. prof. wildlife resources U. Maine, Orono, 1960, 63-66, assoc. prof., 1966-75, prof., 1975; asst. prof. wildlife mgmt. Pa. State U., State College, 1961; prof., head dept. fishery and wildlife scis. N.Mex. State U., Las Cruces, 1976-81, prof. dept. fishery and wildlife scis., 1981—. Contbr. articles to profl. jours. Recipient award of Merit Maine Dept. Inland Fisheries and Game, 1975. Mem. Wildlife Soc., Am. Soc. Mammalogists, Ecol. Soc. Am., Wilson Ornithol. Soc., Western Bird Banding Assn., Bombay Natural History Soc., Internat. Fish and Wildlife Agys., Nat. Wildlife Fedn., N.Mex. Wildlife Fedn., Nat. Wild Turkey Fedn., Ducks Unltd., Thoreau Fellowship, Sigma Xi, Xi Sigma Pi. Current work: Wildlife management in arid ecosystems. Subspecialty: Population biology. Office: Dept Fishery and Wildlife Scis NMex State U Box 4901 Las Cruces NM 88003

SCHENCK, JOHN F., medical researcher; b. Decatur, Ind., June 7, 1939; s. John C. and Mildred H. (Blosser) S.; m. Jane E. Stark, Oct. 12, 1962 (div. 1983); children—Brooke E., Kimberly J., David J. B.S., Rensselaer Poly. Inst., 1961, Ph.D., 1965; M.D., Albany Med. Coll., 1977. Staff scientist Gen. Electric, Syracuse, N.Y., 1965-70, staff mem., Schenectady, N.Y., 1973—; assoc. prof. elec. engring., Syracuse U., 1970-73; mem. med. staff Ellis Hosp., Schenectady, 1980—; adj. prof. radiology U. Pa., Phila., 1982—. Contbr. articles to profl. jours. NSF fellow, 1963-64. Mem. Am. Phys. Soc., IEEE, N.Y. Med. Soc., Sigma Xi. Methodist. Current work: Application of advanced technology to medicine, developing methods including surface coils to enhance the resolution and diagnostic capability of magnetic resonance in aging. Subspecialties: Magnetic resonance imaging; Magnetic physics. Home: 17 Carrie Ct Schenectady NY 12305 Office: Gen Electric Research and Devel Ctr Schenectady NY 12301

SCHENCK, ROBERT ROY, surgeon; b. Brimfield, Ill., Sept. 19, 1931; s. Isaac Barrett and Pearl Irene (Murnan) S.; m. Ruth Mary Helm, June 18, 1955 (div. Jan. 1977); children: Claudia, Lynn, Karen, Heidi, Robert Paul; m. Nanci Whitney, June 13, 1982. B.A., Taylor U., 1951; M.D., U. Ill.-Chgo., 1955. Intern Akron (Ohio) Gen. Hosp., 1955-57; med. missionary Ethiopia Bapt. Gen. Conf., Ambo, 1959-61; staff physician Centerville Clinic, Fredericktown, Pa., 1962-67; resident gen. surgery Western Pa. Hosp., Pitts., 1967-69; resident plastic surgery Columbia-Presbyn. Med. Center, N.Y.C., 1969-71; fellow hand surgery Roosevelt Hosp., N.Y.C., 1971-72; assoc. prof. depts. plastic and orthopedic surgery, dir. sect. hand surgery Rush-Presbyn.-St. Luke's Med. Center, Chgo., 1972—. Guest editor: Replantation and Reconstruction Microsurgery, 1977. Served with USPHS, 1957-59. Mem. Am. Assn. Plastic Surgeons, Am. Soc. Surgery for the Hand, Am. Soc. Plastic and Reconstructive Surgeons. Republican. Club: Union League (Chgo.). Current Work: Microsurgery, basic microvascular amastomotic techniques, replantation, clinical results. Subspecialties: Surgery; Microsurgery. Office: Robert A Schenck & Assocs 1725 W Harrison St Suite 398 Chicago IL 60612

SCHERAGA, HAROLD ABRAHAM, physical chemistry educator; b. Bklyn., Oct. 18, 1921; s. Samuel and Etta (Goldberg) S.; m. Miriam Kurnow, June 20, 1943; children: Judith Anne, Deborah Ruth, Daniel Michael. B.S., CCNY, 1941; A.M., Duke U., 1942, Ph.D., 1946, Sc.D. (hon.), 1961. Teaching, research asst. Duke U., 1941-46; fellow Harvard Med. Sch., 1946-47; instr. chemistry Cornell U., 1947-50, asst. prof., 1950-53, assoc. prof., 1953-58, prof., 1958—, Todd prof. chemistry, 1965—, chmn. dept., 1960-67; vis. assoc. biochemist Brookhaven Nat. Lab., summers 1950, 51, cons. biology dept., 1950-56; vis. lectr. div. protein chemistry Wool Research Labs., Melbourne, Australia, 1959; vis. prof. dept. biophysics Weizmann Inst. Sci., Rehovoth, Israel, 1972-78; vis. prof. Soc. for Promotion Sci., Japan, Aug. 1977; mem. tech. adv. panel Xerox Corp., 1969-71, 74-79; Mem. biochemistry tng. com. NIH, 1963-65; mem. research career award com. NIGMS, 1967-71; commn. molecular biophysics Internat. Union for Pure and Applied Biophysics, 1965-69, mem. commn. macromolecular biophysics, 1969-75, pres., 1972-75, mem. commn. subcellular and macromolecular biophysics, 1975-81; adv. panel molecular biology NSF, 1960-62; Welch Found. lectr., 1962, Harvey lectr., 1968, Gallagher lectr., 1968, Lemieux lectr., 1973, Hill lectr., 1976, Venable lectr., 1981, other lectureships; co-chmn. Gordon Conf. on Proteins, 1963; mem. council Gordon Research Confs., 1969-71. Author: Protein Structure; Theory of Helix-Coil Transitions in Biopolymers; Co-editor: Molecular Biology, 1961—; Mem. editorial bd.: Physiol. Chemistry and Physics, 1969-75, Mechanochemistry and Motility, 1970-71, Thrombosis Research, 1972-76, Biophys. Jour, 1973-75, Macromolecules, 1973-84, Computers and Chemistry, 1974-84, Internat. Jour. Peptide and Protein Research, 1978—, Jour. Computational Chemistry, 1980—, Jour. Protein Chemistry, 1982—; corr.: PAABS Revista, 1971-73; editorial adv. bd.: Biopolymers, 1963—, Biochemistry, 1969-74, 85—. Mem. Ithaca Bd. Edn., 1958-59; Bd. govs. Weizmann Inst., Israel, 1970—; mem. staff Naval Research Lab. Project, Air Force OSRD Project, World War II. Fulbright fellow, Guggenheim fellow Carlsberg Lab., Denmark, 1956-57; Fulbright fellow, Guggenheim fellow Weizmann Inst., Israel, 1963; NIH Spl. fellow Weizmann Inst., 1970; Fogarty scholar NIH, 1984; recipient Townsend Harris medal CCNY, 1970, Chemistry Alumni Sci. Achievement award, 1977; Linderstrom-Lang medal 1983; Kowalski medal 1983. Fellow AAAS; mem. Nat. Acad. Scis., Am. Chem. Soc. (chmn. Cornell sect. 1955-56, mem. exec. com. div. biol. chemistry 1966-69, vice chmn. div. biol. chemistry 1970, chmn. div. biol. chemistry 1971, Eli Lilly award 1957, Nichols medal 1974, Kendall award 1978, Pauling medal 1985), Am. Soc. Biol. Chemists, Biophys. Soc. (council 1967-70), Am. Acad. Arts and Scis., Phi Beta Kappa, Sigma Xi, Phi Lambda Upsilon. Current Work: Physical chemistry of proteins and other macromolecules. Chemistry of blood clotting. Structure of water and dilute aqueous solutions. Subspecialties: Biophysical chemistry; Physical chemistry. Home: 212 Homestead Terr Ithaca NY 14850

SCHERLAG, BENJAMIN JACOB, cardiovascular physiologist; b. Bklyn., Oct. 31, 1932; s. Morris and Anna (Neumann) S.; m. Eleanor Kaufman, Dec. 24, 1960; children—Nancy Beth, Ronald Adam, William Eban, Michael Ara. B.S., CCNY, 1954; M.A., Bklyn. Coll., 1961; Ph.D., SUNY, 1963. Research and tchg. asst. SUNY, Brklyn., 1956-63; research physiologist USPHS, Staten Island, N.Y., 1965-68; cardiovascular physiologist Mt. Sinai Hosp., Miami, 1968-74; assoc. prof. dept. medicine VA Med. Ctr., Miami, 1974-78, cardiovascular physiologist, 1974-78; prof. medicine U. Okla. Health Scis. Ctr., Oklahoma City, 1978—. Author: His Bundle Electrocardiography, 1974. Served with U.S. Army, 1954-56. Recipient Okla. Acad. Sci. Scientist of Yr. award, 1980, VA Med. Ctr. Med. Investigator award, 1980. Fellow Am. Coll. Cardiology; mem. North Am. Soc. Pacing and Electrophysiology (founding mem.), Am. Heart Assn., Am. Physiol. Soc., Am. Fed. Clin. Research, Coll. Physicians and Surgeons Nicaragua (hon. mem.). Jewish. Current work: Electrophysiology of the heart, mechanisms of cardiac arrhythmias in myocardial ischemia and infarction. Subspecialties: Physiology (biology); Cardiology. Office: Univ Okla Health Sci Ctr VA Med Ctr-151F 921 NE 13th St Oklahoma City OK 73104

SCHERRER, JAMES SYDNEY, geologist, consultant; b. Salamanca, N.Y., Dec. 9, 1953; s. Joseph J. and Virginia Scherrer. B.S. in Geol. Scis., SUNY-Geneseo, 1976; M.S. in Energy Mgmt. and Policy, U. Pa., 1981; M.B.A. in Fin., Drexel U., 1984. Tchr. geology Chestnut Hill Acad., Phila., 1976-79; energy analyst WESTEC Services, Inc., Phila., 1980—. Mem. Geol. Soc. Am., Am. Inst. Profl. Geologists, Nat. Water Well Assn. (tech. div.). Republican. Current work: Policy analysis. Subspecialty: Hydrology. Home: 8100 Cherokee St Philadelphia PA 19118

SCHEUERMANN, PETER I., computer scientist; b. Bucharest, Romania, Aug. 28, 1945; s. Salo and Gerda (Metsch) S.; m. Mona M. Scheuermann, Dec. 28, 1973. B.S. in Applied Math, Tel-Aviv U., 1969; Ph.D. in Computer Sci, SUNY-Stony Brook, 1976. Asst. prof. Coll. William and Mary, Williamsburg, Va., 1975-76; asst. prof. Northwestern U., Evanston, Ill., 1976-81, assoc. prof., 1981—; vis. prof. Free U., Amsterdam, 1983. Editor: (with M. Ouksel) Information Systems, Vol. 7, 1982, Improving Database Usability and Responsiveness, 1983, (with C.R. Carlson) Self-Assessment Procedure: Data Base Systems; assoc. editor: (with C.R. Carlson) Internat. Jour. Policy Analysis and Info. Systems. Mem. Assn. Computing Machinery, IEEE, Simulation Council. Current Work: Dynamic structures; distributed database systems, in particular, database machines and query processing. Subspecialties: Database systems; Distributed systems and networks. Office: Dept Elec Engring and Computer Sci Northwestern U Evanston IL 60201

SCHEUING, RICHARD ALBERT, aerospace corporation executive; b. Lynbrook, N.Y., Aug. 19, 1927; s. Emil Conrad and Elise Marie (Blum) S.; m. Doris Elaine Scheuing, May 27, 1950; children—Richard S., Alison I., Christopher J. B.S., M.S. in Aerospace Engring., MIT., 1948; Ph.D. in Aerospace and Astronomy, NYU, 1971; advanced mgmt. program cert. Harvard Bus. Sch., 1982. Researcher aerodynamics Grumman Aerospace Corp., 1948-71, head fluid mechanics research, 1956-71, dep. dir. research, 1961-77; dir. Research Devel. Ctr., 1977—; trustee No. Energy Corp. Active Action for Preservation L.I., Cold Spring Harbor Whaling Mus. MIT scholar. Mem. AIAA, AAAS, Lloyd Harbor Yacht Club, Centerport Yacht Club. Current work: Aerospace engineering sciences, detection physics, fusion and solar energy research. Subspecialties: Aeronautical engineering; Fluid mechanics. Office: Grumman Aerospace Corp M/S A08-35 Bethpage NY 11714

SCHEY, JOHN ANTHONY, mechanical engineering educator, researcher, consultant; b. Sopron, Hungary, Dec. 19, 1922; came to U.S., 1962; s. Mihaly and Terez Hedvig (Topfel) S.; m. Margit Maria Sule, Sept. 25, 1948; 1 son, John Francis. Dip. Metall. Ing., Jozsef Nador Tech. U., Sopron, Hungary, 1946; Cand. Tech. Sci. in Metallurgy, Acad. Scis., Budapest, Hungary, 1953. Supt. metal works Steel and Metal Works, Csepel, Budapest, 1947-51; reader metals tech. Tech. U. Miskolc, Hungary, 1951-56; head dept. fabrication Research Labs., Brit. Aluminum Co., Chalfont Park, Eng., 1957-62; sr. metall. adv. Ill. Inst. Tech. Research Inst., Chgo., 1962-68; prof. metall. engring. U. Ill.-Chgo., 1968-74; prof. mech. engring. U. Waterloo, Ont., Can., 1974—; cons. in field; course dir. Forging Industry Assn. Author: Introduction to Manufacturing Processes, 1977, Tribology in Metalworking: Friction, Lubrication, and Wear, 1983; contbr. numerous articles to profl. publs. Recipient W.H.A. Robertson award Inst. Metals, London, 1966. Mem. Nat. Acad. Engring., Am. Soc. Metals, Soc. Mfg. Engrs. (Gold medal 1974), Sigma Xi. Patentee in field. Current Work: Development of manufacturing processes; tribology of metalworking (friction, lubrication, and wear); interactions between material properties and process conditions in metalworking; social impact of technological advance. Subspecialties: Materials processing; Solid mechanics. Office: U Waterloo Waterloo ON N2L 3G1 Canada

SCHIFTER, CATHERINE CRUTCHFIELD, dental hygiene educator, researcher; b. Abilene, Tex., Sept. 24, 1950; d. James Willard and Josephine (Palmer) Crutchfield; m. Stephan Clay Schifter, Aug. 17, 1974. B.S., Baylor Coll. Dentistry, 1972; M.Ed., U. Houston, 1973; post-grad., U. Pa., 1980—. Cert. dental hygienist. Research asst. Baylor Coll. Medicine, Houston, 1972-73; asso. in dental hygiene U. Pa., Phila., 1973-74, dental hygienist, West Chester, Pa., 1974-75, dental hygienist in periodontal practice, Phila., 1974-78; asst. prof. U. Pa., Phila., 1978-85, clin. asst. prof., 1985—, dir. dental hygiene residencies, 1985—; speaker before profl. groups, 1981—. Mem. editorial bd.: R.D.H, 1981—; contbr. articles to dental jours. Recipient Acad. Effort award Pa. Dental Hygiene Assn., 1981, Earl Banks Hoyt award U. Pa., 1982. Mem. Am. Dental Hygiene Assn., Pa. Dental Hygiene Assn., Am. Assn. Dental Schs., Am. Assn. Dental Research, Internat. Assn. Dental Research, Am. Ednl. Research Assn., Phila. Orch. Assn., Alpha Phi Internat., Sigma Phi Alpha, Phi Delta Kappa. Methodist. Inventor (with others) method of treating chronic inflammatory periodontal disease. Current Work: Use of dark field microscopy in monitoring patient disease/health. Use of dark field microscopy in evaluating effectiveness of antimicrobials. Subspecialty: Periodontics. Home: 1420 Locust St #32K Philadelphia PA 19102 Office: U Pa Sch Dental Medicine 4001 Spruce St Philadelphia PA 19104

SCHILLEBEECKX, DIRK JOHAN, communications company executive, economist; b. St. Nikolas, Belgium, Aug. 3, 1947; came to Can., 1947, naturalized, 1954; s. Koenrad and Andrea (Lammens) S.; m. Anna Joanna Carignan, June 29, 1968; children—Krista, Bret. B.S. in Commerce, U. Montreal, Que., Can., 1968; postgrad., U. Ottawa, Ont., Can., 1976-77. Market analyst Bell Can., Ottawa, 1974-75; mem. sci. staff Bell No. Research Co., Ottawa, 1975-77; product mgr. No. Telecom. Montreal, 1978-79, dir. mktg., 1980-81, Ottawa, 1981-84; v.p., gen. mgr. Communications Systems div. Spar Aerospace, Montreal, 1984—; pres. Comml. Telecommunications Inc., Santa Monica, Calif., 1984—, also dir. Club: Beaconsfield Yacht. Current work: Telecommunications networks and services, satellite communications systems, electronics/digital processing technology. Subspecialty: Telecommunications. Office: Spar Aerospace Ltd 21025 Transcanada Hwy Sainte Anne de Bellevue PQ H9X 3R2 Canada

SCHILLER, ROGER WILLIAM, mechanical engineer, educator; b. Oak Harbor, Ohio, May 25, 1934; s. Harvey William and Elva Christina (Martin) S. B.S., U. Toledo, 1957; M.S., U. Kans., 1959. Registered profl. engr. Ohio. Machime designer Owens Ill. Glass, Toledo, Ohio, 1956-58; instr. U. Kans., Lawrence, 1958-59; Pa. State U., University Park, 1959-66, asst. prof., Reading, 1966-67, Middletown, 1967-71, assoc. prof., 1971—; cons. Instrument Soc., Pitts., 1975-77; reviewer Brooks Cole, Monterey, Pa., 1980—. Editor: Curriculum Guide, 1977. Served to 1st lt. U.S. Army, 1957-64. Mem. Instrument Soc. Am. (pres. sect. 1974-76, sr.), ASME (sec. sect. 1963-66), Am. Soc. Engring. Edn., Sigma Xi (assoc.) Republican. Methodist. Current work: Research in kinematics and dynamics of robot arms. Subspecialties: Mechanical engineering; Robotics. Home: 4210 K Williamsburg Dr Harrisburg PA 17109 Office: Pa State U Capital Campus Middletown PA 17157

SCHILLING, JOHN ALBERT, surgeon; b. Kansas City, Mo., Nov. 5, 1917; s. Carl Fielding and Lottie Lee (Henderson) S.; m. Lucy West, June 8, 1957 (dec.); children: Christine Henderson, Katharine Ann, Jolyon David, John Jay; m. Helen R. Spelbrink, May 28, 1979. A.B. with honors, Dartmouth Coll., 1937; M.D., Harvard U., 1941. Diplomate: Am. Bd. Surgery (chmn. 1969). Intern, then resident in surgery Roosevelt Hosp., N.Y.C., 1941-44; mem. faculty U. Rochester (N.Y.) Med. Sch., 1945-53, asst. prof. surgery, 1955-56; prof. surgery, head dept. U. Okla. Med. Sch., 1956-74; prof. surgery U. Wash. Med. Sch., Seattle, 1974—, chmn. dept., 1975-83; mem. bd. sci. counselors Nat. Cancer Inst.; also mem. diagnosis subcom. breast cancer task force; chmn. adv. com. to surgeon gen. on metabolism of trauma Army Med. Research and Devel. Command; mem. surgery study sect., div. research grants NIH; chief surgery USAF Sch. Aviation Medicine; cons. Surgeon Gen. USAF, 1959-75. Author articles, chpts. in books, abstracts, reports.; Editorial bd.: Am. Jour. Surgery. Served to maj. M.C. USAF, 1953-55. Grantee Army Office Surgeon Gen., 1956—. Mem. A.C.S. (bd. govs., chmn. com. surg. edn. in med. schs.), Am., So., Western, Pan-Pacific, N. Pacific, Pacific Coast surg. assns., Soc. Univ. Surgeons, Am. Assn. Surgery Trauma, Surg. Biology Club, Am. Physiol. Soc., Soc. Surg. Chmn., Am. Trauma Soc., Seattle Surg. Soc., Soc. Exptl. Pathology, Soc. Surgery Alimentary Tract, Explorers Club, Alpha Omega Alpha. Clubs: Yacht (Seattle), University (Seattle). Current Work: Medical education;

surgical research (wounds); clinical surgery (general, gastrointestinal). Subspecialties: Surgery; Cell biology (medicine). Home: 9807 Lake Washington Blvd NE Bellevue WA 98004 Office: Dept Surgery (RF-25) Univ Wash Medical Sch Seattle WA 98195

SCHIPPER, LAWRENCE J., defense systems manufacturing company executive; b. Milw., Oct. 6, 1931; s. William A. and Ann Catherine (Oberbrunner) S.; m. Patricia Theresa Bunce, Nov. 28, 1953; children—William L., Patrick Q., Mark K. Schipper Davis, Lawrence J. II, Leslie Ann, Katherine Anne. B.S.E.E., Marquette U., 1953; M.S.E.E., U. Notre Dame, 1959; postgrad. U. Pa., 1960-64. Jr. engr., assoc. engr., group leader Bendix Aviation Corp., Mishawaka, Ind., 1954-59; various engring. posts Missile and Surface Radar, Govt. Systems div. RCA Corp., Moorestown, N.J., 1959-78, div. v.p., program mgr. naval systems dept., 1978-81, div. v.p., gen. mgr. govt. communications Govt. Systems div., Camden, N.J., 1981-85, div. v.p., gen. mgr. Govt. Communications div., Aerospace and Def., Camden, 1985—. Gen. chmn. United Way of Camden County, 1985—. Mem. Navy League U.S., Am. Soc. Naval Engrs., Assn. U.S. Army, Nat. Security Indsl. Assn., Am. Def. Preparedness Assn., Armed Forces Communications and Electronics Assn., Security Affairs Support Assn., Air Force Assn., Club: Nat. Space. Republican. Roman Catholic. Current work: Management of defense electronics organization. Subspecialty: Electronics. Office: RCA Corp Front and Cooper Sts Camden NJ 08102

SCHLACHTER, ALFRED SIMON, physicist; b. Cedar City, Utah, Feb. 18, 1942; s. Max and Rosel (Rosenfeld) S. A.B., U. Calif. - Berkeley, 1963; M.A., U. Wis., 1965, Ph.D., 1969. Aerospace engr. Ames Research Ctr., NASA, summer 1963; research asst. U. Wis. - Madison, 1963-68; prin. research scientist Honeywell Corp. Research Ctr., Mpls., 1968-70; scientist U. Paris, Orsay, 1971-73, Saclay Nuclear Research Ctr., France, 1971-75; staff scientist Magnetic Fusion Energy Group, Lawrence Berkeley Lab., U. Calif. - Berkeley, 1975—; vis. scientist Ctr. for Nuclear Studies, Fontenay-aux-Roses, France, 1977, Justus-Liebig U., Giessen, W.Ger., 1980-81. Contbr. articles to profl. jours. NSF fellow, 1964; Centre National de la Recherche Scientifique fellow U. Paris, 1971-72; Joliot&Curie fellow Saclay, 1972-73; NATO travel grantee, 1980-81, 85-86; Alexander von Humboldt Stiftung traveling fellow, 1980-81. Mem. Am. Phys. Soc., Optical Soc. Am. Patentee in field. Current Work: Basic research in atomic physics, experimental atomic and molecular physics with applications to fusion energy and diagnostics; particle beams. Subspecialties: Atomic and molecular physics; Fusion. Office: Lawrence Berkeley Lab Univ Calif Berkeley CA 94720

SCHLAFER, DONALD HUGHES, reproductive pathologist, veterinary researcher; b. Sidney, N.Y., July 15, 1948; s. Donald Hughes and Mildred (Gamewell) S.; m. Judith Ann Appleton, Aug. 2, 1981. B.S., Cornell U., 1971; D.V.M., N.Y. State Coll., 1974; M.S., Cornell U., 1975; Ph.D., U. Ga., 1982. Diplomate Am. Coll. Vet. Pathologists, Am. Coll. Theriogenologists. Pvt. practice vet. medicine Guilderland Animal Hosp., Altamont, N.Y., 1975-77; pathology resident U. Ga., Athens, 1977-79; exptl. pathologist Plum Island Animal Disease Ctr., Greenport, N.Y., 1979-82; asst. prof. N.Y. State Coll. Vet. Medicine, Ithaca, 1982—; dir. bovine research ctr. Cornell U., Ithaca, 1982—; cons. in field., Contbr. articles to profl. jours. Mem. Am. Vet. Med. Assn., Soc. Study Reproduction, Soc. Theriogenology, U.S. Animal Health Assn., Am. Assn. Bovine Practitioners. Current work: Reproductive pathology, early embryonic death, placental pathophysiology, foreign animal disease; pathogenesis of infectious abortions, fetal physiology, gnotobiology. Subspecialties: Animal pathology; Theriogenology. Office: 325 VRT NY State Coll Vet Medicine Cornell U Ithaca NY 14853

SCHLAGER, SEYMOUR IRVING, immunologist, cons.; b. Hannover, Germany, Apr. 20, 1949; came to U.S., 1956, naturalized, 1961; s. Conrad and Helen (Topol) S.; m. Diane R. Schlager, Dec. 17, 1971; children: Carin Stephanie, Jason Lee. B.S., U. Ill., Chgo., 1969, M.S., 1973, Ph.D., 1975. Research chemist DeSoto, Inc., Des Plains, Ill., 1969-71; successively staff fellow, sr. staff fellow, cancer expert Lab. of Immunobiology, Nat. Cancer Inst., NIH, Bethesda, Md., 1975-80; assoc. prof. microbiology U. Notre Dame, 1980—; cons. Contbr. articles to profl. jours. Recipient Milan V. Novak award in microbiology U. Ill. Med. Center, 1975, various research grants, 1980-82, 1st prize Sigma Xi Research Forums, 1974, 75. Mem. Am. Assn. Immunologists, Am. Assn. Cancer Research, N.Y. Acad. Scis., AAAS, NIH Alumni Assn. Republican. Jewish. Lodge: B'nai B'rith. Current Work: Cellular immunology, molecular interactions of tumor cells with immune system, tumor cell resistance to immune attack and pharmacol. intervention thereof. Subspecialties: Immunology (medicine); Immunopharmacology. Office: Dept of Microbiology University of Notre Dame Notre Dame IN 46556

SCHLEGEL, RONALD GENE, acoustical and mechanical engineer, aerospace company executive; b. Derby, Conn., Sept. 3, 1936; s. Walter Joseph and Dorothy Louise (Lyon) S.; m. Sandra Webster, Sept. 14, 1957; children: Kenneth Alan, Peter Ronald. B.S. with honors, U. Conn., 1957; M.E., Yale U., 1959. Registered profl. engr., Conn. With Sikorsky Aircraft div. United Technologies Corp., Stratford, Conn., 1957—, program mgr. civil helicopter program, 1974-76, chief acoustics, 1976—; chmn. helicopter noise control com. Aerospace Industries, Inc., Washington, 1982-84; mem. ad hoc com. helicopter acoustics Nat. Acad. Engring., Washington, 1968. Editor: Helicopter Manufacturers' Economic Impact Assessment, 1979; contbr. numerous articles to profl. publs. Mem. planning commn. City of Shelton, Conn., 1960-62, mem. sewer commn., 1964-66, mem. charter revision commn., 1973; lector, spl. minister St. Joseph's Ch., Shelton, 1981—. Mem. Am. Helicopter Soc. (mem. acoustics com. 1970-83), AIAA (mem. aeroacoustics com. 1977-78), Helicopter Assn. Internat. (mem. acoustics com. 1975-83), Soc. Automotive Engring. Republican. Roman Catholic. Club: Seymour Fish and Game (jr. rifle instr. 1970-82). Current Work: Development of technology for the design of helicopters with low internal and external noise levels; work with U.S. and international civil authorities to develop acoustic certification standards for helicopters. Subspecialties: Acoustical engineering; Mechanical engineering. Home: 43 Lady Slipper Dr Shelton CT 06484 Office: United Technologies Corp Sikorsky Aircraft Div North Main St Stratford CT 06601

SCHLENK, HERMANN, biochemistry educator; b. Jena, Germany, July 28, 1914; came to U.S. 1949, naturalized 1952; s. Wilhelm and Mathilde (vonHacke) S.; m. Inge Kaethe Schier, June 29, 1946; children—Thomas, Cornelia. Diplom Chemist U. Berlin, Germany, 1936; Dr. rer. nat., U Munich, Germany, 1939. Research chemist BASF Ludwigshafen, Germany, 1939-44; lectr. U. Wuerzburg, Germany, 1946-49; asst. to assoc. prof. Tex. A&M U., College Station, 1949-52; from asst. to prof. Hormel Inst. U. Minn., Austin, 1953—. Contbr. articles to profl. jours. Mem. Am. Chem. Soc., Am. Soc. Biol. Chemists, Am. Oil Chemists Soc., Sigma Xi. Current work: Biochemistry and function of lipids. Subspecialties: Biochemistry (biology); Organic chemistry. Office: Univ Minn 801 16th Ave NE Austin MN 55912

SCHLESINGER, DAVID HARVEY, biochemist, consultant; b. N.Y.C., Apr. 28, 1939; s. Philip Theodore and Fay (Margolis) S.; children: Sarah Jane, Karen Louise. B.A., Columbia U., 1962; M.S., Albany Med. Coll., 1965; Ph.D., CUNY, 1972. Med. research technician Brookhaven Nat. Labs., Upton, L.I., N.Y., 1965-68; research fellow Harvard Med. Sch. and Mass. Gen. Hosp., Boston, 1972-75, asst. in biochemistry, 1975-77; assoc. prof. U. Ill. Med. Ctr., Chgo., 1977-81; research prof. exptl. medicine and cell biology NYU Med. Ctr., N.Y.C., 1981—; cons. Ortho Pharm., Raritan, N.J., 1978—. Author: Neurohypophysical Peptide Hormones and Other Biologically Active Peptides, 1981. Mem. Am. Physiol. Soc., Am. Soc. Biol. Chemistry, Am. Chem. Soc., N.Y. Acad. Scis. Patentee in field. Current Work: Protein sequencing, peptide synthesis, structure of calcium binding proteins, ubiquitin, thymopoetin, neurophysin, structure determination of porcine corticotropin releasing factor. Subspecialties: Biochemistry (medicine); Neuroendocrinology. Office: Dept Medicine NYU Med Ctr 550 1st Ave New York NY 10016

SCHLESINGER, EDWARD BRUCE, neurol. surgeon; b. Pitts., Sept. 6, 1913; s. Samuel B. and Sara Marie (Schlesinger) S.; m. Mary Eddy, Nov. 14, 1942; children—Jane, Mary, Ralph, Prudence. B.A., U. Pa., 1934, M.D., 1938. Diplomate: Am. Bd. Neurosurgey. Mem. faculty Columbia Coll. Phys. and Surg., N.Y.C., 1946—, prof. clin. neurol. surgery, 1964—, Byron Stookey prof., chmn. dept. neurol. surgery, 1973-80, Byron Stookey prof. emeritus, 1980—; dir. neurol. surgery Columbia Presbyn. Hosp., 1973-80, pres. med. bd., 1976-79; cons. in neurosurgery Presbyn. Hosp., 1980—. Trustee Matheson Found. Fellow N.Y. Acad. Scis. (chmn. Elsberg fellowship com.); mem. Harvey Cushing Soc., Harvey Soc., AAAS, Assn. Research in Nervous and Mental Disease, Neurosurg. Soc. Am. (pres. 1970-71), Soc. Neurol. Surgeons, Am. Assn. Surgery of Trauma, Am. Rheumatism Soc., Am. Coll. Clin. Pharmacology and Chemotherapy, AMA, Eastern Assn. Electroencephalographers, Sigma Xi. Research, publs. on uses, effects of curare in neuromsucualr disease, lesions of central nervous system, localization of brain tumors using radioactive tagged isotopes. Subspecialties: Neuropharmacology; Neurophysiology. Home: Closter Dock Rd Alpine NJ 07620 Office: 710 W 168th St New York NY 10032

SCHLOERB, PAUL RICHARD, surgeon, physiologist; b. Buffalo, Oct. 22, 1919; s. Herman George and Vera Marie (Gross) S.; m. Feb. 25, 1950; children—Ronald G., Patricia J. Schloerb Johnson, Marilyn Schloerb Hock, Dorothy Schloerb Hoban, Paul Richard. A.B., Harvard U., 1941; M.D., U. Rochester, 1944. Diplomate Am. Bd. Surgery. Intern. Strong Meml. Hosp., Rochester, N.Y., 1944-45, resident, 1947-48; resident Peter Bent Brigham Hosp., Boston, 1948-52; from asst. prof. to prof. surgery U. Kans. Med. Ctr., Kansas City, 1953-79, dean for research, 1967-78; prof. surgery U. Rochester, 1979—. Contbr. articles to profl. jours. Served to lt. M.C., USNR, 1945-46, 53-55. NIH grantee, 1956—, Research Career Devel. award, 1962-67. Fellow Am. Surg. Assn., ACS, Internat. Soc. Surgery, AAAS; mem. Am. Physiol. Soc., Soc. Univ. Surgeons, Central Surg. Assn. Republican. Episcopalian. Current work: Pathophysiology and treatment shock; fluid electrolyte derangements; nutritional support and critical care. Subspecialties: Surgery; Physiology (biology). Office: Dept Surgery U Rochester Med Center 601 Elmwood Ave Rochester NY 14642

SCHLOSBERG, RICHARD HENRY, research chemist; b. N.Y.C., May 23, 1942; s. David and Ruth (Helfgott) S.; m. Pamela Alice Graham, Mar. 26, 1967; children—Laura, Jacqueline, Joseph. B.S., Queens Coll., 1963; Ph.D., Mich. State U., 1967. Postdoctoral researcher Case Western Res. U., Cleve., 1967-69; asst. prof. U. Wis.-Whitewater, 1969-73; research assoc. Exxon Research and Engring. Co., Annandale, N.J., 1973-84; research assoc. Exxon Chem. Co., Linden, N.J., 1984—. Editor: Chemistry of Coal Conversion, 1985. Contbr. articles to profl. jours. Patentee in field. Petroleum Research Fund grantee, 1969. Mem. Am. Chem. Soc. (program chmn. div. fuel chemistry 1985), Catalysis Soc. N.Y. Current work: High temperature reaction mechanisms, organic chemistry of complex materials. Subspecialties: Organic chemistry; Fuels. Office: Exxon Chem Co PO Box 536 Linden NJ 07036

SCHLUSSEL, NEIL, space analyst, intelligence analyst; b. Portsmouth, Va., June 26, 1945; s. Nathan and Idarita (Feder) S.; m. Aylin Bromberg, June 18, 1967; children—Daniela, Damian. B.S. in Math., Va. Mil. Inst., 1967; B.S. in System Mgmt., U. So. Calif., 1977. Commd. 2d lt. U.S. Air Force, advanced through grades to lt. col.; orbital analyst surveillance officer Peterson AFB, Colo., 1967-74; minuteman launch control officer Malmstrom AFB, Great Falls, Mont., 1974-77; plans officer advanced command and control Peterson AFB, Colo., 1977-81; surveillance officer Nat. Mil. Command Ctr. JCS, Washington, 1981-83; chief space team Def. Intelligence Agy., Washington, 1983—. Vice pres. W.T. Woodson Band Patrons, Fairfax, Va., 1984—; bd. dirs. Congregation Olam Tikvah, Fairfax, 1984—. Awarded the First Master of Space Def. HQ ADCOM/NORAD, 1974. Mem. Am. Astronautical Soc. Jewish. Subspecialty: Satellite studies. Home: 8504 Litle River Turnpike Annandale VA 22003 Office: DIA/DE-1 Washington DC 20301

SCHMERLING, ERWIN ROBERT, government official; b. Vienna, Austria, July 28, 1929; came to U.S., 1955, naturalized, 1962; 1957. B.A., Cambridge U., 1950, M.A., 1954, Ph.D., 1958; grad., Advanced Mgmt. Program, Harvard, 1969, Fed. Exec. Inst., 1975. Vis. asst. prof. elec. engring. Pa. State U., 1955-57, asst. prof., 1957-60, assoc. prof., 1960-64; program chief ionospheric physics Office Space Sci., NASA Hdqrs., Washington, 1964-70, program chief magnetospheric physics, 1970-76, program chief space plasma physics, 1976-83, asst. dir. space and earth scis. NASA Goddard Space Flight Ctr., 1984—; mem. coms. III and IV Internat. Sci. Radio Union, 1958; sec. U.S. com. III, 1966-69, chmn., 1969-72; mem. Adv. Group Aerospace Research and Devel. Fellow IEEE (wave propagation standards com.); mem. Am. Geophys. Union, AAAS, Sigma Xi. Current Work: Space plasma physics; use of computers for information processing, retrieval and communications. Subspecialty: Information systems (Information science). Office: NASA Goddard Space Flight Ctr Code 630 Greenbelt MD 20771

SCHMID, RUDI RUDOLF, physician, educator, researcher; b. Switzerland, May 2, 1922; came to U.S., 1948, naturalized, 1954; s. Rudolf and Bertha (Schiesser) S.; m. Sonja D. Wild, Sept. 17, 1949; children: Isabelle S., Peter R. B.S., U. Zurich, 1941, M.D., 1947; Ph.D., U. Minn., 1954. Intern U. Calif. Med. Center, San Francisco, 1948-49; resident medicine U. Minn., 1949-52, instr., 1952-54; research fellow biochemistry Columbia U., 1954-55; investigator NIH, Bethesda, Md., 1955-57; assoc. medicine Harvard U., 1957-59, asst. prof., 1959-62; prof. medicine U. Chgo., 1962-66; prof. medicine U. Calif., San Francisco, 1966—, dean Sch. Medicine, 1983—; Cons. U.S. Army Surgeon Gen., USPHS, VA. Mem. editorial bd.: Jour. Clin. Investigation, 1965-70, Jour. Lab. and Clin. Medicine, 1964-70, Blood, 1962-75, Gastroenterology, 1965-70, Jour. Investigative Dermatology, 1968-72, Annals Internal Medicine, 1975-79, Proc. Soc. Exptl. Biology and Medicine, 1976-84. Served with Swiss Army, 1943-45. Fellow AAAS, N.Y. Acad. Scis.; mem. Nat. Acad. Scis., Am. Acad. Arts and Scis., Assn. Am. Physicians, Am. Soc. Clin. Investigation, ACP, Am. Soc. Biol. Chemists, Am. Soc. Exptl. Pathology, Am. Soc. Hematology, Am. Gastroenterol. Assn., Am. Assn. Study Liver Disease (pres. 1965), Internat. Assn. Study Liver (pres. 1980), Leopoldina. Research in metabolism of hemoglobin, heme, porphyrins, bile pigments and liver. Subspecialty: Internal medicine. Home: 211 Woodland Rd Kentfield CA 94904 Office: University of California Med Center San Francisco CA 94143

SCHMIDGALL, ROBERT LEE, chemistry educator; b. Peoria, Ill., Mar. 28, 1943; s. William Henry and Cleona Elizabeth (Ackerly) S.; m. Judith Ann Robins, May 16, 1981. B.A., Bradley U., 1965; Ph.D., Ind. U., 1969; postgrad. Henderson State U., 1978-81. C.P.A., Ark. Chemist, U.S. Dept. Agr., No. Regional Lab., Peoria, Ill., 1963-65; instr. chemistry U. Ark., Fayetteville, 1969-70; prof. chemistry Henderson State U., Arkadelphia, Ark., 1970—. Contbr. articles to profl. jours. Author: Organic Chemistry in the Laboratory, 1979. Mem. Am. Chem. Soc., Am. Inst. C.P.A.'s, Sigma Xi. Republican. Mem. Christian Ch. Current work: Synthesis and characterization of biologically active compounds. Comparative electrophoresis of human/animal blood serums. Subspecialties: Organic chemistry; Biochemistry (biology). Home: Route 1 Box 328 Arkadelphia AR 71923 Office: Henderson State U Box H-7633 Arkadelphia AR 71923

SCHMID-SCHOENBEIN, GEERT WILIFRIED, bioengineer, researcher, educator; b. Ebingen, West Germany, Jan. 1, 1948; s. Ernst and Ursula (Richter) Schmid; m. Renate Elisabeth Klein, June 4, 1976; children—Philip, Mark, Peter. Diploma in Physics, U. Giessen, 1971; M.S. in Bioengring., U. Calif.-San Diego, 1973, Ph.D. in Bioengring., 1976. Research assoc. Columbia U., N.Y.C., 1976-77, sr. research assoc., 1977-79; asst. prof. U. Calif.-San Diego, 1979-84, assoc. prof., 1984—. Mem. Microcirculatory Soc., Am. Phys. Soc., Biorhealogy, Soc., European Soc. Microcirculation (Malphigi award 1982, Abbott award 1984). Current work: Microcirculation, biomechanics, rheology, cell biology. Subspecialty: Biomedical engineering. Office: AMES/Bioengring M-005 U Calif-San Diego LaJolla CA 92093

SCHMIDT, CHARLES ANDREW, See *Who's Who in America*, 43rd edition.

SCHMIDT, JOHN WESLEY, agronomy educator; b. Moundridge, Kans., Mar. 13, 1917; s. John J. and Katie (Sperling) S.; m. Olene Lucile Hall, June 23, 1943; children—Karen, Vicki, Wesley, Loren, Jerold. B.A., Tabor Coll., 1947; M.S., Kans. State U., 1949; Ph.D., U. Nebr., 1952. D.Sci. (hon.), Kans. State U., 1984. Asst. to assoc. agronomist Kans. State U., Manhattan, 1951-54; assoc. prof. U. Nebr., Lincoln, 1954-62, prof. agronomy, 1962—, Regents prof., 1980—. Recipient Alumni Merit award Tabor Coll., 1970; Outstanding Research and Creativity award U. Nebr., 1979; Excellence in Agr. award Nat. Agri-Mktg. Assn., 1984. Fellow Am. Soc. Agronomy; mem. Crop Sci. Soc. Am. (Crop Sci. award 1975, DeKalb-Pfizer Dist. Crop Sci. Career award 1982), Gamma Sigma Delta (Internat. Disting. Service to Agr. award). Republican. Methodist. Current work: Research in wheat breeding, plant genetics. Subspecialties: Agronomy; Plant genetics. Office: Dept Agronomy U Nebr 322 Keim Hall Lincoln NE 68583

SCHMIDT, NATHALIE JOAN, virologist; b. Flagstaff, Ariz., Sept. 24, 1928; d. Joseph Francis and Gertrude Nathalie (Hill) S. B.A., U. Ariz., 1950; M.S, Northwestern U., 1952, Ph.D., 1953. Diplomate: Am. Bd. Med. Microbiology, 1965. Asst. instr. Northwestern U., 1950-53; microbiologist Evanston (Ill.) Hosp., 1953-54; research specialist Virus Lab., Calif. Dept. Health, Berkeley, 1954-81, research scientist, 1981—; lectr. Sch. Pub. Health, U. Calif. - Berkeley, 1971—; cons. NIH. Editor: Diagnostic Procedures for Viral, Rickettsial and Chlamydial Infections, 5th edit, 1979, Jour. Clin. Microbiology, 1975-85; mem. editorial bd.: Intervirology, 1972—, Jour. Immunology, 1973-75, Proc. Soc. Exptl. Biology and Medicine, 1975—; contbr. articles to profl. jours. Recipient Kimble award in lab. methodology Kimble, Inc., 1977; Behring diagnostics award in diagnostic virology/rickettsiology, 1985. Mem. Am. Acad. Microbiology, Am. Assn. Immunologists, Am. Public Health Assn., Am. Soc. Microbiology, N.Y. Acad. Scis., Soc. Exptl. Biology and Medicine. Current Work: Developmental viral diagnosis; immunology of viral diseases; immunology of coxsackievirus, herpes virus and rubella virus infections; immunoassays for viral antigens and antibodies. Subspecialty: Virology (medicine). Office: 2151 Berkeley Way Berkeley CA 94704

SCHMIDT, RICHARD RALPH, developmental immunologist, educator; b. Milw., Mar. 28, 1944; s. Robert Oscar and Jeane Patricia (Oakes) S.; m. Diane Grace Parker, June 19, 1965 (div. 1980); children—Allison J., Garret R.; m. Dulcie Marie Bausch, June 20, 1980; 1 child, Robert Andrew. B.A., U. Wis.-Wilw., 1968; Ph.D., Med. Coll. Wis., 1975. Instr. Jefferson Med. Coll., Phila., 1975-77, asst. prof., 1978-81, assoc. prof., 1982—; anat. cons. Saunders Coll. Pub. Co., Phila., 1983—; manuscript reviewer Teratology Jour., Phila., 1976—, Jour. Am. Coll. Toxicology, Phila., 1983—. Author: (with others) Human Anatomy, 1985. Contbr. articles to profl. jours. Grantee Human Growth Found., 1976, Orthopaedic Research and Edn. Found., 1978-81. Mem. Teratology Soc., AAAS, Immunotoxicology Discussion Group (organizing com.), Sigma Xi. Lutheran. Current work: Immunotoxicology studies of the developing immune system in mammals. Subspecialties: Immunology (agriculture); Toxicology (agriculture). Office: Jefferson Med Coll 1020 Locust St Philadelphia PA 19107

SCHMIDT, ROBERT, engineering educator, editor; b. Chomci, Ukraine, May 18, 1927; came to U.S., 1949; s. Alfred and Kylyna (Konotop); m. Irene Hubertine Bongartz, June 10, 1978; 1 child, Ingbert Robert. Student Technische Hochschule, Karlsruhe, Germany, 1949; B.S., U. Colo., 1951, M.S., 1953; Ph.D., U. Ill., 1956. Draftsman, Kalisch, Poland, 1943-45; research asst. U. Ill., Urbana, 1953-56, asst. prof. engring., 1956-59; assoc. prof. U. Ariz., Tucson, 1959-63; prof. U. Detroit, 1963—, chmn. engring. dept., 1978-80; engr. Corp Engrs. U.S. Army, 1951-52. Editor Indsl. Math. jour., 1969—. Contbr. numerous articles to profl. jours. NSF grantee. Mem. Indsl. Math. Soc., Am. Soc. Engring. Edn., Am. Acad. Mechanics (founder), ASCE, ASME (cert. of recognition 1972), Sigma Xi. Current work: Nonlinear theory of beams, rings, arches, plates and shells; theory of elasticity; direct variational methods of analysis; differential equations. Subspecialties: Solid mechanics; Civil engineering. Office: Engring Bldg U Detroit 4001 W McNichols Rd Detroit MI 48221

SCHMIDT, RUTH A.M., geology educator; b. Bklyn., Apr. 22, 1916; d. Edward and Anna M. (Range) S. A.B., NYU, 1936; A.M., Columbia U., 1939, Ph.D., 1948. X-ray technician L.I. Coll. Hosp., Bklyn., 1936-38; researcher Am. Mus. Natural History, N.Y.C., 1941; geologist U.S. Geol. Survey, Washington, 1943-56, dist. geologist, Anchorage, 1956-63; prof., head dept. geology U. Alaska-Anchorage, Anchorage Community Coll., 1970-84; cons. geologist, Anchorage, 1964—. Author: Geology Color Slide Sets, 1965-68; contbr. articles in field to profl. jours. Trustee Brooks Range Trust, 1973-84; exec. bd. Alaska Ctr. Environment, 1981-83; adviser, sponsor Alaska Conservation Found., 1983—; bd. govs. Arctic Inst. N.Am. Fellow AAAS (past pres. local chpt.), Geol. Soc. Am.; mem. Fedn. Am. Scientists, Soc. Econ. Mineralogists and Paleontologists, Am. Assn. Petroleum Geologists, Alaska Geol. Soc. (hon. mem., past pres.), Am. Inst. Profl. Geologists (cert. profl. geologist), Audubon Soc., Sierra Club, Nat. Parks and Conservation Assn., Sigma Xi (hon.). Current Work: Quaternary micropaleontology Alaska; instructional television delivery of earth science to rural Alaska. Subspecialties: Paleontology, paleoecology; Geology. Office: 1040-C-St Anchorage AK 99501

SCHMIDT, WILLIAM FREDERICK, mechanical engineering educator, researcher; b. Cin., Sept. 15, 1942; 3 children. B.S. in Mech. Engring., U. Ky., 1964; M.S. in Engring., U. Wash., 1966, Ph.D. in Engring. Mechanics, 1968. Engr. Math. Scis. NW, Seattle, 1966-68; asst. prof. mech. engring. U. Maine, Orono, 1968-74, assoc. prof. 1974-80, prof., chmn., 1980-83, prof., chmn., acting dir. Computer Application Network, 1983—. Contbr. articles to profl. jours. Chmn. Sch. Bd., Carmel, Maine, 1974-80; selectman Town of Carmel, 1972-76. Mem. ASME (chmn. region I), Am. Soc. Engring. Edn. (Western Electric Fund award 1981), Tau Beta Pi, Pi Tau Sigma. Current work: Development and application of nonlinear finite element techniques in solid mechanics, computer aided design. Subspecialties: Solid mechanics; Mechanical engineering. Home: 2203 Emma St Fayetteville AR 72701 Office: Dept Mech Engring 204 Mech Engring Bldg U Ark Fayetteville AR 72701

SCHMIDT, WYMAN CARL, research forester; b. Ocheyedan, Iowa, Sept. 9, 1929; s. Carl Edward and Ida Sophie (Bremer) S.; m. Patricia Anne Clark, Mar. 1, 1953; children—Roxi, Carl, Roland, Martin, Kurt. B.S., Mont. State U., 1958; M.S., U. Mont., 1961, Ph.D., 1980. Forester U.S. Forest Service, Dept. Agr., Deadwood, S.D., 1959-60, research forester, Missoula, Mont., 1960-75, research unit leader, Bozeman, Mont., 1975—, dir.'s rep., Bozeman, 1975—. Contbr. articles to profl. and sci. jours. Served with USAF, 1950-54. Recipient Outstanding Performance award Dept. Agr., 1977, 84. Mem. Soc. Am. Foresters, Northwest Sci. Assn., Mont. Acad. Sci. Current work: Silvicultural research of Rocky Mountain coniferous forests with specialties in tree growth, water use relationships, phenology, autecology, insect interactions with silviculture. Subspecialty: Silviculture. Office: Forestry Sciences Lab Mont State U Bozeman MT 59717

SCHMIDT-NIELSEN, KNUT, physiologist, educator; b. Norway, Sept. 24, 1915; came to U.S., 1946, naturalized, 1952; s. Sigval and Signe Torborg (Sturzen-Becker) Schmidt-N. Mag. Scient., U. Copenhagen, 1941, Dr. Phil., 1946. Research fellow Carlsberg Labs., Copenhagen, 1941-44, Carlsberg Labs. (U. Copenhagen), 1944-46; research assoc. zoology Swarthmore (Pa.) Coll., 1946-48; docent U. Oslo, Norway, 1947-49; research assoc. physiology Stanford, 1948-49; asst. prof. Coll. Medicine, U. Cin., 1949-52; prof. physiology Duke, Durham, N.C., 1952—, James B. Duke prof. physiology, 1963—, Harvey Soc. lectr., 1962; Regents' lectr. U. Calif. at Davis, 1963; Brody Meml. lectr. U. Mo., 1962; Hans Gadow lectr. Cambridge (Eng.) U., 1971; vis. Agassiz prof. Harvard, 1972; Mem. panel environmental biology NSF, 1957-61; mem. sci. adv. com. New Eng. Regional Primate Center, 1962-66; mem. nat. adv. bd. physiol. research lab. Scripps Instn. Oceanography, U. Calif. at San Diego, 1963-69, chmn., 1968-69; organizing com. 1st Internat. Conf. on Comparative Physiology, 1972-80; mem. U.S. nat. com. Internat. Union Physiol. Scis., 1966-78, vice chmn. U.S. nat. com., 1969-78, pres., 1980—; mem. subcom. on environmental physiology U.S. nat. com. Internat. Biol. Programme, 1965-67; mem. com. on research utilization uncommon animals, div. biology and agr. Nat. Acad. Scis., 1966-68; mem. animal resources adv. com. NIH, 1968; mem. adv. bd. Bio-Med. Scis., Inc., 1973-74; Chief scientist Scripps Instn. Amazon expdn., 1967. Author: Animal Physiology, 3d. edit, 1970, The Physiology of Desert Animals; Physiological Problems of Heat and Water, 1964, How Animals Work, 1972, Animal Physiology; Adaptation and Environment, 1975, 2d edit., 1979, 3d edit., 1983; sect. editor: Am. Jour. Physiology, 1961-64, 70-76; editor: Jour. Applied Physiology, 1961-64, 70-76; editorial bd.: Jour. Cellular and Comparative Physiology, 1961-66, Physiol. Zoology, 1959-70, Am. Jour. Physiology, 1971-76, Jour. Applied Physiology, 1971-76, Jour. Exptl. Biology, 1975-79, 83—; cons. editor: Annals of Arid Zone, 1962—; hon. editorial adv. bd.: Comparative Biochemistry and Physiology, 1962-63; Contbr. articles to sci. publs. Guggenheim fellow, 1953-54; grantee Office Naval Research, 1952-54, 58-61, UNESCO, 1953-54, Office Q.M. Gen., 1953-54, grantee Office Surgeon Gen., 1953-54, NIH, 1955—, NSF, 1957-61, 59-60, 60-61, 61-63; recipient Research Career award USPHS, 1964. Fellow N.Y. Acad. Sci., AAAS, Am. Acad. Arts and Scis.; mem. Nat. Acad. Scis., N.C. Acad. Sci. (Poteat award 1957), Am. Physiol. Soc., Am. Soc. Zoologists (chmn. div. comparative physiology 1964), Soc. Exptl. Biology, Harvey Soc. (hon.), Royal Danish Acad., Académie des Sciences (France) (fgn. assoc.), Royal Norwegian Soc. Arts and Sci., Norwegian Acad. Scis., Royal Soc. London (fgn.), Physiol. Soc. London (assoc.). Subspecialty: Comparative physiology. Office: Dept Zoology Duke Univ Durham NC 27706

SCHMIEDER, ROBERT WILLIAM, physicist, marine scientist; b. Phoenix, July 10, 1941; s. Otto and Ruby Maybel (Harkey) S.; divorced (div.); children:

Robyn, Russell Otto, Robert Randall. A.B., Occidental Coll., 1963; B.S., Calif. Inst. Tech., 1963; M.A., Columbia U., 1965, Ph.D., 1968. Staff mem. Lawrence Berkeley Lab., 1969-71; instr. physics dept. U. Calif. - Berkeley, 1971-72; mem. tech. staff Sandia Nat. Lab., Livermore, Calif., 1972—. Contbr. articles to sci. jours. Nat. Geog. Soc. grantee, 1979; Explorers Club grantee, 1980; San Francisco Found. grantee, 1981; NOAA grantee, 1981-83. Mem. Am. Phys. Soc., Optical Soc. Am. Patentee in field of nuclear instrumentation. Current Work: Research in combustion physics and chemistry; oceanic research expeditions. Subspecialties: Combustion processes; Atomic and molecular physics. Home: 4295 Walnut Blvd Walnut Creek CA 94596 Office: Div 8513 Sandia Nat Labs Livermore CA 94550

SCHMIT, LUCIEN ANDRÉ , JR., structural engineer; b. N.Y.C., May 5, 1928; s. Lucien Alexander and Eleanor Jessie (Donley) S.; m. Eleanor Constance Trabish, June 24, 1951; 1 child, Lucien Alexander, III. B.S., MIT, 1949, M.S., 1950. Structures engr. Grumman Aircraft Co., Bethpage, N.Y., 1951-53; research engr., aeroelastic and structures lab. MIT, 1954-58; asst. prof. engring. (Case Inst. Tech.), 1958-60, assoc. prof., 1961-63, prof., 1964-70; prof. engring. and applied sci. UCLA, 1970—; mem. sci. adv. bd. USAF, 1977-84. Contbr. numerous articles on analysis and synthesis of structural systems, finite element methods, design of fiber composite components to profl. jours. Fellow ASCE (Walter L. Huber Civil Engring. Research prize 1970), AIAA (assoc., Design Lecture award 1977, Structures, Structural Dynamics and Materials award 1979); mem. ASME, Nat. Acad. Engring., Sigma Xi. Current Work: Methods for optimum and/or balanced design of structural systems subject to static and dynamic load conditions. Subspecialties: Aeronautical engineering; Civil engineering. Home: 712 El Medio Ave Pacific Palisades CA 90272 Office: 4531 K Boelter Hall UCLA Los Angeles CA 90024

SCHMITT, ROLAND WALTER, manufacturing company research executive; b. Seguin, Tex., July 24, 1923; s. Walter L. and Myrtle F. (Caldwell) S.; m. Claire Freeman Kunz, Sept. 19, 1957; children: Lorenz Allen, Brian Walter, Alice Elizabeth, Henry Caldwell. B.A. in Math, U. Tex., 1947, B.S. in Physics, 1947, M.A. in Physics, 1948; Ph.D., Rice U., 1951. With Gen. Electric Co., 1951—, research and devel. mgr. phys. sci. and engring. Gen. Electric Corp. Research and Devel., Schenectady, 1967-74, research and devel. mgr. energy sci. and engring. Gen. Electric Corp. Research and Devel., 1974-78, v.p. corp. research and devel. Gen. Electric Corp. Research and Devel., 1978-82, sr. v.p. corp. research and devel. Gen. Electric Corp. Research and Devel., 1982—; v.p. Indsl. Research Inst.; mem. energy research adv. bd. Dept. Energy, 1977-83. Trustee Northeast Savs. Bank., 1978-84; vice chmn. Bd. dirs., chmn. investment rev. com. N.Y. State Sci. and Tech. Found., 1978-84; bd. govs. Albany Med. Center Hosp., 1979-82; trustee Union Coll., Schenectady, 1981-84, Argonne Univs. Assn., 1979-82, RPI; bd. dirs. Sunnyview Hosp. and Rehab. Center. Served with USAAF, 1943-46. Fellow Am. Phys. Soc., IEEE, AAAS; mem. Am. Inst. Physics (chmn. com. on corp. assocs., mem. governing bd. 1979-83), Nat. Acad. Engring. (council), Nat. Sci. Bd. (chmn.), Dirs. Indsl. Research, Am. Nuclear Soc. Club: Cosmos. Subspecialty: Research management. Office: PO Box 8 Schenectady NY 12301

SCHMITZ, DARREL WAYNE, geologist; b. Eupora, Miss., Dec. 31, 1955; s. Ullin Darrel and Dorothy Jean (Stewart) S.; m. Donna Elizabeth Singleton, May 2, 1981; 1 child, Courtney Elizabeth. B.S. in Geology, Miss. State U., 1980; M.S. in Engring. Sci. and Geology, U. Miss., 1985. Hydrologic asst. technician U.S. Geol. Survey, Baton Rouge, 1974-77; geologist North Am. Exploration, Kaysville, Utah, 1980-82; mud logger and geol. asst. Exploration Services Inc., Tyler, Tex., 1982; geologist Miss. Mineral Resources Inst., Jackson, 1982-83, Miss. Bur. Geology, Jackson, 1983-85, Miss. Bur. Pollution Control, Jackson, 1985—; rep. task force Miss. Automated Resources Info. System, Jackson, 1983—; cons. in field. Compiler color map Econ. Minerals Miss., 1983. Recipient Lithology Log Detail and Accuracy award North Am. Exploration, 1980. Mem. Am. Assn. Petroleum Geologists, Geol. Soc. Am., Minerals and Geotech. Logging Soc., Miss. Acad. Scis., Miss. Geol. Soc. Democrat. Methodist. Current work: Responsible for development and management of Mississippi's groundwater protection program: prevention and control of groundwater contamination, a routine investigative program to pollution incidents, and assessment of potential for groundwater contamination. Subspecialties: Geology; Hydrology. Home: 26 Rockford Ct Brandon MS 39042 Office: Miss Bur Pollution Control 2380 Hwy 80 West Jackson MS 39209

SCHNEIDER, ALLAN FRANK, geology educator; b. Chgo., Feb. 7, 1926; s. Emory F. and Esther M. (Westgard) S.; m. Betty Louise Dorn, Aug. 26, 1950; children—David E., Doris J., James A. B.S., Beloit Coll., 1948; M.S., Pa. State U., 1951; Ph.D., U. Minn., 1957. Geologist U.S. Geol. Survey, Lexington, Ky., 1949-50; instr. Pa. State U., State College, 1950-51, U. Minn., Mpls., 1951-54; geologist Minn. Geol. Survey, Mpls., summers 1951-54; instr. Washington State U., Pullman, 1954-57; asst. prof., 1957-59; geologist Ind. Geol. Survey, Bloomington, 1959-70, map and illustrations editor, 1961-65; assoc. prof. U. Wis.-Parkside, Kenosha, 1970-80, prof. geology, 1980—, coordinator geology program, 1973-75, 80-83, 85—. Author: Pleistocene Geology of Randall Region Central Minnesota, 1961. Editor guidebook, 1967. Contbr. articles to profl. jours. Grantee Geol. Soc. Am., U. Wis., U.S. Dept. Commerce. Fellow Geol. Soc. Am., Ind. Acad. Sci.; mem. Nat. Assn. Geology Tchrs., Am. Quaternary Assn., Wis. Acad. Sci. Arts and Letters, Internat. Glaciol. Soc., Arctic Inst. N. Am., Sigma Xi. Republican. Lutheran. Current work: Stratigraphy and lithology of glacial sediments; late Quaternary history of the Lake Michigan Basin; glacial geology of Minnesota, Indiana, Wisconsin. Subspecialty: Geology. Home: 5136 Cortland Ave Racine WI 53406 Office: U Wis-Parkside Dept Geology Box 2000 Kenosha WI 53141

SCHNEIDER, GERALD ELMORE, mechanical engineering educator, consultant; b. Waterloo, Ont., Can., Aug. 21, 1949; s. Almond Louis and Nelda (Jacobi) S.; m. Joan Diane Illig, June 26, 1968; children: Jeremy Glenn, Joshua James. B.A., U. Waterloo, Ont., Can., 1973, M.A., 1974, Ph.D., 1977. Research asst. U. Waterloo, Ont., Can., 1971-73, project engr., 1973-77, adj. lectr., 1976, asst. prof. mech. engring., 1977-81, assoc. prof., 1981-85, prof., 1985—; cons. Cluff & Cluff Architects, Toronto, Ont., Can., 1980; on-site cons. Aeroject Electro Systems Inc., Azusa, Calif., 1980; cons. Valley Blades Ltd., Waterloo, Ont., 1980-81, Thermo Fluids Research and Devel. Inc., Waterloo, 1980—. Mem. AIAA, ASME. Current Work: Heat transfer, numerical methods, tribology, solution procedures, incompressible fluid flow. Subspecialties: Fluid mechanics; Numerical analysis (computer science). Home: 81 Culpepper Dr Waterloo ON N2L 5K8 Canada Office: Dept Mech Engring U Waterloo University Ave W Waterloo ON N2L 3G1 Canada

SCHNEIDER, HAROLD, engineer; b. Cin., Apr. 8, 1930; s. Kalman and Ethyl (Oscherwitz) S.; m. Joan Shirley Brown, July 3, 1959; children—Lynn D., Steven K. B.S. in Physics, U. Cin., 1951, M.S. in Applied Physics, 1954, Ph.D. in Physics, 1956. Aero. research scientist Lewis Research Ctr., Cleve., 1951-62; staff mem. Lincoln Lab., MIT, Lexington, 1962-72; sr. systems analyst Dynamics Research Corp., Wilmington, Mass., 1972-78; prin. engring. mem. RCA Corp., Morrestown, N.J., 1978; staff engr. Lockheed Missiles and Space Co., Sunnyvale, Calif., 1978—; industry tech. cons. Who's Who in Tech. Today, 1982—. Contbr. articles to tech. publs. Mem. Soc. Indsl. and Applied Math., AIAA, Sigma Xi. Jewish. Current work: Nonlinear systems modelling; optimal estimation-systems identification; optimal control and guidance; 6-degree-of-freedom re-entry body dynamics and aerodynamics modeling, simulation, error analyses; applying unique nonlinear estimation method using spline functions. Subspecialties: Applied mathematics; Aerospace engineering and technology. Home: 855 Clara Dr Palo Alto CA 94303 Office: Missile Systems Div Bld 154 Lockheed Missiles and Space Co Mathilda at 3d St Sunnyvale CA 94086

SCHNEIDER, KENNETH STUART, electrical engineer; b. N.Y.C., Apr. 16, 1945; s. Irving Bernard and Lillian (Goldfein) S.; m. Diane Susan Ertel, June 29, 1969; children—Andrew, Jessica, Rachel. B.S., Cornell U., 1965, M.S.E.E., 1966, Ph.D., 1970. Mem. tech. staff Hughes Aircraft Co., Culver City, Calif., 1970-71, MIT Lincoln Lab., Lexington, Mass., 1971-76; project mgr. Network Analysis Corp., Great Neck, N.Y., 1976-78; pres. Sigcom, Jericho, N.Y., 1978-83; v.p., treas. Telebyte, Greenlawn, N.Y., 1983—, also dir. Contbr. articles to profl. jours. Patentee modem/multiplexer. Chmn. Mass. chpt. Coalition for Democratic Majority, Boston, 1973. Mem. IEEE (chmn. L.I., N.Y. chpt. Quantum Electronics group). Republican. Jewish. Lodges: Masons (sr. deacon), B'nai Brith (v.p. 1972-76). Current work: Modems, lasers; managing research and development of company active in computer and communications equipment business. Subspecialty: Computer engineering. Home: 134 Birchwood Park Dr Jericho NY 11753 Office: Telebyte 270 Pulaski Rd Greenlawn NY 11740

SCHNEIDER, NORMAN RICHARD, veterinarian, educator; b. Ellsworth, Kans., Mar. 28, 1943; s. Henry C. and Irene C. (Ney) S.; m. Karen Marjorie Nelson, July 1, 1968; 1 child, Nelson R. B.S., Kans. State U., 1967, D.V.M., 1968; M.S., Ohio State U., 1972. Diplomate: Am. Bd. Vet. Toxicology. Commd. capt. U.S. Air Force, 1968, advanced through grades to maj., 1976; base veterinarian Goose AB, Labrador, Can., 1968-70; veterinary scientist, toxicologist Armed Forces Radiobiology Research Inst., Bethesda, Md., 1972-76; veterinary toxicologist Aerospace Med. Research Lab., Wright-Patterson AFB, Dayton, 1976-79; assoc. prof., veterinary toxicologist dept. veterinary sci. U. Nebr., Lincoln, 1979—; adj. prof., dept. pharmacodynamics and toxicology U. Nebr. Med. Center, 1982—; chief environ. health services Nebr. Air Nat. Guard, Lincoln, 1979—. Mem. Am. Bd. Vet. Toxicologists, Am. Coll. Vet. Toxicologists, Am. Vet. Med. Assn., Nebr. Vet. Med. Assn., Kans. Vet. Med. Assn., Am. Assn. Vet. Lab. Diagnosticians, Assn. Official Analytical Chemists, Nat. Guard Assn. U.S., Nat. Guard Assn. Nebr., Alliance Air Nat. Guard Flight Surgeons, Air Nat. Guard Environ. Health Assn., Mil. Surgeons U.S., N.Y. Acad. Scis., Council Agrl. Sci. and Tech., Am. Legion, NRA, Alpha Zeta, Phi Zeta. Roman Catholic. Club: FarmHouse. Current Work: Mycotoxins and mycotoxicoses, nitrite/nitrate, pesticides, military munitions, natural toxicants. Subspecialties: Toxicology (agriculture); Diagnostic veterinary toxicology. Home: Rt 1 Box 70 Ceresco NE 68017 Office: Vet Diagnostic Center Lincoln NE 68583

SCHNEIDER, RICHARD JOEL, neurobiologist, translator; b. Bklyn., July 25, 1944; s. Albert and Edith E. (Heltermann) S.; m. Diane J. Shannon, July 31, 1982; children: Kelley, Connie, Keith. Student, Colby Coll., Waterville, Maine, 1961-62; A.B., U. Chgo., 1966; Ph.D., U. Pitts., 1972. Instr. U. Md., Balt., 1971-72, asst. prof., 1972-78; head Lab. Neurosci., Md. Inst. Emergency Medicine, Balt., 1978-81; guest worker NIMH, Bethesda, 1981—; guest prof. Royal Victoria Hosp., McGill U., 1985; cons. Neurosci. Lab., Curtis Hand Ctr., Union Meml. Hosp., Balt. Contbr. articles to profl. jours. Nat. Multiple Sclerosis Soc. grantee, 1978-81; Bressler Research Found. grantee, 1976-80; Curtis Hand Found. grantee, 1980-81; Surgery Research award Plastic Surgery Ednl. Found., 1982; Nat. Media Library Teaching Tape award, 1974. Mem. AAAS, Am. Pain Soc., Balt. Neuroscience Soc., Md. Neurol. Soc., Fedn. Am. Scientists, Internat. Assn. Study Pain, Soc. Neurosci. Current Work: Neurophysiology and neuroanatomy of somatic sensation, pain, demyelinating diseases (Mutiple Sclerosis), neurotransmitters in the somatosensory system; neural prostheses. Subspecialties: Neurobiology; Comparative physiology. Home: 5483 Endicott Ln Columbia MD 21044 Office: Bldg 9 Room INI07 Bethesda MD 20205

SCHNEIDER, ROBERT WILLIAM, mechanical engineering consultant; b. S.I., N.Y., Dec. 30, 1925; s. Otto William and Anna Viola (Androvette) S.; m. Phyllis Mae Rantz, Dec. 24, 1946; children: Craig Robert, Dean Alan, David William. B.S. in Engring, Lehigh U., 1948, M.S. in Engring, 1949. Registered profl. engr., Pa., Ont., Can. Asst. design and metall. engr. Linde Air Products Co., Tonawanda, N.Y., 1949-54; supr. ASME code shop inspection dept. Travelers Indemnity Co., Hartford, Conn., 1954-60; asst. supt. engring. and inspection dept. Oak Ridge Nat. Lab., 1960-68; mgr. engring. Bonney Forge, Allentown, Pa., 1968-81; pres. R.W. Schneider Assocs. (pressure vessels and piping cons.), Allentown, 1981—. Author: An Overview of the Structural Design of Piping Systems, 1978; contbr. articles on design and analysis of pressure vessels and piping to profl. jours. Served to ensign USN, 1943-46, PTO. Merck fellow, 1948-49. Fellow ASME; Mem. Welding Research Council, Nat. Soc. Profl. Engrs., Springhouse Farms Homeowners Assn. Presbyterian. Patentee in field. Current Work: Research and development to investigate stresses in nozzles of pressure vessels and piping due to external loads and internal pressure. Subspecialty: Mechanical engineering. Home and Office: 3918 Lincoln Pkwy W Allentown PA 18104

SCHNEIDER, SAMUEL JAMES, JR., ceramic engineer; b. St. Louis, Sept. 11, 1930; s. Samuel and Dorothy Helen (Pins) S.; m. Joan Carolyn McMahon, Aug. 6, 1955; children—Steven, Michael, Sandra. B.S. in Ceramic Engring., Mo. Sch. Mines, 1952; Profl. Ceramic Engr. (hon.), U. Mo., 1975. Ceramic engr. Laclede Refractory Co., St. Louis, 1952-53; ceramic engr. Inst. Materials Research, Nat. Bur. Standards, Gaithersburg, Md., 1955-72, mgr. energy program, Inst. Materials Research, 1972-78, asst. to dir. Ctr. for Materials Sci., 1978-81, dep. chief inorganic materials div., 1981—. Editor: Science of Ceramic Machining, 1972; Solid State Chemistry, 1972. Contbr. numerous articles to profl. jours. Served with CIC, U.S. Army, 1953-55. Recipient Silver medal Dept. Commerce, 1970, spl. achievement award Nat. Bur. Standards, 1972, 75, 77, 82, 83. Fellow Am. Ceramic Soc., ASTM (award of merit 1984); mem. Nat. Inst. Ceramic Engrs., Keramos. Republican. Presbyterian. Club: Lakewood Country (Rockville, Md.). Current work: Management of research and development; ceramic engineering; ceramic processing and properties; phase equilibria. Subspecialties: Ceramics; High-temperature materials. Home: 5 Marlin Ct Rockville MD 20853 Office: Nat Bur Standards Room A 257 Materials Bldg 223 Gaithersburg MD 20899

SCHNEIDER, STEPHEN HENRY, climatologist; b. N.Y.C., Feb. 11, 1945; s. Samuel and Doris C. (Swarte) S.; m. Cheryl Kay Hatter, Aug. 19, 1978. B.S., Columbia U., 1966, M.S., 1967, Ph.D., 1971. Nat. Acad. Scis., NRC postdoctoral research asso. Goddard Inst. Space Studies NASA, N.Y.C., 1971-72; fellow advanced study program Nat. Center Atmospheric Research, Boulder, Colo., 1972-73, scientist, dep. head climate project, 1973-78, acting leader climate sensitivity group, 1978-80, head visitors program and dep. dir. advanced study program, 1980—; affiliate prof. U. Corp. Atmospheric Research Lamont-Doherty Geol. Obs., Columbia U.; mem. Carter-Mondale Sci. Policy Task Force, 1976; mem. internat. sci. coms. climatic change, energy, food and pub. policy; expert witness congl. coms. Author: (with Lynne E. Mesirow) The Genesis Strategy: Climate and Global Survival, 1976, (with Lynne Morton) The Primordial Bond: Exploring Connections between Man and Nature through Humanities and Science, 1981, (with Randi S. Londer) The Coevolution of Climate and Life, 1984; sci. and popular articles on theory of climate, influence of climate on soc., relation of climatic change to world food, population, energy and environ. policy issues.; Editor: Climatic Change, 1976—, (with W. Bach) Interactions of Food and Climate, 1981, (with R.S. Chen and E. Boulding) Social Science Research and Climate Change: An Interdisciplinary Appraisal, 1983. Current Work: Climatic modeling of paleoclimates and of human impacts on climate; e.g., carbon dioxide increases or aerosols generated by nuclear war. Also popular science writing. Subspecialties: Climatology; Environmental policy. Office: Nat Center Atmospheric Research Box 3000 Boulder CO 80307

SCHNEIDERMAN, HOWARD ALLEN, educator, zoologist; b. N.Y.C., Feb. 9, 1927; s. Louis and Anna (Center) S.; m. Audrey MacLeod, Sept. 16, 1951; children—Anne Mercedes, John Howard. A.B., Swarthmore Coll., 1948; M.A. in Zoology, Harvard U., 1949; Ph.D. in Physiology, Harvard U., 1952; D.Sc. (hon.), La Salle Coll., 1975, Swarthmore Coll., 1982. AEC predoctoral fellow Harvard U., 1949-52, Univ. research fellow, 1952-53; asst. prof. zoology, then asso. prof. Cornell U., 1953-61; prof. biology, chmn. dept. Case Western Reserve U., Cleve., 1961-66, Jared Potter Kirtland Disting. prof. biology, 1966-69, co-dir. devel. biology center, 1961-69; prof. biol. sci., dean sch., dir. Center Pathobiology, U. Calif., Irvine, 1969-79, chmn. dept. developmental and cell biology, 1969-75; sr. v.p. research and devel., Monsanto Co., St. Louis, 1979—, mem. exec. mgmt. com., 1983—; cons. Gen. Med. Sci. Inst., Nat. Inst. Child Health and Devel., NIH, 1961-79; instr. invertebrate zoology Marine Biol. Lab., Woods Hole, Mass., 1956-58, trustee, mem. exec. com., 1966-72; spl. research devel., genetics, insect hormones, and insect physiology. Editorial bd.: Results and Problems of Cell Differentiation; contbr. over 200 articles to profl. jours. Adv. commr. Marshall Scholarship Commn., 1973-77, chmn., 1976-77; trustee Mo. Bot. Garden, 1981—. Served with USNR, 1945-46. NSF sr. fellow Cambridge (Eng.) U., 1959-60. Fellow AAAS, N.Y. Acad. Scis.; mem. Nat. Acad. Sci. (assembly life scis. 1975—), Am. Acad. Arts and Scis., Soc. Exptl. Biology (Eng.), Am. Soc. Zoologists, Entomol. Soc. Am., Lepidopterist Soc., Corp. Marine Biol. Lab., Am. Soc. Naturalists, Soc. Developmental Biology (pres. 1965-66), Internat. Soc. Developmental Biology (dir. 1981—), Genetics Soc. Am., AAUP, Am. Inst. Biol. Scis., Soc. Chem. Industry, Am. Soc. Cell Biology, Japanese Soc. Developmental Biology, Phi Beta Kappa, Sigma Xi. . Address: Dept Research and Devel Monsanto Co 800 N Linderberg Blvd Saint Louis MO 63166

SCHNIEDERJANS, MARC JAMES, management science educator; b. Pocahontas, Ark., Oct. 8, 1950; s. Oliver H. and Florence (Schutte) S.; m. Jill Marlene Schniederjans, Aug. 13, 1971; children—Alexander J., Ashlyn M. B.S., U. Mo., 1972; M.B.A., St. Louis U., 1974, Ph.D., 1978. Program dir. St. Louis U., 1975-78; lectr. U. Mo.-St. Louis, 1976-78, asst. prof. mgmt. sci., 1979-80; asst. prof. decision scis. U. Nebr.-Omaha, 1978-79; asst. prof. mgmt. U. Nebr.-Lincoln, 1981-85, assoc. prof., 1985—; asst. prof. U. Hawaii, Hilo, 1980-81; cons. Blue Hills Homes Corp., St. Louis, 1979, Ralston Purina Corp., St. Louis, 1980, Union Diversified Industries, Lincoln, 1983-84. Author: (with N.K. Kwak) Managerial Applications of Operations Research, 1982; (with N.K. Kwak) Operations Research Applications in Health Care Planning, 1984; Linear Goal Programming, 1984; Introduction to Mathematical Programming, 1985; Case Studies in Decision Support, 1986; contbr. articles to profl. jours. Mem. Am. Inst. Decision Scis., Inst. Mgmt. Scis., Ops. Research Soc. Am., Am. Prodn. and Inventory Soc. Current Work: Developing and applying operations research techniques in micro and macro computer information systems to aid in medical legal and business decision making. Subspecialties: Operations research (mathematics); Information systems, storage, and retrieval (computer science). Home: 5220 S 66th Circle Lincoln NE 68516 Office: Dept of Management University of Nebraska Lincoln NE 68588

SCHNITZER, HOWARD JOEL, physicist, educator; b. Newark, Nov. 12, 1934; s. Albert and Helen (Ehrlich) S.; m. Phoebe Kazdin, May 22, 1966; children: Mark Jacob, Elizabeth Karen. B.S. in Mech. Engring., Newark Coll. Engring., 1955; Ph.D. in Physics, U. Rochester, 1960. Postdoctoral research asso. U. Rochester, 1960-61; mem. faculty Brandeis U., Waltham, Mass., 1961—, prof. physics, 1968—, dept. chmn., 1981-83; vis. prof. Rockefeller U., 1969-70; hon. research asso. Harvard U., 1974, 1976—. Asso. editor: Phys. Rev. Letters, 1978-80. Sloan fellow, 1965-67; Guggenheim fellow, 1983-84. Fellow Am. Phys. Soc.; mem. Sigma Xi. Subspecialties: Particle physics; Theoretical physics. Home: 397 Highland St Newtonville MA 02160 Office: Dept Physics Brandeis Univ Waltham MA 02254

SCHOBER, ROBERT CHARLES, electrical engineer; b. Phila., Sept. 20, 1940; s. Rudolph Ernst and Kathryn Elizabeth (Ehrisman) S.; m. Mary Eve Kanuika, Jan. 14, 1961; children: Robert Charles, Stephen Scott, Susan Marya. B.S. in Engring. (Scott Award scholar), Widner U., 1965; postgrad., Bklyn. Poly. Extension at Gen. Electric Co., Valley Forge, Pa., 1965-67, U. Colo., 1968-69, Calif. State U.-Long Beach, 1969-75, U. So. Calif., 1983-84. Engr. Gen. Electric Co., Valley Forge, 1965-68, Martin Marietta Corp., Denver, 1968-69; sr. engr. Jet Propulsion Lab., Pasadena, Calif., 1969-73; mem. tech. staff Hughes Semiconductor Co., Newport Beach, Calif., 1973-75; prin. engr. Am. Hosp. Supply Corp., Irvine, Calif., 1975-83; sr. staff engr. TRW Systems, Redondo Beach, Calif., 1983-84; cons. Biomed. LSI, Huntington Beach, Calif. Mem. IEEE (student br. pres. 1963-65), Assn. for computing Machinery, Tau Bea Pi. Republican. Patentee cardiac pacemakers. Current Work: Develop large scale integrated circuits which employ and advance the leading edge of technology for biomedical applications including cardiac pacemakers and monitors, implantable and external hearing devices and electronic visual devices; also develop very high speed analog to digital converters and logic in the Gigaherz region. Subspecialties: Integrated circuits; Cardiology. Home: 9411 Tiki Circle Huntington Beach CA 92646 Office: Biomed LSI 22311 Brookhurst St Huntington Beach CA 92646

SCHOCH, ROBERT MILTON, science educator, researcher, consultant; b. Washington, Mar. 30, 1957; s. Milton Ralph and Cornelia Alicia (Goetz) S.; m. Cynthia Benfield Pettit, June 11, 1983; 1 child, Nicholas Robert. B.A. in Anthropology, George Washington U., 1979, B.S. in Geology, 1979; M.S., Yale U., 1981, Ph.D., 1983. Curatorial asst. Peabody Mus., New Haven, 1982-83, research asst., 1983-84; asst. prof. div. sci., coll. basic studies Boston U., 1984—, asst. prof. dept. geology, 1985—; research assoc. Schiele Mus. Natural History, Gastonia, N.C., 1984—; curatorial affiliate Peabody Mus. Natural History, New Haven, 1985—; fossil collecting expdns. to many countries, 1979-84. Author, editor Vertebrate Paleontology, 1984; contbr. articles to profl. jours. Grantee NSF, 1979—. Mem. Paleontol. Soc., Soc. Vertebrate Paleontology, Geol. Soc. Am., Sigma Xi. Current work: Phylogeny reconstruction, especially as related to fossil organisms; evolution of the vertebrates; evolutionary theory. Subspecialties: Paleontology; Evolutionary biology. Office: Div Sci Coll Basic Studies Boston U Boston MA 02215

SCHOELLHORN, ROBERT A., See *Who's Who in America,* 43rd edition.

SCHOEN, GEORGE JANSSEN, mechanical engineer; b. Danbury, Conn., May 7, 1938; s. Ernest George and Alma Lydia (Janssen) S.; m. Barbara Jean Smalley, Sept. 9, 1962; children: Susan E., Cindy-Anne. B.S.M.E., Worcester Poly. Inst., 1960. Application engr. Barden Corp., Danbury, Conn., 1961-74, supr. product engring., 1974-76, supr. product design, 1976-82; adminstr. Barden Corp. (Product Devel. Lab.), 1982—. Served as 1st lt. Signal Corps U.S. Army, 1960-68. Mem. ASME, Sigma Xi. Lutheran. Current Work: Design, use and testing of high precision ball bearings, principally for aerospace and machine tool use. Subspecialty: Mechanical engineering.

SCHOEN, MAX HOWARD, dentist, educator; b. N.Y.C., Feb. 4, 1922; s. Adolph and Ella (Grossman) S.; m. Beatrice Mildred Hoch, Feb. 5, 1950; children: Steven Charles, Karen Ruth. B.S., U. So. Calif., 1943, D.D.S., 1943; M.P.H., UCLA, 1962; D.P.H., U. Calif., Los Angeles, 1969. Diplomate: Am. Bd. Dental Pub. Health. Practice dentistry, Los Angeles, 1947-54, founding partner group dental practice, So. Los Angeles, 1954—; vis. prof. Sch. Dental Medicine, U. Conn., 1972; prof., dean pro-tem, asso. dean Sch. Dental Medicine, State U. N.Y., Stony Brook, 1973-76; prof. preventive dentistry and pub. health U. Calif. Sch. Dentistry, Los Angeles, 1976—, sect. chmn., 1976-82; mem. Com. for Nat. Health Ins.; chmn. dental adv. bd. Headstart, Los Angeles, 1966; cons. in field. Author papers in field. Served to capt. Dental Corps U.S. Army, 1943-46. Fellow Am. Pub. Health Assn.; mem. Inst. Medicine, Am. Dental Assn., Am. Assn. Pub. Health Dentists, Fedn. Dentaire Internat., Am. Assn. Dental Schs., Group Health Assn. Am. Subspecialty: Public health. Home: 5818 Sherbourne Dr Los Angeles CA 90056 Office: Sch Dentistry Univ Calif Los Angeles CA 90024

SCHOENBACH, KARL HEINZ, physicist, electrical engineering educator; b. Peterswald, Germany, Sept. 30, 1941, came to U.S., 1980, m. Gisela Maria Mueller, 1968; children—Stefanie Anja, Sabine Monika. Diploma in Physics, Tech. Hochschule, Darmstadt, Fed. Republic Germany, 1966, Dr. rer. nat., 1970. Research asst. Technische Hochschule, Darmstadt, 1967-72, dozent (asst. prof.), 1972-78; vis. asst. prof. Tex. Tech. U., Lubbock, 1979, asst. prof. elec. engring., 1980-82, assoc. prof., 85; prof. elec. engring. Old Dominion U., Norfolk, Va., 1985—. Contbr. articles to profl. jours. Mem. German Physics Soc., IEEE (sr.), Sigma Xi, Eta Kappa Nu. Current work: Pulsed power physics; opening switches for inductive energy storage; external control of diffuse gas discharges. Subspecialties: Plasma engineering; Electrical engineering. Office: Old Dominion U Dept Elec Engring Norfolk VA 23508

SCHOENING, WILLIAM EDWARD, photographic astronomy researcher; b. St. Louis, Oct. 29, 1941; s. William F. and Catharine S. B.S., Central Meth. Coll., 1964; teaching cert., Central Mo. State Coll., 1965. Tchr. Maplewood (Mo.) Sch. System, 1966-67; photographic researcher Kitt Peak Nat. Obs., 1967—; head Photographic Research Lab., 1967—, sr. research assoc., 1970—. Contbr. articles to sci. jours. Mem. Am. Astron. Soc. (chmn. photo working group 1984—), Ariz. Paper and Photographic Conservation Group. Republican. Methodist. Current Work: Photographic Astronomical photography; emulsion hypersensitizing to reduce exposure times at the telescopes; direct image work with solid state detectors. Subspecialty: Optical astronomy. Home: 542 N Country Club Dr Tucson AZ 85716 Office: 950 N Cherry St Tucson AZ 85726

SCHOKNECHT, JEAN DONZE, mycologist, electron microscopist, educator, researcher; b. Urbana, Ill., Oct. 31, 1943; d. Joseph M. and Genevieve S. (Stanis) Donze. B.S. (Mathew Arnold scholar), U. Ill., 1965, M.S., 1967, Ph.D., 1972. Teaching and research asst. U. Ill., Champaign, Urbana, 1965-71, research assoc., 1972-74; asst. prof. microbiology Ind. State U., Terre Haute, 1974-78, assoc. prof., 1978—; mem. adj. faculty Ind. U. Med. Sch., 1974-78; assoc. mycologist sect. botany and plant pathology Ill. Natural History Survey, Champaign, 1982—; cons. to Western Paper & Mfg. Co.; cons. on fungi in foods Dept. Agr. Contbr. articles to sci. jours. Bd. dirs. Wabash Valley Audubon Soc., 1982-83. NSF grantee, 1980. Mem. Mycol. Soc. Am., Med. Mycol. Soc. Ams., Electroc Microscope Soc. Am., Am. Micros. Soc., Bot. Soc. Am., Brit. Mycol. Soc., Brit. Lichen Soc., Sigma Xi. Club: University (Terre

Haute). Current Work: Ultrastructure, mineral accumulation, utilization, etc. by cells; teaching and research in cell biology, microbiology. Subspecialties: Microbiology; Microscopy. Home: 119 Jackson Blvd Terre Haute IN 47803 Office: Life Scis Dept Ind State U Terre Haute IN 47809

SCHOLL, FREDERICK WILLIAM, electrical engineer; b. Washington, Aug. 22, 1946; s. Herman Frederick and Phoebe (Kent) S.; m. Judith Lois Teitelbaum, May 23, 1978. B.E.E., Cornell U., 1969, Ph.D., 1974. Scientist, Rockwell Internat., Thousand Oaks, Calif., 1974-77, Optical Info. Systems, Elmsford, N.Y., 1977-79; lectr. Columbia U., N.Y.C., 1979-80; adj. assoc. prof. Poly. Inst. N.Y., N.Y.C., 1980—; sr. v.p. Codenoll Tech. Corp., Yonkers, N.Y., 1980—, also dir. Patentee Cleaving laser wafers, device package, light emitting device. Contbr. articles to profl. jours. Mem. IEEE, Tau Beta Pi. Subspecialties: Semiconductors; Fiber optics. Office: Codenoll Tech Corp 1086 N Broadway Yonkers NY 10701

SCHOLZ, LAWRENCE CHARLES, engineer; b. N.Y.C., Aug. 8, 1933; s. Lawrence Henry Scholz and Helen Irene (Westerveldt) Scholz Brodhead; m. Claire Seidner, July 28, 1954; children—Richard L., Karen L. B.E.E., CCNY, 1954, postgrad., 1956-59; postgrad. Ill. Inst. Tech., 1960-64. Design engr. Electron Tube Div. RCA, Harrison, N.J., 1954-60; research physicist Ill. Inst. Tech. Research Inst., Chgo., 1960-64; group leader Vitro Corp., West Orange, N.J., 1964-69; dir. systems analysis ManTech, Livingstone, N.J., 1969-70; engring. mgr. RCA Astro Electronics, Princeton, N.J., 1970-84, div. fellow, 1984—. Editor/Author: Electron Tube Design Handbook, 1961. Contbr. articles to profl. jours. Active Essex council Boy Scouts Am., 1965-75. Recipient Dist. Merit award Boy Scouts Am., 1972. Mem. IEEE, AAAS. Current work: Spacecraft design; systems engineering of satellite systems, especially data management, use of computers in space, automated systems and autonomy or fault tolerance. Subspecialties: Systems engineering; Aerospace engineering and technology. Home: 28 Old Salem Rd West Orange NJ 07052 Office: RCA Astro Electronics Box 800 Princeton NJ 08540

SCHONEWALD-COX, CHRISTINE MICHELINE, research scientist; book series editor; b. Paris, France, May 29, 1950, came to U.S., 1955, naturalized, 1961; d. Hans Emil and Jacqueline (Nuyttens) S.; m. Robert George Cox, Dec., 1979; 1 child, Dominique Nichole. B.A., U. Calif-Davis, 1972; M.S., U. Md., 1974, Ph.D. in Zoology, 1977. Asst. prof. George Mason U., Fairfax, Va., 1977-78; biologist Nat. Park Service, Washington, 1978-83; research scientist, unit coordinator Nat. Park Service, U. Calif.-Davis, 1983—; ecology grad. group faculty U. Calif.-Davis, 1984—; book series editor 1981—; cons. Nat. Acad. Scis. Editor: Genetics and Conservation, 1983. Contbr. articles to profl. jours. Mem. Am. Land Resources Assn. (cons. 1984), Evolution Soc., Calif. Acad. of Scis., Wildlife Soc., Am. Soc. Mammalogists, Am. Land Forum, George Wright Soc. Current work: Conservation biology, socioecology, evolutionary biology and biological and sociological activities occuring across protected habitat boundaries. Subspecialties: Conservation biology; Evolutionary biology. Office: Nat Park Service Wickson Hall Univ Calif Davis CA 95616

SCHOOLEY, DAVID ALLAN, biochemist; b. Denver, Apr. 17, 1943; s. Elmer W. and Gertrude L (Rogers) S.; m. Mary Eleanor Dobbins, Feb. 3, 1968; children—Christine M., Stephen T., Anna K. B.S., N.Mex. Highlands U., 1963; Ph.D., Stanford U., 1968. Fellow U. Fla., Gainesville, 1968-69, Columbia U., N.Y.C., 1969-71; sr. biochemist Zoecon Corp., Palo Alto, Calif., 1971-74, dir. biochemistry, 1974—. Author and co-author book chpts. Contbr. articles to profl. jours. Asst. scoutmaster Boy Scouts Am., Palo Alto, Calif., 1984—. NSF grantee 1974—; N.Mex. Highlands U. scholar, 1962-63; fellow NSF, 1963-67, NIH, 1969-70. Mem. AAAS, Royal Soc. Chemistry, Am. Chem. Soc. (biol. and geochem. divs.). Democrat. Current work: Isolation and identification of insect hormones (peptidic and non-peptidic), hormone metabolism and titers, environmental chemistry. Subspecialties: Biochemistry (biology); Neurochemistry. Home: 3024 Greer Rd Palo Alto CA 94303 Office: Zoecon Corp PO Box 10975 Palo Alto CA 94303

SCHOOLEY, JAMES FREDERICK, physicist; b. Auburn, Ind., Aug. 24, 1931; s. Robert True and Elizabeth (Bierly) S.; m. Mary Alice Hevron, Aug. 1, 1953; children—James Frederick, Therese, Robert, Michael, Mary E., Margaret, Kathleen. A.B. in chemistry, Ind. U., 1953; M.S., U. Calif.-Berkeley, 1955, Ph.D., 1961. Postdoctoral physicist Nat. Bur. Standards, Washington, 1960-62, chief temperature sect., 1974-82, staff physicist, 1962-74, 82—. Contbr. articles to profl. jours. Served to 1st lt. USAF, 1953-57. Recipient Gold medal Dept. Commerce, 1979. Mem. Am. Phys. Soc., Instrument Soc. Am., Sigma Xi. Current work: Research in thermometry. Subspecialty: Low temperature physics. Home: 13700 Darnestown Rd Gaithersburg MD 20878 Office: B128 Physics Bldg Nat Bur Standards Gaithersburg MD 20899

SCHOOLEY, ROBERT TURNER, virology educator, immunologist; b. Washington, Nov. 10, 1949; s. Robert Enoch and Lelia Frances (Barnhill) S.; m. Pamela O. Cook, Mar. 25, 1974; children—Kimberley, Elizabeth. B.S., Washington and Lee U., 1970; M.D., Johns Hopkins U., 1974. Diplomate Am. Bd. Internal Medicine. Resident Johns Hopkins Hosp., Balt., 1974-76; postdoctoral fellow NIH, Bethesda, Md., 1976-79, Mass. Gen. Hosp., Boston, 1979-81; asst. prof. medicine Harvard U. Med. Sch., Boston, 1983—; cons. Millipore Corp., Bedford, Mass., 1983—. Author: Key References in Infectious Diseases, 1982. Contbr. articles to sci. jours. Served with USPHS, 1976-79. Mem. ACP, Am. Assn. Immunologists, AAAS. Congregationalist. Current work: Virology, immunology. Subspecialties: Infectious diseases; Virology (biology). Home: 58 Hobart St Hingham MA 02043 Office: Infectious Disease Unit Mass Gen Hosp Boston MA 02114

SCHOONOVER, MICHAEL WAYNE, research chemist; b. Albion, N.Y., Jan. 24, 1951; s. Theodore Cole and Frances Lillian (Pickett) S.; m. Joy Yukiko Shimabukuro, May 8, 1976. B.S. in Chemistry, U. Rochester, 1973; Ph.D. in Chemistry, 1978; postgrad. Purdue U., 1973-74. Research chemist UOP, Inc., Des Plaines, Ill., 1978-81; group leader Signal UOP Research Ctr., 1981—. Patentee alumina particles mfg. method. Mem. Am. Chem. Soc., Chgo. Catalysis Club (sec.-treas. 1981-82). Current work: Heterogeneous catalyst systems, synthesis and characterization of amorphous and crystalline inorganic oxides. Subspecialties: Catalysis chemistry; Inorganic chemistry. Office: Signal U Research Ctr 50 E Algonquin Rd Box 5016 Des Plaines IL 60017

SCHOWALTER, TIMOTHY DUANE, entomology educator; b. Newton, Kans., Aug. 14, 1952; s. Duane Eugene and Marjorie E. (Fast) S.; m. Catherine Ann Senter, Aug. 4, 1979; children—Shannon Marlene, Corin Michelle. B.A. in Biology and Anthropology, Wichita State U., 1974; M.S. in Biology, N.Mex. State U., 1976; Ph.D. in entomology, U. Ga., 1979. Postdoctoral fellow Tex. A&M U., 1979-81; asst. prof. entomology Oreg. State U., Corvallis, 1981—. Contbr. articles to profl. jours., chpts. to books. Grantee NSF, 1983, Weyerhaeuser Co., 1984. Mem. Nat. Wildlife Fedn., Entomol. Soc. Am. Ecol. Soc. Am., Entomol. Soc. Can. Sigma Xi. Club: Sierra. Current work: Forest entomology; insect plant interactions; insect dispersal, responses to disturbance; herbivore effects on ecosystem nutrient cycling, succession; ecosystem theory. Subspecialties: Population biology; Ecosystems analysis. Office: Dept Entomology Oregon State Univ Corvallis OR 97331

SCHOWALTER, WILLIAM RAYMOND, chemical engineering educator; b. Milw., Dec. 15, 1929; s. Raymond Philip and Martha (Kowalke) S.; m. Jane Ruth Gregg, Aug. 22, 1953; children: Katherine Ruth, Mary Patricia, David Gregg. B.S., U. Wis., 1951; postgrad., Inst. Paper Chemistry, 1951-52; M.S., U. Ill., 1953, Ph.D., 1957. Asst. prof. dept. chem. engring. Princeton U., 1957-63, asso. prof., 1963-66, prof., 1966—, acting chmn. dept. chem. engring., 1971, chmn. dept. chem. engring., 1978—, asso. dean Sch. Engring. and Applied Sci., 1972-77; Sherman Fairchild Disting. scholar Calif. Inst. Tech., 1977-78; vis. fellow U. Salford, Eng., 1974; vis. sr. fellow Sci. Research Council, U. Cambridge, Eng., 1970; cons. to chem. and petroleum cos.; mem. editorial adv. bd. McGraw-Hill Pub. Co., 1964—; co-chmn. Internat. Seminar for Heat and Mass Transfer, 1970; mem. vis. com. for chem. engring. MIT, 1979—, Lehigh U., 1980—, Cornell U., 1983—; mem. evaluation panel Ctr. Chem. Engring., Nat. Bur. Standards, 1982—; mem. commn. engring. and tech. systems NRC, 1983—. Author: Mechanics of Non-Newtonian Fluids, 1978; mem. editorial com.: Ann. Rev. Fluid Mechanics, 1974-80; editorial bd.: Internat. Jour. Chem. Engring., 1974—, Indsl. and Engring. Chemistry Fundamentals, 1975-78, Jour. Non-Newtonian Fluid Mechanics, 1976—, Am. Inst. Chem. Engrs. Jour, 1979-83; Contbr. articles to profl. jours. Served with AUS, 1953-55. Recipient Lectureship award Chem. Engring. div. Am. Soc. Engring. Edn., 1971, Disting. Service citation Coll. Engring., U. Wis.-Madison, 1983; Reilly lectr. in chem. engring. U. Notre Dame, 1985. Mem. Am. Inst. Chem. Engrs. (William H. Walker award 1982), Nat. Acad. Engring., Am. Chem. Soc., Soc. Rheology (exec. com. 1977-79, v.p. 1981-83, pres. 1983—), Sigma Xi, Tau Beta Pi, Phi Lambda Upsilon, Phi Eta Sigma. Subspecialties: Chemical engineering; Industrial engineering. Home: 106 Crestview Dr Princeton NJ 08540

SCHRADER, EDWARD LEON, geologist; b. Vicksburg, Miss., June 19, 1951; s. Edward and Dorothy (Chaney) S.; m. Myra Lee Ladner, June 2, 1973; children: Melanie Denise, Edward Austin. B.S., Millsaps Coll., 1973; M.S., U. Tenn., 1975; Ph.D., Duke U., 1977. Exploration geologist Chevron Minerals, Denver, 1975-76; geochemist Deep Sea Drilling Project, LaJolla, Calif., 1977, 79; project geologist Chevron Resources, Inc., Denver, 1977-78; asst. prof. econ. geology U. Ala., Tuscaloosa, 1978-80; adj. prof., 1980-82; chief geologist J.M. HuberCorp., Macon, Ga., 1981—; vis. lectr. Duke U., spring 1983; Co-chmn. UN sponsored conf., Athens, Greece, 1980. Editor, author: Geology of the Southeastern Clay Belt, 1983. Pres. Baptist Men's Orgn., Ingleside Baptist Ch., Macon, 1982-83; bd. visitors Duke U., 1982-83; mem. program adv. com. U. Ala., Tuscaloosa, 1979-80. HEW grantee, 1975; U.S. Dept. Interior grantee, 1978-80. Mem. Geol. Soc. Am., AIME (co-chmn. Ga. subsect. 1982), Clay Minerals Soc., Soc. Econ. Geologists, Internat. Assn. on the Genesis of Ore Deposits, Phi Beta Kappa, Sigma Xi. Democrat. Current Work: Geochemical and mineralogical analyses of modern and ancient ore forming environments; applications for exploration, also seafloor hotspring chemistry. Subspecialties: Geochemistry; Ore deposit origins, distributions. Home: 390 Lokchapee Dr Macon GA 31210 Office: J M Huber Corp Route 4 Huber Macon GA 31298

SCHRADER, KEITH WILLIAM, mathematics educator, electrical engineer; b. Neligh, Nebr., Apr. 22, 1938; s. william Charles and Gail (Hughes) S.; m. Carol Jeanne Taylor, Dec. 26, 1960 (div. Dec. 1984); children—Jeffrey William, Melinda Sue. B.S., U. Nebr., 1959, M.S., 1961, Ph.D., 1966; postgrad., Stanford U., 1961-63. Engr. Ampex Corp., Red wood City, Calif., 1961, Sylvania Electronic Defense Lab., Mountain View, Calif., 1962-63; asst. prof. dept. math. U. Mo., Columbia, 1966-69, assoc., prof., 1969-78, prof., 1978—, chmn. 1979-82. Contbr. articles to profl. jours. Mem. Columbia Planning and Zoning Commn., 1982—, Columbia Environ. and Energy Commn., 1983-84. Mem. Am. Math. Soc., Math. Assn. Am., Soc. Indsl. and Applied Math., Sigma Xi, Pi Mu Epsilon, Eta Kappa Nu, Sigma Tau, Sigma Phi Epsilon. Libertarian. Current work: Science, mathematics, analysis, ordinary differential equations, boundary value problems. Subspecialties: Analysis; Applied mathematics. Home: 403 Price Ave Columbia MO 65201 Office: Dept Math Univ Mo Columbia MO 65211

SCHRAMM, DAVID NORMAN, astrophysicist, educator; b. St. Louis, Oct. 25, 1945; s. Marvin and Betty (Math) S.; m. Melinda Holzhauer, 1963 (div. 1979); children: Cary, Brett.; m. Colleen Rae, 1980. S.B. in Physics, MIT, 1967; Ph.D. in Physics, Calif. Inst. Tech., 1971. Research fellow in physics Calif. Inst. Tech., Pasadena, 1971-72; asst. prof. astronomy and physics U. Tex., Austin, 1972-74; assoc. prof. astronomy, astrophysics and physics Enrico Fermi Inst. and the Coll., U. Chgo., 1974-77, prof., 1977—, Louis Block prof. phys. scis., 1982—, acting chmn. dept. astronomy and astrophysics, 1977, chmn., 1978—; resident cosmotologist Fermilab, 1982—; cons., lectr. Adler Planetarium; organizer numerous sci. confs.; frequent lectr. in field. Contbr. numerous articles to profl. jours.; co-editor: Explosive Nucleosynthesis, 1973; editor: Supernovae, 1977; assoc. editor: Am. Jour. Physics, 1978—; co-editor: Phys. Cosmology, 1980, Fundamental Problems in Stellar Evolution, 1980, Essays in Nucleosynthesis, 1981; editor: U. Chgo. series Theoretical Astrophysics; Physics Reports, 1981—; editorial bd.: Ann. Revs. Nuclear and Particle Sci., 1976-80; columnist: Outside mag.; co-author: Advanced States of Stellar Evolution, 1977. Nat. Graeco-Roman wrestling champion, 1971; recipient Robert J. Trumpler award Astron. Soc. Pacific, 1974, Gravity Research Found. awards, 1974, 75, 76, 80. Fellow Am. Phys. Soc.; mem. Am. Astron. Soc. (Helen B. Warner prize 1978, exec. com. planetary sci. div. 1977-79, sec.-treas. high energy astrophysics div. 1979-81), Am. Assn. Physics Tchrs. (Richtmeyer prize 1984), Astron. Soc. Pacific, Meteoritical Soc., Internat. Astron. Union, Am. Alpine Club, Austrian Alpine Club, Sigma Xi. Club: Quadrangle. Current Work: The interface of high energy particle physics, nuclear physics and astrophysics. Subspecialties: Cosmology; Theoretical astrophysics. Office: Astronomy and Astrophysics Center Univ Chicago 5640 S Ellis Ave Chicago IL 60637

SCHRAMM, FREDERIC BERNARD, patent lawyer, electrical engineer; b. Cleve., June 3, 1903; s. A. Bernard and Flora Frederica (Leutz) S. B.E.E., Case Inst. Tech., 1925; J.D., George Washington U., 1931; LL.M., Western Res. U., 1955. Registered profl. engr.; registered patent atty. Elec. engr. Gen. Electric Co., Schenectady, N.Y., 1925-31, patent atty., 1931-42; ptnr. Richey & Watts, Cleve., 1942-54, Kendrick, Schramm & Stolzy, Los Angeles, 1954-60, Schramm, Kramer & Sturges, Cleve., 1960-72, Schramm & Knowles, Cleve., 1972—; instr. Fenn Coll., Cleve., 1973-74, Cleve. State U., 1974-75. Author: Handbook on Patent Disputes, 1974; contbr. chpt. to Nurturing New Ideas, articles to Ency. of Patent Practice. Mem. adv. council U.S. Patent Office, Washington, 1954-56; chmn. Lake Erie Council, Am. Youth Hostels, Inc., 1976. Mem. Cleve. Patent Law Assn. (sec. 1960-61), Am. Intellectual Property Assn., IEEE (sr.), Sigma Xi, Tau Beta Pi, Eta Kappa Nu. Club: Torch. Lodge: Kiwanis (chmn. internat. affairs 1982-84). Current work: Development and protection of inventions in the fields of electrical and magnetic measurement. Subspecialties: Electrical engineering; Electronics. Office: 3570 Warrensville Center Rd Cleveland OH 44122

SCHRECK, DAVID MICHAEL, internist, biomedical engineering consultant; b. Paterson, N.J., Jan. 7, 1954; s. Jack Donald and Lenore (Della Rocca) S.; m. Peggy Thielen, Apr. 12, 1980; children—Lauren Nicole, Andrew Joseph. B.S. in Chemistry, Stevens Inst. Tech., 1975, M.S. in Biomed. Engring./Sci., 1975; M.D., Loyola U., Chgo., 1980. Diplomate Am. Bd. Internal Medicine, Nat. Bd. Med. Examiners. Polymer chemist Tenneco Chem. Co., Piscataway, N.J., 1975-76; biomed. engr. C.R. Bard, Inc., Murray Hill, N.J., 1976-77; resident in internal and emergency medicine, Overlook Hosp., Summit, N.J., 1980-84; attending faculty Columbia U. Affiliated Hosp., resident in emergency medicine, 1985; attending physician Holy Name Hosp., Teaneck, N.J., 1985; cons. Biosearch, Inc., 1982-83; cons. Memory Metals, Inc., Stamford, Conn., 1983—; pres. Poly. Med. Assocs., Inc., Summit, 1983—. Patentee method of percutaneous catheterization. Grantee drug design research Merck, Sharp & Dohme Co., 1981. Mem. ACP, Am. Coll. Emergency Physicians, Am. Chem. Soc., AMA, Univ. Assn. for Emergency Medicine. Jewish. Current work: Emergency and critical care medicine; catheter design; medical software/systems development; biopotential signal processing; medical management; drug design. Subspecialties: Internal medicine; Biomedical engineering. Home: 80 Division Ave Summit NJ 07901 Office: Poly Med Assocs 80 Division Ave Summit NJ 07901

SCHREIBER, B. CHARLOTTE, geologist, geology educator; b. N.Y.C., June 27, 1931; d. Herman and Regina (Lukin) Warembat; m. Edward Schreiber; children—Christie Ruth, Sue Anne. A.B., Washington U., St. Louis, 1953; M.S., Rutgers U., 1966; Ph.D., Rensselaer Poly. Inst., 1974. Instr. Columbia U., N.Y.C., 1968, instr. dept. geology, 1969-71, sr. research assoc. Lamont Doherty Geol. Obs., 1981—; instr. dept. geology Queens Coll., CUNY, 1968-69, asst. prof., 1974-77, assoc. prof., 1974-77, assoc. prof., 1978-82, prof., 1982—; cons. Johnson Soils Inc., Palisades Park, N.J., 1968-70; adj. prof. Rice U., 1982-84; cons. Shell Oil Co., Houston, 1982-83. Contbr. articles to profl. jours. NSF fellow 1976; N.Y. State Bus. Womans Assn. scholarship 1972. Mem. Geol. Soc. Am., Soc. Econ. Paleontologists and Mineralogists, Paleontol. Research Found., Internat. Assn. Sedimentologists, Can. Soc. Petroleum Geologists, Petroleum Soc. N.Y., Geol. Soc. London, Am. Assn. Petroleum Geologists (Levorsen award 1975, lectr. 1978—), N.Y. Acad. Scis. (vice chmn. 1980-81, chmn. 1981-82), Houston Geol. Soc., AAUP, Sigma Xi. Current work: Research in evaporites and carbonates on areas in Poland and Italy; writing book on evaporites. Subspecialties: Petrology; Sedimentology. Home: Box 568 Palisades NY 10964 Office: Dept Geology Queens Coll Flushing NY 11367

SCHREIBER, HANS, pathologist, educator; b. Quedlinburg, Germany, Feb. 5, 1944; s. Wolfgang Gotthold and Dorothee Margarete (Zimmermann) S.; m. Karin Kugler, Oct. 28, 1969; children: Dorothee, Ute, Maya. M.D., U. Freiburg, W.Ger., 1969, D.M.Sc., 1969; Ph.D., U. Chgo., 1977. Research staff mem. biology div. Oak Ridge Nat. Lab., 1970-73; med. intern Moabit U. Hosp., Berlin, 1973-74; fellow immunology dept. pathology U. Chgo., 1974-77, asst. prof. pathology, 1977-81, assoc. prof., 1982—, mem. com. immunology, 1977—. Contbr. articles to profl. jours. Recipient Goedecke research prize Med. Faculty U. Freiburg, 1969; German Nat. Found. fellow, 1973; Nat. Cancer Inst. fellow, 1974-77; Nat. Cancer Inst. awardee, 1978—. Mem. Am. Assn. Cancer Research, Am. Assn. Pathologists, Am. Soc. Cytology, Am. Assn. Immunologists. Lutheran. Current Work: Cancer immunology, specific regulation of immune responses. Subspecialties: Immunobiology and immunology; Genetics and genetic engineering (biology). Home: 5467 S Dorchester Ave Chicago IL 60615 Office: La Rabida U Chgo Inst E 65th St at Lake Michigan Chicago IL 60649

SCHREIBER, RICHARD KENT, terrestrial ecologist, research administrator; b. Downs, Kans., June 6, 1943; s. Theodor Edward Otto and Mildred Mary (Coop) S.; m. Linda Ann Kortman, June 2, 1964; children—Robin Kay, Jennifer Nicole. B.S., Fort Hays State U., 1965, M.S., 1969; postgrad. U. Md., 1965-66; Ph.D., U. Idaho, 1973. Research assoc. Oak Ridge Nat. Lab, 1973-78; terrestrial ecologist U.S. Fish and Wildlife Service, Ann Arbor, Mich., 1978-81, acting team leader, 1981-82, supervisory ecologist, Kearneysville, W. Va., 1982—, acting team leader, 1982—; lectr., course unit leader U.S. Forest Service, Marana, Ariz., 1980—; tech. rep. U.S./Can. MOI, Toronto and Washington, 1981—. Contbr. articles to profl. jours. VFW scholar, 1961; PTA scholar, 1963-65; NSF research fellow, 1970-71; Norcus fellow Battelle N.W. Lab., 1972-73. Mem. Am. Soc. Mammalogists (life), Ecol. Soc. Am., Am. Fisheries Soc., Sigma Xi, Phi Sigma, Beta Beta Beta. Democrat. Methodist. Lodges: Kiwanis, Elks. Current work: Bionergetics of vertebrates; biological effects of acidic deposition on terrestrial and aquatic ecosystems; mitigation research; research management. Subspecialties: Ecology (biology); Ecology (environmental science). Office: US Fish and Wildlife Service Box 705 Kearneysville WV 25430

SCHREIBER, SIDNEY S., physician, cell biologist, educator; b. N.Y.C., May 1, 1921; s. Abraham Scheer and Etta Lewin; m. Freda Glass, June 10, 1945; children—Hope, John. B.S., CUNY, 1941; M.S., NYU, 1945, M.D., 1949. Diplomate Am. Bd. Internal Medicine. Tchr. physics Townsend Harris Sch., N.Y.C., 1940-42; lectr. physiology Hunter Coll., N.Y.C., 1960-67; instr. medicine NYU Sch. Medicine, N.Y.C., 1967-71, asst. prof., 1971-74, assoc. prof., 1974-78, prof. 1978—, prin. investigator, dir. research NIH research project on cardiac muscle, 1964—. Editor: Protein Synthesis. Contbr. numerous articles to med. jours., chpts. to books. Served with AUS, 1942-45, ETO. Tremaine scholar, 1939-41. Fellow Am. Coll. Nuclear Physicians, ACP; mem. Internat. Soc. Heart Research, Am. Physiol. Soc., Am. Heart Assn. (editorial bd. Circulation Research 1979—), Phi Beta Kappa, Alpha Omega Alpha. Current work: Study of cardiac muscle cell protein metabolism and influence of stresses as hypertension, anoxia and volume loading on the initiation of the hypertrophy response; study of influence of ethanol intake on cardiac muscle cell metabolism with emphasis on protein synthesis and degradation. Subspecialties: Internal medicine; Cell biology (medicine). Office: Dept Nuclear Medicine VA Med Ctr 24th St and 1st Ave New York NY 10010

SCHREINER, STEPHEN PHILIP, research ecologist; b. Roslyn Heights, N.Y., Sept. 3, 1952; s. Robert Louis Schreiner and Mary Elizabeth (Ogden) Sutcliffe. B.A., Windham Coll., 1974; M.S., U. Ga., 1978; Ph.D., Clemson U., 1983. Grad. asst. U. Ga., Athens, 1975-76, Clemson U., S.C., 1976-83; aquatic ecologist U.S. Army C.E., Vicksburg, Miss., 1984—. Author: (user manual) A User's Guide to Chemical Equilibrium Models, 1983; co-author: (lab. manual) Invertebrate Zoology, 1983; also articles. Mem. Societas Internationalis Limnologiae, Am. Soc. Limnology and Oceanography, Sierra Club, Wilderness Soc., Sigma Xi. Current work: Aquatic ecosystem computer modeling, interactions between physical environment and biota, automated data collection of environmental parameters in the field. Subspecialties: Ecosystems analysis; Ecology (environmental science). Home: 232 Greenbrier Dr Vicksburg MS 39180 Office: US Army Engineers-Waterways Experiment Station PO Box 631 Vicksburg MS 39180-0631

SCHRIEFFER, JOHN ROBERT, physicist; b. Oak Park, Ill., May 31, 1931; s. John Henry and Louise (Anderson) S.; m. Anne Grete Thomsen, Dec. 30, 1960; children: Anne Bolette, Paul Karsten, Anne Regina. B.S., Mass. Inst. Tech., 1953; M.S., U. Ill., 1954, Ph.D., 1957, Sc.D., 1974; Sc.D. (hon.), Tech. U., Munich, Germany, 1968, U. Geneva, 1968, U. Pa., 1973, U. Cin., 1977. NSF postdoctoral fellow U. Birmingham, Eng., Niels Bohr Inst., Copenhagen, 1957-58; asst. prof. U. Chgo., 1958-59; asst. prof., then assoc. prof. U. Ill., 1959-62; mem. faculty U. Pa., Phila., 1962-79, Mary Amanda Wood prof. physics, 1964-79; dir. Inst. Theoretical Physics, U. Calif., Santa Barbara, 1979— Andrew D. White prof.-at large Cornell U., 1969-75. Author: Theory of Superconductivity, 1964. Guggenheim fellow Copenhagen, 1967; Recipient Comstock prize Nat. Acad. Sci.; Nobel Prize for Physics, 1972; John Ericsson medal Am. Soc. Swedish Engrs., 1976; Alumni Achievement award U. Ill., 1979; Nat. Medal of Sci., 1985. Mem. Am. Phys. Soc. (Oliver E. Buckley solid state physics prize 1968), Nat. Acad. Sci., Am. Philos. Soc. Subspecialty: Theoretical physics. Office: Dept Physics U Calif Santa Barbara CA 93106

SCHRIENER, ALEXANDER, JR., geothermal explorationist; b. Arcata, Calif., July 9, 1953; s. Alexander and Phyllis Ann (Jones) S.; m. Margie Lou Abbott, May 15, 1976; children—Alexander Philip, Timothy Matthew. B.S., U. Wash., 1976; M.S., Oreg. State U., 1978. Geologist Noranda Exploration, Juneau, 1976; area geologist No. Calif. geothermal div. Union Oil Co. of Calif., Santa Rosa, 1978—. Contbr. articles to profl. jours. Sr. high youth leader Methodist Ch., Santa Rosa, 1980-82. Mem. Geol. Soc. Am., Soc. Econ. Geologists, Am. Assn. Petroleum Geologists, Soc. Profl. Well Log Analysts. Methodist. Subspecialty: Geothermal power. Office: Geothermal Div Union Oil Co PO Box 6854 Santa Rosa CA 95406

SCHRIER, BRUCE KENNETH, research neurobiologist; b. Kalamazoo, Mar. 26, 1938; s. Neil Mulder and Maurine (Niessink) S.; m. Shirley Fisher, Mar. 7, 1964; children: Jennifer, Peter, Katrin, David, Andrew, Timothy, Abigail. B.A., Coll. Wooster, 1960; M.D., Western Res. U., 1964; Ph.D., Tufts U. Med. Sch., 1967. Researcher in pharmacology Upjohn Co., Kalamazoo, summers 1960-63; NIH postdoctoral fellow Tufts U., Boston, 1964-67; commd. sr. surgeon USPHS, 1967; research assoc. Lab. Biochem. Genetics, Nat. Heart Inst., NIH, Bethesda, Md., 1967-70; research scientist, med. officer Lab. Devel. Neurobiology, Nat. Inst. Child Health and Human Devel., 1970—; fellow Pharmacology Research Assoc. Tng. Program, 1967-69; reviewer in molecular neurobiology NSF; sheep breeder; mem. bd. references Balt. Creation Fellowship. Contbr. chpts., numerous articles to profl. publs. Nat. Inst. Gen. Med. Scis. spl. fellow, 1969-70. Mem. AAAS, Am. Soc. Biol. Chemists, Am. Soc. Pharmacology and Exptl. Therapeutics, Md. Sheep Breeders Assn., Md. Hampshire Sheep Assn. Republican. Current Work: Molecular biology with nervous system expressed genes, fuel and sludge production from poultry manure. Subspecialties: Genetics and genetic engineering (biology); Biomass (agriculture). Home: 1100 Winters Church Rd New Windsor MD 21776 Office: NIH Bldg 36 Room 2A21 Bethesda MD 20892

SCHRIER, DENIS J., industrial immunologist; b. Grand Rapids, Mich., Oct. 29, 1955; s. Jacob and Wilma A. (Simons) S.; m. Linda Jean VandenBerg, Sept. 2, 1977; children—Adam, Caitlin. B.A., Calvin Coll., 1977; Ph.D., Med. coll. Wis., 1980. Sr. scientist Warner-Lambert/Parke-Davis, Ann Arbor, Mich., 1982—. Contbr. articles to profl. jours. Parker B. Francis fellow, 1982—. Mem. Am. Assn. Immunology, Am. Assn. Pathologists, Am. Thoracic Soc. Presbyterian. Subspecialty: Immunopharmacology. Home: 5904 Shagbark Dr Ann Arbor MI 48104 Office: Warner-Lambert/Parke-Davis 2800 Plymouth Rd Ann Arbor MI 48105

SCHRIESHEIM, ALAN, research administrator; b. N.Y.C., Mar. 8, 1930; s. Morton and Frances (Greenberg) S.; m. Beatrice D. Brand, June 28, 1953; children—Laura Lynn, Robert Alan. B.S. in Chemistry, Poly. Inst. Bklyn., 1951; Ph.D. in Phys. Organic Chemistry, Pa. State U., 1954. Chemist Nat. Bur. Standards, 1954-56; with Exxon Research & Engring. Co., 1956-83, dir. corp. research 1975-78; gen. mgr. Exxon engring., 1979-83; sr. dep. lab. dir. Argonne Nat. Lab., 1983-84, lab. dir., 1984—; dir. Heinicke Instrument Co.; Karcher lectr. U. Okla., 1977; Hurd lectr. Northwestern U., 1980; co-chmn. bd. on chem. scis. and tech. NRC, mem. com. to define future role of chemistry; bd. dirs. Petroleum Research Fund; vis. com. chemistry dept. MIT; mem. adv. com. mech. engring. and aerospace dept. Princeton U.; mem. Pure and Applied Chemistry Com.; Del. to People's Republic of China, 1978; mem. U.S. nat. com. Internat. Union Pure and Applied Chemistry; mem. adv. com. process research and devel. Nat. Bur. Standards, 1979-83, mem. bd. assessment of programs, 1983-86; mem. magnetic fusion adv. com. Dept. Energy; mem. adv. com. Div. Phys. Scis. U. Chgo.; mem. sci. adv. bd. Petroform; mem. sci. policy bd. Ctr. for Advanced Materials Lawrence Berkeley Lab. Bd. editors: Chem. Tech.; Author. Fellow N.Y. Acad. Scis.; mem. Am. Chem. Soc. (recipient award petroleum chemistry 1969, chmn. petroleum div., councilor), Am. Petroleum Inst. (com. on refinery equipment), Am. Inst. Chem. Engrs., AAAS, Phi Lambda Upsilon. Club: Cosmos (Washington). Patentee in field. Home: 1440 N Lake Shore Dr Apt 31AC Chicago IL 60610 Office: 9700 S Cass Ave Argonne IL 60439

SCHRODER, DIETER KARL, engineering educator; b. Lubeck, Germany, June 18, 1935, came to U.S., 1964, naturalized, 1976; s. Wilhelm Friedrich and Martha Ida (Werner) S.; m. Beverley Claire Parchment, Aug. 4, 1961; children—Mark, Derek. B. Engring., McGill U., Montreal, Can., 1962, M. Engring., 1964; Ph.D., U. Ill., 1968. Sr. engr. Westinghouse Research Labs., Pitts., 1968-73; fellow engr., 1973-76, adv. engr., 1976-79, mgr., 1979-81; prof. Ariz. State U., Tempe, 1981—. Contbr. articles to profl. jours., chpts. to books; patentee in field. Mem. IEEE (sr.), Electrochem. Soc. Current work: Research in semiconductor materials and devices. Subspecialties: Semiconductors; Microelectronics. Home: 1927 E Bendix Dr Tempe AZ 85283 Office: Ariz State U Dept Elec Engring Tempe AZ 85287

SCHROECK, CALVIN WILLIAM, chemist; b. Erie, Pa., Jan. 30, 1945; s. Norbert Vincent and Josephine Mabel (Tetzlaff) S.; m. Camille Rose Tyczkowski, July 4, 1969; children—Julie Ann, Catherine Marie, Theresa Helen, Jennifer Louise. B.A. in Chemistry, Gannon Coll., 1967; Ph.D. in Organic Chemistry, Wayne State U., 1971. Research chemist Lubrizol Corp., Wickliffe, Ohio, 1971-77, group leader, 1977-81, head. synthesis dept., 1981—. Contbr. articles to profl. jours. Patentee in field. Mem. Am. Chem. Soc., AAAS. Roman Catholic. Current work: Lubricant and fuel additives, industrial specialty chemicals laboratory management, research direction, phosphorus and sulfur chemistry. Subspecialty: Organic chemistry. Office: Lubrizol Corp 29400 Lakeland Blvd Wickliffe OH 44092

SCHROEDER, FRIEDHELM, pharmacologist, membrane researcher, educator; b. Kastorf, E. Ger., July 16, 1947; came to U.S., 1957, naturalized, 1965; s. Helmut R. and Irma Eva (Kaiser) S.; m. Ann Kier, Dec. 9, 1978. B.S. in Chemistry (Univ. scholar), U. Pitts., 1970; Ph.D. in Biochemistry (NSF grad. fellow), Mich. State U., 1974. Am. Cancer Soc. postdoctoral fellow Washington U. Sch. Medicine, St. Louis, 1974-76; asst. prof. pharmacology Sch. Medicine, U. Mo., Columbia, 1976-81, assoc. prof., 1982—; cons. hemotropic disease group (vet. microbiology), 1980—; cons. Miles Research Labs., 1976—; mem. adv. council on Huntington's disease U. Minn., 1980—; abstract presenter at nat. and internat. meetings. Assoc. editor Lipids, 1984—. Contbr. numerous articles to profl. jours. Mem. Am. Soc. for Pharmacology and Exptl. Therapeutics, Am. Soc. Biol. Chemists, Soc. for Neurosci., Am. Oil Chemists Soc., Am. Chem. Soc., Am. Heart Assn., Soc. for Aquatic Vet. Medicine, Mus. Assocs., Friends of Music, Nat. Audubon Soc. Clubs: Spaulding Raquetball, Comic Art. Current Work: Cancer, metastasis, membranes, lipids, fluorescence probes, lipoproteins, atherosclerosis, cholesterol asymmetry, toxicology. Subspecialties: Membrane biology; Biophysical chemistry. Home: Route 2 Carter School Rd Columbia MO 65201 Office: Dept Pharmacology U Mo Sch Medicine Columbia MO 65212

SCHROEDER, JAMES ERNEST, research psychologist; b. Independence, Iowa, Apr. 2, 1947; s. Earl Ernest and Lillian Gertrude (Pahl) S.; m. Elaine Kay Thompson, Dec. 16, 1967; children: Andrew Christopher, James William, Destin Ryan. B.S., U. Iowa-Iowa City, 1969; M.A., U. N.Mex.-Albuquerque, 1971, Ph.D., 1973. Cert. psychologist, Tex. Asst. prof. exptl. psychology Lamar U., Beaumont, Tex., 1973-78, assoc. prof., 1978-80; research psychologist Litton, Ft. Benning, Ga., 1980-81, U.S. Army Research Inst., Ft. Benning, 1980-85; sr. research scientist Southwest Research Inst., San Antonio, 1985—; project mgr. U.S. Army Research Inst. (Videodisc Interpersonal Skills Tng. and Assessment project), 1980-84; mgr. U.S. Army Research Inst. (Multipurpose Arcade Combat Simulator project), 1982-85. Bd. dir. Fairway House, Inc., Beaumont, 1979-80. Recipient Regents Merit award for Excellence in Teaching Lamar U., 1975; U.S. Army Research Inst. award for Sustained Superior Performance, 1982. Mem. Am. Psychol. Assn., Southeastern Psychol. Assn., Southwestern Psychol. Assn., Soc. Applied Learning Technology, Human Factors Soc., Sigma Xi, Beta Theata Pi. Current Work: My interests are in mathematical models for learning and motivation, applying high technology products to training, education and simulation. Subspecialties: Learning; Computer-assisted training and simulation. Home: 15546 Clover Ridge San Antonio TX 78248 Office: 6220 Culebra Rd PO Box Drawer 28510 San Antonio TX 78284

SCHROEDER, LELAND ROY, chemist, educator; b. Caledonia, Minn., June 26, 1938; m. J. Kathleen Ewers, Sept. 10, 1960; children: Todd, Michael. A.B. cum laude in Chemistry, Ripon Coll., 1960; M.S., Lawrence U., 1962; Ph.D. in Organic Chemistry, 1965. Faculty George Washington U., Washington, 1965-66; staff U.S. Army Fgn. Sci. and Tech. Ctr., Washington, 1965-67; faculty Inst. Paper Chemistry, Appleton, Wis., 1967—, prof. chemistry, 1977—, assoc. dean, 1980—. Co-editor: Jour. Wood Chemistry and Tech. Served to capt. U.S. Army, 1965-67. Mem. Am. Chem. Soc., Royal Chemistry Soc., TAPPI. Subspecialties: Organic chemistry; Carbohydrate chemistry. Office: 1042 E South River St Appleton WI 54911

SCHROEDER, LEROY WILLIAM, research chemist; b. Watertown, Wis., July 18, 1942; s. Orie William and Edna G. (May) S.; m. Kay C. Marshek, June 10, 1967; 1 child, Heidi. B.A., Wartburg Coll., 1964; Ph.D., Northwestern U., 1969. NSF-NRC postdoctoral fellow Nat. Bur. Standards, Gaithersburg, Md., 1969-71; research scientist ADA Health Found., Gaithersburg, 1971-73, group leader, 1973-76; chemist FDA, Washington, 1977-80, sr. scientist, Rockville, Md., 1980—. Contbr. numerous articles to profl. jours. Recipient commendable service award FDA, 1981. Mem. Am. Chem. Soc., Am. Crystallographic Assn. Current work: Perturbation of cell function by electromagnetic fields, in particular, cell membrane functions. Subspecialties: Biophysical chemistry; Biophysics (biology). Home: 23000 Timber Creek Ln Clarksburg MD 20871 Office: 12709 Twinbrook Pkwy Rockville MD 20857

SCHROEDER, PETER ALLAN, physics educator; b. Dunedin, N.Z., Dec. 6, 1928; came to U.S. 1961; s. Peter and Gladys (Cross) S.; m. Margaret Gwyneth Taylor, Dec. 5, 1953; children—Judith Ann, Christopher Perran. B.Sc., U. Canterbury, N.Z., 1947; M.Sc., 1949; Ph.D., U. Bristol, Eng., 1955. Lectr. U. Canterbury, Christchurch, 1954-59; post doctoral fellow NRC Can., Ottawa, Ont., 1959-60, research officer, 1960-61; asst. prof. physics Mich. State U., East Lansing, 1961-65, assoc. prof., 1965-68, prof., 1969—; vis. prof. U. Sussex, Eng., 1967-68, Victoria U., Wellington, N.Z., 1974-75, U. Nijmegen, Netherlands, 1982-83. Author: (with others) Thermoelectric Power of Metals, 1976; Thermoelectrity in Metallic Conductors, 1977. Contbr. articles to profl. jours. Chmn. Nuclear War Study Group, Mich. State U., 1981—, chmn. 1984—. Fellow Am. Phys. Soc., Mem. AAUP. Methodist. Current work: Electron transport properties of metals and alloys at low temperatures (especially potassium and alloys); properties of layered matel superlattices. Subspecialties: Condensed matter physics; Low temperature physics. Home: 807 Woodingham Dr East Lansing MI 48823Office: Mich State U Dept Physics and Astronomy East Lansing MI 48824

SCHROER, BERNARD JON, university environmental and energy center director; b. Seymour, Ind., Oct. 11, 1941; s. Alvin J. and Selma A. (Mellencamp) S.; m. Kathleen Dittman, July 5, 1963; children: Shannon, Bradley. B.S. in Engring, Western Mich. U., 1964; M.S. in Engring, U. Ala., 1967; Ph.D., Okla. State U., 1971. Registered profl. engr. Engr. Brown Engring., Huntsville, Ala., 1963-67, Boeing Corp., Huntsville, 1967-70, Computer Sci. Corp., Huntsville, 1970-72; dir. Kenneth E. Johnson Environ. and Energy Ctr., U. Ala., Huntsville, 1972—. Contbr. over 40 sci. articles to profl. publs. NSF grantee, 1971. Mem. Am. Inst. Indsl. Engring. (Outstanding Engr. award 1973, 77), Ala. Soc. Profl. Engrs., Nat. Soc. Profl. Engrs., Soc. Am. Mil. Engrs., Soc. Mfg. Engrs., Ala. Solar Energy Assn., Robotics Internat., Sigma Xi. Democrat. Lutheran. Current Work: Advanced manufacturing; robotics; simulations; information storage and retrieval. Subspecialties: Industrial engineering; Information systems, storage, and retrieval (computer science). Home: 1710 Montdale St Huntsville AL 35801 Office: Kenneth E Johnson Environ and Energy Center Univ Ala Huntsville AL 35899

SCHROHENLOHER, RALPH EDWARD, biochemistry, educator; b. Cin., Aug. 6, 1933; s. Ralph Jacob and Delma Louise (Hagen) S.; m. Sandra Jean Welch, Oct. 30, 1960; children: Robin, John. B.S. in Pharmacy, U. Cin., 1955, Ph.D. in Biochemistry, 1959. Research chemist Nat. Cancer Inst., Hagerstown, Md., 1958-61; asst. prof. medicine U. Ala. Sch. Medicine, Birmingham, 1961-69, assoc. prof., 1969-73, assoc. prof. medicine and pathology, 1973—; guest investigator Rockefeller U., N.Y.C., 1963-64. Contbr. chpts. to books, articles to profl. jours. Nat. Inst. Arthritis and Metabolic Diseases/Nat. Inst. Allergy and Infectious Diseases grantee, 1965-78; Nat. Cancer Inst. grantee, 1975-78. Mem. Am. Assn. Immunologists, Am. Rheumatism Assn., Am. Chem. Soc., AAAS, Sigma Xi. Presbyterian. Current Work: Immunoglobulin structure and function. Research on autoantibodies and immune complexes in connective tissue diseases. Subspecialties: Biochemistry (medicine); Immunology (medicine). Home: 1125 Empire Ln Birmingham AL 35226 Office: U Ala Birmingham Univ Station Birmingham AL 35294

SCHROTH, PETER, ceramic engineer; b. Giessen, Hessen, Germany, May 17, 1931; came to U.S., 1959, naturalized, 1965; s. Erich and Thilde (Binder) S.; m. Ingrid Kiesskalt, Oct. 10, 1959; children—Ursula, Ute, Karin. Ingenieur, 1955; Diplom-Ingenieur, 1957; Doktor-Ingenieur, Technische Hochschule Aachen, Fed. Republic Germany, 1959. Trainee Gen. Refractories, Phila., 1959-61; research engr. Armco Inc., Middletown, Ohio, 1961-64, sr. research engr., 1964-68, supr. research engr., 1968-75, mgr., 1975-85. Co-author: Handbook on Acid Proof Equipment, 1962; Electric Furnace Steelmaking, 1985. Contbr. articles to profl. jours. Fellow Am. Ceramic Soc.,; mem. Nat. Inst. Ceramic Engrs., Am. Iron and Steel Inst. (chmn. refractory com. 1969-71), Am. Foundrymens Soc. (chmn. com. 4-F, 1982-84). Current work: Refractories for iron and steelmaking applications; high technology ceramics for industrial application; properties of graphite electrodes for electric furnace operations. Subspecialties: Ceramic engineering; High-temperature materials. Home: 5995 Kalbfleisch Rd Middletown OH 45042 Office: Armco Inc Research-South Middletown OH 45043

SCHRYER, DAVID RICHARD, research chemist, educator; b. Phila., Feb. 26, 1932; s. William Land and Ella (Jochem) S.; m. Sandra Rose Linzinmeier, Oct. 20, 1962; (div. 1978); children—Aubrina Carole, Eric Richard; m. Jacqueline Lou Hoalt, June 30, 1982. Research chemist NASA, Hampton, Va., 1957—; assoc. adj. prof. St. Leo Coll., Langley AFB Extension, Hampton, 1978—. Editor: Heterogeneous Atmospheric Chemistry, 1982; co-editor; Man's Impact on the Troposphere, 1978; contbr. numerous articles to sci. jours. Recipient spl. achievement award NASA Langley Research Ctr., 1982. Mem. Am. Chem. Soc., AAAS, Mensa. Current work: Chemistry of heterogeneous processes including atmospheric chemistry and catalysis. Subspecialties: Physical chemistry; Heterogeneous processes. Home: 106 Santa Barbara Dr Hampton VA 23666 Office: NASA-Langley Research Ctr Mail Stop 283 Hampton VA 23665

SCHUDA, PAUL FRANCIS, chemist; b. Pitts., Apr. 28, 1952; s. Clemens C. and Eve Frances (Krawczyk) S.; m. Ann Elizabeth DeCamp, Jan. 3, 1981. B.S., U. Pitts., 1973, Ph.D., 1976. NIH postdoctoral fellow MIT, Cambridge, 1977-78; sr. research chemist PPG Industries, Pitts., 1978; asst. prof. U. Md., College Park, 1979-84; sr. research chemist Merck Sharp & Dohme, Rahway, N.J., 1985—. Contbr. articles to profl. jours. Trichothecene Chemistry grantee Dept. Def., 1985. Mem. Am. Chem. Soc., Phi Beta Kappa. Roman Catholic. Current work: Total synthesis of biologically active natural products, development of new synthetic methods. Subspecialties: Organic chemistry; Synthetic chemistry. Office: New Lead Discovery R50G-308 Merck Sharp & Dohme Research Labs PO Box 2000 Rahway NJ 07065

SCHUELER, CARL FREDERICK, electrical engineer mgr., researcher, educator; b. Iowa City, Nov. 10, 1949; s. Fred Warren and Julia (Israel) S.; m. Pamela Rose Ella Eggert, Dec. 15, 1979; children—Janelle, Janessa. B.S., La. State U., 1971, M.S., 1972; M.S., U. Calif.-Santa Barbara, 1977, Ph.D., 1980. Planetarium dir. Troy State U., Montgomery, Ala., 1973; tng. engr. Hughes Aircraft Co., Los Angeles, 1973-75, staff engr., Culver City, Calif., 1979, sr. staff engr., Santa Barbara, 1981-84, dept. mgr., 1984—; instr. Santa Barbara City Coll., 1976-80; lectr. U. Calif.-Santa Barbara, 1980—, cons., 1980—. Author, editor: Landsat Sensor Design, 1983. Contbr. articles to profl. jours. Hughes Aircraft Co. fellow 1979, U.S. Govt. agys. grants 1979—. Mem. IEEE (editor, author Jour. Ultrasonics 1984). Current work: Research and systems engineer for advanced Landsat, ultrasonic imaging, and image processing; manager of industrial research and development programs. Subspecialties: Computer engineering; Graphics, image processing, and pattern recognition. Home: 5871 Connor Ln Goleta CA 93117 Office: Hughes Santa Barbara Research Ctr 75 Coromar Dr Goleta CA 93117

SCHUH, G(EORGE) EDWARD, agricultural development administrator; b. Indpls., Sept. 13, 1930; s. George Edward and Viola (Lentz) S.; m. Maria Ignez, May 23, 1965; children: Audrey, Susan, Tanya. B.S. in Agrl. Edn, Purdue U., 1952; M.S. in Agrl. Econs., Mich. State U., 1954; M.A. in Econs, U. Chgo., 1958, Ph.D., 1961. From instr. to prof. agrl. econs. Purdue U., 1959-79; dir. Center for Public Policy and Public Affairs, 1977-78; dep. undersec. for internat. affairs and commodity programs Dept. Agr., Washington, 1978-79; prof. agrl. and applied econs., head dept. U. Minn., 1979-84; dir. agr. and rural devel. World Bank, Washington, 1984—; program adv. Ford Found., 1966-72; sr. staff economist Pres.'s Council Econ. Adv's., 1974-75; dir. Nat. Bur. Econ. Research, 1977-84; hon. prof. Fed. U. Vicosa, Brazil, 1965; bd. dirs. Econs. Inst., Boulder, Colo., 1979-84. Mpls. Grain Exchange, 1980-83. Author, editor profl. books; contbr. numerous articles to profl. publs. Served with U.S. Army, 1954-56. Fellow Am. Acad. Arts and Scis., Am. Agrl. Econs. Assn. (Thesis award 1962, Published Research award 1971, Article award 1975, Policy award 1979, dir. 1977-80, pres.-elect 1980-81, pres. 1981-82); mem. Internat. Assn. Agrl. Econs., Am. Econ. Assn., Brazilian Soc. Agrl. Economists. Current Work: Economics of technical change and rate of technical change. Subspecialties: Agricultural economics; Resource management. Office: World Bank 1818 H St NW Washington DC 22034

SCHUH, JOSEPH RANDOLPH, biochemist, research scientist; b. Corpus Christi, Tex., Sept. 28, 1947; s. Joseph Wilson and Margaret Katherine (Turner) S.; m. Patricia Denise Waters, Apr. 17, 1971; children—William, Michael, Brian, Kevin, Kathleen. B.S. in Biochemistry, Manhattan Coll., 1973; Ph.D. in Biochemistry, Cornell U., 1978. Am. Cancer Soc. research fellow Calif. Inst. Tech., Pasadena, 1978-80, Boswell research fellow, 1981-82; sr. research chemist Health Care div. Monsanto, St. Louis, 1982—; vis. scientist Washington U., St. Louis, 1984-85; fellow Huntington Inst. Applied Med. Research, Pasadena, 1981-82; cons. Vestar Research, Inc., Pasadena, 1980-82. Contbr. articles to profl. jours., chpt. to book. Served with USMC, 1968-72. Mem. Am. Chem. Soc., Biophys. Soc. Democrat. Current work: Development and application of biophysical methods (e.g. NMR) to study biolog systems. Subspecialties: Biochemistry (medicine); Nuclear magnetic resonance. Home: 2055 Rurline Dr Saint Louis MO 63146 Office: Monsanto 800 N Lindbergh Blvd Saint Louis MO 63167

SCHUHMANN, REINHARDT, JR., metallurgical engineer, emeritus educator, consultant; b. Corpus Christi, Tex., Dec. 16, 1914; s. Reinhardt and Alice (Shuford) S.; m. Betsy Jane Hancock, Aug. 29, 1937; children—Martha S., Alice Schuhman Bishop. Student Calif. Inst. Tech., 1929-31; B.S. in Metall. Engring., Mo. Sch. of Mines, 1933; M.S. in Metall. Engring., Montana Sch. of Mines, 1935; Sc.D., MIT, 1938. Instr. to assoc. prof. MIT, Cambridge, Mass., 1938-54; prof. metall. engring. Purdue U., West Lafayette, Ind., 1954-64, head. Sch. Metall. Engring., 1959-64, Ross Prof. engring., 1964-81, Ross Prof. engring. emeritus, 1981—; Battelle vis. prof. Ohio State U., Columbus, 1966-67; Kroll vis. prof. Colo. Sch. of Mines, 1977; cons. metall. engring. Author: Metallurgical Engineering, 1952. Contbr. articles to profl. jours. Co-inventor Q-S oxygen process, 1976; oxygen sprinkle smelting, 1980. Fellow Metall. Soc. of AIME, (charter), AIME (extractive metallurgy sci. awards 1959, 77, extractive metallurgy lectr. 1965, James Douglas Gold medal 1970, mineral industry edn. award 1975), Am. Soc. for Metals (grade award 1972), AAAS; mem. Nat. Acad. Engring., Am. Chem. Soc. Democrat. Episcopalian. Club: Parlor (pres. Lafayette, Ind. 1963-64). Lodge: Rotary (Lafayette). Current work: Physical chemistry and thermodynamics of pyrometallurgical processes; applications to process design and development, coal gasification and sulfur fixation. Subspecialties: Metallurgical engineering; Physical chemistry. Office: Sch of Materials Engring Purdue U West Lafayette IN 47907

SCHULER, ROBERT HANS, civil engineer, geologist; b. Bad Pymont, Fed. Republic Germany, July 26, 1951; came to U.S., 1955; s. Gerhard George and Johanna (Kroonenberg) S.; m. Marilyn Sue Brown, Nov. 17, 1984; 1 child, Cecily. B.S. in Civil Engring., Tufts U., 1974, B.S. in Geology, 1974. Registered profl. engr., Ky., Okla., Alaska, Va., Md., Fla.; cert. profl. geol. scientist. Design engr. Warren Fondedile, Boston, 1974-76; engr., geologist Ashland Petroleum Co., Ky., 1976-78; civil engr. Ashland Synthetic Fuels, 1978-80; sr. engr. Williams Bros. Engring. Co., Tulsa, 1980-82, sr. geologist, 1982-84; cons. R. W. Tech. Services, N.Y.C., 1983-84; v.p. Testwell-Craig Labs. of Fla., Inc., Miami, 1984—. Mem. ASCE, Am. Inst. Profl. Geologists, Geol. Soc. Am., Am. Cons. Engring. Council, Fla. Engring. Soc., MENSA. Current work: Construction material testing laboratory, researching construction methods and materials. Subspecialties: Materials (engineering); Structural engineering. Home: 270 NE 123d St North Miami FL 33161 Office: Testwell-Craig Labs 7104 NW 51st St Miami FL 33166

SCHULER, ROBERT HUGO, educator, chemist; b. Buffalo, Jan. 4, 1926; s. Robert H. and Mary J. (Mayer) S.; m. Florence J. Forrest, June 18, 1952; children: Mary A., Margaret A., Carol A., Robert E., Thomas C. B.S., Canisius Coll., Buffalo, 1946; Ph.D., U. Notre Dame, 1949. Asst. prof. chemistry Canisius Coll., 1949-53; asso. chemist, then chemist Brookhaven Nat. Lab., 1953-56; staff fellow, dir. radiation research lab. Mellon Inst., 1956-76, mem. adv. bd., 1962-76; prof. chemistry, dir. radiation research lab. Carnegie-Mellon U., 1967-76; prof. chemistry, dir. radiation lab. U. Notre Dame, Ind., 1976—; Sir C.V. Raman vis. prof. U. Madras, India, 1985. Author articles in field. Fellow AAAS; mem. Am. Chem. Soc., Am. Phys. Soc., Chem. Soc., Radiation Research Soc. (pres. 1975-76), Sigma Xi. Club: Cosmos. Current Work: Radiation chemistry and its application to kinetic and structural problems. Subspecialties: Physical chemistry; Radiation chemistry. Office: Radiation Lab U Notre Dame Notre Dame IN 46556

SCHULLER, IVAN KOHN, physicist, consultant; b. Cluj, Rumania, June 8, 1946; came to U.S., 1970; s. Francisco Berla and Iolanda Blum (Kohn) S.; m. Jacqueline Marrieta Scheibel, Mar. 3, 1974; children—Daniel, Jonathan. B.S., U. Chile, 1965, licenciado, 1970; M.S., Northwestern U., 1972, Ph.D., 1976. Research asst. Argonne Nat. Labs., Ill., 1974-76, sr. scientist, group leader, 1978—; adj. prof. UCLA, 1976-78. Contbr. articles to profl. jours. Patentee in field. Recipient Disting. Performance award U. Chgo., 1981; Outstanding New Citizen award Citizenship Council, 1981. Mem. Am. Phys. Soc., IEEE, Metall. Soc., Chilean Phys. Soc., Sigma Xi. Current work: Research in the basic properties and application of novel, thin film and layered materials. Subspecialties: Condensed matter physics; Electronic materials. Home: 6517 Maxwell Dr Woodridge IL 60517 Office: Argonne Nat Labs Bldg 223 Argonne IL 60439

SCHULTES, RICHARD EVANS, botanist, museum executive, educator; b. Boston, Jan. 12, 1915; s. Otto Richard and Maude Beatrice (Bagley) S.; m. Dorothy Crawford McNeil, Mar. 26, 1959; children: Richard Evans II, Neil Parker and Alexandra Ames (twins). A.B., Harvard U., 1937, A.M., 1938, Ph.D., 1941; M.H. (hon.), Universidad Nacional de Colombia, Bogotá, 1953. Plant explorer, NRC fellow Harvard Bot. Mus., Cambridge, Mass., 1941-42, research asso., 1942-53; curator Orchid Herbarium of Oakes Ames, 1953-58, curator econ. botany, 1958—, exec. dir., 1967-70, dir., 1970—; Guggenheim Found. fellow, collaborator U.S. Dept. Agr., Amazon of Colombia, 1942-43; plant explorer in South Am. Bur. Plant Industry, 1944-54; prof. biology Harvard, 1970-72, Paul C. Mangelsdorf prof. natural scis., 1973-81, Edward C. Jeffrey prof. biology, 1981-85, prof. emeritus, 1985—; adj. prof. pharmacognosy U. Ill., Chgo., 1975—; Hubert Humphrey vis. prof. Macalaster Coll., 1979; field agt. Rubber Devel. Corp. of U.S. Govt., in S.Am., 1943-44; collaborator Instituto Argronômico Norte, Belem, Brazil, 1948-50; hon. prof. Universidad Nacional de Colombia, 1953—, prof. econ. botany, 1963; bot. cons. Smith, Kline & French Co., Phila., 1957-67; mem. NIH Adv. Panel, 1964; mem. selection com. for Latin Am. Guggenheim Found., 1964—; chmn. on-site visit U. Hawaii Natural Products Grant NIH, 1966, 67; Laura L. Barnes Annual lectr. Morris Arboretum, Phila., 1969; Koch lectr. Rho Chi Soc., Pitts., 1971, Chgo., 1974; vis. prof. econ. botany, plants in relation to man's progress Jardín Botánico, Medellín, Colombia, 1973; Cecil and Ida H. Green Vis. Lectr. U. B.C., Vancouver, Can., 1974; mem. adv. bd. Fitz Hugh Ludlow Library, San Francisco, 1974—; U.S. nat. coordinator Programa Interciencia Recurses. Author: (with P. A. Vestal) Economic Botany of the Kiowa Indians, 1941, Native Orchids of Trinidad and Tobago, 1960, (with A. F. Hill) Plants and Human Affairs, 1960, rev. edit., 1968, (with A. S. Pease) Generic Names of Orchids—their Origin and Meaning, 1963, (with A. Hofmann) The Botany and Chemistry of Hallucinogens, 1973, rev. edit., 1980, Plants of the Gods, 1979, Plant Hallucinogens, 1976, (with W.A. Davis) The Glass Flowers at Harvard, 1982; contbg. author: Ency. Biol. Scis, 1961, Ency. Brit, 1966, 83, Ency. Biochemistry, 1967, McGraw-Hill Yearbook Sci., Tech, 1971; author numerous Harvard Bot. Mus. leaflets.; Asst. editor: Chronica Botanica, 1947-52; editor: Bot. Mus. Leaflets, 1957—, Econ. Botany, 1962-79; mem. editorial bd.: Lloydia, 1965-76, Altered States of Consciousness, 1973—, Jour. Psychedelic Drugs, 1974—; mem. adv. bd.: Horticulture, 1976-78, Jour. Ethnopharmacology, Bol. Museo Paraense Emelio Goeldi, Belem, Brazil; 1978—; editorial cons. Recurses Biológica Nuevos Boletin, 1984—. Contbr. numerous articles to profl. jours. Mem. governing bd. Amazonas 2000, Bogotá ; assoc. in ethnobotany Museo del Oro, Bogota, 1974—; chmn. NRC panels, 1974, 75; mem. NRC Workshop on Natural Products, Sri Lanka, 1975, participant numerous sems., congresses, meetings. Decorated Orden de la Victoria Regia in recognition of work in Amazon Colombian Govt., 1969, Cruz de Boyacá Govt. of Colombia, 1983, Gold medal for conservation Duke of Edinburgh, 1984. Fellow Am. Acad. Arts, Scis., Am. Coll. Neuropsychopharmacology; mem. Nat. Acad. Sci., Linnean Soc., Academia Colombiana de Ciencias Exactas, Fisico-Quimicas y Naturales, Instituto Ecuatoriano de Ciencias Naturales, Sociedad Científica Antonio Alzate (Mexico), Argentine Acad. Scis., Am. Orchid Soc. (life hon.), Pan Am. Soc. New Eng. (gov.), Am. Soc. Pharmacopia (hon.), Asociación de Amigos de Jardines Botánicos (life), Soc. Econ. Botany (organizer annual meeting 1961, Disting. Botanist of Yr. 1979), New Eng. Bot. Club (pres. 1954-60), Internat. Assn. Plant Taxonomy, Am. Soc. Pharmacognosy, Phytochem. Soc. N.Am., Socieded Colombiana de Orquideologia, Assn. Tropical Biology, Asociación Colombiana de Ingenieros Agrónomos, Sociedad Cubana de Botánica, Explorer's Club, Sigma Xi (pres. Harvard chpt. 1971-72), Beta Nu chpt. Phi Sigma (first hon.). Unitarian (vestryman Kings Chapel 1974-76, 82-85). Current Work: Plants employed as medicines in Amazon; rubber-yielding plants; flora of the northwest Amazon. Subspecialties: Taxonomy; Systematics. Home: 78 Larchmont Rd Melrose MA 02176 Office: Bot Museum Harvard U Cambridge MA 02138

SCHULTHEIS, ROBERT ARTHUR, agricultural engineer; b. Colfax, Wash., Dec. 7, 1955; s. Carroll Anthony and Edna Mae (Morbeck) S.; m. Jennifer Joan Johnmeyer, Oct. 24, 1981. B.S. in Agr. Mechanization, Wash. State U., 1978; M.S. in Agr. Engring., U. Mo., 1980. Foreman Spokane Culvert and Fabricating Co., Wash., 1978, research aide II, Wash. State U., Pullman, 1978-79; grad. research asst. U. Mo., Columbia, 1979-80; agri. engring. specialist Mo. Coop. Extension Service, Marshfield, 1980—, dir. Extension Ctr., 1983—, exec. sec. Springfield Area Irrigation Assn., Marshfield, 1983—. Contbr. articles to profl. jours. Mem. bd. suprs. Ozarks Area Community Action Corp., Webster County, Mo., 1980-84, Soil and Water Conservation Dist., Webster County, 1981-85. Recipient Rookie of Yr. award Mo. Coop. Extension Service, 1982, Pub. Info. award, 1882, 85; scholar Washington Water Power Corp., 1975, Union Pacific R.R., Wash., 1974. Mem. Am. Soc Agri Engrs., Nat. Assn. County Agr. Agts. (pub. relations com. 1983, nat. environ. quality recognition award, 1982), U. Mo. Extension Assn. (profl. improvement com. 1984—), Gamma Sigma Delta, Alpha Zeta. Roman Catholic. Lodge: K.C. Current work: Work 8-county area helping farmers and homeowners solve problems in building construction and ventilation; machinery selection; soil, water and waste management; alternate energy; safety; and agricultural fields. Subspecialties: Agricultural engineering; Extension service. Home: 801 S Locust St Marshfield MO 65706 Office: Mo Cooperative Extension Ser S Hwy A PO Box 7 Marshfield MO 65706

SCHULTZ, ALBERT BARRY, biomechanical engineer, educator, researcher; b. Phila., Oct. 10, 1933; s. George D. and Belle (Seidman) S.; m. Susan Resnikov, Aug. 25, 1955; children: Carl, Adam, Robin. B.S. (Navy ROTC scholar), U. Rochester, 1955; M. Engring, Yale U., 1959, Ph.D., 1962. Asst. prof. U. Del., 1962-65; asst. prof. mech. engring. U. Ill., Chgo., 1965, assoc. prof., 1966-71, prof., 1971-83, dir. Biomechs. Research Lab., 1980-83; Vennema prof. engring. U. Mich., 1983—; chmn. U.S. Nat. Com. on Biomechs., 1982-85. Served with USN, 1955-58. Recipient Research Career award NIH, 1975-80; NIH spl. research fellow, 1971-72; NIH Javits neurosci. investigator award, 1985—. Mem. ASME (chmn. div. bioengring. 1981-82), Am. Soc. Biomech. (pres. 1982-83), Internat. Soc. for Study Lumbar Spine (pres. 1981-82), Phi Beta Kappa, Phi Kappa Phi, Tau Beta Pi. Current Work: Orthopaedic biomechanics; biomechanics of human spine. Subspecialties: Biomedical engineering; Mechanical engineering. Office: Mech Engring Dept U Mich Ann Arbor MI 48109

SCHULTZ, ALFRED BERNARD, physicist; b. New London, Conn., Dec. 28, 1948; s. Nicholas Pershing and Edna Mae (Searchfield) S. Student Sacramento City Coll., 1971-73; B.S., U. Calif.-Davis, 1975; M.S., U. Nev., 1978, Ph.D., 1982. Engr., scientist McDonnell Douglas Co., Huntington Beach, Calif., 1982-83; asst. prof. dept. physics U. Nev., Reno, 1983-84; Weber State Coll., Ogden, Utah, 1984; assoc. researcher Lunar and Planetary Lab., U. Ariz., Tucson, 1984—. Contbr. articles to profl. jours. Served with USAF, 1967-71, Vietnam. Mem. Am. Phys. Soc., Am. Astron. Soc., Astron. Soc. Pacific, Sigma Xi. Current work: Charge-coupled device camera development, apodization applied to telescope resolution. Subspecialties: Planetary science; Optical image processing. Office: Lunar and Planetary Lab Univ of Ariz Tucson AZ 85721

SCHULTZ, ALVIN LEROY, internist, medical educator; b. Mpls., July 27, 1921; s. Maurice Arthur and Elizabeth Leah (Gershin) S.; m. Martha Jean Graham, Aug. 14, 1947; children: Susan Kristine, David Matthew, Peter Jonathan, Michael Graham. B.A., U. Minn.-Mpls., 1943, M.B., 1946, M.D., 1947, M.S., 1952. Diplomate: Am. Bd. Internal Medicine. Instr. medicine U. Minn.-Mpls., 1952-54, asst. prof., 1954-59, assoc. prof., 1959-65, prof., 1965—; asst. chief medicine Mpls. VA Hosp., 1952-54; dir. endocrine clinic U. Minn., 1954-59; dir. medicine and research Mt. Sinai Hosp., Mpls., 1959-65; chief of medicine Hennepin County Med. Ctr., Mpls., 1965; chmn. bd. Hennepin Faculty Assocs., 1983-87. Editor: Jour. Lab. and Clin. Medicine, 1966-69, Modern Medicine, 1960—; editorial bd. Minn. Medicine, 1965—, Data Centrum, 1984—. Contbr. articles profl. jours. Bd. dirs. Planned Parenthood of Minn., 1970-75, Hennepin County Med. Philanthropic Found., 1976—. Served to capt. AUS, 1947-49. Fellow ACP (Minn. gov. 1983-87); mem. Central Soc. Clin. Research, Am. Fedn. Clin. Research, Endocrine Soc., Am. Thyroid Assn., Minn. Med. Assn. (ho. of dels. 1980-85), Hennepin County Med. Soc. (dir. 1977-81), Minn. Assn. Pub. Teaching Hosp. (chmn. bd. 1983-85). Republican. Jewish. Current Work: Thyroid disease, hormonal control lipid metabolism, training of medical students, general internists. Subspecialties: Internal medicine; Endocrinology. Home: 5127 Irving Ave S Minneapolis MN 55419 Office: Hennepin County Med Center 701 Park Ave S Minneapolis MN 55415

SCHULTZ, CLIFFORD WILLIAM, extractive metallurgist; b. Saginaw, Mich., Nov. 26, 1931; s. Leo Asa and Leona Elda (Hagarty) S.; m. Cleone Faye Miller, July 3, 1954; children—Paul H., David T. B.S. in Metall. Engring., Mich. Technol. U., 1953, M.S. in Metall. Engring., 1956; Ph.D. in Mineral Engring., U. Minn., 1975. Metallurgist M.A. Hanna Co., Nashwauk, Minn., 1953-54; instr. Mich. Technol. U., Houghton, 1956-59, asst. dir. mineral research, 1974-80, dir. mineral research, 1980—, adj. prof. metallurgy, 1984—, adj. prof. bus., 1984—; project leader metallurgy U.S. Bur. Mines, Mpls., 1961-65, research leader mining, 1965-74. Contbr. articles to profl. jours. Served with U.S. Army, 1953-55. Reserve Mining Co. fellow, 1959-60. Mem. AIME, Delta Sigma Phi. Republican. Club: Miscowaubik (bd. dirs. 1984—) (Calumet, Mich.). Lodge: Elks. Current work: Mineral processing; mineral economics; coal preparation; oil shale processing. Subspecialty: Metallurgical engineering. Office: Inst of Mineral Research Mich Technol U Houghton MI 49931

SCHULTZ, FREDERICK H. C., physics educator, energy consultant; b. Hanks, N.D., June 11, 1921; s. Herman A. and Helvene G. (Ausl) S.; m. Lila Fay Gregory, Aug. 27, 1949; children: Michael F., Jane F., John F. Ph.B., U. N.D.-Grand Forks, 1942; M.S., U. Idaho-Moscow, 1950; Ph.D., Wash. State U.-Pullman, 1967. Instr. physics Mont. Sch. Mining, Butte, 1950-55; asst. prof. Mont. State U.-Bozeman, 1955-61; physicist U.S. Naval Ordnance Lab., Corona, Calif., summers 1957, 59, 61, 63; asst. prof. Minot (N.D.) State U., 1961-63, Wash. State U., 1963-68; prof. U. Wis.-Eau Claire, 1968—; dir. seismograph sta. U.S. Coast & Geol. Survery, Bozeman, 1955-61; dir. Summer Inst. NSF, Pullman, 1967-68; energy cons. W.C. Wis. Regional Planning Commn., Eau Claire, 1981—. Served with U.S. Navy, 1944-46. Mem. Wis. Assn. Physics Tchrs., Am. Assn. Physics Tchrs., N.Y. Acad. Sci., Optical Soc. Am., Sigma Xi. (local pres. 1979-81). Republican. Lutheran. Current Work: Profession-undergraduate physics teaching; consulting work in energy sources and uses with environmental effects such as acid rain. Subspecialties: Polarized infrared absorption and reflection; Energy sources and uses. Home: 3834 Nimitz St Eau Claire WI 54701 Office: Department Physics University Wisconsin Eau Claire WI 54701

SCHULTZ, FREDERICK JOHN, tobacco company executive; b. Davenport, Iowa, Oct. 12, 1929; s. August William and Alma (Calkins) S.; m. Donna Hansen, July 30, 1955; children—Laurie, Julie, David, James. B.A. in Chemistry, Augustana Coll., Rock Island, Ill., 1952; M.A. in Organic Chemistry, Depauw U., 1956; Ph.D. in Chemistry, State U. Iowa, 1960. Research chemist Lorillard Co., Greensboro, N.C., 1959-62, sr. research chemist, 1962-65, prodn. devel. mgr., 1965-68, dir. research and devel., 1975-79, v.p. research and devel., 1979—; vice chmn. Tobacco Sci. Bd. N.C., 1983—; v.p., bd. dirs. N.C. Tobacco Found., 1982—. Served with U.S. Army, 1953-55. Mem. Am. Chem. Soc., AAAS, Instrument Soc. Am., N.C. Acad. Sci., N.Y. Acad. Sci., Am. Inst. Chemists, Greensboro C. of C., Sigma Xi. Republican. Lutheran. Current work: Analysis of natural products and pyrolysis products; chromatography; spectroscopy; organic synthesis; bioassay methods for tobacco smoke; product development. Subspecialty: Organic chemistry. Office: Lorrillard Co 420 English St Greensboro NC 27405

SCHULTZ, JACK CHARLES, ecology educator; b. Chgo., Jan. 4, 1947; s. Kenneth Frederick and Virginia Marie (Kubes) S.; m. Constance A. McCollum, Sept. 21, 1968 (div. Jan. 1973); m. Martha Jean Richards, May 23, 1982. B.A., U. Chgo., 1969; Ph.D., U. Wash., 1978. Instr. U. Wash., Seattle, 1975-76; research instr. Dartmouth Coll., Hanover, N.H., 1976-78, research asst. prof., 1979-83; vis. fellow Cornell U., Ithaca, N.Y., 1978-79; asst. prof. entomology Pa. State U., University Park, 1983—. Editor: (with Pedro Barbosa) Ecological-Evolutionary Aspects of Pest Outbreaks, 1985. Contbr. articles to profl. jours. NSF grantee, 79, 79—; U.S. Forest Service grantee, 1984—. Mem. Ecol. Soc. Am., Entomol. Soc. Am., Lepidopterists Soc., Soc. Study Evolution, Internat. Chem. Ecology Soc., Am. chem. Soc. Current work: Chemical ecology; plant-insect interactions; plant communication; insect behavior. Subspecialties: Ecology (biology); Integrated pest management. Office: Pesticide Research Lab Pa State U University Park PA 16802

SCHULTZ, JEROLD MARVIN, materials science educator; b. San Francisco, June 21, 1935; s. Ernest Schultz and Florence (Rubin) Schultz Richter; m. Peggy June Ostrom, July 31, 1960; children—Carrie Margaret, Timothy John, Peter Andrew, Anna Christine. B.S., U. Calif.-Berkeley, 1958, M.S., 1959; Ph.D., Carnegie Inst. Tech., 1965. Engr. Westinghouse Research Labs., Pitts., 1959-61; prof. materials sci. U. Del., Newark, 1964—. Author: Polymer Materials Science, 1974; Diffraction for Materials Scientists, 1982. Editor: Properties of Solid Polymeric Materials, 1977. Contbr. articles to profl. jours. Flutist Newark Symphony Orch., 1966—. Recipient Alexander von Humboldt Sr. Am. Scientist award, 1978-79; numerous research grants. Mem. Am. Phys. Soc., Am. Crystallographic Assn., Metall. Soc. Episcopalian. Current work: Polymeric materials: processing, structure, property relationships; composite materials, diffraction methodology. Subspecialties: Polymers (materials science); Composite materials. Office: Dept Chem Engring U Del Newark DE 19716

SCHULTZ, JEROME SAMSON, biochem. engr.; b. Bklyn., June 25, 1933; s. Henry Herman and Sally S.; m. Jane Paula Schwartz, Sept. 1, 1955; children—Daniel Stuart, Judith Susan, Kathryn Ann. B.S. in Chem. Engring, Columbia U., 1954, M.S., 1956; Ph.D. in Biochemistry, U. Wis., 1958. Group leader biochem. research Lederle Labs., N.Y.C., 1958-64; asst. prof. dept. chem. engring. U. Mich., Ann Arbor, 1964-67, assoc. prof., 1967-70, prof., 1970—, chmn. dept., 1977—; vis. prof. physiology U. Nijmegen, Netherlands, 1971-72; sect. head engring. techs. NSF, 1985—. Editorial bd. Biotech.-Bioengring., Jour. New Sci., Biotech. Progress. Contbr. articles to profl. jours. NIH research career devel. awardee, 1970-75. Mem. Am. Chem. Soc. (past chmn. microbial chemistry div.), Am. Inst. Chem. Engrs. (past chmn. food and bioengring. div., Biotech. Research award 1984), Am. Soc. Artifical Internal Organs, AAAS, Sigma Xi, Phi Lambda Upsilon, Tau Beta Pi. Patentee in field. Current Work: Artifical hybrid organs; implantable sensors for metabolites; industrial use of genetic engineering; membranes for separations. Subspecialties: Bioinstrumentation; Enzyme technology. Office: Dept Chem Engring Univ of Mich Ann Arbor MI 48109

SCHULTZ, RICHARD MICHAEL, tumor immunologist; b. Hillsboro, Wis., Mar. 11, 1948; s. Paul Raymond and Thelma Violet (Johns) S.; m. Erika Elisabeth Zander, June 18, 1976. B.S., U. Ill., 1971; postgrad. George Washington U., 1976-77. Research asst. U. Ill. Sch. Vet. Medicine, Urbana, 1971-74; research assoc. Frederick Cancer Research Ctr., Md., 1974; microbiologist Nat. Cancer Inst. NIH, Bethesda, Md., 1974-79; research scientist Eli Lilly & Co., Indpls., 1979—. Author chpts. in books. Contbr. articles to profl. jours. Patentee in field. Mem. Am. Assn. Cancer Research, Am. Assn. Immunologists, Reticuloendothelial Soc. Lutheran. Current work: Regulation of macrophage functional activity; discover autoregulation of macrophage cytotoxic activity by interferons and prostaglandins E. Subspecialties: Immunopharmacology; Cancer research (medicine). Home: 6551 Shelbyville Rd Indianapolis IN 46237 Office: Eli Lilly and Co Dept M931 307 E McCarty St Indianapolis IN 46285

SCHULTZ, SHELDON, physics educator; b. N.Y.C., Jan. 21, 1933; s. Myer and Sarah (Hetson) S.; m. Carolyn Gitterman, Dec. 20, 1953; children—Mark S., Laurie P., David A. M.E., Stevens Inst. Tech., 1954; Ph.D., Columbia U., 1959. Research assoc. Columbia U. Radiation Lab., N.Y.C., 1959-60; asst. prof. physics U. Calif.-San Diego, La Jolla, 1960-67, assoc. prof., 1967-71, prof., 1971—. Alfred P. Sloan Found. fellow, 1964-66; NSF grantee, 1960—. Fellow Am. Phys. Soc.; mem. Am. Vacuum Soc., Sigma Xi, Tau Beta Pi. Current work: Condensed matter physics - spin-glasses, nuclear magnetic resonance, nmr imaging, conduction electron spin resonance, ultra high vacuum, surface physics, and magnetic recording research. Subspecialties: Condensed matter physics; Magnetic resonance imaging. Office: Dept Physics B-019 U Calif San Diego La Jolla CA 92093

SCHULTZ, STANLEY GEORGE, physiologist, educator; b. Bayonne, N.J., Oct. 26, 1931; s. Aaron and Sylvia (Kaplan) S.; m. Harriet Taran, Dec. 25, 1960; children: Jeffery, Kenneth. A.B. summa cum laude, Columbia U., 1952; M.D., N.Y. U., 1956. Intern Bellevue Hosp., N.Y.C., 1956-57, resident, 1957-59; research assoc. in biophysics Harvard U., 1959-62, instr. biophysics, 1964-67; assoc. prof. physiology U. Pitts., 1967-70, prof. physiology, 1970-79; prof., chmn. dept. physiology U. Tex. Med. Sch., Houston, 1979—; cons. USPHS, NIH, 1970—; mem. physiology test com. Nat. Bd. Med. Examiners, 1974-79, chmn., 1976-79. Editor: Jour. Applied Physiology, 1971-75, Physiol. Revs, 1979—; mem. editorial bd.: Jour. Gen. Physiology, 1969—; editorial bd.: Ann. Revs. Physiology, 1974-81; assoc. editor Ann. Revs. Physiology, 1977-81; editorial bd.: Current Topics in Membranes and Transport, 1975—, Jour. Membrane Biology, 1977—; Contbr. articles to profl. jours. Served to capt. M.C. USAF, 1962-64. Recipient Research Career award NIH, 1969-74; overseas fellow Churchill Coll., Cambridge U., 1975-76. Mem. Am. Heart Assn. (established investigator 1964-69), Am. Physiol. Soc., AAAS, Biophys. Soc., Soc. for Gen. Physiologists, Internat. Cell. Research Orgn., Internat. Union Physiol. Scis. (chmn. internat. com. gastrointestinal physiology 1977-80), Phi Beta Kappa, Alpha Omega Alpha. Current Work: Solute transport by epithelial tissues. Membrane transport. Electrophysiology. Subspecialties: Physiology (medicine); Cell biology (medicine). Home: 4955 Heatherglen Dr Houston TX 77096

SCHUMAKER, LARRY LEE, mathematics educator; b. Aberdeen, S.D., Nov. 5, 1939; s. Lee B. and Irene E. (Kelly) S.; m. Gerda Ingeborg Boguszewski, June 15, 1963; 1 child, Anna. B.S., S.D. Sch. Mines, 1961; M.S., Stanford U., 1962, Ph.D., 1966. Vis. prof. U. Munich, Germany, 1974, Free U. Berlin, Germany, 1978-79; research assoc. Math. Research Ctr., U. Wis., Madison, 1966-68, 1973; asst. prof. math. assoc. prof., prof. U. Tex., Austin, 1968-79; prof. Tex. A&M U. College Station, 1980—, dir. Ctr. for Approximation, 1980—. Author: Spline Functions and Basic Theory, 1981; (translator) Approximation Theory by G. Meinandus, 1967. Editor: (with others) Approximation Theory I, 1973, Approximation Theory II, 1976, Approximation Theory IV, 1983. Democratic primary candidate U.S. Senate, S.D., 1980. Recipient research contract NASA, 1981-84; U.S. Air Force grantee, 1968-79. Current work: Theory and applications of spline functions surface fitting, computer-aided design. Subspecialties: Computer-aided design; Applied mathematics. Home: 412 Brady Ln Austin TX 78746 Office: Ctr for Approximation Theory Tex A&M U College Station TX 77843

SCHUMAN, GAIL ISHERWOOD, software engineer, physicist; b. Bayshore, N.Y., Nov. 3, 1947; d. Robert William Isherwood and Lillian Ida (Buttelman) McConlogue; m. Robert Lee Schuman, Aug. 11, 1979; 1 child, Kira Ayn. B.S. in Physics, SUNY-Stony Brook, 1973, B.S. in Applied Math., 1973, M.S. in Applied Math., 1980; M.S. in Physics, Poly. Inst. N.Y., 1982, cert. U.S. energy policy and programs. Physics assoc. Brookhaven Nat. Lab., Upton, N.Y., 1974-77, med. research assoc., 1977-79, instr. technician tng. program, 1978-79; sr. software engr. Grumman Aerospace Corp., Bethpage, N.Y., 1979-85; sr. analyst Photon Research Assocs., Port Jefferson, N.Y., 1985—; active One Mind, speaker's bur. for women in sci. Mem. Service Bur. for Deaf, Nesconset, L.I., N.Y.; Mem. Am. Phys. Soc., Am. Assn. Physics Tchrs., Assn. for Computing Machinery, IEEE Computer Soc., Assn. of Women in Sci. (membership com. L.I. chpt. 1983-84). Democrat. Episcopalian. Current work: Development of automated tools to aid production of software; study of special programming languages, image and signal processing applications. Subspecialties: Software engineering; Programming languages. Office: Photon Research Assocs 640 Belle Terre Rd Port Jefferson NY 11777

SCHUNK, DALE HANSEN, psychology educator, researcher; b. Chgo., Aug. 14, 1946; s. Elmer Charles and Mildred Augusta (Hansen) S.; m. Caryl Cook, 1984. B.S., U. Ill.-Urbana, 1968; M.Ed., Boston U., 1974; Ph.D., Stanford U., 1979. With NATO, Naples, Italy, 1970-74; teaching asst. Stanford U., 1975, research asst., 1975-79; prof. psychology U. Houston, 1979—; ednl. cons. Spring Branch Sch. Dist., Houston, 1981—. Contbr. articles to profl. jours. Served to capt. USAF, 1968-74. USPHS research grantee, 1980, 84; NSF research grantee, 1980, 85; Spencer Found. grantee, 1983, 84. Mem. Am. Psychol. Assn., Am. Ednl. Research Assn., Soc. Research in Child Devel., Southwestern Psychol. Assn., Southwest Ednl. Research Assn., AAAS, N.Y. Acad. Scis., Council Exceptional Children. Current Work: Social learning theory; children's cognitive processes, learning and achievement; motivational processes. Subspecialties: Cognition; Learning. Home: 8711 Ariel St Houston TX 77074 Office: Coll Ed U Houston 4800 Calhoun St Houston TX 77004

SCHUR, PETER HENRY, physician, educator, researcher; b. Vienna, Austria, May 9, 1933; came to U.S., 1939, naturalized, 1946; s. Max and Helen (Kraus) S.; m. Susan D. Dorfman, Sept. 8, 1963 (div. Oct. 1984); children—Diana, Erica. B.S., Yale U., 1955; M.D., Harvard U., 1958. Diplomate Am. Bd. Internal Medicine, Am. Bd. Allergy and Clin. Immunology. Intern Bronx Mcpl. Hosp., N.Y.C., 1958-59, resident in medicine, 1959-62; postdoctoral fellow and asst. hosp. physician Rockefeller U., N.Y.C., 1964-67; instr. and asst. Harvard U., Boston, 1967-69, asst. prof. medicine, 1969-72, assoc. prof., 1972-78, prof., 1978—; clin. instr. Albert Einstein Coll. Medicine, 1961-62, vis. assoc. in medicine, 1964-67; clin. assoc. prof. med. lab. scis. Coll. Pharmacy and Allied Health Professions, Northeastern U., 1983-85; asst. attending physician Bronx Mcpl. Hosp. Ctr., 1964-67; physician Robert B. Brigham Hosp., 1967-81; assoc. in medicine Peter Bent Brigham Hosp., Boston, 1967-70, sr. assoc. in medicine, 1971-81; physician in medicine Brigham and Women's Hosp., 1981—, rhematologist, immunologist, 1981-85; mem. cons. staff various hosps.; mem. sci. com. Mass. Arthritis Found., 1974—; mem. sci. adv. com. Ctr. for Blood Research, Boston; chmn. med. adv. bd., bd. dirs. Mass. Lupus Found., 1975—; bd. dirs. LE Found. Am., 1977—; mem. pub. info. com. Fedn. Am. Socs. Exptl. Biology, 1977—, chmn. pub. info. com., 1979-82; mem. fellowship com. Arthritis Found., 1979-83. Editor: Clinical Management Systemic Lupus Erythematosus, 1983; assoc. editor Blood, 1970-75, Jour. Immunology, 1978-82; editorial bd. Arthritis and Rheumatism, 1976-82, Clin. Immunology and Immunopathology, 1976—, Jour. Clin. and Lab. Immunology, 1977—, Immunologica Clinica, 1978—. Contbr. numerous articles to profl. jours. Treas. PTA, Newton, Mass., 1978—; mem. Newton Democratic City Com., 1970-83. Served as capt. U.S. Army, 1962-64. Helen Hay Whitney Found. fellow, 1964-67; grantee NIH, 1967—. Fellow ACP; mem. Am. Soc. Clin. Investigation, Am. Assn. Immunologists, Am. Fedn. Clin. Research, Am. Rheumatism Assn. (chmn. gen. publ. com. 1975-78), Mass. Med. Soc., New Eng. Rheumatism Soc. (pres. 1976-77), N.Y. Acad. Scis., Assn. Am. Physicians. Current work: Relationships of genetic and immunological factors to clinical manifestations in people with rheumatic diseases, especially systemic lupus erythematosus. Subspecialties: Rheumatology; Immunology (medicine). Home: 16 Manchester Rd Newton MA 02161 Office: Brigham and Women's Hosp 75 Francis St Boston MA 02161

SCHURE, MARK RICHARD, chemist; b. Schenectady, May 28, 1952; s. Robert and Aileen Rosalind (Blumenthal) S. B.S., Northeastern U., 1975; Ph.D., Colo. State U., 1981. Faculty intern U. Utah, Salt Lake City, 1982-83; sr. scientist Digital Equipment Corp., Marlboro, Mass., 1983—. Contbr. articles to profl. jours. Mem. Am. Chem. Soc., Am. Phys. Soc., AAAS, Assn. Computing Machinery, N.Y. Acad. Scis. Current work: Theory of analytical chemical operations, interactive mathematical software, theory of separation processes for polymers and particles. Subspecialties: Analytical chemistry; Software engineering. Office: Digital Equipment Corp 1 Iron Way Marlborough MA 01752

SCHURMAN, DONALD LEE, human factors psychologist, consultant; b. Big Spring, Tex., June 16, 1938; s. Lawrence Logue and Ivis Mae (Martin) S.; m. Kathryn Francis Virnelson, Oct. 26, 1957 (div. 1969); children—Lorelei K., Travis L.E., Yvonne T., Kurt D.; m. Jill Ilene Gelassen, Sept. 10, 1976; 1 child, Aysha. A.B. U. Tex.-Arlington, 1965; Ph.D., U. Ill.-Urbana, 1970. Asst. prof. Emory U., Atlanta, 1969-73; foreman, instrument technician Micromeritics, Inc., Norcross, Ga., 1975-78; prin. scientist Applied Sci. Assocs., Valencia, Pa., 1978-84; sr. scientist Idaho Nat. Engring. Lab., Idaho Falls, 1984—; cons. in field. Contbr. articles to profl. jours. Vestry mem. St. Thomas Ch.-in-the-Fields, Gibsonia, Pa., 1980-81; active Citizens against Pollution, Gibsonia, 1982-83; troop bd. Boy Scouts Am., Gibsonia, 1983. NDEA Title IV fellow, 1965-68. Mem. Human Factors Soc., Psychonomic Soc., Am. Nuclear Soc. (mem. tech. group human factors, exec. com. 1981), IEEE (mem. nuclear power engring. subcom. 7). Episcopalian. Current work: Human factors applications to nuclear power plant operations and maintenance, cognitive models of operator and maintainer behavior, computer simulation of operator behavior. Subspecialties: Human factors engineering; Cognition. Home: 2648 S Higbee Idaho Falls ID 83401 Office: INEL/EG&G Idaho Inc PO Box 1625 Idaho Falls ID 83415

SCHURR, JOHN MICHAEL, chemistry educator, researcher; b. Pittsfield, Mass., Nov. 10, 1937; s. Franklin John Schurr and Pauline Virginia (Dean) Hidden; m. Karen Theresa Martin, Aug. 30, 1958; children—Kerstin Theresa, Rebecca Lynn. B.S., Yale U., 1959; Ph.D., U. Calif.-Berkeley, 1964. Research asst. Oak Ridge Nat. Lab., 1959; postdoctoral fellow U. Oreg., Eugene, 1965-66; asst. prof chemistry U. Wash., Seattle, 1966-72, assoc. prof., 1972-78, prof., 1978—; vis. scientist Swiss Fed. Water Inst., Dubendorf, 1974. Assoc. editor Ann. Rev. Phys. Chemistry, 1976—. Contbr. articles to profl. jours. NSF grantee; NIH grantee. Mem. Biophys. Soc., Am. Phys. Soc., Am. Chem. Soc. Club: Am. Alpine. Current work: Laser photon-correlation techniques; macromolecular Brownian motions; structures and dynamics of DNA; polyelectrolytes. Subspecialties: Biophysical chemistry; Physical chemistry. Home: 7719 Ashworth St N Seattle WA 98103 Office: Dept Chemistry Univ Wash Seattle WA 98195

SCHUSTER, MARVIN MEIER, physician, researcher, educator; b. Danville, Va., Aug. 30, 1929; s. Isaac and Rosel (Katzenstein) S.; m. Lois R. Bernstein, Feb. 19, 1961; children: Roberta, Nancy, Cathy. B.A., B.S., U. Chgo., 1951; M.D., 1955. Diplomate: Am. Bd. Internal Medicine. Intern Kings County Hosp., Bklyn., 1955-56; resident Balt. City Hosp., 1956-58, chief digestive disease div., resident, 1961—, Johns Hopkins Hosp., Balt., 1958-61; prof. medicine and psychiatry Johns Hopkins U. Sch. Medicine, Balt., 1976—. Editor: Gastrointestinal Disorders, 1981; contbr. chpts. to textbooks, articles in field to profl. jours.; mem. editorial bd.: Gastroenterology, 1978-81, Gastrointestinal Endoscopy, 1979-81, Psychosomatics, 1979—. Bd. dirs. Am. Cancer Soc., 1975—, pres. Md. div. 1985, chmn. med. adv. bd. Balt. Ostomy Assn., 1966—. Recipient St. George Disting. Service award Am. Cancer Soc., 1979. Fellow ACP, Am. Psychiat. Assn.; mem. Am. Gastroent. Assn. (chmn. audiovisual com. 1975-78), Am. Soc. Gastrointestinal Endoscopy (governing bd. 1975-78), Am. Physiol. Soc., AAUP. Democrat. Jewish. Current Work: Teaching and research in gastroenterology and application of biofeedback to gastrointestinal control. Subspecialties: Gastroenterology; Psychiatry. Home: 3101 Northbrook Rd Baltimore MD 21208 Office: Baltimore City Hosp 4940 Eastern Ave Baltimore MD 21224

SCHUSTER, ROBERT LEE, engineering geologist; b. Chehalis, Wash., Aug. 29, 1927; s. Rudolph Lester and Helen Aldine (Sonnenberg) S.; m. Patricia Louise McCanney, Feb. 19, 1955; children—Anne, Kathleen, Mark, Richard. B.S., Wash. State U., 1950; M.S., Ohio State U., 1952; M.S., Purdue U., 1958, Ph.D., 1960; Diploma of Imperial Coll. (NSF fellow), U. London, 1965. Registered profl. engr., Ind., Colo.; registered profl. geologist, Idaho. Instr. civil engring. Purdue U., Lafayette, Ind., 1956-60; asso. prof. U. Colo., Boulder, 1960-66, prof., 1966-67; prof., dept. chmn. U. Idaho, Moscow, 1967-74; chief engring. geol. br. U.S. Geol. Survey, Denver, 1974-79, geologist, 1979—. Editor: Landslides--Analysis and Control, 1978. Contbr. articles to profl. jours. Fellow ASCE, Geol. Soc. Am., Geol. Soc. (Gt. Britain); mem. Assn. Engring. Geologists, Internat. Assn. Engring. Geology. Roman Catholic. Current work: Landslide research. Subspecialties: Geology; Civil engineering. Home: 1941 Golden Vue Dr Golden CO 80401 Office: US Geol Survey Box 25046 MS 966 Denver CO 80225

SCHUSTER, TODD MERVYN, biotechnology company executive, biophysics educator; b. Mpls., June 27, 1933; s. David Theodore and Ann (Kaluser) S.; m. Nancy Joanne Mottashed, June 28, 1935; 1 dau., Lela Alexa. Ph.D., Washington U., 1963. Asst. prof. dept. biology SUNY, Buffalo, 1966-70; Assoc. prof. dept. biology U. Conn., Storrs, 1970-75, prof., 1975—, head dept., 1977-81; pres., chief exec. officer Xenogen, Inc., Storrs, 1981—; vis. scientist Max Planck Inst., Goettingen, Germany, 1963-66, 67, 68; vis. prof. chemistry dept. Ind. U., 1976; McCollum-Pratt prof. biology dept. Johns Hopkins U., Balt., 1979-80; mem. NIH grant rev. panels, biophysics and biophys. chemistry panel, 1971-75, Biomed. Scis. Postdoctoral Fellowship Panel, 1976, Sickle Cell Disease Adv. Panel, 1977; mem. biol. instrumentation panel NSF, 1984—. USPHS fellow, 1959-63 63-66. Mem. Am. Chem. Soc., Biophys. Soc., AAAS, Am. Soc. Biol. Chemists. Current Work: Biophysical chemistry, structure and functions of proteins, muscle protein structure, hemoglobin function, mechanisms of virus assembly, rapid reaction kinetics, spectroscopy of biopolymers, research management. Subspecialties: Biophysical chemistry; Molecular biology. Home: 124 Waterville Rd Farmington CT 06032 Office: Xenogen Inc 1764 Storrs Rd Storrs CT 06268

SCHUSTER, WILLIAM STANLEY FALLON, plant ecology researcher, environmental protection specialist; b. Phila., Oct. 15, 1956; s. Edgar Howard and Nancy Louise (Pence) S.; m. Frances Jeanne Fallon, May 26, 1984. B.A., Columbia U., 1978; M.S., Pa. State U., 1983. Preserve caretaker Washington Crossing State Park, Pa., 1979-80; forest ecology researcher Pa. State U., University Park, 1981-83; mem. environ. protection dept. Pa. Dept. Environ. Resources, Greensburg, 1983-84, forester, 1984-85; forest ecology researcher U. Colo., 1985—. Contbr. articles to profl. jours. Acad. scholar Columbia U., 1975-78. Mem. Ecol. Soc. Am., Am. Inst. Biol. Scis. Current work: Forest ecosystem dynamics, ecology of drastically disturbed lands, rocky mountain plant ecology, population and community studies at tree line. Subspecialties: Ecology (biology); Resource conservation. Home: 4825 Thunderbird Circle Apt 25 Boulder CO 80303 Office: Dept EPO Biology Ramaley Bldg U Colo Boulder CO 80309

SCHVANEVELDT, ROGER WAYNE, psychology educator; b. Logan, Utah, Apr. 11, 1941; s. Dee W. Schvaneveldt and Betty (Bench) Schvaneveldt Latimer; m. Ann West, Sept. 26, 1959; 1 child, Susan. B.A., U. Utah, 1963; M.S., U. Wis., 1965, Ph.D., 1967. Asst. prof. SUNY-Stony Brook, 1967-70, assoc. prof., 1970-77; prof. psychology N.Mex. State U., Las Cruces, 1977—. Contbr. articles to profl. jours. Fellow AAAS; mem. Am. Psychol. Assn., Psychonomic Soc., Assn. for Computing Machinery, Cognitive Sci. Soc., Human Factors Soc. Current work: Empirical and theoreticalwork in cognitive modelling and human-computer interaction. Subspecialties: Cognition; Artificial intelligence. Office: Psychology Dept New Mexico State U Box 3452 Las Cruces NM 88003

SCHVARTZMAN, JORGE BERNARDO, cell biologist, researcher; b. Asunción, Paraguay, Dec. 14, 1948; s. Isaac and Olga (Blinder) S.; m. Dora B. Krimer, Jan. 7, 1971; children: Juan Manuel, Daniel Ignacio. Agrl. Engr., U. Nacional de Asunción, 1972; Ph.D., Universidad Politécnica de Madrid, 1978. Research assoc. Instituto de Biología Celular, Madrid, 1976-79, 82—, Brookhaven Nat. Lab., N.Y.C., 1980-82 Current Work: Plant genetics and cytogenetics, DNA replication, damage and repair in higher embryology. Subspecialties: Cell biology; Genome organization.

SCHWAB, ARTHUR WILLIAM, chemist, researcher; b. Mpls., July 17, 1917; s. John Jacob and Effie (Anderson) S.; m. Virginia Ruth Hanson, Sept. 28, 1945; children—Roberta, David, Donald, Sandra. B.S. in Chemistry, U. Minn., 1941; Ph.D., Bradley U., 1952. Chemist U.S. Dept. Agr., Peoria, Ill., 1942—. Patentee in field (14). Contbr. articles to profl. jours. Served with USN, 1945-46. Recipient Superior Service award U.S. Dept. Agr., 1952, cert. of merit, 1963. Mem. Am. Chem. Soc., Am. Oil Chemists Soc. (colloid and surface sci. div.), Am. Contract Bridge League. Congregationalist. Current work: Basic research on micellization and microemulsion chemistry and development of hybrid fuels from renewable agriculture resources. Subspecialties: Organic chemistry; Physical chemistry. Home: 2233 W Albany St Peoria IL 61604 Office: US Dept Agriculture 1815 N University St Peoria IL 61604

SCHWAB, C. WILLIAM, physician. Head div. trauma and emergency medicine U. Medicine and Dentistry of N.J., Piscataway. Subspecialty: Critical care. Office: U Medicine and Dentistry of NJ Div Trauma and Emergency PO Box 101 Piscataway NJ 08854

SCHWABEL, MARY JANE, virologist, nurse; b. Buffalo, Oct. 9, 1946; d. Albert Thomas and Doris Katherine (Schottin) S. B.S., Damen Coll., 1968; M.S., Canisius Coll., 1975; A.A.S. in Nursing, Trocaire Coll., 1983. Cert. in epidemiology, registered nurse, N.Y. Research asst. Erie County Virology Lab., Erie County Med. center, Buffalo, 1968-74, sr. serology technician/supr., 1974-79, chief virologist, 1980—. Author profl. papers. Mem. Western N.Y. Infection Control Soc., Am. Soc. Microbiology, Am. Public Health Assn., N.Y. State Assn. Public Health Labs., N.Y. State Public Health Assn., Erie County Soc. Prevention Cruelty to Animals, North Shroe Animal League, Nat. Antivivisection Soc., Internat. Wildlife Fedn., Nat. Wildlife Fedn., Am. Forestry Assn., Beta Beta Beta. Current Work: Diagnostic virology and infection control. Subspecialties: Virology (biology); Preventive medicine. Office: 462 Grider St Buffalo NY 14215

SCHWAN, HERMAN PAUL, educator, research scientist; b. Aachen, Germany, Aug. 7, 1915; came to U.S., 1947, naturalized, 1952; s. Wilhelm and Meta (Pattberg) S.; m. Anne Marie DelBorello, June 15, 1949; children: Barbara, Margaret, Steven, Carol, Cathryn. Student, U. Goettingen, 1934-37; Ph.D., U. Frankfurt, 1940; Doctor habil. in physics and biophysics, 1946. Research scientist, prof. Kaiser Wilhelm Inst. Biophysics, 1937-47; asst. dir. Kaiser Wilheim Inst. Biophysics, 1945-47; research sci. USN, 1947-50; prof. elec. engring., prof. elec. engring. in phys. medicine, assoc. prof. phys. medicine U. Pa., Phila., 1950—, Alfed F. Moore prof., 1983—, dir. electromed. div., 1952—, chmn. biomed. engring., 1961-73, program dir. biomed. engr. tng. program, 1960-77; vis. prof. U. Calif. at Berkeley, 1956, U. Frankfurt (W.Ger.), 1962; lectr. Johns Hopkins U., 1962-67; W.W. Clyde vis. prof. U. Utah, Salt Lake City, 1980; Fgn. sci. mem. Max Planck Soc. Adv. Research, Germany, 1962—; cons. NIH, 1962—; chmn. nat. and internat. meetings biomed. engring. and biophysics, 1959, 61, 65; mem. nat. adv. council environ. health HEW, 1969-71; mem. Nat. Acad. Scis.-NRC coms., 1968-77, Nat. Acad. Engring., 1975—. Co-author: Advances in Medical and Biological Physics, 1957, Therapeutic Heat, 1958, Physical Techniques in Medicine and Biology, 1963; Editor: Biol. Engring, 1969; Mem. editorial bd.: Environ. Biophysics; Contbr. articles to profl. jours. Recipient Citizenship award Phila., 1952, 1st prize AIEE, 1953, Achievement award Phila. Inst. Elec. Engring. and Electronics, 1963, Rajewsky prize for biophysics, 1974; U.S. sr. scientist award Alexander von Humboldt Found., 1980-81; Biomed. Engring. Edn. award Am. Soc. Engring. Edn., 1983. Fellow IEEE (Morlock award 1967, Edison medal 1983, Centennial award 1984, chmn. and vice chmn. nat. profl. group biomed. engring. 1955, 62-68), AAAS; mem. Bioelectromagnetic Soc. (d'Arsonval award 1985), Am. Standards Assn. (chmn. com. 1961-64), Biophys. Soc. (publicity com., council, constrn. com.), Soc. for Cryobiology, Internat. Fedn. Med., and Biol. Engring., Biomed. Engring. Soc. (dir.), Sigma Xi, Eta Kappa Nu. Current Work: Electrial and acoustic properties of biomatter; biological effects of nonionizing radiation; bioelectrodes, clinical applications of microwaves and ultrasound. Subspecialties: Biophysics (biology); Biomedical engineering. Home: 99 Kynlyn Rd Radnor PA 19087 also 162 59th St Avalon NJ 08202 Office: Dept Bioengring D2 U Pa Philadelphia PA 19104

SCHWANHAUSSER, ROBERT ROWLAND, aerospace engineering company executive; b. Buffalo, N.Y., Sept. 15, 1930; s. Edwin Julius and Helen Putnam (Rowland) S.; m. Mary Lea Hunter, Oct. 17, 1953 (div. 1978); children: Robert Hunter, Mark Putnam; m. Beverly Bohn Allemann, Dec. 31, 1979. S.B. in Aero. Engring, MIT, 1952. Project engr. Continental Aviation & Engring. Co., Detroit, 1954; field service rep. Ryan Aero. Co., San Diego, 1954-56, project engr., 1956-59, program mgr., 1959-62, chief engr., 1962-64, dir. drone programs, 1964-66, v.p. aerospace, 1966-72, exec. v.p. programs, 1972-73, exec. v.p. internat., 1973-75; pres. Condur Aerospace/Condur Engring., San Diego-/El Paso, Calif., 1975-77; v.p. bus. devel. All Am. Engring., Wilmington, Del., 1977-79; v.p. internat. and RPV programs Teledyne Ryan Aero., San Diego, 1979-82; v.p. advanced program Teledyne Brown Engring., Huntsville, Ala., 1982-83; pres. Teledyne CAE, Toledo, Ohio, 1983—. Bd. dirs. Cornerstone Found., Riverside Hosp. Served to 1st lt. USAF, 1952-54. Fellow AIAA (assoc.); mem. Am. Def. Preparedness Assn., Navy League, Nat. Rifle Assn., Nat. Assn. Remotely Piloted Vehicles (trustee 1972—), Theta Delta Chi. Clubs: Inverness, Maumee River Yacht, Greenhead Hunting (founder, pres. San Diego 1937-77). Current Work: Unmanned and manned aircraft and missile systems engineering. Subspecialties: Aeronautical engineering; Aerospace engineering and technology. Office: 1330 W Laskey Rd Toledo OH 43612

SCHWANK, JOHANNES WALTER, chemical engineering educator; b. Zams, Tyrol, Austria, July 6, 1950; came to U.S., 1978; s. Friedrich Karl and Johanna (Ruepp) S.; m. Lynne Violet Duguay, May 11, 1985. Ph.D., U. Innsbruck, Austria, 1978. Research assoc., lectr. U. Mich., Ann Arbor, 1978-80, asst. prof., 1980-84, assoc. prof. chem. engring., 1984—. Contbr. articles to profl. publs. Fulbright-Hays scholar, 1978. Mem. Mich. Catalysis Soc. (pres. 1984—), Am. Chem. Soc., Am. Inst. Chem. Engrs. (affiliate), Materials Research Soc., Verien Osterreichischer Chemiker. Roman Catholic. Current work: Heterogeneous catalysis, surface science, spectroscopy, electron microscopy, chemical sensors. Subspecialties: Catalysis chemistry; Chemical engineering. Office: U Mich 3-14 Dow Bldg Ann Arbor MI 48109

SCHWARCZ, HENRY PHILIP, geology educator; b. Chgo., July 22, 1933; came to Can., 1962; s. Arthur and Zita Elizabeth (Strauss) S.; m. Molly Ann Robinson, Dec. 20, 1964; 1 child, Joshua Arthur. A.B., U. Chgo., 1952; M.S., Calif. Inst. Tech., 1955, Ph.D., 1960. Research fellow Enrico Fermi Inst., U. Chgo., 1960-62; prof.dept. geology McMaster U., Hamilton, Ont., Can., 1962—; vis. prof. Hebrew U. Jerusalem, 1975-76, 82-83. Assoc. editor Geochimica Cosmochimica Acta. Contbr. to publs. in field. Fulbright grantee, 1968. Fellow Geol. Soc. Am., Royal Soc. Can.; mem. Geochem. Soc., Am. Quaternary Assn. Current work: Isotope geochemistry of light elements in rocks, minerals, fossils;dating of archeological sites. Subspecialties: Geochemistry; Archeometry. Office: McMaster Univ Dept Geology Hamilton ON L8S 4M1 Canada

SCHWARTZ, ANTHONY, veterinary surgeon, educator, immunologist; b. Bklyn., July 30, 1940; s. Murray and Miriam Sarah (Wittes) S.; m. Claudia Rosenberg, July 21, 1963; children: Thomas Frederick, Eric Leigh. Student, Mich. State U., 1957-58; D.V.M., Cornell U., 1963; Ph.D., Ohio State U., 1972. Diplomate: Am. Coll. Vet. Surgeons, 1971. Pvt. practice vet. medicine, Huntington, N.Y., 1963-66; resident in surgery Animal Med. Ctr., N.Y.C., 1968-69; resident in surgery Ohio State U., 1969-70, asst. prof., head small animal surgery, 1973; from asst. prof. to assoc. prof. Yale U. Sch. Medicine, 1973-79; from assoc. prof. to prof., chmn. dept. surgery Tufts U. Sch. Vet. Medicine, Boston, 1979—, assoc. dean, 1984—; cons. U.S. Surg. Corp., Norwalk, Conn. Assoc. editor: Yale Jour. Biology and Medicine, 1977-79; sect. editor: Textbook of Small Animal Surgery, 1985; contbr. chpts. to books, articles to profl. jours. Mem. adv. bd. Morris Animal Found., 1981-84. Served to capt., vet. corps. U.S. Army, 1966-68. Recipient 1st prize N.Y. State Vet. Med. Soc., 1963; NIH grantee, 1975-84. Mem. AVMA, AAAS, Am. Assn. Immunologists, Mass. Vet. Med. Assn., N.Y. Acad. Sci., Sigma Xi, Phi Kappa Phi, Phi Zeta. Democrat. Jewish. Current Work: T cell interactions in the immune response. Subspecialties: Immunology (medicine); Immunopharmacology. Office: 200 Westboro Rd North Grafton MA

SCHWARTZ, ARTHUR GERALD, cancer researcher, gerontologist, educator; b. Balt., Mar. 13, 1941; s. Paul and Rose (Goldfinger) S. B.A., Johns Hopkins U., 1961; Ph.D., Harvard U., 1968. Postdoctoral fellow Albert Einstein Coll. Medicine, 1971-72; Asst. prof. microbiology, mem. Fels Research Inst., Temple U., 1972-77, assoc. prof., mem., 1977-85, prof., mem., 1985—; dir. gerontol. research Inst. on Aging, Temple U., 1982—. Contbr. articles to cancer research and gerontology jours. Jane Coffin Childs Meml. Fund fellow U. Oxford, 1968-71. Mem. Am. Assn. Cancer Research, Gerontol. Soc., Phi Beta Kappa. Current Work: Cancer prevention; gerontology; working with naturally occurring adrenal steroid, DHEA, which prevents many types of cancers in laboratory animals and appears to delay aging. Subspecialties: Cancer research (medicine); Gerontology. Home: 220 Locust St Philadelphia PA 19106 Office: Fels Research Institute Temple Med Sch Philadelphia PA 19140

SCHWARTZ, EDITH RICHMOND, medical educator, researcher, administrator; Ph.D., Cornell U. Med. Coll., 1964. Asst. prof. Sch. Medicine, U. Va., Charlottesville, 1972-75, assoc. prof., 1975-78; assoc. prof. dept. orthopedic surgery Sch. Medicine, Tufts U., Boston, 1978-81, prof., 1981—. Bd. dirs. Neighborhood Assn. Back Bay, 1981—. Current work: Biochemical and cell biology research related to osteoarthritis and osteoporosis. Subspecialties: Biochemistry (medicine); Orthopedics. Office: Sch Medicine Tufts Univ 136 Harrison Ave Boston MA 02111

SCHWARTZ, (ELLEN) SHIRLEY ECKWALL, chemist; b. Detroit, Aug. 26, 1935; s. Emil Victor and Jessie Grace (Galbraith) Eckwall; m. Ronald Elmer Schwartz, Aug. 23, 1957; children—Steven Dennis, Bradley Allen, George Byron. B.S. in Chemistry, U. Mich., 1957; B.S. in Math., Detroit Inst. Tech., 1978; M.S. in Chemistry, Wayne State U., 1962, Ph.D. in Chemistry, 1970. Asst. prof. Oakland Community Coll., Auburn Heights, Mich., 1971-73; asst. prof. Detroit Inst. Tech., 1973-79, head div. math.-sci., 1977-79; research staff scientist BASF (Wyandotte Corp., Wyandotte, Mich., 1979-81, sect. head, 1981; staff research scientist Gen. Motors Research Labs., Warren, Mich., 1981—. Author articles in field; contbr. papers to profl. confs., U.S., Eng.; patentee water-based hydraulic fluids, thickened water-based hydraulic fluids, water-based low form hydraulic fluid employing 2-ethylhexanol defoamer, water-based hydraulic fluids having improved lubricity and corrosion inhibiting properties, Can. patents: water-based hydraulic fluids having improved lubricity and corrosion inhibiting properties employing neodecanoic acid, thickened water-based hydraulic fluids. Corr. sec. Childbirth without Pain Edn. Assn., Detroit, 1962, Warren-Centerline Human Relations Council, 1962. named Outstanding Mem. of Faculty, Detroit Inst. Tech., 1976. Mem. Am. Soc. Lubrication Engrs. (bd. dirs. 1985—, chmn. Detroit sect. 1982-83), Soc. Automotive Engrs., Am. Chem. Soc., Tissue Culture Assn., Sigma Xi. Lutheran. Current work: Engine lubrication with alternative fuels, the process of oil aging, water-based lubricants. Subspecialties: Lubrication; Corrosion. Office: Gen Motors Research Labs Warren MI 48090

SCHWARTZ, ILSA ROSLOW, neurobiologist, educator, researcher; b. Bklyn., Aug. 20, 1941; d. David and Lottie (Warshall) Roslow; m. Alan Gordon Schwartz, July 19, 1964; children—Leah Ellen, Seth Roslow. A.B., Vassar Coll., 1962; M.S., Yale U., 1964, Ph.D., 1968. USPHS fellow dept. anatomy Albert Einstein Coll. Medicine, Bronx, N.Y., 1968-69; research assoc. Ctr. for Neural Scis., Bloomington, Ind., 1970-73; asst. prof. anatomy and physiology Ind. U., Bloomington, 1973-75, asst. prof. neural scis., 1973-77, asst. prof. med. scis., 1975-77; vis. research anatomist dept. anatomy UCLA Sch. Medicine, 1976-77, asst. prof. head and neck surgery, 1977-81, assoc. prof., 1981—; mem. communicative disorders rev. com. Nat. Inst. Neurol. and Communicative Disorders and Stroke, Bethesda, Md., 1981-83, chmn., 1983-85. Contbr. articles to profl. jours., chpts. to books. Nat. Inst. Neurol. and Communicative Disorders and Stroke research grantee, 1972-75, 75-78, 78-81, 81-85, 85—; fellow Vassar Coll., 1962-63, NSF, 1962-63, USPHS, 1964-68. Mem. Assn. for Research in Otolaryngology (chmn. long-range planning com. 1984—), Soc. for Neurosci. (chmn. Bloomington chpt. 1975-76), Cajal club, Am. Assn. Anatomists, Assn. for Women in Sci., Women in Neurosci. Jewish. Current work: Neuroanatomy and neurochemistry of the auditory system and the vestibular system; studies of neurotransmitter related properties. Subspecialties: Neurobiology; Morphology. Office: UCLA Sch Medicine Head and Neck Surgery 31-24 Rehab Ctr Los Angeles CA 90024

SCHWARTZ, IRVING LEON, scientist, educator, physician; b. Cedarhurst, N.Y., Dec. 25, 1918; s. Abraham and Rose (Doniger) S.; m. Felice T. Nlerenberg, Jan. 12, 1946; children: Cornelia Ann, Albert Anthony, James Oliver. A.B., Columbia U., 1939; M.D., N.Y.U., 1943. Diplomate: Am. Bd. Internal Medicine. Intern, asst. resident Bellevue Hosp., N.Y.C., 1943-44, 46-47; NIH fellow physiology N.Y.U. Coll. Medicine, 1947-50; Am. Physiol. Soc. Porter fellow, also Gibbs meml. fellow in clin. sci. Rockefeller Inst., N.Y.C., 1950-51, Am. Heart Assn. fellow, 1951-52, asst., then assoc., 1952-58; asst. physician, assoc. physician Rockefeller Inst. Hosp., 1950-58; sr. scientist Brookhaven Nat. Lab., Upton, L.I., N.Y., 1958-61; attending physician Brookhaven Nat. Lab. Hosp., 1958—; research collaborator Brookhaven Nat. Lab., 1961—; Joseph Eichberg prof. physiology, dir. dept. U. Cincinnati Coll. Medicine, 1961-65; dean grad. faculties Mt. Sinai Med. and Grad. Schs., 1965-81; prof. physiology and biophysics, chmn. dept. Mt. Sinai Med. and Grad. Schs. City U. N.Y., 1968-79; exec. officer biomed. scis. doctoral program City U. N.Y., 1969-72, Dr. Harold and Golden Lamport disting. prof., 1979—; dir. Ctr. Peptide and Membrane Research Mt. Sinai Med. Ctr., 1979—; chmn. emeritus dept. physiology and biophysics Mt. Sinai Sch. Medicine, 1979—; dean emeritus Mt. Sinai Grad. Sch. Biol. Scis., 1980—. Contbr. articles to sci. publs. Pres. Life Scis. Found., 1962—. Served from 1st lt. to capt., M.C. AUS, 1944-46. Fellow A.C.P.; mem. Am. Physiol. Soc., Soc. Exptl. Biology and Medicine, Am. Soc. Clin. Investigation, Am. Fedn. Clin. Research, Biophys. Soc., Endocrine Soc., Harvey Soc., Soc. for Neurosci., Am. Heart Assn., John Jay Assos. Columbia Coll., AAAS, N.Y. Acad. Sci., Sigma Xi, Alpha Omega Alpha. Current Work: Conformation and mechanism of action of biologically-active peptides, particularly neurohypophyseal and other peptide hormones, membrane permeability and transport phenomena. Subspecialties: Psychophysiology; Biophysics (physics). Home: 1120 Fifth Ave New York NY 10028 also 9 Thorn Hedge Rd Bellport NY 11713 Office: Mount Sinai Med and Grad Schs City U NY 100th St and Fifth Ave New York NY 10029 also Med Research Center Brookhaven Nat Lab Upton NY 11973

SCHWARTZ, JACOB THEODORE, computer scientist; b. N.Y.C., Jan. 9, 1930; s. Harry and Hedwig (Kurzbartz) S.; m. Frances E. Allen, 1972; children: Rachel, Abby. B.S., CCNY, 1948; Ph.D., Yale U., 1951. Instr. Yale U., 1953-56, asst. prof., 1956-58; assoc. prof. computer sci. NYU, 1957-58; prof. computer sci. dept. Courant Inst. Math. Scis., 1958-59, dir. computer sci. div., 1982-83, chmn. dept., 1969-77; disting. lectr. math. and computer sci. U. Calif.-Santa Barbara, 1978—, MIT, 1980; chmn. computer sci. bd. NRC. Author: 11 books including Lectures on NonLinear Functional Analysis, 1968, Lectures on Differential Geometry and Topology, 1969; Editorial bd.: 11 books including Jour. Computer and Systems Scis, 1980-83, Communications on Pure and Applied Math, 1975-83, Advances in Applied Math, 1980-83; assoc. editor: 11 books including Jour. Programming Langs, 1979-83; Contbr. articles profl. jours. Sloane fellow, 1961-62; recipient Wilbur Cross medal Yale U., 1976, Townsend Harris medal CUNY, 1975, Steele prize Am. Math. Soc., 1981. Mem. Nat. Acad. Scis. Current Work: Algorithms, computer architecture, robotics, programming languages, software engineering, theoretical computer science. Subspecialties: Algorithms; Computer architecture. Home: Finney Farm Rd Croton on Hudson NY 10520 Office: 251 Mercer St New York NY 10012

SCHWARTZ, JAY WILLIAM, engineer; b. Scranton, Pa., Sept. 28, 1934; s. Max and Rose (Grossman) S.; m. Judith Rochelle Konigsberg, June 21, 1970; children—Karen Beth, Michael Paul, Stephen Ross. B.S. in Elec. Engring., U. Pa., 1956; M.S. in Engring., Yale U., 1960, Ph.D., 1964. Mem. tech. staff Inst. Def. Analyses, Arlington, Va., 1963-72; cons. to assoc. dir. for research U.S. Naval Research Lab., Washington, 1972-83; chief scientist, corp. dir. Avtec Systems Inc., Alexandria, Va., 1983—; vis. assoc. prof. Poly. Inst. Bklyn., 1967-68; adj. assoc. prof. George Washington U., Washington, 1972-76. Contbr. articles to profl. jours. Served to lt. USN, 1956-59. Schlumberger fellow, 1960-61. Mem. IEEE (sr.), Internat. Union Radio Sci. (U.S. chmn. Commn C 1985—). Jewish. Club: No. Va. Handball Assn. (v.p., 1984-85). Current work: Space and communication systems; military systems; intersatellite communications; satellite information and control systems and technology; satellite autonomy; fault and error control techniques. Subspecialties: Systems engineering; Telecommunications. Home: 9411 Garden Ct Potomac MD 20854 Office: Avtec Systems Inc 6304 Potomac Ave Alexandria VA 22307

SCHWARTZ, JEFFREY HUGH, physical anthropologist, educator; b. Richmond, Va., Mar. 6, 1948; s. Jack James and Lillian (Feldman) S. B.A., Columbia U., 1969, M.Phil., 1973, Ph.D., 1974; postgrad. Univ. Coll., London, 1971-72. Adj. lectr. Lehman Coll., Bronx, N.Y., 1973-74; asst. prof. anthropology U. Pitts., 1974-81, assoc. prof., 1981—; research assoc. Carnegie Mus. Natural History, Pitts., 1976—, Am. Mus. Natural History, N.Y.C., 1979—. Author: (with I. Tattersall) Evolutionary Relationships of Living Lemurs and Lorises, 1985. Editor: (with H. Rollins) Models and Methodologies in Evolutionary Theory, 1979; mem. editorial bd. Internat. Jour. Primatology, 1978—. Contbr. articles on primate evolution, dental growth and devel. Wenner-Gren Found. travel grantee, 1976; Am. Philos. Soc. travel-research grantee, 1978; NEH research grantee, 1979-81. Mem. Am. Assn. Phys. Anthropologists, AAAS, Soc. Vertebrate Paleontology, Soc. for Study Evolution, Sigma Xi. Democrat. Jewish. Current work: Theoretical and practical issues in determining homology and phylogenetic reconstruction, especially molecular/morphological discrepancies. Subspecialties: Evolutionary biology; Dental growth and development. Home: 4017 Windsor St Pittsburgh PA 15217 Office: Dept Anthropology U Pitts Pittsburgh PA 15260

SCHWARTZ, LELAND DWIGHT, veterinarian, avian pathologist, educator; b. Enid, Okla., July 26, 1925; s. Herbert Elmore and Laura Mabel (Clark) S.; m. Wilma Jo Howe, June 20, 1954; children—Vicki Jeanne, Roger Dwight. D.V.M., Okla. State U., 1953; M.S., U. Ga., 1963. Pvt. practice vet. medicine, Garber, Okla., 1953-55; veterinarian Hartsel Ranch, Colo., 1955-56; vet. insp. U.S. Dept. Agr., Garden City, Kans., 1956-59, poultry insp., Faribault, Minn., 1959-61; instr. U. Ga., Athens, 1961-64; prof. Pa. State U., University Park, 1964-84; prof. vet. medicine Mich. State U., East Lansing, 1984—. Author: Poultry Health Handbook, 1972, 77. Served with USMCR, 1943-46. Recipient Gamebirl Indsl. award Pa. Pa. Game Breeders Assn., 1983; Wildlife Conservation award Pa. Game Commn., 1984; Service award Am. Assn. Extension Vet. Service, 1984. Mem. AVMA, Am. Assn. Avian Pathologists, Am. Assn. Extension Veterinarians (sec.-treas. 1979-84), Pa. Vet. Med. Assn. (Vet. of Yr. award 1984), Am. Poultry Sci. Assn. Current work: Epidemiology poultry health and production in commercial industry operations. Subspecialty: Pathology (veterinary medicine). Home: 3871 Sandlewood Okemos MI 48864 Office: Animal Health Diagnostic Lab Coll Vet Medicine Mich State U PO Box 30076 East Lansing MI 48909

SCHWARTZ, MARSHALL ZANE, pediatric surgeon, educator; b. Mpls., Sept. 1, 1945; s. Sidney Shay and Peggy Belle (Lieberman) S.; m. Michele Carroll Walker, Oct. 16, 1971; children: Lisa, Jeffrey. B.S., U. Minn., 1968, M.D., 1970. Diplomate: Am. Bd. Surgery (cert. pediatric surgery). Instr., Harvard U., Boston, 1978-79; asst. in surgery Children's Hosp. Med. Ctr., Boston, 1978-79; asst. prof. surgery and pediatrics U. Tex. Med. Br., Galveston, 1979-81, assoc. prof., 1981-83, chief pediatric surgery, 1980-83, surgeon-in-chief Child Health Center, 1980-83; assoc. prof. surgery and pediatrics U. Calif.-Davis, 1983—. Author: (with others) Can We Influence Intestine Adaptation, 1983; contbr. articles to profl. jours. Recipient Basil O'Conner Research award March of Dimes Found., 1981; Young Investigator award NIH, 1982; Research award Found. for Children, 1982; James W. McLaughlin Fund award U. Tex., 1983. Fellow ACS, Am. Acad. Pediatrics; mem. AMA, Am. Pediatric Surgery Assn., Assn. Acad. Surgery, Soc. Univ. Surgeons, Am. Gastroenterol. Assn., Pacific Assn. Pediatric Surgeons, AAAS, N.Y. Acad. Sci., Soc. Surgery Alimentary Tract, Sigma Xi. Jewish. Current Work: Functional and immunologic development of the small intestine. The role of gastrointestinal hormones on the function of the small intestine. Subspecialties: Surgery; Physiology (medicine). Office: U Calif Med Ctr 4301 X St Sacramento CA 95817

SCHWARTZ, MISCHA, electrical engineering educator; b. N.Y.C., Sept. 21, 1926; s. Isaiah and Bessie (Weinstein) S.; m. Charlotte Fishman, July 12, 1970; 1 child, David Joshua. B.E.E., Cooper Union, 1947; M.E.E., Poly. Inst. Bklyn., 1949; Ph.D., Harvard U., 1951. Project engr. Sperry Gyroscope Co., Lake Success, N.Y., 1947-52; from asst. prof. to prof. elec. engring. Poly. Inst. Bklyn., 1952-74; prof. elec. engring. and computer sci. Columbia U., N.Y.C., 1974—, dir. Ctr. Telecommunications Research, 1985—; vis. scientist IBM, 1980; cons. Author: Information Transmission, Modulation and Noise, 1969, 3d edit., 1980; Computer Communication Network Design and Analysis, 1977; co-author: Communication Systems and Techniques, 1966; Signal Processing, 1975. Pres. div. Am. Jewish Congress, 1977-80. Served with U.S. Army, 1944-46. Recipient award Australian-Am. Edn. Found., 1975; also others. Fellow IEEE (bd. dirs. 1978-79, pres. Communications Soc. 1984-85, chmn. info. theory group 1964-65; edn. medal 1983, Centennial Hall of Fame 1984), AAAS. Subspecialties: Telecommunications; Distributed systems and networks. Home: 66 Maple Dr Great Neck NY 11021 Office: Columbia U New York NY 10027

SCHWARTZ, MORTIMER LEONARD, medical educator, researcher; b. Newark, Jan. 12, 1915; s. Herman and Rose (Nusbaum) S.; m. Rene Kanengiser, Mar. 25, 1941; children: Gary, Jessica Schwartz Auerbach, Alison. M.D., Eclectic Med. Coll., Cin., 1938. Diplomate: Am. Bd. Internal Medicine, 1954, Cardiovascular Disease, 1962. Intern Alexian Bros. Hosp., Elizabeth, N.J., 1938-39; resident Jersey City Hosp., 1947-48; practice medicine specializing in internal medicine, and cardiovascular disease, N.J., 1940-42, 46-47, 47—; mem. faculty N.J. Med. Sch., Newark, 1958-72; prof. medicine Albert Einstein Coll. Medicine, Bronx, N.Y., 1973-77; chief cardiovascular sect. Bronx Lebanon Hosp., 1972-77; dir. medicine Mountainside Hosp., Montclair, N.J., 1977-80; prof. medicine U. Medicine and Dentistry/N.J. Med. Sch., Newark, 1966-72, 79—; dir. dept. medicine Bergen Pines County Hosp., Paramus, N.J., 1981-84. Served to maj. U.S. Army, 1942-46. Recipient Harry Gold award, 1974. Fellow ACP Am. Coll. Cardiology, Am. Coll. Chest Physicians, Council on Clin. Cardiology of Am. Heart Assn., Am. Coll. Clin. Pharmacology. Current Work: Clinical pharmacology. Subspecialties: Cardiology; Internal medicine. Home: 49 Sommer Ave Maplewood NJ 07040 Office: 51 Sommer Ave Maplewood NJ 07040

SCHWARTZ, ROBERT NELSON, chemist; b. New Haven, Feb. 4, 1940; s. Edward Matthew and Filomena (Celentano) S.; m. Carole Anne Dallape, Mar. 2, 1971; children—Carrie Alison, Dana Ann. B.A., U. Conn., 1962, M.S., 1965; Ph.D., U. Colo., 1969. Postdoctoral fellow U. Ill.-Chgo., 1969-70, asst. prof. chemistry, 1970-76, assoc. prof., 1976-81; vis. prof. UCLA, 1979-81; mem. tech. staff Hughes Research Labs., Malibu, Calif., 1981—; adj. prof. Calif. State U.-Northridge, 1981—. Editor: Time Domain Electron Spin Resonance, 1979. Contbr. articles to profl. jours. Mem. Am. Phys. Soc., N.Y. Acad. Sci., Am. Chem. Soc., Sigma Xi, Phi Lambda Upsilon. Current work: Magnetic resonance; magnetic and optical properties of amorphous solids; nonlinear optical properties of organic materials. Subspecialties: Electron spin resonance; Condensed matter physics. Office: Hughes Research Labs 3011 Malibu Canyon Rd Malibu CA 90265

SCHWARTZ, SANDRA, science and mathematics educator; b. N.Y.C., Jan. 25, 1932; d. Abraham and Pauline (Eisner) Wiener; divorced; children—Rachel Paula Fainman, Abby G. Schwartz. B.S. in Edn., CCNY, 1951; M.S., Rutgers U., 1952; Ph.D., Yale U., 1956. Vis. instr., dep. chmn. Columbia U., 1964-69; adj. asst. prof. Baruch Coll., N.Y.C., 1979-80; instr. Queens Coll., N.Y.C., 1980-81; adj. asst. prof. N.Y. Inst. Tech., 1979—; mem. faculty New Sch., N.Y.C., 1981—. Chmn. LWV, N.Y.C., 1961-63. Fellow Rutgers U., 1951-52, Yale U., 1952-56; research grantee AAUW, 1955-56. Mem. AAAS, Am. Astron. Soc., Planetary Soc., Nat. Space Inst. Current work: Research in radiative transfer; teacher of astronomy, astrophysics (graduate level) space science, physics, mathematics. Subspecialties: Theoretical astrophysics; Satellite studies. Home: 353 E 76th St New York NY 10021 Office: New Sch for Social Research 66 W 12th St New York NY 10011

SCHWARTZ, STEVEN OTTO, physician, hematology educator, researcher; b. Kapolch, Hungary, July 6, 1911; came to U.S., 1923, naturalized, 1929; s. Otto and Henrietta (Lemberger) S.; m. Ruth Deimel, Apr. 24, 1942; children—Kay, Ann, James. B.S., Northwestern U., 1932, M.S., 1935, M.D., 1936. Diplomate Am. Bd. Internal Medicine. Intern Michael Reese Hosp., Chgo., 1935-37, assoc. hematologist, chief hematology clinic of Mandel Clinic, 1938-50; Charlton fellow in hematology Tufts U. Med. Sch., Boston, 1937-38; dir. hematology dept. Cook County Hosp., Chgo., 1938-68; assoc. in medicine Mt. Sinai Hosp., Chgo., 1948-51; attending hematologist West Side VA Hosp., Chgo., 1955-56; cons. hematologist Ill. Masonic Hosp., 1941-84, Highland Park Hosp., 1950-84, Mother Cabrini Hosp., 1951-84, Columbus (medicine). 1955-84, Hines VA Hosp., 1956-84; sr. attending physician Northwestern Meml. Hosp., 1955-84; prof. Cook County Postgrad. Sch., Chgo., 1939-68; asst. prof. U. Ill., 1942-47; prof. Chgo. Med. Sch., 1947-55; assoc. prof. medicine Northwestern U., Chgo., 1955-59, prof., 1959-84, prof. emeritus,

1984—. Asst. editor Blood Jour., 1946-50. Recipient Disting. Service award Columbus-Cuneo-Cabrini Med. Ctr., 1982, Solano medal of honor Quincy Coll., 1966; citation City of Hope Nat. Med. Ctr., 1969; testimonial Cook County Hosp., 1973, Leukemia Research Found., 1976. Fellow ACP, AAAS; mem. AMA, Am. Fedn. Clin. Research, Soc. for Exptl. Biology Medicine, Central Soc. for Clin. Research, Chgo. Soc. Internal Medicine, Internat. Soc. Hematology (charter), European Soc. Hematology (corr.), Acad. Internat. Medicine, Am. Assn. for Cancer Research, Am. Hematology Soc., Ill. Med. Soc. Chgo. Med. Soc. Inst. Medicine Chgo., Sigma Xi. Republican. Jewish. Subspecialty: Virology (medicine). Home: 610 Rice St Highland Park IL 60035

SCHWARTZ, WILLIAM JOSEPH, neurologist, neuroscientist; b. Phila., Mar. 28, 1950; s. Leon and Helene (Siris) S.; m. Randi Joy Eisner, July 1, 1979. Student, U. So. Calif., Los Angeles, 1967-68; B.S. summa cum laude, U. Calif., Irvine, 1971; M.D., U. Calif., San Francisco, 1974. Diplomate: Am. Bd. Psychiatry and Neurology, 1982. Intern U. Calif.-H.C. Moffitt Hosp., San Francisco, 1974-75, resident in neurology, 1978-81; research assoc. Lab. Neurophysiology NIMH, Bethesda, 1975-77, Lab. Cerebral Metabolism, 1977-78; instr. neurology Harvard U., 1981-82, asst. prof. neurology, 1982—; asst.in neurology Mass. Gen. Hosp., 1981-83, asst. neurologist, 1983—; vis. fellow Neuroscis. Inst., N.Y. Contbr. articles in field to profl. jours. Served with USPHS, 1975-78. Recipient Merck Manual award, 1974; Med. Found. Charles A. King Trust fellow, 1981-82; William F. Milton Fund of Harvard U. fellow, 1982; Charles H. Hood Found. fellow, 1982; NINCDS Tchr.-Investigator devel. awardee, 1982—; March of Dimes Basil O'Connor grantee, 1983-85. Mem. Soc. Neuroscience, AAAS, Am. Acad. Neurology, Alpha Omega Alpha. Current Work: Clinical neurology; neural regulation of circadian rhythms. Subspecialties: Neurology; Neuroendocrinology. Office: Neurology Research 4 Mass Gen Hosp Boston MA 02114

SCHWARTZKOPF, STEVEN HENRY, research scientist, consultant; b. Lincoln, Nebr., May 4, 1951; s. Leo Robert and Lydia Katherine (Filbert) S.; m. Johanna Witherspoon, Apr. 2, 1982. B.S., U. Nebr., 1973; M.A., U. Calif.-Davis, 1976, Ph.D., 1978. Teaching asst. U. Calif.-Davis, 1973-76, lectr., 1976-79; research scientist U. N.H., Durham, 1979—, cons. in field. Author: (with P.E. Stofan) A Chamber Design for Closed Ecological Systems Research, 1981. NASA grantee, 1982; U. Calif.-Davis fellow, 1977; Jessie Smith Noyes and Robert Sterling Clark scholar, 1976. Mem. AAAS, Ecol. Soc. Am. Democrat. Lutheran. Inventor plant growth chamber for life support system experimentation-NASA. Current Work: Closed ecological life support systems, controlled environments, develop closed ecological life support systems (CELSS) for outer space life support applications and application to terrestrial agriculture. Subspecialties: Satellite studies; Plant growth. Office: NASA Ames Research Ctr MS 239-10 Moffett Field CA 94035

SCHWARTZMAN, BORIS, prosthodontist; b. Mexico City, Mex., June 27, 1954; s. Moses and Mira (Yasinovsky) S. B.S. Coll. Israelista de Mex, 1972; D.D.S. magna cum laude, Tech. U. Mex., 1976; postdoctoral cert. biomaterial scis., UCLA, 1976-77, splty. cert. in prosthetic dentistry, 1979, splty. cert. in maxillofacial prosthetics, 1980. Practice dentistry specializing in prosthodontics, Mexico City, 1981—; faculty mem. Tech. U. Mex., 1981—; lectr. UCLA, 1981—; expert cons. Calif. Dental Assn., Los Angeles, 1981—. Contbr. chpt. to book, articles and abstracts to profl. jours. Bd. dirs. Jewish Sport Ctr., Mexico City, 1982—. Mem. Am. Acad. Maxillo Facial Prosthetics, Am. Coll. Prosthodontists (hon. mention 1979), Internat. Assn. Dental Research, Am. Acad. Crown and Bridge (Stanley D. Tylman award 1980), Mexican Dental Assn., Atenco Nacional de Ciencias (hon.), Mex. Inst. Culture (hon.). Current Work: Clinical application of prosthetic dentistry, dental biomaterial sciences, research in field. Subspecialty: Prosthodontics. Office: Campos Eliseos 385 B7 piso Mexico City 11560 Mexico

SCHWARZ, ANTON J., research executive; b. Munich, Ger., May 26, 1927; s. Joseph and Therese (Bauer) S.; m. Josephine F. Morrissey, Nov. 15, 1952; children: Theresa, Anton. M.D., Ludwigs Maximilian U., Munich, 1951; grad., Advanced Mgmt. Program, Harvard Bus. Sch., 1972. Intern, resident City Hosp., Munich, St. John's Hosp., L.I., N.Y., Dobbs Ferry Hosp., N.Y., 1951-54; sr. research assoc. U. Cin. Coll. Medicine, 1954-56; dir. virus research Pitman Moore div. Dow Chem. Co., 1965; dir. human health research and devel. Dow Chem. Co., 1965-71, dir. biol. research and devel., dir. biol. labs., 1971-75; med. dir. Dow Europe, 1975-77; dir. corp. med. research Schering-Plough Corp., Bloomfield, N.J., 1977-81, dir. med. sci., 1981—. Contbr. articles to profl. jours. Recipient Order of Merit of Medicine Brazil; Wolverine Frontiersman award State of Mich., 1968. Mem. Soc. Exptl. Biology and Medicine, Am. Assn. Immunologists, N.Y. Acad. Scis., AAAS, AMA. Patentee in field; inventor, developer Schwarz strain further attenuated measles vaccine. Current Work: Direction of research in new drugs and biologicals; evaluation of new products. Subspecialties: Internal medicine; Virology (medicine). Home: 1 Euclid Ave Apt 4A Summit NJ 07901 Office: 2000 Galloping Hill Rd Kenilworth NJ 07033

SCHWARZ, KLAUS W., physicist, researcher; b. Heidelberg, Germany, Mar. 12, 1938; came to U.S., 1949, naturalized, 1956; s. Klaus Schwarz and Else P. (Weber) Campbell; m. Barbara Helen Rice, June 30, 1962; children—Jennifer Ann, Alison Ruth. B.A., Harvard U., 1960; M.S., U. Chgo., 1962, Ph.D., 1967. Research assoc. U. Chgo., 1967-69, asst. prof., 1969-76; research staff mem. IBM Watson Research Ctr., Yorktown Heights, N.Y., 1976—. Contbr. articles to profl. jours. NSF grantee, 1974-76, 79-84. Mem. Am. Phys. Soc., Phi Beta Kappa. Current work: Experimental and theoretical work in superfluid physics and classical fluid mechanics. Subspecialties: Low temperature physics; Fluid mechanics. Office: IBM Watson Research Ctr PO Box 218 Yorktown Heights NY 10598

SCHWARZ, RICHARD ANTON, chemist; b. Lansing, Mich., Oct. 29, 1953; s. William Stanley and Genevieve Louise (McCleary) S.; m. Macy Ann Schwarz, Dec. 30, 1978; children—Elisa Maria, Erika Nicole. B.S., U. S.D., 1976; postgrad. Wright State U., 1976-78. Research chemist Cosden Oil & Chem. Co., Big Spring, Tex., 1978-84, mgr. applications devel., 1984, LaPorte, Tex., 1985—. Contbr. articles to profl. jours. Patentee in field. Mem. Am. Chem. Soc., Soc. Plastics Engrs., Soc. Plastics Industry. Methodist. Current work: Applied polymer science, including formulation, characterization, economics, modelling and equipment design relating to thermoplastics in general. Subspecialty: Polymer chemistry. Address: Cosden Oil and Chem Co Box 1200 Deer Park TX 77536

SCHWARZBECK, CHARLES, clinical psychologist, psychoanalyst, clinical infant researcher; b. N.Y.C., Dec. 21, 1945; s. Charles and June (West) S. A.B., Kenyon Coll., 1967; Ed.M., Boston U., 1970; Ph.D. summa cum laude, U. Tex., Austin, 1976. Intern adult psychiatry Menninger Found., Topeka, Kans., 1974-75; fellow dept. psychiatry Children's Hosp., Washington, 1975-76; chief clin. psychologist Psychiat. Inst., Washington, 1977-82; clin. instr. psychiatry George Washington Sch. Medicine, Washington, 1977-78, clin. prof., 1978-82; clin. investigator NIMH, Bethesda, Md., 1980—; cons. PRETERM Centre for Reproductive Health, Washington, 1980-82; chief cons. Chelsea Sch., Silver Spring, Md., 1977-82. Contbr. chpts., articles in adult, child psychology to research publs. NIMH Infant Study Sect. fellow, 1981-83; NIMH fellow, 1972-74; vis. fellow Tavistock Centre, London, 1976. Mem. Psychologists Interested in Psychoanalysis. Current Work: Clinical infant research in neonates; family and sex therapy; applied research. Home and Office: 35 Wisconsin Circle Chevy Chase MD 20815

SCHWARZSCHILD, ARTHUR ZEIGER, physicist; b. Bklyn., Mar. 24, 1930; s. Myron and Helen (Zeiger) S.; m. Liliane Fuss, June 25, 1952; children—Karen Simon, Roger, Marc. B.A., Columbia U., 1951, M.A., 1952, Ph.D., 1957. Research assoc. Columbia U., N.Y.C., 1958; physicist Brookhaven Nat. Lab., Upton, N.Y., 1958-70, sr. physicist, 1970—, dep. chmn. physics dept., 1978-81, chmn. physics dept., 1981—; cons. NYU, N.Y.C., 1965-80; adj. prof. Pa. State U., 1967; mem. Nuclear Scis. Adv. Com. Dept. Energy, NSF, 1980-83. Contbr. articles to profl. jours. NATO fellow Weizmann Inst. Sci., Israel, 1966. Fellow Am. Phys. Soc., N.Y. Acad. Scis.; mem. AAAS, Sigma Xi. Current work: Heavy ion nuclear physics. Subspecialty: Nuclear physics. Office: Brookhaven Nat Lab Physics Dept Upton NY 11973

SCHWEBEL, SOLOMON LAWRENCE, physics educator; b. N.Y.C., Oct. 21, 1916; s. David and Minnie (Lilienfeld) S.; m. Devora Ruth Denenholz, Sept. 4, 1949; children—Robert Louis, Paul Henry. B.S., CCNY, 1937; M.S., NYU, 1947, Ph.D., 1954. Instr. Bklyn. Coll., 1954-55; staff mem. Lockheed Missile and Space Lab., Palo Alto, Calif., 1955-61; assoc. prof. physics, U. Cin., 1961-64, Boston Coll., Chestnut Hill, Mass., 1964—. Contbr. articles to profl. jours. Served with U.S. Army, 1942-45, PTO. Mem. Am. Phys. Soc., Am. Assn. Physics Tchrs., AAUP, Sigma Xi. Current work: Interaction theory. Subspecialties: Theoretical physics; Relativity and gravitation. Office: Dept Physics Boston Coll Chestnut Hill MA 02167

SCHWEIGHAUSER, CHARLES ARTHUR, astronomer; b. Alton, Ill., June 1, 1936; s. Arthur Albert and Julia (Bezold) S.; divorced; children—Robert, Scott. B.A., Williams Coll., 1958, M.A., 1960. Dir. McDonnell Planetarium, St. Louis, 1961-65; research assoc. Ctr. for Environ. Studies, Williams Coll., Williamstown, Mass., 1967-71; prof. astronomy, dir. obs. Sangamon State U., Springfield, Ill., 1975—, prof. environ. studies and literature, 1973—. Author: Astronomy From A to Z, 1979; Co-author: Astronomy and the Origin of the Earth, 1979, Mem. Am. Astron. Soc., Sigma Xi. Current work: Stellar spectroscopy-stellar classifications; temperatures spectra of peculiar stars; spectra of early-type stars. Subspecialty: Optical astronomy. Home: 413 W Walnut St Chatham IL 62629 Office: Sangamon State U Shepherd Rd Springfield IL 62708

SCHWEITZER, JEFFREY STEWART, physicist, researcher; b. N.Y.C., May 6, 1946; s. Benjamin D. and Bertha (Shavin) S.; m. Judith Louise Mokrzycki, June 27, 1970; 1 child, Julia Seijung. B.S., Carnegie Inst. Tech., 1967; M.S., Purdue U., 1969, Ph.D., 1972. Research fellow in physics Calif. Inst. Tech., Pasadena, 1972-74; scientist Schlumberger-Doll Research, Ridgefield, Conn., 1974—; panel mem. sci. faculty profl. devel. NSF, Washington, 1981. Contbr. articles to profl. jours. Patentee in field. Mem. Am. Phys. Soc. Current work: Nuclear physics, nuclear well logging (especially neutron-induced gamma-ray spectroscopy), nuclear astrophysics. Subspecialties: Nuclear physics; Nuclear well logging. Office: Schlumberger-Doll Research Old Quarry Rd Ridgefield CT 06877-4108

SCHWEIZER, FRANCOIS, astronomer; b. Switzerland, Aug. 16, 1942; s. Hans and Madeleine (Tobler) S.; m. Linda Y., May 25, 1975; children: Briana C., Maia K., Rena. Lizentiat, U. Bern, Switzerland, 1968; M.A. in Astronomy, U. Calif.-Berkeley, 1970, Ph.D. in Astronomy, 1974. Carnegie postdoctoral fellow Hale Obs., Pasadena, Calif., 1974-75; staff astronomer Cerro Tololo Inter-Am. Obs., La Serena, Chile, 1976-81; staff astronomer, dept. terrestrial magnetism Carnegie Instn. of Washington, 1981—. Mem. Schweizerische Astronomische Gesellschaft, Am. Astron. Soc., Astron. Soc. of the Pacific, Internat. Astron. Union. Current Work: Optical studies of colliding and merging galaxies; structure and formation of ellipticals; surface photometry and structure of spiral galaxies. Subspecialties: Optical astronomy; Graphics, image processing, and pattern recognition. Office: 5241 Broad Branch Rd NW Washington DC 20015

SCHWER, ROGER EDWIN, metallurgist; b. Cin., June 14, 1932; s. M. Clayton and Olga Elizabeth (Christenson) S.; m. Margaret Dicken, Jan. 29, 1956; 1 dau., Susan Elizabeth. B.S., Mich. State U., 1954; M.B.A., Seidman Coll. Bus., 1980. Registered profl. engr., Calif. Tech. advisor Revere Copper & Brass, Los Angeles, 1955-56; application engr. Inco Inc., N.Y.C., 1966-72; dir. mktg. Cannon Muskegon Corp., Mich., 1972-80, pres., gen. mgr., 1980—; adj. prof. Seidman Grad. Coll. Bus., 1981—. Contbr. articles to profl. jours. Served to capt. USAF, 1954-57. Mem. Am. Soc. Metals, AIME, Metall. Soc., ASME, Nat. Assn. Corrosion Engrs. Club: Century. Current Work: Development and production of advanced high temperature superalloys; nickel base alloys; for critical gas turbine aerospace applications; single crystal alloys. Subspecialties: Metallurgical engineering; High-temperature materials.

SCHWETMAN, HERBERT DE WITT, JR., computer science researcher, educator; b. Waco, Tex., July 30, 1940; s. Herbert De Witt and Mary Jean (Knight) S.; m. Nanene Gilbert Hall, June 6, 1964; children—John David, Katherine. B.S., Baylor U., 1961; Sc.M., Brown U., 1965; Ph.D., U. Tex., Austin, 1970. Programmer IBM, Yorktown Heights, N.Y., 1964-67; systems programmer U. Tex., Austin, 1967-70; systems analyst Boole & Babbage, Inc., Cupertino, Calif., 1970-72; prof. computer sci. Purdue U., West Lafayette, Ind., 1972-84; mem. tech. staff MCC Corp., Austin, 1984—; Fulbright lectr. U. Helsinki, 1979; lectr. Tech. Transfer Inst., Los Angeles, 1980-85; series editor MIT Press, Cambridge, 1984-85. Mem. Assn. for Computing Machinery (chmn. SIGMETRICS 1981-85), IEEE Computer Soc. Current work: Research on architecture and performance of parallel systems. Subspecialty: Operating systems. Home: 1804 Lost Spring Cove Round Rock TX 78681 Office: MCC Corp 9430 Research Blvd Austin TX 78759

SCHWETMAN, HERBERT DEWITT, physicist, former educator; b. Waco, Tex., Aug. 1, 1911; s. Henry William and Camilla Alice (Henderson) S.; m. Mary Jean Knight, July 29, 1939; children—Herbert Dewitt, John William, Rosemary. B.A., Baylor U., 1932; M.A., U. Tex., 1937, Ph.D., 1952; M.S., Harvard, 1934. Tchr. pub. schs., Brucevill-Eddy, Tex., also, Waco, 1933-41; instr. electrons, research asso. Harvard, 1941-47; asso. prof. physics Baylor U., 1947-52, prof., chmn. dept., 1952-81; cons. in field; sr. nuclear engr., nuclear analysis group Convair, Ft. Worth. Contbr. articles on analogue computers to jours. Fellow AAAS, Tex. Acad. Sci.; mem. AAUP, Am. Assn. Physics Tchrs. (pres. Tex. br.), Am. Phys. Soc., Am. Inst. Physics, Am. Inst. Radio Engrs., Am. Assn. Coll. Profs., Sigma Xi, Sigma Pi Sigma. Baptist.

SCHWICKERT, RUSSELL CHARLES, automotive lighting engineer; b. East Durham, N.Y., July 25, 1927; s. William Jerome and Magdalene Anna (Kircher) S.; m. Eunice Irene England, June 21, 1956 (div. 1964); children—Kathlene, Russell, Christine. B.S.E.E., Ohio No. U., 1955. Laser staff engr. Carson Labs., Inc., Bristol, Conn., 1962-65; laser lab. mgr. Perkin-Elmer Corp., Wilton, Conn., 1965-70; dir. laser engring. Optical Data Processing Inc., New Canaan, Conn., 1970-72; gas discharge lamp engr. Fusion Systems Corp., Rockville, Md., 1972-75; fiber optics mfg. mgr. Amphenol, Danbury, Conn., 1975-78; sr. lamp engr. Wagner Electric Corp., Whippany, N.J., 1978—. Patentee fiber optic connectors, Haolgen lamps. Served with USN, 1946-47. Mem. IEEE, Soc. Mfg. Engrs., N.Y. Acad. Scis. Current work: Computer design of lens, reflector, and filament for desired automotive light distribution; spectroradiometric measurement of gas discharge lamps using an integrating sphere/monochromator characterization. Subspecialty: Fiber optics. Home: 21 Diamond Dr Newton CT 06470

SCHWIMMER, DAVID RICHARD, geology educator, paleontologist; b. N.Y.C., Feb. 8, 1947; s. Louis and Sari Vivien (Wainerdi) S.; m. Gabriele Duhrmann, Dec. 31, 1979; children—Eva Naomi. B.S., U. Wis.-Madison, 1967; M.A., SUNY-Buffalo, 1969; Ph.D., SUNY-Stony Brook, 1973. Profl. registered geologist. Grad. asst. SUNY-Buffalo, Stony Brook, 1967-73; sci. writer World Pub. Co., N.Y.C., 1973-74; sr. geologist Ecology & Environment, Inc., Buffalo, 1974-77; assoc., asst. prof. Columbus Coll., Ga., 1978—; cons. geologist, N.Y.C., Buffalo, Ga., 1974—; tech. photographer Bruce Coleman Inc., N.Y.C., 1974—. Contbr. to numerous sci. and profl. publs. Research grantee Columbus Coll., 1982-84; grantee NATO Advanced Study Conf., 1973; N.Y.S. Research Found. grantee, 1970-72. Current work: Cambrian biostratigraphy and trilobites; Cretaceous reptiles; Cretaceous oysters. Subspecialty: Paleontology. Home: 2407 18th Ave Columbus GA 31901 Office: Dept Chemistry and Geology Columbus Coll Columbus GA 31993

SCHWING, RICHARD CHARLES, environmental engineering researcher; b. Buffalo, Dec. 8, 1934; s. Charles Vincent and Ruth Mary (Geschwender) S.; children—Mark David, Cathryn Lynn; m. Patricia Ann Stevenson, Dec. 17, 1971; stepchildren—Michelle Daane, Michael Daane. B.S. in Chem. Engring., U. Mich., 1957, M.S., 1959, Ph.D., 1963. Sr. research engr. Gen. Motors Research Labs., Warren, Mich., 1963-79, sr. staff research engr., 1979-84, dept. scientist, 1984—. Co-editor: Societal Risk Assessment: How Safe is Safe Enough, 1979; Human Behavior & Traffic Safety, 1985. Contbr. articles to profl. jours. Served to 1st lt. Chem. Corps., U.S. Army, 1962-63. Recipient John M. Campbell award Gen. Motors Research Labs., 1983. Mem. Internat. Assn. for Impact Assessment (pres. 1984-85), Risk Analysis Soc., AAAS, Am. Chem. Soc., Sigma Xi. Unitarian-Universalist. Current work: Methodology of risk-benefit, cost-benefit and cost-effectiveness in areas of environmental impact and traffic safety. Subspecialties: Environmental engineering; Chemical engineering. Home: 145 S Glenhurst St Birmingham MI 48009 Office: Societal Analysis Dept Gen Motors Research Labs Warren MI 48090

SCHWINGER, JULIAN, educator, physicist; b. N.Y.C., Feb. 12, 1918; s. Benjamin and Belle (Rosenfeld) S.; m. Clarice Carrol, 1947. A.B., Columbia U., 1936, Ph.D., 1939, D.Sc., 1966; D.Sc. (hon.), Purdue U., 1961, Harvard, 1962, Brandeis U., 1973, Gustavus Adolphus Coll., 1975; LL.D., CCNY, 1972. NRC fellow, 1939-40; research asso. U. Calif. at Berkeley, 1940-41; instr., then asst. prof. Purdue U., 1941-43; staff mem. Radiation Lab., Mass. Inst. Tech., 1943-46; staff Metall. Lab., U. Chgo., 1943; asso. prof. Harvard, 1945-47, prof., 1947-72, Higgins prof. physics, 1966-72; prof. physics UCLA, 1972-80, Univ. prof., 1980—; Mem. bd. sponsors Bull. Atomic Sci.; sponsor Fedn. Am. Scientists; J.W. Gibbs hon. lectr. Am. Math. Soc., 1960. Author: Particles and Sources, 1969, (with D. Saxon) Discontinuities in Wave Guides, 1968, Particles, Sources and Fields, 1970, Vol. II, 1973, Quantum Kinematics and Dynamics, 1970; Editor: Quantum Electrodynamics, 1958. Recipient C. L. Mayer nature of light award, 1949, univ. medal Columbia U., 1951, 1st Einstein prize award, 1951; Nat. Medal of Sci. award for physics, 1964; co-recipient Nobel prize in Physics, 1965; recipient Humboldt award, 1981; Guggenheim fellow, 1970. Mem. Nat. Acad. Scis., Am. Acad. Arts and Scis., Am. Phys. Soc., Royal Instn. Gt. Britain, ACLU, AAAS, N.Y. Acad. Scis. Subspecialty: Theoretical physics. Office: Dept Physics U Calif Los Angeles CA 90024

SCIAMMARELLA, CESAR AUGUSTO, mechanical engineer, educator, researcher; b. Buenos Aires, Argentina, Aug. 22, 1926; s. Emilio Silvio and Maria Belen (Mansilla) S.; m. Esther Elba Norbis; children: Alejandro, Eduardo, Federico. Diploma in Civil Engring, U. Buenos Aires, 1950; Ph.D., Ill. Inst. Tech., 1960. Prof. mech. engring. U. Buenos Aires, 1955-57, U. Fla., 1961-65, Poly. Inst. Bklyn., 1967-72; prof. Ill. Inst. Tech., 1972—, dir. Exptl. Stress Analysis Lab., Chgo.; vis. prof. Poly. Inst., Milan, Italy, 1979, U. Cagliari, Italy, 1979, Poly. Inst. Lausanne, Switzerland, 1979, U. Poitiers, France, 1980; cons. to govt., pvt. industry. Contbr. articles to profl. jours. Recipient Faculty Research award Sigma Xi, 1966; Outstanding Paper award Acad. Mechanics, 1970; Disting. Services award ASME, 1972; Hetemy award, 1983. Fellow Soc. for Exptl. Mechanics (Frocht award 1980), ASME; mem. Internat. Soc. Optical Engring., ASTM, Gesellschaft für Angewandte Mathematik and Mechanik, Optical Soc. Am., Soc. Photo-optical Instrumentation Engrs., Roman Catholic. Patentee in field. Current Work: Optical techniques applied to stress analysis, mechanics of materials and fracture mechanics, fracture mechanics and fatigue. Subspecialties: Theoretical and applied mechanics; Fracture mechanics. Home: 247 E Chestnut Apt 601 Chicago IL 60611 Office: Dept Mech Engring Ill Inst Tech Chicago IL 60616

SCIANDRA, LUIGI CLAUDIO, mechanical engineer; b. Savigliano, Piedmont, Italy, Dec. 20, 1943; came to U.S., 1981; s. Pietro and Antonietta (Valle) S.; m. Kathleen Marie Daniels, Nov. 13, 1982; 1 child, Claudia Simone. Cadet Naval Acad. Leghorn, Italy, 1963-64; Ph.D., U. Genoa, 1975; M.S., Poly. Inst. Bklyn., 1983. Registered profl. engr. N.Y., Italy; insp. Nat. Bd. Boilder and Pressure Vessels. First engr., Costa Armatori SPA, Genoa, 1965-73; surveyor Am. Bur. Shipping, Genoa, 1974-80, France, 1980-81, sr. surveyor, N.Y.C., 1981-84; prin. engr., N.Y.C., 1985—. Mem. ASME (vice chmn. high pressure systems subcom.), Soc. Naval Architects and Marine Engrs., Am. Welding Soc. (cert. insp.). Served to lt. Italian Navy, 1963-65. Roman Catholic. Current work: Boilers, pressure vessels, tank containers and independent tank for transp. gas, hazardous chemicals; pressure vessels for human occupancy; buckling under external pressure and axial loads; high pressure systems. Subspecialties: Metallurgy; Mechanical engineering. Home: 160 Front St Apt 3C New York NY 10038

SCIFRES, CHARLES JOEL, range scientist, ecology educator, researcher; b. Foster, Okla., June 1, 1941; s. Lloyd Joel and Lois Beryl (Orr) S.; m. Julia Rose Shelton, Dec. 31, 1960; children—Dirk Weldon, Holly Suzanne. A.S., Murray Jr. Coll., 1961; B.S., Okla. State U., 1963, M.S., 1965; Ph.D., U. Nebr., 1968. Instr. U. Nebr., Lincoln, 1965-66; research agronomist Research Service, U.S. Dept. Agr., Lincoln, 1966-68; asst. prof. dept. range sci. Tex. A&M U., Lubbock, 1968-69, College Station, Tex., 1969-72, prof., 1976-82, O'Connor prof., 1982—. Author: Brush Management, 1980. Recipient Disting. Achievement award for research Tex. A&M Former Students, 1980. Mem. Soc. Range Mgmt. (outstanding achievement award 1985), Weed Soc. Am., Ecol. Soc. Am., S.W. Naturalists, Sigma Xi. Current work: Research on range improvement through manipulation of woody plants, shrub ecology and control. Subspecialties: Resource conservation; Ecosystems analysis. Home: 3006 Camelot Bryan TX 77802 Office: Dept Range Sci Tex A&M Univ College Station TX 77843

SCINTA, JAMES, chemical engineer; b. Buffalo, Mar. 15, 1952; s. Vincent T. and Tess (Barr) S.; m. Barbara Ann Goodall, July 25, 1975; children—Patrice Marie, Elizabeth Ann. B.S., Cornell U., 1973; M.S., SUNY-Buffalo, 1975, Ph.D., 1977. Registered profl. engr., Okla. Engr. E.I. DuPont, Niagara Falls, N.Y., 1973; research engr. Phillips Petroleum Co., Bartlesville, Okla., 1977-80, supr., 1980-84, prin. engr., 1984—, supr. catalyst process devel., 1985—. Contbr. articles to profl. jours. Patentee in field. Bd. dirs. Community Action Charitable Found., Bartlesville, 1983—. Mem. Am. Inst. Chem. Engrs., Am. Chem. Soc., Nat. Soc. Profl. Engrs., Jaycees (Officer of Yr. award 1981, Outstanding Local Pres. award 1982, bd. dirs. 1979—). Current work: Catalyst development; process development; scale up; synthetic fuels. Subspecialty: Chemical engineering. Home: 6021 Martin Pl Bartlesville OK 74006 Office: Phillips Research and Development 92 E PRC Bartlesville OK 74004

SCORA, RAINER WALTER, botanist, educator; b. Mokre, Silesia, Poland, Dec. 5, 1928; came to U.S., 1951, naturalized, 1956; s. Paul Wendelin and Helene Maria (Nester) S.; m. Christa Maria Fiala, Sept. 2, 1942; children: George-Alexander, Katharina-Monarda, Peter-Evan. B.S., DePaul U., 1955; M.S., U. Mich., 1958, Ph.D., 1964. Asst. prof. botany U. Calif., Riverside, 1964-70, assoc. prof., 1971-75, prof., 1975—. Author: Interspecific Relationships in the Genus Monarda, 1967; over 75 articles. Served with Signal Corps U.S. Army, 1955-57. Alfred P. Sloan fellow, 1959; recipient Cooley award Am. Inst. Biol. Scis., 1968; NSF fellow, 1963-64. Mem. Phytochem. Soc. N.Am., Internat. Soc. Plant Taxonomists, Internat. Orgn. Plant Biosystematists. Bot. Soc. Am., Sigma Xi, Phi Sigma, Gamma Sigma Delta. Roman Catholic. Current Work: Evolution of plants and their chemical components. Subspecialty: Evolutionary biology. Office: Botany and Plant Sci U Calif Riverside CA 92521

SCORDELIS, ALEXANDER COSTICAS, civil engineering educator; b. San Francisco, Sept. 27, 1923; s. Philip Kostas and Vasilica (Zois) S.; m. Georgia Gumas, May 9, 1948; children: Byron, Karen. B.S., U. Calif., Berkeley, 1948; M.S., M.I.T., 1949. Registered profl. engr., Calif. Structural designer Pacific Gas & Electric Co., San Francisco, 1948; engr. Bechtel Corp., San Francisco, summer 1951, 52, 53, 54, 55; instr. civil engring. U. Calif., Berkeley, 1949-50, asst. prof., 1951-56, asso. prof., 1957-61, prof., 1962—; asst. dean U. Calif. (Coll. Engring.), 1962-65, vice chmn. div. structural engring, structural mechanics, 1970-73; cons. engring. firms, govt. agys. Contbr. articles on analysis and design of complex structural systems, reinforced and prestressed concrete shell and bridge structures to profl. jours. Served to capt., C.E. U.S. Army, 1943-46, ETO. Decorated Bronze Star, Purple Heart; recipient Western Electric award Am. Soc. Engring. Edn., 1978; Axion award Hellenic Am. Profl. Soc., 1979; Best Paper award Canadian Soc. Civil Engring., 1982; K.B. Woods award Nat. Acad. Scis. Transp. Research Bd., 1983. Fellow ASCE (Moissieff award 1976, 81), Am. Concrete Inst.; mem. Internat. Assn. Shell and Spatial Structures, Structural Engrs. Assn. Calif., Nat. Acad. Engring. Subspecialty: Civil engineering. Home: 724 Gelston Pl El Cerrito CA 94530 Office: 729 Davis Hall U Calif Berkeley CA 94720

SCOTT, ALASTAIR IAN, chemistry educator; b. Glasgow, Scotland, Apr. 10, 1928; came to U.S., 1968; s. William and Nell (Newton) S.; m. Elizabeth Wilson Walters, Mar. 4, 1950; children—William Stewart, Ann Walker. B.Sc., Glasgow U., 1949, Ph.D., 1952, D.Sc., 1964; M.A. (hon.), Yale U., 1968. Lectr. organic chemistry Glasgow U., 1957-62; prof. U. B.C., Vancouver, 1962-65, Sussex (Eng.) U., 1965-68, Yale U., 1968-77; Distinguished prof. Tex. A&M U., 1977-80, Davidson prof. sci., 1982—; prof. dept. chemistry U. Edinburgh, Scotland, 1980-82; cons. in field Author: Interpretations of Ultraviolet Spectra of Natural Products, 1964; Contbr. articles to profl. jours. Fellow Royal Soc.; mem. Am. Chem. Soc. (Ernest Guenther award 1976), The Chem. Soc. (Corday-Morgan medal 1964), Biochem. Soc., Swiss Chem. Soc. Current work: Biosynthesis of porphyrins, vitamin B12 and B-lactam antibiotics; biosynthesis of alkaloids using plant tissue culture; application of NMR in biological systems and enzyme mechanism. Subspecialties: Organic chemistry; Nuclear magnetic resonance. Office: Chemistry Dept Texas A&M Univ College Station TX 77843

SCOTT, DAVID, mechanical engineering educator, institute administrator; b. Quebec City, Can., July 15, 1935; s. Gilbert B. and Alberta B. (Sanburn) S.; m. Sylvia Winnifred Shaw, Sept. 1959; children—Penelope Lee, Paul (dec.), Susan Elizabeth, Elspeth (dec.), Douglas Sanborn, Peter David. B.S., Queens U., Kingston, Ont., 1959, M.S., 1963; Ph.D., Northwestern U., 1967. Registered profl. engr., Ont. Supr. Steel Co. of Can., 1959-60; foreman Fiberglas Can., 1960-62; assoc. prof. mech. engring. U. Toronto, Ont., 1966-76, prof., chmn. mechn. engring., 1976-83, exec. dir., chief exec. officer Inst. for Hydrogen Systems, Mississauga, Ont., 1983—; vis. prof. Inst. Sound Vibration Research, U. Southampton, 1974-75. Contbr. articles to profl. jours. Patentee in field. Mem. Ont. Profl. Engrs. Assn. Subspecialty: Fuels and sources. Office: Inst for Hydrogen Systems U Toronto 2480 Dunwin Dr Mississauga ON L5L 1J9 Canada

SCOTT, DAVID BYTOVETZSKI, dental research and forensic odontology consultant; b. Providence, May 8, 1919; (married); 3 children. A.B., Brown U., 1939; D.D.S., U. Md., 1943; M.S., U. Rochester, 1944; Sc.D. (hon.), Med. and Dental Coll. N.J., 1979, U. Louis Pasteur, Strasbourg, France, 1981. Diplomate Am. Bd. Forensic Odontology. Staff Nat. Inst. Dental Research, NIH, Bethesda, Md., 1944-56, chief lab. histology and pathology, 1956-65, dir. inst., 1976-82, now pvt. cons. dental research and forensic odontology; faculty Case Western Res. U., Cleve., 1965-76, Thomas J. Hill Distinguished prof. phys. biology Sch. Dentistry, prof. anatomy Sch. Medicine, 1965-76, dean Sch. Dentistry, 1969-76. Decorated Order Rising Sun (Japan); recipient Arthur S. Flemming award, 1955; award for Research in Mineralization Internat. Assn. Dental Research, 1968; Research Achievement award Mass. Dental Soc., 1978; Fred Birnberg Dental Research award Columbia U., 1978; Callahan Meml. award, 1985. Mem. ADA, Am. Acad. Forensic Sci. (forensic odontology award 1981), Electron Micros. Soc. Am., Internat., Am. colls. dentists, Internat. Assn. Dental Research, Royal Soc. Medicine (hon.). Current Work: Consultant dental research and forensic odontology. Subspecialty: Oral biology. Office: 10448 Wheatridge Dr Sun City AZ 85373

SCOTT, DAVID KNIGHT, nuclear scientist, college administrator; b. North Ronaldsay, Scotland, Mar. 2, 1940; came to U.S., 1973; s. William and Mary Jane (Knight) S.; m. Kathleen Louise Smith, May 28, 1967; children—Wendelin K., Kelvin W.M., Jeremy K. B.Sc. in Physics, U. Edinburgh, Scotland, 1962; Ph.D., U. Oxford, Eng., 1967. Research fellow Balliol Coll. U. Oxford, 1967-73; sr. scientist Lawrence Berkeley Lab., Berkeley, Calif., 1973-79, dir. Cyclotron Lab., 1978-79; Hannah prof. physics and chemistry, Mich. State U., East Lansing, 1979—, assoc. dir. research, 1982-83, assoc. provost, 1983—. Editor: International Conference on Nucleus-Nucleus Collisions, 1983. Contbr. articles to profl. jours. Grierson fellow Edinburgh U., 1958, Chalmers fellow Oxford U., 1962. Fellow Am. Phys. Soc.; mem. Phi Beta Kappa, Phi Kappa Phi, Tau Sigma. Presbyterian. Current work: Studies of nuclear structure and reactions using nucleus-nucleus heavy ion collisions. Subspecialties: Nuclear physics; Nuclear chemistry. Home: 340 Walbridge Dr East Lansing MI 48823 Office: Office of Provost Mich State U East Lansing MI 48824 Also: Nat Superconducting Gyclotron Lab Mich State U East Lansing MI 48824

SCOTT, ELIZABETH LEONARD, statistics educator; b. Ft. Sill, Okla., Nov. 23, 1917; d. Richard C. and Elizabeth (Waterman) S. B.A., U. Calif., Berkeley, 1939, Ph.D., 1949. Research fellow U. Calif., Berkeley, 1939-49, mem. faculty, 1949—, assoc. prof., 1957-62, prof. stats., 1962—, chmn. dept. stats., 1968-73; asst. dean U. Calif. (Coll. Letters and Sci.), 1965-67, co-chmn. group in biostats., 1972—; mem. Commn. on Nat. Stats. Nat. Acad. Scis., 1971-77, Commn. on Women in Sci., 1977-82, Commn. on Applied and Theoretical Stats., 1981-84, Oversight Commn. on Radioepidemiologic Tables, 1983-85. Contbr. articles to sci. pubis. Fellow Royal Statis. Soc. (hon.), Inst. Math. Stats. (pres. 1977-78, mem. council 1971-74, 76-79); mem. Biometric Soc. (council 1978-81), Am. Astron. Soc., Internat. Astron. Union, Internat. Stats. Inst. (v.p. 1981-83), Internat. Assn. Stats. in Phys. Sci. (sci. sec. 1960-72), Bernoulli Soc. (mem. council 1978-81, pres.-elect 1981-83, pres. 1983-85), Astron. Soc. Pacific, AAAS (chmn. sect. U 1970-71, mem. council 1971-76). Research in math. stats. and applications. Subspecialty: Statistics. Home: 34 Tunnel Rd Berkeley CA 94705 Office: Dept Stats U Calif Berkeley CA 94720

SCOTT, GERALD WILLIAM, surgeon, researcher; b. London, Jan. 12, 1931; s. Frederick William and Constance Ella (Burgess) S.; m. Beryl Elizabeth, May 14, 1955; children: Martin, Nigel, Elizabeth, Celia, Ian. M.B., B.S., U. London, 1955. Diplomate: Am. Bd. Surgery. Resident, fellow surgery Mayo Clinic and Grad. Sch. Medicine, Rochester, Minn., 1960-64; practice medicine specializing in surgery, Calgary, Alta., Can., after 1965—; assoc. prof. surgery U. Calgary, after 1968; prof. surgery U. Alta., Edmonton, after 1973; dir. Surg.-Med. Research Inst., 1978—. Served to lt. Royal Navy, 1957-59. Fulbright scholar, 1960; recipient E. Starr Judd award Mayo Found., 1964; Sir Peter Freyer Meml. lectr. U. Coll. Galway, 1983. Fellow Royal Coll. Surgeons Can. (exec. sec. surgery test com.), ACS; mem. Internat. Soc. Gastrointestinal Motility, British Pharmacol. Soc., Western Surg. Assn. Current Work: Function of gallbladder gastrointestinal surgery, gastrointestinal surgery and research. Subspecialty: Gastroenterology. Home: 5511 175th St Edmonton AB T6M 1C3 Canada Office: Surg Med Research Inst 1074B Dentistry/Pharmacy Bld U Alta Edmonto AB T6G 2N8 Canada

SCOTT, IRENA MCCAMMON, physiologist, researcher technical writer; b. Delaware, Ohio, July, 1942; d. James Robert and Gay McCammon; m. John Watson Scott, Dec. 6, 1969. B.S., Ohio State U., 1965; M.S., U. Nev., 1972; Ph.D., U. Mo., 1976. Research assoc. Cornell U., Ithaca, N.Y., 1977-78; asst. prof. St. Bonaventure U., N.Y., 1978-79; research assoc. Ohio State U. Med. Sch., Columbus, 1980—; researcher Battelle Meml. Inst., Columbus, 1980—; campus corr. Popular Mechanics Mag.; cons. in Physiology MuFon. Contbr. articles to sci. jours., poetry to mags. Vol. Ohio State U. Radio Telescope, 1981—. Recipient Bausch & Lomb award, 1965. Mem. Mensa (group coordinator writers' group), Ohio Archeol. Soc., Verse Writers Guild, Am. Physiol. Soc., AAAS, Am. Dairy Sci. Assn., Ohio Hist. Soc., Sigma Xi, Gamma Sigma Delta. Methodist. Club: Olentangy Poets (Delaware). Current Work: Electrophysiological study of the effects of hormones, neurotransmitters and fever producing substances on brain cells. Subspecialties: Neurochemistry; Neurophysiology. Office: Ohio State U 310 Hamilton Hall Columbus OH 43210

SCOTT, MORRIS DOUGLAS, ecologist; b. Mason City, Iowa, Sept. 8, 1945; s. Morris William and Maxine Imogene (Eppard) S.; m. Suvi Annikki Lehtinen, Aug. 12, 1983. B.S., Iowa State U., 1967; Ph.D., Auburn U., 1971. Instr. zoology Auburn U., Ala., 1971-72; asst. prof. So. Ill. U., Carbondale, 1972-74; sr. ecologist Amax Coal Co., Indpls., 1974-75, environ. mgr., Billings, Mont., 1975-77; research assoc. Mont. State U., Bozeman, 1977-80, dir. Inst. Natural Resources, 1980—; cons. mining industry. Editor Conf. Proceedings Plains Aquatic Research, 1983. Contbr. articles to profl. jours. Bd. dirs. Bridger Canyon Property Owners Assn., Bozeman, 1984—. Auburn U. fellow, 1970. Mem. Ecol. Soc. Am., Wildlife Soc., Animal Behavior Soc., Gamma Sigma Delta. Current work: Land use planning systems for microcomputers; wildlife mgmt. on reclaimed surface mines; behavioral ecology of feral dogs; ecology of waterfowl and grouse. Subspecialties: Behavioral ecology; Resource management. Home: 16257 Bridger Canyon Bozeman MT 59715 Office: Inst Natural Resources Mont State Univ Bozeman MT 59717

SCOTT, ROBERT GLENN (BOB), JR., veterinarian, agricultural consultant; b. Denver, Jan. 16, 1926; s. Robert Glenn and Eunice Willard (McCampbell) S.; m. Janice Elizabeth Smith, June 28, 1952 (dec. 1976); children—Robert Glenn, Leslie, David Clinton, April Marie; m. 2d Marie Beard Markey, May 28, 1977. B.A., Colo. State U., 1950, D.V.M., 1951. Ptnr., Brighton Animal Clinic, Colo., 1951-80; v.p. Wagner Indoe Minerals, North Lawrence, Ohio, 1980-81; rep. profl. service Hill's Products Inc., Topeka, Kans., 1981-83; tech. service Pro-Ag Inc., Mpls., 1983—; pres. SJS Dairy, Brighton, Colo., 1960-70; cons. Brookside Farm Lab., New Knoxville, Ohio, 1967-80. Mem. Adams County Dist. 27-J Bd. Edn., Brighton, 1965-71. Served with AUS, 1944-46. Mem. AVMA, Minn. Vet. Med. Assn., Am. Assn. Bovine Practitioners. Presbyterian. Club: Rotary. Current work: Field trials in study of passive immunity using colostrum derivatives. Subspecialty: Preventive medicine (veterinary medicine). Office: Pro Ag Inc 2072 E Center Circle St Minneapolis MN 55441

SCOTT, ROBERT LANE, educator, chemist; b. Santa Rosa, Calif., Mar. 20, 1922; s. Horace Albert and Maurine (Lane) S.; m. Elizabeth Sewall Hunter, May 27, 1944; children—Joanna Ingersoll, Jonathan Armat, David St. Clair, Janet Hamilton. S.B., Harvard U., 1942; M.A., Princeton U., 1944, Ph.D., 1945. Sci. staff Los Alamos Lab., 1945-46; Frank B. Jewett fellow U. Calif. at Berkeley, 1946-48; faculty U. Calif. at. Los Angeles, 1948—, prof. chemistry, 1960—, chmn. dept., 1970-75. Author: (with J.H. Hildebrand) Solubility of Nonelectrolytes, 3d edit. 1950, rev., 1964, Regular Solutions, 1962, Regular and Related Solutions, 1970; Contbr. articles to profl. jours. Guggenheim fellow, 1955; NSF sr. fellow, 1961-62; Fulbright lectr., 1968-69. Fellow Am. Phys. Soc.; Mem. Am. Chem. Soc. (Hildebrand award), AAAS, Royal Soc. Chemistry (London), Sigma Xi. Subspecialty: Physical chemistry. Office: U Calif Dept Chemistry and Biochemistry Los Angeles CA 90024

SCOTT, ROLAND BOYD, pediatrician; b. Houston, Apr. 18, 1909; s. Ernest John and Cordie (Clark) S.; m. Sarah Rosetta Weaver, June 24, 1935 (dec.); children—Roland Boyd, Venice Rosetta, Estelle Irene. B.S., Howard U., 1931, M.D., 1934; Gen. Edn. Bd. fellow, U. Chgo., 1936-39. Diplomate: Nat. Bd. Med. Examiners, Am. Bd. Pediatrics. Faculty Howard U., Washington, 1937—, prof. pediatrics, 1952-77, distinguished prof. pediatrics and child health, 1977—, chmn. dept. pediatrics, 1945-73; dir. Center for Sickle Cell Anemia, 1973—; chief pediatrician Freedmen's Hosp., 1947-73; professorial lectr. in child health and devel. George Washington U. Sch. Medicine, 1971—; staff Children's Hosp., Providence Hosp., Columbia Hosp., D.C. Gen. Hosp., Washington Hosp. Center; cons. in pediatrics to NIH, hosps.; Mem. com. Pub. Health Adv. Council, 1964—, U.S. Children's Bur., 1964—; mem. Nat. Com. for Children and Youth.; mem. sickle cell adv. com. NIH, 1983—. Author: (with Althea D. Kessler) Sickle Cell Anemia and Your Child, (with C.G. Uy) Guidelines For Care of Patients With Sickle Cell Disease; Editor: Procs. 1st Internat. Conf. on Sickle Cell Disease: A World Health Problem, 1979; Mem. editorial bd.: Advances in the Pathophysiology, Diagnosis and Treatment of Sickle Cell Disease, 1982, Clin. Pediatrics, 1962-80, Jour. Nat. Med. Assn, 1978; cons. editor: Medical Aspects of Human Sexuality; editorial bd.: Annals of Allergy, 1977. Recipient Sci. and Community award Medico-Chirurgical Med. Soc. D.C., 1971, Community Service award Med. Soc. D.C., 1972, award for contbns. to sickle cell research Delta Sigma Theta, 1973, 34 years Dedicated and Distinguished Service award in pediatrics dept. pediatrics Howard U., 1973, Faculty award for excellence in research, 1974, certificate of appreciation Sickle Cell Anemia Research and Edn., 1977; Mead Johnson award D.C. chpt. Am. Acad. Pediatrics, 1978; Percy L. Julian award We Do Care, Chgo., 1979; also plaques for work in sickle cell disease various orgns. including Elks, Nat. Assn. Med. Minority Educators, NIH, 1980-82. Mem. AMA, Am. Hematology Soc., Am. Pediatric Soc., Soc. Pediatric Research, Am. Acad. Allergy (v.p. 1966-67), Am. Acad. Pediatrics (mem. com. on children with handicaps, cons. head start program), Am. Fedn. Clin. Research, Nat. Med. Assn. (Distinguished Service medal 1966), AAAS, Internat. Corr. Soc. Allergists, Assn. Ambulatory Pediatric Services, AAUP, Internat. Congress Pediatrics, Am. Coll. Allergists (Distinguished Service award 1977), Can. Sickle Cell Soc. (hon. life), Phi Beta Kappa, Sigma Xi (Percy L. Julian award Howard U. chpt. 1977), Kappa Pi, Beta Kappa Chi, Alpha Omega Alpha, others. Research, publs. on sickle cell anemia, growth and devel. of infants and children, allergy in children. Current Work: Growth and development of children; sickler cell disease and allergic disorders in children. Subspecialties: Allergy; Hematology. Home: 1723 Shepherd St NW Washington DC 20011 Office: 1114 Girard St NW Washington DC 20009

SCOTT, THOMAS RUSSELL, JR., neuroscientist; b. Ridley Park, Pa., Oct. 1,1944; s. Thomas Russell and Cathryn (Steciw) S.; m. Bonnie Kime, June 17, 1967; children: Heather Sheila, Ethan Kime, Heidi Cathryn Molly. B.A. cum laude, Princeton U., 1966; Ph.D., Duke U., 1970. Asst. prof. psychology U. Del., Newark, 1970-75, assoc. prof., 1975-83, prof., 1983—, chairperson dept., 1983—; adj. assoc. prof. physiol. psychology Rockefeller U., N.Y.C., 1980-82; vis. prof. psychology Oxford U., Eng., 1984. Current Work: X. Subspecialty: Neurophysiology. Office: Dept Psycholog U Del Newark DE 19716

SCOTTI, VINCENT GUY, cons. nuclear engr.; b. Villamina, Avelino, Italy, Aug. 1, 1921; came to U.S., 1923; s. Nicholas and Giovanina (Santoro) S.; m. June Kupferschmid, Apr. 4, 1942; m. Hattie E. Tomlin, June 2, 1946 (dec. 1980); children: Vincent Guy, Nicholas, Michael, Richard, Kevin, Barbara. B.A., Boston U., 1950; postgrad., U. Calif., Berkeley, 1956, Ga. Inst. Tech., 1972, Kent State U., 1974. Sr. chemist Tracer Lab., Inc., Boston, 1950-55; asst. project engr. Pratt & Whitney Aircraft Co., East Hartford, Conn., 1955-65; assoc. chemist Argonne Nat. Lab., Ill., 1965; sect. mgr. Battelle Columbus, Ohio, 1969-74; biophysicist Swedish Hosp., Seattle, 1965-66; sr. cons. engr. Combustion Engring. Inc., Windsor, Conn., 1974—. Served with U.S. Navy, 1942-46, PTO. Mem. Am. Nuclear Soc. (exec. com. remote systems tech. div. 1980-82), Fusion Power Assn. Roman Catholic. Current Work: Provide consulting services reactor design (fission) hotcell and fuel fab facilities; fusion reactor components. Subspecialties: Nuclear engineering; Radiochemistry. Office: Combustion Engring Inc 1000 Prospect Hill Rd Windsor CT 06095

SCOVELL, WILLIAM MARTIN, chemist, educator, researcher, cons.; b. Wilkes Barre, Pa., Jan. 16, 1944; s. Glenn W. and Anna M. (Gober) S.; m. Eleanor A. Krehely, July 10, 1965; children: Sherry Diane, William Martin, Jeffrey John. B.S. in Chemistry, Lebanon Valley Coll., 1961-65; Ph.D. in Chemistry, U. Minn., Mpls., 1969. Research chemist E. I. duPont, 1965; postdoctoral fellow Princeton U., 1969-70, instr., 1970-72; asst. prof. chemistry SUNY - Buffalo, 1972-74; assoc. prof. Bowling Green State U., 1974-79, prof., 1979—; adj. prof. Med. Coll. Ohio at Toledo, 1980—. Contbr. articles to profl. jours. Coach Pee Wee Baseball, Biddy basketball; chm. fund dr. for Wood County (Ohio) Arthritis Found., Northwest Ohio chpt. NIH grantee, 1973-76; Am. Cancer Soc. grantee, 1981-83; NIH individual scholar award, 1984-85. Mem. Am. Chem. Soc., Sigma Xi. Methodist. Current Work: Drug and carcinogen interactions with DNA and chromatin; chromatin structure, effect of structural modification on biol functions; laser Raman spectroscopy of DNA and DNA-protein interactions. Subspecialties: Biophysical chemistry; Inorganic chemistry. Home: 1206 Bourgogne Ave Bowling Green OH 43402 Office: Dept Chemistr Bowling Green State U Hayes Hall Bowling Green OH 43403

SCRIBNER, BELDING HIBBARD, nephrology educator; b. Chgo., Jan. 18, 1921; s. Carleton Spear and Mary Elizabeth (Belding) S. A.B., U. Calif.-Berkeley, 1941; M.D., Stanford U., 1945, M.A., U. Minn., 1950; Dr. (hon.) U. Gotteborg, Sweden, 1983, Postgrad. Med. Sch., London, 1985. Intern San Francisco Hosp., 1941, resident in internal medicine, 1942-44; fellow in medicine Mayo Clinic, Rochester, Minn., 1945-51; instr. medicine U. Wash., Seattle, 1951-53, asst. prof., 1953-57, assoc. prof., 1957-68, prof., 1968—, endowed chair in medicine, 1984—. Inventor in field. Served with USN, 1941-44. Markle scholar, 1956. Fellow ACP (Phillips award 1980); mem. Am. Soc. Nephrology (pres. 1981), Am. Assn. Physicians, Am. Soc. Artificial Organs (pres. 1964, Laureate address 1984), Nat. Acad. Medicine. Current work: Hemodialysis; peritional dialysis; hypertension. Subspecialty: Internal medicine. Office: Div Nephrology Mail Stop RM-11 U Wash Seattle WA 98195

SCRIVER, CHARLES ROBERT, physician; b. Montreal, Que., Can., Nov. 7, 1930; s. Walter deM. and Jessie (Boyd) S.; m. E.K. Peirce, Sept. 8, 1956; children: Dorothy, Peter, Julie, Paul. B.A. cum laude, McGill U., Montreal, 1951, M.D.C.M. cum laude, 1955. Intern Royal Victoria Hosp., Montreal, 1955-56; resident Royal Victoria and Montreal Children's hosps., 1956-57, Children's Med. Center, Boston, 1957-58; McLaughlin travelling fellow Univ. Coll., London, 1958-60; chief resident pediatrics Montreal Children's Hosp., 1960-61; asst. prof. pediatrics McGill U., 1961; now prof. genetics (Human Genetics Center); prof. biology (Faculty of Sci.); prof. pediatrics (Faculty of Medicine.); mem. Sci. Council Can., 1984—. Co-author: Amino Acid Metabolism and Its Disorders, 1973; research publs. in field. Recipient Wood Gold medal McGill U., 1955, Borden award Nutrition Soc. Can., 1969, Gairdner Internat. award Gairdner Found., 1979; Markle scholar, 1962-67; Med. Research Council Can. asso., 1968—; Can. Rutherford lectr. Royal Soc. (Eng.), 1983. Fellow Royal Soc. Can. (McLaughlin medal 1981); mem. Can. Soc. Clin. Investigation (pres. 1974-75, G. Malcolm Brown award 1979), Soc. Pediatric Research (pres. 1975-76), Am. Soc. Human Genetics (dir. 1971-74, pres. elect 1985; William Allan award 1978), Am. Soc. Clin. Investigation, Assn. Am. Physicians, Brit. Pediatric Assn. (hon.; 50th Anniversary lectr. 1978), Soc. Francaise de Pediat (hon.), Am. Acad. Pediatrics (Mead Johnson award 1968, Borden award 1973). Current Work: Mendelian and biochemical genetics of membrane transport functions. Prediction and prevention of genetic disease. Subspecialty: Genetics and genetic engineering (medicine). Office: Montreal Children's Hosp Research Inst 2300 Tupper St Montreal PQ H3H 1P3 Canada

SCUDDER, HARVEY ISRAEL, environmental and public health biologist, educator, consultant; b. Wellsburg, N.Y., Jan. 2, 1919; s. Henry Spaulding and Charlotte Evelyn (Draper) S.; m. Florence Viola Graff, June 16, 1945; children: Paul Harvey, Barbara Carol. B.S., Cornell U., 1939; postgrad., N.Y.U., 1939-42; Ph.D., Cornell U., 1953. Commd. scientist, officer USPHS, 1943-66; chief viruses and cancer program Nat. Cancer Inst., NIH, Bethesda, Md., 1959-62, chief research tng. grants br., 1962-65; chief health manpower program USPHS, Washington, 1965-66; head div. biol. and health sci. Calif. State-Hayward, 1967-70, prof. microbiology, 1967-80; research assoc. Calif. Acad. Scis., San Francisco, 1981—; trustee Marine Ecol. Inst., Redwood City, Calif., 1971—; chmn., 1974-78, 79-80, 82—; trustee Moss Landing Marine Labs., Moss Landings, Calif., 1967-70, chmn., 1969-70; chmn. health manpower Alameda County Comprehensive Health Planning Council, Oakland, Calif., 1973-76. Author: Malaria Control Manual, 1982; contbr. articles to profl. jours. Trustee St. Rose Hosp.; adv. com. Fairmont Hosp.; air conservation com. Lung Assn. Alameda County; trustee Alameda County Mosquito Abatement Dist., USPHS. Dupont Corp. fellow, 1939-41. Mem. Am. Pub. Health Assn., Am. Soc. Tropical Medicine and Hygiene, Am. Soc. Microbiology, Entomol. Soc. Am., Am. Mosquito Control Assn., Sigma Xi, Phi Kappa Phi. Republican. Mem. Christian Ch. Club: Pub. Health Service (pres. 1962, treas. 1961-63, dir. 1960-64). Inventor Scudder Fly Grill, 1947. Current Work: Further studies on decision support systems and training for management of malaria control programs in underdeveloped countries for U.S. Agency for International Development; cooperative paleoecological studies of Middle Miocene in southwest Nevada. Subspecialties: Paleontology, paleoecology; Integrated systems modelling and engineering. Home: 7409 Hansen Dr Dublin CA 94568 Office: Dept Biol Scis Calif State U Hayward CA 94542

SCYPINSKI, STEPHEN, analytical chemist; b. Passaic, N.J., Feb. 3, 1957; s. John Stanley and Cecilia (Los) S.; m. Yolanda Alexandra Nargiello, Sept. 12, 1981. B.S. in Chemistry, Seton Hall U., 1979, M.S. in Chemistry, 1982, Ph.D. in Chemistry, 1984. Research chemist Exxon Research and Engring., Linden, N.J., 1979-83; research fellow EPA, Seton Hall U., South Orange, N.J., 1983-84; tech. support chemist, tng. specialist Varian Instrument Group, Florham Park, N.J., 1984—. Contbr. articles to sci. publs. Mem. Am. Chem. Soc., Soc. Applied Spectroscopy (McPherson Student award 1984). Current work: Spectroscopy as applied to chromatographic detection, organized assemblies in analytical chemistry, GC/LC methods and detection. Subspecialty: Analytical chemistry. Home: 42 Starling Dr Branchburg NJ 08876 Office: Varian Instrument Group 25 Hanover Rd Florham Park NJ 07932

SEAB, C(HARLES) GREGORY, astrophysicist; b. Ft. Benning, Ga., May 26, 1950; s. James A. and Ruby (Jones) S.; m. Peggy R. McConnell, May 9, 1979; 1 child, Jenna Rose. B.S., La. State U., 1971, M.S., 1974; Ph.D., U. Colo., 1982. NRC research assoc. NASA Ames Research Ctr., Moffett Field, Calif., 1983-85; asst. astronomer U. Calif.-Berkeley, 1985; postdoctoral assoc. Va. Inst. for Theoretical Astrophysics, Charlottesville, 1985—. Contbr. articles to profl. jours. Nat. Merit scholar, 1967. Mem. Am. Astron. Soc., Phi Kappa Phi. Current work: Theoretical and observational study of dust grains in the interstellar medium, including both galactic and extra-galactic sources. Subspecialties: Theoretical astrophysics; Infrared astronomy. Office: Mail Stop 245-6 NASA Ames Research Ctr Moffett Field CA 94035

SEABORG, GLENN THEODORE, chemistry educator; b. Ishpeming, Mich., Apr. 19, 1912; s. H. Theodore and Selma (Erickson) S.; m. Helen Griggs, June 6, 1942; children: Peter, Lynne Seaborg Cobb, David, Stephen, John Eric, Dianne. A.B., UCLA, 1934; Ph.D., U. Calif.-Berkeley, 1937; numerous hon. degrees; LL.D., U. Mich., 1958, Rutgers U., 1970; D.Sc., Northwestern U., 1954, U. Notre Dame, 1961, John Carroll U.; Duquesne U., 1968, Ind. State U., 1969, U. Utah, 1970, Rockford Coll., 1975, Kent State U., 1975; L.H.D., No. Mich. Coll., 1962; D.P.S., George Washington U., 1962; D.P.A., U. Puget Sound, 1963; Litt.D., Lafayette Coll., 1966; D.Eng., Mich. Technol. U., 1970; Sc.D., U. Bucharest, 1971, Manhattan Coll., 1976. Research chemist U. Calif.-Berkeley, 1937-39, instr. dept. chemistry, 1939-41, asst. prof., 1941-45, prof., 1945-71, univ. prof., 1971, leave of absence, 1942-46, 61-71, dir. nuclear chem. research, 1946-58, 72-75, assoc. dir. Lawrence Berkeley Lab., 1954-61, from 71; chancellor Univ. (U. Calif.-Berkeley), 1958-61, dir. Lawrence Hall of Sci., 1982—; sect. chief metall. lab. U. Chgo., 1942-46; chmn. AEC, 1961-71, gen. adv. com., 1946-50, research nuclear chemistry and physics, transuranium elements.; Chmn. bd. Kevex Corp., Burlingame, Calif., from 1972; Mem. Pres.'s Sci. Adv. Com., 1959-61; mem. nat. sci. bd. NSF, 1960-61; mem. Pres.'s Com. on Equal Employment Opportunity, 1961-65, Fed. Radiation Council, 1961-69, Nat. Aeros. and Space Council, 1961-71, Fed. Council Sci. and Tech., 1961-71, Nat. Com. Am.'s Goals and Resources, 1962-64, Pres.'s Com. Manpower, 1964-69, Nat. Council Marine Resources and Engring. Devel., 1966-71; chmn. Chem. Edn. Material Study, 1959-74, Nat. Programming Council for Pub. TV, 1970-72; dir. Ednl. TV and Radio Center, Ann Arbor, Mich., 1958-64, 67-70; pres. 4th UN Internat. Conf. Peaceful Uses Atomic Energy, Geneva, 1971, also chmn. U.S. del., 1964, 71; U.S. rep. 5th-15th gen. confs. IAEA, chmn., 1961-71; chmn. U.S. del. to USSR for signing Memorandum Cooperation Field Utilization Atomic Energy Peaceful Purposes, 1963; mem. U.S. del. for signing Limited Test Ban Treaty, 1963; mem. commn. on humanities Am. Council Learned Socs., 1962-65; mem. sci. adv. bd. Robert A. Welch Found., from 1957; mem. Internat. Orgn. for Chem. Scis. in Devel., UNESCO, 1980—, chmn., 1981; mem. Nat. Commn. on Excellence in Edn., Dept. Edn., from 1981. Author: (with Joseph J. Katz) The Actinide Elements, 1954, The Chemistry of the Actinide Elements, 1957, The Transuranium Elements, 1958, (with E.G. Valens) Elements of the Universe, 1958 (winner Thomas Alva Edison Found. award), Man-Made Transuranium Elements, 1963, (with D.M. Wilkes) Education and the Atom, 1964, (with E.K. Hyde, I. Perlman) Nuclear Properties of the Heavy Elements, 1964, (with others) Oppenheimer, 1969, (with W.R. Corliss) Man and Atom, 1971, Nuclear Milestones, 1972; editor: Transuranium Elements: Products of Modern Alchemy, 1978; asso. editor: Jour. Chem. Physics, 1948-50; editorial adv. bd.: Jour. Inorganic and Nuclear Chemistry, 1954-82, Indsl. Research, Inc, 1967-75; adv. bd.: Chem. and Engring. News, 1957-59; editorial bd.: Jour. Am. Chem. Soc, 1950-59, Ency. Chem. Tech., from 1975, Revs. in Inorganic Chemistry, from 1977; mem. hon. editorial adv. bd.: Internat. Ency. Phys. Chemistry and Chem. Physics, from 1957; mem. panel: Golden Picture Ency. for Children, 1957-61; mem. cons. and adv. bd.: Funk and Wagnells Universal Standard Ency, 1957-61; mem. Am. Heritage Dictionary Panel Usage Cons, from 1964; contbr. articles to profl. jours. Trustee Pacific Sci. Center Found., 1962-77; trustee Sci. Service, from 1965, pres., from 1966; trustee Am.-Scandinavian Found., from 1968, Ednl Broadcasting Corp., 1970-72; trustee Swedish Council Am., from 1976, chmn. bd. dirs., 1978-82; bd. dirs. World Future Soc., from 1969, Calif. Council for Environ. and Econ. Balance, from 1974; bd. govs. Am. Swedish Hist. Found., 1972—. Recipient John Ericsson Gold medal Am. Soc. Swedish Engrs., 1948; Nobel prize for Chemistry (with E.M. McMillan), 1951; John Scott award and medal City of Phila., 1953; Perkin medal Am. sect. Soc. Chem. Industry, 1957; U.S. AEC Enrico Fermi award, 1959; Joseph Priestley Meml. award Dickinson Coll., 1960; Sci. and Engring. award Fedn. Engring. Socs., Drexel Inst. Tech., Phila., 1962; named Swedish Am. of Year, Vasa Order of Am., 1962; Franklin medal Franklin Inst., 1963; 1st Spirit of St. Louis award, 1964; Leif Erikson Found. award, 1964; Washington award Western Soc. Engrs., 1965; Arches of Sci. award Pacific Sci. Center, 1968; Internat. Platform Assn. award, 1969; Prometheus award Nat. Elec. Mfrs. Assn., 1969; Nuclear Pioneer award Soc. Nuclear Medicine, 1971; Oliver Townsend award Atomic Indsl. Forum, 1971; Disting. Honor award U.S. Dept. State, 1971; Golden Plate award Am. Acad. Achievement, 1972; John R. Kuebler award Alpha Chi Sigma, 1978; Founders medal Hebrew U. Jerusalem, 1981; Henry DeWolf-Smyth award Am. Nuclear Soc., 1982; decorated officier Legion of Honor France; Daniel Webster medal, 1976. Fellow Am. Phys. Soc., Am. Inst. Chemists (Pioneer award 1968, Gold medal award 1973), Chem. Soc. London (hon.), Royal Soc. Edinburgh (hon.), Am. Nuclear Soc., Calif., N.Y., Washington acads. scis., AAAS (pres. 1972, chmn. bd. 1973), Royal Soc. Arts (Eng.); mem. Am. Chem. Soc. (award in pure chemistry 1947, William H. Nichols medal N.Y. sect. 1948, Charles L. Parsons award 1964, Gibbs medal chgo. sect. 1966, Madison Marshall award No. Ala. sect. 1972, Priestley medal 1979, pres. 1976), Am. Philos. Soc., Royal Swedish Acad. Engring. Scis. (adv. council 1980), Am. Nat., Argentine Nat., Bavarian, Polish, Royal Swedish, USSR acads. scis., Royal Acad. Exact, Phys. and Natural Scis. Spain (acad. fgn. corr.), Soc. Nuclear Medicine (hon.), World Assn. World Federalists (v.p. 1980), Fedn. Am. Scientists (bd. sponsors 1980), Deutsche Akademie der Naturforscher Leopoldina (East Germany), Nat. Acad. Pub. Adminstrn., Internat. Platform Assn. (pres. 1981—), Am. Hiking Soc. (dir. 1979—, v.p. 1980), Phi Beta Kappa, Sigma Xi, Pi Mu Epsilon, Alpha Chi Sigma (John R. Kuebler award 1978), Phi Lambda Upsilon (hon.). Clubs: Bohemian (San Francisco); Chemists (N.Y.C.); Cosmos (Washington), University (Washington); Faculty (Berkeley). Co-discoverer elements 94-102, and 106: plutonium, 1940, americium, 1944-45, curium, 1944, berkelium, 1949, californium, 1950, einsteinium, 1952, fermium, 1953, mendelevium, 1955, nobelium,

1958, element 106, 1974; co-discoverer nuclear energy isotopes Pu-239, U-233, Np-237, other isotopes including I-131, Fe-59, Te-99m, Co-60; originator actinide concept for placing heaviest elements in periodic system. Subspecialty: Nuclear chemistry. Office: Lawrence Berkeley Lab U Calif Berkeley CA 94720

SEADLER, STEPHEN EDWARD, management consulting firm executive, social scientist; b. N.Y.C., May 9, 1926; s. Silas Frank and Deborah Amy (Gelbin) S.; m. Ingrid Linnea Adolfsson, Aug. 7, 1954; children—Einar Austin, Anna Carin. A.B. in Physics, Columbia U., 1947, postgrad., 1947; postgrad in physics George Washington U., 1948-50. Elec. engr., polit. sci. educator, social scis. researcher, writer for various cos. and institutions, 1951-65; pres. Internat. Dynamics Corp., Ft. Madison, Iowa, and N.Y.C., 1965-70; mgmt. cons. UNICONSULT, N.Y.C., 1970-73, pres., 1973—; founder ID Ctr., N.Y.C., 1985, pres., 1985—. Contbr. articles to profl. jours. Active, Ideological Def. Ctr., N.Y.C., 1968—. Mem. IEEE Computer Soc., Am. Phys. Soc., N.Y. Acad. of Scis., IEEE, Authors Guild. Unitarian. Lodges: Shriners, Masons. Current work: Development of new social science of ideologics and its mathematical formulation, ideotopology with focus on arms control. Development of the new field of cognition theory in computer science, especially to resolve the null value problem in relational information systems. Subspecialties: Theoretical computer science; Topology and foundations. Office: UNICONSULT 521 Fifth Ave New York NY 10017

SEAGO, JAMES LYNN, JR., biology educator; b. Alton, Ill., June 2, 1941; s. James L. and Dorothy F. (Watkins) S.; m. Katherine A. Brown Fanning, June 18, 1966; m. Jill P. Dabbs Arnold, Dec. 24, 1969; m. Marilyn Ann Meiss, Nov. 25, 1982; children: Kirstjan Erika, Robert Maclean. B.A., Knox Coll., 1963; M.A., Miami U., Oxford, Ohio, 1966; Ph.D. in Botany, U. Ill., Urbana, 1969. Asst. prof. biology SUNY Coll.-Oswego, 1968-74, assoc. prof., 1974—, chmn. dept. biology, 1979-85, also cross country coach; cons. biology. Contbr.: articles to Am. Jour. Botany; reviewer for jour. articles, books. N.Y. State grantee-in-aid, 1971; Nat. Soy Bean Crop Improvement Council grantee, 1976. Mem. Bot. Soc. Am., Torrey Bot. Club, Am. Soc. Agronomy, Sigma Xi. Current Work: Plant root development; cattail growth. Subspecialty: Plant growth. Home: PO Box 316 Dumas Rd Minetto NY 13115 Office: SUNY Dept Biology Piez Hall Oswego NY 13126

SEAGONDOLLAR, LEWIS WORTH, physics educator, nuclear physics researcher; b. Hoisington, Kans., Sept. 30, 1920; s. Fred Lewis and Bessie Estelle (Smilie) S.; m. Winifred Elizabeth Varner, Sept. 5, 1942; children—Bryan Worth, Laruel Jane, Mark Winston. A.B., Kans. State Tchrs. Coll., Emporia, 1941; Ph.M., U. Wis., 1943, Ph.D., 1948. From instr. to prof. physics U. Kans., Lawrence, 1947-65; prof. physics N.C. State U., Raleigh, 1965—, head dept. physics, 1965-75; with U.S. Naval Research Lab., Washington, summers, 1955-58. Contbr. articles to profl. jours. Recipient Outstanding Tchr. award N.C. State U., 1969; Disting. Alumnus award Kans. State Tchrs. Coll., 1971. Fellow Am. Phys. Soc. (regional sec. 1969—); mem. Am. Phys. Soc. (sec. Southeastern sect. 1968—), Health Physics Soc., Sigma Pi Sigma. Democrat. Current work: Van de Graaff generator development; neutron physics; neutron scattering from cryogenic polarized targets. Subspecialty: Nuclear physics. Home: 6853 W Lake Ann Dr Raleigh NC 27612 Office: Dept Physics NC State Univ PO Box 8202 Raleigh NC 27695

SEAMAN, WILLIAM BERNARD, physician; b. Chgo., Jan. 5, 1917; s. Benjamin and Dorothy E. S.; m. Veryl Swick, February 26, 1944; children—Cheryl Dorothy, William David. Student, U. Mich., 1934-37; M.D., Harvard U., 1941. Diplomate: Am. Bd. Radiology. Intern Billings Hosp., U. Chgo., 1941-42; asst. radiology Yale U. Sch. Medicine, 1947-48, instr., 1948-49; instr. radiology Washington U. Sch. Medicine, St. Louis, 1949-51, assoc. prof., 1951-55, prof., 1955-56; prof. radiology, chmn. dept. Coll. Phys. and Surg., Columbia U., 1956—; James Picks prof. emeritus Columbia U., 1982—; dir. radiology service, trustee Presbyn. Hosp., N.Y.C. Served as maj. USAAF, 1942-46; flight surgeon. Recipient W.R. Cannon medal Soc. Gastro-intestinal Radiologists, 1979, Gold medal Am. Coll. Radiology, 1983. Mem. Radiol. Soc. N.A., Am. Roentgen Ray Soc. (pres. 1973-74), Am. Coll. Radiology (pres. 1980-81), Assn. U. Radiologists (pres. 1955-56, Gold medal 1979), N.Y. Roentgen Soc. (pres. 1961-62), N.Y. Gastroent. Soc. (pres. 1965-66), Soc. Chmn. Academic Radiology Depts. (pres. 1967-68). Presbyn. Current Work: Radiology. Subspecialties: Radiology; Diagnostic radiology. Home: 261 Hickory St Tenafly NJ 07670 Office: 622 W 168th St New York NY 10032

SEAMANS, ROBERT CHANNING, JR., astronautical engineering educator; b. Salem, Mass., Oct. 30, 1918; s. Robert Channing and Pauline (Bosson) S.; m. Eugenia Merrill, June 13, 1942; children—Katherine (Mrs. Louis Padulo), Robert Channing III, Joseph, May (Mrs. Eugene Baldwin III), Daniel M. B.S., Harvard U., 1939; M.S., Mass. Inst. Tech., 1942, Sc.D., 1951; grad. exec. program bus. adminstrn., Columbia U., 1959; D.Sc., Rollins Coll., 1962, N.Y.U., 1967; D.Eng., Norwich Acad., 1971, Notre Dame U., 1974, Rensselaer Poly. Inst., 1974, U. Wyo., 1975, George Washington U., 1975, Lehigh U., 1976, Thomas Coll., 1980, Curry Coll., 1981; With Mass. Inst. Tech., 1941-55, successively instr. dept. aero. engring., staff engr. instrumentation lab., asst. prof., project leader instrumentation lab., asso. prof., 1941-50; chief engr. Project Meteor, 1950-53, dir. flight control lab., 1953-55; mgr. airborne systems lab., chief systems engr. airborne systems dept. RCA, 1955-58, chief engr. missile electronics and controls div., 1958-60; asso. adminstr. NASA, 1960-65, dep. adminstr., 1965-68, cons., 1968-69; vis. prof. Mass. Inst. Tech., 1968, Hunsaker prof., 1968-69; sec. air force, 1969-73; pres. Nat. Acad. Engring., 1973-74; adminstr. ERDA, Washington, 1974-77; Henry R. Luce prof. environment and pub. policy Mass. Inst. Tech., Cambridge, 1977-84, dean, 1978-81, sr. lectr. dept. aeronautics and astronautics, 1984—; dir. Charles Stark Draper Lab., Inc., Combustion Engring. Inc., Eli Lilly and Co., Johnny Appleseed's Inc; mem. sci. adv. bd. USAF, 1957-62, asso. adviser, 1963-67. Bd. overseers Harvard U., 1968-74; chmn. bd. Aerospace Corp.; trustee Mus. of Sci., Boston, Sea Edn. Assn., Nat. Geog. Soc., USAF Hist. Found., Carnegie Inst., Washington, Putnam Funds; bd. dirs. Alliance to Save Energy; trustee Woods Hole Oceanographic Instn. Recipient Naval Ordnance Devel. award, 1945; Godfrey L. Cabot award Aero Club New Eng., 1965; Distinguished Service medal NASA, 1965, 69; Robert H. Goddard Meml. trophy, 1968; Distinguished Pub. Service medal Dept. Def., 1973; Exceptional Civilian Service award Dept. Air Force, 1973; Gen. Thomas D. White U.S. Air Force Space Trophy, 1973; Ralph Coats Roe medal ASME, 1977; Achievement award Nat. Soc. Profl. Engrs.; Thomas D. White Nat. Def. award, 1980. Fellow Am. Acad. Arts and Scis., Am. Astron. Soc., IEEE, AIAA (hon., Lawrence Sperry award 1951); mem. Internat. Acad. Astronautics, Am. Soc. Pub. Adminstrn., Nat. Acad. Engring., AAAS, Air Force Acad. Found., Fgn. Policy Assn., Nat. Space Club, Council on Fgn. Relations, Sigma Xi. Clubs: Harvard (Boston); Manchester Yacht (Mass); Essex County (Mass.); Chevy Chase, Metropolitan (Washington). Current work: Technology and institutional management and public policy in aviation, energy, and health care. Subspecialties: Aeronautical engineering; Aerospace engineering and technology. Office: 33-406 Mass Inst Tech Cambridge MA 02139

SEARS, DUANE WILLIAM, immunologist, biochemist; b. Denver, Mar. 23, 1946; s. William A. and Florence E. (Harder) S.; m. Sheryn Elaine Rogers, Dec. 20, 1969; children—Rebecca Anne, David Allen. B.S., Colo. Coll., 1968; M.S., Columbia U., 1974, Ph.D., 1974. Postdoctoral fellow N.Y. Heart Assn.; NIH postdoctoral trainee Albert Einstein Coll. Medicine, 1974-77; assoc. prof. U. Calif.-Santa Barbara, 1977—. Contbr. articles to profl. jours. Served as capt. U.S. Army, 1968-76. Nat. Cancer Inst. grantee, 1978—. Mem. Am. Assn. Immunologists, Am. Chem. Soc., AAAS, N.Y. Acad. Scis. Current Work: Immunogenetic and biochem. analysis of cytotoxic T lymphocytes and K lymphocytes. Subspecialties: Immunogenetics; Transplantation.

SEARS, HENRY FRANCIS, II, oncologic surgeon; b. N.Y.C., July 7, 1940; s. Henry and Mary (Pouch) S.; m. Sarah Day Storm, June 12, 1962; children: David, Nathaniel, H. Christopher. B.A., U. Pa., 1962; M.D., Columbia U., 1966. Diplomate: Am. Bd. Surgery, 1974. Asst. resident in surgery U. Va. Hosp., Charlottesville, 1968-71, chief resident, 1971-72; staff surgeon Bethesda (Md.) Naval Hosp., 1972-74; sr. investigator surgery br. Nat. Cancer Inst., 1974-77; assoc. prof. surgery Harvard New Eng. Deaconess Hosp.; dir. surg. research and edn. Fox Chase Cancer Ctr., Phila., 1977-85; assoc. scientist Wistar Inst., Phila., 1979-85; asst. clin. prof. surgery U. Pa., 1977-85; assoc. prof. clin. surgery Harvard U., 1985—. Contbr. articles to profl. jours. Trustee Kent Sch., Chestertown, Md., 1982—. Served to lt. comdr. USN, 1972-74. Fellow ACS, Phila. Acad. Surgery; mem. Muller Surg. Soc., Assn. Acad. Surgeons, Clinico-Pathologic Soc. Washington, Soc. Surg. Oncology, Am. Assn. Cancer Research. Current Work: Investigation of tumor immunology using monoclonal antibodies to define membrane antigens, circulating antigens and immunodiagnostic and therapeutic potential. Subspecialties: Cancer research (medicine); Surgery. Home: 215 Sunrise Ln Philadelphia PA 19118 Office: New England Deaconess Hosp Boston MA

SEARS, WILLIAM REES, engr., educator; b. Mpls., Mar. 1, 1913; s. William Everett and Gertrude (Rees) S.; m. Mabel Jeannette Rhodes, Mar. 20, 1936; children—David William, Susan Carol. B.S. in Aero. Engring, U. Minn., 1934; Ph.D., Calif. Inst. Tech., 1938. Asst. prof. Calif. Inst. Tech., 1939-41; chief aerodynamics Northrop Aircraft, Inc., 1941-46; dir. Grad. Sch. Aero. Engring., Cornell U., Ithaca, N.Y., 1946-63; dir. Center Applied Math., 1963-67, J.L. Given prof. engring., 1962-74; prof. aerospace and mech. engring. U. Ariz., Tucson, 1974—; Cons. aerodynamics. Author: The Airplane and its Components, 1941; Editor: Jet Propulsion and High-Speed Aerodynamics, vol. VI, 1954, Jour. Aerospace Scis, 1956-63, Ann. Revs. of Fluid Mechanics, Vol. I. Recipient Distinguished Alumnus award U. Minn., 1950; Vincent Bendix award Am. Soc. Engring. Edn., 1965; Prandtl Ring Deutsche Gesellschaft für Luft-und Raumfahrt, 1974; Von Karman lectr. Am. Inst. Aeros. and Astronautics, 1968; F.W. Lanchester lectr. Royal Aero. Soc., 1973; Recipient Von Karman medal AGARD, Von Karman medal NATO, 1977. Fellow Internat. Acad. Astronautics, Am. Acad. Arts and Scis., Am. Inst. Aeros. and Astronautics (hon., G. Edward Pendray award 1975, S.A. Reed aeros. award 1981); mem. Nat. Acad. Engring., Nat. Acad. Engring. Mexico (fgn.), Nat. Acad. Scis., Sigma Xi. Current Work: Wind tunnels. Subspecialties: Aeronautical engineering; Fluid mechanics. Home: 6560 Skyway Rd Tucson AZ 85718 Office: Aerospace and Mech Engring Dept U Ariz Tucson AZ 85721

SEAY, THOMAS AUSTIN, psychologist, educator, consultant; b. Guntersville, Ala., Oct. 5, 1942; s. Barnard Austin and Mary (Croxton) S.; m. Mary Burt, Mar. 4, 1978; children—Michael Alexander, Brian Austin. M.A., Austin Peay State U., 1968; postgrad., U. Del., 1969-70; Ph.D., So. Ill. U., 1973; postgrad., Lehigh U., 1974-75. Lic. psychologist; diplomate Am. Bd. Family Psychology. Tchr. Christian County (Ky.) Sch. System, 1966-67; counselor Cecil County (Md.) Sch. System, 1968-69; asst. prof.psychology Cecil Community Coll., 1969-71; instr. So. Ill. U., Carbondale, 1971-73; researcher Kutztown U., 1973—, asst. prof. counseling psychology, 1973-76, assoc. prof., 1976-80, prof., 1980—; pres., chief exec. officer Community Psychol. Service Cons., Allentown, PA., 1980—; trainer Pa. Dept. Social Welfare, Harrisburg, 1978. Author: Systematic Eclectic Therapy, 1978, (with M. Braswell) Approaches to Counseling and Psychotherapy, 1980, 2d edit., 1984; Counseling; Theory, Practice and Training, 1985—; author test: Counselor R Scale, 1976; editor: Pa. Jour. Counseling, 1978—, Jour. Counseling and Psychotherapy, 1982. Vice chmn. Allentown State Hosp. Patient Rights; bd. dirs. Rape Crisis Council Lehigh Valley, Allentown, Haven House, Council on Drug and Alcohol Abuse, Allentown. Recipient Service award Rape Crisis Council Lehigh Valley, 1980; Md. Dept. Health grantee, 1970; Pa. Dept. Social Welfare Title XX grantee, 1978. Mem. Am. Assn. Marital and Family Therapists (clin.), Am. Psychol. Assn., Am. Ednl. Research Assn., Am. Personnel and Guidance Assn., Am. Acad. Psychologists in Marital, Family and Sex Therapy, Elkton Jaycees (v.p. 1968-71). Lodge: Elks. Current Work: Verbal and nonverbal behavior; prototypes in marital perceptions; therapy styles; personality characteristics of adoptive parents; personality characteristics of alcohol abusers. Subspecialties: Clinical psychology; Social psychology. Home: 1420 Walnut St Allentown PA 18102 Office: Kutztown State Coll Grad Ctr Kutztown PA 19530

SEBEK, OLDRICH KAREL, microbiologist; b. Prague, Czechoslovakia, July 3, 1919, came to U.S., 1947, naturalized, 1955; s. Vaclav and Marie (Sediva) S.; m. Dawn Islea Birch, Apr. 5, 1958; 1 child, Karel William. Sc.D., Charles U., 1946. Asst. in microbiology Charles U., Prague, 1945-47,; postdoctoral fellow J.E. Seagram and Sons, Inc., Louisville, 1947-48, Rutgers U., New Brunswick, N.J., 1948-49, Fordham U., Bronx, N.Y. 1949-50, Ohio State U., Columbus, 1950-52; sr. scientist Upjohn Co., Kalamazoo, Mich., 1952-84; vis. research scientist Western Mich. U., Kalamazoo, 1985—; vis. scientist U. Calif.-Berkeley, 1966-67; vis. prof. Nat. Poly. Inst., Mexico City, 1973; exchange scientist Nat. Acad. Scis., Czechoslovakia, 1980, German Democratic Republic, 1983. lectr. in field. Author: (with others) Genetics of Industrial Microorganisms, 1979. Editor: Applied Microbiology, 1967-71. Contbr. numerous articles to profl. jours. Fellow Am. Acad. Microbiology; mem. Am. Soc. Microbiology (div. agrl. microbiology, fermentation microbiology), Am. Chem. Soc., Soc. Indsl. Microbiology. Current work: Microbial biochemistry; fermentation and biotechnology; biotransformations of natural and synthetic compounds; microbial synthesis; strain improvement. Subspecialties: Microbiology; Enzyme technology. Home: 1002 Short Rd Kalamazoo MI 49008 Office: Dept Biology and Medical Scis Western Mich U Kalamazoo MI 49008

SEBHATU, MESGUN, physics educator, researcher; b. Menoxeito, Ethiopia, Jan. 6, 1946; came to U.S., 1970; s. Sebhatu Bairu and Mehret Tesfay; m. Almaz Yilma, July 21, 1984. B.S. in Physics, Haile Selassie I.U., Ethiopia, 1969; Ph.D. in Physics, Clemson U., 1975. Asst. prof. physics N.C. State U., Raleigh, 1975-76, Pensacola Jr. Coll., Fla., 1976-78; asst. prof. physics Winthrop Coll., Rock Hill, S.C., 1978-84, assoc. prof., 1984—; reviewer Prentice Hall, N.J., 1983—. Contbr. articles to profl. jours. Cottrell research grantee, 1981-83. Mem. Am. Phys. Soc., Am. Assn. Physics Tchrs. Roman Catholic. Current work: Derivation and investigation of two-nucleon potentials from non-linear quantum field theories. Subspecialties: Particle physics; Nuclear physics. Home: 750 Norwood Ave Rock Hill SC 29730 Office: Winthrop Coll 101 Sims Bldg Rock Hill SC 29733

SEBO, STEPHEN ANDREW, electrical engineer, educator, researcher; b. Budapest, Hungary, June 10, 1934; came to U.S., 1967, naturalized, 1976; s. Emery and Elizabeth (Thieben) S.; m. Eva Agnes Vambery, May 25, 1968. M.S.E.E., Budapest Poly. U., 1957; Ph.D. in Elec. Engring, Hungarian Acad. Scis., 1966. Engr. Budapest Electric Co., 1957-61; asst. prof. Budapest Poly. U., 1961-66, assoc. prof., 1966-67; Ford Found. fellow Columbia U., N.Y.C., 1967-68; assoc. prof. elec. engring. Ohio State U., Columbus, 1968-74, prof., 1974—, Am. Electric Power prof. in power systems, 1982—; cons. engr. for electric utilities. Contbr. articles to profl. jours. Recipient MacQuigg award Ohio State U., 1978; Power Educator award Edison Electric Inst., 1981. Mem. IEEE (sr. mem., best paper award 1982), Internat. Conf. on Large High Voltage Electric Systems, Am. Power Conf. Developer/organizer internat. short courses on electric power systems engring. Current Work: Performance of high voltage systems and electric power systems. Subspecialties: Electrical engineering; High voltage. Office: 2015 Neil Ave Columbus OH 43210

SECKAR, JOEL ANDREAS, toxicologist; b. Phila., Feb. 2, 1946; s. Valentine Joseph and Elizabeth Arlene (Andreas) S.; m. Donna Joyce Pruden, June 22, 1968; children—Christina, Janna. B.A., Gettysburg Coll., 1968; Ph.D., U. Cin., 1973; M.S., U. San Francisco, 1983. Sr. research chemist Pennwalt Corp., King of Prussia, Pa., 1973-78, corp. toxicologist, 1978—. Served to 1st lt. U.S. Army, 1973. Mem. Am. Chem. Soc., Soc. Toxicology (Mid-Atlantic sect.), Genetic Toxicology Assn., Soc. Environ. Toxicology and Chemistry. Presbyterian. Current work: Industrial toxicology, contract and design research; advise corporate and divisional management on toxicology matters. Subspecialties: Toxicology (medicine); Environmental toxicology. Home: 3 Barbara Dr Malvern PA 19355 Office: Pennwalt Corp PO Box C 900 1st Ave King of Prussia PA 19406

SECOR, JACK BEHRENT, botany educator, researcher; b. Indpls., Aug. 18, 1923; s. Hugh and Emma (Behrent) S.; B.S., Butler U., 1948; Ph.D., Wash. State U., 1957; postdoctoral Va. Poly. Inst. and State U., 1963-65. Research fellow U. Western Ont., London, Can., 1959-60; instr. Mich. State U., East Lansing, 1960-63; research scientist U. Tex., Austin, 1966-67; asst. prof. to prof. Eastern N.Mex. U., Portales, 1967—; councilor N.Mex. Inst. Chemists, 1976-78. Contbr. sci. articles to jours. Served with U.S. Army, 1942-45, ETO. NSF grantee, 1975. Mem. Ecol. Soc. Am., AAAS, Am. Inst. Biol. Sci., Am. Inst. Chemists, Sigma Xi, Phi Kappa Phi. Current work: Studies of plant communities; seed germination ecology and physiology. Subspecialties: Ecology (biology); Soil science. Home: 804 W 14th Portales NM 88130 Office: Eastern NMex U Dept Life Sci Portales NM 88130

SECORD, DAVID CARTWRIGHT, experimental surgery educator, veterinarian; b. Toronto, Ont., Can., June 6, 1933; s. Alan C. and Geraldine (Cole) S.; m. Susan Haines, May 25, 1957 (div. 1984); children—Lesley, Allison, Heather; m. Joan B. Williamson, Oct. 10, 1984. D.V.M., U. Toronto, 1958, M.V.Sc., 1961. Asst. prof. surgery Faculty Medicine, U. Alta., Edmonton, Can., 1961-64, assoc. prof., 1964-69, assoc. prof., 1969-74, prof., 1974—, dir. med. scis. vivarium, 1961-68, dir. health scis. animal ctr., 1968-79, dir. univ. lab. animal breeding unit, 1973-79, acting dir. surg. Med. Research Inst., 1978-79, dir. Small Animal Research Ctr., 1979—; bd. examiners vet. medicine Province of Alta, 1962—; mem. vet. adv. com. No. Alta. Inst. Tech., 1972—; advisor animal research Province of Alta, 1966, Province of Ont., 1969, U.S.A., 1972; cons. in field; mem. assessment panel Can. Council Animal Care, 1969—; mem. vet. adv. com. Humane Soc. U.S., 1972-74; assoc. veterinarian Edmonton Emergency Vet. Clinic, 1980—. Contbr. articles to profl. jours. Bd. dirs. Edmonton Youth Sci. Found., 1970-74; chmn. vet. div. United Community Fund, 1970-72. Recipient Quill award Can. Assn. Physiotherapy, 1984. Fellow Acad. Surg. Research; mem. Can. Vet. Med. Assn. (Veterinarian of Yr. award 1973), Ont. Vet. Med. Assn., Alta. Vet. Med. Assn. (chmn. advanced edn. com. 1963-67, chmn. lab. animal com. 1970—, Veterinarian of Yr. award 1985), Can. Assn. Lab. Animal Scis. (bd. dirs. 1971-74), Am. Assn. Lab. Animal Scis., AVMA, Am. Soc. Lab. Animal Practitioners, Edmonton Assn. Vet. Practice, Edmonton Vet. Assn. (pres. 1964-65), N.Y. Acad. Scis., Can. Assn. Sport Scis. Anglican. Current work: Research on effects of physical exercise in rats-intracellular basis. Subspecialties: Surgery; Laboratory animal medicine. Office: U Alta Edmonton AB T6G 2G5 Canada

SEDBERRY, GEORGE R., III, marine scientist; b. Tokyo, Sept. 15, 1950 (parents Am. citizens); s. George R. and Jessie M. (Jones) S.; m. Joan I. Kearns; 1 child, Jonathan A. B.S., Old Dominion U., 1972; M.A., Coll. William and Mary, 1975, Ph.D., 1980. Research asst. Va. Inst. Marine Sci., Gloucester Point, 1972-79; asst. marine scientist S.C. Marine Resources, Charleston, 1980—. Contbr. articles to profl. jours. Old Dominion U. scholar. Mem. Am. Soc. Ichthyologists and Herpetologists, Am. Soc. Zoologists, Sigma Xi. Current work: Trophic ecology of marine fishes, commuity ecology of demersal marine fishes, fishery biology, reef ecology. Subspecialties: Ecology (biology); Marine biology. Home: 1299 Relyea Ave Charleston SC 29412 Office: SC Marine Resources Research Inst Box 12559 Charleston SC 29412

SEDINGER, JAMES STONE, ecologist; b. Portland, Oreg., Nov. 28, 1949; s. Lyle Jackson and Marguerite (Newman) S.; m. Constance Margaret Urling, June 13, 1973; 1 child, Benjamin Stone. B.S., U. Wash., 1971; Ph.D., U. Calif.-Davis, 1983. Research biologist U.S. Fish and Wildlife Service, Anchorage, 1984—. Contbr. articles to profl. jours. Mem. AAAS, Am. Ornithologists Union, Am. Soc. Naturalists, Ecol. Soc. Am., Wildlife Soc., Audubon Soc. Current work: Regulation of populations; foraging ecology and nutrition of Arctic geese evolution of life history traits. Subspecialties: Behavioral ecology; Population biology. Office: Alaska Field Station DWRC US Fish and Wildlife Service 1011 E Tudor Rd Anchorage AK 99503

SEDLACEK, WILLIAM ADAM, chemist; b. Glendive, Mont., Feb. 22, 1936; s. Adam and Ena Marie (Boje) S.; m. Nancy Jean Knaus, Sept. 8, 1963 (div. 1978); children—William Brian, Bruce Adam. B.S., U. Wyo., 1958, Ph.D., 1965; postgrad. (fellow) U. Fla., 1965-66. Staff mem. Los Alamos Nat. Lab., 1966—; with Oil Shale and Petroleum Research Sta., U.S. Bur. Mines, Laramie, Wyo., 1960-61. Contbr. articles to profl. jours. Umpire, coach youth baseball, Los Alamos and Boulder, Colo., 1974—. NDEA fellow, 1961-65; NSF fellow, 1965-66. Mem. Am. Chem. Soc., Am. Geophys. Union, Sigma Xi. Republican. Lutheran. Subspecialties: Atmospheric chemistry; Nuclear chemistry. Home: 48 Timber Ridge Los Alamos NM 87544 Office: Los Alamos Nat Lab PO Box 1663 MSJ514 Los Alamos NM 87545

SEDLAK, RICHARD JOHN, electrical engineer; b. New Brunswick, N.J., Mar. 1, 1952; s. Andrew Albert and Helen (Schmidt) S.; m. Roberta Kincaid, May 4, 1980. B.S.E.E. with honors, Lehigh U., 1974. Assoc. mem. tech. staff Solid State div. RCA, Somerville, N.J., 1974-81; prin. engr. Sweda Internat., Pine Brook, N.J., 1981-83; sr. engr. Singer/Kearfott, Wayne, N.J., 1983—. Mem. IEEE, Assn. Computing Machinery, Am. Radio Relay League, Eta Kappa Nu. Republican. Current work: Design testing and downsizing of systems via VLSI technology—structured cells, standard cells, semi-custom integration, fault simulation and automatic pattern generation. Subspecialties: Computer engineering; Microelectronics. Home: 1309 Murray Ave Plainfield NJ 07060 Office: Singer/Kearfott 150 Totowa Rd Wayne NJ 07470

SEEBASS, ALFRED RICHARD, III, aerospace engineer, educator, university dean; b. Denver, Mar. 27, 1936; s. Alfred Richard and Marie Estelle (Wright) S.; m. Nancy Jane Palm, June 20, 1958; children: Erik Peter, Scott Gregory. B.S.E. magna cum laude, Princeton, 1958, M.S.E. (Guggenheim fellow), 1961; Ph.D. (Woodrow Wilson fellow), Cornell U., 1962. Asst. prof. Cornell U., 1962-64, asso. prof., 1964-72, prof., 1972-75, asso. dean, 1972-75; prof. aerospace and mech. engring., prof. math. U. Ariz., Tucson, 1975-81; dean Coll. Engring. and Applied Sci., U. Colo., Boulder, 1981—; cons. in field; mem. coms. Nat. Acad. Engring., Nat. Acad. Sci., NRC, NASA, USAF, Dept. Transp., 1970—; chmn. Aeros. and Space Engring. Bd.; grant investigator NASA, Office Naval Research, Air Force Office Sci. Research, 1966—. Editor: Sonic Boom Research, 1967, Nonlinear Waves, 1974; editorial bd.: Ann. Rev. Fluid Mechanics, Phys. Fluids, AIAA Jour.; Contbg. author: Handbook of Applied Mathematics, 1974; Contbr. articles to profl. jours. Fellow Nat. Acad. Engring., AIAA, AAAS; mem., AAUP, Soc. Indsl. and Applied Math., Sigma Xi, Tau Beta Pi. Subspecialty: Applied mathematics. Office: Coll Engring and Applied Sci U Colo Boulder CO 80309

SEEGER, CHARLES RONALD, geologist, educator; b. Columbus, Ohio, Jan. 31, 1931; s. Karl Elder and Ethel Turney (Jones) S.; m. Barbara Ann Ashley; children—Leslie Ethel, Julie Ann. B.Sc., Ohio State U., 1953; M.S., George Washington U., 1958; Ph.D., U. Pitts., 1966. Engring. geologist Photronix, Inc., Columbus, 1958; ops analyst weapons systems evaluation group Inst. Def. Analyses, Washington, 1958-60; earth scis. analyst Office Naval Intelligence Sci. and Tech. Intelligence Ctr., Washington, 1960-63; instr. George Washington U., Washington, 1962-68; asst. prof. geology and geophysics, Western Ky. U., Bowling Green, 1968-69, assoc. prof., 1969-77, prof., 1977—; vis. lectr. Vanderbilt U. Author: Problems for Exploration Geophysics, 1978; (with others) Geology Field Manual, 1985. Contbr. articles to profl. jours. and meetings. Served with USN, 1953-57. NSF grantee, 1975. Mem. Am. Geophys. Union, Meteoritical Soc., AAUP (chpt. pres. 1971-72), Ky. Acad. Sci. (geology pres. 1978), Geol. Soc. Am., Sigma Xi (pres. Western Ky. U. chpt. 1983-84). Current Work: Tectonic and geophysical studies; cryptoexplosion structural studies; tectonics of central mid-continent. Subspecialties: Tectonics; Geophysics. Home: 630 Ironwood Dr Bowling Green KY 42101 Office: Western Ky U Bowling Green KY 42101

SEEGMILLER, DAVID WILLIAM, chemist, air force officer; b. Nephi, Utah; s. Glen W. and Thelma F. (Park) S.; m. Jean Black, Sept. 1, 1954; children—Donald G., Robert A., Sharon K., Diane L. B.S., Brigham Young U., 1956, M.S., 1958; Ph.D., U. Calif.-Berkeley, 1963. Commd. 2d lt., U.S. Air Force, 1956, advanced through grades to col., 1979; nuclear research officer, McClellan AFB, Calif., 1958-60; prof. chemistry U.S. Air Force Acad., 1962-80; chief scientist European Office of Aerospace Research and Devel., London, 1976-78; chief advanced laser tech. div. Air Force Weapons Lab., Kirtland AFB, N.Mex., 1980-84, chief Aerospace Laser Tech. Office, 1984—; cons. Kaman Scis. Corp., Colorado Springs, Colo., 1964-68; cons. Office of Sci. Advisor, U.S. Mil. Assistance Command, Vietnam, 1968. Patentee high energy batteries. Decorated Air Force Commendation medal with two oak leaf clusters, Air Force Meritorious Service medal with oak leaf cluster; recipient Air Force Systems Command award for Tech. Achievement of Yr., U.S. Air Force Research and Devel. award for Most Outstanding Research of Year. Mem. Am. Chem. Soc., Air Force Assn., Sigma Xi. Mem. Ch. of Jesus Christ of Latter-day Saints. Current work: Principal research in area of high energy batteries and radiochemistry; management of space based laser portion of strategic defense initiatives program. Subspecialty: Physical chemistry. Home: 5300 Van Christoper NE Albuquerque NM 87111 Office: Air Force Weapons Lab AR2 Kirtland AFB NM 87117

SEELER, DAVID CHARLES, veterinary anesthesiologist, educator, researcher; b. Windsor, Ont., Can., July 6, 1953; s. David Clayton and Audrey Catherine (Fisher) S.; m. Helen Elaine Wright, Apr. 26, 1980; 1 child, Jennifer Laura. D.V.M., U. Guelph, Ont., 1978, grad. diploma in anesthesiology, 1979, M.Sc., 1982. Intern U. Guelph, 1978-79; teaching assoc., resident U. Ill., Urbana, 1981-83; asst. prof. anesthesiology Sch. Vet. Medicine, Tufts U., Boston, 1983—; head anesthesia service, staff anesthesiologist Angell Meml. Animal Hosp., Boston, 1983-85. Contbr. chpt., articles to profl. publs. Ont. scholar, 1972; Ont. Govt. scholar U. Guelph, 1980, 81. Mem. AVMA, Can. Vet. Med. Assn., Ont. Vet. Assn., Am. Coll. Vet. Anesthesiologists (diplomate), Internat. Anesthesia Research Soc., Vet. Emergency and Critical Care Soc. Current work: Pharmacokinetics of intravenously administered anesthetics; evaluation of clinical tests for malignant hyperthermia and porcine stress syndrome. Subspecialties: Anesthesiology; Pharmacokinetics. Office: Tufts U Sch Vet Medicine 200 Westborough Rd North Grafton MA

SEELEY, JAMES LEWIS, research chemist; b. Syracuse, N.Y., May 26, 1936; s. Theron Matheson and Elizabeth Lockwood (Cummings) S.; m. Sharon Kay Cadenhead, Feb. 16, 1963; children—Karen Suzanne, James Lewis, Kristine Elizabeth. B.A., Hamilton Coll., 1957; Ph.D., Colo. State U., 1973. Chemist Cowles Chem. Corp. Skaneateles Falls, N.Y., 1957-59, Norwich Pharm. Eaton Labs., N.Y., 1961-63; research chem. engr. GTE Sylvania, Towanda, Pa., 1963-69; grad. research asst. Colo. State U., Ft. Collins, 1969-73; sr. chemist, staff assoc. Ctr. for Indsl. Instl. Devel., U. N.H., Durham, 1973-74; supervising research chemist U.S. Geol. Survey, Menlo Park, Calif., Denver, 1974—; for dir. Ctr. for Maj. Instrumentation, U. N.H., Durham. Author: Emission Spectrometry in Characterization of Solid Surfaces, 1974, instrn. manuals, 1972. Contbr. articles to profl. jours. Bd. dirs. Evergreen Chamber Orch. Soc., 1983-84; scoutmaster Santa Clara County council Boy Scouts Am., Sunnyvale, Calif., 1974-80; vol. Little League, YMCA, Gray Y, Sunnyvale, 1974-80, Amigos de las Americas, 1980-81. Served with USAF, 1959-61. Recipient Leadership award USAF, 1960, Tchng. award USAF Inst., 1961, Superior Achievement award U.S. Geol. Soc., 1982. Mem. Soc. Applied Spectroscopy (pres. Penn-York 1968-69), Am. Chem. Soc., AAAS, Assn. Exploration Geochemists. Republican. Methodist. Current work: Trace inorganic elemental analysis via analytical atomic spectroscopy; primarily optical emission spectrometry as applied to geochemistry. Subspecialties: Analytical chemistry; Geochemistry. Home: 25693 Independence Trail Evergreen CO 80439 Office: US Geol Survey Box 25046 MS 928 DFC Denver CO 80225

SEELY, JOHN HENRY, mechanical engineer, consultant; b. Pensacola, Fla., Sept. 24, 1921; s. John Henry and Eleanor Catherine (Gill) S.; m. Marcella Dennigan, July 4, 1945. M.E., Stevens Inst. Tech., 1949; M.M.E., Syracuse U., 1960; postgrad. (IBM fellow), Stanford U., 1964-65. Registered profl. engr., N.Y. State. Engr. IBM, 1949, engrng. mgr., to, 1976; prof. mech. engrng. Calif. State Poly. U., 1976-82; chmn. dept. mech. engrng. Fla. A&M U.; cons. mech. engrng., Tallahassee, 1982—; lectr., condr. seminars at univs., profl. devel. schs., indsl. cos. Author: (with R. C. Chu) Heat Transfer in Microelectronic Equipment, 1972, Elements of Thermal Technology, 1981; contbr. (with R. C. Chu) articles to profl. jours., mags., meetings. Served to lt. USN, 1942-46, 51-52. Recipient cert. for service to mech. design advs. com. Dutchess Community Coll., 1974, plaque for outstanding service Fla. A&M U. Coll. Sci. and Tech., 1975. Fellow ASME (7 certs. for various activities and com. chairmanships 1967-80, Meritorious Service Citation award Region II 1972, Centennial medallion and cert. 1980). Current Work: Heat Transfer in microelectronic equipment. Subspecialties: Mechanical engineering; Materials. Home: 3042 Shamrock N Tallahassee FL 32308

SEEMAN, NADRIAN CHARLES, biophysics educator; b. Chgo., Dec. 16, 1945; s. Herman and Emma Sylvia (Klaman) S. B.S., U. Chgo., 1966; Ph.D., U. Pitts., 1970. Postdoctoral fellow Columbia U., N.Y.C., 1970-72, MIT, Cambridge, 1972-77; assoc. prof. biophysics SUNY-Albany, 1983—; sr. cons. Molecular Biophysics Tech. Inc., 1983—; cons. Lifecodes, Inc., Elmsford, N.Y., 1983—. Mem. editorial bd. Jour. Biomolecular Structure and Dynamics, 1983—. Contbr. articles to profl. jours. Basil O'Connor fellow; NIH research career devel. award, Mem. Am. Crystallographic Assn., Biophys. Soc., Am. Chem. Soc., AAAS. Current work: Structure, dynamics and applications of nucleic acid branched junction complexes. Subspecialties: Biophysical chemistry; Crystallography. Office: Dept Biology SUNY Albany NY 12222

SEEMUTH, PAUL DOUGLAS, chemist, researcher; b. Tiffin, Ohio, Feb. 19, 1951; s. Jack Richard and Helen Mae (Rumschlag) S.; m. Marilou Elise Moyer, July 25, 1973. B.S., Bowling Green State U., 1973; M.S., Purdue U., 1975; Ph.D., U. Cin., 1978. Postdoctoral fellow Schering-Plough, Bloomfield, N.J., 1978-79; research chemist Ethyl Corp., Ferndale, Mich. and Baton Rouge, 1979-84, E.I. DuPont de Nemours, Greenville, N.C., 1984—; presenter papers at nat. confs. Contbr. articles to profl. jours. Patentee in field. Mem. Am. Chem. Soc. (bd. dirs., pub. relations com. 1979-82, sec. bd. 1982-83). Republican. Roman Catholic. Current work: Fiber surface research. Subspecialties: Organic chemistry; Surface chemistry. Office: EI DuPont de Nemours PO Box 800 Kinston NC 28501

SEETHARAM, BELLUR, biomedical researcher, educator; b. Channarayapatna, Mysore, India, June 3, 1943; came to U.S., 1972; s. Krishna and Gundamma Rao; m. Shakuntla, Mar. 3, 1971; children: Antariksh, Anil. B.S., Mysore U., 1961; M.S., Bangalore U., 1965, Ph.D., 1972. Postdoctoral fellow U. N.Mex., Albuquerque, 1972-74; instr. Washington U., St. Louis, 1974-77; asst. prof. Washington U. (Sch. Medicine), 1977-83, assoc. prof., 1983—. NIH research grantee, 1979. Mem. Am. Gastroent. Assn., Am. Soc. Biochemists, Am. Fedn. Clin. Research. Hindu. Current Work: Study of molecular organization of brush border membrane proteins. Vitamin B_{12} in health and disease. Subspecialties: Biochemistry (medicine); Gastroenterology. Home: 9034 Watsonia Olivette MO 63132 Office: Washington U Sch Medicine 660 S Euclid Saint Louis MO 63110

SEEVERS, ROBERT HARMON, JR., medicinal chemistry researcher, nuclear medicine educator; b. N.Y.C., Nov. 2, 1954; s. Robert Harmon and Hannah Rose (Meller); m. Arlene Renee Kurz, Aug. 11, 1984. B.S., Lehigh U., 1976; Ph.D., U. Mich., 1981. Postdoctoral researcher Argonne Nat. Lab., Ill., 1981-83; radiochemist Michael Reese Hosp., Chgo., 1983—; cons. Cancer Ctr., U. Chgo., 1983—. Contbr. articles to profl. jours. Mem. Am. Chem. Soc., AAAS, Am. Sci. Affiliation, Soc. Nuclear Medicine, Sigma Xi. Baptist. Current work: Teaching radiopharmaceutical chemistry to nuclear medicine and radiology residents; research in technetium and iodinated radiopharmaceuticals. Subspecialties: Medicinal chemistry; Nuclear medicine. Office: Div Nuclear Medicine Michael Reese Hosp and Med Ctr Lake Shore Dr and 31st St Chicago IL 60619

SEFERIS, JAMES CONSTANTINE, chemical engineering educator; b. Athens, Greece, Nov. 3, 1950, came to U.S., 1968. naturalized, 1982; s. Constantine Dimitrios and Roubina L. (Georgoulis) S.; m. Anne V. Moudon, 1982; 1 child, Louiza. B.S. in Chem. Engrng., U. Colo., 1973; Ph.D. in Chem. Engrng., U. Del., 1977. Adj. asst. prof. U. Del., Newark, 1977-78; vis. asst. prof. Drexel U., Phila., 1977; asst. prof. U. Wash., Seattle, 1977-81, assoc. prof., 1981-85, prof. chem. and polymer engrng., 1985—; vis. prof. Nat. Tech. U. of Athens, 1982; dir. U. Wash. Polymeric Composites Lab., Seattle, 1982—; cons. Boeing Co., Seattle, 1977—; cons. E.I. duPont de Nemours, Wilmington, Del., 1979—; cons. Owens-Corning Fiberglas, Granville, Ohio, 1980—. Editor: The Role of the Polymeric Matrix in the Processing and Structural Properties of Composite Materials, 1983; Interrelations between Processing Structure and Properties of Polymeric Materials, 1984; contbr. articles to profl. jours. Recipient First Presdl. Young Investigator award NSF, 1984. Mem. Am. Inst. Chem. Engrs., Am. Chem. Soc., Am. Phys. Soc., Soc. Plastic Engrs., Soc. Advancement of Materials and Processing Engring. Current work: High performance polymer composites; polymer physics and engrng.; processing-structure-property relations of polymers and composites; thermal characterization and rate phenomena. Subspecialties: Composite materials; Polymers (materials science). Home: 1911 N 40th Seattle WA 98103 Office: U Washington Dept Chem Engring Polymeric Composites Lab BF-10 Seattle WA 98195

SEGAL, BARRY M., internist, endocrinologist, educator; b. N.Y.C., Sept. 26, 1934; s. O. Saul and Doris (Eisenberg) S.; m. Susan Betty Grossman, June 17, 1961; children: Jeffrey Howard, Helaine Beth. B.A., Syracuse U., 1956; M.D., SUNY-Syracuse, 1959. Diplomate: Am. Bd. Internal Medicine, Am. Bd. Endocrinology, Am. Bd. Nuclear Medicine. Intern Bellevue Hosp., and Meml. Hosp. Center, N.Y.C., 1959-60, asst. resident in medicine, 1960-61; resident in medicine N.Y. Med. Coll., N.Y.C., 1962-63; vis. fellow in endocrinology Columbia U. Presbyn. Med. Center, N.Y.C., 1963-65; asst. physician Vanderbilt Clinic, Coll. of Physicians and Surgeons, 1965-71; asst. chief endocrinology sect. Westchester County Med. Center, Valhalla, N.Y., 1965; staff mem., cons. Phelps Meml. Hosp., Tarrytown, N.Y., 1965—; program chmn. medicine dept. 1981, chmn. continuing med. edn. com., 1982—; attending staff No. Westchester Hosp., Mt. Kisco, N.Y.; clin. asst. prof. medicine N.Y. Med. Coll., 1971-74, clin. assoc. prof., 1974-84; clin. prof. medicine (endocrinology), 1984—; cons. in endocrinology Peekskill (N.Y.) Community Hosp., 1965—. Contbr. sci. articles to profl. publs. Fellow ACP, Am. Coll. Nuclear Physicians; mem. Westchester Diabetes Assn. (mem. bd. dirs. 1965-70), Am. Diabetes Assn., AMA, Westchester County Med. Soc. (chmn. medicine sect. 1972-77, chief internal medicine sect. 1972-75), Endocrine Soc., Am. Thyroid Assn., Soc. Nuclear Medicine. Current Work: Endocrinology; nuclear medicine. Subspecialties: Endocrinology; Nuclear medicine. Home: 520 Sleepy Hollow Rd Briarcliff NY 10510 Office: 316 Chappaqua Rd Briarcliff NY 10510

SEGAL, BERNARD LOUIS, physician, educator; b. Montreal, Que., Can., Feb. 13, 1929; came to U.S., 1961, naturalized, 1966; s. Irving and Fay (Schecter) S.; m. Idajane Fischman, Feb. 17, 1963; 1 dau., Jody Segal. B.Sc. cum laude, McGill U., 1950, postgrad., 1950-51, M.D., C.M. high standing, 1955. Diplomate: Am. Bd. Internal Medicine. Intern Jewish Gen Hosp., Montreal, 1955-56; resident Balt. City Hosp., 1956-57, Beth Israel Hosp., Boston, 1957-58, Georgetown Med. Center, Washington, 1958-59, St. George's Hosp., London, Eng., 1959-61; practice medicine specializing in internal medicine and cardiology, Phila., 1961—; prof., sr. attending physician medicine Hahnemann Med. Coll., Phila., 1964—, dir. William Likoff Cardiovascular Inst. Author: Auscultation of the Heart, 1965; Editor: Theory and Practice of Auscultation, 1964, Engineering in the Practice of Medicine, 1966, Your Heart, 1972, Arteriosclerosis and Coronary Heart Disease, 1972; Editorial bd.: Am. Jour. Cardiology, 1970—, Clin. Echocardiography, 1978; Contbr. numerous articles on cardiology to med. jours. Fellow ACP, Am. Coll. Cardiology (chmn. scholar-trainee com., trustee 1969-71), Am. Coll. Chest Physicians; mem. N.Y. Acad. Scis., Alpha Omega Alpha. Subspecialties: Cardiology; Internal medicine. Home: 1156 Red Rose Ln Villanova PA 19085 Office: 1320 Race St Philadelphia PA 19102

SEGAL, HAROLD LEWIS, biochemistry researcher and educator; b. N.Y.C., Nov. 18, 1924; s. Charles and Rachel (Finn) S.; m. Norma Caplan, June 15, 1945; children—Robin Ann, Deborah Claire. B.S., Carnegie Mellon U., 1947; M.S., U. Minn., 1949, Ph.D., 1952; Postgrad. UCLA, 1952-54. Asst. prof. U. Pitts. Med. Sch., 1954-59; assoc. prof. St. Louis U. Med. Sch., 1959-64; prof. biochemistry SUNY, Buffalo, 1964—. Mem. editorial bd. Biochemistry, 1978-81, Enzymes, 1980—. Contbr. articles to profl. jours. Served with AUS, 1943-46. Office: Dept Biol Scis SUNY Amherst NY 14260

SEGAL, JOSEPH, biochemist, educator; b. Shaar Ha-Amakim, Israel, Sept. 14, 1946; came to U.S., 1976; s. Mishael and Haya (Lerman) S.; m. Harriet Gildner, Sept. 3, 1975; children—Erin Michelle, Adam Kenneth, Daniel Tal. B.Sch., Hebrew U., Israel, 1970, M.Sc., 1972, Ph.D., 1976. Research fellow in medicine Beth Israel Hosp., Boston, 1976-78; assoc. in medicine Harvard Med. Sch., Boston, 1976-78, instr., 1978-80, asst. prof., 1980—. Leah and Arthur Felix fellow, 1978; Nat. Inst. on Aging grantee, 1979. Mem. Am. Gerontol. Soc., Am. Fedn. for Clin. Research. Current Work: Thyroid hormone: The mechanism of action of thyroid hormone at the plasma membrane level. Aging: The role of endocrine and immune systems in the process of aging. Subspecialties: Biochemistry (biology); Cell biology. Office: U/Beth Israel Hosp 330 Brookline Ave Boston MA 02215

SEGAL, SHOSHANA, molecular biologist; b. Plovdive, Bulgaria, Feb. 27, 1941; came to U.S., 1969, naturalized, 1977; d. Manoach and Sara (Cohen) Ninio; m. David M. Segal, July 18, 1967; children: Ron, Ethan. B.Sc., Hebrew U., Jerusalem, 1965; Ph.D., Georgetown U., 1973. Lab. asst. Weizmann Inst. Sci., Israel, 1961-62, 65-68; fellow Nat. Cancer Inst., NIH, Bethesda, Md., 1973-76, sr. investigator, 1976-80, expert cons., 1980—; supr. students dept. biochemistry Georgetown U., 1981-82. Contbr. in field. Served with Israeli Army, 1959-61. Mem. Am. Soc. Microbiology, Sigma Xi. Current Work: The use of genetic engineering for studying cellular differentiation and regulation of mammalian genes. Subspecialties: Gene actions; Genetics and genetic engineering (biology). Home: 5 Eton Overlook Rockville MD 20850 Office: National Cancer Institute National Institutes Health Bldg 37 Bethesda MD 20205

SEGAR, DOUGLAS ALLAN, technical consulting company executive; b. Liverpool, Eng., Apr. 29, 1944; s. Thomas Harold and Mary (McEvoy) S.; m. Rene Jill, Sept. 10, 1965 (div.); children: Jennifer Kate, Anthony Allan. B.Sc., U. Liverpool, 1965, Ph.D. in Oceanography, 1969. Postdoctoral research fellow Marine Biol. Assn. U.K., Plymouth; asst. prof. Sch. Marine and Atmospheric Scis., U. Miami, Fla., 1970-74; oceanographer NOAA, Rockville, Md., and Miami, 1974-77; profl. staff mem., cons. U.S. Congress Mcht. Marine and Fisheries Com., Washington, 1977-79; pres. SEAMOcean, Inc., Wheaton, Md., 1979—; mem. U.S. Adv. Com. to Internat. Conv. on Prevention of Marine Pollution by Dumping of Wastes and Other Materials, 1981—; congressional rep. U.S. del. Spl. Consultative Meeting Antarctic Treaty, Canberra, Australia, 1978, Buenos Aires, Argentina, 1978, Washington, 1978; cons. EPA, Govt. Poland, 1977. Contbr. articles to profl. jours. Mem. Am. Soc. Limnology and Oceanography (chmn. com. spl. symposia 1977-79), Am. Oceanic Orgn., Am. Geophys. Union, AAAS, Am. Chem. Soc., Optical Soc. Am., N.Y. Acad. Scis., Water Pollution Control Fedn. Current Work: Pollution chemistry, pollution monitoring, optical analysis methods, environmental management.

SEGRÈ, EMILIO, physicist, educator; b. Tivoli, Rome, Italy, Feb. 1, 1905; came to U.S., 1938, naturalized, 1944; s. Giuseppe and Amelia (Treves) S.; m. Elfriede Spiro, Feb. 2, 1936 (dec. Oct. 1970); children: Claudio, Amelia, Fausta; m. Rosa Mines, Feb. 12, 1972. Ph.D., U. Rome, 1928; Dr. honoris causa, U. Palermo, Italy, Gustavus Adolphus Coll., St. Peter, Minn., Tel Aviv U., Hebrew Union Coll., Los Angeles. Asst. prof. U. Rome, 1932-36; dir. physics lab. U. Palermo, Italy, 1936-38; research asst. U. Calif.-Berkeley, 1938-43, prof. physics, 1945-72, emeritus, 1972—, group leader Los Alamos Sci. Lab., 1943-46; hon. prof. San Marcos U., Lima; vis. prof. U. Ill., Purdue U.; prof. physics U. Rome, 1974-75. Recipient Hofmann medal German Chem. Soc., Cannizzaro medal Accad. Lincei; Nobel prize in physics, 1959; decorated great cross merit Republic of Italy; Rockefeller Found. fellow, 1930-31; Guggenheim fellow, 1959; Fulbright fellow. Fellow Am. Phys. Soc.; mem. Nat. Acad. Scis., Am. Philos. Soc., Am. Acad. Arts and Scis., Heidelberg Akademie Wissenschaften, European Phys. Soc., Acad. Scis. Peru, Soc. Progress of Sci. (Uruguay), Società Italiana di fisica, Accad. Naz. Lincei (Italy), Accad. Naz. XL (Italy), Indian Acad. Scis. Bangalore, others. Co-discoverer slow neutrons, elements technetium, astatine, plutonium and the antiproton. Subspecialty: Nuclear physics. Office: Dept Physics U of California Berkeley CA 94720

SEGRE, MARIANGELA, immunology educator; b. Milan, Italy, Oct. 4, 1927; d. Carlo and Armida (Seveso) Bertani; m. Diego R. Segre, July 22, 1952; children: Carlo, Alberto. D.Sc., U. Milan, 1949. Research assoc. U. Milan, 1949-51; vis. investigator Animal Disease Research Lab., Weibridge, Eng., 1951; bacteriologist Montecatini Corp., Milan, 1951-52, Nebr. Dept. Health, 1953-54; research assoc. U. Ill., Urbana, 1963-73; asst. prof. U. Ill. Coll. Vet. Medicine, 1973—. Contbr. articles to profl. jours. Mem. Am. Assn. Immunologists. Current Work: Immunology of aging, cellular immunology. Subspecialty: Immunobiology and immunology. Home: 2010 Boudreau Dr Urbana IL 61801 Office: 2001 S Lincoln Ave Urbana IL 61801

SEGREST, JERE PALMER, pathology and biochemistry educator; b. Dothan, Ala., Aug. 16, 1940; s. Jere Palmer and Grace (Hudgins) Blevins) S.; m. Susan Freeman, Sept. 3, 1966; children: Stuart, Chamberlain, Austin. B.A., Vanderbilt U., 1962, M.D., 1967, Ph.D., 1969. Diplomate: Nat. Bd. Med. Examiners. Intern Vanderbilt U. Hosp., Nashville, 1969, resident, 1970; staff assoc. NIH, Bethesda, Md., 1970-74; resident George Washington U. Hosp., Washington, 1974; assoc. prof. pathology U Ala Med Ctr., Birmingham, 1974-80, prof. pathology, 1980—, prof. biochemistry, 1982—, prof. medicine, 1984—, dir. atherosclerosis research unit, 1983—; mem. molecular cytology study sect. NIH, 1978-82. Served with USPHS, 1970-74. Am. Heart Assn. grantee, 1976-78; NIH grantee, 1976—; NSF grantee, 1976-78; Am. Egg Bd. grantee, 1981-84. Fellow Council on Atherosclerosis, Am. Heart Assn.; mem. Am. Chem. Soc. (com. on profl. tng. 1978-84), Am. Soc. Exptl. Pathology, Am. Soc. Biol. Chemists, Biophys. Soc., Am. Soc. Cell Biology. Democrat. Inventor single vertical spin analysis of plasma lipoproteins. Current Work: Studies of protein-lipid interactions in plasma lipoproteins and biological membranes, roles of plasma lipoprotein in pathophysiology of atherosclerosis. Subspecialties: Biochemistry (medicine); Membrane biology. Home: 3709 Forest Run Rd Birmingham AL 35223 Office: U Ala Med Ctr Volker Hall Room G018 Birmingham AL 35294

SEHGAL, PRAVINKUMAR BHAGATRAM, physician, researcher, educator; b. Bombay, India, Sept. 11, 1949; came to U.S., 1973; m. Shashibala P., Dec. 2, 1972; 1 dau.: Neelima. M.B.B.S. (Nat. Merit Scholar India, Dorabji Tata spl. scholar, J. N. Tata scholar), Seth G. S. Med. Coll., Bombay, 1973; Ph.D., Rockefeller U., 1977. Intern King Edward Meml. Hosp., Bombay, 1971-72; grad. fellow Rockefeller U., 1973-77, postdoctoral fellow, 1977-79, asst. prof. virology, 1979-84, assoc. prof., 1984—. Contbr. numerous articles to profl. jours.; editorial bd.: Jour. Interferon Research, 1980—, Virology, 1983—. Recipient Jr. Faculty Research award Am. Cancer Soc., 1980-82, Career Scientist award Irma T. Hirschl, 1982; Nat. Inst. Allergy and Infectious Diseases grantee, 1979—; Am. Heart Assn. established investigator, 1983—; Nat. Found. Cancer Research, 1984—. Mem. AAAS, Am. Soc. Microbiology, Am. Soc. Virology, N.Y. Acad. Sci., Internat. Soc. Interferon Research, Sigma Xi. Current Work: Human interferons; halobenzimidazole ribosides; regulation gene expression; membrane fusion. Subspecialties: Animal virology; Molecular biology. Office: Rockefeller U 1230 York New York NY 10021

SEIBEL, ERWIN, oceanography educator, researcher; b. Schwientochlowitz, Germany, Apr. 29, 1942; came to U.S., 1952, naturalized, 1957; s. Hugo Josef and Berta Seibel; m. Monique Yvonne LeBras, July 6, 1968; 1 child, Stephanie Karen. B.S., CCNY, 1965; M.S., U. Mich., 1966, Ph.D., 1972. Asst. research oceanographer U. Mich., Ann Arbor, 1972-75, assoc. research oceanographer, asst. dir. sea grant, 1975-78, also sr. scientist on cruises, 1971-78; environ. lab. dir. San Francisco State U., 1978-81, chmn. dept. geoscis., 1981—; mem. sea grante site rev. teams Nat. Sea Grant Program, 1978—; bd. govs. Moss Landing Marine Labs., Calif., 1981—. Contbr. articles on coastal oceanography to profl. publs., 1972—. Developer photogrammetric technique for continuous shoreline monitoring, 1972-78. Adviser MESA program for minority students San Francisco Bay Area, 1981—; vol. Bay Area council Girl Scouts U.S.A., 1982—. Served to capt. C.E., U.S. Army, 1967-71, Vietnam. Recipient Exceptional Merit Service award San Francisco State U., 1984; grantee Am. Electric Power Co., 1972-77, Gt. Lakes Basin Commn., 1975-77. Fellow Geol. Soc. Am., AAAS (symposium coordinator 1983-84); mem. N.Y. Acad Scis, Am. Geophys. Union, Marine Tech. Soc. (pres. San Francisco Bay chpt. 1982-83, exec. sec. Oceans 83, 1982-83), U. Mich. Alumni Assn., Sigma Xi (pres. San Francisco State U. chpt. 1982-84). Current work: Academic administration at departmental and university level; research in coastal sedimentation and coastal dynamics; application of remote sensing techniques to coastal zone; coastal and offshore ice formation and breakup mechanics; coastal pollution. Subspecialties: Oceanography; Coastal zones. Office: San Francisco State U 1600 Holloway Ave San Francisco CA 94132

SEIDE, ROCHELLE KAREN, geneticist, educator, lawyer; b. Bronx, N.Y., Mar. 29, 1948; d. Solomon and Esther Lillian (Berkowitz) S.; m. John Michael Kehoe, June 23, 1974; children—Aaron Michael, Lauren Sarah Renee. B.S. in Bacteriology, Syracuse U., 1968; M.S. in Immunology, L.I. U., 1974; Ph.D. in Human Genetics, CUNY, 1977; J.D., U. Akron, 1984. Bar: Ohio 1984. Research asst. Rockefeller U., N.Y.C., 1969-74; instr. genetics Northeastern Ohio U. Coll. Medicine, Rootstown, 1977-78, asst. prof., 1978-85; mem. grad. sch. faculty Kent State U., Ohio, 1978-85; counselor genetics Children's Hosp., Akron, Ohio, 1979-85; assoc. Brumbaugh, Graves, Donohue & Raymond, N.Y.C., 1985—. Contbr. articles to profl. jours. NSF grantee, 1967—. Mem. Am. Soc. Human Genetics, N.Y. Acad. Sci., AAAS, ABA, Am. Soc. Law and Medicine., Sigma Xi. Current work: Research in medical genetics; molecular basis of and treatment for inherited metabolic diseases particularly Gaucher Disease; genetic counseling; legal aspects of genetic engineering and biotechnology (patent law). Subspecialties: Genetics and genetic engineering (medicine); Cellular engineering. Office: Brumbaugh Graves Donohue & Raymond 30 Rockefeller Plaza New York NY 10112

SEIDELMANN, P. KENNETH, astronomer; b. Cin., June 15, 1937; s. P. Emil and Esther Margaret (Momberg) S.; m. Roberta Jane Buck, Aug. 27, 1960; children: Holly, Alan. B.S. in E.E, U. Cin., 1960, M.S., 1962, Ph.D. in Dynamical Astronomy, 1968. Astronomer Nautical Almanac Office, U.S. Naval Obs., Washington, 1965-73, asst. dir., 1973-76, dir., 1976—; vis. assoc. prof. astronomy U. Md., 1973, 75, 77, 80, 83, 85. Contbr. numerous articles to sci. jours. Served with AUS, 1963-65. Recipient Disting. Alumni award Coll. Engring., U. Cin., 1975. Mem. Am. Astron. Soc., Internat. Astron. Union, Royal Astron. Soc., Inst. Nav., AIAA, AAAS, Sigma Xi. Lutheran. Co-discoverer satellite of Saturn, 1980; prepared star chart for Einstein Monument, Nat. Acad. Scis. grounds. Current Work: Planetary and satellite motions, observations with charge coupled device for astrometry and solar system objects, very large array observations, space telescope. Subspecialties: Planetary science; Optical astronomy. Home: 6539 Windermere Circle Rockville MD 20852 Office: US Naval Observatory Washington DC 20390

SEIDEN, PHILIP EDWARD, physicist; b. Troy, N.Y., Dec. 25, 1934; s. Herman Louis and Freida Ruth (Bress) S.; m. Lois Gotteiner, Sept. 12, 1954; children—Jeffrey Allen, Mark Jay. A.B., U. Chgo., 1954, B.S., 1955, M.S., 1956; Ph.D., Stanford U., 1960. Scientist, Lockheed Missiles Div., Palo Alto, Calif., 1956-59; research assoc. Stanford U., Calif., 1959; mem. research staff IBM Research Ctr., Yorktown Heights, N.Y., 1960—, dir. phys. scis., 1972-76, dir. gen. scis., 1977. Contbr. articles to sci. publs. Fellow Am. Phys. Soc.; mem. Am. Astron. Soc., AAAS, N.Y. Acad. Scis., Sigma Xi. Current work: Magnetism, superconductivity and transport properties of organic metals, structure and evolution of galaxies and propagating star formation. Subspecialties: Theoretical astrophysics; Condensed matter physics. Office: IBM Research Ctr PO Box 218 Yorktown Heights NY 10598

SEIDERS, BARBARA ANN BORNEMEIER, research chemist, technology company executive; b. Wichita, Kans., Mar. 22, 1955; d. Roscoe Paul and Frances Narcissa (Lanning) Bornemeier; m. Reginald Paul Seiders, June 13, 1977; 1 child, Phoebe Alexis. A.B., Dartmouth Coll., 1977; Ph.D., Duke U., 1981. AAAS diplomacy fellow Dept. State, Washington, 1981-82; research chemist U.S. Army Chem. Research and Devel. Ctr., Aberdeen Proving Ground, Md., 1982—. Contbr., co-contbr. chpts. in books, articles to profl. jours. Recruiter, interviewer Dartmouth Coll., 1982—. Assn. Women in Sci. scholar, 1978; Duke U. fellow, 1980. Mem. Am. Chem. Soc., AAAS, Assn. Women in Sci., Drug Info. Assn., Sigma Xi. Republican. Current work: Develop, use quantum chemically derived properties in structure-activity work related to immunology, drug design, molecular design. Subspecialty: Theoretical chemistry. Office: Chem Research & Development Ctr Attn: SMCCR-RSP-C Aberdeen Proving Ground MD 21010

SEIDL, MILOS, physicist, educator; b. Budapest, Hungary, May 24, 1923; came to U.S., 1968, naturalized, 1977; s. Ferdin and Therese (Studinka) S.; m. Vera Hnevsova, Sept. 14, 1960; 1 dau., Kathy. B.Sc., Tech. U. Prague, 1947, Ph.D., 1949, D.Sc., 1963; M.Eng. (hon.), Stevens Inst. Tech., 1979. Research staff Inst. Vacuum Electronics, Prague, Czechoslovakia, 1949-58; sr. scientist Czechoslovakian Acad. Sci., Prague, 1958-68; lectr. Tech. U. Prague, 1960-68; vis. scientist Stanford U., 1968-69; prof. physics Stevens Inst. Tech., 1969—. Recipient Stevens Inst. Tech. J. Davis Meml. Research award, 1978. Fellow Am. Phys. Soc., Am. Vacuum Soc., IEEE, N.Y. Acad. Sci. Presbyterian. Current Work: Interaction of electron beams with plasma; plasma production; ion sources; sputtering of atomic particles from solid surfaces by ion bombardment. Subspecialties: Plasma physics; Plasma engineering. Home: 27 Clinton Ln Wayne NJ 07470 Office: Dept Physics Stevens Inst Tech Hoboken NJ 07030

SEIFER, ARNOLD DAVID, engineer; b. Newark, Apr. 22, 1940; s. Abe W. and Bessie R. (Coopersmith) S. B.S. in Math, Rensselaer Poly. Inst., 1962, M.S. in Math, 1964, Ph.D. in Math, 1968. Research specialist Gen. Dynamics Corp., Groton, Conn., 1967-73; sr. staff mathematician Applied Physics Lab., Laurel, MD., 1973-76; sr. staff engr. Emerson Electric Co., St. Louis, 1976-80; prin. engr. Raytheon Co., Wayland, Mass., 1980—. Contbr. sci. papers to profl. jours. Mem. IEEE (sr.), Soc. Indsl. and Applied Math., Sigma Xi. Current Work: Radar systems analysis and design. Subspecialties: Systems engineering; Applied mathematics. Home: 66 Dinsmore Ave Apt 606 Framingham MA 01701 Office: Raytheon Co Equipment Devel Labs 430 Boston Post Rd Wayland MA 01778

SEIL, FREDRICK JOHN, neuroscientist; b. Nova Sova, Yugoslavia, Nov. 9, 1933; came to U.S., 1938; s. Joseph and Theresa (Krieger) S.; m. Daryle Faith Wolfers, July 2, 1955; children—Jonathan Fredrick, Joel Philip Timothy. Grad. Phillips Acad., 1952; A.B., Oberlin Coll., 1956; M.D., Stanford U., 1960. Intern Kaiser Found. Hosp., San Francisco, 1960-61; resident in neurology Stanford U. Sch. Medicine, Calif., 1961-64; staff neurologist VA Med. Ctr., Palo Alto, Calif., 1969-76; asst. prof. neurology Stanford U., 1969-75; clin. investigator, staff neurologist VA Med. Ctr., Portland, 1976-81, dir. office regeneration research programs, 1981—; assoc. prof. neurology Oreg. Health Scis. U., Portland, 1976-78, prof., 1978—. NIH fellow in neurology Stanford U., 1964-65, Mt. Sinai Hosp. and Albert Einstein Coll. Medicine, N.Y.C., 1965-66. Editor: Nerve, Organ and Tissue Regeneration: Research Perspectives, 1983; contbr. articles to profl. jours. Served to capt. AUS, 1966-68. VA Research

Career Devel. award, 1976-79, grantee, 1970—. Mem. Soc. Neuroscience, Am. Assn. Neuropathologists, Am. Neurol. Assn., Internat. Soc. Devel. Neurosci., Internat. Brain Research Orgn. Democrat. Regeneration and plasticity of the nervous system; nervous system development; mechanisms of demyelination and remyelination; nerve tissue culture. Subspecialties: Regeneration; Neurology. Office: Office of Regeneration Research Programs VA Med Ctr Portland OR 97201

SEINFELD, JOHN HERSH, chemical engineering educator; b. Elmira, N.Y., Aug. 3, 1942; s. Ben B. and Minna (Johnson) S. B.S., U. Rochester, 1964; Ph.D., Princeton U., 1967. Asst. prof. chem. engring. Calif. Inst. Tech., Pasadena, 1967-70, assoc. prof., 1970-74, exec. officer for chem. engring., 1973—, prof., 1974—, Louis E. Nohl prof., 1980—; Allan P. Colburn meml. lectr. U. Del., 1976; Camille and Henry Dreyfus Found. lectr. MIT, 1979; Donald L. Katz lectr. U. Mich., 1981; Reilly lectr. U. Notre Dame. 1983; lectr. U. Rochester, 1985, CUNY, 1985; cons. Chevron Oil Field Research Co.; mem. sci. adv. bd. EPA; trustee CACHE Corp., 1982—; Inst. lectr. Am. Inst. Chem. Engrs., 1980. Author: (with Leon Lapidus) Numerical Solution of Ordinary Differential Equations, 1971; Mathematical Methods in Chemical Engineering, Vol. III, Process Modeling, Estimation and Identification, 1974; Air Pollution: Physical and Chemical Fundamentals, 1975; Lectures in Atmospheric Chemistry, 1980. Assoc. editor: Environmental Science and Technology, 1981—; mem. editorial bd. Computers, Chem. Engring., Jour. Colloid and Interface Sci., 1978—, Advances in Chem. Engring., 1980—, Revs. in Chem. Engring., 1980—, Aerosol Sci. and Tech., 1981—, Large Scale Systems, 1982—; assoc. editor: Atmospheric Environment, 1976—. Bd. dirs. Council for Chem. Research, 1982-83; Recipient Donald P. Eckman award Am. Automatic Control Council, 1970, award Pub. Service medal NASA, 1980; Camille and Henry Dreyfus Found. tchr. scholar grantee, 1972. Mem. Am. Inst. Chem. Engrs. (Allan P. Colburn award 1976), Am. Soc. Engring. Edn. (Curtis W. McGraw research award 1976), Nat. Acad. Engring., Air Polution Control Assn., Am. Chem. Soc., Am. Assn. Aerosol Research (dir. 1983—), Soc. Petroleum Engrs., Sigma Xi, Tau Beta Pi. Home: 121 S Wilson St Unit 101 Pasadena CA 91106 Office: Dept Chem Engring Calif Inst Tech Pasadena CA 91125

SEITER, GARY JOSEPH, electrical engineer; b. Ferguson, Mo., Sept. 18, 1955; s. Curtis Andrew and Marcella Jane (Menetre) S.; m. Lucee Kathleen Bravo, June 25, 1983; stepchildren—Fara Anese Newland, Sean Elliot Newland; 1 child, Olivia Ann. B.S.E.E. with honors, U. Mo.-Rolla, 1978, M.S.E.E., 1980. Research asst. U. Mo.-Rolla, 1978-80; research engr. Advanced Products Research and Devel. Labs., Motorola, Inc., Mesa, Ariz., 1980-84, staff engr. Semicondr. Research and Devel. Lab., Phoenix, 1985—. Mem. IEEE, Eta Kappa Nu. Roman Catholic. Current work: Development of next-generation micro chips utilizing state-of-the-art processes, materials and device engring. Subspecialty: Semiconductors. Home: 1218 W Palo Verde Dr Chandler AZ 85224 Office: Motorola Inc 5005 E McDowell Rd Phoenix AZ 85008

SEITMAN, DAVID T., anesthesiologist; b. Bklyn., Oct. 21, 1952; s. Milton and Shirley Seitman; m. Kathryn Nemiroff, Nov. 20, 1983. B.S.E.E. magna cum laude Princeton U., 1974; M.S. in Biomed. Engring., Case Western Res. U., 1977, M.D., 1981. Diplomate Nat. Bd. Med. Examiners. Intern Presbyn. Med. Ctr., Phila., 1981-82; resident in anesthesia Hosp. of U. Pa., Phila., 1982-84; fellow in anesthesia Hahnemann Hosp., Phila., 1985—; presenter 4th New Eng. Bioengring. Conf., New Haven, 1976. Med. vol. Phila. Spl. Olympics, 1982-83, 1st Aid Mobile Unit Corps, Cleve., 1977-81; water safety, first aid instr. ARC; 1969-83; pres. Lower Merion Ostomy Soc., Bryn Mawr, Pa., 1984-85; judge Delaware Valley Sci. Fair, Phila., 1984. Mem. AMA, Am. Soc. Anesthesiologists, Closed Circuit and Low Flow Anesthesia Systems Soc., Internat. Anesthesia Soc., Internat. Anesthesia Research Soc., Pa. Soc. Anesthesiologists, IEEE, Engring. in Medicine and Biology Soc., Eta Kappa Nu, Tau Beta Pi. Current work: Closed circle and low flow anesthesia; pharmacokinetics; technologic advances in operating room monitoring, record keeping, and anesthesia delivery systems. Subspecialties: Anesthesiology; Biomedical engineering. Home: C620 Presidential Commons Philadelphia PA 19131 Office: Dept Anesthesiology MS 310 Hahnemann Hosp Broad and Vine Sts MS310 Philadelphia PA 19102

SEITZ, FREDERICK, university president emeritus; b. San Francisco, July 4, 1911; s. Frederick and Emily Charlotte (Hofman) S.; m. Elizabeth K. Marshall, May 18, 1935. A.B., Leland Stanford Jr. U., 1932; Ph.D., Princeton U., 1934; Doctorate Hon. Causa, U. Ghent, 1957; D.Sc., U. Reading, 1960, Rensselaer Poly. Inst., 1961, Marquette U., 1963, Carnegie Inst. Tech., 1963, Case Inst. Tech., 1964, Princeton U., 1964, Northwestern U., 1965, U. Del., 1966, Poly. Inst. Bklyn., 1967, U. Mich., 1967, U. Utah, 1968, Brown U., 1968, Duquesne U., 1968, St. Louis U., 1969, Nebr. Wesleyan U., 1970, U. Ill., 1972, Rockefeller U., 1981; LL.D., Lehigh U., 1966, U. Notre Dame, 1962, Mich. State U., 1965, Ill. Inst. Tech., 1968, N.Y. U., 1969; L.H.D., Davis and Elkins Coll., 1970, Rockefeller U., 1981. Instr. physics U. Rochester, 1935-36, asst. prof., 1936-37; physicist research labs. Gen. Electric Co., 1937-39; asst. prof. Randal Morgan Lab. Physics, U. Pa., 1939-41, asso. prof., 1941-42; prof. physics, head dept. Carnegie Inst. Tech., Pitts., 1942-49; prof. physics U. Ill., 1949-57, head dept., 1957-64, dir. control systems lab., 1951-52, dean Grad. Coll., v.p. research, 1964-65; exec. pres. Nat. Acad. Scis., 1962-69; pres. Rockefeller U., N.Y.C., 1968-78; trustee Ogden Corp., 1977—; dir. tng. program Clinton Labs., Oak Ridge, 1946-47; Chmn. Naval Research Adv. Com., 1960-62; vice chmn. Def. Sci. Bd., 1961-62, chmn., 1964-68; sci. adviser NATO, 1959-60; mem. nat. advisory com. Marine Biomed. Inst. U. Tex., Galveston, 1975-77; mem. adv. group White House Conf. Anticipated Advances in Sci. and Tech., 1975-76; mem. advisory bd. Desert Research Inst., 1975-79, Center Strategic and Internat. Studies, 1975—; mem. Nat. Cancer Advisory Bd., 1976-82; Dir. Akzona Inc., Tex. Instruments Inc. Author: Modern Theory of Solids, 1940, The Physics of Metals, 1943, Solid State Physics, 1955. Trustee Rockefeller Found., 1964-77, Princeton U., 1968-72, Lehigh U., 1970-81, Research Corp., 1966-82, Inst. Internat. Edn., 1971-78, Woodrow Wilson Nat. Fellowship Found., 1972—, Univ. Corp. Atmospheric Research, Am. Museum Natural History, 1975—; trustee John Simon Guggenheim Meml. Found., 1973-83, chmn. bd., 1976-83; mem. Belgian Am. Edn. Found.; bd. dirs. Richard Lounsbery Found., 1980—. Recipient Franklin medal Franklin Inst. Phila., 1965; Hoover medal Stanford U., 1968; Nat. Medal of Sci., 1973; James Madison award Princeton U., 1978; Edward R. Loveland Meml. award ACP, 1983; Vannevar Bush award Nat. Sci. Bd., 1983. Fellow Am. Phys. Soc. (pres. 1961); mem. Nat. Acad. Scis., Am. Acad. Arts and Scis., Am. Inst. Mining, Metall. and Petroleum Engrs., Am. Philos. Soc., Am. Inst. Physics (chmn. govorning bd. 1954-59), Inst. for Def. Analysis, Finnish Acad. Sci. and Letters (fgn. mem.), Phi Beta Kappa Assos. Subspecialties: Theoretical physics; Materials. Address: Rockefeller U 1230 York Ave New York NY 10021

SEITZ, JAMES POTTER, electrical manufacturing company executive; b. Phila., Nov. 14, 1922; s. Earl Milton and Laura Mary (Lippincott) S.; m. Edna May Evans, June 12, 1948; children—Barbara Ann, J. David, Robert W. B.S. in Elec. Engring., U. Pa., 1950. Registered profl. engr., N.J. Chief engr. Ajax Magnethermic, Trenton, 1950-60; exec. v.p. Nothelfer Winding Labs, Trenton, 1960-68; pres. NWL Transformers, Bordentown, N.J., 1968—; chmn. bd. Megatran Industries, Prototype Transformer Co., Inc., Megatron Electronic Power, Inc.; dir. Bank of Mid Jersey, Bordentown. Patentee in field. Cubmaster Burlington council Boy Scouts Am., Mount Holly, N.J., 1962-68; mem. Mount Holly Twp. Planning Bd., 1972-78. Served with USN, 1942-46. Republican. Episcopalian. Club: Spray Beach Yacht (commodore 1965-68). Current work: High voltage technology, transformer design, control design, electrical manufacturing. Home: 7 Tulip Tree Dr RD 1 Burlington Twp NJ 08016 Office: NWL Transformers Inc Rising Sun Rd Bordentown NJ 08505

SELBY, THEODORE WILLIAM, research chemist; b. Nebraska City, Nebr. Oct. 19, 1928; s. Theodore Roosevelt and Marge Marie (Bates) S.; m. Jean Gale Campbell, Aug. 18, 1951; children—Kathleen, Mark, Shawn, Diane, Timothy, Scott, Cynthia, Rebecca, Chiara, Douglas. B.S., U. Detroit, 1950; M.S., Wayne State U., 1960, postgrad. 1961-63. Research chemist Gen. Motors Corp., Warren, Mich., 1953-64; automotive research coordinator Dow Chem. Co., Midland, Mich., 1964-71; dir. research and devel. Savant, Inc., Midland, 1969—; mng. dir. Saginaw Valley Inst. Materials, Mich., 1983—; dir. Tannas Co., Midland. Contbr. articles to profl. jours. Developer programmable liquid bath-low temperature viscometric analysis of lubes, 1983. Patentee in field. Named Inventor of Yr., Patent Attys. Assn., 1984. Fellow AAAS; mem. ASTM (spl. award 1982), Soc. Automotive Engrs. (Russell Springer Meml. award 1960, Henry Ford Meml. award 1960), N.Y. Acad. Scis., Am. Soc. Lubrication Engrs., Sigma Xi. Roman Catholic. Current work: Lubricant rheology and tribology. Subspecialties: Physical chemistry; Materials (engineering). Office: Savant Inc 234 E Larkin St Box 111 Midland MI 48640

SELDIN, DONALD WAYNE, physician, educator; b. N.Y.C., Oct. 24, 1920; s. Abraham L. and Laura (Ueberal) S.; m. Muriel Goldberg, Apr. 1, 1943; children: Leslie Lynn, Donald Craig, Donna Leigh. B.A., NYU, 1940; M.D., Yale U., 1943; D.H.L., So. Meth. U., 1977; D.Sci., Med. Coll. Wis., 1980; Docteur honoris causa, U. Paris, 1983. Diplomate: Am. Bd. Internal Medicine (test com. on nephrology 1970-73). Intern New Haven Hosp., Yale U., 1943-44, resident, 1944-46, instr. medicine, 1948-50, asst. prof. internal medicine, 1950-51; mem. faculty U. Tex. Southwestern Med. Sch., Dallas, 1951—, William Buchanan prof. internal medicine, 1969—, chmn. dept. internal medicine, 1952—; chief med. service Parkland Meml. Hosp., Dallas, 1952—; chmn. dept. medicine Lisbon VA Hosp., Dallas; cons. Baylor Hosp., St. Paul's Hosp., Presbyn. Hosp., Dallas; Brooke Army Hosp., Fort Sam Houston, Walter Reed Army Hosp., Washington, also to Surgeon Gen. U.S., Surgeon Gen. USAF, and Eli Lilly Co., 1972—; mem. Bur. Budget, Exec. Office of Pres., 1966-67; chmn. dialysis and transplantation com. of sci. adv. bd. Nat. Kidney Found.; mem. bd. sci. councillors Nat. Inst. Arthritis and Metabolic Diseases, NIH, 1968-71; trustee Rand Corp., 1975-85. Editorial bd.: Jour. Lab. and Clin. Medicine, 1958-60, Nephron, The Clinician, Medicine, Mineral and Electrolyte Metabolism, 1977-79; cons. editor: Am. Jour. Medicine; asso. editor: Kidney Internat., 1973-79; contbr. articles to profl. jours. Served as capt. U.S. Army, 1946-48. Recipient Disting. Achievement award Modern Medicine, 1977; Gold Headed Cane award U. Calif.-San Francisco Sch. Medicine, 1984; Ellen Browning Scripps Soc. medal, 1984; Friedrich Von Muller hon. lectr. U. Munich, 1968. Fellow Royal Soc. Medicine, Am. Acad. Arts and Sci.; mem. Dallas County Med. Soc., Tex. Med. Assn., Dallas Diabetes Assn., So. Soc. Clin. Investigation (pres. 1964, Founders medal 1975), Central Soc. Clin. Research (pres. 1963), AMA, Am. Fedn. Clin. Research, Am. Soc. Clin. Investigation (pres. 1966), Assn. Profs. Medicine (pres. 1971, Robert H. Williams Disting. Chmn. Medicine award 1977), Assn. Am. Physicians (pres. 1980, Kober medal 1985), ACP (master, disting. teaching award 1980), Am. Physiol. Soc., ACP, Am. Soc. Nephrology (pres. 1968, John P. Peters award 1983), Nat. Kidney Found. (David Hume award 1981), Am. Heart Assn., Am. Clin. and Climatol. Assn., Soc. Med. Cons. to Armed Forces, Internat. Soc. Nephrology (councillor 1973-78, pres.-elect 1981, pres. 1984-87), Australian Soc. Nephrology (hon.), Alpha Omega Alpha. Subspecialties: Internal medicine; Nephrology. Office: 5323 Harry Hines Blvd Dallas TX 75235

SELF, HAZZLE LAYAFETTE, animal sci. educator; b. Erath County, Tex., Aug. 1, 1920; s. Hazzle K. and Ethel F. (Dowdy) S.; m. Martha Louise Smith, Oct. 16, 1943; children: Linda Lindell, Debra Parker, Ann Peterson, Michael Self. Cert. animal scientist. Asst. prof. animal husbandry Tarleton State U., 1948-52; asst. prof. U. Wis., 1954-59; prof. Iowa State U., 1961—, state extension swine specialist, 1959-61; dir. Outlying Research Ctr., 1961—. Contbr. to profl. jours. Served with U.S. Army, 1944-46. Recipient Iowa Cattlemen's Assn. Appreciation award, 1971. Mem. Am. Soc. Animal Sci. (Livestock Mgmt. award 1979), Am. Registry Cert. Animal Scientists AAAS, Sigma Xi, Alpha Gamma Rho, Sigma Phi. Methodist. Lodge: Masons. Current Work: Reproductive management in beef cows; feedlot management of cattle; administrative research centers in Iowa; management beef cattle. Subspecialties: Animal physiology; Integrated systems modelling and engineering. Home: Route 2 Box C-38 Hico TX 76457 Office: 20 Curtis Hall Iowa State U Ames IA 50011

SELF, JAMES MAURICE, research chemist, consultant; b. Syracuse, Mo., Aug. 4, 1937; s. James Francis and Opal Irene (Lusk) S.; m. Penny Love Boggs (div. Feb. 1974); children—Pamela, James E., Deborah; m. Lynda Hall, Dec. 11, 1979; 1 stepchild, Johhnna. B.S., Central Mo. State U., 1959; M.S., Ph.D., Oreg. State U., 1964. Sales research chemist E.I. duPont de Nemours, Wilmington, Del., 1966-72; research fellow Mellon Inst., Pitts., 1972-76; tech. dir. Tanner Chem. Co., Greenville, S.C., 1976-82; cons. ABCO Industries, Spartanburg, S.C., 1983-84, research chemist, 1984—; cons. Southeastern Chem., Lenoir, N.C., 1983-84. Contbr. articles to profl. publs. Patentee in field. Officer, Wilmington Civic Assn., 1968-72; mem. dist. com. Boy Scouts Am., 1969-72; pres. local PTA, Wilmington, 1967-72, Pitts., 1972-75; coach Pebble Creek Swim Club, 1976-79. Mem. Am. Chem. Soc., Research Soc. Am., Soc. Plastics Industry. Democrat. Baptist. Current work: Polymerization catalyst, polymer extension and forming, coupling agents for polymer reinforcements. Subspecialties: Composite materials; Inorganic chemistry.

SELIGSON, M. ROSS, psychologist; b. Balt., May 18, 1949; s. Joseph Jerome and Dorothy G. (Greenfeld) S. B.A., U. Md., 1971; Ed.M., Loyola Coll., Balt., 1975; Ph.D., Calif. Sch. Profl. Psychology, 1979. Lic. psychologist, Fla. Clin. psychology intern Long Beach (Calif.) Neuropsychiat. Inst. and Hosp., 1975-76, Orange Coast Coll. Student Health Ctr., Costa Mesa, Calif., 1976-77; psychology field trainee Sect. on Legal Psychiatry UCLA, 1977-78; clin. psychologist Logansport (Ind.) State Hosp. (Isaac Ray Unit), 1978-80, South Fla. State Hosp., Hollywood, 1980—, Counseling Affiliates, Inc., Ft. Lauderdale, 1981—; chmn. exec. com. Am. Med. Health Plan, Miami, 1982—; clin. dir. North Miami Community Mental Health Ctr.; staff writer Women's Issues, Ft. Lauderdale, 1982—; adj. faculty Barry U., 1982—, Nova U., 1982—; cons. Fla. Dept. Health and Rehab. Services. Contbr. articles to profl. jours. Mem. North Area Adv. Bd. of Regional Mental Health Team for Newport Beach, Costa Mesa and Irvine, Calif., 1976. Calif. Sch. Profl. Psychology scholar, 1976; recipient Certificate of Appreciation Am. Bus. Women's Assn., 1982. Mem. Wash. Area Counsel on Alcohol and Drug Abuse, Calif. Psychol. Assn., Am. Psychol. Assn., Fla. Psychol. Assn., Fla. Assn. Practicing Psychologists. Democrat. Jewish. Current Work: Psychological adjustment, social history factors and training performance measures as predictors of suicide prevention. Subspecialty: Clinical psychology. Office: Counseling Affiliates Inc 3891 Stirling Rd #5&6 Fort Lauderdale FL 33312

SELIKOFF, IRVING JOHN, physician; b. Bklyn., Jan. 15, 1915; s. Abraham and Tilli (Katz) S.; m. Celia Shiffrin, Feb. 4, 1946. B.S., Columbia, 1935; M.D., Anderson Coll. Medicine, U. Melbourne, Australia, 1941; Sc.D. (hon.), Tufts U., 1976, Bucknell U., 1979, N.J. State Coll., 1980. Diplomate: Am. Bd. Preventive Medicine. Intern Newark Beth Israel Hosp., 1943-44; asst. morbid anatomy Mt. Sinai Hosp., N.Y.C., 1941, now attending physician community medicine; prof. medicine and community medicine Mt. Sinai Sch. Medicine, City U. N.Y.; prof. environmental medicine, former dir. environmental scis. lab.; resident Sea View Hosp., N.Y.C., 1944-46; cons. medicine Barnert Meml. Hosp., Paterson, N.J.; mem. Nat. Cancer Adv. Bd., from 1979; pres. Collegium Ramazzini, from 1982. Author: The Management of Tuberculosis, 1956, Biological Effects of Asbestos, 1965, Toxicity of Vinyl Chloride and Polyvinyl Chloride, (with D.H.K. Lee) Asbestos and Disease, 1978, Health Hazards of Asbestos Exposure, 1979; also articles profl. jours.; Sr. asso. editor: Mt. Sinai Jour. Medicine, N.Y.C.; editor-in-chief: Am. Jour. Indsl. Medicine, Environ. Research, from 1970. Recipient Lasker award in Medicine, 1955; Ann. Research award Am. Cancer Soc., 1976; Edwards medal Welsh Nat. Sch. Medicine, 1977. Fellow Am. Pub. Health Assn., Am. Coll. Chest Physicians (pres. N.J. chpt. 1954-55); mem. N.Y. Pub. Health Assn. (Haven Emerson award 1975), N.Y. Acad. Scis. (pres. 1969-70, bd. govs. 1970—, Poiley award and medal 1974), AMA, N.J., Passaic County med. socs., Inst. Medicine Nat. Acad. Scis., Soc. Occupational and Environ. Health (pres. 1973-74), Am. Coll. Toxicology (pres. 1980). Research in treatment Tb, 1945; with Dr. Edward H. Robitzek introduced isoniazid and iproniazid, chemotherapy of Tb, 1951-52. Subspecialty: Environmental medicine. Office: Mount Sinai Med Center 10 E 102d St New York NY 10029

SELKURT, EWALD ERDMAN, physiologist, emeritus educator; b. Edmonton, Alta., Can., Mar. 13, 1914; s. Ephraim and Amanda Olga (Stirle) S.; m. Ruth Marion Gesley, June 21, 1941; children: Claire Elaine, Sylvia Anne. B.A., U. Wis., 1937, M.A., 1939, Ph.D., 1941. Instr. physiology N.Y. U. Sch. Medicine, 1941-44; sr. instr. Western Res. U. Sch. Medicine, Cleve., 1944-46, asst. prof., 1946-49, asso. prof., 1949-58; prof., chmn. dept. physiology Ind. U. Sch. Medicine, Indpls., 1958-80, disting. prof., 1976-81, disting. prof. physiology emeritus, 1981—; Centennial vis. prof. physiology Ohio State U. Sch. Medicine, 1970; mem. Josiah Macey Conf. on Kidney, 1949-53, Conf. Shock and Circulatory Homeostasis, 1949-53; mem. subcom. on shock Com. Med. Scis., NRC, 1953-57; mem. cardiovascular study sect. Nat. Heart Inst., NIH, 1963-68; panel mem. evaluation of sci. faculty fellowships NSF, 1963-64; mem. kidney council Internat. Union Service Com., Germany, 1954. Author: Textbook of Physiology, 1963, Basic Physiology for Health Sciences, 1975; cons. editor: Am. Jour. Physiology and Jour. Applied Physiology, 1963-67, 70-73, Am. Heart Jour, 1966-77; procs.: Soc. Exptl. Biology and Medicine, 1967-85, Circulatory Shock, 1974—; Editorial com.: Ann. Rev. Physiology, 1965-69. Active Indpls. Symphonic Chorus. NSF fellow Göttingen, W.Ger., 1964-65. Mem. Am. Soc. Nephrology, AAUP, Am. Heart Assn., Am. Physiol. Soc. (council 1971-74, pres. elect 1975), Harvey Soc., Assn. Chmn. Depts. Physiology (councilor 1967-70, pres. 1971-72, Service award 1979), Soc. Exptl. Biology and Medicine (council 1978-81), Phi Beta Kappa, Sigma Xi, Phi Sigma, Gamma Alpha, Pi Kappa Delta. Lutheran. Club: Singer's (Cleve.). Current Work: Renal blood flow and electrolyte handling; kidney function in hemorrhagic shock; renin production: role of histamine; prostaglandins and renal function. Subspecialties: Nephrology; Physiology (medicine). Home: 3269 W 42d St Indianapolis IN 46208

SELL, JEFFREY ALAN, chemical physicist, researcher; b. Anderson, Ind., Sept. 18, 1952; s. John Millard and Jean Esther (Shake) S.; m. Laura Jane Kyle, May 18, 1973 (div. July 1980); m. Lynne C. Johannesen, Sept. 18, 1982. B.S., Purdue U., 1974; Ph.D., Calif. Inst. Tech., 1978. Staff research scientist physics dept. GM Research Labs., Warren, Mich., 1978—; instr. math. and physics Lawrence Inst. Tech., Southfield, Mich., 1980-82. Contbr. articles to profl. jours. Patentee non-destructive press and oxygen concentration meas in WH bulbs. Mem. Am. Chem. Soc., Am. Phys. Soc., Optical Soc. Am., Combustion Inst., Phi Beta Kappa, Alpha Chi Sigma. Current work: Optical combustion diagnostics, laser spectroscopy, laser photochemistry, heat transfer, transport, thermodynamics, high temperature reactions. Subspecialties: Laser spectroscopy; Laser-induced chemistry. Home: 4348 McNay Ct S West Bloomfield MI 48033 Office: Physics Dept GM Research Labs Warren MI 48090

SELL, JERRY LEE, nutrition educator; b. Adel, Iowa, Feb. 6, 1931; s. Theodore R. and Norma M. (Longmire) S.; m. M. JoAnn Adams, Mar. 8, 1953; children—Roger P., Rex D. B.S., Iowa State U., 1957, M.S., 1958, Ph.D., 1960. Asst. prof. nutrition U. Man., Can., 1960-66; prof. nutrition N.D. State U., Fargo, 1966-76, Iowa State U., Ames, 1976—. Contbr. numerous articles to sci. and tech. jours. Coach, bd. dirs. Fargo Babe Ruth League Baseball, 1969-72; bd. dirs. Fort Richmond Community Ctr., Winnipeg, Man., 1964-66. Grantee USDA, 1971, NIH, 1969, 71. Mem. Am. Inst. Nutrition, Poultry Sci. Assn. (2d v.p. 1984), AAAS, Worlds Poultry Sci. Assn., Council Agrl. Sci. and Tech. Methodist. Current work: Dietary energy sources; energy requirements and metabolism of poultry and mineral requirements and metabolism of poultry. Subspecialty: Animal nutrition. Home: 3602 Oakland St Ames IA 50010 Office: 201 Kildee Hall Iowa State Univ Ames IA 50011

SELL, STEWART, pathology educator; b. Pitts., Jan. 20, 1935; s. Oliver M. and Mary M. (Stewart) S.; m. Patricia D. King, June 20, 1958 (div. Mar. 1985); children—Sherri Lynn Sell Phillips, Stacy Lorraine, Sean Stewart, Stephanie King. B.Sc., Coll. William and Mary, 1956; M.D., U. Pitts., 1960. Diplomate Am. Bd. Pathology, Am. Bd. Lab. Immunology. Intern and resident Mass. Gen. Hosp., Boston, 1960-62; research assoc. NIH, Bethesda, Md., 1962-64; spl. fellow U. Birmingham, Eng., 1964-65; instr., then asst. prof. U. Pitts. Sch. Medicine, 1965-69; asst. prof., then prof. pathology U. Calif.-San Diego Sch. Medicine, 1970-82; prof., chair dept. pathology Sch. Medicine, U. Tex. Health Sci. Ctr., Houston, 1982—; chief autopsy VA Hosp., San Diego, 1981-82; chief pathology Hermann Hosp., Houston, 1982—; cons. VA Hosp., 1971-82. Author: Immunology, Immunopathology and Immunity, 1972. Editor: Cancer Markers I, 1980, II, 1982, III, 1983; Application of Biological Markers to Carcinogen Testing, 1983. Served with USPHS, 1962-64. NIH awardee. Mem. Am. Assn. Immunologists, Am. Soc. Exptl. Pathology, Internat. Soc. Immunology, others. Republican. Mem. Christian Ch. Current work: Carcinogenesis; immunopathology of infectious disease; cell activation; cancer markers. Subspecialties: Immunobiology and immunology; Cancer research (medicine). Home: 2708 Robinhood Houston TX 72005 Office: U Tex Health Sci Ctr PO Box 20708 Houston TX 77025

SELLARS, JOHN RANDOLPH, aerospace executive; b. Fort Stanton, N. Mex., Mar. 1, 1925; s. James Wesley and Ellen (Cavanaugh) S.; m. Ethel Grace Chance, Aug. 12, 1950; children—James D., Mary Ellen, Christopher. B.S. in Elec. Engring., N.Mex. State U., 1945; M.S., U. Mich., 1950, Ph.D., 1952. Research assoc. Johns Hopkins Applied Physics Lab., Silver Spring, Md., 1945-46; asst. prof. U. Mich., Ann Arbor, 1952-55; mem. staff TRW, Redondo Beach, Calif., 1955-58, mgr. aeroscis. lab., 1958-65, mgr. engring. ops., 1965-69, mgr. research and tech. ops., 1969-81, v.p., gen. mgr. energy tech. div., 1981—. Co-inventor manned spacecraft with staged re-entry, 1966. Named Disting. Alumnus U. Mich., 1967, N. Mex. State U., 1982. Democrat. Club: King Harbor Yacht (Redondo Beach, Calif.). Subspecialty: Aeronautical engineering. Office: TRW Electronics and Defense 1 Space Park Redondo Beach CA 90278

SELLERS, GREGORY JUDE, physicist; b. Far Rockaway, N.Y., June 20, 1947; s. Douglas L. and Rita R. (Dieringer) S.; m. Lucia S. Kim, Nov. 26, 1983. A.B. in Physics, Cornell U., 1968; M.S. in Physics, U. Ill., 1970, Ph.D. in Physics, 1975. Sr. scientist B-K Dynamics, Inc., Rockville, Md., 1974-76; with Allied Corp., Morristown, N.J., 1976—, applications physicist, 1977—; dir. Thermo-Tek, Inc., Madison, N.J. Mem. AAAS, Am. Phys. Soc., IEEE, Soc. Plastics Engrs. Co-inventor adhesive bonding metallic glass, electromagnetic shielding, testing of thermal insulation, amorphous antipilferage marker, amorphous spring-shield. Current Work: Development of applications for polymeric materials and glassy metals in the electrical and electronics arena. Subspecialties: Polymers (materials science); Materials. Home: PO Box 296 C Convent Station NJ 07961 Office: Allied Corp PO Box 2332 R Morristown NJ 07960

SELLNER, KEVIN GREGORY, biological oceanographer, educator; b. Albany, N.Y., Oct. 11, 1949; s. Leonard Stanley and Helen Catherine (Prue) S. A.B., Clark U., 1971; M.S., U.S.C., 1973; Ph.D., Dalhousie U., 1978. Asst. curator Acad. Natural Sci., Benedict, Md., 1978—; adj. asst. prof. Chesapeake Biol. Lab., U. Md., Solomons, 1984—; adj. asst. research scientist Chesapeake Bay Inst., Johns Hopkins U., Shady Side, Md., 1984—. Mem. Am. Soc. Limnology and Oceanography, Phycol. Soc. Am., Audubon Soc. Democrat. Current work: Basic research programs to identify and quantify the role of phytoplankton carbon in carbon cycling in estuarine food webs. Subspecialties: Ecology (environmental science); Marine biology. Home: 1422 Snug Harbor Rd Shady Side MD 20764 Office: Acad Natural Scis Benedict Estuarine Research Lab Benedict MD 20612

SELLS, SAUL B., research psychologist, educator, consultant; b. N.Y.C., Jan. 13, 1913; s. Maxwell I. and Dora B. S.; m. Helen Francis Roberts, July 2, 1939 (dec.). A.B., Bklyn. Coll., 1933; Ph.D., Columbia U., 1936; D.Sc. (hon.), Tex. Christian U., 1983. Research asst., instr. edn. research Tchrs. Coll., Columbia U., N.Y.C., 1934-36; instr. psychology Columbia U., N.Y.C., 1935-37; research assoc. Bd. Edn., N.Y.C., 1935-40; lectr. in psychology Grad. Sch., Bklyn. Coll., 1936-37; research analyst Pub. Work Reserve, Washington, 1940-41; chief statistician Office Price Adminstrn., Washington, 1941-46; asst. to pres. A.B. Frank Co., San Antonio, 1946-68; prof., head dept. med. psychology U.S. Air Force Sch. Aerospace Medicine, Randolph AFB, Tex., 1948-58, cons., 1959-62; adj. prof. Trinity U., San Antonio, 1949-55; vis. prof. U. Tex., Austin, 1950-51, Tex. A&M U., College Station, 1984—; prof. psychology Tex. Christian U., Fort Worth, 1958-62, research prof., dir. inst. behavioral research, 1962-83, research prof. emeritus, 1983—; pres. IBR Assocs., 1984—; cons. Nat. Ctr. Health Stats., Washington, 1965-70; mem. research career award com. Nat. Inst. Gen. Med. Sci., NIH, Washington; chmn. personality soc. U.S. Office Edn., Washington; research cons. Am., Eastern, Trans World, Fed. Express, COMAIR, other airlines, 1960—; cons.-reviewer VA, Washington, 1981—, NSF, Washington, 1975—, Can. Sci. Council, Ottawa, 1980-81; pres. Psychology Press, Inc., Brandon, Vt., 1963-68; cons. WHO, Geneva, Switzerland, 1976; mem. Gov.'s Council on Drug Abuse, Austin, Tex., 1980—; mem. adv. com. on research Div. Mental Health and Devel. Disorders, State of Ill., Chgo., 1981—. Cons. editor Psychol. Bull., 1955-58, Jour. Clin. Psychology, 1960—, Psychology in Schs., 1963—; editor Behavioral Research Monographs, 1962—; mng. editor, assoc. editor Multivariate Behavioral Research, 1966—. Chmn. Tarrant County Heart Assn., Fort Worth; mem. Bexar County Mental Health Assn., San Antonio. Recipient Commendation for Meritorious Civilian Service U.S. Air Force, 1955, Pace Setter award Nat. Inst. Drug Abuse, 1978. Fellow Am. Psychol. Assn. (pres. mil. div. 1934), Aerospace Med. Assn. (Longacre award 1956), AAAS; mem. Am. Astronautical Soc. (sr.), Soc. Multivariate Exptl. Psychology (pres. 1964), Am. Ednl. Research Assn., Psychometric Soc., Am. Statis. Assn., Soc. Psychol. Study Social Issues, Southwestern Psychol. Assn. (pres.), Tex. Psychol. Assn. (pres.), Southwest Research Inst. Sigma Xi. Current work: Application of psychology to behavioral problems involving individual and organizational measurement, personnel selection, personality measurement, organizational climate, management strategies, drug and alcohol abuse, air traffic control, aviation space travel and related areas. Subspecialties: Behavioral psychology; Ecology (environmental science). Home: 3850 Overton Park Dr W Fort Worth TX 76109 Office: Tex Christian U PO Box 32902 2800 University Blvd Fort Worth TX 76129

SELM, ROBERT PRICKETT, chemical engineering consultant firm executive; b. Cin., Aug. 9, 1923; s. Frederick O. and Margery Marie (Prickett) S.; children by previous marriage—Rosalie C., Linda R., Robert F., Michael E.; m. Janis Claire Broman, June 25, 1977. B.S., U. Cin., 1949, Chem. Engr., 1959. Registered profl. engr., 19 states; diplomate Am. Acad. Environ. Engrs. Chem. engr. Wilson & Co., Salina, Kans., 1954-67, gen. ptnr., 1967-81, sr. ptnr., 1981—, lab. dir., ptnr.-in-charge Wilson Labs., 1955—. Patentee in field. Served to capt. Ordnance Corps, U.S. Army, 1949-54. Mem. Am. Inst. Chem. Engrs., Am. Chem. Soc., Kans. Engring. Soc., Nat. Soc. Profl. Engrs. Republican. Episcopalian. Club: Salina Country (pres. 1985-86). Lodges: Masons, Elks (exalted ruler 1972-73). Current work: Research into effective chemical processes for treatment trihalomethanes and other toxic byproducts of industrial manufacturing. Subspecialties: Chemical engineering; Water supply and wastewater treatment. Home: 512 Crestwood St Salina KS 67401 Office: Wilson & Co Engrs & Architects PO Box 1648 Salina KS 67402-1648

SELOVE, WALTER, physicist, physics educator; b. Chgo., Sept. 11, 1921; s. Abe and Rose (Feld) S.; m. Fay Ajzenberg, Dec. 18, 1955. B.S., U. Chgo., 1942, Ph.D., 1949. Staff mem. MIT Radiation Lab., Cambridge, 1943-45, physicist Argonne Nat. Lab., Chgo., 1947-50; instr., asst. prof. Harvard U., Cambridge, 1950-56; assoc. prof. physics U. Pa., Phila., 1957-61, prof. 1961—; cons. Congl. Joint Com. on Atomic Energy, 1957-63. Contbr. articles to profl. jours. Patentee in field. NRC fellow, 1946-47; Guggenheim fellow, 1971-72. Fellow Am. Phys. Soc.; mem. Fedn. Am. Scientists (chmn. radiation hazards com. 1957-58; vice chmn. Fedn. 1958), Phi Beta Kappa, Sigma Xi. Current work: Very high energy experimental particle physics, using colliding beams. Subspecialties: Particle physics; Nuclear physics. Office: Physics Dept U Pa Philadelphia PA 19104

SELOVER, THEODORE BRITTON, JR., chemist; b. Cleve., Jan. 13, 1931; s. Theodore Britton and Zelma (Brandt) S.; m Barbara Jean Allen, June 18, 1955; children—Cynthia, Mark, Peter. Sc.B. in Chemistry, Brown U., 1952; M.S. in Chemistry, Western Res. U., 1957. Chemist Standard Oil of Ohio, Cleve., 1952-58, sr. chemist, 1958-66, research assoc., 1966-71, info. specialist, 1971-80, sr. tech. specialist, 1980—; vice chmn. Engring. Socs. Library Bd., N.Y.C., 1983—, mem. adminstrv. bd. Design Inst. for Phys. Properties, N.Y.C., 1982—. Contbr. articles to profl. jours. Patentee in field. Served with U.S. Army, 1952-54. Mem. Am. Inst. Chem. Engrs. (research com.), Am. Chem. Soc., ASTM (com. sec.), Am. Phys. Soc., Am. Ceramic Soc., Brown U. Nat. Alumni Assn., Sigma Xi. Methodist. Current work: Establish and maintain thermophysical property data base for corporate research and engineering staff; information searching and awareness; high temperature chemistry. Subspecialties: Thermodynamics; High temperature chemistry. Home: 3575 Traver Rd Shaker Heights OH 44122 Office: Standard Oil of Ohio Midland Bldg (HB) Cleveland OH 44115

SEMMENS, MICHAEL JOHN, environmental engineering educator, consultant; b. Southampton, Eng., May 28, 1947; s. John Alfred and Cissie Edna (Gibbons) S.; m. Linda Mary Gallagher, Aug. 2, 1968; children—Darius, Bruce. B.S. in Chem. Engring., Imperial Coll., London, 1968; M.S. in Environ. Engring., Harvard U., 1970; Ph.D. in Environ. Engring., Univ. Coll., London, 1973. Project engr. Hazen & Sawyer, N.Y.C., 1968-69; asst. prof. U. Ill., Champaign, 1973-77; assoc. prof. environ. engring. U. Minn., Mpls., 1977—; assoc. prof. U. New South Wales, Sydney, Australia, 1982-83. Contbr. articles to profl. jours. Patentee in field. Recipient Radebaugh award Central States Water Pollution Control Assn., 1976. Mem. Water Pollution Control Found., Am. Waste Water Assn., Assn. Environ. Engring. Profs., Am. Inst. Chem. Engrs., ASCE. Mem. Ch. of England. Club: Harvard. Current work: Ion exchange, adsorption, filtration, coagulation, contaminant removal, resource recovery, wastewater treatment. Subspecialty: Water supply and wastewater treatment. Home: 5029 1st Ave S Minneapolis MN 55419 Office: Environ Engring Program Dept Civil and Mineral Engring U Minn 500 Pillsbury Dr SE Minneapolis MN 55455

SENDAX, VICTOR IRVEN, dentist, researcher, educator; b. N.Y.C., Sept. 14, 1930; s. Maurice and Molly R. S.; m. Deborah DeLand Cobb, Dec. 17, 1969 (div. June 1976); 1 dau., Jennifer Reiland. B.A., Washington Square Coll., NYU, 1951; D.D.S., Coll. Dentistry, 1955; postgrad., Harvard U. Sch. Dental Medicine, Boston, 1969-72. Commr. N.Y. State Dental Service Corp., N.Y.C., 1969-73; pres. Victor I. Sendax, D.D.S. (P.C.), N.Y.C., 1972—, Biodental Research Found., Inc., N.Y.C., 1975—, Sendax Dental Implant Magnetics, Inc. adj. assoc. prof. and dir. implant prosthodontics resident program Columbia U. Sch. Dental and Oral Surgery, 1974—; cons. in field. Author: Magnetic Dental Implants and You, 1985; mem. editorial bd. Oral Implantology, 1979—. Patentee magnetic dental implant retention system. Mem. adv. bd. Hist. Assn., L.I.; bd. dirs. Schola Cantorum, N.Y.C., City Ctr. of Music and Drama, div. Lincoln Ctr. Performing Arts, 1966-85. Served to capt. Dental Corps USAF, 1955-57, Japan.. Recipient spl. recognition for significant contbrs. to dental health Am. Fund Dental Health, Chgo., 1982. Fellow Am. Coll. Dentists Internat. Coll. Dentists, Am. Acad. Implant Dentistry (pres. 1980-81, organizing chmn. 1st workshop-conf. on status of human oral implants 1976); mem. Am. Dental Assn. (ho. of dels. 1969), Am. Assn. Dental Schs. (chmn. spl. interest group on implantology 1982—), Internat. Assn. Dental Research, Am. Assn. Dental Research (implant group). Clubs: The Players (N.Y.C.); United Brothers. Co-inventor anti-calculus agt. Current Work: Research, teaching, and clinical practice related to magnetic implant prosthodontics. Subspecialties: Implantology; Prosthodontics. Home: 70 E 77th St Apt 6A New York NY 10021 Office: Victor I Sendax DDS 30 Central Park S Suite 14B New York NY 10019

SENEFF, JAMES ORIN, civil engineer; b. Odon, Ind., July 22, 1930; s. Ira Benton and Ruth Ada (Evans) S.; m. Mary Cathryn Wadsworth, Dec. 14, 1951; 1 child, Robert. B.S., Rose-Hulman Inst. Tech., 1954. Registered profl. engr., Ind., Fla., Pa. Ill. Chief engr. P.J. Kleiser & Assocs., Terre Haute, Ind., 1960-69, Briley, Wild & Assocs., Ormond Beach Fla., 1978-84, C.E. Burkett & Assocs., Daytona Beach, Fla., 1984-85, Upham, Inc., Ormond Beach, Fla., 1985—; dir. environ. engring. C.E. Williams & Assocs., South Bend, Ind., 1969-76; engring. mgr. ITT Communications Devel. Corp., Palm Coast, Fla., 1976-78. Served with U.S. Army, 1951-53, Korea. Fellow ASCE; mem. Am. Acad. Environ. Engrs. (diplomate), Nat. Soc. Profl. Engrs., Water Pollution Control Fedn., Am. Water Works Assn. Current work: Investigating interrelationships between hydrology and stormwater management; investigations to determine methods to increase ground water yields through improved stormwater management practices. Subspecialties: Water supply and wastewater treatment; Hydrology. Home: 22 Cloverdale Ct S Palm Coast FL 32037 Office: Upham Inc 265 Kenilworth Ave Ormond Beach FL 32074

SENGERS, JAN VINCENT, physicist, educator; b. Heiloo, Netherlands, May 27, 1931; came to U.S., 1963, naturalized, 1977; s. Adriaan and Cornelia Alida (Van Schie) S.; m. Johanna M.H. Levelt, Feb. 24, 1963; children—Rachel, Arjan, Maarten, Phoebe. Candidate, U. Amsterdam, 1952, Doctorandus, 1955, Ph.D., 1962. Physicist, Nat. Bur. Standards, Gaithersburg, Md., 1963—; assoc. prof. physics U. Md., College Park, 1968-74, prof., 1974—; vi.s. prof. Tech. U., Delft, Netherlands, 1974-75. Fellow Am. Phys. Soc., AAAS; mem. ASME, Dutch Phys. Soc., Royal Dutch Acad. Sci. (corr.). Roman Catholic. Current work: Thermophysical properties of fluids. Subspecialties: Statistical physics; Thermodynamics. Home: 110 N Van Buren St Rockville MD 20850 Office: IPST U Md College Park MD 20742

SENHAUSER, DONALD ALBERT, pathology educator; b. Dover, Ohio, Jan. 20, 1927; s. Albert Carl and Maude Anne (Snyder) S.; m. Helen Brown, July 22, 1961; children—William, Norman. B.A., Columbia U., 1948, M.D., 1951. Diplomate Am. Bd. Pathology. Instr., Columbia U., 1955-56; fellow Cleve. Clin. Found., 1956-60, staff physician, 1960-63; assoc. prof. U. Mo., Columbia, 1963-65, prof., 1965-75; dir. pathology services Univ. Hosps., Columbus, Ohio, 1975—; chmn., pres. Univ. Pathology Service, Inc., 1976—. Assoc. editor Am. Jour. Clin. Pathology, 1965-76. Served to lt. USN, 1952-55, Korea. Fellow Am. Soc. Clin. Pathologists; mem. Ohio Hist. Soc., Columbus Art League, Audubon Soc., Coll. Am. Pathologists (bd. govs. 1980—), Am. Assn. Pathologists, Internat. Acad. Pathology, Ohio Soc. Pathologists (bd. govs. 1976—). Republican. Lodge: Masons. Current work: Autoimmune thyroiditis, immunopathology, medical education, laboratory management. Subspecialties: Pathology (medicine); Hematology. Home: 1256 Clubview Blvd N Worthington OH 43085 Office: Dept Pathology Coll of Medicine Ohio State U 333 W 10th Ave Columbus OH 43210

SENICH, GEORGE A., chemist; b. Pitts., Jan. 5, 1953; s. George Albert and Lillian Catherine (Hoellein) S. B.S. Engring., Case Western Res. U., 1974; M.S., U. Mass., Amherst, 1976, Ph.D., 1979. Chemist Nat. Bur. Standards, Washington, 1978-80, research chemist, 1980—. Mem. rev. bd.: Polymer jour, 1979—, Polymer Engring. and Sci. jour, 1980—; contbr. articles to profl jours. Mem. Am. Chem. Soc., Am. Phys. Soc., Chem. Soc. Washington, Younger Chemists Com. D.C., Sigma Xi, Tau Beta Pi. Club: Tip Toppers. Current Work: Diffusion by chromatography with polymers; dynamic mechanical relaxation processes in linear and network polymers; radiation curing kinetics of resins; thermodynamics of oligomer/polymer systems. Subspecialties: Polymer chemistry; Polymers (materials science). Office: Nat Bur Standards Bldg 224 Room B320 Washington DC 20234

SENIOR, THOMAS BRYAN ALEXANDER, electrical engineering educator; b. Menston, Eng., June 26, 1928; came to U.S., 1957; s. Thomas Harold and Emily Dorothy (Matthews) S.; m. Heather Margaret Golby, May 4, 1957; children—Margaret, David, Hazel, Peter. B.Sc., Manchester U., 1949, M.S., 1950; Ph.D., Cambridge U., 1952. Sr. sci. officer Royal Radar Establishment, Malvern, Eng., 1952-57; research scientist U. Mich., Ann Arbor, 1957-59, prof. elec. engring., 1969-84, assoc. chmn., prof. elec. engring. and computer sci., 1984—, dir. radiation lab., 1975—; cons. to industry and govt. agys. Author: (with J.J. Bowman and P.L.E. Uslenghi) Electromagnetic and Acoustic Scattering, 1969; Mathematical Methods in Electrical Engineering, 1985. Editor Radio Sci., 1973-79. Contbr. articles to profl. jours. Fellow IEEE; mem. Internat. Sci. Radio Union (vice chmn. commn. B 1985—, chmn. U.S. nat. com. 1982-84). Current work: Electromagnetic and optical scattering and diffraction; radar systems. Subspecialty: Electrical engineering. Office: Dept Elec Engring and Computer Sci U Mich Ann Arbor MI 48109

SENSIPER, SAMUEL, consulting electrical engineer; b. Elmira, N.Y., Apr. 26, 1919; s. Louis and Molly (Pedolsky) S.; m. Elaine Marie Zwick, Sept. 10, 1950; children—Martin, Sylvia, David. B.S.E.E., MIT, 1939; E.E., Stanford U., 1941; Sc.D., MIT, 1951. Registered profl. engr., Calif. Asst. project engr. to project engr., cons. Sperry Gyroscope, Garden City, N.Y., 1941-51; sect. head, sr. staff cons. Hughes Aircraft, Culver City, Calif., 1951-60; lab. and div. mgr. Space Gen. Corp., Glendale, Calif., 1960-67; lab. mgr. TRW, Redondo Beach, Calif., 1967-70; cons. elec. engr., Los Angeles, 1970-73; 75—; dir. engring. Tranco, Venice, Calif., 1973-75; instr. grad. course U. So. Calif., Los Angeles, 1955-56, 79-80. Contbr. articles to profl. jours. Patentee in field. Recipient cert. of commendation U.S. Navy, 1946; MIT indsl. electronics fellow, 1947, 48. Fellow IEEE, AAAS; mem. Nat. Soc. Profl. Engrs., Assn. Old Crows. Jewish. Current work: Applied research in the application of the microwave frequency range to civilian useage, i.e. satellite communications, article surveillance, etc. Subspecialty: Electronics. Home: 6011 Holt Ave Los Angeles CA 90056 Office: PO Box 3102 Culver City CA 90231

SENTER, PETER DANA, chemist; b. Los Angeles, Nov. 29, 1951; s. Alvin David and Corinne Shirley (Allen) S. A.B., U. Calif.-Berkeley, 1975; M.S., N.C. State U., 1976; Ph.D., U. Ill., 1981. Postdoctoral fellow Max Planck Inst., Gottingen, Fed. Republic Germany, 1981-83; research scientist Dana Farber Cancer Inst., Boston, 1983-85; assoc. dept. pathology Harvard U. Med. Sch., Boston, 1983-85; sr. research scientist Bristol-Myers Co., Syracuse, N.Y., 1985—. Contbr. articles to profl. jours. Alexander von Humboldt fellow 1981-83. Mem. Am. Chem. Soc., AAAS. Jewish. Current work: Preparation of immunotoxins for cancer treatment; chemistry of antibody-toxin and antibody-drug conjugation. Subspecialties: Organic chemistry; Immunobiology and immunology. Office: Bristol Myers Co PO Box 4755 Syracuse NY 13221

SERAYDARIAN, MARIE WARGON, physiology educator, researcher; b. Warsaw, Poland, Jan. 30, 1924; came to U.S., 1949; d. Mieczyslaw and Bronislawa (Diettman) Wargon; m. Krikor Seraydarian, Sept. 24, 1950; children—Ann, Paul. B.A., Am. U., Beirut, 1948, M.A., 1949; Ph.D., Tufts U., 1952. Instr. Sr. Inst., Tufts U., Boston, 1952-56; research assoc. Wayne U., Detroit, 1956-57; research assoc. U. So. Calif., UCLA, Los Angeles, 1957-72; assoc. prof. physiology UCLA, 1972-74, prof., 1974—; dir. edn. abroad program U. Calif.-Bordeaux, France, 1984-86. Contbr. articles to profl. jours. Bd. govs. Family Planning Friends, Los Angeles, 1982—. Research grantee NIH, Am. Heart Assn., also others; named Woman of Sci., UCLA, 1980. Mem. Am. Physiol. Soc., Internat. Soc. for Heart Research, Am. Heart Assn., Cardiac Muscle Soc. Current work: Research in cell biology (physiology), developmental biology, cardiac cells; administration. Subspecialties: Cell and tissue culture; Developmental biology. Home: 2256 Parnell Ave Los Angeles CA 90064 Office: U Calif Ctr for Health Scis Sch Nursing Los Angeles CA 90024

SERAYDARIAN, RAYMOND PAUL, physicist; b. Binghamton, N.Y., May 26, 1952; s. Edward Alfred and Julia Arax (Nakashian) S. B.S., Cornell U., 1974; M. Engring., 1976. Scientist GA Techs., San Diego, 1977—. Mem. Am. Phys. Soc., Cornell Soc. Engrs. Clubs: Friends of Symphony (bd. dirs.) (San Diego), Cornell U. Alumni Assn. (v.p.). Mem. Armenian Apostolic Ch. Current work: Developing hardware to spectroscopically determine the ion temperature in a magnetically confined hydrogen plasma simultaneously at eight separate locations for profile measurement. Subspecialties: Nuclear fusion; Visible and ultraviolet spectroscopy. Office: GA Technologies PO Box 85608 San Diego CA 92138

SERGENT, JERRY ELDEN, microelectronics consultant, packaging engineer; b. Harlan, Ky., Nov. 16, 1939; s. John Marvin and Mary Frances (Peavley) S.; m. Peggy Anita Sanders, May 27, 1980. B.S. in Elec. Engring., U. Cin., 1966, M.S. in Elec. Engring., 1969, Ph.D. in Elec. Engring., 1971. Registered profl. engr., Fla. Engr. Avco Electronics, Cin., 1962-69; lectr. U. Cin., 1967-70; assoc. prof. U. South Fla., Tampa, 1970-79; sr. staff engr. Honeywell Avionics, St. Petersburg, Fla., 1979-80; cons. Sergent & Sergent, St. Petersburg, 1980—. Author: Thick and Thin Film Hybrid Microelectronics, 1979. Contbr. articles to profl. jours. Served with U.S. Army, 1959-61. Recipient spl. tech. achievement award NASA, 1980; spl. tech. award Japan Internat. Soc. Hybrid Microelectronics, 1984. Fellow Internat. Soc. Hybrid Microelectronics (pres. 1979-80), Internat. Electronic Packaging Soc.; mem. IEEE. Current work: Microelectronics packaging, electronic materials, hybrid microelectronics design. Subspecialties: Microelectronics; Electronic materials. Home: 4290 Narvarez Way S Saint Petersburg FL 33712

SEROT, BRIAN DAVID, physicist; b. N.Y.C., Feb. 1, 1955; s. Marvin Michael and Betty (Ernest) S.; m. Alexandra Helena Lampert, Aug. 14, 1976 (div. 1981). B.S., Yale U., 1975; M.S., Stanford U., 1977, Ph.D., 1979. Postdoctoral fellow MIT, Cambridge, Mass., 1979-80; asst. prof. Stanford U., Calif., 1980-83; assoc. prof. Ind. U., Bloomington, 1984—; vis. asst. research physicist Inst. Theoretical Physics, U. Calif.-Santa Barbara, 1982; vis. assoc. physics W.K. Kellogg Rediation Lab., Calif. Inst. Tech., 1983. Author: (with J.D. Walecka) The Relativistic Nuclear Many-Body Problem, 1985; also abstracts and articles. Chaim Weizmann fellow MIT, 1979-80; Alfred P. Sloan Found. fellow, 1982-83, 84—. Mem. Am. Phys. Soc., Sigma Xi, Phi Beta Kappa. Jewish. Current work: Theoretical nuclear physics, the relativistic nuclear many-body problem, electromagnetic and weak interactions with nuclei. Subspecialties: Theoretical physics; Nuclear physics. Office: Ind U Physics Dept Swain Hall W 117 Bloomington IN 47405

SERREZE, HARVEY B., electrical engineer; b. Weymouth, Mass., Dec. 22, 1943; s. Victor Charles and Emily Elizabeth (Martas) S.; m. Judith Marie Delling, Sept. 13, 1970; children—Peter Hawley, Matthew Charles. B.E.E. magna cum laude, Tufts U., 1965, M.E.E., 1968, Ph.D. in Elec. Engring., 1974. Physicist NASA Electronics Research Ctr., Cambridge, Mass., 1968-70; sr. scientist Mobil Solar Energy Corp., Waltham, Mass., 1972-78; dir. research Radiation Monitoring Devices, Inc., Watertown, Mass., 1978-82; research assoc. Stauffer Chem. Co., Elmsford, N.Y., 1982—. Contbr. articles to profl. jours. Mem. IEEE, Sigma Xi, Tau Beta Pi, Eta Kappa Nu. Current work: Research into improved and novel semiconductor device structures utilizing III-V compound materials (e.g. GaAs and InP) and development of processes to fabricate these devices. Subspecialties: Semiconductors; Condensed matter physics. Home: Rural Route 2 Box 366A Pound Ridge NY 10576 Office: Stauffer Chem Co Eastern Research Ctr Grasslands Rd Elmsford NY 10523

SERRIN, JAMES BURTON, educator; b. Chgo., Nov. 1, 1926; s. James B. and Helen Elizabeth (Wingate) S.; m. Barbara West, Sept. 6, 1952; children—Martha Helen, Elizabeth Ruth, Janet Louise. Student, Northwestern U., 1944-46; B.A., Western Mich. U., 1947; M.A., Ind. U., Ph.D., 1951; D.Sc., U. Sussex, 1972. With Mass. Inst. Tech., 1952-54; faculty U. Minn., Mpls., 1955—, prof. math., 1959—; head U. Minn. Sch. Math., 1964-65, Regents prof., 1968—; vis. prof. U. Chgo., 1964, 75, Johns Hopkins U., 1966, Sussex U., 1967-68, 72, 76, U. Naples, 1979. Author: Mathematical Principles of Classical Fluid Mechanics, 1957; Co-editor: Archive for Rational Mechanics and Analysis. Mem. Met. Airport Sound Abatement Council, Mpls., 1969—. Recipient Disting. Alumni award Ind. U., 1979. Fellow AAAS; mem. Nat. Acad. Scis., Am. Math. Soc. (G.D. Birkhoff prize 1973), Math. Assn. Am., Soc. for Natural Philosophy (pres. 1969-70). Current Work: Foundations of continuum mechanics and of thermodynamics, with emphasis on the theoretical roles of energy and entropy, continuum theory of phase transitions in fluids, both in equilibrium and in dynamic situations; nonlinear elliptic partial differential equations. Subspecialties: Applied mathematics; Thermodynamics. Home: 4422 Dupont Ave S Minneapolis MN 55409

SERVOS, KURT, geology educator; b. Anrath, Germany, Dec. 20, 1928; came to U.S., 1939, naturalized, 1945; s. Albert and Ilse S. B.Sc., Rutgers U., 1952; S.M., Yale U., 1954. Registered geologist, Calif. Sr. curator N.Y. State Mus., Albany, 1956-57; asst. prof. mineralogy Stanford U., Calif., 1957-60; asst. prof. geology Calif. State U., Hayward, 1964; geologist Stanford Research Inst., Menlo Park, Calif., 1966-67; prof. geology Menlo Coll., Atherton, Calif., 1967—. Bd. dirs. Pocket Opera Inc., San Francisco, 1980—; cert. ofcl. Athletics Congress, 1980—. Mem. Bay Area Mineralogists (pres. 1982—), Mineral. Soc. Am., Geol. Soc. Am., Deutsche Mineral. Gesellschaft, Am. Crystallographic Assn. Republican. Jewish. Current work: General geology; vulcanology; systematic mineralogy; crystal symmetry; geochemistry. Subspecialties: Geology; Mineralogy. Home: 1281 Mills St Menlo Park CA 94025 Office: Dept Geology Menlo Coll 1000 El Camino Real Atherton CA 94025

SERWER, PHILIP, biochemist, educator; b. N.Y.C., Feb. 5, 1942; s. Zachary Abraham and Blanche (Luria) Berstein; m. Ellen Goldberg, July 25, 1966; children—Zachary, Tamara, Rebecca. A.B. in Physics, U. Rochester, 1963; M.S. in Microbiology, N.Y. Med. Coll., 1967; Ph.D., Harvard U., 1973. Postdoctoral fellow Calif. Tech. Inst., Pasadena, 1973-76; asst. prof. biochemistry Health Sci. Ctr., U. Tex.-San Antonio, 1976-81, assoc. prof., 1981—; cons. Marine Colloids div. FMC, Rockland, Maine, 1981—. Patentee in field. Contbr. articles to profl. jours. Mem. Biophys. Soc., Am. Soc. Biol. Chemists, Electron Microscopy Soc. Am., Electropharesis Soc., Am. Soc. Virology. Subspecialties: Plant growth; Molecular biology. Office: Dept Biochemistry U Tex 7703 Floyd Curl San Antonio TX 78284

SESAK, JOHN ROBERT, control and aerospace engineer; b. Latrobe, Pa., Jan. 19, 1942; s. John and Margaret (Brillo) S. Student St. Vincent Coll., 1960-62; B.S.E.E., Pa. State U., 1965; M.S., U. Conn., 1967; Ph.D., U. Wis., 1974. Sr. engr. Gen. Dynamics Co. div. Convair, San Diego, 1976-79, engring. specialist, 1979-82, sr. engring. specialist, 1982-83, program mgr., 1983—. Inventor flexible satellite control algorithms; model error sensitivity suppression; filter accomodated optical control; originator Nat. Short Course on Flexible Spacecraft Control, 1981. Bd. dirs., v.p. New Thought Episcopal Ch., San Diego, 1979—. Mem. AIAA (guidance and control com. 1981—, council 1982-83, adminstrv. chmn. 1982, Outstanding Contbn. to Aerospace Engring. award San Diego 1979), IEEE, Am. Soc. Engring. Edn. Current work: Application of modern optimal control and estimation theory to complex Engring Systems. Subspecialty: Aerospace engineering and technology. Office: Gen Dynamics Co Convair 5001 Kearnyville Rd PO Box 85357 MZ 21-9530 San Diego CA 92138

SESSLE, BARRY JOHN, dentistry and physiology educator, neuroscience researcher; b. Sydney, Australia, May 28, 1941; came to Can., 1971; s. Frederick George and Sadie Isobel (Lawson) S.; m. Helen Alice Prowse, Aug. 17, 1967 (div.); children—Erica Jane, Claire Marie. B.D.S., Sydney U., 1963, B.Sc., M.D.S., 1965; Ph.D., U. New South Wales, Australia, 1969. Scholar Dental Found., Sydney U., 1963-64; teaching fellow U. New South Wales, 1965-68; vis. assoc. U.S. Nat. Inst. Dental Research, Bethesda, Md., 1968-70; assoc. prof. U. Toronto, Ont., Can., 1971-76, prof. dentistry and physiology, 1976—, chmn. div. biol. scis. Dental Sch., 1978-85, assoc. dean research, 1985—; mem. dental scis. com. Can. Med. Research Council, Ottawa, Ont., 1979-82. Editor: Mastication and Swallowing, 1976; Oro-Facial Pain and Neuromuscular Dysfunction, 1985. Author: The Neural Basis of Oral and Facial Function, 1978. Contbr. articles to profl. jours. Recipient Tchr. award Can. Fund for Dental Edn., 1977; named prin. investigator Can. Med. Research Council, 1971—, NIH, 1974—. Fellow Japan Soc. for Promotion Sci.; mem. Internat. Assn. for Study Pain (sec. Can. 1982—), Soc. for Neurosci., Internat. Assn. for Dental Research (pres. Can. 1977-78, pres. neurosci. group 1985-86, Oral Scis. research award 1976), Internat. Union Physiol. Scis. (sec. oral physiology com. 1983—). Current work: Basic neuroscientific and clinical research of neurophysiological and behavioral aspects of orofacial pain; motor function and dysfunction of craniofacial, jaw and respiratory muscles; administration of biological and clinical science research and teaching. Subspecialties: Neurophysiology; Oral biology. Office: Faculty Dentistry U Toronto 124 Edward St Toronto ON M5G 1G6 Canada

SESSLER, ANDREW MARIENOFF, physicist, researcher; b. Bklyn., Dec. 11, 1928; s. David Sessler and Mary Baron; m. Gladys Lerner, Sept. 23, 1951; children—Daniel Ira, Jonathan Lawrence, Ruth. A.B. in Math. cum laude, Harvard U., 1949; M.A., Columbia U., 1951, Ph.D., 1953. NSF predoctoral fellow Columbia U., 1952-53; NSF postdoctoral fellow Cornell U., 1953-54; visitor Niels Bohr Inst., Copenhagen, 1961; U.S. advisor U.S.-India, Chandigarh, 1966; vis. European Organ. Nuclear Research, 1966-67; physicist Lawrence Berkeley Lab., Berkeley, Calif. 1961-70, 80—, coordinator environ. research, 1970-72, dir., 1973-80; mem. high energy physics adv. panel AEC, 1969-72; mem. Com. on High Energy Physics, 1971-74. Mem. editorial bd. Nuclear Instruments and Methods, 1969—. Contbr. numerous articles to profl. jours. Recipient E.O. Lawrence award AEC, 1970. Fellow Am. Phys. Soc., AAAS; mem. Sigma Xi. Subspecialties: Free-electron lasers; Theoretical physics. Office: Lawrence Berkeley Lab MFE Group Bldg 4 One Cyclotron Rd Berkeley CA 94720

SETH, BALDEV RAJ, civil engineering educator; b. Quetta, India, July 16, 1932; came to U.S., 1978; s. Chaman Lal and Saraswati Devi Seth; m. Shashi Seth, Jan. 30, 1967; 1 child, Brahama. B.Sc. Eng. with honors, Patna U., India, 1956; postgrad. cert. Roorkee U., I.I.T., India, 1958, 67, 68, 72, 74; Ph.D., Ranchi U., India, 1975. Asst. engr. M.P. Electricity Bd., Jabalpore, India. 1957-62; asst. prof. engring. Dayalbagh Engring. Coll., Agra, India, 1962-64, Tuskegee Inst., Ala., 1978-79; assoc. prof. Birla Inst. Tech., Ranchi, India, 1965-78, So. U., Baton Rouge, 1980-83; specialist U.S. Filigree, Tampa, Fla., 1983—. Contbr. articles to profl. publs. Mem. Am. Soc. Engring. Edn., ASCE, Am. Concrete Inst. (com. on creep and shrinkage in concrete, com. on materials research), ASME. Current work: Structural engineering, mechanics, creep stresses. Subspecialties: Civil engineering; Structural engineering.

SETH, SHARAD CHANDRA, computer scientist, electrical engineer. Prof. dept. computer sci. U. Nebr., Lincoln. Subspecialty: Computer engineering. Office: U Nebr Dept Computer Sci Lincoln NE 68508

SETHARES, JAMES COSTAS, physicist, researcher; b. Hyannis, Mass., Dec. 13, 1928; s. Costas H. and Mary S. (Lagos) S.; m. Janet C. Jarvis; children—William, Marilyn, Andrea. B.S. in Elec. Engring., U. Mass., 1959; M.S. in Elec. Engring., MIT, 1962. Physicist Air Force Cambridge Research Lab., Mass., 1962-78, Rome Air Devel. Ctr., Hanscom AFB, Bedford, Mass., 1978—; pres. NDE Assocs. Inc., Burlington, Mass., 1978—. Contbr. articles to profl. jours. Patentee rotation rate sensing and microwave filters and liquid crystal imaging. Bd. dirs. Huntington Disease Found. Am., 1978-82. Served with U.S. Army, 1950-52. Recipient Marcus D. O'Day award Air Force Cambridge Research Labs., 1969. Mem. IEEE (sr. mem.; chmn. ultrasound group 1983). Current work: Development of microwave magnetics technology using thin magnetic films for analog signal processing. Subspecialties: Electrical engineering; Applied magnetics. Home: 131 Bedford St Burlington MA 01803 Office: Rome Air Devel Ctr Hanscom AFB Bedford MA 01731

SETHI, VIDYA SAGAR, cancer pharmacologist; b. Panjab, India, Dec. 1, 1937; came to U.S., 1971, naturalized, 1977; s. Dewan Ch and Ram Rakhi (Wadhwa) S.; m. Hema Lata Amarsingh, Jan. 19, 1969; children: Preeti Seema,

Deepu Shikha. M.Pharmacy, Banaras Hindu U., India, 1960; Ph.D., U. Munich, W.Ger., 1964. Vis. scientist Max Planck Inst. Biochemistry, Munich, 1968-71; head sect. molecular pharmacology Litton Bionetics, Bethesda, Md., 1973-76; research assoc. prof. medicine Bowman Gray Sch. Medicine, Winston-Salem, N.C., 1977—; also dir. Clin. Pharmacology Lab., Oncology Research Center.; Pres. Indo-U.S. Cultural Assn., Winston-Salem, 1981; v.p. Unitarian Universalist Fellowship, Winston-Salem, 1982—. Contbr. articles to profl. jours. Mem. Am. Assn. Biol. Chemists, Am. Assn. Cancer Research, Am. Assn. Pharmacology and Exptl. Therapeutics, Am. Microbiol. Assn., Am. Chem. Soc., AAAS. Democrat. Hindu-Unitarian-Universalist. Current Work: Biochemical, preclinical and clinical pharmacology and metabolism of anticancer drugs. Subspecialties: Cancer research (medicine); Pharmacology. Home: 636 Friar Tuck Rd Winston-Salem NC 27104 Office: Bowman Gray Sch Medicine Winston-Salem NC 27103

SETLIFF, EDSON CARMACK, mycologist; b. Indianola, Miss., Nov. 3, 1941; s. Abram Carmack and Martha (Baumann) S.; m. Dorene Dee Lyon, Aug. 7, 1939; children: Eric John, Alissa Ellen. B.S., N.C. State Coll., 1963; M.F., Yale U., 1964; Ph.D., SUNY-Syracuse, 1970. Vol. U.S. Peace Corps, Arusha, Tanzania, 1964-66; postdoctoral fellow U. Wis., Madison, 1970-73; forest pathologist Cary Arboretum, N.Y. Bot. Garden, Millbrook, N.Y., 1973-77; Coll. Environ. Sci. and Forestry, SUNY-Syracuse, 1977-80; research scientist Forintek Can. Corp., Vancouver, B.C., Can., 1980—; adj. assoc. prof. Vassar Coll., SUNY-Syracuse, U. B.C., Vancouver. Contbr. articles to profl. jours. Mem. Am. Phytopathol. Soc., Mycol. Soc. Am., Central N.Y. Mycol. Soc., Vancouver Mycol. Soc. Patentee in field. Current Work: Fungal taxonomy, forest pathology, wood products pathology, bioconversion of wood wastes into food, alcohol, chemicals, identification of fungi important in forest and biotechnology. Subspecialties: Microbiology; Biomass (agriculture). Office: 6620 NW Marine Dr Vancouver BC V6T 1X2 Canada

SETLOW, RICHARD BURTON, biophysicist; b. N.Y.C., Jan. 19, 1921; s. Charles Meyer and Elsie (Hurwitz) S.; m. Jane Kellock, June 6, 1942; children—Peter, Michael, Katherine, Charles. A.B., Swarthmore Coll., 1941; Ph.D., Yale U., 1947. Asso. prof. Yale U., 1956-61; biophysicist Oak Ridge Nat. Lab., 1961-74, sci. dir. biophysics and cell physiology, 1969-74; dir. U. Tenn.-Oak Ridge Grad. Sch. Biomed. Scis., 1972-74; sr. biophysicist Brookhaven Nat. Lab., Upton, N.Y., 1974—, chmn. biology dept., 1979—, also assoc. dir. life scis.; prof. biomed. scis. U. Tenn., 1967-74; adj. prof. biochemistry State U. N.Y., Stony Brook, 1975—. Author: (with E.C. Pollard) Molecular Biophysics, 1962; editor: (with P.C. Hanawalt) Molecular Mechanisms for Repair of DNA, 1975. Mem. Nat. Acad. Scis., Am. Acad. Arts and Scis., Biophys. Soc. (pres. 1969-70), Comité Internat. de Photobiologie (pres. 1972-76), Radiation Research Soc., Am. Soc. Photobiology, Phi Beta Kappa. Current Work: Damage to DNA and its repair. Repair deficient diseases. Ultraviolet photobiology. Subspecialties: Biophysics (biology); Cancer research (medicine). Home: 57 Valentine Rd Shoreham NY 11786 Office: Biology Dept Brookhaven Nat Lab Upton NY 11973

SETO, JOSEPH TOBEY, microbiologist, educator; b. Tacoma, Aug. 3, 1924; s. T. and K. (Morita) S.; m. Grace K., Aug. 9, 1959; children: Susan Lynn, Steven Fred. B.S., U. Minn., 1949; M.S., U. Wis.-Madison, 1955, Ph.D., 1957. Postdoctoral researcher UCLA Med. Center, 1958-59; asst. prof. San Francisco State U., 1959-60; prof. microbiology Calif. State U.-Los Angeles, 1960—; vis. prof. U. Giessen, Inst. Virology, 1965-66, 72-73, 79-80. Served to sgt. U.S. Army, 1945-46. Recipient United Health Found. award, 1965; WHO award, 1972; Alexander von Humboldt award Humboldt Found., Germany, 1972; Sr. Scientist award NATO, 1979; Deutsche Forschungsgemeinschaft award, 1979. Fellow Am. Soc. Microbiology; mem. N.Y. Acad. Scis., Am. Soc. Microbiology, Soc. Gen. Microbiology, Electron Microscope Soc., AAAS, Japanese Am. Citizens League, Sigma Xi. Current Work: Molecular biology of the pathogenesis of paramyxoviruses and influenza viruses; persistent infections of paramyxoviruses. Subspecialty: Virology (medicine). Office: Dept Microbiology Calif State U Los Angeles CA 90032

SEVERINGHAUS, WILLIAM DANIEL, environmental biologist; b. Ithaca, N.Y., Sept. 15, 1942; s. Charles William and Ethel (Long) S.; m. Mary Catherine Charles, May 27, 1976; children—William Joseph, Steven Nathaniel. A.A.S., Onondaga Community Coll., 1965; B.S., Lambuth Coll., 1968; M.S., Memphis State U., 1969; Ph.D., U. Ill., 1976. Ecologist USA-Constrn. Engring. Research Lab., Champaign, Ill., 1976—; alt. mem. Dept. Def. Natural Resources Group Com., 1983—. Contbr. articles to profl. jours., presentations to profl. societies. Officer, Illini Statesmen Soc. Preservation and Encouragement of Barber Shop Singing in Am., Champaign, 1984-85. Recipient Cert. Appreciation, Vol. Action Ctr., 1983, 84; named Researcher of Yr., USA-CERL, 1983. Mem. Am. Soc. Mammalogists (chmn. resolutions com. 1982-83, poster award winner 1984), Ecol. Soc. Am. (sr. ecologist, appeals com. bd. profl. cert. 1984—), Am. Soc. Naturalists, Soc. Study Evolution, Soc. Systematic Zoology, Tenn. Acad. Sci. Current work: Applications of ecological principles to environmental preservation, conservation, and management. Subspecialties: Ecology (environmental science); Systematics. Home: RR5 Box 3 Mahomet IL 61853 Office: USA-Constrn Engring Research Lab Box 4005 Champaign IL 61820

SEVERNS, MATTHEW LINCOLN, biomedical engineer, researcher; b. Wilmington, Del., Nov. 12, 1952; s. William Harrison and Mary Jeanne (Reeser) S.; m. Dayle Aileen Hulka, Aug. 31, 1974. B.A. magna cum laude, U. Del., 1976; M.E., U. Va., 1978, Ph.D., 1980. Head field ops. Megonigal Electronics, Inc., Stanton, Del., 1975-76; staff engr. Rehab. Engring. Ctr., Charlottesville, Va., 1977; asst. prof. clin. engring. George Washington U. Med. Ctr., Washington, 1980-82; research scientist ARC, Bethesda, Md., 1982—; cons. Del. Assn. Blind Athletes, Wilmington, 1981-83; cons. to industry, 1982—; lectr. NATO Advanced Study Inst., 1983. Contbr. articles to profl. jours. Newcomb fellow U. Va., 1976, predoctoral fellow, NIH, 1977, postdoctoral fellow, 1977-80. Mem. Robotics Internat., Soc. Mfg. Engrs. (sr. mem.), IEEE, AAAS, Internat. Soc. Blood Transfusion, Assn. for Advancement Med. Instrumentation, Soc. for Creative Anachronism (warlord 1981—). Current work: Automation of medical laboratories; applications of robotics in medicine; development of new methods in immunohematology. Subspecialties: Biomedical engineering; Robotics. Home: 2022 Burfoot St Falls Church VA 22043 Office: Am Red Cross Labs 9312 Old Georgetown Rd Bethesda MD 20814

SEVERSON, JAMES ALAN, neurobiologist, educator; b. Ames, Iowa, Jan. 20, 1951; s. Donald Martin and Betty Jean (Duffy) S.; m. Patricia Ann Porter, Aug. 4, 1973; children—Robert Martin, Michael Evan, Ryan James. B.S., Iowa State U., 1973, Ph.D., 1977. Postdoctoral fellow U. So. Calif., Los Angeles, 1977-80, asst. prof. psychiatry Sch. Medicine, 1980—. Mem. AAAS, Soc. for Neurosci., Gerontol. Soc. Am., Sigma Xi, Phi Kappa Phi. Current work: Mechanisms of action of antipsychotics and antidepressants in aging brain. Subspecialties: Neurochemistry; Neuropharmacology. Office: Univ So Calif 1333 San Pablo St Los Angeles CA 90033

SEVIER, JAMES ROLLINS, ceramic tile company executive; b. Asheville, N.C., Jan. 29, 1918; s. Joseph Thomas and Caroline Anne (Rollins) S.; m. Ilma Claire LaBar, Dec. 11, 1941; children—Christy Sevier King, James Rollins, Frank, John. B.S. in Ceramic Engring., N.C. State U., 1941. Plant engr. W.S. George Pottery Co., Cannonburg, Pa., 1946-48; exec. v.p., dir. So. Potteries, Inc., Erwin, Tenn., 1948-57; v.p., dir. Stylon Corp., Florence, Ala., 1957-68; pres. Mosaic Tile Co., Florence, 1968-70; v.p., dir. DCA Devel. Corp., Florence, 1970-73; sr. v.p., dir. Monarch Tile Mfg., Inc., Florence, 1973—. Served to lt. comdr. USNR, 1941-45. Fellow Am. Ceramic Soc. (Hewitt Wilson Meml. award Southeastern sect. 1975); mem. Nat. Inst. Ceramic Engrs. Republican. Methodist. Club: Turtle Point Yacht and Country (Killen, Ala.) (bd. dirs.). Lodges: Elks, Kiwanis (pres. Erwin 1954), Rotary (pres. Florence 1965). Current work: Automating and retrofitting ceramic wall tile plants. Subspecialty: Ceramic engineering. Home: 1842 Hermitage Dr Florence AL 35630 Office: Monarch Tile Mfg Inc 833 Rickwood Rd Florence AL 35630

SEVON, WILLIAM DAVID, geologist; b. Andover, Ohio, July 22, 1933; s. William David and Matilda Ethyl (Smith) S.; m. Joan Eleanor Johnson, Sept. 7, 1957 (div. Mar. 1981); children—Douglass William, David Hugh. B.A., Ohio Wesleyan U., 1955; M.A., U. S.D., 1958; Ph.D., U. Ill., 1961. Geologist Horsethief Canyon Uranium Co., Inc., Salt Lake City, summer 1955, S.D. Geol. Survey, Vermillion, summers 1957-60; lectr. geology U. Canterbury, Christchurch, N.Z., 1961-65; geologist Pa. Geol. Survey, Harrisburg, 1965—. Contbr. articles to profl. jours. Mem. Geol. Soc. Am., Soc. Econ. Paleontologists and Mineralogists, AAAS, Harrisburg Area Geol. Soc., Am. Quaternary Assn., Sigma Xi. Current work: Quaternary geology of Pennsylvania; upper Devonian sedimentology of Pennsylvania; landscape evolution of the Appalachian Mountains. Subspecialty: Geology. Home: 4615 Surrey Rd Harrisburg PA 17109 Office: Pa Geol Survey PO Box 2357 Harrisburg PA 17120

SEVY, ROGER WARREN, pharmacologist, educator; b. Richfield, Utah, Nov. 6, 1923; s. Carl Spencer and Maude (Malmquist) S.; m. Barbara F. Snetsinger, Aug. 16, 1948; children—Pamela Jane, Jonathan Carl. M.S., U. Vt., 1948; Ph.D., U. Ill.-Chgo., 1951; M.D., 1954. Diplomate Nat. Bd. Med. Examiners. Instr. U. Ill.-Chgo., 1951-54; asst. prof. pharmacology Temple U., Phila., 1954-56, prof., 1956—, chmn. dept., 1957-73, dean Med. Sch., 1973-78; adj. prof. Drexel U., Phila. 1966—; cons. Nat. Bd. Med. Examiners, Phila., 1982—. Contbr. articles to profl. jours., chpts. to books. Bd. dirs. St. Christophers Hosp. for Children, Phila., 1974-78. Served with U.S. Army, 1943-46. Mem. Am. Soc. Pharmacology, Am. Physiol. Soc., Endocrine Soc., Coll. Physicians Phila., Sigma Xi, Alpha Omega Alpha. Republican. Current work: Cardiovascular pharmacology; pharmacology of platelets. Subspecialties: Pharmacology; Cellular pharmacology. Home: 242 Mather Rd Jenkintown PA 19046 Office: Temple Univ Sch Med 3420 N Broad St Philadelphia PA 19140

SEWCHOK, MICHAEL GEORGE, chemist; b. Monongahela, Pa., May 2, 1955; s. Pete and Katherine Frances (Secka) S.; m. Susan Scenna, July 19, 1980. B.S., U. Pitts., 1981. Chemist U.S. Dept. Energy, Pitts., 1979-80, Exxon Research and Engring. Co., Annandale, N.J., 1982—. Contbr. articles to profl. jours. Served with U.S. Army, 1974-76. Mem. Am. Chem. Soc. Democrat. Roman Catholic. Current work: Some work on zintl compounds; most of time devoted to porphyrins. Subspecialties: Catalysis chemistry; Inorganic chemistry. Office: Exxon Research and Engring Co Clinton Twp Route 22E Annandale NJ 08801

SEWELL, JOHN IKE, agricultural engineer, educator, researcher; b. Cave Spring, Ga., Aug. 28, 1933; s. Paul C. Sewell and Ila (Jones) Sewell Stargel; m. Rebecca Underwood, July 9, 1960; children—Mary Ila, John Ike II. B.S. in Agrl. Engring., U. Ga., 1954; M.S., N.C. State U., 1958, Ph.D. in Agrl. Engring., 1958. Registered profl. engr., Tenn. Grad. asst., instr. N.C. State U., Raleigh, 1956-62; asst. prof. agrl. engring. U. Tenn., Knoxville, 1962-68, assoc. prof., 1968-74, prof., assoc. head dept. agrl. engring., 1974-77, asst. dean Tenn. Agrl. Expt. Sta., 1977—; farm bldgs. cons. U. Tenn. Inst. Agr., 1964-77. Contbr. articles to profl. jours. Served with U.S. Army, 1954-56; col. Res. (ret.). Recipient Webster Pendergrass Outstanding Service award U. Tenn. Inst. Agr., 1975. Mem. Am. Soc. Agrl. Engrs. (sr.; chmn. Tenn. sect. 1972, chmn. Southeast region 1973, dir. Southeast region 1981-83), Soil Conservation Soc. Am. Club: Knoxville Optimist. Current work: Research in soil sealants, drainage canal design, land grading, infrared remote sensing, water quality, agricultural waste management. Subspecialty: Agricultural engineering. Home: 3109 Ticonderoga Ln Knoxville TN 37920 Office: Tenn Agrl Expt Sta 104 Morgan Hall U Tenn Knoxville TN 37916

SEXSMITH, FREDERICK HAMILTON, chemical company executive; b. Fort Erie, Ont., Can., Mar. 30, 1929; s. Royal Lee and Florence Agnes (Hamilton) S.; children—Malcolm, Katherine. B.A. with honors, Queen's U., Kingston, Ont., 1951, M.A., 1953; Ph.D., Princeton U., 1957; Advanced mgmt. diploma Case-Western Res. U., 1972. Various research, devel. mgmt. positions Johnson & Johnson, Mass. and N.J., 1956-66; mgr. research and devel. Hughson Chems., Lord Corp., Erie, Pa., 1966-79, dir. research Chem. Products Group, 1979-84, div. mgr. elastomer products, 1984—. Patentee in field. Mem. Am. Chem. Soc., Am. Inst. Chemists, Chem. Inst. Can., Fiber Soc., Am. Assn. Textile Chemists and Colorists. Republican. Presbyterian. Lodge: Masons. Current work: Applied polymer chemistry; specialty chemicals for the elastomer processing industries, adhesives for bonding elastomers to metal. Subspecialty: Polymer chemistry. Office: Chem Products Group Lord Corp 2000 W Grandview Blvd Erie PA 16514-0038

SEYDEL, HORST GUNTER, physician, educator; b. Berlin, Germany, Aug. 5, 1929; came to U.S., 1955, naturalized, 1961; m. Emily Meginnity, 1958; children: Edgar, Charlotte, Carolyn. M.D., Goethe U., Frankfurt, Germany, 1955; M.S., Wayne State U., 1961. Intern Md. Gen. Hosp., Balt., 1955-56; resident in oncology Am. Oncologic Hosp., Phila., 1956-57, chief dept. radiation therapy, 1968-75; resident in radiology Wayne State U., Detroit, 1958-61, radiotherapist, 1961-64, U. Md. Sch. Medicine, Balt., 1964-68; cons. radiotherapy Perry Point VA Hosp., Perryville, Md., 1966-68, Prince George Gen. Hosp., Hyattsville, Md., 1966-68, Peninsular Gen. Hosp., Salisbury, Md., 1966-68, Cambridge (Md.) Hosp., 1966-68, St. Joseph Hosp., Balt., 1967-68; radiotherapist No. div. Albert Einstein Med. Ctr., Phila., 1975-77, Thomas Jefferson U. Med. Coll., Phila., 1977-79; cons. radiotherapy Nazareth Hosp., Phila., 1978-79, Chestnut Hill Hosp., Phila., 1978-79; dir. clin. radiation therapy service Harper-Grace Hosps., Detroit, 1979-82, vice chief radiation therapy, 1979-82; clin. prof. radiation oncology Wayne State Sch. Medicine, 1982—; chmn. therapeutic radiology Henry Ford Hosp., Detroit, 1982—. Contbr. articles to profl. jours. Fulbright scholar, 1955-56. Mem. Am. Assn. for Cancer Research, Am. Cancer Soc., Am. Coll. Radiology (accreditation com.), AMA, Am. Radium Soc., Am. Soc. Clin. Oncology, Am. Soc. Therapeutic Radiologists, Mich. State Med. Soc., Mich. State Radiol. Soc., Radiation Therapy Oncology Group (vice chmn. membership com.), Radiol. Soc. N.Am., Southwest Oncology Group (chmn. radiation therapy quality control. com.), Wayne County Med. Soc. Current Work: Clinical cancer research. Subspecialty: Radiology.

SEYFRIED, THOMAS NEIL, neurogenetics educator; b. Flushing, N.Y., July 25, 1946; s. William Edward and Anne Marie (McGuire) S.; m. Karen Elizabeth Seyfried, Apr. 13, 1973; children: Melissa, Nicholas, Edward. B.A., St. Francis Coll., 1968; M.S., Ill. State U., 1973; Ph.D., U. Ill., 1976. Postdoctoral fellow dept. neurology Yale U., New Haven, 1976-79, asst. prof., 1979—. Contbr. articles to profl. jours. Served with U.S. Army, 1969-71; with Res. 1980—. Decorated Bronze Star medal with 2 oak leaf clusters, Air medal, Army Commendation medal; recipient Honored Student award Am. Oil Chemists Soc., 1975; Nat. Research Service fellow NIH, 1976-79; NIH grantee, 1981—; NIH research career devel. award, 1979—. Mem. Genetics Soc. Am., Soc. for Neurosci., Internat. Soc. Neurochemistry, AAAS. Current Work: Cellular localization and function of brain gangliosides; developmental genetics of inherited epilepsy in mice. Subspecialties: Gene actions; Neurochemistry. Home: 40 Union St Foxboro MA 02035 Office: Dept Biology Boston Coll Chestnut Hill MA 02167

SHACKELFORD, SCOTT ADDISON, air force officer, chemist; b. Long Beach, Calif., Aug. 11, 1944; s. Richard Walter and Phyllis Marian (Pearson) S.; m. Alpha Marilyn Coon, Aug. 23, 1969; children—Laura DeAnna, Vicki LeAnna. Student Colo. State U., 1962-64; B.A., Simpson Coll., 1964-66; M.A., No. Ariz. U., 1968; Ph.D., Ariz. State U., 1973. Second lt. U.S. Air Force, 1972, advanced through grades to major, 1985; research chemist F.J. Seiler Research Lab., U.S. Air Force Acad., Colo., 1972-74, research group chief, 1974-77, instr., asst. prof. dept. chemistry and biol. scis., 1977-78; lang. student Nat. Def. Lang. Inst., Monterey, Calif., 1978; exchange scientist DFVLR-Institut fuer Chemische Antriebe und Verfahrenstechnik, Hardthausen A.K., Fed. Republic Germany, 1978-80; research sect. chief Air Force Rocket Propulsion Lab., Edwards AFB, Calif., 1980-84; research liaison officer European Office Aerospace Research and Devel., London, 1984—; sec. Tri-Services Joint Tech. Coordinating Group/Munitions Devel./Working Party for Explosives, Washington, 1975-77; lab. research task mgr. Air Force Office Sci. Research, Washington, 1981-84; nat. propellant survey cons., 1981-82; mem. sci. adv. com. Simpson Coll., Indianola, Iowa, 1983—. Contbr. articles to profl. publs. Patentee in field. Co-mgr. Tee Ball Youth Baseball Team, Fort Collins, Colo., 1964; asst. coach Am. Legion Summer Baseball Team, Pacifica, Calif., 1967, 68; Sunday school tchr. Village Christian Ch., Colorado Springs, Colo., 1976-77; adult class leader Base Protestant Chapel, Edwards, Calif., 1984. Recipient Research and Devel. award U.S. Air Force Chief-of-Staff, 1982, Alumni Achievement award Simpson Coll. Alumni Assn., 1985. Mem. Am. Chemical Soc. (fluorine div.). Mem. Disciples of Christ. Ch. Lodge: Optimists (editor newsletter 1971-72). Current work: In-situ mechanistic studies of thermochemical decomposition and combustion processes with deuterium isotope effects, polynitroaliphatic synthesis, selective organic fluorination with xenon difluoride. Subspecialties: Organic chemistry; High temperature chemistry. Home: 15 Beverley Gardens Wargrave-on-Thames Berkshire England RG10 8ED Office: EOARD Box 14 FPO New York NY 09510

SHADDUCK, JOHN ALLEN, veterinary pathologist; b. Toledo, Ohio, Apr. 22, 1939; s. Hugh Allen and Martha Juliet (Niles) S.; m. Mary Lou Lambdin, Apr. 9, 1960; children: James Allen, Margaret Ann. D.V.M., Ohio State U., 1963, M.Sc., 1965, Ph.D., 1967. NIH postdoctoral fellow Ohio State U., Columbus, 1964-68, asst. prof., 1967-72, asso. prof., 1972-73, U. Tex. Health Scis. Center, Dallas, 1973-80, prof., 1980-81; prof., head dept. vet. pathobiology U. Ill., Urbana-Champaign, 1979-85. Editor: Vet. Pathology, 1979; contbr. articles in field to profl. jours. Grantee NIH, 1970-85; WHO, 1974-85; FDA, 1977-79. Mem. AAAS, Am. Coll. Vet. Pathologists, AVMA, Am. Assn. Pathologists. Current Work: Comparative biology of ocular melanomas; inflammation; endothelial cells; immunology of protozoal diseases; in vitro alternatives to animals. Subspecialties: Pathology (veterinary medicine); Microbiology (veterinary medicine). Office: Dept Vet Pathology 2001 S Lincoln Ave Urbana IL 61801

SHADE, BARBARA JEAN, psychology educator; b. Armstrong, Mo., Oct. 30, 1933; d. Murray Kenneth and Edna Rose (Bowman) Robinson; m. Oscar DePriest Shade, Mar. 22, 1954; children: Christina Marie Shade Jones, Kenneth Eugene, Patricia Louise. B.S., Pittsburg (Kans.) State U., 1955; M.S., U. Wis.-Milw., 1967; Ph.D., U. Wis.-Madison, 1973. Lic. sch. psychologist, Wis. lic. secondary tchr., Wis. Tchr. Milw. Pub. Schs., 1960-68; exec. dir. Dane County Head Start, Madison, Wis., 1969-71; postdoctoral fellow Nat. Endowment Humanities, 1973-74; urban edn. specialist Dept. Public Instrn., Madison, 1974-75; asst. prof. U. Wis., Madison, 1975-81; assoc. prof. ednl. psychology U. Wis.-Parkside, Kenosha, 1981—, chmn. dir. edn., 1984—. Mem. Wis. Gov.'s Policy and Planning Task Force, 1971-72; bd. dirs. St. Mary's Hosp. Med. Center, Madison, 1973-81, chmn. bd., 1979-81; v.p. United Way of Dane County, Madison, 1979; mem. Wis. Humanities Com., 1980—. Recipient Chancellor's Service award U. Wis., Madison, 1980; Gov.'s Employment Tng. Office grantee, 1982; Wis. Center for Endl. Research grantee, 1980-82. Mem. Am. Psychol. Assn., Am. Ednl. Research Assn., AAAS, Delta Sigma Theta. Methodist. Current Work: Study of cultural influences on Afro-American patterns of cognition. Subspecialty: Cognition. Home: 3110 Pelham Rd PO Box 9838 Madison WI 53715 Office: University of Wisconsin-Parkside PO Box 2000 Kenosha WI 53141

SHAFFER, HOWARD JEFFREY, clinical psychologist, consultant, researcher, educator; b. Boston, Sept. 1, 1948; s. Milton and Ruth Ann (Weiner) S.; m. Linda Marie Andrews; 1 son, David Andrew. B.A., U. N.H., 1970; M.S., U. Miami, Coral Gables, Fla., 1972, Ph.D., 1974. Lic. psychologist, Mass., N.H. registered psychologist Nat. Register Health Service Providers in Psychology, 1982. Research dir. Psycho-Social Rehab. Ctr. Dade County (Fla.), Inc., 1974-75; clin. dir. Project Turnabout, Inc., Hingham, Mass., 1975-78, East Boston (Mass.) Drug Rehab. Clinic, 1976-77; dir. spl. consultation and treatment program for women Judge Gould Inst. Human Resources, Inc., Worcester, Mass., 1977-78; dir. narcotics treatment program Drug Problems Resource Center, dept. psychiatry Harvard Med. Sch. at Cambridge (Mass.) Hosp. and North Charles Found. for Tng. and Research, 1978-79, dir. tr., 1979-82; asst. dir. tng. dept. psychiatry Harvard Med. Sch. at Cambridge Hosp., 1982—; mem. adj. faculty U. Miami, 1974; mem. clin. faculty Barry Coll., 1974-75; mem. field faculty Lone Mountain Coll., 1974-75; teaching cons. U. Lowell, 1975-76; clin. assoc. prof. counseling psychology Boston U., 1976-78; instr. psychology dept. psychiatry Harvard Med. Sch. at Cambridge Hosp., 1978-81, asst. prof. psychology, 1982—; mem. faculty Mass. Psychol. Center, Boston, 1980—; mem. council on marijuana and health Nat. Orgn. for Reform Marijuana Laws, 1981—. Contbr. articles, revs., abstracts to profl. publs., presentations in field; editor: a book about drug issues Myths and Realities, 1977, (with M. E. Burglass) Classic Contributions in the Addictions, 1981 (alt. main selection Behavioral Sci. Book Club 1981); (with Harvey Milkman) Addictions; Multidisciplinary Treatments and Perspectives, 1985; assoc. editor: Bull. of Psychologists in Addictive Behavior, 1982—, Jour. Substance Abuse Treatment; guest editor: spl. issue Advances in Alcohol and Substance Abuse, 1983; mem. editorial rev. bd.: spl. issue Jour. Psychoactive Drugs, 1981—, Advances in Alcohol and Substance Abuse, 1982—. Mem. Andover (Mass.) Substance Abuse Com., 1982. Recipient 1st place award U. N.H. Undergrad. Conf. for Psychol. Research, 1969. Mem. Am. Psychol. Assn., AAAS, Soc. Psychologists in Addictive Behavior, Psi Chi, Phi Kappa Phi. Democrat. Jewish. Clubs: Harvard (Boston). Current Work: Cognitive, behavioral, and psychodynamic factors associated with substance use and abuse; the social psychology of psychotherapy; philosophy of science. Subspecialties: Substance use and abuse; Social psychology. Home: 171 Summer St Andover MA 01810 Office: Dept Psychiatry Harvard Med Sch 1493 Cambridge St Cambridge MA 02139

SHAFFER, PAUL RAYMOND, geologist, administrator; b. Fostoria, Ohio, Oct. 18, 1910; s. Joseph William and Estella Haxton (Butler) S.; m. Gene Elizabeth Hoopes, Jan. 16, 1943; children—William H., Elizabeth A. A.B. cum laude, Coll. Wooster, 1935; M.S., Ohio State U., 1937, Ph.D., 1945. Instr. U. N.H., Durham, 1939-40; chief geologist Ranney Water Corp., N.Y.C., 1940-44; assoc. prof. geology Ohio Wesleyan U., 1944-47, head dept. geology, 1944-47; asst. prof. geology U. Ill., Urbana, 1947-48, assoc. prof., 1948-52, prof., 1953-68, assoc. provost for undergrad. affairs, 1963-65; co-dir. 1st Am. Geol. Inst.-Field Inst., Great Britain, summer 1961; program dir. NSF, 1961-62, head internat. sci. devel. sect., office internat. sci. activities, Washington, 1966-67; cons.-dir. Seminar for Secondary Sch. Tchrs., Nigeria, summer 1962; dir. office internat. programs Nat. Assn. State Univs. and Land-Grant Colls., 1968-75. Co-author: (with H. S. Zim) Rocks and Minerals, 1957; (with others) Fossils, 1962; author lab. manuals; also articles on erosion surfaces, shore erosion and glacial stratigraphy. Vice pres. CSC, Marysville, Ohio, 1983—. Recipient Orton award Ohio State U., 1964, Patriotic Civilian Service cert. U.S. Army, 1967. Fellow Geol. Soc. Am., AAAS, Ohio Acad. Sci.; mem. Am. Assn. Petroleum Geologists, Internat. Glaciological Soc., Ill. Acad. Sci., Nat. Assn. Geology Tchrs. (archivist), Sigma Xi, Omicron Delta Kappa, Sigma Phi Epsilon. Current work: Ground water supply; glacial Stratigraphy; development of land forms (geomorphology). Subspecialty: Geology. Home: 518 Hickory Dr Marysville OH 43040

SHAFI, MUHAMMAD IQBAL, biology educator; b. Kanpur, India, Aug. 23, 1943; came to U.S., 1980; s. Mohammad and Ashrafunnisa (Begum) S.; m. Fahmida Iqbal, Dec. 15, 1973; 1 child, Nadeem. B.Sc. with honors, U. Karachi, Pakistan, 1964, M.Sc., 1965; Ph.D., U. Toronto, Ont., Can., 1972. Research asst. Cereal Diseases Research, Murree, Pakistan, 1966-67; biologist Ontario Ministry of Natural Resources, Toronto, 1973-74; ecologist Andre Marsan and Assocs., Montreal, Que., Can., 1975-76; postdoctoral research asst. U. N.B. (Can.), Fredericton, 1977-79; asst. prof. dept. biology Rust Coll., Holly Springs, Miss., 1980—; councillor Karachi U. Student Council Soc., 1962-63. Contbr. articles and guide to profl. jours.; editor: The Botanist jour, 1964-65. Postdoctoral assistantship NRC Can., 1978; U.S. Dept. Edn. grantee, 1981—. Mem. Can. Botanical Soc., Am. Ecol. Soc., Brit. Ecol. Soc., Quebec Assn. Biologists, Internat. Assn. Ecologists. Muslim. Current Work: Fire ecology, fires and weeds, right of way and multiple uses. Subspecialties: Plant cell and tissue culture; Cell and tissue culture. Home: 541 N Randolph St Holly Springs MS 38635 Office: Rust Coll 1 Rust Ave Holly Springs MS 38635

SHAH, BABUBHAI VADILAL, scientist; b. Bombay, India, Feb. 6, 1935; U.S., 1966; m. Ketki Desai, Mar. 10, 1966; children—Parag, Mona. B.Sc. in Math., U. Bombay, 1955, M.Sc. in Stats., 1957, Ph.D., 1960. Research assoc. Iowa State U., Ames, 1959-62; research analyst Karamchand Premchand Ltd., Ahmedabad, India, 1962-66; statistician Research Triangle Inst., Research Triangle Park, N.C., 1966-68, acting mgr., 1968-71, assoc. dir., 1972-75, chief scientist, 1976—; adj. assoc. prof. U. N.C.-Chapel Hill, 1971-79, adj. prof., 1979—. Fellow Am. Statis. Assn., Royal Statis. Soc., Internat. Statis. Inst.; mem. Inst. Math. Stats., Soc. Indsl. and Applied Math., Assn. Computing Machinery, IEEE. Current work: Development of computer language for Statistical and data analysis. Subspecialties: Statistics; Programming languages.

SHAH, KISHORE RAMANLAL, polymer scientist; b. Mysore, India, Feb. 15, 1943; came to U.S., 1967; s. Ramanlal and Kusum Ramanlal Shah; m. Aruna Jain, July 10, 1967; children—Priti, Vinay. B.Sc., U. Bombay, India, 1964, B.Sc. in Tech., 1966; M.S., Lowell Tech. Inst., 1970; Ph.D., U. Md., 1975. Postdoctoral assoc. U. Fla., Gainesville, 1975-76; research assoc. Kendall Co., Lexington, Mass., 1976-84; prin. scientist Instrumentation Lab. Inc., Andover, Mass., 1984-85; mng. polymer research Health-Chem Corp., South Plainfield, N.J., 1985—. Contbr. articles to profl. jours. Patentee in field. Mem. Am. Chem. Soc. Current work: Multicomponent polymer systems, acrylic polymers, adhesives, bioresorbable polymers, biomedical polymer applications-controlled drug delivery systems, soft contact lenses, vascular prosthesis, wound management; synthesis of polypeptides, ionic polymers and hydrogels. Subspecialties: Polymer chemistry; Biomaterials. Home: 568 Cabot Hill Rd Bridgewater NJ 08807 Office: Health-Chem Corp 200 B Corporate Ct South Plainfield NJ 07080

SHAH, RAJIV RAJARAM, applied physicist; b. Maharashtra, India, July 11, 1953; came to U.S., 1972, naturalized, 1976; s. Rajaram Damodar and Kamala (Rajaram) S.; m. Shrida Rajiv, Dec. 18, 1980. B.Sc. in Physics, U. Poona, India, 1972; M.S. in E.E, Rice U., 1974, Ph.D., 1976. Research asst. Rice U., Houston, 1972-76; Dr. Chaim Weizmann postdoctoral research fellow Calif. Inst. Tech., Pasadena, 1976-79; mem. tech. staff Tex. Instruments, Dallas, 1979—. Contbr. articles to profl. jours. Govt. India Nat. Sci. Talent Search scholar, 1969-72. Mem. Am. Phys. Soc., IEEE, Optical Soc. Am., Electrochem. Soc., Am. Vaccum Soc., Materials Research Soc. Developed laser assisted removal of saw damage in silicon slices; apparatus and method for photolithography with phase conjugate optics; reduction in temperature dependence and standard deviation of polysilicon resistors by laser annealing; large crystal growth in polisilicon on oxide or nitride by dual wavelength laser annealing for absorption optimized heating of oxide or nitride; laser processing of PSG, oxide and nitride via absorption optimized selective laser annealing. Current Work: Laser applications, device physics, device processing; laser processing of semiconductor devices, 3-D integration of semiconductor devices, device processing, device physics and device modeling. Subspecialty: Integrated circuits. Home: 2116 Newcombe Dr Plano TX 75075 Office: Texas Instruments MS-82 PO Box 225012 Dallas TX 75265

SHAH, SAIYID MASROOR, medical physicist; b. Rampur, India, Jan. 8, 1938; came to U.S., 1974; s. Syed Maqsood and Noor Jehan (Ali) S.; m. Janice Moore, Aug. 8, 1970. Ph.D., Tex. Tech. U., 1970. Lectr. in physics SRA/DJ Colls., Karachi, 1958-64; asst. prof. physics U. Karachi, 1970-72; assoc. prof. physics Baluchistan U. Quetta, 1972-73; fgn. research fellow Sophia U., Tokyo, 1973-74; postdoctoral research fellow physics M.D. Anderson Hosp., Houston, 1976; med. physicist Rosewood Hosp., Houston, 1976-83, cons., instr. continuing edn. program, 1976-83; med. physicist St. Mary's Med. Ctr., Evansville, Ind., 1984—. Contbr. articles to profl. jours. Japan Soc. for Promotion of Sci. Fgn. Research fellow, 1973; Fulbright Travel scholar, 1964; recipient Am. Friends of Middle East Hon. Mention award, 1969. Mem. Assn. Physicists in Medicine. Muslim. Current Work: Radiation physics; cancer treatment planning; radiation safety; cancer treatment plan optimization for high energy radiation beams, quality control, dosimetry, radiation safety. Subspecialties: Medical physics; Atomic and molecular physics. Home: 7522 Nottingham St Newburgh IN 47630 Office: St Mary's Med Ctr 3700 Washington Ave Evansville IN 47750

SHAH, SUDHIR AMRATLAL, biologist, cancer research scientist; b. Kampala, Uganda, Nov. 23, 1944; came to U.S., 1980, naturalized, 1981; s. Amratlal Tribhovandas and Chandramani (Amratlal) S.; m. Hema Sudhir, Mar. 7, 1972; children: Neha, Reena. B.Sc., U. Bombay, India, 1967; M.Phil., U. London, 1972; Ph.D., U. Newcastle upon Tyne, Eng., 1977; licentiate, Royal Inst. Chemistry, Slough Coll. Tech., Eng., 1969. Tech. officer Chester Beatty Research Inst., London, 1968-72; research assoc. U. Newcastle upon Tyne, 1972-76, research fellow, cancer research unit, 1976-80; guest worker-sr. research assoc. dept. chem. engring. Cancer Research Lab., Carnegie Mellon U., Pitts., 1980-82; tumor biologist-immunopharmacologist biomed. products dept. new tech. research E.I. duPont de Nemours and Co., Inc. North Billerica, Mass., 1983—. Contbr. numerous articles and papers to profl. jours. Brit. Empire Cancer Research Campaign postdoctoral research fellow, 1976-80. Mem. Am. Assn. for Cancer Research, AAAS, Sigma Xi. Current Work: Tumor biology/physiology/immunology, hyperthermia, immunotherapy, chemotherapy and radiotherapy. Metastatic animal tumor models, human cancer cells in culture; diagnostic and therapeutic aspects of monoclonal antibodies. Subspecialties: Cancer research (medicine); Physiology (medicine).

SHAH, SURENDRA POONAMCHAND, civil engineering educator; b. Bombay, India, Aug. 30, 1936; came to U.S., 1959, naturalized, 1966; s. Poonamchand C. and Maniben (Modi) S.; m. Dorothie Crispell, June 9, 1962; children—Daniel S., Byron C. B.Engring., B.V.M. Coll., 1959; M.S., Lehigh U., 1960; Ph.D., Cornell U., 1965. Design engr. Modjeski & Masters, Harrisburg, Pa., 1960-62; faculty mem. U. Ill., Chgo., 1965-81, prof. civil engring., 1973-81; prof. civil engring., grad. coordinator structures program Northwestern U., Evanston, Ill., 1981—; guest prof. MIT, 1969-70, Delft U., Netherlands, 1976-77, Denmark Tech. U., 1984; cons. to industry, U.S.A., Western Europe; keynote speaker at several internat. symposia. Editor: High Strength Concrete, 1980; Fatigue of Concrete Structures, 1982; bd. editors Internat. Jour. Cement Composites, 1980—, Materials and Structures, 1982—, Internat. Jour. Devel. Tech., 1983—, Jour. Ferrocement, 1979—. Contbr. numerous articles to profl. jours. Research grantee NSF, U.S. Army Research Office, U.S. Air Force Office Sci. Research, NATO Sci. Div., 1965—. Fellow Am. Concrete Inst. (pres. Chgo. chpt. 1974); mem. ASTM (tech. com. 1983—, Thompson award 1983), Internat. Union Testing and Research Labs. for Materials and Structures (Gold medal 1980, chmn. tech. com. 1982—), ASCE (chmn. tech. com. 1985—), Prestressed Concrete Inst. (transportation research bd. 1970—). Current work: Principal investigator of 5 research grants on high strength concrete, dynamic loading, fiber reinforced concrete, rock mechanics, fracture mechanics, earthquake design, failure of concrete structures during construction. Subspecialties: Acoustical engineering; Reproductive endocrinology. Home: 2212 McDaniel St Evanston IL 60201 Office: Civil Engring Dept Northwestern U Evanston IL 60201

SHAHADY, EDWARD JOHN, physician; b. Fairmont, W.Va., June 2, 1938; s. Joseph E. and Mary V. (Mallamo) S.; m. Sandra Jean Kovach, Sept. 13, 1958; children—Mary, John, Thomas, Elizabeth, Edward, William. B.S. in Biology, Wheeling Coll., 1960; M.D., W.Va. U., 1964. Diplomate: Am. Bd. Family Practice. Rotating intern Akron (Ohio) City Hosp., 1964-65, resident, 1967-68, practice medicine specializing in family practice, Akron, 1968-70; dir. family practice residency Akron City Hosp., 1970-76; chmn. dept. family practice Northeastern Ohio Univs. Coll. Medicine, 1974-76; prof., chmn. dept. family medicine U. N.C., Chapel Hill, 1976—; football team physician Chapel Hill High Sch., 1979—. Contbr. articles on family medicine and med. edn. to profl. jours. Bd. dirs. Women's Health Counseling Service, Chapel Hill, 1979-80; trustee Child Guidance Center, Akron, 1971-76, Denton House, 1973-76. Served with USN, 1965-67. Recipient Eben J. Carey Phi Chi Meml. award, 1964; Mead Johnson scholar, 1968. Fellow Am. Acad. Family Physicians; mem. N.C. Acad. Family Physicians, Soc. of Tchrs. Family Medicine (chmn. edn. com. 1974-79, pres. 1980-81). Current Work: Sports medicine. Subspecialty: Family practice. Home: 2515 Buxton Ct Chapel Hill NC 27514 Office: Dept of Family Medicine U NC Trailer 15 269H Chapel Hill NC 27514

SHAHINPOOR, MOHSEN, engineering educator; b. Tehran, Iran, Sept. 14, 1943; came to U.S., 1966, naturalized, 1981; s. Ali Asghar and Zarrin (Hajirajabali) S.; m. Jamileh Farahmand, Sept. 9, 1976; children: David, Parsa, Sheerin. B.Sc., Abadan Inst. Tech., 1966; M.Sc., U. Del., 1968, Ph.D., 1970. Assoc. prof. Pahlavi U., Shiraz, Iran, 1972-76, prof., 1976-78, Northwestern U., Evanston, Ill., 1978-79; assoc. prof. Clarkson Coll. Tech., Potsdam, N.Y., 1979-82, prof., chmn. dept. mech. and indsl. engring, 1982—, chmn. solid mechanics, 1982—. Editor-in-chief: Iran Jour. Sci. & Tech, 1975-78; book series: Adv. Mech. Flow Granular Mats, 1982—; contbr. over 150 articles to profl. jours. Named Researcher of Yr. Alborz Found., 1976; Inventor of Yr. Ministry of High Edn., Iran, 1977. Mem. ASME, Am. Acad. Mechanics, Soc. Engring. Sci., AAAS, U.S. Colloid and Surface Sci. Inventor in field. Current Work: Mechanics and flow granular materials, liquid crystals, materials with microstructure, systems analysis and machine design, design of industrial robots. Subspecialties: Mechanical engineering; Materials (engineering). Office: Clarkson Coll Tech Potsdam NY 13676

SHAHRYAR, ISHAQ M., physical chemist; b. Kabul, Afghanistan, Jan. 10, 1936; s. Ahmad Ali and Zahra S. B.S. in Phys. Chemistry, U. Calif., 1961, M.A., 1968. Founder, pres. Solec Internat., Inc. (became subs. Pilkington Bros., P.L.C. of Eng.), Hawthorne, Calif., 1976—; Counsel to chancellor U. Calif., 1981—. Republican. Moslem. Inventor low cost solar cell, 1972; patentee photovoltaics tech., 1977. Current Work: Administration of technology, research and development, manufacturing future solar cell technology. Subspecialty: Solar energy. Office: 12533 Chadron Ave Hawthorne CA 90250*

SHAIKH, ZAHIR AHMAD, toxicologist, educator; b. Jullundur, India, Mar. 31, 1945; s. Zafer Ahmad and Mehmooda Begum (Chohan) S.; m. Mary Butterfield, Aug. 23, 1975; children: Faraz, Kashan, Summur. B.Sc., U. Karachi, Pakistan, 1965, M.Sc., 1967; Ph.D., Dalhousie U., 1972. Research assoc. environ. health U. Okla., Oklahoma City, 1972-73; sr. postdoctoral fellow in toxicology U. Rochester, 1973-75, asst. prof., 1975-81, assoc. prof., 1981-82; assoc. prof. pharmacology and toxicology U. R.I., Kingston, 1982—, chmn., 1985—; spl. reviewer toxicology study sect. NIH, 1983-85, mem. toxicology study sect., 1985—. Contbr. articles to profl. jours. NIH fellow, 1973-75; NIH grantee, 1975—. Mem. Soc. Toxicology (past pres. metals sect.), Soc. Exptl. Biology and Medicine, Am. Soc. Pharmacology and Exptl. Therapeutics, N.Y. Acad. Scis., Tissue Culture Assn., AAAS. Current Work: Heavy metal metabolism and toxicology; role of metallothionein in metal toxicology; detoxification processes; biol. indicators of metal exposure. Subspecialties: Toxicology (medicine); Environmental toxicology. Home: 75 Greenwood Dr Peace Dale RI 02879 Office: Dept Pharmacology and Toxicology U RI Kingston RI 02881

SHALEV, MOSHE, veterinarian, educator; b. Kibbutz Kfar Blum, Upper Galilee, Israel, Oct. 27, 1947; came to U.S., 1971; s. Tuvya and Miriam (Testa) S.; m. Dorothy McCormick, 1978; children—Sarah, Leah, Rachel. B.Sc., Hebrew U., Jerusalem, 1969, M.Sc., 1971; V.M.D., U. Pa., 1975. Diplomate Am. Coll. Lab. Animal Medicine. Clinician, staff cardiologist Women's SPCA, Phila., 1975-76; clin. veterinarian, research assoc. MIT, Cambridge, 1976-80; dir. div. lab. animal medicine Sch. Medicine, U. Pa., Phila., 1980—, asst. clin. prof. human genetics, Sch. Medicine, 1984—; cons. veterinarian Monell Chem. Ctr. for Senses, Phila., 1984, Phila. Coll. Pharmacy and Sci., Phila., 1983—; cons. Am. Assn. for Accreditation of Lab. Animal Care, 1984. Contbr. articles to publs. including Jour. Heredity, Cancer, Jour. AVMA, Lab. Animal, Lab. Animal Sci. NIH research grantee, 1984; basic sci. research grantee Sch. Medicine U. Pa., 1981-84. Mem. AVMA, Am. Assn. for Lab. Animal Sci., Am. Soc. Ultrasound, AASS, Phila. Area and Vicinity Lab. Animal Veterinarians (bd. dirs.). Current work: Laboratory animal medicine, study of aging, vas diferens comparative anatomy, veterinary medicine. Subspecialties: Laboratory animal medicine; Genetics and genetic engineering (medicine). Home: 406 Pembroke Rd Bala Cynwyd PA 19004 Office: Sch Medicine 79 Med Labs 63 Univ Pa Philadelphia PA 19104

SHAMBAUGH, GEORGE ELMER, III, physician, educator, researcher; b. Boston, Dec. 21, 1931; s. George E. and Marietta Moss (Long) S.; m. Katharine Margaret Matthews, Dec. 29, 1956; children: George Elmer IV, Benjamin Albert, Daniel Frederick, James Bradley, Elizabeth Matthews. B.A., Oberlin Coll., 1954; M.D., Cornell U., 1958. Diplomate: Am. Bd. Internal Medicine. Intern Denver Gen. Hosp., 1958-59; resident in internal medicine Walter Reed Gen. Hosp., Washington, 1961-64; research internist Walter Reed Army Med. Ctr., Frederick, Md., 1964-67; fellow in physiologic chemistry U. Wis., Madison, 1967-69; mem. staff endocrinology Northwestern U. Med. Sch., Chgo., 1969—, asst. prof. medicine, 1969-74, assoc. prof. medicine, 1974-81, prof. medicine, 1981—; chief endocrinology and metabolism VA Lakeside Med. Ctr., Chgo., 1974—; attending physician Northwestern Meml. Hosp., Chgo., 1977—. Contbr. chpts. to textbooks, articles to profl. jours. Served to maj. U.S. Army, 1959-67. Schweppe Found. fellow, 1972-74; VA research grantee Chgo., 1975—. Fellow ACP, Inst. Medicine of Chgo.; mem. Am. Fedn. Clin. Research, Sci. Research Soc. Am., Endocrine Soc., Central Soc. for Clin. Research, Am. Thyroid Assn., Am. Inst. Nutrition, Am. Soc. Clin. Nutrition, Am. Physiol. Soc., Sigma Xi. Current Work: Effects of altered nutrition on fetal and neonatal development, including brain, liver, placenta, cell replication, mechanism altered by changing nutrient composition. Subspecialties: Internal medicine; Neuroendocrinology. Home: 530 S Stone Ave La Grange IL 60525 Office: Va Lakeside Med Center 333 E Huron St Chicago IL 60611

SHAMBERGER, RAYMOND JOSEPH, JR., biochemist, clin. chemist, researcher; b. Munising, Mich., Aug. 23, 1934; s. Raymond Joseph and Kathryn Anna S.; m. Barbara Ann Walsh, Jan. 31, 1959; children: Chrissa, Erik, Monica, Kara, Michael, Shannon. B.S., Alma (Mich.) Coll., 1956; M.S., Oreg. State U., 1959; Ph.D., Miami (Fla.) U., 1963. Cert. Am. Bd. Clin. Chemistry, Nat. Registry Clin. Chemistry. Dir. research Sutton Research Corp., Santa Monica, Calif., 1963-64; with Roswell Park Meml. Inst., Buffalo, 1964-69; sect. head enzyme lab. Cleve. Clinic Found., 1969—; prof. clin. chemistry Cleve. State U. Contbr. articles profl. jours. Recipient award Cancer Research, 1981. Mem. Am. Inst. Biol. Sci., N.Y. Acad. Scis., European Assn. Cancer Research, Soc. Geochemistry and Health, Am. Chem. Soc., Am. Assn. Clin. Chemistry, Am. Assn. Cancer Research, Am. Soc. Clin. Pathology, Fedn. Am. Socs. Exptl. Biology, Sigma Xi. Roman Catholic. Patentee in field. Current Work: Mechanisms of cancer formation, enzyme and trace metal chemistry. Subspecialties: Clinical chemistry; Nutrition (biology).

SHAMOIAN, CHARLES A., geriatric psychiatrist, educator, hospt. adminstr.; b. Worcester, Mass., Oct. 5, 1931; s. Garabed and Anna (Varjabedian) S.; m. Paula, Oct. 8, 1961; children: Paula Ann, Charles R. A.B., Clark U., 1950, M.A., 1954; Ph.D., Tufts U., 1961, M.D., 1966. Diplomate: Am. Bd. Psychiatry and Neurology, 1981. Asso. prof. clin. psychiatry and pharmacology Cornell U. Coll. Medicine, N.Y.C., 1979-84, prof. clin. psychiatry, assoc. prof. pharmacology, 1984—; dir. geriatric services N.Y. Hosp.—Cornell Med. Center, White Plains, 1979—. Contbr. articles to sci. jours. Mem. Larchmont Little League. USPHS fellow, 1960-61. Fellow Am. Psychiat. Assn.; mem. Am. Psychopath. Assn., Am. Geriatric Soc., Am. Assn. Geriatric Psychiatry (dir.). Current Work: General psychiatry and geriatric psychiatry; geriatric clinical psychopharmacology, dementia, depression. Subspecialties: Psychiatry; Psychopharmacology. Office: 21 Bloomingdale Rd White Plains NY 10605

SHAMOO, ADIL E(LIAS), biophysicist, educator, researcher; b. Baghdad, Iraq, Aug. 1, 1941; came to U.S., 1964, naturalized, 1973; s. Elias M. Shamoo and Mariam Shamoo Mansour; m. Joan Hutchison, Dec. 16, 1967; children—Abraheem, Zachary, Jessica. B.Sc., U. Baghdad, 1962; M.S., U. Louisville, 1966; Ph.D., CUNY, 1970. Instr. Speed Sch., U. Louisville, 1965-68; asst. in biophysics Mt. Sinai Grad. Sch. Biol. Scis., CUNY, 1968-70, assoc. in biophysics dept. physiology and Grad. Sch., CUNY, 1970-71, asst. prof. physiology Mt. Sinai Sch., 1971-73, mem. grad. faculty in biomed. scis. Grad. Ctr., CUNY, 1972-73; asst. prof. radiation; biology and biophysics U. Rochester, N.Y., 1973-75, assoc. prof., 1975-79; prof. biol. chemistry Med. Sch., U. Md., Balt., 1979—, chmn. dept. biol. chemistry, 1979-82, head membrane biochemistry research lab., 1982—; guest worker labs. biophysics and neurochemistry NIH, Bethesda, Md., 1972-73; cons. Kodak Co., Rochester, 1976-77; guest prof. Max-Planck Inst. for Biophysics, Frankfort, Fed. Republic Germany, summer 1976, 1977-78; grant reviewer for various agys; mem. phys. biochemistry study sect. NIH, New Orleans, 1980; mem. peer rev. com. Md. Heart Assn., 1981-84; speaker, lectr. at numerous seminars, symposiums. Editor: Carriers and Channels in Biological Systems, 1975; Carriers and Channels in Biological Systems—Transport Proteins, 1980; co-editor: Membrane Toxicity, 1977; co-founder, co-editor-in-chief Membrane Biochemistry, 1977—. Contbr. numerous articles to profl. pubIs. Mem. sci. rev. com., chmn. subcom. on spl. edn. Howard County Sch. System, Md., 1984; mem. adv. com., chmn. curriculum com. Howard County Bd. Edn.; soccer coach, 1979—. Grad. fellow U. Louisville, 1964-65; NIH tng. fellow U. Louisville Sch. Medicine, 1967; established investigator Am. Heart Assn., 1976-79; fellow Neurosci. Research Program, Boulder, Colo., summer 1977; grantee NSF, 1973-74, 79-81, 80-81, NIH, 1974-77, 75, 76-79, 78-79, 79-80, ERDA, 1973-77, 76, EPA, 1976, Nat. Inst. Environ. Health Scis., 1976-78, 79-84, Upjohn Internat., Inc., 1976-77, 77-78, Muscular Dystrophy Assn., 1976, 77, 79, 80, 81, 82, Genesee Valley Heart Assn., 1977-78, Dept. Energy, 1977-78, 80-83, Office Naval Research, 1979-81, 80-81, 81-82. Mem. Internat. Soc. Heart Research, Am. Heart Assn. (basic sci. council), Am. Soc. biol. Chemists, Am. Physiol. Soc., Biophys. Soc. (exec. com. bioenergetic subgroup 1980-81, sec.-treas. membrane biophysics group 1983-85, chmn. 1982-83), Am. Biophys. Soc. U.S. Bioenergetics Group, N.Y. Acad. Scis., Sigma Xi, Sigma Pi Sigma, Phi Kappa Phi. Current work: Hormonal regulation of cardiac muscle. Subspecialties: Biophysics (biology); Biochemistry (medicine). Home: 9245 Seawind Ct Columbia MD 21045 Office: Dept Biol Chemistry U Md Sch Medicine 660 W Redwood St Baltimore MD 21201

SHAMOS, MORRIS HERBERT, physics educator; b. Cleve., Sept. 1, 1917; s. Max and Lillian (Wasser) S.; m. Marion Jean Cahn, Nov. 26, 1942; 1 son, Michael Ian. A.B., NYU, 1941, M.S., 1943, Ph.D., 1948; postgrad., MIT, 1941-42. Faculty NYU, 1942—, prof. physics, 1959-83, prof. emeritus, 1983—; chmn. dept. Washington Sq. Coll., 1957-70; sr. v.p. research and devel. Technicon Corp., 1970-75, chief sci. officer, 1975-83, also dir., prin. sci. cons., 1983—; pres. M.H. Shamos & Assocs., 1983—; dir. Sci. Leasing, Inc., 1983—; pres. Protein Databases, Inc., 1984, dir., 1984—; cons. pvt. industry; cons. Armament Center, USAF, 1955-57, Tung-Sol Electric, Inc., 1949-65, Office Pub. Information, UN, 1958, NBC, 1957-67, AEC, 1957-70, N.Y. Eye and Ear Infirmary, 1961-64, 79—, L.I. Jewish Hosp., 1962—, N.Y.C. Health Dept., 1961-70, Technicon Instruments Corp., 1964-70, U.S. Office Edn., 1964-72. Author: Great Experiments in Physics, 1959; Co-editor: Recent Advances in Science, 1956, Industrial and Safety Problems of Nuclear Technology, 1950; cons. editor, Addison-Wesley Pub. Co., 1965-69; Adv. bd.: Jour. Coll. Sci. Teaching, 1971-75, 76-80, Clin. Lab. Guide, Am. Chem. Soc, 1972-76. Dir. tng., N.Y.C. Office Civil Def., 1950-54; subscribing mem. N.Y. Philharmonic Soc.; mem. adv. council Pace U., 1971—, N.Y. Poly. Inst., 1980—, Manhattan Coll., 1983—. Trustee, Hackley Sch., 1971-80, Westchester Arts Council. Fellow N.Y. Acad. Scis. (past chmn. phys. scis., bd. govs. 1977-84, rec. sec. 1978-80, v.p. 1980-81, pres. 1982), AAAS; mem. Nat. Assn. Ednl. Broadcasters, Am. Phys. Soc., IEEE, AAUP, AFTRA, Am. Chem. Soc., Nat. Sci. Tchrs. Assn. Am. (pres. 1967), Assn. Physics Tchrs. Britain, Chemist's Club, Phi Beta Kappa, Sigma Xi, Pi Mu Epsilon, Sigma Pi Sigma. Club: Cosmos. Spl. research atomic and nuclear physics, biophysics. Current Work: Consultant in high technology to the investment community, particulary in health care field. Subspecialties: Biophysics (physics); Bioinstrumentation. Home: 3515 Henry Hudson Pkwy New York NY 10463

SHAN, HSIN-TSAN GRACE, microbiologist; b. Taiwan, June 29, 1950; d. Tse-Wen and Chiung-Hwa (Lin) Lo; m. Ming-chien Shan, Aug. 3, 1974; children: Vivian Yu-Wen, Eric Yu-Sen. M.S., Rutgers U., 1974. Microbiologist SRI Internat., Menlo Park, Calif., 1975-80; mem. sci. staff BNR Inc., Mountain View, Calif., 1980—. Mem. Am. Microbiology Soc., Assn. Computing Machinery. Roman Catholic. Current Work: Computerized analysis methodology for microbiological studies; data base management system. Subspecialties: Microbiology; Database systems. Office: 685A E Middlefield Rd Mountain View CA 94043

SHAN, ROBERT KUOCHENG, biology educator; b. Gaoan, China, Nov. 9, 1927; came to U.S., 1963, naturalized, 1971; s. Shaoyi and Binnan (Lan) S.; m. Lily Chen, Sept. 7, 1963; 1 child, Tony Donguang. B.S., Taiwan Normal U., 1956; M.S., U. B.C., Vancouver, Can., 1962; Ph.D., Ind. U., 1967. Instr., Nat. Taiwan U. Taipei, 1956-59; teaching fellow Dalhousie U. Halifax, Can., 1962-63; research assoc. Ind. U., Bloomington, 1967-69; asst. prof. biology Fairmont State Coll., W.Va., 1969-70, assoc. prof., 1970-72, prof., 1972—. Author: Animal Population Ecology, 1983. Mem. Ecol. Soc. Am., Am. Inst. Biol. Scis., Am. Soc. Limnology and Oceanography, Sigma Xi. Current work: Aquatic community succession to ecological perturbation. Subspecialties: Population biology; Ecosystems analysis. Office: Dept Biology Fairmont State Coll Fairmont WV 26554

SHANDS, JOSEPH WALTER, JR., medical educator, researcher; b. Jacksonville, Fla., Nov. 1, 1930; s. Joseph Walter and Mary Courtney (Harris) S.; m. Elizabeth Anne Rogers, June 15, 1955; children—Walter Elizabeth, Carol, Marian. A.B., Princeton U., 1952; M.D., Duke U., 1956. Intern Duke Hosp., Durham, N.C., 1956-57; resident U. Wash. Hosps., Seattle, 1959-61; asst. prof. microbiology U. Fla., Gainesville, 1965-68, assoc. prof., 1968-70, prof., 1970-76, prof. medicine, chief infectious diseases, 1976—. Editor Infection and Immunity, 1970-79, editor-in-chief, 1979—. Contbr. articles to sci. jours. Served to capt. USMC, 1957-59. Fellow Infectious Diseases Soc.; mem. Am. Soc. Microbiology, Am. Assn. Immunologists, AAAS, Reticuloendothelial Soc., Sigma Xi (assoc.), Alpha Omega Alpha. Current Work: Nature and function of clotting factors made by white blood cells. Subspecialty: Immunotoxicology. Home: 1632 NW 24 St Gainesville FL 32605 Office: U Fla Coll Medicine PO Box U277 Gainesville FL 32610

SHANK, CHARLES VERNON, electrical engineer; b. Mt. Holly, N.J., July 12, 1943. B.S., U. Calif.-Berkeley, 1965, M.S., 1966, Ph.D. in Elec. Engring, 1969. Mem. tech. staff Bell Labs., Holmdel, N.J., 1969—, head dept. quantum physics and electronics, 1976—. Recipient Edward Longstreth medal Franklin Inst., 1983; Morris E. Leeds award IEEE, 1983. Mem. Nat. Acad. Engring. Subspecialty: Electrical engineering. Office: Bell Labs Crawford Corners Rd Holmdel NJ 07733*

SHANK, MAURICE EDWIN, aeronautical engineer; b. N.Y.C., Apr. 22, 1921; s. Edwin A. and Viola (Lewis) S.; m. Virginia Lee King, Sept. 25, 1948; children: Christopher King, Hilary Lee, Diana Lewis. B.S., Carnegie Mellon U., Pitts., 1942; Sc.D., M.I.T., 1949. Registered profl. engr., Mass. Assoc. prof. mech. engring. M.I.T., 1949-60; dir. Advanced Materials Research and Devel. Lab., Pratt & Whitney Aircraft, 1960-70, mgr. materials engring. and research, 1971-72, dir. engring. tech., 1972-80, dir. engine design and structures engring., 1980-81; dir. engring-tech., Pratt & Whitney Engring. Div., United Technologies Corp., East Hartford, Conn., 1981—; mem. aero. adv. com., mem. subcom. aero. propulsion NASA, 1978—, chmn., 1978-81; mem. vis. com. aeros. and astronautics M.I.T., 1979—; mem. vis. com. metallurgy and materials sci. U. Pa., 1970-83. Cons. editor, McGraw-Hill Book Co., 1960—; Contbr. articles to profl. jours. Bd. dirs., mem. exec. com. Coordinating Research Council, 1976—. Served to maj. U.S. Army, 1942-46. Fellow ASME, Metall. Soc. of AIME, AIAA; mem. Conn. Acad. Sci. and Engring., Nat. Acad. Engrs. Current Work: Aeronautical propulsion, analytical and component activities to support present and future engine programs, research and devel. to assure a superior level future technology. Subspecialties: Mechanical engineering; Aeronautical engineering. Office: 400 Main St Mail Stop 162-31 East Hartford CT 06108

SHANK, ROBERT ELY, physician, emeritus preventive medicine educator; b. Louisville, Sept. 2, 1914; s. Oliver Orlando and Isabel Thompson (Ely) S.; m. Eleanor Caswell, July 29, 1942; children: Jane, Robert Oliver, Bruce. A.B., Westminster Coll., 1935; M.D., Washington U., 1939. Diplomate: Am. Bd. Nutrition. Intern, house physician Barnes Hosp., 1939-41; asst. resident physician, asst. in research Hosp. Rockefeller Inst. Med. Research, 1941-46; research asso. div. nutrition and physiology Pub. Health Research Inst. City N.Y., 1946-48; prof. preventive medicine Washington U. Sch. Medicine, 1948-55, Danforth prof. preventive medicine, 1955-83, prof. emeritus preventive medicine, 1983—; Cutter lectr. preventive medicine Harvard, 1964; Mem. food and nutrition bd. NRC, 1949-69; spl. cons. nutrition USPHS, 1949-53; chmn. adv. bd. health and hosps., St. Louis County, 1949-54; med. adv. bd. St. Louis Vis. Nurses Assn., 1950—; mem. com. food and nutrition nat. adv. bd. health services A.R.C., 1950-53; mem. adv. com. metabolism Office Surgeon Gen., 1956-60, mem. adv. com. on nutrition, 1964-72; mem. Am. Bd. Nutrition, 1955-64, sec., treas., 1958-64; mem. Nat. Bd. Med. Examiners, 1957-58; co-dir. nutrition survey NIH, Peru, 1959, N.E. Brazil, 1963; mem. sci. adv. bd. Nat. Vitamin Found., 1958-61; mem. nutrition study sect. NIH, 1964-68, chmn. sect., 1966-68; mem. gastroenterology and nutrition tng. com., 1968-69, mem. nat. adv. child health and human devel. council, 1969-73; mem. clin. application and prevention adv. com. Nat. Heart, Lung and Blood Inst., 1976-80. Author sects. in med. textbooks, sci. paper relating to nutritional, metabolic disorders.; Asso. editor: Nutrition Revs, 1948-58; editorial adv. bd.: Nutrition Today, 1966-76, Hepatology, 1980—. Served as lt. comdr. M.C. USNR, 1942-46. Recipient Alumni Achievement award Westminster Coll., 1970. Fellow Am. Pub. Health Assn. (governing council 1955-56); mem. N.Y. Acad. Scis., Harvey Soc., Am. Soc. Biol. Chemists, Soc. Exptl. Biology and Medicine (council 1952-54), Central Soc. Clin. Research, Am. Soc. Clin. Investigation, Assn. Tchrs. Preventive Medicine (v.p. 1955-57, pres. 1957-58), A.M.A. (council on foods and nutrition 1960-69, chmn. 1963-66), Gerontological Soc., Assn. Am. Physicians, Am. Soc. Clin. Nutrition (council 1963-65, pres. 1967-68), Am. Dietetic Assn. (hon.), Am. Soc. for Study Liver Diseases (council 1963-66, pres. 1966), Am. Heart Assn. (chmn. nutrition com. 1973-76, award of merit 1981), Am. Inst. Nutrition, Sigma Xi, Alpha Omega Alpha. Current Work: Nutrients and aging, cardiovascular disorders and liver disease. Subspecialties: Nutrition (medicine); Preventive medicine. Home: 1325 Wilton Ln Kirkwood MO 63122 Office: 4566 Scott Ave Saint Louis MO 63110

SHANKER, ROY JAMES, natural resources consultant; b. Cleve., July 15, 1948; s. David and Jean (Swartz) S.; m. Rosemary P. Jackson, Mar. 17, 1976 (div. June 1980). S.B., Swarthmore (Pa.) Coll., 1970; M.S., Carnegie-Mellon U., 1972, Ph.D., 1975. Research staff Inst. Def. Analyses, Arlington, Va., 1973-76; prin., ptnr. Resource Planning Assocs., Washington, 1976-80, Hagler Bailly & Co., Washington, 1980-82, pvt. practice natural resources consulting, 1982—; advisor, cons., reviewer Dept. Energy, NSF, Nat. Bur. Standards. Contbr. articles to profl. jours. Mellon fellow, 1970-73. Mem. Ops. Research Soc. Am. (chmn. energy group 1979), Inst. Mgmt. Sci. Republican. Jewish. Current Work: Electric utility system planning (optimal system design and operating). Subspecialties: Regulated utilities; Operations research (mathematics). Home: 1657 Park Rd NW Washington DC 20010

SHANKLIN, DOUGLAS RADFORD, medical educator; b. Camden, N.J., Nov. 25, 1930; s. John F. and Muriel K. (Morgan) S.; m. Virginia A. McClure, Apr. 7, 1956; children: Elizabeth, Leigh, Lois Virginia, John Carter, Eleanor. A.B. in Chemistry, Syracuse U., 1952; M.D., SUNY-Syracuse, 1955. Lic. physician N.Y., Fla., Ill., Tenn. Intern Duke Hosp., Durham, 1955-56, resident in pathology, 1958, SUNY, Syracuse, 1959; instr. to assoc. prof. U. Fla., Gainesville, 1960-67; prof. ob/gyn U. Chgo., 1967-78; exec. dir. Santa Fe Found., Gainesville, 1978-83; prof. pathology U. Tenn., Memphis, 1983—; sr. mem. Marine Biol. Lab., Woods Hole, Mass., 1970—. Author: Maternal Nutrition and Child Health, 1979, Preventive Obstetrics: The Motherwell Experience, 1983, Tumors of Placenta, 1983; chief editor: Jour. Reproductive Medicine, 1970-75. Trustee Coll. Light Opera Co., Falmouth, Mass., 1969—; trustee Hippodrome Theater, Gainesville, 1978—; chmn. Survey Adv. Com., USDA, 1979—. Served to lt. USNR, 1956-58. Named Freeman citizen City Council Glasgow, Scotland, 1981; Best Sci. Tchr. U. Fla., 1967. Mem. Am. Assn. Pathologists, Soc. Pediatric Research, N.Y. Acad. Scis., Sigma Xi. Democrat. Episcopalian. Clubs: Quadrangle (Chgo.); The Barclay. Current Work: Cellular and molecular bases for various neonatal diseases. Subspecialties: Pathology (medicine); Nutrition (medicine). Home: 66 Monroe Ave #1004 Memphis TN 38103 Home: PO Box 3086 Memphis TN 38173 Office: Dept Pathology U Tenn 858 Madison Ave Memphis TN 38163

SHANKS, ROGER D., geneticist, educator; b. Libertyville, Ill., May 30, 1951; s. Douglas and Esther (Sage) S.; m. Wendy D. Shanks, Aug. 28, 1971. B.S., U. Ill., 1974; M.S., Iowa State U., 1977, Ph.D., 1979. Asst. prof. genetics dept. dairy sci U. Ill.-Urbana, 1979-84, assoc. prof. genetics dept. animal scis., 1984—. Contbr. articles to profl. and popular jours. Mem. Am. Agrl. Econs. Assn., AAAS, Am. Dairy Sci. Assn., Am. Genetic Assn., Genetics Soc. Am., Biometric Soc., Alpha Zeta, Gamma Sigma Delta, Phi Kappa Phi. Methodist. Current Work: Quantitative genetics and applied animal breeding; genetic and economic aspects of dairy cattle improvement programs; sire and cow evaluations for multiple traits. Subspecialties: Animal breeding and embryo transplants; Animal genetics.

SHANMUGAM, KEELNATHAM THIRUNAVUKKARASU, microbiologist, educator; b. Keelnatham, India, Oct. 15, 1941; came to U.S., 1965; s. Thirunavukkarasu and Mangayarkarasu T.; m. Valli Narayanasamy, Aug. 27, 1972; 1 son, Nataraj. B.Sc., Annamalai U., 1963; M.Sc., U.P. Agr. U., 1965; Ph.D., U. Hawaii, 1969. Asst. research chemist U. Calif.-San Diego, 1973-75; asst. research agronomist U. Calif.-Davis, 1976-80; asst. research scientist U. Fla., Gainesville, 1980-81, asso. prof. microbiology, 1981—. Mem. Am. Soc. Microbiology. Current Work: Researcher in molecular biology of nitrogen fixation, energetics of nitrogen fixation, molecular biology of hydrogen metabolism and anaerobic metabolism and solar energy conversion; hydrogen metabolism. Subspecialties: Microbiology; Nitrogen fixation. Office: U Fla 1059 McCarty Hall Gainesville FL 32611

SHANNON, CLAUDE ELWOOD, mathematician; b. Petoskey, Mich., Apr. 30, 1916; s. Claude Elwood and Mabel Catherine (Wolf) S.; m. Mary Elizabeth Moore, Mar. 27, 1949; children—Robert, Andrew, Margarita. B.S. in Elec. Engring., U. Mich., 1936, B.S. in Math., 1936; M.S. in Elec. Engring., MIT, 1940, Ph.D. in Math., 1940; M.S. (hon.), Yale U., 1954; D.Sc., U. Mich., 1961, Princeton U., 1962, Edinburgh U. (Scotland), 1964, U. Pitts., 1964, Northwestern U., 1970, U. Oxford (Eng.), 1978, U. East Anglia (Eng.), 1982, Carnegie-Mellon U., 1984. Mem. tech. staff Bell Labs., Murray Hill, N.J., 1940-71; Donner prof. scis. MIT, Cambridge, 1958-78, Donner prof. sci. emeritus, 1978—; dir. Teledyne, Inc., Los Angeles. Author: A Mathematical Theory of Communication; editor: (with J. McCarthy) Automata Studies; also articles. Recipient Noble award AIEE and IRE, 1940; Morris Liebmann Meml. award, 1949; Stuart Ballantine medal Franklin Inst., 1955; Research Corp. award, 1956; medal of honor sp. Rice U., 1962; Mervin J. Kelly award, 1962; Nat. medal Sci., 1966; Golden Plate award Am. Acad. Achievement, 1967; Harvey prize, 1972; Jacquard award Numerical Control Soc., 1978; Harold Fender award U. Pa., 1978; John Fritz medal United Engring. Socs., 1983; Marquis Who's Who Am. Achievement award, 1984; Interface Corp. award, 1985; Audio Engring. Soc. Gold medal, 1985. Mem. Nat. Acad. Engring., Nat. Acad. Scis., Am. Acad. Arts and Scis., Am. Philos. Soc., Deutsche Akademie der Naturforscher Leopoldina, Royal Netherlands Acad. Arts and Scis., Royal Irish Acad., IEEE (Mervin J. Kelly award 1962), Sigma Xi, Tau Beta Pi, Eta Kappa Nu, Phi Kappa Phi. Current work: Research on automata and applications of mathematics. Subspecialties: Applied mathematics; Information systems, storage, and retrieval (computer science).

SHANNON, JACK, engineer, aerodynamics consultant; b. Brenham, Tex., July 19, 1938; s. Aubrey Willys and Josephine Paul (Griffin) S.; children: Mark, John. B.S., U. Tex. Registered profl. engr., Wash. Mem. aerodynamics staff Boeing Co., Seattle, 1961-74; owner, pres. Shannon Engring., Seattle, 1975—. Author test flight documents, and design studies. Inventor Quiet 707. Mem. Soc. Automotive Engrs. Current Work: Low drag high performance airfoils. Aerodynamics and acoustic technology and small technical business growth and management. Subspecialty: Aeronautical engineering. Office: 7675 Perimeter Rd S Suite 200 Seattle WA 98108

SHANNON, ROBERT RENNIE, optical sciences educator, university official; b. Mt. Vernon, N.Y., Oct. 3, 1932; s. Howard A. and Harriebell (Rennie) S.; m. Helen Lang, Feb. 13, 1954; children—Elizabeth, Barbara, Jennifer, Amy, John, Robert. B.S., U. Rochester, 1954, M.A., 1957. Dir. optics lab. ITEK Corp., Lexington, Mass., 1959-69; faculty Optical Scis. Ctr., U. Ariz., Tucson, 1969—, prof. optical scis., 1969, ctr. dir., 1983—; cons. Lawrence Livermore Lab., Calif., 1980—. Editor: Applied Optics and Optical Engineering, vol. 7, 1980, vol. 8, 1981, vol. 9, 1983. Fellow Optical Soc. Am. (pres. 1985), Soc. Photo-Optical Instrument Engrs. (pres. 1979-80, Goddard award 1982). Club: Tucson Soaring (pres. 1976). Current work: Optics and optical engineering including laser applications, optical design and image analysis. Subspecialties: Optical research management; Laser research management. Office: Optical Scis Ctr Univ Arizona Tucson AZ 85721

SHAPERO, DONALD CAMPBELL, physicist, government agency executive; b. Detroit, Apr. 17, 1942; s. Donald Mayer and Lillian Emily (Campbell) S.; m. Diana B. Berner, Dec. 17, 1969 (div.); 1 son, Stephen B.; m. Linda J. Ravdin, Sept. 8, 1985. B.S., MIT, 1964, Ph.D., 1970. Thomas J. Watson fellow IBM Corp., Yorktown Heights, N.Y., 1970-72; asst. prof. physics Am. U., Washington, 1972-73, Catholic U., Washington, 1973-75; exec. dir. Energy Research Adv. Bd. U.S. Dept. Energy, Washington, 1978-79; sr. staff officer Nat. Acad. Scis., Washington, 1975-78, spl. asst. for program coordination, 1979-82; exec. dir. Bd. Physics and Astronomy, Nat. Acad. Scis., 1982—; Exec. sec. com. effects on multiple nuclear weapon detonations Nat. Acad. Scis.-NRC, Washington, 1975-76, exec. sec. geophys. data panel, 1976, exec. sec. panel to assess nat. need for facilities dedicated to prodn. synchrotron radiation, 1976, sr. staff officer geophys. study com., 1976-78; dir. com. sci. and pub. policy nuclear risk survey Nat. Acad. Sci., 1976-78, sr. staff officer for five yr. outlook sci. and tech., 1979-82, sr. staff officer workshop sci. instrumentation, 1982, study dir. physics survey, 1982-85. Contbr. sci. articles to profl. publs. Vice pres. Bethesda Jewish Congregation, 1983-84. NSF fellow, 1964-68; Cottrell Research grantee, 1975. Mem. Am. Phys. Soc. Current Work: Broad interest in science policy, particularly physical sciences and computer science and technology. Subspecialties: Theoretical physics; Particle physics. Home: 7537 Heatherton Ln Potomac MD 20854 Office: Nat Acad Scis 2101 Constitution Ave Washington DC 20418

SHAPIRO, ARTHUR MAURICE, zoology educator; b. Balt., Jan. 6, 1946; s. Bernard Robert and Rose (Pogach) S.; m. Adrienne Ruth Austin, Aug. 3, 1969; 1 child, Austin Warren. B.A., U. Pa., 1966; Ph.D., Cornell U., 1970. Asst. prof. CUNY, S.I., 1970-71; asst. prof. U. Calif.-Davis, 1971-75, assoc. prof., 1975-79, prof., vice chmn. dept. zoology, lectr. entomology, 1980—; cons. U.S. Fish and Wildlife Service, N.Y., Calif., 1970—. Contbr. articles, rev. papers to profl. lit. Grantee: NSF, 1976-79, 84-86, Nat. Geog. Soc., 1976-82. Fellow Explorers Club; mem. AAAS, Soc. for Study Evolution, Ecol. Soc. Am., Lepidopterists Soc. (1st v.p., mem. exec. council 1979-82). Current work: Evolutionary biology, biogeography, biosystematics of the Pierid butterflies; biology of weedy and colonizing organisms; phenotypic plasticity and developmental genetics. Subspecialty: Evolutionary biology. Office: Dept Zoology Univ California Davis CA 95616

SHAPIRO, ASCHER HERMAN, mechanical engineer, educator; b. Bklyn., May 20, 1916; s. Bernard and Jennie (Kaplan) S.; m. Sylvia Charm, Dec. 24, 1939 (div. 1959); children: Peter Mark, Martha Ann, Bernett Mary; m. Regina Julia Lee, June 4, 1961 (div. 1972). Student, CCNY, 1932-35; S.B., MIT, 1938, Sc.D., 1946; D.Sc. honoris causa, Salford U., Eng., 1978, Technion-Israel Inst. Tech., 1985. Asst. mech. engring. MIT, 1938-40, faculty, 1940—, prof. mech. engring., 1952—, prof. charge fluid mechanics div., mech. engring. dept., 1954-65, Ford prof. engring., 1962-75, chmn. faculty, 1964-65, head dept. mech. engring., 1965-74, inst. prof., 1975—; vis. prof. applied thermodynamics U. Cambridge, Eng., 1955-56; Akroyd Stuart Meml. lectr. Nottingham (Eng.) U., 1956; editor Acad. Press, Inc., 1962-65; cons. United Aircraft Corp., M.W. Kellogg Co., Arthur D. Little, Inc., Hardie-Tynes Mfg. Co., Carbon & Carbide Chems. Corp., Oak Ridge, Rohm & Haas Co., Ultrasonic Corp., Jackson & Moreland (Engrs.), Stone & Webster, Bendix Aviation, Oak Ridge Nat. Lab., Acushnet Processing Co., Kennecott Copper Co., Welch Sci., Sargent-Welch, others; served on sub-coms. on turbines, internal flow, compressors and turbines NACA; mem. Lexington Project to study and report on nuclear powered flight to AEC, summer 1948; dir. Project Dynamo to study and report to AEC on technol. and econs. nuclear power for civilian use, 1953, Lamp Wick study Office Naval Research, 1955; mem. tech. adv. panel aeronautics Dept. Def.; cons. ops. evaluation group Navy Dept.; sci. adv. bd. USAF, 1964-66; mem. Nat. Com. for Fluid Mechanics Films, 1962—, chmn., 1962-65, 71—; chmn. com. on ednl. films Commn. on Engring. Edn., 1962-65; dir. lab. for devel. power plants for use in torpedoes Navy Dept., 1943-45; mem. ad hoc med. devices com. FDA, HEW, 1970-72; mem. com. Nat. Council for Research and Devel., Israel, 1971—; mem. com. sci. and pub. policy Nat. Acad. Scis., 1970-74. Author: The Dynamics and Thermodynamics of Compressible Fluid Flow, vol. 1, 1953, vol. 2, 1954, Shape and Flow, 1961, Fluid Dynamics, 39 videotaped lectures and 3-vol. study guide, 1985; also ednl. films and articles, tech. jours. Mem. editorial board: Jour. Applied Mechanics, 1955-56; editorial com.: Ann. Rev. Fluid Mechanics, 1967-71; mem. editorial bd.: M.I.T. Press, 1977—, chmn., 1982—. Mem. Town Meeting Arlington, Mass.; chmn. 1st Mass. chpt. Atlantic Union Com., 1951-52, mem. council, 1954—; bd. govs. Technion, Israel Inst. Tech., 1968—, also chmn. acad. devel. com. Recipient Naval Ordnance Devel. award, 1945; joint certificate outstanding contbn. War and Navy depts., 1947; Richards Meml. award ASME, 1960; Worcester Reed Warner medal, 1965; Fluids Engring. award, 1981; Townsend Harris medal Coll. City N.Y., 1978. Fellow Am. Inst. Aeros. and Astronautics, Am. Acad. Arts and Scis. (councillor 1967-71), ASME; mem. Am. Sci. Films Assn., Nat. Acad. Scis. (com. on sci. and pub. policy 1973-77), Nat. Acad. Engring., Biomed. Engring. Soc. (charter mem. 1968), Am. Soc. Engring. Edn. (Lamme medal 1977), AAAS, Sigma Xi, Tau Beta Pi, Pi Tau Sigma. Clubs: Mass. Inst. Tech. Faculty (Cambridge); Cavendish (Brookline, Mass.). Patentee fluid metering equipment, combustion chambers, propulsion apparatus and gas turbine aux., magnetic disc, magnetic disc storage device, vacuum pump, low-density wind tunnel, recipe calculator. Current Work: Diagnostic and therapeutic devices and systems for the cardiovascular and pulmonary systems. Subspecialties: Biomedical engineering; Fluid mechanics. Office: Mass Inst Tech 77 Massachusetts Ave Cambridge MA 02139

SHAPIRO, BURTON LEONARD, educator; b. N.Y.C., Mar. 29, 1934; s. Nat Lazarus and Fay Rebecca (Gartenhaus) S.; m. Eileen Roman, Aug. 11, 1958; children—Norah Leah, Anne Rachael, Carla Faye. Student, Tufts U., 1951-54; D.D.S., N.Y. U., 1958; M.S., U. Minn., 1962, Ph.D., 1966. Faculty U. Minn. Sch. Dentistry, Mpls., 1962—, asso. prof. div. oral pathology, 1966-70, prof., chmn. div. oral biology, 1970—, prof., chmn. dept. oral biology, 1979, prof. dept. oral pathology and genetics, 1979, prof. dept. lab. medicine and pathology, 1985—, dir. grad. studies, mem. grad. faculty genetics, 1966—, mem. grad. faculty pathobiology, 1979, univ. senator, 1968—; also mem. med. staff U. Minn. Health Scis. Ctr., mem. exec. com. U. Minn. Grad. Sch., mem. Minn. health scis. policy rev. council; hon. research fellow Galton Lab. dept. human genetics Univ. Coll., London, 1974; spl. vis. prof. Japanese Ministry Edn., 1983. Mem. adv. editorial bd.: Jour. Dental Research, 1971—. Contbr. articles to profl. jours. Served to lt. USNR, 1958-60. Am. Cancer Soc. postdoctoral fellow, 1960-62; advanced fellow, 1965-68. Fellow Am. Acad. Oral Pathology, AAAS; mem. Internat. Assn. Dental Research (councilor 1969-72), Am. Soc. Human Genetics, Craniofacial Biology Soc. (pres. 1972), Sigma Xi, Omicron Kappa Upsilon. Current Work: Search for basic defect in cystic fibrosis; explanation of findings in Down syndrome; cell calcium and aging; genetics and human disease. Subspecialties: Genetics and genetic engineering (medicine); Cell and tissue culture. Home: 76 Exeter Pl St Paul MN 55104 Office: Dept Oral Biology Sch Dentistry U Minn Minneapolis MN 55455

SHAPIRO, DONALD MICHAEL, physician; b. Chgo., Jan. 29, 1941; s. Jack Abraham and Helen (Grossman) S.; m. Martha Lee Nazor, Mar. 2, 1979; 1 son, Ryan; children from previous marriage: Steven, Michael, Daniel, Susan. B.S., Roosevelt U., 1963; D.O., Chgo. Coll. Osteopathy, 1968. Diplomate: Am.Bd. Internal Medicine. Intern Detroit Osteo. Hosp., 1968-69, resident in medicine, 1969-70, Wilford Hall Med. Ctr., San Antonio, 1970-73; fellow in hematology-oncology Baylor Coll. Medicine, Houston, 1973-75, practice medicine specializing in hematology, med. oncology, Dayton, Ohio, 1977—; assoc. clin. prof. medicine Wright State U. Medicine, Dayton, 1976—; mil. cons. U.S. Air Force, Dayton, 1975-78. Contbg. editor: Osteo. Physician, 1975-77; contbr. articles to profl. jours. Trustee Miami Valley unit Am. Cancer Soc., Dayton, 1978-79; Trustee Greene County unit, Xenia, Ohio, 1982-84, med. advisor, 1982-84. Served to maj. USAF, 1970-77. Fellow ACP; mem. Am. Soc. Hematology, Am. Soc. Clin. Oncology, Undersea Med. Soc., Am. Osteo. Assn., Ohio Osteo. Assn. (physicians effectiveness com. 1982-83). Current Work: Clinical chemotherapy, undersea medicine, medical education. Subspecialties: Hematology; Chemotherapy. Office: 401 3rd Ave Kingston PA 18704

SHAPIRO, HOWARD MAURICE, physician, researcher; b. Bklyn., Nov. 8, 1941; s. Alfred Lester and Jennie Geraldine (Epstein) S.; m. Leslie Leona Hochberg, June 21, 1964; children: Jill Elise, Peter Jay. A.B., Harvard U., 1961; M.D., NYU, 1965. Asst. research scientist engring. math. N.Y.U., 1962-65; mem. surg. house staff, 1965-67; research assoc., sr. staff fellow Nat. Cancer Inst., NIH, Bethesda, Md., 1967-71; surg. house staff U. Ariz., 1971-72; asst. dir. to dir. clin. research diagnostic products G.D. Searle & Co., 1972-76; cons., inventor, pres. Howard M. Shapiro (M.D., P.C.), West Newton, Mass., 1976—; research assoc. Beth Israel Hosp., 1982—; investigator Ctr. Blood Research, 1983—; lectr. pathology Harvard Med. Sch., 1976—. Served with USPHS, 1967-70. Mem. AAAS, IEEE, Assn. Advancement Med. Instrumentation, Am. Assn. Cancer Research, Am. Soc. Clin. Oncology, Am. Soc. Hematology, Cell Kinetics Soc., Histochem. Soc., Soc. Analytical Cytology. Current Work: Development of biomedical instrumentation for clinical and research laboratories; analytical and quantitative cell biology relating to cell growth control. Subspecialties: Bioinstrumentation; Cancer research (medicine).

SHAPIRO, IRVING MEYER, biochemist; b. London, Oct. 28, 1937; came to U.S., 1969, naturalized, 1977; s. Syd and Betty (Silver) S.; m. Joan Poliner, July 4, 1965; 1 dau., Susan. B.Dental Surgery, U. London, 1961, Ph.D., 1968; M.Sc., U. Liverpool, Eng., 1964. Research fellow Royal Dental Hosp., London, 1966-69; mem. faculty U. Pa. Sch. Dental Medicine, Phila., 1969—, prof., chmn. dept. biochemistry, 1976—. Contbr. articles to profl. jours. Nuffield fellow, 1964-65. Mem. Internat. Assn. Dental Research (Basic Sci. award 1974), AAAS, Am. Soc. Biol. Chemists, Am. Chem. Soc. Current Work: Studies of the mechanisms of biological mineralization. Effects of toxic elements on human populations. Subspecialties: Biochemistry (biology); Environmental toxicology. Home: 555 Haverford Rd Wynnewood PA 19096 Office: Dept Biochemistry Dental Med Sch U Pa Philadelphia PA 19104

SHAPIRO, IRWIN IRA, physicist, educator; b. N.Y.C., Oct. 10, 1929; s. Samuel and Esther (Feinberg) S.; m. Marian Helen Kaplun, Dec. 20, 1959; children: Steven, Nancy. A.B., Cornell U., 1950; A.M., Harvard U., 1951, Ph.D., 1955. Mem. staff Lincoln Lab. MIT, Lexington, 1954-70; Sherman Fairchild Distinguished scholar Calif. Inst. Tech., 1974; Morris Loeb lectr. physics Harvard, 1975; prof. geophysics and physics MIT, 1967-80, Schlumberger prof., 1980—; Paine prof. practical astronomy, prof. physics Harvard U., 1982—; sr. scientist Smithsonian Astrophys. Obs., 1982—; dir. Harvard-Smithsonian Ctr. for Astrophysics, 1983—; cons. NSF. Contbr. articles to profl. jours. Recipient Albert A. Michelson medal Franklin Inst., 1975, award in phys. and math. scis. N.Y. Acad. Scis., 1982; Guggenheim fellow, 1982. Fellow AAAS, Am. Geophys. Union, Am. Phys. Soc.; mem. Am. Acad. Arts and Scis., Nat. Acad. Scis. (Benjamin Apthorp Gould prize 1979), Am. Astron. Soc. (Dannie Heineman award 1983), Internat. Astron. Union, Phi Beta Kappa, Sigma Xi, Phi Kappa Phi. Current Work: Radio and radar techniques: applications to astrometry, astrophysics, geophysics, planetary physics, and tests of theories of gravitation. Subspecialty: Radio and microwave astronomy. Home: 17 Lantern Ln Lexington MA 02173 Office: 60 Garden St Cambridge MA 02138

SHAPIRO, JAMES ALAN, microbial geneticist, educator; b. Chgo., May 18, 1943; s. Henry I. and Soretta Shapiro; m. Joan E. Shapiro, June 14, 1964; children: Jacob N., Danielle E. B.A. magna cum laude, in English Lit, Harvard U., 1964; Ph.D. in Genetics, U. Cambridge, Eng., 1968. Fellow Service de Genetique Cellulaire, Institut Pasteur, Paris, 1967-68; research fellow dept. bacteriology and immunology Harvard U., 1968-70; prof. genetics U. Havana, Cuba, 1970-72; fellow Rosenstiel Basic Med. Scis. Research Center, Waltham, Mass., 1972-73; asst. prof. microbiology U. Chgo., 1973-78, assoc. prof., 1978-82, prof., 1982—; vis. prof. dept. microbiology Tel Aviv (Israel) U., 1980; mem. NSF genetic biology panel, 1981-83. Mem. editorial bd.: Jour. Bacteriology, 1976-84, Enzyme and Microbial Tech, 1981—, Biotech. Series, 1981—; contbr. articles to profl. jours. Current Work: Colony development and social interactions in bacteria, bacterial genetics, transposable elements, hydrocarbon oxidation. Subspecialty: Microbiology. Office: 920 E 58th St Chicago IL 60637

SHAPIRO, JONATHAN SALEM, electrical engineer; b. N.Y.C., July 9, 1943; s. Harold Roland and Pauline (Wolinsky) S.; m. Rosalind Elaine Miller, Jan. 24, 1974; children—Pauline Ingrid Beth. B.E.E. cum laude, CCNY, 1965; M.S.E., Princeton U., 1966, M.A., 1967, Ph.D., 1968. Sr. engr. Microstate Electronics, Murray Hill, N.J., 1968-70; chief elec. engr. Pollution Control Industries, Stamford, Conn., 1970-73; sr. engr. Machlett Labs./Raytheon, Stamford, 1973-74, chief engr., 1974-78, engring. mgr., 1978-84; v.p. tech. AFP Imaging Corp., Elmsford, N.Y., 1984-85; sr. project engr. Philips Med. Systems, Shelton, Conn., 1985—. Contbr. articles to profl. jours. Patentee in field. Mem. IEEE, Am. Phys. Soc., Am. Assn. Physicists in Medicine, Soc. Radiol. Engrs., Sigma Xi, Tau Beta Pi, Eta Kappa Nu. Current work: Design electronic systems for magnetic resonance imaging, film processing and recording/archiving. Subspecialties: Electronics; Imaging technology. Home: 9 Ronald Ln Cos Cob CT 06807 Office: Philips Med Systems 710 Bridgeport Ave Shelton CT 06484

SHAPIRO, LEE TOBEY, planetarium administrator, astronomy educator; b. Chgo., Dec. 12, 1943; s. Sydney Harold and Ruth Iva (Levin) S.; m. Linda Susan Goldman, Aug. 16, 1970; children—Steven Robert, Aaron Edward. B.S. in Physics, Carnegie Inst. Tech., 1966; M.S. in Astronomy, Northwestern U., 1968, Ph.D., in Astronomy, 1974. Lectr. Adler Planetarium, Chgo., 1967-74; asst. prof. to assoc. prof. astronomy Mich. State U., East Lansing, 1974-82, dir. Abrams Planetarium, East Lansing, 1974-82; assoc. prof. U. N.C., Chapel Hill, 1983—; planetarium dir. Morehead Planetarium, Chapel Hill, 1982—. Contbr. articles to profl. jours. Inst. Mus. Services grantee, 1982, 84. Fellow Royal Astron. Soc.; mem. Am. Astron. Soc., Am. Assn. Museums, Internat. Planetarium Soc., Southeast Planetarium Assn. Jewish. Office: Morehead Planetarium U NC Chapel Hill NC 27514

SHAPIRO, MAURICE MANDEL, astrophysicist; b. Jerusalem, Nov. 13, 1915; came to U.S., 1921; s. Asher and Miriam R. (Grunbaum) S.; m. Inez Weinfield, Feb. 8, 1942 (dec. Oct. 1964); children: Joel Nevin, Elana Shapiro Ashley, Raquel Tamar Shapiro Kislinger. B.S., U. Chgo., 1936, M.S., 1940, Ph.D., 1942. Instr. physics and math. Chgo. City Colls., 1937-41; chmn. dept. phys. and biol. scis. Austin Coll., 1938-41; instr. math. Gary Coll., 1942; physicist Dept. Navy, 1942-44; lectr. physics and math. George Washington U., 1943-44; group leader, mem. coordinating council of lab. Los Alamos Sci. Lab., U. Calif., 1944-46; sr. physicist, lectr. Oak Ridge Nat. Lab., Union Carbon and Carbide Corp., 1946-49; cons. div. nuclear energy for propulsion aircraft Fairchild Engine & Aircraft Corp., 1948-49; head cosmic ray br. nucleonics div. U.S. Naval Research Lab., Washington, 1949-65, supt. nucleonics div., 1953-65, chief scientist Lab. for Cosmic Ray Physics, 1965-82, apptd. to chair of cosmic ray physics, 1966-82, chief scientist emeritus, 1982—; lectr. U. Md., 1949-50, 52—, assoc. prof., 1950-51; vis. prof. physics and astronomy U. Iowa, 1981-84; vis. prof. astrophysics U. Bonn, 1982-84; vis. scientist Max Planck Inst. Fur Astrophysik, Munich, 1984-85; Regents' lectr. U. Calif., 1985; cons. Argonne Nat. Lab., 1949; cons. panel on cosmic rays U.S. nat. com. IGY; lectr. physics and engring. Nuclear Products-Erco div. ACF Industries, Inc., 1956-58; lectr. E. Fermi Internat. Sch. Physics, Varenna, Italy, 1962; vis. prof. Weizmann Inst. Sci., Rehovoth, Israel, 1962-63, Inst. Math. Scis., Madras, India, 1971; Inst. Astronomy and Geophysics Nat. U. Mex., 1976; vis. prof. physics and astronomy Northwestern U., Evanston, Ill., 1978; cons. space research in astronomy Space Sci. Bd., Nat. Acad. Scis., 1965; cons. Office Space Scis., NASA, 1965-66; prin. investigator Gemini S-9 Cosmic Ray Expts., NASA, 1964-69, Skylab, 1967-76, Long Duration Exposure Facility, 1977—; mem. Groupe de Travail de Biologie Spatiale, Council of Europe, 1970—; mem. steering com. DUMAND Consortium, 1976—, mem. exec. com., 1979—; lectr. Summer Space Inst., Deutsche Physikalische Gesellschaft, 1972; dir. Internat. Sch. Cosmic-Ray Astrophysics, Ettore Majorana Centre Sci. Culture, 1977—, also sr. corr., 1977—; chmn. U.S. IGY com. on interdisciplinary research, mem. nuclear emulsion panel space sci. bd.; Nat. Acad. Scis., 1959—; chief U.S. rep., steering com. Internat. Coop. Emulsion Flights for Cosmic Ray Research; cons. CREI Atomics, 1959—; vis. com. Bartol Research Found., Franklin Inst., 1967-74; mem. U.S. organizing com. 13th Internat. Conf. on Cosmic Rays; mem. sci. adv. com. Internat. Confs. on Nuclear Photography and Solid State Detectors, 1966—; mem. Com. of Honor for Einstein Centennial, Acad. Naz. Lincei, 1977—. Editorial bd.: Astrophysics and Space Sci, 1968-75; asso. editor: Phys. Rev. Letters, 1977-83; contbr. to: Am. Inst. Physics Handbook. Recipient Distinguished Civilian Service award Dept. Navy, 1967; Guggenheim fellow, 1962-63; medal of Honor Société d'Encouragement au Progrès, 1978; Alexander von Humboldt sr. U.S. scientist award, 1982; Publs. award Naval Research Lab., 1970, 74, 76; Dir.'s Spl. award, 1974. Fellow Am. Phys. Soc. (chmn. organizing com. div. cosmic physics, chmn. 1971-72, com. on publs. 1977—), AAAS, Washington Acad. Scis. (past com. chmn.); mem. Am. Inst. Physics, Research Soc. Am., Am. Astron. Soc. (exec. com. div. high-energy astrophysics 1978—, chmn. 1982), Philos. Soc. Washington (past pres.), Am. Technion Soc. (Washington bd.), Assn. Los Alamos Scientists (past chmn.), Assn. Oak Ridge Engrs. and Scientists (past chmn.), Fedn. Am. Scientists (past mem. exec. com., nat. council), Internat. Astron. Union (organizing com. commn. on high-energy astrophysics), Phi Beta Kappa, Sigma Xi. Research in cosmic radiation: composition, origin, propagation, and nuclear transformations; high-energy astrophysics; particles and fields; nuclear physics; neutron physics and fission reactors, neutrino astronomy. Current Work: Composition, origin; propagation and nuclear transformations of cosmic rays; neutrino astrophysics. Subspecialties: High energy astrophysics; Cosmic ray high energy astrophysics. Office: Code 4154 Naval Research Lab Washington DC 20375

SHAPIRO, STUART LOUIS, astrophysicist; b. New Haven, Conn., Dec. 6, 1947; married. A.B., Harvard U., 1969; M.A., Princeton U., 1971, Ph.D. in Astrophys. Sci., 1973. Lab. instr. physics Harvard Coll., 1967-69; teaching asst. astronomy Princeton U., N.J., 1973; research assoc., Cornell U., Ithaca, N.Y., 1973-75, instr. 1974-75, asst. prof., 1975-78, assoc. prof. astronomy, 1977-84, prof., 1984—. Subspecialty: High energy astrophysics. Office: Cornell U Dept of Astronomy Ithaca NY 14853*

SHAPLEY, LLOYD STOWELL, mathematics educator; b. Cambridge, Mass., June 2, 1923; s. Harlow and Martha (Betz) S.; m. Marian Ludolph, Aug. 19, 1955; children—Peter, Christopher. A.B., Harvard U., 1948; Ph.D. (Grad. Coll. Procter fellow), Princeton U., 1953. Mathematician Rand Corp., Santa Monica, Calif., 1948-50; 54-81; prof. depts. math and econs. UCLA, 1981—; instr. Princeton U., 1952-54; sr. research fellow Calif. Inst. Tech., 1955-56; fellow Inst. Advanced Studies, Hebrew U., Jerusalem, 1979-80; mem. faculty Rand Grad. Inst. for Policy Studies, 1970—. Author: (with S. Karlin) Geometry of Moment Spaces, 1953, (with R. Aumann) Values of Non-Atomic Games, 1974; editor: (with others) Advances in Game Theory, 1964; editorial bd.: Internat. Jour. Game Theory, 1970—, Math. Programming, 1971-80, Jour. Math. Econs., 1973—, Math. Ops. Research, 1975—. Served with AC U.S. Army, 1943-45. Decorated Bronze Star. Fellow Econometric Soc., Am. Acad. Arts and Scis.; mem. Nat. Acad. Scis., Ops. Research Soc. Am., Am. Math. Soc., Math. Programming Soc. Research in game theory, math. econs., polit. sci. Subspecialty: Operations research (mathematics). Office: Dept Math Econs UCLA Los Angeles CA 90024

SHARGEL, LEON DAVID, pharmacologist, educator; b. Balt., Nov. 18, 1941; s. Earl and Irene (Singer) S.; m. Sharon Lee Fine, Mar. 18, 1944; children: Deborah, Jeffrey. B.S. in Pharmacy cum laude, U. Md., 1963; Ph.D. in Pharmacology, George Washington U., 1969. Registered pharmacist. Assoc. research biologist, group leader dept. drug metabolism and disposition Sterling-Winthrop Research Inst., Rensselaer, N.Y., 1969-75; asst. prof. pharmacy and pharmacology Northeastern U. Coll. Pharmacy, Boston, 1975-78, assoc. prof. pharmacy and pharmacology, 1978-82, sect. leader pharmaceutics, 1980-82; assoc. prof. pharmacy and pharmacology, mgr.

biopharm. analysis lab. Mass. Coll. Pharmacy and Allied Health Scis., Boston, 1982—; assoc. dir. Pfeiffer Pharm. Scis. Labs., Inc.; cons. pharm. ind. Contbr. articles, research papers, textbook to sci. lit. Mem. AAAS, Am. Assn. Colls. Pharmacy, Am. Pharm. Assn., Acad. Pharm. Sci., Am. Soc. Pharmacology and Exptl. Therapeutics (div. drug metabolism), Internat. Soc. Study Xenobiotics, Sigma Xi, Rho Chi. Current Work: Drug metabolism and disposition, pharmacokinetics, biopharmaceutics. Subspecialties: Pharmacology; Toxicology (medicine). Office: 179 Longwood Ave Boston MA 02115

SHARMA, GOVIND CHANDRA, plant science educator; b. Udaipur, Rajasthan, India, Mar. 3, 1944; came to U.S., 1964; naturalized, 1980; s. Jagdeesh C. and Manorama (Joshi) S.; m. Prabha Gupta, Aug. 25, 1968; 1 child, Manan. B.S., U. Udaipur, 1964; M.S., U. Fla., 1965, Ph.D., Kans. State U., 1970. Research asst. Pesticide Residue Analysis Lab., U. Fla., Gainesville and Kans. State U., Manhattan, 1965-66; agrl. tng. coordinator Gen. Dynamics Corp., San Diego, 1965-67, U. Wis., Madison, 1965-67; assoc. prof. dept. Natural Resources Ala. A&M U., Normal, 1970-73, prof., chmn., 1973—; cons. Southeast Consortium Internal Devel., Chapel Hill., N.C., 1979, 84. Contbr. articles to profl. jours. Coach Soccer Assn. Youth, 1982. Recipient Marion Meadows award Am. Soc. Hort. Sci., 1970; grantee NASA, TVA, USDA, 1970—. Mem. Am. Soc. Agronomy, Crop Sci. Soc. Am., Am. Soc. Hort. Sci., Huntsville Madison County Bot. Garden Soc. (bd. dirs. 1984). Current work: Plant cell and tissue culture; controlled release fertilizer; plant genetics. Subspecialties: Plant cell and tissue culture; Biomass (agriculture). Home: 2700 Briarwood Huntsville AL 35801-2221 Office: Dept Natural Resource PO Box 183 Ala A&M U Normal AL 35762

SHARMA, JAGDEV MITTRA, veterinary microbiologist, researcher; b. India, June 28, 1941; came to U.S., 1962, naturalized, 1974; s. Hari Ram and Devki S.; m. Sylvia Ann Lemus, June 21, 1969; children: Dave, Susan. B.V.Sc., Punjab U., Hissar, India, 1961; M.S., U. Calif.-Davis, 1964, Ph.D., 1967. Instr. in vet. surgery Punjab U., 1961; jr. specialist U. Calif., Davis, 1962-66, Regents fellow in comparative pathology, 1966-67; poultry pathologist Wash. State U., 1967-71; vet. med. officer Regional Poultry Research Lab., U.S. Dept. Agr., East Lansing, Mich., 1971—; clin. prof. dept. pathology Sch. Vet. Medicine, Mich. State U., East Lansing, 1982—. Contbr. numerous articles to sci. jours. Recipient Cert. of Merit Punjab U., 1961; Outstanding Performance award U.S. Dept. Agr., 1976-77; Achievement award Upjohn Co., 1982. Mem. AVMA, World Vet. Poultry Assn., Am. Soc. Microbiology, Am. Assn. Avian Pathologists, Sigma Xi. Current Work: Pathology and immunology of neoplastic and non-neoplastic diseases of chickens. Subspecialty: Microbiology (veterinary medicine). Home: 4611 Sequoia Trail Okemos MI 48864 Office: 3606 E Mount Hope Rd East Lansing MI 48823

SHARMA, RAGHUBIR PRASAD, toxicologist, educator; b. India, Sept. 7, 1940; came to U.S., 1964, naturalized, 1979; s. Rammurti and Ramdulari S.; m. Lalita Shukla, Dec. 13, 1958; children: Rajesh, Sanjeev. D.V.M., U. Rajasthan, India, 1959; Ph.D., U. Minn., 1968. Diplomate: Am. Bd. Vet. Toxicology, Am. Bd. Toxicology; cert. indsl. hygienist. Clin. practice vet. medicine, 1959-60; instr. pharmacology, U.P. Agrl. U., India, 1960-61, asst. prof., 1961-64; research fellow U. Minn., 1964-69; asst. prof. toxicology Utah State U., Logan, 1969-75, asso. prof., 1975-79, prof., 1979—; cons. in field. Editor: Immunologic Considerations in Toxicology, Vol. I, 1981, Vol. II, 1981; contbr. articles and abstracts to sci. jours. Recipient various research awards USPHS, various research awards State of Utah, pvt. industry. Mem. Soc. Toxicology, Am. Soc. Pharmacology and Exptl. Therapeutics, AVMA, Am. Indsl. Hygiene Assn. Current Work: Immunotoxicology; biochemical mechanisms of toxic action. Subspecialty: Toxicology (medicine). Home: 1375 North 1600 East Logan UT 84321 Office: Utah State U UMC 56 Logan UT 84322

SHARMA, RAM RATAN, physicist; b. Jaipur, India, Oct. 6, 1936; s. Kalyan Mal and Ramanandi Devi S.; m. Shakuntala, July 16, 1967; 1 child, Raja. B.S., U. Rajasthan, 1958; M.S., U. Bombay, 1962; M.A., U. Calif.-Riverside, 1962, Ph.D., 1965. Sci. officer Atomic Energy Establishment, Trombay, Bombay, 1958-62; assoc. prof. U. Ill., Chgo., 1968-72, prof., 1972—; assoc. prof. U. Ill., Urbana, summer 1969; vis. prof. U. Liverpool (Eng.), 1975, Atomic Energy Research Establishment, Harwell, Eng., 1974-75; resident assoc. Argonne Nat. Lab., 1971—. Patentee catalysts for nuclear fusion. Fellow Am. Phys. Soc. Current work: Transition metal ions; excitons; biexcitons in semiconductors; epitaxial recrystallization of amorphous semiconductors; magnetic and optical properties of solids; blood-brain barrier; hemoglobins; isomer shift, phase-transitions in biomembranes, nuclear fusion. Subspecialties: Condensed matter physics; Biophysics (physics). Home: 6809 S Bentley St Darien IL 60559 Office: U Ill Dept Physics Chicago IL 60680

SHARMA, SANSAR C., neurobiologist, educator, researcher; b. Pirthipur, India, Mar. 10, 1938; came to U.S., 1968, naturalized, 1974; s. Ram Rattan and Hukmi Devi S.; m. Janet Phillips, Dec. 4, 1970; children: David, Nina. B.Sc., M.Sc. with honors, Panjab U., 1962; Ph.D. in Physiology, U. Edinburgh Med. Sch., 1967. Teaching asst. Panjab U., 1961-62; research scholar Council for Sci. and Indsl. Research, 1963-64; lectr. zoology, Ambala, India, 1962-63; research scholar U. Edinburgh Med. Sch., 1966-67, postdoctoral fellow, 1967-68; research assoc. Washington U., St. Louis, 1968-72; asst. prof. ophthalmology N.Y. Med. Coll., Valhalla, 1972-77, assoc. prof., 1977-81, prof., 1981—, adj. prof. anatomy, 1981—; summer fellow Marine Biol. Labs., Woods Hole, Mass., 1965. NSF research grantee, 1974-76; Nat. Eye Inst./NIH research grantee, 1975—; NIH research career devel. grantee, 1978-83. Fellow Am. Soc. Exptl. Biology; mem. Soc. for Neurosci., Assn. for Research in Vision and Ophthalmology, Internat. Union Physiologists, Physiol. Soc., Indian Physiol. Soc. Current Work: Genesis of visual pathways; retinotectal connections; study of development and regeneration of visual pathways between the retina and the brain in lower vertebrates. Subspecialties: Comparative neurobiology; Neurophysiology. Office: Dept Opthalmology NY Med Coll Valhalla NY 10595

SHARMA, YADUNANDAN PRASAD, materials and process development engineer; b. Kathura, India, Sept. 7, 1945; came to U.S., 1970, naturalized, 1980; s. Shri Shambhoo Ram and Yashoda (Pandey) P.; m. Archana Bipin Nigam, Jan. 3, 1976; children—Melindah, Vineet. B.Sc., U. Sagar, 1966, M.Sc., 1968; M.S., Fairleigh Dickinson U., 1972; Ph.D., U. Mo., 1977. Tchr., head sci. dept. Abeel High Sch., Hackensack, N.J., 1970-73; O.M. Stewart fellow U. Mo., Columbia, 1973-77; asst. prof., research assoc. U.R.I., Kingston, 1977-81; staff engr. Raytheon Corp., Portsmouth, R.I., 1981—. Contbr. articles to profl. jours. Served with Indian Army, 1964-66. Mem. Am. Phys. Soc., Am. Assn. Physics Tchrs., Am. Inst. Physics. Current work: Development of polymeric materials and processes; solar energy research for space heating and cooling; composite materials investigation and chemical kinetics study using state of the art techniques; microelectronics processing and packaging; non-destructive testing and inspections using ultrasonics and x-ray digital imaging techniques. Subspecialties: Condensed matter physics; Materials processing. Home: 39 John St Portsmouth RI 02871 Office: Raytheon Corp W Main Rd Portsmouth RI 02871

SHARON (SCHWADRON), YITZHAK YAAKOV, physics educator; b. Tel-Aviv, Feb. 29, 1936; came to U.S., 1948; s. Abraham and Dina (Friedenberg) Sharon-Schwadron. A.B. with highest honors, Columbia U., 1958; M.A., Princeton U., 1960, Ph.D., 1966. Asst. Inst. for Advanced Study, Princeton, N.J., 1965-66; asst. prof. physics Northeastern U., Boston, 1966-72; vis. asst. prof. physics Temple U., Phila., 1970-71; assoc. prof. physics Stockton State Coll., Pomona, N.J., 1972-75, prof., 1975—; vis. fellow Princeton U., 1980-82; cons. in field. Contbr. articles to profl. jours. Putnam fellow, 1962-63. Mem. Am. Phys. Soc., Am. Assn. Physics Tchrs., Sigma Xi, Phi Beta Kappa. Jewish. Current work: Nuclear theory, especially nuclear models and the connections between them; shell model; collective model; projected wave functions; physics education. Subspecialty: Nuclear physics. Office: Stockton State Coll Pomona NJ 08240

SHARP, AARON JOHN, botanist, educator; b. Plain City, Ohio, July 29, 1904; s. Prentice Daniel and Maude Katharine (Herriott) S.; m. Cora Evelyn Bunch, July 25, 1929; children: Rosa Elizabeth, Maude Katharine, Mary Martha, Fred Prentice, Jennie Lou. A.B., Ohio Wesleyan U., 1923-27, D.Sc., 1952; M.S., U. Okla., 1927-29; Ph.D., Ohio State U., 1936-38. Botanist technician Nat. Park Service, Great Smoky Mountains Nat. Park, summer, 1934, ranger-naturalist, summers, 1939-41; acting editor The Bryologist, 1943-44, asso. editor, 1938-42, 1945-53, Castanea, 1947-66; instr. summer sch. W.Va. U., 1939-41; instr. U. Tenn., 1929-37, asst. prof., 1937-40, asso. prof., 1940-46, prof., 1946-65, Distinguished Service prof., 1965-74, prof. emeritus, 1974—, curator herbarium, 1949-68, asso. curator, 1968—, head botany dept., 1951-61; mem. staff Hattori Bot. Lab., 1956—; vis. prof. Stanford U., 1951, U. Mich. Biol. Sta., 1954-57, 59-64, U. Minn. Biol. Sta., 1971, U. Mont. Biol. Sta., 1972, Nat. U. Taiwan, 1965, Instituto Universitario Pedagógico Experimental, Maracay, Venezuela, 1976, U. Va. Biol. Sta., 1980; Cecil Billington lectr. Cranbrook Inst. Sci., 1947; vis. lectr. Am. Inst. Biol. Scis., 1967-70; trustee Highlands (N.C.) Biol. Labs., 1934-38, 1948-64, bd. mgrs., 1946-52; sec. of sect. Inter-Am. Conf. on Conservation of Renewable Natural Resources, Denver, 1948; mem. nat. adv. bd. Ministry of Ecology, 1975-81. Contbr.: articles to sci. jours. Ency. Brit; asso. editor: Hattori Bot. Jour., Nichinan, Japan, 1961—. Bd. dirs. Gt. Smoky Mountains Conservation Assn., 1960—, Gt. Smoky Mountains Nat. Hist. Assn., 1979-81, U. Tenn. Arboretum Soc., 1979—. Guggenheim Found. fellow, 1944-46. Fellow AAAS (v.p. 1963); mem. New Eng. Bot. Club, Internat. Soc. Phytomorphologists, Internat. Assn. Plant Taxonomy, So. Appalachian Bot. Club (pres. 1946-47), Sullivant Moss Soc. (pres. 1935), Am. Bryol. and Lichen. Soc., Am. Fern Soc., Bot. Soc. Am. (editorial com. 1948-53, treas. 1957-62, v.p. 1963, pres. 1965, Merit award 1972), Soc. for Study Evolution, Soc. Botánica de México (hon.), Soc. Mexicana de Historia Natural, Tenn. Acad. Sci. (exec. com. 1943-44, v.p. 1952, pres. 1953), Am. Soc. Plant Taxonomists (pres. 1961), Assn. Southeastern Biologists (v.p. 1956, Meritorious Tchr. award 1972), Ecol. Soc. Am. (v.p. 1958-59), Torrey Bot. Club, Nature Conservancy (gov. 1955-61), Am. Soc. Naturalists, AAUP, Bot. Brit. Bryol. Soc., Internat. Soc. Tropical Ecology, Internat. Phycolog. Soc., Nat. Assn. Biology Tchrs., Palynolog. Soc. India, Phycolog. Soc. Am., Systematics Assn., Am. Assn. Stratigraphic Palynol., Soc. Latino-americand de Briologia (hon.), Phi Beta Kappa, Phi Kappa Phi, Sigma Xi, Phi Sigma, Phi Epsilon Phi, Sigma Delta Pi. Club: Explorers. Current Work: Plant geography in relation to geological and environmental factors. Subspecialties: Taxonomy; Ecology (environmental science). Home: 1105 Tobler Rd Knoxville TN 37919 Office: U Tenn Knoxville TN 37916

SHARPLESS, NANSIE SUE, neurochemist, educator; b. West Chester, Pa., Oct. 11, 1932; d. George Roberts and Lorraine Eleanor (Way) S. B.A., Oberlin Coll., 1954; M.S., Wayne State U., 1956, Ph.D., 1970. Med. technologist Henry Ford Hosp., Detroit, 1956-67; research asst., research assoc., sr. research fellow Mayo Clinic/Mayo Found., Rochester, Minn., 1970-74; asst. prof. psychiatry Albert Einstein Coll. Medicine, Bronx, N.Y., 1975-81, assoc. prof. psychiatry and neurology, 1981—, lab. chief clin. neuropsychopharmacology, 1983—. Bd. dirs. Alexander Graham Bell Assn. for Deaf, 1980-83; Pres. Found. Sci. and Handicapped, Inc., 1982-84. Recipient Disting. Alumni award Wayne State U., 1980. Mem. Soc. Neurosci., Internat. Soc. Neurochemistry, Am. Chem. Soc., N.Y. Acad. Scis., AAAS (com. office of opportunities in sci. 1977-85), Am. Assn. Clin. Chemistry, Soc. Exptl. Biology and Medicine. Quaker. Current Work: Basic and clinical research in neurotransmitter chemistry, biogenic amines and neurological and psychiatric disorders. Subspecialties: Neurochemistry; Biochemistry (medicine). Office: 1300 Morris Park Ave Bronx NY 10461

SHARPTON, FRANCIS ARTHUR, physics educator, researcher; b. New Vienna, Ohio, Aug. 2, 1936; m. Wanda Ruth Penland, Dec. 22, 1957; 1 son, Jeffrey. B.S., Coll. Ozarks, 1958; M.S., U. Ark., 1960; Ph.D., U. Okla., 1968. Asst. prof. physics Hendrix Coll., Conway, Ark., 1960-64; assoc. prof. Olivet Nazarene Coll., Kankakee, Ill., 1968-70; prof. physics Northwest Nazarene Coll., Nampa, Idaho, 1970—; researcher U. Ark., 1977; vis. prof. U. Wis., Madison, summers, 1979-85. Contbr. articles to profl. jours. Research Corp. grantee, 1970. Mem. Am. Phys. Soc., Sigma Pi Sigma, Sigma Xi. Mem. Ch. of the Nazarene. Current Work: Physics educator at undergrad. level and carrying on an active research program in atomic physics. Subspecialty: Atomic and molecular physics. Office: Dept Physics Northwest Nazarene College Nampa ID 83651

SHATKIN, AARON JEFFREY, biochemist; b. Providence, July 18, 1934; s. Morris and Doris S.; m. Joan A. Lynch, Nov. 30, 1957; 1 son, Gregory Martin. A.B., Bowdoin Coll., 1956, D.Sc. (hon.), 1979; Ph.D., Rockefeller Inst., 1961. Sr. asst. scientist NIH, Bethesda, Md., 1961-63, research chemist, 1963-68; vis. scientist Salk Inst., La Jolla, Calif., 1968-69; asso. mem. dept. cell biology Roche Inst. Molecular Biology, Nutley, N.J., 1968-73, full mem., 1973-77, head molecular virology lab., 1977—, head dept. cell biology, 1983—; adj. prof. cell biology Rockefeller U.; adj. prof. microbiology N.J. U. Medicine, Princeton U. Mem. editorial bd.: Jour. Virology, 1969-82, Archives of Biochemistry & Biophysics, 1972-82, Virology, 1973-76, Comprehensive Virology, 1974-82, Jour. Biol. Chemistry, 1977-83; editor-in-chief: Molecular and Cellular Biology, 1980—; editor: Advances in Virus Research, 1984—. Served with USPHS, 1961-63. Recipient U.S. Steel Found. prize in molecular biology, 1977; Rockefeller fellow, 1956-61. Fellow N.Y. Acad. Scis.; Mem. Nat. Acad. Scis., Am. Soc. Microbiology, Am. Soc. Biol. Chemists, AAAS, N.Y. Acad. Scis., Harvey Soc. Current Work: Mechanisms of Eukaryotic gene expression structure and function of animal viruses. Subspecialties: Molecular biology; Biochemistry (biology). Home: 4 Tanglewood Rd North Caldwell NJ 07006 Office: Roche Inst Molecular Biology Nutley NJ 07110

SHAUB, WALTER MICHAEL, chemist; b. Mt. Vernon, N.Y., Sept. 21, 1947; s. Charles Arthur and Gertrude Josephine (Houghton) S.; m. Jo Ann Lee Harris, Nov. 29, 1969; children—Walter, Rhiannon. B.S., in Chemistry, SUNY-Cortland, 1969; Ph.D., Cornell U., 1975. Research assoc. NSF-NRC, 1975; research assoc. Naval Research Lab., Washington, 1975-76; research chemist, 1976-81; asst. prof. chemistry George Mason U., Fairfax, Va., 1976-78; research chemist Nat. Bur. Standards, Washington, 1981-83, supr., 1983—, also dir. exploratory fire research; chmn. JANNAF Workshops, Chem. Propulsion Info. Agy., Washington, 1982-84. Inventor dioxin chemsorption technique, 1984 (award 1984). Contbg. author: Dioxins, 1984. Recipient award Am. Inst. Chemists, 1969. Mem. Am. Chem. Soc., ASTM, ASME, Am. Def. Preparedness Assn. Current work: Internationally recognized expert dioxin, dibenzonfuran and related compounds formation, destruction and emission control in thermal environments and in thermal treatment, especially municipal solid waste incineration. Subspecialties: Hazardous waste disposal; Physical chemistry. Home: 2027 Winged Foot Ct Reston VA 22091 Office: Nat Bur Standards Washington DC 20234

SHAW, DENIS MARTIN, geology educator; b. St. Annes, Eng., Aug. 20, 1923; emigrated to Can., 1948; s. Norman Wade and Alice Jane Sylvia (Shackleton) S.; m. Pauline Mitchell, Apr. 6, 1946 (div. 1975); children—Geoffrey, Gillian, Peter; m. Susan L. Evans, Apr. 9, 1976. B.Sc., Emmanuel Coll., Cambridge, Eng., 1943, M.Sc., 1948; Ph.D., U. Chgo., 1951. Lectr. McMaster U., Hamilton, Ont., Can., 1949-51, asst. prof., 1951-55, asso. prof., 1955-60, prof. geology, 1960—, chmn. dept., 1953-59, 62-66, dean grad. studies, 1979-84; asso. prof. ENSGA, U. Nancy, France, 1959-60; Invited prof. Inst. de Minéralogie, U. Genève, 1966-67. Exec. editor: Geochimica et Cosmochimica Acta, 1970—; asso. editor: Handbook of Geochemistry, 1966—; Author: Masson Et Cie, 1964. Served with RAF, 1943-46. Fellow Royal Soc. Can. (W.G. Miller medal 1981); mem. Geol. Assn. Can., Geochem. Soc., Mineral. Assn. Can. (pres. 1964; Past Pres.'s medal 1985), Am. Geophys. Union, AAAS. Current work: Trace element distribution mechanisms in minerals and rocks. Subspecialties: Geochemistry; Petrology. Address: Dept Geology McMaster U Hamilton ON L8S 4M1 Canada

SHAW, MARGERY WAYNE SCHLAMP, physician, lawyer; b. Evansville, Ind., Feb. 15, 1923; d. Arthur George and Louise (Meyer) Schlamp; m. Charles Raymond Shaw, May 31, 1942 (div. Nov. 1972); 1 dau., Barbara Rae. Student, Hanover Coll., 1940-41; A.B. magna cum laude, U. Ala., 1945; M.A., Columbia U., 1946; postgrad., Cornell U., 1947-48; M.D. cum laude, U. Mich., 1957; J.D., U. Houston, 1973; D.Sc. (hon.), U. Evansville, 1977. Intern St. Joseph Mercy Hosp., Ann Arbor, Mich., 1957-58, practice medicine specializing in human genetics, 1958-67, Houston, 1967—; instr. dept. human genetics Med. Sch. U. Mich., 1958-61, asst. prof., 1961-66, asso. prof., 1966-67; asso. prof. dept. biology Grad. Sch. Biomed. Scis., U. Tex., Houston, 1967-69, prof., 1969—; dir. Grad. Sch. Biomed. Scis., U. Tex. (Med. Genetics Center), 1971-79; acting dean Grad. Sch. Biomed. Scis., U. Tex. (Grad. Sch. Biomed. Scis.), 1976-78; mem. genetics study sect. NIH, Bethesda, Md., 1966-70, mem. genetics tng. com., 1970-74, adv. com. to dir., 1979-82; chromosome studies astronauts NASA, 1970-71; mem. med. adv. bd. Nat. Genetics Found., 1972—; research adv. bd. Planned Parenthood, Houston, 1972-79; vis. scholar Yale Law Sch., 1974; vis. prof. Cornell U., 1982—. Asso. editor: Am. Jour. Human Genetics, 1962-68; editorial bd.: Am. Jour. Med. Genetics, 1977—, Am. Jour. Law and Medicine, 1977—; contbr. articles to profl. jours. First aid instr. ARC, 1962-67; unit chmn. United Fund, 1966. Recipient Billings Silver medal AMA, 1966; Achievement award AAUW, 1970-71; Am. Jurisprudence award, 1973. Mem. Am. Soc. Human Genetics (past sec., dir., pres. 1982), Genetics Soc. Am. (sec. 1971-73, pres. 1977-78, Wilhelmene Key award 1977), Tissue Culture Assn. (trustee 1970-72), Environ. Mutagen Soc. (council), Am. Soc. Cell Biology, Phi Beta Kappa, Alpha Omega Alpha. Subspecialties: Genetics and genetic engineering (medicine); Health law. Home: 7469 Brompton Blvd Houston TX 77025 Office: Health Law Inst Sch Pub Health Bldg Room 901 1200 Herman Pressler Dr Houston TX 77030

SHAW, MILTON CLAYTON, mechanical engineering educator; b. Phila., May 27, 1915; s. Milton Fredic and Nellie Edith (Clayton) S.; m. Mary Jane Greeninger, Sept. 6, 1939; children—Barbara Jane, Milton Stanley. B.S. in Mech. Engring, Drexel Inst. Tech., 1938; M.Eng. Sci., U. Cin., 1940, Sc.D., 1942; Dr. h.c., U. Louvain, Belgium, 1970. Research engr. Cin. Milling Machine Co., 1938-42; chief materials br. NACA, 1942-46; with Mass. Inst. Tech., 1946-61, prof. mech. engring., 1953-61, head materials processing div., 1952-61; prof., head dept. mech. engring. Carnegie Inst. Tech., Pitts., 1961-75, univ. prof., 1974-77; prof. engring. Ariz. State U., Tempe, 1978—; Cons. indsl. cos.; lectr. in, Europe, 1952; pres. Shaw Smith & Assos., Inc., Mass., 1951-61; Lucas prof. Birmingham (Eng.) U., 1961; Springer prof. U. Calif. at Berkeley, 1972; Distinguished guest prof. Ariz. State U., 1977; mem. Nat. Materials Adv. Bd., 1971-74; bd. dirs. Engring. Found., 1976, v.p. conf. com., 1976-78. Recipient gold medal Am. Soc. Tool Engrs., 1958; Outstanding Research award Ariz. State U., 1981; Guggenheim fellow, 1956; Fulbright lectr. Aachen T.H., Germany, 1957; OECD fellow to Europe, 1964—. Fellow Am. Acad. Arts and Scis., ASME (Hersey award 1967, Thurston lectr. 1971, meeting theme organizer 1977, hon. 1980; soc. medal 1985), Am. Soc. Lubrication Engrs.; mem. (Nat. award 1964, hon. life); titular mem. Internat. Soc. Prodn. Engring. Research (pres. 1960-61, hon. mem. 1975), Am. Soc. Metals (Wilson award 1971); mem. Am. Soc. for Engring. Edn. (G. Westinghouse award 1956), Soc. Mfg. Engrs. (hon., Gold medal 1970, P. McKenna award 1975, Gold medal 1958, Am. Machinist award 1973, internat. edn. award 1980), Nat. Acad. Engring., Polish Acad. Sci. Current Work: Material processing, brittle fracture tribology; engineering design, materials behavior. Subspecialties: Mechanical engineering; Solid mechanics. Home: 326 E Fairmont Dr Tempe AZ 85282 1540 Spanish Moss Way Flagstaff AZ 86001

SHAW, ROBERT WILSON, physical chemist; b. York, Pa., Jan. 27, 1942; s. Robert Wilson and Harriet Katherine (Thompson) S.; m. Barbara Joanne Ramsay, June 14, 1969; 1 child, Susan Maureen. B.A., Williams Coll., 1964; Ph.D., U. Wash., 1970. Postdoctoral fellow Princeton U., N.J., 1970-73; vis. asst. prof. U. Oreg., Eugene, 1973-75; research chemist EPA, Research Triangle Park, N.C., 1975-82; chief, phys. and analytical chemistry Army Research Office, Research Triangle Park, 1982—; cons. to industry; dir. Am. Inks, Valley Forge, Pa. Contbr. articles to profl. jours. Recipient Silver medal EPA, 1983, Sci. and Tech. Achievement award, 1981, 83, 84; NATO grantee, 1975. Mem. Am. Chem. Soc., Am. Phys. Soc., Phi Beta Kappa. Subspecialties: Physical chemistry; Environmental chemistry. Home: 14 Forest Ridge Pl Durham NC 27705 Office: US Army Research Office PO Box 12211 C&B Research Triangle Park NC 27709-2211

SHAW, WILLIAM WEI-LIEN, microsurgeon, plastic surgeon; b. Kwei-Yang, Kwei-Chow, China, Mar. 12, 1942; came to U.S., 1957, naturalized, 1963; s. Emil and Rosemarie (Lam) S.; m. Margaret Pao, Oct. 19, 1975; children: Emily, Victor. B.A., UCLA, 1964, M.D., 1968. Diplomate: Am. Bd. Surgery, Am. Bd. Plastic Surgery. Surg. resident UCLA Med. Ctr., 1969-70, 73-74, Johns Hopkins Med. Ctr., 1972; plastic surgery resident Inst. Reconstructive Plastic Surgery, NYU Med. Ctr., N.Y.C., 1975-77, instr. surgery, 1977-79, asst. prof. surgery, 1979-83, assoc. prof., 1983—; dir. clin. microsurgery Bellevue (N.Y.) Hosp., 1977—, chief plastic surgery service, 1977—; cons. plastic surgeon VA Hosp., Castle Point, N.Y., 1977—; attending plastic surgeon Manhattan Eye, Ear and Throat Hosp., Univ. Hosp., N.Y. VA Hosp., N.Y. Infirmary/Beekman Downtown Hosp. Served to maj. U.S. Army, 1970-72. Regents scholar UCLA Sch. Medicine, 1963-68; recipient Golden Plate award Am. Acad. Achievement, 1980; Regents Disting. Service award Fairleigh Dickinson U., 1980; U.S. Army Meritorious Service award, 1972. Fellow ACS; mem. Am. Soc. Plastic and Reconstructive Surgeons, Internat. Soc. Reconstructive Microsurgery, Am. Assn. Surgery of Trauma, N.Y. County Med. Soc. Republican. Current Work: Microsurgery in trauma and replantation, tissue preservation and transplantation, breast reconstruction. Subspecialties: Microsurgery; Transplant surgery. Office: 302 E 30th St New York NY 10016

SHAY, WILLIAM ALBERT, mathematics, computer science educator; b. Chgo., Jan. 14, 1949; s. John Joseph and Madeline Ruth (Brandimore) S.; m. Judith Ann, Jan. 8, 1972; 1 son, Daniel John. B.A. in Math., St. Mary's Coll., 1971; M.A. in Math., U. Wis.-Milw., 1973, Ph.D. in Math., 1978. Teaching asst. U. Wis.-Milw., 1971-78, research asst., 1973-74, fellow, 1975, lectr., 1978; asst. prof. math. U. Wis.-Green Bay, 1974-84, assoc. prof., 1984—, dir. computer sci. summer camps, 1980-84. Contbr. articles to profl. jours. Mem. Assn. Computing Machinery, Soc. Indsl. and Applied Math., Math. Assn. Am. Current work: Research in numerical analysis, solutions to partial different equations of fluid dynamics, teaching computer science education, database management, algorithms. Subspecialties: Numerical analysis (computer science); Database systems. Office: Dept Math U Wis-Green Bay Green Bay WI 54301

SHEA, DANIEL JOSEPH, engineering company executive, operations engineering consultant; b. Providence, Dec. 21, 1943; s. Daniel J. and Ann L. (Remillard) S. B.A., U. Louvain, Belgium, 1971, M.A., 1973. Lic. reactor operator, U.S. NRC. Dir. personnel analysis NUS/Halliburton, Rockville, Md., 1975-82; pres. Human Engring. Assocs., Inc., Houston, 1982—; cons. Houston Lighting & Power, La. Power & Ligh, Central Power & Light. Served in USN, 1960-65. Mem. Am. Nuclear Soc. Republican. Roman Catholic. Current Work: Operations safety research relative to light water nuclear power plant operations; integration of hardware design, operating procedure design, job design and training design. Subspecialties: Human factors engineering; Operations research (engineering). Home: 1203 W Bell Houston TX 77019

SHEALY, Y. FULMER, medicinal and organic chemist; b. Chapin, S.C., Feb. 26, 1923; s. L. Yoder and L. Essie (Fulmer) S.; m. Elaine Curtis, Oct. 5, 1950; children—Robin T., Nancy G., Priscilla B. B.S., U. S.C., 1943; Ph.D., U. Ill., 1949. Postdoctoral fellow U. Minn., Mpls., 1949-50; chemist Upjohn Co., Kalamazoo, 1950-56; asst. prof. U. S.C., 1956-57; sr. chemist So. Research Inst., Birmingham, 1957-59, sect. head, 1959-66, head medicinal chem. div., 1966—. Patentee medicinal agents; pioneer in carbocyclic analogs of nucleosides including carbodine; synthesized anti-cancer drug dacarbazine. Contbr. articles to profl. jours. Mem. Am. Chem. Soc., N.Y. Acad. Scis., Internat. Soc. Heterocyclic Chemistry, Pharm. Soc. Japan, AAAS, Sigma Xi, Phi Beta Kappa, Phi Lambda Upsilon, Pi Mu Epsilon. Fellow Acad. Pharm. Scis. Synthesis of reactive compounds for cancer chemotherapy, synthesis of retinoids; Synthesis of antiviral agts. Subspecialties: Drug design; Medicinal chemistry. Southern Research Inst PO Box 55305 Birmingham AL 35255 Office: So Research Inst 2000 9th Ave S Birmingham AL 35255

SHEAR, NATHANIEL, physicist; b. Bklyn., Dec. 20, 1908; s. Victor Jacob and Henrietta Leah (Robinson) S. A.B. with honors, Columbia U., 1930, M.A., 1932. Physicist U.S. Navy, Civil Service, Washington, Phila., Lakehurst, N.J., 1937-44; research physicist div. war research Columbia U., N.Y.C., 1944-46; ops. research analyst MIT Ops. Evaluation Group, U.S. Navy, Washington, 1946-48; physicist Bur. Ships, U.S. Navy, Washington, 1948-51; cons. physicists, Alexandria, Va., 1951-60, U.S. Naval Research Lab., Washington, 1954-60; physicist Emerson Research Lab., Silver Spring, Md., 1960-62; sr. physicist Johns Hopkins U. Applied Physics Lab., Laurel, Md., 1962-66; cons physics, Silver Spring, Md., 1966-69; ops. research analyst Def. Spl. Projects Group, Washington, 1969-72, retired, 1972—. Author sci. reports for, U.S. Navy. Mem. Va. Acad. Sci., Ops. Research Soc. Am., Am. Phys. Soc., U.S. Naval Inst. (assoc.), Phi Beta Kappa. Current Work: Integrating and coordinating scientific papers prepared for the Navy. Subspecialties: Operations research (mathematics); Oceanography. Home: 1401 Blair Mill Rd Apt 612 Silver Spring MD 20910

SHEARER, DAVID ROSS, behavioral medicine specialist, consultant in health psychology; b. Houston, Mar. 2, 1950; s. Hutton A. and Francile (Thompson) S.; m. Penelope Lynn Potter, May 18, 1972 (div. June 1977). B.A., Tex. Christian U., 1972, M.A., 1977; postgrad., Tex. Woman's U., 1975-76, Hawaii Sch. Profl. Psychology, 1983—. Lic. family therapist, Calif. Adolescent team coordinator Psychiat. Inst., Ft. Worth, 1974-75; psychol. asso. Ft. Worth Psychol. Center, 1974-77; psychologist Tex. Dept. Mental Health & Mental Retardation, San Angelo, 1977-78; flight service dir. Am. Airlines, Los

Angeles, 1979-81; behavioral medicine specialist Straub Clinic, Honolulu, 1982—; adj. clin. prof. Antioch U. Hawaii, Honolulu, 1982—. Author: 12 weeks to a Healthier Lifestyle, 1982, Handling Stress at Home and on the Job, 1982, others. Pres. adv. bd. Diamond Head Mental Health Ctr., 1982; Clin research fellow Inst. Child Health, U. Benin, Nigeria, 1978. Mem. Am. Psychol. Assn., Am. Acad. Behavioral Medicine, Acad. Psychologists in Marital, Sex, and Family Therapy, Am. Orthopsychiat. Assn., Am. Soc. Tng. and Devel., Psi Chi. Republican. Episcopalian. Lodge: Masons. Current Work: Behavioral medicine and health psychology, psychology of lifestyle change - psychoneuroimmunology, stress management, instructional systems design. Subspecialties: Preventive medicine; Neuroimmunology. Home: 2452 Tusitala #710 Honolulu HI 96815 Office: Straub Clinic & Hosp Inc 888 S King St Honolulu HI 96813

SHEARER, RUTH EVELYN WHISLER, molecular geneticist; b. Portland, Oreg., Mar. 23, 1930; d. Hugh Levan and Alice Gertrude (Gilstrap) Whisler; m. Jack Eric Shearer, Dec. 29, 1951; children—Daniel Jack, Alice Joy, Donald Hugh, James Edward. B.S., Oreg. State U., 1953; M.S., U. Wash., 1966, Ph.D. in Genetics, 1969, postgrad. in pathology, 1969-71. Head dept. molecular biology Pacific Northwest Research Found., Seattle, 1971-76; asst. mem. Fred Hutchinson Cancer Research Ctr., Seattle, 1973-76; program dir. cancer research Issaquah Health Research Inst., 1976-80; mem. sci. council Pacific Sci. Ctr., Seattle, 1972-77; cons. in genetic toxicology for pub. agys. and citizens groups, 1977—. Contbr. articles to profl. jours. Elected commr. King County Water and Sewer Dist. #82, Wash., 1981—; bd. dirs. Seattle Country Day Sch., 1975-79. Nat. Cancer Inst. postdoctoral fellow, 1969-71; Damon Runyon Meml. Fund grantee for cancer research, 1971-74; Nat. Cancer Inst. grantee, 1973-80. Mem. AAAS, AAUW, Pacific Northwest Assn. Toxicologists, Phi Kappa Phi. . Home and Office: 2017 E Beaver Lake Dr SE Issaquah WA 98027

SHEARIN, NANCY LOUISE, physiology research educator; b. Meridian, Miss., May 17, 1938; d. Robert F. and Ossie (Wall) S. B.S., Millsaps Coll., 1960; M.S., Tenn. Tech. U., 1971; Ph.D., U. Wyo., 1974. Fellow Meml. U. Nfld., St. John's, Can., 1974-76; research assoc. U. Alta., Edmonton, Can., 1976-79; research assoc. dept. physiology U. Utah, Salt Lake City, 1979-82, research instr. gastrointestinal physiology, 1982—. Mem. Am. Physiol. Soc. Current Work: Gastrointestinal motility, ionic flux in smooth muscle, role of prostaglandins in gastrointestinal physiology, direct intracellular measurement (ionselective microelectrode) of ionic activities in colonic smooth muscle. Subspecialties: Physiology (medicine); Gastroenterology. Office: Dept Surgery U Utah Sch Medicine 50 N Medical Dr Salt Lake City UT 84132

SHEEHY, JEROME JOSEPH, electrical engineer; b. Hartford, Conn., Dec. 3, 1935; s. Jeremiah and Anna (Foley) S.; m. Jean Ann Baldassari, Oct. 13, 1962; children—Caroline, Jerome, Daniel, Carlene. B.S.E.E., U. Conn., 1962, M.S.E.E., 1967. Elec. engr. U.S. Naval Underwater Sound Lab., New London, Conn., 1962-69; tech. staff Rockwell Internat., Anaheim, Calif., 1969-74; staff engr. Hughes Aircraft Co., Fullerton, Calif., 1974-83; sr. research engr. Norden Systems, Santa Ana, Calif., 1983—. Contbr. articles to profl. jours. Served with USAF, 1954-57. Mem. Acoustical Soc. Am., IEEE. Democrat. Roman Catholic. Current work: Detection and estimation theory; radar and signal processing; parameter estimation in non-Gaussian noise. Subspecialties: Analysis; Aerospace engineering and technology. Home: 22951 Belquest Dr El Toro CA 92630 Office: Norden Systems 1740 E Garry Santa Ana CA 92705

SHEETZ, DAVID PATRICK, chemical company executive; b. Colebrook, Pa., Dec. 4, 1926; s. David S. and Ella (Youtz) S.; m. Mary Blumer, Feb. 24, 1946; children—Michael, Matthew, Martha. B.S., Lebanon Valley Coll., 1948; M.S. in Phys. Chemistry, U. Nebr., 1951, Ph.D., 1952. In various research and devel. mgmt. positions Dow Chem. Co., Midland, Mich., 1952-67, asst. dir. research and devel. Mich. div., 1967-71, research and devel. dir. Mich. div., 1971-78, v.p., dir. research and devel., 1980—; tech. dir. Dow Chem. U.S.A., Midland, 1978, v.p., dir. research and devel. v.p., dir. research and devel. Dow Chem. Co., 1980—, also dir. 1978-80; Patentee in field. Served with USN, 1945-46. Fellow Am. Inst. Chemists; mem. Am. Chem. Soc., Indsl. Research Inst. (rep.), council for Chem. Research (rep.), Matrix Midland Sci. Com., Sigma Xi. Office: Dow Chem Co 2030 WH Dow Ctr Midland MI 48674

SHEFF, JAMES ROBERT, nuclear and energy engineering educator; b. Colorado Springs, Colo., Nov. 5, 1936; s. Robert Lee and Jessie Marie (Leathers) S.; m. Linda Anne Smith, June 7, 1959 (div. June 1973); children: Robert Benjamin, Nancy Elizabeth (dec.), Natalie Joy, Matthew Garner. B.S.Ch.E., U. Colo., Boulder, 1959; M.S., U. Wash.-Seattle, 1962, Ph.D., 1965; postgrad., Columbia Basin Coll., 1976. Registered profl. engr., Wash. Chem. engr. Gen. Electric Co., Richland, Wash., 1959-60; sr. research engr. Battelle N.W., Richland, 1965-70, WADCO (Westinghouse subs.), Richland, 1970-71; sr. research scientist Battelle-N.W., Richland, 1971-77; prof. nuclear and energy engring. U. Lowell, Mass., 1977—; pres., cons. Desert Ventures, Richland, Wash., 1973-77, Ventures in Energy, Lowell, Mass., 1977-81; cons. Gen. Pub. Utilities-Three Mile Island, Harrisburg, Pa., 1981—; pres., cons. Lowell (Mass.) Tech. Assocs., 1982—. Contbr. articles in field to profl. jours. Mem. Mass. Voice of Energy, Boston, 1977-80. U.S. Dept. Energy grantee, 1977. Mem. Am. Nuclear Soc., Soc. Profl. Well Log Analysts, N.Y. Acad. Scientists, Sigma Xi, Tau Beta Pi, Phi Lambda Upsilon. Club: Toastmasters (Richland, Wash.) (pres. 1965-70). Current Work: Nuclear, wind and geothermal engineering topics, rad waste disposal, reactor physics, windmill design theory, geothermal theory. Subspecialties: Nuclear engineering; Wind power. Home: PO Box 811 Lowell MA 01853 Office: U Lowell 226 Engring Bldg Lowell MA 01854

SHEFFER, RICHARD DOUGLAS, cytogeneticist, educator; b. Portland, Ind., Apr. 19, 1942; s. Elwood Willard and Helen Irene (Hartzell) S.; m. Janet Elston, June 8, 1969; 1 son, Donald Douglas. Student, Ind. U., 1960-63; B.S. with distinction, Purdue U., 1970; Ph.D., U. Hawaii, 1974. Postdoctoral research asso. U. Hawaii, Honolulu, 1974-75; asst. prof. biology U. N.B. (Can.), Fredericton, 1975-76; insr. biology Montclair State Coll., Upper Montclair, N.J., 1976-77; asst. prof. biology Ind. U. N.W., Gary, 1977-81, assoc. prof., 1981—; research assoc. Mo. Bot. Garden, St. Louis, 1979—. Contbr. articles to sci. jours. Served with M.C. U.S. Army, 1964-66. NDEA fellow, 1970-72; Stanley Smith Hort. Trust asst., 1972-74. Mem. AAAS, Genetics Soc. Can., Genetics Soc. Am., Am. Genetics Assn., Am. Soc. Plant Taxonomists, Internat. Assn. Plant Taxonomists, Soc. Study of Evolution, Am. Inst. Biol. Scis., Am. Orchid Soc., Am. Soc. Hort. Sci., Internat. Aroid Soc., N.Y. Acad. Sci., Sigma Xi, Phi Kappa Phi, Gamma Sigma Delta. Current Work: IT*Anthurium cytogenetic and biosystematic studies including chromosome banding, karyotype analysis, chromosomal evolution and meiotic studies of Fone interspecific hybrides to determine interspecific relationships. Subspecialties: Genome organization; Systematics. Home: 208 Shorewood Dr Valparaiso IN 46383 Office: 3400 Broadway Gary IN 46408

SHEFFIELD, JOEL B., biology educator, consultant; b. Bklyn., Dec. 30, 1942; s. Reuben and Gertrude S.; m. Lucy Paige, June 20, 1965; 1 dau., Jennifer. A.B., Brandeis U., 1963; Ph.D., U. Chgo., 1969. Research assoc. Rockefeller U., 1963-64; postdoctoral fellow Netherlands Cancer Inst., 1969-71; asst. mem. Inst. Med. Research, Camden, N.J., 1971-77; asst. prof. biology Temple U., 1977-82, assoc. prof., 1982—Current Work: Developmental cell biology of eye. Subspecialties: Developmental biology; Neurobiology. Office: Dept Biology Temple U Philadelphia PA 19122

SHEINBERG, HASKELL, powder metallurgist, ceramics engineer; b. Houston, Dec. 12, 1919; s. Max and Leona S.; m. Beatrice Freeman, Oct. 13, 1946; children—Michael F., Arthur L. B.S. in Chem. Engring., Rice U., 1941. Progress engr. Consol. Steel Co., Orange, Tex., 1941-43; powder metallurgist Los Alamos Nat. Lab., 1946—; cons., 1980—. Contbr. articles to profl. jours. Patentee in field. Served with U.S. Army, 1943-45. Recipient Disting. Patent award Los Alamos Nat. Lab., 1984; Lab. fellow Los Alamos Nat. Lab., 1982. Fellow Am. Soc. for Metals (pres. N.Mex. 1966-67); mem. Am. Powder Metallurgy Inst., Fine Particle Soc., ASTM, Am. Ceramics Soc. (v.p. N.Mex. 1969-70), Metals Inst. (London), Metall. Soc of AIME. Lodge: B'nai Brith. Current work: Material science with emphasis on refractory metals/compounds, carbon and graphite, refractory ceramics, consulting, powder technology. Subspecialties: Metallurgy; Ceramics. Office: Los Alamos Nat Lab PO Box 1663 G770 Los Alamos NM 97545

SHELLEY, EDWIN FREEMAN, educational administrator, engineering and business consultant; b. N.Y.C., Feb. 19, 1921; s. Robert and Jessie Selma (Sinick) S.; m. Florence W. Dubroff, Aug. 31, 1941; children: Carolyn Shelley LeBel, William Edson. A.B., Columbia U., 1940, B.S.E.E., 1941; cert. advanced mgmt. program, Harvard U., 1957. Flight test engr. Curtiss Wright Corp., Caldwell, N.J., 1941-47; pres., chief engr. Am. Chronoscope Corp., Mt. Vernon, N.Y., 1948-50; v.p., chief engr. Bulova Research and Devel. Labs., Inc., Jackson Heights, N.Y., 1950-57; v.p., dir. advanced programs U.S. Industries, Inc., N.Y.C., 1957-64; pres., chmn. EF Shelley & Co., Inc., N.Y.C. and Washington, 1965-75; dir. center for energy policy and research N.Y. Inst. Tech., 1975—; trustee N.Y. Inst. Tech., Nova U. Mem. adv. bd. N.Y. State Legisl. Commn. on Sci. and Tech., 1977—; pres. Nat. Council on Aging, 1968-72, bd. dirs., 1962-83. Mem. IEEE (sr.), AIAA, AAAS, Newcomen Soc. N.Am. Club: Harvard (N.Y.C.). Patentee in field. Current Work: Information systems, educational technology, flight systems, energy education, consulting for energy-related businesses, educational technology development, flight system development. Subspecialties: Systems engineering; Information systems (Information science). Home: 339 Oxford Rd New Rochelle NY 10804 Office: Center Energy Policy NY Inst Tech Old Westbury NY 11568

SHELLEY, PHILIP EUGENE, environmental engineer, consultant; b. Bristol, Va., Oct. 5, 1935; s. Marion Philip and Mary (Stover) S.; m. Patricia Louise Barnes, May 22, 1959 (div. 1975); children—Pamela Jane, Peter Marvin, Philip Merrill (dec.); m. Sonya Nelson Iverson, June 22, 1976. B.M.E., U. Tenn., 1958, M.S., 1961; Ph.D., Va. Poly. Inst., 1967. Assoc. engr. Union Carbide, Oak Ridge, 1956-61; sr. research scientist Martin-Marietta, Balt., 1961-67; dir. environ. systems EG&G Washington Analytical Service Ctr., Inc., Rockville, Md., 1967—. Author various govt. reports; also contbr. articles to profl. jours. Editor: Dredging and Sediment Control, 1980. Choir dir. First Christian Ch., Blacksburg, Va., 1961; elder First Christian Ch., Balt., 1963-67, North Chevy Chase Christian Ch., Md., 1980—. Recipient Outstanding Publ. award Martin-Marietta, 1965; Tenn. Eastman scholar U. Tenn., Knoxville, 1953; U.S. Steel Found. fellow Va. Poly. Inst., 1960-61. Mem. Am. Geophys. Union, Water Pollution Control Fedn., ASME, Sigma Xi, Tau Beta Pi. Republican. Current work: Characterization, impact assessment, and control of nonpoint source water pollution; water pollution monitoring and data analysis. Subspecialties: Environmental engineering; Hydrology. Home: 11708 Tifton Dr Potomac MD 20854 Office: EG&G Washington Analytical Service Ctr 1396 Piccard Dr Rockville MD 20850

SHELNUTT, JAMES WILLIAM, III, engineering technology educator, consultant; b. Greenville, S.C., Nov. 5, 1938; s. James William and Myrtle Lorene (Baber) S.; m. Evelyn Brown Waldrop, Sept. 11, 1961 (div. Aug. 1981); 1 child, Gregory William. B.M.E., General Motors Inst., Flint, Mich., 1962; M.S. in Systems Engring., Air Force Inst. Tech., Dayton, Ohio, 1966. Registered profl. engr., N.C., Ohio. Process engr. Fisher Body div. Gen. Motors Corp., Flint, 1961-63; project engr. air proving ground ctr. Eglin AFB, Fla., 1963-65; dep. dir. energy conversion lab. Wright Patterson AFB, Ohio, 1967-71; chmn., mech. engr. tech. U. Cin., 1972-78; chmn., engring. tech. U. of N.C.-Charlotte, 1978—; staff assoc. Stanford & Toomey, Cons. Engrs., Charlotte, 1978—. Patentee Scanning Photometer. Commr. Charlotte-Mecklenburg Energy Commn., 1983—. Served to capt. USAF, 1963-71. Mem. ASME (edn. chmn. region IV 1982—), Am. Soc. Engring. Edn., Soc. Mfg. Engrs., ASHRAE (chmn. edn. So. Piedmont chpt., Disting. Service award, 1983), Tau Beta Pi. Democrat. Mem. Unitarian Ch. Current work: Energy use and conservation in buildings; computer modeling of annual energy consumption; manufacturing and mechanical engineering technology; computer integrated manufacturing. Subspecialties: Energy systems in buildings; Mechanical engineering. Office: Dept Engring Tech Univ N C Charlotte NC 28223

SHELOKOV, ALEXIS, physician, vaccine developer; b. Harbin, China, Oct. 18, 1919; came to U.S., 1938, naturalized, 1944; s. Ivan T. and Maria M. (Zolotov) S.; m. Paula Helbig, June 10, 1947; 1 child, Alexis Paul. A.B., Stanford U., 1943, M.D., 1948. Diplomate Am. Bd. Microbiology, Am. Bd. Preventive Medicine. Physiologist climatic research lab. War Dept., 1943-44; research asst. Stanford, 1946-47; house officer Mass. Meml. Hosps., Boston, 1947-50; instr. medicine Boston U. Sch. Medicine, 1948-50; asst. in pediatrics Harvard Med. Sch., 1949-50; clin. instr. medicine Georgetown U., 1953-57; cons. D.C. Gen. Hosp., 1955-57, Gorgas, Coco Solo hosps., C.Z., 1958-61; dir. Middle Am. Research Unit, C.Z., 1957-61; mem. sci. adv. bd. Gorgas Meml. Inst., Panama, 1959-72, 76—; chief lab. tropical virology Nat. Inst. Allergy and Infectious Diseases, NIH, 1959-63; chief lab. virology and rickettsiology Div. Biologics Standards, NIH, 1963-68; officer (med. dir.) USPHS, 1950-68; prof., chmn. dept. microbiology U. Tex. Health Sci. Center, San Antonio, 1968-81; prof. dept. epidemiology Johns Hopkins U. Sch. Hygiene and Public Health, 1981-85, dir. vaccine research Salk Inst., 1981—; mem. U.S. del. on virus diseases to USSR, 1961, chmn. U.S. del. on hemorrhagic fevers, USSR, 1965, 69; exec. council Am. Com. for Arthropod-borne Viruses, 1960-67; panel for arthropod-borne virus reagents. Nat. Inst. Allergy and Infectious Diseases, 1962-66, cons. geog. medicine br., 1972-76; mem. sci. adv. bd. WHO Serum Bank, Yale, 1964-68; cons. Pan Am. Health Orgn., 1958-63, 71, WHO, 1966; mem. commn. on viral infections Armed Forces Epidemiological Bd., 1967-68; mem. virology study sect. div. research grants NIH, 1968-70; mem. viral disease panel U.S.-Japan Coop. Med. Sci. Program, 1971-76; mem. Am. Tropical Medicine del., China; adv. bd. virology CRC Press, 1975-80. Mem. editorial bd.: Am. Jour. Tropical Medicine and Hygiene, 1973—, Jour. Clin. Microbiology, 1976—, Archives of Virology, 1979-81. Trustee Am. Type Culture Collection, 1969-72; bd. sci. counselors Nat. Inst. Dental Research, NIH, 1971-75. Decorated Order Rodolfo Robles (Guatemala). Mem. Am. Assn. Immunologists, Soc. Exptl. Biology and Medicine, Am. Soc. Tropical Medicine and Hygiene, Am. Epidemiologic Soc., AMA, Infectious Disease Soc. Am., Soc. Epidemiological Research, Am. Soc. Microbiology. Current Work: Research and development of viral vaccines. Subspecialties: Virology (medicine); Epidemiology. Home: 7233 Dockside Ln Columbia MD 21045 Office: Salk Inst 9200 Old Annapolis Rd Columbia MD 21045

SHELTON, DAMON CHARLES, nutritionist, biochemist; b. Richland, Ind., Apr. 4, 1922; s. Charles and Opal (Hildebrandt) S.; m. V. Maxine Hall, Dec. 24, 1943; children—Karen, Sandra. B.S. with honors, Purdue U., 1947, M.S., 1949, Ph.D., 1950. Assoc. prof. W.Va. U., Morgantown, 1953-57, prof., 1957-60, assoc. prof. Med. Ctr., 1960-65, prof., 1965-67; mgr. spl. chows research Ralston Purina Co., St. Louis, 1967-75, dir. spl. chows research, 1975—. Served to 1st lt. U.S. Army, 1943-46. Fellow AAAS; mem. Am. Soc. Biol. Chemists, Am. Chem. Soc., Am. Inst. Nutrition, Am. Soc. Microbiology, Am. Assn. Lab. Animal Sci. Current work: Direct research and development activities of laboratory and special chows department. Subspecialties: Animal nutrition; Biochemistry (biology). Home: 9338 Lincoln Dr Saint Louis MO 63127 Office: Ralston Purina Co Checkerboard Sq Saint Louis MO 63164

SHEMIN, DAVID, biochemist, educator; b. N.Y.C., Mar. 18, 1911; s. Louis and Mary (Bush) S.; m. Mildred B. Sumpter (dec. 1962); children: Louise P., Elizabeth; m. Charlotte Norton, Mar. 1963. B.S., CCNY, 1932; A.M., Columbia U., 1933; Ph.D., Columbia, 1938. Asst. prof. biochemistry Columbia, 1945-49, assoc. prof., 1949-53, prof., 1953-68; chmn. dept. biochemistry and molecular biology Northwestern U., Evanston, Ill., 1968—, prof. biochemistry, 1968—. Contbr. articles to sci. publs. Recipient Pasteur medal, Stevens award.; Guggenheim fellow; Commonwealth fellow; Fogarty Internat. scholar, 1981-85. Mem. Nat. Acad. Sci., Am. Acad. Arts and Scis. Current Work: Deputy director of Cancer Center at Northwestern University. Subspecialties: Biochemistry (biology); Enzyme technology. Home: 902 Lincoln St Evanston IL 60201 Office: Dept Biochemistry and Molecular Biology Northwestern U Evanston IL 60201

SHEN, BENJAMIN SHIH-PING, astrophysicist; b. Hangzhou, China, Sept. 14, 1931; s. Nai-cheng and Chen-chiu (Sun) S.; m. Lucia Simpson, July 31, 1971; children—William Li, Juliet Ming. A.B. summa cum laude, Assumption Coll., Mass., 1954, Sc.D. (hon.), 1972; A.M. in Physics, Clark U., 1956; D.Sc. d'Etat in Physics, U. Paris, 1964; M.A. (hon.), U. Pa., 1971. Tchr., Assumption Prep. Sch., Worcester, Mass., 1954-56; asst. prof. physics SUNY-Albany, 1956-59; asso. prof. space sci., dept. aeros. and astronautics Engring. Sch., NYU, 1964-66; asso. prof. U. Pa., Phila., 1966-68, prof., 1968-72, Reese W. Flower prof. astronomy and astrophysics, 1972—, founding chmn. Roundtable on Sci., Industry and Policy, Wharton Sch., 1976—, asso. univ. provost, 1979-80, chmn. council grad. deans, 1979-81, acting univ. provost and chief acad. officer, 1980-81, chmn. dept. astronomy and astrophysics, 1973-79, dir. Flower and Cook Obs., 1973-79, mem. Energy Center, 1976—; cons. Space Sci. Lab., Gen. Electric Co., 1961-68, Am. Inst. Physics, 1965, 72-75, Office of Tech. Assessment, U.S. Congress, 1977-78; sci. and tech. adviser U.S. Senate Budget Com., 1976-77; guest staff mem. Brookhaven Nat. Lab., 1963-64, 65-70; gen. chmn. Internat. Symposium on High-Energy Nuclear Reactions in Astrophysics, 1967; founding chmn. Com. on Public Understanding of Sci., N.Y. Acad. Scis., 1972-75; gen. chmn. Internat. Conf. on Spallation Nuclear Reactions and Their Applications in Astrophysics and Radiotherapy, 1975. Author: Contribution à l'Etude du Passage des Protons dans des Milieux Condensés, 1964; editor, co-author: High-Energy Nuclear Reactions in Astrophysics, 1967; co-editor, co-author: Spallation Nuclear Reactions and Their Applications, 1976; asso. editor: Biosci. Communications, 1974-77; mem. editorial bd.: Earth and Extraterrestrial Scis., 1974-78; asso. editor, 1978-79, Comments on Astrophysics, 1979—; editor: Astron. Series of U. Pa. 1973-79; contbr. articles profl. jours. Mem. Hayden Planetarium com. of bd. trustees Am. Mus. Natural History, N.Y.C., 1978—; mem. sci. adv. bd. Children's TV Workshop, N.Y.C., 1977, 79—; mem. adv. com. Mt. John Obs., N.Z., 1978—. Recipient Cottrell grant Research Corp., 1957-59; Dupont scholar Wesleyan U., 1956; Vermeil medal for sci. Société d'Encouragement au Progrès, France, 1978. Fellow Am. Phys. Soc., AAAS (com. on sci. engring. and pub. policy 1978—, chmn. subcom. on fed. research and devel. budget and policy 1978-81), Royal Astron. Soc. (U.K.), Joint Assn. for Geophysics (U.K.); mem. Am. Astron. Soc., Internat. Astron. Union. Subspecialty: High energy astrophysics. Office: David Rittenhouse Lab E-1 U Pa Philadelphia PA 19104

SHEN, CHIAYI, dental materials educator; b. Taiwan, China, Apr. 27, 1949; came to U.S., 1971; naturalized, 1985; s. Cheng-Kon and Kwan-Ji (Chow) S.; m. Cynthia Hsien Huang, Aug. 16, 1975; 1 child, Shu-Ping. B.S., Chung-Yuan Coll., Taiwan, 1970; M.S., U. Cin., 1974, Ph.D., 1975. Research asst. U. Cin., 1972-75, NIH postdoctoral fellow U. Fla., Gainesville, 1977-79, asst. prof., 1970-85, assoc. prof., 1985—; grad. faculty, U. Fla., Gainesville, 1980—; acting chmn. Dental Biomaterials, 1981-83. Grant Coll. Denistry U. Fla., 1983. Mem. Internat. Dental Research Assn., Am. Assn. Dental Research (pres. chpt. 1980-82), Am. Chem. Soc. Current work: Basic science of failure of dental restorations toward improvement of materials for dental applications; mathematical modeling of fluoride uptake and loss on tooth surface. Subspecialties: Polymers (materials science); Biomedical engineering. Home: 4727 NW 19th Pl Gainesville FL 32605 Office: U Fla Box J446 JHMHC Gainesville FL 32610

SHEN, SIN-YAN, physicist; b. Singapore, Nov. 12, 1949; came to U.S., 1969, naturalized, 1984; s. Shao-Quan and Tien-Siu (Chen) S.; m. Yuan-Yuan Lee, Aug. 4, 1973; children—Jia, Jian. B.Sc. U. Singapore, 1969; M.S. Ohio State U. 1970, Ph.D., 1973. Instr. math. U. Singapore, 1969; asst. prof. physics Northwestern U., Evanston, Ill., 1974-77; faculty assoc. Argonne Nat. Lab., Ill., 1974-77, scientist, 1977—; meeting series reviewer NSF, Washington, 1981—; coordinator Tech. Rev., Argonne, Atlanta, Phoenix, Portland (Oreg.), 1983—. Author: Superfluidity, 1982. Patentee molten liquids, 1974, 1980. Contbr. articles prof. jours. Fulbright scholar U.S. State Dept, 1969; merit scholar Govt. Singapore, 1967; adv. Encyclopedia Brittanica, 1983—. Mem. AAAS, Am. Phys. Soc., Ops. Research Soc. Am. Current work: Renewable energy and materials technologies; industrial sonic technologies; energy policy, planning and economics; acoustics. Subspecialties: Fuels; Acoustics. Home: 2329 Charmingfare Woodridge IL 60517 Office: Argonne Nat Lab 9700 Cass Ave IL 60439

SHEN, TSUNG YING, medicinal chemist; b. Peking, China, Sept. 28, 1924; s. Tsu-Wei and Sien-Wha (Nieu) S.; m. Amy Lin, 1953; children—Bernard, Hubert, Theodore, Leonard, Evelyn, Andrea. B.Sc., Nat. Central U., China, 1946; D.I.C., Imperial Coll., London, 1948; Ph.D., U. Manchester, Eng., 1950, D.Sc. (hon.), 1978. Postdoctoral fellow Ohio State U., 1950; research assoc. MIT, 1952-56; sr. chemist Merck Sharp & Dohme Research Labs., Rahway, N.J., 1956-65, asst. dir. labs., 1965-69, dir., 1969-76, v.p. membrane chem. research, 1976-77, v.p. membrane and arthritis research, 1977—. Editorial bd.: Jour. Medicinal Chemistry, Medicinal Research Revs.; contbr. 150 articles to sci. jours. Recipient Galileo medal U. Pisa, Italy, 1976; Dirs. Sci. award Merck & Co., Inc., 1976; medal of Merit Giornate Mediche Internazionali del Collegium Biologicum Europa, 1977; Rene Descartes Silver medal U. Paris, 1977; Outstanding Patente award N.J. Research and Devel. Council, 1975; Achievement award Chinese Inst. Engrs.-U.S.A., 1984. Mem. Am. Chem. Soc. (Alfred Burger award in Medicinal Chemistry, Am. 1980), N.Y. Acad. Scis., AAAS, Internat. Soc. Immunopharmacology, Acad. Pharm. Scis. (U.S.A.) (hon.). Patentee in field (200). Current Work: Medicinal chemistry and biomembrane research related to anti-inflammatory and immunopharmacological agents. Subspecialties: Synthetic chemistry; Medicinal chemistry. Home: 935 Minisink Way Westfield NJ 07090 Office: PO Box 2000 Rahway NJ 07065

SHEPARD, ROGER NEWLAND, psychologist, educator; b. Palo Alto, Calif., Jan. 30, 1929; s. Orson Cutler and Grace (Newland) S.; m. Barbaranne Bradley, Aug. 18, 1952; children—Newland Chenoweth, Todd David, Shenna Esther. B.A., Stanford U., 1951; Ph.D., Yale U., 1955; A.M. (hon.), Harvard U., 1966. Research asso. Naval Research Lab., 1955-56; research fellow Harvard, 1956-58; mem. tech. staff Bell Telephone Labs., 1958-66, dept. head, 1963-66; prof. psychology Harvard U., 1966-68, dir. psychol. labs., 1967-68; prof. psychology Stanford U., 1968—. Guggenheim fellow Center for Advanced Study in Behavioral Scis., 1971-72; recipient Howard Crosby Warren medal, 1981. Fellow AAAS, Am. Psychol. Assn. (pres. exptl. div. 1980-81, Disting. Sci. Contbn. award 1976); mem. Nat. Acad. Scis., Psychometric Soc. (pres. 1973-74), Psychonomic Soc., Soc. Exptl. Psychologists. Subspecialty: Experimental psychology. Office: Dept Psychology Bldg 420 Stanford U Stanford CA 94305*

SHEPHERD, ALEXANDER M.M., pharmacologist, physician, educator; b. Perth, Scotland, Apr. 26, 1945; came to U.S., 1978. B.Sc., St. Andrews U., Fife, Scotland, 1965, M.B., Ch.B., 1969; Ph.D. in Clin. Pharmacology, U. Dundee, Scotland, 1978. House physician Dundee Royal Infirmary, 1969-70, sr. house physician, 1970-72, registrar in medicine, 1972-73; Med. Research Council fellow in clin. pharmacology U. Dundee, 1973-75, lectr., 1973-75; registrar in internal medicine Ninewells Hosp., Dundee, 1973-75, sr. registrar, 1975-77; asst. prof. pharmacology and medicine U. Tex. Health Sci. Ctr., San Antonio, 1978-83, assoc. prof., 1983—; dir. hypertension service, 1981-, dir. clin. pharmacokinetics, 1981—, chief div. clin. pharmacology, 1983—. Contbr. articles to profl. jours. Lawrence Bequest fellow, 1976-77; grantee Am. Heart Assn.; grantee U. Tex. Health Sci. Ctr.; grantee NIH; grantee Lilly Research Labs.; grantee Bristol Labs.; grantee Marion Labs., others. Mem. Royal Coll. Physicians (U.K.), Am. Fedn. Clin. Research, So. Soc. for Clin. Investigation, Am. Soc. for Pharmacology and Exptl. Therapeutics. Current Work: Clinical pharmacology of Cardiovascular agents; effects of aging on response to cardio-vascular drugs. Subspecialty: Pharmacology. Office: Dept Pharmacology and Medicine U Tex Health Scis Center Room 212B 7703 Floyd Curl Dr San Antonio TX 78284

SHEPHERD, MARK, JR., electronics company executive; b. Dallas, Jan. 18, 1923; s. Mark and Louisa Florence (Daniell) S.; m. Mary Alice Murchland, Dec. 21, 1945; children: Debra Aline (Mrs. Rowland K. Robinson), MaryKay Theresa, Marc Blaine. B.S. in Elec. Engring, So. Meth. U., 1942; M.S. in Elec. Engring, U. Ill., at Urbana, 1947. Registered profl. engr., Tex. With Gen. Elec. Co., 1942-43, Farnsworth Television and Radio Corp., 1947-48; with Tex. Instruments Inc., Dallas, 1948—, v.p., gen. mgr. semicondr.-components div., 1955-61, exec. v.p., chief operating officer, 1961-66, dir., 1963—, pres., chief operating officer, 1967-69, pres., chief exec. officer, 1969-76, chmn. bd., chief exec. officer, 1976-84, chmn., chief corp. officer, 1984-85, chmn., 1985—; dir. RepublicBank Corp., U.S. Steel; mem. internat. council Morgan Guaranty Trust Co.; Mem. Adv. Council on Japan-U.S. Econ. Relations; bd. govs., trustee So. Meth. U.; trustee Com. for Econ. Devel., Am. Enterprise Inst. Pub. Policy Research; councillor Conf. Bd.; mem. adv. council Am. Ditchley Found.; mem. Bus. Council, Dallas Citizens Council; mem. nat. bd. Com. on the Present Danger; mem. Tex. Sci. and Tech. Council. Served to lt. (j.g.) USNR, 1943-46. Fellow IEEE; mem. Soc. Exploration Geophysicists, Newcomen Soc., Council on Fgn. Relations, U.S. Council Internat. Bus. (trustee), Nat. Acad. Engring., Horatio Alger Assn. Disting. Ams., Sigma Xi, Eta Kappa Nu. Subspecialty: Electrical engineering. Office: Texas Instruments Inc PO Box 225474 MS 236 Dallas TX 75265

SHEPPARD, ALBERT PARKER, JR., research administrator, electrical engineering educator, consultant; b. Griffin, Ga., June 6, 1936; s. Albert Parker and Cornelia F. (Cooper) S.; children—Albert Parker, III, Frank P.; m. Eleanor Davis, Feb. 8, 1978; 1 stepchild, Phillip Hancock. B.S. in Physics, Oglethorpe U., 1958; M.S. in Physics, Emory U., 1959; Ph.D. in Elec. Engring., Duke U., 1965. Sr. engr. Martin Marietta Corp., Orlando, Fla., 1960-63; physicist U.S. Army Research Office, Durham, N.C., 1963-65; research engr., div. head Ga. Inst. Tech., Atlanta, 1965-71, chief chem. sci. lab., 1971-72, assoc. dean engring., 1972-74, assoc. v.p. research, 1974—, prof. elec. engring., 1972—;

cons. Whirlpool Corp., St. Joseph, Mich., 1980—, Microwave & Electronics, Inc., Atlanta, 1969—, Swestar, Marietta, Ga., 1983—. Contbr. articles to profl. jours. Patentee in field. Recipient Outstanding Alumni award Oglethorpe U., 1974. Mem. IEEE, Computer Soc. of IEEE, Am. Soc. Engring. Educ., Univs. Space Research Assn., Sigma Xi, Sigma Pi Sigma. Clubs: Ansley Golf (Atlanta); Peachtree World Tennis (Norcross, Ga.). Subspecialties: Electronics; Computer engineering. Home: 3591 Norwich Dr Tucker GA 30084 Office: Vice Pres for Research-0370 225 North Ave NW Ga Inst Tech Atlanta GA 30332

SHEPPARD, LOUIS CLARKE, biomedical engineering educator; b. Pine Bluff, Ark., May 28, 1933; s. Ellis Allen and Louise (Clarke) S.; m. Nancy Louise Mayer, Feb. 8, 1958; children: David, Susan, Lisa. B.S. in Chem. Engring, U. Ark., 1957; diploma, Imperial Coll. Sci. and Tech., London, 1976; Ph.D. in Elec. Engring, U. London, 1976. Devel. staff supr. Diamond Alkali Co., Deer Park, Tex., 1957-63; systems engr. IBM, Houston, 1963-64, staff engr., Rochester, Minn., 1964-66; assoc. prof. surgery U. Ala., Birmingham, 1966—, prof. chmn. dept. biomed. engring., 1979—; dir. acad. computing U. Ala. Med. Ctr., 1981-83; mem. adv. bd. Pharmacontrol, Englewood Cliffs, N.J., 1982—; mem. med. adv. bd. Hewlett Packard, Waltham, Mass., 1980-84; cons. IMED Devel. Corp., San Diego, 1982—, NIH, 1972—; pres. SEACORP; dir. FBK Internat., Birmingham. Contbr. articles to profl. jours. Served with USAR, 1958-66. Recipient various grants. Mem. Am. Inst. Chem. Engrs., IEEE (sr.), Nat. Soc. Profl. Engrs., Cardiovascular Dynamics Soc. (charter), Biomed. Engring. Soc. (bd. dirs.), Instn. Elec. Engrs. (U.K.), Am. Assn. Med. Instrumentation (v.p.), Brit. Computer Soc., Sigma Xi, Tau Beta Pi, Eta Kappa Nu. Current Work: Critical care systems, biomedical instrumentation, computer controlled therapy, infusion devices, drug delivery systems, pharmacodynamics, biological signal analysis, modeling and simulation. Subspecialties: Biomedical engineering; Health services research. Home: 3644 Shamley Dr Birmingham AL 35223 Office: U Ala-Birmingham Univ Sta Birmingham AL 35294

SHEPS, CECIL GEORGE, physician; b. Winnipeg, Man., Can., July 24, 1913; came to U.S., 1946, naturalized, 1956; s. George and Polly (Lirenman) S.; m. Mindel Cherniack, May 29, 1937 (dec. Jan. 1973); 1 son, Samuel B.; m. Ann Shepherd. M.D., U. Man., 1936, D.Sc. (hon.), 1985; M.P.H., Yale, 1947; D.Sc. (hon.), Chgo. Med. Sch., 1970; Ph.D. (hon.), Ben Gurion U. of the Negev, 1983. Intern, St. Joseph's Hosp. Gen. Hosp., Winnipeg; resident Corbett Gen. Hosp., Stourbridge, Eng., Queen Mary's Hosp. for East End, London, Camp Shilo Mil. Hosp., Can., Ft. Osborne Mil. Hosp., Can.; gen. dir. Beth Israel hosp., Boston; also clin. prof. preventive medicine Harvard Med. Sch., 1953-60; prof. med. and hosp. adminstrn. Grad. Sch. Pub. Health, U. Pitts., 1960-65; gen. dir. Beth Israel Med. Center, N.Y.C.; also prof. community medicine Mt. Sinai Sch. Medicine, 1965-68; prof. social medicine U. N.C., Chapel Hill, 1969-79, Taylor Grandy Disting. prof. social medicine, 1980—, dir. Health Services Research Center, 1969-71, vice chancellor health scis., 1971-76; cons. in field, 1947—. Author: Needed Research in Health and Medical Care-A Biosocial Approach, 1954, Community Organization-Action and Inaction, 1956, Medical Schools and Hospitals, 1965, The Sick Citadel: The American Academic Medical Center and the Public Interest, 1983. Chmn. health services research study sect. NIH, 1958-62; cons. med. affairs Welfare Adminstrn., HEW, 1964-67; mem. spl. commn. social scis. NSF, 1968-69; chmn. Milbank Meml. Fund. Commn. on Higher Edn. for Pub. Health, 1972-75. Served as capt. M.C., Royal Can. Army, 1943-46. Mem. Nat. Council Aging (v.p., dir.), Am. Nurses Found. (bd. mem. sec.-treas.), Inst. Medicine, Nat. Acad. Scis. Current Work: Primary care; evaluation of health programs, education for health professions. Subspecialties: Preventive medicine; Epidemiology.

SHERALD, ALLEN FRANKLIN, III, geneticist, educator; b. Frederick, Md., Nov. 15, 1942; s. Allen Franklin Jr. and Betty Eileen (Harrop) S. B.S. cum laude, Frostburg (Md.) State Coll., 1964; Ph.D., U. Va., 1972. Sci. tchr., Montgomery County, Md., 1964-66; postdoctoral trainee Cornell U., Ithaca, N.Y., 1974-76; asst. prof. George Mason U., Fairfax, Va., 1976-80, assoc. prof. biology, 1980—. Contbr. articles to profl. publs. NIH grantee, 1968, 69, 74; George Mason U. research grantee, 1978-81. Mem. AAAS, Genetics Soc. Am., Va. Acad. Scis., ACLU, Sigma Xi, Phi Sigma. Current Work: Control of gene activity in development: sclerotization and coloration of cuticle of Drosophila. Subspecialties: Gene actions; Developmental biology. Home: 9451 Lee Hwy Apt 1209 Fairfax VA 22031 Office: Dept Biology George Mason U Fairfax VA 22030

SHERBON, JOHN WALTER, food science educator; b. Lewiston, Idaho, Oct. 31, 1933; s. Ollis W. and Agnes G. S.; m. Ruth Fern Poppens, Aug. 10, 1957; children—Barbara, William. B.S., Wash. State U., 1955; M.S., U Minn., 1958, Ph.D., 1963. Prof. food sci. Cornell U., Ithaca, N.Y., 1963—Current Work: Investigate rapid methods of food analysis, studies of physical state of fats in foods. Subspecialty: Food science and technology. Office: Cornell U 207 Stocking Hall Ithaca NY 14853

SHERIDAN, PHILIP HENRY, pediatric neurologist; b. Washington, June 29, 1950; s. Andrew James and Mildred Adele (Stohlman) S. B.S. magna cum laude, Yale U., 1972; M.D. cum laude, Georgetown U., 1976. Diplomate Am. Bd. Pediatrics, Am. Bd. Psychiatry and Neurology, Am. Bd. Qualification in Electroencephalography. Resident in pediatrics Children's Hosp. Phila., 1976-79; fellow in pediatric neurology Hosp. of U. Pa., Phila., 1979-82; med. staff fellow NIH, Bethesda, Md., 1982-84, neurologist, epilepsy br. Nat. Inst. Neurol. and Communicative Disorders and Stroke, 1984—, health scientist adminstr., guest worker researcher, 1984—; cons., lectr. Nat. Naval Med. Ctr., Bethesda, 1984—. Contbr. articles on clin. and research neurology to med. jours. Vol. neurologist Bur. Crippled Children, Fairfax, Va., 1984—. Fellow Am. Acad. Pediatrics (neurology sect.); mem. Am. Acad. Neurology, Child Neurology Soc. (ethics com.), Soc. for Neurosci., Am. Epilepsy Soc. (invited book reviewer), Alpha Omega Alpha. Roman Catholic. Current work: Understanding the neurobiological basis for and improving the clinical management of epilepsy and related paroxysmal disorders. Subspecialties: Neurology; Pediatrics. Office: NIH Fed Bldg Room 114 Bethesda MD 20205

SHERIDAN, ROBERT EMMETT, JR., computer scientist, consultant; b. Wilson, Pa., Jan. 18, 1943; s. Robert Emmett and Helen (Somogyi) S. B.S. in Aerospace Engring, Pa. State U., 1965, M.S. in Aerospace Engring, 1968, M.S. in Computer Sci, 1973. Assoc. research engr. Boeing Co., Seattle, 1968-70; sr. exptl. engr. Pratt & Whitney Fla. Research and Devel., West Palm Beach, 1970-71; grad. asst. Applied Research Lab., Pa. State U., 1971-73; program mgr. BDM Corp., Albuquerque, 1974-81, chief scientist, 1983—; prin. scientist BDM Mgmt. Services Co., Killeen, Tex., 1981-83; instr. physics El Paso Community Coll., 1975-76; cons. Trainee NSF, 1965; proposal reviewer research grants, 1979. Mem. AIAA, Assn. Computing Machinery, IEEE Computer Soc., Digital Equipment Computer Users Soc. Democrat. Roman Catholic. Current Work: Modeling and simulation of mathematical and scientific systems, computational fluid mechanics. Subspecialties: Mathematical software; Fluid mechanics. Home: 5528 Amistad NE Albuquerque NM 87111 Office: BDM Corp Albuquerque NM 87106

SHERIDAN, THOMAS BROWN, engineering and applied psychology educator; b. Cin., Dec. 23, 1929; s. Mahlon Brinsley and Esther Anna (Brown) S.; m. Rachel Briggs Rice, Aug. 1, 1953; children—Paul, Richard, David, Margaret. B.S., Purdue U., 1951; M.S., UCLA, 1954; Sc.D., MIT, 1959. Registered profl. engr., Mass. Asst. prof. dept. mech. engring. MIT, Cambridge, 1959-65, assoc. prof., 1965-70, prof., 1970—. Author: (with W.R. Ferrell) Man Machine Systems, 1974; editor: Monitoring Behavior and Supervisory Control, 1976; contbr. articles to profl. jours. Chmn. com. on human factors NRC, Washington, 1984—. Fellow IEEE, Human Factors Soc. Democrat. Current work: Man machine systems models and experiments in power plants, remotely controlled vehicles undersea and in space; human computer interaction. Subspecialties: Human factors engineering; Robotics. Home: 32 Sewall St Newton MA 02165

SHERIF, MOSTAFA HASHEM, engineer, educator; b. Cairo, Sept. 6, 1950, came to U.S., 1975; s. Said Gabr Sherif and Fateia Draz. B.Sc., Cairo U., 1972, M.Sc., 1975; Ph.D., UCLA, 1980. Teaching and research asst. Cairo U., 1972-75; research asst. Tex. Tech. U., Lubbock, 1975-76; teaching fellow UCLA, 1976-80; sr. systems engr. Recognition Systems, Van Nuys, Calif., 1981-82; cons., Los Angeles, 1982-83; mem. tech. staff AT&T Bell Labs., Holmdel, N.J., 1983—. Contbr. numerous articles to profl. jours. Mem. IEEE (sr., mem. chmn. N.J. Shore sect. 1983—), Am. Soc. Biomechanics, Human Factors Soc., AAAS, Sigma Xi. Moslem. Current work: Packet switching; myoelectric signal processing; computer communications; recursive estimation; Box and Jenkins analysis (ARIMA models). Subspecialties: Biomedical engineering; Computer engineering. Home: 83 A White St Eatontown NJ 07724 Office: AT&T Bell Labs Room 3K-311 Crawfords Corner Rd Holmdel NJ 07733

SHERMAN, FRED, molecular biologist, educator; b. Mpls., May 21, 1932; s. Harry and Ann (Kaufman) S.; m. Revina Freeman, July 25, 1958; children: Aaron, Mark, Rhea. B.A., U. Minn., 1953; Ph.D., U. Calif., 1958. Postdoctoral fellow U. Wash., 1959-60, Lab. Genetique Physiol., France, 1960-61; sr. instr. U. Rochester, N.Y., 1961-62, asst. prof., 1962-66, assoc. prof., 1966-71, prof. radiation biology and biophysics, 1971—, prof. and chmn. dept. biochemistry, 1982—, Wilson prof., 1982-; A. Wander Meml. lectr., 1975. NIH fellow, 1959-61; NIH grantee, 1963—. Mem. Genetic Soc. Am., Environ. Mutagen Soc., AAAS, Am. Soc. Microbiology, Biophys. Soc., Nat. Acad. Sci. Current Work: Yeast genetics, gene regulation, gene *protein relationship, mutagensis, recombinant DNA. Subspecialties: Molecular biology; Gene actions. Home: 340 Beresford Rd Rochester NY 14610 Office: Dept RBB U Rochester Med Sch Rochester NY 14642

SHERMAN, GORDON RAE, university computer center ofcl., educator; b. Menomonie, Mich., Feb. 24, 1928; s. Gordon Everett and Myrtle Harriet (Evensen) S.; children: Karen Rae, Gordon Thorstein. B.S., Iowa State U., 1953; Ph.D., Purdue U., 1960. Mem. faculty U. Tenn.-Knoxville, 1960—, prof. computer scis., 1969—, dir. Computing Center, 1960—; cons. U. Santiago (Chile), 1982; mem. People to People Computer Sci. del., USSR, Europe, 1982. Contbr. numerous sci. articles to profl. publs. Del. Knox County (Tenn.) Republican Com., 1968-69. Served with USAF, 1946-49, 50-51. Fellow Brit. Computer Soc.; mem. Data Processing Mgmt. Assn. (Profl. of Yr. award 1979), Assn. for Computing Machinery, Am. Statis. Assn., Operations Research Soc. Am. Republican. Lutheran. Current Work: Discrete optimization; administration of University of Tennessee statewide computer system and network. Subspecialties: Operating systems; Theoretical computer science. Home: 301 Cheshire Dr Apt 105 Knoxville TN 37919 Office: Univ Tenn Computing Center 200 SMC Knoxville TN 37916

SHERMAN, JAMES HOWE, physiology educator; b. Detroit, Mar. 14, 1936; s. Willard H. and Esther M. (Redding) S.; m. Margrit E. Faulk, July 31, 1965; children: Diane, Douglas. B.S., U. Mich., 1957; Ph.D., Cornell U., 1963. Research asst. U. Mich., Ann Arbor, 1963-64, instr., 1964-66, asst. prof., 1966-70, assoc. prof., 1971—; asst. dir. Office Allied Health, 1972-77. Author: Human Physiology, 1970, Human Function and Structure, 1978. Mem. Am. Physiol. Soc., Biophys. Soc., N.Y. Acad. Sci. Current Work: Membrane and muscle physiology. Subspecialties: Physiology (medicine); Cell biology (medicine). Address: Dept Physiology Univ Mich Med Sch Ann Arbor MI 48109

SHERMAN, JOHN FOORD, association official; b. Oneonta, N.Y., Sept. 4, 1919; s. Henry C. and Ruth (Foord) S.; m. Betsy Deane Murray, Feb. 8, 1944; children: Betsy Deane, Mary Ann. B.S., Albany Coll. Pharmacy of Union U., 1949, D.Sc., 1970; Ph.D., Yale U., 1953. With NIH, 1953-74; asso. dir. extramural programs Nat. Inst. Neurol. Diseases and Blindness, 1961-62, Nat. Inst. Arthritis and Metabolic Disease, 1962-63; asso. dir. for extramural programs Office Dir. NIH, 1964-68, dep. dir., 1968-74; v.p. Assn. Am. Med. Colls., Washington, 1974—. Asst. surgeon gen. USPHS, 1964-68; spl. research chemotheraphy and neuropharmacology, research policy and adminstrn.; mem. Nat. Multiple Sclerosis Med. Adv. Bd.; mem. panel on data and studies NRC, 1976—; mem. biomed. library rev. com. NIH. Served with U.S. Army, 1941-46. Decorated Bronze Star; recipient Meritorious Service award USPHS, 1965, Disting. Service award HEW, 1971, Sec.'s Spl. Citation award, 1973, award Nat. Civil Service League, 1973; Disting. Alumnus award Union U.-Pharmacy Coll. Council, 1974. Mem. AAAS, Inst. Medicine, Nat. Acad. Scis., Sigma Xi. Congregationalist. Club: Cosmos.

SHERMAN, LOUIS ALLEN, biophysicist; b. Chgo., Dec. 16, 1943; s. Stanley E. and Sarah S.; m. Debra Meddoff, June 15, 1969; children—Daniel, Jeffrey. B.S., U. Chgo., 1965, Ph.D., 1970. Postdoctoral fellow Cornell U., 1970-72; asst. prof. U. Mo., 1972-77, assoc. prof. div. biol. sci., 1977-83, prof., 1983—, dir. div. biol. sci., 1985—. Contbr. articles to sci. jours. NIH postdoctoral fellow, 1970-72; NIH research grantee, 1975—; grantee U.S. Dept. Agr., Dept. Energy, 1980—. Mem. AAAS, Biophys. Soc., Am. Soc. Microbiology, Am. Soc. Plant Physiologists, Photobiology Soc. Democrat. Jewish. Current Work: Study of the relationship of structure to function in photosynthetic membranes; cloning of photosynthesis genes in cyanobacteria. Subspecialties: Photosynthesis; Molecular biology. Office: U Mo 312 Tucker Hall Columbia MO 65211

SHERMAN, MAX HOWARD, research physicist, energy consultant; b. Los Angeles, Apr. 3, 1954; s. Harry and Claire Rose (Walkin) S.; m. Elizabeth Louise Sherman, Dec. 26, 1977. B.S. in Physics and Chemistry, UCLA, 1975; Ph.D. in Physics, U. Calif.-Berkeley, 1980. Teaching asst. U. Calif.-Berkeley, 1976-77, research assoc., 1977-80; staff scientist Lawrence Berkeley Lab., Calif., 1980—; pres. Harmax Corp., Los Angeles, 1979—; U.S. rep. Annex V of Internat. Energy Agy., London, 1983—. Contbr. articles to sci. jours. Patentee in field. Mem. Am. Phys. Soc., ASHRAE (chmn. SPC 119 1983—), ASTM, AAAS, M.H. De Young Mus. Soc., Calif. Acad. Sci. Exploration, San Francisco Zoo, Am. Contract Bridge League, Sigma Pi Sigma. Current work: Research into air infiltration, heat flow in solids, energy modeling of buildings, group leader of energy performance of buildings group. Office: Lawrence Berkeley Lab 90-3074 Berkeley CA 94720

SHERMAN, S. MURRAY, neurosciences educator; b. Pitts., Jan. 4, 1944; s. Julius Louis and Ida (Schooler) S.; m. Marjorie Jean Ebken, Feb. 1, 1969; children: Erika Kirsten, Benjamin William. B.S. in Biology, Calif. Inst. Tech., 1965; Ph.D. in Anatomy, U. Pa., 1969. Postdoctoral fellow Australian Nat. U., Canberra, 1970-72; asst. prof. physiology U. Va., Charlottesville, 1972-75, assoc. prof., 1975-78, prof., 1978-79; prof. neurobiology and behavior SUNY-Stony Brook, 1979—; Newton-Abraham vis. prof. U. Oxford, 1985-86. Mem. editorial bd.: Physiol. Revs; contbr. chapts. to books, articles to profl. jours. Recipient numerous grants and fellowships Sloan Found., numerous grants and fellowships NIH, numerous grants and fellowships NSF. Mem. Soc. for Neurosci., Am. Assn. Anatomists, Assn. for Research in Vision and Ophthalmology, Cajal Club. Current Work: Postnatal development of mammalian central visual pathways. Subspecialty: Neurobiology. Office: Dept Neurobiology SUNY Stony Brook NY 11794

SHERREN, ANNE TERRY, chemist; b. Atlanta, July 1, 1936; d. Edward Allison and Annie Ayres (Lewis) Terry; m. William Samuel Sherren, Aug. 13, 1966. B.A., Agnes Scott Coll., Decatur, Ga., 1957; Ph.D., U. Fla., Gainesville, 1961. Instr. to asst. prof. chemistry Tex. Woman's U., Denton, 1961-66; assoc. prof. chemistry North Central Coll., Naperville, Ill., 1966-76, prof., 1976—, chmn. dept., 1975-78, 81-84, chmn. sci. div., 1983—; research assoc. Oak Ridge Nat. Lab., summers 1962, 63, Argonne Nat. Lab., summers 1968, 73-80. Mem. Am. Chem. Soc., Am. Inst. Chemists, Nat. Assn. Sci. Tchrs., AAUP, AAAS, Ill. Acad. Sci., Sigma Xi, Iota Sigma Pi (nat. pres. 1978-81), Delta Kappa Gamma. Presbyterian. Current Work: Synthesis of inorganic complex ions and study of related spectra. Subspecialties: Analytical chemistry; Inorganic chemistry. Office: North Central Coll Naperville IL 60566

SHERRIS, JOHN CHARLES, microbiology educator; b. Colchester, Eng., Mar. 8, 1921; came to U.S., 1959, naturalized, 1969; s. Cyril and Dorothy (Sherris); m. Elizabeth, July, 1944; children: Peter, Jacqueline. MRCS, LRCP, 1944; M.B., B.S., U. London, 1948, M.D., 1950; M.D. (hon.), Karolinska Inst., Stockholm, Sweden, 1975. Diplomate: Am. Bd. Pathology, Am. Bd. Med. Microbiology. House surgeon and physician King Edward VII Hosp., Windsor, Eng., 1944-45; trainee, asst. pathologist central lab. Sector V. Ministry Health, 1945-48; sr. registrar in pathology Aylesbury and Dist. Lab., Stoke, Mandeville, Eng., 1948-50, Radcliffe Infirmary, Oxford, Eng., 1950-52; lectr. in bacteriology U. Manchester (Eng.), 1953-56, sr. lectr., 1956-59; dir. clin. microbiology labs. U. Wash. Hosp., 1959-70; assoc. prof. microbiology U. Wash., 1959-63, prof., 1963—, chmn. dept. microbiology and immunology, 1970-80; bd. dirs. Nat. Found. Infectious Diseases. Editor: Cumitech Series, Am. Soc. Microbiology, 1974-80. Fellow Royal Coll. Pathologists, Am. Acad. Microbiology (gov. 1974-78, v.p. 1976-78); mem. Am. Soc. Microbiology (Becton-Dickinson award 1978, pres. 1982-83), Soc. Gen. Microbiology, Can. Soc. Microbiologists, Assn. Clin. Pathologists, Acad. Clin. Lab. Physicians, Scientists, Am. Bd. Med. Microbiology (chmn. 1971-73). Research in antibiotic susceptibility and resistance of bacteria, automation in microbiology. Subspecialty: Microbiology. Home: 10021 Lake Shore Blvd NE Seattle WA 98125 Office: Dept Microbiology and Immunology SC-42 U Wash Seattle WA 98195

SHERRY, SOL, physician, educator; b. N.Y.C., Dec. 8, 1916; s. Hyman and Ada (Greenman) S.; m. Dorothy Sitzman, Aug. 7, 1946; children—Judith Anne, Richard Leslie. A.B., NYU, 1935, M.D., 1939; D.Sc. (hon.), Temple U., 1980. Successively fellow, intern, resident 3d med. div. Bellevue Hosp., N.Y.C., 1939-42, 46; asst. prof. medicine N.Y.U. Coll. Medicine, 1946-51; dir. May Inst. Med. Research, Cin., 1951-54; dir. medicine Jewish Hosp., St. Louis, 1954-58; prof. medicine Washington U. Sch. Medicine, St. Louis, 1958-68, co-chmn. dept., 1964-68; chmn. dept. Temple U. Sch. Medicine, 1968-84, dean, 1984—; dir. Thrombosis Research Center, 1970-79, dir. emeritus, 1979—; Cons. emeritus surgeon gen. army; past chmn. com. thrombolytic agts. USPHS, past chmn. com. on thrombosis; council on thrombosis Am. Heart Assn.; past mem. com. blood, past chmn. task force on thrombosis NRC; mem. Internat. Commn. on Hemostasis and Thrombosis; past chmn. and pres. Internat. Socs. on Thrombosis and Hemostasis; past mem. sci. adv. com. St. Louis Heart Assn., also St. Louis Multiple Sclerosis Soc. Contbr. articles to profl. jours. Mem. bd. Hillel, 1961-67; pres. S.E. Pa. chpt. Am. Heart Assn., 1978-79. Served as flight surgeon USAAF, 1942-46, ETO. Recipient medal for typhus control Lower Bavaria U.S. Army Typhus Commn., 1946; Research Career award USPHS, 1962; Distinghished Achievement award Modern Medicine, 1963; Distinghished Achievement award Modern Medicine A.C.P., 1968; Distinghished Achievement award Modern Medicine Am. Coll. Cardiology, 1971; Distinghished Achievement award Modern Medicine Internat. Soc. Thrombosis and Haemostasis, 1978. Fellow Royal Coll. Physicians; mem. AMA (past mem. and chmn. council drugs, chmn. sect. exptl. medicine and therapeutics), Assn. Am. Physicians, Assn. Profs. Medicine (council 1973-75, pres. 1976), Am. Soc. Clin. Investigation, Am. Heart Assn., Central Soc. Clin. Research (council 1962-64), Am. Physiol. Soc., Soc. Exptl. Biology and Medicine, A.C.P. (master), Phi Beta Kappa, Sigma Xi (pres. Washington U. chpt. 1962-63), Alpha Omega Alpha. Current Work: Primary developer of clot dissolving therapy and its newer applications. Active in organization and conduct of clinical trials evaluating agentsfor prevention or treatment of blood clots. Subspecialties: Hematology; Cardiology. Home: 408 Sprague Rd Narberth PA 19072

SHERTZER, HOWARD GRANT, toxicologist, educator, cons.; b. N.Y.C., Oct. 9, 1945; s. Sidney Maurice and Terry June (Rosenbaum) S.; m. Ellen Lea Asch, June 23, 1968; children—Kyle W., Kevin M. B.S. in Physiology, U. Mich., 1967; Ph.D. in Cell Biology, UCLA, 1973; postdoctoral student in biochemistry, Cornell U., 1975. Asst. prof. cell biology Tex. A&M U., College Station, 1975-79; assoc. prof. toxicology U. Cin. Med. Center, 1979—, also cons. Contbr. numerous articles to sci. jours. Grantee NIH; Grantee Nat. Cancer Inst., 1973—. Mem. AAUP, Am. Soc. Pharmacology and Exptl. Therapeutics, Soc. Toxicology, Internat. Soc. Study Xenobiotics. Current Work: Formation metabolism, toxicity and mechanism of action of chemical carcinogens; biochemical mechanisms of chemoprotection against toxicity, mutagenicity and carcinogenicity. Subspecialties: Cancer research (medicine); Toxicology (medicine).

SHERWIN, JOSEPH RICHARD, physiologist; b. Pitts., Dec. 31, 1944; s. Vincent William and Helen Margaret (Kaza) S.; m. Sarah O'Donnell, Aug. 26, 1978. B.S., Duquesne U., 1966, M.S., 1968; Ph.D., U. Pitts., 1973. Research assoc. U. Pitts., 1973-74, NIH postdoctoral fellow, 1974-76; asst. prof. physiology Jefferson Med. Coll., Phila., 1976-80, assoc. prof., 1980—, assoc. dean, 1984. Dir.-at-large Nat. Hemophilia Found., N.Y.C., 1980. Mem. Am. Physiol. Soc., Endocrine Soc., AAAS, Soc. Exptl. Biology and Medicine, Nat. Council Univ. Research Adminstrn. Democrat. Roman Catholic. Current work: Thyroid gland physiology, regulation of iodine transport. Subspecialties: Physiology (medicine); Endocrinology. Office: Jefferson Med Coll 1020 Locust St Philadelphia PA 19107

SHERWOOD, GERALD E., research engineer; b. Carrollton, Mo., Feb. 19, 1934; s. William Aubrey and Melva Marie (Macoubrie) S.; m. Ethelynn Claudia Hurst, Apr. 9, 1960; children—Brian, Mark. B.S. in Archtl. Engring., U. Colo., 1957. Structural engr. Navy Civil Engring. Lab., Port Hueneme, Calif., 1960-67; engr. Forest Products Lab., Madison, Wis., 1967—. Author: New Life for Old Dwelling, 1975. Contbr. articles to tech. jours. Mem. internat. student com. Intervarsity Christian Fellowship, Madison, 1967—; deacon Assemblies of God Ch., 1973-79. Served with AUS, 1957-59. Mem. ASTM, Am. Soc. Agrl. Engrs. Democrat. Current work: Research in wood as a building material; specialities in condensation control; wind-resistant construction, rehabilitation, light-frametechniques. Home: 1715 Maple St Middleton WI 53562 Office: Forest Products Lab PO Box 5130 Madison WI 53705

SHETLER, STANWYN GERALD, botanist, museum curator, educator; b. Johnstown, Pa., Oct. 11, 1933; s. Sanford Grant and Florence Hazel (Young) S.; m. Elaine Marie Retburg, Feb. 2, 1963; children—Stephen Garth, Lara Suzanne. Student, Eastern Mennonite Coll., 1951-53; B.S. with distinction, Cornell U., 1955, M.S., 1958; Ph.D., U. Mich., 1979. Asst. curator phanerogam dept. botany Smithsonian Instn., Washington, 1962-63, assoc. curator phanerogams, 1963-81, curator phanerogams, 1981—; asst. dir. Nat. Mus. Natural History, 1984—; instr. Dept. Agr. Grad. Sch., 1962-64, 82—, Dept. Agr. Grad. Sch. (Smithsonian Resident Assocs. Program), 1966—; tour leader. Author: The Komarov Botanical Institute: 250 Years of Russian Research, 1967, Variation and Evolution of the Nearctic Harebells, 1982; contbr. numerous tech. and popular sci. articles, revs. to various publs.; editorial bd.: Systematic Botany Monographs, 1981-83. Mem. land use citizens adv. com. Washington Met. Council Govts., 1977-79; mem. open space adv. com. Loudoun County, Va., 1980—. Recipient individual award Piedmont Environ. Council, 1981. Mem. AAAS, Am. Soc. Plant Taxonomists, Am. Inst. Biol. Scis., Bot. Soc. Am., Bot. Soc. Washington (pres. 1983), Internat. Assn. Plant Taxonomy, Nat. Audubon Soc., Audubon Naturalist Soc. Central Atlantic States (dir. 1971-74, 80-85, pres. 1974-77), Washington Biologists Field Club (pres. 1984—), Sigma Xi. Mennonite. Current Work: Systematics and evolution of plant family Campanulaceae; floriistics of temperate N. Am., especially Alaska and central Atlantic region; history of Russian botany; use of info. retrieval in biol. data banking. Subspecialties: Evolutionary biology; Systematics. Home: 142 Meadowland Ln E Sterling VA 22170 Office: Dept Botany Smithsonian Instn NHB 166 Washington DC 20560

SHEVACH, ETHAN MENAHEM, immunologist, physician; b. Brookline, Mass., Oct. 16, 1943; s. Benjamin Jacques and Anne (Pollack) S.; m. Ruth Schneider, May 30, 1967; children: Matthew, Seth. A.B., Boston U., 1967, M.D., 1967. Diplomate: Am. Bd. Internal Medicine. Intern and resident in medicine Bronx Municipal Hosp. Center, N.Y., 1967-69; clin. assoc. Lab. Clin. Investigation, Nat. Inst. Allergy and Infectious Diseases, NIH, Bethesda, Md., 1969-72; sr. staff fellow Lab. Clin. Investigation, Nat. Inst. Allergy and Infectious Diseases, NIH (Lab. Immunology), 1972-73, sr. investigator, 1973—. Served to capt. USPHS, 1973—. Mem. Am. Assn. Immunologists, Am. Soc. Clin. Investigation, Am. Fedn. Clin. Research. Current Work: Immune response gene function; control of immunocompetent cell interactions. Subspecialties: Immunogenetics; Cellular engineering.

SHIBATA, TOMOO, chemist; b. Kokubunjishi, Japan, June 8, 1944; came to U.S., 1967, naturalized, 1985; s. Tadashi and Kimiko (Obi) S.; m. Setsue Hayashi, Aug. 19, 1979; children—Lina, Kayu. B.S., Sophia U., 1967; M.S., Ga. Inst. Tech., 1970; Ph.D., U.S.C., 1982. Mem. research and devel. staff Ricoh, Tokyo, 1973-79; mgr. research and devel. dept. Ricoh Electronics, Santa Ana, Calif., 1982-84, asst. div. mgr., 1984-85, div. mgr., 1985—. Mem. Am. Chem. Soc., N.Y. Acad. Scis., Sigma Xi. Current work: New pressure-sensitive adhesives, emulsion, hotmelt, uv or eb cure types; heat sensitive chemical materials, dye or pigment. Subspecialties: Polymer chemistry; Organic chemistry. Home: 3831 Fern St Irvine CA 92714 Office: Ricoh Electronics Inc 2320 Redhill Ave Santa Ana CA 92705

SHIBIB, MUHAMMED AYMAN, electrical engineer; b. Damascus, Syria, Feb. 14, 1953; came to U.S., 1975, naturalized citizen, 1985; s. Soubhi Taufik and Loutfieh (Shorkatli) S.; m. Reem Estwani, Mar. 30, 1982; children—Dena Reem, Kaream Ayman. B.S., Am. U., Beirut, 1975; M.S., U. Fla.-Gainesville, 1976, Ph.D., 1979. Grad. research asst. U. Fla., Gainesville, 1976-79, research assoc., 1979, vis. asst. prof. elec. engring. dept., 1979-80; mem. tech. staff AT&T Bell Labs., Reading, Pa., 1980—. Contbr. articles to profl. jours. Mem. Am. Phys. Soc., Electrochem. Soc., IEEE (sr.), AAAS, Electron Device Soc. (sr.), N.Y. Acad. Scis. Moslem. Current Work: Research and development in semiconductor device physics and technology of integrated circuits. Subspecialties: Microelectronics; Integrated circuits. Home: 7 Tewkesbury Dr Wyomissing Hills PA 19610 Office: AT&T Bell Labs 2525 N 12th St Reading PA 19604

SHIEH, WEI TONG, metallurgical engineer; b. Keelung, Republic of China, Jan. 22, 1934; came to U.S., 1961; s. Kuo Sian and Wu Mou (Lin) S.; m. Mei Wei Huang, Dec. 30, 1961; children—Karl, Karen, Denise. B.A. in Sci., U. Toronto, 1961; M.S., U. Ill., 1963, Ph.D., 1968. Supr. copper mining Taiwan Gold & Copper Mining Corp., Chinkuashu, Republic of China, 1957-59; research asst. U. Ill., Urbana, 1961-68; research metallurgist Timken Co., Canton, Ohio, 1968-72, leader research mission, research specialist, 1972-77; sr. engr. Gen. Electric Co., Utica, N.Y., 1977—. Contbr. articles to tech. jours. Mem. Am. Welding Soc. (chmn. tech. subcom. CIE 1980—), Nat. Assn. Corrosion Engrs. (mem. tech. com. T9 1978—), ASTM (mem. tech. com. E24, E9 1978—). Current work: Correlations of material microstructure with fracture, fatigue and corrosion; fabrication technology of printed circuit boards, microelectronic chips and packaging; joining of metals to ceramics. Subspecialties: Fracture mechanics; Corrosion. Home: 7 Upper Woods Rd New Hartford NY 13413Office: Gen Electric Co French Rd Utica NY 13503

SHIFFMAN, MAX, mathematician, consultant, researcher; b. N.Y.C., Oct. 30, 1914; s. Nathan and Eva (Krasilchick) S.; m. Bella Manel, June 1938 (div. 1957); children: Bernard, David. B.S., CCNY, 1935; M.S., NYU, 1936, Ph.D., 1938. Instr. in math. St. John's U., N.Y.C., 1938-39, CCNY, 1938-42; mathematician, assoc. prof. NYU, 1941-49; prof. math. Stanford U. (on leave in Washington numerous yrs.), 1949-66, Calif. State U.-Hayward, 1967-81; mathematician, owner Mathematico, San Francisco and Hayward, 1970—; cons. RAND Corp., Santa Monica, Calif., 1951; U.S. Govt., 1962-64; cons. math. logistics George Washington U., 1958-61. Contbr. articles to profl. jours. Recipient award of Merit U.S. Navy, 1945; Blumenthal fellow, 1935-38. Mem. Am. Math. Soc., Soc. Indsl. and Applied Math., Math. Assn. Am. Current Work: Mathematical aerodynamics for airplane wings; stability and instability in variational analysis; measure theory and non-measurable sets; generalized median; topics in algebraic systems. Subspecialties: Analysis; Applied mathematics. Home and Office: 16913 Meekland Ave Apt 7 Hayward CA 94541

SHIH, CHARLES CHIEN, nuclear generation engineer; b. Taipei, Taiwan, June 3, 1950; came to U.S., 1974, naturalized, 1983; s. Tsu-En and Chung-Chueh (Hsu) S.; m. Grace H. Cheng, June 3, 1978. B.S., Nat. Tsing Hua U., 1972; M.S., U. R.I.-Kingston, 1977. Registered profl. engr., Calif. Sr. nuclear engr. Kaiser Engrs., Inc., Oakland, Calif., 1977-80; nuclear generation engr. Pacific Gas & Electric Co., San Francisco, 1980—. Mem. Am. Nuclear Soc., Health Physics Soc. Current Work: Radiological assessment, computer software engineering, nuclear criticality analysis, nuclear radiation analysis, nuclear plant operations support. Subspecialties: Nuclear engineering; Software engineering. Office: Pacific Gas & Electric Co 77 Beale St San Francisco CA 94106

SHIH, DAVID HOUNG-MIN, research chemist; b. Taipei, Taiwan, Dec. 9, 1941; came to U.S., 1967; s. Kwang-chen and Bien-Ewr (Cheng) S.; m. Chyn Shih, June 29, 1968; children—Elizabeth, Connie, Duan. B.S., Nat. Cheng-Kung U., 1965; M.S., Marshall U., 1969; Ph.D., MIT, 1973. Research asst. Dept. Chemistry, Marshall U., Huntington, W.Va., 1967-69; teaching asst. dept. chemistry MIT, Cambridge, 1969-70, research asst., 1970-73; research assoc. MIT, 1973; sr. chemist Merck Sharp & Dohme Research Labs., Rahway, N.J., 1973-78, research fellow, 1978—. Contbr. articles to profl. jours. Patentee in field. Bd. dirs. Chinese Am. Cultural Assn., 1984—. Ashland Oil fellow, 1969. Mem. Am. Chem. Soc., Sigma Xi. Current work: Drug design and synthesis of carbapenem antibotics, structure/activity relationship study of antimicrobial agents; lead optimization of biologically active natural products. Subspecialties: Organic chemistry; Medicinal chemistry. Home: 2 Colby Ct Manalapan NJ 07726 Office: Merck & Co Rahway NJ 07065

SHIH, JASON CHIA-HSING, biotechnology educator, researcher; b. Chien-Cheng, Hunan, China, Oct. 8, 1939; came to U.S., 1969; s. Pang-Fang and Shue-Yin (Shen) S.; m. Jane Chu-Huei Chien, Aug. 31, 1966; children: Giles, Tim. B.S., Nat. Taiwan U., 1963, M.S., 1966; Ph.D., Cornell U., 1973. Lectr. Tunghai U., Taichung, Taiwan, 1966-69; research asst. Cornell U., Ithaca, N.Y., 1969-73, sr. research assoc., 1975-76; research assoc. U. Ill., Champaign-Urbana, 1973-75; asst. prof. N.C. State U., Raleigh, 1976-80, assoc. prof. biotechnology, 1980—; chmn., speaker Poultry Nutrition Conf., 1982; speaker Internat. Seminar Bio-Engergy, U.K., 1982; lectr. Ministry Agr., China, 1982. Pres. Triangle Area Chinese Am. Soc., 1982-83, exec. com., 1979-83; adv. bd. N.C. China Council, 1979—; vis. fellow Univ. Coll. Cardiff, Wales, 1983; Speaker Bio-Energy World Conf., 1984; Speaker, mem. com. 4th Internat. Symposium on Anaerobic Digestion, China, 1985. Research grantee NIH, U.S. Dept. Energy, N.C. Energy Inst., 1977—. Mem. Am. Inst. Nutrition, Am. Chem. Soc., Am. Soc. Microbiology, Poultry Sci. Assn., Phi Kappa Phi. Current Work: Poultry biotechnology: anaerobic digestion of poultry waste for methane production, experimental atherosclerosis: quail model study for atherosclerosis disease. Subspecialties: Biochemistry (biology); Microbiology. Office: Biotechnology Lab Dept Poultry Sci NC State Univ Raleigh NC 27695-7608

SHIH, TSUNG-MING ANTHONY, pharmacologist; b. Taipei, Taiwan, Oct. 8, 1944; came to U.S., 1968, naturalized, 1977; s. Chukun and Jean S.; m. Ming Lin, Sept. 5, 1970; children: Liane, Jason. B.S. in Pharmacy, Kaohsiung (Taiwan) Med. Coll., 1967; Ph.D. in Pharmacology, U. Pitts., 1974. Teaching asst. Columbia U., 1968-69; teaching asst. U. Pitts., 1969-71, research asst. III, 1975-76, research assoc., 1976-78; pharmacologist U.S. Army Med. Research Inst. Chem. Def., Aberdeen Proving Ground, Md., 1978—; dean Chinese Lang. Sch. Balt., 1982-84, prin., 1984—. Contbr. articles to profl. jours. NIH trainee, 1972-74; Western Psychiat. Inst. and Clinic fellow, 1974-76. Mem. N.Y. Acad. Sci., Soc. Neurosci., Am. Chem. Soc., Am. Soc. Neurochemistry, Am. Soc. Mass Spectrometry, AAAS, Sigma Xi. Democrat. Current work: Central neuropharmacological mechanisms of action of organophosphorus anticholinesterases and their treatment compounds; central neurotransmitter system dynamics and interactions. Subspecialties: Neuropharmacology; Neurochemistry. Office: Bldg E-3100 Aberdeen Proving Ground MD 21010

SHIHABI, ZAKARIYA KAMEL, laboratory administrator, pathology educator; b. Jerusalem, Nov. 17, 1939; came to U.S., 1961; s. Kamel and Rueseh Shihabi. B.Sc. in Agr., Alexandria U., Egypt, 1961; M.Sc., Tex. A&M U., 1965; Ph.D. in Biochemistry, U. S.D., 1970. Diplomate Am. Bd. Clin. Chemistry. Postdoctoral fellow Buffalo Gen. Hosp., 1970-72; assoc. lab. dir. Bowman Gray Sch. Medicine, Winston-Salem, N.C., 1972-75, dir., 1975—, assoc. prof. pathology, 1978—. Author: (with Charles Bishop) Blood, 1971. Mem. Am. Assn. Clin. Chemists, Am. Chem. Soc., Nat. Acad. Clin. Biochemists, AAAS, N.Y. Acad. Scis. Democrat. Current work: Developing new tests for clinical diagnosis; automation of laboratory tests. Subspecialties: Clinical chemistry; Biochemistry (biology). Home: 2210 New Castle Winston-Salem NC 27103 Office: Department Pathology Bowman Gray Sch Medicine Winston-Salem NC 27103

SHIN, SUNG-CHUL, materials scientist, researcher; b. Dae-Jeon, Chungchungnam-Do, Korea, July 19, 1952; s. Hyun-Soo and Jai-Soon (Kim) Shin; m. Won-Ki Min, Dec. 20, 1980; 1 child, Jessica. B.S. in Physics, Seoul Nat. U., Korea, 1975; M.S. in Physics, Korean Advanced Inst. Sci. and Tech., Seoul, 1977; Ph.D., Northwestern U., 1984. Researcher, Korean Standards Research Inst., Dae-Duck, 1977-80; lectr. Chungnam Nat. U., Dae-Duck, 1979-80; researcher Eastman Kodak Research Labs., Rochester, N.Y., 1984—; guest researcher Nat. Bur. Standards, Washington, 1977-78. Contbr. articles to profl. jours. Mem. Am. Phys. Soc., Am. Vacuum Soc., Materials Research Soc. Current work: Structural, transport, electronic and superconducting properties of compositionally modulated superlattice films; development of optical recording media and magneto-optical recording media for mass information storage. Subspecialties: Electronic materials; Condensed matter physics. Home: 6 Spanish Trail Apt E Rochester NY 14612 Office: Research Labs Eastman Kodak Co Rochester NY 14650

SHINE, JOHN, molecular geneticist; medical researcher; b. Brisbane, Australia; July 3, 1946; came to U.S., 1984; s. Patrick and Molly Gertrude (Hoare) S.; m. Kathleen Mary Morgan, Feb. 15, 1969; children—Rebecca Kathleen, Michael Patrick. B.Sc. with honors, Australian Nat. U., 1972, Ph.D., 1975. Research fellow Molecular Biology Unit Australian Nat. U., Canberra, 1978-80, fellow dept. genetics, 1980-83, sr. fellow dept. genetics, 1983—, assoc. dir. Centre Recombinant DNA Research, 1983—; adj. prof. medicine U. Calif.-San Francisco, 1985—; v.p. research and devel. Calif. Biotech. Inc., Mountain View, 1984—; cons. Agrigenetics Corp., Boulder, 1982-84, Calif. Biotech. Inc., 1982-84; dir. Biotech. Research Ptnrs., Mountain View, 1984—. Editor Molecular Biology and Medicine, DNA. Patentee; contbr. articles to profl. jours. Recipient Boehringer-Mannheim medal Australian Biochem. Soc., 1980; Gottschalk medal disting. research in biol. med. sci. Australian Acad. Sci., 1982. Current work: Molecular genetics and molecular neurobiology-hypertension and molecular biology of cardiovascular disease. Subspecialties: Molecular biology; Genetics and genetic engineering (medicine). Office: Calif Biotech Inc 2450 Bayshore Frontage Mountain View CA 94043

SHING, YUH-HAN, material scientist, physicist; b. Tungtu, China, June 18, 1941; came to Can., 1965; s. Chih-An and Shin I (Wong) S.; m. Jean Jen Chou, June 24, 1967; children: Mona, Sophia, Lara. B.Sc., Taiwan Normal U., 1963; M.Sc., U. Calgary, Alta., Can., 1969, Ph.D., 1972. Postdoctoral fellow McGill U., 1972-74, research assoc., reader, 1974-76, reader, 1976-79; mem. research staff Xerox Research Ctr., Mississauga, Ont., 1979-80; sr. research scientist ARCO Solar Industries, Woodland Hills, Calif., 1980-82; project leader Atlantic Richfield Co., Los Angeles, 1982—. Contbr. articles to sci. jours. Pres. Conejo Valley Chinese Assn., 1982. NRC of Can. grad. scholar, 1969-72; postdoctoral fellow NRC of Can., 1972-74; recipient grants, 1976-79. Mem. Am. Phys. Soc., IEEE, Electrochem. Soc., Am. Vacuum Soc. Current Work: Photovoltaic energy conversion, thin film semiconductors, compound semiconductors, sputtering processes, semiconductor characterizations, vacuum evaporation, glow discharge, amorphous semiconductors. Subspecialties: Electronic materials; Solar energy. Home: 2134 Calle Riscoso Thousand Oaks CA 91362 Office: Materials Development Lab Atlantic Richfield Co 20717 Prairie St Chatsworth CA 91311

SHINN, MICHAEL HOWARD, chemist; b. Iola, Kans., Dec. 4, 1954; s. Harold Howard and Addie Mae (Kessinger) S.; m. M. Jane Goode, Aug. 7, 1976. B.S., Emporia State U., 1976; M.A., U. Mo., 1979. Research chemist Duval Corp., Tucson, 1979-80, adv. chemist, 1980-82, adv. process chemist, 1982-85, chief chemist, 1985—. Contbr. articles to profl. jours. Mem. Am. Chem. Soc., Am. Inst. Mining Engrs., Soc. Applied Spectroscopy. Lodge: Elks. Current work: Process chemistry; computer simulation and modeling; complex solution equilibria. Subspecialties: Analytical chemistry; Hazardous waste disposal. Office: Duval Corp 4715 E Fort Lowell Tucson AZ 85712

SHINNERS, STANLEY MARVIN, electrical engineer, educator; b. N.Y.C., May 9, 1933; s. Earl and Molly Millie (Platner) S.; m. Doris Pinsker, Aug. 4, 1956; children—Sharon Rose, Walter Jay, Daniel Lawrence. B.E.E., CCNY, 1954; M.S. in Elec. Engring., Columbia U., 1959. Registered profl. engr., N.Y. Equipment engr. Western Electric Co., N.Y.C., 1953-55; staff engr. Otis Elevator Co., Bklyn., 1955-57; project engr. Consol. Avionics, Westbury, N.Y., 1957-58; sr. research sect. head Sperry Systems Mgmt., Great Neck, N.Y., 1958—; adj. prof. elec. engring. Poly. Inst. Bklyn., 1959-68, N.Y. Inst. Tech., Old Westbury, 1972—, Cooper Union, N.Y.C., 1965—. Author: Techniques of Systems Engineering, 1967; Control System Design, 1964; A Guide to Systems Engineering, 1976; Modern Control System Theory, 1978. Recipient Career Achievement medal CCNY, 1980. Fellow IEEE; mem. Am. Soc. for Engring. Edn. Current work: Development of control systems and navigation systems; application of filtering, estimation techniques; application of systems engineering techniques to large computer-controlled systems. Subspecialties: Electronics; Systems engineering. Home: 28 Sagamore Way N Jericho NY 11753 Office: Sperry Systems Mgmt MS K 4 Great Neck NY 11020

SHINNICK, THOMAS MICHAEL, microbiologist, researcher; b. Madison, Wis., Apr. 1, 1953; s. Michael Grant and Cora Adele (Wilson) S.; m. Kathleen Marie McDowell, May 25, 1974. B.S., U. Wis., 1974; Ph.D. (Johnson & Johnson Industries predoctoral fellow, 1977-78), MIT, 1978. Research asst. U. Wis.-Madison, 1973-74; teaching asst. M.I.T., Cambridge, 1975-78; postdoctoral fellow Research Inst. of Scripps Clinic, La Jolla, Calif., 1978-80, asst. mem., 1980—. Contbr. sci. publs. to profl. jours. Helen Hay Whitney Found. fellow, 1978-81. Mem. Am. Soc. Microbiology. Current Work: Control of gene expression; biology of oncogenic viruses. Subspecialties: Molecular biology; Developmental biology. Office: 10666 N Torrey Pines Rd La Jolla CA 92037

SHINOWARA, NANCY LEE, neurobiologist, cell biologist; b. Waynesboro, Va., Aug. 5, 1944; d. George Yukio and Alice Marie (Waterhouse) S. A.B., Mt. Holyoke Coll., 1966; M.A.T., Northwestern U., 1974, Ph.D., 1975. Postdoctoral research fellow div. biology Calif. Inst. Tech., Pasadena, 1974-78; staff fellow Lab. Neuroscis., Gerontology Research Center, Nat. Inst. on Aging, Balt., 1978-81, sr. staff fellow sect. exptl. morphology, 1981—. Contbr. articles on peripheral nerve and synapse, blood-nerve barrier, intercellular junctions in nerve and myelin, freeze-fracture methods, retinal morphology and glucose utilization during aging to profl. jours. Mem. Soc. for Neurosci., Am. Soc. Cell Biology, AAAS, Chesapeake Soc. Electron Microscopy (pres.). Current Work: Functional morphology of the nervous system (peripheral nerve, blood -nerve and blood-ocular barriers, retina) during development and aging with emphasis on cell-cell interactions, cell surfaces, permeability and secretion. Subspecialties: Neurobiology; Cell biology (medicine). Office: Nat Inst Aging Gerontology Research Center Balt City Hosps Baltimore MD 21224

SHIPMAN, CHARLES WILLIAM, chemical engineer, educator; b. Phillipsburgh, N.J., Aug. 29, 1924; s. George Funk and Elizabeth Hope (Johnston) S.; m. Louise Jean Hendrickson, Aug. 31, 1946; children—Nancy Ruth, Jane Louise, Robert Walter George. S.B., MIT, 1948, S.M., 1949, Sc.D., 1952. Registered profl. engr., Mass. asst. prof. U. Del., Newark, 1952-55; research assoc. MIT, Cambridge, 1955-58; from asst. prof. to prof. chem. engring. Worcester Poly. Inst., Mass., 1958-74, dean grad. studies, 1971-74; leader engring. research group Cabot Corp., Billerica, Mass., 1974-77, mgr. engring. analysis sect., 1977-78, asst. dir. corporate research, 1978-80, mgr. carbon blk. RID, 1980—; cons. in field. Contbr. articles to profl. jours. Served cpl. USMC, 1944-46. Mem. Am. Chem. Soc., Am. Inst. Chem. Engrs., Combustion Inst. (bd. dirs. 1958—). Republican. Episcopalian. Current work: Manage research and development involving application of combustion technology to production of fine particles, specifically carbon black. Subspecialties: Chemical engineering; Combustion processes. Home: 105 Spit Brook Rd Apt 14C Nashua NH 03062 Office: Cabot Corp Concord Rd Billerica MA 01824

SHIPMAN, HARRY LONGFELLOW, astrophysicist, educator, researcher; b. Hartford, Conn., Feb. 20, 1948; s. Arthur Leffingwell and Mary Pepperell (Dana) S.; m. Editha Davidson, Apr. 10, 1970; children—Alice Elizabeth, Thomas Nathaniel. B.A. in Astronomy, Harvard U., 1969; M.S. in Astronomy, Calif. Inst. Tech., 1970, Ph.D. in Astronomy, 1971. Programmer Travelers Ins. Co., 1966; research asst. Smithsonian Astrophys. Obs., summers 1968, 69; teaching asst. Calif. Inst. Tech., 1969-71; J. W. Gibbs instr. in astronomy Yale U., 1971-73; asst. prof. physics U. Mo., St. Louis, 1973-74; astronomer McDonnell Planetarium, St. Louis, 1973-74; asst. prof. physics U. Del., 1974-77, assoc. prof., 1977-81, prof., 1981—; Harlow Shapley vis. lectr. Am. Astron. Soc., 1976—; trustee Mt. Cuba Astron. Obs., 1977—; cons. Author: The Restless Universe: An Introduction to Astronomy, 1978, Black Holes, Quasars, and the Universe, 2d edit, 1980; contbr. numerous articles to profl. jours. Guggenheim fellow, 1980-81; NSF grantee, 1974—; NASA grantee, 1976-79, 81—. Mem. Am. Astron. Soc. (edn. officer 1979-85). Am. Assn. Physics Tchrs., AAUP, AAAS, Fedn. Am. Scientists, Internat. Astron. Union, Astron. Soc. Pacific, Phi Beta Kappa, Sigma Xi (sec. U. Del. chpt. 1976-77, v.p. chpt. 1977-79, pres. chpt. 1979-80, chpt. Disting. Scientist award 1981). Current Work: Development numerical simulations of radiative transfer in outer layers of white-dwarf stars; application of these to observations of x-rays and ultraviolet radiation from these stars. Subspecialties: Optical astronomy; Ultraviolet high energy astrophysics. Home: 346 Old Paper Mill Rd Newark DE 19711 Office: Dept Physics U Del Newark DE 19711

SHIPMAN, ROSS LOVELACE, corporate executive, petroleum consultant; b. Jackson, Miss., Nov. 20, 1926; s. William Smylie and Jeanette Scott (Lovelace) S.; m. Lois Pegrim, June 6, 1948; 1 dau., Smylie Shipman Anderson. B.A., U. Miss., 1950. Geologist, Humble Oil & Refining Co., West Tex., 1950-55, petroleum cons., Midland, Tex., 1955-60, Corpus Christi, Tex., 1960-67; asst. exec. dir. Am. Geol. Inst., Washington, 1967-71; assoc. dir. U. Tex. Marine Sci. Inst., Austin, 1971-79; assoc. v.p. for research U. Tex.-Austin, 1979-84; prin. Petroleum Investments/Worldwide, 1975-85; pres., chief exec. officer Live Oak Energy, Inc., Austin, 1985—; mem. Tex. Coastal and Marine Council, 1979-85, U.S.-Mexico Boundary Water Study Program, 1978—; del. Argonne Univs. Assn., Chgo., 1982. Author numerous geol. reports and studies, 1955-; editor, pub.: The AGI Report newsletter, 1968-70; editor: Profl. Geologist, 1975-76. Served to cpl. U.S. Army, 1944-46, PTO. Fellow Geol. Soc. Am., AAAS, Geol. Soc. (London); mem. Am. Assn. Petroleum Geologists (cert. geologist), Am. Inst. Profl. Geologists (cert. profl. geologist, Tex. State pres. 1974, nat. editor 1975-76); Mem. Soc. Ind. Profl. Earth Scientists; mem. Nat. Council Univ. Research Adminstrs.; Mem. Soc. Research Adminstrs. Anglican. Clubs: Corpus Christi Yacht (rear commodore 1965-67), Metropolitan, San Antonio Petroleum. Current Work: Petroleum and mineral exploration and enhanced oil recovery development; international water development. Subspecialties: Geology; Hydrology. Home: Ambiente 1803 Great Oaks Dr Round Rock TX 78681 Office: Live Oak Energy Inc Austin TX 78701

SHIRES, THOMAS KAY, pharmacologist, educator; b. Buffalo, July 12, 1935; s. Frank Alexander and Bessie Cummings (Harder) S.; m. Ann Kirkpatrick, Aug. 27, 1961; children—Cynthia Louise, Heather Ann, Elliot Thomas. A.B., Colgate U., 1957; M.S., U. Okla., 1962, Ph.D., 1965. Instr. depts. anatomy and urology U. Okla. Sch. Medicine, 1965-67, asst. prof., 1967-68; asst. prof. dept. pharmacology U. Iowa Coll. Medicine, Iowa City, 1972-75, assoc. prof., 1975-81, prof., 1981—, assoc. prof. dept. pathology, 1975-77. Author 1 book in field; contbr. articles to profl. jours. Served with U.S. Army, 1958-60. Mem. Am. Soc. Pharmacology and Exptl. Therapeutics, Am. Soc. Cell Biology, Am. Assn. Pathologists, Am. Assn. Cancer Research, N.Y. Acad. Scis., Am. Ornithologists Union, Sigma Xi. Methodist. Current Work: Research into synthesis, degradation and function of the internal cellular membrane system with special concern for neoplastic and toxicologic alterations of the system. Subspecialties: Cell and tissue culture; Molecular pharmacology. Office: Dept Pharmacology U Iowa Coll Medicine Iowa City IA 52242

SHIRKEY, WILLIAM DAN, physicist, engineer, researcher; b. Roswell, N.Mex., Nov. 6, 1951; s. Robert Johnson and Joan (Savage) S. B.S. in Physics, SUNY-Brockport, 1973; M.S. in Physics, Clarkson Coll. Tech., 1980; postgrad., Cornell U. Grad. Sch. Mgmt., 1982-84. Quality assurance engr. Corning Glass Works, Canton, N.Y., 1974-76, sr. process engr., 1979-81, devel. engr., 1981, sr. process and product devel. engr., 1981-82; staff Cornell U. Grad. Sch., 1982—; research asst. Clarkson Coll. Tech., Potsdam, N.Y., 1977-79. Contbr. articles to profl. publs. Mem. Optical Soc. Am., Am. Inst. Physics, Nat. Peace Acad., Amnesty Internat., Sigma Pi Sigma. Current Work: Use of fused silica and low expansion glasses in the fabrication and frit sealing of lightweight mirrors, fusion sealing of lightweight mirrors, astronomical and space use mirror fabrication. Subspecialties: Materials processing; Materials (engineering). Home: 15 Dart Dr Ithaca NY 14850 Office: Corning Glass Works PO Box 28 Canton NY 13617

SHIRLEY, DAVID ARTHUR, research laboratory administrator, chemist, educator; b. North Conway, N.H., Mar. 30, 1934; m. Virginia Schultz, June 23, 1956; children: David N., Diane, Michael, Eric, Gail. B.S. in Chemistry, U. Maine, 1955, Sc.D. (hon.), 1978; Ph.D. in Chemistry (NSF fellow), U. Calif., Berkeley, 1959. From lectr. to prof. chemistry U. Calif., Berkeley, 1960—, vice chmn. dept. chemistry, 1968-71, chmn. dept., 1971-75; assoc. dir. and head materials and molecular research div. Lawrence Berkeley Lab., 1975-80, dir. lab., 1980—. Recipient Ernest O. Lawrence award AEC, 1972; NSF sr. postdoctoral fellow, 1966-67, 70. Fellow Am. Phys. Soc.; mem. Am. Chem. Soc. (Calif. sect. award 1970), AAAS, Nat. Acad. Sci., Am. Acad. Arts and Sci. Subspecialties: Physical chemistry; Surface chemistry. Office: Lawrence Berkeley Lab One Cyclotron Rd Berkeley CA 94720

SHIRLEY, JOSEPH FLOYD, metallurgical engineer; b. Cin., Jan. 28, 1932; s. Joseph Boomer and Luella May (Barnes) S.; m. Nadine Rehm, May 26, 1954; children—Joseph Theodore, William Floyd. B.S. in Metall. Engring., U. Ariz., 1955, M.S. in Metall. Engring., 1958, Ph.D., in Metallurgy, 1969. Research chemist Magma Copper Co., San Manuel, Ariz., 1960-64; pvt. practice metall. cons., Tucson, 1964-72; metall. cons. Mountain States Research and Devel., Tucson, 1972-81, sr. v.p., gen. mgr., 1981—; dir. Mountain States Mineral Enterprises, Tucson. Contbr. articles to profl. jours. Patentee in field. Served to 1st lt. USAF, 1955-57. Mem. AIME, Mining and Metall. Soc. Am., Republican. Presbyterian. Clubs: Mining of Southwest, Old Pueblo (Tucson). Lodge: Masons. Subspecialty: Metallurgical engineering. Office: Mountain States Research and Devel 4370 S Fremont Ave Tucson AZ 85714

SHIVANANDAN, KANDIAH, research physicist; b. Parit Buntar, Malaysia, Aug. 22, 1929; s. Sangrapillai and Vallianaki K.; m. Mary Sheehy, Sept. 21, 1961; children: John, Marianne. B.Sc., U. Melbourne, Australia, 1957; M.S., U. Toronto, 1958; Ph.D., Cath. U. Am., 1966. Physicist M.I.T., Cambridge, Mass., 1957-61; physicist (Goddard Space Flight Ctr.), Greenbelt, Md., 1961-63; research physicist infrared sci. and tech., astronomy/asstrophysics (Naval Research Lab.), Washington, 1963—. Contbr. articles to profl. jours. Optical Soc. Am. fellow, 1965. Mem. Am. Inst. Physics, Indian Inst. Physics, Am. Astron. Soc., Royal Astron. Soc., Internat. Astron. Union. Current Work: Infrared science and technology, astronomy and astrophysics. Subspecialties: Infrared astronomy; Acoustics. Home: 4711 Overbrook Rd Bethesda MD 20816

SHKAROFSKY, ISSIE PETER, physicist; b. Montreal, July 4, 1931; s. Frank and Sylvia (Alpert) S.; m. Agnes Spira, Mar. 10, 1957; children—Marvin David, Sema, Lou Aaron, Aviva Brocha. B.Sc., McGill U., 1952, M.Sc., 1953, Ph.D., 1957. Sr. mem. sci. staff RCA Ltd., Montreal, 1957-73, research/devel. fellow, 1973-76; fellow MPB Technologies, Inc., Ste. Anne de Bellevue, Que., 1977—. Contbr. articles to profl. jours.; author: (with T.W. Johnston and M.P. Bachnyski) The Particle Kinetics of Plasmas, 1966. Fellow Am. Phys. Soc.; mem. Can. Assn. Physicists, Am. Geophys. Union, Assn. Orthodox Jewish Scientists. Current Work: Plasma transport, magnetic fusion, laser fusion, lasers, space physics, ionosphere, troposhere, microwaves, radar, propagation, others. Subspecialties: Plasma physics; Fusion.

SHKEDI, ZVI, physicist; b. Munich, W. Ger., May 24, 1947; came to U.S., 1977, naturalized, 1982; s. Shaul and Fruma (Gerstner) S.; m. Chana S. Nafcha, Aug. 20, 1975; children—Ariel, Michal, Lior, Yael, Eliran. B.Sc. cum laude, Hebrew U. Jerusalem, 1970; M.Sc., Weizmann Inst. Sci., Israel, 1972, Ph.D., 1977. Nuclear research asst. Weizmann Inst., 1970-77; research assoc. Brown U., Providence, 1977-79; mem. tech. staff Monogram Industries, Santa Monica, Calif., 1979-80; project engr. Garrett-AiResearch, Torrance, Calif., 1980—. Contbr. articles to profl. jours. Chaim Weizmann fellow, 1977. Mem. IEEE, Am. Phys. Soc. Current Work: Pressure and temperature transducers, thin films, micro-computer systems. Subspecialties: Aerospace engineering and technology; Solar energy. Office: AiResearch 2525 W 190th St Torrance CA 90509

SHNEIER, MICHAEL OLIVER, computer scientist; b. Johannesburg, Republic of South Africa, Feb. 10, 1951; came to U.S., 1978, naturalized, 1984; s. Lionel Bernard Shneier and Naomi (Heller) Beck; m. Ann Ilene Scher, May 25, 1980. B.Sc. with honors, Witwatersrand U., Johnnesburg, 1974; Ph.D., Edinburgh U., Scotland, 1978. Research assoc. U. Md., College Park, 1978-81; computer scientist Nat. Bur. Standards, Gaithersburg, Md., 1981—; cons. Imtech Inc., Silver Spring, Md., 1979-80. Contbr. articles to profl. jours. Raikes scholar; Julius Robinson scholar; scholar Council for Indsl. Research, U. Witwatersrand. Mem. Assn. for Computing Machinery, IEEE, Soc. for Study Artificial Intelligence and Simulation of Behavior. Current work: Using sensory feedback real-time control of robots in complex environments; algorithms for hierarchical processing of image data; design of fast parallel hardware. Subspecialty: Graphics, image processing, and pattern recognition. Office: Nat Bur Standards Bldg 220 Room B124 Gaithersburg MD 20899

SHNIDER, BRUCE I., physician, educator, researcher; b. Ludzk, Poland, Jan. 20, 1920; came to U.S., 1920, naturalized, 1926; s. Benjamin and Rose (Bornstein) S.; m. Doris Benjamin, June 22, 1942; children—Steven, Marc, Reed. B.S. in Edn, Wilson Tchrs. Coll., 1941; M.D. cum laude, Georgetown U., 1948. Cert. Am. Bd. Internal Medicine. Tchr. D.C. Public Schs., 1941-44; intern D.C. Gen. Hosp., 1948-49, resident in medicine, 1950-51, attending physician, 1958—, dir. tumor service, 1958—, chmn. subcom. ambulatory care, 1970-72, active staff, 1972—; mem. Tumor Bd., 1974-80; asst. resident Georgetown U. Hosp., 1949-50, chief resident, 1951-52; instr. Sch. Medicine, 1952-56, lectr. phys. diagnosis, 1953-61, asst. prof., 1956-61, asst. prof. pharmacology, 1961-63, prof. medicine and pharmacology, 1960-61, prof. medicine, 1966—, prof. pharmacology, 1966-79; asst. dean (Sch. Medicine), 1960-63, assoc. dean, 1963-73, assoc. dean acad. affairs, 1973-79; dir. Cancer Detection Ctr. Hosp., 1952-53; mem. Tumor Bd., 1962-65, cancer coordinator, 1960-65; chmn. cancer edn. com. Vincent T. Lombardi Cancer Ctr., 1971-75, coordinator teaching activities, 1961-79, dir. div. oncology, 1965-79; attending physician Vincent T. Lombardi Cancer Ctr. (Hosp.), 1958—; dir. Georgetown U. Chemotherapy Research program; VA Hosp., 1962-70; head dept. oncology Beilinson Hosp., Petach Tikva, Israel, 1972-74; vis. prof. Tel Aviv U., 1972-73,

Hebrew U., 1979-80; cons. Contbr. articles to profl. jours. Served with USPHS, 1955-57. Fellow ACP, Am. Soc. Clin. Pharmacology and Therapeutics, Am. Coll. Clin. Pharmacology; mem. Med. Soc. D.C., N.Y. Acad. Scis., AAAS, Am. Fedn. Clin. Research, Assn. Am. Med. Colls., AAUP, Am. Assn. Cancer Edn., Georgetown U. Alumni Assn., Royal Soc. Medicine, Southeastern Assn. Cancer Research, Found. Thanatology, AMA, Am. Soc. Preventive Oncology. Subspecialties: Oncology; Chemotherapy. Office: DC General Hospital 19th St and Massachusetts Ave Suite 1505 Washington DC 20003

SHOCH, DAVID EUGENE, physician, educator; b. Warsaw, Poland, June 10, 1918; s. Henry and Hannah (Dembina) S.; m. Gertrude Amelia Weinstock, June 10, 1945; children: James, John. B.S., Coll. City N.Y., 1938; M.S., Northwestern U., 1939, Ph.D., 1943, M.D., 1946. Diplomate: Am. Bd. Ophthalmology (dir., vice chmn. 1978, chmn. 1979). Intern Cook County Hosp., Chgo., 1945-46, resident ophthalmology, 1948-52, practice medicine, specializing in ophthalmology, Chgo., 1952—; asst. prof. ophthalmology dept. Northwestern U., Chgo., 1952-66, prof., 1966—, head dept. ophthalmology, 1966-83; ophthalmology dept. Northwestern Meml. Hosp., Childrens Meml. Hosp., VA Lakeside Hosp., 1966-83. Editorial cons. in ophthalmology: Postgrad. Med; abstract editor: Am. Jour. Ophthalmology. Trustee Assn. U. Profs. (pres. 1973). Opthalmology; bd. dirs., sec. Heed Ophthalmic Found. Served to capt., M.C. AUS, 1946-48. Fellow ACS; mem. AMA, AAAS, Am. Acad. Ophthalmology (sec. for instrn. 1972-78, pres. 1981), Assn. Research in Vision and Ophthalmology, Inst. Medicine Chgo., Chgo. Ophthalmol. Soc. (past pres.), Am. Ophthalmol. Soc. (chmn. council), Pan-Am. Ophthalmol. Soc., French Ophthalmol. Soc., Sigma Xi. Current Work: Cataracts, ophthalmic optics; lens implants. Subspecialty: Ophthalmology. Office: 303 E Chicago Ave Chicago IL 60611

SHOCK, D'ARCY ADRIANCE, engineering consultant; b. Fowler, Colo., June 13, 1911; s. Earl I. and Margaret (Adriance) S.; m. Barbara Beth Lounsbury, Feb. 11, 1955; children: Kathy Beth, David Christopher. B.S. in Chem. Engring, Colo. Coll., 1933; M.A. in Phys. Chemistry, U. Tex., 1946. Registered profl. engr., Okla. Chemist Dow Chem. Co., Midland, Mich., 1933-36; analytical lab. supr. McGean Chem. Co., Cleve., 1936-41; works chemist Internat. Mineras Magnesium Plant, Austin, Tex., 1941-44; Nat. Gasoline Assn. Am. research fellow U. Tex.-Austin, 1945-49; with Continental Oil Co., Ponca City, Okla., 1949-76; dir.-mgr. Corp. Research div. Conoco, Ponca City, 1956-73; mgr. Mining Research div., ret., 1976; cons. on slurry transport and solution mining, Ponca City, 1976—; mem. waste implacement pilot plant panel radioactive waste disposal com. Nat. Acad. Scis., 1976—. Contbr. sci. articles to profl. publs. Mem. Okla. radiation adv. com. Okla. Health Dept., 1956-70. Mem. Nat. Assn. Corrosion Engring., Soc. Petroleum Engrs., AIME, Soc. Mining Engrs. of AIME (disting. mem.). Holder 27 U.S. patents. Current Work: Actively consulting in areas of slurry transport solution mining. Subspecialties: Solution mining; Hazardous waste disposal.

SHOCKLEY, WILLIAM BRADFORD, physicist, emeritus educator; b. London, Feb. 13, 1910; s. William Hillman and May (Bradford) S.; m. Jean A. Bailey, 1933 (div. 1955); children: Alison, William Alden, Richard Condit; m. Emmy Lanning, 1955. B.S., Calif. Inst. Tech., 1932; Ph.D., M.I.T., 1936; Sc.D. (hon.), Rutgers U., 1956, U. Pa., 1955, Gustavus Adolphus Coll., Minn., 1963. Teaching fellow M.I.T., 1932-36; mem. tech. staff Bell Telephone Labs., 1936-42, 45, became dir. transistor physics research, 1954; dir. Shockley Semicondr. Lab.; pres. Shockley Transistor Corp., 1958-60; cons. Shockley Transistor unit Clevite Transistor, 1960-65; lectr. Stanford U., 1958-63, Alexander M. Poniatoff prof. engring. sci. and applied sci., 1963-75, prof. emeritus, 1975—; exec. cons. Bell Telephone Labs., 1965-75; dep. dir. research, weapons systems evaluation group Dept. Def., 1954-55; expert cons. Office Sec. War, 1944-45; vis. lectr. Princeton U., 1946; vis. prof. Calif. Inst. Tech., 1954-55; sci. adv., policy council Joint Research and Devel. Bd., 1947-49; sr. cons. Army Sci. Adv. Panel.; Dir. research Anti-submarine Welfare Ops. Research Group USN, 1942-44. Author: Electrons and Holes in Semiconductors, 1950, (with W. A. Gong) Mechanics, 1966; editor: (with W. A. Gong) Imperfections of Nearly Perfect Crystals, 1952. Recipient medal for Merit; Air Force Assn. citation of honor, 1951; U.S. Army cert. of appreciation, 1953; co-winner (with John Bardeen and Walter H. Brattain) Nobel Prize in Physics, 1956; Wilhelm Exner medal Oesterreichischer Gewerbeverein Austria, 1963; Holley medal ASME, 1963; Calif. Inst. Tech. Alumni Disting. Service award, 1966; NASA cert. of appreciation Apollo 8, 1969; Public Service Group Achievement award NASA, 1969; named to Inventor's Hall of Fame, 1974; named to Calif. Inventor's Hall of Fame, 1983. Fellow AAAS; mem. Am. Phys. Soc. (O.E. Buckley prize 1953), Nat. Acad. Sci. (Comstock prize 1954), IEEE (Morris Liebmann prize 1952, Gold medal, 25th anniversary of transistor 1972, Medal of Honor 1980, Centennial medal and cert. 1984), Sigma Xi, Tau Beta Pi. Holder over 90 patents. Inventor of junction transistor; research on energy bands of solids, ferromagnetic domains, plastic properties of metals; semicondr. theory applied to devices and device defects such as dislocations; fundamentals of electromagnetic energy and momentum; metal tools for sci. thinking; ops. research on human quality problems. Current Work: Statistics of human quality, including I.Q. Subspecialties: Condensed matter physics; Semiconductors. Home: 797 Esplanada Way Stanford CA 94305 Office: Stanford Electronics Labs McCullough 202 Stanford U Stanford CA 94305

SHOEMAKER, DAVID POWELL, chemist, educator; b. Kooskia, Idaho, May 12, 1920; s. Roy Hopkins and Sarah (Anderson) S.; m. Clara Brink, Aug. 5, 1955; 1 son, Robert Brink. B.A., Reed Coll., 1942; Ph.D., Calif. Inst. Tech., 1947. Research asst. Calif. Inst. Tech., 1943-45, NRC fellow, 1945-47, sr. research fellow, 1948-51; fellow John Simon Guggenheim Meml. Found. Inst. Theoretical Physics, Copenhagen, Denmark, 1947-48; asst. prof. chemistry Mass. Inst. Tech., Cambridge, 1951-56, assoc. prof., 1956-60, prof., 1960-70; prof. chemistry Oreg. State U., Corvallis, 1970-84, chmn. dept., 1970-81 prof. emeritus, 1984—; vis. scientist Lab. Cristallographie, CNRS, Grenoble, France, 1967, 78-79; vis. lectr. Kemisk Institut, Aarhus, Denmark, June 1979; cons. Exxon Co. U.S.A., Baton Rouge, 1957—; sec.-treas. U.S.A. Nat. Com. for Crystallography, 1962-64, chmn., 1967-69; mem. vis. com. chemistry dept. Brookhaven Nat. Lab., 1974-79; mem. evaluation panel material scis. div. Nat. Bur. Standards, 1977-79. Author: (with Carl W. Garland, Jeffrey I. Steinfeld, Joseph W. Nibler) Experiments in Physical Chemistry, 1962, 67, 74, 81; Am. co-editor: Acta Crystallographica, 1964-69. Fellow Am. Phys. Soc., AAAS; mem. Am. Chem. Soc., Am. Crystallographic Assn. (pres. 1970), Am. Acad. Arts and Scis., Internat. Union Chrystallography (mem. exec. com. 1972-78), Phi Beta Kappa, Sigma Xi, Phi Lambda Upsilon, Phi Kappa Phi. Current Work: Transition metal alloys, alloy hydrides, zeolites, x-ray diffraction, neutron diffraction. Subspecialties: X-ray crystallography; Solid state chemistry. Home: 3453 NW Hayes Ave Corvallis OR 97330 Office: Dept Chemistry Oreg State U Corvallis OR 97331

SHOEMAKER, EUGENE MERLE, geologist, educator; b. Los Angeles, Apr. 28, 1928; s. George Estel and Muriel May (Scott) S.; m. Carolyn Jean Spellmann, Aug. 18, 1951; children: Christine Carol, Patrick Gene, Linda Susan. B.S., Calif. Inst. Tech., 1947, M.S., 1948; M.A., Princeton U., 1954, Ph.D., 1960; Sc.D., Ariz. State Coll., 1965, Temple U., 1967. Exploration uranium deposits and investigation salt structures Colo. and Utah U.S. Geol. Survey, 1948-50, regional investigations geochemistry, vulcanology and structure Colorado Plateau, 1951-56, research structure and mechanics of meteorite impact and nuclear explosion craters, 1957-60, with E.C.T. Chao, discovered coesite, Meteor Crater, Ariz., 1960, investigation structure and history of moon, 1960-73, established lunar geol. time scale, methods of geol. mapping of moon, 1960, application TV systems to investigation extra-terrestrial geology, 1961—, geology and paleomagnetism, Colo. Plateau, 1969—, systematic search for planet-crossing asteroids, 1973—, geology of satellites of Jupiter and Saturn, 1978, organized br. of astrogeology U.S. Geol. Survey, 1961; co-investigator TV expt. Project Ranger, 1961-65; chief scientist, center of astrogeology U.S. Geol. Survey, 1966-68, research geologist, 1976—, prin. investigator geol. field investigations in Apollo lunar landing, 1965-70, also television expt. Project Surveyor, 1963-68, prof. geology, 1969—, Calif. Inst. Tech., chmn. div. geol. and planetary scis., 1969-72. Recipient (with E.C.T. Chao) Wetherill medal Franklin Inst., 1965; Arthur S. Flemming award, 1966; NASA medal for exceptional sci. achievement, 1967; honor award for meritorious service U.S. Dept. Interior, 1973; Disting. Service award, 1980. Mem. Nat. Acad. Sci., Geol. Soc. Am. (Day medal 1982), Mineral Soc. Am., Soc. Econ. Geologists, Geochem. Soc., Am. Assn. Petroleum Geologists, Am. Geophys. Union, Seismol. Soc. Am., Am. Astron. Soc. (Kuiper prize 1984), Internat. Astron. Union. Subspecialties: Geology; Planetary science. Office: US Geol Survey 2255 N Gemini Dr Flagstaff AZ 86001

SHOFFNER, ROBERT NURMAN, geneticist, educator; b. Junction City, Kans., Mar. 3, 1916; s. Nurman A. and Hazel D. (Cunningham) S.; m. Gladys Marie Shoffner, Sept. 3, 1938; children: R. Kirk, Jane M., Patti I. B.S., Kans. State U., 1940; M.S., U. Minn., 1942, Ph.D., 1946. Instr. animal sci. U. Minn., 1942-46, asst. prof., 1946-49, assoc. prof., 1949-55, prof., 1955—; vis. prof. Iowa State U., 1957, U. Tex., 1969; FAO cons., 1976. Assoc. dir. St. Anthony Park, St. Paul. Fulbright scholar, 1962; recipient Merck Research award, 1982. Fellow Poultry Sci. Assn. (pres. 1966-67), AAAS; mem. Genetic Soc., Genetic Soc. Am., Sigma Xi, Gamma Sigma Delta. Current Work: Animal cytogenetics, genetic modification. Subspecialties: Genetics and genetic engineering (agriculture); Animal breeding and embryo transplants. Home: 2066 Knapp St Saint Paul MN 55108 Office: Dept Animal Science U Minn 1404 Gortner Ave Saint Paul MN 55108

SHOLTIS, JOSEPH ARNOLD, JR., nuclear engineer, air force officer; b. Monongahela, Pa., Nov. 28, 1948; s. Joseph and Gladys Virginia (Frye) S.; m. Cheryl Anita Senchur, Dec. 19, 1970; children: Christian Joseph, Carole Lynne. B.S. in Nuclear Engring, Pa. State U., 1970; M.S., U. N.Mex., 1977, postgrad., 1977-80. Lic. sr. reactor operator U.S. Nuclear Regulatory Commn., 1980. Mathematician, statistician U.S. Bur. Mines, Pitts., 1968-70; commd. officer U.S. Air Force, 1970; advanced through grades to maj., nuclear research officer USAF fgn. tech. div. Wright-Patterson AFB, Dayton, Ohio, 1970-74; sect. chief space nuclear systems analysis Air Force Weapons Lab., Kirtland AFB, N.Mex., 1974-78; mem. tech. staff. advanced nuclear systems safety analyst Sandia Nat. Lab., Albuquerque, 1978-80; chief radiation sources, reactor facilities dir. Armed Forces Radiobiology Research Inst., Bethesda, Md., 1980-84; program mgr. SP-100 space reactor program Air Force Element, Dept. of Energy, Washington, 1984—; faculty Uniformed Services U. of Health Scis., 1983—; cons. in field. Author: handbook LMFBR Accident Delineation, 1980; contbg. author: Military Radiobiology. Mem. N.Mex. gov.'s panel on energy resources, 1976-78; com. chmn. Ft. Detrick Catholic Community; mem. alumni admissions Com. U. Pa. Mem. Am. Nuclear Soc., ASME, AAAS, N.Y. Acad. Scis., Planetary Soc., Scientists and Engrs. for Source Energy, Sigma Xi. Republican. Roman Catholic. Clubs: Fort Detrick (Md.) Rod & Gun, Jefferson's Island. Current Work: Nuclear reactor research, reactor operations, maintenance and upgrade, effects of ionizing radiation on matter, radiation sources development, design and use, reactor safety, risk assessments, reactor regulation Subspecialties: Nuclear engineering; Nuclear physics. Office: Armed Forces Radiobiology Research Inst Bldg 42 Nat Naval Med Ctr Bethesda MD 20814

SHOMER, JOHN EDWARD, electronics engineer, researcher; b. Cleve., Apr. 18, 1909; s. John Edward and Emma Regina (Wetzel) S.; m. Margaret Jeannette Yeager, Sept. 26, 1942; children—Robert Baker, William Edward, James Alan. B.S. in Elec. Engring., Cleve. State U., 1935; postgrad. Case Inst. Tech., 1939-41. Switchboard tester Western Electric Co., Cleve., 1927-32; engr. Cleve. Electric Motor Co., 1936-38; asst. chief electronics engr. Brush Devel. Co., Cleve., 1939-50; sonar engr. Bendix Pacific, North Hollywood, Calif., 1950-52; sonar and radar engr. Stavid Engring., Plainfield, N.J., 1952-58; sr. research specialist systems and radar Boeing Co., Seattle, 1958-69; researcher communication and info. theory, Seattle, 1970—. Patentee in field of electronic engring. and recording. Mem. UN Assn., N.Y.C., Ctr. for study of Democratic Instns., Santa Barbara, Calif. Mem. IEEE (life), Profl. Groups for Communication and Info. Theory. Democrat. Unitarian. Current work: Extension of the original basic work of Claude Shannon and new applications such as the search for extraterrestrial intelligence. Subspecialties: Aerospace engineering and technology; Radio and microwave astronomy. Home: 6578 123d Ave SE Bellevue WA 98006

SHONS, ALAN RANCE, plastic surgeon; b. Freeport, Ill., Jan. 10, 1938; s. Ferral Caldwell and Margaret Zimmerman (Ziegler) S.; m. Mary Ella Misamore, Aug. 5, 1961; children: Lesley Margaret, Susan Campbell. A.B., Dartmouth Coll., 1960; M.D., Case Western Res. U., 1965; Ph.D., U. Minn., 1976. Diplomate: Am. Bd. Surgery, 1975, Am. Bd. Plastic Surgery, 1977. Intern Univ. Hosp., Cleve., 1965-66; surg. resident, 1966-67; research fellow U. Minn., Mpls., 1969-72, surg. resident, 1972-74; dir. U. Minn. (Div. Plastic Surgery), 1976-84, dir. div. plastic and reconstructive surgery Case Western Res. U., 1984—; plastic surgery resident NYU, N.Y.C., 1974-76; chmn. Minn. Com. on Trauma. Author numerous sic. papers and book chpts. Served to capt. USAF, 1967-69. Dartmouth Coll. Wheelcock scholar, 1960. Fellow ACS; mem. Minn. Acad. Plastic Surgeons (pres. 1981-82), Am. Assn. Plastic Surgeons, Am. Assn. Surgery Trauma, Central Surg. Assn., Soc. Head and Neck Surgeons, Plastic Surgery Research Council. Republican. Presbyterian. Current Work: Research on limb transplantation. Subspecialties: Microsurgery; Transplant surgery. Office: University Hospital 2074 Abington Rd Cleveland OH 44106

SHOORE, JOSEPH DAVID, physicist; b. Logan, Utah, Mar. 9, 1938; s. Isadore and Constance (Petersen) S.; m. Rita Fern Finn, June 30, 1960; children: Ginger Fern, David Joseph. B.S. in Physics, Ariz. State U., 1960, M.S., 1963. Registered engr., Calif. Aeronutronic div. Philco-Ford Corp., Newport Beach, Calif., 1963-68; scientist Systems Div., Interstate Electronics Corp., Anaheim, Calif., 1968-69; prin. scientist, prin. test dir. aset facility. McDonnell Douglas Astronautics Corp., Huntington Beach, Calif., 1969—. Contbr. articles in field to profl. jours. Active Boy Scouts Am., 1970—; mem. Newport Beach Sch. Bd. ednl. rev. com., 1981-82. Mem. IEEE, Optical Soc. Am., AAAS, Soc. Information Display. Mormon (high council 1973-82). Current Work: Infrared sensor test and evaluation for space applications; space science, astronomy, remote sensing, cyrogenics/IR detectors. Subspecialties: Infrared astronomy; Infrared spectroscopy.

SHOOT, LYLE EDWARD, ceramic engineer; b. Tuscola, Ill., Feb. 11, 1930; s. Lyle F. and Marjorie M. (Smith) S.; m. Lynn Darrah, Sept. 1, 1951; children—Leslie, Leigh, Lyle Ray, Lloyd. B.S. in Ceramic Engring., Iowa State U., 1952. Ceramic engr. Diamond Ordnance Fuze Lab., Washington, 1952-56; chief engr. Erie Tech. Products, State College, Pa., 1956-63; gen. plant mgr. Radio Materials Co., Chgo., 1963-68; chief engr. Mallory Capacitor Co., Indpls., 1968—. Patentee in field. Fellow Am. Ceramic Soc. (chmn. Ind. sect. 1976); mem. IEEE. Republican. Episcopalian. Current work: Management of development engineering activities related to aluminum and tantalum electrolytic capacitors plus audio signaling devices. Subspecialties: Electronics; Ceramic engineering. Home: 6807 Balfour Ct Indianapolis IN 46220 Office: Mallory Capacitor Co PO Box 372 Indianapolis IN 46206

SHOR, AARON LOUIS, veterinarian, nutritionist; b. N.Y.C., Jan. 13, 1924; s. Harry and Frieda Rachel (Teller) S.; m. Rosalind Darrow, Oct. 2, 1960. B.S., Cornell U., 1947, D.V.M., 1953; M.S., U. Del., 1949. Gen. practice vet. medicine, Jeffersonville and Patchogue, N.Y., 1953-55; mem. clin. devel. staff Am. Cyanamid Co., Kansas City, Mo., Pearl River, N.Y. and Princeton, N.J., 1955-80; mgr. clin. devel. Smith Kline Beckman, West Chester, Pa., 1980—. Contbr. chpts. to books. Mcpl. chmn. Montgomery Twp. Democratic Orgn., Blawenburg, N.J., 1966. Served with U.S. Army, 1943-45. Mem. AVMA (drug availability com. 1979—), Am. Assn. Indsl. Vets. (sec. 1966-71, pres. 1971-72), Poultry Sci. Assn., Am. Soc. Animal Sci. Jewish. Lodge: B'Nai Brith. Current work: Development of new drugs to prevent disease or improve production. Subspecialties: Preventive medicine (veterinary medicine); Animal nutrition. Home: 215 Larchwood Rd West Chester PA 19382 Office: Smith Kline Beckman 1600 Paoli Pike West Chester PA 19380

SHORE, JOSEPH DAVID, biochemistry researcher, research director; b. N.Y.C., Apr. 2, 1934; s. Theodore and Rose (Kaplan) S.; m. Lyla Jeanne Leipzig, Dec. 7, 1968; children—Philip, Elissa. B.S., Cornell U., 1955; M.S. U. Mass., 1957; Ph.D., Rutgers U., 1963. Postdoctoral fellow Nobel Med. Inst., Stockholm, 1964-66; sr. staff investigator Edsel B. Ford Inst., Detroit, 1966-79; head div. biochem. research Henry Ford Hosp., Detroit, 1979—, dir. research, 1982—; adj. prof. biochemistry Wayne State U., Detroit, 1981—. Contbr. articles to profl. jours. Served to 1st lt. U.S. Army, 1957-60. Muscular Dystrophy Assn. fellow 1964-66. Mem. Am. Soc. Biol. Chemists, Am. Chem. Soc., Am. Heart Assn. (council on thrombosis), Internat. Soc. on Thrombosis and Hemostasis. Current work: Enzymology of blood coagulation. Subspecialties: Biochemistry (medicine); Biophysical chemistry. Home: 16 Harbor Ct Grosse Pointe Farms MI 48236 Office: Henry Ford Hosp 2799 W Grand Blvd Detroit MI 48202

SHORT, NICHOLAS MARTIN, geologist; b. St. Louis, Mo., July 18, 1927; s. Harry Elmer and Dorothy May (Martin) S.; m. Eleanor Therese Wilson, June 17, 1961; 1 child, Nicholas Martin. B.S. in Geology, St. Louis U., 1951; M.A. in Geology, Washington U., St. Louis, 1953; postgrad. Pa. State U., 1953-54; Ph.D. in Geology, MIT, 1957. Instr. geology U. Mo., Columbia, 1954; staff geologist Gulf Research and Devel., Pitts., 1957-59; geologist Lawrence Livermore Radiation Lab., Calif., 1959-64; assoc. prof. geology U. Houston, 1964-67; research geologist NASA Goddard Space Flight Ctr., Greenbelt, Md., 1967—; cons. Ecosystems Internat., Crofton, Md., Author: Planetary Geology; Mission To Earth; Volcanic Landforms and Surface Features; Landsat Tutorial Workbook, also others. Contbr. articles to profl. jours. Mem. troop com. Balt. council Boy Scouts Am., 1978-83. Served with U.S. Army, 1945-47. Recipient Exceptional Performance award NASA, 1974; Alumni Merit award St. Louis U., 1975; Lunar Program Prin. Investigator award NASA, 1979. Fellow Geol. Soc. Am.; mem. Planetary Geology Soc. Episcopalian. Current work: Research using remote sensing from satellites on geomorphology, tectonics, and exploration geology. Subspecialties: Geology; Remote sensing (geoscience). Office: NASA Goddard Space Flight Ctr Greenbelt MD 20771

SHORTER, ROY GERRARD, physician, medical educator; b. London, Jan. 11, 1925; came to U.S., 1961, naturalized, 1967; s. Gerrard Anthony and Lily Elizabeth (Parker) S.; m. Rhiannon Morris, May 15, 1948; children—Nicholas Andrew, Lindsay Ann Elizabeth. M.D., U. London, 1952. Cons. physician Mayo Clinic, Rochester, Minn., 1961—, prof. med. and pathology Mayo Med. Sch., Rochester, 1974—. Contbr. articles to profl. jours. Recipient Fulbright travel award, London, 1958, St. Thomas Hosp. Endowment Fund award, London, 1958. Fellow Royal Coll. Pathologists (U.K.), Royal Coll. Physicians; mem. Am. Gastroent. Assn., Brit. Soc. Gastroenterology, Am. Assn. Pathologists, Path. Soc. Gt. Britain and Ireland. Subspecialties: Gastroenterology; Pathology (medicine). Office: Mayo Clinic 200 1st St SW Rochester MN 55905

SHORTHILL, RICHARD WARREN, mechanical engineering educator, researcher, consultant; b. Aberdeen, Wash., Dec. 28, 1928; s. William W. and Elizabeth Ann (Boyle) S.; m. RuthLouise Wood, June 19, 1948 (dec. Aug. 1967); children—David Warren, Ann Louise Shorthill Coffin; m. Ellen L. Eggeleston, June 17, 1968. Student Westminster Coll., 1948; B.A., U. Utah, 1954, Ph.D., 1959. Research physicist Boeing Co., Seattle, 1959-62, sr. research scientist, 1962-74; adj. prof. geophysics U. Utah, Salt Lake City, 1974-80, dir. Geospace Sci. Lab., U. Utah Research Inst., 1974-82, research assoc. prof. mech. engring., 1982—, cons. in radiology, 1981-83; adj. prof. dept. physics, U. Wyo., Laramie, 1982—; cons. on optics and physics Shorthill & Assocs., Salt Lake City, 1974—; cons. on planetology NASA, Washington, 1968-82; sec. Commn. COSPAR, ISC-B of 1972—. Contbr. articles to sci. jours., chpt. to books. Mem. editorial bd. Modern Geology, 1972—, The Earth, Moon and Planets, 1974—. Served with U.S. Army, 1950-52, ETO. Recipient Pub. Service award NASA, 1977, Group Achievement award, 1977. Fellow Soc. Photo-Optical Instrumentation Engrs.; mem. Am. Astron. Soc., Royal Astron. Soc. Can., AAAS, Am. Inst. Physics, AIAA, Sigma Xi, Sigma Pi Sigma. Republican. Presbyterian. Lodge: Masons. Current work: Spectrometric properties (visible and IR) of faint asteroids, CCD-Spectrometer; fiber optic gyroscopes; laser doppler velocity in rotating fluids; electric charge on aerosals; light scattering; lunar photometric and IR properties; applied optics. Subspecialties: Fiber optics; Satellite studies. Home: 4562 Fortuna Way Salt Lake City UT 84124 Office: Dept Mech Engring 3008 Merrill Engring Bldg U Utah Salt Lake City UT 84112

SHORTLIFFE, EDWARD HANCE, medical computer educator, physician; b. Edmonton, Alta., Can., Aug. 28, 1947; came to U.S., 1954, naturalized, 1962; s. Ernest Carl and Elizabeth Joan (Rankin) S.; m. Linda Marie Dairiki, June 21, 1970; 1 dau., Lindsay Ann. A.B., Harvard U., 1970; Ph.D., Stanford U., 1975, M.D., 1976. Diplomate: Am. Bd. Internal Medicine, 1979. Intern Mass. Gen. Hosp., Boston, 1976-77; resident Stanford (Calif.) Hosp., 1977-79, asst. prof. medicine, 1979-85, assoc. prof. medicine, 1985—, asst. prof. computer sci., 1979-85, assoc. prof. computer sci., 1985—; cons. and co-founder Teknowledge, Inc. Contbr. articles on med. computer sci. to profl. jours. Recipient Research Career Devel. award Nat. Library Medicine, 1979-84; Henry J. Kaiser Family Found. Faculty scholar, 1983—; NIH trainee, 1971-76. Fellow Am. Coll. Med. Informatics, ACP; mem. Am. Fedn. Clin. Research, Assn. Computing Machinery (Grace Murray Hopper award 1976), Soc. Med. Decision Making, Am. Assn. Artificial Intelligence. Developer Mycin and Oncocin Med. consultation computer programs. Current Work: Medical computer science, applications of computers to clinical practice, research into development of computer-based clinical decision aids using artificial intelligence techniques. Subspecialties: Internal medicine; Artificial intelligence. Office: TC-135 Stanford Med Sch Stanford CA 94305

SHOUCAIR, FARID SAMI, electrical engineer, researcher; b. Beirut, Aug. 7, 1958; came to U.S., 1976; s. Sami and Eliane (Sehnaoui) S. B.E.E., Columbia U., 1979, S.M.E.E., 1981, Ph.D. in Elec. Engring., 1983. Teaching asst. Columbia U., N.Y.C., 1979-81, research asst., 1981-83; research enr. Schlumberger, Fairchild, Palo Alto, Calif., 1983-85; faculty dept. elec. engring. Yale U., New Haven, 1985—. Mem. IEEE, Eta Kappa Nu. Current work: High temperature LSI and VLSI device and circuit modeling and design (mainly analog circuits); semiconductor devices. Subspecialties: Electrical engineering; Integrated circuits. Home: 888 Park Ave New York NY 10021 Office: Yale U Dept Elec Engring PO Box 2157 Yale Station New Haven CT 06520

SHOUP, ROBERT DONALD, chemist; b. Sinking Spring, Pa., Mar. 14, 1933; s. Evan Lloyd and Mary May (Reeser) S.; 1 child, Thomas Patrick. B.S. in Chemistry, Albright Coll., 1960; Ph.D., U. Pitts., 1964. Research chemist W.R. Grace Co., Columbia, Md., 1964-68; research supr. in phys. chemistry Corning Glass Works, N.Y., 1968—. Contbr. articles to profl. jours. Patentee in field. Scoutmaster Boy Scouts Am., Caton, N.Y., 1977-80; coach Little League Baseball, Painted Post, N.Y., 1973-75. Mem. Am. Chem. Soc., Am. Ceramic Soc. Republican. Methodist. Current work: Colloid and surface chemistry for sol-gel formation of ceramics, glasses and optical waveguide fibers; controlled pore carbon on silica structures via ultraparticle packing prosesses; synthetic processes for mica-like minerals. Subspecialties: Physical chemistry; Surface chemistry. Home: Thurber Rd RD 2 Corning NY 14830 Office: Corning Glass Works SP FR 5-2 Corning NY 14830

SHOUP, WILLIAM DAVID, agricultural engineering educator, consultant; b. Lafayette, Ind., Feb. 7, 1951; s. William E. Shoup and Maxine Ann (Shelton) Brown; m. Roberta Eileen Sikora, July 26, 1981. B.S., Purdue U., 1973, M.S., 1974, Ph.D., 1980; postgrad., Mich. State U., 1974. Sales engr. Internat. Harvester, Chgo., 1974-75; grad. instr. Purdue U., 1975-76; dist. mgr. J. I. Case Co., Indpls., 1977-79, product planning mgr., Racine, Wis., 1979-80; v.p. D2M Corp., Gainesville, Fla., 1980—; asst. prof. agrl. engring. U. Fla., 1980—, cordinator for mechanized agr., 1980—; sr. cons. Harbor Assocs., Boston, 1981—; cons. CMF&Z Corp., Des Moines, 1982-83. Author: books, the most recent being Advanced Farm Machinery Systems, 1982, Technical Machine Sales Management, 1982. Leader 4-H Club, Ind., Fla., 1965—. Named to Outstanding Young Men Am. U.S. Jaycees, 1982. Mem. Am. Soc. Agrl. Engrs. (com. chmn., com. chmn. sect.), Am. Farm Bur. Fedn., Sigma Xi, Alpha Zeta (adv.), Gamma Sigma Delta, Alpha Mu. Club: U. Fla. Faculty. Current Work: Agricultural systems research, technology impact, robotic applications. Subspecialties: Agricultural engineering; Systems engineering. Home: 4106 NW 19th Dr Gainesville FL 32605 Office: U Fla 3 Fazier Rogers Hall Gainesville FL 32611

SHRAUNER, JAMES ELY, physicist, educator; b. Dodge City, Kans., Mar. 10, 1933; s. James Arthur and Mary Ruth (Ely) S.; m. Barbara Wayne Abraham, Oct. 30, 1965; children—Elizabeth, Jay. B.Sc., U. Kans., 1956; M.A., Columbia U., 1958; Ph.D., U. Chgo., 1962. Research assoc. Stanford U., Calif., 1963-65; asst. prof. Washington U., St. Louis, 1965-69, assoc. prof., 1970-77, prof., 1977—; research scientist Los Alamos Nat. Lab., 1974-75, Ames Lab., Iowa, U.S. Dept. Energy, 1978-80; trustee Univs. Research Assocs., Washington, 1978—. Contbr. articles to profl. jours. Fellow Am. Phys. Soc. (com. to revise 1970). Current work: quantum field theory of elementary particle physics; quantum field theory of condensed matter physics. Subspecialties: Particle physics; Theoretical physics. Home: 7452 Stratford St Saint Louis MO 63130 Office: Physics Dept Washington U Saint Louis MO 63130

SHRESTHA, BUDDHI MAN, scientist, cariologist, pathologist and pedodontist; b. Chainpur Bazar, Sankhuwa Sabha, Nepal, Sept. 28, 1936; came to U.S., 1973, also naturalized; s. Lok Man and Subhadra Devi Shrestha. B.D.S., Panjab (India) U., 1963; M.S. in Dental Sci, U. Rochester, 1970, Ph.D. in Pathology, 1980. Cert. pedodontics, clin. intern. Dental surgeon Dept. Health Services, Govt. of Nepal, 1965-73; research assoc. Eastman Dental Ctr. Rochester, N.Y., 1973-74; postdoctoral fellow U. Rochester, 1975-80; scientist, cariologist Oral Health Research Ctr. Sch. Dentistry, Fairleigh Dickinson U.,

Hackensack, N.J., 1981-82, adj. assoc. prof. pathology, 1982-85, dir. div. nutrition and cariology, 1982-85; part-time clin. assoc. prof. oral medicine Coll. Dentistry, NYU, N.Y.C., 1982-85; mem. adv. com. on nutrition edn. in profl. schs. N.Y. Acad. Medicine, 1982-85; cons. pedodontist Anthony L. Jordan Health Ctr., Rochester, N.Y., 1985—. Dental scholar Colombo Plan, 1959-63; research fellow Eastman Dental Ctr., 1968-70; postdoctoral fellow NIH, U. Rochester, 1975-78. Mem. Nepal Med. Assn. (Biratnagar br., hon. joint sec. 1965-67), Nepal Dental Soc. (founding, hon. exec. sec. 1971-73), Internat. Assn. Dental Research, Am. Assn. Dental Research, European Orgn. for Caries Research (sr.). Club: Genesee Golf of Rochester. Patentee method of coating teeth with a durable glaze; inventor UV method for detection and scoring of rat caries. Current Work: Effects of diet and nutrition on dental caries; fluoride and trace elements in prevention of dental caries; cariostatic effects of titanium tetrafluoride; development of prototype rate caries model with improved computerized UV caries scoring system; fluoride and trace elements in prevention and treatment of osteoporosis. Subspecialties: Cariology; Pathology (medicine). Office: Sch Dentistry Fairleigh Dickinson U 110 Fuller Pl Hackensack NJ 07601

SHREVE, GREGORY MONROE, anthropology and computer educator; b. Munich, Bavaria, W.Ger., Aug. 3, 1950; came to U.S., 1964; s. J.L. and Rosa (Zerweiss) S.; m. Joan Marie Nelson, Dec. 29, 1971. B.A., Ohio State U., 1971, M.A., 1974, Ph.D., 1975; cert. advanced study in computer and info. sci, U. Pitts., 1980. Vis. asst. prof. Ohio State U., Columbus, 1975; asst. prof. Kent (Ohio) State U., 1975-80, assoc. prof., 1980—, acad. dean, 1981-85, chmn. acad. computing adv. com., 1983; dir. computer ctr. Kent State U.-Liverpool, 1978-81; vis. prof. Karl Marx U., 1985-86; pres. Logitech, Inc.; cons. BFG Inc., Burton, Ohio, 1982-83. Author: Genesis of Structures in Narrative (2 vols.), 1975, 2d edit., 1983. Pres. Geauga County Arts Council, Chardon, Ohio, 1981-83; mem. steering com. United Way Info. Line, 1981-83. Fellow Am. Anthrop. Assn., Am. Folklore Soc.; mem. Assn. Computing Machinery; installation del. Digital Equipment Users Soc. Current Work: Relationship of software structures to natural language structures; general semiotic structures present in artificial languages and how they relate to natural language systems. Subspecialties: Automated language processing; Distributed systems and networks. Home: 14649 Evergreen Dr Burton OH 44021 Office: Kent State Univ 14111 Claridon-Troy Rd Burton OH 44021

SHRIER, STEFAN, applied mathematician, educator, consultant; b. Mexico City, Nov. 7, 1942; came to U.S., 1943; s. Henry Leon and Mathilda June (Czamanska) S. B.S. in Engring., Columbia U., 1964, M.S. in Ops. Research, 1966; Ph.D. in Applied Math., Brown U., 1977. Chmn. computer sci. program Wellesley Coll., Mass., 1972-75; sr. engr. Booz, Allen & Hamilton, Bethesda, Md., 1977-79; dir. Latin Am. ops. SofTech, Inc., Waltham, Mass., 1979; research staff mem. System Planning Corp., Arlington, Va., 1980-83; tech. dir. Grumman-CTEC, Inc., McLean, Va., 1983—, dir. Lab. for Machine Intelligence and Correlation, 1984—; professorial lectr. stats. George Washington U., Washington, 1981-84, adj. prof. computer and info. systems, 1984-85, professorial lectr. computer and info. systems, 1985—; adj. prof. computer sci. George Mason U., 1985—. Contbr. articles to profl. jours. Fellow Washington Acad. Scis.; mem. Sigma Xi. Current work: Inductive inference and machine learning; research and development in information technologies. Subspecialties: Graphics, image processing, and pattern recognition; Numerical analysis (mathematics). Home: PO Box 19139 Alexandria VA 22320 Office: Grumman-CTEC Inc 6862 Elm St McLean VA 22101

SHRIVASTAVA, RITU, electronics engineer, research and development executive; b. Rajnandgaon, India, Jan. 2, 1951; came to U.S., 1973; s. Kamala Kant and Priamvada (Nigam) S.; m. Poonam Nigam, May 30, 1978; children—Ruchi, Nidhi. B.S., Jabalpur U., India, 1968; B.Engring., Indian Inst. Sci., 1971, M.Engring. 1973; Ph.D. in Elec. Engring., La. State U., 1977. Research asst. La. State U., Baton Rouge, 1973-77, instr., research assoc., 1977-79, vis. asst. prof., 1979-80; project leader CMOS tech. devel. Mostek Corp., Carrollton, Tex., 1980-83; mgr. tech. devel. Cypress Semicondr. Corp., San Jose, Calif., 1983—. Contbr. articles to profl. jours. Patentee in field. Nat. Sci. Talent Search scholar, 1965. Mem. IEEE (sr.), Indian Inst. Sci. Gymkhana (hon. sec. indoor games 1971-72), Phi Kappa Phi, Eta Kappa Nu, Sigma Pi Sigma. Current work: Semiconductor device and process technology development for high performance volatile and nonvolatile CMOS memories. Subspecialties: Microelectronics; Semiconductors. Home: 45131 Manzanita Ct Fremont CA 94539 Office: Cypress Semiconductor Corp 3901 N 1st St San Jose CA 95134

SHRIVER, DAVID ALLEN, gastronintestinal pharmacologist; b. Syracuse, N.Y., May 29, 1942; s. Harry J. and Elixabeth Jane (Allen) Jones; m. Sharon L. Steinberg, Aug. 29, 1964; children—Amy E., Carrie J. Student, Union Coll., Cranford, N.J., 1960-62; B.S., Purdue U., 1966; M.S., U. Iowa, 1968, Ph.D., 1970. Research scientist Wyeth Labs., Inc., 1970-77; research mgr. GI/CN-S/Autonomics Pharmacology Ortho Pharm. Corp., 1977—. Mem. Bd. Edn., Bridgewater-Rariton (N.J.) Sch. Dist. Mem. N.Y. Acad. Sci., Am. Soc. Pharmacology and Exptl. Therapeutics, Phila. Physiol. Soc. Patentee in field. Current Work: Gastrointestinal drug discovery. Subspecialties: Pharmacology; Gastroenterology. Home: 2051 Lynne Way PO Box 8 Martinsville NJ 08836 Office: Ortho Pharm Corp Route 202 PO Box 300 Raritan NJ 08869-0602

SHU, PETER HUA-CHENG, chemist; b. Nanking, China, June 2, 1948; came to U.S., 1971, naturalized, 1984; s. Jyr-Chi and Hwei-Chung (Chang) S.; m. Chun-Wan Liu, Sept. 4, 1978; 1 child, Janet. B.S., Nat. Taiwan U., 1970; M.S., Ohio State U., 1974; M.B.A., SUNY-Albany, 1984; Ph.D., Rensselaer Poly. Inst., 1978. Teaching and research fellow Ohio State U., Columbus, 1971-74; Rensselaer Poly. Inst., Troy, N.Y., 1974-78; postdoctoral research fellow U. Mass., Amherst, 1978-79; project leader, advanced chemist Gen. Electric Co., Selkirk, N.Y., 1979—. Patentee, 1984. Recipient Teaching Officer of Yr. award Chinese Army, 1970; Gen. Electric Co. Mgmt. award, 1983. Mem. Am. Chem. Soc., Am. Phys. Soc., N. Am. Thermal Analysis Soc. Current work: Polymer alloys, blends and composites; plastics fabrication technology; automation/-computerization; thermal analysis; polymer synthesis, modification, characterization and stabilization. Subspecialties: Polymer chemistry; Polymer engineering. Home: 2922 Old State Rd Schenectady NY 12303 Office: Gen Electric Co NPTD 1 Noryl Ave Selkirk NY 12158

SHUBECK, PAUL PETER, biology educator; b. Elizabeth, N.J., Oct. 21, 1926; s. Peter and Mary (Glowacky) S.; m. Mary Pyatak, June 27, 1953; children—Thomas, Mary Ellen. B.S. in Biology, Seton Hall U., 1950; A.M. in Personnel and Guidance, Montclair St. Coll., 1955; Ph.D., in Zoology, Rutgers U., 1967. Diplomate Am. Registry Profl. Entomologists. Tchr. Jefferson High Sch., Elizabeth, N.J., 1951-60; guidance counselor Battin High Sch., Elizabeth, 1961-67; prof. biology Montclair St. Coll., Upper Montclair, N.J., 1967—; research assoc. Naval Research Bur., Washington, 1981; cons. Monsanto Corp., St. Louis, 1980-82. Contbr. articles, reviews to profl. publs. Served to sgt. U.S. Army, 1945-46, PTO. Mem. Entomol. Soc. Am., Am. Entomol. Soc., Coleopterists Soc., N.Y. Entomol. Soc., Sigma Xi. Byzantine Catholic. Current work: Ecology and behavior of carrion beetles (silphidae), population and community studies of aquatic beetles. Subspecialties: Behavioral ecology; Limnology. Office: Montclair State Coll Upper Montclair NJ 07043

SHUBERT, FRED GEORGE, chemist; b. N.Y.C., Feb. 5, 1937; s. John and Jane (Mozemeski) S.; m. Lois Janet DePalma, Nov. 27, 1943; children—Frederick James, Victoria Ann. B.Sc., CUNY, 1972; M.Sc., Fairleigh Dickinson U., 1982. Chief chemist Rexart Chem. Corp., 1955-74; scientist Sun Chem. Corp., Carlstadt, N.J., 1974—. Contbr. articles to profl. jours. Mem. Am. Chem. Soc., Rheology Soc., Adhesion Soc., Tech. Assn. Graphic Arts. Republican. Roman Catholic. Current work: Surface studies of substrates as related to their interaction with printing inks and coatings for the graphic arts industry; rheological studies of flow processes of same materials in extreme low shear region. Subspecialties: Physical chemistry; Surface chemistry. Office: Sun Chem Corp 631 Central Ave Carlstadt NJ 07072

SHUCARD, DAVID WILLIAM, phychiatry educator, researcher; b. Bklyn., July 19, 1939; s. Sidney Leon and Pearl (Kornblatt) S.; m. Mary C. Goldberg, Dec. 24, 1961 (div.); children—Hal Dean, Kevin Allan, Shandel Lyn, Danielle Jean; m. Janet Louise McCloskey, July 10, 1976; children—Laura Wynn, Jennifer May, Stephanie Ann. B.A., U. Colo., 1962; M.S., U. Denver, Ph.D., 1969; postgrad. U. Calif.-San Francisco, 1971. Mem. staff Nat. Jewish Hosp. and Research Ctr., Denver, 1971-76, dir. brain scis. labs., 1976—; asst. prof. phychiatry U. Colo. Med. Sch., Denver, 1971-78, assoc. prof., 1978-84, prof. psychiatry, 1984—; adj. assoc. prof. U. Denver, 1978—. Contbr. articles to profl. jours. Grantee NIH, 1975-76, 78-79, 81—; March of Dimes Found. grantee, 1981—; Office of Naval Research grantee, 1980-84. Mem. Am. Inst. Biol. Scis., Am. Psychol. Assn., EEG Soc., AAAS, Soc. Psychophysiol. Research (chmn. membership com. 1980-84), Alcohol, Drug Abuse and Mental Health Adminstrn. (biol. and neurosci. com. 1979-81, chmn. 1982—), Psi Chi (Denver. pres. 1967-68). Democrat. Current work: Brain-behavior relationships; biological bases of behavior including memory, learning, cognitive development; organization of the brain. Subspecialties: Psychobiology; Neurobiology. Home: 1611 Steele Dr Denver CO 80206 Office: Nat Jewish Hosp and Research Ctr 3800 E Colfax Ave Denver CO 80206

SHUG, AUSTIN LEO, biochemist, researcher, educator, consultant; b. Paterson, N.J., July 23, 1925; s. Leo Austin and Alice (Fiederlein) S.; m. Kathryn Jean Snyder, Sept. 24, 1955; children: Barbara, Mary, Leo. B.S., U. Tenn., 1951, M.S., 1952; Ph.D., U. Wis., 1958. Postdoctoral fellow U. Ind., Bloomington, 1957-59; research assoc. Enzyme Inst. U. Wis., Madison, 1959-60; chemist, prof. neurology dept. U. Wis. and VA Hosp., Madison, 1961—; chemist NIH, Bethesda, Md., 1960-61; part time lab. dir. Metabolic Analysis Labs., Inc., Madison, 1981—; cons. Sigma-Tau Chem. Co., Rome, Italy, 1977—. Contbr. chpts. to books, articles to profl. jours. Served with USN, 1943-46. Grantee NIH, 1975-81, 81—; Grantee VA, 1961—; Grantee Muscular Dystrophy Research Assn., 1982-83. Fellow Am. Inst. Chemists; mem. Am. Soc. Biol. Chemists, Fedn. Am. Socs. for Exptl. Biology, Sigma Xi, Phi Lambda Upsilon. Democrat. Roman Catholic. Current Work: Metabolic control mechanisms, carnitine-linked metabolism, in various diseases such as Ischemia, cardiomyopathy, muscle myopathy, cancer. Subspecialties: Cardiology; Cancer research (medicine). Home: 1201 Shorewood Blvd Madison WI 53705 Office: VA Hosp 2500 Overlook Terr Madison WI 53705

SHUKLA, VIJAI, research geologist; b. Lucknow, India, Jan. 1, 1950; came to U.S., 1974, naturalized, 1985; s. Sri Krishna and Shail (Trivedi) S.; m. Lee Wolpin, June 25, 1978. B.Sc. with honors, Lucknow U. (India), 1972, M.Sc., 1973; M.A., Princeton U., 1976; Ph.D., Rensselaer Poly. Inst., 1980. Teaching asst. Rensselaer Poly. Inst., Troy, N.Y., 1978, research asst., 1979-80; sr. geologist Texaco Research Lab., Houston, 1980—; co-chmn. Sci. Symposium. Contbr. articles to profl. jours. Mem. Soc. Econ. Paleontologists and Mineralogists, Geol. Soc. Am., Am. Assn. Petroleum Geologists, Internat. Assn. Sedimentologists. Current work: Deposition and diagenesis of limestones, delostones, and evaporites. Subspecialty: Sedimentology. Office: Texaco Inc Houston Research Ctr 3901 Briarpark Houston TX 77042

SHUKLA, VISHWA NATH, materials scientist; b. Kanpur, India, July 17, 1947; came to U.S., 1969, naturalized, 1982; s. Raj Kumar and Rani Devi Shukla. B.S., IIT Kanpur (India), 1969; M.S., U. Ill., 1972, Ph.D., 1974. Vis. research prof. Atomic Energy Inst., São Paulo, Brazil, 1974-76; research mgr. Tex. Instruments Inc., Attleboro, 1977—. Contbr. articles to profl. jours. Bd. Edn. India Nat. Merit scholar 1964-69. Mem. Am. Ceramic Soc. (subchmn. publs. com. electronics div.), Materials Research Soc., Nat. Inst. Ceramic Engrs., Internat. Soc. Hybrid microelectronics. Current work: Grainboundary phenomena; conducting oxides; ceramic metal interfaces; hybrid microelectronics. Subspecialties: Ceramics; Electronic materials. Office: Texas Instruments Inc 34 Forest St Attleboro MA 02703

SHULL, PETER OTTO, JR., astrophysicist, educator; b. Summit, N.J., July 24, 1954; s. Peter Otto and Margaret Irma (Billinghurst) S.; A.B., Princeton U., 1976; M.S., Rice U., 1979, Ph.D., 1981. Postdoctoral fellow Max Planck Inst. for Astronomy, Heidelberg, W.Ger., 1982-84, Ariz. State U., Tempe, 1984; asst. prof. physics Okla. State U., Stillwater, 1984—. Major, CAP. Vis. fellow Sci. and Engring. Research Council U. Manchester, (Eng.), 1983, 85. Mem. Am. Astronom. Soc., Sigma Xi. Current work: Structure and kinematics of supernova remnants; evolution of supernova remnants in cloudy media; astrophysical jets. Subspecialties: Optical astronomy; Theoretical astrophysics. Office: Dept Physics Okla State U Stillwater OK 74078

SHULMAN, LAWRENCE EDWARD, biomedical research administrator, rheumatologist; b. Boston, July 25, 1919; s. David Herman and Belle (Tishler) S.; m. Pauline K. Flint, July 19, 1946; 1 son, Lawrence E.; m. Reni Trudinger, Mar. 20, 1959; children—Kathryn Verena, Barbara Corina. A.B., Harvard U., 1941, postgrad., 1941-42; Ph.D., Yale U., 1945, M.D., 1949. Nat. Bd. Med. Examiners. Intern Johns Hopkins Hosp., 1949-50, resident and fellow in internal medicine, 1950-53; dir. connective tissue div. Johns Hopkins U., 1955-75, assoc. prof. medicine, 1964—; assoc. dir. div. arthritis, musculoskeletal and skin diseases NIH, Bethesda, Md., 1976-82, dir., 1982—; chmn. med. adminstrn. com. Arthritis Found., Atlanta, 1974-75, exec. com., 1972-77; dir. Lupus Found. Am., St. Louis, 1977—; med. adv. bd. United. Scleroderma Found., Watsonville, Calif., 1977—. Discoverer: Eosinophilic Fasclitis, 1974, new med. sign friction rubs in scleroderma, 1961. Recipient Sr. Investigator award Arthritis Found., 1957-62, Disting. Service award Arthritis Found., 1979, Herberden medal for research, London, 1975; W.R. Graham Meml. lectr., 1973. Fellow ACP; mem. Am. Fedn. Clin. Research, Am. Rheumatism Assn. (pres. 1974-75), Soc. Clin. Trials, Pan-Am. League Against Rheumatism (pres. 1982-86). Subspecialty: Rheumatology. Office: NIADDK National Institutes of Health Bldg 31 Room 9A35 Bethesda MD 20892

SHULMAN, ROBERT GERSON, biophysics educator; b. N.Y.C., Mar. 3, 1924; s. Joshua S. and Freda (Lipshay) S.; m. Saralee Deutsch, Aug., 1952 (dec.); children: Joel, Mark, James. A.B., Columbia U., 1943, M.A., 1947, Ph.D., 1949. Research assoc. Columbia U. Radiation Lab., N.Y.C., 1949; AEC fellow in chemistry Calif. Inst. Tech., Pasadena, 1949-50; head semicondr. research sect. Hughes Aircraft Co., Culver City, Calif., 1950-53; mem. tech. staff Bell Labs., Murray Hill, N.J., 1953-66, head biophysics research dept., 1966-79; prof. molecular biophysics and biochemistry Yale U., 1979—; Rask Oersted lectr. U. Copenhagen, 1959; vis. prof. Ecole Normale Superieur, Paris, 1962; Appleton lectr. Brown U., 1965; vis. prof. physics U. Tokyo, 1965; Reilly lectr. U. Notre Dame, Ind., 1969; vis. prof. biophysics Princeton U., 1971-72; Regents lectr. UCLA, 1978. Guggenheim fellow in lab. molecular biology MRC Cambridge (Eng.) U., 1961-62; recipient Havinga medal Leiden U., 1983. Mem. Nat. Acad. Scis. Researcher spectroscopic techniques applied to physics, chemistry, biology. Subspecialty: Biophysics (physics). Home: 123 York St New Haven CT 06511 Office: 401 St Roman St Yale U New Haven CT

SHULTZ, LEILA MCREYNOLDS, botanical systematist; b. Bartlesville, Okla., Apr. 20; d. Leo Allen and Odie (Thompson) McReynolds; m. John Stanley Shultz, Dec. 14, 1964; 1 child, Kirsten. B.S., U. Tulsa, 1969; M.A., U. Colo., 1975; Ph.D., Claremont Grad. Sch., 1983. Research assoc. U. Colo., Boulder, 1971-73; asst. curator Intermountain Herbarium, Utah State U., Logan, 1973-78, curator, 1978—; cons. Nat. Wildlife Fedn., Washington, 1974—, U.S. Fish and Wildlife Dept., Washington, 1978—; mem. adv. bd. Utah Botanic Garden, Logan, 1982—. Author: Atlas of Plants of Utah, 1985. Mem. editorial bd. Flora of N.Am. contbr. articles to sci. jours. U. Colo. Walker Van Pier grantee, 1973; Claremont Grad. Sch. fellow, 1980-82. Mem. Am. Bot. Soc., Am. Soc. Plant Taxonomists, Internat. Assn. Plant Taxonomists, Sigma Xi (grantee 1981-82). Current work: Comparative leaf anatomy, flora of intermountain west, sagebrush taxonomy and evolution. Dept Biology UMC 55 Utah State U Logan UT 84322

SHUM, RAYMOND HING-YAN, nuclear scientist, consultant; b. Un Long, Hong Kong, Oct. 24, 1936; came to U.S., 1960, naturalized, 1972; s. Ming Wing and King Fong (Lo) S.; m. Julia Hwa-Yueh Miao, Mar. 4, 1967; children: Wesley, Charlotte, Irene, Margaret. B.Sc. Nat. Taiwan U., Taipei, 1959; M.Sc., U. N.B., 1960; Ph.D., N.C. State U., 1966; M.B.A., U. Chgo., 1973. Registered profl. engr., Pa., N.J., Ill., Idaho. Power system engr. N.B. (Can.) Elec. Power Commn., 1960; teaching asst. N.C. State U., Raleigh, 1960-61, 62-65; asst. prof. Miss. State U., State College, 1960; lectr. Lynchburg (Va.) Coll., 1966-67; prin. engr. B & W Co., Lynchburg, 1966-67; sr. engr. Westinghouse Electric Co., Pitts., 1967-69; nuclear engr. Argonne Nat. Lab. (Ill.), 1969-73; prin. staff engr. P. S. E. & G. Co., Newark, 1973-79; prin. engr. Ebasco Services, Inc., N.Y.C., 1979—; Mem. exec. com. Chinese Am. Acad. and Profl. Assn., N.Y.C., 1979. Mem. Am. Nuclear Soc., N.Y. Acad. Scis., Nat. Taiwan U. Alumni Assn. (exec. adv. 1980). Club: Chgo. Bus. Sch. (N.Y.C.) (communication com. 1976). Current Work: Nuclear power reactor safety analyses, nuclear wate management and electrical power engineering. Subspecialties: Nuclear fission; Electrical engineering. Home: 339 Walnut St Livingston NJ 07039 Office: Ebasco Services Inc 2 World Trade Ctr New York NY 10048

SHUMAKER, DANA EDWARD, physicist; educator; b. New Orleans, Apr. 27, 1946; s. Harry Edward and Janette (Butler) S.; m. Suann Lee Oliver, Oct. 25, 1975; 1 child, Erik Richard. B.S. in Nuclear Engring., U. Fla., 1971; M.S. in Applied Sci., U. Calif.-Davis, 1971, Ph.D. in Applied Sci., 1977. Physicist Lawrence Livermore Nat. Lab., 1977—; lectr. U. Calif.-Davis, 1984—. Contbr. articles to profl. jours. Mem. Am. Phys. Soc., Phi Kappa Phi. Subspecialty: Plasma physics. Home: 2318 Broadmoor St Livermore CA 94550 Office: Lawrence Livermore Nat Lab East Ave Livermore CA 94550

SHUMAN, FREDERICK GALE, meteorologist; b. South Bend, Ind., July 13, 1919; s. Fred William and Catherine (Grimm) S.; m. Elena Fragomeni, June 15, 1946; children: Frederick Gale, Marianne, Deborah Joan. B.S., Ball State U., 1941; M.S., Mass. Inst. Tech., 1948, Sc.D., 1951. Chief computation br. Nat. Meteorol. Center, U.S. Weather Bur., Washington, 1955-58, chief devel. br., 1958-64, dir. center, 1964-81, sr. research meteorologist, 1981—; mem. meteorology group Inst. Advanced Study, Princeton, N.J., 1952-54; vis. prof. N.Y.U., 1961. Served to maj. USAAF, 1941-45. Recipient Meritorious Service award U.S. Dept. Commerce, 1957, gold medal award, 1967; Alumni Distinguished Service award Ball State U., 1965. Fellow Am. Meteorol. Soc. (2d Half Century award 1980); Mem. Am. Geophys. Union, AAAS. Subspecialty: Meteorology. Office: Nat Meteorol Center Nat Weather Service Washington DC 20233

SHUMATE, MONROE WILLIAM, ceramic engineer; b. Charleston, W.Va., Dec. 15, 1952; s. Mack H. and Helen A. (Schafer) S.; m. Patricia Marie Leonard, Aug. 4, 1979. B.S. in Ceramic Engring., U. Ill., 1976, M.S. in Ceramic Engring., 1977. Engr. Johns-Manville Corp., Denver, 1977-80, research engr., 1980-82; sr. research engr. Manville Corp., Denver, 1982-84, project mgr., 1984—, lectr. in field. Patentee (5) hi-temp insulation, 1984. Active Hon. Order Ky. Cols., Louisville, 1979—. Alcoa Found. fellow, 1976-77. Mem. Am. Ceramic Soc. (chmn. Rocky Mountain sect. 1982, program chmn. 1981, sec. 1980), ASTM. Republican. Roman Catholic. Current work: Direct and control development of high-temperature insulations; insulating firebrick, refractory castables, refractory fiber board, and structrual insulations. Subspecialties: Ceramic engineering; High-temperature materials. Home: 7038 S Elizabeth St Littleton CO 80122 Office: Manville Service Corp PO Box 5108 Denver CO 80217

SHUMWAY, NORMAN EDWARD, surgeon, educator; b. Kalamazoo, 1923. M.D., Vanderbilt U., 1949; Ph.D. in Surgery, U. Minn., 1956. Diplomate: Am. Bd. Surgery, Am. Bd. Thoracic Surgery. Intern U. Minn. Hosps., 1949-50, med. fellow surgery, 1950-51, 53-54, Nat. Heart Inst. research fellow, 1954-56, Nat. Heart Inst. spl. trainee, 1956-57; mem. surg. staff Stanford U. Hosps., 1958—, asst. prof. surgery, 1959-61, assoc. prof., 1961-65, prof., 1965—, head div. cardiovascular surgery Sch. Medicine, 1974—; Frances and Charles D. Field prof. Stanford U., 1976—. Served to capt. USAF, 1951-53. Mem. AMA, Soc. Univ. Surgeons, Am. Assn. Thoracic Surgery, Am. Coll. Cardiology, Transplantation Soc., Samson Thoracic Surg. Soc., Soc. for Vascular Surgery, Alpha Omega Alpha. Office: Stanford U Med Ctr Dept Cardiovascular Surgery Stanford CA 94305

SHURSKY, STANLEY JAMES, ocean scientist; b. Liberty, N.Y., Mar. 21, 1952; s. Andrew Stanley and Ruth Mabel (Huschke) S.; m. Joanne Audre Schneider, May 31, 1981. B.S. in Civil Engring., MIT, 1974, M.S. in Ocean Engring., 1975. Project engr. Raytheon Co., Portsmouth, R.I., 1975-78; sr. analyst Syscon Corp., Middletown, R.I., 1978-79, Arcon Corp., Waltham, Mass., 1979-81; sr. scientist Bolt Beranek & Newman, Cambridge, Mass., 1981-85; cons. WPL Inc., Hermosa Beach, Calif.; cons., Mass., 1985—. Mem. IEEE, Soc. Naval Architects and Marine Engring., Beta Theta Pi. Roman Catholic. Club: Goat Island Yacht (Newport). Current work: Naval encounter models, software development, hydrodynamics, corrosion, anechoic coatings. Subspecialties: Systems engineering; Ocean engineering. Home and Office: 1336 Salem St North Andover MA 01845

SHUSTER, JOSEPH, immunologist, researcher; b. Montreal, Que, Can., Jan. 29, 1937; s. Max and Sarah (Fergenbaum) S.; m. Isabel Harriet Esar, Oct. 11, 1964; children—Steven, Alan. B.Sc., McGill U., 1958; M.D., U. Alta., Can., 1962; Ph.D., U. Calif.-San Francisco, 1968; hon. degree U. Uruguay, 1983. Resident in medicine Montreal Gen. Hosp., 1962-64; asst. prof. medicine McGill U., Montreal, 1968-73, assoc. prof., 1973-78, prof., 1978—; dir. Div Clin. Immunology and Allergy, Montreal Gen. Hosp., 1979—; dir. research Montreal Gen. Hosp. Research Inst., 1981—. Recipient Med. Research Scholarship award Med. Research Council, 1968-73, Clin. Research Assoc. award Nat. Cancer Inst., 1974-80. Current work: Tumor markers, immunodeficiency in hemophilia. Subspecialties: Immunology (medicine); Cancer research (medicine). Home: 7 Granville Rd Hampstead PQ H3X 3A9 Canada Office: Montreal Gen Hosp 1650 Cedar Ave Montreal PQ H3G 1A4 Canada

SHUSTERMAN, ALAN JEFFREY, chemistry researcher, educator; b. Los Angeles, May 17, 1955; s. Samuel M. and Shirley (King) S. B.S., Calif. Inst. Tech., 1976; Ph.D., U. Wis., 1981. Lectr. Tel Aviv U., 1983-85; vis. scientist IBM Research Lab., San Jose, Calif., 1984-85; asst. prof. chemistry Pomona Coll., 1985—. Contbr. articles to research jours. NSF fellow, 1976-79; Miller Inst. research fellow, 1980-82; Alon (Israel) fellow, 1983-85. Mem. Am. Chem. Soc. Current work: Physical and chemical properties of organo-transition metal and organo-main metal complexes. Subspecialties: Organometallics; Organic chemistry. Home: 1237 College Ave Claremont CA 91711 Office: Pomona Coll Dept Chemistry Claremont CA 91711

SHUSTOROVICH, EVGENY, chemist; b. Moscow, Mar. 1, 1934; came to U.S. 1977, naturalized, 1983; s. Meer and Rachel (Konnikov) S.; m. Maria Ferber; 1 child, Alexander. Ph.D., Inst. chem. Physics, Moscow, 1960; Dr. Sci. in Chemistry, Inst. Organometallic Compounds, Acad. Scis. of USSR, 1967. Group leader Inst. Gen. Chemistry, Acad. Scis., USSR, Moscow, 1961-77; research assoc. Cornell U., Ithaca, N.Y., 1977-79; Eastman Kodak Co., Rochester, N.Y., 1979—. Author: The Electronic Structure of Polymeric Compounds, 1967; The Chemical Bonding, 1973. Contbr. articles to profl. jours. Recipient C.E.K. Mees award Eastman Kodak Co., 1984. Mem. Am. Chem. Soc. Current work: Theoretical modeling of chemisorption phenomena (heat of chemisorption, adsorbate sites and geometries, barriers for migration and dissociation) especially as related to heterogeneous catalysis. Subspecialties: Theoretical chemistry; Surface chemistry. Office: Research Labs Eastman Kodak Co Rochester NY 14650

SHUTTLEWORTH, DEREK, surface scientist; b. Stalybridge, Eng., Dec. 17, 1953; came to U.S., 1982; s. William and Joan (Henshall) S.; m. Cheryl Ann Williams, Aug. 30, 1980; 1 child, Whitney Joan. B.Sc. with honors, U. Durham, Eng., 1975, Ph.D., 1978. Postdoctoral fellow Xerox Corp., Webster, N.Y., 1978-79; sci. Shell Research Ltd., Chester, Eng., 1979-82; project chemist Texaco Inc., Beacon, N.Y., 1982-84; dir. Polar Materials Inc., Bethlehem, Pa., 1984—. Contbr. articles to profl. jours. Mem. Royal Soc. Chemistry, Am. Vacuum Soc. Current work: Application of surface analytical methods to research problems; study and utilization on plasma polymerization. Subspecialties: Polymers (materials science); Surface chemistry. Office: Polar Materials Inc Ben Franklin Tech Ctr Homer Research Bldg F Bethlehem PA 18016

SIAM, MONIR AHMED, veterinary medicine educator; b. Cairo, Feb. 23, 1938; came to U.S., 1971, naturalized, 1976; s. Ahmed and Aminam (Karkash) S.; m. Alia H. Siam, Aug. 4, 1966; children—Ahmed, Ehab, Tamir. B.V.Sc., Coll. Vet. Medicine, Egypt, 1962, D.M.Sc., 1969. Microbiologist Mt. Sinai Sch. Medicine, N.Y.C., 1971-72; research instr. U. Utah, Salt Lake City, 1972-74; instr. Eastern Wyo. Coll., Torrington, 1975—. Patentee study in gonococcus, 1974. Mem. AVAMA, Wyo. Vet. Med. Assn., Am. Soc. Clin. Pathologists, Am. Soc. Microbiology. Current work: Research for making vaccine for gonococcus from pathogenic strains of gonococcus. Subspecialties: Meteorologic instrumentation; Microbiology (veterinary medicine). Home: 2833 Main St Torrington WY 82240Office: Eastern Wyo College 3200 W C St Torrington WY 82240

SIDBURY, JAMES BUREN, physician; b. Wilmington, N.C., Jan. 13, 1922; s. James Buren and Willie Wellington (Daniel) S.; m. Alice Lucas Rayle, Aug. 29, 1953; children—Anne Mary, Patricia, James, Robert. B.S., Yale U., 1944; M.D., Columbia U., 1947. Intern, then asst. resident in internal medicine Roosevelt Hosp., N.Y.C., 1947-49; intern Johns Hopkins Hosp., 1949-50; asst. resident in pediatrics Univ. Hosp., Cleve., 1950-51; with Communicable Disease Center, USPHS, Atlanta, 1951-53; practice medicine specializing in pediatrics, Wilmington, 1953-54; research fellow Johns Hopkins Hosp., 1955-57; asst. prof. Johns Hopkins U. Med. Sch., 1957-61; asso. prof. pediatrics Duke U. Med. Center, 1961-65, prof., 1965—, dir. clin. research unit, 1961-75;

sci. dir. intramural research program Nat. Inst. Child Health and Human Devel., Bethesda, Md., 1975-82, sr. scientist, 1982—; cons. Lennox Baker Hosp., Durham; lectr. Johns Hopkins Hosp.; clin. prof. pediatrics Uniformed Services U. Health Scis., 1979—; prof. child health and devel. George Washington U. Med Sch., 1977—. Contbr. profl. jours. Served with USNR, 1943-45. Recipient Bicentennial medallion in pediatrics Columbia U. Coll. Physicians and Surg., 1967. Mem. Am. Acad. Pediatrics, Am., So. socs. pediatric research, AAAS, Am. Soc. Human Genetics, Am. Pediatric Soc. Subspecialty: Pediatrics. Home: 5200 W Cedar Ln Bethesda MD 20814 Office: NIH NICHD 10/8C429 Bethesda MD 20205

SIDDIQI, SHAUKAT MAHMOOD, biology educator, taxonomy researcher; b. Gujrat, Pakistan, Mar. 10, 1936; s. Ghulam Haider and Khurshid (Khan) S.; m. Florence Alice Patterson, Sept. 24, 1969; children: John Haider, Javaid E., Jamil J., Jafary A. B.Sc., Peshawar U., Pakistan, 1959, M.Sc., 1961; M.S., Va. State U., 1970; Ph.D., U. S.C., 1980. Acct., Pakistan, 1955-56, lang. interpreter, 1958-59; lectr. Peshawar U., 1961-68; asst. prof. Va. State U., Ettrick, 1969-75; instr. U. S.C., Columbia, 1975-77; assoc. prof. biology Va. State U., 1977—; curator herbarium, 1980—. Sponsor Muslim Fellowship, 1977—. Recipient Belser award U. S.C., 1977; Merit award Peshawar U., 1959; HEW fellow, 1975-77. Mem. Bot. Soc. Am., Am. Soc. Plant Taxonomists, Internat. Assn. Plant Taxonomy, Sigma Xi. Democrat. Moslem. Subspecialties: Taxonomy; Species interaction. Home: 21215 Chesterfield Ave Ettrick VA 23803 Office: Va State U Petersburg VA 23803

SIDDIQUI, SAEED HASAN, electronics engineer; b. Jaipur, Rajasthan, India, June 10, 1945; came to U.S., 1970; naturalized, 1977; s. Ahmed Hasan and Azeezunnisa (Qureshi) S.; m. Martha Jane Brown, June 10, 1973; children—Jeffrey, Michael. B.S., U. Rajasthan, Jaipur, 1964, M.S., 1966; Ph.D. U. Lowell, 1973. Research engr. Tata Inst. Fundamental Research, Bombay, India, 1967-70; sr. engr. Galileo Electro-Optics, Sturbridge, Mass., 1976-78; mem. tech. staff Tex. Instruments Inc., Houston, 1978-79; prin. engr. Digital Equipment Corp., Marlboro, Mass., 1979—. Contbr. articles to profl. jours. Rajasthan State merit scholar, 1965-66. Mem. IEEE. Democrat. Current work: Large scale integrated circuits device physics; reliability of dynamic random access memory devices, dynamic RAMs component engineering. Subspecialties: Integrated circuits; Microelectronics. Home: 164 Nashua Rd Groton MA 01450 Office: Digital Equipment Corp 274 Cedar Hill Rd Marlboro MA 01752

SIDKY, YOUNAN ABDEL-MALIK, scientist; b. Khartoum, Sudan, Feb. 9, 1928; s. Abdel Malik and Iskandara (Abdullah) S.; m. Jan Fahmy, July 30, 1964; children: Emil, Sonya. B.Sc., Cairo U., 1950, M.Sc., 1955; Ph.D., Philipps U., 1956. Demonstrator Cairo U., 1950-60, lectr., 1960-65; research assoc. U. Wis.-Madison, 1965-69, project assoc., 1972-76, assoc. scientist, 1976—; research assoc. U. Alta., Can., 1969-72. Contbr. articles to profl. jours. Mem. Assn. Egyptian-Am. Scholars, Am. Assn. Cancer Research, Am. Assn. Immunologists. Coptic Christian. Current Work: In vivo and in vitro study of lymphocyte and tumor-induced angiogenesis; effects of interferons. Subspecialties: Cancer research (medicine); Immunobiology and immunology. Home: 10 Cheyenne Circle Madison WI 53705 Office: Clinical Science Ctr 600 Highland Ave #K4/444 Madison WI 53792

SIDLINGER, BRUCE DOUGLAS, software engineer; b. Dallas, Mar. 19, 1958; s. Bruce Chester and Joanne (Leonard) S.; m. Sarah Lynne Jennings. B.S., Trinity U., San Antonio, 1982, diploma cum laude, 1982. Sci. programmer Recognition Equipment, Irving, Tex., 1975-76; software engr. Tex. Instruments, Dallas, 1976-77; dir. new products Alcor Inc., San Antonio, 1977-80, research scientist, 1980-82, dir. research, 1982-83, v.p. research and engring., 1983-84, exec. v.p., 1984-85, dir., 1985—; pres. Sidlinger Computer Corp., 1985—. Trinity U. Pres.'s scholar, 1980. Mem. Digital Equipment Corp. Users Soc. (San Antonio chmn. 1985—, So. region coordinator 1985—), Upsilon Pi Epsilon (local pres. 1981-82), Aircraft Owners and Pilots Assn., Soaring Soc. Am., Seaplane Pilots assn., Porsche Club Am., Alpha Chi. Republican. Patentee exercise trampoline; inventor stepper motor indicator. Current Work: Integrated display software systems, computer time standards, process control systems, computer-aided designing/drafting. Subspecialties: Operating systems; Graphics, image processing, and pattern recognition. Home: 14713 Babcock Rd Apt 7419 San Antonio TX 78256 Office: Sidlinger Computer Corp 4335 NW Loop 410 Suite 209 San Antonio TX 78229

SIDOROWICZ, KENNETH JOSEPH, mechanical engineer, consultant; b. Topeka, Sept. 28, 1951; s. Norbert Joseph and Florence Matilda (Malnar) S.; 1 child, Andrew Joseph. B.Arch., Kans. State U., 1969, M.S. in Applied Mechanics/Mech. Engring, 1976; postgrad. in bus. administrn, U. Kans. Regents Ctr., Overland Park, 1980—. Registered profl. engr., Kans., Mo. Engr. Kansas City div. Bendix Corp., Mo., 1977-79, 80-82; mech. engr. Black & Veatch Cons. Engrs., Overland Park, 1979; engr. King Radio Corp., Olathe, Kans., 1979-80; assoc. cons. Wagner-Hohns-Inglis-Inc., Kansas City, Mo., 1982; ptnr. GJS Cons., Kansas City, Mo., 1983—. Mem. Westwood Hills Homeowners Assn. Mem. ASME (assoc.). Democrat. Roman Catholic. Current Work: Structural engineering, finite element method, thermal shock phenomenon, structural engineering consulting. Subspecialties: Theoretical and applied mechanics; Laser welding stress analysis. Home: 14350 Gardner Rd Gardner KS 66030 Office: 3217 Gillham Rd Suite 100 Kansas City MO 64109

SIDWELL, ROBERT WILLIAM, scientist, educator; b. Huntington Park, Calif., Mar. 17, 1937; s. Robert Glen and Eva Amalie (Gordy) S.; m. Rhea Julander, May 31, 1957; children: Richard Dale, Jeanette Kathleen, David Eugene, Cynthia Diane, Michael Jason, Robert Odell. B.S., Brigham Young U., Provo, Utah, 1958; M.S., U. Utah, 1961, Ph.D., 1963. Head serology, ricketts and virus research Epizoology Lab., U. Utah, 1958-63; head virus div. So. Research Inst., Birmingham, Ala., 1963-69; head dept. virology ICN Nucleic Acid Research Inst., Irvine, Calif., 1969-72, head div. chemotherapy, 1972-75, dir. inst., 1975-77; prof. animal, dairy and vet. scis. Utah State U., Logan, 1977—; mem. faculty U. Ala. Med. Sch., 1968-69, speaker in field. Editorial bd.: Antimicrobial Agts. and Chemotherapy, 1972—, Chemotherapy, 1974, Jour. Antiviral Research, 1980—; Contbr. articles to profl. jours. Mem. Nibley (Utah) City Planning and Zoning Commn., 1978—; mem. steering com. Irvine Sch. Bd., 1972, chmn. health edn. awareness forum, 1975. Scholar Order Eagles, 1954; Scholar Dept. Interior, 1954. Mem. AAAS, Am. Assn. Immunologists, Soc. Exptl. Biology and Medicine, Internat. Soc. Chemotherapy, Inter-Am. Soc. Chemotherapy (trustee, co-chmn. virus sect.), Am. Soc. Microbiology, Am. Soc. Virology, Sigma Xi. Current Work: Chemotherapy and immunotherapy of viral diseases, effects of nutrition and specific nutritional factors on sensitivity to viral infection, major interest in the antiviral drug, ribavirin. Subspecialties: Virology (biology); Virology (veterinary medicine). Home: 162 Quarter Circle Dr Nibley UT 84321 Office: Dept Biology Utah State U Logan UT 84322

SIEBERT, JOSEPH ROBERT, pediatric anatomist; b. Bradford, Pa., Dec. 12, 1947; s. Wilbur Joseph and Lois Virginia (Brown) S. B.A., U. Pitts., 1969, M.S., 1975; M.A., U. Wash., 1984, Ph.D., 1985. Research assoc. dept. surgery U. Pitts. Sch. Medicine, 1971; anatomist dept. pathology Children's Hosp., Pitts., 1972-77; anatomist dept. labs. Children's Orthopedic Hosp. and Med. Ctr., Seattle, 1977—. Contbr. articles to profl. jours. Mem. Am. Assn. Phys. Anthropologists, Teratology Soc., Soc. for Pediatric Pathology. Democrat. Presbyterian. Clubs: Mountaineers, U. Wash. Yacht. Current work: Developmental biology of the craniofacial complex, morphology of congenital anomalies. Subspecialties: Anatomy and embryology; Dental growth and development. Office: Children's Orthopedic Hosp and Med Ctr Dept Labs PO Box C-5371 Seattle WA 98105

SIEDLER, ARTHUR JAMES, educator; b. Milw., Mar. 17, 1927; s. Arthur William and Margaret (Stadler) S.; m. Doris Jean Northrup, Feb. 23, 1976; children—William, Nancy Siedler Wilhite, Sandra Siedler Lowman, Roxanne Rose Butler, Randy Rose, Rick Rose. B.S., U. Wis., 1951; M.S., U. Chgo., 1956, Ph.D., 1959. Chief div. biochemistry and nutrition Am. Meat Inst. Found., Chgo., 1959-64; group leader Norwich (N.Y.) Pharmacal Co., 1964-65, chief physiology sect., 1965-69, chief biochemistry sect., 1969-72; acting dir. div. nutritional scis. U. Ill., Urbana, 1978-81; prof., head dept. food sci., prof. U. Ill. (Sch. Basic Med. Scis. and Nutritional Scis.), 1972—. Served with USCG, 1945-46, PTO. NIH research grantee, 1960-63; Nat. Livestock and Meat Bd. grantee, 1959-64. Mem. Inst. Food Technologists, Am. Chem. Soc., Am. Inst. Nutrition, Am. Heart Assn., Assn. Vitamin Chemists (past pres. 1962), Am. Dairy Sci. Assn., Am. Assn. Cereal Chemists, Council for Agrl. Sci. and Tech., N.Y. Acad. Sci., Sigma Xi. Clubs: Rotary, Isaak Walton, Moose. Patentee in field. Current Work: Mode of anti bacterial activity of nitrite; food additives. Subspecialties: Food science and technology; Biochemistry (biology). Home: 8 Stanford Pl Champaign IL 61820 Office: 567 Bevier Hall 905 S Goodwin Urbana IL 61801

SIEGEL, ERIC DAVID, computer networking educator; b. N.Y.C., Oct. 30, 1950; s. Elwood and Shirley (Adelson) S. B.S., Cornell U., 1972, M.E.E., 1974. Tech. staff mem. Mitre Corp., Bedford, Mass. and McLean, Va., 1974-82; staff cons. Network Strategies, Inc., Burke, Va., 1982-84; instr. Systems Tech. Forum, Burke, 1983—; sr. tng. analyst Tandem Computers, Inc., Reston, Va., 1984—. Contbr. articles to Datamation Mag. Mem. IEEE, Assn. Computing Machinery, Eta Kappa Nu. Democrat. Jewish. Current work: Data communications, network protocols, computer network performance and security. Subspecialties: Distributed systems and networks; Telecommunications. Home: 8370 Greensboro Dr Apt 424 McLean VA 22102 Office: Tandem Computers Inc 12100 Sunrise Valley Dr Reston VA 22091

SIEGEL, IVENS AARON, pharmacologist; b. Bay Shore, N.Y., Jan. 28, 1932; s. Nathan and Rose S.; m. Naomi Mary; children: Elizabeth, Sondra, Maria. B.S., Columbia U., 1953; M.S., U. Kans., 1958; Ph.D., U. Cin., 1962. Asst. prof. SUNY at Buffalo, 1962-68; assoc. prof. U. Wash., 1968-72, prof., 1972-79; prof., chmn. dept. pharmacology U. Ill., Urbana, 1979—. Served with U.S. Army, 1954-56. Mem. Am. Soc. Pharmacology and Exptl. Therapeutics, Internat. Assn. Dental Research. Jewish. Current Work: Transport in salivary glands and oral mucosa. Subspecialties: Pharmacology; Oral biology. Home: 910 W Park Champaign IL 61821 Office: 506 S Matthew Ave Urbana IL 61801

SIEGEL, MELVIN WALTER, physicist; b. N.Y.C., May 26, 1941; s. Moses and Mae (Sager) S.; m. Jane A.L. Licht, Aug. 18, 1968. B.A., Cornell U., 1962; M.S., U. Colo., 1967, Ph.D., 1970. Postdoctoral fellow U. Va., Charlottesville, 1970-72; asst. prof. SUNY Buffalo, 1972-74; staff scientist Extranuclear Labs., Inc., Pitts., 1974-78, research devel. mgr., 1978-82; sr. research scientist The Robotics Inst., Carnegie-Mellon U., Pitts., 1982—; cons., patentee in field. Contbr. articles to profl. jours. Vol. Peace Corps, Ghana, 1962-64. Recipient I-R 100 awards, 1978, 79, I-R 100 awards Indsl. Research/Devel. Mag. Mem. AAAS, Am. Phys. Soc., ASTM, N.Y. Acad. Sci., Am. Soc. Mass Spectrometry, Soc. Analytical Chemists Pitts., Am. Assn. Artificial Intelligence, Spectroscopy Soc. Pitts. Patentee in field. Current Work: Application of advanced sensor technology, microprocessor control, artificial intelligence to robotics and systems. Subspecialties: Robotics; Artificial intelligence. Home: 5232 Westminster Pl Pittsburgh PA 15232 Office: Robotics Inst Carnegie Mellon Univ Pittsburgh PA 15213

SIEGEL, MICHAEL ELLIOT, physician, educator, researcher; b. N.Y.C., May 13, 1942; s. Benjamin and Rose (Gilbert) S.; m. Marsha Rose Snower, Mar. 20, 1966; children: Herrick Jove, Meridith Ann. A.B., Cornell U., 1964; M.D., Chgo. Med. Sch., 1968. Diplomate: Nat. Bd. Med. Examiners. Intern Cedars-Sinai Med. Ctr., Los Angeles, 1968-69; resident in radiology, 1969-70; NIH fellow in radiology Temple U. Med. Ctr., Phila., 1970-71; NIH fellow in nuclear medicine Johns Hopkins Sch. Medicine, Balt., 1971-73, asst. prof. radiology, 1972-76; assoc. prof. radiology, medicine U. So. Calif., Los Angeles, 1976—, co-dir. nuclear cardiology, 1976—, dir. cardiovascular nuclear medicine, 1981—, dir. div. nuclear medicine, 1982—; dir. div. nuclear medicine Kenneth Norris Cancer Hosp. and Research Ctr., Los Angeles, 1983—; dir. nuclear medicine, cons. Orthopaedic Hosp., Los Angeles, 1981—; cons. Intercommunity Hosp., Covina, Calif., 1981—, Rancho Los Amigos Hosp., Downey, Calif., 1976—. Author: Textbook of Nuclear Medicine, 1978, Vascular Surgery, 1983; editor: Nuclear Cardiology, 1981, Vascular Disease: Nuclear Medicine, 1983. Coach Little League, Beverly Hills; mem. Maple Ctr., Beverly Hills. Served as maj. USAF, 1974-76. Mem. Soc. Nuclear Medicine (sci. exhbn. com. 1978-79, program com. 1979-80, Silver medal 1975), Am. Coll. Nuclear Medicine (sci. investigator 1974, 76, nominations com. 1980, program com. 1983), Soc. Magnetic Resonance in Medicine, Radiol. Soc. N.Am., Soc. Nuclear Magnetic Resonance Imaging. Lodge: Friars So. Calif. Inventor pneumatic radiologic pressure system. Current Work: Development of nuclear medicine techniques to: evaluate cardiovascular disease and diagnose and treat cancer, development of nuclear magnetic resonance (NMR) as a clinical imaging. Subspecialties: Nuclear medicine; Radiology. Office: U So Calif Med Ctr PO Box 693 1200 N State St Los Angeles CA 90033

SIEGEL, ROBERT, research scientist; b. Cleve., July 10, 1927; s. Morris and Mollie (Binder) S.; m. Elaine Jane Jaffe, July 19, 1951; children—Stephen David, Lawrence Charles. B.S., Case Inst. Tech., 1950, M.S., 1951; Sc.D., MIT, 1953. Research engr. Gen. Electric Co., Schenectady, 1953-54, Knolls Atomic Power Lab., Schenectady, 1954-55; research scientist NASA Lewis Research Ctr., Cleve., 1955—. Author: Thermal Radiation Heat Transfer, 1972, 2d edit., 1981. Contbr. articles to profl. jours. Served with AUS, 1945-47; ETO. Fellow ASME (Heat Transfer Meml. award 1970, assoc. editor Jour. Heat Transfer 1973-83), Sigma Xi, Tau Beta Pi. Republican. Jewish. Current work: Thermal radiation heat transfer, heat conduction, freezing and melting, convection heat transfer. Subspecialty: Fluid mechanics. Home: 3052 Warrington Rd Shaker Heights OH 44120 Office: NASA Lewis Research Ctr 21000 Brookpark Rd Cleveland OH 44135

SIEGEL, STUART ELLIOTT, physician; b. Plainfield, N.J., July 16, 1943; s. Hyman and Charlotte (Freidberg) S.; m. Linda Wertkin, Jan. 20, 1968; 1 son, Joshua. B.A., Boston U., 1967, M.D., 1967. Diplomate: Am. Bd. Pediatrics, Am. Bd. Pediatric Hematology/Onbcology. Intern U. Minn. Hosp., 1967-68, resident, 1968-69; clin. assoc. NIH, Bethesda, Md., 1969-72; asst. prof. U. So. Calif., Los Angeles, 1972-76, assoc. prof., 1976-81, prof. pediatrics, 1981—; head div. hematology/oncology Children's Hosp., Los Angeles, 1976—; cons. in field. Editorial bd.: Current Concepts in Pediatric series, 1981—; reviewer: Jour. Pediatrics, 1980—, Med. and Pediatric Oncology, 1978—, Am. Jour. Pediatric Hematology-Oncology, 1981—, Jour. Nat. Cancer Inst, 1981—; contbr. numerous articles to profl. jours. Pres. So. Calif., Children's Cancer Services, Inc., 1978—; participant Nat. Leukemia Broadcast Council Radiothon, 1978-80, mem. adv. bd., 1978—; adv. bd. Leukemia Soc. Am., 1978—. Served with USPHS, 1969-72. NIH grantee, 1975-77; USPHS grantee, 1974—; Am. Cancer Soc. grantee, 1977-80; Nat. Cancer Inst. grantee, 1979-82; others. Mem. Los Angeles County Med. Soc., Los Angeles Pediatric Soc., Western Soc. Pediatric Research, AMA, AAAS, Am. Assn. Cancer Research, Am. Soc. Hematology, Am. Soc. Microbiology, Am. Soc. Clin. Oncology, Am. Soc. Pediatric Hematology-Oncology, Am. Assn Cancer Edn., Soc. Pediatric Research. Current Work: Clinical pediatric cancer research. Subspecialties: Pediatrics; Oncology. Office: 4650 Sunset Blvd Los Angeles CA 90027

SIEKEVITZ, PHILIP, cell biologist; b. Phila., Feb. 25, 1918; s. Joseph and Tillie (Kaplan) S.; m. Rebecca Burstein, Aug. 7, 1949; children: Ruth, Miriam. B.S. in Biology, Phila. Coll. Pharmacy and Scis., 1942, Ph.D. (hon.), 1972; Ph.D. in Biochemistry, U. Calif.-Berkeley, 1949; Ph.D. (hon.), U. Stockholm, 1974. USPHS fellow Mass. Gen. Hosp., 1949-51; fellow oncology McArdle Lab., U. Wis., 1951-54; mem. faculty Rockefeller U., 1954—, now prof. cell biology.; mem. molecular biology panel NSF, 1964-67; panel Internat. Cell Research Orgn., 1963-79; bd. dirs., treas., chmn. Scientists Com. Pub. Information N.Y., 1962-80; bd. dirs. N.Y. Univs. Com., 1965-70; council Am. Fedn. Scientists, 1967-68. Author: (with A. Loewy) Cell Structure and Function, 2d edit, 1969; editor: Jour. Cell Biology, 1962-65, Jour. Cellular Physiology, from 1970, Biosci., Jour. Exptl. Zoology, 1969-73, Biochim. Biophysica Acta; mem. editorial bd.: Jour. Cell Sci. Served with USAAF, 1942-45. Mem. Am. Soc. Biol. Chemists, Am. Soc. Cell Biology (pres. 1966-67), AAAS, Am. Acad. Arts and Scis., Am. Inst. Biol. Scientists, N.Y. Acad. Scis. (governing bd. from 1973, pres. 1976), Nat. Acad. Scis., Sigma Xi. Subspecialty: Cell biology. Office: Dept Cell Biology Rockefeller U 1230 York Ave New York NY 10021*

SIERACKI, LEONARD MARK, research/development company executive.; b. Hartford, Conn., Apr. 15, 1941; s. Joseph and Lillian (Golec) S.; m. Martha Elaine Shermeth, Sept. 12, 1964; children: Jeffrey Mark, Jennifer Elaine, Julie Elaine. B.M.E., Cath. U. Am., 1963, M.M.E., 1970; M. Adminstrv. Sci., Johns Hopkins U., 1977. Registered profl. engr., Md. Aerospace engr. Harry Diamond Labs., Washington, 1963-67; sr. project mgr. Hydrospace Research Corp., Rockville, Md., 1967-70; dir. applied mechanics div. Columbia Research Corp., Gaithersburg, Md., 1970-74; pres. Lorelei Corp., Gaithersburg, 1974-77, Tritec Inc., Columbia, Md., 1977—; cons. in field. Contbr. articles to profl. jours.; author: Handbook of Fluidic Sensors, 1977; prin. author: Submarine Cabled Systems Design and Planning Manual, 1976. Mem. Am. Assn. Small Research Cos., Am. Def. Preparedness Assn. Roman Catholic. Patentee in field. Current Work: Biomedical engineering as related to respiratory devices. Subspecialties: Fluid mechanics; Ocean engineering. Home: 9421 Kilimanjaro Rd Columbia MD 21045 Office: Tritec Inc PO Box 56 Columbia MD 21045

SIERAKOWSKI, ROBERT LEON, engineer. Chmn. dept. of civil engring. Ohio State U. Subspecialty: Theoretical and applied mechanics. Office: Ohio State U Dept Civil Engring Columbus OH 43210*

SIESS, CHESTER PAUL, educator; b. Alexandria, La., July 28, 1916; s. Leo C. and Adele (Liebreich) S.; m. Helen Kranson, Oct. 5, 1941; 1 dau., Judith Ann. B.S., La. State U., 1936; M.S., U. Ill., 1939, Ph.D., 1948. Party chief La. Hwy. Commn., 1936-37; research asst. U. Ill., 1937-39; soil engr. Chgo. Subway Project, 1939-41; engr., draftsman N.Y.C. R.R. Co., 1941; mem. faculty U. Ill., 1941—, prof. civil engring., 1955-78, emeritus, head dept. civil engring., 1973-78; Mem. adv. com. on reactor safeguards Nuclear; Regulatory Commn., 1968—, chmn., 1972. Recipient award Concrete Reinforcing Steel Inst., 1956. Mem. ASCE (hon. mem., Research prize 1956, Howard medal 1968, Reese award 1970), Nat. Acad. Engring., Am. Concrete Inst. (pres. 1974—, Wason medal 1949, Turner medal 1964, hon. mem.), Reinforced Concrete Research Council (chmn. 1968-80, Boase award 1974), Internat. Assn. Bridge and Structural Engring., Sigma Xi, Tau Beta Pi, Phi Kappa Phi, Omicron Delta Kappa, Gamma Alpha, Chi Epsilon. Research reinforced and prestressed concrete structures and hwy. bridges. Current Work: Pathology of structural concrete; safety of nuclear power plants. Subspecialties: Civil engineering; Nuclear engineering. Home: 805 Hamilton Dr Champaign IL 61820 Office: Newmark Lab 208 N Romine St Urbana IL 61801

SIGAL, NOLAN HOWARD, immunologist; b. Rochester, Pa., Dec. 3, 1949; s. Saul M. and Ann (Siegel) S.; m. Elaine Cohen, June 20, 1971; children—Joshua, Yaron, Adam. A.B., Princeton U., 1971; Ph.D., U. Pa., 1976, M.D., 1977. Postdoctoral fellow U. Pa., Phila., 1976-77; resident physician Children's Hosp. of Phila., 1977-80; asst. prof. U. Toronto, Ont., Can.; 1980-83; scientist Research Inst., Hosp. for Sick Children, Toronto, 1980-83, cons., 1983—; dir. cellular immunology Merck Sharp & Dohme Research Labs., Rahway N.J., 1983—. Med. Research Council Can. scholar, 1981. Mem. Am. Assn. Immunologists, Phi Beta Kappa, Sigma Xi. Jewish. Current work: Development of new therapeutic agents which affect regulatory cell interactions within the immune system; B cell activation; B cell repertoire. Subspecialties: Immunobiology and immunology; Immunopharmacology. Office: Merck Sharp & Dohme Research Labs PO Box 2000 Rahway NJ 07065

SIGINER, AYDENIZ, engineering educator, researcher; b. Ankara, Turkey, July 10, 1943; came to U.S., 1976; s. Kazim Musa and Emine (Turkoz) S. Dr.Sc., Tech. U. Istanbul, Turkey, 1971; Ph.D., U. Minn., 1981. Asst. prof. civil engring. Tech. U. Istanbul, 1971-73; research and teaching assoc. U. Minn., Mpls., 1976-81; asst. prof. engring. mechanics U. Ala., Tuscaloosa, 1981—. Author: Handbook of Hydraulics, 1971, Problems in Hydraulics, 1978. Served to lt. C.E. Turkish Army, 1975. Sci. and Tech. Research Council Turkey fellow, 1969-71; recipient Henry Charles Ratcliff award U. Ala., 1983. Mem. ASME, NY Acad. Scis., Soc. Engring. Sci., Sigma Xi. Current Work: Research in mechanics of non-Newtonian fluids and fluid Mechanics in general. Subspecialties: Fluid mechanics; Theoretical and applied mechanics. Home: 4317 Crabbe Rd Northport AL 35476 Office: Dept Engring Mechanics U Ala Box 2908 University AL 35486

SIGMAN, CAROLINE COMPTON, scientific information consultant, toxicology consultant; b. Dayton, Mar. 6, 1946; d. Justin Sinclair and Lillian (Franke) Compton; m. Kenneth Jay Sigman, June 1, 1968; 1 child, Ryan Compton. B.A. in Chemistry, Wellesley Coll., 1968; M.S. in Biochemistry, Northwestern U., 1971, Ph.D., 1972. Info. scientist, supr. G.D. Searle, Skokie, Ill., 1973-75; sr. biochemist, dir. chem. biol. info. program SRI Internat., Menlo Park, Calif., 1976—; instr. toxicology San Jose State U., Calif., 1984. Mem. Am. Chem. Soc., Environ. Mutagen Soc., AAAS, Genetic and Environ. Toxicology Assn. No. Calif. (sec.-treas. 1982-84, pres-elect 1985), Sigma Xi. Current work: Development of expert systems and relational data base systems on biological effects of chemicals; genetic toxicology. Subspecialties: Information systems (Information science); Environmental toxicology. Home: 1285 Hamilton Ave Palo Alto CA 94301 Office: SRI Internat 333 Ravenswood Ave Menlo Park CA 94025

SIGURDSSON, HARALDUR, geology educator; b. Stykkisholmur, Iceland, May 31, 1939; came to U.S., 1974; s. Sigurdur Steinthorsson and Anna Oddsdottir; children—Bergljot, Ashildur. B.Sc., Queens U., Belfast, No. Ireland, 1966; Ph.D., Durham U., Eng., 1970. Lectr. U. W.I., Trinidad, 1970-74; assoc. prof. Grad. Sch. Oceanography, U. R.I., Kingston, 1974-80, prof., 1980—. NSF grantee. Mem. Am. Geophys. Union, Geol. Soc. Am., Explorer's Club, Iceland Geosci. Soc. Current work: Petrology of igneous rocks; volcanic processes. Subspecialties: Volcanology; Sea floor spreading. Office: Grad Sch Oceanography Univ RI Kingston RI 02881

SILAS, CECIL JESSE, chemical engineer, petroleum company executive. Chmn., chief exec. officer Phillips Petroleum Co. Subspecialty: Chemical engineering. Office: Phillips Petroleum Co Phillips Bldg Bartlesville OK 74004*

SILBERBERG, DONALD H., neurologist, educator; b. Washington, Mar. 2, 1934; s. William Aaron and Leslie Frances (Stone) S.; m. Marilyn Alice Damsky, June 7, 1959; children: Mark, Alan. M.D., U. Mich., 1958; M.A. hon.), U. Pa., 1971. Diplomate: Am. Bd. Neurology. Mem. faculty dept. neurology U. Pa. Sch. Medicine, Phila., 1963—, prof., 1971—, chmn. dept., 1982—; mem. numerous govtl. and pvt. non-profit health agy. coms. Contbr. articles to profl. jours.; mem. editorial bd.: Annals of Neurology, 1981—. Served with USPHS, 1951-61. Mem. Am. Acad. Neurology, Am. Neurol. Assn., Am. Assn. Neuropathologists, Assn. Research in Nervous and Mental Disease, Internat. Brain Research Orgn., Internat. Soc. Neurochemistry, Soc. Neurosci., Tissue Culture Assn. Current Work: Etiology and pathogenesis of demyelinating disease; normal development of and role of the oligodendrocyte in myelination, demyelination and remyelination; studies of myelination in vitro in organ cultures of mammalian CNS. Subspecialties: Neurology; Neurobiology. Office: 3400 Spruce St Philadelphia PA 19104

SILBERBERG, REIN, research physicist, educational administrator; b. Tallinn, Estonia, Jan. 15, 1932; s. Juri and Elisabeth (Linkvest) S.; m. Ene-Liis, Aug. 28, 1965; children: Hugo, Ingrid. Ph.D. in Physics, U. Calif. Berkeley, 1960. Grad. research asst. U. Calif. Berkeley, 1957-60; NRC-NAS postdoctoral research assoc. Naval Research Lab., Washington, 1960-62, research physicist, 1962-81; acting chief scientist Lab. for Cosmic Ray Physics, 1981-82, dep. br. head gamma and cosmic ray astrophysics, 1985—; asst. dir. Internat. Sch. Cosmic Ray Astrophysics. Contbr. chpts to books, articles to sci. publs. Active Philos Soc., Washington. Recipient Naval Research Lab. publ. award, 1970, 75, 76; Meritorious Civil Service award U.S. Navy, 1980; Sigma Xi pure sci. award, 1981. Fellow Am. Phys. Soc.; mem. Am. Astron. Soc., Internat. Astron. Union, Am. Geophys. Union, Radiation Res. Soc., Sigma Xi. Current Work: Cosmic-ray transformations, nuclear astrophysics, neutrino astrophysics, nuclear spallation cross sections, active galactic nuclei. Subspecialties: Cosmic ray high energy astrophysics; Nuclear physics. Home: 7507 Hamilton Spring Bethesda MD 20817 Office: Naval Research Lab Code 4154 Washington DC 20375

SILK, JOHN KEVIN, physicist; b. Cambridge, Mass., May 6, 1939; s. John Leo and Margaret Mary (Lynch) S.; m. Laura Pearce Wright, Nov. 26, 1960; children—Catherine Christy, Sean Conroy. A.B., Harvard U., 1960; Ph.D., MIT, 1969. Asst. engr. Raytheon Co., Walthmanm, Mass., 1960-64; research asst. MIT, Cambridge, 1964-69; sr. staff scientist Am. Sci. and Engring., Inc., Cambridge, 1969—. Contbr. articles to profl. jours. Mem. Am. Phys. Soc. Current work: X-rayoptics, radiographic nondestructive testing, security screening, solar x-ray astronomy. Home: 37 Pine St Wellesley MA 02181 Office: Am Sci and Engring Fort Washington Cambridge MA 02139

SILLMAN, ARNOLD JOEL, physiology educator, scientist; b. N.Y.C., Oct. 10, 1940; s. Philip and Anne L. (Pearlman) S.; m. Jean Fletcher Van Keuren, Sept. 26, 1969; children: Andrea Jose, Diana Van Keuren. B.A., UCLA, 1963, M.A., 1965, Ph.D., 1968. Asst. prof. ophthalmology UCLA, 1969-73; asst. prof. U. Calif., Davis, 1975-78, assoc. prof., 1978-85, prof., 1985—; asst. prof U. Pitts., 1973-75; cons. Bio-Med. Sci. Assocs., Davis. Contbr. articles to profl. jours. USPHS trainee, 1966-67; NSF fellow, 1967-68; Fight For Sight, Inc. fellow, 1968-69. Mem. Assn. Research in Vision and Ophthalmology. Jewish. Current Work: Physiology, biochemistry and biology of the vertebrate visual system with special interest in the visual pigments, adaptation and transduction in photoreceptors; current research concerns the photoreceptors and visual pigments of reptiles and amphibians. Subspecialties: Neurophysiology; Amphibiology (biology). Home: 1140 Los Robles St Davis CA 95616 Office: University of California Department of Animal Physiology Davis CA 95616

SILSBY, GRAHAM FORBES, mech. engr., govt. researcher; b. Richmond, Va., Apr. 7, 1943; s. Howard Wiswell II and Eleanor (Foltz) S.; m. Patricia Shields; m. Louise Rose, May 12, 1979; 1 son, Jeffrey Allen Shumate. B.S.M.E., Carnegie Inst. Tech., 1965; B.S.C.E., Johns Hopkins U., 1978. Jr. mech. engr. Farrington Electronics Inc., Springfield, Va., 1965-66; mech. engr. U.S. Army Nuclear Def. Lab., Edgewood Arsenal, Md., 1966-68, Dept. of Army—U.S. Army Nuclear Def. Lab., Edgewood Arsenal, 1968-72; research mech. engr. Dept. of Army—Ballistic Research Lab., Aberdeen Proving Ground, Md., 1972—. Mem. corp. bd. United Ch. of Christ Bd. for Homeland Ministries, N.Y.C., 1975-81. Served with U.S. Army, 1966-68. Recipient Am. Spirit Honor medal Citizen's Com. for Army Navy and Air Force, 1967. Mem. ASME. Current Work: Mechanics of high speed impact; research into mechanics of interaction of kinetic energy penetrators and armors at ordnance and increased velocities. Subspecialty: Mechanical engineering.

SILVEIRA, MILTON ANTHONY, engineer; b. Mattapoisett, Mass., May 4, 1929; s. Antone and Carolinda (Avila) S.; m. Joan Weninger, Dec. 23, 1983; children by previous marriage—Leland Reed, Douglas Stewart, Carolyn Marie, Robert Scott. B.S., U. Vt., 1951, Ph.D., 1977. M.S., U. Va., 1960; postgrad. Va. Poly. Inst., U. Houston, 1963. Research intern NACA/Langley, Hampton, Va., 1951; chief engring. U.S. Army, St. Louis, 1951-55; with vibration flutter br. NACA/Langley, Hampton, 1955-61, acting head loads br., NASA/Langley, 1961-63, dept. chief aerodynamics br., Manned Space Ctr., Houston, 1963-64, program mgr. Little Joe II, 1964-65, br. head aerodynameic br., 1965-67, asst. to dir. engring. Johnson Space Ctr., Houston, 1967-68, chief engring. analysis, 1968-69, mgr. space shuttle engring., 1969-73, dept. mgr. orbiter project, 1973-81, asst. to dep. adminstr. hdqrs., Washington, 1981-83, chief engr., 1983—. Served to capt. U.S. Army, 1951-55. Mem. AIAA. Subspecialty: Aerospace engineering and technology. Home: 7213 Evans Mill Rd McLean VA 22101 Office: NASA 600 Independence Ave Washington DC 20546

SILVER, DONALD, educator, surgeon; b. N.Y.C., Oct. 19, 1929; s. Herman and Cecilia (Meyer) S.; m. Helen Elizabeth Harnden, Aug. 9, 1959; children: Elizabeth Tyler, Donald Meyer, Stephanie Davies, William Paige. A.B., Duke U., 1950, B.S. in Medicine, M.D., 1955. Diplomate Subsplty. Bd. Gen. Vascular Surgery of Am. Bd. Surgery, Am. Bd. Thoracic Surgery. Intern Duke Med. Center, 1955-56, asst. resident, 1958-63, resident, 1963-64; mem. faculty Duke Med. Sch., 1964-75, prof. surgery, 1972-75; cons. Watts Hosp., Durham, 1965-75; cons. VA Hosp., Durham, 1970-75, chief surgery, 1968-70; prof. surgery, chmn. dept. U. Mo. Med. Center, Columbia, 1975—; cons. Harry S. Truman VA Hosp., Columbia, 1975—; mem. bd. sci. advisers Cancer Research Center, Columbia, 1975—; mem. surg. study sect. A NIH. Contbr. articles to med. jours., chpts. to books. Served with USAF, 1956-58. James IV Surg. traveler, 1977. Fellow ACS, Deryl Hart Soc.; mem. Am., Mo. med. assns., Boone County Med. Soc., AAAS, Internat. Cardiovascular Soc., Soc. Univ. Surgeons, Am. Heart Assn. (Mo. affiliate research com.), Soc. Surgery Alimentary Tract, Assn. Acad. Surgery, So. Thoracic Surg. Assn., Internat. Soc. Surgery, Soc. Vascular Surgery, Midwestern Vascular Surg. Soc. (pres.), Am. Assn. Thoracic Surgery, Am., Central, Western surg. assns., Phi Beta Kappa, Alpha Omega Alpha. Current Work: Quantitation of peripheral blood flow; intravascular fibrinolysis; heparin-induced anti-platelet antibodies. Subspecialties: Surgery; Physiology (medicine). Home: 1050 W Covered Bridge Rd RD 3 Columbia MO 65203 Office: Dept Surgery M580 Univ Mo Med Center Columbia MO 65212

SILVER, GARY LEE, chemist; b. Fort Benning, Ga., Nov. 22, 1936; s. Samuel Fayette and Elisabeth Annette (Cloud) S.; m. Marcine Jeanette Robohm, Nov. 29, 1968; 1 child, Meredith Jeanette. B.S., MIT, 1959; Ph.D., U. N.C., 1963. Sr. chemist Monsanto Research Corp. Mound Lab., Miamisburg, Ohio, 1963-80, fellow, 1980—. Contbr. articles to profl. jours. Mem. Am. Chem. Soc., Am. Inst. Chemists. Current work: Chemistry: actinides, particularly plutonium, lanthanides, nuclear waste treatment, numerical methods in chemistry. Subspecialties: Inorganic chemistry; Numerical analysis (mathematics). Home: 294 Linden Dr Centerville OH 45459 Office: Monsanto Research Corp Mound Ave Miamisburg OH 45342

SILVER, HENRY K., pediatrician, educator; b. Phila., Apr. 22, 1918; s. Samuel and Dora (Kreitzer) S.; m. Harriet Ashkenas, June 15, 1941; children: Stephen, Andrew. B.A., U. Calif., Berkeley, 1938, M.D., 1942. Diplomate: Am. Bd. Pediatrics. Intern U. Calif. Hosp., San Francisco, 1941-42; resident Children's Hosp., Phila., 1942-43; instr., then asst. prof. pediatrics U. Calif. Med. Sch., San Francisco, 1946-52; assoc. prof. Yale Med. Sch., 1952-57; prof. pediatrics U. Colo. Med. Sch., Denver, 1957—, assoc. dean admissions, 1977—; clin. prof. nursing U. Colo. Sch. Nursing, 1976—. Co-author: Healthy Babies-Happy Parents, 1958, Current Pediatric Diagnosis and Treatment, 8th edit., 1984, Handbook of Pediatrics, 14th edit., 1983. Rosenberg Found. fellow, 1945-47; recipient George Armstrong award Ambulatory Pediatric Assn., 1972; Martha May Eliot award Am. Pub. Health Assn., 1974; Eleanor Roosevelt Humanitarian award Denver chpt. Hadassah, 1973. Mem. Inst. Medicine of Nat. Acad. Sci., Am. Acad. Pediatrics, Western Soc. Pediatric Research (Ross award in edn. 1962), Soc. Pediatric Research, Am. Pediatric Soc., Sigma Xi, Alpha Omega Alpha. Developer of first nurse practitioner program and child health associate program in U.S.; first to describe Silver's Syndrome, 1953, Deprivation Dwarfism, 1967. Current Work: Development of health manpower programs and health education. Subspecialty: Pediatrics. Home: 135 S Ivy St Denver CO 80224 Office: 4200 E 9th Ave Denver CO 80262

SILVER, HULBERT KEYES BELFORD, physician; b. Montreal, Que., Can., July 15, 1941; s. Arthur Desraeli and Norah Joanna (Belford) S.; m. Susan Daphne Andrew, Oct. 8, 1967; children: Hulbert, Signe, William. B.Sc., Bishop's U., Lennoxville, Que., 1962; M.D., McGill U., Montreal, 1966, Ph.D., 1974. Asst. prof. UCLA Sch. Medicine, 1973-76; asst. prof. medicine U. B.C., Vancouver, 1976-79, assoc. prof., 1979-85, prof., 1985—; med. oncologist Cancer Control Agy. B.C., 1976—. Contbr. articles to profl. jours. Served with Royal Can. Air Force, 1960-62. Recipient medal in medicine Royal Coll. Physicians and Surgeons Can., 1975. Fellow ACP, Royal Coll. Physicians and Surgeons Can.; mem. Am. Soc. Clin. Oncology, Am. Assn. Cancer Research, Can. Oncology Assn., Internat. Soc. Interferon Research Current Work: Tumor markers, biologic response modifiers, immunology. Subspecialties: Cancer research (medicine); Oncology. Office: Cancer Control Agy British Columbia 600 W 10th Ave Vancouver BC V5Z 4E6 Canada

SILVER, LARRY BERNARD, psychiatrist; b. Washington, Mar. 24, 1934; s. Abraham and Ida (Baker) S.; m. Clara Meyerovitch, Sept. 1, 1957; children—Caren Lee, Marla Lynn, Dana Lise. B.S., George Washington U., 1956; M.D., Howard U., 1960. Am. Bd. Psychiatry and Neurology. Intern D.C. Gen. Hosp., 1960-61; resident Georgetown Med. Ctr., 1963-65; fellow in child psychiatry Children's Hosp. of D.C., 1965-67; prof. psychiatry. prof. pediatrics, chief child psychiatry Rutgers Med. Sch., New Brunswick, N.J., 1971-79; assoc. dir. NIMH, Rockville, Md., 1979-81, dep. dir., 1981—; clin. prof. psychiatry Georgetown U. Med. Ctr., Washington, 1971—. Contbr. articles to profl. publs. Served to capt. AUS, 1961-63. Recipient NIMH Career Tchr. award, 1968-70, USPHS Superior Service award, 1981. Fellow Am. Psychiat. Assn., Am. Acad. Child Psychiatry (sec. 1977-81); mem. Am. Coll. Psychiatrists. Current work: Learning disabilities, attention deficit disorders. Subspecialty: Psychiatry. Home: 11518 Gauguin Ln Potomac MD 20854 Office: NIMH Office of the Director 5600 Fishers Ln Rockville MD 20857

SILVER, ROBERT BENJAMIN, biochemistry educator, biomed. researcher; b. Chgo., Aug. 9, 1950; s. Seymour Martin and Mary (Brodsky) S. B.S. in Biology, Ill. Inst. Tech., 1973; Ph.D. in Zoology, U. Calif.-Berkeley, 1977. Am. Cancer Soc. postdoctoral research fellow dept. biochemistry U. Calif.-Berkeley, 1977-80, lectr., 1978-79; asst. prof. biochemistry dept. biochemistry Univ. Health Scis., Chgo. Med. Sch., 1981—, dir. electron microscope lab.; cons. in field. Contbr. articles on biochemistry to profl. jours. Am. Cancer Soc. grantee, 1981-83; Chgo. Heart Assn. grantee, 1981-83; STEPS fellow Marine Biol. Lab., Woods Hole, Mass., 1983. Mem. Am. Soc. Cell Biology, Soc. for Devel. Biology, Am. Soc. Zoologists, AAAS, Sigma Xi. Current Work: Role of membranes and calcium regulation in the assembly and functioning of the mitotic apparatus in cell division. Subspecialties: Cell and tissue culture; Cancer research (medicine). Office: 3333 N Green Bay Rd North Chicago IL 60064

SILVERMAN, ALBERT JACK, psychiatrist, educator; b. Montreal, Que., Can., Jan. 27, 1925; came to U.S., 1950, naturalized, 1955; s. Norman and Molly (Cohen) S.; m. Halina Weinthal, June 22, 1947; children: Barry Evan, Marcy Lynn. B.Sc., McGill U., 1947, M.D., C.M., 1949; grad., Washington Psychoanalytic Inst., 1964. Diplomate: Am. Bd. Psychiatry and Neurology. Intern Jewish Gen. Hosp., Montreal, 1949-50; resident psychiatry Colo. U. Med. Center, 1950-53, instr., 1953; from assoc. to assoc. prof. psychiatry Duke Med. Center, 1953-63; prof. psychiatry, chmn. dept. Rutgers U. Med. Sch., 1964-70; prof. psychiatry U. Mich. Med. Sch., Ann Arbor, 1970—, chmn. dept., 1970-81; cons. to area hosps. Mem. biol. scis. tng. rev. com. NIMH, 1964-69, chmn., 1968-69, mem. research scientist devel. award com., 1970-75, chmn., 1973-75; mem. merit rev. bd. in behavioral scis. VA, 1975-78, chmn., 1976-78; Bd. mgrs. N.J. Neuropsychiat. Inst., 1965-69; trustee N.J. Fund Research and Devel. Nervous and Mental Diseases, 1965-67; bd. dirs. N.J. Mental Health Assn., 1964-69; mem. behavioral sci. com. Nat. Bd. Med. Examiners, 1978-82, mem. behavioral scis. task force, 1983-84, chmn. behavioral scis. test com., 1984—; mem. small grant research com. NIMH, 1982—. Cons. editor: Psychophysiology, 1970-74, Psychosomatic Medicine, 1972—; Contbr. articles in field. Served as capt. M.C. USAF, 1955-57. Fellow Am. Coll. Psychiatry (charter), Am. Psychiat. Assn. (chmn. council on med. edn. 1970-75), Am. Acad. Psychoanalysis, Am. Coll. Neuropsychopharmacology; mem. Am. Psychosomatic Soc. (council 1964-68, 70-74, pres. 1976-77), N.J. Psychoanalytic Soc. (trustee 1968-70), Assn. Research Nervous and Mental Diseases, N.J. Neuropsychiat. Assn. (council 1966-69), Group Advancement Psychiatry (chmn. com. psychopathology 1968-74), Soc. Psychophys. Research, Soc. Biol. Psychiatry, Mich. Psychiat. Soc. (council 1975-77), Mich. Psychoanalytic Soc. Current Work: Psychophysical differences in field dependency; brain lateralization; pre-clinical and clinical psychiatric studies. Subspecialties: Psychiatry; Psychophysiology. Home: 19 Regent Dr Ann Arbor MI 48104

SILVERMAN, HIRSCH LAZAAR, clinical and forensic psychologist; b. N.Y.C., June 19, 1915; s. Herman Bear and Ida (Mackta) S.; m. Mildred Friedlander, Mar. 1, 1942; children: Hyla Susan. Morton Maier, Stuart Edward. B.Sc., CCNY, 1936, M.Sc., 1938; M.A., NYU, 1947; Ph.D., Yeshiva U., 1951; M.A., Seton Hall U., 1956; D.Sc. (hon.), Lane Coll., 1962; LL.D., Fla. Meml. Coll., 1965; L.H.D., Ohio Coll. Podiatric Medicine, 1972. Diplomate: Am. Bd. Profl. Psychology, Am. Bd. Forensic Psychology, Am. Acad. Behavioral Medicine., Am. Acad. Neuropsychology, Am. Assn. Clin. Counselors, Am. Bd. Vocat. Experts, Am. Bd. Family Psychology; cert. profl. psychotherapist cert. family psychologist. Asst. prof. philosophy and psychology, chmn. dept. Philosophy Mohawk Coll., 1946-48; ednl. and vocational cons., psychol. lab. Stevens Inst. Tech., 1948-49; asst. prof. psychology Rutgers U., 1949-53; asst. to supt. schs., dir. psychol. services Nutley (N.J.) Bd. Edn., 1953-59; chmn. dept. ednl. and sch. psychology Yeshiva U. Grad. Sch., 1959-61, prof. psychology grad. div., 1959-65; prof. ednl. adminstrn., chmn. dept. Seton Hall U., 1965-80, prof. emeritus, 1980—; research clin. psychologist Columbus Hosp., Newark, 1963-72; psychol. cons. N.J. Rehab. Hosp., East Orange, N.J.; vis. prof. psychology Lane Coll., 1961—, Fla. Meml. Coll., 1961—; research clin. psychologist N.Y. Med. Coll., 1961-65; clin. psychologist, med. staff St. Vincent's Hosp., Montclair, N.J.; v.p. Am. Bd. Forensic Psychology, 1978-80. Assoc. editor, Am. Assn. Clin. Counselors; Author 16 books, numerous articles in field. Chmn. N.J. Bd. Marriage Counsel Examiners, 1968-74; mem. N.J. Mental Health Council, 1966-69; mem. N.J. Bd. Psychol. Examiners, 1975-84, chmn., 1979-82; mem. nat. adv. com. White House Conf. on Families. Bd. dirs. Family Service Bur., Newark, 1961-82; mem. Mental Health Adv. Bd. Freeholders, Essex County, N.J., 1984—; mem. Commn. on Developmentally Disabled, Metro-West Fedn., N.J., 1984—. Served with U.S. Army, 1942-46. Decorated Army Commendation medal; grand cross St. John of Jerusalem; Maltese cross Order St. John Denmark. Fellow Coll. Preceptors Eng., Philos. Soc. Eng. (hon. v.p.), Royal Soc. Health, Royal Soc. Arts, Gerontological Soc., Am. Acad. Forensic Scis., Acad. Forensic Psychologists, AAAS, Assn. Advancement Psychotherapy, Am. Assn. Social Psychiatry, Am. Orthopsychiat. Assn., Assn. Advancement Psychotherapy, Am. Psychol. Assn., Am. Med. Writers Assn., Am. Pub. Health Assn., Am. Assn. Psychiat. Services for Children, Royal Soc. Medicine, World Acad. Art and Sci.; mem. N.J. Assn. Marriage and Family Counselors (pres. 1967-70), Acad. Psychology in Marital Therapy (pres. 1964-67), Essex County Psychol. Assn. (exec. com., sec., editor), Internat. Council Psychologists (treas. 1971-73), Am. Coll. Psychology (adv. bd.), Phi Beta Kappa, Sigma Xi, Psi Chi, Phi Sigma Tau, Kappa Delta Pi, Phi Delta Kappa. Current Work: Psychotherapy; forensic psychology; marital therapy; clinical psychology; humanities; psychopoetry and psycho-diagnostic assessments; lecturing and teaching in psychological services. Subspecialties: Cognition; Neuropsychology. Home: 123 Gregory Ave West Orange NJ 07052 Office: NW Corner Northfield and Gregory Aves West Orange NJ 07052

SILVERMAN, JOSEPH, educator, scientist; b. N.Y.C., Nov. 5, 1922; s. Jakob and Mary (Chechick) S.; m. Joan Aline Jacks, Jan. 14, 1951; children: Joshua Henry, David Avrom. B.A., Bklyn. Coll., 1944; A.M., Columbia U., 1948, Ph.D., 1951. Head research dept. Walter Kidde (nuclear labs.), Garden City, N.Y., 1952-54; v.p., tech. dir. RAI Research Corp., L.I. City, N.Y., 1954-59; assoc. prof. chemistry State U. N.Y., Stony Brook, 1959-60; prof. dept. chem. engring. U. Md., College Park, 1960—; dir. Inst. Phys. Sci. and Tech., 1976-83, Spitz Space Systems, Inc., 1970—, Applied Tech. Corp., 1981—, RAI Research Corp., 1954-70; cons. Danish AEC, Indsl. Research Inst., Japan, Boris Kidric Inst., Yugoslavia, Bechtel Co., IAEA, Vienna; disting. vis. prof. Tokyo U., 1974; gen. chmn. 2d Internat. Meeting on Radiation Processing, Miami, Fla., 1978, 3d Tokyo, 1980. Editor: Internat. Jour. Applied Radiation and Isotopes, 1973-78, Internat. Jour. Radiation Engring, 1970-73, Trans. 1st Internat. Meetings on Radiation Processing, 1977, 2d, 1979, 3d, 1981; mem. editorial adv. bd.: Radiation Physics and Chemistry, 1978—. Served with AUS, 1944-46. Research fellow Brookhaven Nat. Lab., 1949-51; Guggenheim fellow, 1966-67. Fellow Nordic Soc. Radiation Chemistry and Tech., Am. Phys. Soc., Am. Nuclear Soc. (Radiation Industry award 1975); mem. Am. Inst. Chemists, Am. Chem. Soc., Sigma Xi. Club: Cosmos. Current Work: Applied radiation chemistry of vinyl monomers and polymers; radiation source technology. Subspecialties: Polymer chemistry; Nuclear engineering. Home: 320 Sisson St Silver Spring MD 20902 Office: Dept Chem and Nuclear Engring U Md College Park MD 20742

SILVERMAN, PAUL HYMAN, university president, zoologist; b. Mpls., Oct. 8, 1924; s. Adolph and Libbie (Idelkope) S.; m. Nancy Josephs, May 20, 1945; children: Daniel Joseph, Claire Storms. B.S., Roosevelt U., 1949; M.S. in Parasitology and Ecology, Northwestern U., 1951; D.Sc., U. Liverpool, 1968, Ph.D. in Parasitology and Epidemiology, 1955. Research fellow Malaria Research Sta., Hebrew U., Israel, 1951-53; sr. sci. officer dept. parasitology Moredun Inst., Edinburgh, Scotland, 1956-59; head dept. immunoparasitology Allen & Hanbury, Ltd., Ware, Eng., 1960-62; prof. zoology and vet. pathology and hygiene U. Ill., Urbana, 1963-72, chmn. dept. zoology, 1964-65, head dept. zoology, 1965-68; sr. staff mem. Ctr. for Zoonoses Research, 1964; prof. biology, head div. natural scis. Temple Buell Coll., Denver, 1970-71; prof. biology, chmn. dept. biology, acting v.p. research, v.p. research and grad. affairs, assoc. provost for acad. services and research U. N.Mex., 1972-77; provost for research and grad. studies SUNY, Central Adminstrn., Albany, 1977-79; pres. Research Found., SUNY, Albany, 1979-80, U. Maine, Orono, 1980—; adj. prof. U. Colo., Boulder, 1970-72; Fulbright prof. zoology Australian Nat. U., Canberra, 1969; faculty appointee Sandia Corp., Dept. Energy, Albuquerque, 1974-81; project dir. research in malaria immunology and vaccination AID, 1965-76; project dir. research in Helminth immunity USPHS, NIH, 1964-72; sr. cons. Ministry Edn. and Culture, Brazil, 1975—; bd. dirs. Inhalation Toxicology Research Inst., Lovelace Biomed. and Environ. Research Inst., Albuquerque, 1977—; mem. N.Y. State Gov.'s High Tech. Opportunities Task Force; chmn. research and rev. com. N.Y. State Sci. and Tech. Found.; bd. advs. Lovelace-Bataan Med. Ctr., Albuquerque, 1974-77; chmn. Commn. on Instns. Higher Edn. North Central Assn. Colls. and Secondary Schs., 1974-76, cons. examiner, 1964—. Contbr. chpts. to books, articles to profl. jours.; mem. editorial bd. profl. jours. Bd. dirs. Historic Albany Found. Served with AUS, 1943-46. Fellow Royal Soc. Tropical Medicine and Hygiene, N.Mex. Acad. Scis.; mem. Am. Soc. Parasitologists, Am. Soc. Immunologists, Brit. Soc. Parasitology (council), Brit. Soc. Immunologists, Soc. Gen. Microbiology, Soc. Parotozoologists, Am. Soc. Zoologists, Am. Inst. Biol. Scis., AAAS, N.Y. Acad. Scis., N.Y. Soc. Tropical Medicine, Sigma Xi, Phi Kappa Phi. Subspecialties: Immunology (agriculture); Parasitology. Home: U Maine President's House Orono ME 04469 Office: U Maine 209 Alumni Hall Orono ME 04469

SILVERMAN, RICHARD BRUCE, chemistry educator; b. Phila., May 12, 1946; s. Philip and S. Ruth (Simon) S.; m. Barbara Kesner, Jan. 9, 1983; children: Matthew, Margaret, Philip. B.S., Pa. State U., 1968; A.M., Harvard U., 1972, Ph.D., 1974. NIH postdoctoral fellow Brandeis U., Waltham, Mass., 1974-76; asst. prof. Northwestern U., Evanston, Ill., 1976-82, assoc. prof. chemistry, 1982—. Contbr. articles to profl. jours. Patentee (2). Served with U.S. Army, 1969-71. Recipient Research Career Devel. award NIH, 1982-87; Young Faculty award E. I. duPont de Nemours & Co., 1976; Alfred P. Sloan research fellow, 1981-85. Mem. Am. Chem. Soc., Am. Soc. Biol. Chemistry, AAAS. Current Work: Medicinal and bioorganic chemistry, mechanism of action and design of drugs, specific enzyme inhibition, enzyme mechanisms. Subspecialties: Medicinal chemistry; Biochemistry (biology). Office: Dept Chemistry Northwestern U Evanston IL 60201

SILVERN, LEONARD CHARLES, systems engineering company executive; b. N.Y.C., May 20, 1919; s. Ralph and Augusta (Thaler) S.; m. Gloria Marantz, June, 1948 (div. 1968); 1 son, Ronald; m. Elisabeth Beeny, Aug., 1969 (div. 1972). B.S., L.I.U., 1946; M.A., Columbia U., 1948, Ed.D., 1952. Registered profl. engr., Calif. Tech. tng. supr. U.S. Dept. Navy, N.Y.C., 1939-49; tech. tng. dir. State Div. Safety, Albany, N.Y., 1949-55; head engring., psychologist Rand Corp., MIT Lincoln Lab., Lexington, Mass., 1955-56; research engr., dir. Hughes Aircraft Co., Culver City, Calif., 1956-62; dir. engring. lab. Northrop Corp., Hawthorne, Calif., 1962-64; prin. scientist, v.p., pres. Edn. and Tng. Consultants Co., Los Angeles, 1964-80; v.p. Systems Engring. Labs. div. ETC Co., Sedona, Ariz., 1980—; adj. prof. U. So. Calif., 1957-65; vis. prof. UCLA, 1963-72; cons. Hdqrs. USAF Air Tng. Command, Randolph Air Force Base, 1964-68, U. Hawaii, 1970-74, Centro Nacional de Productividad, Mexico City, 1973-75. Author, editor: book series Systems Engineering of Education, 1964—; contbg. editor: book series Educational Technology mag, 1968-73, 1981-84; reviewer Computing Revs., 1962—. Contbr. articles to profl. jours., chpts. to books. Dist. ops. officer Los Angeles County Sheriff's Dept. Disaster Commn., 1973-75, dist. communications officer, 1975-76. Served with USNR, 1944-46. Mem. IEEE (sr.), Am. Psychol. Assn., Soc. Wireless Pioneers, Quarter Century Wireless Assn., Friendship Veterans Fire Engine Co., Am. Radio Relay League, Radio Amateur Satellite Corp., Ariz. Archeol. Soc., Verde Valley Archeol. Soc., Sierra Club. Club: Westerners. Current Work: Developing computer-controlled radio communications systems incorporating 3D cartography, meteorological satellite data, and technical data bases including space science, geoscience, social and behavioral science, military and political science, energy science and electronics; communications worldwide. Subspecialties: Systems engineering; Computer engineering. Office: Systems Engring Labs Sedona AZ 86336

SILVERSTEIN, EMANUEL, medical and biochemistry educator; b. N.Y.C., Feb. 14, 1930; s. Israel Suris and Rose (Rubock) S.; m. Shoshana Tubi, Mar. 25, 1965; children—Roselle Rama, Daniel Doron. B.S., CCNY magna cum laude, 1950; M.D., SUNY-Downstate Med. Ctr., 1954; Ph.D., U. Minn., 1963. Intern, U. Minn. Hosps., Mpls., 1954-55, research in medicine, 1958-59; intern in pathology Yale U. Hosp., New Haven, 1955-56; research assoc. NIH, NIAMD, Bethesda, Md., 1956-58; postdoctoral fellow U. Minn., Mpls., 1959-63; postdoctoral fellow dept. biology MIT, Cambridge, 1963-64; asst. prof. SUNY-Downstate Med. Ctr., Bklyn., 1964-69, assoc. prof., 1970-76, prof. medicine and biochemistry, 1977—. Contbr. articles to med. and sci. jours. Served with USPHS, 1956-58. Grantee: NIH, NSF, Am. Cancer Soc., Health Research Council N.Y.C., Damon Runyon, 1965—; Am. Cancer Soc. grantee, 1959-64. Fellow N.Y. Acad. Medicine; mem. Am. Soc. Biol. Chemists, Am. Assn. Pathologists, Am. Chem. Soc., AAAS. Jewish. Current work: Mechanisms of disease, enzyme mechanism, genetic disease and therapy, molecular mechanisms of behavior. Subspecialties: Molecular biology; Internal medicine. Home: 175 Adams St Brooklyn NY 11201 Office: SUNY-Downstate Med Ctr 450 Clarkson Ave Brooklyn NY 11203

SIMHA, ROBERT, educator; b. Vienna, Aug. 4, 1912; s. Mercado and Mathilde S.; m. Genevieve Martha Cowling, June 7, 1941. Student, Poly. Inst., Vienna, 1930-31; Ph.D., U. Vienna, 1935. Research assoc. U. Vienna, 1935-38, Columbia U., 1939-41; mem. faculty Poly. Inst. Bklyn., 1941-42, Howard U., 1942-45; cons., coordinator Polymer Research, Nat. Bur. Standards, 1945-51; mem. faculty N.Y. U., 1951-58, U. So. Calif., 1958-67; prof. macromolecular sci. Case Western Res. U., Cleve., 1968—; cons. in field. Contbr. articles to profl. jours. Lalor Found. fellow, 1940; J.F. Kennedy Meml. Found. fellow, 1966; British Sci. Research Council fellow, 1967; recipient Meritorious Service award U.S. Dept. Commerce, 1949; Superior Accomplishment award Nat. Bur. Standards, 1950. Fellow AAAS, Am. Inst. Chemistry, Am. Phys. Soc. (High Polymer Physics prize 1981), N.Y. Acad. Scis. (A. Cressy Morrison prize in natural sci. 1948), Washington Acad. Sci. (Disting. Service to Sci. award 1946); mem. AAUP, Am. Chem. Soc., Soc. Rheology (Bingham medal 1973), Sigma Xi. Current Work: Research on physics and physical chemistry of macromolecular systems. Subspecialties: Polymer chemistry; Polymer physics. Office: Dept Macromolecular Science Case Western Res U Cleveland OH 44106

SIMINOVITCH, LOUIS, scientist, educator; b. Montreal, Que., Can., May 15, 1920; s. Nathan and Golda (Watchman) S.; m. Elinore Esther Faierman, July 2, 1944; children—Harriet Jean, Katherine Ann, Margo Ruth. B.Sc., McGill U., 1941, Ph.D., 1944. Mem. staff Nat. Research Council Can., 1944-47; Canadian Royal Soc. fellow Pasteur Inst., Paris, 1947-49; mem. staff Centre Nationale de la Recherche Scientifique, 1949-53; Nat. Cancer Inst. Can. fellow U. Toronto, Ont., Can., 1953-56, asso. prof. microbiology, 1956-60, asso. prof. med. biophysics, 1958-60, prof. microbiology, 1960-67, prof. med. biophysics, 1960—, univ. prof., 1976—, asso. prof. pediatrics, 1972-78, chmn. dept. cell biology, 1966-73, med. genetics, 1973—; dir. research Mt. Sinai Hosp., Toronto, 1983—; head microbiology sect. biol. research div. Ont. Cancer Inst., Toronto, 1957-63, head div. biol. research, 1963-69; geneticist-in-chief Hosp. Sick Children, Toronto, 1970—; mem. program com. Am. Assn. Cancer Research, 1964-68; mem. virology and rickettsiology sect. NIH, 1966-68; mem. health research com. Ont. Council Health, 1966—; mem. long-range planning com. Nat. Research Council Can., 1966; mem. research adv. group Nat. Cancer Inst. Can., 1969-74, chmn., 1970-72, bd. dirs., 1975—, pres., 1982; bd. dirs. Canadian Weizmann Inst. Sci., 1972—; mem. adv. bd. Ont. Mental Health Found., 1974—; chmn. Ont. Health Research and Devel. Com., 1974—; task force on genetic services Ont. Ministry Health, 1976—; mem. Ont. Task Force On Health Research Requirements, 1974-76; chmn. com. on guidelines for Recombinant DNA, Med. Research Council Can., 1975—; bd. dirs. Mount Sinai Hosp., Toronto, 1975—; mem. United Ch. Can. Gen. Council Commission on Genetic Engring., 1974—; bd. advisors Clin. Research Inst. Montreal Center Bioethics, 1976—; chmn. adv. com. on genetic services Ont. Ministry Health, 1976—; G. Malcolm Brown Meml. lectr. Royal Coll. Physicians and Surgeons, 1978; bd. dirs. Ont. Cancer Treatment and Research Found., 1979—; mem. Alfred P Sloan, Jr., Selection Com. Gen. Motors Cancer Research Found., 1980—; nat. bd. dirs. Canadian Cancer Soc., 1981—. Editor: Virology, 1960—, Bacteriological Revs., 1969-72, Jour. Molecular and Cellular Biology, 1980—; founding mem., pres. editorial bd.: Science Forum, 1968—; mem. editorial bd.: Cell, 1973—, Somatic Cell Genetics, 1974—, Jour. Cytogenetics and Cell Genetics, 1974—, Mutation Research, 1976—, Jour. de Microscopie et de Biologie Cellulaire, 1976, Cancer Genetics and Cytogenetics, 1979—, Jour. Cancer Surveys, 1980—; Contbr. numerous articles to sci. jours. Decorated officer Order of Can.; recipient Queen Elizabeth II Silver-Jubilee award, 1977; Izaak Walton Killam meml. prize, 1981; Wightman award Gardner Found., 1981; Research grantee Med. Research Council, 1958, Nat. Cancer Inst. Can., 1974, NIH, 1972. Fellow Royal Soc. Can. (Centennial medal 1967, Flavell e Medal 1978), Royal Soc. (London); mem. Can. Soc. Cell Biology (pres. 1967), AAAS. Subspecialty: Genetics and genetic engineering (medicine). Home: 106 Wembley Rd Toronto ON M6C 2G6 Canada Office: Dept Medical Genetics U Toronto Toronto ON M5S 1A8 Canada

SIMITSES, GEORGE JOHN, mechanical and aerospace engineer, educator, researcher, consultant; b. Athens, Greece, July 31, 1932; s. John G. and Vasilike G. (Goutoufas) S.; m. Nena E. Simitses, Sept. 11, 1960; children: John G., William G., Alexandra. Student, U. Tampa, 1951-52; B.S. in Aero. Engring. Ga. Inst. Tech., 1955, M.S. in Aero. Engring, 1956; Ph.D. in Aeros. and Astronautics, Stanford U., 1965. Research engr. Ga. Inst. Tech. Exptl. Sta., 1956; instr. Ga. Inst. Tech., 1957-59, asst. prof., 1959-66, assoc. prof., 1966-74, prof. engring. sci. and mechanics, 1974—, cons. to industry; summer faculty assoc. Lockheed-Ga. Co., 1958, 60, 61, 65. Author: Elastic Stability of

Structures, 1976; contbr. numerous articles on structural analysis, stability and optimization. Fellow AIAA (assoc.); mem. ASME, Structural Stability Research Council, Hellenic Soc. Theoretical and Applied Mechanics (founding mem.), Am. Acad. Mechanics, Soc. Engring. Sci., Sigma Xi (Ga. Inst. Tech. chpt. Sustaining Research award 1980, best paper award 1985). Greek Orthodox. Current Work: Structural stability under static and dynamic loads of arches, frames, plates and shells of various constrns. (metallic and fiber reinforced composites). Subspecialties: Theoretical and applied mechanics; Aerospace engineering and technology. Home: 1389 Spalding Dr NE Atlanta GA 30338 Office: care Ga Inst Tech ESM Atlanta GA 30332

SIMKIN, THOMAS EDWARD, geologist; b. Auburn, N.Y., Nov. 11, 1933; s. William Edward and Ruth Helen (Commons) S.; m. Sharon Marie Russell, July 3, 1965; children—Shona Kathleen, Adam Javier. B.S., Swarthmore Coll., 1955; Ph.D., Princeton U., 1964. Instr. SUNY, Birghamton, 1964-65; postdoctoral fellow U. Chgo., 1965-67; supr. geology Smithsonian Oceanographic Sorting Ctr., Washington, 1967-71; curator Nat. Mus. Natural History, Smithsonian Instn., Washington, 1972—; sec. for the Americas (sci.) Charles Darwin Found. for Galapagos Isles, 1970. Author: (with others) Volcanoes of the World, 1981; (with F.S. Fiske) Krakatau, 1983. Contbr. articles to profl. jours. Mem. Arlington County (Va.) Environ. Improvement Commn., 1981—. Served with U.S. Coast and Geodetic survey, 1956-58. NSF grantee; Smithsonian Instn. grantee. Mem. AAAS, Am. Geophys. Union, Internat. Assn. Volcanology (editor Catalog of Active Volcanoes of the World 1980—), Fedn. Am. scientists. Subspecialties: Petrology; Sedimentology. Office: NHB Stop 119 Smithsonian Instn Washington DC 20560

SIMMONS, GEORGE ALLEN, mineral company executive; b. Birmingham, Ala., May 2, 1926; s. George Allen and Stella Lee (Reid) S.; m. Marilyn Naome Boyer, June 9, 1951; children—Roger Allen, Gaile Lynette, Elaine Denise. B.S. cum laude, Birmingham So. Coll., 1947; M.S., Ohio State U., 1949, Ph.D., 1952. Asst. then assoc. prof. Birmingham So. Coll., 1949-55, asst. prof. Purdue U., West Lafayette, Ind., 1952-53; mgr. research services Pitts. Plate Glass, 1955-61, coordinator melting, 1961-62; special projects chief Owens Illinois-Toledo, 1962-66, tech. dir. new product devel., 1966-69, sr. mktg. mgr., 1969-71; tech. dir. Dominion Glass Co., Mississauga, Ont., Can., 1971-76; sr. v.p. research and devel. Thatcher Glass Co., Elmira, N.Y., 1976-81; tech. dir. Ga. Marble Co., Atlanta, 1981—. Author: Silicates: Glasses, Rocks and Ferrous Slags, 1963. Contbng. chpts. to books in field. Patentee in field. Contbr. articles to profl. jours. DuPont fellow, 1952. Fellow Am. Inst. Chemists, Am. Chem. Soc., Ceramic Soc; mem. Can. Ceramic Soc. (div. dir. 1971-76), Phi Beta Kappa Omicron Delta Kappa, Delta Sigma Phi. Unitarian. Current work: Polymer composites; surface chemistry and coatings; ultrafine grinding. Subspecialties: Inorganic chemistry; Materials processing. Office: Ga Marble Co 2575 Cumberland Pkwy NW Atlanta GA 30339

SIMMONS, RALPH OLIVER, physics educator; b. Kensington, Kans., Feb. 19, 1928; s. Fred Charles and Nellie (Douglass) S.; m. Janet Lee Lull, Aug. 31, 1952; children: Katherine Ann, Bradley Alan, Jill Christine, Joy Diane. B.A., U. Kans., 1950; B.A. (Rhodes scholar), Oxford U., 1953; Ph.D., U. Ill., 1957. Research assoc. U. Ill., Urbana, 1957-59, faculty physics, 1959—, assoc. prof., 1961-65, prof. physics, 1965—, head physics dept., 1970—; vis. scientist Ctr. for Study Nuclear Energy, Mol, Belgium, 1965; mem. governing bd. Internat. Symposia on Thermal Expansion, 1970-82; vis. scientist Ctr. Very Low Temperatures, Grenoble, France, 1984; cons. Argonne Nat. Lab., 1978—, Los Alamos Nat. Lab., 1983—, Fla. State U. Bd. Regents, 1984; chmn. Office of Phys. Scis., NRC, 1978-81; mem. Assembly of Math. and Phys. Scis., 1978-81, Geophysics Research Bd., 1978-81; trustee Argonne Univs. Assn., 1979-83. Mem. internat. adv. bd.: Jour. Physics C (Solid State Physics), 1971-76; mem. editorial bd.: Physical Review B, 1978-81. Sr. postdoctoral fellow NSF, 1965. Fellow Am. Phys. Soc. (vice chmn., chmn. div. solid state physics 1975-77), AAAS (chmn. sect. B physics 1985-86); mem. Am. Crystallographic Assn., Am. Assn. Physics Tchrs., Am. Soc. Engring. Edn., Phi Beta Kappa, Sigma Xi, Pi Mu Epsilon. Research on atomic defects in solids, neutron scattering, quantum solids, molecular crystals, crystal dynamics, radiation damage. Current Work: Condensed matter physics, low temperature physics. Subspecialties: Condensed matter physics; Low temperature physics. Home: 1005 Foothill Dr Champaign IL 61821

SIMMONS, WILLIAM HOWARD, biochemistry and biophysics educator, researcher; b. Mansfield, Ohio, May 15, 1947; s. Harold Eugene and Mildred Eileen (Patterson) S. B.A., Wittenberg U., 1969; M.S., Bowling Green State U., 1973; postgrad., Ohio State U., 1975-76; Ph.D., U. Ill. Med. Ctr., 1979. Teaching asst. Bowling Green (Ohio) State U., 1971-75; research asst. Ohio State U., Columbus, 1975-76; research asst. U. Ill. Med. Ctr., Chgo., 1976-79, research assoc., 1979-81; asst. prof. biochemistry and biophysics Loyola U. Med. Ctr., Maywood, Ill., 1981—. Contbr. articles to profl. jours. NIH research grantee, 1981—. Mem. Am. Soc. Biol. Chemists, Am. Chem. Soc., N.Y. Acad. Scis., AAAS, Sigma Xi. Lutheran. Current Work: Purification and characterization of enzymes which metabolize biologically active peptides. Purification of new brain peptides. Behavioral effects of peptides. Subspecialties: Biochemistry (biology); Physiology (biology). Home: 225 Homestead Rd La Grange Park IL 60525 Office: Dept Biochemistry and Biophysics Loyola U Med Center 2160 S 1st Ave Maywood IL 60153

SIMMS, JAMES ROBERT, physicist; b. Vinita, Okla., Dec. 5, 1924; s. Paul Otto and Meda (Hall) S.; m. Pauline Sue Blackwell, Aug. 12, 1950 (dec. 1969); 1 child, Suzanne Marie; m. Lanita Jayne Thiessen, Nov. 30, 1974. B.S. in Engring. Physics, U. Okla., 1950. Registered profl. engr., Md. Electronic engr. The Martin Co., Balt., 1950-56; systems engr. The Martin Co., Denver, 1956-61; mgr. electronics and systems engring. Fairchild, Hagerstown, Md., 1961-63; sr. tech. staff ITT Intelcom, Baileys Cross Roads, Va., 1963-67; program mgr. Systems Research Corp., Washington, 1967-70, dir. ops., 1970-71; program mgr. Gen. Elec., Valley Forge, Pa., 1971-73; cons. pvt. practice, Clarksville, Md., 1973-75; sr. assoc. Booz, Allan & Hamilton, Bethesda, Md., 1975-83; pres. Simms Industries Inc., Clarksville, 1983—; dir. Electronic Learning Facilitators, Bethesda, 1984. Author: A Measure of Knowledge, 1971, The Limits of Behavior: A Quantitative Social Theory, 1983. Contbr. articles to profl. jours. Inventor correlation missile guidance system. Bd. dirs. So. Howard County Democratic Club, Md., 1980—, pres., 1979; county coordinator Com. to Elect Congresswoman Byron, 1978, 80, 82. Served with USN, 1943-46. Mem. IEEE, Soc. Gen. Systems Research, Am. Soc. Cybernetics, World Future Soc. Methodist. Current work: Quantitative casual methodologies and theories in behavioral, social and political science; technology forecasting and assessment; communications; information systems; design of organizations; systems research and analysis. Subspecialties: Systems engineering; Information systems (Information science). Home: 7413 Meadow View Circle Clarksville MD 21029 Office: Simms Industries Inc 7413 Meadow View Circle Clarksville MD 21029

SIMON, ALBERT, physicist, engineer, educator; b. N.Y.C., Dec. 27, 1924; s. Emanuel D. and Sarah (Leitner) S.; m. Harriet E. Rubinstein, Aug. 17, 1947 (dec. June 1970); children: Richard, Janet, David; m. Rita Shiffman, June 11, 1972. B.S., CCNY, 1947; Ph.D., U. Rochester, 1950. Registered profl. engr., N.Y. State. Physicist Oak Ridge Nat. Lab., 1950-54, asso. dir. neutron physics div., 1954-61; head plasma physics div. Gen. Atomic Co., San Diego, 1961-66; prof. dept. mech. engring. U. Rochester, N.Y., 1966—, prof. physics, 1968—, chmn. dept. mech. engring., 1977-84; mem. Inst. for Advanced Study, Princeton, 1974-75; sr. vis. fellow U.K. Sci. Research Council, Oxford U., 1975. Author: An Introduction to Thermonuclear Research, 1959; contbr. to: Ency. Americana, 1964, 74; Editor: Advances in Plasma Physics, 1967—. John Simon Guggenheim fellow, 1964-65. Fellow Am. Phys. Soc. (chmn. plasma physics exec. com. 1963-64); mem. ASME, Am. Soc. Engring. Edn. (chmn. nuclear engring. div. 1985-86). Current Work: Theoretical studies on plasma behavior in fusion devices; both magnet confinement and inerial confinement. Subspecialties: Nuclear fusion; Nuclear engineering. Home: 263 Ashley Dr Rochester NY 14620

SIMON, BARRY, mathematician, physicist, educator; b. Bklyn., Apr. 16, 1946; s. Hy and Minnie (Landa) S.; m. Martha Katzin, Jan. 24, 1971; children: Rivka, Benjamin, Zvi, Aryeh. B.A., Harvard U., 1966; Ph.D., Princeton U., 1970. Instr. depts. math. and physics Princeton (N.J.) U., 1969-70, asst. prof., 1970-72, assoc. prof., 1972-76, prof., 1976-81; prof. math. and theoretical physics Calif. Inst. Tech., 1981-84, IBM prof. math. and theoretical physics, 1984—. Author 8 books in field; contbr. articles to profl. jours.; editor: Wadsworth Advanced Mathematics Book Series, 1980—, Mathematical Notes series, 1980—; asso. editor: Jour. Operator Theory, 1979—, Communications in Math. Physics, 1979—, Duke Math. Jour, 1980—. Recipient medal Internat. Acad. Atomic and Molecular Sci., 1981, Stampacchia prize, 1982. Fellow Am. Phys. Soc.; mem. Am. Math. Soc. (council 1976-78, program com. for nat. meetings 1980-82; nominating com. 1984-85). Current Work: Research in mathematical physics, especially the theory of Schrodinger operators and the statistical mechanics of lattice gases. Subspecialty: Theoretical physics. Office: Calif Inst Tech 253-37 Pasadena CA 91125

SIMON, MELVIN I., biologist. Prof. div. biology Calif. Inst. Tech. Elected mem. Nat. Acad. Scis., 1985. . Office: Calif Inst Tech Div Biology Pasadena CA 91125

SIMON, MYRON SYDNEY, chemist, industrial researcher; b. Burlington, Vt., Sept. 23, 1926; s. Louis Ableheim and Gertrude Gussie (Yette) S.; m. Rose Reguera, Aug. 30, 1950; children—Laurel, Amy, Ethan. A.B., Harvard U., 1946, M.A., 1948, Ph.D., 1949. Scientist, Polaroid Corp., Cambridge, Mass., 1949-52, group leader, 1953-59, mgr., 1960-70, assoc. dir., 1970-84, research fellow, 1984. Author sci. papers. Patentee in field. Mem. Am. Chem. Soc. (chmn. Northeastern sect. 1985—), Assn. Harvard Chemists, Phi Beta Kappa. Current work: Invent and develop photographic processes to generate color photographs using silver halide and non-silver halide technologies. Subspecialties: Organic chemistry; Synthetic chemistry. Home: 20 Somerset Rd West Newton MA 02165 Office: Polaroid Corp Research Div 730 Main St-5A Cambridge MA 02139

SIMON, SHERIDAN ALAN, physicist, educator; b. Buffalo, Apr. 20, 1947; s. Aaron and Sylvia Shirley (Greenfeld-Ray) S.; m. Rose Anne Schrader, July 19, 1970. B.S., U. Rochester, 1969, M.A., 1971, Ph.D., 1978. Teaching asst. U. Rochester, N.Y., 1969-74, research assoc., 1978; instr. SUNY-Geneseo, 1971, 72; vis. scientist NASA-Langley, Hampton, Va., 1981; assoc. prof. physics Guilford Coll., Greensboro, N.C., 1974—; dir. Tri-Coll. Obs., Snow Camp, N.C., 1977—; textbook reviewer Prentice-Hall, Inc., 1980—. Author: The Astronomy Disk, 1983; Unprintable Physics, 1983; The Physics Disk, 1984. Recipient Excellence in Teaching award Guilford Coll., 1976; Research Corp. grantee, 1977; Burroughs Wellcome grantee, 1978. Mem. Am. Phys. Soc., Am. Astron. Soc., Am. Assn. Physics Tchrs., Sigma Xi. Current work: Physics research involving undergraduates, educational software for college level science and mathematics students, science fiction writing, editing texts. Subspecialties: Theoretical astrophysics; Software engineering. Home: 5723-A Bramblegate Rd Greensboro NC 27409 Office: Guilford Coll Friendly Rd Greensboro NC 27410

SIMONDS, J(OHN) TODD, sociologist; b. Pitts., Sept. 29, 1946; s. John Ormsbee and Marjorie Clara (Todd) S.; m. Juliet Lea Hillman, Apr. 9, 1970; children—Dylan, Talbott, Henry. A.B., Princeton U., 1968; M.A. in Edn., U. Pitts., 1972, M.A. in Sociology, 1976. Prin. research asst. Learning Research and Devel. Ctr., U. Pitts., 1970-74, research assoc. Urban Research Ctr., 1975-78; research assoc. Tech. Soc. Inst., U. Pitts., 1979-80; exec. dir. World Ctr. for Computers and Human Resources, Paris, 1983-84; assoc. dir. Robotics Inst., Carnegie-Mellon U., Pitts., 1981—. Trustee, Chatham Coll., Buhl Sci. Ctr., Carnegie Mus. Natural History, 1981-83, St. Edmund's Acad., 1976-83. Democrat. Clubs: Pitts. Golf (dir. 1978-83), Rolling Rock, Fox Chapel Golf. Current work: Social impact of technology; research management. Subspecialty: Robotics. Office: Robotics Inst Carnegie Mellon U Schenley Park Pittsburgh PA 15213

SIMONETTI, JOSEPH LAWRENCE, test engineer; b. Plainfield, N.J., Apr. 12, 1952; s. John Joseph and Philomena Rose (Mone) S. B.S.M.E., Rutgers Coll. Engring., 1976; B.A. in Psychology, Rutgers U., 1976; grad. Aircraft Accident Investigation Sch., U. So. Calif., 1985. Test engr. Pratt and Whitney Aircraft, East Hartford, Conn., 1976, Sikorsky Aircraft, Stratford, Conn., 1976-77; test engr. level IV Avco Lycoming, Stratford, from 1977, now Sr. test engr. NSF grantee, 1975. Mem. ASME, Soc. Automotive Engrs., Aircraft Owners and Pilots Assn., Pi Tau Sigma. Club: Flying Eagles (Stratford). Current Work: Flight and ground testing of high by-pass ratio turbofan engines; aircraft powerplants. Subspecialties: Mechanical engineering; Aerospace engineering and technology. Office: 550 S Main St Stratford CT 06497

SIMONIAN, SIMON JOHN, surgeon, educator; b. Antioch, French Ter., Apr. 20, 1932; came to U.S., 1965, naturalized, 1976; s. John Simon and Marie Cecile (Tomboulian) S.; m. Arpi Ani Yeghiayan, July 11, 1965; children: Leonard Armen, Charles Haig, Andrew Hovig. M.D., U. London, 1957; B.A. with honors, St. Edmund Hall, U. Oxford, Eng., 1964; M.A., U. Oxford, Eng., 1969; Sc.M., Harvard U., 1967, Sc.D., 1969. Diplomate: Am. Bd. Surgery, Brit. Bd. Surgery. Intern Edinburgh (Scotland) Royal Infirmary, 1957-58, resident, 1961-62; clin. clk. Nat. Hosp. London, 1958; resident Edinburgh Western Gen. Hosp., 1958-59, Birmingham Accident and Burns Hosp., U. Birmingham, Eng., 1959-60; demonstrator dept. anatomy Edinburgh U., 1960-61; research fellow in pathology Harvard U., Boston, 1965-68; resident in surgery Boston City Hosp., 1970-74; dir. surg. immunology, asst. in surgery Brigham and Womens Hosp., Boston, 1968-70; attending surgeon in transplantation and gen. surgery services U. Chgo. Hosp. Med. Ctr., 1974-78; instr., asso. in surgery Harvard Med. Sch., 1968-70, vis. prof., 1982; asst. prof. surgery, mem. com. immunology U. Chgo., 1974-78; head div. renal transplantation Hahnemann U. Sch. Medicine, 1978—, prof. surgery, 1978—; surg. dir. End Stage Renal Disease Program, 1980—; dir. Transplantation Program, 1983—; lectr. in field.; vis. prof. Vanderbilt U., 1968, UCLA, 1977, U. Cambridge, 1977, Karolinska Inst., 1977, U. Stockholm, 1977, Med. Coll. Pa., 1980, 81, 85, U. Pa., 1981, 85, U. Athens, 1981, Tufts U., 1982, U. Oxford, 1982. Editorial bd. Issues in Transplantation. Contbr. articles to profl. jours. and books. Co-founder Armenian Youth Soc., Eng., 1953, pres., 1953-54; co-founder Armenian Studies program U. Chgo., 1975; bd. govs. Friends Sch., London, 1964-65; Mass. del. Armenian Assembly, Washington, 1970-74. Nairn scholar, 1949-52; Middlesex scholar, 1952-57; recipient Suckling prize, 1957; Brit. Med. Research Council award, 1962-64; NIH award, 1965-70; Alt prize, 1973; Thompson award, 1974-77; Johnson award, 1975-77; named outstanding new citizen of 1976-77 Washington. Fellow Royal Coll. Surgeons Edinburgh, A.C.S., Phila. Acad. Surgery (ann. orator 1984); mem. AAAS, Royal Coll. Surgeons of Eng., Nat. Assn. Armenian Studies and Research, Am. Armenian Med. Assn. (co-founder 1972, treas. 1972-74), Armenian Med. and Dental Assn. Greater Phila. (pres. 1983-85), Assn. Acad. Surgery, Transplantation Soc. (editorial bd. 1968-70, membership com. 1980-82), Am. Fedn. Clin. Research, N.Y. Acad. Scis., Am. Soc. Transplant Surgeons (founding mem. 1974, membership com. 1984—), Phila. Acad. Scis. (co-chmn. membership com. 1980—), Greater Delaware Valley Soc. Transplant Surgeons (pres. 1982-85), Phila. County Med. Soc. (rep. City Ctr. br. 1981-83, pres. 1984, bd. dirs. 1985), Pa. Med. Soc., AMA, Am. Technion Soc., Am. Soc. Artificial Organs, Internat. Cardiovascular Spc., End Stage Renal Disease Network 24 (mem. med. rev. bd. 1980-82), AAUP, Sigma Xi. Clubs: Harvard (Phila.), Med. (Phila.). Current Work: Organ transplantation surgery, biology, immunology and prosthetic surgery. Subspecialties: Transplant surgery; Transplantation. Office: 230 N Broad St Philadelphia PA 19102

SIMONS, ROY KENNETH, pomology educator, researcher; b. Kincheloe, W.Va., Dec. 26, 1920; s. Basil E. and Essie M. (Currey) S.; m. Frances Jensen, June 12, 1953; children: Janet Simons Orashan, Kenneth B. B.S., M.S., W.Va. U., 1947; Ph.D., Mich. State U., 1951. Instr. U. Del., Newark, 1947-48; grad. asst. Mich. State U., East Lansing, 1948-51; prof. horticulture U. Ill.-Urbana, 1951—. Contbr. numerous articles on pomology to profl. jours. Served with AUS, 1942-45. Rootstock Research Com. grantee, 1980-81; Hort. Research Inst. grantee, 1981. Fellow AAAS, Am. Soc. for Hort. Sci. (Stark award 1967, Hurov award 1977, 78); mem. Internat. Soc. Hort. Sci., Internat. Dwarf Fruit Tree Assn. (sec. rootstock research com.), Am. Pomological Soc., Ill. Hort. Soc., Mich. Hort. Soc. Current Work: Pomology, fruit growth as related to cultural practices, morphology anatomy of specific plant parts and dwarfing rootstock evaluations. Subspecialties: Ecosystems analysis; Cell biology (medicine). Home: 1517 Alma Dr Champaign IL 61820 Office: 1707 S Orchard St Urbana IL 61801

SIMPSON, JOANNE MALKUS, meteorologist; b. Boston, Mar. 23, 1923; d. Russell and Virginia (Vaughan) Gerould; m. Robert H. Simpson, Jan. 6, 1965; children by previous marriage—David Starr Malkus, Steven Willem Malkus, Karen Elizabeth Malkus. B.S., U. Chgo., 1943, M.S., 1945, Ph.D., 1949. Instr. physics and meteorology Ill. Inst. Tech., 1946-49, asst. prof., 1949-51; meteorologist Woods Hole Oceanographic Instn., 1951-61; prof. meteorology UCLA, 1961-65; dir. exptl. meteorology lab. NOAA, Dept. Commerce, Washington, 1965-74; prof. environ. scis. U. Va., Charlottesville, 1974-76, W.W. Corcoran prof. environ. scis., 1976-81; head Severe Storms br. Goddard Lab. Atmospheric Scis., NASA, Greenbelt, Md., 1981—. Author: (with Herbert Riehl) Cloud Structure and Distributions Over the Tropical Pacific Ocean; assoc. editor: Revs. Geophysics and Space Physics, 1964-72, 75-77; contbr. articles to profl. jours. Mem. Fla. Gov.'s Environ. Coordinating Council, 1971-74. Recipient Disting. Authorship award NOAA, 1969; Silver medal, 1967, Gold medal, 1972 both from Dept. Commerce; Community Headliner award Women in Communications, 1973; Profl. Achievement award U. Chgo. Alumni Assn., 1975; Exceptional Sci. Achievement award NASA, 1982; named Woman of Yr. Los Angeles Times, 1963; Guggenheim fellow, 1954-55. Fellow Am. Meteorol. Soc. (Meisinger award 1962, Rossby Research medal 1983, council 1975-77, 79-81, exec. com. 1977, 79-81); mem. Weather Modification Assn. (Vincent J. Schaefer award 1979), Royal Meteorol. Soc., Nat. Weather Assn., Phi Beta Kappa, Sigma Xi. Current work: Precipitating cumulus cloud systems; severe storms; tropical meteorology. Subspecialties: Meteorologic instrumentation; Remote sensing (atmospheric science). Home: 6200 Westchester Park Apt 517 College Park MD Office: Lab Atmospheric Scis Goddard Space Flight Center NASA Greenbelt MD 20771

SIMPSON, JOHN A., government laboratory executive. Dir. mfg. engring. ctr. Nat. Engring. Lab., Dept. Commerce, Gaithersburg, Md. Subspecialty: Manufacturing engineering. Office: Nat Engring Lab Mfg Engring Ctr Route 270 Gaithersburg MD 20234

SIMPSON, LARRY DEAN, medical physicist; b. Satanta, Kans., Sept. 3, 1944; s. Melvin LeRoy and Dorothy Lorraine (Moody) S.; m. Sara Margaret Frandle, Aug. 14, 1965; 1 child, Rustin Dean. A.B., U. Kans., 1966, M.S. in Radiation Biophysics, 1969, Ph.D., 1971. Radiol. health traineeship div. radiol. health USPHS, Dept. Radiation Biophysics, U. Kans., Lawrence, 1967-71; postdoctoral fellow in med. physics Meml. Sloan-Kettering Cancer Ctr., N.Y.C., 1971, asst. physicist dept. med. physics, 1971-72, asst. attending physicist dept. med. physics, 1973-79, assoc. attending physicist, 1979-81; asst. prof. radiology Cornell U. Grad. Sch. Med. Scis., 1979-81; dir. med. physics sect. div. radiation oncology, assoc. prof. radiology, asst. prof. radiation, biology and biophysics U. Rochester Cancer Ctr., Rochester, N.Y., 1981—. Contbr. numerous articles to profl. jours. Mem. Health Physics Soc., Am. Assn. Physics Tchrs., AAAS, Am. Soc. Therapeutic Radiologists (mem. sci. program com., mem. com. on radiation therapy technologists' affairs), Am. Assn. Physicists in Medicine (bd. dirs., fin. com., publs. com., chmn. sci. program com., mem. sci. council, chmn. continuing edn. com.), Radiol. Soc. N.Am., Am. Coll. Radiology, Radiation Therapy Oncology Group (mem. med. physics com.), Sigma Xi. Current Work: Optimization of radiation use in diagnosis, cure and research of cancer. Director radiation physics and radiation biophysics activities allied to cancer radiation treatments. Subspecialties: Cancer research (medicine); Biophysics (physics). Office: U Rochester Cancer Center 601 Elmwood Ave Box 647 Rochester NY 14642

SIMPSON, RICHARD KENDALL, JR., physician, surgeon, researcher; b. Atlanta, Sept. 10, 1953; s. Richard Kendall and Juliet Hodges (Rowsey) S. B.A., Coker Coll., 1975; Ph.D., Med. U. S.C., 1980, M.D., 1982; postgrad., Warnborough Coll., Oxford, Eng., 1974. Diplomate: Nat. Bd. Med. Examiners. Teaching asst. dept. physiology Med. U. S.C., Charleston, 1976-80, research assoc., 1980—83, intern in neurology, 1982-83; resident neurosurgery dept. neurosurgery Baylor Coll. Medicine, Houston, 1983-89; cons. Spinal Cord Injury Research, Charleston, S.C., 1980-83; grant reviewer NSF, Charleston, 1981—. Author: Peripheral Nerve Fiber Group and Spinal Corp Pathway Contributions to the Somatosensory Evoked Potential, 1980. Mem. Am. Med. Polit. Action Com., 1983. Watson fellow Coker Coll., 1974. Mem. AMA, Am. Physiol. Soc., Soc. Neurosci., Digital Equipment Computer Users Soc., N.Y. Acad. Sci., Sigma Xi, Alpha Omega Alpha, S.C. Soc. Neurosci., S.C. Acad. Sci. Episcopalian. Current Work: Evaluation and management of patients with spinal cord and closed head injury utilizing somatosensory and corticomotor evoked potentials, the pathophysiology of central nervous system trauma, the neurophysiological mechanisms of evoked potential production. Subspecialties: Neurosurgery; Neurophysiology. Home: 5540 Aspen St Houston TX 77081 Office: Dept Neurosurgery Baylor Coll Medicine 1200 Moursund Ave Houston TX 77030

SIMPSON, W(ILBURN) DWAIN, computer science company executive, physicist; b. Lone Grove, Okla., Oct. 4, 1937; s. Joseph Charles and Ruby Wilma (Smith) S.; m. Ann Marie Coratello, Aug. 27, 1967; children—Ketah Marie Elizabeth, Rebecca Elizabeth. B.S., U. Miss., 1959, M.S., 1961; M.A., Rice U., 1963, Ph.D., 1965. Research assoc. Rice U., Houston, 1965-67; assoc. physicist Brookhaven Nat. Lab., N.Y., 1967-69; founder, v.p., sec. Periphonics Corp., Bohemia, N.Y., 1969-80, Alta Tech. Inc., Stamford, Conn., 1980-85; founder, pres. W.D. Simpson Tech. Inc., Wilton, Conn., 1985—; seminar lectr. Ayentka, Bay Shore, N.Y., 1980-81. Patentee in field. NASA fellow, 1963. Mem. Assn. Computing Machinery, IEEE, Am. Phys. Soc., N.Y. Acad. Scis., AAAS. Democrat. Methodist. Current work: Computer system memories, voice/analog storage, telecommunications, data compression and security, magnetic and optical storage of data, computer systems analysis, system design consultation. Subspecialties: Distributed systems and networks; Nuclear physics. Home: 124 Catalpa Rd Wilton CT 06897 Office: WD Simpson Technology Inc Box 482 Wilton CT 06897

SINCLAIR, ROLF MALCOLM, physicist; b. N.Y.C., Aug. 15, 1929; s. Nathan and Elizabeth (Stout) S.; m. Margaret Lee Andrews, June 13, 1959 (div. 1978); children—Elizabeth Ann, Andrew Caisley. B.S., Calif. Inst. Tech., 1949; M.A., Rice U., 1951, Ph.D., 1954. Physicist, Westinghouse Research Labs., 1953-56; vis. scientist U. Hamburg, Fed. Republic Germany, 1956-57, U. Paris, 1957-58, U.K. Atomic Energy Authority, Culham Lab., Eng., 1965-66; research physicist Princeton U., N.J., 1958-69; program dir. NSF, Washington, 1969—; rep. U.S. solar eclipse expdn. to India, 1980; mem. Solstice Project, 1978—; cons. to industry, 1960-69. Patentee in field. Fellow Am. Phys. Soc. (panel pub. affairs), AAAS (sec. physics sect. 1972—; mem. council 1972-73); mem. Sigma Xi. Current work: Plasma physics; thermonuclear fusion research and development; archaeology and archaeoastronomy in the U.S. southwest. Subspecialties: Nuclear fusion; Archaeoastronomy. Office: NSF Washington DC 20550

SINDELAR, WILLIAM FRANCIS, physician, researcher; b. Cleve., Mar. 13, 1945; s. William Frank and Josephine Ann (Storkan) S.; m. Aleta Beth Merkel, May 8, 1982. B.A., Western Res. U., 1967, M.A., 1968, Ph.D., 1970, M.D., 1971. Diplomate: Am. Bd. Surgery, 1979. Mem. faculty Western Res. U., Cleve., 1966-67, Marine Biol. Lab., Woods Hole, Mass., 1966-67; jr. house officer in surgery Johns Hopkins U., Balt., 1971-73; fellow in surgery NIH, Bethesda, Md., 1973-75; sr. house officer in surgery U. Md., Balt., 1975-77; sr. surgeon Nat. Cancer Inst., NIH, Bethesda, 1977—; cons. in surgery U. Md. Contbr. articles on cancer biology, immunobiology and clin. treatment to profl. jours. Commd. sr. surgeon USPHS, 1973—. Mem. ACS, Am. Assn. for Cancer Research, Am. Soc. Clin. Oncology, Am. Soc. for Cell Biology, Am. Radium Soc., Assn. for Acad. Surgery, Soc. of Surg. Oncology, Phi Beta Kappa, Alpha Omega Alpha. Current Work: Development of new clinical cancer treatment; basic research in cancer immunobiology, surgical oncology, cancer research, immunobiology. Subspecialties: Surgery; Immunobiology and immunology. Office: Surgery Br Nat Cancer Inst NIH Bethesda MD 20205

SINFELT, JOHN HENRY, chemist; b. Munson, Pa., Feb. 18, 1931; s. Henry Gustave and June Lillian (McDonald) S.; m. Muriel Jean Vadersen, July 14, 1956; 1 son, Klaus Herbert. B.S., Pa. State U., 1951; Ph.D., U. Ill., 1954, D.Sc. (hon.), 1981. Research engr. Exxon Research Engring. Co., Linden, N.J., 1954-57, sr. research engr., 1957-62, research asso., 1962-68, sr. research asso., 1968-72, sci. advisor, 1972-79, sr. sci. advisor, 1979—; vis. prof. chem. engring. U. Minn., 1969; Lacey lectr. Calif. Inst. Tech., 1973; Reilly lectr. U. Notre Dame, 1974; Francois Gault lectr. catalysis Council Europe Research Group Catalysis, 1980; Mobay lectr. in chemistry U. Pitts., 1980; disting. vis. lectr. in chemistry U. Tex., 1981; Robert A. Welch Found. lectr. Confs. on Chem. Research, 1981; Camille and Henry Dreyfus lectr. UCLA, 1982. Contbr. articles to sci. jours. Recipient Dickson prize Carnegie-Mellon U., 1977; Internat. prize for new materials Am. Phys. Soc., 1978; Nat. Medal of Sci., 1979; Chem. Pioneer award Am. Inst. Chemists, 1981; Perkin medal for outstanding contbns. to applied chemistry Soc. Chem. Industry, 1984. Fellow Am. Acad. Arts and Scis.; mem. Am. Inst. Chem. Engrs. (Alpha Chi Sigma award 1971, Profl. Progress award 1975), Am. Chem. Soc. (Carothers lectr. Del. sect. 1982, Petroleum Chemistry award 1976), Catalysis Soc. (Emmett award 1973), Nat. Acad. Scis., Nat. Acad. Engring. Methodist. Inventor polymetallic cluster catalysts used commercially in petroleum reforming.

Current Work: Heterogeneous catalysis; bimetallic cluster catalysts; catalysis of hydrocarbon reactions on metals; structure of metal catalysts. Subspecialty: Catalysis chemistry. Office: Exxon Research Engineering Co Clinton Township Route 22 East Annandale NJ 08801

SINGER, ISADORE MANUAL, mathematician; b. Detroit, May 4, 1924; m. 1944; 3 children. B.S., U. Mich., 1944; M.S., U. Chgo., 1948, Ph.D. in Math., 1950. Moore instr. math. MIT, 1950-52, from asst. prof. to prof. math., 1956-77; asst. prof. UCLA, 1952-54; vis. asst. prof. Columbia U., N.Y.C., 1954-55; mem. Inst. advanced Study, 1955-56; prof. math U. Calif.-Berkeley, 1977—; first holder MacArthur chair MIT, 1984—. Recipient Nat. medal of Sci. 1985; Bocher prize Am. Math. soc., 1969. Mem. Nat. acad. Scis. Office: Dept Math U Calif Berkeley CA 94720*

SINGER, MAXINE FRANK, biochemist; b. N.Y.C., Feb. 15, 1931; d. Hyman S. and Henrietta (Perlowitz) Frank; m. Daniel Morris Singer, June 15, 1952; children: Amy Elizabeth, Ellen Ruth, David Byrd, Stephanie Frank. A.B., Swarthmore Coll., 1952, D.Sc. (hon.), 1978; Ph.D., Yale U., 1957; D.Sc., Wesleyan U., 1977, U. Md.-Baltimore County, 1985. USPHS postdoctoral fellow NIH, Bethesda, Md., 1956-58, research chemist (biochemistry), 1958-74; head sect. on nucleic acid enzymology Nat. Cancer Inst., 1974-79; chief Lab. of Biochemistry, Nat. Cancer Inst., 1979—; Regents vis. lectr. U. Calif., Berkeley, 1981; Bd. dirs. Found. for Advanced Edn. in Scis., 1972-78, 85—; mem. sci. council Internat. Inst. Genetics and Biophysics, Naples, Italy, 1982—. Editor: Jour. Biol. Chemistry, 1968-74, Sci. mag, 1972-82; chmn. editorial bd. Proc. Nat. Acad. Scis., 1985—. Contbr. articles to scholarly jours. Trustee Wesleyan U., Middletown, Conn., 1972-75; trustee Yale Corp., New Haven, 1975—; bd. govs. Weizmann Inst. Sci., Rehovot, Israel, 1978—. Recipient award for achievement in biol. scis. Washington Acad. Scis., 1969, award for research in biol. scis. Yale Sci. and Engring. Assn., 1974, Superior Service Honor award HEW, 1975, Dirs. award NIH, 1977, Disting. Service medal HHS, 1983. Fellow Am. Acad. Arts and Scis.; mem. AAAS, Am. Soc. Biol. Chemists, Am. Soc. Microbiologists, Am. Chem. Soc., Inst. Medicine (Nat. Acad. Scis.), Nat. Acad. Scis. (council 1982-85). Current Work: Organization and function of highly-repeated DNA sequences; relation between host and viral genomes. Subspecialties: Genome organization; Molecular biology. Home: 5410 39th St NW Washington DC 20015 Office: Bldg 37 4E-28 Bethesda MD 20205

SINGER, TIMOTHY JAMES, aviation psychologist, consultant; b. Champaign, Ill., June 3, 1947; s. Robert Roy and Earline Elizabeth (Harris) S.; m. Ann Kathleen Widmer, Jan. 14, 1978; children: Rachael Linn, Lindsay. B.A., Reed Coll., Portland, Oreg., 1973; M.S., Yale U., 1975, M. Phil., 1976, Ph.D., 1977. Commd. lt. comdr. USNR, 1980—; Clin. psychology resident Wilford Hall U.S. Air Force Med. Ctr., San Antonio, 1976-77; chief mental health service U.S. Air Force Hosp., Loring AFB, Jaine, 1977-80; flight surgeon trainee Naval Aerospace Med. Inst., Pensacola, Fla., 1980-81, spl. project officer operational psychology, 1981; aviation safety researcher COMNAVAIRPAC, San Diego, 1981—, aircraft accident investigator, 1981—; adj. asst. prof. George Washington U. Med. Sch., 1981—. Author U.S. Navy med. trg. manuals; contbr. articles in field to profl. jours. Decorated U.S. Air Force Commendation Medal, Armed Forces Expeditionary Medal. Mem. Aerospace Med. Assn., Am. Psychol. Assn., Assn. Aviation Psychologists, Am. Soc. Clin. Hypnosis, Human Factors Soc., Yale Sci. and Engring. Assn., Phi Beta Kappa. Club: Yale (San Diego). Current Work: Research and development, testing and evaluation in the military aviation community; special interests in man-machine integration, human-computer interface, maximization of aircrew performance and safety, and the application of human factors research methods to advanced aviation technology projects. Subspecialties: Aerospace engineering and technology; Human factors engineering. Home: 9939 Oviedo St San Diego CA 92129 Office: COMNAVAIRPAC (code 0143C) NAS North Island San Diego CA 92135

SINGH, BRAMAH NAND, cardiologist, educator, researcher; b. Suva, Fiji, Mar. 3, 1938; came to U.S., 1975; s. Shri Ram and Janki S.; m. Roshni Ram, Dec. 11, 1964; children: Pramil, Nalini, Sanjiv. B.Med.Sc., U. Otago, N.Z., 1961, M.B.Ch.B., 1963; Ph.D., U. Oxford, Eng., 1971; postgrad. (fellow) Harvard U. Med. Sch., 1971-72; M.D., U. Otago, 1975. Sr. lectr. medicine U. Auckland (N.Z.) Sch. Medicine, 1972-75; dir. inpatient cardiology Cedars-Sinai Med. Ctr., Los Angeles, 1976-78; assoc. prof. medicine UCLA, 1976-80, prof. medicine, 1980—; dir. cardiovascular research lab. VA Hosp., Los Angeles, 1978—; Mem. cardiology adv. com. Nat. Heart, Lung and Blood Inst., 1979-83. Contbr. numerous articles to profl. jours.; Editor: Calcium Antagonists, 1984; editorial bd. numerous med. jours. Am. Heart Assn. grantee, 1978—. Fellow Royal Coll. Physicians (London), Am. Coll. Cardiology; mem. Royal Australasian Coll. Physicians. Current Work: Cardiovascular research into the mechanisms and control of disturbances of cardiac rhythm and conduction and the biology of myocardial ischemia. Subspecialty: Cardiology. Home: 16979 Encino Hills Dr Encino CA 91436 Office: UCLA Los Angeles CA 90073

SINGH, JARNALL, biologist, educator, environ. researcher; b. Amritsar, Punjab, India, Oct. 26, 1941; came to U.S., 1965, naturalized, 1978; s. Mihan and Basant (Kaur) S.; m. Brijindar Kaur, June 26, 1968; children: Harpreet, Vijaypreet. B.S. in Agr, Punjab U., Chandigarh, India, 1961; M.S., Punjab Agrl. U., Ludhiana, India, 1964; Ph.D., Kans. State U., 1968. Asso. prof. biology Stillman Coll., Tuscaloosa, Ala., 1969-81, prof., 1981—, chmn. div. math. and sci., 1970-73, prin. investigator minority biomed. research support program, 1974—. Author: Simple Laboratory Exercises for General Biology, 1982; contbr. articles to profl. jours. Mem. Tuscaloosa Clean Air Com., 1970-74. Recipient Dedication to Equal Opportunity in Edn. award United Negro Coll. Fund, 1973; Oak Ridge Assoc. Univs. fellow, 1973; United Negro Coll. Fund fellow, 1979; Nat. Health Research Service fellow, 1983-84. Mem. AAAS, AAUP, Inst. Environ. Scis. Democrat. Current Work: Research on the teratogenicity of protein deficient diets mycotoxins and air pollutant gases such as carbon monoxide, sulphur dioxide and nitrogen dioxide. Subspecialties: Environmental toxicology; Teratology. Office: Stillman Coll 3700 15th St Tuscaloosa AL 35403

SINGH, JOGESHWAR PREET, civil engineer, seismologist, consultant, researcher; b. Patiala, Panjab, India, Jan. 3, 1944; came to U.S., 1965; s. Rajkumar Hazura Singh and Ratnagar Kaur; m. Parmjit Singh, Aug. 13, 1967; children—Harman Preet, Prabh Sharan. Student Panjab U., 1958-60; B.S. in Civil Engring., Panjabi U., Patiala, Panjab, 1964; M.S. in Soil Mechanics, U. Calif.-Berkeley, 1966, Ph.D. in Earthquake Engring., 1980. Registered civil engr., Calif. Sr. engr. Dames & Moore, San Francisco, 1966-80; prin. engr., prin. seismologist, dir. newtech. Harding Lawson Assocs., Novato, Calif., 1980—. Author, editor numerous articles in seismology, earthquake engring, geotech. engring. Founding dir. Guru Gobind Singh Internat. Hosp. Found., Milw.; v.p., sec. Sikh Ctr. San Francisco Bay Area, El Sobrante, Calif., 1970, 76-79; v.p. western region Sikh Council N.Am., Richmond Hill, N.Y., 1980. Recipient Outstanding Immigrant award Internat. Inst. of East Bay, Oakland, Calif., 1980. Mem. ASCE, Seismol. Soc. Am., Structural Engrs. Assn. Calif., ASME (mem. Arctic subcom. off-shore mechanics and Arctic engring. div.), Earthquake Engring. Research Inst. (mem., lectr. continuing edn. com.), ASTM (chmn. subcom. 1972-76). Current work: Geotechnical engineering; arctic engineering; engineering seismology; earthquake engineering; risk engineering. Subspecialties: Civil engineering; Seismology. Home: 23 Red Arrow Ct El Sobrante CA 94803 Office: Harding Lawson Assocs 7655 Redwood Blvd Novato CA 94948

SINGH, RAJ NARAIN, engineering research and development engineer, consultant to industry; b. Hardasipur, India, Apr. 14, 1946; came to U.S., 1969, naturalized 1981; s. Lakshmi Narain and Prabhawati S.; m. Satya Prabha, June 18, 1974; children—Richa, Meha, Shubha. B. Tech., Indian Inst. Tech., Kanpur, India, 1967; M.S., U. Man. 1969; Ph.D., MIT, 1972. Fellow U. Man., Winnipeg, 1968-69; research asst. MIT, Cambridge, 1969-72, staff div. sponsored research, 1972-73; ceramist Argonne Nat. lab., Ill., 1973-79; mem. tech. staff Gen. Electric Co., Schenectady, N.Y., 1979—, mem. battery process selection team, 1983—. Patentee in field. Contbr. articles to profl. jours. Mem. Hindu Temple Sco., Latham, N.Y., 1979—. Recipient Disting. Service award Argonne Nat. Lab., 1979, Bronze Patent medallion Gen. Electric, 1983; U. Man. fellow, 1968, MIT research assistantship, 1969-72. Mem. Am. Ceramic Soc., Inst. Ceramic Engrs. Club: Whitney (Schenectady). Current work: Development of new metallization for VLSI circuits of tomorrow, new ceramic materials for electronic and high-temperature applications, research and development on novel material processing techniques. Subspecialties: Ceramics; Microchip technology (materials science). Home: 31 Shelburne Ct Schenectady NY 12309 Office: Gen Electric R&D K-1 4A32 PO Box 8 Schenectady NY 12301

SINGH, RAJENDRA, electrical engineering educator, researcher; b. Saharanpur, India, July 13, 1946; came to U.S., 1979; s. Kartar Singh and Savitri Devi; m. Reeta Sinha, Aug. 15, 1976; children—Rupalika, Rupangini. B.S. in Physics, Agra U., India, 1965; M.S. in Electronics, Meerut U., India, 1968; M.S. in Super Conductivity, Dalhousi U., Can., 1974; Ph.D. in Solar Cells, McMaster U., Can., 1979. Lectr. Meerut U., India, 1968-73; vis. asst. prof. U. Waterloo, Ont., Can., 1979; vis. asst. prof. Colo. State U., Ft. Collins, 1979-80; sr. research scientist Energy Conservation Devices, Troy, Mich., 1980-82; assoc. prof. elec. engring. and computer sci. U. Okla., Norman, 1982—; cons. Howard U., Washington, 1978-79, Arco Solar, Inc., Chatsworth, Calif., 1983—. Patentee; contbr. articles to profl. jours. Vol. Can. Red Cross, Hamilton, 1977-79. Recipient Faculty Excellence award U. Okla., 1983-84, award Outstanding Instrn. and Service, 1984, Young Faculty Devel. award, 1984. Mem. IEEE (sr., Disting. Lectr. award 1983). Hindu. Current work: Microelectronics (gate dielectrics for very large scale intergration), high temperature electronics, solar cells, nuclear detectors, molecular computors. Subspecialties: Microelectronics; Microchip technology (materials science). Home: 514 Midland Dr Norman OK 73069 Office: U Okla Sch Elec Engring 202 W Boyd #219 Norman OK 73019

SINGH, SHIVA PUJAN, microbiologist, microbiology educator; b. Tulsipur Majha, Gonda, India, July 15, 1947; came to U.S., 1971, naturalized, 1977; s. Ram Bahadur and Dukhana (Devi) S.; m. Patricia Ann Gangloff, Sept. 12, 1973; children: Suman R., Raj K. B.S., Pant U., Pantnagar, India, 1969, M.S., 1971; Ph.D., Auburn U., 1976. Grad. asst. Pant U., 1969-71, Auburn U., 1971-75; research assoc. Tuskegee Inst., 1976; acting head gen. biology Ala. State U., 1978, asst. prof., 1976-82, assoc. prof. microbiology, 1982-84, assoc. prof., coordinator biomed. research, 1984—, program dir. minority biomed. research support program, 1984—. Argonne Nat. Lab. Faculty Research Fellowship awardee, 1979; NIH grantee, 1984—; Ala. Research Inst. grantee, 1984—. Mem. AAAS, Am. Soc. Microbiology, Ala. Acad. Sci. Democrat. Hindu. Current Work: Molecular architecture and functioning of envelope proteins of gram negative bacteria; preparation and use of monoclonal antibodies for detection and identification of baculoviruses. Subspecialties: Microbiology; Virology (biology). Home: 2186 W Aberdeen Dr Montgomery AL 36116 Office: Ala State U 915 S Jackson St Montgomery AL 36195

SINGHAKOWINTA, AMNUAY, physician, oncologist, educator; b. Thailand, Oct. 25, 1939; s. Prasong and Chu S.; m. Boonploog Tancharoenpol, June 20, 1965; children: Pearl, Ann. M.D., U. Med. Sci., Bangkok, Thailand, 1963. Diplomate: Am. Bd. Internal Medicine, Am. Bd. Med. Oncology. Instr. Wayne State U., Detroit, 1971, asst. prof. med. oncology, 1972-75, assoc. prof., 1976—; vice-chief oncology dept. Harper-Grace Hosp., Detroit, 1975—. Contbr. chpts. to books. Fellow ACP; mem. Am. Assn. Cancer Research, Am. Soc. Clin. Oncology. Buddhist. Current Work: Breast cancer research and treatment; steroid receptors and cancer. Subspecialties: Cancer research (medicine); Receptors. Home: 2875 Homewood Troy MI 48098 Office: 785 N Lapeer Rd Lake Orion MI 48035

SINGHAL, ANIL KUMAR, mech. engr.; b. Gwalior, India, Oct. 17, 1947; came to U.S., 1969, naturalized, 1982; s. Uma Shanker and Shri Kumari (Goel) S.; m. Maria Da Graca Singhal, Dec. 1, 1980; 1 son: Neel Shanker. B.S.M.E. (Merit scholar), Birla Inst. Tech. and Sci., Pilani, India, 1969; M.S.I.E., U. Houston, 1971. Registered profl. engr., Tex., La. Project engr., supr. engring. Graver Tank & Mfg. Co. div. Aerojet Gen. Corp., 1971-80; lead engr. Foster Wheeler Corp., 1980-81; sr. mech. engr. Bechtel Pet Corp., 1981-82; mgr. equipment design Sci. Design Corp., Houston, 1982-83. Mem. ASME, Cryogenic Soc. Am., Tex. Soc. Profl. Engrs., La. Soc. Profl. Engrs. Project dir. devel. of light weight aluminum floating roof for tanks storing volatile substances. Current Work: Process equipment design, study of various metals of construction, process equipment design and engineering management. Subspecialties: Mechanical engineering; Cryogenics. Home: 11211 Wood Lodge Houston TX 77077

SINGHVI, SAMPAT MANAKCHAND, pharmacist, researcher; b. India, Oct. 14, 1947; came to U.S., 1968, naturalized, 1971; s. Manakchand R. and Jayanta (Balai) S.; m. Usha S. Singhvi, July 17, 1971; children: Nikhil, Nilima. B.Pharm., Birla Inst. Tech. and Sci., Pilani, India, 1967; M.S., Phila. Coll. Pharmacy and Sci., 1970; Ph.D., SUNY, Buffalo, 1974; M.B.A., Rider Coll., 1979. Research investigator, Squibb Inst. Med. Research, Princeton, N.J., 1974-78, sr. research investigator, 1978-79, research group leader, 1979—. Contbr. articles on drug metabolism, biopharmaceutics, pharmacokinetics and pharm. analysis to profl. jours. Mem. Am. Pharm. Assn., Acad. Pharm. Scis., Am. Soc. Pharmacology and Exptl. Therapeutics, Drug Metabolism Discussion Group, Rho Chi. Current Work: Pharmacokinetics, pharmacodynamics, biopharmaceutics, and drug metabolism in animals and man. Subspecialty: Pharmacokinetics. Office: PO Box 4000 Princeton NJ 08540

SINHA, BIKASH KUMAR, mechanical engineer, researcher; b. Patna, Bihar, India, Dec. 14, 1947; came to U.S., 1970; s. Kedar Nath and Shanti S.; m. Asha Sinha, Jan. 14, 1976; children—Monica, Seema. B.Sc. with honors, St. Xavier's Coll., 1965; B.Tech. with honors, Indian Inst. Tech., Kharagpur, 1968; M.A. Sci., U. Toronto, 1970; Ph.D., Rensselaer Poly. Inst., Troy, N.Y., 1973. Postdoctoral fellow McGill U., Montreal, 1973-74; vis. asst. prof., sr. research assoc. Rensselaer Poly. Inst., 1975-79; mem. profl. staff, program leader Schlumberger-Doll Research, Ridgefield, Conn., 1979—. Contbr. articles to profl. jours. Patentee stress compensated quartz resonators, surface acoustic wave sensors. Mem. IEEE, Tau Beta Pi. Current work: Research interests include wave propagation in piezoelectric solids, electroacoustic devices for applications in the design of resonators, transducers, pressure and temperature sensors. Subspecialties: Theoretical and applied mechanics; Acoustics. Home: 39 Topledge Rd West Redding CT 06896 Office: Schlumberger-Doll Research Old Quarry Rd Ridgefield CT 06877

SINK, JOHN DAVIS, biochemist, educator, consultant; b. Homer City, Pa., Dec. 19, 1934; s. Aaron Tinstman and Lauella Bell (Davis) S.; m. Claire Kaye Huschka, June 13, 1964; children—Kara Joan, Karl John. B.S. in Animal-Vet. Sci., Pa. State U., 1956, M.S. in Biophysics, 1960, Ph.D. in Biochemsitry and Animal Sci., 1962; Ed.D., U. Pitts., 1985. Adminstrv. officer, exec. asst. to Pa. Sec. Agr., Harrisburg, 1962; prof., group leader depts. food, dairy and animal sci., Inst. Policy Research and Evaluation, Pa. State U., 1962-79; postdoctural fellow in biochemistry U. Wis.-Madison, 1965; joint planning, evaluation staff officer Sci. and Edn. Adminstrn., USDA, Washington, 1979-80; exec. asst., naval rep. to gov. and adj. gen. State of W.Va., Charleston, 1981-84; prof., chmn. animal and vet. sci. W.Va. U., Morgantown, 1980-82, prof., chmn. agrl. biochemistry, 1980-84, prof., chmn. food sci. and nutrition, 1980—; mem. nat. adv. council Nat. Commn. Higher Edn. Issues, 1980-82; mem. nat. adv. bd. Am. Security Council, 1981; cons. in field. Vice pres. Coll. Area Council Chs., 1966-69; active Central Pa. Heart Assn., 1969-79, Blair County-Altoona Council Civil Def., 1969-75, Centre Community Hosp. Corp., 1969-79; bd. dirs. Wesley Found., 1974-79, numerous others. Served to capt. USNR, 1956—. Recipient Dekalb Accomplishment award, 1952, Pa. Acad. Sci. Darbaker prize, 1967; U. Wis. fellow, 1964-65; Senatorial scholar, 1952-56; Pa. Meat Packers' Assn. scholar, 1958-62. Fellow Am. Inst. Chemists, AAAS, Inst. Food Technologists; mem. Am. Meat Sci. Assn. (bd. dirs. 1971-73, pres. 1974-75), W.Va. Cattleman's Assn. (bd. dirs. 1981-83), W.Va. Poultry Assn. (bd. dirs. 1980-83), Am. Assn. Higher Edn., Am. Assn. U. Adminstrs (editorial bd. jour. 1985), Biophys. Soc., Am. Chem. Soc., Acad. Polit. Sci., Am. Soc. Animal Sci. (editorial bd. jours. 1979-82), Soc. Research Adminstrs. (editorial bd. jour. 1982), U.S. Naval Inst. (life), Naval Res. Assn. (life), Res. Officers Assn. U.S. (life), Navy League U.S., Armed Forces Communications Electronics Assn., Sigma Xi, Phi Lambda Upsilon, numerous others. Democrat. Methodist. Lodges: Masons, Shriners, Elks. Current work: Muscle biology; growth biodynamics; science, technology and public policy; higher education administration. Subspecialties: Biochemistry (biology); Food science and technology. Home: PO Box 4275 Morgantown WV 26504 Office: W Va U PO Box 6108 Morgantown WV 26506-6108

SINKOVICS, JOSEPH G., oncologist, virologist, educator; b. Budapest, Hungary, June 17, 1924; came to U.S., 1956; s. Joseph and Maria (Rajnocha) S.; divorced (div.); children: Geza, Eszter. M.D., Petrus Pazmany U. Hungary, 1948. Diplomate: Am. Bd. Internal Medicine. Prof. medicine U. Tex.-M.D. Anderson Hosp., Houston, 1972-79, chief sect. tumor virology and immunology, 1968-79, cons. oncology, 1979—; prof. virology Baylor Coll. Medicine, Houston, 1980—, pvt. practice med. oncology, hematology, infectious diseases and internal medicine. Author: Die Grundlagen der Virusforschung, 1956, Medical Oncology, 1979, (with J.E. Harris) The Immunology of Malignant Disease, 1976; contbr. articles to profl. jours. Fellow ACP; mem. Am. Soc. Clin. Oncology, Am. Assn. Cancer Research, Am. Soc. Microbiology, Infectious Diseases Soc. Am., others. Club: Doctors (Houston). Current Work: Cancer immunology and immunotherapy. Cancer cell culture. Chemoimmunotherapy of human cancer. Subspecialties: Cancer research (medicine); Infectious diseases. Home: 2336 N Braeswood Blvd Houston TX 77030 Office: 909 Frostwood Suite 153 Houston TX 77024

SINSHEIMER, ROBERT LOUIS, university chancellor; b. Washington, Feb. 5, 1920; s. Allen and Rose (Davidson) S.; m. Flora Joan Hirsch, Aug. 8, 1943 (div. 1972); children—Lois Sinsheimer Wickstrom, Kathy Sinsheimer Vandegriff, Roger A.; m. Karen Current, Aug. 1, 1981. S.B., MIT, 1941, S.M., 1942, Ph.D., 1948; D.Sc. (hon.), St. Olaf Coll., 1974, Northwestern U., 1976. Research assoc. MIT, 1948-49; assoc. prof. Iowa State Coll., Ames, 1949-55, prof. biophysics, 1955-57, Calif. Inst. Tech., Pasadena, 1957-77, chmn. biology, 1968-77; chancellor U. Calif.-Santa Cruz, 1977—; cons. Sloan Found., N.Y.C. Contbr. over 200 articles to profl. jours. Named Calif. Scientist of Yr., 1968; recipient Beijerinck virology medal Royal Netherlands Acad. Scis., 1969. Mem. Nat. Acad. Scis. (chmn. procs. 1972-81), Jane Coffin Childs Meml. Fund for Med. Research (bd. dirs. 1974-82), Am. Acad. Arts and Scis. (pres. 1970-71), Biophys. Soc. Subspecialties: Molecular biology; Genetics and genetic engineering (biology). Office: Univ Calif 296 McHenry Library Santa Cruz CA 95064

SINTETOS, ANTHONY LEE, physician, physiologist; b. Washington, Jan. 26, 1953; s. Peter Theodore and Gloria Theresa (Pensiero) S.; B.S., U. Md., 1975; M.S. with distinction, Georgetown U., 1976, M.D., 1981, Ph.D., 1981. Diplomate Am. Bd. Internal Medicine. Intern, Duke Med. Ctr., Durham, N.C., 1981-82, resident, 1982, asst. chief resident, 1982-83, fellow in cardiology, 1983—; cardiology cons. Cabarrus Meml. Hosp., Concord, N.C., 1984—. Contbr. articles to profl. jours. NIH grantee, 1984. Mem. Am. Physiol. Soc., Am. Coll. Cardiology, AMA. Roman Catholic. Current work: Pursuing the description of the natural history of supraventricular tachycardias in humans and designing clinical therapies with novel antiarrhythmic agents. Subspecialties: Cardiology; Physiology (medicine). Home: 2106 Front St E2 Durham NC 27705 Office: Duke Univ Med Ctr Box 31114 Durham NC 27710

SIPPLE, WILLIAM STANTON, ecologist, educator; b. Camden, N.J., Nov. 16, 1939; s. Gordon Harris and Beulah (Stetser) S.; m. Geraldine Anne Ruggiano, June 18, 1966; children—Michael, Michele, Sean. B.S. in Biology, Glassboro State Coll., 1969; M.Regional Planning, U. Pa., 1971; Doctoral program plant ecology U. Md., 1973-78; natural resources planner Md. Dept. Natural Resources, Annapolis, 1971-79; instr. grad. sch. U.S. Dept. Agr., Washington, 1972—; ecologist U.S. EPA, Washington, 1979—; cons. in field. Contbr. articles to profl. jours. and chpts. to books. Mem. Ecol. Soc. Am., Nat. Assn. Environ. Profls., Soc. Wetland Scientists, Phila. Bot. Club, So. Appalachian Bot. Club, The Nature Conservancy, Audubon Wildlife Soc., Internat. Assn. Aquatic Plant Biologists, Sigma Xi. Current work: Plant taxonomy, wetland ecology, wetland management, wetland characterization and delineation. Subspecialties: Taxonomy; Ecology (biology). Home: 503 Benforest Dr Severna Park MD 21146 Office: US EPA 401 M St Washington DC 20460

SIRGY, MAGDY JOSEPH, marketing and psychology educator; b. Cairo, May 31, 1952; came to U.S., 1970, naturalized, 1972; s. Joseph Ibrahim and Odette Mikaheel (Hosni) S.; m. Karen Sue Cornett, Nov. 15, 1973; children—Melissa Jane, Danielle Odette. B.A. in Psychology, UCLA, 1974; M.A., Calif. State U., 1977; Ph.D., U. Mass., 1979. Interogator/interpreter U.S. Mil. Intelligence, Schofield, Hawaii, 1971-73; personnel analyst Calif. State Employment Dept., Los Angeles, 1975; teaching asst. Calif. State U.-Long Beach, 1975-77; teaching assoc. U. Mass., Amherst, 1977-79; asst. prof. Va. Poly. Inst. and State U., Blacksburg, 1979-85, assoc. prof., 1985—; research cons. Mktg. & Mgmt. Research Assocs., Greensboro, 1980. Author: Social Cognition and Consumer Behavior, 1983; Marketing as Social Behavior, 1984; Self-Congruity, 1985; contbr. articles to profl. jours. Served with U.S. Army, 1971-73. Va. Tech. Honors Program grantee, 1981; Va. Tech. Learning Resource Ctr. grantee, 1980-81; Calif. State U. scholar, 1979. Mem. Am. Psychol. Assn., Assn. Consumer Research, Acad. Mktg. Sci., Soc. General Systems Research, Am. Acad. Advt., Social Mktg. Assn. Current Work: Examination of personality variables (e.g. self-concept, achievement motivation) and other social psychol. variables in relation to economic behavior. Subspecialties: Social psychology; Consumer psychology. Home: 2102 Birch Leaf Ln Blacksburg VA 24060 Office: Va Poly Inst and State Univ Blacksburg VA 24061

SIRI, WILLIAM EMIL, energy analyst, consultant; b. Phila., Jan. 2, 1919; s. Emil M. and Caroline (Schaedel) S.; m. Margaret Jean Brandenburg, Dec. 3, 1949; children—Margaret Lynn, Ann Kathryn. B.S., U. Chgo., 1942; postgrad. U. Calif.-Berkeley, 1946-50. Registered profl. engr., Calif. Research engr. Baldwin Corp., Phila., 1942; staff physicist Lawrence Berkeley Lab., U. Calif.-Berkeley, 1943-73, sr. scientist, 1974-82, sr. scientist emeritus, 1982—; cons. in field, 1983—. Author: Isotopic Tracers and Nuclear Radiations, 1949. Contbr. articles to profl. jours., sci. papers on biophysics and energy analysis. Pres., Sierra Club, San Francisco, 1964-68, bd. dirs., 1954-74; pres. Save San Francisco Bay Assn., Berkeley, 1968—; bd. dirs. 7 other environ. orgns., 1964—. Recipient Hubbard medal Nat. Geog. Soc., 1963; cert. of merit Explorers Club, 1964; William E. Colby award Sierra Club, 1975; Sol Feinstone Environ. award SUNY, 1977. Mem. Am. Phys. Soc., Biophys. Soc., Am. Assn. Physicist in Medicine, AAAS, Sigma Xi. Democrat. Current work: Integrated energy analysis, energy conservation. Home: 1015 Leneve Pl El Cerrito CA 94530 Office: Lawrence Berkeley Lab U Calif Berkeley CA 94720

SIRICA, ALPHONSE EUGENE, cancer researcher, educator; b. Waterbury, Conn., Jan. 16, 1944; s. Alphonse Eugene and Elena Virginia (Mascolo) S.; m. Annette Marie Murray, June 9, 1984; 1 child, Gabrielle Theresa. B.A., St. Michaels Coll., Winooski Park, Vt., 1965; M.S., Fordham U., 1968; Ph.D. in Biomed. Scis, U. Conn., 1976. Research asso., supr. drug evaluation div. Microbiol. Assocs., Cancer Chemotherapy Research Lab., Bethesda, Md., 1969-71; postdoctoral trainee dept. oncology McArdle Lab. for Cancer Research, U. Wis.-Madison, 1976-79; asst. prof. anatomy and hepatic pathology U. Wis. Med. Sch., 1979-84; assoc. prof. pathology and internal medicine Med. Coll. Va./Va. Commonwealth U., 1984—. Contbr. articles to profl. jours. Nat. Cancer Inst. grantee, 1981-83, 84—. NIH grantee, 1981-84. Mem. AAAS, Am. Assn. Cancer Research, Am. Assn. Pathologists, N.Y. Acad. Scis., Tissue Culture Assn., Am. Soc. Cell Biology. Current Work: Chemical hepatocarcinogenesis, pathobiology of liver neoplasms, regulatory mechanisms controlling hepatocyte differentiation and proliferation, liver cell culture. Subspecialties: Cancer research (medicine); Pathology (medicine). Office: Med Edn Bldg Room 4019 Richmond VA 23298

SIRIGNANO, WILLIAM ALFONSO, aerospace and mechanical scientist; b. Bronx, N.Y., Apr. 14, 1938; s. Anthony P and Lucy (Caruso) S.; m. Molly Van Leeuwen, Oct. 29, 1966 (div. 1975); 1 dau., Monica Ann; m. Lynn Haisfield, Nov. 26, 1977; 1 dau., Jacqueline Hope. B.Aero.Engring., Rensselaer Poly. Inst., 1959; Ph.D., Princeton U., 1964. Mem. research staff Guggenheim Labs., aerospace, mech. scis. dept. Princeton U., 1964-67, asst. prof. aerospace and mech. scis., 1967-69, assoc. prof., 1969-73, prof., 1973-79, dept. dir. grad. studies, 1974-78; George Tallman Ladd prof., head dept. mech. engring. Carnegie-Mellon U., 1979-84; dean Sch. Engring., U. Calif., Irvine, 1985—; cons. industry and govt., 1966—; mem. emissions control panel Nat. Acad. Scis., 1971-73; lectr. and cons. NATO adv. group on aero. research and devel., 1967, 75, 80; mem. NASA Space Applications Adv. Com., 1985—; mem. acad. adv. council Indsl. Research Inst., 1985—; chmn. nat. and internat. tech. confs. Assoc. editor: Combustion Sci. and Tech, 1969-70; contbr. articles to nat. and internat. profl. jours., also research monographs. United Aircraft research fellow, 1973-74. Mem. Combustion Inst. (treas. internat. orgn. and chmn. Eastern sect.), Soc. Indsl. Applied Math., AIAA, ASME. Current Work: Turbulent reacting flows; spray combustion; fuel-droplet heating and vaporization; ignition, combustion of pulverized coal; combustion instability, fire safety. Subspecialties: Combustion processes; Fluid mechanics. Home: 3 Gibbs Ct Irvine CA 92715 Office: U Calif Irvine Sch Engring Irvine CA 92717

SISMANIS, ARISTIDES, otolaryngologist, educator; b. Athens, Greece, Nov. 6, 1949; came to U.S., 1973, naturalized, 1982; s. Dimitrios and Stella (Petropoulos) S.; m. Anna Rozaki, Mar. 10, 1974; children: Stamatina,

Dimitrios, John. M.D., Med. Sch. Athens, 1973. Intern. in gen. surgery Maimonides Hosp., Bklyn., 1973-74; resident in surgery Bklyn. Jewish Hosp., 1974-75; resident in otolaryngology L.I. Coll. Hosp., Bklyn., 1975-78; also Univ. Hosp., Jamaica Plains (N.Y.) VA Hosp.; fellow in head and neck surgery Boston U., 1978-79; fellow in otology and neurotology Otology Group, Nashville, 1979-80; assoc. prof. otolaryngology Med. Coll. Va. Hosp., Va. Commonwealth U., Richmond, 1980—. Contbr. numerous med. articles to profl. publs. Fellow ACS, Am. Acad. Otolaryngology; mem. AMA (Physician's Recognition award 1980, 82). Current Work: Otology, otorhinolaryngology. Subspecialty: Otorhinolaryngology. Home: 1917 Windingridge Dr Richmond VA 23233 Office: MCV Sta Box 146 Richmond VA 23298

SISSON, THOMAS RANDOLPH CLINTON, medical educator; b. Winnipeg, Man., Can., Jan. 22, 1920; s. Lorne Randolph Clinton and Edna (Wilson) S.; m. Shirley Anne Robson, May 5, 1945; children: Geoffrey R.L., Peter A.W., Paul C.R. A.B., Colgate U., 1941; M.D., Temple U., 1944. Diplomate: Am. Bd. Pediatrics. Intern St. John's Riverside Hosp., Yonkers, N.Y., 1944-45; resident U. Rochester Med. Center, 1946-48, sr. instr. pediatrics, obstetrics, 1953-59; asso. dir. clin. research Geigy Pharm., Ardsley, N.Y., 1960-64; asso. prof. pediatrics Albert Einstein Coll. Medicine, Bronx, 1959-65; assoc. prof. Loma Linda U., 1965-67; prof. pediatrics, dir. neonatal research Temple U., Phila., 1967-78; clin. prof. pediatrics Rutgers U., Piscataway, N.J., 1978—; prof. pediatrics UMD/N.J. Med. Sch., Newark, 1985—; chmn. dept. pediatrics Raritan Bay Health Service Corp., Perth Amboy, N.J., 1978-84; dir. neonatal research Newark Beth Israel Med. Ctr., 1984—; mem. com. on photobiology NAS/NRC, 1972-76; cons. NIH, 1972—. Contbr. articles to profl. jours.; editorial bd.: Clin. Pediatrics, 1976—. Served to comdr. USNR, 1950-52, 45-46, PTO. Buswell Faculty fellow, 1956-59. Fellow Am. Acad. Pediatrics, Am. Coll. Nutrition; mem. Am. Soc. Photobiology (councillor 1972-76), Soc. Pediatric Research, Am. Inst. Nutrition, Internat. Soc. Chronobiology, Am. Fedn. Clin. Research, Alpha Omega Alpha. Anglican. Current Work: Photobiology, iron and bilirubin metabolism, neonatal nutrition chronobiology Subspecialties: Neonatology; Nutrition (medicine). Address: Dept Pediatrics Newark Beth Israel Med Ctr 201 Lyons Ave Newark NJ 07112

SITES, KENNETH RONALD, electrical engineer, physicist; b. Waynesboro, Pa., July 7, 1939; s. Arthur Kenneth and Nellie Irene (Reid) S.; m. Sharon Ann Reynolds, Oct. 30, 1967 (div. Mar. 1973); children—Mitzi Kay, Dana Lee; m. Mary D. Mulkey, Mar. 19, 1973. B.S. in Physics, U. Nev.-Las Vegas, 1977. Electronics technician EGG Inc., Las Vegas, 1962-67, electronics engr., 1968-74; mgr. Nuclear Inst. div. Sci. Applications Internat. Corp., Las Vegas, 1975—. Mem. Republican Presdl. Task Force, Washington, 1983-84, Nat. Rep. Com., Washington, 1984. Served with USAF, 1957-61. Mem. IEEE, Instrument Soc. Am., Soc. of Photo-Optical Instrumentation Engrs. Presbyterian. Current work: Instrumentation and analysis of nuclear cratering dynamics, radiation effects in electronics systems, underground nuclear test programs, high explosives simulation test programs. Subspecialties: Nuclear physics; Electrical engineering. Home: 5353 Auborn Ave Las Vegas NV 89108 Office: Sci Applications Internat Corp 3351 S Highland Dr Suite 206 Las Vegas NV 89109

SIURU, WILLIAM DENNIS, JR., retired air force officer, engineering consultant; b. Detroit, Jan. 29, 1938; s. William D. and Bertha S. (Lindfors) S.; m. Nancy K. Watson, June 22, 1962; children: Brian, Andrea. B.S. in Mech. Engring, Wayne State U., 1960; M.S. in Aero. Engring, Air Force Inst. Tech., 1964; Ph.D., Ariz. State U., 1975. Registered profl. engr., Ohio, Colo. Commd. 2d lt. U.S. Air Force, 1960, advanced through grades to col., 1984; project engr. devel. planning (Air Force Space Div.), Los Angeles, 1964-68; chief space launch systems br. fgn. tech. div., Wright-Patterson AFB, Ohio, 1968-71; chief support tech br. Air Force Rocket Propulsion Lab., Edwards AFB, Calif., 1974-76; asst. prof. dept. engring. U.S. Mil. Acad., West Point, N.Y., 1976-79; comdr. Frank J Seiler Research Lab. (U.S. Air Force Acad.), Colo., 1979-83; dir. flight systems engring. Wright-Patterson AFB, Ohio, 1983—. Contbr. numerous articles on engring. to profl. jours. Decorated Legion of Merit. Mem. AIAA (sr.). Current Work: Consultant; freelance journalist. Subspecialties: Aeronautical engineering; Mechanical engineering.

SIVAK, ANDREW, life scis. mgr., researcher; b. New Brunswick, N.J., May 31, 1931; s. Andrew and Isabelle (Paragh) S.; m. Mary Margaret Donohue, May 24, 1958; children: Thomas, Gustav. B.S., Rutgers U., 1952, M.S., 1957, Ph.D., 1960. Staff biochemist Arthur D. Little, Inc., Cambridge, Mass., 1961-63, sr. staff, 1975-77, sect. mgr. bio/med. research tech., 1977—, v.p., 1979—; research dir. Bio/Dynamics, Inc., East Millstone, N.J., 1963-64; research assoc. Inst. Environ. Medicine, N.Y. U. Med. Ctr., 1964-68, asst. prof., 1968-71, assoc. prof., 1971-74; vis. lectr. M.I.T., 1975—. Contbr. articles to profl. jours. Served with USNR, 1952-72. USPHS fellow, 1960-61. Mem. Am. Coll. Toxicology, Am. Assn. Cancer Research, AAAS, Am. Soc. Cell Biology, Am. Soc. Microbiology, Environ. Mutagen Soc., Soc. Toxicology, Tissue Culture Assn., Sigma Xi. Current Work: Carcinogenesis, tumor promotion, genetic toxicology, risk assessment. Subspecialties: Cell biology; Toxicology (medicine). Office: Acorn Park Cambridge MA 02140

SIVERTSON, JOHN NEILOS, statistician; b. Everett, Mass., Dec. 28, 1915; s. John S. and Margaret S.; m. Annette Thurston, Apr. 20, 1939; children: Carol Sivertson Rooney, John N. B.A., Northeastern U., 1938; M.S., Rutgers U., 1972. Food chemist First Nat. Stores, Inc., Somerville, Mass., 1938-39; chemist Lever Bros. Co., Cambridge, Mass. and Balt., 1939-40, Am. Smelting & Refining Co., Balt., 1940-42; chemist So. Acid & Sulphur Co., Port Arthur, Tex., 1942-48, Memphis, 1942-48, Pasadena, Tex., 1942-48, Johnson & Johnson, New Brunswick, N.J., 1948-67, mgr. stats. and computer ops., 1967-79, cons., 1979—; assoc. J. A. Keane & Assocs., Princeton, N.J., 1979—; pres. Warren (N.J.) Statis. Services, 1982—. Pres. Edison Twp. Republican Club, 1960; v.p. Warren Twp. Bd. Health, 1963-67. Mem. Am. Chem. Soc., Am. Soc. Quality Control, Am. Statis. Assn., Biometric Soc. Current Work: Experimental design, computers in quality control; biostatistics, non-parametric statistics. Subspecialties: Statistics; Analytical chemistry. Address: 7 Katherine Dr RD 1 Warren NJ 07060

SIX, HOWARD RONALD, microbiology educator; b. Princeton, W.Va., Jan. 5, 1942; s. Howard Berkeley and June Joan (Pruitt) S.; m. Bobbye June Young, Feb. 14, 1964; children: Robert H., Kimberley G. B.A., David Lipscomb Coll., Nashville, 1963; Ph.D., Vanderbilt U., 1972. Postdoctoral fellow in pharmacology Washington U., St. Louis, 1972-74; research assoc. in molecular biology Vanderbilt U., Nashville, 1974-75; asst. prof. microbiology and immunology Baylor Coll. Medicine, Houston, 1975-82, assoc. prof., 1982—; adj. assoc. prof. immunology program U. Tex. Sch. Biomed. Scis., Houston, 1982—. Co-editor: Liposomes and Immunobiology, 1980; author articles. Mem. Am. Soc. for Microbiology, Am. Assn. Immunologists, Infectious Disease Soc. Am., Am. Assn. Virologists, Soc. for Exptl. Biology and Medicine. Current Work: Immunity to influenza virus; liposomes as adjuvants; antigenic variation, viral immunology, liposomes, immunobiology and vaccines. Subspecialties: Infectious diseases; Microbiology.

SIZEMORE, ROBERT CARLEN, immunologist; b. Lexington, Ky., Sept. 30, 1951; s. Dewey and Juanita (Peel) S. B.S. with honors, U. Ky., 1973, M.S., 1975; Ph.D., U. Louisville, 1982. Postdoctoral research assoc. U. Miss. Med. Ctr., Jackson, 1982-84; div. dir. cellular immunology II, Imreg Inc., New Orleans, 1984—; adj. asst. prof. Tulane U. Sch. Medicine, 1985—. Contbr. articles to profl. jours. Mem. Am. Soc. Tropical Medicine and Hygiene, Internat. Soc. Devel. and Comparative Immunology, Alpha Epsilon Delta. Current work: Immunoparasitology; comparative immunology; phylogeny of lymphocyte heterogeneity; immunomodulators from human white blood cells. Subspecialties: Immunology (medicine); Immunopharmacology. Office: Imreg Inc 144 Elk Pl Suite 1400 New Orleans LA 70112

SKALAFURIS, ANGELO JAMES, applied mathematician, engr., researcher; b. Pitts., Dec. 9, 1931; s. James Thomas and Katherine (Marinos) S.; m. Marie Consuelo Guerrero, Aug. 12, 1967 (div.); 1 child, Christopher. B.S., Ill. Inst. Tech., 1954; M.S., U. Chgo., 1958; Ph.D., Brandeis U., 1963. Registered profl. engr., N.Y., Pa., D.C. Research physicist U. Chgo., 1954-55; nuclear engr. G.L. Martin, Balt., 1956-57; ops. research analyst Caywood Schiller, Chgo., 1958; cons. Allied Research Assocs., Boston, 1959-60; research physicist Harvard Obs., 1960-63; Fulbright prof. U. Athens, U. Paris, 1963-64; research assoc. Space Inst., NASA, N.Y.C., 1965-66; prof. physics CCNY, 1967-69; prof. math. Bartol Research Found., Swarthmore, Pa., 1970-72; sr. research assoc. SUNY, Albany, 1972-74; sr. staff researcher Naval Research Lab., Washington, 1974—; chmn. bd. Modular Cogeneration Corp. Contbr. chpts. to books, articles to profl. jours. Nat. Acad. Scis. fellow, 1965-66. Mem. ASME, Am. Phys. Soc., Am. Astron. Soc. Current Work: Infra-red image processing, computor simulations, artificial intelligence, cogeneration and solar energy systems. Subspecialties: Systems engineering; Applied mathematics. Home: 2401 Calvert St NW Washington DC 20008 Office: Naval Research Lab Code 5307 Washington DC 20375

SKALAK, RICHARD, engineering educator; b. N.Y.C., Feb. 5, 1923; s. Rudolph and Anna (Tuma) S.; m. Anna Lesta Allison, Jan. 24, 1953; children—Steven, Thomas, Martha, Barbara. B.S., Columbia U., 1943, C.E., 1946, Ph.D., 1954. Registered profl. engr., N.Y. Instr. civil engring. Columbia U., N.Y.C., 1948-54, asst. prof., 1954-60, assoc. prof., 1960-64, prof., 1964-77, James Kip Finch prof. engring. mechanics, 1977—, dir. Bioengring. Inst., 1978—; dir. Am. Bur. Med. Research Advancement in China, 1979—. Editor Jour. Circulation Research, 1982—. Contbr. articles to profl. jours. Bd. dirs. Inst. Applied Biotech., Gothenburg, Sweden, 1976—. Served with USN, 1944-46. Recipient Great Tchr. award Columbia U., 1973. Fellow Am. Acad. Mechanics, ASME (editor jour., Centennial Service award 1980); mem. ASCE, Soc. Rheology, AAAS, Am. Heart Assn., Microcirculatory Soc., Soc. Engring. Sci. (bd. dirs. 1984—), Internat. Soc. Biorheology (editor jour.), Red Cell Club, Biomed. Engring. Soc. (bd. dirs. 1980-84), Cardiovascular System Dynamics Soc., Am. Soc. Engring. Edn., Am. Physiol. Soc., Internat. Assn. Hydraulic Research, N.Y. Acad. Scis., Sigma Xi, Tau Beta Pi. Current work: teaching and research in biomechanics. Subspecialty: Biomedical engineering. Home: 345 Magnolia Pl Leonia NJ 07605 Office: Columbia U 620 Mudd Bldg New York NY 10027

SKALKA, HAROLD WALTER, medical educator, ophthalmologist; b. N.Y.C., Aug. 22, 1941; s. Jack and Sylvia Skalka; m. Barbara Jean Herbert, Oct. 2, 1965; children—Jennifer, Gretchen, Kirsten. A.B. with distinction, Cornell U., 1962; M.D., NYU, 1966. Lic. physician, N.Y., Calif., Ala.; diplomate Am. Bd. Ophthalmology. Intern Greenwich Hosp., Conn., 1966-67; resident in ophthalmology Bellevue Hosp., Univ. Hosp., Manhattan VA Hosp., 1967-70; fellow in retinal physiology and ultrasonography NYU Med. Ctr., 1970-71; asst. prof. combined program in ophthalmology U. Ala. in Birmingham-Eye Found. Hosp., Birmingham, 1973-75, assoc. prof., 1975-80, prof., 1980—, acting chmn. combined program in ophthalmology, 1974-76, chmn., 1981—; assoc. prof. dept. medicine Sch. Medicine, U. Ala.-Birmingham, 1980—; mem. med. adv. com. Jefferson County System. Contbr. articles to profl. jours. Served to maj. M.C., USAF, 1971-73. Fellow ACS; mem. Am. Acad. Ophthalmology and Otolaryngology, AMA, Am. Inst. Ultrasound in Medicine, Internat. Soc. for Clin. Electrophysiology of Vision, Internat. Soc. on Metabolic Eye Disease, Assn. for Research in Vision and Opththalmology, AAUP, Am. IntraocularImplant Soc., Am. Assn. Ophthalmology, Pan Am. Assn. Ophthalmology, So. Med. Assn., Ala. Acad. Ophthalmology, Med. Assn. State Ala., Jefferson County Med. Soc., Contact Lens Assn. Ophthalmologists, Ala. Ultrasound Soc., Royal Soc. Medicine, N.Y. Acad. Scis., AAAS, Societas Internationalis pro Diagnostica Ultrasonica Ophthalmologia (regional rep. on exec. bd.), Ala. Wildlife Fedn., Ala. Sight Conservation Assn. Lodge: Lions. Current work: Evaluation of visual function; contrast sensitivity changes in disease states; metabolic cataracts and lens biochemistry. Office: 1720 University Blvd Birmingham AL 35233

SKARDA, ROMAN THOMAS, veterinary and anesthesiology educator; b. Bitterfeld, Germany, Mar. 9, 1944; s. Hubert Ludwig and Viktoria Catherina (Liska) S.; m. Nicole Coderey, Sept. 5, 1975; children: Michael, Amanda, Emmanuelle. Eidg Fachpreufung fuer Tieraerzte, U. Zurich, 1969, M., 1972, Habilitation, 1984. Diplomate Am. Coll. Vet. Anesthesiologists. Asst. prof. vet. anesthesiology Ohio State U., Columbus, 1975—; oberassistent U. Zurich, 1984. Contbr. articles to profl. jours., chpts. in textbooks. Served to capt., inf. Swiss Army, 1963-85. Recipient Rotary Found. award and postgrad. scholarship, 1974-75. Mem. Gruetli Soc., Internat. Orgn. Christian Businessmen, Phi Zeta., AVMA (autotutorial excellence award 1981), Am. Soc. Vet. Anesthesiology, Am. Assn. Equine Practitioners, Assn. Swiss Officers. Liberal. Roman Catholic. Club: Swiss Home Assn. Current Work: Local anesthesia in veterinary medicine, neuroanatomy, neurophysiology, pharmacology, spinal and epidural anesthesia in cows and horses, new techniques. Subspecialties: Veterinary anesthesiology; Anesthesiology. Home: 5048-K Cobblestone Dr Columbus OH 43220 Office: 1935 Coffey Rd Columbus OH 43210

SKARE, KEVIN LYNN, biochemical pharmacologist; b. Murray, Utah, May 19, 1954; s. Orville Marvin and Elaine Audrey (Anderson) S.; m. Julie Ann Wiklund, Aug. 22, 1981. B.S., U. Wyo., 1976; Ph.D., U. Wis., 1981. Staff scientist Procter and Gamble, Cin., 1981-84, group leader, 1984-85, sect. head, 1985—. Contbr. articles to profl. jours. Babcock fellow, 1977; U. Wis. fellow 1978, 79, 80. Mem. AAAS, Am. Chem. Soc., Ohio Valley Soc. Toxicology, N.Y. Acad. Sci., Sigma Xi, Phi Kappa Phi, Gamma Sigma Delta. Current work: Development of therapeutic approaches to arthritis and other inflammatory diseases; toxicological evaluation of experimental drugs. Subspecialties: Biochemistry (medicine); Toxicology (medicine). Home: 5971 Red Oak Dr Fairfield OH 45014 Office: Procter and Gamble Box 39175 Cincinnati OH 54247

SKELLEY, GEORGE CALVIN, JR., animal scientist, educator; b. Boise City, Okla., Jan. 28, 1937; s. George Calvin and Catherine Bell (May) S.; m. Aletha Clair Brown, June 22, 1958; children: Mary Laura, Martha Alice. B.S., Okla. Panhandle State U., 1958; M.A., U. Ky., 1960, Ph.D., 1963. Research assoc. U. Ky., 1958-62; asst. prof. animal sci. Clemson U., 1962-67, assoc. prof., 1967-72, prof., 1972—; cons. in field. Contbr. numerous articles, abstracts to profl. jours., 1962—; author numerous research series' publs., exptl. sta. circulars and bulls. Named to Honor Roll of Profs. Clemson U., 1981, 82. Mem. Am. Soc. Animal Sci. (cert. animal scientist), Am. Meat Sci. Assn., Inst. Food Technologists, Block and Bridle (hon.), Sigma Xi, Alpha Zeta (hon.), Gamma Sigma Delta. Republican. Methodist. Lodge: Kiwanis. Current Work: Nutrition and treatment of beef and pork on meat. Subspecialties: Animal nutrition; Food science and technology. Home: 112 Knight Circle Clemson SC 29631 Office: Dept Animal Sci Clemson U Clemson SC 29631

SKELTON, DENNIS LEE, optical systems engr.; b. Pontiac, Mich., June 17, 1951; s. Walter Kenneth and Phyllis Elaine (Walter) S. B.S., U. Mich., 1973; M.S., U. Colo., 1978. Observer Radio Astronomy Obs., U. Mich., Ann Arbor, 1974; research asst. Lab. for Atmospheric and Space Physics, U. Colo., Boulder, 1975-78; systems engr., electro-optics design (Ball Aerospace Systems Div.), Boulder, 1978-82; staff optical engr. optical systems engring. Itek Optical Systems, Lexington, Mass., 1982—. Mem. Am. Astron. Soc., Soc. Photo-optical Instrumentation Engrs. Methodist. Current Work: Solar physics, stellar atmospheres, radiative transfer, the design and operation of scientific instrumentation for aerospace applications. Subspecialties: Solar physics; Optical engineering.

SKINNER, BRIAN JOHN, educator, geologist; b. Wallaroo, South Australia, Dec. 15, 1928; came to U.S., 1958, naturalized 1963; s. Joshua Henry and Joyce Barbara Lloyd (Prince) S.; m. Helen Catherine Wild, Oct. 9, 1954; children—Adrienne Wild, Stephanie Wild, Thalassa Wild. B.Sc., U. Adelaide, Australia, 1950; A.M., Harvard U., 1952, Ph.D., 1955. Lectr. U. Adelaide, 1955-58; research geologist U.S. Geol. Survey, 1958-62, chief br. exptl. geochemistry and mineralogy, 1962-66; prof. geology and geophysics, chmn. dept. Yale U., New Haven, 1966-73, Eugene Higgins prof., 1972—; Hugh Exton McKinstry Meml. lectr. Harvard U., 1978; Alex L. du Toit lectr. Combined Socs. South Africa, 1979; Cecil H. and Ida Green lectr. U. B.C., 1983; Thayer Lindsley Meml. lectr. Soc. Econ. Geologists, 1983; Mem. exec. com. div. earth scis. NRC, 1966-69; chmn. com. mineral resources and the environment Nat. Acad. Scis.-NRC, 1973-75; mem. Lunar Sample Analysis Planning Team, 1968-70, Lunar Sci. Rev. Bd., 1971-72, U.S. Nat. Com. for Geochemistry, 1966-67, U.S. Nat. Com. for Geology, 1973-77; cons. Office Sci. and Tech. Policy, 1977-80, NSF, 1977—; dir. Econ. Geology Pub. Co.; Chmn. governing bd. Am. Jour. Sci., 1972—. Author: Earth Resources, 1969, 77, Man and the Ocean, 1973, Physical Geology, 1974, 77, Rocks and Rock Minerals, 1979; editor: Econ. Geology, 1969—, Oxford Univ. Press Monographs in Geological Sciences, 1979—; editorial bd.; Am. Scientist, 1974—. Trustee Hopkins Grammar Sch., 1978-83. Guggenheim fellow, 1970; recipient Disting. Contbns. award Assn. Earth Sci. Editors, 1979; Silver medal Soc. Econ. Geologists, 1981. Fellow Geol. Soc. Am. (pres. 1984-85, councillor 1976-78, chmn. spl. publs. com. 1980-81, chmn. com. on coms. 1983); mem. Geochem. Soc. (pres. 1972-73), Conn. Acad. Sci. and Engring. (div. chmn. 1978-80, council 1982—). Current work: Origin, distribution of, and exploration for mineral deposits; geochemistry of sulfide minerals. Subspecialties: Geochemistry; Mineralogy. Home: PO Box 894 Woodbury CT 06798

SKINNER, BURRHUS FREDERIC, psychologist, educator; b. Susquehanna, Pa., Mar. 20, 1904; s. William Arthur and Grace (Burrhus) S.; m. Yvonne Blue, Nov. 1, 1936; children—Julie (Mrs. Ernest Vargas), Deborah (Mrs. Barry Buzan). A.B., Hamilton Coll., 1926, Sc.D., 1951; M.A., Harvard, 1930, Ph.D., 1931; Sc.D., N.C. State U., 1960, U. Chgo., 1967, U. Mo., 1968, Alfred U., 1969, U. Exeter, Eng., 1969, Ind. U., 1970, McGill U., 1970, C.W. Post Center L.I. U., 1971, Dickinson Coll., 1972, Lowell Technol. Inst., 1974, Nasson Coll., 1976, Harvard U., 1985; Litt.D. (hon.), Ripon Coll., 1957, Tufts U., 1977; L.H.D., Rockford Coll., 1971, Framingham (Mass.) State Coll., 1972, U. Md.-Balt. County, 1973, New Coll., Hofstra U., 1974, Exptl. Coll. Inst. Behavioral Research, 1974, Johns Hopkins U., 1979; LL.D., Ohio Wesleyan U., 1971, Hobart and William Smith Coll., 1972, Western Mich. U., 1976; D.Soc.Sci., U. Louisville, 1977, D.Laws, Keio U., Tokyo, 1979. Research fellow NRC, Harvard, 1931-33; jr. fellow Harvard Soc. Fellows, 1933-36; instr. psychology U. Minn., Mpls., 1936-37, asst. prof., 1937-39, asso. prof., 1939-45; conducted war research sponsored by Gen. Mills, Inc., 1942-43; prof. psychology, chmn. dept. Ind. U., 1945-48; William James lectr. Harvard, 1947, prof. psychology, 1948-57, Edgar Pierce prof., 1958-74, prof. emeritus, 1974—. Author: Behavior of Organisms, 1938, Walden Two, 1948, Science and Human Behavior, 1953, Verbal Behavior, 1957, (with C.B. Ferster) Schedules of Reinforcement, 1957, Cumulative Record, 1959, rev. 1961, 72, (with J.G. Holland) The Analysis of Behavior, 1961, The Technology of Teaching, 1968, Contingencies of Reinforcement: A Theoretical Analysis, 1969, Beyond Freedom and Dignity, 1971, About Behaviorism, 1974, Particulars of My Life, 1976, Reflections on Behaviorism and Society, 1978, The Shaping of a Behaviorist, 1979, Notebooks, 1980; Enjoy Old Age, 1983; (with M.E. Vaughan) A Matter of Consequences, 1983; Upon Further Reflection, 1986. Recipient disting. sci. contbn. award, 1958, Nat. medal Sci., 1968, Gold medal Am. Psycol. Assn., 1971, Joseph P. Kennedy, Jr. Found. award, 1971; Guggenheim fellow, 1944-45. Fellow Royal Soc. Arts; mem. Am. Psychol. Assn., A.A.A.S., Nat. Acad. Sci., Am. Acad. Arts and Scis., Swedish, Brit., Spanish psychol. socs., Am. Phil. Soc., Phi Beta Kappa, Sigma Xi. Home: 13 Old Dee Rd Cambridge MA 02138

SKINNER, DANIEL ZOLEK, plant pathologist; b. Jackson, Mich., June 23, 1955; s. Lester Harvey and Stasia (Wszolek) S.; m. Julie Anne Knauer, Jan. 2, 1975; 1 child, Emily Elizabeth. B.A., St. Cloud State U., 1978; M.S., Kans. State U., 1983. Research technician Kans. State U., Manhattan, 1979—. Contbr. articles to profl. jours. Scholar biology dept. St. Cloud State U., 1977. Mem. Am. Phytopathol. Soc., Am. Genetic Assn., Phi Kappa Phi. Current work: Qualitative and quantitative host-parasite genetics, particularly with respect to effects of epistasis. Subspecialties: Plant genetics; Plant pathology. Home: 2122 Prairie Field Pl Manhattan KS 66502 Office: Dept Plant Pathology 404 Throckmorton Hall Kans State U Manhattan KS 66506

SKINNER, THOMAS PAUL, computer science educator, consultant; b. N.Y.C., May 17, 1944; s. Harold P. and Blanche A. (Schifferdecker) S.; m. Linda Joan Grillo, June 5, 1971; children—Kristin Lin, Erin Ann. S.B., MIT, 1966; M.S., Worcester Poly. Inst., 1978; Ph.D., Boston U., 1982. Mem. research staff MIT Project MAC, Cambridge, Mass., 1966-71; sr. engr. Urban Scis., Inc., Wellesley, Mass., 1971-72; treas., prin. engr. Systems of Security Inc., Boston, 1972-78; pres. Microcom Assocs., Framingham, Mass., 1978—; asst. prof. computer sci. Boston U., 1979—. Contbr. articles to profl. jours. Mem. IEEE, IEEE Computer Soc., Assn. Computing Machinery. Current Work: Microprocessor-based distributed systems; microprocessors; computing networks; distributed operating systems; personal computing; computer architecture systems. Subspecialties: Operating systems; Distributed systems and networks. Home: 15 Rolling Dr Framingham MA 01701 Office: Boston U 755 Commonwealth Ave Room B4 Boston MA 02215

SKIPSKI, VLADIMIR P(AVLOVICH), research biochemist, educator; b. Ugrojedy, Ukraine, Russia, Oct. 15, 1913; s. Pavel G. and Anna I. (Novickova) S.; m. Irene A. Lysloff, Sept. 5, 1959 (div.); 1 son: Pavel V. M.S. equivalent, Kiev State U., 1938; Ph.D. equivalent, Inst. Exptl. Biology and Pathology, Kiev, 1941; Ph.D., U. So. Calif., 1956. Research assoc. Kavir Research Inst., Santa Barbara, Calif., 1950-51; research assoc. Sloan Kettering Inst. Cancer Research, N.Y.C., 1956-59, assoc., 1960-69, asoc. mem., 1970-82, head lab., 1979-82; asst. prof. biochemistry Cornell U. Grad. Sch. Med. Scis., 1960-70, assoc. prof., 1970-82. Contbr. to books, articles in field. Swift and Co. fellow, 1951-56; Damen Runyen Meml. Fund for Cancer Research grantee, 1971-73; NIH grantee, 1974-82. Mem. Am. Soc. Biol. Chemists, Am. Physiol. Soc., Biochem. Soc. Gt. Britain, Soc. Gen. Physiologists, Am. Assn. Cancer Research, Harvey Soc., N.Y. Lipid Research Club, Soc. Complex Carbohydrates, AAAS, Sigma Xi. Greek Orthodox. Current Work: Effect of malignant tumors upon glycosphingolipid protiles in host blood serum; possible role of glycosphingolipids and glycoproteins in formation of metastases. Subspecialties: Biochemistry (biology); Cancer research (medicine). Home: 148 Wallace Ave Mount Verno NY 1055

SKLAR, JEFFREY L., biomedical research scientist. Asst. prof. dept. pathology Stanford U. Sch. Medicine, Calif. . Office: Stanford U Sch Medicine Dept Pathology Stanford CA 94305

SKOLNICK, PHIL, neuropharmacologist; b. N.Y.C., Feb. 26, 1947; s. David Louis and Gertrude (Gewirtzman) S. B.S. summa cum laude, L.I. U., 1968; Ph.D. in Pharmacology, George Washington U. Sch. Medicine, 1972. USPHS trainee in pharmacology/toxicology, 1968-71; teaching fellow George Washington U., 1971-72; staff fellow NIH, Bethesda, Md., 1972-75, sr. staff fellow, 1975-77, pharmacologist, sr. investigator, 1977-83, chief sect. neurobiology; 1983—; Am. Coll. Neuro-Psychopharmacology, Soc. Neurosci. nat. and internat. lectr. in field. Contbr. articles to profl. publs. Mem. Am. Soc. Pharmacology and Exptl. Therapeutics, Internat. Soc. Neurochemistry, Soc. Biol. Psychiatry (A.E. Bennett award 1980), Am. Coll. Neuro-psychopharmacology, Soc. Neurosci. Patentee (with S. Paul) radioreceptor assay for benzodiazepines in plasma; Solowey award in neuroscis., 1983; Disting. Service award Washington Acad. Scis., 1984; Inventor's award U.S. Dept. Commerce, 1984. Current Work: Investigation of neurochemical bases of anxiety and sleep disorders. Research on anxiety, sleep disorders, benzodiazepines, adenosine receptors, neurotransmitters. Subspecialties: Neuropharmacology; Psychopharmacology. Office: NIH Bldg 4 Room 212 Bethesda MD 20205

SKOLNIK, MERRILL I., electrical engineer; b. Balt., Nov. 6, 1927; s. Samuel and Mary (Baker) S.; m. Judith Magid, June 4, 1950; children—Norma Jean, Martin Allen, Julia Anne, Ellen Charlotte. B.Engring., Johns Hopkins U., 1947, M.S. in Engring., 1949, D.Eng., 1951. Research scientist Johns Hopkins U., Balt., 1947-54, vis. prof., 1973-74; engring. specialist Sylvania Electric, Boston, 1954; staff mem. MIT Lincoln Lab., Lexington, 1954-59; research mgr. Electronic Communications, Timonium, Md., 1959-64, Inst. Def. Analyses, Arlington, Va., 1964-65; supr. radar div. Naval Research Lab., Washington, 1965—; mem. bd. visitors Engring. Sch. Duke U., Durham, N.C., 1977—. Author: Introduction to Radar Systems, 1962, 2d edit., 1980, Radar Handbook, 1970. Recipient Heinrich Hertz premium Instn. Electronic and Radio Engrs., London, 1964, Disting. Civilian Service award U.S. Navy, 1982—; Disting. Alumnus award Johns Hopkins U., 1979; named to Soc. of Scholars, Johns Hopkins U., 1975. Fellow IEEE (Harry Diamond award 1983, Centennial award 1984). Current work: Radar, antennas, electronic systems, gaseous electronics. Subspecialties: Electronics; Systems engineering. Home: 8123 McDonogh Rd Baltimore MD 21208 Office: Naval Research Lab Radar Div Washington DC 20375

SKORYNA, STANLEY CONSTANTINE, b. Warsaw, Poland, Sept. 4, 1920; s. Constantine Gregory and Alexandra Lydia (Fabian) S.; m. Jane Marie Polud, Aug. 8, 1970 (dec.); children: Christopher, Richard, Elizabeth. M.D., U. Vienna, 1943; M.Sc., McGill U., 1950, Ph.D., 1963. With McGill U., 1947—; dir. Gastrointestinal Research Lab., 1959—, Rideau Inst. Advance Research Ctr. for Behavioral and Phys. Scis., Newboro, Ont., Can., 1969—; dir. med. expdn. to Easter Island, 1964-65. Author: Pathophysiology of Peptic Ulcer, 1964, Intestinal Absorption of Trace Elements, 1970, Handbook of Stable Strontium, 1981; creative works include Inside Mara, 1981, Rideau Lakes-A Ballet, 1982. Recipient Outstanding Citizenship award Montreal Citizenship Council, 1965; recipient Outstanding Achievement award McGill Grad. Soc., 1965; medalist in surgery Royal Coll. Physicians and Surgeons Can., 1957. Fellow ACS; mem. Can. Physiol. Soc., Am. Physiol. Soc., Am. Assn. Cancer Research, Can. Med. Assn., Soc. Exptl. Biology, Am. Gastroent. Assn. Roman

Catholic. Clubs: McGill Univ, Royal Montreal Curling. Current Work: Gastrointestinal pathophysiology; trace elements; alternate energy sources; cancer research. Subspecialties: Physiology (medicine); Surgery (veterinary medicine). Office: 740 Penfield Ave Donner Bldg McGill U Montreal PQ H3A 1A4 Canada

SKOTHEIM, TERJE ASBJORN, physicist; b. Molde, Norway, June 7, 1949; s. Ole and Liv Solveig (Rodal) S.; m. Ellen Dolsa, May 1, 1972; children: Jan Marcel, Suzanne. B.S., MIT, 1972; Ph.D., U. Calif.-Berkeley, 1979. Postdoctoral fellow CNRS-Meudon, France, 1979-80; vis. research scientist U. Linköping, Sweden, 1980-81; physicist Brookhaven Nat. Lab., Upton, N.Y., 1981—. Contbr. articles to profl. jours.; editor: Handbook of Conducting Polymers, 1984. Mem. Am. Phys. Soc., Norwegian Phys. Soc., Patentee in field. Current Work: Synthesis and characterization of highly conducting and semiconducting polymers, applications of conducting polymers to electronic and energy conversion devices and catalysis; surface science. Subspecialties: Polymers (materials science); Polymer physics. Office: Brookhaven Nat Lab Bldg 815 Upton NY 11772

SKURLA, GEORGE MARTIN, aerospace company executive; b. Newark, July 2, 1921; m. Marie Brignoli; children: George Martin, Thomas Michael, Martin John, James Mathew. B.S. in Aero. Engring., U. Mich., 1944; postgrad., Harvard U. Bus. Sch., 1973; D. Aviation Mgmt. (hon.), Embry-Riddle Aero. U., 1983. With Grumman Aerospace Corp., Bethpage, N.Y., 1944—, v.p., 1970-74, pres., chief operating officer, from 1974, chmn. bd., chief exec. officer, from 1976, now pres.; dir. Grumman Corp.; chmn. bd. Grumman Houston Corp., Grumman St. Augustine Corp., Grumman Tech. Services Inc.; dir. LITCO Bancorp., L.I. Trust Co. Mem. pres.'s adv. council for L.I. Poly. Inst. N.Y.; trustee Urban League of L.I., U.S.S. Intrepid Mus., Fla. Inst. Tech., Adelphi U., Nat. Aviation Mus. Found.; mem. nat. adv. council Ariz. Heart Inst.; bd. dirs. L.I. Assn., Air Force Acad. Found. Recipient Disting. Citizen award Suffolk County council Boy Scouts Am., 1977, Tree of Life award Jewish Nat. Fund, 1983; named Outstanding Man of Year in Aviation Mgmt. Roth Grad. Sch. Bus. Adminstrn., L.I. U., 1976; Disting. Citizen of Yr. Dowling Coll., 1980; recipient L.I. Tech. Leadership award Poly. Inst. N.Y., 1982. Fellow AIAA; mem. Soc. Logistics Engrs. (Founders medal 1977), Air Force Assn. (Ira Eakerfellow Iron Gate chpt. 1983, Man of Yr., H.H. Arnold chpt. 1975), Am. Def. Preparedness Assn. (exec. com.), Assn. U.S. Army, Nat. Space Club (bd. govs.), Assn. Nav. Aviation (dir.), Navy League U.S. (life). Subspecialty: Aerospace engineering and technology. Office: Grumman Aerospace Corp 1111 Stewart Ave Bethpage NY 11714

SKY-PECK, HOWARD H., biochemist, educator; b. London, July 24, 1923; s. Harry H. and Rebecca B. (Silverman) Sky-P.; m. Bernice Mogg, Dec. 20, 1952; children: Stephen, Kathryn, Constance. B.S., U. Calif., 1949; M.S., U. So. Calif., 1951, Ph.D., 1956. Asst. prof. U. Ill., 1958-62, assoc. prof., 1962-68, prof., 1968-71; dir. clin. chemistry Presbyn.-St. Luke's Hosp., Chgo., 1967-75, dir. cancer research lab., 1956-70; prof. biochemistry Rush Med. Coll., Chgo., 1971—, chmn. dept. biochemistry, 1971-80. Contbr. articles to profl. jours. Served to lt. col. U.S. Army, 1942-46. Am. Cancer Soc., Nat. Cancer Inst., NIH grantee. Mem. Nat. Acad. Clin. Biochemistry, Am. Assn. Cancer Research, AAAS, Internat. Union Against Cancer, Royal Soc. Medicine, Am. Assn. Clin. Chemistry, Sigma Xi. Democrat. Episcopalian. Current Work: Distribution of trace elements in human cancer tissues and their effect on genetic control of nucleic acids; comparison between normal and tumor subcellular distribution of trace elements and kinetics of biological function. Subspecialties: Biochemistry (medicine); Cancer research (medicine). Home: 187 Olmsted Rd Riverside IL 60546 Office: Dept Biochemistry Rush Med Coll Chicago IL 60612

SLACK, NELSON HOSKING, biostatistician; b. Burlington, Vt., Feb. 7, 1935; s. Errol Carlton and Ivy (Hosking) S.; m. Patricia Jane Billow, Sept. 10, 1960; children: Gregory and Gordon (twins), Brian. B.S., U. Vt., 1957; M.S., Rutgers U., 1963, Ph.D., 1964. Cancer research scientist Roswell Park Meml. Inst., Buffalo, 1964-67, sr. cancer research scientist, 1967-70, asso., 1970—, dep. dir. clin. trials nat. prostatic cancer project, 1977-84, staff dept. biomath., 1984—; asst. prof. Grad. Sch. RPMI div. SUNY, Buffalo, 1969—. Contbr. numerous articles to profl. jours. Served with U.S. Army, 1957-59. Recipient G. H. Waker prize U. Vt., 1957. Mem. Am. Statis. Assn., Soc. for Clin. Trials, AAAS, Sigma Xi. Current Work: Chemotherapy clin. trials; disease-related factors. Subspecialties: Statistics; Cancer research (medicine). Office: 666 Elm St Buffalo NY 14263

SLACK, STEPHEN THOMAS, med. physicist, radiation safety officer; b. Lawrence, Mass., Nov. 3, 1941; s. Kenneth Francis and Leona Gertrude (Hmurciak) S. B.A., Marist Coll., Poughkeepsie, N.Y., 1964; Ph.D., Pa. State U., 1974. Cert. therapeutic med. physics and diagnostic med. physics. Am. Bd. Radiology. Tchr. Central Catholic High Sch., Wheeling, W.Va., 1962-64; physics instr. Emmanuel Coll., Boston, 1972-74; postdoctoral fellow U. Calif., San Francisco, 1974-75; chief med. physics and radiation safety, assoc. prof. dept. radiology, radiation safety officer W.Va. U., Morgantown, 1977—. Active Common Cause. Mem. Am. Assn. Physicists in Medicine, Health Physics Soc., Am. Phys. Soc., Am. Assn. Physics Tchrs., AAAS. Democrat. Roman Catholic. Subspecialties: Medical physics; Radiation safety. Office: Dept Radiology WV Univ Med Center Morgantown WV 26506

SLADE, BERNARD NEWTON, electrical engineer; b. Sioux City, Iowa, Dec. 21, 1923; s. William Charles and Katherine (Slotsky) S.; m. Margot Friedlein, Aug. 18, 1946; children—Steven P., Eric J. B.S.E.E., U. Wis., 1948; M.S., Stevens Inst. Tech., 1954. Research devel. engr. RCA Corp., Harrison, N.J., Princeton, N.J., 1948-56; mgr. component product ops., then corp. dir. mfg. tech. IBM Corp., Armonk, N.Y., 1956-84; sr. cons. Arthur D. Little, Inc., Cambridge, Mass., 1984—; guest lectr. Harvard Bus. Sch., 1983—, Stanford U., 1984. Co-author: Winning the Productivity Race, 1985. Patentee in field. Contbr. articles to profl. jours. Served to 2d lt. AUS, 1943-46. Mem. IEEE (sr.), Sigma Xi. Current work: consulting in industrial productivity, development and manufacturing. Subspecialties: Semiconductors; Integrated circuits. Home: 12 Merry Hill Rd Poughkeepsie NY 12603 Office: Arthur D Little Inc Acorn Park Cambridge MA 02140

SLADEK, CELIA DAVIS, neuroscientist, educator; b. Denver, Mar. 25, 1944; d. C. Willard Davis and Mildred Davis TeSelle; m. John R. Sladek, Jr., May 23, 1970; children: Jonathan, Stefan, Jessica. B.A., Hastings (Nebr.) Coll., 1966; M.S., Northwestern U., 1968, Ph.D., 1971. Asst. prof. physiology U. Ill., 1970-73; research assoc. U. Rochester, N.Y., 1974-76, asst. prof. neurology, neurobiology and anatomy, 1976-80, assoc. prof., 1980—. Editor: Brain Research Bull, 1980—; mem. editorial adv. bd.: Peptides, 1980—; contbr. articles in field to profl. jours. Grantee Nat. Inst. Arthritis Metabolism, 1977—, Nat. Inst. Heart Lung, 1982—; recipient Research Career Devel. award Nat. Inst. Neurol. and Communicable Disorders and Stroke, 1977-82. Mem. N.Y. Acad. Sci., Neuroscience Soc., Am. Assn. Anatomists, Endocrine Soc. Current Work: Regulation of vasopressin and oxytocin release research using radioimmunoassay, organ and tissue culture and electrophysiological techniques. Subspecialties: Neuroendocrinology; Neuropharmacology. Office: 601 Elmwood Ave Rochester NY 14642

SLAMINSKI, JOHN MICHAEL, mechanical engineer; b. Tucson, Sept. 9, 1938; s. Harold Charles and Clara Elizabeth (Damron) S.; m. Dorothy Ann Cawthrone, Dec. 20, 1959; children—Cathi, Debra; m. Janet Marie Barrie, Sept. 1, 1984. B.S. in Mech. Engring., U. Ariz., 1961; M.S. in Mech. Engring., U. So. Calif., 1965; postgrad. UCLA, 1968-70. Registered profl. engr., N.Mex. Research engr. Rocketdyne div. Rockwell Internat. Corp., Canoga Park, Calif., 1961-71; br. chief EPA, Research Triangle Park, N.C., 1971-72; supr. Pub. Service Co. N.Mex., Albuquerque, 1972-75; energy program mgr. Naval Civil Engring. Lab., Port Hueneme, Calif., 1975-79; dep. project mgr. Solar Ten Megawatt Project, Barstow, Calif., 1979-83; program mgr. San Francisco ops. office Dept. Energy, 1983—; cons. in field; dir. Biomex Corp., Alpine, Calif. Inventor lightweight, low-cost solar collector. Basketball and track coach Newbury Park Athletic Assn., Calif., 1979-82. Served with USAF, 1958. Airesearch Mfg. Co. scholar, 1961; Rocketdyne fellow, 1969. Mem. ASME (tech. program chmn. 1979), Tau Beta Pi. Democrat. Roman Catholic. Current work: Space shuttle and other advanced liquid rocket engines; economically sound sulfur dioxide absorber system; ten megawatt solar electric power plant; tech. analysis of solar and wind energy systems. Subspecialties: Aerospace engineering and technology; Combustion processes. Home: 13567 Bear Valley Rd Moorpark CA 93021 Office: Dept Energy PO Box 1446 Canoga Park CA 91304

SLAUGHTER, JOHN BROOKS, university administrator; b. Topeka, Mar. 16, 1934; s. Reuben Brooks and Dora (Reeves) S.; m. Ida Bernice Johnson, Aug. 31, 1956; children—John Brooks, Jacqueline Michelle. Student, Washburn U., 1951-53; B.S.E.E., Kans. State U., 1956; M.S. in Engring, UCLA, 1961; Ph.D. in Engring. Scis, U. Calif., San Diego, 1971; D.Engring. (hon.), Rensselaer Poly. Inst., 1981, D.Sc. (hon.), U. So. Calif., 1981, Tuskegee Inst., 1981, U. Md., College Park, 1982, U. Notre Dame, 1982, U. Miami, 1983, U. Mass., 1983, Wayne State U., 1983, Eastern Mich. U., 1983, Tex. So. U., 1984. Registered profl. engr., Wash. Electronics engr. Gen. Dynamics Convair, San Diego, 1956-60; with Naval Electronics Lab. Center, San Diego, 1960-75, div. head, 1965-71, dept. head, 1971-75; dir. applied physics lab. U. Wash., 1975-77; asst. dir. NSF, Washington, 1977-79, dir., 1980-82; acad. v.p., provost Wash. State U., 1979-80; chancellor U. Md., College Park, 1982—; dir., vice chmn. San Diego Transit Corp., 1968-75; mem. com. on minorities in engring. Nat. Research Council, 1976-79; mem. Commn. on Pre-Coll. Edu. in Math., Sci., and Tech. Nat. Sci. Bd., 1982-83; dir. Monsanto Co., Balt. Gas and Electric. Editor: Jour. Computers and Elec. Engring, 1972—. Bd. dirs. San Diego Urban League, 1962-66, pres., 1964-66; mem. Pres.'s Com. on Nat. Medal Sci., 1979-80; trustee Rensselaer Poly. Inst., 1982; bd. dirs. Annenberg Sch. Communication, Corp. Pub. Broadcasting. Naval Electronics Lab Center fellow, 1969-70; Recipient Engring. Alumnus award UCLA, 1978; Disting. Service award NSF, 1979, Disting. Service in Engring. award Kans. State U., 1981; named UCLA Engring. Disting. Alumnus of Year, 1978, U. Calif.-San Diego Disting. Alumnus of Year, 1982, Disting. Alumnus, Washburn U., 1985. Fellow IEEE (chmn. com. on minority affairs 1976-80), AAAS (dir. 1983—); mem. Nat. Acad. Engring., Tau Beta Pi, Eta Kappa Nu, Alpha Phi Alpha. Subspecialties: Computer engineering; Control systems theory. Office: Univ of Maryland Office of Chancellor College Park MD 20742

SLAYTON, DONALD KENT, astronaut; b. Sparta, Wis., Mar. 1, 1924; s. Charles Sherman and Victoria Adelia (Larson) S.; m. Marjory Lunney, May 15, 1955 (div.); 1 son, Kent Sherman; m. Bobbie Osborn, Oct. 8, 1983. B.Aero. Engring., U. Minn., 1949; Sc.D. (hon.), Carthage Coll., 1960, D.Eng., Mich. Tech. Inst. Served to capt., pilot USAAF, 1942-46; engr. Boeing Aircraft Co., 1949-51; commd. capt. USAF, 1951, advanced to maj., 1959, resigned, 1963; fighter pilot, maintenance officer, Germany, 1952-55, fighter test pilot, Edwards AFB, Cal., 1955-59; joined Project Mercury, manned space flight, NASA, 1959, chief astronaut, 1962-63, dir. flight crew ops., 1963-74; mem. crew Apollo-Soyuz pilot docking module, 1975; mgr. Space Shuttle Approach and Landing Test, 1975-77, Space Shuttle Orbital Flight Test, 1978-82; pres. Space Services Inc., 1982—. Fellow Soc. Exptl. Test Pilots, AIAA, Am. Astronautical Soc.; mem. Order of Daedalians, Am. Fighter Aces, Houston C. of C. Current work: Aerospace engineering. Subspecialty: Aerospace engineering and technology. Office: 7015 Gulf Freeway Suite 140 Houston TX 77087

SLAYTON, MICHAEL HENRY, physicist; b. Moscow, May 10, 1947; came to U.S., 1979; s. Henry Boris and Rozalia M. (Rovinskaya) S.; m. Lana Assorova, Dec. 14, 1974; 1 child, Julia Michell. B.Sc., Kiev's State U. Russia, 1971, M.Sc., 1971; Ph.D., Paton's Research Inst. of Acad. Sci., Russia, 1978. Research engr. Paton's Research Inst., Kiev, 1968-71, group leader, 1972-78; chief project engr. Keramos, Inc., Indpls., 1979-82; v.p. research and devel. Etalon, Inc., Indpls., 1982—; pres. Ultrasound Devel., Indpls., 1982—; cons. Purdue U., West Lafayette, Ind., 1983—. Contbr. articles to profl. jours. Mem. IEEE, IEEE Sonic and Ultrasonic Group, Am. Soc. Nondestructive Testing, Ind. Soc. Ultrasound, Am. Inst. Ultrasound in Medicine. Club: Russian (pres. 1981-82). Current work: Research and development of ultrasonic transducers for medical imaging and non-destructive testing; development of ultrasonic instruments and systems for industrial and medical applications. Subspecialties: Acoustics; Ceramics. Home: 1726 Trace Ln Indianapolis IN 46260 Office: Etalon Inc 5332 W 79th St Indianapolis IN 46268

SLEMON, GORDON RICHARD, electrical engineering educator; b. Bowmanville, Ont., Can., Aug. 15, 1924; s. Milton Everitt and Selena (Johns) S.; m. Margaret Jean Matheson, July 9, 1949; children: Sally, Stephen, Mark, Jane. B.A.Sc., U. Toronto, 1946, M.A.Sc., 1948; D.I.C., Imperial Coll. Sci., London (Eng.) U., 1951, Ph.D., 1952, D.Sc., 1968. Asst. prof. elec. engring. N.S. Tech. Coll., Can., 1953-55; assoc. prof. U. Toronto, Ont., Can., 1955-63, prof., 1964—, chmn. dept. elec. engring., 1966-76; dean U. Toronto (Faculty of Applied Sci. and Engring.), 1979—; chmn. bd. Micro-electronics Devel. Ctr., 1984—; Colombo plan adviser, India, 1963-64; pres. Elec. Engring. Consociates, 1976-79. Author: (with J.M. Ham) Scientific Basis of Electrical Engineering, Magnetoelectric Devices, (with A. Straughen) Electric Machinery; (with Dewan and Straughen) Power Semiconductor Devices. Contbr. articles to profl. jours. Chmn. bd. Innovations Found., 1980—. Recipient excellence in teaching award Western Electric, 1965. Fellow Engring. Inst. Can., Inst. Elec. Engrs., IEEE; mem. Am. Soc. for Engring. Edn., others. Patentee in field. Current Work: Variable-speed drives for industry and transportation. Subspecialties: Electrical engineering; Electrical propulsion. Home: 40 Chatfield Dr Don Mills ON Canada Office: Faculty Applied Sci and Engring Univ Toronto Toronto ON Canada

SLEPIAN, DAVID, mathematician, communications engr.; b. Pitts., June 30, 1923; s. Joseph and Rose Grace (Myerson) S.; m. Janice Dorothea Berek, Apr. 18, 1950; children—Steven Louis, Don Joseph, Anne Maria. Student, U. Mich., 1941-43; M.A., Harvard U., 1947, Ph.D., 1949. With AT&T Bell Labs., Murray Hill, N.J., 1950-83, head math studies dept., 1970-83; prof. elec. engring. U. Hawaii, Honolulu, 1970-81; McKay prof. elec. engring. U. Calif., Berkeley, 1957-58, regents lectr., 1977. Contbr. articles to profl. jours. Served with U.S. Army, 1943-46. Fellow IEEE (Alexander Graham Bell award 1981), Inst. Math. Statistics, AAAS; mem. Nat. Acad. Scis. Nat. Acad. Engring., Soc. Indsl. and Applied Math. Patentee in field. Subspecialties: Probability; Electrical engineering. Home: 212 Summit Ave Summit NJ 07901

SLEVIN, JOHN THOMAS, neurologist, pharmacology educator; b. Parkersburg, W.Va., Dec. 15, 1948; s. John Marshall and Mary Belle (Kysor) S.; m. Barbara Nyere, June 26, 1971; children: John Robert, Amie Elizabeth. B.A., Johns Hopkins U., 1970; M.D., W.Va. U., 1975. Intern in medicine W.Va. U. Hosp., Morgantown, 1975-76; resident in neurology U. Va. Hosp., Charlottesville, 1976-79; fellow in neuropharmacology Johns Hopkins U., Balt., 1979-81; asst. prof. neurology U. Ky. Med. Ctr. Lexington, 1981, asst. prof. pharmacology, 1982—; staff neurologist VA Med. Ctr. Lexington, 1981; research assoc. Sanders Brown Multidisciplinary Ctr. Gerontology. NIH postdoctoral fellow, 1979-81; tchr.-investigator devel. awardee, 1982—; So. Med. Assn. med. student scholar, 1971-72; Klingman lectr. U. Va., 1983. Mem. Am. Acad. Neurology, AAAS, Soc. Neurosci., Sigma Xi. Current Work: Aging and development of the nervous system, epilepsy, excitatory amino acid neurotransmitters, neuropharmacology of the basal ganglia. Subspecialties: Neurology; Neuropharmacology. Home: 3317 Lyon Dr Lexington KY 40513 Office: Dept Neurology Univ Ky Med Center Lexington KY 40536

SLICHTER, CHARLES PENCE, physicist, educator; b. Ithaca, N.Y., Jan. 21, 1924; s. Sumner Huber and Ada (Pence) S.; m. Gertrude Thayer Almy, Aug. 23, 1952 (div. Sept. 1977); children: Sumner Pence, William Almy, Jacob Huber, Ann Thayer; m. Anne FitzGerald, June 7, 1980; children—Daniel H., David P. A.B., Harvard U., 1946, M.A., 1947; Ph.D., Harvard, 1949. Research asst. Underwater Explosives Research Lab., Woods Hole, Mass., 1943-46; mem. faculty U. Ill. at Urbana, 1949—, prof. physics, 1955—, prof. Center for Advanced Study, 1968—; Morris Loeb lectr. Harvard U., 1961; dir. Polaroid Co.; mem. Pres.'s Sci. Adv. Com., 1964-69, Com. on Nat. Medal Sci., 1969-74, Nat. Sci. Bd., 1975-84, Pres.'s Com. Sci. and Tech., 1976. Author: Principles of Magnetic Resonance, 1963, rev. edit., 1978; Contbr. articles to profl. jours. Mem. corp. Harvard U.; former trustee, mem. corp. Woods Hole Oceanographic Instn. Recipient Langmuir award Am. Phys. Soc., 1969; Alfred P. Sloan fellow, 1955-61. Mem. Nat. Acad. Scis., Am. Acad. Arts and Scis., Am. Philos. Soc. Current Work: Nuclear magnetic resonance, electron spin resonance, experimental solid state physics. Subspecialties: Condensed matter physics; Magnetic physics. Home: 61 Chestnut Ct Champaign IL 61821

SLICHTER, WILLIAM PENCE, chemist; b. Ithaca, N.Y., Mar. 31, 1922; s. Sumner Huber and Ada (Pence) S.; m. Ruth Kaple, June 17, 1950; children—Nancy, Carol, Catherine, Margaret. B.A., Harvard U., 1944, M.A., 1949, Ph.D., 1950. Mem. tech. staff Bell Telephone Labs., Murray Hill, N.J., 1950—, head chem. physics research dept., 1958-67, chem. dir., 1967-73, exec. dir. research-materials sci. and engring. div., 1973—; mem. adv. coms. Nat. Bur. Standards, NSF, NASA, Harvard U., Northwestern U., Dartmouth Coll., Rutgers U., SUNY, Albany. Served to lt. U.S. Army, 1943-46. Fellow Am. Phys. Soc. (award in high polymer physics 1970), Am. Acad. Arts and Scis.; mem. Nat. Acad. Engring., Am. Chem. Soc., Electrochem. Soc., AAAS, Sigma Xi. Research on molecular motion and structure in high polymers, nuclear magnetic resonance spectrosocopy. Subspecialties: Kinetics; Nuclear magnetic resonance. Home: 55 Van Doren Ave Chatham NJ 07928 Office: Bell Telephone Labs Murray Hill NJ 07974

SLIKKER, WILLIAM, JR., pharmacologist, toxicologist; b. Bakersfield, Calif., Apr. 3, 1950; s. William and Hazel Marie (Marchant) S.; m. Cristine Blozan, July 4, 1975; children—Annamarie, William III. B.A. in Biology, U. Calif., Santa Barbara, 1972, M.A. in Biol. Scis, 1974; Ph.D. in Pharmacology/-Toxicology, U. Calif., Davis, 1978. Jr. staff fellow drug research and evaluation program and perinatal research program Nat. Center for Toxicol. Research, FDA, USPHS, Jefferson, Ark., 1978-79, supervisory pharmacologist, pharmacodynamics br., div. reproductive and devel. toxicology, 1979—, acting br. chief pharmacodynamics br., 1979-80, chief, 1980—; adj. assoc. prof. dept. pharmacology and interdisciplinary toxicology and pediatrics U. Ark. for Med. Sci., Little Rock, 1980—; adj. assoc. prof. dept. medicinal chemistry U. Tenn., Memphis, 1982—. Contbr. articles to profl. jours. Recipient award for outstanding achievement in study of estrogen metabolism FDA, 1979. Mem. AAAS, Am. Soc. for Study Xenobiotics (charter), Am. Soc. Pharmacology and Exptl. Therapeutics. Current Work: Understanding the influence of metabolism and disposition of chems. on their resultant developmental toxicology; investigating estrogens, glucocorticoids and ethanol; developmental neuropharmacology/neurotoxicology and behavioral toxicology. Subspecialties: Pharmacology; Teratology. Office: Pharmacodynamics Br Div Teratogenesis Research Nat Center for Toxicological Research Jefferson AR 72079

SLINEY, DAVID HAMMOND, med. physicist; b. Washington, Feb. 21, 1941; s. David Xavier and Ida Lee (Echols) S.; m. Carol Ann Scott, Feb. 19, 1966; children: Sean Scott, David Scott, Stephen Paul. B.S. in Physics, Va. Poly. Inst. and State U., 1963; M.S. in Physics and Radiol. Health, Emory U., 1965. Chief laser br. laser microwave div. U.S. Army Environ. Hygiene Agy., Aberdeen Proving Ground, Md., 1965—; cons. to WHO, others. Author: (with M. Wolbarsht) Safety with Lasers and Other Optical Sources, 1980; editor: (with M. Wolbarsht) Health Physics Jour, 1976—; contbr. (with M. Wolbarsht) articles to profl. jours. Served to capt. Med. Service Corps U.S. Army, 1965-67. Fulbright fellow Yugoslavia, 1976; recipient decoration for meritorious civilian service Dept. of Army, 1978. Mem. Optical Soc. Am., Health Physics Soc., Laser Inst. Am. (chmn. laser safety com., dir.), Soc. Photo-optical Instrumentation Engrs., Am. Conf. on Govtl. Hygienists, Assn. for Research in Vision and Ophthalmology, others. Unitarian. Current Work: Evaluation of health hazards from lasers; establishment of safety standards for lasers and other optical sources; vision research and ocular effects of lasers. Subspecialties: Laser medicine; Biophysics (physics). Home: 406 Streamside Dr Fallston MD 21010 Office: Laser Microwave Div USAEHA Aberdeen Proving Ground MD 21010

SLOCUM, JONATHAN, machine translation investigator. Researcher Linguistics Research Ctr., U. Tex., Austin. Subspecialty: Automated language processing. Office: U Tex Linguistics Research Ctr Austin TX 78712

SLOMIANY, BRONISLAW LESZEK, biochemist, researcher; b. Wlodzimierz Wolynski, Poland, Dec. 12, 1941; came to U.S., 1966; s. Feliks and Eugenia (Murdzia) S.; m. Amalia Niewieczerzal, May 27, 1967; children: Lee, Beatrix, Mark. M.S., U. Lodz, 1966; Ph.D., N.Y. Med Coll., 1971. Postdotoral fellow Yeshiva U., 1971-72; research asst. prof. biochemistry N.Y. Med. Coll., Valhalla, 1972-74, research assoc. prof., 1974-78, research prof., 1979—; head gastroenterology research lab. Met. Hosp. N.Y. Med. Coll., 1979—. Contbr. articles sci. jours., chpts. to books. NIH research grantee, 1978, 81. Mem. Am. Soc. Biol. Chemists, Soc. Complex Carbodydrates, N.Y. Acad. Scis., AAAS. Roman Catholic. Current Work: Lipids, glycolipids, glycoproteins, mucous secretions, gastrointestinal tract, salivary secretions in health and disease. Subspecialties: Gastroenterology; Oral biology. Home: 130 Ridge Rd Rutherford NJ 07070 Office: New York Medical College Valhalla NY 10595

SLOWINSKI, DAVID ALLEN, software engineer; b. Willimantic, Conn., Sept. 1, 1953; s. Emil John, Jr. and Emily (Dayton) S. B.S. in Computer Sci., Mich. State U., 1976, M.S. in Computer Sci., 1980. Cert. data processor Inst. for Cert. Computer Profls. Systems analyst Burroughs Corp., Lansing, Mich., 1973-77; sr. software engr. Cray Research Inc., Chippewa Falls, Wis., 1977—; adj. instr. U. Wis.-Eau Claire, 1983—. Mem. IEEE, CAP (mission pilot 1982—). Current work: Operating system support for high performance I/O on supercomputers; optimization tools and methods for large applications programs. Subspecialties: Operating systems; Computer architecture. Home: Route 5 Box 583 Oakwood Pl Chippewa Falls WI 54729 Office: Cray Research Inc Hwy 178 N Chippewa Falls WI 54729

SLUTSKY, ROBERT ALLEN, cardiology and radiology educator, researcher; b. Bklyn., Jan. 22, 1949; s. Abraham Morris and Evelyn (Morris) S.; m. Elizabeth Cass, June 9, 1974; children: Anna Elizabeth, Nicholas Robert. B.A., Tufts U., 1970; M.D., UCLA, 1974. Diplomate: Am. Bd. Internal Medicine. Inter, resident in medicine U. Calif.-San Diego, 1974-77, research fellow in medicine, 1977-79, fellow in cardiology, 1979-81, asst. prof. medicine and radiology, 1981—; cons. radiology and medicine San Diego VA Med. Ctr., 1981—. Contbr. numerous articles profl. jours. Mem. Uptown Democratic Club, San Diego, 1982—. Grantee Am. Heart Assn.; Grantee Am. Lung Assn.; Grantee Distilled Spirits Council U.S.A. Fellow ACP, Am. Coll. Cardiology; mem. Radiol. Soc. N.Am., Soc. Nuclear Medicine, Am. Fedn. Clin. Research. Jewish. Current Work: Application of new imaging modalities to cardiopulmonary physiology. Subspecialties: Cardiology; Imaging technology. Home: 1913 Fort Stockton Dr San Diego CA 92103 Office: U Calif Med Sch 225 W Dickinson St San Diego CA 92103

SMAGORINSKY, JOSEPH, meteorologist; b. N.Y.C., Jan. 29, 1924; s. Nathan and Dinah (Azaroff) S.; m. Margaret Knoepfel, May 29, 1948; children: Anne, Peter, Teresa, Julia, Frederick. B.S., N.Y. U., 1947, M.S., 1948, Ph.D., 1953; Sc.D. (hon.), U. Munich, Ger., 1972. Research asst., instr. meteorology N.Y. U., 1946-48; with U.S. Weather Bur., 1948-50, 53-65, chief gen. circulation research sect., 1955-63; meteorologist Inst. Advanced Study, Princeton, N.J., 1950-53; acting dir. Inst. Atmospheric Scis., Environ. Scis. Services Adminstrn., Washington, 1965-66; dir. Geophys. Fluid Dynamics Lab., Environ. Scis. Services Adminstrn.-NOAA, Washington and Princeton, 1964-83; Vice chmn. U.S. Com. Global Atmospheric Research Program, Nat. Acad. Sci., 1967-73, 80—, officer, 1974-77, mem. climate bd., 1978—, chmn. com. on internat. climate programs, 1979, bd. internat. orgns. and programs, 1979-83, chmn. climate research com., 1981—; chmn. joint organizing com. Global Atmospheric Research Program, Internat. Council Sci. Unions/World Meteorol. Orgn., 1976—, officer, 1967—; chmn. Joint Sci. Com. World Climate Research Program, 1980-81; chmn. climate coordinating forum Internat. Council Sci. Unions, 1980-84; vis. lectr. with rank of prof. Princeton U., 1968-83, vis. sr. fellow, 1983—. Contbr. to profl. publns. Served to 1st lt. USAAF, 1943-46. Decorated Air medal; recipient Gold medal Dept. Commerce, 1966; award for sci. research and achievement Environ. Sci. Services Adminstrn., 1970; Buys Ballot Gold medal Royal Netherlands Acad. Arts and Scis., 1973; IMO prize and Gold medal World Meteorol. Orgn., 1974. Fellow Am. Meteorol. Soc. (pres.-elect 1985—, councilor 1974-77, asso. editor jour. 1965-74, Meisinger award 1967, Wexler Meml. lectr. 1969, Carl-Gustaf Rossby Research Gold medal 1972, Cleveland Abbe award for disting. service to atmospheric sci. 1980, presdl. award 1980, Symons meml. gold medal 1981); mem. Royal Meteorol. Soc. (Symons Meml. lectr. 1963). Current Work: Geophysical fluid dynamics and thermodynamics; geophysical applications of high speed computers; atmospheric general circulation and theory of climate; atmospheric predictability. Subspecialties: Climatology; Meteorology. Home: 21 Duffield Pl Princeton NJ 08540 Office: Geol and Geophys Scis Guyot Hall Princeton Univ Princeton NJ 08540

SMALE, JOHN GRAY, diversified industry executive; b. Listowel, Ont., Can., Aug. 1, 1927; s. Peter John and Vera Gladys (Gray) S.; m. Phyllis Anne Weaver, Sept. 2, 1950; children—John Gray, Catherine Anne Smale Caldemeyer, Lisa Beth, Peter McKee. B.S., Miami U., Oxford, Ohio, 1949, LL.D., 1979; LL.D., Kenyon Coll., Gambier, Ohio, 1974; D.Sc. (hon.), DePauw U., 1983; D.C.L., St. Augustine's Coll., 1985. With Vick Chem. Co., 1949-50, Bio-Research, Inc., N.Y.C., 1950-52; pres. Procter & Gamble Co., 1974—, dir., 1972—, chief exec., 1981—; mem. internat. council Morgan Guaranty Trust Co.; dir. Eastman Kodak Co., Gen. Motors Corp.; bd. dirs. Listed Co. Adv. Com., N.Y. Stock Exchange. Chmn. bd. dirs. United Negro Coll. Fund, United Way Am.; mem. nat. adv. bd. Goodwill Industries Am., Inc.; trustee Kenyon Coll., Cin. Inst. Fine Arts; mem. Cin. Bus. Com.; mem. Bus. and Profl. Friends

Com., Nat. Ctr. State Cts. Served with USNR, 1945-46. Mem. Grocery Mfrs. Am. (bd. dir.), Conf. Bd., Bus. Council (exec. com.), Bus. Roundtable. Clubs: Commercial, Commonwealth, Queen City, Cincinnati Country. . Office: PO Box 599 Cincinnati OH 45201

SMALL, HENRY GILBERT, information scientist; b. Chgo., June 17, 1941; s. Gilbert and Gladys (Quinn) S.; m. Lois Gootnick, July 3, 1971; 1 child, Matt. B.A. in Chemistry, U. Ill., 1963; M.A., U. Wis., 1966, Ph.D., 1971. Research assoc. Am. Inst. Physics, N.Y.C., 1969-70; acting dir. Ctr. for History of Physics, AIP, N.Y.C., 1971-72; dir. grant research Inst. for Sci. Info., Phila., 1972-80, dir. corp. research, 1980—; sr. fellow Hist. Sci., U. Pa., Phila., 1974-79; editor newsletter Soc. for Social Study of Sci., 1977-81; editorial bd. Scientometrics, 1979—. Editor compilation: Physics Citation Index: 1920-1929, 1980. Contbr. articles to profl. jours. Mem. sci. and arts com. Franklin Inst., 1985—. U. Wis. fellow, 1967-68. Mem. Am. Soc. Info. Sci., Soc. for Social Study of Sci. (council 1979-81), History of Sci. Soc., AAAS, Phi Beta Kappa. Current work: Information science, bibliometrics, citation analysis, knowledge bases, cognitive science, artificial intelligence, computer graphics. Home: 105 Rolling Rd Bala Cynwyd PA 19004 Office: Inst for Sci Info 3501 Market St Philadelphia PA 19104

SMALLEY, LARRY LEE, physics educator; b. Grand Island, Nebr., Aug. 7, 1937; s. Lionel Mullen and Grace B. (Reinecke) S.; m. Katherine F. Davenport, Nov. 16, 1957; children: Larry L, Daco S., Audrey M. B.S., U. Nebr., 1959, M.S., 1964, Ph.D., 1967. Grad. asst. U. Nebr., Lincoln, 1962-67; nuclear engr., Hallam Nuclear Power Facility, Nebr., 1964; faculty U. Ala., Huntsville, 1967—, prof. physics, 1980—, chmn. dept., 1972-85; space scientist NASA-Marshall Space Flight Ctr., Huntsville, 1979—. Contbr. articles to profl. jours. Served to lt. USN, 1959-62. Nat. Acad. Sci./NRC sr. research assoc. NASA, 1974-75; Humboldt fellow, 1977-78. Mem. Am. Phys. Soc., Sigma Xi, Pi Mu Epsilon, Phi Sigma Iota. Current Work: Extensions of general relativity to microscopic spacetime; gauge theories of gravitation; discrete geometry; post-Newtonian approximations. Subspecialties: Relativity and gravitation; Cosmology. Office: Dept Physics U Ala Huntsville AL 35899

SMALLWOOD, DONALD LEE, mechanical engineer; b. Scott County, Va., Oct. 22, 1940; s. Robert Lee and Della Mae (Vineyard) W.; m. EllaWeis Davis, Nov. 24, 1967; 1 dau., Natoka Lee. B.S.M.E., U. Cin., 1977. Registered profl. engr., Ohio, Ky., Fla., Wash. Electronic designer PMC Designing, Cin., 1965-67; designer Dover Corp., Cin., 1967-73; sr. engr. Xomox Corp., Cin., 1973—. Patentee flapper check valve; flotation check valve. Apptd. Ky. State Adv. Panel for Exceptional Children, 1978-81; mem. Louisville Dept. Advocacy Com., 1978-79. Mem. ASME, ASTM. Baptist. Clubs: Greater Cincinnati Amateur Radio, No. Ky. Amateur Radio. Lodge: Masons. Current work: Devices to permit the physically impaired to drive an auto by other than hand controls; developed method of seismically qualifying large overhanging valve actuator masses; designed special wheelchair front platform. Subspecialties: Mechanical engineering; Rehabilitation Engineering. Home: 2282 Galaxy Dr Fort Mitchell KY 41017 Office: Xomox Corp 4444 Cooper Rd Cincinnati OH 45242

SMARR, LARRY LEE, astrophysicist, computer center director; b. Columbia, Mo., Oct. 16, 1948; m. 1973; 2 children. B.A., U. Mo., 1970, M.S., 1970; M.S., Stanford U., 1972; Ph.D. in Physics, U. Tex., 1975. Lectr. astrophysics, dept. astrophys. sci. Princeton U., 1974-75, research asst. Obs., 1975-76; research affiliate dept physics Yale U., 1978-79; jr. fellow dept. physics and astronomy Harvard Soc. Fellows, 1976-79; asst. prof. depts. astronomy and physics U. Ill., Urbana, 1979-81, assoc. prof., 1981-85, prof., 1985—; dir. Nat. Ctr. for Supercomputing Applications, 1985—; physicist B Div. Lawrence Livermore Nat. Lab., 1976-79, cons. 1976—; vis. fellow Cambridge U., 1978. Assoc. editor Jour. Computing Physics, 1977-80. Alfred P. Sloan fellow, 1980-84; Max Planck Inst. for Physics and Astrophysics fellow, 1982, 83. Subspecialty: High energy astrophysics. Office: U Ill Nat Ctr for Supercomputing Applications Urbana IL 61801

SMIKA, DARRYL EUGENE, soil scientist; B. Hill City, Kans., July 1, 1933; s. Fred and Verna Marie (Tuttle) S.; m. Darlene Faye Wilson, Aug. 16, 1956 (div.); children—Rejeana, Thayne, Lavona, Tava. B.S., Kans. State U., 1956, M.S., 1956, Ph.D., 1969. Farm planner Soil Conservation Service, Dept. Agr., Lakin, Kans., 1956-57; soil scientist Agrl. Research Service, Dept. Agr., Mandan, N.D., 1957-60, North Platte, Nebr., 1961-73, Akron, Colo., 1973—, research leader, 1979—. Recipient cert. of merit Dept. Agr., 1982; Disting. Service award Gt. Plains Agrl. Council, 1984. Fellow Am. Inst. Chemists; mem. Am. Soc. Agronomy, Can. Soc. Soil Sci., Soil Sci. Soc. Am. (chmn. div. 6 1984), Soil Conservation Soc. Am. (commendation award 1981, pres. Colo. chpt. 1984), Internat. Soil Tillage Research Orgn., C. of C. Akron. Methodist. Lodge: Lions (pres. Akron 1978-79), Masons. Current work: Soil and water conservation management for crop production in no-till systems. Subspecialties: Soil science; Agronomy. Office: Central Great Plains Research Station 40335 County Rd GG Akron CO 80720

SMILEY, CHARLES JACK, geologist, educator; b. Mt. Vernon, Wash., Dec. 2, 1924; s. Charley and Julia Carolina (Watson) S.; m. Marguerite Clayton, Aug. 24, 1954; children: John, Sharifah. B.A., Western Wash. Coll., 1951; Ph.D., U. Calif.-Berkeley, 1960, M.A., 1954. Asst. prof. geology Macalester Coll., St. Paul, 1956-61; fellow Harvard U., 1961-62; asst. prof. geology U. Idaho, Moscow, 1962-65, assoc. prof., 1965-67, prof., 1967—; assoc. dean U. Idaho (Coll. Mines and Earth Resources), 1976-80; dir. U. Idaho (Tertiary Research Ctr.), 1980—; investigator in No. Alaska Arctic Inst. N.Am./U.S. Office Naval Research, 1956-67; lectr. Author: The Ellensburg Flora of Washington, 1963; Editor, contbr.: Later Cenozoic History of the Pacific North west, 1985; contbr. articles to sci. jours. Served in USN, 1943-47, 51-52. NSF fellow, 1954-55; Fulbright prof. U. Malaya, Kuala Lumpur, 1968-69; NSF vis. scientist Japan, 1973; research assoc. U. Calif. Mus. Palentology, Berkeley, 1985—. Mem. Am. Assn. Petroleum Geologists, Explorers Club, Bot. Soc. Am., Paleobot. Soc., Geol. Soc. Am., AAAS (adv. bd. Pacific div. 1983—), Sigma Xi. Phi, Kappa Phi. Current Work: Cretaceous and tertiary floras: taxonomy, systematics, biostratigraphy, paleoecology; research and consulting on Cretaceous floras of western North America; research on Miocene Clarkia compression flora of northern Idaho. Subspecialties: Paleontology; Evolutionary biology. Home: 2100 Robinson Lake Rd Moscow ID 83843 Office: U Idaho Moscow ID 83843

SMILEY, PARKER CLARK, mechanical engineer; b. Boone, Iowa, Oct. 17, 1931; s. Paul Parsons and Ruth Louise (Clark) S.; m. Dorothy Jean Strader, July 18, 1959; children: Scott Parker, Kevin David. B.S., U. Calif.-Berkeley, 1959, M. Engring., 1960. Mech. engr. Lawrence Livermore (Calif.) Nat. Lab., 1960-65; mech. engr. Physics Internat. Co., San Leandro, Calif., 1965-67, sr. mech. engr., 1967-81, sr. staff engr., 1981—. Contbr. articles to profl. jours., confs. Served with USN, 1951-55. Mem. ASME. Patentee temperature compensated hydraulic valve, lever motion multiplier driven by electroexpansive material, spring diaphragm, pump systems. Current Work: Piezoelectric actuators; ceramics; plastics; mechanical design and development of vacuum tubes for high voltage electron accelerators. Subspecialties: Biomedical engineering; Ceramic engineering. Home: 6693 Saroni Dr Oakland CA 94611 Office: 2700 Merced St San Leandro CA 94577

SMILEY, TERAH LEROY, geosciences educator; b. Oak Hill, Kans., Aug. 21, 1914; s. Terah Edward and Frances Angelina (Huls) S.; m. Marie Lemley, July 1935; 1 dau., Terrie Lucille Scheele; m. Winifred Whiting Lindsay, June 10, 1947; children: John, Maureen, Kathlyn; 1 stepdau., Margaret Ann Taylor. Student, U. Kans., 1934-36; M.A., U. Ariz., 1949. With U.S. Nat. Park Service, 1939-41, U.S. Immigration Service, 1941-42; research Lab. of Tree-Ring, U. Ariz., Tucson, 1946-60, dir., 1958-60, dir. geochronology labs., 1957-67, head dept. geochronology, 1967-70, prof. geosciences, 1970-83; Gen. chmn. Internat. Conf. on Forest Tree Growth, Tucson, 1960; vice chmn. U.S. Com. on Internat. Assn. for Quaternary Research, Nat. Acad. Sci., 1961-66; gen. chmn. First Internat. Conf. on Palynology, Tucson, 1962; mem. U.S. Com. on Internat. Hydrological Decade, Nat. Acad. Sci., 1964-66; gen. chmn. Internat. Conf. on Arid Lands, Tucson, 1969. Editor: (with James H. Zumberge) Polar Deserts and Modern Man, 1974, The Geological Story of the World's Deserts, 1982; co-editor, contbr.: Landscapes of Arizona: The Geological Story, 1984. Contbr. articles to profl. jours. Served with USNR, 1942-45. Research fellow Clare Coll., Cambridge, U., 1970; vis. prof. Kvartärgeologiska Institutionen, Uppsala (Sweden) U., 1970-71; hon. v.p. 2d Internat. Conf. on Palynology, Utretch, 1966. Fellow Geol. Soc. Am., AAAS, Ariz. Acad. Sci.; mem. Am. Meteorol. Soc., Tree-Ring Soc., Ariz. Geol. Soc. (past pres.), Ariz. Archeol. Soc. (past pres.), Sigma Xi. Current Work: Role of geology in past climates; geological story of world's deserts , formation of landscapes in Arizonas. Home: 2732 N Gill Ave Tucson AZ 85719

SMITH, ALBERT CHARLES, biologist; b. Springfield, Mass., Apr. 5, 1906; s. Henry Joseph and Jeanette Rose (Machol) S.; m. Nina Grönstrand, June 15, 1935; children: Katherine (Mrs. L.J. Campbell), Michael Alexis; m. Emma van Ginneken, Aug. 1, 1966. A.B., Columbia U., 1926, Ph.D., 1933. Asst. curator N.Y. Bot. Garden, 1928-31, asso. curator, 1931-40; curator herbarium Arnold Arboretum of Harvard U., 1940-48; curator div. phanerogams U.S. Nat. Mus., Smithsonian Instn., 1948-56; program dir. systematic biology NSF, 1956-58; dir. Mus. of Natural History, Smithsonian Instn., 1958-62, asst. sec., 1962-63; prof. botany, dir. research U. Hawaii, Honolulu, 1963-65, Gerrit Parmile Wilder prof. botany, 1965-70, prof. emeritus, 1970—; Ray Ethan Torrey prof. botany U. Mass., Amherst, 1970-76, prof. emeritus, 1976—; editorial cons. Pacific Tropical Bot. Garden, Hawaii, 1977—; bot. expdns., Colombia, Peru, Brazil, Brit. Guiana, Fiji, West Indies, 1926-69; del. Internat. Bot. Congresses, Amsterdam, 1935, Stockholm, 1950; v.p. systematic sect., Montreal, 1959, Internat. Zool. Congress, London, 1958. Author: Flora Vitiensis Nova: a New Flora of Fiji, Vol. I, 1979, Vol. II, 1981, Vol. III, 1985; also tech. articles.; Editor: Brittonia, 1935-40, Jour. Arnold Arboretum, 1941-48, Sargentia, 1942-48, Allertonia, 1977—; editoral com.: International Code Botanical Nomenclature, 1954-64. Bishop Museum fellow Yale U., 1933-34; Guggenheim fellow, 1946-47; Robert Allerton award for excellence in tropical botany, 1979. Fellow Am. Acad. Arts and Scis., Linnean Soc. London; mem. Bot. Soc. Am., Assn. Tropical Biology (pres. 1967-68), Internat. Assn. Plant Taxonomy (v.p. 1959-64), Nat. Acad. Scis., Fiji Soc. (hon.). Club: Washington Biologists' Field (pres. 1962-64). Current Work: Angiosperm flora of southwestern pacific; evolution and phytogeography of angiosperms. Subspecialties: Evolutionary biology; Systematics. Office: Dept of Botany Univ of Hawaii Honolulu HI 96822

SMITH, BARRY HAMILTON, neurosurgeon, neuro-oncologist, neuroscience researcher, medical foundation director; b. Orange, N.J., Oct. 6, 1943; s. Kenneth Wright and Harriet Kathryn (Barr) S.; m. Carley Eldredge, Dec. 18, 1969; children: Christopher, Sara. B.A., Harvard U., 1965; Ph.D. (NIMH fellow), M.I.T., 1968; M.D. (Life Ins. Med. Research Fund med. scientist fellow), Cornell U., 1972. Intern N.Y. Hosp., N.Y.C., 1971-72, asst. resident and fellow in surgery, 1972-75, asst. resident and fellow in neurosurgery, 1973-75; staff scientist neuroscis. research program M.I.T., 1975, program dir., 1976-78; resident in neurosurgery Mass. Gen. Hosp., Boston, 1975-78; dep. chief surg. neurology br. Nat. Inst. Neurol. Communicative Disorders and Stroke, Bethesda, Md., 1976-77, dep. chief, 1978-83; neurosurgeon, mem. Sloan Kettering Cancer Ctr., 1983-85; med. dir. Dreyfus Med. Found., 1983—. Contbr. articles to sci. publs. Served with USPHS, 1978-83. Recipient EEO award Nat. Inst. Neurol. Communicative Disorders and Stroke, 1980; Commendation medal USPHS, 1982; ACS Schering scholar, 1975. Mem. AAAS, AMA, Soc. for Neurosci., Electron Microscopy Soc. Am., Internat. Brain Research Orgn., N.Y. Acad. Scis., Phi Beta Kappa, Sigma Xi, Alpha Omega Alpha. Current Work: Neurooncology; cellular growth control and differentiation; image analysis; chemotherapy agent evaluation; neuronal regeneration. Subspecialties: Neurosurgery; Cancer research (medicine). Home: 40 E 94th St New York NY 10128 Office: Dreyfus Med Found 767 5th Ave New York NY 10021

SMITH, BRADFORD A., astronomer. Prof. dept. planetary sci. U. Ariz., Tucson. Subspecialty: Planetary science. Office: U Ariz Dept Planetary Sci Tucson AZ 85721

SMITH, BRUCE DAVID, archaeologist; b. Iowa City, Iowa, Mar. 24, 1946; s. Goldwin Albert and Emily Corina (Bateman) S.; m. Martha Mary Johnson, Sept. 22, 1973; children—David Vernon, Jonathan Oliver. A.B., U. Mich., 1968, M.A., 1970, Ph.D., 1973. Asst. prof. Loyola U. Chgo., 1973-74, U. Ga., Athens, 1974-77; assoc. curator Nat. Mus. Natural History, Smithsonian Instn., Washington, 1977-81, curator, 1981—; pres. Southeastern Archaeol. Conf., 1981-83. Author: Prehistoric Patterns of Human Behavior, 1978; Mississippian Exploitation of Animals, 1975. Editor: Mississippian Settlement Patterns, 1978; Mississippian Emergencies, 1985. Mem. Soc. Am. Archaeology (sec.), AAAS, Soc. for Ethnobiology, Southeastern Archaeol. Conf. Current work: Origins of agriculture in eastern N.Am.; origins of ranked agricultural societies in eastern U.S.; prehistoric subsistence and settlement patterns. Subspecialty: Paleobiology. Home: 2404 Daphne Ln Alexandria VA 22306 Office: Anthropology/Nat Mus Natural History Smithsonian Instn Washington DC 20560

SMITH, C. WILLIAM, engineering educator; b. Christiansburg, Va., Jan. 1, 1926; s. Robert Floyd and Ollie May (Surface) S.; m. Doris Burton, Sept. 9, 1950; children: Terry J., David B. B.S. in Civil Engring, Va. Poly. Inst., 1946, M.S., 1949. Registered profl. engr., Va. Teaching fellow Va. Poly. Inst. and State U., Blacksburg, 1947, instr., 1948, asst. prof., 1949-53, assoc. prof., 1954-58, prof., 1958-81, alumni disting. prof., 1981—; cons. Kollmorgen Corp., Redstone Arsenal, Western Electric Co., Brunswick Corp., Am.-Marietta Corp., Radford Arsenal, Litton Industries, Rubatex Inc., Masonite Corp., W.Va. Paper & Pulp Co. Editor: Fracture Mechanics, Vol. II; regional editor Internat. Jour. Theoretical and Applied Fracture Mechanics. Contbr. numerous articles to tech. jours.; chpts. to books. NSF grantee, 1976—; NASA grantee, 1973-76; Dept. Def. grantee, 1968-78; Oak Ridge Nat. Lab. grantee, 1975-78; Delft U. Tech. grantee, 1976-78. Fellow Soc. Exptl. Stress Analysis; mem. ASME, Soc. Exptl. Stress Analysis, Soc. Engring. Sci., Am. Soc. Engring. Edn., ASTM, Internat. Assn. Structural Mechanics in Reactor Tech. Christian. Current Work: Application of optical methods to three dimensional cracked body problems. Subspecialties: Fracture mechanics; Solid mechanics. Home: 107 College St Christiansburg VA 24073 Office: Va Poly Inst and State U Dept Engring Sci and Mechanics Blacksburg VA 24061

SMITH, CASSANDRA L., molecular biologist, researcher; b. N.Y.C., May 25, 1947; divorced. B.A. in Biology, W.Va. U., 1969, M.S. in Med. Microbiology, 1971; Ph.D. in Genetics, Tex. A&M U., 1974. Postdoctoral fellow Pub. Health Research Inst., NIH, 1974-78; research assoc. in chemistry and biology Columbia U., N.Y.C., 1978-82, research assoc. in human genetics and devel., 1982—. Mem. Am. Soc. Microbiology, Genetics Soc. Am. Subspecialties: Genetics and genetic engineering (biology); Molecular biology. Office: Dept Human Genetics and Devel Columbia U 701 W 168th St New York NY 10032

SMITH, CHARLES IRVEL, medicinal chemistry educator; b. Balt., Aug. 22, 1923; s. Louis Eldon and Lillian Marie (Akehurst) S.; m. Millicent Lois Yamin, Aug. 11, 1950; children: Carol Lois, Barbara Anne, Alan Craig. B.S., U. Md., 1944, Ph.D., 1950. Instr. physiol. chemistry dept. Sch. Medicine, Johns Hopkins U., Balt., 1950-52; sr. research scientist sect. drug metabolism pharmacology Squibb Inst. Med. Research, New Brunswick, N.J., 1952-60; assoc. prof. medicinal chemistry Coll. Pharmacy, U. R.I.-Kingston, 1960-74, prof., 1974—, chmn. dept., 1975-82. Contbr. articles to profl. jours. Served to lt. (j.g.) USNR, 1944-46. Recipient William Simon Gold medal Sch. Pharmacy, U. Md., 1944; U.S. AEC grantee, 1962-63. Fellow AAAS; mem. Am. Chem. Soc., Sigma Xi, Rho Chi, Kappa Psi. Current Work: Synthesis, analysis, metabolism of drugs including radiopharms. Subspecialties: Medicinal chemistry; Nuclear medicine. Home: 6 Nichols Rd Kingston RI 02881 Office: Coll Pharmacy U RI Kingston RI 02881

SMITH, CLIFFORD WINSTON, botanist, educator; b. Hereford, Eng., Mar. 10, 1938; s. Clifford Richard Joseph and Elizabeth (Winstone (Smith)) S. B.Sc. with honors, Univ. Coll. North Wales, 1962; M.Sc., U. Manchester, Eng., 1963, Ph.D., 1965. Research assoc. Princeton U., 1966-67; from asst. prof. to assoc. prof. botany U. Hawaii-Manoa, 1967—; field assoc. Bishop Mus., Honolulu, 1978—; dir. coop. nat. parks resources studies unit U. Hawaii-Manoa, 1975—. Author sci. articles. Mem. Big Bros., Volincor Hawaii. Served as cpl. Royal Army Service Corps, 1956-58. Nat. Park Service grantee, 1975—; U.S. Fish and Wildlife grantee, 1979—; Nature Conservancy grantee, 1980-81. Mem. Bot. Soc. Am., Mycol. Soc. Am., Am. Bryological and Lichenological Soc., Brit. Lichen Soc., Audubon Soc., Am. Mus. Natural History. Roman Catholic. Current Work: Taxonomy and ecology of Hawaiian lichens; resource management of Hawaiian national parks. Subspecialties: Taxonomy; Ecology (environmental science). Home: 1205 Manulani St Kailua HI 96734 Office: 3190 Maile Way Honolulu HI 96822

SMITH, DALE WILFORD, planetarium director, astronomer, educator; b. Amsterdam, N.Y., May 9, 1948; s. George Wilford and Florence Lucille (Wessels) S. A.B. Colgate U., 1970; M.S., U. Wash., 1973, Ph.D., 1978. Instr., Bellevue Community Coll., Wash., 1977-80; vis. asst. prof. Western Wash. U., Bellingham, 1980-81, Colgate U., Hamilton, N.Y., 1981-83; asst. prof., dir. planetarium Bowling Green State U., Ohio, 1983—; cons. U. Utah, Salt Lake City, 1978—. NASA and NSF grantee, 1978—. Mem. Am. Astron. Soc., Internat. Planetarium Soc., Great Lakes Planetarium Assn. Methodist. Current work: Asteroids, outer planet satellites. Subspecialty: Planetary science. Home: 135 Crim St Bowling Green OH 43402 Office: Dept Physics and Astronomy Bowling Green U Bowling Green OH 43403

SMITH, DAVID WILLIAM, chemist; b. Winchester, Ind., Mar. 18, 1948; s. William Harrold and Sara Lee (Kramer) S.; m. Vicki Sue McNiece, Mar. 9, 1949; children—Scot, Amy. B.S., Ball State U., 1972; Ph.D., U. Cin., 1981. Mgr. customer service United Parcel Service, Indpls., 1969-75; supr. lab. Cin. Gen. Hosp., 1976-80; researcher U. Cin. Med. Ctr., 1980-81; sr. scientist Bristol-Myers Co., Evansville, Ind., 1981—. Author: Neurosciences, 1983. Mem. Westside Improvement Assn., Evansville, 1981—, Evansville-Vanderberg Sch. Corp. PTA, 1981—. U. Cin. scholar, 1976-81. Mem. Am. Chem. Soc., Am. Coll. Clin. Pathologists, AAAS, Phi Lambda Upsilon. Current work: Antidepressants; analgesia; drug design; synthetic organic chemistry; computer science programming and applications. Subspecialties: Medicinal chemistry; Information systems, storage, and retrieval (computer science). Home: 6500 Middle Mt Vernon Rd Evansville IN 47712 Office: Pharm Div Bristol Myers Co Evansville IN 47721

SMITH, DEAN F., astrophysicist; b. Los Angeles, July 25, 1942; s. Emmett F. and Mildred (Graveline) S.; m. Zdenka A. Kopal, Sept. 1, 1967; children: Helena D., Lara M. B.S., M.I.T., 1964; M.S. in Applied Physics, Stanford U., 1966, Ph.D. in Astrophysics, 1969. Postdoctoral fellow U.S.-USSR Cultural Exchange Program, 1969-70; mem. staff Nat. Ctr. for Atmospheric Research, Boulder, Colo., 1970-78; sr. research assoc., lectr. dept. astro-geophysics U. Colo., Boulder, 1978-82; staff scientist Berkeley Research Assoc., Berkeley, Calif., 1982—; cons. physics dept. U. Calif., Irvine.; Invited visitor Max-Planck Inst. fur Extraterrestrishe Physik, Garching, W.Ger., 1975-76, Acad. Scis. USSR, 1980. Contbr. numerous articles to sci. jours. Mem. Internat. Astron. Union, Internat. Radio Sci. Union, Internat. Assn. Geomagnetism and Aeronomy, Am. Astron. Soc., Am. Phys. Soc. Club: American Alpine. Current Work: Pulsar and planetary magnetospheres; solar flares and coronal loops; particle acceleration in astrophysics. Subspecialties: Theoretical astrophysics; Solar physics. Office: PO Box 241 Berkeley CA 94701

SMITH, DONALD EUGENE, space tracking systems manager, consultant; b. Arcadia, Ohio, Sept. 18, 1934; s. Clyde Verlin and Evangeline (Smith) S.; m. Ieada Maggard, July 28, 1956; children—Margaret, Michael, Mark. B.S. in Phys. Sci., Ohio State U., 1959; M.S. in System Mgmt., George Washington U., 1973. Head dept., electronics engr. Columbus Tech. Inst., Ohio, 1964-66; sr. engr. tracking systems Bendix Field Engring. Corp., Columbia, Md., 1967-68, supr. tracking engr., 1968-71, mgr. engring., 1971-77, gen. mgr. network support, 1977-81, v.p. space ops., 1981—. Served with U.S. Army, 1953-55. Mem. AIAA, U.S. Space Found., Nat. Space Club, Am. Astron. Soc. Current work: Reviewing management systems (including use of expert systems) to increase productivity in labor intensive areas of space tracking and data handling. Subspecialties: Aerospace engineering and technology; Optical image processing. Home: 9538 Pamplona Rd Columbia MD 21045 Office: Bendix Field Engring Corp 1 Bendix Rd Columbia MD 21045

SMITH, EMIL L., biochemist, consultant; b. N.Y.C., July 5, 1911; s. Abraham and Esther (Lubart) S.; m. Esther Press, Mar. 29, 1934. B.S., Columbia U., 1931, Ph.D., 1936. Guggenheim fellow, 1938-40; fellow Rockefeller Inst., N.Y.C., 1940-42; biochemist E. R. Squibb & Sons, New Brunswick, N.J., 1942-46; prof. biochemistry Sch. Medicine U. Utah, 1946-63; prof., chmn. dept. biochemistry UCLA Sch. Medicine, 1963-79, prof. emeritus, 1979—; cons. in field; cons. NIH, Nat. Acad. Scis. Co-author: Principles of Biochemistry, 7th edit, 1983; contbr. numerous articles on biochemistry to profl. jours. Mem. Nat. Acad. Scis. Current Work: Protein chemistry and biology. Subspecialties: Biochemistry (biology); Molecular biology. Office: Dept Biochemistry UCLA Sch Medicine Los Angeles CA 90024

SMITH, EMIL RICHARD, pharmacologist, educator; b. Bridgewater, Mass., July 25, 1931; s. Emil Hilding and Sadie Eleanor (Riesberg) S.; m. Alice Jeanette Pike, July 29, 1956; children—Judith, Peter, David, Catherine, Margaret. B.S., Northeastern U., 1954; M.S., Tufts U., 1956; Ph.D., 1958. Postdoctoral fellow U. Buffalo, 1958-60; assoc. research biologist Sterling Drug Co., Renssalaer, N.Y., 1960-62; research pharmacologist Mason Research Inst., Worcester, Mass., 1962-67, dir. chem. carcinogenesis, 1972-75; head gen. pharmacology Astra Pharm. Products, Worcester, 1967-72; assoc. prof. pharmacology U. Mass. Med. Sch., Worcester, 1975—. Mem. Am. Soc. Pharmacology and Exptl. Therapy, Soc. Toxicology. Current work: Drugs effecting autonomic nervous system and cardiovascular system; environmental toxicology, especially chemicals causing cancer. Subspecialties: Pharmacology; Toxicology (medicine). Home: 5 Bryant Ave Shrewsbury MA 01545 Office: Dept Pharmacology U Mass Med Sch 55 Lake Ave N Worcester MA 01605

SMITH, ERIC PETER, statsitics educator, consultant; b. Phila., Nov. 20, 1953; s. William Stinger and Virginia (Jacobs) S.; m. Leslie Hager, Sept. 8, 1980; 1 child, Elliot. B.S., U. Ga., 1975; M.S., U. Wash., 1982, Ph.D., 1982. Research asst. U. Wash., Seattle, 1978; asst. prof. stats. Va. Poly. Inst. and State U., Blacksburg, 1982—. Contbr. articles to profl. jours. Mem. Biometric Soc., Am. Statis. Assn., Ecol. Soc. Am., Sigma Xi, Mu Sigma Rho. Current work: Applied statistics, environmental statistics, multivariate methods. Subspecialties: Statistics; Population biology. Office: Va Poly Inst and State U Dept Statistics Balcksburg VA 24061

SMITH, FRANK ACKROYD, biochem. toxicologist, educator, consultant; b. Winnipeg, Man., Can., Feb. 14, 1919; s. Frank and Doris A. S.; married, Apr. 15, 1944; children: Susan J., Deborah A. B.A., Ohio State U., 1940, M.S., 1941, Ph.D., 1944. With Mellon Inst., Pitts., 1944; with Manhattan Project, U. Rochester, N.Y., 1944-46, with atomic energy project, 1946—; instr. toxicology U. Rochester (Sch. Medicine and Dentistry), 1946-54, asst. prof., 1954-58, assoc. prof., 1958-85, prof. emeritus, 1985—, ad hoc cons. to govt. and industry. Author: (with Dr. Harold C. Hodge) Fluorine Chemistry, Vol. 4, 1965, (with Dr. Hodge and Dr. P.S. Chen) Fluorine Chemistry, Vol. 3, 1963; contbr. articles to profl. jours. Recipient (with Dr. Harold C. Hodge) Adolph Kammer award Am. Occupational Med. Assn., 1978. Mem. Am. Chem. Soc., Am. Indsl. Hygiene Assn., Am. Soc. Pharmacology and Exptl. Therapeutics, Soc. Toxicology (charter), AAAS, AAUP, N.Y. Acad. Scis., Sigma Xi. Current Work: Biochemical toxicology of inorganic, organic fluorides, organic solvents especially as related to occupational exposure. Subspecialty: Toxicology (medicine). Office: U Rochester Sch Medicine and Dentistry Dept Radiation Biology & Biophysics Rochester NY 14642

SMITH, GEORGE DAVID, research scientist; b. Youngstown, Ohio, Aug. 24, 1941; s. George William and Doris May (Fultz) S.; m. Elizabeth Margaret Bellion, June 4, 1963; children—Trevor D., Todd D. B.S., Westminster Coll., 1963; Ph.D., Ohio U., 1968. Research assoc. Mont. State U., Bozeman, 1968-74; assoc. research scientist Med. Found. Buffalo, 1974—; asst. research prof. Roswell Park Meml. Inst., Buffalo, 1982—. Contbr. articles to profl. jours. Mem. Am. Crystallographic Assn., Am. Chem. Soc., AAAS, Sigma Xi. Current work: Structure determination and correlation to activity of biologically important compounds such as insulin, analgetics and ionophores. Subspecialties: X-ray crystallography; Biophysics (biology). Home: 93 Warren Ave Kenmore NY 14217 Office: Med Found Buffalo Inc 73 High St Buffalo NY 14203

SMITH, GERALD RALPH, microbiologist, researcher; b. Vandalia, Ill., Feb. 19, 1944. B.S., Cornell U., 1966; Ph.D., M.I.T., 1970. Postdoctoral fellow dept. biochemistry U. Calif.-Berkeley, 1970-72, U. Geneva, Switzerland, 1972-75; asst. prof. biology Inst. Molecular Biology, U. Oreg., Eugene, 1975-80, assoc. prof., 1980-82; assoc. mem. Fred Hutchinson Cancer Research Center, Seattle, 1982—. Contbr. articles to profl. jours. Helen Hay Whitney fellow, 1970-73; Swiss Nat. Sci. Found. fellow, 1973-75; recipient NIH Research Career Devel. award, 1980-84. Mem. AAAS, Genetics Soc. Am., Am. Soc. Microbiology. Current Work: Molecular basis of genetic recombination; regulation of gene expression. Subspecialties: Molecular biology; Gene actions. Address: 1124 Columbia St Seattle WA 98104

SMITH, HARLAN JAMES, educator, astronomer; b. Wheeling, W.Va., Aug. 25, 1924; s. Paul Elder and Anna Persis (McGregor) S.; m. Joan Greene, Dec. 21, 1950; children: Nathaniel, Sarah (dec.), Julia, Theodore, Hannah. A.B., Harvard, 1949, M.A., 1951, Ph.D., 1955; D.Phys. Sci. (hon.), Nicholas Copernicus U., Torun, Poland, 1973; D.Phys. Sci., Denison U., 1983. Research asst. astronomy, teaching fellow and research fellow Harvard, 1946-53; from instr. to asso. prof. astronomy Yale, 1953-63; prof. astronomy, chmn. dept., 1963-78; also dir. McDonald Obs., U. Tex., 1963—; mem. (Space Sci. Bd.), 1977-79. Co-editor: Astron. Jour, 1960-63. Served as weather observer USAAF, 1943-46. George R. Agassiz research fellow Harvard Obs., 1952-53. Fellow AAAS; Mem. Am. Astron. Soc. (acting sec. 1961-62, chmn. planetary div. 1974-75, council 1975-78, v.p. 1977-79), Royal Astron. Soc., Am. Geophys. Union, Asso. Univs. Research in Astronomy (chmn. bd. 1980—), AAAS, Internat. Astron. Union, Sigma Xi. Current Work: Quasars; precise radial velocities, instrumentation; large telescopes. Subspecialties: Optical astronomy; Planetary science. Home: 2705 Pecos St Austin TX 78703

SMITH, IAN CORMACK PALMER, biophysicist; b. Winnipeg, Man., Can., Sept. 23, 1939; s. Cormack and Grace Mary S.; m. Eva Gunilla Landvik, Mar. 27, 1965; children—Brittmarie, Cormack, Duncan, Roderick. B.S., U. Man., 1961, M.S., 1962; Ph.D., Cambridge U., England, 1965. Fellow Stanford U., 1965-66; mem. research staff Bell Telephone Labs., Murray Hill, N.J., 1966-67; prin. research officer div. biol. scis. Nat. Research Council, Ottawa, 1967—; adj. prof. chemistry and biochemistry Carleton U., 1973—; adj. prof. chemistry and biochemistry U. Ottawa, 1976—; adj. prof. biophysics U. Ill., Chgo., 1974-80; allied scientist Ottawa Civic Hosp. Contbr. chps. to books, articles in field to profl. jours. Recipient Barringer award Can. Spectroscopy Soc., 1979. Fellow Chem. Inst. Can. (Merck award 1978, Labatt award 1984), Royal Soc. Can.; mem. Am. Chem. Soc., Biophys. Soc., Canadian Biochem. Soc. (Ayerst award 1978), AAAS. Current work: Application of nuclear magnetic resonance to problems in biology, biotechnology and medicine. Subspecialties: Biophysics (biology); Nuclear magnetic resonance. Office: Division of Biological Sciences National Research Council Ottawa ON K1A 0R6 Canada

SMITH, JACKSON BRUCE, physician, immunology researcher; b. Mt. Holly, N.J., Mar. 2, 1938; s. Jackson Burdette and Cynda Bruce (Hughes) S.; m. Penelope Lynne Prusa, June 7, 1963; children: Jackson Bruce, Joshua, Brian. B.S., Wake Forest U., 1960; M.D., Bowman Gray Sch. Medicine, 1965. Intern Pa. Hosp., Phila., 1965-66; resident, 1966-67, Hosp. of U. Pa., 1967-68; clin. research fellow Inst. Cancer Research, Phila., 1967-69; fellow Univ. Coll. London, 1972-74; research physician Inst. Cancer Research, Phila., 1974-81; assoc. prof. medicine Jefferson Med. Coll., Phila., 1981-85, prof., 1985—. Contbr. articles to profl. jours. Served with U.S. Navy, 1969-72. NIH grantee, 1979—; Am. Cancer Soc. grantee, 1978-81, 84—. Mem. AAAS, Am. Assn. Immunologists, Am. Assn. Cancer Research, ACP. Democrat. Current Work: Lymphocyte interactions and immune system regulation; biological research; cell interactions immune regulation, autoimmunity, cancer. Subspecialties: Internal medicine; Immunology (medicine). Home: 7939 Montgomery Ave Elkins Park PA 19117 Office: 1015 Walnut St Philadelphia PA 19107

SMITH, JAMES GILBERT, engineering educator; b. Benton, Ill., May 1, 1930; s. Jesse and Ruby Frances (Darnell) S.; m. Barbara Ann Smothers, July 29, 1955; 1 child, Julie. B.S. in Elec. Engring., U. Mo.-Rolla, 1957, M.S., 1959, Ph.D., 1967. Engr. Emerson Electric, St. Louis, 1957; engr. Boeing Co., Wichita, Kans., summers 1958-62; instr. then asst. prof. U. Mo., Rolla, 1959-66; prof. So. Ill. U., Carbondale, 1966—, chmn. dept. elec. sci. and systems engring., 1971-80. Contbr. articles to profl. jours. Served with U.S. Army, 1951-53, Korea. NSF fellow. Mem. IEEE (sr.), Am. Soc. Engring. Edn., (chmn. Ill., Ind. sect.), AAAS, Phi Kappa Phi, Tau Beta Pi, Eta Kappa Nu. Lodge: Rotary (Carbondale) (dir. 1983—). Current work: Electromagnetics; lightning and lightning protection; electrical properties of the earth. Subspecialties: Electrical engineering; Meteorologic instrumentation. Office: Dept Elec Engring So Ill U Carbondale IL 62901

SMITH, JESSE GRAHAM, JR., physician, educator; b. Winston-Salem, N.C., Nov. 22, 1928; s. Jesse Graham and Pauline Field (Griffith) S.; m. Dorothy Jean Butler, Dec. 28, 1950; children: Jesse Graham, Cynthia Lynn, Grant Butler. B.S., Duke U., 1962, M.D., 1951. Diplomate: Am. Bd. Dermatology (dir. 1974-83, pres. 1980-81). Intern VA Hosp., Chamblee, Ga., 1951-52; resident in dermatology Duke U., 1954-56, assoc. prof. dermatology, 1960-62, prof., 1962-67; resident U. Miami, 1956-57, asst. prof., 1957-60; prof. dermatology Med. Coll. Ga., 1967—, chmn. dept. dermatology, 1967—, acting chmn. dept. pathology, 1973-75, acting v.p. devel., 1984-85; chief staff Talmadge Meml. Hosp., Augusta, Ga., 1970-72; mem. advisory council Nat. Inst. Arthritis, 1975-79. Contbr. chpts. in books.; Mem. editorial bd.: Archives of Dermatology, 1963-72, Jour. Investigative Dermatology, 1966-67, Jour. AMA, 1974-80, So. Med. Jour., 1976—; editor: Jour. Am. Acad. Dermatology, 1978—; Contbr. articles to profl. jours. Served with USPHS, 1952-54. Fellow A.C.P., Royal Soc. Medicine; mem. Am. Dermatol. Assn. (sec. 1976-81, pres. 1981-82), Soc. Investigative Dermatology (dir. 1964-69, pres. 1979-80), Am. Acad. Dermatology (dir. 1971-74, 78—), Southeast Dermatolo. Assn. (sec. 1970-71, pres. 1975-76), Ga. Soc. Dermatology (pres. 1979-80), So. Med. Assn. (chmn. sect. dermatology 1973-74), AMA (chmn. sect. dermatology 1981-85), Assn. Profs. Dermatology (dir. 1976-77, 80-82, pres. 1984-86), Med. Research Found. Ga. (dir. 1967—, pres. 1974-75), Alpha Omega Alpha. Current Work: Connective tissue and aging. Subspecialty: Dermatology. Home: 606 Scotts Way Augusta GA 30909 Office: Medical College of Georgia Augusta GA 30912

SMITH, JOE MAUK, educator; b. Sterling, Colo., Feb. 14, 1916; s. Harold Rockwell and Mary Calista (Mauk) S.; m. Essie Johnstone McCutcheon, Dec. 23, 1943; children—Rebecca K., Marsha Mauk. B.S., Calif. Inst. Tech., 1937; Ph.D., Mass. Inst. Tech., 1943. Chem. engr. Texas Co., Standard Oil Co. of Calif., 1937-41; instr. chem. engring. Mass. Inst. Tech., 1943; asst. prof. chem. engring. U. Md., 1945; prof. chem. engring. Purdue U., 1945-56; dean Coll. Tech., U. N.H., 1956-57; prof. chem. engring. Northwestern U., 1957-59, Walter P. Murphy prof. chem. engring., 1959-61; prof. engring. U. Calif., 1961—, chmn. dept. chem. engring., 1964—; hon. prof. chem. engring. U. Buenos Aires, Argentina, 1964—; Fulbright lectr., Eng., Italy, Spain, 1965, and, Argentina, 1963, 65, Ecuador, 1970; Mudaliar Meml. lectr. U. Madras, India, 1967; UNESCO cons., Venezuela, 1972—. Author: Introduction to Chemical Engineering Thermodynamics, 3d edit, 1975, Chemical Engineering Kinetics, 1956, 3d edit., 1981. Guggenheim research award for study in Holland; also Fulbright award, 1953-54. Mem. Am. Chem. Soc., Am. Inst. Chem. Engrs. 77 (Walker award 1960, Wilhelm award 1977), Nat. Acad. Engring., Sigma Xi, Tau Beta Pi. Subspecialties: Chemical engineering; Petroleum engineering. Home: 760 Elmwood Dr Davis CA 95616

SMITH, JOHN BRYAN, pharmacologist, educator, researcher, cons.; b. Darlington, Eng., June 17, 1942; came to U.S., 1971; s. Robert Frederick and Phoebe (Mulhatton) S.; m. Angela Jane Fogg, Sept. 9, 1967; children: Timothy, Susanne. Ph.D. in Biochemistry, London U., 1971. Mem. staff Cardeza Found. for Hematologic Research, Thomas Jefferson U., Phila., 1971-82, mem. faculty dept. pharmacology, 1971-82, prof., 1981-82; prof. pharmacology and thrombosis Temple U., Phila., 1982—; asst. dir. Temple U. (Center for Thrombosis Research), 1982—. Contbr. over 100 articles to profl. jours. NIH grantee, 1982—. Mem. Am. Soc. Pharmacology and Exptl. Therapeutics, AAAS, Royal Inst. Chemistry, Chem. Soc., Sigma Xi. Patentee in field. Current Work: Prostaglandins and inhibition of platelet involvement in thrombosis. Subspecialties: Cellular pharmacology; Hematology. Office: SCOR Temple U Med Sch 3400 N Broad St Philadelphia PA 19140

SMITH, JOHN PHILIP, psychologist; b. N.Y.C., Dec. 14, 1933; s. Philip and Anna Josephine (Burke) S.; m. Sylvia Ann Esposito, Dec. 18, 1965; children: Richard, Kevin, Amy. A.B., Fordham U., 1954, M.A., 1958, Ph.D., 964. Lic. psychologist, N.Y. State. Psychologist in pvt. practice, Yonkers, N.Y., 1971—. Served to 1st lt. U.S. Army, 1954-56. Mem. Am. Psychol. Assn., Sigma Xi. Current Work: Elaboration of natural, absolute ethics; establishment of scientific basis for law. Subspecialties: Behavioral psychology; Social psychology. Office: 5 Seminary Ave Yonkers NY 10704

SMITH, JOSEPH LORENZO, physician, educator, cons.; b. Green River, Wyo., Oct. 15, 1946; s. Joseph Franklin and Vera (Robinson) S.; m. Judy Peterson, Aug. 8, 1969; children: Joseph Lorenzo II, A. Theodore, Brett Lowell, Heather, Megan, Jason Jon. B.S. magna cum laude, U. Utah, 1970; M.D., Cornell U., 1972. Diplomate: Am. Bd. Internal Medicine, also Sub-Bd. Infectious Diseases and Pulmonary Diseases, Am. Bd. Med. Examiners. Internal medicine intern Pa. State U. Hershey Med. Ctr., 1972-73, resident in internal medicine, 1973-74; epidemiologist Phoenix labs. div. Bur. Epidemiology, Ctr. for Disease Control, USPHS, 1974-76; postdoctoral fellow div. infectious diseases Stanford (Calif.) U. Sch. Medicine, 1976-78; practice medicine specializing in infectious diseases, Ogden, Utah, 1979-81; clin. instr. medicine U. Utah, Salt Lake City, 1979-81, postdoctoral fellow div. respiratory, critical care and occupational medicine (respiratory), LDS Hosp. and U. Utah, 1981-83; asst. prof. medicine Wayne State U., Detroit, 1983-84; assoc. dir. critical care medicine Harper Hosp., Detroit, 1983-84; assoc. Critical care Medicine, Thoracic Medicine, Infectious Diseases, Geisinger Med. Ctr., Danville, Pa., 1984—; Tb cons. Utah Dept. Health, 1979-83; cons. in infection control McKay Dee Hosp., Ogden, 1981-83. Contbr. articles and abstracts to sci. jours. Fellow ACP, Am. Coll. Chest Physicians; mem. Am. Soc. Microbiology. AMA, Soc. Critical Care Medicine, Infectious Disease Soc. Am., Am. Thoracic Soc., Pa. Med. Assn., Montour County Med. Soc., Alpha Epsilon Delta, Phi Kappa Phi. Current Work: Sepsis, septic shock, infectious disease, respiratory failure. Subspecialties: Critical care; Pulmonary medicine. Office: Geisinger Med Ctr Danville PA 17822

SMITH, KEVIN RICHARD, mech. engr.; b. Kansas City, Mo., Oct. 7, 1953; s. Richard Frazier and Betty Jean (Waters) S.; m. Cathy Lynne Nelson, Aug. 8, 1976. B.S., U. Kans., Lawrence, 1975. Designer Burnett Instruments Co., Lawrence, Kans., 1973-75; product design engr. Dazey Products Co., Kansas City, Mo., 1975-77; mech. project engr., engring. computer system mgr. King Radio Corp., Olathe, Kans., 1977—. Recipient Mech. Design award Kans. U. Endowment Assn., 1973. Mem. ASME. Presbyterian. Patentee in field. Current Work: Computer aided engineering design and management in electronic/electromechanical industry, computer graphics, engineering data base applications. Subspecialties: Mechanical engineering; Computer-aided design. Office: 400 N Rogers Rd Olathe KS 66062

SMITH, KIRBY, psychophysiologist, research administrator; b. Des Moines, Feb. 6, 1926; s. Charles Norris and Louise Ann (Spillers) S.; m. D. Joan Groves, June 28, 1958; children—Andrew, Gillian, Gavin. B.A., U. Chgo., 1950; M.A., Temple U., 1952; M. Phil., Columbia U., 1956. Research psychologist E. Pa. Psychiat. Inst., Phila., 1956-64, med. research scientist, 1964-81; pres., dir. Icans, Inc., Phila., 1981—; assoc. dir. Biokinetics Research Labs., Temple U., Phila., 1981—; cons. Dept. Neurology and Psychiatry Woman's Med. Coll. Pa., 1965-70, Phila. Gen. Hosp., 1974-77, U. Pa. Sch. Medicine, Dept. Psychiatry, 1974-82, Dept. Neurology and Psychiatry Phila. Coll. Osteopathic Medicine, 1980-83. Contbr. chpts. to books, articles to profl. jours. Recipient Travel award NSF, 1966; Med. Research Scientist Achievement award Commonwealth of Pa., 1975-80; Ben Franklin Partnership award, 1984; various grants, 1955—. Mem. Soc. Research Adminstrs., IEEE, Engring. in Medicine and Biology Soc., Computer Soc., Soc. Psychophysiol. Research, Am. Psychol. Assn., Soc. Behavioral Medicine. Current work: Physiological correlates of behavioral and perception processes; non-invasive and remote monitoring of neurophysiological and psychomotor processes. Subspecialties: Physiological psychology; Biomedical engineering. Office: Biokinetics Research Labs Temple U 048-00 Philadelphia PA 19122

SMITH, LEONARD CHARLES, chemist, educator; b. Spokane, Wash., Jan. 31, 1921; s. Leonard Charles and Edith L. (McLellan) S.; m. Mary Elaine Rush, Oct. 1, 1945; children: David E., L. Frederic, Steven M., Peter D., Andrew I. A.B., U. Mont., Missoula, 1943; Ph.D., U. Ill., Urbana, 1949. Instr. in exptl. medicine Northwestern U. Med. Sch., 1950-51, instr. in biochemistry, 1952-56; research biochemist Hines (Ill.) VA Hosp., 1949-56; asst. prof. biochemistry U. S.D. Sch. Medicine, 1956-57, assoc. prof., 1957-62, prof., 1962-66; prof. chemistry Ind. State U., 1966; vis. lectr. Glasgow (Scotland) U., 1961-62, cons. to pub. cos. Contbr. articles to profl. publs. Mem. Chem. Soc. (U.K.), Soc. Exptl. Biology and Medicine, AMA, Am. Chem. Soc., Sigma Xi, Phi Sigma, Pi Mu Epsilon. Lodges: Masons; Shriners. Current Work: Research in amino acid metabolism. Subspecialties: Biochemistry (biology); Nutrition (biology).

SMITH, LEWIS WILBERT, animal scientist; b. York, Pa., Jan. 13, 1937; s. George Wilbert and Eleonora (Masimore) S.; m. Kay Elizabeth Vorhees, Feb. 1, 1963; children—Scott H., Paige E. B.S., U. Md., 1959, M.S., 1961, Ph.D., 1968. Grad. asst. U. Md., College Park, 1959-61; dairy husbandman Agrl. Research Ctr., U.S. Dept. Agr., Beltsville, Md., 1961-71, research animal scientist, 1971-75, supr. research animal scientist, 1975-79, chmn. animal sci. inst., 1979—; cons. Ceres Ecology Corp., Fort Collins, Colo., 1974-76, FAO Headquarters, Rome, 1976; vice leader U.S. Waste Mgmt. Team, USSR, 1975; mem. CAST task force, 1978. Contbr. articles to profl. publs., chpts. to books. Served to 2d lt. USPHD, 1962-64. Mem. Am. Dairy Sci. Assn. (mem. subcom. on environ. quality 1978-81), Am. Soc. Animal Sci. (mem. animal waste mgmt. com. 1970-73, chmn. 1972-73), Council for Agrl. Sci. and Tech., Sigma Xi, Gamma Delta Sigma. Current work: Donduct research in dynamics of forage fiber digestion in ruminants and manager of large group of scientists conducting animal production research. . Home: 406 Neale Ct Silver Spring MD 20901 Office: USDA-ARS Animal Sci Inst Bldg 200 Room 217 BARC-East Beltsville MD 20705

SMITH, LOREN MICHAEL, wildlife ecology educator; b. Davenport, Iowa, Sept. 26, 1956; s. Wendell Leigh and Helen Marie (Giltner) S.; m. Janiece Marie Becker, Dec. 19, 1976. B.S., N.E. Mo. State U., 1977; M.S., S.D. State U., 1980; Ph.D., Utah State U., 1983. Cert. wildlife biologist Wildlife Soc. Curator herpetology exhibit N.E. Mo. State U., Kirksville, 1976-77; research technician Iowa Conservation Commn., Chariton, 1978; research asst. S.D. State U., Brookings, 1978-80, Utah State U., Logan, 1980-83; research assoc. Savannah River Ecol. Lab., Aiken, S.C., 1983-84; asst. prof. wildlife ecology Tex. Tech. U., Lubbock, 1984—; chmn. environ. quality Interagy. Playa Lakes Disease Council, Lubbock, 1984—. Contbr. articles to profl. jours. Research grantee prairie chicken Eli Lilly Inc., 1984, wintering waterfowl Savannah River Ecol. Lab., 1984, wintering brant Atlantic Flyway Council, 1984, banding analysis U.S. Fish and Wildlife Service, 1984, others. Mem. Inst. Ecology, Ecol. Soc. Am., Wildlife Soc. (chmn. publs. Tex. chpt. 1984—, Tex. rep. 1984—), Am. Ornithologists Union, Soc. Wetland Scientists. Current work: Wetland ecology, biomass relationships, wildlife habitat in wetlands, prairie ecosystems, vertebrate effects on ecosystems. Subspecialties: Ecosystems analysis; Behavioral ecology. Home: 5735 92d St Lubbock TX 79424 Office: Dept Range and Wildlife Tex Tech U Lubbock TX 79409

SMITH, LYNWOOD HERBERT, nephrologist, educator; b. Kansas City, Mo., Aug. 2, 1929; s. Lynwood Herbert and Arline Estel (Chandler) S.; m. Margery Davis Waddell, Dec. 15, 1951; children: Michael Chandler, Katherine Ann, Philip Waddell, Martha Lynn. B.S., U. Kans., 1951, M.D., 1960. Intern Met. Gen. Hosp., Cleve., 1961-62; resident internal medicine Mayo Grad. Sch., Rochester, Minn., 1962-64; research fellow Johns Hopkins U., Balt., 1964-65; cons. nephrology/urology Mayo Clinic, Rochester, Minn., 1965—, dir. urulithiasis research, 1966—, prof. medicine, 1977—. Contbr. articles to profl. jours. Mem. vestry St. Luke's Episcopal Ch., Rochester, 1972-75. Served to lt. (j.g.) USN, 1952-56. Mayo Grad. Sch. travel grantee, 1965; named Tchr. of Yr., 1982. Mem. Am. Soc. Nephrology, Internat. Soc. Nephrology, ACP, Central Soc. Clin. Research, Am. Clin. and Climatol. Assn., Alpha Omega Alpha, Omicron Delta Kappa, Beta Theta Pi, Sigma Xi. Republican. Current Work: Basic and clinical research relating to formation of urinary calculi, crystal formation and inhibition and calcium matabolism. Subspecialties: Nephrology; Internal medicine. Home: 4912 Weatherhills Dr SW Rochester MN 55901 Office: Mayo Clinic 200 First St SW Rochester MN 55905

SMITH, MICHAEL ROBERT, engineer; b. Tela, Honduras, Aug. 24, 1937; came to U.S., 1951; s. Ike Morgan and Edith (Hudson) S.; m. Suzanne Hudgins, Aug. 20, 1960; children—Stephen Michael, Monica Ruth, Meryl Andrea. B.M.E., Ga. Inst. Tech., 1959, M.Nuclear Engring., 1961; Ph.D., Case Inst. Tech., 1965. Mem. tech. staff Hughes Research Labs., Malibu, Calif., 1965-68; v.p., dir. research Britt Corp., W. Los Angeles, 1968-73; sr. staff engr. Singer Librascope, Glendale, Calif., 1973-78; pres. Exocor Tech., Inc., Thousand Oaks, Calif., 1978—; pres. Spectra-Med Co., Thousand Oaks, 1974—; lectr. in field. Contbr. articles to profl. jours. Patentee in field. Mem. IEEE, Soc. Photo-Optical Instrumentation Engrs., Sigma Xi, Pi Tau Sigma, Pi Kappa Alpha. Current work: Development of laser surgical devices and inspection systems utilizing electro-optical devices. Address: 752 N Woodlawn Dr Thousand Oaks CA 91360

SMITH, OTTO J.M., electrical engineering educator; b. Urbana, Ill., Aug. 6, 1917; s. Otto Mitchell and Mary Catherine (Carr) S.; m. Phyllis Pearl Sterling, Sept. 3, 1941; children: Candace Smith Shock, Otto J.A., Sterling Barton, Stanford. B.S. in Chemistry, Okla. State U., 1938; B.S. in Elec. Engring, U. Okla., 1938; Ph.D. in Elec. Engring, Stanford U., 1941. Registered profl. engr., Calif. Research asst. Stanford U., 1938-41; instr. elec. engring. Tufts U., Medford, Mass., 1941-43; asst. prof. elec. engring. U. Denver, 1943-44; prof. electronics Instituto Tecnologico de Aeronautica, Sao Jose dos Campos, Sao Paulo, Brazil, 1954-56; sr. research fellow in econs. and engring. Monash U., Melbourne, Australia, 1966-67; prof. elec. engring. and computer scis. U. Calif.-Berkeley, 1947—; dir. Wind Electric Systems, Inc. Author: Feedback Control Systems, 1958; contbr. articles to profl. jours. Dist. commr. Boy Scouts Am., 1949-53. Guggenheim fellow Tech. Hoch. Darmstadt, W.Ger., 1960. Fellow AAAS, IEEE; mem. Am. Soc. for Engring. Edn., Soc. for Social Responsibility in Sci., Soc. for Social Responsibility in Engring., AAUP, Fedn. Am. Scientists, Union Concerned Scientists, Internat. Solar Energy Soc., No. Calif. Solar Energy Assn. Democrat. Methodist. Club: City Commons (Berkeley). Patentee solar power, wind power, variable speed generators, stepping motors, heliostats, others. Current Work: Design of solar-electric plants and wind turbines. System optimization, economic planning, appropriate technology, power system stabilization, automatic control, measurements. Subspecialties: Solar energy; Wind power. Home: 612 Euclid Ave Berkeley CA 94708 Office: Dept EECS U Calif Berkeley CA 94720

SMITH, PETER WILLIAM, quantum electronics scientist; b. London, Nov. 3, 1937; naturalized Can. citizen; m. Jacqueline Marie Smith, June 18, 1966; children: Christal, Dawn Noelle. B.Sc., McGill U., Montreal, Que., Can., 1958, M.Sc., 1961, Ph.D., 1963. Mem. tech. staff Bell Labs., Holmdel, N.J., 1963-83; dist. research mgr. Bell Communications Research, Red Bank, N.J., 1984—; vis. MacKay prof. U. Calif., Berkeley, 1970; vis. research scientist Laboratoire D'Optique Quantique, Ecole Polytechnique, Palaiseau, France, 1978-79. Contbr. numerous articles on quantum electronics to profl. jours.; editorial bd.: Comtex Sci, 1982-84. Bd. dirs. Monmouth Arts Found., Red Bank, N.J. Recipient Sr. Scientist award NATO, 1979. Fellow IEEE, Optical Soc. Am.; mem. Am. Phys. Soc. Patentee in field. Current Work: Quantum electronics research in optical switching and optical signal processing. Subspecialties: Laser research; Optical signal processing. Office: Bell Communications Research Navasink Research Center Red Bank NJ 07701

SMITH, PHILIP MEEK, organization executive; b. Springfield, Ohio, May 18, 1932; s. Clarence Mitchell and Lois Ellen (Meek) Dudley. B.S., Ohio State U., 1954, M.A., 1955. Mem. staff U.S. Nat. Com. for Internat. Geophys. Yr., Nat. Acad. Scis., 1957-58; program dir. NSF, 1958-63, dir. ops. U.S. Antarctic Research Program, 1964-69, dep. head div. polar programs, 1969-73; chief gen. sci. br. Office Mgmt. and Budget, Exec. Office of the Pres., 1973-74; exec. asst. to dir. NSF and sci. advisor to the Pres., also exec. sec. Pres.' Com. Nat. Medal of sci., 1974-76; assoc. dir. Office sci. and Tech. Policy, Exec. Office of Pres., 1976-81; spl. asst. to chmn. Nat. Sci. Bd., 1981; exec. officer Nat. Research Council-Nat. Acad. scis., Washington, 1981—; corp. mem. Woods Hole Oceanographic Instn., 1983—; pres. Cave Research Found., Yellow Springs, Ohio, 1957-63; chmn. tech. panels Fed. Coordinating Council Sci., Engring. and Tech., 1976-80. Author: (with others) Defrosting Antarctic Secrets, 1962; The Frozen Future, a Prophetic Report from Antarctica, 1973; Contbr. articles to profl. jours. Bd. dirs. Washington Project for the Arts, 1983—, Washington Sculptors Group, 1983—. Served to 1st lt. Transp. Corp, U.S. Army, 1955-57. Recipient Meritorious Service medal NSF, 1972. Mem. AAAS, Am. Mgmt. Assn., Antarctican Soc., Western River Guides Assn. Clubs: Cosmos (Washington); Am. Alpine (N.Y.C.). Office: Nat Research Council Nat Acad Scis 2101 Constitution Ave NW Washington DC 20418

SMITH, RALPH EARL, microbiologist; b. Yuma, Colo., May 10, 1940; s. Robert Conrad and Esther Clara (Schwarz) S.; m. Sheila Lee Kondy, Aug. 26, 1961; 1 dau., Andrea Denise. B.S., Colo. State U., 1961; Ph.D., U. Colo. Med. Sch., 1968. USPHS postdoctoral fellow Duke U. Med. Ctr., Durham, N.C., 1968-70, asst. prof. dept. microbiology and immunology, 1970-74, assoc. prof., 1974-80, prof., 1980-82; prof., chmn. dept. microbiology and environ. health Colo. State U., Ft. Collins, 1983—; cons. Bellco Glass, Inc., Vineland, N.J., 1977-80. Contbr. articles to profl. jours. Asst. scoutmaster Boy Scouts Am., 1972-82. Eleanor Roosevelt fellow Internat. Union Against Cancer, 1978-79. Mem. Am. Soc. Microbiology, N.Y. Acad. Scis., Am. Soc. Virology, Am. Assn. Immunologists, Am. Assn. Avian Pathologists. Democrat. Methodist. Patentee in field. Current Work: Isolated avian leukosis viruses which had limited oncogenic spectra; characterized virus causing bone tumors in chickens; isolated viruses causing obesity and lung tumors in chickens. Subspecialties: Virology (medicine); Microbiology (medicine). Office: Dept Microbiology and Environ Health Colo State U Fort Collins CO 80523

SMITH, RAYMOND VIRGIL, mechanical engineer, consultant; b. Esbon, Kans., Nov. 17, 1919; s. John Nathan and Iva Irene S.; m. Mary W. Smith, June 12, 1948 (div. 1974); children—Stanley, Teresa Madden, Timothy, Robert; m. Rita Pratt, Dec. 22, 1974. Registered profl engr., Colo. Engr., Boeing Aircraft Co., Seattle, 1941-44, 48-49; instr. Colo. Sch. Mines, 1949-52; research engr. Sandia Corp., Albuquerque, 1952-53; asst. prof. N.Mex. State U., 1953-54; assoc. prof. U. Utah, 1954-57, Colo. State U., 1957-61; engr., sect. chief Nat. Bur. Standards, Boulder, Colo., 1961-71; prof. mech. engring. Wichita State U., 1971-84; mech. engring. cons., Wichita, Kans., 1984—. Contbr. numerous articles to tech. jours. Served with USAAF, 1944-45. Recipient Tech. Utilization award, NASA, 1972. Mem. ASME, Pi Tau Sigma. Current work: Two-phase flow, rehabilitation engineering, history of technology. Subspecialty: Fluid mechanics. Office: 5 Crestview Lakes Wichita KS 67220

SMITH, RICHARD GRAHAM, engineer, government executive; b. Durham, N.C., Oct. 22, 1929; s. Marvin George and Eva Jean (Dye) S.; m. Anna Louise Self, June 6, 1953; children—Carol, Lisa Anne, Richard G., Jr. B.S.E.E., Auburn U., 1951; Sc.D. (hon), Fla. Inst. Tech., 1981, Auburn U., 1983. Various positions Marshall Space Flight Ctr., Huntsville, Ala., 1960-71, mgr. Saturn Program, 1971-74, dir. sci. and engring., 1974-75, dep. dir., 1975-78; dep. assoc. adminstr. for space transp. systems NASA hdqrs., Washington, 1978-79; dir. John F. Kennedy Space Ctr. NASA, Fla., 1979—. Fellow Am. Astronautical Soc.; mem. Auburn U. Alumni Engring. Council and Research Council. Subspecialty: Aerospace engineering and technology. Office: NASA Kennedy Space Center FL 32899

SMITH, ROBERT DAVID, computer science educator, consultant, researcher; b. Erie, Pa., Dec. 7, 1937; s. Ira E. and Rozella (Zimmerman) S.; m. Vilma J. Monserrate, Aug. 28, 1966; children: Roger, Victor, Elena. B.S., Gannon Coll., 1959; M.S., Pa. State U., 1964, Ph.D., 1966. Instr. Pa. State U., University Park, 1962-66, asst. prof., 1966-68; assoc. prof. computer sci. Kent State U., Ohio, 1968-72, prof., 1972—; researcher, cons. McDermott/Babock, Alliance, Ohio, 1968—; research and devel. Goodyear Aerospace, Akron, Ohio, 1974—; mgmt. devel. exec. Akron City Hosp., 1980—; with Rehab. Services Adminstrn., 1979—; faculty Ohio Bankers Assn., Columbus, 1971—. Co-author: Personnel Management: A Computer Approach, 1970, Systems Analysis and Design, 1976, Personnel Management: A Human Resource System, 1982. Mem. Diocesan Bd. Edn., Youngstown, Ohio, 1982—. Served to lt. U.S. Army, 1960-62. Ford Found. grantee, 1974; Bur. Vocat. Rehab. Ohio grantee, 1981. Mem. Am. Soc. Personnel Adminstrn. (adv. 1977, Nat. Merit award 1980). Roman Catholic. Current Work: Computer systems in banking; research and development management; management of technological innovation. Subspecialties: Information systems, storage, and retrieval (computer science); Human resource information systems. Home: 1587 Morris Rd Kent OH 44240 Office: Kent State U Kent OH 44242

SMITH, ROBERT JOHNIE, grain/feed company executive, veterinarian, researcher; b. Kansas City, Mo., Aug. 22, 1935; s. Johnie Alfred and Opal Grace (King) S.; m. Reta Mae Christman, June 11, 1958; children—Melissa L., Kyle E., Brian E. B.S. in Agr., U. Mo., 1960, D.V.M., 1960. Pvt. practice vet. medicine specializing in large animals, Polo, Mo., 1960-77; staff veterinarian MFA Inc., Columbia, Mo., 1977-80, mgr. tech. services, 1980-83; mgr. animal health research Continental Grain Co., Chgo., 1983-84, mgr. tech. services, 1984—. Animal health columnist Today's Farmer, 1980-83. Co-organizer 1st Caldwell County Fair, Mo., 1976. Mem. AVMA, Mo. Vet. Med. Assn., Am. Assn. Bovine Practitioners, Am. Assn. Indsl. Veterinarians. Lodge: Masons. Current work: Animal health research; training sales force; preventive medicine; animal health workshops; technical writing; personnel management.

Subspecialties: Preventive medicine (veterinary medicine); Animal nutrition. Home: 1009 Juniper Pkwy Libertyville IL 60048

SMITH, ROBERT L., auditory neurophysiologist, educator; b. N.Y.C., Mar. 29, 1941; s. Abe J. and Bertha (Rosenthal) S.; m. Carolee Gelman, Nov. 16, 1968; children: Jana, Shayna, Marnina. B.E.E., CCNY, 1962; M.S.E.E., N.Y.U., 1966; Ph.D., Syracuse U., 1973. Devel. engr. Wheeler Labs., Great Neck, N.Y., 1962-64; lectr. elec. engring. CCNY, N.Y.C., 1964-66; instr. elec. and computer engring. Syracuse (N.Y.) U., 1970-74, asst. prof. sensory scis., 1974-80, assoc. prof., 1980-85, prof., 1985—. Contbr. articles to profl. publs. Recipient Career devel. award NIH, 1979—; NSF grantee, 1981—. Fellow Accoustical Soc. Am.; mem. Soc. Neurosci., Assn. Research in Otolaryngology, N.Y. Acad. Scis., Sigma Xi, Eta Kappa Nu, Tau Beta Pi. Jewish. Current Work: Investigation the encoding and transmission of information in auditory nervous system. Recording and analyzing responses to sound of single cells in cochlea, cochlear nerve and nucleus, and modelling of results. Subspecialties: Neurophysiology; Sensory processes. Home: 3 Haverhill P1 Dewitt NY 13214 Office: Inst Sensory Research Syracuse U Syracuse NY 13210

SMITH, ROGER POWELL, pharmacologist, toxicologist, educator, researcher, cons.; b. Hokuchin, Korea, July 16, 1932; s. Burton Powell and Mary Hannah (McMullen) S.; m. Rena Joan Pointer, Nov. 1, 1956; children: Sam F., Joan B., Ben H. B.S., Purdue U., 1953, M.S., 1955, Ph.D., 1957; M.A. (hon.), Dartmouth Coll., 1975. Lic. pharmacist, N.H. Instr. dept. pharmacology and toxicology Dartmouth Med. Sch., Hanover, N.H., 1960-63, asst. prof., 1963-68, assoc. prof., 1968-73, prof., 1973—, chmn. dept., 1976—; adj. prof. Vt. Law Sch., South Royalton, 1981—, Dartmouth Coll., 1983—. Author: (with others) Clinical Toxicology of Commercial Products, 1984; contbr. (with others) articles to profl. jours. Committeeman Cub Scouts, Boy Scouts Am., Hanover Youth Hockey Assn.; deacon Ch. of Christ, Hanover. Served with Med. Service Corps. U.S. Army, 1957-60. USPHS career devel. award, 1966-71; Nat. Air Pollution Control Adminstrn. grantee, 1962-70; Nat. Heart, Lung and Blood Inst. grantee, 1970—. Mem. AAAS, Soc. Toxicology, Am. Soc. Pharmacology and Exptl. Therapeutics, Soc. Exptl. Biology and Medicine, Sigma Xi. Republican. Club: Hanover Country. Current Work: Biochemical toxicology of cytochrome oxidase inhibitors, chemically induced damage to red blood cells, toxicology of vasodilator agents, pharmacology of vascular smooth muscle and platelet aggregation. Subspecialties: Toxicology (medicine); Pharmacology. Home: 12 Kingsford Rd Hanover NH 03755 Office: Dept Pharmacology and Toxicology Dartmouth Med Sch Hanover NH 03756

SMITH, SAMUEL HOWARD, plant pathologist, university administrator; b. Salinas, Calif., Feb. 4, 1940; s. Adrian Reed and Elsa Rose (Jacop) S.; m. Patricia Ann Walter, July 8, 1960; children: Samuel Howard, Linda M. B.S., U. Calif.-Berkeley, 1961, Ph.D., 1964. NATO postdoctoral fellow Glasshouse Crops Research Inst., Sussex, Eng., 1964-65; asst. prof. plant pathology U. Calif.-Berkeley, 1965-69; assoc. prof. plant pathology Pa. State U.-Arendtsville, 1969-71, assoc. prof., University Park, 1971-74, prof., 1974-85, head dept. plant pathology, 1976-81, dean Coll. Agr., 1981-85, dir. Agrl. Expt. Sta., and dir. Coop. Extension Service, 1981-85; pres. Wash. State U., 1985—. Contbr. articles to profl. jours. Mem. Am. Phytopathol. Soc., AAAS, Am. Inst. Biol. Scis., Am. Mushroom Inst. Subspecialties: Plant pathology; Plant virology. Home: NE 755 Campus Pullman WA 99163 Office: 422 French Adminstrn Bldg Pullman WA 99164-1048

SMITH, SHELDON MAGILL, physicist, astronomer; b. St. Paul, Apr. 19, 1931; s. Sheldon Holloway and Sarah Alice (Matteson) S.; children: Sheldon, Jennifer, Christina. B.S., U. Calif.-Berkeley, 1953; M.A. in Physics, U. Calif.-Davis, 1962; postgrad., Stanford U., 1965-66. Research scientist NASA Ames Research Center, Moffett Field, Calif., 1962—, sr. research scientist, 1979—. Contbr. articles to sci. jours. Vice pres. Stanford NACCP, 1972-73; asst. scoutmaster Boy Scouts Am., 1976-78. Served to lt. USNR, 1954-64. Mem. Am. Astron. Soc., AAAS, Optical Soc. Am., Sigma Pi. Democrat. Episcopalian. Clubs: Toastmasters, Almaden Cycle Touring (v.p. 1981—). Lodge: Masons. Designer spl. instrumentation for several solar eclipse expdns.; developer (with Peter Sturrock) of magnetic field configuration of solar streamers. Current Work: Space shuttle infrared telescope facility; study and design of far-infrared attenuating coatings to reduce stray light in the SIRTF telescope. Far-infrared reflectance; scattering; optical constants; photometry; spectroscopy. Subspecialties: Solar physics; Infrared astronomy. Office: NASA-Ames Research Center MS 245-6 Moffett Field CA 94036

SMITH, THOMAS LLOYD, horticulturist, educator; b. Cin., July 29, 1946; s. Lloyd Damon and Aline Elizabeth (Rust) S.; m. Susan Sprow, Mar. 1, 1969; children: David Thomas Maguire, Lisa Suzanne Rust, Kathleen Elizabeth Rust. B.S., U. Cin., 1968; M. in Forest Sci, Yale U., 1970, postgrad., 1971. Grad. asst. Yale U., 1970-71; v.p. Spring Grove Cemetery, Cin., 1972—; lectr. horticulture U. Cin., 1973—; pres. Flora Therapy, Inc., Cin., 1979-81. Bd. dirs. Civic Garden Ctr. Greater Cin., 1980-83, Urban Forestry Dept. Parks, Cin., 1981—. Mem. Profl. Grounds Mgmt. Soc. (chmn. nat. conv. 1983), So. Ohio Profl. Grounds Mgmt. Soc., Ohio Forestry Assn., Ohio Nurseryman's Assn., Beta Theta Pi. Clubs: Diogenes (Cin.), Yale Alumni (Cin.). Current Work: Involved with urban forest resource management of both developed and undeveloped grounds within the largest nonprofit cemetery in the United States; specific interests have included tree physiology and air pollution/photosynthetic tolerance of certain plant materials. Subspecialties: Plant growth; Urban forest resource management. Office: Spring Grove Cemetery 4521 Spring Grove Ave Cincinnati OH 45232

SMITH, THOMAS WOODWARD, cardiologist, educator; b. Akron, Ohio, Mar. 29, 1936; s. Luther David and Beatrice Pearl (Woodward) S.; m. Sherley Goodwin, Sept. 13, 1958; children: Julia Goodwin, Geoffrey Woodward, Allison Lloyd. A.B., Harvard U., 1958, M.D. magna cum laude, 1965. Diplomate: Am. Bd. Internal Medicine, 1971. Intern, then resident in medicine Mass. Gen. Hosp., Boston, 1965-67, clin. fellow in cardiology, 1967-69, Nat. Heart and Lung asso. program dir. myocardial infarction research unit, 1972-74, Inst. spl. fellow, 1969-71; instr. medicine Harvard Med. Sch., 1969-71, asst. prof. medicine, 1971-73, assoc. prof. medicine, 1973-79, prof. medicine, 1979—; chief of cardiology Peter Bent Brigham Hosp., 1974—; cons. Children's Hosp. Med. Center, 1975—, Mass. Gen. Hosp., 1977—, Sidney Farber Cancer Inst., 1978—. Served to lt. (j.g.) USN, 1958-61. Mem. Fellow Am. Coll. Cardiology, ACP; mem. Am. Heart Assn. (council clin. cardiology, council basic sci., council circulation), Am. Fedn. Clin. Research, Paul Dudley White Soc., AAAS, Am. Soc. Pharmacology and Exptl. Therapeutics, Am. Soc. Clin. Investigation, Assn. Univ. Cardiologists, Am. Physiol. Soc., Assn. Am. Physicians, Soc. Gen. Physiologists. Current Work: Investigative cardiology and cardiovascular pharmacology. Cardiac glycoside mechanisms of action; antibody reversal of toxicity; receptor and inotropic state control in cardiac muscle. Subspecialties: Cardiology; Internal medicine. Office: Cardiovascular Div Brigham and Women's Hosp 75 Francis St Boston MA 02115

SMITH, WAYNE D., electrical engineer; b. Ingram, Tex., Apr. 14, 1933; children: Michelle, Leisa, Mathew; m. Beverly Smith, July 3, 1975; children: Drew, D.R., Dana. B.A. in Psychology, Tex. Christian U., 1962. Photographer Swayze Studio, Kerrville, Tex., 1949-52; Humrro pilot adviser Dept. Def. Washington, 1957-61; engr. Ling Temco Vought Co., Dallas, 1961-65; engr. mgr. Boeing Co., Seattle, 1965—; mgr. crew systems research Boeing Comml. Airplane Co., Seattle, 1967—. Served with U.S. Army, 1953-57. Fellow AIAA. Democrat. Baptist. Lodge: Moose. Current Work: Controls and displays systems development, crew interface performance test and evaluation, crew workload evaluation. Subspecialties: Electronics; Human factors engineering. Home: 2929 76th SE Apt 412 Mercer Island WA 98040 Office: Boeing Co PO Box 3707 Seattle WA

SMITH, WESLEY HAROLD, physics researcher, physics educator; b. San Francisco, June 14, 1954; s. Harold Allison and Anita (Koyrn) S.; m. Stephanie Joy Sligh, Jan. 1, 1983; 1 child, Jennifer A. A.B., Harvard U., 1975, A.M., 1976; Ph.D., U. Calif.-Berkeley, 1981. Grad. research assoc. Lawrence Berkeley Lab., Calif., 1976-81; research assoc. Nevis Labs, Irvington, N.Y., 1981-82; asst. prof. physics Columbia U., N.Y.C., 1982—. Recipient Presdl. Young Investigator award NSF, 1983. Mem. Am. Phys. Soc. Current work: High energy neutrino physics research in structure functions, neutral currents, dimuons, rare phenomena, teaching premedical physics at Columbia University. Subspecialty: Particle physics. Home: Yorktown 2D Scarsdale Country Estates Scarsdale NY 10583 Office: Nevis Labs Columbia U PO Box 137 Irvington NY 10533

SMITH, WILLIAM BOYCE, statistics educator, consultant; b. Port Arthur, Tex., Sept. 7, 1938; s. Benjamin Thomas and Eula (Wactor) S.; m. Patricia Rutherford, Apr. 12, 1963; children: Leah Ann, Scott Andrew, Angela Rae. B.S. in Math., Lamar U., 1959; M.S. in Math., Tex. A&M U., 1960, Ph.D. in Stats. (NDEA fellow), 1967; postgrad., Rice U., 1960-62. Asst. prof. math. Lamar U., 1962-64; mathematician Sandia Corp., summers 1961-62; asst. prof. to prof. stats. Tex. A&M U., 1967—, asst. deanColl. Sci., 1972-77; head dept. stats. (Tex. A&M U.), 1977—, legal cons., researcher. Contbr. articles profl. jours. Baseball coach, football ofcl.; mem. S.W. Football Ofcls. Assn. Ctr. Energy and Mineral Resources grantee, 1979-82; grantee NASA, 1969-71, 82—. Fellow Japanese Soc. Promotion of Sci.; mem. Am. Statis. Assn, Math. Assn. Am., Biometric Soc., Sigma Xi. Methodist. Current Work: Multivariate statistical methods —development and application. Subspecialty: Statistics. Home: 1040 Rose Circle College Station TX 77840 Office: Dept Statistics Tex A&M U College Station TX 7784

SMITH-VANIZ, WILLIAM REID, electrical engineer; b. Memphis, Feb. 16, 1925; s. William Reid and Louise (McDowell) S.; m. Joan James Pollard, Oct. 20, 1951; children—Alison, William, Thomas, Jane. S.B., MIT, 1947, S.M., 1952. Elec. engr. MIT, Cambridge, Mass., 1949-52; elec. engr., v.p. Trak Electronics, Wilton, Conn., 1952-65; sr. scientist Perkin-Elmer, Wilton, 1965-68; elec. engr., v.p. Product Devel. Service, Fairfield, Conn., 1968—. Patentee in fields of communications, info. processing and interferometry. Served with USN, 1944-46. Mem. IEEE, Sigma Xi. Current work: Microcomputer applications and operating systems; instrumentation and control. Subspecialties: Computer engineering; Software engineering. Home: 14 Pasture Ln Darien CT 06820 Office: Product Devel Services Inc 2000 Black Rock Turnpike Fairfield CT 06430

SMOLENSKY, MICHAEL HALE, physiology educator, chronobiology researcher; b. Chgo., May 10, 1942; s. Louis Rosenzweig and Lottie (Benditson) Smolensky-Rosenzweig; m. Michele Tauber, Aug. 17, 1963 (div. Apr. 1978); 1 child, Susan; m. Nita Beth Gathing, Oct. 18, 1980; children: Brian Burroughs, Melissa. B.S. in Zoology, U. Ill., 1964, M.S. in Physiology, 1964, Ph.D. in Physiology, 1971. Asst. prof. U. Tex. Sch. Pub. Heatlh, Houston, 1970-74, assoc. prof. environ. physiology, 1974—; research assoc. McGovern Allergy Clinic, Houston, 1972—; research cons. Tex. Allergy Research Found., Houston, 1974—. Co-author: Biological Rhythms and Medicine, 1983; co-editor: Chronobiology in Allergy and Immunology, 1977, Recent Advances in the Chronobiology of Allergy and Immunology, 1980, Internat. Jour. Chronobiology, 1983, Ann. Rev. of Chronopharmacology, 1984—. Mem. Cypress Creek Emergency Med. Service, Houston, 1974-77. Grantee NASA; grantee Nat. Inst. Occupational Safety and Health. Mem. Internat. Soc. Chronobiology (dir. 1982—, mem. organizing com. internatl. confs.), Soc. Menstrual Cycle Research (dir. 1976-77), Montreux Internat. Conf. of Biol. Rhythms and Medications (sec.-treas. 1983—), AAAS, Sigma Xi. Current work: Chronobiology, environmental physiology, environmental and occupational heatlh, public health, pharmacology, toxicology. Subspecialties: Physiology (biology); Chronobiology. Office: U Tex Sch Pub Health Health Sci Ctr at Houston Houston TX 77225

SMOLUCHOWSKI, ROMAN, physicist, educator; b. Zakopane, Austria, Aug. 31, 1910; came to U.S., 1935, naturalized, 1946; s. Marian and Sophia (Baraniecka) S.; m. Louise Catherine Riggs, Feb. 3, 1951; children—Peter, Irene. M.A., U. Warsaw, 1933; Ph.D., U. Groningen, Holland, 1935. Mem. Inst. Advanced Study, Princeton, 1935-36, instr., research asso. physics dept., 1939-41; prof. solid state scis. head solid state and materials program Princeton U., 1960-78; research asso., head physics sect. Inst. Metals, Warsaw, 1936-39; research physicist Gen. Electric Research Labs., Schenectady, 1941-46; asso. prof., staff Metals Research Lab., Carnegie Inst. Tech., 1946-50, prof. physics and metall. engring., 1950-56, prof. physics, 1956-60; prof. astronomy and physics U. Tex., Austin, 1978—; vis. prof. Internat. Sch. Solid State Physics, Mol, Belgium, 1963, Faculté des Sciences, Paris, 1965-66; lectr. Sch. Planetary Physics, Super-Besse, France, 1972; Fulbright prof. Sorbonne, Paris, 1955-56; lectr. Internat. Sch. Solid State Physics, Varenna, Italy, 1957, U. Liège, Belgium, 1956; vis. prof. NRC of Brazil, 1958-59, Tech. U. Munich, 1974; mem. solid state panel Research and Devel. Bd., Dept. Def., 1949, sec. panel, 1950-61; mem. tech. adv. bd. Aircraft Nuclear Propulsion, 1950; chmn. com. on magnetism Office Naval Research, 1952-56; chmn. com. on solids NRC, 1950-61, chmn. solid state scis. panel, 1961-67, chmn. div. phys. scis., 1969-75; mem. space sci. bd. Nat. Acad. Scis., 1969-75, mem. physics Survey, 1963-66, 1969-72; adv. com. metallurgy Oak Ridge Nat. Lab., 1960-62, mem. com. on planetary and lunar exploration, 1980-84. Author: (with Mayer and Weyl) Phase Transformations in Nearly Perfect Crystals, 1952, (with others) Molecular Science and Molecular Engineering, 1959, The Solar System—Sun, Planets and Life, 1983; editor: (with N. Kurti) Monograph Series on Solid State, 1957, (with W. Brinkman and E. Burstein) Comments in Solid State Physics, (with M. Glazer) Phase Transitions; co-editor: Ices in the Solar System; editor-in-chief: Crystal Lattice Defects and Amorphous Materials, Semiconductors and Insulators; asso. editor: Fundamentals of Cosmic Physics; Contbr. articles to profl. jours. Chmn. bd. trustees Simon's Rock Coll., 1971-72. Guggenheim Meml. fellow, 1974; fellow Churchill Coll. Cambridge U., Eng., 1974. Fellow Am. Phys. Soc. (chmn. div. solid state physics 1944-46), Am. Acad. Arts and Scis.; mem. AAAS, Internat. Astron. Union, Finnish Acad. Scis. and Letters, Am. Astron. Soc., Mex. Acad. Engring., Brazilian Acad. Scis., Sigma Xi, Alpha Sigma Mu, Pi Mu Epsilon. Current work: Theory of defects in solids. Heat transport in porous crystalline and amorphous cometary solids. Formation of H2. Resonance phenomena in the solar system. Subspecialties: Condensed matter physics; Planetary science. Home: 1401 Ethridge Ave Austin TX 78703 Office: U Tex Dept Physics and Astronomy Austin TX 78712

SMYTH, KERMIT CAMPBELL, chemist; b. Portland, Maine, Jan. 16, 1946; s. Duncan and Jean (Corthell) S.; married; 1 dau., Kirsten. B.A., Amherst Coll., 1968; Ph.D., Stanford U., 1972. Mem. tech. staff Bell Labs., Murray Hill, N.J., 1972-74; research chemist, head exploratory fire research group Nat. Bur. Standards, Gaithersburg, Md., 1974—. Contbr. articles to profl. jours. Recipient Bronze medal Dept. Commerce, 1981. Mem. Am. Phys. Soc., Sigma Xi, Phi Beta Kappa. Current Work: Application of laser-based optical diagnostic methods to study the chemistry of soot formation in flames. Subspecialties: Laser spectroscopy; Atomic and molecular physics. Office: Nat Bur Standards Bldg 224 Rm B260 Gaithersburg MD 20899

SNEDDON, LEIGH, physics educator; b. Newcastle, New South Wales, Australia, Oct. 26, 1952; came to U.S., 1979; s. William Kevin and Valerie Elizabeth (Coulcher) S.; m. Beatriz Alba Del Rio, Aug. 9, 1981. B.S. with 1st class honors, U. Sydney, Australia, 1974; M.S., U. New South Wales, 1975; Ph.D., Oxford U., England, 1978. Research assoc. Oxford U., 1978-79, Princeton U., N.J., 1979-82; asst. prof. Brandeis U., Waltham, Mass., 1982—; cons. in field; invited speaker numerous nat. and internat. orgns. Contbr. numerous articles to profl. jours. Mem. Am. Phys. Soc. Current work: Theory of electrical conductivity, particularly nonlinear effects, due to charge density waves in solids; general nonlinear dynamics; quantum properties of solids; statistical physics. Subspecialties: Condensed matter physics; Theoretical physics. Office: Martin Fisher Sch Physics Brandeis Univ 415 South St Waltham MA 02254

SNELL, GEORGE DAVIS, geneticist; b. Bradford, Mass., Dec. 19, 1903; s. Cullen Bryant and Katharine (Davis) S.; m. Rhoda Carson, July 28, 1937; children: Thomas Carleton, Roy Carson, Peter Garland. B.S., Dartmouth Coll., 1926; M.S., Harvard U., 1928, Sc.D., 1930; M.D. (hon.), Charles U., Prague, 1967; LL.D. (hon.), Colby Coll., 1982; Sc.D., Dartmouth Coll., 1974, Gustavus Adolphus Coll., 1981, U. Maine, 1981, Bates Coll., 1982, Ohio State U., 1984. Instr. zoology Dartmouth Coll., 1929-30, Brown U., 1930-31; asst. prof. Washington U., St. Louis, 1933-34; research asso. Jackson Lab., 1935-56, sr. staff scientist, 1957—, emeritus, 1969—, sci. adminstr., 1949-50. Co-author: Histocompatibility, 1976; also sci. papers in field; editor: The Biology of the Laboratory Mouse, 1941. Recipient Bertner Found. award in field cancer research, 1962; Griffin award Animal Care Panel, 1962; career award Nat. Cancer Inst., 1964-68; Gregor Mendel medal Czechoslovak Acad. Scis., 1967; Internat. award Gairdner Found., 1976; Wolf Found. prize in medicine, 1978; award Nat. Inst. Arthritis and Infectious Disease-Nat. Cancer Inst., 1978; Nobel prize in physiology or medicine (with Dausset and Benacerraf), 1980; NRC fellow U. Tex., 1931-33; NIH health research grantee for study genetics and immunology of tissue transplantation, 1950-73 (allergy and immunology study sect. 1958-62); Guggenheim fellow, 1953-54. Mem. Nat. Acad. Scis., Transplantation Soc., Am. Acad. Arts and Sci., French Acad. Scis. (fgn. asso.), Am. Philos. Soc., Brit. Transplantation Soc. (hon.), Phi Beta Kappa. Current Work: Writing . Home: 21 Atlantic Ave Bar Harbor ME 04609

SNELL, JACK EASTLAKE, federal agency administrator; b. Evanston, Ill., Nov. 29, 1935; s. Clarence Eastlake and Ruth (Meloy) S.; m. Elizabeth Kercher, Oct. 15, 1966; children—Jeffrey Eastlake, Julie Elizabeth. B.S.E. with honors in Aero. Engring., Princeton U., 1957; M.S. in Indsl. Engring., Northwestern U., 1965; Ph.D. in Civil Engring., Northwestern U., 1966; grad., Fed. Exec. Inst., 1979. Aircraft maintenance engr. Pan Am. World Airways, N.Y.C., 1960; asst. prof. transp. engring., and dir. Transp. and Urban Systems Lab., Princeton U., 1966-71; chief bldg. service systems sect. Nat. Bur. Standards, Washington, 1971-73, asst. chief bldg. environ. div., 1973-74; chief Office Energy Conservation, 1974-76; dir. Office Energy Programs, 1976-81; dir. Ctr. Fire Research Nat. Engring. Lab., 1981—; mem. various fed. interagy. energy task forces, 1973-79; steering com. Intersoc. Energy Conversion Engring. Conf.; mem. Md. Gov.'s Sci. Adv. Council, 1976—; chmn. U.S.-Japan Panel on Fire Research and Safety. Contbr. articles to profl. jours. Served to 1st lt. USAF, 1953-60. Recipient Silver medal dept. Commerce, 1975. Charter mem. U.S. Sr. Exec. Service.; Mem. ASME (chmn. advanced energy systems div. 1981), Nat. Fire Protection Assn. (chmn. toxicity adv. com.), AAAS, Sigma Xi, Chi Epsilon. Presbyterian. Office: National Bureau of Standards Washington DC 20234

SNELL, TERRY WAYNE, biology educator, researcher; b. Miami, Fla., Dec. 23, 1948; s. William Madison and Sophie (Horowitz) S.; m. Sandra Jeanne Malafronte, Feb. 25, 1984. A.S., Miami-Dade Community Coll., 1968; B.S., Fla. So. Coll., 1970; M.S., U. South Fla., 1973, Ph.D., 1977. Postdoctoral research assoc. U. South Fla., Tampa, 1977; asst. prof. biology Wright State U., Dayton, Ohio, 1977-78; asst. prof. biology U. Tampa, 1978-82, assoc. prof., 1982—. Contbr. articles to profl. jours. Grantee NSF, 1980, 83-86, Binat. Agrl. Research and Devel. Fund, 1980-83. Mem. Genetics Soc. Am., Soc. for Study Evolution, AAAS, Sigma Xi. Subspecialties: Evolutionary biology; Population biology. Office: Div Sci and Math U Tampa 401 W Kennedy Blvd Tampa FL 33606

SNIDER, JOSEPH LYONS, physicist; b. Boston, June 10, 1934; s. Joseph Lyons and Greta (Wood) S.; m. Ann Lackritz Fuller, June 27, 1981; children: Karen, Benjamin. B.A., Amherst Coll., 1956; Ph.D., Princeton U., 1961. Instr., research fellow in physics Harvard U., 1961-64, asst. prof. physics, 1964-69; assoc. prof. physics Oberlin (Ohio) Coll., 1969-75, prof., 1975—. Mem. AAAS, Am. Phys. Soc., Am. Astron. Soc., Am. Assn. Physics Tchrs., AAUP. Current Work: Solar rotation and oscillation, teaching relativity and gen. physics. Subspecialties: Solar physics; Relativity and gravitation. Office: Dept of Physics Oberlin College Oberlin OH 44074

SNOW, JOEL ALAN, government executive; b. Brockton, Mass., Apr. 1, 1937; s. George Herbert and Mary Wilson (Sproul) S.; m. Laetita Harrer, June 27, 1959; children—Jonathan Edward, Nicholas Harrer. B.A., U. N.C., 1958; M.A., Washington U., St. Louis, 1964, Ph.D., 1967. Program dir. theoretical physics NSF, Washington, 1969-71, dep. asst. dir., 1971-74, dir. planning and resource mgmt., 1974-76; sr. policy analyst Exec. Office Pres., Washington, 1976-77; assoc. dir. research policy U.S. Dept. Energy, Washington, 1977-81, dir. sci. and tech. affairs, 1981—. Contbr. numerous articles to profl. jours. Served to lt. U.S. Navy, 1958-64. Recipient Meritorious Service award NSF, 1974; award William A. Jump Found., 1975; Arthur S. Flemming award U.S. Jaycees, 1976. Fellow AAAS (judge AAAS-Westinghouse Sci. Writing 1969—); mem. Am. Phys. Soc., World Future Soc., Sigma Xi. Current work: Responsible for scientific advice to Sec. of Energy through Energy Research Advisory Board; advise on research policy for U.S. Dept. Energy; speeches and policy statements on government research policy. Subspecialties: Condensed matter physics; Energy research management. Office: Office Energy Research US Dept Energy 1000 Independence Ave SW Washington DC 20585

SNOW, WILLIAM ROSEBROOK, physicist, technical adminstrator; b. N.Y.C., Jan. 6, 1930; s. William Boring and Genevieve (Rosebrook) S.; m. Phyllis Dodson, Aug. 25, 1951; children: William Dodson, David James. B.S. in Physics, Stanford U., 1952; M.S. in Physics, U. Wash., 1964, Ph.D., 1966. Reactor physicist Gen. Electric Co., Hanford, Wash., 1952-54; physicist Precision Tech., Inc., Calif., 1954-58; staff assoc. Gen. Atomic, 1958-62; research staff Aerospace Corp., Calif., 1966-68; asst. prof. physics U. Mo., Rolla, 1968-73, assoc. prof., 1973-78; staff scientist Pacific Western Systems, Inc., Mountain View, Calif., 1978-81, tech. dir., 1981—. Contbr. articles in field to profl. jours. Mem. Am. Phys. Soc., Am. Vacuum Soc., Electrochemical Soc., Sigma Xi. Current Work: Negative ion charge transfer, molecular beams, plasma enhanced chem. vapor deposition. Subspecialties: Atomic and molecular physics; Plasma physics. Office: 505 E Evelyn Ave Mountain View CA 94041

SNYDER, ANN CATHERINE, physical education educator; b. Lansing, Mich., July 16, 1951; d. Warren G. and Ann Catherine (Dearing) S. B.S., Western Mich. U., 1973; M.Ed., Bowling Green State U., 1975; M.A., Mich. State U., 1979; Ph.D., Purdue U., 1982. Asst. prof. phys. edn. Ball State U., Muncie, Ind., 1982—. Contbr. articles to profl. jours. Research grantee Internat. Inst. Sports Medicine, 1984-85. Mem. Am. Coll. Sports Medicine (bd. dirs. 1982-84, pres.-elect regional chpt. 1984-85), AAHPERD Muncie Jaycee Women (pres. 1984-85). Methodist. Current work: Determination of mechanisms involved in exercise training adaptations, specifically, occurances of athletic amenorrhea and muscle soreness. Subspecialty: Physiology (biology). Home: Rural Route 9 PO Box 189 Muncie IN 47302 Office: Ball State U Human Performance Lab Muncie IN

SNYDER, ARNOLD PETER, biochemist, researcher; b. Sellersville, Pa., Jan. 28, 1952; s. Arnold Carson and Elfriede Martha (Gunther) S. B.A., Mansfield U. Pa., 1974; student SUNY-Buffalo, 1974-75; Ph.D., Pa. State U., 1981. Fellow Pa. State U., University Park, 1975-81; research biochemist Chem. Research and Devel. Ctr., Aberdeen Proving Ground, Md., 1982—. Contbr. articles to profl. jours. Patentee in field. Recipient Army Research and Devel. Achievement award U.S. Army, 1984. Mem. Am. Chem. Soc., AAAS, Am. Soc. Microbiology, N.Y. Acad. Sci., Sigma Xi. Lutheran. Current work: Basic and applied research in rapid, spectroscopic and mass spectrometry techniques (triple quadrupole, atmospheric pressure ionization, pyrolysis) in the detection and identification of microorganisms, fluorescence and excitation laser applications in biochemistry and neurophysiology. Subspecialties: Analytical microbiology; Laser biochemistry. Home: 422 Campus Hills Dr Bel Air MD 21014 Office: AMCCOM Chemical Research and Devel Ctr SMCCR-RSL Aberdeen Proving Ground MD 21010

SNYDER, FRED LEONARD, biochemist; b. New Ulm, Minn., Nov. 22, 1931; s. George B. and Lillian R. (Meyer) S.; m. Joy D. Synder, Nov. 22, 1978; children: Vicki, David, Jon. Ph.D., U. N.D., 1958. Chief scientist med. and health sci. div. Oak Ridge Assos. Univs., Tenn., 1958-75; faculty U. Tenn.—Oak Ridge Grad. Sch. Biomed. Scis., 1972—, asst. chmn. med. and health sci. div., 1975-79, assoc. chmn., 1979—; prof. biochemistry U. Tenn. Center for Health Scis., Memphis, 1964—; prof. medicinal chemistry U. N.C., Chapel Hill, 1966—, chmn., 1981-82; mem. Am. Cancer Soc. adv. com. on biochemistry and chem. carcinogenesis, 1979-82. Editorial bd.: Reviews on Cancer, 1973-78, Biochimica Biophys. Acta, 1972-78, Archives of Biochemistry and Biophysics, 1972-78, Jour. Lipid Research, 1966—; asso. editor: Cancer Research, 1971-78; contbr. articles to profl. jours. & Lipid biochemistry, membranes, biol. chem. mediators. Nat. Heart Inst. fellow, 1955-58. Mem. Am. Soc. Biol. Chemists, Am. Assn. Cancer Research, Soc. Exptl. Biology and Medicine, Sigma Xi. Subspecialty: Biochemistry (biology). Office: ORAU PO Box 117 Oak Ridge TN 37830

SNYDER, FREEMAN WOODROW, retired plant physiologist; b. Phila., Dec. 6, 1917; s. Freeman and Mary Anna (Shaffer) S.; m. Elizabeth Fink, Aug. 6, 1938; children: Robert Gordon, Barbara Naneen Snyder St. John. B.S., U. Idaho, 1938; Ph.D., Cornell U., 1950. Asst. agronomist U. Ark., Fayetteville, 1950-53; adj. asst. prof. adj. assoc. prof. crop and soil scis. Mich. State U., East Lansing, 1957-75; plant physiologist U.S. Dept. Agr., East Lansing, 1953-75, Beltsville, Md., 1975-83. Contbr. article to profl. jours. Served with AUS, 1943-46. Mem. AAAS, Am. Inst. Biol. Scis., Crop Sci. Soc. Am., Am. Soc. Plant Physiologists, Am. Soc. Sugarbeet Technologists. Current Work: Use of physiological and morphological characteristics to increase yield of alfalfa, sugarbeet and other crops; partitioning of the photosynthate. Subspecialties: Plant physiology (biology); Plant physiology (agriculture).

SNYDER, GLENN JACOB, mechanical engineer; b. Akron, Ohio, Aug. 1, 1923; s. George and Henrietta Louise (Ley) S.; m. Donna Lou Jones, Oct. 11, 1927; children: Gavin Jay, Leslie Marie, Adrianne Lee, Jeffrey David. B.S.M.E., Ohio U., 1949; postgrad. in thermodynamics, Akron U., 1950; postgrad. in mech. engring, U. Va., 1961-64; postgrad. in bus. adminstrn, Lynchburg Coll., 1965-69. Registered profl. engr., Ohio, Va. Plant engr. Ohio Boxboard Co., Rittman, 1950-52; sr. plant engr. Goodyear Aerospace Corp., Akron, 1952-55; group supr. remote handling and maintenance equipment design Nuclear Power Generation div. Babcock and Wilcox Co., Lynchburg, Va., 1955-61, unit mgr. reactor vessel, structural internals and rod drive mechanisms design, 1961-79, prin. engr. advanced reactor unit on liquid metal fast breeder reactor, large devel. plant, 1979-84; pub. speaker, trainer on nuclear power generation and other subjects. Deacon, elder Rivermont Presbyterian Ch., 1959—; Meml. Bible Plan rep. Gideons Internat., Lynchburg North Camp, 1976—. Served as staff sgt. U.S. Army, 1943-46, PTO. Mem. ASME (chmn. Va. sect. 1979-80, 82-83), Nat. Soc. Profl. Engrs., Soc. Mfg. Engrs., Am. Nuclear Soc. Republican. Clubs: Lynchburg, Babcock & Wilcox, Toastmasters. (area gov. 1978-79). Current Work: Mechanical engineering consultant to nuclear power, aerospace, rubber and plastics industries. Subspecialties: Mechanical engineering; Systems engineering. Home: 3300 Woodridge Pl Lynchburg VA 23503 Office: PO Box 1260 Lynchburg VA 24505

SNYDER, JAMES JACOB, physicist; b. Lyons, N.Y., Jan. 19, 1940; s. Howard Lincoln and Mary (Donnelly) S.; m. Asta-Marie Schulze, Jan. 11, 1964; children—Anne-Marie, Kevin Howard. B.S. in Math., SUNY-Stony Brook, 1969, Ph.D. in Elec. Engring., 1973. Postdoctoral fellow Nat. Bur. Standards, Boulder, Colo., 1973-75, physicist, Gaithersburg, Md., 1975—; cons. U.N. Devel. Program, Beijing, China, 1984; vis. scientist Centre National de la Recherche Scientifique, 1978-79. Editor: Laser Character and Control, 1986. Contbr. articles to profl. jours. Inventor and patentee in field. Served with U.S. Army, 1959-62. Recipient Spl. Achievement award Dept. Commerce, 1977, Inventor Incentive award, 1980; cert. of recognition Nat. Bur. Standards, 1982. Mem. Optical Soc. Am. Current work: Laser physics, laser metrology, interferometry, digital electronics and computers. Subspecialty: Laser spectroscopy. Office: NBS Physics A141 Gaithersburg MD 20899

SNYDER, JAMES NEWTON, physicist, computer scientist, educator; b. Akron, Ohio, Feb. 17, 1923; s. Louis Emery and Mary (Sullivan) S.; m. Betty Jane Cooper, July 28, 1944; 1 son, James Newton. B.S., Harvard, 1945, M.A., 1947, Ph.D., 1949. Mem. faculty physics dept. U. Ill. at Urbana, 1949—; asso. prof. Digital Computer Lab., 1957-58, prof., 1958-70, prof. computer sci. and physics, head dept. computer sci., 1970—; head computer div. Midwestern U. Research Assn., Madison, Wis., 1956-57. Contbr. articles to profl. jours. Mem. Am. Phys. Soc., A.A.A.S., Assn. Computing Machinery, I.E.E.E., Phi Beta Kappa, Sigma Xi. Subspecialty: Administration. Home: 2304 S Vine St Urbana IL 61801

SNYDER, SOLOMON HALBERT, psychiatrist-pharmacologist; b. Washington, Dec. 26, 1938; s. Samuel Simon and Patricia (Yakerson) S.; m. Elaine Borko, June 10, 1962; children—Judith Rhea, Deborah Lynn. Student, Georgetown U., 1955-58, M.D. cum laude, 1962; D.Sc. (hon.), Northwestern U., 1981. Intern Kaiser Found. Hosp., San Francisco, 1962-63; research asso. NIMH, Bethesda, Md., 1963-65; resident psychiatry Johns Hopkins Hosp., Balt., 1965-68; asso. prof. psychiatry and pharmacology Johns Hopkins Med. Sch., 1968-70, prof., 1970-77, Disting. Service prof. psychiatry and pharmacology, 1977-80, Disting. Service prof. neurosci., psychiatry, and pharmacology, 1980—, dir. dept. neurosci., 1980—; NIH lectr., 1979. Author: Uses of Marijuana, 1971, Madness and the Brain, 1973, Opiate Receptor Mechanisms, 1975, The Troubled Mind, 1976, Biologic Aspects of Mental Disorder, 1980; editor: Perspectives in Neuropharmacology, 1971, Frontiers in Catecholamine Research, 1973, Handbook of Psychopharmacology, 1974; contbr. articles to profl. jours. Served with USPHS, 1963-65. Recipient Outstanding Scientist award Md. Acad. Scis., 1969; John Jacob Abel award Am. Pharmacology Soc., 1970; A.E. Bennett award Soc. Biol. Psychiatry, 1970; Gaddum award Brit. Pharm. Soc., 1974; F.O. Schmitt award in neuroscis. MIT, 1974; Nicholas Giarman lecture award Yale U., 1975; Rennebohm award U. Wis., 1976; Salmon award, 1977; Stanley Dean award Am. Coll. Psychiatrists, 1978; Harvey Lecture award, 1978; Lasker award, 1978; Wolf prize, 1983; Dickson prize, 1983; Einstein award for research in psychiatry Albert Einstein Coll. Medicine, 1985. Fellow Am. Coll. Neuropsychopharmacology (Daniel Efron award 1974), Am. Psychiat. Assn. (Hofheimer award 1972), Am. Acad. Arts and Scis.; mem. Psychiat. Research Soc., Nat. Acad. Scis., Soc. for Neuroscis. (pres. 1979-80), Am. Soc. Biol. Chemists, Am. Pharmacology Soc. Subspecialties: Psychopharmacology; Neuropharmacology. Office: Johns Hopkins U Med Sch Dept Neurosci Baltimore MD 21205*

SNYDERMAN, SELMA E(LEANORE), physician, educator; b. Phila.; d. Harry Samuel and Rose (Koss) S.; m. Joseph Schein, Aug. 4, 1939; children—Roland Milo Hyatt, Oliver Douglas. A.B., U. Pa., 1937, M.D., 1940. Diplomate Am. Bd. Pediatrics, Am. Bd. Clin. Nutrition. Intern Albert Einstein Med. Ctr., Phila., 1940-42; resident Bellevue Hosp., N.Y.C., 1943-45, fellow, 1946-47; asst. prof. pediatrics NYU, N.Y.C., 1950-57, assoc. prof., 1957-67, prof., 1967—, dir. metabolic disorders ctr., 1967—; assoc. prof. U. Tex. Med. Br., Galveston, 1952-53; mem. nutrition study sect. NIH, Bethesda, 1973-77; field reviewer FDA, Washington, 1983. Contbr. numerous articles on amino acid metabolism and metabolic disorders to profl. jours. Recipient Career Scientist award Health Research Council, 1961-75. Mem. Soc. Pediatric Research, Am. Pediatric Soc., Am. Acad. Pediatrics (amino acid com. 1975-79, Borden award 1975), Soc. for Inherited Metabolic Disorders (v.p. 1978—, pres. 1979—), Soc. for Study Inborn Errors Metabolism, Phi Beta Kappa. Jewish. Current work: Amino acid metabolism; inherited metabolic errors; nutritional requirements. Subspecialties: Pediatrics; Biochemistry (medicine). Home: 300 Central Park W New York NY 10024 Office: NYU Med Ctr 550 1st Ave New York NY 10016

SOBOL, BRUCE J., physician, researcher, consultant; b. N.Y.C.; s. Ira J. and Ida (Gelula) S.; m. Barbara Gordon, Apr. 30, 1951; children—Peter G., Scott D. B.S., Swarthmore Coll.; M.D., NYU. Diplomate Am. Bd. Internal Medicine. Intern Bellevue Hosp., N.Y.C., 1950-51, resident, 1951-52; resident in cardiology VA Hosp., Boston, 1952-53; fellow N.Y. Heart Assn. at Bellevue Hosp., N.Y.C., 1953-55; dir. cardiopulmonary lab N.Y. Med. Coll., Valhalla, 1959-78, prof. medicine, 1970-78, research prof. medicine, 1978—; dir. med. research Boehringer Ingelheim, Ridgefield, Ct., 1978-83; attending physician Westchester County Med. Ctr., Valhalla, 1959-84; cons. Danbury Hosp., Ct., 1979—, Burke Rehab. Hosp., White Plains, N.Y., 1978—. Contbr. articles to profl. jours. Served to pfc. U.S. Army, 1943-45; ETO. Grantee Am. Thoracic Soc., N.Y. State Dept. Health, Westchester Heart Assn. Fellow N.Y. Acad. Scis., ACP, Am. Coll. Chest Physicians, Am. Coll. Allergy. Current work: Consultant pharacueticals, pharmaeutical research and advertising, medical instrumentation, new chemical entities. Subspecialties: Pulmonary medicine; Cardiology. Office: B & B Assocs 275 Ridgebury Rd Ridgefield CT 06877

SOCOLOW, ROBERT HARRY, scientist, engineering educator; b. N.Y.C., Dec. 27, 1937; s. A. Walter and Edith (Gutman) S.; m. Elizabeth Anne Sussman, June 10, 1962 (div. Apr. 27, 1982); children: David, Seth. B.A., Harvard U., 1959, M.A., 1961, Ph.D., 1964. Asst. prof. physics Yale U., New Haven, 1966-71; assoc. prof. mech. and aerospace engring. Princeton U. (N.J.), 1971-77, prof. mech. and aerospace engring., 1977—; mem. Inst. Advanced Study, Princeton, 1971; dir. Center for Energy and Environmental Studies, Princeton, 1978—. Author: (with John Harte) Patient Earth, 1971, (with K. Ford, G. Rochlin, M. Ross) Efficient Use of Energy, 1975, (with H.A. Feiveson, F.W. Sinden) Boundaries of Analysis: An Inquiry into the Tocks Island Dam Controversy, 1976, Saving Energy in the Home: Princeton's Experiments at Twin Rivers, 1979. Mem. Council Fedn. Am. Scientists, 1981—. John Simon Guggenheim fellow, 1976-77; German Marshall Fund fellow, 1976-77; Yale Jr. Faculty fellow, 1970-71; NSF Postdoctoral fellow, 1964-66; NSF Predoctoral fellow, 1960-64. Fellow Am. Phys. Soc., Fedn. Am. Scientists, AAUP, AAAS. Jewish. Current Work: Energy use in buildings, energy policy, global resources. Home: 37 Laurel Rd Princeton NJ 08540 Office: H102 Engineering Quad Princeton Univ Princeton NJ 08544

SOFFEN, GERALD ALAN, government official; b. Cleve., Feb. 7, 1926. B.A., UCLA, 1949; M.S., U. So. Calif., 1956; Ph.D.; USPHS fellow 1958-59, Princeton U., 1960, NYU, 1960-61. Sr. scientist Jet Propulsion Lab. Calif. Inst. Tech., 1961-79; former chief scientist Viking project NASA, Langley Research Center, Hampton, Va.; dir. NASA Life Scis., from 1979; now assoc. dir. space and earth scis. Goddard Space Flight Ctr., Greenbelt, Md. Served with AUS, 1944-46. Mem. AAAS. Subspecialty: Government space program administration. Office: NASA Space Flight Ctr Greenbelt MD 20771

SOFFER, BERNARD H., physicist; b. Bklyn., Mar. 2, 1931; s. Meyer and Sabina (Adlersheim) S.; m. Reba Nussbaum; 1 son: Roger. B.S., Bklyn. Coll., 1953; M.S., M.I.T., 1958. Staff mem. Lab. for Insulation Research, M.I.T., 1958-59; mem. tech. staff Hughes Research Lab., Malibu, Calif., 1959-61; sr. scientist Korad Corp., Santa Monica, Calif., 1961-69, sr. staff physicist, 1969—. Contbr. articles to profl. jours. Served with U.S. Army, 1953-55. Fellow Optical Soc. Am.; mem. IEEE (sr.), Am. Phys. Soc., Sigma Xi. Patentee in field. Current Work: Research and development in optical signal and image processing and devices. Subspecialty: Optical signal processing. Home: 665 Bienveneda Ave Pacific Palisades CA 90272 Office: 3011 Malibu Canyon Rd Malibu CA 90265

SOFIA, ROBERT DUANE, pharmaceutical company executive, pharmacologist; b. Ellwood City, Pa., Oct. 8, 1942; s. Mario and Clara (Mancini) S.; m. Shirley Ann., Sept. 11, 1965; children: Robert, Maria, Tricia, Joella. B.S., Geneva Coll., 1964; M.S., Fairleigh-Dickinson U., 1969; Ph.D. (NIH predoctoral trainee), U. Pitts., 1971. Research biologist dept. pharmacology and exptl. therapeutics Lederle Labs., Inc., Pearl River, N.Y., 1964-67; research assoc. dept. pharmacology Union Carbide Corp., Tuxedo, N.Y., 1967-69; investigator Pharmakon Labs., Scranton, Pa., 1969, supr., 1969-71, cons., 1971; sr. pharmacologist Wallace Labs. div. Carter-Wallace, Inc., Cranbury, N.J., 1971-73, dir. dept. pharmacology and toxicology, 1973-76, v.p. biol. research, 1976-80, v.p. research and devel., 1980-82, v.p. preclin. research, 1982—; co-adj. lectr. continuing edn. Rutgers U. Coll. Pharmacy, New Brunswick, N.J., 1973, 77, vis. assoc. prof. pharmacology, 1979-84; mem. tech., merit rev. panel Nat. Inst. Neurol. and Communicative Disorders and Stroke, 1979. Contbr. numerous abstracts, articles to profl. jours. Mem. AAAS, N.Y. Acad. Scis. (Pulmonary Research Group), Soc. Neurosci., Inflammation Research Assn. (pres. 1975-78), Internat. Assn. for Study Pain (founding), Am. Soc. Pharmacology and Exptl. Therapeutics, Soc. Toxicology, Eastern Pain Assn. (charter), Physiol. Soc. Phila., Am. Chem. Soc., Am. Rheumatism Assn., Am. Assn. Lab. Animal Sci. (Wallace Labs. rep. 1977—), Research and Devel. Council N.J. (Carter-Wallace rep. 1977—), European Biol. Research Assn. (assoc.), Am. Pain Soc. (charter), Soc. Research Administrs., Internat. Soc. for Study Xenobiotics (charter), Sigma Xi. Current Work: Research adminstrn. Subspecialties: Pharmacology; Toxicology (medicine). Office: Wallace Labs Half Acre Rd Cranbury NJ 08512

SOGAH, DOTSEVI YAO, chemical company executive, researcher; b. Tegbi, Ghana, Apr. 19, 1945; came to U.S. 1971; s. Kodzo Ahiatsi and Fiawosinu (Kwawudzo) S.; m. Monica Adzo Selonmey, July 15, 1973; children—Senanu, Dodzie, Esinam. B.Sc. first class, U. Ghana, Legon-Accra, 1970, B.Sc. with honors, 1971; M.S., UCLA, 1974, Ph.D., 1975. Postdoctoral fellow U. Calif., Santa Barbara, 1975-77; research assoc. UCLA, 1977-80, vis. prof., 1978-80; research chemist DuPont Co., Wilmington, Del., 1981-83, group leader, 1983-84, research supr., 1984—. Contbr. articles to profl. jours.; patentee in field. British Commonwealth fellow, 1971, AID fellow, 1971-75; recipient Wadell prize U. Ghana, 1974; named one of 100 Outstanding/Brightest Scientists in Am., Sci. Digest, 1984. Mem. N.Y. Acad. Scis., Internat. Soc. African Scientists (bd. dirs. 1982-84, chmn. projects com., 1985—), Am. Chem. Soc. (chmn. membership com. Del. 1984—), Sigma Xi. Roman Catholic. Current work: Polymer synthesis, kinetics and mechanisms, organosilicon chemistry, polymers for biomedical applications, drug delivery systems, synthetic enzymes and enzyme models. Subspecialties: Polymer chemistry; Organic chemistry. Home: 2518 Channin Dr Wilmington DE 19810 Office: Central Research and Devel Dept E I duPont de Nemours & Co Inc Experimental Sta Wilmington DE 19898

SOGANDARES-BERNAL, FRANKLIN, biology educator, researcher, consultant; b. Ancon, C.A., Panama, May 12, 1931; came to U.S., 1951; s. Anastasio and Blanca Helena Bernal-Almillategui; m. Lucy Ann McAlister, 1960 (div. 1982); children: Franklin McAlister, Maria Helena, John Francis Marion. B.S., Tulane U., 1954; M.S., U. Nebr., Lincoln, 1955, Ph.D., 1958. Instr., asst. prof., prof. Tulane U., New Orleans, 1959-71, coordinator sci. planning, 1965-68; prof., chmn. zoology U. Mont., Missoula, 1971-72, prof. microbiology, 1972-74; prof. biology So. Meth. U., Dallas, 1974—, chmn. biology, 1974-76; cons. in pathology Baylor U. Med. Center, Dallas, 1974—, med. staff affiliate, 1978—, dir. Ctr. Infectious Diseases Research; research affiliate Nebr. State Mus., Lincoln, 1972—, pvt. practice cons. immunologist, Dallas, 1978—; sci. adv. bd. EPA, Washington, 1980-82. Contbr. articles to profl. jours. Mem. Am. Soc. Parasitologists (council 1970-73, editorial bd 1964-67, H.B. Ward medal 1969), Am. Assn. Pathologists, Soc. Wildlife Diseases, Conf. Biol. Editors, N.Y. Acad. Scis., Am. Soc. Zoologists, Nat. Rifle Assn. (life). Democrat. Current Work: Consultant in parasitology and immunopathology, pathology; research parasitic disease and tropical medicine, antigen fractionation, Chagas Disease, cerebral cysticercosis diagnosis. Subspecialties: Parasitology; Pathology (medicine). Home: 10622 Royal Chapel Dr Dallas TX 75229 Office: Southern Meth Univ Dallas TX 75275

SOHN, HONG YONG, b. Kaesung, Kyunggi-do, Korea, Aug. 21, 1941; came to U.S., 1966; s. Chong-ku and Soon-Deuk (Woo) S.; m. Victoria Ngo, Jan. 8, 1971; children—Berkeley Jihoon, Edward Jihyun. B.S. in Chem. Engring., Seoul Nat. U., 1962; M.Sc., U. N.B., 1966; Ph.D., U. Calif.-Berkeley, 1970. Engr., Cheil Sugar Co., Pusan, Korea, 1962-64, Can. Starch Co., Cardinal, Ont., 1966; research assoc. SUNY-Buffalo, 1971-73; research engr. DuPont Co., Wilmington, Del., 1973-74; prof. metallurgy and fuels engring. U. Utah, Salt Lake City, 1974—; cons. Lawrence Livermore Nat. Lab., others. Co-author: (with J. Szekely and J.W. Evans) Gas Solid Reactions, 1976. Editor: Rate Processes of Extractive Metallurgy, 1976, others. Contbr. articles to profl. jours. Patentee in field. Bd. dirs. Asian Ass. Utah, 1984—. Recipient Tchr. Scholar award Camille and Henry Dreyfus Found., 1977; Alcoa Found. grantee, 1982; Fulbright Disting. lectr., 1983; NSF grantee, 1975-85; Dept. Energy grantee, 1976-81; Dept. Interior grantee, 1979-83, others. Mem. Metall. Soc. of AIME, Am. Inst. Chem. Engrs. Current work: Extractive metallurgy; fluid solid reaction engring; combustion of solids; oil shale conversion. Subspecialties: Metallurgy; Chemical engineering. Office: Univ Utah 417 Browning Bldg Salt Lake City UT 84112-1183

SOKOL, ROBERT JAMES, researcher, medical educator, obstetrician-gynecologist; b. Rochester, N.Y., Nov. 18, 1941; s. Eli and Mildred (Levine) S.; m. Roberta Sue Kahn, July 26, 1964; children: Melissa Anne, Eric Russell, Andrew Ian. B.A. with highest distinction, U. Rochester, 1963, M.D. with honors, 1966. Diplomate Am. Bd. Ob-Gyn, 1972, Am. Bd. Maternal-Fetal Medicine, 1975. Resident in ob-gyn Barnes Hosp./Washington U., St. Louis, 1966-70; Buswell fellow in maternal-fetal medicine Strong Meml. Hosp./U. Rochester, 1972-73; asst. prof. Cleve. Met. Gen. Hosp./Case Western Res. U., 1973-77, co-program dir. perinatal clin. research ctr., 1973-81, assoc. prof., 1977-81, prof., 1981-83, assoc. dir. dept. ob-gyn, 1981-83, program dir. perinatal clin. research ctr., 1982-83; prof., chmn. dept. ob-gyn Wayne State U., Detroit, 1983—, mem. grad. faculty dept. physiology, 1984—; chief ob-gyn Hutzel Hosp., 1983—; dir. C.S. Mott Ctr. for Human Growth and Devel., 1983—; cons. Nat. Inst. Child Health and Human Devel., Nat. Inst. Alcohol Abuse and Alcoholism, Ctr. Disease Control, NIH, Health Resources and Services Adminstrn.; asso. examiner Am. Bd. Ob-Gyn; mem. alcohol psychosocial research rev. com. Nat. Inst. Alcohol Abuse and Alcoholism. Reviewer profl. jours.; contbr. articles to sci. jours., chpts. to books. Served from capt. to maj. USAF, 1970-72. Grantee NIH; grantee Nat. Inst. Alcohol Abuse and Alcoholism, others. Mem. Soc. Perinatal Obstetricians, Perinatal Research Soc., Soc. Gynecologic Investigation, Research Soc. on Alcoholism, Assn. Profs. Gynecology and Obstetrics, Behavioral Teratology Soc., Am. Pub. Health Assn., Royal Soc. Medicine, Central Assn. Obstetricians and Gynecologists, Am. Coll. Obstetricians and Gynecologists, Phi Beta Kappa, Sigma Xi, Alpha Omega Alpha. Current Work: Perinatal risk assessment database management and statistical analysis; alcohol-related birth defects; low birth weight risks and outcomes; algorithmic diagnosis and management; fetal risks of ultrasound exposure. Subspecialties: Maternal and fetal medicine; Database systems. Home: 5200 Rector Ct Bloomfield Hills MI 48013 Office: 4707 Saint Antoine Detroit MI 48201

SOKOLOFF, JEFFREY BRUCE, physicist; b. N.Y.C., Oct. 7, 1941; s. Jack and Charlotte (Jaraslow) S.; m. Miriam Kandler, June 30, 1968; children—Eva Meira, Leah Judith, Shoshana Rachel. B.S., Queens Coll., 1965; Ph.D., MIT, 1967. Research assoc. Brookhaven Nat. Lab., Upton, N.Y., 1967-69; asst. prof. Northeastern U., Boston, 1969-74, assoc. prof., 1974-79, prof. physics, 1979—; vis. scientist Bar: Ilan U., Ramat, Israel, 1971, Weitzmann Inst., Rehovot, Israel, 1980; com. for Conf. on Magnetism and Magnetism Materials, Boston, 1973. Contbr. articles to profl. jours. Grantee U.S. Dept. Energy, 1979—, NSF, 1979—. Mem. Am. Phys. Soc. Current work: Condensed matter physics; sliding charge density waves, quantum hall effect electronic structure in incommensurate periodic potentials, itinerant electron theory of magnetism. Subspecialty: Condensed matter physics. Home: 21 Hancock Rd Brookline MA 02146 Office: Northeastern U Boston MA 02115

SOKOLOFF, LOUIS, physiologist, neurochemist; b. Phila., Oct. 14, 1921; (married); 2 children. B.A., U. Pa., 1943, M.D., 1946. Intern Phila. Gen. Hosp., 1946-47; research fellow in physiology U. Pa. Grad. Sch. Medicine, 1949-51, instr., then asso., 1951-56; asso. chief, then chief sect. cerebral metabolism NIMH, Bethesda, Md., 1953-68, chief lab. cerebral metabolism, 1968—. Chief editor: Jour. Neurochemistry, 1974-78. Served to capt. M.C. U.S. Army, 1947-49. Recipient F.O. Schmitt medal in neurosci., 1980; Albert Lasker clin. med. research award, 1981. Mem. Am. Physiol. Soc., Assn. Research Nervous and Mental Diseases, Am. Biophys. Soc., Am. Acad. Neurology, Am. Neurol. Assn., Am. Soc. Biol. Chemists, Am. Soc. Neurochemistry, U.S. Nat. Acad. Scis. Subspecialty: Physiology (biology). Address: NIMH Bethesda MD 20892

SOLBERG, RUELL FLOYD, JR., mechanical engineer; b. Norse, Tex., July 27, 1939; s. Ruel Floyd and Ruby Mae (Rogstad) S.; m. Laquetta Jane Massey, Oct. 3, 1959; children: Chandra Dawn Solberg Hamilton, Marla Gaye. B.S., U. Tex., 1962, M.S., 1967; M.B.A., Trinity U., San Antonio, 1977. Registered profl. engr., Tex. Research engr. assoc. II, acoustics div. Def. Research Lab., Austin, Tex., 1962-65, research engr. assoc. III, 1965-67, asst. supr. mech. engring. sect., 1966-67; research engr., dept. applied electromagnetics S.W. Research Inst., San Antonio, 1967-70, sr. research engr., 1970-74, sr. research engr. electromagnetics div., 1974-75, sr. research engr. dept. electromagnetic engring., 1975—, tech. asst. Applied Mechanics Revs., 1980-83. Co-author: The Solbergs from Norway to Texas, 1979; contbr. articles to profl. jours. Charter mem. Norwegian Soc. Tex., Nordland Heritage Found. (charter mem.), Bosque Meml. Mus. Served with U.S. Army. Howell Instruments scholar, 1961. Mem. ASME (Charles E. Balleisen award 1976, 78, council cert. 1977, 79, 80, 81, Centennial medal 1980, Centennial award 1980, Bd. Govs. cert. 1982, 83, 84, 85), Nat. Soc. Profl. Engrs., Tex. Soc. Profl. Engrs., Consumer Products Tech. Group, Human Factors Soc., Soc. Allied Weight Engrs., Instrument Soc. Am., Tex. Engring. Found., Sigma Xi, Tau Beta Pi, Pi Tau Sigma, Sigma Iota Epsilon. Patentee in field. Current Work: Measurement of weight (mass) in space flight; zero gravity effects in space flight; electromechanical research and development; structural optimization; environmental effects; theoretical and experimental analysis; response of structures to periodic and impulsive loading. Subspecialties: Mechanical engineering; Theoretical and applied mechanics. Home: 5906 Forest Cove San Antonio TX 78240 Office: PO Drawer 28510 San Antonio TX 78284

SOLBERG, WILLIAM KNOTT, dentistry educator; b. Parkers Prairie, Minn., Apr. 11, 1936; s. Francis Alvin and Gladys Louise (Knott) S.; divorced; 1 child, Peter. B.A., Carleton Coll., 1958; D.D.S., U. Minn., 1962, M.S.D., 1966. Prof. dentistry UCLA, 1968—, chmn. sect. gnathology and occlusion Sch. Dentistry, 1968—, also mem. Dental Research Inst.; postdoctoral fellow USPHS, Copenhagen, 1967-68; dir. Temporomandibular Joint and Facial Pain Clinic, 1968—; Editor: Temporomandibular Joint Problems: Biologic Diagnosis and Treatment, 1980; Abnormal jaw Mechanics, 1984. Mem. Am. Acad. Craniomandibular Disorders (pres. 1985), Internat. Assn. Dental Research, Colombian Soc. Prosthodontics (hon.), Omicron Kappa Upsilon. Current work: Human studies involving temporomandibular joint dysfunction, mandibular behavior, and orofacial pain. Subspecialty: Temporomandibular joint and facial pain. Office: 43009 Ctr For Health Scis UCLA Los Angeles CA 90024

SOLIMAN, MAGDI RAMZI ISKANDAR, pharmacology educator; b. Alexandria, Egypt, June 30, 1942; came to U.S., 1980; s. Ramzi Iskandar and Nouzha (Chafik) S.; m. Salwa Halim, Sept. 17, 1967; children—George, Suzette. B.S. in Pharmacy, Faculty of Pharmacy, Alexandria, 1964, M.S. in Pharmacology, 1968; Ph.D. in Pharmacology, U. Ga., 1972; postgrad. Pa. State U., 1972-74. Instr. pharmacology Faculty of Pharmacy, Alexandria, 1964-69; teaching asst. pharmacy, U. Ga., Athens, 1969-72; research assoc. Hershey Med. Ctr., Pa., 1972-74; assoc. prof. Faculty of Pharmacy, 1974-80; assoc. prof. pharmacy, Fla. A&M U., Tallahassee, 1980—, dir. chronopharmacology research lab., 1982—. Contbr. articles to med. jours., chpt. to book. Mem. Egyptian Pharm. Soc., Egyptian Pharmacological Soc., Am. Soc. for Pharmacology and Exptl. Therapeutics (affiliate), Sigma Xi, Phi Kappa Phi, Rho Chi. Mem. Coptic Orthodox Ch. Current work: Teaching and research in areas of pharmacology, drug metabolism, toxicology and neuropharmacology. Subspecialties: Molecular pharmacology; Neuropharmacology. Home: 4144 Tralee Rd Tallahassee FL 32308Office: Coll of Pharmacy Fla A&M U Tallahassee FL 32307

SOLINGER, ALAN MICHAEL, physician, rheumatologist/immunologist; b. Cin., Nov. 27, 1948; s. Frank and Ruth (Schuhmann) S. B.A. in Chem. Biology, Columbia U., 1970; M.D., U. Cin., 1974. Diplomate: Am. Bd. Internal Medicine. Intern in internal medicine U. Mo., 1974-75, resident in internal medicine, 1975-76; research fellow div. rheumatology-clin. immunology U. Calif.-San Francisco, 1978-81; asst. prof. medicine div. immunology U. Cin., 1981—; travel scholar Internat. League Against Rheumatism, Paris, 1981. Contbr. articles, chpts. to profl. publs. Served with USPHS, 1976-78. Recipient Arthritis Investigator award Arthritis Found., 1982-85; Nat. Arthritis Found. clin. fellowship grantee, 1978-81; No. Calif. Arthritis Found. project grantee, 1980-81. Fellow ACP; mem. AAAS, Am. Assn. Immunologists, Am. Fedn. Clin. Research, AMA (Calif. house staff 1978-81), Am. Rheumatism Assn. (Anglo-U.S. fellow 1985, Sr. Rheumatology Scholar award 1981), N.Y. Acad. Scis., Ohio Rheumatism Soc. (exec. com.), Greater Cin. Rheumatism Soc. (pres. 1982—), Sigma Xi. Democrat. Jewish. Subspecialties: Immunogenetics; Rheumatology. Office: 7462 MSB U Cin Med Center 231 Bethesda Ave Cincinnati OH 45267

SOLLINGER, HANS WERNER, physician, educator; b. Munich, Germany, Aug. 30, 1946; came to U.S., 1976, naturalized, 1979; s. Johann and Maria S.; m. Mary Lou Lang, Mar. 16, 1976; children: Nicola, Christina. M.D., U. Munich, 1973, Ph.D., 1975. Intern U. Munich Hosp., 1973-74; resident U. Wis. Hosp.-Madison, 1976-80; research assoc. U. Munich, 1974-75; postdoctoral fellow U. Wis.-Madison, 1975-77; asst. prof. U. Wis. Hosp., 1980—; dir. Tissue Typing Labs., 1981—. Recipient Max-Kade Found. research award, 1975; Deutsche Forschungsgemeinschaft research award, 1976. Mem. Internat. Transplantation Soc., Am. Soc. Transplant Surgeons, Madison Surg. Soc., Assn. Acad. Surgery, Soc. Univ. Surgeons. Current Work: Transplantation immunology, pancreas transplantation, tissue typing. Subspecialties: Surgery; Transplant surgery. Office: Dept Surgery U Wis Hosp 600 Highland Ave Madison WI 53792

SOLLNER, TRAUGOTT CARL LUDWIG GERHARD, electrical engineering educator; b. Nashville, Oct. 14, 1943; s. Traugott Carl Ludwig Gerhard and Araminta Louise (Henrichsen) S.; m. Patricia Mae Roberson, Mar. 21, 1947. B.S., Ga. Inst. Tech., 1967; Ph.D., U. Colo., 1974. Postdoctoral fellow U. London, 1974-76; faculty research assoc. U. Mass., 1976-80, asst. prof., 1980-82; cons. Lincoln Lab., M.I.T., 1977-82, staff, 1982—. Contbr. articles to prof. jours. NASA grantee, 1980-81; Raytheon grantee, 1980-82. Mem. IEEE, Am. Inst. Physics, Internat. Astron. Union. Current Work: Quantum physics; birth of stars. Subspecialties: Condensed matter physics; Semiconductors. Home: 24 Mason St Winchester MA 01890 Office: MIT Lincoln Lab Lexington MA 02173

SOLNIT, ALBERT JAY, medical educator, child psychiatrist; b. Los Angeles, Aug. 26, 1919; s. Benjamin and Bertha (Pavin) S.; m. Martha Benedict, 1949; children—David, Ruth, Benjamin, Aaron. B.A. in Med. Scis., U. Calif., 1940, M.A. in Anatomy, 1942, M.D., 1943; M.A. (hon.), Yale U., 1964. Rotating intern L.I. Coll. Hosp., 1944, asst. resident in pediatrics, 1944-45; resident in pediatrics and communicable diseases U. Calif.-San Francisco Hosp., 1947-48; asst. resident dept. psychiatry and mental hygiene Yale U., New Haven, 1948-49, sr. resident, 1949-50, fellow in child psychiatry, 1950-52, instr. pediatrics and psychiatry, 1952-53, asst. prof., 1953-60, assoc. prof., 1960-64, prof., 1964-70, Sterling prof., 1970—, dir. Child Study Ctr., 1966-83; tng. and supervising analyst Western New Eng. Inst. Psychoanalysis, 1962—, N.Y. Psychoanalytic Inst., 1962—; chmn. Ctr. for Study Edn., Instn. for Social and Policy Studies, Yale U., 1971-73; Sigmund Freud Meml. prof. Univ. Coll.,

London, 1983-84; WHO prof. psychiatry and human devel.U. Negev, Beer-Sheva, Isarel, 1973; sci. adviser Ctr. for Preventive Psychiatry, White Plains, N.Y., 1970; mem. adv. bd. Action for Children's TV, Newtonville, Mass., 1973; mem. div. med. scis. Assembly Life Scis. NRC, 1974; cons. div. mental health service program NIMH, 1974. Bd. dirs. Human Services Inst. for Children and Families, Washington, 1973. Author: (with M.J.E. Senn) Problems in Child Behavior and Development, 1968; (with A. Freud, J. Goldstein) Beyond the Best Interests of the Child, 1973; and Before the Interests of the Child, 1979; (with S. Goldstein) Divorce and Your Child, 1984. Editor: (with S. Provence) Modern Perspectives in Child Development, 1963; mng. editor Psychoanalytic Study of the Child, 1971; mem. editorial bd. Pediatrics, 1968-76, Am. Jour. Psychiatry, 1974—, Jour. Am. Acad. Child Psychiatry, 1975, Psychiatry in Medicine, Internat. Jour. Med. Psychology and Psychiatry in the Gen. Hosp., 1969; mem. editorial adv. bd. Internat. Ency. Psychiatry, Psychoanalysis and Psychology, 1972—; mem. Am. editorial com. Israel Annals of Psychiatry and Related Disciplines, 1969—. Served with USAAF, 1945-47. Mem. Am. Orthopsychiatry Assn., Am. Psychiat. Assn., Am. Psychoanalytic Assn. (past pres.), Am. Acad. Child Psychiatry (past pres.), Internat. Assn. Child Psychiatry and Allied Professions (pres. 1974-78), Am. Pediatric Soc., Am. Assn. Child Psychoanalysis (past pres.), Am. Acad. Pediatrics, AAAS, Internat. Psycoanalytic Assn., N.Y. Psychoanalytic Soc., Soc. Profs. Child Psychiatry. Subspecialty: Psychiatry. Office: 333 Cedar St New Haven CT 06510

SOLOMON, DAVID HARRIS, educator, physician; b. Cambridge, Mass., Mar. 7, 1923; s. Frank and Rose (Roud) S.; m. Ronda L. Markson, June 23, 1946; children: Patricia Jean (Mrs. Richard E. Sinaiko), Nancy Ellen. A.B., Brown U., 1944; M.D., Harvard U., 1946. Intern Peter Bent Brigham Hosp., Boston, 1946-47, resident, 1947-48, 50-51; fellow endocrinology New Eng. Center Hosp., Boston, 1951-52; faculty UCLA Sch. Medicine, 1952—, prof. medicine, 1966—, vice chmn. dept. medicine, 1968-71, chmn. dept., 1971-81; chief med. service Harbor Gen. Hosp., Torrance, Calif., 1966-71; cons. Wadsworth VA Hosp., Los Angeles, 1952—, Sepulveda VA Hosp., 1971—; cons. metabolism tng. com. USPHS, 1960-64, endocrinology study sect., 1970-73; mem. dean's com. Wadsworth, Sepulveda VA hosps. Contbr. numerous articles to profl. jours. Mem. Assn. Am. Physicians, Am. Soc. Clin. Investigation, Am. Fedn. Clin. Research, Am. Physiol. Soc., Western Soc. Clin. Research (councillor 1963-65), Endocrine Soc., Am. Diabetes Assn., Am. Thyroid Assn. (pres. 1973-74), Soc. Exptl. Biology and Medicine, ACP (master), Am. Geriatrics Soc. (bd. dirs.), Inst. Medicine Nat. Acad. Scis., AAAS, Assn. Profs. Medicine (pres. 1980-81), Western Assn. Physicians (councillor 1972-75, pres. 1983-84), Phi Beta Kappa, Sigma Xi, Alpha Omega Alpha. Current Work: Treatment of hyperthyroidism; thyroid hormone methabolism in sickness, health and aging. Subspecialties: Endocrinology; Gerontology. Home: 863 Woodacres Rd Santa Monica CA 90402 Office: Dept Medicine UCLA Sch Medicine Los Angeles CA 90024

SOLOMON, RICHARD LESTER, educator; b. Boston, Oct. 2, 1918; s. Frank and Rose (Roud) S.; children by previous marriage—Janet Ellen, Elizabeth Grace. A.B., Brown U., 1940, M.Sc., 1942, Ph.D., 1947. Instr. psychology Brown U., 1946; asst. prof. Harvard U., 1947-50, asso. prof., 1950-57, prof. social psychology, 1957-60; prof. psychology U. Pa., Phila., 1960-74, James M. Skinner Univ. prof. sci., 1975-85, James M. Skinner prof. emeritus, 1985—; Staff OSRD, 1942-45. Mem. Am. Psychol. Assn., Eastern Psychol. Assn. (past pres.), Psychonomic Soc. (past chmn. governing bd.), Am. Acad. Arts and Scis., Soc. Exptl. Psychologists, AAAS, Nat. Acad. Sci., Phi Beta Kappa, Sigma Xi. Subspecialty: Experimental psychology. Address: Box 2075 Conway NH 03818

SOLOMON, SIDNEY, physiologist, educator; b. Worcester, Mass., Feb. 22, 1923; s. Samuel and Bessie (Grace) S.; m. Mina Libyan Kramer, Dec. 28, 1947; children—Anne Faye, Susan Judith. B.S., U. Mass.-Amherst, 1948; Ph.D., U. Chgo., 1952. Instr., Med. Coll. Va., Richmond, 1952-54, asst. prof., 1954-60, assoc. prof., 1960-63; prof., chmn. dept. physiology U. N.Mex.-Albuquerque, 1963-78, prof., 1978—; cons. Phillip Morris, Inc., 1959-63, 79-83, NSF, 1963-66, 79-83, program dir., 1968-69. Contbr. numerous articles to sci. jours. Mem. Am. Assn. Profs. for Peace in Middle East, 1978-82. Served with USMCR, 1942-45. Recipient N.M. Kidney Found. Med. award, 1984. Mem. Am. Physiol. Soc., Soc. Exptl. Biol. and Medicine, Biophys. Soc., Soc. Nephrology, Democrat. Jewish. Current work: Development of the kidney; regulation of the kidney; epithelial transport; comparative physiology. Subspecialty: Physiology (medicine). Home: 3406 D Indian School Rd NE Albuquerque NM 87106 Office: U NMex Sch Medicine 915 Stanford Ave NE Albuquerque NM 87131

SOLOMONOW, MOSHE, bioengineering scientist; b. Tel-Aviv, Israel, Oct. 24, 1944; s. Johnathan and Eva (Ephraim) S.; m. Susanne Elisabeth Nickerson, May 21, 1982; children—Deborah Leigh, Esther Monique. B.S., Calif. State U., 1970, M.S., 1972; Ph.D., UCLA, 1976. Asst. prof. UCLA, 1976-80; assoc. prof. Tulane U., New Orleans, 1980-83; dir. of bioengring. La. State U. Med. Ctr., New Orleans, 1983—; cons. VA, Washington, 1977—, La. Dept. of Health, Baton Rouge, 1981—, La. Ctr. of Cerebral Palsy, New Orleans, 1981—. Contbr. articles to technical jours. Mem. bd. mem. United Cerebral Palsy of Greater New Orleans, 1982—; cons. Area Agency on Aging, Los Angeles, 1980. Served to sgt. Israeli Army, 1962-65. Mem. IEEE (sr. mem.), Biomed. Engring. Soc. (sr. mem.), Am. Congress of Physical Medicine, Orthopedic Research Soc. Current work: Biomechanics of movement, orthopaedic rehabilitation, neuromuscular physiology. Subspecialties: Biomedical engineering; Neurophysiology. Home: 3380 State St Dr New Orleans LA 70125 Office: La State U Med Ctr 1542 Tulane Ave New Orleans LA 70112

SOLON, LEONARD R(AYMOND), radiation physicist; b. White Plains, N.Y., Sept. 11, 1925; s. Morris and Rebecca (Bobrov) S.; m. Charlotte Rothman, June 30, 1946; children: Miriam, Matthew, Emily. B.A., Hamilton Coll., 1947; M.S., Rutgers U., 1949; Ph.D., N.Y.U., 1960. Cert. health physicist Am. Bd. Health Physics. Physicist Nuclear Devel. Assocs., 1950-52; asst. chief, then chief radiation br. AEC Health and Safety Lab., N.Y.C., 1952-60; dir. applied nuclear tech. Tech. Research Group, Inc., 1960-62; cons. Burns & Roe, Servo Corp. of Am., 1962-64; mgr. research and devel. Del Electronics Corp., Mount Vernon, N.Y., 1964-67; founder, exec. v.p., tech. dir. Hadron, Inc., 1967-75; dir. Bur. Radiation Control, N.Y.C. Dept. Health, 1975—; successively lectr., adj. asst. prof., adj. assoc. prof. dept. environ. medicine N.Y.U. Med. Ctr., 1955—; prof. health physics Mcht. Marine Acad., Kings Point, N.Y., 1963. Contbr. articles to profl. jours. Served with inf. AUS, 1944-46, ETO. Decorated Combat Infantryman's badge, Bronze Star medal; recipient Southworth prize in physics Hamilton Coll., 1947; cert. of appreciation EPA, 1979. Mem. Conf. Radiation Control Program Dirs., AAAS, Am. Nuclear Soc., Health Physics Soc., Am. Phys. Soc., N.Y. Acad. Scis., Radiol. and Med. Physics Soc. N.Y., Phi Beta Kappa. Current Work: Environmental standards and public health control for ionizing and non-ionizing radiation, biomedical laser applications; radiation emergency management; nuclear disarmament and proliferation. Subspecialties: Health physics; Laser medicine. Home: 28 Pilgrim Ave Yonkers NY 10710 Office: 65 Worth St New York NY 10013

SOLOWAY, ALBERT HERMAN, chemist, college dean; b. Worcester, Mass., May 29, 1925; s. Bernard and Mollie (Raphaelson) S.; m. Barbara Berkowicz, Nov. 29, 1953; children—Madeleine Rae, Paul Daniel, Renee Ellen. Student, U.S. Naval Acad., 1945-46; B.S., Worcester Poly. Inst., 1948; Ph.D., U. Rochester, 1951. Postdoctoral fellow Nat. Cancer Inst. at Sloan-Kettering Inst., N.Y.C., 1951-53; research chemist Eastman Kodak Co., Rochester, N.Y., 1953-56; asst. chemist Mass. Gen. Hosp., Boston, 1956-61, assoc. chemist, 1961-73; asso. prof. med. chemistry Northeastern U., Boston, 1966-68, prof. medicinal chemistry, chmn. dept., 1968-71, prof. medicinal chemistry and chemistry, chmn. dept. medicinal chemistry and pharmacology, 1971-74; dean Coll. Pharmacy and Allied Health Professions, 1975-77; dean Coll. Pharmacy, prof. medicinal chemistry Ohio State U., Columbus, 1977—; pres. Cambridge (Mass.) Med. Tech. Corp., 1960-61, v.p., 1961-74, dir., 1960-74. Author research medicinal chemistry. Served with USNR, 1944-45. Fellow AAAS, Acad. Pharm. Soc.; Mem. Am. Chem. Soc., Am. Pharm. Assn., Am. Assn. Coll. Pharmacy, Ohio Pharm. Assn., Am. Assn. Cancer Research. Jewish (trustee temple 1969-77, v.p., 1970-73). Current Work: Design of new structures and new approaches to chemoradiotherapy and chemoimmunotherapy of cancer. Subspecialties: Medicinal chemistry; Cancer research (medicine). Office: 500 W 12th Ave Columbus OH 43210

SOLTERO, RAYMOND ARTHUR, limnologist, educator; b. Milw., July 20, 1943; s. Harry R. and Marion J. (Ott) S.; m. Marlene G. Thompson; children—Douglas R., Kirsten M., Tamara J. B.S., Mont. State U., 1966, M.S., 1968, Ph.D., 1971. Teaching asst. Mont. State U., Bozeman, 1967-69; prof. biology Eastern Wash. U., Cheney, 1971—. Contbr. articles to profl. jours. Councilman, City of Cheney, 1975-83. Recipient Trustee's medal Eastern Wash. U., 1982. Mem. Am. Soc. Limnology and Oceanography, Northwest Sci. Assn. (pres. 1985), N. Am. Lake Mgmt. Soc., Sigma Xi. Lodge: Rotary (pres. Cheney-Medical Lake 1982-83). Current work: Lake and stream restoration, eutrophication processes. Subspecialty: Limnology. Office: Dept Biology Eastern Wash U Cheney WA 99004

SOMANI, SATU MOTILAL, pharmacology educator; b. Hingoli, Maharashtra, India, Mar. 14, 1937; s. Motilal and Tulsibai (Tapdia) S.; m. Shipra S. Somani, Nov. 5, 1966; children—Indira, Sheila. B.Sc., Osmania U., 1956; M.Sc., Poona U., 1959; M.S., Duquesne U., 1964; Ph.D., Liverpool U., 1969. NIH fellow U. Pitts., 1969-70, instr., 1970-71, asst. prof., 1971-74; assoc. prof. So. Ill. U. Sch. Medicine, Springfield, 1974-82, prof. pharmacology and toxicology, 1982—; Ellis T. Davies fellow Liverpool U., Eng., 1967-69; scientist Nuclear Sci. & Engring. Corp., Pitts., 1964-66. Author: Environmental Toxicology, 1981. Health Sci. Research Found. grantee, 1971-74; Ill. EPA grantee, 1977-79; Am. Heart Assn. grantee, 1982-84; Dept. Army grantee. Mem. Soc. Toxicology, Am. Soc. Pharmacology and Exptl. Therapeutics, Am. Soc. Clin. Pharmacology, Am. Chem. Soc. (treas. 1979, chmn. 1981), N.Y. Acad. Sci., Sigma Xi. Clubs: Cosmopolitan (pres. 1963), Toastmasters. Current work: Anticholinesterase metabolism and pharmacokinetics in rat and man; theophylline and caffeine disposition and its relationship to control of apnea; effect of exercise on caffeine pharmacokinetics in lean and obese volunteers; indentification of organic discharges in industrial waste waters and their mutagenicity. Subspecialties: Pharmacology; Toxicology (medicine). Home: 81 Interlacken Springfield IL 62704 Office: So Ill U Sch Medicine 801 N Rutledge St Springfield IL 62702

SOMASUNDARAN, PONISSERIL, mineral and chemical engineering educator, consultant; b. Annallur, India, June 28, 1939; came to U.S., 1961, naturalized, 1979; s. M.G. Kumara Pillai and K.P. (Lakshmikutty) Amma; m. Usha Nair, May 26, 1966; 1 child, Tamara. B.S., Kerala U., India, 1958; B.E., Indian Inst. Sci., Bangalore, 1961; M.S., U. Calif.-Berkeley, 1962, Ph.D., 1964. Research engr. Internat. Minerals & Chem., Skokie, Ill., 1965-67; research chemist R.J. Reynolds Inc., Winston-Salem, N.C., 1967-70; assoc. prof. engring., Columbia U., N.Y.C., 1970-78, prof., 1978-83, La Von Duddleson Krumb prof., 1983—; cons., IBM, Exxon, Sohio, Colgate and others. Editor-in-chief Colloids and Surfaces Jour., 1980; assoc. editor Minerals and Metall. Processing; contbr. articles to profl. jours. Patentee in field. Dir. Vols. in Service to Edn., Hartford, Conn., 1973—, Fedn. Indian Assns., N.Y., 1976—; pres. Kerala Samajam Greater N.Y., 1975. Recipient Dist. Achievement in Engring. award Assn. Indians North Am., 1980. Fellow Inst. Mining and Metallurgy-London, Nat. Acad. Engring.; mem. Soc. Mining Engrs. (bd. dirs. 1981, Antoine M. Gaudin award, 1982, Mill Man of Distinction 1983, dist. mem.), Am. Inst. Chem. Engrs., Am. Chem. Soc., Fine Paritcle Soc., Internat. Assn. Colloid and Surface Sci. Current work: Surface and colloid chemistry of minerals and petroleum. Subspecialties: Surface chemistry; Metallurgical engineering. Home: 748 Broadway Ave Nyack NY 10960 Office: Columbia U 911 SW Mudd Bldg New York NY 10027

SOMERO, GEORGE NICHOLLS, biology educator; b. Duluth, Minn., July 30, 1940; s. George T. and Mary E. (Nicholls) S.; m. Meredith Gould, June 8, 1968 (div. Nov. 1982). B.A., Carleton Coll., 1962; Ph.D., Stanford U., 1967. Postdoctoral fellow U. B.C., Vancouver, 1967-70; prof. biology Scripps Instn. Oceanography, La Jolla, Calif., 1970—, chmn. marine biology research div., 1983—. Author: Biochemical Adaptation, 1984. Fellow AAAS. Current work: Biochemistry of environmental adaptation. Subspecialty: Marine biology. Office: U Calif-San Diego Marine Biology Research Div Scripps Instn of Oceanography La Jolla CA 92093

SOMLYO, AVRIL VIRGINIA, physiologist, researcher; b. Sask., Can., Apr. 9, 1939; d. Frederick William and Miriam Virginia (MacDougal) Russell; m. Andrew Paul Somlyo, May 25, 1961; 1 son, Andrew Paul. B.A., U. Sask., 1959, M.Sc., 1961; Ph.D., U. Pa., 1976. Co-prin. investigator dept. pathology and Pa. Muscle Inst. Presbyn. U. Pa. Med. Center, Phila., 1968-79, asso. research prof., 1978-82, research prof. physiology, 1982—. Contbr. articles to profl. jours. Mem. Biophys. Soc., Soc. Gen. Physiologists, Am. Soc. Pharmacology and Exptl. Therapeutics. Anglican. Current Work: Muscle physiology, blood vessels, excitation-contraction coupling, electron optical techniques, electron probe analysis, in situ elemental localization. Subspecialties: Cell biology (medicine); Biophysics (physics). Office: Pa Muscle Inst Univ Pa Med Sch Philadelphia PA 19104

SOMMER, NOEL FREDERICK, plant pathologist; b. Scio, Oreg., Jan. 21, 1920; s. John Frederick and Anna Effie (Holt) S.; m. Connie Inez Truxillo, May 1, 1946; 1 son, Gary Frederick. B.S., Oreg., State U., 1941; M.S., U. Calif.-Davis, 1952, Ph.D., 1955. Plant pathologist USDA, Raleigh, N.C., 1955-56; pomologist U. Calif.-Davis, 1956-80, chmn. dept. pomology, 1975-81, postharvest pathologist, 1981—; cons. Hawaii Dept. Agr., 1970, TRC Corp., 1973, Alexander and Baldwin Corp., 1975-76, Banco de Mexico, 1980, Bakki Steamship Co., 1981, UN Devel. Program-India, 1982; participant AID Devel. Project-Egypt, 1977-81. Contbr. articles to profl. jours. Served to maj. F.A. AUS, 1941-46. Fellow Institut Nationale de la Recherche Agronomique French Ministry of Agr., 1968-69; recipient Bronze medal Chambre d'Agriculture du Vaucluse, France, 1978. Mem. Mycol. Soc. Am., Am. Soc. Microbiology, Am. Phytopath. Soc., Am. Soc. Hort. Sci. Current Work: Prevention of losses in perishable raw food commodities through research in the teachnology of handling, storage and transportation and the suppression of microbial activity. Subspecialties: Plant pathology; Postharvest pathology. Office: Dept Pomology Univ Calif Davis CA 95616

SOMMERS, SHELDON CHARLES, pathologist; b. Indpls., July 7, 1916; s. Charles Birk and Leonore (Dickey) S.; m. Edith, Nov. 9, 1943. S.B., Harvard U., 1937, M.D., 1941. Diplomate: Am. Bd. Pathology. Intern U. Chgo. Clinics, 1941-42; resident on pathology New Eng. Deaconess Hosp., Boston, 1946-48, Free Hosp., also Boston Lying-In Hosp., Boston, 1948-49, Henry Ford Hosp., Detroit, 1949-50; staff pathologist New Eng. Deaconess Hosp., Boston, 1950-53; lab. dir. Mass. Meml. Hosps., Boston, 1953-61, Scripps Meml. Hosp., LaJolla, Calif., 1961-63; asso. dir., lab. dir. Delafield Hosp., N.Y.C., 1963-68; lab. dir. Lenox Hill Hosp., N.Y.C., 1968-81; sci. dir. Council Tobacco Research U.S., 1981—; clin. prof. pathology Columbia U. Coll. Phys. and Surg., U. So. Calif. Med. Sch.; cons. in field. Author numerous papers in field.; Co-editor: Pathology Annual. Chmn. N.Y. State Mental Hygiene Med. Rev. Bd., 1976-85. Served to capt. M.C. AUS, 1942-46. Decorated Silver Star, Bronze Star; Croix de Guerre. Mem. Am. Assn. Pathologists, Coll. Am. Pathologists, Am. Soc. Clin. Pathologists, Internat. Acad. Pathology, Arthur Purdy Stout Soc. Surg. Pathology (pres. 1983-85), N.Y. County Med. Soc., N.Y. Pathol. Soc. (pres. 1976). Clubs: Harvard (N.Y.C.); Knickerbocker Country (Tenafly, N.J.). Subspecialties: Pathology (medicine); Cancer research (medicine).

SOMORJAI, GABOR A(RPAD), chemist, educator; b. Hungary, May 4, 1935; came to U.S., 1957, naturalized, 1962; s. Charles and Livia (Ormos) S.; m. Judith K., Sept. 2, 1957; children: Nicole, John. Ph.D. in Chemistry, U. Calif.-Berkeley, 1960. Mem. research staff IBM Research, 1960-64; prin. investigator materials research div. Lawrence Berkeley Lab., 1964—; asst. prof. chemistry U. Calif.-Berkeley, 1964-67, assoc. prof., 1967-72, prof., 1972—, Miller prof., 1978; cons. in field. Author: Principles of Surface Chemistry, 1972, Chemistry in Two Dimensions, Surface, 1981; contbr. numerous articles to profl. jours. Recipient Kokes award Johns Hopkins U., 1976, Emmett award Am. Catalysis Soc., 1977; Guggenheim fellow, 1969. Fellow Am. Phys. Soc., AAAS; mem. Nat. Acad. Scis., Am. Acad Arts and Scis., Am. Chem. Soc. (Colloid and Surface Chemistry award 1981). Current Work: Surface chemistry; the surface science of heterogeneous catalysis. Subspecialties: Catalysis chemistry; Surface chemistry. Home: 665 San Luis Rd Berkeley CA 95707 Office: Dept Chemistry U Calif Berkeley CA 94720

SONDEL, PAUL M., immunologist, pediatric hematologist-oncologist; b. Milw., Aug. 14, 1950; s. Robert F. and Audrey J. (Dworkus) S.; m. Sherie A. Katz, Jan. 1, 1973; children: Jesse Adam, Beth Leah, Elana Rose. B.S. with honors, U. Wis.-Madison, 1971, Ph.D. in Genetics, 1975; M.D. magna cum laude, Harvard U., 1977. Diplomate: Am. Bd. Pediatrics. Postdoctoral research fellow Sidney Farber Cancer Ctr., Boston, 1975-77; intern U. Minn. Hosp., Mpls., 1977-78; resident in pediatrics U. Wis. Hosp., Madison, 1978-80; asst. prof. depts. pediatrics, human oncology and genetics U. Wis. Med. Sch., Madison, 1980—. Contbr. articles to profl. jours. Co-chmn. Madison Gan Ha Yeled Nursery Sch. Com. J.A. and G.L. Hartford Found. fellow, 1981-84; Leukemia Soc. Am. scholar, 1981-86; Nat. Cancer Inst. grantee, 1982—; Am. Cancer Soc. grantee, 1982-87. Mem. Internat. Transplantation Soc., Am. Assn. Immunologists, Am. Fedn. Clin. Research, Soc. Pediatric Research. Jewish. Current Work: Using in vitro techniques to study the immune responses of fresh and cloned human T lymphocytes to histocompatible tumor cells. Subspecialties: Immunogenetics; Oncology. Office: 600 Highland Ave Madison WI 53792

SONES, JR. F. MASON, heart surgeon, medical researcher. With dept. cardiology Cleve. Clinic. Recipient Lasker med. research award, 1983. Subspecialty: Cardiac surgery. Office: Cleve Clinic Dept Cardiology 9500 Euclid Ave Cleveland OH 44106

SONG, CHANG WON, radiobiology educator, consultant; b. Korea, Apr. 10, 1932; came to U.S., 1959, naturalized, 1978; s. Jong Joo and So Soon (Kim) S.; m. Jai Kang, May 12, 1934; 3 children. B.S. in Chemistry, Seoul Nat. U., 1957; M.S. in Biochemistry, Korea U., Seoul, 1959; Ph.D. in Radiobiology, U. Iowa, 1964. Radiobiologist Albert Einstein Med. Center, Phila., 1964-69; asst. prof. Med. Coll. Va., 1969-71; asst. prof. radiobiology U. Minn., Mpls., 1971-75, assoc. prof., 1975-79, prof., 1979—; dir. Radiobiology Lab., 1971—; vis. prof. grantee Korean Dept. Sci. and Tech., 1972. Contbr. numerous articles to profl. jours. Nat. Cancer Inst. grantee, 1972—; Am. Cancer Soc. grantee, 1974-76. Mem. Radiation Research Soc., Am. Assn. Cancer Research, AAAS, Cell Kinetic Soc. Current Work: Role of blood flow, po2 and pH in treatment of cancer with radiation or hyperthermia; chemical sensitization of tumor cells to radiation and hyperthermia. Subspecialties: Cancer research (medicine); Biophysics (biology). Home: 9359 Hyland Creek Circle Bloomington MN 55437 Office: U Minn Box 494 Med Sch Minneapolis MN 55455

SONG, LEILA SHIA, chemistry educator; b. Chen-kiang, China, May 27, 1947; d. Chien-Kuang and Yu-Lien Tu Shia; m. Yih H-Song, Sept. 6, 1974; children: Priscilla, Berwin. B.S. in Chem. Engring, Nat. Taiwan U., Taipei, 1970; M.A. in Chemistry, SUNY-Plattsburgh, 1973. Teaching asst. Nat. Taiwan U., 1970-71; research asst., lab. instr. SUNY-Plattsburgh, 1971-73, Tufts U., Medford, Mass., 1973-75; research chemist Thermo Electron Co., Waltham, Mass., 1976-78; adj. prof. N.J. Inst. Tech., Newark, 1979—. Contbr. articles to profl. jours. Current Work: Environmental carcinogenic research. Subspecialties: Environmental chemistry; Chemical engineering. Office: Dept Chemistry NJ Inst Tech 323 High St Newark NJ 07102

SONNEMANN, HARRY, electrical engineer; b. Munich, Germany, Sept. 3, 1924; came to U.S., 1938, naturalized, 1944; s. Leopold and Emmy (Markus) S.; m. Shirley E. Battles, Nov. 25, 1949; children—Carol Jean, Joyce Elaine, Patricia Ann. B.S., Poly. Inst. Bklyn., 1954. Research electroence-phalography, 1944-47; asst. to dir. electronics dept. AEC contract, Columbia U., 1947-50; supr. electronics shop Columbia Hudson Labs., 1951-53, head electronics dept., 1954-59; asst. dir. Project Artemis, 1959-64, 1961-64; asst. dir. field engring. Advanced Research Projects Agy., Nuclear Test Detection Office, 1964-67; acting dep. dir. Nuclear Test Detection Office, 1967-68; spl. asst. in electronics to asst. sec. navy for research and devel. Navy Dept., 1968-76, spl. asst. to asst. sec. navy for research and devel., 1976-77; asst. to chief engr. NASA, 1977-78, dep. chief engr., 1978-85, asst. chief engr., 1985—; chmn. Dept. Def. Tactical Satellite Exec. Steering Group, 1968-69, chmn. Dept. Def. nav. satellite exec. steering group, 1969-70, 72-73. Treas. Art League, No. Va., 1967-68; pres. Rotunda Condominium Unit Owners Assn., 1982—. Clubs: Washington Figure Skating (dir. 1968-73, treas. 1969-72), Ice of Washington (pres. 1974-76). Home: 8360 Greensboro Dr McLean VA 22102 Office: 600 Independence Ave Washington DC 20546

SONNENBERG, STEPHEN ARNOLD, petroleum geologist, researcher; b. Billings, Mont., Mar. 17, 1952; s. Frank Payler and Mary Anne (Case) S.; m. Jane Phillips, June 19, 1976; 1 child, William Case. B.S., Tex. A&M U., 1974, M.S., 1975; Ph.D., Colo. Sch. Mines, 1981. Geologist, Gulf Oil, Oklahoma City, 1974; teaching and research asst. Tex. A&M U., College Station, 1974-75; geologist Exxon Co., U.S.A., Houston, 1976-78; research asst. Colo. Sch. Mines, Golden, 1978-81, adj. asst. prof., 1982; geologist Bass Enterprises, Denver, 1981—. Author: Tectonics, Sedimentation and Petroleum Potential, Northern Denver Basin, 1981. Contbr. articles to profl. jours. Recipient Award of Excellence, Soc. Tech. Communications Writers, 1982. Mem. Am. Assn. Petroleum Geologists (cert., ho. of dels. 1984—), Rocky Mountain Assn. Geologists (sec. 1984), Am. Inst. Profl. Geologists (cert.), Colo. Sci. Soc., Geol. Soc. Am. Clubs: Petroleum, Athletic, (Denver). Current work: Stratigraphy, sedimentology and tectonics and their applications in petroleum geology. Subspecialties: Geology; Sedimentology. Home: 1875 Glen Dale Dr Lakewood CO 80215 Office: Bass Enterprises 1512 Larimer St 1000 Writer Sq Denver CO 80202

SONNENFELD, GERALD, microbiologist, educator; b. N.Y.C., Oct. 14, 1949; s. Otto and Ann (Perelman) S.; m. Elaine Marie Budd, May 6, 1978; 1 child, Jennifer Lyn. B.S., CCNY, 1970; Ph.D., U. Pitts. Sch. Medicine, 1975. Postdoctoral fellow Stanford (Calif.) U. Sch. Medicine, 1976-78; assoc. guest worker biomed. research div. NASA-Ames Research Ctr., Moffett Field, Calif., 1976-78; asst. prof. dept. microbiology and immunology U. Louisville Sch. Medicine, 1978-83, assoc. prof., 1983—. Sect. editor immunology, mem. editorial bd.: Jour. Interferon Research; contbr. articles to sci. jours. Trustee, head profl. edn. com. Ky. chpt. Leukemia Soc. Am. Recipient Esther Teplitz award U. Pitts. Sch. Medicine, 1974; NIH trainee, 1970-75; grantee NASA, Ky. Tobacco and Health Research Inst. Mem. Internat. Soc. Interferon Research (charter), Soc. Gravitational Biology, Am. Assn. Immunologists, Am. Soc. Microbiology, Sigma Xi. Current Work: Regulation of immune response by interferon; interactions between carcinogens and interferon. Subspecialties: Immunotoxicology; Infectious diseases. Office: U Louisville Sch Medicine Louisville KY 40292

SONTAG, MARC ROBERT, medical physicist; b. Bklyn., June 1, 1950; s. Howard Monroe and Marjorie Louise (Seldowitz) S.; m. Robin Joy Sontag, July 3, 1977; children—Lisa Michelle, Brian Nathaniel. B.S., Bucknell U., 1972, M.S., 1974; Ph.D., U. Toronto, 1979. Med. physicist, instr. radiation therapy Thomas Jefferson U., Phila., 1979; med. physicist, asst. prof. U. Pa. Med. Sch., Phila., 1980—; pres. Micro Med. Physics and Engring. Co., Cherry Hill, N.J., 1981—. Contbr. articles to profl. jours. Mem. Am. Assn. Physicists in Medicine, Am. Soc. Therapeutic Radiologists, AAAS, N.Y. Acad. Sci. Current Work: Methods of radiation dose calculations. Subspecialty: Radiology. Office: Dept Radiation Therapy Hosp U Pa Box 522 34th and Spruce Sts Philadelphia PA 19104

SOO, SHAO LEE, mechanical engineer, educator; b. Peking, China, Mar. 1, 1922; came to U.S., 1947, naturalized, 1962; s. Hsi Yi and Yun Chuan (Chin) S.; m. Hermia G. Dan, June 7, 1952; children—Shirley A., Lydia M., David D. B.S., Nat. Chiaotung U., 1945; M.S., Ga. Inst. Tech., 1948; Sc.D., Harvard U., 1951. Engr. China Nat. Aviation, Calcutta and Shanghai, 1945-47; lectr. Princeton (N.J.) U., 1951-54, asst. prof., 1954-57, assoc. prof. mech. engring., 1957-59; prof. mech. engring. U. Ill., Urbana, 1959—; dir. S. L. Soo Assocs., Ltd., Urbana, 1980—; cons. NASA, NIH, Dept. Energy, EPA, NATO; mem. sci. adv. bd. EPA, 1976-78; adv. energy transp. World Bank, 1979; dir. Internat. Powder Inst., 1976—; NATO AGARD lectr.; Fulbright-Hays disting. lectr., 1974—, lectr. Chinese Acad. Sci., 1980. Author 5 books on thermodynamics, energy conversion and multiphase flow; mem. editorial bd.: Internat. Jour. Multiphase Flow, 1972—, Jour. Pipelines, 1980—, Internat. Jour. Sci. and Engring., 1983; contbr. numerous articles to profl. jours. Recipient Applied Mechanics Rev. award, 1972, Disting. Lecture award Internat. Pipeline Assn., 1981; ALCOA Found. research award, 1985. Fellow ASME; mem. ASEE, Combustion Inst., Fine Particle Soc. (chmn. fluidized beds com.), Sigma Xi, Pi Tau Sigma (hon.). Methodist. Patentee in field (5). Current Work: Basic differential-integral equations of multiphase flow; pneumatic transport systems; and slurry pipeline systems; computer modeling for nuclear reactor safety and energy policy. Subspecialty: Fluid mechanics. Home: 2020 Cureton Dr Urbana IL 61801 Office: 1206 W Green St Urbana IL 61801

SOPER, HENRY VICTOR, scientist, educator; b. Glen Ridge, N.J., Mar. 10, 1945; s. Kenneth L. and Sylvia (Caldwell) S. B.A., Yale U., 1966; M.A., U. Conn., 1972, Ph.D., 1974. Neurophysiologist Brain Research Inst., UCLA, 1974-76, NIH fellow psychology dept., 1976-78; intern, fellow in neuropsychology Camarillo (Calif.) State Hosp. Neuropsychiat. UCLA, 1982-83, fellow faculty neuropsychiatry, 1983—; research assoc., lectr. U. Ill.-Chgo., 1978-82; dir. U. Ill.-Chgo. (Neurobehavior Lab.), 1978-81; dir. Exptl. Epilepsy Lab.,

UCLA, Brain Research Inst., Los Angeles, 1974-78; manuscript reviewer Am. Psychol. Assn., Washington, 1974-75. Contbr. articles to profl. jours.; author: Behind the Laws of Rugby, 1979. Served to 1st lt. U.S. Army, 1966-68, Vietnam. Alcohol, Drug Abuse and Mental Health Adminstrn. fellow, 1976. Mem. AAAS, Internat. Primatological Soc., Am. Assn. Primatologists, Am. Psychol. Assn., Soc. Neurosci., N.Y. Acad. Sci., Sigma Xi, U.S.A. Rugby Football Union (referee nat. com. 1979-82). Current Work: Functions of the cerebral association cortices in man and monkeys; assessment of higher cortical dysfunction in man and subsequent rehabilitation, neurological bases of autism, mental retardation, other disorders, human cerebral organization. Subspecialties: Neuropsychology; Physiological psychology. Home: Box A-326 Camarillo CA 93011 Office: UCLA NPI Research Program PO Box A Camarillo CA 93010

SORACE, RONALD EUGENE, engineer, educator; b. Elgin, Ill., Feb. 12, 1946; s. Larry Eugene and Sylvia Virginia (Tuggle) S.; m. Christine Francis Popp, July 23, 1968 (div. 1979); children—Ronald Eugene Jr., Robert Louis; m. Penny Lee Scholl, Dec. 23, 1979 (div.). B.S. in Math., U. Md.-Coll. Pk., 1968, M.S. in Physics, 1974; Ph.D. in Engring., UCLA, 1981. Mathematician Naval Ordance Lab., Silver Spring, Md., 1968-74; programming staff Compu-Net, Los Angeles, 1974-75; supr. tech. Librascope, Glendale, Calif., 1975-81; mem. tech. staff Bell Labs., Murray Hill, N.J., 1981-83, TRW Electronic Systems Group, Redondo Beach, Calif., 1983—; faculty engring. Calif. State U., Los Angeles, 1983—, UCLA, 1984—. Contbr. articles to profl. jours. Mem. IEEE (program chmn. 1984—). Current work: Satellite communications; stochastic processes; detection, modulation and filtering. Subspecialties: Systems engineering; Applied mathematics.

SORGENTI, HAROLD ANDREW, petroleum and chemical company executive; b. Bklyn., May 28, 1934; s. Louis J. and Lucille (Sisti) S.; m. Ann Rusnack, June 30, 1962; children—Elizabeth, Lucille. B.S.Ch.E., CCNY, 1956; M.S. Ohio State U., 1959. Research engr. Battelle Meml. Inst., Columbus, Ohio, 1956-59; with Atlantic Richfield Co., 1959—, v.p. research and engring., products div., 1975-76; sr. v.p., 1978-79; v.p. chem. devel. ARCO Chem. Co., Phila., 1976-78, pres., 1979—; dir. Provident Mut. Life Ins. Co., Phila. Nat. Bank., Core States Fin. Corp., Greater Phila. First Corp., O'Brien Energy Products. Bd. dirs. Phila. Orch. Assn., Pa. Acad. bd. govs. Winterthur Mus.; Bd. dirs. Phila. Coll. Art, St. Joseph's U.; mem. Bus. Council of Pa., Gov.'s Pvt. Sector Initiatives Task Force. Mem. Am. Chem. Soc., Am. Inst. Chem. Engrs., Soc. Chem. Industry, Ohio State U. Alumni Assn., CCNY Alumni Assn., Greater Phila. C. of C. (dir.). Clubs: Union League (Phila.); Sunday Breakfast. Office: ARCO Chem Co 1500 Market St Philadelphia PA 19101

SORGER, GUNTHER URBAN, electronic instrument company executive, electrical engineer; b. Riedlingen, Germany; s. Urban and Katherine (Kohnle) S.; m. Ursula Margarete Etter, Jan. 20, 1956; children—Stephan G., Philip O., Alex G. Vordiplom in Physics, Technische U., Stuttgart, W.Ger., 1948, Diploma in Physics, 1951, Ph.D. in Elec. Engring., 1953. Dir. research Weinschel Engring., Gaithersburg, Md., 1954-68; dir. research and devel. electronic instrumentation div. Singer Co., Bridgeport, Conn., 1968-71, Palo Alto, Calif., 1971-75; tech. cons., Menlo Park, Calif., 1975-78; dir. research and devel. ctr., electronic instrumentation div. Eaton Corp., Sunnyvale, Calif., 1979-84, v.p. research and devel., electronic instrumentation div., 1984—; adj. prof. elec. engring. George Washington U., Washington, 1960-68. Contbr. articles on relaxation effects in ferromagnetic materials, microwave measurements to profl. jours. Patentee microwave measurement techniques, automatic microwave connections, RF digital Fourier analyses, low frequency ferromagnetic resonance filter. Past coach Am. Youth Soccer Orgn., Portola Valley, Calif., 1971—. Fellow IEEE. Republican. Roman Catholic. Subspecialty: Electronics. Office: Eaton Corp Electronic Instrumentation Div 612 N Mary Ave Sunnyvale CA 94080

SOROKIN, PETER PITIRIMOVICH, physicist; b. Boston, July 10, 1931; s. Pitirim Alexandrovich and Elena Petrovna (Baratynskaya) S.; m. Anita J. Schell, Oct. 1, 1977; 1 child, Elena P. A.B., Harvard U., 1952, M.S., 1953, Ph.D., 1958. Research physicist IBM Watson Research Center, Yorktown Heights, N.Y., 1957—. Contbr. articles in quantum electronics to profl. jours. Recipient Michelson medal Franklin Soc., 1974; R.W. Wood award Optical Soc. Am., 1978; Harvey prize, 1983; IBM fellow, 1968—. Mem. Nat. Acad. Sci. (Comstock award 1983), Am. Acad. Sci., N.Y. Acad. Sci. Patentee laser devices. Current Work: Atomic and molecular physics; laser spectroscopy. Subspecialties: Atomic and molecular physics; Laser spectroscopy. Home: PO Box 225 Millwood NY 10546 Office: IBM Watson Research Center PO Box 218 Yorktown Heights NY 10598

SOSKEL, NORMAN TERRY, physician; b. Norfolk, Va., Sept. 1, 1948; s. Fred and Ruth (Chapel) S.; m. Judith Anne Barrie, Apr. 9, 1980; 1 son, Daniel Aaron. B.A., U. Va., 1970, M.D., 1974. Med. intern Hosp. of St. Raphael, New Haven, 1974-75; resident in medicine Salem (Va.) Hosp., 1975-76, U. Va. Hosp., Charlottesville, 1976-77; pulmonary fellow U. Utah Sch. Medicine, Salt Lake City, 1977-80, asst. prof. medicine, 1982—. Recipient Paderewski medal Am. Fedn. Music Tchrs., 1967; NIH grantee, 1980—. Mem. Am. Thoracic Soc., Am. Fedn. Clin. Investigation, Nat. Speleological Soc., AAAS, N.Y. Acad. Sci., Sigma Xi. Current Work: Mechanisms of producing lung injury with specific interest in connective tissue macromolecules. Mechanisms of modulating lung injury. Subspecialties: Internal medicine; Pulmonary medicine. Office: Div Respiratory Critical Care and Occupational Medicine Room 3E544 U Utah Med Center 50 N Medical Dr Salt Lake City UT 84132

SOSSAMON, DAVID BAINE, software engineer/executive; b. Balt., Aug. 10, 1957; s. Oscar Baine and Bessie Pearl (Graeber) S. Student Peabody Inst. Music, Md. Inst. Art; B.S.E.E., Johns Hopkins U., 1979. Systems engr. Hewlett-Packard, Rockville, Md., 1979-81; dir. telecommunications div. Research & Data Systems Corp., Lanham, Md., 1982—. Mem. IEEE, Assn. Computing Machinery. Club: BMW Car Club Am. Current work: Marketing; project management of software/systems design for satellite communications; expertise in both FDM and TDMA technologies. Subspecialties: Software engineering; Telecommunications. Home: 1617 19th St NW Washington DC 20009 Office: Research & Data Systems Inc 10300 Greenbelt Rd Lanham MD 20706

SOURES, JOHN MICHAEL, physicist, technical executive; b. Galatz, Rumania, Jan. 2, 1943; came to U.S., 1954, naturalized 1960; s. Michael John and Dia (Petrakis) S.; m. Diana Carrousos, June 29, 1969; children—Mandy, Nicholas, Eleni, Alexander. B.S. in Physics, U. Rochester, 1965, M.S. in Mech. and Aerospace Sci., 1967, Ph.D., 1970. Research assoc. Lab. for Laser Energetics, Rochester, N.Y., 1970-72, sr. scientist, 1972—, group leader, 1975-81, exptl. div. dir., 1979—, dep. dir., 1983—. Contbr. articles to profl. jours. NASA trainee, Rochester, N.Y., 1967-69. Mem. AAAS, Optical Soc. Am., N.Y. Acad. Sci., Am. Phys. Soc. Republican. Greek Orthodox. Current work: Applications of high-power lasers to inertial fusion and x-ray laser research. Subspecialties: Laser fusion; Plasma (energy science and technology). Office: Lab for Laser Energetics 250 River Rd Rochester NY 14623

SOURKES, THEODORE LIONEL, biochemistry educator; b. Montreal, Que., Can., Feb. 21, 1919; s. Irving and Fannie (Golt) S.; m. Shena Rosenblatt, Jan. 17, 1943; children: Barbara, Myra. B.Sc., McGill U., 1939, M.Sc. magna cum laude, 1946; Ph.D., Cornell U., 1948. Asst. prof. pharmacology Georgetown U. Med. Sch., 1948-50; research asso. dept. enzyme chemistry Merck Inst. Therapeutic Research, Rahway, N.J., 1950-53; sr. research biochemist Allan Meml. Inst., Montreal, 1953-65, dir. lab. neurochemistry, 1965—; mem. faculty McGill U., Montreal, 1954—, prof. biochemistry, 1965—, assoc. dean of medicine for research Faculty Medicine, 1972-75. Mem. Que. Med. Research Council, 1971-77; sr. fellow Parkinson's Disease Found., N.Y.C., 1963-66. Author: Biochemistry of Mental Disease, 1962, Nobel Prize Winners in Medicine and Physiology, 1901-1965, 1967. Fellow Royal Soc. Can.; mem. Canadian Biochem. Soc., Pharmacol. Soc. Can., Canadian Coll. Neuropsychopharmacology (Heinz Lehmann award), Am. Soc. Biol. Chemists, Am. Soc. Pharmacology and Exptl. Therapeutics, Am. Soc. Neurochemistry, Internat. Soc. Neurochemistry, Internat. Brain Research Orgn., Canadian Soc. Study History and Philosophy Sci., Sigma Xi. Research and publs. on drugs for treatment high blood pressure; 1st basic research on methyldopa; elucidation of role of dopamine and other monamines in nervous system; biochemical and histological bases of Parkinson's disease, biochemistry of mental depression, pathways of stress in the nervous system. Subspecialties: Neurochemistry; Biochemistry (medicine). Home: 4645 Montclair Ave Montreal PQ H4B 2J8 Canada

SOUSA, WAYNE PHILIP, zoology educator; b. White Plains, N.Y., Nov. 24, 1951; s. Joseph Arthur and Dayne (McGeihan) S. B.S., U. R.I., 1973; M.A., U. Calif.-Santa Barbara, 1975, Ph.D., 1977. Asst. prof. dept. zoology U. Calif., Berkeley, 1977-83, assoc. prof., 1983—, vice chmn. dept. zoology, 1985—. Mem. editorial bd. The Veliger, 1982—. Contbr. articles to profl. jours. Mem. Ecol. Soc. Am. (Mercer award 1981), AAAS, Western Soc. Naturalists, Am. Soc. Zoologists, Am. Soc. Parasitologists, Calif. Malacozoological Soc. Current work: Experimental marine ecology; ecology of host-parasite interactions. Subspecialty: Ecology (biology). Office: Dept Zoology U Calif Berkeley CA 94720

SOUTH, HUGH MILES, engineering administrator; b. Houston, Nov. 10, 1947; s. Hugh Wilson and Lala (Miles) S.; m. Marilyn Morrell, Oct. 1, 1976. B.A., Rice U., 1971; Ph.D., Johns Hopkins U., 1981. Instr. engring. Johns Hopkins Evening Coll., Balt., 1972-76; sr. engr. Johns Hopkins Applied Physics Lab., Laurel, Md., 1976-79, Span Lab. supr., 1979-85, supr. signal processing group, 1985—; instr. Whiting Sch. Engring., Johns Hopkins U., 1985—. Contbr. articles to profl. jours. Mem. IEEE, European Soc. for Signal Processing, Acoustical Soc. Am. (assoc.), Phi Beta Kappa, Sigma Xi, Tau Beta Pi. Democrat. Current Work: Signal processing hardware/software systems, signal processing algorithms, ultrasonic waves. Subspecialties: Electrical engineering; Acoustics. Home: 7242 Lasting Light Way Columbia MD 21045 Office: Johns Hopkins Applied Physics Lab Johns Hopkins Rd Laurel MD 20707

SOWERS, JOSEPH LOUIS, computer scientist, educator; b. Phila., Nov. 20, 1946; s. Joseph Louis and Edith Frances (Ober) S.; m. Louise Ann Schissler, Aug. 18, 1949; children: Matthew Sean, Kerri Leigh. A.B., Rutgers U., 1968; M.A., Temple U., 1971, Ph.D., 1978. Lab. instr. Temple U., Phila., 1968-69; instr. physics Rutgers U.-Camden, N.J., 1969-74, programmer analyst (CCIS), 1974-82, asst. prof. computer scis., 1982—. Contbr. articles to profl. jours. Mem. Am. Astron. Soc., Am. Phys. Soc., U.S. Coast Guard Aux., Am. Assn. Physics Tchrs., Soc. Computer Simulation. Republican. Roman Catholic. Current Work: Researcher in computer simulation. Subspecialties: Simulation; Programming languages. Office: Dept Computer Sci Rutgers U Camden NJ 08102

SPACHNER, SHELDON ARTHUR, metalforming process and systems development executive; b. Chgo., Mar. 28, 1924; s. Arthur and Sadie (Cohen) S.; m. Ruth Joy Kraus, Oct. 24, 1959; 1 child, Carol Jo. B.S. in Physics, Northwestern U., 1948, M.S., 1949; postgrad. U. Md., 1949-53; Ph.D. in Metall. Engring., Ill. Inst. Tech., 1958. Sr. scientist RCA, Harrison, N.J., 1966-67; prin. scientist, asst. chief engr. Gulf & Western Advanced Devel. and Engring. Ctr., Swarthmore, Pa., 1967-80, devel. chief engr., 1980; v.p. tech. G&W Advanced Fuels Tech., Bridgeport, N.J., 1980-82; pres. Tech. Devel. Enterprises, Media, Pa., 1982—. Patentee metalforming machinery and metall. processes, 1955-77; contbr. articles to profl. jours. Served with U.S. Army, 1942-45. Mem. Am. Soc. Metals. Current work: Management of primary metallurgical process production systems development. Subspecialty: Metallurgical engineering.

SPAET, THEODORE HERZL, physician, educator; b. N.Y.C., June 24, 1920; s. Morris and Frances (Rosenberg) S.; m. Amy Abrams, Apr. 23, 1941 (dec. Dec. 1970); children—Linda Sue Spaet Tetzlaff, Barbara Lynne Spaet Pratzel; m. Mona Lois Kropatkin, Aug. 6, 1971; 1 child, Susan Miriam. B.A., U. Wis., 1942; M.D., N.Y. Med. Coll., 1945. Diplomate Am. Bd. Internal Medicine. Intern then asst. resident Montefiore Hosp., N.Y.C., 1945-49, head hematology, prof. medicine, 1956—; asst. resident Morrisania Hosp., N.Y.C., 1949-50; hematology fellow New England Med. Ctr., Boston, 1950-51; instr. then asst. prof. Stanford U. Med. Sch., San Francisco, 1951-55; assoc. prof. pathology Coll. Physicians and Surgeons, N.Y.C., 1956-66; cons. Bronx and Manhattan VA Hosps., N.Y.C., 1961—; assoc. seminar on biomaterials Columbia U., N.Y.C., 1966—. Editor book series in field. Contbr. numerous articles to profl. jours. Served to 1st lt. USMC, 1946-48. Mem. Am. Assn. Physicians, Am. Physiol. Soc., Am. Heart Assn., Soc. Exptl. Biology and Medicine, Am. Soc. Hematology, Internat. Soc. Hematology, Internat. Soc. Thrombosis and Haemostasis (chmn. 1979-81), Edward Kowalsky Meml. Lctr. award 1977). Current work: Hemostasis and atherosclerosis. Subspecialties: Hematology; Physiology (biology). Office: Montefiore Med Ctr 111 E 210th St Bronx New York NY 10467

SPALDING, DONALD HOOD, plant pathologist, researcher; b. Pawtucket, R.I., Dec. 1, 1925; s. John Davis and Mildred Idella (Hood) S.; m. Marion Elizabeth Headley, Jan. 30, 1953; children: Darcy Elizabeth, Donna Jane. A.B. in Biology, Brown U., 1950; M.A. in Bacteriology, U. Kans., 1953; Ph.D. in Plant Pathology, Wash. State U., 1960. Microbiologist Dow Chem. Co., Midland, Mich., 1953-57; research asst. Wash. State U., Pullman, 1957-60; research plant pathologist Agr. Research Service, U.S. Dept. Agr., Wenatchee, Wash., 1960-61, Beltsville, Md., 1961-71, Subtropical Hort. Research Sta., Miami, Fla., 1971—. Served with USN, 1943-46, PTO. Mem. Am. Phytopathol. Soc., Am. Soc. for Hort. Sci., Fla. Hort. Soc. Presbyterian. Current Work: Head agriculture research station for plant introduction and evaluation, research on biology and control of insects and market quality; research on postharvest technology for fruits and vegetables. Subspecialty: Plant pathology. Home: 17500 SW 89th Ct Miami FL 33157 Office: 13601 Old Cutler Rd Miami FL 33158

SPARACINO, JACK ROBERT, human resources researcher and consultant, psychologist; b. N.Y.C., Nov. 4, 1950; s. Robert R. and Marguerite (Riff) S. B.A., Syracuse U., 1972; Ph.D., U. Chgo., 1978. Lectr. U. Chgo., 1977-78; instr. Roosevelt U., Chgo., 1974-78; sr. research assoc. Ohio State U., 1980-81; assoc. project dir. Yankelovich, Skelly and White, Inc., Stamford, Conn., 1982—; cons. Columbus (Ohio) Quality of Working Life Program, 1979-81; adj. asst. prof. Ohio State U., 1980-81. Contbr. articles to profl. jours. Mem. Am. Psychol. Assn. Current Work: Currently working with Yankelovich, Skelly, and White's human resource research and consulting group; organizational personality psychology and the psychology of work behavior are my primary research areas; my firm now offers full service research and consulting capabilities and continues to conduct groundbreaking studies. Subspecialty: Social psychology. Home: 73 Willuwbrook Ave Stamford CT 06902 Office: Yankelovich Skelly and White Inc 969 High Ridge Rd Stamford CT 06905

SPARKS, DAVID LEE, neuroscientist, educator; b. Guntersville, Ala., Dec. 22, 1937; s. Houston Lee and Ruth Bertha (Mooney) S.; m. Betty Ann Ellis, Aug. 31, 1963; children: Steven Edward, Robert Gregory, Michael Scott. B.A., U. Ala., 1959, M.A., 1962, Ph.D., 1963. USPHS postdoctoral research fellow U. Miss. Med. Sch., 1963-65; instr. psychiatry U. Ala., Birmingham, 1965-67, asst. prof., 1967-69, assoc. prof. psychology, 1969-72, prof., 1972-73, chmn. dept., 1969-72, prof. psychology and neurosci., 1973-81, prof. physiology and biophysics, 1981—, prof. neurosci., 1981—, Univ. scholar, 1974-81. Mem. editorial bd.: Revs. Oculomotor Research; contbr. articles to sci. jours. NIMH grantee, 1966-71; Nat. Eye Inst. grantee, 1973—. Mem. AAAS, Assn. Research in Vision and Ophthalmology, Soc. Neurosci. Current Work: Neural control of eye movements; motor physiology; sensory physiology; teaching medical and dental students; research; graduate education. Subspecialties: Physiological psychology; Neurophysiology. Home: 3501 Old Leeds Ct Birmingham AL 35213 Office: Dept Physiology U Ala Birmingham AL 35294

SPARKS, HARVEY VISE, JR., physiologist; b. Flint, Mich., June 22, 1938; s. Harvey Vise and Ellen Louise (Paschall) S.; m. Barbara M. Taylor, Jan. 17, 1969; children—Matthew Taylor, Catherine Elliott, Wendy Sue, Harvey Vise. Student, U. Mich., 1956-59, M.D., 1963. Postdoctoral fellow dept. physiology Harvard Med. Sch., Boston and; U. Goteborg, Sweden; instr. U. Mich., 1966-67, asst. prof. physiology, 1967-70, asso. prof., 1970-74, prof., 1974-78; asst. to dean U. Mich. (Med. Sch.), 1970-71, asst. dean, 1971-72; prof., chmn. dept. physiology Mich. State U., 1979—; mem. survey team, liaison com. on med. edn. AMA and; Am. Assn. Med. Colls.; mem. rev. teams NIH. Author: Casebook of Physiology, 1973; contbr. numerous articles to profl. jours.; editor: (with others) Handbook of Physiology, 1979. Recipient Meritorious Service award Mich. Heart Assn., 1962; Borden award for med. student research, 1963; Mich. Heart Assn. student fellow, 1962-63; John and Mary Markle scholar, 1967-72; USPHS postdoctoral fellow, 1963-66; U. Mich. student research fellow, 1960-61; USPHS grantee, 1963—. Mem. Am. Physiol. Soc. (editorial bd. Am. Jour. Physiology 1974—), AAAS, Microcirculatory Soc., Soc. Exptl. Biology and Medicine, Am. Heart Assn. (council circulation), Mich. Heart Assn., Am. Coll. Sports Medicine, Victor Vaughn Soc., Alpha Omega Alpha, Phi Kappa Phi. Current Work: Cononary blood flow, capillary transport, exercise myocardial ischemia. Subspecialties: Physiology (medicine); Cardiology. Home: 7996 Lovejoy Rd Perry MI 48872 Office: Dept Physiology Giltner Hall Mich State U East Lansing MI 48824

SPARKS, RONALD WAYNE, physicist; b. Wilmington, N.C., Apr. 14, 1955; s. William Marcellis and Sarah Lois S.; m. Cheryl Hawes, Nov. 24, 1979; children: Xylia Maxine, Adam Tobias. B.S. in Physics, U. N.C.-Wilmington, 1979. Salesman Sears Roebuck & Co., Wilmington, N.C., 1975-79; physicist Inst. for Marine Bio-Med. Research, Wrightsville Beach, N.C., 1979; tchr. chemistry, physics, math, electronics New Hanover County Bd. Edn., Wilmington, 1979-80; analyst Talbert, Cox & Assocs. Inc. (Cons. Engrs.), Wilmington, 1980-81; application engr. Climate Control, Wilmington, 1982—; energy cons., cons. physicist. Mem. Am. Phys. Soc., Forum of Physics and Soc. Seventh-day Adventist. Subspecialty: Enhanced heat transfer.

SPEAR, NORMAN EBERMAN, psychology educator; b. Canton, Ohio, Oct. 15, 1937; s. Jesse B. and Florence (Eberman) S.; m. Linda Patia, June 14, 1977; children: Amanda Teri, Jennifer Lee. B.S., Bowling Green State U., 1959, M.S., 1961; Ph.D., Northwestern U., 1963. Asst. prof. psychology Rutgers U., 1963-65, assoc. prof., 1965-69, prof., 1969-74; disting. prof. psychology SUNY-Binghamton, 1974—, chmn. dept., 1976-78; vis. cons. U. So. Calif., 1971; vis. prof. Oxford U., 1973-74. Author: (with others) Learning and Memory, 1977, Processing Memories, 1978; editor: (with B.A. Campbell) Ontogeny of Learning and Memory, 1979, (with R.R. Miller) Information Processing in Animals, 1981, (with R. Isaacson) The Expression of Knowledge, 1982; (with R. Kail) Comparative Perspectives on Development of Memory; (with R. Miller) Conditioned Inhibition, 1985; contbr. articles to profl. jours. NIMH career devel. awardee, 1970-74; NIMH, NSF grantee, 1963—. Mem. Am. Psychol. Assn., Soc. for Neurosci., Psychonomic Soc. (bd. govs. 1985—), Midwestern Psychol. Assn. (sec.-treas. 1985—), Eastern Psychol. Assn. (bd. dirs. 1981-84, 85—), Internat. Soc. Devel. Psychobiology Soc. Stimulus Properties of Drugs, Sigma Xi. Subspecialties: Learning; Developmental psychology. Home: 201 African Rd Vestal NY 13850 Office: Dept Psychology SUNY Binghamton NY 13901

SPECIALE, ROSS ALDO, scientist, researcher; b. Palermo, Sicily, Italy, July 24, 1927; came to U.S., 1970; s. Pietro Sebastiano and Rosalia (Trizzino) S.; m. Louisa Maria Robiins, Mar. 6, 1962; children: Paul, Claudia, Alexander. Ph.D. in Elec. Engring., Politecnico di Milano, Italy, 1955. Microwave engr. Magneti Marelli, Milan, 1955-58; elec. engr. Laben, Milan, 1958-62; sr. scientist Philips N.V., Eindhoven-Holland, 1962-70, Tektronix, Inc., Beaverton, Oreg., 1970-77, TRW Elec. Systems Group, Redondo Beach, Calif., 1977—. Sr. mem. IEEE; mem. Am. Math. Soc., Soc. Indsl. and Applied Math., Assn. Computing Machinery. Subspecialties: Electronics; Computer-aided design. Home: 639 Camino de Encanto Redondo Beach CA 90277 Office: TRW Electronics and Defense Sector One Space Park Dr Redondo Beach CA 90278

SPECTOR, ANDREW LAWRENCE, biomedical engineer; b. Bklyn., Mar. 10, 1947; s. William and Miriam (Jankelowitz) S.; m. Ann Denise Fogle, July 5, 1981. B.A. in Math., NYU, 1969, B.E. in Elec. Engring., 1969; postgrad. U. Pa., 1969-72; M.S. in Bioengring., U. So. Calif., 1974. Elec. engr. U.S. Naval Air Devel. Ctr., Warminster, Pa., 1969-74; research assoc. Children's Hosp. Los Angeles, 1973-74; chief biomed. engr. VA Med. Ctr., Palo Alto, Calif., 1974-83, systems mgr., 1983—; instr. Foothill Community Coll., Los Altos Hills, Calif., 1976; chmn. VA Task Group on Ultrasound Instrumentation, 1974-76, chmn. No. Calif.-Nev. Biomed. Engring. Com., 1976-83; cons. to med. device and health care industries. Contbr. to tech. lit. Univ. scholar NYU, 1964-69, N.Y. State Regents scholar, 1964-69; fellow U.S. Naval Air Devel. Ctr., 1972-74. Mem. IEEE (chmn. Santa Clara Valley bioengring. group 1978-79), Profl. and Tech. Consultants Assn. (assoc.), Tau Beta Pi, Eta Kappa Nu. Current work: Clinical engineering for health care industry; design of computer based medical devices and systems. Subspecialties: Biomedical engineering; Biomedical engineering. Office: PO Box 2350 Stanford CA 94305

SPECTOR, IRA CHARLES, electrical engineer, electronics and semiconductors analyst; b. Allentown, Pa., June 4, 1956; s. Herbert Hyman and Bernice (Rudman) S.; M.D. Yager, Jan. 4, 1985. B.S. in Physics, Washington U., St. Louis, 1978, B.E.E., 1978; M.B.A., Drexel U., 1983. Registered engr.-in-tng., Pa. Teaching asst., research asst. Washington U., 1975-78; with Air Products & Chems., Inc., Allentown, Pa., 1977—, prin. contract research and devel. specialist, 1981-84, electronics bus. analyst, 1983—; entrepreneur, Allentown, 1979—; com. mem. Engr.'s Joint Planning Council, Allentown, Bethlehem, and Easton, Pa., 1983. Alexander S. Langsdorf fellow, Dean's scholar Washington U., 1974. Mem. IEEE, Nat. Contract Mgmt. Assn. (v.p. chpt. 1982-83), Am. Inst. Chem. Engrs., Am. Mgmt. Assn., Am. Soc. Metals, Engr.'s Club Lehigh Valley (v.p. 1985-86). Current work: Development and marketing of new technologically based products; strategic planning of technology-based ventures. Co-developer QMAC-TM Network for semiconductor industry process control. Coordinator liquid phase methanol PDU, LaPorte, Tex.. Home: 3076 Whitehall St Allentown PA 18104 Office: Air Products and Chems Inc PO Box 538 Allentown PA 18105

SPECTOR, REYNOLD, pharmacologist, physician, educator; b. Stoneham, Mass., Nov. 3, 1940; s. Asher and Esther (Karelitz) S.; m. Michiko, Mar. 1, 1973; children: Regine Amy, June Thalia. B.A., Harvard U., 1962; M.D., Yale U., 1966. Diplomate: Am. Bd. Internal Medicine, 1973. Intern and resident Peter Bent Brigham Hosp., Boston, 1966-68, 70-71; instr. Harvard U. Med. Sch., 1971-74, asst. prof., 1974-78, assoc. prof., 1978; prof. internal medicine and pharmacology U. Iowa, 1978—, dir. divs. clin. pharmacology and gen. medicine, 1978—, dir. Clin. Research Ctr., Poison Control Ctr., 1985—. Contbr. numerous articles to profl. jours. Served to maj. M.C. U.S. Army, 1968-70. NIH grantee, 1974—. Mem. Assn. Am. Physicians, Am. Soc. Clin. Investigation, Am. Soc. Pharmacology and Exptl. Therapeutics, Am. Coll. Clin. Pharmacology, Central Soc. Clin. Research, Assn. Am. Physicians, Am. Fedn. Clin. Research. Club: Hasty Pudding (Cambridge, Mass.). Patentee in field. Current Work: Blood-brain barrier; vitamin and drug transport in brain; DNA synthesis in brain; treatment of poisoned patients. Subspecialties: Neurochemistry; Pharmacology. Office: Univ Hosps/clinics Univ Iowa E331 B4 GH Iowa City IA 52242

SPEIS, THEMIS P., government official; b. Pa., Nov. 17, 1930; s. Philip T. and Athena (Katinos) S.; m. Mary Kanacopoulos, Nov. 17, 1971. B.S. Ch.E., U. Pitts., 1956, M.S.M.E., 1966; Ph.D. in Nuclear Engring, U. Md., 1975. Engr. Blaw-Knox Chem. Co., Pitts., 1956-58; sr. engr. Westinghouse Electric Co., Pitts., 1958-67; sr. engr. Atomic Energy Commn., Washington, 1967-74, branch chief, 1974-81; asst. dir. NRC, Washington, 1981-83, dir. div. safety tech., 1983—. Contbr. articles in field to profl. jours. Mem. Am. Nuclear Soc., AAAS. Greek Orthodox. Current Work: Manage and direct activities of the NRC division responsible for the identification and solution of technical issues relating to nuclear power plant safety and the assessment of nuclear power plant risks using probabalistic risk assessment techniques and methods. Subspecialties: Nuclear engineering; Nuclear power plant risk assessment. Home: 14 Watchwater Way Rockville MD 20850 Office: US NRC Washington DC 20555

SPELLMAN, DONALD JEROME, consulting engineer; b. Galesburg, Ill., Sept. 9, 1941; s. Walter Anthony and Verla Mae (Lorance) S.; m. Sharon A. McMahan, Mar. 3, 1962; children: Mark Raymond, Lisa Mae. B.S. in E.E, Purdue U., 1967; M.S. in Ocean Engring, U. R.I., 1974. Enlisted in U.S. Navy, advanced through grades to lt. comdr., 1980; ops. Officer Submarine Group 8, Naples, Italy, 1978-80; ret., 1980; project mgr. Gas Cooled Reactor Assoc., La Jolla, Calif., 1980-82; sr. cons. engr. Advanced Sci. and Tech. Assocs., Solana Beach, Calif., 1982—. Contbr. in field. Vol. Pete Wilson Senatorial Campaign, San Diego, 1982. Recipient Navy Achievement medal Sec. Navy, 1980. Mem. Am. Nuclear Soc. (exec. com. 1982), San Diego Voice Energy. Republican. Episcopalian. Club: San Diego Yacht. Current Work: Completed two years research engineering on hi temperature gas cooled reactors, currently with consulting firm at San Onofre nuclear generating station. Subspecialties: Nuclear engineering; Electronics. Home: 3751 Jennings St San Diego CA 92106 Office: Advanced Science and Technology Associates 337 S Cedros Ave Suite J Solana Beach CA 92075

SPENCE, JANET TAYLOR, psychology educator; b. Toledo, Aug. 29, 1923; d. John Crichton and Helen (Hodge) Taylor; m. Kenneth W. Spence, Dec. 27, 1959. A.B., Oberlin Coll., 1945, D.Sc. (hon.), 1985; postgrad. Yale U., 1945-46; Ph.D., U. Iowa, 1949. Instr. psychology Northwestern U., Evanston, Ill., 1949-51, asst. prof., 1951-57, assoc. prof., 1957-60; research psychology VA

Hosp., Iowa City, Iowa, 1960-64; prof. psychology and ednl. psychology U. Tex., Austin, 1964—, chmn. psychology, 1969-73, Ashbel Smith prof. psychology, 1979—; fellow Center for Advanced Study in Behavioral Scis., 1978-79. Author: (with others) Elementary Statistics, 4th edit., 1983, (with R.L. Helmreich) Masculinity and Femininity, 1978; editor: (with K.W. Spence) Learning and Motivation, Vol. I, 1967, Vol. II, 1968, (with G. Bower) Vol. III, 1969; (with H.H. Kendler) Essays in Neobehaviorism, 1971, Contemporary Psychology, A Jour. of Revs, 1974-79; Achievement and Achievement Motives. Bd. dirs. Social Sci. Research Council, 1975-77. Recipient Gold medal Hollins Coll., 1970; Ford Found. fellow, 1974-75. Mem. Am. Psychol. Assn. (dir. 1977-79, 83-85, pres. 1984), Psychonomic Soc. (mem. governing bd. 1978-83), Soc. Exptl. Social Psychologists, Soc. Exptl. Psychology, AAAS (chmn. sect. on psychology 1983), Southwestern Psychol. Assn. (pres. 1972), Am. Acad. Arts and Scis. Current work: Contributions of intrinsic and extrinsic achievement motives to achievement behaviors and career success; psychological aspects of masculinity and femininity. Subspecialty: Social psychology. Office: U Tex Austin TX 78712

SPENCER, EDSON WHITE, electronics company executive. Chmn., chief exec. officer Honeywell, Inc., Mpls. Subspecialty: Electronics. Office: Honeywell Inc Honeywell Plaza Minneapolis MN 55408*

SPENCER, EDWARD G., physicist, researcher; b. Lynchburg, Va., July 21, 1920; s. William Henry and Helen Guerrant (Hilldrup) S.; m. Necia Bernice Jellison, Feb. 17, 1946; children—Edward G., Jr., Thomas J. B.S.E. in Physics, George Washington U., 1945; M.A. in Physics, Boston U., 1950; postgrad. U. Md., 1950-54. Radio engr. Naval Research Labs., Washington, 1943-46, physicist, 1949-53; physicist Cambridge Air Force Research Labs., 1946-49, Diamond Ordnance Fuze Labs (formerly Nat. Bur. Standards), Washington, 1953-58; AT&T Bell Labs, Murray Hill, N.J., 1958—. Co-editor Conf. Magnetism and Magnetic Materials, N.Y.C., 1964-68; editorial bd. Jour. Applied Physics and Applied Physics Letters, 1965-69, Electronics Letters, London, 1965-75. Contbr. articles to profl. jours. Patentee in field. Recipient Achievement award Dept. of Army Research and Devel., 1955, 57. Fellow Am. Phys. Soc. Republican. Methodist. Current work: Condensed matter physics; superconducting thin films of metals and alloys; metal-insulator transition. Subspecialties: Condensed matter physics; Electronic materials. Home: 76 Roland Rd Murray Hill NJ 07974 Office: AT&T Bell Labs 600 Mountain Ave Murray Hill NJ 07974

SPENCER, JAMES ALPHUS, plant pathologist; b. Clayton, Okla., Nov. 5, 1930; s. James E. and Lola Lea (Booth) S.; children from previous marriage: James Timothy, Jeannie Alexander, Jay Barton. M.S., U. Ark., 1962; Ph.D., N.C. State U., 1966. Agrl. research technician U. Ark., 1957-62; agrl. research technician USDA, N.C. State U., Raleigh, 1962-66; plant pathologist Miss. State U., State College, 1967—. Contbr. articles to profl. jours. Served with AUS, 1953-55. Mem. Am. Phytopath. Soc., Am. Rose Soc., Gamma Sigma Delta. Mem. Ch. of Christ. Club: Kiwanis. Current Work: Woody ornamental diseases; especially rose blackspot. Subspecialty: Plant pathology. Office: Drawer PG Mississippi State MS 29762

SPENCER, LORRAINE BARNEY, biologist, educator; b. Ogden, N.Y., Jan. 26, 1924; d. Elmer Cecil and Edna Justine (Zinter) Barney; m. Richard Earl Spencer, Sept. 12, 1942 (div.); children: Linda, Susan, Deborah, Nancy. B.S. (Dana fellow), Guilford Coll., 1966; M.A. (scholar), Wake Forest U., 1970, Ph.D., 1973. Instr. in biology lab. Wake Forest U., 1968-72, research fellow, 1972-73; adj. prof. Guilford Coll., 1974; assoc. prof. biology St. Augustine's Coll., Raleigh, N.C., 1974—. Contbr. articles to Jour. Phycology. Mem. So. Appalachian Bot. Club, Phycological Soc. Am., Bot. Soc. Am., Assn. S.E. Biologists, Am. Inst. Biol. Scis., Sigma Xi. Current Work: Preparation monograph on genus zephyranthes north of S.Am. (with others). Subspecialties: Systematics; Taxonomy. Home: 315 White Oak Dr Cary NC 27511 Office: Saint Augustine's Coll Raleigh NC 27611

SPENCER, ROBERT FREDERICK, neuroanatomist; b. Jamaica, N.Y., Oct. 20, 1949; s. Lincoln Ryder and Roberta Florence (Johnson) S.; m. Patricia Caldwell Ducker, July 9, 1977. B.Sc., Boston U., 1971; Ph.D., U. Rochester Med. Sch., 1974. USPHS postdoctoral research fellow Inst. Neurol. Scis., U. Pa. Med. Sch., Phila., 1974-77; asst. prof. anatomy Med. Coll. Va., Richmond, 1977-82, assoc. prof., 1982—; vis. assoc. prof. Uniformed Services U. Health Scis. Med. Sch., Bethesda, Md., 1982—. Contbr. articles to profl. jours. Nat. Eye Inst. grantee, 1978—. Mem. Am. Assn. Anatomists, Soc. Neurosci., Assn. Research in Vision and Ophthalmology, N.Y. Acad. Scis., Internat. Brain Research Orgn., Richmond Engrs., Cajal Club, Sigma Xi. Methodist. Current Work: Anatomy and physiology of oculomotor system; synaptic transmission; axoplasmic transport; neurotransmitters, excitatory and inhibitory synaptic mechanisms, innervation and structure of extraocular muscle. Subspecialties: Anatomy and embryology; Neurobiology. Home: 5203 Devonshire Rd Richmond VA 23225 Office: Dept Anatomy Med Coll VA PO Box 709 Richmond VA 23298

SPENSER, IAN DANIEL, chemistry educator; b. Vienna, Austria, June 17, 1924; m. Anita Fuchs, Sept. 5, 1951; children—Helen Ruth, Paul Andrew. B.Sc. in Chemistry, U. Birmingham (Eng.), 1948; Ph.D. in Biochemistry, U. London, 1952, D.Sc., 1969. Demonstrator in biochemistry King's Coll., U. London, 1948-52, asst. lectr. in biochemistry Med. Coll. St. Bartholomew's Hosp., 1952-54, lectr., 1954-57; postdoctoral fellow div. pure chemistry NRC Can., Ottawa, Ont., 1953-54; asst. prof. biochemistry McMaster U., Hamilton, Ont., Can., 1957-59, assoc. prof., 1959-64, prof., 1964-68, prof. chemistry, 1968—; Akademischer Gast Laboratorium fur Organische Chemie/Eidenossische technische Hochschule, Zurich, Switzerland, 1971; vis. prof. Inst. Organic Chemistry Tech. U. Denmark, Lyngby, 1977, Institut fur Organische Chemie, Universitat Karlsruhe (W. Ger.), 1981. Research in biosynthesis of alkaloids, biosynthesis of vitamin B1 and vitamin B6. Recipient Sr. Scientist award NATO, 1980, Can.-Japan Exchange award, 1982-83. Fellow Royal Soc. Can., Royal Inst. Chemistry, Chem. Inst. Can. (John Labatt Ltd. award 1982-83), Royal Soc. Chemistry (U.K.); mem. Biochem. Soc., Can. Biochem. Soc., Am. Soc. Biol. Chemists, Phytochem. Soc. N.Am. Office: Dept Chemistry McMaster U Hamilton ON L8S 4M1 Canada

SPERBER, DANIEL, physics educator, researcher; b. Vienna, Austria, May 8, 1930; came to U.S., 1955, naturalized, 1967; s. Emmanuel and Aniela Hanah (Lieberman) S.; m. Ora Yuval, Nov. 30, 1963; 1 child, Ron E. MS.C., Hebrew U., Jerusalem, 1954; M.A., Princeton U., 1957, Ph.D., 1960. Sr. physicist Ill. Inst. Tech. Research Inst., Chgo., 1964-66, sci. adviser, 1966-67; assoc. prof. physics Ill. Inst. Tech., Chgo., 1964-67; assoc. prof. physics Rensselaer Poly. Inst., Troy, N.Y., 1967-72, prof., 1972—; Nordita prof., Copenhagen, 1973-74; vis. prof. Niel Bohr Inst., Copenhagen, 1975-78; research prof. G.S.I., Darmstadt, Fed. Republic Germany, 1983. Contbr. articles to profl. jours. Served to capt. Israel Air Force, 1948-50. NATO fellow, 1976. Fellow Am. Physical Soc.; mem. N.Y. Acad. Scis., Sigma Xi. Democrat. Jewish. Current work: Application of group theory to quantum mechanics, atomic and nuclear thoretica spectroscopy, theory of heavy ion physics and mathematical physics. Subspecialties: Nuclear physics; Theoretical physics. Home: 1 Taylor Ln Troy NY 12180 Office: Rensselaer Poly Inst Troy NY 12181

SPERRY, ROGER WOLCOTT, neurobiologist, educator; b. Hartford, Conn., Aug. 20, 1913; s. Francis B. and Florence (Kraemer) S.; m. Norma G. Deupree, Dec. 28, 1949; children: Glenn Tad, Janeth Hope. B.A., Oberlin Coll., 1935, M.A., 1937, D.Sc. (hon.), 1982; Ph.D., U. Chgo., 1941, D.Sc. (hon.), 1977; D.Sc. (hon.), Cambridge U., 1972, Kenyon Coll., 1979, Rockefeller U., 1980. Research fellow Harvard and Yerkes Labs., 1941-46; asst. prof. anatomy U. Chgo., 1946-52, sect. chief Nat. Inst. Neurol. Diseases of NIH, also asso. prof. psychology, 1952-53; Hixon prof. psychobiology Calif. Inst. Tech., 1954-84, prof. emeritus, 1984—; research brain orgn. and neural mechanism. Contbr. articles to profl. jours., chpts. to books.; Editorial bd.: Behavioral Biology. Recipient Oberlin Coll. Alumni citation, 1954; Howard Crosby Warren medal Soc. Exptl. Psychologists, 1969; Calif. Scientist of Year award Calif. Mus. Sci. and Industry, 1972; award Passano Found., 1973; Albert Lasker Basic Med. Research award, 1979; co-recipient William Thomas Wakeman Research award Nat. Paraplegia Found., 1972, Claude Bernard sci. journalism award, 1975, Disting. research award Internat. Visual Literacy Assn., 1979; Wolf Found. prize in medicine, 1979; Nobel prize in physiology or medicine, 1981. Fellow AAAS, Am. Acad. Arts and Scis., Am. Psychol. Assn. (recipient Distinguished Sci. Contbn. award 1971); mem. Royal Acad. (fgn. mem.), Nat. Acad. Scis., Am. Physiol. Soc., Am. Assn. Anatomists, Internat. Brain Research Orgn., Soc. for Study of Devel. and Growth, Psychonomic Soc., Am. Soc. Naturalists, Am. Zool. Soc., Soc. Developmental Biology, Am. Philos. Soc. (Lashley prize 1976), Am. Neurol. Assn. (hon.), Soc. for Neurosci., Internat. Soc. Devel. Biologists, AAUP, Pontifical Acad. Scis., Sigma Xi. Subspecialty: Psychobiology. Office: Calif Inst Tech Pasadena CA 91125

SPICER, WILLIAM EDWARD, III, educator, physicist; b. Baton Rouge, Sept. 7, 1929; s. William Edward II and Kate Crystal (Watkins) S.; m. Cynthia Stanley, June 12, 1951 (div. 1969); children: William Edward IV, Sally Ann; m. Diane Lubarsky, Apr. 24, 1969; 1 dau., Jacqueline Kate. B.S., Coll. William and Mary, 1949, MIT, 1951; M.S., U. Mo., 1953, Ph.D., 1955; D.Tech. (hon.), U. Linköping, Sweden, 1975. Scientist, RCA Labs., Lawrence Radiation Lab., U. Calif.-Livermore, 1961-62; mem. faculty Stanford U., 1962—, prof. elec. engring. and materials sci. engring., 1965—, prof. by courtesy applied physics, 1976—, Stanford Ascherman prof. engring., 1978—; dep. dir. Stanford Synchrotron Radiation Lab., 1973-75, cons. dir., 1975—; cons. to govt. and industry, 1962—; mem. solid state scis. panel Nat. Acad. Sci.-NRC, 1965-73; cons., vis prof. Chinese univ. devel. project World Bank-Fudan U., 1983; mem. panel atomic and molecular physics div. Nat. Bur. Standards, 1966-73, chmn., 1971-73; mem. adv. group election devices Dept. Def., 1975-82; fellow Churchill Coll., Cambridge U., Eng., 1979. Editorial bd.: Jour. Crystal Growth, 1981—, Thin Solid Films, 1985; author publs. theory and experiment solid state and surface physics and chemistry, photoemission, optical properties solids, electronic structure metals, semiconductors, insulators. Bd. dirs. Princeton (N.J.) YMCA, 1960-62. Recipient Achievement award RCA, 1957, 60; named Scientist of Yr., Indsl. Research and Devel. mag., 1981; Guggenheim fellow, 1978-79. Fellow IEEE, Am. Phys. Soc. (Oliver Buckley Solid State Physics prize 1980); mem. Am. Vacuum Soc. (chmn. electronics material div. 1978-79, dir. 1978-80, trustee 1981—; Medard W. Welch award 1984), Phi Beta Kappa, Sigma Xi. Current Work: Fundamentals of surface and interface applications to microchip technology; applications of synchrotron radiation. Subspecialties: Condensed matter physics; Microchip technology (engineering). Home: 785 Mayfield Rd Stanford CA 94305 Office: McCullough Bldg Stanford Univ Stanford CA 94305

SPIEGEL, STANLEY LAWRENCE, mathematics educator, researcher; b. N.Y.C., Oct. 27, 1935; s. Sidney Daniel and Gertrude (Milsky) S.; m. Diana Lees, Aug. 13, 1972; children: David Solomon, Sarah Caren; 1 dau. from previous marriage, Stephanie Berit. B.S., NYU, 1957; A.M., Harvard U., 1959, Ph.D., 1966. Postdoctoral fellow meteorology dept. MIT, Cambridge, 1966-68; research assoc. math. dept. Northeastern U., Boston, 1969-73; sr. scientist EG&G Environ. Cons., Waltham, Mass., 1978-79, cons., 1978—; prof. math. U. Lowell, Mass., 1973—; cons. Tri-Con Assocs., Cambridge, Mass., 1980—. Contbr. articles to profl. jours. Mem. Town Meeting, Brookline, Mass., 1981—. Summer faculty research fellow; Air Force Office Sci. Research, 1981, 82; research grantee, 1982, 85—. Mem. Am. Geophys. Union, Am. Meteorol. Soc., N.Y. Acad. Scis., Sigma Xi, Pi Mu Epsilon. Jewish. Current Work: Development and implementation of a computer algorithm to detect charging of spacecraft at geosynchronous and low earth orbits in real time, error analysis of a multi layer, spectral global numerical weather prediction model. Subspecialty: Satellite studies. Home: 39 Stetson St Brookline MA 02146 Office: Math Dept U Lowell 1 University Ave Lowell MA 01854

SPIEGEL, ZANE, consulting ground-water hydrologist, hydrology educator; b. Middletown, N.Y., Nov. 6, 1926; s. Nathan and Anna Rebecca (Mayer) S.; m. Maryanne Geissler, Dec. 19, 1959; children: Austin Gregory, Evan Nathaniel. Student, Lafayette Coll., 1944-46; B.S. in Gen. Sci, U. Chgo., 1949, M.S. in Geology, 1952; Ph.D. in Earth Sci, N.Mex. Inst. Mining and Tech., 1962. Registered profl. engr., N.Mex., N.Y., Mass., Conn., Ohio. Geologist U.S. Geol. Survey, Albuquerque, 1949-53; water resource engr. N.Mex. State Engr. Office, Santa Fe, 1954-58, 66-71; Fulbright Commn. lectr., Arequipa, Peru, 1958-59; postdoctoral fellow Harvard U., 1962-63; vis. prof. Imperial Coll. Tech., London, 1963-64; project mgr. UN Spl. Fund, San Juan, Argentina, 1964-66; prin. Zane Spiegel, 1971—, cons. hydrologist, Santa Fe, 1971—; vis. lectr. U. Minn.-Mpls., 1967-68, N.Mex. Inst. Mining and Tech., 1971; course coordinator Coll. Santa Fe, 1974-77, 85; assoc. prof. Ohio State U., 1980-82; hydrology advisor City/County Planning Commn., Santa Fe, 1970-71; extramural reviewer of research proposals EPA, 1973-77. Author: Geology and Groundwater of Northeast Socorro County, New Mexico, 1958, Hydraulics of Certain Stream-Connected Aquifer Systems, 1962, (with B. Baldwin) Geology and Water of Santa Fe Area, New Mexico, 1963; hydrology advisor to: film When the Rivers Run Dry, 1979. Served with AUS, 1945-46. Lafayette Coll. scholar, 1944-46; NSF coop. fellow, 1960-61. Fellow Geol. Soc. Am., ASCE; mem. Am. Geophys. Union, Nat. Water Well Assn., Assn. Geologists for Internat. Devel. Republican. Unitarian. Current Work: Rehabilitation of brine-contaminated aquifers; diversion of stream flow by wells; aquifer-stream modelling and management; waste spray irrigation; equilibrium theory. Subspecialties: Hydrology; Resource management. Home and Office: Zane Spiegel PO Box 1541 Santa Fe NM 87504

SPIELVOGEL, LAWRENCE GEORGE, consulting engineer; b. Newark, N.J., June 2, 1938; s. Joseph and Fanny (Ravitz) S. B.S. in Mech. Engring, Drexel U., 1962. Registered profl. engr. in 49 states. Asst. post engr. Walter Reed Army Med. Ctr., 1963-65; engr. Utility Survey Corp., Chgo., 1965-66; assoc. Robert G. Werden & Assocs., Inc., Jenkintown, Pa., 1959-70; pres. Lawrence G. Spielvogel, Inc., Wyncote, Pa., 1970—; vis. lectr. Yale U., 1975-81. Author: Energy Management Handbook, 1982. Served to 1st lt. U.S. Army, 1963-65. Mem. ASHRAE (Disting. Service award 1975, award of merit 1976, best jour. award 1980, 81, Crosby Field award 1981), Illuminating Engring. Soc., Am. Cons. Engrs. Council, ASME, Internat. Solar Energy Soc., Chartered Instn. Bldg. Services (Eng.). Current Work: Energy use in buildings. Subspecialty: Mechanical engineering. Address: Wyncote House Wyncote PA 19095

SPIESS, FRED NOEL, oceanographer, educator; b. Oakland, Calif., Dec. 25, 1919; s. Fred Henry and Elva Josephine (Monck) S.; m. Sarah Scott Whitton, July 25, 1942; children: Katherine Spiess Dallaire, Mary Elizabeth Spiess DeJong, John Frederick, Helen Spiess Shamble, Margaret Josephine. A.B., U. Calif., Berkeley, 1941, Ph.D., 1951; M.S., Harvard U., 1947. With Marine Phys. Lab., U. Calif., San Diego, 1952—, dir., 1958-80; dir. U. Calif. Inst. Marine Resources, 1980—; dir. Scripps Inst. Oceanography, La Jolla, 1964-65, prof. oceanography, 1961—; Mem. com. on geodesy Nat. Acad. Scis., 1980—. Served with USNR, 1941-46, 53. Decorated Silver Star medal, Bronze Star medal; recipient John Price Wetherill medal Franklin Inst., 1965; Compass Disting. Scientist award Marine Technol. Soc., 1971; Robert Dexter Conrad award U.S. Sec. of Navy, 1974; Newcomb Cleveland prize AAAS, 1981. Fellow Acoustical Soc. Am., Am. Geophys. Union (Maurice Ewing award 1983); mem. Marine Tech. Soc., Phi Beta Kappa, Sigma Xi. Current Work: Studies of the sea floor; development of seafloor work technology. Subspecialties: Oceanography; Ocean engineering. Home: 9450 La Jolla Shore Dr La Jolla CA 92037 Office: Scripps Inst Oceanography U Calif San Diego La Jolla CA 92093

SPIESS, LURETTA D(AVIS), biologist, educator; b. Chgo., Feb. 3, 1927; d. Arthur G. and Luretta E. (Lindefield) Davis; m. Eliot B., June 23, 1951; children: Arthur Eliot, Bruce Davis. A.B. cum laude, Radcliffe Coll., 1949; Ph.D., Harvard U., 1953. Instr. Northwestern U., 1968-70, sr. research asso. in biology, 1978—, lectr. in biology, 1978—; asst. prof. Lake Forest Coll., 1970-78. Contbr. numerous articles to profl. jours. NSF grantee, 1979, 82. Mem. Bot. Soc. Am., Am. Soc. Plant Physiologists, Bryological Soc. Am. Current Work: Physiology and devel. of moss; role of bacterial assns. Subspecialties: Developmental biology; Plant growth. Home: 1153 Asbury Ave Winnetka IL 60093 Office: Northwestern U Hogan Hall Evanston IL 60201

SPIGLANIN, THOMAS ARTHUR, chemistry researcher; b. Los Angeles, May 20, 1958; s. Edward and Anna Marie (Schneider) S.; m. Vivian Lee Messer, Aug. 26, 1977; 1 child, Kimberly Ann. B.S., U. Calif.-Riverside, 1980; Ph.D., Wesleyan U., 1984. Mem. chemistry staff Wesleyan U., Middletown, Conn., 1984—. Mem. Am. Phys. Soc., Am. Chem. Soc. Current work: Elucidating the basis of photochemical, energy transfer and relaxation phenomena in molecules using laser one-and two-photon spectroscopy. Subspecialties: Physical chemistry; Laser photochemistry. Office: Chemistry Dept Wesleyan U Middletown CT 06457

SPILKER, BERT, pharmacologist, researcher, educator, physician; b. Washington, July 3, 1941; s. Victor and Sara (Robbins) S.; m. Arlene Titow, July 27, 1967; children: Adam, Karen. Ph.D. in Pharmacology, SUNY Downstate Med. Center, Bklyn., 1967; M.D., U. Miami, 1977. Resident in internal medicine Brown U. Med. Sch., Providence, 1977-78; with Pfizer Ltd., Kent, Eng., 1969-70, Phillips-Duphar B.V., Weesp, Netherlands, 1970-72, Sterling-Winthrop Research Inst., Rensselaer, N.Y., 1972-75, JRB Assos., Inc., McLean, Va., 1978-79; pvt. practice medicine specializing in internal medicine, Reston, Va., 1978-79; sr. clin. research scientist Burroughs-Wellcome Co., Research Triangle Park, N.C., 1979—; clin. asst. prof. medicine, adj. assoc. prof. pharmacology, researcher U. N.C. Med. Sch., Chapel Hill, 1979—. Contbr. articles to profl. jours. Mem. Am. Soc. Pharmacology and Exptl. Therapeutics, Am. Epilepsy Soc., Am. Soc. Clin. Pharmacology and Therapeutics, Am. Pain Soc. Current Work: Clinical pharmacology and development of new drugs in various areas, especially neurology. Subspecialties: Internal medicine; Pharmacology. Home: 2556 Booker Creek Rd Chapel Hill NC 27514 Office: 3030 Cornwallis Rd Research Triangle Park NC 27709

SPILLER, GENE ALAN, nutritionist, clinical human nutrition research consultant; b. Milan, Italy, Feb. 19, 1927; came to U.S., 1950, naturalized, 1962; s. Silvio and Beatrice (Galli) S. D.Chemistry, U. Milan, 1949; M.S., U. Calif.-Berkeley, 1968, Ph.D. in Nutrition, 1972. Cons. nutrition research and edn., Los Angeles, 1952-65; research chemist U. Calif., Berkeley, 1966-67, assoc. specialist physiology dept., 1968-72; prin. scientist, head nutritional physiology Syntex Research, Palo Alto, Calif., 1972-80, cons. clin. nutrition research, Los Altos, Calif., 1981—; lectr. Mills Coll., Oakland, Calif., 1971-81, Foothill Coll., Los Altos, 1974—. Editor: Fiber in Human Nutrition, 1976, Topics in Dietary Fiber, 1978, Medical Aspects of Dietary Fiber, 1980, Nutritional Pharmacology, 1981; The Methylxanthines Beverages and Foods, 1984; reviewer papers: Am. Jour. Clin. Nutrition, 1976-83. Mem. Am. Inst. Nutrition, Am. Soc. Clin. Nutrition, Brit. Nutrition Soc., Am. Assn. Cereal Chemists. Club: Alpine Hills. Current Work: Research in human nutrition; principal investigator in human nutrition studies; dietary fiber and carbohydrates effect on human health; role of lesser known food components in nutrition; non-human primates as models for human nutrition. Subspecialties: Nutrition (medicine); Physiology (medicine). Office: PO Box 123 Los Altos CA 94022

SPINDEL, WILLIAM, scientist, administrator; b. N.Y.C., Sept. 9, 1922; s. Joseph and Esther (Goldstein) S.; m. Louise Phyllis Hoodenpyl, July 30, 1967; children: Robert Andrew, Lawrence Marshall. B.A., Bklyn. Coll., 1944; M.A., Columbia U., 1947, Ph.D., 1950. Jr. scientist Los Alamos Lab, Manhattan Dist., 1944-45; instr. Poly. Inst., Bklyn., 1949-50; asso. prof. State U. N.Y., 1950-54; research asso., vis. prof. Columbia, 1954-57, vis. prof., sr. lectr., 1962-74; asso. prof. then prof. Rutgers U., 1957-64; prof., chmn. dept. chemistry Belfer Grad. Sch. Sci., Yeshiva U., 1964-74; exec. sec., office chemistry and chem. tech. Nat. Acad. Scis.-NRC, 1974—, also staff dir. bd. on chem. scis. and tech., 1974—; vis. Am. scientist, Yugoslavia, 1971-72. Contbr. articles to profl. jours. Served with AUS, 1943-46. Guggenheim fellow, 1961-62; Fulbright Research scholar, 1961-62. Fellow AAAS; mem. Am. Chem. Soc., Am. Phys. Soc. Club: Cosmos. Patentee in field. Current Work: Science policy studies in the chemical sciences; needs and scientific opportunities in chemical sciences, and potential of chemical sciences for solution of social needs. Subspecialties: Physical chemistry; Science policy, chemical science administration. Home: 6503 Dearborn Dr Falls Church VA 22044 Office: Nat Acad Scis 2101 Constitution Ave Washington DC 20418

SPINKA, HAROLD MATTHEW, JR., physicist, educator; b. Chgo., Apr. 2, 1945; s. Harold M. and Dorothy Jean (Wellman) S.; m. Katherine Marie Wick, Feb. 24, 1973; children—Christine, Thomas. B.A., Northwestern U., 1966; Ph.D., Calif. Inst. Tech., 1970. Postdoctoral fellow Argonne Nat. Lab., Ill., 1970-73. physicist, 1976—; adj. asst. prof. UCLA, 1973-76. Mem. Am. Phys. Soc., Phi Beta Kappa, Sigma Xi. Current works: Spin effects in nucleon-nucleon and meson-nucleon scattering at high and intermediate energies, nuclear astrophysics. Subspecialties: Particle physics; Nuclear physics. Home: 635 S Loomis Naperville IL 60540 Office: Argonne Nat Lab 9700 S Cass Ave Argonne IL 60439

SPIRO, CLIFFORD LAWRENCE, chemist, scientist; b. Bronx, N.Y., Apr. 9, 1954; s. Frank Kamak and Naomi (Domash) S.; m. Rhoda Quisenberry, May 9, 1980; children—Ian Scott, Miranda Lee. B.S. with honors in Chemistry, Stanford U., 1976; Ph.D. in Inorganic Chemistry, Calif. Inst. Tech., 1980. Staff scientist Gen. Electric Corp. Research and Devel., Schenectady, N.Y., 1980—; lectr. in field. Contbr. articles to profl. jours. Patentee in field. Recipient Patent and Publ. award Gen. Electric, 1983; Earl S. Anthony fellow, 1976. Mem. Am. Chem. Soc. (cert., fuel inorganic, and petroleum divs.), Capital Dist. Mineral Club (program chmn.). Current work: Coal science; new techniques to study coal; modelling, EXAFS spectroscopy, computed tomography, benefication, catalysis. Subspecialties: Inorganic chemistry; Coal. Office: Gen Electric Corp Research and Devel Bldg K1-4B24 Schenectady NY 12345

SPIRO, JULIUS, electronic engineer; b. N.Y.C., Nov. 20, 1921; s. Sam and Helen (Schild) S.; m. Gertrude Bauer, Oct. 27, 1946; children—George William, Rochelle G. B.S. CCNY, 1953. Engr. Nevis labs. Columbia U., N.Y.C., 1947-53, Hudson labs., N.Y.C., 1953-54; sr. engr. Brookhaven Nat. Lab., Upton, N.Y., 1954—. Contbr. articles to profl. jours. Served to capt. U.S. Army, 1943-46. Sr. mem. IEEE. Current work: Design and construction of particle-accelerators. Subspecialties: Electrical engineering; Particle physics. Home: 101 Gillette Ave Patchoque NY 11772 Office: Brookhaven Nat Lab Upton NY 11973

SPISAK, JOHN FRANCIS, metallurgist, minerals company executive; b. Cleve., Mar. 27, 1950; s. Ernest L. and Adele M. (Chipko) S.; m. Barbara Ann Heisman, June 10, 1972; 1 son, John Stefan. B.S. in Chemistry and Biology with honors, Purdue U., 1972. Research engr. Anaconda Co., Tucson, 1972-79; chief metallurgist Fed. Am. Uranium, Riverton, Wyo., 1979-80, Anschutz Mining Corp., Denver, 1980—; lectr. Colo. Sch. Mines, Golden, 1982—. Author: Metallurgical Effluents-Growing Challenges for Second Generation Treatment, 1979, Solvent Extraction of Copper from Smelter Dust Treatment Liquirs with ACORGA P-5100, 1981, Recovery of Cobalt, Nickel and Copper from the Madison Mine, 1983. Recipient Presdl. Service award Purdue U., 1972. Mem. AIME, Am. Inst. Biol. Scis., Am. Chem. Soc., Purdue U. All-Am. Club. Republican. Roman Catholic. Lodge: Purdue Elks. Current Work: Metallurgical process design and development; bioprocessing of heavy metals; process design management; financial analyses; biometallurgical process development; biotechnology company formation. Subspecialties: Metallurgical engineering; Integrated systems modelling and engineering. Home: 8224 Everett St Arvada CO 80005 Office: 555 17th St Suite 2400 Denver CO 80202

SPITAL, ROBIN DAVID, physicist; b. N.Y.C., Oct. 29, 1948; s. Max and Elaine (Steinberg) S. A.B., Harvard U., 1969; M.S., Cornell U., 1972, Ph.D., 1974. Asst. prof. physics Ill. State U., Normal, 1974-75; cons. scientist Pfizer Med. Systems, Columbia, MD., 1976-81; prin. devel. engr. AAI Corp., Cockeysville, Md., 1981—. Contbr. articles to profl. jours. Mem. Am. Phys. Soc., Am. Assn. Physicists in Medicine, Phi Beta Kappa. Club: Marshall Chess (N.Y.C.). Current Work: Researcher in computer simulation of tactical environment for military training, medical and theoretical physics. Subspecialties: Theoretical physics; Software engineering. Office: AAI Corp PO Box 6767 Baltimore MD 21204

SPITSBERG, VITALY LEV, biochemistry educator; b. Kazatin, USSR, July 27, 1938; came to U.S., 1975, naturalized, 1981; s. Lev Israel and Anna Efim (Rubchinsky) S.; m. Margarita Bakaeva, Sept., 1960 (div. 1970); 1 son, Vladimir; m. Natalia Krasnova, Nov. 19, 1971; 1 son, Andrey. M.D., Moscow First Med. Inst., 1961; Ph.D., Inst. Biophysics, Moscow, 1966. Jr. scientist Inst. Med. Chemistry, Moscow, 1961-62; sr. scientist Inst. Molecular Biology, Moscow, 1966-71, Inst. Devel. Biology, Moscow, 1971-74; asst. research prof. St. Louis U., 1981-82; vis. research prof. U. Nebr.-Lincoln, 1982—; project assoc. Northwestern U. Med. Sch., 1975; project assoc. Inst. Enzyme Research, U. Wis.-Madison, 1976, research assoc. dept. pharmacology, 1977-78; research assoc. Syracuse U., 1978-79; sr. research assoc. St. Louis U., 1979-81. NSF grantee, 1982. Mem. Am. Soc. Biol. Chemists, N.Y. Acad. Scis. Current Work: Oxidative phosphorylation, photosynthesis, biochemical evolution, cell biology. Subspecialties: Biochemistry (biology); Biochemical evolution. Home: 1205 S 20th St Lincoln NE 68502 Office: U Nebr-Lincoln 705 Hamilton Hall Lincoln NE 68588

SPITZER, ADRIAN, pediatrics educator, pediatrician; b. Bucharest, Rumania, Dec. 21, 1927; came to U.S., 1963, naturalized, 1968; s. Osias and Sophia S.; m. Carole Zelter, Oct. 30, 1951; 1 son, Vlad. B.S., Matei Basarab Lyceum, Bucharest, 1946; M.D., Med. Sch. Bucharest, 1952. Intern White Plains (N.Y.)

Hosp., 1964-65; resident in pediatrics Med. Coll. Pa., Phila., 1965-66; asst. prof. pediatrics Albert Einstein Coll. Medicine, 1968-72, assoc. prof., 1972-76, prof., dir. div. nephrology, 1976—; mem. gen. medicine B study sect. NIH, 1976-80; mem. sub-bd. in pediatric nephrology Am. Bd. Pediatrics, 1977-83, chmn., 1981-82; mem. com. health and sci. affairs Nat. Kidney Found., 1978-80, mem. sci. adv. bd., 1982. Assoc. editor: Pediatric Kidney Disease, 1980; editor: The Kidney During Development, 1982. NIH spl fellow, 1968; NIH Fogarty sr. internat. fellow, 1982; NIH grantee, 1968—; Health Research Council N.Y. grantee, 1978—; Nat. Kidney Found. grantee, 1970—. Fellow Am. Acad. Pediatrics; mem. Am. Physiol. Soc., Am. Soc. Nephrology, Am. Soc. Pediatric Nephrology (council 1976-83, pres. 1981-82), Soc. Pediatric Research, Intersoc. Council Research of Kidney and Urinary Tract (sec.-treas. 1984—), Am. Pediatric Soc. Current Work: Developmental renal physiology; kidney disease in children. Subspecialties: Pediatrics; Nephrology. Home: 27 Sycamore Ln Irvington NY 10533 Office: Albert Einstein Coll Medicine 1410 Pelhm Pkwy S Bronx NY 10461

SPITZER, JOHN J., physiology educator; b. Baja, Hungary, Mar. 9, 1927; came to U.S., 1952; s. Sigmund and Irene (Roheim) S.; m. Judy A. Gottfried, June 30, 1951; children—Peter G., Juliet I. Student U. Budapest Sch. Medicine, 1945, U. Vienna Sch. Medicine, 1949; M.D., U. Munich, 1950. Instr., Dalhousie U., Halifax, N.S., 1951-52; asst. prof. physiology Fla. State U.-Tallahassee, 1952-54; research scientist N.Y. State Dept. Health, Albany, 1954-57; asst. prof. Hahnemann Med. Coll., 1957-58, assoc. prof., 1958-61, prof., 1961-73; prof., head dept. physiology La. State U. Med. Ctr., New Orleans, 1973—. Contbr. numerous articles to sci. jours. NIH Program Project grantee, 1984. Mem. Am. Physiol. Soc., Internat. Soc. Heart Research, Shock Soc., AAAS, Soc. Exptl. Biology and Medicine. Jewish. Current work: Shock and trauma; metabolism; myocardian metabolism and function. Subspecialty: Physiology (medicine). Home: 5687 Evelyn Ct New Orleans LA 70124 Office: La State Med Ctr 1901 Perdido St New Orleans LA 70112

SPITZER, LYMAN, JR., astronomer; b. Toledo, June 26, 1914; s. Lyman and Blanche C. (Brumback) S.; m. Doreen D. Canaday, June 29, 1940; children: Nicholas, Dionis, Lutetia, Lydia. A.B., Yale U., 1935, D.Sc., 1958; postgrad., Cambridge (Eng.) U., 1935-36; Ph.D., Princeton U., 1938, D.Sc., 1984; Case Inst. Tech., 1961, Harvard U., 1975, Princeton U., 1984; LL.D., Toledo U., 1963. Nat. research fellow Harvard U., 1938-39; instr. physics and astronomy Yale U., 1939-42; scientist spl. studies group div. war research Columbia U., 1942-44, dir. sonar analysis group, 1944-46; assoc. prof. astrophysics Yale U., 1946-47; prof. astronomy, chmn. dept. and dir. obs. Princeton U., 1947-79, Charles A. Young prof. astronomy, 1952-82, chmn. research bd., 1967-72; dir. Princeton U. (Project Matterhorn), 1953-61; chmn. exec. com. (Plasma Physics Lab.), 1961-66; prin. investigator Princeton telescope on Copernicus satellite; trustee Woods Hole Oceanographic Inst., 1946-51; mem. com. on undersea warfare NRC, 1948-51; mem. Yale U. Council, 1948-51; chmn. Scientists Com. on Loyalty Problems, 1948-51. Author: Physics of Fully Ionized Gases, 1956, 62, Diffuse Matter in Space, 1968, Physical Processes in the Interstellar Medium, 1978, Searching between the Stars, 1982; editor: Physics of Sound in the Sea, 1946; contbr. articles to profl. jours. Recipient Rittenhouse medal, 1957; Exceptional Sci. Achievement medal NASA, 1972; Bruce Gold medal, 1973; Henry Draper gold medal, 1974; James C. Maxwell prize, 1975; Disting. Pub. Service medal NASA, 1976; Nat. Medal of Sci., 1980; Janssen medal, 1980; Franklin medal, 1980. Fellow Am. Phys. Soc.; mem. Nat. Acad. Sci., Am. Acad. Arts and Scis., Am. Philos. Soc., Am. Astron. Soc. (past pres.), Royal Astron. Soc. (assoc., gold medal 1978), Am. Geophys. Union, Astron. Soc. Pacific, Royal Soc. Scis. (Liege) (fgn. corr. mem.). Unitarian. Club: Am. Alpine; Alpine (London). Current Work: Chairman of AURA's Space Telescope Institute Council, with administrative oversight of Space Telescope Science Institute; member of various committees for Space Telescope. Subspecialties: Optical astronomy; Theoretical astrophysics. Home: 659 Lake Dr Princeton NJ 08540

SPITZER, ROGER EARL, physician, medical educator; b. Washington, June 20, 1935; s. Ronald Heller and Mildred Edith (Jaffee) S.; m. Rosalie J. Gutride, June 10, 1962; children: Scott, Neal, Amy. B.S., George Washington U., 1958; M.D., Howard U., 1962. Diplomate Am. Bd. Pediatrics, Am. Bd. Pediatric Nephrology. Instr. chemistry George Washington U., Washington, 1956-58; asst. prof. pediatrics U. Cin., 1969-73; assoc. prof. pediatrics SUNY Upstate Med. Ctr., Syracuse, 1973-77, prof., 1977—, dir. pediatric nephrology, 1978—; adv. Central N.Y. Kidney Disease Soc. Contbr. articles to profl. jours. NIH fellow; USPHS grantee; Am. Cancer Soc. grantee. Mem. Am. Soc. Nephrology, Soc. Pediatric Research, Am. Pediatric Soc., Am. Assn. Immunologists. Democrat. Jewish. Current Work: Glomerulonephritis and the complement system; pediatric kidney disease, mechanisms of complement activity and the role of complement in leukemia. Subspecialties: Nephrology; Immunology (medicine). Home: 104 E Genesee Pkwy Syracuse NY 13214 Office: 750 E Adams St Syracuse NY 13210

SPITZER, WILLIAM GEORGE, material scientist, physics educator, university administrator; b. Los Angeles, Apr. 24, 1927; s. Max and May Lea (Axleband) S.; m. Jeanette Dorothy Navsky, June 23, 1949; children—Matthew Laurence, Margaret Ilene. B.A., UCLA, 1949; M.S., U. So. Calif., 1952; Ph.D., Purdue U., 1957. Mem. tech. staff Bell Telephone Lab., Murray Hill, N.J., 1957-62, Bell & Howell Research Ctr., Pasadena, Calif., 1962-63; prof. material sci. and physics U. So. Calif., Los Angeles, 1963—, chmn. dept. materials sci., 1967-69, physics dept., 1969-72, 78-81, dean grad. studies, vice provost for research, 1983—. Contbr. numerous articles to profl. jours., chpt. to books. Served with AUS, 1945-46. Fellow Am. Phys. Soc.; mem. IEEE (sr.). Subspecialties: Electronic materials; Condensed matter physics. Office: U So Calif University Park Adminstrn Bldg Room 102 Los Angeles CA 90089

SPIZIZEN, JOHN, microbiology educator; b. Winnipeg, Man., Can., Feb. 7, 1917; s. Nathan and Sarah (Frankel) S.; m. Louise Myers, 1968; 1 son, Gary. B.A., U. Toronto, 1939; Ph.D., Calif. Inst. Tech., 1942. Assoc. prof. microbiology Western Res. U., 1954-61; prof., head dept. microbiology U. Minn.-Mpls., 1961-65; mem., chmn. dept. microbiology Scripps Clinic and Research Found., La Jolla, Calif., 1966-79; prof., head dept. microbiology U. Ariz.-Tucson, 1979—; mem. bd. sci. advisors La Jolla Cancer Research Found., 1978—. Co-author: Medical Microbiology, 1984; contbr. numerous articles to sci. jours. Vice-chmn. personnel com. Am. Cancer Soc., 1980—. Served to capt. AUS, 1943-47. Current work: Genetics and genetic engineering; genetics of bacilli; infecticidal toxins produced by bacilli. Subspecialties: Microbiology; Genetics and genetic engineering (biology). Office: Dept Microbiology and Immunology U Ariz Tucson AZ 85724

SPLINTER, WILLIAM ELDON, agricultural engineer; b. North Platte, Nebr., Nov. 24, 1925; s. William John and Minnie (Calhoun) S.; m. Eleanor Love Peterson, Jan. 5, 1953; children: Kathryn Love, William John, Karen Ann, Robert Marvin. B.Sc., U. Nebr., 1950; M.Sc., Mich. State U., 1951, Ph.D., 1955. Instr. agrl. engring. Mich. State U., 1953-54; asso. prof. biology and agrl. engring. N.C. State U., 1954-61, prof., 1961-68; prof., George W. Holmes Disting. prof., head dept. agrl. engring. U. Nebr., 1968—; cons. engr. Mem. exec. bd.; Am. Assn. Engring. Socs. Contbr. articles tech. jours. Served with USNR, 1946-51. Recipient Massey Ferguson Ednl. award; named to Nebr. Hall of Agrl. Achievement. Fellow Am. Soc. Agrl. Engrs. (pres., adminstrv. council), AAAS; mem. Nat. Acad. Engring., Soc. Automotive Engrs., Am. Soc. Engring. Edn., Nat. Soc. Profl. Engrs., Sigma Xi, Sigma Tau, Sigma Pi Sigma, Pi Mu Epsilon, Gamma Sigma Delta, Phi Kappa Phi, Beta Sigma Psi. Patentee in field. Current Work: Measurement and computer modeling of plant growth. Subspecialty: Agricultural engineering. Home: 7105 N Hampton St Lincoln NE 68520

SPLITTSTOESSER, DON FREDERICK, microbiology educator; b. Norwalk, Wis., Aug. 17, 1927; s. Frederick A. and Martha (Rosenwald) S.; m. Clara Mae Quinnell, Mar. 28, 1959. B.S., U. Wis., 1951, M.S., 1952, Ph.D., 1956. Asst. prof. Cornell U., Geneva, N.Y., 1958-64, assoc. prof., 1964-69, prof. microbiology, 1969—, chmn. dept. food sci. and tech., 1982—; mem., chmn. food protection com. NRC, 1979—; chmn. Gordon Research Conf., 1984. Author, editor: Food Microbiology; Public Health and Spoilage Aspects, 1976. Chmn. Zoning Bd. of Appeals, Geneva, 1972-83. Served to 1st lt. Med. Service Corps, U.S. Army, 1956-58. Fellow Inst. Food Technologists; mem. Am. Soc. Enologists (chmn. eastern sect. 1979-80). Democrat. Clubs: Geneva Country, Finger Lakes Torch (pres., sec.-treas.) (Geneva). Office: Dept Food Sci and Tech Cornell U Geneva NY 14456

SPOELHOF, CHARLES P., photographic company executive; b. Hackensack, N.J., Aug. 6, 1930; s. Charles and Elizabeth (Keegstra) S.; m. Kay, June 11, 1953; children: Beth, Philip, Gordon, Ronald. Student in engring., Calvin Coll., 1948-51; U. Mich., 1953, B.S. in Engring. Math, 1953, M.S. in Physics, 1954; postgrad. in optics, U. Rochester, 1954-55; postgrad. in advanced engring. studies, MIT, 1965-66. With Apparatus Div., Eastman Kodak Co., Rochester, N.Y., 1954—; dir. research and engring. Apparatus Div., Eastman Kodak Co. (U.S. and Can. Photog. div.), 1973-75, mgr. bus. and profl. products, 1975-82; v.p., asst. gen. mgr. Kodak Apparatus Div., 1982—, v.p., dir. tech. assessment, comml. and info. systems, 1985—. Bd. dirs. N.Y. State Epilepsy Assn. Recipient Apollo Achievement award NASA, 1970. Mem. Nat. Acad. Engring., Optical Soc. Am., Soc. Photog. Scientists and Engrs., Rochester C. of C., Rochester Acad. Sci., Phi Kappa Phi. Mem. Christian Reformed Ch. Patentee wide angle optical system. Current Work: Management of development and production of photographic apparatus. Subspecialties: Optical engineering; Systems engineering. Office: 901 Elmgrove Rd Rochester NY 14650

SPOERI, RANDALL KEITH, statistics and operations research educator, consultant, administrator; b. Cleve., June 12, 1946; s. Theodore Warren and Marion (Barrick) S.; m. Kathleen Loma Bryden, Aug. 31, 1968 (div. 1981); 1 child Jennifer Anne; m. Deborah Jean Hammett, June 20, 1981; 1 son, Jason Randall. B.S. in Math, Calif. Poly. State U., 1968; M.S. in Stats, Tex. A&M U., 1970, Ph.D. in Stats, 1976. Spl. asst., math. statistician Bur. of Census, Washington, 1976-80, quantitative methods research br. chief, 1980; assoc. prof. stats. and ops. research U.S. Naval Acad., 1980-83; statis. cons. Md. Energy Adminstrn., 1980-83; adj. prof. U. Md., 1978—; statis. cons. Ctr. Mgmt. and Policy Research, Inc., Washington, 1980-83, Trident Engring., Inc., Annapolis, Md., 1982-83; assoc. exec. dir. Am. Statis. Assn., Washington, 1983—. Author, editor: Operations Research, 1972. Served to 1st lt. U.S. Army, 1970-72. Decorated Army Commendation Medal; recipient Outstanding Performance rating Bur. of Census, 1978. Mem. Am. Statis. Assn., Ops. Research Soc. Am., Inst. Mgmt. Scis., Mil. Ops. Research Soc., Phi Kappa Phi, Omega Rho, Mu Sigma Rho. Republican. Current Work: Development and innovative application of statistical and operations research methodologies; computer technology to support diverse problem areas such as military tactics, educational and association administration, census data use, ecology and engineering. Subspecialties: Statistics; Operations research (mathematics). Home: 929 Burnett Ave Arnold MD 21012 Office: 806 15th St NW Suite 640 Washington DC 20005

SPOHN, HERBERT EMIL, psychologist; b. Berlin, Germany, June 10, 1923; s. Herbert F. and Bertha S.; m. Billie M. Powell, July 28, 1973; children—Jessica, Madeleine. B.S.S., CCNY, 1949; Ph.D., Columbia U., 1955. Research psychologist VA Hosp., Montrose, N.Y., 1955-60, chief research sect., 1960-64; sr. research psychologist Menninger Found., Topeka, 1965-80, dir. hosp. research, 1979—, dir. research dept., 1981—; mem. mental health small grant com. NIMH, 1972-76, mem. treatment assessment rev. com., 1983—. Author: (with Gardner Murphy) Encounter with Reality, 1968; contbr. articles to profl. jours; assoc. editor: Schizophrenia Bull, 1970—. Served with AUS, World War II. USPHS grantee, 1964—. Mem. Am. Psychol. Assn., AAAS, N.Y. Acad. Sci., Phi Beta Kappa, Sigma Xi. Current Work: Experimental psychopathology treatment evalation research. Subspecialties: Psychopharmacology; Experimental psychopathology. Office: Menninger Found Box 829 Topeka KS 66601

SPOMER, LOUIS ARTHUR, plant physiology researcher, educator; b. Denver, Apr. 17, 1940; s. Peter John and Thelma Pauline (Johnson) S.; m. Wilma Elise Price, Aug. 26, 1962; children—Paul Arthur, William Ryan, Mark Andrew. B.S., Colo. State U., 1963; M.S., Cornell U., 1967, Ph.D., 1969. Research asst. Cornell U., Ithaca, N.Y., 1965-69; staff officer, meteorologist Deseret Test Ctr., Ft. Douglas, Utah, 1969-71; phys. scientist, 1971; asst., then assoc. prof. plant physiology U. Ill., Urbana, 1971-80, prof., 1981—. Served to capt. U.S. Army, 1969-71. Mem. Am. Soc. Horticulture Sci., Am. Soc. Agronomy, Soil Sci. Soc. Am. Current work: Determination of environmental control of plant growth; study of plant water requirement. Subspecialty: Plant physiology (agriculture). Home: 704 Burkwood Dr Urbana IL 61801 Office: U Ill 1107 W Dorner Dr Urbana IL 61801

SPRADLING, ALLAN C., molecular biologist. Mem. staff Carnegie Inst. Washington. Recipient (with Gerald Rubin) U.S. Steel Found. award Nat. Acad. Scis., 1985. Subspecialty: Molecular biology. Office: Carnegie Inst Washington Dept Embryology Baltimore MD 21210

SPRAGUE, CHARLES CAMERON, college president; b. Dallas, Nov. 14, 1916; s. George Able and Minna (Schwartz) S.; m. Margaret Frederica Dickson, Sept. 7, 1943; 1 dau., Cynthia Cameron. B.B.A., B.S., D.Sc., So. Meth. U., D.Sc. (hon.), 1966; M.D., U. Tex., 1943. Intern U.S. Naval Med. Center, Bethesda, Md., 1943-44; resident Charity Hosp., New Orleans, 1947-48, Tulane U. Med. Sch., 1948-50; Commonwealth research fellow in hematology Washington U. Sch. Medicine, St. Louis, also Oxford (Eng.) U., 1950-52; mem. faculty Med. Sch. Tulane U., 1952-67, prof. medicine, 1959-67; dean Med. Sch. Tulane U. (Sch. Medicine), 1963-67; prof., dean U. Tex. Southwestern Med. Sch., Dallas, 1967-72; pres. U. Tex. Health Sci. Center, Dallas, 1972—; Mem. Nat. Adv. Council, 1966-70; mem. adv. com. to dir. NIH, 1973—; chmn. Gov.'s Task Force Health Manpower, 1981, Gov.'s Med. Edn. Mgmt. Effectiveness Com.; chmn. allied health edn. adv. com., coordinating bd. Tex. Coll. and Univ. System. Served with USNR, 1943-47. Recipient Ashbel Smith Distinguished Alumnus award U. Tex. Med. Br., 1967; Distinguished Alumnus award So. Meth. U., 1965; recipient Sports Illustrated Silver Anniversary award, 1963. Mem. Assn. Am. Med. Colls. (chmn. council deans 1970, chmn. exec. council and assembly 1972-73), Am. Soc. Hematology (pres. 1968), Assn. Acad. Health Ctrs. (bd. dirs. 1982—). Subspecialties: Medical administration; Hematology. Office: U Tex Health Sci Center 5323 Harry Hines Blvd Dallas TX 75235

SPRAGUE, JAMES MATHER, medical scientist, educator; b. Kansas City, Mo., Aug. 31, 1916; s. James P. and Lelia (Mather) S.; m. Dolores Marie Eberhart, Nov. 25, 1959; 1 child, James B. B.S., U. Kans., 1938, M.A., 1940; Ph.D., Harvard U., 1942; A.M. (hon.), U. Pa., 1971. From asst. to asst. prof. anatomy Hopkins Med. Sch., 1942-50; asst. prof. to prof. anatomy U. Pa. Med. Sch., Phila., 1950—, chmn. dept., 1967-76, Joseph Leidy prof. anatomy, 1973—, dir. Inst. Neurol. Sci., 1973-80; chmn. faculty senate U. Pa. Med. Sch. (Inst. Neurol. Sci.), 1963; vis. prof. Northwestern U., 1948, Rockefeller U., 1955, Cambridge U., 1956, U. Pisa, 1966, 74-75; sci. cons. NIH, 1957-60. Co-editor: Progress in Psychobiology and Physiological Psychology, 1966-85, assoc. editor: Acta Neurobiol. Exper., 1976; contbr. articles to profl. jours. Recipient Macy faculty award, 1974-75; Guggenheim fellow, 1948-49. Mem. Am. Assn. Anatomists (v.p. 1976-78), Japanese Assn. Anatomists (hon.), Soc. Neurosci., Nat. Acad. Sci. Democrat. Current Work: Neutral mechanisms of visually-guided behavior- attentions; pereption; discrimination activity. behavior. Subspecialties: Neurobiology; Anatomy and embryology. Home: 631 Moreno Rd Narberth PA 19072 Office: Dept Anatomy Sch Med U Pa Philadelphia PA 19104

SPRATT, JAMES LEO, pharmacologist; b. Chgo., Jan. 27, 1932; s. William and Margaret (Callahan) S.; children: James, Sheila. A.B., U. Chgo., 1953, Ph.D., 1957, M.D., 1961. Asst. prof. pharmacology U. Iowa, Iowa City, 1961-65, asso. prof., 1965-71, prof., 1971—. Contbr. articles to sci. jours. Recipient Research Career Devel. award USPHS, 1963-68; Markle scholar, 1963-68. Mem. Am. Chem. Soc., AAAS, Am. Soc. Exptl. Pharmacology and Therapeutics. Current Work: Metabolism and actions of cardiac and neuropharmacological agents. Subspecialty: Pharmacology.

SPRATT, JOHN STRICKLIN, surgeon; b. San Angelo, Tex., Jan. 3, 1929; s. John Stricklin and Nannie Lee (Morgan) S.; m. Beverly Jane Winfiele, Dec. 27, 1951; children: John Arthur, Shelley Winfiele, Robert Stricklin. B.S., So. Meth. U., 1976; M.S.P.H., U. Mo., Columbia, 1970; M.D., U. Tex. Southwestern Med. Sch., 1952. Diplomate: Am. Bd. Surgery. Intern, resident in surgery Barnes Hosp., Washington U., St. Louis, 1952-59; faculty U. Mo., 1961-76, U. Louisville, 1976—; prof. surgery, adj. prof. community heals, asso. Systems Sci. Inst., J. Graham Brown Cancer Center, 1979—; chief surgeon Ellis Fischel State Cancer Hosp., Columbia, 1961-76. Author numerous books and articles. Served to capt. USNR, 1952—. Nat. Cancer Inst. grantee, 1958-76. Mem. Am. Surg. Assn., A.C.S. (fellow), SAR, Naval Order. Baptist. Clubs: Rotary (Louisville); Cosmos (Washington). Current Work: Cancer, surgery, epdiemiology, med. edn., med. econs. Subspecialties: Surgery; Cancer research (medicine). Office: J Graham Brown Cancer Center 529 S Jackson St Louisville KY 40202

SPREITZER, ROBERT JOSEPH, geneticist; b. Cleve., Apr. 12, 1952; s. Charles Joseph and Sophia Amelia (Zelasko) S.; m. Nancy Jean Pitts, June 3, 1978. B.S. cum laude, Cleve. State U., 1974; Ph.D. (NIH fellow), Case Western Res. U., 1979. Research assoc. in agronomy U. Ill., Urbana, 1979-80, vis. scholar, 1980-82; research assoc. molecular biology U. Geneva, 1982—. Rockefeller Found. postdoctoral fellow, 1980-82; EMBO fellow, 1982; Swiss NSF fellow, 1982—. Mem. AAAS, Am. Soc. Plant Physiologists, Bot. Soc. Am. Current Work: Research in chloroplast genetics, genetics of photosynthesis, Chlamydomonas genetics, molecular biology RUBP carboxylase. Subspecialties: Genetics and genetic engineering (biology); Photosynthesis. Office: Dept Biologie Moléculaire Univ Genéve 30 Quai Ernest-Ansermet CH-1211 Genéve 4 Switzerland

SPREMULLI, LINDA LUCY, chemistry educator, consultant; b. Corning, N.Y., Sept. 6, 1947; d. Paul Francis and Gertrude Lollabella (Haspeslaph) S. B.A. in Chemistry, U. Rochester, 1969; Ph.D. in Biochemistry, M.I.T., 1973. Postdoctoral fellow Clayton Found. Biochem. Inst., U. Tex., Austin, 1973-76; asst. prof. dept. chemistry U. N.C., Chapel Hill, 1976-81, assoc. prof., 1981—, cons. Contbr. research papers to profl. publs. NIH. Research grantee Eli Lilly Corp., 1980-82. Mem. AAAS, Assn. Women in Sci., Am. Chem. Soc., Am. Soc. Microbiology, Am. Soc. Biol. Chemists. Current Work: Mechanism of protein biosynthesis. Subspecialties: Biochemistry (biology); Molecular biology.

SPRIGGS, RICHARD MOORE, ceramic materials administrator, scientific management executive; b. Washington, Pa., May 8, 1931; s. Lucian Alexander and Kathryn (Aber) S.; m. Patricia Anne Blaney, Aug. 1, 1953; children—Carolyn, Richard Jr., Alan. B.S., Pa. State U., 1952; M.S., U. Ill., 1956, Ph.D., 1958. Sr. research engr. Ferro Corp., Cleve., 1958-59; group leader Avco Corp., Wilmington, Mass., 1959-64; prof. Lehigh U., Bethlehem, Pa., 1964-80, v.p. adminstrn., 1972-78; sr. staff officer NRC, Washington, 1980—, staff dir., 1984—; dir. Precision Magnetics & Ceramics, Inc., Gonic, N.H., Pensacola, Fla., Potter Instrument Co., Gonic; cons. various corps. and govt. agys., 1964—. Contbr. articles to profl. jours. Patentee in field. Pres. YMCA, Bethlehem, Pa., 1977-78. Served to lt. USNR, 1952-56. Recipient numerous research grants, 1972-80. Fellow Am. Ceramic Soc. (pres. 1984-85, Ross Coffin Purdy award, Hobart M. Kraner award), Inst. Ceramics; mem. Nat. Inst. Ceramic Engrs., Internat. Inst. for Sci. of Sintering. Club: Rotary (pres. 1985-86) (Bailey's Crossroads, Va.). Current work: Processing, structure and behavior of advanced ceramic materials. Subspecialties: Ceramics; Ceramic engineering. Home: 1722 Tamerisk Ct Vienna VA 22180 Office: Nat Research Council JH 817 2101 Constitution Ave NW Washington DC 20418

SPRINGER, DONALD HAROLD, software engr.; b. Rochester, Pa., Jan. 2, 1942; s. Harold L. and Anna (Fatula) S.; m. Judy Clarissa, Apr. 10, 1970; children: Clarissa, Jonathan, Joel, Stephen. B.A., San Diego State U., 1966; M.S., Calif. State U., Hayward, 1973; M.B.A., U. Santa Clara, 1976, postgrad., 1977. Assoc. engr. Advanced Memory Systems, Sunnyvale, Calif., 1971-75; systems programmer Diablo Systems, Hayward, Calif., 1975-76; software engr. Anderson-Jacobson, San Jose, Calif., 1976-78; software engr. advanced tech. and applications div. Boeing Artificial Intelligence Ctr., Seattle, 1978; mem. adj. faculty dept. software engring. Seattle U. Grad. Sch. Engring., 1981—. Served with USN, 1966-70. Mem. Assn. Computing Machinery (nat. recognition service), IEEE. Current Work: Applied research in artificial intelligence, particularly knowledge acquisition for distributed expert systems. Subspecialties: Software engineering; Distributed systems and networks.

SPRINGER, JOSEPH TUCKER, biology educator; b. Lo-Ping, Kiang Si, China, Aug. 9, 1949; s. Charles Oliver and Marion E. (Tucker) S.; m. Elaine Castle, Oct. 15, 1978. B.A., Knox Coll., 1971; M.S., Wash. State U., 1976, Ph.D., 1977. Cert. wildlife biologist, Nebr. Wildlife ecologist Wyo. Game and Fish Dept., Laramie, 1977-79; asst. prof. biology Kearney (Nebr.) State Coll., 1979-85, assoc. prof., 1985—; research ecologist/cons. Nature Conservancy, 1980; research program dir. NSF, Kearney, 1981; research cons. Nat. Audubon Soc., 1982. Author: Interactions Between and Some Ecological Aspects of Coyotes and Mule Deer, 1982; What Every Zoologist Should Know, 1984. Weekly columnist Wildlife Conservation Notes. Contbr. articles to profl. jours.; editor: Jour. Wildlife Mgmt, 1980—, Wildlife Soc. Bull, 1980—. Coordinator Recycle for Wildlife, Kearney, 1981, 82; instr. Elder Hostel, Minden, 1982—. NSF grantee, 1969; Sloan Found. grantee, 1970; others. Mem. Am. Soc. Mammalogists, Nat. Audubon Soc. (chpt. v.p., conservation chmn.), Nat. Wildlife Fedn., Wildlife Soc. (chpt. exec. bd.), Pacific N.W. Bird and Mammal Soc. Democrat. Current Work: Behavioral ecology of coyotes; effects of prairie fires on small mammal populations. Subspecialties: Ecology (environmental science); Population biology. Office: Dept Biology Kearney State Coll Kearney NE 68849-0531

SPRINKLE, FREDRICK PRESTON, veterinarian; b. Marion, Va., Apr. 24, 1953; s. Lewis Barton and Delphine Madge (McMillan) S.; m. Deborah Lynn Romans, June 19, 1976; 1 child, Daniel Bascom. B.S., E. Tenn. State U., 1975; M.S., Auburn U., 1977, D.V.M., 1982. Field veterinarian U. Ky., Lexington, Ky., 1984; resident veterinarian Spendthrift Farm, Lexington, Ky., 1984—; tchr. Midway Coll., Ky., 1984—. Contbr. articles to profl. jours. Mem. AVMA, Ky. Vet. Med. Assn. Republican. Baptist. Current work: Providing veterinary health care for some of the most expensive thoroughbred horses in the world. Subspecialty: Preventive medicine (veterinary medicine). Address: Box 621 Iron Works Pike Lexington KY 40511

SPROTT, JULIEN CLINTON, physics educator; b. Memphis, Sept. 16, 1942; s. Frank Wilson and Ila (Tidwell) S. B.S., MIT, 1964; M.S., U. Wis., 1966, Ph.D., 1969. Research physicist Oak Ridge Nat. Lab., 1970-72; prof. physics U. Wis.-Madison, 1972—; cons. McDonnell Douglas Corp., St. Louis, 1977-80; cons. TRW, El Segundo, 1979; cons. Argonne Nat. Lab., Ill., 1979-80. Author: Introduction of Modern Electronics, 1981. Fellow Am. Phys. Soc. Current work: Heating and confinement of plasmas in magnetic mirrors and toroidal confinement devices; extraterrestrial plasmas. Subspecialties: Plasma physics; Electronics. Home: 5002 Sheboygan Ave #207 Madison WI 53705 Office: Dept Physics U Wis Madison WI 53706

SPROUSE, KENNETH MICHAEL, engineer; b. Los Angeles, Sept. 1, 1952; s. George Mason and Olivia Elizabeth (Mallacove) S.; m. Deborah Louise Crump, June 17, 1978. B.S. in Mech. Engring. with high honors, U. Calif.-Santa Barbara, 1974; M.S. Mech. Engring., U. Calif.-Berkeley, 1975; J.D., Loyola Law Sch., 1985. Registered profl. engr., Calif. Teaching, research asst. U. Calif., Berkeley, 1974-75; mem. tech. staff Rockwell Internat., Canoga Park, Calif., 1975-82, mgr. functional unit, 1982, mgr., project engr., 1983—. Contbr. numerous articles to profl. jours. Patentee in field. Chmn. youth com. Emmanuel Lutheran Ch., North Hollywood, Calif., 1979, big brother, 1976, mem. ch. council, 1980. Placed 4th nat. design competition Lincoln Arc Welding Found., 1974. Mem. ASME (outstanding student scholar petroleum div., 1973), Am. Inst. Chem. Engrs. (referee jour. 1981—), ABA. Republican. U. Calif. Alumni Assn. (Santa Barbara; bd. dirs. Los Angeles chpt. 1976-78). Current work: R&D synfuels, coal combustion, solar, nuclear fuels processing, pollution. Tech. and soc.: adminstrv. law, legislation, politics. Subspecialties: Coal; Mechanical engineering. Home: 18213 Osborne St Northridge CA 91325 Office: Rockwell Internat Rocketdyne Div 6633 Canoga Ave Canoga Park CA 91304

SPRUNG, DONALD WHITFIELD LOYAL, physicist, university dean; b. Kitchener, Ont., Can., June 6, 1934; s. Lyall McCauley and Doreen Bishop (Price) S.; m. Hannah Sueko Nagai, Dec. 12, 1958; children—Anne Elizabeth, Carol Hanako. B.A., U. Toronto, 1957; Ph.D., U. Birmingham, Eng., 1961, D.Sc., 1977. Instr. Cornell U., 1961-62; mem. research staff Mass. Inst. Tech., 1964-65; asst. prof. physics McMaster U., Hamilton, Ont., 1962-66, asso. prof., 1966-71, prof., 1971—; dean Faculty of Sci., McMaster U. (Faculty of Sci.), 1975-84; vis. prof. U. Tuebingen, Ger., 1980-81. Contbr. numerous articles to physics jours.; mem. editorial bd.: Canadian Jour. Physics, 1975-80. C.D. Howe Meml. fellow Institut de Physique Nucleaire, Orsay, France, 1969-70; Japan-Can. Exchange Fellow, 1985-86. Fellow Royal Soc. Can.; mem. Canadian Assn. Physicists (Herzberg medal 1972), Am. Phys. Soc., Inst. Physics (London). Current Work: Models of the nucleon-nucleon interaction; Hartree-Fock calculations of nuclear structure, electron scattering from nuclei, structure of the deuteron. Subspecialties: Nuclear physics; Theoretical physics. Home: 15 Little John Rd Dundas ON L9H 4G5 Canada Office: Dept Physics GSB-114 McMaster Univ Hamilton ON L8S 4M1 Canada

SPRUNT, EVE SILVER, research geophysicist; b. Bklyn., July 9, 1951; d. Aaron B.Z. and Ruth (Chew) Silver; m. Hugh H. Sprunt, Jr., Jan. 2, 1973; children—Alexander Dalziel, Elsa Dunbar. S.B., MIT, 1972, S.M., 1973; Ph.D., Stanford U., 1977. Research assoc. Stanford U., Calif., 1976-78; assoc. Mobil Research and Devel., Dallas, 1978—. NSF fellow, 1973. Mem. Am. Geophys. Union, Soc. Exploration Geophysicists, Soc. Core Analysts (founder), Soc. Petroleum Engrs., Geol. Soc. Am., Soc. Profl. Well Log Analysts. Libertarian. Current work: Core analysis, in situ stress determination, natural and induced fracturing. Subspecialties: Geophysics; Petroleum engineering. Home: 3508 Watercrest Farmers Branch TX 75234 Office: Mobil Research and Devel 13777 Midway Dallas TX 75234

SQUILLANTE, MICHAEL ROBERT, chemist; b. Boston, Dec. 12, 1948; s. Alexander Nicholas and Eileen Barbara (Twomey) S.; m. Lynda Dee Barrows, Oct. 12, 1982; 1 child, Michael Steven. Ph.D., Tufts U., 1980. Staff Scientist Radiation Monitoring Devices, Watertown, Mass., 1980-81, sr. scientist, 1982-83, dir. research, 1983—. Contbr. articles to profl. jours. Patentee in field. Mem. Am. Chem. Soc., Am. Assn. Crystal Growth. Current work: Solid state nuclear and optical sensors; crystal growth of electronic materials and semiconductors, research management. Subspecialties: Electronic materials; Inorganic chemistry. Home: 2 Leslie Rd Waltham MA 02154 Office: Radiation Monitoring Devices 44 Hunt St Watertown MA 02172

SQUIRES, ARTHUR MORTON, chemical engineering educator; b. Neodesha, Kans., Mar. 21, 1916; s. Charles Loren and Vera Amber (Moore) S. A.B. in Chemistry with distinction, U.Mo., 1938; Ph.D. in Phys. Chemistry, Cornell U., 1947. Process design engr. M.W. Kellogg Co., N.Y.C., 1942-46; dir. process analysis Union Carbide Co., Oak Ridge, 1945-46; asst. dir. process devel. Hydrocarbon Research, Inc., N.Y.C., 1946-50; dir. process devel., 1950-59; cons. to chem. process industry, N.Y.C., 1959-67; prof. chem. engring. CCNY, 1967-76, Va. Poly. Inst. and State U., Blacksburg, 1976—. Author: The Tender Ship: Governmental Management of Technological change, 1985. Contbr. articles to profl. jours. Patentee in field. Fellow Am. Acad. Arts and Scis., AAAS; mem. Nat. Acad. Engring., Am. Chem. Soc. (Henry H. Storch award, fuel chemistry div. 1973), Am. Inst. Chem. Engrs., ASME. Current work: Shallow gas- and vibro-fluidized beds: heat transfer; use for chemical reaction and waste heat recovery; use as micro-reactors to simulate large gas-fluidized beds. Subspecialties: Chemical engineering; Coal. Office: Dept Chem Engring Va Poly Inst and State U Blacksburg VA 24061

SQUIRES, RICHARD FELT, neuropharmacologist, neurochemist, biochemist; b. Sparta, Mich., Jan. 15, 1933; s. Monas Nathan and Dorothy Lois (Felt) S.; m. Else Saederup; 1 child: Iben Saederup. B.S. in Chemistry, Mich. State U., 1958. Dir. dept. biochemistry A/S Ferrosan, Soeborg, Denmark, 1963-78; group leader CNS Research Lederle Labs., Pearl River, N.Y., 1978-79; prin. investigator Rockland Research Inst., Orangeburg, N.Y., 1979—. Contbr. articles in field to profl. jours. Mem. Soc. Neurosci., Am. Soc. Biol. Chemists, Internat. Soc. Neurochemistry, Internat. Soc. Psychoneuroendocrinology, European Neurosci. Assn., Collegium Internationale Neuro-Psychopharmacologicum, Am. Soc. Neurochemistry. Current Work: Benzodiazepine, GABA, Picrotoxin receptors in brain, characterization of receptors in CNS, devel. of novel psychotropic agts., neurol. and psychiat. disorders. Subspecialties: Neuropharmacology; Neurochemistry. Home: 10 Termakay Dr New City NY 10956 Office: Rockland Research Institute Orangeburg NY 10962

SREENIVASAN, S. RANGA, physicist; b. Mysore, India, Oct. 20, 1933; emigrated to Can., 1966, naturalized, 1974; s. H. Sreenivasachari and Alamelammal (Rangaswami) S.; m. Claire Selma Julie de Reineck, Oct. 16, 1963; children: Gopal, Govind, Gauri, Gayatri, Aravind. B.Sc. with honors in Physics, U. Mysore, 1950, B.Sc. (hons.) in Math, 1952, Ph.D. in Theoret. Physics, 1958. Research fellow Harvard U., 1958-61; research asso. NASA, Goddard Inst. Space Studies, N.Y.C., 1961-64; vis. scientist Max Planck Inst, Munich, W.Ger., 1964-66; research fellow U. Calgary, Alta., Can., 1966-67, asst. prof. physics, 1967-68, asso. prof., 1968-74, prof., 1974—; vis. prof. Royal Inst. Tech., Stockholm, Sweden, 1974-75. Mem. Internat. Astronom. Union, Am. Geophys. Union, Am. Phys. Soc., Am. Astron. Soc., Am. Meteorol. Soc. Current Work: Stellar structure and evolution; solar physics; stellar atmospheres; interstellar medium; plasma astrophysics; controlled thermonuclear fusion. Subspecialties: Theoretical astrophysics; Plasma physics. Home: 2110-30 Ave SW Calgary AB T2T 1R4 Canada Office: 2500 University Dr NW Calgary AB T2N 1N4 Canada

SRINIVASAN, BRIHMADESAM NARASIMHAN, chemist; b. Coimbatore, India, Jan. 21, 1935; came to U.S., 1963, naturalized, 1975; s. Brihmadesam Sivarama Sastri and Lakshmi (Venkatachalam Iyer) Narasimha Iyer; m. Savithri Sivaramakrishna Iyer, May 21, 1971; children—Narasimhan, Ramakrishnan. B.Sc. with honors, Annamalai U., 1957; Ph.D., La. State U., 1967. Sci. officer Bhabha Atomic Research Ctr., India, 1957-63; vis. asst. prof. La. State U., Baton Rouge, 1967-69; research assoc. Northeastern U., Boston, 1970-72; staff assoc. Forsyth Dental Ctr., Boston, 1972-77; research assoc. Boston Biomed. Research Inst., 1977-81; chemist U.S. FDA, Winchester, Mass., 1983—. Contbr. articles to profl. jours. Mem. exec. council New Eng. Hindu Temple, Boston, 1978—. Mem. Indian Sci. Congress, Am. Chem. Soc., Assn. Ofcl. Analytical Chemists. Current work: Pharmaceutical analysis, carcinogenic hydrocarbons, dental chemistry, electronic spectroscopy, luminescence. Subspecialties: Physical chemistry; Analytical chemistry. Home: 61 Pitt Rd Framingham MA 01701 Office: FDA 109 Holton St Winchester MA 01890

SRIRAM, K(AUSHIK) P., geophysicist; b. New Delhi, Nov. 6, 1944; s. K.R. Padmanabha and Pankajam Aiyangar; m. Carolyn Marzec, Sept. 8, 1967 (div. dec. 1979); 1 child, Chandra Lekha m. Lyn Robertson, Mar. 26, 1982. B.Tech., Indian Inst. tech., Bombay, 1965; M.S., Rice U., 1966, Ph.D., 1967. Geophysicist Shell Devel. Co., Houston, 1967-72, 74-81, 84—, Shell Oil Co., Denver, 1972-74, Pecten Internat. Co., Houston, 1981-84. Mem. IEEE, Soc. Exptl. Geohysicists (research com.), Houston Grand Opera Guild. Current work: Interpretation of lithology from compressional and shear velocity measurements. Subspecialties: Geophysics; Applied mathematics. Home: 5712 Innsbruck Bellaire TX 77401 Office: Shell Devel Co PO Box 481 Houston TX 77001

SRIVASTAVA, SATISH KUMAR, geologist; b. Sitapur, Uttar Pradesh, India, June 28, 1935; came to U.S., 1970, naturalized, 1979; s. Hazari Lal and Sheopiari S.; m. Rosalind Ann Catterall, July 14, 1970. Ph.D. in Geology, U. Alta. (Can.), Edmonton, 1968. Research asst. Forest Research Inst. Dehradun, India, 1954-57; sr. tech. asst. Oil and Gas Commn., Dehradun, 1957-68; Killam postdoctoral fellow dept. botany U. B.C. (Can.), Vancouver, 1968-70; research geologist Chevron Oil Field Research Co., La Habra, Calif., 1970-80, sr. research geologist, 1980—. Contbr. numerous articles on palynology to nat., internat. profl. jours. Fellow Geol. Assn. Can., Linnean Soc. London, Indian Assn. Palynostratigraphers (pres. 1984, 85); mem. Am. Assn. Stratigraphic Palynologists, Am. Assn. Petroleum Geologists, Soc. Econ. Paleontologists and Mineralogists, Am. Bot. Soc., Internat. Orgn. Palaeobotany, Palynological Soc. India (life). Current Work: Fossil spore-pollen taxonomy; biostratigraphy; paleoecology; evolution; study of palynology applied to oil exploration. Subspecialties: Paleontology; Paleontology, paleoecology. Home: 3054 S Blandford Dr Rowland Heights CA 91748 Office: 3282 Beach Blvd La Habra CA 90631

STAATS, JOAN, medical librarian; b. Chgo., July 31, 1921; d. Walter J. and Betty (Pischel) S. B.S. in Psychology, U. Ill., 1943, M.S. in Zoology, 1947. Asst. in labs. Wilson & Co., 1943-44; exptl. pharmacologist Armour Pharm. Co., 1944-45; teaching asst. U. Ill.-Urbana, 1945-46, acting instr., 1946-47; med. librarian Jackson Lab., Bar Harbor, Maine, 1949-84, staff scientist, 1955-76, sr. staff scientist, 1976-84, sr. staff emeritus, 1984—. Contbr. articles to sci. jours. Corporator, bd. dirs. Jesup Meml. Library, Bar Harbor, 1964—. Mem. AAAS, Genetics Soc. Am., Med. Library Assn., AAUW, Health Sci. Libraries and Info. Coop. (founding), North Atlantic Health Sci. Libraries (founding). Episcopalian. Current Work: Mammalian genetics, bibliographic research. Home: Dix Point Rd West Tremont MA 04690 Office: Jackson Lab Bar Harbor ME 04609

STABA, EMIL JOHN, pharmacognosy educator; b. N.Y.C., May 16, 1928; s. Frank and Marianna T. (Mack) P.; m. Joyce Elizabeth Ellert, June 19, 1954; children—Marianna, Joanna, Sarah Jane, John, Mark. B.S. cum laude, St. John's U., 1952; M.S., Duquesne U., 1954; Ph.D., U. Conn., 1957. Asst. prof. U. Nebr., 1957-60, prof., chmn. dept., 1968; prof., chmn. dept. pharmacognosy U. Minn., 1968—; Cons. econ. plants, plant tissue culture U.S. Army Q.M. Corps; Cons. drug plants, plant tissue culture NASA; cons. Korean govt., food and pharm. industry.; Con. aquatic vis. prof. Dalhousie U., 1983; mem. natural products revision com. U.S. Pharmacopeia, 1980—; mem. life sci. adv. com. NASA, 1984-86. Mem. editorial bd. Jour. Plant Cell, Tissue and Organ Culture, 1980—. Served with USNR, 1945-46, PTO. Sr. fgn. fellow NSF, Poland, 1969; Fulbright fellow Germany, 1970; CSIR-NSF fellow India, 1973; PCSIR-NSF fellow Pakistan, 1978. Fellow AAAS; mem. Am. Soc. Pharmacognosy (pres. 1971-72), Am. Assn. Colls. Pharmacy (chmn. tchrs. sect. 1972-73, dir. 1976-77), Tissue Culture Assn. (pres. plant sect. 1972-74), Am. Pharm. Assn. and Acad. (chmn. pharmacognosy and nat. products 1977—), Soc. Econ. Botany. Current Work: Medicinal and economic plant cell and organ culture; aquatic plant chemistry and herbs. Subspecialties: Plant cell and tissue culture; Pharmacognosy. Home: 2840 Stinson Blvd NE Minneapolis MN 55418

STABLER, TIMOTHY ALLEN, biology educator; b. Port Jervis, N.Y., Sept. 27, 1940; s. Ralph Allen and Marjorie (Hoyt) S. B.A., Drew U., 1962; M.A., DePauw U., 1964; postgrad., Albany Med. Coll., 1964-65; Ph.D., U. Vt., 1969. Postdoctoral fellow U. Minn., Mpls., 1968-69; asst. prof. Hope Coll., Holland, Mich., 1969-71; postdoctoral fellow Boston U. Med. Sch., 1971-73; asst. prof. Ind. U. N.W., Gary, 1973-76, assoc. prof. biology, 1976—, chmn. dept., 1983-85, health profl. adv., 1973—. Mem. Am. Soc. Zoologists, Nat. Assn. Advs. Health Profession (dir. 1980—), Central Assn. Advs. Health Profession (treas. 1978—), Ind. Acad. Sci., N.Y. Acad. Sci., Tissue Culture Assn. (midwest br.). Methodist. Current Work: Cell culture of endocrine cells and histochemical cell indentification. Subspecialties: Cell and tissue culture; Developmental biology. Home: 1901 Alice St Valparaiso IN 46383 Office: Ind U NW 3400 Broadway Gary IN 46408

STACH, JOSEPH, electrical engineer; b. Wallington, N.J., Aug. 21, 1938; s. Joseph and Anna Stach; m. Kathleen Joan Kobscenski, May 11, 1963; children—Kevin J., Marcy A. B.S.E.E., N.J. Inst. Tech., 1960; M.S.E.E., Pa. State U., 1962, Ph.D., 1966. Mem. tech. staff Bell Telephone Labs., Allentown, Pa., 1966-67; prof. elec. engring. Pa. State U., 1967-84; exec. dir. Mass. Microelectronics Ctr., Westboro, 1984—; cons. in field; dir. Machine Tech. Inventor in field. Contbr. articles to profl. jours. Mem. IEEE, Electrochem. Soc. Subspecialties: Microelectronics; Integrated circuits. Home: 376 Commercial St Boston MA 02109 Office: Mass Microelectronics Ctr PO Box 663 Westboro MA 01581

STACH, ROBERT WILLIAM, biochemist; b. Chgo., Feb. 12, 1945; s. Edward Edwin and Chrystal Julia S. (Schwieger) S.; m. Bettie Marie Jones, Jan. 29, 1966; 1 dau., Jeannette Lynn. B.A., Ill. Wesleyan U., 1967; Ph.D. in Organic Chemistry, U. Wis.-Madison, 1972. Postdoctoral trainee Stanford U. Sch. Medicine, 1972-74; asst. prof. dept. biochemistry SUNY Upstate Med. Center, Syracuse, 1974-80; assoc. mem. faculty Center for Neurobehavioral Scis., 1979—, adj. assoc. prof. dept. anatomy, 1980—, assoc. prof. dept. biochemistry, 1980—; adj. assoc. prof. U. Tex. Med. Br., Galveston, 1982-83. Contbr. articles to profl. jours. NIH grantee, 1975—. Mem. N.Y. Acad. Scis., AAAS, Soc. Neurosci., Am. Soc. Biol. Chemists, Internat. Soc. Neurochemistry, Am. Soc. Neurochemistry, Sigma Xi. Republican. Methodist. Current Work: Developmental neurobiochemistry growth and development, sensory and sympathetic nervous systems, receptors, peptide hormones. Subspecialties: Neurobiology; Neurochemistry. Home: 10 Juniper Liverpool NY 13090 Office: 766 Irving Ave Syracuse NY 13210

STACHEL, JOHN JAY, physicist, educator; b. N.Y.C., Mar. 29, 1928; s. Jacob Abraham and Bertha S.; m. Eveleyn Lenore Wassermann, Feb. 8, 1953; children—Robert, Laura, Deborah. B.S., CCNY, 1956; M.S., Stevens Inst. Tech., 1959, Ph.D., 1962. Instr. physics Lehigh U., Bethlehem, Pa., 1959-61, U. Pitts., 1961-62, research assoc., U. Pitts., 1962-64; asst. prof. physics Boston U., 1964-69, assoc. prof., 1969-72, prof., 1972—, dir. Inst. Relativity Studies. Editor: Selected Papers Leon Rosenfeld, 1979; Foundations of Space-Time Theories, 1977; Collected Papers of Albert Einstein. Grantee NSF, NEH. Mem. Fedn. Am. Scientists, AAUP. Subspecialties: Relativity and gravitation; Theoretical physics. Office: Boston U Dept Physics Boston MA 02215

STADLER, HENRY LEWIS, scientist, engineer; b. Columbia, Mo., Mar. 28, 1923; s. Lewis John and Cornelia Field (Tuckerman) S.; m. Carol Maier, Sept. 20, 1947; children—Jane T., John A., Sarah L. Student, Calif. Inst. Tech., 1942, U. Mo., 1942-43, 46; A.B., Harvard U., 1948; S.M., U. Chgo., 1951, Ph.D., 1954. Teaching asst. U. Mo., Columbia, 1942-43; research asst. U. Chgo., 1949-51, 53-54; mem. tech. staff Bell Telephone Labs., Murray Hill, N.J., 1954-60; scientist, mgr. Ford Motor Co., Dearborn, Mich., 1960-80; office dir. vehicle and engine research U.S. Dept. Energy, Washington, 1980-82; mem. tech. staff Jet Propulsion Lab., Pasadena, Calif., 1982—; vis. scientist U. Tokyo, 1965-66. Patentee exhaust gas oxygen sensor. Ward chmn. Democratic Party, Ann Arbor, 1963-69; city councilman City of Ann Arbor, 1969-71. Served to 1st lt. USAF, 1943-46. Mem. Am. Physical Soc., IEEE, Soc. Automotive Engrs. (session organizer 1984), Am. Ceramic Soc. (electronics award 1978). Current work: Ceramic engines, engine control devices and systems, ferro-electrics, high field effects. Subspecialties: Condensed matter physics; Ceramic engineering. Home: 324 Knight Way La Canada CA 91011 Office: Jet Propulsion Lab Calif Inst Tech 4800 Oak Grove Dr Pasadena CA 91109

STADTMAN, EARL REECE, biochemist; b. Carrizozo, N.Mex., Nov. 15, 1919; s. Walter William and Minnie Ethyl (Reece) S.; m. Thressa Campbell, Oct. 19, 1943. B.S., U. Calif., Berkeley, 1942, Ph.D, 1949. With Alcan Hwy. survey Public Rds. Adminstrn., 1942-43; research asst. U. Calif., Berkeley, 1938-49, sr. lab. technican, 1949; AEC fellow Mass. Gen. Hosp., Boston, 1949-50; chemist lab. cellular physiology Nat. Heart Inst., 1950-58, chief enzyme sect., 1958-62, chief lab. biochemistry, 1962—; Biochemist Max Planck Inst., Munich, Germany, Pasteur Inst., Paris, 1959-60; faculty dept. microbiology U. Md.; prof. biochemistry grad. program dept. biology Johns Hopkins U.; adv. com. Life Scis. Research Office, Am. Fedn. Biol. Sci., 1974-77; Bd. dirs. Found. Advanced Edn. Scis., 1966-70, chmn. dept. biochemistry, 1966-68; biochem. study sect. research grants NIH, 1959-63. Editor: Jour. Biol. Chemistry, 1960-65, Current Topics in Cellular Regulation, 1968—, Circulation Research, 1968-70; exec. editor: Archives Biochemistry and Biophysics, 1960—, Life Scis, 1973-75, Procs. Nat. Acad. Sci, 1975-81, Trends in Biochem. Research, 1975-78; editorial adv. bd.: Biochemistry, 1969-76, 81—. Recipient medallion Soc. de Chemie Biologique, 1955, medallion U. Pisa, 1966, Presdl. rank award as Disting. Sr. Exec., 1981. Mem. Am. Chem. Soc. (Paul Lewis Lab. award in enzyme chemistry 1952, exec. com. biol. div. 1959-64, chmn. div. 1963-64, Hillebrand award 1969), Am. Soc. Biol. Chemists (publs. com. 1966-70, council 1974—, Merck award 1983), Nat. Acad. Scis. (award in microbiology 1970), Am. Acad. Arts and Scis., Am. Soc. Microbiology, Washington Acad. Scis. (award biol. chemistry 1957, nat. medal sci. 1979, meritorious exec. award 1980). Current Work: Regulation of cellular metabolilsm; enzyme chemistry. Subspecialties: Biochemistry (biology); Microbiology. Home: 16907 Redland Rd Derwood MD 20855 Office: Nat Heart and Lung Inst Bethesda MD 20014

STADTMAN, THRESSA CAMPBELL, biochemist, microbiologist, researcher; b. Sterling, N.Y., Feb. 12, 1920; d. Earl and Bessie (Waldron) Campbell; m. Earl Reece Stadtman, Oct. 19, 1943. B.S., Cornell U., 1940, M.S., 1942; Ph.D., U. Calif.-Berkeley, 1949. Research assoc. U. Calif.-Berkeley, 1943-46; research asst. Harvard U. Med. Sch., 1949-50; biochemist Nat. Heart Inst., NIH, Bethesda, Md., 1950—; sect. chief lab. biochemistry Nat. Heart, Lung, Blood Inst., 1974—; lectr. in field; mem. U.S. nat. com. Internat. Union Biochemistry, 1976-82; mem. U.S. nat. com. Internat. Union Microbiology, 1982—. Contbr. numerous articles, revs. on amino acid metabolism, vitamin B12-dependent enzymes, methane biosynthesis, selenium dependent enzymes and seleno tRNAs to profl. publs. Recipient Hillebrand award Chem. Soc. Washington, 1979, Superior Service award USPHS, 1980; Helen Hay Whitney fellow Oxford (Eng.) U., 1954-55; Rockefeller Found. fellow U. Munich, W.Ger., 1959. Mem. Nat. Acad. Scis., Am. Soc. Biol. Chemists (sec. and program chmn. 1979-81), Am. Chem. Soc., Am. Soc. Microbiology, Am. Acad. Arts and Scis. Current Work: Selenium biochemistry. Subspecialties: Biochemistry (biology); Microbiology. Office: NIH Bldg 3 Room 108 Bethesda MD 20205

STAEHLE, CHARLES MICHAEL, marine/ocean engineer, consultant; b. Lovell, Wyo., Oct. 4, 1938; s. Eddie Leroy and Frances Lenora (Glenn) S.; m. Margaret Elizabeth Allen, Jan. 21, 1963 (div. July 1982); children: Cynthia Marie, Mark Allen. B.S. in Physics, U. Okla., 1963. Project engr. oceanic div. Westinghouse Corp., Annapolis, Md., 1970-77; tech. mgr. NOAA, Washington, 1977-82; mgr. spl. programs Perry Offshore, Inc., Riviera Beach, Fla., 1982—. Pres. Chase Creek Civic Assn., Arnold, Md., 1975. Served to lt. comdr. USN, 1958-70; to capt. Res. 1970—. Mem. Soc. Naval Architects and Marine Engrs., Marine Tech. Soc. (underwater physics com. 1981—, marine mining and minerals com. 1983—), Deep Submersible Pilots Assn., Naval Res. Assn., Navy Submarine League. Republican. Episcopalian. Lodges: Masons; Shriners. Current Work: Ocean engineering and marine technology, particularly as applied to the deep ocean and sea bed; research on marine minerals survey and recovery, nuclear waste disposal and related marine ecological technology. Subspecialties: Ocean engineering; Systems engineering. Home: 8716 Satalite Terr Lake Park FL 33403 Office: Perry Offshore Inc PO Box 10297 275 W 10th St Riviera Beach FL 33404

STAHL, CHARLES DREW, engineering educator, consultant; b. Altoona, Pa., Aug. 28, 1923; s. C. Asher and Anna M. (Leinhoff) S.; m. Barbara M. Morrison, Aug. 14, 1948; 1 son, Kevin M. B.S., Pa. State U., 1947, M.S., 1950, Ph.D., 1953. Registered profl. engr., Pa. Research assoc. Pa. State U., 1947-49; reservoir engr. Mobil Internat., 1958-59; assoc. prof. Pa. State U., University Park, 1959-61, prof. dept. petroleum and natural gas engring., 1962-83, head dept., 1962—; cons. to major oil cos., also Commonwealth of Pa. Contbr. articles to profl. jours. Recipient Wilson award Pa. State U., 1981. Mem. Soc. Petroleum Engrs. of AIME, Am. Petroleum Inst. Republican. Current Work: Tertiary recovery of petroleum; flow and displacement of oil in porous media by use of micellar and other soluble fluids. Subspecialties: Petroleum engineering; Fluid mechanics. Home: 209 Norle St State College PA 16801 Office: 101 Mineral Sci Bldg University Park PA 16802

STAHL, FRANKLIN WILLIAM, biologist; b. Boston, Oct. 8, 1929; married; 2 children. A.B., Harvard U., 1951, Ph.D. in Biology, U. Rochester, 1956; Sc.D., (hon.) Oakland U., Research fellow biology Calif. Inst. Tech., Pasadena, 1955-58; assoc. prof. zoology U. Mo., 1958-59; assoc. prof. biology U. Oreg., 1959-70, prof., 1970—, research assoc. Inst. Molecular Biology, 1959—. MacArthur Found. fellow, 1985. Mem. Nat. Acad. Scis. Subspecialty: Molecular biology. Office: U Oreg Inst Molecular Biology Eugene OR 97403*

STAHL, JOEL S., plastics company executive; b. Youngstown, Ohio, June 10, 1918; s. John Charles and Anna (Nadler) S.; m. Jane Elizabeth Anglin, June 23, 1950; 1 son, John A. B.Ch.E., Ohio State U., 1939. Mgr. spl. products, coordinator sales, mfg. and transp. Ashland Oil, Inc., Ky., 1939-50; pres., gen. mgr. Cool Ray Co., 1950-51; pres. Stahl Industries, Inc., Youngstown, Ohio, 1951—. Bd. dirs. Boardman Civic Assn. Mem. Soc. Plastics Engrs. (chmn. plastics in bldg. sect.), Soc. Plastics Industry, ASTM. Republican. Christian Scientist. Clubs: Circumnavigators (N.Y.C.); Berlin Yacht (North Benton, Ohio). Lodge: Shriners. Patentee in field. Current Work: Plastics in building construction, plastic foam core panels and fire resistant plastic products for building construction. Subspecialties: Polymer chemistry; Polymers (materials science). Home: 746 Golfview Ave Youngstown OH 44512 Office: 9th Floor Dollar Bank Bldg Youngstown OH 44503

STAHL, RAYMOND EARL, chemist, researcher; b. Chgo., Feb. 21, 1936; s. Arthur Daniel and Gladys Hazel (Lockwood) S. Ph.B. in Chemistry and Math, Northwestern U., 1971. Group leader Morton Chem. Co., Elk Grove Village, Ill., 1962-65; tech. dir. Am. Indsl. Finishes, Chgo., 1965-67; formulator DeSoto, Inc., Chgo., 1956-62, research assoc., 1967-73, Midland div. Dexter Corp., Waukegan, Ill., 1973—; cons. superior system devel. Fellow Am. Inst. Chemists; mem. Am. Chem. Soc., Am. Inst. Physics, Am. Phys. Soc., AAAS, Fedn. Socs. for Coating Tech., Math. Assn. Am., Am. Statis Assn., Assn. Computer Users, Am. Mgmt. Assn., Ill. State Acad. Sci., Nat. Rifle Assn., Ill. State Rifle Assn. Republican. Current Work: Increasing productivity in the laboratory; maximization of computer utilization where ever applicable; statistical design of experiments and analysis of data. Subspecialties: Mathematical software; Statistics. Office: Dexter Corp Midland Div E Water St Waukegan IL 60085

STAHR, HENRY MICHAEL, chemist, educator; b. White, S.D., Dec. 10, 1931; s. George Conrad and Kathryn Evelyn (Smith) S.; m. Irene Frances Sondey, July 27, 1952; children: Michael, John, Mary, Patrick, Matthew. B.S., S.D. State U., 1956; M.S., Union Coll., 1961; postgrad., U. S.C., 1961-63, U. Richmond, 1965-68; Ph.D., Iowa State U., 1976. Analyst, sr. devel. chemist Gen. Electric, 1956-65; research chemist, sr. scientist Philip Morris Research, Richmond, Va., 1965-69; asst. prof. chemistry Iowa State U., 1969-76, assoc. prof., 1976-82, prof., 1982—, chief chemist, 1969—. Contbr. to profl. jours. Mem. Ogden Sch. Bd., 1977—. Served with USMC, 1949-53. Mem. Am. Chem. Soc., Microchem. Soc., Electrochem. Soc., Am. Soc. Mass Spectroscopy, Am. Acad. Vet. and Comparative Toxicology, Am. Assn. Vet. Lab. Diagnosticians, Soc. Applied Spectroscopy, Am. Lab. Mgrs. Assn. Democrat. Roman Catholic. Lodges: Lions; KC; Am. Legion. Current Work: Method development for toxic substances, utilization of modern instrumentation for objective biomedical information; research on toxic substances. Subspecialties: Analytical chemistry; Toxicology (agriculture). Home: Route 1 Box 180 Ogden IA 50212 Office: Iowa State U 1636 Coll Vet Medicine Ames IA 50011

STAKGOLD, IVAR, educator; b. Oslo, Norway, Dec. 13, 1925; came to U.S., 1941, naturalized, 1947; s. Henri and Rose (Wishengrad) S.; m. Alice Calvert O'Keefe, Nov. 27, 1964; 1 dau., Alissa Dent. B.Mech. Engring., Cornell U., 1945, M.Mech. Engring., 1946; Ph.D., Harvard U., 1949. Instr., then asst. prof. Harvard, 1949-56; head math. and logistics brs. Office Naval Research, 1956-59; faculty Northwestern U., 1960-75, prof. math. and engring. scis., 1964-75, chmn. engring. scis., 1969-75; prof., chmn. math. U. Del., 1975—; mem. U.S. Army basic research com. NRC, 1977-80; mem. com. on applications of math. Nat. Acad. Scis.-NRC, 1982—; vis. faculty Math. Inst., Oxford (Eng.) U., 1973, Univ. Coll., London, 1978, Victoria U., Wellington, N.Z., 1981, Ecole Polytechnique Federale de Lausanne, Switzerland, 1981. Author: Boundary Value Problems of Mathematical Physics, vols. I and II, 1967, Green's Functions and Boundary Value Problems, 1978; asso. editor: Am. Math. Monthly, 1975-80, Jour, Applicable Analysis, 1977—, Internat. Jour. Engring. Sci, 1977—, Jour. Integral Equations, 1978—. Mem. Soc. Indsl. and Applied Math. (trustee 1976—, chmn. 1979-85). U.S. rep. World Bridge Championships, 1959, 60; holder 7 nat. bridge championships. Current Work: Nonlinear boundary value problems. Subspecialty: Applied mathematics. Home: 13 Fairfield Dr Newark DE 19711

STALEY, FREDERICK JOSEPH, research mathematician; b. Terre Haute, Ind., June 28, 1944; s. Harold Joseph and Catherine (Roetker) S.; m. Pamela Kay Pierce, Nov. 17, 1966 (div. 1972); m. Carol Heineman, Jan. 2, 1980. B.S., SUNY, Albany, 1978; M.S. in Physics, Colo. State U., 1980. Self-employed as research mathematician, Ft. Collins, Colo., 1980—. Author monographs. Mem. Am. Phys. Soc. Current Work: Research on the foundations of mathematics and on the applications of mathematics to new fields; catastrophe physics. Subspecialties: Foundations of mathematics; Psychophysics. Home and Office: 600 Blevins Ct Fort Collins CO 80521

STALEY, RALPH HORTON, chemist; b. Boston, Mar. 15, 1945; s. Carroll Hallowell and Patricia Lewis (Horton) S. A.B., Dartmouth Coll., 1967; Ph.D., Calif. Inst. Tech., 1976. Asst. prof. chemistry M.I.T., 1975-81; group leader, central research and devel. dept. E. I. DuPont de Nemours & Co., Wilmington, Del., 1981—. Contbr. revs., numerous articles to profl. jours. Mem. Am. Chem. Soc. Subspecialties: Physical chemistry; Catalysis chemistry. Home: 7 Stage Rd Newark DE 19711 Office: DuPont Co E356 Wilmington DE 19898

STALKER, KENNETH WALTER, mechanical engineer; b. St. John, Kans., Oct. 3, 1918; s. Walter Richard and Bertha (Bisset) S.; m. Eva Leona Stalker, Feb. 7, 1947. B.A., U. Colo., 1941; LL.B., LaSalle U., 1955; postgrad., Coll. Engring. U. Ark., 1964-66. Prodn. mgr. Wright Mfg. Co., Erie, Pa., 1942-45; process engr. DeLaval Steam Turbine Co., Trenton, 1946-51; mfr. mfg. engring and process devel. Gen. Electric Co., Cin., 1950-59; mgr. engring. Goodman Mfg. Co., Chgo., 1959-64; cons. engr. Gen. Electric Co., Cin., 1966-81, Pratt & Whitney Aircraft Co., West Palm Beach, Fla., 1981—. Chmn. Republican Precinct Com., Chgo., 1963-64. Recipient William Badger award Gen. Electric Co., 1970; Appreciation awards Pratt & Whitney Aircraft, 1984, 85. Mem. ASME. Presbyterian. Lodges: Masons; Shriners. Patentee hot isostatic pressing of castings, inertia welding, using plasma guns to fabricate components, coldformed components for aircraft engines. Current Work: Devel. of mfg. processes for future products to improve design and achieve lower cost production, including mining machinery, aircraft engines, missiles, space vehicles. Subspecialties: Mechanical engineering; Metallurgical engineering.

STALLARD, RICHARD ELGIN, dentist, health administrator; b. Eau Claire, Wis., May 30, 1934; s. Elgin Gale and Caroline Francis (Betz) S.; m. Norma Ann Woock, Oct. 15, 1956 (dec. 1973); children: Rondi Lynn, Alison Judith; m. Jaxon Shirley Sandlin, May 2, 1974; 1 son, Elgin Sandlin. B.S., U. Minn., 1956, D.D.S., 1958, M.S., 1959, Ph.D., 1962. Co-dir. periodontal research Eastman Dental Center, Rochester, N.Y., 1962-65; prof., head dept. periodontology Sch. Dentistry, U. Minn., Mpls., 1965-68, adj. prof. public health, 1976—; asst. dir. (Eastman Dental Center), 1968-70; prof. anatomy Boston U. Sch. Medicine, 1970-74; asst. dean Sch. Grad. Dentistry, dir. clin. research center Boston U. Sch. Grad. Dentistry, 1970-74; dental dir., head dept. periodontology Group Health Plan, Inc., St. Paul, 1974-79; exec. v.p., dental dir. Minndent, Inc., Mpls., 1980-82; pres. R.E. Stallard & Assocs., Mpls., 1982—; cons. USAF, 1968—, U.S. Navy, 1971-75; mem. tng. grant com. NIH/Nat. Inst. Dental Research, 1969-72; edn. cons. Project Vietnam, AID, Saigon, 1969-74; mem. grants and allocations com. Am. Fund for Dental Health, 1976—. Author preventive dentistry textbook, articles in profl. jours. Recipient Meritorious Achievement citation for dental research and edn. Boston U., 1970. Fellow Am., Internat. colls. dentists, Acad. Gen. Dentistry, Internat. Coll. Oral Implantology (pres. 1980-81); mem. Am. Acad. Periodontology (pres. 1974), Am. Acad. Dental Group Practice, Fedn. Dentaire Internationale, Royal Soc. Medicine (Eng.), Am. Acad. Dental Radiology, Det Danske Akademi Oral Implantologi (Denmark), Am. Acad. Dental Spltys. (pres. 1971-75), Am. Pub. Health Assn., Omicron Kappa Upsilon, Sigma Xi. Club: Alumni (Mpls.). Current Work: Research and education into the cause and prevention of dental disease and the replacement of portions of the dental apparatus lost through disease or accident by means of transplants or implants. Subspecialties: Implantology; Preventive dentistry. Home: 4200 W 44th St Edina MN 55424 Office: 7645 Metro Blvd Minneapolis MN 55435

STALLCUP, ODIE TALMADGE, animal scientist, educator; b. Paragould, Ark., Dec. 2, 1918; s. Woodford and Lissie (Cunningham) S.; m. LaRue McDaniel, June 3, 1947; children—Alice Kay, James Odie, John Wesley. B.S.A., U. Ark., 1943; A.M., U. Mo., 1947; Ph.D., 1950. Instr. U. Ark., Fayetteville, 1945-46; instr. U. Mo., Columbia, 1947-50; assoc. prof. U. Ark., Fayetteville, 1950-55, prof. animal sci., 1955—, Univ. Prof., 1985, interim head dept. animal sci., 1981. Served to capt. U.S. Army, 1942-45, ETO. Recipient merit cert. Am. Forage and Grassland Council, 1981; John W. White award U. Ark., 1981. Fellow AAAS; mem. Am. Dairy Sci. Assn. (pres. so. sect. 1969-70), Soc. for Study Reproduction (charter), Am. Soc. Animal Sci. Histochem. Soc. Democrat. Mem. Ch. Nazarene. Lodge: Rotary (dir. 1964). Current work: Nutrition and physiology of ruminants with emphasis on forage utilization, nitrogen metabolism; growth and development in bovidae. Subspecialties: Animal nutrition; Animal physiology.

STALLONES, REUEL ARTHUR, college dean; b. North Little Rock, Ark., Oct. 10, 1923; s. Wilner Leroy and Jet (Wilson) S.; m. E. Joyce Graves, Aug. 14, 1945 (div. 1977); children—Jorel, Loran, Jared. Student, Visalia Jr. Coll., 1941-42, Ripon Coll., 1943-44, U. Mich., 1944-45; M.D., Case-Western U., 1949; M.P.H., U. Calif. at Berkeley, 1952. Intern Letterman Hosp., San Francisco, 1949-50; asst. chief dept. epidemiology Walter Reed Army Inst. Research, Washington, 1954-56; lectr., prof. U. Calif. at Berkeley, 1956-68; prof., dean Sch. Pub. Health, U. Tex. at Houston, 1968—. Served with AUS, 1943-46, 49-56. Fellow Am. Pub. Health Assn., Am. Coll. Preventive Medicine, AAAS; mem. Am. Epidemiology, Assn. Tchrs. Preventive Medicine, Inst. of Medicine, Hamann Soc., Delta Omega, Sigma Xi. Current work: Epidemiological theory and methods. Subspecialty: Epidemiology. Home: 9427 Bassoon Houston TX 77025

STALLWORTH, CHARLES DOROTHEA, JR., psychologist; b. Riderwood, Ala., July 4, 1940; s. Charles D. and Annie (Horn) S. B.S., Tenn. State U., Nashville, 1963, M.S., 1966; postgrad, Calif. Sch. Profl. Psychology, 1977-79, U. Ky., 1980, Internat. Coll., 1981-82, U. South Ala., summer 1967, Tuskegee Inst., summer 1968, Auburn U., summer 1969, Harvard U., summer 1975. Psychiat. asst. Hubbard Hosp., Nashville, 1964-66; counselor, math tchr. North Central High Sch., Chatom, Ala., 1969-70; supr. adult edn. Washington County Bd. Edn., Chatom, 1968-70; dir. counseling ctr. Albany State Coll., Ga., 1970—; cons. Peace Corps, 1979-82. Bd. dirs. Dougherty County CODAC, Inc., Albany, 1973-77, Albany Area Council V.D. Control, 1975-77. Recipient grants HEW, 1970-77, grants U.S. Office Edn., 1972. Mem. Am. Psychol. Assn. (assoc.), Alpha Phi Alpha. Democrat. Baptist. Current Work: Impact of the affective domain on learning outcomes and on the application of cognitive therapies as a means of controlling negative effects. Subspecialties: Behavioral psychology; Cognition. Home: 805 E 4th Ave Albany GA 31705 Office: Ctr Student Devel Albany State Coll Albany GA 31705

STALNAKER, JOHN MARSHALL, emeritus educational corporation administrator; b. Duluth, Minn., Aug. 17, 1903; s. William Edward and Sara (Tatham) S.; m. Ruth Elizabeth Culp, July 29, 1933 (dec. Apr. 1968); children: John Culp, Robert Culp, Judith S. Aycock.; m. Edna Remmers, Aug. 21, 1969. B.S. with honors, U. Chgo., 1925; A.M. in Psychology, 1928; LL.D., Purdue U., 1956, Centre Coll., 1960. Tchr. rural sch., Hardisty, Alta., Can., 1922; tchr. math., sci. Harvard Sch. for Boys, 1925-26; instr. psychology, spl. research asst. to pres., 1926-30; asst. prof. edn. and psychology (on leave) Purdue U., 1930-31; dir. attitude measurement, athletic survey U. Minn., 1930-31; examiner (instr.) bd. exams. U. Chgo., 1931-36, asst. prof., 1936-37, assoc. prof., 1937-44; prof. Princeton U., 1944-45; research assoc. Coll. Entrance Exam Bd., 1936-37, cons. examiner, 1937-42, assoc. sec., 1942-45, dir. Navy test research unit, 1942-45; contractor's tech. rep. for N.D.R.C. project N-106, 1942-45; dir. Army-Navy Coll. Qualifying Test, 1943-45; dean students, prof. psychology Stanford, 1945-49; prof. psychology, coordinator psychol. scis. and services Ill. Inst. Tech., 1949-51; cons. Fund for Advancement Edn., 1952-55, NSF, 1952-56; dir. studies Assn. Am. Med. Colls., 1949-55; pres. Nat. Merit Scholarship Corp., 1955-69, pres. emeritus, hon. dir., 1969—; mem. bd. North Shore Mental Health Assn., 1967-70; mem. Northfield Twp. Mental Health Adv. Bd., 1978-79, Ill. Bd. Higher Edn., 1969-75; trustee, dir. Pepsi-Cola Scholarship Bd., 1945-54; mem. adv. com. Fgn. Service Exam. Dept. State, 1941-51; sci. adv. bd. to Chief of Staff, USAF, 1950-53; mem. bd. fgn. scholarships Dept. State, 1962-67, chmn., 1962-65. Contbr. articles to ednl., psychol. jours. Recipient Certificate Merit Pres. U.S., 1948, Distinguished Civilian Service award Sec. Navy, 1946; citation for outstanding contbn. to edn. Nat. Assn. Secondary Sch. Prins., 1970; Distinguished Service medal Coll. Entrance Exam. Bd., 1976. Fellow Am. Psychol. Assn.; mem. Psychometric Soc., Am. Edn. Research Assn., Phi Beta Kappa, Sigma Xi, Tau Kappa Epsilon. Clubs: Univ. (Chgo.); Cosmos (Washington). Current Work: Discovery and stimulation of gifted and talented. Subspecialty: Statistics. Home: 3839 Tangier Terr Sarasota FL 33579

STAMBAUGH, JOHN EDGAR, JR., physician, researcher; b. Everett, Pa., Apr. 30, 1940; s. John Edgar and Rhoda Irene (Becker) S.; m. Shirley Fultz, Sept. 15, 1940; children: Bambi, Michele, Michael, Heather. B.S., Dickinson Coll., 1962; M.D., Jefferson Med. Coll., 1966, Ph.D. in Pharmacology, 1968. Intern Thomas Jefferson Univ. Hosp., 1966-67, resident in medicine, 1968-70, fellow in oncology, 1970-72; asst. prof. pharmacology Jefferson Med. Coll., Phila., 1968-70, assoc. prof., 1970-82, prof., 1982—, asst. prof. medicine, 1972—, practice medicine specializing in oncology and hematology, Woodbury, N.J., 1972—; research clin. pharmacology Chronic Pain Ctr., Haddon Heights, N.J., 1982—. Contbr. articles on drug kinetics, analgesic trials, Phase I and II trials of antineoplastics, antibiotics, antiemetics and analgesics to profl. jours. Fellow Am. Soc. Exptl. Biology; mem. AMA, Am. Soc. Clin. Pharmacology, Am. Soc. Clin. Oncology, Am. Assn. Cancer Research, Am. Pain Soc., Internat. Pain Soc., Eastern U.S. Pain Soc., Am. Assn. Clin. Research, Sigma Xi. Current Work: Cancer chemotherapy, chronic pain therapy, drug kinetics. Subspecialties: Internal medicine; Pharmacokinetics. Office: 119 White Horse Pike Haddon Heights NJ 08035

STAMOUDIS, VASSILIS CHRISTOS, environmental scientist, consultant; b. Proti, Greece, Apr. 6, 1944; came to U.S. 1969, naturalized 1977; s. Christos Panayotis and Catherine (Voyadgis) S.; m. Lia Antonopoulou, June 23, 1968; children—Catherine-Xenia, Xenia-Christina. B.S. in Chemistry, U. Athens, Greece, 1967; Ph.D. in Organic Chemistry, Mich. State U., 1973. Grad. asst. in chemistry Mich. State U., East Lansing, 1969-73; postdoctoral fellow in chemistry Northwestern U., Evanston, Ill., 1973-75; asst. prof. marine sci. Coll. William and Mary, Gloucester Point, Va., 1975-78; assoc. marine scientist Va. Inst. Marine Sci., Gloucester Point, 1975-78; asst. environ. scientist Argonne Nat. Lab., Ill., 1978-81, environ. scientist, 1981—, acting leader geochemistry sect., 1985—; cons. U. Mich., Ann Arbor, 1981—, Tex. A & M U., College Station, 1983; adj. prof. environ. chemistry Sch. Pub. Health, U. Mich., 1985—; reviewer various jours. and orgns. and sci. meetings, 1978—. Contbr. articles to profl. jours. Bd. dirs. St. Athanasios Greek Orthodox Ch., Aurora, Ill., 1981—; pres. St. Athanasios Greek Sch., Aurora, 1982—. Served with Greek Arty., 1967-69. U.S. Dept. Energy grantee Argonne Nat. Lab., 1978—; Am. Petroleum Inst. grantee Va. Inst. Marine Sci., 1975-78; EPA grantee Va. Inst. Marine Sci., 1975-76; NIH grantee Northwestern U., 1973-75. Mem. Am. Chem. Soc., N.Y. Acad. Sci., Va. Acad. Sci., Soc. Applied Spectroscopy, Am. Soc. Mass Spectroscopy. Current work: Project leader several long-range interdisciplinary research programs to study health and environmental effects of energy-related industrial plants, state-of-the-art chemical and toxicological characterization of energy-related natural and synthetic (coal-conversion and shale oil) materials, health and environmental distribution, fate and effects of complex energy-related mixtures, evaluating of synfuel wastewater treatment trains, computer applications in analytical, environmental organic chemistry, chemical structure/toxicological activity relationships; photolytic and partitioning behavior of polycyclic aromatic compounds, aromatic amines, and phenols in agueous coal-oil systems. Subspecialties: Environmental chemistry; Organic chemistry. Home: 11S544 Webster Ln Naperville IL 60565 Office: Argonne Nat Lab Energy and Environ Systems Div Bldg 362 Geochemistry Sect 9700 S Cass Ave Argonne IL 60439

STANFORD, ROBERT ERNEST, operations research analyst; b. Montgomery, Ala., May 26, 1944; s. Robert Ernest and Carolyn Ann (Wagner) Stanford Van Ryzin; m. Janet Lee Zicarelli, Dec. 4, 1982. B.A., U. of South, Sewanee, Tenn., 1965; M.S., Ga. Inst. Tech., 1967; Ph.D., U. Calif.-Berkeley, 1971. Lectr. Calif. State U., Hayward, 1971-73; U. Calif.-Berkeley, 1973-74, U. Calif.-Riverside, 1974-76; asst. prof. Auburn U., Ala., 1976-79, assoc. prof., 1980-81; assoc. prof. ops. research U. Ala., Birmingham, 1982—; research assoc. U.S. Naval Postgrad. Sch., Monterey, Calif., 1979. Contbr. articles to profl. jours. NASA/Am. Inst. Indsl. Engring. fellow, 1977. Mem. Ops. Research Soc. Am., Inst. Mgmt. Sci., Sigma Pi Sigma. Current Work: Manpower system models, applied stochastic processes, decision support systems, productivity of white collar labor, quality control analysis. Subspecialties: Operations research (engineering); Operations research (mathematics). Home: 2615 Montevallo Rd Birmingham AL 35223 Office: Dept Econs Univ Ala Birmingham AL 35294

STANG, PETER JOHN, chemistry educator; b. Nurnberg, Germany, Nov. 17, 1941; came to U.S., 1956, naturalized, 1963; s. John and Margaret (Pollman) S.; m. Christine S. Schirmer, June 12, 1969; children: Antonia, Alexandra. B.S., DePaul U., 1963; Ph.D., U. Calif.-Berkeley, 1966. Instr. Princeton U., N.J., 1968-69; asst. prof. U. Utah, Salt Lake City, 1969-75, assoc. prof., 1975-79, prof. chemistry, 1979—. Editorial adviser: Acad. Press; Author: Vinyl Cations, 1979; assoc. editor: Jour. Am. Chem. Soc, 1982—. Recipient Alexander von Humboldt Sr. U.S. Scientist award, 1977; JSPS fellow, 1985, Lady Davis fellow, Israel, 1986. Mem. Am. Chem. Soc., Chem. Soc. (London), AAAS. Current Work: Mechanistic organic chemistry: unsaturated reactive intermediates; vinyl cations, carbenes, dication ether salts; antitumor agents, organometallic chemistry. Subspecialty: Organic chemistry. Office: Chemistry Department U. of Utah Salt Lake City UT 84112

STANGE, JAMES HENRY, architect; b. Davenport, Iowa, May 25, 1930; s. Henry Claus and Norma Strange; m. Mary Suanne Peterson, Dec. 12, 1954; children: Wade Weston, Drew Dayton, Grant Owen. B.Arch., Iowa State U., 1954. Lic. architect, Nebr., Iowa, Kans., Mo., Okla. Designer Davis & Wilson, Lincoln, Nebr., 1954-62, v.p., 1962-68; v.p., sec. Davis/Fenton/Stange/Darling, Lincoln, 1968-76, pres., 1976-78, pres., chmn. bd., 1978—. Archtl. works include Lincoln Hosp, 1974, Hastings YMCA, 1980, Nebr. Wesleyan U. Theatre, 1980, Bryan Hosp, 1982, others. Pres. Lincoln Ctr. Assn., 1979; pres. Capitol Assn. Retarded Citizens, 1972; vice chmn. United Way. Recipient numerous design awards AIA. Mem. AIA, Nebr. Soc. AIA (pres. 1968, dir. 1964-65), Am. Assn. Health Planners, Lincoln C. of C. (dir.), Interfaith Forum on Religion, Art, Architecture. Republican. Presbyterian. Clubs: Crucible, 12, Hillcrest Country (past pres.), Executive (past pres.). Current Work: Passive solar system integration and application to existing or new structure; integration of structures into existing environmental conditions. Subspecialties: Solar energy; Environmental engineering. Home: 3545 Calvert Lincoln NE 68506 Office: 211 N 14th Lincoln NE 68508

STANISLAO, JOSEPH, college dean, industrial engineering educator; b. Manchester, Conn., Nov. 21, 1928; s. Edguardo and Rose (Zacarro) S.; m. Bettie Chode Carter, Sept. 12, 1960. B.S., Tex. Tech U., 1957; M.S., Pa. State U., 1959; Sc.D. in Engring., Columbia U., 1970. Registered profl. engr., Mass. Asst. engr. Naval Ordance Research Lab., University Park, Pa., 1958-59; asst. prof. indsl. engring. N.C. State U., Raleigh, 1959-61; dir. research Darlington Fabrics, Pawtucket, R.I., 1961-62; from asst. prof. to prof. U. R.I., Kingston, 1962-71; prof. indsl. engring., dept. chmn. Cleve. State U., 1971-75; dean, prof. indsl. engring. N.D. State U., Fargo, 1975—; cons. engr. Bulova Watch Div., Lincoln, R.I., 1965-68, Internat. Tool, Inc., Warwick, R.I., 1968-71, Asian Productivity Orgn., Tokyo, Republic of China, India, 1972-75, Gateway Industries, Inc., Bloomington, Minn., 1981-83. Author: (with others) Maintenance System and Appliance, 1979; Production Handbook, 3d edit., 1972. Contbr. numerous articles to profl. jours. Scoutmaster Exeter council Boy Scouts Am., R.I., 1965-68; mem. Gov.'s Club, Fargo, N.D., 1982; mem. Republican voting drive, Fargo, 1984. Served as sgt. USMC, 1948-51. Recipient Order of Engr., Cleve. State U., 1972; Recognition award U.S. Air Force, 1979, Air Force ROTC Appreciation award, 1982. Mem. ASME (program chmn. 1971-72), Am. Inst. Indsl. Engrs. (sr., v.p. 1964-65), Am. Soc. Engring. Edn. (campus coordinator 1979-81), Sigma Xi, Tau Beta Pi (faculty advisor 1978-79). Roman Catholic. Lodges: Lions (com. chmn. 1978-82), Elks. Current work: Established engineering computer center with Control Data Corporation, North Dakota Economic Commission and North Dakota State University, 1985. Subspecialties: Industrial engineering; Robotics. Home: 3520 Longfellow Rd Fargo ND 58102 Office: ND State U Coll Engring and Architecture Fargo ND 58105

STANLEY, DANIEL JEAN, geological oceanographer, marine sedimentologist; b. Metz, France, Apr. 14, 1934; came to U.S., 1941, naturalized, 1946; s. Paul Emile and Madeleine (Simon) S.; m. Anne Marie Pavloff, July 1, 1960 (div. July 1982); children—Marc Michel, Eric Paul, Nathalie Anne. B.S., Cornell U., 1956; M.S., Brown U., 1958; D.Sc., U. Grenoble, France, 1961. Research geologist French Petroleum Inst., Paris, 1958-61; asst. dir. Waterways Experiment Sta., U.S. Army C.E., Vicksburg, Miss., 1961-63; asst. prof. U. Ottawa, Ont., Can., 1963-64; postdoctoral fellow Woods Hole Oceanographic Instn., 1964; assoc. prof. Dalhousie U., Halifax, N.S., Can., 1964-66; curator, sr. oceanographer Smithsonian Instn., Washington, 1966—, dir. Mediterranean Basin project, 1976—; adj. prof. dept. geology U. Maine, Orono, 1973—; vis. prof. French Petroleum Inst., Paris, 1974—; cons. offshore petroleum Govt. of Tunisia, 1978-81; legal adviser, sci. expert, marine scis. Internat. Ct. Justice, The Hague, 1981. Author: The Mediterranean Sea—A Natural Sedimentation Laboratory, 1972; Marine Sediment Transport and Environmental Management, 1976; The Shelfbreak: Critical Interface on Continental Margins, 1983; Geological Evolution of the Mediterranean Basin, 1985, others. Editor books on marine geology; mem. editorial bds. profl. jours. Contbr. articles to profl. jours. Served to capt. C.E., U.S. Army, 1961-63. Grantee: Smithsonian Instn., Nat. Geog., 1967-74, Nat. Acad. Sci., 1976. Fellow Geol. Soc. Am., AAAS; mem. Internat. Assn. Sedimentologists, Soc. Econ. Paleontology Mineralogists, Am. Assn. Petroleum Geologists. Republican. Clubs: Cosmos, Jefferson Island (Washington). Current work: Origin of continental margins, with special interest in U.S. Atlantic margin and Mediterranean (work on land and offshore). Subspecialties: Sedimentology; Oceanography. Office: Div Sedimentology E-109 NMNH Smithsonian Instn Washington DC 20560

STANNARD, JAMES NEWELL, radiation biologist and toxicologist, educator; b. Owego, N.Y., Jan. 2, 1910; s. Jay Ellis and Miriam (Newell) S.; m. Grace L. Kingsley, Aug. 7, 1935; 1 child, Susan L. Stannard Stumpf. A.B., Oberlin Coll., 1931; M.A., Harvard U., 1934, Ph.D., 1935. Asst. in gen. physiology Harvard U., Cambridge, Mass., 1932-35; instr. physiology U. Rochester, N.Y., 1935-39, asst. prof. radiation biology and biophysics, 1947-49, assoc. prof., 1949-59, prof., 1959-75, emeritus prof., 1975—, prof. pharmacology and toxicology, 1952-75, emeritus prof., 1975—, assoc. dean for grad. studies, 1959-75; adj. prof. community medicine and radiology U. Calif. San Diego, La Jolla, 1977—; asst. prof. pharmacology Emory U., 1939-41; sr. pharmacologist to prin. physiologist NIH, 1941-47; vis. prof. U. Calif. Med. Ctr., San Francisco, 1954; cons. Battelle Pacific NW Lab., others; mem. task group Internat. Commn. on Radiol. Protection; chmn., mem. sci. coms., life mem. Nat. Council on Radiation Protection and Measurements; mem. adv. bd. Hanford Environ. Health Found. Author: Radioactivity and Health-A History, 1985; author, editor: Handbook of Experimental Pharmacology, vol. 36, 1973; editor: Radioisotopes in the Aquatic Environment, 1976; contbr. sci. articles to profl. jours. Sec. bd. dirs. Oaks North Mgmt. Corp. Number 1, San Diego. Served to lt. USN, 1944-46. Recipient cert. of appreciation HEW, 1970, AEC, 1975, EPA, 1977. Mem. Am. Indsl. Hygiene Assn., AAAS, Am. Soc. Pharmacology and Exptl. Therapeutics, Am. Physiol. Soc., Radiation Research Soc., Health Physics Soc. (dir. 1965-71, pres. 1969-70, editor, mem. editorial bd. 1975-81, Disting. Achievement award 1977), Biophys. Soc., Soc. Gen. Physiologists, Phi Beta Kappa, Sigma Xi. Presbyterian. Current work: Writing, editing, teaching and national committee operations in field of biological effects and metabolism of radionuclides, basic radiobiology, standard setting. Subspecialties: Radiation biology; Toxicology (agriculture). Home: 17441 Plaza Animado Apt 132 San Diego CA 92128 Office: U Calif-San Diego M-022 La Jolla CA 92093

STANNARD, JAN GREGORY, dental materials educator, chemurgist; b. Detroit, Dec. 30, 1953; s. Frank Kempster and Edith (Olmsted) S.; m. Roberta Anne Salay, Sept. 5, 1981. B.S. in Med. Chemistry, U. Mich., 1976, M.S. in Polymer Chemistry, 1978, Ph.D. in Macromolecular Sci. and Engring. and Dental Materials, 1981. Chemist Dow Chem. Co. U.S.A., Midland, Mich., 1972-74; praktikant Hoffman-LaRoche, Basel, Switzerland, 1974-75; research assoc. U. Mich., 1974-78; asst. prof. dental materials U. Nebr.-Lincoln, 1981—; co-owner Design Interactions, Lincoln, 1981—; cons. in field. Contbr. articles to profl. jours.; author 2 patent disclosure documents. Recipient Dept. Commerce award, 1971, USN Sci. award, 1971, Internat. Sci. and Engring. award Sci. Service, 1971, Mich. Soc. Profl. Engrs. award, 1972, award of Excellence Gen. Motors, 1972, Key to City of Flint Mich., 1972; Westinghouse Sci. Talent Search Scholar, 1972; Welch sci. scholar, 1972; Nat. Research Service award Nat. Inst. Dental Research, 1977-81. Mem. Internat. Assn. Dental Research, N.Y. Acad. Sci., Nebr. Acad. Sci., Mich. Sci. Research Club, Assn. Study of Higher Edn., Sigma Xi. Current Work: Biomedical research; development and testing of new biocompatible materials and devices for internal and external interfacing. Subspecialty: Biomaterials. Home: 5523 S 31-12 Lincoln NE 68516 Office: Dental Materials U Nebr Lincoln NE 68583

STANTON, GLENNON JOHN, microbiologist, educator, researcher; b. Rock Springs, Wyo., Nov. 18, 1931; s. Glennon George and Nan (Wortheim) S.; m. Beverly M. Doak; children: James, Lori, Barbara, Michael, Shauna. B.A., Stanford U., 1956; Ph.D., U. Utah, 1967. Asst. prof. microbiology U. Tex. Med. Br., Galveston, 1967-77, assoc. prof., 1977-81, prof., 1981—; cons. in field. Contbr. to profl. jours., books, 1964—. USPHS grantee, 1976—. Mem. Am. Soc. Microbiology, Ocular Microbiology and Immunology Group, Assn. for Research and Vision in Ophthalmology. Current Work: Host defenses and viral pathogenesis; interferons; lymphokines; lymphokine induced cell communication; leukocyte defenses against viral disease and cancer. Subspecialties: Immunobiology and immunology; Virology (biology). Home: 9214 San Jose Texas City TX 77590 Office: Dept Microbiology U Tex Med Br Galveston TX 77550

STANTON, ROBERT JAMES, JR., geology educator, researcher; b. Los Angeles, June 17, 1931; s. Robert James and Audrey (Franke) S.; m. Patricia Ann Burns, Sept. 13, 1953; children—John, Carol. B.S. in Geology, Calif. Inst. Tech., 1953, Ph.D., 1960; M.A., Harvard U., 1956. Research geologist Shell Devel. Co., Houston, 1959-67; assoc. prof. geology Tex. A&M U., Coll. Sta., 1967-72, prof. geology, 1972—, head geology dept., 1979-83. Author: (with others) Paleoecology, Concepts and Applications, 1981. Contbr. articles to profl. jours. Fellow Geol. Soc. Am.; mem. Paleontol. Soc., Soc. Econ. Paleontols. and Mineralogists (Best Paper Pub. Jour. Paleontology, 1970), Internat. Paleontol. Union. Republican. Presbyterian. Current work: Development of techniques and criteria and their application to determine ancient environments from paleontologic data. Subspecialties: Paleontology, paleoecology; Paleobiology. Home: 3609 Sunnybrook Bryan TX 77802 Office: Dept of Geology Tex A&M Univ College Station TX 77843

STAPLES, RICHARD CROMWELL, plant biochemist; b. Hinsdale, Ill., Jan. 29, 1926; s. George Allen and Ruth (Larken) S.; m. Mildred J. Durdik, Aug. 7, 1954; children: Cynthia, Laura, Robert. B.S., Colo. State U., 1950; A.M., Columbia U., 1954, Ph.D., 1957. With Boyce Thompson Inst. Plant Research, Cornell U., Ithaca, N.Y., 1952—, program dir. plant stress, 1966—; vis. scientist dept. biochemistry U. Wis.-Madison, 1961-62; policy analyst Policy Research and Analysis Div., NSF, 1975-76. Editor: (with G.A. Toenniessen) 3 books in field including Plant Disease Control, 1981; contbr. (with G.A. Toenniessen) articles to profl. jours. Served with USN, 1944-46, 50-52. Alexander von Humboldt Found. sr. U.S. scientist awardee, 1980; Humboldt awardee Institut für Biologie III, Aachen, W.Ger., 1981-82. Mem. Am. Soc. Plant Physiologists, Am. Phytopath. Soc. Current Work: Basic research on sensing in fungi especially development of infection structures in the rust fungi. Subspecialties: Plant pathology; Plant physiology (biology). Office: Boyce Thompson Inst Tower Rd Ithaca NY 14850

STAPLETON, LEROY EARL, therapist, clinical psychologist, foundation executive; b. Harlan, Ky., Nov. 9, 1923; s. William Jesse and Joyce Mae (Belcher) S.; m. Mary Lillian Wynn, May 8, 1945; children: Teresa Dwen, Earl Patrick, Carrie Ellen. B.E., U. Nebr.-Omaha, 1957; M.A., Stanford U., 1959; Ph.D., Fla. State U., 1973. Lic. psychologist, Fla. Commd. 2d lt. U.S. Air Force, 1942, advanced through grades to lt. col., 1961, served as pilot, navigator, radar operator, bombardier, gunner, mechanic, performance engr., Eng., Africa, Pacific Islands, ret., 1966; prof. Troy State U., Ft. Walton Beach, Fla., 1973-75; dir. curriculum Air U., USAF, Montgomery, Ala., 1964-67; dir. psychol. services Okaloosa Bd. Edn., Ft. Walton Beach, 1968-77; psychologist, Ft. Walton Beach, 1979-81; pres. Child Family Research Found., Ft. Walton Beach, 1978—; pres., chmn. bd. Fla. Research Found., Ft. Walton Beach, 1978-83; clin. psychologist Fla. Regional Found., Ft. Walton Beach, 1975—; devel. and learning psychologist Okaloosa Bd. Edn., 1968-75; bio-astronautics psychologist USAF Proving Ground, Ft. Walton Beach, 1963-64. Author, creator gravitational bomb table, USAF, 1952; author, designer: Learning Disability Mental Analysis Profile for Children, 1975 (bd. edn. recognition 1975, spl. proclamation Bd. Edn. Okaloosa County 1975). Founder Fla. Regional Family Life Child Devel. Research Found., Ft. Walton Beach, 1978; bd. dirs. Mental Health Clinic, 1970-75, Fla. Crime Commn., Panhandle, 1973-75. Recipient Disting. Flying award USAF, 1952-53, Disting. Educator award Okaloosa County Bd. Edn., 1975. Mem. Fla. Assn. Practicing Psychologists (pres. 1979-81), Am. Psychol. Assn., Fla. Psychol. Assn., Fla. Assn. Sch. Psychologist Ethics (exec. bd. 1970-72), Am. Contract Bridge League (advanced sr. sr. 1963-83), Psi Chi. Methodist. Lodges: Masons; Shriners. Featherweight boxing champion USAF, 1943. Current Work: Deep sleep hypnotherapy; hypnotherapy as a functional study of retardation, regression study in behavioral trauma. Subspecialties: Behavioral psychology; Neuropsychology. Home: 583 Pocahontas Dr Fort Walton Beach FL 32548 Office: Fla Regional Family-Life Child Devel Research Found 2000 Lewis Turner Blvd Fort Walton Beach FL 32548

STARFIELD, BARBARA HELEN, physician, educator; b. Bklyn., Dec. 18, 1932; d. Martin and Eva (Illions) S.; m. Neil A. Holtzman, June 12, 1955; children—Robert, Jon, Steven, Deborah. A.B., Swarthmore Coll., 1954; M.D., SUNY, 1959; M.P.H., Johns Hopkins U., 1963. Teaching asst. in anatomy Downstate Med. Center, N.Y.C., 1955-57; intern in pediatrics Johns Hopkins U., 1959-60, resident, 1960-62, dir. pediatric med. care clinic, 1963-66, dir. community staff comprehensive child care project, 1966-67, dir. pediatric clin. scholars program, 1971-76, asso. prof. pediatrics, 1973—, prof. health policy, 1975—; cons. HEW. Contbr. articles to profl. jours.; Mem. editorial bd.: Med. Care, 1977-79, Pediatrics, 1977-83, Internat. Jour. Health Services, 1978—, Med. Care Rev, 1980—. Recipient Dave Luckman Meml. award, 1958; HEW Career Devel. award, 1970-75. Mem. Nat. Acad. Sci. Inst. Medicine (governing council 1981-83), Am. Pediatric Soc., Soc. Pediatric Research, Internat. Epidemiologic Assn., Ambulatory Pediatric Assn. (pres. 1980), Am. Public Health Assn., Sigma Xi, Alpha Omega Alpha., Nat. Acad. Sci. Inst. Medicine (governing bd. NRC 1983). Current Work: Cost effectiveness of care; health needs-care of population subgroups; primary care delivery; epidemiology of child health problems. Subspecialties: Health services research; Epidemiology. Office: 615 N Wolfe St Baltimore MD 21205

STARK, JACK ALAN, clinical psychologist, educator; b. Hastings, Nebr., Sept. 20, 1946; s. Arlen Odale and Mary Virginia (Dryden) S.; m. Shirley A. Theis, Aug. 1, 1970; children: John, Nick, Suzanne. B.A., St. Francis Coll., Milw., 1968; M.A., U. Nebr., 1970, Ph.D., 1973. Lic. psychologist and rehab. counselor, Nebr. vocat. expert Social Security Adminstrn. Secondary tchr. Lincoln Parochial Schs., 1968-70, sch. psychologist, 1970-71, counseling psychologist, 1971-73; assoc. prof. med. psychology, dir. family rehab. U. Nebr. Med. Ctr., Omaha, 1973—; dir. U. Nebr. Med. Ctr. (Ctr. Comprehensive Rehab), 1978-82, U. Nebr. Med. Ctr. (Prevocat. and Vocat. Edn. for Spl. Needs Youth), 1982—. Editor: Curative Aspects of Mental Retardation—Biomedical and Behavioral Aspects, 1983, Mental Illness in Mental Retardation, 1983: (with others) Prevocational and Vocational Education for Special Needs Youth: A Blueprint for the 1980s, 1983, (with others) International Handbook of Community Services, 1984 (with others) Community Services for the Mentally Retarded, 1985. Contbr articles to jours., presentations to confs., chpts. to books. Tng. grantee HEW, 1968-70; recipient Outstanding Profl. Employee award Greater Omaha Assn. for Retarded Citizens, 1979. Mem. Am. Assn. Mental Deficiency (v.p. vocat. rehab. 1982-84), Assn. for Advancement Community Services (v.p. 1979—). Democrat. Roman Catholic. Current Work: Psychology, mental retardation, behavioral medicine. Subspecialties: Behavioral psychology; Health services research. Home: 306 Heavenly Dr Omaha NE 68154 Office: U Nebr Med Ctr 444 S 41st St Omaha NE 68131

STARNES, WILLIAM HERBERT, JR., research chemist; b. Knoxville, Tenn., Dec. 2, 1934; s. William Herbert St. and Edna Margaret (Osborne) S. B.S. with honors, Va. Poly Inst., 1955; Ph.D., Ga. Inst. Tech., 1960. Research chemist Esso Research & Engring. Co., Baytown, Tex., 1960-62, sr. research chemist, 1962-64, section head, 1964-65, research specialist, 1965-67, research assoc., 1967-71; instr. and research assoc. dept. chemistry U. Tex., Austin, 1971-73; mem. tech. staff AT&T Bell Labs., Murray Hill, N.J., 1973—; vis. scientist Tex. Acad. Scis., 1964-67. Mem. adv. bd. and bd. reviewers Jour. Vinyl Tech., 1981-83. Contbr. articles to profl. jours. NSF fellow 1958-60; recipient Profl. Progress award Soc. Profl. Chemists and Engrs. 1968, Disting. Tech. Staff award AT&T Bell Labs. 1982. Fellow AAAS, Am. Inst. Chemists (life); mem. Am. Chem. Soc. (bd. dirs. southeastern Tex. sect. 1970, speakers bur. div. polymer chemistry 1976—), N.Y. Acad. Scis., Sigma Xi, Phi Kappa Phi, Phi Lambda Upsilon (pres. Va. Poly. Inst. chpt. 1954-55). Current work: Degradation, stabilization, flammability, microstructures, and polymerization mechanisms of synthetic polymers, especially poly (vinyl chloride); free radical chemistry; carbon-13 nuclear magnetic resonance and organic synthesis. Subspecialties: Organic chemistry; Polymer chemistry. Office: AT&T Bell Labs 600 Mountain Ave Room 7D-226 Murray Hill NJ 07974

STARR, CHAUNCEY, research institute executive; b. Newark, Apr. 14, 1912; s. Rubin and Rose (Dropkin) S.; m. Doris Evelyn Debel, Mar. 20, 1938; children: Ross M., Ariel E. E.E., Rensselaer Poly. Inst., 1932, Ph.D., 1935, D.Engring. (hon.), 1964; D.Engring. (hon.), Swiss ETH, 1980. Research fellow physics Harvard, 1935-37; research asso. Mass. Inst. Tech., 1938-41; research physicist D.W. Taylor Model Basin, Bur. Ships, 1941-42; staff radiation lab. U. Calif., 1942-43, Tenn. Eastman Corp., Oak Ridge, 1943-46, Tenn. Eastman Corp. (Clinton Labs.), 1946; chief spl. research N. Am. Aviation, Inc., Downey, Calif., 1946-49, dir. atomic energy research dept., 1949-55, v.p., 1955-66; gen. mgr. N. Am. Aviation, Inc. (Atomics Internat. div.), 1955-60, pres. div., 1960-66; dean engring. U. Calif. at Los Angeles, 1966-73; cons. prof. Stanford, 1974—; pres. Electric Power Research Inst., 1973-78, vice chmn., 1978—; Dir. Atomic Indsl. Forum. Contbr. sci. articles to profl. jours. Decorated Legion of Honor France).; recipient Henry D. Smyth award Atomic Indsl. Forum, 1983. Fellow Am. Nuclear Soc. (past pres.), Am. Phys. Soc., AAAS (dir.); mem. AIAA (sr.), Am. Power Conf., Nat. Acad. Engring., Am. Soc. Engring. Edn., Royal Swedish Acad. for Engring. Scis., Eta Kappa Nu, Sigma Xi. Current Work: Risk assessment; impact of energy supply on society. Subspecialties: Fuels and sources; Nuclear fusion. Home: 95 Stern Ln Atherton CA 94025

STARR, RICHARD CAWTHON, botany educator; b. Greensboro, Ga., Aug. 24, 1924; s. Richard Neal and Ida Wynn (Cawthon) S. B.S. in Secondary Edn, Ga. So. Coll., 1944; M.A., George Peabody Coll., 1947; postgrad. (Fulbright scholar), Cambridge (Eng.) U., 1950-51; Ph.D., Vanderbilt U., 1952. Faculty, Ind. U., 1952—, prof. botany, 1960-76, founder, head culture collection algae, 1953-76; prof. botany U. Tex.-Austin, 1976—; Head course marine botany Marine Biol. Lab., Woods Hole, Mass., 1959-63. Algae sect. editor: Biol. Abstracts, 1959—; editorial bd.: Jour. Phycology, 1965-68, 76—, Archiv für Protistenkunde; assoc. editor: Phycologia, 1963-69; Contbr. articles to profl. jours. Trustee Am. Type Culture Collection, 1962-68, 80—. Guggenheim fellow, 1959; sr. fellow Alexander von Humboldt-Stiftung, 1972-73. Fellow AAAS, Ind. Acad. Sci.; mem. Nat. Acad. Scis. (Gilbert Morgan Smith award 1985), Am. Inst. Biol. Scis. (governing bd. 1976-77, exec. com. 1980—), Bot. Soc. Am. (sec. 1965-69, v.p. 1970, pres. 1971, Darbaker prize 1955), Phycological Soc. Am. (past pres., v.p., treas.), Soc. Protozoologists, Internat. Phycological Soc. (sec. 1964-68), Brit. Phycological Soc., Akademie der Wissenschaften zu Göttigen (corr.), Sigma Xi. Current Work: Cultivation of algae; sexual reproduction and cell differentiation in colonial green algae; viral infections in algae. Office: Dept Botany Univ Texas Austin TX 78712

STARRFIELD, SUMNER GROSBY, astronomer; b. Los Angeles, Dec. 29, 1940; s. Harold Earnest and Eve (Grosby) S.; m. Susan Lee Hutt, Aug. 6, 1966; children: Barry, Brian, Sara. B.A., U. Calif., Berkeley, 1962; M.A., UCLA, 1966, Ph.D., 1969. Lectr. Yale U., 1967-69, asst. prof., 1969-71; fellow IBM Watson Research Center, 1971-72; asst. prof. physics and astronomy Ariz. State U. Tempe, 1972-75, assoc. prof., 1975-80, prof., 1981—; vis. staff mem. Los Alamos Nat. Lab., 1975—. Contbr. articles to profl. jours. NSF grantee, 1975—; NASA grantee, 1979—; U.S. Israel Binat. Found. grantee, 1981-84. Mem. Internat. Astron. Union, Am. Astron. Soc., Royal Astron. Soc., Astron. Soc. Pacific. Democrat. Club: Puli. Current Work: Hydrodynamic stellar evolution, evolution of nova outburst, nucleo synthesis in stars, white dwarf pulsations. Subspecialties: Theoretical astrophysics; High energy astrophysics. Office: Dept Physics Ariz State U Tempe AZ 85281

STARY, FRANK EDWARD, chemistry educator; b. St. Paul, Minn., Jan. 3, 1941; s. Frank C. and Elaine E. (Anderson) S.; m. Sonja G. Dalsbo, Aug. 30, 1964. B.Chem., U. Minn., 1963; Ph.D., U. Cin., 1969. Fellow, instr. U. Calif., Irvine, 1969-72; research assoc. U. Mo., 1972-74; asst. prof. chemistry Maryville Coll., St. Louis, 1974-78, assoc. prof., 1978-81, prof., 1982—; cons in field. Contbr. articles to profl. jours. Recipient Disting. Teaching award Maryville Coll., 1981. Mem. Am. Chem. Soc., Sigma Xi, Phi Lambda Upsilon, St. Louis Audio Soc. Current Work: Pulsed magnetic resonance on solids, chem. lasers, chemiluminescence of polymers. Subspecialties: Nuclear magnetic resonance; Polymer chemistry. Office: 13550 Conway Rd Creve Coeur MO 63141

STARZL, THOMAS EARL, physician, educator; b. Le Mars, Iowa, Mar. 11, 1926; s. Roman F. and Anna Laura (Fitzgerald) S.; m. Barbara Brothers, Nov. 27, 1954 (div.); children—Timothy, Rebecca, Thomas.; m. Joy D. Conger, Aug. 1, 1981. B.A., Westminster Coll., 1947, D.Sc. (hon.), 1965; M.A., Northwestern U., 1950, Ph.D., 1952, M.D., 1952; D.Sc. (hon.), N.Y. Med. Coll., 1970, Med. Coll. Wis., 1981, Northwestern U., 1982, Bucknell U., 1985, Muhlenberg Coll., 1985; LL.D., U. Wyo., 1971, Westmar Coll., 1974; M.D. (hon.), U. Louvain, Belgium, 1985. Faculty Northwestern U. Med. Sch., 1958-61; faulty U. Colo. Med. Sch., Denver, 1962-80, prof. surgery, 1964-80, chmn. dept., 1972-80; prof. surgery U. Pitts., 1981—; mem. staffs Presbyn. Hosp., Univ. Hosp., Children's Hosp. of Pitts., Pitts. VA Hosp. Author: Experience in Renal Transplantation, 1964, Experience in Hepatic Transplantation, 1969; Contbr. articles to profl. jours. Recipient award Westminster Coll., 1965, Achievement award Lund U., 1965; Eppinger award Soc. Internat. de Chirurgie, 1965; Eppinger prize, Freiburg, 1970; William S. Middleton award for outstanding research in VA system, 1968; Merit award Northwestern U., 1969; Disting. Achievement award Modern Medicine, 1969; Creative Council award U. Colo., 1971; Colo. Man of Yr. award, 1967; Brookdale award AMA, 1974; David Hume Meml. award Nat. Kidney Found., 1978; Pitts. Man of Yr. award, 1981; Markle Scholar, 1958. Fellow ACS (Sheen award 1982), Am. Acad. Arts and Scis., Royal Coll. Surgeons Eng. (hon.); mem. Soc. Univ. Surgeons, Soc. Vascular Surgery, Am. Surg. Assn., Transplantation Soc., Surg. Soc. Lyon (fgn. hon.), Deutsche Gesellschaft für Chirurgie, numerous others. Subspecialties: Surgery; Transplant surgery. Office: Dept Surgery U Pittsburgh Sch Medicine 1084 Scaife Hall Pittsburgh PA 15261

STASZESKY, FRANCIS MYRON, consultant; b. Wilmington, Del., Apr. 16, 1918; s. Frank J. and Ruth (Jones) S.; m. Barbara F. Kearney, May 30, 1943; children—Francis Myron, John B., Barbara J., Faith A., Paul D. B.S. in Mech. Engring, Mass. Inst. Tech., 1943, M.S. in Mech. Engring, 1943. Mech. engr. Union Oil Co. Calif., Los Angeles, 1943-45; with E.I. duPont de Nemours Co., Wilmington, Del., 1946-48; joined Boston Edison Co., 1948, supervising engr. design and constrn., 1948-57, supt. engring. and constrn. dept., 1957-64, v.p., asst. to pres., 1964-67, exec. v.p., 1967-79, pres., chief operating officer, 1979-83, cons., 1983—; dir. Boston Edison Co., 1968-83; dir. Shawmut Corp., Shawmut Bank Boston N.A. Fellow ASME; mem. IEEE, Nat. Acad. Engring., Engring. Soc. New Eng. (pres. 1961-62). Clubs: Algonquin (Boston); Brae Burn Country. Current Work: Independent consultant to corporate management in capital intensive industry and on issues of future energy supply. Subspecialties: Electrical engineering; Energy consulting. Address: 144 Chestnut Circle Lincoln MA 01773

STAUB, RICK WALTER, genetics educator, researcher; b. Waukesha, Wis., Feb. 15, 1952; s. Frank Paul and Betty Ann (Evans) S.; m. Cynthia Jean Harrison, Aug. 12, 1983. B.S., U. Wis., 1974; M.S., U. Ariz., 1978, Ph.D., 1984. Cyotgeneticist U. Ariz., Tucson, 1978-82; instr. genetics Carleton Coll., Northfield, Minn., 1982-84, asst. prof., 1984—. Mem. AAAS, Am. Genetic Assn., Genetics Soc. Am., Sigma Xi. Current work: Investigation of the influences of B chromosomes on the genome and cellular physiology of maize. Subspecialties: Plant genetics; Genome organization. Home: 1739 Roosevelt Dr Northfield MN 55057 Office: Biology Dept Carleton Coll Northfield MN 55057

STAUBUS, JOHN REGINALD, dairy sci. educator; b. Cissna Park, Ill., Mar. 21, 1926; s. Raymond Reginald and Anna Evelyn (Newell) S.; m. Lorene Lawrence, Sept. 8, 1951; 1 dau., Anna Marie Staubus Jones. B.S., U. Ill., 1950, M.S., 1956, Ph.D., 1959. Mortgage rep. Phoenix Mut. Life Ins. Co., 1951-54; research assoc. dept. dairy sci. U. Ill., 1954-60; asst. prof. dairy sci. Ohio State U., 1960-64, assoc. prof., 1964-69, prof., 1969—. Served with C.E. U.S. Army, 1945-47. Mem. Am. Dairy Sci. Assn., Am. Soc. Animal Sci., AAAS. Methodist. Current Work: Ruminant nutrition and management teaching. Subspecialties: Animal nutrition; Microbiology.

STAVELY, JOSEPH RENNIE, plant pathologist; b. Wilmington, Del., May 28, 1939; s. Joseph Glover and Susan Frances S.; m. Nancy Carol Gall, Aug. 15, 1965; 1 son, Joseph Carl. B.S., U. Del., 1961; M.S., U. Wis., 1963, Ph.D., 1965. Grad. research asst. U. Wis., Madison, 1961-65, postdoctoral NIH research fellow, 1965-66; research plant pathologist tobacco Agrl. Research Services, U.S. Dept. Agr., Beltsville, Md., 1966-80; research plant pathologist beans Agrl. Research Services, U.S. Dept. Agr. (Applied Plant Pathology Lab.), 1980—. Contbr. articles to profl. jours. Vestryman St. Philip's Episcopal Ch., Laurel, Md., 1977-80; Webelos leader Cub Pack 1349, Silver Spring, Md., 1981-82. NIH postdoctoral research grantee, 1965-66; U.S. Dept. Agr. research grantee, 1980—. Mem. Am. Phytopath. Soc. (pres. Potomac div. 1980), Am. Genetic Assn., Am. Soc. Hort. Sci., Crop Sci. Soc. Am. Episcopalian. Current Work: Research on pathogen variability, host-pathogen relationships, and disease resistance in beans, including breeding for disease resistance. Subspecialties: Plant pathology; Plant genetics. Office: Applied Plant Pathology Lab Bldg 004 BARC-W US Dept Agr Beltsville MD 20705*

STEAD, FREDERICK LEE, geologist, consultant; b. Toledo, Dec. 20, 1923; s. Jay Wheeler and Ona K. (Grunder) S.; m. Betty Ellen Leonard, Feb. 4, 1946; children—Michele Lee Stead Lamar, Patricia Lance Stead Sullivan, Ashley Summers, Frederick Lee. B.A., Coll. of Wooster, 1947; M.A., U. Tex., 1950. Lic. geologist, Calif. Instr. geology U. Tex. Austin, 1948-50; dist. geologist Continental Oil Co., Midland, Tex., 1951-54; div. mgr. Ada Oil Co., Midland, 1954-56; chief geologist McAlester Fuel Co., Magnolia, Ark., 1956-60; cons. geologist Los Angeles and Denver, 1960-77; pres. F.L. Stead & Assocs., Inc., Dallas, 1977—; guest lectr. Ark. State Coll., Magnolia, 1957-58; cons. geologist, Magnolia, 1960-62, Houston, 1965-67, Los Angeles, 1968-70; pres. Gt. Lakes Gas Corp., Dallas, 1963-64, Tri-Coast Petroleum, Inc., Los Angeles, 1970-73, Helmet Petroleum, Denver, 1975-76. Contbr. articles to profl. jours. Ark. state chmn. Boys Clubs Am., 1965-66, Magnolia pres., 1967; elder Presbyterian Ch.; bd. dirs. Parkland Residential Sch., El Toro, Calif. Served as 2d lt. USAAF, 1943-45. Fellow Geol. Soc. Am., mem. Am. Assn. Petroleum Geologists, Am. Inst. Profl. Geologists (pres. Calif. sect. 1975, nat. v.p. 1977), Soc. Econ. Paleontologists and Mineralogists, Soc. Mining Engrs. AIME, Petroleum Club Denver, Petroleum Club Dallas, Energy Club Dallas, Sigma Gamma Epsilon. Republican. Current work: Natural gas exploration and development. Subspecialties: Geology; Petroleum geology. Office: FL Stead & Assocs Inc Box 740128 Dallas TX 75374

STEADMAN, JAMES ROBERT, plant pathologist, researcher, educator; b. Cleve., Feb. 7, 1942; s. Jerry E. and Theresa H. (Dunne) S.; m. Sharon A., Mar. 21, 1964; children: Cyndy, Leslye, Tracey, Jason. B.A., Hiram Coll., 1964; M.S., U. Wis., Madison, 1968, Ph.D. in Plant Pathology, 1969. Wis. Alumni Research Found. fellow U. Wis., 1964-65; NIH predoctoral fellow, 1965-69; assoc. prof. plant pathology U. Nebr., Lincoln, 1969—; cons. on bean diseases, vegetable prodn. problems, Australia, U.S., Latin Am. Contbr. numerous articles to sci. jours. Chmn. bd. trustees Nebr. San. and Improvement Dist. 2. Dept. Interior Water Resources grantee, 1972-77; Dept. Agr. Regional Research grantee, 1977-85; Union Pacific Found. grantee, 1980-83; Dept. Agr.-AID Title VII Internat. Program grantee, 1981-85. Mem. Am. Phytopath. Soc., Internat. Soc. Plant Pathology, Bean Improvement Coop., Sigma Xi. Current Work: Epidemiology and control of bean and other vegetable diseases; research, some teaching on epidemiology of plant diseases, primarily beans and cucurbits. Subspecialty: Plant pathology. Office: 406 H Plant Sci Hall U Nebr Lincoln NE 68583

STEADMAN, STEPHEN GEOFFREY, physicist; b. Rochester, N.Y., June 28, 1942; s. Luville T. and Elizabeth (Genung) S.; m. Brigitte M. Kreuzer, Aug. 1, 1975; children—Claudia, Mark. B.S., U. Rochester, 1964; M.S., Rutgers U., 1966, Ph.D., 1969. Asst. prof. MIT, Cambridge, 1975-79, assoc. prof. physics, 1979-82, sr. research scientist, 1982—; chmn. exec. com. Outside Users, Brookhaven Heavy-ion Facility, 1980-84; mem. exec. com. of users Holifield Heavy-ion Research Facility, Oak Ridge, 1984-86, chmn., 1985; mem. exec. com. of users Nat. Superconducting Cyclotron Lab. Mich. State U., 1981. Editor: Fusion Reactions Below The Coulomb Barrier, 1985. Contbr. articles to profl. jours. Mem. Am. Phys. Soc. Am. Assn. Physics Tchrs., AAAS. Episcopalian. Current work: Reaction mechanisms in relativistic heavy-ion nuclear physics. Subspecialty: Nuclear physics. Home: 91 Common St Watertown MA 02172 Office: Room 26-411 MIT Cambridge MA 02139

STEARNS, MARY BETH, physicist; b. Mpls.; m. Martin Stearns; children: Daniel, Richard. Ph.D., Cornell U., 1952. Research assoc. Carnegie Inst. Tech., 1952-57; scientist Gen. Atomic, 1957-60; staff scientist Ford Motor Co., Dearborn, Mich., 1960-81; prof. physics Ariz. State U., Tempe, 1981—; cons. in field. Contbr. articles to profl. jours. Recipient von Humboldt award, W.Ger., 1984. Fellow Am. Phys. Soc., IEEE, Sigma Xi. Current Work: Electronic structure of transition metals compositionally modulated thin films, EXAFS structure analysis, ferromagnetism. Subspecialties: Condensed matter physics; Magnetic physics. Office: Dept Physics Arizona State U Tempe AZ 85287

STEBBING, NOWELL, cell biologist, virologist; b. Copenhagen, Sept. 5, 1941; came to U.S., 1979; s. Lionel Charles and Margarita (Behrenz) S.; m. Birgit Evjen, Sept. 29, 1973; children—Clare Hunter, Zoe Elizabeth, Benjamin. B.Sc., Edinburgh U., Scotland, 1964, Ph.D., 1968. Demonstrator, Edinburgh U., 1967-69; dir. biology Searle Research Labs., High Wycombe, U.K., 1969-79, Genentech Inc., San Francisco, 1979-82; v.p. Amgen, Inc., Thousand Oaks, Calif., 1982—. Contbr. articles to tech. jours. Mem. Am. Soc. Microbiology, Endocrine Soc., Am. Soc. Pharmacology Exptl. Therapeutics, Am. Assn. Immunologists, Fedn. Am. Scientists. Current work: Preclinical and clinical assessment of recombinant DNA derived peptides, interferons, vaccines, erythropoietin; control mechanisms in cellular physiology. Subspecialties: Molecular pharmacology; Virology (medicine). Home: 2821 N Redondo Ave Camarillo CA 93010 Office: Amgen Inc 1900 Oak Terrace Ln Thousand Oaks CA 91320

STEBBINS, GEORGE LEDYARD, emeritus genetics educator; b. Lawrence, N.Y., Jan. 6, 1906; s. George Ledyard and Edith Alden (Candler) S.; m. Margaret Chamberlaine, June 14, 1931 (div. 1958); children: Edith Candler, Robert Lloyd, George Ledyard (dec.); m. Barbara Jean Brumley, July 27, 1958. A.B., Harvard U., 1928, A.M., 1939; Ph.D., Harvard, 1931. Instr. biology Colgate U., 1931-35; jr. geneticist U. Calif., Berkeley, 1935-39, asst. prof. genetics, 1939-40, asso. prof., 1940-47, prof., 1947-50, prof. genetics, Davis, 1950-73, prof. emeritus, 1973—. Author: Processes of Organic Evolution, 1966, The Basis of Progressive Evolution, 1969, Chromosomal Evolution in Higher Plants, 1971, Flowering Plants: Evolution above the Species Level, 1974, others. Guggenheim fellow, 19S4, 60-61; recipient Verrill medal Yale U., 1968; Gold medal Linnean Soc. London, 1973; Nat. Medal of Sci., 1980. Mem. Soc. Study of Evolution (pres. 1950), Bot. Soc. Am. (pres. 1962), Am. Soc. Naturalists (pres. 1969), Calif. Native Plant Soc. (pres. 1966-72), Western Soc. Naturalists (pres. 1976), Internat. Union Biol. Scis. (sec. gen. 19S9-64), Nat. Acad. Scis., Am. Philos. Soc., Am. Acad. Arts and Scis., Genetics Soc. Am., Royal Swedish Acad. Scis., German Leopoldina Acad., Phi Beta Kappa, Sigma Xi. Democrat. Unitarian. Current Work: Evolution of higher plants, especially origin of species and of asexual reproduction. Subspecialty: Evolutionary biology. Office: Dept Genetics U Calif Davis CA 95616

STECK, THEODORE LYLE, physician; b. Chgo., May 3, 1939; s. Irving E. and Mary L. S.; children: David B., Oliver M. B.S. in Chemistry, Lawrence Coll., 1960; M.D., Harvard U., 1964. Intern Beth Israel Hosp., Boston, 1964-65, fellow, 1965-66; research asso. Nat. Cancer Inst., NIH, Bethesda, Md., 1966-68, Harvard U. Med. Sch., Boston, 1968-70; asst. prof. medicine U. Chgo., 1970-74, asst. prof. biochemistry and medicine, 1973-74, asso. prof., 1974-77, prof., 1977—, chmn. dept. biochemistry, 1979-84. Current Work: Structure and function of biological membranes. Subspecialties: Biochemistry (biology); Membrane biology. Office: 920 E 58th St Chicago IL 60637

STECKEL, RICHARD J., physician, educator; b. Scranton, Pa., Apr. 17, 1936; s. Morris Leo and Lucille (Yellin) S.; m. Julie Raskin, June 16, 1960; children—Jan Marie, David Matthew. B.S. magna cum laude, Harvard U., 1957, M.D. cum laude, 1961. Diplomate: Am. Bd. Radiology. Intern UCLA Hosp., 1961-62; resident in radiology Mass. Gen. Hosp., Boston, 1962-65; clin./research asso. Nat. Cancer Inst., 1965-67; mem. faculty UCLA Med. Sch., 1967—, prof. radiol. scis. and radiation oncology, dir. Jonsson Comprehensive Cancer Center, 1974—; pres. Assn. Am. Cancer Insts., 1981. Author two books, over seventy articles in field of radiology and cancer diagnosis. Fellow Am. Coll. Radiology; mem. Radiol. Soc. N. Am., Am. Roentgen Ray Soc. Current Work: New diagnostic methods for cancer. Subspecialties: Diagnostic radiology; Cancer research (medicine). Home: 248 24th St Santa Monica CA 90402 Office: Louis Factor Health Scis Bldg UCLA Center Health Scis Los Angeles CA 90024

STECKER, FLOYD WILLIAM, astrophysicist; b. N.Y.C., Aug. 12, 1942; s. Norman and Helen Lilian (Stern) S.; m. Dorothy Ruth Bick, July 4, 1965; children: Benjamin, Jonathan. B.S., M.I.T., 1963; M.A., Harvard U., 1965, Ph.D., 1968. Research asst. Lab. for Nuclear Sci., M.I.T., 1962-63, teaching asst., 1963; physicist Harvard-Smithsonian Center for Astrophysics, Cambridge, 1963-66, predoctoral intern, 1966-67; Nat. Acad. Sci. postdoctoral research asso. NASA Goddard Space Flight Center, 1967-68, astrophysicist, 1968-77; sr. astrophysicist Lab. High Energy Astrophysics, 1977—. Author: Cosmic Gamma Rays; contbr. articles to profl. jours. Recipient NASA Medal for exceptional sci. achievement, 1973. Fellow Am. Phys. Soc.; mem. Internat. Astron. Union (Commn. on Galactic Structure, Commn. on Cosmology), Am. Astron. Soc., Sigma Xi. Current Work: High energy astrophysics, cosmic ray astrophysics, gamma ray astrophysics, galactic structure, cosmology. Subspecialties: Theoretical astrophysics; Cosmology. Address: Code 660 NASA Goddard Space Flight Center Greenbelt MD 20771

STEELE, GERALD HICKS, chemist; b. Murray Ky., June 24, 1948; s. Carlos Maston and Jean (Hicks) S.; m. Diane Lyons, Jan. 17, 1975 (div. 1984); m. Barbara Socha, Mar. 9, 1985. B.A., cum laude, Murray State U., 1970. Cert. chemist, Ky. Devel. chemist Ebonite, Inc., Hopkinsville, Ky., 1971-73; materials chemist Victor-Dana, Chgo., 1973-74; research chemist Joanna Western Mills, Chgo., 1974-76; chief chemist Debeers Labs. Inc., Addison, Ill., 1976-79; adhesives chemist ESCHEM, Inc., Downers Grove, Ill., 1979-83; sr. research chemist Dexter-Midland, Waukegan, Ill., 1983—. Mem. Am. Chem. Soc. Current work: FDA acceptable food contact coatings, application of new polymer developments. Subspecialty: Organic chemistry. Home: 514 Lakehurst Rd Apt 2R Waukegan IL 60085 Office: Dexter-Midland 1 E Water St Waukegan IL 60085

STEELE, GLENN DANIEL, JR., surg. oncologist, immunologist; b. Balt., June 23, 1944; s. Glenn Daniel and Alice E. S.; m. Lisa LaBoissiere, Nov. 19, 1977; children: Joshua, Kirsten, Lara. B.A., Harvard U., 1966; M.D., N.Y.U., 1970; Ph.D., U. Lund, Sweden, 1975. Diplomate: Am. Bd. Surgery, 1977. Instr. surgery Harvard Med. Sch., 1976-78, asst. prof. surgery, 1978-81, assoc. prof. surgery, 1981-84, McDermott prof. surgery, chmn. dept. surgery New Eng. Deaconess Hosp., 1985—; surg. oncology Sidney Farber Cancer Inst., 1978-79, asst. physician in surg.oncology, 1979—; assoc. in surgery Brigham and Women's Hosp., Boston, 1976-84. Contbr. articles to profl. jours. Nat. Cancer Inst. grantee. Fellow ACS; mem. Am. Assn. Immunologists, Boston Surg. Soc., Fedn. Am. Socs. Exptl. Biology, Soc. Surg. Oncology, Soc. Univ. Surgeons, Phi Beta Kappa, Alpha Omega Alpha. Clubs: Denver Athletic, Boston Tennis and Racquet. Current Work: Clinical oncology and research in tumor biology; clinical specialist in surgical oncology and research in carcinogenesis and immunologic manipulation in attempts to develop effective immunotherapy; chairman National Large Bowel Organ Systems Project, NCI; chairman surgery committee Gastro-Intestinal Study Group. Subspecialties: Surgical oncology; Cellular engineering. Office: 110 Francis St Boston MA 02215

STEELE, JOHN HYSLOP, marine scientist, oceanographic institute administrator; b. Edinburgh, U.K., Nov. 15, 1926; s. Adam and Annie H.; m. Margaret Evelyn Travis, Mar. 2, 1956; 1 son, Hugh. B.Sc., Univ. Coll., London U., 1946, D.Sc., 1964. Marine scientist Marine Lab., Aberdeen, Scotland, 1951-66, sr. prin. sci. officer, 1966-73, dep. dir., 1973-77; dir. Woods Hole Oceanographic Instn., Mass., 1977—, vis. research fellow, 1958, lectr. marine biol. lab., 1967; vis. prof. U. Miami, 1961; mem. NSF panel for internat. Decade of Ocean Exploration, 1972-73, Council Marine Biol. Assn. of U.K., 1974-76, Council Scottish Marine Biol. Assn., 1974-78; mem. Bd. Ocean Sci. and Policy Nat. Research Council; corp. mem. Marine Biol. Lab., Woods Hole, Mass. Author: The Structure of Marine Ecosystems, 1974; Contbr. articles to profl. jours. Served with Brit. Royal Air Force, 1947-49. Recipient Alexander Agassiz medal Nat. Acad. Sci., 1973. Fellow Royal Soc. Edinburgh, Royal Soc. London, Am. Acad. Arts and Scis. Subspecialty: Oceanography. Office: Woods Hole Oceanographic Instn Woods Hole MA 02543

STEELE, OLIVER LEON, plant geneticist, consultant; b. Bloomington, Ill., Apr. 8, 1915; s. Blondee Wood and Mary Vance (Eagle) S.; m. Ruth Holbert, June 21, 1941; children: David, Dennis, Nancy Steele Brokaw. B.S., Ill. Wesleyan U., 1940, Sc.D. (hon.), 1967. Mgr. research dept. Funk Seeds Internat., Bloomington, Ill., 1940-52, assoc. research dir., 1952-57, research dir., 1957-78, v.p., 1963-78, research cons., 1978—; cons. in field. Elder 2d Presbyterian Ch, Bloomington. Mem. AAAS, Am. Soc. Agronomy, Genetics Soc., Am. Genetic Assn. Republican. Lodge: Rotary. Current Work: Cytoplasm interactions; seed improvement in South Asia. Subspecialty: Plant genetics.

STEELMAN, ROBERT JOE, oral and maxillofacial surgeon; b. Richland, Wash., Apr. 11, 1949; s. Earl and Betty Catherine (Young) S.; m. Marie Carol Hobson, Dec. 20, 1980. A.A.S., Columbia Basin Coll., Pasco, Wash., 1969; B.A., U. Wash., 1972; A.M., Washington U., St. Louis, 1974, D.M.D., 1982. Ecology researcher Washington U., 1974-76, med. researcher, 1976-78; resident in oral and maxillofacial surgery Emory U., Atlanta, 1982—. Contbr. articles to profl. jours. Mem. ADA, Am. Assn. Dental Research, Sigma Xi, Omicron Kappa Upsilon. Current Work: Long term effects of therapeutic radiation to the temporomandibular joint and associated structures. Subspecialty: Oral and maxillofacial surgery. Office: Emory U 1462 Clifton Rd Atlanta GA 30322

STEELY, H(ENRY) THOMAS, JR., molecular biologist; b. Dallas, June 5, 1952; s. Henry Thomas and Margaret Ann (Truitt) S.; m. Alice Mae Weaver, Aug. 10, 1974. B.A. in Psychology, U. Tex., 1976; M.S. in Molecular Biology, U. Tex.-Dallas, 1978, Ph.D. in Molecular Biology, 1984. Research asst. U. Tex.-Dallas, 1976-80, postdoctoral fellow, 1985—. Mem. AAAS, Biophys. Soc., Fedn. Am. Scientists. Methodist. Current work: Biophysical properties of viruses, nucleic acids, and proteins. Subspecialties: Molecular biology; Biophysics (physics). Home: 1806 Sherwood Pl Carrollton TX 75006 Office: Dept Molecular Biology U Tex-Dallas PO Box 688 Richardson TX 75083-0688

STEEVES, RICHARD ALLISON, radiation oncologist; b. Fredericksburg, Va., Feb. 2, 1938; s. William Horace and Doris Calkin (Cole) S.; m. Eliane Monique Brunet, Sept. 29, 1965; children: Pascal, Colin, Rachel. M.D., U. Western Ont., 1961; Ph.D., U. Toronto, Ont., Can., 1966. Diplomate: Am. Bd. Radiology. Postdoctoral fellow McMaster U., Hamilton, Ont., 1966-67; assoc. cancer research scientist Roswell Park Meml. Inst., Buffalo, 1967-72; assoc. prof. Albert Einstein Coll. Medicine, Bronx, N.Y., 1972-80; asst. prof. U. Wis.,

Madison, 1980-82, dir. div. radiation oncology, 1982—; dep. dir. Wis. Clin. Cancer Center, 1982—. Contbr. numerous articles to profl. jours. Recipient Rowntree prize U. Western Ont., 1961; Nat. Cancer Inst. grantee, 1972-82. Mem. AAAS, Am. Assn. Cancer Research, Am. Soc. Microbiology, Am. Soc. Therapeutic Radiologists, Exptl. Aircraft Assn. Unitarian. Current Work: Role of hyperthermia in treatment of cancer. Subspecialties: Oncology; Cancer research (medicine). Office: 600 Highland Ave K4/B100 Madison WI 53792

STEFANINI, MARIO, pathologist; b. Chieri, Piedmont, Italy, June 11, 1920; s. Eleuterio and Marie Therese (Trivereau) S.; m. Elizabeth Shields Just, Feb. 12, 1949; children: Marie Therese, Virginia Elizabeth. M.D., U. Rome, 1939; M.Sc., Marquette U., 1947. Diplomate: Am. Bd. Pathology. Asst. physician New Eng. Med. Ctr., Boston, 1949-55; dir. research St. Elizabeth Hosp., Boston, 1956-61; assoc. pathologist St. Joseph Hosp., Chgo., 1962-65; pathologist St. Elizabeth Hosp., Danville, Ill., 1966-79, Humana Hosp. Clinch Valley, Richlands, Va., 1979—; cons. VA Hosp., Boston, 1950-61; asst. prof. Tufts U. Sch. Medicine, 1950-52, prof. medicine, 1952-61. Author: The Hemorrhagic Disorders, 1955, 2nd edit. 1962; editor series: Progress in Clin. Pathology, 1966-81. Served to capt. USAF, 1941-45. Recipient Piccinini prize, 1946; Cert. of Merit Nat. Gastroent. Assn., 1948; Cert. of Merit AMA, 1952; 1st prize Am. Assn. Blood Banks, 1952, 56; Nuffield medal Royal Soc. London, 1979; USPHS sr. research fellow, 1947-49; Damon Runyon clin. Cancer fellow, 1950-52; established investigator Am. Heart Assn., 1952-58. Fellow Internat. Soc. Hematology, Coll. Am. Pathologists, Am. Coll. Nuclear Medicine, Am. Soc. Exptl. Pathology; mem. Coll. Nuclear Physicians, Am. Soc. Clin. Investigation. Roman Catholic. Current Work: Techniques for preparation and transfusion of human platelets; introduction of proteolytic enzymes; discovery of the syndrome of DIC (disseminated intravascular coagulation); present interest: treatment of malignancies through immune technology. Subspecialties: Pathology (medicine); Chemotherapy. Home: 723 Cresswood Dr Richlands VA 24641 Office: Humana Hospital Clinch Valley Community 2949 W Front St Richlands VA 24641

STEFANO, GEORGE B., neurobiologist, researcher; b. N.Y.C., Sept. 11, 1945; s. George and Agnes (Hendrickson) S.; m. Judith Mary Stefano, Aug. 24, 1968; 1 child, Michelle Laura. Ph.D., Fordham U., 1973. Mem. faculty N.Y.C. Community Coll., 1972-79, Medgar Evers Coll., CUNY, 1979-82; assoc. prof. cell biology, chmn. dept. biol. sci. SUNY-Old Westbury, 1982-85, asst. v.p. research, 1985—; pres., dir. East Coast Neurosci. Found., Dix Hills, N.Y., 1977-82; research coordinator dept. anesthesiology St. Joseph Hosp. and Med. Ctr., Paterson, N.J., 1979-82. Contbr. articles to sci. jours. Nat. Acad. Scis. grantee, 1978, 80; NIMH grantee, 1979-83; project dir. ADA MHA-MARC, 1983—. Mem. Soc. Neurosci., N.Y. Acad. Sci., Gerontol. Soc. Am., AAAS. Current Work: Opioid mechanisms in neural tissues; characterization and demonstration of opiate binding sites and pharmacological effects in neural tissues. Subspecialties: Neurobiology; Molecular pharmacology.

STEHLIN, JOHN SEBASTIAN, JR., surgical oncologist; b. Brownsville, Tenn., June 16, 1923; s. John Sebastian and Princess (King) S.; divorced; 1 child, Mary Cleary. M.D., Med. Coll. Wis., 1947; B.S. (hon.), U. Notre Dame; D.S. (hon.), Oral Roberts U. Diplomate Am. Bd. Surgery. Intern, then resident Milw. Hosp., 1947-48, 49-52; resident in pathology Bapt. Hosp., Memphis, 1948-49; surgery fellow Lahey Clinic, Boston, 1952-53, 56-57; sr. surgery fellow U. Tex Anderson Hosp. and Tumor Inst., Houston, 1955-56, surg. staff, 1957-67, asst. prof. surgery, postgrad. sch., 1957-60, asst. surgeon, 1957-60, assoc. prof., 1961-63, assoc. prof. grad. sch. biomed. scis., 1963-67, assoc. surgeon, 1961-67; clin. assoc. prof. Baylor Coll. Medicine, 1967—; surg. staff St. Joseph Hosp., Houston, 1967—; hon. prof. U. Republic Uruguay, 1965; founder, sci. dir. Stehlin Found. Cancer Research. Contbr. numerous articles to profl. jours. Served to capt. USAF, 1953-55. Decorated Commendation Ribbon USAF; recipient Nat. Humanitarian award B'nai B'rith, 1982. Mem. Am. Assn. Cancer Research, AAAS, ACS, AMA, Cancer Assn. Argentina (hon.), Cancer Soc. Chile (hon.), Harris County Med. Soc., Houston Surg. Soc., Internat. Platform Assn., N.Y. Acad. Scis., Pan Am. Med. Assn., Salem Surg. Soc. (hon.), Soc. Dermatology Uruguay (hon.), Soc. Surg. Oncology Inc., Southwestern Surg. Congress, So. Med. Assn., Surg. Soc. Chile (hon.), Tex. Med. Assn., Tex. Surg. Soc., Western Surg. Assn., Royal Soc. Medicine (affiliate). Current work: Oncology cancer research; surgery. Subspecialties: Oncology; Surgery. Office: 1315 Calhoun Suite 1800 Houston TX 77002

STEHNEY, ANN KATHRYN, mathematician; b. Oak Ridge, June 30, 1946; d. Andrew Frank and Virginia Lorraine (Allen) S.; children—Jessica Stehney Charlap, Emily Elizabeth Stehney Charlap. A.B., Bryn Mawr Coll., 1967; M.S., SUNY-Stony Brook, 1969; Ph.D., 1971. Asst. prof. math. Wellesley Coll., Mass., 1971-77, assoc. prof., 1977-83, prof., 1983—, dir. ednl. research and devel., 1976-78, chmn. dept. math., 1977-78, 1980-81; vis. scholar Enrico Fermi Inst., U. Chgo., 1974-75; vis. assoc. prof. SUNY, Stony Brook, 1981-82; mem. research staff communications research div. Inst. for Def. Analyses, Princeton, N.J., 1983—. Editor: (with others) Selected Papers in Geometry, 1979. Contbr. articles, reviews to profl. jours. Mem. Math. Assn. Am. (chmn. editorial com. on geometry 1975-78), Am. Math. Soc., Sigma Xi. Club: Bryn Mawr (Princeton and Boston). Current work: Analysis and statistical studies in communications, applied linear algebra and combinatorics. Subspecialty: Applied mathematics. Office: Inst for Def Analyses Thanet Rd Princeton NJ 08540

STEIHAUG, TROND, mathematical science educator; b. Lillehammer, Norway, Aug. 6, 1950; came to U.S., 1977, naturalized, 1977; s. Arne and Signe S.; m. Nina Naess, Aug. 19, 1972; children: Ole Martin, Espen. Candidatus Magisterii, U. Oslo, 1973, Candidatus Realium, 1975; M.A., Yale U., 1980, Ph.D., 1981. Asst. prof. math. sci. U. Oslo, 1976-77; research assoc. Chalmers U. Tech., Gothenburg, Sweden, 1977; asst. prof. math. sci. Rice U., 1981—; cons. Mobil Co., Dallas. Mem. Soc. Indsl. and Applied Math., ACM, Ops. Research Soc. Am., Math. Programming Soc. Current Work: Large scale nonlinear programming. Subspecialties: Numerical analysis (computer science); Operations research (mathematics). Office: Rice U Math Sci Dept PO Box 1892 Houston TX 77251

STEIN, DAVID ERIC, air force officer, physicist; b. Jacksonville, Fla., Jan. 13, 1950; s. Stanley W. and Dorothy J. (Lilley) S.; m. Joanne Marie Knott, Nov. 4, 1983. B.S., U. Fla., 1971, M.S., 1977, postgrad.; grad. Air Command and Staff Coll., 1982. Research and teaching asst. U. Fla., Gainesville, 1971-76; commd. lt. U.S. Army, 1977; commd. capt. U.S. Air Force, 1979; physicist Rome Air Devel. Ctr., Griffiss AFB, N.Y., 1979-81, MIT Lincoln Lab., Hanscom AFB, Mass. and Holloman AFB, N.Mex., 1981-82, 6585th Test Group, Holloman AFB, N.Mex., 1983—; part-time coll. faculty, 1982—. Contbr. articles to profl. jours. Mem. U.S. Congl. Adv. Bd. of Am. Security Council, Washington and Boston, 1981—. Mem. Am. Phys. Soc., Am. Assn. Physics Tchrs., Res. Officers Assn., IEEE, Air Force Assn. Republican. Current work: Electromagnetic scattering and radar backscatter, to include use of quantum-mechanics formalism in electromagnetic scattering, polarimetry, glint, surface waves and other scattering mechanisms, measurement problems. Subspecialties: Theoretical physics; Electrical engineering. Office: 6585th Test Group Holloman AFB NM 88330

STEIN, GEORGE NATHAN, radiologist, educator; b. Phila., Aug. 11, 1917; s. Samuel M. and Marie B. S.; m. Hazel Gloria Gould, Aug. 18, 1948; children—Stephen G., Eric J., James M. B.A., U. Pa., 1938; M.D., Jefferson Med. Coll., 1942; postgrad., Sch. Medicine, U. Pa., 1946. Asso. radiologist Grad. Hosp. U. Pa., 1948-60, asst. dir. dept. radiology, 1960-71; dir. dept. radiology Presbyn. U. Pa. Med. Center and prof. radiology U. Pa., 1971—; Prof. extraordinaire Javeriana U., Bogota, Colombia, 1960; cons. VA Hosp., Wilmington, Del., 1968-70. Author 3 books.; Contbr. numerous articles to profl. jours. Served with M.C. AUS, 1943-46. Fellow Am. Coll. Radiology; mem. Phila. Roentgen Ray Soc. (pres. 1968-69), Am. Roentgen Ray Soc., Tex. Radiol. Soc. (hon.), Philadelphia County, Pa. State med. socs., Radiol. Soc. N.Am., AMA. Subspecialties: Gastroenterology; Diagnostic radiology. Home: 544 Howe Rd Merion Station PA 19066 Office: 51 N 39th St Philadelphia PA 19104

STEIN, IRA DAVID, physician; b. N.Y.C., Mar. 13, 1955; s. Harry S. and Freida (Lagman) S.; m. Shirley B. Miller, Aug. 16, 1958; children: Joel, Tamara Judith, Shira Robin. B.S. in Biology, Rutgers U., 1956; M.D., George Washington U., 1960. Intern USPHS Hosp., San Francisco, 1960-61; resident in internal medicine VA Hosp., Coral Gables, Fla., 1963-66; USPHS fellow Mt. Sinai Hosp. Services, City Hosp. Ctr., Elmhurst, N.Y., 1966-68, clin. asst. hematology, 1968-69; staff physician VA Hosp., East Orange, N.J., 1969-81, chief of medicine, Erie, Pa., 1981—; asst. prof. medicine Coll. Medicine and Dentistry N.J., Newark, 1969-75, assoc. prof. medicine, 1975-81. Contbr. chpt. to book. Served with USPHS, 1961-63. Fellow ACP; mem. AAAS, Am. Soc. Clin. Research, Am. Soc. Hematology, Sigma Xi. Democrat. Jewish. Current Work: Metabolic diseases of bones and their structural and mechanical consequences. Subspecialty: Hematology. Home: 135 E 38th St Blvd Erie PA 16501 Office: VA Med Ctr 135 E 38th St Blvd Erie PA 16501

STEIN, JEFFREY LEE, marine biologist, researcher; b. Tokyo, Mar. 28, 1955; came to U.S., 1955; s. David Jack and Nobuko (Takamura) S.; B.S., Calif. State U., 1979, M.S., 1983. Research assoc. Occidental Coll., Los Angeles, 1979—; cons. Vantuna Research Group, Los Angeles, 1979—. Mem. AAAS, Western Soc. Naturalists. Current work: The influence of subtidal hydrothermal vents on invertebrate community ecology, the role of sulfur-oxidizing bacteria in the nutrition of subtidal invertebrates. Subspecialty: Marine biology. Office: Occidental Coll Dept Biology 1600 Campus Rd Los Angeles CA 90041

STEIN, KONRAD MARK, physics educator; b. Prarie View, Tex., Sept. 14, 1952; s. Andrew Mark and Ruth Katherine (Hall) S. B.S., U. Calif.-San Diego, 1974; Ph.D., U. Calif.-Riverside, 1982; M.S., Calif. State U.-Los Angeles, 1978. Systems engr., Jet Propulsion Lab., Pasadena, Calif., 1974-77; instr. physics Riverside City Coll., Calif., 1978-80, Calif. State U., 1980-81; prof. physics Goldenwest Coll., Huntington Beach, Calif., 1983—; vis. prof. physics Qing Hua U., Beijing, People's Republica China, 1984-85. Mem. Am. Phys. Soc., N.Y. Acad. Scis. Current work: Phase transitions and quantum effects in superconductors and superfluids by the functional integral method. Subspecialty: Condensed matter physics. Home: 4821 Parkglen Ave Los Angeles CA 90043 Office: Golden West Coll 15744 Golden West St Huntington Beach CA 92647

STEIN, RICHARD STEPHEN, chemistry educator; b. N.Y.C., Aug. 21, 1925; s. Isidor and Florence (Lewengood) S.; m. Judith Elma Balise, May 27, 1951; children—Linda Ann, Anne Marie, Carol Joan, Lisa Jean. B.S., Poly. Inst. Bklyn., 1945; M.A., Princeton U., 1948, Ph.D., 1949. Postdoctoral fellow Cambridge U., 1948-49; research asso. Princeton U., 1949-50; asst. prof. U. Mass., Amherst, 1950-57, asso. prof., 1957-59, prof., 1959-61, Commonwealth prof., 1961-80, Goessman prof. chemistry, 1980—, founder, dir. Polymer Research Inst., 1961—; cons. Monsanto Co., Johnson & Johnson, Xerox Corp., Upjohn Corp., Exxon Corp., Raychem Corp. Co-editor: Electromagnetic Scattering, 1967, Structure and Properties of Polymer Films, 1973; author numerous sci. articles. Recipient Internat. award Soc. Plastics Engrs., 1969, Bingham award Rheology Soc., 1972. Mem. Am. Chem. Soc. (Bordon award 1972, Polymer Chemistry award 1983), Am. Phys. Soc. (award in high polymer physics 1976), Rheology Soc., AAAS, AAUP, Sigma Xi. Founder sci. rheo-optics of polymers. Subspecialty: Polymer chemistry. Office: U Mass Dept Chemistry Amherst MA 01002

STEIN, SCOTT ALLEN, consulting engineer; b. Detroit, June 12, 1953; s. Wesley Herman and Rachel Lenore (Allen) S. B.S., U. Mich., 1977, M.S., 1982. Asso. systems programmer Burroughs Corp., Plymouth, Mich., 1978-80, systems programmer, Paoli, Pa., 1980-81, sr. systems programmer, 1981-82, project systems programmer, 1982-84; cons. engr. Honeywell Info. Systems, Phoenix, 1984—. Mem. Fedn. Am. Scientists, Assn. Computing Machinery, IEEE. Current Work: Networking architectures, distributed processing, communications protocols, protocol representation, distributed operating systems. Subspecialties: Distributed systems and networks; Operating systems. Office: PO Box 8000 AZ 13-H32 Phoenix AZ 85066

STEINBACH, ARDEN LYNN, physicist; b. Austin, Minn., Apr. 24, 1948; s. Merton Elger and Anna Marie (Plagge) S.; m. Suzanne Barbara Fields, June 17, 1972; children—Carl, Elizabeth. B.S. in Physics, Calif. Tech., 1970; Ph.D. in Applied Physics, Stanford U., 1978. Postdoctoral fellow IBM Research Lab., San Jose, Calif., 1976-78; research fellow Fritz Haber Inst., Berlin, Fed. Republic Germany, 1978-80; vis. asst. prof. elec. engring. U. Ill., Urbana, 1981-82; asst. prof. applied physics, elec. engring. Oreg. Grad. Ctr., Beaverton, 1982-84; pres. Oreg. Applied Research, Portland, 1984—. Contbr. articles to profl. jours. Mem. Am. Phys. Soc.; Optical Soc. Am., Sigma Xi. Current work: Neutron microscopy, x-ray microscopy and holography, three dimensional imaging, radiation damage, gamma-ray laser, computer simulation. Subspecialties: Microscopy; Medical physics. Home: 8405 SW 89th Ave Portland OR 97223 Office: Oreg Applied Research 11855 SW Ridgecrest Dr Beaverton OR 97005

STEINBACK, KATHERINE ELLEN, biochemist, educator; b. Berkeley, Calif., July 10, 1949; d. Edward William and Vera Madeline (Art) S. B.A., U. Calif.-Berkeley, 1971; M.A., Ph.D., Harvard U., 1977. Postdoctoral fellow U. Ill., Urbana, 1977-80; asst. prof. Wellesley Coll., Mass., 1980-81; vis. asst. prof. plant research lab. Mich. State U., East Lansing, 1981-82; staff sci. Advanced Genetic Sci. Inc., Oakland, Calif., 1982—; cons. Advanced Genetic Sci. Inc., Oakland, 1981-82. Contbr. articles to profl. jours. Mem. Am. Soc. Plant Physiologists, Weed Sci. Soc. Am., Internat. Weed Sci. Soc., Am. Chem. Soc. (pesticide div.), Sigma Xi. Current work: Mechanism of herbicide action and herbicide resistance in plants; characterization of stress damage in plants and recovery from stress as related to the photosynthetic apparatus. Subspecialties: Biochemistry (biology); Photosynthesis. Office: Advanced Genetic Sci Inc 6701 San Pablo Ave Oakland CA 94608

STEINBERG, ELLIS PHILIP, chemistry administrator, researcher; b. Chgo., Mar. 26, 1920; s. Solomon and Sarah (Saphir) S.; m. Esther Abraham, Dec. 16, 1944; children—Sheryl Diane, David Alan, Deborah Leah. S.B., U. Chgo., 1941, Ph.D., 1947. Govt. chemist Elwood Ordnance, Joliet, Ill., 1941-43; research chemist, Manhattan Project, Chgo., 1943-46; chemist Argonne Nat. Lab., Ill., 1947-58, sr. chemist, 1958—, sect. head, 1974-82, dir. chem. div., 1982—. Contbr. articles to profl. jours. Guggenheim fellow, 1952-58. Mem. Energy Task Force, Village Park Forest, Ill., Environ. Conservation Commn., Am. Chem. Soc. (div. chmn. 1974-75), Am. Phys. Soc., AAAS, Sigma Xi. Jewish. Club: Park Forest Racquet. Lodge: B'nai B'rith. Current work: Nuclear fission and high energy nuclear reactions; administration of chemistry research. Subspecialty: Nuclear chemistry. Office: Argonne Nat Lab 9700 S Cass Ave Argonne IL 60439

STEINBERG, FREDERICK, mathematician, engineering research analyst; b. Bklyn., Feb. 20, 1924; s. Ephriam and Helen (Steinberg) S. B.S. in Sci, L.I. U., 1949; M.A. in Math, NYU, 1951; diploma in local govt., U. Calif.-Berkeley, 1971. Cert. secondary sch. teaching, N.Y., Calif. Mathematician Aerojet-Gen. Corp., Azusa and Sacramento, Calif., 1951-58; data systems analyst TRW Systems, Inc., Los Angeles, 1958-62; research analyst N.Am. Rockwell/Space, Downey, Calif., 1962-66; ops. researcher Lockheed Missiles & Space Co., Sunnyvale, Calif., 1966-70; data systems analyst Space Group Hughes Aircraft Co., Los Angeles, 1973-81, Hughes Aircraft Co. (Electro-Optical and Data Systems Group), El Segundo, Calif., 1981—; tchr., cons. Santa Clara Unifed Sch. Dist., 1970-71; mgmt. systems analyst City Adminstrv. Office, City of Los Angeles, 1972. Served in USAAF, 1943-46. N.Y. State Bd. Edn. scholar, 1946. Mem. AIAA, IEEE (sr.). Republican. Jewish. Clubs: Mulholland (Los Angeles); NYU (N.Y.C.). Current Work: Electro-optical (laser) engineering applications to tactical weapon systems, computer reporting systems for management visibility and control. Subspecialties: Operations research (engineering); Systems engineering. Home: 933 N Cedar St 13 Inglewood CA 90302 Office: Hughes Aircraft Co Bldg El 2000 El Segundo Blvd El Segundo CA 90245

STEINBERG, ROBERT, mathematician. Prof. dept. math. UCLA. Elected mem. Nat. Acad. scis., 1985. . Office: Dept Math UCLA Los Angeles CA 90024*

STEINER, BRUCE WATSON, materials scientist; b. Oberlin, Ohio, May 14, 1931; s. Luke Eby and Helen Annette (Watson) S.; m. Ruth Piette, Jan. 1, 1960; children: Jonathan, Miriam. A.B., Oberlin Coll., 1953; Ph.D., Princeton U., 1956. Research assoc. U. Chgo., 1958-61; research scientist Nat. Bur. Standards, 1961-69; chief Interdiv. Nat. Bur. Standards Task Group for the Candella, 1969-71, research scientist, 1971-74, program analyst office of the dir., 1974-76; program officer atomic and material physics NSF, 1976-78; chmn. energy standards planning task force Nat. Bur. Standards, 1977; spl. asst. for long range planning Center for Material Sci., 1977-85, inorganic materials div., 1985—; chmn. U.S. Nat. Com., Internat. Com. for Optics. Contbr. articles to profl. jours. Fellow Optical Soc. Am., Am. Inst. Chemists; mem. Am. Phys. Soc., Am. Chem. Soc., AAAS, N.Y. Acad. Scis. Current Work: Development of programs in materials for advanced optics. Home: 6624 Barnaby St NW Washington DC 20015 Office: Nat Bur Standards Gaithersburg MD 20899

STEINER, DONALD FREDERICK, biochemist, physician, educator; b. Lima, Ohio, July 15, 1930; s. Willis A. and Katherine (Hoegner) S. B.S. in Chemistry and Zoology, U. Cin., 1952; M.S. in Biochemistry, U. Chgo., 1956, M.D., 1956; D.Med.Sci. (hon), U. Umea, 1973, U. Ill., 1984. Intern, King County Hosp., Seattle, 1956-57; USPHS postdoctoral research fellow, asst. medicine U. Wash. Med. Sch., 1957-59, asst. medicine, med. resident, 1959-60; mem. faculty U. Chgo. Med. Sch., 1960—, A.N. Pritzker prof. biochemistry and medicine, 1971—, chmn. dept. biochemistry, 1973-79; Jacobaeus lectr., Oslo, 1970, E.F.F. Copp Meml. lectr., La Jolla, Calif., 1971. Co-editor: The Endocrine Pancreas, 1972, discoverer proinsulin. Recipient Gairdner award, Toronto, 1971; Hans Christian Hagedorn medal Steensen Meml. Hosp., Copenhagen, 1970; Lilly award, 1969; Ernst Oppenheimer award, 1970; Diaz-Cristobal award Internat. Diabetes Fedn., 1973; Banting medal Am. Diabetes Assn., 1976, Brit. Diabetes Assn., 1981; Passano award, 1979; Wolf prize in Medicine, 1985. Mem. Nat. Acad. Scis., Am. Soc. Biol. Chemists, AAAS, Biochem. Soc., Am. Diabetes Assn. (50th Anniversary medallion 1972), Am. Acad. Arts and Scis., Sigma Xi, Alpha Omega Alpha. Club: Innominates (U. Chgo.). Current work: Production of insulin and related hormones; processing of peptide precursors; gene abnormalities in diabetes. Subspecialties: Endocrinology; Genetics and genetic engineering (medicine). Home: 2626 N Lakeview Ave Apt 2508 Chicago IL 60614

STEINER, ROBERT FRANK, physical biochemist, educator; b. Manila, Philippines, Sept. 29, 1926; came to U.S., 1933; s. Frank and Clara Nell (Weems) S.; m. Ethel Mae Fisher, Nov. 3, 1956; children: Victoria, Laura. A.B., Princeton U., 1947; Ph.D., Harvard U., 1950. Chemist Naval Med. Research Inst., Bethesda, Md., 1950-70, chief lab. phys. biochemistry, 1965-70; prof. chemistry U. Md., Balt., 1970—, chmn. dept. chemistry, 1974—; mem. biophysics study sect. NIH, 1976. Author: Life Chemistry, 1968, Excited States of Proteins and Nucleic Acids, 1971, The Chemistry of Living Systems, 1981, Excited States of Biopolymers, 1983; editor: Jour. Biophys. Chemistry, 1972—. Served with AUS, 1945-47. Recipient Superior Civilian Achievement award Dept. Def., 1966; NSF research grantee, 1971; NIH research grantee, 1973. Fellow Washington Acad. Sci.; mem. Am. Soc. Biol. Chemists. Club: Princeton (Washington). Current Work: Physical properties of proteins and nucleic acids; fluorescence; allosteric enzymes. Subspecialties: Biophysical chemistry; Biochemistry (biology). Home: 2609 Turf Valley Rd Ellicott City MD 21043 Office: 5401 Wilkens Ave Baltimore MD 21228

STEINER, ROBERT VICTOR, physicist, educator; b. San Francisco, May 19, 1956; s. Eric Edwin and Rita (Lucas) S. B.S., U. Calif.-Berkeley, 1978; M.S., M. Phil., Yale U., 1980, Ph.D., 1985. Teaching fellow Yale U., New Haven, 1978-79, research asst., 1980-85; mem. tech. staff MIT, Cambridge, 1983—. Contbr. articles to physics jours. Mem. Am. Phys. Soc. Current work: Experimental elementary particle physics; investigations of Quantum number flow in strong interactions, identification of relativistic charged particles, flavor correlations between final state particles. Subspecialty: Particle physics. Office: Dept Physics Yale U 217 Prospect St New Haven CT 06520

STEINER, WILLIAM WALLACE MOKAHI, population geneticist, consultant; b. Honolulu, Nov. 16, 1942; s. Charles William and Florence Wahine O'Mau Haleakala (Vera Cruz) S.; m. Judith Ann Matthews, June 26, 1964; children: Angela June, Shawna Lynne. A.S., Boise State Coll., 1964; B.A., U. Hawaii, 1970; Ph.D., 1974. Research asst. Hawaii Internat. Biol. project, Honolulu, 1972-74; asst. prof. dept. genetics U. Ill., Urbana, 1974-81; assoc. research scientist Ill. Natural History Survey, Champaign, 1981—; cons. S.E. Asian Ministers of Edn. Orgn., 1981—. Lead editor: Recent Developments in the Genetics of Insect Disease Vectors, 1982; contbr. articles to profl. jours. Grantee Hasselblad Found., Sweden, 1981-83; Grantee Dept. Energy and Natural Resources, 1982-84; Grantee Rockefeller Found., 1980; Grantee NIH, NSF, 1976-78. Mem. Genetics Soc. Am., Am. Genetics Assn., AAAS, Soc. Study Evolution, Am. Mosquito Control Assn. Roman Catholic. Current Work: Conducting research in the areas of genetics of insect disease vectors and conservation of genetic resources in natural populations; major interests ecological genetics, genetic biochemical polymorphisms, environment-genotype interaction. Subspecialties: Genetics and genetic engineering (biology); Systematics. Office: Ill Natural History Survey 607 E Peabody St Champaign IL 61820

STEINFELS, GEORGE FRANCIS, pharmacologist; b. Newark, June 22, 1954; s. George G. and Helen (Skutack) S.; m. Alison B. Barnat, Aug. 20, 1978. B.A. in Biology, Johns Hopkins U., 1976; Ph.D., U. Md., Balt., 1980. Instr. pharmacology, research asst. U. Md. Sch. Pharmacy, Balt., 1977-80; vis. research fellow dept. psychology Princeton U., 1980—. Contbr. articles to profl. jours. Issac E. Emerson fellow, 1979; NIH fellow, 1981; Am. Phils. Soc. grantee, 1981. Mem. Am. Soc. Pharmacology and Exptl. Therapeutics, Soc. Neurosci., AAAS, N.Y. Acad. Scis., Brit. Brain Research Assn., European Brain and Behavior Soc., Rho Chi. Club: River Rd. Rangers' Soccer (New Brunswick, N.J.). Current Work: Effects of psychoactive drugs on brain and behavior; neurophysiological recording of single cells in behaving animals; drug addiction in experimental animals/neurophysiology and pharmacology of sleep. Subspecialties: Pharmacology; Neuropharmacology. Home: Faculty Rd Hibben Apt 5F Princeton NJ 08540 Office: Princeton U Dept Psychology Green Hall Princeton NJ 08544

STEINITZ, LOUIS JOSEPH, mech. engr.; b. Balt., Sept. 17, 1920; s. Louis Adam and Elizabeth Mary (Benda) S.; m. Helen Mary, June 12, 1948; children: Mary Ellen, Kathleen, Paul, Louis, Anne. B.S.M.E., U. Md., 1950; B.S.E.E., Johns Hopkins U., 1960. Registered profl. engr., Md. Mech. engr. Indsl. Research Labs., Balt., 1950-55, Aeronca Mfg. Corp., Balt., 1955-65; sr. staff engr. Communications div. Bendix, Balt., 1965—. Adv. Balt. council Boy Scouts Am. Served with USN, 1943-46. Mem. ASME, Soc. Automotive Engrs. Club: KC. Subspecialty: Mechanical engineering. Home: 1229 Gleneagle Rd Baltimore MD 21239 Office: 1300 E Joppa Rd Baltimore MD 21204

STEINMAN, CHARLES ROBERT, medical educator, researcher; b. N.Y.C., Sept. 3, 1938; s. Alan and Estelle S.; m. Heidi Sims Fiske, Jan. 8, 1978. A.B., Princeton U., 1959; M.D., Columbia U., 1963. Staff assoc. NIH, Bethesda, Md., 1965-67; fellow in rheumatology Columbia U., N.Y.C., 1967-68, 69-70; asst. prof. Mt. Sinai Sch. Medicine, N.Y.C., 1970-77, assoc. prof., 1977-83; prof. medicine SUNY-Downstate Med. Ctr., Bklyn., 1983—. Served to lt. comdr. USPHS, 1965-67. Mem. Am. Rheumatology Assn., N.Y. Rheumatology Assn., Am. Assn. Immunology, Harvey Soc., AAAS, N.Y. Acad. Scis. Current work: Research and teaching in rheumatology with special interest in immunology and molecular biology. Subspecialties: Internal medicine; Immunology (medicine). Office: SUNY-Downstate Med Ctr PO Box 42 450 Clarkson Ave Brooklyn NY 11203

STEINMAN, STUART LEONARD, emergency physician, biomedical engineering researcher; b. N.Y.C., July 7, 1951; s. Beartram Quat and Dorothy (Baum) S. B.S., M.E., Tufts U., 1972; M.D., SUNY-Stony Brook, 1976. Intern Highland Hosp., Oakland, Calif., 1976-77; attending physician emergency room Lincoln Hosp., Bronx, N.Y., 1978-80; instr. emergency medicine N.Y. Med. Coll., 1979-80; gen. practice medicine, Bklyn., 1980-82; emergency room physician Meml. Hosp. of Green County, Catskill, N.Y., 1982-83, chief emergency dept. 1983-84; attending physician, assoc. dir. emergency dept. Marlborough Hosp., Mass., 1984—; spl. lectr. dept. community medicine SUNY-Stony Brook, 1980; med. dir. Crown Heights summer program, Bklyn., 1981. Mem. IEEE, Engring. in Medicine and Biology, N.Y. Acad. Scis., Am. Coll. Emergency Physicians, AMA. Jewish. Current work: Development of software for emergency room diagnosis and treatment combining elements of artificial intelligence, data base management and algorithms in real time interactive mode. Subspecialties: Critical care; Artificial intelligence.

STEINWAY, WILLIAM JOSEPH, electrical engineer; b. Los Angeles, Jan. 20, 1944; s. Elmo V. and Frances (Kautzman) S.; m. Sherry Jane Andrews, Mar. 22, 1969; children—Keith, David, Diana. B.S.E.E., Loyola U., 1966; M.S.E.E., U. Ariz.-Tucson, 1968; Ph.D., So. Methodist U., 1971. Mem. tech. staff MIT Lincoln Lab, Lexington, Mass., 1971-79; sr. research engr. Ga. Tech./EES, Atlanta, 1979-83; v.p. Gulf Applied Research, Marietta, Ga., 1983—; chmn. bd. Spectrum Research Group, Marietta, 1984—; cons. Ga. Tech./Radar Lab., Atlanta, 1983—. Contbr. articles to profl. jours. Recipient Cert. of Recognition for creative devel. and tech. NASA, 1982. Mem. IEEE, ASTM, Eta Kappa Nu. Republican. Episcopalian. Current work: Research and development in electromagnetics, applications of radar technology to measurements, instrumentation and testing. Remote sensing using electromagnetics (radar). Subspecialties: Electrical engineering; Electronics. Home: 4535 Kings Lake Dr Marietta GA 30067 Office: Gulf Applied Research 2260 Northwest Pkwy Suite S Marietta GA 30067

STEITZ, JOAN ARGETSINGER, molecular biophysics and biochemistry educator; b. Mpls., Jan. 26, 1941; d. Glenn D. and Elaine A. (Magnusson) Argetsinger; m. Thomas A. Steitz, Aug. 20, 1966; 1 son, Jonathan. B.S., Antioch Coll., Yellow Springs, Ohio, 1963; Ph.D., Harvard U., 1967. Asst. prof. molecular biophysics and biochemistry Yale U., New Haven, 1970-74, assoc. prof., 1974-78, prof., 1978—. Editorial bd.: Molecular/Cell Biology; contbr. numerous articles to profl. jours. NSF fellow, 1967-69; Jane Coffin Childs fellow, 1969-70; NIH grantee, 1979—; recipient Passano Found. Young Scientist award, 1975, Eli Lilly award, 1976, U.S. Steel Found. award in molecular biology, 1982. Fellow AAAS, Am. Acad. Arts and Scis.; mem. Nat. Acad. Scis., Am. Soc. Biol. Chemists. Current Work: Structure and function of small ribonucleoprotein complexes from Eukaryotes, control of transcription and translation, RNA processing. Subspecialties: Molecular biology; Gene actions. Office: Molecular Biophysics and Biochemistry Yale U PO Box 3333 New Haven CT 06510

STEMMLER, EDWARD JOSEPH, physician, university dean; b. Phila., Feb. 15, 1929; s. Edward C. and Josephine (Heitzmann) S.; m. Joan C. Koster, Dec. 27, 1958; children: Elizabeth, Margaret, Edward C., Catherine, Joan. B.A., La Salle Coll., Phila., 1950; M.D., U. Pa., 1960; Sc.D. (hon.), Ursinus Coll., 1977, LaSalle Coll., 1983. Diplomate: Am. Bd. Internal Medicine. Intern U. Pa. Hosp., 1960-61, med. resident, 1961-63, fellow in cardiology, 1963-64, chief med. resident, 1964-65, chief med. outpatient dept., 1966-67; chief of medicine U. Pa. Med. Service, VA Hosp., Phila., 1967-73; cons. pulmonary disease VA Hosp., Phila., 1973—, mem. deans com., 1974—; cons. pulmonary disease Phila. Gen. Hosp., 1973-76; NIH postdoctoral research trainee, dept. physiology Grad. Div. Medicine, U. Pa., 1965-67, instr. medicine, 1964-66, asso. in medicine, 1966-67; asso. in physiology Grad. Div. Medicine, 1967-72, asst. prof. medicine, 1967-70, asso. prof., 1970-74, prof., 1974—, Robert G. Dunlop prof., 1981—; asso. dean Univ. Hosp. (Sch. Medicine), 1973, asso. dean student affairs, 1973-75, acting dean, 1974-75, dean, 1975—; dir. Rorer Group, Inc.; Mem. Gov.'s Com. on Health Edn., 1974-76; mem. Nat. Bd. Med. Examiners, 1974-76; mem. ednl. policy com. Nat. Fund for Med. Edn., 1975-77; mem. policy governing bd. Advanced Tech. Ctr. Southeastern Pa., 1975-77; mem. long range planning project Nat. Library Medicine Panel 5, 1985; mem. Commonwealth Fund Task Force on Acad. Health Ctr., 1984. Contbr. articles to med. jours. Chmn. Pa. Dean's Com., 1976—; bd. govs. Mid-Eastern Regional Med. Library Services, 1977—, chmn., 1978-81; mem. bd. visitors U. Pitts. Sch. Medicine, 1980—. Served with Chem. Corps U.S. Army, 1951-53. Decorated Commendation medal; recipient Frederick A. Packard award, 1960, Albert Einstein Med. Center staff award, 1960, Roche award, 1960. Fellow ACP (treas., chmn. investment com. 1975-80, master 1985); mem. AMA (health policy agenda), Phila. County Med. Soc., Am. Heart Assn., Am., Pa. thoracic socs., Am. Fedn. for Clin. Research, Assn. Am. Med. Colls. (ad hoc external exam. rev. com. 1980—, exec. council 1980—, council of deans adminstrv. bd. 1980—, chmn. council of deans 1983-84, chmn. elect 1985), Coll. of Physicians of Phila. (bd. censors 1979—, council 1979—), Laennec Soc., Am. Clin. and Climatological Soc., John Morgan Soc., Alpha Omega Alpha. Republican. Mem. Christian Ch. Subspecialties: Internal medicine; Pulmonary medicine. Home: 139 E Wynnewood Rd Merion PA 19066 Office: 36th and Hamilton Walk U Pa Philadelphia PA 19104

STENCHEVER, MORTON ALBERT, physician, educator; b. Paterson, N.J., Jan. 25, 1931; s. Harold and Lena (Suresky) S.; m. Diane Bilsky, June 19, 1955; children: Michael A., Marc R., Douglas A. A.B., NYU, 1951; M.D., U. Buffalo, 1956. Intern Mt. Sinai Hosp., 1956-57; resident obstetrics and gynecology Columbia-Presbyn. Med. Center, N.Y.C., 1957-60; asst. prof., Oglebey Research fellow Case-Western Res. U., Cleve., 1962-66, asso. prof. dept. reproductive biology, 1967-70; dir. Case-Western Res. U. (Tissue Culture Lab.), 1965-70; coordinator Case-Western Res. U. (Phase II Med. Sch. program), 1969-70; prof., chmn. dept. obstetrics-gynecology U. Utah Med. Sch., Salt Lake City, 1970-77, U. Wash. Sch. Medicine, Seattle, 1977—; test com. chmn. for Ob-Gyn Nat. Bd. Med. Examiners, 1979-82. Author: Labor: Workbook in Obstetrics, 1968, Human Sexual Behavior: A Workbook in Reproductive Biology, 1970, Human Cytogenics: A Workbook in Reproductive Biology, 1973, Introductory Gynecology: A Workbook in Reproductive Biology, 1974; Contbr. articles to profl. jours. Served to capt. USAF, 1960-62. Fellow Am. Coll. Obstetricians and Gynecologists (com. on residency edn. 1974-80, learning resource commn. 1980—, vice chmn. 1982-83, chmn. prolog self-assessment program 1982—), Am. Assn. Obstetricians and Gynecologists, Am. Gynecol. Soc., Pacific Coast Ob-Gyn Soc.; mem. Assn. Profs. Gynecology and Obstetrics (chmn. steering com. teaching methods in obstetrics and gynecology 1970-79, v.p. 1975—, pres. 1983-84), AMA, AAAS, Pacific Northwest Obstetrics-Gynecology Soc., Wash. State Med. Assn., Seattle Gynec. Soc. (v.p. 1981, pres.-elect 1982, pres. 1982-83), Pacific Coast Obstet.-Gynecol. Soc., Am. Soc. Human Genetics, Central Assn. Obstetrics and Gynecology, Soc. Gynecologic Investigation, Wash. State Obstet. Soc., Tissue Culture Assn., N.Y. Acad. Sci., Utah Obstetrics-Gynecology Soc., Utah State Med. Assn., Teratology Soc. Current Work: Reproductive genetics including male fertility problems; sperm penetration assay. Subspecialties: Obstetrics and gynecology; Perinatal diagnosis and therapy. Home: 8301 SE 83d St Mercer Island WA 98040 Office: Dept Obstetrics and Gynecology U Wash Sch Medicine Seattle WA 98105

STENGER, RALPH L., JR., scientific company executive, physicist; b. Wheeling, W.Va., Mar. 14, 1942; s. Ralph Lawrence and Gladys Johana (Kalkreuth) S.; m. Lynne Kathryn Milonas, June 19, 1971; children—Christopher Nicholas, Kathryn Marie. B.S. in Physics, St. Joseph's U., 1964; M.S. in Physics, W.Va. U., 1966, Ph.D. in Physics, 1970; M.B.A., U. Pitts., 1980. Instrument analyst, instr. W.Va. U., Morgantown, 1967-69; research physicist Gulf Research & Devel. Co., Pitts., 1969-73, section dir., 1973-80, mgr. research info. systems, 1980-83, mgr. research support service, 1983-85; coordinator, tech. cons. Chevron, USA, Denver, 1985—. Patentee in field. Bd. dirs. Riverview Sch. Dist., Oakmont, Pa., 1981, v.p., 1983-85; sr. physics div. judge Buhl Sci. Ctr., Pitts., 1972-85. Mem. Am. Phys. Soc., Instrument Soc. Am., Am. Mgmt. Assn., Am. Chem. Soc., Soc. Exploration Geophysicists, Sigma Pi Sigma. Republican. Roman Catholic. Current work: Application of instrumentation and computing technologies to manufacturing process automation, minerals exploration, materials characterization and research information acquisition and retrieval. Subspecialties: Information systems (Information science); Computer engineering. Home: 19 Clare Ct Castle Pines N Castle Rock CO 80104 Office: Chevron USA PO Box 599 Denver CO 80201

STENT, GUNTHER SIEGMUND, molecular biologist, educator; b. Berlin, Germany, Mar. 28, 1924; came to U.S., 1940, naturalized, 1945; s. George and Elizabeth (Karfunkelstein) S.; m. Inga Loftsdottir, Oct. 27, 1951; 1 son, Stefan Loftur. B.S., U. Ill., 1945, Ph.D., 1948; (hon.) D.Sc., York U., Toronto, Ont., Can., 1984. Research asst. U. Ill., 1945-48; research fellow Calif. Inst. Tech., 1948-50, U. Copenhagen, Denmark, 1950-51, Pasteur Inst., Paris, France, 1951-52; asst. research biochemist U. Calif., Berkeley, 1952-56, faculty, 1956—, prof. molecular biology, 1959—, prof. arts and scis., 1967-68, chmn. molecular biology, 1980—, dir. virus lab., 1980—; Document analyst U.S. Field Intelligence Agy. Tech., 1946-47; mem. genetics panel NIH, 1959-64, NSF, 1965-68. Author: Papers On Bacterial Viruses, 2d edit, 1966, Molecular Biology of Bacterial Viruses, 1963, Phage and the Origin of Molecular Biology, 1966, The Coming of the Golden Age, 1969, Function and Formation of Neural Systems, 1977, Morality as a Biological Phenomenon, 1978, Paradoxes of Progress, 1978, Molecular Genetics, 2d edit, 1978; Mem. editorial bd.: Jour. Molecular Biology, 1965-68, Genetics, 1963-68, Zeitschrift für Vererbungslehre, 1962-68, Ann. Revs. Genetics, 1965-69, Ann. Revs. Microbiology, 1966-70; Contbr. numerous sci. papers to profl. lit. Merck fellow NRC, 1948-54; sr. fellow NSF, 1960-61; Guggenheim fellow, 1969-70. Mem. Am. Acad. Arts and Scis., Soc. Neurosci., Nat. Acad. Scis., Am. Philos. Soc. Current Work: Developmental neurobiology; history and philosophy of science. Subspecialties: Neurobiology; Molecular biology. Home: 145 Purdue Ave Berkeley CA 94708

STEPHENS, JOHN JOSEPH, JR., research metallurgist; b. Canton, Ohio, Sept. 11, 1955; s. John Joseph and Anna Louise (Roberts) S. B.A. in Physics, Cornell U., 1977; M.S. in Metallurgy and Materials, Stevens Inst. Tech., 1980; Ph.D. in Materials Sci. and Engring., Stanford U., 1984. Research technician Exxon Research & Engring. Co., Linden, N.J., 1977-80; research asst. Stanford U., 1980-84; mem. tech. staff Sandia Nat. Lab., Albuquerque, 1985—. Bd. dirs., pres. 410 Sheridan Homeowners' Assn., Palo Alto, Calif., 1981-83. Mem. Am. Soc. for Metals (travel fellow 1983), AIME. Current work: High temperature alloys, structure-property relations of oxide disperson strengthened alloys, small-angle X-ray scattering applications in metallurgy. Office: Sandia Nat Lab Div 1832 PO Box 5800 Albuquerque NM 87110

STEPHENS, PHILIP JOHN, biologist, educator, researcher; b. London, Apr. 24, 1951; s. Gerwyn Lougher and Elizabeth (Morgan) S.; divorced; children: Charles Andrew, David Philip. B.Sc., London U., 1972; Ph.D., Aberdeen U., Scotland, 1977. Alfred P. Sloan research fellow U. Va., Charlottesville, 1975-78, postdoctoral fellow, 1978-79; postdoctoral research fellow U. Toronto, Ont., Can., 1979-80; Grass Found. research fellow Woods Hole (Mass.) Biol. Lab., Mass., 1980; asst. prof. dept biology Villanova (Pa.) U., 1980-84, assoc. prof., 1984—. Contbr. articles to sci. jours. Whitehall Found. grantee, 1981-87; NSF grantee, 1982-85. Mem. Soc. Neurosci. Current Work: Nerve and muscle physiology; temperature effects on neuromuscular physiology; nerve-muscle interactions during development; axon firing mechanisms. Subspecialty: Neurophysiology. Office: Villanova U Villanova PA 19085

STEPHENS, TRENT DEE, anatomy educator; b. Wendell, Idaho, Aug. 14, 1948; s. Herbert Raymond and Phyllis (Behunin) S.; m. Kathleen Rae Brown, Sept. 4, 1971; children: Summer, Rhett Dee, Brittani, Derek Ray, Blake Christopher. B.S., Brigham Young U., 1973, M.S., 1974; Ph.D., U. Pa., 1977. Sr. fellow U. Wash., Seattle, 1977-79, research assoc., 1979-81; asst. prof. anatomy Idaho State U., Pocatello, 1981—. Author: Atlas of Human Embryology, 1980. Rotary Found. grantee, 1973-74; NIH fellow, 1974-77; Poncin scholar, 1977-79. Mem. Teratology Soc., Am. Assn. Anatomists, Idaho Acad. Sci., AAAS. Mormon. Current Work: Morphogenesis, pattern formation, comparative embryology, limb field induction and placement, comparative and evolutionary morphogenesis. Subspecialties: Anatomy and embryology; Teratology. Home: 4441 N Williamsburg Ln Pocatello ID 83204 Office: Dept Biol Scis Idaho State U Pocatello ID 83209

STEPHENSON, THOMAS EDGAR, engineer, physicist; b. Dahlgren, Ill., Oct. 19, 1922; s. Simon Gilmore and Lilly May (Atchisson) S.; m. Helen Julia Mizzoni, June 8, 1946; children—Thomas Paul, Joan Priscilla, Timothy James, Michael David. B.S. in Physics, So. Ill. U., 1945; M.S. in Physics, U. Tenn., 1950. Assoc. scientist Republic Aviation Corp., Farmingdale, N.Y., 1957-65; assoc. physicist Brookhaven Nat. Lab., Upton, N.Y., 1965-70; project engr. S.M. Stoller Corp., N.Y.C., 1970-73; Nuclear licensing engr. VEPCO, Richmond, Va., 1973-76; sr. nuclear engr. Burns & Roe, Inc., Oradell, N.J., 1976-80; nuclear licensing engr. Stone & Webster Engring. Corp., N.Y.C., 1980—; adj. assoc. prof. physics L.I. U., Greenvale, N.Y., 1968-70. Contbg. author: Recent Research in Molecular Beams, 1959; Nuclear Orientation, 1963. Contbr. articles to profl. jours. Served to sgt. U.S. Army, 1943-46; ETO, PTO. Mem. Am. Phys. Soc., Am. Nuclear Soc. Episcopalian. Current work: Licensing of nuclear power stations, nuclear safety evaluations for nuclear power stations, nuclear shielding and radiation dose assessment. Subspecialties: Nuclear engineering; Nuclear physics. Home: 16 Briarfield Ln Huntington NY 11743 Office: Stone & Webster Engring Corp 1 Penn Plaza New York NY 11743

STEPLEWSKI, ZENON, research scientist, educator; b. Komorki, Poland, Sept. 27, 1929; came to U.S., 1974; s. Wojciech and Caroline (Pawlik) S.; m. Wilhelmina Lercher, July 7, 1955 (div. 1982); children—Beata, Andrzej; m. Maria-Anna Obrocka, Mar. 2, 1983. M.D., Silesian Med. Sch., Poland, 1960, D. Med. Sci., 1963; D.Sc., Polish Acad. Sci., 1970. Assoc. prof. Inst. Oncology, Gliwice, Poland, 1963-66; vis. scientist Wistar Inst., Phila., 1966-68; head tumor virus lab. Inst. Oncology, Gliwice, 1969-73; assoc. scientist Wistar Inst., 1974-77, assoc. prof., 1977-83, prof., 1984—. Editor: Hybridoma, 1981—; Monoclonal Antibody News, 1981—. Recipient Genetics and Virology Cancer award Nat. Cancer Inst., 1977, Consol. Basic Cancer Research Program award, 1978, Monoclonal Antibodies in Cancer Therapy award, 1983, Human Melanoma and Tumor Specific Monoclonal Antibodies award, 1980. Mem. Am. Cancer Soc., European Assn. Cancer Research, AAAS, Am. Assn. Cancer Research. Current work: Cancer diagnosis, cancer immunotherapy: hybridoma technology, monoclonal antibodies; human effector cells active in immunotherapy. Subspecialties: Cancer research (medicine); Cellular engineering. Office: Wistar Inst 36th St at Spruce Philadelphia PA 19104

STERLING, RAYMOND LESLIE, civil engineer, educator, researcher, cons.; b. London, Apr. 19, 1949; came to U.S., 1966; s. Richard Howard and Joan Valeria (Skinner) S.; m. Linda Lee Lundquist, Aug. 7, 1970 (div. Sept. 1982); children: Paul Nathan, Juliet Paige, Erika Joy; m. Janet Marie Kjera, Aug. 20, 1983; 1 stepchild, Zoey Kjera Cohen. B. Civil and Structural Engring., U. Sheffield, Eng., 1970; M.S. in Geol. Engring, U. Minn., 1975, Ph.D. in Civil Engring, 1977. Registered profl. engr., Minn. Civil engr. Egil Wefald & Assocs., Mpls., 1969-71; structural engr. Husband & Co., Sheffield, 1971-73, Setter, Leach & Lindstrom, Inc., Mpls., 1976-77; asst. prof. civil and mineral engring. dept. U. Minn., Mpls., 1977-83, assoc. prof., 1983—; dir. Underground Space Ctr., 1977—; prin. cons. Itasca Cons. Group, Inc., Mpls., 1981—; mem. U.S. Nat. Com. on Tunneling Tech., 1985—. Author: Earth Sheltered Housing Design, 1979, Earth Sheltered Housing: Code, Zoning and Financing Issues, 1980, Earth Sheltered Community Design, 1981 (Assn. Am. Pubs. architecture and urban planning book of yr. 1981), Earth Sheltered Residential Design Manual, 1982; Underground Building Design, 1983. Mem. Mpls. Energy Futures Com., 1981-82. Mem. ASCE (Young Engr. of Yr. award Minn. sect. 1982), Instn. Structural Engrs. (U.K.), Instn. Civil Engrs. (U.K.), Nat. Soc. Profl. Engrs., Internat. Solar Energy Soc., Am. Underground Space Assn. Club: Mpls. Engrs. Current Work: Use of underground space for land and energy conservation research, underground space use, earth sheltered buildings, passive energy conservation building techniques. Subspecialties: Underground engineering; Earth-sheltered buildings. Home: 4933 Dupont Ave S Minneapolis MN 55409 Office: 128 Pleasant St SE Minneapolis MN 55455

STERN, ARTHUR PAUL, electronic products and systems company executive; b. Budapest, Hungary, July 20, 1925; came to U.S., 1951; s. Leon and Bertha (Frankfurter) S.; m. Edith M. Samuel, Sept. 17, 1952; children—Daniel, Claude, Jacqueline. Dipl. Elec. Engring., Swiss Fed. Inst. Tech., 1948; M.E.E., Syracuse U., 1955. Mgr.-elect Devices and Applications Lab., Gen. Electric Co., Syracuse, 1957-61; dir. engring. Martin Marietta Corp., Balt., 1961-64; dir. ops. Bunker Ramo Corp., Canoga Park, Calif., 1964-66; v.p., gen. mgr. Magnavox Advanced Products div., Torrance, Calif., 1966-79, pres. Magnavox Advanced Products and Systems Co., 1980—, dir. Magnavox Govt. and Indsl. Electric Co., Ft. Wayne, Ind., 1975—; non-resident mem. staff MIT, Syracuse, 1956-59. Co-author: Transistor Circuit Engineering, 1957; Handbook of Automation, Computation and Control, 1961; contbr. articles to tech., sci. jours. Patentee in field. Fellow IEEE (Centennial medal 1984), AAAS. Jewish. Current work: Research in gaseous discharges; research and advanced development in solid state circuits; technical management; general management. Subspecialties: Electrical engineering; Electronics. Home: 606 N Oakhurst Dr Beverly Hills CA 90210 Office: Magnavox Advanced Products and Systems Co 2829 Maricopa St Torrance CA 90503

STERN, ROBERT MORRIS, psychology educator; b. N.Y.C., June 18, 1937; s. Irving Dan and Nellie (Wachstetter) S.; m. Wilma Olch, June 19, 1960; children—Jessica Leigh, Alison Rachel. A.B., Franklin and Marshall Coll., 1958; M.S., Tufts U., 1960; Ph.D., Ind. U., 1963. Research assoc. dept. psychology Ind. U., 1963-65; asst. prof. psychology Pa. State U., 1965-68, assoc. prof., 1968-73, prof., 1973—, head dept. psychology, 1978—. Author: (with W.J. Ray) Biofeedback, 1977; (with W.J. Ray and C.M. Davis) Psychophysiological Recording, 1980; (with K.L. Koch) Electrogastrography, 1985. Contbr. articles to profl. jours. Recipient Nat. Media award Am. Psychol. Found., 1978. Mem. Am. Psychol. Assn., Eastern Psychol. Assn., Internat. Orgn. Psychophysiology, Am. Gastroent. Assn., Soc. Psychophysiol. Research. Current work: Gastrointestinal functioning in humans and health, disease and behavior. Subspecialties: Physiological psychology; Gastroenterology. Home: 1360 Greenwood Circle State College PA 16803 Office: 417 Moore Bldg Pennsylvania State Univ University Park PA 16802

STERN, WARREN CHARLES, pharm. co. exec., psychopharmacologist, cons.; b. Bronx, N.Y., June 1, 1944; s. Julius and Eleanor (Fox) S.; m. Carol Joy, June 13, 1965; children: Andrew, Douglas, Gregory. B.S., Bklyn. Coll., 1965; Ph.D., Ind. U., Bloomington, 1969. Postdoctoral fellow Boston State Hosp., 1969; postdoctoral fellow Worcester (Mass.) Found. Exptl. Biology, 1970, staff scientist, 1971-75; neuropharmacologist Squibb Inst. Med. Research, Princeton, N.J., 1976; head sect. psychiatry dept. clin. research Burroughs Wellcome Co., Research Triangle Park, N.C., 1976—; research scientist D. Dix Hosp.; adj. asso. prof. Sch. Pharmacy, U. N.C. Contbr. numerous articles on neurosci., psychopharmacology, biol. psychiatry to profl. jours.; regional editor: Pharmacology, Biochemistry and Behavior, 1975—, Drug Devel. Research, 1981—. Recipient First prize Psychopharmacology div. Am. Psychol. Assn., 1971. Mem. Am. Soc. Pharm. and Exptl. Therapeutics, Biol. Psychiatry, AAAS, New Clin. Drug Eval. Unit. Current Work: Clin. devel. new psychiat. drugs; animal neuropharmacology; human and animal psychopharmacology. Subspecialties: Neuropharmacology; Psychopharmacology. Home: 8904 Willow Wood Ct Raleigh NC 27612 Office: Burroughs Wellcome Co Research Triangle Park NC 27709

STERNHAGEN, CHARLES JAMES, therapeutic radiologist; b. Glasgow, Mont., Oct. 15, 1933; s. Joseph Peter and Mary Catherine (Carignan) S.; m. Marlene Linda Keubler, Dec. 19, 1952; children: Charlene, Charles, Linda, Joseph, William, Marc, Donald, Bernard, Mary, Scott, Catherine, Marleen. B.A., Carroll Coll., Helena, Mont., 1956; M.D., Loyola U., 1959. Intern St. Joseph Hosp., South Bend, Ind., 1959-60; resident U. Okla., Oklahoma City, 1969-72; instr. environ. health U. Okla. Health Scis. Ctr., Oklahoma City, 1968-72, instr. radiation oncology, 1972; asst. prof. radiology Cancer Research and Treatment Ctr., U. N.Mex.-Los Alamos Sci. Lab., 1971-75, assoc. prof., 1976-78; chief radiation oncology Lovelace Bataan Med. Center, Albuquerque, 1972-78; dir. Cancer Therapy Ctr., Providence Hosp., Anchorage, 1978—; Pres.-elect State of Alaska div. Am. Cancer Soc., 1982; state surgeon N.Mex. N.G., 1973-76. Contbr. articles to profl. jours. Served to col. USAR, 1964-82. Lederly research fellow, 1956; recipient various grants. Fellow Am. Pub. Health Assn., Royal Soc. Health (London); mem. Am. Endocurietherapy Soc., Am. Soc. Preventive Oncology, Okla. Acad. Environ. Health Scis., Alaska State Med. Assn. (councillor, conv. chmn.), Am. Soc. Therapeutic Radiologists, Am. Coll. Radiology, Am. Soc. Clin. Oncology, Am. Roentgen Ray Soc., Am. Assn. for Cancer Research, Health Physics Soc. (ethics com.), Internat. Radiation Protection Assn., Radiation Research Soc., Radiol. Soc. N.Am., Am. Radium Soc., N.Mex. Soc. Radiology, AMA, Anchorage Med. Soc., AAAS. Current Work: Particles and radiation therapy; the negative Pi-meson research efforts in cancer; hyperthermia and cancer research; nasopharyngeal cancer research in Alaska natives. Subspecialties: Oncology; Cancer research (medicine). Home: 8421 Pioneer Dr Anchorage AK 99504 Office: 3200 Providence Blvd Anchorage AL 99504

STERNICK, EDWARD SELBY, med. physicist; b. Cambridge, Mass., Feb. 10, 1939; s. Charles and Adele N. (Stengel) S.; married; children: Heidi, Jennifer, Peter. B.S., Tufts U., 1960; M.A., Boston U., 1963; Ph.D., UCLA, 1968. Diplomate: Am. Bd. Radiology. Research scientist NASA, Ames Research Center, Moffett Field, Calif., 1962-63; NIH fellow UCLA, Los Angeles, 1964-67; dir. med. physics Dartmouth-Hitchcock Med. Center, Hanover, N.H., 1968-78; dir. med. physics div. Tufts-New Eng. Med. Center, Boston, 1978—; assoc. prof. therapeutic radiology and diagnostic radiology Tufts U. Sch. Medicine, Boston, 1978—. Mem. Am. Assn. Physicists in Medicine, Health Physics Soc., Am. Coll. Radiology, Radiol. Soc. N.Am., Soc. Nuclear Medicine, Sigma Xi. Unitarian. Current Work: Applications of computer tech. to medicine. Office: Med Phys Div 171 Harrison Ave Boston MA 02111

STERNLICHT, BENO, technical director. Vice chmn., tech. dir. Mechanical Tech. Inc., Latham, N.Y. Subspecialty: Mechanical engineering. Office: Mech Tech Inc 968 Albany-Shaker Rd Latham NY 12110*

STERN-TOMLINSON, WENDY BARBARA, neurophysiologist; b. Bronx, N.Y., Jan. 12, 1943; d. Aaron and Hannah (Katz) S.; m. Charles D. Yingling, July 3, 1964; 1 dau., Arden; m. Christopher J. Tomlinson, June 28, 1975; 1 dau., Stephanie. Student, Barnard Coll., 1960-61; B.A., Rice U., 1964, Ph.D., 1976. Research asst. N.Y. U. Med. Sch., N.Y.C., 1966-69; research assoc. dept. biology Tufts U., Medford, Mass., 1974-76; postdoctoral fellow dept. physiology U. Pa. Sch. Medicine, Phila., 1978-82; postgrad. research biologist, dept. biology U. Calif.-San Diego, La Jolla, 1982—. Contbr. articles to sci. jours. NIH fellow, 1978-81; NSF fellow, 1977; Whitehall Found. grantee, 1982—. Mem. AAAS, Soc. Neurosci., Assn. Women in Sci., Women in Neurosci. Current Work: Neural circuitry underlying behavior in invertebrates. Subspecialties: Neurobiology; Neurophysiology. Office: U Calif La Jolla CA 92093

STEUER, ANTON FRANCIS, cell biologist; b. Reading, Pa., Oct. 23, 1947; s. Anton and Rose (Schroeder) S.; m. Mary Kathryn Steuer, Dec. 18, 1971; children: Andre, Shaun. B.S., Allentown Coll., Center Valley, Pa., 1969; M.S., Cath. U. Am., Washington, 1972, Ph.D., 1974. Teaching asst. Cath. U. Am., 1971-73; dir. dept. cell biology Biotech Research Labs., Inc., Rockville, Md., 1974—; lectr. gen. biology Dunbarton Coll., 1972. Contbr. articles and abstracts to profl. jours. Mem. Tissue Culture Assn., Am. Assn. Cancer Research, Am. Soc. Microbiology, Sigma Xi. Current Work: Hybridoma research, devel. of biol. detection systems. Subspecialty: Cell and tissue culture. Office: Biotech Research Labs 1600 E Gude Dr Rockville MD 20850

STEVENS, CHARLES F., neurobiologist, educator; b. Chgo., Sept. 1, 1934; m. Jane Robinson; 3 children. B.A., Harvard U., 1956; M.D., Yale U., 1960; Ph.D., Rockefeller U., 1964. Asst. prof. dept. physiology and biophysics U. Wash. Sch. Medicine, 1963-68, asso. prof., 1968-72; guest investigator Lorentz Inst. Theoretical Physics, Leiden (Netherlands) U., 1969-70; prof. dept. physiology Yale U. Sch. Medicine, New Haven, 1975-83, prof., chmn. sect. molecular neurobiology, 1983—. Author: Neurophysiology: A Primer, 1966; contbr. articles to profl. jours. Subspecialties: Neurophysiology; Biophysics (biology). Office: Sect Molecular Neurobiology Yale School Medicine 333 Cedar St PO Box 3333 New Haven CT 06510

STEVENS, DONALD MEADE, physicist; b. Lynchburg, Va., May 9, 1947; s. Samuel Meade and Emma (Huff) S.; m. Mary Anne Henry, June 20, 1970; B.S. in Physics, Va. Poly. Inst. and State U., 1969, M.S. in Physics, 1970, Ph.D. in Physics, 1974. Research asst. Va. Poly. Inst. and State U., Blacksburg, 1969-74; guest research assoc. Brookhaven Nat. Lab., Upton, N.Y., 1969-73; vis. physicist Fermi Nat. Lab., Batavia, Ill., 1973-74; sr. research engr. Babcock & Wilcox, Lynchburg, 1974-79, group supr., 1979—. Gulf Oil fellow, 1971. Mem. Am. Phys. Soc., IEEE, ASME, ASTM. Baptist. Lodge: Lions (Amherst) (sgt. at arms 1984-85). Current work: Materials science-non destructive evaluation and diagnostics. Subspecialties: Acoustics; Graphics, image processing, and pattern recognition. Office: Babcock & Wilcox PO Box 239 Lynchburg VA 24505

STEVENS, GWENDOLYN RUTH, psychology educator; b. Los Angeles, Feb. 29, 1944; d. Oscar and Alice (Whalen) S.; m. David Nichols, Feb. 24, 1962 (div.); children: Lorin Ann, Stephen Forrest; m. Sheldon Gardner, Oct. 24, 1972. B.A., Calif. State U.-Los Angeles, 1973, M.A., 1974; Ph.D., U. Calif.-Riverside, 1978. Instr. Tri-Community Nursery, Coving, Calif., 1964-67; instr. psychology East Los Angeles Community Coll., 1975, Cypress Community Coll., Calif., 1975, Whittier Coll., Calif., 1976; asst. prof. psychology Southeast Mo. State U., Cape Girardeau, 1978-82; assoc. prof. psychology dept. humanities U.S. Coast Guard Acad., New London, Conn., 1982—; cons. Calif. Grad. Inst., Orange, 1975-78; research dir. Client Assistance, Downey, Calif., 1975-77; research asst. Rancho Los Amigos Hosp., Downey, 1973-75; counselor Luth. Family Service, Cape Girardeau, 1978-81, Student Devel. Ctr., 1977-80. Author: Women in Psychology, vol. I and II, 1981, Care and Cultivation of Parents, 1979; History of Psychology in Vienna, 1922-1938; contbr. articles to profl. jours. Southeast Mo. State U. scholar, 1981. Mem. Am. Psychol. Assn., Internat. Council Psychology, Internat. Assn. for History of Social Scis. Libertarian. Current Work: Gender roles, attribution process, psychometric properties of attitude scales, history of women in psychology. Subspecialty: Social psychology. Home: 29 Denison Ave Mystic CT 06355 Office: Dept Humanities US Coast Guard Acad New London CT 06320

STEVENS, JAMES EVERELL, physicist; b. Ann Arbor, Mich., May 4, 1950; s. Everell D. and Naomi C. (Graese) S.; m. Anne C. Stevens, Dec. 22, 1972. B.S.E., U. Mich., 1972, Ph.D., 1980. Programmer, Shared Applications, Inc., Ann Arbor, 1973-76; physicist Plasma Physics Lab., Princeton U., 1980—. Mem. Am. Phys. Soc. (Excellence in Plasma Physics Research award 1984), IEEE, Sigma Xi. Current work: Radio frequency heating and current drive in plasmas for fusion research. Subspecialties: Plasma physics; Fusion. Office: Plasma Physics Lab PO Box 451 Princeton NJ 08540

STEVENS, ROY HARRIS, microbiologist, dentist; b. N.Y.C., Jan. 8, 1948; s. Daniel and Gladys (Sporn) S.; m. Jeanne Marie Connors, Sept. 14, 1971; 1 dau., Jocelyn Natalie. B.A., Adelphi U., 1969; M.S., Rutgers U., 1972; D.D.S., Columbia U., 1976; Cert. in Endodontics, U. Pa., 1985. Resident dental service Beth Israel Med. Ctr., N.Y.C., 1976-77; postdoctoral fellow dept. microbiology Dental Sch., U. Pa., Phila., 1977-79, research assoc., 1979-80, research asst. prof., 1980—. Author: Host-Parasite Interactions in Periodontal Disease, 1982; contbr. articles to profl. jours. Nat. Inst. Dental Research/NIH grantee, 1978—. Mem. Am. Soc. Microbiology, Internat. Assn. Dental Research. Jewish. Current Work: Oral microbiology, interaction of oral microorganisms on host tissues. Subspecialties: Oral biology; Microbiology. Home: 4 Winfield Dr Berlin NJ 08009 Office: Dept Microbiology Sch Dental Medicine Univ Pa 4001 Spruce St Philadelphia PA 19104

STEVENSON, ROBERT EDWIN, biological resources company executive, consultant; b. Columbus, Ohio, Dec. 2, 1926; s. Arthur Edwin and Mary Lucille (Beman) S. B.Sc., Ohio State U., 1947, M.Sc., 1950, Ph.D., 1954. Diplomate Am. Bd. Microbiology in Pub. Health and Med. Lab. Virology. Head, tissue culture Tissue Bank, U.S. Navy Med. Sch., Bethesda, Md., 1958-60; chief viral carcinogenesis br. Nat. Cancer Inst., Bethesda, 1960-67; mgr. biol. scis. Union Carbide Corp., Tarrytown, N.Y., 1967-72; v.p., gen. mgr. Litton Bionetics, Frederick, Md., 1972-80; dir. Am. Type Culture Collection, Rockville, Md., 1980—; pres. BioResources Labs. Inc., Rockville, 1983—; cons. indsl. biosafety com. Genex Corp., Rockville, 1980—; cons. biotech. tech. adv. com. Office Tech. Assessment, Washington, 1985—, U.S. Dept. Commerce, Washington, 1985—. Editor: Uses and Standardization of Vertebrate Cell Cultures, 1985. Fellow Inst. for Soc., Ethics and Life Scis.; mem. Tissue Culture Assn., Am. Soc. for Microbiology, Soc. for Cryobiology, Am. Assn. Tissue Banks. Republican. Episcopalian. Club: Cosmos (Washington). Subspecialty: Cell and tissue culture. Office: Am Type Culture Collection 12301 Parklawn Dr Rockville MD 20852

STEVER, HORTON GUYFORD, scientific consultant, corporation director; b. Corning, N.Y., Oct. 24, 1916; s. Ralph Raymond and Alma (Matt) S.; m. Louise Risley Floyd, June 29, 1946; children—Horton Guyford, Sarah, Margarette, Roy. A.B., Colgate U., 1938, Sc.D. (hon.), 1958; Ph.D., Calif. Inst. Tech., 1941; LL.D., Lafayette Coll., U. Pitts., 1966, Lehigh U., 1967, Allegheny Coll., 1968, Ill. Inst. Tech., 1975; D.Sc., Northwestern U., 1966, Waynesburg Coll., 1967, U. Mo., 1975, Clark U., 1976, Bates Coll., 1977; D.H., Seton Hill Coll., 1968; D.Engring., Washington and Jefferson Coll., 1969, Widener Coll., Poly. Inst. Bklyn., 1972, Villanova U., 1973, U. Notre Dame, 1974; D.P.S., George Washington U., 1981. Mem. staff radiation lab. MIT, Cambridge, 1941-42, asst. prof., 1946-51, assoc. prof., 1951-56, prof. aero. engring., 1956-65, head depts. mech. engring., naval architecture, marine engring., 1961-65, assoc. dean engring., 1956-59, exec. officer guided missiles program, 1946-48; chief scientist USAF, 1955-56; pres. Carnegie-Mellon U., Pitts., 1965-72; dir. NSF, Washington, 1972-76; sci. adviser, chmn. Fed. Council Sci. and Tech., 1973-76; dir. Office Sci. and Tech. Policy, sci. and tech. adviser to Pres., 1976-77; sci. cons., corp. dir., 1977—; dir. TRW, Schering-Plough Corp., Goodyear Tire & Rubber Co.; mem. secretariat guided missiles com. Joint Chiefs of Staff, 1945; sci. liaison officer London Mission, OSRD, 1942-45; mem. guided missiles tech. evaluation group Research and Devel. Bd., 1946-48; mem. sci. adv. bd. to chief of staff U.S. Air Force, 1947-69, chmn., 1962-69, mem. steering com. tech. adv. panel on aeros. Dept. Def., 1956-62; chmn. spl. com. space tech. NASA, chmn. research adv. com. missile and spacecraft aerodynamics, 1959-65; mem. Nat. Sci. Bd., 1970-72, mem. ex-officio, chmn. exec. com., 1972-75; mem. Def. Sci. Bd.; mem. adv. panel U.S. Ho. of Reps. Com. Sci. and Astronautics; mem. Pres.'s Commn. on Patent System, 1965-67; chmn. U.S.-USSR Joint Commn. Sci. and Tech. Cooperation, 1973-77, Fed. Council Arts and Humanities, 1972-76, Pres.'s Com. Nat. Sci. Medal, 1973-77. Author: Flight, 1965. Contbr. articles to profl. publs. Past trustee Colgate U., Shady Side Acad., Sarah Mellon Scaife Found., Buckingham Sch., trustee Univ. Research Assn., 1977—, pres., 1982-85; trustee Woods Hole Oceanographic Instn., 1980—, Univ. Assn. Armosperic Research, 1980-83; bd. dirs. Saudi Arabia Nat. Ctr. Sci. and Tech., 1977-81; bd. govs. U.S.-Israel Binat. Sci. Found., 1972-76. Recipient Pres.'s cert. of merit, 1948, Exceptional Civilian Service award U.S. Air Force, 1956, Scott Gold medal Am. Ordnance Assn., 1960, Disting. Pub. Service medal Dept. Def., 1969; comdr. Order of Merit (Poland). Fellow AIAA (hon., pres. 1960-62), Royal Aero. Assn., Am. Acad. Arts and Scis., AAAS, Am. Phys. Soc.; mem. Nat. Acad. Engring. (chmn. aero. and space engring. bd. 1967-69 fgn. sec. 1984—, nat. conf. bd., sr. exec. council), Nat. Acad. Scis. (chmn. assembly engring. 1979-83), Phi Beta Kappa, Sigma Xi, Sigma Gamma Tau, Tau Beta Pi. Episcopalian. Clubs: Cosmos (Washington); Bohemian (San Francisco); Century Assn. (N.Y.C.). Current work: Scientific consultant; corporate director. Subspecialties: Aeronautical engineering; Aerospace engineering and technology. Office: Nat Acad Engring 2101 Constitution Ave NW Washington DC 20418

STEWART, DAVID HARRY, management consulting firm executive; b. Detroit, Oct. 16, 1939; s. Versile Harry and Alice Louise (Jackson) S.; m. Donna O.T. Lee, Jan. 5, 1980; 1 son, Eric Edward. B.A. in Philosophy, Calif. State U.-Long Beach, 1962. Computer programmer Aeronutronics, Newport Beach, Calif., 1959-63, Iowa State U., Ames, 1963-65; computer scientist Sch. Medicine U. So. Calif., Los Angeles, 1965-69; dept. head Rand Corp., Santa Monica, Calif., 1969-80; pvt. practice cons., Alexandria, Va., 1980-82; v.p. Viar and Co., Inc., Alexandria, 1982—; vis. fellow U. Copenhagen, Denmark, 1971. Bd. dirs. Los Angeles Regional Family Planning, 1976-77; mem. fiscal adv. com. Santa Monica Sch. Bd., 1980. Fellow Inst. for Advancement of Engring. (life), Phi Sigma Tau (life); mem. Assn. Computing Machinery, IEEE Computer Soc. (chpt. pres. 1978-80). Democrat. Club: Palos Verdes Yacht. Current Work: Decision support systems, office automation, complex textual data bases, chemical data bases, structured office practices. Subspecialties: Information systems, storage, and retrieval (computer science); Database systems. Home: 7202 Rebecca Dr Alexandria VA 22307 Office: Viar and Co Inc 300 N Lee Alexandria VA 22314

STEWART, DAVID JAMES, medical oncologist, educator; b. Ottawa, Ont., Can., May 15, 1950; s. Archibald McDiarmid and Mary Iris (Keenan) S.; m. Nancy Isobel Merab Hall, July 26, 1975; children—Adam Matthew, Megan Lynn. M.D., Queen's U., Kingston, Can., 1974. Diplomate Am. Bd. Med. Oncology. Intern in medicine McGill U., Montreal, Can., 1974-75; resident Royal Victoria Hosp., 1975-76; fellow in oncology M.D. Anderson Hosp. and Tumor Inst., Houston, 1976-78, faculty assoc. and instr. dept. devel. therapeutics, 1978-79, asst. prof., asst. internist, 1979-80; med. oncologist Ont. Cancer Treatment and Research Found., Ottawa, 1980—; clin. asst. prof. U. Ottawa, 1980-84, clin. assoc. prof. medicine, 1984—. Contbr. numerous articles to profl. jours. and books. Queen's U. Provincial scholar for Ont., 1968, W.W. Near and Susan Near scholar 1969, 72, 73, Roberta Mcculloch scholar in English, 1969, Isaac Cohen scholar in microbiology, 1972, Rueben Wells Leonard scholar, Frederick Henry Loughes scholar, 1973; recipient Plunkett prize for Proficiency in Clin. Medicine, 1974. Fellow Royal Coll. Physicians Can.; mem. Ont. Med. Assn., Can. Oncology Soc., Can. Med. Protective Assn., Am. Soc. Clin. Oncology, Am. Assn. Cancer Research. Current work: Chemotherapy of brain tumors, chemotherapy uptake into tissues, phase I-II studies, chemotherapy pharmacokinetics, intraarterial chemotherapy, hairy cell leukemia. Subspecialties: Chemotherapy; Pharmacology. Home: 207 Glebe Ave Ottowa ON K1S 2C8 Canada Office: Ont Cancer Found Clinic Gen Hosp div 501 Smyth Rd Ottawa ON K1H 8L6 Canada

STEWART, DONALD MARTIN, plant pathologist; b. Rembrandt, Iowa, Jan. 20, 1908; s. Alexander Porter and Nellie Louise (Martin) S.; m. Marion Grace Christiansen, May 14, 1938; children: Margo Jeanne Gardner, Bonnie Ann. B.S., U. Minn., 1931, Ph.D., 1953. Jr. forester Bur Entomology and Plant Quarantine, U.S. Dept. Agr., 1933-35; dist. leader White Pine Blister Rust Control, Duluth, Minn., 1935-51; research plant pathologist U. Minn., St. Paul, 1951-70; project mgr. field crops productivity FAO/UN Devel. Project, Cairo, Egypt, 1970-74; profl. cons. plant scis. dept. U. Ariz., Tucson, 1977—; agronomist USAID, North Yemen, 1977-78. Contbr. articles in field to profl. jours. Recipient Cert. of Merit U.S. Dept Agr., 1958, cert. of tng., 1963, cert. of appreciation, 1974; cert. of appreciation Mpls. Pub. Schs., 1968-69; Fulbright-Hays research and lectr. grantee Romania, 1965. Mem. Am. Phytopath. Soc., Minn. Archaeol. Soc. (pres. 1965), Sigma Xi. Presbyterian. Lodge: Masons. Current Work: Development of new field crops. Subspecialties: Plant genetics; Plant cell and tissue culture. Home: 9476 E Shiloh St Tucson AZ 85710

STEWART, IVAN, biochemist, plant physiologist; b. Stanton, Ky., July 24, 1922; s. Alexander T. and Clemma (Lacy) S.; m. Gladys White, Aug. 30, 1947; children—Alice Stewart O'Hara, Sarah Stewart Godwin, Charles I. B.S., U. Ky., 1948, M.S., 1949; Ph.D., Rutgers U., 1951. Asst. prof. U. Fla., Lake Alfred, 1951-56, assoc. prof., 1956-61, prof. biochemistry, 1961—. Contbr. articles to profl. publs., chpts. in books. Served to 1st lt. U.S. Army, 1942-46, ETO, PTO. Fellow Am. Soc. Hort. Sci.; mem. Am. Chem. Soc., AAAS. Current work: Investigation of endogenous plant growth hormones, especially in developing emmunoassays and methods of extraction and measuring. Subspecialties: Biochemistry (biology); Plant physiology (agriculture). Home: 1851 Peninsular Dr Haines City FL 33844 Office: U Fla 700 Experiment Sta Rd Lake Alfred FL 33850

STEWART, JAMES EDMUND, III, nuclear engineer, consultant; b. Bristol, Tenn., Aug. 17, 1943; s. James Edmund and Jane Reeve (Booher) S.; m. Peggy Elizabeth Adams, Dec. 30, 1966; children: Margaret Ann, James E. B.S., U. Tenn., 1966; M.E., U. Va., 1970, Ph.D., 1974. Assoc. and lead engr. Babcock & Wilcox Co., Lynchburg, Va., 1966-69; teaching asst. U. Va., Charlottesville, 1970-71; reactor engr. AEC, Washington, 1972-73; staff member and project leader Los Alamos Nat. Lab., 1974—; cons. Los Alamos Tech. Assocs., 1976—; Principal investigator neutron monitoring for centrifuge enrichment plant inspections, 1979-83. Author: (with T. D. Reilly, et al) Passive Nondestructive Assay of Fissionable Material, 1982-83. Mem. Am. Nuclear Soc., Inst. Nuclear Materials Mgmt., AAAS, Sigma Xi. Current Work: Monte Carlo modeling of particle transport processes, non-destructive assay instrumentation development and training for international safeguards and nuclear materials accountability, radiation shielding. Subspecialties: Nuclear fission; Nuclear engineering. Office: Los Alamos Nat Lab PO Box 1663 MS #540 Los Alamos NM 87545

STEWART, JOHN ALVIN, public health physician, educator; b. Hamden, N.Y., July 25, 1934; s. Alvin W. and Pearl M. (McCague) S.; m. Madeline J. Stewart, Dec. 28, 1956; children: Bruce, Rebecca, Steven, Gary. A.B., Houghton Coll., 1956; M.D., U. Rochester, 1961, M.S., 1968. Diplomate: Am. Bd. Pediatrics. Intern Cleve. Met. Gen. Hosp., 1961-62, resident in pediatrics, 1962-64; instr. pediatrics Emory U., Atlanta, 1964—; acting chief, virus reference unit Center for Disease Control, Atlanta, 1966-67, asst. chief, virology sect., 1967-68, chief perinatal virology unit, 1968-73, asst. chief, perinatal virology br., 1973—. Served to lt. comdr. USPHS, 1964-67. Mem. Am. Soc. Microbiology, Ga. Acad. Pediatrics. Current Work: Researcher in rapid diagnosis of perinatal viral infection. Subspecialties: Microbiology (medicine); Preventive medicine. Office: Center for Disease Control Bldg 7-240 Atlanta GA 30333

STEWART, KENT KALLAM, chemistry educator; b. Omaha, Sept. 5, 1934; s. George Franklin and Grace (Sledge) S.; m. Margaret Reiber, June 10, 1956; children—Elizabeth, Cynthia, Richard, Robert. Student, U. Chgo., 1951-53; A.B., U. Calif.-Berkeley, 1956; Ph.D. Fla. State U., 1965. Guest investigator Rockefeller U., N.Y.C., 1965-67, research assoc., 1967-68, asst. prof., 1968-79; research chemist U.S. Dept. Agr., Beltsville, Md., 1970-75, lab. chief Nutrient Composition Lab., 1975-82; prof., head dept. food sci. and tech. Va. Poly. Inst. and State U., Blacksburg, 1982—, also prof. biochemistry and nutrition, 1985—. Author articles and book chpts.; patentee in field. Served to capt. USMCR, 1956-59. Mem. Inst. Food Technologist, Am. Chem. Soc., AAAS, Assn. Ofcl. Analytical Chemists, Sigma Xi. Current work: Analytical chemistry of foods; chemical composition of foods; automated chemical analysis; flow injection analysis. Subspecialties: Analytical chemistry; Food science and technology. Home: 14 Shawnee Trail Blacksburg VA 24060 Office: Va Poly Inst and State U Dept Food Sci and Tech Blacksburg VA 24061

STEWART, LARRY GENE, psychologist, consultant; b. San Angelo, Tex., Oct. 9, 1937; s. John Summers and Bertha Irene (Barnes) S.; m. Shirley Hosephine Hanrahan, Dec. 30, 1958 (div. 1974); children: Lamar Gregory, Lee Garrett. B.S., Gallaudet Coll., 1957; M.Ed., U. Mo., 1963; Ed.D., U. Ariz., 1970. Lic. psychologist, Calif., Ariz., Tex., sch. psychologist, Ariz. Assoc. prof. U. Ariz., Tucson, 1972-75, research specialist, 1976-79, pvt. practice psychology, Tucson, 1973-79; exec. dir. Tex. Comm. for Deaf, Austin, 1979-80; pvt. practice psychology, Huntington Beach, Calif., 1980—; forensic psychologist Los Angeles, Orange County, Superior Cts. So. Calif., 1980—; cons. psychologist Dayle McIntosh Center, Garden Grove, Calif., 1980—, Calif. State U.-Northridge, 1981—, Drs. Hosp. Lakewood, Calif., 1983—; rehab. cons. various state and fed. agys., 1970—. Author: Hearing Impaired Developmentally Disabled Children and Adults, 1980, Guide on Hearing Impaired Developmentally Disabled for State Development Disability Councils, 1978; contbr. chpt. to book in field. Co-innovator Ariz. Council for the Deaf, Phoenix, 1974-75, Greater Kansas City Adv. Council for the Deaf, 1965, Greater Tucson Adv. Council for the Deaf, 1972-73. HEW grantee, 1970-71, 74, 74-76, 76-79. Mem. Profl. Rehab. Workers with Adult Deaf (pres. 1973-75), Am. Psychol. Assn., Calif. Psychol. Assn. Current Work: Research: forensic psychological assessment methods, techniques, instruments with deaf individuals, neuropsychological assessment of deaf individuals having additional impairments affecting learning, communication, and adjustment. Subspecialty: Neuropsychology. Office: 5200 Warner Ave Suite 109 Park Pl Huntington Beach CA 92649

STEWART, ROBERT MURRAY, JR., educator; b. Washington, May 6, 1924; s. Robert Murray and Emily (Smith) S.; m. Patricia Mary Alberding, June 27, 1945; children—Martha Murray, Scott Robert. Student, U. Utah, 1941-43; B.S. in Elec. Engring, Iowa State Coll., 1945, Ph.D. in Physics, 1954. Faculty Iowa State U., 1946—, research asso., 1948-53, asst. prof. physics, 1953, asso. prof. physics, elec. engring., 1956-60, prof. physics, elec. engring., 1960—; research scientist AEC, Ames Lab., 1963-73, chief engr. cyclone digital computer, 1956-66; asso. dir. Iowa State U. Computation Center, 1963—, prof. and chmn. computer sci. dept., 1969—; pres. Computer Sci. Bd., 1976-77; cons. Midwest Research Inst., Kansas City, Mo., Collins Radio Corp., Cedar Rapids, Iowa, Dept. Meteorology and oceanography Tex. A. and M. Coll., Nat. Acad. Sci., Electronic Assos., Inc.; vis. scientist NSF, Assn. for Computing Machinery, Coll. Cons. Service. Mgmt. bd. YMCA, Snow Mountain Ranch, 1969-77; Bd. dirs. Ames Town and Gown Chamber Music Soc., 1973-77; pres. bd. dirs. Story County Youth and Shelter Service, 1975—. Served as ensign USNR, 1945-46. Mem. Assn. Computing Machinery, Am. Phys. Soc., IEEE (adminstrv. com. profl. group on electronic computers 1962-64), Iowa Acad. Sci., Osborn Research Club (chmn. 1971), Am. Fedn. Information Processing Socs. (mem. edn. com.), YMCA of Rockies (dir. 1977—), Ames Soc. for Arts (pres. 1970), UN Assn. (bd. dirs. Ames chpt.), Sigma Xi (pres. Iowa State U. chpt. 1974-75). Chief investigator NSF sponsored time sharing computer research, 1968-78; designer, implementer computer control system for expts. Ames Lab. Research Reactor AEC, 1963-73. Current Work: Distributed microprocessor systems. Subspecialties: Computer architecture; Distributed systems and networks. Home: 3416 Oakland Ames IA 50010

STEWART, RONALD LEROY, ceramic scientist; b. Tarentum, Pa., Oct. 3, 1949; s. William Leroy and Betty Mae (Mentch) S.; m. Pamela Ann Falise, Aug. 20, 1971; children—Douglas, Lauren. B.S., Pa. State U., 1971, Ph.D., 1981. Ceramic engr. Brockway Glass Co., Inc., Pa., 1971-74, PPG Industries, Inc., Pitts., 1974-75; sr. scientist-ceramics Corning Glass Works, N.Y., 1980—. Contbr. articles to tech. jours. Mem. Am. Ceramic Soc., ASTM, AAAS, Nat. Inst. Ceramic Engrs., Sigma Xi. Current work: Development and mechanical characterization of fiber-reinforced glass-ceramic composites; microstructure and mechanical behavior of glass-ceramics. Subspecialties: Ceramics; Composite materials. Home: 741 Cardinal Ln RD 1 Elmira NY 14903 Office: Corning Glass Works SP-FR-51 Corning NY 14831

STEWART, WARREN EARL, chemical engineer, educator; b. Whitewater, Wis., July 3, 1924; s. Earl Austin and Avis (Walker) S.; m. Jean Durham Potter, May 24, 1947; children—Marilyn, David, Douglas, Carol, Margaret, Mary Jean. B.S. in Chem. Engring., U. Wis., 1945, M.S., 1947, Sc.D., Mass. Inst. Tech., 1951. Project chem. engr. Sinclair Research Labs., Harvey, Ill., 1950-56; cons. Sinclair and Atlantic Richfield Research Labs., 1956-83; asst. prof. chem. engring. dept. U. Wis., Madison, 1956-58, assoc. prof., 1958-61, prof., 1961—, McFarland-Bascom prof., 1983—, chmn. dept., 1973-78; Cons. Engelhard Industries, Inc., Newark, 1956-58; instr. spl. courses transport phenomena Chemstrand Corp., Pensacola, Fla., 1962, Nat. U. La Plata, Argentina, 1962, Esso Research & Engring. Co., 1963, 66, Phillips Petroleum Co., 1963, Am. Inst. Chem. Engrs., 1965, 68, 69, Inst. Tec. Celaya (Mex.), 1983, U. Nacional Autonoma de Mex., 1985. Author: (with R.B. Bird and E.N. Lightfoot) Transport Phenomena, 1960, Special Topics in Transport Phenomena, 1965 (with Bird, Lightfoot and Chapman) Lectures in Transport Phenomena, 1969; Editorial adviser: Latin Am. Jour. Chem. Engring. and Applied Chemistry; assoc. editor: Computers and Chem. Engring. Served to ensign USNR, 1944-46. Recipient Benjamin Smith Reynolds teaching award, 1981. Fellow Am. Inst. Chem. Engrs. (computing and systems tech. div. award 1985); mem. Am. Chem. Soc., Am. Soc. for Engring. Edn. (lectr. chem. engring. div. 1983), Phi Beta Kappa, Sigma Xi, Alpha Chi Sigma (research award 1981), Phi Eta Sigma, Tau Beta Pi, Phi Lambda Upsilon, Phi Kappa Phi. Conglist. (deacon, moderator). Subspecialty: Chemical engineering. Office: U Wis Dept Chem Engring Madison WI 53706

STICHT, FRANK DAVIS, med. and dental educator, pharmacologist; b. Plattsburg, Miss., June 14, 1919; s. Frank and Nannie Pearl (Davis) S.; m. Sarah Catherine Tabor, May 6, 1941; children: Sarah Elizabeth, Rebekah Lois. B.S. in Pharmacy, U. Miss., 1948; D.D.S., Baylor U., 1956; M.S., U. Tenn., 1965. Lic. dentist and pharmacist, Miss. Pvt. practice dentistry, 1956-58; USPHS postdoctoral research fellow U. Tenn. Center for Health Scis., 1959-61, faculty, 1961-84; prof. pharmacology U. Tenn. Center for Health Scis. (Coll. Medicine), 1979-84, emeritus prof. pharmacology, 1984—, researcher in cardiovascular pharmacology, 1959-84; adj. prof. Sou Coll. Optometry, 1984—. Served with USN, 1942-45; to 1st lt. U.S. Army, 1950-52. Mem. Am. Soc. Pharmacology and Exptl. Therapeutics, Sigma Xi. Baptist. Current Work: Research in pharmacology of antihypertensive drugs. Teacher of pharmacology to optometry students. Home: 6092 Ridgewyck Dr Apt 1 Memphis TN 38115 Office: Dept Biomed Scis Sou Coll Optometry Memphis TN 38104

STICKNEY, ROBERT ROY, educator; b. Mpls., July 2, 1941; s. Roy E. and Helen Doris (Nelson) S.; m. LuVerne C. Whiteley, Dec. 29, 1961; children: Robert Roy, Marolan Margaret. B.S., U. Nebr., 1967; M.A., U. Mo., 1968; Ph.D., Fla. State U., 1971. Cert. fisheries scientist. Research assoc. Skidaway Inst. Oceanography, Savannah, Ga., 1971-73, asst. prof., 1973-75, Tex. A&M U., College Station, 1975-78, assoc. prof., 1978-83, prof., from 1983; chmn. S-168 Com., So. Regional Coop. Research Project, from 1981; now prof. Sch. Fisheries, U. Wash., Seattle Author: Principles of Warmwater Aquaculture, 1979; contbr. articles to profl. jours. Served with USAF, 1959-63. Named Tex. Aquaculturist of Yr. Am. Fisheries Soc., 1979. Mem. Am. Fisheries Soc. (pres. fish culture sect. 1983-84), Am. Inst. Fish Research Biologists (Tex. div. dir.), Am. Inst. Nutrition, AAAS, Tex. Acad. Sci., Am. Soc. Limnology and Oceanography. Current Work: Nutritional/environ. requirements of freshwater/marine fishes. Emphasis on lipid and fatty acid requirements of fish. Office: U Wash Sch Fisheries Seattle WA 98195

STILLE, JOHN KENNETH, chemistry educator; b. Tucson, May 8, 1930; s. John Rudolph and Margaret Victoria (Sakrison) S.; m. Dolores Jean Engelking, June 7, 1958; children: John Robert, James Kenneth. B.S., U. Ariz., 1952, M.S., 1953; Ph.D., U. Ill., 1957. Instr. organic chemistry U. Iowa, Iowa City, 1956-59, asst. prof., 1959-63, asso. prof., 1963-65, prof., 1965-77, Colo. State U., Ft. Collins, 1977—; guest prof. Royal Inst. Tech., Stockholm, 1969; cons. E.I. duPont de Nemours & Co., Inc. Author: Introduction to Polymer Chemistry, 1962, Industrial Organic Chemistry, 1968; Editor: Condensation Monomers (vol. 27 High Polymers), Jour. Am. Chem. Soc., 1982—; Asso. editor: Macromolecules, 1968-82; editorial bd.: Jour. Macromolecular Sci; adv. bd.: Jour. Polymer Sci. Served to lt. comdr. USNR, 1953-55. Fellow Chem. Soc. London; mem. Am. Chem. Soc. (chmn. polymer div. 1975, award in polymer chemistry 1982), Phi Lambda Upsilon, Alpha Chi Sigma, Soc. Sigma Xi. Current Work: Organometallic chemistry; mechanisms and organic synthesis catalyzed by transition metals; polymer synthesis; structure property relationships. Subspecialties: Organic chemistry; Polymer chemistry. Home: 1523 Miramont St Fort Collins CO 80524 Office: Dept Chemistry Colo State U Fort Collins CO 80523

STILLER, CALVIN RALPH, medical scientist-clinician, educator, business executive; b. Naicam, Sask., Can., Feb. 12, 1941; s. Carl Hilmer and Mildred Ruth (Parson) S.; m. Marlene Catherine Onn, Sept. 1, 1962; children: Cynthia, Robert, Denise, Troy, Debra, Timothy. Student, U. Sask., 1958-60, M.D., 1965; postgrad, U. Western Ont., Can., 1965-71, U. Alta., Can., 1971-72. Chief Nephrology and transplantation Univ. Hosp., London, Ont., 1972—; dir. transplantation immunology, asst. prof. medicine U. Western Ontario, London, 1972-81, prof., 1982; chmn. Centre for Transplant Studies, London, 1981; chmn. bd. Diversicare Corp., London, 1982; vis. prof., Europe, Africa, N.Am. Mem. editorial bd.: Exec. Congress Immunology, 1983—; contbr. articles to profl. jours; editor and co-editor three books. Bd. dirs. Kidney Found. Can.; active United Way, Can. Diabetes Assn., Borrd-Mission Services of London, Child Care Internat. Recipient Med. Research Council of Can. award, 1973-83; Optimists Internat. Humanitarian award, 1983. Fellow Royal Coll. Physicians (Can.); mem. Royal Coll. Physicians and Surgeons (Can.), Can. Soc. Nephrology (bd. dirs.), Internat. Soc. Nephrology, Internat. Transplantation Soc. (chmn. com.), Can. Med. Assn., Can. Soc. Clin. Investigators. Club: London. Current Work: Immune monitoring, immunogenetics and immunosuppression; induction of tolerance and immunosuppression by biologic and pharmocologic (cyclospurine) means in transplantation (renal, cardiac, hepatic, pancreatic); immune probes in autoimmune disease; lymphokines and control of immune response. Subspecialties: Transplantation; Nephrology. Office: University Hospital STE 2R34 London ON N6G 2K3 Canada

STILLER, DAVID MARTIN, hydrogeologist; b. Franklin, Pa., Feb. 5, 1947; s. Martin William and Violet (Beith) S.; m. Victoria MacLean, Aug. 12, 1975. B.S., U. Wyo., 1972, M.A., 1975; postgrad. U. Calgary, Alta., Can., 1975-76, 78-79. Geologist, Wold Minerals, Casper, Wyo., 1975; hydrologist Lt. Gov.'s Office, Helena, Mont., 1976-78, Hydrometrics, Helena, 1980-81; hydrologist, pres. Stiller & Assocs., Helena, 1981—; cons., Helena, 1978-80. Contbr. articles to profl. publs. Served to sgt. USMC, 1968-70. Mem. Nat. Water Well Assn., Am. Geophys. Union, Mont. Mining Assn., Assn. Environ. Scientists and Adminstrs. Clubs: Outing (Laramie, Wyo.) (v.p. 1972-73); Mont. Mountain Mushers (Helena) (pres. 1980, 82). Current work: Direct hydrologic investigations of hazardous waste sites, coal and precious metals mines in Pacific Northwest. Subspecialties: Hydrology; Hazardous waste disposal. Office: Stiller & Assocs Inc 130 Neill Ave Helena MT 59601

STILLINGER, FRANK HENRY, chemist; b. Boston, Aug. 15, 1934; s. Frank Henry and Gertrude (Metcalf) S.; m. Dorothea Anne Keller, Aug. 18, 1956; children—Constance Anne, Andrew Metcalf. B.S., U. Rochester, 1955; Ph.D., Yale U., 1958. NSF postdoctoral fellow Yale U., 1958-59; with Bell Telephone Labs., Murray Hill, N.J., 1959—, head chem. physics dept., 1976-79; disting. lectr. chemistry dept. U. Md., 1981; mem. evaluation panel Nat. Bur. Standards, 1975-78; Mem. adv. com. for chemistry NSF, 1980—; mem. Nat. Acad. Sci., 1984—. Asso. editor: Phys. Rev; Contbr. articles to profl. jours. Welch Found. fellow, 1974; Recipient Elliott Cresson medal Franklin Inst., 1978. Fellow Am. Phys. Soc.; mem. AAAS, Sigma Xi. Club: Early Am. Coppers Inc. Current work: Theoretical study of liquids, glasses and surfaces, fundamental studies in chemical quantum theory. Subspecialties: Statistical mechanics; Theoretical chemistry. Home: 216 Noe Ave Chatham NJ 07928 Office: 600 Mountain Ave Murray Hill NJ 07974

STILLWAGON, GARY BOULDIN, radiation protection physicist; b. Memphis., Dec. 30, 1951; s. Jack Wright and Ida Jean (Bouldin) S.; m. Leta Fern Miller, Jan. 20, 1979. B.S. in Physics, Ga. Inst. Tech., 1974, M.S. in Nuclear Engring, 1975, Ph.D., 1978. Cert. Health Physics Bd., Part I, Nat. Bd. Med. Examiners, Parts I and II. Med. physicist Meth. Hosp., Memphis, 1974; research asst. Ga. Inst. Tech., Atlanta, 1975-78; radiation safety officer, and physicist VA Med. Center, Memphis, 1978-80, cons. radiation safety, 1980—; cons. in radiation safety to various area hosps. Contbr. articles to profl. jours. Active Boy Scouts Am., Bapt. Ch. Sunday Sch. Dept. Energy fellow, 1976-78. Mem. Health Physics Soc., Am. Assn. Physicists in Medicine, Am. Nuclear Soc., AAAS, AMA, Sigma Xi. Republican. Current Work: In-situ dosimetry of internally deposited alpha emitters. Internal dosimetry. Radiation protection. Home: 772 Metcalf Pl Memphis TN 38104 Office: 1030 Jefferson Ave Memphis TN 38104

STINCHCOMB, THOMAS GLENN, physicist; b. Tiffin, Ohio, Sept. 12, 1922; s. George Alfred and Ruth Elise (Branch) S.; m. Maxine Orr Kohler, Nov. 22, 1945; children: James A., William J., David G., Dan T. B.S., Heidelberg Coll., 1944; S.M. (univ. fellow, 1946-47), U. Chgo., 1948, Ph.D., 1951. Grad. teaching asst. U. Chgo., 1947-48; research asst. U. Chgo. High Altitude Cosmic-Ray Lab., Climax, Colo., 1948-51; full time vis. prof. radiology dept. U. Chgo., 1976-77, vis. research asso. part time radiology dept.,

1977—; asst. prof. physics dept. State U. Wash., Pullman, 1951-54; prof. physics dept. Heidelberg Coll., Tiffin, Ohio, 1954-61; sr. physucist Ill. Inst. Tech. Research Inst., Chgo., 1961-68; prof. physics dept. DePaul U., Chgo., 1968—, chmn., 1968-76, head div. natural scis. and math., 1984—. Contbr.: articles to profl. publs. including Radiation Research. Pres. Lincoln Sch. PTA, Tiffin, 1959-60; lay adv. council Evanston Twp. High Sch., 1966-69; bd. deacons St. Paul's United Ch. of Christ, 1976-82; bd. dirs. Com. for Nuclear Overkill Moratorium, 1976—; treas. Chgo. Area Faculty for a Freeze on Nuclear Arms Race, 1981-85, bd. dirs., 1985—. Served to lt. j.g. USNR, 1943-46. Recipient Admiral's award U.S. Naval Acad., 1944; Award of Merit, Chgo. Assn. Tech. Socs., 1985; mem. honor soc. Heidelberg Coll., 1943. Mem. Am. Assn. Physics Tchrs., Am. Assn. Physicists in Medicine, Am. Nuclear Soc., Physics Club Chgo. (dir. 1976—, pres. 1974-76), Chgo. Assn. Technol. Socs. (treas. 1981—), Sigma Xi, Sigma Pi Sigma. Democrat. Current Work: Radiation physics (cosmic-rays, neutrons, gamma-rays, applications to medicine, nuclear-weapon effects). Neutron beam therapy for cancer, dosimetry, neutron and gamma-ray microdosimetry, exptl. and theoretical, radiation protection against neutrons. Home: 429 Grant Pl Apt D Chicago IL 60614 Office: 2219 N Kenmore St Chicago IL 60614

STINNETT, JIMMY DWIGHT, immunologist, educator, researcher; b. Athens, Ala., Dec. 11, 1949; s. Billy Joe and Hazel Willowdean (Lovell) S.; m. Mary Virginia Smith, May 30, 1970; 1 dau.: Suzanne Michelle. B.S. in Microbiology, U. Ala., 1971; Ph.D., U. Ga., 1974. Postdoctoral research fellow Med. Coll. Va., Richmond, 1974-75; mem. faculty U. Cin. Med. Ctr., 1975—, assoc. prof. research surgery and microbiology, 1979—, assoc. dir. surg. immunobiology lab., 1975—; dir. basic research Cin. unit Shriners Burns Inst., 1979—. Mem. editorial bd.: Jour. Bacteriology, 1977-79, Jour. Reticuloendothelial Soc, 1982—; contbr. chpts. to books, articles to profl. jours. Served to maj. USAF, 1973-82. USPHS grantee. Mem. Am. Soc. Microbiology, Reticuloendothelial Soc., Am. Assn. Immunologists, Internat. Soc. Immunopharmacology, N.Y. Acad. Scis., Sigma Xi. Baptist. Current Work: Infections in immunocompromised patients, modification by nutrition and immunomodulators; infection, immunology, immunocompromised, immunomodulators, nutrition, burns, trauma. Subspecialties: Immunopharmacology; Nutrition (medicine). Office: 231 Bethesda Ave Cincinnati OH 45267

STITH, WILLIAM JOSEPH, biomedical engineer; b. Oklahoma City, Feb. 7, 1942; s. Joseph B. and Lera O. (Hall) S.; m. Linda Elizabeth Back, July 30, 1966; children: Debra E., William Joseph, David V. B.A. in Chemistry, Phillips U., 1964; Ph.D. in Biochemistry, 1972. Sr. cell physiologist Fenwal div. Baxter Travenol Labs., Round Lake, Ill., 1973-77, sect. mgr., 1976-77; with Med. Engring. Corp., Racine, Wis., 1977-81, v.p. sci. affairs, 1980-81; gen. mgr. bioengring. dept. Lord Corp., Erie, Pa., 1981-84; dir. clin. research Am. Med. Electronics, Dallas, 1985—. Contbr. articles to profl. jours. Served to lt. comdr. Med. Service Corps U.S. Navy, 1965-69. Mem. Am. Soc. Quality Control, Sigma Xi. Baptist. Current Work: Development of new biomedical devices for orthopedic health care field. Subspecialties: Biomaterials; Orthopedics. Home: 3101 Hidden Cove Plano TX 75075 Office: 4125 Keller Springs Rd Dallas TX 75244

STIVEN, ALAN ERNEST, zoologist, ecologist, educator; b. St. Stephen, N.B., Can., Nov. 12, 1935; came to U.S., 1962, naturalized, 1977; s. Alan J. and Edith G. S.; m. Julia Ann Heeb, Aug. 18, 1972; 1 son, Alan; children by previous marriage—Terry Kim. B.S., U. N.B., 1957; M.A., U. B.C., 1959; Ph.D., Cornell U., 1962. Asst. prof. zoology U. N.C., 1962-66, assoc. prof., 1966-71, chmn. biology curriculum, 1968-70, prof., chmn. ecology curriculum, 1971—, chmn. dept. zoology, 1967-72, acting chmn., 1979-80. Editor: Ecology and Ecol. Monographs, 1967-73; contbr. articles scholarly jours. Mem. Chapel Hill Bd. Adjustment, 1973-76. NSF research grantee, 1962-82; NIH tng. grantee, 1966-70. Mem. Ecol. Soc. Am., Am. Soc. Naturalists, Brit. Ecol. Soc., Japanese Soc. Population Ecology, Estuarine Research Fedn. Current work: Population biology, ecological genetics of marine bivalves and higher altitude fauna. Community ecology, experimental benthic research. Subspecialties: Ecology (biology); Evolutionary biology. Office: Univ NC Dept Biology Coker Hall 010A Chapel Hill NC 27514

STOBO, WAYNE THOMAS, marine biologist; b. Sudbury, Ont., Can., June 16, 1944. B.Sc., Laurentian U., 1965; M.Sc., U. Ottawa, 1971; Ph.D., Dalhousie U., 1972. Research biologist Dept. Fisheries of Can., St. Andrews, N.B., 1972-76, sect. head, population dynamics, Dartmouth, N.S., 1976-82; div. chief, marine fish div. Dept. Fisheries and Oceans Can., Dartmouth, 1983-84, research scientist, 1984—. Author: (with Stobo and McLaren) The Ipswich Sparrow, 1975. Current work: Migratory patterns and stock structure of seals and marine fin fish species; biology of grey and harbor seals. Subspecialties: Fishery biology; Marine biology. Office: Marine Fish Div Bedford Inst Oceanography PO Box 1006 Dartmouth NS B2Y 4A2 Canada

STOCK, RODNEY DENNIS, computer engineer; b. N.Y.C., July 21, 1947; s. Dennis and Norma Elizabeth (Waymouth) S. Student, Northeastern U., Boston, 1969. Jr. engr. NASA, Boston, 1967; technician Adage Corp., Boston, 1967-68; test engr. Electronic Image Systems, Boston, 1969; design engr. automated material handling Mobility Systems, Santa Clara, Calif., 1970-72; programmer Teleterminal Analysis Center, Memorex Corp., Santa Clara, 1972-73; project engr. flight simulators Evans and Sutherland Computer Corp., Salt Lake City, 1973-76; sr. engr. Ampex Video Art System, Ampex Corp., Redwood City, Calif., 1978-80; graphics engr., mgr. advanced image synthesis computer for movies) Lucasfilm, Ltd., San Rafael, Calif., 1980—. Mem. IEEE, Assn. Computing Machinery, Soc. Motion Picture and TV Engrs. Club: Sierra (San Francisco). Patentee in field. Current Work: Computer graphics hardware, computer graphics algorithms, 3-D computer graphics, computer architecture, image processing, digital video, parallel processing, local area networks. Subspecialties: Graphics, image processing, and pattern recognition; Computer architecture. Office: PO Box 2009 San Rafael CA 94912

STOCKINGER, SIEGFRIED LUDWIG, consultant; b. Yokohama, Japan, Feb. 3, 1943; came to U.S., 1952; s. Alois and Maria (Brokamp) S.; m. Bernadette Kulesz, Oct. 16, 1965; 1 son, Trevor. B.S. in Mech. Engring, Stevens Inst. Tech., 1965; M.S. in Environ. Engring, Loyola U., Los Angeles, 1973. Registered profl. engr., Calif., N.J., N.Y., N.C. Engr. electric boat div. Gen. Dynamics Corp., Groton, Conn., 1965-68; research and devel. labs. Mobil Chems., Edison, N.J., 1968-69; sect. mgr. Litton Ship Systems, Los Angeles, 1969-73; chief engr. Cosmodyne, Torrance, Calif., 1973-76; cons., Los Angeles, 1976-77; sr. supr. Ebasco Services, Inc., N.Y.C., 1977—. Contbr. writings in field to profl. publs. Active Republican Club, Short Hills, N.J., 1980—, USCG Aux., Redondo Beach, Calif., 1970-72, Eagle Scout. Mem. ASME, Am. Nuclear Soc., Alpha Sigma Phi (v.p. 1964). Roman Catholic. Club: Racquets (Short Hills, N.J.). Current Work: Chemical engineering and advanced technology applications in radioactive waste management and chemical process applications for treating effluents from nuclear operations. Subspecialties: Environmental engineering; Chemical engineering.

STOCKMAYER, WALTER HUGO, chemist; b. Rutherford, N.J., Apr. 7, 1914; s. Hugo Paul and Dagmar (Bostroem) S.; m. Sylvia Kleist Bergen, Aug. 12, 1938; children—Ralph, Hugh. S.B., MIT, 1935, Ph.D., 1940; B.Sc. (Rhodes scholar), Oxford U., 1937; hon. doctorate, U. Louis-Pasteur, Strasbourg, France, 1972; L.H.D. (hon.), Dartmouth Coll., 1983. Instr. MIT, 1939-41, asst. prof., 1943-46, asso. prof., 1946-52, prof., 1952-61; prof. chemistry Dartmouth, 1961-79, prof. emeritus, 1979—; instr. Columbia, 1941-43; cons. E.I. duPont de Nemours & Co., Inc., 1945—; vis. com. Nat. Bur. Standards, 1979-84. Contbr. articles on phys. and macromolecular chemistry to sci. jours. Guggenheim fellow, 1954-55; hon. fellow Jesus Coll., Oxford, Eng., 1976; Alexander von Humboldt fellow W. Ger., 1978-79; Recipient MCA Coll. Chemistry Tchr. award, 1960. Fellow Am. Acad. Arts and Scis., Am. Phys. Soc. (Polymer Physics prize 1975); mem. Am. Chem. Soc. (asso. editor Macromolecules 1968-74, 76—, chmn. polymer chem. div. 1968, Polymer Chemistry award 1965, Peter Debye award 1974), Nat. Acad. Scis. (exec. com. assembly math. phys. sci. 1974-77), Sigma Xi. Club: Appalachian Mountain. Current Work: Polymer chemistry, polymer physics. Subspecialties: Physical chemistry; Polymer chemistry. Home: Norwich VT 05055

STOCKWELL, CHARLES WARREN, neurophysiologist; b. Port Angeles, Wash., Dec. 31, 1940; s. Frank Edward and Esther Marie S.; m. Marsha Jo Stockwell, Aug. 23, 1966; children: Laura, Frank. B.A., Western Wash. U., 1964; M.A., U. Ill., 1966, Ph.D., 1968. Research psychologist Naval Aerospace Med. Inst., Pensacola, Fla., 1968-72; asst. prof. Ohio State U., Columbus, 1972-77, assoc. prof. otolaryngology, 1977-83, prof. 1983-84; prof. Wayne State U., Detroit, 1984—. Author: Manual of Electronystagmograph, 1976, 2d edit., 1980, ENG Workbook, 1983; Contbr. articles to profl. jours. Served with AUS, 1968-72. Mem. Assn. Research in Otolaryngology, Barany Soc., Soc. Neurosci. Current Work: Vestibular physiology. Subspecialties: Neurophysiology; Otorhinolaryngology. Home: 284 Merriweather Rd Grosse Pointe MI 48236 Office: 5D Univ Health Ctr 4201 St Antoine Detroit MI 48201

STODDARD, PATRICIA ANN, medical technologist, chemistry educator; b. Albert Lea, Minn., Apr. 5, 1930; d. Armond William and Lois Roberta (Remo) Olson Armstrong; m. Charles Gilbert Stoddard, Jan. 7, 1966; m. William Anton Hoogendijk, July 16, 1949 (div. Dec. 1964); 1 son, Christopher John. A.Sc., Clackamas Community Coll., 1973; B.A., Linfield Coll., 1976. Med. technologist King County Blood Bank, Seattle, 1962-63; surg. research technician Bishop Eye Research, Seattle, 1964-65; gen. supr. Willamette Falls Hosp., Oregon City, Oreg., 1965-68; adj. asst prof. U. Portland, Oreg., 1977—; dir. Willamette Animal Lab., Corbett, Oreg., 1969—. Author: Veterinarian Medicine for Small Animal Clinician, 1976, 77. Instr. ARC, Vancouver, Wash., 1979—; flotilla comdr. Coast Guard Aux., Vancouver, 1984. Mem. Am. Med. Technologists (Nat. Achievement award 1972, 74), Am. Soc. Microbiologists, Am. Inst. Biol. Sci., Am. Chem. Soc. (exec. bd. Portland sect. 1982—), Iota Sigma Phi. Republican. Episcopalian. Club: Dolphin Yacht (Camas, Wash.). Current Work: Developed the first effect fungus vaccine to treat as well as prevent microsporim canis in cats and dogs and aspergillus fumigatus for birds, producer of many veterinarian vaccines for domestic animals. Subspecialties: Microbiology (veterinary medicine); Immunology (agriculture). Home: PO Box 828 Camas WA 98607 Office: Willamette Animal Lab 26610 E Crown Point Hwy Corbett OR 97019

STODDARD, STEPHEN DAVIDSON, engineer, banker, state legislator; b. Everett, Wash., Feb. 8, 1925; s. Albert and Mary Louise (Billings) S.; m. Joann Elizabeth Burt, June 18, 1949; children—Dorcas Ann Avery, Stephanie Kay. B.S. in Ceramic Engring., U. Ill., 1950. Registered profl. engr., N.M. Asst. ceramic engr. Coors Porcelain Co., Golden, Colo., 1950-52; section leader ceramics, powder-metallurgy Los Alamos Sci. Lab. U. Calif., N.Mex., 1952-80; pres., treas. Materials Tech. Assocs., Inc., Los Alamos, 1978—; dir. Bank of Los Alamos. Co-author book chpts. on nuclear fuels, ceramics. Patentee in field. Contbr. articles to tech. jours. Municipal judge, county commr. Los Alamos, Santa Fe, and Standovol counties; state senator State of N.Mex. Served to capt. U.S. Army Corp of Engrs, 1943-46, ETO. Recipient Graves-Walker award Nat. Inst. Ceramic engrs., 1984. Fellow Am. Ceramics Soc. (pres. 1976-77, named Nation's Outstanding Ceramic Engr., 1964, disting. life mem.). Republican. Episcopalian. Lodges: Kiwianis, Elks, Masons, Shriners. Current work: Materials engineering and processing for hostile environments especially high temperatures, corrosive and radio active environments. Subspecialties: Ceramics; High-temperature materials. Home: 326 Kimberly Lane Los Alamos NM 87544 Office: Materials Tech Assocs Inc PO Box 11 Los Alamos NM 87544

STOEBE, THOMAS GAINES, dean, materials science and engineering educator; b. Upland, Calif., Apr. 26, 1939; s. Wallace Theodore and Martha Thomas (Gaines) S.; m. Janet Dumm Jenkins, Aug. 7, 1982; children—Brian, Paul, Diane. B.S., Stanford U., 1961, M.S., 1963, Ph.D., 1965. Postdoctoral fellow Imperial Coll., London, 1965-66; asst. prof. U. Wash., Seattle, 1966-69, assoc. prof., 1969-75, prof., 1975—, assoc. dean, 1982—; vis. prof. U. Sao Paulo, Brazil, 1972-73; mem. bd. Wash. State TV System, Pullman, 1984—; mem. bd. Wash. MESA program, Seattle, 1984—. Contbr. articles to profl. jours. Patentee direct response dosimeter, 1975. Spl. fellow AEC, 1962-65. Mem. Am. Soc. Engring. Edn. (Young Faculty award 1972, Western Electric award 1977), Metall. Soc. of AIME (sect. chmn. 1973), Am. Phys. Soc., Am. Ceramic Soc., Sigma Xi. Current work: Luminescent materials, luminescent dosimetry, solid state electronics, lattice defect properties of materials. Subspecialties: Electronic materials; Integrated circuits. Office: U Wash 371 Loew Hall FH-10 Seattle WA 98195

STOERMER, EUGENE FILMORE, biologist, ecologist; b. Webb, Iowa, Mar. 7, 1934; s. E. Filmore and Agnes Elizabeth (Ekstrand) S.; m. Barbara Purves Ryder, Aug. 13, 1960; children—Eric Filmore, Karla Jean, Peter Emil. B.S., Iowa State U., 1958, Ph.D., 1963. Research fellow Acad. Natural Sci., Phila., 1958-59; postdoctoral fellow Iowa State U., Ames, 1963-65; assoc. research scientist U. Mich., Ann Arbor, 1965-71, research scientist, 1971—; Nat. Research Council of Sweden research fellow U. Lund, 1984. Served with U.S. Army, 1954-56. Mem. Phycological Soc. Am. (assoc. editor 1978), Internat. Assn. for Gt. Lakes Research (mem. editorial bd. 1980), Am. Soc. Limnology and Oceanography. Current work: Computer assisted systematic analysis, reconstruction of lake history, and applications of quantitative cytology to ecological problems. Subspecialties: Systematics; Limnology. Home: 4392 Dexter Rd Ann Arbor MI 48103 Office: Gt Lakes Research Div U Mich Ann Arbor MI 48109

STOFAN, ANDREW J., government research institute director. Dir. NASA Lewis Research Ctr., Cleve. Subspecialty: Aerospace engineering and technology. Office: NASA Lewis Research Ctr Office of the Dir Cleveland OH 44135

STOHS, SIDNEY JOHN, pharmacologist, educator; b. Ludell, Kans., May 24, 1939; s. John and Lydia (Holtz) S.; m. Susan Joan Stehl, Sept. 4, 1960; children: Sarah E., Timothy W. B.S. with distinction, U. Nebr., 1962, M.S., 1964; Ph.D., U. Wis., 1967; fellow, Karolinska Inst., Stockholm, 1975-76. Registered pharmacist, Nebr. Asst. prof. U. Nebr., 1967-71, asso. prof., chmn. dept. medicinal chemistry, 1971-74; prof., chmn. dept. medicinal chemistry U. Nebr. (Med. Center), 1974-78, prof., chmn. dept. biomedical chemistry, 1978—. Contbr. over 150 articles to profl. jours. Pres. First Lutheran Ch., 1979-81, 85—. NIH fellow, 1962-64, 64-67; recipient Outstanding Tchr. award U. Nebr., 1981, Alumni Faculty Outstanding Research award, 1985. Mem. Am. Pharm. Assn., Acad. Pharm. Sci., Am. Chem. Soc., Am. Soc. Pharmacognosy, AAAS, Am. Assn. Colls. Pharmacy, Drug Metabolism Group, Am. Soc. Pharmacology and Exptl. Therapeutics, Internat. Union Pharmacology, Internat. Soc. Study of Xenobiotics, Sigma Xi, Rho Chi. Republican. Current Work: Drug metabolism; molecular mechanisms of aging; chemical carcinogenesis and xenobiotic toxicity. Subspecialties: Medicinal chemistry; Molecular pharmacology. Office: U Nebr Med Center Omaha NE 68105

STOLINSKY, DAVID C., physician; b. Fargo, N.D., Nov. 19, 1934; s. Aaron and Rose Charlotte (Meblin) S.; m. Stefanie Auerbach, May 17, 1966. A.B. with honors, U. Calif., Berkeley, 1955; M.D., U. Calif., San Francisco, 1958. Intern U. Calif., San Francisco, 1958-59; resident Mt. Zion and San Francisco Gen. Hosps., 1959-61; fellow in hematology U. Calif., San Francisco, 1961-63; asst. research physician Cancer Research Inst., 1965-66; fellow in med. oncology U. So. Calif., Los Angeles, 1963-65, asst. prof. medicine, 1966—. Contbr. chpts. to books, articles to profl. jours. Served to lt. comdr. USPHS, 1963-65. Mem. Am. Assn. Cancer Research, Am. Soc. Clin. Oncology, Am. Fedn. Clin. Research, Western Cancer Study Group (sec. 1968-76), Phi Beta Kappa, Phi Delta Epsilon. Current Work: Clinical trials of chemo- and immunotherapy in patients with cancer. Subspecialties: Cancer research (medicine); Chemotherapy. Office: 1200 N State St Los Angeles CA 90033

STOLL, ROGER G., pharmaceutical manufacturing company executive; b. Berlin, May 12, 1942; came to U.S. 1949, naturalized, 1955. B.S. in Pharmacy, Ferris State Coll., 1965; Ph.D. in Biopharmaceutics, U. Conn., 1970; postdoctorate U. Mich., 1970-72. Monitor clin. bioavailability Upjohn Co., Kalamazoo, 1972-76; dir. clin. pharmacology Arnar-Stone lab., McGaw Park, Ill., 1976-79; dir. research and devel. Am. Critical Care, McGaw Park, 1979-80, v.p. research and devel., 1980-82, pres., 1982—. Author: Modern Pharmaceutics, 1979; (monographs) Bioavilability of Drug Products, 1978; Productivity in Pharmaceutical Research and Development, 1981. Chmn. fund drive Jr. Achievement, Chgo., 1982—; mem. exec. com. U. Wis. Found., Madison, 1984; ruling elder ch., Lake Forest, (Ill.), 1984—. Sterling-Winthrop research fellow 1968-70. Mem. Am. Pharm. Assn. (program chmn. 1981), Am. Soc. Clin. Pharmacology and Therapeutics, Pharm. Mfrs. Assn. (bd. dirs. 1983—), Sigma Xi, Rho Chi. Current work: Set strategic business directions for a research and development based pharmaceutical manufacturer. Subspecialty: Pharmaceutical research and development. Office: Am Critical Care div of Am Hosp Supply Corp 1600 Waukegan Rd McGaw Park IL 60085

STOLTENBERG, CARL HENRY, university dean; b. Monterey, Calif., May 17, 1924; s. George L. and Eloise (Hyatt) S.; m. Rosemary Johnson, Apr. 20, 1973; children by previous marriage—Bruce C., Gail L., Susan I., Paul L., Shirley J.; stepchildren—Michael Johnson, Jillean Johnson. B.S., U. Calif. at Berkeley, 1948, M.F., 1949; Ph.D., U. Minn., 1952. Instr. U. Minn., 1949-51; asst. prof. Duke, 1951-56; forest economist U.S. Forest Service, Washington, 1956; chief div. forest econs. research N.E. Forest Expt. Sta., Forest Service, U.S. Dept. Agr., Upper Darby, Pa., 1956-60; head dept. forestry Iowa State U., 1960-67; dean Oreg. State U. Sch. Forestry, Corvallis, 1967—; Mem. adv. bd. Coop. for Research, U.S. Dept. Agr., 1963-67, mem. adv. com. for state and pvt. forestry, 1970-74; mem. Oreg. Bd. Forestry, 1967—, chmn., 1974-84; bd. dirs. Resources for Future, 1980—. Author: Research Planning for Resource Decisions, 1970. Served with AUS, 1943-45; ETO. Mem. AAAS, Soc. Am. Foresters (past mem. council, com. chmn.), Forest Products Research Soc., Am. Econ. Assn., Sigma Xi, Xi Sigma Pi. Methodist. Current work: Management of forest resources research and education. Subspecialties: Agricultural economics; Resource management. Home: 7890 NW Ridgewood Dr Corvallis OR 97330 Office: Forest Research Lab Oreg State U Sch Forestry Corvallis OR 97331

STOMMEL, HENRY MELSON, oceanographer; b. Wilmington, Del., Sept. 27, 1920; m. Elizabeth Huntington Brown, 1950; children—Elijah, Matthew, Abigail. B.S., Yale U., 1942, D.Sc. (hon.), 1970; D.Sc. (hon.), Gothenburg U., 1964, U. Chgo., 1970. Instr. math. and astronomy Yale U., 1942-44; research assoc. phys. oceanography Oceanographic Inst., Woods Hole, Mass., 1944-59, oceanographer, 1978—; prof. oceanography MIT, 1959-60, prof., 1963-78; prof. Harvard U., 1960-63. Author: Science of the Seven Seas, 1945; The Gulf Stream, 1955; (with Elizabeth Stommel) Volcano Weather: The Story of 1816, The Year Without a Summer, 1983. Recipient Crafoord prize, 1983. Mem. Nat. Acad. Sci. (Agassiz medal 1979), Am. Astron. Soc., Am. Soc. Limnology and Oceanography, Am. Acad. Arts and Scis., Am. Geophys. Union (Bowie medal 1982). Subspecialty: Oceanography. Office: Woods Hole Oceanographic Inst Woods Hole MA 02543*

STONE, EDWARD CARROLL, JR., physicist; b. Knoxville, Iowa, Jan. 23, 1936; s. Edward Carroll and Ferne Elizabeth (Baber) S.; m. Alice Trabue Wickliffe, Aug. 4, 1962; children: Susan, Janet. A.A., Burlington Community Coll., 1956; M.S. (NASA fellow), U. Chgo., 1959, Ph.D., 1964. Research fellow in physics Calif. Inst. Tech., Pasadena, 1964-66, sr. research fellow, 1967, mem. faculty, 1967—, prof. physics, 1976—, chmn. div. physics, math. and astronomy, 1983—, Voyager project scientist, 1972—; cons. Office of Space Scis., NASA, 1969—, mem. adv. com. outer planets, 1972-73, mem. high energy astrophysics mgmt. ops. group, 1976—, mem. cosmic ray program working group, 1980-82; editorial bd. Space Sci. Instrumentation, 1975-81, Space Sci. Revs., 1982—, Astrophysics and Space Sci., 1982—; mem. high energy astrophysics mgmt. operating working group Office of Space Scis., NASA Solar System Exploration Com., 1983; mem. com. on space astronomy and astrophysics Space Sci. Bd., 1979-82. Recipient medal for exceptional sci. achievement NASA, 1980, also; Disting. Service medal, 1981; Am. Edn. award, 1981; Dryden award, 1983; Space sci. award AIAA, 1984; Sloan Found. fellow, 1971-73. Fellow Am. Phys. Soc. (chmn. cosmic physics div. 1979-80, exec. com. 1974-76), Am. Geophys. Union, AIAA (assoc.); mem. Am. Astron. Soc. (com. mem. div. planetary scis. 1981-84), Nat. Acad. Scis., Am. Assn. Physics Tchrs., AAAS; corr. mem. Internat. Acad. Astronautics. Current Work: Experimental studies of galactic and solar cosmic rays and planetary magnetospheres. Scientific coordination of outer planet exploration. Subspecialties: Cosmic ray high energy astrophysics; Planetary science. Office: 103-33 E Bridge Lab Calif Inst Tech 1201 E California Blvd Pasadena CA 91125

STONE, GREGORY MICHAEL, research engineer, business executive; b. Hartford, Conn., July 31, 1959; s. George William and Patricia Gertrude (Fitton) S. A.B., Loyola U., Chgo., 1981; postgrad., Pacific Western U., 1982. Electronic system design engr. Barrett Electronics Corp., Northbrook, Ill., 1977-80; cons. engr. Tyndale-Dausen, Ltd., Mundelein, Ill., 1977-80, Sachs/-Freeman Assocs., Inc., Northbrook, 1980—; mng. dir., chief scientist Stone Industries Inc., Mundelein, 1982—, also dir.; dir. Consol. News Service Ltd. Mem. IEEE, Soc. Am. Mil. Engrs., Soc. Cable TV Engrs., Amateur Radio Satellite Corp., Soc. Automotive Engrs., Radio Club Am., Midwest Intersystem Repeater Assn., John Birch Soc., SAR, Mayflower Soc. Republican. Current Work: Audio frequency bandwidth compression; magnetic anomolie detection communications systems design; radio frequency propagation empirical research. Subspecialties: Electronics; Robotics. Home: 1112 Regency Ln Libertyville IL 60048 Office: PO Box 485 Mundelein IL 60060

STONE, JACK LEE, electrical engineer; b. Taylor, Tex., July 12, 1941; s. Jack Edgar and Ludie Ceclia (Kovar) S.; m. Valene Joyce Koss, June 15, 1966; children—Adrienne Kathleen, Jonathan Edward, Megan Marie. B.S.E.E., U. Tex., 1963, M.S.E.E., 1964, Ph.D. in Elec. Engring., 1968. Registered profl. engr., Tex. Asst. prof. U. Tex., Austin, 1968-69; from asst. prof. to assoc prof. Tex. A&M U., College Station, 1969-78; sr. scientist Solar Energy Research Inst., Golden, Colo., 1978-80, branch chief, 1980-82, dept. div. dir., 1982—; vis. scientist Inaoe, Puebla, Mex., 1972-73. Inventor in field. Contbr. chpt. to book. Mem. IEEE, Am. Phys. Soc., Electorchem. Soc., Tau Beta Pi, Eta Kappa Nu, Sigma Xi, Pi Eta Sigma. Roman Catholic. Current work: Applied superconductivity; intergrated circuits; photovoltaics; amorphous materials. Subspecialties: Electrical engineering; Solar energy. Home: 8410 W 5th Pl Lakewood CO 80226 Office: 1617 Cole Blvd Golden CO 80401

STONE, JULIAN, physicist; b. N.Y.C., Apr. 12, 1929; s. Harry and Etta (Fishman) S.; m. Florence Pistreich, June 16, 1951; children: David, Hillary, Robert. B.S., CCNY, 1950, M.S., 1951; Ph.D., N.Y.U., 1958. Material scientist Naval Material Lab., 1952; tutor CCNY, 1952-53, 1956-57; assoc. dir. Hudson Labs., Columbia U., 1953-69; mem. tech. staff Bell Labs., Holmdel, N.J., 1969—. Assoc. editor Optics Letters. Contbr. numerous articles on optics and acoustics to tech. jours. Fellow Optical Soc. Am. Current Work: Fiber optics and lasers. Subspecialties: Fiber optics; Laser spectroscopy.

STONE, MARVIN JULES, hematologist-oncologist, educator; b. Columbus, Ohio, Aug. 3, 1937; s. Roy J. and Lillian (Bedwinek) S.; m. Jill Ruth Feinstein, June 29, 1958; children—Nancy Lillian, Robert Howard. Student Ohio State U., 1955-58; M.S., U. Chgo., 1962, M.D. with honors, 1963. Diplomate Am. Bd. Internal Medicine, Am. Bd. Hematology, Am. Bd. Med. Oncology. Clin. assoc. NIAMD-NIH, Bethesda, Md., 1965-68; fellow hematology-oncology U. Tex. Southwestern Med. Sch., Dallas, 1969-70, instr. internal medicine, 1970-71, asst. prof., 1971-73, assoc. prof., 1974-76; chief oncology, dir. immunology Baylor U. Med. Ctr., Dallas, 1976—; clin. prof. internal medicine U. Tex. Health Sci. Ctr., Dallas, 1976—; dir. Sammons Cancer Ctr., Baylor U. Med. Ctr., 1976—; adj. prof. biology So. Methodist U., Dallas, 1977—. Contbr. articles to profl. jours. Bd. dirs. Leukemia Soc. Am., Dallas, 1971—, Baylor Research Found., 1984—; pres. Am. Cancer Soc., Dallas, 1978-80; mem. adv. bd. Lupus Found. Am., Dallas, 1982—. Served to lt. comdr. USPHS, 1965-68. ACP postgrad. scholar, 1968-69; established investigator Am. Heart Assn., 1970-75. Fellow ACP; mem. Am. Soc. Hematology, Internat. Soc. Hematology, Am. Assn. Immunologists, Am. Assn. Cancer Research, Am. Soc. Clin. Oncology, Sigma Xi, Phi Beta Kappa. Current work: Immunochemistry; monoclonal immunoglobulins; multiple myeloma; related plasma cell dyscrasias; monoclonal antibodies to lung cancer antigens. Subspecialties: Cancer research (medicine); Immunology (medicine). Office: Baylor U Med Ctr 3500 Gaston Ave Dallas TX 75246

STONE, WILLIAM HAROLD, geneticist, educator; b. Boston, Dec. 15, 1924; s. Robert and Rita (Scheinberg) S.; m. Elaine Morein, Nov. 24, 1947; children: Susan Joy, Debra M.; m. Carmen Maqueda, Dec. 22, 1971; 1 son, Alexander R.M. A.B., Brown U., 1948; M.S., U. Maine, 1949; Ph.D., U. Wis., 1953; Sc.D. (hon.), U. Cordoba, Spain, 1984. Research asst. Jackson Meml. Lab., Bar Harbor, Maine, 1947-48; faculty dept. genetics U. Wis., Madison, 1949-83, prof., 1961-83, prof. med. genetics, 1964-83; Cowles Disting. prof. dept. biology Trinity U., San Antonio, 1983—; staff scientist S.W. Found. for Biomed. Research, San Antonio, 1983—; adj. prof. dept. cellular structural biology U. Tex. Health Sci. Ctr., 1985; NIH fellow Calif. Inst. Tech., 1960-61; mem. panel blood group experts FAO, 1962-67, program dir. immunogenetics research, Spain, 1971-74; mem. NIH study sect. on gen. med. sci., 1984; mem. tech. adv. com. grants program in biotech. U.S. Dept. Agr., 1985; mem. sci. adv. bd. Tex. Research and Tech. Found. Author: Immunogenetics, 1967; Contbr. articles to profl. jours. Recipient I.I. Ivanov medal USSR, 1974. Mem. Am. Inst. Biol. Scis., NRC, Assembly Life Scis., Nat. Acad. Scis., AAAS, Am. Soc. Immunologists, Am. Genetics Assn., Am. Aging Soc., Genetics Soc., Am. Soc. Human Genetics, Research Soc. Am., Internat. Soc. Transplant, Am. Soc. Animal Sci., Internat. Primatological Soc., Sigma Xi, Gamma Alpha., Beta Beta Beta. Current Work: Immuno genetics in mammals. Subspecialties:

Animal genetics; Immunology (agriculture). Office: Dept Biology Trinity U San Antonio TX 78284

STONE, WILLIAM ROSS, physicist, high technology research and development company executive; b. San Diego, Aug. 26, 1947; s. William Jack and Winifred (Beckcom) S.; m. Susan L. Lane, Aug. 8, 1970; 1 dau., Ann Michele. B.A., U. Calif.-San Diego, La Jolla, 1967, M.S., 1973, Ph.C., 1978, Ph.D., 1978. Research asst. U. Calif.-San Diego, 1967-69; sr. physicist Gulf Gen. Atomic, La Jolla, 1969-73; sr. scientist Megatek Corp., San Diego, 1973-80; prin. physicist, leader computer ctr. and inverse scattering group IRT Corp., San Diego, 1980—; pres. Stoneware Ltd., La Jolla, 1976—. Contbr. numerous articles to profl. publs.; editor: New Methods for Optical, Quasi-Optical, Acoustic, and Electromagnetic Synthesis, 1981; editor, columnist: IEEE Antennas and Propagation Soc, 1980—. Mem. adminstrv. bd. First United Methodist Ch., San Diego, 1964—, trustee, chmn. fin. com., 1975-80; trustee Samaritan Ctr. Recipient medal San Diego Soc. Tech. Writers and Pubs., 1962. Mem. Internat. Radio Sci. Union (mem. U.S. nat. com. Commn. B. 1979—), U.S. Nat. Com. of Union Radio Scientifique Internationale (assoc. mem. Commn. G. 1979—), IEEE (profl. activities coordinator 1969—), Optical Soc. Am., Acoustical Soc. Am., Soc. Exploration Geophysicists, AAUP. Democrat. Current Work: Fundamental research in inverse scattering theory, its application to seismic exploration, radar, sonar, and optical remote probing; basic and applied research in electromagnetic field theory. Subspecialties: Theoretical physics; Electronics. Home: 1446 Vista Claridad La Jolla CA 92037 Office: IRT Corp 3030 Callan Rd San Diego CA 92121

STONEBRAKER, JEFFREY SCOT, military officer; b. Freeport, Ill., Sept. 21, 1959; s. Russell Oliver Stonebraker and Patricia Gladys (Strangberg) Smith; m. Nancy Christiana Popham, Dec. 18, 1982. B.E.E., U. South Fla., 1983. Elec. engring. tutor, radar systems officer, Project Thrust, U.S. Air Force, Hill AFB, Utah, 1983—. Cert. engr.-in-tng. Mathcounts vol. Utah State Profl. Engrs., Ogden, 1984; youth bowling coach Hill AFB, 1983-84; squadron athletic rep. 1954 Radar Evaluation Squadron, 1983-84. Serving as 2d lt. USAF, 1983—. Recipient Internat. Youth in Achievement award Am. Biog. Inst., 1980; named to Nat. Dean's List Ednl. Communication, Inc., 1978-79. Mem. IEEE, IEEE Aerospace Electronic Systems Soc., Nat. Soc. Profl. Engrs., Armed Forces Communications and Electronics Assn., Tau Beta Pi, Phi Kappa Phi. Republican. Club: Officers (Hill AFB). Current work: Designs complex test plans to evaluate operational capabilities and limitations of air defense radar systems worldwide. Subspecialty: Systems engineering. Home: 3061B Concord St Hill AFB UT

STONER, MARTIN FRANKLIN, plant pathology educator, cons.; b. Pasadena, Calif., Jan. 19, 1942; s. Robert Chester and Genevieve Virginia (Perrin) S.; m. Darleen Kay Roberts, June 13, 1963. B.S., Calif. State Poly. Coll., 1963; Ph.D., Washington State U., 1967. Research asst. Wash. State U., Pullman, 1963-67; asst. prof. Calif. State Poly. U., Pomona, 1967-70, assoc. prof., 1970-75, prof. plant pathology and mycology, 1975—, plant pathologist, 1967—; vis. prof., researcher plant pathology U. Hawaii, Honolulu, 1980-81. Named Disting. Alumnus in Sci. Calif. State Poly. U., 1982; Hawaii Ecosystems Analysis Project, Internat. Biol. Program, NSF grantee, 1972-75. Mem. Am. Phytopath. Soc. (pres. Pacific div. 1980-81), AAAS, Bot. Soc. Am., Mycological Soc. Am., Am. Theater Organ Soc. Current Work: Applications of soil mycology and plant pathology in agrotech. transfer systems; innovative methods for assessment of fungi in soil ecosystems; integrated mgmt. plant diseases with spl. emphasis on cultural factors; post-harvest pathology; myco ecology and biotechnology of sewage sludge processing and utilization. Subspecialties: Plant pathology; Integrated systems modelling and engineering. Office: 3801 W Temple Ave Pomona CA 91768

STORK, GILBERT (JOSSE), chemistry educator; b. Brussels, Belgium, Dec. 31, 1921; s. Jacques and Simone (Weil) S.; m. Winifred Stewart, June 9, 1944; children: Diana, Linda, Janet, Philip. B.S., U. Fla., 1942; Ph.D., U. Wis., 1945; D.Sc. (hon.), Lawrence Coll., 1961, U. Paris, 1979, U. Rochester, 1982. Sr. research chemist Lakeside Labs., 1945-46; instr. chemistry Harvard, 1946-48, asst. prof., 1948-53; asso. prof. Columbia, 1953-55, prof., 1955-67, Eugene Higgins prof., 1967—, chmn. dept., 1973-76; plenary lectr. numerous internat. symposia. Vis. lectr. Swiss Am. Found. Sci. Exchange, 1959; Coover lectr., 1958, Folkers lectr.; Bachmann lectr., 1962, Treat B. Johnson lectr.; Frank Burnet Dains lectr., 1964; Kharasch vis. prof. U. Chgo.; Foster lectr. U. Buffalo, 1966; vis. scholar Fisk U., 1967; T. Dale Stewart lectr.; distinguished vis. prof. U. Iowa, 1968; Seydell Wooley lectr. Ga. Inst. Tech.; Karl Pfister lectr. Mass. Inst. Tech.; Robert Gnehm lectr. ETH, Zurich, 1969; Univ. lectr. U. Western Ont., 1974; Phi Lambda Upsilon lectr. Johns Hopkins, 1974; Centenary lectr. Brit. Chem. Soc., 1975; Tishler lectr. Harvard, 1975; John Howard Appleton lectr. Brown U.; Distinguished vis. lectr. U. Rochester; Benjamin Rush lectr. U. Pa., 1976; Royal Australian Chem. Inst. lectr., 1977; McElvain vis. scholar U. Wis., 1977; Debye lectr. Cornell U., 1977; Alexander Todd vis. prof. Cambridge (Eng.) U., 1979; Sandin lectr. U. Alta., 1980; Frank Mathers lectr. U. Ind., 1981; Greater Manchester lectr., 1982; Lemieux lectr. U. Ottawa, 1982; H. Martin Friedman lectr. Rutgers U., 1982; disting. lectr. U. Tex., 1983; Mack lectr. Ohio State U., 1983; H. C. Brown lectr. Purdue U., 1984; Warner Lambert Disting. lectr. U. Mich., 1985; cons. Syntex, Internat. Flavors and Fragrances; chmn. Gordon Steroid Conf., 1958-59; bd. editors Jour. Organic Chemistry, 1955-61. Hon. adv. editor: Tetrahedron Letters, Nouveau Jour. de Chimie, Heterocycles; Editorial bd.: Accounts of Chem. Research, 1968-71. Recipient Baekeland medal, 1961; Harrison Howe award, 1962; Edward Curtis Franklin Meml. award Stanford, 1966; award for creative work in synthetic organic chemistry Am. Chem. Soc., 1967; Gold medal Synthetic Chems. Mfrs. Assn., 1971; Nebr. award, 1973; Roussel prize in steroid chemistry, 1978; Linus Pauling award, 1983; Edgar Fahs Smith award, 1982; Willard Gibbs medal, 1982; Nat. medal of sci., 1982; Guggenheim fellow, 1959. Fellow Am. Acad. Arts and Scis., Nat. Acad. Scis. (award in chem scis. 1982), Royal Soc. Chemistry (hon.); mem. Chemist Club (hon.), Am. Chem. Soc. (award in pure chemistry 1957, Nichols medal 1980, Arthur C. Cope award 1980, chmn. organic chemistry div. 1967), Pharm. Soc. Japan (hon.). Subspecialty: Organic chemistry. Home: 459 Next Day Hill Englewood NJ 07631 Office: Columbia U New York NY 10027

STORM, DAVID ANTHONY, chemist; b. Bridgeton, N.J., Nov. 8, 1938; s. Francis Anthony and Gertrude (Robbinson) S.; m. Joanne Runk, Sept. 9, 1961; children: John, Elaine. B.S., Lehigh U., 1960; Ph.D. in Chemistry, Poly. Inst. Bklyn., 1970; Ph.D. in Chem. Engring, Stanford U., 1978. Engr. Celanese Corp. Am., Houston, 1960-65; research assoc. U. Tex., Dallas, 1971-75; sr. research engr. Halcon Research and Devel., Montavle, N.J., 1978-81; group leader Texaco, Inc., Beacon, N.Y., 1981-83, research coordinator, 1983—. Contbr. articles to profl. jours. NASA grad. trainee Poly. Inst. Bklyn., 1967-69; NSF grad. trainee, 1969-70; Robert A. Welch Found. fellow U. Tex., 1971-75. Mem. Am. Chem. Soc., Am. Inst. Chem. Engrs., Am. Phys. Soc., ASTM, N.Y. Acad. Scis., Sigma Xi. Presbyterian. Patentee in field. Current Work: Surface chemistry, catalysis chemistry, inorganic chemistry, chemical engineering, solid state chemistry. Subspecialties: Catalysis chemistry; Chemical engineering. Home: 35 Valley View Terrace Montvale NJ 07645 Office: PO Box 509 New Tech Research Beacon NY 12508

STORM, ROGER S., oil company executive, chemical engineer; b. Buffalo, Jan. 6, 1943; s. Bernard and Lorraine S.; m. Elizabeth Storm, Aug. 8, 1964; children—Jonathan, Sarah, Jessica. B.A., SUNY-Buffalo, 1964, Ph.D., 1969. Sr. research assoc. Carborundum Co., Niagara Falls, N.Y., 1969-73, sr. devel. assoc., 1973-80, project mgr., 1980-81, mgr. advanced processing, 1981-84; dir. research and devel. Sohio Engineered Materials Co., Niagara Falls, 1984—. Contbr. articles to profl. jours. Patentee in field. Mem. Am. Ceramic Soc., Am. Chem. Soc., Am. Mgmt. Assn. Current work: Directing the efforts of a sector laboratory to provide a diversification into a wide range of cermaic materials including structural, fibers, coatings and composites. Subspecialties: Ceramics; Physical chemistry. Office: Sohio PO Box 832 Niagara Falls NY 14302

STORMONT, CLYDE JUNIOR, immunogeneticist, educator; b. Viola, Wis., June 25, 1916; s. Clyde James and Lulu Elizabeth (Mathews) S.; m. Marguerite Butzen, Aug. 31, 1940; children: Bonnie Lu, Michael Clyde, Robert Thomas, Charles James, Janet Jean. B.A. in Zoology, U. Wis., 1938, Ph.D. in Genetics, 1947. Instr., lectr., then asst. prof. U. Wis., 1946-50; asst., then asso., then prof. dept. vet. microbiology U. Calif., Davis, 1950-60, prof. dept. reprodn., 1973-82, prof. emeritus, 1982, dir. serology lab., 1952-81; chmn. Stormont Labs., Inc., Woodland, Calif., 1981—. Contbr. numerous articles to sci. jours. Served with USNR, 1944-46, PTO. Fulbright fellow N.Z., 1949-50; Ellen B. Scripps fellow San Diego Zool. Soc., 1956-57, 64-65. Mem. AAAS, Am. Genetics Assn., Am. Assn. Immunologists, Am. Soc. Naturalists, Genetics Soc. Am., Am. Soc. Human Genetics, Soc. Exptl. Biology and Medicine, Internat. Soc. Animal Bloodgroup Research, Am. Buffalo Assn., Nat. Buffalo Assn.; mem. N.Y. Acad. Scis.; Mem. Sigma Xi. Current Work: Immunogenetic analysis of antigenic determinants which characterize the membrane of blood cells (erythrocytes, lymphocytes and platelets). Subspecialties: Animal genetics; Immunology (agriculture). Home: Route 1 Box 264 Winters CA 95694 Office: 1237 E Beamer St Suite D Woodland CA 95695

STOROZUM, STEVEN LEE, fiber optics company executive, electrical engineer; b. St. Louis, Jan. 14, 1954; s. Henry and Marcella (Goldstein) S. A.B. in Physics, Washington U., St. Louis, 1975; M.S. in Elec. Engring., Carnegie-Mellon U., 1976; postgrad. in Elec. Engring. Va. Inst. Tech., 1978-79. Assoc. in engring. Ill. Inst. Tech. Research Inst. Electromagnetic Compatibility Analysis Ctr., Annapolis, Md., 1977; applications engr. electro-optical products div. ITT, Roanoke, Va., 1977-79; sr. engr. electronics McDonnell Aircraft Co., St. Louis, 1979-82; mgr. local network systems Am. Photonics, Inc., Brookfield Ctr., Conn., 1982—; speaker at profl. confs., 1980—. Contbr. articles to profl. jours. Mem. IEEE, IEEE Quantum Electronics Soc. (assoc. editor newsletter 1981—), Optical Soc. Am., Am. Phys. Soc. Current work: Developing fiber optic local area networks and systems; finding new applications for fiber optic technology. Subspecialties: Fiber optics; Distributed systems and networks. Office: Am Photonics Inc PO Box 289 Brookfield Center CT 06805

STOTHERT, JOSEPH CLARKE, JR., physician, educator; b. Springfield, Mass., Dec. 8, 1948; s. Joseph Clarke and Elizabeth (Wootherspoon) S.; married, Jan. 4, 1980. B.A., MacMurray Coll., 1970; M.D., St. Louis, U., 1974; Ph.D., U. Wash., 1984. Diplomate Am. Bd. Surgery, Am. Bd. Med. Examiners. Intern St. Louis U. Hosps., 1974-75, resident 1975-79, asst. prof. surgery, 1982—, asst. prof. physiol., 1982—, dir. Trauma Div. Emergency Room, 1982—, dir. Med. Air Rescue Corps, 1982—; assoc. chief surgery St. Louis City Hosp., 1982—. Contbr. articles to profl. jours. Grantee, NIH, Inst. Med. Edn. Research. Fellow NIH, 1979-82; mem. ACS, Am. Physil. Soc. (assoc.), Assn. Acad. Surgery, Va. Mason Research Ctr. (affiliate), AAAS, St. Louis Med. Assn., Mo. State Med. Assn., Gateway Vascular Soc., Aerospace Med. Assn., Am. Coll. Emergency Room Physicians, Soc. Critical Care Medicine. Current work: Trauma related subjects; pulmonary physiology; lung injury; lymph fistulae models; Adult Respiratory Distress Syndrome. Office: Dept Surgery 1325 S Grand Saint Louis MO 63104

STOTT, DONALD FRANKLIN, geologist; b. Reston, Man., Can., Apr. 30, 1928; s. Franklin Brisbin and Catherine Alice (Parker) S.; m. Margaret Elinor Hutton, Oct. 8, 1960; children: Glenn, David, Donald. B.Sc. with honors, U. Man., 1953, M.Sc., 1954; M.Sc., Princeton U., 1956, Ph.D., 1958. Jr. geologist Consol. Mining and Smelter Co., 1952, Calif. Standard Oil Co., summer 1953; research geologist Geol. Survey Can., 1957-66, head mesozoic stratigraphy sect., 1967-72, head regional geology subdiv., 1972-73; dir. Inst. Sedimentary and Petroleum Geology, Calgary, Alta., 1973-80, research scientist, 1980—. Contbr. articles to profl. jours. Recipient Willet G. Miller medal Royal Soc. Can., 1983. Fellow Geol. Assn. Can., Geol. Soc. Am.; mem. Can. Soc. Petroleum Geologists (v.p. 1977, pres. 1978), Soc. Econ. Paleontologists, Sigma Xi. Subspecialty: Geology. Office: 3303 33d St NW Calgary AB T2L 2A7 Canada

STOUT, BENJAMIN BOREMAN, university dean; b. Parkersburg, W.Va., Mar. 2, 1924; s. Clarence P. and Laurane (Boreman) S.; m. Phyllis Ingraham, Sept. 4, 1945; children—Susan L., David F., Bruce D. B.S. in Forestry, W.Va. U., 1947; M.Forestry, Harvard U., 1950; Ph.D., Rutgers U., 1967. Forester, Pond & Moyer Co., Ithaca, N.Y., 1947-48; silviculturist Harvard U., Cornwall, N.Y., 1950-58; prof. Rutgers U., New Brunswick, N.J., 1958-78; dean of forestry U. Mont., Missoula, 1978—; mem. Coop. Forestry Research Adv. Council, U.S. Dept. Agr., Washington, 1983—. Editor: Forests in Here and Now, 1981. Contbr. articles to sci. publs. Mem., officer Cornwall Bd. Edn., 1950s. Served to 2d lt. U.S. Army, 1943-45, ETO. Decorated Bronze Star. Mem. Soc. Am. Foresters (sec., chmn. 1948—), AAAS, Ecol. Soc. Am., Sigma Xi. Club: Missoula Country (pres. 1984). Current work: Research administration and management of forest systems. Subspecialties: Silviculture; Biostatistics. Office: Sch Forestry U Mont Missoula MT 59812

STOUT, LANDON CLARKE, JR., physician, pathologist, educator; b. Kans. City, Mo., Feb. 20, 1933; s. Landon Clarke and Mildred Ann (Buckner) S.; m. Martha Ann McKone, May 1, 1954 (div. 1975); children—Lynn, Clinton, Karen, Halsted; m. Elaine Marie Farrell, Feb. 28, 1981. B.S., U. Md. Coll. Pk., 1953; M.D., U. Md., 1957. Diplomate Am. Bd. Pathology. Asst. prof. medicine, U. Okla., Okla. City, 1963-72; asst. prof. pathology U. Okla., Okla. City, 1968-71; assoc. prof., 1971-72; assoc. prof. U. Tex. Med. Branch, Galveston, 1972-74, prof. pathology, 1974—; interim chmn. pathology U. Okla. Med. Ctr., Okla. City, 1970-72; dir. autopsy U. Tex. Med. Branch, Galveston, 1972-77; dir. residency program U. Tex. Med. Branch, Galveston, 1975—. Contbr. articles to profl. jours. Grantee NIH, John A. Hartford Found. Fellow Am. Heart Assn., Am. Coll. Physicians, Am. Gastroent. Assn., Am. Assn. Pathologists, Internat. Acad. Pathology. Current work: Diabetic micro angiopathy; diffuse intimal thickening in animal and human aortas. Subspecialty: Pathology (medicine). Office: U Tex Med Branch Dept Pathology Galveston TX 77550

STOUT, ROBERT DANIEL, educator, univ. dean emeritus; b. Reading, Pa., Jan. 2, 1915; s. Harry Herbert and Anna (Guldin) S.; m. Elizabeth Allwein, Aug. 16, 1939; 1 dau., Elizabeth Ann. B.S., Pa. State U., 1935; M.S., Lehigh U., 1941, Ph.D., 1944; D.Sc., Albright Coll., 1967. Metall. engr. Carpenter Steel Co., 1935-39; faculty Lehigh U., Bethlehem, Pa., 1939—, prof. metallurgy, 1950—; dean Lehigh U. (Grad. Sch.), 1960-80, dean emeritus, 1980—; Metall. cons. Author: Weldability of Steels, 1953, 71; Contbr. articles to profl. publs. Fellow Am. Soc. Metals (Stoughton Teaching award 1952, White Disting. Teaching award 1974); mem. Am. Welding Soc. (pres. 1972-73, Lincoln gold medal 1943, Adams lectr. 1960, Sparagen award 1964, Thomas award 1973, Jennings award 1974, Am. del. Internat. Inst. Welding 1955—, Houdremont lectr. 1970), Am. Soc. Engring. Edn., Sigma Xi. Current Work: Metallurgical effects of welding; mechanical properties of welded alloy steels used for pressure vessels and cryogenic applications. Subspecialties: Metallurgical engineering; Fracture mechanics. Home: 141 E Market St Bethlehem PA 18018

STOWE, BRUCE BERNOT, biologist, educator, plant biochemist; b. Neuilly-sur-Seine, France, Dec. 9, 1927; s. Lel and Ruth Florida (Bernot) S.; m. Elizabeth Louise Kwasny, June 23, 1951; children: Mark Kwasny, Eric Bernot. B.Sc., Calif. Inst. Tech., 1950; A.M., Harvard U., 1951, Ph.D., 1954; M.A. (hon.), Yale U., 1971. NSF fellow Univ. Coll. North Wales, 1954-55; instr. biology Harvard U., Cambridge, Mass., 1955-58, tutor biochem. scis., 1956-58, lectr. botany, 1958-59; asst. prof. botany Yale U., New Haven, 1959-63, assoc. prof. biology, 1963-71, prof. biology, 1971—, prof. forestry, 1974—; dir. Marsh Bot. Garden, 1975-78, 82; vis. prof. U. Osaka, Japan, 1972, 73, Waite Agrl. Research Inst., U. Adelaide, South Australia, 1972-73, external examiner various Can. and Indian univs.; cons. plant biochemistry to industry. Contbr. articles to sci. jours.; editorial bd.: Plant Physiology, 1965-84; editorial com.: Ann. Rev. Plant Physiology, 1968-73. Served with Signal Corps U.S. Army, 1946-47. AEC fellow, 1951-53; Lalor Found. fellow, 1953-54; Guggenheim fellow, 1965-66. Fellow AAAS; mem. Am. Soc. Plant Physiologists (exec. com. 1960-65, sec. 1963-65, trustee 1970-72, 75-77), AAUP (chpt. exec. com. 1963-75, chpt. sec.-treas. 1969-75, chpt. pres. 1966-68), Am. Soc. Biol. Chemists, Am. Soc. Plant Physiology, Bot. Soc. Am., Phytochem. Soc., Soc. Plant Growth Regulation, Soc. Developmental Biology, Soc. Gen. Physiology, Fedn. Am. Scientists, Am. Inst. Biol. Scis., Biochem. Soc. (U.K.), Soc. Exptl. Biology (U.K.), Soc. Physiol. Végétale (France), Soc. Botanique de France, Scandinavian Soc. Plant Physiology, Japanese Soc. Plant Physiology, Sigma Xi, Australian Soc. Plant Physiology, Sigma Xi. Democrat. Current Work: Biochemistry and physiology of plant hormones and membranes; physiologically active lipids; membrane modelling by bioassay; computer correlations of biological data and molecular models; computer aids to handicapped. Subspecialties: Plant physiology (biology); Biochemistry (biology). Home: 161 Grand View Ave Hamden CT 06514 Office: 46A Kline Biology Tower Yale U Box 6666 New Haven CT 06511

STOWELL, ROBERT EUGENE, pathologist, medical educator, administrator, researcher, consultant; b. Cashmere, Wash., Dec. 25, 1914; s. Eugene Frances and Mary (Wilson) S.; m. Eva Mae Chambers, Dec. 1, 1945; children: Susan Jane, Robert Eugene. Student, Whitman Coll., 1932-33; A.B. with honors, Stanford U., 1936, M.D., 1941; Ph.D. (Univ. fellow), Washington U., St. Louis, 1944. Diplomate: Am. Bd. Pathology. Asst. resident in pathology Barnes, McMillan, Children's hosps., St. Louis, 1942-43, resident, 1943-44; research assoc. Barnard Free Skin and Cancer Hosp., St. Louis, 1942-48; instr. pathology Washington U. Sch. Medicine, St. Louis, 1943-45, asst. prof., 1945-48, assoc. prof., 1948; chmn. dept. oncology U. Kans. Med. Center, 1948-51, prof. pathology and oncology, 1948-59, dir. cancer research, 1948-59, chmn. dept. pathology and oncology, 1951-59, pathologist-in-chief, 1951-59; sci. dir. Armed Forces Inst. Pathology, Washington, 1959-67; vis. prof. pathology U. Md., 1960-67; chmn. dept. pathology U. Calif. Sch. Medicine-Davis, 1967-69; asst. dean U. Calif. Sch. Medicine-Davis (Sch. Medicine), 1967-72, prof. pathology, 1967-82, emeritus prof. pathology, 1982—; acting dir. Nat. Ctr. Primate Biology, 1968-69, dir., 1969-71; dir. div. pathology Sacramento Med. Center, 1967-69, mem. numerous adv. coms. and cons. to govt. Contbr. articles in pathology to med. jours. Recipient Meritorious Service award Dept. Army, 1963, Exceptional Civilian Service award, 1965. Mem. AAAS, Am. Assn. Cancer Research, Am. Assn. Pathologists and Bacteriologists (pres. 1970-71), AMA, Am. Soc. Clin. Pathologists, Am. Soc. Exptl. Pathology (pres. 1964-65), Assn. Am. Med. Colls., Calif. Med. Soc., Calif. Soc. Pathologists, Coll. Am. Pathologists, Histochem. Soc., Internat. Acad. Pathology (pres. 1959-60), Radiation Research Soc., Soc. Cryobiology (bd. govs. 1968-71), Soc. Exptl. Biology and Medicine, Yolo County Med. Soc., Phi Beta Kappa, Sigma Xi, Alpha Omega Alpha. Current Work: Human and experimental pathology; pathology education and administration; cancer research; consultant. Subspecialties: Pathology (medicine); Cancer research (medicine). Home: PO Box 3061 El Macero CA 95618 Office: Dept Pathology Sch Medicine U Calif Davis CA 95616

STRADER, HERMAN LEE, biology educator; b. Danville, Va., Aug. 9, 1920; s. Wesley Samuel and Margaret (Clark) S.; m. Edna Mae Mitchell, Nov. 27, 1948. B.S. in Biology, Va. Union U., 1946; M.S., Columbia U., 1952, Ed.D., 1965. Lab. asst. dept. biology Va. Union U., Richmond, 1945-46, instr., 1948-50, asst. prof., 1952-60, assoc. prof., 1960-72, prof., 1972—; sci. cons. Richmond Pub. Schs., Va., 1972-80. Author: A Program of Conservation Education, 1970. Mem. Falls of the James Environ. Com., Richmond, 1978-82. Danforth Found. fellow, 1958; United Negro Coll. Fund fellow, 1963; Nat. Wildlife Found. fellow, 1965; Macy Found. fellow, 1972. Mem. Am. Inst. Biol. Scis., Bot. Soc. Am., AAAS, Nat. Sci. Tchrs. Assn., Ecol. Soc. Am., Beta Kappa Chi. Baptist. Current Work: General biology, ecology and comparative anatomy. Subspecialties: Ecology (environmental science); Plant growth. Home: 2209 Northumberland Ave Richmond VA 23220 Office: Va Union U Dept Biology 1500 N Lombardy St Richmond VA 23220

STRAHLENDORF, JEAN CAROL, neurophysiologist and neuropharmacologist, researcher; b. Houston, Jan. 29, 1949; d. Albert Henry and Willyne Ruth (Vidrine) Roberts; m. Howard Kurt Strahlendorf, June 9, 1973. B.S. in Pharmacy cum laude, U. Houston, 1972; M.S. in Pharmacology, Phila. Coll. Pharmacy and Sci., 1974, Ph.D. in Pharmacology, 1978. Registered pharmacist, Tex. Teaching asst., instr. Phila. Coll. Pharmacy and Sci., 1972-74; grad. instr. U. Pa., Phila., 1976-77; lectr. Tex. Tech U. Sch. Medicine, Lubbock, 1977-80, postdoctoral fellow, 1979-80, NIH postdoctoral fellow, 1979-80, asst. prof. Health Scis. Ctr., 1980—. Author: Neural Control of Circulation, 1980; Mouse in Biomedical Research, 1982; Progress in Clinical and Biological Research, 1981, Progress in Clinical and Biological Research, vol. 68, 1981. Contbr. articles to profl. jours. Speaker research awareness Tex. affiliate, Am. Heart Assn., Lubbock, 1982—. Harrison Meml. fellow in pharmacology, 1976-77; grantee Am. Heart Assn., 1983-85, NIH, 1983—. Mem. Soc. Neurosci., West Tex. Soc. Neurosci. (sec. 1981-84, pres. 1985—), Am. Physiol. Soc., Sigma Chi, Rho Chi. Current work: Neurotransmitter and neuromodulator systems in the central nervous system. Subspecialties: Neurophysiology; Neuropharmacology. Home: 6803 1st St Route 8 Lubbock TX 79407 Office: Tex Tech U Health Scis Ctr Dept Physiology Lubbock TX 79430

STRAIN, BOYD RAY, botany educator, director of phytotron; b. Laramie, Wyo., July 19, 1935; s. Harold Ray and Elizabeth Alzina (Redd) S.; m. Joan Marie Bacon, June 8, 1958; children—Robert Jay, Katherine Kay. B.S. in Edn., Black Hills State Coll., 1960; M.S., U. Wyo., 1961; Ph.D., UCLA, 1964. Asst. prof. U. Calif.-Riverside, 1964-69; assoc. prof. botany Duke U., Durham, N.C., 1969-77, prof., 1977—; vis. research prof. Nuclear Research Ctr., Julich, Federal Republic Germany, 1975-76; adj. prof. Desert Research Inst., Reno, Nev., 1984. Editor: Vegetation and Environment, 1974. Contbr. articles to profl. jours. Served with U.S. Army, 1955-58, Korea. NSF grantee, 1965—. Mem. Ecol. Soc. Am. (council 1978-80), Am. Inst. Biol. Scis. (bd. govs 1981—), AAAS (rep. biology sect. 1982-84). Current work: Physiological ecology of plants; plant responses to environmental stress; plant response to atmospheric CO2 increase. Subspecialties: Ecology (biology); Botany. Office: Duke U Dept Botany Durham NC 27706

STRAIN, JOHN WILLARD, aerospace company executive, consultant; b. Ottumwa, Iowa, Dec. 31, 1929; s. John Wells and Agnes Gertrude (Kearns) S.; m. Elizabeth LaVonne Moment, Dec. 27, 1952 (dec. 1969); children: James Anthony, Mary Therese, Michael Douglas, Meagan Kathleen. B.A., U. No. Iowa, 1952. Rocket power plant engr. White Sands Proving Ground, Las Cruces, N.Mex., 1954-55; mgr. Lockheed Missile & Space Co., Santa Cruz, Calif., 1960-63, Sunnyvale, Calif., 1947-73, RPV Aquila chief test engr., 1975-79, factory test mgr., 1979-82, div. mgr., 1982—; owner Indsl. Systems Co., Sunnyvale, 1976—. Assoc. editor: Missile Away Mag, 1954-55. Bd. dirs. San Jose Civic Light Opera, 1972; leader Boy Scouts Am., San Jose, 1964. Served with U.S. Army, 1952-54. Recipient Alumni Service award U. No. Iowa, 1981. Fellow AIAA (assoc.); mem. Inst. Environ. Scis. (sr.), Assn. Unmanned Vehicle Systems (treas. 1982-83), AAAS, Nat. Mgmt. Assn. Republican. Roman Catholic. Current Work: Development and test of remotely piloted vehicles with integrated datalink, video sensor, laser capabilities. Subspecialties: Aerospace engineering and technology; Combustion processes. Home: 626 Oneida Dr Sunnyvale CA 94087 Office: Lockheed Missiles and Space Co 1111 Lockheed Way Sunnyvale CA 94086

STRAIN, PRISCILLA LOGAN, geologist, curator; b. Weehawken, N.J., Aug. 15, 1952; d. Robert James and Mildred (Kidd) S. B.A., Smith Coll., 1974. Research asst. Nat. Air & Space Mus., Smithsonian Instn., Washington, 1974-79, geologist, 1979-82, geologist/exhibit curator, 1982—. Contbr. articles to profl. jours. Mem. Geol. Soc. Am. Current work: Lunar geology, remote sensing. Subspecialties: Planetology; Remote sensing (geoscience). Office: Center for Earth and Planetary Studies Nat Air and Space Mus Washington DC 20560

STRANDBERG, GERALD WILLIAM, microbiologist; b. Oak Park, Ill., Oct. 13, 1939. B.S. in Biology, Loyola U., Chgo., 1961; M.S. in Bacteriology, U. Wis.-Madison, 1963, Ph.D. in Bacteriology, 1966. Lab. technician Luth. Gen. Hosp., Park Ridge, Ill., 1959-61; research asst. dept. bacteriology U. Wis.-Madison, 1961-66; research microbiologist No. Region Research Ctr., Peoria, Ill., 1966-76; staff microbiologist Oak Ridge Nat. Lab., 1976—. Contbr. articles to profl. jours. Mem. Am. Soc. Microbiology, Soc. Indsl. Microbiology, AAAS, Am. Chem. Soc., Sigma Xi. Current work: Applied microbiology, bioprocess research and development, microbial production of fuels and chemicals, environmental control technology. Subspecialties: Microbiology; Applied microbiology. Home: 11534 Monticello Dr Farragut TN 37922 Office: Oak Ridge Nat Lab PO Box X Oak Ridge TN 37831

STRANZ, DAVID DONALD, research chemist, computer scientist; b. Balt., May 6, 1953; s. Donald Walter and Shirley Mae (Loeffler) S.; m. Jane Ellen Rhodes, Sept. 4, 1981. B.S. in Chemistry, U. Md., 1976, Ph.D. in Phys. Chemistry, 1980. Computer specialist NSF, Washington, 1977-81; research chemist Shell Devel. Co., Modesto, Calif., 1981—. Contbr. articles to profl. jours. Mem. Soc. Applied Spectroscopy, Coblentz Soc., Assn. Computing Machinery, Computer Soc. of IEEE. Current work: Applications of vibrational spectroscopy to molecular structure determination and quantitative analysis. Surface characterization by microscopic infrared imaging and computer graphics-based image processing. Subspecialties: Analytical chemistry; Graphics, image processing, and pattern recognition. Office: Shell Devel Co Biol Scis Research Ctr PO Box 4248 Modesto CA 95352

STRAUB, RICHARD OTTO, psychology educator, experimental psychologist; b. Renton, Wash., May 10, 1954; s. Lee Fred and Phyllis Joan (Sullivan) S.; m. Pamela Lee Hanlon, July 31, 1977; 1 son, Jeremy Alan. B.S., Fla. So. U., 1975; M.A., Columbia U., 1976, M.Phil., 1978, Ph.D., 1979. Faculty fellow Columbia U., 1975-79; research asst. N.Y. State Psychiat. Inst., N.Y.C.,

1976-77; asst. prof. psychology U. Mich., Dearborn, 1979—; cons., reviewer Worth Pubs., N.Y.C. Editor: Readings in the Psychobiology of Motivation, 1982; contbr. in field. NIMH fellow, 1977; recipient Disting. Tchr. award U. Mich., 1982. Mem. Am. Psychol. Assn., Mich. Acad. Sci., Arts and Letters, Psi Chi, Omicron Delta Kappa. Current Work: The development of an animal model of coronary-prone behavior and selectively-bred substrains of coronary-prone and coronary-resistant animals as a vehicle for behavioral, genetic and pathophysiological research into the etiology of type A behavior and precursors to coronary heart disease. Subspecialties: Psychobiology; Learning. Home: 19398 Ingram Livonia MI 48152 Office: U Mich 4901 Evergreen Rd Dearborn MI 48128

STRAUSS, BERNARD S., educator, geneticist; b. N.Y.C., Apr. 18, 1927; s. Joseph and Kate (Silk) S.; m. Carol Maxine Dunham, Sept. 8, 1949; children: Leslie Joan Travis, David Wilson, Paul Leonard. B.S., CCNY, 1947; Ph.D., Calif. Inst. Tech., 1950; postdoctoral fellow, U. Tex., 1950-52. Teaching asst. Calif. Inst. Tech., 1947-48; asst. prof. Syracuse U., 1952-56, assoc. prof., 1956-60; research assoc. Brookhaven Nat. Lab., 1954-55; assoc. prof. U. Chgo., 1960, prof. microbiology, 1965-84, prof. molecular genetics and cell biology, 1984—, chmn. com. genetics, 1962-76, chmn. dept. microbiology, 1969-84, dean basic sci. div. biol. Sci., 1985—; vis. prof. U. Sydney, 1967, Hadassah Med. Sch., Hebrew U., Jerusalem, 1975, 81; Mem. genetics tng. com. NIH, 1962-66, 70-73. Editorial bd.: Cancer Research, Mutation Research. Served with U.S. Mcht. Marine, 1945-47. Fulbright, Guggenheim fellow Osaka U., Japan, 1958-59. Mem. Am. Soc. Biol. Chemists, Am. Assn. Cancer Research, Genetics Soc. Am., Am. Soc. Microbiology, Phi Beta Kappa, Sigma Xi. Current Work: Molecular mode of action of mutagenic and carcinogenic agents. Subspecialties: Molecular biology; Cancer research (medicine). Home: 5431 S Ridgewood Ct Chicago IL 60615

STRAUSS, BRUCE PAUL, metallurgical engineer; b. Elizabeth, N.J., Aug. 19, 1942; s. Edward and Sylvia (Levine) S.; m. Judi Ann Schleiner, Sept. 5, 1964 (div. Apr. 1978); m. Suzanne Felice Louise Geller, Oct. 30, 1983; children—Lori, Lisa. S.B., MIT, 1964, Ph.D., 1967; M.B.A., U. Chgo., 1972. Registered profl. engr., Ill., Mass. Sr. engr. AVCO Everett Research Labs., Mass., 1967-68; physicist Argonne Nat. Lab., Ill., 1968-69; scientist, asst. div. dir. Fermi Lab., Batavia, Ill., 1969-79; sr. prin. engr., engring. mgr. Magnetic Corp. Am., Waltham, Mass., 1979—; cons. in field; active various profl. confs., 1974-82. Contbr. articles to profl. publs. Patentee in field. Mem. Am. Soc. Metals, Am. Phys. Soc., Sigma Xi. Current work: Development of advanced superconductors, superconducting magnets and associated technologies. Subspecialties: Superconductors; Materials (engineering). Home: 330 Clark Rd Brookline MA 02146 Office: Magnetic Corp Am 179 Bear Hill Rd Waltham MA 02154

STRAUSS, ELLIOTT WILLIAM, educator biology and medicine, researcher; b. Bklyn., Jan. 25, 1923; s. Joseph Maxwell and Sophie (Rapoport) S.; m. Margaret Crane, Dec. 9, 1951 (dec. 1983); children—William, Monica, Nicholas; m. Gloria Dinella, Aug. 9, 1984. A.B., Columbia Coll., 1943; M.D., NYU, 1949; M.A. (hon.), Brown U., 1968. Resident in pathology VA Hosp., S.W. Med. Sch., Dallas, 1950-54; assoc. medicine Harvard Med. Sch., Boston, 1957-59, research fellow anatomy, 1959-61, assoc. pathology, 1961-65; prof. pathology U. Colo., Denver, 1965-67, Brown U., Providence, 1968—; cons. in field. Served to lt. USNR, 1954-56. Current work: Gastroenterology; lipid transport. Subspecialties: Biochemistry (medicine); Microscopy. Home: 48 Reservoir St Cambridge MA 02138

STRAUSS, PHYLLIS R., biochemist, educator; b. Worcester, Mass., Mar. 19, 1943. A.B., Brown U., 1964; Ph.D., Rockefeller U., 1971. Research fellow Harvard U., 1971-73; asst. prof. Northeastern U., Boston, 1973-78, assoc., 1978-84, prof., 1984—; cons. Nat. Cancer Inst., Bethesda, Md., 1983, Alta. Heritage Found., Calgary, Can., 1982, Human Nutrition Ctr. Tufts U., Boston, 1981—. Contbr. articles to profl. jours. Recipient Research Career Devel. award, NIH, 1978-83; grantee NSF, NIH, Office Naval Research, Am. Cancer Soc. Mem. Am. Soc. Biol. Chemists, Am. Assn. Immunologists, N.Y. Acad. Sci., Am. Soc. Cell Biologists (com. program, 1984, Travel award, 1984). Current work: Replication intermediates in euraryotic cells. Subspecialty: Biochemistry (biology). Office: Northeastern U Dept Biology 360 Huntington Ave Boston MA 02115

STRAUSS, WALTER ALEXANDER, mathematician, educator; b. Aachen, Germany, Oct. 28, 1937; came to U.S., 1940; s. Charles and Johanna (Goldschmidt) S.; m. Phyllis Romanoff; children: Charles, Nathaniel. A.B., Columbia U., 1958; M.S., U. Chgo., 1959; Ph.D., MIT, 1962. NSF postdoctoral fellow U. Paris, 1962-63; vis. asst. prof. Stanford (Calif.) U., 1963-66; assoc. prof. Brown U., Providence, 1966-71, prof. math., 1971—. Mem. editorial bd.: Jour. Differential Equations, 1978—; contbr. articles to profl. jours. Fulbright lectr. U.S. State Dept., Rio de Janeiro, 1967; Guggenheim fellow, 1971; Japan Soc. Promotion Sci. fellow, 1972. Mem. Am. Math. Soc., Soc. Indsl. and Applied Math. Current Work: Nonlinear wave equations;scattering theory. Subspecialty: Applied mathematics. Office: Brown U Providence RI 02912

STRAUSSNER, JOEL HARVEY, psychologist, researcher; b. Bklyn., Apr. 7, 1947; s. William Gabriel and Henrietta Beth (Edelson) S.; m. Shulamith Lala Ashenberg, Dec. 28, 1969; children—Adam Ashenberg, Savina Beth Ashenberg. M.S., CCNY, 1972, 75; M.S. in Humanities, Yeshiva U., 1977, cert., 1977, Ph.D., 1982. Cert. sch. psychologist, N.Y. cert. tchr. K-6, N.Y. State. Tchr. N.Y.C. Bd. Edn., 1969-72, spl. edn., 1972-73; clin. psychology intern N.J. Dept. Human Services, Trenton, 1976-77; sch. psychologist Bur. Child Guidance N.Y.C., 1978-80; sch. psychologist, com. handicapped N.Y.C. Bd. Edn., 1980—; reading cons. N.Y. League for Hard of Hearing, N.Y.C., 1972-73; learning disabilities cons. W. H. Solan, Teaneck, N.J., 1973-75, St. Joseph's Home, Peekskill, N.Y., 1978; dir. St. Philips Child and Adolescent Ctr., 1985—; dir. child and adolescent services Whitestone (N.Y.) Counseling Ctr., 1981—. Contbr. articles to profl. jours. N.J. Dept. Human Services jr. fellow, 1977. Mem. Am. Psychol. Assn. (award of research competency div. 16 1982), N.Y. Soc. Clin. Psychologists, Internat. Reading Assn. Current Work: Investigation of differences in adult problem solving styles and subsequent results on adult's behavior, relationship of problem solving behavior and its effect susceptibility to the expectancy phenomenon; also investigating cross-cultural educational issues of newly-arrived immigrants. Subspecialties: Cognition; Educational psychology. Home: 124 W 79th St New York NY 10024 Office: NYC Bd Edn 801 Park Pl Brooklyn NY 11216

STREET, ROBERT LYNNWOOD, civil and mechanical engineer; b. Honolulu, Dec. 18, 1934; s. Evelyn Mansel and Dorothy Heather (Brook) S.; m. Norma Jeanette Ensminger, Feb. 6, 1959; children: Brian Clarke (dec.), Deborah Lynne, Kimberley Anne. M.S., Stanford U., 1957, Ph.D. (NSF grad. fellow 1960-62), 1963. Mem. faculty Stanford U. Sch. Engring., 1962—, prof. civil engring., asso. chmn. dept., 1970-72, chmn. dept., 1972-80, prof. fluid mechanics and applied math., 1972—; asso. dean research Sch. Engring., 1971-83, acting vice provost, dean research, 1979, vice provost for acad. computing and info. systems, 1983; vis. prof. U. Liverpool, Eng., 1970-71; trustee Univ. Corp. Atmospheric Research, 1983, chmn. sci. programs evaluation com., 1981, chmn. audit com.; cons. in field. Author: The Analysis and Solution of Partial Differential Equations, 1973; co-author: Elementary Fluid Mechanics, 6th edit, 1982; asso. editor: Jour. Fluids Engring, 1978-81; author articles in field; mem. editorial bds. profl. jours. Served as officer C.E., USN, 1957-60. Sr. postdoctoral fellow Nat. Center Atmospheric Research, 1978-79; fellow N.E. Asia-U.S. Forum on Internat. Policy Stanford U. Mem. Am. Soc. Engring. Edn., ASCE (chmn. publs. com. hydraulics div. 1978-80, Walter Huber prize 1972), ASME, Am. Geophys. Union, Phi Beta Kappa, Sigma Xi, Tau Beta Pi. Current Work: Fluid mechanics; experimental studies and numerical simulation of turbulent stratified flows in nature, ground water hydrology; numerical simulation modeling of hazardous waste transport. Subspecialties: Fluid mechanics; Hydrology. Office: Dept Civil Engring Stanford Univ Stanford CA 94305

STREETEN, BARBARA ANNE WIARD, ophthalmologist, educator, researcher; b. Candia, N.H., Mar. 3, 1925; d. Robert Campbell and Gertrude Sarah (Matheson) Wiard; m. David Henry Palmer Streeten, Aug. 2, 1952; children: Robert, Elizabeth, John. A.B., Tufts U., 1945, M.D., 1950. Diplomate: Am. Bd. Ophthalmology. Instr. U. Mich. Med. Sch., Ann Arbor, 1956-60; from asst. prof. to prof. ophthalmology and pathology Upstate Med. Ctr., Syracuse, N.Y., 1964—, dir. eye pathology lab., 1966—; study sect. on vision Nat. Eye Inst., NIH, 1977-80, bd. sci. counselors, 1982-86. Editorial bd.: Investigative Ophthalmology and Visual Sci, 1979-82; editorial adv.: Opthalmology, 1982—; contbr. articles to sci. jours., chpts. to books. NIH grantee, 1975—. Fellow Am. Acad. Ophthalmology; mem. Am. Ophthal. Soc., Am. Assn. Ophthalmic Pathologists (charter) (pres. 1984), Verhoeff Soc. (pres.), Eastern Ophthalmic Pathology Soc., Assn. Research in Vision and Ophthalmology (sect. chair 1976), Phi Beta Kappa, Alpha Omega Alpha. Episcopalian. Current Work: Ultrastructure, immunology and biochemistry of extracellular matrix related to ophthalmic disease. Subspecialties: Ophthalmology; Pathology (medicine). Home: 334 Berkeley Dr Syracuse NY 13210 Office: 766 Irving Ave Syracuse NY 13210

STREGOWSKI, THOMAS JOHN, mech. engr., cons.; b. New Britain, Conn., Jan. 31, 1948; s. Stanley J. and Catherine (Holyst) S.; m. Elva G. Stregowski, Apr. 22, 1972; 1 son: Christopher. B.S.M.E., U. Conn., 1971, postgrad., 1972-77. Registered profl. engr., Conn. Advanced mfg. engr. Colt Firearms; mfg. engr. Arrow-Hart; engr. Supr. Plessey Ltd.; project engr. Union Carbide Corp., East Hartford, Conn., 1978—, cons. engring.; pres. Conn. Joint Fedn. Recipient Lyman Johnson Meml. award Am. Soc. Non-Destructive Testing, 1971. Mem. Nat. Soc. Profl. Engrs., Conn. Soc. Profl. Engrs., Soc. Am. Value Engrs. (pres. chpt. 1979-81), ASME. Democrat. Roman Catholic. Club: Timberlin Men's Golf. Current Work: Process capabilities of LLDPE versus LDPE resins and their relative strengths. Subspecialties: Materials processing; Materials (engineering). Home: 189 Patterson Way Berlin CT 06037 Office: 88 Long Hill St East Hartford CT 06108

STREICHER, EUGENE, scientist, administrator; b. N.Y.C., Oct. 25, 1926; s. Samuel and Lucy (Carlin) S.; m. Janet Reid Hutcheson, Aug. 9, 1973; 1 son, William Leigh. B.A., Cornell U., 1947, M.A., 1948; Ph.D., U. Chgo., 1953. Physiologist med. div. Army Chem. Ctr., Edgewood, Md., 1948-50; physiologist, health scientist adminstrn. NIH, Bethesda, Md., 1954—, program dir. fundamental neuroscis., 1979—. Served with USN, 1945-46. Mem. Soc. for Neurosci., Am. Neuropath. Assn., AAAS, Soc. Exptl. Biology and Medicine. Subspecialties: Neurochemistry; Neurobiology. Office: NIH Federal Bldg Bethesda MD 20205

STREITWIESER, ANDREW, JR., chemistry educator; b. Buffalo, June 23, 1927; s. Andrew and Sophie (Morlock) S.; m. Mary Ann Good, Aug. 19, 1950 (dec. May 1965); children—David Roy, Susan Ann; m. Suzanne Cope Beier, July 29, 1967. A.B., Columbia, 1949, M.A., 1950, Ph.D., 1952; postgrad. (AEC fellow), Mass. Inst. Tech., 1951-52. Faculty U. Calif. at Berkeley, 1952—, prof. chemistry, 1963—; cons. to industry, 1957—. Author: Molecular Orbital Theory for Organic Chemists, 1961, Solvolytic Displacement Reactions, 1962, (with J.I. Brauman) Supplemental Tables of Molecular Orbital Calculations, 1965, (with C.A. Coulson) Dictionary of Pi Electron Calculations, 1965, (with P.H. Owens) Orbital and Electron Density Diagrams, 1973, (with C.H. Heathcock) Introduction to Organic Chemisty, 3d edit, 1985; also numerous articles.; Co-editor: Progress in Physical Organic Chemistry, 11 vols., 1963-74. Recipient Humboldt Found. Sr. scientist award, 1976, Humboldt medal, 1979. Fellow AAAS; mem. Am. Chem. Soc. (Calif. sect. award 1964, award in Petroleum Chemistry 1967, Norris award in phys. organic chemistry 1982), Royal Soc. Chemistry, AAAS, Nat. Acad. Scis., Am. Acad. Arts and Scis., Phi Beta Kappa, Sigma Xi. Research on organic reaction mechanisms, application molecular orbital theory to organic chemistry, effect chem. structure on carbon acidities, rare earths organometallic chemistry. Subspecialties: Organic chemistry; Organometallics. Office: Dept Chemistry U Calif Berkeley CA 94720

STRELKAUSKAS, ANTHONY JAMES, cellular immunologist; b. Newark, N.J., Apr. 25, 1944; s. Anthony and Stephanie (Nowselski) S.; m. Jennifer Dianne Snow, July 11, 1970; children: Jennifer E., Daniel A. B.A., U. Calif.-Riverside, 1971; M.S., U. Wyo., 1973; Ph.D., U. Ill., 1976. Postdoctoral fellow Harvard Med. Sch., 1976-78; research assoc. Farber Cancer Ctr., 1978-79; asst. prof. Med. U. S.C., Charleston, 1979-81, assoc. prof. immunology and microbiology, 1981—; assoc. prof. pediatrics Med. U.S.C., 1982—. Served with USMC, 1962-67. Mem. Am. Assn. Immunologists, Am. Soc. Microbiologists, Soc. Exptl. Biology and Medicine, AAAS. Current Work: Molecular mechanisms of cellular interactions and immunoregulation; construction of human hybridoma clones for dissection of human immune response thereby facilitating understanding of immunological diseases. Subspecialties: Immunobiology and immunology; Genetics and genetic engineering (biology). Home: 26 27th Ave Isle of Palms SC 29451 Office: Med U SC 171 Ashley Ave Charleston SC 29425

STRICKLER, STEWART JEFFERY, chemist; b. Mussoorie, U.P., India, July 12, 1934; s. Herbert J. and Martha T. (Stewart); m. Carol A. Sayles, June 27, 1959; children: Janet Carol, Peter Herbert. B.A., Coll. of Wooster, 1956; Ph.D., Fla. State U., 1961. Lectr. Rice U., Houston, 1962-63; asst. prof. U. Colo., Boulder, 1963-68, assoc. prof., 1968-73, prof., 1973, chmn. dept. chemistry, 1974-77; hon. fellow Australian Nat. U., Canberra, 1972-73. Contbr. articles to profl. jours. Mem. Am. Chem. Soc., Am. Phys. Soc., AAAS. Republican. Presbyterian. Current Work: Research in molecular spectroscopy, quantum chemistry, photochemistry, solar energy conversion. Subspecialties: Physical chemistry; Photochemistry. Home: 1690 Wilson Ct Boulder CO 80302 Office: Chemistry Dept U Colo Boulder CO 80309

STROBEL, RUDOLF GOTTFRIED KARL, biochemist; b. Kiessling, Germany, Feb. 7, 1927, came to U.S., 1958, naturalized, 1968; s. Karl M. and Frida L. (Weber) S.; m. Josephine M. Haunschild, Sept. 2, 1958; children—Wolfgang R., Christine B., Oliver K., Roland W. Batchelor, U. Munich, Bavaria, 1953, Masters, 1956, Ph.D., 1958. Biochemist, Proctor & Gamble Co., Cin., 1958-75, group leader, 1975-81, sect. head, 1981—. Patentee emulsion chemistry, apparatus, and flavor chemistry. Mem. Am. Chem. Soc., Assn. Sci. Internat. du Café, AAAS, Internat. Apple Inst. Current work: Skin morphology; flour rheology-emulsion technology; microbiological metabolism; protein analyses synthesis; browning reaction; flavor chemistry; separation technology; coffee, tea, fruit juice technology. Subspecialties: Biochemistry (biology); Food science and technology. Office: Proctor & Gamble Co Ctr Hill Rd Cincinnati OH 45224

STROBER, SAMUEL, immunologist, educator; b. N.Y.C., May 8, 1940; s. Julius and Lee (Lander) S.; m. Myra Hoffenberg, June 23, 1963; children: Jason, Elizabeth. A.B in Liberal Arts, Columbia U., 1961; M.D. magna cum laude, Harvard U., 1966. Intern Mass. Gen. Hosp., Boston, 1966-67; resident in internal medicine Stanford (Calif.) U. Hosp., 1970-71; research fellow Peter Bent Brigham Hosp., Boston, 1962-63, 65-66, Oxford (Eng.) U., 1963-64; research assoc. Lab. Cell Biology, Nat. Cancer Inst., NIH, Bethesda, Md., 1967-70; instr. medicine Stanford U., 1971-72, asst. prof., 1972-78, assoc. prof. medicine, 1978-82, chief div. immunology, 1978—, prof. medicine, 1982—; investigator Howard Hughes Med. Inst., Miami, Fla., 1976-81. Assoc. editor: Jour. Immunology, 1981—, Transplantation, 1981—; contbr. articles to profl. jours. Served with USPHS, 1967-70. Recipient Leon Riznick Meml. Research prize Harvard U., 1966, Career Devel. award Nat. Insts. Allergy and Infectious Diseases, 1971-76. Mem. Am. Assn. Immunology, Am. Soc. Clin. Investigation, Am. Rheumatism Assn., Alpha Omega. Current Work: Immunobiology and immunology, transplantation, cellular engineering. Subspecialties: Immunobiology and immunology; Immunology (medicine). Office: Stanford University School of Medicine Stanford CA 94305

STROJNY, NORMAN, analytical chemist, researcher; b. Edwardsville, Pa., June 14, 1943; s. John and Blanche (Stawarz) S.; m. Elaine Kupchik, June 24, 1967 (div. 1982). B.S., Wilkes Coll., 1966; M.A., Montclair State Coll., 1974; Ph.D., Rutgers U., 1980, postgrad., 1982—. Jr. chemist Hoffman LaRoche Inc., Nutley, N.J., 1965-80, sr. scientist, 1980-85; mem. governing bd. Eastern Analytical Symposium, 1984. Contbr. articles to profl. jours. Mem. Am. Chem. Soc., Am. Pharm. Assn., Am. Inst. Chemists, Soc. Applied Spectroscopy (chmn. N.Y. sect. 1984-85), Sigma Xi. Current work: Determination of drugs and biotransformation products in biological fluids, high performance liquid chromatograph and fluorescence and uv absorption spectrophotometry. Subspecialty: Analytical chemistry. Home: PO Box 1234 Clifton NJ 07012

STROM, JOEL ANDREW, cardiologist, educator; b. N.Y.C., Sept. 14, 1943; s. Irving and Sophie (Shreefter) S.; m. Jane Rosemarie Golin, June 18, 1967; children: Rebecca Nan, Jessica Marie. B.S. in Engring, Cornell U., 1965, M.S. in Engring. Physics, 1966; M.D., SUNY, 1970. Diplomate: Am. Bd. Internal Medicine, 1973, Am. Bd. Cardiovascular Disease, 1977. Intern in medicine Upstate Med. Ctr., Syracuse, N.Y., 1970-71, resident, 1971-73; fellow in cardiology Cornell Med. Ctr., N.Y.C., 1973-74; research med. officer Brooks AFB, San Antonio, 1974-76; fellow in cardiology Albert Einstein Coll. Medicine, Bronx, N.Y., 1976-77, asst. prof. medicine and radiology, 1978-83, assoc. prof. medicine, 1983—, dir. clin. cardiac labs., assoc. attending physician. Contbr. articles to sci. publs. Frieda and Herman Saporta cardiology fellow, 1980. Fellow N.Y. Cardiologic Soc.; mem. Am. Heart Assn., N.Y. Acad. Sci., AAAS, Am. Fedn. Clin. Research. Jewish. Current Work: Cardiac ultrasound. Subspecialties: Cardiology; Imaging technology. Home: 24 Wildwood Dr Dix Hills NY 11746 Office: Hosp Albert Einstein College Medicine 1600 Tenbroeck Ave Bronx NY 10461

STROM, TERRY BARTON, physician, educator; b. Chgo., Nov. 30, 1941; s. David and Sylvia D. (Abelson) S.; m. Margot Stern, Aug. 2, 1964; children: Adam Frederick, Rachel Fan. M.D., U. Ill., 1966. Diplomate: Am. Bd. Internal Medicine, 1970. Intern U. Ill. Hosp., Chgo., 1966-67; resident Beth Israel Hosp., Boston, 1970-71, dir. clin. immunology, 1985—; mem. task force on organ transplantation U.S. Dept. Health Social Services instr. medicine Harvard U. Med. Sch., Boston, 1973-75, asst. prof., 1978, assoc. prof., 1978—; med. dir. renal transplant service, co-dir. lab. immunogenetics and transplantation Brigham and Women's Hosp., Boston, 1973-85. Contbr. over 200 articles to sci. jours. Served to capt. USAF, 1968-70. NIH awardee, 1976; also grantee. Mem. Am. Soc. Clin. Investigation, Transplantation Soc., Am. Assn. Immunologists, Union Concerned Scientists, Am. Soc. Nephrology, Internat. Soc. Nephrology. Democrat. Jewish. Current Work: Immunology (cellular and transplantation). Subspecialty: Transplantation. Home: 22 Kennard Rd Brookline MA 02146 Office: 330 Brookline Ave Boston MA 02215

STROMER, MARVIN HENRY, cell biologist, researcher, educator; b. Readlyn, Iowa, Sept. 1, 1936; s. Roy Henry and Luella (Klemp) S.; m. Shirley Louene Roepke, Apr. 3, 1960; 1 son, Craig. B.S. in Animal Sci. (Nat. Merit scholar, George Gund scholar), Iowa State U., Ames, 1959, B.S. in Agrl. Edn, 1959, Ph.D. in Cell Biology, 1966. With product devel. dept. George A. Hormel & Co., Austin, Minn., 1959-62; research in biochemistry Iowa State U., 1962-66, assoc. prof., 1968-76, prof., 1976—; postdoctoral fellow biochemistry Carnegie-Mellon U., 1966-68; vis. lectr. Tex. A&M U., 1971; vis. prof. U. Ariz., 1979-80; Humboldt fellow, vis. scientist Max Planck Inst. Med. Research, Heidelberg, W.Ger., 1974-75. Contbr. articles, revs. and abstracts to profl. jours., chpts. in books. Served with Army NG, 1959-65. Mem. Am. Soc. Cell Biology, Electron Microscopy Soc. Am., Biophys. Soc., Am. Heart Assn. (pres. Iowa affiliate 1984-86), Iowa Microbeam Soc. (pres. 1984-85), Sigma Xi, Alpha Zeta. Republican. Lutheran. Current Work: Ultrastructure and biochemistry of striated and smooth muscle and other movement systems. Subspecialties: Cell biology; Biochemistry (biology). Office: Muscle Biology Group Iowa State University Ames IA 50011

STRONG, DOUGLAS MICHAEL, researcher; b. Newport, Wash., Sept. 4, 1941; s. George and Dorothea (Rednour) S.; m. Geraldine O'Melveny, Jan. 30, 1965; children: Michael Phillip, David Richard, Patricia Anne. B.S., Gonzaga U., 1963; Ph.D., Med. Coll. Wis., 1973. Med. technologist Am. Soc. Clin. Pathology.; Supr. hematology Blood Bank U.S. Naval Hosp., Phila., 1965-67; clin. chemist Med. Tech. Sch., U.S. Naval Hosp., Gt. Lakes, Ill., 1967-69; chief clihn. immunology-histocompatability lab. Naval Med. Research Inst., Bethesda, Md., 1973-78, dep. chmn., 1978-79, head transplant research br., 1979-82; program mgr., fleet health care systems Naval Med. Research and Devel. Command, Bethesda, 1982—; asso. prof. Uniformed Services U., 1979—. Contbr. numerous articles to profl. jours. Soccer coach Wheaton Boys Club, 1973-78, Montgomery and Rockville United Soccer Clubs, 1978—. Served to comdr. USN, 1965—. Mem. Naval Med. Research Inst., Soc. Cryobiology (editorial bd. 1980—), Am. Soc. Clin. Histocompatability Testing, Assn. Immunology, Transplantation Soc., Am. Assn. Tissue Banks. Roman Catholic. Current Work: Cell and tissue antigens, hybridoma tech., genetic engring. Subspecialties: Transplantation; Marrow transplant. Home: 8 Atwell Ct Potomac MD 20854 Office: Code 45 Naval Med R & D Command Betheda MD 20814

STROSCIO, MICHAEL ANTHONY, physicist; b. Winston-Salem, N.C., June 1, 1949; s. Anthony and Norma Lee (Sidbury) S.; m. Lucy Chadbourn Worth, Aug. 29, 1970; children—Elizabeth de Clare, Charles Marshall Sidbury. B.S. in Physics, U. N.C., 1970; M. In Philosophy and Physics, Yale U., 1972, Ph.D. in Physics, 1974. Physicist Los Almos Sci. Lab., 1975-78; sr. staff mem. Johns Hopkins U. Applied Physics Lab., Laurel, Md., 1978-80; program mgr. electromagnetic research Air Force Office Sci. Research, Dept. Def., Washington, 1982-83, spl. asst. research dir. Office of Under Sec. Def., 1982-83; policy analyst White House Office Sci. and Tech. Policy, Washington, 1983-85; dir. laser fusion experiments Dept. Energy, 1983-85; program mgr. micro electronics Army Research Office, 1985—; referee Phys. Rev. Letters Am. Inst. Physics, N.Y.C., 1977—, Nuclear Fusion IAEA, Vienna, Austria, 1978—. Author: Positronium: A Review of the Theory, 1975. Patentee in field. Contbr. articles to profl. jours. Served to capt. USAF, 1974-75. Research Initiative grantee Los Alamos Nat. Lab., 1977. Mem. Yale Sci. and Engring. Assn. (exec. bd. 1983—), IEEE (sr.; exec. sec., com. plasma scis. applications), Am. Phys. Soc., Am. Geneal. Soc., Phi Beta Kappa. Current work: Microelectronics and atomic physics. Subspecialties: Microelectronics; Atomic and molecular physics. Home: 1001 Serendipity Ln Chapel Hill NC 27514 Office: US Army Research Office Research Triangle Park NC 27709

STRYER, LUBERT, biochemist, educator; b. Tientsin, China, Mar. 2, 1938. B.S. with honors, U. Chgo., 1957; M.D., magna cum laude, Harvard U., 1961. Helen Hay Whitney fellow Harvard U., also Med. Research Council Lab., 1961-63; from asst. prof. to asso. prof. biochemistry Stanford U., 1963-69; prof. molecular biophysics and biochemistry Yale U., 1969-76; Winzer prof. cell biology Stanford U. Sch. Medicine, 1976—, chmn. dept. structural biology, 1976-79; cons. NIH, NRC.; mem. sci. adv. bd. Jane Coffin Childs Fund, Research to Prevent Blindness. Mem. editorial bd.: Jour. Molecular Biology, 1968-72, Jour. Cell Biology, 1981-83; assoc. editor: Annual Revs. Biophysics and Bioengineering, 1970-76. Recipient Am. Chem. Soc. award in biol. chemistry Eli Lilly & Co., 1970. Fellow Am. Acad. Arts and Scis., Nat. Acad. Scis.; mem. Am. Chem. Soc., Am. Soc. Biol. Chemists, Biophys. Soc., Phi Beta Kappa. Current work: Molecular basis of visual excitation. Fluorescence spectroscopy. Membrane receptors. Protein structure and dynamics. Subspecialties: Biochemistry (biology); Cell biology. Office: Fairchild Center Stanford Sch Medicine Stanford CA 94305

STUART, ROBERT JAMES, exploration geologist; b. San Juan, P.R., Apr. 6, 1935; s. Lyman James and Winona King (McCulley) S.; m. Alice Joyce Schwarz, Sept. 9, 1961; children—Lisa Marie, Brian James, Michael Glen. B.S. in Geology, So. Methodist U., 1959; M.A. in Geology, Bowling Green State U., Ohio, 1962. Geologist Bear Creek Mining Co., Denver, 1962-72; chief geologist Freeport Indonesia, Inc., Irian Jaya, New Guinea, 1972-76; sr. geologist Freeport Exploration Co., Reno, Nev., 1976—. Com. mem., asst. scoutmaster Catalina and Nev. area councils Boy Scouts Am., 1977—(Recognition awards 1982, 83, 84). Served with USN, 1954-56. Mem. Am. Inst. Profl. Geologists, AIME, Soc. Econ. Geologists, Geol. Soc. Am., N.Mex. Geol. Soc. (sec. 1965). Republican. Lodge: Elks. Current work: Economic mineral geologist; exploration and mining. Subspecialty: Geology. Home: 339 South Spring Creek Pkwy Elko NV 89801 Office: Mountain City Star Route Elko NV 89801

STUART, WILLIAM DORSEY, JR., geneticist, educator; b. St. Louis, Mar. 28, 1939; s. William Dorsey and Alice Margueritte (Holleman) S. B.A. in Chemistry, Fla. State U., 1969, M.S. in Genetics; Univ. fellow, 1970, Ph.D. in Biochem. Genetics, 1973. Technologist Virology Lab., Mt. Sinai Hosp., N.Y.C., 1960-64; NIH predoctoral trainee Fla. State U., 1970-73; NIH postdoctoral fellow dept. biology Stanford (Calif.) U., 1973-76; research fellow in human genetics depts. pediatrics and genetics U. Melbourne, Australia, 1976-78; asst. prof. genetics Sch. Medicine, U. Hawaii, Honolulu, 1978-83, assoc. prof., 1983—; cons. CETUS Corp., Berkeley, Calif., 1980-82; founder Hawaii Biotech. Group, Honolulu, 1982—. Contbr. articles to sci. jours. Mem. Genetics Soc. Am., Am. Soc. Microbiology, Genetics Soc. Australia, Sigma Xi, Phi Eta Sigma. Current work: Human and fungal biochemical and cytological genetics. Subspecialties: Genetics and genetic engineering (biology); Immunocytochemistry. Home: 3061 Pualei Circle Apt 105 Honolulu HI 96815 Office: Dept Genetics U Hawaii at Manoa Honolulu HI 96822

STUBBERUD, ALLEN ROGER, scientist; b. Glendive, Mont., Aug. 14, 1934; s. Oscar Adolph and Alice Marie (LeBlanc) S.; m. May B. Tragus, Nov. 19, 1961; children—Peter A., Stephen C. B.S. in Elec. Engring, U. Idaho, 1956; M.S. in Engring, UCLA, 1958, Ph.D., 1962. From asst. prof. to asso. prof. engring. UCLA, 1962-69; prof. elec. engring. U. Calif., Irvine, 1969—(on leave), asso. dean engring., 1972-78, dean engring., 1978-83; chief scientist U.S. Air Force, 1983—. Author: Analysis and Synthesis of Linear Time Variable Systems, 1964, (with others) Feedback and Control Systems, 1967; asso. editor: Jour. Astron. Sci; contbr. articles to profl. jours. Fellow IEEE, AIAA (asso.); mem. Ops. Research Soc. Am., Sigma Xi, Sigma Tau, Tau Beta Pi, Eta Kappa Nu. Current work: Estimation, control theory, signal processing. Subspecialties: Electrical engineering; Aerospace engineering and technology. Home: 19352 Sierra Soto Rd Irvine CA 92715

STUCKI, JACOB CALVIN, pharmaceutical research administrator; b. Neillsville, Wis., Nov. 30, 1926; m. 1948; 3 children. B.S., U. Wis.-Madison, 1948, M.S., 1951, Ph.D. in Zoology, Physiology, 1954. Research asst. U. Wis.-Madison, 1950-54; endocrinologist William S Merrell Co., 1954-57; research assoc., 1957-60, dept. head endocrinology, 1960-61, mgr. pharmacology research, 1961-68, dir. research planning and adminstrn. pharm. research and devel., 1968-79, dir. adminstrn. and support ops., 1979-81; v.p. pharm. research The Upjohn Co., Kalamazoo, 1981—. Subspecialty: Pharmaceutical research and development. Office: The Upjohn Co Pharm Research and Devel Lab 301 Henrietta St Kalamazoo MI 49001*

STUCKY, GALEN DEAN, chemist; b. McPherson, Kans., Dec. 17, 1936; married; 2 children; B.S., McPherson Coll., 1957; Ph.D. in Chemistry, Iowa State U., 1962. Fellow in physics MIT, 1962-63, NSF fellow Quantum Chem. Inst., Fla., 1963-64; from asst prof. to assoc prof. chemistry U. Ill., Urbana, 1964-72, prof. 1972-79; group leader Sandia Nat. Lab., N.Mex., 1979-81; group leader Central Research and Devel. Dept., E. I. Du Pont de Nemours and Co., Inc., Wilmington, Del., 1981-85; prof. chemistry U. Calif., Santa Barbara, 1985—. Subspecialties: Organometallics; Inorganic chemistry. Office: Dept Chemistry Univ Calif Santa Barbara CA 93106

STUESSY, TOD FALOR, plant systematist; b. Pitts., Nov. 18, 1943; s. Haydn and Mary Louise (Falor) S.; m. Carol Liebe, June 15, 1968 (div.); children: Mary Elizabeth, Alan Briscoe. B.A., DePauw U., 1965; Ph.D., U. Tex., Austin, 1968. Asst. prof. botany Ohio State U., 1968-71, 72-74, assoc. prof., 1974-78, prof., 1979—; Maria Moors Cabot postdoctoral fellow Harvard U., 1971-72; assoc. dir. Systematic Biology Program, NSF, Washington, 1978-79; dir. Ohio State U. Herbarium, 1980—. Contbr. numerous articles on plant systematics to profl. jours. NSF grantee, 74-82; Sigma Xi grantee, 1968; Nat. Geog. Soc. grantee, 1975; Am. Philos. Soc. grantee, 1969. Mem. AAAS, Am. Soc. Plant Taxonomy, Assn. Tropical Biology, Bot. Soc. Am., Calif. Bot. Soc., Classification Soc., Internat. Assn. Plant Taxonomy, Soc. Study Evolution, Southwestern Assn. Naturalists, Soc. Systematic Zoology. Methodist. Current Work: Systematic and evolutionary studies of flowering plants; compositae, herbarium, Latin Am., Juan Fernandez Islands, cladistics, Chile. Subspecialty: Systematics. Office: Dept Botany Ohio State U 1735 Neil Ave Columbus OH 43210

STUMPE, WARREN ROBERT, manufacturing company executive; b. Bronx, N.Y., July 15, 1925; s. William A. and Emma J. (Mann) S.; m. Jean Marie Mannion, June 5, 1952; children: Jeffrey, Kathy, William. B.S., U.S. Mil. Acad., 1945; M.S., Cornell U., 1949; M.S. in Indsl. Engring, N.Y. U., 1965. Registered profl. engr., N.Y., Fla., Wis. Commd. 2d lt., C.E. U.S. Army, 1945, advanced through grades to capt., 1954; with (65th Engr. Bn.), 1945-48; asst. prof. mechanics U.S. Mil. Acad., 1951-54; resigned, 1954; from capt. to col. Res., 1958-79; dep. gen. mgr., gen. engring. div. AMF, Stamford, Conn., 1954-63; exec. v.p. Dortech, Inc., Stamford, 1963-69; dir. systems mgmt. group Mathews Conveyor div. REX, Darien, Conn., 1969-71; dir. research and devel. Rexnord, Inc., Milw., 1971-73, v.p. corp. research and tech., from 1973, v.p. bus. devel. sector, from 1981, now v.p., chief tech. officer; civilian aide to sec. army for, State of Wis. Contbr. articles to profl. jours. Founder, pres. No. Little League, Stamford, 1965-69; pres. Turn of River Jr. High Sh. PTA, 1967-68; vice chmn. for Wis. Dept. Def., Nat. Com. Employer Support Guard and Res.; bd. regents Milw. Sch. Engring.; mem. liaison council Coll. Engring., U. Wis., also mem. indsl. adv. council; mem. Wis. Gov.'s Task Force on Energy. Mem. Am. Water Pollution Control Fedn., Process Equipment Mfrs. Assn., Indsl. Research Inst. (v.p., dir.), West Point Soc. N.Y. (career adv. bd.), West Point Soc. Wis., Tau Beta Pi, Phi Kappa Phi. Clubs: Wisconsin, Ozaukee Country. Current Work: Responsible for all company-wide technology activities which includes bringing to marketplace a product line of imaging recognition equipment. Subspecialties: Mechanical engineering; Systems engineering. Office: PO Box 2022 Milwaukee WI 53201

STUMPF, WALTER ERICH, anatomist, pharmacologist, educator; b. Oelsnitz/Vogtland, Ger., Jan. 10, 1927; came to U.S., 1963; m. Ursula Emily Schwinge, May 20, 1961; children: Andrea, Martin, Carolin, Silva. Student, U. Leipzig, Germany, 1946-50; M.D. summa cum laude, Humboldt U., Berlin, 1952; Ph.D. in Pharmacology, U. Chgo., 1967. Intern Charite Hosp., Humboldt U., 1952-53, resident in neurology and psychiatry, 1954-57; trainee in psychotherapy and psychoanalysis Inst. Psychotherapy, Berlin, 1954-56; teaching asst. in clin. neurology Humboldt U., 1956-57; resident dept. neurology and psychiatry U. Marburg, W.Ger., 1958-60, Lab. Isotope Research and Radiobiology, U. Marburg, 1961-62; research assoc. dept. pharmacology U. Chgo., 1963-67, asst. prof. pharmacology, 1963-64, 67-70; assoc. prof. anatomy and pharmacology U. N.C., Chapel Hill, 1970-73, prof., 1973—; vis. psychiatrist Maudsley Hosp., London, 1959; vis. prof. Max-Planck Inst. Cell Biology, Wilhelmshaven, Germany, 1975; vis. prof. clin. morphology U. Ulm, Ger., 1981; research scientist, child devel. Biol. Research Center, N.C. Meml. Hosp.; assoc. mem. Carolina Population Center, Chapel Hill; cons. in field; mem. council, exec. com. Inst. Lab. Animal Resources, NRC, Nat. Acad. Scis., 1978-81. Author: Autoradiography of Diffusible Substances, 1969; Anatomical Neuroendocrinology, 1975. Mem. editorial bd. Jour. Histochemistry and Cytochemistry, Exptl. Aging Research. Coordinating editor Cell and Tissue Research. Contbr. articles chpts. to profl. jours. Berlin Labs. fellow, 1968-69. Mem. AAAS, Am. Assn. Anatomists, N.Y. Acad. Scis., Soc. Exptl. Biology and Medicine, Internat. Brain Research Orgn., Am. Soc. Zoologists, Histochem. Soc. (council 1977-81), Internat. Soc. Psychoneuroendocrinology, Am. Chem. Soc., Soc. Neurosci., Internat. Soc. Xenobiotics (charter). Design cryosption pump, Harris wide range cryostat. Current Work: Steroid hormone receptors; brain; pituitary; autoradiography; immunohistochemistry; peptide hormones. Subspecialties: Neuroendocrinology; Cytology and histology. Home: Route 5 Box 380 Chapel Hill NC 27514 Office: U NC Dept Anatomy 111 Swing Bldg Chapel Hill NC 27514

STURROCK, PETER ANDREW, astrophysicist; b. Grays, Eng., Mar. 20, 1924; U.S. citizen; married; 3 children. B.A., Cambridge U., 1945, M.A., 1948, Ph.D., in Math., 1951. Harwell sr. fellow Atomic Energy Research Estab., Eng., 1951-53; fellow St. John's Coll., Cambridge U., 1952-55; Ford fellow in plasma physics, Europe Orgn. Nuclear Research, Switzerland, 1958-59; research assoc. microwaves Stanford U., Calif., 1955-58, research assoc., 1959-60, prof. engring. sci. and applied physics, 1961-66, chmn. inst. plasma research, 1964-74, prof. space sci. and astrophysics dept. applied physics, 1966—; cons. Varian Assocs., Calif., 1957-64, NASA Ames Research Ctr., 1962-64; mem. phys. sci. com. NASA, 1975-77, chmn. study group anomalous phenomena, AIAA, 1975—. Recipient Gavity Found. Prize, 1967. Subspecialties: Theoretical astrophysics; Plasma physics. Office: Stanford U Dept Applied Physics Stanford CA 94305*

STURTEVANT, FRANK MILTON, pharmaceutical company executive; b. Evanston, Ill., Mar. 8, 1927; s. Frank Milton and Marguerite Marie (Walsh) S.; m. Ruthann Patterson, Mar. 18, 1950; children: Jill Diane Sturtevant Rovani, Jan Kimberly Sturtevant Cassidy. B.A. cum laude, Lake Forest Coll., 1948; M.S., Northwestern U., 1950, Ph.D., 1951. Grad. asst. in biol. scis. Northwestern U., Evanston, 1949-51; sr. investigator div. biol. research G.D. Searle & Co., Chgo., 1951-58, asso. dir. research and devel., 1972-80; dir. Office Sci. Affairs, 1980—; sr. pharmacologist Research and Devel. div. Smith, Kline and French Labs., Phila., 1958-60; sr. research fellow in biochemorphology Mead Johnson Research Center, Evansville, Ind., 1960-64, dir. dept. neuro- and psychopharmacology, 1963-64, dir. sci. and regulatory affairs, 1963-72, Cons. editor: Internat. Jour. Chronobiology, Internat. Jour. Fertility; contbr. over 100 articles to profl. jours. Bd. govs. Lake Forest Coll. Served with U.S. Army, 1945-46. Fellow AAAS; mem. Am. Fertility Soc., Soc. Advancement Contraception, Fallopius Soc. (treas.), Pacific Coast Fertility Soc., Internat. Soc. Reproductive Medicine, Drug Info. Assn. (charter), Internat. Soc. Chronobiology, Am. Coll. Toxicology (charter), Internat. Union Pharmacology (sect. toxicology), Am. Soc. Exptl. Therapeutics, Soc. Exptl. Biol. Medicine (emeritus), Sigma Xi. Current Work: Biometrics, chronopharmacokinetics. Subspecialties: Reproductive biology (medicine); Chronobiology. Home: 1868 Mission Hills Ln Northbrook IL 60062 Office: GD Searle & Co 4901 Searle Pkwy Skokie IL 60077

STURTEVANT, JULIAN MUNSON, biophysical chemistry researcher; b. Edgewater, N.J., Aug. 9, 1908; s. Edgar Howard and Bessie Fitch (Skinner) S.; m. Elizabeth Caroline Reihl; children—Ann, Bradford. A.B., Columbia U., 1927; Ph.D., Yale U., 1931; D.Sc. (hon.), Ill. Coll., 1962, U. Regensburg, W.Ger., 1978. Mem. faculty Yale U., New Haven, 1931-77, prof. biophys. chemistry, 1952-77, sr. research scientist,1977—; staff mem. radiation lab. MIT, Cambridge, Mass., 1943-46; Alexander von Humboldt sr. scientist U. Regensburg, W.Ger., 1978-79. Author: (with Ernest C. Pollard) Microwaves and Radar Electronics, 1950. Contbr. sci. articles to profl. jours. Recipient Huffman award U.S. Calorimetry Conf., 1964; William Clyde DeVane medal Yale U., 1978; Innovator in Biochemistry award Va. Med. Coll., 1984. Fellow Am. Acad. Arts and Scis.; mem. Nat. Acad. Scis. Democrat. Current work: Thermodynamics of biochemical and biological processes. Subspecialties: Biophysical chemistry; Thermodynamics. Office: Kline Chemistry Lab Yale Univ 225 Prospect St New Haven CT 06520

STURTEVANT, RUTHANN PATTERSON, anatomist; b. Rockford, Ill., Feb. 7, 1927; d. Joseph Hyelmun and Virginia (Wharton) Patterson; m. Frank M. Sturtevant, Mar. 18, 1950; children—Barbara (dec.), Jill Sturtevant Rovani, Jan Sturtevant Cassidy. B.S., Northwestern U., 1949, M.S., 1950; Ph.D., U. Ark., 1972. Instr., Ind. State U., Evansville, 1965-72; asst. prof. Ind. U. Sch. Medicine, Evansville, 1972-74; lectr. Northwestern Med. Sch., Chgo., 1974-75; asst. prof. anatomy Loyola U. Med. Sch., Maywood, Ill., 1975-81, assoc. prof., 1981—. Contbr. articles to profl. jours. NIH grantee, 1981, 83; Potts Found. grantee, 1983. Mem. Am. Assn. Anatomists, Internat. Soc. Chronobiology, Internat. Soc. Biomed. Research on Alcoholism, Am. Soc. Pharmacology and Exptl. Therapeutics. Current work: Chronopharmacokinetics of ethanol; fetal alcohol syndrome; chronotoxicity of ethanol to developing cerebellar cells. Subspecialties: Anatomy and embryology; Chronobiology. Home: 1868 Mission Hills Ln Northbrook IL 60062 Office: Loyola U Med Ctr 2160 S 1st Ave Maywood IL 60153

SU, CHE, pharmacologist; b. Taipei, Taiwan, June 12, 1932; came to U.S., 1961, naturalized, 1971. Ph.D., UCLA, 1965. Asst. to assoc. prof. UCLA, 1967-78; prof. So. Ill. U. Sch. Medicine, Springfield, 1978-85, Disting. prof., 1985—. Mem. Am. Pharmacol. Soc. Current Work: Presynaptic receptors in hypertension; purinergic mechanisms in blood vessels. Subspecialty: Pharmacology. Home: 66 W Hazel Dell Ln Springfield IL 62707 Office: So Ill U Sch Medicine 801 N Rutledge Springfield IL 62702

SU, KUNG-YEN, electrical and semiconductor engineer, researcher; b. Kaohsiung, Taiwan, Republic of China, Jan. 17, 1950; came to U.S., 1974, naturalized 1985; s. Lien-Hsin and Shiang (Chao) S.; m. Heuy-Ching Lin, Aug. 15, 1974; children—Cynthia, Jennifer. B.S. in Elec. Engring., Nat. Chiao-Tung U., Taiwan, 1972; M.S. in Elec. Engring., U. Calif.-Santa Barbara, 1976, Ph.D., 1981. Registered profl. engr., Calif. Sr. process engr. Fairchild Semiconductor, San Jose, Calif., 1981-83; sect. head process engring. Signetics Corp., San Jose, 1983; prin. process device engr. Data Gen., San Jose, 1983—. Patentee doping of poly resistor by out diffusion, 1983; contbr. articles to profl. jours. Chiao-Tung U. fellow, 1972-74. Mem. IEEE, Chinese Engring Assn. (chmn. 1978-81). Current work: Device characteristics, device modeling, process simulation and integration. Subspecialty: Semiconductors. Home: 1540 Guadalajara Dr San Jose CA 95120

SU, LAO-SOU, physical chemist, physicist; b. Kao hsiung, Taiwan, Republic of China, Dec. 13, 1932; came to U.S., 1962; m. Hui-mei Su, Jan. 29, 1966; children—Peggy Ann, Lester Kinker. B.S., Taiwan Nat. Normal U., 1957; Ph.D., Ind. U., 1967. Postdoctoral research assoc. U. Mich., Ann Arbor, 1967-69; sr. research scientist S.C. Johnson & Son, Inc., Racine, Wis., 1969—. Contbr. articles to profl. jours. Mem. Am Chem. Soc., Electrochem. Soc. Current work: Molecular modeling by computational chemistry, corrosion of pressurized system, dielectric spectra of polymer and biological tissue, electrical aspect of colloidal interface, and other surfactant mixtures. Subspecialties: Physical chemistry; Biophysical chemistry. Home: 5541 Sandhill Rd Racine WI 53402 Office: SC Johnson and Son Inc 1525 Howe St Racine WI 53403

SU, STANLEY Y. W., database systems educator; b. Taiwan, Feb. 18, 1940; came to U.S., 1963; m. Siew Phek; 2 children. B.A. in Fgn. Lang. and Lit., Tamkang Coll. of Arts and Scis., Taiwan, 1961; B.A. in Math., U. Wis.-Madison, 1964, M.S. in Computer Scis., 1965, Ph.D. in Computer Scis., 1968. Project asst. U. Wis.-Madison, 1964-66, research asst., 1966-68; mathematician Rand Corp., Santa Monica, Calif., 1968-70; prof. computer sci. U. Fla., Gainesville, 1970—, dir. Database Systems Research and Devel. Ctr., 1977—. Assoc. editor: Transactions on Software Engring., 1981—. Current work: Database machines, integrated manufacturing, CAD, CAM. Subspecialties: Software engineering; Computer-aided design. Office: U Fla 512 Weil Hall Gainesville FL 32611

SUBBIAH, RAVI MANDEPANDA THIMMIAH, biochemistry educator, researcher; b. Mercara, Mysore, India, June 30, 1942; came to U.S., 1970; s. Mandepanda C. and Bolamma (Kanda) Thimmiah; m. Deachu Muddayya, Jan. 15, 1972; children: Jeevan, Rekha. B.S., U. Mysore, Mercara, India, 1961; M.S., U. Baroda, India, 1964; Ph.D., U. Toronto, 1970. Research fellow Mayo Clinic, Rochester, Minn., 1970-72, research assoc., 1972-74, cons., 1974-78, asst. prof., 1975-78; assoc. prof. U. Cin. Med. tr., 1978-81, prof. exptl. medicine, 1981—, dir. lipid biochemistry, 1978—, dir. lipids-nutrition tng. program, 1980—. Editorial bd.: Proc. Soc. Exptl. Biology and Medicine, Atherogenese, 1983—; contbr. articles to profl. jours. Recipient First prize Govt. Coll., Mercara, India, 1959-61; NIH research grantee, 1974-83. Fellow Council Arteriosclerosis; mem. Am. Inst. Nutrition, Am. Chem. Soc., Am. Oil Chemists Soc., Soc. Exptl. Biology and Medicine. Current work: Atherosclerosis, cholesterol metabolism, bileacids, prostaglandins. Subspecialty: Biochemistry (medicine). Home: 4036 Ridgedale Dr Cincinnati OH 45247 Office: U Cin Med Center 234 Goodman St Cincinnati OH 45267

SUBRAMANIAN, SETHURAMAN, chemist, researcher; b. Mattur, Madras, India, May 16, 1940; came to U.S., 1970, naturalized, 1978; s. P. and Rajalakshmi (Panchanathan) Sethuraman; m. Ananthi Gopalakrishnan, Jan. 29, 1969; children—Sumathi, Sukanya, Mekhala. B.Sc., Madras U., Trichy, 1960, M.Sc., 1965; Ph.D., Indian Inst. Tech., Kanpur, 1969; M.B.A., Ind. U., 1985. Postdoctoral fellow VA Hosp., Kansas City, Mo., 1970-74; research physicist Naval Med. Research Inst., Bethesda, Md., 1974-75; vis. scientist NIH, Bethesda, Md., 1975-82; research scientist Miles Labs., Elkhart, Ind., 1982-84, sr. research scientist, 1984—. Contbr. chpts., articles to profl. publs. Mem. Am. Chem. Soc. (chmn.-elect St. Joseph Valley sect.), Am. Soc. Biol. Chemists, Miles Sci. Forum (chmn. 1984). Current work: Purification and separation of proteins and enzymes; enzyme engineering; protein structure, function and thermodynamics relationships; affinity separation methods; chemical and physical enzymology. Subspecialties: Enzyme technology; Biophysical chemistry. Home: 54648 Glenwood Park Dr Elkhart IN 46514 Office: Miles Labs PO Box 932 Elkhart IN 46515

SUCIU, SPIRIDON N., electric co. ofcl.; b. Flint, Mich., Dec. 11, 1921; s. Nicholas and Mary (Moian) S.; m. Jean E. Suciu, Aug. 27, 1949; children: Nancy Susan, Barbara Jean, Richard Spiridon, James Nicholas, Ronald Edward. B.S.M.E., Purdue U., 1944, M.S.M.E., 1949, Ph.D., 1951. Registered profl. engr., Ohio. Mgr. applied research and aerodynamic design Aircraft Engine Bus. div. Gen. Electric Co., Cin., 1958-67; mgr. design tech. operation Aircraft Engine div., Cin., 1967-71; gen. mgr. GTPD Engring. dept., Gas Turbine Products div., Schenectady, N.Y., 1971-76; mgr. energy tech. operation Energy Systems and Tech. div., Schenectady, 1976-78; gen. mgr. Neutron Devices dept. Aerospace Bus. Group, St. Petersburg, Fla., 1978—; chmn, air breathing propulsion com. NASA; mem. Air Force Sci. Adv. Bd. Mem. Suncoast Chamber Adv. Council, Com. of 100. Served to ensign USNR, 1944. Recipient Akroyd Stuart award Royal Aero. Sco., 1972. Mem. ASME, AIAA, Am. Mgmt. Assn. Club: Eastlake Woodlands Golf and Racquet. Current Work: Management of high technology businesses, general manager research, development, manufacturing advanced electro-mechanical devices. Research on aircraft engine design, heavy duty gas turbine design, properties and chem. composition of cumbustion products, residual fuels, solubility of gases. Subspecialties: Mechanical engineering; Electrical engineering.

SUCKEWER, SZYMON, physicist; b. Warsaw, Poland, Apr. 10, 1938; U.S. citizen. M.S., Moscow U., 1962; Ph.D. in Plasma Physics, Inst. Nuclear Research, Warsaw, 1966, Hibilitation, 1971. Head spectros. lab plasma physics, Inst. Nuclear Research, 1966-69; pvt. researcher, 1969-71; assoc. prof. Inst. Nuclear Research, Warsaw U., 1971-75, mem. staff, 1975-77, research physicist, 1977-80; sr. research physicist Plasma Physics Lab., Princeton U., N.J., 1980—, leader x-ray laser research group, 1980—. Subspecialty: X-ray lasers. Office: Princeton U Plasma Physics Lab PO Box 451 Princeton NJ 08544*

SUDAN, RAVINDRA NATH, physicist, educator; b. Chineni, Kashmir, India, June 8, 1931; came to U.S., 1958, naturalized, 1971; s. Brahm Nath and Shanti Devi (Mehta) S.; m. Dipali Ray, July 3, 1959; children: Rajani, Ranjeet. B.A. with first class honors, U. Punjab, 1948; diploma, Indian Inst. Sci., 1952, Imperial Coll., London, 1953; Ph.D., U. London, 1955. Engr., Brit. Thomson-Houston Co., Rugby, Eng, 1955-57; Engr. Imperial Chem. Industries, Calcutta, India, 1957-58; research asso. Cornell U., Ithaca, N.Y., 1958-59, asst. prof. elec. engring., 1959-63, assoc. prof., 1963-68, prof., 1968-75, IBM prof. engring., 1975-85; dir. Lab. Plasma Studies, 1975-85; dep. dir. Cornell Theory Ctr., 1985—; cons. Lawrence Livermore Lab., Los Alamos Sci. Lab., Sci. Applications Inc., Physics Internat. Co.; vis. research asso. Stanford U., summer 1963; cons. U.K. Atomic Energy Authority, Culham Lab., summer 1965; vis. scientist Internat. Center Theoretical Physics, Trieste, Italy, 1965-66, summers 1970, 73, Plasma Physics Lab. Princeton U., 1966-67, Inst. for Advanced Study, Princeton, N.J., spring 1975; head theoretical plasma physics group U.S. Naval Research Lab., 1970-71, sci. adviser to dir., 1974-75; chmn. Ann. Conf. on Theoretical Aspects of Controlled Fusion, 1975, 2d Internat. Conf. on High Power Electron and Ion Beam Research and Tech., 1977. Mem. editorial bd.: Nuclear Fusion, 1976-84, Physics of Fluids, 1973-76, Comments on Plasma Physics, 1973—; co-editor: Handbook of Plasma Physics; contbr. over 100 articles to sci. jours. Fellow Am. Phys. Soc., IEEE; mem. Sigma Xi. Patentee (with S. Humphries, Jr) intense ion beam generator. Current Work: Physics and technology of high powered charged particle beams; high energy particle accelerators; plasma confinement for nuclear fusion and spaceplasma physics. Subspecialties: Plasma physics; Nuclear fusion. Office: 290 Grumman Hall Cornell Univ Ithaca NY 14853

SUDILOVSKY, OSCAR, pathologist, educator; b. Rosario, Argentina, Nov. 8, 1933; s. Malquiel and Esther (Busel) S. M.D., U. Littoral, Rosario, Argentina, 1959; Ph.D., Case Western Res. U., Cleve., 1972. Chief tissue culture lab. U. Littoral, 1959-62; hon. fellow McArdle Lab. Cancer Research, U. Wis., Madison, 1969-71; asst. prof. pathology, also dir. Autopsy Service Univ. Hosps. of Cleve., 1970-76, assoc. prof., also dir. Tissue Culture Lab. 1976—; dir. Hybridoma Facility, 1982—, assoc. prof. environ. health sci., 1985—; mem. pathology B study sect. NIH. Contbr., articles to profl. jours. Nat. Council Sci. and Tech. Research (Argentina) fellow, 1959; NIH spl. research fellow, 1967-71. Mem. Am. Assn. Cancer Research, Tissue Culture Assn., Am. Assn. Pathologists, AAAS. Current Work: Hepatocarcinogenesis, hybridomas and monoclonal antibodies; somatic cell genetics. Subspecialties: Cancer research (medicine); Pathology (medicine). Office: 2085 Adelbert Rd Cleveland OH 44106

SUDWEEKS, EARL MAX, nutritionist; b. Richfield, Utah, Dec. 27, 1933; s. Alton D. and Olive (Lewis) S.; m. Dorene Collett, June 30, 1960; children—Jed, Karen, Ruth, Earlene, Susan, William, Marie, Nanette, David. B.S., Utah State U., 1960, M.S., 1962; Ph.D., N.C. State U., 1972. Research asso. Utah State U., Logan, 1962-65, county agt., 1965-68; research asst. N.C. State U., Raleigh, 1968-72; asst. prof. ruminant nutrition U. Ga., Experiment, 1972-80; dir. nutrition Watkins, Inc., Winona, Minn., 1980-81, Profl. Products, Saulk City, Wis., 1981; extension dairy specialist, Tex. A&M U., Overton, 1981—; cons. in field. Served to cpl. U.S. Army, 1953-55. Grantee U.S. Dept. Agr. Coop. States Research Service, 1979, Hoffman-La Roche, 1983, Tex. Agr. Experiment Sta., 1983. Mem. Am. Dairy Sci. Assn. (com. 1981—), Am. Soc. Animal Sci. (com. 1981—), Am. Inst. Nutrition, Nutrition Today Soc., Sigma Xi. Club: Toastmasters. Mormon. Current work: Forage and fiber in the ruminant. Subspecialties: Animal nutrition; Nutrition (medicine). Home: Route 4 Box 173 Kilgore TX 75662 Office: Tex A&M Agr Research and Extension Ctr PO Box 220 Overton TX 75684

SUEDFELD, PETER, educator, psychologist; b. Budapest, Hungary, Aug. 30, 1935; emigrated to U.S., 1948, naturalized, 1952; s. Leslie John and Jolan (Eichenbaum) Field; m. Gabrielle Debra Guterman, June 11, 1961 (div. 1980); children: Michael Thomas, Joanne Ruth, David Lee. Student, U. Philippines, 1956-57; B.A., Queens Coll., 1960; M.A., Princeton U., 1962, Ph.D., 1963. Research assoc. Princeton; lectr. Trenton State Coll., 1963-64; vis. asst. prof. psychology U. Ill., 1964-65; asst. prof. psychology Univ. Coll. Rutgers U., 1965-67, assoc. prof., 1967-71, prof., 1971-72, chmn. dept., 1967-72; prof., head dept. psychology U. B.C., Vancouver, 1972-84, dean grad. studies, 1984—; cons. in field. Author: Restricted Environmental Stimulation: Research and Clinical Applications, 1980; editor: Attitude Change: The Competing Views, 1971, Personality Theory and Information Processing, 1971, The Behavioral Basis of Design, 1976, Jour. Applied Social Psychology, 1975-82; Contbr. articles to profl. jours. Served with U.S. Army, 1955-58. NIMH grantee, 1970-72; Can. Council grantee, 1973—; Nat. Research Council Can. grantee, 1973—; NIH grantee, 1980-83. Fellow Can., Am. psychol. assns., Acad. Behavioral Medicine Research; mem. N.Y. Acad. Scis., AAAS, Psychonomic Soc., Soc. Exptl. Social Psychology, Phi Beta Kappa, Sigma Xi. Current Work: Behavioral, cognitive, attitudinal and biological effects and uses of reduced stimulation (habit modification, isolated areas, solitary confinement); effects of and adaptation to extreme and unusual environments/experiences; cognitive complexity of information processing and decision-making as a function of international crisis, governmental disruption, and personal life experiences. Subspecialties: Behavioral psychology; Cognition. Office: Dept Psychology U BC Vancouver BC Canada

SUGARBAKER, EVERETT VAN DYKE, surgeon/oncologist; b. N.Y.C., Aug. 6, 1940; s. Everett D. and Geneva I. (Van Dyke) S.; m. Catherine M. Mongiello, Sept. 16, 1968; children: Everett M., Kathryn A. B.S., Wheaton Coll., 1962; M.D., Cornell U., 1966. Resident in gen./thoracic surgery Mass. Gen. Hosp., Boston, 1966-68, 70-74; fellow surg. oncology M.D. Anderson Hosp., Houston, 1974-75; assoc. prof. surgery/oncology U. Miami (Fla.) Sch. Medicine, 1978-80; dir. surg. oncology Miami Cancer Inst., 1980—; pres. Surg. Oncology Assocs., Inc., Miami, 1980—; dir. dept. pathology Oncology Labs. div. Cedar Health Care Ctr., Miami; staff Mercy Hosp., Miami North Shore Hosp., Miami, Victoria Hosp., Miami. Contbr. articles to profl. jours. Served to lt. comdr. USPHS, 1968-70. Recipient Mo. Med. Soc. Sci. award, 1958; Wheaton Coll. scholar, 1960; Polk prize in surgery Cornell Med. Coll., 1966; ACS fellow, 1979; cert. of merit. Am. Cancer Soc., 1979-82; others. Fellow ACS; mem. Mass. Med. Soc., Assn. for Acad. Surgery, Dade County Med. Assn., Fla. Med. Assn., Am. Assn. Cancer Research, Am. Soc. Clin. Oncology, Am. Radium Soc., AMA, Soc. Surg. Oncology, Surg. Hist. Soc., Soc. Univ. Surgeons, Soc. Head and Neck Surgeons, AAAS, Miami Cancer Inst., Northwestern Med. Assn., Internat. Assn. Breast Cancer Research, others. Republican. Current Work: Cancer biology and metastasis research. Subspecialties: Surgery; Oncology. Home: 6916 Sunrise Terr Coral Gables FL 33133 Office: 1399 SW 1st Ave Miami FL 33131

SUGIHARA, TERUO, biologist; b. Kearny, N.J., June 19, 1949; s. Kyuichi and Shinobuko (Yamaguchi) S.; m. Lois-Anne Burek, July 30, 1976; A.B., in Biology, Lafayette Coll., 1971; Ph.D. in Ecology, Rutgers U., 1981. Research asst. Rutgers U., 1972-77; cons. Betz Converse Murdoch, Plymouth, Meeting, Pa., 1979; project leader Rutgers U., 1977-80; sr. environ. specialist N.J. Dept. Environ. Protection, Trenton, 1981-84; biologist U.S. Army C.E., Phila., 1984—. Author and editor tech. bulletin, 1979. Served to 1st lt. U.S. Army, 1972. Mem. Am. Soc. Limnology and Oceanography, Ecol. Soc. Am., Am. Inst. Biol. Sci., Estuarine Research Fedn., N.J. Acad. Sci. Presbyterian. Current work: Impact assessment of projects on environment; mitigation of project impacts; wetland boundary determination. Subspecialty: Ecology (biology). Home: 245 Cattell Ave West Collingswood NJ 08107 Office: US Army CE Environ Res Br Custom House 2d and Chestnut Sts Philadelphia PA 19106

SUH, NAM PYO, educator; b. Seoul, Korea, Apr. 22, 1936; came to U.S., 1954, naturalized, 1963; s. Doo Soo and Joon Joo (Lee) S.; m. Young Ja Surh, June 24, 1961; children—Mary M., Helen H., Grace J., Carolina Y. S.B., MIT, 1959, S.M., 1961; Ph.D., Carnegie-Mellon U., 1964. Devel. engr. Guild Plastics Inc., Cambridge, Mass., 1958-60; sr. research engr., project mgr. USM Corp., Beverly, Mass., 1961-65; asst. prof. U. S.C., Columbia, 1965-68, assoc. prof., 1968-69; assoc. prof. mech. engring. MIT, Cambridge, 1970-75, prof., 1975—; dir. MIT (Lab. Mfg. and Productivity), 1977—, MIT (Industry Polymer

Processing Program), 1973—; chmn. bd. Axiomatics Corp., Sudbury, Mass.; dir. Surftech Corp., Hollis, N.H., Intelitec Corp., Billerica, Mass. Author: (with A.P.L. Turner) Mechanical Behavior of Solids, 1975; editor: (with N. Saka) Fundamentals of Tribology, 1980, (with N. Sung) Science and Technology of Polymer Procs, 1979, The Delamination Theory of Wear, 1977. Chmn. bd. Korean-Am. Soc. New Eng., 1979. Recipient Best Paper award Soc. Plastics Engrs., 1981; Citation Classic Inst. for Sci. Info., 1981; USM Corp. fellow, 1962-63. Mem. ASME (Gustus L. Larson Meml. award 1976, Blackall award 1982), Sigma Xi, Pi Tau Sigma, Phi Kappa Phi. Methodist. Patentee in field. Subspecialty: Mechanical engineering. Office: Room 35-234 Mass Inst Tech Cambridge MA 02139

SUKOW, WAYNE WILLIAM, physicist, researcher; b. Merrill, Wis., Dec. 9, 1936; s. William A. and Sylvia (Buntrock) S.; m. Carol J. Nelson, June 20, 1959; children—Catherine Anne, David Wayne. B.S. in Physics and Biology, U. Wis.-River Falls, 1959; M.S. in Nuclear Physics, Case Western Res. U., 1963; Ph.D. in Chem. Physics, Wash. State U., 1974. Research assoc. Los Alamos N.M. Sci. Lab., N.Mex., summer 1964; physicist, applied research group 3M Co., St. Paul, 1967; vis. asst. prof. Wash. State U.-Pullman, summer 1974, U. Oreg.-Eugene, summer 1976; prof. physics U. Wis.-River Falls, 1973-84; exec. dir. W. Central Wis. Consortium, River Falls, Wis., 1984—; sci. coordinator K-12, Wis. Sch. Evaluation Consortium, Madison, Wis., 1983—; textbook reviewer Wadsworth Pub. Co., Belmont, Calif., 1980—; evaluator faculty coll. U. Wis. system, Madison, 1980. Contbr. articles to sci. jours. Mem., chmn. River Falls Bd. Edn., 1981—; mem. governing bd. Growth, Learning, Enrichment Enterprise, Kenosha, Wis., 1977-84. NSF Sci. Faculty Fellow awardee, 1970-72. Mem. Biophys. Soc., Wis. Assn. Physics Tchrs. (past pres.), Am. Assn. Physics Tchrs., Sigma Pi Sigma, Phi Kappa Phi. Lutheran. Clubs: St. Croix Rockhounds, Minn. Mineral. Current work: Protein-small ligand interactions, electron spin resonance applied to biological macromolecules and detergent systems, photoelectron microscopy of biological surfaces. Subspecialties: Molecular biology; Biophysics (physics). Home: 1027 W Maple St River Falls WI 54022 Office: West Central Wisconsin Consortium 410 S 3d St River Falls WI 54022

SUKUP, JAMES WALTER, geologist; b. Chgo., Mar. 4, 1953; s. John Peter and Janet Laura (Greger) S.; m. Mary Helen Vinich, Sept. 30, 1979; children—Dawn Marie, Ann Bernice. B.S. in Geology, Ind. U., 1975; M.S. in Geology, U. Wyo., 1978. Geologist, Rocky Mountain Energy, Broomfield, Colo., 1978-82, project geologist, 1982—. Mem. Geol. Soc. Am., Paleontol. Soc., Wyo. Geol. Assn., Soc. Econ. Mineralogists and Paleontologists. Republican. Roman Catholic. Current work: Reconnaissance and exploration for and development of uranium ore-bodies within the western United States. Subspecialties: Sedimentology; Paleontology. Home: 10751 Routt St Westminster CO 80020 Office: Rocky Mountain Energy 10 Longs Peak Dr Box 2000 Broomfield CO 80020

SULLIVAN, CARL ROLLYNN, JR., fisheries scientist, association executive; b. Marietta, Ohio, Feb. 20, 1926; s. Carl Rollynn and Grace Roberta (Bengel) S.; m. Dolores Marion Cortes, Sept. 12, 1950; children—Carl R., Michael Dexter, Peter Augustin. B.S. in Forestry, W.Va. U., 1950; M.S. in Hydrobiology Ohio State U., 1953. Asst. fish chief W.Va. Conservation Commn., Charleston, 1953-55; pub. relations dir., land mgr. Kaser Aluminum, Ravenswood, W.Va., 1955-61; dir. W.Va. Centennial Commn., Charleston, 1961-63; dir. Alaska Centennial Commn., Anchorage, 1964-67; owner Sullivan Services, Anchorage, 1967-72; exec. sec. Sport Fishing Inst., Washington, 1972-75; dir. Am. Fisheries Soc., Bethesda, Md., 1975—. Founder, editor Fisheries, 1975—. Commr., W.Va. Dept. Natural Resources, 1981—; mem. Outer Continental Shelf Policy Com., Dept. Interior, Washington, 1984—, Mid-Atlantic Regional Tech. Working Group, 1978—; mem. Rigs to Reefs Com., and Wetlands Com., 1980—; vice chmn. Renewable Natural Resource Found. Served with U.S. Army, 1944-46. Recipient Gulf Conservation award, Gulf Oil Co., 1984, Disting. Service award Am. Fisheries Soc., 1983, 84. Mem. Am. Fisheries Soc., Am. League Anglers and Boaters (pres.), Planetary Soc., Wildlife Soc., Coastal Soc. Conservative. Club: Izack Walton League. Current work: involved with directing professional society activities, legislative initiatives, conservation programs, editing, aquatic resource policy. Subspecialties: Marine biology; Limnology. Home: Box 58 Route 2 Charles Town WV 25414 Office: Am Fisheries Soc 5410 Grosvenor Ln Bethesda MD 20814

SULLIVAN, CAROLE A., radiation therapist, educator; b. Chgo., Nov. 16, 1941; d. John Norman and Arlene Mary (Narducy) S. M.Ed., U. Okla., 1982. Cert. in radiation therapy U. Chgo. Hosps. Chief technologist Radiation Therapy Ctr., U. Chgo. Hosps., 1963-67; dosimetrist, chief technologist Radiation Therapy Ctr. Northwestern Meml. Hosp., Chgo., 1968-73; tech. dir. Radiation Therapy Ctr., Univ. Hosp., Okla. U. Health Scis. Center, Oklahoma City, 1973—; assoc. prof., dir. radiation therapy program Coll. Allied Health, U. Okla., Oklahoma City, 1973-78, prof. chmn. dept. radiologic tech., 1980—; cons. ednl. accreditation, adminstrn. of health care facilities. Contbr. articles to profl. jours. Bd. dirs. Children's Tomorrow House Okla. Fellow Am. Soc. Radiologic Tech.; mem. Am. Assn. Physicists in Medicine, Okla. Acad. Scis., AAUP, Assn. Univ. Radiologic Technologists, Phi Delta Kappa. Roman Catholic. Current Work: Radiation biology-radiation exposure. Specific interest in the long term effects of chronic long term radiation exposure to radiation workers such as physicians and technologists. Subspecialties: Radiation oncology; Medical physics. Home: 1118 Bedford Dr Oklahoma City OK 73116 Office: PO Box 26901 Dept Radiologic Tech Coll Allied Health Room 441 Oklahoma City OK 73190

SULLIVAN, DENNIS, mathematics educator; b. Port Huron, Mich., Feb. 12, 1941. B.A., Rice U., 1963; Ph.D., Princeton U., 1965; hon. degree U. Warwick, Coventry, Eng., 1984. Lectr., assoc. prof. Princeton U., N.J., 1967-69; prof. math. MIT, Cambridge, Mass., 1972-73; professeur permanent Inst. des Hautes Etudes, Bures-sur-Yvette, France, 1974; Einstein prof. sci. Queens Coll. and CUNY Grad. Sch., N.Y.C., 1981—. Recipient Oswald Veblen prize Am. Math. Soc., 1971; Elie Cartan prix en geometrie French Acad. Sci., 1981. Mem. Nat. Acad. Sci., Nat. Acad. Sci. Brazil (corr.). Current work: Part of mathematics concerned with simple (numerical) processes which develop intricatepatterns and structure after many iterations. Office: Einstein Chair Dept Math CUNY Grad Ctr 33 W 42d St New York NY 10036

SULLIVAN, EDWARD MAURICE, chemist; b. Balt., Aug. 24, 1950; s. Maurice Henry and Jean Caroline (Harvey) S.; m. Patricia Nancy Groff, Dec. 21, 1974. B.S., Frostburg State Coll., 1974. Corp. ops. staff Carling Nat. Brewery, Balt., 1975-76, quality control mgr., 1976-77, master brewer, 1977-78; tech. adviser BBL Microbiology, Cockeysville, Md., 1978-80; quality assurance mgr. Lever Brothers, Inc., Balt., 1980—. Served with USAR, 1970-76. Mem. Am. Chem. Soc., Master Brewers Assn. Am., Am. Oil Chemists Soc. Subspecialties: Quality assurance; Physical chemistry. Home: 108 Cloverhill Rd Pasadena MD 21122 Office: Lever Brothers Inc 5300 Holabird Ave Baltimore MD 21224

SULLIVAN, FRANCIS EDWARD, mathematician, educator; b. Bklyn., May 12, 1941; s. Francis Edward and Beatrice (DeLucca) S.; m. Mary Alyce Lennon, May 10, 1969. B.S. in Physics, Pa. State U., 1962; M.S. in Math., U. Pitts., 1964, Ph.D. in Math., 1968. Mathematician, Gulf Research and Devel. Co., Pitts., 1963-66; vis. prof. computer sci. Chalmers, Gothenburg, Sweden, 1971-73; chmn. math. and computer sci. Catholic U., Washington, 1973-82, adj. prof., 1985; mathematician Nat. Bur. Standards, Gaithersburg, Md., 1978—, chief sci. computing div., 1982—; vis. prof. math. Catholic U. Netherlands, Nijmegen, 1980. Contbr. articles to profl. publs. Curriculum cons. St. Jerome Sch., Hyattsville, Md., 1979-84. Mem. Soc. Indsl. and Applied Math. Roman Catholic. Current work: Supercomputer algorithms for condensed matter; data structures and algorithm design; applications of non-linear functional analysis; scientific administration. Subspecialties: Applied mathematics; Algorithms. Home: 10402 Nolan Dr Rockville MD 20850 Office: Ctr Applied Math Nat Bur Standards Gaithersburg MD 20899

SULLIVAN, HUGH RICHARD, JR., chemist, pharmacologist; b. Indpls., Apr. 8, 1926; s. Hugh Richard and Josephine Cecelia (Gill) S.; m. Betty Catherine Smith, Oct. 5, 1924; children: Hugh R., Kathleen, Mark K., Marianne, Kevin J. B.S. in Organic Chemistry, Notre Dame U., 1948; M.S., Temple U., 1954. Assoc. research chemist Mobil Oil Co., Paulsboro, N.J., 1948-51; assoc. research chemist Lilly Research Labs., Indpls., 1951-58, research chemist, 1958-67, sr. research chemist, 1967-69, research scientist, 1969-72, research assoc., group leader, 1972—. Contbr. articles to profl. jours. Served with USN, 1944-46. Mem. AAAS, Am. Soc. Mass Spectrometry, N.Y. Acad. Scis., Am. Soc. Pharmacology and Exptl. Therapeutics. Democrat. Roman Catholic. Club: KC. Patentee in field. Current Work: Drug Metabolism and pharmacokinetic research. Subspecialty: Pharmacokinetics. Home: 7135 Kingswood Circle Indianapolis IN 46256 Office: Lilly Research Labs 307 E McCarty St Indianapolis IN 46285

SULLIVAN, JAY MICHAEL, medical educator; b. Brockton, Mass., Aug. 3, 1936; s. William Dennis and Wanda Nancy (Kelpsh) S.; m. Mary Suzanne Baxter, Dec. 30, 1964; children: Elizabeth, Suzanne, Christopher. B.S. cum laude, Georgetown U., 1958, M.D. magna cum laude, 1962. Diplomate: Nat. Bd. Med. Examiners, Am. Bd. Internal Medicine. Nat. Heart Inst. fellow, 1964; Med. Found. research fellow, 1967. Med. intern Peter Bent Brigham Hosp., Boston, 1962-63, resident, 1963-64, 66-67, chief resident, 1969-70, fellow in cardiology, 1964-66, dir. hypertnesion unit, 1970-74; preceptorship in biol. chemistry Harvard Med. Sch., Boston, 1967-69, asst. prof. medicine, 1970-74; dir. med. services Boston Hosp. for Women, 1973-74; prof. medicine, chief div. cardiovascular diseases U. Tenn. Coll. Medicine, Memphis, 1974—, vice-chmn. dept. medicine, 1982—; mem. staff City of Memphis, VA, Bapt. Meml. hosps., U. Tenn. Medical Center-Wm. F. Bowld Hosp.; mem. med. adv. bd. Council for High Blood Pressure Research; cons. Nat. Heart, Lung and Blood Inst., 1974—, U.S. VA, 1983—. Contbr. articles to sci. jours. Served with M.C., U.S. Army, 1963-70. Fellow ACP, Am. Coll. Cardiology, Council on Circulation of Am. Heart Assn.; mem. Assn. Univ. Cardiologists, Internat. Soc. Hypertension, Am. Fedn. Clin. Research, Am. Heart Assn. (pres. chpt. 1982-83), AAAS, Alpha Omega Alpha, Sigma Xi, Alpha Sigma Nu. Roman Catholic. Club: Racquet of Memphis. Current Work: Pathophysiology and hemodynamics of hypertension. Subspecialty: Cardiology. Home: 6077 Maiden Ln Memphis TN 38117 Office: 951 Court Ave Room 353D Memphis TN 38163

SULLIVAN, KATHRYN D., geologist, astronaut. Astronaut NASA Johnson Space Ctr; Houston; mem. Nat. Commn. Space, 1985—. Subspecialties: Astronautics; Mineralogy. Office: NASA Johnson Space Ctr Astronaut Office Houston TX 77058*

SULLIVAN, NEIL MAXWELL, oil and gas company executive; b. McKeesport, Pa., May 25, 1942; s. Thomas James and Jane Mason (Ginn) S.; m. Margaret Pedrick, Aug. 10, 1974; children—Margaret Blair, Mason Pedrick. B.S., Dickinson Coll., 1970; postgrad. Tulane U., 1970-74. Exploration geologist Bass Enterprises, Midland, Tex., 1976-77; dist. geologist ATAPCO, Midland, 1977-78; div. geologist Anadarko Prodn. Co., Midland, 1978-79, chief geologist, 1979-80, v.p. exploration, regional mgr., 1980-82; exploration ops. mgr. Valero Producing Co., San Antonio, 1982—. Editor: Guadalupian Delaware Mountain Group of West Texas and Southeast New Mexico, 1979; Ancient Carbonate Reservoirs and Their Modern Analogs, 1977; Petroleum Exploration in Thrust Belts and Their Adjacent Forelands, 1976. Bd. dirs. Permian Basin Grad. Ctr., Midland, Tex., 1979; com. chmn. Mus. of Southwest, Midland, 1978; mem. Gulf of Mexico regional tech. working group com. Outer Continental Shelf Adv. Bd., 1985—. Served with USAF, 1964-68. Mem. Geol. Soc. Am., Am. Assn. Petroleum Geologists (chmn. Dist. 20), Am. Petroleum Inst. (com. on stats. of drilling 1984—), West Tex. Geol. Soc., South Tex. Geol. Soc., Soc. Econ. Paleontologists and Mineralogists (pres. Permian Basin sect. 1979-80). Republican. Episcopalian. Lodge: Elks. Current work: Synthesis of remote sensing, surface, subsurface and geophysical data in structural and stratigraphic analysis of petroleum productive and potentially productive basins and trends with emphasis on prospecting by environmental-sedimentologic modeling of subtle traps. Subspecialties: Geology; Sedimentology.

SULLIVAN, NEIL SAMUEL, physicist, researcher, educator; b. Wanganui, Wellington, N.Z., Jan. 18, 1942; came to U.S., 1983; s. Reynold Richard and Edna Mary (Alger) S.; m. Robyn Annette Dawson, Aug. 28, 1965; children—Raoul Samuel, Robert Alexander and David Charles (twins). B.Sc. with 1st class honors, U. Otago, N.Z., 1964, M.Sc. in Physics, 1965; Ph.D. in Physics, Harvard U., 1972. Postdoctoral research Centre d'Etudes Nucleaires, Saclay, France, 1972-74, research physicist, 1974-82; prof. physics U. Fla., Gainesville, 1982—. Contbr. numerous articles on quantum solids and nuclear magnetism to profl. jours., 1971—. Recipient prix Saintour, College de France, Paris, 1978, prix LaCaze, Academie des Sciences, Paris, 1982; Fulbright exchange grantee, 1965; Frank Knox Meml. fellow Harvard U., Cambridge, Mass., 1965-67. Mem. Inst. Physics, Societe Francaise de Physique, European Phys. Soc., Am. Phys. Soc., AAAS. Current work: Investigation of fundamental properties of solid hydrogen and solid helium at very low temperatures; studies of molecular motions using nuclear magnetic resonance; orientational disorder in molecular crystals. Subspecialties: Condensed matter physics; Low temperature physics. Home: 4244 NW 76 Terr Gainesville FL 32606 Office: U Fla 215 Williamson Hall Gainesville FL 32611

SULLIVAN, ROGER JOHN, engineer, physicist; b. Newport, R.I., Feb. 8, 1941; s. John Francis Jr. and Barbara (Williams) S.; m. Susan Dulaney Goodpaster, Aug. 27, 1966; children—Andrew, Barbara, Catherine. B.S. in Physics, MIT, 1962, Ph.D. in Physics, 1969. Scientist, Ill. Inst. Tech. Research Inst., Chgo., 1969-73; sr. scientist System Planning Corp., Arlington, 1973—. Contbr. reports, articles to prof. publs. Exec. sec. Am. Strategic Defense Assn., Arlington, Va., 1982-84. Mem. Am. Astron. Soc. Republican. Current work: Design of radar signal-processing algorithms, civil defense and strategic arms analysis, planetary science, x-ray astronomy. Subspecialties: Electrical engineering; Planetary science. Home: 371 N Edison St Arlington VA 22203 Office: System Planning Corp 1425 N Quincy St Arlington VA 22207

SUMMERFIELD, MARTIN, physicist; b. N.Y.C., Oct. 20, 1916; s. Jacob and Augusta (Tobias) S.; m. Eileen Budin, Aug. 31, 1945; 1 dau., Jacqueline. B.S., Bklyn. Coll., 1936; M.S., Calif. Inst. Tech., 1938, Ph.D., 1941. Asst. chief Air Corps Jet Propulsion Project, Calif. Inst. Tech., 1940-43, chief, rocket research div., 1945-49; chief, rocket devel. div. Aerojet Engring. Corp., Azusa, Calif., 1943-45; mem. subcom. on fuels NACA, 1948-49, subcom. on combustion, 1949-50; prof. jet propulsion Princeton U., 1951-78, prof. emeritus, 1978—; Astor prof. applied sci. N.Y.U., 1978-80; tech. dir. Project Squid, 1949-51; chief scientist Flow Industries Inc., 1975-78; pres. Princeton Combustion Research Labs., 1978—; editor Aeros. Publ. Program, 1949-52; editor-in-chief Jour. Am. Rocket Soc., 1951-57; editor Jet Propulsion; also tech. editor Astronautics, 1957-63; editor AIAA series on Progress in Astronautics and Aeros., 1960—; editor-in-chief Astronautica Acta, 1964-69; cons. U.S. Army Research Office, 1968-71; mem. adv. com. chem. propulsion NASA, 1968-71; chmn. com. on fire toxicity hazards of materials NRC, 1984—, mem. com. on energetic materials NRC, 1984—. Recipient Pendray award, 1954; Wyld award, 1977. Fellow AAAS, AIAA (v.p. 1963-65), Am. Rocket Soc. (pres. 1962-63); mem. Internat. Acad. Astronautics, Nat. Acad. Engring. ASME (Heat Transfer award 1978), Internat. Astronautical Fedn. (v.p. 1963-65), Sigma Xi. Patentee on rocket motors and related devices. Current work: Flammability of fuels, fire toxicity, experimental methods, rocket engines, interior ballistics of guns. Subspecialty: Combustion processes. Office: Princeton Combustion Research Labs Monmouth Junction NJ 08852

SUMMERS, GEORGE DONALD, technical company consultant; b. Eldorado, Ill., Jan. 16, 1927; s. Arthur W. and Georgia Pearl (Horn) S.; m. Margot Gene Sturken, Dec. 28, 1949; children: Emmy L., Susan H.; m. Sachiko Orui, Aug. 1, 1977. B.S., U.S. Mil. Acad., 1949; postgrad., Army schs., 1949-50, 54-55. Registered profl. engr. Project engr. Am. Bosch Arma Corp., Garden City, N.Y., 1956-58; program mgr. Fairchild Industries (formerly Republic Aviation), Mineola and Farmingdale, N.Y., 1958-72; with Atlantic Research Corp., Alexandria, Va., 1972—, v.p., 1980-84, cons., 1984—. Served to capt. F.A. U.S. Army, 1949-56. Recipient 100 award Indsl. Research publ., 1974. Mem. IEEE, AIAA, AAAS, Am. Soc. Artificial Internal Organs, Armed Forces Communications and Electronics Assn., Assn. U.S. Army, Air Force Assn., U.S. Naval Inst., Assn. Unmanned Vehicles, Am. Def. Preparedness Assn., Soc. Info. Display, Mensa, Intertel. Patents, publs. in biomed., aerospace systems, and communications fields. Current Work: Application of science and technology to solve problems such as systems engring. Subspecialty: Systems engineering. Home: 10402 Hollyoak Pl Fairfax VA 22032 Office: Atlantic Research Corp 5390 Cherokee Ave Alexandria VA 22312

SUMMERS, WILLIAM KOOPMANS, neuropsychiatrist, educator; b. Jefferson City, Mo., Apr. 14, 1944; s. Joseph Steward and Amy (Koopmans) S.; m. Angela Forbes Taveras, Oct. 24, 1972; children: Lawrence Pierce, Elisabeth Stuart, Wilhelmina Derek. B.A., U. Mo., 1966; M.D., Washington U.-St. Louis, 1971. Intern Barnes Hosp.-Washington U., St. Louis, 1971-72, resident in medicine and psychiatry, 1970-76; instr. dept. psychiatry and medicine Washington U., St. Louis, 1971-76; asst. prof. psychiatry, internal medicine U. Pitts., 1976-77, asst. dir. disorder clinic, 1976-77; asst. prof. psychiatry, internal medicine U. So. Calif., Los Angeles, 1977-82, ward chief med. center, 1977-81; asst. prof. research dept. psychiatry UCLA, 1982—. Contbr. articles to profl. jours. Markle Found. fellow Washington U., 1971. Mem. ACP, Am. Fedn. Clin. Research, Soc. Biol. Psychiatry. Republican. Episcopalian. Current Work: General studies of neuropsychiatry and specific study of clinical central nervous system acetylcholine mechanisms. Subspecialties: Neuropharmacology; Internal medicine. Office: 624 W Duarte Rd Arcadia CA 91006

SUMMIT, ROGER KENT, information systems and services company executive; b. Detroit, Oct. 14, 1930; s. Paul Maurice and Mildred Suzanne S.; m. Virginia Buckhorn, Aug. 8, 1964; children: Jennifer Lee, Scott Wesley. A.B., Stanford U., 1952, M.B.A., 1957, Ph.D., 1965. Research scientist Lockheed Research Lab., Palo Alto, Calif., 1965-72; mgr. DIALOG info. retrieval service Lockheed Corp., Palo Alto, 1972-77, pres. DIALOG Info. Services, Inc., 1981—; dir. Lockheed Info. Systems, Palo Alto, 1977-81; mem. sci. and tech. info. working group Dept. Commerce and M.I.T.; mem. public-pvt. sector relations task force Nat. Commn. on Libraries and Info. Sci.; trustee Engring. Index, Inc., mem. adv. bd. Internat. Acad. at Santa Barbara, 1982. Contbr. to profl. publs. Served to lt. (j.g.) USN, 1952-55. Recipient Spl. Invention award Lockheed Corp.; award for achievement in library and info. tech. ALA; Hon. fellow Inst. Info. Scientists Gt. Britain. mem. Info. Industry Assn. (dir., Info. Product of Year award 1975, Hall of Fame award 1982), Assn. Info. and Dissemination Centers (v.p. 1975-76), Am. Soc. Info. Sci., IEEE, AAAS (council 1982—). Inventor aerospace bus. environment simulator, DIALOG info. retrieval lang. Subspecialties: Information systems, storage, and retrieval (computer science); Information systems (Information science). Office: 3460 Hillview Ave Palo Alto CA 94304

SUMNERS, CAROLYN TAYLOR, museum administrator, investigator; b. Chattanooga, Mar. 7, 1948; d. Robert Armstrong and Eunice (Kenney) T.; m. Robert William Sumners, Dec. 27, 1970 (div.); children: Robert William, Jonathan Taylor. B.A. in Physics Astronomy magna cum laude, Vanderbilt U., 1969; Ed.D., U. Houston, 1979. Lectr. astronomy Burke Baker Planetarium, Houston, 1970-73, curator, 1973-78; curator astronomy Houston Mus. Natural Sci., 1978-81, dir. astronomy and physics, 1982—; co-prin. investigator Informal Sci. Study U. Houston, 1980—; tchr., cons. Kinkaid/Houston Sci. and Math. Inst. for Gifted Minority Students. Author articles, physics textbooks, elem. sci. textbooks. Woodrow Wilson fellow, 1978; recipient citation for excellence in energy edn. Tex. Edn. Agy., 1982. Mem. Met. Assn. Tchrs. Sci., Am. Assn. Physics Tchrs., Am. Astron. Soc., Nat. Sci. Tchrs. Assn., Internat. Solar Energy Soc., Planetary Soc., Houston Astron. Soc. Current Work: Development of astronomy data center mini-computer software package; implementation of an astronomy bulletin board system; development of a radio remote-computer controlled robot. Subspecialties: Optical astronomy; Solar energy. Home: 9238 Westwood Village Dr Houston TX 77036 Office: 1 Hermann Circle Dr Houston TX 77030

SUN, ALBERT YEN, geologist; b. State College, Pa., Feb. 7, 1956; s. Shiou Chuan and E-tu (Zen) S. B.A., Cornell U., 1978; M.S., U. Wis.-Madison, 1980, Ph.D., 1984. Geologist, ARCO Exploration Co., Dallas, 1984—. Mem. Geol. Soc. Am., Am. Geophys. Union, Sigma Xi. Current work: Structural geology and tectonics; petroleum exploration. Subspecialty: Tectonics. Office: ARCO Exploration PO Box 2819 Dallas TX 75221

SUN, ALBERT YUNG-KWANG, biochemistry and neurochemistry educator; b. Amoy, Fukien, Peoples Republic of China, Oct. 13, 1932; came to U.S., 1959, naturalized, 1972; s. Pehcheng and SuiHo Kuo Wu; m. Grace Yen-Chi Cheung Sun, May 9, 1964; 1 child, Aggie Yee-Chun. B.S. in Agrl. Chemistry, Nat. Taiwan U., Taipei, 1957; Ph.D. in Biochemistry, Oreg. State U., 1967. Postdoctoral research assoc. Case-Western Res. U., Cleve., 1967-68; sr. research scientist Cleve. Psychiat. Inst., 1968-74; project dir. Ohio Mental Health Research Ctr., Cleve., 1972-74, research prof. neurochemistry, assoc. prof. biochemistry U. Mo., Columbia, 1974—; mem. adv. panel NSF, Washington, 1984—. Editor: Neural Membranes, 1983. Advisor, Chinese Christian Fellowship Group, Columbia, 1974—. Grantee Nat. Inst. Alcohol Abuse and Alcoholism, 1974-78, 82—, Nat. Inst. Neurol. Com. Disease and Stroke, 1975-79, Nat. Cancer Inst., 1979-83. Mem. Research Soc. Alcoholism, Am. Soc. Neurochemistry, Internat. Soc. Neurochemistry, Am. Soc. Neurosci., Am. Soc. Biol. Chemists, Am. Chem. Soc. Current work: Structure-functional relationship of neural membranes using biochemical and biophysical approaches, study on the effect of aging and alcohol on membrane systems in the brain. Subspecialties: Biochemistry (medicine); Neurochemistry. Home: Route 12 Box 335 Columbia MO 65203 Office: Univ Mo Sinclair Research Farm Columbia MO 65203

SUN, CHANG-TSAN, engineering educator; b. Shenyang, China, Feb. 20, 1928; came to U.S., 1958, naturalized, 1969; s. Yao-Tsung and Chung-Shuan (Lee) S.; m. Jenny M. Lin, Aug. 17, 1963; children: Barry I-Lung, Karen I-Teh, Nancy I-Huei. B.S., Taiwan U., 1953; M.S., Stevens Inst. Tech., 1960; D. Engring., Yale U., 1964. With Iowa State U., Ames, 1965-77; with Gen. Motors Research Labs., Warren, Mich., 1977-79; prof. dept. engring. scis. U. Fla., Gainesville, 1979—. Contbr. articles to sci. jours. Mem. ASTM, ASME. Republican. Subspecialties: Solid mechanics; Fracture mechanics. Office: Dept Engring Scis U Fla Gainesville FL 32611

SUN, GRACE YAN CHI, educator, researcher; b. Hong Kong, Oct. 4, 1939; came to U.S., 1957; d. Paul and Mei-Sin (Lau) Cheung; m. Albert Y. Sun, May 9, 1964; 1 dau., Aggie. B.S., Seattle Pacific U., 1961; Ph.D., Oreg. State U., Corvallis, 1966. Research scientist Cleve. Psychiat. Inst., 1966-74; asst. prof. dept. chemistry U. Mo., Kansas City, 1974-75, assoc. prof. dept. biochemistry, Columbia, 1978-85, prof., 1985—; research prof. Sinclair Research Farm, Columbia, 1975—. Mem. Am. Soc. Neurochemists, Internat. Soc. for Neurochemists, Neurosci. Soc., Fedn. Am. Socs. for Exptl. Biology, Internat. Soc. for Neurochem. Research in Neurochem. Alcoholism. Current Work: Membrane phospholipid metabolism. Subspecialties: Neurochemistry; Biochemistry (medicine). Home: Box 335 Route 12 Columbia MO 65201 Office: Sinclair Research Farm Univ Missouri Columbia MO 65201

SUN, JOHN, aerodynamics engineer, researcher, educator, consultant; b. Shanghai, China, Mar. 20, 1942; came to U.S., 1965; s. Cheung and Wan-Ching (Chang) S.; m. Michele T. Tollie, Sept. 1, 1973; children: Stephanie Francis, Valerie Michele, Gregory William. B.S., Provincial Taiwan Cheng Kung U., 1964; M.S. in Aerospace Engring, Va. Poly. Inst. and State U., 1969, Ph.D. in Engring. Mechanics, 1976. Grad. teaching asst. Va. Poly. Inst. and State U., Blacksburg, 1965-66; aerospace engr. Naval Surface Weapons Ctr., Dahlgren, Va., 1967-80; sr. staff engr. Missile Systems Group, Hughes Aircraft Co., Canoga Park, Calif., 1980-85; engr. specialist sr. Aircraft Group, Northrop Corp., Ventura, Calif., 1985—. Contbr. articles to profl. publs. Recipient awards Naval Surface Weapons Ctr., 1976, 77, 78, 81, awards Hughes Aircraft Co., 1981, 82, 83, 84, 85. Assoc. fellow AIAA; mem. Nat. Honor Soc. Aerospace Engring., Naval Aeroballistic Com. Navy/Dept. Def. Patentee controlled store separation system. Current Work: researcher, developer state-of-the-art missile aerodynamics predicition computer code for generalized missiles configuration, radar cross-sections, designs for new missiles, aerial target aircraft and tactical air vehicles. Subspecialty: Aeronautical engineering. Home: 664 San Telmo Circle Newbury Park CA 91320 Office: Northrop Aircraft Group Ventura Div Newburg Park CA 91320

SUN, MIKE, potato specialist, plant pathologist; b. Taiwan, Feb. 2, 1938; s. A. T. and Y. T. (Lieu) S.; m. Anna Wei, Oct. 7, 1967; children: Joannie, Theodore. Ph.D. in Plant Pathology, N.C. State U., 1971. Postdoctoral fellow N.C. State U., 1971-73; assoc. plant pathologist Asian Vegetable Research and Devel. Ctr., Taiwan, 1973-75; research assoc. Mich. State U., 1976-78; potato specialist, extension plant pathologist Mont. State U., 1978—Current Work: Research on potato diseases and potato seed improvement; certify potato seed. Subspecialties: Plant virology; Plant cell and tissue culture. Home: 1710 Park View Pl Bozeman MT 59715 Office: Potato Laborator Montana State University Bozeman MT 59717

SUND, ELDON H(AROLD), chemist, educator, consultant; b. Plentywood, Mont., June 6, 1930; s. Lawrence and Ethel May (Andersen) S.; m. Roberta Faulkner, July 13, 1933; children: Sharon Ellen, Elizabeth Dianne, Phillip Lawrence, Nancy Annemarie. B.S., U. Ill., Urbana, 1952; Ph.D., U. Tex., Austin, 1960. Research chemist E. I. duPont de Nemours & Co., Wilmington, Del., 1959-66; asst. prof. chemistry Ohio No. U., 1966-67; prof. Midwestern

State U., Wichita Falls, Tex., 1967—, Hardin prof., 1975, chmn. dept. chemistry, 1983—. Contbr. articles to profl. jours., 1970—. Served to 1st lt. USAF, 1952-56. NSF grantee, 1968-70; Robert A. Welch Found. grantee, 1970—. Mem. Am. Chem. Soc., Internat. Soc. Heterocyclic Chemistry, AAAS, Tex. Acad. Sci., Sigma Xi. Lutheran. Patentee in field. Current Work: Synthesis of heterocyclic ketones capable of undergoing enol-keto tautomerism. Subspecialties: Organic chemistry; Synthetic chemistry. Office: 3400 Taft Blvd Wichita Falls TX 76308

SUNDE, MILTON L., poultry science educator, administrator; b. Volga, S.D., Jan. 7, 1921; s. Andrew Carl and Clara Josephine (Mehl) S.; m. Clara Josephine (Mehl) S.; m. Genevieve Claire, Dec. 29, 1946; children—Roger, Scott, Robert. B.S., S.D. State Coll., 1947; M.S., U. Wis., 1949, Ph.D., 1950. Asst. field mgr. S.D. Poultry Improvement, Brookings, 1946-47; instr. to assoc. prof. U. Wis., Madison, 1949-57, prof., 1957—; chmn. poultry sci. dept., 1964-66, 1971—; mem. research council U.S. Brewers Assoc., 1970-80. Author: Nutrition Requirements of Poultry, 1978. Served to capt. inf. U.S. Army, 1942-46, ETO. Recipient Coll. Agr. Teaching award U. Wis., 1974. Fellow Poultry Sci. Assn. (pres. 1967-68, Am. Feed Mfg. Research award 1961, Ralston Purina Teaching award 1962); mem. Am. Poultry Hist. Soc. (pres. 1978-80), World's Poultry Sci. Assn. (U.S. Br. pres. 1984—), Am. Chem. Soc. Lutheran. Lodge: Sertoma Club (pres. 1966). Current work: Amino acids-vitamins, energy metabolism, zinc nutrition. Subspecialties: Animal nutrition; Nutrition (biology). Home: 1111 Starlight Dr Madison WI 53706 Office: Poultry Sci Dept Univ Wis 1675 Observatory Dr Madison WI 53706

SUNDELL, KENT ALLAN, oil company executive, geological consultant; b. Olathe, Kans., July 5, 1955; s. Allan Richard and Joyce (Jensen) S.; m. Margaret Bertolino, Aug. 31, 1980; 1 child, Jessica Ann. B.S. in Geology, U. Wyo., 1977, M.S. in Geology, 1980; Ph.D. in Geology, U. Calif.-Santa Barbara, 1985. Geol. cons. W.G.M. Minerals Co., Anchorage, 1977; teaching asst. U. Wyo., Laramie, 1978-80; teaching asst., assoc., U. Calif.-Santa Barbara, 1980-82; founder, chmn., geologist Ram Oil Co., Inc., Casper, Wyo., 1980—; geol. cons., Casper, 1982—. Contbr. articles to profl. publs. Grantee Geol. Soc. Am., 1980, 81, 82. Mem. Geol. Soc. Am., Wyo. Geol. Assn., Sigma Xi. Current work: Ancient volcanic rocks and petroleum potential of the Absaroka Range, Wyo. Subspecialties: Geology; Volcanology. Office: Ram Oil Co Inc PO Box 1543 Casper WY 82602

SUNG, ZINMAY RENEE, plant cell genetics educator; b. Shanghai, China, Feb. 14, 1947; came to U.S., 1968; d. Feng-en and DiLee (Fan) S.; m. Nelson N.H. Teng, Mar. 12, 1974. B.S., Nat. Taiwan U., 1967; Ph.D., U. Calif.-Berkeley, 1973. Research asst. Max Planck Inst. Cell Physiology, Berlin, 1967-68; research asst. U. Calif.-Berkeley, 1968-73; research assoc. MIT, Cambridge, 1973-76; asst. prof. dept. genetics and dept. plant pathology U. Calif.-Berkeley, 1976-82, assoc. prof., 1982—; cons. Cetus Corp., Berkeley, 1982—. Mem. Am. Soc. Plant Pathologists, Am. Soc. Developmental Biologists, Am. Soc. Plant Physiologists. Current Work: Plant somatic genetics, developmental biology of plants, genetic engineering of plant via tissue culture manipulations. Subspecialty: Plant physiology (agriculture). Office: Dept Genetics and Dept Plant Pathology U Calif Berkeley CA 94720

SUNG HO, (SALK), physicist, educator; b. Seoul, Korea, Apr. 14, 1939; came to U.S., 1964, naturalized, 1982; s. Chin S. and Kuk J. (Shin) Suck; m. Jung J. Yeon, Apr. 3, 1942; children: Tom T., Bob S. M.S., U. Houston, 1968; Ph.D., U. Tex.-Austin, 1972. Research assoc. U. Tex.-Austin, 1972-76; research asst. prof. U. Mo.-Rolla, 1977-82, research assoc. prof. physics and cloud physics, 1982—. Contbr. numerous articles to profl. jours. NSF fellow, 1980-82. Mem. Am. Phys. Soc., Sigma Xi, Phi Kappa Phi. Current Work: Molecular reaction dynamics (rearrangement collision theory); conductivity of organic crystals; atmospheric nucleation and radiation; air pollution. Subspecialties: Atomic and molecular physics; Polymer physics. Home: 1114 Sycamore St Rolla MO 65401 Office: U Mo Rolla MO 65401

SUNKARA, SAI PRASAD, tumor biologist; b. Valivarthi Padu, India, June 18, 1948; came to U.S., 1975, naturalized, 1979; s. Sanyasi Rao and Nancheramma (Ambati) S.; m. Kusuma A. Sunkara, Aug. 8, 1974; children: Haritha, Srinivas. B.S., A.P. Agrl. U., Bapatla, India, 1969; M.S., U.P. Agrl. U., Pantnagar, India, 1971; Ph.D., Indian Inst. Sci., Bangalore, 1975. Fellow M.D. Anderson Hosp. and Tumor Inst., Houston, 1976-78, asst. prof., 1978-80; sr. research biochemist Merrell Dow Research Ctr., Cin., 1980-82, research leader, 1982-84, group leader, 1984—. Contbr. articles to profl. jours. Recipient Indian Nat. Sci. Acad. Young Scientist award, 1976; Indian Inst. Sci. Hanumantha Rao Meml. award, 1976. Mem. Am. Soc. Cell Biology, Am. Assn. Cancer Research. Current Work: To understand the biochemical differences between normal and tumor cells in order to design effective anti cancer drugs; tumor cell biology; biochemical regulation of DNA synthesis and mitosis; interferon; polyamine metabolism in normal and tumor cells. Subspecialties: Cancer research (medicine); Cell biology (medicine). Office: 2110 E Galbraith Rd Cincinnati OH 45215

SUOMI, STEPHEN JOHN, psychology researcher, educator; b. Chgo., Dec. 16, 1945; s. Verner E. and Paula A. (Meyer) S.; m. Karen Francis Basele, Nov. 1, 1975. B.A., Stanford U., 1968; M.A., U. Wis.-Madison, 1969, Ph.D., 1971. Research assoc. U. Wis.-Madison, 1971-75, asst. prof. psychology, 1975-79, assoc. prof., 1979-83, prof., adj. prof., 1984—; chief Lab. Comparative Ethology, Nat. Inst. Child Health and Human Devel., NIH, 1983—; asst. dir. research in primate behavior NIMH, 1984—; cons. BBC, Italian Nat. TV; Prokasy lectr. U. Utah, 1983; lectr. Nat. Ctr. Clin. Infant Programs, 1984, Georgetown U. ann. symposium, 1985. Assoc. editor Psychiatry, 1985—. Contbr. chpts. to books and articles to profl. jours. Mem. gov. selection com. Nat. Youth Sci. Camp, 1981. NIH fellow, 1970; Effron lectr. Am. Coll. Neuropsychopharmacology, 1981; recipient Excellence in Teaching award U. Wis., 1982. Mem. Internat. Primatol. Soc., Soc. Research in Child Devel. (governing council 1985-92), Am. Soc. Primatologists (editorial bd. jour. 1981—), Am. Psychol. Assn., Animal Behavior Soc., Internat. Soc. Developmental Psychobiology, Internat. Soc. Study Behavioral Devel., Internat. Soc. Research in Emotions. Lutheran. Current Work: Study of primate psychobiological and social development, focusing on genetic environmental transactions, developmental continuities and individual differences, creation of primate models of human development. Subspecialties: Psychobiology; Developmental psychology. Office: Lab Comparative Ethology NIH Bldg 31 Room B2B-15 9000 Rockville Pike Bethesda MD 20892

SUR, MRIGANKA, neuroscientist, educator; b. Fatehgarh, Uttar Pradesh, India, Sept. 1, 1953; s. Arun Kumar and Anika (Ghose) S.; m. Abha Jain, Dec. 18, 1974; 1 child, Samir. B.Tech., Indian Inst. Tech., Kanpur, 1974; M.S., Vanderbilt U., 1975, Ph.D., 1978. Research assoc. Vanderbilt U., Nashville, 1978-80; research asst. prof. SUNY-Stony Brook, 1980-83; asst. prof. neuroanatomy Yale U., New Haven, 1983—; referee neurosci. jours.; ad. hoc reviewer NSF. Contbr. sci. papers to profl. lit. Recipient Herrick award Am. Assn. Anatomists, 1983; Sloan Research fellow, 1985-87; grantee NIH, 1983—, NSF, 1985—. Mem. Soc. Neurosci. Current work: Structure and function of sensory systems in mammalian brain; information processing in neural circuits. Subspecialties: Neurobiology; Neurophysiology. Home: 103 Thornton St Hamden CT 06517 Office: Sect Neuroanatomy Yale U Sch Medicine 333 Cedar St New Haven CT 06510

SURKO, CLIFFORD MICHAEL, physicist; b. Sacramento, Oct. 11, 1941; s. Vlaho John and Alma Beatrice (Horan) S.; m. Pamela T. Hansen, Jan. 30, 1965; children: Michael, Leslie. A.B. in Physics and Math, U. Calif.-Berkeley, 1964, Ph.D. in Physics, 1968. Research asst. U. Calif.-Berkeley, 1968-69; mem. tech. staff Bell Labs., Murray Hill, N.J., 1969-82, head semicondr. and chem. physics research dept., 1982—; vis. research scientist Ecole Polytechnique, Palaiseau, France, 1979, Plasma Fusion Center, M.I.T., Cambridge, 1978-85. Contbr. articles to profl. jours. Mem. Am. Phys. Soc., AAAS, Phi Beta Kappa, Sigma Xi. Episcopalian. Patentee in field. Current Work: Light scattering from waves and fluctuations in tokamak plasmas and fluid turbulence. Subspecialties: Plasma physics; Condensed matter physics. Office: Bell Labs Room 1D432 Murray Hill NJ 07974

SUSLICK, KENNETH SANDERS, chemistry educator, consultant; b. Chgo., Sept. 16, 1952; s. Alvin and Edith (Paul) S.; m. Adele Mazurek. B.S., Calif. Inst. Tech., 1974; Ph.D., Stanford U., 1978. Chemist Lawrence Livermore Lab., Calif., 1974-75; asst. prof. chemistry U. Ill., Urbana, 1978-84, assoc. prof., 1984—. Editor: The Effects of Ultrasound, 1985. Contbr. articles to profl. jours. Sloan Found. fellow, 1985-87; NIH Research Career Devel. award, 1985—. Fellow Royal Soc. Arts (Silver medal 1974); mem. Am. Chem. Soc. Current work: Bioinorganic: synthetic analogs of heme proteins; metalloporphrins; organometallic: chemical effects of ultrasound; sonochemistry; sonocatalysis. Subspecialties: Inorganic chemistry; Catalysis chemistry. Office: Dept Chemistry U Ill 505 S Mathews Urbana IL 61801

SUSSKIND, LEONARD, physicist. With dept. physics Stanford U., Calif. . Office: Stanford U Dept Physics Stanford CA 94305

SUTER, ROBERT BOWEN, biology educator, researcher; b. Boston, Nov. 29, 1946; s. John Wallace and Antoinette (Brown) S.; m. Valerie Lyn Jackson, June 22, 1968; children—Nathaniel Wallace, Katherine Jackson. B.A., Swarthmore Coll., 1968; Ph.D., Ind. U., 1977. Asst. prof. biology Vassar Coll., Poughkeepsie, N.Y., 1977-85, assoc. prof. biology, 1985—; vis. asst. prof. biology The Rockefeller U., Millbrook, N.Y., 1982-83; dir. Vassar Ecol. Preserve Vassar Coll., Poughkeepsie, 1978—. Contbr. articles to profl. jours. Trustee Bulls Head-Oswego Mts. Religious Soc. Friends, Clinton Corners, N.Y., 1982-84. Mem. Ecol. Soc. Am., Animal Behavior Soc., Am. Arachnological Soc. Democrat. Current work: Agonistic interactions, chemical communication, courtship, and behavioral thermoregulation of arthropods. Subspecialties: Behavioral ecology; Ethology. Home: 63 Titusvilk Rd Poughkeepsie NY 12603Office: Vassar Coll Raymond Ave Poughkeepsie NY 12601

SUTHERLAND, GEORGE LESLIE, chemical company executive; b. Dallas, Aug. 13, 1922; s. Leslie and Madge Alice (Henderson) S.; m. Mary Gail Hamilton, Sept. 9, 1961 (dec. 1984); children—Janet Leslie, Gail Irene, Elizabeth Hamilton. B.A., U. Tex., Austin, 1943, M.A., 1947, Ph.D., 1950. With Am. Cyanamid Co., various locations, 1951—, asst. dir. research and devel., Princeton, N.J., 1969-70, dir. research and devel., agr. div., 1970-73; v.p. med. research and devel. Pearl River, N.Y., 1973—; dir. med. research div. Am. Cyanamid Co., Pearl River, N.Y., 1978—, dir. chem. research div., 1980-81. Served with USN, 1944-46. Mem. Assn. Research Dirs. (pres. 1975-76), AAAS, Am. Chem. Soc., Royal Soc. Chemistry. Home: 42 Sky Meadow Rd Suffern NY 10901 Office: Lederle Labs Med Research Div Middletown Rd Pearl River NY 10965

SUTHERLAND, JAMES MILTON, chemist; b. Lebanon, Va., Jan. 2, 1954; s. Milton Lewis and Jean (Jones) S.; m. Rebekah Jeree Ernst, Aug. 6, 1976; children—Timothy James, Jeremy Robert. B.S. in Chemistry and Biology, Emory and Henry Coll., 1976. Quality control chemist Morrison Molded Fiberglass Co., Bristol, Va., 1976-77; grad. asst. E. Tenn. State U., Johnson City, 1977-79; assoc. engr. Westinghouse Electric Corp., Abingdon, Va., 1979-84, engr., 1984—. Named Engr. of Yr., Wire div. Westinghouse Electric Corp., 1981. Mem. Am. Chem. Soc., Am. Soc. Metals, Nat. Elec. Mfrs. Assn. (chmn. environ. affairs magnet wire sect. 1984—). Current work: Applications of computer-aided chemistry in characterization, manufacturing and processing of polymeric wire coatings; non destructive testing of metals. Subspecialties: Analytical chemistry; Polymer engineering. Home: Rt 2 Box 394E Abingdon VA 24210 Office: Westinghouse Electric Corp PO Box 869 Abingdon VA 24210

SUTNICK, ALTON IVAN, medical school administrator, physician; b. Trenton, N.J., July 5, 1928; s. Michael and Rose (Horwitz) S.; m. Mona Reidenberg, Aug. 17, 1958; children—Amy, Gary. B.A., U. Pa., 1950, M.D., 1954. Diplomate Am. Bd. Internal Medicine. Intern Hosp. of U. Pa., Phila., 1954-55, resident, 1955-57; resident Wishard Meml. Hosp., Indpls., 1957-58, 60-61; from instr. to assoc. prof. medicine Temple U. and U. Pa., Phila., 1962-75; prof. medicine, sr. v.p. health affairs and dean Med. Coll. of Pa., Phila., 1975—; assoc. dir. Inst. for Cancer Research, Phila., 1971-75; dir. clin. devel. Am. Oncologic Hosp., Phila., 1973-75; cons. WHO, SE Asia, 1979-81; mem. Gov's Task Force on Cancer Control, 1974-76; bd. govs. Health Systems Agy., Southeastern Pa., 1981—, exec. com., 1983—; mem. Mayor's Commn. on Health in 80's, Phila., 1982-83. Editor: Oncologic Medicine, 1976. Mem. editorial bd. various profl. jours. Contbr. articles to profl. jours. Recipient Torch of Learning award Am. Friends of Hebrew U., 1981. Mem. Assn. Am. Med. Colls. (council of deans), Pa. Council Deans (treas. 1975—), Council of Deans Pvt. Free Standing Med. Schs. (chmn. 1983), AMA (award in Medicine 1976), Phi Beta Kappa, Alpha Omega Alpha. Current work: Discovered association of Hepatitis B Surface Antigen with hepatitis; performed first studies of pulmonary surfactant in adult human lung disease; developed cancer screening system based on risk status. Subspecialty: Internal medicine.

SUTTON, HARRY ELDON, geneticist, educator; b. Cameron, Tex., Mar. 5, 1927; s. Grant Edwin and Myrtle Dovie (Fowler) S.; m. Beverly Earlene Jewell, July 7, 1962; children: Susan Elaine, Caroline Virginia. B.S. in Chemistry, U. Tex., Austin, 1948, M.A., 1949; Ph.D. in Biochemistry, U. Tex., 1953. Biologist U. Mich., 1952-56, instr., 1956-57, asst. prof. human genetics, 1957-60; assoc. prof. zoology U. Tex., Austin, 1960-64, prof., 1964—, chmn. dept. zoology, 1970-73, assoc. dean Grad. Sch., 1967-70, 73-75, v.p. for research, 1975-79; mem. adv. council Nat. Inst. Environ. Health Scis., 1968-72, council sci. advs., 1972-76, Bd. Radiation Effects Research, 1985-87; mem. various coms. Nat. Acad. Scis.-NRC; cons. in field; bd. dirs. Associated Univs. for Research in Astronomy, 1975-79, Argonne Univs. Assn., 1975-79, Univ. Corp. for Atmospheric Research, 1975-79, Associated Western Univs., 1978-79. Author: Genes, Enzymes, and Inherited Disease, 1961; An Introduction to Human Genetics, 1965, 4th edit., forthcoming; Genetics: A Human Concern, 1985; editor: First Macy Conference on Genetics, 1960; Mutagenic Effects of Environmental Contaminants, 1972; Am. Jour. Human Genetics, 1964-69. Trustee S.W. Tex. Corp. Public Broadcasting, 1977-80, sec., 1979-80; bd. dirs. Ballet Austin, 1978-84. Served with U.S. Army, 1945-46. Mem. Am. Soc. Human Genetics (dir. 1961-69, pres. 1979), Genetics Soc. Am., Am. Soc. Biol. Chemists, Am. Chem. Soc., Tex. Genetics Soc. (pres. 1979), Environ. Mutagen Soc., AAAS, Am. Genetic Assn. Club: Headliners (Austin). Research, publs. in human genetics. Current Work: Environmental and human somatic mutation; effects of mutation on enzyme function. Subspecialties: Gene actions; Environmental toxicology. Home: 1103 Gaston Ave Austin TX 78703 Office: Dept Zoology U Tex Austin TX 78712

SUYDAM, PETER R., clinical engineer, consultant; b. Jersey City, Apr. 1, 1945; s. Stedman Mills and Winifred M. (Murphy) S.; m. Patricia Cunniff, Feb. 2, 1970 (dec. 1976); m. Jaimy Slifka, Feb. 11, 1978; children—Rycken Stedman, Stephen Michael. Student in engring. Rensselaer Poly. Inst.; student in pre-medicine, psychology, U. Rochester; B.S. in Bio-Engring., U. Ill.-Chgo., 1975. Cert. clin. engr.; cert. health care safety profl. Dir. clin. engring. Rush-Presbyn.-St. Luke's Med. Ctr., Chgo., 1975-81; pres. Syzygy, Inc., Chgo., 1978-81; lead auditor quality assurance Callaway Nuclear Power Plant, Union Elec. Co., St. Louis, 1981-84; sr. cons. Ellerbe Assocs., Inc., Mpls., 1984—; staff cons. Joint Commn. on Accreditation for Hosps., Chgo., 1978-81; mem. tech. com. Safe Use of Electricity in Patient Care Areas of Health Care Facilities; mem. Bd. Examiners for Clin. Engring. Cert., 1980; com. mem. Midwest Med. Group Standards, Chgo. Hosp. Council, 1976-81. Contbr. articles to profl. jours. Served with USN, 1967-73. Mem. Assn. Advancement Med. Instrumentation (elec. safety com. 1980—), AAAS, IEEE (chpt. chmn. group on engring. in medicine and biology), Instrument Soc. Am., Am. Hosp. Assn., Nat. Space Inst., Nat. Fire Protection Assn. (health care, elec. and engring. sects.), Am. Soc. Hosp. Engrs., Am. Soc. Quality Control. Current work: Biotechnology applications in medicine and industry; quality assurance-all fields. Subspecialties: Biomedical engineering; Biomedical engineering. Office: Ellerbe Inc One Appletree Sq Minneapolis MN 55420

SUZUKI, JON BYRON, periodontist, immunologist, educator, consultant; b. San Antonio, July 22, 1947; s. George K. and Ruby K. (Kanaya) S. B.A., Ill. Wesleyan U., 1968; Ph.D., Ill. Inst. Tech., 1972; S.M., Am. Acad. Microbiology, 1973; D.D.S., Loyola U.-Chgo., Maywood, Ill., 1978; cert., U. Md.-Balt., 1980. Diplomate: Am. Acd. Microbiology. Instr. Columbia Coll. Physicians and Surgeons-St. Luke's Hosp., N.Y.C., 1971-73; dir. med. tech. U. Hawaii, Honolulu, 1973-74; instr. microbiology Loyola U.-Chgo., Maywood, 1974-78; NIH fellow periodontics U. Wash., Seattle, 1978-80; mem. adv. council NASA, Houston, 1976-85; assoc. prof. microbiology and periodontics U. Md., Balt., 1980—; lectr. periodontics and oral pathology, instr. pre-clin. endodontics, adv. grad. oral biology program Loyola U., Maywood, Ill., 1974—, pvt. practice dentistry, Ill., Wash., Md., 1978-82, pvt. practice periodontics, Towson, Md., 1982—. Author: Clinical Laboratory Methods, 1974, Soft Tissue Curettage, 1979; contbr. articles to profl. jours. Instr. cardiopulmonary resuscitation Am. Heart Assn.; water safety instr., sr. lifesaver ARC. Recipient Outstanding Alumnus of Year award Ill. Wesleyan U., 1977; Pres. medallion St. Apollonia Guild, Loyola U. Chgo., 1978; Gold Key medallion, 1978; Dean's Spl. Recognition award Loyola U.-Chgo., 1978; Disting. Service award St. Apollonia Jesuit Nat. Bd., 1978; Research award NASA, 1980; Excellence in Dentistry award Bd. Trustees, Loyola U.-Chgo., 1981; Achievement award Dentsply Internat. Clinicians, 1982; Omicron Kappa Upsilon-Am. Fund for Dental Health Charles Craig scholar, 1980-82. Mem. Internat. Assn. Dental Research, Internat. Soc. Biophysicists, Internat. Soc. Endocrinologists, Am. Acad. Microbiology, Am. Acad. Periodontology (First place Orban prize 1982), Am. Dental Assn. (Henry M. Thornton SCADA fellow 1978), Am. Acad. Oral Pathology (Oral Pathology award 1977), AAAS, AAUP, Am. Assn. Dental Research (pres. Md.), Greater Washington Soc. Periodontology (pres.), Am. Inst. Biol. Scis., Am. Soc. Microbiology, Soc. Indsl. Microbiology, Western Soc. Periodontology, N.Y. Acad. Scis., Sigma Xi, Blue Key, Omicron Kappa Upsilon (pres.). Current Work: Biology of immunodeficient patients, periodontal disease-microbiology and immunology. Subspecialties: Periodontics; Immunology (medicine). Office: 1819 Thornton Ridge Rd Baltimore MD 21204

SUZUKI, KINUKO, neuropathologist, educator, researcher; b. Hyogo, Japan, Nov. 10, 1933; came to U.S., 1961; s. Saburo and Tamae Ikeda; m. Kunihiko Suzuki, Dec. 17, 1960; 1 child, Jun. Grad. Sch. Sci., Osaka City U., Japan, 1955, M.D., Sch. Medicine, 1959; M.A. (hon.), U. Pa., 1971. Diplomate in anat. pathology and neuropathology Am. Bd. Pathology. Intern Resident Montefiore Hosp., N.Y.C., 1961-64; asst. prof. Albert Einstein Coll. Medicine, N.Y.C., 1968-69, assoc. prof., 1972-76, prof. pathology, 1976—; asst. prof. U. Pa., Phila., 1969-70, assoc. prof. pathology, 1970-72; attending neuropathologist Bronx Mcpl. Hosp. Ctr., N.Y., 1972—, Hosp. of Albert Einstein Coll. Medicine, Bronx, 1972—; cons. in neuropathology Bronx Lebanon Hosp., 1977—. Author numerous sci. book chpts. and articles. NIH research grantee, Bethesda, Md., 1969—. Mem. Am. Assn. Neuropathologists, Soc. Neurosci., Am. Soc. Neurochemistry, Internat. Soc. Developmental Neurosci. Subspecialty: Neurobiology. Office: Albert Einstein Coll Medicine 1300 Morris Park Ave Bronx NY 10461

SUZUKI, TATEYUKI, engineering educator; b. Kawagoe, Saitama, Japan, Apr. 28, 1945; s. Sentaro and Michiyo (Akiyama) S.; m. Kumiko Takaichi, Aug. 23, 1982; 1 child, Ayako. B.S. in Engring., U. Tokyo, 1968, M.S. in Engring., 1970, Dr.Eng., 1973. Research fellow dept. aeros. U. Tokyo, 1973-74, lectr. dept. mechanics, Kawagoe, Japan, 1974-76; lectr. U. Saitama, Urawa, Japan, 1974—; research assoc. NASA-Ames Research Center, Moffett Field, Calif., 1976-77; assoc. prof. dept. mechanics Saitama Inst. Tech., Okabe, Japan, 1978-85, prof. gas dynamics, 1985—. Author: Characteristics of a Blast Wave over Dust Deposit, 1982; contbr. articles to profl. jours. Recipient research prizes Japan Pvt. Sch. Promotion Found., 1981, 82, 83; recipient research prizes Japan Securities Found., 1982. Mem. Kanto Inst. Engring. Edn., AIAA, Japan Soc. Mech. Engring. Buddhist. Current Work: Interaction of a shock wave with dust deposit; ignition of hydrogen injected into a stagnant region behind a reflected shock; ignition and combustion of coal particles. Subspecialties: Fluid mechanics; Combustion processes. Home: 15-12 Minami-Torimachi Kawagoe 350 Japan Office: Saitama Inst Tech 1690 Fusaiji Okabe 369-02 Japan

SVARRER, ROBERT W., research engineer, engineering educator; b. Bklyn., Mar. 3, 1932; s. Viggo A. and Emily E. (Marr) S.; m. Rita Rose Bruno, May 4, 1958; children: Donna Rose, Scott Christopher. A.A.S., N.Y. Inst. Tech., 1963, B.S., 1967. Product engr. Reeves Instrument Co., Garden City, N.Y., 1959-64; sr. engr. Bendix Corp., Teterboro, N.J., 1964-75; faculty mem. Tech. Career Inst., N.Y.C., 1975-81; asst. prof. County Coll. Morris, Randolph, N.J., 1981-82; chmn. sci. and tech. Hudson County Community Coll., Jersey City, N.J., 1982—; adj. faculty mem. Stevens Inst. Tech., Hoboken, N.J., 1979—; research electronics engr. Office Naval Research, Arlington, Va., 1980—; Aux. police lt. N.Y.C. Police Emergency Div., 1956-70. Served to sgt. USMC, 1949-55; to lt. col. USMCR, 1956—. Mem. AIAA, Am. Soc. Engring. Edn., IEEE, Assn. Computing Machinery, N.Y. Acad. Scis., Marine Corps Res. Officers Assn., Marine Corps Aviation Assn. Designer and co-designer of avionic systems for helicopters and fighter/attack aircraft, automatic flight systems for DC-10s. Current Work: Digital avionic systems, computer systems, computer technology, and computer science education and research. Subspecialties: Computer engineering; Computer architecture. Home: 5 Martin Pl Fairfield NJ 07006 Office: Hudson County Community Coll Jersey City NJ 07306

SWAIMAN, KENNETH FRED, pediatric neurologist, educator; b. St. Paul, Nov. 19, 1931; s. Lester J. and Shirley (Ryan) S.; married; children: Lisa, Jerrold, Barbara, Dana. B.A. magna cum laude, U. Minn., 1952, B.S., 1953, M.D., 1955. Diplomate: Am. Bd. Psychiatry and Neurology, Am. Bd. Pediatrics. Intern Mpls. Gen. Hosp., 1955-56; resident in pediatrics U. Minn., 1956-58, neurology, 1960-63; asst. prof. pediatrics, neurology U. Minn. Med. Sch., Mpls., 1963-66, assoc. prof., 1966-69, prof., dir. pediatric neurology, 1969—, exec. officer dept. neurology, 1977—, mem. internship adv. council exec. faculty, 1966-70; cons. pediatric neurology Hennepin County Gen. Hosp., Mpls., St. Paul-Ramsey Hosp., St. Paul Children's Hosp., Mpls. Children's Hosp.; mem. human devel. study sect. NIH, 1976-79, guest worker, 1978-81. Author: (with Francis S. Wright) Neuromuscular Diseases in Infancy and Childhood, 1969, Pediatric Neuromuscular Diseases, 1979, (with Stephen Ashwal) Pediatric Neurology Case Studies, 1978, 2d edit., 1984; editor: (with John A. Anderson) Penylketonuria and Allied Metabolic Diseases, 1966, (with Francis S. Wright) Practice Pediatric Neurology, 1975, 2d edit., 1982; mem. editorial bd.: (with Francis S. Wright) Annals of Neurology, 1977-82, Neurology Update, 1977-82, Pediatric Update, 1977—, Brain and Devel. (jour. Japanese Soc. Child Neurology), 1980—, Neuropediatrics, 1982—; contbr. (with Francis S. Wright) articles to profl. jours. Nat. Inst. Neurologic Diseases and Blindness fellow, 1960-63. Fellow Am. Acad. Pediatrics, Am. Acad. Neurology (rep. to nat. council Nat. Soc. Med. Research); mem. Soc. Pediatric Research, Central Soc. Clin. Research, Central Soc. Neurol. Research, Internat. Soc. Neurochemistry, Am. Neurol. Assn., Minn. Neurol. Soc., AAAS, Midwest Pediatric Soc., Am. Soc. Neurochemistry, Child Neurology Soc. (1st pres. 1972-73, Hower award 1981), Internat. Assn. Child Neurologists (exec. com. 1975-79), Profs. Child Neurology (1st pres. 1978-80), Phi Beta Kappa, Sigma Xi. Current Work: Metabolism of developing brain; cerebral iron metabolism; childhood neuromovement disorders. Subspecialties: Neurology; Developmental neuroscience. Office: U Minn Med Sch Dept Pediatric Neurology Minneapolis MN 55455

SWAKON, DOREEN H.D., animal scientist, educator; b. Berwyn, Ill., Oct. 9, 1953; d. Darrell L. and Elaine D. (Jensen) Downer; m. Lawrence W. Swakon, Nov. 30, 1974; 1 dau., Casey Laine. B.S. with high honors in Agr, U. Ill., 1975; M.S., U. Fla., 1977, Ph.D. in Animal Sci.-Nutrition, 1980. Grad. research asst. U. Fla., Gainesville, 1975-80; assoc. prof. animal sci. Tex. A&I U., Kingsville, 1980—; dir. Forage Testing Lab., 1981-85. Contbr. articles to profl. jours. Recipient Am. Forage and Grassland Council Young Scientist award, 1980. Mem. Am. Soc. Animal Sci., Range Mgmt. Soc., Am. Forage and Grassland Council, Tex. Forage and Grassland Council, AAAS, Council for Agrl. Sci. and Tech. Lutheran. Current Work: Forage quality evaluation and utilization by ruminants and other herbivores. Subspecialties: Animal nutrition; Agronomy. Home: 11121 Timbergrove Corpus Christi TX 78410 Office: Tex A&I U Coll Agr Box 156 Kingsville TX 78363

SWALIN, RICHARD ARTHUR, educator; b. Mpls., Mar. 18, 1929; s. Arthur and Mae (Hurley) S.; m. Helen Marguerite Van Wagenen, June 28, 1952; children: Karen, Kent, Kristin. B.S. with distinction, U. Minn., 1951, Ph.D., 1954. Research assoc. Gen. Electric Co., 1954-56; mem. faculty U. Minn., Mpls., 1956-77, prof., head Sch. Mineral and Metall Engring., 1962-68, asso. dean Inst. Tech., 1968-71, dean Inst. Tech., 1971-77; acting dir. Space Sci. Center, 1965; v.p. tech. Eltra Corp., N.Y.C., 1977-80; v.p. research and devel. Allied Corp., Morristown, N.J., 1980-84; dean Coll. Engring. and Mines, U. Ariz., Tucson, 1984—, dir. tech. innovation, 1985—; guest scientist Max Planck Inst. für Phys. Chemie, Göttingen, Germany, 1963, Lawrence Radiation Lab., Livermore, Cal., 1967; Cons. to govt. and industry. Dir. Medtronic Corp.; dir. BMC Industries. Author: Thermodynamics of Solids, 2d edit, 1972; Contbr. articles to profl. jours. Trustee Midwest Research Inst., 1975-78, Sci. Mus. Minn., 1973-77. Recipient Disting. Teaching award Inst. Tech., U. Minn., 1967; NATO sr. fellow in sci., 1971. Mem. AAAS, Am. Phys. Soc., Sigma Xi, Tau Beta Pi, Phi Delta Theta, Gamma Alpha. Current Work: Management of college activities; stimulation of industry, university relations. Subspecialty: Metallurgy. Home: 5260 Circulo Sobrio Tucson AZ 85718 Office: Coll Engring Bldg 72 U Ariz Tucson AZ 85721

SWAN, RICHARD GORDON, mathematics educator; b. N.Y.C., Dec. 21, 1933; s. A. Gordon and Rose (Nespor) S.; m. Erdmuthe J.D.B. Plesch-Ritz, Mar. 18, 1963; children—Adrian Alexander, Irit Alexandra. Grad. Phillips Exeter Acad., 1951; A.B., Princeton U., 1954, Ph.D., 1957. Instr. math. U. Chgo., 1958-60, asst. prof., 1960-62, assoc. prof., 1962-65, prof., 1965—, Louis Block prof., 1983—. Author: Theory of Sheaves, 1964; Algebraic K-Theory, 1968; K-Theory of Finite Groups and Orders. Editor Am. Jour. Math., 1977-83, Jour. of Algebra, 1981—. Contbr. articles to profl. jours. Alfred P. Sloan fellow, 1961-65. Mem. Nat. Acad. Scis., Am. Math. Soc. (Cole prize 1970), Math. Assn. Am., N.Y. Acad. Scis., AAAS, Sigma Xi. Current work: Projective modules, algebraic K-Theory, homological algebra. Subspecialty: Algebra and number theory. Office: U Chgo 5734 University Ave Chicago IL 60637

SWANN, GORDON ALFRED, geologist; b. Palisade, Colo., Sept. 21, 1931; s. Alfred Mead and Glava Beatrice (Wing) S.; m. Joan Dell Steinebaugh, Dec. 21, 1975. B.A., U. Colo., 1958, Ph.D., 1962. Geologist U.S. Geol. Survey, Flagstaff, 1963—, dep. asst. chief geologist, 1975-85. prin. investigator Apollo lunar geology NASA, 1970-72; adj. prof. No. Ariz. U., Flagstaff, 1978—. Author: Geology of Apollo 14, 1976; also articles on lunar geology. Co-editor: Geology of Northern Arizona, 1974. Served with USN, 1952-56. Recipient Exceptional Sci. Achievement award NASA, 1971, Profl. Excellence award Am. Inst. Profl. Geologists, 1972; grantee Geol. Soc. Am., 1961. Fellow Geol. Soc. Am.; mem. Sigma Xi. Methodist. Lodges: Masons (sr. warden 1985), Order Eastern Star (patron 1982). Current work: Precambrian geology; lunar geology. Subspecialties: Geology; Tectonics. Home: 814 W Murray Flagstaff AZ 86001 Office: US Geol Survey 2255 N Gemini Dr Flagstaff AZ 86001

SWANSON, DAVID HENRY, economist, educator; b. Anoka, Minn., Nov. 1, 1930; s. Henry Otto and Louise Isabell (Holiday) S.; m. Suzanne Nash, Jan. 19, 1952; children: Matthew David, Christopher James. B.A. in Econs, St. Cloud State Coll., 1953; M.A. in Econs, U. Minn., 1955. Economist area devel. dept. No. States Power Co., Mpls., 1955-56, staff asst., v.p. sales, 1956-57, economist indsl. devel. dept., 1957-63; dir. area devel. dept. Iowa So. Utilities Co., Centerville, 1963-67, dir. econ. devel. and research, 1967-70; dir. New Orleans Econ. Devel. Council, 1970-72; div. mgr. Kaiser Aetna, New Orleans, 1972-73; dir. corp. research United Services Automobile Assn., San Antonio, 1973-76; pres. Lantern Corp., San Antonio, 1974-79; administr. bus. devel. State of Wis., Madison, 1976-78; dir. Center Indsl. Research and Service, Iowa State U., Ames, 1978—; mem. mktg. faculty Coll. Bus. Adminstrn., Iowa State U., 1979—; mem. adv. council Iowa State U. (Coll. Engring.), 1978—; dir. Applied Strategies Internat. Ltd., 1983—; Mem. adv. council Center Indsl. Research and Service, 1967-70. Contbr. numerous tech. articles to profl. publs. Vice chmn. Planning Commn. Roseville, Minn., 1961; mem. Iowa Airport Planning Council, 1968-70; mem. adv. council Office Comprehensive Health Planning, 1967-70; mem. Dist. Export Council, 1978—; mem. region 7 adv. council SBA, 1978—; dir. Mid-Continent Research and Devel. Council, 1980-84, Iowa Devel. Commn., 1982-83; chmn. Iowa del. White House Conf. on Small Bus., 1980, Gov.'s Task Force on High Tech., 1982, Gov.'s High Tech. Commn., 1983, Gov.'s High Tech. Council, 1983—; mem. adv. com. U. New Orleans, 1972-73; county fin. chmn. Republican Party, 1966-67; mem. bd. dirs. Greater New Orleans Urban League, 1970-73; v.p. Iowa Sister State Friendship Com. Served with USAF, 1951-52. Mem. Small Bus. Inst. Dirs. Assn., Nat. Assn. Mgmt. Tech. Assistance Centers (pres. 1985), Tech. Transfer Soc. (bd. dirs. 1984—), Internat. Council Small Bus., Fed. Lab. Consortium, Indsl. Policy Council, Nat. Univ. Edn. Assn. Republican. Episcopalian. Lodges: Rotary; Toastmasters (past pres.). Subspecialty: Technology transfer administration. Home: 1007 Kennedy Dr Ames IA 50010 Office: Center Indsl Research and Service Iowa State Univ Ames IA 50011

SWANSON, DON RICHARD, university dean; b. Los Angeles, Oct. 10, 1924; s. Harry Windfield and Grace Clara (Sandstrom) S.; m. Patricia Elizabeth Klick, Aug. 22, 1976; children—Douglas Alan, Richard Brian, Judith Ann. B.S., Calif. Inst. Tech., 1945; M.A., Rice U., 1947; Ph.D., U. Calif., Berkeley, 1952. Physicist U. Calif. Radiation Lab., Berkeley, 1947-52, Hughes Research and devel. Labs., Culver City, Calif., 1952-55; research scientist TRW, Inc., Canoga Park, Calif., 1955-63; prof. Grad. Library Sch., U. Chgo., 1963—, dean, 1963-72, 77-79; mem. Sci. Info. Council, NSF, 1960-65; mem. toxicology info. panel Pres.'s Sci. Advisory Com., 1964-66; mem. library vis. com. Mass. Inst. Tech., 1966-71; mem. com. on sci. and tech. communication Nat. Acad. Scis., 1966-69. Editor: The Intellectual Founds. of Library Education, 1965, The Role of Libraries in the Growth of Knowledge, 1980; co-editor: Operations Research: Implications for Libraries, 1972, Management Education: Implications for Libraries and Library Schools, 1974; mem. editorial bd.: Library Quarterly, 1963—; Contbr.: chpt. to Ency. Brit, 1968—; sci. articles to profl. jours. Trustee Nat. Opinion Research Center, 1964-73; Research fellow Chgo. Inst. for Psychoanalysis, 1972-76. Served with USNR, 1943-46. Mem. Assn. Am. Library Schs., Am. Soc. for Info. Sci. Current Work: Communication to public of science information; microcomputer applications to library problems. . Home: 5825 Dorchester Ave Apt 14E Chicago IL 60637 Office: Grad Library Sch U Chgo 1100 E 57th St Chicago IL 60637

SWANSON, GEORGE ALBERT, wildlife and aquatic biologist; b. St. Paul, Dec. 5, 1929; s. George Alexandra and Alice Standish (Chandler) S.; m. Marlyn Marie Jones, Aug. 6, 1952; children—Sandra Marie, Lorie Alice. A.A., U. Minn., 1956; B.S., U. Minn.-St. Paul, 1959. Cert. profl. wildlife biologist. Fishery research biologist North Central Reservoir Investigations, Yankton, S.D., 1962-66; aquatic research biologist No. Prairie Wildlife Research Ctr., Jamestown, N.D., 1966-82, wildlife research biologist, 1982—. Patentee automatic plankton sampling system. Contbr. articles to profl. jours., chpts. to books. Served to sgt. USAF, 1950-54. Recipient Incentive award U.S. Fish and Wildlife Service, 1965, Spl. Achievement award, 1976, 81. Mem. Wildlife Soc., Ecol. Soc., Am. Soc. Limnology and Oceanography, Am. Benthological Soc., Am. Fisheries Soc. Lutheran. Club: Jamestown Eagles. Current work: Waterfowl ecology and wetland ecology design; supervise research investigations of prairie waterfowl and their aquatic habitats. Subspecialties: Ecology (biology); Ecosystems analysis. Home: 1727 4th Ave NE Jamestown ND 58401 Office: No Prairie Wildlife Research Ctr PO Box 1747 Jamestown ND 58401

SWANSON, PAUL NORMAN, physicist; b. San Mateo, Calif., June 29, 1936; s. Arnold C. and Velma G. (Dubois) S.; m. Sandra J. Berube, Dec. 28, 1960; children: Kyle, Brian. B.S., Calif. State Poly. U., 1962; Ph.D., Pa. State U., 1968. Faculty dept astronomy Pa. State U., State College, 1968-75; mem. tech. staff, group supr. Jet Propulsion Lab., Calif. Inst. Tech., Pasadena, 1975-85, mgr. microwave observational systems sect., 1985—. Contbr. articles to profl. publs. Served with USN, 1954-58. NASA grantee, 1965-68. Mem. AAAS, Am. Astron. Soc., Sigma Xi, Aircraft Owners and Pilots Assn. Current Work: Submillimeter astronomy from space; space science and technology, astronomy, project management. Subspecialties: Aerospace engineering and technology; Radio and microwave astronomy. Home: 3338 Los Olivos La Crescente CA 91214 Office: 4800 Oak Grove Dr Pasadena CA 91103

SWANSON, ROBERT A., genetic engineering company executive; b. N.Y.C., Nov. 29, 1947; s. Arthur John and Arline (Baker) S.; m. Judy Church, Sept. 2, 1980. S.B., M.I.T., 1970, S.M. in Mgmt, 1970. Asst. treas. Citicorp Venture Capital Ltd., N.Y.C., 1970-74; partner Kleiner & Perkins Venture Capital Partnership, San Francisco, 1975; chief exec. Genentech, Inc., South San Francisco, Calif., 1976—. Mem. corp. MIT, 1985—; bd. dirs. San Francisco Mus. Modern Art, San Francisco Ballet Assn., Tech. Ctr. Silicon Valley. Named Entrepreneur of Year Chgo. Research Dirs. Assn., 1981; Gold medal as Chief Exec. Biotech. Industry, Wall Street Transcript, 1984. Mem. Am. Chem. Soc., Royal Swedish Acad. Engring. Scis., AAAS, Am. Soc. Microbiology. Subspecialty: Genetics and genetic engineering (biology). Office: 460 Point San Bruno Blvd South San Francisco CA 94080

SWANSON, WILLIAM MASON, aluminum company executive; b. Chgo., Jan. 12, 1932; s. C. William and Lois A. (Rieff) S.; m. Joan Emily Krause, Aug. 2, 1952; children: Roger, Jill Champion, Daniel, Jeff, Paul. B.S. in Chem. Engring., Purdue U., West Lafayette, Ind., 1953; M.B.A., U. Chgo., 1969. Petrochem. process devel. ofcl. UOP, Inc., Des Plaines, Ill., 1961-66; mgr. mktg. Process div. Japan UOP, Inc., 1966-69; dir. mktg. Process div. Far East UOP, Inc., 1969-72; v.p. Mgmt. Services div. UOP, Inc., Des Plaines, 1972-74, v.p., gen. mgr. Minerals Scis. div., Tucson, 1974-82; pres. Toth Aluminum Corp., New Orleans, 1982—; seminar participant. Contbr. articles to profl. jours. Leader, Boy Scouts Am.; pres. bd. Adlai E. Stevenson High Sch., Prairie View, Ill.; active United Way, Tucson, 1980-82. Named Exec. of Week, Sta. WGSO News Radio, New Orleans, 1982. Mem. AIME, Am. Chem. Soc., Am. Petroleum Inst., Can. Inst. Mining, Beta Gamma Sigma. Patentee in field. Current Work: Production of aluminum trichloride and silicon tetrachloride by carbo-chlorination from clay, recovery of high purity nickel and cobalt through ammoniacal leaching and solvent extraction. Subspecialties: Chemical engineering; Metallurgy. Home: 645 Carmenere S Kenner LA 70065 Office: 3101 W Napoleon Ave 200 Metairie LA 70001

SWARIN, STEPHEN JOHN, chemistry researcher; b. Plainfield, N.J., July 24, 1945; s. Stephen A. and Margaret K. (Beksvoort) S.; m. Ruth A. Shea, Aug. 23, 1969; children—Douglas, Gregory. A.B. in Chemistry, Lafayette Coll., 1967; M.S. in Chemistry, U. Mass., 1969, Ph.D., 1972. Assoc. sr. research scientist Gen. Motors Research Lab., Warren, Mich., 1972-76, sr. staff research scientist, 1976—; lectr. in field. Contbr. articles to profl. jours. Served to capt. U.S. Army, 1971-72. Fellow NDEA, Polaroid Found. Mem. Am. Chem. Soc., Anachems, Sigma Xi, Phi Kappa Phi. Current work: Polymer characterization and environmental analysis by chromatographic and mass spectrometic methods; research and development management utilizing motivation, team development, communication. Subspecialties: Analytical chemistry; Polymers (materials science). Office: Gen Motors Research Lab Warren MI 48090

SWARM, RICHARD LEE, physician; b. St. Louis, June 9, 1927; s. Clarence Lee and Elsie Viola (Parker) S.; m. Pauline Kirksey Alexander, Dec. 28, 1950; children: Lee Ann, Robert Alexander. B.A., Washington U., 1949, B.S., 1950, M.D., 1950. Diplomate: Am. Bd. Pathology. Intern, resident, chief resident and instr. pathology Washington U., St. Louis, 1950-54; assoc. prof. pathology U. Cin., 1965-68; pathologist Hoffmann LaRoche Inc. (Research Div.), Nutley, N.J., 1968-82, dir. exptl. pathology and toxicology, 1968-75, assoc. dir. exptl. therapeutics, 1975-82; sr. cons., dir Health Sci. Assocs., Ridgewood, N.J., 1982—; assoc. prof. pathology Coll. Physicians and Surgeons, Columbia U., N.Y.C., 1970—. Contbr. articles to profl. jours. Served with USPHS, 1954-65. Am. Cancer Soc. clin. fellow, 1953; grantee Am. Cancer Soc., 1965-68; grantee USPHS, 1965-68. Mem. Am. Assn. Pathologists, AAAS, Am. Assn. for Cancer Research, AMA, Am. Soc. Clin. Pathologists, Coll. Am. Pathologists, Internat. Acad. Pathology, N.Y. Acad. Sci., Radiation Research Soc., Soc. Cryobiology, Soc. Toxicology, Soc. Toxicologic Pathologists, Sigma Xi, Phi Delta Theta. Current Work: Study of neoplasms in man and animals, particularly bone tumors; human and experimental cancer pathology; chemotheray and drug development; data management by computer. Subspecialties: Pathology (medicine); Toxicology (medicine). Office: PO Box 808 Ridgewood NJ 07451

SWARTS, E(LYWN) LOWELL, physical chemist; b. Hornell, N.Y., Feb. 26, 1929; s. Elwyn D(evillo) and Anna Gertrude (Zimmerman) S.; m. Rachel Anne Homet, Aug. 28, 1954; children—Heidi J., Andrew L., Adam J. A.B., Hamilton Coll., 1949; Ph.D., Brown U., 1954. Research assoc. Alfred U., N.Y., 1953-56; research chemist Knolls Atomic Power Lab., Schenectady, N.Y., 1956-57, Gen. Electric Co., Cleve., 1957-59; staff scientist glass research and devel. ctr. PPG Industries Inc., Pitts., 1959—. Contbr. articles to profl. jours. Fellow Am. Ceramic Soc.; mem. Am. Chem. Soc., Soc. Analytical Chemists Pitts., Soc. Glass Tech. Unitarian-Universalist. Current work: Physical chemistry of glass-making, glass-molten glass equilibria, analysis of glass surfaces. Subspecialties: Physical chemistry; Analytical chemistry. Home: 625 Ravencrest Rd Pittsburgh PA 15215 Office: PPG Industries Inc Box 11472 Pittsburgh PA 15238

SWARZ, JEFFREY ROBERT, filtration and membrane company executive, neuroscientist; b. Newark, Nov. 9, 1949; s. Irvin Brad and Blanche S. (Marcus) S.; m. Kathy Helen Kafer, June 20, 1976. B.S. with honors, U. Calif.-Irvine, 1971; Ph.D. (NIMH trainee 1971-74, NIH fellow 1975-76), U. Rochester, 1976. Postdoctoral fellow in neurovirology Johns Hopkins U. Sch. Medicine, 1976-79; staff fellow Infectious Disease br. NIH, Bethesda, Md., 1979-80; dir. biotech. group Teknekron Research Inc., McLean, Va., 1980-81; pres. AgroBiotics, Inc., Balt., 1981-82, Urbana, Ill., 1981-82; sr. scientist Pall Corp., Glen Cove, N.Y., 1982-83, sr. mktg. mgr. biotech., 1983—; cons. U.S. Senate Subcom. on Sci., Tech. and Space, 1979-80. Author: (with others) Genetic Engineering: Issues and Trends, 1982; contbr. numerous articles to profl. jours. Recipient Undergrad. Research award Bank of Am., 1970-71, Nat. Research Service award, 1976-79. Mem. Neurosci. Soc., Am. Chem. Soc., Soc. Indsl. Microbiology. Democrat. Jewish. Current Work: Membrane application to diagnostic tests, and affinity chromatography; cell harvesting and cell concentration. Subspecialties: Genetics and genetic engineering (agriculture); Neurobiology.

SWEAT, ROBERT LEE, veterinarian, virologist; b. Lamar, Colo., June 8, 1931; s. James B. and Ora L. (Wile) S.; m. Barbara J. Shaffer, Mar. 15, 1953; children—Michael J., Deborah L. B.S., Colo. State U., 1954, D.V.M., 1956; M.S., U. Nebr., 1962, Ph.D., 1966. Vet. virologist U. Nebr., Lincoln, 1958-66, Norden Labs., Lincoln, 1967; vet. med. scientist U. Idaho, Caldwell, 1968-70; vet. virologist Fort Dodge Lab., Iowa, 1970—. Vet. rep. Nebr. State Bd. Health, Lincoln, 1966-67; bd. trustees Sioux Fall Coll., S.D., 1983—. Served to capt. U.S. Army, 1956-58. Mem. Am. Vet. Med. Assn., Iowa Vet. Med. Assn., Am. Assn. Bovine Practitioners, AAAS. Baptist. Current work: Veterinary virology and immunology. Subspecialties: Virology (veterinary medicine); Preventive medicine (veterinary medicine). Home: 1371 N 14th St Fort Dodge IA 50501 Office: Fort Dodge Labs PO Box 518 Fort Dodge IA 50501

SWEDLOW, JEROLD LINDSAY, mechanical engineer; b. Denver, Aug. 31, 1935; s. Jack and Evelyn Lillian (Weinstein) S.; m. Patricia L. Lauer, Mar. 25, 1959; children: Jason, Pamela, Kathryn. B.S., Cal. Inst. Tech., 1957; M.S., Stanford U., 1960; Ph.D., Calif. Inst. Tech., 1965. Research fellow Calif. Inst. Tech., 1965-66; research scientist U.S. Steel Co., 1966; mem. faculty Carnegie Mellon U., Pitts., 1966—, prof. mech. engring., 1973—, assoc. dean engring., 1977-79; sr. vis. fellow Imperial Coll., London, 1973-74. Contbr. articles to profl. jours.; editor: reports of current research Internat. Jour. Fracture, 1969—. Trustee, 1st v.p. First Unitarian Ch. Pitts., 1979-82. Recipient Philip M. McKenna Meml. award Kennametal, Inc., 1978, Ralph Coats Roe award Am. Soc. Engring. Edn., 1981. Fellow AAAS, AIAA (assoc.), ASME, ASTM (award of merit 1983), mem. Internat. Congress Fracture (founding). Democrat. Current Work: Elastic-plastic fracture of metals. Subspecialties: Solid mechanics; Fracture mechanics. Office: Dept Mech Engring Carnegie Mellon U Pittsburgh PA 15213

SWEENEY, PATRICK J., computer software consultant; b. N.Y.C., Feb. 8, 1954; s. Thomas John and Eileen (McCaffrey) S.; m. Karin Kathleen A'Hearn, Mar. 17, 1979; 1 son, Timothy. B.S. in Computer Sci, SUNY, Stony Brook, 1974; M.S. in Computer Sci, Columbia U., 1980; M.B.A., NYU, 1984. Computer software cons. Digital Equipment Corp., N.Y.C., 1975—. Vol. U.S. Peace Corps, Togo, West Africa, 1974-75. Mem. IEEE Computer Soc., Assn. Computing Machinery. Subspecialties: Distributed systems and networks; Software engineering. Home: 39-59 59th St Woodside NY 11377 Office: Digital Equipment Corp 1 Pennsylvania Plaza New York NY 10119

SWEENEY, URBAN JOSEPH, corporation librarian, information services consultant; b. v. St. John, N.B., Can., Jan. 18, 1922; came to U.S., 1927; s. Urban James and Dorothy Elizabeth (Murray) S.; m. Margaret Stretz, Jan. 12, 1952; children: Dennis, Steven, Edward, Mark, Barbara. B.S., NYU, 1955; M.L.S., Pratt Inst., 1956. Cert. profl. librarian, N.Y. cert. coll. tchr., Calif. Asst. librarian Sperry Gyroscope Corp., Lake Success, N.Y., 1956-58; chief librarian Republic Aviation Corp., Farmingdale, N.Y., 1958-66, Gen. Electronics, Rochester, N.Y., 1966-71, Convair div. Gen. Dynamics, San Diego, 1971—, library cons., 1976—. Author: Initialisms of Science and Technology Organizations, 1978. Served with USAAF, 1941-45. Mem. Spl. Libraries Assn. (pres. San Diego chpt. 1973-74, chmn. aerospace div. 1978-80, award 1980), AIAA, Assn. Computing Machinery. Republican. Roman Catholic. Current Work: On-line information, retrieval and microcomputer applications. Subspecialties: Information systems, storage, and retrieval (computer science); Information systems (Information science). Home: 7311 Borla Pl Carlsbad CA 92008 Office: Gen Dynamics Convair Div PO Box 85386 San Diego CA 92138

SWEET, ALEXANDER, microelectronics consultant, educator; b. Providence, July 5, 1943; s. Norman Allen and Caroline Elizabeth (Cunn) S.; m. C. Frances MacIver, July 12, 1980; children—Kaatje, John, Martin, Melinda, Andy, Jill. B.S. in E.E., Worcester Poly. Inst., 1966; M.S. in Physics/E.E., Cornell U., 1968, Ph.D., 1970. Sr. research engr. Monsanto Co., St. Louis, 1970-71; group leader Microwave Assocs., Burlington, Mass., 1971-75; mem. tech. staff Varian Assocs., Palo Alto, Calif., 1975-77; sect. head Watkins Johnson Co., Palo Alto, 1977-79; microelectronics cons., Menlo Park, 1979—; course instr. Tech. Service Corp., Silver Spring, Md., 1981—. Contbr. articles to profl. jours. Mem. IEEE (IEEE-MTT Microwave prize, 1977). Democrat. Episcopalian. Current work: GaAs integrated circuits; hybrid microwave and circuits and subsystems; microwave instruments; the physics of information. Subspecialties: Microchip technology (engineering); Integrated circuits. Office: Palo Alto CA 94303

SWEET, ROBERT MAHLON, biophys. chemist; b. Omaha, Sept. 21, 1943; s. Mahlon and Elizabeth K. S.; children: Anna, Charles, Joseph. B.S., Calif. Inst. Tech., 1965; Ph.D., U. Wis.-Madison, 1970. Research fellow Med. Research Council, Cambridge, Eng., 1970-73; asst. prof. chemistry UCLA, 1973-81, specialist in molecular biology, 1981-83; scientist Brookhaven Nat. Lab., Upton, N.Y., 1983—. Mem. Am. Crystallographic Assn., Sigma Xi. Current Work: Study of protein structure and function; x-ray diffraction studies of light-harvesting systems from photosynthetic organisms; application of synchrotron radiation to macromolecular x-ray crystallography Subspecialties: Biophysical chemistry; X-ray crystallography. Office: Dept Biology Brookhaven Nat Lab Upton NY 11973

SWENSON, CLAYTON A., physicist, educator; b. Mpls., Nov. 11, 1923; s. Nels and Anna (Roth) S.; m. Heather M.F. Gell, Sept. 2, 1950 (dec. 1977); children—Anna, Paul, Wendy; m. Ruth B. Wildman, Jan. 1, 1980. B.S., Harvard, 1944; D.Phil., Oxford U., 1949. Mem. staff Los Alamos Sci. Lab., 1944-46; instr. Harvard, 1949-52; Div. Indsl. Cooperation staff mem. Mass. Inst. Tech., 1952-55; prof. physics, disting. prof. scis. and humanities, sr. physicist Ames Lab., U.S. Dept. Energy, Iowa State U., 1955—; chmn. dept. physics Iowa State U., 1975-82; mem. cons. com. on thermometry Internat. Com. on Weights and Measures. Fellow Am. Phys. Soc.; mem. Am. Assn. Physics Tchrs., AAAS, Phi Beta Kappa, Sigma Xi. Research, publs. in solid state physics with emphasis on low temperature and high pressure and combinations of these; publs. on understanding of elementary solids (inert gases and alkali metals) at low temperatures, devel. temperature scales below 30K. Subspecialties: Condensed matter physics; Low temperature physics. Home: 2102 Kildee St Ames IA 50010

SWENSON, DONALD OTIS, mechanical engineer; b. Manhattan, Kans., Feb. 19, 1937; s. Donald D. and Florence (Knapp) S.; m. Harriett Swenson; 4 children. B.S. in Mech. Engring, U. Kans., 1963; M.S., 1965, Ph.D., 1967. Registered profl. engr., Ariz., Calif., Fla., Kans., Minn., Mo., Nebr., Nev., N.D., Utah, Wis. Sr. research assoc. Pratt and Whitney div. United Aircraft Corp., East Hartford, Conn., 1967-71; cons. engr. Black & Veatch Engrs.-Architects, Kansas City, Mo., 1971—. Co-author 5 books. Contbr. articles to profl. jours. Served with USN, 1955-59. Summerfield scholar, 1961-63; NDEA fellow, 1963-66; U. Kans. fellow, 1966-67. Fellow ASME; mem. ASTM, Air Pollution Control Assn., Sigma Xi, Tau Beta Pi, Pi Tau Sigma, Sigma Tau. Roman Catholic. Current Work: Air pollution control systems, fabric filters and electrostatic precipitators, flue gas scrubbers, spray dryer absorbers. Subspecialties: Mechanical engineering; Gas cleaning systems.

SWENSON, GEORGE WARNER, JR., electronics engineer, radio astronomer, educator; b. Mpls., Sept. 22, 1922; s. George Warner and Vernie (Larson) S.; m. Virginia Laura Savard, June 26, 1943 (div. 1970); children: George Warner III, Vernie Laura, Julie Loretta, Donna Joan; m. Joy Janice Locke, July 2, 1971. B.S., Mich. Coll. Mining and Tech., 1944, E.E., 1950; M.S., Mass. Inst. Tech., 1948; Ph.D., U. Wis., 1951. Asso. prof. elec. engring. Washington U., St. Louis, 1952-53; prof. U. Alaska, 1953-54; asso. prof. Mich. State U., 1954-56; faculty U. Ill., Urbana, 1956—, prof. elec. engring. and astronomy, 1958—, acting head dept. astronomy, 1970-72, head dept. elec. engring., 1979-85; dir. Vermilion River Obs., 1968-81; Vis. scientist Nat. Radio Astronomy Obs., 1964-68; cons. to govt. agys. and other sci. bodies. Author: Principles of Modern Acoustics, 1953, An Amateur Radio Telescope, 1980; Interferometry and Synthesis in Radio Astronomy, 1986. Contbr. articles to profl. jours. Guggenheim fellow, 1984. Fellow IEEE, AAAS; mem. Nat. Acad. Engring., Internat. Sci. Radio Union (mem. U.S. nat. com. 1965-67, 80-82), Internat. Astron. Union, Sigma Xi, Eta Kappa Nu, Tau Beta Pi, Phi Kappa Phi. Current Work: Radio astronomy instruments, antennas, electrical engineering education and research. Subspecialties: Acoustics; Optics. Home: 1107 Kenwood Rd Champaign IL 61821 Office: U Ill 1406 W Green St Urbana IL 61801

SWETS, JOHN ARTHUR, scientist; b. Grand Rapids, Mich., June 19, 1928; s. John A. and Sara Henrietta (Heyns) S.; m. Maxine Ruth Crawford, July 16, 1949; children—Stephen Arthur, Joel Brian. B.A., U. Mich., 1950, M.A., 1953, Ph.D., 1954. Instr. psychology U. Mich., Ann Arbor, 1954-56; asst. prof. Mass. Inst. Tech., Cambridge, 1956-60, asso. prof., 1960-63; v.p. Bolt Beranek & Newman Inc., Cambridge, 1964-69, sr. v.p., 1969-74, gen. mgr. research, devel. and cons., dir., 1971-74, chief scientist, 1975—; Mem. corp. Edn. Devel. Center, Newton, Mass., 1971-75; Vis. research fellow Philips Labs., Netherlands, 1958; Regents' prof. U. Calif., 1969; mem. com. on quantitative scis. in the med. area Harvard U., 1982-84; sci. adv. bd. Navy Personnel Research and Devel. Ctr., 1983-85; chmn. NRC com. on techniques for enhancement of human performance, 1985-87; cons. NIH, 1975—; mem. NRC panel on accuracy of polygraph lie detection, 1984—, mem. vision com., com. on hearing and bioacoustics Nat. Acad. Sci.-NRC. Author: (with D.M. Green) Signal Detection Theory and Psychophysics, 1966, (with R.M. Pickett) Evaluation of Diagnostic Systems: Methods From Signal Detection Theory, 1982; Editor: Signal Detection and Recognition by Human Observers, 1964, (with L.L. Elliott) Psychology and the Handicapped Child, 1974. Bd. dirs. Unitarian Cooperative Nursery Sch., Lexington, Mass., 1958-59; trustee Lexington Home for Aged, 1966-69; mem. corp. Winchester (Mass.) Hosp., 1981-84. Fellow AAAS (council 1986—), Acoustical Soc. Am. (exec. council 1968-71), Am. Psychol. Assn.; mem. Soc. Exptl. Psychologists (Howard Crosby Warren medal 1985, chmn. 1986, exec. com. 1986—), Psychonomic Soc., Psychometric Soc., Evaluation Research Soc., Soc. for Med. Decision Making (editorial bd. 1980-85), Sigma Xi, Sigma Alpha Epsilon. Conglist. (moderator). Clubs: Winchester Country, Cosmos. Current work: Decision making, pattern recognition, enhancement of human performance, evaluation of diagnostic systems, computer-assisted instruction. Subspecialties: Psychophysics; Sensory processes. Office: 50 Moulton St Cambridge MA 02138

SWIFT, ROBERT ANTON, metallurgical engineer, research administrator; b. Hempstead, N.Y., Jan. 21, 1940; s. William A. and Anna D. (Bartosh) S.; m. Christiane Marchionda, Nov. 30, 1963; children—Joseph W., Robert C., Tracey D. B. Metallurgical Engring., Poly. Inst. Bklyn., 1961; M.Materials Engring., Drexel Inst. Tech., 1969; Ph.D., Drexel U., 1974. Devel. engr. Martin Marrietta Co., Balt., 1964-65; research engr. IRC, Inc., Phila., 1965-67; research engr. Lukens Steel Co., Coatesville, Pa., 1967-76, supr. metallurgical div., 1976-81, supr. product research, 1981-84, supr. product research and devel., 1984-85; mgr. mfg. tech. and process devel. space systems div. Gen. Electric Co., Valley Forge, Pa., 1985—. Editor: Recent Advanced in Cr-Mo Steels, 1984. Contbr. articles to profl. jours. Pres., South Brandywine PTA, Coatesville, 1976; mem. Coatesville Long Range Planning Com., 1977. Served to 1st lt. U.S. Army, 1961-63. Mem. Am. Welding Soc., Am. Soc. Metals, ASME, Metal Properties Council (chmn. several task groups). Roman Catholic. Current work: Composites, electronic components, space hardware. Subspecialties: High-temperature materials; Materials processing. Office: Gen Electric Co Space Systems Div Valley Forge PA

SYDORAK, JAROSLAVA KUZMYCZ, quality control exec.; b. Mittenwald, Germany, Oct. 14, 1946; came to U.S., 1949, naturalized, 1975; d. George C. and Valentine P. (Dziwak) Kuzmycz; m. Mark Zenobius Sydorak, June 15, 1968; children: Larissa, Darya. B.S., Queens Coll., CUNY, 1967; M.A., CUNY, 1971. Import-export liaison dir. Podarogift, USSR, 1968-69; researcher in immunologic reactions Rockefeller U., N.Y.C., 1970-77; quality assurance mgr. Diagnostic Tech., Hauppauge, N.Y., 1977-81, product mgr., 1981—. Mem. Am. Soc. for Quality Control, N.Y. Acad. Scis., Ukrainian Inst. Am. Current Work: Introduction of monoclonal antibody techniques into clinical laboratory testing. Subspecialties: Hematology; Neuroimmunology. Home: 66 Richards Rd Port Washington NY 11050 Office: 240 Vanderbilt Pkwy Hauppauge NY 11788

SYED, IBRAHIM BIJLI, medical physicist, educator; b. Bellary, India, Mar. 16, 1939; came to U.S., 1969, naturalized, 1975; s. Ahmed Bijli and Mumtaz Begum (Maniyar) S.; m. Sajida Shariff, Nov. 29, 1964; children: Mubin, Zafrin. B.S., Mysore U., 1960, M.S., 1962; D.Sc., Johns Hopkins U., 1972 Ph.D. (hon.), Marquis Giuseppe Scicluna Internat. U., Madrid, 1985. Diplomate: Am. Bd. Radiology, Am. Bd. Health Physics. Postgrad. trainee WHO, Bhabha Atomic

Energy Research Ctr., Bombay, India, 1963-64; med. physicist, radiation safety officer Victoria Hosp., India, 1964-67, Bowring & Lady Curzon Hosp. and Postgrad. Med. Research Inst., Bangalore, India, 1964-67, Halifax (N.S., Can.) Infirmary, 1967-69; con. med. physicist, radiation safety officer Ministry of Govt. of Karnataka, India, 1964-67, Bangalore Nursing Home, 1964-67, Mercy Hosp., Springfield, Mass., 1973-79, Wing Meml. Hosp., Palmer, Mass., 1973-79; dir. med. physics, radiation safety officer Baystate Med. Center, Springfield, Mass., 1973-79; med. physicist, radiation safety officer VA Med. Center, Louisville, 1979—; assoc. prof. Springfield Tech. Community Coll., Mass., 1973-79; asst. clin. prof. nuclear medicine U. Conn. Health Scis. Ctr., 1974-79; prof. medicine and nuclear medicine tech. U. Louisville Sch. Medicine, 1979—; guest examiner Am. Bd. Radiology; mem. panel oral examiners Am. Bd. Health Physics; Ph.D. thesis examiner U. Delhi. Contbr. numerous articles to sci. jours. Pres. Springfield Islamic Center, 1973-79, India Assn., Louisville, 1980-81; v.p. Islamic Cultural Assn., Louisville, 1979-80, trustee, 1980—; vice chmn. bd., 1980-84, chmn. bd., 1984—. Author: Radiation Safety for Allied Health Professionals; mem. editorial bd.: Jour. Islamic Med. Assn, 1981—; contbr. 100 articles to sci. jours. Trustee India Community Found. Louisville, 1980—; bd. dirs. Child Guidance Clinic, Springfield, 1973-79, Heritage Corp., Louisville, 1981—, others; active Am. Cancer Soc., Heart Fund. Recipient Disting. Community Service award India Community Found., 1982. Fellow Inst. Physics (U.K.), Am. Inst. Chemists, Royal Soc. Health, Am. Coll. Radiology; mem. Am. Coll. Nuclear Medicine, Health Physics Soc., N.Y. Acad. Scis., Ky. Med. Assn., Jefferson County Med. Soc., Assn. Med. Physicists of India (life), Am. Assn. Physicists in Medicine, Soc. Nuclear Medicine, Nat. Assn. Ams. of Asian Indian Descent (chmn. state pub. relations com. 1982—). Moslem. Current work: Theory of limitations, radio-pharmaceutical development. Home: 7102 Shefford Ln Louisville KY 40222 Office: 800 Zorn Ave Louisville KY 40202

SYKES, LYNN RAY, geologist, educator; b. Pitts., Apr. 16, 1937; s. Lloyd Ascutney and Margaret (Woodburn) S. B.S. (Proctor & Gamble scholar) and; M.S., Mass. Inst. Tech., 1960; Ph.D. in Geology, Columbia, 1964. Phys. sci. aide geophys. lab. U.S. Geol. Survey, Silver Spring, Md., summer 1956; participant summer coop. program Geophys. Service Inc., Dallas, 1958; Summer Research fellow Woods Hole (Mass.) Oceanographic Inst., 1959; research asst. Lamont-Doherty Geol. Observatory Columbia, 1961-64, research asso. in seismology, 1964-66, adj. asst. prof. geology Columbia, 1966-68, asst. prof., 1968-69, asso. prof., 1969-73, prof., 1973-78, Higgins prof. geology, 1978—, mem. univ. com. on acad. priorities, 1977-79; research geophysicist earth scis. labs. U.S. Dept. Commerce, 1966-68; Mem. panel polar geophysics Nat. Acad. Scis., 1968; adv. com. to ESSA Research Labs., 1968-69; mem. subcom. geodesy and cartography applications steering com. NASA, 1968-70; mem. com. on world-wide standardized network Nat. Acad. Scis./NRC, 1969, com. seismology, 1972-73, panel earthquake prediction, 1973-75; organizing sec. Internat. Symposium Mech. Properties and Processes of Mantle of Internat. Upper Mantle Com., 1970; mem. panel on deep crustal drilling in marine areas JOIDES, 1970-71; advisor N.Y. State Geol. Survey and N.Y. State Environ. Protection Agy., 1970-80; mem. U.S. Geodynamics Panel on Mid-Atlantic Ridge, 1971-72; mem. working group U.S./USSR Joint Program for Earthquake Prediction, 1973-77; mem. U.S. Del. on Earthquake Prediction to USSR, fall, 1973; mem. adv. com. on proposals for earthquake prediction U.S. Geol. Survey, 1974, adv. panel earthquake hazards program, 1977-82; mem. U.S. Tech. Del. for talks on treaty on Threshold Limitations Underground Nuclear Explosions, Moscow, USSR, summer, 1974; mem. rev. panel earth scis. NSF, 1974-77; mem. study groups on plate interiors and Cocos and Caribbean plates U.S. Geodynamics Com.; mem. U.S. Seismology Group to People's Republic of China, fall, 1974; vis. prof. Earthquake Research Inst. of Tokyo (Japan) U., fall 1974; Fairchild vis. scholar Calif. Inst. Tech., 1982; vis. fellow Clare Hall, Cambridge U., 1983; mem. com. acad. priorities Columbia U., 1977-78. Contbg. author: History of the Earth's Crust, 1968, Geodynamics of Iceland and the North Atlantic Area, 1974, Encounter with the Earth, 1975; Assoc. editor: Jour. Geophys. Research, 1968-70; Contbr. numerous articles to profl. jours. Pres. Far West 77th St. Block Assn., N.Y.C., 1973-74. Recipient H. O. Wood award in seismology Carnegie Instn. of Washington, 1967-70, Edward John Noble Leadership award during first three years grad. study; Sloan fellow, 1969-71; NSF grantee; AEC grantee; Air Force Office Sci. Research, NASA, N.Y. State Sci. and Tech. Found. grantee; N.Y. State Atomic and Space Devel. Authority grantee; U.S. Geol. Survey, Sloan Found. grantee. Fellow Am. Geophys. Union (Macelwave award to Outstanding Young Geophysicist for 1970, Walter H. Bucher medal for original contbns. to basic knowledge of Earth's crust 1975, pres. sect. tectonophysics 1972-74, pres. sect. on seismology 1984—), Seismol. Soc. Am., Geol. Soc. Am., Geol. Soc. London; mem. Nat. Acad. Scis., Am. Acad. Arts and Scis., Royal Astron. Soc., Soc. Exploration Geophysicists, N.Y. Acad. Scis. (pres. geol. sect. 1970-71). Research includes maj. contbns. on plate tectonics, earthquake prediction and discrimination of underground nuclear explosions from earthquakes. Current work: Earthquake prediction; verification of a comprehensive nuclear test ban treaty; prevention of nuclear war. Subspecialties: Seismology; Tectonics. Home: Box 248 Washington Spring Rd Palisades NY 10964 Office: Lamont-Doherty Geol Observatory Columbia U Palisades NY 10964

SYMES, MARION ERNEST, research chemist; b. Granger, N.Y., Nov. 3, 1920; s. Harry Grant and Nina Slater (Swartz) S. B.S. in Chemistry, Rochester Inst. Tech., 1975. Dairy farmer, Walworth, N.Y., 1938-63; mechanic Borden Co., Fairport, N.Y., 1963-65; lab technician Eastman Kodak, Rochester, N.Y., 1965-75, research chemist, 1975—. Treas., Walworth Fire Dept., N.Y., 1977-80, 84; bd. dirs. Palmyra Vol. Ambulance, N.Y., 1980-84. Mem. Am. Chem. Soc. Current work: Characterizing and correlating the physical and tensile properties of polymers with their wear and abrasion. Subspecialties: Physical chemistry; Polymer chemistry. Home: 3855 Walworth-Ontario Rd Walworth NY 14568 Office: Eastman Kodak Co 343 State St Rochester NY 14650

SYNEK, M., physics educator, researcher; b. Prague, Czechoslovakia, Sept. 18, 1930; came to U.S., 1958, naturalized 1963; s. Frantisek and Anna (Kokrment) S.; m. Rosemarie Wahl, June 12, 1965; children—Mary Rose, Thomas Robert. Indsl. chemist Tech. Sch., Prague, 1946-50; cert. in liberal arts, Prague, 1951; M.S. in Physics with distinction, Charles U., Prague, 1956; Ph.D. in Physics, U. Chgo., 1963. Analytical chemist Indsl. Medicine Inst., Prague, 1950-51; research physicist Acad. of Scis., Prague, 1956-58; from asst. to assoc. prof. De Paul U., Chgo., 1962-67; prof. Tex. Christian U., Ft. Worth, 1967-71; lectr., researcher U. Tex.-Austin, 1971-75; tenured faculty U. Tex.-San Antonio, 1975—; sci. advisor Tex. Edn. Agy., Austin, 1971-73, U. Tex., 1971-73. Contbr. articles to sci. jours. Campaigner United Way, San Antonio, 1975—. Research grantee Robert A. Welch Found., 1968-71, 1976-83. Fellow AAAS, Am. Phys. Soc., Tex. Acad. Sci.; mem. AAUP, Am. Assn. Physics Tchrs., Am. Chem. Soc., Czechoslovak Nat. Council (dist. sec. Chgo. 1961-63), Sigma Xi (life), Sigma Pi Sigma. Roman Catholic. Current work: Laser-active ions of lanthanides and the laser-crystal energy efficiency; laser fusion; space lasers. The extra-terrestrial intelligence probability. Subspecialties: Laser-active materials; Intelligent life in the universe. Home: 5300 NW Loop 410 San Antonio TX 78229 Office: U of Tex San Antonio TX 78285

SYVERTSEN, JAMES PATRICK, plant physiology educator, researcher; b. Oxnard, Calif., Nov. 20, 1948; s. Clarence Wilbur and Yvette (Michaud) S.; m. Linda Kay Farron, Oct. 28, 1978. B.A., Calif. State U.-Fullerton, 1970, M.A., 1973; Ph.D., N.Mex. State U., 1977. Postdoctoral fellow U. Fla., Gainesville, 1977-78, asst. prof. plant physiology U. Fla.-Lake Alfred, 1978-83, assoc. prof., 1983—. Contbr. chpt., numerous articles to profl. publs. Mem. Am. Soc. Hort. Sci. (chmn. photosynthesis working group 1984), Ecol. Soc. Am., Am. Soc. Plant Physiology. Current work: Water relations; photosynthesis. Subspecialties: Plant physiology (agriculture); Ecology (biology). Office: U Fla 700 Exptl Station Rd Lake Alfred FL 33850

SYVERTSON, CLARENCE ALFRED, aerospace engineering consultant; b. Mpls., Jan. 12, 1926; s. Alfred and Esther Louise (Goertemiller) S.; m. Helen Hammond Gonnella, May 4, 1953 (dec. May 1981); 1 dau., Marguerite Louise; m. JoAnn Mary Caruso, May 8, 1982. B. Aero. Engring., U. Minn., 1946, M.S., 1948; postgrad., Stanford U., 1950-57; grad., Advanced Mgmt. Program, Harvard U., 1977. Research scientist Ames Aero. Lab., NACA, Moffett Field, Calif., 1948-58; exec. dir. Joint Dept. Transp./NASA Civil Aviation Research and Devel. Policy Study, 1970-71; with Ames Research Center, NASA, Moffett Field, 1958-84, dep. dir., 1969-78, dir., 1978-84; cons. prof. Stanford U., 1985—. Mem. adv. bd. Coll. Engring., U. Calif., Berkeley; mem. engring. adv. council San Jose (Calif.) State U.; mem. adv. council, dept. aerospace engring. and mechanics U. Minn. Served with U.S. Army, 1946-47. Recipient invention and contbn. award NASA, 1964, Exceptional Service medal, 1971, Disting. Service medal, 1984, Outstanding Achievement award U. Minn., 1982, Commanders award for civilian service U.S. Army, 1984. Fellow AIAA (Lawrence Sperry award 1957), Am. Astronautical Soc.; mem. Nat. Acad. Engring. Current work: Consultant in space systems design, advanced scientific computer systems. Subspecialties: Aeronautical engineering; Aerospace engineering and technology. Home: 15725 Apollo Heights Ct Saratoga CA 95070

SZABO, ALEXANDER, physicist; b. Copper Cliff, Ont., Can., Mar. 13, 1931; s. John and Anna (Fazekas) S.; m. Ethel Jessica Semmens, Sept. 21, 1957; children—Susan, John, Eleanor, Jennifer. B.Sc., Queen's U., 1953; M.Sc., McGill U., 1955; Ph.D., Tohoku U., Sendai, Japan, 1970. Research officer Nat. Research Council Can., Ottawa, 1955—, now sr. research officer. Inventor frequency selective optical memory. Japan Soc. for Promotion of Sci. fellow, 1985. Mem. Optical Soc. Am. Current work: Study of optical homogeneous linewidths in low temperature solids using coherent transient, fluorescence line narrow and hole-burning techniques. Subspecialties: Laser spectroscopy; Laser data storage and reproduction. Office: Nat Research Council of Can Bldg M-50 Montreal Rd Ottawa ON K1A OR8 Canada

SZABO, KALMAN TIBOR, reproductive physiologist, toxicologist; b. Abda, Hungary, July 29, 1921; came to U.S., 1957; s. Kalman Tibor and Helen Anna (Natz) S.; m. Edith Patka, Dec. 26, 1944; children—Claire, Helen. B.S., U. Budapest, Hungary, 1947; M.S., Rutgers U., 1962; M.S., U. Vienna, 1971, D.Sc., 1973. Sr. scientist, unit head Smith Kline & French Labs., Phila., 1967-69, sr. investigation group leader, 1969-70, asst. dir. toxicology, 1971-72, assoc. dir. toxicology, 1972-81, dir. toxicology, 1981-82, dir. reproductive toxicology, 1982—; research assoc. prof. pediatrics Med. Coll., Thomas Jefferson U., Phila., 1974—. Contbr. articles to profl. jours. Reviewer Jour. Teratology, 1970—. Patentee in field. Mem. Am. Coll. Toxicology, Behavioral Teratology Soc., European Teratology Soc., Internat. Acad. Environ. Safety, Soc. Toxicology, Teratology Soc., Soc. Study Reprodn. Current work: Experimental teratology; embryology of congenital malformations; role of maternal and embryonic nutritional factors in teratogenesis; reproductive toxicology. Subspecialties: Reproductive biology; Teratology. Home: 215 Morris Rd Ambler PA 19002 Office: Smith Kline & French Labs 1500 Spring Garden St Philadelphia PA 19101

SZABO, SANDOR, research pathologist; b. Ada, Yougslavia, Feb. 9, 1944; s. Gyorgy and Ilona (Komlos) S.; m. Ildiko Mecs, Feb. 19, 1972; children: Peter, David. M.D., U. Belgrade, Yugoslavia, 1968; M.Sc., U. Montreal, Que., Can., 1971, Ph.D., 1973. Intern U. Belgrade Med. Sch. and Med. Center, Senta, Yugoslavia, 1968-69; vis. scientist Inst. Exptl. Medicine and Surgery, U. Montreal, 1969-70; resident in pathology Peter Bent Brigham Hosp.-Harvard U. Med. Sch., Boston, 1973-77; research fellow Harvard U. Med. Sch., 1975-77, asst. prof. pathology, 1977-81, assoc. prof., 1981—. Contbr. over 200 articles to sci. jours. Recipient Physician's Recognition award AMA, 1976; Milton Fund award Harvard U., 1978; NIH award, 1980. Mem. Am. Assn. Pathologists, Royal Coll. Pathologists, Am. Soc. Pharmacology and Exptl. Therapeutics, Soc. Exptl. Biology and Medicine, Am. Gastroent. Assn., Endocrine Soc., N.Y. Acad. Scis., others. Roman Catholic. Current Work: Studying pathogenesis of chemically-induced diseases. Subspecialties: Pathology (medicine); Gastroenterology. Home: 46 Clearwater Rd Brookline MA 02167 Office: 75 Francis St Boston MA 02115

SZABO, TIBOR, veterinarian; b. Szentes, Hungary, Sept. 14, 1935; came to U.S. 1957, naturalized, 1962; s. Gyula and Clara (Kocziszky) S.; m. Georgette Monostory, Oct. 1, 1968 (div. 1983); m. Ruth Simon, Feb. 16, 1984. D.V.M., U. Ga., 1963; M.P.H., Columbia U., 1975. Lic. vet., N.Y. Treatment room vet. Am. Soc. for the Prevention to Cruelty to Animals, N.Y.C., 1963-66; staff vet. Mt. Sinai Hosp., N.Y.C., 1966-68, chief vet., 1968-70; asst. dir. ctr. for lab. animal scis., Mt. Sinai Sch. Medicine, N.Y.C., 1970-73, assoc. dir. 1973—; cons. vet. Beth Israel Med. Ctr., N.Y.C., 1972—, Orthopedic Inst. N.Y.C., 1972—, City Hosp. Ctr., Elmhurst, N.Y., 1972—. Contbr. articles to profl. jours. Bd. dirs. Bide-A-Wee Home Assn., N.Y.C., 1968—, v.p., 1983—. Rockefeller Found. scholar, 1957. Mem. Am. Vet. Med. Assn., N.Y. Acad. Scis., Am. Pub. Health Assn., Am. Assn. Lab. Animal Scis., Am. Soc. Lab. Animal Practitioners. Republican. Current work: Managing a laboratory animal science department. Subspecialties: Laboratory animal medicine; Preventive medicine (veterinary medicine). Home: 110-40 72d Ave Forest Hills NY 11375

SZAL, MARCEL MICHAEL, radiological physicist, biologist; b. McKees Rocks, Pa., Nov. 21, 1954; s. Valerian F. and Florence (Drost) S.; m. Kathleen Ann Koczur, June 20, 1981. M.S., U. Pitts., 1981. Radiol. physicist Mid-East Center for Radiol. Physics, Allegheny Gen. Hosp., Pitts., 1980—. Mem. Nuclear Medicine Soc., Health Physics Soc., Am. Assn. Physicists in Medicine. Current Work: Radiation oncology. Subspecialties: Cancer research (medicine); Radiology. Home: 238 Helen St McKees Rocks PA 15136 Office: 320 E North Ave Pittsburgh PA 15212

SZALECKI, WOJCIECH JOSEF, chemistry researcher; b. Kutno, Lodz, Poland, Mar. 18, 1935; came to U.S., 1969; s. Mieczyslaw and Julia (Wojciechowska) S.; m. Zofia Fortuna, Nov. 10, 1959 (div. Mar. 1974); 1 child, Dorota; m. Danuta Grad, Dec. 10, 1977; 1 child, Adam. M.S., U. Lodz, 1959, Ph.D., 1968. Fellow, Wayne State U., Detroit, 1969-70; research assoc., adj. U. Lodz, 1970-79; research assoc. U. Colo., Boulder, 1979-82, prof. research assoc., 1982-83; research chemist Molecular Probes, Junction City, Oreg., 1983—; abstractor Chem. Abstracts Service, Columbus, Ohio, 1970-82. Patents, publs. in chem. field. Fellow Am. Inst. Chemists; mem. Polish Chem. Soc., Am. Chem. Soc. Current work: Organic synthesis (especially new methods), structure determination chromatography, spectroscopy. Subspecialties: Synthetic chemistry; Analytical chemistry. Home: 4109 Jessen Dr Eugene OR 97402 Office: Molecular Probes Inc 27450 Lawrence Rd Junction City OR 97448

SZCZEPANSKI, MAREK MICHAL, veterinarian; b. Warsaw, Poland, June 8, 1941, came to Can., 1968, naturalized, Can. citizen, 1973; s. Zygmunt and Krystyna (Bulak) S.; m. Ewelina Rodziewicz, Sept. 23, 1980; 1 child. D.V.M., U. Warsaw, Poland, 1967; D.V.P.H., U. Toronto, Ont., Can., 1972. Research asst. McGill U., Montreal, Que., Can., 1968-80; research fellow U. Toronto, 1970-72; assoc. vet. Lakeshore Vet. Hosp., Port Credit, Ont., 1973-75; dir. animal care, asst. prof. physiology Faculty of Medicine, Meml. U. Newfoundland, Can., 1975-80; dir. lab. animal scis., asst. prof. physiology Northeastern Ohio U. Coll. Medicine, Rootstown, 1980—. Mem. Am. Assn. Lab. Animal Scis., No. Ohio Br. Am. Assn. Lab. Animal Scis., (bd. dirs. 1982-83), Ont. Vet. Assn., Geauga County Vet. Med. Assn. Roman Catholic. Current work: Pathophysiology of esophagus; experimental surgery; laboratory animal sciences. Subspecialties: Laboratory animal medicine; Surgery (veterinary medicine). Home: 411 Vine St Kent OH 44240 Office: NE Ohio U Coll Medicine 4209 State Route 44 Rootstown OH 44272

SZEBEHELY, VICTOR G., aerospace engineer; b. Budapest, Hungary, Aug. 10, 1921; s. Victor and Vilma (Stockl) S.; m. Jo Betsy Lewallen, May 21, 1970; 1 dau., Julia. M.E., U. Budapest, 1943, Ph.D. in Engring, 1945. Asst. prof. U. Budapest, 1945-47; research asso. State U. Pa., 1947-48; asso. prof. Va. Poly. Inst., 1948-53; research asso. Model Basin, U.S. Navy, 1953-57; research mgr. Gen. Electric Co., 1957-62; asso. prof. astronomy Yale U., 1962-68; prof. aerospace engring. U. Tex., Austin, 1968—, chmn. dept., 1977-81, L.B. Meaders prof. engring., 1978-82, D.D. Cockrell prof. engring., 1982-85, R. B. Curran chair of engring., 1985—; cons. NASA-Johnson Space Center. Author 17 books; contbr. numerous articles on space research, celestial mechanics and ship dynamics to profl. jours. Knighted by Queen Juliana of Netherlands, 1956. Fellow AIAA, AAAS; mem. Am. Astron. Soc. (Brouwer award div. dynamical astronomy 1977), Internat. Astron. Union (pres. commn. on celestial mechanics), Nat. Acad. Engring. Current work: Aerospace engineering, satellites, orbit computations. Subspecialties: Aerospace engineering and technology; Astronautics. Home: 2501 Jarratt Ave Austin TX 78703 Office: Dept Aerospace Engring and Engring Mechanics U Texas Austin TX 78712

SZEBENYI, EMIL STEVEN, cancer researcher, corporation president; b. Budapest, Hungary, June 9, 1920; came to U.S., 1957, naturalized, 1962; s. Edmund and Franciska (Jalovits) S.; m. Clasa Goots de Jaszo, Apr. 21, 1944; children: Thomas, Andrew, Steve. Diploma agr., zootechnic, Poly. U., Budapest, 1942, doctorate in zoo-genetics, 1943. Asst. prof. animal genetics Agrl. U., Godollo, Hungary, 1950-51, assoc. prof., 1952-56; asst. prof. Fairleigh Dickinson U., Rutherford, N.J., 1962-69, assoc. prof., 1969-73, prof., 1973—, chmn. dept. biol. scis., 1971-80; pres. Alfacell Corp., Bloomfield, N.J., 1982—. Author: Atlas of Macaca Mulatta, 1969, Atlas of Developmental Embryology, 1979, Anatomy of Squalus Acautias, 1982, Anatomy of Felis domestica, 1982. Mem. presdl. task force Republican Party, 1980—. Mem. Soc. Developmental Biology, Am. Soc. Zoology, Am. Soc. Morphogenesis, Am. Assn. Lab. Animal Sci., AAAAS, Sigma Xi. Current Work: Cancer; antitumor agents. Subspecialties: Cancer research (veterinary medicine); Animal breeding and embryo transplants. Home: 5 Stephen Pl Little Falls NJ 07424 Office: Alfacell Corp 225 Belleville Ave Bloomfield NJ 07003

SZEKELY, JULIAN, materials engineering educator; b. Budapest, Hungary, Nov. 23, 1934; came to U.S., 1966, naturalized, 1975; s. Gyula and Ilona (Nemeth) S.; m. Elizabeth Joy Pearn, Mar. 2, 1963; children—Richard J., Martin T., Rebecca J., Matthew T., David A. B.Sc., Imperial Coll., London, 1959; Ph.D., D.I.C., 1961, D.Sc., 1972. Lectr. metallurgy Imperial Coll., 1962-66; asso. prof. chem. engring. State U. N.Y. at Buffalo, 1966-68, prof., 1968-76; dir. Center for Process Metallurgy, 1970-76; prof. materials engring. Mass. Inst. Tech., Cambridge, 1976—, assoc. dir. Ctr. for Materials Processing, 1982—; cons. to govt. and industry. Author: (with N.J. Themelis) Rate Phenomena in Process Metallurgy, 1971, (with W.H. Ray) Process Optimization, 1973, (with J.W. Evans and H.Y. Sohn) Gas-Solid Reactions, 1976, Fluid Flow Aspects of Metals Processing, 1979; Editor: Ironmaking Technology, 1972, The Steel Industry and the Environment, The Steel Industry and The Energy Crisis, 1975, The Future of the World's Steel Industry, 1976, Alternative Energy Sources for the Steel Industry, 1977; Contbr. articles to profl. jours. Recipient Jr. Moulton medal Brit. Inst. Chem. Engrs., 1964; Extractive Metallurgy Div. Sci. award Am. Inst. Mining and Metall. Engrs., 1973; also Mathewson Gold medal, 1973; Howe Meml. lectr., 1979; Sir George Beilby Gold medal Brit. Inst. Chem. Engrs.-Soc. Chem. Industry-Inst. Metals, 1973; Curtis McGraw research award Am. Soc. Engring. Edn., 1974; Profl. Progress award Am. Inst. Chem. Engrs., 1974; John Simon Guggenheim fellow, 1974. Mem. Nat. Acad. Engring. Current work: Materials processing at high temperatures in crystal growth and in microgravity. Office: Room 4-117 Dept Materials Sci and Engring Mass Inst Tech Cambridge MA 02139

SZENT-GYORGYI, ALBERT, biochemist; b. Budapest, Hungary, Sept. 16, 1893; came to U.S., 1947, naturalized, 1955; s. Nicholas and Josephine (Lenhossek) Szent-G.; 1 dau., Cornelia Szent-Gyorgyi Pollit. M.D., U. Budapest, 1917; Ph.D., Cambridge U., Eng., 1927. Prof. med. chemistry Szeged, 1931-45; prof. biochemistry U. Budapest, 1945-47; sci. dir. Nat. Found. Cancer Research Marine Biol. Labs., Woods Hole, Mass., 1947—. Author: Oxidation, Fermentation, Vitamins, Health and Disease, 1939, Muscular Contraction, 1947, The Nature of Life, 1947, Contraction in Body and Heart Muscle, 1953, Bioenergetics, 1957, Submolecular Biology, 1960, Bioelectronics, 1968, The Crazy Ape, 1970, What Next?, 1971, The Living State, 1972, Electronic Biology and Cancer, 1976, The Living State and Cancer, 1978. Recipient Nobel prize in medicine, 1937, 55, Lasker award Heart Association, 1954. Mem. Acad. Scis. Budapest (pres.), Nat. Acad. Budapest (v.p.), Nat. Acad. Scis., Council of Edn. (chmn.). Subspecialty: Cancer research (medicine). Office: Marine Biological Labs PO Box 187 Woods Hole MA 02543

SZEWCZYK, ALBIN ANTHONY, aerospace and mech. engr., educator, researcher, cons.; b. Chgo., Feb. 26, 1935; s. Andrew Aloysius and Jean Cecelia (Wojcik) S.; m. Barbara Valerie, June 16, 1956; children: Karen Marie Szewczyk Finkenbinder, Lisa Anne, Andrea Jean Szewczyk Harman, Terese Helene. B.S.M.E., U. Notre Dame, 1956, M.S.M.E., 1958; Ph.D., U. Md., 1961. Mem. tech. staff Aerospace Corp., El Segundo, Calif., summer 1962; asst. prof. aerospace and mech. engring. U. Notre Dame, 1962-65, assoc. prof., 1965-67, prof., 1967—, chmn. dept. aerospace and mech. engring., 1978—; cons. Argonne Nat. Lab., cons. as expert witness. Research numerous publs. in field. Office Naval Research grantee, 1967-72; NSF grantee, 1971-85. Mem. Am. Phys. Soc., ASME, AIAA. Roman Catholic. Clubs: Univ. (Notre Dame, Ind.); South Bend (Ind.) Country. Current Work: Experimental fluid mechanics; bluff body flows. Subspecialties: Mechanical engineering; Fluid mechanics. Office: Dept Aerospace and Mech Engring Notre Dame Notre Dame IN 46556

SZILAGYI, MIKE NICHOLAS, engineer, physicist, educator; b. Budapest, Hungary, Feb. 4, 1936; came to U.S., 1981; s. Karoly and Ilona (Abraham) S.; m. Larissa Dorner, Feb. 23, 1957; m. Julia Levai, May 31, 1975; children: Gabor, Zoltan Charles. M.Sc. with honors in Engring.-Physics, Poly. U. Leningrad, 1954-60; Ph.D., Electrotech. U. Leningrad., 1965; D.Tech., Tech. U., Budapest, 1965; D.Sc., Hungarian Acad. Sci., 1979. Research asst. dept. phys. electronics Poly U. Leningrad, 1958-60; research assoc. Research Inst. Tech. Physics, Hungarian Acad. Sci., Budapest, 1960-66; sci. adviser Nat. Research Inst. Neurosurgery, Budapest, 1966-70; chief research scientist, head Lab. Electron Optics, Tech. U., Budapest, 1966-71; prof. physics, head dept. phys. scis. K. Kando Coll. Elec. Engring., Budapest, 1971-79, rector, 1971-74; guest prof. Aarhus U., Denmark, 1979-81; vis. sr. research assoc. engring. physics Cornell U., Ithaca, N.Y., 1981-82; prof. elec. and computer engring. U. Ariz., Tucson, 1982—; vis. prof. U. Heidelberg, 1984. Author: Introduction to the Theory of Space Charge Optics, 1974, Fachlexikon Physik, 1977, others; Contbr. articles to profl. jours. Mem. Am. Phys. Soc., IEEE (sr.), Danish Phys. Soc., Danish Engring. Soc., European Soc. Stereotactic and Functional Neurosurgery, J. Neumann Soc. Computer Sci., L. Eötvös Phys. Soc. (Brody prize 1964). Current Work: Teaching and research in electron and ion optics, focused ion beams, microfabrication of integrated circuits, physical electronics, expert systems. Subspecialties: Computer-aided design; Artificial intelligence. Office: University of Arizona Dept Elect and Computer Engineering Tucson AZ 85721

SZLYK, PATRICIA CAROL, research physiologist, biochemist; b. Worcester, Mass., Dec. 24, 1952; d. Stanley John and Felicia Geraldine (Kislak) Szlyk. B.A. summa cum laude in Biochemistry, Elmira Coll., 1974; Ph.D. with distinction in Physiology, SUNY-Buffalo, 1980; postgrad. Clark U., 1974-75. Research asst. Worcester Found. Exptl. Biology, Shrewsbury, Mass., 1974-75; predoctoral trainee physiology SUNY-Buffalo, 1975-80; lectr. physiology Queen's U., Kingston, Ont., Can., 1980-83; Heart Found. fellow Can. Heart Found., Kingston, 1980-83; research physiologist heat research, U.S. Army Research Inst. Environ. Medicine, Natick, Mass., 1983—; contract officers tech. rep. Inst. Chem. Def., Edgewood, Md., 1984—; mem. animal use com. USARIEM, 1983—, reviewer research contract property, 1983—. Contbr. articles to sci. jours.; author poem: As I Lay Dying (Nat. Poetry Press award 1973, Pegasus 1974). Dir., coach Girls' Softball and Basketball Leagues, Holden, Mass., 1967-74; tutor high sch. equivalency tests, N.Y. Neighborhood Corp., Elmira, N.Y., 1973-74; asst. leader Girl Guides of Can., Kingston, Ont., 1982-83. Recipient Research award Sigma Xi, 1980; Elmira Coll. merit scholar, 1971-74; Can. Heat Found. fellow, 1980-83. Mem. Am. Physiology Soc., Can. Physiology Soc., N.Y. Acad. Scis., Phi Beta Kappa, Sigma Xi, Tri-Beta Nat. Biol. Honor Soc. Democrat. Roman Catholic. Current work: Mechanisms regulating circulatory, respiratory, and thermal responses to environmental stresses; function of peripheral chemoreceptors in cardiovascular and respiratory control. Subspecialties: Physiology (medicine); Health services research. Home: 7 Cumberland Circle Holden MA 01520 Office: Heat Research USARIEM Natick MA 01760

TAAM, RONALD EVERETT, astrophysics educator, researcher; b. N.Y.C., Apr. 24, 1948; s. Lawrence and Julia (Louie) T.; m. Rosa Wen Mei Yang, Oct. 19, 1974; children—Jonathan, Alexander. B.S., Poly. Inst. N.Y., 1965-69; M.A., Columbia U., 1971, Ph.D., 1973. Postdoctoral fellow U. Calif., Santa Cruz, 1973-76; lectr. U. Calif., Berkeley, 1976-78; asst. prof. Northwestern U., Evanston, Ill., 1978-83, assoc. prof., 1983—. Contbr. articles profl. jours. Mem. Am. Astron. Soc., Am. Phys. Soc., Royal Astron. Soc. Current work: The emphasis of my research is to provide a foundation upon which one can understand the nature, origin, and evolution of close binary systems. Subspecialty: Theoretical astrophysics. Home: 30 Williamsburg Ln Evanston IL 60203 Office: Northwestern Univ Dept Physics and Astronomy Evanston IL 60201

TABACHNICK, JOSEPH, biochemist, molecular biologist; b. N.Y.C., May 14, 1919; s. Harry Tabachnick and Sarah Tabachnick Berman; m. Brunhild Stark, Dec. 21, 1961; children—Lysa, Maynard. B.S., U. Calif.-Berkeley, 1942, M.S., 1946, Ph.D. in Comparative Biochemistry, 1949. Head hormone receptor lab., dept. chemistry Albert Einstein Med. Ctr., Phila., 1941. Current work: Health and science publications in skin biochemistry, cell-kinetics, enzyme chemistry; assay and research with breast tumor steroid receptors. Subspecialties: Biochemistry (biology); Biochemistry (medicine). Office: Hormone Receptor Lab Albert Einstein Med Ctr Philadelphia PA 19141

TABAK, MARK DAVID, research executive; b. Phila., Dec. 2, 1937; s. Jules and Ruth T.; m. Margaret J. Tabak; children—Alison, Carolyn. B.S.E.E. with distinction, U. Pa., 1959; M.A.E.E. (ITT fellow, NSF coop. fellow), Princeton U., 1962; Ph.D. in Elec. Engring, Princeton U., 1965. Sr. scientist, project leader photocondr. physics Xerox Research Labs., 1965-70, mgr. photocondr. and insulator physics, 1970-72, mgr., 1972-73, mgr. imaging sci. lab., 1973-77; mgr. advanced marking program, research and devel. group Xerox Corp., 1977-78; v.p., mgr. Webster Research Center, Xerox Corp., Rochester, N.Y., 1978-84, v.p., gen. mgr. electronic pub. bus. unit, San Diego, 1984-85, v.p. tech. transfer, corp. research group, Palo Alto, Calif., 1985—. Program chmn. 3d Internat. Conf. Electrophotography, 1977; gen. chmn. 4th Internat. Conf. Electrophotography, 1981. Contbr. articles to sci. jours. Bd. dirs. So. Meth. U. Found. Sci. and Engring. Mem. IEEE (sr.), Am. Phys. Soc., Soc. Photog. Engrs. and Scientists, Sigma Xi, Tau Beta Pi, Eta Kappa Nu. Current work: Identification and quantification of the business potential for corporate research developed technology. Subspecialties: Semiconductors; Condensed matter physics. Home: 16244 Ave Florencia Poway CA 92064 Office: PARC 3333 Coyote Hill Rd Palo Alto CA 94304

TABASHNIK, BRUCE ELLIOT, ecologist, educator; b. Detroit, Oct. 31, 1954; s. David M. and Phyllis (Zieve) T.; m. Rowena H. Krakauer, Dec. 26, 1982. B.S., U. Mich., 1975; Ph.D., Stanford U., 1981. Postdoctoral research assoc. Mich. State U., East Lansing, 1981-83; asst. prof. insect ecology U. Hawaii, Honolulu, 1983—; cons. Thomas Reid Assocs., Palo Alto, Calif., 1980-81, Consortium for Internat. Crop Protection, Berkeley, Calif., 1985—. Contbr. articles to profl. jours. NSF fellow, 1976-80; NIH trainee, 1980-81. Mem. AAAS, Ecol. Soc. Am., Entomol. Soc. Am., Soc. for Study of Evolution, Hawaiian Entomol. Soc., Rocky Mountain Biol. Lab. Current work: Evolution of insecticide resistance, insect population biology, plant-herbivore interactions, computer-aided pest mgmt. Subspecialties: Evolutionary biology; Ecology (biology). Address: Univ Hawaii Dept Entomology Honolulu HI 96822

TABER, JOSEPH J., petroleum engineering and research educator; b. Adena, Ohio, Feb. 6, 1920; s. William Pickett and Sarah (Negus) T.; m. Catharine Holsinger, June 11, 1947; children—Deborah, J(oseph) John, Thomas, Catharine. B.S., Muskingum Coll., 1942; Ph.D., U. Pitts., 1955. Asst. prof. naval sci. U.S. Navy and Ohio State U., Columbus, 1946; instr. chemistry Washington and Jefferson Coll., Washington, Pa., 1946-50; Proctor & Gamble jr. research fellow U. Pitts., 1950-54, faculty mem., 1964-76, prof. chemistry, to 1976; sr. project chemist Gulf Research and Devel. Co., Pitts., 1954-64; dir. N.Mex. Petroleum Recovery Research Ctr., N.Mex. Inst. Mining and Tech., Socorro, 1976—; mem. com. on enhanced oil recovery Interstate Oil Compact Commn., Oklahoma City, 1980—. Contbr. chpts. to books, sci. articles to profl. jours. Patentee in field improved oil recovery. Judge elections Glenshaw Election Bd., Pa., 1967-76. Recipient Disting. Service award Muskingum Coll., 1983. Mem. AAAS, Soc. Petroleum Engrs.-AIME, Am. Chem. Soc., Socorro C. of C., Sigma Xi, (pres. 1979-80), Phi Lambda Upsilon. Served to lt. USNR, 1943-46. Republican. Quaker. Lodge: Rotary. Current work: Research and development on enhanced oil recovery including multi-phase flow in porous media, liquid-vapor phase behavior and fluid-solid interactions. Subspecialties: Petroleum engineering; Surface chemistry. Office: N Mex Petroleum Recovery Research Ctr N Mex Inst Mining and Technology Socorro NM 87801

TABER, ROBERT IRVING, pharmacologist; b. Perth Amboy, N.J., June 28, 1936; married; children: Scott and Stacy (twins), Jennifer. B.S., Rutgers U., 1958; Ph.D., Med. Coll. Va., 1962. Pharmacologist research div. Schering Plough Pharm., Bloomfield, N.J., 1962-66, sr. pharmacologist, 1967-71, mgr. pharmacology, 1971-74, assoc. dir. biol. research, 1974-77, dir. biol. research, 1977-82; dir. pharm. research DuPont Pharms., Glenolden, Pa., 1982—. Mem. AAAS, Am. Coll. Neuropsychopharmacology, Am. Soc. Pharmacology and Exptl. Therapeutics, Acad. Pharm. Sci., Am. Pharm. Assn. Subspecialty: Pharmacology. Home: 120 Guernsey Rd Swarthmore PA 19081 Office: Du Pont Co Glenolden Lab Glenolden PA

TABER, STEVE, bee geneticist, researcher; b. Columbia, S.C., Apr. 17, 1924; s. Stephen and Bessie (Ray) T.; m. Martha Polenz, Dec. 10, 1945 (div. Apr. 1970); children—Caroline, Stephen, Louis, Ray, Eugenie; m. Bonnie Cornett, June 14, 1970; children—Guyle, Brian, Sarah. B.S., U. Wis.-Madison, 1949. Apiculturist, Div. Bee Culture, Baton Rouge, 1950-65, Agr. Research Service, U.S. Dept. Agr., Tucson, 1965-79; research dir. Taber Apiaries, Vacaville, Calif., 1979—. Contbr. articles on bee behaviors to profl. jours. Contbr. monthly column Am. Bee Jour., Bee Behaviour. Served as aviation cadet U.S. Navy, 1943-45. Mem. AAAS, Entomology Soc. Am., Internat. Bee Research Assn., Am. Bee Fedn., Am. Genetic Assn. Liberal. Current work: Bee genetics and bee breeding. Subspecialty: Animal genetics. Home and office: 3639 Oak Canyon Ln Vacaville CA 95688

TABER-MAIER, KATHERINE HELEN, neuroscientist, nuclear magnetic resonance researcher; b. Oakland, Calif., Aug. 17, 1951; d. Richard Douglass and Barbara (Fleming) Taber; m. Herbert Norton Maier, Mar. 23, 1980; 1 child, Matthew Paul Benedict. B.S., U. Calif.-Irvine, 1973; M.S., U. Fla., 1977; Ph.D., U. Tex.-Houston, 1982. Teaching asst. U. Fla., Gainesville, 1976-77, U. Tex., Houston, 1978; research assoc. dept. neurology Baylor Coll. Medicine, Houston, 1982-84, research assoc. nuclear magnetic resonance lab., 1984—. Contbr. articles to profl. jours. Recipient 2d place award Grad. Student div. Eastern Student Research Forum, 1977, 3d place Neurosci. div. Nat. Student Research Forum, 1977; grantee Hoffman-LaRoche, Inc., 1978; predoctoral fellow NIMH, 1980. Mem. Soc. for Neurosci. Current work: Application of proton nuclear magnetic resonance imaging and phosphorus, hydrogen, and carbon spectroscopy to the study of in vivo brain functioning in man and animals in normal and disease states. Subspecialties: Neurophysiology; Nuclear magnetic resonance. Home: 19 Wolly Bucket Pl Woodlands TX 77380 Office: Baylor Coll Medicine Nuclear Magnetic Resonance Ctr 9450 Grogans Mill Rd Woodlands TX 77380

TACHE, YVETTE FRANCE, neuro-gastroenterologist, medical educator; b. Lyon, Rhone, France, Feb. 1, 1945; came to U.S., 1982; d. Lucien Joseph and Jeanne Marthe (Fouillat) Laurent; m. Jean Arthur Tache, June 20, 1970 (dec. 1979); children: Stephanie, Veronique. Baccalaureat, Lycée Tarare, 1965; Maitrise, Faculty Scis. U. Claude Bernard, Lyon, France, 1968, D.E.A., 1969; Ph.D., Faculty Medicine U. Montreal, 1974. Asst. research prof. U. Montreal, Que., Can., 1977-78, asst. research prof., 1980-81, assoc. research prof., 1981-82; vis. scientist Salk Inst., La Jolla, Calif., 1978-80; assoc. prof. in residence UCLA, 1982-85, prof. medicine, 1985—; external referee Med. Research Council Que., 1981—, mem. selection com., 1982. Vice pres. Hans Selye Found. External referee specialized sci. jours., U.S., 1977—; contbr. writings to publs. Fellow Med. Research Council Que., 1974-78; fellow Med. Research Council, 1974-78; Centennial fellow, 1978-80; scholar, 1980-82 research grantee Med. Research Council Que.; research grantee Med. Research Council Can.; research grantee NIH, 1977. Mem. Internat. Soc. Psychoneuroendocrinology, Endocrine Soc., Soc. Neurosci., Am. Physiol. Soc., Am. Gastroent. Soc., Brain Research Inst., Acad. Behavioral Med. Research N.Y. Acad. Sci. Current Work: Independent research on brain control of gastric function. Subspecialties: Gastroenterology; Neurophysiology. Home: 1180 McClellan Dr Los Angeles CA 90049 Office: CURE VA Wadsworth Bldg 115 Room 217 Los Angeles CA 90073

TACKEL, IRA STUART, clinical engineer, microcomputer and biomedical consultant; b. N.Y.C., Apr. 3, 1954; s. Herman William and Aida (Link) T.; m. Sherry Dee Melker, Aug. 28, 1977; children—Elana Rachael, Joshua Chad. B.S., Rensselaer Poly. Inst., 1976, M.Engring., 1977. Mech. engr. Olin Corp., Lake Charles, La., 1974; biomed. engr. VA Hosp., Albany, N.Y., 1976-77; clin. engr., dept. dir. Hosp. of U. Pa., Phila., 1977-85; dept. dir. biomed. instrumentation Thomas Jefferson U. Hosp., Phila., 1985—; cons. Biosonics, Phila., 1982—, Integrated Tech. Resource Corp., Ft. Washington, Pa., 1983—; adj. faculty Temple U., Phila. Mem. editorial bd. Emergency Care Research Inst., 1982—. Mem. Phila. Area Med. Instrumentation Assn. (pres. 1982-84), IEEE, Assn. for Advancement of Med. Instrumentation (chmn. edn. com.). Democrat. Jewish. Subspecialties: Biomedical engineering; Biomedical engineering. Home: 1327 Barton Dr Fort Washington PA 19034 Office: Thomas Jefferson Univ Hosp 561 Thompson bldg Philadelphia PA 19107

TACKER, JR. WILLIS ARNOLD, biomedical engineering, cardiovascular physiology researcher; b. Tyler, Tex., May 24, 1942; s. Willis Arnold Sr. and Willie M. (Massey) T.; m. Martha McClelland, Mar. 18, 1967; children—Sarah Mae, Betsy Jane, Katherine Ann. B.S. in Biology, Baylor U., 1964, M.D., Ph.D., 1970. Intern Mayo Clinic, Rochester, Minn., 1970-71; gen. practice medicine, Prudhoe Bay, Alaska, 1971; physiology instr. Baylor Coll. Medicine, Houston, 1971-73, asst. prof., 1973-74; vis. asst. prof. Biomed. Engring. Ctr., Purdue U., West Lafayette, Ind., 1974-76, prof., 1979—. Contbr. articles to profl. publs., chpts. to books. Patentee in field. Mem. Am. Physiol. Soc., Assn. Advancement Med. Instrumentation, Ind. State Med. Assn., Tippecanoe County Med. Soc. Baptist. Current work: Biomedical engineering; cardiovascular physiology and medical education. Home: 300 Forest Hill Dr West Lafayette IN 47906 Office: Purdue Univ A A Potter Bldg Room 204 West Lafayette IN 47907

TAENZER, JON CHARLES, robot research scientist, consultant; b. Chgo., Nov. 10, 1942; s. Roderick Bendix and Marcella Ida (Galle) T.; m. Anita Jeanette Sanner, Aug. 10, 1969; 1 child, Bryce Jon. B.E.E., Purdue U., 1964; M.E.E., Stanford U., 1966, Ph.D., 1971. Research engr. Hewlett-Packard, Palo Alto, Calif., 1965; sr. engr. SRI Internat., Menlo Pk., Calif., 1972-79; dir. engring. Diasonics Inc., Milpitas, Calif., 1979-80; staff scientist SRI Internat., 1980-83; sr. scientist Adept Tech. Inc., Sunnyvale, Calif., 1983—; cons. in field. Patentee (13). Atholl McBean Postdoctoral fellow SRI, 1970; recipient Inventor awards SRI, 1971-83. Mem. IEEE, Tau Beta Pi, Eta Kappa Nu. Current work: High speed, high precision robotic mechanisms, machine vision, automated speech recognition, medical ultrasound imaging, medical blood flow measurement, audio music reproduction. Subspecialties: Robotics; Ultrasound.

TAFT, WILLIAM HARRISON, geologist; b. San Mateo, Calif., Sept. 21, 1931; s. Foster Harrison and Dorris (Callaghan) T.; m. Constance Ann Polk, May 10, 1952; 11 children. A.A., Menlo Coll., 1954; B.S., Stanford U., 1957; M.A., U. S.D., 1958; Ph.D., Stanford U., 1962. Asst. prof. geology U. South Fla., Tampa, 1963-65, asst. dean acad.affairs, 1965-76, dir. grad. studies, dir. research 1976-78; pres. Mote Marine Lab., Sarasota, Fla., 1978-83; chmn. bd., pres. Gulf Coast R & D Lab., Sarasota, 1984—. Contbr. articles to profl. jours. Served to 1st lt. C.E., U.S. Army, 1952-53. Republican. Roman Catholic. Current work: Red tide research; applied environmental science. Subspecialty: Genetics and genetic engineering (biology). Office: Gulf Coast R & D Lab PO Box 31166 Sarasota FL 33582

TAI, CHEN-YU, physicist; b. Hofei, An-Whi, China, Sept. 4, 1945; s. Tseng-Hsi and Wen-Min (Chang) T.; m. Ping-Kuang Ku, Dec. 29, 1971; children: Yunsian Tai, Jan-Sian Tai. B.S., Nat. Taiwan U., 1968; M.A., Columbia U., 1971, M.Phil., 1973, Ph.D., 1974. Postdoctoral fellow U. B.C., Vancouver, 1974-76, research assoc., 1976-79; asst. prof. physics U. Toledo, 1979-83, assoc. prof. physics, 1983—. Contbr. articles to profl. jours. NSF grantee, 1981—. Mem. Am. Phys. Soc., Sigma Xi. Current Work: Coherent spectroscopy, nonlinear optics, atomic and molecular structure. Subspecialty: Atomic and molecular physics. Office: Dept Physics and Astronomy Univ Toldeo 2801 W Bancroft St Toledo OH 43606

TAI, PETER YAI-PO, plant geneticist; b. Chutung, Republic of China, July 6, 1937; came to U.S., 1964, naturalized, 1975; s. Yu Shu and Chomay (Liao) T.; m. Rosie Shwu-ing Peng, Jan. 30, 1964; children—Robert H., Thomas H. B.S., Nat. Taiwan U., Taipei, Republic of China, 1961; M.S., Tex. A&M U., 1966; Ph.D., Okla. State U., 1972; postdoctoral fellow, Ga. Peanut Commn., 1972-73. Research asst. Ga. Exptl. Sta., 1972-75; research geneticist Coastal Plain Exptl. Sta., Tifton, Ga., 1975-77; research geneticist plants Sugarcane Field Sta., Agrl. Research Service, U.S. Dept. Agr., Canal Point, Fla., 1977—. Contbr. articles to profl. jours. Mem. U.S. Sugar Corp. scholarship com., Clewiston, Fla., 1978—. Mem. Crop Sci. Soc. Am., Am. Soc. Agronomy, Am. Genetic Assn., AAAS, Am. Sugar Cane Technologists. Current work: Sugarcane genetics and breeding; intergeneric hybridization; pollen storage; cold tolerance in sugarcane; selection methodology. Subspecialty: Plant genetics. Home: 214 2d St PO Box 411 Canal Point FL 33438 Office: US Dept Agr-Agrl Research Service Sugarcane Field Sta Star Rt Box 8 Canal Point FL 33438

TAI, SELWYN CLARKE, podiatric physician and surgeon; b. Hong Kong, Oct. 31, 1950, came to U.S., 1962, naturalized, 1972; s. Enshui and Jean (Wong) T.; m. Helen Lim, June 2, 1979; 1 child, Gabriel. B.S. in Engring., U. Pa., 1974; D. Podiatric Medicine, Ohio Coll. Podiatric Medicine, 1980. Project engr. ECRI, Plymouth Meeting, Pa., 1974-76; resident Vancouver Gen. Hosp., B.C., Can., 1980-81; chief exec. officer Community Foot and Ankle Clinic, 1981—, dir., Renton, Wash., 1981—, Federal Way, Wash., 1984—. Mem. Am. Podiatric Med. Assn., Wash. State Podiatric Med. Assn., Internat. Coll. Podiatric Laser Surgery, Acad. of Ambulatory Foot Surgery, IEEE, Am. Pub. Health Assn., Greater Renton C. of C. Current work: Biomedical research; computer application to medical and related use; podiatric laser surgery. Subspecialties: Podiatric medicine and surgery; Laser medicine. Home: PO Box 1762 Bellevue WA 98009 Office: Community Foot and Ankle Clinic Capitol Square 720 S 320th St Federal Way WA 98003

TAI, TSZE CHENG, aerodynamicist, research scientist; b. Shaoxiang, Chekiang, China, Apr. 29, 1933; came to U.S., 1963, naturalized, 1972; m. Shih Lin Sun, Aug. 27, 1965; children: Kuangheng, Kuangkai, Kuangshin. M.S., Clemson U., 1965; Ph.D., Va. Poly. Inst., 1968. Aircraft insp. Taoyuan Airbase, Taoyuan, Taiwan, 1958-63; research asst. Clemson U., 1963-65; grad. asst. Va. Poly. Inst., 1965-67, instr., 1967-68; research scientist Naval Ship Research and Devel. Ctr., Bethesda, Md., 1968—; chmn. panel U.S. Navy Aeroballistics Com., Washington, 1978-81; lectr. von Karman Inst. Fluid Dynamics, Belgium, 1980; Prin. Potomac (Md.) Chinese Sch., 1981-82. Recipient Eugene Brooks award Naval Ship Research and Devel. Center, 1979. Assoc. fellow AIAA; mem. Sigma Xi (chmn. awards com. 1979-80). Current Work: Research in transonic aerodynamics and three-dimensional flow separation. Subspecialties: Fluid mechanics; Aerospace engineering and technology. Home: 10705 Tara Rd Potomac MD 20854 Office: David Taylor Naval Ship Research and Devel Center Code 166.3 Bethesda MD 20084

TAI, YUAN-HENG, research physiologist; b. Quinming, Yunnan, China, Aug. 14, 1941; came to U.S., 1965; s. Pei-Chih and I-Yun (Chou) T.; m. Chung-Yui Betty Li, Mar. 25, 1972; children—Katherine Chi, Kenneth C. B.S., Nat. Taiwan U., 1963; M.Phil., Yale U., 1969, Ph.D., 1971. Postdoctoral assoc. Yale U., New Haven, 1971-74, research assoc., 1974-76; research physiologist Walter Reed Army Research Inst., Washington, 1976—. Contbr.: articles to profl. jours. including Gastroenterology. Mem. Am. Physiol. Soc., Biophys. Soc., N.Y. Acad. Scis. Current Work: Membrane physiology and biophysics, particularly the transport mechanisms of electrolytes and non-electrolytes across biological membranes. Subspecialties: Physiology (medicine); Biophysics (physics). Home: 5417 Wehawken Rd Bethesda MD 20816 Office: Walter Reed Army Inst Research Washington DC 20307

TAINTOR, JERRY FRANK, dental educator, researcher; b. Trenton, Aug. 10, 1942; s. Aubra Ray and Frances Lilly (Marek) Nooncaster; m. Mary Jane McComas, Feb. 1, 1965. B.S., Okla. State U., 1965; D.D.S., U. Mo.-Kansas City, 1967; M.S., U. Iowa, 1975. Asst. prof. Med. Coll. Ga., 1975-76, U. Nebr.-Lincoln, 1976-79; assoc. prof. endodontics, chmn. dept. UCLA, 1979—; cons. Sepulveda VA Hosp., Los Angeles, 1982—. Author: (with J.I. Ingle) Endodontics, 1982; contbr. (with J.I. Ingle) numerous articles to profl. jours. Bd. dirs. Am. Cancer Soc., Alaska, 1971. Med. Coll. Ga. grantee, 1975-76; U. Nebr. grantee, 1977-78. Fellow So. Calif. Acad. Endodontics; mem. AAUP (v.p. UCLA chpt. 1981-82, pres. 1982-83), Am. Assn. Endodontics (chmn. com. 1979—), ADA, Clyde Davis Endodontic Study Club (sec. 1977-80). Democrat. Presbyterian. Current Work: Research on pulpal biology. Subspecialty: Endodontics. Home: 5021 Tilden Ave Sherman Oaks CA 91423 Office: UCLA Sch Dentistry Center Health Scis Los Angeles CA 90024

TAJIMA, TOSHIKI, plasma physicist, educator; b. Nagoya, Japan, Jan. 18, 1948; came to U.S., 1973; s. Hidetoshi and Fumiko (Tsuda) T.; m. Fumiko Chiba, July 7, 1973; children—Mika, Yuhki. B.S., U. Tokyo, 1971, M.S., 1973; Ph.D., U. Calif.-Irvine, 1975. Teaching cert. Ministry of Edn. Japan. Asst. research physicist UCLA, 1976-80, asst. group leader, 1977-80, assoc. research physicist, 1980; asst. prof. physics U. Tex., Austin, 1980-85, assoc. prof., 1985—; vis. scientist Los Alamos Nat. Lab., 1983—; cons. Western Research Corp., San Diego, Calif., 1978—. Author: Computational Plasma Physics, 1985. Japan Soc. Promotion of Sci. fellow, 1973-75; NSF grantee, 1980-87. Mem. Am. Phys. Soc., Phys. Soc. Japan, Am. Geophys. Union, NRC. Club: Lost Creek Country (Austin). Current work: Plasma physics in general; in particular nonlinear plasma physics, computer simulation, applications to fusion, solar physics, geophysics. Subspecialties: Plasma physics; Solar physics. Office: Dept Physics Inst Fusion Studies Univ Texas Austin TX 78712

TAKAHASHI, HIRONORI, physicist; b. Tokyo, June 5, 1942; came to U.S., 1965; s. Hideo and Fumi (Kojima) T. B. Engring., Keio U., Tokyo, 1965; M.S., MIT, 1967, Sc.D., 1970. Alexander vonHumboldt postdoctoral fellow U Stuttgart, Fed. Republic Germany, 1971-72, vis. lectr., 1972-73; postdoctoral fellow Princeton U., N.J., 1973-75, research staff mem., 1975-79, 80—; mem. research staff MIT, Cambridge, 1979-80. Mem. Am. Phys. Soc. Current work: Plasma physics; controlled thermonuclear fusion research; plasma waves; equilibrium and stability of magnetically confined plasmas; tokamaks. Subspecialty: Plasma physics. Office: Plasma Physics Lab Princeton U Princeton NJ 08544

TAKAHASHI, JOSEPH S., neuroscience educator; b. Tokyo, Dec. 16, 1951 (parents Am. citizens); s. Shigeharu and Hiroko (Hara) T. B.A. in Biology, Swarthmore Coll., 1974; Ph.D., U. Oreg., 1981. Research assoc. NIMH, Bethesda, Md., 1981-83; asst. prof. dept. neurobiology, physiology Northwestern U., Evanston, Ill., 1983—. Contbr. articles to profl. jours. Fellow USPHS, 1975-76, 79-81, NSF, 1976-79, NIH, 1981-83, Alfred P. Sloan, 1983-85; Searle scholar, 1985-88; NSF Presdl. young investigator, 1985-90. Mem. AAAS, Soc. Neurosci., Assn. Research Vision and Opthalmology. Current work: Cellular regulation of circadian rhythms and photoreception. Subspecialties: Neurobiology; Chronobiology. Office: Dept Neurobiology and Physiology Northwestern U Hogan Hall Evanston IL 60201

TAKAHASHI, YASUSHI, physics educator; b. Osaka, Japan, Dec. 12, 1924; s. Momochi and Chise (Miyata) T.; m. Elizabeth Mary Maclaughlin, Sept. 15, 1959; children—Atsushi Mark, Hiroshi Jerome. B.Sc., Nagoya U., Japan, 1951, D.Sc., 1954. Research assoc. U. Rochester, N.Y., 1954, State U. Iowa, 1955-57; postdoctoral fellow Nat. Research Council Can., 1954-55; research assoc. Dublin Inst. for Advanced Studies, Ireland, 1957-58, asst. prof., 1958-60, prof., 1960-68; prof. dept. physics U. Alta., Edmonton, 1968—, dir. Theoretical Physics Inst., 1969-72, 83—; vis. prof. Inst. for Solid State Physics, U. Tokyo, 1972-73; sr. research fellow, dept. physics Imperial Coll., Eng., 1980; vis. prof. dept. physics Tsukuba U., Japan, 1980-81. Author: Introduction to Field Quantization, 1969; Renormalization Theory I, 1973; Renormalization Theory II, 1973; Quantum Field Theory for Solid State Physicists, Vol. I, 1974, Vol. II, 1976; Analytical Dynamics, 1978; Path from Classical to Quantum Fields, 1979; Analytical Dynamics of Classical Fields, 1982. Contbr. articles to profl. jours. Fellow Am. Phys. Soc.; mem. Royal Irish Acad. Shinto. Current work: Quantum field theory and many-body problems. Subspecialty: Theoretical physics. Office: Theoretical Physics Inst Dept Physics U Alberta Edmonton AB T6G 2J1 Canada

TAKANO, MASAHARU, physical chemist, researcher; b. Tainan, Taiwan, Jan. 20, 1935; came to U.S., 1967, naturalized, 1973; s. Syuzo and Misao (Rengakuji) T.; m. Hiroko Takenoshita, Aug. 28, 1965; children—Kentaro, Jojiro, Miwako. B.S., Hokkaido U., Sapporo, Japan, 1957; M.S., U. Tokyo, 1959, D.Sc., 1963. Research cons. Takasago Rubber Industry, Tokyo, 1959-63; sr. research chemist Monsanto Co., St. Louis, 1967-68, research specialist, 1968-79, sr. research specialist, 1979—. Contbr. articles to profl. jours. Patentee in field. Mem. Japanese Am. Citizens League, St. Louis, 1970—, bd. dirs., 1974, 75; mem. Japan Am. Soc. St. Louis. Japan Soc. for Promotion of Sci. Postdoctoral fellow U. Tokyo, 1962-63; Nat. Research Council Can. fellow McGill U., 1963-65; NIH fellow McGill U., 1965-67. Fellow Am. Inst. Chemists (cert.); mem. Am. Chem. Soc., Am. Phys. Soc., AAAS, N.Y. Acad. Scis., Soc. Rheology, Fine Particle Soc., Japan Soc. Polymer Sci., Japan Soc. Materials Sci., Sigma Xi. Buddhist. Current work: Physical chemistry; polymers; composites; development of industrial process; biotechnologies; international trade of technologies; international business and communications. Subspecialties: Physical chemistry; Chemical engineering. Home: 13146 Roundstone Ct Saint Louis MO 63146 Office: Monsanto Co 800 N Lindbergh Blvd Saint Louis MO 63167

TAKEDA, HARUNORI, physicist; b. Tokyo, Sept. 10, 1948; s. Masami and Mikiko (Hayaski) T.; m. Young-Ja Choi, Dec. 25, 1976; children—Theodore, Miyuki. B.S. in Physics, Waseda U., Tokyo, 1971; Ph.D. in Physics, U. Pa., 1978. Postdoctural appointee Argonne Nat. Lab., Ill., 1978-80, asst. physicist, 1981; research scientist KMS Fusion, Inc., Ann Arbor, Mich., 1982-84; staff physicist Los Alamos Nat. Lab., N.Mex., 1985—. Contbr. articles to tech. jours. Mem. Am. Phys. Soc., IEEE. Current works: Particle accelerator related design and accelerator theory; free electron laser. Subspecialties: Free-electron lasers; Fusion. Home: 682 Callecita Jicarilla Sante Fe NM 87505 Office: Los Alamos Nat Lab PO Box 1663 MS-H829 Los Alamos NM 87545

TAKEMOTO, DOLORES JEAN, educator biochemistry, researcher; b. Indpls., May 5, 1949; d. Joseph Paul and Anna Marie (Zimmermann) Feld; m. Larry Jun Takemoto, Sept. 2, 1972; children—Michelle, Lauren. B.S., Ball State U., 1971; M.S., Colo. State U., 1973; Ph.D., U. So. Calif., 1979. Postdoctoral fellow Kans. State U., Manhattan, 1979-82, research asst. prof., 1982-84, asst. prof., 1984—. Contbr. chpts. to books, articles to profl. jours. Active United Campus to Prevent Nuclear War, Washington, 1984. Recipient Am. Cancer Soc. postdoctoral fellow, 1979-81; Leukemia Soc. Spl. fellow, 1981-83; Tech. Transfer award Internat. Union Against Cancer, Eng., 1984. Mem. Assn. Research Vision and Ophthalmology, Am. Assn. Cancer Research. Democrat. Lutheran. Current work: Biochemistry of retinal rod outer segments and retinal degenerations; development of immune response modifiers. Subspecialties: Biochemistry (biology); Membrane biology. Office: Kans State U Dept Biochemistry Willard Hall Manhattan KS 66506

TAKEUCHI, TAKAO, physics educator; b. Nagoya, Japan, Feb. 16, 1945; came to U.S., 1970; s. Masataka and Kinko (Owaki) T.; m. Keiko Fukuda, Dec. 26, 1983. B.S., Nagoya U., 1967; M.S., Kanazawa U., Japan, 1970; Ph.D., U. N.C., 1976. Asst. prof. physics N.C. Central U., Durham, 1977-82; SUNY-Alfred, 1983—. Author: Advances in Ceramics, 1984. Mem. Am. Phys. Soc., Phys. Soc. Japan. Current work: Solid state physics, education and research. Subspecialty: Condensed matter physics. Home: 2 Hillcrest Ct Alfred NY 14802 Office: Dept Physics SUNY Alfred NY 14802

TALBOT, LEE MERRIAM, ecologist; b. New Bedford, Mass. Aug. 2, 1930; s. Murrell Williams, and Zenaida (Merriam) T.; m. Martha Walcott Hayne, May 16, 1959; children—Lawrence Hayne, Russell Merriam. Cert., Deep Springs Coll., 1949; B.A., U. Calif., 1953, M.A., Ph.D., 1963. Biologist, Arctic Research Lab., Point Barrow, Alaska, 1951; staff ecologist Internat. Union for Conservation of Nature and Natural Resources, Brussels, 1954-56; dir. East African research project Nat. Acad. Scis., Govts. of Kenya and Tanzania, 1959-63; wildlife and ecology advisor UN Spl. Fund, Africa, 1963-64; dir. S.E. Asia project Internat. Union for Conservation Nature and Natural Resources, 1965-66; ecologist, field rep. for internat. affairs Smithsonian Instn., Washington, 1966-70, research assoc., 1970-78; sr. scientist, dir. internat. affairs Pres.'s Council on Environ. Quality, Washington, 1970-78; hon. cons. World Wildlife Fund Internat., Morges, Switzerland, 1973, dir. conservation, spl. sci. advisor, 1978-80; dir. gen. Internat. Union for Conservation Nature and Natural Resources, Geneva, 1980-83; research fellow East-West Environment and Policy Inst., Honolulu, Washington, 1983—; vis. fellow World Resources Inst., Washington, 1984—; sr. sci. advisor Internat. Council Sci. Unions, Paris, 1978-83; cons. World Bank, Washington, 1984, UN orgns., Nat. Acad. Scis., African, Am., Asian, Australian, European govts., other non-govt. orgns., industries, 1956—. Author: Wildebeest in Masailand, 1963; documentary film, Man, Beast and the Land, 1968; New Principles for Conservation of Living Resources, 1978, others. Contbr. numerous monographs, sci. and tech. articles to profl. jours. and popular mags. Pres., Cornwell Homeowners Assn. No. Va., 1973-76; pack chmn. Boy Scouts Am., Geneva, 1979-82; capt. Westmoreland Citizens Watch Assn., No. Va., 1984. Served to lt. USMCR, 1953-54. Recipient Fgn. Field Research award Nat. Acad. Scis., 1959, Union Wildlife Found. award U. Calif., 1962, Outstanding Publ. award Sports Car Club Am., 1962, Albert Schweitzer medal Animal Welfare Inst., 1975; named to Order of Lion, Republic of Senegal, 1981; hon. fellow Population Reference Bur., Washington, 1975. Fellow Acad. Medicine, AAAS, N.Y. Zool. Soc., Royal Geog. Soc. (London), Royal Soc. Arts (London); mem. Am. Inst. Biol. Scis. (Disting. Service award 1979), Am. Soc. Mammalogists (life), Internat. Assn. Ecology, Wildlife Soc. (life mem., Outstanding Publ. award 1963), Fauna Soc. (London) (v.p. 1976—), Zool. Soc. Korea (hon.), Explorers Club, Sigma Xi. Clubs: Cosmos (Washington); Boone and Crockett (v.p. 1972-78). Current work: Incorporating environmental concerns in economic development; environmental assessment; development of environmental policy; maintenance of biological diversity including endangered species conservation; living resource management. Subspecialties: Ecology (environmental science); Resource conservation. Home: 6656 Chilton Ct McLean VA 22101 Office: World Resources Inst 1735 New York Ave NW Washington DC 20006

TALBOT, RICHARD BURRITT, veterinary medicine educator; b. Waterville, Kans., Jan. 4, 1933; s. Roy Benjamin and Aleta Maude (Stone) T.; m. Mary Jane Hensley, May 24, 1953; children—Richard Lee, Andrea Jean. B.S., Kans. State U., 1954, D.V.M., 1958; Ph.D., Iowa State U., 1963. From instr. to assoc. prof. Iowa State U., Ames, 1958-65; prof. physiology, chmn. dept. physiology U.Ga., Athens, 1965-67, prof. physiology, dean Coll. Vet. Medicine, 1967-74; prof. physiology Va. Poly. Inst. and State U., Blacksburg, 1974—, dean Coll. Vet. Medicine, 1974-84, dean emeritus, 1984—; dir. Hazleton Labs. Corp., Vienna, Va., 1st Va. Bank of S.W., Roanoke; cons. FDA, Washington, 1980—. Editor Jour. Vet. Med. Edn., 1978—. Commr., Boy Scouts Am. NIH postdoctoral fellow Baylor Coll. Medicine, Houston, 1960. Mem. AVMA, Am Physiol. Soc., Assn. Am. Vet. Med. Colls., Am. Soc. Vet. Physiologists and pharmacologists, Va. Vet. Med. Assn. Republican. Presbyterian. Lodges: Rotary, Ruritan. Subspecialties: Veterinary physiology; Toxicology (medicine). Home: Route 2 Box 561 Newport VA 24128 Office: VA Poly Inst and State U Coll Vet Medicine Va Tech Campus Blacksburg VA 24061

TALBOT, JR. TIMOTHY RALPH, physician, educator; b. Berkeley, Calif., July 14, 1916; s. Timothy Ralph and Caroline Eleanor (Lowe) T.; m. Mary Wallace Robinson, Oct. 16, 1943; children—Timothy R., Mary Talbot Havens, William R., Lucy Talbot Myers, David Campbell. A.B., U. Pa., 1937, M.D., 1941. Diplomate Am. Bd. Internal Medicine. Intern Pa. Hosp., 1941-42; asst. resident in medicine Boston U., 1946-48; asst. mem. Sloan Kettering, N.Y.C., 1948-51; asst. prof. U. Pa., Phila., 1951-65, assoc. prof. medicine, 1966—; Nat. Cancer Inst. fellow Chester Beatty Research Inst., London, 1956-57; dir. Inst. Cancer Research, Phila., 1957-74; pres. Fox Chace Cancer Ctr., Phila., 1974-81, emeritus, 1981—. Contbr. articles on med. sphere to profl. jours. Active, Diversified Community Services, Phila., 1952-83; mem. Pa. Sci. Adv. Com., 1966-75; mem. Pa. Cancer Control Prevention and Research Adv. Bd., 1980—; chmn. cancer control grant rev. com. Nat. Cancer Inst., 1974-78; mem. task force on HMOs, Nat. Exec. Service Corps, 1981-84. Served to lt. comdr. USNR, 1942-46. Mem. Assn. Am. Cancer Inst. (founding mem., pres. 1968-81), AAAS. Club: Union League. Current work: Creation and development of Fox Chase Cancer Center in Philadelphia. Subspecialties: Cancer research (medicine); Oncology. Office: Fox Chase Cancer Ctr 7701 Burholme Ave Philadelphia PA 19111

TALIAFERRO, CHARLES MILLARD, plant geneticist, educator; b. Leon, Okla., Mar. 1, 1940; s. Benjamin Ernest and Haughty (Davis) T.; m. Anna Kathrine Young; children—Michael Brent, Jason O'Neal, Mark Allen. B.S. in Agronomy, Okla. State U., 1962; M.S. in Agronomy, Tex. A&M U., 1965, Ph.D. in Plant Breeding and Genetics, 1966. Research agronomist USDA Agrl. Research Service, Tifton, Ga., 1965-68; asst. prof. agronomy, Okla. State U., Stillwater, 1968-71, assoc. prof., 1971-76, prof., 1976—; King lectr. U. Ark., Fayetville, 1984. Contbr. articles to sci. jours. NDEA fellow, 1962. Mem. Am. Soc. Agronomy, Am. Genetics Assn., Am. Forage and Grasslands Council, So. Pasture and Forage Crop Assn. (chmn. 1974), Sigma Xi. Democrat. Baptist. Current work: Breeding of improved grasses for herbage and turf; study of inheritance and genetic control of plant characters related to varietal performance; development of improved breeding procedures. Subspecialties: Plant genetics; Agronomy. Home: 1402 N Jardot St Stillwater OK 74075 Office: Agronomy Dept Okla State U Stillwater OK 74078

TALLAN, NORMAN M., defense materials laboratory administrator, materials researcher; b. Newark, Sept. 24, 1932; s. Max and Anna (Barer) T.; m. Joan Judith Harnett, Aug. 24, 1958; children—Mitchell, Eric, Mark, Daniel. B.S. in Ceramics, Rutgers U., 1954; M.S. in Ceramic Engring., Ohio State U., 1955; Ph.D. in Ceramics, Alfred U., 1959. Sr. scientist Aerospace Research Labs., Wright-Patterson AFB, Ohio, 1969-70, dir. metals and ceramics lab., 1970-75; sr. scientist Air Force Materials Lab., Wright-Patterson AFB, 1975-78; chief scientist Aero. Labs, Materials Lab., Wright-Patterson AFB, 1978-82, chief metals and ceramics div., 1983—; asst. dep. for advanced tech. Office Asst. Soc. of U.S. Air Force, Washington, 1982-83. Editor: Electrical Conductivity of Ceramics, 1974. Contbr. articles on defect structure and transport properties of ceramics to profl. jours. Fellow Am. Ceramic Soc. (Ross Coffin Purdy award 1967); mem. Am. Phys. Soc., Sigma Xi. Current work: Research and development related to materials for aircraft, missile and space structures, high temperature materials for turbine engines, processing science, mechanics of materials, NDE. Subspecialties: Materials (engineering); Ceramics. Home: 3743 Greenbay Dr Dayton OH 45415 Office: AFWAL Materials Lab AFWAL/MLL Wright-Patterson AFB Dayton OH 45433

TALLENT, WILLIAM HUGH, research administrator, biochemist; b. Akron, Ohio, May 28, 1928; s. Charles Othar and Agnes Annette (Johnson) T.; m. Joy Anne Redfield, Aug. 23, 1952; children—Elizabeth Ann, Cinda Marie, Raymond Charles. B.S. in Chemistry, U. Tenn., 1949, M.S. in Organic Chemistry, 1950; Ph.D. in Biochemistry, U. Ill., 1953. Research chemist Nat. Heart Inst., Bethesda, Md., 1953-57, G.D. Searle & Co., Skokie, Ill., 1957-64; supr. research chemist No. Regional Research Ctr., U.S. Dept. Agr., Peoria, Ill., 1964-75, dir., 1975-83, dep. adminstr. Northeastern Region Agrl. Research Service, Beltsville, Md., 1983-84, asst. adminstr., 1984—; U.S. del. FAO-WHO-Codex Vege Prot Com., 1980—. Contbr. articles to profl. jours. Recipient Disting. Service to Agr. award Ill. chpt. Gamma Sigma Delta, 1979. Mem. AAAS, Am. Chem. Soc., Am. Oil Chemists Soc. (assoc. editor jour. 1970-83, World Conf. chmn. 1980, treas. 1982-84), Inst. Food Technologists, Soc. Econ. Botany (council chmn. 1974-76, Disting. Econ. Botanist 1981). Current work: Coordination of cooperative research and other interactions between the Agricultural Research Service and industry, academe and other government agencies. Subspecialties: Food science and technology; Biochemistry (biology). Office: US Dept Agr Agrl Research Service Room 358-A Admintrn Bldg Washington DC 20250

TALLEY, ROBERT LEE, researcher; b. Eureka, Kans., Nov. 25, 1933; s. Kenneth Carl and Adelaide Jean (Welsh) T.; m. Ann Quarles Wallace, Dec. 19, 1956; children—Robert Sean, Christopher Wallace, James Quarles, Timothy Welsh. B.A., U. Kans., 1955; M.A., 1956; student SUNY-Buffalo, 1963-74. Research physicist Cornell Aero. Lab., Buffalo, 1961-67, head kinetics sect., 1967-70; mem. product devel. group Calspan Corp., Buffalo, 1971-74; tech. dir. Pelorex Corp., Buffalo, 1974-75; sr. research physicist Falcon Research, Buffalo, 1976-83; prin. physicist Veritay Tech., Inc., East Amherst, N.Y., 1983—; cons. Pelorex Corp., Buffalo, 1970-74. Contbr. articles to profl. jours.; patentee in field. Bd. dirs. Elma-Marilla-Wales Jr. Football, N.Y., 1975-78; coach Little League Baseball, Amherst, N.Y., 1969-74, Little League Football, Amherst, 1970-74. Served to lt. USN, 1956-61. Mem. Am. Astron. Soc., N.Y. Acad. Scis., Am. Def. Preparedness Assn., Sigma Xi, Phi Beta Kappa, Sigma Pi Sigma (sec. 1956), Pi Kappa Alpha (v.p. 1955). Republican. Episcopalian. Current work: Research in advanced ordnance systems, materials and processes including: liquid propellant and high velocity guns; caseless, smart and ablative ammunition; improved barrels,; transient combustion processes; internal ballistics; thermal, wear, erosion and corrosion phenomena; terminal effects; and diagnostic instrumentation. Subspecialties: Aerosol and small macroscopic particle physics; Combustion processes. Home: S 2221 Eastwood Rd East Aurora NY 14052 Office: Veritay Tech Inc 4845 Millersport Hwy East Amherst NY 14051-305

TALLEY, THOMAS JAMES, electrical engineer, researcher, consultant; b. Fort Worth, Oct. 30, 1945; s. Paul Judson and Mary Irene (Conner) T.; m. Linda Jean Dugger, May 15, 1970; children—John Paul, Jo Ann. B.E.E., Tex. A&M U., 1971, M.S., 1979, D.Engring., 1982. Registered profl. engr., Tex. Engr., Tex. Elec. Service Co., Fort Worth, 1972-80; sr. systems research and devel. specialist Rockwell Internat., Richardson, Tex., 1980-81; lead elec. engr. TMI Engring. Group, Comanche Peak/Glen Rose, Tex., 1981-82; asst. to project gen. mgr. Comanche Peak Nuclear Facility, Glen Rose, 1982-83; mgr. research Tex. Utilities Generating Co., Dallas, 1983—. Mem. devel. team for arcing fault detection system (Outstanding Engring. Achievement award Nat. Soc. Profl. Engrs. 1981). Adviser Longhorn council Boy Scouts Am., 1976. Served with USAF, 1964-68. Mem. IEEE, Tesco Amateur Radio Assn. (pres. 1975-76), Cleburne Amateur Radio Assn. (pres. 1982-83), Sigma Xi (assoc.), Eta Kappa Nu. Lodge: Masons. Current work: Internal telecommunications consulting and management. Research administration and following-steering comittees, task forces chairman and member. Subspecialties: Electrical engineering; Computer engineering. Office: Tex Utilities Generating Co 400 N Olive LB 81 Dallas TX 75201

TALMAGE, DAVID WILSON, physician, medical educator, university administrator; b. Kwangju, Korea, Sept. 15, 1919; s. John Van Neste and Eliza (Emerson) T.; m. LaVeryn Marie Hunicke, June 23, 1944; children: Janet, Marilyn, David, Mark, Carol. Student, Maryville (Tenn.) Coll., 1937-38; B.S., Davidson (N.C.) Coll., 1941; M.D., Washington U., St. Louis, 1944. Intern Ga. Baptist Hosp., 1944-45; resident medicine Barnes Hosp., St. Louis, 1948-50, fellow medicine, 1950-51; asst. prof. pathology U. Pitts., 1951-52; asst. prof., then assoc. prof. medicine U. Chgo., 1952-59; prof. medicine U. Colo., 1959—, prof. microbiology, 1960—, chmn. dept., 1963-65, assoc. dean, 1966-68, 83—, dean, 1969-71; dir. Webb-Waring Lung Inst., 1973-83; mem. nat. council Nat. Inst. Allergy and Infectious Diseases, NIH, 1963-66, 73-77. Author: (with John Cann) Chemistry of Immunity in Health and Disease; editor: Jour. Allergy, 1963-67, (with M. Samter) Immunological Diseases. Served with M.C. AUS, 1945-48. Markle scholar, 1955-60. Mem. Am. Acad. Allergy (pres.), Am. Assn. Immunologists (pres.), Am. Acad. Arts and Scis., Nat. Acad. Scis., Inst. Medicine, Phi Beta Kappa. Current Work: Transplantation and tumor immunology. Subspecialties: Immunobiology and immunology; Allergy. Office: U Colo Sch Medicine Denver CO 80262

TALTY, ROBERT DEAN, research company executive; b. Mpls., Oct. 2, 1924; s. Clifford William and Carol esther (Butterworth) T.; m. Dorothy Melva Willis, Dec. 21, 1953. B.S. in Chem. Engring., U. Kans., 1949; Ph.D. in Chem. Engring., U. Del., 1953; M.B.A., So. Ill. U., 1976. Registered profl. engr., Ill. Research engr. Amoco Oil, Whiting, Ind., 1953-57; sr. engr. Monsanto, Pensacola, Fla., 1957-63; tech. mgr. Teepak, Inc., Danville, Ill., 1963-79; br. mgr. Dept. Energy, Grand Forks, N.D., 1979-81; pres. Heat Transfer Research, Inc., South Pasadena, Calif., 1981—. Contbr. articles to profl. jours. Patentee in field. Served with U.S. Army, 1943-46, ETO. Mem. Am. Inst. Chem. Engrs., Am. Chem. Soc., Sigma Xi, Tau Beta Pi, Sigma Pi Sigma. Club: Toastmasters. Lodge: Elks. Subspecialty: Chemical engineering. Office: Heat Transfer Research Inc 1499 Huntington Dr Suite 409 South Pasadena CA 91030

TALUKDAR, SAROSH N., electrical and computer engineering educator; b. Poona, India, Apr. 22, 1942; came to U.S., 1964, naturalized, 19; s. Naval and Roshen T. B.Tech., Madras, India, 1964; M.S. in Elec. Engring., Purdue U., 1966, Ph.D., 1970. Sr. staff engr. McGraw-Edison Co., Canonsburg, Pa., 1969-76; asst. prof. Carnegie Mellon U., Pitts., after 1974, assoc. prof., 1981, prof. elec. and computer engring., 1981—, dir. Design Research Ctr., 1983—; cons. in field. Assoc. editor IEEE Transactions on CAD, 1980-83. Sr. mem. IEEE. Current work: Computer aided design, expert systems, intelligent computer aided instruction. Subspecialties: Electrical engineering; Computer-aided design. Office: Elec and Computer Engring Dept Carnegie-Mellon U Pittsburgh PA 15213

TAM, ANDREW CHING, physicist; b. Canton, Kwangtung, China, Oct. 13, 1944; came to U.S., 1970, naturalized, 1984; s. Simon and Grace Tam; m. Eugenia U. Yip, Mar. 3, 1970; children—Miriam, Adela. M.Sc., U. Hong Kong, 1970; Ph.D., Columbia U., 1975. Asst. prof. Columbia U., N.Y.C., 1977-78; mem. tech. staff Bell Telephone Lab., Murray Hill, N.J., 1978-79; mem. research staff IBM Research Lab, San Jose, Calif., 1979-85, mgr., 1985—. Contbr. chpt. to book. Mem. Am. Phys. Soc., Optical Soc. Am. Roman Catholic. Current work: Laser applications; optics; ultrasonics; photoacoustics. Subspecialties: Atomic and molecular physics; Acoustics. Office: IBM Research Lab Dept KO6-282 San Jose CA 95193

TAM, STEVE YIK-KAI, chemist; b. Hong Kong, May 31, 1947; came to U.S. 1974, naturalized 1979; s. Pak-Him and Wai-Hing (Gum) T.; m. Judy Sabina Chan, May 19, 1973; children—Jeffrey K., Jonathan K. B.Sc. cum laude, Chinese U. Hong Kong, 1968; Ph.D., U. Waterloo, Ont., Can., 1974. Postdoctoral fellow Sloan Kettering Inst. for Cancer Research, Rye, N.Y., 1974-75, research assoc., 1975-79; sr. scientist Hoffman La Roche Inc., Nutley, N.J., 1979—. Contbr. articles to profl. jours. Mem. Am. Chem. Soc., N.Y. Acad. Scis., Sigma Xi. Current work: Use of carbohydrate chemistry in the synthesis of natural products and medicinally useful compounds. Subspecialty: Organic chemistry. Office: Chem Research Dept Bldg 76 Hoffmann La Roche Inc Nutley NJ 07110

TAMARIN, ROBERT HARVEY, population biologist, educator; b. Bklyn., Dec. 14, 1942; s. Leon and Zelda R. (Hirsch) T.; m. Virginia M. Londy, May 31, 1968; children: David L., Bonnie. B.S., CUNY, 1963; Ph.D., Ind. U., 1968. Postdoctoral fellow U. Hawaii, 1968-70; research assoc. Princeton U., 1970-71; asst. prof. Boston U., 1971-77, assoc. prof. biology, 1977-83, prof. biology, 1983—. Author: Population Regulation, 1978, Principles of Genetics, 1985, Biology of New World Microtus, 1985, also articles, abstracts, book revs. NIH grantee, 1972-76, 78-81, 85—; NSF grantee, 1981-84. Mem. AAAS, Am. Soc. Mammalogists, Am. Soc. Naturalists. Current Work: Population regulation in small animals; behavior, genetics, demography, reproductive physiology of island and mainland voles; sociobiology using radionuclides. Subspecialties: Population biology; Evolutionary biology. Office: Dept Biology Boston U Boston MA 02215

TAMM, IGOR, biologist, educator; b. Tapa, Estonia, Apr. 27, 1922; came to U.S., 1945, naturalized, 1954; s. Alexander and Olga T.; m. Olive Emma Pitkin, May 9, 1953; children—Carol, Eric, Ellen. Student, Tartu (Estonia) U., 1942-43, Karolinska Inst., Stockholm, 1944-45; M.D. cum laude, Yale U., 1947. Intern, then asst. resident in medicine Grace-New Haven Community Hosp. Univ. Service, 1947-49; also asst. in medicine Yale U. Med. Sch.; mem staff and faculty Rockefeller Inst., N.Y.C., 1949—, prof., sr. physician, 1964—; chmn. bd. sci. cons. Sloan-Kettering Inst., 1972-73; chmn. task force virology Nat. Inst. Allergy and Infectious Diseases, 1976-78; Centennial lectr. U. Ill., 1968. Author, editor papers and jours. in field. Recipient Alfred Benzon Found. prize, 1967, Sarah L. Poiley Meml. award N.Y. Acad. Scis., 1977. Fellow N.Y. Acad. Scis., AAAS; mem. Am. Soc. Microbiology, Am. Assn. Immunology, Soc. Exptl. Biology and Medicine, Am. Soc. Clin. Investigation, Am. Acad. Microbiology, Am. Soc. Cell Biology, Soc. Gen. Microbiology, Assn. Am. Physicians, Nat. Acad. Scis., Harvey Soc. (pres. 1974-75), Sigma Xi, Alpha Omega Alpha. Current Work: Interferon action; cell cycle and motility; cytoskeleton; effects of transforming viruses and growth factors on cells; RNA transcription; DNA replication. Subspecialties: Virology (biology); Cell biology. Office: 1230 York Ave New York NY 10021

TAMMINGA, CAROL ANN, psychiatrist, educator; b. Grand Rapids, Mich., Jan. 26, 1946; d. Samuel William and Freda (Hekman) T.; m. James Harmon Hengeveld, Mar. 30, 1967 (div. Jan. 1975); children—Cristan Fredericka, Bonnie Michelle. B.A., Calvin Coll., 1966; M.D., Vanderbilt Sch. Medicine, 1971. Diplomate Am. Bd. Psychiatry. Asst. prof. U. Chgo., 1975-78; guest worker Nat. Inst. Mental Health, Bethesda, Md., 1978-79; assoc. prof. psychiatry U. Md., Balt., 1979-85, prof., 1985—; guest scientist Nat. Inst. Neurol. and Communicative Diseases and Stroke, NIH, 1979—; cons. in field. Contbr. multiple articles to profl. jours. Recipient Sandoz award for psychiatric research U. Chgo., 1975, McAlpin award Nat. Assn. Mental Health, 1979; fellow Vivian Allen, 1968-71, Found. For Research Psychiatry, 1975-76; Beauchamp scholar, 1971. Mem. Am. Psychiatric Assn., Internat. Psychoneuroendocrine Soc., AAAS, Soc. Neurosci., Biol. Psychiatry, Am. Coll. Neuropharmacology. Current work: Study of pathophysiology of schizophenia and strategies for pharmacotherapy; role of neuropeptide systems in human brain function. Subspecialties: Psychopharmacology; Neuropharmacology. Office: Box 3235 Baltimore MD 21184

TAMURA, TSUNENOBU, nutrition researcher, educator; b. Tokyo, Dec. 15, 1938; came to U.S., 1969; s. Shiro and Miwa (Sasaki) T.; m. Atsuko Ohnuma, Sept. 30, 1973; children—Yoshiko, Nobunori. M.D., Fukushima Med. Coll., Japan, 1964; D. Med. Scis., Tohoku U., Sendai, Japan, 1973. Research biochemist U. Calif.-Berkeley, 1970-73, asst. research biochemist, 1976-78; adj. asst. prof. U. Calif.-Davis, 1978-82; asst. prof. nutrition scis. U. Ala., Birmingham, 1982—. Contbr. articles to profl. jours. Nat. Council on Alcoholism fellow, 1978-79; NIH grantee, 1984—. Mem. Am. Inst. Nutrition, Am. Soc. Clin. Nutrition, Am. Fedn. Clin. Research, Research Soc. Alcoholism, N.Y. Acad. Scis. Current work: Folate metabolism, vitamin and trace mineral interactions, zinc nutrition and perinatal nutrition. Subspecialties: Nutrition (medicine); Pediatrics. Home: 2209 Pine Crest Dr Birmingham AL 35216 Office: U Ala Dept Nutrition Scis Birmingham AL 35294

TAN, ENG MENG, biomedical scientist; b. Seremban, Maalysia, Aug. 26, 1926; came to U.S., 1950; s. Ming Kee and Chooi Eng (Ang) T.; m. Liselotte Filippi, June 30, 1962; children: Philip, Peter. B.A., Johns Hopkins U., 1952, M.D., 1956. Asst. prof. Washington U. Sch. Medicine, St. Louis, 1965-67; assoc. mem. Scripps Clinic and Research Found., LaJolla, Calif., 1967-70, mem., 1970-77, dir. autoimmune disease ctr., 1982—; prof. U. Colo. Sch. Medicine, Denver, 1977-82; chmn. allergy and immunology research com. NIH, Bethesda, Md., 1980-82; mem. nat. arthritis adv. bd. HHS, Washington, 1981-85. Contbr. chpts. to books, articles to profl. jours. Named to Nat. Lupus Hall of Fame, 1984. Mem. Arthritis Found. (pres. San Diego chpt. 1974-75), Am. Rheumatism Assn. (chmn. lupus com. 1980-82, pres. 1984-85), United Scleroderma Found. (ann. award 1982), Assn. Am. Physicians, Am. Soc. Clin. Investigation, Western Assn. Physicians (v.p. 1980-81), Am. Assn. Immunologists (hon.), Argentina Rheumatism Assn. (hon.), Australian Rheumatism Assn. Patentee in field. Current Work: Characterization of autoantibodies in autoimmune diseases; systemic lupus erythematosus, scleroderma, sjogren's syndrome, myositis and mixed connective tissue disease; relationship of autoantibodies to pathogenesis. Subspecialties: Cell biology (medicine); Rheumatology. Home: 8303 Sugarman Dr La Jolla CA 92037 Office: Scripps Clinic and Research Found 10666 N Torrey Pines Rd La Jolla CA 92037

TANAKA, KAY, genetics educator, physician; b. Osaka, Japan, Mar. 2, 1929; came to U.S., 1969; s. Kumaji and Fusa (Nakamae) Tanaka; m. Tomoko Hasegawa, Nov. 3, 1954; children—Atau, Elly Margaret. M.D., U. Tokyo, 1956; Dr. Med. Scis., 1962; M.A. (hon.), Yale U., 1983. Vis. asst. prof. Baylor Med. Sch., Houston, 1963-64; research fellow Harvard U. Med. Sch., Boston, 1964-67, asst. prof. medicine, 1969-73; asst. in medicine Tokyo U., 1967-69; sr. research scientist Yale U., New Haven, 1973-82, prof. human genetics, 1982—; mem. biochemistry study sect. NIH, Bethesda, Md., 1982—. Grantee NIH, 1971—, March of Dimes, 1974—. Mem. Am. Soc. Biol. Chemists, Soc. Inborn Metabolic Disorders, Am. Soc. Mass Spectrometry, Am. Soc. Human Genetics. Current work: Inborn metabolic disorders. Subspecialties: Genetics and genetic engineering (medicine); Biochemistry (medicine). Office: Dept Human Genetics Yale U Sch Medicine 333 Cedar St New Haven CT 06510

TANAKA, NOBUMASA, microbiologist, consultant; b. Tokyo, May 23, 1935; came to U.S., 1965; s. Taisuke and Misawo (Nozawa) T.; m. Yoko Kaminaga, Oct. 23, 1961. B.A., U. Tokyo, 1961; M.S., U. Wis., 1971, Ph.D., 1973. Researcher Kyowa Hakko Kogyo, Co., Tokyo, 1961-65; research assoc. molecular biology U. Wis., Madison, 1973-75, project assoc. Food Research Inst., 1975-79, asst. scientist Food Research Inst., 1979-85; chief cons. U.S.-Japan Sci. Communications, Madison, 1983—. Researcher and developer microbial production of ATP, 1965 (recipient Dir. award 1966). Contbr. articles to profl. jours. Fulbright grantee Japan-U.S. Ednl. Commn., 1965. Mem. Am. Soc. for Microbiology, Internat. Assn. Milk, Food and Environ. Sanitarians, Inst. Food Technologist, Jour. Food Protection (editorial bd. 1984—). Current work: Safety of food (microbiological) especially clostridium botulinum. Better communication between scientists of the U.S. and Japan. Subspecialties: Microbiology; Biochemistry (biology). Home and Office: 72 Paxwood Rd Delmar NY 12054

TANAKA, STEPHANIE MASAE, geologist; b. St. Louis, Oct. 13, 1958; d. George Masayuki and Mitzi Mitzue (Nakao) T. B.S., U. Mo.-Rolla, 1981. Geologist oil shale Phillips Petroleum Co., Lexington, Ky., 1980, Denver, 1981; geologist oil and gas Cities Service Co., Tulsa, 1982-83; geologist minerals Amselco Exploration Inc., St. Peters, Mo., 1983-84, Phoenix, 1985—. Mem. Am. Assn. Petroleum Geologists, Geol. Soc. Am., Sigma Gamma Epsilon, Alpha Chi Sigma. Lutheran. Current work: Geological exploration for base and precious metal deposits in the continental U.S. Subspecialties: Geology; Tectonics. Office: Amselco Exploration Inc 17602 N Black Canyon Hwy Suite 105 Phoenix AZ 85023

TANDBERG-HANSSEN, EINAR ANDREAS, astronomer, physicist; b. Bergen, Norway, Aug. 6, 1921; s. Birger and Mona (Meier) T.-H.; m. Erna, June 22, 1951; children: Else Bartels, Karin Willoughby. Ph.D., U. Oslo, 1960. Research assoc. U. Oslo, 1954-57, lectr., 1959-61; research assoc. High Altitude Obs., Boulder, Colo., 1957-59, mem. sr. research staff, 1961-74; sr. research scientist NASA/Marshall Space Flight Center, Huntsville, Ala., 1974—, 83, dep. dir. Space Sci. Lab., 1983—; adj. prof. physics U. Ala., Huntsville, 1976—. Author: Radioastronomy, 1961, Solar Activity, 1967, Solar Prominences, 1974; contbr. numerous articles on astronomy, solar physics to sci. jours. Recipient Exceptional Service medal NASA, 1979. Mem. Norwegian Acad. Sci., Geophysics Research Bd., Internat. Astron. Union, Am. Astron. Soc. Lutheran. Current Work: Nature of solar activity, solar flares prominences, solar magnetic fields. Subspecialties: Solar physics; Optical astronomy. Home: 4010 Granada Dr Huntsville AL 35802 Office: ES01 NASA Marshall Space Flight Center Huntsville AL 35812

TANG, M CHUNG-MUH, meteorologist; b. Tungkang, China, Oct. 20, 1936; came to U.S., 1962, naturalized, 1977; s. Shih-Ai and Kim (Lee) T.; m. Lanling Mao, Nov. 27, 1965; children—Henry, Eugene. B.S., Nat. Taiwan U., China, 1959; M.A., UCLA, 1965, Ph.D., 1970. Research asst. Taiwan Rain S Stimulation Inst., China, 1961-62; UCLA Meteorology, 1962-70; research assoc. Yale U., New Haven, 1970-75; asst. prof. Drexel U., Phila., 1975-80; cons., research scientist Univs. Space Reseach Assn., Columbia, Md., 1980—. Treas. Chinese Sch. Greater Phila., Radnor, Pa., 1979-80. Chinese Cultural and Natural Sci. scholar, 1956. Mem. Am. Meteorol. Soc., AAAS, Meteorol. Soc. Japan, Sigma Xi. Democrat. Current work: Research on evolution of cloud pattern and latent heat release in baroclinic waves with application of satellite data. Subspecialties: Meteorology; Synoptic meteorology. Home: 241 Marple Rd Haverford PA 19041 Office: Univs Space Research Assn Am City Bldg Suite 311 Columbia MD 21044

TANG, DENNY DUAN-LEE, electrical engineer; b. Kwang Tung, Republic of China, 1946; came to U.S. 1969; naturalized 1982; s. Sik Ling and Pick-kwan (Tseng) T.; m. Kaolin Chiong; children—Minchene, Minyee, Weishene. B.S. Nat. Chen-Kung U., Taiwan, Rep. China, 1968; M.S., U. Conn., 1971; Ph.D., U. Mich., 1975. Research staff mem. IBM T.J. Watson Research Ctr., Yorktown Heights, N.Y., 1975-82, mgr., 1982—. Patentee in field. Contbr. articles to engring. jours. Mem. IEEE (sr.). Current work: Microwave semiconductor devices and circuits, bipolar integrated circuit design theory and scaling. Subspecialties: Microchip technology (engineering); Integrated circuits. Office: IBM TJ Watson Research Ctr PO Box 218 Yorktown Heights NY 10598

TANG, IGNATIUS NING-BANG, research chemical engineer; b. Nankin, Kiangsu, China, July 7, 1933; came to U.S., 1958, naturalized, 1972; s. Hung-Ching and Wen-Shung (Shih) T.; m. Carol Yu Lin, Oct. 30, 1962; children—Marion, Alice. B.S. in Chem. Engring., Nat. Taiwan U., 1955; M.S. in Chem. Engring., U. N.D., 1960; postgrad. in chem. engring., NYU, 1961-63; M.S. in Applied Math., SUNY-Stony Brook, 1978, Ph.D. in Applied Math., 1982. Chem. Engr. Taiwan Fertilizer Corp., 1956-58; research chem. engr. Brookhaven Nat. Lab., Upton, N.Y., 1964—. Contbr. articles to tech. jours. Mem. Am. Chem. Soc., N.Y. Acad. Sci., Am. Assn. for Aerosol Research. Republican. Roman Catholic. Current work: Deliquescence properties of hygroscopic aerosols, thermodynamics of concentrated electrolyte solutions, phase transition and reaction kinetics. Subspecialties: Atmospheric chemistry; Chemical engineering. Home: 27 Suffolk Down Box 156 Shoreham NY 11786 Office: Brookhaven Nat Lab Bldg 815 Upton NY 11973

TANG, JOHN CHU-TAY, genetic engineer; b. Ling-Shen, China, Mar. 15, 1944; came to U.S., 1973, naturalized, 1985; s. Yao-Nang and Po-In (Chen) T.; m. Teresa Yen-Rong Wu, Sept. 1, 1976; children—Michelle, Christopher. B.S., Nat. Chung-Hsing U., Taiwan, Republic of China, 1966; M.S., Inst. Biochemistry, Nat. Defense Med. Ctr., Taiwan, 1970; Ph.D., CUNY, 1978. Instr. Nat. Maritime U., Taiwan, 1967-68; lectr. Inst. Biochemistry, Nat. Defense Med. Ctr., Taiwan, 1970-73, Nat. Normal U., Taiwan, 1972-73; adj. lectr. CUNY, N.Y.C., 1973-77; postdoctoral fellow Harvard Med. Sch., Boston, 1977-81; research scientist Biogen Research Corp., Cambridge, Mass., 1981—. Contbr. articles to profl. jours. Served to 2d lt. Chinese Air Force, 1966-67. Mem. N.Y. Acad. Sci., Am. Soc. Biol. Chemists, Am. Chem. Soc., Am. Soc. Microbiology, Sigma Xi. Current work: Purification and characterizations of tissue plasminogen activators produced by recombinant DNA technology in E. coli and mammalian cells, refolding of recombinant proteins extracted from E. coli, exploring second generation products through genetic engineering, developing enzyme-immunoassays for screening and quantitation of recombinant products, studies on serine protease and its inhibitors. Subspecialties: Genetics and genetic engineering (biology); Biomedical engineering. Home: 118 Evelyn Rd Newton MA 02168 Office: Biogen Research Corp 14 Cambridge Ctr Cambridge MA 02142

TANG, JOHN THEODORE, physicist, conputer research specialist; b. Shanghai, China, July 5, 1947; came to U.S.; s. John Lai Boon and May (Kaung) T.; m. Angela Chow, Oct. 24, 1970; 1 child, Josephine. B.S. in Physics,

UCLA, 1969, M.S. in Physics, 1970, Ph.D. in Physics, 1974. Teaching asst. UCLA, 1970, research asst., 1971-72, research assoc. elec. engring. dept., 1972-74; research asst. Los Alamos Sci. Lab., 1971-72; tech. staff TRW Inc., Los Angeles, 1975—. Contbr. articles to profl. jours. Mem. Am. Phys. Soc., AAAS, Sigma Pi Sigma. Democrat. Methodist. Current work: Experimental and computational physics pertaining to the development of advanced isotope separation process; also, computer systems development to automate data acquisitions and process control. Subspecialty: Plasma physics. Home: 28622 Leacrest Dr Rancho Palos Verdes CA 90274 Office: TRW Inc 1 Space Pk Redondo Beach CA 90278

TANG, LUCIA CHIA-LU, chemist; b. Tsingtao, China, Dec. 20, 1938; came to U.S., 1964; naturalized, 1973; d. George C. and Tze Hua (Chu) Yang; m. Tsou-liang Tang, Dec. 17, 1966; children—Tina S., Tricia S. B.A., Radford U., 1966; M.S., U. Conn., 1970. Textile engr. Bur. commodity, Taipei, Taiwan, Republic of China, 1963-64; clin. chemist U. Md. Hosp., Balt., 1967-68, analytical chemist Strasburger and Siegel, Balt., 1968; teaching asst. U. Conn., Storrs, 1968-70; chemist Bur. Lab., Dept. Human Resources, Washington, 1971-74, Library of Congress, Washington, 1974—. Patentee in field. Contbr. articles to profl. jours. Recipient Honorable Mention award Assn. Am. Pubs. Mem. Am. Chem. Soc., Capital Chemists Assn., Women Chemists Assn. Current work: Stabilization of paper artifacts through metal borohydride; developing analytical techniques for conservation science; effect of metal on paper permanence and artifacts. Subspecialty: Analytical chemistry.

TANG, RUEN C., educator; b. Chenkiang, China, Oct. 31, 1934; came to U.S., 1963; s. Ping H. and I-Chen (Shen) T.; m. Anna C.Y. Huang, Dec. 25, 1960; children: Gina, Sophia, Jayne. B.S., Nat. Chung-Hsing U., 1957; Ph.D., N.C. State U., 1968. Forester Taiwan Forest Bur., China, 1959-63; research asst. N.C. State U., Raleigh, 1963-67; research assoc. U. Ky., Lexington, 1968-69, asst. prof., 1970-74, assoc. prof., 1974-77; prof. Auburn U., Ala., 1978—; cons. Forest Products Industries, Ky., Ala., 1968—; adviser on wood sci. Miss. State U., Starkville, 1979—. Contbr. numerous articles to profl. jours. Mem. Soc. Wood Sci. and Tech., Soc. Exptl. Stress Analysis, Soc. Exptl. Mechanics, Brit. Soc. Strain Measurement, Ala. Acad. Sci., Soc. Am. Foresters, Forest Products Research Soc. (chmn. Physics sect. 1977-78), Am. Forest Assn., ASTM, AAAS, Internat. Assn. Math. Modeling, Soc. Computer Simulation, Sigma Xi, Gamma Sigma Delta, Xi Sigma Pi. Confusianist. Current Work: Anisotropic elasticity, composite materials, fiber mechanisms, wood engineering, timber physics, computer simulation and modeling. Subspecialties: Theoretical and applied mechanics; Composite materials. Home: 687 Longweed Rd Lexington KY 40503 Office: Sch of Forestry Auburn U Auburn AL 36849

TANGHERLINI, FRANK ROBERT, physics educator, researcher; b. Boston, Mar. 14, 1924; s. Emiliano Francisco Tangherlini and Rosa (Robinson) LeClaire; m. Jane Kjaergaard Kjems, Jan. 2, 1960 (div. 1979); children—Arne Emil, Timothy Roland, Daniel Mark, Niels Louis. S.B. cum laude with honors in Physics, Harvard U., 1948; M.S. in Physics, U. Chgo., 1952; Ph.D. in Physics, Stanford U., 1959. Research engr. Gen. Dynamics Co., San Diego, 1953-55; teaching fellow Stanford U., Calif., 1955-58; NSF postdoctoral fellow Niels Bohr Inst., Copenhagen, 1958-59, Istituto di Fisica Teorica, Naples, Italy, 1959-60; research assoc. Inst. Field Physics, U. N.C., Chapel Hill, 1960-61; asst. prof. Duke U., Durham, N.C., 1961-64; assoc. prof. physics George Washington U., 1964-66, Coll. of the Holy Cross, Worcester, Mass., 1967—; vis. scientist Danish Space Research Orgn., Lyngby-Denmark, 1966-67, Internat. Ctr. for Theoretical Physics, Trieste, Italy, 1973-74. Author: An Introduction to the General Theory of Relativity, 1961. Contbr. numerous articles to physics jours. Chmn. Cub Scouts, Auburn, Mass., 1972-73, 74-78; committeeman Boy Scouts Am., Auburn, 1975-78; coach Jr. Soccer Team, 1977-79. Served with AUS, 1943-46; ETO. Mem. Am. Phys. Soc. (particles and fields div.), AAUP, Sigma Xi. Club: Harvard (Worcester). Current work: Dimensionality of space, classical electron, quantum optics, particle masses, spin and isospin, foundations of relativity, general relativity, gravitation and cosmology, complementarity. Subspecialties: Relativity and gravitation; Theoretical physics. Office: Coll Holy Cross College St Worcester MA 01610

TANGNER, CECIL HERMAN, JR., veterinary surgeon, orthopedic researcher; b. Oklahoma City, Okla., Mar. 11, 1952; s. Cecil Herman and Mildred Susan (Cook) T.; m. Ellen Kay Blackburn, Aug. 15, 1981; 1 child, John Clayton. B.S., Okla. State U., 1976, D.V.M., 1978; M.S., Tex. A&M U., 1982. Diplomate Am. Coll. Vet. Surgeons. Vet. intern Tex. A&M U., College Station, 1978-79, surg. resident, 1979-82, asst. prof. vet. medicine, 1983—; asst. prof. La. State U., Baton Rouge, 1982-83; cons. Austin Vet. Surg. Clinic, Tex., 1981—. Author, editor: Operative Techniques in Small Animal Surgery, 1984. Contbr. articles to profl. pubs. T.C. Johnson scholar Tex. Vet. Medicine Assn., 1982; grad. grantee Tex. A&M U., 1982. Mem. Am. Coll. Vet. Surgeons, AVMA, Vet. Orthopedic Soc., Am. Animal Hosp. Assn., Tex. Vet. Med. Assn. Republican. Methodist. Current work: Research interests include orthopedics, canine coxal joint and prosthetic joint implantation. Subspecialty: Surgery (veterinary medicine). Office: Tex A&M U Coll Vet Medicine Dept Small Animal Medicine and Surgery College Station TX 77843

TANIELIAN, MINAS HAGOP, research scientist; b. Athens, Greece, Mar. 5, 1951; came to U.S., 1970, s. Hagop and Zumrut (Yakoupian) T.; B.A. in Physics, U. Chgo., 1974, M.S., 1975, Ph.D., 1981. Research scientist Gould Research Ctr., Rolling Meadows, Ill., 1981—, project mgr., 1984. Contbr. articles to profl. jours. Mem. Am. Phys. Soc., Am. Vacuum Soc. Current work: Research interest centers around the physics of thin films, their preparation, analysis and physical properties (mainly transport properties). Main materials: semiconductors. Subspecialties: Condensed matter physics; Microchip technology (materials science). Home: 1326 E Algonquin Rd Schaumburg IL 60195 Office: Gould Research Center 40 Gould Center Rolling Meadows IL 60008

TANIMOTO, STEVEN LARRY, computer scientist, educator; b. Chgo., May 18, 1949; s. Taffee Tadashi and Mary-Mae Muriel (Whistler) T.; m. Gunnel Birgitta Neander, Sept. 19, 1981; 1 child, Elise. A.B., Harvard U., 1971; M.S.E., Princeton U., 1973, M.A., 1974, Ph.D., 1975. Asst. prof. computer sci. U. Conn., Storrs, 1975-77; asst. prof. U. Wash., Seattle, 1977-81, assoc. prof., 1981—. Editor: Structured Computer Vision, 1980; assoc. editor Pattern Recognition, 1983—. NSF grantee, 1983, 84. Mem. Computer Soc. of IEEE (assoc. editor Transactions Pattern Analysis and Machine Intelligence, 1982—). Assn. Computing Machinery, Am. Assn. Artificial Intelligence. Current work: Image processing with pyramidal data structures and architecture; iconic programming systems; inference methods in artificial intelligence. Subspecialties: Graphics, image processing, and pattern recognition; Artificial intelligence. Office: Univ Wash Computer Sci FR-35 Seattle WA 98195

TANKUS, HARRY, mechanical engineer; b. Bialystok, Poland, Aug. 23, 1921; came to U.S., 1929, naturalized, 1929; s. Isador and Sima (Siegel) T.; m. Lila Beverly Lee, Sept. 9, 1947; children—Rolana, Ilyce. Cert. in Engring., Armour Tech., Inst., Chgo., 1942; postgrad. U. Ill.-Chgo., 1966. Dept. head inspection div. aircraft Buick div. Gen. Motors Corp., Melrose Park, Ill., 1942-44; with Crane Packing Co., Morton Grove, Ill., 1947—, v.p. engring., 1953-64, v.p. product sales, 1971-76, pres., 1976-82; chmn. bd. John Crane-Houdaille, Morton Grove, 1982—; v.p. Houdaille Ind., 1982—. Contbr. articles to profl. jours. Patentee (15) in field. Trustee, Skokie Valley Hosp., Ill., 1981—; pres. United Way Skokie Valley, 1983; bd. dirs. Oakton Community Coll. Ednl. Found., Des Plaines, Ill., 1977, pres., 1979-82; bd. dirs. United Way Suburban Chgo., 1983—; alumni bd. dirs. Ill. Inst. Tech., 1980—. Mem. Nat. Fluid Power Conf. (bd. govs. 1967-82, gen. chmn. 1970), Am. Soc. Lubrication Engrs. (pres. 1975). Subspecialty: Fluid mechanics. Home: 415 Sunset Dr Wilmette IL 60091 Office: John Crane-Houdaille Inc 6400 Oakton St Morton Grove IL 60053

TANNEN, RICHARD LAURENCE, physician, educator; b. N.Y.C., Aug. 31, 1937; s. Harold and Fannie (Rosenberg) T.; m. Elizabeth Harriman, Aug. 8, 1964; children—Bradford, Whitney, Alison. Student Vanderbilt U., Nashville, 1954-57; M.D., U. Tenn., 1960. Surg. intern U. Fla., Gainesville, 1960-61; med. intern Peter Bent Brigham Hosp., Boston, 1961-62, jr. resident medicine, 1962-63, sr. resident medicine, 1965-66; research fellow New Eng. Med. Ctr., Boston, 1963-65; research internist Dept. Metabolism, Walter Reed Army Inst. Research, Washington, 1966-69; asst. medicine Harvard Med. Sch., Boston, 1965-66; asst. prof., co-dir. nephrology unit dept. medicine U. Vt., Burlington, 1969-73, assoc. prof., dir. nephrology unit, 1973-78, acting assoc. chmn. dept. medicine, 1975-76; vis. scientist dept. clin. biochemistry Radcliffe Infirmary, Oxford, Eng., 1976-77; mem. faculty U. Mich. Med. Sch., Ann Arbor, 1978—, prof., dir. nephrology div., 1978—; mem. faculty U. Mich. Med. Sch., Ann Arbor, 1978—, prof. dept. physiology, 1982—, assoc. dean hosp. affairs, 1982—; cons. to various hosps.; lectr, speaker numerous orgns. Guest editor Symposium of Potassium Homeostasis, Kidney Internat. II, 1977. Contbr. numerous chpts. in books, articles to various publs. Mem. sci. adv. bd. Kidney Found. Mich., 1978—; mem. sci. adv. bd. Nat. Kidney Found., 1980—, mem. exec. com. sci. adv. bd., 1982—, chmn. sci. adv. bd., 1983, region III v.p., 1984; mem. exec. com. Council Kidney in CV Diseases, Am. Heart Assn., 1982—. Served to major USAR, 1966-69. USPHS grantee, 1970—, Am. Heart Assn., 1973-80. Fellow ACP; mem. Am. Fedn. Clin. Research, Am. Soc. Nephrology, Council Circulation, Am. Heart Assn., Internat. Soc. Nephrology, Am. Soc. Clin. Investigation, Central Soc. Clin. Research, Assn. Am. Physicians. Subspecialties: Nephrology; Physiology (medicine). Office: Univ of Michigan Nephrology Div Ann Arbor MI 48109

TANNENBAUM, MICHAEL J(AY), physicist; b. N.Y.C., Mar. 10, 1939; s. Morris and Ann T.; m. Barbara C. Moshinsky, July 15, 1973; children—Nina Fay, Lisa Marie. A.B. magna cum laude, Columbia U., 1959, M.A., 1960, Ph.D., 1965. Vis. scientist CERN (European Orgn. for Nuclear Research), Geneva, Switzerland, 1965-66, attache scientifique, 1973-84; asst. prof., assoc. prof. Harvard U., Cambridge, Mass., 1966-71; assoc. prof. Rockefeller U., N.Y.C., 1971-80; physicist Brookhaven Nat. Lab., Upton, N.Y., 1980—. Author articles in field; inventor coherently hardened photon beam. Ernest Kempton Adams fellow, 1965; NSF fellow, 1959-63, 66; Alfred P. Sloan Found. fellow, 1967-69. Fellow Am. Phys. Soc.; mem. Am. Assn. Physics Tchrs., AAAS, N.Y. Acad. Scis., Phi Beta Kappa. Jewish. Current work: Fundamental interactions of quarks, gluons, leptons and photons; high energy heavy in collisions; superconducting accelerator magnet. Subspecialty: Particle physics. Home: 9 Buena Vista Rd Port Jefferson NY 11777 Office: Physic Dept Brookhaven Nat Lab Bldg 510A Upton NY 11973

TANNENWALD, PETER ERNEST, research physicist; b. Keil, Germany, Mar. 30, 1926; came to U.S., 1940, naturalized 1945; s. Bruno and Alma (Mendel) T.; A.B. in Physics, U. Calif.-Berkeley, 1947, Ph.D., 1952. Staff U. Calif. Radiation Lab., Berkeley, 1950-52; Lincoln Lab. MIT, Lexington, 1952—, asst. head solid state div., 1963-65, assoc. head, 1965-74, sr. staff mem., 1974—. Served with AUS, 1945. Fellow Am. Phys. Soc.; mem. Phi Beta Kappa. Current work: Submillimeter quantum electronics, far infared detection and heterodyning, semiconductor devices for millimeter waves. Subspecialties: Quantum electronics; Condensed matter physics. Office: Lincoln Lab MIT Lexington MA 02173

TANNER, ANTHONY CHARLES, physical chemistry educator; b. St. Louis, Oct. 8, 1948; s. Charles Edward and Marie Josephine (Nicoletti) T. A.B., Washington U., St. Louis, 1970; Ph.D., Brandeis U., 1975. Fischbach fellow, research fellow Israel Inst. Tech., Haifa, 1975-77; research assoc. Fla. State U., Tallahassee, 1977-81; research fellow U. Waterloo, Ont., Can., 1981-82; vis. asst. prof. Hiram Coll., Ohio, 1982-83, Colby Coll., Waterville, Maine, 1983-84; asst. prof. chemistry Austin Coll., Sherman, Tex., 1984—. Contbr. articles to sci. jours., chpts. to books. Mem. Am. Chem. Soc., Am. Phys. Soc., Am. Assn. Physics Tchrs. Current work: Quantum chemistry, Van der Waals forces, X-ray scattering. Subspecialty: Theoretical chemistry. Home: 915 S Travis St Sherman TX 75090 Office: Austin Coll Sherman TX 75090

TANNER, DAVID BURNHAM, physicist, educator; b. Norfolk, Va., Mar. 12, 1945; s. James Taylor and Nancy Burnham (Sheedy) T.; m. Marcia Carol Haney, July 29, 1972; children—James Daniel, Michael Gregory. B.A., U. Va., 1966, M.S., 1967; Ph.D., Cornell U., 1972. Postdoctoral assoc. U. Pa., Phila., 1972-74; asst. prof. Ohio State U., Columbus, 1974-79, assoc. prof., 1979-82; prof. physics U. Fla., Gainesville, 1982—; cons. Xerox Corp., Rochester, N.Y., 1978—. Author: (with others) Review of 1-Dimensional Systems, 1982. Editor: Electrical Transport and Optical Properties of Inhomogeneous Media, 1978. Contbr. articles to profl. jours. Treas. Cub Scout Pack 511, Gainesville, 1984-85. Grantee Dept. Energy, 1978-82, NSF, 1981-82, 82-84. Mem. Am. Phys. Soc. Democrat. Episcopalian. Current work: Optical properties of solids, particularly for infrared spectroscopy; electronic properties of conducting polymers, composite systems, and one-dimensional materials. Subspecialties: Condensed matter physics; Solid state chemistry. Home: 3619 NW 38th St Gainesville FL 32606 Office: U Fla Physics Dept 205 Williamson Gainesville FL 32611

TANNER, JOHN EYER, JR., nuclear safety analyst; b. Cleve., Apr. 30, 1930; s. John Eyer Tanner and Irene (Goodfellow) Rogers; m. Martha Jane Hester, July 2, 1966; children—Clare, Bryce, Craig. A.B., Oberlin Coll., 1951; M.S., Ind. U., 1954; Ph.D., U. Wis.-Madison, 1966. Postdoctoral asst. Pa. State U., University Park, 1966-68, Max Planck Inst. Med. Research, Heidelberg, Fed. Republic of Germany, 1968-69; sr. scientist Ford Motor Co., Dearborn, Mich., 1969-71; research chemist Naval Weapons Support Ctr., Crane, Ind., 1971-79; criticality safety analyst Westinghouse Co., Idaho Falls, Idaho, 1979—. patentee pyrotechnics. Contbr. articles to profl. jours. Served with U.S. Army, 1954-56. Mem. Am. Chem. Soc., Am. Nuclear Soc., Am. Phys. Soc. Unitarian. Current work: Nuclear criticality analysis applied to nuclear fuel reprocessing. Subspecialties: Nuclear magnetic resonance; Physical chemistry. Home: 2175 Tasman Ave Idaho Falls ID 83401 Office: WINCO CPP PO Box 4000 Idaho Falls ID 83403

TANNER, WILLIAM FRANCIS, JR., geologist, educator; b. Milledgeville, Ga., Feb. 4, 1917; s. William Francis and Robbie Belle (Carter) T.; m. Julia Katherine Rigby, July 17, 1938; children—William Francis III, Bruce, Julianne. B.A., Baylor U., 1937; M.A., Tex. Tech U., 1939; Ph.D., Okla. U., 1953. Asst. prof. geology Okla. Bapt. U., Shawnee, 1946-51; spl. instr. Okla. U., Norman, 1951-54; geologist Shell Oil Co., Denver, 1954; vis. prof. geology Fla. State U., Tallahassee, 1954-56, assoc. prof., 1956-66, prof., 1966-74, regents prof., 1974—. Editor Coastal Research, 1962—; (series) Coastal Sedimentology, 1977—. Author books and articles. Served with USNR, 1941-45. Fellow AAAS, Geol. Soc. Am. Baptist. Current work: Evolution of coasts, sediment transport in fluid systems, paleogeography and paleoclimatology, interaction of sedimentation and tectonics. Subspecialties: Sedimentology; Coastal zones. Office: Fla State U Tallahassee FL 32306

TANNOCK, IAN FREDERICK, physician, cancer research scientist; b. Hatfield, Hertshire, Eng., Nov. 22, 1943; emigrated to Can., 1974, naturalized, 1979; s. Archibald A. and Freda A.G. (Rickels) T.; m. Rosemary Tannock, May 20, 1967; children: Stuart, Lisa, Steven. B.A., Cambridge (Eng.) U., 1965; Ph.D., Inst. Cancer Research, London, 1968; M.D., U. Pa., 1974. Postdoctoral fellow M.D. Anderson Hosp., Houston, 1968-70; vis. scientist Radiobiol. Inst. T.N.O., Rijswijk, Netherlands, 1971; resident in internal medicine and med. oncology U. Toronto, 1974-78; staff physician, sr. scientist Ont. Cancer Inst., Princess Margaret Hosp., Toronto, 1978—; mem. Nat. Cancer Inst. Can. Grants panel, 1982-85; mem. exptl. therapeutics study sect. NIH, 1980-84. Contbr. articles to profl. jours. Mem. Am. Soc. Clin. Oncology, Am. Assn. Cancer Research, Radiation Research Soc., Cell Kinetics Soc. Current Work: Clinical and experimental studies of drug treatment of solid tumors, biology of human tumors. Subspecialties: Cancer research (medicine); Chemotherapy. Office: Ontario Cancer Institute Department Medicine 500 Sherbourne St Toronto ON M4X 1K9 Canada

TANSEY, MICHAEL ANSELME, clinical psychologist, biofeedback clinician; b. Frankfurt, Germany, Feb. 4, 1948; naturalized, 1948; s. Frank Vincent and Ginette (Tommassini) T.; m. Mary Loretta Glod, June 19, 1971; children: Jennifer, Michael, Matthew. B.A. in Psychology, Seton Hall U., South Orange, N.J., 1970; M.A. in Psychology, Fairleigh Dickinson U., Teaneck, N.J., 1972; Ph.D. in Clin. Psychology, Calif. Sch. Profl. Psychology, Fresno, Calif., 1976. Lic. clin. psychologist, N.J. Pres. Michael A. Tansey (P.A.), Union, N.J., 1978—; co-dir., owner T.H.E. Biofeedback and Counselling Assocs., Hightstown, N.J., 1981—; teaching fellow Fairleigh Dickinson U., 1971. Mem. Am. Psychol. Assn., N.J., Psychol. Assn., Biofeedback Soc. N.J. Lodge: K.C. Current Work: The remediation of learning disabilities via the direct enhancement of discrete neural discharge over the Rolandic cortex of the brain. Subspecialties: Neuropsychology; Biofeedback. Home: 2297 Camplain Rd Somerville NJ 08876 Office: 2810 Morris Ave Union NJ 07083

TANTTILA, WALTER HJALMER, physics educator; b. Sax, Minn., Nov. 21, 1922; s. Herman and Rose Amelia (Koskenniska) T.; m. Catherine Patricia Turner, May 10, 1964; children—Shelly, Amelia, Lisa, Reino; m. Inez Lyman, June 21, 1951 (div. 1962); children—Patricia, Harvey, Margaret. B.Chem. Engring., U. Minn., 1948, M.A., 1950; Ph.D., U. Wash., 1955. Instr., Tchrs. Coll., Winona, Minn., 1950-51; research physicist Mps. Honeywell, 1951-52; asst. prof. Mich. State U., East Lansing 1955-58; mem. faculty U. Colo., Boulder, 1958—, assoc. prof., 1958-60, prof. physics, 1964—; cons. Martin Marietta Corp., Denver, 1962-64. Contbr. articles to profl. jours. Served with USCGR, 1943-46. Fulbright fellow, Turku, Finland, 1966-67. Mem. Am. Phys. Soc. Current work: Amorphous materials; computer simulation, nuclear magnetic resonance and positron annihilation techniques. Subspecialties: Condensed matter physics; Statistical physics. Office: Dept Physics Univ Colo Campus Box 390 Boulder CO 80309

TAO, LI-CHUNG, research scientist, mechanical engineer; b. WuChen, China, Dec. 20, 1932; came to U.S., 1957, naturalized, 1969; s. Yao-Kai and Kuang-Show (Hu) T.; m. Cecilia Chiang, June 17, 1961; children: Jeffrey, Angela. Ph.D., Yale U., 1968. Sr. research engr. Gen. Tire & Rubber Co., Akron, Ohio, 1968-71, research scientist, 1971-77; sr. engr. Bechtel Power Corp., Gaithersburg, Md., 1977-84; sr. staff engr. Pub. Service Electric & Gas Co., 1984—. Mem. ASME, Soc. Rheology. Current Work: Engineering mechanics activities in BWR Mark I containment. Subspecialties: Solid mechanics; Composite materials. Home: 709 Hope Ln Gaithersburg MD 20878 Office: Hancocks Bridge NJ 08038

TAPLEY, BYRON DEAN, aerospace engineer; b. Charleston, Miss., Jan. 16, 1933; s. Ebbie Byron and Myrtle (Myers) T.; m. Sophia Philen, Aug. 28, 1959; children—Mark Byron, Craig Philen. B.S., U. Tex., 1956, M.S., 1958, Ph.D., 1960. Research engr. Structural Mechanics Research Lab., U. Tex., Austin, 1954-58, instr. dept. mech. engring., 1958, prof. dept. aerospace engring. and engring. mechanics, 1960—, chmn. dept., 1966-77; adv. scientist Structural Mechanics Research Lab., U. Tex. (Lockheed Missile and Space Vehicle div.), Sunnyvale, Calif., 1961, W.R. Woolrich prof. engring., 1974-84, Clare Cockrell Williams centennial chair in aerospace engring., 1984—, dir. Ctr. Space Research, 1982—; cons. NASA Manned Spacecraft Center, 1965—, mem. adv. com. on guidance control and nav., 1966-67, com. on space research, panel I, 1974—, chmn. region IV, engring. council on profl. devel., 1974—; mem. com. geodesy NRC, 1979-83; mem. aero. and space engring. bd. NRC, 1981-85, also mem. com. on earth scis. Editor: Celestial Mech. Jour, 1976-79; assoc. editor: Jour. Guidance and Control, 1978-79; asso. editor: Geophys. Revs, 1979—. Mem. ASME, Am. Acad. Mechanics, Am. Astronautics Soc., Soc. Engring. Sci., Am. Inst. Aeros. and Astronautics (chmn. com. on astrodynamics 1976-78), IEEE, Am. Geophys. Union (pres. Am. Astron. Soc., AAAS, Internat. Astron. Union (chmn. 1981—), Sigma Xi, Pi Tau Sigma, Sigma Gamma Tau, Phi Kappa Phi, Tau Beta Pi. Current Work: Estimation theory; satellite geodesy, satellite oceanography and remote sensing; application of satellite remote sensed data to study of earth. Subspecialties: Aerospace engineering and technology; Satellite studies. Home: 3100 Perry Ln Austin TX 78731

TARAMAN, KHALIL SHOWKY, manufacturing engineering educator, consultant; b. Cairo, Egypt, July 10, 1939; came to U.S., 1967, naturalized, 1975; s. Showky K. and Saadat M.A. (Ghany) T.; m. Sanaa R. Taraman, July 4, 1968; children: Shaoky, Sharief, Mona. B.S.M.E., Ain Shams U., Egypt, 1964, M.S.M.E., 1967; M.S. (WARF fellow), U. Wis., 1969; Ph.D. (fellow), Tex. Tech U., 1971. Registered profl. engr., Calif.; cert. mfg. engr. Instr., research fellow Tex. Tech U., 1969-70; asst. prof. U. Detroit, 1970-73, assoc. prof., 1973-77, dir. mfg. engring. isnt., 1975, prof., chmn. dept. mech. engring., 1977—, sr. tech. cons., research supr. corps. Editor: Computer Aided Design/Computer Aided Manufacturing, 1980; CAD/CAM Integration, 1985; contbr. articles to profl. jours. Named Eminent Engr. Tau Beta Pi, 1982. Mem. Soc. Mfg. Engrs. (internat. dir., chpt. chmn. 1975-76, chmn. material removal council 1979-84, resolution of appreciation 1977, 79, 80), ASME, Am. Soc. Engring. Edn., Am. Egyptian Scholars, Pi Tau Sigma, Alpha Pi Mu. Current Work: Manufacturing engineering systems and its productivity, material removal. Subspecialties: Mechanical engineering; Materials processing. Office: 4001 W McNichols Rd Detroit MI 48221

TARANIK, JAMES VLADIMIR, geoscience and mineral engineering educator, researcher; b. Los Angeles, Apr. 23, 1940; s. Vladimir James and Jeanette Downing (Smith) T.; m. Colleen Sue Glessner, Dec. 4, 1971; children—Debra Lynn, Dan Lee. B.S., Stanford U., 1964; Ph.D., Colo. Sch. Mines, 1974. Cert. profl. geologist, photogrammetrist. Prof. geology U. Iowa, Iowa City, 1971-79; chief of remote sensing Iowa Geol. Survey, Iowa City, 1971-74; prin. scientist U.S. Geol. Survey, Sioux Falls, S.D., 1975-79; branch chief NASA Hdqrs., Washington, 1979-82; dean, prof. Mackay Sch. Mines, Reno, Nev., 1982—; dir. Alhambra Mines, Inc., Reno, Gen. Minerals Am., Reno, Geosat Com., San Francisco. Contbr. numerous articles to profl. jours. Served to capt. USAR, 1965-67, Vietnam. Named mem. sci. team SIR-B Mission, NASA, 1984; prin. investigator AIS Program, NASA, 1984, Landsat AO Program, 1985; recipient NASA Exceptional Sci. Achievement award, 1982, U.S. Geol. Survey Special Achievement award, 1978. Fellow AAAS, Explorers Club, Geol. Soc. Am.; mem. Internat. Acad. Astronautics, Am. Geophys. Union, Am. Astronautical Soc. (sr.), Am. Assn. Petroleum Geologists, Soc. Exploration Geophysicists, AIME, IEEE, AIAA, Am. Inst. Profl. Geologists (pres. Nev. sect.), Internat. Soc. Rem. Sensing and Photogrammetry (chmn. working group VII-5). Current work: Electromagnetic remote sensing techniques applied to mineral and energy exploration, engring. and environmental geology, and geohydrology. Computer analysis of multispectral remote sensing data. Subspecialties: Remote sensing (geoscience); Geophysics. Home: 3075 Susileen Dr Reno NV 89509 Office: Mackay Sch of Mines U Nev Reno NV 89557

TARBELL, DEAN STANLEY, chemistry educator; b. Hancock, N.H., Oct. 19, 1913; s. Sanford and Ethel (Millikan) T.; m. Ann Hoar Tracy, Aug. 15, 1942; children: William Sanford, Linda Tracy, Theodore Dean. A.B., Harvard U., 1934, M.A., 1935, Ph.D., 1937. Postdoctoral fellow U. Ill., 1937; mem. faculty U. Rochester, 1938—, successively instr., asst. prof., asso. prof., 1938-48, prof. chemistry, 1948-62, Charles Frederick Houghton prof. chemistry, 1960—, chmn. dept., 1964—; Disting. prof. chemistry Vanderbilt U., 1967—, Branscom disting. prof., 1975-76, disting. prof. emeritus, 1981—; Guggenheim fellow and vis. lectr. chemistry Stanford U., 1961-62; Fuson lectr., 1972; cons. USPHS, Army Q.M.C.; mem. various sci. adv. bds. to govt. agencies. Author research papers in field, history of chemistry; author: (with Ann T. Tarbell) Roger Adams, Scientist and Statesman, 1981. Recipient Herty medal, 1973; Guggenheim fellow, 1946-47. Mem. Nat. Acad. Sci., Am. Chem. Soc. (chmn. div. history of chemistry 1980-81), Chem. Soc. London, Am. Acad. Arts and Scis., History of Sci. Soc. Current Work: Structure of antibiotics; mechanism of organic reactions, history of chemistry. Subspecialty: Organic chemistry. Home: 6033 Sherwood Dr Nashville TN 37215

TAREN, JAMES ARTHUR, neurosurgeon; b. Toledo, Nov. 10, 1924; s. Joseph Clarence and Mary Frances (Walker) Taren Lewis. B.S., U. Toledo, 1948; M.D., U. Mich., 1952. Diplomate Am. Bd. Neurosurgery. Intern, Univ. Hosp., Ann Arbor, 1952-53, resident in neuro-surgery, 1953-54, 56-57; resident Children's Hosp., Peter Bent Brigham, 1965; instr. U. Mich. Med. Sch., Ann Arbor, 1958, asst. prof., 1959-62, assoc. prof. neurosurgery, 1962-67, prof., 1967—; fellow in surgery Boston Children's Hosp./Harvard U., 1954-55; assoc. dean U. Mich. Med. Sch., 1978—, dir. neurobehavioral sci., 1977-78; dir. Lab. Brain Tumor Research, 1984—; vis. prof. Karolinska Inst., Stockholm, 1980, Hosp. Foch, Paris, 1966, 74, 80. Author, editor: Correlative Neurosurgery, 3d edit., 1981; contbr. articles to profl. jours. Served with USN, 1943-45. NIH fellow, 1958. Mem. Am. Assn. Neurol. Surgeons, Congress Neurol. Surgery, Am. Assn. Med. Colls., Internat. Soc. Stereotaxic Surgery, Am. Soc. Stereotaxic Surgery, RCP (Eng.). Current work: Brain tumor research; radio isotopes; immunology brain tumors. Subspecialties: Neurosurgery; Oncology. Office: Univ Hosp Sect Neuroscience Ann Arbor MI 48104

TARGOWSKI, STANISLAW PYTKOWSKI, veterinarian, microbiologist; b. Nagorzyce, Poland, Nov. 13, 1940; came to U.S. 1967, naturalized s. Waclaw Pytkowski and Maria (Targowski) Targowski. m. Hanna Targowski, Dec. 28, 1970. D.V.M., U. Warsaw, Poland, 1963; M.S., U. Wis., 1969, Ph.D., 1972. Diplomate of Am. Coll. Vet. Microbiologists. Research asst. U. Wis., Madison, 1967-72; research assoc. Purdue U., Lafayette, Ind., 1972-74; asst. prof. SUNY, Buffalo, 1974-78; assoc. prof. Ohio State U., Columbus, 1978-82; research leader Nat. Animal Disease Ctr., Ames, 1982—. Contbr. articles to profl. jours. and books. Grantee Am. Cancer Soc., 1976-80, NIH, 1980-83, USDA-Sci., Edn. and Adminstrn., 1979-83. Mem. Am. Assn. Immunologists, N.Y. Acad. Sci., Am. Vet. Med. Assn., Am. Coll. Vet. Microbiology (bd. govs. 1982—). Democrat. Roman Catholic. Current work: Immunology of neoplastic and infectious diseases, reproductive immunology, embryo transplants and phagocytosis. Subspecialties: Microbiology (veterinary medicine); Infectious diseases. Home: RR 1 Ames IA 50010 Office: Nat Animal Disease Ctr Dayton Ave PO Box 70 Ames IA 50010

TARJAN, ROBERT ENDRE, computer scientist, educator; b. Pomona, Calif., Apr. 30, 1948. B.S. in Math, Calif. Inst. Tech., 1969; M.S. in Computer Sci, Stanford U., 1971, Ph.D. in Computer Sci, 1972. Asst. prof. computer sci. Cornell U., 1972-74; Miller research fellow U. Calif.-Berkeley, 1973-75; from asst. prof. to assoc. prof. computer sci. Stanford U., 1974-81; mem. tech. staff Bell Labs., Murray Hill, N.J., from 1980; adj. prof. NYU, 1981-85; prof. Princeton U., 1985—. Recipient Nevanlinna prize Internat. Math. Union, 1983. Subspecialties: Algorithms; Group theory, data structures. Office: Princeton U Dept Math Princeton NJ 08544*

TARNOWSKI, STANLEY JOSEPH, JR., biochemist; b. St. Louis, Sept. 17, 1953; s. Stanley Joseph and Dolores Marjorie (Caldwell) T.; m. Deborah Kay Young, Aug. 14, 1974; children—Megan Suzanne, Matthew Caldwell. B.S., Southeast Mo. State U., 1975; Ph.D., U. Tenn., 1979. Postdoctoral fellow Roche Inst. Molecular Biology, Nutley, N.J., 1979-81; sr. scientist Hoffmann-LaRoche, Inc., Nutley, 1981-82, research group chief, 1982-84, research sect. chief, 1984-85; dir. process devel. Interferon Scis., Inc., New Brunswick, N.J., 1985—; adj. asst. prof. Fairleigh-Dickinson U., 1983—. Contbr. articles to profl. jours. Patentee in field. U. Tenn. fellow, 1975-79; grantee Sigma Xi, Research Soc. N.Am., 1977, Am. Cancer Soc. U. Tenn., 1978. Mem. Am. Chem. Soc., Am. Assn. Advancement Sci., Sigma Xi. Roman Catholic. Current work: Development of isolation and purification processes for the recovery of pharmacologically active polypeptides produced by recombinant DNA technology, the effects of site-specific mutagenesis of DNA on the structure, function of proteins and enzymes. Subspecialties: Biochemistry (biology); Enzyme technology. Home: 50 Dutch Rd East Brunswick NJ 08816 Office: Interferon Scis Inc 783 Jersey Ave New Brunswick NJ 08901

TARNOWSKI, THOMAS LYNN, research chemist; b. San Diego, May 6, 1950; s. Donald Vincent and Elma Lynn (Castle) T. B.A., U. Minn., 1972; Ph.D., UCLA, 1976. Vis. scientist Syva Co., Palo Alto, Calif., 1979-80, sr. chemist, 1980-84; research group leader Syva/Syntex Diagnostics, Palo Alto, 1984—. Contbr. articles to tech. publs. Nat. Merit scholar, 1968-72; fellow, NSF, 1972-75, NIH, 1979. Mem. Am. Chem. Soc. Current work: Applications of organic chemistry, photochemistry, biochemistry to needs in clinical diagnostics and medical areas. Subspecialties: Organic chemistry; Clinical chemistry. Office: Syva Co/Syntec Diagnostics PO Box 10058 Palo Alto CA 94303

TARR, MELINDA JEAN, immunotoxicologist, veterinary pathologist; b. San Francisco, Aug. 18, 1948; d. Cedric Winship and Janis Arlene (White) T. B.S., U. Calif., Davis, 1971, D.V.M., 1973; M.S., Ohio State U., 1976; Ph.D., 1979. Cert. Am. Coll. Vet. Pathology. Pvt. practice vet. medicine, Sebastopol, Calif., 1973-74; resident in equine medicine and surgery Ohio State U., Columbus, 1974-76, NIH postdoctoral trainee, fellow, 1976-79, research assoc., dept. vet. pathobiology, 1979-81, asst. prof., 1981—. Contbr. articles to profl. jours. Mem. Internat. Soc. for Immunopharmacology, Am. Assn. Vet. Immunologists, AVMA, Calif. Vet. Med. Assn. Current Work: Immunotoxicology, immunopharmacology, immunopathology, comparative pathobiology. Subspecialties: Immunotoxicology; Immunopharmacology. Office: Dept Veterinary Pathobiology Ohio State U 1925 Coffey Rd Columbus OH 43210

TARTER, C. BRUCE, physicist; b. Louisville, Sept. 26, 1939; s. Curtis B. and Marian Turner (Cundiff) T.; m. Jill Cornell Tarter, June 6, 1964; 1 dau.: Shana. B.S., M.I.T., 1961; Ph.D., Cornell U., 1967. Sr. scientist aero. div. Philco Ford, Newport Beach, Calif., 1967; mem. staff Lawrence Livermore Nat. Lab., 1967-69, group leader, 1969-74, dep. head theoretical physics div., 1974-78, head theoretical physics div., 1978—; lectr. dept. applied sci. U. Calif., Davis, 1970—. Contbr. articles to profl. jours. Mem. Am. Phys. Soc., Am. Astron. Soc., Internat. Astron. Union, Sigma Xi. Current Work: Theoretical astrophysics, properties of matter at high temperatures and densities. Subspecialties: Theoretical astrophysics; Statistical physics.

TARTER, JILL CORNELL, research astronomer; b. New Rochester, N.Y., Jan. 16, 1944; d. Richard Janney and Elizabeth (Johnston) Cornell; m. Curtis Bruce Tarter, June 6, 1964 (div. 1976); 1 child, Shana; m. William John Welch, July 4, 1980; stepchildren—Eric, Ruth Leslie, Jeanette. B.Engring. Physics, Cornell U., 1966; M.A. in Astronomy, U. Calif.-Berkeley, 1971, Ph.D. in Astronomy, 1975. Asst. research astronomer U. Calif., Berkeley, 1971-83, assoc. research astronomer, 1983—; resident research assoc. Nat. Acad. Sci.-NRC, NASA, Ames Research Ctr., 1975-77; mem. Arecibo sci. adv. com. Arecibo Obs., P.R., 1981-84. Contbr. articles to profl. jours. and chpts. to books. Mem. Am. Astron. Soc. (Shapley lectr. 1983-85), Internat. Astronom. Union, Internat. Union on Radio Sci., Internat. Acad. Astronautics (chmn. Communication with Extraterrestrial Intelligence rev. symposia 1982-85). Current work: Strategies and observations in search for extraterrestrial intelligence; brown dwarf stars; star formation; water masers; astronomical observations relating to origin and evolution of biogenic elements and compounds. Subspecialties: Radio and microwave astronomy; Search for extraterrestrial intelligence. Office: NASA-Ames Research Ctr. SETI Program Office Mail Stop 229-8 Moffett Field CA 94035

TARTOF, DAVID, rheumatologist, immunologist, educator, researcher; b. Detroit, Sept. 15, 1945; s. Herman Harry and Margaret (Bensie) T.; m. Linda Abbey Yee, May 9, 1970; children—Rachel Yee, Sara Yee. B.S., Mich. State U., 1966; M.D., U. Mich., 1970; Ph.D., U. Chgo., 1978. Diplomate Am. Bd. Internal Medicine, Am. Bd. Rheumatology. Intern in medicine U. Ill. Hosp., Chgo., 1970-71, resident in medicine, 1973-75; research fellow U. Chgo., 1975-78, fellow in rheumatology, 1978-80, asst. prof. medicine, 1980—; mem. med. adv. bd. Ill. chpt. Lupus Found., Chgo., 1983—. Contbr. articles on cellular immunology to profl. jours. Served to capt. M.C., U.S. Army, 1971-73; Vietnam. Andrew Mellon Found. Fellow 1980; Chgo. Community Trust grantee, 1982. Mem. Am. Assn. Immunologists, Am. Rheumatism Assn., Sigma Xi. Current work: Investigation of cells and factors involved in human delayed type hypersensitivity response; cellular immunity in autoimmune diseases. Subspecialties: Rheumatology; Immunobiology and immunology. Home: 1640 E 50th St Apt 18 B Chicago IL 60615 Office: U Chgo Dept Medicine Box 404 5841 S Maryland Ave Chicago IL 60637

TASK, HARRY LEE, research physicist; b. Chgo., May 31, 1946; s. Harry John and Christine Virginia (Rozell) T.; m. Marjorie F. Howard, Apr. 4, 1970; 1 child, Christine Marie. B.S. in Physics, Ohio U., 1968; M.S. in Physics, Purdue U., 1971; M.S., U. Ariz., 1978, Ph.D. in Optical Scis, 1978; M.S. in Mgmt. of Tech., 1985. Optical scis. researcher human engring. div. Air Force Aerospace Med. Research Lab., Wright-Patterson AFB, Ohio, 1971—. Contbr. articles to profl. jours. Pres. Multi-Metrics Inc., Dayton, Ohio, 1982—. Served with USAF, 1969-70. Mem. Optical Soc. Am., Human Factors Soc. Patentee in optico-visual devices field, vision and vision measurement devices. Current Work: Display image quality, night vision and night lighting, night vision goggles, aircraft transparency evaluation. Subspecialty: Optical engineering. Office: AFAMRL/HEF Wright-Patterson AFB OH 45433

TASKER, JOHN BAKER, veterinary medicine educator, university dean; b. Concord, N.H., Aug. 28, 1933; s. John Baker and Catherine Mabel (Baker) T.; m. Grace Ellen Elliott, June 17, 1961; children—Sybil Alice, Sarah Catherine, Sophia Ethel. D.V.M., Cornell U., 1957, Ph.D., 1963. Diplomate Am. Coll. Vet. Pathologists. Instr. Cornell U., Ithaca, N.Y., 1960-61, assoc. prof., 1967-69, prof., 1969-78; assoc. prof., asst. prof. Colo. State U., Ft. Collins, 1963-67; prof., assoc. dean La. State U., Baton Rouge, 1978-84; prof., dean Mich. State U., East Lansing, 1984—; cons. in field. Editor Veterinary Clinics of Northern America, 1976. Served to 1st lt. U.S. Army, 1958-60. Recipient Norden Teaching award Vet. Coll., Cornell U., 1977, Outstanding Instr. award Vet. Coll., Colo. State U., 1967. Mem. AVMA, Mich. Vet. Med. Assn., Am. Coll. Vet. Pathologists (examiner 1972-74), Am. Soc. Vet. Clin. Pathology (pres. 1971-72), Assn. Am. Vet. Medicine Colls. Current work: Hematology, clinical chemistry. Subspecialties: Pathology (veterinary medicine); Veterinary medicine education. Office: Coll Vet Medicine Mich State U A-133 E Fee Hall East Lansing MI 48824

TATCHYN, ROMAN OREST, research scientist; b. Hanover, Pa., Oct. 28, 1949; s. William and Stephanie (Maykowska) T. B.S.E.E., Princeton U., 1976; M.S.E.E., Stanford U., 1977, EE. Adminstrn., 1981, Ph.D., 1982, postgrad. in linguistics. Research asst. Stanford Electronics Lab., Calif., 1977-82, research scientist Stanford Synchrotron Radiation Lab., 1982—; cons. in field. Contbg. author: X-ray Microscopy, 1984. Contbr. articles to profl. jours. Recipient John Ogden Bigelow award in elec. engring. Princeton U., 1976; Dartmouth U. grad. fellow, 1979. Patentee in field. Mem. IEEE, SPIE, AVS. Club: Princeton of N.Y. Current work: Undulators, X-ray lasers, diffraction optics, quantum physics, systems theory, translation linguistics. Subspecialties: X-Ray Optics; Electrical engineering. Home: 2533 Alma St Palo Alto CA 94301 Office: Stanford Synchroton Radiation Lab 2575 Sand Hill Rd Stanford CA 94305

TAUBE, HENRY, chemistry educator; b. Sask., Can., Nov. 30, 1915; came to U.S., 1937, naturalized, 1942; s. Samuel and Albertina (Tiledetski) T.; m. Mary Alice Wesche, Nov. 27, 1952; children: Linda, Marianna, Heinrich, Karl. B.S., U. Sask., 1935, M.S., 1937, LL.D., 1973; Ph.D., U. Calif., 1940; Ph.D. (hon.), Hebrew U. of Jerusalem, 1979; D.Sc. (hon.), U. Chgo., 1983, Poly. Inst. N.Y., 1984, SUNY, 1985. Instr. U. Calif., 1940-41; instr., asst. prof. Cornell U., 1941-46; faculty U. Chgo., 1946-62, prof., 1952-62, chmn. dept. chemistry, 1955-59; prof. chemistry Stanford U., 1962—, chmn. dept., 1971-74; Baker lectr. Cornell U., 1965. Recipient Harrison Howe award, 1961; Chandler medal Columbia U., 1964; F.P. Dwyer medal U. N.S.W., Australia, 1973; Nat. medal of Sci., 1976, 77; Allied Chem. award for Excellence in Grad. Teaching and Innovative Sci., 1979; Nobel Prize in Chemistry, 1983; Bailar medal U. Ill., 1983; Robert A. Welch Found. Award in chemistry, 1983; Guggenheim fellow, 1949, 55. Mem. Am. Acad. Arts and Scis., Nat. Acad. Scis. (award in chem. scis. 1983), Am. Chem. Soc. (Kirkwood award New Haven sect. 1965, award for nuclear application in chemistry 1955, Nichols medal N.Y. sect. 1971, Willard Gibbs medal Chgo. sect. 1971, Distinguished Service in Advancement Inorganic Chemistry award 1967, T.W. Richards medal NE sect. 1980, Monsanto Co. award in inorganic chemistry 1981, Linus Pauling award Puget Sound sect. 1981, Priestley medal 1985), Royal Physiographical Soc. of Lund, Nat. Acad. Scis., Am. Philos. Soc., Royal Danish Acad. Scis. and Letters, Phi. Beta Kappa, Sigma Xi, Phi Lambda Upsilon (hon.). Current Work: Reactivity of inorganic substances; electron transfer reactions; mixed-valence molecules; systematic study of back-bonding. Subspecialties: Inorganic chemistry; Kinetics.

TAUBMAN, MARTIN ARNOLD, dental research scientist, immununologist; b. N.Y.C., July 10, 1940; s. Herman and Betty (Berger) T.; m. Joan Petra Mikelbank, May 31, 1965; children—Benjamin, Joel. B.S., Bklyn. Coll., 1961; D.D.S., Columbia U., 1965; Ph.D., SUNY-Buffalo, 1970. Head, dept. immunology Forsyth Dental Ctr., Boston, 1970—; assoc. clin. prof. oral biology, pathophysiology Harvard Sch. Dental Medicine, Boston, 1980—. Contbr. articles to profl. jours. NIH grantee, 1971—; NIH Career Devel. awardee, 1971-76. Mem. Internat. Assn. Dental Research, Am. Assn. Immunologists. Current work: Immunological aspects of dental diseases. Subspecialties: Oral biology; Immunology (medicine). Office: Forsyth Dental Ctr 140 Fenway St Boston MA 02115

TAUC, JAN, physics educator; b. Pardubice, Czechoslovakia, Apr. 15, 1922; came to U.S., 1969, naturalized, 1978; s. Jan and Josefa (Semonska) T.; m. Vera Koubelova, Oct. 18, 1947; children: Elena (Mrs. Milan Kokta), Jan. Ing.Dr. in Elec. Engring, Tech. U. Prague, 1949; RNDr., in Physics, Charles U., Prague, 1956; Dr.Sc. in Physics, Czechoslovak Acad. Scis., 1956. Scientist microwave research Sci. and Tech. Research Inst., Tanvald and Prague, 1949-52; head semiconductor dept. Inst. Solid State Physics, Czechoslovak Acad. Scis., 1953-69; prof. exptl. physics Charles U., 1964-69, dir. Inst. Physics, 1968-69; mem. tech. staff Bell Telephone Labs., Murray Hill, N.J., 1969-70; prof. engring. and physics Brown U., 1970—, L. Herbert Ballou prof. engring. and physics, 1983—, dir. Materials Research Lab., 1983—; dir. E. Fermi Summer Sch., Varenna, Italy, 1965; vis. prof. U. Paris, 1969, Stanford U., 1977, Max Planck Inst. Solid State Research, Stuttgart, Germany, 1982; UNESCO fellow, Harvard, 1961-62. Author: Photo and Thermoelectric Effects in Semiconductors, 1962, also numerous articles.; Editor: The Optical Properties of Solids, 1966, Amorphous and Liquid Semiconductors, 1974; co-editor: Solid State Communications, 1963—. Recipient Nat. prize Czechoslovak Govt., 1955, 69; Sr. U.S. Scientist award Humboldt Found., 1981. Fellow Am. Phys. Soc. (Frank Isakson prize 1982), AAAS; founding mem. European Phys. Soc.; corr. mem. Czechoslovak Acad. Scis., 1963-71. Current Work: Electronic and optical properties of amorphous semiconductors; picosecond relaxation processes. Subspecialties: Condensed matter physics; Semiconductors. Office: Div Engring Brown Univ Providence RI 02912

TAYLOR, AUBREY ELMO, physiologist, educator; b. El Paso, Tex., June 4, 1933; s. Virgil T. and Mildred (Maher) T.; m. Mary Jane Davis, Apr. 4, 1953; children—Audrey Jane Hildebrand, Lenda Sue Brown, Mary Ann Smith. B.A. in Math. and Psychology, Tex. Christian U., 1960; Ph.D. in Physiology, U. Miss., 1964; Postdoctoral fellow biophysics lab. Harvard U. Med. Sch., Boston, 1965-67; from asst. prof. to prof. dept. physiology U. Miss. Coll. Medicine, Jackson, 1967-77; prof., chmn. dept. physiology U. South Ala. Coll. Medicine, Mobile, 1977—; mem. pulmonary score com. Nat. Heart, Lung and Blood Inst., 1976. Author 4 books. Contbr. chpts. to books, articles to profl. jours. Assoc. editor Jour. Applied Physiology, 1984—; mem. editorial bd. Circulation Research, Am. Jour. Physiology, Microvascular Research, Microcirculatory and Lymphatic Research. Served with U.S. Army, 1953-55. NIH grantee, 1967—; Lederle Faculty award, 1967-70. Fellow Am. Heart Assn. (circulation and cardiopulmonary council 1985—, chmn. So. and regional rev. com. 1977-81); mem. Am. Physiol. Soc. (council 1984—), Microcirculatory Soc. (council 1977-81, pres. 1981-83, Landis award 1985), AAAS, Lymphology Soc., N.Y. Acad. Scis., Biophys. Soc., Sigma Xi. Democrat. Presbyterian. Current work: Cardio-pulmonary physiology; fluid balance, edema, microcirculation and capillary exchange of solute and water. Subspecialties: Physiology (medicine); Pulmonary medicine. Home: 11 Audubon Pl Mobile AL 36606 Office: U So Ala Coll Medicine MSB 3024 Mobile AL 36688

TAYLOR, BARRY NORMAN, physicist; b. Phila., Mar. 27, 1936; s. Morris and Sarah (Weiss) T.; m. Sheila Anne Cohen, Dec. 28, 1958; children—Deborah Susan, David Joel, Denise Beth. A.B., Temple U., 1957; M.S., U. Pa., 1960, Ph.D., 1963. Instr., then asst. prof. physics U. Pa., 1963-66; mem. tech. staff RCA Research Labs., Princeton, N.J., 1966-70; chief absolute elec. measurements sect., then chief electricity div. Nat. Bureau Standards, D.C., 1970—; instr. Rider Coll., Trenton, N.J., 1969-70. Author: Fundamental Constants and Quantum Electrodynamics, 1969. Co-editor: Precision Measurement and Fundamental Constants, 1971, 1984. Contbr. articles to profl. jours. Recipient Sci. award RCA, 1969, Silver medal Dept. Commerce, 1975, John Price Wetherill medal Franklin Inst., 1975. Fellow Am. Phys. Soc., IEEE, Washington Acad. Scis.; mem. Sigma Xi. Current work: Least squares adjustments of fundamental constants, data analysis techniques; precision electrical measurements; fundamental constant determinations. Subspecialties: Low temperature physics; Electrical engineering. Home: 11908 Tallwood Ct Potomac MD 20854 Office: Nat Bur Standards Bldg 220 Room B258 Gaithersburg MD 20899

TAYLOR, BERNARD FRANKLIN, laboratory administrator, educator; b. Charles Town, W.Va., Mar. 21, 1930; s. Beverly Douglas and Harriet Elizabeth (Dotson) T.; m. Sylvia Adora Spriggs, Jan. 28, 1957; children: Bernard Franklin, Michael Lensen. B.S. in Biology cum laude, Storer Coll., 1952; postgrad., Bluefield State Coll., 1951; M.S. in Microbiology and pub. health, Mich. State U., 1959; postgrad., Rider Coll., 1961, Trenton Jr. Coll., 1964; Ph.D. in Microbiology, Rutgers U., 1972; M.A. in Adminstrn, Rider Coll., 1980. Cert. Inst. Med. Research, Camden, N.J. 1974. Bacteriologist Bur. Virology, Dept. Health, State of Mich., Lansing, 1954-56, virologist, 1956-59; instr. sci., coach football Elizabeth City (N.C.) State Tchrs. Coll., 1959-60; virologist div. labs. Dept. Health State of N.J., 1960-61, sr. virologist, 1961-62, prin. virologist, 1962-67, chief virologist, 1967-79, dir. pub. health lab. service div. pub. health and environ. labs., 1979—; med. technologist Helene Fuld Hosp., Trenton, 1961-64; co-adj. dept. biology Trenton State Coll., 1972—; co-adj. Mercer County Community Coll., 1981—; resource mgmt. officer Office Def. Resources, Nat. Def. Exec. Res., Region III, Phila. Contbr. articles to profl. jours. Mem. juvenile cof. com. County of Mercer (N.J.); chmn. United Way campaign N.J. Dept. Health, 1973; asst. scoutmaster troop 31 Boy Scouts Am., Charles Town, 1949. Recipient Ella P. Stewart Biology award, 1952. Mem. Am. Soc. Microbiologists, Am. Acad. Microbiology, Am. Assn. for Lab. Animal Sci., Found. Infectious Disease, Assn. State and Territorial Pub. Health Lab. Dirs., Am. Soc. Pub. Adminstrs., Am. Pub. Health Assn., N.Y. Acad. Scis., Sigma Xi, Beta Kappa Chi, Alpha Phi Alpha. Democrat. Lodge: Masons. Current Work: Immunology as a sero-diagnostic tool. Subspecialties: Virology (biology); Microbiology. Home: 438 Walnut Ave Trenton NJ 08609 Office: CN 360 New Jersey State Department Health Trenton NJ 08625

TAYLOR, CHARLES LAVERNE, geologist, engineer; b. Hughes Springs, Tex., Apr. 18, 1931; s. Fonnie C. and Bernice (Rankin) T.; m. Lois Marie Bright, Aug. 9, 1957; children—Laurie Marie Taylor Agnello; Charles LaVerne. B.S. in Geology, San Diego State U., 1958. Registered geologist, Calif., Oreg.; cert. engring. geologist, Calif., Oreg. Jr. engring. geologist Dept. Water Resources, Sacramento, 1958-59; assoc. engring. geologist Woodward-Clyde Cons., San Francisco, 1959-84; v.p., prin. engring. geologist Geomatrix Cons. Inc., San Francisco, Oakland, 1984—. Contbr. articles and geol. studies to profl. publs. Com. mem. Calif. Seismic Safety Commn., Assn. Bay Area Govt., various others. Served with USAF, 1950-54. Recipient Spl. Service award Woodward-Clyde Cons., 1981. Mem. Assn. Engr. Geologists (chmn. San Francisco sect. 1976), Earthquake Engring. Research Inst., Seismol. Soc. Am., Geol. Soc. Am., Am. Pub. Works Assn. Republican. Mem. Christian Missionary Alliance. Clubs: E. Bay Engrs., E. Bay Structural Engrs. Current work: Slope stability investigations, assessment of active faults, site assessments for civil engineering and hazardous waste projects. Subspecialties: Geology; Tectonics. Home: 2608 Fahey Ct Pinole CA 94564 Office: Geomatrix Cons Inc 1330 Broadway Suite 811 Oakland CA 94612

TAYLOR, CHARLES PRICE, JR., neurobiologist, researcher; b. Fort Knox, Ky., Aug. 15, 1954; s. Charles Price and Diane (Danforth) T.; m. Judith Jill Armstrong, June 18, 1977; children—Nathan Armstrong T., Emily Melissa T. B.A. in Zoology, U. Tex., 1975; Ph.D. in Neurobiology, U. Calif.-Berkeley, 1980. NIH postdoctoral fellow Tulane U. Med. Ctr., New Orleans, 1980-82; sr. scientist Parke-Davis Research, Ann Arbor, Mich., 1982—, chmn. anticonvulsant project team, 1983—. Contbr. articles to sci. jours. Mem. Soc. for Neurosci., Am. Epsilepsy Soc., Phi Beta Kappa. Current work: Discovery of anticonvulsant drugs and the neurophysiology of mammalian central nervous system. Subspecialties: Neurophysiology; Neuropharmacology. Home: 513 McKinley St Chelsea MI 48118 Office: Warner-Lambert/Parke-Davis Pharm Research 2800 Plymouth Rd Ann Arbor MI 48105

TAYLOR, CHARLES RICHARD, biology educator; b. Phoenix, Sept. 8, 1939; s. Norman W. and Rosalind E. (Gregory) T.; m. Ann Boyd, June 7, 1969; children—Gregory, Caitlin. B.S., Occidental Coll., 1960; A.M., Harvard U., 1962, Ph.D., 1963. Research officer East African Vet. Research Orgn., Muguga, Kenya, 1963-68; hon. lectr. East African U., Nairobi, Kenya, 1963-68; Research assoc. Harvard U., Cambridge, Mass., 1963-68, faculty mem., 1970—, prof. biology, 1973—; research assoc. Duke U., Durham, N.C., 1968-70. Contbr. numreous sci. articles to profl. jours. Editorial bd. Jour. Exptl. Biology, 1984—. Mem. Am. Physiol. Soc. (editorial bd. Jour. 1977—), Am. Soc. Zoology, Internat. Commn. on Comparative Physiology (chmn. 1977—). Current work: Energetics and mechanics of locomotion, design of respiratory system. Subspecialties: Animal physiology; Physiology (biology). Home: 329 Silver Hill Rd Concord MA 01742 Office: Concord Field Station-Harvard U Old Causeway Rd Bedford MA 01730

TAYLOR, DENNIS RILEY, research chemist; b. Eureka, Calif., May 5, 1941; s. Walter Riley and Lenora May (Viale) T.; m. Georgie Ann Cherry, July 17, 1965; children—Noelani Ann, Sean Riley. A.A., Am. River Jr. Coll., 1961; B.S., U. Calif.-Davis, 1963; Ph.D., U. Oreg., 1967. Sr. chemist, research chemist Texaco, Inc., Beacon, N.Y., 1968-74; mgr. research and devel. Filtrol, Inc., Los Angeles, 1974-80, Harshaw/Filtrol, Pleasanton, Calif., 1980—. Contbr. articles to profl. jours. Patentee in field. Mem. Am. Oil Chemists Soc. (treas. 1984—), Calif. Catalysis Soc. (treas. 1983—), Clay Minerals Soc. Current work: Catalysis and surface chemistry; interactions of organic molecules with oxides, silicates, clay minerals; development and formulation of catalysts and absorbent clays; synthesis and modification of zeolites and clays. Subspecialties: Surface chemistry; Catalysis chemistry. Office: Harshaw/Filtrol Partnership Div Kaiser Aluminum and Chem 6177 Sunol Blvd Pleasanton CA 94566

TAYLOR, DUNCAN PAUL, pharmaceutical company executive, neuropharmacologist; b. Bremerton, Wash., Feb. 4, 1949; s. Alan Earl and Barbara Eleanor (Thiel) T.; m. Jeanne Louise Damgaard, Apr. 8, 1972; 1 child, Aubrey Elizabeth. B.S., Calif. Inst. Tech., 1971; Ph.D., Oreg. State U., 1977. Technician analytical services Carnation Co. Research Labs., 1967-70; vol. U.S. Peace Corps, St. Johns, Antigua, W.I., 1971-73; grad. research, teaching asst. dept. biochemistry and biophysics Oreg. State U., Corvallis, 1973-77; research assoc. sect. on biochemistry and pharmacology, biol. psychiatry br. NIMH, Bethesda, Md., 1977-79; scientist, neuropharmacologist biol. research, pharm. div. Mead Johnson & Co., Evansville, Ind., 1979-80, research assoc., 1980, sr. scientist, 1980-82; sr. scientist group leader, neuropharmacologist preclin. central nervous system research, pharm. research and devel. div. Bristol-Myers Co., Evansville, 1982-83, sr. research scientist, mgr., 1983-85, research fellow, 1985—; participant Gordon Research Confs., 1977, 83, NATO Advanced Study Inst., 1977; grant reviewer sect. on biol. instrumentation Div. Physiology, Cellular and Molecular Biology, NSF, 1981, Neurobiology Program, 1982. Contbr. articles, abstracts, reports to profl. lit. Recipient Nat. Research Service award Nat. Inst. on Drug Abuse, 1977-79; NSF fellow, 1965, 70, Cold Spring Harbor Labs. fellow, 1974; Carnation Co. scholar, 1967-70, Calif. State scholar, 1967, 68, 70. Mem. Am. Chem. Soc., AAAS, Am. Soc. for Neurochemistry, Soc. for Exptl. Biology and Medicine, Am. Soc. for Pharmacology and Exptl. Therapeutics, Fedn. Am. Scientists, Soc. for Neurosci., Brit. Brain Research Assn., European Brain and Behavior Soc., Biophys. Soc., Fedn. Am. Socs. for Exptl. Biology, Sigma Xi, Phi Lambda Upsilon. Democrat. Methodist. Current work: Receptors in nervous tissue membranes; receptor coupling to second messengers; linkage of changes in receptors to pathology, behavior; etiology, expression and pharmacotherapy of psychiatric disorders. Subspecialties: Neuropharmacology; Neurochemistry. Home: 112 Ryan Ln Evansville IN 47712 Office: Pharmaceutical Research and Development Div Bristol-Myers Co Evansville IN 47721

TAYLOR, EDWARD CURTIS, chemist; b. Springfield, Mass., Aug. 3, 1923; s. Edward Curtis and Margaret Louise (Anderson) T.; m. Virginia Dion Crouse, June 29, 1946; children—Edward Newton, Susan Raines. Student, Hamilton Coll., 1942-44, D.Sc. (hon.), 1969; A.B., Cornell U., 1946, Ph.D., 1949. Postdoctoral fellow Nat. Acad. Scis., Zurich, Switzerland, 1949-50; DuPont postdoctoral fellow chemistry U. Ill., 1950-51, faculty, 1951-54, asst. prof. organic chemistry, 1952-54; faculty Princeton U., 1954—, prof. chemistry, 1964—, A. Barton Hepburn prof. organic chemistry, 1966—, chmn. dept. chemistry, 1974-79; vis. prof. Technische Hochschule, Stuttgart, Germany, 1960, U. East Anglia, 1969, 71; Distinguished vis. prof. U. Buffalo, 1968, U. Wyo., 1977; Backer lectr. U. Groningen, Holland, 1969; mem. chemistry adv. com. Office Sci. Research, USAF, 1962-73, Cancer Chemotherapy Nat. Service Center, 1958-62; cons. research divs. Procter & Gamble, 1953—, Eastman Kodak Co., 1965-83, Tenn. Eastman Co., 1968-83, Eli Lilly & Co. 1970—, Burroughs Wellcome Co., 1984—. Author: (with McKillop) Chemistry of Cyclic Enaminonitriles and o-Aminonitriles, 1970, Principles of Heterocyclic Chemistry; film course, 1974; editor: (with Raphael, Wynberg) Advances in Organic Chemistry, vols. I-V, 1960-65, (with Wynberg) vol. VI, 1969, vols. VII-IX, 1970-79, (with W. Pfleiderer) Pteridine Chemistry, 1964, (with A. Weissberger) The Chemistry of Heterocyclic Compounds, 1968—, General Heterocyclic Chemistry, 1968—; organic chemistry editorial adviser, Intersci. Pubs., 1968—; mem. editorial adv. bd.: Jour. Medicinal Chemistry, 1962-66, (with A. Weissberger) Jour. Organic Chemistry, 1971-75, Synthetic Communications, 1971—, Heterocycles, 1973—, Chem. Substructure Index, 1971—. Recipient research awards Smith Kline & French Found., 1955, Hoffmann-LaRoche Found., 1964, 65, Ciba Found., 1971; sr. faculty fellow Harvard U., 1959, Disting. Hamilton award, 1977; Guggenheim fellow, 1979-80; recipient U.S. sr. scientist prize Alexander von Humboldt Found., 1983. Fellow N.Y. Acad. Scis., Am. Inst. Chemists; mem. Am. Chem. Soc. (award for creative work in synthetic organic chemistry, 1974, chmn. organic chemistry div. 1976-77), German Chem. Soc., Chem. Soc. London, Phi Beta Kappa, Sigma Xi, Phi Kappa Phi. Subspecialties: Organic chemistry; Synthetic chemistry. Office: Princeton U Dept Chemistry Princeton NJ 08540

TAYLOR, ERIC ROBERT, chemistry educator, researcher; b. Quincy, Mass. B.S. Ohio State U., 1972; Ph.D., Rutgers U., 1981. Postdoctoral research assoc. Rensselaer Poly. Inst., Troy, N.Y., 1981-84; asst. prof. chemistry U. Southwestern La., Lafayette, 1984—. Contbr. articles to profl. jours. Served with U.S. Army, 1972-76. Mem. Biophys. Soc., N.Y. Acad. Sci., Sigma Xi. Current work: Conformational interaction of nucleic acids with other species (drugs, protein, etc.); DNA theoretical denaturation pathways. Subspecialties: Biochemistry (biology); Biophysics (biology). Office: Dept Chemistry U Southwestern La Lafayette LA 70504

TAYLOR, GARY, physicist; b. London, Sept. 23, 1952; came to U.S., 1977; s. Iris Taylor; m. Wendy Collins, Sept. 26, 1983. B.S. in Physics, Manchester U., Eng., 1974; M.S. in Plasma Physics, Oxford U., Eng., 1975, D.Phil., 1977. Postdoctoral research assoc. Plasma Physics Lab., Princeton U., N.J., 1977-79, research physicist, 1979—. Mem. Am. Phys. Soc. Current work: Application of laser and microwave techniques to the study of high temperature plasmas in magnetic confinement fusion experiments; energy confinement in large tokamak machines. Subspecialties: Nuclear fusion; Plasma physics. Home: 31 Federal City Rd Ewing NJ 08638 Office: Plasma Physics Lab Princeton U Princeton NJ 08544

TAYLOR, GEORGE WILLIAM, electrical engineer, electronics company executive; b. Perth, Australia, June 16, 1934; came to U.S., 1962, naturalized, 1968; s. George William and Myrtle (Spigl) T.; m. Cynthia Hatch, Aug. 24, 1957; children: Susan, George William, Deborah, Felicity. B.E.E. with honors, U. Western Australia, 1957, D.Eng., 1981; Ph.D., U. London, 1961. Registered profl. engr., Australia, Eng. Lectr. U. Sydney, Australia, 1961-62; mem. tech. staff RCA Labs., Princeton, N.J., 1962-70; exec. v.p. research and engring. Princeton Materials Research, 1970-75; pres. Princeton Resources, Inc., 1975—, dir., 1975—; dir. Cottesloe Corp., Perth, Aberdare Co., Princeton, Abbotsford Co., Launceston, Tasmania, Australia. Author: Polar Dielectrics and Their Applications, 1979; editor: Ferroelectrics Jour, 1970—, Ferroelectrics Letters, 1981—, Display and Imaging Technology Jour, 1982—; contbr. over 50 sci. articles to profl. publs. Recipient RCA Labs. Achievement award, 1966; Hackett Overseas scholar, 1958-59; CSIRO Overseas scholar, 1960; NSF fellow, 1976. Fellow Instr. Elec. Engrs. (London), Inst. Engrs. (Australia); mem. IEEE (sr.), Am. Phys. Soc., Soc. for Info. Display, Sigma Xi. Episcopalian. Holder 15 patents. Current Work: Piezoelectronics, ferroelectrics; electronic displays; liquid crystals. Subspecialties: Electronics; Electronic materials. Office: Box 211 Princeton NJ 08540

TAYLOR, GERALD REED, JR., physics educator, researcher; b. Bloxom, Va., Apr. 17, 1937; s. Gerald Reed and Sarah (Hartman) T.; m. Susan Shrieves, Nov. 27, 1960; children—Gerald Reed III, John William. B.S. in Physics, Va. Polytech. Inst., 1959, M.S. in Physics, 1961; Ph.D. in Physics, U. Va., 1967. Research physicists Union Carbide Corp., Tonowanda, N.Y., 1967-69; assoc. prof. James Madison U., Harrisonburg, Va., 1969-80, prof., 1980—; dir. Vis. Scis., Richmond Va., 1977-79, Va. Acad. Sci. Co-author: Boron, Vol. 2, 1965; contbr. articles to profl. jours. Mem. Am. Physical Soc., Am. Assn. Physics Tchrs., Va. Acad. Sci. (chmn., sec., editor), Sigma Xi, Sigma Pi Sigma. Methodist. Lodge: Kiwanis (past scholarship com. chmn.). Current work: Confinement and diagnostics in multidipole plasmas, transport properties in ferromagnetic materials at low temperatures, teaching and computer applications in physics. Subspecialties: Low temperature physics; Plasma physics. Home: 1110 S Dogwood Dr Harrisonburg VA 22801

TAYLOR, HERBERT LYNDON, component engineer; b. Van Alstyne, Tex., Aug. 11, 1931; s. Herbert Lonnie and Eula Estelle (Grissom) T.; m. Barbara Ruth Luther, Nov. 24, 1956; children—Karen Lynette, Harmon Luther. B.A. in Physics, Austin Coll., 1951; M.A. in Physics, Rice U., 1952, Ph.D. in Physics, 1955. Registered profl. engr., Tex. Mem. tech. staff Tex. Instruments, Dallas, 1955-63; assoc. prof. elec. engring. U. Tex., Austin, 1963-80; mgr. failure analysis Mostek-United Tech., Carrollton, Tex., 1980-81; component engr. Rockwell Internat., Richardson, Tex., 1983—. Patentee Intracranial pressure sensor system, 1979; contbr. articles to profl. jours. Precinct participant Republican Party, Dallas, 1982—; Jr. Achievement counselor, Dallas and Richardson, 1983—. Mem. Am. Phys. Soc., IEEE, Electrochem. Soc., Am. Vacuum Soc., Internat. Soc. Hybrid Microelectronics. Republican. Presbyterian. Current work: Lightwave communication, non-destructive testing. Subspecialties: Electrical engineering; Integrated circuits. Home: 7014 Mason Dells Dr Dallas TX 75230

TAYLOR, HUGH PETTINGIL, JR., See *Who's Who in America,* 43rd edition.

TAYLOR, JACK E., physicist; b. Emporia, Kans., s. John and B. (Brown) T.; m. Marion Jeanne Pearsall, Feb. 13, 1948; children—Joan A., Jeannette A. Ph.B., U. Wis., Madison, 1946, M.S., 1948, Ph.D., 1951. Research assoc. Gen. Electric Research Lab., Schenectady, 1951-61; sr. research staff G.D. Electronics Div., Rochester, N.Y., 1961-70; sr. research staff integrated circuit fabrication Stromberg Carlson Co., Rochester, 1970-81; unit head integrated circuit fabrication Eastman Kodak Co., Rochester, 1981—. Served to lt (j.g.) USNR, 1943-47, PTO. Mem. IEEE (sr. mem.). Current work: Materials and technology for fabrication of integrated circuits. Home: 31 Old Pond Rd Rochester NY 14625 Office: US Apparatus Div Eastman Kodak 901 Elmgrove Rd Rochester NY 14650

TAYLOR, LARRY DON, mechanical engineer; b. Oklahoma City, Apr. 24, 1959; s. Donald Gene and Billie Jean (Craig) T. B.S., Okla. State U., 1981. Mech. engr. Sun Exploration and Prodn. Co., Houston, 1981-84, project engr. platform installation, 1984—. Vol. worker Com. to Re-elect K. Whitmire, Houston, 1983. Mem. ASME (assoc.), Proctor Plaza Civic Club, Houston Heights Assn. Methodist. Current work: Design of production facilities for offshore production platforms; environmental impact of offshore facilities. Subspecialties: Petroleum engineering; Offshore technology. Office: Sun Exploration and Prodn Co PO Box 1501 Houston TX 77251

TAYLOR, LEONARD STUART, electrical engineering educator, consultant; b. N.Y.C., Dec. 28, 1928; s. Jacob and Elizabeth Taylor; m. Lillian Rachel Schland, Apr. 11, 1954; children—Robin Jolie, Allyn Lise. A.B., Harvard Coll., 1951; M.S., N.Mex. State U., 1956, Ph.D., 1960. Electronics engr. Raytheon Mfg. Co., Bedford, Mass., 1951-55; electronics scientist U.S. Dept. Def., White Sands, N.Mex., 1958-60; physicist Gen. Electric Co., Phila., 1960-62; assoc. prof. Case-Western Res. U., Cleve., 1963-67; prof. elec. engring. U. Md., College Park, 1967—; cons. Ford Found., Mexico City, 1963-64; sr. Fulbright lectr. U. Madrid, 1962-63. Patentee in field. Contbr. articles to profl. jours. Recipient Disting. Alumnus award N.Mex. State U., 1971. Fellow IEEE; mem. Am. Phys. Soc., Optical Soc. Am., Bioelectromagnetics Soc. Current work: Electromagnetic theory, biomedical applications of electromagnetic radiation, optical engring. Subspecialties: Biomedical engineering; Electrical engineering. Office: Elec Engring Dept Univ Md College Park MD 20742

TAYLOR, LLOYD DAVID, research chemist, chemistry educator; b. Boston, Jan. 11, 1933; s. Lloyd Septimus and Emily Nathalie (LeBlanc) T.; m. Marianne Therese Cassie, June 29, 1957; children—Lloyd D. III, Julianne M., Lisa D. B.S., Boston Coll., 1954; Ph.D., MIT, 1958. Scientist Polaroid Corp., Cambridge, Mass., 1958-65, group leader, 1965-69, mgr. polymer research, 1969-80, dir. chem. research, 1980-83, sr. research fellow, 1980—; adj. prof., Boston Coll., Chestnut Hill, Mass., 1982—. Contbr. articles to profl. jours. Patentee (70) in field. Town mtg. mem. Lexington, Mass., 1977-82. Served to capt. U.S. Army, 1958. Mem. Am. Chem. Soc., Am. Inst. Chemists (cert.), Soc. Photo Sci. and Engring. Roman Catholic. Club: Charles River Yacht (Cambridge). Lodge: Elks. Current work: Polymer chemistry, new polymer synthesis, photographic chemistry, critical phenomena of polymer solutions, diffusion. Subspecialties: Polymer chemistry; Organic chemistry. Home: 1 Maureen Rd Lexington MA 02173 Office: Polaroid Corp 730 Main St 5A Cambridge MA 02139

TAYLOR, LYLE HERMAN, physicist, researcher; b. Paton, Iowa, Oct. 23, 1936; s. Hilles J. and Alma (Friedrichs) T.; m. Jane K. Easley, Sept. 27, 1959; children—Steven, Alan, Susan, Kevin, Brian. B.S., Iowa State U., 1958; M.S., N.Mex. State U., 1961; Ph.D., U. Kans., 1967. Sr. scientist White Sands Missile Range, N. Mex., 1958-61, Midwest Research Inst., Kansas City, Mo., 1961-64; sr. scientist Westinghouse Electric Co., Pitts., 1967-84, George Westinghouse research fellow, 1984—. Patentee lasers. Mem. Am. Phys. Soc. Presbyterian. Lodge: Lions (pres. 1978-79). Current work: Infrared laser devel.; inertial confinement fusion reactor studies; theory of molecular vibrations; laser-material interactions. Subspecialties: Atomic and molecular physics; Fusion. Home: 3317 Benden Dr Murrysville PA 15668 Office: Westinghouse Research and Devel Ctr 1310 Beulah Rd Pittsburgh PA 15235

TAYLOR, NORMAN LINN, agronomy educator, researcher; b. Augusta, Ky., July 18, 1926; s. Norman Bruce and Mabel Angela (Newland) T.; m. Evelyn Osborne, Mar. 30, 1951; children—Sharon, Norman, Clayton, Steven, Kathryn. B.S., U. Ky., 1949, M.S., 1951; Ph.D., Cornell U., 1953. Grad. asst. U. Ky., Lexington, 1949-51, asst. agronomist, 1953-57, assoc. agronomist, 1957-60, assoc. prof., 1960-65, prof., 1965—; grad. asst. Cornell U., Ithaca, N.Y., 1951-53. Editor: Clover Science & Technology, 1985. Contbr. articles to profl. jours., chpts. to books. Recipient cert. merit Am. Forest & Grassland Council, 1973, research award U. Ky., 1982. Fellow Am. Soc. Agronomy; mem. Am. Genetics Assn., Genetics Soc. Can. Democrat. Presbyterian. Current work: Breeding and genetics of Trifolium (clover). Subspecialties: Agronomy; Genetics and genetic engineering (biology). Office: Dept Agronomy Univ Ky Lexington KY 40546

TAYLOR, RALPH DALE, research engineering executive; b. Boonville, Mo., Dec. 24, 1945; s. Ralph and Florence Lucy (Gerke) T.; m. Jennie Sue Antte, Sept. 3, 1973; children—Jennifer Lee and Nathan Ralph. B.S.E.E., U. of Mo.-Rolla, 1968; M.S.E.E., U. Mo., Columbia, 1971; M.B.A., U. Mo.-Kansas City, 1977. Registered profl. engr. Engr., Bendix, Kansas City, Mo., 1968-77; mgr. research and devel. Dit-MCO, Kansas City, 1977—; adj. prof. U. Mo., Columbia. Contbr. articles to profl. jours. Mem. IEEE, Beta Gamma Sigma. Democrat. Baptist. Current work: Automatic test, systems, optical image acquisition, artifical intelligence. Home: Rural Route 1 Lone Jack MO 64070 Office: Dit-MCO Internat 5612 Brighton Terr Kansas City MO 64131

TAYLOR, R(AYMOND) DEAN TAYLOR, low temperature physicist, researcher; b. Okemah, Okla., Aug. 18, 1928; s. H(enry) Ray and Vera (Bay) T.; m. Janis Dexter T.; June 24, 1961; children—Scott Edward, Kay Suzanne. B.S., Kans. State Coll., 1950; Ph.D., Rice U., 1954. Mem. staff Los Alamos Nat. Lab., N.Mex., 1954-72, assoc. group leader, 1973-80, dep. group leader, 1981—. Contbr. articles to profl. jours. Mem. Am. Phys. Soc., Sigma Xi. Current work: Magnetism, superconductivity, Mossbauer effect, high pressure physics, ultralow temperatures, thermometry. Subspecialties: Low temperature physics; Condensed matter physics. Office: Los Alamos Nat Lab PO Box 1663 MS K764 Los Alamos NM 87545

TAYLOR, ROBERT COOPER, chemistry educator; b. Colorado Springs, Colo., May 5, 1917; s. Clarence Egbert and Marjorie Caroline (Cooper) T.; m. Evelyn Letitia Seeley, Dec. 27, 1942; children—David Robert, Donald Cooper. A.B., Kalamazoo Coll., 1941; Ph.D., Brown U., 1947. Chemist Brown U., Providence, 1942-45, instr., 1947-49; instr. U. Mich., Ann Arbor, 1949-53, asst. prof., 1953-58, assoc. prof., 1958-63, prof. chemistry, 1963—, assoc. chmn. dept. chemistry, 1967—; cons. Council on Library Resources, Barrow Lab., 1974-77; vis. sci. Los Alamos Nat. Lab., N.Mex., 1974. Contbr. articles to profl. jours. NRC fellow. Mem. Am. Chem. Soc. (councillor 1974—), Am. Phys. Soc., AAAS, Sigma Xi. Current work: Infrared and Raman spectroscopic methods applied to problems of molecular structure; molecular parameters and force constants; correlation of molecular parameters with chemical properties. Subspecialties: Spectroscopy and molecular structure; Physical chemistry. Home: 850 Heatherway Ann Arbor MI 48104 Office: U Mich Dept Chemistry Ann Arbor MI 48109

TAYLOR, ROBERT JOE, ecologist academic; b. Pomona, Calif., May 1, 1945; s. Thaddeus T. and Bertha B. (Gordon) T.; m. Susana V. Englander, Sept. 9, 1967; children—Jonathan and Peter. A.B., Stanford U., 1967; M.A., U. of Calif.-Santa Barbara, 1970, Ph.D., 1972. Research assoc. Princeton U., N.J., 1971-72; asst. prof. U. of Minn., Mpls., 1972-78; assoc. prof. Clemson U., S.C., 1978—; dir. Clemson Environ. Research Ctr., 1985—. Contbr. articles to prof. jours. Mem. Am. Soc. of Naturalists, British Ecol. Soc., Animal Behavior Soc., Ecol. Soc. of Am., Japanese Soc. for Population Ecology. Democrat. Current work: Population dynamics of predotor-prey systems; theoretical studies of pursuit and evasion; theory of wildlife harvesting; theoretical biogeography. Subspecialties: Behavioral ecology; Theoretical ecology. Home: Star Rte 1 Six Mile SC 29682 Office: Dept Biological Scis Long Hall Clemson Univ Clemson SC 29631

TAYLOR, ROBERT P., mechanical engineering educator; b. Columbus, Miss., Oct. 22, 1951; s. Robert Penn and Catherine (Barton) T. B.S. in Mech. Engring., Miss. State U., 1973, Ph.D., in Mech. Engring., 1983; M.S. in Mech. Engring., Purdue U., 1975. Sr. engr. Texaco, Inc., Houston, 1975-78; research asst. Miss. State U., 1979-81, instr., 1981-83, asst. prof., 1984—. Contbr. articles to profl. jours. Purdue U. fellow, 1973; recipient U.S. Air Force contract. Mem. AIAA, ASME, Sigma Xi, Phi Kappa Phi, Tau Beta Pi. Current work: Development of predictive models for fluid flow over rough surfaces. Subspecialties: Fluid mechanics; Mechanical engineering. Office: Dept Mech Engring PO Drawer ME Mississippi State MS 39762

TAYLOR, ROGER NORRIS, immunologist, cons., researcher, writer, educator; b. Farmington, Utah, Oct. 23, 1941; s. Norris John and Josephine (Hardy) T.; m. Sydney Moulton, Apr. 1, 1965; children: Michael, Stephen, Reuben, Melissa, Marcus, Benjamin, Lettitia. B.S., U. Utah, 1969, M.S., 1971, Ph.D., 1974. Clin. and research microbiologist VA Hosp., Salt Lake City, 1969-72; teaching assoc. U. Utah Coll. Medicine, 1970-74; microbiologist, lab improvement Utah Div. Health, Salt Lake City, 1972-74; chief diagnostic immunology Ctrs. for Diseases Control, Atlanta, 1975—; cons., tchr. in field. Author monographs, also numerous articles. Scouting coordinator, mem. dist. scout com., mem. dist. scout tng. com. and tng. staff DeKalb dist. Atlanta Area Council Boy Scouts Am.; Tucker (Ga.) stake primary scouting dir. Mormon Ch. Served to cpl. USMC, 1960-64. Recipient Order of Arrow award Boy Scouts Am., 1981, Scouters' Tng. award, 1981, Woodbadge, 1981, On My Honor award, 1981, Dist. award of merit, 1982; USPHS vol. award, 1985. Mem. Am. Acad. Microbiology, Am. Bd. Bioanalysis, Nat. Com. Clin. Lab. Standards, N.Y. Acad. Sci., Sigma Xi. Current Work: Measurement and improvement of laboratory proficiency with immunologic tests; proficiency testing; immunology; quality control; laboratory improvement; serology; biometrics. Subspecialties: Immunology (medicine); Health services research. Home: 308 Westwind Dr Lilburn GA 30247 Office: 1600 Clifton Rd Bldg 6 Room 319 Atlanta GA 30333

TAYLOR, ROGER WILLIAM, research institute administrator; b. St. Louis, Dec. 5, 1950; s. James W. and Sallie L. (Rogers) T.; m. Patricia R. Weis, Aug. 31, 1979; children—Amber Weis, Alexander Weis. B.A. in Physics, Colo. Coll., 1973; M.S. in Mech. Engring., U. Ariz., 1976. Research analyst Ariz. Pub. Service, Phoenix, 1977-78; staff engr. Solar Energy Research Inst., Golden, Colo., 1978-80; project mgr. Electric Power Research Inst., Palo Alto, Calif., 1980—. Current work: Photovoltaic and other solar technology development; integration of solar systems into electric utilities. Subspecialty: Solar energy. Office: Electric Power Research Inst 3412 Hillview Ave Palo Alto CA 94303

TAYLOR, THOMAS ALAN, scientist, researcher; b. Portland, Oreg., May 25, 1941; s. Thomas L. and Lucille E. (Davis) T.; m. Melaine Everly McVay, June 19, 1965; children—James Miles, Thomas Jarard. B.S. in Materials Sci., Stanford U., 1963, M.S., 1965, Ph.D., 1968. Sr. scientist Union Carbide, Indpls., 1968-72, research assoc., 1972-77, cons., 1977-82, mgr. materials devel., 1982—. Patentee in field (2 U.S., 1 French, 1 German). Contbr. numerous articles to profl. jours. Mem. Am. Soc. Metals (chmn. Indpls., 1982), AIME. Republican. Current work: Coatings for high temperature components to protect them from oxidation, sulfidation or act as thermal barrier. Coatings for wear in high temperature nuclear applications. Subspecialties: High-temperature materials; Ceramics. Office: Union Carbide 1500 Polco St Indianapolis IN 46224

TAYLOR, WILLIAM FRANCIS, chemical engineer; b. Washington, Apr. 20, 1931; s. Samuel Hunter and Marie (Loebel) T.; m. Marianne Fazzini, Apr. 8, 1961; children—Patricia C., Barbara A., Margaret M. B.Chem.Engring., Cath. U. Am., 1953; M.S., Ohio State U., 1957; M.S. in Statistics, Rutgers U., 1962; Sc.D., Stevens Inst. Tech., 1967. Registered profl. engr., Ohio. Engr., Goodyear Tire & Rubber Co., Akron, Ohio, 1953-54; research engr. Exxon Research & Engring. Co., Linden, N.J., 1957-71, sr. research engr., 1971-75, engring. assoc., 1975-82, sr. engring. assoc., 1982—; leader aviation alt. fuel adv. com. Coordinating Research Council Atlanta, 1980—. Contbr. articles to profl. jours. Patentee in field. Served with U.S. Army, 1954-56. Mem. Am. Inst. Chem. Engrs., Am. Chem. Soc., Sigma Xi. Current work: Aviation fuel research, fuel autoxidative stability, synthetic fuel research. Subspecialties: Fuels; Chemical engineering. Home: 1598 Brookside Rd Mountainside NJ 07092 Office: Exxon Research and Engring Products Research Div Linden NJ 07036

TAYLOR, WILLIAM LEROY, physical chemist, educator; b. Cin., July 16, 1931; s. William Leroy and Helen Louise (Koch) T.; m. Kathleen Bouchette Nelson, Aug. 23, 1952; children—William, Andrew, Daniel, Robert, Anthony, Thomas. Chem. E., U. Cin., 1954, Ph.D., 1961. Registered profl. engr., Ohio. Sr. research chemist Monsanto Research Corp. Mound, Miamisburg, Ohio, 1961-63, group leader, 1963-74, sci. fellow, 1974—; prof. chemistry U. Cin., 1984—. Contbr. articles to profl. jours. Patentee in field. Served to 1st lt. U.S. Army, 1954-57. Proctor & Gamble fellow, 1960-61; recipient Disting. Engring. Alumnus award U. Cin., 1978. Mem. Am. Phys. Soc., Am. Chem. Soc. Sigma Alpha Epsilon. Presbyterian. Clubs: Hyde Pk. Golf and Country (Cin.) (gov. 1973-75, sec. 1974-75), Camargo Racquet. Current work: Transport and thermodynamic properties of atoms, molecules, and isotopes. Subspecialty: Atomic and molecular physics. Home: 7250 Cayuga Dr Cincinnati OH 45243 Office: Monsanto Research Corp Mound PO Box 32 Miamisburg OH 45342

TCHEN, TCHE-TSING, biochemist, educator; b. Bejing, China, Oct. 1, 1924; s. Tze-fan and T.R. (Tsou) Cheng; m. Ina Lin Tchen, Dec. 25, 1960; children—Terence, Vincent. Chem. engr., Aurora U., Shanghai, China, 1948; Ph.D., U. Chgo., 1954. Research assoc. Harvard U., 1955-58; assoc. prof. biochemistry Wayne State U., Detroit, 1958-61, prof., 1961—; mem. physiol. chemistry study sect. NIH, Bethesda, Md., 1960-65; mem. research com. Am. Heart Assn., 1966-70. Mem. editorial bd. Jour. Biol. Chemistry, Archives of Biochemistry and Biophysics, Endocrine Research Communication. Mem. Am. Soc. Biol. Chemists. Current work: Organelle translocations, cytoskelton, protein kinases. Subspecialties: Biochemistry (medicine); Cell biology. Office: Dept Chemistry Wayne State U Detroit MI 48202

TEAGUE, JAMES RALPH, engineering manager laser technology; researcher; b. Asheville, N.C., Mar. 16, 1946; s. James Millard and Helena (Ward) T.; m. Elizabeth Ann Hoffert, Nov. 17, 1984; children—Jeff, Jason. B.S. in Physics, U. N.C., 1967; M.S. in Physics, N.Mex. Highlands U., 1968; Ph.D. in Physics, U. Mo., 1971. Group leader McDonnell-Douglas, St. Louis, 1971-79; tech. mgr. Internat. Laser Systems, Orlando, Fla., 1979-80; group leader, Harris Corp., Melbourne, Fla., 1980-82; v.p. Newport Electro-Optics, Melbourne, 1982-84; mem. tech. staff Rockwell Missile Systems Div., Duluth, Ga., 1984—; adj. prof. Fla. Inst. Tech., Melbourne, 1980-82; cons. Control Laser, Orlando, 1982-84. Contbr. writings to publs. in field; patentee electro-optics, acousto-optics, laser tech. Mem. Optical Soc. Am., Laser Inst. Am., Soc. Photo-optical Instrumentation Engrs., Am. Phys. Soc., Sigma Xi. Club: Kiwanis. Research or work interests: laser technology including optics design, acousto-optics, electro-optics, detectors, infrared detection, electro-optics modeling, system analysis. Subspecialties: Laser technology; Optical signal processing. Home: 1442 Hartman Trail Lilburn GA 30247 Office: Rockwell Missile Systems Div 1800 Satellite Blvd Duluth GA 30136

TEAL, JOHN M., marine ecologist; b. Omaha, Nov. 9, 1929; s. Clarence William and Valentine (Moline) T.; m. Mildred Mann, Dec. 30, 1950 (div. 1978); children—Eric, Tanya; m. Susan Blackmore Peterson, June 4, 1979. A.B., Harvard U., 1951, Ph.D., 1955. Research assoc. U. Ga., Sapelo Island, 1955-59; asst. prof. Dalhousie U., Halifax, N.S., Can., 1959-61; asst. scientist Woods Hole Oceanograhic Inst., Mass., 1961-65, assoc. scientist, 1965-71, sr. scientist, 1971—; dir. conservation Law Found. New Eng., Boston. Author: Portrait of an Island, 1964; Life and Death of the Salt Marsh, 1969; The Sargasso Sea, 1975. Contbr. numerous articles to profl. jours. Mem. Am. Soc. Limnology and Oceanography, Ecol. Soc. Am., AAAS. Current work: Salt marsh ecology and geochemistry, hydrocarbon biogeochemistry. Subspecialties: Ecology (biology); Environmental chemistry. Home: 567 New Bedford Rd Rochester MA 02770 Office: Woods Hole Oceanograhic Inst Woods Hole MA 02543

TEDDLIE, CHARLES BENTON, education research consultant, social psychologist; b. Winnfield, La., July 30, 1949; s. Charles Ray and Blanche (Wilson) T.; m. Susan Elizabeth Kochan, June 19, 1982; m. Karen Antoinette Lafontaine, Dec. 1972 (div. 1974). B.S. cum laude, La. State U., 1972; M.A. in Social Psychology, U.N.C.-Chapel Hill, 1977, Ph.D., 1979. Vis. asst. prof. La. State U., Baton Rouge, 1979, adj. asst. prof., 1980-85; asst. prof. U. New Orleans, 1980—; internal research cons. La. State Dept. Edn., Baton Rouge, 1980-85; pres. La Data, Baton Rouge, 1980—. Contbr. articles to profl. jours.; editorial cons.: Personality and Social Psychology Bull, 1980, Population: Behavioral, Social and Environ. Issues, 1977-79, Representative Research in Social Psychology, 1973-79. Mem. Democratic Socialist Organizing Com., 1980—. Recipient Paul C. Young award La. State U., 1971-72. Mem. Am. Ednl. Research Assn., Am. Psychol. Assn., Assn. Instl. Research, SAS Users Group Internat., Phi Kappa Phi. Democrat. Current Work: Forecasting educational enrollment and policy trends, school efficiency and effectiveness studies, racial differences in social perception, self disclosure, information systems, communications research. Subspecialties: Social psychology; Information systems (Information science). Home: 9065 Redbud Baton Rouge LA 70815 Office: Dept Ednl Leadership and Foundations Univ New Orleans New Orleans LA 70148

TEDROW, PAUL MULLER, physicist; b. Ware, Mass., Apr. 5, 1940; s. N. Paul and Edna (Zimmerman) T.; m. Prabha Kumbhare, Mar. 26, 1970, children—Usha Beth, John Rahul. B.S., MIT, 1961; Ph.D., Cornell U., 1966. Postdoctoral assoc. Cornell U., Ithaca, N.Y., 1966-67; research scientist nat. magnet lab. MIT, Cambridge, Mass., 1967—. Contbr. articles to profl. jours. Fellow Am. Phys. Soc. Subspecialties: Condensed matter physics; Low temperature physics. Office: Nat Magnet Lab MIT Cambridge MA 02139

TEEGARDEN, KENNETH JAMES, optics educator, university institute executive; b. East Chicago, Ill., May 13, 1928; s. Joseph Archibald and Lillian Maud (Collins) T.; m. Judith Darnell, Jan. 24, 1959; children—Josephine, Christina, Henry. A.B., U. Chgo., 1947, B.S., 1950; M.S., U. Ill., 1951, Ph.D., 1954. Research assoc. U. Rochester, N.Y., 1954-58, asst. prof, 1956-58, assoc. prof., 1958-60, sr. research assoc., 1961-66, prof. optics, 1966—, dir. Inst. Optics, 1981—, NY. State Ctr. for Advanced Optical Tech., 1982—; cons. Eastman Kodak Co., Rochester, 1966-76. Referee: Phys. Rev. and Phys. Rev. Letters, 1980—; U.S. editor Optica Acta, 1983—; mem. internat. adv. bd. Marquis Who's Who, 1983—. Fellow Optical Soc. Am. (Alfred Sloan Found. fellow 1961, mem. Max Born Medal com. 1984-85, Newport Research Award com. 1984), Am. Phys. Soc.; mem. N.Y. State Acad. Sci., Sigma Xi. Club: Rochester Yacht. Current work: Electro-optics, gradient index optics, lasers, optical materials. Subspecialty: Optical research management. Office: Inst of Optics Univ Rochester Rochester NY 14627

TEEM, JOHN MCCORKLE, astronomy association administrator; b. Springfield, Mo., July 23, 1925; s. Lon Vester and Judith (McCorkle) T.; m. Sylvia Victoria Konvicka, July 11, 1953; children—Judith Majka Donald, Paul Norman. A.B., Harvard U., 1949, M.A., 1951, Ph.D., 1954. Sr. research fellow Calif. Inst. Tech., Pasadena, 1954-60; v.p., chief scientist Electro Optical Systems, Pasadena, 1960-67; dir. tech. staff of research and devel. Xerox Corp., Stamford, Conn., 1967-72; asst. gen. mgr., dir. phys. research U.S. AEC, Washington, 1973-75; asst. adminstr. Energy Research and Devel. Adminstrn., Washington, 1975-76; pres. Assn. Univs. for Research in Astronomy, Washington, 1977—; dir., cons. Nat. Patent Devel. Corp., N.Y.C., 1978-80; dir. Technion, Inc., Irvine, Calif. Served with U.S. Army, 1943-46. Fairchild Disting. scholar Calif. Inst. Tech., 1976-77. Fellow AAAS; mem. Am. Astron. Soc., Am. Phys. Soc. Democrat. Roman Catholic. Current work: Operating national astronomical centers. Subspecialty: Astronomical research administration. Office: Assn Univs for Research in Astronomy 2100 Pennsylvania Ave NW 820 Washington DC 20037

TEEVAN, RICHARD COLLIER, psychology educator; b. Shelton, Conn., June 12, 1919; s. Daniel Joseph and Elizabeth (Hallowell) T.; m. Virginia Agnes Stehle, July 28, 1945; children—Jan Elizabeth, Kim Ellen, Clay Collier, Allison Tracy. B.A., Wesleyan U., Middletown, Conn., 1951; M.A., U. Mich., 1952, Ph.D., 1955. Rubber buffer Sponge Rubber Product Co., Derby, Conn., 1939-41; with U. Mich., 1951-57, teaching fellow, 1951-53, instr., 1953-57; asst. prof. Smith Coll., 1957-60; assoc. prof. Bucknell U., 1960-64, prof., 1964-69; chmn. psychology, prof. SUNY-Albany, 1969—. Author: Reinforcement, 1961, Instinct, 1961, Color Vision, 1961, Measuring Human Motivation, 1962, Theories of Motivation in Learning, 1964, Theories of Motivation in Personality and Social Psychology, 1964, Motivation, 1967, Fear of Failure, 1969, Readings in Elementary Psychology, 1973; contbr. articles to sci. jours. Served to capt. AUS, 1941-47; prisoner of war 1943-45, Ger. Office Naval Research grantee, 1958-72; recipient Lindbach award Bucknell U., 1966. Mem. Am. Psychol. Assn., Eastern Psychol. Assn., AAUP, AAAS, Phi Beta Kappa, Sigma Xi. Current Work: Fear of failure in achievement situations, in women, need for achievement, projective measurement of motivation. Subspecialties: Social psychology; Cognition. Address: 45 Pine St Delmar NY 12054 Office: Dept Psychology SUNY 1400 Washington Ave Albany NY 12222

TEFFT, MELVIN, physician, radiologist; b. Boston, Dec. 15, 1932; s. Louis and Anna (Krivian) T. A.B., Harvard U., 1954; M.D., Boston U., 1958. Diplomate Am. Bd. Radiology. Resident in radiology Mass. Meml. Hosp., Boston, 1959-62, fellow in radiation therapy, 1962-64, cons. radiology, 1964-71; cons. radiology Lemuel Shattuck Hosp., Boston, 1962-70; assoc. Peter Bent Brigham Hosp., Boston, 1966-70; chief div. radiotherapy and nuclear medicine Children's Hosp. Med. Ctr., Boston, 1967-70; assoc. attending radiotherapist Meml. Sloan-Kettering Cancer Ctr., 1970-71, attending radiotherapist, 1973-75, dir. of med. edn. dept. radiation therapy, 1973-75; assoc. mem. dept. pediatrics R.I. Hosp., Providence, 1975—, radiotherapist, 1975—; instr. Harvard Med. Sch., Cambridge, Mass., 1966-67, clin. assoc. radiology, 1967-69, asst. prof. radiology, 1969-70, asst. prof. radiotherapy, 1971-72, assoc. prof., 1972-73; assoc. prof. therapeutic radiology Tufts Med. Ctr., Boston, 1969-70; assoc. prof. radiology Cornell U. Med. Sch., N.Y.C., 1970-71, prof. radiology, 1973-75; prof. radiation medicine Brown U., Providence, 1975—; chmn. dept. radiation therapy R.I. Hosp.-Brown U., Providence, 1984—. Mem. editorial bd. Am. Jour. Pediatric Hematology-Oncology, 1974—, Med. and Pediatric Oncology, 1984. Chmn. radiation safety com. Boston Lying-In Hosp., 1966-70; sec. radiation safety com. Children's Hosp. Med. Ctr., 1962-67, chmn., 1967-70; chmn. com. for protocol rev. Meml. Sloan-Kettering Cancer Ctr., 1973-75, mem. action com., 1974-75; mem. pediatric oncology task force com. R.I. Hosp., 1975. Mem. Am. Acad. Pediatrics (exec. com. 1979-82, chmn. 1981-83), AAAS, Am. Assn. Cancer Research, Am. Assn. Physicists in Medicine, Am. Cancer Soc., Am. Coll. Nuclear Medicine, Am. Coll. Radiology, AMA, Am. Radium Soc., Am. Soc. Clin. Oncology, Am. Soc. Preventive Oncology, Am. Soc. Therapeutic Radiologists, European Soc. Pediatric Radiology, Internat. Soc. Pediatric Oncology (North Am. coordinator), Internat. Soc. Pediatric Radiology, Mass. Med. Soc., New Eng. Cancer Soc., New Eng. Soc. Radiation Oncology (pres. 1979-80), N.Y. Acad. Scis., Providence Med. Assn., R.I. Cancer Control Program., R.I. Med. Soc., Soc. Pediatric Radiology, Soc. Nuclear Medicine. Club: Harvard (N.Y.C., Boston). Subspecialties: Oncology; Radiology. Office: R I Hosp Dept Radiation Therapy 593 Eddy St Providence RI 02902

TEHON, STEPHEN WHITTIER, research engineer; b. Shenandoah, Iowa, Oct. 20, 1920; s. Leo Roy and Mary Viola (Bruner) T.; m. Betty Irene Albright, Oct. 24, 1942; children—Chloe Ann, Susan, Rebecca, Penelope, Candace. B.S. in Engring. Physics, U. Ill., 1942, M.S. in Elec. Engring., 1946, Ph.D. in Elec. Engring., 1958. Sr. engr. Curtiss-Wright, Columbus, Ohio, 1946-47; instr. elec. engring. U. Ill., Urbana, 1947-52; sr. engr., cons. engr. G.E. Electronics Lab., Syracuse, N.Y., 1952-66; research engr. Tecumseh Products, Ann Arbor, Mich., 1966-67; cons. engr., prin. staff scientist G.E. Electronics Lab., Syracuse, 1967—; adj. prof. U. Mich., Ann Arbor, 1966-67; Syracuse U., 1977—; vis. prof. Clarkson Coll., Potsdam, N.Y., 1979. Author: (with others) Electronics Engineers Handbook, 1975, 1982; Amplifier Handbook, 1966; Solid State Magnetic and Dielectric Devices, 1959. Patentee in field. Served to lt., USNR, 1942-45, PTO. Fellow IEEE. Current work: Application of piezoelectric polymers to sensors in sonar systems, aircraft instruments and machine automation. Subspecialties: Acoustics; Polymer engineering. Home: 6056 Pine Grove Rd Clay NY 13041 Office: Electronics Lab Gen Electric Co Electronics Park 3-107 Syracuse NY 13221

TEJADA, FRANCISCO, physician, med. researcher; b. Moyobamba, Peru, July 25, 1942; s. Francisco Tejada Rojas and Semiramis Reategui Tuesta; m. Barbara Ann Kotowski, Feb. 1, 1970; children: Ana Maria, Semiramis, Barbara Lee, Francisco, James. B.S., Universidad Nacional Mayor de San Marcos, Lima, 1961; M.D., Peruvian U. Cayetano Heredia, 1967. Diplomate: Am. Bd. Internal Medicine. Sr. cancer research internist Nat. Cancer Inst., NIH, 1973-75; asst. prof. George Washington U., 1974-75; asst. prof. medicine and oncology U. Miami, 1975-80; asst. to dir. U. Miami (Comprehensive Cancer Center), 1975-80, assoc. prof. oncology and otolaryngology, 1980—; head med. oncology div. Miami Cancer Inst., 1980—; cons. in field. Contbr. articles to profl. jours. Mem. community health assn., 1980—. Recipient Hipolito Unanue Inst. award, 1969; grantee NIH, 1976-79, 78—; grantee Lilly Research Lab., 1978-79. Mem. Peruvian Coll. Physicians, ACP (fellow), Am. Assn. Cancer Research, AM. Soc. Hematology, Am. Soc. Clin. Oncology, Cell Kinetic Soc., AAAS. Roman Catholic. Current Work: Cell kinetics of solid tumors and its pertubation by drugs and radiation. Subspecialties: Cancer research (medicine); Cell study oncology. Home: 1550 SW 132d St Miami FL 33156 Office: 1321 NW 14th St Miami FL 33136

TEJWANI, GOPAL DAS, physics researcher; b. Hyderabad, India, Dec. 5, 1945; came to U.S., 1968, naturalized, 1983; s. Tahikandas N. and Kishibai (Jaromal) T.; m. Roop Hukmani, Mar. 12, 1976. B.Tech. in Mech. Engring., Indian Inst. Tech., Kanpur, 1967; M.S., SUNY-Stony Brook, 1969, Ph.D., 1971; M.B.A., Washington U., St. Louis, 1984. Research assoc. U. Tenn., Knoxville, 1971-73; postdoctoral fellow Ames Lab., Iowa, 1974-75, asst. chemist, 1976-78; asst. prof. S.D. Sch. Mines, Rapid City, 1979-82; research physicist U. Denver, 1984—. Contbr. articles to profl. jours. Govt. India Nat. Merit scholar Indian Inst. Tech., Kanpur, 1961-67; NATO scholar Advanced Study Inst., Antigonish, N.S., Can., 1978; dean's merit scholar Washington U., 1982-84. Mem. ASME, Am. Phys. Soc. Democrat. Current work: Atmospheric spectroscopy; infrared quantitative spectroscopy; atmospheric radiative energy balance. Subspecialties: Atomic and molecular physics; Mechanical engineering. Home: 1111 Ash St Apt 402 Denver CO 80220 Office: U Denver Dept Physics Denver CO 80208

TELESCO, CHARLES MICHAEL, astronomer; b. Trenton, N.J., Oct. 18, 1946; s. Charles Edward and Aileen Mary (Harle) Watters; m. Patricia Gaynor Telesco, Mar. 6, 1982. A.S. in Physics, Palm Beach Jr. Coll., 1966; B.S. in Physics, Case Western Res. U., 1969; M.S. in Physics, Purdue U., 1971; M.S. in Astronomy, U. Chgo., 1975, Ph.D. in Astronomy, 1977. Postdoctoral research fellow Ctr. for Space Research, M.I.T., 1977-78; asst. astronomer U. Hawaii; also staff astronomer NASA Infrared Telescope Facility, Honolulu, 1979-82; NRC research assoc. Space Sci. div. Astrophys. Expts. br. NASA Ames Research Ctr., Moffett Field, Calif., 1982-83; space scientist Space Sci. Lab NASA Marshall Space Flight Ctr., Huntsville, Ala., 1983—. Contbr. articles to sci. jours. Mem. Am. Astron. Soc., Astron. Soc. of Pacific. Current Work: Extragalactic infrared emission; infrared instrumentation; star formation. Subspecialty: Infrared astronomy. Home: 13029 Camelot Dr Huntsville AL 35803 Office: Space Sci Lab NASA Marshall Space Flight Mail Stop ES-63 Huntsville AL 35812

TELESHAK, STEPHEN, metall. engr., cons.; b. Monessen, Pa., May 10, 1922; s. Konstantin and Tekla (Kostura) Telischak; m. Alice Marie Feldman; 1 dau.: Tekla. B.S. in Metall. Engring, U. Pitts., 1949. Registered profl. engr., Pa., Tex., La. Mgr. metall. dept. Pitts. Testing Lab., 1952-74; owner, prin. Teleshak Metall. Lab., New Orleans, 1974—. Served with AUS, 1942-46. Mem. Am. Soc. Metals, ASME, Am. Welding Soc., ASTM, Am. Soc. Nondestructive Testing, Electron Microscope Soc. Am., Nat. Assn. Corrosion Engrs, VFW. Subspecialties: Metallurgy; Failure anaylsis. Home: 113 Eden Isles Dr Slidell LA 70458 Office: 4315 Royal St New Orleans LA 70117

TELETZKE, GERALD HOWARD, engineer; b. Beaver Dam, Wis., Mar. 22, 1928; s. Gerhardt Charles and Helen Ida (Mohr) T.; m. Elaine M. Gloudemann, June 21, 1952; children—Gary, Barbara Ann. B.S. in Civil Engring., U. Wis.-Madison, 1952, M.S. in Civil Engring., 1953, Ph.D., 1956. Registered profl. engr., Wis. Assoc. prof. Purdue U., West Lafayette, Ind., 1956-59; dir. research and devel., Palatine, Ill., 1959-61; engr. Zimpro Inc., Rothschild, Wis., 1961-65, exec. v.p., 1965-69, pres., 1969—; dir. Nat. Water Alliance, Washington, 1983—; mem. mgmt. adv. group EPA, Washington, 1982—. Patentee environ. control systems. Mem. Wausau Sch. Bd., Wis., 1970-73. Served to maj. U.S. Armed Forces, 1945-49. Recipient Disting. service citation U. Wis. Coll. Engring., 1984. Mem. Am. Acad. Environ. Engrs. (diplomate), Am. Inst. Chem. Engrs., ASCE. Clubs: Wausau, Wausau Country. Current work: Sludge management, water reclamation, toxic and hazardous waste control. Subspecialties: Environmental engineering; Hazardous waste disposal. Home: 1403 Stark St Wausau WI 54401 Office: Zimpro Inc Rothschild WI 54474

TELKES, MARIA, scientist, engr., educator; b. Budapest, Hungary, Dec. 12, 1900; came to U.S., 1925, naturalized, 1937; d. Aladar and Maria (Laban) T. Ph.D., U. Budapest, 1924. Research asst. U. Budapest, 1923-24; biophysicist Cleve. Clinic, 1925-37; research engr. Westinghouse Research Labs., 1937-39; research asso. Mass. Inst. Tech., 1939-53; project dir. Coll. Engring., N.Y.U., 1953-58; research dir. solar energy lab. Princeton (div. Curtiss-Wright Co.), 1958-60; dir. research and devel. Cryo-Therm Co., 1961-64; head solar energy applications lab. MELPAR, Inc. (subsidiary Westinghouse Air-Brake Co.), 1965-69; chief scientist Inst. Direct Energy Conversion, U. Pa., Phila., 1970-72; adj. prof., cons. energy conversion Inst. of Energy Conversion, U. Del., 1972-77; dir. solarthermal storage devel. Am. Technol. U., Killeen, Tex., 1977-80; cons., 1980—. Contbr. numerous articles to profl. jours., chpts. in books. Mem. Solar Energy Soc. (dir., C.G. Abbott award), Am. Chem. Soc., Soc. Women Engrs. (hon. life, recipient 1st award 1952), Hellenic Soc. Solar Energy (hon., Quarter Century award), Nat. Acad. Sci./NRC. Specializes in solar energy research Specializes in solar energy research. Current Work: Solar energy conversion, thermal energy storage. Subspecialties: Inorganic chemistry; Physical chemistry. Office: NAHB Research Found PO Box 1627 Rockville MD 20850

TELLEP, DANIEL MICHAEL, aerospace company executive; b. Forest City, Pa., Nov. 20, 1931; s. John M. and Mary J. (Yusko) T.; m. Patricia Godfrey Taylor, Sept. 5, 1970; children—Theresa, Mary, Susan, Patricia. Student San Diego State U., 1950-51; B.S. in Mech. Engring. with highest honors, U. Calif.-Berkeley, 1954, M.S. in Mech. Engring., 1955; A.M.P., Harvard U., 1971. Sr. scientist Lockheed Missiles and Space Co., Sunnyvale, Calif., 1955-57, head thermal research, 1958-61, mgr. missile thermodynamics, Missile Systems div., 1961-62, mgr. launch and entry thermodynamics, 1962-66, chief Poseidon reentry systems, mgr. reentry systems engring., 1966-69, chief engr., 1969-75, v.p., asst. gen. mgr., Advanced Systems div., 1976-83, exec. v.p., 1983-84, v.p. Lockheed Corp., 1983—, pres. Lockheed Missiles and Space Co., 1984—; cons. in field. Exec. sponsor to 12 Jr. Achievement cos., Sunnyvale, Calif., 1976-78, 84-85; bd. regents Inst. Med. Research, San Jose, Calif., 1979-82; campaign mem. United Way of Santa Clara County, 1983-84; adv. bd. mem. U. Santa Clara Sch. Engring., 1983—, U. Calif.-Berkeley, 1984-85; mem. pres.'s adv. bd. San Jose State U., 1984-88. Fellow AIAA (Lawrence B. Sperry award 1964, fluid mech. com. 1960-63, planning staff strategic scis. meeting 1967, adv. council San Francisco sect. 1984—); mem. Nat. Acad. Engring., Sigma Xi, Pi Tau Sigma, Tau Beta Pi. Subspecialties: Mechanical engineering; Fluid mechanics. Office: Lockheed Missiles and Space Co Inc 1111 Lockheed Way Sunnyvale CA 94089

TELLER, CECIL MARTIN, II, research institute executive; b. Galveston, Tex., Oct. 25, 1939; s. Cecil Martin and Laura Mary (Adascheck) T.; m. Valerie Diana Klossner, June 18, 1966; children: Cecil Martin III, Diana Lynn. B.S.M.E., U. Tex.-Austin, 1964, M.S.M.E., 1966, Ph.D., 1971. Registered profl. engr., Tex. Engr., scientist Def. Research Lab.; Engr., scientist U. Tex., Austin, 1965-66, research engr. dept. mech. engring., 1970-71; mgr. materials tech. sect. dept. applied sci. Tracor, Inc., Austin, 1972-74; dep. br. chief U.S. Govt., Washington, 1974-77; mgr. nondestructive evaluation research instrumentation research div. Southwest Research Inst., San Antonio, Tex., 1977-83; tech. dir. Tex. Research Inst., Austin, 1983—. Contbr. articles to profl. jours. Served to lt. Civil Engr. Corps USNR, 1966-69. Cameron Iron Works fellow, 1969-71. Mem. ASME, Am. Soc. Metals, Am. Soc. Nondestructive Testing, Tau Beta Pi, Pi Tau Sigma, Phi Kappa Phi. Mem. Ch. of Christ. Current Work: Materials testing and characterization, nondestructive evaluation; technical direction and management of a wide variety of research and development contracts in materials, chemistry and mechanical engineering. Subspecialties: Mechanical engineering; Materials (engineering). Office: 9063 Bee Caves RD Austin TX 78733

TELLER, EDWARD, physicist; b. Budapest, Hungary, Jan. 15, 1908; naturalized, 1941; s. Max and Ilona (Deutch) T.; m. Augusta Harkanyi, Feb. 26, 1934; children: Paul, Susan Wendy. Student, Inst. Tech., Karlsruhe, Ger., 1926-28, U. Munich, 1928; Ph.D., U. Leipzig, Ger., 1930; D.Sc. (hon.), Yale U., 1954, U. Alaska, 1959, Fordham U., 1960, George Washington U., 1960, U. So. Calif., 1960, St. Louis U., 1960, Rochester Inst. Tech., 1962, PMC Colls., 1963, U. Detroit, 1964, Clemson U., 1966, Clarkson Coll., 1969; LL.D., Boston Coll., 1961, Seattle U., 1961, U. Cin., 1962, U. Pitts., 1963, Pepperdine U., 1974, U. Md. at Heidelberg, 1977; D.Sc., L.H.D., Mt. Mary Coll., 1964; Ph.D., Tel Aviv U., 1972; D.Natural Sci., DeLaSalle U., Manila, 1981; D. Med. Sci. (n.c.), Med. U. S.C., 1983. Research assoc., Leipzig, 1929-31, Goettingen, Ger., 1931-33, Rockefeller fellow, Copenhagen, 1934; lectr. U. London, 1934-35; prof. physics George Washington U., Washington, 1935-41, Columbia, 1941-42; physicist U. Chgo., 1942-43, Manhattan Engr. Dist., 1942-46, Los Alamos Sci. Lab., 1943-46; prof. physics U. Chgo., 1946-52; prof. physics U. Calif., 1953-60, prof. physics-at-large, 1960-70, Univ. prof., 1970-75, prof. emeritus, chmn. dept. applied sci., Davis and Livermore, 1963-66; asst. dir. Los Alamos Sci. Lab., 1949-52; cons. Livermore br. U. Calif. Radiation Lab., 1952-53; assoc. dir. Lawrence Livermore Lab., U. Calif., 1954-58, 60-75; dir. Lawrence Livermore Radiation Lab., U. Calif., 1958-60, now dir. emeritus, cons.; concerned with planning and prediction function atomic bomb and hydrogen bomb, Manhattan Dist. of Columbia, 1942-46; also Metall. and Lab. of Argonne Nat. Lab., U. Chgo., 1942-43, 46-52, and Los Alamos, N.Mex., 1943-46, Radiation Lab., Livermore, Calif., 1952-75; sr. research fellow Hoover Instn. War, Revolution and Peace, Stanford U., 1975—; mem. sci. adv. bd. USAF; mem. White House Sci. Council; mem. adv. bd. Fed. Emergency Mgmt. Agy.; bd. dirs. Assn. to Unite the Democracies; past mem. gen. adv. com. AEC; former mem. President's Fgn. Intelligence Adv. Bd. Author: (with Francis Owen Rice) The Structure of Matter, 1949, (with A.L. Latter) Our Nuclear Future, 1958, (with Allen Brown) The Legacy of Hiroshima, 1962, The Reluctant Revolutionary, 1964, (with G.W. Johnson, W.K. Talley, G.H. Higgins) The Constructive Uses of Nuclear Explosives, 1968, (with Segre, Kaplan and Schiff) Great Men of Physics, 1969, The Miracle of Freedom, 1972, Energy: A Plan for Action, 1975, Nuclear Energy in the Developing World, 1977, Energy from Heaven and The Earth, 1979, The Pursuit of Simplicity, 1980. Past bd. dirs. Def. Intelligence Sch., Naval War Coll.; bd. dirs. Fed. Union, Hertz Found., Am. Friends of Tel Aviv U.; sponsor Atlantic Union, Atlantic Council U.S., Univ. Ctrs. for Rational Alternatives; mem. Com. to Unite Am., Inc.; bd. govs. Am. Acad. Achievement. Recipient Joseph Priestley Meml. award Dickinson Coll., 1957, Harrison medal Am. Ordnance Assn., 1955; Albert Einstein award, 1958; Gen. Donovan Meml. award, 1959; Midwest Research Inst. award, 1960; Research Inst. Am. Living History award, 1960; Golden Plate award Am. Acad. Achievement, 1961; Gold medal Am. Acad. Achievement, 1982; Thomas E. White and Enrico Fermi awards, 1962; Robins award of Am., 1963; Leslie R. Groves Gold medal, 1974; Harvey prize in sci. and tech. Technion Inst., 1975; Semmelweiss medal, 1977; Albert Einstein award Technion Inst., 1977; Henry T. Heald award Ill. Inst. Tech., 1978; Gold medal Am. Coll. Nuclear Medicine, 1980; A.C. Eringen award, 1980; fellow Hudson Inst.; named ARCS Man of Yr., 1980, Disting. Scientist, Nat. Sci. Devel. Bd., 1981; Paul Harris award Rotary Found., 1980; Disting. Scientist Phil-Am. Acad. Sci. and Engring., 1981; Lloyd Freeman Hunt Citizenship award, 1982; Nat. medal of Sci., 1983; Joseph Handleman prize, 1983. Fellow Am. Nuclear Soc., Am. Phys. Soc., Am. Acad. Arts and Scis.; mem. Nat. Acad. Scis., Am. Geophys. Union, Soc. Engring. Scis., Internat. Platform Assn. Current Work: Research on chemistry; molecular and nuclear physics, quantum mechanics, thermonuclear reactions, applications of nuclear energy, astrophysics, spectroscopy of polymatomic molecules, theory of atomic nuclei. Subspecialties: Nuclear physics; Theoretical physics. Office: Hoover Instn Stanford CA 94305 PO Box 808 Livermore CA 94550

TELLER, RAYMOND GENE, chemist; b. Chgo., Oct. 6, 1946; s. Winthrop Edward and Elaine (Witten) T.; m. Jennifer Stevenson, Aug. 25, 1979; children—Justin, Sean. B.S., U. Ill.-Chgo., 1969; Ph.D., U. So. Calif., 1978. Postdoctorial fellow UCLA, 1978-79; chemist Argonne Nat. Lab., Ill., 1979-82; project leader Standard Oil Sohio, Cleve., 1982—; cons. Dahlman Assn., Braham, Minn., 1981. Contbr. numerous articles to profl. jours. Mem. Aurora Community Theater, Ohio, 1983—. James scholar U. Ill., 1966-69; Walter C. Hamilton fellow Brookhaven Nat. Lab., 1976. Mem. Am. Chem. Soc., Am. Crystallographic Assn., Argonne Users Com. Current work: X-ray and neutron crystallography; solid state science; heterogeneous catalysis, the relation between structure and activity for solid state catalysts. Subspecialties: Crystallography; Catalysis chemistry. Office: Sohio Research Ctr 4440 Warrensville Cleveland OH 44128

TEMIN, HOWARD MARTIN, scientist, educator; b. Phila., Dec. 10, 1934; s. Henry and Annette (Lehman) T.; m. Rayla Greenberg, May 27, 1962; children: Sarah Beth, Miriam Judith. B.A., Swarthmore Coll., 1955, D.Sc. (hon.), 1972; Ph.D., Calif. Inst. Tech., 1959; D.Sc. (hon.), N.Y. Med. Coll., 1972, U. Pa., 1976, Hahnemann Med. Coll., 1976, Lawrence U., 1976, Temple U., 1979, Med. Coll. Wis., 1981. Postdoctoral fellow Calif. Inst. Tech., 1959-60; asst. prof. oncology U. Wis., 1960-64, asso. prof., 1964-69, prof., 1969—, Wis. Alumni Research Found. prof. cancer research, 1971-80, Am. Cancer Soc. prof. viral oncology and cell biology, 1974—, H.P. Rusch prof. cancer research, 1980—, Steenbock prof. biol. scis., 1982—; mem. NIH (virology study sect.), 1971-74, mem. dir.'s adv. com., 1979-83; mem. Nat. Cancer Inst. (spl. virus cancer program tumor virus detection segment working group), 1972-73; sponsor Fedn. Am. Scientists, 1976—; sci. adv. Stehlin Found., Houston, 1972—; mem. Waksman award com. Nat. Acad. Sci., 1976-81; mem. U.S. Steel award Com., 1980-83, chmn., 1982. Assoc. editor: Jour. Cellular physiology, 1966-77, Cancer Research, 1971-74; mem. editorial bd.: Jour. Virology, 1971—, Intervirology, 1972-75, Proc. Nat. Acad. Scis, 1975-80, Archives of Virology, 1975-77, Ann. Rev. Gen., 1983, Molecular Biology and Evolution, 1983—. Pub. Health Service Research Career Devel. awardee Nat. Cancer Inst., 1964-74; co-recipient Warren Triennial prize Mass. Gen. Hosp., 1971, Gairdner Found. Internat. award, 1974, Nobel Prize in medicine, 1975; recipient Med. Soc. Wis. Spl. commendation, 1971; Papanicolaou Inst. PAP award, 1972; M.D. Anderson Hosp. and Tumor Inst. Bertner award, 1972; U.S. Steel Found. award in Molecular Biology, 1972; Theobald Smith Soc. Waksman award, 1972; Am. Chem. Soc. award in Enzyme Chemistry, 1973; Modern Medicine award for Distinguished Achievement, 1973; Harry Shay Meml. lectr. Fels Research Inst., 1973; Griffuel prize Assn. Devel. Recherche Cancer, Villejuif, 1972; G.H.A. Clowes lectr. award Assn. Cancer Research, 1974; NIH Dyer lectr. award, 1974; Harvey lectr., 1974; Charlton lectr. Tufts U., 1976; Hoffman-LaRoche lectr. Rutgers U., 1979; Albert Lasker award in basic med. sci., 1974; Lucy Wortham James award Soc. Surg. Oncologists, 1976; Alumni Disting. Service award Calif. Inst. Tech., 1976; Gruber award Am. Acad. Dermatology, 1981; Bitterman Meml. lectr., 1984; Cetus lectr. U. Calif., 1984; Dupont lectr. Harvard U., 1985; Japanese Found. for Promotion of Cancer Research lectr., 1985. Fellow Am. Acad. Arts and Scis.; fellow Wis. Acad. Sci., Arts and Letters; mem. Nat. Acad. Scis., Am. Philos. Soc. Current Work: Molecular biology and genetics; virus evolution and variation. Subspecialties: Animal virology; Genetics and genetic engineering (biology). Office: McArdle Lab 450 N Randall St U Wis Madison WI 53706

TEMKIN, RICHARD JOEL, physicist; b. Boston, Jan. 8, 1945; s. Max. O. and Lillian G. T.; m. Carol Fay, May 28, 1972; children—Daniel James, Jessica Beth, Mark David. B.A., Harvard Coll., 1966; Ph.D., MIT, 1971. Research fellow Harvard U., Cambridge, Mass., 1971-74; research scientist MIT Nat. Magnet Lab., Cambridge, 1974-80; group leader MIT Plasma Fusion Ctr., Cambridge, 1980—; mem. gyrotron rev. com. U.S. Dept. Energy, 1980—; mem. organizing com. Internat. Conf. IR and MM Waves, 1981—. Editor Digest of Eighth Internat. Conf. IR and MM Waves; assoc. editor Internat. Jour. IR and Millimeter Waves, 1980—. IBM fellow, 1972-74. Mem. Am. Phys. Soc., Fusion Power Assocs. (affiliate). Current work: High frequency gyrotron research; plasma diagnostics, plasma heating, far infrared laser research. Subspecialties: Plasma physics; Atomic and molecular physics. Home: 35 O'Rourke Path Newton Centre MA 02159 Office: Plasma Fusion Ctr MIT NW16-138 Cambridge MA 02139

TEMPEL, ANN, neuroscientist, educator, researcher; b. N.Y.C., Jan. 9, 1953; d. Abraham and Rosa (Schattner) T. B.A., CCNY, 1975; Ph.D. in Physiol. Psychology, CUNY, 1982. Lectr. CCNY, 1976-81; postdoctoral fellow Albert Einstein Coll. Medicine, N.Y.C., 1981-84, lectr., 1982-83. Contbr. articles to profl. jours. Recipient New Investigator award. Mem. AAAS, Internat. Soc. Neurosci., Brit. Brain Research Assn. (hon.), European Brain and Behavior Soc. (hon.). Current work: Molecular mechanisms underlying brain opiate receptor regulation and neuroanatomical, behavioral and functional correlates of regulation of brain opiate receptors. Subspecialties: Neuropharmacology; Opiate receptor regulation. Home: 98-01 67th Ave Queens NY 11374 Office: Albert Einstein Coll Dept Neurosci 1300 Morris Park Ave Bronx NY 10461

TEMPLE, WALLEY JOHN, general and oncological surgeon, educator; b. Ann Arbor, Mich., May 8, 1946; s. Victor Clarence and Marna (Walley) T.; m. Doreen H. Farley, Sept. 3, 1966; children: Lara, Claire, Philip, Martha. M.D., Queen's U., Kingston, Ont., Can., 1970; postgrad., U. Man. (Can.), Winnipeg, 1976. Intern Health Scis. Center, 1972-76; fellow in surg. oncology U. Miami, Fla., 1976-78, asst. prof. surgery, 1979-82, assoc. prof., 1982—; mem. surg. staff VA Hosp., Miami, 1979—, Jackson Meml. Hosp., Miami, 1981—; mem. surg. com. Southeastern Cancer Study Group, 1981—. Am. Cancer Soc. fellow, 1978-79, 80-83. Fellow Royal Coll. Physicians and Surgeons Can., ACS; mem. Soc. Surg. Oncology, Soc. Head and Neck Surgeons. Methodist. Current Work: Tumor immunology cell cycle kinetics; clinical trials melanoma and colon cancer. Subspecialties: Surgery; Oncology. Home: 7301 SW 113th St Miami FL 33156 Office: Univ Miami Sch Medicine 1600 NW 10th Ave Miami FL 33101

TEMPLES, TOM J., geologist; b. Anderson, S.C., Mar. 24, 1954; s. Tom Vassar and Retha (Ethridge) T.; m. Debbie Rabideau, Aug. 11, 1979; 1 child, Christopher. B.S., Clemson U., 1976; M.S., U. Ga., 1978. Exploration geologist Texaco, Houston, 1978-81, project mgr., Tulsa, 1981-84, Denver, 1984—. Contbr. articles to profl. jours. Mem. Am. Assn. Petroleum Geologists, Soc. Exploration Geologists, Am. Geophys. Union, Geol. Soc. Am. Republican. Episcopalian. Current work: Carbonate geochemistry, exploration for hydrocarbons in carbonates; risk analysis in petroleum exploration, budget and strategic planning. Subspecialties: Geology; Geochemistry. Home: 10056 E Caley Pl Englewood CO 80111 Office: Texaco PO Box 2100 Denver CO 80201

TENEDORIO, JAIME GONSALVES, semiconductor process engineer, researcher; b. New Bedford, Mass., June 18, 1957; s. Antonio DeSousa and Arminda (Gonsalves) T.; m. Abigail Lee O'Connell, June 24, 1978. B.S., Cornell U., 1978, M.Engring., 1979, Ph.D.E.E., 1982. Research and devel engr. Narda Microwave, San Jose, Calif., 1982-84; mgr. product devel. Harris Microwave Semiconductor, Milpitas, Calif., 1984—. Mem. IEEE. Roman Catholic. Club: No. Calif. Karate Assn. (Mountain View). Current work: Gallium arsenide field effect transistor and microwave monlithic integrated circuit development process development and device design. Subspecialties: Microchip technology (engineering); Semiconductors. Office: Harris Microwave Semiconductor 1530 McCarthy Blvd Milpitas CA 95035

TENG, LEE CHANG-LI, research and development director, physics researcher; b. Peiping, Hopei, China, Sept. 5, 1926; came to U.S., 1947, naturalized, 1962; s. Tsuey Ying and Chien Min (Ho) T.; m. Nancy Lai-Shen Huang, Sept. 21, 1961; 1 child, Michael Nan-Hao. B.S., Fujen U., Peiping, China, 1946; M.S., U. Chgo., 1948, Ph.D., 1951. Teaching asst. U. Chgo., 1948-49, Cyclotron asst., 1949-51, profl. lectr., 1964-67; asst. prof. U. Minn., 1951-53; assoc. prof. Wichita State U., 1953-55; leader accelerator theory group particle accelerator div. Argonne Nat. Lab., 1955-62, div. dir., 1962-67; head accelerator theory sect. accelerator div. Fermi Nat. Accelerator Lab, Batavia, Ill., 1967-72, head advanced projects dept. accelerator div., 1974-79, assoc. div. head, 1972—; prof. (hon.), Beijing Normal U., China, 1982; dir. Synchrotron Radiation Research Ctr, Taiwan, 1983—; cons. in field; chmn. confs., workshops, summer studies, schs., coms. Contbr. articles to profl. jours. Recipient Gold Medal of Achievement, Chinese Ministry Edn., Taiwan, 1956, Disting. Service award Immigrants Service League, Chgo., 1963. Fellow Am. Phys. Soc. (exec. com. 1980-82); mem. Academia Sinica, AAUP, Inst. for High Energy Physics Chinese Acad. Sci. (hon. advisor 1980—), Fu Jen Alumni Assn. (hon. chmn. 1984), Chinese Student and Alumni Assn. (Chgo. chpt. pres. 1973-74, Sigma Xi, Phi Tau Phi. Republican. Current work: Research and development of new methods of particle acceleration; design, construction of particle accelerators, thermo-nuclear devices. Subspecialty: Particle physics. Home: 400 E Eighth St Hinsdale IL 60521 Office: Fermi Nat Accelerator Lab PO Box 500 Batavia IL 60510

TENNANT, WILLIAM EMERSON, technical science executive, physicist; b. Washington, Oct. 8, 1945; s. Richard Stacus and Mary Anne (Chiles) T.; m. Margaret Avis Hinman, Sept. 7, 1968; children—Jessica Faris, Elizabeth Ashton, Richard Shelton. A.B. in Physics with high honors, Harvard U., 1967; Ph.D. in Solid State Physics, U. Calif.-Berkeley, 1974. Mem. tech. staff Rockwell Internat. Sci. Ctr., Thousand Oaks, Calif., 1973-80, mgr., 1980—. Contbr. numerous articles to profl. jours. Mem. IEEE, (sr.), Am. Phys. Soc., Sigma Xi. Current work: Infrared detector materials, infrared imaging devices, optical and electrical properties of semiconductors, opto electronics, electro optics, materials characterization. Subspecialties: Semiconductors; Condensed matter physics. Home: 227 Cedar Heights Dr Thousand Oaks CA 91360 Office: Rockwell Internat Sci Center 1099 Camino Dos Rios Thousand Oaks CA 91360

TENNEY, AGNES, chemistry educator; b. Boston, Nov. 23, 1942. A.B., Regis Coll., 1967; Ph.D., Ind. U., 1975. Systems analyst Ind. U., Bloomington, 1973-77, vis. asst. prof. chemistry, 1976-77; asst. prof. chemistry U. Portland, 1977-81, assoc. prof., 1981—. Mem. Am. Chem. Soc. (chmn. Portland sect. 1983—), Am. Phys. Soc., Hydrogen Energy Internat. Current work: Hydrogen as alternative fuel; computer interfacing in undergrad laboratories. Subspecialty: Theoretical chemistry. Office: Univ Portland 5000 N Willamette Blvd Portland OR 97225

TENNEY, STEPHEN MARSH, physiologist, educator; b. Bloomington, Ill., Oct. 22, 1922; s. Harry Houser and Caroline (Marsh) T.; m. Carolyn Cartwright, Oct. 18, 1947; children: Joyce B., Karen M., Stephen M. A.B., Dartmouth Coll.; M.D., Cornell U.; Sc.D. (hon.), U. Rochester. Instr. medicine U. Rochester Sch. Medicine, 1951-54, instr. physiology, 1953-54, asst. prof. physiology and medicine, 1954-56, asso. prof., 1956; prof. physiology Dartmouth Med. Sch., Hanover, N.H., 1956—, dean, 1960-62, acting dean, 1966, 73—, dir. med. scis., 1957-59, chmn. dept. physiology, 1956-77, Nathan Smith prof. physiology, 1974—; med. dir. Parker B. Francis Found., 1975-83; exec. v.p. Puritan-Bennett Found., 1984—; Chmn. physiology study sect. NIH, 1962-65; tng. com. Nat. Heart Inst., 1968-71; mem. exec. com. NRC; mem. physiology panel NIH study Office Sci. and Tech.; mem. regulatory biology panel NSF, 1971-75; chmn. bd. sci. counselors Nat. Heart and Lung Inst., 1974-78; chmn. Commn. Respiratory Physiology Internat. Union Physiol. Scis. Asso. editor: Jour. Applied Physiology, 1976—, Handbook of Physiology; editorial bd.: Physiol. Revs., Respiratory Physiology, Circulation Research. Contbr. articles to sci. jours. Served with USNR, 1947-49; sr. med. officer Shanghai. Markle scholar in med. sci., 1954-59. Fellow Am. Acad. Arts and Scis., AAAS; mem. Inst. Medicine of Nat. Acad. Scis., Am. Physiol. Soc., Am. Soc. Clin. Investigation, N.Y. Acad. Scis., Gerontol. Soc., Am. Heart Assn., Assn. Am. Med. Colls., Sigma Xi. Current Work: Control of breathing; comparative respiratory physiology; high altitude. Subspecialty: Physiology (biology).

TENOPIR, CAROL, library science educator; b. Whittier, Calif., Sept. 17, 1952; d. George Kenneth and Jane Ann (Longwell) T.; m. Gerald Wayne Lundeen, Aug. 7, 1979. B.A., Whittier Coll., 1974.; M.S., Calif. State U., 1976; Ph.D., U. Ill., 1984. Supervisory librarian Cibbarelli & Assocs., Huntington Beach, Calif., 1976-78, v.p. ops., 1978-79; library systems librarian U. Hawaii, Honolulu, 1979-81, asst. prof. library and info. sci., 1983—; research asst. Coordinated Sci. Lab., Urbana, Ill., 1981-83. Editor column Library Jour., 1983—; (with others) Directory of Information Management Software, 1983. Contbr. articles to profl. jours. Recipient Berner Nash award U. Ill., 1984. Mem. Am. Soc. Info. Sci., ALA, Hawaii Library Assn., Spl. Libraries Assn., Assn. Records Mgrs. and Admistrs. Current work: full text databases; online database searching; information management database design and construction. Subspecialties: Information systems (Information science); Database systems. Home: 308 Opihikao Pl Honolulu HI 96825 Office: U Hawaii 2550 The Mall Honolulu HI 96822

TEPAS, DONALD IRVING, psychologist, educator; b. Buffalo, Apr. 7, 1933; s. Irving Carl and Dorothy Winofred (Scheuerle) T.; m. Susan Marion Krum, Aug. 1,. 1959; children—Matthew, Katherine. B.A., U. Buffalo, 1955; Ph.D., SUNY-Buffalo, 1963. Research scientist Walter Reed Army Inst. Research, Washington, 1959-62; sr. prin. research scientist staff Honeywell, Inc., Mpls., 1962-66; prof. St. Louis U., 1966-79; prof. psychology Ill. Inst. Tech., Chgo., 1978-85, chmn. dept., 1978, 81; prof. psychology U. Conn., 1985—; dir., Dir. Indsl./Orgnl. Psychology, 1985—; instr., adminstrv. asst. U. Buffalo, 1957-59; asst. research prof. U. Minn., Mpls., 1963-66; cons. Nat. Inst. Occupational Safety and Health, Cin., 1980—; mgr. Work Systems Research, Chgo., 1981—. Contbr. articles to profl. jours. Editor (with others): Biological Rhythms, Sleep and Shift Work, 1981. Mem. adminstrv. bd. Martin Luther King-Franz Fanon Community Mental Health Clinic, St. Louis, 1974-76. Recipient award for excellence St. Louis Assn. Black Psychologists, 1976, citation for excellence in research St. Louis U., 1977. Fellow Am. Psychol. Assn., AAAS; mem. Soc. Computers in Psychology (pres. 1972-73), Sleep Research Soc. (exec. com. 1984—), Permanent Commn. and Internat. Assn. on Occupational Health (sci. com. on night and shift work 1979—). Current work: Research on and evaluation of alternative work systems; human sleep and wakefulness; computer applications in life sciences. Subspecialty: Human factors engineering.

TEPERA, JOSEPH EDWARD, structural engineer, research and development executive; b. Houston, Feb. 19, 1938; s. Joseph Frank and Helen Agnes (Ctvrtnik) T.; m. Martha Sue Gordon, Mar. 31, 1962; children—Joseph A., Janet E., Susan K., Nancy E., Michael F., James G., Mark T., Mary R., Steven P. B.S. in Aerospace Engring., U. Tex., 1961, M.S. in Engring. Mechanics, 1969; Ph.D. in Engring. Mechanics, 1971. Registered profl. engr., Tex. Structural engr. Gen. Dynamics, Ft. Worth, 1963-68. mem. tech. staff Tex. Instruments, Dallas, 1970-78; v.p. tech. services Fibergrate Corp., Dallas, 1978—; cons. structural engring., Dallas, 1976—. Organizer St. Jude Catholic Ch., Allen, Tex., 1981; mayor pro tem Lucas City Council, Tex., 1973-77. Served to lt. (j.g.) USN, 1961-63, PTO, to comdr. Res. Mem. ASME, ASCE. Current work: Composite materials structures based on fiberglass reinforcements, thermoset plastics, inorganic aggregrates. Subspecialties: Solid mechanics; Structural engineering. Home: Route 1 Box 317 Van Alstyne TX 75095 Office: Fibergrate Corp 4112 Billy Mitchell Addison TX 75234

TEPLEY, NORMAN, physicist, educator; b. Denver, Dec. 14, 1935; s. David Jack and Ida Elizabeth (Cohan) T.; m. Elaine Tepley, Nov. 29, 1939; children: Jamina Esther, Philip Scot, Alan Joseph. B.S. in Physics, M.I.T., 1957; postgrad., Columbia U., 1957-59; Ph.D. in Physics, M.I.T., 1963. Asst. prof. physics Wayne State U., Detroit, 1963-69; assoc. prof. physics Oakland U.-Rochester, Mich., 1969-77, prof., 1977—, acting chmn. dept. physics, 1981—; vis. prof. U. Lancaster (U.K.), 1970; faculty research participant Argonne (Ill.) Nat. Lab., 1971. Contbr. articles to profl. jours. Faculty Research fellow Wayne State U., 1965; AFOSR Research grantee, 1964-69; Research Corp. grantee, 1971; Mich. Heart Assn. research grantee, 1975-79. Mem. Am. Phys. Soc., AAAS, Sigma Xi. Current Work: Biomagnetism including magnetocardiography, magnetoplethysmography, cell magnetism, low temperature physics including superconductivity, Fermi surfaces. Subspecialty: Low temperature physics. Office: Dept of Physics Oakland University Rochester MI 48063

TEPOORTEN, BERNARD A., osteo. medicine educator; b. Pontiac, Mich., Apr. 28, 1927; s. Bernard Angus and Ada Lucile (Thurman) TeP.; m. Nancy Louise Fish, Jan. 18, 1959 (div. Jan. 1969); m. Elizabeth Ann Klock, Nov. 21, 1969; children: Michael, Leslie. B.S., Mich. State U., 1952; D.O., Kirksville Coll. Osteo. Medicine, 1956. Pvt. practice osteo. medicine and surgery, Kezar Falls, Maine, 1957-59, Tucson, 1959-75; prof., div. chmn. U. Osteo. Medicine and Health Scis., Des Moines, 1975—. Contbr. articles to profl. jours. Served with U.S. Army, 1945-47, ETO. Fellow Am. Acad. Osteopathy; mem. Ariz.Acad. Applied Osteopathy (pres. 1960-62), Am. Osteo Assn., Polk County Osteo. Assn. Republican. Roman Catholic. Subspecialty: Family practice. Home: 3200 John Lynde Rd Des Moines IA 50312 Office: U Osteo Medicine and Health Scis 3200 Grand Ave Des Moines IA 50312

TEPPER, LLOYD BARTON, physician, corporate executive, environmental researcher, educator; b. Los Angeles, Dec. 21, 1931; married, 1957; 2 children. A.B., Dartmouth Coll., 1954; M.D., Harvard U., 1957, M.I.H., 1960, Sc.D. in Occupational Medicine, 1962. Diplomate: Am. Bd. Preventive Medicine. Fellow Mass. Gen. Hosp., Boston, 1958-60, MIT, Cambridge, 1959-61; physician Eastman Kodak Co., 1961-62, AEC, 1962-65; assoc. dir. occupational medicine and inst. environ. health Kettering Lab., U. Cin., 1965-72; assoc. prof. environ. health U. Cin., 1965-71, prof., 1971-72, assoc. prof. medicine, 1969-72; assoc. commr. sci. FDA, 1972-76; corp. med. dir. Air Products & Chem., Inc., Allentown, Pa., 1976—; adj. prof. environ. medicine U. Pa., 1977—. Editor: Jour. Occupational Medicine, 1979—. Fellow Am. Acad. Occupational Medicine (pres. 1980-81), Am. Occupational Medicine Assn. Subspecialties: Toxicology (medicine); Environmental medicine. Office: Air Products & Chem Inc PO Box 538 Allentown PA 18105*

TERAMURE, ALAN HIROSHI, botany educator, researcher; b. Los Angeles, Dec. 26, 1948; s. Kuniyoshi and Mineko (Nakamura) T.; m. Karen Lee Mc Knight, Aug. 10, 1974. Student, U. Dundee (Scotland), 1970-71; B.A., Calif. State U.-Fullerton, 1971, M.A., 1973; Ph.D. Duke U., 1978. Postdoctoral research assoc. U. Fla.-Gainesville, 1977-78; vis. asst. prof. Utah State U., Logan, 1979; asst. prof. U. Md.-College Park, 1979-82, assoc. prof. botany, 1982—; guest prof. U. Karlsruhe, W. Ger., 1982; cons. EPA, Washington, 1984. Contbr. articles to profl. jours. Recipient Faculty Devel. award U. Md., 1980-83; research grantee EPA, 1980-85, NASA, 1984. Mem. Ecol. Col. Am., Botanical Soc. Am., Am. Soc. Plant Physiologists, Sigma Xi, Phi Kappa Phi. Republican. Methodist. Current work: The effect of environmental stress (UV-B radiation, water, mineral, light, salt) on plant growth and development, plant adaptations to light and water stress. Subspecialties: Theoretical ecology; Plant physiology (agriculture). Office: U Md Dept Md College Park MD 20742

TERMAN, DAVID STEPHEN, physician, researcher, educator; b. N.Y.C., Oct. 23, 1940; s. Joseph and Pearl (Scharfman) T.; m. Naomi Sue Auerbach, Sept. 17, 1967; children: Erica, Jennifer. B.A., Syracuse U., 1962; M.D., Georgetown U., 1966. Intern in internal medicine U. Ala. Med. Center, Birmingham, 1966-67, resident in internal medicine, 1967-68; fellow in nephrology U. Colo. Med. Center, Denver, 1968-69, fellow in immunology, 1969-71, asst. prof. medicine, 1973-76; assoc. prof. Baylor U. Coll. Medicine, Houston, 1978—, dir. cancer biology program, 1982—; cons. biologic response modifiers program NIH, Washington, 1982—; dir. cancer immunology program Methodist Hosp., Houston, 1980—. Assoc. editor: Internat. Jour. Artificial Organs, 1977, Plasma Therapy, 1979—; contbr. articles to profl. jours. Served to maj. USAF, 1971-73. Recipient Research Career Devel. award NIH, 1978-83; clin. investigator VA, 1973-76. Mem. Am. Soc. Clin. Investigation, So. Soc. Clin. Investigation, AAAS, Am. Fedn. Clin. Research, AMA. Jewish. Subspecialties: Cancer research (medicine); Immunology (medicine). Office: Baylor Coll Medicine 1200 Moursund Ave Houston TX 77030

TERMINE, JOHN DAVID, biomedical research administrator; b. Bklyn., Sept. 25, 1938; s. Charles A. and Mary R. (Fiore) T.; m. Virginia A. Galvin, Dec. 26, 1961; children—Mary, John, Theresa, Anne. B.S., St. John's U., 1960; M.S., U. Md., 1963; Ph.D., Cornell U. Med. Coll., 1966. Asst. prof. biochemistry Cornell U. Med. Coll., N.Y.C., 1968-70; spl. research fellow Nat. Inst. Dental Research, NIH, Bethesda, Md., 1970-73, research biochemist, 1973-78, chief skeletal material biochemistry sect., 1978-83, chief mineralized tissue research br., 1983—. Contbr. articles to profl. jours., chpt. to books. Recipient NIH Dirs.' award, 1983. Fellow AAAS (sec. dental sect. 1973-76); mem. Am. Soc. Bone and mineral Research (councilor 1983—), Am. Soc. Biol. Chemists, Orthopaedic Research Soc., Internat. Assn. for Dental Research (pres. mineralized tissue group 1974-76). Roman Catholic. Current work: Molecular and cell biology of bone and tooth tissue in normal and disease states. Subspecialties: Biochemistry (medicine); Oral biology. Home: 6013 Kingsford Ct Bethesda MD 20817 Office: Mineralized Tissue Research Br Nat Inst Dental Research NIH Bldg 30 Room 106 Bethesda MD 20205

TERNER, JAMES, physical chemist, educator; b. Reading, Berkshire, Eng., Mar. 27, 1951; came to U.S., 1955, naturalized 1960; s. Charles naturalized, Ruth Hilde (Cohn) T.; m. Ellen Cindy Shapiro, July 1, 1979. B.A., Brandeis U., 1973; Ph.D., UCLA, 1979. NIH postdoctoral fellow Princeton U., N.J., 1979-81; asst. prof. phys. chemistry Va. Commonwealth U., Richmond, 1981—. Contbr. articles to profl. jours. NSF grad. trainee, 1978; Alfred P. Sloan fellow, 1985-87. Mem. Biophys. Soc., Am. Chem. Soc., Coblentz Soc., Inter-Am. Photochem. Soc. Jewish. Current work: Time-resolved resonance Raman Spectroscopy of chemical transients. Subspecialties: Laser spectroscopy; Physical chemistry. Home: 505 Ridgeley Ln Richmond VA 23229 Office: Va Commonwealth U Chemistry Dept Richmond VA 23284

TERRELL, (NELSON) JAMES, physicist, astrophysicist; b. Houston, Aug. 15, 1923; s. Nelson James and Gladys Delphine (Stevens) T.; m. Elizabeth Anne Pearson, June 9, 1945; children: Anne, Barbara, Jean. B.A. (Graham Baker scholar), Rice U., 1944, M.A. (Rice U. fellow 1946-48), 1947, Ph.D. in Physics (AEC fellow), 1950. Research asst. in physics Rice U., Houston, 1950; asst. prof. physics Western Res. U., Cleve., 1950-51; staff mem. Los Alamos Nat. Lab., 1951—; vis. prof. N. Mex. Highlands U., Las Vegas, summer 1959; vis. staff mem. Lawrence Radiation Lab., U. Calif., Berkeley, summer 1963. Contbr. articles to sci. jours.; co-producer computer-generated movie on x-ray sky, 1982. Served from pvt. to 1st lt., Signal Corps AUS, 1944-46. Fellow AAAS, Am. Phys. Soc.; mem. Internat. Astron. Union, Am. Astron. Soc., Los Alamos Choral Soc., Phi Beta Kappa, Sigma Xi. Club: Los Alamos Ski. Current Work: X-ray astronomy, Gamma-burst astronomy, quasar theory, Fourier analysis, special and general relativity. astrophysics. Subspecialties: High energy astrophysics; Theoretical astrophysics. Home: 85 Obsidian Loop Los Alamos NM 87544 Office: Los Alamos Nat Lab Mail Stop D436 Los Alamos NM 87545

TERZIAN, YERVANT, educator; b. Alexandria, Egypt, Feb. 9, 1939; came to U.S., 1960, naturalized, 1971; s. Bedros and Maria (Kiriakaki) T.; m. Araxy Hovsepian, Apr. 16, 1966; children: Sevan, Tamar. B.Sc., Am. U. Cairo, 1960; M.Sc., Ind. U., 1963; Ph.D., 1965. Staff Nat. Radio Astronomy Obs., 1963-65; Staff Cornell U. Arecibo Obs., Ithaca, N.Y., 1965-67, prof. astronomy, chmn. dept., 1967—; vis. prof. astronomy U. Montreal, 1973, U. Salonica, 1974. Contbr. articles to profl. jours.; editor: Interstellar Ionized Hydrogen, 1968, Planetary Nebulae Observations and Theory, 1978, Cosmology and Astrophysics, 1982. Mem. Internat. Astron. Union, Internat. Union Radio Sci., Am. Astron. Soc. Current Work: Radio astronomy, specialist in physics of interstellar medium. Subspecialties: Radio and microwave astronomy; High energy astrophysics. Home: 109 Brandywine Dr Ithaca NY 14850 Office: Space Scis Bldg Cornell Univ Ithaca NY 14853

TESTA, JOSEPH ROBERT, cancer cytogeneticist, educator; b. Norwalk, Conn., Apr. 28, 1947. B.S., So. Conn. State U., 1969, M.S., 1973; Ph.D., Fordham U., 1976. Assoc. in research Yale U., New Haven, 1975-76; research assoc. U. Chgo., 1976-80; chief cytogenetics unit Nat. Cancer Inst., Balt. Cancer Program, 1980-81; assoc. prof. U. Md., Balt., 1982—, chief sect. cancer genetics, 1981—; cons., lectr. Johns Hopkins Oncology Ctr., Balt., 1983—. Contbr. articles to profl. jours. Leukemia Soc. Am. fellow, 1982-84, scholar, 1984—; Nat. Cancer Inst. grantee, 1984—. Mem. AAAS, Am. Assn. Cancer Research, Am. Soc. Human Genetics, N.Y. Acad. Scis., Phi Beta Kappa, Sigma Xi. Current work: Role clonal chromosome abnormalities in malignancy related to cell phenotype, drug resistance, alterations cellular oncogenes. Subspecialties: Cancer research (medicine); Genetics and genetic engineering (medicine). Office: U Md Cancer Ctr 655 W Baltimore St Baltimore MD 21201

TEW, KENNETH DAVID, molecular pharmacologist, researcher; b. Dumbarton, Scotland, Apr. 20, 1952; came to U.S., 1977; s. Kenneth William and Britalena (Jamieson) T. B.Sc., U. Wales, Swansea, 1973; Ph.D., U. London, 1977. Research assoc. depts. medicine and biochemistry Georgetown U., 1977-79, instr. medicine, 1979-80, asst. prof., medicine and biochemistry, 1980-85; head basic pharmacology program Vincent T. Lombardi Cancer Ctr., 1983-85; mem. Fox Chase Cancer Ctr., assoc. prof. U. Pa., Phila., 1985—. Specialist editor Pharmacology and Therapeutics. Contbr. to books, also articles to profl. jours. Active Am. Cancer Soc. Nat. Cancer Inst. grantee, 1980—. Mem. Am. Assn. Cancer Research, Am. Soc. Cell Biology, AAAS., Am. Soc. Pharmacology and Exptl. Therapeutics. Club: Old Red Rugby Football (Washington). Current Work: Nuclear structure and drug mechanisms of action; application of molecular biology to pharmacology; anticancer drugs, drug resistance, carcinogenisis, European cancer research. Subspecialties: Molecular pharmacology; Cancer research (medicine). Office: Fox Chase Cancer Ctr 7701 Burholme Ave Philadelphia PA 19111

THEOHARIDES, THEOHARIS CONSTANTIN, pharmacologist, physician, educator; b. Thessaloniki, Greece, Feb. 11, 1950; s. Constantin A. and Marika (Krava) T.; m. Efthalia I. Triarchou, July 10, 1981. Diploma with honors, Anatolia Coll., 1968; B.A. with honors, Yale U., 1972, M.S., 1975, M.Phil., 1975, Ph.D. in Pharmacology, 1978, M.D., 1983. Asst. in research biology Yale U., 1968-71, asst. in research pharmacology, 1973-78, research assoc. faculty clin. immunology, 1978-83; asst. prof. biochemistry and pharmacology Tufts U., 1983—, dir. med. pharmacology, 1985—; spl. instr. modern Greek Yale U., 1974, 77; vis. faculty Aristotelian U. Sch. Medicine, Thessaloniki, 1979. Author book on pharmacology; contbr. numerous articles to profl. jours. Bd. dirs., v.p. for relations with Greece, Krikos, 1978-79; trustee Anatolia Coll., 1984-85. Recipient Theodore Cuyler award Yale U., 1972; George Papanicoalou Grad. award, 1977; Med. award Hellenic Med. Soc. N.Y., 1979, 83; M.C. Winternitz prize in pathology Yale U., 1980; others. Mem. Hellenic Biochem. and Biophys. Soc., AMA, AAUP, N.Y. Acad. Scis., Am. Inst. History Pharmacy, AAAS, Soc. Health and Human Values, Am. Assn. History Medicine, Am. Soc. Cell Biology, Soc. Neurosci., Am. Fedn. Clin. Research, Conn. Acad. Arts and Scis., Am. Soc. Pharmacology and Exptl. Therapeutics, Hellenic Soc. Cancer Research, Hellenic Soc. Med. Chemistry, Internat. Soc. Immunopharmacology, Am. Soc. Microbiology, Am. Assn. Immunologists, Internat. Soc. History of Medicine, Assn. Greeks at Yale (pres. 1982-83), New Eng. Hellenic Med. Soc. (sec. 1985), Hellenic Sci. Assn. Boston (bd. dirs. 1985), Internat. Anatolia Alumni Assn. (sec. 1984-85) Sigma Xi. Current Work: Mechanisms of release of secretory products; hormonal induction of ornithine decarboxylase and membrane functions of polyamines; pathophysiology of mast cells. Subspecialties: Endocrinology; Cellular pharmacology. Home: 61 N Washington St Apt 5A Boston MA 02114 Office: Dept Biochemistry and Pharmacology Tufts U 136 Harrison Ave Boston MA 02111

THEON, JOHN SPERIDON, meteorologist; b. Washington, Dec. 12, 1934; s. Lewis and Merope (Xydias) T.; m. Joanne Edens, July 31, 1965; children—Christopher James, Catherine. B.S. in Aero. Engring, U. Md., 1957; B.S. in Meteorology, Pa. State U., 1959, M.S., 1962; Ph.D. in Engring. Sci. and Mechanics, U. Tenn., 1985. Aero. engr. Douglas Aircraft Co., Santa Monica, Calif., 1957-58; engr. U.S. Naval Ordnance Lab., White Oak, Md., 1962; research meteorologist NASA Goddard Space Flight Center, Greenbelt, Md., 1962-74, head meteorology br., 1974-77; asst. chief Lab. for Atmospheric Scis., 1977-78, Nimbus project scientist, 1972-78, Landsat discipline leader meteorol. investigations, 1974-78; mgr. global weather research program NASA Hdqrs., Washington, 1978-82, chief Atmospheric Dynamics and Radiation br., 1982—, Spacelab 3 program scientist, 1979-85. Contbr. articles to profl. jours. Served with USAF, 1958-60. Recipient Nimbus F Instrument Team award NASA-Goddard, 1976, Exceptional Performance award, 1978. Mem. Am. Meteorol. Soc., Am. Geophys. Union, AAAS, Sigma Xi. Presbyterian. Current Work: Responsible for synthesizing, planning, executing and evaluating a broad research and development program in remote sensing of the atmosphere and applying resulting satellite data to problems in meteorology and climatology. Subspecialties: Remote sensing (atmospheric science); Meteorology. Home: 6801 Lupine Ln McLean VA 22101 Office: 600 Independence Ave Washington DC 20546

THIER, SAMUEL OSIAH, physician, educator; b. Bklyn., June 23, 1937; s. Sidney and May Henrietta (Kanner) T.; m. Paula Dell Finkelstein, June 28, 1958; children—Audrey Lauren, Stephanie Ellen, Sara Leslie. Student, Cornell U., 1953-56; M.D., State U. N.Y., Syracuse, 1960. Diplomate: Am. Bd. Internal Medicine (bd. dirs. 1977-85, exec. com. 1981-85, chmn. 1984-85). Intern Mass. Gen. Hosp., Boston, 1960-61, asst. resident, 1961-62, sr. resident, 1964-65, clin. and research fellow, 1965, chief resident, 1966; clin. asso. Nat. Inst. Arthritis and Metabolic Diseases, 1962-64; from instr. to asst. prof. medicine Harvard U. Med. Sch., 1967-69; asst. in medicine, chief renal unit Mass. Gen. Hosp., Boston, 1967-69; asso. prof., then prof. medicine U. Pa. Med. Sch., 1969-72, vice chmn. dept., 1971-74; asso. dir. med. services Hosp. U. Pa., 1969-74; David Paige Smith prof. internal medicine, 1978-81, Sterling prof. medicine, 1981—; chmn. dept. Yale U. Sch. Medicine, 1975—; chief medicine Yale-New Haven Hosp., 1975—, bd. dirs., 1978-85, Hospice, Inc., 1976-82. Mem. editorial bd.; New Eng. Jour. Medicine, 1978-81; Contbr. articles to med. jours. Mem. adv. com. to the dir. NIH, 1980-84. Served with USPHS, 1962-64. Recipient Christian R. and Mary F. Lindback Found. Distinguished Teaching award, 1971. Fellow ACP (bd. regents 1982-85); mem. Assn. Am. Med. Colls. (adminstrv. bd. council acad. socs.), John Morgan Soc., Am. Fedn. Clin. Research (pres. 1976-77), Am. Soc. Nephrology, Am. Physiol. Soc., Inst. Medicine, Nat. Acad. Scis., Internat. Soc. Nephrology, Assn. Profs. Medicine, Assn. Am. Physicians, Interurban Clin. Club, Alph Omega Alpha. Current work: Renal pathophysiology. Subspecialties: Internal medicine; Nephrology. Home: 8 Spector Rd Woodbridge CT 06525 Office: PO Box 3333 New Haven CT 06510

THIESSEN, HENRY ARCHER, physicist, researcher; b. Dumont, N.J., Nov. 8, 1940; s. Henry B. and Alice K. (Leon) T.; m. Challis Ann Lefton, July 14, 1962; 1 child Paul Archer. B.S., Calif. Tech. Inst., 1961, M.S., 1962, Ph.D., 1967. Staff mem. MP div. Los Alamos Nat. Lab., N.Mex., 1966-72, group leader, 1972-83, asst. div. leader, 1983—. Fellow Am. Phys. Soc. Current work: Accelerator design, nuclear physics with high energy pions, protons, and kaons. Subspecialties: Nuclear physics; Particle physics. Office: Los Alamos Nat Lab Mail Stop H847 Los Alamos NM 87545

THIGPEN, JAMES TATE, physician, oncology educator; b. Columbia, Miss., June 6, 1944; m. Louisa Berdie Kessler, June 14, 1969; children: Monroe Tate, James Howard, Samuel Calvin, Richard Allen, David Albert. B.S., U. Miss., 1964, M.D., 1969. Intern Strong Meml. Hosp., U. Rochester, N.Y., 1969-70; resident U. Miss. Sch. Medicine, 1970-71, fellow dept. hematology, 1971-73, assoc. prof., dir. div. med. oncology dept. internal medicine, 1973-85, prof., 1985—. Fellow ACP; mem. AMA, Miss. Med. Assn., Central Med. Soc., Jackson Acad. Medicine, Miss. Acad. Scis., S.W. Oncology Group, Gynecologic Oncology Group, Am. Fedn. Clin. Research, Am. Assn. Cancer Edn., Am. Soc. Clin. Oncology, Am. Assn. Cancer Research, Am. Soc. Hematology. Baptist (deacon 1978— , Sunday sch. tchr. 1979—). Subspecialties: Oncology; Gynecological oncology. Home: 1135 Briarwood Dr Jackson MS 39211 Office: 2500 N State St Jackson MS 39216

THIND, GUADARSHAN SINGH, medical educator, hypertensionologist, consultant; b. Lyallpore, Punjab, India, Oct. 17, 1940; came to U.S., 1962; s. S. Manmohan Singh and Ajaib Kaur (Jawanda) T.; m. Rajinder K. Sekhon, June 26, 1967; children—Gurpreet Kaur, Gurbir Singh. F.Sc., Punjab U., 1957, M.D., M.B.B.S., 1962; M.S., U. Pa., 1966. Diplomate Am. Bd. Internal Medicine. Rotating intern Rajindra Hosp. of Govt. Med. Coll., Patiala, India, 1962; mixed med. intern Albert Einstein Med. Ctr., Phila., 1963-64; resident in internal medicine Grad. Hosp. U. Pa., 1968-70, fellow in cardiology, 1964-68, instr. cardiology, 1966-70, assoc. in cardiology, 1969, assoc. in medicine, 1970, asst. prof., 1971-72; asst. prof. medicine Washington U., St. Louis, 1972-76; assoc. prof. medicine U. Louisville, 1976-85, prof., 1985—, dir. hypertension unit, 1976—; chmn. med. adv. com. high blood pressure program Jefferson County Health Dept., 1982—; mem. adv. bd. Louisville-Jefferson County Health Dept. Hypertension Program, 1982—. Contbr. articles & abstracts to sci., med. jours. Investigative work presented at sci. meetings. Cons. manuscript reviewer Am. Jour. Cardiology, Hypertension, Archives of Internal Medicine, 1977-84. Heart Assn. Southeastern Pa. research fellow, 1969-70. Fellow ACP, Am. Coll. Cardiology; mem. Am. Physiol. Soc., N.Y. Acad. Scis., Am. Heart Assn., AAAS, Am. Fedn. Clin. Research, Ky. Heart Assn., Internat. Study Group Research in Cardiac Metabolism, Jefferson County Med. Soc., Am. Assn. Advancement of Tension Control, Sigma Xi. Current work: Pathophysiology of hypertension and newer pharmacologic treatments of hypertension. Subspecialties: Cardiology; Hypertension. Home: 17603 Pope Dale Rd Louisville KY 40223 Office: U Louisville Health Scis Ctr Hypertension Unit 530 S Jackson St Louisville KY 40292

THIRION, JEAN-PAUL JOSEPH, geneticist, educator; b. Metz, France, July 30, 1939; emigrated to U.S., 1963, naturalized, 1972; s. Paul Roger and Anne-Marie Josephine (Averlant) T.; m. Nancy Ouei, Oct. 12, 1967; children: Daniel, Philippe. Diplome d'Ingénieur, ENSIC, Nancy, France, 1963; Ph.D., U. Wis., 1966; Doctorat-ès-Sciences, U. Paris, 1969. Chargé de recherce CNRS, France, 1967-76; asst. prof. dept. microbiology U. Sherbrooke, Que., Can., 1972-76, assoc. prof., 1976-82, prof., 1982—. Fulbright fellow, 1962-66; MRC-Can. scholar, 1972-77; Chercheur scholar, 1977—. Current Work: Somatic cell genetics, DNA recombinant. Subspecialties: Genetics and genetic engineering (agriculture); Genetics and genetic engineering (medicine).

THIRUMALAI, KUPPUSAMY, government executive; b. Madras, India, Mar. 15, 1938; came to U.S., 1967; s. Alagirisamy and Elluthai K.; m. Padma Veeraswami; 3 children. B.E. in Mining Engring., Coll. Engring., Madras, 1960; Diploma Engring., Mining Acad. Freiberg, Germany, 1963, D. Geotech. Engring., 1966. Head lab. Minn. Bur. Mines, Mpls, 1967-74; coordinator Mining Enforcement and Safety Adminstrn., Washington, 1974-80; mgr. Rockwell Internat., Richland, Wash., 1980-82; program dir. NSF, Washington, 1982—; exec. dir. Sci. and Tech. Inst., Inc., Fairfax, Va., 1984—. Contbr. articles to profl. jours. Recipient Rock Mechanics award Nat. Acad. Scis., 1973, numerous awards Dept. Interior, Dept. labor. Mem. presdl. task force Republican Party, Washington, 1985. Mem. Earthquake Engring. Research Inst., AIME, Internat. Soc. Rock Mechanics, Inter Agy. Com. for Disaster Mitigation. Current work: Earthquake, ground stability, underground construction designing, hazard mitigation, health and safety, education and training, rock mechanics, nuclear waste disposal, hazardous waste disposal. Office: NSF 1800 G St NW Washington DC 20550

THODE, HENRY GEORGE, scientist, educator; b. Dundurn, Sask., Can., Sept. 10, 1910; s. Charles Herman and Zelma Ann (Jacoby) T.; m. Sadie Alicia Patrick, Feb. 1, 1935; children: John Charles, Henry Patrick, Richard Lee. B.Sc., U. Sask., 1930, M.Sc., 1932, LL.D., 1958; Ph.D., U. Chgo., 1934; D.Sc. (hon.), U. Toronto, 1955, U. B.C., 1960, Acadia U., 1960, Laval U., 1963, Royal Mil. Coll. Can., 1964, McGill U., 1966, Queen's U., 1967, York U., 1972, McMaster U., 1973; LL.D. (hon.), U. Regina, 1983. Research asst. chemistry Columbia, 1936-38; research chemist U.S. Rubber Co., Passaic, N.J., 1938-39;

asst. prof. chemistry McMaster U., 1939-42, asso. prof. chemistry, 1942-44, prof. chemistry, 1944-79, prof. emeritus, 1979—; head dept. chemistry, 1948-52, dir. research, 1947-61; prin. Hamilton Coll., 1949-63, v.p., 1957-61, pres. and vice chancellor, 1961-72; Research asso. atomic energy project NRC, 1943-46; Sr. Fgn. Scientist fellow NSF, 1970; mem. commn. on atomic weights Internat. Union Pure and Applied Chemistry, 1963-79; mem. Can. nat. com. to Internat. Union Pure and Applied Chemistry, 1975-80; dir. Atomic Energy Can. Ltd., 1966-81, Stelco Inc. Mem. editorial adv. bd.: Jour. Inorganic and Nuclear Chemistry, 1954—, Earth and Planetary Sci. Letters, 1965—; Contbr. numerous articles in field. Bd. govs. Ont. Research Found., 1955-82; bd. dirs. Western N.Y. Nuclear Research Centre, 1965-73, Royal Bot. Gardens, 1961-72. Decorated mem. Order Brit. Empire, companion Order Can.; recipient medal Chem. Inst. Can., 1957; Shell Can. merit fellow, 1974. Fellow Royal Soc. Can. (pres. 1959-60, Tory medal 1959, Centenary medal 1982), Chem. Inst. Can. (hon., pres. 1951-52), Royal Soc. (London), Geol. Soc. Am. (Day medal 1980). Office: Nuclear Research Bldg McMaster Univ 1280 Main St W Hamilton ON L8S 4K1 Canada

THOM, RONALD MARK, marine biologist, researcher; b. Long Beach, Calif., June 6, 1948; s. Harlan Mark and Ruth Mabel (Harris) T.; m. Susan Kathleen Wray, July 10, 1971; children—Andrew Mark. A.S. in Biology, Long Beach City Coll., 1969; B.A. in Biology, Calif. State Univ., 1971; M.A. in Biology, Long Beach State U., 1976; Ph.D. in Fisheries, U. Wash., 1978. Biologist Los Angeles County, Calif., 1971-74; research asst. U. Wash., 1974-78; fisheries biologist U.S.C.E., Seattle, 1979-82; research scientist U. Wash., 1982—; sci. adv. Kitsap County, Wash., 1983, Seattle Mayor's Office, 1983-84; mem. tech. adv. com. Puget Sound Initiative, U.S. EPA. Mem. AAAS, Ecol. Soc. Am., Phycological Soc. Am., Internatl. Phycological Soc., Estuarine Research Fed. Roman Catholic. Club: Shotokan Karate (Seattle). Current work: Quantitative benthic algal ecology; wetlands restoration, benthic marine primary production. Subspecialties: Ecology (biology); Marine biology. Office: Fisheries Research Inst WH-10 U Wash Seattle WA 98195

THOMAS, ADRIAN WESLEY, agricultural scientist; b. Edgefield, S.C., June 23, 1939; s. Hasting Adrian and Nancy Azalena (Bridges) T.; m. Martha Elizabeth McAllister, July 12, 1964; children—Wesley Adrian, Andrea Elizabeth. B.S.A.E., Clemson U., 1962, M.S.A.E., 1965; Ph.D., Colo. State U., 1972. Agrl. engr. USDA Research Service, Tifton, Ga., 1965-69, Ft. Collins, Colo., 1969-72, Watkinsville, Ga., 1972-78, research leader, 1978-84, acting dir. lab., 1984—; cons. Agr. Research Service Dept. State, 1981; adviser, lectr. in field. Mem. Am. Soc. Agrl. Engrs., Am. Soc. Agronomy, Soil Conservation Soc. Am., Soil Sci. Soc. Am., So. Assn. Agrl. Scientists, Sigma Xi, Alpha Epsilon, Gamma Sigma Delta, Phi Kappa Phi. Lutheran. Current work: Planning risk strategies for conservation production systems in the southeastern U.S. Subspecialties: Agricultural engineering; Integrated systems modelling and engineering. Office: US Dept Agr Research Service PO Box 555 Watkinsville GA 30677

THOMAS, III ALEXANDER EDWARD, organic chemist, research administrator; b. Chgo., May 3, 1930; s. Alexander E. Jr. and Ethel (Bauer) T.; m. Mary Ann Weiner, Apr. 7, 1956; children—Carol Ann, Laura Jean, Joanne Marie. B.S. in Chemistry, U. Ill.-Urbana, 1955; M.S. in Organic Chemistry, DePaul U., 1961. Research chemist Glidden Co., Chgo., 1955-58; sect. head analytical chemistry Durkee Foods div./Glidden Co., Chgo., 1958-66; mgr. chem. research Durkee div./SCM Corp., Strongsville, Ohio, 1967-72, mgr. applications research, 1972-78, assoc. dir. applied sci., 1978—. Contbr. articles to profl. jours. Served with U.S. Army, 1952-54. Mem. Am. Chem. Soc., Am. Oil Chemists Soc. Republican. Roman Catholic. Current work: Product development food and food ingredients. Subspecialty: Food science and technology. Office: Durkee Foods div SCM Corp 16651 Sprague Rd Strongsville OH 44136

THOMAS, CARLTON EUGENE, electrical engineer; b. Cleve., Dec. 16, 1939; s. Clyde and Laura Bernice (Miles) T.; m. Anne Edna Todd, Jan. 28, 1961; children: Scott, Todd, Julie, Penny. B.S.E.E., U. Mich., 1961, M.S.E.E., 1963, Ph.D., 1971. Research scientist Conductron Corp., Ann Arbor, Mich., 1962-67; head advanced optics KMS Industries, Ann Arbor and Van Nuys, Calif., 1967-72; dir. laser and optics div. KMS Fusion, Ann Arbor, 1972-81; group leader photoengring., also tech. dir. sovonics solar systems with Energy Conversion Devices Co. (Troy, Mich.), Standard Oil Co. (Ohio), Cleve., 1981—. Contbr. articles to profl. jours. Bd. dirs. Ann Arbor YMCA, 1979-80; mem. Interfaith Council for Peace, Ann Arbor, 1976-81. Mem. Fedn. Am. Scientists, AAAS, Sigma Xi. Methodist. Patentee in lasers and optics fields. Current Work: Development of inexpensive photovoltaic solar cell systems based on amorphous silicon technology. Subspecialty: Solar energy. Home: 2681 Rochester St Shaker Heights OH 44122 Office: 4440 Warrensville Center Rd Cleveland OH 44119

THOMAS, CHARLES SAMUEL, physical therapist, educator; b. Nazareth, South India, June 25, 1920; came to U.S., 1946, naturalized, 1954; s. Edward and Sellammal (Monicham) T.; m. Virginia Mae Learned, June 18, 1940; children: Dale, Carol. B.A., Pacific Union Coll., 1949; B.S., Loma Linda U., 1952; M.A., Stanford U., 1959; Ph.D., Clairemont Grad. Sch., 1966. Staff therapist White Meml. Hosp., 1952-54; instr. Sch. Phys. Therapy, Loma Linda U., Calif., 1954-58, asst. phys. medicine, 1958-63, developer home rehab. program, dept. phys. medicine and rehab., 1962-64, instr. div. pub. health, 1966; asst. prof. pub. health practice Sch. Phys. Therapy, Loma Linda U. (Sch. Pub. Health), 1967-69; asst. prof. health edn. Sch. Phys. Therapy, Loma Linda U. (Sch. Health), 1970-71, asst. prof. preventive care, 1971-74, asst. prof. health sci., 1974-75, assoc. prof., 1975-82, assoc. prof. emeritus, 1982—; rehab. cons. Thailand Refugees UN, 1982. Seventh-day Adventist. Current Work: Developing hydrotherapy for home and simple treatments for home. Subspecialty: Health services research. Office: 4027 W George St Banning CA 92220

THOMAS, CLAUDE EARLE, plant pathologist, researcher; b. Spartanburg, S.C., Dec. 4, 1940; s. John E. and Bertha Leola (Holder) T.; m. June Gilliam Oakman, Aug. 27, 1960; children: Christopher Lee, Matthew Earle, Andrew Beauregard. A.B., Wofford Coll., 1962; M.S., Clemson Coll., 1964; Ph.D., Clemson U., 1966. NDEA grad. fellow Clemson U., 1962-65, sr. grad. teaching asst., 1965-66; research plant pathologist Subtropical Research Lab., Agrl. Research Service, Dept. Agr., Weslaco, Tex., 1966-82, U.S. Vegetable Lab., Charleston, S.C., 1982—; vis. mem. grad. faculty Tex. A&M U., 1978-82; adj. prof. Clemson U., 1983—. Contbr. articles to profl. jours., 6 germ plasm releases, 4 vegetable cultivar releases. Mem. Am. Phytopath. Soc., Am. Soc. Hort. Sci., Cucurbit Genetics Coop., Tex. Vegetable Assn. Baptist. Lodge: Rotary. Current Work: Foliar diseases of vegetable crops (especially cucurbits); germ plasm enhancement for disease resistance; nature and mechanisms of disease resistance. Subspecialty: Plant pathology. Office: 2875 Savannah Hwy Charleston SC 29407

THOMAS, DAN MCDOUGAL, physicist; b. Wiesbaden, Fed. Republic Germany, Oct. 13, 1954; s. Thomas Elihue and Yvonne June (McDougal) T.; m. Mary Catherine Prouty, Sept. 4, 1982. B.S. in Physics, Emory U., 1976; M.S. in Physics, U. Tex., Austin, 1979, Ph.D. in Physics, 1983. Research assoc. physics dept. U. Tex., Austin, 1977-82; guest scientist Oak Ridge Nat. Lab., 1979-82; sr. scientist GA Techs., Inc., San Diego, 1983—. Contbr. articles to profl. jours. Kenneth W. Finkel Meml. scholar Emory U., 1975. Mem. Am. Phys. Soc. (plasma div., electron-atom div.), Am. Nuclear Soc. Current work: Plasma diagnostics for controlled fusion research, understanding the physics of ion sources and neutral particle production. Subspecialties: Nuclear fusion; Atomic and molecular physics. Home: 6307 Connie Dr San Diego CA 92115 Office: GA Technologies Inc PO Box 85608 San Diego CA 92138

THOMAS, DONALD CHARLES, univ. dean, microbiologist, educator; b. Cin., Sept. 26, 1935; s. Howard G. and Elsie M. (Sack) T.; m. Barbara J., Sept. 2, 1957; children: Mark, Matthew, Michael. B.S., Xavier U., Cin., 1957; M.S., U. Cin., 1959; Ph.D., St. Louis U., 1968. Asst. dir. Surg. Bacteriology Labs. dept. surgery U. Cin., 1959-61; instr. in biology Villa Madonna Coll., 1961-63; instr. depts. med. microbiology and pediatrics Coll. Medicine, Ohio State U., 1968-69, asst. prof. med. microbiology and pediatrics, 1969-72, asst. prof. pediatrics, adj. asst. prof. med. microbiology, and asso. dir. div. program devel. assistance, 1972-77; dir. contracts and grants mgmt. Sch. Medicine, adj. assoc. prof. microbiology and immunology Sch. Medicine and Coll. Sci. and Engring., Wright State U., 1977-78; assoc. prof. pathology Sch. Medicine and Coll. Sci. and Engring., Wright State U. (Sch. Medicine), 1978—; assoc. prof. microbiology and immunology Sch. Medicine and Coll. Sci. and Engring., Wright State U. (Coll. Sci. and Engring.), 1978—, dir. univ. research services, 1978—; asst. dean for research Sch. Medicine and Coll. Sci. and Engring., Wright State U. (Sch. Grad. Studies), 1979-80, assoc. dean for research, 1980-83, acting dean, 1980-83, dean, 1983—, vice provost research, 1984—; mem. vis. faculty Princeton U., 1979; mem. bd. advisers St. Leonard Coll., 1980—; 2d v.p., mem. exec. com. Trustee Hospice Dayton (Ohio), Inc., 1981—; cons. Econ. Task Force for Social Justice, sponsored by Archdiocese Cin., Office Social Action and World Peace, 1981—. Author: (with others) Molecular Basis of Viral Carcinogenesis in Exploitable Molecular Mechanisms and Neoplasia, 1969; contbr. (with others) chpt., articles to profl. publs. Mem. steering com. Consortium for Cancer Control in Ohio, 1978—, mem. eval. com., 1980—; mem. pilot research com. Ohio div. Am. Cancer Soc., 1979-82; mem. regents adv. com. for grad. studies Ohio Bd. Regents, 1980—; mem. Gov.'s Tech. Task Force; trustee Miami Valley Small Bus. Incubator, 1985. Ohio Dept. Econ. and Community Devel., 1982. Grantee Nat. Inst. Allergy and Infectious Disease, 1968-72; Grantee others. Mem. Am. Soc. Microbiology, AAAS, Fedn. Am. Scientists, Soc. Research Adminstrs., Nat. Council Univ. Research Adminstrs., Soc. Univ. Pat. Adminstrs., Nat. Soc. Med. Research, Licensing Execs. Soc. Club: Dayton Execs. Current Work: diagnostic virology; molecular aspects of virus replication; pathogenesis of virus diseases; devels. in tumor viruses. Subspecialties: Virology (biology); Microbiology.

THOMAS, EDWARD DONNALL, physician, educator; b. Mart, Tex., Mar. 15, 1920; s. Edward E. and Angie (Hill) T.; m. Dorothy Martin, Dec. 20, 1942; children: Edward Donnall, Jeffery A., Elaine. B.A., U. Tex., 1941, M.A., 1943; M.D., Harvard U., 1946. Diplomate: Am. Bd. Internal Medicine. NRC fellow medicine dept. biology MIT, 1950-51; instr. medicine Harvard Med. Sch., Boston; also hematologist Peter Bent Brigham Hosp., 1953-55; research asso. Cancer Research Found., Children Med. Center, Boston, 1953-55; physician in chief Mary Imogene Bassett Hosp., also asso. clin. prof. medicine Coll. Physicians and Surgeons, Columbia U., 1955-63; prof. U. Wash. Sch. Medicine, Seattle, 1963—. Mem. Am. Soc. Clin. Investigation, Assn. Am. Physicians, Am. Soc. Hematology, Am. Fedn. Clin. Research, Internat. Soc. Hematology, Nat. Acad. Scis., Am. Assn. Cancer Research, Western Assn. Physicians, Am. Soc. Clin. Oncology, Transplantation Soc. Research and numerous publs. on hematology, marrow transplantation, biochemistry and irradiation biology. Subspecialties: Marrow transplant; Oncology. Office: Fred Hutchinson Cancer Research Center 1124 Columbia St Seattle WA 98104

THOMAS, FAIRWELL, biochemist, researcher; b. Kerala, India, Apr. 8, 1941; came to U.S., 1969; s. Thomas Puthiyathu and Ammukutty (Alexios) T.; m. Philsamma Vetticad, Apr. 17, 1971; children—Beena Fairwell, Neena Fairwell. B.S., St. Berchman's Coll., Kerala, 1960; M.S., U. Saugor, Rewa, India, 1963; Ph.D., Nat. Chem. Lab., U. Poona, 1967. Instr. Loyola Coll., Madras, India, 1960-61; lectr. Christian Med. Coll., Vellore, India, 1963; research fellow Nat. Chem. Lab., Poona, 1964-69; research assoc. U. Ga., Athens, 1969-72, Yale Med. Sch., New Haven, 1970; research chemist NIH, Bethesda, 1972—. Mem. Am. Soc. Mass Spectrometry, Assn. Scientists of Indian Origin in Am. Republican. Roman Catholic. Current work: Primary structure and synthesis of proteins and peptides, applications of mass spectrometry in biological chemistry. Subspecialties: Biochemistry (biology); Organic chemistry. Home: 5812 Kingswood Rd Bethesda MD 20814 Office: NIH Bldg 10 Room 7N117 Bethesda MD 20205

THOMAS, GARETH, materials science and mineral engineering educator; married; 1 child. B.Sc. with honors in Metallurgy, U. Wales, 1952; Ph.D., Cambridge U., 1955, Sc.D., 1969. Mem. faculty U. Calif.-Berkeley, 1960—, prof. dept. materials sci. and mineral engring., 1966—, assoc. dean grad. div., 1968-69, asst. to chancellor, 1969-72, sr. faculty scientist materials and molecular research div., sci. dir. Nat. Ctr. Electron Microscopy, 1981—; cons., lectr., vis. prof. in field. Author several books in field. Contbr. chpts. to books, articles to profl. jours. Mem. exec. adv. bd. Ency. Phys. Sci. and Tech., 1984. Patentee in field. Vice chmn. Materials Adv. Bd., Taiwan; mem. fund-raising com. TMS-AIME Found. of the Future. ICI fellow, Cambridge U., 1956-59; vis. scientist Alcoa Research Labs., New Kensington, Pa.; Guggenheim fellow, 1971-72; recipient numerous awards and grants in field including: Alexander von Humboldt Sr. Scientist award Max Planck Inst., Suttgart, Fed. Republic Germany, 1981. Fellow Am. Soc. Metals, Royal Microscopical Soc. (U.K.), AIME (bd. dirs. Metall. Soc. 1977-80); mem. Nat. Acad. Scis., Nat. Acad. Engring., Acta Metallurgica (bd. dirs. 1979-82, chmn. bd. govs. 1982-85), Electron Microscopy Soc. Am. (pres. 1975), Internat. Fedn. Electron Microscopy Soc. (sec.-gen. 1974—). Current work: Physical metallurgy and ceramics; electron diffraction and microscopy. Subspecialty: Metallurgy. Office: U Calif Dept Materials Sci and Mineral Engring 284 Hearst Mining Bldg Berkeley CA 94720

THOMAS, GARLAND LEON, physicist, remote sensing consultant; b. Topeka, Aug. 29, 1920; s. Jasper McKinley and Margaret Mae (Hickman) T.; m. Kathleen Hickey, Aug. 29, 1948; children—John, Patricia, LiLi. B.S., Drury Coll., 1942; A.M., U. Mo., 1948, Ph.D., 1954. Fellow engr. Westinghouse Atomic Power Co., Pitts., 1953-59; assoc. prof. physics Drury Coll., Springfield, Mo., 1959-66, Fla. Inst. Tech., Melbourne, 1966-71; remote sensing cons. Brevard County Planning Dept., Merrit Island, Fla., 1971-79; prin. engr. Planning Research Corp., Ebon Research Systems, Kennedy Space Center, Fla., 1979-85, NASA, Safety Engring. Office, 1985—. Patentee in nuclear reactor field. Served to lt. comdr. USNR, 1944-46. Mem. Am. Phys. Soc., Am. Soc. Photogrammetry, Am. Nuclear Soc., Biophys. Soc., Am. Assn. Physics Tchrs. Republican. Mem. Christian Ch. (Disciples of Christ). Club: Melbourne Yacht. Current work: Scientific problems in aerospace safety. Subspecialties: Aerospace engineering and technology; Remote sensing (geoscience). Home: 1208 E River Dr #102 Melbourne FL 32901 Office: NASA Safety Engring Office Kennedy Space Center FL 32815

THOMAS, GARY CHARLES, mechanical engineering consultant, educator; b. Buffalo, June 17, 1942; s. Charles Dellinger and Rosemary (Bowen) T.; m. Marilou E. Layton, Nov. 23, 1966; children—Joseph Charles, Courtney Layton. B.S. in Mech. Engring., U. Mich.-Ann Arbor, 1967; M.B.A., U. Santa Clara, 1972. Registered profl. engr., Calif. Engr., Beckman Instruments, Palo Alto, Calif., 1969-72; mgr. ramp engring. FMC Corp., San Jose, Calif., 1972-77; sr. project engr. Kaspar Instruments, Mountain View, Calif., 1977-78; mgr. systems engring. Coherent, Palo Alto, Calif., 1978-80, XMR, Santa Clara, Calif., 1983; sole practice cons. mech. engring., Los Altos, Calif., 1980—; asst. prof. mech. engring. San Jose State U., 1981—. Co-author: Lasers-Operation, Equipment, Application and Design, 1980. Patentee hydraulic lubrication of high-speed spindle, 1977. Mem. ASME, Beta Gamma Sigma. Current work: Design of CO2 lasers, surgical and industrial laser systems; design of satellite receiving stations for data and video teleconferencing system. Subspecialty: Mechanical engineering. Home: 1195 St Charles Ct Los Altos CA 94022

THOMAS, GEORGE JOSEPH, JR., chemistry educator, research scientist; b. New Bedford, Mass., Dec. 24, 1941; m. Martha Ann Sheehan, July 2, 1966; children: Elizabeth Ann, George Joseph, Jeanine Marie. B.A., Boston Coll., 1963; Ph.D., MIT, 1967. Research fellow King's Coll., London, 1967-68; asst. prof. Southeastern Mass. U., North Dartmouth, 1968-71, assoc. prof., 1971-74, prof. chemistry, 1974—; vis. scientist dept. biology Osaka (Japan) U., 1975-76, MIT, Cambridge, 1982-83; chmn. biophys. chemistry study sect. NIH, Bethesda, Md., 1979-83. Editorial bd.: Biophys. Jour, 1982—; contbr. articles to sci. publs. Mem. Sch. Com. Westport, Mass., 1978-84, chmn., 1982-83; trustee Westport Free Public Library, 1975-78. Recipient Coblentz award Coblentz Soc., 1976. Mem. AAAS, Biophys. Soc. Current Work: Structure and assembly of viruses and nucleoproteins; vibrational spectroscopy of nucleic acids and proteins. Subspecialties: Biophysical chemistry; Laser spectroscopy. Office: Southeastern Mass U Dept Chemistry North Dartmouth MA 02747

THOMAS, H. RONALD, chemist; b. Auburn, Ind., June 9, 1942; s. Herbert Ronald and Margaret Lonise (Sheely) T.; m. Louise; children: Jason, Morganna. M.Sc., U. Durham, Eng., 1975, Ph.D., 1977. Mem. sci. staff Xerox Corp., 1967-82; sr. research scientist Pfizer, Inc., 1982—; adj. prof. chem. engring. U. Wash., 1982—; instr. Am. Chem. Soc. courses, 1979—; cons. Center Adhesion, Va. Inst. Tech., 1982—. Co-editor: Characterizations of Polymer Molecular Structure by Photon, Electron and Ion Probes, 1981; contbr. articles to profl. jours. Inst. Petroleum grantee, 1975-76; Xerox Corp. grantee, 1974-77. Mem. Am. Chem. Soc., Am. Phys. Soc. Current Work: Surface chemistry and surface physics on polymer and inorganic surfaces. Subspecialties: Surface chemistry; Polymer physics. Home: 4105 N Delaware Dr Easton PA 18042 Office: 640 N 13th St Easton PA 18042

THOMAS, JOHN HOWARD, engring. educator, astrophysicist; b. Chgo., Apr. 9, 1941; s. William Whitney and Dorothy L. T.; m. Lois Moffit, Aug. 11, 1962; children: Jeffrey, Laura. B.S., Purdue U., 1962, M.S., 1964, Ph.D. in Engring. Scis, 1966. Registered profl. engr., N.Y. NATO postdoctoral fellow U. Cambridge, Eng., 1966-67; mem. faculty U. Rochester, N.Y., 1967—, prof. mech. and aerospace scis., 1981—; assoc. dean grad. studies U. Rochester (Coll. Engring. and Applied Scis.), 1981—; vis. scientist Max-Planck Inst. for Physics and Astrophysics, Munich, W. Ger., 1973-74. Contbr. articles to profl. jours. NSF, NASA, U.S. Air Force grantee. Mem. Am. Astron. Soc., Internat. Astron. Union, Am. Phys. Soc., Am. Geophys. Union, ASME, Am. Acad. Mechanics, Am. Soc. Engring. Edn. Current Work: Theoretical research in solar physics, especially sunspots; geophysical and astrophysical fluid dynamics; applied mathematics. Subspecialties: Solar physics; Fluid mechanics. Office: Coll Engring and Applied Sci U Rochester Rochester NY 14627

THOMAS, JOHN JOSEPH, chemistry researcher, environmental educator; b. Boston, Apr. 24, 1936; s. John Jefferson and Margaret Isabelle (Haver) T.; m. Betty Jane Ericson, Nov. 6, 1966. B.S., Boston Coll., 1959, M.S., 1961; Ph.D., U. N.H., 1966. Research chemist Rachelle Labs., Long Beach, Calif., 1966-69; research assoc. U. Mich., Ann Arbor, 1969-71; research prof. Fla. Inst. Tech., Melbourne, 1971—. Contbr. articles to profl. jours. Recipient Creative Tech. award NASA, 1980, 83. Mem. Am. Chem. Soc., AAAS. Democrat. Current work: Diagnostic systems for influenza; biomass to liquid fuels and chemicals; environmental carcinogenesis; waste conversion to commercial products; toxic gas cleaning systems. Subspecialties: Clinical chemistry; Biomass (energy science and technology). Home: 419 Bridgetown Ct Satellite Beach FL 32937 Office: Med Research Inst Fla Inst Tech 3325 W New Haven Ave Melbourne FL 32901

THOMAS, JOHN RICHARD, chemist; b. Anchorage, Ky., Aug. 26, 1921; s. John R. and Mildred (Woods) T.; m. Beatrice Ann Davidson, Dec. 7, 1944; children—Jonnie Sue Jacobs, Richard G. B.S., U. Calif., Berkeley, 1943, Ph.D., 1947. With U.S. AEC, 1949-51; research chemist Chevron Research Co., Richmond, Calif., 1948-49, sr. research asso., 1951-60, sr. research scientist, 1961-67; mgr. research and devel. Ortho div. Chevron Chem. Co., Richmond, 1967-68; asst. sec. Standard Oil Co., Calif., 1968-70; pres. Chevron Research Co., 1970—; v.p. petroleum research Chevron Corp.; dir. Cetus Corp. Contbr. articles to profl. jours. Mem. Am. Chem. Soc., AAAS, Indsl. Research Inst., Soc. Automotive Engrs. Republican. Patentee in field. Current work: Petroleum research. Home: 847 McEllen Way Lafayette CA 94549 Office: Chevron Research Co 576 Standard Ave Richmond CA 94802

THOMAS, LEO JOHN, manufacturing company executive; b. St. Paul, Oct. 30, 1936; s. Leo John and Christal (Dietrich) T.; m. Joanne Juliani, Dec. 27, 1958; children—Christopher, Gregory, Cynthia, Jeffrey. B.S., U. Minn., 1958; M.S., U. Ill., 1960, Ph.D., 1962. With Eastman Kodak Co., Rochester, N.Y., 1961—, asst. dir. research labs., 1975-77, dir., from 1977, v.p., 1977-78, sr. v.p., from 1978, now v.p., gen. mgr. life scis. div.; bd. dirs. N.Y. State Sci. and Tech. Found., Indsl. Research, Indsl. Research Inst.; mem. founding com. Chem. Research Council; dir. Security Trust Co., Rochester. Mem. Am. Inst. Chem. Engrs., Soc. Photog. Scientists and Engrs., Soc. Motion Picture and TV Engrs., N.Y. Acad. Scis., Rochester C. of C. Subspecialty: Chemical engineering. Office: Eastman Kodak Co 343 State St Rochester NY 14650

THOMAS, LEWIS, physician, educator; b. Flushing, N.Y., Nov. 25, 1913; s. Joseph S. and Grace Emma (Peck) T.; m. Beryl Dawson, Jan. 1, 1941; children: Abigail Luttinger, Judith, Eliza. B.S., Princeton U., 1933, Sc.D. (hon.), 1976; M.D., Harvard U., 1937; M.A., Yale U., 1969; Sc.D. (hon.), U. Rochester, 1974, U. Ohio at Toledo, 1976, Columbia U., 1978, Meml. U. Nfld., 1978, U. N.C., 1979, Worcester Found., 1979, Williams Coll., 1982, Conn. Coll., 1983, U. Wales, 1983; LL.D. (hon.), Johns Hopkins U., 1976, Trinity Coll., 1980; L.H.D. (hon.), Duke U., 1976, Reed Coll., 1978; Litt.D. (hon.), Dickinson Coll., 1980, Ursinus Coll., 1981, SUNY-Stony Brook, 1983; D.Mus. (hon.), New Eng. Conservatory Music, 1982; D.H.L. (hon.), NYU Sch. Medicine, 1983; Litt.D. (hon.), Drew U., 1983. Intern Boston City Hosp., 1937-39, Neurol. Inst., N.Y.C., 1939-41; Tilney Meml. fellow Thorndike Lab., Boston City Hosp., 1941-42; vis. investigator Rockefeller Inst., 1942-46; asst. prof. pediatrics Med. Sch. Johns Hopkins, 1946-48; asso. prof. medicine Med. Sch. Tulane, 1948-50, prof. medicine, 1950; prof. pediatrics and medicine, dir. pediatric research labs. Heart Hosp., U. Minn., 1950-54; prof., chmn. dept. pathology N.Y. U. Sch. Medicine, 1954-58, prof., chmn. dept. medicine, 1958-66, dean, 1966-69; prof., chmn. dept. pathology Yale, 1969-72; dean Yale Sch. Medicine, 1972-73; prof. medicine, pathology Med. Sch. Cornell U., N.Y.C., from 1973; prof. biology Med. Sch. Cornell U. (Grad. Sch. Med. Sci.), from 1973; adj. prof. Rockefeller U., from 1975; pres., chief exec. officer Meml. Sloan-Kettering Cancer Center, N.Y.C., 1973-80, chancellor, 1980-83, pres. emeritus, 1984—; Univ. prof. SUNY-Stony Brook Health Scis. Ctr., 1984—; dir. 3d and 4th med. divs. Bellevue Hosp., 1958-66, pres. med. bd., 1963-66; cons. Manhattan VA Hosp., 1954-69; cons. to surgeon gen. Dept. Army, surgeon gen. USPHS; mem. pathology study sect. NIH, 1954-58, nat. adv. health council, 1958-62, nat. adv. child health and human devel. council, 1963-67; mem. commn. on streptococcal disease Armed Forces Epidemiological Bd., 1950-62; mem. Pres.'s Sci. Adv. Com., 1967-70, mem. council and governing bd., from 1979; chmn. overview cluster subcom. Pres.'s Biomed. Research Panel, 1975-76; mem. Tech. Assessment Adv. Council, from 1980. Mem. Bd. Health, N.Y.C., 1956-69; mem. bd. sci. consultants Sloan-Kettering Inst. Cancer Research, 1966-72; bd. dirs. Josiah Macy Jr. Found., from 1975; bd. sci. advisers Mass. Gen. Hosp., 1970-73, Scripps Clinic and Research Found., 1969-78; bd. dirs., research council Public Health Research Inst. of City N.Y., 1964-69; bd. overseers Harvard Coll., 1976-82; mem. sci. adv. com. Sidney Farber Cancer Inst., from 1978; mem. council Grad. Sch. Bus. and Public Adminstrn., Cornell U., 1978-82; mem. awards assembly Gen. Motors Cancer Research Found., from 1978; Asso. fellow Ezra Stiles Coll. Yale U. Author: Lives of a Cell, 1974, Medusa and the Snail, 1979, The Youngest Science, 1983, Late Night Thoughts on Listening to Mahler's Ninth Symphony, 1983; mem. editorial bd.: Inflammation. Contbr. articles to Jour. Devel. and Comparative Immunology, Daedalus, Cellular Immunology, Am. Jour. Pathology. Trustee N.Y.C.-Rand Inst., 1967-71, The Rockefeller U., from 1975, Draper Lab., 1975-81, John Simon Guggenheim Meml. Found., from 1975, Mt. Sinai Sch. Medicine, from 1979, Ednl. Broadcasting Co., 1977-83, Menninger Found., from 1980; bd. dirs. Lounsbery Found., from 1982; chmn. bd. Monell Chem. Senses Ctr., from 1982; mem. bd. advisors Kennedy Inst. Ethics, Georgetown U., from 1982; Trustee Nat. Hospice, from 1978, Sidney Farber Cancer Inst., from 1978; mem. bd. overseers U. Pa. Sch. Nursing, from 1983; mem. adv. council program in history of sci. Princeton U., from 1982. Served as lt. comdr. M.C. USNR, 1941-46. Recipient Distinguished Achievement award Modern Medicine, 1975; Nat. Book award for arts and letters, 1975; Honor award Am. Med. Writers Assn., 1978; Med. Edn. award AMA, 1979; Bard award in medicine and sci. Bard Coll., 1979; Am. Book award, 1981; St. Davids Soc. award, 1980; Recipient Woodrow Wilson award Princeton U., 1980, award Cosmos Club, Washington, 1982. Fellow Am. Acad. Arts and Scis., Am. Rheumatism Assn.; mem. Nat. Acad. Scis., Am. Acad. and Inst. Arts and Letters, Am. Philos. Assn., Am. Soc. Exptl. Pathology, Practitioners Soc., Am. Acad. Microbiology, Peripatetic Clin. Soc., Am. Soc. Clin. Investigation, Am. Assn. Immunologists, Friends of History of Sci. Soc. (council from 1982), Soc. Am. Bacteriologist, Assn. Am. Physicians (Kober medal 1983), Am. Pediatric Soc., N.Y. Acad. Scis., Harvey Soc. (councillor), Scientist's Inst. for Pub. Info (chmn. bd. from 1982, award for excellence in sci. communication), AAUP, Soc. Exptl. Biology and Medicine, Am. Soc. Clin. Oncology, Council on Fgn. Relations, Interurban Clin. Club, Phi Beta Kappa, Alpha Omega Alpha. Clubs: Harvard (N.Y.C.); Century Assn. Subspecialty: Internal medicine. Office: SUNY Stony Brook Health Scis Ctr Sch Medicine Stony Brook NY 11794

THOMAS, MATHEW, materials scientist, ceramic engineer; b. Tiruvalla, Kerala, India, Aug. 26, 1938; came to U.S., 1971; s. Mannancheril Varughese and Rachel Valliaparampil (Mathew) T.; m. Elizabeth Thekkeparampil Chacko, Oct. 4, 1976; children—Jessvin Mathew, Shinu Rachel. B.S., U. Kerala, 1960, M.S., 1961; Ph.D., U. Ottawa, Ont., Can., 1970. Postdoctoral fellow U. Sask., Saskatoon, Can., 1970-71; vis. lectr. Mosul U., Iraq, 1972-74; faculty Rensselaer Poly. Inst., Troy, N.Y., 1974-79; mgr. materials tech. Cerac Inc., Milw., 1979-80; sr. materials engr. Avco Lycoming Div., Stratford, Conn., 1980-81; cons. engr. Ceramics & Composites Tech., Orange, Conn., 1982—; cons. Therm Inc., Ithaca, N.Y., 1984—. Co-inventor implantable bioceramic, 1976. Contbr. numerous articles to sci. jours. Mem. bd. edn. Congregational Ch., West Haven, Conn., 1984-86. Kerala U. scholar, 1956-60. Mem. Am. Ceramic Soc. (New Eng. chpt.), Sigma Xi. Current work: Research and development of high performance ceramic materials for high temperature, energy related, biomedical and electronic applications. Subspecialties: Ceramics; Biomaterials. Home: 27 Ridge Ct E West Haven CT 06516 Office: Ceramics & Composites Tech PO Box 845 Orange CT 06477

THOMAS, ROBERT JAMES, biologist, educator; b. Flint, Mich., July 5, 1949; s. Allan James and Ruth Pauline (Brandt) T. B.A., U. Mich., 1971; Ph.D., U. Calif., Santa Cruz, 1975. Asst. prof. biology Bates Coll., Lewiston, Maine, 1975-82, assoc. prof., 1982—, chmn. dept. biology, 1983—. Contbr. articles to sci. jours. NSF grantee, 1985-87; Cottrell Coll. Sci. grantee, 1983-85. Mem. Bot. Soc. Am., Am. Soc. Plant Physiologists, Am. Bryol. and Lichenol. Soc., Internat. Assn. Bryologists. Current Work: Physiology and development of bryophytes, including culture, hormone effects on growth, tropisms, protoplast isolation and transport studies. Subspecialties: Plant physiology (biology); Plant growth.

THOMAS, WILLIAM ERIC, biochemist; b. Nashville, Aug. 2, 1951; s. Andrew Johnson and Alphonsa Lucille (Williams) T.; m. Linda Love, Aug. 25, 1973; 1 dau., Kimberly Monique. B.S., Tenn. State U., 1973, M.S., 1975; Ph.D., Meharry Med. Sch., 1980. Postdoctoral research fellow Harvard Med. Sch., Boston, 1980—. Contbr. articles to profl. jours. Mem. Soc. for Neurosci., AAAS. Current Work: Study of cerbral cortical neurotransmitters, cerebral cortical tissue culture, neurotransmitter metabolism. Subspecialties: Neurochemistry; Biochemistry (biology). Home: 15 Pasadena Rd Dorchester MA 02121 Office: Dept Neurobiology Harvard Med Sch Boston MA 02115

THOMASON, HARRY JACK LEE, JR., mechanical engineer; b. Washington, Apr. 12, 1953; s. Harry Emitte and Hattie Cornelia (Davis) T.; m. Ema Jean Bulaon, Dec. 15, 1974. A.A., Prince Georges Community Coll., 1973; B.S., U. Md., 1975. Cons. Thomason Solar Homes Inc., Ft. Washington, Md., 1975-79, v.p., 1979-84; mech. engr. Naval Surface Weapons Ctr., Dahlgren, Va., 1984—; instr. solar house heating and cooling George Washington U., Washington, 1974-75. Patentee in field. Recipient 1st place environ. award Isaac Walton League, 1971, spl. awards Washington Soc. Engrs., 1971, IEEE, 1971. Mem. ASME. Current work: Development of domestic hot water analysis program for solar simulation; interest in energy conservation. Subspecialties: Solar engineering; Fuels and sources. Home: 609 Cedar Ave Fort Washington MD 20744 Office: Naval Surface Weapons Ctr Dahlgren VA 22448

THOMPSON, ALVIN JEROME, physician, gastroenterologist; b. Washington, 1924; m. Faye Grindle; children—Michael, Donna, Kevin, Susan, Gail. Student Howard U., 1940-43, M.D., 1946, B.S., 1981. Diplomate Am. Bd. Internal Medicine. Commd. 1st lt., U.S. Army, 1943, advanced through grades to maj., Res., ret., 1959; intern St. Louis City Hosp. (Phillips), 1946-47, resident, 1947-51; chief med. service Ramey AFB Hosp., 1951-53; gastroenterologist VA Hosp., Seattle, 1953-57, attending physician, 1957—; practice medicine specializing in internal medicine, gastroenterology, 1957—; mem. attending staff Providence Hosp., Swedish Hosp. Med. Ctr., 1957—; attending physician U. Hosp., Harborview Med. Ctr., 1957—; active numerous med. coms. Contbr. articles to profl. jours. Pres. bd. dirs. East Madison YMCA, 1956; trustee Seattle Urban League, 1958-59, Travelers Aid Soc., 1960-64, Civic Unity Com., 1960-64, Anti-Tb. League, 1961-62, Seattle Ballet Assn., 1968-69, Pacific Sci. Ctr. Found., 1980—; vestry Christ Ch., Seattle, 1958-60; mem. Emmanuel Ch., Mercer Island, 1963—; mem. fair housing com. City of Mercer Island, 1961—; mem. and case mem. Gilbert and Sullivan Soc., 1954-57; mem. adv. com. Salvation Army, 1979-82, chmn. human services com., 1979-82; co-chmn. King County Medic I Com., 1979. Recipient Outstanding Contbns. in Health award Nat. Assn. Med. Minority Educators, 1983. Mem. ACP (gov. for Wash. and Alaska 1974-78), AMA, Am. Gastroenterologic Assn., Am. Soc. for Gastroenterologic Assn., Am. Soc. for Gastrointestinal Endoscopy, North Pacific Soc. Internal Medicine, Am. Soc. Internal Medicine, Inst. of Medicine, Nat. Acad. Scis., Nat. Med. Assn., Wash. State Med. Assn. (trustee 1969-70, pres. 1977-78, chmn. exec. com. 1978-79), Wash. State Soc. Internal Medicine (pres. 1970-71), King County Med. Soc. (pres. 1974), Seattle Acad. Internal Medicine (sec.-treas. 1970-71, pres. 1972-73, Robert H. Williams award 1979), Seattle C. of C. (trustee 1976-80, health care policy com. 1976—, council for corporate responsibility 1983), NAACP, Seattle Mountineers. Lodge: Rotary. Subspecialty: Internal medicine. Office: 1001 Broadway Seattle WA 98122

THOMPSON, BENNY LOUIS, energy engineering co. exec.; b. Seminole, Okla., July 1, 1928; s. Kermit Louis and Pauline (Forbes) T.; m. Joanne Crowell, Mar. 23, 1957 (div.); children—Pamela, Dianne, Janice, Steven. Student, San Jose State U., 1947-48, Pierce Coll., Woodland Hills, Calif., 1957-58. Pres. Thomco Equipment Engring. Co., San Fernando, Calif., 1952-65; owner B&K Auto Parts, Marysville, Calif., 1965-71; pres. Ben Thompson Design Corp., Yuba City, Calif., 1971—, Biomass Corp., Yuba City, 1978—; cons. for low BTU gas engine conversion systems. Vice chmn. Sutter County Bicentennial Commn., 1976; mem. Sutter County Republican Central Com. Served with USN, 1948-52. Recipient Sutter County Clean Air award, 1974. Lodges: Lions; Shriners; Masons. Patentee automatic plowing systems, specialized boring systems for problem soils, compacting system for problem soils. Current Work: Broadest application of producer gas to power mechanical systems. Designed and built new design meat processing plant for Vel Pero Mandox Meat Co. Designed and supervised dismantling and erection procedures for Raft River Idaho geothermal isobutane energy plant for Nev. Geothermal Enterprises. Subspecialties: Gasification; Gas cleaning systems. Home and Office: 7655 Oroville Hwy Marysville CA 95901

THOMPSON, BRIAN JOHN, college dean, optics scientist; b. Glossop, Derbyshire, Eng., June 10, 1932; came to U.S., 1962; s. Alexander William and Edna May (Gould) T.; m. Joyce Emily Cheshire, Mar. 31, 1956; children: Karen Joyce, Andrew Derrick. B.Sc.Tech., U. Manchester, Eng., 1955, Ph.D., 1959. Demonstrator in physics Faculty of Tech., U. Manchester, 1955-56, asst. lectr., 1957-59; lectr. physics U. Leeds, Eng., 1959-62; sr. physicist Tech. Ops., Inc., Burlington, Mass., 1963-65, dir. optics dept., 1965-67; mgr. West. tech. dir. Tech. Ops., Inc., (Beckman & Whitley div.), 1967-68; prof. Inst. Optics, U. Rochester, N.Y., 1968—, Wm. F. May prof. engring., 1982—, dir., 1968-75; dean Inst. Optics, U. Rochester (Coll. Engring. and Applied Sci.), 1974—. Am. editor: Optica Acta, 1974—; Asso. editor: Optics Communications, 1974—, Optical Engring., 1973—; editorial adv. bd.: Laser Focus, 1967—; internat. editor: Optics and Laser Tech., 1970—; contbr. articles to profl. jours. Served with Brit. Army, 1950-52. Fellow Optical Soc. Am. (dir. 1969-72, exec. com. 1970-73, asso. editor Jour. 1966-77), Inst. Physics and Phys. Soc. (Gt. Britain), Soc. Photo-Optical Instrumentation Engrs. (pres. 1974, 75-76, Pres.'s award 1967, Pezzuto award 1978, Kingslake medal 1978); mem. Am. Phys. Soc., AAAS, N.Y. Acad. Scis. Mem. Christ Ch. Current Work: Holographic particle size and velocity measurements; phase microscopy, image processing; design of coherent optical systems. Subspecialties: Optical engineering; Holography. Home: 9 Esternay Ln Pittsford NY 14534 Office: Univ of Rochester Office of the Provost Rochester NY 14627

THOMPSON, DAVID ALFRED, industrial engineer; b. Chgo., Sept. 9, 1929; s. Clifford James and Christobel Eliza (Sawin) T.; married; children—Nancy, Brooke, Lynda, Diane, Kristy. B.M.E., U. Va., 1951; B.S. in Indsl. Engring., U. Fla., 1955; M.S. in Engring., U. Fla., 1956; Ph.D., Stanford U., 1961. Registered profl. engr., Calif. Research asst. U. Fla. Engring. and Industries Exptl. Sta., Gainesville, 1955-56; instr. indsl. engring. Stanford U., 1956-58, acting asst. prof., 1958-61, asst. prof., 1961-64, assoc. prof., 1964-72, prof., 1972—, prof., assoc. chmn. dept. indsl. engring., 1972—; prin. investigator NASA Ames Research Ctr., Moffatt Field, Calif., 1974—; cons. Dept. of State, Fed. EEO Commn.; maj. U.S. and fgn. cos.; cons. emergency communications ctr. design Santa Clara County Criminal Justice Bd., 1975, Bay Area Rapid Transit Control Ctr., 1977. Dir., editor: documentary film Rapid Answers for Rapid Transit, Dept. Transp., 1974. Contbr. articles to profl. jours. Editorial adv. bd.: Computers and Graphics, 1970—. Reviewer: Indsl. Engring. and IEEE Transactions, 1972. Served to lt. USNR, 1951-54. HEW grantee, 1967-70. Mem. Am. Inst. Indsl. Engrs., Human Factors Soc., IEEE, Am. Soc. Engring. Edn., Am. Soc. Info. Sci., MTM Assn. Standards and Research, Am. Robotics Soc., Soc. Info. Display. Subspecialty: Industrial engineering. Office: Dept Indsl Engring and Engring Mgmt Stanford U Stanford CA 94305

THOMPSON, DAVID JEROME, chemical company executive; b. Sand Creek, Wis., July 21, 1937; s. Marshall T. and Bernice (Severson) T.; m. Virginia Ruth Williams, Aug. 11, 1962; children: Keith D., Craig M. B.S., U. Wis.-Madison, 1960, M.S., 1961, Ph.D., 1963; M.B.A., U. Chgo., 1975. Research biochemist Internat. Minerals & Chem. Corp., Libertyville, Ill., 1964-68, supr. animal research, 1968-69, mgr. tech. service, Mundelein, Ill., 1969-78, dir. tech. service, 1978-79, sales mgr., 1979-81, v.p. sci. and tech., Northbook, 1981-84, v.p., gen. mgr. Sterwin div., 1984—; cons. Am. Assn. Feed Control Ofcls., 1974-85, NRC, Nat. Acad. Sci., 1976-80; chmn. Nutrition Council of Am. Feed Mfrs. Assn. Co-author: Mineral Tolerance of Domestic Animals, 1980; contbr. articles to jours. and papers to internat. confs. Mem. AAAS, N.Y. Acad. Sci., Am. Inst. Nutrition, Poultry Sci. Assn., Am. Dairy Sci. Assn., Am. Soc. Animal Sci., Nutrition Today Soc., Am. Chem. Soc., Council for Agrl. Sci. and Tech., Sigma Xi, Gamma Alpha. Current Work: General management. Subspecialties: Animal nutrition; Biochemistry (biology). Home: 826 Fairway Libertyville IL 60048 Office: Internat Minerals & Chem Corp 2315 Sanders Rd Northbrook IL 60062

THOMPSON, EDWARD IVINS BRADBRIDGE, cell and molecular biologist; b. Burlington, Iowa, Dec. 20, 1933; s. Edward Bills and Lois Elizabeth (Bradbridge) T.; m. Lynn Taylor Parsons, June 27, 1957; children: Elizabeth Lynn, Edward Ernest Bradbridge. B.A. with distinction, Rice U., 1955; postgrad., Cambridge (Eng.) U., 1957-58; M.D., Harvard U., 1960. Diplomate: Nat. Bd. Med. Examiners. Intern then resident in internal medicine Presbyn. Hosp., Columbia U. Med. Ctr., N.Y.C.; commd. USPHS, 1962; research asst. NIMH, 1962-64; research scientist Nat. Inst. Arthritis and Metabolic Diseases, 1964-68, Nat. Cancer Inst., 1968-73; chief sect. biochemistry gene expression Nat. Cancer Inst. Lab. Biochemistry, 1973-84; I.H. Kempner prof. human genetics, chmn. dept. human biol. chemistry and genetics, also dir. div. human genetics, prof. internal medicine U. Tex. Med. Br., Galveston, 1985—; attending physician endocrine service Nat. Naval Med. Ctr., 1978-80; chmn. Task Force Hormones and Cancer, 1978-80; mem. faculty Found. Advanced Edn. in Scis.; mem. com. on revision U.S. Pharmacopeial Conv., 1980-85. Author articles in field; editor-in-chief Molecular Endocrinology, 1985—; editor: Regulation of Gene Expression, 1973, Gene Expression and Carcinogenesis in Cultured Liver, 1975, Steroid Receptors and the Management of Cancer, 1979; editorial bd. Jour. Steroid Biochemistry; assoc. editor Cancer Research. Active local Girl Scouts, Rice U. Alumni Fund. Hohenthal scholar, 1955; Harvard U. Med. Sch. scholar, 1955-57; Maco Stewart fellow, 1955-57; John Parker fellow, 1957-58. Mem. Am. Chem. Soc., Am. Soc. Cell Biology, Am. Assn. Cancer Research, Am. Soc. Biol. Chemists, Am. Cancer Soc. (adv. com. on biochemistry and chem. carcinogenesis 1982—), Endocrine Soc., Phi Beta Kappa, Alpha Omega Alpha. Club: Bob Smith Yacht. Current Work: Steroid hormone effects on cells and gene expression. Subspecialties: Cell and tissue culture; Genetics and genetic engineering (medicine). Office: Dept Human Biol Chemistry and Genetics U Tex Med Br Route F-45 Galveston TX 77550

THOMPSON, ELIZABETH BARNES, research biologist; b. San Antonio, June 15, 1942; d. Virgil Everett and Mildred Louise (Adlof) Barnes; m. Hugh Walter Thompson, June 18, 1964; 1 dau., Victoria Mireille. B.A., Radcliffe Coll., 1964; Ph.D., Cornell U. Grad. Sch. Med. Scis., 1971. Instr. dept. physiology NYU Med. Sch., 1971-74; asst. dept. neurobiology and behavior Pub. Health Research Inst. City N.Y., 1971-74; instr. physiology Coll. Physicians and Surgeons, Columbia U., N.Y.C., 1974-77, asst. prof., 1977-78, asst. prof. physiology and asst. prof. anatomy, 1978-80; vis. scientist Population Council Ctr. for Biomed. Research, Rockefeller U., N.Y.C., 1980—. Contbr. articles to profl. jours. NIH grantee, 1975-81; Career Devel. award, 1975-80; NSF grantee, 1979—. Mem. Am. Soc. Cell Biology, Soc. Neurosci., N.Y. Soc. Electron Microscopists. Current Work: Ultrastructure of identified synapses in Aplysia which exhibit behaviorally relevant plasticity, development of techniques to mark uniquely identified synaptic contacts for study with light and electron microscopes. Subspecialties: Neurobiology; Cell biology. Office: 1230 York Ave New York NY 10021

THOMPSON, FRED CLAYTON, electronics engineering company executive; b. Snowshoe Pa., Feb. 26, 1928; s. Clayton Alfred and Edna Pearl (Oswalt) T.; m. M. Joan Bender, June 21, 1952; children—Marjorie A., Richard C., Scott D., Carol A. B.S.E.E., Pa. State U., 1950, M.S.E.E., 1958. Radar systems designer Martin Co., Balt., 1952-54; dir. electronic systems Hab-Singer, State College, Pa., 1954-68; v.p. electronics Locus, Inc., State College, 1968-80, pres., 1980—; regional dir. Mellon Bank Central, State College; dir. Penn Tran, Inc., Bellefonte, Pa., Patentee in field. Served with U.S. Army, 1950-52. Mem. IEEE, SPEBQSA (pres. chpt. 1975, 83), Tau Beta Pi, Eta Kappa Nu. Lodges: Masons, Elks. Current work: Electronic systems development in the areas of electronic defense and telecommunications. Subspecialty: Electronics. Office: Locus Inc PO Box 740 State College PA 16801

THOMPSON, GEORGE ALBERT, geophysics educator; b. Swissvale, Pa., June 5, 1919; s. George A. and Maude A. (Harkness) T.; m. Anita Kimmell, July 20, 1944; children: Albert J., Dan A., David C. Pa. State U., 1941; M.S., MIT, 1942; Ph.D., Stanford U., 1949. Geologist, geophysicist U.S. Geol. Survey, 1942-76; asst. prof. Stanford, 1949-55, assoc. prof., 1955-60; prof. geophysics Stanford U., 1960—, Otto N. Miller prof. earth scis., 1980—, chmn. geophysics dept., 1967—, geology dept., 1979-82. Served from ensign to lt. (j.g.) USNR, 1944-46. Recipient G.K. Gilbert award in seismic geology, 1964, George P. Woollard award, 1983; NSF postdoctoral fellow, 1956-57; Guggenheim fellow, 1963-64. Fellow AAAS, Geol. Soc. Am., Geophys. Union; mem. Seismol. Soc. Am., Soc. Exploration Geophysicists, Soc. Econ. Geologists. Current Work: Geophysics of the continental lithosphere(crust and upper mantle) based on seismic reflection, refraction and gravity data. Subspecialties: Geophysics; Tectonics. Home: 421 Adobe Pl Palo Alto CA 94306 Office: Geophysics Dept Stanford U Stanford CA 94305

THOMPSON, GREGORY ROBERT, ceramic engineer; b. Phila., Oct. 1, 1955; s. Robert Marshall and Mary Catherine (Haney) T.; m. Lilies Soesilowaty, Dec. 16, 1984. B.A. in Geology, Rutgers Coll., 1978; M.S. in Ceramic Engring., Rutgers U., 1981. Instr. lab. Rutgers U., New Brunswick, N.J., 1978-80, research intern, 1978-79, research fellow, 1979-80, guest lectr., 1983-84; ceramist Am. Standard Inc., New Brunswick, 1981-84, plant ceramic engr., Jakarta, Indonesia, 1984—. HEW mineral fellow, 1979; N.J. State scholar, 1974. Mem. Am. Ceramic Soc. (vice chmn. Trenton sect. 1985—), Nat. Inst. Ceramic Engrs., Ceramic Assn. N.J., Keramos, Soc. Exptl. Stress Analysis, Brit. Soc. Strain Measurement, Chi Phi (trustee Delta chpt.). Roman Catholic. Current work: Characterization and utilization of local raw materials in ceramic formulations; the analysis of stresses developed during the firing of ceramic materials. Subspecialty: Ceramic engineering. Office: Am Standard Inc Internat and Export Div PO Box 2003 New Brunswick NJ 08903

THOMPSON, JACK MANSFIELD, JR., mechanical engineer; b. Hartford, Conn., Mar. 30, 1951; s. Jack Mansfield and Sarah Gertrude (Matthews) T. B.S. in Engring, Cornell U., 1973, M.M.E., 1974. Engr. Gleason Works, Rochester, N.Y., 1973; project mgr., sr. tech. cons. Structural Dynamics Research Corp., Milford, Ohio, 1974-84, Robotics Research Corp., Milford, 1984—. Contbr. articles to profl. jours. Recipient award Lincoln Arc Welding Found., 1973, 1978. Mem. ASME, Soc. Automotive Engring., Delta Tau Delta. Current Work: State of the art mechanical and structural design, specializing in composite materials and robotics. Subspecialties: Mechanical engineering; Robotics.

THOMPSON, JAMES BURLEIGH, JR., geologist, educator; b. Calais, Maine, Nov. 20, 1921; s. James Burleigh and Edith (Peabody) T.; m. Eleanora Mairs, Aug. 3, 1957; 1 son, Michael A. A.B., Dartmouth, 1942, D.Sc. (hon.), 1975; Ph.D., Mass. Inst. Tech., 1950. Instr. geology Dartmouth, 1942; research asst. Mass. Inst. Tech., 1946-47, instr., 1947-49; instr. petrology Harvard, 1949-50, asst. prof., 1950-55, asso. prof. mineralogy, 1955-60, prof., 1960-77, Sturgis Hooper prof. geology, 1977—; guest prof. Swiss Fed. Inst. Tech., 1977-78. Served to 1st lt. USAAF, 1942-46. Guggenheim fellow, 1963; Sherman Fairchild distinguished scholar Calif. Inst. Tech., 1976. Fellow Mineral. Soc. Am. (pres. 1967-68, recipient Roebling medal 1978), Geol. Soc. Am. (A.L. Day medal 1964), Am. Acad. Arts and Scis.; mem. AAAS, Am. Geophys. Union, Nat. Acad. Scis., Geochem. Soc. (pres. 1968-69), Sigma Xi. Current Work: Metamorphic petrology; regional geology of appalachians. Subspecialties: Petrology; Mineralogy. Office: Harvard U Cambridge MA 02138

THOMPSON, JAMES EARL, analytical chemist, Researcher; b. Akron, Ohio, Jan. 16, 1954; s. Earl John and Theresa Ann (Justin) T. B.A., Hiram Coll., 1976; M.S., Purdue U., 1979, Ph.D., 1982. Preparation asst. Hiram Coll. Chem. Dept., Ohio, 1973-76; teaching asst. Purdue U., West LaFayette, Ind., 1976-77, lab. supr. gen. chem., 1977-78; sr. research and devel. chemist Standard Oil Co., Cleve., 1982—. Contbr. articles to profl. jours. Mem. Am. Chem. Soc. (analytical chem. div.), AAAS, Cleve. Area Forth Interest Group, Nat. Geog. Soc., Phi Lambda Upsilon. Republican. Current work: Automation of laboratory instrumentation to increase productivity, multi-wavelength spectroscopy. Subspecialties: Analytical chemistry; Programming languages. Home: 631-C Lee Rd Apt #1230 Bedford OH 44146 Office: Standard Oil of Ohio Research Ctr 4440 Warrensville Ctr Rd Cleveland OH 44128

THOMPSON, JOSEPH KYLE, chemist; b. Columbus, Ohio, Oct. 2, 1920; s. Harry Alexander and Mary Olive (Kyle) T.; m. Jean Appleton, Apr. 14, 1956; children—John, James, Jeffrey. B.S., Sterling Coll., Kans., 1942; M.A., U. Kans., 1949, Ph.D., 1950; D.Sc. (hon.) Sterling Coll., 1967. Research chemist Naval Research Lab., Washington, 1942-46, 50—. Contbr. articles to profl. jours. Served with U.S. Navy, 1944-45. Fellow Am. Inst. Chemists; mem. Am. Chem. Soc. Republican. Presbyterian. Current work: Environmental science, air purification. Subspecialty: Physical chemistry. Home: 6106 Baxter Dr Suitland MD 20746

THOMPSON, KEITH FRANCIS MACKECHNIE, petroleum geochemist; b. Romford, Eng., Mar. 16, 1933, came to U.S., 1966; s. Alexander William and Rose Mary (Davis) T.; m. Jo J. Jones, Oct. 3, 1981; children—Kathryn M., Gregory R., Rebecca E., Gwendolynne R., Monica C. B.S., U. Manchester, Eng., 1955; Ph.D., MIT, 1966. Geologist Iraq Petroleum Co., Basrah, 1955-59; geologist Brit. Petroleum Co., Alaska, 1960-61; research sci. Sinclair Research Inc., Tulsa, 1966-69; research geochemist Atlantic Richfield Co., Dallas, 1969-75; prin. research geochemist Arco Oil and Gas Co., Dallas, 1975-82, research assoc., 1982-85; research scientist Houston Area Research Ctr., 1985—. Contbr. articles to profl. jours. Fellow Geol. Soc. London; mem. Geochem. Soc., Am. Chem. Soc. Current work: Application of carbon isotopes, biomarkers and hydrocarbon composition to petroleum evaluation and correlation; utilization of light hydrocarbons in petroleum exploration; aromatization of petroleum. Subspecialties: Geochemistry; Geology. Home: 500 Middlefork Irving TX 76063 Office: Dept Oceanography Tex A&M U College Station TX 77843

THOMPSON, KENNETH LANE, computer scientist; b. New Orleans, Feb. 4, 1943; s. Lewis Elwood and Anna Hazel (Lane) T.; m. Bonnie Perlmutter, July 2, 1967; 1 son, Corey Allen. B.S. in Elec. Engring. U. Calif., Berkeley, 1965, M.Sc., 1966. Mem. tech. staff Bell Telephone Labs., Murray Hill, N.J., 1966—. Co-author: UNIX Time Sharing System, 1974, Belle-World Champion Computer Chess Program, 1980. Recipient Priore award IEEE, 1982. Mem. Nat. Acad. Engring., Assn. Computing Machinery, AAAS. Subspecialty: Distributed systems and networks. Office: Bell Labs Murray Hill NJ 07974*

THOMPSON, LARRY FLACK, chemist, polymer engineer; b. Union City, Tenn., Aug. 31, 1944; s. Rufus Russell and Polly (Flack) T.; m. Joan Bondurant, Aug. 31, 1965; children—Tony, Allen. B.S. in Secondary Edn. Tenn. Tech. U., 1966, M.S. in Chemistry, 1968; Ph.D., U. Mo—Rolla, 1970. Mem. tech. staff AT&T Bell Labs., Murray Hill, N.J., 1971-79, dept. head, 1979—. Editor: Introduction to Microlithography, 1982; Introduction to Materials for Microlithography, 1984. Patentee in field. Indsl. Research Council grantee, 1977. Mem. Am. Chem. Soc. (chmn. div. Polymeric Materials: Sci. and Engring. 1979). Current work: Polymer materials for microlithography; new processes for semi-conductor fabrication. Subspecialties: Polymer chemistry; Microchip technology (materials science). Home: 1511 Longhill Rd Millington NJ 07946 Office: AT&T Bell Labs 6C302 600 Mountain Ave Murray Hill NJ 07974

THOMPSON, MARY EILEEN, chemist, educator; b. Mpls., Dec. 21, 1928; d. Albert Charles and Mary Blanche (McAvoy) T. B.A., Coll. St. Catherine, 1953; M.S., U. Minn., Mpls., 1958; Ph.D., U. Calif., Berkeley, 1964. Joined Sisters of St. Joseph of Carondolet, Roman Catholic Ch., 1950; tchr. chemistry and math. Derham Hall High Sch., St. Paul, 1953-56, 58-9; instr. dept. chemistry lab. Coll. St. Catherine, 1953-56, instr., 1964-65, asst. prof. chemistry, 1965-69, assoc. prof., 1969-78, prof., 1978—, chairperson dept. chemistry, 1969—; cons. Center Edni. Affairs, Argonne Nat. Lab., 1968-71. Research Corp. grantee, 1981. Mem. Am. Chem. Soc., Chem. Soc. London, AAAS, Midwestern Assn. Chemistry Tchrs. in Liberal Arts Colls., N.Y. Acad. Scis., Nat. Sci. Tchrs. Assn., Phi Beta Kappa, Sigma Xi. Current Work: Separation and characterizations of Cr(III) hydolytic polymers; oxidation-reduction kinetics of inorganic complexes; superoxo complexes of Co(III): synthesis, characterizations. Subspecialties: Inorganic chemistry; Physical chemistry. Home: 1132 Grand Ave Saint Paul MN 55105 Office: 2004 Randolph Ave Saint Paul MN 55105

THOMPSON, RICHARD CLAUDE, chemistry educator; b. Kansas City, Mo., Mar. 12, 1939; s. Claude S. T.; m. Jeannette E. Thompson, Mar. 30, 1969. B.S., U. Chgo., 1961; Ph.D., U. Md., 1965. Resident research assoc. Argonne Nat. Lab. (Ill.), 1965-66; asst. prof. (Ill. Inst. Tech.), 1966-67; with U. Mo., 1967—, prof. chemistry, 1977—. Contbr. articles to profl. jours. Mem. Am. Chem. Soc., Sigma Xi, Alpha Chi Sigma. Current Work: Mechanisms of inorganic reactions. Subspecialties: Inorganic chemistry; Kinetics.

THOMPSON, RICHARD DAVID, chemist; b. Ely, Minn., Nov. 30, 1936; s. Theodore and Naomi Marcella (Kurvinen) T.; m. Shirley Ann Solberg, Sept. 15, 1962; 1 child, David. Assoc. Sci., Vermilion Coll., 1956; B.A., Mankato State U., 1964; M.S., U. Minn., 1972. Research asst. Archer-Daniels-Midland Co., Mpls., 1958-60, Armed Forces Inst. Pathology, Washington, 1960-62; analytical chemist U.S. FDA, Mpls., 1964-72, pharm. analyst, 1972—; cons. VA Hosp., Mpls., 1973. Contbr. articles to profl. jours. Served with U.S. Army, 1960-62. Mem. Am. Chem. Soc., Assn. Ofcl. Analytical Chemists (referee), Acad. Pharm. Scis., Minn. Chromatography Forum, Brass, Inc. (percussion dir. 1964-70). Democrat. Lutheran. Lodges: Masons (32 degree), Shriners. Current work: Pharmaceutical analysis, high-pressure liquid chromatography (HPLC) of pharmaceuticals, drug decomposition, drug metabolism. Subspecialties: Analytical chemistry; Medicinal chemistry. Home: 4740 York Ave S Minneapolis MN 55410 Office: US FDA 240 Hennepin Ave Minneapolis MN 55401

THOMPSON, RICHARD FREDERICK, psychobiology educator; b. Portland, Oreg., Sept. 6, 1930; s. Frederick Albert and Margaret (St. Clair) T.; m. Judith K. Pedersen, June 22, 1960; children: Kathryn M., Elizabeth K., Virginia, St. Clair. B.A., Reed Coll., 1952; M.S., U. Wis.-Madison, 1953, Ph.D., 1956. Faculty mem. U. Oreg. Med. Sch., Portland, 1959-67, prof. med. psychology, 1965-67; prof. psychobiology U. Calif.-Irvine, 1967-73, 75-80; prof. psychology Harvard U., Cambridge, Mass., 1973-74; prof. psychology, human biology Stanford (Calif.) U., 1980—; mem. exec. com. Assembly of Behavioral and Social Sci., NRC, from 1977. Author: Foundations of Physiological Psychology, 1967; contbr. articles in field to profl. lit.; editor Jour. Comparative and Physiological Psychology, from 1981; regional editor: Behavioral Brain Research, from 1979; assoc. editor: Ann. Revs. of Neurosci, from 1980. Recipient Research Scientist Career award NIMH, 1967-77; fellow Center for Advanced Studies in Behavioral Sci., Stanford U., 1978-79. Fellow Am. Psychol. Assn. (pres. Div. 6 1972, Disting. Sci. Contbn. award 1977); mem. Nat. Acad. Scis., Soc. Exptl. Psychologists, Psychonomic Soc. (gov. bd. 1972-77, chmn. 1976). Current Work: Brain mechanisms of learning and memory. Subspecialties: Psychobiology; Neurophysiology. Home: 1097 Cathcart Way Stanford CA 94305 Office: Psychology Dept Stanford U Stanford CA 94305

THOMPSON, RICHARD ROGERS, geologist; b. Rochester, Pa., Nov. 14, 1930; s. Charles Vance and Josephine Ruth (Rogers) T.; m. Ellen Kristina Hammar, Mar. 27, 1954; 1 child, Jennifer Ann. B.S. in Geology, Antioch Coll., 1954; Ph.D. in Geology, Pa. State U., 1961. Research assoc. Pa. State U., University Park, 1960-62; engr., supr., asst. sect. mgr. coal and coke research Bethlehem Steel Corp., Pa., 1962-76, sect. mgr., 1976-77, sect. mgr. basic studies and raw materials research, 1977-82, tech. cons. research and natural resources, 1982-84, mgr. domestic metall. coal and coke sales, 1984—. Contbr. articles to profl. jours. Dir. Leevalle Sch. for Brain Damaged Children, Bethlehem, 1969-74; dir. Bethlehem YMCA, 1974-79; deacon, elder First Presbyn. Ch., Bethlehem, 1970-79. Mem. Iron and Steel Soc. (regional tech. meeting award 1970), AIME (chmn. iron making div. 1985-86), Geol. Soc. Am., Internat. Com. Coal Petrology, AAAS, N.Y. Acad. Sci., Soc. Organic Petrologists, Eastern States Blast Furnace and Coke Oven Assn. Club: Bethlehem Steel (Hellertown, Pa.). Current work: Coal and coke sales and utilization. Subspecialty: Coal. Home: 2621 Nottingham Rd Bethlehem PA 18017 Office: Bethlehem Steel Corp 18th Floor Martin Tower Bethlehem PA 18016

THOMPSON, RODGER IRWIN, astrophysicist, educator, cons.; b. Texarkana, Tex., Aug. 9, 1944; s. William B. and Pearle J. (Goodman) R. S.B. in Physics, M.I.T., 1966, Ph.D. in Physics, 1970. Asst. prof. optical sci. U. Ariz., Tucson, 1970-71, asst., then assoc. prof. astronomy, 1971-81, prof. astronomy, astronomer, 1981—. Contbr. articles and papers to sci. lit. Mem. curriculum com. Tucson Unified Sch. Dist., 1979—. NSF research grantee. Mem. Internat. Astron. Union, Am. Astron. Soc., Am. Phys. Soc. Current Work: Infrared astronomy applied to star formation; accretion disks in star formation. Subspecialties: Infrared astronomy; Theoretical astrophysics. Office: Steward Obs U Ariz Tucson AZ 85721

THOMPSON, SYLVESTER, industrial mathematician; b. Osceola, Ark., Apr. 9, 1948; s. Raymond Alton and Ola Francis (Maynard) T.; m. Judy Faye Finch, Dec. 23, 1977; children: Michael Lee, David Eric. A.B. in Math, U. Mo.-Columbia, 1970, A.M. in Math, 1971, Ph.D. in Math, 1974; M.Engring. Adminstrn., George Washington U., 1984. Asst. prof. U.S.C., 1974-76; prin. mathematician Babcock and Wilcox, Lynchburg, Va., 1976-85, leader sci. software support project, 1985—. Contbr. articles to profl. publs. NSF fellow, 1970-74. Mem. Soc. Indsl. and Applied Math. (jour. referee 1978-79), Assn. Computing Machinery, Internat. Assn. Math. and Computers in Simulation, Internat. Assn. Math. Modelling, Soc. Computer Simulation (jour. referee), Am. Mgmt. Assn. Unitarian. Current Work: Mathmatical software, mathematical software libraries, numerical solution of ordinary differential equations; continuous simulation. Subspecialties: Applied mathematics; Numerical analysis (computer science). Home: 118 Hazleton Ln Oak Ridge TN 37830 Office: Martin-Marietta Energy Systems PO Box Y Bldg 9207A MS-2 Oak Ridge TN 37831

THOMPSON, THOMAS WILLIAM, astronomer; b. Canton, Ohio, May 25, 1936; s. Clifford Earl and Doris Marie (Flickinger) T.; m. Alicia Kathleen, July 16, 1966; children: Kimberly Robin, Marisa Lynn. B.S., Case Inst. Tech., 1958; M.S., Yale U., 1959; Ph.D., Cornell U., 1966. Research assoc. Arecibo Obs., Arecibo, P.R., 1966-69; mem. tech. staff Jet Propulsion Lab., Pasadena, Calif., 1969-76, scientist, 1982—; staff scientist Planetary Sci. Inst., Pasadena, 1977-81. Contbr. articles to profl. jours. Mem. Internat. Astron. Union, Am. Geophys. Union, IEEE, Sigma Xi. Current Work: Radar astronomy; radar remote sensing. Subspecialties: Planetology; Remote sensing (geoscience). Home: 3043 Cloudcrest Rd La Crescanta CA 91214

THOMPSON, WILLIAM WARREN, educator, educationalpsychology consultant; b. Londonderry, No. Ireland, Nov. 8, 1944; emigrated to Can., 1977; s. John and Ivy (Fulton) T.; m. Rebecca Louise Chapman, June 29, 1974; 1 dau., Stephanie Sara. B.A., Trinity Coll., Dublin, 1966, M.A., 1969; M.Ed., Queens U., Belfast, No. Ireland, 1968, Ph.D., 1971. Registered psychologist, N.S., N.B. Sch. psychologist County Derry Schs., Londonderry, 1971-72, Argyllshire Schs., Dunoon, 1972-73, Isle of Wight (U.K.) Schs., 1973-74; sr. clin. psychologist Wessex Unit, Portsmouth, Eng., 1974-77; dir. pupil evaluation Sch. Dist. 20, Saint John, N.B., Can., 1977-80; assoc. prof. Mt. Saint Vincent U., Halifax, N.S., Can., 1980—, coordinator sch. psychology, 1982—. Author: Children and Their Problems, 1977; Contbr. chpts. to books, articles to profl. jours. Mem. com. Saint John Family Services, 1978. Mem. Brit. Psychol. Soc., Can. Psychol. Assn., Am. Psychol. Assn., Nat. Assn. Sch. Psychologists, Assn. Psychologists of N.S. (exec. sec. 1980—). Conservative. Presbyterian. Current Work: Environmental influences on educational performance; effective school psychology delivery systems; behavioral approaches to the treatment of teenage obesity. Subspecialties: Behavioral psychology; Educational psychology. Home: Box 505 Waverley NS B0N 2S0 Canada Office: Mount Saint Vincent Univ Bedford Hwy Halifax NS B3M 2S6 Canada

THOMPSON, WILMER LEIGH, pharmacologist, critical care physician; b. Shreveport, La., June 25, 1938; s. Wilmer Leigh and Mary Bissell (McIver) T.; m. Maurice Eugenie Horne, Mar 29, 1957; 1 dau., Mary Linton Bounetheau. B.S., Coll. Charleston, S.C., 1958; M.S., Med. U. S.C., 1960, Ph.D. in Pharmacology, 1963; M.D., Johns Hopkins U., 1965. Diplomate: Am. Bd. Internal Medicine. Osler med. resident Johns Hopkins U., Balt., 1965-67, 69-70; staff assoc. NIH, Bethesda, Md., 1967-69; asst. prof. medicine and pharmacology Johns Hopkins U., 1970-74; also dir. med. critical care Johns Hopkins Hosp.; prof. medicine, assoc. prof. pharmacology, dir. clin. pharmacology, dir. critical care and drug info. Case Western Res. U and Univ. Hosps. Cleve., 1974-82; exec. dir. clin. investigation and regulatory affairs Lilly Research Labs., Eli Lilly & Co., Indpls., 1982—. Contbr. 165 articles to profl. jours. Served as sr. surgeon USPHS, 1967-69. Burroughs Wellcome scholar, 1975-80; Pharm. Mfrs. Assn. faculty awardee, 1971-74; Sir Henry Hallett Dale lectr. Johns Hopkins U., 1981; Frohlich vis. prof. Royal Soc. Medicine Found., London, 1981. Fellow ACP; mem. Soc. Critical Care Medicine (pres. 1982), Central Soc. Clin. Research, Am. Soc. Pharmacology and Exptl. Therapeutics, Am. Soc. Clin. Pharmacology and Therapeutics, Council Clin. Pharmacology, Phi Beta Kappa, Alpha Omega Alpha. Episcopalian. Developed hydroxyethyl starch, an artificial blood; tapmot, an emetic for poisoning. Current Work: Drug development. Subspecialties: Pharmacology; Internal medicine. Home: 1024 Indianpipe Circle Carmel IN 46032 Office: Lilly Corp Ctr Indianapolis IN 46285

THOMPSON, WOODROW BURR, Quaternary geologist; b. Plymouth, N.H., Dec. 10, 1946; s. George Arthur and Bertha May (Monroe) T.; m. Louise May Latty, Aug. 8, 1970; 1 child, Larissa Michelle. B.A., Dartmouth Coll., 1968; M.S., U. Vt., 1971; Ph.D., Ohio State U., 1975. Cert. profl. geologist, Maine. Geologist U.S. Geol. Survey, Conn., 1968-73, 78-79; dir. bedrock and surficial geology div. Maine Geol. Survey, Augusta, 1975—. Author: Surficial Geologic Handbook for Coastal Maine, 1979; editor: Late Pleistocene History of Northeastern New England and Adjacent Quebec, 1985; chief editor and compiler state geologic map: Surficial Geologic Map of Maine, 1985, also articles. Served with USNG, 1968-74. Recipient U.S. Antarctic Service medal. Mem. Geol. Soc. Am., Am. Quaternary Assn., Mineral. Assn. Can., Geol. Soc. Maine. Democrat. Current work: Glacial history and stratigraphy of the New England region, including till stratigraphy and deglaciation history. Subspecialties: Geology; Glacial stratigraphy. Office: Maine Geol Survey State House Sta 22 Augusta ME 04333

THORMAR, HALLDOR, virologist; b. Iceland, Mar. 9, 1929; came to U.S., 1967; s. Thorvardur and Olina Marta Jonsdottir; m. Lilja Asdis, Dec. 25, 1962; children: Sigridur, Asdis Birna, Olina Marta. Mag. Scient. in Cell Physiology, U. Copenhagen, 1956, Dr. phil. in Virology, 1966. Research scientist Inst. Exptl. Pathology, U. Iceland, Reykjavik, 1958-60, 62-65, 66-67, Statens Serum Inst., Copenhagen, 1960-62, Centro do Virologia, IVIC, Caracas, Venezuela, 1965-66; chief research scientist Inst. Basic Research in Mental Retardation, S.I., N.Y., 1967—. Contbr. numerous articles on cell biology and virology to profl. jours. Mem. Am. Soc. Microbiology, N.Y. Acad. Scis. Current Work: Pathogenesis of viral infections of the central nervous system. Subspecialty: Virology (biology). Home: 8 Galewood Dr Holmdel NJ 07733 Office: 1050 Forest Hill Rd Staten Island NY 10314

THORNBURG, DALE LYNN, mechanical engineer, power plant designer; b. Tucson, Oct. 2, 1925; s. Martin Lynn and Lucille (Bitting) T.; m. Frances Pauline Whelan, Dec. 26, 1950; children—Marcia Susan Thornburg Lemons, Bruce Lynn. B.S.M.E., U. Ariz., 1950. Registered profl. engr., Ariz. Jr. engr. Ariz. Pub. Service Co., Phoenix, from 1950, now cons. sr. engr. Served with U.S. Army, 1943-46, ETO. Mem. ASME, Theta Tau. Current work: Fossil power plant design. Subspecialty: Mechanical engineering. Office: Ariz Pub Service Co PO Box 21666 Phoenix AZ 85036

THORNE, KIP STEPHEN, physicist, educator; b. Logan, Utah, June 1, 1940; s. David Wynne and Alison (Comish) T.; m. Linda Jeanne Peterson, Sept. 12, 1960 (div. 1977); children: Kares Anne, Bret Carter; m. Carolee Joyce Winstein, July 7, 1984. B.S. in Physics, Calif. Inst. Tech., 1962; A.M. in Physics (Woodrow Wilson fellow, Danforth Found. fellow), Princeton U., 1963, Ph.D. in Physics (Danforth Found. fellow, NSF fellow), 1965, postgrad. (NSF postdoctoral fellow), 1965-66; D.Sc. (hon.), Ill. Coll., 1979; Dr.h.c., Moscow U., 1981. Research fellow Calif. Inst. Tech., 1966-67, asso. prof. theoretical physics, 1967-70, prof., 1970—, William R. Kenan, Jr. prof., 1981—; Fulbright lectr., France, 1966; vis. asso. prof. U. Chgo., 1968; vis. prof. Moscow U., 1969, 75, 78, 81, 82; vis. sr. research asso. Cornell U., 1977; adj. prof. U. Utah, 1971—; mem. Internat. Com. on Gen. Relativity and Gravitation, 1971-80, Com. on U.S.-USSR Coop. in Physics, 1978-79, Space Sci. Bd., NASA, 1980-83. Co-author: Gravitation Theory and Gravitational Collapse, 1965, Gravitation, 1973. Alfred P. Sloan Found. Research fellow, 1966-68; John Simon Guggenheim fellow, 1967; recipient Sci. Writing award in physics and astronomy Am. Inst. Physics-U.S. Steel Found., 1969. Mem. Nat. Acad. Scis., Am. Acad. Arts and Scis., Am. Astron. Soc., Am. Phys. Soc., Internat. Astron. Union, AAAS, Sigma Xi, Tau Beta Pi. Current Work: Research in theoretical physics and astrophysics with emphasis on gravitation, black holes, gravitational waves, experimental tests of general relativity and quantum mechanical aspects of high-precision measurements. Subspecialties: Theoretical physics; Theoretical astrophysics. Office: 130-33 Calif Inst Tech Pasadena CA 91125

THORNTON, GUNNAR, engineering consultant, nuclear engineer; b. Oppegaard, Norway, Apr. 8, 1920; came to U.S., 1922, naturalized, 1937; s. Jens and Ingeborg (Herstad) T.; m. Nancy Alice Williamson, Nov. 22, 1948; children: Leslie Ann, Eleanor Jean, John Lauritz, Douglas Gunnar. B.S. in Engring, Tufts U., 1947; M.A. in Physics, Harvard U., 1948. Engr. U. Calif., Los Alamos, N.Mex., 1944-46; engr. physicist Fairchild Co., Oak Ridge, 1948-51; corp. engring. cons. Gen. Eelectric Co., Schenectady, N.Y., 1965—, engring. mgr., Evendale, Ohio, 1951-65. Author: (with D.C. Layman) Remote Handling of Mobile Nuclear Systems, 1965. Served with C.E. U.S. Army, 1942-46. Mem. Am. Nuclear Soc. Current Work: Corporate staff review of major technical projects; aerospace nuclear propulsion. Home: 1017 Onondaga Rd Schenectady NY 12309 Office: 1 River Rd Bldg 36 517 Schenectady NY 12345

THORNTON, WILLIAM E., astronaut, physician; b Faison, N.C., Apr. 29, 1929; m. Elizabeth Jennifer Fowler; 2 sons. B.S., U. N.C., 1952, M.D., 1963. Dir. electronics div. Del Mar Engring. Labs., Los Angeles, 1956-62; instr. U. N.C. Med. Sch., 1963-64; intern Wilford Hall, USAF Hosp., Lackland AFB, San Antonio, 1964-65; with aerospace med. div. Brooks AFB, San Antonio, 1965-67; scientist-astronaut NASA, 1967—; instr. dept. medicine U. Tex. Med. Br., from 1977. Decorated Legion of Merit; Recipient Exceptional Service, Exceptional Sci. Achievement awards NASA. Subspecialty: Space medicine. Address: Johnson Manned Spacecraft Center NASA Houston TX 77058*

THORSON, ROBERT MARK, geology educator, geologist; b. Edgerton, Wis., Oct. 6, 1951; s. Theodore W. and Margaret (Andersen) T.; m. Kristine Hoy, Aug. 21, 1977; children: Karsten, Adam. B.S. summa cum laude, Bemidji State U., 1973; M.S., U. Alaska-Fairbanks, 1975; Ph.D., U. Wash., Seattle, 1979. Geologist Arctic Environ. Project, U.S. Geol. Survey, Menlo Park, Calif., 1975-76, Puget Sound ESA Project, Seattle, 1976-81; asst. prof. geology U. Wis., Oshkosh, 1979-80; asst. prof. geology, geology/geophysics program U. Alaska, Fairbanks, 1980-84, chmn. office quaternary studies, 1981-84; dir. U. Alaska (Alaska Tephrochronology Ctr.), 1982-84; head surficial geology U. Alaska Mus., Fairbanks, 1982-85; assoc. prof. geology and geophysics U. Conn., Storrs, 1985—. Pres. Unitarian-Universalist Assn. Fairbanks, 1982. Alaska Council on Sci. and Tech. grantee, 1982. Mem. AAAS, Geol. Soc. Am. (Penrose Bequest grant 1974), Am. Quarternary Assn., Soc. Archeol. Scis., Alaska Geol. Soc., Alaska Quarternary Group. Unitarian/Universalist. Club: Scandinavian Fraternity Am. Current Work: Arctic and subarctic geomorphology, quaternary paleogeography, paleoclimatology and paleoenvironments, volcanic hazards research, environmental problems associated with permafrost, early man chronology and stratigraphy, glacier processes and hazards. Subspecialties: Geology; Geological hazards. Home: Ithaca Rd University Heights Fairbanks AK 99701 Home: 9 Storrs Heights Rd Storrs CT 06268 Office: Dept Geology and Geophysics U Conn Storrs CT 06268

THRODAHL, MONTE CORDEN, retired chemical company executive; b. Mpls., Mar. 25, 1919; s. Monte Conrad and Hilda (Larson) T.; m. Josephine Crandall, Nov. 6, 1948; children: Mark Crandall, Peter Douglas. B.S., Iowa State U., 1941. With Monsanto Co., St. Louis, 1941-84, gen. mgr. internat. div., 1964-66, v.p., 1965-74, dir., 1966-84, group v.p. tech., 1974-79, sr. v.p., 1979-84, ret., 1984. Bd. dirs., mem. exec. com. Webster Coll. Fellow Am. Inst. Chemists, Am. Inst. Chem. Engrs.; mem. Am. Chem. Soc., Am. Inst. Chem. Engrs., Nat. Acad. Engring., Comml. Devel. Assn., AAAS, Soc. Chem. Industry, Alpha Chi Sigma. Clubs: Old Warson Country (St. Louis), St. Louis (St. Louis). Subspecialty: Chemical research management. Home: No 36 Briarcliff Ladue MO 63124 Office: 7811 Carondelet Ave Saint Louis MO 63105

THROWER, PETER ALBERT, materials science educator; b. Norfolk, Eng., Jan. 9, 1938; came to U.S., 1969; s. Cyril Albert and Lilian Clara (Howes) T.; m. Christine Ruth Bailey, Aug. 20, 1960 (div. 1985); m. Carol Ann Black, Apr. 19, 1985. B.A., Cambridge U., Eng., 1960, M.A., 1963, Ph.D., 1969. Sr. sci. officer U.K. Atomic Energy Authority, Harwell, Eng., 1960-69; prof. materials sci. Pa. State U., University Park, 1969—; cons. in field. Editor jour. Carbon, 1983—. Editor monograph series Chemistry and Physics of Carbon, 1973—. Mem. Am. Carbon Soc. (exec. com. 1983—), Am. Soc. Metals. Current work: Structure-property relationships in carbon materials, use of carbon/carbon components in advanced applications. Subspecialties: Materials; Composite materials. Home: 1659 Cherry Hill Rd State College PA 16803 Office: Pa State U 117 Steidle Bldg University Park PA 16802

THULIN, FREDERICK ADOLPH, JR., architect, design engineer; b. Oak Park, Ill., July 17, 1925; s. Frederick Adolph, Sr. and Ruth Priscilla (Fraser) T.; m. Adelaide Ann Peterson, Aug. 18, 1945; children—Frederick, Kristin, Mary, Margaret, Francis, Peter, Andrea, Charles, Joseph, James, Kathleen, Suzanne, Patricia. B.S.M.E., Northwestern U., 1948; B.S. in Architecture, Chgo. Tech. Coll., 1953; postgrad., Ill. Inst. of Tech., 1967-69. Registered prof. engr., Ill. Registered prof. architect, Ill., Wis. Div. engr. Underwriters Labs., Inc., Chgo., 1948-53; ptnr. architectural engineering firm Thulin and Woods, Chgo., 1953-63; architect Austin Co., Chgo., 1959; architect, engr. U.S. Gypsum Co. USG Corp. Des Plaines, Libertyville, Ill., 1963—; sole practice, Mt. Prospect, Ill., 1963—; mem. com. NSF, 1981; dir. Applied Design Assocs., Mt. Prospect. Patentee in field. Commr., Weller Creek Drainage Dist., Arlington Heights, Ill., 1959-73; treas. Elk Grove Twp. Registered Democratic Organization, Mt. Prospect, 1960-64; bd. dirs. Williams Mil. Acad., Wheaton, Ill., 1970-74. Served with Mcht. Marine, 1945-46. Mem. AIA (chmn. Chgo. chpt. housing com. 1964-68), Earthquake Engring. Research Inst., Northwestern Engring. Alumni Assn. (v.p., dir. 1976—), Phi Eta Sigma, Pi Mu Epsilon, Pi Tau Sigma, Theta Xi (dir., v.p. alum corp. 1965—). Republican. Roman Catholic. Club: Swedish (Chgo.). Current work: Seismic performance of building systems, design of light steel structures, computer aided design. Subspecialties: Structural engineering; Software engineering. Home: 4 South Owen St Mount Prospect IL Office: USG Corp Research Ctr 700 N Hwy 45 Libertyville IL 60048

THURMAN, RONALD GLENN, pharmacologist, consultant, educator; b. Carbondale, Ill., Nov. 25, 1941; s. Glenn and Melba T. T. B.S. in Pharmacy, St. Louis Coll. Pharmacy, 1963; Ph.D. in Pharmacology, U. Ill., 1968. Postdoctoral fellow dept. biophysics and phys. biochemistry Johnson Research Found., U. Pa., 1968-69, asst. prof. biochemistry and biophysics, 1972-77; postdoctoral fellow Inst. Physiol. Chemistry and Phys. Biochemistry, U. Munich, W.Ger., 1969-72; assoc. prof. pharmacology U. N.C., Chapel Hill, 1977-82, prof., 1982—, reviewer, cons. Editor: (with Williamson, Drott and Chance) Alcohol and Aldehyde Metabolizing Systems, Vol. I, 1974, Vol. II, 1977, Vol. III, 1977, Vol. IV, 1980; contbr. numerous articles to sci. jours. Recipient Research Career Devel. award Nat. Inst. Alcohol Abuse and Alcoholism, 1973-83; Alexander von Humboldt postdoctoral fellow, 1970-71. Mem. Soc. Toxicology, Research Soc. on Alcoholism, Internat. Soc. Biomed. Research on Alcoholism, N.Y. Acad. Scis., Am. Soc. Biol. Chemists, Am. Soc. Cancer Research, Am. Soc. Pharmacology and Exptl. Therapeutics, Internat. Council Alcohol and Addictions, Argentine Soc. Pathology (life). Current Work: Regulation of hepatic carbohydrate and mixed-function oxidation, methods development for carcinogen metabolites, control of hepatic ethanol metabolism, drug and alcohol metabolism. Subspecialty: Pharmacology. Home: Route 2 Box 735A Chapel Hill NC 27514 Office: University of North Carolina 1124 Faculty Lab Office Bldg Chapel Hill NC 27514

THYVELIKAKATH, GEORGE XAVIER, chemistry educator; b. Cochin, India, Apr. 29, 1943; came to U.S., 1967; s. Anne Joseph (Chakiamury) T.; married; children—Mary, George, Manakil. B.Sc. in Chemistry, Kerala U., Cochin, India, 1965; M.S. in Chemistry, U. Southwestern La., 1971; Ph.D. in Chemistry, Okla. State U., 1975. Postdoctoral fellow U. Ark., Fayetteville, 1975-76, vis. asst. prof. chemistry, 1976-77; asst. prof. chemistry Oral Roberts U., Tulsa, 1977-80, assoc. prof., 1980-83, prof., 1983—; vis. prof. Northeastern Okla. State U., Tahlequah, 1978; cons. Metal Cleaning Corp., Tulsa, 1980-81; chem. lab. tech. staff Tulsa Jr. Coll., 1983—, adv. com. mem., 1983—. Author: Basic Organic Chemistry Laboratory Procedures, 1980; Cancer: Its Causes and Chemistry of Selected Anticancer Drugs, 1984. Contbr. articles to profl. jours. Convenor, Indian Nat. Congress Party Election Com., A Pallurathy, India, 1965; bd. dirs. Royal Oaks Condominium Homeowners Assn., Tulsa, 1980-82. Fellow Dow Research Corp., 1974, Gulf, 1975; recipient Outstanding Faculty award U. Ark., 1976-77, Oral Roberts U., 1979-80, Cert. Meritorious Service Okla. Sci. Tchrs. Assn., 1978; 1st recipient Performance award Oral Roberts U., 1984-85. Mem. Am. Chem. Soc. (sec. Tulsa sect. 1979-80, chmn. Tulsa sect. 1983), Okla. Acad. Sci. (chmn. sci. edn. sect. 1978—), Soc. Magentic Resonance Imaging, Sigma Xi, Phi Lambda Epsilon, Alpha Epsilon Delta. Roman Catholic. Club: Diana Arts (Kumbalanghy, Cochin) (pres. 1964-65). Current work: Cancer chemotherapy, mechanistic and systematic approach to drug design, complexation studies of medically important compounds, NMR studies for the detection of cancer, heart disease, etc.; NMR imaging of oil, water, and gas in rock samples, organic water and air pollutants, pesticides and herbicides; philosophy of education, professional ethics and human nature. Subspecialties: Organic chemistry; Nuclear magnetic resonance. Home: 6611 S Zunis Ave Tulsa OK 74136 Office: Oral Roberts U Natural Sci Dept 7777 S Lewis Ave Tulsa OK 74171

TIBBETTS, GARY GEORGE, physicist; b. Omaha, Oct. 12, 1939; s. Donald and DeLois Julene (Black) T.; m. Patricia Avis Andreasen, Aug. 1, 1964; children—Margaret, Elizabeth, Katherine. B.S., Calif. Inst. Tech., Pasadena, 1961; M.S., U. Ill., 1963, Ph.D., 1967. Guest scientist Tech. U., Munich, Fed. Republic Germany, 1967-69; staff research scientist physics dept. Gen. Motors Research Lab., Warren, Mich., 1969—. Mem. Am. Phys. Soc., Am. Carbon Soc. Subspecialties: Condensed matter physics; Materials. Home: 1177 Chesterfield St Birmingham MI 48009 Office: Gen Motors Research Lab Dept Physics Warren MI 48090

TIDBALL, CHARLES STANLEY, computer scientist, medical educator, physician; b. Geneva, Apr. 15, 1928; came to U.S., 1935; s. Charles Taylor and Adele (Desmaison) T.; m. M. Elizabeth Peters, Oct. 25, 1952. B.A., Wesleyan U., 1950; M.S., U. Rochester, 1952; Ph.D., U. Wis., 1955; M.D., U. Chgo., 1958. Asst. research prof. physiology George Washington U., Washington, 1959-63, assoc. prof., 1963-64, prof., 1964-65, Henry D. Fry prof. physiology, 1965-84, prof. edn., 1982-84, prof. computer medicine Med. Ctr., 1984—; cons. Clin. Ctr., NIH, Bethesda, Md., 1977-78; Walter Reed Army Inst. of Research, Washington, 1970-71. Author computer software Tidball Learning library, 1973—. Editor: Frontiers in Teaching Physiology, 1981; editor Jour. Computer-Based Instruction, 1974—. Contbr. articles to profl. jours. Trustee Wilson Coll., Chambersburg, Pa., 1983—; mem. Cathedral Choral Soc., Washington, 1962—; lay reader, clergy asst. Cathedral Ch. St. Peter and St. Paul, Washington, 1967—; vol. YMCA, Washington, 1968—; bd. dirs. Cathedral West Condominium, Washington, 1983—. Recipient Sci. Achievement award Washington Acad. Scis., 1967; Outstanding Service award Met. YMCA, 1974, 76, 79. Mem. Am. Physiol. Soc., Assn. Devel. Computer Based Instructional Systems, Assn. Computing Machinery, AAUP. Republican. Episcopalian. Current work: Computer assisted instruction, computer graphics, medical risk factor analysis, bio-electric impedance, design of small-scale computer networks. Subspecialty: Preventive medicine. Home: 4100 Cathedral Ave NW Washington DC 20016 Office: Dept Computer Medicine George Washington U Med Ctr 2300 K St NW Washington DC 20037

TIEDEMANN, EDWARD ERIC, nuclear engineer, researcher; b. Belleville, Ill., Feb. 9, 1954; s. Charles Edwin and Delores Ruth (Davidson) T.; m. Mary Ann Edwards, Apr. 24, 1977; 1 child, Brent Edward. B.S.M.E., U. of Ill., 1976. Registered prof. engr., Ill. Construction engr. Ill. Power Co., Havana, 1976-78, project mgmt. engr., Clinton, 1978—. Donor, U. of Ill. Grants-In-Aid, Urbana, 1984. James scholar U. Ill., 1972. Mem. ASME, Ill. Soc. Profl. Engrs. Republican. Current work: The study of interactions of radiation with matter in quantum physics; neutron attenuation and cross-sections of nuclei. Subspecialties: Nuclear engineering; Human factors engineering. Home: 804 Hillside Dr Monticello IL 61856 Office: Ill Power Co 500 S 27th St Decatur IL 62525

TIEN, CHANG LIN, engineering educator; b. Wuhan, China, July 24, 1935; came to U.S., 1956, naturalized, 1969; s. Yun Chien and Yun Di (Lee) T.; m. Di Hwa Liu, July 25, 1959; children: Norman Chihnan, Phyllis Chihping, Christine Chihyih. B.S., Nat. Taiwan U., 1955; M.M.E., U. Louisville, 1957; M.A., Ph.D., Princeton U., 1959. Acting asst. prof. dept. mech. engring. U. Calif.—Berkeley, Berkeley, 1959-60, asst. prof., 1960-64, asso. prof., 1964-68, prof., 1968—, dept. chmn., 1974-81, vice chancellor for research, 1983—; tech. cons. Lockheed Missiles & Space Co., Gen. Electric Co. Contbr. articles to profl jours. Guggenheim fellow, 1965. Fellow ASME (Max Jakob Meml. award ASME—Am. Inst. Chem. Engrs. 1981, Heat Transfer Meml. award 1974, Larson Meml. award 1975), AIAA (Thermophysics award 1977); mem. Nat. Acad. Engring. Current Work: Thermal radiation transport; heat transport in porous media; heat transfer in multiphase systems. Subspecialties: Heat transfer; Thermophysics. Home: 1451 Olympus Ave Berkeley CA 94708 Office: Dept Mech Engring U Calif Berkeley CA 94720

TIEN, H. TI, biophysicist, educator; b. Peking, China, Feb. 1, 1938; m. Joseleyne Slade, Jan. 31, 1953; children—Stephen, Robbins, Adrienne, Jennifer. B.S. in Chem. Engring, U. Nebr.; Ph.D. in Chemistry, Temple U., 1963. Chem. engr. Allied Chem. Corp., 1953-57; med. scientist Ea. Pa. Psychiat. Inst., Phila.; prof. biophysics, chmn. dept. Mich. State U., East Lansing, 1978—. Author: Bilayer Lipid Membranes: Theory and Practice, 1974; contbr. numerous articles internat. jours. Grantee NIH, 1964—; Grantee NSF, 1977-79; Grantee Dept. Energy, 1980-82. Mem. Am. Chem. Soc., AAAS, Biophys. Soc. Current Work: Membrane biophysics, electrochem. solar cells, PGV cells, energy transduction including solar, primary events in photosynthesis and vision. Subspecialties: Solar energy; Biophysics (biology). Office: Biophysics Dept Michigan State U East Lansing MI 48824

TIEN, PING KING, electronic engineer; b. Chekieng, China, Aug. 2, 1919; came to U.S., 1947; s. N.S. and Y.S. (Chao) T.; m. Nancy N.Y. Chen, Apr. 19, 1952; children: Emily Ju-Psia, Julia Ju-Wen. M.S., Stanford U., 1948, Ph.D., 1951. Head dept. high speed electronics. Bell Telephone Labs., Holmdel, N.J., 1952—. Contbr. sci. and tech. articles to profl. jours. Recipient Achievement award Chinese Inst. Engrs., 1966; AT&T Bell Labs. fellow, 1983. Fellow IEEE (Morris N. Liebmann award 1979), Optical Soc. Am.; mem. Nat. Acad. Sci., Nat. Acad. Engring. Patentee in field. Current Work: Advanced research in opto electronics for optical communication. Subspecialties: Fiber optics; Microelectronics. Home: 9 Carolyn Ct Holmdel NJ 07733 Office: Bell Labs Holmdel NJ 07733

TIFFNEY, BRUCE HAYNES, research biologist, educator; b. Sharon, Mass., July 3, 1949; s. Wesley Newell and Sarah (Cousins) T. B.A. cum laude, Boston U., 1971; Ph.D., Harvard U., 1977. Asst. prof. dept. biology Yale U., New Haven, 1977-82, assoc. prof., 1982—; curator Paleobot. and Herbarium Collections Peabody Mus. Natural History, 1977—. Contbr. articles to sci. jours. Mem. Bot. Soc. Am., Geol. Soc. Am., Internat. Assn. Plant Taxonomists, Assn. Tropical Biology, Internat. Orgn. Paleobotany, New Eng. Bot. Club, Tertiary Research Group. Current Work: Study of evolution of vascular land plants, especially angiosperms, with emphasis on contribution of paleobotany to general evolutionary theory. Subspecialties: Paleobiology; Evolutionary biology. Office: Dept Biology Yale U Box 6666 New Haven CT 06511

TIFFNEY, WESLEY NEWELL, JR., botanist, environmental consultant; b. Springfield, Mass., June 10, 1940; s. Wesley Newell and Sarah Margaret (Cousins) T. B.S. Ed., Boston U., 1963; M.S. in Botany, U. N.H., 1965, Ph.D. in Bot. Ecology, 1972. Instr. biology U. Mass., Boston, 1967-72, developed teaching and research field sta., Nantucket Island, 1969-74, dir., 1974—, asst. prof. biology, 1972-74; chmn. Internat. Conf. Georges Bank Oil, 1982; co-dir. Calif. Offshore Petroleum Conf., 1985; environ. cons.; dir. Harbor Fuel Corp. Contbr. articles to sci. jours. Mem. Am. Soc. Environ. Edn. (trustee, v.p. programs), Am. Bot. Soc., Brit. Ecol. Soc., Torrey Bot. Club, New Eng. Bot. Club, Nantucket Hist. Assn. (life), Nantucket Maria Mitchell Assn. (life, chmn. natural scis. com., v.p.), Sigma Xi. Current Work: Nitrogen fixation, coastal ecology, health ecology. Subspecialties: Nitrogen fixation; Ecology (environmental science). Home and office: U Mass Nantucket Field Sta Box 756 Nantucket MA 02554

TIGNER, MAURY, physicist; b. Middletown, N.Y., Apr. 22, 1937; married; 2 children. B.S., Rensselaer Poly. Inst., 1958; Ph.D. in Physics, Cornell U., 1963. Research assoc., Cornell U., Ithaca, N.Y., 1963-68, sr. research assoc. in physics, 1968-77, prof. physics and mem. staff Lab. Atomic and Solid State Physics, 1977—; dir. research and devel. superconducting super collider project U.S. Dept. Energy. Subspecialty: Accelerator physics. Office: Dept Physics Cornell U Ithaca NY 14853*

TILAK, MANOHAR ANANT, chemist, evolution theorist; b. Dhulia City, India, Nov. 20, 1925; came to U.S., 1962; s. Anant Vishwanath and Annapurna (Barve) T. B.S., Benares Hindu U. (India), 1959; M.S., Tech. U. (Germany), 1959, Ph.D., 1961. Research chemist Max Planck Inst., Munich, West Germany, 1961-62; research assoc. U. Med. Sch., Pitts., 1962-64, Brookhaven Nat. Lab., Upton, N.Y., 1964-66; research chemist Eli Lilly Research Lab., Indpls., 1966—. Mem. Am. Chem. Soc., India Sci. News Assn. (life mem.), Indian Assn. History and Philosophy Sci. (life mem.). Current work: Biochemistry, analysis of evolutionary phenomena, Macroperspectives of interactive continuums, evolutionary meaning of exponentiation of rate of change; originated the concepts of evoluon theory and evolutionary phase changes. Subspecialty: Biochemistry (medicine). Home: 572 Banbury Rd Noblesville IN 46060 Office: Eli Lilly and Co Dept MC 797 Bldg 88/4 Indianapolis IN 46285

TILL, GERD OSKAR, pathologist; b. Neudek, Sudetenland, Germany, Dec. 12, 1939; came to U.S., 1980; s. Oskar and Maria (Rieger) T.; m. Anita Zimmer, Sept. 30, 1966; children: Joachim, Christopher. M.D., U. Freiburg, 1967; Dr. med. habil., U. Heidelberg, 1978. Postdoctoral fellow U. Conn., Farmington, 1972-73; Wissenschaftlicher Angestellter, U. Heidelberg, W. Ger., 1973-78, privat-dozent, 1978-80; assoc. prof. pathology U. Mich., Ann Arbor, 1980—. Author: (with K. Rother) Komplement: Biochemie und Pathologie, 1974; editor: (with H.U. Keller) Leukocyte Locomotion and Chemotaxis, 1983; also articles. Mem. Am. Assn. Pathologists, Am. Assn. Immunologists, Am. Burn Assn., German Soc. Immunology, German Soc. Cell Biology. Current Work: Regulatory processes in inflammation; complement biology; leukocyte functions; thermal injury. Subspecialties: Pathology (medicine); Immunobiology and immunology. Home: 2009 Shadford Rd Ann Arbor MI 48104 Office: Dept Pathology U Mich 1315 Catherine Rd Ann Arbor MI 48109

TILLEY, JEFFERSON WRIGHT, organic chemist, drug designer; b. Detroit, Dec. 13, 1946; s. George Cook and Barbara (Wright) T.; m. Katherine Mighell, Jan. 31, 1970; children—Molly Ann, Jennifer Scott. B.S. in Chemistry, Harvey Mudd Coll., 1968; Ph.D. in Chemistry, Caltech., 1972. Sr. chemist Hoffmann-LaRoche, Nutley, N.J., 1972-76, Basle, Switzerland, 1976-78, asst. group chief, Nutley, 1978-80, group chief, 1980-83, sr. group chief, 1983—. Contbr. articles to tech. jours. Patentee in field. Firefighter and company officer North Caldwell Vol. Fire Dept., N.J., 1972—. Mem. Am. Chem. Soc., N.Y. Acad. Scis. Club: Bell and Siren (Newark) (treas. 1975-76). Current work: Design and synthesis of new drug candidates with emphasis on potential cardiovascular or bronchopulmonary utility. Subspecialties: Organic chemistry; Medicinal chemistry. Office: Hoffman-LaRoche Inc Kingsland Rd Nutley NJ 07110

TILLMAN, JAMES EDWARD, geologist, oil and gas explorationist; b. Balt., Dec. 23, 1949; s. James Rogers and Joyce (Hall) T.; m. Kathryn Bell, Mar. 9, 1974; children—Anna Elizabeth, Leigh Bonner. B.A., Franklin and Marshall Coll., 1971; M.S., Syracuse U., 1973. Cert. Am. Inst. Profl. Geologists. Project mgr. Dames & Moore, Cranford, N.J., 1973-78; mem. faculty Johns Hopkins U., Laurel, Md., 1978-81; sr. cons. H.J. Gruy & Assocs., Arlington, Va., 1981-82; pres. Target Exploration, Columbia, Md., 1982—, also dir.; dir. Tiara Am., N.Y.C. Contbr. articles to prof. jours. Chmn. Md. Commn. Energy Sources, Annapolis, 1982. Mem. Am. Assn. Petroleum Geologists, Geol. Soc. Am., Ind. Oil and Gas. Assn. W.Va. and Mich., Assn. Geochem. Explorationists, Appalachian Petroleum Club Washington. Current work: Development and utilization of geochemical techniques for surface detection of oil and gas reservoirs. Subspecialties: Geochemistry; Tectonics. Home: 4851 Manor Ln Ellicott City MD 21043 Office: Target Exploration Inc Suite 216 5513 Twin Knolls Rd Columbia MD 21045

TILSON, HUGH ARVAL, JR., neurotoxicologist; b. Plainview, Tex., July 24, 1946; s. Hugh Arval, Sr., and Olive Aileen (Hewett) T.; m. Beverly June Crosby, Aug. 26, 1966 (div. Dec. 1980); m. Gaylia Jean Harry, Aug. 7, 1981. B.A., Tex. Tech. U., 1968; Ph.D., U. Minn., 1972. Research assoc. Mich. State U., East Lansing, 1972-73; sr. research scientist Bristol Labs., Syracuse, N.Y., 1973-76; pharmacologist Nat. Inst. Environ. Health Scis., Research Triangle Park, N.C., 1976—. Mem. Soc. Neurosci., Soc. Teratology, Am. Soc. Pharm. Exptl. Therapy. Democrat. Unitarian. Current work: Research on neural effects of neurotoxic agents with special interest in mechanism of action of organochlorine and related chemicals. Subspecialties: Neurotoxicology; Environmental toxicology. Home: 2616 Salisbury Plain Raleigh NC 27612 Office: Nat Inst Environ Health Scis PO Box 12233 Research Triangle Park NC 27709

TILTON, RONALD GENE, physiologist; b. Kearney, Nebr., Apr. 19, 1949; s. Dean S. and Roberta J. (Patterson) T.; m. Kathleen Ellen Brune, Aug. 6, 1983; 1 child, Paul Dean. B.S., U. So. Fla., 1971; Ph.D., Washington U., St. Louis, 1977. Research fellow Washington U., St. Louis, 1977-78, cardiology fellow, 1978-79, research instr., 1979—. Mem. Am. Diabetes Assn., Am. Heart Assn., Am. Soc. Cell Biology, Internat. Acad. Pathology, Microcirculatory Soc. Democrat. Methodist. Current work: Effects of diabetes and myocardial infarction on the structural and functional integrity of the coronary vasculature. Subspecialties: Cardiology; Pathology (medicine). Office: Dept Pathology Washington U 660 S Euclid Ave Saint Louis MO 63110

TIMBERLAKE, WILLIAM EDWARD, biologist, educator; b. Washington, May 2, 1948; s. George Taylor and Helen Doris (Nelson) T.; m. Sally Price, Aug. 23, 1969; children: Martha Anne, Nathan William. B.S., SUNY-Syracuse, 1970, Ph.D., 1973. Asst. prof. dept. biology Wayne State U., Detroit, 1974-79, assoc. prof., 1979-81; assoc. prof. dept. plant pathology U. Calif.-Davis, 1981-83, prof., 1983—. Mem. Mycol. Soc. Am., Genetics Soc. Am., AAAS. Current Work: Gene control during fungal and plant development. Subspecialties: Developmental biology; Gene actions. Office: Dept Plant Pathology U Calif Davis CA 95616

TIMIAN, ROLAND GUSTAV, plant pathologist; b. Langdon, N.D., Mar. 5, 1920; s. Gustav Albert and Adelena (Sueltz) T.; m. Frances Anna Newman, Mar. 17, 1949; children: James, Carol, Yvonne, Steven, Paulette. B.S., N.D. State U., 1949, M.S., 1950; Ph.D., Iowa State U., 1953. Research plant pathologist Agr. Research Service, USDA, Fargo, 1953—; adj. prof. N.D. State U., Fargo, 1960—. Contbr. articles to profl. jours.; editor: Barley Newsletter, 1977-80. Mem. Nat. Barley Improvement Com., 1979—. Served with USN, 1942-45. Decorated D.F.C., Air medal (5). Mem. Am. Phytopath. Soc., N.D. Acad. Sci., Sigma Xi, Gamma Sigma Delta. Lutheran. Current Work: Host-virus interactions. Subspecialties: Plant virology; Plant pathology. Home: 2305 10th St Fargo ND 58102 Office: ND State U Fargo ND 58105

TIMMERHAUS, KLAUS DIETER, college dean; b. Mpls., Sept. 10, 1924; s. Paul P. and Elsa L. (Bever) T.; m. Jean L. Mevis, Aug. 3, 1952; 1 dau., Carol Jane. B.S. in Chem. Engring, U. Ill., 1948, M.S., 1949, Ph.D., 1951. Registered profl. engr., Colo. Process design engr. Calif. Research Corp., Richmond, 1952-53; extension lectr. U. Calif., Berkeley, 1952; mem. faculty U. Colo., 1953—, prof. chem. engring., 1961—, assoc. dean engring., 1963—; dir. engring. research center U. Colo. (Coll. Engring.), 1963—, chmn. aerospace dept., 1979-80; cryogenic engr. lab. Nat. Bur. Standards, Boulder, summers 1955, 57, 59, 61; lectr. UCLA, 1961-62; sect. head engring. div. NSF, 1972-73; cons. in field. Bd. dirs. Colo. Engring. Expt. Sta., Inc., Engring. Measurements Co, both Boulder. Editor: Advances in Cryogenic Engineering, vols. 1-25, 1954-80; co-editor: Internat. Cryogenic Monograph Series, 1965—. Served with USNR, 1944-46. Recipient Distinguished Service award Dept. Commerce, 1957; Samuel C. Collins award outstanding contbns. to cryogenic tech., 1967; George Westinghouse award, 1968; Alpha Chi Sigma award chem. engring. research, 1968; Meritorious Service award Cryogenic Engring. Conf., 1967; U. Colo. R.L. Stearns Profl. Achievement award, 1981; Disting. Pub. Service award NSF, 1984. Fellow AAAS; mem. Nat. Acad. Engring., Am. Astron. Soc., Am. Inst. Chem. Engrs. (v.p. 1975, pres. 1976, Founders award 1978, Eminent Chem. Engr. award 1983), Am. Soc. for Engring. Edn. (3M Chem Engring. div. award 1980), Internat. Inst. Refrigeration (v.p. 1979—), Cryogenic Engring. Conf. (chmn. 1956-67), Sigma Xi (dir. 1981—), Sigma Tau, Tau Beta Pi, Phi Lambda Upsilon. Current Work: Cryogenic refrigeration; heat transfer and thermodynamic properties. Subspecialties: Chemical engineering; Cryogenics. Home: 905 Brooklawn Dr Boulder CO 80303

TIMMERMAN, ROBERT WILSON, mech. engr. and researcher; b. Abington, Pa., July 27, 1944; s. Clarence Arthur and Mildred Wilson (Slack) T.; m. Nancy Jean Spinka, Sept. 28, 1974. Student, Wesleyan U., 1961-62; B.S., Cornell U., 1965, M.E., 1966; postgrad., Northwestern U., 1971-72, U. Pa., 1972-74. Registered profl. engr., Mass., Pa. Project engr. Monsanto Co., Springfield, Mass., 1966-68; engr. Stone & Webster Engring. Co., Boston, 1968-71, United Engrs. & Constructors, Boston, 1974-75; sr. engr. R.W. Beck & Assocs., Wellesley, Mass., 1975-77; founder, prin. R.W. Timmerman & Assocs., Boston, 1977—. Mem. ASME (chmn. Boston sect. 1979-80), ASHRAE (assoc.), Assn. Energy Engrs. (cert. energy mgr.), Internat. Dist. Heating Assn. Presbyterian. Patentee in heating field. Current Work: District heating, cogeneration, waste heat utilization. Subspecialty: Mechanical engineering. Home and Office: 25 Upton St Boston MA 02118

TING, ROBERT YEN-YING, physicist, researcher; b. Kwei-yang, China, Mar. 8, 1942; came to U.S., 1965, naturalized, 1975; s. Chi-yung and Shiu-fang (Yang) T.; m. Teresa Y. Chen, June 3, 1967; children—Paul, Peggy. B.S., Nat. Taiwan U., 1964; M.S., MIT, 1967; Ph.D., U. Calif.-San Diego, 1971. Research staff MIT, Cambridge, 1967-68; research engr. Naval Research Lab., Washington, 1971-77, head plymer mechanics sect., 1977-80, head materials research, Orlando, Fla., 1980—; asst. prof. George Washington U., Washington, 1972-74, assoc. prof., 1974-80. Author: Polyelectrolytes & Application, 1975; Resins for Aerospace, 1980; Adhesive Joints, 1984. Contbr. articles to profl. jours. Recipient Outstanding Performance award Naval Research Lab., 1973, 76, Merit Performance award Naval Research Lab., 1982, 83, 84. Mem. Ching-Hwa Sino-Am. Assn., Am. Chem. Soc., Am. Chem. Engring. Inst., Acoustical Soc. Am. Current work: Underwater acoustic materials, dynamic mechanical property, polymer, ceramic, composites, ferroelectricity, elastomer, adhesion. Subspecialties: Acoustics; Materials (engineering). Office: PO Box 8337 Orlando FL 32856-8337

TING, SAMUEL CHAO CHUNG, physicist, educator; b. Ann Arbor, Mich., Jan. 27, 1936; s. Kuan H. and Jeanne (Wong) T.; m. Susan Carol Marks, Apr. 28, 1985 children—Jeanne Min, Amy Min. B.S. in Engring., U. Mich., 1959, M.S., 1960, Ph.D., 1962, Sc.D. (hon.), 1978. Ford Found. fellow CERN (European Orgn. Nuclear Research), Geneva, 1963; instr. physics Columbia U., 1964, asst. prof., 1965-67; group leader Deutsches Elektronen-Synchrotron, Hamburg, W.Ger., 1966; asso. prof. physics M.I.T., Cambridge, 1967-68, prof., 1969—, Thomas Dudley Cabot Inst. prof., 1977—; program cons. Div. Particles and Fields, Am. Phys. Soc., 1970. Asso. editor: Nuclear Physics B, 1970; contbr. articles to profl. jours.; editorial bd.: Nuclear Instruments and Methods. Recipient Nobel prize in physics, 1976; Am. Acad. Sci. and Arts fellow, 1975; Ernest Orlando Lawrence award U.S. Govt., 1976; Eringen medal Soc. Engring. Sci., 1977. Mem. Nat. Acad. Sci., Pakistani Acad. Sci., Pakistani Acad. Sci. (fgn. mem.), Academia Sinica (Taiwan) (fgn. mem.). Subspecialty: Nuclear physics. Office: Dept Physics Mass Inst Tech 51 Vassar St Cambridge MA 02139

TING, YU-CHEN, geneticist; b. Henan, China, Oct. 3, 1920; s. Chin-Yung and Yi-Yung (Wang) T.; m. Jovina Y.H. Chen, June 25, 1960; children: Andrew, Claire. B.S., Henan U., China, 1944; M.S.A., Cornell U., 1951; Ph.D., La. State U., 1954. Postdoctoral fellow Harvard U., 1955-62; asst. prof. genetics Boston Coll., 1962-64, assoc. prof., 1964-67, prof., 1967—. Contbr. articles to profl. jours. Bd. dirs. Nat. Assn. Chinese Ams., Boston. Research collaborator Brookhaven Nat. Lab., 1963-65; Nat. Acad. Scientists sr. fellow, 1979. Mem. Am. Genetics Assn., Genetics Soc. Am., AAAS, Bot. Soc. Am., New Eng. Bot. Club. Current Work: Researcher in cytogenesis of maize and its relatives, fine structure of meiotic chromosomes, plant cell and tissue culture. Subspecialties: Cell and tissue culture; Genetics and genetic engineering (agriculture). Home: 230 Bonad Rd Brookline MA 02167 Office: Dept Biology Boston Coll Chestnut Hill MA 02167

TINKHAM, MICHAEL, physicist, educator; b. Green Lake County, Wis., Feb. 23, 1928; s. Clayton Harold and LaVerna (Krause) T.; m. Mary Stephanie Merin, June 24, 1961; children: Jeffrey Michael, Christopher Gillespie. A.B., Ripon (Wis.) Coll., 1951, Sc.D. (hon.), 1976; M.S., MIT, 1951; Ph.D., 1954; M.A. (hon.), Harvard, 1966. NSF postdoctoral fellow at Clarendon Lab., Oxford (Eng.) U., 1954-55; successively research physicist, lectr., asst. prof., asso. prof., prof. physics U. Calif. at Berkeley, 1955-66; Gordon McKay prof. applied physics Harvard U., 1966—, prof. physics, 1966-80, Rumford prof. physics, 1980—, chmn. physics dept., 1975-78; cons. to industry, 1958—; participant internat. seminars and confs. Mem. commn. on very low temperatures Internat. Union Pure and Applied Physics, 1972-78. Author: Group Theory and Quantum Mechanics, 1964, Superconductivity, 1965, Introduction to Superconductivity, 1975; also numerous articles. Served USNR, 1945-46. Recipient award Alexander von Humboldt Found. U. Karlsruhe, W. Ger., 1978-79; NSF sr. postdoctoral fellow Cavendish lab.; vis. fellow Clare Hall Cambridge (Eng.) U., 1971-72; Guggenheim fellow, 1963-64. Fellow Am. Phys. Soc. (chmn. div. solid state physics 1966-67, Buckley prize 1974, Richtmyer lectr. 1977), AAAS; mem. Am. Acad. Arts and Scis., Nat. Acad. Scis. Current Work: Superconducting Josephson junctions and nonequilibrium superconductivity. Subspecialties: Low temperature physics; Superconductors. Home: 98 Rutledge Rd Belmont MA 02178 Office: Physics Dept Harvard Univ Cambridge MA 02138

TINOCO, IGNACIO, JR., biophysical chemist; b. El Paso, Tex., Nov. 22, 1930; married; 1 child. B.S., U. N.Mex., 1951, Sc.D., 1972; Ph.D. in Chemistry, U. Wis.-Madison, 1954. Research fellow chemistry Yale U., 1954-56; from instr. to assoc. prof. chemistry U. Calif.-Berkeley, 1956-66, prof., 1966—. Recipient Nat. Medal of Sci., 1985. Subspecialty: Biophysical chemistry. Office: U Calif Dept Chemistry Berkeley CA 94720*

TIPLER, FRANK JENNINGS, III, mathematical physicist, educator; b. Andalusia, Ala., Feb. 1, 1947; s. Frank Jennings Jr. and Anne (Kearley) T.; m. Jolanta Rokicka, Nov. 23, 1984. S.B., MIT, 1969; Ph.D., U. Md., 1976. NSF research mathematician U. Calif.-Berkeley, 1976-79; sr. research fellow Oxford (Eng.) U., 1979; research assoc. U. Tex.-Austin, 1979-81; assoc. prof. math. physics Tulane U.-New Orleans, 1981—; sr. research fellow U. Sussex, 1985. Author: l'Homme et le Cosmos, 1984; The Anthropic Cosmological Principle, 1985. Editor: Essays in General Relativity: A Festschrift for Abraham H. Taub, 1980; contbr. numerous articles to sci. publs. Mem. Am. Phys. Soc., Royal Astron. Soc., Internat. Soc. Gen. Relativity and Gravitation, Sigma Xi. Current Work: Research on topics in global general relativity: quantum cosmology, physics of black holes, and long-time evolution of the Universe. Subspecialties: General relativity; Cosmology. Home: 3915 St Charles Ave Apt 515 New Orleans LA 70115 Office: Tulane Univ 312 Gibson Hall New Orleans LA 70118

TIRAS, HERBERT GERALD, engineering company executive; b. Houston, Aug. 11, 1924; s. Samuel Louis and Rose (Seibel) T.; m. Aileen Wilkenfeld, Dec. 14, 1955; children: Sheryle, Leslie. Student Tex. A&M U., 1941-42; B.S., U. Houston, 1965; postgrad. Nat. Def. U., 1984. Registered prof. engr., Calif. Mfg. engr. Reed Roller Bit, Houston, 1942-60; pres. Tex-Truss, Houston, 1960-77; chief exec. officer OMNICO, Houston, 1977—; nat. dir. Coll. and Univ. Mfg. Ednl. Council, 1978—; resources dir., Region VI Fed. Emergency Mgmt. Agy., 1982—; mem. Nat. Def. Exec. Res. Mem. Soc. Mfg. Engrs. (cert. in mfg. mgmt., gen. mfg. engring. and robotics; named to Profl. Devel. Honor Roll), Robot Inst. Am., Robotics Internat., Marine Tech. Soc., Nat. Soc. Profl. Engrs., Machine Vision Assn. Lodge: Masons, Shriners. Patentee in field. Current Work: Application of robotics and remote sensing to sub-sea mining. Subspecialties: Robotics; Remote sensing (geoscience). Home: 9703 Runnymeade Houston TX 77096

TISCHLER, HERBERT, geology educator; b. Detroit, Apr. 28, 1924; s. Louis and Hermine (Leb) T.; m. Annette Zeidman, Aug. 10, 1954; children—Michael A., Robert D. B.S. in Geology, Wayne State U., 1950; M.A. in Paleontology, U. Calif.-Berkeley, 1955; Ph.D. in Geology, U. Mich., 1961. Instr. Wayne State U., Detroit, 1956-58; assoc. prof. No. Ill. U., DeKalb, 1958-65; prof., chmn. dept. earth scis. U. N.H., Durham, 1965—; NSF Sci. Faculty fellow Columbia U., N.Y.C., 1964-65. Co-dir. No. New Eng. Jr. Sci. and Humanities Symposium, U. N.H., 1979—; trustee Mt. Washington Obs., N.H., 1980—. Fellow Geol. Soc. Am.; mem. Am. Assn. Petroleum Geologists, Paleontological Soc., Nat. Assn. Geology Tchrs. (pres. New Eng. sect. 1969-70), Sigma Xi. Subspecialties: Paleontology; Stratigraphy. Office: Dept Earth Scis U NH Durham NH 03824

TISCHLER, MARC ELIOT, biochemistry educator, researcher; b. N.Y.C., Nov. 10, 1949; s. Henry M. and Harriet (Green) T.; m. Meryl Green, Aug. 5, 1979; children—Rebecca, Laura. B.A., Boston U., 1971; M.S., U. S.C., 1973; Ph.D., U. Pa., 1977. Postdoctoral fellow Harvard Med. Sch., Boston, 1977-79; asst. prof. U. Ariz. Sch. Medicine, Tucson, 1979-85, assoc. prof., 1985—. Mem. phys. edn. com. Jewish Community Ctr., Tucson. Am. Heart Assn. established investigator, 1982—; Muscular Dystrophy Assn. fellow, 1978-79; Am. Heart Assn. fellow, 1977-78. Mem. Biophys. Soc., Am. Physiol. Soc., Am. Heart Assn., Am. Soc. Biol. Chemists. Jewish. Current Work: Regulation of protein degradation in muscle by hormones and the response of this process and other aspects of muscle metabolism to fasting, diabetes, trauma and muscle disuse. Subspecialties: Biochemistry (biology); Biochemistry (medicine). Office: U Ariz Sch Medicine Tucson AZ 85724

TISHLER, MAX, chemist; b. Boston, Oct. 30, 1906; s. Samuel and Anna (Gray) T.; m. Elizabeth M. Verveer, June 17, 1934; children—Peter Verveer, Carl Lewis. B.S., Tufts Coll., 1928; M.A., Harvard U., 1933, Ph.D., 1934; D.Sc., Tufts U., 1956, Bucknell U., 1962, Phila. Coll. Pharmacy, 1966, U. Strathlyde, Glasgow, 1969, Rider Coll., 1970, Upsala Coll., 1972, Fairfield U., 1972, Wesleyan U., 1981; D.Eng., Stevens Inst. Tech., 1966. Teaching asst. Tufts Coll., 1924; Austin teaching fellow Harvard, 1930-34, research asso., 1934-36, instr. chemistry, 1936-37; research chemist Merck & Co., Inc., 1937-41, head sect. process devel., 1941-44, dir. devel. research, 1944-51, asso. dir. research and devel., 1951-54, v.p. sci. activities, chem. div., 1954-56; pres. Merck & Co., Inc. (Merck, Sharp & Dohme Research Lab. div.); pres. Merck & Co., Inc. (Merck Inst. Therapeutic Research), 1956-69, sr. v.p. research and devel., 1969-70; Rennebohm lectr. sch. pharmacy U. Wis., 1963; prof. chemistry Wesleyan U., Middletown, Conn., 1970-72, Univ. prof. scis., 1972-75, Univ. prof. scis. emeritus, 1975—, chmn. dept. chemistry, 1973-75; Mem. vis. com. dept. chemistry Harvard U., 1965-71, Sch. Pub. Health, 1963-69; mem. vis. com. dept. chem. engring. M.I.T.; trustee, chmn. vis. com. dept. chemistry Tufts U.; trustee Union (N.J.) Coll., 1965-70; assoc. trustee sci. U. Pa., 1960-65, 70; adv. council Newark Coll. Engring., 1956-59; adminstrv. bd. Tufts New Eng. Med. Center, adv. bd. Coll., 1964-68; adv. com. biol. scis. Princeton U., 1972-75. Author: (with J.B. Conant) Chemistry of Organic Compounds, 1937, Streptomycin, (with S. A. Waksman), 1949; co-chmn. study group, author: Chemistry in the Economy, 1973; Editorial bd.: Organic Syntheses, 1953-61, Separation Science, Clin. Pharmacology and Therapeutics; editor: Organic Syntheses, 1960-61. Bd. dirs. Merck & Co. Found.; bd. govs. Weizmann Inst.; mem. nat. adv. council Hampshire Coll., 1964-68; bd. visitors Faculty Health Scis., SUNY, Buffalo, 1965-68; trustee Royal Soc. Medicine Found., 1965-69; bd. sci. advisers Sloan Kettering Inst., 1974—. Recipient Merck & Co., Inc. Bd. Dirs. Sci. award (resulting in establishment Max Tishler Vis. Lectureship at Harvard and Max Tishler Scholarship (ann.) at Tufts Coll., 1951; medalist Indsl. Research Inst., 1961; medalist Soc. Chem. Industry, 1963; Julius W. Sturmer Meml. Lecture award Phila. Coll. Pharmacy, 1964; Chemistry lectr. Royal Swedish Acad. Engring. Scis., 1964; Kauffman Meml. lectr. Ohio State U., 1967; Chem. Pioneer award Am. Inst. Chemists, 1968; Gold medal, 1977; DuPont lectr. Dartmouth; Priestley medalist Am. Chem. Soc., 1970; Found. Patent award, 1970; Eli Whitney award Conn. Patent Law Assn., 1974; New Brunswick lectr. Am. Soc. Microbiology, 1974; C. Chester Stock award contbns. Sloan-Kettering Inst. Cancer Research, 1984. Fellow N.Y. Acad. Sci., Royal Soc. Chemistry (hon.), Chem. Soc. London, Am. Inst. Chemists, Soc. Chem. Industry (chmn. Am. sect. 1966, hon. v.p. 1968), AAAS, Acad. Pharm. Scis. of Am. Pharm. Assn. (hon. mem.), Conn. Acad. Sci. and Engring.; mem. Am. Acad. Arts and Scis., Indsl. Research Inst., Nat. Acad. Scis., Am. Chem. Soc. (chmn. dir. organic chemistry 1951, pres. 1972, bd. dirs. 1973), Swiss Chem. Soc., Conn. Acad. Scis. and Engring., Harvard Assn. Chemists, Société Chimique de France (hon.), Phi Beta Kappa, Sigma Xi, Pi Lambda Phi (Big Pi award 1951). Club: Chemists (N.Y.C.) (hon.). Patentee in field. Current Work: Synthesis of bioisoteres of l-amino acids and of small peptides containing these bioisoteres and to test them for possible therapeutic or enzyme inhibiting activities. Subspecialties: Organic chemistry; Medicinal chemistry. Home: 6 Red-Orange Rd Middletown CT 06457

TISI, GENNARO MICHAEL, physician, educator; b. N.Y.C., Sept. 26, 1935; s. Arthur Rocco and Anna Rose (Guerriero) T.; m. Margaret Anne Coniglare, Sept. 8, 1957; children—Judith Anne, Steven Arthur, Karen Eliaabeth. B.S., Fordham U., 1956; M.D., Gerogetown U., 1960. Diplomate Am. Bd. Internal Medicine. Intern, Georgetown U. Hosp., Washington, 1960-61, resident in medicine, 1963-65, pulmonary fellow, 1965-67; research pulmonary fellow U. Calif., San Francisco, 1967-68; dir. Lab. Pulmonary Function U. Calif., San Diego, 1968-73, asst., then assoc. prof., 1973-85, prof. medicine, 1985—, dir. Ednl. Clin. Service, 1982—; chief pulmonary sect. VA Hosp., San Diego, 1972-82; cons. U.S. Naval Hosp., Pendleton, Calif., 1971—. Author: Pulmonary Physiology in Clinical Medicine, 1980. Editor: Clinical Topics in Internal Medicine, 1982. Contbr. articles to profl. jours. Served to lt. M.C., USN, 1961-63. Recipient pulmonary acad. award NIH, 1981-85. Fellow ACP; mem. Western Soc. Clin. Research, Am. Physiol. Soc., Am. Fedn. Clin. Research, Alpha Omega Alpha. Roman Catholic. Current work: Staging of lung cancer; medical pulmonary education; pulmonary physiology; pulmonary mechanics; clinical research in pulmonary disease. Subspecialties: Pulmonary medicine; Internal medicine. Office: Pulmonary Div H-772D 225 Dickinson St San Diego CA 92103

TIVIN, FRED, analytical chemist, research executive; b. Chgo., Sept. 28, 1937; s. Edward and Min (Stone) T.; m. Sandra Sue Tivin, Dec. 12, 1941; children: David Scott, Mark Ingram, Brian Joseph. B.A., Kalamazoo Coll., 1958; M.S., U. Ill., 1960, Ph.D., 1963. Research chemist Exxon Co., 1963-66; with Procter & Gamble Co., Cin., 1966—, dir. analytical devel. and quality assurance, 1979—. Contbr. articles to profl. jours. Mem. Am. Chem. Soc., AAAS, Am. Soc. Quality Control, Sigma Xi, Phi Lambda Upsilon. Current Work: Separations, pharmaceutical product development, director of analytical development, quality assurance, and regulatory affairs for pharmaceutical product development. Subspecialties: Analytical chemistry; Pharmaceutical quality assurance. Office: PO Box 39175 Cincinnati OH 45247

TJIOE, SARAH ARCHAMBAULT, pharmacologist, educator; b. Phila., Oct. 12, 1944; d. Alfred and Joanna (Pomicter) Archambault; m. Gim Beng Tjioe, Aug. 19, 1967; children: Susan, James. B.A., U. Pa., 1966, Ph.D., 1971. Postdoctoral fellow Ohio State U., 1971-72, instr., 1972-75, asst. prof., 1975—. Pharm. Mfrs. Assn. Found. fellow, 1972-74. Mem. Neurosci. Soc., Am. Soc. Pharmacology and Exptl. Therapeutics. Current Work: Developing brain and effect of drugs on developing nerve. Subspecialties: Neurochemistry; Neuropharmacology. Office: 333 W 10th Ave Columbus OH 43210

TOBACK, F(REDERICK) GARY, physician, educator; b. Bklyn., Oct. 23, 1941; s. Israel Henry and Evelyn Adele (Friedman) T.; m. Phyllis Ruby Brooks, June 9, 1963; children—David Andrew, Alison Rachel, Jonathan Daniel. A.B. cum laude, Columbia U., 1963; M.D., N.Y. Sch. Medicine, 1967; Ph.D. in Biochemistry, Boston U., 1974. Diplomate Am. Bd. Internal Medicine. Intern and resident Cleve. Met. Gen. Hosp., 1967-69; research assoc. Boston U. Sch. Medicine, 1970-73; clin. fellow Harvard U. Med. Sch. and Beth Israel Hosp., Boston, 1974; asst. prof. medicine U. Chgo., 1974-79; assoc. prof., 1980-85, prof., 1985—. Contbr. articles to profl. jours. Fin. sec. Congregation Rodfei Zedek, Chgo., 1983—. Served with USN, 1979-80. Fellow Nat. Kidney Found., USPHS; Am. Cancer Soc. scholar; named Established Investigator, Am. Heart Assn. 1980-85; grantee Chgo. Heart Assn., Am. Heart Assn., USPHS. Mem. Am. Soc. Clin. Investigation, Am. Physiol. Soc., Central Soc. Clin. Research, Am. and Internat. Soc. Nephrology, Sci. Councils Am. Heart Assn. Jewish. Current work: Research mechanisms of growth regulation in kidney epithelial cells. Subspecialties: Cell biology; Nephrology. Office: U Chgo Sch Medicine 5841 S Maryland Ave Box 453 Chicago IL 60637

TOBE, STEPHEN SOLOMON, educator, physiologist; b. Niagara-on-the-Lake, Ont., Can., Oct. 11, 1944; s. John Harold and Rose (Bolter) T.; m. Martha, Oct. 19, 1969. B.Sc., Queen's U., Kingston, Ont., 1967; M.Sc., York U., Downsview, Ont., 1969; Ph.D., McGill U., Montreal, Que., Can., 1972. Research fellow Agrl. Research Council, U. Sussex, U.K., 1972-74; asst. prof. dept. zoology U. Toronto, 1974-78, assoc. prof., 1978-82, prof., 1982—. Contbr. articles to profl. jours. NRC of Can. bursary, 1968-70; scholar, 1970-72; postdoctoral fellow, 1972-74; E.W.R. Steacie Meml. fellow Natural Scis. and Engring. Research Council, 1982-84; recipient C. Gordon Hewitt award Entomol. Soc. Can., 1982. Fellow Royal Entomol. Soc. London; mem. AAAS, Am. Soc. Zoologists, Biochem. Soc., Can. Soc. Zoologists, Entomol. Soc. Can., Entomol. Soc. Ont., Soc. for Endocrinology, Soc. for Exptl. Biology, Sigma Xi. Current Work: Invertebrate endocrinology. Regulation of hormone biosynthesis and control of hormone titre in insects. Role of hormones in reproduction of invertebrates. Hormonal regulation of metamorphosis insects. Mode of action of hormone agonists/antagonists. Subspecialties: Physiology (biology); Reproductive biology. Home: 55 Marmot St Toronto ON M4S 2T4 Canada Office: Dept Zoology U Toronto 25 Harbord St Room 537 Toronto ON M5S 1A1 Canada

TOBIAS, CHARLES WILLIAM, chemical engineer, educator; b. Budapest, Hungary, Nov. 2, 1920; came to U.S., 1947, naturalized, 1952; s. Karoly and Elizabeth (Milko) T.; m. Marcia Rous, Sept. 10, 1950 (dec. Jan. 1981); children—Carla, Eric, Anthony.; m. Katalin Voros, June 19, 1982. Dipl. in chem. engring., U. Tech. Scis., Budapest, 1942, Ph.D., 1946. Registered profl. engr., Calif. Research, devel. engr. United Incandescent & Elec. Co., Ltd., Ujpest, Hungary, 1942-47; instr. phys. chemistry U. Tech. Scis., 1945-46; mem. faculty U. Calif.-Berkeley, 1947—, prof. chem. engring., 1960—, chmn. dept., 1967-72; faculty sr. scientist Lawrence Berkeley Lab., 1954—; assoc. research prof. Miller Inst. Basic Sci., 1958-59. Editor: (with Paul Delahay and Heinz Gerischer) Advances in Electrochemistry and Electrochemical Engineering, 1961—; editorial bd.: Jour. Applied Electrochemistry. Fellow AAAS; mem. Am. Chem. Soc., Am. Inst. Chem. Engrs. (Alpha Chi Sigma award 1983), Am. Soc. Engring. Edn., Electrochem. Soc. (assoc. editor Jour. 1955—, v.p. 1967-70, pres. 1970-71, Acheson award 1972, Henry B. Linford award for disting. teaching 1982, hon. mem. 1977—), Nat. Acad. Engring., Internat. Soc. Electrochemistry (v.p. 1975-76, pres. 1977-78), Deutsche Bunsen-Gesellschaft, Sigma Xi. Researcher numerous publs. on mass and charge transport in electrochem. systems, design of electrolytic processes, batteries and fuel cells, electrolysis in non-aqueous solvents. Subspecialty: Chemical engineering. Home: 524 Moraga Way Orinda CA 94563 Office: Dept Chem Engring U Calif Berkeley CA 94720

TOBIAS, LAWRENCE DAMIAN, pharmacologist; b. south Amboy, N.J., July 23, 1947; s. Charles George and Irene Patricia (Biesiada) T.; m. Mary-Margaret Bergamini, June 20, 1970 (div. Nov. 1984); 1 child, Malinda. B.A., U. Pa., 1969; M.Sc., U.S. Fla., 1971; M.B.A., Fairleigh Dickinson U., 1983. Research scientist, Hoffmann-LaRoche, Nutley, N.J., 1972—. Contbr. articles to profl. jours. Mem. Mem. Am. Chem. Soc., AAAS, Delta Mu Delta. Democrat. Roman Catholic. Current work: Currently interested in the pathophysiology of asthma and other bronchopulmonary diseases, and the development of biotechnological discoveries into useful products. Subspecialties: Pharmacology; Genetics and genetic engineering (medicine). Home: 20 Douglas Rd Glen Ridge NJ 07028 Office: Hoffmann-La Roche Inc 340 Kingsland St Nutley NJ 07110

TOBIN, ALLAN JOSHUA, biology educator, administrator; b. Manchester, N.H., Aug. 22, 1942; s. Maurice and Eve (Alter) T.; m. Elaine Munsey, Apr. 7, 1968 (div.); m. Janet Ruth Hadda, Mar. 22, 1981; children—David, Adam. B.S., MIT, 1963; Ph.D., Harvard U., 1969. Asst. prof. biology Harvard U., Cambridge, Mass., 1971-75, UCLA, 1975-81, assoc. prof. biology, 1981—; sci. dir. Hereditary Disease Found., Santa Monica, Calif., 1979—. Recipient Faculty Teaching award dept. biology UCLA, 1979. Mem. Soc. for Neurosci., AAAS. Current work: Molecular neurobiology. Subspecialties: Molecular biology; Neurobiology. Office: Dept Biology UCLA 405 Hilgard Ave Los Angeles CA 90024

TOBIN, GORDON ROSS, plastic surgeon; b. Twin Falls, Idaho, Jan. 6, 1943; s. Gordon Ross and Garnett Othalia (Peterson) T.; m. Elisabeth Ann Pelcher, Dec. 21, 1968; children: Christopher Ross, Anne Elise. A.B., Whitman Coll., 1965; M.D., U. Calif.-San Francisco, 1969. Diplomate: Am. Bd. Surgery, Am. Bd. Plastic Surgery. Intern San Francisco Gen. Hosp., 1969-70; resident U. Ariz. Affiliated Hosps., Tucson, 1970-76; practice medicine, specializing in plastic surgery, Louisville, 1977—; asst. prof. surgery U. Calif.-Irvine, 1976-77; assoc. prof. surgery U. Louisville, 1977-86, prof. surgery, 1986—; dir. U. Louisville (Plastic Surgery Research Lab.), 1977—. Paralized Vets of Am. grantee, 1975; Am. Cancer Soc. grantee, 1980. Fellow ACS; mem. Am. Assn. Plastic Surgeons, Soc. Univ. Surgeons, Plastic Surgery Research Council, Am. Soc. Plastic and Reconstructive Surgeons, Southeastern Soc. Plastic and Reconstructive Surgeons, Ky. Soc. Plastic and Reconstructive Surgery (pres. 1983), Sigma Xi, Delta Tau Delta. Democrat. Presbyterian. Current Work: Myology, microneurovascular anatomy, collagen biochemistry, soft tissue microcirculatory physiology, central nervous system wound healing, tissue transfer, burn physiology, implantable biomaterials, medical education. Subspecialties: Surgery; Anatomy and embryology. Home: 2413 Tavener St Louisville KY 40222 Office: Dept Surgery Univ Louisville 530 S Jackson St Louisville KY 40292

TOBLER, WALDO RUDOLPH, geography educator, cartographer; b. Portland, Oreg., Nov. 16, 1930; s. Verner and Hanny (Urech) T.; m. Dorothy Weix, Dec. 27, 1957 (div. Sept. 1979); children—Eric, Stephen; m. Rachel Mendenhall, Sept. 16, 1982. B.A., U. Wash., 1955, M.A., 1957, Ph.D., 1961. Asst. planner Pierce County, Tacoma, Wash., 1958-59; asst. prof. U. Mich., Ann Arbor, 1961-64, assoc. prof., 1965-68, prof., 1969-77; prof. dept. geography U. Calif.-Santa Barbara, 1977—; vis. prof. U. Minn., Mpls., 1968, U. Zurich, Switzerland, 1973; research scientist Internat. Inst. for Applied Systems Analysis, Austria, 1975; chmn. Math. Social Sci. Bd., 1974. Contbr. articles to profl. jours. Served with U.S. Army, 1948-52. Mem. Assn. Am. Geographers (Meritorious Service award 1968), Assn. Computing Machinery, Am. Statis. Assn., Population Assn. Am., Am. Congress on Surveying and Mapping, Nat. Acad. Scis., Am. Geog. Soc. (hon.), Sierra Club, Phi Beta Kappa, Sigma Xi, Phi Kappa Phi. Club: Swiss (pres. 1980-82, treas. 1983-85) (Santa Barbara). Current work: Modelling geographical movement, map projections, cartographic algorithms, geographical information systems. Subspecialties: Mathematical geography; Graphics, image processing, and pattern recognition. Office: Dept Geography U Calif Santa Barbara CA 93106

TODARO, GEORGE JOSEPH, pathologist; b. N.Y.C., July 1, 1937; s. George J. and Antoinette (Piccinni) T.; m. Jane Lehv, Aug. 12, 1962; children: Wendy C., Thomas M., Anthony A. B.S., Swarthmore Coll., 1958; M.D., N.Y. U., 1963. Intern N.Y. U. Sch. Medicine, N.Y.C., 1963-64, fellow in pathology, 1964-65, asst. prof. pathology, 1965-67; staff assoc. Viral Carcinogenesis br. Nat. Cancer Inst., Bethesda, Md., 1967-70, head molecular biology sect., 1969-70; chief Viral Carcinogenesis br. Nat. Cancer Inst. (Lab. Viral Carcinogenesis), 1970-83; sci. dir. Oncogen, Seattle, 1983—; faculty mem. Genetics Program, George Washington U.; prof. pathology U. Wash., Seattle, 1983—. Editor: Cancer Research, 1973—, Archives of Virology, 1976—, Jour. Biol. Chemistry, 1979—; contbr. articles to profl. jours. Served as med. officer USPHS, 1967-69. Recipient Borden Undergrad. Research award, 1963, USPHS Career Devel. award, 1967, HEW Superior Service award, 1971, Gustav Stern award for virology, 1972, Parke-Davis award in exptl. pathology, 1975; Walter Hubert lectr. Brit. Cancer Soc., 1977. Mem. Am. Soc. Microbiology, Am. Assn. Cancer Research, Soc. Exptl. Biology and Medicine, Am. Soc. Biol. Chemists, Am. Soc. Clin. Investigation. Subspecialty: Cancer research (medicine). Home: 1940 15th Ave E Seattle WA 98112 Office: Oncogen 3005 1st Ave Seattle WA 98121

TODD-SPRING, DEBORAH ANN, engineer, consultant; b. Long Island City, N.Y., June 18, 1955; d. Ralph and Mae W. (Milligan) T.; m. S.F. Spring, June 4, 1985. B.S. in Mech. Engring, Union Coll., 1976; M.S. in Mech. Engring, Rensselaer Poly. Inst., 1978; M.B.A., Harvard U., 1985. Registered profl. engr., N.Y. Mech. design engr. Large Steam Turbine div. Gen. Electric Co., Schenectady, 1976-78, mech. engr. projects engring ops., 1978-79, project engr. dept. internat. projects, N.Y.C., 1980-83; mech. engr. Gibbs & Hill, Inc., N.Y.C., 1979-80; lectr. in field. Recipient Gen. Electric Co. Top Young Engrs. award, 1982. Mem. Nat. Soc. Profl. Engrs., ASME, Tau Beta Phi. Republican. Clubs: Appalachian Mountains, Appalachian Trail Conf. Current Work: Optimization of power plant cycles; waterhammer; water treatment control and supervision of architect-engr. firms performing proposal/contract engring. on internat. and domestic power plant projects. Subspecialties: Power engineering; Systems engineering. Home: 6 Lorne Grove Camberwell 3124 Victoria Australia

TODOROVIC, RADMILO ANTONIJE, veterinarian, technical development executive; b. Zabojnica, Yugoslavia, Oct. 30, 1927; came to U.S., 1960, naturalized, 1963; s. Antonije Ilija and Rajka (Otasevic) T.; m. Lillian Djukic, June 9, 1960; children—Jovan, Ilija, Joan, Jane. D.V.M., U. Belgrade, Yugoslavia, 1953; M.S., U. Wis., 1963; Ph.D., U. Ill., 1967. Diplomate Am. Coll. Vet. Medicine. Veterinarian, Vetinary Hosp., Bare-Knic, Yugoslavia, 1953-55; asst. prof. U. Belgrade, 1955-60; veterinarian Am. Breeders, Madison, Wis., 1960-63; dir. Ctr. Tropical Agri., Cali, Colombia, 1968-78; assoc. prof. Tex. A&M U., College Station, 1968-80; mgr. research and devel. Internat. Minerals & Chem. Corp., Terre Haute, Ind., 1980—, research veterinarian, 1983—; research veterinarian Colombian Inst. of Agr., Bogota, 1968-72; cons. U.S. Aid-Vet. Dept., Lima, Peru, Micronesia, 1969-73; invited speaker World Vet. Congress, 1970, 75 and Agrl. Seminar, China, 1984. Contbr. over 120 articles to profl. jours. and textbooks. Postdoctoral fellow North Atlantic Treaty Pact. Mem. Am. Vet. Med. Assn., Ill. Soc. for Med. Research, Conf. on Research Workers in Animal Diseases, Soc. of Protozoologists, Assn. of Univ. Profs., AAAS, Latin Am. Assn. for Agrl. Scis., Colombian Vet. Med. Assn., N.Y. Acad. Scis., Soc. Tropical Vet. Medicine, Ind. State Vet. Med. Assn., Smithsonian Assocs., U.S. Animal Health Assn., Am. Assn. Industrial Vets., Sigma Xi, Phi Sigma, Phi Zeta. Current work: Veterinary science, parasitology, immunology, reproduction, nutrition, tropical diseases, control of internal and external parasites. Home: 1355 Winterberry Ct Terre Haute IN 47802 Office: Internat Minerals & Chem Corp PO Box 207 Terre Haute IN 47808

TOGA, ARTHUR WARREN, neuroscientist, consultant; b. Boston, July 19, 1952; s. Carl J. and Elayne B. (Ullian) T.; m. Deborah Ruth Luten, Oct. 22, 1983. B.S. U. Mass., 1974; M.S., St. Louis U., 1976, Ph.D., 1978. Asst. prof. neurology Washington U. Sch. Med., St. Louis, 1981—; mgr., application engring. APTEC Computer Systems, Portland, Oreg., 1984—. Mem. Am. Psychol. Assn., AAAS, Soc. Neurosci., Nat. Computer Graphics Assn., Assn. for Computing Machinery. Current work: Biomedical imaging; image processing; auto/adiogryly. Subspecialties: Neurophysiology; Graphics, image processing, and pattern recognition. Office: Dept Neurology Washington Univ Sch of Med 660 South Euclid Saint Louis MO 63110

TÖKÉS, ZOLTÁN ANDRÁS, biochemistry educator; b. Budapest, Hungary, May 14, 1940; s. Elemér and Marianne (Tilzer) T.; m. Dorcas-May Vanian; children: Krisztina, Géza. B.Sc., U. So. Calif., 1964; Ph.D. in Biochemistry, Calif. Inst. Tech., 1971. Lectr. U. Malaya Sch. Medicine, Kuala Lumpur, Malaysia, 1971-72; ind. investigator Basel Inst. for Immunology, Switzerland, 1972-74; asst. prof. biochemistry U. So. Calif. Sch. Medicine, Los Angeles, 1974-79, assoc. prof., 1980—; dir. cell culture and tumor marker labs. U. So. Calif. Sch. Medicine (Comprehensive Cancer Ctr.), 1977—. Contbr. articles to profl. jours. Nat. Cancer Inst. grantee. Mem. Am. Soc. Biol. Chemists, Am. Assn. Cancer Research, Am. Assn. Pathologists, Am. Soc. Cell Biology, N.Y. Acad. Scis. Patentee in field. Current Work: Detection of cell surface changes due to malignancy and other pathological conditions; molecular basis of cell-cell recognition. Subspecialties: Biochemistry (biology); Cancer research (medicine). Office: 1303 N Mission Rd Los Angeles CA 90033

TOLBERT, LESLIE PAGE, neurobiologist, educator; b. Boston, May 13, 1951; m. Paul A. St. John; children—Lindsay, Alexander. A.B., Radcliffe Coll., 1973; Ph.D., Harvard U., 1978. Postdoctoral fellow Harvard Med. Sch., Boston, 1978-81; research assoc. Harvard U., Cambridge, Mass., 1981-82; asst. prof. Georgetown U., D.C., 1982—. Contbr. articles to profl. jours. Mem. Soc. Neurosci., Am. Assn. Anatomists, AAAS. Current work: Interactions among nerve cells and nonneuronal cells during development of nervous system; structure, function and development of synaptic networks. Subspecialties: Neurobiology; Developmental biology. Office: Dept Anatomy Georgetown U Sch Medicine 3900 Reservoir Rd NW Washington DC 20007

TOLBERT, NATHAN EDWARD, biochemist, educator; b. Twin Falls, Idaho, May 19, 1919; married. B.S., U. Calif.-Berkeley, 1941; M.S., U. Wis., 1948, Ph.D., 1950. Research assoc. dept. viticulture U. Calif.-Davis, 1941-43; biochemist sci. adminstrn., div. biology and medicine AEC, Washington, 1950-52; profl. collaborator U.S. Dept. Agr. Bur. Plant Industry, Beltsville, Md., 1951-52; sr. biochemist biology div. Oak Ridge Nat. Lab., 1952-58; prof. biochemistry Mich. State U., East Lansing, 1958—. Patentee plant growth regulators. Mem. editorial bd. Archives Biochemistry and Biophysics, Plant Physiology, Phtyochemistry; contbr. articles to profl. jours. Grantee NSF, NIH, Mich. State U. Mem. Nat. Acad. Sci., Am. Soc. Biol. Chemists, Am. Soc. Plant Physiology, Am. Chem. Soc., Am. Inst. Biol. Scis., AAAS, Plant Growth Regulator Working Group, Fulbright Alumni Assn., Sci. Socs. Presidents, Sigma Xi. Current work: Photosynthetic carbon metabolism; photorespiration; peroxisomes. Subspecialty: Plant physiology (biology). Office: Dept Biochemistry Mich State U East Lansing MI 48824

TOLCHINSKY, PAUL D., psychologist; b. Cleve., Sept. 30, 1946; s. Sanford M. and Frances (Klein) T.; m. Laura S. Schermer, Nov. 2, 1968; children: Heidi E., Dana M. B.A., Bowling Green State U., 1971; Ph.D., Purdue U., 1978. Trainer Detroit Bank & Trust Co., 1971-73; cons. Babock & Wilcox, Barberton, Ohio, 1973-75, Gen. Foods Corp., West Lafayette, Ind., 1975-77; prof. psychology U. Akron, Ohio, 1978-81; pres. Creative Work-Life, Shaker Heights, Ohio, 1979—; cons. in field; prof. Bowling Green (Ohio) State U., 1980-82. Contbr. articles to profl. jours. Served with U.S. Army, 1966-69. Bowling Green State U. research grantee, 1971; David Ross grantee Purdue Found., 1977-78. Mem. Acad. Mgmt., Am. Psychol. Assn., Am. Mgmt. Assn. Democrat. Jewish. Current Work: Improving orgnl. effectiveness and efficiency thru use of behavioral and socio-tech. sci. applications. Subspecialty: Behavioral psychology. Office: 3310 Warrensville Rd Shaker Heights OH 44122

TOLEDO-PEREYRA, LUIS HORACIO, surgeon, educator; b. Nogales, Ariz., Oct. 19, 1943; s. Jose Horacio and Elia Elvira (Pereyra) Toledo; m. Marjean May, Mar. 21, 1974; children—Alexander Horacio, Suzanne Elizabeth. B.S. magna cum laude, Regis Coll., Hermosillo, Mex., 1960; M.D. with high honors, U. Mex., Mexico City, 1967, M.S. in Internal Medicine, 1970; Ph.D. in Surgery, U. Minn., 1976, Ph.D. in History of Medicine, 1984. Rotating intern Juarez Hosp., Mexico City, 1966; resident in internal medicine Nat. Inst. Nutrition, Mexico City, 1968-70; resident in gen. surgery U. Minn., Mpls., 1970-76; resident in thoracic and vascular surgery U. Chgo., 1976-77; dir. surg. research Henry Ford Hosp., Detroit, 1977-79; chief transplantation, dir. surg. research Mt. Carmel Mercy Hosp., Detroit, 1979—; prof. health scis. Mercy Coll., Detroit, 1983—; cons. Hutzel Hosp., Detroit, 1983—, Providence Hosp., Southfield, Mich., 1983-84. Editor: Organ Procurement and Preservation for Transplantation, 1982; The Pancreas: Principles of Medical and Surgical Practice, 1984; Immunology Essentials of Surgical Practice; mem. editorial bd. Dialysis and Transplantation, 1979—. Contbr. numerous articles to sci. jours. Patentee in field. Recipient Outstanding Achievement award U. Mex., 1961, 64, 67, Cecil Lehman Mayer Research award Am. Coll. Chest Physicians, 1975. Mem. Am. Soc. Transplant Surgeons, Am. Assn. Acad. Surgery (Resident Research award 1974), Am. Soc. Immunologists, Am. Soc. Artificial Internal Organs, Fedn. Socs. Exptl. Biology. Clubs: Grosse Pointe Yacht (Mich.). Current work: Transplant immunology; organ preservation; artificial internal organs; 19th century English medical history; the work of Sydney Ringer. Subspecialties: Transplant surgery; Artificial organs and prostheses. Home: 93 Lothrop Grosse Pointe Farms MI 48236 Office: Mt Carmel Mercy Hosp 6071 W Outer Dr Detroit MI 48235

TOLLNER, ERNEST WILLIAM, agricultural engineering researcher, educator; b. Maysville, Ky., July 14, 1949; s. Ernest Edward and Ruby (Henderson) T. B.S.A.E., U. Ky., 1972, M.S.A.E., 1974; Ph.D., Auburn U., 1980. Grad. asst. U. Ky., Lexington, 1972-74, research specialist, 1974-76; grad. asst. Auburn U., Ala., 1977-80; asst. prof. agrl. engring. U. Ga.-Griffin, 1980—; proposal reviewer Univ. Council on Water Relations, Lincoln, Nebr., 1983; participant U. Ga. Research Found., Cambridge, Eng., 1984. Contbr. articles to profl. jours. Patentee penetrometer for simulating plant roots. Mem. Am. Soc. Agrl. Engrs. (tech. reviewer 1980—, vice chmn. PM 45 soil dynamics com. 1984), Soil Conservation Soc. Am. (tech. reviewer 1983—, subcom. chmn. SW223 erosion research com. 1984). Current work: Characterizing and improving soil physical properties related to crop growth through reforestation, crop residue management, waste application, legumes and other cultural practices and erosion prevention. Subspecialties: Agricultural engineering; Environmental engineering. Home: 36 Johnson Rd Orchard Hill GA 30266 Office: Agrl Engring Dept Ga Expt Sta Experiment GA 30212

TOLMAN, EDWARD LAURIE, biochem. pharmacologist; b. Chelsea, Mass., Oct. 9, 1942; s. Max and Frances (Baker) T.; m. Anita Young, June 25, 1967; 1 dau., Jennifer. B.A., U. Mass., 1964, M.A., 1965; Ph.D., SUNY, Syracuse, 1970. Postdoctoral fellow Hershey Med. Center, 1969-72; sr. scientist Lederle Labs., 1972-76, project leader, 1977-78, group leader, 1978-80; sect. head biochem. pharmacology Ortho Pharm. Corp., Raritan, N.J., 1980-84, asst. dir. biochem. pharmacology/microbiology, 1984—; adj. asst. prof. human biochemistry Fairleigh Dickinson U. Sch. Dentistry, 1979—. Contbr. articles to profl. jours. Mem. Am. Soc. Pharmacology and Exptl. Therapeutics, Am. Diabetes Assn., Soc. Exptl. Biology and Medicine, Am. Chem. Soc., N.J. Acad. Sci., Sigma Xi. Current work: Prostaglandins, inflammation, diabetes drug discovery; research administration. Subspecialties: Cellular pharmacology; Biochemistry (medicine). Office: Biochem Research Ortho Pharm Corp Raritan NJ 08869

TOM, BALDWIN H., immunologist, conference developer and consultant; b. San Francisco, Sept. 19, 1940; s. Fred and Lily (Wong) T.; m. Madeline R. Nobori, June 13, 1964; children: Darren, Alyson. B.A. in Biochemistry, U. Calif.-Berkeley, 1963; M.S., U. Ariz., 1967, Ph.D. in Microbiology and Immunology, 1970. Research fellow in immunology Stanford U. Med. Sch., 1970-73; asst. prof. Northwestern U. Med. Sch., 1973-77; asst. prof., supr. Human Tumor Immunobiology Lab., U. Tex. Med. Sch.-Houston, 1977-83, assoc. prof. biochemistry, molecular biology, surgery, 1983—; chmn./organizer Nat. Symposium on Liposomes and Immunobiology, 1980, Nat. Symposium on Hybridomas and Cellular Immortality, 1981, Internat. Beijing Symposium on Interaction Traditional Chinese Medicine and Western Medicine: Impact on Immunology, 1983. Author: books, including Hybridomas and Cellular Immortality; contbr. numerous articles, chpts. to profl. publs. Recipient Research Career Devel. award Nat. Cancer Inst., 1979; Stanford U. Dean's fellow, 1970; Internat. Union Against Cancer exchange fellow, 1981. Mem. Am. Assn. Immunologists, Am. Assn. Cancer Research, Soc. Exptl. Biology and Medicine, N.Y. Acad. Scis., Fedn. Am. Scientists, Sigma Xi, Beta Beta Beta. Presbyterian. Patentee cellular prodn. of carcinoembryonic antigen. Current Work: Molecular immunology of human cancers. Subspecialties: Cancer research (medicine); Cellular engineering. Office: U Tex Med Sch MSMB 6240 Houston TX 77030

TOMANEK, ROBERT JOSEPH, anatomy scientist, educator; b. Omaha, Apr. 5, 1937; s. Joseph and Marie (Zatocil) T.; m. Rita Rose Svoboda, Aug. 12, 1961; children—Lisa Rose Evans, Paul Joseph, Ann Marie. B.S., U. Omaha, 1959; Ph.D., U. Iowa, 1967. Asst. prof. anatomy Simon Fraser U., Burnaby, B.C., 1967-70; NIH postdoctoral fellow U. Iowa, Iowa City, 1971-72, asst. prof., 1972-76, assoc. prof., 1976-82, prof. anatomy, 1982—; ad hoc reviewer NIH, 1982-84. Assoc. editor Anatomical Record, 1980—; reviewer numerous sci. jours.; contbr. articles to sci. jours. Mem. Am. Physiol. Soc., Am. Heart Assn., Am. Assn. Anatomists, Am. Soc. Cell Biology, Internat. Soc. Heart Research. Democrat. Roman Catholic. Current work: Heart in hypertension; myocyte ultrastructure; coronary vessels and ventricular function. Subspecialties: Cytology and histology; Cell biology (medicine). Office: Dept Anatomy U Iowa Coll Medicine Iowa City IA 52242

TOME, RICHARD EARLE, mechanical engineer; b. Berea, Ohio, Mar. 1, 1936; s. Lloyd Edward and Ruth Helen (Blazek) T.; m. Eileen Costolo, July 1, 1961; children: Brian, Kevin, Kari. B.A., Baldwin Wallace Coll., 1959; B.S.M.E., Columbia U., 1959; M.S.M.E., Case Inst. Tech., 1961. Registered profl. engr., Pa. Grad. asst. dept. mech. engring. Case Inst. Tech., 1959-61; mech. engr. water reactor divs. Westinghouse Electric Corp., Pitts., 1961—, fellow engr. in primary components engring., plant engring. div., 1976—. Author numerous company publs. Ruling elder First Presbyterian Ch., Murrysville, Pa., 1978—; adult committeman Troop 205 Westmoreland-Fayette council Boy Scouts Am., 1981-84. Mem. ASME (cert. for services in devel. standards and codes 1978, mem. Working Group on Vessel Design of Sect. III Nuclear Power Plant Components of Boiler and Pressure Vessel Code 1963—). Republican. Inventor self adjustable reactor vessel head insulation, improved reactor vessel head removable insulation. Current Work: Design, analysis and fabrication of pressurized water nuclear power plant reactor vessels and reactor coolant loop piping. Subspecialty: Mechanical engineering. Home: 3710 Gleneagle Dr Murrysville PA 15668 Office: Westinghouse Electric Corp Plant Engring Div PO Box 355 Pittsburgh PA 15230

TOMEI, L. DAVID, cell physiologist; b. Williamsport, Pa., Apr. 27, 1945; s. Louis J. and Florence V. (Orbanac) T.; m. Angela M. Huber, Sept. 3, 1966; m. Louise M. Bartels, July 27, 1978; children: Annette, Monica, Maria, David, Victoria. B.S., Canisius Coll., 1968; M.S., SUNY, Roswell Park Meml. Inst., Buffalo, 1970, Ph.D., 1974. Research chemist Agrl. Research Service, U.S. Dept. Agr., Plum Island Animal Disease Ctr., 1974-75; assoc. dir. research Don Monti Leukemia Found.; career scientist dept. medicine North Shore Univ. Hosp., L.I., N.Y., 1975-76; sr. cancer research scientist Roswell Park Meml. Inst., Buffalo., 1976-80; Comprehensive research scientist Ohio State U. Cancer Ctr., Columbus, 1980—. Contbr. articles to profl. jours. Mem. Am. Assn. Cancer Research., Cell Kinetics Soc. Current Work: Regulation of the phenotypic expression of malignancy cell cycle control; information transfer, cell culture, image analysis, laser optics, high speed scanning. Subspecialties: Cell study oncology; Optical image processing. Office: Ohio State U Comprehensive Cancer Center Suite 302 410 W 12th Ave Columbus OH 43210

TOMLINSON, RICHARD LEE, nuclear physicist; b. Davenport, Iowa, July 16, 1929; s. Thell Dodson and Ayliffe Hazel (Lewis) T.; m. Carol Jeanette Nyre, July 11, 1959; children: Kari Lee, Kyle Marie. B.S., Lake Forest Coll., 1951; postgrad., U. Calif., Berkeley, 1955-56; cert. bus., Diablo Valley Coll., Pleasant Hill, Calif., 1976. Physicist Gen. Electric Co., Richland, Wash., 1951-55, N. Am. Aviation Co., Canoga Park, Calif., 1955-62; physicist Aerojet-Gen. Corp., San Ramon, Calif., 1962-74; mgr. reactor ops. Aerotest Ops. Inc., San Ramon, 1974-78, Westinghouse Hanford Co., Richland, Wash., 1978—. Author: Nuclear Reactor Operator Training Manual, 1983. Mem. Am. Nuclear Soc., Am. Soc. Non-Destructive Testing, ASTM. Current Work: Design, construction, operation of reactor facilities for commercial and government use for neutron radiography applications. Subspecialties: Nuclear engineering; Nuclear fission. Office: Westinghouse Hanford Co PO Box 1970 Richland WA 99352

TOMLINSON, W. JOHN, physicist; b. Phila., Apr. 3, 1938; s. W. John and Olive (Greatorex) T.; m. Barbara Kellog, June 10, 1963; 1 child, Robin B. S.B., M.I.T., 1960, Ph.D. in Physics, 1963. Mem. tech. research staff Bell Telephone Labs., Holmdel, N.J., 1965-81, supr. optical disk rec. group, 1981-83; dist. research mgr. lightwave component tech. research Bell Communications Research, Red Bank, N.J., 1984—. Served to capt. U.S. Army, 1963-65. Mem. Optical Soc. Am., Am. Phys. Soc. Current Work: Optical disk recording technology and media; nonlinear optics. Subspecialties: Optics research; Laser data storage and reproduction. Home: 22 Indian Creek Rd Holmdel NJ 07733 Office: Bell Communications Research 331 Newman Springs Rd Red Bank NJ 07701

TOMONTO, CHARLES VINCENT, metallurgist, researcher; b. Troy, N.Y., Aug. 24, 1958; s. James Robert and Irene (Terenzio) T. B.S. in Mech. Engring., U. Miami, 1980; M.S. in Materials Engring., Rensselaer Poly. Inst., 1983, Ph.D. in Materials Engring., 1986. Project engr., co-op Cordis Corp., Miami, Fla., 1978-80; researcher Rensselaer Poly. Inst., Troy, 1980-86, Communications Unltd., Raleigh, N.C., 1983-86. Recipient C. Edward Anderson award Faculty Dept. Mech. Engring., U. Miami, 1980. Mem. Am. Soc. Metals, ASME (student pres. 1979-80), AIME, Tau Beta Pi, Pi Tau Sigma. Current work: Ultrasonic testing of premartensitic effects in Fe-Ni-Cr-C alloys. Subspecialties: Metallurgical engineering; Non-destructive testing. Home: 198 Pawling Ave Apt 12 Troy NY 12180Office: Rensselaer Poly Inst MRC 168 Troy NY 12181

TOMREN, DOUGLAS ROY, optical physicist; b. Buffalo, July 16, 1945; s. Raymond Henry and Dorothy Gertrude (Berg) T.; m. Linda Sue Kenne, Aug. 24, 1971; children: Holly Ann, Erik Roy, Michael Douglas. B.S. in Physics, UCLA, 1967; postgrad., Optical Scis. Center, U. Ariz., 1971. Mem. tech. staff RCA, Burlington, Mass., 1967-69; laser engr. Martin Marietta Co., Orlando, Fla., 1969; holographer TRW, Redondo Beach, Calif., 1972-76, laser effects physicist, 1976—, project mgr., 1978—. Mem. 4th dist. adv. council City of Long Beach, Calif., 1979—. Mem. Optical Soc. Am., AIAA. Democrat. Methodist. Current Work: Laser effects testing, laser research and development; applied research in nonlinear optical phenomena, development and testing of laser hardened materials. Subspecialties: Laser research; Holography. Office: TRW One Space Park R1/1112 Redondo Beach CA 90278

TONDA, RICHARD DALE, mechanical engineer; b. Oskaloosa, Iowa, Apr. 12, 1952; s. Richard William and Betty Lee (Trinkle) T.; m. Vicki Lynn Sterling, Aug. 5, 1972; children—Richard Aaron, Heather Richelle. B.M.E., Gen. Motors Inst., 1975; M.S. in Engring. Mechanics, Mich. State U., 1976; Ph.D., Tex.A&M U., 1985. Registered profl. engr., Tex. Jr. engr. Oldsmobile div. Gen. Motors Corp., Lansing, Mich., 1974-75; research asst. Mich. State U., East Lansing, 1975-76; asst. prof. Coll. Engring., Tex. A&M U., College Station, 1976-79; head, proving grounds Tex. Transp. Inst., Tex. A&M U. System, College Station, 1978-80; mgr. materials and structures lab. Tex. Transp. Inst., Tex. A&M U., College Station, 1983-84, mgr. automotive research program, 1980—; dir. Engitech, Inc., College Station. Author: Graphics for Engineers III, 1978. Mem. Soc. Automotive Engrs., Tex. Soc. Profl. Engrs. (chpt. pres. 1983-84, Outstanding Young Engr. 1984). Republican. Methodist. Lodge: Masons. Current work: Research in automotive emissions and fuel economy, vehicle handling and design; work in area of solid mechanics research into constitutive behavior of high-performance, fiber-reinforced composites, especially as they apply to determining and predicting fracture behavior of the composite. Subspecialties: Mechanical engineering; Composite materials. Office: Texas Transp Inst Texas A&M U College Station TX 77843

TONEGAWA, SUSUMU, biology educator; b. Nagoya, Japan, Sept. 5, 1939; came to U.S., 1963; s. Tsutomu and Miyoko (Masuko) T. B.S., Kyoto U., Japan, 1963; Ph.D., U. Calif.-San Diego, 1968. Research asst. U. Calif.-San Diego, 1963-64, teaching asst., 1964-68; mem. Basel Inst. Immunology, Switzerland, 1971-81; prof. biology MIT, Cambridge, 1981—. Editorial bd.: Jour. Molecular and Cellular Immunology. Recipient Cloetta prize, 1978, Avery Landsteiner prize Gesselschaft fur Immunologie, 1981, Louisa Gross Horwitz prize Columbia U., 1982, award Gardiner Found. Internat., Toronto, Can., 1983; Order of Culture of Japan, 1984; named Person with Cultural Merit Japanese Govt., 1983. Hon. mem. Am. Assn. Immunologists, Scandinavian Soc. Immunology. Current work: Understanding of the molecular and cellular mechanisms of immune recognitions by recombinant DNA and related technologies. Subspecialties: Immunobiology and immunology; Molecular biology. Office: MIT 77 Massachusetts Ave Cambridge MA 02139

TOOME, VOLDEMAR, chemist; b. Parnu, Estonia, Sept. 10, 1924; came to U.S. 1957, naturalized, 1963; s. Jakob and Anna (Palberg) T.; m. Hedwig Lager, July 16, 1952; children—Birgit Kai. M.S. in Pharmacy, U. Bonn, 1948, M.S. in Chemistry, 1952, Ph.D. in Phys. Chem., 1954. Sci. asst. U. Bonn, W.Ger., 1954; dept. head E. Merck, A.G., Darmstadt, W.Ger., 1954-57; sr. chemist Hoffman-La Roche, Inc., Nutley, N.J., 1958-65, research fellow, 1966-72, group chief, 1973-78, sr. group chief, 1979—. Contbr. numerous articles to profl. jours. and book. Patentee in field. Mem. Am. Chem. Soc., AAAS, N.Y. Acad. Scis., Sigma Xi. Current work: Molecular spectroscopy, analytical and physical chemistry, physical organic chemistry, electrochemistry, automation of analytical and service laboratories, microchemistry, etc. Subspecialties: Physical chemistry; Analytical chemistry. Home: 18 Carrie Ct Nutley NJ 07110

TOOMEY, JOHN PATRICK, III, electrical engineer; b. Beverly, Mass., Feb. 21, 1942; s. John Patrick, II and Thelma Elizabeth (Detour) T.; m. Phyllis Chandler Bailey, Aug. 15, 1964; 1 child, Michael. B.S.E.E., Merrimack Coll., 1964; M.S.E.E., U. R.I., 1966, Ph.D. in Elec. Engring., 1970. Registered profl. engr., Mass. Instr. elec. engring. U. R.I., Kingston, 1969-70; mem. tech. staff Bell Labs., Whippany, N.J., 1970-74, Sperry Research Ctr., Sudbury, Mass., 1974-83; prin. engr. Raytheon Co., Wayland, Mass., 1983-84, sect. mgr., 1984—; lectr. in elec. engring. Grad. Sch. of Engring. Northeastern U., Boston, 1982—. Contbr. articles to profl. jours. NASA fellow, 1967; NSF trainee, 1968. Mem. IEEE (sr. mem.), Am. Assn. for Artificial Intelligence. Current work: Radar and sonar signal and information processing, detection and estimation, decision theory, pattern recognition. Subspecialties: Systems engineering; Radar, sonar. Office: Raytheon Co 430 Boston Post Rd Wayland MA 01778

TOOMEY, JOSEPH EDWARD, JR., chemist; b. Somerville, N.J., Aug. 8, 1943; s. Joseph Edward Sr. and Waunetta Erma (Shaffer) T.; m. Barbara Joan Forrest, Nov. 4, 1967; children—Rose Katherine, Sean Patrick, Amanda Helen, Kathleen Waunetta. B.S. in Chemistry, Rider Coll., 1970; Ph.D. in Organic Chemistry, Purdue U., 1975. Research chemist Reilly Tar & Chem. Corp., Indpls., 1975-81, group leader, 1981-83, sect. head, 1983—. Author: Advances in Heterocyclic Chemistry, 37, 1984. Patentee in field. Advisor Jr. Achievement, Indpls., 1979. Served to EO3 USMC, 1961-65. Mem. AAAS, Am. Chem. Soc. Republican. Clubs: Circle of Janus (Indpls.), IDEA Parent Group (Indpls.). Current work: Industrial chemistry, electroorganic synthesis, bioactive organics, herbicides, insecticides, biocides, pyridine chemistry, hetrocyclic chemistry, plant growth regulators. Subspecialty: Organic chemistry. Home: 2035 Rosedale Dr Indianapolis IN 46227 Office: Reilly Tar & Chem Corp 1500 S Tibbs Ave Indianapolis IN 46241

TOOMRE, ALAR, theoretical astronomer, mathematics educator; b. Rakvere, Estonia, Feb. 5, 1937; came to U.S., 1949, naturalized, 1955; s. Elmar and Linda (Aghen) T.; m. Joyce Stetson, June 14, 1958; children: Lars, Erik, Anya. B.S. in Aero. Engring, MIT, 1957, B.S. in Physics, 1957; Ph.D., Manchester (Eng.) U., 1960. Instr. math. MIT, Cambridge, 1960-62, asst. prof., 1963-65, assoc. prof., 1965-70, prof. applied math., 1970—; fellow Inst. Advanced Study, Princeton, N.J., 1962-63; vis. assoc. Calif. Inst. Tech., Pasadena, 1969-70. Guggenheim fellow, 1969-70; Fairchild scholar Calif. Inst. Tech., 1975; MacArthur fellow, 1984—. Fellow AAAS; mem. Am. Astron. Soc., Internat. Astron. Union, Math. Assn. Am., Am. Acad. Arts and Scis., Nat. Acad. Scis. Current Work: Research in dynamics of galaxies. Subspecialty: Applied mathematics. Office: Room 2-371 MIT Cambridge MA 02139

TOP, FRANKLIN HENRY, JR., physician, army officer, researcher; b. Detroit, Mar. 1, 1936; s. Franklin Henry and Mary (Madden) T.; m. Lois Elizabeth Fritzell, Sept. 23, 1961; children—Franklin Henry III, Brian Nelson, Andrew Madden. B.S., Yale U., 1957, M.D., 1961. Pediatric intern, resident U. Minn. Hosps., Mpls., 1961-64; commd. capt. U.S. Army, 1966, advanced through grades to col., 1974; chief dept. virology SEATO Med. Research Lab., Bangkok, Thailand, 1970-73; chief dept. virus diseases Walter Reed Army Inst. Research, Washington, 1973-76, dir. div. communicable diseases and immunology, 1976-78, dep. dir. inst., 1978-81, dir., commandant, 1983—; comdr. U.S. Army Inst. Chem. Defense, Aberdeen Proving Ground, Md., 1981-83; mem. microbic and infectious disease adv. com. NIH, Bethesda, Md., 1976-80. Contbr. articles to profl. jours. Decorated Legion of Merit with oak leaf cluster. Mem. Infectious Diseases Soc. Am., AMA, Am. Soc. Tropical Medicine and Hygiene, AAAS, Alpha Omega Alpha. Current work: Management of research and development of military importance, including development of drugs and vaccines against bacterial, viral, and parasitic diseases; medical defense against chemical agents and military occupational hazards. Subspecialties: Virology (medicine); Pediatrics. Office: Dir Walter Reed Army Inst Research Washington DC 20307-5100

TOPPER, YALE J., biochemist; b. Chgo., Aug. 11, 1916; s. Ben and Aida T.; m. Hildegrad P. Pokorny, Oct. 12, 1956; children—David, Nina, James, Ethan. B.S., Northwestern U., 1942; M.A., Harvard U., 1943, Ph.D., 1947. Research fellow dept. biochemistry Harvard U., 1946-48; assoc. Public Health Research Inst., City of N.Y., 1948-53; fellow Am. Heart Assn., Mass. Gen. Hosp., Boston, 1953-54; with Nat. Inst. Arthritis, Diabetes, Digestive and Kidney Diseases, NIH, Bethesda, Md., 1954-83, chief sect. intermediary metabolism, 1983—, chief sect. developmental biology. Contbr. articles to profl. jours. Mem. Am. Soc. Biol. Chemists, Endocrine Soc. Current Work: Hormone-dependent gene expression. Subspecialties: Developmental biology; Cell and tissue culture. Home: 11608 Danville Dr Rockville MD 20852 Office: NIH Bethesda MD 20205

TOPPING, JOHN ALLAN, technology planner, glass technologist; b. Preston, Eng., June 20, 1943; came to U.S., 1977; s. Allan and Kathleen Hadfield (Sewell) T.; m. Frances Mary Swain, Sept. 9, 1967; children—Karen Elizabeth, Allan Geoffrey. B.Sc., Durham U. (Eng.), 1965; Ph.D., Sheffield U. (Eng.), 1968. Research scientist G.E.C. Hirst Research Centre, Wembley, Eng., 1968-70; assoc. research scientist Ont. Research Found., Toronto, 1970-73, research scientist, 1973-75, sr. research scientist, 1975-77; sr. research scientist Ferro Corp. Tech. Centre, Independence, Ohio, 1977-80; group leader, 1980-83, mgr. tech. planning, 1983—. Patentee in field (5). Contbr. articles to profl. jours. Vol. YMCA, Northfield, Ohio. Current work: Technology classification and trend analysis; technology surveillance, scanning, monitoring; analysis of research and development programs, projects; information. Subspecialty: Ceramics. Home: 73 Sandy Hill Rd Northfield OH 44067 Office: Ferro Corp 7500 E Pleasant Valley Rd Independence OH 44131

TORIGOE, RODNEY YOSHITO, clinical psychologist; b. Honolulu, Feb. 1, 1945; s. Samuel Yoshio and Sueko Thelma (Inakazu) T.; m. Bess Misao, Aug. 7, 1971; children—Tiffany Kikue Nakamura, Troy Yoshio. B.A., U. Hawaii, 1968; M.A., U. Colo., 1973, Ph.D., 1976. Diplomate: Am. Acad. Behavioral Medicine. Affirmative action officer Western Interstate Commn. for Higher Edn., Boulder, Colo., 1973-74; psychology assoc. Ariz. State Hosp., Phoenix, 1975-76; clin. psychologist VA, Phoenix, 1976-78, chief, Honolulu, 1978—, chief psychology service, 1980—; asst. clin. prof. psychology U. Hawaii, 1980—, asst. clin. prof. psychiatry, 1981—. Pres. bd. dirs. House, Inc., 1981-82; mem. Neighborhood Bd. Hawaii, 1981-82. NIMH fellow, 1971-72; recipient recognition award Western Interstate Commn. for Higher Edn., 1974. Mem. Am. Psychol. Assn., Hawaii Psychol. Assn. (treas. Honolulu 1981-82), Am. Assn. Sex Educators, Counselors, and Therapists, Biofeedback Soc. Am., Am. Assn. Marriage and Family Therapy, Internat. Council Psychologists. Democrat. Buddhist. Current Work: Sexual therapy, paradoxical maxims, sexuality for the aged, respiration and biofeedback, medical psychology. Office: VA OPC PO Box 50188 Honolulu HI 96850

TORMEY, DOUGLASS C., oncology researcher; b. Madison, Wis., Sept. 2, 1938; s. Weston C. and Marion D. (Douglass) T.; m. Patricia Bevington, Jan. 25, 1964; children: Bruce, Paula, Marc. B.S., U. Wis., 1960, M.D., 1964, M.S., 1964, Ph.D., 1969. Intern U. Calif. Med. Ctr., San Francisco, 1964-65, resident, 1965-66; postdoctoral fellow U. Wis. Med. Ctr., Madison, 1966-69; fellow in oncology Roswell Park Meml. Inst., Buffalo, 1969-70; staff oncologist Walter Reed Gen. Hosp., Washington, 1970-72; with NIH, Bethesda, Md., 1972-76; cons. in research, cell physiology, dept. biol. scis. George Washington U., Washington, 1974-76; assoc. prof. dept. human oncology U. Wis. Med. Sch., Madison, 1976-82, assoc. prof. dept. medicine, 1976-82, prof. depts. human oncology and medicine, 1982—; cons. William S. Middleton Meml. VA Hosp., Madison, 1979—. Contbr. articles to profl. jours. Served to maj. U.S. Army, 1970-72; to sr. surgeon USPHS, 1972-76. Recipient Borden award, 1964; Am. Cancer Soc. postdoctoral fellow, 1967-69; grantee NIH; grantee pharm. industry. Mem. AAAS, Am. Assn. for Cancer Research, Am. Soc. Hematology, Am. Soc. Clin. Oncology, Am. Fedn. Clin. Oncologic Socs., Cell Kinetic Soc., Am. Fedn. for Clin. Research, Internat. Assn. for Breast Cancer Research, Sigma Xi, Nu Sigma Nu. Current Work: Therapeutic research in clinical oncology. Subspecialties: Oncology; Cancer research (medicine). Office: 600 Highland Ave K4/632 CSC Madison WI 53792

TORNABENE, HUGH SALVATORE, physics educator; b. Liverpool, Eng., Dec. 27, 1932; came to U.S., 1965; s. John and Nora (Green) T.; m. Cathy McPherson, July 20, 1982; children—Laurence, Valerie. B.S. 1st class, U. Liverpool, 1953, Ph.D., 1957; M.Div., Woodstock Coll., 1968, S.T.M., 1969. Demonstrator, U. Liverpool, 1955-56; sci. officer U.K.A.E.A., Harwell, Eng., 1956-59; chmn. dept. physics St. Ignatius Coll., London, 1963-65; research fellow Woodstock Coll., Balt., 1965-69; prof. physics Bowie State Coll., Md., 1969—. Mem. AAUP, Am. Phys. Soc., U. of Liverpool Phys. Soc. Democrat. Current work: Extensive air showers, ultrahigh energy gamma rays. Subspecialties: Particle physics; Cosmic ray high energy astrophysics. Home: 6020 Westchester Park Dr #TI College Park MD 20740 Office: Dept Sci Bowie State Coll Bowie MD 20715

TORR, MARSHA RUSSELL, space science physicist, educator; b. Pretoria, South Africa, Dec. 4, 1942; d. John Russell and Joan Ereina Marshall (Vercueil) Harding; m. Douglas G. Torr, Dec. 15, 1965. B.Sc. in Physics with distinction, Rhodes U., Grahamstown, S. Africa, 1963, B.Sc. with honors, 1964, M.Sc. in Physics with distinction, 1966, Ph.D. in Physics, 1969. Jr. lectr. Rhodes U., 1965; lectr. physics U. Witwatersrand, S.Africa, 1966-67; sr. chief research officer South African Council Sci. and Indsl. Research, 1968-81; vis. fellow Yale U., 1973-74; assoc. research scientist U. Mich., 1974-80; prof. physics Utah State U., 1980-85; chief atomic physics and aeronomy br. Marshall Space Flight Ctr., NASA, Huntsville, Ala., 1985—; mem. various coms. Spacelab 1; mission scientist Earth Observations Mission I. Assoc. editor: Jour. Geophys. Research-Space Physics, 1982-85; contbr. numerous articles profl. jours. NASA grantee; NSF grantee. Mem. Am. Geophys. Union, Optical Soc. Am., AIAA. Current Work: Study of physics and chemistry of near-earth environment (atmosphere/ionosphere/magnetosphere) by theoretical and experimental techniques; development of remote sensing instrumentation with which to probe this region. Subspecialties: Aeronomy; Satellite studies. Office: Space Sci Lab ES55 NASA Marshall Space Flight Center Huntsville AL 35812

TORRES-MEDINA, ALFONSO, veterinary science educator; b. Colombia, Aug. 28, 1945; came to U.S., 1978; s. Alfonso Torres-Rudas and Maria Elena Medina de Torres; m. Maria Cecilia Cuervo, Aug. 26, 1972; children: Julian, Marcela. D.V.M., Nat. U. Colombia, 1968; M.S., U. Nebr., 1971, Ph.D., 1973. Asst. instr. Sch. Vet. Medicine, Nat. U. Colombia, Bogota, 1969; asst. prof. dept. vet. sci. U. Nebr.-Lincoln, 1973-75, 78-81, assoc. prof., 1981—; new products mgr. for Latin Am. Ames Co. div. Miles Labs. Inc., 1976-78. Contbr. articles to profl. jours. FAO-UN postgrad. fellow, 1971-73. Mem. Conf. Research Workers in Animal Diseases, Sigma Xi, Gamma Sigma Delta. Roman Catholic. Current Work: Viral enteric infections of newborn animals (calves, piglets, and human). Subspecialties: Virology (veterinary medicine); Pathology (veterinary medicine). Office: U Nebr 126 VBS Dept Veterinary Sci Lincoln NE 68583

TORREY, JOHN GORDON, forestry educator, plant physiologist; b. Phila., Feb. 22, 1921; s. Wiliam Edward and Elsie (Gordon) T.; m. Norah Jamison Lea-Wilson, June 1949; children—Jennifer, Joanna, Susan, Sarah, Carolyn. B.A., Williams Coll., 1942; M.A., Harvard U., 1947, Ph.D., 1950. Instr., U. Calif.-Berkeley, 1949-51, asst. prof., 1951-56, assoc. prof., 1956-60; prof. botany, dept. biology Harvard Forest, Harvard U., Petersham, Mass., 1960-71, Harvard U., Cambridge, Mass., 1971—, dir. Harvard Forest, 1984—; dir. Cabot Found., Harvard U., 1966-76. Author: (with L. Machlis) Plants in Action, 1956; Development in Flowering Plants, 1967. Editor: (with D.T. Clarkson) The Development and Function of Roots, 1976. Contbr. articles to sci. jours. Served to capt. Med. Adminstrv. Corps, U.S. Army, 1943-46, ETO. Merck sr. postdoctoral fellow, 1956-57; Guggenheim fellow, 1965-66; Fulbright sr. research scholar, 1984. Mem. Am. Acad. Arts and Scis., Nat. Acad. Scis. Current work: Symbiotic nitrogen-fixing trees; culture of Frankia. Subspecialty: Forestry. Office: Harvard Forest Harvard U Petersham MA 01366

TORRIANI, ANNAMARIA GORINI, educator; b. Milan, Italy, Dec. 19, 1918; came to U.S., 1955, naturalized, 1962; d. Carlo and Ada (Forti) T.; m. Luigi Gorini, Dec. 6, 1959; 1 son: Daniel. Ph.D., U. Milan, 1942. Research assoc. Instituto Chimica e Biochimica, G. Ronzoni, Milan, Italy, 1942-48; charge de recherche dept. cellular physiology Institut Pasteur, Paris, 1948-56; Fulbright postdoctoral fellow dept. microbiology N.Y.U., 1956-58; research assoc. Harvard Med. Sch., Boston, 1958-59; research assoc. biology dept. Harvard U., 1959-60; research assoc. M.I.T., Cambridge, 1960-71, assoc. prof. microbiology, 1971-76, prof., 1976—. Contbr. articles to profl. jours. Mem. Am. Soc. Microbiology, Genetics Soc. Am. Subspecialties: Microbiology; Molecular biology. Home: 115 Longwood Ave Brookline MA 02146 Office: Dept Biology Mass Inst Tec Cambridge MA 02139

TORTORICI, MARIANNE RITA, radiological scientist, educator; b. Waterbury, Conn., May 22, 1947; d. Anthony and Carmela Emily (DiNapoli) T. B.S., Incarnate Word Coll., San Antonio, 1972; M.Ed., U. Nev.-Las Vegas, 1975, M.S., 1985; Ed.D., U. Houston, 1979. Staff radiographer St. Raphael's Hosp., New Haven, Conn., 1968-72, Santa Rosa Med. Ctr., San Antonio, 1972; dir. Sch. Radiol. Tech., North Country Community Coll., Saranac Lake, N.Y., 1972-74; prof., U. Nev., Las Vegas, 1974—, chmn. dept. radiol. scis., 1974-84; lectr. U. Calif.-Santa Barbara Extension, Barstow, Calif., 1980; lectr. Western Intercollegiate Consortium on Edn. in Radiol. Tech., Reno, 1981, v.p., 1980-82; accrediting visitor AMA, Chgo., 1982—. Author: Fundamentals of Angiography, 1983, also lab. manuals.; Contbr. articles to profl. jours. Mem. Nev. Soc. Radiologic Tech. (pres. 1976-77, dir. 1977-78), Am. Soc. Radiologic Technologists (counselor 1974-76), Phi Kappa Phi, Alpha Beta Gamma. Current Work: Radiographic techniques and quality control, angiography, education. Subspecialty: Diagnostic radiology. Home: 4139 Newcastle Las Vegas NV 89103 Office: Dept Radiologic Scis U Nevada 4505 Maryland Pkwy Las Vegas NV 89154

TOTH, ATTILA, obstetrician/gynecologist; b. Szekszard, Hungary, Mar. 19, 1940; came to U.S., 1968, naturalized, 1977; s. Sandor and Ibolya (Tarjani) T.; m. Constance Wesley Brooks, Mar. 20, 1980. M.D., U. Budapest, 1964. Diplomate: Am. Bd. Pathology, Am. Bd. Obstetrics and Gynecology. Research fellow Cleve. Clinic, 1968-69; intern Mt. Sinai Hosp., N.Y.C., 1969-70, resident in pathology, 1970-73; asst. prof. Mt. Sinai Med. Sch., N.Y.C., 1973-74; resident obstetrics/gynecology N.Y. Hosp./Cornell, N.Y.C., 1974-77, asst. prof., attending, 1977-83, assoc. prof., 1983—; dir. MacLeod Lab. Infertility, N.Y.C., 1977—. Contbr. articles to profl. jours. Mem. Am. Fertility Soc., Am. Soc. Andrology. Republican. Mem. Dutch Reform Ch. Current Work: Role of infection in male/female reproductive performance. Subspecialties: Obstetrics and gynecology; Pathology (medicine). Home: 436 E 69th St Apt 8C New York NY 10021 Office: New York Hosp Cornell Med Center 525 E 68th St New York NY 10021

TOTH, JOSEPH WILLIAM, geodetic analyst; b. Phila., Mar. 7, 1951; s. Joseph Francis and Mary Veronica (McCovick) T. B.A., U. Pa., 1973; M.A., Temple U., 1979. Research asst. Temple U., Phila., 1975-78; sr. math. analyst Bendix Field Engring. Co., Greenbelt, Md., 1979—. Author: Geodetic Locations For SSO Support, 1980; (quar. manual) NASA Directory of Station Location-Updates, 1979-85; also articles on sta. coordinates for shuttle ops. Phila. Bd. Edn. scholar U. Pa., 1969-73; NSF grantee, 1977. Mem. Am. Geophys. Union, Geol. Soc. Am. Roman Catholic. Current work: Provide geodetic analysis and software support for Flight Dynamic division of Goddard Space Flight Center. Subspecialties: Geodetic analysis; Software engineering. Home: 198 Easton S Apt 202 Laurel MD 20707 Office: Bendix Field Engring Corp-TDG Aerospace Bldg 10210 Greenbelt Rd Seabrook MD 20801

TOTH, MARGO IRENE, geologist; b. St. Albans, N.Y., May 27, 1953; d. Kenneth Dean and Virgina Naomi (Mount) T. B.A., U. Calif.-Santa Barbara, 1975; M.S., U. Colo., 1979, Ph.D., 1983. Geologist, U.S. Geol. Survey, Denver, 1975—. Contbr. articles to profl. jours. Scholar Soroptomist Soc., 1983, Am. Businesswoman's Assn., 1982. Mem. Geol. Soc. Am. Current work: Petrology of the bitterroot lobe of the Idaho batholith; mineralization of granite systems; rhyolite ash flows of Eastern Nevada. Subspecialties: Petrology; Geology. Office: US Geol Survey Denver Fed Ctr MS 922 Box 25046 Denver CO 80225

TOU, JAMES CHIEH, chemist; b. Jiangsu, China, Apr. 25, 1936, came to U.S., 1962, naturalized, 1973; s. Ching-huang and Kuey-jong (Chen) T.; m. Jane Ying-ching Hu, Mar. 21, 1964; children—Jarvis, Joseph, Juliana. B.Sc., Taiwan Normal U., Nat. Republic of China, 1961; Ph.D., U. Utah, 1965. Sr. research chemist Dow Chem. Co., Midland, Mich., 1970-73, research specialist, 1973-78, assoc. scientist, 1978-81, sr. assoc. scientist, 1981-84, research scientist, 1984—. Contbr. articles to profl. jours. Served to 1st lt. Chinese Army, 1961-62. Mem. Am. Chem. Soc., Am. Soc. Mass. Spectrometry, ASTM, Sigma Xi (award 1977). Roman Catholic. Current work: Mass spectrometry; thermal analysis; trace analysis; chemical kinetics. Subspecialties: Analytical chemistry; Physical chemistry.

TOUGH, ALLEN M(AC NEILL), psychology educator; b. Montreal, Que., Can, Jan. 6, 1936; s. David Lloyd and Margaret Phyllis (Allen) T.; m. Elaine Posluns, June 10, 1981; children: (by previous marriage) Susan Anne, Paul Allen. B.A., U. Toronto, 1958, M.A., 1962; Ph.D., U. Chgo., 1965. Tchr. Scarborough (Ont.) Bd. Edn., 1959-61; asst. prof. U. Toronto, Ont., 1964-66; asst. to full prof. adult learning and future studies Ont. Inst. Studies in Edn. and U. Toronto, 1966—; cons. editor Adult Edn. Jour., 1967-73; conf. chmn. Nat. Seminar Adult Edn. Research, Toronto, 1969; v.p. UNESCO Meeting, Paris, 1979; cons. Nat. Inst. Edn., 1978-79. Author: Learning Without a Teacher, 1967, Adult's Learning Projects, 2d edit, 1979, Expand Your Life, 1980, Intentional Changes, 1982. Kellogg Found. fellow, 1962; Can. Council scholar, 1964; Ont. Inst. grantee, 1966-77. Mem. Am. Psychol. Assn., World Futures Studies Fedn., World Future Soc., Brit. Interplanetary Soc. Current Work: Long-term futures for humankind and extraterrestrial civilizations. Subspecialties: Learning; Developmental psychology. Office: Ont Inst Studies in Edn 252 Bloor St W Toronto ON M5S 1V6 Canada

TOURANGEAU, PHILLIP CLIFFORD, environmental scientist, researcher; b. Syracuse, N.Y., Oct. 31, 1942; s. Donald John and Ruth (Mahaney) T. B.A., U. Mont., 1971. Research assoc. U. Mont., Missoula, 1969-81, acting lab. dir., 1981—. Contbr. articles to profl. jours. Chmn. Health Air Pollution Control. Bd., Missoula, 1980-84. Served with U.S. Army, 1963-66. Mem. AAAS, Air Pollution Control Assn., Sigma Xi. Democrat. Current work: Environmental biology, air-water pollution, inorganic toxics, laboratory/field experimental design, laboratory/field quality control and quality assurance, data analysis, policy and legislation. Subspecialty: Ecology (environmental science). Office: Botany Dept U Mont Missoula MT 59812

TOURTELLOTTE, MILLS CHARLTON, mechanical and electrical engineer; b. Great Falls, Mont., Dec. 26, 1922; s. Nathaniel Mills and Frances Victoria (Charlton) T.; m. Dorothy Elsie Gray, Sept. 16, 1947; children—Jane Tourtellotte Collins, Kathryn Tourtellotte Bauman, Thomas. B.S., Ill. Inst. Tech., 1947, M.S., 1952. Registered profl. engr., Ill., Mich., Tex. Engr., Automatic Electric Co., Chgo., 1947-49, Inland Steel Co., East Chicago, Ind., 1952-56, Quanex Corp., Rosenberg, Tex., 1956—; fallout shelter analyst Fed. Emergency Mgmt., Washington, 1970—. Contbr. papers to tech. lit. Patentee mech. and elec. devices. Election judge Ft. Bend County Republican Party, 1965; chmn. 4H Adult Leaders Assn., 1968. Named Friend of 4H, Ft. Bend County Extension Service, 1968. Mem. Nat. Soc. Profl. Engrs., ASME, Tex. Soc. Profl. Engrs. (edn. chmn. 1969), Fluid Power Soc., Am. Soc. for Engring. Edn. (industry chmn. 1969), Assn. Iron and Steel Engrs. (life), VFW (life, quartermaster 1984). Methodist. Current work: Tubular highway break-away signs, tubular towers, underground vertical heat exchanger, electromechanical automatic circuitry. Subspecialties: Electrical engineering; Mechanical engineering. Home: 1114 Inwood Dr Richmond TX 77469 Office: Gulf States Tube Div Spur 529 and Scott Rd Rosenberg TX 77471

TOURTELLOTTE, WALLACE WILLIAM, neurologist, educator; b. Great Falls, Mont., Sept. 13, 1924; s. Nathaniel Mills and Frances Victoria (Charlton) T.; m. Jean Esther Toncray, Feb. 14, 1953; children: Wallace William, George Mills, James Millard, Warren Gerard. B.S. in Anatomy, U. Chgo., 1945, Ph.B., 1945, Ph.D. in Neurochem. Pharmacology, 1948, M.D., 1951. Diplomate: Am. Bd. Psychiatry and Neurology; lic. physician, N.Y., Mich., Calif. Intern Strong Meml. Hosp., U. Rochester (N.Y.) Sch. Medicine and Dentistry, 1951-52; resident in neurology U. Mich. Med. Ctr. Hosp., Ann Arbor, 1954-57; postdoctoral research dept. pharmacology U. Chgo. Toxicity Lab., 1948-51, instr. pharmacology, 1948-51; from asst. prof. to prof. neurology U. Mich., Ann Arbor, 1957-71; prof.-in-residence dept. neurology UCLA, 1971—, vice chmn. dept. neurology, 1971—; chief neurology service VA Wadsworth Med. Ctr., Los Angeles, 1971—; dir. neurology resident tng. program, dir. multiple sclerosis treatment ctr., co-dir. memory enhancement clinic, dir. Parkinson's disease ctr., dir. neurofunction lab., dir. Nat. Neurol. Research Bank, 1971—; dir. NMSS Human Speciman Bank; of Am., 1976—; cons. dept. consumer affairs Bd. Med. Quality Assurance, 1980—; cons. and lectr. in medicine; mem. numerous research coms. and orgns. Co-author 3 books including: Post-Lumbar Puncture Headaches, 1964; Multiple Sclerosis (textbook); Quantitative Evaluation of Neurological Functions (2 vols.); contbr. articles on cerebrospinal fluid, multiple sclerosis, neurochemistry, neuroimmunology, molecular virology to profl. jours. and books. Mem. sci. adv. com. Internat. Maltese Mus. Fine Art. Served with M.C., USN, 1952-54. Recipient Disting. Alumni Service award U. Chgo., 1982; Fellow Am. Acad. Neurology (sect. neuropharmacy 1981—, S. Weir Mitchell neurology research award 1959), ACP, Am. Neurol. Assn.; mem. AAAS, World Fedn. Neurology (founding mem., multiple sclerosis research com. 1970—), Family Survival Project (mem. sci. adv. council 1982—), Am. Bd. Neurology and Psychiatry (asst. examiner 1965—), Internat. Soc. Neurochemistry (founding mem.), World Assn. Neurol. Commns. (founding mem.; neurochemistry commn. 1965—), Am. Soc. Pharmacology and Exptl. Therapeutics, Am. Therapeutic Soc., Am. Soc. Neurochemistry (founding mem.; exec. com. 1968), Fedn. Western Socs. of Neurol. Sci. (program chmn. 1973), Assn. Am. Med. Colls., AAUP (VA com. 1980—), Nat. Multiple Sclerosis Soc. (nat. med. adv. bd. 1968—, So. Calif. chpt. 1976—, Hope Chest award 1982), Internat. Fedn. Multiple Sclerosis Socs. (adv. bd. 1972—), Soc. Neurosci., Am. Assn. Neuropathologists (assoc. mem.). Clubs: Pasadena Wine and Food Soc, Soc. Med. Friends of Wine, Confrerie de la Chaine des Rotisseur (chevalier), Argentier du Baillage de Los Angeles (vice chancelier), La Chaine, Les Amis du Vin, Vigneron d'Honneur du Cru Morgan, Academie des Vins du Mts. Daphne. Current Work: Organic neurology; establishment of a neuro-function lab. to quantitate the neurologic exam.; collection and distribution of control and neurological tissues for basic scientists; treatment of Parkinson's disease; non-medical treatment of dementia; treatment and prevention of multiple sclerosis; molecular virology evoked responses and subclinical lesions. Subspecialties: Neurology; Neurophysiology. Home: 1140 Tellem Dr Pacific Palisades CA 90272 Office: VA Med Ctr-West Los Angeles Wilshire and Sawtelle Blvds Los Angeles CA 90073

TOUSEY, RICHARD, physicist; b. Somerville, Mass., May 18, 1908; s. Coleman and Adella Richards (Hill) T.; m. Ruth Lowe, June 29, 1932; 1 dau., Joanna. A.B., Tufts U., 1928, Sc.D. (hon.), 1961; A.M., Harvard, 1929; Ph.D., 1933. Instr. physics Harvard, 1933-36, tutor div. phys. scis., 1934-36; research instr. Tufts U., 1936-41; physicist U.S. Naval Research Lab. optics div., 1941-58, head instrument sect., 1942-45, head micron waves br., 1945-58, head rocket spectroscopy br., atmosphere and astrophysics div., 1958-67, space sci. div., 1967-78, cons., 1978—; Mem. com. vision Armed Forces-NRC, 1944—; line spectra of elements com. NRC, 1960-72; mem. Rocket and Satellite Research Panel, 1958—; mem. astronomy subcom. space sci. steering com. NASA, 1960-62, mem. solar physics subcom., 1969-71; prin. investigator expts.

including Skylab; mem. com. aeronomy Internat. Union Geodesy and Geophysics, 1958—; U.S. nat. com. Internat. Commn. Optics, 1960-66; mem. sci. steering com. Project Vanguard, 1956-58; mem. adv. com. to office sci. personnel Nat. Acad. Scis.-NRC, 1969-72. Contbr. articles to sci. jours. and books. Bayard Cutting fellow Harvard, 1931-33, 35-36; recipient Meritorious Civilian Service award U.S. Navy, 1945; E.O. Hulburt award Naval Research Labs., 1958; Progress medal photog. Soc. Am., 1959; Prix Ancel Soc. Francaise de Photographie, 1962; Henry Draper medal Nat. Acad. Scis., 1963; Navy award for distinguished achievement in sci, 1963; Eddington medal, 1964; NASA medal for exceptional sci. achievement, 1974; George Darwin lectr. Royal Astron. Soc., 1963. Fellow Am. Acad. Arts and Scis., Am. Phys. Soc., Optical Soc. Am. (dir. 1953-57, Frederic Ives medal 1960), Am. Geophys. Union; mem. Internat. Acad. Astronautics, Nat., Acad. Scis., Am. Astron. Soc. (v.p. 1964-66, Henry Norris Russell lectr. 1966), Soc. Applied Spectroscopy, AAAS, Am. Geophys. Union, Philos. Soc. Washington, Internat. Astron. Union, Nuttall Ornithol. Club, Audubon Naturalists Soc., Phi Beta Kappa, Sigma Xi, Theta Delta Chi. Current Work: Consultant in space research; solar physics, optics, spectroscopy. Subspecialties: Satellite studies; Solar physics. Home: 7725 Oxon Hill Rd Oxon Hill MD 20745 Office: US Naval Research Lab Washington DC 20375

TOWBIN, ABRAHAM, researcher, medical legal consultant; b. Cripple Creek, Colo., Apr. 26, 1916; s. Mike and Esther (Jaffee) T.; m. Margret Mary Towbin, Sept. 17, 1942; 1 dau.: Mary Kathryn Towbin Potere. B.S., U. Denver, 1936; M.D., U. Colo., 1940. Cert. Am. Bd. Pathology, Am. Bd. Neuropathology. Intern N. Hudson Hosp., Weehawken, N.J., 1941-42; resident N.Y.C. Hosp., 1945-48; instr. pathology Ohio State U., 1948-51, asst. prof., 1951-54, assoc. prof., 1954-55; assoc. prof. pathology SUNY, Bklyn., 1955-57; Fulbright research scholar Max Planck Inst., Munich, W.Ger., 1957-58; prof. pathology Chgo. Med. Sch., 1959-62; pathologist NIH collaborative perinatal project, dept. neuropathology Harvard U., 1962-65; pathologist, clinician Mass. Dept. Mental Health, 1965-80; med. dir. Mental Retardation Research Inst., Danvers, Mass., 1980—. Contbr. numerous articles to profl. jours. Served to col., M.C. U.S. Army, 1942-65. Mem. Am. Assn. Pathology, Am. Assn. Neuropathologists. Jewish. Current Work: Research in perinatal brain damage and its sequels: Mental retardation, cerebral palsy, epilepsy, psychopathy; fetal-neonatal brain damage; psychopathy. Subspecialties: Pathology (medicine); Maternal and fetal medicine. Home: 18 Inis Circle West Newton MA 02165 Office: Mental Retardation Research Inst 30 Centre St Danvers MA 01923

TOWER, RAYMOND CAMILLE, See *Who's Who in America,* 43rd edition.

TOWN, DONALD EARL, systems analyst, consultant; b. Forestville, N.Y., Dec. 5, 1949; s. Earl Grover and Violet Grace (Kear) T. B.A., DePauw U., 1971; M.S., Ohio State U., 1973; Ph.D., Brown U., 1978. Teaching asst. Ohio State U., 1971-73; research asst. Brown U., 1975-78; asst. prof. Wellesley Coll., 1980; research mathematician Thomte & Co., Inc., Boston, 1978-80; staff systems analyst Dynamics Research Corp., Wilmington, Mass., 1980—; cons. Thomte & Co., Inc. Coach Wellesley Coll., 1979—. Mem. IEEE, Am. Math. Soc.., Soc. Indsl. and Applied Math., Am. Statis. Assn., Math. Assn. Am., Phi Beta Kappa, Sigma Xi, Sigma Pi Sigma. Democrat. Methodist. Club: Providence Turners. Current Work: Software quality metrics using applied mathematical techniques from statistics and pattern theory. Subspecialties: Statistics; Software engineering. Home: 15 Leamington Rd Brighton MA 02135 Office: Dynamics Research Corp 60 Concord St Wilmington MA 01887

TOWNES, CHARLES HARD, physics educator; b. Greenville, S.C., July 28, 1915; s. Henry Keith and Ellen Sumter (Hard) T.; m. Frances H. Brown, May 4, 1941; children: Linda Lewis, Ellen Screven, Carla Keith, Holly Robinson. B.A., B.S., Furman U., 1935; M.A., Duke U., 1937; Ph.D., Calif. Inst. Tech., 1939. Mem. tech. staff Bell Telephone Lab., 1939-47; asso. prof. physics Columbia U., 1948-50, prof. physics, 1950-61; exec. dir. Columbia Radiation Lab., 1950-52, chmn. physics dept., 1952-55; provost and prof. physics Mass. Inst. Tech., 1961-66, Inst. prof., 1966-67; v.p., dir. research Inst. Def. Analyses, Washington, 1959-61; Univ. prof. U. Calif. at Berkeley, 1967—; Guggenheim fellow, 1955-56; Fulbright lectr. U. Paris, 1955-56, U. Tokyo, 1956; lectr., 1955, 60; dir. Enrico Fermi Internat. Sch. Physics, 1963; Richtmeyer lectr. Am. Phys. Soc., 1959; Scott lectr. U. Cambridge, 1963; Centennial lectr. U. Toronto, 1967; Lincoln lectr., 1972-73, Halley lectr., 1976; R.M. Petrie lectr. Canadian Astron. Soc., Toronto, 1985; dir. Perkin-Elmer Corp., Gen. Motors Corp.; mem. Pres.'s Sci. Adv. Com., 1966-69, vice chmn., 1967-69; chmn. sci. and tech. adv. com. for manned space flight NASA, 1964-69; mem. Pres.'s Com. on Sci. and Tech., 1976. Author: (with A.L. Schawlow) Microwave Spectroscopy, 1955; author, co-editor: Quantum Electronics, 1960, Quantum Electronics and Coherent Light, 1964; editorial bd.: (with A.L. Schawlow) Rev. Sci. Instrument, 1950-52, Phys. Rev, 1951-53; bd.: (with A.L. Schawlow) Phys., Rev, 1951-53, Jour. Molecular Spectroscopy, 1957-60, Procs. Nat. Acad. Scis, 1978—; contbr. articles to sci. publs. Trustee Calif. Inst. Tech., Carnegie Instn. of Washington, Pacific Sch. Religion; mem. corp. Woods Hole Oceanographic Instn. Recipient numerous hon. degrees and awards, including; Nobel prize for physics, 1964; Stuart Ballantine medal Franklin Inst., 1959, 62; Thomas Young medal and prize Inst. Physics and Phys. Soc., Eng., 1963; Disting. Public Service medal NASA, 1969; Wilhelm Exner award Austria, 1970; Niels Bohr Internat. Gold medal, 1979; Nat. Sci. medal, 1983; named to Nat. Inventors Hall of Fame, 1976, Engring. and Sci. Hall of Fame, 1983. Fellow Am. Phys. Soc. (council 1959-62, 65-71, pres. 1967, Plyler prize 1977), Optical Soc. Am. (hon., Mees medal 1968), IEEE (medal of honor 1967), Calif. Acad. Scis.; mem. Am. Philos. Soc., Am. Astron. Soc., Am. Acad. Arts and Scis., Nat. Acad. Scis. (council 1969-72, 78-81, chmn. space sci. bd. 1970-73, Comstock award 1959), Société Française de Physique (council 1956-58), Royal Soc. (fgn.), Pontifical Acad. Scis. Patentee masers and lasers; research nuclear and molecular structure, quantum electronics, interstellar molecules, radio and infrared astrophysics. Current Work: Microwave physics, laser physics and quantum electronics, nuclear and molecular structure, and astrophysics particularly infrared and microwave astronomy. Subspecialties: Infrared astronomy; Atomic and molecular physics. Office: Dept Physics U Calif at Berkeley Berkeley CA 94720

TOWNSEND, FRANK MARION, pathologist, educator; b. Stamford, Tex., Oct. 29, 1914; s. Frank Marion and Beatrice (House) T.; m. Gerda Eberlen, Nov. 1940 (div. June 1944); 1 child, Frank Marion; m. Ann Graf, Aug. 25, 1951; 1 child, Robert N. Student San Antonio Coll., 1931-32, U. Tex., 1932-34; M.D., Tulane U., 1938. Diplomate Am. Bd. Pathology. Intern So. Bapt. Hosp., New Orleans, 1938, N.Y. Polyclinic Hosp., N.Y.C., 1939-40; instr. pathology Washington U., St. Louis, 1945-47; instr. clin. pathology U. Nebr., Omaha, 1947-48; assoc. prof. U. Tex. Med. Br., Galveston, 1949-57; dir. lab. Tex. Dept. Health, San Antonio, 1965-72; prof., chmn. dept. pathology U. Tex. Health Sci. Ctr., San Antonio, 1972—; cons. VA; mem. Armed Forces Epidemiology Bd., Washington, 1983—; bd. govs. Armed Forces Inst. Pathology, Washington. Mem. editorial bd. Tex. Medicine, 1980—. Contbr. articles to sci. lit., chpts. to books. Active local Boy Scouts Am., 1966-72; mem. wastewater com. City of San Antonio, 1974—. Served to col. USAF, 1950-65. Decorated D.S.M., Legion of Merit; recipient Founder's medal Assn. Mil. Surgeons U.S., Washington, 1959. Fellow Am. Soc. Clin. Pathologists (Ward Burdick award 1983), ACP, Coll. Am. Pathologists (regional commr. 1970—, ednl. cons., regional commr. lab accreditation program), Aerospace Med. Assn. (Moseley award 1962), Internat. Acad. Aerospace Medicine; mem. AMA, Internat. Acad. Pathologists, Am. Assn. Pathologists, Acad. Clin. Lab. Physicians and Scientists, Tex. Med. Assn. (chmn. disaster med. care Bexar County 1972-78). Baptist. Current work: Clinical pathology, aerospace accident investigation, improvement and accreditation of clinical laboratories. Subspecialties: Pathology (medicine); Space medicine. Home: 10406 Mount Marcy St San Antonio TX 78213 Office: Dept of Pathology U of Tex Health Sci Ctr 7703 Floyd Curl Dr San Antonio TX 78284

TOWNSEND, JOHN WILLIAM, JR., physicist, aerospace company executive; b. Washington, Mar. 19, 1924; s. John William and Elenore (Eby) T.; m. Mary Irene Lewis, Feb. 7, 1948; children: Bruce Alan, Nancy Dewitt, John William III, Megan Lewis. B.A., Williams Coll., 1947, M.A., 1949, Sc.D., 1961. With Naval Research Lab., 1949-55, br. head, 1955-58; with NASA, 1958-68, dep. dir. Goddard Space Flight Ctr., 1965-68; dep. adminstrn. Environmental Scis. Services Adminstrn., 1968-70; asso. adminstr. Nat. Oceanic and Atmospheric Adminstrn., 1970-77; pres. Fairchild Space and Electronics Co., 1977-82; v.p. Fairchild Industries, 1979—; pres. Fairchild Space Co., 1983-85; sr. v.p. Fairchild Industries, 1985—; chmn. mgmt. bd. Am. Satellite Co., 1985—; mem. U.S. Rocket, Satellite Research Panel, 1950—. Author numerous papers, reports in field. Pres. town council, Forest Heights, Md., 1951-55. Served with USAAF, 1943-46. Recipient Profl. Achievement award Engrs. and Architects Day, 1957; Meritorious Civilian Service award Navy Dept., 1957; Outstanding Leadership medal NASA, 1962; Distinguished Service medal, 1971; recipient Arthur S. Fleming award Fed. Govt., 1963. Fellow Am. Meteorol. Soc., AIAA, AAAS; mem. Am. Phys. Soc., Nat. Acad. Engring., Am. Geophys. Union. Internat. Astronautical Fedn. (mem. internat., acad. astronautics), Sigma Xi. Subspecialties: Aerospace engineering and technology; Remote sensing (geoscience). Home: 15810 Comus Rd Clarksburg MD 20871

TOWNSEND, LAWRENCE WILLARD, theoretical physicist, physics educator; b. Jacksonville, Fla., May 13, 1947; s. Willard Hyram and Marion Patricia (McCann) T.; m. Linda Susan Summerlin, June 5, 1969; children—Laura Suzanne, David Matthew, Jeremy Peter. B.S., U.S. Naval Acad., 1969; M.S., U.S. Naval Postgrad. Sch., 1970; Ph.D., U. Idaho, 1980. Commd. ensign U.S. Navy, 1969, advanced through grades to lt. comdr., 1977, served as nuclear submarine officer, engr.; lectr. in physics U. Idaho, Moscow, 1978-79; research asst. prof. physics Old Dominion U., Norfolk, Va., 1980; research scientist NASA Langley Research Ctr., Hampton, Va., 1981—; adj. faculty Old Dominion U., 1981—. Contbr. articles to profl. jours. Recipient Spl. Achievement award NASA Langley Research Ctr., 1984; Whittenberger fellow, 1979-80. Mem. Am. Phys. Soc., AIAA, Full Gospel businessmen's Fellowship Internat. (dir. Charleston, S.C. chpt. 1975-76, pres. Pullman, Wash. chpt. 1979, v.p. 1978, 80, treas. Newport News, Va. chpt. 1983, v.p. 1984, pres. 1985), Sigma Xi. Republican. Current work: Principal investigator for NASA Space Radiation Protection research program; specialize in relativistic heavy ion physics including nuclear fragmentation, pi meson production processes, transport in extended matter, and health physics effects. Subspecialties: Nuclear physics; Theoretical physics. Office: NASA Langley Research Ctr Mail Stop 160 Hampton VA 23665

TOWNSEND, LEROY B., chemistry educator; b. Lubbock, Tex., Dec. 20, 1933; s. L.B. and Ocie Mae (McBride) T.; m. Sammy Lee Beames, Sept. 15, 1953; children—Lisa Loree, Byron. B.A. in Chemistry and Math., N.Mex. Highlands U., 1955, M.S. in Chemistry, 1957; Ph.D. in Chemistry, Ariz. State U., 1965. Assoc. prof. medicinal chemistry U. Utah., Salt Lake City, 1971-75, adj. prof. chemistry, 1975-78, prof. med. chemistry, 1975-78; prof. medicinal chemistry U. Mich., Ann Arbor, 1979—, prof. chemistry, 1979—, chmn., program dir. medicinal chemistry, 1979—; mem. exec. and adv. coms. 9th Internat. Congress Heterocyclic Chemistry, Tokyo, 1983; mem. adv. com. Comprehensive Cancer Ctr., Brown U., Providence, R.I., 1983. Contbr. articles to profl. jours. Mem. Cancer Research Com., U. Mich., Devel. Treatments for Rare Genetic Diseases Com., U. Mich. Grantee Am. Cancer Soc., Nat. Cancer Inst., WHO, various pharm. firms. Mem. Internat. Soc. Heterocyclic Chemistry (treas. 1973-77, pres-elect 1978-79, pres., 1980-81). Subspecialties: Organic chemistry; Cancer research (medicine). Home: 1400 Folkstone Ct Ann Arbor MI 48105 Office: U Mich Coll Pharmacy Ann Arbor MI 48109

TOWNSEND, MARJORIE RHODES, aerospace engineer, business executive; b. Washington, Mar. 12, 1930; d. Lewis Boling and Marjorie Olive (Trees) Rhodes; m. Charles Eby Townsend, June 7, 1948; children: Charles Eby Jr., Lewis Rhodes, John Cunningham, Richard Leo. B.E.E., George Washington U., 1951. Registered profl. engr., D.C. Electronic scientist Naval Research Lab., Washington, 1951-59; research engr. to sect. head NASA-Goddard Space Flight Ctr., Greenbelt, Md., 1959-65, tech, asst. to chief systems div., 1965-66, project mgr. small astronomy satellites, 1966-75, project mgr. applications explorer missions, 1975-76, mgr. preliminary systems design group, 1976-80, aerospace and electronics cons., Washington, 1980-83; v.p. systems devel. Space Am., 1983-84; aerospace cons., Washington, 1984—. Decorated knight Order Italian Republic, 1972; recipient Fed. Woman's award, 1973; award Culture Assn. EUR, Rome, 1974; Engr. Alumni Achievement award George Washington U., 1975; Gen. Alumni Assn. Achievement award, 1976; Exceptional Service medal NASA, 1971; Outstanding Leadership medal, 1980. Fellow IEEE (chmn. Washington sect. 1974-75, program chmn. 1971), AIAA (nat. capitol sect. council 1973-75, 79-83, chmn. nat. capitol sect. 1985-86), Washington Acad. Sci. (pres. 1980-81); mem. AAAS (council del. 1985—), N.Y. Acad. Sci., Am. Geophys. Union, Soc. Women Engrs., Sigma Kappa, DAR, Daus. Colonial Wars, Daughters 1812, Mensa. Republican. Episcopalian. Patentee digital telemetry system. Current Work: Aerospace consulting. Subspecialties: Aerospace engineering and technology; Electronics. Home: 3529 Tilden St NW Washington DC 20008

TRACHTENBERG, EDWARD NORMAN, chemistry educator; b. N.Y.C., Dec. 8, 1927; s. Jacob M. and Eva (Adwokat) T.; m. Victoria A. Gotsky, Aug. 21, 1954; children: Ellen C. Guilbert, Judith Ann, Richard Bruce. A.B., N.Y.U., 1949; A.M., Harvard U., 1951, Ph.D., 1953. Postdoctoral fellow U. Colo., 1952-53; instr., then asst. prof. Columbia U., 1953-58; successively asst. prof., assoc. prof., prof. chemistry Clark U., Worcester, Mass., 1958—; cons. Radiation Applications, Inc., 1956-61, E.F. Drew and Co., 1958-62. Contbr. articles to profl. jours. Mem. Worcester Democratic Com., 1972—, Mass. Dem. Platform Com., 1972-76; mem. exec. com. Citizens for Participation in Polit. Action, 1972—, treas., 1976—. Served with USAAF, 1946-47. NSF sci. faculty fellow, 1967-68. Mem. Am. Chem. Soc., Am. Inst. Chemists, Chem. Soc. London, Civil Liberties Union Mass. (exec. com. 1968-74, 81-85), N.E. Assn. Advisors Health Professions (exec. com. 1983—). Current Work: Mechanisms of organic reactions. Subspecialty: Organic chemistry. Home: 28 S Lenox St Worcester MA 01602 Office: Chemistry Dept Clark U Worcester MA 01610

TRACY, JOSEPH CHARLES, electronics researcher; b. Wilkes Barre, Pa., Jan. 15, 1943; s. J. Charles and Susanne (Kelly) T.; m. Charlotte Shaw, June 25, 1966; children—Marla, Justin, Greg. B.E.E., Rensselaer Poly. U., 1964; Ph.D. in Applied Physics, Cornell U., 1968. Postdoctoral fellow N.Am. Rockwell, Thousand Oaks, Calif., 1968-69, mem. tech. staff, 1969-70; mem. materials sci. research dept. Bell Telephone Labs., Murray Hill, N.J., 1970-73; supr. research physicist Gen. Motors Research Labs, Warren, Mich., 1973-75, asst. head physics dept., 1975-82, head, electronics dept., 1982—. Trustee, Village of Romeo, Mich., 1975-78; pres. Romeo Community Sch. Bd., 1982-83, v.p., 1981, trustee, 1980. Chmn. NAS Evaluation Panel Nat. Bur. Standards, 1980-82, mem. 1977-82. Fellow Am. Phys. Soc.; mem. Am. Vacuum Soc., AAAS, Soc. Automotive Engrs., Tau Beta Pi. Current work: Overall responsibility for research programs in areas of microelectronics, transducers, circuits and communications and control systems. Subspecialty: Electronics. Office: Electronics Dept Gen Motors Research Labs Warren MI 48090-9057

TRAFICANTE, DANIEL DOMINICK, chemist; b. Hoboken, N.J., Nov. 20, 1933; s. Paul and Mary T.; m. Doris Marilyn Poley, Aug. 20, 1955 (div. 1983); children—Daniel D., Mark S., Christopher, Dawn; m. Margaret Mary Kelly, May 19, 1984. B.S., Syracuse U., 1955; Ph.D., MIT, 1962. Commd. 2d lt. U.S. Air Force, 1956, advanced through grades to capt. 1967, resigned, 1967; dir. undergrad. labs. MIT, Cambridge, 1968-70, dir. nuclear magnetic resonance lab., 1970-78; dir. nuclear magnetic resonance lab. Yale U., New Haven, 1978-81; dir. Nuclear Magnetic Resonance Inst., Cranford, N.J., 1981-83; dir. chem. instrumentation NSF, Washington, 1983-85; research fellow, dir. life scis. nuclear magnetic resonance consortium Monsanto Co., Chesterfield, Mo., 1985—; dir. Nuclear Magnetic Resonance Concepts. Author: Chemistry, 1978. Contbr. articles to profl. jours. Mem. Am. Chem. Soc. Current work: Development and applications of new techniques in nuclear magnetic resonance for solving chemical problems. Subspecialties: Nuclear magnetic resonance; Organic chemistry. Home: 15776 Summer Ridge Dr Chesterfield MO 63017 Office: Monsanto Co Life Scis Nuclear Magnetic Resonance Consortium 700 Chesterfield Village Pkwy Chesterfield MO 63017

TRAFTON, LAURENCE MUNRO, astronomer; b. Boston, July 31, 1938; s. Hurbert and Vesta Estelle (Trafton) Meara. B.S., Calif. Inst. Tech., 1960, M.S., 1961, Ph.D., 1965. Research scientist U. Tex., Austin, 1973—, spl. research assoc., 1969-73; physicist GS-13 Air Force Weapons Lab., Albuquerque, 1968-69. Served as 1st lt. USAF, 1965-68. Mem. Internat. Astron. Union, Am. Astron. Soc., AAAS. Congregationalist. Club: Northcross Figure Skating (Austin, Tex.). Current Work: Atmospheres of the major planets, observational astronomy, spectroscopy, planetary atmospheres, solar system studies. Subspecialty: Planetary atmospheres. Home: 1208 A Elm St Austin TX 78703 Office: Astronomy Dept U Tex RLM 16 342 Austin TX 78712

TRAJMAR, SANDOR, scientist; b. Bogacs, Hungary, Sept. 7, 1931; came to U.S., 1957, naturalized, 1962; s. Gyula and Maria (Balazs) T.; m. Magdolna Csanak, Feb. 1, 1930; 1 son, Peter. Dipl. Phys. Chemistry, L. Kossuth U., Hungary, 1955; Ph.D. in Phys. Chemistry, U. Calif., Berkeley, 1961. Research chemist N. Hungarian Chem. Works, Miskolc, 1955-57, Stauffer Chem. Co., Richmond, Calif., 1957-58; research asst. Lawrence Radiation Lab., U. Calif., Berkeley, 1959-61; sr. scientist Jet Propulsion Lab., Calif. Inst. Tech., Pasadena, 1961-80, research fellow div. chemistry, 1965-69, sr. research fellow, 1970-72, sr. research scientist, head Electron Collision group, 1970—. Contbr. articles to profl. jours. Recipient NASA medal for exceptional sci. achievement, 1973. Fellow Am. Phys. Soc.; mem. Am. Chem. Soc. Current Work: Research and supervision of research in electron collision physics and spectroscopy. Subspecialties: Atomic and molecular physics; Physical chemistry. Home: 400 S Parkwood Ave Pasadena CA 91107 Office: 4800 Oak Grove Dr Pasadena CA 91109

TRAMILL, JAMES LOUIS, psychology educator; b. Clarksville, Tenn., July 25, 1945; s. Louis Howell and Mable (Clark) T.; m. P. Jeannie Kleinhammer, May 19, 1982; 1 child, Lacey. B.S., Austin Peay State U., 1967, M.A., 1977; Ph.D., U. So. Miss., 1981. Instr. psychology Austin Peay State U., Clarksville, 1977-78; asst. prof. ednl. psychology Wichita (Kans.) State U., 1980-84, assoc. prof., 1984—. Contbr. articles to profl. jours. Mem. Am. Psychol. Assn., Soc. Research in Child Devel., Am. Ednl. Research Assn., Assn. Psychology and Edn. Research in Kans. (pres. 1981-83), Kans. Acad. Sci. (jour. editor 1980-83). Current Work: Behavioral and physiological effects of ethanol challenges, cognitive development, sex roles, ego development, life span. Subspecialties: Developmental psychology; Physiological psychology. Office: Wichita State U Instructional Services 28 Wichita KS 67208

TRAMONTOZZI, LOUIS ROBERT, electrical engineer; b. Boston, Mar. 24, 1958; s. Fiore and Concetta (Antonellis) T. B.S. in E.E., U. Lowell, 1980; M.S. in Microwave Engring., U. Mass., 1984. Programmer, Army Materials and Mechanics Research Ctr., Watertown, Mass., 1975-77; assembler Omni-Spectra, Waltham, Mass., 1978; engr. Raytheon, various locations, 1980—. Contbr. articles to profl. jours. Jacob Ziskind fellow U. Lowell, 1980. Mem. IEEE, Am. Radio Relay League, Eta Kappa Nu. Roman Catholic. Current work: Research in microwave solid state amplifiers and/or MMIC technology at microwave frequencies. Subspecialties: Fracture mechanics; Software engineering. Home: 48 Bridge St Watertown MA 02172 Office: Raytheon 131 Spring St Lexington MA 02173

TRAN, NANG TRI, electrical engineer, physicist; b. Binh Dinh, Vietnam, Jan. 2, 1948; came to U.S., Mar., 1979; s. Cam Tran and Cuv Thi Nguyen; m. Thu-Huong Thi Tong, Oct. 14, 1982; 1 child, Helen T. B.S.E.E., Kyushu Inst. Tech., Kitakyushu, Japan, 1973, M.S.E.E., 1975; Ph.D., U. of Osaka Prefecture, Sakai, Japan, 1978. Research assoc. U. of Calif.-Irvine, 1979 research scientist Sharp Electronics, Irvine, 1979-80; sr. research scientist Arco Solar Industries, Chatsworth, Calif., 1980-84; research specialist 3M Co., St. Paul, 1985—. Contbr. articles to profl. jours. Scholarship fellow Vietnamese Govt., Japan, 1968-73, grad. scholarship fellow Rotary Internat., Japan, 1973-75, predoctoral fellow Japanese Govt., 1975-78. Mem. IEEE, Am. Vacuum Soc., Japan Soc. of Applied Physics, Japan Soc. of Physics. Current work: Thin film solar cells; sputtering, chemical vapor deposition and other vacuum technique. Electroluminescent displays semi conductor device physics. Subspecialties: Electronic materials; Materials processing. Office: 3M Ctr 201-1E-23 Saint Paul MN 55144

TRAPASSO, LOUIS MICHAEL, geography and geology educator; b. Niagara Falls, N.Y., Apr. 25, 1953; s. Domenick and Maria (Minervini) T. B.A., SUNY-Buffalo, 1975; M.A., Ind. U., 1977; Ph.D., Ind. State U., 1980. Teaching asst. dept. geography Ind. U., Bloomington, 1975-77; research asst. geography/geology dept. Ind. State U., Terre Haute, 1977-80; assoc. prof. dept. geography/geology Western Ky. U., Bowling Green, 1980—; advisor Nat. Assn. Ptnrs. of the Alliance, Holcomb Research Inst., Indpls., 1981. Contbr. Ency. of Climatology and lab. exercise manual. Contbr. chpt. to book and articles to profl. jours. Dames and Moore project grantee, 1983; Shell and Assocs. project grantee, 1985. Mem. Assn. Am. Geographers, Am. Meteorol. Soc., AAAS, Ky. Acad. Sci., Internat. Graphoanalysis Soc., Ky.-Ecuador Ptnrs., Sigma Xi, Gama Theta Upsilon (v.p. 1979-80). Democrat. Roman Catholic. Current Work: Climate and the human body, climatic changes, climate and crime, environmental perception and environmental systems, thunderstorm trigger mechanisms. Subspecialties: Climatology; Remote sensing (atmospheric science). Office: Dept Geography/Geology Western Ky U Bowling Green KY 42101

TRAUB, ROGER DENNIS, neurologist; b. Washington, Feb. 26, 1946; s. Robert and Renee Charlotte (Gluck) T.; m. Stephanie Kinter, May 4, 1974; 1 son: Matthew. A.B., Princeton U., 1967; M.D., U. Pa., 1972. Research assoc. NIH, Bethesda, Md., 1973-75; research staff mem. IBM Watson Research Lab., Yorktown Heights, N.Y., 1975—; resident in neurology Neurol. Inst. N.Y., 1978-81; asst. prof. clin. neurology Columbia U., 1981-84, adj. assoc. prof. neurology, 1984—. Contbr. articles to profl. jours. Mem. Soc. Neurosci., Am. Acad. Neurology. Current Work: Cellular mechanisms of epilepsy, neurophysiology of hippocampus, computer simulation, dementia. Subspecialties: Neurophysiology; Neurology. Office: IBM Watson Research Center Yorktown Heights NY 10598

TRAVIS, LARRY DEAN, space scientist; b. Burlington, Iowa, July 29, 1943; s. Dean Frank and Martha Virginia (Logsdon) T. B.A., U. Iowa, 1965, M.S., 1967; Ph.D., Pa. State U., 1971. Asst. prof. physics Pa. State U., University Park, 1971-73; sr. sci. analyst Computer Scis. Corp., N.Y.C., 1973-74, GTE Info. Systems, N.Y.C., 1974-77, Sigma Data Services Corp., N.Y.C., 1977-78; space scientist NASA Goddard Inst. for Space Studies, N.Y.C., 1978—. Contbr. articles to profl. jours. Recipient Exceptional Sci. Achievement medal NASA, 1980. Mem. Am. Astron. Soc., Am. Geophys. Union, AAAS, Sigma Xi. Current Work: Remote sensing and analysis of planetary atmospheres. Subspecialties: Planetary atmospheres; Satellite studies. Office: 2880 Broadway New York NY 10025

TRAYNHAM, RICHARD NEVILLE, clinical psychologist; b. Seattle, Oct. 14, 1947; s. David James and Merceile Lois (Neville) T.; m. Billie J. Holmquist, June 19, 1967; children: William, Amy. B.A., Western Wash. U., 1971; M.A., U. Ark., 1974, Ph.D., 1977. Lic. clin. psychologist, Mont. Psychology technician VA Hosp., Hampton, Va., 1971-72; psychologist Warm Springs (Mont.) State Hosp., 1976-77, research dir., 1977-78; dir. clin. GTU, 1978-79, pvt. practice clin. psychology, Bozeman, Mont., 1978—; cons. Gov.'s Office, Mont. Mental Disabilities Bd. of Visitors, 1978—, Mont. State Prison, 1978-80; clin. psychologist Mont. State U., 1980-81. Contbr. articles to profl. jours. Team cons. Gallatin County Child Abuse, Bozeman, 1979—. Mem. Am. Psychol. Assn., Biofeedback Soc. Am., Assn. for Transpersonal Psychology, Assn. Rural Mental Health, Internat. Ctr. for Social Gerontology. Current Work: Provide evaluation, treatment and consulting to nontraditional mental health delivery system in rural catchment area; research in the integration of transpersonal approaches with biofeedback and health psychology areas. Subspecialty: Clinical psychology. Home: 504 Henderson St Bozeman MT 59715 Office: 111 S Tracy Ave Bozeman MT 59715

TREACY, MICHAEL MATTHEW JOHN, petrochemical research engineering company physicist; b. Londonderry, Northern Ireland, Oct. 13, 1954; s. Mathew John and Mary (Boshell) T.; m. Linda Louise Hutchings, May 4, 1985. M.A., St. John's Coll., U. Cambridge, 1976, Ph.D., 1979. Postdoctoral researcher IBM Corp., Yorktown Heights, N.Y., 1980-81; engr. Centre National d'Etudes des Telecommunications, Bagneux, Paris, 1981-82; sr. physicist Exxon Chems., Annandale, N.J., 1982-84, Exxon Research & Engring. Co., 1984—. Contbr. articles to profl. jours. Fellow Royal Micros. Soc.; mem. Am. Phys. Soc., Am. Chem. Soc., AAAS. Roman Catholic. Current work: Application of electron microscopical techniques to the characterization of heterogeneous catalysts and surface structures. Subspecialties: Condensed matter physics; Electronic materials. Home: 6 Dennis Ave High Bridge NJ 08829 Office: Exxon Research & Engring Co Route 22E Annandale NJ 08829

TREHUB, ARNOLD, psychologist; b. Malden, Mass., Oct. 19, 1923; s. Clarence and Rose (Issner) T.; m. Elaine Dorothy Epstein, Aug. 12, 1950; children: Craig, Aaron, Lorna. B.A., Northeastern U., 1949; M.A., Boston U., 1951, Ph.D., 1954. Research psychologist Mass. Gen. Hosp., Boston, 1953-54, VA Med. Center, Northampton, Mass., 1954-82; adj. prof. U. Mass., Amherst, 1972—. Served with AC U.S. Army, 1943-46. Mem. Soc. Neurosci., N.Y. Acad. Scis., AAAS. Current Work: Neuronal mechanisms for cognitive processes, brain, cognition, synapse, perception, learning, memory, vision, imagination. Subspecialties: Cognition; Neurophysiology. Home: 145 Farview Way Amherst MA 01002 Office: U Mass Dept Psychology Amherst MA 01003

TRENCH, WILLIAM FREDERICK, mathematics educator; b. Trenton, N.J., July 31, 1931; s. George Daniel and Anna Elizabeth (Taylor) T.; m. Beverly Joan Busenshut, Nov. 22, 1980; m. Lucille Ann Marasco, Dec. 26, 1954; (div. Dec. 1978); children—Joseph William, Randolph Clifford, John Frederick, Gina Margaret. B.A., Lehigh U., 1953; M.A., U. Pa., 1955, Ph.D., 1958. Instr. elec. engring. U. Pa., 1953-56; mathematician Gen. Electric Co., Phila., 1956-57; engring. specialist Philco Corp., Phila., 1957-59; engr. RCA, Moorestown, N.J., 1959-64; assoc. prof. math. Drexel U., Phila., 1964-67, prof. math, 1967—. Author: Advanced Calculus, 1978; (with others Elementary Multivariable Calculus, 1971, Elementary Multivariable Calculus with Linear Algebra and Series, 1972; contbr. articles to profl. jours. Mem. Am. Math. Soc, Math. Assn. Am., Soc. Indsl. and Applied Math. Current work: Ordinary differential equations, numerical linear algebra; special functions. Subspecialties: Analysis; Applied mathematics. Home: 32 Rockwood Rd Levittown PA 19056 Office: Dept Math Drexel U Philadelphia PA 19056

TRETTER, MARIETTA JOAN, business statistics and computer science educator, researcher; b. Pueblo, Colo., Dec. 16, 1944; d. Vincent Joseph and Lena (Oberto) T. A.A., Pueblo Jr. Coll., 1964; B.S., U. So. Colo., 1965; M.S., U. Wis.-Madison, 1969, Ph.D., 1973. Programmer 1st Nat. Bank of Pueblo, 1965-66; instr. data processing Albuquerque Tech. Vocat. Inst., 1966-67; research asst. U. Wis.-Madison, 1969-75; asst. prof. mgmt. sci. Pa. State U., 1975-81; assoc. prof. bus. analysis Tex. A&M U., 1981—; cons. load research. Author: Software Interval Arithmetic, 1981. Mem. Soc. Indsl. and Applied Math. (vis. lectr. 1981), Inst. Math. Stats., Am. Statis. Assn. Current Work: Distribution functions in applied statistics, interval arithmetic, symbolic manipulation, continued fractions, special functions, graphics. Subspecialties: Mathematical software; Applied mathematics. Office: Dept Business Analysis and Research Texas A&M U College Station TX 77843

TREVES, SAMUEL BLAIN, educator, geologist; b. Detroit, Sept. 11, 1925; s. Samuel and Stella (Stork) T.; m. Jane Patricia Mitoray, Nov. 24, 1960; children—John Samuel, David Samuel. B.S., Mich. Technol. U., 1951; postgrad. (Fulbright scholar), U. Otago, New Zealand, 1953-54; M.S., U. Idaho, 1953; Ph.D., Ohio State U., 1959. Geologist Ford Motor Co., 1951, Idaho Bur. Mines and Geology, 1952, Otago Catchment Bd., N.Z., 1953-54; mem. faculty U. Nebr., Lincoln, 1958—, prof. geology, 1966—, chmn. dept., 1964-70, 74—; curator geology Nebr. State Mus., 1964—; expdns. to, Antarctica and Greenland, 1960, 61, 63, 65, 70, 72, 73, 74, 75, 76. Fellow Geol. Soc. Am.; mem. Am. Mineral. Soc., Royal Soc. New Zealand, Nat. Assn. Geology Tchrs., Am. Polar Soc., AAAS, Sigma Xi, Tau Beta Pi, Sigma Gamma Epsilon. Club: Explorers. Research and publs. on geology of igneous and metamorphic rocks of Idaho, N.Z., Mich., Antarctica, Greenland, emphasis on origin of Precambrian granite complexes and volcanology. Current Work: Investigation of mineral phases of alkaline basalts from Antarctica and precambrian of Nebraska. Subspecialties: Petrology; Tectonics. Home: 1710 B St Lincoln NE 68502

TREVORROW, LAVERNE EVERETT, chemist; b. Moline, Ill., Nov. 1, 1928; s. Barney Thomas and Winona Marie (Jones) T.; m. Marjorie Jane Anderson, Aug. 12, 1950; children—Tristram, Cindy. A.B., Augustana Coll., 1950; M.S., Okla. State U., 1952; Ph.D., U. Wis.-Madison. Chemist Argonne Nat. Lab., Ill., 1955—. Mem. Am. Chem. Soc. Current work: Chemistry of metallic florides; transition metals actinides; disposal of radioactive wastes; dev. nuclear fuel reprocessing. Subspecialties: Inorganic chemistry; Hazardous waste disposal. Office: Argonne Nat Lab 9700 S Cass Ave Argonne IL 60439

TREYBIG, JAMES B., computer company executive. Pres., Tandem Computers Inc., Cupertino, Calif. . Office: Tandem Computers Inc 19333 Vallco Pkwy Cupertino CA 95014*

TRIFFET, TERRY, research engineer, educator; b. Enid, Okla., June 10, 1922; m. Millicent McMaster, May 26, 1946; children: Patricia A., Terrence P., Melanie K. B.A., U. Okla., 1945; B.S., U. Colo., 1948, M.S., 1950; Ph.D. in Structural Mechanics, Stanford U., 1957. Instr. engring. U. Colo., Boulder, 1947-50; gen. engr. rocket and guided missile research U.S. Naval Ordnance Test Sta., 1950-55; gen. engr. radiol. research, head radiol. effects br. U.S. Naval Radiol. Def. Lab., 1955-59; assoc. prof. applied mechanics Mich. State U., East Lansing, 1959-63, prof. mechanics and material sci., 1963-76; assoc. dean research Coll. Engring., U. Ariz., Tucson, 1976—; cons. U.S. Dept. Def., 1959-65, Battelle Meml. Inst., 1965-68, Lear-Siegler, Inc., 1965—. Australian Research Com. grantee, 1966-67, 72-73. Mem. Am. Phys. Soc., Am. Math. Soc., Soc. Engring. Sci., Soc. Indsl. and Applied Math, IEEE. Current Work: Mathematical mechanics, software engineering, neural modeling. Subspecialties: Theoretical and applied mechanics; Artificial intelligence. Office: Coll Engring U Ariz Dean's Office Tucson AZ 85721

TRIGG, MICHAEL EDWARD, pediatric oncologist, pediatric hematologist; b. Hartford, Conn., Aug. 18, 1949; s. Vincent Paul and Jean (Greenberg) T. B.A. with honors, Trinity Coll., 1971; M.D. with distinction, George Washington U., 1975. Diplomate: Nat. Bd. Med. Examiners. Student scientist lab. gen. and comparative biochemistry NIMH, Bethesda, Md., 1972-75; resident in pediatrics Northwestern U., Children's Mem. Hosp.-Prentice Maternity Ctr., Evanston, (Ill.) Hosp., 1975-78; cons. Prentice Maternity Ctr., Chgo., 1977-78; clin. assoc. pediatric oncology br. Nat. Cancer Inst., Bethesda, 1978-80; pediatrician Washington Adventist Hosp., Takoma Park, Md., 1978-80; guest worker Nat. Cancer Inst., 1980—; asst. prof. pediatrics U. Wis.-Madison, 1980—; assoc. mem. Wis. Clin. Cancer Ctr., Madison, 1982—; sci. dir. Molecular Medicine, Bethesda, 1980—, Inst. Immuno-oncology and Genetics, Bethesda, 1981—. Contbr. numerous articles to profl. jours. Served with USPHS, 1978-80. NIH tng. grantee, 1972; recipient William Beaumont Med. Research award, 1974; Ronald M. Ferguson prize, 1971; Am. Cancer Soc. Jr. Faculty fellow. Jr. fellow Am. Acad. Pediatrics; mem. William Beaumont Med. Soc., So. Med. Assn., Am. Soc. Clin. Oncology, Am. Soc. Pediatric Hematology/Oncology, Am. Assn. Cancer Research, Midwest Soc. Pediatric Research, Children's Cancer Study Group, Phi Beta Kappa, Alpha Omega Alpha. Current Work: Serotherapy, malignant tumors, allogeneic and autologous bone marrow transplantation; allogeneic transplantation with T-lymphocyte depletion. Subspecialties: Marrow transplant; Immunopharmacology. Home: 7359 Tree Ln Madison WI 53717 Office: U Wis Dept Pediatrics 600 Highland Ave Madison WI 54792

TRIMBERGER, STEPHEN MATHIAS, software designer; b. New Brunswick, N.J., Aug. 30, 1955; s. Leon Paul and Carol Mae (Eberhardy) T. B.S., Calif. Inst. Tech., 1977, Ph.D., 1983; M.S., U. Calif.-Irvine, 1979. Dep. dir. silicon structures project Calif. Inst. Tech., Pasadena, 1980-81; CAD software cons., Pasadena, 1979-83; project leader VLSI Tech., Inc., San Jose, Calif., 1982-84, supr. advanced CAD software, 1984—; chmn. IEEE Design automatic standards subcom. working group and circuit and phys. design, 1985—. Contbr. articles to profl. jours. Mem. IEEE, Assn. Computing Machinery. Current work: computer aided design of integrated circuits, especially silicon compilation. Subspecialties: Integrated circuits; Computer-aided design. Address: VLSI Tech Inc MS30 1109 McKay Dr San Jose CA 95131

TRIPATHI, RAMESH CHANDRA, ophthalmology educator, ophthalmologist and pathologist; b. Jamira, India, July 1, 1936; came to U.S., 1977; s. Arjun and Gandhari T.; m. Brenda Jennifer Lane, May 20, 1969; children: Anita, Paul. I.Sc., Lucknow (India) Christian Coll., 1954; M.B., B.S., Argra Med. Coll., 1959; M.S. in Ophthalmology, Lucknow U., 1963; M.Surgery; Ph.D., U. London, 1970. Diplomate: ophthalmology Exam. Bd. Eng., Royal Coll. Pathologist Eng. Intern GSVM Med. Coll. Hosps., Kanpur, 1959-60, Lucknow U., 1959-60; resident, 1960-63; fellow Univ. Eye Clinic, Ghent, Belgium, 1964; registrar S.W. Middlesex Hosps., Isleworth, Middlesex, Eng., 1965-67; lectr. U. London, 1967-70, sr. lectr., 1970-77; cons. pathologist and ophthalmologist Moorfields Eye Hosp., London, 1972-77; prof. ophthalmology U. Chgo., 1977—, sec. dept., 1977—; mem. med. staff U. Chgo. (Med. Ctr.), 1977—, cons. pediatric tumor bd., 1978-80; prof. U. Chgo. (The Coll.), 1978—. Exec. editor: Exptl. Eye Research, 1973—; editorial bd.: Ophthalmic Research, 1974—, Lens Research, 1983—; sect. editor: Cornea, 1981—; assoc. editor: Afro-Asian Jour. Ophthalmology, 1981—; contbr. chpts. to books and articles to profl. jours. Council mem. Friends of India Soc. Internat., Chgo., 1982. Med. Research Council grantee, 1972-75; Nat. Eye Inst. grantee, 1977—; recipient Ophthalmology prize Royal Soc. Medicine, 1971, Royal Eye London prize Ophtalmol. Soc., 1976. Fellow Royal Soc. Medicine, Am. Acad. Opthalmology, Internat. Coll. Surgeons, Royal Coll. Physicians and Surgeons; mem. AMA, Physiol. Soc. London, Fedn. Am. Soc. Exptl. Biologists, Assn. Indians in Am. (co-chmn. med. council Chgo. 1983). Club: Quadrangle (Chgo.). Current Work: Authored more than 170 scientific publications and 20 book chapters encompassing medical and biological fields of morphology, pathophysiology, clinical and experimental ophthalmology, genetics, cell biology, tissue culture, electron microscopy, immunopathology. Subspecialties: Ophthalmology; Pathology (medicine). Home: 5545 S Harper Ave Chicago IL 60637 Office: U Chicago 939 E 57th St Chicago IL 60637

TRIPATHY, SUKANT KISHORE, physicist; b. Chakradharpur, Bihar, India, Aug. 4, 1952; came to U.S., 1976, naturalized, 1981; s. Jyotish Chandra and Usha Rani (Pani) T.; m. Susan Jean Thomson, Sept. 5, 1981. B.S., Indian Inst. Tech., 1972, M.S., 1974; Ph.D., Case Western Res. U., 1980. Research fellow Indian Inst. Tech., Kharagpur, 1974-76; grad. fellow Case Western Res U., Cleve., 1976-80; mem. tech. staff GTE Labs., Inc., Waltham, Mass., 1981-83, tech. mgr., 1983—. Contbr. articles to profl. jours. Recipient Nat. Sci. award Nat. Council India, 1969, Talent Search award, 1969. Mem. Am. Phys. Soc., Am. Chem. Soc., Sigma Xi. Current Work: Structural studies in polymeric and composite systems having interesting electrical electronic and optical properties; theoretical modelling and statistical mechanics of chain molecules. Subspecialty: Polymer physics. Home: 34 Dartmouth St Arlington MA 02174 Office: 40 Sylvan Rd Waltham MA 02254

TRIVEDI, MANMOHAN MANUBHAI, electrical and computer engineering educator; b. Wardha, India, Oct. 4, 1953; s. Manubhai J. and Tanugauri M. Trivedi; m. Nayana N. Mehta, Aug. 22, 1982. B.E.E. with honors, Birla Inst. Tech. and Sci., Pilani, India, 1974; M.E.E., Utah State U., 1976, Ph.D. in Elec. Engring., 1979. Jr. engr. Uranus Electronics, Surat, India, 1974; teaching asst. elec. engring. Utah State U., Logan, 1975-76, research asst. space dynamics lab., 1976-79; assoc. prof. elec. and computer engring. La. State U., Baton Rouge, 1979—, also mem. Faculty Senate, 1984—; session chmn. internat. confs. on computer vision, artificial intelligence, robotics. Editor spl. issue on artificial intelligence Optical Engring. jour., 1986. Contbr. articles to profl. jours. Pres. India Assn., Utah State U., 1977; conf. co-chmn. Applications of Artificial Intelligence, Arlington, Va., 1985—. Mem. IEEE, Soc. Photo-Optical Engrs., Pattern Recognition Soc., Am. Soc. Photogrammetry, Am. Assn. Artificial Intelligence, Sigma Xi, Phi Kappa Phi, Tau Beta Pi. Current work: Development of algorithms for automatic interpretation of high resolution aerial scenes; interests are computer vision, artificial intelligence, image analysis, industrial automation, remote sensing. Subspecialties: Computer engineering; Graphics, image processing, and pattern recognition. Home: 327 McDonald Ave Baton Rouge LA 70808 Office: Dept Elec and Computer Engring South Campus Dr La State U Baton Rouge LA 70803

TRIVELPIECE, ALVIN WILLIAM, physicist, government official; b. Stockton, Calif., Mar. 15, 1931; s. Alvin Stevens and Mae (Hughes) T.; m. Shirley Ann Ross, Mar. 23, 1953; children: Craig Evan, Steve Edward, Keith Eric. B.S., Calif. Poly. Coll., San Luis Obispo, 1953; M.S., Calif. Inst. Tech., 1955, Ph.D., 1958. Fulbright scholar Delft (Netherlands) U., 1958-59; asst. prof., then asso. prof. U. Calif. at Berkeley, 1959-66; prof. physics U. Md., 1966-76; on leave as asst. dir. for research div. controlled thermonuclear research AEC, Washington, 1973-75; v.p. Maxwell Labs. Inc., San Diego, 1976-78; corp. v.p. Sci. Applications, Inc., La Jolla, Calif., 1978-81; dir. Office of Energy Research, U.S. Dept. Energy, Washington, 1981—. Author: Slow Wave Propagation in Plasma Wave Guides, 1966, (with N.A. Krall) Principles of Plasma Physics, 1973; also articles. Named Disting. Alumnus Calif. Poly. State U., 1978; Guggenheim fellow, 1966. Fellow Am. Phys. Soc., AAAS, IEEE; mem. Am. Nuclear Soc., Ams. for Energy Independence, AAUP, N.Y. Acad. Scis., Am. Assn. Physics Tchrs., Sigma Xi. Clubs: Cosmos, Capital Hill. Patentee in field. Current Work: Properties of plasmas, waves-experimental/theoretical, fusion-confinement, heating, stability, transport, nonneutral plasmas-experimental, accelerators: cyclotron wave. Subspecialties: Plasma physics; Plasma (energy science and technology). Office: US Dept Energy 1000 Independence Ave SW Washington DC 20585

TROPF, WILLIAM JACOB, physicist; b. Chgo., Jan. 14, 1947; s. William Jacob and Ardith Shirley (Clausen) T.; m. Cheryl Lynn Griffiths, Aug. 31, 1968; 1 son, Andrew Zachary. B.S., Coll. William and Mary, 1968; Ph.D., U. Va., 1973. Project dir. B-K Dynamics, Inc., Rockville, Md., 1973-76; prin. staff physicist, supr. electrooptics group Applied Physics Lab., Johns Hopkins U., Laurel, Md., 1977—. Served with USAR, 1968-78. Mem. Am. Phys. Soc., Optical Soc. Am., Sigma Xi, Sigma Pi Sigma. Home: 13060 Saint Patricks Ct Highland MD 20707 Office: Johns Hopkins Rd Laurel MD 20777

TROPP, BURTON E., biochemistry educator, biochemical researcher; b. N.Y.C.; s. Sol and Renee (Rosenthal) T.; m. Roslyn Goldman, June 22, 1965; children—Jonathan, Matthew, Paul. B.S. in Chemistry, Bklyn. Coll., 1961; Ph.D. in Biochemistry and Molecular Biology, Harvard U., 1966. Research fellow Harvard U. Med. Sch., 1965-67; asst. prof. chemistry Richmond Coll., CUNY, S.I., 1967-70; asst. prof. chemistry Queens Coll. CUNY, 1970-72, assoc. prof., 1972-75, prof., 1975—. Contbr. articles to sci. jours.; patentee in field. Mem. Am. Chem. Soc., Am. Soc. Biol. Chemists, Am. Soc. Microbiologists, AAAS, Sigma Xi. Current work: Control and Regulation of Phosphoglyceride metabolism. Subspecialties: Biochemistry (biology); Microbiology. Office: Dept Chemistry Queens Coll Flushing NY 11367

TROSKO, JAMES EDWARD, educator; b. Muskegon, Mich., Apr. 2, 1938; s. Andrew and Christina (Nemeth) T.; m. Beverly Kay Dowell, Sept. 3, 1960; 1 son, Philip Randal. B.A., Central Mich. U., 1970; M.S., Mich. State U., 1962, Ph.D., 1963. Postdoctoral fellow Oak Ridge Nat. Lab., 1963-66; asst. prof. Mich. State U., East Lansing, 1966-71, assoc. prof., 1971-75, prof., 1975—; vis. prof. McArdle Lab. Cancer Research U. Wis., 1972-73. Contbr. numerous articles to profl. jours. NDEA fellow, 1960-63; Nat. Cancer Inst. research career devel. award, 1972-77; Searle award U.K. Environ. Mutagen Soc., 1979. Mem. Am. Assn. Cancer Research, Genetic Soc. Am., AAAS, Toxicology Soc., Environ. Mutagen Soc., Tissue Culture Assn., Sigma Xi. Current Work: Genetic causes of chronic diseases. Subspecialties: Cancer research (medicine); Genetics and genetic engineering (medicine).

TROST, BARRY MARTIN, chemist, educator; b. Phila., June 13, 1941; s. Joseph and Esther T.; m. Susan Paula Shapiro, Nov. 25, 1967; children: Aaron David, Carey Daniel. B.A. cum laude, U. Pa., 1962; Ph.D., MIT, 1965. Mem. faculty U. Wis., Madison, 1965—, prof., chemistry, 1969—, Evan P. and Marion Helfaer prof. chemistry, from 1976, now Vilas research prof. chemistry; cons. Merck, Sharp & Dohme, E.I. duPont de Nemours.; Chem. Soc. centenary lectr., 1982. Author: Problems in Spectroscopy, 1967, Sulfur Ylides, 1975; editor: Structure and Reactivity Concepts in Organic Chemistry series, 1972—; asso. editor: Jour. Am. Chem. Soc, 1974-80; editorial bd.: Organic Reactions Series, 1971—; contbr. numerous articles to profl. jours. NSF fellow, 1963-65; Sloan Found. fellow, 1967-69; Am. Swiss Found. fellow, 1975—; recipient Dreyfus Found. tchr.-scholar, award, 1970; Am. Chem. Soc. pure chemistry award, 1977; Creative work in synthetic organic chemistry award, 1981; Baekeland medal, 1981; named Chem. Pioneer Am. Inst. Chemists, 1983. Mem. Am. Chem. Soc., Nat. Acad. Scis., Am. Acad. Arts and Scis., AAAS, Chem. soc. London. Subspecialties: Organic chemistry; Synthetic chemistry. Home: 209 N Whitney Way Madison WI 53705 Office: Dept Chemistry U Wis Madison WI 53706

TROWBRIDGE, RICHARD STUART, research scientist; b. Cambridge, Mass., Apr. 3, 1942; s. Walter Henry and Lamia Andree (Sanderson) T.; m. Sue Hitchcock Trowbridge, June 12, 1965; 1 son, John Richard. B.S., U. Mass., 1964, M.S., 1966, Ph.D., 1971. Research scientist dept. virology N.Y. State Inst. Basic Research in Mental Retardation, S.I., 1970-72, sr. research scientist, 1972-77, research scientist III, 1980-81, research scientist IV, 1981—; grants adminstr., dir. Research Found. Mental Hygiene, Inc., S.I., 1977-80. Contbr. articles to profl. jours. Mem. exec. bd. S.I. Council Boy Scouts Am., 1981—; v.p. Meals on Wheels S.I., Inc., 1981-82, pres., 1982-83; bd. dirs. Camp Fire of N.Y., Inc., 1985—. NIH grantee, 1974-80. Mem. Am. Soc. Microbiology, Tissue Culture Assn., N.Y. Acad. Sci. Lodge: Rotary. Current Work: Virus-host cell interactions which culminate in persistent infections of the central nervous system. Subspecialties: Cell and tissue culture; Virology (biology). Home: PO Box 805 Staten Island NY 10314 Office: 1050 Forest Hill Rd Staten Island NY 10314

TROWN, PATRICK WILLOUGHBY, pharmaceutical company research executive, immunobiologist; b. Birmingham, Eng., Mar. 17, 1937; came to U.S., 1962; s. Ronald Hugh and Evelyn Mary (Willoughby) T.; m. Marie-Claire Allain Labbe, Aug. 18, 1962; children: Christopher, Nicolas. B.A. with honors, Oxford (Eng.) U. Oriel Coll., 1960, M.A., 1962, D.Phil., 1962. Research scientist Lederle Labs., Pearl River, N.Y., 1964-69; chief research group Hoffmann-La Roche, Inc., Nutley, N.J., 1969-76, asst. dir. dept. chemotherapy, 1976-78, assoc. dir. dept. chemotherapy, 1978-80, dir. dept. immunotherapy, 1980-84, dir. dept. exptl. oncology and virology, 1984—; vis. asst. prof. molecular biology Albert Einstein Coll. Medicine. Contbr. articles to profl. jours. Mem. Am. Assn. Cancer Research, Internat. Soc. Immunopharmacology. Current Work: Biology of interferons and other lymphokines; antitumor chemotherapy and immunotherapy. Subspecialties: Cancer research (medicine); Chemotherapy. Office: Hoffmann-La Roche Inc Kingsland Ave Nutley NJ 07110

TROY, FREDERIC ARTHUR, II, medical biochemistry, educator, enologist; b. Evanston, Ill., Feb. 16, 1937; s. Charles McGregor and Virginia (Minto) T.; m. Linda Ann, Mar. 23, 1959; children: Karen M., Janet R. B.S., Washington U., St. Louis, 1961; Ph.D., Purdue U., 1966. Am. Cancer Soc. postdoctoral fellow dept. physiol. chemistry Johns Hopkins U. Sch. Medicine, 1966-68; asst. prof. biol. chemistry U. Calif. Sch. Medicine, Davis, 1968-74, assoc. prof., 1974-80, prof., 1980—, co-prin. investigator tumor biology tng. program, 1972; vis. research prof. dept. tumor biology Karolinska Inst. Med. Sch., Stockholm, 1976-77; cons. NIH, NSF, Damon Runyon-Walter Winchell Cancer Fund; cons. basic med. sci. rev. bd. VA. cons. enology; tchr. wine chemistry. Contbr. rev. article, numerous research articles to profl. jours. Recipient Research Career Devel. award NIH, 1975-80; Am. Cancer Soc.-Eleanor Roosevelt-Internat. Cancer fellow awarded by Union International Contre le Cancer, Geneva, 1976-77; NIH grantee, 1968—. Mem. Am. Soc. Biol. Chemists, Am. Soc. Cancer Research, Biochem. Soc. (London), Am. Chem. Soc., Biophys. Soc., Am. Soc. Microbiology, Am. Soc. Enologists, Soc. Complex Carbohydrates, N.Y. Acad. Scis., AAAS, Sigma Xi. Current work: Membrane chemistry; biosynthesis of glycoconjugales; research on molecular structure of cell membranes of human tumor cells for understanding relevance of cell surface changes to metastatic and invasive potential of tumor in vivo. Subspecialties: Cancer research (medicine); Membrane biology.

TROYER, ALVAH FORREST, seed corn company executive, plant breeder; b. LaFontaine, Ind., May 30, 1929; s. Alvah Forrest and Lottie (Waggoner) T.; m. Joyce Wigner, Sept. 22, 1950; children—Anne, Barbara, Catherine, Daniel. B.S., Purdue U., 1954; M.S., U. Ill.-Champaign-Urbana, 1956; Ph.D., U. Minn., 1964. Research assoc. U. Ill.-Champaign-Urbana, 1955-56; research fellow U. Minn.-St. Paul, 1956-58; research sta. mgr. Pioneer Hi-Bred Internat., Inc., Mankato, Minn., 1958-65, research coordinator, 1965-77; dir. research and devel. Pfizer Genetics, St. Louis, 1977-81, v.p. research and devel., St. Louis, 1981-82, v.p. research and devel. DeKalb-Pfizer Genetics, DeKalb, Ill., 1982—. Contbr. numerous articles to various publs.; developer widely grown hybrids. Served with U.S. Army, 1951-53; Korea. Fellow Am. Soc. Agronomy; mem. AAAS, Am. Seed Trade Assn., Crop Sci. Soc. Am., N.Y. Acad. Sci., Sigma Xi, Gamma Sigma Delta, Alpha Zeta, Lambda Chi Alpha, Gamma Alpha. Methodist. Lodge: Masons. Subspecialty: Plant genetics. Home: 611 Joanne Lane DeKalb IL 60115 Office: DeKalb-Pfizer Genetics 3100 Sycamore Rd DeKalb IL 60115

TROZZOLO, ANTHONY MARION, chemist; b. Chgo., Jan. 11, 1930; s. Pasquale and Francesca (Vercillo) T.; m. Doris C. Stoffregen, Oct. 8, 1955; children: Thomas, Susan (Mrs. Bruce Hecklinski), Patricia, Michael, Lisa, Laura. B.S., Ill. Inst. Tech., 1950; M.S., U. Chgo., 1957, Ph.D., 1960. Asst. chemist Chgo. Midway Labs., 1952-53; assoc. chemist Armour Research Found., Chgo., 1953-56; mem. tech. staff Bell Labs., Murray Hill, N.J., 1959-75; Charles L. Huisking prof. chemistry U. Notre Dame, 1975—; vis. prof. Columbia U., N.Y.C., 1971, U. Colo., 1981, Katholieke Universiteit Leuven, Belgium, 1983; vis. lectr. Academia Sinica, Beijing, Hofei, Singapore, 1984. AEC fellow, 1951, NSF fellow, 1957-59; Phillips lectr. U. Okla., 1971; P.C. Reilly lectr. U. Notre Dame, 1972; C.L. Brown lectr. Rutgers U., 1975; Sigma Xi lectr. Bowling Green U., 1976, Abbott Labs., 1978; M. Faraday lectr. No. Ill. U., 1976; F.O. Butler lectr. S.D. State U., 1978; Chevron lectr. U. Nev.-Reno, 1983. Asso. editor: Jour. Am. Chem. Soc, 1975-76; editor: Chem. Reviews, 1977-84; editorial adv. bd.: Accounts of Chem. Research, 1977—; contbr. articles to profl. jours. Fellow N.Y. Acad. Scis. (Halpern award in Photochemistry 1980), AAAS, Am. Inst. Chemists; mem. Am. Chem. Soc. (Disting. Service award St. Joseph Valley sect. 1979, Coronado lectr. 1980), AAUP, Sigma Xi. Roman Catholic. Patentee. Current Work: Physical organic chemistry: detection and characterization of reactive intermediates: laser photochemistry: photodegradation of polymers. Subspecialties: Photochemistry; Solid state chemistry. Home: 1329 E Washington St South Bend IN 46617 Office: U Notre Dame Notre Dame IN 46556

TRUBATCH, JANETT, university administrator, researcher, consultant; b. N.Y.C., Oct. 13, 1942; d. Louis L. and Lee J. (Jacobs) Rosenberg; m. Sheldon L. Trubatch, Aug. 26, 1962; children: A. David, Beth, Ruth Shoshana, Joel. B.Sc., Poly. Inst. N.Y., 1962; Ph.D., Brandeis U., 1968. Asst. prof. physics Calif. State U., Los Angeles, 1967-68; postdoctoral fellow Calif. Inst. Tech., 1968-73; asst. prof.-physiology N.Y. Med. Coll., 1973-77; program dir. neurobiology NSF, Washington, 1977-79; assoc. research prof. physiology George Washington U., 1979-80; health sci. adminstr. neurol. disorders program Nat. Inst. Neurol. and Communicative Disorders and Stroke, Bethesda, Md., 1980-85; assoc. v.p. research, dir. research adminstrn. U. Chgo., 1985—, acting dep. dir. neurol. disorders program, 1981-82; legis. fellow Office of Senator Inouye, 1981-83; guest speaker Nobel Symposium on Chem. Neurotransmission, Stockholm, 1980. Contbr. chpts. to books. Recipient Outstanding Performance award NSF, 1979, NIH, 1983; Whitehall Found. grantee, 1976-80; NSF grantee, 1976-81. Mem. Am. Phys. Soc., Soc. Neurosci., AAAS, Sigma Xi, Sigma Pi Sigma. Current Work: Mechanisms of synaptic transmission; synaptic plasticity and correlates of learning; basic mechanisms underlying neurological disorders. Subspecialties: Neurobiology; Neurophysiology. Office: Dir Research Adminstrn U Chgo 970 E 58th St Chicago IL 60637

TRUDEAU, FRANCIS BERGER, physician; b. Saranac Lake,N.Y., July 21, 1919; s. Francis B. and Helen G. (Garretson) T.; m. Jean Douglas Moore, Oct. 31, 1942 (div. 1960); children—Jean, Garret, Michelle; m. Ursula Wyatt Johnston, Nov. 1961. B.A., Yale U., 1942; M.D., Columbia U., 1950. Intern, Bellevue Hosp., N.Y.C., 1950-51, resident, 1951-52; resident Royal Victoria Hosp., Montreal, Que., Can., 1952-53; founder, pres. Trudeau Inst., Inc., Saranac Lake, N.Y.,1954—, Med. Assocs. P.C., Saranac Lake, 1971-80; physician U.S. Ski Team, 1977—; sch. and sports physician Saranac High Sch., 1980—; sr.med. officer Nordic events 1980 Winter Olympics, Lake Placid, N.Y.; bd. dirs. Am. Heart Assn., 1960-61. Contbr. articles on med. aspects of sports to ski mags. Warden St. John's in the Wilderness, Paul Smiths N.Y., 1958—; bd. dirs. Adirondack Council. Served to lt. USNR, 1942-46, ETO. Recipient citation in medicine St. Lawrence U., 1981; Bertrand Snell award Clarkson U., 1982. Fellow Am. Coll. Medicine, Am. Coll. Sports Medicine. Republican. Episcopalian. Club: Yale (N.Y.C.). Subspecialty: Sports medicine. Office: Trudeau Inst Inc Saranac Lake NY 12983

TRULLINGER, STEVEN EUGENE, physics educator, consultant; b. Eugene, Oreg., Sept. 21, 1950; s. Lawrence Eugene and Maureen (Barrows) T.; m. Nancy Cornelia Scott, Aug. 22, 1970 (div. June 1982); children—Valerie Lynn, Cynthia Ann, Joseph Scott; m. Marjorie Lou Dorsey, July 31, 1982; 1 dau., Tamra Lee. B.A., U. Calif.-Irvine, 1972, M.A., 1974, Ph.D., 1975. NSF postdoctoral fellow Cornell U., Ithaca, N.Y., 1975-76; asst. prof. physics U.So. Calif., Los Angeles, 1976-82, assoc. prof., 1982—; mem. Inst. for Theoretical Physics, Santa Barbara, Calif., 1981; cons. to industry and govt.; collaborator Los Alamos Nat. Lab., 1979—. Contbr. numerous articles to profl. jours. U. Calif.-Irvine pres.'s research fellow, 1972-73; Alfred P. Sloan fellow, 1980-84. Mem. Am. Phys. Soc. Democrat. Current work: Theoretical investigations of nonlinear, particle-like waves (solitons) in condensed matter systems such as low-dimensional conductors and magnets. Subspecialty: Condensed matter physics. Office: U So Calif Dept Physics University Park Los Angeles CA 90089

TRYBUS, RAYMOND J., research administrator, clinical psychologist; b. Chgo., Jan. 9, 1944; s. Fred and Cecilia (Liszka) T.; m. Sandra A. Noone, Aug. 19, 1967; children: David, Nicole. B.S., St. Louis U., 1965, M.S., 1970, Ph.D., 1971. Lic. psychologist, Md., D.C. Clin. psychologist Jewish Vocat. Service, St. Louis, 1968-71; clin. psychologist Gallaudet Coll., Washington, 1971-72, research psychologist, 1972-74, dir. demographic studies, 1974-78; dir. Gallaudet Coll. (Rehab. Engring. Ctr.), 1982—; dean Gallaudet Research Inst., 1978—; cons. Mental Health Ctr. for Deaf, Laurel, Md., 1982—, Congl. Research Service, 1982—. Editor, contbg. author: The Future of Mental Health Services for the Deaf, 1978. Grantee NIMH; Grantee Spencer Found.; Grantee Tex. Edn. Agy.; Grantee W.K. Kellogg Found. Mem. Internat. Assn. Study of Interdisciplinary Research, Am. Psychol. Assn., Soc. Research Adminstrs., AAAS, von Bekesy Soc. (sect. chair 1982—). Roman Catholic. Current Work: Development and management of interdisciplinary research on deafness, prevention of deafness, restoration of hearing, accommodation to deafness. Subspecialty: Sensory processes. Home: 8806 Altimont Ln Chevy Chase MD 20815 Office: 800 Florida Ave NE Washington DC 20002

TRYON, EDWARD POLK, physics educator; b. Terre Haute, Ind., Sept. 4, 1940; s. Philip Freeland and Elizabeth Marsh (Banker) T. A.B., Cornell U., 1962; Ph.D., U. Calif., Berkeley, 1967. Research asso. Columbia U., N.Y.C., 1967-68, asst. prof., 1968-71; asst. prof. physics Hunter Coll., CUNY, 1971-73, assoc. prof., 1974-79, prof., 1979—(on leave 1977-78); vis. mem. Inst. Advanced Study, Princeton, 1977-78. Contbr. articles to profl. jours. Cornell nat. scholar, 1958-62; hon. Woodrow Wilson fellow, 1962-64; NSF fellow, 1962-64; CUNY scholar, 1982-83. Mem. Am. Phys. Soc., N.Y. Acad. Scis., Phi Beta Kappa, Sigma Xi (nat. lectr. 1982-84), Phi Kappa Phi. Originator quantum fluctuation theory for creation of universe from nothing, 1973. Current Work: Creation of universe from nothing as quantum fluctuation, particle theory. Subspecialties: Cosmology; Particle physics. Office: Dept Physics Hunter Coll New York NY 10021

TRZASKO, JOSEPH ANTHONY, psychologist, educator; b. Jamaica, N.Y., June 4, 1946; s. Joseph Anthony and Lottie Marion (Nadraus) T.; m. Ann Elizabeth Kidd, June 26, 1971; 1 child, Joshua Damon. B.A. cum laude, U. N.H., 1967; M.A., U. Vt., 1969, Ph.D., 1972. Dir. instl. testing and research Mercy Coll., Dobbs Ferry, N.Y., 1969-80, prof. psychology, 1969—; staff psychologist St. Dominic's Intermediate Care Facility, Blauvelt, N.Y., 1980—; cons. staff psychologist Jewish Guild for The Blind, N.Y.C., 1982—; postdoctoral intern Colo. Dept. Instns., Wheat Ridge, 1980; adj. prof. L.I. U., Dobbs Ferry, N.Y., 1978—; project dir. U.S. Office Edn. Career Edn. Grant, 1976-77; cons. psychologist, Somers, N.Y., 1983—. NDEA fellow, 1967-69; NSF grantee Edn. Commn. of States, 1976. Mem. Internat. Council Psychologists, Am. Psychol. Assn., Am. Ednl. Research Assn., AAUP, Westchester County Psychol. Assn., Psi Chi, Pi Gamma Mu, Kappa Delta Pi. Current Work: Development of procedures for the establishment of intermediate care facilities for mentally retarded and developmentally disabled. Subspecialty: Behavioral psychology. Home: 30 Lake Dr Somers NY 10589 Office: Mercy Coll 555 Broadway Dobbs Ferry NY 10522

TSAI, JAMES HSI-CHO, entomology educator; b. Fuzhou, Fujian, China, June 10, 1934; came to U.S., 1964, naturalized, 1973; s. Chuan Li and Chu Yin (Chen) T.; m. Sue Cheng, June 15, 1959; children: Cynthia H., Julie C. M.S., Mich. State U., 1967, Ph.D., 1969. Entomologist Internat. Inst. Tropical Agr., Ibadan, Nigeria, 1969-70; research assoc. dept. entomology Mich. State U., East Lansing, 1970-72; asst. prof. entomology U. Fla., Ft. Lauderdale, 1973-78, assoc. prof., 1978-84, prof., 1984—. Contbr. articles to profl. jours. Hort. Research Inst. grantee, 1975, 76, 79; NSF grantee, 1976-85; Nat. Acad. Scis. grantee, 1980. Mem. Internat. Orgn. Citrus Virologists, Internat. Orgn. Mycoplasmology, Am. Phytopathol. Soc., Entomol. Soc. Am. Republican. Current Work: Conducting research on plant mycoplasmal and virus diseases. Subspecialties: Plant virology; Plant pathology. Home: 6491 Plantation Rd Plantation FL 33317 Office: University of Florida 3205 SW College Ave Fort Lauderdale FL 33314

TSANG, ALFRED KWONG-Y, immunologist; b. Hong Kong, June 23, 1945; s. Chi Keung and Shui Hing (Lee) T.; m. Susan J. Tsang, May 13, 1972. B.S., Chinese U. Hong Kong, 1966; M.S., Bowling Green State U., 1969, Ph.D. (univ. fellow), 1974. Research asst. biol. sci. Bowling Green (Ohio) State U., 1973-74; postdoctoral research assoc. dept. surgery Med. Coll. Ohio, 1974-75, instr., 1975-77, asst. prof., 1977-79; instr. immunology Med. U. S.C., Charleston, 1979-81, asst. prof., 1981—. Recipient Merrill Chase prize in cellular immunology, 1982; Nat. Cancer Inst. grantee, 1981-84. Mem. Am. Acad. Microbiology, Am. Soc. Microbiologists, Electron Microscopy Soc. Northwestern Ohio, AAAS, Am. Assn. Immunologists, Sigma Xi. Current Work: Tumor immunology, clinical immunology. Subspecialties: Cancer research (medicine); Immunology (medicine). Office: Dept Immunology Med U SC Charleston SC 29425

TSANG, DEAN ZENSH, electrical engineer; b. Detroit, Aug. 13, 1952; s. Chi Mou Tsang and Chin Nien (Chow) T. S.B.E.E., MIT, 1974; M.S., U. Ill., 1976; Sc.D., MIT, 1981. Engring. aide LTV Aerospace, Sterling Heights, Mich., 1973; research asst. MIT Lincoln Lab., Lexington, Mass., 1975-80, staff mem., 1981—. Contbr. articles to profl. jours. Mem. IEEE, Sigma Xi (bd. electors). Club: MIT. Current work: Design, fabrication and study of semiconductor injection lasers, especially modulation characteristics and Q-switching behavior. Subspecialties: Semiconductor lasers; Semiconductors. Home: 34F Beacon Village Burlington MA 01803 Office: MIT Lincoln Lab 244 Wood St Lexington MA 02173

TSANG, JOSEPH CHIAO-LIANG, biochemistry educator; b. Hong Kong, Oct. 11, 1936; s. Anthony Hee-Wing and Mo-Ching (Kiang) T.; m. Linda Gail Hansford, June 2, 1969. B.S. in Chemistry, U. Okla.-Norman, 1962; M.S. in Biochemistry, U. Okla.-Oklahoma City, 1965, Ph.D., 1968. Primary sch. master Tung Wah Sch. Systems, Hong Kong, 1956-59; teaching and research asst. dept. chemistry Iowa State U.-Ames, 1962-63; NIH predoctoral fellow Western Res. U., Cleve., 1963-64; research asst. Okla. Med. Research Found., Oklahoma City, 1964-68; vis. prof. biochemistry dept. biochemistry U. Hong Kong, 1983-84; prof. chemistry Ill. State U.-Normal, 1968—, joint prof. biol. sci., 1971—; concurrent prof. biochemistry Jinan U., Guangzhou, China, 1980—; vis. prof. biochemistry dept. biochemistry, Hong Kong, 1985—. Contbr. numerous articles to sci. jours. Brown-Hazen Research grantee, 1969-71; NSF grantee, 1972, Ill. Heart Assn. Research grantee, 1973. Anglican. Current Work: Biosynthesis of prodigiosin, an antibiotic pigment from Serratia marcescens, a gram (-) bacterium; metal complexes of prodigiosin; antibiotic resistance mechanisms in S. marcescens. Subspecialties: Biochemistry (biology); Biochemistry (medicine). Home: 1317 E Washington St Bloomington IL 61701 Office: Dept Chemistry Ill State Univ Normal-Bloomington IL 61761

TSAY, YIH TSONG, computer science educator, researcher; b. Tungshan, China; Oct. 1, 1948; came to U.S., 1975; s. Pao Tai and Chiao Yun (Chen) T. B.S., Cheng Kung U., Republic of China, 1970; M.S., U. Houston, 1975, Ph.D., 1983. Design engr. Chung Shan Inst., Lungtan, Republic of China, 1971-74, system engr., 1976-77, project supr., 1977-79; research asst. U. Houston, 1980-83, asst. prof., 1983—; cons. U.S. Army Missile Command, Redstone Arsenal, Ala., 1975, U.S. Army Armament Command, Dover, N.J., 1981. Author: Algebraic Theory for Structural Analysis and Design of Multivariable Control Systems, 1983. Contbr. articles to profl. jours. Mem. IEEE, Assn. Computing Machinery, Mathematical Assn. Am., Soc. Indsl. and Applied Math. Current work: Symbolic and algebraic computation and applications; analysis and design algorithms; algebraic structure and algorithms for analysis and design of multivariable systems. Subspecialties: Mathematical software; Systems engineering. Office: U Houston Univ Park Computer Sci Dept 4800 Calhoun Blvd Houston TX 77004

TSE, HARLEY Y., immunologist, educator; b. China, July 17, 1947; s. Ton-cheuk and Hou-Ying (Choy) T.; m. Kwai-Fong Chui, Jan. 13, 1979; children—Kevin Y., Alan C. B.S. with honors, Calif. Inst. Tech., 1972; Ph.D., U. Calif.-San Diego, 1977. Fellow Arthritis Found., NIH, Bethesda, Md., 1977-80; sr. research immunologist Merck Sharp & Dohme Research Lab., Rahway, N.J., 1980-83, head immunogenetics,1983-84, research fellow, 1983—; adj. asst. prof. Columbia U., 1981-84, adj. assoc. prof., 1984—. Contbr. articles to profl. jours. Bd. dirs. Chinese Social Service Center, San Diego, 1975. Calif. Biochem. Research fellow, 1975; Arthritis Found. fellow, 1977-80. Mem. Am. Assn. Immunologists, Am. Assn. Lab. Animal Sci. Roman Catholic. Current Work: Mechanisms of immune regulation and immune recognition. Subspecialty: Immunobiology and immunology. Home: 11 Dana Ct Princeton NJ 08540 Office: Dept Immunology MSDRL PO Box 2000 Rahway NJ 07065

TSENG, AMPERE AN-PEI, mechanical engineer, educator; b. Kiangsi, China, Jan. 21, 1946; came to U.S., 1971, naturalized, 1983; s. Chi-Kung and Ai-Chung; m. Maggie Shih-Ying Yang, Aug. 9, 1975; children: Claire, Karen, Miles. Coll. Diploma, Taipei (Taiwan) Inst. Tech., 1966; M.S., U. Ill., Urbana, 1974; Ph.D., Ga. Inst. Tech., 1978. Mech. engr. Taitan (Taiwan) Industries Pty. Ltd., 1967-71; structural engr. Westinghouse Electric Corp., Tampa, Fla., 1977-79; staff engr. Martin Marietta Labs., Balt., 1979-84; assoc. prof. mech. engring. Drexel U., Phila., 1985—. Contbr. articles to profl. jours., confs.; reviewer: Iron and Steel Engr., Nuclear Engring. and Design, ASME Transactions, Internat. Jour. Fracture. Mem. ASME, AIME, Soc. Mfg. Engrs. (sr.), Soc. Engring. Sci. Current Work: Numerical simulation of metal forming processes; computer-aided design and manufacturing; fracture mechanics; finite element method; nuclear pressure vessel analysis. Subspecialties: Solid mechanics; Fracture mechanics. Home: 27 Timothy Ave Kendall Park NJ 08824 Office: Dept Mech Engring and Mechanics Drexel U Philadelphia PA 19104

TSENG, JEENAN, immunologist, researcher; b. Taipei, Taiwan, China, Oct. 24, 1940; came to U.S., 1970, naturalized, 1978; s. Hualin and Wen Chang T.; m. Leeying Hsu, Dec. 24, 1974; children: Ann, Sharon. B.S., Kaohsiung Med. Coll., Taiwan, 1965; M.S., Nat. Taiwan U., 1967; Ph.D., U. Ill.-Chgo., 1974. Instr. bacteriology and immunology Nat. Taiwan U., 1966-67; asst. investigator Vets. Gen. Hosp., Taipei, 1968-70; instr. U. Ill., Chgo., 1972-74; fellow Johns Hopkins U., 1975-79; acting chief dept exptl. pathology Walter Reed Army Inst. Research, Washington, 1981-83, chief dept. exptl. pathology, 1983—. Contbr. articles to profl. jours. NIAID fellow, 1978. Mem. Am. Soc. Microbiology; Mem. Am. Assn. Immunologists, N.Y. Acad. Scis. Current Work: Migration and differentiation of lymphoid and nonlymphoid cells; development of mucosal immunity to microbial infections. Subspecialties: Immunobiology and immunology; Microbiology (medicine). Office: Dept Exptl Pathology Walter Reed Army Inst Research Dahlia St and 14th St Washington DC 20307

TSIN, ANDREW TSANG CHEUNG, physiology educator; b. Hong Kong, July 19, 1950; came to U.S., 1979, naturalized, 1982; s. Sai Nin and Choi Pang (Tsang) T.; m. Wendy Lu Wickstrom, Jan. 20, 1979. B.Sc., Dalhousie U., Halifax, N.S., Can., 1972; M.Sc., U. Alta., Can., 1975, Ph.D., 1979. Research assoc. U. Alta., Edmonton, 1973-79; postdoctoral fellow Baylor Coll. Medicine, Houston, 1979-81; asst. prof. life scis. U. Tex., San Antonio, 1981—, adj. asst. prof. ophthalmology U. Tex. Health Scis. Ctr., San Antonio, 1984—. Contbr. articles to profl. jours. Med. Research Council fellow, 1979-82; Alta. Heritage Found. med. research fellow, 1981-82. Mem. AAAS, N.Y. Acad. Scis., Assn. Research Vision and Ophthalmology, Am. Soc. Zoologists, Soc. Neurosci., Biophys. Soc., Tex. Acad. Sci. Current work: Visual mechanisms of the eye. Subspecialties: Comparative neurobiology; Physiology (biology). Office: U Tex-San Antonio Div Life Scis San Antonio TX 78285

TSITLIK, JOSHUA E., biomedical engineer, researcher; b. Zhitkovichi, Belorussia, USSR, Nov. 22, 1939; came to U.S., 1976; s. Anatoli and Dina (Kunda) T.; m. Victoria Plaks, Jan. 6, 1968; 1 child, Ann. M.S. in Elec. Engring., Leningrad Poly. Inst., USSR, 1964, Ph.D. in Elec. Engring., 1972; M.S. in Clin. Engring., Johns Hopkins Sch. Medicine, 1980. Various positions in engring. and metrology, USSR, 1964-76; research asst., assoc. Johns Hopkins U. Sch. Medicine, Balt., 1977-80, instr. biomed. engring. and medicine, 1980-84, asst. prof., 1984—. Translation editor Jour. of Engring. Cybernetics, 1982-84. Author of abstracts, book chpt., articles. Patentee in field. Bd. dirs. Levindale Hebrew Geriatric Ctr. and Hosp., Balt. 1982-84. NIH grantee, 1984. Mem. IEEE (sr.), Biomed. Engring. Soc., Cardiovascular System Dynamics Soc. Democrat. Jewish. Lodge: B'nai B'rith. Current work: Mechanics of cardiopulmonary interaction, cardiopulmonary resuscitation, measurements (pressure and flow) in biomedical research. Subspecialties: Biomedical engineering; Cardiology. Home: 121 Northway Rd Reisterstown MD 21236 Office: Johns Hopkins U Sch of Medicine 600 N Wolfe St Baltimore MD 21205

TS'O, PAUL ON-PONG, biophysical chemist, educator; b. July 17, 1929. B.S., Lingnan U., 1949; M.S., Mich. State U., 1951; Ph.D., Calif. Inst. Tech., 1955. Teaching asst. Calif. Inst. Tech., 1952-55, research fellow biology div., 1955-61, sr. research fellow, 1961-62; asso. prof. biophys. chemistry dept. radiol. scis. Johns Hopkins U., Balt., 1962-67, prof., 1967-73; prof., dir. div. biophysics Johns Hopkins U. (Sch. Hygiene and Public Health), 1973—, prof. dept. environ. health scis. div. environ. health biology, 1980—; cons. Nat. Cancer Inst., 1972-75; mem. study sect. A on biophysics and biophys. chemistry NIH, 1976-80; mem. Clearinghouse on Environ. Carcinogens, Nat. Cancer Inst., 1976-80; mem. European expert com. on biophysics UNESCO. Editor: Basic Principles in Nucleic Acid Chemistry, Vol. I and II, 1974, The Molecular Biology of the Mammalian Genetic Apparatus, Vol. I and II, 1977; co-editor: The Nucleohistones, 1964, Chemical Carcinogenesis, Part A and Part B, 1974, Polycyclic Hydrocarbons and Cancer: Environment, Chemistry and Metabolism; and Molecular and Cell Biology, Vol. 1 and 2, 1978, Vol. 3, 1981, Carcinogenesis: Fundamental Mechanisms and Environmental Effects, 1980; mem. editorial bd.: Molecular Pharmacology, 1964—, Biophys. Jour, 1969-72, Biochimica et Biophysica Acta, 1971-81, Cancer Rev, 1973—, Jour. Environ. Health Scis, 1976-81; asso. editor: Cancer Research, 1975—; mem. editorial adv. bd.: Biochemistry, 1966-74, Biopolymers, 1979—; contbr. over 240 articles and revs. to profl. jours. Named Md. Chemist of Yr., 1981. Fellow AAAS; mem. Biophys. Soc. (chmn. public sci. policy com. 1972-76, council mem. 1975-78, exec. bd. 1975), Am. Soc. Biol. Chemists, Am. Soc. Microbiology, Am. Soc. Cell Biology, Biology Alliance for Public Affairs (chmn. organizing com. 1973-76), Am. Assn. Cancer Research, Am. Chem. Soc., Academia Sinica, European Acad. Arts, Scis. and Humanities, Sigma Xi. Current Work: Nucleic acid chemistry and biology; nuclear magnetic resonance in biochemical research; chemical and viral carcinogenesis, interferon research,cellular research on aging and differentiation; application of recombinant DNA techniques in cell biology. Subspecialty: Biophysics (biology). Office: Div Biophysics Johns Hopkins U Sch Hygiene and Public Health Baltimore MD 21205

TSO, WAI KEUNG, civil engineering educator, consultant; b. Hong Kong, Apr. 5, 1937; s. Ta-Ming and Mon-Ha (Lau) T.; m. Aline Min Peng, Sept. 15, 1965; 1 child, Alexander Wing-Yuen. B.Sc. in Engring., London U., 1959; M.S., Calif. Inst. Tech., 1960, Ph.D., 1964. Registered profl. engr., Ont. Sr. engr. Northrop Corp., Hawthorne, Calif., 1964-65; asst. prof. civil engring. McMaster U., Hamilton, Ont., Can., 1965-69, assoc. prof., 1969-75, prof., 1975—. Mem. ASCE, Can. Soc. Civil Engring. Current work: Earthquake engineering, structural dynamics and vibrations. Subspecialties: Structural engineering; Solid mechanics. Office: Dept Civil Engring McMaster Univ Hamilton ON L8S 4L7 Canada

TSOI, MANG-SO, immunologist; b. Hong Kong, Dec. 13, 1934; s. Sui-Po and King-Chong (Chan) Leung; married; children—Douglas, Kenneth. B.S., Whitworth Coll., Spokane, 1961; M.S., U. Wash., 1963, Ph.D., 1966. Tchr. sub-insp. schs. Edn. Dept., Hong Kong, 1956-59; research assoc. dept. microbiology U. Wash., 1966-67; research assoc. Virginia Mason Research Ctr., Seattle, 1971-72; research assoc. dept. medicine U. Wash., 1972-75, research asst. prof., 1975-79, research assoc. prof. dept. medicine, 1979—; assoc. mem. Fred Hutchinson Cancer Research Ctr., 1979—. Contbr. articles to profl. jours. Am. Cancer Soc. grantee; Nat. Cancer Inst. grantee. Mem. Am. Assn. Immunologists, Reticuloendothelial Soc., N.Y. Acad. Scis., AAUP, Sigma Xi. Current Work: Study of immunological mechanisms of graft-versus-host disease and graft host tolerance; immunology of cellular interactions in patients after bone marrow transplantation. Subspecialties: Transplantation; Cellular engineering. Office: 1124 Columbia St Seattle WA 98104

TSONG, TIEN TZOU, physicist, educator; b. Taichung, Taiwan, China, Sept. 6, 1934; came to U.S., 1962, naturalized, 1974; m. Miaw Fan, Mar. 24, 1964; children—Jing, Lily, Edith. B.S., Nat. Taiwan Normal U., 1959; M.S. Pa. State U., 1964, Ph.D., 1966. Research assoc. Pa. State U.-University Park, 1967-69, asst., then assoc. prof., 1969-75, prof., 1975—; dir. Field Emission Lab., University Park, Author: (with others) Field Ion Microscopy Principals and Applications, 1969; Field Ion Microscopy Field Ionization and Field Evaporation, 1973. Fellow Am. Physical Soc.; mem. Am. Vacuum Soc. Current work: Atomic processes on solid surfaces; field ion emission; atom probe field ion microscopy; structures of surfaces. Subspecialty: Condensed matter physics. Office: 104 Davey Lab University Park PA 16802

TSUCHIYA, TAKUMI, genetics educator, researcher; b. Ajimu-cho, Japan, Mar. 10, 1923; s. Torao and Masao Tsuchiya; m. Chiyoko Fukushima, Feb. 20, 1953; children—Keiko, Noriko. B. Agr., Gifu U. (Japan), 1943; B. Agr., Kyoto U. (Japan), 1947, D. Agr., 1960. Asst. prof. Beppu U., Japan, 1950-57; cytegeneticist Kihara Inst. Biol. Research, Yokohama, Japan, 1957-63; cytogeneticist Children's Hosp., Winnipeg, Man., Can., 1964-65; research assoc. U. Man., Winnipeg, 1965-68; prof. Colo. State U., Ft. Collins, 1968—; dir. Barley Genetics Stock Ctr. World, Ft. Collins, 1969—. Editor-in-chief Barley Genetics Newsletter, 1971—. Contbr. chpts. to books, articles to profl. jours. Chmn. Internat. Com. Barley Genetics, 1969—, Genetics Com. Am. Barley Research Workers Conf., 1969—. Fellow Am. Soc. Agronomy; mem. Am. Genetic Assn., Genetics Soc. Can., Botanical Soc. Am., Internat. Soc. Cytology (standing collaborator), Sigma Xi, Phi Kappa Phi, Gamma Sigma Delta. Current work: Plant genetics especially chromosome engineering in genetics and plant breeding; germplasm preservation and related genetic researches of plants; tissue and cell structures in plant genetics and breeding. Subspecialties: Plant genetics; Plant cell and tissue culture. Home: 1617 Lakeridge Ct Fort Collins CO 80521 Office: Dept Agronomy Colo State U Fort Collins CO 80523

TU, SHU-I, research chemist; b. Chungking, China, Jan. 3, 1943; came to U.S., 1966, naturalized, 1975; s. Show-Mei and I-Fan (Hu) T.; m. Jenny Gin-I Chang, July 18, 1969; 1 child, Stephen. B.S., Nat. Tawian U., 1965; M.Philosophy, Yale U., 1968, Ph.D., 1969. Research assoc. Yale U., New Haven, 1969-72; research asst. prof. SUNY, Buffalo, 1972-74; asst. prof. SUNY, Stony Brook, 1974-81; research chemist USDA, Phila., 1981—. Contbr. numerous articles to profl. jours. Dir. parents activity Li-Ming Chinese Culture Assn., Phila., 1984-85. Served as 2d lt. Chinese Army, 1965-66. Fellow SUNY, 1975, Yale U., 1966; grantee NSF, 1978-80, NIH, 1975-77. Mem. N.Y. Acad. Sci., Biophys. Soc., Am. Chem. Soc., Sigma Xi. Current work: Mechanism of energy transduction processes in biological systems, ion transport processes between soil and roots interphase, structure and function of subcellular biomembranes. Subspecialties: Biophysical chemistry; Membrane biology. Home: 1025 Adams Ct Warrington PA 18976 Office: 1600 E Mermaid Lane Philadelphia PA 19118

TUCKER, ALLEN BROWN, JR., computer science educator; b. Worcester, Mass., Feb. 19, 1942; s. Allen B. and Louise (Woodberry) T.; m. Maida Somerville, Dec. 19, 1965; children—Jennifer, Brian. B.A. in Math., Wesleyan U., 1963; M.S. in Computer Sci., Northwestern U., 1968, Ph.D., 1970. Systems analyst Norton Co., Worcester, 1963-67; asst. prof. U. Mo.-Rolla, 1970-71, Georgetown U., Washington, 1971-76, assoc. prof., dir., 1976-83; MacArthur prof. chmn. computer sci. dept. Colgate U., Hamilton, N.Y., 1983—; dir. acad. computer ctr. Georgetown U., 1976-83. Author: Programming Languages, 1985, Text processing, 1979, Apple Pascal, 1982. Budget com. chmn. St. Thomas Ch., Hamilton, 1984—. NSF grantee, 1984—; MacArthur Found. endowed profl. chmn., 1983—. Mem. Assn. Computing Machinery, N.Y. Acad. Sci., AAAS, Sigma Xi. Current work: Research in computer applications and theoretical issues in natural language understanding, programing language design and automata theory. Subspecialties: Programming languages; Automated language processing. Office: Colgate Univ Computer Sci Dept Hamilton NY 13346

TUCKER, GAIL SUSAN, cell biologist, educator; b. N.Y.C., Aug. 30, 1945; d. Albert Eugene and Frances Anna (Kennedy) T. B.A., Mercy Coll., Dobbs Ferry, N.Y., 1967; Ph.D., U. Kans.-Lawrence, 1973. Postdoctoral, Columbia U., 1973-75; vis. instr. Mercy Coll., 1973-75; research assoc. U. Miami, Fla., 1976-80, research asst. prof. Sch. Medicine, 1980—; trainee Harvard U., 1980; cons. Dade County Pub. Sch. System, Miami. Contbr. articles to profl. jours. Vol., Meals on Wheels, Lawrence, Kans., 1970-72. Fla. Lions Eye Bank fellow, 1978; United Way Dade County grantee, 1978, NIH grantee, 1979, 80. Mem. Am. Soc. Cell Biology, Assn. Research in Vision and Ophthalmology, Soc. Neurosci., Women in Eye Research (pres. 1980-83), AAAS. Club: Zonta (Miami, treas. 1981-82, v.p. 1982-83, pres. 1984-85). Current work: Morphometry of the developing retina in the normal and visually deprived cat; retinal correlates in human eye disease and in the aging human. Subspecialties: Developmental biology; Neurobiology. Home: 2121 N Bayshore Dr Apt 1104 Miami FL 33137 Office: Bascom Palmer Eye Inst D-880 Univ Miami Sch Medicine 1638 NW 19th Ave Miami FL 33136

TUCKER, JOHN R., physicist, electrical engineering educator; b. Seattle, Mar. 26, 1944; s. Clarence Estes and Florence Ann (Robinson) T. B.S. in Physics, Calif. Inst. Tech., 1966; A.M. in Physics, Harvard U., 1967, Ph.D. in Physics, 1972. Resident visitor, cons. Bell Telephone Labs., Murray Hill, N.J., 1970-71; research assoc. dept. physics, Brown U., Providence, 1971-72; mem. tech. staff Aerospace Corp., El Segundo, Calif., 1973-80; sr. NRC assoc. NASA Inst. Space Studies, N.Y.C., 1980; assoc. prof. elec. engring., U. Ill., Urbana, 1981—. Author: The Quantum Response of Nonlinear Tunnel Junctions as Detectors and Mixers, 1983; (with M.J. Feldman) Quantum Detection at Millimeter Wavelengths, 1985. NSF fellow Harvard U., 1967-71. Mem. Am. Phys. Soc. Current work: Quantum tunneling and detection at millimeter wavelengths, charge-density wave conduction in quasi-one-dimensional crystals. Subspecialties: Condensed matter physics; Low temperature physics. Office: Dept Elec Engring U Ill 1406 W Green St Urbana IL 61801

TUCKER, MARC STEPHEN, computer research administrator, consultant; b. Boston, Nov. 15, 1939; s. David Jones and Natalie (Croman) T.; m. Linda Beth Hepler, Sept. 27, 1964 (div. 1973); children: Matthew, Joshua. A.B., Brown U., 1961; M.S., George Washington U., 1982. Lighting dir., camera, sta. WGBH-TV, Boston, 1962-64, asst. dir. edn. div., 1964-66; asst. to pres. Edn. Devel. Ctr., Newton, Mass., 1966-71; asst. dir. NWREL, Portland, Oreg., 1971-72; assoc. dir. Nat. Inst. Edn., Washington, 1972-81; dir. Project on Info. Tech. and Edn., Washington, 1981—; cons. Cresap, McCormick, Washington, 1982, Vanderbilt U., 1982, BRS, Albany, N.Y., 1982, U. Pa., 1982. Chmn., pres. Brass Chamber Music Soc. Annapolis, 1980-81, mem. sch. bd., Bedford, Mass., 1971. Mem. AAAS, Assn. Computing Machinery, Assn. for Pub. Policy Analysis and Mgmt. Democrat. Current Work: Public policy on use of computers and telecommunications technology in schools, colleges and universities. Development of improved hardware, software and management systems for education applications. Subspecialties: Information systems (Information science); Information systems, storage, and retrieval (computer science). Home: 510 2d St Annapolis MD 21403 Office: Project on Info Tech and Edn Suite 301 1001 Connecticut Ave NW Washington DC 20036

TUCKER, ROBERT J., research chemist, administrator; b. Newark, Aug. 3, 1940; s. Matthew Martin and Blanche Margaret (Wetmore) T.; m. Patricia Ann Pavloski, Sept. 14, 1963; children—Robert, John Brian, Matthew Martin. B.S., Rutgers U., 1962; postgrad. MIT, 1962-63. Research chemist Am. Cyanamid Co., Bound Brook, N.J., 1963-74, sr. research chemist, 1974-82, tech. dir., 1982—; tech. cons. Glendale Optical Co., Woodbury, N.Y., 1978-82. Patentee in field. Mem. Environ. Commn., Hackettstown, N.J., 1973-76; bd. dirs. N.J. Eye/Ear Mobile Inst., Scotch Plains, 1982; Henry Rutgers scholar, 1961. Mem. Am. Chem. Soc., Am. Welding Soc. (v.p. 1982-84, vice chmn. 1978—), Phi Beta Kappa. Republican. Roman Catholic. Lodge: Lions (v.p. 1980-84) (Hackettstown). Current work: Currently working on outdoor and thermal stabilization of polymers, laser eye protective filters, specialty optical filters mar resistant coatings. Subspecialties: Polymer chemistry; Optical engineering. Office: Am Cyanamid Co Easton Turnpike Bound Brook NJ 08805

TUCKER, WALLACE HAMPTON, astrophysicist; b. McAlester, Okla., Nov. 4, 1939; s. Charles B. and Josephine E. T.; m. Karen A. Slagle; children: Kerry, Stuart. B.S. in Math, U. Okla., 1961, M.S., 1962; Ph.D. in Physics, U. Calif., San Diego, 1966. Instr., research assoc. Cornell U., 1966-67; asst. prof. Rice U., Houston, 1967-69; sr. staff scientist Am. Sci. and Engring., Inc., 1969-72, cons., 1972-76; astrophysicist Smithsonian Astrophys. Obs., Cambridge, Mass., 1976—; lectr. U.S. Internat. U., 1979-80, U. Calif., Irvine, 1980—. Mem. Am. Astron. Soc., AAAS, Soc. Sci. Exploration, Astron. Soc. Pacific, Internat. Astron. Union. Subspecialties: High energy astrophysics; X-ray high energy astrophysics. Home: PO Box 266 Bonsall CA 92003

TULP, ORIEN LEE, nutrition and food sciences educator, researcher, health services officer; b. Newark, July 15, 1936; s. Harry Carlton and Helen Gertrude (Myers) T.; m. Patricia Jane Clouse, Nov. 9, 1957; children—David A., Bona J., Susan L. A.A. in Med. Tech., Carnegie Coll., 1958; B.S., U. Vt., 1968, M.S., 1970, Ph.D., 1974. Med. tech., asst. lab. chief Kerbs Meml. Hosp., St. Albans, Vt., 1958-63; med. tech. Med. Ctr. Hosp. Vt., Burlington, 1963-68; research asst. U. Vt. Med. Sch., Burlington, 1963-74, research assoc., 1974-83; vis. assoc. prof. Colby Coll., Waterville, Maine, 1981-83; assoc. prof. Drexel U., Phila.,

1983—; lt. col., health services officer U.S.N.G., Winooski, Vt., 1960-84; vis. prof. dept. nutrition U. Del., Newark, 1984; cons. Wyeth Labs., Radnor, Pa., 1984, Weight Control Program Office of Surgeon Army N.G., Washington, 1983-85. Contbr. articles to profl. jours. Asst. scoutmaster Champlain council Boy Scouts Am., Milton, Vt., 1974-80; mem. legis. com. Vt. State Legis., Montpelier, 1977; asst. med. dir. Internatl. Winter Spl. Olympics, Stowe, Vt., 1981. Recipient citation merit Muscular Dystrophy Assn., Burlington, 1980. Mem. AAAS, Am. Inst. Nutrition, The Nutrition Soc. Great Britain, Am. Fedn. Clin. Research (sr.), N.Y. Acad. Sci., Assn. Mil. Surgeons U.S., Am. Chem. Soc. Baptist. Current work: Nutrition, metabolism, obesity and diabetes (clinical and experimental) using animal models, thermogenesis and energy balance; insulin-independent diabetes. Subspecialties: Nutrition (medicine); Biochemistry (medicine). Home: 115 Bishop Hollow Rd Media PA 19063 Office: Dept Nutrition and Food Scis Drexel U 32d and Chestnut St Philadelphia PA 19104

TUMA, SAMIR NAIF, physician, researcher; b. Acco, Israel, Feb. 17, 1940; came to U.S., 1975; s. Naif J. and Miriam I. T.; m. Grace I. Anfous, May 9, 1970; children: Mona, Noha. M.D., Hebrew U., Jerusalem, 1968. Intern Rambam Univ. Hosp., Haifa, Israel, 1968-69, resident internal medicine, 1969-72, fellow in nephrology, 1972-74, sr. nephrologist, 1974-75; cons. physician Rotchild U. Hosp., Haifa, 1974-75; instr. medicine U So. Calif. Med. Ctr., Los Angeles, 1975-78; asst. prof. Medicine Baylor Coll. Medicine, Houston, 1978—; Co-establisher dialysis units Evangilican Mission, Nablis, West Bank, Israel, 1972-75, Nicosea Gen. Hosp., Nicosea, Cypress, 1973-74, Ramallah New Hosp., West Bank, Israel, 1973-74; cons. physician Nat. Israeli Radio, Jerusalem, 1972-75. Founder, 1st and 2d pres. Arab Am. Med. Assn., Houston, 1979; mem. Nat. Council High Edn., Tel Aviv, 1974. Recipient Tavori award Hebrew U., 1968. Mem. Internat. Soc. Nephrology, Am. Fedn. Clin. Research, Am. Soc. Nephrology, AAUP, N.Y. Acad. Sci. Club: Eliaho Hanovi (warden 1974-75). Current Work: Clinical nephrology, parathyroid hormone and uremia toxicity. Subspecialties: Nephrology; Internal medicine. Home: 10915 Paulwood St Houston TX 77071 Office: Baylor Coll Medicine 1200 Moursund Ave Houston TX 77030

TUMBLESON, M.E., physiological chemist, educator; b. Mountain Lake, Minn., Mar. 13, 1937; s. Leonard Orville and Marie Kathryn (Meyer) T.; married; children: Elise Marie, Eric Jon, Ellen Rae. B.S., U. Minn., 1958, M.S., 1961, Ph.D., 1964. Asst. prof. vet. physiology U. Mo., Columbia, 1966-69, assoc. prof., 1969-80; prof. vet. biomed. sci., research prof. Sinclair Research Farm, 1980—. Contbr. numerous articles and sci. abstracts to profl. jours. Nat. bd. dirs. Alpha Gamma Rho. Recipient Disting. award in research Gamma Sigma Delta, 1980. Fellow Gerontol. Soc.; mem. Am. Inst. Nutrition, Am. Soc. Animal Sci., Am. Soc. Biol. Chemists, Am. Soc. Clin. Nutrition, Am. Soc. Neurochemistry, Am. Soc. Vet. Physiologists and Pharmacologists, Nat. Council on Alcoholism, Soc. Exptl. Biology and Medicine, Sigma Xi. Current Work: Alcohol metabolism in mammals during devel. and aging. Subspecialties: Biochemistry (medicine); Nutrition (biology). Home: Route 10 Box 41 Columbia MO 65202 Office: Coll Vet Medicine U MO Columbia MO 65211

TUMMALA, RAO RAMAMOHANA, scientist; b. India, Feb. 15, 1942; came to U.S., 1967; s. Venkataswara Rao and Subbamma (Paladugu) T.; m. Anne Mitran, Dec. 30, 1966; children—Dinesh, Vijay, Suneel. B.S., Andhra, Waltair, India, 1961; B.E., Indian Inst., Bangalore, India, 1963; M.S., Queens U., Kingston, Can., 1964; Ph.D., U. Ill., 1969. Research scientist RMC, Kingston, 1964-65; process engr. Norton Co., Niagara Falls, N.Y., 1965-67; adv. engr. IBM, East Fishkill, N.Y., 1969-74; adviser U. Ill.-Urbana, 1980-83; IBM fellow IBM, 1984—. Contbr. articles to profl. publs. Patentee in field. Fellow Am. Ceramic Soc.; mem. Materials Research Soc. Subspecialty: Ceramic engineering. Home: 13 Shadybrook Ln Hopewell Junction NY 12533 Office: IBM Corp East Fishkill NY 12533

TUMMALA, V. M. RAO, operations research and information systems educator; b. Pedalimgala, India, Sept. 10, 1937; came to U.S., 1961; s. Veeraiah and Subbamma T.; m. Parvati, May 12, 1955; children: Chandrasekhar, Prabhakhar, Sreenidhi. B.A., Andhra U., Waltair, India, 1957; M.A., Gujarat U., Ahmedabad, India, 1959; M.S., Mich. State U., 1962, Ph.D., 1968. Asst. prof. U. Detroit, 1967-70, assoc. prof., 1970-75, prof., area coordinator, 1977-81; prof. ops. research and info. systems Coll. Bus., Eastern Mich. U., Ypsilanti, 1976-77, 81—, head dept. ops. research and info. systems, 1981—. Author: Decision Analysis with Business Applications, 1974, Modern Decision Models, 1975; editor.: Procs. of 1981 Midwest conf, Am. Inst. Decision Scis. Contbr. articles to profl. jours. Pres. Telugu Assn. N.Am., Detroit, 1979-81; v.p. Mich. chpt. India League Am., 1980-85, pres., 1985—. Mem. Am. Stats. Assn., Inst. Mgmt. Scis., Am. Inst. Decision Scis., Soc. Risk Analysis. Current Work: Multi-attribute utility; subjective probability; risk; uncertainty; hierarchical decision making; Bayesian inference. Subspecialties: Statistics; Information systems (Information science). Home: 2103 Glencoe Hills Apt 5 Ann Arbor MI 48104 Office: Dept Ops Research and Info Systems Coll Bus Eastern Mich U Ypsilanti MI 48197

TURCHIN, VALENTIN FEDOROVICH, computer science educator; b. Podolsk, USSR, Feb. 14, 1931; came to U.S., 1978; s. Fedor Vassilievich and Lubov Dmitrievna (Bagler) T.; m. Tatiana I. Novikova, Sept. 26, 1956; children: Peter, Dimitri. B.S., Moscow U., 1952; Ph.D., Inst. for Physics and Energy, Obninsk, USSR, 1958. Sr. scientist Inst. Physics and Energy, 1953-64, Inst. Applied Math., Moscow, 1964-73; assoc. research scientist Courant Inst. Math. Scis., N.Y.C., 1978-79; prof. computer sci. CCNY, CUNY, 1979—. Author: Slow Neutrons, 1965, The Phenomenon of Science, 1977, The Inertia of Fear and the Scientific Worldview, 1981. Chmn. Moscow chpt. Amnesty Internat., 1974-77. NSF grantee, 1980-87. Mem. Assn. Computing Machinery. Current Work: Computers, artificial intelligence, philosophy of science, foundations of mathematics. Subspecialties: Artificial intelligence; Programming languages. Home: 188 Hiawatha Blvd Oakland NJ 07436 Office: Computer Sci Dept CCNY New York NY 10031

TURCO, SALVATORE JOSEPH, biochemistry educator; b. New Kensington, Pa., Sept. 16, 1950; s. Antonio Salvatore and Elvira (Pate) T.; m. Cathy Jane Hummel, Dec. 22, 1973; children: Jason Christopher, Joseph Matthew. B.S., Ind. U., 1972; Ph.D., U. Pitts., 1972-76. Postdoctoral fellow M.I.T., Cambridge, 1976-78; asst. prof. biochemistry U. Ky., Lexington, 1978—. NIH award, 1983-88; grantee, 1980-87; Am. Cancer Soc. grantee, 1980-81; Leukemia Soc. Am. fellow, 1977-78. Mem. N.Y. Acad. Scis., Soc. Complex Carbohydrates, AAAS, Am. Soc. Biol. Chemists. Republican. Methodist. Current Work: Structure, function and biosynthesis of complex carbohydrate-containing macromolecules and the involvement of these substances in abnormal states. Subspecialties: Biochemistry (medicine); Biochemistry (biology). Home: 2908 E Hills Dr Lexington KY 40502 Office: U Ky Dept Biochemistry Lexington KY 40536

TURCOTTE, DONALD LAWSON, educator; b. Bellingham, Wash., Apr. 22, 1932; s. Lawson Phillip and Eva (Pearson) T.; m. Joan Meredith Luecke, May 17, 1957; children—Phillip Lawson, Stephen Bradford. B.S., Calif. Inst. Tech., 1954, Ph.D., 1958; M.Aero.Engring., Cornell U., 1955. Asst. prof. aero. engring. U.S. Naval Postgrad. Sch., Monterey, Calif., 1958-59; asst. prof. aero. engring. Cornell U., Ithaca, N.Y., 1959-63, asso. prof., 1963-67, prof., 1967-73, prof. geol. scis., 1973—, chmn., 1981—. Author: (with others) Statistical Thermodynamics, 1963, Space Propulsion, 1965, Geodynamics, 1982. Trustee U. Space Research Assn., 1975-79. NSF sr. postdoctoral research fellow, 1965-66; Guggenheim fellow, 1972-73. Mem. Am. Geophys. Union, Am. Phys. Soc., Geol. Soc. Am. (Day medal 1982), Seismol. Soc. Am. Club: Ithaca Country. Current Work: Mantle convection, sedimentary basins, stress in earth, faulting. Subspecialties: Geophysics; Tectonics. Home: 703 Cayuga Heights Rd Ithaca NY 14850 Office: Snee Hall Cornell U Ithaca NY 14853

TURCOTTE, JEREMIAH GEORGE, physician, educator; b. Detroit., Jan. 20, 1933; s. Vincent Joseph and Margaret Campau (Meldrum) T.; m. Claire Mary Lenz, July 5, 1958; children—Elizabeth Margaret, John Jeremiah, Sarah Lenz, Claire Meldrum. B.S. with high distinction, U. Mich., 1955, M.D. cum laude, 1957. Diplomate: Am. Bd. Surgery. Intern U. Mich. Med. Center, 1957-58, resident in surgery, 1958-60, 61-63; research asst. USPHS grant U. Mich. surgery dept., 1960-61; mem. faculty U. Mich. Med. Sch., 1963—, prof. surgery, 1971—, chmn. dept. surgery, 1974—, head sect. gen. surgery, 1974-81; sci. adv. bd. Mich. Kidney Found. Contbr. to med. jours. Recipient Henry Russell award U. Mich., 1970. Fellow A.C.S.; mem. Transplantation Soc. Mich. (pres. 1973-75), Assn. Academic Surgeons, Am. Surg. Assn., Soc. Univ. Surgeons. Internat. Transplantation Soc., Central Surg. Assn., Western Surg. Assn., Soc. Surgery Alimentary Tract, Am. Soc. Transplant Surgeons (pres. 1979-80), Frederick A. Coller Soc. (pres. 1982-83), Am. Trauma Soc. (a founder). Roman Catholic. Subspecialties: Surgery; Transplant surgery. Home: 769 Heatherway St Ann Arbor MI 48104 Office: Univ Hosp B3912 Box 17 1405 E Ann St Ann Arbor MI 48109

TUREK, JEFFERY LEE, sytems engineer; b. Toledo, Oct. 3, 1946; s. Robert Otis and Eve (Stribrny) T.; m. Patricia Jean Skilinchar, Feb. 8, 1969 (div. Oct. 1982). B.A., Washington and Jefferson Coll., 1968; M.S., Va. Poly. Inst. and State U., 1977, Ph.D., 1980. Research assoc. Va. Poly. Inst. and State U., Blacksburg, 1978-80, mgr. research and devel., 1981—; assoc. Systems Research & Applications, Arlington, Va., 1980-81. Served in USN, 1968-74. Assoc. mem. Am. Inst. Indsl. Engrs., Ops. Research Soc. Am. Current Work: Fuzzy sets, optimal stopping theory, risk analyses, human factors and their integration into a decisionsupport system aimed at practical, effective management of large research and development programs. Subspecialty: Information systems (Information science). Home: Rt 1 Box 57-F Newport VA 24128 Office: 106 Faculty St Blacksburg VA 24061

TUREKIAN, KARL KAREKIN, geology educator; b. N.Y.C., Oct. 25, 1927; s. Vaughan Thomas and Victoria (Guleserian) T.; m. Arax Roxanne Hagopian, Apr. 22, 1962; children: Karla Ann, Vaughan Charles. A.B., Wheaton (Ill.) Coll., 1949; M.A., Columbia U., 1951, Ph.D., 1955. Lectr. geology Columbia U., 1953-54, research asso., 1954-56; faculty Yale U., 1956—, prof. geology and geophysics, 1965-72, Henry Barnard Davis prof. geology and geophysics, 1972—, chmn. dept., 1982—; curator meteorites Peabody Mus., 1964—; cons. Pres.'s Commn. Marine Sci. Engring. and Resources, 1967-68; oceanography panel NSF, 1968-70; NASA exobiology panel NASA, Am. Inst. Biol. Scientists, 1966-69; U.S. nat. com. for geochemistry NAS-NRC, 1970-73, mem. climate research bd., 1977-80, ocean sci. bd., 1979-82; mem. group experts sci. aspects Marine Pollution UN, 1971-73. Author: Oceans, 1968, 2d edit., 1976, Chemistry of the Earth, 1972, (with B.J. Skinner) Man and the Ocean, 1973, (with C.L. Drake, J. Imbrie and J.A. Knauss) Oceanography, 1978; editor: Late Cenozoic Glacial Ages, 1971, Jour. Geophys. Research, Oceans and Atmospheres, 1969-75, Earth Planet Sci. Letters, 1975—; asso. editor: Geochim. et Cosmochim. Acta, 1967-70, Jour. Geophys. Research, 1967-69; editor: Discovery, Yale Peabody Mus., 1978-81; contbr. articles to profl. jours. Served with USNR, 1945-46. Guggenheim fellow, 1962-63. Fellow Geol. Soc. Am., Meteoritical Soc., Am. Geophys. Union, AAAS; mem. Nat. Acad. Scis., Am. Chem. Soc., Geochem. Soc. (pres. 1975-76), Sigma Xi. Current Work: Marine and surficial geochemistry, geochemistry of planetary evolution. Subspecialty: Geochemistry. Home: 555 Skiff St North Haven CT 06473 Office: Dept Geology and Geophysics Yale U Box 6666 New Haven CT 06511

TURIN, GEORGE LEWIS, engineering educator, university dean; b. N.Y.C., Jan. 27, 1930; s. Meyer and Lillian (Podolsky) T.; m. Helen Green, Sept. 11, 1964; children—David, Abigail. S.B., MIT, 1952, S.M., 1952, Sc.D., 1956. Mem. staff Philco Corp., Phila., 1949-52, MIT Lincoln Lab., Lexington, 1952-56, Hughes Aircraft Co., Los Angeles, 1956-60; prof. engring. U. Calif.-Berkeley, 1960—, chmn. dept. elec. engring. and computer sci., 1980-83; dean Sch. Engring. and Applied Sci. UCLA, 1983—; cons. in field; dir. Tera Corp., Berkeley. Author: Notes on Digital Communication, 1969. Editor: Notes on System Science, 1969-75. Contbr. articles to profl. jours. Fellow Guggenheim Found., 1966, Sci. and Engring. Research Council (U.K.), 1983. Fellow IEEE; mem. Nat. Acad. Engring. Democrat. Jewish. Current work: Statistical communication theory and applications; mobile radio channels and systems; communication networks. Subspecialties: Electrical engineering; Information systems (Information science). Home: 763 San Diego Rd Berkeley CA 94707 Office: Sch Engring and Applied Sci UCLA 7400 Boelter Hall Los Angeles CA 90024

TURINSKY, PAUL JOSEF, nuclear engineering educator; b. Hoboken, N.J., Oct. 20, 1944; s. Paul Josef and Wilma Ann (Budig) T.; m. Karen Ann DeLuca, Aug. 20, 1966; children: Grant Dean, Beth Noelle. B.S. in Chem. Engring, U. R.I., 1966; M.S. in Nuclear Engring, U. Mich., 1967, Ph.D. in Nuclear Engring, 1970; M.B.A., U. Pitts., 1979. Asst. prof. nuclear engring. and sci. Rensselear Poly. Inst., Troy, N.Y., 1971-73; sr. nuclear design engr. Water Reactor div. Westinghouse Electric Corp., Pitts., 1973-75, lead nuclear design engr., 1975-76, fellow nuclear design engr., 1976, mgr. nuclear design group, 1976-78; mgr. core devel., 1978-80; prof. nuclear engring. N.C. State U., Raleigh, 1980—, head nuclear engring. dept., 1980—; cons. in field. Contbr. sci. articles to profl. publs. Recipient Meritorious Service citation Westinghouse Electric Corp., 1974; AEC fellow, 1966-69. Mem. Am. Nuclear Soc., (Mark Mills award 1971), Am. Soc. Engring. Edn., AAAS, Beta Gamma Sigma, Sigma Xi., Tau Beta Pi, Phi Kappa Phi. Current Work: Applications of mathematical optimization techniques to nuclear fuel cycle management; computer simulation of nuclear power plant's neutronic and thermal-hydraulic behaviors on multi-CPU/rector pipeline computer architectures. Subspecialties: Nuclear fission; Fluid mechanics. Office: NC State Univ 1110 Burlington Engring Labs Raleigh NC 27695-7909

TURKEVICH, ANTHONY LEONID, chemist, educator; b. N.Y.C., July 23, 1916; s. Leonid Jerome and Anna (Chervinsky) T.; m. Ireene Podlesak, Sept. 20, 1948; children: Leonid, Darya. B.A., Dartmouth Coll., 1937, D.Sc., 1971; Ph.D., Princeton U., 1940. Research assoc. spectroscopy physics dept. U. Chgo., 1940-41; asst. prof., research on nuclear transformations Enrico Fermi Inst. and chemistry dept., 1946-48, asso. prof., 1948-53, prof., 1953—, James Franck prof. chemistry, 1965-70, Distinguished Ser. prof., 1970—; war research Manhattan Project, Columbia U., 1942-43, U. Chgo., 1943-45, Los Alamos Sci. Lab., 1945-46; Participant test first nuclear bomb, Alamagordo, N.Mex., 1945, in theoretical work on and test of thermonuclear reactions, 1945—, chem. analysis of moon, 1967—; cons. to AEC Labs.; fellow Los Alamos Sci. Lab., 1972—. Del. Geneva Conf. on Nuclear Test Suspension, 1958, 59. Recipient E.O. Lawrence Meml. award AEC, 1962; Atoms for Peace award, 1969. Fellow Am. Phys. Soc.; mem. Am. Chem. Soc. (nuclear applications award 1972), AAAS, Nat. Acad. Scis., Am. Acad. Arts and Scis., Royal Soc. Arts (London), Phi Beta Kappa. Clubs: Quadrangle, Cosmos. Subspecialties: Nuclear chemistry; Space chemistry. Office: 5640 S Ellis Ave Chicago IL 60637*

TURKINGTON, ROBERT (ROY) ALBERT, botany educator, plant population biologist; b. Portadown, No. Ireland, Apr. 8, 1951; came to Can., 1976, naturalized, 1981; s. Joseph Henry and Elizabeth Edna (Thompson) T.; m. Evelyn Robinson, Sept. 13, 1975; children—Alistair, Andrea. B.Sc., New U. Ulster, Coleraine, No. Ireland, 1972; Diploma in Ecology, Univ. Coll. N. Wales, Bangor, 1974, Ph.D., 1975. Postdoctoral fellow U. WesternOnt., London, 1976-77; asst. prof. botany dept., U. B.C., Vancouver, 1977-83, assoc. prof., 1983—. Contbr. articles in field to various publs. Recipient Bilateral Exchange award Royal Soc. London, 1985. Mem. Brit. Ecol. Soc., Ecol. Soc. Am., Can. Bot. Assn. Baptist. Current work: Biology of plant populations in pastures; the evolutionary consequences of competition among pasture species; rhizobium-legume symbiosis; genecology; population differentiation. Subspecialty: Population biology. Office: Botany Dept U BC Vancouver BC V6T 2B1 Canada

TURLAPATY, PRASAD DURGA MALLIKHARJUNA VARA, pharmacologist, clinical researcher; b. Vijayawada, India, June 1, 1942; came to U.S., 1967; s. Sangameswara Rao and Visalakshmi (Nidumolu) T.; m. Snehalatha D. Kurapati, Sept. 3, 1972; 1 dau., Neelima. M. Pharmacy, Andhra (India) U., 1965; Ph.D. in Pharmacology, U. Hawaii, 1971. Postdoctoral fellow dept pharmacology U. Tex. Health Sci. Ctr., 1972-74; Sci. officer Jipmer, Pondicherry, India, 1975-77; instr. dept. physiology Downstate Med. Center N.Y., Bklyn., 1977-78, asst. prof., 1978-80; clin. investigative assoc. Ives Labs., N.Y.C., 1980-81, sr. clin. investigative assoc., 1982-83; asst. dir. clin. research Am. Critical Care, Chgo., 1983-85, assoc. dir. clin. research, 1985—. Contbr. articles to profl. publs. Recipient Gold medals Andhra U., 1964, 65; awards Dept. state, East-West Ctr., Honolulu, 1967-69. Mem. Am. Physiol. Soc., Am. Soc. Pharmacology and Exptl. Therapeutics, Am. Soc. Microbiology, N.Y. Acad. Scis. Current Work: Physiology and pharmacology of vascular smooth muscle in hypertension and diabetes; role of magnesium deficiency; clinical research on new drugs in hypertension, angina, arrhythmia, congestive heart failure. Subspecialties: Pharmacology; Physiology (medicine). Home: 1102 Whitman Rd Vernon Hills IL 60061 Office: 1600 Waukegan Rd McGraw Park IL 60085

TURNER, BRUCE JAY, biologist, educator; b. Bklyn., Sept. 19, 1945; s. Frederic Alexander and Lillian (Lindenberg) T.; m. Barbara Anne Bush, Dec. 18, 1972; children: Jonathan, Mikaila. B.S., Bklyn. Coll., 1966; M.A., UCLA, 1967, Ph.D., 1972. Postdoctoral fellow Neuropsychiatric Inst., UCLA, 1972-74; research assoc. Rockefeller U., N.Y.C., 1974-76; vis. research scientist Mus. Zoology, U. Mich., Ann Arbor, 1976-78; asst. prof. zoology dept. biology Va. Poly. Inst. and State U., Blacksburg, 1978-84; assoc. prof., 1984—; cons. in field. Contbr. articles to profl. jours. N.Y. State Regents scholar, 1962-66; USPHS fellow, 1968-70; NSF grantee, 1976, 79; Nat. Geog. Soc. grantee, 1980; NSF grantee, 1985. Mem. Am. Soc. Naturalists, Soc. for Study Evolution, Soc. Ichthyologists and Herpetologists, Soc. for Systematic Zoology, Genetics Soc. Am., Am. Fisheries Soc., Am. Genetics Assn., AAUP. Current Work: Elucidation of factors determining genetic differentiation of fish populations. Subspecialties: Evolutionary biology; Systematics. Office: Va Poly Inst and State Univ Dept Biology Blacksburg VA 24061

TURNER, DEREK TERENCE, materials science educator, researcher; b. London, Dec. 19, 1926; came to U.S., 1962, naturalized, 1973; s. Henry Godfrey and (Ellen Grant) T.; m. Anais Quevedo, Aug. 6, 1954; children: Luis, Christine. B.Sc., London U., 1951; A.I.R.I., Nat. Coll. Rubber Tech., London, 1952; Ph.D., London U., 1957. Research chemist Brit. Insulated Callenders Cables, London, 1952-55; sr. chemist British Rubber Producers Research Assn., Welwyn Garden City, 1955-62, Camille Dreyfus Lab., Research Triangle Inst., N.C., 1962-68; prof. metall. engring. Drexel U., Phila., 1968-71; prof. oral biology U. N.C., Chapel Hill, 1971-80, prof. operative dentistry, 1980—. Contbr. articles to profl. jours. Served to lt. U.S. Army, 1945-48. Mem. Am. Phys. Soc., Soc. Rheology, Am. Chem. Soc., Soc. Biomaterials, Internat. Assn. Dental Research. Current Work: Design of composite materials to restore teeth, work on coupling agents and on satisfactory service performance in an aqueous environment, structure and properties of highly crosslinked glassy polymers. Subspecialties: Polymer chemistry; Materials. Home: 230 Wild Turkey Trail Chapel Hill NC 27514

TURNER, EARL JAMES, civil engineer; b. Marine, Ill., Feb. 11, 1918; s. James Robert and Emma (Suter) T.; m. Marjorie M. Hunziker, Feb. 22, 1944 (dec.); children: James Allen, John Earl, Gary Lee. B.S. in Civil Engring, Washington U., St. Louis, 1943. Registered profl. engr., Mo. Archtl. draftsman Mo. Pacific R.R., 1946-48; structural engr. sect. spl. structures Sverdrup & Parcel & Assocs., Inc., St. Louis, 1948—, project engr., 1955—. Served to 1st lt. inf. U.S. Army, 1944-46. Decorated Bronze Star. Mem. ASCE (chmn. com. aerodynamics Aerospace Div.), Nat. Soc. Profl. Engrs., Am. Concrete Inst., ASME, Res. Officers Assn. Mem. United Ch. of Christ. Current Work: Project engineer. Subspecialties: Civil engineering; Aerospace engineering and technology. Office: 801 N 11th Blvd Saint Louis MO 63101

TURNER, MALCOLM ELIJAH, JR., educator, biomathematician; b. Atlanta, May 27, 1929; s. Malcolm Elijah and Margaret (Parker) T.; m. Ann Clay Bowers, Sept. 16, 1948; children: Malcolm Elijah IV, Allison Ann, Clay Shumate, Margaret Jean; m. Rachel Patricia Farmer, Feb. 1, 1968; children—Aleta van Riper, Leila Samantha, Alexis St. John, Walter McCamy. Student, Emory U., 1947-48; B.A., Duke U., 1952; M.Exptl. Stats., N.C. State U., 1955, Ph.D., 1959. Analytical statistician Communicable Disease Center, USPHS, Atlanta, 1953; research asso. U. Cin., 1955, asst. prof., 1955-58; asst. statistician N.C. State U., Raleigh, 1957-58; assoc. prof. Med. Coll. Va., Richmond, 1958-63, chmn. div. biometry, 1959-63; prof., chmn. dept. statistics and biometry Emory U., Atlanta, 1963-69; prof., chmn. dept. biomath., prof. biostats. and math. U. Ala., Birmingham, 1970-82, prof. biostats. and biomath., 1982—; instr. summers Yale U., 1966, U. Calif., Berkeley, 1971, Vanderbilt U., 1975; prof. U. Kans., 1968-69; vis. prof. Atlanta U., 1969; cons. to industry. Contbr. articles to profl. jours. Fellow Am. Statis. Assn., AAAS, Ala. Acad. Sci.; mem. Biometric Soc. (mng. editor Biometrics 1962-69), Soc. for Math. Biology, Soc. for Indsl. and Applied Math., AMA (affiliate), Mensa, Sigma Xi, Phi Kappa Phi, Phi Delta Theta, Phi Sigma. Current Work: Math. biology, inductive inference. Subspecialties: Applied mathematics; Statistics. Home: 1734 Tecumseh Trail Pelham AL 35124

TURNER, MORTIMER DARLING, government executive; b. Greeley, Colo., Oct. 24, 1920; s. Clarence Earnest and Satis May (Darling) T.; m. Laura Mercedes Perez y Mende, Jan. 18, 1945 (dec.); children—Sylvia Turner Goff, Ylla Turner Romdell, Robert; m. Joanne Kay Church, Dec. 5, 1965; 1 child, Christopher Scott Dort. B.S., U. Calif.-Berkeley, 1943, M.S., 1954; postgrad. Va. Poly. Inst., 1943-44; Ph.D., U. Kans., 1972. Registered geologist, Calif.; cert. engring. geologist. Asst. mining geologist Calif. Div. Mining and Geology, San Francisco, 1948-54; state geologist Econ. Devel. Adminstrn., Santurce, P.R., 1954-59; program mgr. div. polar programs NSF, Washington, 1959—, program mgr. polar earth scis., 1965—; assoc. prof. geology George Washington U., Washington, 1972—; ptnr., cons. JCT Enterprises, Silver Spring, Md., 1980—; cons. Caribbean region, 1955—. Editor: (with others) Clays and Clay Technology, 1955; Permafrost, 1973; Geology of the Trans-Antarctic Mountains, Antarctica, 1982. Served with U.S. Army, 1943-46. Recipient Manuela Perez award Govt. of P.R., 1955; Commendation Cert. NSF, 1960, Antartic medal NSF, 1960, Group Achievement award NASA, 1984. Fellow Geol Soc. Am.; mem. Antarctican Soc. (pres. 1982-84), Caribbean Geol. Conf. (organizing com. 1957-60), Internat. Geol. Congress (v.p. 1956), Nat. Conf. Clays and Clay Tech. (organizing com. 1949-54). Current work: Research by U.S. in Antartica, tectonic development of Caribbean area, economic geology of industrial minerals, entry of early man in Americas. Subspecialty: Geology. Office: Div Polar Programs NSF 1800 G St NW Washington DC 20550

TURNER, ROBERT EUGENE, marine science educator; b. Niskayuna, N.Y., Apr. 7, 1945; s. Robert and Emily Elizabeth (Connell) T.; B.A., Monmouth Coll., 1967; M.S. in Biology, Drake U., 1969; Ph.D. in Zoology, U. Ga., 1974. Research assoc. La. State U., Baton Rouge, 1974, asst. prof. in marine sci., 1975-78, assoc. prof., 1978-83, prof., 1983—. Editor: 3rd Coastal Marsh Estuary Management Symposium, 1979; Wetlands: Ecology and Management, 1982. NSF fellow, 1972-74; mem. Nat. Acad. Exchange Program Nat. Acad. Scis., 1979. Mem. Am. Soc. Limnology and Oceanography, INTECOL (chmn. wetland working group), Am. Fisheries Soc., Ecolog. Soc. Am. Current work: Wetland ecology and fisheries, environmental management, resource management in developing countries. Subspecialties: Ecology (environmental science); Coastal zones. Office: La State U Dept Marine Scis Baton Rouge LA 70803

TURNER, TERRY TOMO, reproductive physiologist, researcher, educator; b. Moultrie, Ga., Nov. 1, 1945; s. Otis Guy and Donita Maxine (Murphy) T.; m. Susan Stegall, Sept. 22, 1965; children—Heather Lynn, Patrick Lee. B.S.A., U. Ga., 1967, M.S., 1972, Ph.D., 1974. Postdoctoral fellow U. Tex.-San Antonio, 1975; instr. U. Va., Charlottesville, 1976-77, asst. prof. urology, 1977-83, assoc. prof., 1983—. Author: (under name David Donovan) Once A Warrior King, 1985. Contbr. numerous articles to profl. jours. Chmn. World Hunger and Disaster Relief Com., Charlottesville, 1980-84. Served to capt. U.S. Army, 1967-70, Vietnam. Decorated Bronze Star; Cross of Gallantry (Vietnam); NIH grantee, 1980, 82, 84. Mem. Am. Soc. Andrology (exec. council 1979-83), Soc. for Study Reprodn., Soc. for Study Fertility, Am. Physiol. Soc., AAAS. Democrat. Baptist. Club: Greencroft (Charlottesville). Current work: Physiology of the testis and epididymis; androgen microenvironment of testis; effect of varicocele on testis function; development of alloplastic spermatocele; effect of testicular torsion on reproductive function; control of sperm motility in male tract. Subspecialties: Reproductive biology; Urology. Office: Dept Urology U Va Sch Medicine Charlottesville VA 22908

TURRO, NICHOLAS JOHN, chemistry educator; b. Middletown, Conn., May 18, 1938; s. Nicholas John and Philomena (Russo) T.; m. Sandra Jean Misenti, Aug. 6, 1960; children—Cynthia Suzanne, Claire Melinda. B.A., Wesleyan U., 1960, D.Sc. (hon.), 1984; Ph.D., Calif. Inst. Tech., 1963. Postdoctoral research assoc. Harvard U., 1963-64; instr. Columbia U., N.Y.C., 1964-65, asst. prof., 1965-67, assoc. prof., 1967-69, prof. chemistry, 1969—, William P. Schweitzer prof. chemistry, 1982—, chmn. chemistry dept., 1981-84; Guggenheim fellow Oxford U.; Sherman Fairchild vis. scholar, Calif. Inst. Tech., 1984-85; cons. E.I. duPont de Nemours and Co., Inc. Author: Molecular Photochemistry, 1965, (with G.S. Hammond, J.N. Pitts, D.H. Valentine) Survey of Photochemistry, vol. 1, 1968, vol. 2, 1970, vol. 3, 1971, (with A.A. Lamola) Energy Transfer and Organic Photochemistry, 1971, Modern Molecular Photochemistry, 1978; Editorial bd.: (with A.A. Lamola) Jour. Organic Chemistry, 1974—Recipient Eastman Kodak award for excellence in grad. research; Mem. Nat. Acad. Sci., Am. Chem. Soc. (editorial bd. Jour. 1985—), Am. Acad. Arts and Scis., Am. Chem. Soc. (Fresenius award 1973, award for pure chemistry 1974), Chem. Soc. (London), N.Y. Acad. Scis. (Freda and Gregory Halpern award in photochemistry 1977), Am. Soc. Photochemistry and Photobiology, Internat. Solar Energy Soc., Phi Beta Kappa, Sigma Xi. Current Work: Molecular photochemistry; chemiluminescent organic reactions; small ring compounds; energy transfer mechanisms; laser application to photochemical problems; models for solar energy capture and storage; fluorescence probes of micelles and biological membranes; photochemistry in polymers; reactions of molecular oxygen. Subspecialty: Photochemistry. Home: 125 Downey Dr Tenafly NJ 07670

TUTTLE, JEREMY BALLOU, neuroscientist, researcher, educator; b. N.Y.C., Oct. 9, 1947; s. John Bauman and Charlotte Marion (Root) T.; m. Sara Jane Stasko, Mar. 26, 1971. A.B., U. Rochester, 1969; Ph.D. in Physiology (fellow), Johns Hopkins U., 1977. Research asst. Sloan-Kettering Inst., N.Y.C., summers 1966-68; postdoctoral fellow physiology sect. biol. sci. group U. Conn., Storrs, 1976-79, Spinal Cord Injury Found. fellow, 1980, asst. prof. in residence physiology sect. biol. scis. group, 1980-84; asst. prof. physiology U. Va. Sch. Medicine, 1984—. Contbr. articles to sci. jours. Nat. Inst. Neurol. Communicative Disease and Stroke nat. research service awardee, 1976-79; research career devel. awardee, 1981—. Mem. Soc. for Neurosci., AAAS, N.Y. Acad. Scis., Johns Hopkins U. Med. and Surg. Assn., Sigma Xi. Current Work: Cellular neurophysiology; trophic interactions of neural tissue in cell culture; neuronal cell culture; neural circuit formation; pharmacology of excitable cells. Subspecialties: Neurobiology; Neurophysiology. Home: 900 Stillwater Ln Earlysville VA 22936 Office: U Va Sch Medicine Box 449 Charlottesville VA 22908

TUUL, JOHANNES, physics educator, researcher; b. Tarvastu, Viljandi, Estonia, May 23, 1922; came to U.S., 1956, naturalized, 1962; s. Johan and Emilie (Tulf) T.; m. Marjatta Murtoniemi, July 14, 1957 (div. Aug. 1971); children: Melinda, Melissa; m. Sonia Esmeralda Manosalva, Sept. 15, 1976; 1 son, Johannes. B.S., U. Stockholm, 1955, M.A., 1956; Sc.M., Brown U., 1957, Ph.D., 1960. Research physicist Am. Cyanamid Co., Stamford, Conn., 1960-62; sr. research physicist Bell & Howell Research Center, Pasadena, Calif., 1962-65; asst. prof., assoc. prof. Calif. State Poly. U., Pomona, 1965-68; vis. prof. Pahlavi U., Shiraz, Iran, 1968-70; chmn. phys. earth sci. Calif. State Poly. U., Pomona, 1971-75, prof. physics, 1975—, mem. acad. senate, 1981—; cons. Bell & Howell Research Center, Pasadena, Calif., 1965, Teledyne Co., Pasadena, 1968; guest researcher Naval Weapons Center, China Lake, Calif., 1967, 72. Author: Physics Made Easy, 1974; contbr. articles in field to profl. jours. Pres. Group Against Smoking Pollution, Pomona Valley, Calif., 1976; foster parent Foster Parents Plan, Inc., Warwick, R.I., 1964—; block capt. Neighborhood Watch, West Covina, Calif., 1982-85. Brown U. fellow, 1957; U. Namur (Belgium) research grantee, 1978; Centre Nat. de la Recherche Scientifique research grantee, 1979; recipient Humanitarian Fellowship award Save the Children Fedn., 1968. Mem. Am. Phys. Soc., AAAS (life), Am. Assn. Physics Tchrs., N.Y. Acad Scis. Republican. Roman Catholic. Current Work: Research in the area of energy conservation and new energy technologies. Subspecialties: Condensed matter physics; Surface chemistry. Office: Calif State Poly U 3801 W Temple Ave Pomona CA 91768

TVERSKY, AMOS, cognitive psychologist; b. Haifa, Israel, Mar. 16, 1937; came to U.S., 1977; s. Yosef and Jenny (Ginzburg) T.; m. Barbara Gans, Aug. 30, 1966; children—Oren, Tal, Dona. B.A., Hebrew U., Jerusalem, 1961; Ph.D., U. Mich., 1965. Lectr., prof. Hebrew U., 1966-77; prof. psychology Stanford U., Calif., 1978—. Author: (with others) Mathematical Psychology, 1970; The Foundations of Measurement, 1971; Judgement Under Uncertainty, 1982. Recipient MacArthur prize MacArthur Found., 1984, Disting. Sci. award Am. Psychol. Assn., 1982. Mem. Am. Acad. Scis., Nat. Acad. Sci., Soc. Exptl. Psychologists. Subspecialty: Cognition. Office: Stanford U Bldg 420 Stanford CA 94305

TWEEDLE, CHARLES DAVID, anatomy educator; b. Astoria, Oreg., Jan. 22, 1944; s. David Charles and Opal Iona (Keen) T.; m. Carmen Celia Umpierre Norat, Dec. 22, 1982. B.A., U. Oreg., 1966, M.A., 1967; Ph.D., Mich. State U., 1970. Postdoctoral fellow Yale U., New Haven, 1970-72; research assoc. dept. zoology Mich. State U., East Lansing, 1972-73, asst. prof. dept. biomechanics, 1973-76, assoc. prof. dept. anatomy, 1976-84, prof., 1984—. Contbr. articles to profl. jours. Research grantee Muscular Dystrophy Assn., 1973-75, NSF, 1976-80, NIH, 1980—, Am. Osteo. Assn., 1975-77, 82-84. Mem. Soc. for Neurosci., AAAS, Am. Assn. Anatomists, Am. Soc. Zoologists. Democrat. Club: Capital. Current work: Role of glia in normal neuronal activity; synaptic plasticity during physiological conditions. Subspecialties: Neurobiology; Neuroendocrinology. Office: Dept Anatomy Mich State U East Lansing MI 48824

TWEEDY, BILLY G., biochemist, plant pathologist, chemical company executive; b. Cobden, Ill., Dec. 31, 1934; s. Amos Glenn and Lona Clara (Klughart) T.; m. Patsy Ann Glasco, Dec. 28, 1957; children: Patricia Lynn, Glenna Jean, Carol Jane. B.S., So. Ill. U., 1956; M.S., U. Ill., 1959, Ph.D., 1961. Asst. plant pathologist Boyce Thompson Inst., Yonkers, N.Y., 1961-65; mem. faculty dept. plant pathology U. Mo., Columbia, 1965-73, prof., 1973; prin. plant pathologist U.S. Dept. Agr., Washington, 1971-72; mgr. residue investigations CIBA-Geigy Corp., Greensboro, N.C., 1973-78, dir. biochemistry, 1978—; project leader U.S.-USSR Bilateral Agreement on Integrated Pest Mgmt. Contbr. chpts. to books, articles to profl. jours. Mem. Am. Phytopathol. Soc., Am. Chem. Soc., Weed Sci. Soc., AAAS, Internat. Congress Plant Protection (standing com.), Sigma Xi, Gamma Sigma Delta. Baptist. Current Work: Administrator in area of biochemistry of pesticide in plants, soil and animals. Subspecialties: Biochemistry (biology); Plant pathology. Home: 111 Crest Hill Rd Jamestown NC 27282 Office: PO Box 18300 Greensboro NC 27419

TWERSKY, VICTOR, See *Who's Who in America,* 43rd edition.

TWISS, PAGE CHARLES, geology educator; b. Columbus, Ohio, Jan. 2, 1929; s. George Ransom and Blanche (Olin) T.; m. Nancy Homer Hubbard, Aug. 29, 1954; children—Stephen Ransom, Catherine Grace, Thomas Stuart. B.S. in Geology, Kans. State U., 1950, M.S., 1955; Ph.D., U. Tex. at Austin, 1959. Mem. faculty dept. geology Kans. State U., Manhattan, 1959—, assoc. prof., 1964-69, prof., 1969—, also head dept., 1968-77; geologist agrl. research service U.S. Dept. Agr., 1966-68; research scientist U. Tex., Austin, 1966-67. Contbr. articles to profl. jours. Chmn. Manhattan Council Human Relations, 1960-61; vice pres. Riley County Democratic Club, 1970-71; mem. Dem. Precinct Com., Manhattan, 1970-72, 74-80. Served with USAAF, 1951-53. Fellow Pan Am. Petroleum Found., 1957-58; Shell Found. fellow, 1958-59. Fellow Geol. Soc. Am. (chmn. South Central sect. 1972-73, sec.-treas. 1980—); mem. Am. Assn. Petroleum Geologists (geologic maps com. 1968-70), Soc. Econ. Paleontologists and Minerologists, Kans. Acad. Sci. (mem. research awards com. 1966—, assoc. editor 1977—), AAAS, Clay Minerals Soc., Kans. Geol. Soc., W. Tex. Geol. Soc., Am. Soc. Agronomy, Soil Sci. Soc. Am., Internat. Soc. Soil Sci., Internat. Assn. Sedimentologists, Assn. Internationale pour l'Etude des Argiles, Am. Quaternary Assn., AAUP (chpt. v.p. 1971-72, chpt. pres. 1972-73), Nat. Assn. Geology Tchrs., Mineral. Soc. Am., Sigma Xi, Sigma Gamma Epsilon, Gamma Sigma Delta. Club: Mason. Current Work: Origin, distribution, and classification of silica bodies (phytoliths)in plants, atmospheric dust deposition and composition, petrology and geochemistry of sandstone, carbonate rocks, and ignimbrites. Subspecialties: Geology; Sedimentology. Home: 2327 Bailey Dr Manhattan KS 66502

TYLER, GEORGE LEONARD, electrical engineer, radio astronomer; b. Bartow, Fla., Oct. 18, 1940; married; 2 children. B.S., Ga. Inst. Tech., 1963; M.S., Stanford U., 1964, Ph.D. in Elec. Engring, 1967. Research assoc. Stanford U., 1967-79, research engr., 1969-71; sr. research assoc. Stanford U. (center Radar Astronomy), 1971-74, adj. prof. elec. engring., 1974-82; prof. elec. engring. Stanford U., 1982—; team leader Voyager Radio Sci. Team, NASA, from 1979. Recipient NASA Exceptional Sci. Achievement medal, 1977, 81. Mem. IEEE, Am. Astron. Soc., Am. Geophys. Union, Internat. Astron. Union, Internat. Union Radio Sci. Subspecialty: Radio and microwave astronomy. Office: Ctr Radar Astronomy Stanford U Stanford CA 94305

TYLER, TIPTON RANSOM, toxicologist; b. Milw., Jan. 3, 1941; s. Ransom and Margerite (Struble) T.; m. Barbara Ann Manville, Apr. 21, 1962; children: Timothy, Gregory, Jennifer. B.S., Colo. State U., 1963, Ph.D., 1968; M.S., N.C. State U., 1965. Diplomate: Am. Bd. Toxicology. Sr. research chemist Merck Sharp & Dohme Research Labs., Rahway, N.J., 1968-73; asst. prof. animal sci. U. Ill., Urbana, 1974-75; sr. scientist, chem. hygiene fellow Bushy Run Research Lab., Carnegie-Mellon U., Pitts., 1976-81; asst. corp. dir. applied toxicology Union Carbide Corp., Danbury, Conn., 1981—; adj. assoc. prof. toxicology dept. pharmacology Sch. Pharmacy, U. Pitts., 1979-83; adj. prof. toxicology W.Va. Coll. Grad. Studies, 1982-84. Contbr. articles to sci. jours. Mem. Soc. Toxicology, Am. Soc. Pharmacology and Exptl. Therapeutics, Am. Coll. Toxicology, Am. Chem. Soc. Current Work: Metabolism of chemicals and foreign compounds. Subspecialties: Toxicology (medicine); Pharmacokinetics. Office: PO Box 8361 South Charleston WV 25303

TYNDALL, BRUCE MAPES, mathematics educator, automotive analysis consultant and researcher; b. Iowa City, June 16, 1930; s. Edward Philip Theodore and Irene Beatrice (Mapes) T.; m. Antoinette van der Berg, Aug. 22, 1957; children: Suzanne, Juliet. B.A., U. Iowa, 1955, M.S., 1956; student, Roosevelt U., 1950-51; Ph.D. equivalent Faculty Com. on Tenure and Promotion, U. New Haven, 1976. Cons. actuary Huggins & Co., Phila., 1956-57; instr. Elizabethtown Coll., 1957-59, asst. prof. math., 1959-61, assoc. prof., 1961; instr. in mechanics Johns Hopkins U., 1961-63; cons. actuary Monumental Life Ins. Co. and O. Herschman Assocs., Balt., 1963-65; assoc. prof. math. U. New Haven, 1965-76, prof., 1976—; cons. automotive analysis Bruce Tyndall Assocs., Guilford, Conn., 1963—; pres. Tyndall Motor Car Co., Guilford, 1973—. Co-founder, co-editor: Essays in Arts and Scis, 1970—; inventor new forms of math. analysis, aluminum frame for impact absorption. Concert oboist, numerous concerts, East Coast, 1960-81; pianist, tchr. U. N.H. Served to cpl. U.S. Army, 1952-54. Recipient Author's award Automotive Industries jour., 1964; Outstanding Tchr. award U. New Haven, 1975. Mem. Soc. Indsl. and Applied Math., Soc. Automotive Engrs., Soc. Logistics Engrs. (chmn. chpt. 1982-84), Soc. Automotive Historians, Internat. Double Reed Soc. Current Work: Nonlinear differential equations with new forms of analytical solutions and approximation methods; numerous applications to impact, mortality, music, automotive and neuroscience. Subspecialties: Applied mathematics; Materials. Office: Dept Math U New Haven West Haven CT 06516

TYRE, TIMOTHY EDWARD, psychologist, hospital program administrator; b. Oak Park, Ill., Mar. 12, 1947; s. Edward William and Shirley (Litton) T.; m. Marilyn Yanchar, Dec. 28, 1969; children: Emily, Lisa, Kateri, Sean. B.A., St. Mary's Coll., Winona, Minn., 1969; M.A., Xavier U., Cin., 1971; Ph.D., U. Wis.-Milw., 1973. Dir. Children's Clinic, Archdiocese Milw., 1973-75; asst. dir. dept. psychol. services Norris Health Center, U. Wis.-Milw., 1975-77; pvt. clin. practice psychology, Waukesha, Wis., 1977—; dir. Pain Clinic, Waukesha Meml. Hosp., 1979—; dir. cancer research program West Allis (Wis.) Hosp., 1981—; cons. psychology dept. phys. medicine St. Luke's Hosp., Milw., 1977—; chmn. Wis. Bd. Examiners in Psychology, Madison, 1980—. Research publs. in field. Mem. Soc. Clin./Cons. Psychology State Wis. (pres. 1978-79), Am. Psychol. Assn., Wis. Psychol. Assn. (pres. Div. I 1978-79), Soc. Behavioral Medicine, Soc. Clin. and Exptl. Hypnosis. Republican. Roman Catholic. Current Work: Management of chronic pain-both benign and malignant; psychological variables active in neoplastic disease. Subspecialties: Cancer research (medicine); Behavioral psychology. Home and Office: 1519 Summit Ave Waukesha WI 53186

TYRRELL, JAMES, chemistry educator; b. Kilsyth, Scotland, Apr. 19, 1938; came to U.S., 1967, naturalized, 1977; s. Thomas and Jean (Bauld) T.; m. Karine Babrowski, Nov. 4, 1940; 1 son: Dalton; m. Neena Lynne Summers, Sept. 9, 1955. B.Sc. with honors, U. Glasgow, Scotland, 1960; Ph.D., 1963. Teaching postdoctoral fellow dept. chemistry McMaster U., Hamilton, Ont., Can., 1963-65; postdoctoral fellow div. pure physics NRC, Ottawa, Ont., Can., 1965-67; asst. prof. dept. chemistry So. Ill. U., Carbondale, 1967-72, assoc. prof., 1972-80, prof., 1980—, chmn. dept., 1982—. Mem. Am. Chem. Soc., Sigma Xi. Democrat. Current Work: AB initio molecular orbital calculations on complexes of transition metals and small gaseous molecules. Subspecialties: Theoretical chemistry; Physical chemistry. Home: 1433 E Walnut St 7 C Carbondale IL 62901 Office: So Ill U Dept Chemistry Carbondale IL 62901

TYSON, ROBERT KARL, physicist; b. Reading, Pa., Mar. 28, 1948; s. William Karl and Elizabeth (Drenning) T.; m. Suzanne Marie Walton, July 10, 1971; children—Kia Nicole, Andrew James. B.S., Pa. State U., 1970; M.S., W.Va. U., 1976, Ph.D., 1978. Research asst. W.Va. U. Sch. Medicine, 1974-78; sr. exptl. engr. Pratt & Whitney Aircraft, West Palm Beach, Fla., 1978-79; pres. Ankia Research, Jupiter, Fla., 1983—; sr. systems engr. United Techs. Research Ctr., West Palm Beach, 1979—; cons., lectr. in field. Contbr. articles to profl. jours. Judge of elections City of Morgantown, W.Va., 1976; youth football coach Jupiter-Tequesta Athletic Assn., 1978; deacon 1st United Ch. of Christ, 1984—. Served to lt. (j.g.) USN, 1970-74. Recipient Outstanding Tchr. Asst. award Coll. of Arts and Sci., 1978. Mem. Am. Assn. Physicists in Medicine, Soc. Photo-optical Instrumentation Engrs., Optical Soc. Am., Tech. Mktg. Soc. Am., Sigma Pi Sigma. Democrat. Mem. Christian Ch. Current work: Development of high energy laser beam control systems and technology; analysis of diffraction and atmospheric turbulence; development of computer simulations and engineering software. Subspecialties: Theoretical optics; Mathematical software. Home: 1255 Holly Cove Dr Jupiter FL 33458 Office: United Techs Research Ctr Optics & Applied Tech Lab PO Drawer 4181 West Palm Beach FL 33402

TYTELL, MICHAEL, anatomist, educator; b. N.Y.C., Jan. 3, 1948; s. Samuel and Ida Rachel (Smoller) T.; m. Frances Wilke, Mar. 3, 1973; children: Eric Daniel, Alison Rebecca. B.A., Queens Coll., 1969; M.S., Purdue U., 1973; Ph.D., Baylor Coll. Medicine, 1977. NIH postdoctoral fellow Case Western Res. U., Cleve., 1977-79, sr. research assoc., 1979-80; asst. prof. dept. anatomy Bowman Gray Sch. Medicine, Wake Forest U., Winston-Salem, N.C., 1980—. Contbr. articles to profl. jours. NSF grantee, 1982-84. Mem. AAAS, Soc. Neurosci., Am. Soc. Neurochemistry, Am. Soc. Cell Biology, N.Y. Acad. Scis., Planetary Soc., Sigma Xi. Jewish. Current Work: Transport of proteins within axons of nerve cells; research on cell biology of neurons. Subspecialties: Cell biology; Neurobiology. Office: Dept Anatomy Bowman Gray Sch Medicine Winston Salem NC 27103

TZENG, OLIVER CHUN SHUN, psychology educator; b. Taiwan, Dec. 1, 1939; s. Pen-Yeo and Jin-Mei T.; m. Diana Yu-Maan, Sept. 3, 1969; children: Bertrand JePing, Sophia SeaPing. B.Ed., Taiwan Normal U., 1966; M.S., U. Wis.-Menomonie, 1969; Ph.D., U. Ill., 1972. Asst. prof. U. Wis.-Menomonie, 1972; research asst. prof. U. Ill., 1972-76; asst. prof. Purdue U., Indpls., 1976-77, assoc. prof., 1978-81, prof., 1981—, dir. grad. applied social psychology, 1980—; advisor Taiwan Ministry of Edn., 1982-83; research advisor Taiwan Inst. Tchrs. Inservice, 1981—; dir. Osgood Lab. for Cross-cultural Research, 1982—. Contbr. chpts. to books, articles to profl. jours. U.S. Army grantee, 1977-79; Spencer Found. grantee, 1977-79; Conrail grantee, 1978-81. Mem. Am. Psychol. Assn., Soc. Intercultural Edn., Tng. and Research, Psychometric Soc., Soc. for Cross-cultural Research, Sigma Xi. Current Work: Cross-cultural social and personality research, inter-group relations, inter-cultural training, psychosemantics, quantitative methodologies, and applied social psychology. Subspecialty: Cross-cultural Psychology; Psychosemantics. Home: 3019 Lehigh Ct Indianapolis IN 46268 Office: Purdue Univ 1201 E 38th St Indianapolis IN 46223

TZIANABOS, THEODORE, microbiologist, researcher; b. Manchester, N.H., Feb. 12, 1933; s. Arthur and Marika (Tsoulhidou) T.; m. Irene Davis, Aug. 11, 1962; children: Suzanne Tresselt, Peter T. B.A., U. N.H., 1955, M.S., 1959; Ph.D. (Lotta Crabtree fellow), U. Mass., 1965. Researcher U. N.H., 1955-57; microbiologist virus serology Mass. Dept. Pub. Health, Boston, 1958-59; research instr. U. Mass., 1961-65; postdoctoral resident Ctr. Disease Control, Atlanta, 1965-67, rickettsiologist, viral and rickettsial zoonoses br., viral disease div., 1972—; research microbiologist research and devel. U.S. Army Labs., Ft. Detrick, Md., 1967-70, Beckman Instruments, Atlanta, 1970-72. Contbr. numerous articles to profl. jours. Mem. Am. Soc. Microbiology, Am. Soc. Tropical Medicine and Hygiene (trustee Am. Type Culture Collection), Am. Acad. Microbiology, Atlanta Photog. Soc. (pres. 1981-82), Am. Soc. Rickettsiology, Sigma Xi. Greek Orthodox. Current Work: Research in rickettsiology—reagents, structure and function. Subspecialties: Microbiology; Virology (biology). Office: 1600 Clifton Rd Atlanta GA 30333

UBELAKER, DOUGLAS HENRY, museum curator, anthropologist; b. Everest, Kans., Aug. 23, 1946; s.Henry Edward and Wilma Ann (Stabler) U.; m. Maruja Andrade, Nov. 12, 1975; children—Max Henry, Lisa Ann. B.A. with honors, U.Kans., 1968, Ph.D., 1973. Curator dept. anthropology Smithsonian Instn., Washington, 1973-80, 85—, chmn. dept.anthropology, 1980-85; cons. forensic anthropologist FBI, Washington, 1977—. Author: Demographic Reconstruction, 1973; Human Skeletal Remains, 1978; The Ayalan Cemetery, 1981; Plains Indian Studies, 1982. Served with U.S. Army, 1969-71. mem. Anthrop. Assn., Am. Assn. Phys. Anthropologists, Soc. Am. Archaeology, Am. Acad. Forensic Scis., Plains Anthrop. Assn. Current work: Forensic anthropology; prehistoric biology of new world; physicalanthropology; demography; bone biology; paleopathology. Subspecialties: Paleobiology; Forensic anthropology. Office: Dept Anthropology Nat Mus Natural History Smithsonian Institution Washington DC 20560

UBERALL, HERBERT MICHAEL STEFAN, physicist, educator, consultant; b. Neunkirchen, Austria, Oct. 14, 1931, came to U.S., 1953, naturalized, 1963; s. Michael and Stefanie (Hacker) U.; m. Reyna Tosta; children—Bernadette, Bertrand. Ph.D. sub-auspiciis praesidentis in Theoretical Physics, U. Vienna, Austria, 1953; Ph.D. in Theoretical Physics, Cornell U., 1956. Research fellow Nuclear Physics Research Lab., U. Liverpool, Eng., 1956-57; Ford Found. fellow CERN, Geneva, 1957-58; research physicist Carnegie Inst. Tech., Pitts., 1958-60; asst. prof. U. Mich., Ann Arbor, 1960-64; assoc. prof. Catholic U., Washington, 1964-65, prof. physics, 1965—; cons. Conductron Corp., Ann Arbor, 1961-64, Naval Research Lab., Washington, 1966—, Naval Surface Weapons Ctr., Silver Spring, Md., 1976-82. Author: (2 vols.) Electron Scattering from Complex Nuclei, 1971; (with F. Cannata) Giant Resonance Phenomena, 1980. Editor: (with A.W. Sáenz) Long-Distance Neutrina Detection, 1979; Coherent Radiation Sources, 1985. Recipient Publs. award Naval Research Lab., 1978; Achievement award Washington Acad. Scis., 1984. Fellow Am. Phys. Soc., Acoustical Soc. Am.; mem. IEEE, Internat. Union Radio Scis., AAUP. Current work: Study of resonance phenomena in acoustics/radar/non-destructive testing (ultrasonics)/and nuclear physics. Subspecialties: Acoustics; Nuclear physics. Home: 5101 River Rd Apt 1417 Bethesda MD 20816 Office: Dept Physics Catholic U Washington DC 20064

UCHUPI, ELAZAR, oceanographic, scientist, researcher; b. Oct. 31, 1928. B.S., CCNY, 1952; M.S., U. So. Calif., 1954, Ph.D., 1962. Research asst. U. So. Calif., Los Angeles, 1955-62; research asst. Woods Hole Oceanographic Instn., Mass., 1962-64, assoc. scientist, 1965-79, sr. scientist, 1979—; mem. working group 41, Sci. Com. for Ocean Research, 1973-74; mem. steering com. Relief Map of World's Oceans, U.S. Oceanographic Office; mem. Joint Oceanographic Instns. Site Survey Panel, 1978—, mem. Gulf of Mexico Panel deep fault sampling, 1972-74. Mem. editorial staff Marine Geology, 1971-75, Offshore Mag., 1972-74. Contbr. articles to profl. publs. Recipient Cert. Recognition, Nat. Assn. Geology Tchrs., Inc., Crustal Evolution Edn. Project, 1979, medal Offshore Mag., 1974. Fellow Geol. Soc. Am.; mem. Am. Assn. Petroleum Geologists (bull. editorial staff 1972-78, Cert. Recognition 1969), Soc. Econ. Paleontologists and Mineralogists, Sigma Xi. Current work: Geology of ocean basins. . Office: Woods Hole Oceanographic Instn Dept Geology and Geophysics Woods Hole MA 02543

UDA, ROBERT TAKEO, aerospace engineer, consultant, researcher; b. Honolulu, Hawaii, Aug. 1, 1942; s. Masao and Irene Kuualoha (Waipa) U.; m. Karen Elizabeth Rowland, June 8, 1968; children—Atom Richard, Marc Edward, Heather Ann. M.S. in Astronautics USAF Inst. Tech., WPAFB, Dayton, Ohio, 1968; B.S. in Aerospace Engring., U. Okla., 1966; M.A. in Mgmt., U. Redlands, 1982; Exec. Program diploma UCLA, 1982. Astronautical devel. engr. USAF, 1966-74; lead sr. design engr. Planning Research Corp., Kennedy Space Ctr., Fla., 1974-76, prin. engr., 1976-77; sr. preliminary design engr. UTC Hamilton Standard Div., Windsor Locks, Conn., 1977-78; project engr. TRW, Inc., Redondo Beach, Calif., 1978-79; program mgr. HR Textron Inc., Valencia, Calif., 1979-80, product line mgr., Pacoima, Calif., 1980-82, gen. mgr. accessory products group, 1982-83; v.p., gen. mgr. N. Am. Mfg. Corp., Spanish Fork, Utah, 1983; pres. Systems Tech. Services, Canyon Country, Calif., 1983; chmn., pres., chief exec. officer Apollo Systems Tech., Inc., Canyon Country, 1984—. Contbr. articles to profl. jours. Com. mem. Cedarcreek Sch. PTA; com. mem. Gt. Western council Boy Scouts Am.; Stake High councilor Los Angeles-Santa Clarita Stake of Mormon Ch., Canyon Country, 1984—. Served to capt. USAF, 1966-74. Recipient Outstanding Nat. Dir. award Calif. Jaycees, 1973-74; named Jr. Officer of Yr. Space and Missile Systems Orgn., El Segundo, Calif., 1971. Fellow Brit. Interplanetary Soc.; assoc. fellow AIAA; mem. Am. Astron. Soc., Air Force Assn., Am. Def. Preparedness Assn., Am. Mgmt. Assns., Tech. Mktg. Soc. Am., Sigma Tau, Alpha Sigma Phi. Current work: Risk assessment and analysis; system requirements analysis; system engineering management planning, physical security, threat analysis, vulnerability and survivability, human factors engineering, configuration management. Subspecialties: Aerospace engineering and technology; Systems engineering. Home: 19544 Delight St Canyon Country CA 91351 Office: Apollo Systems Tech Inc 27141 Hidaway Ave Suite 205 Canyon Country CA 91351

UDAGAWA, TAKESHI, physicist, educator; b. Tokyo, May 3, 1932; s. Moheiji and Toruko (Yamazaki) U.; m. Yukiko Amano, Mar. 21, 1960; children—Yoichi, Taturo. B.S., Tokyo Inst. Sci., 1957; M.S., Tokyo U. Edn., 1959, Ph.D., 1962. Instr. Tokyo Inst. Tech., 1962-64; research assoc. Fla. State U., Tallahassee, 1964-66; research scientist Niels Bohr Inst., Copenhagen, 1966-68; assoc. prof. physics Kyoto U., Japan, 1968-70; asst. prof. U. Tex., Austin, 1970-74, assoc. prof., 1974-81, prof., 1981—. Mem. Am. Phys. Soc., Japan Phys. Soc. Current work: Nuclear reaction and structure theories. Subspecialty: Nuclear physics. Home: 8501 Millway Austin TX 78758 Office: U Tex Dept Physics Austin TX 78712

UDVARDY, MIKLOS DEZSO FERENC, Giological sciences educator; b. Debrecen, Hungary, Mar. 23, 1919; came to U.S., 1958; s. Miklos and Eliz U.; m. Maud Emelie Bjorklund, Feb. 11, 1951; children—Beatrix U., M. Andrew P., Monica L. Diploma natural scis. chemistry and geography U. Debrecen-Hungary, 1941, Ph.D., 1942. Biologist Hungarian Inst. Ornithology, Budapest, 1942-45; researcher Hungarian Biol. Research Inst., 1946-48; research assoc. U. Helsinki, Finland, 1948-49, U. Uppsala, Sweden, 1950; asst. curator Swedish Mus. Natural History, Stockholm, 1951; asst. to assoc. prof. U. B.C., Vancouver, 1952-66; prof. biol. scis. Calif. State U., Sacramento, 1966—; cons. Internat. Union Conservation of Nature Morges, Switzerland, 1980—; adv. bd. Wilhelminenberg Biol. Sta., Wienna, Austria, 1963—, Point Reyes Bird Obs., Bolinas, Calif., 1977—. Contbr. articles to profl. jours. Author: Dynamic Zoogeography, 1969; Audubon Soc. Guide to Birds of N. Am., 1977; Biogeographical Provinces of the World, 1975, 78. Recipient numerous research grants. Fellow AAAS, Am. Ornithologists Union; mem. Argentinian Ornithologists Soc. (hon.), Finnish Ornithol. Soc. (hon.), others. Republican. Roman Catholic. Current work: Ecol. distbn. of Pacific seabirds-mapping of the biogeographical provinces of the world for conservation purposes for UNESCO and UNEP, IUCN. Subspecialty: Behavioral ecology. Address: Dept Biol Scis Calif State Univ Sacramento CA 95819

UDWADIA, FIRDAUS ERACH, civil engineer, educator; b. Bombay, India, Aug. 28, 1947; came to U.S., 1968, s. Eruch Rustom and Perin (Lentin) U.; m. Farida Gagrat, June 1, 1977; children—Shanaira, Zubin. B.Tech., Indian Inst. Tech., 1968; M.S., Calif. Inst. Tech., 1969, Ph.D., 1972. Mem. faculty applied sci. Calif. Inst. Tech., Pasadena, 1972-74; asst. prof. U. So. Calif., Los Angeles, 1974-77, assoc. prof., 1977-82, prof., 1983—; cons. Avery Internat. Research, Pasadena, 1980, Argonne Nat. Labs., Chgo., 1982, Jet Propulsion Lab., Pasadena, 1978—. Reviewer, referee various sci. jours. Contbr. poetry to jours., sci. articles to profl. jours. Recipient Outstanding Tech. Contbns. award NASA, 1983, Disting. Alumnus award Indian Inst. Tech., 1983; numerous research grants NSF. Mem. ASCE (com. on dynamics, probabilistic methods), Seismol. Soc. Am., Soc. Applied and Indsl. Math., Am. Acad. Mechanics, Earthquake Research Inst. Current work: Research in the areas of earthquake engineering, applied mechanics, biomechanics, applied mathematics. Subspecialties: Theoretical and applied mechanics; Biomedical engineering.

UEDA, ISSAKU, educator, anesthesiologist; b. Tokyo,; came to U.S., 1968; s. Ichiro and Yoshiko (Uchiyama) U.; m. Setsuko Hirama, Dec. 8, 1955; children—Shunsaku, Marie Anna. M.D., Keio U., 1948, Ph.D., 1960. Diplomate Am. Bd. Anesthesiology. Asst. prof. U. Utah, Salt Lake City, 1971-72, assoc. prof., 1972-76, prof. anesthesiology, 1978—; prof. U. Kans., Kansas City, 1976-78; med. investigator VA Med. Ctr., Salt Lake City, 1978-83. Mem. AMA, Am. Chem. Soc., Am. Soc. Anesthesiologists. Current work: Molecular mechanisms of anesthesia, thermodynamics and statis. mechanics of anesthetic-macromolecular interactions. Subspecialties: Anesthesiology; Surface chemistry. Home: 1447 Ambassador Way E Salt Lake City UT 84108 Office: Anesthesia VA Med Ctr Salt Lake City UT 84148

UEDA, TETSUFUMI, research scientist, educator; b. Osaka, Japan, July 11, 1940; came to U.S., 1966, naturalized, 19; s. Ryuji and Takao (Hamaguchi) U.; m. Yasuko Amano, Jan. 11, 1970; children: Jane Kiyoko, Judy Yoshiko. B.S. in Chemistry, Kyoto (Japan) U., 1966; Ph.D. in Biol. Chemistry, U. Mich., 1971. Mem. faculty Yale U., 1971-78, NIH fellow, 1974-76, research assoc., 1976-78; asst. prof. U. Mich., Ann Arbor, 1978-81, assoc. prof., 1981—, asst.

research scientist, 1978-81, assoc. research scientist, 1981—. Contbr. numerous articles to profl. publs. NIH grantee, 1979-82; NSF grantee, 1982—; U. Mich. Rackham Grad. Sch. grantee, 1981. Mem. Am. Soc. Biol. Chemists, Am. Soc. Neurochemistry, Internat. Soc. Neurochemistry, Soc. Neurosci., N.Y. Acad. Sci. Current Work: To understand the molecular mechanism and regulation of excitatory amino acid synaptic transmission and the role of protein phosphorylation in the synaptic events. Subspecialties: Neurochemistry; Neurobiology. Home: 3474 Richmond Ct Ann Arbor MI 48105 Office: Univ Mich Mental Health Research Inst 205 Washtenaw Pl Ann Arbor MI 48109

UHL, CHARLES H., botanical cytologist; b. Schenectady, May 28, 1918; s. Harry C. and Florence H. U.; m. Natalie Whitford, Aug. 15, 1945; children: Jean, Mary, Charles H., Elizabeth. B.A., Emory U., 1939, M.S., 1941; Ph.D., Cornell U., 1947. Assoc. prof. botany Cornell U., Ithaca, N.Y., 1952-85, prof. emeritus, 1985—. Served to lt. U.S. Navy, 1942-45. Mem. AAAS, Bot. Soc. Am., Genetics Soc., Soc. Study of Evolution, Internat. Assn. Plant Taxonomy. Current Work: Hybrids and cytotaxonomy of American crassulaceae; chromosome pairing. Subspecialty: Evolutionary biology. Home: 1504 Hanshaw Rd Ithaca NY 14850 Office: Sect Plant Biology Cornell U Ithaca NY 14853

UHLANER, JULIUS EARL, psychologist, educator; b. Vienna, Apr. 22, 1917; came to U.S., 1928, naturalized, 1928; s. Benjamin and Ethel Uhlaner; m. Vera Kolar, Sept. 3, 1949; children—Carole Jean, Lorraine Marie Hendrickson, Robert Theodore. B.S., CCNY, 1938; M.S. in Psychology and Stats., Iowa State U., 1941; Ph.D. in Psychology, NYU, 1947. Asst. dir. tng. N.Y. State Div. Vet. Affairs, 1946-47; tech. dir. U.S. Army Research Inst., Arlington, Va., 1947-78; chief psychologist U.S. Army, 1964-78; adj. prof. George Washington U., D.C., 1961—; v.p. Perceptronics, Inc., Woodland Hills, Calif., 1978-81, now dir.; pres. Uhlaner Cons., Encino, Calif., 1981—; dir. Starpak, Ann Arbor, Mich., 1980—; mem. Def. Adv. Com., Washington, 1981-85. Author: Psychological Research in National Defense Today, 1964. Cons. editor: Jour. Applied Psychology, 1970-82. Mem. Reagan Task Force, Washington, 1982. Served with USAF, 1944-46. Recipient Washington Acad. Scis. award, 1976, Predls. Mgmt. Improvement award U.S. Pres., 1976. Fellow Am. Psychol. Assn. (pres. mil. psychology div. 1969-70), Human Factors Soc., Internat. Assn. Applied Psychology, Ops. Research Soc. Am. Club: Cosmos (Washington). Subspecialty: Behavioral psychology. Home: 4258 Bonavita Dr Encino CA 91436 Office: Uhlaner Cons 4258 Bonavita Dr Encino CA 91436

UHLENBECK, KAREN K., mathematician, educator; b. Cleve., Aug. 24, 1942; married, 1965. B.A., U. Mich., 1964; Ph.D. in Math, Brandeis U., 1968. Instr. math. MIT, 1968-69; lectr. U. Calif.-Berkeley, 1969-71; asst. prof. math. U. Ill., Urbana, 1971-76; assoc. prof. U. Ill.-Chgo., 1976-78, prof., 1978-83; mem. faculty U. Chgo., 1983—. Sloan fellow, 1974-76; MacArthur fellow, 1983. Mem. Am. Math. Soc., Assn. Women in Math. Office: U Chgo Dept Math Chicago IL 60637*

UHLENHUTH, EBERHARD HENRY, psychiatrist, educator; b. Balt., Sept. 15, 1927; s. Eduard Carl Adolph and Elisabeth (Baier) U.; m. Helen Virginia Lyman, June 20, 1952; children—Kim, Karen, Eric. B.S., Yale U., 1947; M.D., Johns Hopkins U., 1951. Intern, Harborview Hosp., Seattle, 1951-52; resident in psychiatry Johns Hopkins U., Balt., 1952-56, Balt. Psychoanalyt. Inst., 1957-66; instr. psychiatry Johns Hopkins U., Balt., 1956-59, asst. prof. psychiatry, 1959-67, assoc. prof. psychiatry, 1967-68, U. Chgo., 1968-73, prof. psychiatry, 1973—, prof. clin. pharmacology, 1975—, acting chmn. psychiatry, 1983—; mem. clin. psychopharmacology research rev. com. NIMH, Bethesda, 1968-72; mem. psychopharmacology adv. com. FDA, Bethesda, 1974-78; mem. adv. group Treatment of Depression Collaborative Research Program, NIMH, 1978—. Mem. editorial bd. Jour. Affective Disorders, 1978—; Psychiatry Research, 1979—, Jour. Human Stress, 1982—. Contbr. numerous articles to sci. jours. Career tchr. trainee USPHS, 1957-59, Research Career Devel. awards, 1962-68; recipient Research Scientist award, 1976-81, Assoc. Clin. Psychiatrists award, 1958. Fellow Am. Coll. Neuropsychopharmacology (v.p. 1983, pres.-elect 1985), Am. Psychiat. Assn.; mem. Coll. Internat. Neuro-Psychopharmacologicum, Psychiat. Research Soc., AAAS. Current work: Depression, anxiety, diagnosis, pharmacologic treatment, psychotherapeutic treatment. Subspecialties: Psychiatry; Psychopharmacology. Office: Univ Chicago 5841 S Maryland Ave Chicago IL 60637

UHLIR, DONALD ANDREW, developmental engineer; b. Summit, N.J., July 5, 1957; s. Arthur and Cristina Ingeborg (Nuernburger) U., Jr. B.S. in Chem. Engring., Rensselaer Poly. Inst., 1979; M.S. in Chem. Engring., Tufts U., 1985. Materials engr. U.S. Army Materials and Mechanics Research Ctr., Watertown, Mass., 1980-85; sr. engr. Convair div. Gen. Dynamics, San Diego, 1985—. Patentee in field. Mem. Am. Chem. Soc., Soc. for Advancement of Material and Process Engring., Soc. Plastics Engrs. Current work: High temperature composite materials processing research. Subspecialties: Materials (engineering); Composite materials. Home: 9121 Togan Ave San Diego CA 92129 Office: Convair Div Gen Dynamics PO Box 85357 MZ41-6850 San Diego CA 92129

UHLMANN, DONALD ROBERT, materials science educator; b. Chgo., Sept. 22, 1936; s. Martin S. and Helen G. (Hannigan) U.; m. Eulalie T. Harvey, Aug. 30, 1958; children—Donald R., Eugenie V., Angelique T., Melie C., Aurelie C., Elise V. B.S., Yale U., 1958; Ph.D., Harvard U., 1963. Postdoctoral fellow Harvard U., Cambridge, Mass., 1963-65; asst. prof. materials sci. MIT, Cambridge, 1963-68, assoc. prof., 1968-74, prof., 1974-83, Cabot prof. materials, 1983—; dir. Exolon-ESK Corp., Tonawanda, N.Y., Donnelly Inc., Holland, Mich., Permattach Diamond Tool Co., Milford, N.H. Author: (with others) Introduction to Ceramics, 1976; Editor: (with others) Elasticity and Strength in Glasses, 1980; Glass Forming Systems, 1983; Glass Processing I, 1984. Guggenheim fellow, 1981. Fellow Am. Ceramic Soc. (F.H. Norton award 1979, George W. Morey award 1981; Sosman lectr. 1983); mem. Am. Phys. Soc., Soc. Glass Tech., AIME, Nat. Inst. Ceramic Engrs. Current work: Structure, properties and processing of ceramics (especially glasses) and polymers; ceramics derived from metal-organic polymers. Subspecialties: Ceramics; Polymers (materials science). Office: MIT 13-4005 Cambridge MA 02139

UHR, JONATHAN W., medical educator; b. N.Y.C., Sept. 8, 1927; s. Jacques S. and Mary (Wetsman) U.; children—Jacqueline, Sarita. A.B., Cornell U., 1948; M.D., N.Y. U., 1952. Assoc. prof. medicine N.Y. U. Sch. Medicine, N.Y.C., 1962-68, prof. medicine, 1968-72; vis. prof. Yale U., New Haven, Conn., 1970-71; prof., chmn. microbiology dept. U. Tex. Health Sci. Ctr., Dallas, 1972—; head U.S.-Japan panel of the cooperative sci. program in immunology, 1984. Assoc. editor: Advances in Immunology, 1984. Served with USN, 1945-46. Recipient Mary Nell and Ralph B. Rogers prof. in immunology, 1982; achievement award, U.Y. U. Alumni, 1978, medal of the Faculty, Med. Sch. Montpellier, France, 1984. Mem. Nat. Acad. Sci., Am. Assn. Immunologists (pres. 1983-84). Current work: Medical microbiology; cellular immunology; immunology of cancer. Subspecialty: Immunology (medicine). Office: Univ Texas Health Sci Ctr Dept Microbiology 5323 Harry Hines Blvd Dallas TX 75235

UHRIG, ROBERT EUGENE, engineer, utility company executive; b. Raymond, Ill., Aug. 6, 1928; s. John Matthew and Anna LaDonna (Fireman) U.; m. Paula Margaret Schnepf, Nov. 27, 1954; children: Robert John, Joseph Charles, Mary Catherine, Charles William, Jean Marie, Thomas Paul, Frederick James. B.S. with honors, U. Ill., 1948; M.S. Iowa State U, 1950, Ph.D., 1954; grad. Advanced Mgmt. Program, Harvard U., 1976. Registered profl. engr., Iowa, Fla. Instr. engring. mechanics Iowa State U., 1948-51; asso. engr., research asst. Inst. Atomic Research (at univ.), 1951-54, asso. prof. engring. mechanics and nuclear engring., also group leader, 1956-60; prof. nuclear engring., chmn. dept. U. Fla., Gainesville, 1960-68, on leave, 1967-68; dean Coll. Engring., 1968-73; dep. asst. dir. research Dept. Def., Washington, 1967-68; dir. nuclear affairs Fla. Power & Light Co., Miami, 1973-74, v.p. for nuclear affairs, 1974-75, v.p. nuclear and gen. engring., 1976-78, v.p. advanced systems and tech., 1978—; Miami. Rep. Dept. Def. to com. on acad. sci. and engring. Fed. Council Sci. and Tech., 1967; chmn. engring. adv. com. NSF, 1972-73; bd. dirs. Engring. Council Profl. Devel., 1968-72; mem. commn. edn. for engring. profession Nat. Assn. State Univs. and Land Grant Colls., 1969-72. Author: Random Noise Techniques in Nuclear Reactor Systems, 1970, trans. into Russian, 1974. Served to 1st lt. USAF; instr. engring. mechanics U.S. Mil. Acad. 1954-56. Recipient Sec. of Def. Civilian Service award, 1968, Outstanding Alumni award U. Ill. Coll. Engring., 1970, Alumni Profl. Achievement award Iowa State U., 1972, President's medallion U. Fla., 1973; Disting. Achievement citation Iowa State U. Alumni Assn., 1980. Fellow Am. Nuclear Soc. (chmn. edn. com. 1962-64, chmn. tech. group for edn. 1964-66, dir. 1965-68, exec. com. of bd. 1966-68), ASME (Richards Meml. award 1969), AAAS; mem. Am. Soc. Engring. Edn. (pres. S.E. sect. 1972-73, chmn. nuclear engring. div. 1966-67, research award S.E. sect. 1962), John Henry Newman Honor Soc., Sigma Xi, Tau Beta Pi, Pi Mu Epsilon, Pi Tau Sigma, Phi Kappa Phi. Current Work: Primarily concerned with utility research and development (coal-liquid mixtures, load management etc.), nuclear licensing of power plants, environmental affairs and quality assurance. Subspecialty: Nuclear engineering. Home: 3900 County Line Rd #11-D Tequesta FL 33458 Office: Fla Power & Light Co PO Box 14000 Juno Beach FL 33408

UICKER, JOSEPH BERNARD, mechanical engineer; b. State College, Pa., Mar. 29, 1940; s. John Joseph and Elizabeth Josephine (Flint) U.; m. Mary Catherine Howze, June 12, 1965 (div. 1970); children—Patricia, Suzanne; m. Janet Ann Ballman, Sept. 22, 1973. B.S. in Mech. Engring., U. Detroit, 1963, M.S., 1965. Registered profl. engr., Mich. Dir. profl. staff Smith Hinchman & Grylls, Detroit, 1964—. Served to capt. U.S. Army, 1966-67. Mem. ASHRAE, Nat. Soc. Profl. Engrs., ASME, Soc. Am. Mil. Engrs., Engring. Soc. Detroit. Club: Detroit Athletic. Current work: Design of mechanical systems for major building projects specializing in hospitals and research laboratories. Subspecialties: Mechanical engineering; Environmental engineering. Home: 14585 Lamphere Detroit MI 48223 Office: Smith Hinchman & Grylls 455 W Fort St Detroit MI 48226

UITTO, JOUNI JORMA, physician, educator; b. Helsinki, Finland, Sept. 15, 1943; came to U.S., 1971; s. Jorma Armas and Lea Julia (Tanner) U.; m. Elaine Mei-Li Tan, Aug. 6, 1982; children—Jari Ilmari, Jessica Jaime Su-Lin. M.D., Ph.D., U. Helsinki, 1970. Instr. biochemistry U. Helsinki, 1967-71; asst. prof. biochemistry Rutgers U., Piscataway, N.J., 1972-75; instr. medicine Washington U., St. Louis, 1975-78, asst. prof. medicine and biochemistry, 1978-80; prof. medicine UCLA, 1980—, assoc. chief, dir. research dermatology div. Harbor-UCLA Med. Ctr., Torrance, Calif., 1980—. Co-editor: The Molecular Pathology of the Extracellular Matrix, 1985. Contbr. numerous articles to sci. jours., chpts. to books. NIH Research Career Devel. awardee, 1978-83. Mem. Soc. Investigative Dermatology, Am. Fedn. Clin. Research, Am. Soc. Biol. Chemists, Am. Acad. Dermatology, Am. Soc. Clin. Investigation. Current work: Connective tissue biochemistry; metabolism of collagen and elastin; connective tissue aberrations in diseases. Subspecialties: Dermatology; Biochemistry (medicine). Office: Harbor-UCLA Med Ctr 1000 W Carson St Torrance CA 90509

UKACHUKWU, VICTORIA CHIKAODILI, research chemist; b. Nigeria, Mar. 29, 1953; d. Denis Obeke and Patience E. (Udechukwu) U. B.S., U. Ibadan, Nigeria, 1975; Ph.D., Ga. Inst. Tech., 1984. Asst. lectr. Coll. of Arts and Sci., Zaria, Nigeria, 1975-78; grad. asst. U. Md., Baltimore County, Balt., 1978-79, postdoctoral research assoc. 1984—; grad. asst. Ga. Inst. Tech., Atlanta, 1979-83. Mem. Am. Chem. Soc. Current work: Investigation of solution chemistry of various model vinyl and aryl expoxides. Subspecialty: Organic chemistry. Office: Dept Chemistry U Md Baltimore County Baltimore MD 21228

UKLEJA, PAUL, physicist; b. Chgo., Nov. 22, 1946; s. Frank Stanley Joseph and Louise Anita (Charbonnier) U.; m. Diana Lynn Shiphorst, July 22, 1967; 1 child, Niklos. B.A., New Coll., 1967; M.S., U. Chgo., 1969; Ph.D., Kent State U., 1976. Vol. Peace Corps., Malta, 1970-73; postdoctoral fellow Kent State U., Liquid Crystal Inst., Kent, Ohio, 1976-78; asst. prof. Southeastern Mass. U., North Dartmouth, Mass., 1978—. Contbr. articles to profl. jours. Kent State U. fellow, 1975-76. Mem. Am. Phys. soc., Am. Assn. Physics Tchrs., Biophys. Soc., Internat. Soc. Magnetic Resonance. Current work: Diffusion, order and molecular motions in liquid crystals; NMR, physics education. Subspecialty: Condensed matter physics. Home: 204 Maple St New Bedford MA 02740 Office: Southeastern Mass U Physics Dept North Dartmouth MA 02747

ULABY, FAWWAZ TAYSSIR, electrical engineering educator; b. Damascus, Syria, Feb. 4, 1943; s. Tayssir and Moukarram U.; m. Mary Ann Hammond, Aug. 28, 1968; children: Neda Elizabeth, Aziza Marie, Laith Arthur. B.S. in Physics, Am. U. Beirut, 1964; M.S.E.E., U. Tex.-Austin, 1966, Ph.D., 1968. Assoc. research engr. U. Tex., 1966-68, coordinator millimeter wave sci. lab., 1968; asst. prof. elec. engring. U. Kans., Lawrence, 1968-69, assoc. prof., 1971-76, prof., 1976-84, assoc. dir. remote sensing lab., 1969-71, dir. lab., 1971-84, J.L. Constant Disting. prof., 1980-84; prof. elec. engring. U. Mich., Ann Arbor, 1985—. Contbr. over 135 articles to sci./tech. jours.; co-author: Microwave Remote Sensing: Active and Passive, 3 vols; assoc. editor: Manual of Remote Sensing, 1983. Recipient Chancellor's award U. Kans., 1980. Fellow IEEE (Centennial medal 1984); mem. IEEE Geosci. and Remote Sensing Soc. (Outstanding Service award 1982, Disting. Achievement award 1983, disting. lectr., 1985, editor GRS Transaction 1985-88, pres. 1979-81), URSI, Internat. Soc. Photogrammetry, Am. Soc. Photogrammetry (Presdl. citation for meritorious service 1984), Am. Soc. Engring. Edn., Am. Geophys. Union, AIAA, Eta Kappa Nu (Holmes MacDonald award 1975), Sigma Xi, Tau Beta Pi. Current Work: Radar remote sensing; microwave radiometry; antennas; microwave communications systems; radar systems. Subspecialties: Electrical engineering; Remote sensing (geoscience). Home: 2049 Winsted Ann Arbor MI 48103 Office: Radiation Lab 4072 E Engring U Mich Ann Arbor MI 48109

ULINSKI, PHILIP STEVEN, neuroanatomist; b. Detroit, Feb. 17, 1943; s. Steven Stanley and Helen Veronica (Kudej) U.; m. Lee Anna Richards, Mar. 19, 1965; children—Shari, Candi, Steven. B.S., Mich. State U., 1964, M.S., 1967, Ph.D., 1969. Asst. prof. Oberlin Coll., Ohio, 1969-70, Loyola U., Maywood, Ill., 1970-74; asst. prof. U. Chgo., 1975-78, assoc. prof., 1979—. Author: Dorsal Ventricular Ridge, 1983. Mem. Am. Soc. Zoologists, Am. Assn. Anatomists, Soc. Neurosci., Assn. for Research in Vision and Ophthalmology. Current work: Organization of forebrain, visual system, nervous system of reptiles. Subspecialties: Neurobiology; Comparative neurobiology. Home: 5345 S Hyde Park Chicago IL 60615 Office: Dept Anatomy Univ Chicago 1025 E 57th St Chicago IL 60637

ULLAND, PAUL DAVID, electrical engineer; b. Austin, Minn., Sept. 15, 1944; s. Palmer Anton and Myrtle Gladys (Rolfson) U.; m. Judy Kay Noble, May 29, 1967; children—Dorinda Lee, Karsten Paul, Justin Robert. B.S.E.E., Northwestern U., 1966; M.S.E.E., Iowa State U., 1967. Devel. engr. Northrop Corp., Newbury Park, Calif., 1967-71; sr. engr. The Trane Co., La Crosse, Wis., 1971-73, engring. mgr., 1973-81, project mgr., 1981—. Patentee in field. Key leader 4-H Club, La Crescent, Minn., 1984—. Mem. IEEE. Lutheran. Lodge: Lions Internat. (La Crescent) (treas. 1977-79). Current work: Application of electronics to the control of heating, ventilating and air conditioning (HVAC) equipment and building systems. Subspecialties: Electronics; Electrical engineering. Home: 562 Hickory Lane La Crescent MN 55947 Office: The Trane Co 20th and Horton Sts La Crosse WI 54601

ULMER, GENE C., geochemistry educator; b. Cin., Jan. 28, 1937; s. Howard S. and Mildred (Miller) U.; m. Dagmar Ingrid, Dec. 26, 1960; children—Alexander, Susan, Erika, Kirk. B.S. in Chemistry, U. Cin., 1958; Ph.D., Penn. State U., 1964. Ceramic engr. Bethlehem Steel, Pa., 1964-69; assoc. prof. Temple U., Phila., 1969-74, prof. geochemistry, 1974—; sci. witness Fed. Ct. Dist. Ohio, 1975, 78. Author, editor: Research Techniques in High Pressure and High Temperature, 1971. Editor: (with others) Lunar Science Volumes, 1977. Co-patentee micropore refractories, Vol. Long-Range Twp. Planning, Warrington, Pa., 1978-79; water supply cons. Citizens Group, Warrington, 1981. Grantee NSF, Rockwell. Mem. Am. Geophys. Union, Am. Ceramic Soc. (abstractor), Am. Mineral. Soc. (publs. com.). Current work: Volcanology; igneous ore deposits; spinel crystal chemistry; diamond genesis; geologic evaluation of nuclear waste sites; energy reserves. Subspecialties: Petrology; Geochemistry. Home: 2207 Blackhorse Dr Warrington PA 18976 Office: Temple U Geology Dept 13th & Norris Sts Philadelphia PA 19122

ULMER, MELVILLE PAUL, physics and astronomy educator, researcher; b. Washington, Mar. 12, 1943; s. Melville Jack and Naiomi Louise (Zinken) U.; m. Patricia Elifson, Dec. 12, 1947; children: Andrew Todd, Jeremy John, Rachel Ann. B.A., Johns Hopkins U., 1965; Ph.D., U. Wis., Madison, 1970. Asst. research physicist U. Calif., San Diego, 1970-74; astrophysicist Harvard-Smithsonian Center for Astrophysics, 1974-76; asst. prof. dept. physics and astronomy Northwestern U., 1976-82, assoc. prof., 1982—. Contbr. articles to profl. jours. NASA grantee, 1976. Mem. Am. Astron. Soc., Roya Astron. Soc., Internat. Astron. Union, Am. Physical Soc. Current Work: X-ray astronomy, clusters of galaxies, x-ray instrumentation, gamma ray astronomy. Subspecialties: X-ray high energy astrophysics; Gamma ray high energy astrophysics. Home: 2021 Noyes St Evanston IL 60201 Office: Dept Physics and Astronomy Northwestern U Evanston IL 60201

ULRICH, HENRI, chemical company executive, organic chemist; b. Rheinsberg, Germany, May 4, 1925; came to U.S., 1954, naturalized, 1964; s. Hermann and Ella (Seeling) U.; m. Franziska Schimitzek, June 2, 1954; children—Stefan, Tomas, Barbara, Bertram. Ph.D. summa cum in Organic Chemistry, Humboldt U. (Berlin), 1954. Group leader chem. research Upjohn Co., North Haven, Conn., 1959-62, head organic chemistry, 1962-65, mgr. chem. research, 1965-74, group mgr. chem. research and devel., 1974-76, dir. DSG labs., 1976-81, v.p. DSG labs., 1982—; supervisory bd. Upjohn Polymer BV, Delfzijl, Netherlands, 1975—; bd. dirs. Kasei Upjohn Co., Tokyo, 1975—; adj. prof. Wesleyan U., Middletown, Conn., 1979—. Author: Cycloaddition Reactions of Reterocumulenes, 1967; The Chemistry of Imidoyl Halides, 1968; Introduction to Industrial Polymers, 1982. Mem. Am. Chem. Soc., Gesellschaft Deutcher Chemiker. Current work: Polyurethanes, isocyanate chemistry. Subspecialty: Organic chemistry. Office: Upjohn Co 410 Sackett Point Rd North Haven CT 06473

ULRICH, ROBERT DAVID, polymer scientist, researcher; b. Pitts., Oct. 25, 1945; s. Robert Louis and Aligene (Wall) U.; m. Mary Diane Quane, June 6, 1966 (div. Oct. 1975); m. Gail G. Grant, Oct. 2, 1976; children—Michael Glenn Walker, Melissa Jill Walker. B.A., Claremont McKenna Coll., 1967; M.S., U. Mass., 1970, Ph.D., 1972. Photog. engr. Eastman Kodak Co., Rochester, N.Y., 1967-68; sr. research physicist Monsanto Textile Co., Pensacola, Fla., 1972-75, group supr., 1975-77; mgr. product tech. Plastics div. Gen. Electric, Selkirk, N.Y., 1977-81, mgr. engring., Bridgeport, Conn., 1981-83; dir. new tech. Ethicon div. Johnson & Johnson, Somerville, N.J., 1983—. Patentee in field. Contbr. articles to profl. jours. NDEA fellow. Mem. Am. Chem. Soc. Republican. Baptist. Club: Executive (Pensacola). Current work: Application of polymers to surgical repair of soft tissue. Subspecialties: Polymers (materials science); Artificial organs and prostheses. Office: Ethicon Inc Route 22 Somerville NJ 08876

ULTMANN, JOHN ERNEST, physician, educator, researcher; b. Vienna, Jan. 6, 1925; s. Oskar and Hedwig (Schechter) U.; m. Ruth E. Layton, May 25, 1952; children—Monica, Michelle, Barry. Student, Oberlin Coll., 1946-48; M.D., Columbia U., 1952. Diplomate Am. Bd. Internal Medicine. Intern N.Y. Hosp.-Cornell Med. Ctr., N.Y.C., 1952-53, resident, 1953-55; Am. Cancer Soc. fellow in hematology Columbia U., N.Y.C., 1955-56; practice medicine specializing in internal medicine N.Y.C., 1956-68, Chgo., 1968—; prof. medicine U. Chgo., 1970—, also dir. Cancer Research Ctr., dean for research and devel.; mem. staff Francis Delafield Hosp., 1955-68, Presbyn. Hosp., 1959-68, Bellevue Hosp., 1961-68; career scientist Health Research Council, N.Y.C., 1959-68; cons. Harlem Hosp., N.Y.C., 1966-68; chmn. bd. sci. counselors, div. cancer treatment Nat. Cancer Inst., NIH, 1976-80; mem. Ill. Gov.'s Adv. Bd. Cancer Control, 1976—; bd. dirs. at-large Ill. div. Am. Cancer Soc., 1976-79; trustee, officer Ill. Cancer Council, 1975—; chmn. selections com. Bristol-Myers Award for Distinguished Achievement in Cancer Research, 1976-77, mem., 1977-85; mem. fed. funds com. Health Systems Agy., Chgo., 1979-81; chmn. Ill. Coop. Oncology Network, 1981. Assoc. editor Cancer Research, 1974-81; mem. editorial bd. Annals Internal Medicine, 1974-77, Blood, 1975-77; cons. editor Am. Jour. Medicine, 1975—. Contbr. articles to profl. jours. Served with U.S. Army, 1943-46. Fellow ACP, Inst. Medicine Chgo.; mem. Am. Soc. Clin. Oncology (bd. dirs. 1978-80, pres. 1982-83), Assn. Am. Cancer Insts. (bd. dirs. 1974-77, pres. 1984-85, chmn. bd. 1985—, by-laws com. 1981), Am. Assn. Cancer Research (awards com. 1981-82), Am. Fedn. Clin. Research, Soc. Study Blood, Internat. Soc. Hematology, Am. Soc. Hematology, AAUP, AAAS, Harvey Soc., Chgo. Soc. Internal Medicine, Central Soc. Clin. Research, Sociedad Chilena de Cancerologia, Sociedad Chilena de Hematologia, Phi Beta Kappa, Alpha Omega Alpha. Current work: Lymphoma, Hodgkin's disease, leukemia, cancer, pathophysiology staging and treatment. Subspecialties: Cancer research (medicine); Chemotherapy. Office: 5841 S Maryland Ave Chicago IL 60637

UMEK, ANTHONY M., company administrator; b. New Kensington, Pa., Apr. 17, 1947; s. Anthony and Veronica (Yugovich) U.; m. Kristy S. Kocher, July 9, 1977. B.S. in Mech. Engring, Carnegie-Mellon Inst., 1969; M.B.A., U. Pitts., 1971. Engr. Westinghouse Electric Corp., Madison, Pa., 1970-74; mgr. line Westinghouse Hanford Co., Richland, Wash., 1974-80, dept. mgr., 1981—. Author: Non-Lethal Weapon, 1969; Contbr. articles to profl. jours. Karate instr. YMCA; pres. Tri-City Estates Water Dist. Mem. ASME (mem. energy com., chmn. pub. affairs com.), Am. Nuclear Soc., Am. Mgmt. Assn. Roman Catholic. Current Work: Manager of an engineering and startup testing department, in charge of nuclear reactor related facilities. Subspecialties: Mechanical engineering; Nuclear fission. Office: Westinghouse Hanford Co Box 1970 Richland WA 99352

UMLAND, ERIC ALEXANDER, physicist; b. Emporia, Kans., Apr. 28, 1956; s. James Frederick and Mabel Charlotte (Kappelmann) U.; m. Jaye Sherri Schoengold, Oct. 12, 1980. B.S. in Physics, MIT, 1978; M.S. in Physics, Rice U., 1980, Ph.D., 1982. Grad. research assoc. Rice U., Houston, 1978-82, research fellow, 1982-83; Bantrell research fellow Calif. Inst. Tech., Pasadena, 1983—. Contbr. articles to physics jours. McCollum, fellow, 1981; recipient R.L. Chouke award Rice U., 1980, H.A. Wilson award Rice U., 1983. Mem. Am. Phys. Soc., Caltech Flying Club (asst. treas. 1984—). Current work: Lattice gauge theory; high energy electron scattering; QCD quark models; charge symmetry breaking in nuclei. Subspecialties: Theoretical physics; Particle physics. Home: 1974 E Beverly Dr Pasadena CA 91104 Office: Calif Inst Tech MS 106-38 Pasadena CA 91125

UMMINGER, BRUCE LYNN, science administrator, biology educator; b. Dayton, Ohio, Apr. 10, 1941; s. Frederick William and Elnora Mae (Waltemathe) U.; m. Judith Lackey Bryant, Dec. 17, 1966; children: Alison Grace, April Lynn. B.S., Yale U., 1963, M.S., 1966, M.Phil., 1968, Ph.D., 1969. Asst. prof. biol. sci. U. Cin., 1969-73, assoc. prof. biol. sci., 1973-75, acting head biol. sci., 1973-75, prof. biol. sci., 1975-81, dir. grad. affairs biol. sci., 1978-79; program dir. NSF, Washington, 1979-84, dep. div. dir., 1984-85, acting div. dir., 1985—; mem. Space Shuttle Proposal Rev. Panel, NASA, 1978; mem. adv. screening com. in life scis. Council Internat. Exchange of Scholars, 1978-81; liaison rep., adv. council Nat. Heart, Lung and Blood Inst., Bethesda, Md., 1979—; adv. bd. Campbell Comml. Coll., Cin., 1977-79. Assoc. editor: Jour. Exptl. Zoology, 1977-79; editorial adv. bd.: Gen. and Comparative Endocrinology, 1982. Mem. world mission com. Ch. of the Redeemer, New Haven, 1967-68; mem. Sunday sch. steering com. Calvary Episcopal Ch., Cin., 1972-73, sr. acolyte, 1972-77. Recipient George Rieveschl, Jr. univ. research award U. Cin., 1973, fellow grad. sch., 1977—; NSF grantee, 1971, 73, 76; fellow, 1964; Nat. Acad. Scis. travel grantee, 1974. Fellow AAAS (council 1980-83), N.Y. Acad. Scis; mem. Am. Physiol. Soc. (comparative physiology sect. program officer 1978-81, program exec. com. 1983—), Am. Soc. Zoologists (sec. 1979-81), Sigma Xi (pres. chpt. 1977-79, Disting. Research award 1973). Clubs: Yale of Washington (New Haven), Mory's Assn. (New Haven). Lodge: Masons. Current Work: Comparative physiology, endocrinology, biochemistry; research into fish systems, and administration of federal funding programs to assure health of science in these areas. Subspecialties: Comparative physiology; Endocrinology. Home: 4087-B S Four Mile Run Dr Arlington VA 22204 Office: Div Cellular Bioscis NSF 1800 G St NW Washington DC 20550

UMSAWASDI, THEERA, physician, educator; b. Bangkok, Thailand, Oct. 13, 1942; s. Manit and Priub (Jaiprasart) U.; m. Chantana Wisoopakan, Jan. 20, 1967; children: Alyssa, Charlie, Marisa. M.D., Faculty of Medicine-Siriraj Hosp., Bangkok, Thailand, 1965. Diplomate: Medicine, Thailand, 1965. Intern Faculty of Medicine-Siriraj Hosp., 1965-66; instr. Faculty of Medicine-Siriraj Hosp. (Cancer Inst.), 1972-77; resident in medicine Bangkok Sanatorium Hosp., 1966-67; intern St. John Hosp., Detroit, 1967-68; resident in medicine Sinai Hosp., Detroit, 1968-69; fellow in med. oncology U. Miami (Fla.) Sch. Medicine, 1977-79; project investigator U. Tex.-M.D. Anderson Hosp. and Tumor Inst., Houston, 1969-72, asst. prof. internal medicine, 1979—. Contbr. numerous sci. articles and abstracts to profl. publs. Mem. AMA, Tex. Med. Assn., Harris County Med. Assn., Am. Assn. Cancer Research, Am. Soc. Clin. Oncology., N.Y. Acad. Scis. Current Work: Chemotherapy and combined modality in treatment of lung cancer. Subspecialty: Oncology. Office: 6723 Bertner Ave Houston TX 77030

UNDERDAHL, NORMAN RUSSELL, microbiologist, educator; b. Freeborn County, Minn., June 5, 1918; s. Knut O. and Maria (Stoa) U.; m. Bernice Eleanor Nagle, Aug. 29, 1948; 1 dau., Kimbra. B.A., St. Olaf Coll., Northfield,

Minn., 1941; M.S., U. Minn., Mpls., 1948. With Hormel Inst., U. Minn., Austin, 1946-55; asst. prof. vet. sci. U. Nebr., 1955-61, assoc. prof., 1961-68, prof., 1968—; cons. pharm. cos. Author: Specific Pathogen-Free Swine, 1973; contbr. numerous articles profl. jours. Served with USNR, 1942-46, PTO. Mem. Am. Legion., Nebr. Vet. Med. Assn. (hon.), Nebr. Specific—Pathogen-Free Accrediting Assn. (service award), Nat. Specific-Pathogen—Free Accrediting Assn. (service award), AVMA (assoc.), Am. Soc. Microbiology, Nat. Swine Repopulation Assn., Assn. Gnotobiology, Sigma Xi, Gamma Sigma Delta. Patentee breeder for raising surgically obtained pigs; co-developer specific-pathogen-free methods for obtaining and rearing surgically obtained pigs. Current Work: Use of probiotics as a preventive measure of enteric diseases, effect of combination of bacterial organisms on pneumonia in swine. Subspecialties: Microbiology; Preventive medicine (veterinary medicine). Home: 935 N 67th St Lincoln NE 68505 Office: Dept Veterinary Science U Nebr Lincoln NE 68583

UNDERHILL, EARL MARVIN, electrical engineer, former company executive; b. N.Y.C., Aug. 15, 1913; s. Edward Marvin and Henrietta Catherine (Green) U.; m. Virginia Margaret Jones, Jan. 6, 1940; children—Edward William, Alan Richard. Engr. Weston Electric Instrument Corp., Newark, 1937-39; chief engr. Cinaudagraph Corp., Stamford, Conn., 1939-46; mgr. engring. Crucible Steel Co. of Am., Harrison, N.J., 1946-67; plant mgr. Ind. Gen. Corp., Valparaiso, 1967-77; cons. Pfizer Corp., Valparaiso, 1977-79. Editor: Permanent Magnet Handbook, 1957; contbr. articles to profl. jours. Pres. Upper Ridgewood Tennis Club, 1950-52. Mem. IEEE (sr.). Republican. Presbyterian. Subspecialties: Applied magnetics; Applied mathematics. Address: Route 5 Box 605 Knox IN 46534

UNDERWOOD, ARTHUR LOUIS, JR., chemist, educator; b. Rochester, N.Y., May 18, 1924; s. Arthur Louis and Grace (Porter) U.; m. Elizabeth Emery, June 30, 1948; children: Paul W., Robert E., Susan E. B.S. in Chemistry, U. Rochester, 1944, Ph.D. in Biochemistry, 1951. Research assoc. U. Rochester Atomic Energy Project, 1946-51; research assoc. in chemistry M.I.T., 1951-52; asst. prof. chemistry Emory U., 1952-58, assoc. prof., 1958-62, prof., 1962—; research assoc. in chemistry Cornell U., 1959-60; vis. prof. Mont. State U., summers 1979-82. Author: (with R.A. Day, Jr.) Quantitative Analysis, 1980; research, numerous publs. in field. Served with USN, 1944-46. Mem. AAAS, Am. Chem. Soc., Phi Beta Kappa, Sigma Xi. Current Work: Studies on Micelles, particularly the effects of organic counterions on micellar parameters. Subspecialties: Biochemistry (biology); Analytical chemistry. Home: 1354 Springdale Rd NE atlanta GA 30306 Office: Dept Chemistry Emory U Atlanta GA 30322

UNGAR, EDWARD WILLIAM, research organization executive; b. N.Y.C., Feb. 6, 1936; s. Morris and Elizabeth (Czitrom) U.; m. Lois Cramer, July 9, 1978; children—Michele Ruth, Mark Steven, Elizabeth Ann. B.M.E., CCNY, 1957; M.S., Ohio State U., 1959, Ph.D., 1966. Mem. research staff Battelle Columbus Labs., Ohio, 1957-66, div. chief, 1966-70, sect. mgr., 1970-73, dept. mgr., 1973-76, assoc. dir., 1976-78, dir., 1978-85; v.p. indsl. bus. devel. Battelle Meml. Inst., 1978—. Mem. Devel. Com. for Greater Columbus; mem. Dean of Engring. Adv. Bd. Ohio State U.; mem. Columbus Area C. of C. Discover Columbus Campaign Task Force. Mem. ASME, AAAS, Am. Def. Preparedness Assn., Newcomen Soc., Sigma Xi, Pi Tau Sigma, Tau Beta Pi. Subspecialty: Research and development management. Office: 505 King Ave Columbus OH 43201

UNGAR, IRWIN A., botany educator; b. N.Y.C., Jan. 21, 1934; s. Isidor and Gertrude (Feigeles) U.; m. Ana del Cid, Aug. 10, 1959; children: Steven, Sandra, Sharon. B.S., CCNY, 1955; M.S., U. Kans., 1957, Ph.D., 1961. Instr. dept. botany U. R.I., Kingston, 1961; asst. prof. dept. biology Quincy (Ill.) Coll., 1962-66; prof. dept. botany Ohio U., Athens, 1975—; research assoc. Centre National de la Recherche Scientifique, 1972-73. Contbr. articles to profl. jours. NSF grantee, 1963-65, 67-69, 74-76, 76-78, 80—. Mem. Bot. Soc. Am., Ecol. Soc. Am., AAAS, Sigma Xi. Jewish. Current Work: Ecology of halophytes. Subspecialty: Ecology (environmental science). Office: Dept Botany Ohio U Athens OH 45701

UNGER, BRIAN WILLIAM, computer science educator; b. Milw., Apr. 12, 1940; s. William J. and Lucile F. (Lenz) U.; m. Marilynn M. Zimmerman, Aug. 18, 1972 (div. 1980); m. Sheila Ann Robinson, June 24, 1983; children—Neal Anthony, Claire Lucile, Naomi Teresa. B.S. in Engring., Loyola U., Los Angeles, 1962; M.S.E.E., U. So. Calif., 1965; Ph.D. in Info. and Computer Sci., U. Calif.-San Diego, 1972. Engr., Aerojet Gen. Corp., Downey, Calif., 1963-65; group engr. Teledyne Ryan Aerospace, San Diego, 1965-68; pres. Synectics, Inc., San Diego, 1968-72; prof. computer sci. U. Calgary, Alta., Can., 1972—; vis. scientist Nanjing U., China, Royal Inst. Tech., Sweden, Zilog Corp., Calif., 1979-80. Contbr. articles to profl. jours. Mem. Soc. Computer Simulation (bd. dirs. 1981—), IEEE (chmn. Alta. sect. 1983-84), Software Research and Devel. Group (exec. dir. 1984—). Current work: Distributing computing and intelligence, simulation, software development. Subspecialty: Distributed systems and networks. Office: U Calgary Software Research and Devel Group 2500 University Dr NW Calgary AB T2N 1N4 Canada

UNGER, STEFAN HOWARD, scientist; b. Glen Ridge, N.J., June 23, 1944; s. Jerome Gordon and Florence Pearl (Lief) U.; m. Arlene Klein, Aug. 19, 1979; 1 child, Max. B.S., U. Rochester, 1966; Ph.D., MIT, 1970. Postdoctoral tng. Eidgenossische Technische Hochschule, Zurich, 1970-72, Pomona Coll., Claremont, Calif., 1972-74; staff research I Syntex Research, Palo Alto, Calif., 1974-77, sr. staff researcher II, 1979-81, prin. scientist, 1981—; cons. in field. Contbr. chpts. to books and articles to profl. jours. Patentee in field. NIH fellow, 1967-68. Mem. Am. Chem. Soc. Clubs: Stanford for IBM PC, Homebrew Computer (Palo Alto). Current work: Computerized drug design; quantitative structure activity relationships statistics and computer graphics used for drug design; physical-organic chemistry; computer program for recombinant DNA sequence analysis. Subspecialties: Drug design; Medicinal chemistry. Home: 2250 Webster St Palo Alto CA 94301 Office: Syntex Research R6-123 3401 Hillview St Palo Alto CA 94301

UNO, HIDEO, pathologist, researcher; b. Tokyo, Nov. 28, 1929; came to U.S., 1970; s. Yoshinori and Hana U.; m. Shoko Ohashi, Apr. 1, 1956; children: Takeshi, Yayoi. M.D., Yokohama (Japan) Med. Coll., 1955, Ph.D., 1961. Asst. prof. Yokohama City U., 1961-64, assoc. prof., 1968-70; instr. Jefferson Med. Coll., Phila., 1964-66; vis. scientist Oreg. Primate Research Center, Beaverton, 1966-68, scientist, 1970-79; sr. scientist Wis. Primate Research Center, Madison, 1979—. Grantee Oreg. Med. Found., 1976; Upjohn Co., 1982. Mem. Am. Assn. Pathologists, Am. Assn. Anatomists, Soc. Investigative Dermatology, Internat. Acad. Pathology, Japanese Soc. Histochemistry and Cytochemistry (counselor). Buddhist. Club: Internat. House of Japan (Tokyo). Current Work: Comparative pathology of nonhuman primates (aging), peptides in sensory autonomic nerve systems, effect of Minoxidil on alopecia. Subspecialties: Neuroendocrinology; Gerontology. Home: 3722 Ross St Madison WI 53705 Office: Wis Regional Primate Research Center U Wis 1223 Capitol Ct Madison WI 53715-1299

UNRUH, WILLIAM GEORGE, physics educator; b. Winnipeg, Man., Can., Aug. 28, 1945. B.Sc with honors, U. Man., 1967; M.A., Princeton U., 1969, Ph.D., 1971. NRC Can. fellow in physics U. London, 1971-72; Miller fellow in physics U. Calif.-Berkeley, 1973-74; asst. prof. applied math. McMaster U., Hamilton, Ont., Can., 1974-76; asst. prof. physics U. B.C., Vancouver, 1976-80, assoc. prof., 1980-82, prof., 1982—. Recipient Rutherford medal Royal Soc. Can., 1982, Herzberg medal Can. Assn. Physics, 1983; Sloan fellow, 1978; Seacie fellow NSERC, 1984-86; Steacie prize, 1984; Can.-U.K. Rutherford lectr., 1985. Fellow Royal Soc. Can. Current Work: The relation of quantum mechanics and gravity to each other. Subspecialties: Relativity and gravitation; Theoretical physics. Office: Physics Dept Univ BC Vancouver BC V6T 2A6 Canada

UNTERSTEINER, NORBERT, science adminstrator, educator; b. Meran, Italy, Feb. 24, 1926; s. Raimund and Anna (Sperk) U.; m. Krystyna Untersteiner, Aug. 11, 1980. Dr.phil., U. Innsbruck, Austria, 1950; Dozent, U. Vienna, 1960. Asst. prof. U. Vienna, 1951-56; research meteorologist Central Inst. Meteorology and Geodynamics, Vienna, 1957-62; research assoc. prof. U. Wash., 1962-67, prof. atmospheric scis. and geophysics, 1967—; dir. Polar Sci. Center. Contbr. articles to profl. jours. Decorated Hon. Cross for Arts and Scis. Austria, 1959; recipient Antarctic Service Medal U.S. Govt., 1967, numerous research grants. Mem. AAAS, Am. Geophys. Union, Internat. Glaciol. Soc., Comite Arctique International, German Polar Soc., Norsk Polar Club. Current Work: Air-sea interaction at high latitudes, climatic change, research planning and coordination including field work and theoretical analysis. Subspecialties: Oceanography; Climatology. Home: 7412 E Greenlake Dr N Seattle WA 98115 Office: U Wash Applied Physics Lab Seattle WA 98105

UNWIN, STEPHEN CHARLES, research scientist; b. Bromley, Kent, Eng., Sept. 8, 1953; s. Thomas Eric and Barbara Jean (Herrington) U. B.A. with honors in Physics and Theoretical Physics, Cambridge U., Eng., 1976, Ph.D. in Radio Astronomy, 1979, M.A., 1980. Staff scientist radio astronomy Owens Valley Radio Obs., Calif. Inst. Tech., 1979—. Contbr. articles to profl. jours. Mem. Am. Astron. Soc., Royal Astron. Soc. Current Work: Research in radio astronomy using interferometric methods. Mapping of compact radio sources; study of kinematics and spectra of variable sources. Subspecialty: Radio and microwave astronomy. Office: Owens Valley Radio Calif Inst Tech Mail Code 105-24 Pasadena CA 91125

UPATNIEKS, JURIS, research engineer; b. Riga, Latvia, May 7, 1936; s. Karlis and Eleonora (Jegers) U.; m. Ilze Induss, July 13, 1978; children: Ivars, Ansis. B.E.E., U. Akron, 1960; M.S.E., U. Mich., 1965. Jr. engr. Goodyear Aircraft Corp., Akron, 1957-59; research engr. Environ. Research Inst. Mich., Ann Arbor, 1960—; adj. assoc. prof. elec. and computing engring. dept. U. Mich., 1974—. Contbr. articles to profl. jours. Served to lt. U.S. Army, 1961-62. Recipient Holley medal ASME, 1976; R.W. Wood prize Optical Soc. Am., 1976. Fellow Optical Soc. Am., Soc. Photog. Instrument Engrs.; mem. IEEE, Am. Latvian Assn. Patentee in field. Current Work: Coherent optics, holography, optical data processing research. Subspecialties: Holography; Optical signal processing. Office: PO Box 8618 Ann Arbor MI 48107

UPGREN, ARTHUR REINHOLD, JR., astronomer, educator; b. Mpls., Feb. 21, 1933; s. Arthur Reinhold and Marion Elizabeth (Andrews) U.; m. Joan Josephine Koswoski, Jan. 7, 1967; 1 dau., Amy Joan. B.A., U. Minn., 1955; M.S., U. Mich., 1958; Ph.D., Case Inst. Tech., 1961. Research assoc. Swarthmore Coll., 1961-63; astronomer U.S. Naval Obs., Washington, 1963-66; asst. prof. astronomy Conn. Wesleyan U., Middletown, 1966-73, assoc. prof., 1973-81; Van Vleck prof. astronomy, dir. Wesleyan U. (Van Vleck Obs.), 1981—; vis. prof. Yale U., 1979-80. Contbr. numerous articles to profl. jours. Mem. Internat. Astronom. Union, Am. Astronom. Soc., Royal Astronom. Soc., Sigma Xi. Current Work: Galactic structure, astrometry. Subspecialty: Optical astronomy. Office: Van Vleck Observatory Wesleyan U Middletown CT 06457

UPTON, ARTHUR CANFIELD, pathologist, educator; b. Ann Arbor, Mich., Feb. 27, 1923; s. Herbert Hawkes and Ellen (Canfield) U.; m. Elizabeth Bache Perry, Mar. 1, 1946; children: Rebecca A., Melissa P., Bradley C. Grad., Phillips Acad., Andover, Mass., 1941; B.A., U. Mich., 1944, M.D., 1946. Intern Univ. Hosp., Ann Arbor, 1947, resident, 1948-49; instr. pathology U. Mich. Med. Sch., 1950-51; pathologist Oak Ridge Nat. Lab., 1951-54, chief pathology-physiology sect., 1954-69; prof. pathology SUNY Med. Sch. at Stony Brook, 1969-77, chmn. dept. pathology, 1969-70; dean Sch. Basic Health Scis., 1970-75; dir. Nat. Cancer Inst., Bethesda, Md., 1977-79; prof., chmn. dept. environ. medicine N.Y. U. Med. Sch., N.Y.C., 1980—; Mem. various coms. nat. and internat. orgns. Asso. editor: Cancer Research; mem. editorial bd.: Internat. Union Against Cancer. Served with AUS, 1943-46. Recipient Ernest Orlando Lawrence award for atomic field, 1965; Comfort-Crookshank award for cancer research, 1979. Mem. Am. Assn. Pathologists and Bacteriologists, Internat. Acad. Pathology, Radiation Research Soc. (councilor 1963-64), Internat. Assn. Radiation Research (v.p. 1979-83, pres. 1983—), Radiation Research Soc. (pres. elect 1964-65, pres. 1965-66), Am. Assn. Cancer Research (pres. 1963-64), Am. Soc. Exptl. Pathology (pres 1967-68), AAAS, Gerontol. Soc., Sci. Research Soc. Am., Soc. Exptl. Biology and Medicine, Phi Beta Kappa, Phi Gamma Delta, Alpha Omega Alpha, Nu Sigma Nu. Subspecialty: Pathology (medicine). Home: 3 Washington Square Village New York NY 10012 Office: NY U Sch Medicine 550 1st Ave New York NY 10016

UPTON, CHARLES JOSEPH, chemist; b. Doylestown, Pa., Oct. 1, 1947; s. Clarence and Regina Elizabeth (Peters) U.; m. Dorothy Hahn, Dec. 27, 1969; children—Kevin, Janet. B.S., Del. Valley Coll., 1969; Ph.D., Duquesne U., 1973. Postdoctoral research assoc. U. Ill., Urbana, 1973-74; sr. research chemist Monsanto Co., St. Louis, 1974-79; mgr. coating imaging and graphic arts Champion Internat., West Nyack, N.Y., 1979—. Patentee in non-phosphate detergent builders. Mem. Am. Chem. Soc., Tech. Assn. Pulp and Paper Industry, Sigma Xi. Current work: Study of paper coatings and coating methods for improved impact and non-impact printing techniques. Subspecialty: Organic chemistry. Home: 82 B Station Rd Rock Tavern NY 12575 Office: Champion Internat West Nyack NY 10994

URANO, MUNEYASU, radiation biologist, educator; b. Osaka, Japan, Apr. 21, 1936; came to U.S., 1977, naturalized, 1978; s. Iekazu and Shizuyo (Hirata) U.; m. Michiyo, Mar. 2, 1963; children: Shin-ichi, Jun. M.D., Kyoto (Japan) Prefectural U. Medicine, 1961, Ph.D., 1968. Intern Kyoto Prefectural U. Medicine, 1961-62, resident, 1962-66, asst. prof., 1968-71; sr. researcher and staff radiologist Nat. Inst. Radiol. Scis., Chiba, Japan, 1971-77; asst. radiation biologist Mass. Gen. Hosp., Boston, 1977-81, assoc. radiation biologist, 1982—; asst. prof. radiation biology Harvard U. Med. Sch., Boston, 1977-82, assoc. prof., 1983—. Contbr. articles to profl. jours. Nat. Cancer Inst. grantee, 1979—; Internat. Union against Cancer fellow, 1982. Fellow Japanese Soc. for Promotion Cancer Research; mem. Radiation Research Soc., Am. Soc. Therapeutic Radiology and Oncology, N.Am. Hyperthermia Group, Cancer Research, AAAS. Current Work: Hyperthermia; thermal effect on animal malignant and normal tissues; hyperthermia combined with radiation or chemotherapy; proton radiation biology. Subspecialties: Oncology; Cancer research (medicine). Home: 3 Laurel Hill Ln Winchester MA 01890 Office: Mass Gen Hosp Cox 7 Fruit St Boston MA 02114

URQUHART, JAMES BURWELL, III, research engineer, thermodynamicist, computer systems consultant; b. Pitts., Mar. 18, 1944; s. James Burwell Jr. and Eva Marie (Williams) U.; m. Eleanor Mack, July 29, 1967; children—Susan, Melanie, Katherine. B.S.M.E. magna cum laude, Duke U., 1966; M.S.M.E., Ga. Inst. Tech., 1968. Registered profl. engr., Fla. Research engr. Boeing Co., Huntsville, Ala., 1968-72, Pratt & Whitney, West Palm Beach, Fla., 1972-79, 85—, United Tech. Research Ctr., West Palm Beach, 1979-85; engring. cons., 1974—; computer cons., Lake Park, Fla., 1979-85; chmn. bd. Computer Applications, Inc. Contbr. articles to profl. jours. Patentee in field. Recipient commendation NASA/Boeing Co., 1971. Mem. Phi Beta Kappa, Sigma Xi, Tau Beta Pi, Pi Mu Epsilon, Pi Tau Sigma. Episcopalian. Current work: Computer modelling of complex physical systems such as high energy laser's optical cavity and rocket engine transients. Subspecialties: Mechanical engineering; Laser wave optics. Home: 4754 Holly Dr Palm Beach Gardens FL 33410 Office: Pratt & Whitney PO Box 2691 West Palm Beach FL 33402

URQUHART, JOHN, physiologist; b. Pitts., Apr. 24, 1934; s. John and Wilma Nelda (Martin) U.; m. Joan Cooley, Dec. 28, 1957; children—Elizabeth Urquhart Wynne, Robert Malcolm, Thomas Jubal. B.A. with honors, Rice U., 1955; M.D. with honors, Harvard U., 1959. Teaching fellow Harvard U., 1956-61; intern in surgery Mass. Gen. Hosp., Boston, 1960-61, resident, 1960-61; USPHS sr. asst. surgeon, investigator NIH, Bethesda, Md., 1961-63; from asst. prof. to prof. physiology U. Pitts., 1963-70; prof. biomed. engring. U. So. Calif., Los Angeles, 1970-71; prin. scientist ALZA Corp., Palo Alto, Calif., 1971-78, dir. biol. scis., 1971-74, pres. research div., 1974-78, dir., 1976-78, chief scientist, v.p., 1978-82, sr. v.p., prin. scientist, 1978—; adj. prof. pharmacology U. Calif., 1984—; vis. prof. pharmacology Riksuniversiteit Limburg, The Netherlands, 1984; trustee GMI Engring. and Mgmt. Inst., Flint, Mich. mem. various coms. U. Pitts., U. Edinburgh; dir. sci. advisors Crump Inst. Med. Engring.; cons. in field. Author: Risk Watch-The Odds of Life, 1984. Contbr. articles to profl. jours. Mem. editorial bd. Am. Jour. Physiology, 1970-76, Jour. Applied Physiology, 1970-76, Endocrinology, 1973-78, Metabolism, 1971—, Drug Info. Service Jour., 1983—. Patentee in field. Mem. Boyleston Med. Soc., Am. Physiol. Soc. (Bowditch lectr. 1969), Endocrine Soc. (Upjohn award, 1962), Biomed. Engring. Soc. (pres. 1976), Internat. Soc. Chronbiology, Am. Social Health Assn. (bd. dirs. 1983—), Internat. Soc. Neuroendocrinology, Phi Beta Kappa, Sigma Xi, Alpha Omega Alpha. Club: Saturday Morning (Palo Alto). Current work: Cardiovascular physiology; medical education, organ perfusion; experimental surgery; experimental design; pharmacokinetics; pharmacodynamics. Subspecialties: Endocrinology; Epidemiology. Office: ALZA Corp 950 Page Mill Rd PO Box 10950 Palo Alto CA 94303

URRY, VERN WILLIAM, research psychologist; b. Salt Lake City, Sept. 20, 1931; s. Herbert William and Emma Irene (Swaner) U.; m. Billie Jeanne Nevius, Sept. 24, 1957; 1 child, Gloria Jeanne. B.A., U. Utah, 1955, M.S., 1962; Ph.D., Purdue U. (1970.). Research psychologist U.S. Army Enlisted Eval. Ctr., Ft. Benjamin Harrison, Ind., 1961-67; head systems and programming Measurement and Research Ctr., Purdue U., West Lafayette, 1967-70; asst. dir. Bur. Testing U. Wash., 1970-72; personnel research psychologist U.S. Office Personnel Mgmt., Washington, 1972—. Author: Tailored Testing and Its Theory and Practice, 1983. Served with U.S. Army, 1952-54. Recipient cert. achievement U.S. Army Enlisted Eval. Ctr., 1967. Mem. AAAS, Am. Psychol. Assn., Md. Psychol. Assn., Psychometric Soc., Internat. Platform Assn., N.Y. Acad. Scis., Phi Kappa Phi. Current Work: Research in tailored testing, a computerized mode of personnel or psychological testing, including the development of statistical models and the derivation of algorithms. Subspecialties: Test theory; Algorithms. Home: 3301 Accolade Dr Clinton MD 20735 Office: Office of Staffing Policy US Office of Personnel Mgmt 1900 E St NW Washington DC 20415

URSCHEL, STEPHEN FRANCIS, geologist, researcher; b. Albany, N.Y., Nov. 28, 1958; s. Robert John and Frances Eleanor (Galvin) U. Student U. Central Fla., 1976-79; B.S., SUNY-Albany, 1982; M.S., Rensselaer Poly. Inst., 1984. Teaching asst. Rensselaer Poly. Inst., Troy, N.Y., 1983, research asst., 1983-84; research assoc. Northeastern Sci. Found., Troy, 1984—. Mem. Am. Assn. Petroleum Geologists (jr.), Geol. Soc. Am., Soc. Econ. Paleontologists and Mineralogists, Electron Microscopy Soc., Sigma Gamma Epsilon (v.p. Delta Theta chpt. 1983-84). Republican. Roman Catholic. Current work: Carbonate sedimentology related to petroleum reservoir exploration and evaluation. Subspecialties: Sedimentology; Petroleum engineering. Home: 4 Seeley Dr Albany NY 12203

URSIC, STANLEY JOHN, research hydrologist, forester; b. Milw., Apr. 2, 1924; s. Stanley and Jennie (Rupnik) U.; children—Michael, Steven, Mark. B.S., U. Minn.-St. Paul, 1949; M.F., Yale U., 1950. Project leader, prin. research hydrologist So. Forest Expt. Sta., Forest Hydrology Lab., U.S. Dept. Agr., Oxford, Miss., 1951—; Assoc. editor So. Jour. Applied Forestry, 1967—. Contbr. articles to profl. jours. Served with U.S. Army, 1942-45, ETO. Decorated Bronze Star. Mem. Soc. Am. Foresters (cert.), Am. Inst. Hydrology. Current work: Research: forest land hydrology, watershed management, land rehabilitation, atmospheric deposition. Subspecialties: Hydrology; Resource management. Home: 1031 Zilla Avent Dr Oxford MS 38655 Office: US Dept Agr Forest Service So Forest Expt Sta Forest Hydrology Lab Oxford MS 38655

USDANSKY, STEVEN IRA, geology educator; b. N.Y.C., Dec. 12, 1955; s. Isadore and Sonia Helen (Namenwirth) U.; m. Janet Yvonne Smith, Sept. 10, 1983. B.S. cum laude, UCLA, 1976; Ph.D., U. Minn., 1981. Tchg. assoc. U. Minn.-Morris, 1980; asst. prof. geology, U. Ala., 1981-85; asst. prof. geoscis. Murray State U., 1985—. Mem. Ala. Acad. Sci. (chmn. geology sect. 1984-85), Geol. Soc. Am., Am. Geophys. Union, AAAS, Mineral. Soc. Am. Current work: Petrogenesis of peraluminous granitoids of the Northern Alabama Piedmont, development of computer programs to construct geologic cross sections based on geometric models of structures. Subspecialty: Petrology. Home: 2206 Gatesborough Circle Murray State U Murray KY 42071 Office: Dept Geoscis Murray State U Murray KY 42071

USSAILIS, JAMES STEWART, research scientist, engineer; b. Boston, Sept. 9, 1939; s. James I. and Myrtle T. (MacQuarrie) U.; m. Carolyn M. Marchant, Jan. 1, 1966 (dec. June 1981); children—Catherine E., James S., Jr. B.S., U. Mass., 1969, M.S., 1972. Technician, designer Automatic Radio Mfg. Co., 1958-61; technician MIT Lincoln Lab., 1961-67, 78; instr. physics U. Mass., 1969-72; engr. periscope VHF/UHF systems, electro-optical div. Kollmorgen Corp., Northampton, Mass., 1972-77; task leader on radar simulator project Ga. Inst. Tech., 1977-78, research scientist, 1978-83; mem. tech. staff Mitre Corp., Bedford, Mass., 1983—. Contbr. research reports to tech. lit. Served with USNG, 1961-67. Mem. Am. Geophys. Union, IEEE, Am. Radio Relay League (life). Lodge: Masons. Current work: Electromagnetic propagation, polarimetric backscatter from meteorological targets, polarimetric radar system design, microwave system and antenna system engineering. Subspecialties: Electromagnetic propagation; Meteorologic instrumentation. Home: 24 O'Donnell Dr Northampton MA 01060 Office: Mitre Corp PO Box 208 Bedford MA 01730

USSERY, LARRY EUGENE, nuclear chemist; b. Macon, Ga., Dec. 13, 1955; s. Eugene and Susie Evelyn (Whitfield) U.; m. Debora Mae Bender, June 9, 1984. B.S. in Chemistry and Physics, Mercer U., 1978; Ph.D. in Chemistry, Fla. State U., 1982. Postdoctoral appointment Fla. State U. and Lawrence Livermore Nat. Lab., Los Alamos, 1982-84, Los Alamos Nat. Lab., 1984—. Contbr. articles to profl. jours. Bd. dirs. Los Alamos Civitan, 1984. Mem. Am. Chem. Soc., Am. Phys. Soc., Gamma Sigma Epsilon. Republican. So. Baptist. Current work: Low energy nuclear structure studies; in-beam gamma ray and internal conversion electron spectroscopy; pion induced single and double charge exchange reactions. Subspecialties: Nuclear chemistry; Nuclear physics. Home: PO Box 153 Los Alamos NM 87544 Office: Los Alamos Nat Lab MS-H824 Los Alamos NM 87545

UTLAUT, WILLIAM FREDERICK, electrical engineer; b. Sterling, Colo., July 26, 1922; s. Frederick Ernst and Francis Ruth Hanna U.; m. Jeanne Elizabeth Pomeroy, Aug. 4, 1946; children—Mark William, Niles Frederick, Paige Elizabeth. Utlaut Hodges. B.S.E.E., U. Colo., 1944, M.S.E.E., 1950, Ph.D. in Elec. Engring, 1966; diploma, Naval Radar Sch., 1945. Engr. Gen. Electric Co., Schenectady, 1946-48, Nat. Bur. Standards, Boulder, Colo., 1952-53; instr. U. Colo., 1948-52, 53-54; dir. Nat. Telecom and Info. Adminstrn., Inst. for Telecommunication Scis., U.S. Dept. Commerce, Boulder, 1954—; chmn. U.S. study group 1, Internat. Radio Consultative Com., 1975-81, mem. U.S. nat. com., 1970-81; mem. electromagnetic wave propagation panel, adv. group aerospace research and devel. NATO, 1978-81; chmn. tech. com. Integrated Services Digital Network Standards, Exchange Carriers Standards Assn./Am. Nat. Standards Inst., 1984—. Guest co-editor spl. joint issue: IEEE Trans. on Spectrum Mgmt, 1981, IEEE Trans. on Communications, 1975; guest editor spl. issue: Radio Sci, 1974; contbr. numerous articles to profl. jours. Bd. dirs. YMCA, 1955—; mem. bd. mgmt. 1st Congl. Ch., 1960-66, 78—; mem. engring. devel. council U. Colo., 1969-81. Served in USN, 1943-46. Recipient Gold medal U.S. Dept. Commerce, 1971; Disting. Engring. Alumnus award U. Colo., 1973. Fellow IEEE (policy bd. Communications Soc.), Internat. Sci. Radio Union. Current Work: Radio spectrum utilization and management improvement; radio propagation research; telecommunication system international standards development. Subspecialty: Telecommunications. Office: 325 Broadway Boulder CO 80303

UTTING, KENNETH, software engineer; b. Riverhead, N.Y., Mar. 6, 1959; s. Walter Arthur and Nancy Rita (Ballirano) U. B.S.E., Princeton U., 1981. Software engr. Sanders Assoc., Nashua, N.H., 1981—. Mem. Assn. Computing Machinery. Current Work: Computer graphics, image processing, computer animation. Subspecialties: Graphics, image processing, and pattern recognition; Artificial intelligence. Home: 160 Central St Hudson NH 03051

UYEKI, EDWIN M., pharmacology educator; b. Seattle, Mar. 12, 1928; s. Roger R. and Chisato (Hirai) U.; m. Aiko Harada, Sept. 16, 1951; children—Teresa, William, Amy. A.B., Kenyon Coll., 1949; Ph.D., U. Chgo., 1953. Assoc. prof. dept. pharmacology Kans. U. Med. Ctr., Kansas City, 1965-71, prof. pharmacology, 1971—. Contbr. articles to profl. jours. NIH, NIEHS grantee, 1965—, others. Mem. Am. Soc. Pharmacology and Exptl. Therapeutics, Am. Soc. Cell Biology, Radiation Research Soc., Tissue Culture Assn., AAAS. Unitarian. Current work: Cell proliferation and cell differentiation; genotoxicity of drugs and toxicants; SCE; cytometric analysis of cells and chromosomes; cellular deoxytide levels. Subspecialties: Cellular pharmacology; Neurobiology. Home: 6000 W 87th St Overland Park KS 66207 Office: Kansas U Med Ctr 39th St and Rainbow Kansas City KS 66103

UYENO, EDWARD TEISO, psychopharmacologist; b. Vancouver, B.C., Can., Mar. 1921; came to U.S., 1958; s. Ritsuichi and Kuye (Matsumiya) U.; m. Dorothy Hill, Apr. 27, 1969. B.A., U. Toronto, 1947, M.A., 1952, Ph.D., 1958. Research asst. U. Toronto, 1955-57; research assoc. Stanford (Calif.) U., 1958-61; psychopharmacologist Stanford Research Inst., 1961-76; S.R.I. Internat., 1977—. Author numerous sci. articles, also chpts. in books. NIMH grantee, 1963-66, 68-70, 71-73, 71-74; USPHS grantee, 1984—. Mem. Am. Soc. Pharmacology and Exptl. Therapeutics, Western Pharmacology Soc., Am. Psychol. Assn., Can. Psychol. Assn., Psychonomic Soc., Internat. Primatol.

Soc., Behavior Genetics Assn. Current Work: Evaluation of new analgesics, antidepressants, antianxiety agents, memory enhancers. Behavioral toxicology, behavioral pharmacology. Bioassay of anesthetics, stimulants, sedatives, neurotoxicants and neuropeptides. Subspecialties: Psychopharmacology; Behavioral psychology. Office: SRI Internat Life Sci Div 333 Ravenswood Ave Menlo Park CA 94025

UZMAN, BETTY GEREN, pathologist; b. Fort Smith, Ark., Nov. 17, 1922; d. Benton Asbury and Myra Estelle (Petty) Geren; m. L. Lahut Uzman, Dec. 17, 1955 (dec.); 1 dau., Betty Tuba. Student, Fort Smith Jr. Coll., 1939-40; B.S., U. Ark., 1942; M.D., Washington U., 1945; postgrad., M.I.T., 1948-49; M.A. (hon.), Harvard U., 1967. Intern Childrens Hosp., Boston, 1945-46; resident in pathology Barnes Hosp., St. Louis, 1946-48; Am. Cancer Soc. research fellow MIT, Cambridge, Mass., 1948-50; chief biol. ultrastructure and exptl. pathology Children's Cancer Research Found., Boston, 1950-71; instr. Harvard Med. Sch., Boston, 1949-53, assoc., 1953-56, research assoc., 1956-67, assoc. prof., 1967-71, prof., 1971-72; head research dept. Sparks Regional Med. Center, Fort Smith, 1972-74; prof. pathology La. State U., Shreveport, 1972-74, U. Tenn., Memphis, 1977—; assoc. chief staff research VA, Shreveport, 1974-77; staff pathologist VA, Memphis, 1977—; chief field ops., spl. asst. to dir. VA Central Office, Washington, 1978-79, dir. med. research services, 1979-80; chmn. pathology A Study sect. NIH, 1973-76; cons. to sci. dir. Children's Cancer Research Found., Boston, 1971-73; mem. adv. com. on prevention, diagnosis and treatment Am. Cancer Soc., 1970-73, 77-80; disting. vis. investigator Inst. Venezolano Investigación Científicas, Caracas, 1972-74; mem. adv. council Instituto Internacionale de Estudios Avanzados, Caracas, 1980—. Decorated Order of Andres Bello 1st class Venezuela; recipient Weinstein award United Cerebral Palsy, 1964; Am. Cancer Soc. research fellow, 1948-50. Mem. AAAS, Am. Soc. Cell Biology, Soc. Devel. Biology, Am. Acad. Neurology (assoc.), Am. Soc. Neurochemistry (assoc.), Electron Microscope Soc., Am., Internat. Acad. Pathology, Am. Assn. Neuropathology (assoc.), Soc. Neuroscience, Am. Assn. Cancer Research. Current Work: Nerve structure; peripheral nerve regeneration. Subspecialties: Pathology (medicine); Regeneration. Home: Apt 1411 109 N Main St Memphis TN 38103 Office: 1030 Jefferson Ave Memphis TN 38104

VACHON, REGINALD IRENEE, technological company executive, aerospace engineer; b. Norfolk, Va., Jan. 29, 1937; s. Rene Albert and Regina (Galvin) V.; m. Mary Eleanor Grigg, Jan. 16, 1960; children—Reginald Irenee, Jr., Eleanor Marie. B.M.E., Auburn U., 1958, M.S., 1960; student U.S. Naval Acad., 1954-55; Ph.D., Okla. State U., 1963; LL.B., Jones Law Sch., 1969. Bar: Ala. 1971. Registered profl. engr., Ala., Ga., Miss., La. Engr., Hayes Internat., 1958; instr. research asst. Auburn U., 1958-60, research assoc., 1961, assoc. prof., 1963-66, prof., 1966-78; research and devel. engr. E.I. DuPont, 1960; aerospace engr., technologist NASA Marshall Space Flight Ctr., summers 1964, 65; pres. Vachon Nix & Assocs., Norcross, Ga., 1977—; pres. VNA Systems Inc., 1981—; chmn. bd. Optimal Systems Internat., Inc., 1969—; chief operating officer Thacker Orgn. Inc., 1981—. Contbr. articles to profl. jours. Served with U.S. Army, 1960-61. Fellow ASME; mem. AIAA, Nat. Soc. Profl. Engrs., ABA, Ala. Bar Assn. Roman Catholic. Club: Cosmos (Washington). Patentee in field. Current work: Systems design, energy systems, vision systems. Subspecialty: Mechanical engineering. Home: 1414 Epping Forest Atlanta GA 30319 Office: PO Box 467069 Atlanta GA 30346

VADALA, FRANK ROCCO, fundraising counselor, environmentalist; b. Syracuse, N.Y., Jan. 26, 1942; s. Frank Dominick IV and Natalie Marie (Silino) V.; m. Gloria Frances Todaro, Sept. 16, 1967; children—Lori Ann, Frank Patrick, Wendy Lynn, Stephanie Catherine. B.A. in Bus. Adminstrn. and Environ. Sci., Columbia Pacific U. Ptnr. Vad's Sport Shop, Syracuse, 1962-70, pres., 1970-77; owner, operator Hackle & Tackle Co., Central Square, N.Y., 1973-83, Action Line Products Co., Central Square, 1978-83; pres. Frank Vadala Assocs., Syracuse, 1979—; dir. devel. Catskill Fly Fishing Ctr., 1983; pub. sport fishing catalogs, 1973-82. Editor Iroquois Guardian, 1973-76; assoc. pub., new products editor Iroquois Report, 1971. Mem. Nat. Soc. Fund Raising Execs. (cert. fund raising exec., nat. bd. dirs. 1984, exec. officer central N.Y. chpt. 1984, membership coordinator 1984—), Trout Unltd. (charter life, founder various bodies, nat. bd. dirs. at large 1979—, Northeast regional v.p. 1983—, nat. membership chmn. 1981-83, bd. dirs. N.Y. State council 1972—, 1st v.p. N.Y. State Council 1976-81, N.Y. state chmn. conservation fund 1981—, founder Iroquois chpt. 1969, exec. officer chpt. 1969-71, bd. dirs. chpt. 1969-76, chpt. adv. bd. 1976—, bd. dirs. Catskill Fly Fishing Ctr. 1981-82, author membership guide 1982, contbg. editor Actionline, Lines to Leaders 1982-83, Nat. Membership award 1971, N.Y. State Membership award 1973, Iroquois chpt. Man of Yr. 1975, Nat. Conservationist of Yr. award 1978, Nat. Service award 1981, 82, Northwest Steelhead Salmon Council Spl. Recognition award 1982), Associated Photographers Internat., Nat. Sporting Goods Assn. (sports age retail panel 1964-67), Izaak Walton League, Conservation Edn. Assn., Nat. Rifle Assn. (life), Nat. Wildlife Assn., Global Tomorrow Coalition. Democrat. Roman Catholic. Current work: Developing an environmental education fund to educate and encourage citizens to think and act responsibly so they may protect the natural resources for present and future generations. Subspecialty: Ecology (environmental science). Home: 106 Grandy Dr Liverpool NY 13088 Office: Frank Vadala Assocs 2827 James St Suite 210 Syracuse NY 13206

VADAS, ROBERT LOUIS, marine biology educator; b. New Brunswick N.J., Aug. 5, 1936; s. Louis I. and Mary Anne (Gurkovich) V.; m. Patricia Ann Bulgreen, July 8, 1961; children—Robert L., Sharon Lynn, Brent Kevin. B.S., Utah State U., 1962; Ph.D., U. Wash., 1968. Mem. faculty, researcher U. Maine, Orono, 1967—, prof. botany, oceanography and zoology, 1977—, chmn. dept. botany and plant pathology, 1983—. Baseball coach Babe Ruth League, Orono, 1979, 80; hockey coach Pee Wee League, Orono, 1981, 82. Served with USMC, 1954-57. Mem. Ecol. Soc. Am., Phycological Soc. Am., Internat. Phycological Soc. Current work: Marine plant-herbivore interactions, population ecology and genetics, community ecology. Subspecialties: Ecology (biology); Phycology. Office: Dept Botany and Plant Pathology U Maine Orono ME 04469

VAETH, JOSEPH GORDON, government official; b. N.Y.C., Feb. 12, 1921; s. Joseph Anthony and Sara (Billard) V.; m. Joanne Corell, Dec. 30, 1950; 1 son, Gordon Corell. A.B., N.Y. U., 1941. Instr. Adm. Billard Acad., New London, Conn., 1941-42, Lawrenceville (N.J.) Sch., 1946-47; project engr., tech. programs officer U.S. Naval Tng. Device Center, 1947-54, head new weapons and systems div., 1954-58; tech. staff mem. for man-in-space Advanced Research Projects Agy., Def. Dept., 1958-60; mgr. Washington operations Reflectone Electronics, Inc., 1960-62; asst. to dir. Nat. Weather Satellite Ctr. U.S. Weather Bur., 1962-63; mgr. TIROS (operational satellite system engring. div.), 1963-66; dir. system engring. Nat. Environ. Satellite Service, Environ. Sci. Services Adminstrn., 1966-70, Nat. Oceanic and Atmospheric Adminstrn., 1970-80; dir. satellite ops. Nat. Earth Satellite Service, 1980—. Author: Weather Eyes in the Sky, 1965, 200 Miles Up, 1951, Graf Zeppelin, 1958, To the Ends of the Earth, 1962, Langley: Man of Science and Flight, 1966, The Man Who Founded Georgia, 1968; also numerous articles.; Contbr. to: Ency. Brit. Served as officer USNR, 1942-46. Fellow Am. Inst. Aeros. and Astronautics (asso.); mem. British Interplanetary Soc., U. S. Naval Inst., Lighter-than-Air soc. Episcopalian. Club: Cosmos. Subspecialty: Satellite studies. Office: NOAA Environ Satellite Data and Info Service Fed Bldg #4 Suitland MD 20233

VAFAI, KAMBIZ, researcher, mechanical engineering educator, consultant; b. Tehran, Iran, July 16, 1953; came to U.S., 1971, naturalized; s. Abbas and Mansoureh (Emami) V.; m. Parisa Foroutan, Aug. 12, 1981. B.S., U. Minn., 1975; M.S., U. Calif.-Berkeley, 1977, Ph.D., 1980. Researcher U. Calif.-Berkeley, 1975-80; fellow Harvard U., Cambridge, Mass., 1980-81; cons., summer staff Battelle Meml. Inst., Columbus, Ohio, 1982—; asst. prof. Ohio State U., Columbus, 1981—, mem. mech. engring. grad. com. and doctoral com. 1982—, joint researcher with Bell Labs. and Owens Corning Fiberglas, 1985—. Reviewer for various jours. Contbr. articles to profl. jours. Earle C. Anthony fellow, 1975-76; Mary Ann Wheeler scholar, 1975-76. Mem. ASME (chmn. and mem. various coms. Nat. and Central Ohio chpts.), AIAA (chmn. various sessions, mem. thermophysics tech. com.), Pi Tau Sigma, Tau Beta Pi. Current work: Multiphase flow, heat and mass transfer in porous media, fundamentals of transport processes in porous media, heat transfer in electronic components and geologic media. Subspecialties: Heat transfer; Fluid mechanics. Office: Mech Engring Dept 206 W 18th Ave Ohio State U Columbus OH 43210

VAGELOS, PINDAROS ROY, biomedical research executive; b. Westfield, N.J., Oct. 8, 1929; s. Roy John and Marianthi (Lambrinides) V.; m. Diana Touliatos, July 10, 1955; children: Randall, Cynthia, Andrew, Ellen. A.B., U. Pa., 1950; M.D., Columbia U., 1954; D.Sc. (hon.), Washington U., 1980, Brown U., 1982, U. Medicine and Dentistry N.J., 1985. Intern medicine Mass. Gen. Hosp., 1954-55, asst. resident medicine, 1955-56; surgeon Lab. Cellular Physiology, NIH, 1956-59; surgeon Lab. Biochemistry, 1959-64, head sect. comparative biochemistry, 1964-66; prof. biochemistry, chmn. dept. biol. chemistry Washington U. Sch. Medicine, St. Louis, 1966-75, dir. div. biology and biomed. scis., 1973-75; sr. v.p. research Merck, Sharp & Dohme Research Labs., 1975-76, pres., 1976—; corp. sr. v.p. Merck & Co., Inc., 1982-84, exec. v.p., 1984-85, pres., chief exec. officer, 1985—; mem. molecular biology study sect. NIH, 1967-71, mem. physiol. chemistry study sect., 1973-75; mem. commn. on human resources NRC, 1973-76, Inst. Medicine, Nat. Acad. Scis., 1974—. Mem. editorial bds. jours. in field. Mem. Am. Chem. Soc. (chmn. div. biol. chemistry 1973, award enzyme chemistry 1967), Am. Soc. Biol. Chemists, A.A.A.S., Nat. Acad. Scis., Am. Acad. Arts and Scis. Discoverer of acyl-carrier protein. Subspecialty: Biomedical research management. Home: 10 Canterbury Ln Watchung NJ 07060

VAICAITIS, RIMAS, engineering educator, researcher, consultant; b. Sakei, Lithuania, Apr. 30, 1941; came to U.S., 1960; s. Kostas and Valerija V.; m. Jone A., June 19, 1965; children—Rima, Krista. B.S., U. Ill., 1967, M.S., 1968, Ph.D., 1970. Asst. prof. engring. Columbia U., N.Y.C., 1970-75, assoc. prof., 1975-80, prof., 1980—, dir. Inst. Flight Structures, 1977—; vis. scholar Princeton U. (N.J.), 1972; research engr. NASA, Hampton, Va., 1976-77, 83-84; cons. U.S. Air Force, U.S. Army, NASA, Nat. Bur. Standards. Pres. PTA, Maironis Sch., Bklyn., 1980-82. Named Outstanding Young Alumnus, U. Ill., 1977, Disting. Alumnus, 1984; grantee NASA, NSF, Nat. Bur. Standards, Sloan Found., 1981—. Mem. ASCE, AIAA. Roman Catholic. Current work: Structural dynamics, random vibrations, fluid-solid interactions, wind engineering, structural acoustics. Subspecialties: Aeronautical engineering; Civil engineering. Home: 14 Mallard Dr West Nyack NY 10994 Office: Dept Civil Engring Columbia U New York NY 10027

VAIL, SIDNEY LEE, research chemist; b. New Orleans, Aug. 10, 1928; s. Sidney Lee and Mabel Claire (Moore) V.; m. Mary Margaret Smith, May 16, 1953; children—Mary Kathleen, Richard Lee, Fay Ellen, Ann Margaret. B.S. in Chemistry, Tulane U., 1949, Ph.D. in Organic Chemistry, 1965; M.S. in Chemistry, La. State U., 1951. Chemist Dow Chem. Co., Freeport, Tex., 1951-53; sr. chemist Am. Cyanamid, Fortier, La., 1955-59; research leader U.S. Dept. Agr., Agrl. Research Service, New Orleans, 1959—; adj. prof. textile chemistry N.C. State U., Raleigh, 1979-83; exchange scientist Shirley Inst., Manchester, Eng., 1965-66. Contbr. articles to profl. jours. Patentee in field. Served with U.S. Army, 1953-55. Recipient Disting. Service award U.S. Dept. Agr., 1964. Mem. Am. Chem. Soc., Weed Sci. Soc. Am., Sigma Xi. Democrat. Episcopalian. Current work: Petrochemicals based on ethylene, bioactive (natural and synthetic) chemicals, textile chemistry; flameproofing and durable press finishing, weed control. Subspecialties: Organic chemistry; Synthetic chemistry. Office: Southern Regional Research Ctr PO Box 19687 New Orleans LA 70179

VAISHNAV, DINESH DIVAKARRAI, microbiologist; b. Junagadh, India, Sept. 21, 1948; came to U.S., 1970, naturalized, 1982; s. Divakarrai Jadavrai and Jankkumari Vaishnav; m. Nila Dinesh, Mar. 13, 1977; 1 child, Tej Dinesh. B.Sc., S. Gujarat U., Navsari, India, 1969; M.S., Miss. State U., 1973, Ph.D., 1977. Grad. research asst. dept. microbiology, Miss. State U., Starkville, 1970-77; asst. prof. natural and applied sci., Selma U. Ala., 1977-80; research scientist U. Wis.-Superior, 1980—. Contbr. articles to sci. publs. Mem. Am. Soc. Microbiology, Soc. Indsl. Microbiology. Current work: Relationship between chemical structure and biodegradation of xenobiotic compounds. Subspecialties: Microbiology; Biochemistry (biology). Office: Ctr for Lake Superior Environ Studies U Wis Superior WI 54880

VAISHNAV, RAMESH NAVALSHANKER, engineering educator; b. Jamnagar Gujarat, India, Apr. 2, 1934; came to U.S., 1957; s. Navalshanker Pranshanker and Harbala (Buch) V.; m. Marianne Pollich, Aug. 22, 1964. B.Sc., Gujarat U., India, 1952, M.E., 1955; M.S. in Engring., U. Mich.-Ann Arbor, 1958; Ph.D., U. Ill., 1961. Registered Profl. Engr., Md. Divisional overseer Pub. Works Dept., Junagadh, India, 1955-56; research asst. U. Mich.-Ann Arbor, 1957; structural engr. VIS Assocs., Cin., 1957-58; research assoc. U. Ill.-Urbana, 1958-61; prof. Catholic U. Am., 1961—; guest scientist NIH, Bethesda, Md., 1967-80; con. NIH, 1970—, others, 1961—. Co-author: Basic Hemodynamics and Its Role in Diseases Processes, 1980. Contbr. articles to sci., tech. jours. Fellow ASME; mem. Am. Acad. Mechanics, AAAS, N.Y. Acad. Scis., Soc. Rheology, Internat. Soc. Biorheology, Soc. Engring. Sci., Soc. Natural Philosophy, Internat. Soc. Math. Modelling, Cardiovascular System Dynamics Soc., Washington Soc. Engrs., Sigma Xi, Tau Beta Pi. Current work: Theoretical and experimental research in various aspects of mechanics; particular interest in the application of modern techniques in characterization of finite deformations of biological and other materials. Subspecialties: Theoretical and applied mechanics; Biomedical engineering. Home: PO Box 2129 Gaithersburg MD 20879 Office: Catholic Univ Am 620 Michigan Ave NE Washington DC 20064

VAISHNAVA, PREM PRAKASH, physics educator, researcher; b. Jodhpur, India, Oct. 10, 1942; came to U.S., 1980; s. Hari Ram and Shanti D. (Sharma) V.; m. Manju Lata, Feb. 19, 1973; children—Sanjay, Ajay, Prashant. B.S., Jodhpur U., 1963, M.S., 1965, Ph.D., 1976. Asst. prof. solid state physics Jodhpur U., 1965-77; research assoc. Heriot-Watt U., Edinburgh, Scotland, 1978-80; asst. prof. physics W.Va. U., Morgantown, 1980-83; assoc. prof. physics No. Ill. U., DeKalb, 1983—; vis. scientist Argonne Nat. Lab., Ill., 1983—. Contbr. articles to profl. publs. Mem. Am. Phys. Soc., Materials Research Soc., Sigma Xi. Current work: Mossbauer spectroscopic and EXAFS characterization of superconducting materials; Auger, LEED and EELS characterization of epitaxially grown thin films on various single crystals. Subspecialties: Condensed matter physics; Low temperature physics. Home: 201 River Dr DeKalb IL 60115 Office: Dept Physics No Ill U DeKalb IL 60115

VAKS, YEFIM ELIAS, biostatistician; b. Moscow, USSR, May 5, 1935; came to U.S., 1980; s. Elias Samuel and Ida (Mozel) V.; m. Laura M. Smakhtin, Dec. 17, 1960; children—Ilya, Michael. M.S. in Elec. Engring., Moscow Power Engring. Inst., 1960; Ph.D., Moscow Inst. Tech., 1967. Jr. scientist Central Research Inst. Textile Industries, Moscow, 1956-60, sr. scientist, 1960-69, dept. head, 1969-78; analytical engr. Bogue Electric Mfg. Co., Paterson, N.J., 1981-83; biostatistician Technicon Instrument Corp., Tarrytown, N.Y., 1983—; chmn. sect. Moscow House for Sci. and Tech. Propaganda, 1972-75; mem. sci. and tech. councils on indsl. automation USSR Ministry Light Industries, 1975-78. Author: Yarn Tension Measurement, 1966. Patentee in instrumentation and control. Contbr. articles to profl. jours. Recipient Bronze medal, 1973, Silver medal, 1974, 75, USSR Exhbn. Econ. Achievements. Mem. Am. Statis. Assn., Am. Soc. Quality Control, Soc. Indsl. and Applied Math. Current work: Algorithms for medical blood analyzers; electrical circuit analyses; experimental design and statistical analysis. Subspecialties: Statistics; Electrical engineering. Home: 620 N Columbus Ave Mt Vernon NY 10552 Office: Technicon Instruments Corp 511 Benedict Ave Tarrytown NY 10591

VALASSI, KYRIAKE VLASSIOS, nutritional biochemistry educator; b. Salonika, Greece, May 15, 1917; came to U.S., 1947, naturalized, 1962; s. Spyros and Maria (Kirkos) Kostouros. B.S. Syracuse U., 1950, M.S., Cornell U., 1952; Ph.D., Oreg. State U., 1956. Prof. nutritional biochemistry Catholic U. Am., Washington, 1956—; cons. Office Internat. Research, NIH, Bethesda, Md., 1960-69, Ctr. Disease Control, Atlanta, 1967-73, PanAm. Health Orgn., Washington, 1972-74, FDA, Washington, 1982, Nat. Acad. Pediatrics, Chgo., 1982. Contbr. articles to profl. jours. Recipient Benemerenti medal Cath. U. Am., 1984; Nat. Library Medicine grantee, 1976. Mem. Am. Inst. Nutrition for Exptl. Biology, Am. Dietetic Assn., Parenteral Enteral Nutrition Soc., Washington Nutrition Group Inc., Nat. Nutrition Consortium. Current work: Nutrition and cancer - dietary assessment. Subspecialties: Biochemistry (biology); Food science and technology. Home: 2700 Virginia Ave NW #605 Washington DC 20037 Office: Cath U Am Washington DC 20064

VALDES, JAMES JOHN, neurotoxicologist, cons.; b. San Antonio, Apr. 25, 1951; s. Fernando and Barbara Marie (Sachtleben) V.; m. Leslie Elizabeth Valdes, June 6, 1981. B.S., Loyola U., Chgo., 1973; M.S., Trinity U., 1976; Ph.D. (chemistry of Behavior fellow), Tex. Christian U., 1979; postdoctoral fellow, Johns Hopkins U., 1979-81. Instr. Tex. Christian U., Ft. Worth, 1978-79; phys. scientist toxicology br. Aberdeen Proving Ground, Md., 1982-85, pharmacologist biotechnology div., 1985—; instr. environ. psychobiology, cons. neurochemistry and biostats. Johns Hopkins U.; instr. physiol. psychology and pharmacology Hood Coll., 1982-83. Assoc. editor: Neurobehavioral Toxicology and Teratology, 1982; contbr. articles profl. jours. Grantee U.S. Army Research Office, 1982-85; Grantee Dept. Def. Chem. Systems Lab., 1982-83. Mem. Soc. Neurosci., AAAS, Brit. Brain Research Assn., European Brain and Behavior Soc. Current work: Neurotransmitter compensatory mechanisms and recovery of central nervous system function after toxic insult, neurochemical effects of mycotoxins, immobilization of receptor proteins in artificial membranes. Subspecialties: Neuropharmacology; Toxicology (medicine). Office: Biotechnology Div CRDC Aberdeen Proving Ground MD 21010

VALEGA, THOMAS MICHAEL, health science administrator; b. Linden, N.J., May 23, 1937; s. Paul and Ann (Bakalar) V.; m. Margo Orr, Aug. 30, 1958; children—Margaret, Thomas Michael, Vinson, Catherine. B.S., Rutgers U., 1959, Ph.D., 1963. Chemist U.S. Dept. Agr., Beltsville, Md., 1963-67; grants assoc. NIH, Bethesda, Md. 1968, health scientist Nat. Inst. Environ. Health Scis., 1969, health scientist adminstr. Nat. Inst. Arthritic and Metabolic Diseases, 1969-72, Nat. Inst. Dental Research, 1972-84, spl. asst. for manpower and devel. tng., 1984—. Mem. Soc. Biomaterials (spl. award 1984), AAAS, Internat. Assn. Dental Research, Am. Acad. Implant Dentistry Research Found., Am. Acad. Dental Materials, Md. Ornithol. Soc. (pres. 1969-71). Current work: Administration of dental research manpower development and training; administration of dental research on dental materials and implants. Subspecialties: Dental materials; Implantology. Home: 19005 Willow Grove Rd Olney MD 20832 Office: NIH Nat Inst Dental Research WB-510 Bethesda MD 20205

VALENCIS, JANET MARGARET, mechanical engineer; b. Waterbury, Conn., Nov. 22, 1958; d. Walter Joseph and Margaret (O'Dea) V.; m. Dennis Joseph Dell'Accio, June 26, 1982. B.S. in Mech. Engring., U. Hartford, 1980. Secondary power plant reliability engr. Northeast Utilities, Berlin, Conn., 1980-81, engring., dataprocessing liason engr., 1981—. U. Hartford scholar, 1976-80; Nat. Assn. Women in Constrn. scholar, 1977-79. Mem. Soc. Women Engrs. (sec.-treas. 1978-80), Pi Tau Sigma (v.p. 1979-80), Kappu Mu. Roman Catholic. Subspecialties: Mechanical engineering; Database systems. Home: 136 Maplewood Ave Hartford CT 06119 Office: Northeast Utilities 107 Sheldon St Hartford CT

VALENT, FRANCIS SAMUEL, ceramic engineer; b. Frankfort, N.Y., Mar. 13, 1949; s. Samuel Joseph and Wanda (Skibinski) V.; m. Pamela Theresa Kaminsky, Sept. 11, 1982; 1 dau., Nicole Ashley. A.Engring., Mohawk Valley Community Coll., 1970; B.S., Alfred U., 1973. Ceramic engr. Cerac, Inc., Milw., 1974-76; sr. process engr. Ceradyne, Inc., Santa Ana, Calif., 1976—. Mem. Am. Ceramic Soc., Nat. Inst. Ceramic Engrs. Current work: Development of techniques to hot press complex shaped parts. Subspecialties: Ceramic engineering; High-temperature materials. Home: 2508-A W MacArthur Blvd Santa Ana CA 92704 Office: Ceradyne Inc 3030-A S Redhill Ave Santa Ana CA 92705

VALENTINE, DANIEL THOMAS, chemical engineering educator; b. Bklyn., Dec. 24, 1946; s. John James and Sixta (Montiel) V.; m. Mary Christine Ullrich, Dec. 16, 1967; 1 dau., Clara Montiel. B.S.M.E., Rutgers U., 1968, M.S., 1970; Ph.D., Cath. U. Am., 1982. Research asst. Rutgers U., New Brunswick, 1968-70; mech. engr. David W. Taylor Naval Ship Research and Devel. Ctr., Bethesda, Md., 1970-77; research assoc. prof. Stevnes Inst Tech., Hoboken, N.J., 1977-80; v.p. Hydrodynamics Research Assocs., Inc., Rockville, Md., 1980-83; assoc. prof. Clarkson U., Potsdam, N.Y., 1983—; co-owner, dir. Hydrodynamics Research Assocs., Rockville, Md., 1980—; cons. ORI Inc., Silver Spring, 1980-82. Contbr. articles to profl. jours. NSF grantee, 1984. Mem. ASME, Soc. Indsl. and Applied Math, Soc. Naval Architects and Marine Engrs., Sigma Xi. Current work: Buoyancy induced flows; comutational fluid dynamcis; geophysical flows, computer aided design; marine hydrodynamics. Subspecialties: Mechanical engineering; Fluid mechanics. Home: 10 Waverly St Potsdam NY 13676 Office: Clarkson U Dept Mech Engring Potsdam NY 13676

VALENTINE, JAMES WILLIAM, geology educator, paleontologist; b.Los Angeles, Nov. 10, 1926; s. Adelbert Cuthbert and Isabel (Davis) V.; m. Grace Whysner, 1957 (div. 1971);children—Anita, Ian; m. Cathryn Alice Campbell, Sept. 30, 1978; 1 child, Geoffrey. B.A., Phillips U., 1950; M.A., UCLA, 1954, Ph.D., 1958. Asst. prof. U.Mo., Columbia, 1958-64; assoc. prof. U. Calif.-Davis, 1964-68, prof., 1968-77; prof. dept. geology U. Calif.-Santa Barbara, 1977—. Author: Evolutionary Paleoecology, 1972; (with Dobzhansky, Ayala and Stebbins) Evolution, 1977; (with Ayala) Evolving, 1979. Contbr. articles to profl. jours. Served with USNR, 1944-46, PTO. Guggenheim fellow, 1968-69; grantee NSF, 1981—, NASA, 1981-83. Fellow Am. Acad. Arts and Scis., AAAS, Geol. Soc. Am.; mem. Nat. Acad. Scis., Paleontol. Soc. (pres. 1974-75). Current work: The origin, regulation and extinction of organic diversity; the origin of phyla. Subspecialty: Paleontology. Office: U Calif Dept Geology Santa Barbara CA 93106

VALENTINE, MARTIN DOUGLAS, physician, researcher, educator; b. Greenwich, Conn., Apr. 13, 1935; s. Emanuel Henriques and Betty (Resnick) V.; m. Leah Helen David, June 16, 1957; children: Mark D., Daniel S., Rachel L., Joshua R. B.S., Union Coll. Schenectady, 1956; M.D., Tufts U., 1960. Diplomate: Am. Bd. Internal Medicine, Am. Bd. Allergy and Immunology. Research fellow Harvard U.-Mass. Gen. Hosp., 1965-66, Peter Bent Brigham Hosp., 1966-68, Robert Breck Brigham Hosp., 1966 68; jr. assoc. in medicine Peter Bent Brigham Hosp.-Harvard U., 1968-70; asst. prof. medicine Johns Hopkins U., 1970-77, assoc. prof., 1977—. Mem. editorial bd.: Jour. Allergy and Clin. Immunology, 1980-85; contbr. articles to profl. jours. Served to capt. USAF, 1962-64. Nat. Inst. Allergy and Infectious Disease grantee, 1978—. Mem. Am. Acad. Allergy, Am. Assn. Immunologists, Am. Thoracic Soc. Current Work: New methods in treatment and prevention of insect allergy. Subspecialties: Allergy; Immunology (medicine). Office: 5601 Loch Raven Blvd Baltimore MD 21239

VALENTY, VIVIAN BRIONES, chemist; b. Concepcion, Tarlac, Philippines, Dec. 15, 1944; came to U.S., 1966; naturalized, 1973; d. Eleuterio Santos and Felisa Policarpio Briones; m. Steven Jeffrey Valenty, Aug. 23, 1969; children—Jeffrey Alexander, Elise Arielle. B.S. in Chemistry, Mapua Inst. Tech., Manila, 1964; Ph.D., Pa. State U., 1971. Research asst. Internat. Rice Research Inst., Los Banos, Laguna, Philippines, 1964-66; asst. prof. Skidmore Coll., Saratoga Springs, N.Y., 1975-77; research scientist N.Y. State Dept. Health, Albany, 1977-81; sr. research chemist A.E. Staley Mfg. Co., Decatur, Ill., 1981-83; research chemist Gen. Electric Co., Waterford, N.Y., 1983—. Contbr. articles to profl. jours. Patentee in field. Mem. Am. Chem. Soc. (treas. 1981-83), AAAS. Soc. Photo-Optical Instrumentation Engrs.; Sigma Xi. Subspecialty: Organic chemistry. Home: 2631 Rosendale Rd Schenectady NY 12309 Office: Gen Electric Co Hudson River Rd Waterford NY 12188

VALENZUELA, PABLO DE TARSO, genetic engineering company executive; b. Santiago, Chile, June 13, 1941; came to U.S., 1967, naturalized, 1976; s. Fernando Valenzuela and Carmen Valdes; m. Dec. 13, 1968; children—Fernando, Andres, Javier. M.S. in Biochemistry, U. Chile, 1965; Ph.D. in Biochemistry, Northwestern U., 1970. Asst. prof. Cath. U., Santiago, Chile, 1971-74, prof. biochemistry, 1974-75; adj. assoc. prof. U. Calif.-San Francisco, 1977-78, adj. assoc. prof., 1978-81; v.p., research dir. Chiron Corp., Emeryville, Calif., 1981—. Mem. editorial bd. Jour. DNA, N.Y.C., 1984, Jour. Vaccine, Surrey, Eng., 1985. Contbr. articles to sci. jours. Mem. Chilean Biol. Soc., Chilean Biochem. Soc., Am. Soc. Biol. Chemists. Current work: Genetic engineering, Hepatitis B vaccines, molecular genetics. Subspecialty: Biochemistry (biology). Office: Chiron Corp 4560 Horton St Emeryville CA 94608

VALFER, ERNST SIEGMAR, management scientist, psychologist, consultant; b. Frankfurt, Ger., July 4, 1925; came to U.S., 1941; s. Hermann Heinrich and Frieda (Kahn) V.; m. Lois Brandwynne, July 8, 1961; children: Rachel, Lilah. A.A., San Francisco City Coll., 1948; B.S., U. Calif.-Berkeley, 1950, M.S., 1952, Ph.D., 1965. Diplomate Am. Bd. Profl. Psychology; lic. psychologist, Calif. registered profl. engr., Calif. Supt. indsl. planning U.S. Navy, Alameda, Calif., 1952-57; research scientist, dir. NRC-Nat. Acad. Scis., San Francisco and Washington, 1957-62; assoc. research engr. U. Calif.-Berkeley, 1961-64, sr. lectr., research engr., 1965-67, cons. in pvt. practice, Berkeley, 1981; adj. sr. fellow UCLA, 1973—; dir. mgmt. sci. staff. U.S. Dept. Agr.-Forest Service, Berkeley, 1962—; Western bd. mem. Am. Bd. Profl.

Psychology, 1980—; cons. numerous pvt., govt. and acad. orgns.; examiner Calif. State Bd. Profl. Engrs., Sacramento, 1967-69. Contbr. articles to profl. jours., chpts. to books. Chmn. Agy. Jewish Edn., 1982-85; bd. dirs. Tehiyah Sch., Berkeley, 1979-83, various ednl., charitable, and civic orgns. in San Francisco Bay Area, 1970—. Served to lt. AUS, 1944-46, ETO. Recipient citation Pres. of Nat. Acad. Scis.-NRC, 1961-62, recognition Am. Inst. Indsl. Engrs., 1958, various awards Dept Agr.-Forest Service, 1970s. Mem. Inst. Indsl. Engrs. (sr.), Am. Psychol. Assn., Inst. Mgmt. Scis., Am. Bd. Profl. Psychology, Sigma Xi. Jewish. Current Work: Multi-disciplinary approach to complex decision making in large organizations, organizational adaptation to major technological and social changes. Subspecialties: Social psychology; Human factors engineering. Home: 2621 Rose St Berkeley CA 94708 Office: Dept Agriculture Forest Service PO Box 245 Berkeley CA 94701

VALLEE, BERT LESTER, biochemist, physician, educator; b. Hemer, Westphalia, Germany, June 1, 1919; came to U.S., 1938, naturalized, 1948; s. Joseph and Rosa (Kronenberger) V.; m. Natalie T. Kugris, May 29, 1947. Sc.B., U. Berne, Switzerland, 1938; M.D., NYU Coll. Medicine, 1943; A.M. (hon.), Harvard, 1960. Research fellow Harvard Med. Sch., Boston, 1946-49, research assoc., 1949-51, assoc., 1951-56, asst. prof. medicine, 1956-60, assoc. prof., 1960-64, prof. biol. chemistry, 1964-65, Paul C. Cabot prof. biol. chemistry, 1965-80, Paul C. Cabot prof. biochem. scis., 1980—; research assoc. dept. biology Mass. Inst. Tech., Cambridge, from 1948; physician Peter Bent Brigham Hosp., Boston, 1961-80; biochemist-in-chief Brigham & Women's Hosp., Boston, from 1980; sci. dir. Biophysics Research Lab., Harvard Med. Sch., Peter Bent Brigham Hosp., 1954-80; head Center for Biochem. and Biophys. Scis. and Medicine, Harvard Med. Sch. and Brigham & Women's Hosp., from 1980. Author book.; Contbr. articles and chpts. to sci. publs. Founder, trustee Boston Biophysics Research Found., from 1957; founder, pres. Endowment for Research in Human Biology, Inc., from 1980. Recipient Buchman Meml. award Calif. Inst. Tech., 1976; Linderstrøm-Lang award and gold medal, 1980; William C. Rose award in biochemistry, 1982. Fellow AAAS, Nat. Acad. Scis., Am. Acad. Arts and Scis., N.Y. Acad. Scis.; mem. Am. Soc. Biol. Chemists, Am. Chem. Soc. (Willard Gibbs gold medal 1981), Optical Soc. Am., Biophys. Soc., Swiss Biochem. Soc. (hon. fgn. mem.), Royal Danish Acad. Scis. and Letters, Alpha Omega Alpha. Subspecialty: Biophysical chemistry. Office: Harvard Med Sch 25 Shattuck St Boston MA 02115

VALLENTYNE, JOHN REUBEN WAY (JOHNNY BIOSPHERE), ecologist, environmental educator; b. Toronto, Ont., Can., July 31, 1926; s. Harold James and Alice Mary (Laurie) V.; m. Ann Vera Tracy, Aug. 30, 1947; children—Peter Lloyd, Stephen Way, Jane Leslie, Ann Marie, Geoffrey Gordon. B.A. with honors, Queen's U., 1949; Ph.D., Yale U., 1953. Lectr., asst. prof. Queen's U., Kingston, Ont., 1952-58; assoc. prof., prof. biology Cornell U., Ithaca, N.Y., 1958-66; sci. leader Freshwater Inst., Winnipeg, Man., Can., 1966-72, sr. scientist, 1972-77; sr. scientist Can. Centre Inland Waters, Burlington, Ont., 1977—; v.p. World Council for Biosphere, 1984—. Author: The Algal Bowl, 1974. Advisor Great Lakes research Internatl. Joint Commn., Windsor, Ont., 1972-82. Served with Can. Army, 1943-45. Guggenheim fellow, 1964-65. Mem. Internat. Assn. Limnology (pres. 1974-80), Can. Soc. Environ. Biologists (pres. 1980-82), Rawson Acad. Aquatic Sci. (chmn. 1980-83). Club: Tennis (Burlington). Current work: Environmental education. Subspecialties: Ecology (environmental science); Limnology. Home: 341 Newbold Ct Burlington ON L7R 2Y5 Canada Office: Can Centre for Inland Waters PO Box 5050 Burlington ON L7R 4A6 Canada

VALLERA, DANIEL ATTILIO, therapeutic radiology, laboratory medicine and pathology educator, cancer and transplantation researcher; b. East Liverpool, Ohio, Oct. 13, 1951; s. Jesse Anthony and Mary Sue (Frank) V. B.S., Ohio State U., 1973, M.S., 1975, Ph.D., 1978. Asst. prof. therapeutic radiology, lab. medicine, pathology U. Minn., Mpls., 1980-84, assoc. prof., 1984—. Minn. Med. Found. grantee, 1982; Leukemia Soc. Am. scholar, 1983; recipient Am. Cancer Soc. Jr. faculty award, 1983, Hubert H. Humphrey cancer research award, 1981. Mem. Am. Assn. Immunologists, Transplantation Soc., Assn. Minn. Immunologists. Roman Catholic. Current work: Experimental bone marrow transplantation and cancer research involving a new class of agents (antibodies linked to toxins); transplantation and tumor immunology. Subspecialties: Immunotoxicology; Cancer research (medicine). Office: Dept Therapeutic Radiology Univ Minn Box 367 Mayo Meml Bldg Minneapolis MN 55455

VALSAMAKIS, EMMANUEL ANTHONY, scientist; b. Istanbul, Turkey, May 11, 1933; came to U.S., 1955; s. Anthony Valsamakis and Alexandra (Horianou) Vale; m. Aliki Apostolides, Jan. 31, 1960; children—Tony, Alexandra. B.S. in E.E., Robert Coll., Istanbul, 1955; M.E.E., Rensselaer Poly. Inst., Troy, N.Y., 1958, Ph.D., 1963. Research scientist Grumman Aircraft, Bethpage, N.Y., 1962-67; adv. physicist IBM Corp., Hopewell Junction, N.Y., 1967-75, research staff mem., Yorktown Heights, N.Y., 1976-80, devel. engr., Hopewell Junction, 1980-81, adv. engr., 1982—. Contbr. articles to profl. jours. Patentee in field. Mem. IEEE, Am. Phys. Soc., N.Y. Acad. Scis., Sigma Xi, Tau Beta Pi. Subspecialties: Integrated circuits; Semiconductors. Office: IBM Corp Route 52 Facility Hopewell Junction NY 12533

VALVANI, SHRI CHAND, research scientist; b. Jacobabad, India, Mar. 20, 1940; came to U.S., 1966, naturalized, 1980; m. Swerun K. Singh; children—Sanjay, Rajeev, Reena. B.S. in Pharmacy, U. Saugar, India, 1965; M.S., U. Mich., 1969, Ph.D., 1970. Scientist Upjohn Co., Kalamazoo, Mich., 1970-72, research scientist, 1973-79, sr. research scientist, 1979-83, research head, 1983-85, assoc. dir., 1985—. Editor: Physical Chemical Properties of Drugs, 1980. Mem. Acad. Pharm. Scis., Am. Chem. Soc., Sigma Xi, Phi Lambda Upsilon, Phi Lambda Upsilon. Current work: Research and development of drug delivery systems, formulation, stability and information systems. Subspecialties: Drug delivery systems; Drug design. Office: Upjohn Co Pharmacy Research Kalamazoo MI 49001

VALYI, EMERY I., machinery company executive; b. Murska Sobota, Yugoslavia, July 14, 1911; came to U.S., 1940, naturalized, 1946; s. Alexander and Elizabeth (Arvay) V.; m. Ilsabe von Behr; children: Katherine, Thomas. M.E., Swiss Fed. Inst. Tech., 1933, D.Sc., 1937. Research engr. Swiss Fed. Inst. Testing Materials, 1934-37; metall. engr. Injecta, Ltd., Switzerland, 1937-40; mgr. die casting machine div. Press Mfg. Co., Mt. Gilead, Ohio, 1940-42; v.p. Sam Tour Co., N.Y.C., 1942-45; pres. ARD Corp., Yonkers, N.Y., 1945-62; cons. maj. U.S., fgn. corps., 1972-80; pres. tpT Machinery Corp., Norwalk, Conn., 1974—. Contbr. numerous articles to profl. jours. Mem. Am. Inst. Mech. Engrs., Soc. Plastics Industry, Soc. Plastics Engrs., ASME, Am. Inst. Chemists. Patentee in field. Current Work: Conversion process for polymers. Subspecialties: Materials processing; Polymers (materials science). Office: 3 Eversley Ave Norwalk CT 06851

VAN ALFEN, NEAL K., biologist, educator, cons.; b. Ogden, Utah, July 17, 1943; s. Gerrit Johan and Marguerite (Noorda) Van A.; m. Susan Duffin, Dec. 18, 1965; children: Peter, Anne, David, Christina. Ph.D., U. Calif.-Davis, 1972. Asst. plant pathologist Conn. Agrl. Expt. Sta., New Haven, 1972-75; asst. prof. biology Utah State U., 1975-78, assoc. prof., 1978-82, prof., 1982—; cons. Kennecott Corp., 1976—. Research, publs. in field. NSF grantee, 1976-78, 78-79, 81-84; Dept. Agr. Competitive Research Grants Office grantee, 1978-80, 80-82, 82-84; Dept. Agr. Forest Service grantee, 1979-82, 1981-83; Dept. Interior Park Service grantee, 1979-81. Mem. Am. Phytopath. Soc., Am. Soc. Plant Physiologists. Current Work: Mechanisms of pathogen virulence; biochemistry and genetics of virulence expression by plant pathogens. Subspecialties: Plant pathology; Genetics and genetic engineering (biology). Office: Dept Biology UMC 45 Utah State U Logan UT 84322

VAN ALLEN, JAMES ALFRED, physicist, educator; b. Mt. Pleasant, Iowa, Sept. 7, 1914; s. Alfred Morris and Alma E. (Olney) Van A.; m. Abigail Fithian Halsey, Oct. 13, 1945; children: Cynthia Olney Van Allen (Schaffner), Margot Isham, Sarah Halsey, Thomas Halsey, Peter Cornelius. B.S., Iowa Wesleyan Coll., 1935, Sc.D., 1951; M.S., U. Iowa, 1936, Ph.D., 1939; Sc.D., Grinnell Coll., 1957, Coe Coll., 1958, Cornell Coll., 1959, U. Dubuque, 1960, U. Mich., 1961, Northwestern U., 1961, Ill. Coll., 1963, Butler U., 1966, Boston Coll., 1966, Southampton Coll., 1967, Augustana Coll., 1969, St. Ambrose Coll., 1981. Research fellow, physicist dept. terrestrial magnetism Carnegie Instn., Washington, 1939-42; physicist, group and unit supr., applied physics lab. Johns Hopkins, 1942, 1946-50, organizer, leader sci. expdns. study cosmic radiation, Peru, 1949, Gulf of Alaska 1950, Greenland 1952, 57, Antarctica 1957; Carver prof. physics, head dept. U. Iowa, 1951-85; Regents fellow Smithsonian Instn., 1981; research asso. Princeton, 1953-54; dir. Iowa Electric Light and Power Co., 1st Nat. Bank Iowa City; Devel. radio proximity fuze Nat. Def. Research Council, OSRD; pioneer high altitude research with rockets, satellites and space probes. Contbg. author: Physics and Med. of Upper Atmosphere, 1952, Rocket Exploration of the Upper Atmosphere; author: Origins of Magnetospheric Physics, 1983; Editor: Scientific Uses of Earth Satellites, 1956; asso. editor: Jour. Geophysical Research, 1959-64, Physics of Fluids, 1958-62; Contbr. numerous articles to sci. jours. Served as lt. comdr. U.S. Navy, 1942-46; ordnance and gunnery specialist, combat observer. Received C.N. Hickman medal for devel. Aerobee rocket Am. Rocket Soc., 1949; physics award Washington Acad. Sci., 1949; Guggenheim Meml. Found. research fellow, 1951; space flight award Am. Astronautical Soc., 1958; Louis W. Hill space transp. award Inst. Aero. Scis., 1959; Elliot Cresson medal Franklin Inst., 1961; John A. Fleming award Am. Geophys. Union, 1963, 64; Golden Omega award Elec. Insulation Conf., 1963; comdr. Order du Merit Pour la Recherche et L'Invention, 1964; Iowa Broadcasters Assn. award, 1964; Fellows award of merit Am. Cons. Engrs. Council, 1978. Fellow Am. Rocket Soc., IEEE, Am. Phys. Soc., Am. Geophys. Union (pres. 1982-84); mem. Iowa Acad. Sci., Nat. Acad. Scis., Internat. Acad. Astronautics (founding mem.), Am. Philos. Soc., Am. Astron. Soc., Royal Astron. Soc. (U.K.) (gold medal 1978), Am. Acad. Arts and Scis., Sigma Xi, Gamma Alpha. Presbyn. Club: Cosmos (Washington). Discoverer radiation belts around earth. Subspecialties: Cosmic ray high energy astrophysics; Satellite studies. Office: 203 Physics Bldg U Iowa Iowa City IA 52242

VANALSTYNE, FREDERICK EARL, engineering geologist; b. Gloversville, N.Y., June 12, 1945; s. Willard S. VanAlstyne and Helena B. (Gifford) Bona; 1 child, Laura Ann. B.S. in Edn., Norwich U., 1967. Cert. profl. geol. scientist. Jr. engrng. geologist N.Y. State Dept. Transp., Albany, 1967-68; jr. engrng. geologist N.Y. State Dept. Environ. Conservation, Albany, 1970-72, asst. engrng. geologist, 1972-73, sr. engrng. geologist, 1973-75, assoc. engrng. geologist, 1975—, chief geotech. services, 1983—. Served to 1st lt. U.S. Army, 1968-70. Mem. Am. Inst. Profl. Geologists, Geol. Soc. Am., Nat. Water Well Assn., Internat. Assn. Water Pollution Research and Control. Lodge: Masons. Current work: Ground water resource evaluation and management. Subspecialty: Hydrology. Home: 35 Ruggles Rd Saratoga Springs NY 12866 Office: NY State Dept Environ Conservation 50 Wolf Rd Albany NY 12233

VAN ALTEN, PIERSON JAY, immunologist, educator; b. Grand Rapids, Mich., Feb. 21, 1928; s. Daniel and Anna (Zuidema) Van A.; m. Lucille Westendorp, June 30, 1953; children—Faith, Daniel. B.A., Calvin Coll., 1950; M.S., Mich. State U., 1955, Ph.D., 1958. Research fellow UCLA, 1958-60; asst. prof. anatomy U. Ill.-Chgo., 1960-63, assoc. prof., 1964-73, prof., 1973—; vis. prof. U. Minn., Mpls., 1966-67; guest prof. U. Bern (Switzerland), 1973-74; mem. research com. Am. Cancer Soc., Chgo., 1975—; mem. staff life sci. research office Fedm. Am. Socs. Exptl. Biology, Bethesda, Md., 1975-81. Contbr. articles to profl. jours., chpts. to books. Served to sgt. U.S. Army, 1951-53. Grantee United Cerebral Palsy, 1965-68, John Hartford Found., 1973-76, Nat. Cancer Inst., 1976-82; fellow Am. Cancer Soc., 1973-74. Mem. Reticuloendothelial Soc. (treas. 1978-80), Am. Soc. Immunologists (rep. to Life Scis. Research Office 1975-81), Am. Soc. Anatomists (1st place speech award), Transplantation Soc., AAAS. Christian Reformed. Subspecialties: Immunobiology and immunology; Developmental biology. Home: 140 Fairview Elmhurst IL 60126 Office: U Ill Coll Medicine PO Box 6998 Chicago IL 60680

VANAMAN, THOMAS C., biochemist, educator; b. Louisville, Ky., Aug. 12, 1941; s. Sherman Benton and Thelma Cecilia (Clark) V.; m. Gretchen L. Biles; children: Thomas Randolph, John Tyler, Maripat, Steven. B.S. in Chemistry, U. Ky., 1964; Ph.D., Duke U., 1968; postgrad., Stanford U., 1968-70. Asst. prof. microbiology and immunology Duke U., 1970-75, assoc. prof., 1975-79, prof., 1979-83, dir. Basic Research Comprehensive Cancer Center, 1981-83; prof., chmn. biochemistry U. Ky. Med. Ctr., Lexington, 1983—; mem.-at-large Nat. Am. Heart Assn. grant rev. panel, 1982-86; mem. molecular cytology study sect. NIH, 1981-85; mem. at large nat. grant rev. panel Am. Heart Assn., 1982-86. Mem. editorial bd.: Jour. Biol. Chemistry, 1981-85. Contbr. in field. Served with USAR, 1961-67. Recipient Josiah Macy faculty scholar award, 1977-78; grantee in field. Mem. Am. Soc. Biol. Chemistry, N.Y. Acad. Sci., AAAS. Current Work: Protein chemistry, cell regulation, 2d messenger signalling systems. Subspecialties: Biochemistry (medicine); Biochemistry (biology). Office: Dept Biochemistry U Ky Med Ctr Lexington KY 40536

VANATTA, JOHN CROTHERS, III, physiology educator, researcher; b. Lafayette, Ind., Apr. 22, 1919; s. John Crothers Jr. and Ida Lahr (Raub) V.; m. Carol Lee Geisler, July 30, 1944; children—Lynn Ellen, Paul Richard. A.B. in Chemistry, Ind. U., 1941; M.D., 1944. Diplomate Am. Bd. Internal Medicine. Intern, then resident Wayne County Gen. Hosp., Detroit, 1944-47; fellow Southwestern Med. Coll., Dallas, 1947-49; instr. in physiology Southwestern Med. Sch., U. Tex., 1949-50, asst. prof., 1950-53, assoc. prof., 1953-57, prof., 1957—; cons. div. nuclear edn. AEC, Washington, 1964-67; adj. prof. So. Meth. U., Dallas, 1969-81. Author: (with others) Moyer's Fluid Balance, 2d edit. 1976, 3d edit., 1982; (programmed text) Oxygen Transport, Hypoxia and Cyanosis, 1974. Councilman, First United Luth. Ch., Dallas, 1950—, v.p., 1974, 79; pres. Luth. Health Care Council, Dallas, 1980-81. Served to lt. (j.g.) MC, USNR, 1945-46. Mem. Am. Physiol. Soc., AMA, Soc. Exptl. Biology and Medicine, Sigma Xi. Republican. Current work: Epithelial transport of ions, electrolyte metabolism. Subspecialties: Physiology (medicine); Membrane biology. Home: 10416 Remington Ln Dallas TX 75229 Office: Univ Tex Health Sci Ctr Physiology Dept 5323 Harry Hines Blvd Dallas TX 75235

VAN BEAUMONT, KAREL WILLEM, physiology educator, researcher; b. Amsterdam, The Netherlands, Sept. 26, 1930; came to U.S. 1957. naturalized 1967; s. Cornelis Karel and Anna Marie (Meilink) Van B.; m. Sheila Irene Lindsay, June 26, 1959; children—Eric Franklin, Roy William. Master's P.E., U. Louvain, Belgium, 1956; M.S. in Physiology, U. Ill., 1962; Ph.D. in Physiology, Ind. U., 1965. Instr. physiology Ind. U., Bloomington, 1964-66; research physiologist Proctor & Gamble, Cin., 1966-68; asst. prof. physiology St. Louis U., 1968-73, assoc. prof., 1973—. Contbr. articles to profl. jours. Field hockey coach 1980 U.S. Women's Olympic team, 1980. Fellow Am. Coll. Sports Medicine; mem. Am. Physiol. soc., Sigma Xi. Current work: Exercise and environmental physiology, thermoregulation, hematology, cyclic activity of sweat glands, thermoregulation problems in paraplegics, burn patients, cutaneous sensations during exercise. Subspecialty: Physiology (medicine). Office: St Louis Univ Sch Med 1402 S Grand Blvd Saint Louis MO 63104

VAN BIBBER, KARL ALBERT, physicist; b. New London, Conn., Dec. 5, 1950; s. Max Arnold and Sylvia Dora (Silverio) Van B. B.S. in Physics and Math., MIT, 1972, Ph.D. in Physics, 1976. Instr. MIT, Cambridge, 1976-77; research assoc. Lawrence Berkeley Lab., Calif., 1977-79; asst. prof. physics Stanford U., Calif., 1980-85; physicist Lawrence Livermore Nat. Lab., 1985—. Contbr. articles to profl. jours. Alfred P. Sloan Found. fellow, 1982—. Mem. Am. Phys. Soc., Sigma Xi, Phi Beta Kappa (exec. com. Stanford U. 1982—). Roman Catholic. Current work: Electromagnetic nuclear physics; study of the nuclear response function; heavy ion nuclear physics. Subspecialty: Nuclear physics. Home: 600 21st Ave San Francisco CA 94121 Office: Dept Physics Stanford U Stanford CA 94305

VANBLARICOM, GLENN RICHARD, marine ecologist; b. Shelton, Wash., Apr. 16, 1949. B.S. in Oceanography and Zoology magna cum laude, U. Wash., Seattle, 1972; Ph.D. in Oceanography, U. Calif.-San Diego, 1978. Wildlife biologist U.S. Fish and Wildlife Service, San Simeon, Calif., 1977—, research assoc. Inst. for Marine Studies, U. Calif.-Santa Cruz, 1984—; mem. Species Survival Commn., Internat. Union for Conservation of Nature and Natural Resources, Gland, Switzerland, 1981—. Contbr. articles to profl. jours. Mem. Phi Beta Kappa, Phi Eta Sigma. Current work: Experimental and descriptive analysis of roles of marine mammals in coastal ecosystems; effects of offshore oil development on coastal ecosystems. Subspecialties: Ecology (biology); Marine biology. Office: US Fish and Wildlife Service Inst for Marine Studies Applied Scis Bldg U Calif Santa Cruz CA 95064

VAN BRUNT, RICHARD JOSEPH, physicist; b. Jersey City, May 11, 1939; s. Martin Joseph and Dorothy (Arnold) Van B.; m. Virginia Wargelin, Sept. 1, 1962; 1 child, Nicholas. B.S. in Physics, Math., U. Fla.-Gainesville, 1961; M.S. in Physics, U. Fla., 1964; Ph.D., U. Colo., 1969. Research-teaching asst. U. Fla., 1961-64; physicist Nat. Bur. Standards, Washington, 1961-64, research physicist, 1978—; research asst. Joint Inst. Lab. Astrophysics, Nat. Bur. Standards, U. Colo., Boulder, 1964-69, research physicist, 1975-78; asst. prof. physics U. Va., Charlottesville, 1969-75; faculty fellow NASA-Goddard Space Flight Ctr., Greenbelt, Md., 1974. Contbr. chpts. to books and numerous articles in field to profl. jours. Recipient Bronze medal U.S. Dept. Commerce, 1984. Mem. Am Phys. Soc., Am. Assn. Physics Tchrs., IEEE, AAAS. Current work: Conducting basic research on physics of electric discharges in gases, plasma chemistry and atomic and molecular ionization and collision processes; responsible for high-voltage ac calibration service at Nat. Bur. Standards. Subspecialties: Atomic and molecular physics; Plasma physics. Office: Nat Bur Standards Bldg 200 Room B344 Gaithersburg MD 20899

VAN BURKALOW, ANASTASIA, geology and geography educator, researcher; b. Buchanan, N.Y., Mar. 16, 1911; d. James Turley and Mabel Ritchie (Ramsay) Van B. B.A. magna cum laude, Hunter Coll., 1931; M.A., Columbia U., 1933, Ph.D., 1944. Research asst. Columbia U., N.Y.C., 1934-37; research and editorial asst. Am. Geog. Soc., N.Y.C., 1945-48; from tutor to full prof. Hunter Coll. of CUNY, 1938-45, 1948-75, prof. emeritus, 1976—; cons. geologist E.I. duPont de Nemours, Wilmington, Del., 1945-59. Editor: Megalopolis (Jean Gottman), 1961; Jour. Geol. Edn., 1954-57; contbg. editor Geog. Rev., 1949-72. Contbr. articles to profl. jours. Kemp fellow, 1937-38. Fellow Geol. Soc. Am., N.Y. Acad. Scis. (sec. geology sect. 1955-57), AAAS, Am. Geog. Soc.; mem. Assn. Am. Geographers, Nat. Council Geog. Edn., Am. Geophys. Union. Current work: Research in medical geography. Subspecialty: Geomorphology; Medical geography. Home and Office: 160 E 95th St New York NY 10128

VAN CAMPEN, LYNN, pharmaceutical scientist; b. Bryn Mawr, Pa., Feb. 1, 1948; d. Berington Rathbun and Mary (Walton) Van C. B.S. in Chemistry, Mary Washington Coll. U. Va., 1969; M.S. in pharmacy, U. Wis.-Madison, 1979, Ph.D., 1981. Research technician Pfizer, Inc., Groton, Conn., 1970-76; sr. scientist Boehringer Ingelheim Pharm., Inc., Ridgefield, Conn., 1981—; mem. U. Wis. Extension Planning com. Nat. Indsl. Pharm. Research Conf., Madison, 1982—; mem. task force on acad. programming Am. Pharm. Assn., Acad. Pharm. Sci., Washington, 1984—; Contbr. articles to profl. jours. Town chmn. Am. Cancer Soc., Groton, Conn., 1973-74, unit chmn., New London County, Conn., 1975; Jr. Achievement leader, Groton, 1972. Fellow Am. Found. Pharm. Edn., 1977-80. Mem. Am. Pharm. Assn. (Ebert prize, 1984), Am. Chem. Soc., Acad. Pharm. Scis., Sigma Xi., Rho Chi. Republican. Club: Danbury Health and Racquetball. Current work: Pharmaceutical solids characterization and formulation; nature of hygroscopicity; kinetics of deliquescence; thermal analysis; solid state stability. Subspecialties: Drug delivery systems; Drug design. Home: Fanton Rd Danbury CT 06811 Office: Boehringer Ingelheim Pharm Inc 90 E Ridge PO Box 368 Ridgefield CT 06877

VANDEBERG, JOHN LEE, geneticist; b. Appleton, Wis., June 14, 1947; s. Gale LeRoy and Zona Idell (Raine) VandeB.; m. Jane Frances Barr, Mar. 29, 1975; children: Jason Cash, James Robert. B.S., U. Wis., 1969; B.Sc. with honors, La Trobe U., Australia, 1970; Ph.D., Macquarie U., Australia, 1975. Research assoc., postdoctoral fellow lab. genetics U. Wis., Madison, 1975-79, asst. scientist lab. genetics and Wis. Regional Primate Research Ctr., 1979-80; dir., assoc. scientist dept. genetics Southwest Found. Biomed. Research, San Antonio, 1980—; asst. prof. dept. pathology and dept. cellular and structural biology U. Tex. Health Sci. Ctr., San Antonio, 1980—82, assoc. prof., 1982—; mem. internat. awards rev. group NIH, 1981-83; mem. com. animal models and genetic stocks NRC, 1982—; mem. sci. adv. council Tex. Research and Tech. Found., 1985—. Contbr. articles to profl. jours. Recipient award of Merit Gamma Sigma Delta, 1967; Fulbright fellow, 1969-70. Mem. AAAS, Tex. Genetics Soc., Genetics Soc. Am., Am. Heart Assn., Sigma Xi. Current Work: Biochemical genetics of mammals; genetic control of heart disease. Subspecialty: Genetics and genetic engineering (biology). Office: PO Box 28147 San Antonio TX 78284

VANDE HEY, ROBERT CLARENCE, biology educator; b. Hollandtown, Wis., July 19, 1924; s. Peter Joseph and Odelia Mary (Meulenmans) V.; B.A., St. Norbert Coll., 1946; M.S., U. Notre Dame, 1957, Ph.D., 1961. Ordained priest Roman Cath. Ch., 1949. Instr. Southeast Cath. High Sch., Phila., 1949-55, St. Norbert Coll., De Pere, Wis., 1955-56, 1961-62; mem. faculty St. Norbert Coll., De Pere, 1962—, asst. prof., 1962-69, assoc. prof. biology, 1969—. Research fellow NIH, Mainz, Germany, 1963-64. Mem. AAAS, Entomol. Soc. Am., Am. Mosquito Control Assn., Delta Epsilon Sigma, Sigma Xi. Lodge: KC (De Pere, Wis.). Current work: Genetic variability and control of mosquitoes, especially Aedes aegypti and Culex pipiens. Subspecialties: Genetics and genetic engineering (biology); Parasitology. Home: 103 Grant St De Pere WI 54115 Office: St Norbert Coll De Pere WI 54115

VAN DE KAR, LOUIS D., pharmacologist, educator; b. Amsterdam, Netherlands, Apr. 15, 1947; came to U.S., 1975; s. Abraham and Marianne (Barend) Van de K.; m. Susan Lynn Schmitt, Oct. 28, 1978. B.A. in Chemistry, U. Amsterdam, 1971, M.S. in Biochemistry, 1974; Ph.D., U. Iowa, 1978. Postdoctoral fellow U. Calif.-San Francisco, 1978-81; asst. prof. Loyola U., Maywood, Ill., 1981—. Contbr. articles to profl. jours. Fullbright Hays Found. fellow, 1975, NIH postdoctoral fellow, 1980. Mem. Am. Soc. Pharmacology Exptl. Therapeutics, Am. Physiol. Soc., Soc. Neurosci., Internat. Soc. Neuroendocrinology. Current work: Role of brain neurotansmitters in regulation of secretion of renin from the kidney and prolactin and croticosterone; pharmacology of brain serotonin and catecholamines; mechanism of stress induced renin and prolactin secretion. Subspecialties: Neuroendocrinology; Neuropharmacology. Office: Loyola U Chgo Pharmacology 2160 S 1st Ave Maywood IL 60153

VANDELL, WILLIAM RONALD, semiconductor device design engineer, electrical engineer; b. Royal Oak, Mich., May 31, 1957; s. William Alden and Nancy Ruth (Shaffer) VanD.; m. Lori Lee Gorman, Aug. 27, 1977; children—Emily, Wesley. B.S.E.E., Mich. Tech. U., 1979. Mem. tech. staff device design discrete semiconductor Gen. Elec. Co., Syracuse, N.Y., 1979-82, project mgr. advance device design, 1982—. Contbr. articles to profl. jours. Inventor in field. Mem. IEEE, Eta Kappa Nu. Current work: State of the art power semiconductor technology including discrete components, high voltage IC's, subsystems. Subspecialties: Semiconductors; Computer-aided design. Office: Gen Electric Electronics Park Bldg 7 Box 2 Syracuse NY 13221

VAN DE MARK, MICHAEL ROY, chemistry educator; b. Pigeon, Mich., May 21, 1950; s. Roy Donald and Alice Elizabeth (Gremel) Van De M.; m. Suzan Elaine Yelek, Nov. 26, 1976. B.S., Saginaw Valley State Coll., 1972; Ph.D., Texas A&M U., 1976. Assoc. prof., dir. grad. studies in chemistry U. Miami, Coral Gables, Fla., 1978-85, U. Mo.-Rolla, 1986—. Contbr. numerous articles to profl. jours. Mem. Am. Chem. Soc. (Miami subsect. sec./treas. 1979, chmn.-elect 1980, chmn. 1981), Electrochem. Soc., Phi Lambda Upsilon, Sigma Xi. Current Work: Polymer adsorption on surfaces for electrode modification and corrosion inhibition through chelating adsorbed polymers. In addition am involved in synthetic organic electrochemistry and polymer synthesis. Subspecialties: Polymer chemistry; Surface chemistry. Home: 9800 SW 80 Dr Miami FL 33173 Office: U Mo-Rolla Dept Chemistry Rolla MO 65401

VAN DEMARK, NOLAND LEROY, physiologist, educator; b. Columbus Grove, Ohio, July 6, 1919; s. Daniel Leroy and Mary Frances (Bogart) V.; m. Beda Alta Basinger, Aug. 18, 1940; children: Gary Lee, Judy Beth, Linda Kay. B.S., Ohio State U., 1941, M.S., 1942; Ph.D., Cornell U., 1948. Asst. animal husbandry Ohio State U., 1941-42; vitamin chemist, div. plant industry Ohio Dept. Agr., 1942; livestock specialist U.S. Allied Commn. Austria, 1946-47; asst. animal husbandry Cornell U., 1942-44, 48; from asst. prof. to prof. physiology, dept. dairy sci. U. Ill., 1948-64; prof. dairy sci., chmn. dept. Ohio State U. and Ohio Agrl. Research and Devel. Center, 1964-73; dir. research N.Y. State Coll. Agr. and Life Scis.; dir. Cornell U. Agr. Expt. Sta., Ithaca, 1974-81, prof. animal sci., 1974-83, prof. emeritus, 1983—; Disting. Bicentennial prof. U. Ga., winter 1985; cons. on reproductive biology study sect. Nat. Inst. Child Health, 1966-70. Author: (with G. W. Salisbury) Physiology of Reproduction and Artificial Insemination of Cattle, 1961, 78; co-editor, contbr. to: The Testis, 3 vols, 1970. Mem. bd. Community Sch. Dist. 4, Champaign, Ill., 1956-64. Served to 2d lt., inf. and CIC AUS, 1944-46. Recipient Borden award in dairy sci., 1959; Alpha Zeta Outstanding Agr. Tchr. award U. Ill., 1960; Italian Master Pioneer Gold Medal award 5th Internat. Congress Reprodn., Trento, 1964; Ivanov Centennial medal Russia, 1975. Fellow AAAS; mem. Am. Physiol. Soc., Soc. Study Fertility, Am. Dairy Sci. Assn. (chmn. prodn. sect. 1969-70, dir. 1971-74), Soc. for Study Reprodn. (v.p. 1968-69, pres. 1969-70, dir. 1970-71), Am. Soc. Animal Sci., Sigma Xi, Gamma Sigma Delta. Methodist (lay leader). Current Work: Research management and nurturing individual creativity. Subspecialty: Animal physiology. Office: 8801 Leesville Rd Raleigh NC 27612

VAN DEN BERGH, SIDNEY, astronomer; b. Wassenaar, Netherlands, May 20, 1929; emigrated to U.S., 1948; s. Sidney J. and Mieke (van den Berg) vandenB.; m. Gretchen Krause; children by previous marriage: Peter, Mieke, Sabine. Student, Leiden (Netherlands) U., 1947-48; A.B., Princeton U., 1950; M.Sc., Ohio State U., 1952; Dr. rer. nat., Goettingen U., 1956. Asst. prof. Perkins Obs., Ohio State U., Columbus, 1956-58; research assoc. Mt. Wilson Obs., Palomar Obs., Pasadena, Calif., 1968-69; prof. astronomy David Dunlap Obs., U. Toronto, Ont., Can., 1958-77; dir. Dominion Astrophys. Obs., Victoria, B.C., 1977—; dir. Can.-France-Hawaii Telescope Corp. Mem. Am., Royal astron. socs., Royal Soc. Can. Current Work: Galaxies, super noval; star clusters. Subspecialty: Optical astronomy. Home: 418 Lands End Rd Sidney BC Canada Office: Dominion Astrophysic Observatory Victoria BC Canada

VANDEN BOUT, PAUL ADRIAN, astronomer; b. Grand Rapids, Mich., June 16, 1939; s. Adrian and Cornelia (Peterson) Vanden B.; m. Rachel Ann Eggebeen, Sept. 1, 1961; children—Thomas, David. A.B., Calvin Coll., 1961; Ph.D., U. Calif.-Berkeley, 1966. Teaching research asst. U. Calif.-Berkeley, 1961-66, postdoctoral, 1966-67; postdoctoral, asst. prof. Columbia U., N.Y.C., 1967-70; from asst. prof. to prof. astronomy U. Tex., Austin, 1970-84; dir. Nat. Radio Astronomy Obs., Charlottesville, Va., 1985—. Contbr. articles to profl. jours. Fulbright fellow, 1977. Mem. Am. Astron. Soc., Am. Phys. Soc., Internat. Astron. Union, Internat. Radio Sci. Union, AAAS. Current work: Interstellar medium, galactic molecular clouds, star formation. Subspecialty: Radio and microwave astronomy. Office: Nat Radio Astronomy Obs Edgemont Rd Charlottesville VA 22903

VANDENDORPE, MARY MOORE, psychology educator; b. Chgo., June 2, 1947; d. Era William and Mary (Dobis) Moore; m. James Edward Vandendorpe, Aug. 16, 1969; 1 child, Laura. A.B., St. Louis U., 1969; M.S., Ill. Inst. Tech., 1975, Ph.D., 1980. Adj. instr. Ill. Inst. Tech., Chgo., 1975; adj. instr. Lewis U., Romeoville, Ill., 1975-80, asst. prof., 1980—, chmn., 1985—; adult officer, asst. historian Ill. Jr. Acad. Sci., Champaign, 1973-75. Author: History of the Illinois Junior Academy of Science, 1974, Faculty Student Interaction and Undergraduate Careers, 1975, Student Nurses and the Aged, 1980. Mem. Legis. Ednl. Network of DuPage, Naperville, Ill., 1982—; active Naperville Heritage Soc., 1982—, Naperville Humane Soc., 1980—; mem. Naper Carriage Homeowners; bd. dirs. Music Theatre Chgo., 1972-74. Mem. Am. Psychol. Assn., Gerontol. Soc., Chgo. Psychol. Assn. (mem. council 1979-82, pres. 1982-83), Psi Chi, Gamma Pi Epsilon. Current Work: Development of work and family attitudes; human information processing; attitudes towards aging and death. Subspecialties: Developmental psychology; Cognition. Office: Lewis Univ Romeoville IL 60441

VANDERBILT, VERN CORWIN, research engineer; b. Toledo, Feb. 23, 1946; s. Vern Corwin and Gwendolyn (Curry) V.; m. Anne Symon, Aug. 8, 1968 (div. 1984). B.S. in Elec. Engring., Purdue U., 1968, M.S. in Elec. Engring., 1971, Ph.D., 1976. Registered profl. engr., Ind. Postdoctoral fellow Lab. for Applications of Remote Sensing, Purdue U., West Lafayette, Ind., 1977-79, research engr., 1980—; cons. Dynamic Precision Controls, Hagerstown, Ind., 1969-72. Contbr. articles to profl. jours. Chmn. bd. Internat. Ctr., West Lafayette, 1984, vice chmn. programs, 1983, pres. European Club, 1980-84. Mem. IEEE, Am. Soc. Photogrammetry, Am. Inst. Physics, Sigma Xi. Clubs: Purdue Scuba (pres.), Aviation Tech. Flying (v.p. 1974) (West Lafayette). Current work: Optical engineering, remote sensing research, radiation transfer in plant canopies, optical polarization. Subspecialties: Electrical engineering; Remote sensing (geoscience). Home: 1291 Cumberland West Lafayette IN 47906 Office: Lab for Applications of Remote Sensing Purdue U West Lafayette IN 47905

VANDER MEER, ROBERT KENNETH, research chemist; b. Chgo., Nov. 29, 1942; s. Robert Valentine and Marian Kelso (MacBratney) V.; m. Penelope Rae Miller, June 20, 1964; children—Jeffrey Scott, Elizabeth Vanessa. B.A., Blackburn Coll., 1964; M.S., John Carroll U., 1966; Ph.D., Pa. State U., 1972. Asst. prof. U. South Pacific, Suva, Fiji Islands, 1972-76; postdoctoral fellow Cornell U., Ithaca, N.Y., 1976-77; research chemist U.S. Dept. Agr., Agrl. Research Service, Gainesville, Fla., 1977—. Contbr. articles to profl. jours. Inventor method for control of insects. Recipient Superior Service award U.S. Dept. Agr., Gainesville, Fla., 1982; postdoctoral fellow Am. Cancer Soc., Cornell U., 1976-77. Mem. Am. Chem. Soc., Royal Chem. Soc. (Eng.), Entomol. Soc. Am., Fla. Entomol. Soc., Fla. Acad. Scis., Sigma Xi. Current work: Deciphering the chemical codes used by insects to affect intra-species behavior and inter-species behavior, primarily with fire ant, trail pheromones and queen related pheromones. Subspecialties: Organic chemistry; Ethology. Home: 3712 NW 16th Blvd Gainesville FL 32605 Office: US Dept Agr Agrl Research Service PO Box 114565 Gainesville FL 32604

VANDERMEULEN, DAVID LEE, research scientist; b. Des Moines, Sept. 29, 1948; s. Herman Christian and Elma Louise (LeCocq) VanderM.; m. Carol Jean Morelli, Sept. 1, 1979; 1 child, David Christian. B.A. in Physics, Central Coll., 1970; Ph.D. in Biophysics, U. Ill., 1977. Research assoc. U. Ill. Med. Ctr., Chgo., 1977-83; research scientist Baylor Research Inst., Dallas, 1984—. Contbr. articles to profl. jours. Research fellow Muscular Dystrophy Assoc., 1980-81. Mem. Biophys. Soc., Sigma Xi. Republican. Mem. Assembly of God Ch. Current work: Biochemistry and biophysics of muscle proteins utilizing spectroscopic techniques. Subspecialties: Biochemistry (biology); Biophysics (biology). Office: Baylor Research Inst Pathology Dept 3500 Gaston Ave Dallas TX 75246

VAN DER POEL, JAN M., electrical engineer; b. Geldrop, The Netherlands, Dec. 3, 1929, came to U.S., 1957, naturalized, 1978; s. Cornelius and Helena (Wouts) V.; m. Elizabeth J. Rouleaux; Jan. 19, 1957; children—John A., Ronald F., Andrew P., Raina E. Student Philips Nyverheids Sch. and Hogere Technische Sch., Eindhoven, Holland. Electrician, Philips, Holland, 1947-48, design engr., 1954-57; mfg. engr. Western Elec., Kearny, N.J., 1957-61; engr., mgr. of engrs. Ferroxcube, Saugerties, N.Y., 1961—. Contbr. articles to profl. jours. Served to 1st lt. Dutch Army, 1953-54. Mem. IEEE (sr.). Republican. Roman Catholic. Current work: Use of ferrite components in the design of magnetic devices. Subspecialty: Applied magnetics. Office: Ferroxcube Div 5083 Kings Hwy Saugerties NY 12477

VANDERSLICE, THOMAS AQUINAS, computer manufacturing company executive; b. Phila., Jan. 8, 1932; s. Joseph R. and Mae (Daly) V.; m. Margaret Hurley, June 9, 1956; children: Thomas Aquinas, Paul Thomas Aquinas, John Thomas Aquinas, Peter Thomas Aquinas. B.S. in Chemistry and Philosophy, Boston Coll., 1953; Ph.D. in Chemistry and Physics, Catholic U. Am., 1956. With Gen. Electric Co., 1956—, gen. mgr. electronic components bus. div., 1970-72, v.p., 1970—, group exec. spl. systems and products group, Fairfield, Conn., 1972-77; sr. v.p., sector exec. Gen. Electric Co. (Power Systems Sector), 1977-79, exec. v.p., sector exec., 1979; pres., chief operating officer, dir. Gen. Telephone & Electronics Corp., Stamford, Conn., 1979—; pres., chief exec. officer Apollo Computer, Inc., Chelmsford, Mass., 1984—; dir. Texaco Inc., Emery Worldwide. Co-author: Ultra High Vacuum and Its Applications, 1963; reviser: Scientific Foundations of Vacuum Technique, 1960; Contbr. to profl. jours. Trustee Boston Coll., Com. Econ. Devel.; mem. steering com. Econ. Policy Council UNA. Fulbright scholar, 1953-56; recipient Golden Plate award Acad. Achievement, 1963; Bicentennial medallion Boston Coll., 1976. Mem. Nat. Acad. Engring., Conn. Acad. Sci. and Engring., Am. Vacuum Soc., ASTM, Am. Chem. Soc., Am. Inst. Physics, Sigma Xi, Tau Beta Pi, Alpha Sigma Nu, Sigma Pi Sigma. Clubs: Conn. Golf (Easton, Conn.); Patterson (Fairfield). Patentee low pressure gas measurements and analysis, gas surface interactions and elec. discharge. Subspecialty: Electrical research; manufacturing management. Office: Apollo Computer Inc 330 Billerica Rd Chelmsford MA 01824

VANDER SLUIS, KENNETH L., physicist; b. Holland, Mich., Dec. 19, 1925; s. Leonard and Jennie (Vander Woude) Vander S.; m. Joan Harvie, June 14, 1962; children: Lisa Joan, Stephen Harvie, David Kenneth. Student, U. Notre Dame, 1945-46; B.S., Baldwin Wallace Coll., 1947; M.S., Pa. State U., 1950, Ph.D. in Physics, 1952. Physicist Oak Ridge Nat. Lab., 1952—. Subspecialty: Laser systems. Address: 954 West Outer Dr Oak Ridge TN 37830

VAN DER VOO, ROB, geology educator, geophysics research; b. Utrecht, Netherlands, Aug. 4, 1940; came to U.S., 1970; s. Maximiliaan and Johanna Hendrika (Baggerman) Van Der V.; m. Tatina M.C. Graafland, Mar. 26, 1966; children—Serge Nicolas, Bjorn Alexander. B.Sc., U. Utrecht, Netherlands, 1961, M.Sc. in Geology, 1965, M.Sc. in Geophysics, 1969, Ph.D., 1969. Vis. asst. prof. U. Mich., Ann Arbor, 1970-72, asst. prof., 1972-75, prof. geology, 1979—, chmn., 1981—. Contbr. articles to profl. jours. Recipient Russell award U. Mich., 1976. Fellow Am. Geophys. Union, Geol. Soc. Am.; mem. Royal Acad. Scis. Netherlands (corr.), Geologische Vereinigung, Royal Geol. Mining Soc. Netherlands. Current work: Paleomagnetism and tectonics and applications to structural geology and geodynamics. Subspecialties: Tectonics; Geophysics. Home: 909 5th St Ann Arbor MI 48103 Office: U Mich Dept Geol Scis Ann Arbor MI 48109

VANDER WOUDE, JACK CLARENCE, retired manufacturing company executive; b. Chgo., Oct. 27, 1918; s. George and Gertrude (Vander Meer) Vander W.; m. Jeannette Helen Uddenberg, July 27, 1946; children—Jean Helen, Lois Claire, Richard John, Robert Charles. A.B., Calvin Coll., 1939; B.S., Ill. Inst. Tech., 1941. Chem. engr. Tenn. Eastman Co., Kingsport, 1941-50; dept. supt. Tex. Eastman Co., Longview, 1950, asst. div. supt., 1961, works mgr., 1968, v.p., works mgr., 1970, v.p., asst. mgr., 1972, pres., 1975-83; mem. adv. council Engring. Found., Coll. Engring., U. Tex., Austin, 1977—. Bd. dirs. Tex. Ind. Coll. Fund, 1979-85, Civic Music Assn., Longview, 1951—; founding pres. Longview Mus. and Art Center, 1972-74; bd. dirs. Good Shepherd Med. Center, 1976—; pres. bd. trustees, 1981; dir. First Nat. Bank of Longview; bd. dirs. Greater Longview United Way, 1962-81. Served with USN, 1944-46. Mem. Am. Chem. Soc., Am. Inst. Chem. Engrs., Alpha Chi Sigma, Phi Lambda Upsilon, Tau Beta Pi. Presbyterian. Clubs: Pinecrest Country, Summit. Patentee in field. . Home: 7 Bramlette Pl Longview TX 75601

VAN DER ZIEL, JAN PETER, solid state physicist; b. Eindhoven, Netherlands, Aug. 17, 1937; came to U.S., 1950; s. Aldert and Jantina J. (de Wit) van der Z.; m. Madeline J. Lange, Sept. 11, 1965; children—Nancy J., Peter G. B.S. in Elec. Engring., U. Minn., 1959; M.S., Harvard U., 1961, Ph.D., 1964. Post-doctoral fellow Harvard U., Cambridge, Mass., 1964-65; mem. tech. staff AT & T Bell Labs., Murray Hill, N.J., 1965—. Contbr. chpts. to books, articles to profl. jours. Mem. IEEE (sr.), Am. Phys. Soc. Congregationalist. Current work: Semiconductor lasers for optical communications. Subspecialties: Semiconductor lasers; Condensed matter physics. Office: AT & T Bell Labs 600 Mountain Ave Murray Hill NJ 07974

VANDESTEEG, GREGG ALAN, laboratory administrator, organic chemist; b. Melrose, Minn., Feb. 20, 1949; s. Gerald Henry and Vernette Margaret (Carlson) V.; m. Marcia Marie White, May 31, 1971; children—Michelle, Nathan. B.A. in Chemistry, St. Olaf Coll., 1971; Ph.D. in Organic Chemistry, U. Minn., 1976. Research chemist central research 3M, St. Paul, 1976-78, supr. chem. research central research, 1978-81, mgr. materials research I & C sector, 1981-83, product devel. mgr. dental products div., 1983-84, lab. mgr. dental products div., 1984—. Patentee in field. Mem. Am. Chem. Soc., AAAS, Internat. Assn. Dental Research, U. Minn. Inst. Tech. Alumni Soc. (dir. 1978-83, pres. 1984). Club: St. Paul Curling. Current work: Materials research in dental composite restoratives and agents which bond to tooth structure; silicones, fluorochemicals. Subspecialties: Organic chemistry; Dental materials. Office: Dental Products Lab 3M Ctr 260-2B-09 Saint Paul MN 55144

VAN DE VAART, HERMAN, physicist; b. Arnhem, Netherlands, Apr. 11, 1934; came to U.S., 1960; s. Herman and Elizabeth (Sinke) Van De V.; m. Tania Skrinnikov, June 22, 1982. M.S., Inst. Tech., Delft, Netherlands, 1958, Ph.D., 1967. Research staff mem. Sperry Research Ctr., Sudbury, Mass., 1962-73, dept. mgr., 1973-81, dir. applied physics lab., 1981-84; dir. research Sawtek, Orlando, Fla., 1984; mgr. electronics and optical physics Allied Corp., Morristown, N.J., 1985—. Contbr. articles to sci. jours.; patentee in field. Served to 1st lt. Dutch Army, 1958-60. Mem. IEEE (sr. mem.; pres. Group on Sonics and Ultrasonics 1984—, sec., treas. 1981-84), Am. Phys. Soc. Current work: Materials, ultrasonics, optics, magnetics. Subspecialties: Electronics; Magnetic physics. Office: Allied Corp PO Box 1021 R Morristown NJ 07960

VAN DE WALLE, CHRIS GILBERT, electrical engineer, researcher; b. Gent, Belgium, May 10, 1959; came to U.S., 1982; s. Gaston Eduard and Louise Armanda (DeMoor) Van De W. Degree in Elec. Engring., Rijksuniversiteit Gent, 1982; M.S.E.E., Stanford U., 1983. Research asst. Stanford U., Calif., 1983—; cons. Xerox, Palo Alto, Calif., 1984—. Recipient City of Gent prize, 1982. Mem. Flemings in the World, Koninklijke Vlaamse Ingenieursvereniging, IEEE, Am. Phys. Soc. Current work: Density functional calculations of solid state materials and applications to interfaces. Subspecialties: Condensed matter physics; Semiconductors. Home: 728 Mayfield Ave Stanford CA 94305 Office: Stanford Electronics Labs McCullough 238 Stanford CA 94305

VAN DE WATER, THOMAS ROGER, scientist, laboratory administrator, medical educator; b. Oceanside, N.Y., Dec. 6, 1939; s. Lynn Patterson and Leonora (Winterson) Van De W.; m. Jeanette Adele Vilece, July 11, 1964; children: Ann Marie, Thomas Scott, Christopher Michael, Elizabeth Adele. A.A.S. in Forestry, Pauls Smiths Coll., 1959; B.S. in Biology, Western Carolina U., 1961; M.S., Hofstra U., 1965; Ph.D. in Biology, N.Y. U., 1976. Research assoc. Yale U. Sch. Medicine, 1964-65; research scientist N.Y. U. Med. Sch., 1966-68; research assoc., instr. Albert Einstein Coll. Medicine, 1968-75, asst. prof. otolaryngology and neurosci., 1976-81, assoc. prof., 1981—; vis. prof. Karolinska Inst., Stockholm, 1976-77; cons. communications disorders panel NIH, Washington; dir. Devel. Otobiology Lab., Bronx, N.Y., 1976—; spl. reviewer grant study sect. NIH, Bethesda, Md., 1982-83; invited lectr. Chaba sect. Nat. Acad. Sci., 1979; participant Nobel Symposium, 1985. Regional rep. Catholic Charismatic Renewal, Nassau County, N.Y., 1980-82; field cons. Nassau County council Boy Scouts Am., 1981; bd. dirs. Cath. Fellowship, 1977-82. Served with U.S. Army, 1962. Swedish Med. Research Council grantee, 1976-77; NIH grantee, 1980-85; March of Dimes Birth Defects Found. grantee, 1983, 85; Am. Otol. Found. grantee, 1983. Mem. N.Y. Acad. Sci., Am. Assn. Anatomists (pres. Morphogenesis Club 1983-84), Assn. Research in Otolaryngology, Internat. Soc. Devel. Neurosci., Soc. Developmental Biology (organizer symposium). Current Work: Investigation of tissue interactions during development of inner ear that result in normal and abnormal morphogenesis employing techniques of organ culture, ultrastructure, biochemistry, teratology, genetic mutations and immunocytochemistry. Subspecialties: Cell and tissue culture; Developmental biology. Home: 262 Pennsylvania Ave Freeport NY 11520 Office: Albert Einstein Coll Medicine 1300 Morris Park Ave Bronx NY 10461

VAN DILLA, MARVIN ALBERT, biophysicist; b. N.Y.C., June 18, 1919; s. Albert and Hattie (Isenberg) Van D.; children from previous marriage—Teresa, Peter, Laura, Wendy. B.S., CCNY, 1939; Ph.D., MIT, 1951. Sr. scientist U. Utah, Salt Lake City, 1951-57, Los Alamos Nat. Lab., 1957-72; sect. leader Lawrence Livermore Lab., Calif., 1972-82, sr. scientist, 1983—; sabbatical U. Calif., Berkeley, 1982-83. Editor: Flow Cytometry: Instrumentation and Data Analysis, 1985. Mem. AAAS, Soc. Analytical Cytology. Democrat. Unitarian. Current work: Flow cytometry and sorting; instrumentation and applications to cell biology, cytogenetics, cell kinetics, cancer; genetic engineering; gene library construction; biotechnology. Subspecialties: Biophysics (biology); Genetics and genetic engineering (biology). Office: Biomed Scis Div Lawrence Livermore Nat Lab Livermore CA 94550

VAN DOLAH, ROBERT FREDERICK, marine ecologist, institute administrator; b. Portland, Oreg., Nov. 4, 1949; s. Robert Wayne and Elizabeth (Becker) Van D.; m. Frances Matthews, May 26, 1979; 1 child, Elizabeth Rebecca. B.S., Marietta Coll., 1971; M.S., U. Md., 1975, Ph.D., 1977. Teaching asst. U. Md., College Park, 1971-77; asst. marine scientist S.C. Marine Resources Research Inst., Charleston, 1978-84, assoc. marine scientist, 1984, asst. dir., 1984—. Contbr. sci. papers to profl. lit. Recipient Von Alexander biol. award Tau Kappa Epsilon; Messerly biol. award Marietta Coll. Mem. Ecol. Soc. Am., Southeastern Estuarine Research Soc., Estuarine Research Fedn., Sigma Xi, Beta Beta Beta. Current work: Population and community ecology with emphasis on regulatory processes operating in marine and estuarine systems. Subspecialties: Ecology (biology); Marine biology. Home: 809 S Channel St Charleston SC 29412 Office: SC Marine Resources Research Inst PO Box 12559 Charleston SC 29412

VAN DRIEL, HENRY MARTIN, physicist, educator; b. Breda, Netherlands, Dec. 27, 1946; s. John Cornelis and Anna Marie (Marijnissen) Van D.; m. Christine Marie Dent, June 27, 1970; children: Martin, Katherine, Peter. B.Sc., U. Toronto, 1970, M.Sc., 1971, Ph.D., 1975. Research assoc. U. Ariz., 1975-76; asst. prof. physics U. Toronto, 1976-81, assoc. prof., 1982-85, prof., 1985—; cons. optics cos. Contbr. articles to profl. jours. Mem. Can. Assn. Physics, Optical Soc. Am., Am. Phys. Soc. Roman Catholic. Current Work: Laser interactions with semiconductors. Subspecialty: Condensed matter physics. Home: 386 Clarksville Ct Mississauga ON L5A 1G8 Canada Office: Dept Physics U Toronto Toronto ON M5A 1A7 Canada

VAN DYKE, MILTON DENMAN, aeronautical engineering educator; b. Chgo., Aug. 1, 1922; s. James Richard and Ruth (Barr) Van D.; m. Sylvia Jean Agard Adams, June 16, 1962; children: Russell B., Eric J., Nina A., Brooke A. and Byron J. and Christopher M. (triplets). B.S., Harvard U., 1943; M.S., Calif. Inst. Tech., 1947, Ph.D., 1949. Research engr. NACA, 1943-46, 50-54, 55-58; vis. prof. U. Paris, France, 1958- 59; prof. aero. Stanford, 1959—; cons. aerospace industry, 1949—; pres. Parabolic Press. Author: Perturbation Methods in Fluid Mechanics, 1964, An Album of Fluid Motion, 1982. Served with USNR, 1944-46. Guggenheim and Fulbright fellow, 1954-55. Mem. Am. Acad. Arts and Scis., Nat. Acad. Engring., Am. Phys. Soc., Phi Beta Kappa, Sigma Xi, Sierra Club. Current Work: Perturbation methods in fluid mechanics. Subspecialties: Fluid mechanics; Aeronautical engineering. Office: Div Applied Mechanics Stanford Univ Stanford CA 94305

VAN DYKE, THOMAS ELLIOTT, periodontist, researcher; b. Rockville Centre, N.Y., July 14, 1947; s. Charles Henry and Eleanor Frances (Schmeis) Van D.; m. Barbara Rowdybush, Aug. 30, 1969; children—Charles Brinton, William Heaney. B.A. in Natural Sci., Case Western Res. U., 1969, D.D.S., 1973; M.S. in Oral Scis., SUNY-Buffalo, 1979, cert. periodontology, 1980, Ph.D. in Oral Biology, 1982. Clin. research instr. SUNY-Buffalo, 1976-80, clin. asst. prof., 1980-82; asst. prof. Emory U., Atlanta, 1982—; assoc. dir. Perio research Ctr, Atlanta; dir. Grad. Periodontics, Atlanta; guest researcher Ctrs. Disease Control, Atlanta. Contbr. articles to profl. jours. Served to major, U.S. Army, 1973-76. Recipient Balint Orban Meml. prize, 1981. Mem. Am. Assn. for Dental Research, Internat. Assn. for Dental Research, Am. Acad. of Periodontology, Ga. Soc. of Periodontology, Am. Soc. Microbiologists, Psi Omega (pres. chpt. 1972-73). Current work: Neutrophil biology; molecular biology of neutrophil function; pathogenesis of periodontal disease. Subspecialties: Periodontics; Oral biology. Office: Dept Periodontology Emory Dental Sch 1462 Clifton Rd NE Atlanta GA 30322

VANE, SYLVIA BRAKKE, anthropologist; b. Fillmore County, Minn., Feb. 28, 1918; d. John T. and Hulda Christina (Marburger) Brakke; m. Arthur Bayard Vane, May 17, 1942; children—Ronald Arthur, Linda Joyce, Laura Mae. A.A., Rochester Jr. Coll., 1937; B.S. with distinction, U. Minn., 1939; postgrad. Radcliffe Coll., 1944; M.A., Calif. State U., 1975. Cons., Sonoma Engring. & Research, Santa Rosa, Calif., 1971-75; cons. in inter-ethnic relations, Menlo Park, 1975-78; v.p. Cultural Systems Research, Inc., Menlo Park, 1978—; pres. Ballena Press, Menlo Park, 1981—; cons. in cultural resource mgmt., various cos. Author: (with Lowell John Bean) Primary Resources: California Indians, 1976, Cahuilla and Santa Rosa Mountain Region, 1981. Contbr. articles to profl. jours. Bd. dirs. Sequoia Area council Girl Scouts U.S.A., 1954-62, Community Com. for Internat. Students, Stanford U., 1964, 77; bd. dirs. San Mateo County chpt. LWV, 1958-68, pres., 1965-66. Fellow Soc. for Applied Anthropology, Am. Anthropol. Assn., Southwestern Anthropol. Assn. (past bd. dirs.), Soc. for Am. Archaeology. Republican. Mem. United Ch. of Christ. Current work: Analysis of water supply and irrigation systems on Southern California Indian reservations and effect on ecological system as whole; interdisciplinary studies of human occupation in two canyons Palm Springs, California. Subspecialties: Resource management; Ecosystems analysis. Home: 823 Valparaiso Ave Menlo Park CA 94025 Office: Cultural Systems Research Inc 823 Valparaiso Ave Menlo Park CA 94025

VAN ECHO, DAVID ANDREW, medical oncologist, educator; b. Ft. Wayne, Ind., July 19, 1947; s. Andrew and Elizabeth Jane (Lauer) Van E.; m. M. Kathleen Barry, Apr. 17, 1971; children—David C., Matthew A., Kyra N. B.A., Xavier U., 1969; M.D., U. Md., 1973. Diplomate Am. Bd. Internal Medicine, Am. Bd. Medical Oncology. Intern. U. Md., 1973-74, resident, 1974-75, asst. prof. medicine, 1979, assoc. prof. oncology Cancer Ctr., 1981—, assoc. prof. medicine, 1983—; clin. assoc. Balt. Cancer Research Program, Div. Cancer Treatment, Nat. Cancer Inst., 1975-77, investigator, 1977-78, sr. investigator, 1978-81, cons. grants and rev. br., 1983—; chief sect. med. oncology Balt. VA Med. Ctr., 1982-84, mem. Tumor Bd., 1982; prin. investigator phase II studies in acute leukemia, primary liver cancer, breast and non-Hodgkin's lymphoma, 1981, vice chmn. chemotherapy com. 1982. Contbr. chpts. to books and numerous articles to profl. jours. Served with USPHS, 1975-80. Mem. Am. Soc. Clin. Oncology, Am. Assn. Cancer Research. Subspecialties: Oncology; Cancer research (medicine). Office: Univ Maryland Cancer Ctr 22 S Greene St Baltimore MD 21201

VANFLEET, HOWARD BAY, physics educator; b. Salt Lake City, June 5, 1931; s. Willard and Celia May (Bay) V.; m. Helen Haacke, Sept. 17, 1954; children—Pamela, Vennette, Howard, James, May Lyn, David, Richard. B.S., Brigham Young U., 1955; Ph.D., U. Utah, 1961. Nuclear engr. Gen. Dynamics, Fort Worth, 1956-57; prof. physics, chmn. dept. physics and astronomy Brigham Young U., Provo, Utah, 1960—; sr. research physicist Fort Monmouth, N.Y., 1966-67; vis. prof. Am. U., Cairo, Egypt, 1973-74. Contbr. articles to profl. publs. Served to cpl. U.S. Army, 1952-54, Korea. Grantee U.S. Air Force Office Sci. Research, 1962-64, 64-66, NSF, 1969-77; faculty fellow Brigham Young U., 1964-65, 68-69; recipient Karl G. Maeser Research and Creative Arts award Brigham Young U., 1973. Mem. Am. Phys. Soc., Am. Assn. Physics Tchrs., Sigma Xi, Sigma Pi Sigma. Subspecialty: Condensed matter physics. Home: 1722 N 1500 E Provo UT 84604 Office: Brigham Young U Dept Physics and Astronomy Provo UT 84602

VAN HOUTEN, JUDITH LEE, geneticist, educator; b. Paterson, N.J., Apr. 26, 1948; d. Charles D. and Jean T. Post; m. John C. Van Houten, Dec. 23, 1967; 1 dau., June H. Student, Elizabethtown Coll., 1965-68, U. Del., 1969-70; B.S., Pacific Luth. U., 1972; Ph.D., U. Calif., Santa Barbara, 1976. NIH postdoctoral researcher dept. pharmacology U. B.C., 1977-79; vis. asst. prof. U. Iowa, Iowa City, 1979-80; asst. prof. dept. zoology U. Vt., Burlington, 1980—. Contbr. articles to profl. publs. Grantee NIH; Grantee NSF. Mem. Soc. Neurosci., Am. Soc. Cell Biology, European Chemoreception Research Orgn., Assn. Chemoreception Scis., N.Y. Acad Scis., AAAS, Soc. Protozoologists, Sigma Xi. Current Work: Chemoreception and related membrane phenomena in normal and mutant paramecia. Research in genetic dissection, membrane biology, ciliary motility, sensory transduction im microorganisms; teaching of general, neurobehavioral, cell cycle and developmental genetics. Subspecialties: Membrane biology; Gene actions. Office: Dept Zoology U Vt Burlington VT 05405

VAN HOVEN, GERARD, physics educator; b. Los Angeles, Nov. 23, 1932; s. Aaron and Josephine (Hoppenjans) Van H.; m. Barbara Hoxie, Dec. 29, 1956; children: Enid, Ian. B.S., Calif. Inst. Tech., 1954; Ph.D., Stanford U., 1963. Mem. tech. staff Bell Telephone Labs., 1954-56; electron physicist Gen. Electric Co., Palo Alto, Calif., 1956-63; research assoc. W.W. Hansen Labs. Physics, Stanford U., 1963-65; research physicist Inst. Plasma Research, 1965-68; asst. prof. to assoc. prof. U. Calif.-Irvine, 1968-79, prof. physics, 1979—; Fulbright fellow Vienna Tech. U., 1963-64; cons. Gen. Electric Co., 1963-65, Varian Assocs., 1965-68, Smithsonian Astrophys. Obs., 1975, Aerospace Corp., 1975-77; Langley-Abbot vis. scientist Ctr. Astrophysics, Harvard U., 1975; vis. astrophysicist Oss Astrofisico Arcetri, 1976, 82. Contbr. articles to profl. jours. Mem. Am. Phys. Soc., Am. Astron. Soc., Internat. Astron. Union. Current Work: Plasma instabilities in solar physics. Subspecialties: Plasma physics; Theoretical astrophysics. Office: Dept Physics U Calif Irvine CA 92717

VANKO, DAVID ALAN, geologist, educator; b. Balt., Oct. 31, 1954; s. John James and Audrey (Buechler) V.; m. Carol Appleby, Aug. 25, 1979. B.A. and M.A. with honors, Johns Hopkins U., 1976; Ph.D., Northwestern U., 1982. Postdoctoral fellow Washington U. and McDonnell Ctr. for Space Scis., St. Louis, 1982-83; asst. prof. geology Ga. State U., Atlanta, 1983—. Contbr. articles to profl. jours., 1982—. Pres.'s fellow Northwestern U., Evanston, Ill., 1977. Mem. Geol. Soc. Am., Mineral Soc. Am., Can. Mineral. Assn., Am. Geophys. Union, AAAS. Democrat. Current work: Petrology of igneous and metamorphic ocean crustal rocks; hydrothermal fluid-rock interaction. Subspecialties: Petrology; Sea floor spreading. Office: Ga State U Dept Geology Atlanta GA 30303

VAN LANDINGHAM, SAMUEL LEIGHTON, environmentalist, geologist, consultant, researcher; b. Iraan, Tex., Aug. 25, 1935; s. Grady Richard and Winnie (Fry) Van L.; m. Becky Jean Ball, Dec. 28, 1967. B.S. in Geology, Tex. Tech U., 1958; A.B. in Botany, U. Kans., 1960, M.A. in Botany, 1963; Ph.D. in Biology, U. Louisville, 1966. Geologist Nelson Creek Mining Co., Rapid

City, S.D., 1963; teaching asst. U. Louisville, 1963-66; asst. prof. biology Northeast La. U., Monroe, 1967-70; aquatic biologist Mich. Dept. Natural Resources, Lansing, 1972-73; research diatomist, research assoc. Calif. Acad. Scis., San Francisco, 1973-78; cons. environmentalist and geologist, Cin., 1970—; cons., expert witness AT&T Co., Pillsbury, Madison and Sutro, San Francisco, 1974-75; cons. U.S. EPA, Cin., 1972-82, U.S. Geol. Survey, Menlo Park, Calif., 1975-77, State of Calif., Sacramento, 1975-76. Author, editor: Geology of World Gem Deposits, 1985; Economic Evaluation of Mineral Property, 1983; Catalogue of the Fossil and Recent Genera and Species of Diatoms, 8 vols., 1967-79; author: Guide to the Identification, Environmental Requirements and Pollution Tolerance of Blue Green Algae, 1982; Jessup fellow Acad. Natural Scis. of Phila., 1962; McHenry fellow Acad. Natural Scis. of Phila., 1963; NSF grantee, 1969-70, 73-78. Mem. Geol. Soc. Am., Soc. Ind. Profl. Earth Scientists (earth scientist), Los Angeles Self Realization Fellowship. Zen Buddhist and Hindu. Current work: Biological water quality appraisal and surveillance; tertiary non-marine stratigraphy of the Great Basin; ecology, paleoecology, and stratigraphy of non-marine diatoms; non-marine diatom index fossils; economic evaluation of diatomite deposits. Subspecialties: Limnology; Paleontology. Office: Sam L Van Landingham Cons Environmentalist/Geologist 3741 Woodsong Dr Cincinnati OH 45239

VAN LINT, VICTOR ANTON JACOBUS, physicist; b. Samarinda, Borneo, Indonesia, May 10, 1928; came to U.S., 1937; s. Victor J. and Margaret (DeJager) Van L.; m. M. June Woolhouse, June 10, 1950; children—Lawrence, Kenneth, Linda, Karen. B.S., Calif. Inst. Tech., Pasadena, 1950, Ph.D., 1954. Instr., Princeton U., 1954-55; staff mem., Gen. Atomic, San Diego, Calif., 1957-74; pvt. practice physics cons., San Diego, 1974-75; staff mem. Mission Research Corp., San Diego, 1975-82, 83—; spl. asst. to dep. dir. sci. and tech. Def. Nuclear Agy., Washington, 1982-83. Author, editor: Radiation Effects in Electronic Materials, 1976. Contbr. articles to profl. jours. Served with U.S. Army, 1955-57. Recipient Pub. Service award NASA, 1981. Fellow IEEE. Republican. Mem. Ch. of Christ. Current work: Radiation effects in semiconductors, insulators and gases; electromagnetic effects in plasmas and electromagnetic coupling. Subspecialties: Nuclear physics; Electrical engineering. Home: 1032 Skylark Dr La Jolla CA 92037

VAN LOON, GLEN RICHARD, physician, scientist; b. Petrolia, Ont., Can., Mar. 1, 1940; came to U.S., 1983; s. John E. and Margaret B. (Thomson) Van L.; m. Joye L. Gerry, June 30, 1962. B.S., McMaster U., Hamilton, Ont., 1961; M.D., U. Toronto, 1965; Ph.D., U. Calif.-San Francisco, 1970. Intern Toronto Gen. Hosp., 1965-66, resident, 1971-72; jr. asst. resident Royal Victoria Hosp., Montreal, 1966-67; fellow in endocrinology Vanderbilt U., 1970-71; asst. prof. medicine and physiology U. Toronto, 1972-79, assoc prof., 1979-82; prof. medicine U. Ky., Lexington, 1982—; staff physician Toronto Gen. Hosp., 1972-80, U. Ky. Med. Ctr., Lexington, 1983—, VA Med. Ctr., Lexington, 1983—. Contbr. articles to profl. jours. and books. Fellow Royal Coll. Physicians Can.; mem. Am. Fedn. Clin. Research, Am. Soc. Pharmacology and Exptl. Therapeutics, Am. Physiol. Soc., Endocrine Soc., Soc. Neurosci., Am. Soc. Clin. Investigation, Central Soc. Clin. Research, Internat. Soc. Neuroendocrinology. Current Work: interest: Endogenous opioid peptides, catecholamines, AcTH, regulation of responses to stress. Subspecialties: Neuroendocrinology; Neuropharmacology. Home: Route 4 Keene Pike Nicholasville KY 40356 Office: VA Medical Center (111) Lexington KY 40511

VANMARCKE, ERIK HECTOR, civil engineering educator; b. Menen, Belgium, Aug. 6, 1941; came to U.S., 1965, naturalized, 1976; s. Louis Eugene and Rachel Louisa (van Hollebeke); m. Margaret Maria Delesie, May 25, 1965; children—Lieven, Ann, Kristien. B.S., U. Louvain, Belgium, 1965; M.S., U. Del., 1967; Ph.D., in Civil Engring., MIT, 1970. From instr. to prof. civil engring. MIT, Cambridge, 1969-85, Gilbert W. Winslow Career Devel. prof., 1974-77, dir. civil engring. systems group, 1976-80; prof. Princeton U., 1985—; cons. Office Sci. and Tech. Policy, 1978-80; cons. various govt. agencies and engring. firms. Author: Random Fields: Analysis and Synthesis, 1983; Editor: Structural Safety Jour., 1981. Recipient ASCE Raymond C. Reese Research award, 1975, Walter C. Huber Research prize, 1984. Mem. Am. Geophys. Union, Seismol. Soc. Am., Internat. Soc. Soil Mechanics and Found. Engring., Sigma Xi. Subspecialties: Civil engineering; Probability. Home: 16 Deer Run Wayland MA 01778

VAN METTER, RICHARD LAWRENCE, imaging scientist; b. Yonkers, N.Y., Mar. 8, 1949; s. Russell Leslie and Mary (Sharkey) Van M.; m. Patricia Love Popowich, Aug. 23, 1969; children—Kristen, James, Johann, Jill. B.S., Manhattan Coll., 1971; Ph.D., U. Rochester, 1978. Sr. research physicist Eastman Kodak Co., Rochester, N.Y., 1977—. Mem. Am. Phys. Soc., (mem. exec. com. N.Y. state sect. 1982—), Soc. Photog. Scientists and Engrs. (jour. hon. mention 1982), Royal Photographic Soc. Current work: Imaging science, analysis and modeling of photographic and electronic imaging systems, particularly in terms of overall imaging efficiency and signal-to-noise. Subspecialty: Imaging technology. Home: 1151 Woodbridge Ln Webster NY 14580 Office: Eastman Kodak Co 2000 Lake Ave Rochester NY 14650

VANN, DOUGLAS CARROLL, immunologist; b. Coronado, Calif., May 3, 1939; s. John W. and Marjorie Douglas (Gillie) V.; m. Caroline Bragg, July 1, 1961 (div. 1974); 1 child, Michael. A.B., U. Calif.-Berkeley, 1960, Ph.D., U. Calif.-Santa Barbara, 1966. Postdoctoral fellow Oak Ridge Nat. Labs., Tenn., 1966-68, Scripps Clinic and Research Found., LaJolla, Calif., 1968-70; asst. then assoc. prof. U. Hawaii, Honolulu, 1970-81; owner Joy of Learning, Honolulu, 1981-83; sr. scientist Hawaii Biotech., Aiea, 1983—. Mem. Am. Assn. Immunologists. Current work: Immunotoxins; immunoassays. Subspecialties: Immunology (agriculture); Animal genetics. Home: 98-1617 Apala Loop Alia HI 96701 Office: Hawaii Biotech Group Inc 99-193 Aiea Heights Dr Alea HI 96701

VAN NAGELL, JOHN RENSSELAER, JR., physician, educator; b. N.Y.C., Sept. 16, 1939; s. John Rensselaer and Rosamond Porter (Musgrave) van N.; m. Elizabeth Clemens Gay, June 10, 1965; children: John, Lucy, Elizabeth Knox. B.A., Harvard Coll., 1961; M.D., U. Pa., 1967. Diplomate: Am. Bd. Ob-Gyn. Am. Cancer Soc. fellow in gynecologic oncology, 1971-73; asst. prof. U. Ky. Med. Center, 1971-74, assoc. prof. gynecologic oncology, 1974-76, prof., dir. gynecologic oncology div., 1978—, Am. Cancer Soc. prof. clin. oncology, 1980—. Contbr. articles to profl. jours.; Author: Modern Concepts of Gynecologic Oncology, 1982. Bd. dirs. Ephraim McDowell Cancer Center, Lexington; trustee U. Ky. Hosp., 1978—. Served with USNR, 1968-75. Mem. Am. Assn. Cancer Research, Am. Assn. Clin. Oncology, Soc. Pelvic Surgeons, Soc. Gynecologic Oncology, Internat. Soc. Pathologists, Alpha Omega Alpha. Republican. Episcopalian. Clubs: Fly (Boston); Idle Hour Country, Iroquois Hunt (Lexington). Current Work: Tumor markers in gynecologic malignancies; in vitro chemotherapy testing. Subspecialties: Gynecological oncology; Cancer research (medicine). Home: 226 Henry Clay Blvd Lexington KY 40502 Office: 800 Rose St Lexington KY 40536

VAN NIEUWENHUIZEN, PETER, physicist; b. Utrecht, Netherlands, Oct. 26, 1938; came to U.S. 1973. Ph.D. in Physics, Utrecht U., 1971. Fellow CERN, Switzerland, 1969-70, research asst., 1970-71; Joliot-Curie fellow, U. Paris, 1971-73; research asst. Brandeis U., 1973-75; prof. physics SUNY-Stony Brook, 1975—. Contbr. articles to profl. jours. Co-inventor of supergravity theory. Subspecialties: Particle physics; Relativity and gravitation. Address: SUNY-Stony Brook Dept Physics Stony Brook NY 11794

VANONI, VITO AUGUST, hydraulic engineer; b. Calif., Aug. 30, 1904; s. Battista and Mariana V.; m. Edith Maria Fuacinella, June 23, 1934. B.S. in Civil Engring, Calif. Inst. Tech., 1926, M.S. in Civil Engring, 1932, Ph.D., 1940. Supr. research lab. U.S. Soil Conservation Service, Pasadena, Calif., 1935-47; asst. prof. hydraulics Calif. Inst. Tech., 1942-49, asso. prof., 1949-55, prof., 1955-74, prof. emeritus, 1974—. Contbr. numerous articles on hydraulics and sedimentation to profl. jours.; editor: Sedimentation Engineering, 1975. Mem. ASCE (hon.), Internat. Assn. Hydraulic Research, Nat. Acad. Engring., Sigma Xi. Current Work: River mechanics. Subspecialty: Civil engineering. Home: 3545 Lombardy Rd Pasadena CA 91107 Office: 1201 E California St Pasadena CA 91125

VAN OSTENBURG, DONALD ORA, physics educator, researcher; b. Grand Rapids, Mich., July 19, 1929; s. Orie and Jane (Versluis) Van Oostenbrugge; m. Betty Jean Roskamp, Aug. 31, 1951; children—Suzanne Lynn, Donald Mark. A.S., Grand Rapids Jr. Coll., 1949; B.S., Calvin Coll., 1951; M.S., Mich. State U., 1953, Ph.D., 1956. Assoc. scientist Armour Research Found., Chgo., 1956-59, Argonne Nat. Lab., Ill., 1959-70; prof. physics DePaul U., Chgo., 1970—; pres. Central State Univs., Inc., DeKalb, Ill., 1982. Contbr. articles to profl. jours. Fellow Am. Phys. Soc.; mem. Am. Sci. Affiliation, Sigma Xi, Sigma Pi Sigma, Pi Mu Epsilon. Mem. Reformed Ch. Am. Current work: Nuclear magnetic resonance research. Subspecialty: Condensed matter physics. Home: 12537 E Navajo Dr Palos Heights IL 60463 Office: DePaul U Dept Physics 2219 N Kenmore Chicago IL 60614

VAN PATTER, DOUGLAS MACPHERSON, physicist, educator, researcher; b. Montreal, Que., Can., July 4, 1923; came to U.S., 1946; s. Hugh Stanley and Jean Macdowell (Macpherson) Van P.; m. J. Annabel Knowles, May 27, 1950; children—Scott, Kenneth, Bruce, Laurie. B.Sc. with honors, Queen's U., Kingston, Ont., Can., 1945; Ph.D. in Nuclear Physics, MIT, 1949. Jr. research physicist Can. Atomic Energy Project, Chalk River, 1945-46; research assoc. dept. physics MIT, Cambridge, 1949-52; asst. prof. physics U. Minn., Mpls., 1952-54; sr. physicist, prof. Bartol Research Found., U. Del., Newark, 1954—; chmn. subcom. on nuclear constants, NRC-Nat. Acad. Sci., Washington, 1958-65; mem. adv. council for engring. Queen's U., 1966-68; vis. prof. Nuclear Physics Inst., Frankfurt, Federal Republic Germany, 1972. Editor: (with others) Nuclear Research with Low Energy Accelerators, 1967. Contbr. articles to profl. jours. Fellow APS; mem. Meteoritical Soc., AAAS. Current work: Nuclear structure, nuclear reactions, radioactivity; statistical reaction theory; proton microprobe for compositional analysis. Subspecialties: Nuclear physics; Geochemistry. Home: 97 Sproul Rd Springfield PA 19064 Office: Bartol Research Found Univ Del Newark DE 19716

VAN PELT, LLOYD FRANKLIN, veterinarian; b. Brownsdale, Minn., June 23, 1930; s. Robert Luman and Tilda (Guttormson) Van P.; m. Constance Jean Rasmusson, Nov. 21, 1951; children—Lee Ann, Lynn Marie, Lori Jean. D.V.M., U. Minn., 1959. Diplomate Am. Coll. Lab. Animal Medicine. Dist. veterinarian Dept. Los Angeles County, South Gate, Calif., 1960-64; attending veterinarian Los Angeles County Harbor Gen. Hosp., Torrance, Calif., 1964-70, sr. veterinarian, 1970-72, chief veterinarian, 1972-74, dir. Veterinary Service, Los Angeles County Harbor/UCLA Med. Ctr., 1974-80; ptnr. Lincoln Ave. Animal Hosp., Orange, Calif., 1964-66; lectr. dept. pathology Sch. Medicine, UCLA, 1969-80; dir. Ctr. Exptl. Animal Resources, Northwestern U., 1980—, assoc. prof. dept. microbiology-immunology Med. and Dental Sch., 1981—; site visitor Am. Assn. Accreditation of Lab. Animal Care, 1971—, mem. council on accreditation, 1977-80, trustee, 1981—; cons. animal medicine VA Med. Ctr., Hines, Ill., 1982—, VA Lakeside Med. Ctr., Chgo., 1982—, Am. Dental Research Inst., Chgo., 1982—, Children's Meml. Hosp., Chgo., 1982—. Contbr. articles to sci. jours. Served AUS, 1949-52. Recipient Research grants, NIH, HEW, 1967-70. Mem. Am. Assn. Lab. Animal Sci. (Chgo. br.), Am. Soc. Lab. Animal Practitioners, AVMA, Ill. State Vet. Med. Assn., Northwestern Apple Computer Users Group. Republican. Lutheran. Current work: Clinical methods for the evaluation of male and female reproductive competence in laboratory monkeys, and insemination by intraperitoneal injection; effective animal care delivery and administration in the institutional setting. Subspecialty: Laboratory animal medicine. Office: Northwestern U 303 E Chicago Ave Chicago IL 60611

VAN RIPER, CHARLES, III, research scientist, educator; b. Mahopac, N.Y., Sept. 24, 1943; s. Charles II and Dorothy (Wilson) van R.; m. Sandra Jean Guest, June 4, 1977; children—Charles IV, Jacqueline Ellen, Kimberly Ann, Carena Jollene. B.S., Colo. State U., 1966, M.S., 1967; Ph.D., U. Hawaii, 1978. Teaching asst. dept. zoology U. Hawaii, Honolulu, 1972-74, research asst., 1974-75; wildlife biologist Dept. Interior, Honolulu, 1975-76; asst. researcher U. Hawaii, 1977-79; unit leader Nat. Park Service, 1979—; adj. prof. U. Calif.-Davis, 1980—; dir. Coop. Parks Studies Unit, Davis, 1979—. Author: A Field Guide to the Mammals of Hawaii, 1982. Editor: Proceedings of 2d Biennial Conference of NPS Research, 1985. Contbr. articles to profl. jours. Leader Boy Scouts Am., Mahopac, 1968—; leader 4-H Club, Davis, 1980—. Grantee U. Hawaii, 1977-80; Hawaii Audubon Soc., 1978, Ctr. for Field Research, 1978-80, World Wildlife Fund Research, 1979; Frank M. Chapman Meml. Fund, 1979, Sigma Xi, 1979; Office Manpower Resources, 1979-80; Opportunity Program for Ecol. Research, 1980; Nat. Pk. Service, 1980; Nat. Geog. Soc., 1980-81, Earthwatch and C.F.R., 1981-82, U.S. Dept. Interior, 1981-83, Man and the Biosphere, 1982-85, U.S. Dept. Interior, 1983-86, Hewlett Found. Research, 1984-85; Spl. Merit award U.S. Fish and Wildlife Service, 1980. Life mem. Am. Ornithological Union (career opportunity com. 1984-85), Cooper Ornithological Soc. (bd. dirs. 1985—); mem. Wildlife Disease Assn. Ecol. Soc. Am. Clubs: Nat. Wildlife (regional rep. 1979-80); Yolo Sportsman (Davis). Current work: Avian breeding systems; island biogeographe; endangered species; epidemiology of avian diseases. Subspecialties: Ecology (biology); Epidemiology. Home: Route 1 Box 776C Woodland CA 95695 Office: Inst Ecology U Calif-Davis 2148 Wickson Hall Davis CA 95616

VAN ROOSBROECK, WILLY WERNER, physicist, researcher; b. Antwerp, Belgium, Aug. 10, 1913; came to U.S., 1916, naturalized, 1921; s. Gustave Leopold and Marie Joanna (DeGraef) van R.; m. Marjorie Anna Covert, Oct. 7, 1945 (dec. 1982). A.B., Columbia U., 1934, M.A. in Physics, 1937. Mem. tech. staff Bell Labs., Murray Hill, N.J., 1937-78. Contbr. articles to profl. jours. Patentee semiconductor device and optical fiber prodn. principles. Fellow Am. Phys. Soc.; mem. AAAS, N.Y. Acad. Sci., Phi Beta Kappa. Current work: Theoretical semiconductor physics; formulation and applications of basic equations governing transport and recombination of current carriers in semiconductors; theory for recombination and switching properties of amorphous and relaxation semiconductors. Subspecialties: Condensed matter physics; Theoretical physics. Home: 19 Whittredge Rd Summit NJ 07901

VAN RYZIN, ROBERT JOSEPH, research institute veterinary pathologist; b. Milw., Feb. 20, 1929; s. Gerald Sylvester and Lydia (Mathey) Van R.; m. Margaret Bielinski, Sept. 9, 1950; children—Peter, Anne, Joan, Helen, Paul, John, Mary, William, Jean. B.S. in Agr., U. Wis., 1951; D.V.M., Iowa State U., 1955. Diplomate Am. Coll. Vet. Pathologists, Am. Bd. Toxicology. Instr., Mich. State U., 1957-59; pathologist Norwich Pharm. Co. N.Y., 1956-62; head pathology/toxicology Sandoz, Inc., East Hanover, N.J., 1962—; mem. rev. com. Pharm. Mfrs. Assn. Found. Fellowship awards, 1982—. Contbr. articles, abstracts to profl. lit. Served to 1st lt. AUS, 1955-57. Mem. Soc. Toxicology, Internat. Acad. Pathology, Nat. Agrl. Chem. Assn. (toxicology com. 1974-85), Pharm. Mfrs. Assn. (drug safety com. 1975-80), Soc. Toxicologic Pathologists (pres. Wenonah, N.J. 1984-85, editorial bd. 1980-86), AVMA, N.J. Vet. Med. Assn. (exec. com. Govern Soc. 1983-86). Republican. Roman Catholic. Club: Summit Nature (editor 1983-86) (N.J.). Current work: Safety assessment of chemicals being developed as drugs or other uses - pesticides; directing laboratory that studies agents in laboratory animals-toxicity studies. Subspecialties: Pathology (veterinary medicine); Pharmaceutical toxicology. Home: 403 Woodland Rd Madison NJ 07940 Office: Sandoz Research Inst Route 10 East Hanover NJ 07936

VAN SLYKE, RICHARD MAURICE, telecommunications researcher and educator; b. Manila, Philippines, Aug. 17, 1937; came to U.S., 1937; s. Francis Allen and Dorthy Elisabeth (Quigley) Van S.; m. Irene Van Veen, Dec. 22, 1969. B.S. in Physics, Stanford U., 1959; Ph.D. in Engring. Sci., U. Calif.-Berkeley, 1965. Assoc. prof. U. Calif., Berkeley, 1965-69; v.p. Network Analysis Corp., Great Neck, N.Y., 1969-80; prof. Steven Inst. Tech., Hoboken, N.J., 1980-83; dir. Ctr. for Advanced Tech. in Telecommunications, Bkyn., 1983—. Assoc. editor Networks Jour., 1970—. Mem. IEEE (sr.), Assn. Computer Machinery, Ops. Research Soc. Am., Soc. Indsl. and Applied Math. Democrat. Current work: Design and analysis algorithms for telecommunication network design. Subspecialties: Telecommunications; Operations research (mathematics). Home: 208 Bergen St Brooklyn NY 11217 Office: Ctr for Advanced Tech in Telecommunications 333 Jay St Brooklyn NY 11201

VAN TIL, ALAN EVERETT, chemist; b. Hammond, Ind., Oct. 8, 1942; s. Edward R. and Cornelia Philippina (Feikema) van T.; m. Glennyce Faye den Besten, Aug. 14, 1971; children—Evelyn Rae, Andrew Glen, Audrey Anne, Carolyn Beth. B.S. in Chemistry, Purdue U., 1967; Ph.D., Iowa State U., 1976. Tchr. high sch., Hammond, 1967-69; research chemist Signal Universal Oil Products (now Signal Research Ctr.), Des Plaines, Ill., 1975-81, assoc. scientist, 1981-82, scientist, 1982—. Patentee in field. Contbr. articles to profl. jours. Served to sgt. U.S. Army, 1961-67. Mem. Am. Chem. Soc., Am. Vacuum Soc., Materials Research Soc., Calorimetry Conf., Air Pollution Control Assn. Republican. Christian Reformed. Current work: Thermal analysis and calorimetry; ultraviolet-visible spectroscopies; instrumental design and technique development; magnetic and electronic property measurements; air pollution control techniques. Subspecialties: Analytical chemistry; Combustion processes. Home: 321 S Cherry St Itasca IL 60143 Office: Signal Research Ctr 50 UOP Plaza Des Plaines IL 60016

VAN UITERT, LEGRAND GERARD, chemist; b. Salt Lake City, May 6, 1922; s. Antone and Lambertha Maria (Groeneveld) Van U.; m. Marion Emma Woolley, June 8, 1945; children: Robert, Bonnie, Craig. B.S., George Washington U., 1949; M.S., Pa. State U., 1951, Ph.D., 1952. Union Carbide fellow Pa. State U., 1951-52; materials scientist Bell Telephone Labs., Murray Hill, N.J., 1952—; cons. to materials adv. bd. Nat. Acad. Sci. Served with USN, 1940-46. Co-recipient W.R.G. Baker award IEEE, 1971; recipient H. N. Potts award Franklin Inst., 1975; award Indsl. Research Inst., 1976; internat. award for new materials Am. Phys. Soc., 1981. Mem. Nat. Acad. Engring., Am. Chem. Soc. (award for creative invention 1978), Sigma Xi. Research on microwave ferrites, lasers, bubble domain memory, electro, non-linear and acusto-optic materials, luminescence, optical fibers, crystal growth, passive displays, correlation of films for semiconductor processing and properties of matter. Current Work: Inovative semiconductor processing, optical fibers; luminescence and the correlation of physical properties of crystals and glasses. Subspecialty: Materials. Home: 2 Terry Dr Morristown NJ 07960 Office: Bell Labs Murray Hill NJ 07974

VAN VALIN, CHARLES CARROLL, research chemist; b. Wakefield, Nebr., Aug. 10, 1929; s. Carroll Dean and May Evelyn (Brodersen) V.; m. Ann E. Tichy, June 3, 1954. B.A., Wayne State Tchrs. Coll., 1951; M.S., U. Colo., 1958. Tchr. Ralston Pub. Schs., Nebr., 1953-54; technician Nat. Bur. Standards, Boulder, Colo., 1955-57; chemist Shell Chem. Co., Denver, 1957-58; research chemist Gt. Western Sugar Co., Denver, 1958-60; U.S. Dept. Interior, Denver, 1961-66, U.S. Dept. Commerce, Boulder, 1966—. Contbr. articles to profl. jours. Served to cpl. U.S. Army, 1951-53. Mem. Am. Chem. Soc., Am. Geophys. Union, AAAS, Sigma Xi. Lodge: Mason. Current work: Acid rain research; chemical and physical processes of the formation and removal of aerosols in the atmosphere; microphysics and microchemistry in clouds. Subspecialties: Atmospheric chemistry; Analytical chemistry. Home: 925 Gilbert St Boulder CO 80302 Office: U S Dept Commerce NOAA 325 Broadway Boulder CO 80303

VAN VLACK, LAWRENCE HALL, materials engineering educator, engineering firm executive; b. Atlantic, Iowa, 1920; s. Claude H. and Ruth L. (Stone) Van V.; m. Frances E. Runnells, June 27, 1943; children—Laura, Bruce. B.S., Iowa State U., 1942; Ph.D., U. Chgo., 1950. Registered profl. engr., Mich. Ceramist, U.S. Steel Corp., Chgo., 1943-52, metallurgist, Pitts., 1952-53; faculty U. Mich., Ann Arbor, 1953—, prof. metall. engring., 1958—, chmn. dept., 1966-73; prin. L.H. Van Vlack, P.E., Ann Arbor, 1953—. Author books including: Elements of Materials Science, 1959, 5th edit., 1985, Physical Ceramics for Engineers, 1964; Textbook of Materials Technology, 1973; Nickel Oxide, 1980; Materials for Engineering, 1982. Contbr. numerous tech. papers to profl. lit. Served with USNR, 1945-46. Fellow Am. Soc. Metals (Gold medal 1984), Am. Ceramic Soc. (chmn. Mich. sect. 1960), AAAS; mem. Am. Inst. Metall. Engrs., Brit. Ceramic Soc. Methodist. Current work: Nonmetallic inclusions in metals. Subspecialties: Materials (engineering); Ceramics. Home: 2115 Nature Cove Apt 309 Ann Arbor MI 48104 Office: Dept Metall Engring Univ Mich Ann Arbor MI 48109

VAN VLIET, CAROLYN MARINA, educator, physicist; b. Dordrecht, Netherlands, Dec. 27, 1929; emigrated to U.S., 1960, naturalized, 1967; d. Marinus and Jacoba (de Lange) Van V.; divorced; children: Elsa Marianne, Mark Edward, Cynthia Joyce, Renata Annette Carolina. B.S., Free U. Amsterdam, Netherlands, 1949, M.A., 1953, Ph.D. in Physics, 1956. Research fellow Free U. Amsterdam, 1950-54, research asso., 1954-56, asst. dir., 1958-60; postdoctoral fellow U. Minn., Mpls., 1956-57, mem. faculty, 1957-58, 60-70, prof. elec. engring. and physics, 1965-70; sr. research mem., prof. Centre Recherches Math. U. Montreal, Que., 1969—; vis. prof. U. Fla., 1974, 4-6 months annually, 78—. Contbg. author: Fluctuation Phenomena in Solids, 1965; author numerous articles. Research grantee NSF; Research grantee Air Force OSR; Research grantee Nat. Sci. and Engring. Research Council, Ottawa. Fellow Am. Sci. Affiliation; mem. Am., European, Canadian phys. socs., IEEE (sr.). Current Work: Nonequilibrium statistical mechanics; theoretical solid state physics; fluctuations and stochastic processes; solid state device theory. Subspecialties: Semiconductors; Statistical physics. Home: 920 Van Dyck Ave Brossard Montreal PQ J4W 2E6 Canada

VAN WINKLE, EDGAR WALLING, electrical engineer, computer consultant; b. Rutherford, N.J., Oct. 12, 1913; s. Winant and Jessie Walcott (Mucklow) Van W.; m. Jessie Stetler, Apr. 23, 1938; children—Barbara, Catrina, Cornelia. B.E.E., Rutgers U., 1936; M.S. in Indsl. Engring., Columbia U., 1943, P.E. in Indsl. Engring., 1966. Registered profl. engr., N.J. Elec. engr. A.B. Dumont Labs. Passaic, N.J., 1943-48; chief engr. Facsimile Electronics, Passaic, 1948-52; cons. Bur. Ships, Washington, 1952; asst. sr. staff scientist Bendix Corp., Teterboro, N.J., 1952-67; sr. staff scientist Conrac Corp., West Caldwell, N.J., 1967-78; pres. Empac, Inc., Rutherford, N.J., 1979—. Author profl. papers. Contbr. articles to profl. jours. Patentee in field. Ruling elder Presbyterian Ch., Rutherford, 1984—. Mem. IEEE (life, treas. artificial intelligence sect. North N.J. Chpt. 1982-84), Bendix Mgmt. Club (life), North N.J. Automatic Control Group (chmn. 1967-68), Met. Engring. Mgmt. (chmn. 1966-67), Mensa, Holland Soc., Delta Phi. Republican. Current work: Artificial intelligence and robotics. Subspecialties: Artificial intelligence; Mathematical software. Home and Office: 439 Edgewood Pl Rutherford NJ 07070

VAN ZYTVELD, JOHN BOS, physics educator, researcher solid state physics; b. Hammond, Ind., Nov. 12, 1940; s. Cornelius Jacob and Catherine (Bos) VanZ.; m. Carol Ann Vander Slik, Dec. 30, 1961; children—Jennifer Sue, Eric James, Sara Lynne. A.B., Calvin Coll., Grand Rapids, Mich., 1962; M.S., Mich. State U., 1964, Ph.D., 1967. Postdoctoral fellow U. Sheffield, Eng., 1967-68; asst. to assoc. to prof. physics Calvin Coll., Grand Rapids, Mich., 1968, 72, 76—; sr. postdoctural fellow U. Leicester, England, 1974-75; sr. Fulbright lectr. Yarmouk U., Jordan, 1980-81; assoc. program dir. and program dir. solid state physics NSF, Washington, 1983-85; mem., chmn. sci. adv. com. Congressmen G.R. Ford, R. VanderVeen, H. Sawyer, Grand Rapids, 1972-78. Contbr. articles to tech. jours. Grantee NSF, 1977—, Research Corp. 1969-76. Fellow Am. Sci. Affiliation; mem. Am. Phys. Soc., AAAS, Am. Assn. Physics Tchrs., Christian Reformed. Current work: Electronic properties of liquid and solid metals and alloys at high temperatures. Subspecialty: Condensed matter physics. Office: Dept Physics Calvin Coll Burton St SE Grand Rapids MI 49506

VARGA, JANOS M., biochemist, researcher; b. Hungary, June 19, 1935; s. Janos and Maria (Toth) V.; m. Eva Pierrou, Oct. 15, 1969; children: Daniel, Paul, Elisabet. B.S., U. Tech., Budapest, 1959; Ph.D., U. Sci., Budapest, 1966. Research assoc. Inst. Pharmacology, Budapest, 1960-67; research asso. Royal Inst. Tech., Stockholm, 1967-69; sect. head dept. biochemistry, Uppsala, Sweden, 1970; postdoctoral asso. Yale U., 1971-74, asst. prof., 1974-76, asso. prof., 1976—; vis. scientist Inst. Microbiol. Chemistry, Rome, 1963-64. Contbr. numerous articles to profl. jours. Postdoctoral fellow USPHS, 1971-74; Research Career Devel. award, 1976-81. Mem. Am. Assn. Immunologists, Internat. Pigment Cell Soc. Patentee in field. Current Work: Chemistry, specificity and cell cycle dependence on cell surface receptors in eukaryotic cells. Subspecialties: Receptors; Immunology (agriculture).

VARGAS, JOHN DAVID, mathematics educator, text reviewer and writer; b. Bronx, N.Y., Nov. 9, 1947; s. Paul and Elsie (Withenshaw) V.; m. Kathy Mary Capasso, June 8, 1974; 1 child, Stephen John. B.S., Hunter Coll., 1969; M.S., N.Y. U., 1971, Adelphi U., 1982; Ph.D., Adelphi U., 1983. Instr. Hostos Community Coll. CUNY, Bronx, N.Y., 1972-77, asst. prof., 1977-80; asst. prof. math. Mercy Coll., Dobbs Ferry, N.Y., 1980-85, assoc. prof., 1985—; text reviewer Prentice Hall, Englewood Cliffs, N.J., 1982, Acad. Press, N.Y.C., 1980-82. Co-author: Solutions Manual - Calculus, 1984. Served with Army N.G., 1969-75. Teaching fellow N.Y. U., 1969-71; Sloan Found. fellow Adelphi U., 1975-77. Mem. Soc. Indsl. and Applied Math., Math. Assn. Am., Am. Math. Soc., N.Y. Acad. Scis., N.Y. State Math. Assn. Two-Yr. Colls. (campus rep.), Pi Mu Epsilon. Democrat. Roman Catholic. Current Work: Application of integral transform techniques to solve problems in wave propagation. Subspecialties: Applied mathematics; Solid mechanics. Home: 36 Irving Ave Floral Park NY 11001 Office: Mercy Coll 555 Broadway Dobbs Ferry NY 10522

VARGAS, LUIS ALBERTO, organic synthesis chemist, educator; b. Iquique, Chile, Nov. 14, 1936; came to U.S., 1968, naturalized, 1977; s. Alfredo Vargas and Ana Rosa Perez; m. Marta Gonzalez, Sept. 14, 1968 (dec. 1980); 1 child, Luis Alfredo. M.S., Universidad Catolica, Chile, 1959; Ph.D. in Chemistry, Universidad Madrid, Spain, 1963. Adj. prof. Universidad Madrid, 1961-63; organic chemistry prof. Universidad Catolica, Valparaiso, Chile, 1964-68, chmn. dept. chemistry, 1965-68; lectr. chemistry NYU, N.Y.C., 1969-70, vis. faculty mem., 1969-70; research chemist L.I. Jewish Med. Ctr., N.Y., 1970—, dir. chemistry research, 1972—. Contbr. articles to profl. jours. Universidad Catolica fellow, 1960-63; research grantee L.I. Jewish Med. Ctr., 1980—. Mem. Am. Chem. Soc. Roman Catholic. Current work: Synthesis, biological activities: nucleotides, nucleosides, phospholipids; organophosphorus, organosilicon chemistry: reactivity, reaction mechanism. Subspecialties: Organic chemistry; Synthetic chemistry. Home: 9 Michael Ln New Hyde Park New York NY 11040 Office: L I Jewish Med Ctr New Hyde Park New York NY 11042

VARKEY, ALEXANDER, biology educator; b. Tiruvalla, Kerala, India, July 27, 1934; came to U.S., 1966, naturalized, 1982; s. Puthenparampil and Karukakkalathil (Aley) V.; m. Mercy Alexander Varkey, Nov. 26, 1962; 1 son, Daniel. B.Sc., St. Berchmans' Coll., India, 1954; M.Sc., Agra Coll., India, 1958; Ph.D., La. State U., 1973. Lectr. U. Kerala, 1958-59; head biology Cuttington Coll., Monrovia, Liberia, 1961-66; instr. St. Thomas Coll., St. Paul., 1967-68; teaching asst. La. State U., Baton Rouge, 1968-73; asst. prof. W.Va. Wesleyan Coll., Buckhannon, 1973-77; prof. Liberty Bapt. Coll., Lynchburg, Va., 1977—; research asst. Govt. India Dept. Fisheries, Mandapam, 1959-61. Author: A Laboratory Study of Vertebrate Zoology, 1982, Comparative Cranial Myology of North American Natricine Snakes, 1979. Recipient Merit cert. Cuttington Coll., 1966. Mem. Am. Soc. Zoologists, Herpetol. League, Soc. Study of Amphibians and Reptiles. Baptist. Current Work: Cranial myology of snake genus Helicops, Conophanes. Subspecialties: Morphology; Systematics. Home: 103 Hillview Dr Lynchburg VA 24502 Office: PO Box 2000 C Lynchburg VA 24506

VARKI, AJIT POTHAN, biochemist, medical researcher; b. Golden Rock, Madras, India, Jan. 4, 1952; s. Mathew and Anna (Joseph) V.; m. Nissi Mary Loenen, June 9, 1974; 1 dau., Sarah Anna. M.B.B.S., Christian Med. Coll., Vellore, India, 1975. Diplomate Am. Bd. Internal Medicine. Rotating intern Christian Med. Coll. Hosp., Vellore, 1974-75; resident med. officer dept. medicine Malankara Mission Hosp., Kolenchery, Kerala, India, 1975; research asst. biochemistry research labs. U. Nebr. Med. Ctr., Omaha, 1976; resident in medicine Episcopal Hosp., Temple U., Phila., 1976-77; resident in internal medicine U. Nebr. Med. Ctr., 1977-78; fellow in hematology/oncology Washington U. Sch. Medicine, St. Louis, 1978-82, instr. medicine dept. internal medicine, 1980-82; asst. prof. medicine U. Calif.-San Diego, 1982—. Contbr. articles to profl. jours. Mem. Am. Fedn. Clin. Research, Am. Soc. Biochemists, ACP. Current work: Structural studies of the oligosaccharide units of glycoproteins aimed at understanding the biological roles of the sugar. Subspecialties: Membrane biology; Cancer research (medicine). Office: Cancer Ctr T-011 U Calif-San Diego La Jolla CA 92093

VARLEY, RONALD ARTHUR, nuclear engineer; b. Buffalo, Aug. 26, 1949; s. Arthur and Jeanette Louise (Black) V.; m. Rejenia Ann McKinney, Sept. 28, 1969; children: Heather Lynn, Dawn Marie. Student, Naval Nuclear Power Sch., 1970-71. Tng. engr. Westinghouse Hanford Co., Richland, Wash., 1977-81; sr. emergency planning specialist Energy Cons., Inc., Harrisburg, Pa., 1981-83; sr. engr. EDS Nuclear, Melville, N.Y., 1983—; Adv., bd. dirs. Columbia Basin Coll., Pasco, Wash., 1977-81. Served with USN, 1969-77. Mem. Am. Nuclear Soc., Scientists and Engrs. for Secure Energy. Current Work: Developing emergency planning concepts, programs, procedures and facilities for the nuclear energy. Subspecialties: Nuclear engineering; Nuclear fission. Home: 20 Wilson St Port Jefferson Station NY 11776 Office: EDS Nuclear 225 Broad Hollow Rd Melville NY 11747

VARMA, ARVIND, chemical engineering educator, researcher; b. Ferozabad, India, Oct. 13, 1947; came to U.S., 1968, naturalized, 1979; s. Hans Raj and Vijay L. (Jhanjhee) V.; m. Karen K. Guse, Aug. 7, 1971; children: Anita, Sophia. B.S. in Chem. Engring, Panjab U., Chandigarh, India, 1966; M.S. in Chem. Engring, U. N.B. (Can.), Fredericton, 1968; Ph.D. in Chem. Engring, U. Minn.-Mpls., 1972. Asst. prof. U. Minn.-Mpls., 1972-73; sr. research engr. Union Carbide Corp., Tarrytown, N.Y., 1973-75; asst. prof. chem. engring. U. Notre Dame, 1975-77, assoc. prof., 1977-80, prof., 1980—, chmn. dept. chem. engring., 1983—; vis. prof. U. Fla., 1980, U. Wis.-Madison, 1981; Chevron vis. prof. Calif. Inst. Tech., 1982. Research numerous publs. in field; editor: (with R. Aris) The Mathematical Understanding of Chemical Engineering Systems, 1980. Mem. Am. Inst. Chem. Engrs., Am. Chem. Soc., Sigma Xi. Current Work: Chemical and catalytic reaction engineering; kinetics and catalysis; mathematical modeling. Subspecialty: Chemical engineering. Home: 1721 E Cedar South Bend IN 46617 Office: Dept Chem Engring U Notre Dame Notre Dame IN 46556

VARMA, ASHA, chemist; b. Bareilly, India, Mar. 19, 1942; d. Gulzari Mall and Javitri Devi V.; m. Vinod Shanker Agarwala, Feb. 14, 1967; children—Veena Vinod Agarwala, Vinay Agarwala. B.Sc., Bareilly Coll., Agra U., India, 1958, M.Sc., 1960; Ph.D., Benaras Hindu U., Varanasi, India, 1963. Cert. profl. chemist. Research fellow Benaras Hindu U., 1960-64; sr. research fellow Nat. Chem. Lab., Poona, India, 1964-66; asst. dir. Forensic Sci. Lab., Sagar, India, 1966-68; postdoctoral fellow U. Conn., Storrs, 1966-67; research assoc. Materials Inst. U. Conn., 1973-75; supr. analytical labs. Lab. for Research on Structures of Matter, U. Pa., Phila., 1977-82; team leader Code 6062, Naval Air Devel. Ctr., Warminster, Pa., 1983—. Author: Handbook of Atomic Absorption, 2 vols., 1984. Contbr. 30 articles to tech. jours. Fellow Am. Inst. Chemists; mem. Am. Chem. Soc., Coblentz Soc., Soc. Applied Spectroscopy, Thermal Analysis Forum, Nat. Wildlife Fedn. (assoc.), Am. Mus. Natural History (assoc.). Current work: Metallic and non-metallic trace contaminants, inductively coupled plasma emission, flame and furnace atomic absorption, gas chromatography (capillary), Fourier transform infrared spectroscopy, thermal analysis. Subspecialties: Analytical chemistry; Atomic spectroscopy. Office: Naval Air Devel Ctr Code 6062 Warminster PA 18974

VARMUS, HAROLD ELIOT, microbiologist, educator; b. Oceanside, N.Y., Dec. 18, 1939; s. Frank and Beatrice (Barasch) V.; m. Constance Louise Casey, Oct. 25, 1969; children—Jacob Carey, Christopher Isaac. A.B., Amherst Coll., 1961, D.Sc. (hon.), 1984; M.A., Harvard U., 1962; M.D., Columbia U., 1966. Lic. physician, Calif. Intern, resident Presbyterian Hosp., N.Y.C., 1966-68; clin. assoc. NIH, Bethesda, Md., 1968-70; lectr. dept. microbiology U. Calif.-San Francisco, 1970-72; asst. prof. U. Calif., San Francisco, 1972-74, assoc. prof., San Francisco, 1974-79, prof., San Francisco, 1979—, Am. Cancer Soc. research prof., 1984—; cons. Chiron Corp., Emoryville, Calif. Editor: Readings in Tumor Virology, 1983; assoc. editor: Cell Jour.; editor Molecular and Cellular Biology Jour.; mem. editorial bd.: Cancer Surveys. Named Calif. Acad. Sci. Scientist of Yr., 1982; co-recipient Lasker Found. award, 1982, Passano Found. award, 1983, Armand Hammer Cancer prize, 1984. Mem. Am. Soc. Virology, Am. Soc. Microbiology, AAAS, Nat. Acad. Scis. Democrat. Subspecialties: Cancer research (medicine); Virology (biology). Home: 956 Ashbury St San Francisco CA 94117 Office: U Calif Med Sch Dept Microbiology Parnassus Ave San Francisco CA 94143

VARNEY, ROBERT NATHAN, physicist; b. San Francisco, Nov. 7, 1910; s. Frank Hastings and Emily Patricia (Rhine) V.; m. Astrid Margareta Riffolt, June 19, 1948; children—Nils Roberts, Natalie Rhine. A.B. with highest honors in Physics, U. Calif.-Berkeley, 1931, M.A. in Math., 1932, Ph.D., in Physics, 1935; D.Sc. (hon.), U. Innsbruck, Austria, 1983. Instr. physics U. Calif.-Berkeley, 1935-36, NYU, 1936-38; from asst. prof. to prof. physics Washington U., St. Louis, 1938-64; sr. mem. research lab., sr. sci. cons. Lockheed Missiles & Space Co., Palo Alto, Calif., 1964-75, ret., 1975; mem. tech. staff Bell Telephone Labs., 1951-52; guest prof. atomic physics U. Innsbruck, 1977-78, Author: Lecture Notes in Engineering Physics, 1948-56, 2 edits. Contbr. articles to profl. jours. and chpts. to books. Served to comdr. USNR, 1941-45. Recipient Cross of Honor, Austria, 1981; fellow NSF, 1958-59, NCR, 1975-76; Fulbright lectr. Bd. Fgn. Scholarships, 1971-72, 76-77. Fellow Am. Phys. Soc., AAAS; mem. Am. Assn. Physics Tchrs. Current work: Electric breakdown in gases. Subspecialties: Atomic and molecular physics; Plasma physics. Home: 4156 Maybell Way Palo Alto CA 94306

VARSHNEY, PRAMOD KUMAR, electrical and computer engineering educator, consultant; b. Allahabad, India, July 1, 1952; came to U.S., 1970; s. Raj Kumar and Narvada Devi (Varshney) V.; m. Anju Varshney, Aug. 9, 1978; children—Lav, Kush. B.S., U. Ill., 1972, M.S., 1974, Ph.D., 1976. Asst. prof. elec. and computer engring. Syracuse U., N.Y., 1976-80, assoc. prof., 1980—; cons. in field. Contbr. articles to profl. jours. Air Force Office Sci. Research-/Southeastern Ctr. for Elec. Engring. Edn. fellow, 1979. Mem. IEEE, Am. Soc. Engring. Edn., Tau Beta Pi. Current work: Statistical communication theory; information theory applications to computer science; testing and reliability. Subspecialty: Computer engineering. Home: 312 Haddonfield Dr Dewitt NY 13214 Office: Elec and Computer Engring Dept Syracuse Univ Syracuse NY 13210

VARSHNEY, RAMESH CHANDRA, engineer, researcher; b. Hathras, India, July 28, 1938; s. Babulal and Maha Devi Arya; m. Jaishree Gupta, Nov. 14, 1967; children—Rachna, Rahul. B.Sc., U. Rajasthan, (Jaipur, India), 1960, M.Sc. in Physics, 1963; M. Tech. in Elec. Engring., B.I.T.S. (India), 1967; Ph.D. in Elec. Engring., U. Waterloo, 1971. Instr. elec. engring. U. Waterloo, Ont., Can., 1971-72; design engr. Burrough Corp., San Diego, 1972-74; mgr. Fairchild Research and Devel., Palo Alto, Calif., 1974-78; adv. engr. IBM, Fishkill, N.Y., 1978-79; mgr. Fairchild Semicondr., San Jose, Calif., 1979-83; pres. Inova Corp., Campbell, Calif., 1983—. Patentee in field (25). Contbr. articles to profl. jours. Recipient Tech. achievement award Fairchild Camera and Instrument Co., 1983, Scientist award, 1980. Mem. IEEE, Am. Phys. Soc., Electro-chem. Soc. Current work: Redundancy and ultra large scale integration. Subspecialties: Semiconductors; Integrated circuits. Home: 6041 Crossmont Ct San Jose CA 95120 Office: Inova Microelectronics Corp 1400 Dell Ave Campbell CA 95008

VARY, JAMES CORYDON, biochemistry educator; b. Flint, Mich., Feb. 24, 1939; s. Edwin Phelps and Mary (Burns) V.; m. Patricia Susan Potter, Jan. 20, 1967; children—Catherine, James C., Jr. B.A., Brown U., 1961; M.S., U. Wis., 1964, Ph.D., 1967. Postdoctoral fellow Stanford U., Calif., 1967-69; asst. prof. U. Ill., Chgo., 1969-74, assoc. prof., 1974-79, prof. biochemistry, 1979—. Contbr. articles to profl. jours. Named Prof. of Yr., Sch. Dentistry U. Ill. at Chgo., 1975, Disting. tchr. Grad. Coll., 1982, 84. Mem. Am. Soc. Microbiology, Am. Soc. Biol. Chemists, Fed. Am. Scientists, AAAS, Sigma Xi. Current work: Mechanism of bacterial spore germination. Subspecialties: Biochemistry (biology); Microbiology. Home: 315 W Prairie St Wheaton IL 60187 Office: Dept Biochemistry 1853 W Polk St Univ Ill Chicago IL 60617

VARY, JAMES PATRICK, physics educator; b. Savanna, Ill., May 23, 1943; s. Willis L. and Ethice K. (McCabe) V.; m. Audrey Maria Zarba, June 11, 1966; children—William James, Brian Edward. B.S., Boston Coll., 1965; M.Ph., Yale U., 1968, Ph.D., 1970. Research assoc. MIT, Cambridge, 1970-72; asst. physicist Brookhaven Nat. Lab., Upton, N.Y., 1972-74, assoc. physicist, 1974-75; asst. prof. physics Iowa State U., Ames, 1975-77, assoc. prof., 1977-81, prof., 1981—; dir. nuclear theory program Ames Lab., 1977-82. Contbr. over 75 articles to sci. jours. Alexander von Humboldt fellow, 1979. Mem. Am. Phys. Soc., AAAS, Sigma Xi. Current work: Nuclear structure and nuclear reactions, especially related to intermediate and high-energy experiments; models of nuclei based on quarks and gluons. Subspecialties: Nuclear physics; Particle physics. Office: Dept Physics Iowa State U Ames IA 50011

VASIL, INDRA KUMAR, research biologist, educator, cons.; b. Basti, U.P., India, Aug. 31, 1932; came to U.S., 1962, naturalized, 1974; s. Lal Ch and Pushpalata (Abrol) V.; m. Vimla Negi, May 15, 1959; children: Kavita, Charu. B.S., Banaras Hindu U., 1952; M.S., U. Delhi, 1954, Ph.D., 1958. Assoc. prof., prof. botany U. Fla., Gainesville, 1967-79, grad. research prof. botany, 1979—; cons. Contbr. over 150 articles on biology to profl. jours. Recipient Sr. U.S. Scientist award (Humboldt award) Fed. Republic Germany, 1975-76. Mem. Bot. Soc. Am., Internat. Assn. Plant Tissue and Cell Culture, Internat. Assn. Plant Morphologists, Nat. Geog. Soc., AAAS. Current work: Plant cell and tissue culture for genetic improvement of crop plants. Subspecialties: Genetics and genetic engineering (agriculture); Plant cell and tissue culture. Home: 4901 NW 19th Pl Gainesville FL 32605 Office: Dept Botany U Fla Gainesville FL 32611

VASINGTON, FRANK DANIEL, biochemistry educator; b. Norwich, Conn., Nov. 3, 1928; s. Savino and Carmela (Tempesta) V.; m. Margaret Elizabeth Campbell, Aug. 16, 1952 (div. 1984); children—Lynn Marie, Gail Ellen, Mark Daniel, Philip Kevin. B.A., U. Conn.-Storrs, 1950, M.S., 1952; Ph.D., U. Md. Sch. Medicine, Balt., 1955. Asst. prof. Sch. Medicine. U. Md.-Balt., 1955-57; postdoctoral research fellow Nat. Found. for Infantile Paralysis, McCollum Pratt Inst., Johns Hopkins U., Balt., 1957-59, asst. prof. Johns Hopkins U. Sch. Medicine, 1959-64; assoc. prof. biochemistry U. Conn.-Storrs, 1964-68, prof., 1968—, head biol. scis. group, 1967-70, head biochemistry and biophysics sect., 1967-76, assoc. dean Coll. Liberal Arts and Scis., 1976-78, assoc. v.p. acad. affairs, 1978-82. Contbr. articles to sci. jours., chpts. to books. NIH grantee, 1964-69; NSF grantee, 1969-71, 85—, U. Conn. Research Found. grantee, 1971-76. Mem. Am. Chem. Soc., Am. Soc. Biol. Chemists, AAAS, Conn. Acad. Arts and Scis. Democrat. Roman Catholic. Current work: Biosynthesis and turnover of biological membranes, secretion, transport processes across biological membranes. Subspecialties: Biochemistry (biology); Membrane biology. Home: 293 Stearns Rd Willimantic CT 06226 Office: U Conn Box U-125 75 N Eagleville Rd Storrs CT 06268

VASKO, FRANCIS JOSEPH, management scientist, educator; b. Bethlehem, Pa., Mar. 23, 1952; s. Frank Benedict and Ann Elizabeth (Holva) V.; m. Nancy Louise Rosenberger, July 1, 1978. B.S. in Math. Edn., Kutztown U., 1974; M.S. in Math., Lehigh U., 1976, M.S. in Indsl. Engring./Ops. Research, 1978, Ph.D., in Indsl. Engring./Ops. Research, 1983. Tchr., Northampton Sch. Dist., Pa., 1975-77; adj. prof. Northampton County Area Community Coll., 1976; engr. Bethlehem Steel Corp., Pa., 1978-81, asst. research engr., 1981-83, research engr., 1983—; adj. prof. Allentown Coll., Center Valley, Pa., 1985—. Contbr. articles to tech. jours. Active Hellertown Hist. Soc., Pa., Friends of Pa. Stage Co., Allentown, Friends of Pa. Sinfonia, Allentown. Recipient D.J. Blickwede Research Recognition award Bethlehem Steel Corp., 1983. Mem. Math. Programming Soc., Inst. Mgmt. Scis., Soc. Indsl. and Applied Math. Roman Catholic. Current work: Design and development of highly efficient and practical computer-based optimization models for strategic planning, production planning and resource allocation. Subspecialties: Operations research (engineering); Systems engineering. Home: 510 Ellen St Hellertown PA 18055 Office: Bethlehem Steel Corp Homer Labs Bethlehem PA 18016

VASSALLE, MARIO, physiology educator, physician; b. Viareggio, Lucca, Italy, May 26, 1928; came to U.S., 1958, naturalized, 1973; s. Giuseppe and Antonietta V.; m. Anna Maria Petrucci, Sept. 7, 1959; children: Andrew G., Alessandra A., Massimo B., Roberto M., Francesca A. M.D. cum laude, U. Pisa, 1953, diploma in cardiology cum laude, 1955. Diplomate: in medicine, Italy. Intern dept. medicine, cardiology U. Pisa Med. Sch., 1953-55, asst. dept. med. pathology, 1956-58; acting chief resident in medicine French Hosp., N.Y.C., 1958-59; trainee cardiovascular research and tng. program, dept. physiology Med. Coll. Ga., Augusta, 1959-60; fellow physiology SUNY-Downstate Med. Ctr., Bklyn., 1960-61, N.Y. Heart Assn. fellow, 1961-62, faculty mem., 1964—, prof. physiology, 1971—; NIH fellow U. Bern, Switzerland, 1962-64; vis. prof. U. Ferrara, Italy, 1971, U. Vt., 1978; bd. dirs. N.Y. Heart Assn., N.Y.C., 1980-84; mem. study sect. NIH, Bethesda, Md., 1981-85. Editor: Research in Physiology, 1971, Cardiac Physiology for the Clinician, 1976, Excitation and Neural Control of the Heart, 1982; assoc. editor: Am. Jour. Physiology - Heart and Circulatory Physiology, 1976-80; editorial bd.: Circulation Research, 1974-80, European Jour. Pharmacology, 1985—, Jour. Electrocardiology, 1985—. editorial cons. several jours.; contbr. chpts. to books, numerous articles, abstracts, revs. in field to profl. jours. Fulbright travel grantee, 1958; recipient French Hosp. Alumni award, 1959, A. and A. Sinsheimer Fund award, 1966-71, N.Y. Health Research Council award, 1972-75. Mem. Am. Physiol. Soc., N.Y. Acad. Scis., Am. Heart Assn. (bd. dirs.), AAAS, Harvey Soc., Cardiac Muscle Soc., Cardiac Electrophysiol. Group (pres. 1972-73), Internat. Study Group for Research in Cardiac Metabolism, Sigma Xi. Roman Catholic. Current Work: Study of normal and abnormal cardiac automaticity with various techniques. Subspecialty: Physiology (medicine). Home: 104 Huntington Rd Port Washington NY 11050 Office: Dept Physiology SUNY-Downstate Med Ctr Box 31 450 Clarkson Ave Brooklyn NY 11203

VATSIS, KOSTAS PETROS, pharmacologist, educator; b. Patras, Greece, May 6, 1945; came to U.S., 1962, naturalized, 1983; s. Petros Dennis and Eugenia (Konstantinopoulou) V. B.S., Calif. State U.-Long Beach, 1967, M.S., 1969; Ph.D., Coll. Medicine, U. Ill., Chgo., 1975. Lectr. U. Mich., Ann Arbor, 1976-78; asst. prof. pharmacology Northwestern U., Chgo., 1978-84, assoc. prof., 1984—; cons. U. Ill. Coll. Medicine, Chgo., 1976—. Contbr. articles to profl. jours. Mem. Am. Soc. Pharm. Exptl. Therapeutics, Soc. Toxicology, Am. Chem. Soc., Sigma Xi. Democrat. Greek Orthodox. Current work: Physico-chemical characterization and enzymology of hepatic microsomal electron transport systems involved in the biotransformation of physiologically important compounds (prostaglandins) and xenobiotics (drugs, environmental pollutants). Subspecialties: Biochemistry (medicine); Molecular pharmacology. Home: 3950 N Lake Shore Dr Apt #C-1315 Chicago IL 60613 Office: Dept Pharmacology Northwestern U Med Sch 303 E Chicago Ave Chicago IL 60611

VAUGHAN, JOHN HEATH, physician, medical researcher; b. Richmond, Va., Nov. 7, 1921; s. Warren Taylor and Emma (Heath) V.; m. Marjorie Seybold; children: John, Nancy, David, Margaret. A.B. cum laude, Harvard U., 1942, M.D., 1945. Diplomate: Am. Bd. Internal Medicine. Intern Peter Bent Brigham Hosp., Harvard U. Med. Sch., Boston, 1945-46, research fellow, 1948-50, sr. asst. resident in medicine, 1950-51; asst. prof. medicine Med. Coll. Va., Richmond, 1953-58; assoc. prof. medicine, asst. prof. bacteriology and immunology U. Rochester (N.Y.) Med. Sch., 1958-63, prof. medicine, head immunological and infectious diseases, 1963-70; adj. prof. medicine U. Calif.-San Diego, La Jolla, 1970—; chmn. clin. divs. Scripps Clinic and Research Found., La Jolla, 1970-74, chmn. dept. clin. research, 1974-77, head div. clin. immunology, 1977—. Editor: Immunological Diseases, 3d edit, 1978, Dermatology in General Medicine, 1971; contbr. articles to profl. jours. Served with U.S. Army, 1946-48. NRC fellow, 1951-53. Mem. Am. Acad. Allergy (pres. 1966-67), Am. Assn. Immunologists, Am. Clin. and Climatological Assn., ACP, Am. Fedn. for Clin. Research, Am. Rheumatism Assn. (pres. 1970-71), Am. Soc. for Clin. Investigation, Assn. Am. Physicians, Infectious Diseases Soc., San Diego County Med. Soc., Western Assn. Physicians, Western Soc. for Clin. Research, Alpha Omega Alpha. Current Work: Emphasis on etiology and pathogenesis of rheumatoid arthritis, a disease apparently involving an abnormal immunity to the Epstein-Barr virus. Subspecialties: Allergy; Immunology (medicine). Office: 10666 N Torrey Pines Rd La Jolla CA 92037

VAUGHAN, RICHARD DUGGER, environmental engineer; b. Evanston, Ill., Dec. 18, 1926; s. Merlon Gilchrist Vaughan and Beatrice Vivian (Dugger) Gill; m. Laura May Henderson, Sept. 15, 1951; children—Cynthia Lynn, Robert Bruce, Kathryn Ann. B.S. in Civil Engring., Ga. Inst. Tech., 1951; M.S. in Pub. Health, U. Mich., 1962, M.A. in Engring., 1962. Registered profl. engr., Tex. Commd. engring. officer and ensign USPHS, 1951, advanced through grades to rear adrm. 1971; v.p. Engring. Sci., Washington, 1971-72, ret., 1972; dir. environ. affairs and quality asssurance ITT Community Devel. Corp., Palm Coast, Fla., 1973—. Pres. Civic Music, Inc., Daytona Beach, Fla., 1980-84; pres., v.p. Daytona Playhouse, 1975-78, 1984; bd. dirs. Daytona Beach Symphony Soc., Daytona Beach, 1980—, Embry-Riddle Aero. U., Daytona Beach, 1980—. Decorated Commendation medal USPHS, Washington, 1964; Meritorious Service medal USPHS, 1970; recipient William Gibson award U. Mich., 1962. Fellow Am. Pub. Health Assn.; mem. Am. Acad. Environ. Engrs. (trustee 1981-84), Am. Pub. Works Assn., Fed. Pollution Control Assn., Fla. Pub. Health Assn., Phi Kappa Phi, Delta Omega, Chi Epsilon. Democrat. Methodist. Club: MOWW (Palm Coast, Fla) Lodge: Lions. Current work: Environmental engineering and environmental health. Subspecialties: Environmental engineering; Resource management. Home: 956 Ginger Circle Ormond Beach FL 32074 Office: ITT Community Devel Corp Executive Offices Palm Coast FL 32051

VAUGHAN, WILLIAM WALTON, atmospheric scientist; b. Clearwater, Fla., Sept. 7, 1930; s. William Walton and Ella Vermelle (Warr) V.; m. Wilma Geraldine Stapleton, Dec. 23, 1951; children: Stephen W., David A., William D., Robert T. B.S., U. Fla., 1951; grad. cert. Fla. State U., 1952; Ph.D., U. Tenn., 1976. Sci. asst. Air Force Armament Center, Eglin AFB, Cert. cons. meteorologist. Fla., 1955-58; Army Ballistic Missile Agy., Huntsville, Ala., 1958-60; chief aerophysics and astrophysics br. Marshall Space Flight Center, NASA, Huntsville, 1960-64, chief aerospace environ. div., 1964-76, chief atmospheric scis. div., 1976—. Contbr. articles to profl. jours. Bd. dirs. Huntsville Youth Orch. Served with USAF, 1951-55. Recipient Exceptional Service medal NASA, 1971. Mem. Am. Meteorol. Soc., AIAA (Losey Atmospheric Scis. award 1980), Am. Geophys. Union, AAAS, Sigma Xi. Current Work: Atmospheric dynamics and space technology applications to atmospheric science problems; natural environment inputs for aerospace engineering applications, space-based sensor and payload development. Subspecialties: Meteorology; Aerospace engineering and technology. Office: Marshall Space Flight Center NASA Atmospheric Scis Div Huntsville AL 35812

VAUGHN, CLARENCE BENJAMIN, oncologist; b. Phila., Dec. 14, 1928; s. Albert and Aretha (Johnson) V.; m. Sara, Sept. 25, 1953; children—Steven, Annette, Carl, Ronald. B.S. in Chemistry and Math., Benedict Coll., 1951; M.S. in Chemistry, Howard U., 1955, M.D., 1957; Ph.D. in Physiol. Chemistry, Wayne State U., 1965. Research physician Milton A. Darling Meml. Ctr., Detroit, 1964-70, clin. dir., 1970-72; med. dir. oncology program Providence Hosp., Southfield, Mich., 1973—; clin. assoc. prof. Wayne State U., Detroit, 1978—; mem. NIH, CCOP ad hoc rev. com. Nat. Cancer Inst., Washington, 1982—. Contbr. articles to profl. jours. Served to col. USAF, 1958—. Recipient U.S. Air Force Commendation medal, 1972, 79, Outstanding AFRES Aerospace Physician award, 1974, Meritorious Service award, 1981; named Command Flight Surgeon of Yr., 1980. Mem. Southwest Oncology Group (prin. investigator), Nat. Med. Assn., AMA, AAAS. Subspecialties: Oncology; Chemotherapy. Office: Providence Hosp 16001 W Nine Mile Rd Southfield MI 48075

VAUGHN, MICHAEL THAYER, physicist, educator; b. Chgo., Aug. 6, 1936; s. Charles LeClaire and Kathleen (Thayer) V.; m. Gudrun Royek, Sept. 11, 1971 (dec. 1984). A.B., Columbia U., 1955; Ph.D., Purdue U., 1960. Research assoc., instr. U. Pa., Phila., 1959-62; asst. prof. Ind. U., Bloomington, 1962-64; assoc. prof. Northeastern U., Boston, 1964-73, prof. physics, 1973—; vis. sci. Argonne Nat. Lab., Ill., 1967; vis. prof. Tex. A&M U., College Station, 1975; sr. vis. fellow U. Southampton, Eng., 1979. Contbr. articles to profl. jours. Mem. Am. Phys. Soc. (div. particles and fields). Current work: Unified gauge theories; renormalization group analysis; group theoretical methods. Subspecialties: Particle physics; Theoretical physics. Home: 190 Forest St Needham MA 02192 Office: Northeastern U Physics Dept Boston MA 02115

VAUPEL, DONALD BRUCE, pharmacologist; b. Hackensack, N.J., Aug. 30, 1942; s. Donald Fackert and Ruth Irma (Guenther) V.; m. Susan Skinner, Aug. 12, 1967; children: Lisa Marie, Jonathan Bruce. B.A., Wittenberg U., 1964; M.S., U. Ky., 1970, Ph.D., 1974. Chemist quality control sect. Am. Cyanamid Co., Lederle Labs., Pearl River, N.Y., 1964-66; pharmacologist neuropsychopharmacology sect. Nat. Inst. on Drug Abuse, Addiction Research Ctr., Lexington, Ky. and Balt., 1972—; asst. adj. prof. dept. pharmacology U. Ky. Coll. Medicine. Contbr. articles on pharmacology to profl. jours. Mem. Am. Soc. Pharmacology and Exptl. Therapeutics, Sigma Xi. Episcopalian. Current Work: Evaluating the pharmacology of drugs of abuse, especially hallucinogens, opiates, and amphetamines, and determining their abuse liability on the basis of pharmacologic equivalence. Subspecialty: Neuropharmacology. Home: 900 Fairway Dr Towson MD 21204 Office: PO Box 5180 Baltimore MD 21224

VAURIO, JUSSI KALERVO, nuclear engineer, research administrator; b. Lapua, Finland, Mar. 4, 1940; came to U.S., 1975; s. Juho Kullervo and Rauha Anni (Hietala) V.; m. Eija K. Hyotylainen, June 27, 1963; children: Sari, Katja, Lena. Diploma engr., Tech. U., Helsinki, 1967, licentiate of tech., 1970, D.S. in Tech, 1971. Tchr., lectr. Tech. U., Espoo, Finland, 1965-72; operating engr. Reactor Lab., Espoo, 1966-68; researcher, engr. Tech. Research Ctr. of Finland, Espoo, 1968-72; nuclear engr. Imatra Power Co., Helsinki, 1972-75; nuclear engr. Argonne (Ill.) Nat. Lab., 1975-80, program mgr., 1980—; alternate mem. Radioation Protection Commn., Helsinki, 1967-69. Editor: Dictionary Nuclear Engineering Terms, 1972; contbr. articles to profl. jours. Bd. dirs. Student Congregation, Espoo, 1965, League Finnish Am. Socs., Chgo., 1978-82; mem. engring. bd. City of Espoo, 1973-75. Served to lt. Finnish Army, 1959-60. Finnish Cultural Found. fellow, 1969; Emil Aaltonen Found. fellow, 1970; grantee, 1968; Jenny and Antti Wihuri Found. fellow, 1971. Mem. Finnish Nuclear Soc., Am. Nuclear Soc., Soc. Risk Analysis. Lutheran. Club: Coalition Party (Espoo). Current Work: Reliability analysis models and methods, probabilistic risk assessment, man-machine interface technology methodology. Subspecialties: Nuclear engineering; Probability. Office: Argonne National Laboratory Bldg 207 9700 S Cass Ave Argonne IL 60439

VAVRA, TERRY GWYN, advertising agency executive; b. Los Angeles, Mar. 22, 1941; s. Marvin Joseph and Gwen Charlotte (Filipy) V.; m. Linda Faye Dallas, Dec. 19, 1970; children: Stacy Dallas, Kerry Lynn, Tammy Gwen. B.S., UCLA, 1964, M.S., 1967; Ph.D. in Mktg, U. Ill., Champaign, 1973. Dir. news audience research NBC, N.Y.C., 1972-77; group research dir. Kenyon & Eckhardt Advt., N.Y.C., 1977-79; dir. research Batten, Barton, Durstine & Osborn, Internat., N.Y.C., 1979-81; dir. mktg./research Levine, Huntley, Schmidt & Beaver, N.Y.C., 1981—; cons. Rolls-Royce Motors, Lyndhurst, N.J. Commr.-soccer Allendale (N.J.) Athletic Assn., 1982—; treas. Bergen Highland United Methodist Ch., Upper Saddle River, N.J., 1979-81. Recipient Pub. Service award Retinitis Pigmentosa Found., 1981. Mem. Am. Psychol. Assn., Am. Mktg. Assn., Assn. for Consumer Research, Psychometric Soc. Republican. Current Work: Quantification of the impact of brand image on brand selection in consumer purchasing of package goods; micro computers for collecting survey data. Home: 4 Michele Ct Allendale NJ 07401

VAZIRI, NOSTRATOLA DABIR, internist, nephrologist, educator; b. Tehran, Iran, Oct. 13, 1939; came to U.S., 1969, naturalized, 1977; s. Abbas and Tahera V. M.D., Tehran U., 1966. Diplomate: Am. Bd. Internal Medicine, Am. Bd. Nephrology. Intern Cook County Hosp., Chgo., 1969-70; resident Berkshire Med. Ctr., Pittsfield, Mass., 1970-71, Wadsworth VA Med. Ctr., 1971-72, UCLA Med. Ctr., 1972-74; prof. medicine U. Calif.-Irvine, 1979—, chief nephrology div., 1977—, dir. hemodialysis unit, 1977—; vice chmn. dept. medicine, 1982—; mem. sci. adv. council Nat. Kidney Found., 1977—. Contbr. numerous articles to med. jours. Recipient Golden Apple award, 1977; named outstanding tchr. U. Calif-Irvine, 1975, 78, 79, 80, 82. Fellow ACP; mem. Am. Soc. Nephrology, Am. Soc. Artificial Organs, Am. Soc. Clin. Research, Am. Paraplegia Soc., Alpha Omega Alpha. Current Work: Pathophysiology of end-stage renal disease particularly in spinal cord injured patients, active in field acid-base metabolism, blood coagulation, and development of new dialysis modalities. Subspecialties: Internal medicine; Nephrology. Home: 66 Balboa Coves Newport Beach CA 92663 Office: Div Nephrology Dept Medicine Room C351 Med Sci I U Calif Irvine CA 92717

VEBLEN, THOMAS THORSTEIN, educator, researcher; b. Seattle, Nov. 15, 1947; s. Robert Alfred and Lois Aileen (Oglesbee) V.; m. Arlene Shui-Yuen Tseu, June 28, 1969; children—Kari Elizabeth, Conner Thorstein. B.A., U. Calif.-Berkeley, 1969; M.A., 1970, Ph.D., 1975. Vis. prof. Universidad Austral, Valdivia, Chile, 1975-79; research fellow Forest Research Inst., Christchurch, N.Z., 1979-81; asst. prof. U. Colo.-Boulder, 1981-83, assoc. prof., 1983—. Contbr. articles to profl. jours. Vol. Smithsonian-Peace Corps, Valdivia, 1975-79; bd. dirs. Internat. Mountain Soc., Boulder, 1982—, Ctr. Andean Studies, Boulder, 1984—. Recipient Postdoctoral fellow Nat. Research Adv. Council, N.Z., 1979-81; Research Assoc. award Inst. Arctic Alpine, 1982—; Nat. Geog. Soc. grantee, 1983; Colo. Commn. Higher Edn. grantee, 1982; Guggenheim Found. fellow, 1985-86. Mem. Ecol. Soc. Am., Brit. Ecol. Soc., Assn. Am. Geography, Internat. Assn. Vegetation Sci., AAAS. Democrat. Current work: Research on forest structure and dynamics, particularly in relation to disturbance; fieldwork in southern Andes and Rocky Mountains. Subspecialty: Ecology (biology). Home: 4170 Hunt Ct Boulder CO 80303 Office: Dept Geography U Colo Campus Box 260 Boulder CO 80309

VEHAR, GORDON ALLEN, biochemist; b. Cleve., Apr. 26, 1948; s. Victor Andy and Georgian Marie (Krause) V.; m. Janet Kaye Cox, Dec. 30, 1977. B.S., Bowling Green State U., 1970; Ph.D., U. Cin., 1976. Postdoctoral fellow U. Wash., Seattle, 1975-80; sr. scientist Genentech, Inc., South San Francisco, Calif., 1980—. Current work: Hematology: protein biochemistry of proteins of fibrinolysis and hemophilia. Subspecialty: Biochemistry (biology). Office: Genentech Inc 460 Point San Bruno Blvd South San Francisco CA 94080

VEIDIS, MIKELIS VALDIS, material scientist, chemist; b. Riga, Latvia, Jan. 25, 1939; came to U.S., 1969, naturalized, 1976; s. Andrejs and Milda (Skolins) V.; m. Brigita Edite Liliensteins, Jan. 27, 1963; children—Valda, Andris, Martins. B.S., U. Queensland, Australia, 1963, M.S., 1967; Ph.D., U. Waterloo Ont., Can., 1969. Chemist Dept. Health, Brisbane, Australia, 1963-67; research fellow Harvard U., Cambridge, Mass., 1969-71; metallurgist Wakefield Corp., Mass., 1971—; supr. materials lab. Unitrod Corp., Mass., 1985—. Contbr. articles to profl. jours. Mem. Royal Australia Chem. Inst. (assoc.), Am. Chem. Soc. Current work: X-ray crystallography, powder metallurgy, analytical chemistry. Subspecialties: Crystallography; Metallurgy. Home: 71 Walnut Hill Rd Newton MA 02161 Office: Wakefield Corp 29 Foundry St Wakefield MA 01880

VEIS, ARTHUR, biochemistry educator; b. Pitts., Dec. 23, 1925; s. Fred M. and Sarah (Landis) V.; m. Eve Zenner, June 24, 1951; children: Judith, Sharon, Deborah. B.S., U. Okla., 1947; Ph.D., Northwestern U., 1951. Instr. phys. chemistry U. Okla., 1951-52; research chemist Armour & Co., Chgo., 1952-60, head phys. chemistry dept., 1959-60; spl. instr. Crane Jr. Coll., Chgo., 1955-56, Loyola U., Chgo., 1957-58; mem. faculty Northwestern U. Med. Sch., Chgo., 1960—, prof. biochemistry, 1965—; asst. dean Northwestern U. Med. Sch. (Grad. Sch.), 1968-70; asso. dean Northwestern U. Med. Sch. (Grad. Sch. and Med. Sch.), 1970-76, chmn. dept. oral biology, 1977—; Disting. vis. prof. U. Adelaide, Australia, 1980; chmn. Gordon Conf. on Structural Macromolecules: Collagen, 1981; chmn. Gordon Conf. on Bones and Teeth, 1985; chmn. dental insts. and spl. projects adv. com. Nat. Inst. Dental Research, 1974-78; mem. pathobiochemistry study sect. NIH, 1983—. Author: Macromolecular Chemistry of Gelatin, 1964; Editor: Biological Polyelectrolytes, 1970, Chemistry and Biology of Mineralized Connective Tissues, 1981; also articles. Editor-in-chief Connective Tissue Research. Served with USNR, 1943-46. Recipient Fogarty Sr. Internat. Scholar award, 1977; Guggenheim fellow, 1967; Case Centennial scholar, 1980; award Internat. Assn. Dental Research, 1981. Mem. Am. Chem. Soc., Am. Soc. Biol. Chemists, Biophys. Soc., N.Y. Acad. Scis., Sigma Xi, Phi Lambda Upsilon. Patentee in field. Current Work: Research in connective tissue biology, particulary collagen structure and biomineralization. Subspecialties: Biochemistry (biology); Biophysical chemistry. Home: 7633 Lowell St Skokie IL 60076 Office: 303 E Chicago Ave Chicago IL 60611

VEITH, FRANK JAMES, surgeon, educator; b. N.Y.C., Aug. 29, 1931; married, 1954; 4 children. A.B., Cornell U., 1952, M.D., 1955. NIH fellow Harvard U. Med. Sch., 1963-64; asst. prof. surgery Cornell U., 1964-67; assoc. prof. Albert Einstein Coll. Medicine, 1967-71, prof. surgery, 1971—; co-dir. kidney transplant unit Montefiore Hosp., N.Y.C., 1967—, assoc. attending surgeon, 1967-71, attending surgeon and chief vascular surgery, 1972—; cons. Heart-Lung Project Com., 1971—. Recipient Career Scientist award Health Research Council, City of N.Y. and Montefiore Hosp., 1965-72; Markle scholar in acad. medicine Cornell U., Albert Einstein Coll. Medicine and Montefiore Hosp., 1964-69. Mem. Soc. Univ. Surgeons, Soc. Vascular Surgery, Am. Assn. Thoracic Surgery, Am. Surg. Assn., Transplantation Soc. Subspecialty: Transplant surgery. Office: Dept Surgery Montefiore Hosp and Med Ctr New York NY 10467*

VEIZER, JÁN, geologist, geology educator; b. Pobedim, Czechoslovakia, June 22, 1941; s. Viktor and Brigita (Brandsteter) V.; m. Elena Ondrus, July 30, 1966; children—Robert, Andrew Douglas. P.G., Comenius U., Bratislava, Czechoslovakia, 1964, Dr. rer. nat., 1968; C.Sc., Slovak Acad. Sci., Bratislava, 1968; Ph.D., Australian Nat. U., Canberra, 1971. Lectr. Comenius U., 1963-66; research scientist Slovak Acad. Sci., 1966-71; vis. asst. prof. UCLA, 1972; vis. scientist U. Göttingen, 1972-73, Humboldt fellow, 1980; research scientist U. Tübigen, 1973; prof. U. Ottawa, Ont., Can., 1973—; vis. fellow Australian Nat. U., 1979; vis. scholar Northwestern U., Evanston, Ill., 1983—; cons. NASA, Houston, 1983—. Contbr. articles to profl. jours. Served to jr. lt. Med. Service Corps. Army of Czechoslovakia, 1965-66. Can.-France fellow Nat. Sci. Engring. Research Council, 1980-81. Fellow Geol. Soc. Am., Geol. Assn. Can.; mem. Geochem. Soc. Am. Roman Catholic. Club: Skying (Ottawa). Current work: Evolution of earth, atmosphere, oceans, life; environment; sedimentary geochemistry; diagenesis. Subspecialties: Geochemistry; Sedimentology. Home: 580 Duff Crescent Ottawa ON K1J 7C5 Canada Office: Derry Lab Dept Geology U Ottawa Ottawa ON K1N 6N5 Canada

VELARDO, JOSEPH THOMAS, molecular biologist, endocrinologist, curricula consultant; b. Newark, Jan. 27, 1923; s. Michael Arthur and Antoinette (Iacullo) V.; m. Forresta M. Monica Power, Aug. 12, 1948 (dec. July 1976). A.B., No. Colo. U., 1948; S.M., Miami U., 1949; Ph.D., Harvard U., 1952. Teaching research fellow Harvard, 1949-52, research fellow in biology and endocrinology, 1952-53; research asso. in pathology Sch. Medicine, 1953-54; research asso. in surgery, 1954-55; asst. in surgery Peter Bent Brigham Hosp., Boston, 1954-55; asst. prof. anatomy and endocrinology Yale Sch. Medicine, 1955-61; prof. anatomy, chmn. dept. N.Y. Med. Coll., N.Y.C., 1961-62; cons. N.Y. Fertility Inst., 1961-62; dir. Inst. for Study Human Reprodn., Cleve., 1962-67; prof. biology John Carroll U., Cleve., 1962-67; mem. research and edn. divs. St. Ann Obstetric and Gynecologic Hosp., Cleve., 1962-67, head dept. research, 1964-67; prof. anatomy dept. Stritch Sch. Medicine Loyola U., Chgo., 1967—, chmn., 1967-73; mem. med. adv. bd. Barren Found., 1973—, cons. internat. basic and biomed. curricula, 1973—; hon. v.p. research and devel. and edn. Universal Research Systems, Warren-Niles, Ohio, 1973—. Editor, contbr. to: Endocrinology of Reproduction, 1958; editor, contbr. to: Essentials of Human Reproduction, 1958; cons. editor, co-author: The Uterus, 1959; contbg. author: The Ovary, 1963, The Ureter, 1967, rev. edit., 1981; co-editor, contbr.: Biology of Reproduction, Basic and Clinical Studies, 1973; Co-author: Histochemistry of Enzymes in the Female Genital System, 1963. Served with USAAF, 1943-45. Recipient award Lederle Med. Fac. Awards Com., 1955-58; named hon. citizen of Sao Paulo Brazil, 1972; U.S. del. Vatican 6th Internat. Congress on Animal Reprodn., 1964. Fellow AAAS, N.Y. Acad. Scis., Gerontol. Soc., Pacific Coast Fertility Soc. (hon.); mem. Am. Assn. Anatomists, Am. Soc. Zoologists, Am. Physiol. Soc., Endocrine Soc., Soc. Endocrinology (Gt. Britain), Soc. Exptl. Biology and Medicine, Am. Soc. Study Sterility (Rubin award 1954), Internat. Fertility Assn., Pan Am. Assn. Anatomy, Midwestern Soc. Anatomists (pres. 1973-74), Mexican Soc. Anatomy (hon.), Sigma Xi, Kappa Delta Pi, Phi Sigma, Gamma Alpha, Alpha Epsilon Delta. Club: Harvard (Chgo.). Current Work: Hormonal effects on cellular mechanisms, effects of hormones on reproductive mechanisms. Subspecialties: Cell biology (medicine); Neuroendocrinology. Home: E Wilson Ave and Cherry Ln Old Grove East Lombard IL 60148 Office: 607 E Wilson Rd Lombard IL 60148

VELASCO-SUAREZ, MANUAL M., physician, surgeon; b. San Cristobal las Casas, Chiapas, Mex., Dec. 28, 1915; s. José Manual Velasco Balboa and María (Suarez) Velasco-S.; m. Elvira Siles, Mar. 1, 1946; children: Jose Manual, María Cristina, Guadalupe, Jess Agustín, Francisco Javier, Juan Antonio, María de Lourdes, Elvira, Lucía Angélica, Teresita, Agnes. M.C., Universidad Nacional Autónomo de Mex., 1939. Resident U. Iowa, 1940; resident in neurology, neurol. surgery Harvard U., 1941-42; resident in neuropathology, neurol. surgery; Mass. Gen. Hosp.; neurosurgeon Hosp. Juarez, Mexico City, 1947-58; head neuropsychiat. dept. S.S.A., nat. health agy., Mexico City, 1953-59; head neurology and neurosurgery Hosp. Juarez, from 1958; dir. Inst. Nacional de Neurología, 1959—; prof. Universidad Nacional Autónomo de Mex., 1944—; chief prof. neurology and neurosurg. group; now pres. Academia Nacional de Ciencias de Mex. Fellow ACS, Am. Psychiat. Assn.; mem. Liga Mex. Contra la Epilepsia (founding pres.), Mex. Soc. Neurology and Psychiatry (pres.), World Group of Experts on Epilepsy (pres. 1968), other Mex., fgn. and internat. orgns. Subspecialty: Neurosurgery. Office: Academia Nacional de Ciencias Apdo M 77-98 Mexico 1 DF Mexico*

VELK, ROBERT JAMES, psychologist, consultant, researcher; b. Chgo., Feb. 27, 1938; s. Jerry E. and Sylvia B. (Vladar) V.; m. Vera Anne Kraml, Nov. 25, 1961; children—Robert Frank, Cheryl Anne. A.A. in Edn., Morton Coll., 1956; B.B.A., Northwestern U., 1963, M.B.A., 1968; M.A. in Expl. Psychology, Rutgers U., 1980, Ph.D. in Psychology, 1983. Asst. mgr. product decoration Meyercord Co., Carol Stream, Ill., 1960-68; dir. mktg. Kepner-Tregoe, Inc., Princeton, N.J., 1968-73; pres. Creative Leadership Inc., Princeton, 1973-82, Cognitive Sci. Corp., Ft. Collins, Colo., 1982—. Authored atty. gen.'s sr. exec. seminar U.S. Dept. Justice, program in problem-solving, decision-making and planning Johns Hopkins Med. Inst. Mem. Am. Soc. Tng. and Devel., Nat. Soc. for Performance and Instruction, Am. Psychol. Assn., AAAS. Republican. Club: Gideon's Internat. (Trenton, N.J.) (chaplain 1979). Current work: Conceptual and perceptual determinants of accuracy in recognition and recall of symbolic and nonsymbolic stimuli; expert and novice problem-solving/decision-making in applied settings. Subspecialty: Cognition. Home: 305 Stove Prairie Rd Bellvue CO 80512Office: Cognitive Sci Corp PO Box 1487 Ft Collins CO 80522

VELTRI, ROBERT WILLIAM, microbiologist; b. McKeesport, Pa., Dec. 1, 1941; s. Anthony and Desdemona (D'Innocenzo) V.; m. Suzanne Jones, Apr. 10, 1961; children: Anthony J., Katherine M. (dec.). A.B., Youngstown State U., 1963; M.S. in Microbiology, W.Va., U., 1965, Ph.D., 1968. Asst. prof., dir. research depts. otolaryngology and microbiology W.Va. U. Med. Ctr., Morgantown, 1968-72, assoc. prof., dir. research, 1972-76, prof., dir. research, 1976-81; dir. research and devel. immunology-serology Diagnostics div. Cooper Biomed., Inc., Malvern, Pa., 1982-84; pres. Am. Biotech. Co., 1984—; regional lab. dir. Nat. Found. for Cancer Research, 1980—. Contbr. articles to profl. jours. Bd. dirs. Monongahela County (W.Va.) unit Am. Cancer Soc., 1979-81, bd. dirs. W.Va. state unit, 1980-81. Grantee Deafness Research Found., 1971-74; Grantee Nat. Cancer Inst., 1974-78, 80-83. Fellow Am. Acad. Microbiology; mem. AAAS, Am. Assn. Immunologists, Am. Assn. Cancer Research, Soc. Infectious Diseases, Am. Soc. Microbiology, Sigma Xi. Republican. Roman Catholic. Current Work: Development of new in vitro diagnostic tests for cancer and infectious diseases; cancer research on human tumor markers; investigations on new immune modulatory and anti-cancer agents produced by participating scientists of the National Foundation for Cancer Research. Subspecialties: Immunology (medicine); Cancer research (medicine). Home: 19005 Glendower Rd Gaithersburg MD 20879 Office: 7658 Standish Pl Suite 107 Rockville MD 20855

VENEZIA, WILLIAM ALBERT, scientist; b. Portchester, N.Y., Jan. 22, 1947; s. Caesar A. and Alice (Schrader) V.; m. Ingrid Marie Johnson, Mar. 21, 1970; children: Anthony, Kristine. A.S., Broward Community Coll., 1967; B.S., Fla. Atlantic U., 1970; M.S., Clemson U., 1971, Ph.D., 1975. Sr. staff engr. Johns Hopkins U., Laurel, Md., 1975-80; assoc. prof. ocean engrng. Fla. Atlantic U., Boca Raton, 1980-81; prin. scientist Gen. Offshore Corp., Fort Lauderdale, Fla., 1981-84; adj. prof. Nova U., Fort Lauderdale, 1981—; cons. Johns Hopkins U. Applied Physics Lab., Laurel, Md., 1980-81; mem. tech. com. Naval Sea Systems Command, Washington, 1981—; dir. master's research Fla. Atlantic U., Boca Raton, 1980-81; cons. Naval Surface Weapons Center, Fort Lauderdale, Fla., 1980-84, tech. mgr., 1984—; mem. Citizen Ambassador Program People to People Coastal Zone Mgmt. del. to Japan and People's Republic of China, 1985. Mem. Allview Arrowhead Civic Assn., Columbia, Md., 1975-80. NSF trainee, 1970-75; Fla. Atlantic U. research grantee, 1981; Fla. Inst. Oceanography research grantee, 1981; Johns Hopkins U. research grantee, 1981. Mem. Marine Tech. Soc. (chmn. student chpt. 1968-70). Republican. Roman Catholic. Current Work: Applied ocean science, working in areas of fiber optics in ocean systems, ocean surveillance, and state of the art ocean system development. Subspecialties: Ocean engineering; Offshore technology. Home: 375 NW 35th Ln Boca Raton FL 33431 Office: Naval Surface Weapons Ctr 1650 SW 39th St Fort Lauderdale FL 33315

VENKATARAMIAH, AMARANENI, environ. physiologist; b. Atmakur, India, Aug. 16, 1928; came to U.S., 1969; s. A. and A. (Lakshvamma) Rangaiah; m. Swarajyam Kurra, June 9, 1949; children: Sulochana, Rao, Bharadwaj, Kumar, Sujatha. B.S. in Biology and Chemistry, Andhra U., Waltair, India, 1955; M.A. in Zoology, Sri Venkateswara U., Tirupati, India, 1957, Ph.D. in Eco-Physiology, 1965. Lectr. Andhra Loyola Coll., Vijayawada, India, 1957-61, Sri Venkateswara U., 1965-66; research fellow Council of Sci. and Indsl. Research, New Delhi, India, 1966-67; head physiology sect. Gulf Research Lab., Ocean Springs, 1969—; adj. prof. biology U. So. Miss., Hattiesburg, 1978—. Contbr. articles to profl. jours. Dept. Army grantee, 1970-77; Dept. Energy grantee, 1978-82; other grants. Mem. AAAS, Am. Soc. Zoologists, Gulf Estuarine Research Soc., Miss. Acad. Scis., Inc., World Mariculture Soc. Patentee in field. Current Work: Physiological ecology of marine animals with emphasis on osmoregulation and metabolic problems, crustacean aquaculture, toxicological effects of discharges from the ocean thermal energy conversion plants on marine animals. Subspecialties: Comparative physiology; Ocean energy conversion. Home: 219-1/2 Halstead Rd PO Drawer AG Ocean Springs MS 39564 Office: Gulf Coast Research Lab East Beach Dr Ocean Springs MS 39564

VENKATESAN, VALADI NATARAJ, research engineer; b. Madras, India, Jan. 23, 1946; came to U.S., 1973, s. V.S. and Janaki (Mahadevan) Natarajan; m. Jeyashree Viswanathan, Feb. 26, 1982; 1 child, Naren N. B.E., U. Annamalai, India, 1968; M. Tech., Indian Inst. Tech., Madras, 1970; Ph.D., U. Utah, Salt Lake City, 1979. Postdoctoral fellow U. Utah, 1979-80; research engr. Mobil Research & Devel. Corp., Dallas, 1980—. Contbr. articles to profl. jours. Patentee in field. Mem. Am. Chem. Soc., Am. Inst. Chem. Engrs., Soc. Petroleum Engrs. Current work: Development of processes for enhanced oil recovery; process variables studies as related to thermal EOR processes. Subspecialties: Petroleum engineering; Chemical engineering. Office: Mobil Research & Devel Corp 13777 Midway Rd Dallas TX 75234

VENTER, J. CRAIG, research scientist, biochemist, educator; b. Salt Lake City, Oct. 14, 1946; s. John and Elizabeth (Wisdom) V.; m. Claire M. Fraser, Oct. 10, 1981; 1 son: Christopher. B.A., U. Calif., San Diego, 1972, Ph.D. in Physiology and Pharmacology, 1975. Postgrad. research pharmacologist and chemist U. Calif., San Diego, 1975-76; asst. prof. pharmacology and therpaeutics SUNY, Buffalo, 1976-81; assoc. prof. biochemistry SUNY (Sch. Medicine), 1981-82; assoc. chief molecular immunology Roswell Park Meml. Inst., Buffalo, 1982-84; adj. prof. biochem. pharmacology SUNY-Buffalo, 1983-85; chief sect. receptor biochemistry NIH, NINCDS, Bethesda, Md., 1984—; indsl. cons. Contbr. articles to sci. jours. Served with MC USN, 1965-68, Vietnam. NIH grantee, 1977-84; Am. Heart Assn. grantee, 1977-82; Pharm. Mfrs. Assn. grantee, 1977. Mem. Am. Soc. Exptl. Biology. Current Work: Neurotransmitter receptor purification; monoclonal antibodies; autoimmune receptor diseases (asthma), radiation inactivation. Subspecialties: Biochemistry (medicine); Receptors. Office: Sect Receptor Biochemistry NINCDS NIH Bethesda MD 20892

VENTURA, WILLIAM PAUL, pharmacologist, educator; b. Braddock, Pa., Dec. 1, 1942; s. Piero and Matilda (Rogym) V.; m. Marion R. Simpson, Apr. 3, 1942; children—Alexander, Christine. B.Sc., Duquesne U., Pitts., 1964, M.Sc., 1966; Ph.D., N.Y. Med. Coll., 1969; M.B.A., Pace U., 1981. Instr. to asst. prof. N.Y. Med. Coll., Valhalla, 1969-73; prof. pharmacology Pace U., Pleasantville, N.Y., 1974—, chmn. dept. biol. scis., 1985—. Contbr. articles to profl. jours. Scoutmaster Tappanzee Council, Boy Scouts Am., Briarcliff, N.Y., 1984—. NIH postdoctorial fellow; grantee NSF, Lalor Found. Mem. various socs. in field. Current work: Reproductive pharmacology; physiology teratology. Subspecialties: Pharmacology; Toxicology (medicine). Office: Pace Univ Pleasantville NY 10570

VERAY, FRANCISCO X., cardiology educator, history of medicine and philosophy researcher; b. Yauco, P.R., Mar. 9, 1933; s. Francisco Veray-Marin and Margarita Torregrosa; m. Maria del Pilar Mazo Franco, Sept. 13, 1959; children: Carmen, Francisco X III, Maria-Jose, Carlos-Jaime. B.S., U. P.R.-Rio Piedras, 1953, Instituto Balmes, Barcelona, Spain, 1956; M.D., U. Barcelona, 1959. Rotating intern Damas Hosp., Ponce, P.R., 1959-60; resident in internal medicine VA Hosp., Ft. Howard, Md., 1962-64; pres. elect., dir., exec. com. P.R. Heart Assn., 1983; fellow in cardiology dept. medicine Univ. Hosp., Rio Piedras, P.R., 1964-66; assoc. in medicine dept. medicine Recinto de Ciencias Medicas, Rio Piedras, 1966-68, asst. prof. medicine, 1968-70, assoc. prof., 1977; med. dir. coronary care unit Univ. Hosp., Recinto de Ciencias Medicas, Rio Piedras, 1972—. Author: Betances, El Medico, 1969. Sec. P.R. Heart Assn., 1969, exec. com., 1969-73, pres. elect, dir., exec. com., 1983; pres. com. history and cultural Asociacion Medica de Puerto Rico, 1974-80. Served to 1st lt. USAR, 1953-60. Fellow Am. Coll. Chest Physicians, Am. Coll. Angiology (assoc.); mem. N.Y. Acad. Scis., Sociedad Cardiologia P.R. (sec. 1969-70), Hastings Ctr., AAAS, Am. Soc. Internal Medicine, Am. Soc. Clin. Research, AAUP. Roman Catholic. Current Work: History of medicine and philosophy, heart disease in pregnancy, beta blockers chronic use after acute myocardial infarction. Subspecialties: Cardiology; Internal medicine. Office: Dept of Medicine Recinto de Ciencias Medicas University of Puerto Rico Rio Piedras PR 00936

VERBALIS, JOSEPH GEORGE, physician, researcher, educator; b. Plymouth, Pa., July 14, 1949; s. Anthony Charles and Michalene (Margavage) V.; m. Virginia Dale Steen, Nov. 10, 1973; children—Alyssa Denise, Michael Joseph. A.B., Princeton U., 1971; M.D., U. Pitts., 1975. Diplomate. Am. Bd. Internal Medicine. Intern and resident in internal medicine Hosp. of U. Pa., Phila., 1975-78; fellow in endocrinology U. Pitts., 1978-80, asst. prof. medicine, 1980—. Mem. ACP, Am. Fedn. Clin. Research, Endocrine Soc., Soc. for Neurosci., Sigma Xi, Alpha Omega Alpha. Episcopalian. Current work: Neuroendocrinology; neurohypophysis; regulation of pituitary function; disorders of body fluid balance. Subspecialties: Neuroendocrinology; Internal medicine. Office: Univ Pitts 930 Scaife Hall Pittsburgh PA 15261

VERCELLOTTI, JOHN RAYMOND, laboratory research executive; b. Joliet, Ill., May 2, 1933; s. Joseph Francis and Mary Therese (Walowski) V.; m. Sharon Cecile Verget, Sept. 3, 1966; children: Ellen, Paul. B.A. with distinction, St. Bonaventure U., Olean, N.Y., 1955; postgrad., Cath. U. Am., 1955-58, U. Pitts., 1958; M.Sc., Marquette U., 1960; Ph.D., Ohio State U., 1963. Resident research assoc. fellow Ohio State U., Columbus, 1963-64; asst. prof. chemistry Marquette U., Milw., 1965-67; assoc. prof. U. Tenn., Knoxville, 1969-70; assoc. prof. Va. Poly. Inst. and State U., Blacksburg, 1970-73, prof., 1973-79; research dir. V-Labs., Inc., Covington, La., 1979-85; research leader So. Regional Research Ctr., U.S. Dept. Agr., New Orleans, 1985—. Contbr. articles on chemistry to profl. jours. NSF grantee, 1971-74; U.S. Dept. Agr. grantee, 1973-76; NATO grantee, 1978-80; Crinos Pharm. grantee, 1980-83. Fellow Am. Inst. Chemists, Royal Soc. Chemistry London; mem. Am. Soc. Biol. Chemists, Am. Chem. Soc., Sigma Xi. Democrat. Roman Catholic. Current Work: Research on chemistry and biochemistry of the carbohydrates, enzymology of glycosidic linkages, fermentations and organic synthesis. Subspecialties: Biochemistry (medicine); Organic chemistry. Home: 215 E 4th Ave Covington LA 70433 Office: So Regional Research Ctr US Dept Agr PO Box 19687 New Orleans LA 70179

VERDIER, PETER HOWARD, research chemist; b. Pasadena, Calif., Feb. 16, 1931; s. Albert Russell and Margaret Blossom (Buck) V. B.S., Calif. Inst. Tech., 1952; Ph.D., Harvard U., 1957. Research assoc. in chemistry MIT, Cambridge, 1957-58; research fellow in chemistry Harvard U., Cambridge, 1958-59; research chemist Union Carbide Corp., Tarrytown, N.Y., 1959-64, staff cons., N.Y.C., 1964-65; research chemist Nat. Bur. Standards, Gaithersburg, Md., 1965-70, 75—, chief molecular characterization, 1970-74. Contbr. articles to profl. jours. Fellow Am. Phys. Soc. Current work: Macromolecular dynamics and structure; high-polymer solution properties. Subspecialties: Polymer physics; Physical chemistry. Office: Nat Bur Standards Gaithersburg MD 20899

VEREBEY, KARL G., clin. pharmacologist, educator; b. Budapest, Hungary, Mar. 12, 1938; came to U.S., 1956, naturalized, 1963; s. Karoly and Etelka (Szabo) V.; m. Debra M. Adler, Feb. 22, 1962; children: Todd, Marc. A.A. in Humanities, Eotvos J. Gimnazium, 1956; B.A. in Physiology, Hunter Coll., 1965; M.A. in Molecular Biology, CUNY, 1968; Ph.D. in Pharmacology and Biochemistry, Cornell U., 1972. Cert. clin. lab. dir. Am. Bd. Bioanalysis. Research assoc. in neurology and pharmacology Cornell U. Med. Coll., N.Y.C., 1972-73; dir. clin. pharmacology N.Y. State Div. Substance Abuse Services, Bklyn., 1973—; research prof. psychiatry N.Y. Med. Coll., 1977—; assoc. prof. psychiatry SUNY Downstate Med. Sch., Bklyn., 1979—; clin. lab. dir. Psychiat. Diagnostic Labs. Am., Summit, N.J., 1982—; mem. exec. com. Council Research Scientists, N.Y. State, 1980—, Drug Abuse Adv. Council N.Y. State, 1984. Contbr. over 75 articles to sci. publs. Served with U.S. Army, 1961-63. USPHS fellow, 1972-73; Nat. Inst. Drug Abuse grantee, 1974-77, 79-81. Mem. Am. Soc. Pharmacology and Exptl. Therapeutics, N.Y. Acad. Scis. Current Work: Development of sensitive analytic methods for drugs in body fluids, evaluate plasma levels vs. behavioral responses; experiments in pharmacodynamics correlated with psychopharmacology. Subspecialties: Pharmacology; Toxicology (medicine). Office: 80 Hanson Pl Brooklyn NY 11217

VERGHESE, CHACKO PERAKATHU, research scientist; b. Kozhencherry, Kerala, India, Feb. 8, 1945; came to U.S., 1969, permanent resident, 1972; s. Chacko Manil and Thankamma (Sara) V.; m. Kumari Daniel, Sept. 21, 1972; children—Tikku Jacob, Tisha Sarah. B.S. in Chemistry, Union Christian Coll., Alwaye, Kerala, India, 1968, M.S. in Chemistry, Roosevelt U., 1972. Research assoc. Copernicus Med. Research Ctr., Chgo., 1971-72; research specialist Henry Ford Hosp., Detroit, 1973-80; research analyst Duke Med. Ctr., Durham, N.C., 1980-83; research scientist Burroughs Wellcome, Research Triangle Park, N.C., 1983—. Contbr. articles to profl. jours. Roosevelt U. grad. fellow, 1970-71; Witco Chem. scholar, 1969-70. Mem. Am. Chem. Soc., Am. Assn. for Clin. Chemistry. Republican. Episcopalian. Current work: Design and conduct pharmacokinetic and metabolic studies of drugs for human use; develop and apply analytical methods for quantitation of drugs in biological fluids and tissues. Subspecialties: Medicinal chemistry; Drug metabolism. Office: Burroughs Wellcome Co 3030 Cornwallis Rd Research Triangle Park NC 27709

VERINK, ELLIS DANIEL, JR., metallurgical engineering educator; b. Peking, Feb. 9, 1920; s. Ellis Daniel and Phoebe Elizabeth (Smith) V.; m. Martha Eulala Owens, July 4, 1942; children: Barbara Ann, Wendy Susan. B.S. in Metall. Engring, Purdue U., 1941; M.S. in Metall. Engring, Ohio State U., 1963, Ph.D. in Metall. Engring, 1965. Registered profl. engr., Fla., Pa., Calif. Engr., mgr. chem. sect. Alcoa, New Kensington, Pa., 1946-59, mgr. chem. and petroleum industry sales, Pitts., 1959-62; mem. faculty U. Fla., Gainesville, 1965—, prof. metall. materials engring, 1973—, chmn. materials sci. and engring. dept., 1973—, Disting. Service prof., 1984—; pres. Materials Cons., Inc., Gainesville, 1970—; cons. in field; chmn. Gordon Research Conf. on Corrosion, New London, N.H., 1978. Contbr. over 70 articles to tech. publs. Pres. bd. dirs. YMCA, Gainesville. Served to comdr. USNR, 1941-46. Recipient Tchr.-Scholar of Yr. award U. Fla., 1979, Disting. Alumnus award Ohio State U., 1982. Mem. AIME (pres. Metall. Soc. 1985), ASTM (Sam Tour award 1978), Am. Welding Soc., Electrochem. Soc., Am. Soc. for Metals, Nat. Assn. Corrosion Engrs. (bd. dirs. 1984—; Willis Rodney Whitney award 1982). Republican. Presbyterian. Lodges: Masons; Shiners; Kiwanis. Current Work: Improving the ability to predict corrosion behavior of alloys through electrochemical and complementary methods, thereby increasing cost effectiveness of research. Subspecialties: Corrosion; Materials (engineering). Home: 4401 NW 18th Pl Gainesville FL 32605 Office: Materials Sci and Engring Dept Univ Fla Gainesville FL 32611

VERMA, DESH PAL SINGH, molecular biology educator, researcher, consultant; b. Tikri, India, Mar. 2, 1944; came to Can., 1967, naturalized, 1977; s. Baljeet Singh and Atalkaur Verma; m. Indra Verma, Jan. 5, 1965; children—Hiram, Surya. B.Sc., Meerut Coll., Agra U., India, 1962, M.Sc., 1964; Ph.D., U. Western Ont., 1970. Postdoctoral researcher Cancer Inst., Phila.; research assoc. McGill U., Montreal, Que., Can., 1972-74, asst. prof. molecular biology, 1974-78, assoc. prof., 1978-83, prof., 1983—, dir. Centre Plant Molecular Biology, 1985—; cons. Allied Chems., Syracuse, N.Y., 1982-85, Allelix, Inc., Mississauga, Ont., Can., 1982—. Co-author: Genes Involved in Microbe-Plant Interactions, 1984. Contbr. numerous articles to profl. jours. Patentee in rhizobium/soybean, 1983. Recipient C.D. Nelson award, 1984; NSERC grantee, 1974—, 83—; Rockefeller Found. grantee, 1979-81; NSERC-Steacie fellow, 1981-83. Mem. Internat. Soc. Plant Molecular Biology (bd. dirs. 1982-86), Am. Soc. Plant Physiologists (editorial bd.), Montreal Molecular Biology Assn. (pres. 1980-81), Can. Soc. Plant Physiologists, Am. Soc. Cell Biologists. Current work: Molecular biology of symbiosis/-pathogenicity in plants, regulation of gene expression, gene transfer, nitrogen fixation, plant biotechnology. Subspecialties: Molecular biology; Plant genetics. Office: McGill U Centre Plant Molecular Biology 1205 Dr Penfield Ave Montreal PQ H3A 1B1 Canada

VERMA, RAM SAGAR, geneticist, educator; b. India, Mar. 3, 1946; s. Gaya Prasad and Moonga Devi V.; m. Shakuntala Devi, May 4, 1962; 1 child, Harendra Kumar. B.Sc. in Agr, Agra U., India, 1965, M.Sc. in Agr, 1967; Ph.D. in Cytogenetics, U. Western Ont., Can., 1972. Plant breeder dept. genetics and plant breeding Govt. Agrl. Coll., Janpur, India, 1965-67; teaching asst. U. Western Ont., 1967-73, research asst. dept. plant scis., 1967-73; research assoc. dept. pediatrics U. Colo., Denver, 1973-74, fellow, 1974-76; instr. dept. medicine SUNY-Downstate Med. Ctr., Bklyn., 1976, asst. prof., 1976-79, assoc. prof., 1979—; assoc. dir. cytogenetics Jewish Hosp. and Med. Ctr., Bklyn., 1976-78, chief cytogenetics, 1978-79, chief div. cytogenetics, 1980—; mem. cytogenetic adv. com. for prenatal diagnosis lab. N.Y.C. Dept. Health, 1978—. Contbr. numerous articles to profl. jours. Fellow N.Y. Acad. Scis.; mem. Am. Soc. Cell Biology, AAAS, Am. Fedn. Clin. Research, Am. Genetic Assn., Am. Soc.. Human Genetics, European Soc. Human Genetics, Genetic Soc. Am., Genetic Soc. Can., Internat. Assn. Human Biologists, Indian Soc. Human Genetics, Soc. Exptl. Biology and Medicine. Subspecialties: Animal genetics; Biofeedback. Home: 42-70 65th Pl Woodside NY 11377 Office: 555 Prospect Pl Brooklyn NY 11238

VERNARDAKIS, THEODORE GALACTION, chemist; b. Limassol, Cyprus, Nov. 14, 1942; came to U.S., 1961, naturalized, 1977; s. Galaction George and Eleni Michael (Konstanti) V.; m. Mary Louise Kolentse, May 11, 1974. B.S., Coll. of Emporia., 1965; M.S., Okla. State U., 1968, Ph.D., 1972. Research assoc. U. Cin., 1972-77; chemist Borden Chem. Co., Cin., 1978-79; sr. chemist, group leader Sun Chem. Corp., Cin., 1979—. Contbr. articles to profl. jours. Mem. Am. Chem. Soc., Sigma Xi, Phi Lambda Upsilon. Current work: Pigment research and development; the application of physicochemical techniques in characterization of organic pigments with emphasis on their morphological, particulate and surface properties. Subspecialties: Physical chemistry; Surface chemistry. Home: 5394 Sidney Rd Cincinnati OH 45238 Office: Sun Chem Corp 4625 Este Ave Cincinnati OH 45232

VERNICK, ARNOLD SANDER, environmental engineer; b. N.Y.C., May 2, 1933; s. Joseph Leon and Beatrice (Carlin) V.; m. Lynne Beatrice Bowin, Sept. 16, 1962; children—Jeffrey Francis, Kenneth Charles. B.S., Queens Coll., 1956; B.C.E., Columbia U., 1956; M.S., NYU, 1970. Registered profl. engr., N.J., N.Y. Project engr. Esso Standard Oil Co., Linden, N.J., 1956-62; civil engr. Alexander Potter Assocs., N.Y.C., 1962-63; dist. engr. Gulfstan Corp., Middlesex, N.J., 1963-64; sanitary engr. Chem. Constrn. Corp., N.Y.C., 1964-66, Gibbs & Hill, N.Y.C., 1966-68; mgr. environ. engring. Burns & Roe Indsl. Services Corp., Oradell, N.J., 1968—. Author: (with others) Handbook of Industrial Wastes Pretreatment, 1980. Editor: Handbook of Wastewater Treatment Processes, 1981. Contbr. articles to profl. jours. Served with AUS, 1958, to comdr. USPHS Res. Corp. Fellow ASCE; mem. Nat. Soc. Profl. Engrs., Am. Acad. Environ. Engrs. (diplomate), Am. Water Works Assn., Air Pollution Control Assn., Water Pollution Control Fedn., Tau Beta Pi. Current work: Manage a staff of professionals engaged in wastewater treatment, water supply, solid waste management, air pollution abatement and hazardous waste disposal for both governmental and industrial clients. . Home: 602 James Ln River Vale NJ 07675 Office: Burns & Roe Indsl Services Corp 700 Kinderkamack Rd Oradell NJ 07649

VERRIEST, ERIK ISIDOOR, electrical engineering educator, researcher; b. Roeselare, West Flanders, Belgium, Mar. 19, 1950; came to U.S., 1974, permanent resident, 1981; s. Julien Henri and Rosa (Dezeure) V.; m. Katherine Hanson, May 13, 1983; 1 child, Kirstin Marieke. Candidate in chem. engring. State U. Ghent, Belgium, 1970, Elec. Engr., 1973; M.E.E., Stanford U., 1975, Ph.D. in Elec. Engring., 1980. Teaching and research asst. controls lab. and hybrid computer ctr. State U. Ghent, 1973-74; research asst. Stanford U., Calif., 1975-79; asst. prof. elec. engring. Ga. Inst. Tech., Atlanta, 1980—; cons., vis. prof. U. South Fla., Tampa, 1980. Belgian Am. Ednl. Found. Inc. Francqui fellow, 1974. Mem. IEEE, AAUP, Planetary Soc., Belgian Math. Soc., AAAS, Sigma Xi. Current work: Systems modeling and model reduction estimation and filtering; effects of finite wordlength in digital machines. Subspecialties: Electrical engineering; Systems engineering. Office: Ga Inst Tech Sch Elec Engring Atlanta GA 30332

VERRILLO, RONALD THOMAS, sensory scientist, researcher; b. Hartford, Conn., July 31, 1927; s. Francesco Paul and Angela (Forte) V.; m. Violet Verrillo, June 3, 1950; children: Erica, Dan, Thomas. B.A., Syracuse U., 1952; Ph.D., U. Rochester, 1958. Asst. prof. Syracuse U., 1957-62, research assoc., 1959-63, research fellow, 1963-67, assoc. prof., 1967-74, prof., 1977—; assoc. dir. Inst. Sensory Research Syracuse U., 1980-84, dir., 1984—; vis. prof. Karolinska Inst., Stockholm, 1977. Contbr. numerous articles in field to profl. jours. Served with USN, 1945-46. Am. Found. Blind fellow, 1956; NATO fellow Oxford U., 1970-71; NSF grantee, 1967-72, 84—; NIH grantee, 1972—; recipient research award Am. Personnel and Guidance Assn., 1961. Fellow Acoustical Soc. Am.; mem. Psychonomic Soc., Eastern Psychol. Assn., Soc. Neurosci., N.Y. Acad. Sci., Internat. Assn. Study Pain, Am. Pain Soc., Sigma Xi (recipient Research award 1982). Current Work: Cutaneous sensory systems; sensory, cutaneous, mechanoreceptor, psychophysics. Subspecialties: Sensory processes; Psychophysics. Home: 312 Berkeley Dr Syracuse NY 13210 Office: Inst Sensory Research Syracuse U Syracuse NY 13210

VERRY, WILLIAM ROBERT, systems engineer; b. Portland, Oreg., July 11, 1933; s. William Richard and Maurine Houser (Braden) V.; m. Bette Lee Ronspiess, Nov. 20, 1955 (div. 1981); children: William David, Sandra Kay Verry Londregan, Steven Bruce, Kenneth Scott; m. Jean Elizabeth Morrison, Oct. 16, 1982; step-children: Lucinda Jean Hale, Christine Carol Hale Fortner, Martha Jean Johnson, Brian Kenneth Lackey, Robert Morrison Lackey. B.A., Reed Coll., 1955; B.S., Portland State U., 1957; M.A., Fresno State U., 1960; Ph.D., Ohio State U.-Columbus, 1972. Instr. chemistry Reedley (Calif.) Coll., 1957-60; ops. research analyst Naval Weapons Center, China Lake, Calif., 1960-63; ordnance engr. Honeywell Ordnance, Hopkins, Minn., 1963-64; sr. scientist Litton Industries, St. Paul., 1964-67; project mgr. Tech. Ops., Inc., Alexandria, Va., 1967-70; research assoc. Ohio State U., Columbus, 1970-72; prin. engr. Computer Sci. Corp., Falls Church, Va., 1972-77; mem. tech. staff MITRE Corp., Albuquerque, 1977—. Mem. Ops. Research Soc. Am. Current Work: Systems engineering of simulations on a Joint Test Force designing and implementing a state-of-the-art simulation of command control and communications (C3) in the airland battle using current combat and C3 simulations as components. Subspecialties: Operations research (engineering); Systems engineering. Home: 5209 Mesa del Oso NE Albuquerque NM 87111 Office: MITRE Corp PO Box 5520 Kirtland AFB NM 87185

VERSTANDIG, CHARLES COLEMAN, radiologist; b. Noddle, Miss., Sept. 26, 1905; s. Hermann Verstandig and Helene Schmidt; m. W. Dower, June 7, 1937 (dec. June 1965); children—Lee Lovely, Davyne Elaine. Student Ala. Poly., Auburn, 1936; M.D., U. Tenn., 1939. Diplomate Am. Bd. Radiology. Intern, St. Joseph Hosp., Paterson, N.J. and St. Raphael Hosp., New Haven, Conn.; resident Wright Hosp., Houston and John Gaston Hosp., Memphis; radiologist Meriden Hosp., Conn., 1947-52, Hasonic Hosp., Wallingford, Conn., 1951—, Conn. Valley Hosp., Middletown, Conn., 1952-67; practice medicine specializing in radiology, New Haven, 1942; cons. in field. Mem. Bd. Edn. Town of Hamden, Conn., 1954. Served to col. U.S. Army, 1939-46; ETO. Recipient Disting. Alumni award U. Tenn. Fellow AMA, Am. Coll. Radiology, Royal Coll. Surgeons, Am. Coll. Cardiology, New Eng. Roentgen Ray Soc.; mem. Soc. Nuclear Medicine, Biophys. Soc. Lodge: Masons. Current work: Geriatrics. Subspecialties: Diagnostic radiology; Nuclear medicine. Home: 19 Filbert St Hamden CT 06517 Office: Radiologic Inst Suite 112 2 Church St S New Haven CT 06519

VESEL, RICHARD WARREN, engineering products company executive; b. Wickliffe, Ohio, Sept. 1, 1954; s. Clarence George and Wanda Jacqueline (Purpura) V.; m. Nancy Hallam, Aug. 13, 1982. B.S.E.E., Case Western Res. U., 1976, M.S.E.E., 1978. Registered profl. engr. Ohio. Pres. Method Systems Inc., Euclid, Ohio, 1976—; supr. engring. Bailey Controls Co., Wickliffe, 1978-83. Mem. IEEE, Am. Nuclear Soc. Republican. Developer vortex shedding Flowmeter with optical transducer, 1982, optical communications loop terminal module, 1982. Current Work: Empirically derived algorithms for vision based decisions. Subspecialties: Graphics, image processing, and pattern recognition; Robotics. Home: 1755 Duffton Ln Painesville OH 44077 Office: 3511 Lost Nation Rd Willoughby OH 44094

VESELL, ELLIOT SAUL, pharmacologist, educator; b. N.Y.C., Dec. 24, 1933; s. Harry and Evelyn (Jaffe) V.; m. Kristen Peery, Mar. 24, 1968; children: Liane, Hilary. A.B. magna cum laude, Harvard Coll., 1955; M.D. magna cum laude, Harvard U., 1959. Intern in pediatrics Mass. Gen. Hosp., 1959-60; research assoc. in human genetics, asst. physician Rockefeller Inst., 1960-62; asst. resident in medicine Peter Bent Brigham Hosp., 1962-63; clin. assoc. Nat. Inst. Arthritis and Metabolic Disease, 1963-65; head. sect. pharmacogenetics Lab. Chem. Pharmacology, Nat. Heart Inst., 1965-69; prof. pharmacology, genetics and medicine, also chmn. dept. pharmacology Coll. Medicine, Pa. State U., Hershey, 1969—, Evan Pugh prof., 1981—; Julius W. Sturmer Meml. lectr. Phila. Coll. Pharmacy and Sci., 1980; Frohlich prof. Royal Soc. Medicine, 1985. Contbr. articles to profl. publs. Mem. Am. Soc. Pharmacology and Exptl. Therapeutics (therapeutics award 1971, Harry Gold award 1985), Soc. Exptl. Biology and Medicine (Samuel J. Meltzer award 1967), Am. Soc. Clin. Investigation, Am. Coll. Clin. Pharmacology, Assn. Am. Physicians, Am. Soc. Clin. Pharmacology and Therapeutics. Jewish. Clubs: Cosmos (Washington); Century Assn. (N.Y.C.). Current Work: Molecular and clinical pharmacology; effects of heredity and environmental factors on the disposition of drugs. Subspecialties: Pharmacology; Genetics and genetic engineering (medicine). Office: Pa State U Coll Medicine PO Box 850 Hershey PA 17033

VEST, ANTHONY LEON, nuclear engineering services executive; b. Kingsport, Tenn., Aug. 26, 1947; s. Landon Leon and Helen Maige (Payne) V.; m. Nancy Ann Morton, Sept. 27, 1970; 1 dau., Shannon Tamralyn. B.S. in Mech. Engring, U. Tenn.-Knoxville, 1969, M.B.A., 1984. Field engr. Gen. Electric Co., Atlanta, 1969-70, requisition engr., Knoxville, 1970-71, nuclear test engr., Cordova, Ill., 1971-72, shift engr., Morris, Ill., 1972-73, outage coordinator, Waterford, Conn., 1972-73, pre-op test coordinator, Auburn, Nebr., 1973-74, project mgr., Vidalia, Ga., 1974-75, mgr. nuclear operating plant, Chattanooga, 1975-80, mgr. nuclear plant services, Atlanta, 1980—; founder, pres. Onsite Engring. and Mgmt., Inc., 1985—. Speaker Scientists and Engrs. for Secure Energy, N.Y.C., 1981; mem. Save the Ocoee River Com., Chattanooga, 1981, Citizens Tax Relief Com., Atlanta, 1981, Feed the Hungry, 1980. Recipient Managerial award Gen. Electric Co., 1974, Brass Ring award, 1973. Mem. Am. Nuclear Soc., Elfur Soc. Republican. Methodist. Clubs: Atlanta Track; Tennessee Valley Canoe (Chattanooga) (editor 1979-80). Current Work: Improvement in the construction, startup and operation of nuclear power facilities. Development of new maintenance equipment and techniques to provide improved safety, reliability and availability. Subspecialty: Nuclear fission. Home: 495 N Link Rd Alpharetta GA 30201 Office: Gen Electric Co 22 Technology Park Norcross GA 30092

VEST, CHARLES MARSTILLER, mechanical engineer, educator, college dean; b. Morgantown, W.Va., Sept. 9, 1941; s. Marvin Lewis and Winifred Louise (Buzzerd) V.; m. Rebecca McCue, June 8, 1963; children: Ann Kemper, John Andrew. B.S.M.E., W.Va. U., 1963; M.S.E., U. Mich., 1964, Ph.D., 1967. Asst. prof. mech. engring. U. Mich., 1968-72, assoc. prof., 1972-77, prof., 1977—; head interferometric holography group U. Mich. (Willow Run Labs.), 1970-73; assoc. dean for acad. affairs U. Mich. (Coll. Engring.), 1981—; vis. assoc. prof. Stanford U., 1974-75; honored guest Universidad Nacional de La Plata, Argentina, 1979. Author: Holographic Interferometry, 1979; contbr. articles on applied optics, fluid mechanics and heat transfer to profl. jours. Recipient Class of '38E Service award U. Mich., 1972. Fellow Optical Soc. Am. (assoc. editor jour. 1982-83); mem. ASME, Sigma Xi, Tau Beta Pi, Pi Tau Sigma. Current Work: Applied optics, holographic interferometry, computer tomography, holographic nondestructive testing, heat transfer, fluid mechanics. Subspecialties: Holography; Mechanical engineering. Home: 910 Kuebler Dr Ann Arbor MI 48103 Office: Dept Mech Engring U Mich Ann Arbor MI 48109

VEZIROGLU, TURHAN NEJAT, mechanical engineer, educator, researcher, cons.; b. Istanbul, Turkey, Jan. 24, 1924; came to U.S., 1962, naturalized, 1983; s. Abdul Kadir and Ferruh (Burun) V.; m. Bengi Isikli, Mar. 17, 1960; children: Emre Alp, Oya Sureyya. A.C.G.I. in Mech. Engring, City and Guilds Coll., London, 1946; B.Sc. with honors, U. London, 1947, Ph.D. in Heat Transfer, 1951; D.I.C., Imperial Coll., London, 1948. Engring, apprentice Alfed Herbert Ltd., Coventry, Eng., 1945; project engr. Office of Soil Products, Ankara, Turkey, 1954-56; tech. dir. M.K.V. Constrn. Co., Istanbul, Turkey, 1957-61; assoc. prof. mech. engring. U. Miami, Coral Gables, Fla., 1962-65, prof., 1966—, dir. grad. studies in mech. engring., 1965-71, chmn. dept. mech. engring., 1971-75; assoc. dean for research U. Miami (Sch. Engring. and Architecture), 1975-79; dir. Clean Energy Research Inst. U. Miami, 1974—; UNESCO cons. on energy; invited lectr. in heat transfer and energy. Contbr. numerous articles on thermal contact conductance, two-phase flow instabilities, solar energy and hydrogen energy systems to profl. jours; editor 20 conf. procs. Pres. Learning Disabilities Found., Miami, Fla., 1972-73, adv., from 1974. Served to 1st lt. Ordnance Service Turkish Army, 1952-53. Recipient Turkish Presdl. Sci. award, 1975. Fellow Instn. Mech. Engrs., ASME, AAAS; mem. Am. Soc. Engring. Edn., AAUP, Am. Nuclear Soc., Internat. Solar Energy Soc., Soc. Engring. Sci., AIAA, Internat. Assn. Hydrogen Energy (editor Internat. Jour. Hydrogen Energy from 1976, pres. from 1975), Sigma Xi. U. London chess champion, 1948. Current Work: Two-phase flow instabilities; thermal contact conductance; solar energy applications; hydrogen energy system. Subspecialties: Mechanical engineering; Fuels and sources. Office: U Miami Coral Gables FL 33124

VICENTE, PETER JAMES, psychologist, educator; b. Phila., May 12, 1947; s. James and Ana Rosa (Mendoza) V.; m. Margaret Ann Duddy, Dec. 27, 1969; children: Sean, Brian, Kevin. B.A., LaSalle Coll., 1969; M.A., Ohio State U., 1971, Ph.D., 1975. Diplomate: Diplomate Am. Bd. Prof. Neuropsychology, 1983. Dir. dept. psychol. services Ohio State U. Hosps., Columbus, 1976-80; dir. div. rehab. psychology Ohio State U. Coll. Medicine, 1976-80, clin. asst. prof., 1980—; clin. assoc. prof. Wright State U Sch. Profl. Psychology, Dayton, Ohio, 1981—; dir. dept. health psychology indsl. Commn. of Ohio, Columbus, 1980—; mem. profl. adv. bd. Nat. Head Injury Found. (Ohio chpt.), 1983-85. Co-editor: Foundations of Clinical Neuropsychology. Recipient Outstanding Profl. Contbns. award Nat. Acad Neuropsychologists, 1981. Fellow Nat. Acad. Neuropsychologists (v.p. 1982-84); mem. Ohio Acad. Neuropsychologists (pres. 1979-83), Internat. Neuropsychology Soc., Am. Psychol. Assn., Ohio Psychol. Assn. Current Work: Comprehensive bio-psycho-social assessment and treatment of industrially injured or diseased workers and their return to productivity. Subspecialty: Neuropsychology. Home: 208 Erie Rd Columbus OH 43214 Office: Indsl Commn Ohio 107 N High St Columbus OH 43215

VICK, ROBERT LORE, physiologist, educator; b. Courtland, Miss., Sept. 1, 1929; s. Atheral Sylvester and Gladys Rane (Monteith) V.; m. Blanche Rose Ross, May 29, 1953; 1 child, Suzanne. B.S. in Pharmacy, U. Miss., 1952, M.S., 1954; Ph.D., U. Cin., 1957. Asst. prof. Southwest Okla. State Coll., Weatherford, 1953; instr. pharmacy U. Miss., University, 1953-54; fellow NIH, Cin., 1955-57; instr. physiology SUNY-Syracuse, 1958-61; asst. then assoc. prof. Baylor Coll. Medicine, Houston, 1961-72, prof., 1972—. Author, editor: Contemporary Medical Physiology, 1984. Recipient Career Devel. award NIH, 1967-72. Mem. Am. Physiological Soc., Am. Soc. Pharmacology and Exptl. Therapeutics, Soc. Exptl. Biology and Medicine, AAAS. Scientific Methodist. Current work: Currents and potentials underlying repetitive activity of the heart; extra-renal control of plasma potassium. Subspecialties: Physiology (medicine); Pharmacology. Home: 5151 Grape Rd Houston TX 77096 Office: Baylor Coll Medicine 1 Baylor Plaza Houston TX 77030

VICKERS, STANLEY, biochemical pharmacologist, researcher; b. Blackpool, Lancashire, Eng., Sept. 27, 1939; came to U.S., 1962, naturalized, 1979; s. Norman Stanley and Hannah (Snape) V. B.Sc., London U., 1962; Ph.D., SUNY-Buffalo, 1967. Fellow U. Kans., 1966-69; sr. research pharmacologist Merck & Co., West Point, Pa., 1969-71, research fellow, 1971-81, sr. research fellow, 1981—. Contbr. articles to profl. jours. Mem. Am. Soc. Pharmacology and Exptl. Therapeutics, Am. Chem. Soc., N.Y. Acad. Sci. Current Work: Absorption, distribution and metabolism of drugs, assays of therapeutic concentration of drugs. Subspecialties: Pharmacokinetics; Biochemistry (biology). Home: Box 243 RD 2 Slotter Rd Perkasie PA Office: Merck Institute for Therapeutic Research Bldg 44A West Point PA 19486

VICTORY, HAROLD DEAN, JR., mathematics educator; b. Longview, Tex., Aug. 11, 1946; s. Harold Dean and Elizabeth Hunt (Benson) V. A.B. in Math., Rice U., 1968; M.S. in Applied Math., Purdue U., 1970, Ph.D. in Applied Math., 1974. Grad. teaching asst. math. Purdue U., West Lafayette, Ind., 1968-74; lectr. math. Tex. Tech U., Lubbock, 1974-76, asst. prof., 1976-80, assoc. prof., 1980—. Guest editor Progress in Nuclear Energy, 1981; assoc. editor Transport Theory and Statis. Physics, 1982—; referee Jour. Math. Physics, Jour. Math. Analysis and its Applications. Contbr. articles to profl. jours. NSF trainee, 1970-74; faculty participant Assoc. Western Univs., 1977; Alexander von Humboldt Research fellow U. Frankfurt and U. Kaiserslautern, Fed. Republic Germany, 1982-84. Mem. Am. Math. Soc., Soc. Indsl. and Applied Math. (referee Jour. on Numerical Analysis), Am. Nuclear Soc., Phi Kappa Phi. Republican. Episcopalian. Current work: Mathematical study of analytical and numerical techniques for solving transport equations arising in the kinetic theory of gases and in the general area of plasma physics; the structure of positive operators on Banach lattices. Subspecialties: Applied mathematics; Numerical analysis (mathematics). Home: 5302 11th St Apt 128 Lubbock TX 79416 Office: Tex Tech Univ Dept Math Lubbock TX 79409

VIECHNICKI, DENNIS JOHN, ceramic engineer; b. Passiac, N.J., Dec. 25, 1940; s. John Victor and Emily (Serafin) V.; m. Barbara Austen Bradshaw, Sept. 11, 1965; children—John, Peter, Joe, Katherine. B.S. in Ceramic Sci., Rutgers U., 1962; Ph.D. in Ceramics, Pa. State U., 1966. Sr. scientist Westinghouse Research & Devel. Ctr., Pitts., 1966; project officer U.S. Army Materials and Mechanics Research Ctr., Watertown, Mass., 1966-68, research ceramic engr., 1968-81, chief processing and applications br., 1981—; NSF-CNRS exchange scientist Centre D'Etudes de Chimie Metallurgique, Vitry-sur-Seine, France, 1972-73. Contbr. articles to sci. jours. Patentee in field. Coach, tournament dir. Wellesley United Soccer Club, Mass., 1967—. Recipient Research and Devel. Achievement awards Dept. Army, 1971, 79. Fellow Am. Ceramic Soc. (chmn. New Eng. sect. 1974). Clubs: Wellesley Tennis Assn., Chatham Yacht (Mass.) (mem. bldg. and grounds com.). Current work: Ceramic materials processing; structural and ballistic properties of ceramics. Subspecialties: Ceramics; Ceramic engineering. Home: 5 Poplar Rd Wellesley MA 02181 Office: US Army Materials and Mechanics Research Ctr Arsenal St Watertown MA 02172

VIEST, IVAN M(IROSLAV), consulting structural engineer; b. Bratislava, Czechoslovakia, Oct. 10, 1922; came to U.S., 1947, naturalized, 1955; s. Ivan and Maria (Zacharova) V.; m. Barbara K. Stevenson, May 23, 1953. Ing., Slovak Tech. U., Bratislava, 1946; M.S., Ga. Inst. Tech., 1948; Ph.D., U. Ill., 1951. Registered profl. engr., Pa. Research asst. U. Ill., Urbana, 1948-50, research asso., 1950-51, research asst. prof., 1951-55, research asso. prof., 1955-57; bridge research engr. Am. Assn. State Hwy. Ofcls.; rd. test Nat. Acad. Scis., Ottawa, Ill., 1957-61; structural engr. Bethlehem Steel Corp., Pa., 1961-67, sr. structural cons., 1967-70, asst. mgr. sales engring. div., 1970-83, cons. structural engr., 1983—; lectr. in field. Author: Composite Construction, 1958. Recipient Constrn. award Engring. News Record, 1972. Fellow Am. Concrete Inst. (Wason Research medal 1956); mem. ASCE (hon., Research prize 1958, v.p. 1973-75), Am. Iron and Steel Inst., Internat. Assn. Bridge and Structural Engring., Nat. Acad. Engring., Transp. Research Bd., AAAS. Club: Saucon Valley Country (Bethlehem). Research, numerous publs. on various steel and concrete structures, especially bridges and bldgs., to profl. jours. Current Work: Structural aspects of bridges; buildings and other civil engineering structures. Subspecialties: Civil engineering; Theoretical and applied mechanics. Office: PO Box 1428 Bethlehem PA 18016

VIETTI, TERESA JANE, physician, pediatrics educator, researcher; b. Fort Worth, Nov. 5, 1927; d. William Victor and Grace (Christian) V. B.A., Rice U., 1949; M.D., Baylor U., 1953. Intern, resident, chief resident St. Louis Children's Hosp., 1953-56, dir. hematology, oncology, 1970—; resident fellow in hematology Children's Hosp. Mich., 1956-58; instr. pediatrics Wayne State U., Detroit, 1958, Southwestern Med. Sch., Dallas, 1958-60; asst. prof. pediatrics Washington U., St. Louis, 1961-65, assoc. prof., 1965-72, prof., 1972—. Author: Clinical Pediatric Oncology, 1984. Contbr. articles to profl. jours. Recipient Disting. Alumnus award Rice U., 1982. Mem. Am. Assn. for Cancer Research, Internat. Soc. Hematology, Am. Soc. Clin. Oncology, Am. Acad. Pediatrics, Alpha Omega Alpha. Subspecialties: Oncology; Hematology. Office: Washington U Sch Medicine 400 S Kings Hwy Saint Louis MO 63110

VIGIL, MANUEL GILBERT, mechanical engineer; b. Medanales, N.Mex., Oct. 1, 1941; s. Manuel Juan and Georgia S. (Sisneros) V.; m. Barbara Josephine Vigil, Aug. 10, 1963; children: Mark Matthew, Gilbert Emmanuel. B.S.M.E., N.Mex. State U., Las Cruces, 1966; M.S.M.E., U. N.Mex., Albuquerque, 1968. Project design engr. Sandia Nat. Labs., Albuquerque, 1966—. Contbr. articles to profl. jours. Mem. ASME, Am. Nuclear Soc. Democrat. Roman Catholic. Club: Pajarito Classic T-Bird. Subspecialties: Fluid mechanics; Mechanical engineering. Home: 3325 June St NE Albuquerque NM 87111 Office: PO Box 5800 KAFB Albuquerque NM 87185

VIJAYAKUMAR, RAJAGOPAL, mechanical engineer, environmental consultant, particle technologist; b. Madras, India, Jan. 8, 1950; came to U.S., 1975; s. A.V. and Bhama (Rajan) Rajagopal; m. Sarojini Sockalingam, June 21, 1972; children—Vinod, Gayathri, Savithri. B.E., U. Madras, 1971; M.S. in Mech. Engring., U. Minn., 1977, Ph.D., 1982. Mgmt. trainee Eswaran & Sons, Madras, 1971-73; works engr. Torrance & Sons, Madras, 1973-75; grad. asst. U. Minn., Mpls., 1976-82; project engr. EMSI Combustion Engring. (formerly Rockwell Internat.), Newbury Park, Calif., 1982—. Contbr. articles to profl. jours. Recipient Nat. Rowing Championship awards Amateur Rowing Assn. of East India, 1973, 74. Mem. Air Pollution Control Assn.; assoc. mem. ASME (bd. dirs. San Francisco Valley sect. 1983-84). Hindu. Club: Madras Boat (capt. 1974). Current work: Particulate control; waste incineration; particle system design/modeling; atmosphere corrosion. Subspecialties: Environmental engineering; Mechanical engineering. Office: EMSI Combustion Engring 2421 W Hillcrest Dr Newbury Park CA 91320

VIJAYENDRAN, BHEEMA RAO, chemist; b. Bangalore, Mysore, India, June 16, 1941; came to U.S., 1966, naturalized, 1980; s. Bheema Rao and Saroja (Rao) Sirsi; m. Levi E. Cuico, Aug. 8, 1970; children—Ravi, Anil. B. Tech., U. Madras, India, 1963, M.Tech., 1966; Ph.D., U. So. Calif., 1969; M.B.A., U. New Haven, 1977. Postdoctoral fellow R.J. Reynolds Co., Winston-Salem, N.C., 1969-70; research chemist Pitney Bowes, Stamford, Conn., 1970-76;

project mgr. Celanese, Summit, N.J., 1976-78, Louisville, 1978-83; research assoc. Air Products and Chems. Inc., Allentown, Pa., 1983—; vis. prof. Ind. U.-New Albany, 1981-83. Contbr. articles to profl. jours. Patentee in field. Coordinator youth activities YMCA, Allentown, 1983—. Fellow Council Sci. and Industry, India, 1963-66, NIH, 1967-69. Mem. Am. Chem. Soc., TAPPI, Petroleum Engrs. Assn., Plastics Soc., N.Y. Acad. Sci., Sigma Xi. Current work: Surface, colloid and polymers technologies related to coatings, adhesives, oil field chemicals, water soluble polymers and food packaging. Subspecialties: Polymer chemistry; Surface chemistry. Home: 4702 Parkview Dr N Emmaus PA 18049 Office: Air Products and Chems PO Box 538 Allentown PA 18105

VIJH, ASHOK KUMAR, chemistry educator, researcher; b. Multan, India (now Pakistan), Mar. 15, 1938; s. Bishamber Nath and Prem Lata (Bahl) V.; m. Danielle Blais; 1 son, Aldous Ian. B.Sc. with honors, Panjab U., India, 1960, M.Sc. with honors, 1961; Ph.D., Ottawa U., 1966. Group leader Inst. Research Hydro-Quebec, 1969-74, program leader, 1975-81, maitre-de-research, 1973—; vis. prof., thesis dir. INRS-Energie, U. Que., 1970—. Author: Electrochemistry of metal and semiconductors, 1973. Editor series: Oxides and Oxide Films. Editorial bd.: Materials Chemistry and Physics, Applied Physics Communication, Surface Tech., Jour. Power Sources, Progress Batteries and Solar Cells, New Materials and New Processes. Contbr. over 200 articles to profl. jours. Fellow Royal Soc. Chemistry, Chem. Inst. Can. (Noranda lectr. 1979), IEEE, Inst. Physics, Royal Soc. Can.; mem. Electrochem. Soc. (Lash Miller award 1973), Association Canadienne Française pour l'Avancement des Sciences (Archambault prize and medal 1984). Current Work: Electrochemistry; materials science; surface chemistry. Subspecialties: Physical chemistry; Surface chemistry. Office: 1800 Montee St Varennes PQ J0G 2P0 Canada

VILCEK, JAN TOMAS, medical educator, researcher; b. Bratislava, Czechoslovakia, June 17, 1933; s. Julius and Friderika (Fischer) V.; m. Marica Gerhath, July 28, 1962. M.D., Comenius U. Med. Sch., Bratislava, 1957; C.Sc., Inst. Virology Czechoslovak Acad. Sci., Bratislava, 1962. Asst. dept. microbiology Comenius U., 1953-57; research assoc. Inst. Virology Czechoslovak Acad. Sci., 1957-59, fellow, 1959-62, head lab., 1962-64; asst. prof. microbiology NYU, 1965-68, assoc. prof., 1968-73, prof., 1973—; chmn. Am. Cancer Soc. Adv. Com. on Microbiology and Virology. Author: Interferon, 1969; editor: (with T.C. Merigan and I Gresser) Regulatory Functions of Interferon, 1980, (with R. Kono) The Clinical Potential of Interferons, 1982; (with E. DeMaeyer) Interferons and the Immune System, 1984; editor-in-chief: Archives of Violgy, 1975-84; mem. editorial bd.: Infection and Immunity, 1983—, Applied Biochemistry and Biotechnology, 1981—, Jour. of Interferon Research, 1981—, Interferon, 1979—, Virology, 1979-81; contbr. numerous articles to profl. jours. USPHS grantee, 1965—, 76—; recipient USPHS Career Devel. award, 1968-73. Mem. Soc. Gen. Microbiology London, Am. Soc. Microbiology, AAAS, N.Y. Acad. Sci., Am. Assn. Immunologists, Council Biology Editors, Am. Soc. Virology, Internat. Soc. Interferon Research. Current Work: Properties of interferons and their functions; soluble mediators of the immune responses; biological response modifiers. Subspecialties: Microbiology; Immunobiology and immunology. Office: Dept Microbiology NYU Sch Medicine 550 1st Ave New York NY 10016

VILENKIN, ALEXANDER, physics educator; b. Kharkov, Russia, May 13, 1949; came to U.S., 1976; s. Vladimir L. and Fira J. (Goldstein) V.; m. Inna Simone, Oct. 2, 1973; 1 dau., Alina. Diploma physics, Kharkov State U., 1971; Ph.D., SUNY-Buffalo, 1977. Physics lab. asst. elem. sch., Kharkov, 1973-74; research assoc. Case Western Res. U., Cleve., 1977-78; asst. prof. physics Tufts U., Medford, Mass., 1978-83, assoc. prof., 1983—. Contbr. articles to physics jours. Served with Russian Bldg. Service, 1972-73. Tufts U. fellow, 1981; recipient Young Presdl. Investigator award NSF, 1984, grantee, 1982—. Mem. Am. Phys. Soc. Current work: Cosmological evolution of vacuum domain walls and strings, galaxy formation, inflationary cosmological scenario, quantum origin of the universe. Subspecialties: Cosmology; Relativity and gravitation. Home: 12 Appletree Ln Lexington MA 02173Office: Dept Physics Tufts U Medford MA 02155

VILKKI, ERKKI UUNO, astronomer; b. Soanlahti, Finland, July 5, 1922; came to U.S., 1967; s. Uuno and Bertta (Takkinen) V.; m. Josette Boulanger, June 20, 1952; 1 dau., Ann. Student, Nav. Sch. Rauma, Finland, 1947-48, 51-52; Sea Capt., Nav. Sch. Kotka, Finland, 1959. With Scandinavian Mcht. Marine, 1945-62; collaborator Pic du Midi Obs., Hautes Pyrénées, France, 1964-66; observer-research technician Yerkes Obs., Williams Bay, Wis., 1967-73, asst. astronomer, 1973-78, assoc. astronomer, 1979-85, astronomer, 1985—. Contbr. articles to profl. jours. Served with Finnish Army, 1941-44. Mem. Am. Astron. Soc. Current Work: Trigonometric stellar parallaxes; photographic observations of double stars. Subspecialty: Optical astronomy. Office: Yerkes Obs Williams Bay WI 53191

VILLA-KOMAROFF, LYDIA, molecular biology educator; b. Las Vegas, Aug. 7, 1947; d. John and Drucilla (Jaramillo) V.; m. Anthony L. Komaroff, June 18, 1970. Student, U. Wash., 1965-68; B.A. cum laude, Goucher Coll., 1970; Ph.D., M.I.T., 1975. Postdoctoral fellow Harvard U., Cambridge, Mass., 1975-78; vis. postdoctoral fellow, Cold Spring Harbor, N.Y., 1976-77; asst. prof. molecular genetics/gene structure U. Mass. Med. Sch., Worcester, 1978-82, assoc. prof., 1982-85; assoc. prof. dept. neuro-pathology Harvard Med. Sch., 1985—; sr. research assoc. Children's Hosp. Med. Ctr., Boston, 1985—; mem. mammalian genetics study sect. NIH, 1982-84. Contbr. articles to profl. jours. Helen Hay Whitney fellow, 1975-78; Basil O'Conner Starter grantee Nat. Found. March of Dimes, 1981-83. Mem. Am. Soc. Cell Biology, AAAS, N.Y. Acad. Scis., Fedn. Am. Scientists, Assn. Women in Sci., Soc. Advancement Chicanos and Native Ams., Sigma Xi. Subspecialties: Genetics and genetic engineering (agriculture); Genome organization. Office: Dept Neurosci Enders 3 Children's Hosp Med Ctr 300 Longwood Ave Boston MA 02115

VILLERE, KAREN R., astrophysicist; b. Teaneck, N.J., Apr. 9, 1944; d. Peter N. and Alice E. (Hall) Heere; m. Gary L. Villere, Aug. 28, 1967. B.A. summa cum laude, U. Pa., 1965; M.A., U. Calif.-Berkeley, 1968; Ph.D., U. Calif.-Santa Cruz, 1976. Research scientist Sci. Applications Inc., Palo Alto, Calif., 1974-76; Nat. Acad. Scis., NRC resident research assoc. NASA Ames Research Center, Moffett Field, Calif., 1977-79, asst. research astronomer, 1979—, U. Calif.-Santa Cruz, 1979—. Woodrow Wilson fellow, 1965. Mem. Am. Astron. Soc., Astron. Soc. Pacific. Current Work: Stellar evolution, star formation. Subspecialty: Theoretical astrophysics. Home: 226 Flynn Ave Mountain View CA 94043 Office: NASA Ames Research Center MS 245-3 Moffett Field CA 94035

VINCENZI, FRANK FOSTER, pharmacologist, educator; b. Seattle, Mar. 14, 1938; s. Frank and Thelma Charlotte (McAllister) V.; m. Judith I. Heimbigner, Aug. 27, 1960; children: Ann, Franklin, Joseph. B.S. magna cum laude in Pharmacy, U. Wash., 1960, M.S. in Pharmacology, 1962, Ph.D., 1965. Research asst. dept. pharmacology U. Wash., 1963-65, USPHS trainee, 1965, asst. prof., 1967-72, assoc. prof., 1972-80, prof., 1980—, acting chmn., 1975-77, vice chmn., 1977—. Author revs. and articles in field. Mem. exec. com., bd. dirs. Wash./Alaska chpt. Cystic Fibrosis Found., 1977-80, chmn. med. adv. com., 1977-80. Mem. AAAS, Am. Soc. Pharmacology and Exptl. Therapeutics, Internat. Soc. Biorheology, Biophys. Soc., Cardiac Muscle Soc., Red Cell Club, Soc. Exptl. Biology and Medicine, Sigma Xi, Phi Beta Kappa, Kappa Psi. Subspecialties: Molecular pharmacology; Pharmacology. Home: 3205 109th St SE Bellevue WA 98004 Office: U Washington Pharmacology SJ-30 Seattle WA 98195

VINEYARD, GEORGE HOAGLAND, physicist; b. St. Joseph, Mo., Apr. 28, 1920; s. George Hoagl and Mildred M. (Barkley) V.; m. Phyllis Ainsworth Smith, Feb. 3, 1945; children: John H., Barbara Gale. B.S., MIT, 1941, Ph.D., 1943; Sc.D. (hon.), L.I. U., 1977. Mem. staff Radiation Lab. MIT, 1943-45; mem. faculty U. Mo., Columbia, 1946-54, prof., 1952-54; mem. staff Brookhaven Nat. Lab., Upton, N.Y., 1954—, sr. physicist, 1960—, chmn. dept. physics, 1961-66, dep. dir. lab., 1966-72, dir. lab., 1973-81; cons. to govt. and industry; fellow Poly. Inst. N.Y., from 1978; vis. com. Materials Sci. Center, Cornell U., 1964-67; mem. vis. com. dept. physics MIT, 1969-73, dept. nuclear engring., from 1983; mem. pres.'s sci. and ednl. adv. com. Lawrence Berkeley Lab., U. Calif., 1977-81; adv. com. Nat. Magnet Lab., 1963-67; adv. com. math. and phys. scis. NSF, 1966-71, chmn., 1971; mem. sci. policy bd. Stanford Synchrotron Radiation Project, 1977-81; mem. solid state sci. panel NRC, from 1954, chmn., 1965-71, chmn. solid state scis. com., 1970-72; chmn. panel condensed matter physics survey com. Nat. Acad. Scis., 1969-72; mem. materials research council Def. Advanced Research Projects Agy., from 1967; chmn. nat. allocations com. J. von Neumann Ctr. for Computation, 1985—; mem. ad hoc com. U.S. participation Internat. Atomic Energy Agy., 1970-72. Co-editor: series Documents in Modern Physics, 1964-78; bd. assoc. editors: Am. Jour. Physics, 1948-50, Phys. Rev, 1959-61; bd. editors: Physics, 1964-68, Jour. Computational Physics, 1966-79, Physics and Chemistry of Liquids, from 1968; editor Phys. Rev. Letters, 1983—. Bd. dirs. L.I. Action Com., 1979-82; mem. adv. com. on sci. and tech. N.Y. State Legis. Commn., from 1980. Recipient award for disting. contbns. to higher edn. Stony Brook Found., 1975. Fellow Am. Acad. Arts and Scis., Am. Phys. Soc. (chmn. div. solid state physics 1972-73, councillor at large 1974-79, chmn. div. condensed matter physics 1984-85), AAAS; mem. L.I. Assn. Commerce and Industry (dir. from 1975), Sigma Xi. Current Work: Research in Physics of condensed matter. Subspecialties: Condensed matter physics; Theoretical physics. Office: Brookhaven Nat Lab Upton NY 11973

VINEYARD, JERRY D., geologist, state official; b. Dixon, Mo., Mar. 26, 1935; s. Henry and Bessie Florence (Geisler) V.; m. Helen Louise Anderson, Nov. 24, 1960; children—Monica Lynne. Vanessa Anne. B.A., U. Mo., 1958, A.M., 1963. Cert. profl. geologist. Instr. geology and geography Met. Jr. Coll., Kansas City, Mo., 1960-63; chief info. services Mo. Geol. Survey, Rolla, 1963-79, asst. state geologist, 1979—; dir. water resources research Mo. Div. Geology and Land Survey, Rolla, 1981—; dir. Geology Devel. Bd., Columbia. Author: Springs of Missouri, 1974. Illustrator/contbr. Geologic Wonders and Curiosities, 1979. Bd. dirs. Mo. chpt. Nature Conservancy, St. Louis, 1975. Served to lt. (j.g.) USN, 1958-60. Named Pub. Ofcl. of Yr. Ozark chpt. Sierra Club, 1972. Recipient Bretz award Mo. Speleological Survey, 1977. Fellow Geol. Soc. Am., Nat. Speleological Soc. (cert. of merit 1969); mem. Am. Inst. Profl. Geologists, Mo. Acad. Sci., Assn. Mo. Geologists. Baptist. Current work: Research in the geology and hydrology of carbonate karst terranes. Subspecialties: Geology; Hydrology. Home: 2 Valley Rd Saint James MO 65559 Office: Mo Div Geology and Land Survey Fairgrounds Rd Rolla MD 65401

VINING, LEO CHARLES, microbiologist. Prof. biology Dalhousie U., Halifax, N.S., Can. Recipient John Labott award Chem. Inst. Can., 1985. Subspecialty: Bio-organic chemistry. Office: Dalhousie U Dept Biology Halifax NS B3H 4H6 Canada

VINOGRADOV, ALEKSANDRA M., civil engineering educator; b. Chernovtsy, Ukraine, USSR, Sept. 23, 1940; emigrated to Can., 1977; d. Mark and Malya (Litvin) Endelshtein; m. Oleg Vinogradov, Apr. 7, 1963; 1 son, Mark. M.Sc., Lvov (USSR) State U., 1962; Ph.D., Leningrad State U., 1972. Registered prof. engr. Engr. Design Inst. Coal Industry, Lugansk, USSR, 1962-66; research engr. Nat. Research Inst. Hydraulic Engring., Leningrad, USSR, 1971-77; research assoc. dept. civil engring. U. Calgary, Alta., Can., 1977-80, asst. prof., 1980—. Research fellow Natural Scis and Engring. Research Council, Can., 1980. Mam. Canadian Soc. Civil Engring., Am. Soc. Engring. Sci., Canadian Assn. Univ. Tchrs. Current Work: Creep of structures, stability of structures, interaction problems, ice mechanics. Subspecialties: Civil engineering; Solid mechanics. Home: 180 Ranch Estates Rd NW Calgary AB T3G 2A9 Canada Office: U Calgary 2500 University Dr NW Calgary AB T2N 1N4 Canada

VINSON, JOHN WILMOT, computer chemist; b. Shanghai, China, May 16, 1946; came to U.S., 1954; s. John Walker and Mary Lucy (Boone) V.; m. Karen Lee Strickler, Aug. 12, 1972; B.S., Mich. State U., 1968; Ph.D., U. Calif.-Berkeley, 1973. Postdoctoral fellow, Harvard U., Cambridge, Mass., 1973-77; scientist Warner Lambert/Parke Davis, Ann Arbor, Mich., 1977-80, sr. scientist, 1980-82, research assoc., 1982—. Elder 1st Presbyterian Ch., Stockbridge, Mich., 1984. Mem. Am. Chem. Soc., AAAS, Phi Beta Kappa, Sigma Xi. Current work: Use of computer for drug design; molecular modeling; quantitative structure activity relations; user-friendly databases; pattern recognition. Subspecialties: Drug design; Information systems, storage, and retrieval (computer science). Home: 212 W Main Box 301 Stockbridge MI 49285 Office: Warner Lambert/Parke Davis 2800 Plymouth Rd Ann Arbor MI 48105

VINYARD, TIMOTHY WAYNE, biological technician, botanical educator, researcher; b. Herlong, Calif., Apr. 25, 1958; s. Jack Leo and Kate M. (Slattery) V.; m. Laura Jean Coulter, May 28, 1983. B.S. in Biology, Mo. So. State Coll., 1980, B.S.E. in Biology, 1983; M.A. in Botany, U. No. Colo., 1982. Cert. secondary biology tchr., Mo. Environ. cons. Mo. So. State Coll., Joplin, 1978-80; teaching fellow U. No. Colo., Greeley, 1980-82; biol. technician Dept. Interior, Diamond, Mo., 1982-84, resource mgmt. technician Nat. Park Service, 1984—; head lichen research Dept. Interior, Pipestone, Minn., 1983-84. Co-author research report. Pres., Newman Soc., Joplin, 1980. Mem. Colo.-Wyo. Acad. Sci., Ecol. Soc. Am., Audubon Soc., Sigma Xi, Tri Beta Lambda Sigma Tau. Republican. Roman Catholic. Current work: Corticolous lichen identification; prairie restoration; integrated pest management. Subspecialties: Ecology (environmental science); Ecology (biology). Home: PO Box 525 Joplin MO 64801 Office: Carver Nat Monument PO Box 38 Diamond MO 64840

VIOLA, ALFRED, educator; b. Vienna, Austria, July 8, 1928; came to U.S., 1940, naturalized, 1945; s. Isidore and Greta (Broch) V.; m. Joy Darlene Winkie, Oct. 19, 1963. B.A., Johns Hopkins U., 1949, M.A., 1950; Ph.D., U. Md., 1955. Research assoc., vis. instr. biochemistry Boston U., 1955-57; asst. prof. Northeastern U., Boston, 1957-62, assoc. prof., 1962-68, prof. chemistry, 1968—; vis. prof. U. Munich, 1977, Monash U., Melbourne, Australia, 1984. Contbr. articles to profl. jours. Mem. Am. Chem. Soc., Sigma Xi. Current Work: Reaction mechanisms, thermal rearrangements of organic compounds, stereochemistry of transition states, thermal reactions of acetylenic and allenic compounds, unimolecular kinetics. Subspecialty: Organic chemistry. Home: 14 Glover Rd Wayland MA 01778 Office: Dept Chemistry Northeastern U Boston MA 02115

VIOLA, VICTOR E., JR., chemistry educator; b. Abilene, Kans., Apr. 8, 1935; s. Victor E. and Frances Nadine (Holmes) V.; m. Nancy Jean Weaver, Dec. 29, 1962; children—Charles, Randall, Gina. A.B., Kans. U., 1957; Ph.D., U. Calif.-Berkeley, 1961. Research assoc., instr. U. Calif.-Berkeley, 1961-62; research assoc. Centre Europeene Recherche Nucleaire, Geneva, 1963-64, Argonne Nat. Lab., Ill., 1964-66; asst., assoc., then prof. U. Md., College Park, 1966-80; prof. chemistry Ind. U., Bloomington, 1980—; mem. program adv. com. Los Alamos Nat. Lab., 1983—; mem. user's exec. com. Nat. Superconducting Cyclotron, East Lansing, Mich., 1979-81, mem. program adv. com., 1984-86; mem. user's exec. com. Oak Ridge Nat. Lab., 1979-81, Lawrence Berkeley Lab., 1975-78, Nuclear Sci. Rev. Com., Lawrence Berkeley Lab. Contbr. articles to profl. jours. Author: Heart of Matter, 1973, 2d edit., 1980. Guggenheim grantee, 1980-81; U. Md. research grantee, 1979; NSF, Ford Found. fellow, 1963-64; Woodrow Wilson fellow, 1958-61, others. Mem. Am. Chem. Soc. (chmn. 1980—), Am. Phys. Soc., AAUP, Phi Beta Kappa, AAAS, Sigma Xi. Democrat. Club: Bloomington Track. Current work: Studies of nuclear reactions at low to intermediate energies; nuclear astrophysics; nuclear systematics; fission. Subspecialty: Nuclear physics. Office: Dept Chemistry Ind U Bloomington IN 47405

VIOLATO, CLAUDIO, psychology educator; b. Valdagno, Vicenza, Italy, May 23, 1952; emigrated to Can., 1958; s. Efrem and Marianna (Battistin) V. B.Sc., U. B.C., 1976, M.A., 1978; Ph.D., U. Alta., 1982. Instr. Kwantlen Coll., Surrey, B.C., 1981-82; asst. prof. psychology U. Victoria, B.C., 1982—; cons. sch. dists. Contbr. articles to profl. jours. Mem. Can. Psychol. Assn., Am. Psychol. Assn., Can. Soc. Study of Edn., Can. Assn. Ednl. Psychologists. Roman Catholic. Current Work: Personality organization and stability, IQ testing and assessment, creativity and giftedness, memory processes. Subspecialties: Developmental psychology; Social psychology. Home: 1576 Midgard Ave Apt 308 Victoria BC V8P 2Y1 Canada Office: Dept Psychol Founds U Victoria Victoria BC V8W 2Y2 Canada

VISHER, GLENN SHILLINGTON, oil properties corporation executive, lecturer; b. Evansville, Ind., May 20, 1930; s. John William and Marguerite Ruth (Miller) V.; m. Bettye Ruth Gentry, Oct. 17, 1953; children: Christine Ann, Lynn Ellen, Sara Catherine. B.S., U. Cin., 1952; M.S., Northwestern U., 1958, Ph.D., 1960. Cert. profl. geol. scientist. Exploration geologist Shell Oil Co., Casper, Wyo., 1958-60; research geologist Sinclair Oil Co., Tulsa, 1960-66; prof. U. Tulsa, 1966-80; pres. Geol. Services and Ventures, Inc., Tulsa, 1980—, BNJ Oil Properties, Inc., Tulsa, 1981—; lectr. continuing edn. Oil & Gas Cons. Internat., Tulsa, 1969—; convenor, rapporteur symposia, profl. confs. Contbr. writings to profl. publs. Pres. Tulsa chpt. ACLU, 1976; v.p. Okla. chpt. ACLU, 1964-66; mem. budget exec. com. United Way, Tulsa, 1974-78. Served as 1st lt. USAF, 1952-54. Fellow AAAS, Geol. Soc. Am.; mem. Soc. Econ. Paleontologists and Mineralogists, Am. Assn. Petroleum Geologists (lectr. Tulsa 1973-75), Internat. Assn. Sedimentologists. Democrat. Unitarian. Current Work: Developing scientific and stratigraphic bases for petroleum exploration; use of tectonic, geomorphic, geochemical, sedimentologis processes to predict hydrocarbon occurrences. Subspecialties: Sedimentology; Oceanography. Home: 2920 E 73rd St Tulsa OK 74136

VISOTSKY, HAROLD MERYLE, educator, physician; b. Chgo., May 25, 1924; s. Joseph and Rose (Steinberg) V.; m. Gladys Mavrich, Dec. 18, 1955; children: Jeffrey, Robin. Student, Herzl Coll., Chgo., 1943-44, Baylor U., 1944-45, Sorbonne, 1945-46; B.S., U. Ill., 1947, M.D. magna cum laude, 1951. Intern Cin. Gen. Hosp., 1951-52; resident U. Ill., Ill. Research and Ednl. Hosp., also Neuropsychiat. Inst., Chgo., 1952-55; asst. prof. U. Ill. Coll. Medicine, 1957-61, asso. prof. psychiatry, 1965-69, dir. psychiat. residency tng. and edn., 1955-59; prof., chmn. dept. psychiatry and behavioral scis. Northwestern U. Med. Sch., Chgo., 1969—; dir. Psychiat. Inst., chmn. dept. psychiatry Northwestern Meml. Hosp.; sr. attending Evanston Hosp.; Polio respiratory center psychiat. cons. Nat. Found. Infantile Paralysis, U. Ill., 1955-59; dir. mental health Chgo. Bd. Health div. mental health services, 1959-63; dir. Ill. Dept. Mental Health, 1962-69; examiner Am. Bd. Psychiatry and Neurology, 1964—; dir. Center Mental Health and Psychiat. Services, Am. Hosp. Assn., 1979—; mem. 1st U.S. mission on mental health to USSR State Dept. Mission, 1967; chmn. task force V Joint Commn. on Mental Health of Children, 1967—; mem. adv. com. on community mental health service Nat. Inst. Mental Health, 1965—; mem. profl. adv. com. Jerusalem Mental Health Center; profl. adv. group Am. Health Services, Inc.; adv. com. Joint Commn. Accreditation Hosps., Council Psychiat. Facilities; mem. spl. panel mental illness for bd. dirs. ACLU; rector Lincoln Acad. of Ill. Faculty Social Service; mem. select com. psychiat. care and evaluation HEW; mem. faculty Practising Law Inst.; bd. overseers Spertus Coll. Judaica, Chgo., 1981—. Contbr. articles to psychiat. jours., chpts. psychiat. textbooks. Trustee Erikson Inst. Early Edn., Ill. Hosp. Assn., Mental Health Law Project, Washington. Served with AUS, 1942-46. Decorated D.S.C., Purple Heart, Bronze Star; recipient Edward A. Strecker award Inst. Pa. Hosp., 1969; Med. Alumnus of Year award U. Ill., 1976; Disting. Service award Chgo. chpt. Anti-Defamation League; Disting. Service award B'nai B'rith, 1978. Fellow Am. Orthopsychiat. Assn. (dir. v.p. 1970-71, pres. 1976), Am. Psychiat. Assn. (chmn. council on mental health services 1967—, v.p. 1973-74, sec. 1981—, chmn. council nat. affairs 1975-78, com. on abuse of psychiatry and psychiatrists), AAAS, Am. Coll. Psychiatrists (charter, bd. regents 1976-79, v.p. 1980, pres. 1983-84, Bowis award 1981), Chgo. Inst. Medicine; mem. Am. Assn. Chmn. Dept. Psychiatry, Am. Assn. Social Psychiatry (v.p. 1976), Council Med. Splty. Socs., AMA, Ill. Psychiat. Soc. (pres. 1965-66), Am. Coll. Psychoanalysts. Current Work: Health care planning; stess research. Subspecialty: Psychiatry. Home: 1128 Ridge Ave Evanston IL 60202 Office: 320 E Huron St Chicago IL 60611

VISWANATHAN, K., consulting engineer; b. Calicut, Kerala, India, Apr. 28, 1944; came to U.S., 1971; s. V. Thangam and V. Kirshnan; m. Annapoorni, Nov. 15, 1974; children—Balakrishnan, Gayathri. B.E., Birla Inst. Tech. and Sci., Pilani, India, 1966; M.S. in Indsl. Engring, Texas A&M U., 1972. Mech. engr. Brown & Root, Inc., Houston, 1972-74, sr. engr., 1980—; process engr. Wright Engr., Ltd., Vancouver, B.C., Can., 1974-76; design engr. Spraymould Ltd., Cambridge, Ont., Can., 1977-78, Shawinigan Energy Cons., Toronto, Ont., Can., 1978-80. Patrol leader Boy Scouts, 1960; active player Tamilnadu Cricket and Football Assn., 1966, all India; active United Way Campaigns, Houston, 1982. Sr. mem. Inst. Indstl. Engrs.; assoc. mem. Ops Research Soc. Am.; mem. Alpha Pi Mu, Phi Kappa Phi. Hindu. Clubs: Soccer (Missouri City, Tex.) (player coach 1982—); Century (College Station, Tex.). Current Work: Planning and control; equipment and systems design. Subspecialties: Mechanical engineering; Materials handling. Home: 3126 Cherry Creek Dr Missouri City TX 77459

VITERBI, ANDREW JAMES, business executive; b. Bergamo, Italy, Mar. 9, 1935; came to U.S., 1939, naturalized, 1945; s. Achille and Maria (Luria) V.; m. Erna Finci, June 15, 1958; children—Audrey, Alan, Alexander. S.B., MIT, 1957, S.M., 1957; Ph.D., U. So. Calif., 1962. Research group supr. C.I.T. Jet Propulsion Lab., 1957-63; mem. faculty Sch. Engring. and Applied Sci., UCLA, 1963-73; assoc. prof. Sch. Engring. and Applied Sci., UCLA, 1965-69, prof., 1969-73; exec. v.p. Linkabit Corp., 1973-82; pres. M/A-Com Linkabit, Inc., 1982-84; chief scientist M/A-Com, Inc., 1984-85; vice chmn. Qualcomm, Inc., 1985—; cons. sci. adv. panel U.S. Army, 1968-74; adj. prof. U. Calif., San Diego, 1975-85, prof. elec. engring. and computer sci., 1985—; chmn. U.S. Commn. C, URSI, 1982; vis. com. dept. elec. engring. and computer sci. MIT. Author: Principles of Coherent Communication, 1966, (with J.K. Omura) Principles of Digital Communication and Coding, 1979; bd. editors: Proc. IEEE, 1968-77; Mem. bd. editors: Information and Control, 1967, Transactions on Info. Theory, 1972-75. Recipient award for valuable contbns. to telemetry, space electronics and telemetry group IRE, 1962; best original paper award Nat. Electronics Conf., 1963; outstanding paper award, info. theory group IEEE, 1968; Christopher Columbus Internat. Communications award, 1975; Aerospace Communication award AIAA, 1980. Fellow IEEE (past chmn. info. theory group, Alexander Graham Bell medal 1984); mem. Nat. Acad. Engring. Subspecialty: Telecommunications. Office: 10555 Sorrento Valley Rd San Diego CA 92121

VITKOVITSKY, IHOR MYRON, federal government physicist; b. Lviv, Ukraine, July 4, 1932; came to U.S., 1949, naturalized, 1954; s. Roman and Irene (Korol) V.; m. Tamara Baczynsky, June 13, 1959; 1 child, Donna R. B.S., U. Rochester, 1955; M.S., U. Md., 1963. Physicist, Naval Power Plant, Indian Head, Md., 1955-57, research physicist Naval Research Lab., Washington, 1957-70, sect. head high voltage tech., 1970-76, br. head plasma tech., 1976-83, assoc. dir. plasma phys. div., 1983—; cons. Scires, Inc., Washington, 1966-69, Power Conversion Tech., San Diego, 1979-82. Author: High Power Switching, 1985. Contbr. articles to profl. jours. Patentee in field. Sec., Ukrainian Washington Fed. Credit Union, 1982-84. Recipient Publ. award Naval Research Lab., 1972, 77, Outstanding Performance award, 1977, 80, 84, Achievement in Pulse Power award Def. Nuclear Agy., 1976. Mem. Am. Phys. Soc., AAAS, Ukrainian Engring. Soc. Am., Inst. Elec. Engring., Ukrainian Assn. Washington (v.p. 1983-84), Sigma Xi. Democrat. Ukrainian Catholic. Current work: Research on intense charged particles beams, high energy plasma, energy channeling and propagation and high power inductive storage; multi-disciplinary aspects of applying research to problems of interest to military technology and energy development. Subspecialties: Plasma physics; Electrical engineering. Office: Plasma Physics Div Naval Research Lab Washington DC 20375-5000

VITOLA, JACK JOSEPH, electrical engineer, research executive; b. Long Branch, N.J., May 15, 1931; s. John Paul and Yolanda Ann (Marinaro) V.; m. Maria Elisa Coll, July 22, 1967; children—Lisa Ann, Bernadette. B.S. in Elec. Engring., Rutgers U., 1958; M.S. in Engring. Mgmt., Columbia Pacific U., 1980. Project engr. Wheelock Signals, Inc., Long Branch, 1958-66, engring. dir., 1966-79; v.p. engring. HI-G Research and Engring. Corp., Bloomfield, Conn., 1979-81; product mgr. Magnecraft Electric Co., Chgo., 1981-84; dir. research, devel. and engring. Eureka X-Ray Tube Co. div. Litton Industries, Chgo., 1984—. Patentee audible signal device, 1964, vibrating mechanism, 1966, miniature magnetic latch relay, 1982. Served with U.S. Army, 1952-54. Coll. Relay Engring. fellow Nat. Assn. Relay Mfrs., Okla. State U., 1970. Mem. IEEE (sec.-treas. 1968-72), Nat. Elec. Mfrs. Assn. (chmn. audible signal group 1973-76), Am. Mgmt. Assn., Cath. War Vets. (post comdr. 1960-61). Republican. Roman Catholic. Current work: Vacuum technology, materials science, electron beam engineering, filmless radiography, dielectric and insulation engineering. Subspecialties: CAT scan; Electrical engineering. Home: 301 Apple Hill Ln Streamwood IL 60103

VIVEROS, OSVALDO HUMBERTO, neurobiologist, educator; b. Santiago, Chile, May 14, 1937; s. Humberto and Elena (Letelier) V.; m. Yolanda Faune, Mar. 24, 1964; children: Cristian, Claudia, Cristobal. M.D., U. Chile, 1962. Research fellow dept. physiology and biophysics U. Chile Med. Sch., 1962-65; research assoc. dept. physiology and pharmacology Duke U. Med. Center, Durham, N.C., 1966-67, USPHS postdoctoral fellow dept. biochemistry, 1967-69, Fulbright-Hays scholar dept. biochemistry, 1971; assoc. prof. dept. physiology and biophysics U. Chile Med. Sch., 1970-71; prof. dept. neurobiology Cath. U. Chile, Santiago, 1971-74; vis. scientist Lab. Clin. Scis., NIMH, Bethesda, Md., 1974-77; group leader dept. medicinal biochemistry Wellcome Research Labs., Research Triangle Park, N.C., 1977—; adj. assoc. prof. dept.

pharmacology Duke U. Med. Center; reviewer div. physiology, cellular and molecular biology NSF. Contbr. articles to profl. jours.; mem. editorial and adv. bd.: Molecular Pharmacology, 1978—. Mem. Colegio Medico de Chile, Sociedad de Biologia de Chile, Latinoamerican Pharmacological Soc., Internat. Brain Research Orgn., Soc. Neurosci., N.C. Soc. Neuroscis. (pres. 1985—), Am. Soc. Pharmacology and Exptl. Therapeutics, Am. Soc. Neurochemistry. Club: Duke Faculty (Durham, N.C.). Current Work: Catecholamine and opiod peptide biosynthesis, storage, secretion; co-transmission, epinephrine, norepinephrine, enkephalins, sympathetic system, adrenal medulla, adrenal cortex, tetrahydrobiopterin, pterins, excitation-secretion coupling. Subspecialties: Neurobiology; Neuroendocrinology. Office: 3030 Cornwallis Rd Research Triangle Park NC 27709

VLATTAS, ISIDOROS, organic chemist, research scientist; b. Chios, Greece, Apr. 28, 1935, came to U.S. 1966, naturalized 1972; s. Ioannis and Aggela (Binikos) V.; m. Argyro Koufopantelis, May 7, 1967; children—John, Angela, Christina. Diploma, U. Athens, Greece, 1959; Ms.D., U. B.C. 1963, Ph.D., 1966. Postdoctoral fellow Syntex Corp., Palo Alto, Calif., 1966-67, Harvard U., Cambridge, Mass., 1967-69; researcher Geigy Corp., Ardsley, N.Y., 1969-71; organic chemist, sr. research scientist, Ciba-Geigy Corp., Summit, N.J., 1971—. Mem. Am. Chem. Soc. Democrat. Christian Orthodox. Current work: Syntesis or organic medicinal compounds. Subspecialties: Synthetic chemistry; Medicinal chemistry. Home: 131 Butler Pkwy Summit NJ 07901 Office: Ciba-Geigy Corp Morris Ave Summit NJ 07901

VLAY, GEORGE JOHN, engring. mgmt. exec.; b. Buffalo, Dec. 1, 1927; s. John and Victoria (Mili) V.; m. Betty Jo Wayland, July 21, 1949; children: Vanessa Michele, Susan Victoria, George John. B.S.E.E., U. Buffalo, 1953, postgrad., 1954-56. Registered profl. engr., Okla. Project engr. R.B. Warman, Inc., Buffalo, 1954-56, Aero Comdr., Inc., Norman, Okla., 1956-61, GTE/Sylvania, Williamsville, N.Y., 1961-66; mgr. advanced communication systems Philco-Ford Corp., Palo Alto, Calif., 1966-77; with Ford Aerospace & Communications Corp., Palo Alto, 1977—, dir. tech. affairs, 1982—; Mem. tech. council Electronics Industry Assn., Washington, 1978—. Served to sgt. USAF, 1946-49. Mem. IEEE (sr.), AIAA (space Systems com. 1976-78), Armed Forced Communications and Electronics Assn., Air Force Assn., Navy League, Am. Def. Preparedness Assn., Nat. Security Indsl. Assn. Republican. Methodist. Current Work: Advanced communication satellite systems. Computer aided engineering, design, test and manufacturing. Subspecialties: Aerospace engineering and technology; Satellite studies. Home: 32 Yerba Buena Ave Los Altos CA 94022Office: Ford Aerospace & Communication Corp 3939 Fabian Way Palo Alto CA 94303

VOADEN, DENYS JOHN, organic chemist; b. Okehampton, Devon, Eng., Apr. 15, 1926; came to U.S., 1959; naturalized, 1964; s. Arthur and L. Betsy V. B.Sc., Oxford U., 1954, M.A., 1956, D.Philosophy, 1957. Sci. officer Imperial Chem. Industries Ltd., Manchester, Eng., 1956-57; postdoctoral chemist U. Southampton, Eng., 1957-59, Fordham U., N.Y., 1959-60, U. Mass., Amherst, 1960-65; research chemist U.S. Dept. Agr. Beltsville, Md., 1965-71, 1973—; pesticide expert Food and Agr. Orgn. of UN, Cairo, 1971-73. Author: (with C.W. Cain) Military A/C of the USSR, 1952. Contbr. articles to profl. jours. Served to cpl. M.C. Royal Army, 1946-48. Mem. Royal Soc. Chemistry, Soc. Chem. Industry, Am. Chem. Soc., Monogolia Soc. Inc. (v.p.) Current work: Synthesis of organic chemicals; structure activity relations; isolation and identification of natural products as pest control agents. Subspecialties: Organic chemistry; Integrated pest management. Office: US Dept Agr Research Ctr Room 303 Bldg 306 Beltsville MD 20705

VODKIN, MICHAEL HAROLD, geneticist; b. Boston, Dec. 4, 1942; s. Hyman Roy and Eva (Weiner) V.; m. Lila Ott, June 28, 1975. B.S., Boston Coll., 1964, M.S., 1969; Ph.D., U. Ariz., Tucson, 1971. Postdoctoral fellow Cornell U., Ithaca, N.Y., 1972-74; asst. prof. U. S.C., Columbia, 1974-79; staff fellow NIH, Bethesda, Md., 1979-81; NRC sr. staff fellow U.S. Army Med. Research Inst. Infectious Diseases, Ft. Detrick, Md., 1981-83, research chemist, 1983—. NIH grantee, 1975-79. Mem. Genetics Soc. Am., Am. Soc. Microbiology, Sigma Xi. Jewish. Current Work: Cloning of prokaryotic genomes. Subspecialties: Genetics and genetic engineering (biology); Genome organization. Home: 900 Laredo Rd Silver Spring MD 20901 Office: USAMRIID Fort Detrick MD 21701

VOEHEES, CHARLES VAN, psychologist, pediatrics research educator; b. Columbus, Ohio, Oct. 9, 1948; s. Charles and Leona M. (Beany) V.; m. Elizabeth Mollnow, Nov. 10, 1982; children—Darcy M., Collin V. B.A. with honors, U. Cin., 1971; M.A., Vanderbilt U., 1973; Ph.D., 1976. Lic. psychologist, Ohio. Research scholar Inst. Developmental Research, Cin., 1976-78; asst. prof. U. Cin., Ohio, 1978-82, assoc. prof., 1982—; dir. lab. Inst. Dev. Research, Cin., 1980—. Contbr. articles to profl. jours.; chpts. to books. Grantee NSF, NIH, FDA. Mem. Behavioral Teratology Soc. (pres. 1984-85), Soc. for Neuroscis., Teratology Soc., Behavioral Toxicology Soc., Internat. Soc. Developmental Psychobiology. Current work: Behavioral teratology; research on how drugs and environ. chemicals damage the brain before birth. Subspecialties: Psychobiology; Teratology. Office: Inst Developmental Research Dept Pediatrics and Developmental Biology Elland and Bethesda Aves Cincinnati OH 45229

VOGEL, CHARLES LEWIS, physician, oncology educator; b. Belle Harbor, N.Y., Nov. 6, 1938; s. Samuel and Sylvia (Love) V.; married; children: Stacey Lynn, Brian Arnold. A.B., Princeton U., 1960; M.D., Yale U., 1964. Diplomate: Nat. Bd. Med. Examiners, Am. Bd. Internal Medicine. Intern, med. resident Grady Meml. Hosp., Atlanta, 1964-66; clin. assoc. medicine br., solid tumor service Nat. Cancer Inst., Bethesda, Md., 1966-69; sr. investigator Nat. Cancer Inst., 1969-73; assoc. prof. medicine Emroy U., Atlanta, 1973-75; assoc. prof. oncology U. Miami, Fla., 1975-82; prof., 1982—; chief div. breast cancer, clin. dir. Comprehensive Cancer Ctr., State of Fla., 1980—; sci. advisor Solid Tumor Center of Uganda Cancer Inst., 1969-73; cons. in field. Contbr. articles to profl. jours. Served with USPHS, 1966-73. Mem. Am. Assn. Cancer Research, Am. Soc. Clin. Oncology, Fla. Soc. Clin. Oncologists. Current Work: Breast cancer research/chemotherapy. Subspecialties: Chemotherapy; Cancer research (medicine). Home: 1420 NE 101st St Miami Shores FL 33183 Office: 1475 NW 12 Ave PO Box 016960 Miami FL 33101

VOGEL, EVA MILAR, chemist; b. Kezmarok, Czechoslovakia, Aug. 5, 1946; came to U.S., 1969, naturalized, 1977; d. Andrej and Ruta (Hermanstadt) Milar; m. Gerald Carl Vogel, Sept. 4, 1972; children—Peter Roman, Michael Henry. M.S., Slovak Tech. U., 1969. Mem. tech. staff Bell Telephone Labs., Murray Hill, N.J., 1970-83, Bell Communication Research, 1984—. Contbr. articles to profl. jours. Mem. Am. Ceramic Soc., Internat. Confed. for Thermal Analysis. Club: Murray Hill Canoe. Current work: Novel processing of electronic ceramics and glasses; research activities in ionic conductors and ferrites, synthesis and characterization of the intrinsic properties of glasses. Subspecialties: Ceramics; Materials processing. Office: Bell Communication Research 600 Mountain Ave 6D-329 Murray Hill NJ 07974

VOGEL, JAMES ALAN, research physiologist, administrator; b. Snohomish, Wash., Dec. 22, 1935; s. Otto Wilhelm and Elva (Conrad) V.; m. Catherine Lucy Castano, Aug. 1, 1959; children—Jean L., Susan E., Stephen A. B.S., Wash. State U., 1957; Ph.D., Rutgers U., 1961. Research physiologist U.S. Army Med. Research Nat. Lab., Denver, 1961-67, U.S. Army Research Inst. Environ. Medicine, Natick, Mass., 1967—, dir. exercise physiol. div., 1973—. Editor: Biochemistry of Exercise, 1983. Contbr. numerous articles to sci. jours. Served to capt. M.C., U.S. Army, 1961-63. Recipient Sr. Exec. Service award Dept. Army, 1981. Fellow Am. Coll. Sports Medicine; mem. Am. Physiol. Soc., Group on Phys. Fitness (North Atlantic Treaty Orgn. study group) (vice chmn. 1980—). Democrat. Lutheran. Current work: Applied exercise physiology and physical work performance, medical problems related to physical training. Subspecialty: Physiology (medicine). Office: US Army Research Inst Environ Medicine Natick MA 01760

VOGEL, THOMAS TIMOTHY, surgeon, educator, physiologist; b. Columbus, Ohio, Feb. 1, 1934; s. Thomas A. and Charlotte (Hogan) V.; m. Darina Kelleher, May 29, 1965; children: Thomas Timothy, Catherine Darina, Mark Patrick, Nicola Marie. A.B., Coll. Holy Cross, 1955; M.S., Ohio State U., 1960, Ph.D., 1962; M.D., Georgetown U., 1965. Diplomate: Nat. Bd. Med. Examiners, Am. Bd. Surgery. Intern Georgetown and D.C. Gen. hosps., 1965-66; resident Ohio State Univ. Hosps., 1966-70; instr. physiology Ohio State U., Columbus, 1960-62, instr. surgery, 1969-70, clin. asst. prof. surgery, 1974—. Contbr. articles to profl. jours. Fellow ACS; mem. Am. Physiol. Soc. (assoc.), Fedn. Am. Socs. Exptl. Biology, Soc. Acad. Surgery, Am. Soc. Parenteral and Enteral Nutrition, Am. Trauma Soc., AMA, Ohio Med. Assn., Ohio Acad. Sci., Sigma Xi. Lodge: Rotary. Current Work: Cardiovascular, endocrine and gastrointestinal physiology and surgery, nutrition of the hospitalized patient. Subspecialties: Surgery; Physiology (medicine). Home: 247 S Ardmore Rd Columbus OH 43209 Office: 621 S Cassingham Rd Columbus OH 43209

VOGELMAN, JOSEPH HERBERT, scientific engineering company executive; b. N.Y.C., Aug. 18, 1920; s. Jacob Vogelman and Sabina (Weingarten) Vogelman Holstein; m. Norma Schneider, Dec. 8, 1946; children—Jeffrey Allan, Leslie Sue, Linda Leigh. B.S., CCNY, 1940; M.E.E., Poly. Inst. Bklyn., 1948, D.Elec. Engring., 1957. Registered profl. engr., N.Y., N.J. Project engr. Signal Corps Engr. Labs., Belmar, N.J., 1943-45; chief devel. br. Watson Labs., Eatontown, N.J., 1945-50; chief scientist Rome Air Devel. Ctr., Griffiss AFB, N.Y., 1951-52, chief electronic warfare lab., 1953-56, dir. communications, 1956-59; v.p., dir. Capehart Corp., N.Y.C., 1959-64; dir. electronics Chromalloy Am. Corp., N.Y.C., 1964-67, gen. mgr. pocket fone div., 1966-67, v.p., 1967-73; v.p., dir. Cro-Med. Bionics Corp., 1968-73; vice chmn. bd., dir. Laser Link Corp., 1968-73; chief scientist, dir. Orentreich Found. for Advancement Sci., 1973—; pres. Vogelman Devel. Corp., 1973—; dir. Compupix Tech. Inc., Boca Raton, Fla., 1983-85, chmn. tech. adv. com., 1983—; cons. in field. Contbr. numerous articles to profl. jours. and encys. Patentee in field. Vice pres., Bnai Zion, L.I., N.Y., 1980—. Served with U.S. Army, 1942-43. Recipient Outstanding Performance award U.S. Air Force, 1957. Fellow IEEE (mem. Dist. I Bd. 1960-62), AAAS; mem. N.Y. Acad. Scis., Societe Francaise de Electroniciens et des Radioelectricines, Sigma Xi, Eta Kappa Nu. Republican. Jewish. Subspecialties: Biomedical engineering; Software engineering. Home: 48 Green Dr Roslyn NY 11576

VOGL, OTTO, polymer science and engineering educator; b. Traiskirchen, Austria, Nov. 6, 1927; came to U.S., 1953, naturalized, 1959; s. Franz and Leopoldine (Scholz) V.; m. Jane Cunningham, June 10, 1955; children: Eric, Yvonne. Ph.D., U. Vienna, 1950; Dr. rer. nat. h.c., U. Jena, 1983. Instr. U. Vienna, 1948-55; research asso. U. Mich., 1953-55, Princeton U., 1955-56; scientist E.I. Du Pont de Nemours & Co., Wilmington, Del., 1956-70; prof. polymer sci. and engring. U. Mass., 1970-83, prof. emeritus, 1983—; Herman F. Mark porf. polymer sci. Poly. Inst. N.Y., 1983—; guest prof. Kyoto U., 1968, 80, Osaka U., 1968, Royal Inst. Stockholm, 1971, U. Freiburg, Germany, 1973, U. Berlin, 1977, Strasbourg U., 1976, Tech. U. Dresden, 1982; guest Soviet Acad. Sci., 1973, Polish Acad. Sci., 1973, 75, Acad. Sci. Rumania, 1974, 76; cons. in field. Chmn. com. on macromolecular chemistry Nat. Acad. Sci. Author: Polyaldehydes, 1967, (with Furukawa) Polymerization of Heterocyclics, 1973, Ionic Polymerization, 1976, (with Simionescu) Radical Co and Graftpolymerization, 1978, (with Donaruma) Polymeric Drugs, 1978, (with Donaruma and Ottenbrite) Polymers in Biology and Medicine, 1980, (with Goldberg and Donaruma) Targeted Drugs, 1983; contbr. articles to profl. jours. Recipient Fulbright award, 1976; Humboldt award, 1977; Japan Soc. Promotion of Sci. sr. fellow, 1980. Fellow Am. Chem. Soc. (chmn. div. polymer chemistry 1974, chmn. Connecticut Valley sect. 1974), Am. Inst. Chemists AAAS; mem. Austrian Chem. Soc., Japanese Soc. Polymer Sci., Acad. Sci. German Democratic Republic (fgn.), Acad. Sci. Austria (fgn.). Current Work: Polymer science and engineering, polymer synthesis, polymeric drugs, polymeric stabilizers, optically active polymers, ring opening polymerization aldehyde polymerization. Subspecialty: Polymer chemistry. Home: 349 Oxford Rd New Rochelle NY 10804 Office: Poly Inst NY Brooklyn NY 11201

VOGT, ROCHUS EUGEN, physicist, educator; b. Neckarelz, Germany, Dec. 21, 1929; came to U.S., 1953; s. Heinrich and Paula (Schaefer) V.; m. Micheline Alice Yvonne Bauduin, Sept. 6, 1958; children: Michele, Nicole. Student, U. Karlsruhe, Germany, 1950-52, U. Heidelberg, Germany, 1952-53; S.M., U. Chgo., 1957, Ph.D., 1961. Mem. faculty dept. physics Calif. Inst. Tech., Pasadena, 1962—, assoc. prof., 1965-70, prof., 1970-82, R. Stanton Avery Disting. Service prof., 1982—, chmn. faculty, 1975-77, chmn. div. physics, math. and astronomy, 1978-83, v.p. and provost, 1983—, chief scientist Jet Propulsion Lab., 1977-78; acting dir. Owens Valley Radio Obs., 1980-81. Fellow Am. Phys. Soc.; mem. Am. Assn. Physics Tchrs., AAAS, Sigma Xi. Research in astrophysics. Subspecialties: Cosmic ray high energy astrophysics; Gamma ray high energy astrophysics. Office: Calif Inst Tech 206-31 Pasadena CA 91125

VOGT, STEVEN SCOTT, astrophysicist; Rock Island, Ill., Dec. 20, 1949; s. Calvin Roy and Jeanne (Josephson) V.; m. Zarmina Dastagir, June 15, 1980; 1 dau., Crystal. A.B. in Physics and Astronomy, U. Calif.-Berkeley, 1972; M.A., U. Tex.-Austin, 1975, Ph.D. in Astronomy, 1978. Research asst. astronomy dept. U. Tex.-Austin, 1972-78; asst. astronomer, asst. prof. Lick Obs.,U. Calif.-Santa Cruz, 1978-84, assoc. prof./assoc. astronomer, 1984—; cons. in field. Contbr.: articles to publs. including Nature. Recipient acad. fellowships; grantee NSF; grantee NASA. Mem. Am. Astron. Soc., Astron. Soc. of Pacific, Internat. Astron. Union. Current Work: Development of solid state array detectors for low light level astronomical research; spectroscopy and direct imaging. Subspecialty: Optical astronomy. Office: Natural Sci II U Calif Santa Cruz CA 95064

VOLANAKIS, JOHN EMMANUEL, immunology educator, researcher; b. Thessaloniki, Greece, Mar. 17, 1938; came to U.S., 1968; s. Emmanuel John and Cleo (Agathonos) V.; m. JoAnne Somerville, May 16, 1970; children: Manolis, Marina. M.D., U. Thessaloniki, 1962; D.Med., U. Athens, 1968. Fellow in rheumatology Metropolitan Gen. Hosp., Cleve., 1968-71; instr. medicine U. Ala. in Birmingham, 1971-73, asst. prof. medicine and pathology, 1973-77, assoc. prof. medicine, 1977-83, prof. medicine, 1983—, assoc. prof. pathology and microbiology, 1977-85, prof. pathology and microbiology, 1985—; vis. scientist U. Utrecht, Netherlands, 1978; mem. study sect. NIH, Bethesda, Md., 1981—. Editor: C-Reactive Protein and the Plasma Protein Response to Tissue Injury, 1982; assoc. editor: Jour. Immunology, 1982—. NIH fellow, 1978. Mem. Am. Assn. Immunologists, Am. Rheumatism Assn., AAAS, Sigma Xi. Current Work: Biochemistry and biology of complement and acutephase proteins. Subspecialties: Immunology (medicine); Biochemistry (biology). Home: 3432 Old Wood Ln Birmingham AL 35243 Office: Univ Ala in Birmingham Univ Sta THT 437 Birmingham AL 35294

VOLCANI, BENJAMIN ELAZARI, microbiology educator; b. Ben-Shemen, Israel, Jan. 4, 1915; came to U.S., 1956, naturalized, 1963; s. Isaac and Sarah (Krieger) V.; m. Eleanor Toni Solomons, Mar. 14, 1948; 1 son, Yanon. M.Sc., Hebrew U., 1936, Ph.D., 1941. Vis. scientist Inst. Tech. Delft, Netherlands, 1937-38, U. Utrecht, Netherlands, 1938-39; staff Sieff Research Inst., Weizmann Inst. Sci., Israel, 1939-58, head sect. microbiology, 1948-58; research fellow plant nutrition U. Calif.-Berkeley, 1945-46, Hopkins Marine Sta., Stanford (Calif.) U., 1946-47, Calif. Inst. Tech., Pasadena, 1947-48, U. Wis.-Madison, 1948; research assoc. Inst. Pasteur, Paris, 1951; research assoc. biochemistry virus lab. U. Calif.-Berkeley, 1957-59; vis. prof. Tenovus Cancer Inst., Cardiff, Wales, 1972-73; prof. microbiology U. Calif. Scripps Inst. Oceanography, La Jolla, 1959—; NASA cons., 1966. Editorial bd.: Ann. Rev. Microbiology, 1962-67, 78, Sci. Total Environ, 1975-79, Bioinorganic Chemistry, 1976-78; Contbr. articles to profl. jours. NSF fellow, 1960-70; NIH-/USPHS fellow, 1960—; Elsa U. Pardee Found. grantee, 1971-75. Mem. Am. Soc. Microbiology, Am. Soc. Cell Biology, Western Soc. Naturalists, So. Calif. Soc. Electron Microscopy, Soc. Gen. Microbiology (U.K.). Current Work: Role of silicon in cellular metabolism and diseases; molecular biology of silicon. Subspecialties: Microbiology; Biochemistry (biology). Home: 6708 Muirlands Dr La Jolla CA 92037 Office: Univ Calif Scripps Inst Oceanography La Jolla CA 92093

VOLD, BARBARA SCHNEIDER, research biochemist, consultant; b. Oakland, Calif., Jan. 3, 1942; d. Julius Mackey and Thea Elfrieda (Riedel) Schneider. B.A. in Zoology with distinction, U. Calif., Berkeley, 1963; M.S. (univ. fellow), U. Ill., Urbana, 1964, Ph.D. in Cell Biology (NIH predoctoral fellow), 1967. Postdoctoral fellow M.I.T., Cambridge, 1967-68; postdoctoral fellow Scripps Clinic and Research Found., La Jolla, Calif., 1968-69, research assoc., 1969-70, staff assoc., 1970-76; sr. biochemist SRI Internat., Menlo Park, Calif., 1977—; cons. NIH, 1973-77. Contbr. articles to profl. publs. NIH postdoctoral fellow, 1967-69; research career devel. awardee, 1971-76; NIH research grantee, 1970—; research grantee NSF, 1977-79, 80-82. Mem. Am. Soc. Biol. Chemists, Am. Soc. Microbiology, Phi Beta Kappa. Patentee in field. Current Work: Structure and function of transfer ribonucleic acids; sequence of tRNA and tRNA genes; differentiation in Bacillus subtilis; function of modified nucleosides; immunoassays and monoclonal antibodies to nucleosides. Subspecialties: Molecular biology; Biochemistry (biology). Office: Biomed Research SRI Interna 333 Ravenswood Ave Menlo Park CA 9402

VOLICER, LADISLAV, pharmacologist, physician; b. Prague, Czechoslovakia, May 21, 1935; s. Ladislav and Vilma (Molnarova) V.; m. Olga Holeckova, July 14, 1959; children: Irena, Katerina; m. Beverly Beers, May 20, 1972; children: Susan, Marika, Nadine. M.D. with honors, Charles U., Prague, 1959; Ph.D., Czechoslovak Acad. Scis., 1964. Resident Hosp. Jindrichuv Hradec, Czechoslovakia, 1959-61; vis. assoc. Nat. Heart Inst., NIH, Bethesda, Md., 1965-66; research assoc. Inst. Pharmacology, Czechoslovak Acad. Sci., Prague, 1966-68; research asst. prof. pharmacology U. Munich, W.Ger., 1968-69; from asst. prof. to prof. pharmacology Boston U., 1969—, asst. prof. medicine, 1974—, prof. psychiatry, 1985—; clin. pharmacologist E. N. Rogers Meml. VA Hosp., Bedford, Mass., 1978-85, chief clin. pharmacology sect., 1985—; mem. Mass. Drug Formulary Commn., 1977-83. Editor/co-editor books in field; contbr. articles to sci. jours. Merck faculty devel. awardee, 1971-72; Nat. Inst. Alcoholism grantee, 1972-78; Nat. Inst. Drug Abuse grantee, 1973-77; VA grantee, 1978—, others. Mem. Am. Soc. Pharmacology and Exptl. Therapeutics, Research Soc. Alcoholism, Soc. Neurosci. Unitarian. Club: Masaryk (Boston). Current Work: Research on pharmacology of alcoholism, Alzeimer disease, and aging; teaching. Subspecialties: Pharmacology; Gerontology. Home: 11 Beverly Rd Bedford MA 01730 Office: 200 Springs Rd Bedford MA 01730

VOLKMAN, ALVIN, educator, physician; b. Bklyn., June 10, 1926; s. Henry Phillip and Sarah Lucille (Silverstein) V.; m. Carol Ann Fishel, Jan. 27, 1973; children: Jeffrey C., Natalie F.; married; children from previous marriage: Karl F., Nicholas J., Rebecca J. Evans, Margaret R. Werrell, Deborah A. Falls. B.S., Union Coll., Schenectady, 1947; M.D., SUNY, Buffalo, 1951; D.Phil., Oxford U., 1963. Diplomate: Am. Bd. Pathology, 1959. Intern Mt. Sinai Hosp., Cleve., 1951-52; research fellow anatomy Western Res. U. Sch. Medicine, Cleve., 1952-54; resident, sr. resident in pathology Peter Bent Brigham Hosp., Boston, 1956-59, asst. in pathology, 1959-60; teaching fellow pathology Harvard Med. Sch., 1956-69; asst. prof. pathology Columbia U. Coll. Physicians and Surgeons, 1960-66; asst. to assoc. mem. Trudeau Inst., Saranac Lake, N.Y., 1960-77; prof. pathology East Carolina U. Sch. Medicine, Greenville, N.C.; mem. immunol. scis. study sect. NIH, 1974-79, chmn., 1977-79; cons. NIH; pathologist Pitt County Meml. Hosp., Greenville. Contbr. chpts. to books, articles to profl. jours. Served to lt. USNR, 1954-56. Mem. Am. Assn. Immunologists, Am. Soc. Microbiology, Am. Soc. Hematology, Reticuloendothelial Soc., N.Y. Acad. Scis., AAAS. Jewish. Current Work: Origin, population regulation and functions of mononuclear phagocytes; regulation of population renewal and origins of functional diversity among subpopulations of mononuclear phagocytes. Subspecialties: Immunobiology and immunology; Infectious diseases. Office: Dept Pathology East Carolina U Sch Medicine Greenville NC 27834

VOLLENWEIDER, RICHARD, eutrophication expert. Sr. scientist Can. Ctr. for Inland Waters, Burlington, Ont., Can. Subspecialty: Ecology (environmental science). Office: Can Ctr for Inland Waters Burlington ON L7R 3X7 Canada

VOLLHARDT, KURT PETER CHRISTIAN, chemistry researcher, consultant, educator; b. Madrid, Spain, Mar. 7, 1946; came to U.S., 1972. Ph.D., Univ. Coll., London, 1972. Prof., U. Calif.-Berkeley, 1974—; cons. in field. Author: Aromatizität, 1973. Contbr. articles to profl. jours. Fellow A.P. Sloan Found., 1976-80, Camille and Henry Dreyfus Tchr.-Scholar, 1978-83. Recipient Adolf Windaus Medal, 1983; Named One of 100 Top Young Scientists in Am., Sci. Digest, 1984. Mem. Am. Chem. Soc., German Chem. Soc., Brit. Chem. Soc. Current work: Synthetic and mechanistic organic and organometallic chemistry. Subspecialty: Organometallics. Office: Dept Chemistry U Calif Berkeley CA 94720

VOLLMER, JAMES, physicist, consultant; b. Phila., Apr. 19, 1924; s. Edward Lawrence and Elizabeth (MacMichael) V.; m. Mary Ann Campolieto, Nov. 16, 1946; children—Jamie, Kurt Kimarie. B.S., Union Coll., 1946; M.A., Temple U., 1951, Ph.D., 1956; A.M.P., Harvard U., 1971. Instr. physics Temple U., Phila., 1946-51; research group leader Honeywell Corp., Phila., 1951-59; research dir. RCA Corp., Camden, N.J., 1959-71, v.p., gen. mgr., Cherry Hill, N.J., 1971-79, group v.p.-sr. v.p., 1979-84; pres. James Vollmer Assocs., Haddonfield, N.J., 1984—; chmn. bd. Bartol Research Found., Newark, Del.; dir. Franklin Inst., Phila. Contbr. articles to profl. jours. Patentee in field. Trustee, West Jersey Health System, Camden, N.J., 1979—; bd. dirs. World Affairs Council Phila., 1980, Greater Phila. C. of C., 1981. Fellow IEEE (Centennial medal 1984), AAAS; mem. Am. Phys. Soc., N.Y. Acad. Scis., Phi Beta Kappa, Sigma Xi, Eta Kappa Nu. Clubs: Tavistock Country, Seaview Country, Tequesta Country. Current work: Management of high technology based enterprises. Subspecialties: Electronics; Systems engineering. Home and Office: 609 Centre St Haddonfield NJ 08033

VOLSKY, DAVID JULIAN, biochemistry and pathology educator; b. Wroclaw, Poland, Nov. 10, 1948; came to U.S., 1981; s. Izaak and Ilana (Forc) V.; m. Barbara Paszt, Nov. 11, 1972; children: Karin, Nelly. B.Sc., Ben-Gurion U., 1972; M.Sc., Hebrew U., 1975, Ph.D., 1979. Teaching asst. Hebrew U., Jerusalem, 1976-78, teaching instr., 1978-79; postdoctoral researcher Karolinska Inst., Stockholm, 1979-81; asst. prof. pathology and biochemistry U. Nebr. Med. Center, Omaha, 1981-83, asso. prof., 1983—, mem. peer rev. com., 1982. Recipient Landau Prize in biochemistry, 1978; European Molecular Biology Orgn. fellow, 1978, 79-81; NIH grantee, 1981—. Mem. Am. Soc. Biol. Chemistry, Internat. Assn. Comparative Research on Leukemia and Related Diseases, Am. Soc. Microbiology, AAAS. Current Work: Tumor biology and virology; molecular mechanisms of cell transformation; DNA microinjection; membrane biology; receptors, reconstitution of membranes; AIDS. Subspecialties: Biochemistry (biology); Molecular biology. Home: 3363 S 115th St Omaha NE 68144 Office: Univ Nebr Med Center Molecular Biology Lab Swanson Ctr 42nd and Dewey Ave Omaha NE 68105

VONA, DANIEL O'NEAL, III, physics educator, criminal justice expert, international trade executive; b. Vona, Colo., Mar. 8, 1939; s. Daniel O'Neal and Helen Rutledge (Robbins) V.; m. Barbara Ann Kulacki, June 19, 1965 (div. 1981); children—Daniel O'Neal, IV, Andrew Kulacki; m. Mary Giles Stevenson, Mar. 23, 1982; 1 son, Leal Stevenson. B.A., St. John's Coll. of Annapolis, 1957; B.Litt., Oxford U., 1971, D.Phil., 1973; M.S., Fordham U., 1969, Ph.D., 1979. Asst. prof. physics Fordham U., N.Y.C., 1973-76; assoc. prof. physics John Jay Coll., CUNY, 1980—; dir. Agromar Corp., N.Y.C., Phoenix Oil Corp., Denver, Sonoma Trust, London. Author: The Universe Around Us, 1975; All About Eavesdropping-Senate Select Sub-Committee on Wiretapping and Electronic Surveillance, 1974. Contbr. articles to profl. jours. Spl. asst. police commr. for internal affairs, N.Y.C. Police Dept., 1973-75; dep. police commr. for adminstrn., chmn. Police Pension Fund, 1975-78. Recipient Nat. Commendation medal SAR, 1976; fellow Internat. Sch. Physics, Varenna, Italy, 1972, 75, Internat. Sch. Cosmology, Erice, Sicily, 1974, AAAS/NSAF 1982. Mem. Am. Phys. Soc., AAAS, N.Y. Acad. Sci., Colo. Hist. Soc., Oxford Soc. Club: United Oxford and Cambridge (London). Current work: Mathematical physics; nuclear structure; gen. relativistic cosmology; large scale nuclear structure calculations. Subspecialties: Theoretical physics; Cosmology. Office: John Jay Coll CUNY Room 2321 444 W 56th St New York NY 10021

VON BAEYER, HANS CHRISTIAN, theoretical physicist, educator, researcher; b. Berlin, Apr. 6, 1938; married; 4 children. A.B., Columbia U., 1958; M.Sc., U. Miami, 1961; Ph.D. in Physics, Vanderbilt U., 1964. Research assoc. in physics McGill U., Montreal, Que., Can., 1964-65, asst. prof., 1965-68; from asst. prof. to assoc. prof. Coll. William and Mary, Williamsburg, Va., 1968-75, prof. physics, 1975—, chmn. dept. physics, 1972-78; dir. Va. Assoc. Research Campus, 1979-85; vis. prof. Tri-Univ Meson Facility and Simon Fraser U., 1978-79. Author: Rainbows, Snowflakes, and Quarks, 1984. Contbg. editor The Sciences. Fellow Am. Phys. Soc.; mem. Fedn. Am. Scientists, AAUP, Southeastern Univs. Research Assn. (sec. 1980—). Subspecialty: Theoretical physics. Office: Dept Physics Coll William and Mary Williamsburg VA 23185

VON BERNUTH, ROBERT DEAN, engineering educator, researcher; b. Del Norte, Colo., Apr. 14, 1946; s. John D. and Bernice H. (Dunlap) von B.; m. Judy M. Wehrman, Dec. 29, 1969; children: Jeanie D., Suzann S. B.S., Colo. State U., Fort Collins, 1968; M.S., U. Idaho-Moscow, 1970; M.B.A., Claremont Grad. Sch., 1980; Ph.D., U. Nebr.-Lincoln, 1982. Registered profl. engr., Nebr., Calif. Nuclear power engr. Betis Atomic Power Labs., Idaho Falls, Idaho, 1973-74; product mgr. Rain Bird Sprinkler Mfg., Glendora, Calif.,

1974-80; instr. U. Nebr., Lincoln, 1980-82; assoc. prof engring. U. Tenn., Knoxville, 1982—; prin. von Bernuth Agrl., Knoxville, 1982-85. Served with USN, 1969-73. Decorated D.F.C. (2); named Hon. Engr. Colo. Engring. Council, 1968. Mem. Am. Soc. Agr. Engrs., Irrigation Asn., Am. Mktg. Assn., Internat. Commn. Irrigation and Drainage, Sigma Xi, Alpha Zeta, Omicron Delta Kappa, Tau Beta Pi, Kappa Mu Epsilon, Gamma Sigma Delta. Republican. Patentee in field. Current Work: Research on irrigation and erosion of agricultural soils, application of economics and statistics to analysis and synthesis of problems associated with irrigation and erosion; measurement of size and velocity of falling water droplets. Subspecialty: Agricultural engineering. Office: Agr Engring Dept U Tenn Knoxville TN 37901-1071

VON FRAUNHOFER, JOSEPH ANTHONY, biomaterials science educator; b. London, Eng., Nov. 9, 1940; came to U.S., 1978; s. Hans and Jessie Josephine (Schoen) von F.; m. Anne Marsom, Sept. 7, 1962 (div. 1979); children: Nicola Anne, Michael Anthony. B.S., U. London, Eng., 1963, M.S., 1967; Ph.D., Council Nat. Acad. Awards, London, 1969. Chartered chemist chartered engr. Sci. officer Brit. Rail Research Div., London, 1963-64; scientist Harris Plating Ltd., London, 1964-65; sr. officer research div. Gas Council, London, 1965-70; sr. lectr., dept. chmn. Inst. Dental Surgery, U. London, 1970-78; prof. biomaterials sci. U. Louisville, 1978—. Author: Potentiostat and Its Applications, 1972, Concise Corrosion Science, 1974, Paint Formulation, 1981, Protective Paint Coatings for Metals, 1976, Concise Paint Technology, 1977, Instrumentation in Metal Finishing, 1975, Basic Metal Finishing, 1976, Statistics in Medical, Dental and Biological Studies, 1976, Scientific Aspects of Dental Materials, 1975; contbr. chpts. to books, over 180 sci. articles to profl. publs. Fellow Royal Soc. Chemistry, Instn. Corrosion Sci. and Tech. (sec. 1977-78), Acad. Dental Materials; mem. Instn. Metallurgists. Club: Chemical (London). Current Work: Biomaterials, wear and degradation of materials in the biosystem. Chemistry and metallurgy of corrosion of metals and alloys in the biosystem and in engineering. Protective coatings for metals against corrosion. Subspecialties: Biomaterials; Corrosion. Home: 2032 Eastern Pkwy Louisville KY 40204 Office: Health Scis Center Dental Sch Univ Louisville Louisville KY 40204

VON GIERKE, HENNING EDGAR, government official, educator; b. Karlsruhe, Germany, May 22, 1917; came to U.S., 1947, naturalized, 1977; s. Edgar and Julie (Braun) Von G.; married; 2 children. Dipl. Ing., Karlsruhe Tech., 1943, Dr. Engr., 1944. Asst. in acoustics Karlsruhe Tech., 1944-47, lectr., 1946; cons. Aerospace Med. Research Labs, Wright-Patterson AFB, Ohio, 1947-54, chief bioacoustics br., 1954-63, dir. biodynamics and bionics div., 1963—; asso. prof. Ohio State U., 1963—; clin. prof. Wright State U., 1980—; mem. com. hearing and bioacoustics Armed Forces NRC, 1953, bio-astronaut, com., 1959-61; mem. adv. com. flight medicine and biology NASA, 1960-61. Author numerous tech. publs., book chpts. Recipient Dept. Def. Disting. Civilian Service award, 1963; Hubertus Strughold medal, 1980; H.R. Lissner award ASME, 1983. Fellow Acoustical Soc. Am. (pres. 1979-80), Aerospace Med. Assn. (v.p. 1966-67, E. Liljenkrantz award 1966, A.D. Tuttle award 1974), Inst. Environ. Scis. (hon.), Internat. Acad. Aviation and Space Medicine; mem. Inst. Noise Control Engring., Biomed. Engring. Soc., Internat. Acad. Astronautics, Nat. Acad. Engring. Researcher in bioacoustics, acoustics, biomechanics and bioengring. Current Work: Biodynamics; effects of acceleration and weightlessness on safety, health and performance; injury protection; bioacoustics. Subspecialties: Biomedical engineering; Human factors engineering. Home: 1325 Meadow Ln Yellow Springs OH 45387 Office: Biodynamics and Bionics Div Air Force Aerospace Med Research Lab Wright-Patterson AFB OH 45433

VON HIPPEL, PETER HANS, chemistry educator; b. Goettingen, Germany, Mar. 13, 1931; came to U.S., 1937, naturalized, 1942; s. Arthur Robert and Dagmar (franck) von H.; m. Josephine Baron Raskind, June 20, 1954; children: David F., James A., Benjamin J. B.S., MIT, 1952, M.S., 1953, Ph.D., 1955. Phys. biochemist Naval Med. Research Inst., Bethesda, Md., 1956-59; from asst. prof. to assoc. prof. biochemistry Dartmouth, 1959-67; prof. chemistry, mem. Inst. Moledular Biology U. Oreg., 1967—; dir. inst. Inst. Moledular Biology of U. Oreg., 1969-80; chmn. dept. chemistry U. Oreg., 1980—; mem. study sect. USPHS, 1963-67; chmn. biopolymers Gordon Conf., 1968; mem. trustees' vis. com. biology dept. MIT, 1973-76; mem. bd. sci. counsellors Nat. Inst. Arthritis, Metabolic and Digestive Diseases, NIH, 1974-78; mem. council Nat. Inst. Gen. Med. Scis., NIH, 1982-85. Editorial bd.: Jour. Biol. Chemistry, 1967-73, 76-82, Biochem. Biophys. Acta, 1965-70, Physiological Reviews, 1972-77, Biochemistry, 1977-80; Contbr. articles to profl. jours. and books. Served as lt. M.S.C. USNR, 1956-59. NSF predoctoral fellow, 1953-55; NIH postdoctoral fellow, 1955-56; NIH sr. fellow, 1959-67; Guggenheim fellow, 1973-74. Fellow Am. Acad. Arts and Scis.; mem. AAAS, Am. Chem. Soc., Am. Soc. Biol. Chemists (mem. council 1983-86), Biophys. Soc. (mem. council 1970-73, pres. 1973-74), Nat. Acad. Scis., Soc. Gen. Physiology, Fedn. Am. Scientists, Sigma Xi. Current Work: Protein-nucleic acid intreaction; regulation of gene expression; DNA replecation; mRNA transcription. Subspecialties: Molecular biology; Biophysical chemistry. Home: 1900 Crest Dr Eugene OR 97405

VON LEDEN, HANS, surgeon, laryngologist, educator; b. Breslau, Prussia, Nov. 20, 1918; s. Peter Paul and Elizabeth (Freter) von L.; m. Mary Louise Shine, Jan. 10, 1948; children: Jon Eric, Lisa Maria. M.D., Loyola U., Chgo., 1941. Diplomate Am. Bd. Otolaryngology. Intern Mercy Hosp.-Loyola U. Clinics, 1941-42; resident Presbyn. Hosp.-Rush Med. Coll., Chgo., 1942-43; fellow in otolaryngology Mayo Found., Rochester, Minn., 1943-44; asst. Mayo Clinic, 1945; instr. Loyola U., 1947-51; asst. prof. to assoc. prof. Northwestern U. Med. Sch., Chgo., 1951-61; assoc. prof. UCLA, 1961-66; prof. U. So. Calif., Los Angeles, 1966—; med. dir. Inst. Laryngology and Voice Disorders, 1966—; cons. U.S. Navy, 1947—, W.Ger., 1960—; cons. Lenox Hill Hosp., N.Y.C., 1968—, Juilliard Sch. Music, 1969—; mem. adv. staff Gov. Ill., 1953-61. Author: (with Rand and Rinfret) Cryosurgery, 1968, (with Cahan) Cryogenics in Surgery, 1971; contbr. articles, chpts. to med. publs.; author sci. films; chief editor: ORL Digest; editorial bd. med. jours. Col., a.d.c. Gov. La., 1976—. Served to lt. USNR, 1945-46. Recipient numerous awards, including Minerva award Third Internat. Festival for Medico-Sci. Films, 1957; Bucranio award U. Padua, 1958; Gold medal Italian Red Cross, 1959; award of Honor Am. Acad. Ophthalmology and Otolaryngology, 1959; Casselberry award Am. Laryngol. Assn., 1962; Manuel Garcia prize Internat. Assn. Logopedics and Phoniatrics, 1968; Gutzmann medaille Deutsche Gesellschaft fur Otorhinolaryngologie, 1980. Fellow ACS, Internat. Coll. Surgeons (past pres. U.S. sect., internat. bd. govs., hon. fellow), Am. Acad. Otolaryngology (life), AAAS, Am. Soc. Head and Neck Surgery (sr.), Am. Acad. Facial Plastic and Reconstructive Surgery (dir. 1962-76), Am. Speech and Hearing Assn. (life), Collegium Medicorum Theatri (hon. pres.), Am. Coll. Cryosurgery, Academia Peruana de Cirugia (hon.); mem. AMA (Hektoen medal 1960, Sci. Achievement award 1980), Calif. Med. Assn. (past del.), Los Angeles County Med. Assn. (past pres., past chmn., trustee), Am. Council Otolaryngology (dir. 1973-76), Am. Fedn. Clin. Research, Assn. Mil. Surgeons U.S. (life), Soc. Med. Cons. to Armed Forces, Pan Am. Assn. Otorhinolaryngology and Bronchoesophagology (sec. gen. 1966-80, pres. 1980-82, cons. 1982—), Pacific Coast Oto-Ophthal. Soc., Paracelsus Soc. (past pres.), Los Angeles Soc. Otolaryngology, Bay Dist. Surg. Soc., Westwood Acad. Medicine and Dentistry (past pres.), Mil. Order World Wars (comdr., comdr. in chief 1962-63), Sigma Xi; hon. mem. Soc. Mil. Otolaryngologists, Deutsche Gesellschaft fur Hals-Nasen-Ohren-Heilkunde, Kopf-und Hals-Chirurgie, Japan Soc. Oto-Rhino-Laryngology, Sociedad Mexicana de Otorrinolaringologia, Sociedad Colombiana de Otorrinolaringologia y Bronco-Esofagologia, Asociacion Argentina de Logopedia, Foniatria y Audiologia, Sociedad Chilena de Otorrinolaringologia, Sociedad Peruana de Otorrinolaringologia y Broncoesofagologia, Sociedad de Otorrinolaringologia de El Salvador, Sociedad Panamena de Otorrinolaringologia, Dallas So. Clin. Soc., Greek Soc. Noise Pollution Research; corr. mem. Dansk Oto-Laryngologisk Selskab, Sociedad Cubana de Cancerologia. Republican. Roman Catholic. Clubs: Marines Meml. (San Francisco); Army and Navy (Washington). Current Work: Physiology and pathology vocal system; development of new technics and instruments for the diagnosis and treatment of laryngeal diseases and voice disorders. Office: Inst Laryngology and Voice Disorders 10921 Wilshire Blvd Los Angeles CA 90024

VON TERSCH, LAWRENCE WAYNE, educator; b. Waverly, Iowa, Mar. 17, 1923; s. Alfred and Martha (Emerson) Von T.; m. LaValle Sills, Dec. 17, 1948; 1 son, Richard George. B.S., Iowa State U., 1943, M.S., 1948, Ph.D., 1953. From instr. to prof. elec. engring. Iowa State U., 1946-56; dir. computer lab. Mich. State U., 1956—, prof. elec. engring., chmn. dept., 1958-65, asso. dean engring., 1965-68, dean, 1968—. Author: (with A. W. Swago) Recurrent Electrical Transients, 1953. Mem. IEEE; Mem. Sigma Xi, Tau Beta Pi, Eta Kappa Nu, Phi Kappa Phi, Pi Mu Epsilon. Subspecialties: Computer engineering; Electrical engineering. Home: 4282 Tacoma Blvd Okemos MI 48864 Office: Coll Engring Michigan State U East Lansing MI 48823

VON TIESENHAUSEN, GEORG F., research engineer space missions; b. Riga, Latvia, May 18, 1914; came to U.S., 1953; s. Marion (Cowan) von T.; m. Asta E. Esch, Mar. 16, 1943; children—Evamaria, Georg, Jutta. B.S. in Mech. Engring., Ingenieur Schule (Germany), 1943. Group chief German Rocket Devel., Peenemunde, Germany, 1943-45; devel. engr. Utersen Mach. Fab. Natlapa, Uetersen, W. Ger., 1945-53; br. chief Army Ballistic Missle Agy., Huntsville, Ala., 1953-60; group chief NASA Marshall Space Flight Ctr., Huntsville, 1960-71, asst. dir. advanced system office, 1971—. Patentee: Saturn launch mechanism, 1964, landing device, 1966, space beam connector, 1981, satellite designer. Contbr. articles to profl. jours. Counselor, HELP Line, Huntsville, 1970-72; organist Holy Spirit Ch., Huntsville, 1972-79. Democrat. Episcopalian. Current work: Robotics, artificial intelligence, space tethers, human factors, computer science. Subspecialty: Aerospace engineering and technology. Office: NASA Marshall Space Flight Ctr Huntsville AL 35812

VOOK, RICHARD WERNER, physics educator, researcher; b. Milw., Aug. 2, 1929; s. Fred Ludwig and Hedwig Anna (Werner) V.; m. Julia Deskins, Sept. 7, 1957; children: Katherine, Elizabeth, Richard, Frederick. B.A., Carleton Coll., 1951; M.S. in Physics, U. Ill., 1952, Ph.D. in Physics, 1957. Staff physicist IBM Research Lab., Yorktown Heights, N.Y., 1957-61; sr. research physicist Franklin Inst. Research Labs., Phila., 1961-65; assoc. prof. Syracuse (N.Y.) U., 1965-70, prof. materials sci., 1970-84, prof. physics, 1984—. Contbr. articles, revs. to profl. publs. Recipient Pfeil medal and prize Metals Soc. Gt. Britain, 1983. Mem. Am. Phys. Soc., Am. Vacuum Soc., Electron Microscope Soc. Am., Metall. Soc. of AIME, Phi Beta Kappa, Sigma Xi, Pi Mu Epsilon. Republican. Lutheran. Current Work: Epitaxy, catalysis, electrical contact phenomena, tribology, electron microscopy (scanning and transmission), electron diffraction (low and high energy), Auger electron spectroscopy, X-ray diffraction and spectroscopy. Subspecialty: Thin films and surfaces. Home: 5592 Sentinel Heights Rd Nedrow NY 13120 Office: Syracuse U 409 Link Hall Syracuse NY 13210

VOS, KENNETH DEAN, chemist, manufacturing company executive; b. Iowa, Nov. 13, 1935; s. Peter G. and Henrietta (Groenendyk) V.; m. Irene Marskamp, June 15, 1960; children—Julie Elizabeth Vos Yanker, Peter Dean. B.A., Central Coll., Iowa, 1957; Ph.D., Mich. State U., 1963; student bus. adminstrn. U. Wis.-Milw., 1970-72. Research assoc. Los Alamos Nat. Lab., N.Mex., 1960; staff assoc. Gulf Gen. Atomic, San Diego, 1963-68; dir. research and devel. S. C. Johnson and Son, Racine, Wis., 1968—. Contbr. articles to profl. jours. Patentee in field. Bd. dirs. Racine Area United Way, 1984—, mem. budget and agy. relations coms., 1980—; past bd. dirs. Racine Christian Reformed Ch., local schs. Mem. Chem. Specialties Mfrs. Assn. (bd. dirs. 1983—, first Charles E. Allderdice award 1982), Proprietary Assn. (Sci. affairs com. 1984—), Am. Chem. Soc., Am. Phys. Soc., AAAS, N.Y. Acad. Sci. Republican. Current work: physical chemistry, safety, regulatory. Office: S C Johnson and Son Inc 1525 Howe St Racine WI 53403

VOSBURGH, KIRBY GANNETT, research manager, scientist; b. Pasadena, Calif., May 27, 1944; s. Kirby A. and Lois Elinor (Gannett) V.; m. Kaye Barber, June 24, 1967; children—Jennett, Kirby. B.S., Cornell U., 1965, M.S., 1967, Ph.D., Rutgers U., 1971. Postdoctoral student, Princeton U. (N.J.), 1971-72; physicist, Gen. Electric, Schenectady, 1972-76, br. mgr., 1976-84, lab. mgr., 1984—. Author writings in field; patentee higher energy radiation detector, method of making integrated circuits utilizing ion implantation and selective epitaxial growth. Deacon Reformed Ch. Am. Mem. IEEE, Am. Phys. Soc. Current work: Research and Development management, solid state electronics, medical, energy physics. Office: Gen Electric PO Box 8 Schenectady NY 12301

VOVIS, GERALD FRANCIS, geneticist; b. Chgo., Feb. 15, 1943; s. Frank Joseph and Elsie Mary (Mucha) V.; m. Carol Ann Klail, Aug. 21, 1965. B.A., Knox Coll., 1965; Ph.D., Case Western Res. U., 1971. Research assoc., dept. genetics Rockefeller U., N.Y.C., 1970-76, asst. prof., 1976-80; sr. research scientist, core tech. Collaborative Research Inc., Waltham, Mass., 1980—82, EMIA research and devel. program mgr., Lexington, Mass., 1982-83, dir. RFLP devel., Waltham, Mass., 1983-85, dir. Prourokinase project, Lexington, 1985—. Mem. Am. Soc. Biol. Chemists, AAAS, Am. Soc. Microbiology, Genetics Soc. Am., N.Y. Acad. Sci., Sigma Xi. Current Work: Research in structure and function of nucleic acids, control of gene expression, expression of foreign genes in yeast and mammalian cells, production and process development of thrombolytic reagents. Subspecialties: Molecular biology; Genetics and genetic engineering (biology). Office: 128 Spring St Lexington MA 02173

VUILLEUMIER, FRANCOIS, evolutionary biologist, biogeographer; b. Berne, Switzerland, Nov. 26, 1938; came to U.S., 1961; s. Willy Georges and Denise Genevieve (Privat) V.; m. Bonita Rae Johnson, Mar. 15, 1972 (div. 1982); children—Alexis, Claire; m. Rebecca Branch Finnell, Feb. 26, 1983; 1 child, Isabelle. Lic. Scis. Naturelles, U. Geneva, 1961; Ph.D., Harvard U., 1967. Instr. biology U. Mass.-Boston, 1966-67, asst. prof., 1967-70, assoc. prof., 1971; prof. U. Lausanne, 1971-72, dir. Inst. Ecology, 1971-72; prof. U. Paris, 1973-74; sr. fellow Marine Biology Lab., Roscoff, France, 1972-73; assoc. curator Am. Mus. Natural History, N.Y.C., 1974-79, curator, 1979—; adj. prof. Queens Coll., 1979—; vis. prof. U. Andes, Merida, Venezuela, 1981. Contbr. articles to profl. jours. Mem. editorial bd. La Terre et la Vie, 1972—, Systematic Zoology, 1974-77, Jour. Biogeography, 1974—, Alauda, 1975-76, Curator, 1976-77, Natural History Mag., 1979-80, Oecologia Generalis, 1979—, Acta Oecologica, 1984—, Acta Zoologica Mexicana, 1984—. Fellow Am. Ornithologists Union; mem. AAAS, Am. Soc. Naturalists, Ecol. Soc. Am., Societe de biogeographie, Societe nationale de protection de la nature d'acclimatation de France, Societe ornithologique de France. Subspecialties: Evolutionary biology; Biogeography. Office: Am Mus Natural History Central Park West at 79th St New York NY 10024

WACHS, ISRAEL EPHRAIM, chemical engineer, researcher; b. Tel Aviv, Israel, Jan. 28, 1950; came to U.S. 1958, naturalized 1963; s. Muni and Rose (Wites) W.; m. Gale Sharon Gavil, Dec. 29, 1973; children—Heidi Laura, David Jacob. B.E. in Chem. Engring., CCNY, 1973; M.S. in Chem. Engring., Stanford U., 1974, Ph.D. in Chem. Engring., 1977. Research scientist Exxon Research and Engring. Co., Annandale, N.J., 1977—; lectr. U. Conn., Storrs, 1980-82, Princeton U., 1984. Contbr. articles to profl. jours. Patentee(9) in field. N.Y. State Regents scholar, 1968-73, Tremaine Baruch scholar CCNY, 1968-73; Stanford U. grad. fellow, 1973-74. Mem. Am. Chem. Soc. (symposia chmn. 1982, 85), Catalysis Soc. N.Y., Am. Inst. Chem. Engrs., N. Am. Catalysis Soc. (symposium chmn. 1983). Current work: Synthesis, physical and chemical characterization, and surface chemistry of atomically dispersed metal oxides on oxide substrates (supported metal oxides). Subspecialties: Materials; Surface chemistry. Home: 340 Rolling Knolls Way Bridgewater NJ 08807 Office: Corp Research Sci Labs Exxon Research and Engring Co Rt 22 E Annandale NJ 08801

WACHTER, WILLIAM JOHN, research and development director; b. Alliance, Ohio, July 22, 1923; s. Ferdin and Helen Alberta (Ormesher) W.; m. Barbara Lee Keep, Oct. 8, 1950; children: William John, Gretchen Lee, Heidi Ann, Frederica Jo, Annelies. B.S.ME., U. Pitts., 1946; M.S.A.E., Case Western Res. U., 1955. Cert. profl. engr., Pa. Mem. staff Lord Mfg., Erie, Pa., 1947-50; staff engr., vibration cons. NASA, Cleve., 1950-53; mgr. applied physics projects Crush Beryllium Co., Cleve., 1953-55; engr. fellow Westinghouse Electric Corp., Bettis Atomic Power Lab., West Mifflin, Pa., 1955-67; pres., prin. cons. Wachter Assocs. Inc., Gibsonia, Pa., 1967-81; mgr. research and devel. U.S. Tool & Die, Gibsonia, 1981—. Fellow Am. Chem. Soc.; mem. ASME, Am. Nuclear Soc. Patentee in field (50). Current Work: Designing high burnup nuclear fuel rods; developing new concepts in nuclear spent fuel storage. Subspecialties: Nuclear fission; Nuclear fusion. Home: 411 English Rd Wexford PA 15090 Office: US Tool & Die 5410 Rt 8 North Gibsonia PA 15090

WACHTMAN, JOHN BRYAN, JR., ceramic scientist, educator; b. Conway, S.C., Feb. 6, 1928; s. John Bryan and Ruby Lee (Moore) W.; m. Edith Virginia Matheny, Aug. 27, 1955. B.S. in Physics, Carnegie-Mellon U., 1948, M.S., 1949; Ph.D., U. Md., 1961. Research assoc. Carnegie-Mellon U., 1949-51; with Nat. Bur. Standards, Dept. Commerce, Washington, 1951-83, sect. chief, 1962-68, chief inorganic materials div., 1968-78, dir. center Materials Sci., 1978-82; dir. Ctr. Ceramics Research Rutgers U., 1983—; vis. prof. materials sci. Northwestern U., 1971; mem. advisory com. Ames Lab, AEC, 1973-74; program mgr. Congl. Office Tech. Assessment, 1974-75; mem. ceramic advisory bd. U. Ill., 1973-75, Alfred U., 1974-83, Pa. State U., 1976-83, Northwestern U., 1977-82, MIT, 1978-82, SUNY, Stony Brook, 1979; mem. Nat. Materials Advisory Bd., 1976-79; chmn. Henniher Conf. Nat. Materials Policy, 1976; program chmn. Internat. Materials Congress, 1979. Editor: (with A.D. Franklin) Mass Transport in Oxides, 1966, Mechanical and Thermal Properties of Ceramics, 1969; series editor: Ceramics and Glass: Science and Technology, 1969—; contbr. articles to profl. jours. Trustee Orton Found., Columbus, Ohio, 1968-82. Recipient gold medal Dept. Commerce, 1971; Samuel Wesley Stratton award Nat. Bur. Standards, 1975. Fellow Am. Ceramic Soc. (trustee 1969-72, pres. 1978-79), Fedn. Materials Soc. (pres. 1976, Hobart N. Craner award in ceramics 1978); mem. Nat. Acad. Engring. Current work: Microstructure and mechanical properties of ceramics. Subspecialties: Ceramics; Condensed matter physics. Home: 20 Independence Ct Piscataway NJ 08854 Office: Center Ceramics Research Rutgers U Box 909 Piscataway NJ 08854

WACKER, WARREN ERNEST CLYDE, physician, health service administrator, researcher; b. Bklyn., Feb. 29, 1924; s. John Frederick and Kitty Dora (Morrissey) W.; m. Ann Romeyn MacMillan, May 22, 1948; children—Margaret Morrissey, John Frederick. Student Georgetown U., 1946-47; M.D., George Washington U., 1951; M.A. (hon.), Harvard U., 1968. Diplomate Am. Bd. Internal Medicine Intern, resident George Washington U. Hosp., 1951-53; resident Peter Bent Brigham Hosp., Boston, 1953-55; from instr. to assoc. prof. med. Harvard U., Boston, 1957-71, Henry K. Oliver prof. hygiene, Cambridge, Mass., 1971—; trustee Risk Mgmt. Found., Cambridge, 1978—; dir. Millipore Corp., Bedford, Mass., Applied Mgmt. Systems, Burlington, Mass. Co-author: Metallo proteins, 1970; author: Magnesium and Man, 1980. Editor, sec. bd. Biochemistry Jour., 1962-76; editor Magnesium Jour., 1982—. Contbr. articles to profl. jours. and books. Trustee Brigham and Women's Hosp., Boston, 1976—, Harvard Community Health Plan, Boston, 1971-84. Served to 1st lt. U.S. Army, 1942-45, ETO. Decorated Air medal, D.F.C. Nat. Found. Infantile Paralysis fellow, 1955-57; Howard Hughes Med. Found. investigator, 1957-68; named Disting. Alumnus George Washington Med. Found., 1963; recipient cert. merit Am. Soc. Magnesium Research, 1985. Fellow ACP; mem. Am. Soc. Clin. Investigation, Am. Soc. Biol. Chemists, Biochem. Soc. London, Am. Coll. Health Assn. (pres. 1981-82), Am. Coll. Nutrition, Sigma Xi, Alpha Omega Alpha. Democrat. Episcopalian. Clubs: Harvard (Boston); Cosmos (Washington). Current work: The role of metals in biological systems, application of biological technology to medicine and industry, health service research, development of alternative delivery stems, cost assessment and control. Subspecialties: Biochemistry (medicine); Internal medicine. Home: 87 Perry St Brookline MA 02146 Office: Harvard University Health Services 75 Mt Auburn St Cambridge MA 02138

WACKERS, FRANS JOZEF THOMAS, cardiology educator, researcher; b. Echt, Netherlands, May 29, 1939; came to U.S., 1977; s. Thomas F. and Miep (Koopman) W.; m. Marjan A. Meyer, Sept. 29, 1972; children: Michiel, Paul. M.D., U. Amsterdam, 1970, Ph.D., 1970. Diplomate: Netherlands Bd. Internal Medicine, Netherlands Bd. Cardiology. Intern U. Amsterdam, 1965-66, 69-70, resident in medicine, 1972-74, fellow in cardiology, 1974-77; asst. prof. cardiology Yale U., 1977-81; assoc. prof. cardiology U. Vt.-Burlington, 1981-84, dir. nuclear cardiology, 1981-84; assoc. prof. cardiology and radiology Yale U., 1984—. Editor: Thallium-201 Myocardial Imaging, 1978, Myocardial Imaging in CCU, 1980. Fellow Am. Coll. Cardiology (editorial bd. jour.); mem. Am. Fedn. Clin. Research, Soc. Nuclear Medicine. Current Work: Nuclear cardiology; noninvasive assessment of cardiac function and perfusion (T1-201, Tc-99m, Au-195m), Quantitative analysis. Subspecialties: Cardiology; Nuclear medicine. Office: Yale U Cardiology New Haven CT 06510

WADDELL, WILLIAM JOSEPH, toxicology educator; b. Commerce, Ga., Mar. 16, 1929; s. John D. and Lillian M. (Vollrath) W.; m. Aubrey A. Christie, Dec. 22, 1951 (div. Jan. 1974); children—William, James, Martin, Amy; m. Grace C. Marlowe, Oct. 19, 1974. A.B. in Chemistry, U. N.C.-Chapel Hill, 1951, M.D., 1955. Lic. physician, N.C. Asst. prof. U. N.C.-Chapel Hill, 1958-62, assoc. prof., 1962-69, prof., 1969-72; prof. pharmacology U. Ky., Lexington, 1972-77; prof., chmn. dpt. pharmacology and toxicology U. Louisville Sch. Medicine, 1977—; disting. vis. prof. Sch. Medicine, U. N.C., 1979; cons. to industry. Mem. editorial bd. Drug Metabolism and Disposition, Toxicology & Applied Pharmacology. Contbr. chpts. to books, articles to sci. jours. Recipient Centennial Alumnus award U. N.C.-Chapel Hill, 1979. Mem. Am. Soc. Pharmacology and Exptl. Therapeutics (chmn. ednl. affairs com.), Am. Physiol. Soc., Am. Teratology Soc., Soc. Toxicology, Soc. Exptl. Biology and Medicine. Current work: Mechanisms of chemical carcinogenesis. Subspecialties: Pharmacology; Toxicology (medicine). Home: 6604 Gunpowder Ln Prospect KY 40059 Office: U Louisville Med Sch Louisville KY 40292

WADDINGTON, CECIL JACOB, astrophysicist, educator; b. Cambridge, Eng., July 6, 1929; came to U.S., 1957, naturalized, 1973; s. Conrad H. and Cecil E. (Lascelles) W.; m. Jean C. Bassett Webb, Sept. 15, 1956. B.Sc. with honors, U. Bristol, Eng., 1952, Ph.D., 1955. Royal Soc. research student, 1955-59; research assoc. U. Minn., 1957-58; lectr. U. Bristol, 1959-61; vis. prof. Goddard Space Sci. Ctr., 1959; assoc. prof. U. Minn., 1961-69, prof. physics, 1969—; vis. prof. Imperial Coll., London, 1971-72. Contbr. articles to profl. jours. Served with Royal Elec. and Mech. Engrs., 1947-49. Recipient NASA Exceptional Sci. Achievement Medal, 1980. Fellow Am. Phys. Soc.; mem. Am. Astron. Soc., AAAS, Internat. Astron. Union. Current Work: Mass, charge, and energy spectra of cosmic ray nuclei observed from balloons and satellites. The characteristics of high energy nucleus-nucleus interactions using cosmic ray and artificially accelerated nuclei. Subspecialties: Cosmic ray high energy astrophysics; Nuclear physics. Office: U Minn 116 Church St SE Minneapolis MN 55455

WADE, ADELBERT ELTON, pharmacologist, educator, researcher; b. Hilliard, Fla., Apr. 29, 1926; s. Adelbert Elton and Esther (Sundberg) W.; m. Mary Lucy Wade, Jan. 22, 1950; children: William Elton, James Howard. B.S. in Pharmacy, U. Fla., 1954, M.S. in Pharmacology, 1956, Ph.D. in Pharmacology, 1959. Instr. U. Fla., 1954-56; asst. prof. U. Ga., Athens, 1959-62, assoc. prof., 1962-67, prof., 1967—, head dept. pharmacology, 1968—, research in field. Contbr. articles to profl. jours. Served with USN, 1944-46. Recipient Creative Research award U. Ga., 1981; NIH grantee, 1972—. Mem. Am. Soc. Pharmacology and Exptl. Therapeutics, Internat. Soc. Biochem. Pharmacology, Soc. Exptl. Biol. Medicine. Democrat. Baptist. Club: Torch (Athens). Current Work: Drug activity enzymes in the initiation and promotion of chemically induced cancer. Subspecialties: Molecular pharmacology; Cancer research (medicine). Office: Univ of Ga Sch of Pharm GA 30802

WADE, JAMES JOSEPH, medicinal chemist; b. St. Paul, Jan. 7, 1946; s. Ralph Robert and Marjorie (Durbin) W.; m. Elizabeth Rose Weber, Apr. 4, 1970; children—Daniel, Michael, Kristin. B.A., Coll. St. Thomas, 1968; Ph.D., U. Minn., 1972. NIH postdoctorate U. Rochester, N.Y., 1972-73; sr. medicinal chemist Riker Labs 3M Co., St. Paul, 1973-76, research specialist, 1976-83, sr. research specialist, 1983—. Contbr. articles to profl. jours. Patentee in field. Mem. Am. Chem. Soc. Current work: Design and synthesis of organic compounds as potential drug candidates; heterocyclic chemistry; new synthetic methods; branchodilator drugs. Subspecialties: Organic chemistry; Synthetic chemistry. Home: 1385 N Hallmark Ave Saint Paul MN 55119 Office: Riker Labs 3M Co 270-2S-06 3M Ctr Saint Paul MN 55144

WADE, PETER ALLEN, chemistry educator; b. Taunton, Mass., Nov. 12, 1946; s. Lawrence Wade and Elizabeth E. (Caddell) Barr; m. Joann Frances Kearnan, Aug. 5, 1967; 1 child, Jennifer. B.S., Lowell Tech. Inst., 1968; Ph.D., Purdue U., 1973. Asst. prof. chemistry Drexel U., 1976—. Contbr. articles to profl. jours. IBM fellow, 1975-76. Mem. Am. Chem. Soc. Club: Phila. Organic Chemists (chmn.). Current work: Cycloaddition reactions; new synthetic methods; natural product synthesis; reactive intermediates; nitro compounds. Subspecialties: Organic chemistry; Organometallics. Home: 2104 Haverford Rd Ardmore PA 19003 Office: Drexel Univ Chemistry Dept Philadelphia PA 19104

WADE, THOMAS EDWARD, electrical engineer, educator, researcher, engineering administrator; b. Jacksonville, Fla., Sept. 14, 1943; s. Wilton Fred and Alice Lucyle (Hedge) W.; m. Ann Elizabeth Chitty, Aug. 6, 1966; children—Amy Renee, Nathan Thomas, Laura Ann. B.S.E.E., U. Fla.-Gainesville, 1966, M.E.E., 1968, Ph.D., 1974. Interim asst. prof. U. Fla.-Gainesville, 1974-76; prof. elec. engring. Miss. State U., Starkville, 1976-85, assoc. dean. U. South Fla., Tampa, 1985—, also exec. dir. Ctrs. Engring. Devel. and Research;

solid state circuit specialist Applied Micro-Circuits Corp., San Diego, Calif., 1981-82; cons. in field. Author: Polyimides for VLSI Applications, 1984. Contbr. articles to profl. jours. Vol., United Fund, Miss. State U., 1983-85. Recipient Outstanding Engrng. Teaching award Coll. Engrng. U. Fla., 1976, Cert. of Recognition NASA, 1981, 82, 83, Outstanding Research award Sigma Xi, 1984. Mem. IEEE (guest editor periodical 1982, gen. chmn. Internat. VLSI Multilevel Interconnection Conf. 1984, 85), Am. Soc. Engrng. Edn., AAAS, Internat. Soc. Hybrid Microelectronics, Soc. Photo Optical Instrumentation Engrng. Current work: Solid state microelectronics, VLSI multilevel interconnection systems, fluctuation phoenomena in semiconductors and solid state devices, novel device and fabrication characterization. Subspecialties: Microelectronics; Microchip technology (materials science). Home: 16219 W Course Dr Tampa FL 33624 Office: Coll of Engrng Office of Dean 4202 Fowler Ave Tampa FL 33620

WADLEIGH, CECIL HERBERT, retired physiologist; b. Oct. 1, 1907; s. Hazel Carl and Lucy (Whitehead) W.; m. Clarice Lucille Bean, Sept. 18, 1930; children—Evelyn Estelle, Carolyn Priscilla, Stanley Firth, Elaine Lucille. B.S., U. Mass., 1930; D.Sc. (hon.), 1974; M.S., Ohio State U., 1932; Ph.D., Rutgers U., 1935. Asst. prof. plant physiology U. Ark., Fayetteville, 1936-41; sr. plant physiologist U.S. Solinity Lab., Riverside, Calif., 1941-51; head physiologist U.S. Agrl. Research Ctr., Beltsville, Md., 1951-55; dir. soil and water research div., USDA, Beltsville, 1955-70, sci. adviser, 1971, retired, 1971; mem. White House Panel in Indus. Basin of Pakistan, 1961-63; mem. Com. on Watershed Hydrology, White House Office Sci. and Tech., 1961-62; mem. Com. Water Resources Research, 1963-69, mem. Com. on Environ. Quality, 1967-69; ofcl. del U.S. Dept. Agr. to White House Conf. on Conservation, 1963, Dept. Agr. Bilateral Conf. on Environ. Protection, Pilsen, Czechoslovakia, 1973; cons. Lake Verret Watershed Planning Group, La., 1971-76. Contbr. articles to profl. publs. Recipient Disting. Service award U.S. Dept. Agr., 1967. Fellow Soil Conservation Soc. Am. (Hugh Hammond Bennett award 1976), Am. Soc. Agronomy; mem. Am. Soc. Plant Physiology (pres. 1951-52), Nat. Acad. Scis., Am. Soc. Hort. Sci. Current work: plant physiology, soil conservation, horticulture. Subspecialties: Plant physiology (agriculture); Resource conservation. Home: 5621 Whitefield Chapel Rd Lanham MD 20706

WADSWORTH, MILTON ELLIOT, metallurgy educator; b. Salt Lake City, Feb. 9, 1922; s. Thomas Guy and Agnes (Flockhart) W.; m. Mirian M. Bailey, Nov. 19, 1943; children—Cristine, Kathryn, Jane, Amy, Leslie, Margaret. B.S., U. Utah, 1948, Ph.D., 1951; Dr. h.c., U. Liege, Belgium, 1979. Registered profl. engr., Utah. From instr. to disting. prof. U. Utah, Salt Lake City, 1948—, chmn. dept. metallurgy, 1955-66, 70-76, assoc. dean Coll. Engrng., 1973-74, assoc. dean Coll. Minds, 1976-83, dir. Mining and Minerals Research Inst., 1979-80, dean Coll. Mines and Mineral Industries, 1983—. Contbr. articles to profl. publs. Served to 1st lt. U.S. Army, 1943-45. Recipient Disting. Research Prof. award U. Utah, 1972-73, Disting. Teaching award U. Utah, 1978. Fellow AIME (Best Paper award 1957, lectr. 1969, Arthur F. Taggert award 1973, 77, James Gouglas Gold medal 1978, Disting. Mem. award 1978, Henry Krumb lectr. 1979, 25 Yr. Membership cert. 1981, Mineral Industry Edn. award 1981, Antoine M. Gurdin award 1984); mem. Am. Soc. Metals (disting. mem., 25 Yr. award 1983), Cam. Inst. Mining and Metallurgy, Am. Chem. Soc., Electrochem. Soc., Sigma Xi, Phi Kappa Phi, Tau Beta Pi, Alpha Sigma Mu (disting. mem.). Current work: Surface chemistry of mineral systems in mineral dressing and extractive metallurgy processes, hydrometallurgy, intermediate temperature processes such as roasting, decomposition and reduction, the application of reaction rate kinetics in determination of mechanisms in extractive metallurgy processes and electrochemistry as applied to metals extraction. Subspecialty: Metallurgical engineering.

WADSWORTH, WILLIAM BINGHAM, geology educator, researcher; b. Cortland, N.Y., Dec. 4, 1934; s. Welland Bingham and Jeanne Kathryn (Jenkins) W.; m. Martha Kikuyo Nakao, June 23, 1962; children—W. Bryan, Kyle Evan. A.B., Brown U., 1957; M.S., Northwestern U., 1963, Ph.D., 1966. Asst. prof. geology U. S.D., Vermillion, 1963-66; asst. prof. geology Idaho State U., Pocatello, 1966-69, assoc. prof., 1969-72; assoc. prof., chmn. dept. geology Whittier Coll., Calif., 1972-78, prof., chmn. dept., 1978—; cons. FMC Corp., Pocatello, 1968-71. Contbr. articles, abstracts to profl. publs. Served with U.S. Army, 1957-59. NSF fellow, 1971-72. Fellow Geol. Soc. Am.; mem. Am. Geophys. Union, Mineral. Soc. Am., Soc. Econ. Paleontologists and Mineralogists (treas. Pacific sect. 1978-80), Internat. Assn. Math. Geologists, AAAS, Nat. Assn. Geology Tchrs., AAUP, Sigma Xi. Current work: Porphyry-copper host plutons, mechanics of ore-fluid separation from Magma; modal analysis of granites by x-ray diffraction; quantitative textural analysis of igneous rocks. Subspecialties: Petrology; Mineralogy. Home: 2967 Sisal Pl Hacienda Heights CA 91745 Office: Whittier Coll Dept Geology Whittier CA 90608

WAELSCH, SALOME GLUECKSOHN, genetics educator; b. Danzig, Germany, Oct. 6, 1907; came to U.S., 1933, naturalized, 1938; d. Ilyia and Nadia Gluecksohn; m. Heinrich B. Waelsch, Jan. 8, 1943; children—Naomi Barbara, Peter Benedict. Student, U. Konigsberg, Ger., U. Berlin; Ph.D., U. Freiburg, Ger., 1932. Research assoc. in genetics Columbia U., 1936-55; assoc. prof. anatomy Albert Einstein Coll. Medicine, 1955-58, prof., 1958-63, prof. genetics, 1963—, chmn. dept. genetics, 1963-76; mem. study sects. NIH. Fellow Am. Acad. Arts and Scis.; mem. Nat. Acad. Scis., Am. Soc. Zoologists, Am. Assn. Anatomists, Genetics Soc., Soc. Devel. Biology, Am. Soc. Naturalists, Am. Soc. Human Genetics, Sigma Xi. Research, numerous publs. on devel. genetics. Subspecialties: Gene actions; Developmental biology. Office: Dept Genetics Albert Einstein Coll Medicine 1300 Morris Park Ave Bronx NY 10461

WAGENKNECHT, JOHN HENRY, chemical manufacturing company research scientist; b. Washington, Iowa, Jan. 30, 1939; s. Herman Frederick and Anna Marie (Jenkins) W.; m. Joan Barbara Schilthuis, Aug. 20, 1960; children—Jill Helene, John Edward, Jason Hugh. A.B., Monmouth Coll., 1960; Ph.D., U. Iowa, 1964. Sr. research chemist Monsanto Co., St. Louis, 1964-71, research specialist, 1971-74, sci. fellow, 1974—. Contbr. numerous articles to profl. jours. Patentee in field. Active God's Green Acre Assn., Webster Groves, Mo., 1976—. Mem. Am. Chem. Soc., Internat. Soc. Electrochemistry, Electrochem. Soc. (sec. Organic and Biol. Div. 1976-78, treas., 1976-78, vice chmn. 1978-80, chmn. 1980-82, editor Jour. 1984—). Current work: Synthesis by electrochemistry; mechanisms of electro-organic reactions; electroanalytical chemistry. Subspecialty: Organic chemistry. Home: 934 Wood Ave Kirkwood MO 63122 Office: Monsanto Co 800 N Lindbergh Blvd Saint Louis MO 63167

WAGERS, ROBERT SHELBY, research electrical engineer; b. Covington, Ky., Jan. 25, 1943; s. Isaac S. and Hazel M. (Eissner) W.; m. Judy Anne Hipke, Aug. 16, 1969. A.A., Phoenix Jr. Coll., 1963; B.S.E.E., Ariz. State U., 1966, M.S.E.E., 1966; postgrad. Oxford U., 1966-67; Ph.D., Stanford U., 1972. Engr., Gen. Electric Co., Phoenix, 1964-66; research mgr. Tex. Instruments, Dallas, 1972-76; asst. prof. Princeton U., N.J., 1976; research mgr. Tex. Instruments, 1977—. Assoc. editor IEEE Trans Sonics and Uultrasonics, 1981-84. Contbr. articles to profl. jours., chpts. to books. Patentee in field (9). Rhodes scholar, 1966. Fellow IEEE (Best Paper award 1976; tech. program chmn. symposium 1982). Current work: Wide-band signal processing with electronic devices, especially surface acoustic wave devices. Subspecialties: Electrical engineering; Acoustics. Home: 921 Forreston Dr Richardson TX 75080 Office: Texas Instruments PO Box 225936 Dallas TX 75265

WAGGONER, PAUL EDWARD, agricultural scientist, agricultural experiment station administrator; b. Appanoose County, Iowa, Mar. 29, 1923; s. Walter Loyal and Kathryn (Maring) W.; m. Barbara Ann Lockerbie, Nov. 3, 1945; children: Von Lockerbie, Daniel Maring. S.B., U. Chgo., 1946; M.S., Iowa State Coll., 1949, Ph.D., 1951. With Conn. Agrl. Exptl. Sta., New Haven, 1951—, vice dir., 1969-72, dir., 1972—; lectr. Sch. Forestry Yale U., 1962—; dir. N.E. Bancorp Inc., Union Trust Co. Contbr. articles to profl. jours. Served to 1st lt. USAAF, 1943-46. Guggenheim fellow, 1963. Fellow Am. Soc. Agronomy, AAAS, Am. Phytopath. Soc.; mem. Am. Acad. Arts and Sci., Am. Meterol. Soc. (award outstanding achievement biometeorology 1967), Am. Soc. Plant Physiology, Nat. Acad. Sci., Conn. Acad. Sci. and Engring. (v.p. 1976—). Club: Grad. (New Haven). Current Work: Effect of weather on plants and insects; epidemiology of plant disease. Subspecialties: Plant pathology; Integrated systems modelling and engineering. Home: 314 Vineyard Rd Guilford CT 06437 Office: 123 Huntington St New Haven CT 06511

WAGMAN, ALTHEA M.I., research psychophysiologist, educator; b. Knoxville, Tenn., Dec. 22, 1933; d. David Gerard and Althea Devecmon (Wimbrough) Iliff; m. William D. Wagman, June 5, 1954; children: Althea Susan, David Wolfe, Ida Lee. B.S., Coll. William and Mary, 1954; M.S., Columbia U., 1958; Ph.D., So. Ill. U., 1966. Lic. psychologist, Md. Lectr. So. Ill. U., Carbondale, 1961-72; asst.prof. Towson (Md.) State U., 1967-69, assoc. prof., 1969-71; research scientist State of Md., 1971-77; research assoc. in psychiatry Md. Psychiat. Research Center U. Md. Med. Sch., Balt., 1977-83; prof. Loyola Coll., Balt., 1980; research assoc. prof. U. Md. Med. Sch., Balt., 1983—; chmn. Tng. Adv. Bd. Psychology Md. Dept. Mental Hygiene. Contbr. articles to profl. jours. Recipient Disting. Psychologist award Md. Psychol. Assn., 1984; USPHS fellow, 1964-66; grantee; NIH; NIMH. Mem. Am. Psychol. Assn., Soc. Neurosci., Soc. Psychophysiol. Research. Democrat. Current Work: Evoked potentials in schizophrenia. Subspecialties: Psychophysiology; Neuropsychology. Home: 1533 Park Ave Baltimore MD 21217 Office: Box 3235 Baltimore MD 21228

WAGMAN, GERALD H(OWARD), microbial biochemist, antiobiotics researcher; b. Newark, N.J., Mar. 4, 1926; s. David and Sophie (Milinsky) W.; m. Rhoda Kirschner, Dec. 9, 1948; children—Jan D., Neil M. B.S. in Chemistry, Lehigh U., 1946; M.S. in Chemistry, Va. Poly. Inst. and State U., 1947. Tech. research asst. Squibb Inst., New Brunswick, N.J., 1947-49, research asst., 1954-57; mgr. indsl. electronics Yankee Radio Corp., N.Y.C., 1950-54; assoc. biochemist Schering Corp., Bloomfield, N.J., 1957-58; biochemist, 1958-65; sr. biochemist, 1966-68, sect. leader, 1969-70, mgr. antibiotics dept., 1970-74, assoc. dir. microbiol. scis., 1974-77, assoc. dir., head screening lab., 1977-78, dir. microbial strain lab., 1979-84, dir. antibiotic isolation, 1984—; mem. cert. adv. bd. Nat. Cert. Commn. in Chemistry and Chem. Engring., 1985—. Sr. author: Chromatography of Antibiotics, 1973, 2d edit., 1984. Co-editor: Antibiotics: Isolation, Separation and Purification, 1978. Contbr. numerous articles to sci. jours. Numerous patents in field. Various offices Highview Acres Civic Assn., East Brunswick, N.J., 1957-75; communications officer East Brunswick Civil Def., 1958-76; sci. adv. com. East Brunswick Bd. Edn., 1963-65; bd. dirs. Tamarack North Homeowners Assn., 1982-83, others. Fellow Am. Inst. Chemists; mem. Am. Chem. Soc., Am. Soc. Microbiology, AAAS, Soc. Indsl. Microbiology, N.Y. Acad. Scis., Royal Soc. Chemistry (chartered chemist), Sigma Xi. Current work: Chemical screening and classification of antibiotics and other fermentation products. Subspecialty: Organometallics. Home: 17 Crommelin Ct East Brunswick NJ 08816 Office: Schering Corp 60 Orange St Bloomfield NJ 07003

WAGNER, AUBREY JOSEPH, energy consultant; b. Hillsboro, Wis., Jan. 12, 1912; s. Joseph Michael and Wilhelmina Johanna (Filter) W.; m. Dorothea Johanna Huber, Sept. 9, 1933; children: Audrey Wagner Elam Joseph M., James R., Karl E. B.S.C.E. magna cum laude, U. Wis., 1933; LL.D. (hon.), Newberry Coll., 1966; Ph.D. in Public Adminstrn. (hon.), Lenoir-Rhyne Coll., 1970. Registered profl. engr., Tenn. With TVA, 1934-78, asst. gen. mgr., Knoxville, 1951-54, gen. mgr., 1954-61, bd. dirs., 1961-62, chmn. bd., 1962-78, cons. energy and resource-use matters, Knoxville, Tenn., 1978—; seminar lectr., Pakistan, 1967, Salzburg, Austria, 1968; bd. dirs. U.S. Nat. Com. of World Energy Conf., 1975-84. Contrbr. chpts. numerous articles to various nat., regional publs. Bd. dirs. Citizens for Home Rule, Knoxville, 1975-84. Recipient Walter H. Zinn award Am. Nuclear Soc., 1978; named Engr. of Distinction Tenn. Technol. U., 1981. Mem. Tenn. Soc. Profl. engrs., Nat. Soc. Profl. Engrs., Nat. Acad. Engring., Explorers Club, Lambda Chi Alpha (Order of Achievement). Lutheran. Current Work: Working actively as proponent of nuclear energy and especially breeder reactor. Subspecialties: Civil engineering; Nuclear engineering.

WAGNER, CARL ERNEST, physicist, consultant; b. Berkeley Twp., N.J., July 10, 1940; s. Lawrence Frederick and Dorothy Eistetter (Ayars) W.; m. Barbara Jean Carter, Apr. 8, 1979; children—Laura Christine, David Nicholas. S.B., MIT, 1961, Sc.D., 1970. Research and teaching asst. MIT, Cambridge, 1962-69; physicist U.S. Naval Research Lab., Washington, 1970-75; sr. scientist Sci. Applications, Inc., LaJolla, Calif., 1975-81, also cons.; chief physicist Inesco, Inc., La Jolla, 1981-84; sr. physicist TRW, Redondo Beach, Calif., 1984—; cons. Energy Applications & Systems, Inc., Carlsbad, Calif., 1984. Contbr. articles to profl. jours. Alfred P. Sloan scholar MIT, 1957; U.S. Intercollegiate Chess Champion, 1967. Mem. Am. Phys. Soc., Am. Nuclear Soc., Fusion Power Assocs., Sigma Xi. Presbyterian. Current work: Controlled fusion, plasma physics and engineering, computational physics, compact Tokamak fusion reactors and ignition experiments. Subspecialties: Nuclear fusion; Plasma engineering. Office: TRW R1/2128 1 Space Park Redondo Beach CA 90278

WAGNER, CARMEN MACHADO, immunologist; b. Rio de Janeiro, Brazil, Sept. 12, 1946; d. Alipio Severiano and Carmen (dos Santos) Machado; m. Brian Frederick Wagner, Jan. 31, 1976. B.S., U. Ariz., 1975, Ph.D., 1981. Research assoc. U. Estado da Guanabara, Rio de Janeiro, 1975; teaching asst. U. Ariz., Tucson, 1976-80, research assoc., 1980-83; asst. med. research prof. Duke U., Durham, N.C., 1984-85; cons. in field, 1985; with Wagner Computer Systems Tucson, 1985—. Contbr. articles to profl. jours. Recipient Mayor's award City of Tucson, 1975. Mem. N.Y. Acad. Scis., AAAS, Am. Soc. Immunology, Assn. for Devel. Computer-Based Inst. Systems, Computer Users in Edn., Tucson Computer Soc., Phi Kappa Phi. Current work: Applications of biotechnology in medicine including role of immunologic mediators in glomerulonephritis; applications of computers in the health field. Subspecialties: Cellular engineering; Cell and tissue culture. Office: Wagner & Assocs 2330 E Edison St Tucson AZ 85719

WAGNER, DANIEL HOBSON, mathematician; b. Jersey Shore, Pa., Aug. 24, 1925; s. Hobson Charles and Kathryn (Eyer) W.; m. Mary Emma Mertz, Sept. 9, 1949; children—David Hobson, Christopher Daniel, Thomas John, Elizabeth Ann. B.S., Haverford Coll., 1947; Ph.D., Brown U., 1951. Sci. staff mem. ops. eval. group MIT, Washington, 1951-56; supr. math. analysis sect. Burroughs Research Ctr., Paoli, Pa., 1956-58; ptnr. Kettelle and Wagner, Paoli, 1958-63; lectr. Swarthmore Coll., Pa., 1958; pres. Daniel H. Wagner Assocs., Paoli, 1963—; task group chmn. Adv. Group on Reliability of Electronic Equipment, 1956; mem. com. on tng. in applied math. Nat. Acad. Scis., 1977-78. Contbr. articles to profl. jours. Mem. exec. com. Chester County Republican Com., Pa., 1960-63; pres. Chester County Young Republicans, 1960. Served with USNR 1943-45. Mem. Am. Math. Soc. (council 1979-81), Math. Assn. Am., Ops. Research Soc. Am., Mil. Ops. Research Soc. (bd. dirs. 1978-79). Presbyterian. Current work: Measurable selection theory optimization theory, group theory. Subspecialties: Operations research (engineering); Applied mathematics. Office: Daniel H Wagner Assocs Station Square One Paoli PA 19301

WAGNER, GEORGE JOSEPH, plant biochemist, educator; b. Buffalo, Sept. 15, 1943; s. George and Helen (Gyvlavics) W.; m. Beverly J. Davis, Sept. 10, 1970; children Jenny Lynn, Kristen Mary, Katherine Marie. B.A., SUNY-Buffalo, 1970, M.A., 1971, Ph.D., 1974. Research assoc. Brookhaven Nat. Lab., Upton, N.Y., 1974-77, asst. scientist, 1977-79, assoc. scientist, 1979-83; assoc. prof. plant physiology, biochemistry U. Ky., Lexington, 1983—. Served as sgt. USAF, 1970-72. Mem. Am. Soc. Plant Physiologists (exec. com. 1979-81, chmn. 1981, grantee 1975), AAAS, Phytochem. Soc. N.Am. (exec. com. 1984—, sec. 1984—). Current work: Cell biology of intracellular transport and accumulation in plants; physiology and biochemistry of toxic metal accumulation in plants; toxicology of plant-derived metals in animals. Subspecialties: Plant physiology (agriculture); Toxicology (agriculture). Office: Univ Ky Agronomy Dept N212 Agr Sci Ctr N Lexington KY 40546

WAGNER, HERMAN LEON, physical chemist, researcher; b. N.Y.C., Mar. 21, 1921; s. Max and Regina (Hahn) W.; m. Jean March, June 25, 1954 (dec. Dec. 1976); 1 child, Nancy. B.S., CCNY, 1942; M.S., Bklyn. Poly. Inst., 1946; Ph.D., Cornell U., 1950. Research chemist S.A.M. Labs., N.Y.C., 1942-46, E.I. duPont, Phila., 1951-55, M.W. Kellogg Co., Jersey City, 1955-57, Celanese Corp., Summit, N.J., 1957-68, Nat. Bur. Standards, Gaithersburg, Md., 1968—. Contbr. articles to profl. jours. Patentee in field. Mem. Am. Chem. Soc., ASTM (sect. chmn. 1979-85), Phi Beta Kappa, Sigma Xi. Current work: Viscosity and molecular weight methods of polymer chemistry; physical chemistry of high polymers; gel permeation chromatography; ultra-high molecular weight polyethylene; viscosity-molecular weight relationships; polymer standard reference materials. Subspecialties: Polymers (materials science); Polymer chemistry. Home: 5457 Marlin St Rockville MD 20853 Office: Nat Bur Standards Bldg 224 Room B320 Gaithersburg MD 20899

WAGNER, JAMES BRUCE, JR., solid state science educator; b. Hampton, Va., July 28, 1927; s. James Bruce and Mary (Hudgins) W.; m. Phyllis M. Mountjoy, Sept. 5, 1951; children: James Bruce III, Ashley Stephen, Rebecca Bland. B.S. in Chemistry, U.Va., 1950, Ph.D. in Chemistry, 1955. Research assoc. MIT, Cambridge, 1954-56; asst. prof. metallurgy Pa. State U., State College, 1956-58, Yale U., New Haven, 1958-62; assoc. prof. materials sci. Northwestern U., Evanston, Ill., 1962-65, prof., 1965-77; dir. Northwestern U. (Materials Research Lab.), 1972-76; mem. faculty Ariz. State U., Tempe, 1977—, prof. solid state sci., 1977—; dir. Ariz. State U. (Center for Solid State Sci.), 1980-84, affiliate prof. physics and mech. and aerospace engring., 1981—, prof. chemistry, 1981—; Ford. Found. residency in engring. Motorola, Inc., Phoenix, 1968-69. Mem. Electrochem. Soc. (pres. 1983), Am. Phys. Soc., Metall. Soc. AIME. Episcopalian. Current Work: Solid state electrolytes; diffusion in non-stoichiometric compounds; high temperature corrosion. Subspecialties: Ceramics; Solid state chemistry. Office: Center for Solid State Sci Ariz State Univ Tempe AZ 85287

WAGNER, JOHN GARNET, pharmacology educator, researcher; b. Weston, Ont., Can., Mar. 28, 1921; came to U.S., 1949; s. Herbert William and Coral (Cates) W.; m. Eunice Winona Kelsey, July 4, 1946; children—Wendie Lynn, Linda Beth. B.Pharm., U. Toronto, 1947; B.S. in Pharmacy, U. Sask., 1948, B.A., 1949; Ph.D., Ohio State U., 1952, Sc.D., 1980. Research scientist Upjohn Co., Kalamazoo, 1953-56, head pharm. research sect., 1956-63, sr. research scientist, 1963-68, cons., 1968—; prof. pharmacy, asst. dir. research and devel. pharm. services Univ. Hosp., U. Mich., Ann Arbor, 1968-72, prof. pharmacy, staff mem. Upjohn Ctr. for Clin. Pharmacology, 1973-82, Albert B. Prescott prof. pharmacy, 1982—, staff mem. Upjohn Ctr. Clin. Pharm., 1973—; cons. Warner Lambert Labs., Ann Arbor, 1983—, Key Pharms., Miami, Fla., 1980—. Author: Biopharmaceutics and Relevant Pharmacokinetics, 1971; Fundamentals of Clinical Pharmacokinetics, 1975. Contbr. articles to profl. jours. Patentee in field. Recipient William E. Upjohn award, 1960; Centennial Achievement award Ohio State U., 1970; Host-Madsen medal Fedn. Internat. Pharmaceutique, 1972; Propter merita medal Czechoslovakian Med. Soc., 1974; Volwiler Research Achievement award Am. Assn. Colls. Pharmacy, 1983. Served with RCAF, 1941-45. Fellow Acad. Pharm. Scis. (stimulation research award 1983, Pharmaceutics award 1984), AAAS; mem. Am. Pharm. Assn. (Ebert prize 1961), Am. Fedn. Clin. Research, Am. Soc. Clin. Pharmacology and Therapeutics, Am. Soc. Pharmacology and Exptl. Therapeutics, N.Y. Acad. Scis., Internat. Soc. Study of Xenobiotics. Home: 2142 Spruceway Ln Ann Arbor MI 48103 Office: Upjohn Ctr Clin Pharmacology U Mich Med Ctr Ann Arbor MI 48109

WAGNER, JOSEPH EDWARD, veterinarian, educator; b. Dubuque, Iowa, July 29, 1938; s. Jacob Edward and Leona (Callahan) W.; D.V.M., Iowa State U., 1963; M.P.H., Tulane, U., 1964; Ph.D., U. Ill.-Urbana, 1967. Diplomate Am. Bd. Animal Medicine. Research assoc. Tulane, New Orleans, 1963-64. U. Ill., Urbana, 1964-67; asst. prof. U. Kans., Kansas City, 1967-69, assoc. prof., 1969-72; professor U. Mo., Columbia, 1972—. Editor: The Biology of the Guinea Pig, 1976. Co-author: The Biology and Medicine of Rabbits and Rodents, 1978, 1983. Mem. AVMA, Am. Coll. Lab. Animal Medicine (bd. dirs.), Am. Assn. Lab. Animal Sci. (pres. 1979-80). Home: 2801 West Blvd A3 Columbia MO 65203 Office: Coll Vet Medicine Columbia MO 65211

WAGNER, LORRY YALE, energy company executive, research engineer; b. Miami Beach, Fla., June 24, 1951; s. Morris Maxwell and Thelma (Portman) W.; m. Joanne Elaine Gold, Jan. 6, 1973 (div. Nov. 1975); m. Susan Lee Hogan, Oct. 6, 1979. B.S. in Engring, Purdue U., 1973, M.S. in Nuclear Engring, 1975, Ph.D., 1981. Research instr. Purdue U., West Lafayette, Ind., 1974-81; pres. Phillips Electric Co., Cleve., 1981-83, pres. 1983—; P.E. Energy Resources, Cleve., 1981—, Remote Sensors, Inc., Cleve.; exec. v.p. Redmond Waltz Electric Co., Cleve., 1981-83, pres., 1983—. Contbr. articles to profl. jours. Coach West Lafayette Swim Club, 1974-81, Lafayette Jefferson High Sch., 1978-81, Purdue U., 1976-78, Cleveland Heights (Ohio) Community Services, 1982-85; women's coach Cleve. State U., 1985—. Mem. Am. Nuclear Soc., Assn. Energy Engrs., Nat. Soc. Profl. Engrs., AAAS, Order of the Engr., Tau Beta Pi. Club: University (Cleve.). Current Work: Integrating/designing automation equipment for computer control of industrial facilities, design/implementation of computer controlled energy management systems. Subspecialty: Systems engineering. Home: 2977 Coleridge Rd Cleveland Heights OH 44118 Office: Phillips Electric Energy Resources 4126 St Clair Ave Cleveland OH 44103

WAGNER, LOUIS FRANK, research chemist, lawyer; b. Elmhurst, N.Y., Mar. 11, 1952; s. Louis M. and Amelia S. (Sickar) W.; m. Zoe E. Keim, Oct. 1, 1983. B.A., Washington and Jefferson Coll., 1974; M.S., U. Pitts., 1977; J.D., U. Akron, 1983. Research chemist, patent info. specialist Standard Oil Ohio, Cleve., 1977—; sole practice law, Cuyahoga Falls, Ohio, 1983—. Patentee in field. Mem. Am. Chem. Soc., ABA, Ohio Bar Assn., Akron Bar Assn. Current work: Oxidative heterogeneous catalysis in the areas of hydrocarbon upgrading and synthetic fuels. Subspecialty: Inorganic chemistry. Home: 707 Chestnut Blvd Cuyahoga Falls OH 44221 Office: Standard Oil Ohio 4440 Warrensville Ctr Rd Cleveland OH 44128

WAGNER, MELVIN PETER, research chemist; b. Hastings, Nebr., Nov. 16, 1926; s. Carl and Caroline (Pittz) W.; m. Ruth M. Hilt, Aug. 29, 1953; children—Joan, Mark, Martha, John, MaryLynne. B.S. in Chemistry, Creighton U., 1950, M.S. in Chemistry, 1952; Ph.D. in Polymer Sci., U. Akron, 1960. Research chemist PPG Industries, Barberton, Ohio, 1952-60, sr. research chemist, 1960-61, research supr., 1961-65, sr. research supr., 1965-78, research scientist, 1978—; lectr. Akron U./Akron Rubber Group, 1960—. Mem. editorial bd. Rubber Revs., 1982—. Contbr. articles to profl. jours., chpt. to book. Patentee in field. Mem. Am. Chem. Soc. (hon. mention best paper Rubber div. 1976, 79), ASTM, Soc. Plastics Engrs. Current work: Filler reinforcement (elastomers), rubber chemistry, polymer characterization, structure/property relationship (polymers) silica surface chemistry, organosilene chemistry. Subspecialties: Polymer chemistry; Polymers (materials science). Office: Chem Div PPG Industries Inc 95 Columbia Ct Barberton OH 44203

WAGNER, RAYMOND LEE, systems engineer; b. Kansas City, Mo., Aug. 21, 1946; s. Albert Louis and Esther Pauline (Anderson) W.; m. Cheri Charlene Adams, Aug. 28, 1969; children: Richard Lamar, Frederek Prescot. A.B., Rice U., 1968; Ph.D., U. Tex. Austin, 1972. Asst. prof. astronomy U. Wash., Seattle, 1972-74; asst. prof. astronomy and physics La. State U., Baton Rouge, 1974-78; sr. astrodynamics software engr. Ford Aerospace & Communications Corp., Colorado Springs, Colo., 1979-81, prin. software engr., 1981-83, supr. security engring., 1983—. Contbr. articles to profl. jours. Cabot scholar Rice U., 1964-68; NSF summer fellow, 1970; U. Tex. fellow, 1970-72. Mem. Am. Astron. Soc., AIAA, Internat. Astron. Union, Sigma Xi, Phi Kappa Phi. Current Work: Secure systems, formal specification and verification, astrodynamics, astrophysics, command and control. Subspecialties: Cryptography and data security; Software engineering. Home: 2610 Black Diamond Terr Colorado Springs CO 80918 Office: State Hwy 83 Colorado Springs CO 80908-3699

WAGNER, WARREN HERBERT, botanist. Prof. botany, prof. natural resources U. Mich., Ann Arbor. Elected mem. Nat. Acad. Scis., 1985. Subspecialty: Botany. Office: U Mich Dept Botany Ann Arbor MI 48109

WAGNER, WILLIAM CHARLES, veterinarian; b. Elma, N.Y., Nov. 12, 1932; s. Frederick George and Doris Edna (Newton) W.; m. Donna Ann McNeill, Aug. 14, 1954; children: William Charles, Elizabeth Ann, Victoria Mary, Kathryn Farrington. D.V.M., Cornell U., 1956, Ph.D., 1968. Gen. practice vet. medicine, Interlaken, N.Y., 1956-57; research veterinarian Cornell U., 1957-65, NIH postdoctoral fellow dept. animal sci., 1965-68; asst. prof. vet. medicine Vet. Med. Research Inst., Iowa State U., Ames, 1968-69, asso. prof., 1969-74, prof., 1974-77; prof. physiology, head dept. vet. bioscis. U. Ill.-Urbana, 1977—; gen. sec. Internat. Congress on Animal Reprodn., Urbana, 1984. Pres. Ames Community Theater, 1972-73, 76-77. Recipient Alexander von Humboldt U.S. Scientist award Humboldt Stiftung, Freising-Weihenstephan, W. Ger., 1973-74; Fulbright research prof. fellow, W. Ger., 1984-85. Mem. Am. Coll. Theriogenologists (diplomate), AVMA, Physiol. Soc., Am. Soc. Animal Sci., Soc. Study Reprodn., Soc. Study Fertility, N.Y. Acad. Scis., Sigma Xi, Phi Kappa Phi, Phi Zeta, Gamma Sigma Delta, Alpha Zeta. Lutheran. Current Work: Effects of stress on reproduction; prolactin regulation; fetal endocrinology. Subspecialties: Reproductive biology; Animal physiology. Home: 306 W Florida Ave Urbana IL 61801 Office: U Ill Coll Vet Medicine Urbana IL 61801

WAGNER, WILLIAM GERARD, university dean, physicist; b. St. Cloud, Minn., Aug. 22, 1936; s. Gerard C. and Mary V. (Cloone) W.; m. Janet Agatha Rowe, Jan. 30, 1968 (div. 1978); children—Mary, Robert, David, Anne; m. Christiane Jeanne le Guen, Feb. 21, 1985. B.S., Calif. Inst. Tech., 1958, Ph.D., 1962. Cons. Rand Corp., Santa Monica, Calif., 1960-65; sr. staff physicist Hughes Research Lab., Malibu, Calif., 1960-69; asst. prof. physics U. Calif.-Irvine, 1965-66; assoc. prof. physics U. So. Calif., Los Angeles, 1966-69, prof. depts. elec. engring. and physics, 1969—, dean div. natural scis. and math. Coll. Letters, Arts and Scis., 1973—, spl. asst. automated record services, 1975-81; chmn. bd. Malibu Securities Corp., Los Angeles, 1971—; cons. Janus Mgmt. Corp., Los Angeles, 1970-71, Croesus Capital Corp., Los Angeles, 1971-74; allied mem. Pacific Stock Exchange, 1974-82; fin. and computer cons. Hollywood Reporter, 1979-81. Contbr. articles to profl. jours. NSF fellow, Howard Hughes fellow; Richard Chase Tolman postdoctoral fellow, 1962-65. Mem. Am. Phys. Soc., Fin. Mgmt. Assn., Nat. Assn. Security Dealers, Sigma Xi. Subspecialty: Information systems (Information science). Home: 2828 Patricia Ave Los Angeles CA 90064 Office: 201 Adminstrn Bldg Univ So Calif Los Angeles CA 90089

WAGNER-BARTAK, CLAUS GUNTHER JOHANN, advanced technology executive; b. Munich, Bavaria, Ger., Sept. 9, 1937; emigrated to Can., 1974; s. Friedrich and Johanna A. (Trinschek) Wagner-B.; m. Maria Helene Reich, Aug. 23, 1969; children: Natalie, Nicolaus, Nadine. B.S., Ludwig-Maximilian U., Munich, 1962, M.S., 1966, Ph.D., 1969. Cert. physics and engring, Ger., Ont. Research engr. Siemens Co., Munich, 1962; research asst. U. Munich, 1966-69; aerospace engr and project mgr. Junkers, Messerschmitt-Boelkow-Blohm Co., Munich, 1969-74; program mgr. and program dir. Spar Aerospace Ltd., Toronto, Ont., 1974-80, v.p. and gen. mgr., 1980-81, v.p. research and tech., 1982-83; pres. Energy Dynamics, Inc., Toronto, 1983—; mng. dir. Project Research Ltd., Woodbridge, Ont. Recipient NASA Pub. Service medal, 1982; Group Achievement awards NASA-Kennedy Space Ctr. and Johnson Space Ctr., 1982; NASA Astronaut award, 1983. Sr. mem. Robotics Internat.; mem. AIAA, Assn. Profl. Engrs. Ont. (Engring. medal 1982), Am. Soc. Quality Control. Club: Bd. Trade (Toronto). Current Work: Developments in advanced technology; systems for aerospace, electronics and manufacturing industries; developments of robotics systems; operations research; computer science. Subspecialties: Aerospace engineering and technology; Robotics. Home: 32 Woodgreen Dr Woodbridge ON L4L 3B3 Canada Office: Energy Dynamics Inc 100 Strada Dr Woodbridge ON L4L 4L5 Canada

WAGONER, ROBERT VERNON, astrophysicist; b. Teaneck, N.J., Aug. 6, 1938; s. Robert Vernon and Marie Theresa (Clifford) W.; m. Lynne Ray Moses, Sept. 2, 1963; children: Alexa Frances, Kim Stephanie. B.M.E., Cornell U., 1961; M.S., Stanford U., 1962, Ph.D., 1965. Research fellow in physics Calif. Inst. Tech., 1965-68, Sherman Fairchild Disting. scholar, 1976; asst. prof. astronomy Cornell U., 1968-71, asso. prof., 1971-73; asso. prof. physics Stanford U., 1973-77, prof., 1977—; George Ellery Hale Disting. vis. prof. U. Chgo., 1978; mem. Com. on Space Astronomy and Astrophysics, 1979-82. Contbr. articles on theoretical astrophysics and gravitation to profl. publs., mags.; co-author Cosmic Horizons. Sloan Found. research fellow, 1969-71; Guggenheim Meml. fellow, 1979; NSF grantee, 1973—. Fellow Am. Phys. Soc.; mem. Am. Astron. Soc., Internat. Astron. Union, Sigma Xi, Tau Beta Pi, Phi Kappa Phi. Patentee in field. Current Work: Supernova atmospheres, sources of gravitational radiation, early universe. Subspecialties: Theoretical astrophysics; Relativity and gravitation. Home: 984 Wing Pl Stanford CA 94305

WAHBA, GRACE, statistics educator, applied mathematician; b. Washington; d. Harry and Anne Goldsmith; 1 child, Jeffrey Wahba. B.A., Cornell U.; M.A., U. Md.; Ph.D., Stanford U., 1966. Research mathematician Ops. Research, Inc., 1957-61; systems analyst IBM, 1961-66; research assoc. Stanford U., Calif., 1966-67; vis. prof. stats. dept., summers 1969-71, 73, 75, 77-78; prof. stats. U. Wis., Madison, 1967—; vis. prof. Math. Inst., Oxford U., Eng., 1974-75; vis. prof. math. Weizman Inst., Israel, 1975, Technion, Israel, 1980, Australian Nat. U., Canberra, 1984, U. Calif.-Santa Cruz, Math. Scis. Research Inst., Berkeley, Calif., 1983, Math. Research Ctr., Madison, 1968, 72, 76. Contbr. articles to profl. jours. Fellow Inst. Math. Stats. (council), Am. Statis. Soc.; mem. Internat. Statis. Inst., Am. Meteorol. Soc., Soc. Indsl. and Applied Math. (council). Current work: Mathematical methods for the analysis of data from remote sensing experiments in meteorology and medicine; spline models with applications to forecasting, risk analysis, economic modelling, multivariate functional estimation. Subspecialties: Statistics; Applied mathematics. Office: U Wis Dept Statistics 1210 W Dayton St Madison WI 53706

WAHL, FLOYD MICHAEL, geologist, professional association executive; b. Hebron, Ind., July 7, 1931; m. Dorothy W. Daniel; 4 children. A.B., DePauw U., 1953; M.A., U. Ill., 1957, Ph.D., 1958. Instr., U. Ill.-Urbana, 1958-59, research asst. prof., 1959-60, from asst. prof. to assoc. prof., 1960-69; prof. geology U. Fla., Gainesville, 1969—, chmn. dept., 1969-73, dir. div. phys. sci. and math., 1971-73, assoc. dean Grad. Sch. and assoc. dir. research, 1973-79, 80-81, acting dean grad. study and research, 1979-80; exec. dir. Geol. Soc. Am., Boulder, Colo., 1982—. Fellow Geol. Soc. Am.; mem. Mineral. Soc. Am., Geochem. Soc., Clay Minerals Soc., Am. Inst. Profl. Geologists, Soc. Econ. Paleontologists and Mineralogists, Sigma Xi. Current work: Clay mineralogy and sedimentary geochemistry; phase changes in minerals at elevated temperature. Subspecialties: Mineralogy; Geochemistry. Office: Geol Soc Am PO Box 9140 Boulder CO 80301

WAHNSIEDLER, WALTER EDWARD, chemist, researcher; b. Evansville, Ind., Jan. 23, 1947; s. Walter Joseph and Mildred (Brown) W.; m. Sandra Lee Oldham, Jan. 9, 1969; 1 dau., Brooke. Student U. Evansville, 1965-67; B.S. in Chemistry, Purdue U., 1968; Ph.D. in Chem. Physics, 1974. Research assoc. Northwestern U., Evanston, Ill., 1974; scientist Aluminum Co. of Am., New Kensington, Pa., 1974-77, sr. scientist, 1977-80, staff scientist, 1980—. Contbr. articles to profl. jours. Patentee in field. NSF fellow 1969. Mem. Am. Chem. Soc., Sigma Xi. Presbyterian. Current work: chemistry and physics of Hall process and Bayer process; numerical modeling; thermodynamics; chemical kinetics; heat and mass transfer. Subspecialties: Physical chemistry; Numerical analysis (computer science). Office: Aluminum Co of Am Alcoa Tech Ctr Alcoa Center PA 15069

WAID, MARGARET COWSAR, petroleum company executive; b. Baton Rouge, Feb. 21, 1941; d. Chester Meredith and Margaret Josephine (Ingalls) C.; m. Charles Carter Waid, Mar. 16, 1963; children—James Bryan, Gordon Chester. B.S., La State U., 1961, M.S., 1963; Ph.D., Tex. Tech U., 1971. Asst. prof. math. U. Del.-Newark, 1972-77, assoc. prof., 1977-81; vis. assoc. prof. U. Tex., Austin, 1979-80; sr. devel. engr. Schlumberger Well Services, Houston, 1981-84; supr. software and analysis NL Sperry Sun, Sugar Land, Tex., 1984, mgr. prodn. services, 1984—. Contbr. articles to profl. jours. Leader 4H, 1977-79. Mem. Soc. Indsl. and Applied Math. (pres. Tex. Okla. sect. 1984-85), Assn. Women in Math, Soc. Petroleum Engrs., Soc. Profl. Well Log Analysts, AAUP, Sigma Xi. Democrat. Club: Bay Area Racquet (Houston). Lodge: Eastern Star. Current work: Mathematical analysis of pressure transient well testing. Subspecialties: Applied mathematics; Petroleum engineering. Office: NL Sperry Sun PO Box 69 Sugar Land TX 77487

WAINERDI, RICHARD ELLIOTT, medical center administrator; b. N.Y.C., Nov. 27, 1931; s. Harold Roule and Margaret (Greenhut) W.; m. Angela Lampone, June 2, 1956; children—Thomas Joseph, James Cooper. B.S. in Petroleum Engring, Okla. U., 1952; M.S., Pa. State U., 1955, Ph.D., 1958. Registered profl. engr., Tex. Research asst., fellow petroleum engring. Pa. State U., 1953-55; mem. faculty Tex. A. and M. U., College Station, 1957-77, prof. chem. engring., 1961-77, asso. v.p. acad. affairs., 1974-77, also founder, head activation analysis lab., 1957-77; sr. v.p. 3D/Internat., Houston, 1977-82; pres. Gulf Research & Devel. Co. div. Gulf Oil Corp., Houston, 1982-84; pres., chief exec. officer Tex. Med. Ctr., Houston, 1984—; coordinator nuclear activities Dresser Industries Inc., Dallas, 1956-57; head Nuclear Sci. Center Tex. Engring. Experiment Sta., 1957-59; adv. dir. First Nat. Bank, Bryan, Tex. Regional editor: Internat. Jour. Radioanalytical Chemistry; contbg. editor: Producers Monthly, 1957-69; asso. editor: Radiochemical and Radioanalystical Letters; mem. editorial adv. bd.: Talanta jour, 1969; Author: Modern Methods of Geochemical Analysis; Contbr. to profl. jours. Mem. Tex. Energy Adv. Com., 1964—. Served with USAF, 1952-53. Recipient 1st place presentation award Am. Inst. Chem. Engrs. and Chem. Inst. Can., 1961, disting. research award Tex. A. and M. U., 1962, George Hevesy medal, 1977, and others. Mem. Am. Nuclear Soc. (chmn. isotopes and radiation div. 1964), Internat. Union Pure and Applied Chemistry, Am. Soc. Engring. Edn., Am. Chem. Soc., Sigma Xi, Tau Beta Pi, Phi Kappa Phi, Sigma Tau, Pi Epsilon Tau, Phi Eta Sigma. Club: Petroleum of Houston. Patentee in field. Home: 1635 Warwickshire Dr Houston TX 77077 Office: Tex Med Ctr 406 Jesse H Jones Library Bldg Houston TX 77030

WAINWRIGHT, STANLEY DUNSTAN, biologist, educator; b. Cottingham, Eng., Apr. 15, 1927; s. Stanley and Hannah (Dunstan) W.; m. Lillian Karelltz, Mar. 10, 1952; children: David Stanley, Peter Francis. B.A. with 1st class honors, Cambridge (Eng.) U., 1947; Ph.D. in Biochemistry, London U., 1950. Exchange research scholar Pasteur Inst., Paris, 1950-51; research assoc. zoology dept. Columbia U., N.Y.C., 1951-52; NRC fellow in biology Atomic Energy of Can. Ltd., Chalk River, Ont., 1952-54; research assoc. microbiology dept. Yale U., New Haven, 1954-56; career research investigator, research prof. biochemistry Dalhousie U., Halifax, N.S., 1956—. Author: Control Mechanisms and Protein Synthesis, 1972. Mem. Can. Fedn. Biol. Socs. (bd. dirs. 1979-82), Can. Soc. Cell Biology (past pres.), Can. Biochem. Soc. (past councillor), Am. Soc. Cell Biology, Genetics Soc. Am., AAAS, Am. Inst. Biol. Scis., Sigma Xi. Current Work: Molecular biology of chick pineal 'clock'. Subspecialties: Chronobiology; Neurobiology. Home: 21 Torrington Dr Halifax NS B3M 1Y5 Canada Office: Biochemistry Dept Dalhousie U Halifax NS B3H 4H7 Canada

WAIT, JAMES RICHARD, electrical engineering educator, research scientist, consultant; b. Ottawa, Ont., Can., Jan. 23, 1924; s. George Enoch and Doris Lillian (Browne) W.; m. Gertrude Laura Norman, June 16, 1951; children—George, Laura. B.A.Sc., U. Toronto, Ont., 1948, M.A.Sc., 1949, Ph.D., 1951. Registered profl. engr., Ont.; chartered engr., U.K. Research scientist Can. Def. Research Lab., Ottawa, 1952-55, U.S. Dept. Commerce Labs., Boulder, Colo., 1955-80; prof. elec. engring. and geosci. U. Ariz., Tucson, 1980—; cons. Schlumberger-Doll Labs., Ridgefield, Conn., Mission Research Corp., Santa Barbara, Calif., Naval Ocean System Ctr., San Diego. Author: Electromagnetic Radiation from Cylindrical Structures, 1959; Electromagnetic Waves in Stratified Media, 1970; Electromagnetic Wave Theory, 1985, Electromagnetics and Plasmas, 1968; GeoElectromagnetism, 1982. Contbr. numerous articles to profl. jours. Served with Can. Army, 1942-45. Recipient Gold medal Dept. Commerce, 1959, Flemming award, 1964, achievement award NOAA 1977, Balth van der Pol award Union Radio Sci., 1978. Fellow IEEE (Harry Diamond award 1964, Centennial medal 1984, Achievement award Geosci Soc. 1985); mem. Nat. Acad. Engr., Soc. Exploration Geophysicists, Am. Geophys. Union. Current work: Application of electromagnetic wave theory to problems in environmental science, communications, radar, and optics. Subspecialty: Electrical engineering. Home: 2210 E Waverly Tucson AZ 85719 Office: Dept Elec Engring U Ariz Tucson AZ 85721

WAITE, DANIEL ELMER, oral surgeon; b. Grand Rapids, Mich., Feb. 19, 1926; s. Charles Austin and Phoebe Isabel (Smith) W.; m. Alice Darlene Carlile, June 20, 1948; children—Christine Ann, Thomas Charles, Peter Daniel, Julie Marilyn, Stuart David. A.A., Graceland Coll., 1948; D.D.S., State U. Iowa Coll. Dentistry, 1953; M.S., Grad. Coll., 1955, certificate oral surgery, certificate residency univ. hosps., 1955. Diplomate: Am. Bd. Oral Surgery. Resident oral surgery State U. Iowa Hosps., 1953-55; instr. oral surgery State U. Iowa Coll. Dentistry, 1955-56, asst. prof., 1956-57, asso. prof., acting head dept. oral surgery, 1957-59, prof. head dept., 1959-63; mem. staff Mayo Clinic, Mayo Grad. Sch. Medicine, Rochester, Minn., 1963-68; prof., also chmn. div. oral surgery U. Minn., 1968-84; chmn. dept. oral and maxillofacial surgery, asst. dean hosp. affairs Baylor Coll. Dentistry; vis. prof. U. Adelaide, Australia, 1980. Author: Textbook of Practical Oral Surgery, 1972, 2d edit., 1978; Contbr. numerous articles to profl. jours. Active People to People Found.; served with Project HOPE, Peru, 1962, Sri Lanka, 1969, Egypt, 1975; Trustee Graceland Coll., Lamoni, Iowa, 1970-78, Park Coll., Parkville, Mo., 1972-78; bd. dirs. Hennepin County unit Am. Cancer Soc., 1970-73. Served with USAAF, 1944-46; sr. dental surgeon USPHS(R). Recipient Novice award Internat. Assn. Dental Research, 1955; named Man of Yr. U. Minn. Sch. Dentistry Century Club, 1980. Fellow Am. Coll. Dentists, Am. Soc. Oral Surgeons; mem. Midwestern Soc. Oral Surgeons, Ia. Soc. Oral Surgeons (sec. 1958-61, pres. 1962), Minn. Soc. Oral Surgeons (pres. 1974), Am. Dental Assn., Internat. Assn. Dental Research (sec. Ia. sect. 1957-62), Sigma Xi, Omicron Kappa Upsilon. Mem. Reorganized Ch. of Jesus Christ of Latter Day Saints. (patriarch, mem. med. council). Subspecialty: Oral and maxillofacial surgery. Home: 9334 Raeford Dr Dallas TX 75243

WAITE, PAUL JUNIOR, climatologist; b. New Salem, Ill., June 21, 1918; s. Wesley Philip and Edna Viola (Bartlett) W.; m. Margaret Elizabeth Cresson, June 13, 1943; children: Carolyn, Lawrence. B.Ed., Western Ill. State U., 1940; M.S., U. Mich.-Ann Arbor, 1966. Sci. tchr., coach Ill. Schs., 1938-39, 40-42, 46-48; meteorologist Nat. Weather Service, Kansas City, Mo., 1948-51, 52-56, Chgo., 1948-51, 52-56, state climatologist, Des Moines, Madison, Wis., 1956-59, 59-74; dep. project mgr. NOAA, Johnson Space Center, Houston, 1974-76; state climatologist Iowa Dept. Agr., Des Moines, 1976—; adj. prof. Drake U., Des Moines, 1970—; collaborator Iowa State U., Ames, 1959-73; asst. dir. Iowa Weather Service, Des Moines, 1959-70, dir., 1970-73. Author: series Climate of Iowa, 1979—; contbr. articles in field to profl. jours. Served to 1st lt. USAF, 1942-46, 51-52. Recipient Group Achievement award NASA, 1976. Fellow Iowa Acad. Sci. (pres. elect 1985, Disting. Service award 1983); mem. Am. Assn. State Climatologists (pres. 1977-78), Am. Meteorol. Soc., AAAS, Nat. Weather Assn. Republican. Mem. Evangelical Free Ch. Club: Toastmasters (Des Moines) (pres. 1981-82). Lodge: Masons. Current Work: Applied climatology. Subspecialty: Climatology. Home: 6657 NW Timberline Dr Des Moines IA 50313 Office: Iowa Dept Agr Room 10 Municipal Airport Des Moines IA 50321

WAITZMAN, DONALD ANTHONY, chemical engineer; b. New Orleans, May 17, 1924; s. Samuel D. and Mollie A. (Dietlein) W.; m. Mary Ann Stroble; children: Paul D., Donald Anthony, Charles S., Caroline D. Waitzman Beck, Marianne Waitzman Stanhope. B.S. in Chem. Engring, Auburn U., 1948. Registered profl. engr., Ala. Technician City Service Refining Corp., Lake Charles, La., 1948-51, Stone & Webster Engring. Corp., Boston, 1951-53; asst. project engr. Rust Engring. Co., Birmingham, Ala., 1953-56; v.p. D.B. Gooch Assocs., Inc., Birmingham, 1956-60; sales engr. Crandall Engring. Co., Birmingham, 1960-62, project engr. chem. devel. div. design br., 1962-75; mgr. ammonia from coal projects, chem. devel. div. TVA, Muscle Shoals, Ala., 1975—. Contbr. numerous articles to sci. publs. Served to 1st lt. USAAF, 1943-45. Decorated Air medal with two oak leaf clusters. Mem. Am. Chem. Soc., Am. Inst. Chem. Engrs., Nat. Mgmt. Assn., Sigma Alpha Epsilon. Roman Catholic. Club: Florence Golf and Country. Current Work: In responsible charge of project to obtain technical and economic information from prototype plant that substitutes coal for natural gas for the production of ammonia, and synthetic fuel gas. Subspecialties: Fuels and sources; Agricultural engineering. Home: 515 Windsor St Florence AL 35630 Office: TVA Chem Devel Div Ammonia from Coal Projects Muscle Schoals AL 35660

WAITZMAN, MORTON BENJAMIN, educator; b. Chgo., Nov. 8, 1923; s. Joseph and Anna (Glickman) W.; m. Aviva Shedroff, June 9, 1949; children: Sherri, Brad, Rhonda. B.S., U. Miami, Fla., 1948; M.S., U. Ill., 1950, Ph.D., 1953. Instr. dept. pharmacology Case Western Res. U., Cleve., 1954-59, asst. prof., 1959-62; asst. prof. dept. physiology Emory U., Atlanta, 1962-67; assoc. prof., dir. Emory U. (Lab. Ophthalmic Research), 1962-68, prof., dir., 1968—. Editorial bd.: Metabolic, Pediatric and Systemic Ophthalmology, 1982—; contbr. articles to profl. jours. Chmn. tech. adv. com. Citizens for Clean Air of Atlanta, 1971. NIH grantee, 1962. Mem. Assn. for Research in Vision and Ophthalmology, AAAS, Internat. Soc. Metabolic Eye Diseases, Am. Physiol. Soc., AAUP, Internat. Physiol. Soc., Sigma Xi, Phi Sigma. Current Work: Metabolic aspects of blood-tissue transport and vascular permeability, especially involving diabetes, glaucoma and inflammation. Subspecialties: Physiology (biology); Ophthalmology. Home: 1137 Mason Woods Dr Atlanta GA 30329 Office: Lab for Ophthalmic Research Box 23579 Emory U Atlanta GA 30322

WAKEHAM, STUART GLENWOOD, chemist, researcher; b. Charlottesville, Va., Dec. 17, 1948; s. Helmut Richard Rae and Kathleen (Ferguson) W.; m. Brenda Lynn Smith, Aug. 21, 1971; 1 child, Ryan. B.A., Coll. of Wooster, 1970; M.S., U. Wash., 1970, Ph.D., 1976. Asst. scientist Woods Hole Oceanographic Instn., Mass., 1978-82, assoc. scientist, 1982—. Contbr. articles to sci. jours. Mem. Am. Chem. Soc., AAAS, Am. Soc. Limnology and Oceanography, European Assn. Organic Geochemists. Current work: Geochemistry of organic compounds in the marine environment, sources, transformations, fates of compounds. Subspecialties: Geochemistry; Environmental chemistry. Home: 65 Belvidere Rd Falmouth MA 02540 Office: Chemistry Dept Woods Hole Oceanographic Instn Woods Hole MA 02543

WAKELAND, HOWARD LESLIE, engineering educator; b. Minonk, Ill., July 22, 1927; s. Fred R. and Florence E. (Downend) W.; m. Betty Droy, June 6, 1948 (dec. 1983); children—Lezlie, Craig, Todd, Marta; m. Joyce Irene Odell, Aug. 30, 1984. B.S.A.E., U. Ill., 1950, M.S.A.E., 1954. Instr. agrl. engring. U. Ill., Urbana, 1951-54, asst. prof., 1954-59, assoc. prof., 1954-68, prof., 1968—, asst. dean, 1954-66, assoc. dean, 1966—; bd. dirs. Accreditation Bd. for Engring. and Tech., 1974—. Recipient Disting. Service award Cons. Engring. Council Ill., 1981. Fellow Am. Soc. Engring. Edn.; mem. Ill. Soc. Profl. Engrs., Nat. Soc. Profl. Engrs., AAAS, Am. Soc. Agrl. Engrs. Jr. Engring. Tech. Soc. (bd. dirs. 1972—), Assn. for Internat. Practical Tng. (bd. dirs.). Lodge: Rotary (pres. Urbana 1974-75). Subspecialty: Engineering education. Home: 2213 Combes Ave Urbana IL 61801 Office: U Ill 1308 W Green St Urbana IL 61801

WAKIL, SALIH JAWAD, biochemistry educator; b. Kerballa, Iraq, Aug. 16, 1927; s. Jawad and Milook (Attraqchi) W.; m. Fawzia Bahrani, Nov. 30, 1952; children—Sonya, Aida, Adil, Youssef. B.Sc., Am. U. Beirut, 1948; Ph.D., U. Wash., 1952. Research fellow U. Wash., Seattle, 1949-52, U. Wis., Madison, 1952-56, asst. prof., 1956-59; asst. prof. biochemistry Duke U., Durham, N.C., 1959-60, assoc. prof., 1960-65, prof., 1965-71; prof., chmn. dept. biochemistry Baylor Coll. Medicine, Houston, 1971—. Recipient Paul Lewis award in enzyme chemistry, 1967; Guggenheim fellow, 1968-69; Disting. Duke Med. Alumnus award, 1973. Current work: Fatty acid metabolism and regulation of enzymes. Mechanism in fatty acid synthases. Subspecialties: Biochemistry (biology); Membrane biology. Home: 414 Thamer Cir Houston TX 77024 Office: Biochemistry Dept Baylor Coll Medicine One Baylor Plaza Houston TX 77030

WALBA, DAVID MARK, chemistry educator; b. Oakland, Calif., June 29, 1949; s. Harold and Beatrice (Alpert) W.; m. Cassandra B. Geneson, Oct. 30, 1981; 1 son, Paul. B.S. in Chemistry, U. Calif.-Berkeley, 1971; Ph.D. in Chemistry, Calif. Inst. Tech., 1975. Postdoctoral fellow UCLA, 1975-77; asst. prof. chemistry U. Colo., Boulder, 1977-83, assoc. prof., 1983—. Contbr. articles to profl. jours. NIH fellow, 1976-77; A. P. Sloan fellow, 1982-84; Camille and Henry Dreyfus Tchr.-Scholar, 1983-85. Mem. Am. Chem. Soc., Sigma Xi. Current Work: Organic chemistry, natural products total synthesis, host-guest chemistry, and topological stereochemistry. Subspecialty: Organic chemistry. Office: U Colo Dept Chemistry PO Box 215 Boulder CO 80309

WALD, FRITZ VEIT, solar energy company exeuctive, chemist; b. Dieringhausen, Germany, Apr. 28, 1933; came to U.S., 1963, naturalized, 1969; s. Eugen and Elli (Veit) W.; m. Doris Herberg, Mar. 21, 1959; children—Kristin Dorothea, Andrea Elisabeth, Katja Fredericke. B.S., Sch. Tech. Chemistry, Cologne, W.Ger., 1955. Tech. chemist Doerrenberg Steel Works, Ruenderoth, Fed. Republic Germany, 1955-57; research asst. solid state chemistry Philips, Central Labs., Aachen, Fed. Republic Germany, 1957-61; research metallurgist Frigistors Ltd., Montreal, Que., Can., 1961-63; sr. scientist, head materials sci. dept. Tyco Labs. Inc., Waltham, Mass., 1963-75; dir. research Mobil Solar Energy Corp., Waltham, 1975—; dir., adviser Radiation Monitoring Devices Inc., Watertown, Mass., 1976—. Contbr. chpt. to book, sci. articles to profl. jours. Patentee in field. Mem. Am. Chem. Soc., Metall. Soc., Electrochem. Soc., Materials Research Soc., Internat. Metallographic Sco. (sr.). Lutheran. Current work: Direct energy conversion methods using solid state devices, in particular solar energy conversion to electricity by photovoltaic means. Subspecialty: Solar energy. Office: Mobil Solar Energy Corp 16 Hickory Dr Waltham MA 02254

WALD, GEORGE, biochemist; b. N.Y.C., Nov. 18, 1906; s. Isaac and Ernestine (Rosenmann) W.; m. Frances Kingsley, May 15, 1931 (div.); children: Michael, David; m. Ruth Hubbard, 1958; children: Elijah, Deborah. B.S., N.Y. U., 1927; M.A., Columbia U., 1928, Ph.D., 1932; M.D. (hon.), U. Berne, 1957; D.Sc., Yale U., 1958, Wesleyan U., 1962, N.Y. U., 1965, McGill U., 1966, Amherst Coll., 1968, U. Rennes, 1970, U. Utah, 1971, Gustavus Adolphus U., 1972, U. León, Nicaragua, 1984 D.H.L., Kalamazoo Coll., 1984. NRC fellow at Kaiser Wilhelm Inst., Berlin and Heidelberg, U. Zurich, U. Chgo., 1932-34; tutor biochem. scis. Harvard U., 1934-35, instr. biology, 1935-39, faculty instr., 1939-44, asso. prof. biology, 1944-48, prof., 1948—, Higgins prof. biology, 1968-77, prof. emeritus, 1977—; vis. prof. biochemistry U. Calif., Berkeley, summer 1956; Nat. Sigma Xi lectr., 1952; chmn. divisional com. biology and med. scis. NSF, 1954-56; Guggenheim fellow, 1963-64; Overseas fellow Churchill Coll., Cambridge U., 1963-64; participant U.S.-Japan Eminent Scholar Exchange, 1973; guest China Assn. Friendship with Fgn. Peoples, 1972; v.p. Permanent Peoples' Tribunal, Rome, 1980—. Co-author: General Education in a Free Society, 1945, Twenty Six Afternoons of Biology, 1962, 66, also sci. papers on vision and biochem. evolution. Recipient Eli Lilly prize Am. Chem. Soc., 1939; Lasker award Am. Pub. Health Assn., 1953; Proctor medal Assn. Research in Ophthalmology, 1955; Rumford medal Am. Acad.; Arts and Scis., 1959; Ives medal Optical Soc. Am., 1966; Paul Karrer medal in chemistry U. Zurich, 1967; co-recipient Nobel prize for physiology, 1967; T. Duckett Jones award Helen Hay Whitney Found., 1967; Bradford Washburn medal Boston Mus. Sci., 1968; Max Berg award, 1969; Priestley medal Dickinson Coll., 1970. Fellow Nat. Acad. Sci., Am. Acad. Arts and Scis., Am. Philos. Soc. Subspecialties: Biochemistry (biology); Biophysics (biology). Home: 21 Lakeview Ave Cambridge MA 02138

WALD, NIEL, physician, medical educator; b. N.Y.C., Oct. 1, 1925; s. Albert and Rose (Fischel) W.; m. Lucienne Hill, May 24, 1953; children—David, Phillip, A.B., Columbia U., 1945; M.D., NYU, 1948. Intern, resident Lincoln Hosp., NYU div. Goldwater Meml. Hosp., Beth Israel Hosp., N.Y.C., 1948-52; sr. hematologist Atomic Bomb Casualty Commn., Hiroshima, Japan, 1954-57; head biologist health physics div. Oak Ridge Nat. Lab., 1957-58; practice medicine specializing in radiation medicine and cytogenetics, Pitts., 1958—; mem. faculty U. Pitts. Grad. Sch. Pub. Health and Med. Sch., 1958—, prof. radiation medicine, 1962—, prof. radiology, 1965—, chmn. dept. occupational health, 1975-76, chmn. dept. indsl. environ. health scis., 1976-77; dir. radiation medicine Presbyn. U. Hosp., 1966—; cons. U.S. Nuclear Regulatory Commn., mem. adv. panel decontamination of Three Mile Island Nuclear Power Station Unit 2, 1981—; cons. U.S. Navy, nuclear industries and utilities; chmn. radiol. health study sect. USPHS, 1967-71; mem. Nat. Council Radiation Protection and Measurements, 1969-81, assoc. mem., 1981—; mem. Pa. Gov.'s Adv. Com. on Atomic Energy Devel. and Radiation Control, 1966-84, chmn., 1974-76. Contbr. numerous articles to profl. jours. Served to capt. M.C., USAF, 1952-54. Mem. Health Physics Soc. (pres. 1973-74), Am. Pub. Health Assn. (governing council 1971-73, program devel. bd. 1973-74), Radiation Research Soc. (assoc. editor jour. 1965-68), Soc. Nuclear Medicine (assoc. editor jour. 1959-69), Am. Soc. Human Genetics, Am. Occupational Med. Assn., AAAS, AMA, Internat. Soc. Hematology. Current work: Medical management of radiation accidents, clinical cytogenetics, radiation biology and radiation protection. Subspecialty: Radiation biology. Office: Grad Sch Pub Health U Pitts A 512 Pittsburgh PA 15261

WALDBAUER, GILBERT PETER, entomology educator, behavioral ecology researcher; b. Bridgeport, Conn., Apr. 18, 1928; s. George Henry and Hedwig Martha (Gribisch) W.; m. Stephanie Margot Stiefel, Jan. 2, 1955; children—Gwen Ruth, Susan Martha. B.S., U. Mass., 1953; M.S., U. Ill., 1956, Ph.D., 1960. Asst. prof. entomology U. Ill.-Urbana, 1961-65, assoc. prof., 1966-71, prof., 1972—; researcher Instituto Colombiano Agropecuario, Palmira, Colombia, 1971, Internat. Rice Research Inst., Manila, Philippines, 1978-79. Contbr. articles to prof. jours. Served with U.S. Army, 1946-47. Grantee NSF, 1982-84, U.S. Dept. of Agrl., 1982-83—. mem. Entomol. Soc. Am., Ecol. Soc. Am., Entomol. Soc. Washington, Great Lakes Entomol. Soc. Current work: Mimicry, life histories, insect-host plant interactions. Subspecialty: Behavioral ecology. Home: 1806 Maynard Dr Champaign IL 61821 Office: Dept Entomology U of Ill 320 Morrill Hall 505 S Goodwin Urbana IL 61801

WALDMANN, THOMAS ALEXANDER, immunology researcher, physician; b. N.Y.C.; s. Charles and Elizabeth (Sipos) W.; m. Katharine Emory Spreng, Mar. 29, 1958; children: Richard Allen, Robert James, Carol Ann. A.B., U. Chgo., 1951; M.D., Harvard U., 1955. Diplomate: Am. Bd. Allergy and Immunology. Med. Intern Mass. Gen. Hosp., Boston, 1955-56; clin. assoc. Nat. Cancer Inst., NIH, Bethesda, Md., 1956-58, sr. investigator, 1958-68, head immunophysiology sect., 1968-73, chief metabolism br., 1972—; cons. WHO, FTC, FDA; William Dameseek vis. prof. Tufts Med. Sch., Boston, 1983;

Welcome vis. prof. U. Calif.-Irvine, 1984. Author 1 book, over 400 sci. articles. Bd. dirs. Found. Advanced Edn. in the Scis., Bethesda, 1981—. Recipient Michael Heidelberger award Columbia U., 1976; Henry Stratton medal Am. Soc. Hematology, 1977; named Man of Yr. Leukemia Soc. Am., 1980; G. Burroughs Mider lectr. NIH, 1980, Nat. Acad. Scis. Fellow Am. Acad. Allergy-Immunology (Bela Schick award 1977); mem. Am. Soc. Clin. Investigation (editorial bd. 1975-80), Am. Assn. Physicians (Kroc lectr. 1980), Am. Assn. Immunology (assoc. editor jour. 1982, Honor lectr 1981), Internat. Plasma Protein Study Group (dir., sec. 1970-75). Democrat. Clubs: NIH Camera (pres. 1970), Silver Spring (Md.) Camera. Discoverer intestinal lymphanglectasia, 1961, allergic gastroenteropathy, 1963, human suppressor T cells in immunodeficiency (Henry Berton award), 1977. Current Work: Analysis of the regulatory mechanisms that control the human immune response and the disorders in these mechanisms in immunodeficiency diseases and cancer; special emphasis on use of recombinant DNA technology to study arrangement of immuoglobulin T-cell receptor and interleukin-2 receptor. genes and on studies of suppressor and helper T lymphocytes. Subspecialties: Immunology (medicine); Cancer research (medicine). Home: 3910 Rickover Rd Silver Spring MD 20902 Office: 9000 Rockville Pike Bethesda MD 20205

WALDO, GEORGE VAN PELT, JR., engineering physicist; b. Montgomery, Ala., July 20, 1940; s. George Van Pelt and Martha Katheryn (Vickery) W.; m. Nancy Arlene Hershberger, Jan. 28, 1966. A.B., Johns Hopkins U., 1961; Ph.D. in Physics, U. Md., 1972. Physicist David Taylor Naval Ship Research and Devel. Ctr., Bethesda, Md., 1962—, prin. investigator, 1968—. Contbr. articles to profl. jours. Mem. Am. Phys. Soc., Sigma Xi, Sigma Pi Sigma. Current work: Statistical mechanics of phase transitions; cavitation induced by shock waves; interaction of shock waves with structures; Monte-Carlo simulation of ship vulnerability; perturbation theory of phase transitions; underwater explosions. Subspecialties: Fluid mechanics; Statistical physics. Home: 11502 Alma St Silver Spring MD 20902 Office: David Taylor Naval Ship Research and Devel Ctr Bethesda MD 20084

WALDRON, JOSEPH ANTHONY, psychologist, educator; b. Batavia, N.Y., Oct. 3, 1943; s. Elsworth Thomas and Dolores Agnes (Kanaley) W.; m. Irene Montgomery, Oct. 31, 1966; children: Wendy June, Joelle Dolores, Elizabet Hannah. B.A., SUNY-Buffalo, 1972; M.A., Ohio State U., 1973, Ph.D., 1975. Lic. psychologist, Ohio registered Nat Register Health Service Providers. Psychologist, dept. head Ohio Youth Commn., Columbus, 1975-77; chief psychologist Mahoning County Diagnostic and Evaluation Clinic, Youngstown, Ohio, 1977-78; assoc. prof. dept. criminal justice, dir. Forensic Research Lab. Youngstown State U., 1978—; owner Towne Square Psychol. Services, Inc., Canfield, Ohio, 1971—; pres. Mahoning Valley Acad. Psychology, 1981-82; founder, dir. Integrated Profl. Systems Inc., Austintown, Ohio, 1981-82; cons. to local and state agencys. Author manuals and computer programs; contbr. articles to profl. jours. Mem. Youth Services Council, Youngstown, 1979; bd. dirs. Gateways to Better Living, 1980-81. State of Ohio grantee, 1980-82. Mem. Am. Psychol. Assn., Ohio Psychol. Assn., Acad. Criminal Justice Scis., AAAS, Sigma Xi. Current Work: Construction of microcomputer programs to be used for psychometric assessments, test scoring, and test interpretation. Home: 266 Bradford Dr Canfield OH 44406 Office: Forensic Research Lab Youngstown State U Youngstown OH 44555

WALDRON, KENNETH JOHN, mechanical engineering educator, researcher; b. Sydney, Australia, Feb. 11, 1943; came to U.S. 1974; s. Edward Walter and Maurine Florence (Barrett) W.; m. Manjula Bhushan, July 3, 1968; children—Andrew, Lalitha, Paul. B.Engring., U. Sydney, Australia, 1963, M. Engring. Sci., 1965; Ph.D., Stanford U., 1969. Registered profl. engr., Tex. Acting asst. prof. Stanford U., 1968-69; lectr. to sr. lectr. U. New South Wales, Australia, 1969-74; assoc. prof. U. Houston, 1974-79; assoc. prof. to prof., Nordholt prof. Ohio State U., Columbus, 1979—. Contbr. numerous articles to profl. jours. Mem. ASME (design div. com. 1981—), Soc. Mfg. Engrs., Soc. Automotive Engrs. (Teetor award 1977), Am. Soc. Engring. Educ. Current work: Robotic mobility, computer coordinated mechanical systems, mechanism design. Subspecialties: Robotics; Computer-aided design. Office: Dept Mech Engring Ohio State U Columbus OH 43210

WALECKA, JOHN DIRK, physicist. Prof. dept. physics Stanford U., Calif. Subspecialty: Nuclear physics. Office: Stanford U Dept Physics Stanford CA 94305

WALGENBACH-TELFORD, SUSAN CAROL, physiology educator, researcher; b. Sacramento, June 29, 1952; d. Mart Gilbert and Susan Margaret (Gloden) Walgenbach; m. Gordon Laing Telford, May 29, 1983. B.S. in Physiology, U. Calif.-Davis, 1974, Ph.D. in Physiology, 1979. Teaching asst. U. Calif.-Davis, 1974-75, assoc. in physiology, 1975-76, postgrad. researcher, 1976-79; NIH postdoctoral fellow Mayo Clinic, Rochester, Minn., 1979-82; instr. Mayo Med. Sch., Rochester, 1981-83; asst. prof. anesthesia and physiology Med. Coll. Wis., Milw., 1983—. Contbr. articles to sci. jours. Recipient Irving I. Hertzendorf award dept. physiology, U. Calif. 1979; NIH grantee, 1979-82. Mem. Am. Physiol. Soc., Soc. Exptl. Biology and Medicine, AAAS, N.Y. Acad. Scis. Current work: Neural control of circulation, cardiopulmonary control mechanisms during exercise and environmental stress, hypertension. Subspecialties: Physiology (medicine); Physiology (biology). Office: Med Coll Wis VA Med Ctr RS 151 Wood WI 53193

WALI, MOHAN KISHEN, environmental science educator; b. Kashmir, India, Mar. 1, 1937; came to U.S., 1969, naturalized, 1975; s. Jagan Nath and Somavati (Wattal) W.; m. Sarla Safaya, Sept. 25, 1960; children: Pamela, Promod. B.Sc., U. Jammu and Kashmir, India, 1957; M.Sc., U. Allahabad, India, 1960; Ph.D., U. B.C., Can., 1970. Lectr. S.P. Coll., Srinagar, Kashmir, 1963-65; research fellow U. Copenhagen, 1965-66; grad. fellow U. B.C., Vancouver, 1967-69; asst. prof. biology U. N.D., Grand Forks, 1969-73, assoc. prof., 1973-79, prof., 1979-83, Hill research prof., summer 1973; dir. U. N.D. (Forest River Biology Area Field Sta.), 1970-79; dir. U. N.D. (Project Reclamation), 1975-83, spl. asst. to pre. univ., 1977-83; prof., dir. grad. program environ. sci. SUNY-Syracuse, 1983—; staff ecologist Grand Forks Energy Research Lab., U.S. Dept. Interior, part-time 1974-75. Contbr. articles to profl. jours.; editor: Some Environmental Aspects of Strip-Mining in North Dakota, 1973, Prairie: A Multiple view, 1975, Practices and Problems of Land Reclamation in Western North America, 1975, Ecology and Coal Resource Development, 1979; sr. editor: Reclamation Rev, 1976-80; chief editor, 1980-81, Reclamation & Revegetation Research, 1982—. Vice-chmn. N.D. Air Pollution Adv. Council. Recipient Outstanding Research award Sigma Xi-U. N.D., 1975; B.C. Gamble Disting. Teaching and Service award, 1977. Mem. Ecol. Soc. Am. (chmn. sect. internat. activities 1980—), Brit. Ecol. Soc., Can. Bot. Assn. (dir. ecology sect. 1976-79, v.p. 1982-83), Torrey Bot. Club, AAAS, Am. Soc. Agronomy, Am. Inst. Biol. Sci. (gen. chmn. ann. meeting), Internat. Assn. Ecology, Internat. Soc. Soil Sic., N.D. Acad. Sci. (chmn. editorial com. 1979-81), Sigma Xi (nat. lectr. 1983-85). Subspecialties: Ecology (environmental science); Ecosystems analysis. Office: Coll Environ Sci & Forestry SUNY Syracuse NY 13210

WALIA, AMRIK SINGH, surgery educator, immunologist; b. Punjab, India, Aug. 6, 1947; came to U.S., 1970; s. Harkishan Singh and Harbhajan K. (Sumitra) Ahluwalia; m. Shammi A. Chadha, Jan. 6, 1974; children: Jasmeet Singh, Shalini R. B.Sc., Punjab U., 1965; M.Sc., Meerut U., India, 1968; Ph.D., Loyola U., New Orleans, 1975. Prin. investigator alcoholism research VA Med. Ctr., Birmingham, Ala., 1982—; research asst. prof. surgery U. Ala.-Birmingham, 1980—; assoc. scientist U. Ala.-Birmingham (Comprehensive Cancer Ctr.), 1980—. U. Ala.-Birmingham Cancer Ctr. Faculty Devel. grantee, 1980-81; research fellow Nat. Cancer Inst., 1977-80; grantee Internat. Union Against Cancer, Sweden, 1978. Mem. Am. Assn. Immunologists, N.Y. Acad. Scis., Sigma Xi. Current Work: Immunology and effects of alcohols, retinoids, divalent cations, trace metals on immune response; T cells, B cells, immune complex receptors, complement receptors. Subspecialties: Immunology (medicine); Cancer research (medicine). Home: 500 Cedar St Birmingham AL 35206 Office: Dept of Surgery University of Alabama Birmingham AL 35294

WALKER, CEDRIC FRANK, biomedical engineering educator, consultant; b. Los Angeles, Jan. 26, 1950; s. Edmund Frank and Charlotte (Frisch) W.; m. Julia Ingraham, June 14, 1985. B.S., Stanford U., 1972, M.S., 1972; Ph.D., Duke U., 1978. Cert. Am. Bd. Clin. Engring. Asst. prof. biomed. engring. Tulane U., New Orleans, 1977-82, assoc. prof., 1982—, asst. chmn., 1980—. Mem. IEEE (sr. mem.) editorial bd. 1974-78), Assn. for Advancement Med. Instrumentation, Sigma Xi, Tau Beta Pi. Current work: Electrode design, implantable neurological stimulator design. Subspecialties: Bioinstrumentation; Biomedical engineering. Office: Dept Biomed Engring Tulane U New Orleans LA 70118

WALKER, CLAY BROWN, microbiologist; b. Union, W.Va., Aug. 5, 1947; s. Dewey Clay and Ruth A. (Brown) W.; m. Linda Lee Lemons, June 14, 1969; 1 child, Michael Clay. B.S. in Biology, Va. Poly. Inst. and State U., 1972, Ph.D. in Microbiology, 1977. Post-doctoral fellow Forsyth Dental Ctr., Boston, 1977-79, mem. staff, 1979-81; asst. prof. U. Fla., Gainesville, 1981-83, assoc. prof., 1983—. Contbr. articles to profl. jours. Served to 1st lt. U.S. Army, 1967-70, Vietnam. Mem. Am. Soc. Microbiology, Am. Assn. Dental Research, Internat. Assn. Dental Research. Democrat. Current work: Periodontics, oral biology, microbiology, pharmacokinetics, pharmacology Subspecialties: Microbiology (medicine); Pharmacokinetics. Home: 4202 NW 67th Terr Gainesville FL 32606 Office: Periodontal Disease Research Ctr U Fla Box J424 JHMHC Gainesville FL 32610

WALKER, DAN BERNE, biology educator, researcher; b. Connersville, Ind., Apr. 18, 1945; s. Merrell C. and Cathryn R. (Burkhart) W.; m. Denise G. Garriott, June 15, 1969; m. Susan S. Schroeder, May 29, 1982. A.B., Ind. U., 1968; Ph.D., U. Calif., Berkeley, 1974. Lectr. botany dept. U. Calif., Berkeley, 1973-74; asst. prof. botany U. Ga., Athens, 1974-78, UCLA, 1978—; cons. Contbr. articles to profl. jours. Recipient Outstanding Instr. award U. Ga., 1977. Mem. AAAS, Bot. Soc. Am., Am. Soc. Plant Physiologists, Soc. Devel. Biology, Electron Microscopy Soc. Am. Current Work: Epidermal morphogenesis and pattern formation in plants, differentiation and dedifferentiation in epidermal and subepidermal plant cells, pattern formation in plant tissues. Subspecialties: Plant growth; Developmental biology. Office: Biology Dept U Calif Los Angeles CA 90024 Office: Biology Dept U Calif Los Angeles CA 90024

WALKER, DAVID, geology educator; b. Troy, N.Y., Aug. 9, 1946; s. Roland and Vivian V. (Tombetta) W. A.B., Oberlin Coll., 1968; A.M., Harvard U., 1970, Ph.D., 1972. Geol. researcher Harvard U., 1972-82; prof. geology Lamont-Doherty Geol. Obs., Columbia U., Palisades, N.Y., 1982—; Fairchild disting. scholar Calif. Inst. Tech., 1982; Assoc. editor: Basaltic Volcanism on the Terrestrial Planets, 1981, Jour. Geophys. Research, 1981-83. Contbr. articles to profl. jours. Recipient NASA Group Achievement award, 1983; grantee NSF, NASA, Dept. Energy, 1970-84. Fellow Mineral. Soc. Am.; mem. Am. Geophys. Union, Geochem. Soc. (Clarke medal 1975), Meteoritical Soc., Geol. Soc. Am. Current work: Experimental petrology of geological materials; evolution of planets. Subspecialties: Petrology; Planetology. Home: 379 Ferdon Ave Piermont NY 10968 Office: Lamont-Doherty Geol Obs Palisades NY 10964

WALKER, DAVID HUGHES, pathologist, educator, research rickettsiologist; b. Nashville, May 31, 1943; s. William Walter and Sara Elizabeth (Huddleston) W.; m. Marjorie Ruth Blum, May 31, 1968; children—Jesse Jospeh, Andrew Julius. B.A., Davidson Coll., 1965; M.D., Vanderbilt U., 1969. Diplomate Am. Bd. Pathology. Intern, Peter Bent Brigham Hosp., Boston, 1969-70, resident in pathology, 1969-73; research med. officer Ctr. for Disease Control, Atlanta, 1973-75; asst. prof. pathology U. N.C., Chapel Hill, 1975-80, assoc. prof., 1980—; investigator NIH, 1979-82, 84—, U.S. Army Med. Research and Devel. Command, 1983-86. Contbr. numerous articles, revs., chpts. to profl. publs. Served to surgeon USPHS, 1973-75. Grantee NIH, 1979-82, 84—. Fellow Infectious Diseases Soc. Am.; mem. Am. Assn. Pathologists, Am. Soc. Rickettsiology and Rickettsial Diseases, Internat. Acad. Pathology, Am. Soc. Tropical Medicine and Hygiene. Current work: Pathogenesis, immunology and diagnosis of Rocky Mountain spotted fever, boutonneuse fever, and other rickettsioses; basic rickettsiology of Rickettsia rickettsia. Subspecialties: Pathology (medicine); Infectious diseases. Home: 410 Whitehead Circle Chapel Hill NC 27514 Office: U NC Dept Pathology 228-H Chapel Hill NC 27514

WALKER, ERIC ARTHUR, consulting engineer, institute executive; b. Long Eaton, Eng., Apr. 29, 1910; came to U.S., 1923, naturalized, 1937; s. Arthur and Violet Elizabeth (Haywood) W.; m. L. Josephine Schmeiser, Dec. 20, 1937; children: Gail (Mrs. Peter Hearn), Brian. B.S., Harvard U., 1932, M.S., 1933, Sc.D., 1935; LL.D., Temple U., 1957, Lehigh U., 1957, Hofstra Coll., 1960, Lafayette Coll., 1960, U. Pa., 1960, U. R.I., 1962; L.H.D., Elizabethtown Coll., 1958; D.Litt., Jefferson Med. Coll., 1960; D.Sc., Wayne State U., 1965, Thiel Coll., 1966, U. Notre Dame, 1968, U. Pitts., 1970. Registered profl. engr., Pa. Instr. math. Tufts Coll., 1933-34, asst. prof., assoc. prof. elec. engring., 1935-38, head elec. engring. dept., 1935-40, U. Conn., 1940-43; assoc. dir. Harvard U. Underwater Sound Lab., 1942-45; dir. Ordnance Research Lab., Pa. State U., 1945-52, head elec. engring. dept., 1945-51; dean Coll. Engring., Pa. State U. 1951-56, dir. Ordnance Research Lab., v.p. univ., 1956, pres., 1956-70; v.p. sci. and tech. Aluminum Co. Am., 1970-76. Exec. sec. Research and Devel. Bd., Dept. Def., 1950-51; cons. NRC, 1949-50; mem. and past chmn. com. on undersea warfare; chmn. Pres.'s Com. on Tech. and Distbn. Research for Benefit of Small Bus., 1957; mem. nat. sci. bd. NSF, 1962-68, chmn. nat. sci. bd., 1966-68; chmn. Naval Research Adv. Com., 1963-65, 71-76, Army Sci. Adv. Panel, 1956-58; vice chmn. Pres.'s Com. Scientists and Engrs., 1956-58; adv. panel on engring. and tech. manpower Pres.'s Sci. Adv. Com.; mem. Gov.'s Com. of 100 for Better Edn., 1960-61; bd. dirs. Engring. Found.; chmn. bd. Inst. for Def. Analyses, 1976—. Contbr. to tech. mags. United bd. visitors U.S. Naval Acad., 1958-60, U.S. Mil. Acad., 1962-64. Recipient Horatio Alger award, 1959, Tasker H. Bliss award Am. Soc. Mil. Engrs., 1959; Golden Omega award Am. Inst. E.E and Nat. Elec. Mfg. Assn., 1962; DoD Pub. Service medal, 1970; Presdl. citation, 1970. Fellow IEEE, Am. Acoustical Soc., Am. Inst. E.E., Am. Phys. Soc.; mem. Am. Inst. Physics, Am. Soc. Engring. Edn. (Lamme award 1965, pres. 1961-62), Pa. Assn. Colls. and Univs. (pres. 1950-60), Middle States Assn. Colls. and Secondary Schs. (commn. higher edn. 1958-61), Engrs. Joint Council (pres. 1962-63), Nat. Assn. State Univs. and Land-Grant Colls. (exec. com. 1958-62), Nat. Acad. Engring. (pres. 1966-70), Am. Acad. Arts and Scis., Newcomen Soc., Royal Soc. Arts, Sigma Xi, Tau Beta Pi, Phi Kappa Phi. Clubs: Duquesne, Cosmos. Current Work: New processes and products. Subspecialties: Electrical engineering; Acoustical engineering. Home: 904 Outer Dr State College PA 16801

WALKER, GEORGE PINCKNEY, III, geologist, consultant; b. El Paso, Tex., June 28, 1934; s. George Pinckney, Jr. and Helen (Griffith) W.; m. Estella Jeanne Livingston, Sept. 4, 1955; children—George Pinckney, Charlisa Ann, Betsy Kim. Degree in Petroleum Engring., Colo. Sch. Mines, 1956; M.A. in Geology, U. Tex., Austin, 1967. Jr. petroleum engr. to dist. petroleum engr. Tenneco Oil Co., Tex., Kans. and La.; geologist sr. grade to div. geologist AMOCO Prodn. Co., Midland, Ft. Worth, Houston, Tex., 1966-80; cons. geologist, owner Walker Exploration Co., Sattler, Tex., 1980—. First vice chmn. Lafayette Republican Club, La., 1963; mem. Rep. Parish Exec. Com., Lafayette, 1963-64; candidate for Police Juror, Lafayette Parish, 1964. Mem. Am. Assn. Petroleum Geologists, Soc. Ind. Petroleum Earth Sci., Geol. Soc. Am., W. Tex. Geol. Soc., Soc. Econ. Paleontologists and Mineralogists, Soc. Petroleum Engrs., Soc. Econ. Geophysicists, Soc. Profl. Wireline Log Analysts, Am. Petroleum Inst. (adv. bd., 3d vice chmn. 1962-64), Am. Inst. Profl. Geologists. Episcopalian. Current work: Petroleum exploration. Subspecialties: Petroleum geology; Petroleum engineering. Home: Route 5 Box 637 A Canyon Lake TX 78130 Office: Walker Exploration Co PO Box 2022 Sattler TX 78130

WALKER, JAMES ROY, microbiologist, educator; b. Chestnut, La., Nov. 8, 1937; s. Clint Cortez and Annie Mae (Holland) W.; m. Barbara Ann Fess, Aug. 9, 1959; children: James Bryan, Melinda Lee. B.S., Northwestern State U., La., 1960; Ph.D., U. Tex., Austin, 1963. Postdoctoral research assoc. Princeton U., 1965-67; asst. prof. microbiology U. Tex., 1967-71, assoc. prof., 1971-78, prof., 1978—, chmn. dept., 1981—; research assoc. in biochemistry and molecular biology Harvard U., 1972-73. Served with U.S. Army, 1963-65. NIH, NSF, Am. Cancer Soc. fellow; various grants. Mem. Am. Soc. for Microbiology, Genetics Soc. Am. Current Work: Biochemical and genetic studies on chromosome replication and regulation of cell division in Escherichia coli. Subspecialties: Genetics and genetic engineering (biology); Molecular biology. Home: 8504 Greenflint Ln Austin TX 78759 Office: Dept Microbiology U Tex Austin TX 78712

WALKER, JERRY TYLER, plant pathologist; b. Cin., Sept. 7, 1930; s. Wallace Burch and Edith Tyler W.; m. Mary Bridges, Sept. 26, 1930; children: Robert William, Ann Elizabeth. A.B., Miami U., Oxford, Ohio, 1952; M.Sc., Ohio State U., Columbus, 1957, Ph.D., 1960. Research assoc. Ohio Agrl. Research and Devel. Ctr., Wooster, 1959-61; plant pathologist Bklyn. Bot. Garden, 1961-69; chmn. Kitchawan Field Sta., Ossining, N.Y., 1968-69; prof., dept. head U. Ga., Ga. Agrl. Expt. Sta., 1969—. Contbr. articles to profl. jours. Served with Chem. Corps U.S. Army, 1953-55. Mem. Am. Phytopathol. Soc., Soc. Nematologists, Internat. Soc. Arboriculture, Sigma Xi. Episcopalian. Lodges: Rotary. Current Work: Air pollution effects on plants, nematology, diseases of ornamentals. Subspecialty: Plant pathology. Office: Ga Agrl Expt Sta Experiment GA 30212

WALKER, KENNETH RUSSELL, geology educator; b. Spartanburg, S.C., June 21, 1937; s. Henry Robert and Sarah Elmina (Russell) W.; m. Susan Schreiber, May 1, 1964 (div. 1974); children—Leslie, Sarah, Mary. B.S., U. N.C., 1959, M.S., 1964; M.Ph., Yale U., 1967, Ph.D., 1969. Asst. prof. U. Tenn., Knoxville, 1968-73, assoc. prof., 1973-77, prof. geology, 1977-82, dept. head, 1977—, Carden prof., 1982—; cons. Oak Ridge Nat. Lab., Tenn., 1983—, various oil cos., Houston, 1978—. Contbr. articles to profl. jours. Served to capt. USAF, 1961-66. Grantee NSF, Mobil Found. Fellow Geol. Soc. Am. (sect. vice chmn., 1984-85); mem. Paleontol. Soc. (co-editor, council mem. 1982—), Soc. Econ. Paleontologists and Mineralogists, Internat. Assn. Paleontology. Democrat. Unitarian. Current work: Ordovician System of Appalachians; basin analysis in Precambrian and Paleozoic sequences; paleocommunity analysis; geohistory analysis. Subspecialties: Sedimentology; Paleontology, paleoecology. Office: U Tenn Dept Geol Sci Knoxville TN 37996

WALKER, ROBERT MOWBRAY, educator, physicist; b. Phila., Feb. 6, 1929; s. Robert and Margaret (Seivwright) W.; m. Alice J. Agedal, Sept. 2, 1951 (div. 1973); children: Eric, Mark; m. Ghislaine Crozaz, Aug. 24, 1973. B.S. in Physics, Union Coll., 1950, D.Sc., 1967; M.S., Yale, 1951, Ph.D., 1954; D.h.c., Université de Clermont-Ferrand, 1975. Physicist Gen. Electric Research Lab., Schenectady, 1954-62, 63-66; McDonnell prof. physics Washington U., St. Louis, 1966—; dir. McDonnell Center for Space Scis., 1975—; Vis. prof. U. Paris, 1962-63; adj. prof. metallurgy Rensselaer Poly. Inst., 1958, adj. prof. physics, 1965-66; vis. prof. physics and geology Calif. Inst. Tech., 1972, Phys. Research Lab., Ahmedabad, India, 1981, Institut d'Astrophysique, Paris, 1981; Pres. Vols. for Internat. Tech. Assistance, 1960-62, 65-66, founder, 1960, bd. dirs., 1961—; mem. Lunar Sample Analysis Planning Team, 1968-70, Lunar Sample Rev. Bd., 1970-72; adv. com. Lunar Sci. Inst., 1972-75; mem. temporary nominating group in planetary scis. Nat. Acad. Scis., 1973-75, bd. on sci. and tech. for internat. devel., 1974-76, space bd. 1977-80, com. planetary and lunar exploration, 1978—; mem. Task Force on Sci. Uses of Space Station, 1985-86; Bd. dirs. Univs. Space Research Assn., 1969-71; Sigma Xi nat. lectr., 1984-85. Recipient Distinguished Service award Am. Nuclear Soc., 1964, Yale Engring. Assn. award for contbn. to basic and applied sci., 1966, Indsl. Research awards, 1964, 65; Exceptional Sci. Achievement award NASA, 1970; E.O. Lawrence award AEC, 1971; NSF fellow, 1962-63. Fellow Am. Phys. Soc., Meteoritical Soc., AAAS, Am. Geophys. Union; mem. Am. Astron. Soc., Nat. Acad. Scis. Research and publs. on cosmic rays, nuclear physics, geophysics, radiation effects in solids, particularly devel. solid state track detectors and their application to geophysics and nuclear physics problems; discovery of fossil particle tracks in terrestrial and extra-terrestrial materials and fission track method of dating; application of phys. scis. to art and archaeology; fission track method of dating; discovery of extremely heavy (Z greater than 30) cosmic rays; and infrared measurements of interplanetary dust collected in the stratosphere and in near earth orbit. Subspecialty: Geophysics. Home: 3 Romany Park Ln Olivette MO 63132

WALKER, THOMAS EUGENE, federal government biochemist; b. Glendale, Calif., Feb. 1, 1948; s. Robert Eugene and Vada Mae (Styles) W.; m. Robin Dee Russell, Sept. 22, 1973. B.A., Westmar Coll., 1969; Ph.D., U. Iowa, 1974. Postdoctoral fellow Mich. State U., East Lansing, 1974-75; NIH postdoctoral fellow Los Alamos Nat. Lab., 1975-77, staff mem., 1977—. Mem. Am. Chem. Soc., AAAS. Democrat. Methodist. Club: Amateur Radio (Los Alamos). Current work: Synthesis and nuclear magnetic resonance spectroscopy of compounds of biological interest labeled with stable isotopes. Subspecialties: Biochemistry (biology); Nuclear magnetic resonance. Home: 65 Kachina Los Alamos NM 87544 Office: INC-4 MS-C345 Los Alamos National Lab Los Alamos NM 87545

WALKUP, JOHN FRANK, electrical engineer, educator; b. Oakland, Calif, Feb. 7, 1941; s. Francis Milton and Mabel Doreen (Lishman) W.; m. Patricia Ann Hagbom, June 26, 1965; children: Mary Kathleen, Amy Christine, Rebecca Joy. B.A., Dartmouth Coll., 1962, B.E.E., 1963; M.S., Stanford U., 1965, Engr., 1969, Ph.D., 1971. Registered profl. engr., Tex. Research asst. Stanford Electronics Labs., Stanford U., 1963-71; asst. prof. elec. engring. Tex. Tech. U., Lubbock, 1971-76, assoc. prof., 1976-81, prof., 1981-85, P.W. Horn prof., 1985—, assoc. dean engring., 1982-83; cons. in field. Author articles. Recipient Goodrich prize Dartmouth Coll., 1963; Halliburton award for excellence in teaching Tex. Tech U., 1980; Pres.'s award for excellence in teaching, 1981. AT&T Found. award for teaching, 1985. Fellow Optical Soc. Am.; sr. mem. IEEE; mem. Soc. Photo-Optical Instrumentation Engrs., Am. Soc. Engring. Edn., Sigma Xi. Current Work: Optical information processing, image processing, communication theory, electrical engineering education. Subspecialties: Optical signal processing; Graphics, image processing, and pattern recognition.

WALL, FREDERICK THEODORE, chemistry educator; b. Chisholm, Minn., Dec. 14, 1912; s. Peter and Fanny Maria (Rauhala) W.; m. Clara Elizabeth Vivian, June 5, 1940; children: Elizabeth Wall Ralston, Jane Vivian Wall-Meinike. B.Chemistry, U. Minn., 1933, Ph.D., 1937. Instr. chemistry U. Ill., 1937-39, assoc., 1939-41, asst. prof., 1941-43, asso. prof., 1943-46, prof. chemistry, 1946-64, acting dean grad. coll., 1951-52, head div. phys. chemistry, 1953-56, dean grad. coll., 1955-63; prof., chmn. dept. chemistry U. Calif., Santa Barbara, 1964-66, vice chancellor research, 1965-66; vice chancellor grad. studies and research, prof. chemistry U. Calif. at San Diego, 1966-69; exec. dir. Am. Chem. Soc., Washington, 1969-72; prof. chemistry Rice U., Houston, 1972-78, San Diego State U., 1978-81, U. Calif., San Diego, 1982—; Pres. Assn. Grad. Schs., 1961; trustee Inst. Def. Analyses, 1962-64; Mem. governing bd. Nat. Acad. Scis.-NRC, 1963- 67; mem. adv. com. for math. and phys. scis. NSF, 1964-68, chmn., 1967; chmn. bd. trustees Univs. Space Research Assn., 1970-73, chmn. council instns., 1974; mem. sci. adv. com. U. Calif. concerning Los Alamos and Livermore Labs., 1972-80. Author: Chemical Thermodynamics, 1958; Editor: Jour. Phys. Chemistry, 1965-69; Contbr. articles on phys. chemistry of polymers and statis. mechanics to sci. jours. Mem. Am. Chem. Soc. (Pure Chemistry award 1945, dir. 1962-64), Finnish Chem. Soc. (corr.), Am. Acad. Arts and Scis., Nat. Acad. Scis., Am. Phys. Soc., AAAS, Sigma Xi, Phi Kappa Phi, Phi Lambda Upsilon (hon.). Current Work: Statistical mechanics of polymer systems, thermodynamics. Subspecialties: Physical chemistry; Theoretical chemistry. Home: 2468 Via Viesta La Jolla CA 92037

WALL, JOHN FURMAN, army officer; b. Boise, Idaho, Oct. 19, 1931; s. John Furman and Helen Eulalie (Northrop) W.; m. Suzanne McHenry Jones, June 30, 1956; children—John Furman, Henry Pickett, Wright Northrop. B.S. in Mil. Sci., U.S. Mil. Acad., 1956; M.S. in Engring., Princeton U., 1961; Ph.D. in Civil Engring., Cornell U., 1972; J.D., George Washington U., 1980. Registered profl. engr. Tex.; registered profl. engr. La. Commd. 2d lt. U.S. Army, advanced through grades to lt. gen., 1985, dist. comdr. 2d Engr. Group, Seoul, 1975-76, dist. engr. C.E., Ft. Worth, 1976-79; asst. dir. mil. programs Office Chief Engrs., Washington, 1979-80; dir. civil works U.S. Army, 1982—, asst. comdr., 1982—; project mgr. Israeli Air Base program, Tel-Aviv, 1980-82; South Atlantic div. engr., Atlanta, 1982. Decorated Legion of Merit, Def. Superior Service medal, Bronze Star for valor, Air medal with two oak leaf clusters, Meritorious Service medal; Army Disting. Service medal; recipient Peace medal Ministry of Def. Israeli Def. Forces, 1982. Mem. ASCE, Soc. Am. Mil. Engrs. (gen. Wheeler medal 1982), U.S. Assn. Army, Soc. of Cincinnati. Republican. Episcopalian. Club: St. Crispians (pres.). Lodges: Masons; Shriners; Lions; Nat. Sojourners. Home: 16 A Fort Myer VA Office: CG US Army Strategic Def Command Arlington VA 22215

WALL, ROBERT ECKI, science administrator; b. Aurora, Ill., Aug. 1, 1935; s. Clifford Nathan and Mildred (Ecki) W.; m. Carol Porta, May 29, 1963; children: Laura, Andrea, Jason. B.A., Carleton Coll., 1957; Ph.D., Columbia U., 1965. Research assoc. Columbia U., 1965-66; sci. officer Office Naval Research, Washington, 1966-70; program dir. NSF, Washington, 1970-75, sect. head, 1975—. Mem. Am. Geophys. Union, AAAS, Geol. Soc. Am. Current Work: Technical administration of $55 million grants program supporting research largely in academic institutions in physical, chemical and biological oceanography and submarine geology and geophysics. Subspecialties: Oceanography; Geophysics. Office: NSF 1800 G St NW Washington DC 20550

WALL, THOMAS RANDOLPH, molecular biologist, educator; b. Lakeland, Fla., Mar. 23, 1943; s. Adolph Shirley and Elsie Mae (Griffin) W.; m. Joyce Ann Seder, Dec. 18, 1965 (div. May 1970); m. Betty Ettman, June 11, 1977; children—Gavin Stuart Ettman, Ethan Grant Ettman. A.B., U. South Fla., 1965; Ph.D., Ind. U., 1970; postgrad. Columbia U., 1970-72. USPHS fellow Ind. U., Bloomington, 1966-70; Damon Runyon Meml. Fund fellow Columbia U., N.Y.C., 1970-72, research assoc. dept. biol. scis. Columbia U., 1970-72; asst. prof. dept. microbiology and immunology UCLA Sch. Medicine, 1972-78, assoc. prof., 1978-79, prof., 1979—; founder, dir. INGENE, Inc., Santa Monica, Calif., 1980—. Contbr. articles to sci. jours. Mem. editorial bds. Jour. Immunology, 1982—, Jour. Molecular and Cellular Immunology, 1983—. Mem. Am. Assn. Immunologists. Current work: Molecular biology. Subspecialties: Genetics and genetic engineering (agriculture); Immunology (agriculture). Home: 5106 Van Noord Sherman Oaks CA 91423 Office: Molecular Biology Inst UCLA Los Angeles CA 90024

WALLACE, BONNIE ANN, biophysics educator; b. Greenwich, Conn., Aug. 10, 1951; d. Arthur Victor and Maryjane Ann W. B.S. in Chemistry, Rensselaer Poly. Inst., 1973; M. Philosophy, Yale U., 1975, Ph.D. in Molecular Biophysics and Biochemistry, 1977. Postdoctoral research fellow Harvard Med. Sch., Boston, 1977-79; asst. prof. dept biochemistry and molecular biophysics Columbia U., N.Y.C., 1979—; vis. scientist MRC Lab. Molecular Biology, Cambridge, Eng., 1978. Contbr. numerous articles to profl. jours. Jane Coffin Childs fellow, 1977-79; recipient Irma T. Hirschl award, 1980-84. Mem. N.Y. Acad. Scis. (chmn. biophysics sect. 1983—), Biophys. Soc. (nat. council, Dayhoff award 1985), Am. Chem. Soc., Am. Crystallographic Assn., Sigma Xi, Phi Lamda Upsilon. Current work: Biophysics; structure and function of membrane proteins; spectroscopy; electron microscopy; x-ray crystallography. Subspecialties: Biophysical chemistry; Biophysics (biology). Office: Dept Biochemistry and Molecular Biophysics Columbia Univ 630 W 168th St New York NY 10032

WALLACE, DOUGLAS CECIL, geneticist, educator; b. Cumberland, Md., Nov. 6, 1946; s. David H. and Elizabeth M. W. B.S., Cornell U., 1968; M.Ph., Yale U., 1972, Ph.D., 1975. Research microbiologist USPHS, Gig Harbor, Wash., 1968-70; fellow in microbiology Yale U., 1970-75, postdoctoral fellow in human genetics, 1975-76; asst. prof. genetics Stanford (Calif.) U., 1976-83; prof. biochemistry, assoc. prof. pediatrics in med. genetics Emory U., Atlanta, 1983—. Mem. Am. Soc. Human Genetics, Am. Soc. Microbiology, AAAS, Sigma Xi. Current Work: Organelle genetics. Subspecialties: Genetics and genetic engineering (biology); Molecular biology. Office: Emory U Sch Medicine Atlanta GA 30322

WALLACE, GARN ARTHUR, agricultural manufacturer executive; b. Logan, Utah, Mar. 3, 1944; s. Arthur and Elna (Kemp) W.; Sherry Lee Olson, Aug. 2, 1947; children—Holly, Karyl, Michael, Laura, John, Elizabeth. B.S. in Chemistry, Brigham Young U., 1968; Ph.D. in Biochemistry, UCLA, 1972; postdoctorate UCLA Sch. Medicine, 1972-74. Research biochemist surgery UCLA, 1974, Lab. Biomedical and Environ. Sci., 1974-80; gen. mgr. Complete Green Co., Los Angeles, 1980—; cons. L.L. Co., Los Angeles, 1980—. Contbr. articles to profl. jours.; patentee soil structure (pending). Western Los Angeles phys. facilities mgr. Mormon Ch., Calif., 1977—; envoy, rep. Mormon Ch., Paris, 1963-66. Fellow UCLA Sch. Medicine, 1972-74. Mem. Am. Chem. Soc., Sigma Xi, Phi Kappa Phi. Republican. Current work: Maximal crop yields; potentialities by nutrient balance; chelated plant nutrients; soil structure and reducing limiting factors; hydroponic production nutrients; biological control mechanisms. Subspecialties: Nutrition (biology); Biochemistry (biology). Home: 1647 Manning Ave Los Angeles CA 90024 Office: Complete Green Co 2066 Westwood Blvd Los Angeles CA 90025

WALLACE, HAROLD JAMES, JR., physician, oncologist; b. Hadley Falls, Mass., Aug. 15, 1930; s. Harold James and Evelyn (Mason) W.; m. Dorothy Green, July 4, 1959; children—Harold James III, Elizabeth Marie, John Hill. B.A., U. Vt., 1954, M.D., 1958. Diplomate Am. Bd. Internal Medicine, Am. Bd. Oncology. Intern Mary Fletcher Hosp., Burlington, Vt., 1958-59, resident, 1959-62; asst. prof. medicine U. Vt., Burlington, 1964-70; assoc. chief medicine Roswell Park Meml. Inst., Buffalo, 1970-75; chief cancer control, 1976-79; chief treatment br. Nat. Cancer Inst., Bethesda, Md., 1975-76, cons. cancer control, 1982—; oncologist Rutland Regional Med. Ctr., Vt., 1979—; chmn. Green Mountain Oncology Group, Rutland, 1983—; pres. Vt. div. Am. Cancer Soc. 1982-84. Pres. Rutland Area Hospice, 1984. Recipient Div. Service award Am. Cancer Soc., 1970. Fellow ACP; mem. Am. Soc. Clin. Oncology, Am. Assn. Cancer Research, Am. Assn. Cancer Edn., Alpha Omega Alpha. Current work: Clinical cancer research and treatment in collaboration with the Vermont Regional Cancer Center, Eastern Cooperative Oncology Group and National Surgical Adjuvant Breast Project. Subspecialties: Chemotherapy; Cancer research (medicine). Home: 12 Granview Terr Rutland VT 05701 Office: Green Mountain Oncology Group 92 Allen St Rutland VT 05701

WALLACE, JOHN ROBERT, microelectronics executive, integrated circuit design consultant; b. Columbus, Ohio, Aug. 22, 1948; s. Robert Edward and Nora Joan (Wright) W.; m. Shirley Gale Hengst, May 25, 1969 (div. 1976); m. Christine Gale Connors, June 26, 1976; children—Melissa Erin, Chelsea Lin, Mathew Robert. B.S.E.E., Rice U., 1969, M.E.E., 1970. Project engr. Garrett Comtronics, San Diego, 1971-73, Western Digital, Costa Mesa, Calif., 1973-75; pres. Precision Micro Design, Santa Cruz, Calif., 1975-78; dir. western devel. ctr. Perkin-Elmer, Santa Cruz, 1978-81; program mgr. Intel, Chandler, Ariz., 1981-82; pres. Ford Microelectronics, Inc., Colorado Springs, Colo., 1982—; chmn. microelectronics com. U. Colo. Engring. Council, Colorado Springs, 1983—. Mem. IEEE. Presbyterian. Current work: Captive semiconductor resource; development of gallium arsenide digital IC's for commercial market. Subspecialties: Integrated circuits; Microchip technology (engineering). Home: 27 Broadmoor Hills Dr Colorado Springs CO 80906 Office: Ford Microelectronics Inc 10340 State Hwy 83 Colorado Springs CO 80908

WALLACE, ROBERT BRUCE, JR., computer software consultant; b. Ft. Bragg, N.C., Dec. 4, 1955; s. Robert Bruce and Bertha Jane (Bell) W. B.S. in Math. and Computer Sci, Fla. State U., 1977. Cons. Leon County Schs., Tallahassee, 1977-78; systems analyst STAR Operating Systems Group, Control Data Corp., Sunnyvale, Calif., 1978; project mgr. MAXBASIC, Nat. Info. Systems, Cupertino, Calif., 1978-79; mgr. software devel. Personal Software Inc., Sunnyvale, 1979-80; cons. Aydin Energy Div., Palo Alto, Calif., 1980-81, GenRad, Milpitas, Calif., 1981, OMEX, Santa Clara, Calif., 1981-82, Mgmt. Blueprint Software, Los Gatos, Calif., 1982-84, Applicon, Santa Clara, 1985, Hewlett Packard, Cupertino, Calif., 82; chief exec. officer PolyGlot, Inc., San Jose, Calif., 1981—; faculty Northeastern U., 1985. Contbr. articles to mag. Nat. Merit scholar. Mem. Assn. Computing Machinery, Profl. and Tech. Cons. Assn. Created game Asteroids in Space, 1980. Current Work: Increase ease of use and flexibility of computer systems/human interfaces with application of artificial intelligence techniques and high order languages. Subspecialties: Software engineering; Programming languages. Office: PolyGlot Inc 6030 Calle de Suerte San Jose CA 95124

WALLACE, ROBERT EARL, geologist, government administrator; b. N.Y.C., July 16, 1916; married, 1945; 1 child. B.S., Northwestern U., 1938; M.S., Calif. Inst. Tech., 1940, Ph.D. in Structural Geology and Vertebrate Paleontology, 1946. Geologist U.S. Geol. Survey, 1942—, chief southwestern br., 1960-65, regional geologist, 1970-73; chief scientist Office Earthquakes, Volcanoes and Engring., Menlo Park, Calif., 1973—; from asst. prof. to assoc. prof. Wash. State U., 1946-51; vis. lectr. Stanford U., 1960; mem. Nat. Earthquake Prediction Evaluation Council; chmn. U.S./USSR Environ Agreement, U.S. Working Group Earthquake Prediction; mem. engring. criteria rev. bd. San Francisco Bay Conservation and Devel. Commn., from 1978, chmn., from 1981. Fellow Geol. Soc. Am.; mem. Soc. Econ. Geology, Seismol. Soc. Am., Earthquake Engring. Research Inst. Subspecialties: Geology; Tectonics. Office: US Geol Survey Menlo Park CA 94025*

WALLER, BRUCE FRANK, cardiologist, med. researcher and educator; b. Austin, Minn., Oct. 18, 1947; s. Frank Joseph and Marcella Marie (Greenlee) W.; m. Nancy Lynn Morton, Aug. 26, 1978. B.A. in Biology, B.A. in Math, B.A. in German; B.A. in Chemistry, Luther Coll., 1969; M.D., U. Minn., 1973, M.S., 1976. Diplomate: Am. Bd. Internal Medicine, Am. Bd. Cardiovascular Diseases. Intern in medicine Mayo Clinic, Rochester, Minn., 1973-74, resident in medicine, 1974-76; fellow in cardiology Georgetown U., Washington, 1976-78, asst. prof. medicine (cardiology), 1979-82; staff assoc. Nat. Heart, Lung and Blood Inst., NIH, Bethesda, Md., 1978-82; assoc. prof. medicine and pathology Ind. U., Indpls., 1983—; cons. cardiology Silver Spring (Md.) Ultrasound, 1978-82; cons. cardiac pathology D.C. VA Hosp., Washington, 1979-82, Riley Children's Hosp., Indpls., 1982—, St. Vincent Hosp., Indpls., 1982—. Co-author: monograph Exercise and Sudden Death, 1982. Served to lt. comdr. USPHS, 1978-82. Recipient Edgar Van Allen award Am. Heart Assn., Mayo Clinic, 1973. Fellow Am. Coll. Cardiology, ACP, Am. Coll. Chest Physicians, Am. Heart Assn.-Clin. Council Cardiology; mem. Internat. Acad. Pathology, Am. Coll. Sports Medicine. Presbyterian. Current Work: Clinical and morphologic correlation in congenital and acquired diseases of the cardiovascular system. Subspecialties: Cardiology; Pathology (medicine). Office: Ind U Sch Medicine 926 W Michigan Indianapolis IN 46223

WALLERSTEIN, ROBERT SOLOMON, psychiatrist; b. Berlin, Germany, Jan. 28, 1921; s. Lazar and Sarah (Guensberg) W.; m. Judith Hannah Saretsky, Jan. 26, 1947; children—Michael Jonathan, Nina Beth, Amy Lisa. B.A., Columbia, 1941, M.D., 1944; postgrad., Topeka Inst. Psychoanalysis, 1951-58. Asso. dir., then dir. research Menninger Found., Topeka, 1954-66; chief psychiatry Mt. Zion Hosp., San Francisco, 1966-78; tng. and supervising analyst San Francisco Psychoanalytic Inst., 1966—; clin. prof. U. Calif. Sch. Medicine, Langley-Porter Neuropsychiat. Inst., 1967-75, prof., chmn. dept. psychiatry, also dir. inst., 1975—; vis. prof. psychiatry La. State U. Sch. Medicine, also New Orleans Psychoanalytic Inst., 1973-73, Pahlavi U., Shiraz, Iran, 1977, Fed. U. Rio Grande do Sul, Porto Alegre, Brasil, 1980; Mem., chmn. research scientist career devel. com. NIMH, 1966-70; Fellow Center Advanced Study Behavioral Scis., Stanford, Calif., 1964-65, 81-82. Author books and, monographs.; Mem. editorial bd. 8 profl. jours.; Contbr. articles to profl. jours. Served with AUS, 1946-48. Recipient Heinz Hartmann award N.Y. Psychoanalytic Inst., 1968; Distinguished Alumnus award Menninger Sch. Psychiatry, 1972; J. Elliott Royer award U. Calif. at San Francisco, 1973. Fellow Am. Psychiat. Assn., A.C.P., Am. Orthopsychiat. Assn.; mem. Am. Psychoanalytic Assn. (pres. 1971-72), Internat. Psychoanalytic Assn. (v.p. 1977—), Group Advancement Psychiatry, Phi Beta Kappa, Alpha Omega Alpha. Current Work: Psychotherapy research into processes and outcomes of psychotherapy and psychoanalysis psychotherapy supervision; nature of supervision process. Subspecialty: Psychiatry. Home: 290 Beach Rd Belvedere CA 94920 Office: Langley-Porter Neuropsychiat Inst 401 Parnassus St San Francisco CA 94143

WALLIN, JACK ROBB, plant pathologist; b. Omaha, Nov. 21, 1915; s. Carl A. and Elizabeth Josephine (Smith) W.; m. Janet Mary Melhus, Sept. 25, 1937; children: Jack I.M., Robb M. B.S., Iowa State U., 1939, Ph.D., 1944. Research grad. asst. U. Mo., Columbia, 1939-40, prof. plant pathology, 1975—; research grad. asst. Iowa State., Ames, 1941-44, research asst. prof., 1944-47; research plant pathologist U.S. Dept. Agr., Agrl. Research Service Iowa State U., Ames, 1947—, U.S. Dept. Agr. Research Service U. Mo., Columbia, 1947-75. Recipient William F. Petersen award Internat. Soc. Biometeorology, 1966; Iowa State U. Pres. grantee, 1966-67. Mem. Internat. Soc. Plant Pathology, Am. Phytopath. Soc., Mo. Acad. Sci., Sigma Xi, Gamma Sigma Delta. Republican. Presbyterian. Lodge: Rotary. Patentee in field. Current Work: Host plant resistance to plant diseases in corn search for genetic control in corn to aspergillus flavus, corn viruses, low level of aflatoxin in corn, stewart's wilt, other pathogens. Subspecialties: Plant pathology; Plant genetics.

WALLING, CHEVES THOMSON, chemistry educator; b. Evanston, Ill., Feb. 28, 1916; s. Willoughby George and Frederika Christina (Haskell) W.; m. Jane Ann Wilson, Sept. 17, 1940; children—Hazel, Rosalind, Cheves, Janie, Barbara. A.B., Harvard U., 1937; Ph.D., U. Chgo., 1939. Research chemist E.I. duPont de Nemours & Co., Wilmington, Del., 1939-43, U.S. Rubber Co., Passaic, N.J., 1943-49; research assoc. Lever Bros. Co., Cambridge, Mass., 1949-52; prof. Columbia U., N.Y.C., 1952-70; disting. prof. U. Utah, Salt Lake City, 1970—. Author: Free Radicals in Solution, 1957; also tech. papers. Fellow AAAS; mem. Nat. Acad. Scis., Am. Acad. Arts and Scis., Am. Chem. Soc. (Norris award 1970, Lubrizol award 1984). Current work: Physical organic chemistry, reaction mechanisms, free radical reactions, polymer chemistry, chemical education. Subspecialty: Organic chemistry. Office: U Utah Dept Chemistry Salt Lake City UT 84112

WALLS, BETTY L., psychologist, consultant; b. Kansas City, Mo., Oct. 26, 1932; d. Austin Truman Webb and Gladys O. (Gillespie) Webb Morrison; m. William C. Walls, Apr. 6, 1954 (div. Jan. 1961); 1 son, Paul Kevin. R.N. diploma, Kansas City (Mo.) Gen. Hosp., 1957; B.A., U. Mo.-Kansas City, 1967, M.A., 1971, Ph.D. with distinction, 1974. Lic. psychologist, Mo. cert. psychologist, Kans. Pvt. practice clin. psychology, Kansas City, Mo., 1972—; lectr. U. Mo.-Kansas City, 1973—; chmn. dept. psychology Park Coll., 1972-80; contract psychologist Catholic Charities, Kansas City, 1980-84; vis. prof. psychology U. Mo.-Kansas City, 1980-83; lectr. Rockhurst Coll., 1980, Benedictine Coll., 1980. Author: test bank for Byrne Introduction to Psychology, 1975. Bd. dirs. Alcoholism Recovery, Kansas City, 1974—; v.p. bd. dirs. Operation Discovery, 1975-82; v.p. Sherwood Ctr., 1978-83; cons. Kansas City Regional Assn. Mental Retardation, 1978-82. Named Outstanding Tchr. U. Mo.-Kansas City, 1973, Outstanding Tchr. Park Coll., 1980. Mem. Am. Psychol. Assn., N.Y. Acad. Sci., Assn. Behavior Analysts, AAAS, Am. Assn. Tension Control, Mo. Psychol. Assn., Greater Kansas City Psychol. Assn., Psi Chi. Democrat. Methodist. Clubs: Cotton Eyed Joe (Kansas City), Sugar Shack (Kansas City). Current Work: Child development, fetal development, acquisition of various curricular material, reinforcement theory. Subspecialties: Behavioral psychology; Learning. Home: 8019 Kenwood Kansas City MO 64131 Office: U Mo 51st and Rockhill Kansas City MO 64110 Also: 7711 State Line Kansas City MO 64124

WALLS, RICHARD ALAN, geologist, oil and gas exploration company executive; b. Fairborne, Ohio, Dec. 3, 1948; s. Teddy Kieling and Anna Alfrieda (Brisley) W. B.S., Morehead State U., 1971; M.S., U. N.C., 1973; Ph.D., McGill U., 1977. Registered profl. geologist. Exploration geologist Columbia Gas and Transmission Corp., Charleston, W.Va., 1971-72; lectr. McGill U., Montreal, Que., Can., 1975-76; sr. exploration geologist Shell Can. Ltd., Calgary, Alta., Can., 1977-79, Can. Hunter Exploration Co., Calgary, 1979-80; v.p. Petrosec Exploration Ltd. Calgary, 1980-83; pres. KenTex Oil Corp., Houston, 1983—, also dir.; dir. Aritex Resources Ltd., Vancouver, B.C., Can. Contbr. articles to profl. jours. Vice pres. Post Grad. Students Soc., Montreal, 1975. Named H.W. Straley III Outstanding Geology alumnus Morehead State U., 1982. Mem. Geol. Soc. Am., Can. Soc. Petroleum Geologists, Soc. Econ. Paleontologists and Mineralogists. Roman Catholic. Current work: Reservoir properties of carbonate rocks; petroleum occurrences in eocene formations of Texas. Subspecialties: Sedimentology; Geochemistry. Home: 9449 Briar Forest Dr 1907 Houston TX 77063 Office: KenTex Oil Corp 9430 Old Katy Rd Suite 206 Houston TX 77055

WALQUIST, ROBERT LOUIS, business executive, electrical engineer. Vice pres. SDI program exec. TRW Electronics and Def. Redondo Beach, Calif. Subspecialties: Aerospace engineering and technology; Electrical engineering. Office: TRW Electronics and Def One Space Park Redondo Beach CA 90278*

WALSER, MACKENZIE, physician, educator; b. N.Y.C., Sept. 19, 1924; s. Kenneth Eastwood and Jean (Mackenzie) W.; m. Lynne Margaret White, Aug. 8, 1965; children—Karen D., Jennifer McK., Cameron M., Eric H. Grad., Phillips Exeter Acad., 1941; A.B., Yale, 1944; M.D., Columbia, 1948. Diplomate: Am. Bd. Internal Medicine. Intern Mass. Gen. Hosp., Boston, 1948-49, asst. resident in medicine, 1949-50; resident Parkland Hosp., Dallas, 1950-52; staff mem. Johns Hopkins Hosp., Balt., 1957—; instr. U. Tex. at Dallas, 1950-51, asst. prof., 1951-52; investigator Nat. Heart Inst., Bethesda, Md., 1954-57; asst. prof. pharmacology Johns Hopkins Med. Sch., 1957-61, asso. prof., 1961-70, prof., 1970—, asst. prof. medicine, 1957-64, asso. prof., 1964-74, prof., 1974—; Med. dir. USPHS, 1970—, pharmacology study sect., 1968-72. Co-author: Mineral Metabolism, 2d edit, 1969, Handbook of Physiology, 1973, The Kidney, 1976, 2d edit., 1981, also articles; co-editor: Branched-Chain Amino and Ketoacids, 1981; Nutritional Management: The Johns Hopkins Handbook, 1984. Served with USNR, 1942-45; to lt. M.C. USNR, 1952-54. Recipient Research Career Devel. award USPHS, 1959-69. Mem. Am. Soc. Clin. Investigation, Assn. Am. Physicians, Am. Fedn. Clin. Research, AAAS, Am. Physiol. Soc., AAUP (pres. Johns Hopkins 1970), Am. Soc. Pharmacology and Exptl. Therapeutics (Exptl. Therapeutics award 1975), Am. Soc. Nephrology, Am. Soc. Clin. Nutrition. Club: Century Assn. Current Work: Amino acid and protein metabolism and disorders thereof. Subspecialties: Nephrology; Nutrition (medicine). Home: 7513 Club Rd Ruxton MD 21204 Office: Johns Hopkins U Sch Medicine Baltimore MD 21205

WALSH, JACQUELINE ANN, systems engineer, consultant; b. Denver, Sept. 9, 1951; d. John James and Shyla Darlene (Burke) W. Student, S.D. State U., 1969-70; B.S. in Computer Sci, Iowa State U., 1973; postgrad., U. Minn., 1973-74, U. Houston, 1976-77. Computer programmer Sperry Univac Def. Systems, Eagan, Minn., 1973-75, Lockheed Electronics, Houston, 1975-77; sr. systems analyst Sperry Univac, Blue Bell, Pa., 1977-80; sr. systems engr. Space Systems div. Gen. Electric Co., Valley Forge, Pa., 1980-83; data processing consultant Sperry Computer Systems, Blue Bell, Pa., adr3—. Recipient commendation Lockheed Electronics, 1976, commendation NASA, 1976. Mem. Assn. for Computing Machinery. Current Work: Distributed systems and network communications. Primary interest in operating systems internals and in inter computer communications. Interest in new micro processor technologies. Subspecialties: Operating systems; Computer architecture. Home: PO Box 306 Warrington PA 18976 Office: Sperry Computer Systems PO Box 500 Blue Bell PA 19424

WALSH, JOHN STUART, chemist; b. La Jolla, Calif., July 23, 1955; s. Eugene Arthur and Mary Beverly (Catto) W. B.Pharm. with honors, U. London, 1976; M.S., U. Kans., 1978. Staff chemist Merck & Co., Rahway, N.J., 1979-82, research chemist, 1982—. Contbr. articles to sci. jours. Patentee derivatives of CO76 compounds. Mem. Am. Chem. Soc. (div. med. chemistry). Republican. Roman Catholic. Current work: Drug metabolism; metabolite isolation and structure determination; enzyme mechanisms; isotope effects, nitro imidazole chemistry and metabolism. Subspecialties: Medicinal chemistry; Biochemistry (biology). Home: 2202 Village Dr Avenel NJ 07001 Office: Merck & Co R80A11 PO Box 2000 Rahway NJ 07065

WALSH, PATRICK CRAIG, urologist; b. Akron, Ohio, Feb. 13, 1938; s. Raymond Michael and Catherine N. (Rodden) W.; m. Margaret Campbell, May 23, 1964; children—Christopher, Jonathan, Alexander. A.B., Case Western Res. U., 1960, M.D., 1964. Intern in surgery Peter Bent Brigham Hosp., Boston, 1964-65, asst. resident in surgery, 1965-66; asst. resident in pediatric surgery Children's Hosp. Med. Center, Boston, 1966-67; resident in urology U. Calif.-Los Angeles Med. Center, 1967-71; dir. Brady Urol. Inst., urologist-in-chief Johns Hopkins Hosp., Balt., 1974—; prof., dir. dept. urology Johns Hopkins U. Sch. Medicine, 1974—. Contbr. articles to med. jours. Served to comdr. M.C. USN, 1971-73. Mem. Soc. Univ. Surgeons, Am. Assn. Genito-Urinary Surgeons, Clin. Soc. Genito-Urinary Surgeons, Am. Urol. Assn., Endocrine Soc., Alpha Omega Alpha. Roman Catholic. Current work: Carcinoma of the prostate; benign prostatic hyperphasia; steroid hormone receptors. Subspecialties: Urology; Endocrinology. Home: 13910 Cuba Rd Cockeysville MD 21030 Office: John Hopkins Hosp Baltimore MD 21205

WALSH, PATRICK ROBERT, neurosurgeon, researcher; b. St. Paul, May 29, 1948; s. Robert Jerome and Arlene Delores (Krenz) W.; m. Patricia Ann Kane, Dec. 23, 1968; children—Brian Patrick, Monica Lee. Student St. Mary's Coll., Winona, Minn., 1966-69; M.D., Med. Coll. Wis., Milw., 1973, Ph.D. in Anatomy, 1984. Diplomate Am. Bd. Neurol. Surgery; lic. physician, Wis. Intern Med. Coll. Wis. Affiliated Hosps., Milw., 1973-74, resident in neurosurgery, 1974-78; asst. prof. neurosurgery Med. Coll. Wis., 1978-84, assoc. prof., 1984—; attending neurosurgeon Milwaukee County Med. Ctr., Wood VA Hosp.; attending neurosurgeon Froedtert Meml. Luth. Hosp., 1978-84, co-dir. Neurosci. ICU, 1980-84; cons. staff Sacred Heart Rehab. Hosp., Milw., 1983—. Author articles and book chpts. on neuroanatomy, neuropathology, neurophysiology, mechanisms of nervous system injury, stereotactic neurosurgery, microvascular neurosurgery, neurodiagnostic imaging. Recipient Outstanding Research award Lakeside Labs., Milw., 1973, Outstanding Clin. Achievement award Upjohn Pharms., 1973; postdoctoral fellow Paralyzed Vets. Am., 1978-80; NIH grantee, 1984. Fellow ACS; mem. Am. Assn. Neurol. Surgeons, Congress Neurol. Surgeons, AMA, Wis. Med. Assn., Milwaukee County Med. Soc. (del.), Am. Soc. Stereotactic and Functional Neurosurgery, Biophys. soc., Neuroelectric Soc. (nat. adv. bd.), Soc. for Neurosci., Soc. for Neurosurg. Anesthesia and Neurol. Supportive Care, Am. Guild Organists, Alpha Omega Alpha. Independent. Roman Catholic. Current work: Biophysical and ultrastructural alterations of myelinated axons associated with traumatic conductive blockade, including mathematical modelling; electrophysiologic monitoring of clinical traumatic and ischemic diseases (multimodal intensive care); biomechanics and epidemiology of spinal disorders; stereotactic, spinal and microvascular neurosurgery. Subspecialties: Neurophysiology; Neurobiology. Home: 18170 Midland Pl Brookfield WI 53005 Office: Dept Neurosurgery Milwaukee County Med Complex 8700 W Wisconsin Ave Milwaukee WI 53226

WALSH, TED WILLIAM, analytical environmental chemist; b. Cleve., Oct. 1, 1950; s. John Robert and Dorothy Ellen (Brady) W. B.S. in Biology, Ashland Coll., 1972, B.S. in Chemistry, 1972; M.S. in Chemistry, U. Hawaii, 1975. Lab. asst. Ashland Coll., Ohio, 1970-72; teaching asst. U. Hawaii, Honolulu, 1973-75; research assoc. Hawaii Inst. Marine Biology, Kaneohe, 1976—, sr. chemist analytical services, 1979—; water quality cons. System Culture Corp., Kahuku, Hawaii, 1977-78; cons. on ocean thermal energy conversion U. Calif.-Berkeley, Kona, Hawaii, 1984. Author: Environmental Impact Survey, Tarawa Atoll, 1981; Environmental Sewage Discharge, Kaneohe Bay, 1981; Ocean Thermal Energy - Seawater Chemistry, 1985; Seawater Nutrient Analysis, 1985. Instr. YMCA Camp, Cleve., 1966-67, swim coach, 1966-68. Ashland Coll. swimming scholar, 1968-70, biology and chem. sci. scholar, 1970-72. Lutheran. Clubs: Cleve. Swim; Honolulu Body Surfing. Current work: Analytical method development-environmental, water, soils, etc., chemistry; water quality; oceanography; aquaculture; impact survey chemistry; nutrient chemistry. Subspecialties: Environmental chemistry; Oceanography. Home: 2868 Ala Ilima Apt 1406 Honolulu HI 96818 Office: Hawaii Inst Marine Biology U Hawaii Room 619 Marine Sci Bldg Honolulu HI 96822

WALSH, WILLIAM KERSHAW, textile chemistry educator, researcher; b. Columbus, Ohio, Sept. 29, 1932; s. Merrick Kershaw and Genevieve (McCaw) W.; m. Josie Lea Shearin, Jan. 30, 1970; 1 child, Genevieve Shearin. B.S., U. S.C., 1954; Ph.D., N.C. State U., 1967. Engr. Celanese Co., Rock Hills, S.C., 1959-60; asst. prof. textile chemistry N.C. State U. Sch. Textiles, Raleigh, 1967-72, assoc. prof., 1972-77, prof., 1977—, asst. dean research, 1980-81, assoc. dean research, 1981—. Contbr. articles to profl. jours., chpts. to books. Patentee delayed cure with ionizing radiation, method for decreasing flamability of cellulosic fabrics. Served to 1st lt. USAF, 1954-58. NSF grantee. Mem. Am. Chem. Soc., Am. Assn. Textile Chemists and Colorists, AAAS, Sigma Xi. Current work: Radiation curing of polymers; physical properties of polymers; moisture transport and comfort. Subspecialties: Polymers (materials science); Polymer chemistry. Home: 224 E Park Dr Raleigh NC 27605Office: NC State U Sch Textiles Box 8301 Raleigh NC 27695-8301

WALTER, DONALD KENNETH, government official; b. Phila., May 28, 1931; s. Edwin B. and Catherine M. (Albert) W.; m. Katherine Steiner (div.); m. Ann Laing, July 6, 1962; 1 child, Debra Ann. B.S. in Civil Engring., Drexel Inst. Tech., 1953; M.S. in Civil Engring., Drexel U., 1965. Registered profl. engr., Pa., Md. Commd. officer U.S. Army, 1953, advanced through ranks to lt. col., 1980; real estate officer U.S. Hdqrs. Area Command, Saigon, Vietnam, 1966-67; logistics officer Engring. Command, Frankfurt, W. Ger., Germany, 1967-69; facility engr., Würtzburg, W. Ger., 1969-71, Fort Detrick, Md., 1971-73; retired, 1973; city engr., Annapolis, Md., 1973-75; div. dir. mcpl. waste U.S. Dept. Energy, Washington, 1975—. Contbr. chpts. to books, articles to profl. jours. Decorated Legion of Merit medal, 1973. Mem. ASME, Soc. Am. Mil. Engrs., ASTM, Nat. Soc. Profl. Engrs., Md. Soc. Profl. Engrs. (pres. Annapolis chpt. 1979). Republican. Lutheran. Lodge: Rotary (pres. 1982). Current work: Manage varied research programs to convert municipal wastes to energy; research includes mechanical, thermal and biochemical systems; maintain current knowledge of institutional aspects of energy. Office: US Dept of Energy CE323 Energy from Municipal Waste 1000 Independence Ave SW Washington DC 20585

WALTER, GILBERT GUSTAV, mathematics educator, researcher; b. Ottawa, Ill., Nov. 24, 1930; s. Gustav Gottlieb and Christiana (Berner) W.; m. Edith Gertrude Weege, Feb. 1, 1958; children—Natalia, Pierre, Mark. B. Indsl. Engring., Gen. Motors Inst., 1953; B.S. in Elec. Engring., N.Mex. State U., 1956; M.S. in Math., U. Wis.-Madison, 1959, Ph.D. in Math., 1962. Project engr. A.C. Electronics, Milw., 1956-57; vis. prof. U. Agraria, Lima, Peru, 1968-69, U. Calif.-San Diego, La Jolla, 1965-66; instr. to prof. math., U. Wis.-Milw., 1961—, chmn. dept. math., 1973-75, coordinator applied math and physics, 1975—. Author numerous research articles. Treas., Amnesty Internat. Group #106, Milw., 1981—. Served to cpl. U.S. Army, 1953-55. Mem. Am. Math. Soc., Inst. Math. Stats., Soc. Indsl. and Applied Math. Current work: Sturm-Liouville problems, estimation of prior distribution, structure of compartmental models, regulation of fisheries. Subspecialties: Analysis; Statistics. Home: 2122 E Edgewood Ave Milwaukee WI 53211 Office: U Wis-Milw Dept Math Box 413 Milwaukee WI 53201

WALTER, THOMAS HARRY, podiatric surgeon, educator; b. Allentown, Pa., Feb. 16, 1950; s. John Harold and Mae (Grammes) W. B.A., Pa. State U., 1971; D.P.M., Pa. Coll. Podiatric Medicine, 1978. Intern Parkview Hosp., Phila., 1978-79, resident, 1979-80; research fellow, instr. surgery Pa. Coll. Podiatric Medicine, Phila., 1980-81; fellow U. Md. Hosp. and Trauma Ctr., 1981-82; research cons. Sutter Biomech. Corp., San Diego, 1981—, sole practice, Phila. and New London, Conn., 1982—; dir. Broad St. Hosp. Pediatric Edn., Phila., 1983—, asst. dir. research tng. program, 1983—. Fellow Am. Podiatry Assn.; mem. Conn. podiatry Assn., Hartford County Podiatry Assn., Phila. Bone Club, Bioelec. Repair and Growth Stimulation Soc. Republican. Current Work: Advances in podiatric surgery; research in electrical bone stimulation. Subspecialties: Orthopedics; Bioelectricity. Home: 12 Water St Apt B-4 Mystic CT 06355 Office: Dept Podiatric Surgery Pa Coll Podiatric Medicine 8th & Race Sts Philadelphia PA 19107

WALTERS, DOUGLAS BRUCE, chemist; b. Bklyn., Apr. 6, 1942; s. Eugene Thomas and Bertha (Beckroge) W.; m. Carole Lowe, Sept. 13, 1969 (div. 1980); 1 child, Patricia Jean. B.S., L.I. Univ., 1963, M.S., 1965; Ph.D., U. Ga., 1971. Chemist, EPA, Athens, Ga., 1970-71, Agrl. Research Service, U.S. Dept. Agr., Athens, 1971-77; tech. program mgr. Nat. Inst. Environ Health Scis. HEW, Research Triangle Park, N.C., 1977-80, head chem. health and safety Nat. Toxicology Program, Dept. Health and Human Services, Research Triangle Park, 1980—. Editor: Safe Handling of Chemical Carcinogens Vol I, II, 1980; Health and Safety for Toxicity Testing, 1984; Chemistry for Toxicity Testing, 1984; Compendium of Safety Data Sheets for Research and Industrial Chemicals, Vol. I, II, III, 1985. Contbr. articles to profl. jours. Patentee in field. Mem. Am. Chem. Soc. (chem. health and safety div. sec. 1980-83, chmn. 1983-84), Am. Chem. Soc. Northeast Ga. (sect. chmn. 1976), Am. Indsl. Hygiene Assn., Mensa. Mem. Unity Ch. Current work: Chemical health and safety, industrial hygiene, analytical chemistry, environmental chemistry, food chemistry. Subspecialties: Chemical health and safety; Analytical chemistry. Home: 6807 Breezewood Rd Raleigh NC 27607 Office: Nat Toxicology Program Box 12233 Research Triangle Park NC 27709

WALTERS, JAMES CARTER, geology educator, researcher; b. Zeeland, Mich., June 27, 1948; s. Jerome C. and Dorothy F. (Bowens) W.; m. Bonnie J. Kuhlman, June 11, 1971; children—Jennifer, Kyle. B.A., Grand Valley State Coll., 1970; M. Phil., Rutgers U., 1973, Ph.D., 1975. Teaching fellow Fairleigh Dickinson U., Madison, N.J., 1974-75; asst. prof. geology U. No. Iowa, Cedar Falls, 1975-82, assoc. prof., 1982—; research assoc. The Center for Northern Studies, Wolcott, Ver., 1975—. Contbr. numerous articles to profl. jours. Grantee Nat. Park Service, 1977-82. Fellow Geol. Soc. Am., Iowa Acad. Sci. (pres. 1980); mem. Am. Quaternary Assn., Sigma Xi, Sigma Gamma Epsilon (v.p. central province 1978—). Lodge: Lions (bd. dirs. 1982-84). Current work: Quaternary geology, periglacial geomorphology. Subspecialties: Geology; Arctic studies. Home: 802 Latham Pl Cedar Falls IA 50613 Office: Dept Earth Sci U Northern Iowa Cedar Falls IA 50614

WALTERS, RONALD ARLEN, molecular biologist; b. Greeley, Colo., Apr. 25, 1940; s. Reuben and Esther Marie (Anderson) W.; m. Geraldine Jane Huck, Aug. 16, 1969; children—Christian Grant, Colin Jeremy. B.S., Colo. State U., 1962, M.S., 1964, Ph.D., 1967. Engr., Gen. Electric Co., Richland, Wash., 1962-63; staff mem. Los Alamos Nat. Lab., 1967-80, dep. group leader, 1980-82, group leader, 1982-84, asst. to assoc. dir., 1984—; mem. biotech. task force Office of Pres., U. Calif.-Berkeley, 1984—. Contbr. chpts. to books, articles to profl. jours. Mgr. Little League, Los Alamos, 1983—; pack chmn. Great S.W. council Boy Scouts Am., Los Alamos, 1984; mem. exec. council United Ch., Los Alamos, 1984. Recipient Disting. Performance award Los Alamos Nat. Lab., 1981. Mem. Am. Chem. Soc., AAAS, Am. Soc. Biol. Chemists, Radiation Research Soc., Biophys. Soc., Sigma Xi. Republican. Presbyterian. Current work: Study of induced gene expression, molecular basis of neoplasia, molecular biological effects of ionizing radiation, nucleotide structure and function of genes. Subspecialties: Molecular biology; Gene actions. Home: 545 Totavi St Los Alamos NM 87544 Office: Los Alamos Nat Lab ADCEL MS-A102 Los Alamos NM 87545

WALTERS, SANDRA JEAN, research chemist; b. Canton, Ohio, Jan. 12, 1939; d. Carl A. and Irene Harriet (Baer) Brehm; m. Paul Alden Walters, Aug. 29, 1959. B.Sc. in Chemistry, Kent State U., 1960; postgrad. Akron U., 1961-62. Chemist Goodyear Tire & Rubber Co., Akron, Ohio, 1960-73, sr. research chemist, 1973—. Contbr. articles to profl. journs. Patentee polymer sci. field. Mem. Am. Chem. Soc., Tire Soc. (rubber div.). Club: Ninety-Nines. Current work: Basic research in polymer physics. Subspecialties: Polymer chemistry; Polymer physics. Home: 4099 Ellsworth Rd Stow OH 44224 Office: Goodyear Tire & Rubber Co D/410B 142 Goodyear Blvd Akron OH 44316

WALTKING, ARTHUR ERNEST, chemist; b. N.Y.C., Nov. 7, 1937; s. Ernest Conrad and Jennie Violet (Gilles) W.; m. Kathryn Martha Schraut, June 4, 1961; children—Claire Virginia, Adrienne Rosa. B.A., Lehigh U., 1959. Chemist Best Foods div. CPC Internat., Bayonne, N.J., 1959-66, group leader analytical research, 1966-67, sect. leader analytical service, Union, N.J., 1967-72, mgr. analytical services, 1972-79, assoc. research scientist, 1979-84, prin. materials scientist, 1984—; rep. IUPAC Commn. on Oils, Fats and Derivatives, 1980—. Contbr. articles to profl. jours. Patentee in field. Mem. council Good Shepherd Luth. Ch., 1980-82. Recipient Golden Peanut award Nat. Peanut Council, 1971. Mem. Am. Oil Chemists Soc. (chmn. flavor, bio methods and hydro oils coms. 1976-82, chmn. mycotoxin com. 1984—, rep. to joint mycotoxin com.), Assn. Ofcl. Analytical Chemists (liaison to Am. Oil Chemists Soc. 1980—, food I com. 1981—), Soc. Rheology, N.Am. Thermal Analysis Soc., Am. Chem. Soc. Current work: Methodology for analysis of food products for mycotoxins, flavor volatiles, texture, rheological properties, essential fatty acids and polymers. Subspecialties: Analytical chemistry; Physical chemistry. Home: 482 Rock Rd Glen Rock NJ 07452 Office: Best Foods Div CPC Internat 1120 Commerce Ave Union NJ 07083

WALTON, LEWIS ANTHONY, nuclear engineer; b. Wilmington, Del., Nov. 22, 1945; s. Warren and Helen (Harvilchuck) W.; m. Barbara Rae Brown, Oct. 22, 1969; children: Thomas Anthony, David Richard. B.S., Rensselaer Poly. Inst., 1967. Registered profl. engr., Va. Jr. engr. Boeing Aircraft, Seattle, 1967-71; engr. Getty Oil Co., Rockville, Md., 1971-73; engr. Babcock & Wilcox, Lynchburg, Va., 1973-74, sr. engr., 1974-79, supervisory engr., 1979—; cons. engr., Forest, Va., 1978—. Contbr. articles to tech. jours. Treas. Forest PTA, 1982, pres., 1983. N.Y. State Regents scholar, 1963. Mem. Am. Nuclear Soc. (newsletter com. 1981—, program com. 1982—, pub. info. com. Va. sect. 1981), AIAA (sect. vice-chmn. 1964-66, chmn. 1966-67). Patentee in field. Current Work: Performance of materials and design in light water reactor cores (fuel elements) - advanced designs and performance models; high level waste disposal studies. Subspecialties: Mechanical engineering; Materials (engineering). Home: 102 Lake Ridge Dr Forest VA 24551 Office: PO Box 1260 Lynchburg VA 24505

WALTON, PAUL TALMAGE, geologist; b. Salt Lake City, Feb. 4, 1914; s. Paul and Margaret (Watts) W.; m. Helen E. Baer, July 3, 1944; children: Holly, Paul, Ann. B.S. in Geol. Enging, U. Utah., 1935, M.S. in Geology, 1940; Ph.D., M.I.T., 1942. Cert. Am. Inst. Profl. Geologists. With U.S. Dept. Agr., Utah, 1935-38; geologist and geophysicist Standard Oil Calif., Saudi Arabia, 1938-39; exploration geologist Rocky Mountain area Tex. Co., 1942-44; div. geologist Pacific Western Oil Corp. div. Getty Oil Co., Rocky Mountains and Saudi Arabia, 1944-49; geologist, partner Morgan-Walton Oils, Rocky Mountains, 1949-55, Walton-Kearns, 1955-57; partner Paul T. Walton & Assocs., Salt Lake City, 1957—; cons. bd. dirs. Jackson Hole Land Trust. Contbr. to profl. bulls. and guidebooks. Mem. Am. Assn. Petroleum Geologists, Am. Inst. Profl. Geologists, Geol. Soc. Am., Am. Geol. Inst., Ind. Petroleum Assn. Am., others. Current Work: Exploration for oil and gas. Subspecialty: Geology. Home: 2591 Brentwood Dr Salt Lake City UT 84121 Office: 1102 Walker Ctr Salt Lake City UT 84111

WALTON, ROBERT EUGENE, agriculture company executive; b. Shattuck, Okla., Jan. 15, 1931; s. Lonnie J. and Marguerite Ruth (Rose) W.; m. Janice Carolyn Graning, Sept. 5, 1959; children—Cynthia Claire, Robert Eugene Jr., John Randolph. B.S. in Agr., Okla. State U., 1952, M.S. in Animal Breeding, 1956; postgrad. Royal Agr. U., Uppsala, Sweden, 1952-53; Ph.D. in Animal Breeding and Genetics, Iowa State U., 1961; postgrad. Harvard U., 1970. Gen. mgr. West Hide Farms, Hereford, Eng., 1953-54; asst. prof. U. Ky., Lexington, 1958-62; geneticist Am. Breeder's Service, DeForest, Wis., 1962-65, dir. mktg. div., 1965-67, exec. v.p., 1967-68, pres., 1968—; dir. First Wis. Bank, Madison, Am. Genetics, Inc., Middleton, Wis., World Dairy Expo, Madison. Developer genetic evaluation system, 1962, cattle breeding system, 1968. Bd. dirs., v.p. United Way of Dane County (Wis.), 1983—. Served to capt. U.S. Army, 1957-62. Recipient Disting Animal Sci. grad. award Okla State U., 1975; award of Distinction U. Wis., 1980; Agri-Bus. award Nat. Agrl. Mktg. Assn., 1985; named All-Time Great Dairyman Internat. Stockman's Sch., 1983, Exec. of Yr. Sales and Mktg. Club, 1984; Industry Person of Yr. World Dairy Expo, 1982. Mem. Am. Soc. Animal Sci., Am. Dairy Sci. Assn., Dairy Shrine, Nat. Assn. Animal Breeders (pres. 1972-74), Cert. Semen Services (pres. 1977-79), Greater Madison C. of C. (bd. dirs. 1985). Republican. Methodist. Club: Madison. Lodge: Rotary. Subspecialty: Animal breeding and embryo transplants. Office: Am Breeders Service PO Box 459 DeForest WI 53532

WALTON, THOMAS EDWARD, veterinarian, researcher; b. McKeesport, Pa., Dec. 2, 1940; s. Thomas Edward and Matilda Lucy W.; children: Anne Louise, Leigh Ellen. D.V.M., Purdue U., 1964; Ph.D., Cornell U, 1968. NIH trainee in microbiology Cornell U., 1964-68; research microbiologist Middle Am. research unit HEW-USPHS-NIH-Nat. Inst. Allergy and Infectious Diseases, Ancon, C.Z., 1968-69, research vet. med. officer, 1969-72; vet. med. officer Agrl. Research Service, U.S. Dept. Agr., Arthropod-borne Animal Diseases Research Lab., Denver, 1972-74, research leader, 1974—. Contbr. articles to profl. jours. Recipient cert. merit Dept. Agr., 1974, 77, 82, Sci. and Edn. Adminstr. Dir.'s award, 1981. Mem. Am. Com. Arthropod-borne Viruses, Am. Soc. Tropical Medicine and Hygiene, AVMA, Am. Soc. Virology, Nat. Assn. Fed. Veterinarians, U.S. Animal Health Assn. Club: Optimists (Lakewood, Colo.). Current Work: Vet. medicine, arbovirology, research mgmt. Subspecialties: Microbiology (veterinary medicine); Virology (veterinary medicine). Office: PO Box 25327 Denver CO 80225

WALTON, VINCENT MICHAEL, electrical engineer; b. Spokane, Wash., Oct. 23, 1949; s. Norman John and Elsie (Swanson) W.; m. Mary Elizabeth McGuire, Mar. 9, 1984. A.S., Olympic Coll., 1970; B.S. in Elec. Engring., U. Wash., 1973, M.S. cum laude, 1975; postgrad. Stanford U., 1977-78. Engr. trainee Puget Sound Naval Shipyard, Bremerton, Wash., 1969-73; mem. tech. staff Boeing Aerospace Co., Seattle, 1973-75; dept. staff engr. TRW, Redondo Beach, Calif., 1975-82; prin. engr. Measurement Analysis Corp., Torrance, Calif., 1982-84; pres. VMW Systems Dynamics, Federal Way, Wash., 1984-85; lead engr. Boeing Mil. Airplane Co., Seattle, 1985—. Contbr. articles to profl. jours. Mem. IEEE, AIAA, Aeronautics and Astronautics Soc. Republican. Lutheran. Club: TRW ski. Current work: Research and development in aerospace automatic digital control systems. Subspecialties: Systems engineering; Aerospace engineering and technology. Home and Office: 419 SW 322d St Federal Way WA 98023

WAMPLER, JOHN EDWARD, biochemistry educator; b. Knoxville, Tenn., Sept. 9, 1944; s. Ward Edward and Mary Alice (McSween) W.; m. Alma Jean Phibbs, June 12, 1965; 1 child, Sandra Jean. B.S. in Chemistry, U. Tenn., 1966, Ph.D., 1969. Research assoc. U. Ga., Athens, 1970-72, asst. prof., 1972-77, assoc. prof., 1977-82, prof. biochemistry, 1982—; founding ptnr. On-Line Instrument Systems, Athens, 1975-81. Editor Analytical Instrumentation Jour., 1984. Contbr. articles to profl. jours. Grantee NSF, 1974-83, NIH, 1974—. Mem. Soc. for Applied Spectroscopy, Am. Soc. for Photobiology, Am. Soc. Biol. Chemists, AAAS, Am. Chem. Soc. Current work: Applications of on-line computer control and data aquisition to measurements of spectra and images of ultra weak light sources; studies of bioluminescence and stimulus/response coupling in single living cells. Subspecialties: Biochemistry (biology); Biomedical engineering. Office: Univ GA Dept Biochemistry Athens GA 30602

WAN, FREDERIC YUI-MING, applied mathematician; b. Shanghai, China, Jan. 7, 1936; s. Wai-Nam and Olga Pearl (Jung) W.; m. Julia Y.S. Chang, Sept. 10, 1960. S.B., M.I.T., 1959, S.M., 1963, Ph.D., 1965. Mem. staff M.I.T. Lincoln Lab., Lexington, 1959-65; instr. math. M.I.T., Cambridge, 1965-67, asst. prof., 1967-69, assoc. prof., 1969-74; prof. math., dir. Inst. Applied Math. and Stats., U. B.C., Vancouver, 1974-83; prof. applied math. and math. U. Wash., Seattle, 1983—, chmn. applied math., 1984—; cons. indsl. firms and govt. agys. Mem. M.I.T. Ednl. Council for B.C Area of Can. Contbr. articles to profl. jours. Sloan Found. fellow, 1973; Killam sr. fellow, 1979. Fellow Am. Acad. Mechanics; mem. Soc. Indsl. and Applied Math., Can. Applied Math. Soc. (council 1980-83, pres. 1983-84), Can. Math. Soc., AAUP, ASME, Sigma Xi. Current work: Foundations of theory of plates and shells, finite deformations problems; optimal control problems in economics of forestry, land and other exhaustible resources; biomechanics of neurons and other cell bodies; asymptotic and numerical solutions. Subspecialties: Applied mathematics; Theoretical and applied mechanics. Office: Dept Applied Math U Wash FS-20 Seattle WA 98195

WANAT, STANLEY FRANK, chemist; b. Nanticoke, Pa., Dec. 31, 1939; s. Stanley John and Irene Rita (Sobolewski) W.; m. Joy Marilyn Edmonds, July 25, 1964; children—Brian, Jill. A.B., Rutgers U., 1963; M.S., Seton Hall U., 1969, Ph.D., 1971. Chemist Shell Chem. Co., Princeton, N.J., 1964-65; instr. Union County Coll., Cranford, N.J., 1965-66; chemist CIBA/GEIGY Corp., Summit, N.J., 1966-69; instr. Union County Regional, Berkeley Heights, N.J., 1971-73; group leader Am. Hoechst Corp., Somerville, N.J., 1974—. Contbr. articles to profl. jours. Patentee in field. Pres. Babe Ruth Baseball Athletic Congress, Scotch Plains, N.J., 1983-84. Served with USNG, 1958-66. Mem. Am. Chem. Soc. Roman Catholic. Current work: Photosensitive coatings, metal or composite substrates for graphic arts applications. Subspecialties: Organic chemistry; Photochemistry. Office: Am Hoechst Corp 50 Meister Ave Branchburg NJ 08876

WANDERER, PETER JOHN, JR., physicist; b. Monroe, La., Aug. 5, 1943; s. Peter John and Marjorie Ellen (Hoepfner) W.; m. Judith Anne Porter, Sept. 16, 1972; children—Maryellen, Michael, Jonathan. B.S., U. Notre Dame, 1965; Ph.D., Yale U., 1970. Postdoctoral researcher Cornell U., Ithaca, N.Y., 1970-73, U. Wis.-Madison, 1973-75; staff physicist Brookhaven Nat. Lab., Upton, N.Y., 1975—. Contbr. articles to Encyclopedia International. Mem. Am. Phys. Soc. Current work: Construction of superconducting magnets for particle accelerators, neutrino interactions. Subspecialties: Magnetic physics; Particle physics. Home: 20 Harvard Rd Shoreham NY 11786 Office: Brookhaven Nat Lab Bldg 902B Upton NY 11973

WANG, ANDREW CHI MO, electrical engineer; b. Nanking, China, July 11, 1937; came to U.S., 1960; naturalized, 1972; s. Tao Yuan and Chun Chih (Wei) W.; m. Janet Chueh, Aug. 25, 1962; children—Justin, Patrick, Karen. B.S.E.E., Taiwan U., Taipei, 1958; M.S.E.E., U. Calif.-Berkeley, 1962; Ph.D., Stanford U., 1970. From design to staff engr. IBM, San Jose, Calif., 1962-72; vis. assoc. prof. Taiwan U., 1970-71; mgr. to dir. component tech. Amdahl Corp., Sunnyvale, Calif., 1972-85; co-founder, chmn. Saratoga Semiconductor Corp., Cupertino, Calif., 1985—. Founder, bd. dirs. Penninsula Refuge Relief Fund, San Francisco, 1979. Mem. IEEE, Chinese Inst. Engrs. Current work: High performance logic gate arrays and memories for high speed mainframes. Subspecialty: Microelectronics. Office: Saratoga Semiconductor Corp 10500 Ridgeview Ct Cupertino CA 95014

WANG, CARL CHANG-TAO, engineering company executive, consultant; b. Hankow, Hubei, China, Dec. 2, 1935; came to U.S., 1955; s. Joseph Teh-Fong and Mona Ming-Yun (Chen) W.; m. Linda Yun-Hsieu, July 23, 1962; children—Paul, Andrew, David. B.S. in Elec. Engring., U. Ill., 1958, M.S. in Elec. Engring., 1959, Ph.D. in Elec. Engring., 1964; postgrad. Columbia U. Coll. Physicians and Surgeons, 1967-69. Mem. research staff IBM Research, Yorktown Heights, N.Y., 1964-67; chief engr. Med. Inst. Labs, Fort Lee, N.J., 1967-69; sect. mgr. Micro-Bit Corp., Lexington, Mass., 1969-75; v.p. research and devel. Berkeley Bio-Engring., San Leandro, Calif., 1975-79; v.p. sci. and tech. Cooper Med. Device Corp., San Leandro, 1979-81; pres. Mid Labs, San Leandro, 1981—; cons. in field. Contbr. in field. Pres. Chinese Cultural Assn., Urbana, Ill., 1963-64; prin. Chinese Lang. Sch., Lexington, Mass., 1970-75; mem. Catholic Peace Group, Piedmont, Calif., 1984. NIH grantee, 1984. Mem. IEEE, Assn. for Advancement of Med. Instrumentation. Current work: Instrumentation for microsurgery; endo-surgical devices; percutaneous surgical devices; diagnostic and therapeutic instruments. Subspecialties: Bioinstrumentation; Biomedical engineering. Office: Med Instrument Device Labs 2458 Verna Ct San Leandro CA 94577

WANG, CHARLES P., aerospace scientist, educator; b. Shanghai, China, Apr. 25, 1937; s. Kuan Ying and Pinglu (Ming) W.; m. Lilly L. Lee, June 29, 1963. B.S., Taiwan U., 1959; M.S., Tshinghua U., 1961; Ph.D., Calif. Inst. Tech., 1967. Lectr. Taiwan U., Taipei, 1961-62; Inst. scholar Calif. Inst. Tech., Pasadena, 1963-67; mem. tech. staff Bellcomm, Washington, 1967-69; research engr. U. Calif., San Diego, 1969-74; adj. prof., 1979—; sr. scientist Aerospace Corp., Los Angeles, 1976—. Assoc. editor AIAA Jour., 1981-84; Contbr. articles to profl. jours. Assoc. fellow AIAA; fellow IEEE; mem. Am. Phys. Soc., Am. Optical Soc., Chinese Engrs. and Scientist Assn. So. Calif. (pres., chmn. bd.), Sigma Psi. Democrat. Club: Manhattan Beach (Calif.) Badminton. Current Work: Laser development and applications, gasdynamics, plasmadynamics, gas lasers, chemical laser, quantum electronics, excimer lasers, laser remote sensing, laser wavefront sensor. Subspecialties: Aeronautical engineering; Laser research. Home: 28509 Seamont Dr Palos Verdes CA 90274 Office: 2350 E El Segundo Blvd El Segundo CA 90045

WANG, CHEH CHENG, mechanical engineer; b. Chuan Chow, Fukien, China, Mar. 3, 1930; came to U.S., 1963, naturalized, 1976; s. Pi-Chen and Ling-Fung (Lee) W.; m. Esther Chun-Mei Chu, Aug. 12, 1967; children—Albert, Edward, Sophia. Diploma Engring., Nanking Inst. Tech., Peoples Republic of China, 1953; M.Sc., U. Calif.-Berkeley, 1965; Ph.D., U. Sheffield, Eng., 1976. Registered mech. engr., Wash. Lectr. Xian Inst. Aero. Engring., Peoples Republic of China, 1953-58; prin. designer V.K. Song & Co., Ltd., Hong Kong, 1959-62; asst. chief engr. Fulton Shipyard, Antioch, Calif., 1963-67; sr. mech. engr. Lockheed Shipbuilding, Seattle, 1967-68; chief mech. engr. Interactive Tech. Inc., Santa Clara, Calif., 1971-72; sr. staff engr. Central Engring. Labs., FMC Corp., Santa Clara, 1972—; cons. in field. Contbr. articles to profl. jours. Mem. ASME (sec. Ditto, Santa Clara Valley sect. 1980-81), Am. Acad. Mechs., Soc. Indsl. and Applied Maths., Nat. Soc. Profl. Engrs., Calif. Soc. Profl. Engrs. Republican. Current work: Gear dynamics, applied numerical methods; computer aided engineering in solid mechanics areas; modeling and simulation of mechanical systems. Subspecialties: Mechanical engineering; Computer-aided design. Home: 1479 San Marcos Dr San Jose CA 95132 Office: Central Engring Labs FMC Corp 1185 Coleman Ave Santa Clara CA 95052

WANG, CHIA PING, research physicist, educator; b. Philippines, Sept. 1; came to U.S., 1963, naturalized, 1972; s. Guan Can and Tah (Lin) W. B.Sc., U. London, 1950; M.Sc., U. Malaya, 1951; Ph.D. in Physics, Univs. of Malaya and Cambridge, 1953; D.Sc. in Physics, U. Singapore, 1972. Asst. lectr. U. Malaya, 1951-53; assoc. prof. Nankai U., Tientsin, 1954-56, prof. physics, 1956-58, head electron physics div., 1955-58, mem. steering com. nuclear physics div., 1958; head electron physics div. Lanchow Atomic Project, 1958; sr. lectr., prof. physics, acting head depts. physics and math. U. Hong Kong and Chinese U. of Hong Kong, 1958-63; research assoc. Lab. Nuclear Studies, Cornell U., Ithaca, N.Y., 1963-64; assoc. prof. space sci. and applied physics Cath. U. Am., 1964-66; assoc. prof. physics Case Inst. Tech. and Case-Western Res. U., Cleve., 1966-70; vis. scientist, vis. prof. U. Cambridge, U. Leuven (Belgium), U.S. Naval Research Lab., U. Md., and MIT, 1970-75; research physicist U.S. Army Natick (Mass.) Research and Devel. Labs., 1975—. Contbr. articles to sci. jours., chpts. in books. Recipient Outstanding Performance award Dept. of Army, 1980, Quality Increase award, 1980. Mem. Am. Phys. Soc., Inst. Physics London, AAAS (life), N.Y. Acad. Scis., Sigma Xi. First to convert picosecond time interval into pulse height, 1963; deduced from more than 50 expts. the many-subunit structure of the nucleon and other hadrons in 1968; deduced the 3-quark-meson-cloud nucleon substructure from high-energy electron (1970), neutrino (1971), and meson and proton (1972) collision experiments in 1970-72; formulated gen. integral survival fraction of bacteria during heat sterilization, 1978. Current Work: Particle interactions, radiation, heat transfer, laser interferometry, computers sci., director, planner, conductor research and development. Subspecialties: Particle physics; Thermal physics. Home: 28 Hallet Hill Rd Weston MA 02193 Office: US Army Natick Research and Development Laboratories Natick MA 01760

WANG, CHIA-LIN JEFFREY, chemist; b. Han-Kow, China, June 24, 1949; came to U.S., 1973; s. Tze-Ching and Ding-Shi (Liao) W.; m. Wen-Ying Sophia Lee, Dec. 15, 1973. B.S., Nat. Taiwan U., 1971; Ph.D., U. Pitts., 1977. Research assoc. U. Pitts., 1977, Harvard U., Cambridge, Mass., 1978-79; research chemist Du Pont Co., Wilmington, Del., 1979—. Contbr. chpt. to book. Patentee in field. Mem. Am. Chem. Soc. Current work: Synthesis of biologically interesting compounds. Subspecialties: Organic chemistry; Synthetic chemistry. Home: 115 Wynnwood Dr Wilmington DE 19810 Office: Du Pont Co Exptl Sta 353/345 Wilmington DE 19898

WANG, CHIH-CHUN, research scientist, consultant, educator; b. Peking, China, Oct. 9, 1932; came to U.S. 1958, naturalized 1970; s. Hsi-Whan and Hilda (Yang) W.; m. Betty Rei-Chi Tung, Mar. 29, 1969; children—Joyce S., Francis P., Bessie. B.S., Nat. Taiwan U., 1955; M.S., Kans. State U., 1959; Ph.D., Colo. State U., 1962. Postdoctoral assoc. U. Kans., Lawrence, 1963; mem. tech. staff RCA Labs, Princeton, N.J., 1963-66, research leader, 1966-73, fellow tech. staff. 1973—; cons. space materials program NASA, Washington, 1977-79; hon. prof. univ. devel. program for China, NSF, Washington, 1984—. Author: Characterization of Epitaxial Semiconductor Films, 1976. Editor: Heteroepitaxial Semiconductors for Electronic Devices, 1978. Contbr. articles to profl. jours. Patentee in field. Recipient numerous Outstanding Achievement awards RCA Labs. Mem. Am. Chem. Soc., Electrochem. Soc. (divisional editor jour. 1979—), Am. Physics Soc., Am. Vacuum Soc., ASTM, Sigma Xi, Sigma Pi Sigma, Phi Lambda Upsilon. Current work: Synthesis and characterization of electronic materials including semiconductors, phosphors, dielectrics, ferromagnetics, single crystal growth, chemical vapor depositions, photoconductive TV pick up devices, CRT materials and technology. Subspecialties: Solid state chemistry; Electronic materials. Home: 41 Maple Stream Rd East Windsor NJ 08520 Office: RCA Labs David Sarnoff Research Ctr Princeton NJ 08540

WANG, CHING-PING SHIH, physics educator; b. Shanghai, China, Feb. 16, 1947; came to U.S., 1969, naturalized, 1981; d. Bin and Han-Tsing (shih) Chang; m. Hung-Tai Wang, June 5, 1971; 1 child, Eric H. B.S., Tung-Hai U., Taichung, Taiwan, 1969; M.S., La. State U., 1971, Ph.D., 1974. Postdoctoral fellow La. State U., Baton Rouge, 1974-76, Northwestern U., Evanston, Ill., 1976-79; asst. prof. physics U. Md., College Park, 1979—. Contbr. articles to profl. jours. Recipient Alan Berman research publ. awards Naval Research Lab., 1984; grantee Office Naval Research, 1979-85, NSF, 1984-85. Mem. Am. Phys. Soc. Democrat. Improvements and applications of the density functional theory; magnetic, structural and superconducting properties of solid; semi-conductors; heavy fermions; quantum hall effects; surface and interfaces. Subspecialties: Condensed matter physics; Magnetic physics. Home: 5531 Charles St Bethesda MD 20814 Office: Dept Physics & Astronomy Univ Md College Park MD 20742

WANG, CHING-TSO, chemist; b. Hsilou, Taiwan, Oct. 22, 1931; came to U.S., 1960; s. Zuei-Chang and Kun (Lin) W. B.S., Cheng Kung U., Republic of China, 1957; M.S., Baylor U., 1964; Ph.D., Rutgers U., 1983. Tech. assoc. Taiwan Indsl. Research Inst., Taipei, 1950-53; chem. engr. Taiwan Fertilizer Co., Hsinchu, 1959-60; research asst. Inst. Molecular Evolution, Coral Gables, Fla., 1965-68; organic chemist Schwarz BioResearch, Inc., Orangeburg, N.Y., 1968-70; scientist Hoffmann-La Roche Inc., Nutley, N.J., 1970—. Contbr. articles to profl. jours. Served to 2d lt. Republic of China, 1957-59. Baylor U. research fellow, 1963. Mem. Am. Chem. Soc., Sigma Xi. Current work: Chem. synthesis of biologically active peptides and study of its structure-activity relationship; glyoxalase I-active site amino acid residues and activation and inhibition studies. Subspecialties: Synthetic chemistry; Enzyme technology. Office: Hoffmann La Roche Inc 340 Kingsland St Nutley NJ 07110

WANG, CHI-SUN, biochemist; b. Shanghai, China, Oct. 8, 1942; came to U.S., 1968, naturalized, 1977; s. Po-Jong and Yu-Fu (Yang) W.; m. Nancy Tao, Oct. 27, 1973; 1 child, Christy Pei-Ling. B.S., Nat. Taiwan U., 1966; Ph.D., U. Okla., 1971. Staff scientist Okla. Med. Research Found., Oklahoma City, 1974-75, asst. mem., 1975-82, assoc. mem., 1982—; assoc. prof. dept. biochemistry and molecular biology U. Okla. Sch. Medicine, Oklahoma City, 1985—. Contbr. articles to profl. jours. Mem. Am. Chem. Soc., AAAS, Am. Heart Assn., Am. Soc. Biol. Chemists, Am. Oil Chemists Soc. Current work: Lipoprotein metabolism. Subspecialties: Biochemistry (biology); Kinetics. Home: 11813

Oldwick Circle Oklahoma City OK 73132 Office: Oklahoma Med Research Found 825 NE 13th St Oklahoma City OK 73104

WANG, DALTON TA TUNG, biochemist, educator, consultant; b. Peking, China, Nov. 11, 1925; came to U.S., 1961, naturalized, 1974; m. Olia Ai. B.A., Fu-jen U., Peking, 1947; B.S.A., U. Sask., 1952, M.Sc., 1954; Ph.D., McGill U., 1957. Research assoc. U. Man., Winnipeg, Can., 1957-60; postdoctoral fellow U. Wis., Madison, 1961-63; sr. biochemist Boyce Thompson Research Inst., Yonkers, N.Y., 1963-70; research assoc. Purdue U., West Lafayette, Ind., 1971-73; asst. prof. Rockefeller U., N.Y.C., 1973-79; assoc. prof. biochemistry SUNY Downstate Med. Ctr., Bklyn., 1979—; adj. prof. Nankai U., Tienjing, People's Republic China, 1982—; cons. Shenyang Research Inst. Chem. Industry, Shenyang, People's Republic China, 1984—. Mem. Am. Chem. Soc., Am. Soc. for Biol. Chemists N.Y. Acad. Scis., Am. Soc. for Microbiology, Sigma Xi. Subspecialties: Biochemistry (biology); Enzyme technology. Home: 412-25 N Broadway Yonkers NY 10701 Office: SUNY Downstate Med Ctr 450 Clarkson Ave Brooklyn NY 11203

WANG, HOWARD HAO, biophysicist, educator; b. Shanghai, China, Jan. 24, 1942; came to U.S., 1957 naturalized, 1963; s. Charles Y.C. and Lola Wang; m. Judith A. Wang, Aug. 17, 1963; children—Maureen S., Kevin L. B.S., Calif. Inst. Tech., 1963; Ph.D., UCLA, 1968. Chemist Lawrence Radiation Lab., Berkeley, Calif., 1968-69; neuroscientist MIT, Cambridge, 1969-70; prof. biophysics U. Calif.-Santa Cruz, 1970—. Mem. Biophys. Soc., Soc. for Neurosci., Am. Assn. Anatomists. Current work: Molecular pharmacology of synaptic receptors, neurobiology of information storage and retrieval. Subspecialties: Membrane biology; Neurobiology. Office: Dept Biology U Calif Natural Scis II Bldg Santa Cruz CA 95064

WANG, JAMES CHENG-KOUNG, material scientist, researcher; b. Shanghai, China, Feb. 25, 1946; came to U.S., 1968, naturalized, 1983; B.S. in Mech. Engring., Nat. Taiwan U. 1967; M.S. in Materials Sci., SUNY-Stony Brook, 1971, Ph.D. in Materials Sci., 1978. Guest research assoc. Brookhaven Nat. Lab., Upton, N.Y., 1972-74; heat transfer engr. Pullman-Kellogg, Hackensack, N.J., 1974-79; research metallurgist SCM Corp., Cleve., 1979-84; mgr. Union Carbide Corp., Greenville, S.C., 1984—. Patentee. Recipient Tech. Excellence award. Mem. Am. Soc. Metals (founder Electronics Material Cleve. chpt. 1984), Am. Powder Metallurgy Inst. (officer 1983-84), Am. Ceramic Soc. Current work: Powder metallurgy, electrochemical processes, electronics materials, dielectric thin films, product reliability. Subspecialties: Metallurgy; Electronic materials. Office: Union Carbide Corp PO Box 5928 Greenville SC 29606

WANG, JERRY HSUEH-CHING, medical biochemistry educator, scientist; b. Nanking, China, Feb. 12, 1937; came to Can., 1965; s. Ta Chung and Hsueh Ping (Lee) W.; m. Teresa Hsing Lew; children—Melissa Yi, Emily Yi. B.S., Nat. Taiwan U., Taipei, 1958; Ph.D., Iowa State U., 1965. Research asst. Iowa State U., Ames, 1963-65; postdoctoral fellow div. bioscis. Nat. Research Council, Ottawa, Can., 1965-66; asst. prof. dept. biochemistry U. Man. Winnipeg, Can., 1966-71, assoc. prof., 1971-78, prof., 1978-82; prof. med. biochemistry Alta. Heritage Found for Med. Research; med. scientist dept. med. biochemistry U. Calgary, Alta., Can., 1982—, chmn. cell regulation group, 1983—; vis. prof. U. Calif.-Davis, 1973-74; cons. NIH, Bethesda, Md., 1979-80; lectr. numerous univs. world-wide. Mem. editorial bd. Jour. Archives Biochemistry and biophysics, 1980—, Cell Calcium Jour., 1981—, Jour. Biol. Chemistry, 1982—; mem. adv. bd. Biochem. Jour., 1985—. Contbr. articles to profl. jours. Recipient John Zubek Meml. award U. Man. 1973, Disting. Alumnus award Iowa State U., 1978, Research Inst.Med. Research award U. Man., 1979, Gairdner Internat. award, 1981, Alta. Heritage Found. Med. Research Med. Scientist award, 1982; scholar Proctor and Gamble, 1962-63; fellow U.S. State Dept., 1961-62, Nat. Research Council, 1965-66; grantee Fulbright Found., 1961, Med. Research Council Can., 1967-86, Nat. Cancer Inst. Can., 1967, 68; Alta. Heritage Found., 1982-87, Muscular Dystrophy Assn. Can., 1967-82, Can. Diabetic Assn., 1979-80, Alta. Cancer Bd., 1983-85; others. Mem. Am. Soc. Biol. Chemists, Can. Biochem. Soc., Chinese Biochem. Soc., Royal Soc. Can. Current work: Protein - protein interaction, allosteric interaction, and covalent modification in enzyme-regulation. Cellular regulator system involving phosphotyrosyl proteins, structure-function relationships in regulatory enzymes, biochemical mechanisms of Ca2+ and cyclic nucleotides relationships in regulatory. Subspecialty: Biochemistry (medicine). Office: Dept Med Biochemistry U Calgary 3330 Hospital Dr NW U Calgary Calgary AB T2N 4N1 Canada

WANG, LEON RU-LIANG, civil engineering educator, researcher; b. Canton, China, June 15, 1932; came to U.S., 1959, naturalized, 1966; s. Huai-Kao and Yuan-Chin (Ho) W.; m. Joyce C. C. Tien, July 22, 1961; children—Frank, Mark, Cindy. B.S., Cheng-Kung U., Tainan, Republic of China, 1957; M.S., U. Ill., 1961; D.Sc., MIT, 1965. Registered profl. engr., N.Y., Okla. Asst. prof. civil engring. Rensselaer Poly. Inst., Troy, N.Y., 1965-69, assoc. prof., 1969-80; prof. U. Okla., Norman, 1980-84; prof., chmn. dept. civil engring. Old Dominion U., Norfolk, Va., 1984—; ptnr. Wang & Assocs., Norfolk, 1980—. Editor Proc. of Wind Engineering, 1981; Proc. of Joint U.S.-Taiwan-Seminar of Multiple Hazard Research, 1984. Fellow ASCE; mem. Am. Soc. Engring. Edn., Am. Concrete Inst., Earthquake Engring. Research Inst. Current work: Structural engineering, earthquake engineering, lifeline earthquake engineering, civil engineering. Subspecialties: Structural engineering; Solid mechanics. Office: Old Dominion Univ Hampton Blvd Norfolk VA 23508

WANG, NAI-YI, chemist, researcher; b. Gwei-Lin, China, June 27, 1940; came to U.S., 1967; s. Shih-Ying and Man-Yu (Ma) W.; m. Sandra Hsiao Ma, Aug. 19, 1969; children—Linda, Andrew. B.S., Taiwan Normal U., 1964; M.S., Nat. Taiwan U., 1966; Ph.D., SUNY-Buffalo, 1972. Sr. chemist USV Pharm. Corp., Tuckahoe, N.Y., 1975-77; vis. assoc. prof. Nat. Taiwan U., Taipei, 1977-79; research investigator Squibb Inst. for Med. Research, Princeton, N.J., 1981-83; research chemist Abbott Labs., North Chicago, Ill., 1983—. Author publs., patentee in field. USPHS research fellow, 1976. Mem. Am. Chem. Soc. Current work: Organic synthesis of biologically active substances and therapeutic drug monitoring. Subspecialty: Organic chemistry. Home: 305 E Walker Pl Mundelein IL 60060 Office: Abbott Labs Routes 137 and 43 North Chicago IL 60064

WANG, NANCY, cytogeneticist, researcher; b. Anwei, China, Sept. 2, 1944; came to U.S., 1966; d. Ho-I and Wen-Yen (Chiou) Tang; m. Tingchung Wang, Mar. 29, 1967; children—Jessie, Melissa. B.S., Nat. Taiwan U., 1966; M.S., U. Minn., 1968, Ph.D., 1978. Diplomate Am. Bd. Med. Genetics. Jr. scientist dept. animal scis. U. Minn.-St. Paul, 1969-73; asst. scientist in neurosurgery U. Minn., Mpls., 1974-77, instr. lab. medicine and pathology, 1978-79, asst. prof., 1980-82, dir. Tumor Cytogenetics Lab., 1980-82; asst. prof. pathology Tulane U. Med. Sch., New Orleans, 1982-83, assoc. prof., 1983—, dir. Oncocytogenetics Lab., 1982—. Mem. Am. Assn. Cancer Research, Am. Soc. Human Genetics. Current work: Chromosomal evolution during tumor progression and mutastasis. Subspecialties: Cancer research (medicine); Genetics and genetic engineering (medicine). Home: 2661 Hyman Pl New Orleans LA 70114 Office: Human Genetics Program Tulane U Med Sch 1430 Tulane Ave New Orleans LA 70112

WANG, PAO-KUAN, meteorology educator; b. Tainan, Taiwan, Dec. 1, 1949; came to U.S., 1973; s. Shou and Luan-Chao (Chiu) W.; m. Li-Bi C. Wang, Aug. 28, 1976; children: Lawrence Chang-Yung, Victor Chang-Mien. B.S., Nat. Taiwan U., 1971; M.S., UCLA, 1975, Ph.D., 1978. Research atmospheric physicist UCLA, 1978-80, adj. asst. prof., 1980; asst. prof. meteorology U. Wis., Madison, 1980-84, assoc. prof., 1984—. Contbr. articles to profl. jours. EPA grantee, 1982; NSF grantee, 1982. Fellow Royal Meteorol. Soc. (Eng.); mem. Am. Meteorol. Soc., Am. Geophys. Union, AAAS. Current work: Microphysics of clouds and precipitation, cloud dynamics, aerosol physics, atmospheric chemistry, particle technology, atmospheric electricity, historical climatology and climatic change. Subspecialties: Meteorology; Atmospheric chemistry. Office: Dept Meteorology U Wis 1225 W Dayton St Madison WI 53706

WANG, PATRICK SHEN-PEI, computer specialist; b. Shanghai, China, Dec. 27, 1946; came to U.S., 1972; s. Yung-hsi and Su-jen (Lo) W.; m. Yuan-fang Tung, July 30, 1972; children: Da-yuan, Da-wen. B.S.E.E., Nat. Chiao Tung U., 1968; M.S.E.E., Nat. Taiwan U., 1971; M.S.I.C.S., Ga. Inst. Tech., 1974; Ph.D., Oreg. State U., 1978. Asst. prof. U. Oreg, Eugene, 1976-80; sr. mem. tech. staff GTE Labs., Waltham, Mass., 1980-82; adj. assoc. prof. Boston U., 1982—; software engring. specialist Wang Labs., Lowell, Mass., 1982—; prof. Northwestern U., 1983. Editor: Artificial Intelligence, 1983. NSF grantee, 1979, 80, 81; Steward grantee, 1979; Chung Shan scholar award, 1971. Sr. mem. IEEE Computer Soc.; Mem. Assn. for Computing Machinery, Pattern Recognition Soc., Chinese Computer Soc. Patentee in field. Subspecialties: Software engineering; Graphics, image processing, and pattern recognition. Home: 7 Ledgelawn Ave Lexington MA 02173 Office: Wang Labs Lowell MA 01851

WANG, PAUL KENG-CHIEH, electrical engineer, educator; b. Nanking, China, July 23, 1934; came to U.S., 1949, naturalized, 1973; B.E.E. with honors, Calif. Inst. Tech., 1955, M.E.E., 1956; Ph.D., U. Calif.-Berkeley, 1960. Research staff IBM Research Lab., San Jose, Calif., 1959-64; asst. prof. U. So. Calif., Los Angeles, 1964-67; prof. elec. engring. UCLA, 1967—; cons. Jet Propulsion Lab., Pasadena, Calif., 1981—. Contbr. articles to profl. jours. Mem. IEEE (sr.; best paper award 1964), AIEE (best paper award 1963), Am. Math. Soc., Am. Phys. Soc., Soc. for Indsl. and Applied Math. Current work: Control of distributed-parameter systems with applications to control of plasmas and large space structures; nonlinear system theory; robotics. Subspecialties: Systems engineering; Robotics. Office: Dept Elec Engring U Calif Los Angeles CA 90024

WANG, PONG-SHENG, computer scientist; b. Taipei, Taiwan, Sept. 13, 1950; s. Man-po and Chin-Fan (Yin) W.; m. Ai-chu Yeh, Feb. 20, 1950; children: Annie An-Li, Charles Li-cheng. B.S., Nat. Taiwan U., Taipei, 1972; M.S., Ind. U., Bloomington, 1976; Ph. D., Ohio State U., Columbus, 1980. Assoc. instr. Ind. U., Bloomington, 1974-76; programmer/analyst Shoe Corp. Am., Columbus, Ohio, 1976-77; grad. research assoc. Ohio State U., Columbus, 1976-80; prin. research scientist Honeywell, Mpls., 1980-83; staff programmer IBM, San Jose, Calif., 1983-84, adv. programmer, 1984—. Mem. IEEE, Assn. Computing Machinery. Current Work: Storage Management systems. Subspecialties: Distributed systems and networks; Computer architecture. Home: 741 Mairwood Ct San Jose CA 95120 Office: 555 Bailey Ave D28-D20 San Jose CA 95150

WANG, RICHARD HSU-SHIEN, chemist; b. Anqing, Anhui, China, Jan. 2, 1932; came to U.S., 1959; s. Chung and Ging-Wen (Hsia) W.; m. Josephine Sun, Aug. 11, 1962; children—Joseph, Christine, Dorothy. B.S., Nat. Taiwan U., Taipei, 1956; M.S., U. Ill., 1961; Ph.D., U. Kans., 1968. Research asst., Nat. Taiwan U., 1958-59; research asst. Natural History Survey of Ill., Urbana, 1961-63; research chemist Tenn. Eastman Co., Kingsport, 1968-74, sr. research chemist, 1975—. Contbr. articles to profl. jours. Patentee in field. Mem. Am. Chem. Soc., Phi Lambda Upsilon. Current work: Stabilization of polymer against light and oxidation; organic synthesis; lignin chemistry; free radical reactions. Subspecialties: Organic chemistry; Polymer chemistry. Home: 1414 Fairidge Dr Kingsport TN 37664 Office: Tenn Eastman Co Lincoln St Kingsport TN 37662

WANG, RONG, materials scientist; b. Szechwan, China, Aug. 3, 1939; came to U.S., 1963, naturalized, 1967; s. Sun Hsu and Min Lang (Wang) W.; m. Dora Fan, Apr. 12, 1941; 1 son, Wilson. B.S. in Chem. Engring, Cheng Kung U., Tainan, Taiwan, 1961; M.S. in Chem. Engring, U. Tex., 1964, Ph.D. in Materials, 1967. Research fellow MIT, Cambridge, 1967-68; asst. prof. materials and chem. engring. U. So. Calif., Los Angeles, 1968-73; sr. research scientist Battelle Meml. Inst. Pacific N.W. Lab, Richland, Wash., 1973-85; project mgr. advanced materials div. Flow Industries, Seattle, 1985—; cons. in field. Contbr. over 60 tech. articles to profl. publs. Mem. Am. Crystallographic Assn., Am. Soc. Engring. Edn., Am. Ceramic Soc., Materials Research Soc., Electrochem. Soc., Nat. Assn. Corrosion Engrs. Current Work: Glassy stainless steel coatings; alloy phase stability; non-equilibrium phases; electrochemical and photoelectrochemical properties of materials, corrosion and corrosion prevention techniques. Subspecialties: Metallurgy; Corrosion. Home: 2453 Catalina St Richland WA 99352 Office: Flow Industries 21414 68th Ave South Kent WA 98032

WANG, RU TSANG, physicist, researcher; b. Changhua, Taiwan, Sept. 13, 1928; came to U.S. 1959; naturalized 1975; s. Lun-Kuei and Pan (Lang) W.; m. Nancy Pi-Shan Yuan, Mar. 12, 1955; children—James J., Theodore. B.S. in Physics, Taiwan U., 1950; Ph.D. in Physics, Renesslaer Poly. Inst., 1968. Research asst. Renesslaer Poly. Inst., Troy, N.Y., 1968-70, Dudley Obs., Albany, N.Y., 1970-76, SUNY-Albany, 1977-80; assoc. research scientist U. Fla., Gainesville, 1981—, mgr., dir. Microwave Lab., 1982—. Mem. IEEE, Am. Assn. for Aerosol Research, Optical Soc. Am. Current work: Electromagnetic scattering, wave propagation, interaction of electromagnetic waves and matter. Office: Space Astronomy Lab U Fla 1810 NW 6th St Gainesville FL 32609

WANG, SHING CHUNG, electrical engineer; b. Hsinchu, Taiwan, Nov. 20, 1934; came to U.S., 1967, naturalized, 1978; s. Wan Jen and Yu (Chen) W.; m. Chu Mei Kuo, Jan. 21, 1958; children: Jean, Philip, Fanny, Charlie. B.S., Taiwan U., 1957; M.S., Tohoku U., 1965; Ph.D. (scholar), Stanford U., 1971. Assoc. prof. elec. engring. Chiao Tung U., Hsinchu, Taiwan, 1965-67; research assoc. Microwave Lab., Stanford U., 1971-74; sr. research scientist Xerox Corp., Pasadena, Calif., 1974-85; sr. staff scientist Lockheed Missiles & Space Co., Palo Alto, Calif., 1985—. Contbr. articles in field to profl. jours. Japanese Govt. scholar, 1963-65. Mem. So. Calif. Taiwanese Assn. (chmn. bd. 1979-80), Optical Soc. Am., IEEE, Quantum Electronics and Application Soc., Sigma Xi. Buddhist. Patentee in field. Current Work: Laser technology and optoelectronics; semiconductor lasers and integrated optics. Subspecialties: Semiconductor lasers; Optical signal processing. Office: 3251 Hanover St Palo Alto CA 94304

WANG, SHYH, electrical engineer, educator; b. Wusih, Jiangsu, China, June 15, 1925; s. Chung Chuan and Pao Chen (Wong) W.; m. Dila Ben, Nov. 23, 1962. B.S., Chiao-tung U., Shanghai, China, 1945; M.A., Harvard U., 1949, Ph.D., 1951. Research fellow Harvard U., 1951-53; sr. engr., engring. specialist Sylvania Electric Products, GTE, 1953-58; assoc. prof. elec. engring. and computer scis. U. Calif., Berkeley, 1958-64, prof., 1964—; cons. in field. Author: Solid State Electronics, 1965; contbr. articles to profl. jours. Guggenheim Found. fellow, 1964-65; hon. prof. Jilin U., Changchun, China, 1985. Fellow IEEE, Optical Soc. Am.; mem. Am. Phys. Soc. Patentee in field. Current Work: Research in integrated and guided-wave optics, semiconductor lasers, electrical and optical properties of III-V Compound semiconductors, microelectronic devices of III-V Compounds; development of semiconductor lasers and integrated optic devices for optical signal processing. Subspecialties: Optical signal processing; Semiconductors. Home: 8636 Thors Bay Rd El Cerrito CA 94530 Office: U Calif 571 Cory Hall Berkeley CA 94720

WANG, TAITZER, biochemist, educator; b. Pingtung, Taiwan, Feb. 2, 1939; s. Jen-huey and Juey-hua (Su) W.; m. Judy Chang; children—Frances, Martha, Iris. B.S., Nat. Taiwan U., 1961; Ph.D., Rice U., 1967. Assoc. prof. pharmacology and cell biophysics U. Cin. Med. Coll., 1977—. NIH grantee, 1983—. Mem. AAAS, Am. Chem. Soc., Am. Soc. Biol. Chemists, Am. Heart Assn., Biophys. Soc., N.Y. Acad. Scis. Current work: Biomedical research in cation transport. Subspecialties: Biochemistry (medicine); Neurochemistry. Home: 450 Flemridge Ct Cincinnati OH 45231 Office: Dept Pharmacology and Cell Biophysics U Cin Coll Medicine 231 Bethesda St Cincinnati OH 45267

WANG, TEEN-MEEI THOMAS, dental educator; b. Shia-Man, Fu-Chieng, China, Sept. 10, 1945; s. Jit-Liang and Yu-Ying (Lin) W.; m. Chun-Meei Su, Jan. 29, 1975; children: Yie-Shuan, Yie-Ding. B. Dental Surgery, Nat. Def. Med. Center, Taipei, Taiwan, 1969; Ph.D., U. Utah, 1974. Teaching asst. Nat. Def. Med. Center, Taipei, 1969-72, asso. prof., 1974-79, prof., 1973-80; teaching asst. U. Utah, Salt Lake City, 1972-74; vis. research prof. Office of Continuing Edn., Baylor U. Med. Center, Dallas, 1980-81; prof. dept. dentistry, dean Sch. Dentistry China Med. Coll., Taichung, Taiwan, 1980—; cons. dept. dentistry Tri-Service Gen. Hosp., Taipei. Author: Basic Neuroanatomy, 1976, Clinical Neuroanatomy and Neurophysiology, 1979; editor-in-chief: Oral Sci. Bimonthly, 1981; adv. editor: Chinese Dental Jour, 1982—, China Dental Mag, 1982—. Served to lt. col. Chinese Army, 1963-79. Recipient Excellent Tchr. award Nat. Def. Med. Center, Taipei, 1976; Nat. Sci. Council Republic of China scholar, 1972-74; China Med. Coll. fellow, 1980; R. Jackson Found. fellow, 1981. Fellow Internat. Coll. Dentists; mem. Internat. Assn. Dental Research, Taipei Dental Assn. Republic of China, Dental Assn. Republic of China (trustee and editor-in-chief 1977-81), Chinese Med. Assn. Club: Fgn. Affairs (Taipei). Current Work: Cell Kinetics and Morphometrics studies of the effects of mitogenic agents upon hard tissue and periodontal ligament following orthodontic tooth movement; pulp response to dental materials. Subspecialties: Dental growth and development; Anatomy and embryology. Home: 2/F 34 Alley 5 Lane 626 Ding-chow Rd Taipei 107 TaiwanOffice: School of Dentistry China Medical College 91 Sheh-Shih Rd Taichung 400 Taiwan

WANG, TSEN CHEN, chemical engineer, consultant, researcher; b. Taiwan, Apr. 26, 1943; came to U.S., 1967, naturalized, 1973; s. Ken Sun and Lain (Chou) W.; m. Huei Li Lee, Aug. 29, 1970; children—Clifford, Sean. B.S., Chun Yuan U., Taiwan, 1966; M.S., U. Iowa, 1969, Ph.D., 1972. Registered profl. engr. Fla. Research chemist Dunn Edward Co., Los Angeles, 1969; presdl. intern. Smithsonian Instn., Fort Pierce, Fla., 1972-73; chem. engr. Harbor Branch Found., Fort Pierce, 1973-79, chief chem. engr., 1979—; cons. City of Vero Beach, Fla., 1982—, Piper Aircraft Corp., Vero Beach, 1981—. Contbr. articles to profl. jours. Grantee City of Vero Beach, 1982—, Piper Aircraft 1981—, State of Fla., 1984—. Mem. Am. Inst. Chem. Engrs., Am. Chem. Soc., Am. Water Works Assn., AAAS. Current work: Life support and environmental control systems, water and wastewater treatment groundwater contaminations, environmental impact and monitoring. Pollution control. Subspecialties: Water supply and wastewater treatment; Environmental chemistry. Office: Harbor Branch Found Inc Rural Route 1 Box 196 Fort Pierce FL 33450

WANG, TSUEY TANG, research scientist; b. Tainan, Taiwan, Nov. 12, 1932; came to U.S., 1958, naturalized, 1971; s. Shih Neng and Tsun (Chen) W.; m. Margaret Mei-Tieh Lin, June 12, 1965; children: David, Marjorie, Vanessa. B.Sc., Cheng-Kung U., Tainan, 1955; M.Sc., Brown U., 1961, Ph.D., 1965. Research group leader Poly. Inst. N.Y., 1965-66, asst. prof. applied mechanics, 1966-67; mem. tech. staff AT&T Bell Labs., Murray Hill, N.J., 1967—; mem. Ph.D. thesis rev. com., dept. mechanics and materials Rutgers U., Piscataway, N.J., 1982-83. Contbr. numerous articles to profl. publs. Fellow Am. Phys. Soc.; mem. Am. Acad. Mechanics, N.Y. Acad. Scis., Am. Chem. Soc., Soc. Rheology. Patentee in field. Current Work: Piezoelectricity in polymers; relaxation and mechanical properties of polymers; structure-properties of polymer thin films. Subspecialties: Polymer physics; Theoretical and applied mechanics. Office: 600 Mountain Ave Murray Hill NJ 07974

WANG, WEI-CHYUNG, climatologist; b. Zhangjiakou, China, May 7, 1943; came to U.S., 1968, naturalized, 1977; s. Kuang-Fa and Wan-Zen (Huang) W.; m. Chao-Hsien Tien, June 19, 1971; children—Brian Ming-Yu, Emily Hungyu. B.S., Nat. Cheng Kung U., 1965; M.S., SUNY-Buffalo, 1970; D.Eng. Scis., Columbia U., 1973. NRC-Nat. Acad. Sci. research assoc. Goddard Inst. Space Studies/NASA, N.Y.C., 1973-75; assoc. sr. research scientist Sigma Data, Inc., N.Y.C., 1975-80; mgr. climate programs Atmospheric and Environ. Research Inc., Cambridge, Mass., 1980—. Contbr. articles to profl. jours. Mem. Am. Meteorol. Soc., Am. Geophys. Union. Current work: Development of climate models and analysis of climate data to investigate the potential climatic effects due to increase of atmospheric pollutants. Subspecialties: Climatology; Meteorology. Office: Atmospheric and Environ Research Inc 840 Memorial Dr Cambridge MA 02139

WANG, WEN I., physicist; b. Taipei, Taiwan, June 11, 1953; came to U.S., 1977; s. Chen S. and Dee F. (Hsu) W.; m. Jeannette C. Wang, June 16, 1981; children—David, Stanley. B.S., Nat. Taiwan U., 1975; M.E.E., Cornell U., 1979, Ph.D., 1981. Mem. research staff Rockwell Internat., Thousand Oaks, Calif., 1981-82, IBM, Yorktown Heights, N.Y., 1982—. Mem. Am. Phys. Soc., IEEE. Current work: Semiconductor physics, optical properties, lasers. Subspecialties: Semiconductors; Atomic and molecular physics. Office: Thomas J Watson Research Ctr IBM PO Box 218 Yorktown Heights NY 10598

WANGSNESS, PAUL JEROME, animal nutrition educator; b. Madison, Wis., Mar. 27, 1944; s. Leonard J. and Gladys E. Wangsness; m. Sally I. Martalock, May 27, 1967; children—Jonathan, Sarah. B.S. in Agr., U. Wis., 1966; Ph.D. in Nutrition, Iowa State U., 1971, Ph.D. in Physiology, 1971. Postdoctoral scholar Pa. State U., University Park, 1971-72, asst. prof. animal nutrition, 1972-75, assoc. prof., 1975-80, prof., 1980—, dept. head, 1980—; lectr., cons. various cos. and univs.; mem. rev. teams U.S. govt. and univs., Mass., Ohio, Va., 1981-83. Contbr. articles to profl. jours. Grantee, 1976-83. Named Outstanding Young Scientist, Am. Dairy and Animal Sci. Assn. Mem. Am. Soc. Animal Sci. (editorial bd. 1978-81), Am. Dairy Sci. Assn., Am. Inst. Nutrition, AAAS, Council Agrl. Sci. and Tech. Lutheran. Current work: Nutritional, genetic and endocrine factors affecting food intake and nutrient utilization. Subspecialties: Animal nutrition; Animal physiology. Home: 1046 Greenfield Circle State College PA 16801 Office: Dairy and Animal Sci Dept Pa State U 324 Henning Bldg University Park PA 16802

WANN, LEE SAMUEL, cardiologist, educator, echocardiographic researcher; b. Crawfordsville, Ind., July 28, 1946; s. Raymond Woodrow and Ora Lee (Riepie) W.; m. Mary Alice Fifer, June 8, 1968; children: Randie Leigh, Carrie Lynn. A.b., Ind. U.-Bloomington, 1968; M.D., Ind. U.-Indpls., 1971. Diplomate: Am. Bd. Internal Medicine. Intern Ind. U.-Indpsl., Hosps., 1971-72, resident, 1972-75, fellow in cardiology, 1975-77; asst. prof. medicine Ind. U.-Indpls., 1977-79; asst. prof. Med. Coll. Wis., 1979-81, assoc. prof., 1981—; research assoc. Krannert Inst. Cardiology, Indpls., 1977-79; dir. echocardiographic labs. Milw. County Med. Complex and Wood VA Med. Ctr., Milw., 1979—; mem. adv. com. Clin. Research Ctr., Milw., 1979-81. Contbr. chpts. to books. Am. Heart Assn. fellow, 1976; VA grantee, 1980; NIH grantee, 1981. Fellow Am. Coll. Cardiology, Council Clin. Cardiology of Am. Heart Assn.; mem. ACP, Am. Inst. Ultrasound in Medicine, Am. Fedn. Clin. Research, Am. Soc. Echocardiography (dir. 1982—). Current Work: Clinical research in field of echocardiograph, including digital image processing, development of ultrasonic contrast agents, and hemodynamic modeling. Subspecialties: Cardiology; Internal medicine. Home: 4751 N Cumberland Blvd Whitefish Bay WI 53211 Office: Cardiology Div Med Coll Wis 8700 W Wisconsin Ave Milwaukee WI 53226

WANNER, ADAM, physician, educator; b. Budapest, Hungary, Apr. 16, 1940; s. Heinrich and Helen (Simon) W.; m. Doris Baechli, May 31, 1966; children—Kathrin, Daniel. M.D., U. Basel, Switzerland, 1966. Diplomate Am. Bd. Internal Medicine. Asst., Turgauisch Schaffhausische Heilstaette, Tb sanatorium, Davos, Switzerland, 1966-67; intern Phila. Gen. Hosp.; resident in medicine Kantons-Spital Aarau, Switzerland, 1968-70; pulmonary fellow Mt. Sinai Med. Ctr., Miami Beach, Fla., 1970-72, assoc. div. pulmonary disease, 1972-75, co-chief, 1975-78, med. dir. respiratory therapy dept., 1975-79, dir. pulmonary function lab., 1975-78, chief div. pulmonary disease, 1978—; from asst. to prof. medicine U. Miami Sch. Medicine, Fla., 1974—, chief pulmonary div., 1983—; mem. study sect. NIH, 1984; mem. residency review com. Accreditation Council for Grad. Med. Edn., 1984; mem. merit rev. bd. for respiration VA Med. Research Service, 1984. Mem. editorial bd. Pulmonary Medicine, 1978-79, Current Revs. in Respiratory Therapy, 1980-82, Jour. Applied Physiology, 1980-84, Am. Rev. Respiratory Disease, 1980—, Respiration, 1984—, Pediatric Pulmonology. Grantee NIH, Fla. Lung Assn., Nat. Research Soc. Assn., Gen. Motors Corp., Electric Power Research Inst. Fellow ACP, Am. Coll. Chest Physicians; mem Am. Thoracic Soc., Am. Physiol. Soc., European Soc. Clin. Respiratory Physiology, Brit. Thoracic Soc., Fla. Thoracic Soc. (pres.). Current work: Pulmonary defense mechanisms, pulmonary circulation asthma. Subspecialties: Internal medicine; Pulmonary medicine. Home: 1660 S Treasure Dr Miami Beach FL 33141

WARCHOL, JOSEPH FREDERICK, organic chemist, researcher; b. Central Falls, R.I., Dec. 4, 1941; s. Frederick Anthony and Catherine (Plosaj) W.; m. Sandra Ann Rangatore, Aug. 12, 1967; children—Joseph Frederick, Michael Samuel. B.S. in Chemistry, Providence Coll., 1964; M.S. in Chemistry, Niagara U., 1966; Ph.D. in Chemistry, St. Johns U., 1970. Group leader Oakite Products, Berkley Heights, N.J., 1970-75, GAF Corp., Wayne, N.J., 1975-77; tech. dir. E.F. Houghton & Co., Valley Forge, Pa., 1977—. Patentee in field. Mem. Am. Chem. Soc., Roman Catholic. Current works: Synthesis and development of polymer and amphipathic systems for use in industrial applications including tribology and detergent systems. Subspecialties: Surface chemistry; Polymer chemistry. Home: 214 Horseshoe Rd Norristown PA 19403 Office: EF Houghton & Co Madison & Van Buren Ave Valley Forge PA 19482

WARD, ANGUS LORIN, wildlife research biologist; b. Willard, Utah, Oct. 26, 1923; s. Angus Parsons and Mona (Baird) W.; m. Jean Lowe, June 30, 1947; children—Gregory Lorin, Amy Lynn. B.S. in Wildlife Mgmt., Utah State U., 1950. Laborer, biologist U.S. Fish and Wildlife Service, Bear River Refuge, 1950-51, clk., biologist, Aransas Nat. Refuge, 1951-52, wildlife research biologist, Gainesville, Fla., 1952-54, Denver, 1954-66; wildlife research biologist U.S. Forest Service, Laramie, Wyo., 1966—. Served with USN, 1943-46. Mem. Wildlife Soc. Mormon. Current work: Big game wildlife research biology.

Subspecialties: Behaviorism; Ecology (biology). Office: Rocky Mountain Research Sta 222 S 22d St Laramie WY 82070

WARD, F(RASER) PRESCOTT, biotechnologist, wildlife ecologist; b. Lancaster, Pa., Aug. 22, 1940; s. Grant Weirbach and Esta Mae (McCaa) W.; m. Laurel Edith Syda, Sept. 29, 1984; children by previous marriage—Christopher Aaron, Carolyn Ann, Daniel Prescott. Student Pa. State U., 1958-61; V.M.D., U. Pa., 1965; Ph.D., Johns Hopkins U., 1979. Vet. practitioner Tredyffrin Vet. Hosp., Paoli, Pa., 1965-66; chief ecology br. U.S. Army, Aberdeen Proving Ground, Md., 1969-81, chief toxicology br., 1981-82, chief scientist, 1982-84, chief biotech. div., 1984—; project coordinator U.S./USSR Conv. on Protection of Nature, 1973—; research assoc. Sch. Hygiene and Pub. Health, Johns Hopkins U., Balt., 1979—. Contbr. articles to profl. publs. Served to capt. Vet. Corps, U.S. Army, 1966-69. Recipient William H. Walker award Chem. Research Ctr., 1982, U.S. Army Research and Devel. Achievement award, 1984. Mem. Am. Inst. Biol. Scientists, Raptor Research Found., Sigma Xi. Current work: Biotechnology in chemical defense; population ecology of peregrine falcons. Subspecialties: Biomaterials; Ecology (environmental science). Home: 137 E Broadway Bel Air MD 21014 Office: Chief Biotech Div Research Directorate Chem Research and Devel Ctr Aberdeen Proving Ground MD 21010

WARD, H. BLAIR, JR., manufacturing engineer; b. Cranston, R.I., Sept 7, 1935; s. H. Blair and Edwinna Mary (Wilson) W.; m. Marilyn Eileen Hughes, Feb. 15, 1974; children: Michelle, Kristi, Kelly. Tool engring. diploma (Imperial Oil scholar), Ryerson Poly. Inst., Toronto, Ont., Can., 1958. Registered profl. engr., Calif., Pa. Tool engr. Automatic Elec., Brockville, Ont., 1958-60; mfg. engr. Moog, East Aurora, N.Y., 1960-66; project engr. A. Smith, Erie, Pa., 1966-71; mfg. engr. Talon, Meadville, Pa., 1971-81; mgr. mfg. engring. Leech Tool & Die, Meadville, 1981—. Mem. Soc. Mfg. Engrs. (cert. mfg. engr.), Nat. Soc. Profl. Engrs., ASME, Soc. Automotive Engrs. Patentee zipper mfg.; developer high speed automatic molding processes, high speed automatic stamping and forming processes and equipment. Current Work: Developed manufacturing processes for consumer products in high-volume miniature sizes—in both polymers and metals. Subspecialties: Materials processing; Polymers (materials science). Home: 1 Box 291 Guys Mills PA 16327 Office: Leech Tool & Die RD 7 Meadville PA 16355

WARD, JOHN ROBERT, physician, rheumatologist, researcher; b. Salt Lake City, Nov. 23, 1923; s. John I. and Clara A. W.; m. Norma Harris, Nov. 5, 1948; children—John Harris, Pamela Ward Proctor, Robert Scott, James Alan. B.S., U. Utah, 1944, M.D., 1946; M.P.H., U. Calif.-Berkeley, 1967. Diplomate Am. Internal Medicine. Intern, Salt Lake County Gen. Hosp., Salt Lake City, 1947-48, resident, 1949-51; research fellow dept. physiology U. Utah, 1948-49; clin. and research fellow Mass. Gen. Hosp., Boston, 1955-57; practice medicine specializing in internal medicine, 1957-84; prof. dept. medicine U. Utah Coll. Medicine, Salt Lake City, 1957—, chief div. rheumatology, 1957—. Contbr. numerous articles to med. jours., chpts. to books. Recipient Modern Med. Monograph award, 1958; NIH grantee, 1976—, Nora Eccles Treadwell Found. grantee, 1980—; VaLois grantee, Egbert 1983—. Fellow ACP (gov. 1979); mem. Western Soc. Clin. Research, Western Assn. Physicians, Am. Rheumatism Assn. Roman Catholic. Current work: Clinical trials, experimental models of arthritis, immunogenetics. Subspecialties: Rheumatology; Internal medicine. Home: 1249 East 3770 South Salt Lake City UT 84106 Office: U Utah Med Ctr 50 N Medical Dr Salt Lake City UT 84132

WARD, JOHN WESLEY, pharmacologist; b. Martin, Tenn., Apr. 8, 1925; s. Charles Wesley and Sara Elizabeth (Little) W.; m. Martha Isabelle Hendley, Dec. 7, 1947; children: Henry Russell, Judith Carol, Charles Wesley, Richard Little. A.A., George Washington U., 1948, B.S., 1950, M.S., 1955; Ph.D., Georgetown U., 1959. Research asso. in pharmacology Hazleton Labs., Falls Church, Va., 1950-55, head dept. pharmacology, 1955-58, chief depts. biochemistry and pharmacology, 1958-59; with A. H. Robins Co., Richmond, Va., 1959—, dir. biol. research, 1978-80, dir. research, 1980—, v.p. research, 1982—; lectr. in pharmacology Med. Coll. Va., 1960-64, adj. assoc. prof. pharmacology, 1982—; guest lectr. Seminar on Good Lab. Practices, FDA, Washington, 1979, Chgo., 1979, San Francisco, 1979. Contbr. articles on pharmacology, toxicology and medicinal chemistry to profl. publs. Served with USMC, 1943; Served with USN, 1944-46; Served with U.S. Army, 1944. Mem. AAAS, N.Y. Acad. Sci., Va. Acad. Sci., Am. Chem. Soc., Soc. Toxicology (charter), Internat. Soc. Registered Toxicologists and Pharmacologists (charter), Am. Soc. Pharmacology and Exptl. Therapeutics, Internat. Soc. Toxicology and Pharmacology (charter), Pharm. Mfrs. Assn. (chmn. color additive toxicology com. 1978—), Am. Assn. for Accreditation Lab. Animal Care (chmn. bd. trustees 1976-80), Sigma Xi. Clubs: Willow Oaks (Richmond); Cosmos (Washington), Masons (Washington). Patentee in field. Current Work: Cardiovascular, central nervous system, gastrointestinal, inflammation, allergy; directs research and development in medicinal chemistry, pharmacology, molecular biology, drug metabolism, toxicology and pathology. Subspecialties: Pharmacology; Toxicology (medicine). Home: 10275 Cherokee Rd Richmond VA 23235 Office: 1211 Sherwood Ave Richmond VA 23220

WARD, JOHN WILLIAM, physical chemistry researcher; b. Moline, Ill., Oct. 16, 1929; s. William Ewald and Violet Xenia (Nordquist) W.; m. Nima Diane Copeland, June 4, 1954; children—William, David, Daniel, Michael. B.A., Augustana Coll., 1952; M.S., Washington U., St. Louis, 1956; Ph.D., U. N.Mex., 1966. Staff mem. Los Alamos Nat. Lab., 1956—. Contbr. chpts. to books, articles to profl. jours. Bd. dirs. Los Alamos Choral Soc., Los Alamos Concert Assn., N.Mex. Symphony. Recipient von Humboldt prize Alexander von Humboldt Stiftug, 1972; Lab. fellow, 1983. Fellow Am. Inst. Chemists (pres. 1975); mem. Am. Chem. Soc., Am. Vacuum Soc., Catgut Acoustical Soc. Lutheran. Current work: High temperature properties, solid-state and surface properties of actinide metals, alloys and compounds; properties of metal hydrides. Subspecialties: Surface chemistry; Solid state chemistry. Home: 25 Turquoise St Los Alamos NM 87544 Office: Los Alamos Nat Lab MST-13 MS E 511 Los Alamos NM 87545

WARD, LOUIS EMMERSON, retired physician; b. Mt. Vernon, Ill., Jan. 19, 1918; s. Henry Ben Pope and Aline (Emmerson) W.; m. Nan Talbot, June 5, 1942; children—Nancy, Louis, Robert, Mark; m. Marian Mansfield, 1979. A.B., U. Ill., 1939; M.D., Harvard, 1943; M.S. in Medicine, U. Minn., 1949. Intern Ill. Research and Ednl. Hosp., Chgo., 1943; fellow medicine Mayo Found., 1946-49; cons. medicine, rheumatology Mayo Clinic, 1950-83, chmn. bd. govs., 1964-75; dir. Bankers Life, Des Moines. Contbr. articles to profl. jours. Vice chmn. bd. trustees Mayo Found., 1964-76; past bd. dirs. Fund for Republic; bd. dirs. Center for Study Democratic Instns.; past bd. dirs. Arthritis Found.; mem. Nat. Council Health Planning and Devel., 1976-83. Recipient U. Ill. Alumni Achievement award, 1968; recipient disting. alumnus award Mayo Found., 1983. Mem. Inst. Medicine (Nat. Acad. Scis.), AMA, Am. Rheumatism Assn. (pres. 1969-70), Nat. Soc. Clin. Rheumatologists (pres. 1967-69), Central Soc. Clin. Research, Minn., Zumbro Valley med. socs., So. Minn. Med. Assn., Phi Beta Kappa, Sigma Xi, Alpha Omega Alpha, Phi Delta Theta. Current Work: Clinical investigation in rheumatic diseases. Subspecialties: Internal medicine; Rheumatology. Home: 30 Raeburn Ct Port Ludlow WA 98365

WARD, OSCAR G., JR., cytogeneticist, researcher; b. Denver, Feb. 16, 1932; s. Oscar G. and Elizabeth M. W.; m. Lea E. Ramirez, July 16, 1955; children: Oscar G., Anne E. B.S., U. Ariz., Tucson, 1958, M.S., 1960; Ph.D., Purdue U., 1966. Instr. biol. scis. Purdue U., 1960-64, David Ross research fellow, 1964-66; asst. prof. biology U. Ariz., Tucson, 1966-74, lectr., 1974-77, assoc. prof. dept. ecology and evolutionary biology, 1977—, chmn. com. on genetics, 1984—; sr. internat. fellow PHS Universidad Nacional Autonoma de Mexico, 1980. Served with USMC, 1951-54. NSF grantee, 1976-77; Fogarty Internat. Center and NIH sr. internat. fellow grantee to Mex., 1980. Mem. AAAS, Am. Soc. Human Genetics, Genetics Soc. Am., Am. Genetics Assn., Am. Soc. Mammalogists, Sigma Xi, Tau Beta Pi. Current Work: Plant and animal cytogenetics, emphasis on mammalian systems; Karyotype evolution in rodents and canids. Subspecialties: Genome organization; Evolutionary biology. Office: Dept Ecology/Evolutionary Biology Univ Ariz Tucson AZ 85721

WARD, PATRICK E., pharmacologist; b. Warren, Ohio, Mar. 2, 1947; s. Donal L. and Virginia (Kania) W.; divorced (div.); 1 son, Christopher M. B.A., Kent State U., 1969; M.S., Miami U., Oxford, Ohio, 1971; Ph.D., Cambridge (Eng.) U., 1974. NIH postdoctoral fellow dept. pharmacology U. Tex. Health Sci. Center, Dallas, 1974-77, asst. prof., 1977-80; assoc. prof. dept. pharmacology N.Y. Med. Coll., Valhalla, 1980—, dir. grad. program pharmacology, 1980—; established investigator Am. Heart Assn., 1978-83. Contbr. articles to profl. jours. Mem. Am. Soc. Pharmacology and Exptl. Therapeutics, Am. Heart Assn. (council for high blood pressure research). Current Work: Metabolism of vasoactive peptides and their relationship to blood pressure regulation and hypertension. Subspecialties: Cellular pharmacology; Molecular pharmacology. Office: Dept Pharmacology New York Med Coll Valhalla NY 10595

WARD, PETER ALLAN, pathologist, educator; b. Winsted, Conn., Nov. 1, 1934; s. Parker J. and Mary Alice (McEvoy) W. B.S., U. Mich., Ann Arbor, 1958, M.D., 1960. Diplomate: Am. Bd. Anat. Pathology. Intern Bellevue Hosp., 1960-61; resident U. Mich. Hosp., Ann Arbor, 1961-63; chief immunobiology br. Armed Forces Inst. Patholgy, Washington, 1967-71; prof. dept. pathology, chmn. dept. U. Conn. Health Center, Farmington, 1971-80; prof., chmn. dept. pathology U. Mich., Ann Arbor, 1980—; interim dean U. Mich. (Med. Sch.), 1982-85; cons. VA Hosp., 1980-84; mem. research rev. com. Nat. Heart, Lund, Blood Inst., NIH, Bethesda, Md., 1978-84; bd. dirs. Univ. Associated for Research and Edn. in Pathology, Inc., 1978—; chmn., bd. mem. sci. adv. bd. Armed Forces Inst. Pathology, Washington, 1981-83; mem. patholgy A study sect. NIH, Bethesda, Md., 1972-76, chmn., 1976-78. Served to capt., M.C. U.S. Army, 1965-67. Recipient Borden Research award U. Mich. Med. Sch., Ann Arbor, 1980; recipient Research and Devel. award U.S. Army, 1969, Meritorious Civilian Service award Dept. Army, 1970, Park-Davis award Am. Soc. Exptl. Pathology, 1971. Mem. Am. Assn. Pathologists (pres. 1978-79), Am. Soc. Clin. Investigation, Am. Assn. Immunologists, Assn. Pathology Chmn., Mich. Soc. Pathologists. Current Work: Basic clinical biomedical research. Subspecialty: Pathology (medicine). Home: 2815 Washenaw Ave Ann Arbor MI 48104 Office: Med Sci I 1315 Catherine Rd M5240 Ann Arbor MI 48109

WARD, ROBERT C., numerical analyst, researcher; b. Sparta, Tenn., Dec. 7, 1944; s. James C. and Mary E. (Pharris) W.; m. C. Gayle Gillen, Sept. 3, 1965; children—Kimberly M., Jonathan R. B.S., Tenn. Tech. U., 1966; M.S., Coll. of William and Mary, 1969; Ph.D., U. Va., 1974. Aerospace technologist NASA Langley Research Ctr., Hampton, Va., 1966-74; mathematician Union Carbide Corp., Oak Ridge, 1974-82; mgr. Oak Ridge Nat. Lab., 1982—. Contbr. articles to profl. jours. Mem. Soc. for Indsl. and Applied Math. (program com. 1984—), Assn. for Computing Machinery, AAAS, Sigma Xi. Current work: Manager of research in applied mathematics, statistics, and computer science; researcher in numerical linear algebra and parallel computation. Subspecialties: Numerical analysis (mathematics); Mathematical software. Office: Oak Ridge Nat Lab PO Box Y Bldg 9207-A Oak Ridge TN 37831

WARD, ROBERT CARL, engineering educator, researcher; b. Swansea, Great Britain, July 4, 1944; came to U.S., 1946; s. Leon Otho and Marjorie Irene (Batchelar) W.; m. Brenda Elsa Linden, Aug. 27, 1966; children—Stephanie, Justin, Ryan. B.S., Miss. State U., 1966; M.S., N.C. State U., 1968, Ph.D., 1970. Asst. prof. Colo. State U., Ft. Collins, 1970-75, assoc. prof., 1975-80; prof., 1980—, acting dept. head, 1982-83; vis. researcher Danish Water Quality Inst., Horsholm, Denmark, 1976; cons. N.Z. Govt., Hamilton, 1983-84, Resource Cons. Inc., Ft. Collins, 1981-83. Author: Water Quality Monitoring, 1983. Contbr. articles to profl. jours. Recipient Durrell Disting. Service award Colo. State U., 1974. Mem. Am. Soc. Agrl. Engrs. (Countryside Engr. award 1976), Water Pollution Control Fed., Nat. Water Well Assn., Am. Geophys. Union, Am. Water Resources Assn. Democrat. Episcopalian. Current work: Research, teaching and consulting in water quality management and hydrology, particularly with respect to the design of water quality monitoring systems. Subspecialties: Environmental engineering; Resource management. Office: Agrl and Chem Engr Dept Colo State U Fort Collins CO 80523

WARD, THOMAS EDMUND, physicist; b. Los Angeles, Nov. 10, 1944; s. Eugene and Cleo Madeline (Carpenter) W.; m. Marsha Mae Waren, Oct. 21, 1967 (div. 1974); 1 child, Marnie Lianne. B.S. in Chemistry and Edn., N.E. State Coll., Okla., 1965; M.S. in Nuclear Chemistry, U. Ark., 1969, Ph.D. in Nuclear Chemistry, 1970. Research asst. U. Ark., Fayetteville, 1965-70; postdoctoral researcher Brookhaven Nat. Lab., Upton, N.Y., 1970-72, assoc. physicist, 1985—; vis. assoc. chemist, 1972-75; staff scientist Ind. U. Cyclotron Facility, Bloomington, 1972-85; vis. faculty mem. chemistry dept., 1980-85, editor Cyclotion Facility newsletter, 1978-85. Contbr. articles to profl. jours. Fellow Am. Inst. Chemists; mem. Am. Chem. Soc., Am. Phys. Soc., N.Y. Acad. Scis., Sigma Xi. Democrat. Current work: Nuclear science in basic research and applied research in medicine, materials science, environment and space sciences. Subspecialties: Nuclear chemistry; Nuclear physics. Home: 210 S Country Rd Bellport NY 11713 Office: Dept Nuclear Energy Brookhaven Nat Lab Upton NY 11973

WARD, WALTER F(REDERICK), physiology educator; b. Darlington, Wis., June 23, 1940; s. Harry Hovey and Hazel Gladys (Hansen) W.; m. Patricia Ann Hauser, Dec. 1958; children—Elizabeth Ann, Daniel Harry, Diane Lynn. B.Sc., U. Wis.-Platteville, 1964; Ph.D., Marquette U., 1970. USPHS postdoctoral fellow Brown U., Providence, 1970-73; research asst. prof. Pa. State U.-Hershey, 1973-78; asst. prof. physiology U. Tex. Health Scis. Ctr., San Antonio, 1978-82, assoc. prof., 1982—. NIH grantee, 1981-84, 83-87. Mem. Am. Physiol. Soc., Am. Diabetes Assn., Gerontol. Soc. Am., AAAS. Democrat. Lutheran. Current work: Insulin internalization and degradation; protein metabolism in aging. Subspecialties: Physiology (medicine); Endocrinology. Home: 5910 Forest Rim San Antonio TX 78240 Office: U Tex Health Sci Ctr 7703 Floyd Curl Dr San Antonio TX 78284

WARDELL, JOE RUSSELL, JR., pharmacologist, researcher, pharmacist; b. Omaha, Nov. 11, 1929; s. Joe Russell and Marie H. (Waugh) W.; children—Michael R., Susan E., John D.; m. Doris Erway, Aug. 27, 1983. B.S. in Pharmacy, Creighton U., 1951; M.S., U. Nebr., 1959, Ph.D. in Physiology and Pharmacology, 1962. Registered pharmacist, Nebr., Iowa. Retail pharmacist Omaha, 1953-56; grad. asst. U. Nebr., 1956-59, instr., 1959-62; with Smith, Kline and French Labs., Phila., 1962—, dir. new compound evaluation and licensing, 1981—. Contbr. articles to profl. jours. Patentee in field. Mem. Washington Square Civic Assn., Phila., 1984—; asst. scout master Boy Scouts Am., 1968-74. Served with U.S. Army, 1951-53. Mem. AAAS, N.Y. Acad. Scis., Am. Acad. Allergy, Am. Soc. Pharmacology and Exptl. Therapeutics. Current work: Respiratory; bronchodilators; cardiovascular; dopamine; pharmaceutical licensing. Subspecialties: Pharmacology; Pharmacological research and administration. Office: Smith Kline and French Labs 1500 Spring Garden St Philadelphia PA 19101

WARDER, RICHARD CURREY, JR., mechanical and aeronautical engineering educator; researcher; b. Nitro, W.Va., Sept. 30, 1936; s. Richard Currey and Edith Irene (Moser) W.; m. Carolyn Stickler, Mar. 7, 1964 (div. 1978); children—Jennifer, Jeffrey; m. Marjorie Dianne Forney, Jan. 10, 1980. B.S., S.D. Sch. Mines, 1958; M.S., Northwestern U., 1959, Ph.D., 1963. Asst. prof. mech. engring. Northwestern U., Evanston, Ill., 1963-65; sr. staff engr., mgr. energy processes research Litton Industries, Beverly Hills, Calif., 1965-68; program mgr., head resources research NSF, Washington, 1974-76; assoc. prof., prof. dept. mech. and aero. engring. U. Mo., Columbia, 1968—; reviewer govt. and tech. publs. Bd. dirs. Columbia Montessori Soc., 1971-73; pres. Columbia Soccer Club, 1976-80; referee adminstr. Central Mo. div. U.S. Soccer Fedn., 1979—. Fellow AIAA (assoc.); mem. AAAS, ASME, Am. Phys. Soc., Am. Soc. Engring. Edn. Republican. Methodist. Current work: Theoretical and experimental research in aerosol mechanics. Subspecialties: Mechanical engineering; Fluid mechanics. Home: 516 Stalcup St Columbia MO 65203 Office: Dept Mech and Aero Engring U Mo Columbia MO 65211

WARD-MCLEMORE, ETHEL, geophysicist; b. Sylvarena, Miss., Jan. 22, 1908; d. William Robert and Frances Virginia (Douglas) W.; m. Robert Henry McLemore, June 30, 1935; 1 child, Mary Frances McLemore Guyton. B.A., Miss. Woman's Coll., 1928; M.A., U. N.C., 1929; postgrad. U. Chgo., 1931, Colo. Sch. of Mines, 1941, So. Meth. U., 1962. Teaching fellow U. N.C., 1928-29; head math. dept. Scooba Jr. Coll., Miss., 1929-30; instr. math. and chemistry Miss. State Coll. for Women, 1930-33; research mathematician Humble Oil & Refinery Co., Houston, 1933-37; research geophysicist United Geophys. Co., Pasadena, Calif., 1941-46; cons. geophysics, Dallas, 1946—; dir. Geol. Info. Library of Dallas. Contbr. articles to profl. jours. Mem. Am. Math. Soc., Math. Assn. Am., Am. Chem. Soc., Soc. Indsl. and Applied Math., Am. Geophys. Union, Soc. Exploration Geophysicists, Seismol. Soc. Am., Inst. Math. Statistics, Tex. Acad. Sci. (bd. dirs. 1982—). Current work: Seismic velocity probability studies, Huygens principle and reflection coefficients; Eulerian equations of energy and fluid dynamics. Subspecialties: Statistics; Geophysics. Home and Office: 11625 Wander Ln Dallas TX 75230

WARFIELD, JOHN NELSON, electrical engineering educator, management researcher; b. Sullivan, Mo., Nov. 21, 1925; s. John D. and Flora A. (L) W.; m. Rosamond Arline Howe, Feb. 2, 1948; children: Daniel, Nancy, Thomas. A.B., U. Mo.-Columbia, 1948, B.S.E.E., 1948, M.S.E.E., 1949; Ph.D., Purdue U., 1952. Mem. Faculty U. Mo.-Columbia, 1948, Pa State U., University Park, 1949-55, U. Ill.-Urbana, 1955-57, Purdue U., Lafayette, Ind., 1957-58, U. Kans., Lawrence, 1958-65; dir. research Wilcox Electric Co., Kansas City, Mo., 1965-66; sr. research leader Battelle Meml. Inst., Columbus, Ohio, 1966-74; prof. U. Va., Charlottesville, 1975-83, Forsyth prof. elec. engring., 1975-83; dir. Center Interactive Mgmt., 1981-83; sr. mgr. Burroughs Corp., 1983-84; Univ. prof., dir. Inst. Info. Tech., George Mason U., Fairfax, Va., 1984—; cons. consensus methodologies, orgn. design, long-range planning. Author 4 books, numerous articles. Founding editor Systems Research, 1983—. Served in U.S. Army, 1944-46. RCA fellow NRC, 1951-52; recipient Western Electric Fund award Midwest sect. Am. Soc. Engring. Edn., 1966. Fellow IEEE (cert. for outstanding service 1973, Centennial medal 1984); mem. Soc. Gen. Systems Research (pres. 1982-83), Acad. Polit. Sci., Am. Mgmt. Assns., World Future Soc. Patentee (2). Current Work: Research on interactive management, including developing and testing consensus methodologies, and creating productive environments for holding meetings. Subspecialties: Systems engineering; Foundations of computer science. Home: 4308 Wakefield Dr Annandale VA 22003 Office: George Mason U 219 Thompson Hall Fairfax VA 22030

WARGA, JACK, mathematics educator, researcher; b. Warsaw, Poland, Dec. 5, 1922; came to U.S., 1943; s. Herman and Czarna (Lichtenstein) W.; m. Faye Kleinman, Feb. 27, 1949; children—Charna Ruth Warga Schakow, Arthur David. B.A. in Physics, Carleton Coll., 1944; Ph.D. in Math., NYU, 1950. Chief engring. computing sect. Republic Aviation Corp., Farmingdale, N.Y., 1952-53; head math. dept. Burroughs Corp., Pasadena, Calif., 1954-56; Weizmann Meml. fellow Weizmann Inst. Sci., Rehovot, Israel, 1956-57; mgr. math. dept. Avco R&D, Wilmington, Mass., 1957-66; prof. math. Northeastern U., Boston, 1966—. Author: Optimal Control of Differential and Functional Equations, 1972; also research articles. Served with U.S. Army, 1944-56, ETO. Fellow AAAS; mem. Am. Math. Soc., Soc. Indsl. and Applied Math. Current work: Optimal control, optimization and nonsmooth analysis Subspecialties: Analysis; Applied mathematics. Home: 233 Clark Rd Brookline MA 02146 Office: Northeastern U 360 Huntington Ave Boston MA 02115

WARLTIER, DAVID CHARLES, physician, pharmacologist, educator; b. Hartford, Conn., Mar. 28, 1947; s. Benjamin Charles and Arline (Brown) W.; children—Candice, Charles, Kristin, Karin. B.S., Carroll Coll., 1969; Ph.D., Med. Coll. Wis., 1976, M.D., 1982. Asst. prof. pharmacology Med. Coll. Wis., Milw., 1978-82, assoc. prof., 1982—. Contbr. articles to profl. jours. Bd. dirs. Milw. Kickers Soccer Club, 1978—. NIH grantee, 1978—. Am. Heart Assn. grantee, 1982—. Mem. Am. Heart Assn., N.Y. Acad. Scis., Am. Physiol. Soc., AMA, Am. Soc. Pharmacology and Exptl. Therapeutics. Current work: Basic research in pathophysiology and pharmacology of the coronary circulation and myocardial ischemia. Subspecialties: Pharmacology; Cardiology. Office: Dept Pharmacology Med Coll Wis 8701 W Watertown Plank Rd Milwaukee WI 53226

WARNAT, WINIFRED IRENE, educational researcher, social psychologist; b. Grosse Pointe, Mich., Feb. 8, 1943; d. Rudolf P. W. and Frieda (Lupp) W.; m. Henry Godfrey Scharles, Nov. 29, 1968 (div. 1976). B.A., Fla. Atlantic U., 1965, M.Ed., 1967; Ph.D., Am. U., 1971. Spl. edn. tchr. Deerfield Beach (Fla.) Jr. High Sch.; vocat. rehab. counselor, Ft. Lauderdale, Fla.; dir. placement Gallaudet Coll., Washington, 1963-68; asst. dean advanced studies and research Grad. Sch. Arts and Scis., clin. prof. dept. pediatrics and child health Coll. Medicine, prof./chair dept. curriculum and instrn. Sch. Edn., Howard U., Washington, 1969-77; research p Am. U., Washington, 1977-81, dir. Adult Learning Potential Inst., 1977-81; dir. Nat. Center Teaching and Learning, Eastern Mich. U., Ypsilanti, 1981—; lectr., speaker. Contbr. chpts. to books, articles to profl. jours. Mem. Montgomery County Commn. for Women, Md., 1974-76. Grantee Charles Stewart Mott Found., 1981-83; Grantee U.S. Office Edn., 1975-77, 77-80, 75-76, 74-76; others. Mem. Am. Ednl. Research Assn., Am.Psychol. Assn., Robotics Internat./Soc. Mfg. Engrs., N.Am. Soc. Corp. Planners. Current Work: High technology and changing character of works. Robotics education and human factors; training and employment of youth displaced workers, women, minorities, and older workers; gender and technology; adult learning and development. Subspecialties: Robotics; Learning. Office: Eastern Mich U 111 King Hall Ypsilanti MI 48197

WARNER, RAY ALLEN, physicist, researcher; b. Davis, Calif., May 5, 1938; s. William Lorenzo and Fern Edna (Squires) W.; m. Judith Rita Sauve, July 30, 1965. B.S. in Engring. Physics, U. Calif.-Berkeley, 1961; Ph.D., in Physics, U. Calif.-Davis, 1969. Research asst. U. Calif.-Davis, 1964-69; research assoc. Mich. State U., East Lansing, 1969-72, asst. prof. physics and chemistry, 1972-77; sr. research scientist Battelle Northwest, Richland, Wash., 1977—. Contbr. articles in field to profl. jours. Served to 2d lt. U.S. Army, 1961-62. Mem. Am. Phys. Soc., AAAS, Sigma Xi, Tau Beta Pi. Current work: Experimental research in nuclear fission and in the spectroscopy of short-lived radio nuclides; development of analytical instrumentation for the detection of trace quantities of toxic elements. Subspecialties: Nuclear physics; Analytical chemistry. Home: Route 1 Box 1234A Benton City WA 99320 Office: Pacific Northwest Lab Battelle Blvd Richland WA 99352

WARRELL, RAYMOND PAUL, physician, educator; b. Ardmore, Pa., Sept. 2, 1949; s. Raymond Paul and Katherine Elizabeth (Donnelly) W.; m. Loretta Marie Itri, Aug. 12, 1981. B.S. in Chemistry, Emory U., 1971; M.D., Med. Coll. Ga., 1975. Diplomate Am. Bd. Internal Medicine. Intern Maimonides Med. Ctr., Bklyn., 1975-76; resident in medicine SUNY-Stony Brook, 1976-78; fellow in med. oncology Meml. Sloan-Kettering Cancer Ctr., N.Y.C., 1978-80, attending physician, 1980—; asst. prof. Cornell U. Med. Coll., N.Y.C., 1980—. Contbr. articles to profl. jours. Patentee gallium compounds for calcium disorders. Bd. dirs. Connaught Tower Corp., N.Y.C., 1982—. Jr. faculty fellow Am. Cancer Soc., 1982-85. Mem. Am. Fedn. Clin. Research, Am. Soc. Clin. Oncology, Am. Assn. Cancer Research. Current work: New drug evaluation in hematologic cancer; inhibition of bone resorption from metastasis; coagulation and metastasis. Subspecialties: Cancer research (medicine); Chemotherapy. Office: Meml Sloan-Kettering Cancer Ctr 1275 York Ave New York NY 10021

WARREN, HOLLAND DOUGLAS, research physicist; b. Wilkes County, N.C., July 31, 1932; s. Henry Harrison and Nannie (Shaver) W.; m. Nancy Wall, May 21, 1955; children: Douglas Alan, Jill Jeneen, Karen Kay. B.S. in Math, Wake Forest U., 1959; M.S. in Physics, U. Va., 1961, Ph.D. in Physics, 1963. Research assoc. U. Va., summers 1960-62; devel. physicist Celanese Corp., Charlotte, N.C., 1963-64; sr. physicist Babcock & Wilcox Co., Lynchburg, Va., 1964-69, research specialist, 1969—. Contbr. numerous articles to profl. jours. Served with USN, 1951-55. Mem. Am. Phys. Soc., Am. Nuclear Soc., Phi Beta Kappa, Sigma Mu Epsilon. Republican. Baptist. Patentee in field. Current Work: Theoretical and experimental development of self-powered instrumentation for application inside the cores of nuclear power plants (incore instrumentation). Subspecialties: Nuclear engineering; Nuclear physics. Office: Babcock & Wilcox Co PO Box 11165 Lynchburg VA 24506

WARREN, KENNETH S., physician; b. N.Y.C., June 11, 1929; m. Sylvia Marjorie Rothwell, Feb. 14, 1959; children: Christopher Harwood, Erica Marjorie. A.B., Harvard U., 1951, M.D., 1955. Intern, Harvard service Boston City Hosp., 1955-56; research asso. Lab. Tropical Diseases, NIH, Bethesda, Md., 1956-62; asst. prof. medicine Case Western Res. U., 1963-68, assoc. prof., 1968-75, prof., 1975-77, prof. library sci., 1974-77; dir. health scis. Rockefeller Found., N.Y.C., 1977—; cons. WHO; mem. Inst. Medicine, Nat. Acad. Scis. Author: Schistosomiasis: The Evolution of a Medical Literature. Selected Abstracts and Citations, 1852-1972, 1973, Geographic Medicine for the Practitioner, 1978, Scientific Information Systems and the Principle of Selectivity, 1980, Coping with the Biomedical Literature, 1981, Immunology of Parasitic Diseases, 1983, Tropical and Geographical Medicine, 1984; contbr. numerous articles to profl. jours. Recipient Career Devel. award NIH, 1966-71. Fellow ACP; mem. Am. Soc. Clin. Investigation, Assn. Am. Physicians, Am. Assn. Immunologists, Am. Assn. Study Liver Diseases, Am. Soc. Tropical Medicine and Hygiene (Bailey K. Ashford award 1974), Infectious Diseases Soc. Am. (Squibb award 1975), Royal Soc. Tropical Medicine and Hygiene. Patentee diagnostic methods, drugs. Subspecialties: Immunology (medicine); Tropical medicine. Office: 1133 Ave of Americas New York NY 10036

WARSHAW, RHODA, psychologist; b. N.Y.C., Nov. 17, 1930; d. Irving and Celia (Edlin) Adelstein; m. Seymour Warshaw, 1950 (div. 1972); children: Lynne, Sheryl, Michael. B.A., Hunter Coll., 1951; M.S., Queens Coll., 1971; Ph.D., Fordham U., 1978. Tchr. Long Beach (N.Y.) Pub. Schs., 1956-61 62-71; sch. psychologist Yonkers (N.Y.) Pub. Sch., 1971-72, Smithtown (N.Y.) Pub. Schs., 1974—; psychotherapist Commack (N.Y.) Cons. Ctr., 1979-85. Mem. Nassau County Psychol. Assn., Am. Psychol. Assn., N.Y. State United Tchrs., Nat. Assn. Sch. Psychologists. Current Work: Counseling, also diagnosis, and remediation of learning disorders. Subspecialties: Developmental psychology; Learning. Home: 22 Linden St Great Neck NY 11021 Office: 22 Linden St Great Neck NY 11021 Also: Smithtown Pub Schs Smithtown NY 11787

WARTH, JAMES ARTHUR, hematologist, educator; b. N.Y.C., Apr. 30, 1942; s. Peter and Anne (Furgang) W.; m. Maria Archer Russell, May 3, 1969; children—David, Andrew. B.S., Tufts U., 1963, M.D., 1967. Diplomate Am. Bd. Internal Medicine, Am. Bd. Hematology. Intern Albany Med. Ctr. Hosp., N.Y., 1967-68; resident Tufts U.-Boston City Hosp., 1971-72; USPHS fellow in hematology Tufts U., Boston, 1973-74; NIH spl. fellow in hematology Tufts New England Med. Ctr., Boston, 1974-76, instr. medicine, 1974-77; asst. physician, hematologist Harvard U., Cambridge, Mass., 1976-77; asst. prof. medicine Wayne State U., Detroit, 1977-84, dept. medicine-hematology Tufts-New England Med. Ctr. Hosp., Boston, 1984—; advisor, mem. com. NIH, Bethesda, Md., 1980-83, cons., 1980-82. Contbr. articles to profl. jours. Served to maj. U.S. Army, 1969-71. Recipient Traineeship award USPHS-NIH, 1973-74. Fellow ACP; mem. Am. Fed. Clin. Research, Am. Soc. Hematology. Current work: Research on erthrocyte physiology including sickle cell anemia, calmodulin, density ultracentrifugation, intraerythrocyte PH, zinc deficiency, oxidant induced damage; physiology of dark adaptation. Subspecialties: Hematology; Physiology (medicine). Office: Hematology Div Box 826 New England Med Ctr Hosp 171 Harrison Ave Boston MA 02111

WARTIK, THOMAS, college dean; b. Cin., Oct. 1, 1921; s. Abraham and Lena (Monnes) W.; m. Louise Dreifus, Apr. 8, 1952; children: Nancy, Steven Philip. A.B., U. Cin., 1943; Ph.D., U. Chgo., 1949. Chemist, Manhattan project U. Chgo., 1944-46; faculty Pa. State U., University Park, 1950—, prof. chemistry, 1960—, chmn. dept., 1960-71; dean Pa. State U. (Coll. Sci.), 1971—; Vis. scientist U. Calif. Radiation Labs., 1957, 59, 61; cons. in field. Mem. adv. bd. Petroleum Research Fund, Am. Chem. Soc., 1968-71; mem. Fulbright Scholar Selection Com. in Chemistry, 1966-72, chmn., 1969-72; mem. N.Y. State Doctoral Evaluation Com., 1974; chmn. chemistry vis. com. Tex. A. and M. U., 1979—; mem. council Am. Colls. Selection Com. Nat. Sci. Bd., 1983. Contbr. profl. articles to jours.; Editor: Borax to Boranes, 1961. Fellow AAAS; mem. Am. Chem. Soc. (councillor 1967-69), Phi Beta Kappa, Sigma Xi. Club: Lake Glendale Sailing (dir.). Subspecialty: Inorganic chemistry. Home: 333 S Allen St Apt 602 State College PA 16801 Office: 211 Whitmore Lab University Park PA 16802

WARWICK, PETER DELAWET, sedimentary geologist, educator; b. Clinton, N.C., Sept. 21, 1955; s. Lawet Osbie and Mary Danzle (Bass) W. B.S., N.C. State U., 1977, M.S., 1982; Ph.D., U. Ky., 1985. Tchr., Wake County Schs., Raleigh, N.C., 1978-80; geologist U.S. Geol. Survey, Denver, summers 1981, 83, 84; instr. geology U. Ky., Lexington, 1982-85; research assoc. Nat. Research Council-U.S. Geol. Survey, 1985—. Contbr. articles to sci. jours. Recipient Pirtle award U. Ky., 1983; Geol. Survey-Wyo. grantee, 1984. Mem. Geol. Soc. Am. (Rocky Mountain Coal scholar 1984), Am. Soc. Petroleum Geologists (Pres.'s award for best paper 1985). Clubs: Grad. Assocs. (pres. 1982-83, rep. 1983-84) (U. Ky.). Current work: Development of depositional models for coal and coal-bearing rocks. Subspecialties: Sedimentology; Petrology. Office: US Geol Survey 956 National Ctr Reston VA 22092

WARZECHA, LADISLAUS WILLIAM, electrical aerospace equipment manufacturing corporation executive; b. Cuero, Tex., Jan. 23, 1929; s. Vincent William and Suzie (Dreymala) W.; m. Elinor Ryan, Oct. 9, 1954; children: Janet, Carol, Gary. B.S., U. Tex., 1948. With Gen. Electric Co., since 1948—, mgr. systems engring., Phila., 1956-62, gen. mgr. NASA Houston programs, 1962-73, ground systems dept., 1973-77, space systems ops., 1977-79, gen. mgr. re-entry systems, Phila., 1980-83, v.p. def. systems, 1984—. Contbr. articles to profl. jours. Bd. dirs. United Way, 1975-77. Mem. AIAA, IEEE, Am. Astronautical Soc., Am. Mgmt. Assn. Roman Catholic. Clubs: Waynesborough Country, Pelican Bay Golf and Country. Subspecialties: Systems engineering; Electrical engineering. Home: 1056 Beaumont Rd Berwyn PA 19312 Office: Gen Electric Co Valley Forge Space Center Philadelphia PA 19101

WASHBURN, JOHN GARRETT, medical and dental equipment consulting designer, dental researcher; b. Los Angeles, June 3, 1924; s. John Garrett and Rachel Gwendolyn (Struble) W.; m. Lavina S. Roloson, 1945 (div. 1954). Student, Pasadena (Calif.) City Coll., 1941-42, Coll. St. Thomas, St. Paul, 1942-43, U. So. Calif., 1943-45, UCLA, 1949-51. Pvt. practice med. and dental equipment consulting designer, Alhambra, Calif., 1969-82; project engr. Unitek Corp., Monrovia, Calif., 1968-69; cons. The Birtcher Corp., El Monte, Calif., 1971—. Founder, chmn. Commn. for the Reestablishment of Mountain Lion Hunting in Calif., 1977-82. Served with USNR, 1942-45. Mem. Internat. Assn. Dental Research, Am. Assn. Dental Research. Current Work: Design electromedical equipment (cardiology, intensive care, electro-surgery); design dental equipment, instruments and materials; dental materials research. Subspecialties: Biomedical engineering; Dental materials. Home: 207 S Cordova St Alhambra CA 91801

WASHINGTON, LINDA PHAIRE, cell biologist, educator; b. N.Y.C., Aug. 11, 1948; d. Charles Oliver and Grace Matilda (Bryan) Phaire; m. Joey Lee Washington; children—Kamau, Imani. B.S., Boston U., 1970; Ph.D., CCNY, 1975; postgrad. Rockefeller U., 1977, Cath. U., 1983. Asst. prof. Hunter Coll., N.Y.C., 1976-77, Howard U., Washington, 1977-79; assoc. prof. Tuskegee Inst., Ala., 1979-81, prof. immunology, 1981—, biomed. research cons., 1982-83, dir. various programs including, Natural Sci. Research & Devel., Carver Research Found., 1981—, Cell Culture Sci. Ctr., 1981—, cons. NIH, 1983—; panel mem. program NSF, 1983-84. Contbr. articles to profl. jours. Dancer Tuskegee City Dance Theatre, 1981-84. Recipient Disting. Scholar award United Negro Coll. Fund, 1984-85, Outstanding Sci. award Atlanta Minority Women in Sci., 1984, Outstanding Faculty award Tuskegee Inst., 1981, Murray J. Steele Award N.Y. Heart Assn., 1975. Mem. Am. Soc. Cell Biologists, N.Y. Acad. Sci., Am. Soc. Microbiology, Fedn. for Am. Soc. Exptl. Biologists, Sigma Xi. Mem. Christian Ch. Current work: Use of monoclonal antibody biotechnology to study the structure and function of cytoskeleton of macrophages and to develop reagents useful in control of malaria. Subspecialties: Cell and tissue culture; Immunobiology and immunology. Office: Tuskegee Inst Carver Research Found Tuskegee Institute AL 36088

WASHINGTON, WARREN MORTON, meteorologist; b. Portland, Oreg., Aug. 28, 1936; s. Edwin and Dorothy Grace (Morton) W.; m. LaRae Herring, July 30, 1959 (div. Aug. 1975); children: Teri, Kim, Marc, Tracy; m. Joan Ann, July 3, 1978. B.S. in Physics, Ore. State U., 1958, M.S. in Meteorology, 1960; Ph.D. in Meteorology, Pa. State U., 1964. Sr. scientist Nat. Center Atmospheric Research, Boulder, Colo.; affiliate prof. meteorology oceanography U. Mich. at Ann Arbor, 1968-71; mem. Nat. Adv. Com. for Oceans and Atmospheres, 1978-84. Contbr. articles to meteorol. jours. Mem. Boulder Human Relations Commn., 1969-71; mem. Gov.'s Sci. Adv. Com., 1975-78. Fellow Am. Meteorol. Soc., AAAS; mem. Am. Geog. Union. Current Work: Computer modeling of earth's climate. Home: 1480 Landis Ct Boulder CO 80303 Office: PO Box 3000 Boulder CO 80307

WASHOM, BYRON JOHN, energy research and development executive; b. Bethesda, Md., Mar. 24, 1949; s. Paul S. and Doris I. (Lee) W. B.S., U. So. Calif., 1971, M.B.A., 1972; postgrad., MIT, 1976. Coordinator Sea Grant Program, U. So. Calif., 1972-75, sr. research assoc., 1975-77; mgr. tech. and policy Fairchild-Stratos, Manhattan Beach, Calif., 1977-80; pres. Advance Corp., El Segundo, Calif., 1980—; cons. UN, 1980-81, U.S. Congress, 1976-77, MIT, 1976-78, Fairchild Industries, 1976-77; testified before Congress, 1977-83; mem. solar research and devel. panel Energy Research Adv. Bd., Washington. Mem. Renewable Energy Inst. (dir.), Solar Energy Industry Assn., Marine Tech. Soc., Soc. Naval Architects and Marine Engrs. (assoc.), Tech. Mktg. Soc. Am. Presbyterian. Current Work: Parabolic dish Stirling solar electric systems sponsored by Dept. of Energy; established record conversion efficiencies of sunlight to electricity of 29%, 1982. Subspecialties: Solar energy; Systems engineering. Home: 3616 Manhattan Ave Manhattan Beach CA 90266 Office: Advanco Corp 999 N Sepulveda Blvd Suite 314 El Segundo CA 90245

WASLENCHUK, DENNIS GRANT, geochemical oceanographer, environmental chemist, geotechnical engineer; b. Calgary, Alta., Can., Aug. 18, 1951; s. Nick and Minnie Ellen (Gardner) W.; m. Lorraine Rose Letourneau, Aug. 26, 1972. B.Sc., U. B.C., 1973; M.Sc., U. Ottawa, 1975; Ph.D., Ga. Inst. Tech., 1977. Research asst. Skidaway Inst. Oceanography, Savannah, Ga., 1975-77; lectr., research asst. Ga. Inst. Tech., Atlanta, 1975-76; asst. prof. U. Conn., Groton, 1977-84; dir., chief scientist Aquademia, cons. oceanography, geohydrology and hazardous wastes, New London, Conn., 1979-85; sr. environ. geologist Haley & Aldrich, Inc., cons. geotech. engrs., geologists, and hydrogeologists, Glastonbury, Conn., 1985—; task force leader Conn. Hazardous Waste Mgmt. Service, 1984—; advisor, Marine Commerce and Devel. Com., New London, 1982-85. NSF grantee, 1981-83. Mem. Am. Geophys. Union, Geochem. Soc., AAAS, N.Y. Acad. Scis. Current Work: The natural processes and human activities that exert controls on seawater chemistry, especially the influences of industrial waste, aquatic organisms and hydrodynamics on the minor elements of the coastal ocean, lakes and rivers; hazardous waste site investigations and remedial engineering, research and development hazardous waste management policy. Subspecialties: Oceanography; Geochemistry. Home and Office: 50 Center St New London CT 06320

WASS, HANNELORE LINA, psychology educator; b. Heidelberg, Ger., Sept. 12, 1926; came to U.S., 1957; d. Hermann and Mina (Lasch) Kraft; m. Harry H. Sisler, Apr. 1, 1978; 1 son, Brian C. B.A., Tchrs. Coll., Heidelberg, 1951; M.A., U. Mich., 1960, Ph.D., 1968. Supervising tchr. U. Chgo. Lab. Sch., 1960-61, U. Mich. Lab. Sch., Ann Arbor, 1958-60, 63; asst. prof. Eastern Mich. U., Ypsilanti, 1964-69; prof. U. Fla., Gainesville, 1969—. Author: (with others) Death Education - An Annotated Resource Guide, Vol. I, 1980, Vol. II, 1985; Helping Children Cope with Death, 1982, 2d edit., 1984; Childhood and Death, 1984; editor, co-author: (with others) Dying-Facing the Facts, 1979; founder, editor jour. Death Studies. Mem. adv. bd. Compassionate Friends, Gainesville, 1982—, Meml. Soc., 1978—, Hospice, 1982—. EDPA fellow, 1968; Research award U. Fla., 1972; Fla. Dept. Health and Rehab. Services grantee, 1978. Mem. Am. Psychol. Assn., Fourm Death Edn. and Counseling (dir. 1977-80, program dir. 1979), Internat. Workgroup on Death, Dying and Bereavement, Gerontol. Soc., So. Gerontol. Soc. Current Work: Children's and adults' concepts and ideas about death; death education for parents, teachers, children, health professionals, evaluation of educational gerontology programs effectiveness, bereavement, hospice work. Home: 6014 NW 54th Way Gainesville FL 32606 Office: U Fla 1418 Norman Hall Gainesville FL 32611

WASSERBURG, GERALD JOSEPH, educator, geologist; b. New Brunswick, N.J., Mar. 25, 1927; s. Charles and Sarah (Levine) W.; m. Naomi Z. Orlick, Dec. 21, 1951; children—Charles David, Daniel Morris. B.Sc. in Physics, U. Chgo., 1951, M.Sc. in Geology, 1952, Ph.D., 1954; D. honoris causa, U. Brussels, 1985. Cons. Argonne Nat. Lab., 1952-55; research asso. Inst. Nuclear Studies, Chgo., 1954-55; mem. faculty Calif. Inst. Tech., 1955—, prof. geology and geophysics, 1962—; vis. prof. U. Kiel, Germany, 1960, Harvard, 1962, U. Bern, Switzerland, 1966, Swiss Fed. Tech. Inst., 1967. Served with AUS, 1943-46. Decorated Purple Heart, Combat Inf. Badge.; Recipient Group Achievement award NASA, 1969, Exceptional Sci. Achievement award, 1970, Disting. Pub. Service medal, 1972, Disting. Pub. Service medal with cluster, 1978; J.F. Kemp medal Columbia U., 1973; Leonard medal Meteoritical Soc., 1975; V.M. Goldschmidt medal Geochem. Soc., 1978; John D. MacArthur lectr. Nat. Acad. Scis., 1982; Regents fellow Smithsonian Instn., 1982; Wollaston medal Geol. Soc. London, 1985; Sr. U.S. Scientist award Alexander von Humboldt-Stiftung, 1985. Fellow Am. Acad. Arts and Scis., Am. Geophys. Union (Harry H. Hess medal 1985), Geol. Soc. Am. (Arthur L. Day medal 1970); mem. Nat. Acad. Sci. (chmn. com. lunar and planetary exploration 1975-78, Arthur L. Day prize and lectureship 1981, J. Lawrence Smith medal 1985), Am. Philos. Soc. Subspecialties: Coastal zones; Geophysics. Home: 2100 Pinecrest Dr Altadena CA 91001 Office: Div Geol and Planetary Scis Cal Inst Tech Pasadena CA 91125

WASSERMAN, JACK FREDERICK, biomedical engineering educator; b. Dayton, Ohio, July 29, 1941; s. Lee Simon and Louise (Cockerill) W.; m. Susan Ainsworth, Sept. 4, 1965 (div. 1975); children—Frederick, Andrea; m. Elizabeth M. McClain, July 29, 1978; 1 child, Michel. B.S. in Aero. Engring., Purdue U., 1964; M.S. in Mech. Engring., U. Cin., 1971, Ph.D. in Mech. Engring., Biomed. Engring., 1975; A.S. in Physician Assisting, Cin. Tech., 1977. Registered profl. engr., Ohio. Structural engr. Lockheed Aircraft Co., Atlanta, 1964-65; design engr. Gen. Electric Co., Cin., 1965-71; research assoc. U. Cin., 1971-79; assoc. prof. biomed. engring., U. Tenn.-Knoxville, 1979—, cons. dept. orthopedics, 1979-82, cons. Surg. Appliance Co., Cin., 1979-82, dept. neurosurgery U. Pitts., 1983—. Contbr. articles to sci. publs. Patentee acoustic detection method for cerebral aneurysms. Recipient Young Engr. award Gen. Electric Co., 1969, Excellence in Teaching award Phi Eta Sigma, U. Tenn., 1982, Outstanding Tchr. award dept.-engring. sci. and mechanics U. Tenn., 1984, Hesler award U. Tenn. Alumni Soc., 1984-85. Mem. Am. Soc. Engring. Educators, ASME (membership devel. chmn. 1982—), Orthopaedic Research Soc. Republican. Methodist. Current work: Spinal biomechanics; vibration-human performance interaction; bioacoustics; modal analysis; bioelectric healing. Subspecialties: Biomedical engineering; Computer-aided design. Home: 4512 Westover Terrace Knoxville TN 37914 Office: Dept Engring Sci and Mechanics 310 Perkins Hall U Tenn Knoxville TN 37996-3030

WASSERMAN, MARTIN ALLAN, pharmacologist, pharmacist; b. Newark, N.J., Nov. 20, 1941; s. Charles and Betty (Schneider) W.; m. Cheryl Elyse Price, June 22, 1966; children: Dana Beth, Rick Darrin. B.S., Rutgers U., 1963; M.A. in Pharmacology, U. Tex. Med. Br., Galveston, 1971, Ph.D. in Pharmacology, 1972. Registered pharmacist, N.J., Tex., Mich. Pharmacist Shor's Med. Service Ctr., Elizabeth, N.J., 1964-68; research scientist Upjohn Co., Kalamazoo, Mich., 1972-81; asst. dir. pharmacology SK&F Labs., Phila., 1981-82; dir. pharmacology Smith Kline & French Labs., Phila., 1982—; instr. pharmacology Kalamazoo Valley Community Coll., 1978-81. McLaughlin fellow, 1969-72; recipient Mead-Johnson excellence of research award, 1971. Mem. Am. Soc. Pharmacology and Exptl. Therapeutics, Am. Lung Assn., Sigma Xi. Jewish. Current Work: Research in asthma and other lung diseases, protaglandins, thromboxanes, leukotrienes, calcium antagonists. Subspecialties: Pharmacology; Physiology (biology).

WASSERMAN, ZELDA RAKOWITZ, computational chemist, researcher; b. N.Y.C., July 19, 1935; d. Samuel and Flora Blanche (Weisberg) Rakowitz; m. Edel Wasserman, Jan. 29, 1955; children—Stephen Rak, Diane Carol Wasserman Feldman. A.B., Radcliffe Coll., 1956; M.S., Rutgers U., 1965. Mem. tech. staff Bell Labs., Murray Hill, N.J., 1965-81; mem. sci. staff E.I. duPont de Nemours & Co., Wilmington, Del., 1981—. Contbr. articles to profl. jours., chpts. to books. Mem. Am. Chem. Soc., Assn. for Computing Machinery. Current work: Computational chemistry; molecular modeling, simulation, molecular orbital calculations. Subspecialties: Theoretical chemistry; Mathematical software. Home: 1904 Academy Pl Wilmington DE 19806 Office: E I duPont de Nemours & Co Exptl Sta Wilmington DE 19898

WATANABE, KOUICHI, pharmacologist, educator; b. Manchuria, Japan, Aug. 26, 1942; s. Tetsuya and Mine W.; married; children: Toshikazu, Yoshihiro, Motohiro; m. Sumiko Abe, Aug. 18, 1977. B.S., Tokyo Coll. Pharmacy, 1966; M.S., Osaka U., 1968; Ph.D., 1971. Vis. fellow reprodn. research br. Nat. Inst. Child Health and Devel., NIH, Bethesda, Md., 1971-73; vis. scientist dept. pharmacology Coll. Medicine, Howard U., Washington, 1973-75, asst. prof., 1975-83; asst. prof. pharmacology U. Hawaii, 1983—. Contbr. articles to sci. jours. Am. Cancer Soc. grantee, 1980-81. Mem. Am. Soc. Pharmacology and Exptl. Therapeutics, N.Y. Acad. Scis. Current Work: Mechanism of action of various antineoplastic agents on calmodulin. Vinca alkaloids found to be calmodulin inhibitors. Suggested that amounts of calmodulin its binding proteins may be endogenous regulators of antineoplastic action or transport of these drugs. Subspecialties: Chemotherapy; Molecular pharmacology. Home: 35-4 Sakaecho Kitaku Tokyo Japan Office: 1960 East West Rd Honolulu HI 96822

WATERS, DAVID JOHN, molecular virologist; b. San Diego, Nov. 24, 1942; s. John David and Jane (Bates) W.; m. Marjorie, Mar. 17, 1962; children: Jeanne Louise, Marie Annette. B.S., San Diego State U., 1965,66; Ph.D., U. Kans., 1972. NIH trainee, dept. microbiology U. Kans., Lawrence, 1969-72; NIH multiple sclerosis research fellow Wistar Inst., Phila., 1973-74, asst. prof., 1974-78; asst. dir. sci. Mass. Biol. Labs., Boston, 1978—; asst. prof. medicine Tufts U., Boston, 1979—; lectr. dept. med. microbiology and immunology Harvard U. Med. Sch., Boston, 1981—. Contbr. articles to profl. jours. Chmn. Norfolk (Mass.) Bd. Health, 1980—. Mem. Am. Soc. Microbiology, Soc. Gen. Microbiology. Current Work: Research on the genetic and molecular biology of varicellazoster, protein fractionation of coagulant proteins from human plasma. Subspecialties: Virology (biology); Molecular biology. Office: Massachusetts Biological Labs 375 South St Boston MA 02130

WATKINS, DAVID HYDER, surgeon; b. Denver, Nov. 26, 1917; s. David Milroy and Mary Rose (Hyder) W.; m. Lucile Maxine Pingel, Sept. 27, 1941; children: John David Hyder, Bryan David Pingel. A.B., U. Colo., 1937, M.D., 1940; M.S. in Surgery, U. Minn., 1947, Ph.D., 1949. Diplomate: Am. Bd. Surgery, Am. Bd. Thoracic Surgery. Intern U. Iowa Hosps., Iowa City, 1940-41; resident Mayo Clinic, Rochester, Minn., 1942-44, asst. surg. staff, 1945-49; instr. surgery Ohio State U., Columbus, 1949-50; asso. prof. surgery U. Colo., Denver, 1951-56, prof., 1956-67, practice medicine specializing in surgery, Des Moines, 1967—; mem. staff Iowa Meth Hosp., Broadlawns Hosp., VA Hosp.; clin. prof. surgery U. Iowa, Iowa City, 1967—. Contbr. articles in field to med. jours. Fellow A.C.S.; mem. Am. Assn. for Thoracic Surgery, Central, Western surg. assns., S.W. Surg. Congress, Soc. Univ. surgeons, Societe Internationale de Chirurgie, Am. Heart Assn., Am. Coll. Cardiology, Am. Coll. Chest Physicians, Am. Fedn. for Clin. Research, Am. Geriatrics Soc., Am. Soc. for Artificial Internal Organs, Priestley Soc., S.R., Phi Beta Kappa, Sigma Xi, Alpha Omega Alpha. Club: Univ. (Denver). Current Work: Development of acute and subactue devices for assisted circulation. Subspecialties: Surgery; Artificial organs and prostheses. Home: 6039 N Waterbury Rd Des Moines IA 50312 Office: 1200 Pleasant St Des Moines IA 50308

WATKINS, LOUIE W(ILLARD), composite materials engineer; b. Wilmington, N.C., May 18, 1940; s. L.W. and Jean P. W. B.S. in Product Design, N.C. State U., 1963. Registered profl. mech. engr., Mass. Engr. Rockwell Mfg. Co., Raleigh, N.C., 1965-68; sr. engr. Data Packaging Co., Cambridge, Mass., 1968-73; product mgr. Emerson & Cuming Inc., Canton, Mass., 1973-78; tech. dir. W. R. Grace & Co., Canton, 1978—. Patentee in field. Served to 1st lt. U.S. Army, 1963-65. Mem. ASME, Marine Tech. Soc. Current work: Syntactic foam buoyancy systems for deepsea exploration; fiber-reinforced plastics for ballistic protection and aerospace. Subspecialties: Mechanical engineering; Composite materials. Office: Emerson & Cuming/W R Grace 869 Washington St Canton MA 02021

WATKINS, PAUL ROGER, accounting educator; b. Cedar City, Utah, Jan. 14, 1944; s. David Crockett and Ella (Sagers) W.; m. Sheila Victoria Cunningham, June 22, 1972; children: Jennifer, Kimberly, Michael, Jeremy. B.S., Ariz. State U., 1974, M.B.A., 1975, Ph.D., 1980. Systems cons. A-M Internat., Phoenix, 1968-73; v.p., controller O. Sullivan Woodside, Phoenix, 1973-76; research asst. Ariz. State U., Tempe, 1976-77, faculty assoc., 1977-78; asst. prof. dept. Sch. of Acctg. U. So. Calif., Los Angeles, 1978-84, assoc. prof., 1984—. Mem. Am. Acctg. Assn., Am. Inst. Decision Scis., Am. Assn. Artificial Intelligence, Inst. Mgmt. Scientists, Inst. Mgmt. Accts., Beta Gamma Sigma, Theta Tau. Republican. Mormon. Current Work: Research in human judgement and decision making also info. systems, expert systems and artificial intelligence. Subspecialties: Cognition; Information systems, storage, and retrieval (computer science). Home: 31871 Via Puntero San Juan Capistrano CA 92675 Office: University of Southern California Grad School Business Los Angeles CA 90089

WATNEY, WILLARD LYNN, geologist, administrator, researcher; b. Mason City, Iowa, Mar. 6, 1948; s. Willard Vincent and Lucille Mae (Radloff) W.; m. Karen Louise Amundson, Dec. 28, 1970; 1 child, Chris. A.A., N. Iowa Area Community Coll., 1968; B.S. with distinction, Iowa State U., 1970, M.S., 1972; Ph.D., U. Kans., 1985. Petroleum geologist Chevron, U.S.A., New Orleans, 1972-76; research assoc. Kans. Geol. Survey, Lawrence, 1976-81, chief geologic investigations, 1981—; cons. petroleum geologist, Lawrence, 1981—; petroleum geologist Univs. Field Staff Internat. and U.S. AID (Bangladesh Energy Project), Hanover, N.H., 1982. Author: Cyclic Sedimentation, 1980. Author, Compiler: Core Studies in Kansas, 1984. Contbr. articles to profl. jours. Oil cos. grantee, 1982, 84. Mem. Am. Assn. Petroleum Geologists, Soc. Econ. Paleontologists and Mineralogists (pres. midcontinent sect. 1985—), Soc. Profl. Well Log Analysts, Soc. Petroleum Engrs., Kans. Geol. Soc. Current work: Carbonate sedimentology and diagenesis of upper Pennsylvanian of Midcontinent; basin analysis; characterization of petroleum reservoirs. Subspecialties: Sedimentology; Fuels. Office: Kans Geol Survey 1930 Constant Ave Campus W Lawrence KS 66044

WATRAS, RONALD EDWARD, chemistry educator; b. Bayonne, N.J., Feb. 3, 1943; s. Edward T. and Mae T. (Bonczek) W.; m. Margaret M. Korneluk, July 9, 1966; children: Mary Lynn, Sandra Dawn, Rhonda. B.S., No. Mich. U., 1968; M.S. in Chemistry, U. Ariz., 1972, M.Ed., 1973; D.A. in Chemistry, U. No. Colo., 1979. Cancer researcher E.R. Squibbs, New Brunswick, N.J., 1963-64; commd. 2d lt. U.S. Air Force, 1968, advanced through grades to maj., 1983, missile combat crew comdr., 1968-74; asst. prof. chemistry U.S. Air Force Acad., Colorado Springs, Colo., 1974-79, assoc. prof., 1979-80; assoc. prof. chemistry U.S. Naval Acad., Annapolis, 1981-84; ret. USAF, 1984; internat. Baccalaureate chemistry tchr., 1985—; dir. State of Colo. Dept. Energy, Citizens Workshops on Energy, 1978-80. Mem. Am. Chem. Soc., Nat. Sci. Tchrs. Assn., Md. Sci. Tchrs. Assn., Soc. Coll. Sci. Tchrs., Internat. Union Pure and Applied Chemistry. Roman Catholic. Current Work: Chemical and energy education, chemical demonstrations. Subspecialties: Chemical education; Energy education. Office: Science Dept Chandler Sr High Sch Chandler AZ 85224

WATSON, ANNETTA PAULE, scientist, researcher; b. Pleasure Ridge Park, Ky., May 2, 1948; d. Harvey Paul and June Antoinette (Shelton) W.; m. Robert John Luxmoore, Oct. 18, 1975. B.S., Purdue U., 1970; Ph.D., U. Ky., 1976. Research cons. environ. sci. div. Oak Ridge Nat. Lab., 1975-76, research assoc. health and safety research div., 1977-83, mem. research staff, 1983—; vis. scientist CSIRO, Western Australia, 1976; mem. adv. com. Sci. for Citizens, NSF, Washington, 1978-79. Author numerous articles and tech. reports. Mem. adv. com. rural abandoned mine program U.S. Soil Conservation Service, Nashville, 1979—; mem. task force on energy and jobs for minorities and women Nat. Urban Coalition, 1980-82; bd. dirs. Appalachia-Sci. in Pub. Interest, Livingston, Ky., 1981—. Radiation Sci. and Protection fellow Oak Ridge Assoc. Univs., 1973-75. Mem. AAAS, Am. Council Reclamation Research, Ecol. Soc. Am., Sigma Xi. Current work: Human ecology; assessment of occupational and public health/safety impacts of energy development and drinking water. Subspecialties: Ecology (environmental science); Epidemiology. Office: Health and Safety Research Div Bldg 4500S PO Box X Oak Ridge National Lab Oak Ridge TN 37831

WATSON, DONALD CHARLES, cardiovascular surgeon; b. Fairfield, Ohio, Mar. 15, 1945; s. Donald Charles and Priscilla (Hirons) W.; m. Susan Prince, June 23, 1973; children: Moira Huntington, Katherine Anne, Kirsten Prince. B.S., B.A., Lehigh U., 1968; M.S., Stanford U., 1969; M.D., Duke U., 1972. Diplomate: Am. Bd. Surgery, Am. Bd. Thoracic Surgery, Nat. Bd. Med. Examiners. Resident Stanford U. Med. Ctr., 1972-1974, 76-78, chief resident, 1978-80; clin. assoc., acting attending Nat. Heart and Lung Inst., NIH, Bethesda, Md., 1974-76; cardiovascular surgeon Children's Hosp., Washington, 1980—; asst. prof. surgery George Washington U., 1980—. Served to lt. comdr. USPHS, 1974-76. NSF fellow, 1968-69; Smith Kline & French fellow, 1968. Fellow Am. Coll. Chest Physicians, Am. Coll. Cardiology; mem. A.C.S., Assn. for Acad. Surgery, Am. Fedn. Clin. Research. Republican. Presbyterian. Current Work: Surgical treatment of pediatric cardiovascular diseases. Preservation and transplantation of the mammalian heart. Subspecialties: Cardiac surgery; Transplant surgery. Home: 10908 Roundtable Ct Rockville MD 20852 Office: Children's Nat Med Center 111 Michigan Ave NW Washington DC 20010

WATSON, DONALD RALPH, architect, educator, writer; b. Providence, Sept. 27, 1937; s. Ralph Giles and Ethel Mae (Fletcher) W.; m. Marja Helena Watson, Sept. 9, 1966 (div. 1984); children: John Petrik, Elise. A.B., Yale U., 1959, B.Arch., 1962, M.E.D., 1969. Architect Peace Corps, 1962-64; cons. Govt. of Tunisia, 1964-65; prin., pvt. practice as architect, Branford, Conn., 1967—; vis. prof. Yale Sch. Architecture; cons. UN, World Bank, other internat. orgns. Author Designing and Building a Solar House, 1977, Energy Conservation Through Building Design, 1979, Climatic Design, 1983; editor: Advances in Solar Energy, 1982—. Bd. dirs. Save the Children Fedn., 1979-82. AMAX/ACSA research fellow, 1967-69; Rockefeller Found. fellow, 1978; recipient various prizes in architecture. Fellow AIA; mem. Am. Solar Energy

Soc. Current Work: Building energy conservation, solar building design. Subspecialty: Solar energy. Office: PO Box 401 Guilford CT 06437

WATSON, EDWARD FISK, civil engineer; b. N.Y.C., Mar. 14, 1929; s. Edward Fisk and Dorothy Emeline (Beakes) W.; m. Sophie Louisa Pirone, Jan. 10, 1954; children—Bonnie, Laura, Donna, Julie, Sharon, Edward, Steven. B.C.E., Cornell U., 1951; M.P.A., SUNY-Brockport, 1984. Registered profl. engr., N.Y., Pa. From constrn. insp. to project engr. Chester Engrs., Pitts., 1953-64; supt. water and sewers City of Batavia, N.Y., 1964-66, cons. 1966-68; asst. dir. water City of Rochester, N.Y., 1966-67, dep. commr. environ. services, 1980—; vice chmn. Rochester Pure Waters Dist., 1975—. Contbr. articles to profl. publs. Mem. ch. choir, Pitts. and Rochester, 1957; mem. troop com. Otetiana council Boy Scouts Am., 1980—, chmn., 1984. Served to 1st lt. U.S. Army, 1951-53. Recipient Merit award City Rochester, 1982, 83, 84. Fellow ASCE; mem. Am. Acad. Environ. Engrs. (diplomate), Nat. Soc. Profl. Engrs., Monroe Profl. Engrs. Soc. (bd. dirs. 1982—), Am. Water Works Assn., Rochester Engring. Soc., Am. Pub. Works Assn. (sec. 1973, v.p. 1974, 75, pres. 1976, 77, chpt. del. 1978, 79, 84, spl. merit award 1982), N. Am. Snow conf. (gen. chmn. 1977), Inst. Water Resources (exec. council 1978-84, v.p. 1981-82, pres. 1982-83). Current work: Water meter maintenance, use of the tandem meter test at the customer's site to determine economic time to service meter. Subspecialties: Civil engineering; Water supply and wastewater treatment. Home: 422 Yarmouth Rd Rochester NY 14610 Office: City of Rochester 300 B City Hall 30 Church St Rochester NY 14614

WATSON, GARY EDWARD, mechanical engineer, educator; b. Grand Rapids, Mich., Sept. 20, 1947; s. Gerald and Lorraine (Siegle) W.; m. Patricia O'Connor, Aug. 11, 1970; children—Colleen, Andrew, Brian. B.S., Western Mich. U., 1970; M.B.A., Ind. Northern U., 1976. Registered profl. engr., Mich., Wis. Reliability engr. Am. Chain and Cable Co., Adrian, Mich., 1970-73; quality engr. Diamond Reo Trucks, Lansing, Mich., 1973; project engr. Yardman, Jackson, Mich., 1974-75; product engr. Teledyne Water Pik, Fort Collins, Colo., 1975-77; engring. mgr. Western Products, Milw., 1977-79, v.p., engr., 1979—. instr. Am. Soc. for Quality Control, Milw., 1976—. Guest editor newspaper Tech. Today, 1977. Patentee in field. Bd. dirs. St. James, Mequon, Wis., 1982-83. Recipient Cost Reduction award Diamond Reo Trucks, 1973, Spl. Service award Nat. Truck Equipment Assn., 1979. Mem. Soc. of Automotive Engrs. (recipient Outstanding Younger mem. 1984, mem. governing bd. 1979—), ASTM (mem. plastics com. 1973). Roman Catholic. Current work: Principal work is in the area of new product development and quality improvement programs. Subspecialties: Mechanical engineering; Polymers (materials science). Home: 2115 West Glen Oaks Ln Mequon WI 53092Office: Western Products Div Doulgas Dynamics Inc 7777 N 73d St Milwaukee WI 53223

WATSON, JAMES DEWEY, educator, molecular biologist; b. Chgo., Apr. 6, 1928; s. James Dewey and Jean (Mitchell) W.; m. Elizabeth Lewis, 1968; children: Rufus Robert, Duncan James. B.S., U. Chgo., 1947, D.Sc., 1961; Ph.D., Ind. U., 1950; D.Sc., 1963; LL.D., U. Notre Dame, 1965; D.Sc., L.I. U., 1970, Adelphi U., 1972, Brandeis U., 1973, Albert Einstein Coll. Medicine, 1974, Hofstra U., 1976, Harvard U., 1978, Rockefeller U., 1980, Clarkson Coll., 1981, SUNY, 1983. Research fellow NRC, U. Copenhagen, 1950-51; Nat. Found. Infantile Paralysis fellow Cavendish Lab., Cambridge U., 1951-53; sr. research fellow biology Calif. Inst. Tech., 1953-55; asst. prof. biology Harvard, 1955-58, asso. prof., 1958-61, prof., 1961-76; dir. Cold Spring Harbor Lab., 1968—. Author: Molecular Biology of the Gene, 1965, 2d edit., 1970, 3d edit., 1976, The Double Helix, 1968, (with John Tooze) The DNA Story, 1981, (with others) The Molecular Biology of the Cell, 1983. Hon. fellow Clare Coll., Cambridge U.; Recipient (with F. H. C. Crick) John Collins Warren prize Mass. Gen. Hosp., 1959; Eli Lilly award in biochemistry Am. Chem. Soc., 1959; Albert Lasker prize Am. Pub. Health Assn., 1960; with F.H.C. Crick Research Corp. prize, 1962; with F.H.C. Crick and M.H.F. Wilkins Nobel prize in medicine, 1962; Presdl. medal of freedom, 1977. Mem. Royal Soc. (London), Nat. Acad. Scis. (Carty medal 1971), Am. Philos. Soc., Danish Acad. Arts and Scis., Am. Assn. Cancer Research, Am. Acad. Arts and Sci., Am. Soc. Biol. Chemists. Subspecialty: Molecular biology. Home: Bungtown Rd Cold Spring Harbor NY 11724

WATSON, JOHN THOMAS, medical research institute administrator, cardiovascular physiologist; b. Indpls., Jan. 9, 1940; s. Myron Thomas and Catherine (Butz) W.; m. Marilyn Cornelia Caplinger, May 9, 1964 (div. June 1983); children—Stuart Thomas, Julie Ann. B.S. in Mech. Engring., U. Cin., 1962; M.S. in Mech. Engring., So. Meth. U., 1966; Ph.D., U. Tex.-Dallas, 1972. Student engr. Indpls. Power and Light Co., 1957-59; design cons. Nat. Cash Register Co., Dayton, Ohio, 1959-62; systems engr. Ling-Temco-Vought Co., Dallas, 1962-66; teaching asst. dept. physiology U. Tex. Southwestern Med. Sch., Dallas, 1966-69, adj. instr., 1969-71, instr. thoracic and cardiovascular surgery, physiology, 1971-74, asst. prof. surgery and physiology, 1974-76; chmn. grad. studies program in biomed. engring. U. Tex. Health Sci. Ctr., Dallas, 1974-76, mem. faculty Grad. Sch. Biomed. Scis., 1974-76; chief devices and tech. br. Nat. Heart, Lung and Blood Inst., NIH, Bethesda, Md., 1976—, chmn. interagy. tech. com. working group on cardiovascular biomed. engring., 1977—, dep. dir. cardiology Inst., 1984—; exec. sec. U.S./USSR Artificial Heart Agreement, 1977—; invited mem. nominating com. for Nobel Prize in Physiology or Medicine, 1978—. Editor: Congestive Heart Failure, 1982; Noninvasive Techniques for Assessment of Atherosclerosis, 1982. Mem. editorial bd. Artificial Organs, 1980—. Contbr. articles to profl. jours. Tchr., adminstr., mem. choir Presbyterian Ch., Bethesda and Dallas, 1964—; pres. Farmland Athletic Assn., Bethesda, 1984; coach youth soccer, Bethesda, 1970—, youth basketball, Bethesda, 1978—. USPHS spl. fellow NIH, 1970. Mem. Am. Soc. Artificial Internal Organs, ASME, Am. Fedn. Clin. Research, Am. Heart Assn., Internat. Soc. Artificial Organs. Club: Old Farm (Rockville, Md.) (bd. dirs.). Current work: Cardiovascular physiology; artificial heart; imaging, and biomaterials. Subspecialties: Physiology (medicine); Artificial organs and prostheses. Office: Nat Heart Lung and Blood Inst Federal Bldg Room 312 Bethesda MD 20205

WATSON, KENNETH MARSHALL, marine physical laboratory administrator, educator; b. Des Moines, Sept. 7, 1921; s. Louis Erwin and Irene Nellie (Marshall) W.; m. Elaine Carol Miller, Mar. 31, 1946; children—Ronald M., Mark Louis. B.S., Iowa State U., 1941; Ph.D., U. Iowa, 1948. D.Sc. (hon.), Ind. U., 1976. Mem. staff Lawrence Berkeley Lab., Calif., 1948-51; asst. prof. Ind. U., Bloomington, 1951-53; assoc. prof. U. Wis., Madison, 1953-57; prof. Lawrence Berkeley Lab., U. Calif.-Berkeley, 1957-81, prof. physics, 1957-81; prof., dir. Marine Phys. Lab., Scripps Instn. Oceanography, U. Calif.-San Diego, 1981—; trustee La Jolla Inst., Calif., 1975—; mem. Jason com. Mitre Corp., Washington, 1981—; cons. Sci. Applications Inc., La Jolla, 1981—. Author: (with Goldberger) Collision Theory, 1964; Gas Dynamics, 1968; Many Particle Dynamics, 1969; (with Flatte) Sound Transmission, 1979. Fellow Am. Phys. Soc.; mem. Nat. Acad. Sci., Am. Geophy. Union, Acoustical Soc. Am. Methodist. Club: San Diego Yacht. Current work: Ocean energy transport. Subspecialties: Oceanography; Theoretical physics. Home: 2191 Caminito Circulo Norte La Jolla CA 92037 Office: Marine Phys Lab Scripps Instn Oceanography U Calif La Jolla CA 92093

WATSON, RONALD ROSS, immunology and nutrition researcher, educator; b. Tyler, Tex., Dec. 9, 1942; s. Roscoe Derrick and Ellen (Kemp) W.; m. Anita Ann Hebert, May 27, 1966; children—Jon Brent Derrick, Britton Kemp, Bethany Lynne, Cali Annette. Student U. Idaho, 1960-62, 64-65; B.S. in Chemistry, Brigham Young U., 1966; Ph.D. in Biochemistry, Mich. State U., 1971; postgrad. Sch. Pub. Health, Harvard U., 1972. Fellow Sch. Pub. Health, Harvard U., Boston, 1971-73; asst. prof. Med. Sch. U. Miss., Jackson, 1973-74, Ind. U. S Medicine, Indpls., 1974-78; assoc. prof. Purdue U., West Lafayette, Ind., 1978-82; research assoc. prof. U. Ariz. Med. Sch., Tucson, 1982—; collaborating scientist in nutrition and immunology Internat. Ctr. for Med. Research, Cali, Colombia, 1973-80; v.p. health research Mariposa Found. for Conservation, Inc., Moscow, Idaho, 1980—. Editor: Handbook of Nutrition in Elderly, 1984; Malnutrition, Immunity and Disease, 1984. Served to maj. USAR, 1977—. Recipient Future Leaders award Nutrition Found., 1978. Mem. Am. Assn. Immunology, Am. Inst. Nutrition (pub. affairs com. 1980-82), Fedn. Am. Socs. Exptl. Biology (pub. affairs com. 1980-82), Am. Soc. Clin. Nutrition, N.Y. Acad. Sci. Mormon. Current work: Cancer prevention by immunomodulation with nutrients; cellular immunology; alcohol immunoalteration; international nutrition. Subspecialties: Immunobiology and immunology; Nutrition (biology). Office: Ariz Health Sci Ctr Dept Family and Community Medicine Tucson AZ 85724

WATT, DORIS JANE, biology educator; b. Bentonville, Ark., Apr. 19, 1950; d. George Everett and Carrie Edith (Pippin) Taylor. B.S., U. Ark., 1972, M.S., 1975; postgrad. U. Md., 1974-76; Ph.D., U. Okla., 1983. Lectr. U. Okla., Norman, 1981; instr. St. Mary's Coll., Notre Dame, Ind., 1982-83, asst. prof. biology, 1983—; cons. Senegal environ. assessment study Gannet, Flemming, Corddry & Carpenter, Inc., Harrisburg, Pa., 1980. Contbr. articles to profl. jours. Mem. Am. Ornithologists Union, Wilson Ornithol. Soc., Cooper Ornithol. Soc., Animal Behavior Soc., Northeastern Bird-Banding Assn., Okla. Ornithol. Soc. (editor 1979-82), Audubon Soc; Sigma Xi. Current work: Avian behavioral ecology, dominance relationships, plumage variation, individual adaptave strategies in groups, roosts, flocks. Subspecialties: Behavioral ecology; Ornithology. Home: 1219 White Oak Dr South Bend IN 46617 Office: Saint Mary's Coll Dept Biology Notre Dame IN 46556

WATT, MAMADOU HAMÉ, water resources center director, researcher; b. Dakar, Senegal, Aug. 30, 1943; came to U.S., 1973; s. Aliou A. and Kadiaka (Diallo) W.; children—Hamet, Tijan. M.S. in Mechanics, U. Grenoble, France, 1969, Doctorate in Fluid Mechanics, 1972. Sr. Assoc. Planning Research Ctr., McLean, Va., 1977-79; prof. U. of D.C., 1979—; dir. Water Research Ctr., Washington, 1979—; commr. Interstate Commn. on Potomac River Basin, Rockville, Md.; pres. Water and Energy Mgmt. Services, Washington, 1983. Mem. Am. Water Resources Assn., Internat. Water Resources Assn. Current work: Water research management; water quantity and quality research; resources planning and management training. Energy resources and international applications of water and energy systems. Subspecialties: Resource management; Solar energy. Office: Water Resources Research Ctr U of DC 4200 Connecticut Ave NW Washington DC 20008

WATTENDORF, FRANK LESLIE, engineer; b. Boston, May 23, 1906; s. Frank Michael and Helen Ruth (Hurley) W.; m. Glenn Rogers, Jan. 11, 1941; 1 son, Roger Frank. A.B., Harvard U., 1926; M.S., M.I.T., 1928; Ph.D., Calif. Inst. Tech., 1933. Cert. profl. engr., Ohio. Guggenheim research fellow Calif. Inst. Tech., Pasadena, 1930-34; chief research engr. Metropolitan Water Dist., Hydraulic Research Labs., 1934-36; prof. aero. engring. Peiping (China) U., 1936-38; dir. wind tunnels Wright Field, Dayton, Ohio, 1939-45; civilian chmn. planning group Air Engring. Devel. Center (now Arnold Engring. Devel. Center), Tullahoma, Tenn., 1945-50, dep. chief sci. adv., 1950-52; dir. adv. group Aero. Research & Devel., NATO, Paris, 1952-63, vice chmn., 1963-68, hon. vice chmn., 1968—; cons. in field. Fellow AIAA, Royal Aero. Soc.(Eng.); mem. Internat. Council Aero. Scis. (founder), ASME, Am. Phys. Soc., Air Force Assn., Assn. Francais Technique de l'Aeronautique et de l'Espace(-France), Deutsche Gesellschaft fur Luft und Raumfahrt(Ger.), Gen. Assembley Von Karman Inst.(Belgium). Co-inventor Multi-component Gas Compressor, 1982; designer China's first large wind tunnel. Current Work: Aerospace engineering and technology. Subspecialty: Aerospace engineering and technology. Home: 3005 P St NW Washington DC 20007

WATTS, MICHELLE MARIE, chemist; b. Cleve., Oct. 31, 1951; d. Samuel Purcell and Winifred Marie (Dominick) W. B.S. in Chemistry, Bowling Green State U., 1974; M.B.A. in Mktg., Xavier U., 1980. Chemist Ashland Chem. Co., Dublin, Ohio, 1974-79, Sherex Chem. Co., Dublin, 1980—. Patentee in field. Vol. Scioto Village, Powell, Ohio, 1980-81; tutor Upward Bound, Ohio Wesleyan U., 1983-85. Mem. Am. Chem. Soc., AIME, Am. Mgmt. Assn., Nat. Assn. Female Execs., Alpha Kappa Alpha. Club: Pentax Owners. Current work: Effects of surface active agents on selected mineral particles during various processing stages. Subspecialties: Organic chemistry; Metallurgy. Office: 2081 Sprucefield Rd Columbus OH 43229

WATTS, TANIA HELEN, biochemist; b. Amersham, Eng., Sept. 17, 1957; came to U.S., 1983; d. Albert James and Irene Naomi Sophie (Kirstein) W.; m. Jean Gariepy, Aug. 18, 1984. B.S., U. Alta., Can., 1979, Ph.D., 1983. Postdoctoral fellow Stanford U., Calif., 1983—. Recipient Merit award Soc. Chem. Industry, 1979; Med. Research Council of Can. fellow, 1983—. Mem. Am. Biophys. Soc., Can. Biochem. Soc. Current work: Model membranes in studies of cell surface recognition in the immune system; purification and functional reconstitution of membrane proteins. Subspecialties: Membrane biology; Biochemistry (biology). Office: Stanford U Dept Chemistry Stanford CA 94305

WAUGH, JOHN STEWART, chemist, educator; b. Willimantic, Conn., Apr. 25, 1929; s. Albert E. and Edith (Stewart) W.; children: Alice Collier, Frederick Pierce. A.B., Dartmouth Coll., 1949; Ph.D., Calif. Inst. Tech., 1953. Research fellow physics Calif. Inst. Tech., 1952-53; mem. faculty Mass. Inst. Tech., 1953—, prof. chemistry, 1962—, Albert Amos Noyes prof., 1973—; Vis. prof. U. Calif.-Berkeley, 1963-64; Robert Welch Found. lectr., 1968; Falk-Plaut lectr. Columbia U., 1973; DuPont lectr. U. S.C., 1974; Lucy Pickett lectr. Mt. Holyoke Coll., 1978; Reilly lectr. U. Notre Dame, 1978; Spedding lectr. Iowa State U., 1979; McElvain lectr. U. Wis., 1981; Vaughan lectr. Rocky Mountain Conf., 1981; G.N. Lewis meml. lectr. U. Calif., 1982; Dreyfus lectr. Dartmouth Coll., 1984; sr. fellow Alexander von Humboldt-Stiftung; also vis. prof. Max Planck Inst., Heidelberg, 1972; vis. scientist Harvard U., 1976, G.B. Kistiakowsky lectr., 1984; Adv. prof. East China Normal U., Shanghai, 1984; Joliot-Curie prof. École Superieure de Physique et Chemie, Paris, 1985; mem. chemistry adv. panel NSF, 1966-69, vice chmn., 1968-69; mem. rev. com. Argonne Nat. Lab., 1970-74; mem. sci. and edn. adv. com. Lawrence Berkeley Lab., 1980—; exchange visitor USSR Acad. Scis., 1962, 75; mem. vis. com. Tufts U., 1966-69, Princeton, 1973-78; mem. fellowship com. Alfred P. Sloan Found., 1977-82. Author: New NMR Methods in Solid State Physics, 1978; Editor: Advances in Magnetic Resonance, 1965—; assoc. editor: Jour. Chem. Physics, 1965-67, Spectrochimica Acta, 1964-78; editorial bd.: Chem. Revs., 1978-82. Recipient Irving Langmuir award, 1976, Gold Pick Axe award, 1976; Pitts. award Spectroscopic Soc. Pitts., 1979; Wolf prize, 1984, Pauling medal, 1984; Sloan fellow, 1958-62; Guggenheim fellow, 1963-64, 72. Fellow Am. Acad. Arts and Scis., Am. Phys. Soc. (chmn. div. chem. physics 1983-84); mem. Nat. Acad. Scis., AAAS, Phi Beta Kappa, Sigma Xi. Current Work: Nuclear magnetic resonance, especially in solids and at low temperatures. Subspecialties: Physical chemistry; Magnetic resonance. Home: Conant Rd Lincoln MA 01773 Office: 77 Massachusetts Ave Cambridge MA 02139

WAY, JAMES LEONG, educator, pharmacologist/toxicologist; b. Watsonville, Calif., Mar. 21, 1927; s. Wong Bung Whee and Shew Lay Har; m. Helen Wong, Mar. 21, 1932; children: Lani, Jon, Lori. B.S. in Chemistry, U. Calif., Berkeley, 1951; Ph.D. in Pharmacology, George Washington U., 1955. Instr. pharmacology U. Wis., Madison, 1958-59, asst. prof., 1959-62; assoc. prof. Med. Coll. Wis., Milw., 1962-67; prof. Wash. State U., Pullman, 1957-82; Sheiton prof., Tex. A&M U., College Station, 1982—; vis. scientist Nat. Inst. Med. Research, London, 1973-75; vis. prof. Nat. Def. Med. Ctr., Taipei, Taiwan, 1981-82; mem. toxicology data bank com. Nat. Library Medicine, 1977—; mem. sci. adv. bd. Nat. Ctr. Toxicology and Research, 1979-82, mem. exec. council, 1980-82; mem. pesticide div. U.S. Dept. Agr., 1973-76; mem. toxicology study sect. NIH, 1974-78, mem. com. effect chems. in health Dept. fisheries, Washington, 1978—. Contbr. articles to profl. jours., chpts. to books. Greenwalde scholar, 1949-50; Baxter N.Am. fellow, 1951-52; Nat. Cancer Inst. fellow, 1952-1955, 55-57; NAt. Inst. Gen. Med. Sci. fellow, 1957-58; NIH spl. research fellow, 1974-75; NSF vis. scientist, 1981-82. Mem. Am. Soc. Pharmacology and Exptl. Therapeutics, Soc. Toxicology, Western Pharmacology Soc. (pres. 1978), Am. Chem. Soc., AAAS, N.Y. Acad. Scis., Soc. Biology and Exptl. Medicine, Am. Whitewater Assn., Nat. Ski Assn. Current Work: Pharmacology and toxicology of cyanide, alkylphosphate antagonists, selective fish toxicants. Subspecialties: Toxicology (medicine); Pharmacology. Home: 18 Forest Dr College Station TX 77840 Office: Dept Pharmacology Tex A&M U Coll Medicine College Station TX 77843

WAY, RICHARD A(LVORD), nuclear engineer; b. Erie, Pa., Mar. 10, 1956; s. Robert Bailey and Audrey (Booth) Chase W. B.S., Rensselaer Poly. Inst., 1978. Field engr. Gen. Electric Co., Oak Brook, Ill., 1978-79, constrn. engr., Monroe, Mich., 1979, Perry, Ohio, 1979-80; instr. Boiling Water Reactor Tng. Ctr., Tulsa, 1980-81, startup engr. startup/testing ops., Marseilles, Ill., 1981—. Vol. Joliet Area Operation Snowball, 1982. Mem. Am. Nuclear Soc. Republican. Lutheran. Club: Rugby (Cleve.); Rugby (Tulsa). Current Work: Providing supervision and technical direction to utility personnel on the startup and testing of LaSalle 1, the first domestic operating BWR/5. Subspecialties: Nuclear engineering; Nuclear fission. Office: Gen Electric Co DA & ESO 8157 Cass Ave Darien IL 60559

WAYLAND, RUSSELL GIBSON, JR., geologist, engineer, consultant; b. Treadwell, Alaska, Jan. 23, 1913; s. Russell Gibson and Fanchon Dudley (Borie) W.; m. Mary Mildred Brown, May 19, 1943 (div. 1964); children—Nancy Wayland Opal, Paul Russell; m. Virginia Bradford Phillis, Dec. 24, 1965. B.S., U. Wash., 1934; M.S., U. Minn., 1935, Ph.D., 1939; A.M., Harvard U., 1937. Cert. profl. geologist, Va. Instr. and research asst. U. Minn.-Mpls., 1934-39; geologist U.S. Geol. Survey, Washington, 1939-42, 52-80; Washington rep. Am. Inst. Profl. Geologists, Arlington, Va., 1982—; commr. Va. Oil & Gas Conservation Commn., Richmond, Va., 1982—, Allied High Commn., Federal Republic Germany, 1945-52. cons. Minerals Mgmt. Service, Washington, 1980-82, Bur. Land Mgmt., Washington, 1982-83. Contbr. articles to profl. jours. Served to lt. col. U.S. Army, 1942-46. Recipient Disting. Service award Dept. Interior, 1968. Fellow Mineral Soc. Am., AAAS; mem. Am. Inst. Profl. Geologists, AIME, Assn. Engring. Geologists, Soc. Econ. Geologists, Geol. Soc. Am., Am. Assn. Petroleum Geologists. Episcopalian. Club: Cosmos (Washington). Current work: Washington representative of the American Institute of Professional Geologists concerned with federal legislation and regulations concerning or affecting geologists. Subspecialty: Petroleum engineering. Home and Office: 4660 N 35th St Arlington VA 22207

WAYNE, STEVEN FALKO, materials engr., researcher; b. Manchester, N.H., Aug. 2, 1951; s. Lacon McCauley and Lillian Adrienne (Provencher) W.; m. Elizabeth Biase, June 29, 1979; 1 son, David Thomas. B.S.E. in Mech. Engring, U. Conn., 1977, M.S. in Material Sci, 1980. Engring. aide Naval Underwater Systems Center, New London, Conn., 1972-73; research asst., dept. mech. engring. and Inst. Materials Sci. U. Conn., Storrs, 1976—. Contbr. articles to profl. jours., confs. Recipient Soc. Mfg. Engrs. award, 1972, Soc. Nondestructive Testing award, 1972. Mem. ASME, Am. Soc. Metals, AIME, AAUP. Democrat. Roman Catholic. Current Work: Tribology research,. alloy (carbide and nitride) devel., conservation of strategic materials. Subspecialties: Metallurgical engineering; Allergy. Home: Box 416 Long Hill Rd Andover CT 06232 Office: U Conn Inst Materials Sci U-136 Storrs CT 06268

WEATHERFORD, CHARLES ALBERT, physicist, educator; b. Mobile, Ala., June 23, 1947; s. Charles William and Mildred Laverne (Wells) W.; m. Virginia Sara Weatherford, Aug. 16, 1982. B.S. in Physics, La. State U., 1969, Ph.D., 1974. Prof. physics Fla. A&M U., Tallahassee, 1974—. Author: ETO Multicenter Molecular Integrals; contbr. articles to profl. jours. NSF fellow, 1980. Mem. Am. Phys. Soc., N.Y. Acad. Scis., AAAS. Democrat. Current Work: Electron-molecule scattering; applied math teaching, research in electron-molecule scattering, applied math, computer modeling. Subspecialties: Atomic and molecular physics; Physical chemistry.

WEATHERSBY, A(UGUSTUS) BURNS, entomologist-parasitologist; b. Pinola, Miss., May 19, 1913; s. Augustus Benton and Louis Jane (Burns) W.; m. Olive Pearl Hammons, Apr. 8, 1945; children: Richard Michael, Robert Benton. B.S., La. State U., 1938, M.S., 1940, Ph.D., 1954; postgrad., George Washington U., 1950-53. Lab. instr. La. State U., Baton Rouge, 1938-40; asst. entomologist at large La. Dept. Agr., Baton Rouge, 1940-42; commd. ensign U.S. Navy, 1942, advanced through grades to comdr., 1957, ret., 1962; faculty U. Ga., Athens, 1962—, prof. entomology, 1964-84, emeritus, 1984—. Contbr. articles to profl. jours. on susceptibility of mosquitoes. Recipient Excellence in Teaching award U. Ga., 1981. Fellow Royal Soc. Tropical Medicine and Hygiene; mem. Am. Soc. Parasitologist, Am. Soc. Tropical Medicine and Hygiene, Entomol. Soc. Am. (Disting. Achievement award 1983), Southeastern Soc. Parasitologists, Sigma Xi, Phi Kappa Phi, Phi Sigma Gamma, Sigma Sigma Delta. Baptist. Current Work: Teaching entomology and research on susceptibility of mosquitoes to malaria, mosquito immunity, cryobiology. life cycles of plasmodium and time-lapse photography. Subspecialty: Entomology. Home: 210 Bishop Dr Athens GA 30606 Office: U Ga Athens GA 30602

WEAVER, CARSON EDGAR, semiconductor development engineer; b. Hellertown, Pa., Nov. 4, 1930; s. Edgar Peter and Theresa Helen (Schratt) W.; m. Charlotte Bernice Kauffman, July 13, 1956; children—Kerry Lee, Debra Ann. Student electronic tech. U.S. Navy Electronic Sch., 1948-49, chem. engring. Lowell Tech., 1962-63, indsl. mgmt. U. R.I., 1968, computer sci., Middlesex Community Coll., 1983. Field engr. IBM, Bethlehem, Pa. and Phila., 1952-53; devel. engr. Gahagan Inc., Bethlehem and Centerdale, R.I., 1953-59; microwave devel. engr. Sylvania Electric Co., Woburn, Mass., 1959-64; devel. engr. to wafer fabrication mgr. Amperex Electronic Co., Cranston, R.I., 1964-69; product engring. mgr. Quantum Sensing Co., Bohemia, N.Y., 1969-70; sr. engr. Semicon, Inc., Burlington, Mass., 1972-77; devel. engr. Unitrode Corp., Watertown, Mass., 1977—. Patentee in field. Served with USN, 1948-52, PTO. Mem. IEEE (sr.). Current work: Semiconductor devices, device design (materials, process and packaging DC through microwave frequencies). Subspecialties: Materials processing; Electronic materials. Home: 20 Dike Ct Tewksbury MA 01876 Office: Unitrode Corp 580 Pleasant St Watertown MA 02172

WEAVER, CHRISTOPHER SCOT, research scientist; b. N.Y.C., Feb. 6, 1951; s. Richard B. and Mildred J. (Stier) W. B.A., Hobart Coll., 1973; M.A., M.S., Wesleyan U., 1975, C.A.S., 1976; postgrad., Columbia U., 1977-79. Mgr. tech. research ABC, N.Y.C., 1977-79; v.p. sci. and tech. Nat. Cable TV Assn., Washington, 1979-81; v.p. videodisc research and devel. VML Labs., Rockville, Md., 1982-85; prin. Media Tech. Assocs., Ltd., Bethesda, Md., 1981—; instr. Aikido, Wesleyan U., Middletown, Conn., 1974; mem. Internat. Electrotech. Commn., Geneva, 1979-81; vis. scholar research program on communications policy MIT, 1981—; mem. tech. advisor subcom. on communications U.S. Congress, 1981-83. Author: Aikidosho, 1975; mem. editorial bd.: Internat. Videotex/Teletext News, Washington, 1981-85. Mem. IEEE (cable subcom. 1979-82), Soc. Motion Picture and TV Engrs. (new tech. com. 1979—), Soc. Info. Display, Am. Nat. Standards Inst. (com. V98 1979-81), Soc. Photo Optical Instrumentation Engrs. Current Work: Engaged in the development of advanced videodisc, broadband, and computer applications. Subspecialties: Information systems, storage, and retrieval (computer science); Laser data storage and reproduction. Office: 9208 Burning Tree Rd Bethesda MD 20817

WEAVER, JAMES CLYDE, chemist, researcher; b. Abingdon, Va., June 21, 1944; s. Arthur Chester and Dorothy Ernestine (McCracken) W.; m. Susan Marie Benson, Aug. 19, 1973; children—Christopher James, Todd Andrew. B.S., Emory & Henry Coll., 1965; M.S., U. Tenn., 1981. Research lab. technician Tenn. Eastman Co., Kingsport, 1965-67, chemist, 1967-76, research chemist, 1976-81; sr. research chemist Eastman Chems. Div., Kingsport, 1981—. Patentee in field. Mem. Soc. Plastics Engrs. (v.p. 1983-84, pres. 1984—, dir. 1982—), Am. Chem. Soc. Current work: Fundamental and applied research in polymer characterization, blends, reinforced and filled plastics; property-structure relationships; injection molding, extrusion and coextrusion. Subspecialties: Polymer engineering; Polymers (materials science). Home: 3922 Skyland Dr Kingsport TN 37664 Office: Eastment Chemicals Div Bldg 150A PO Box 1972 Kingsport TN 37662

WEAVER, MICHAEL JOHN, plant pathologist, pesticide coordinator; b. Greenville, Pa., July 30, 1952; s. Wayne Alvin and Virginia Grace (Malizia) W.; m. Nancy Jean Schiefferle, July 26, 1975; children—Jennifer Christine, Patrick Michael. B.S., Edinboro (Pa.) State Coll., 1974; M.S., W.Va. U., 1977; Ph.D., Va. Poly. Inst. and State U., 1982. Grad. asst., pesticide and chem. office W.Va. U., W.Va. Coop. Ext. Service, Morgantown, 1975-77; grad. asst. chem., drug and pesticide unit Va. Poly Inst. and State U., 1977-80; extension coordinator chem., drug and pesticide unit Va. Poly Inst. and State U. (Coll. Agr. and Life Scis.), 1980—, research assoc. in plant pathology, 1980-83, asst. prof., 1983—; state pesticide applicator tng. coordinator, state liaison rep. Inter-regional Research Project 4, Pesticide Impact Assessment Program. Mem. Am. Phytopathological Soc. Current Work: Advanced methods to disseminate pesticide information, interactive video and computer-assisted training systems, expert systems, computerized pesticide information systems, plant stress pathology, grape pathology, pesticide research. Subspecialties: Plant pathology; Agriculture information systems. Office: Chem Drug and Pesticide Uni Va Poly Inst and State U 139 Smyth Hall Blacksburg VA 24061

WEBB, JOHN DAY, III, chemist; b. Washington, Nov. 30, 1949; s. John Day and Marjorie (Gash) W. B.A. in Chemistry, U. Colo.-Denver, 1973; B.Sci., U. Colo.-Boulder, 1977; M.S., U. Denver, 1982. Chemist Protex Industries, Inc., Denver, 1973-75; teaching asst. U. Colo.-Boulder, 1975-77; process engr. Shell Chem. Co., Marietta, Ohio, 1977-78; sr. chemist Solar Energy Research Inst., Golden, Colo., 1978—. Patentee concrete coating compound, 1975. Prin. author book chpt. Polymers in Solar Energy Utilization, 1983. Mem. Am. Chem. Soc. Democrat. Club: Sierra (Denver). Current work: Photo chemistry thin polymer films on elemental or oxidized metallic surfaces. Subspecialties:

Solar energy; Polymer chemistry. Home: 13251 W 20th Ave Golden CO 80401 Office: Solar Energy Research Inst 1617 Cole Blvd Golden CO 80401

WEBB, THOMAS EVAN, biochemistry educator, researcher; b. Edmonton, Alta., Can., Mar. 4, 1932; came to U.S., 1970, naturalized, 1967; s. Donald John and Sarah Jane (McMinis) W.; m. Ellen Adair Armstrong, Sept. 4, 1961; children—Linda Carol, Sharon Laura. B.Sc., U. Alta., 1955, M.Sc., 1957; Ph.D., U.Toronto, Ont., Can., 1961. Asst. prof. biochemistry U. Man., Winnipeg, Can., 1965-67; McGill U., Montreal, Que., Can., 1967-70; assoc. prof. Ohio State U., Columbus, 1970-74, prof. biochemistry, 1984—, staff scientist Comprehensive Cancer Ctr., 1976—. Contbr. articles to profl. publs. Patentee in field. Grantee Nat. Cancer Inst., Dept. Health and Human Services, 1970-84. Mem. Am. Assn. Cancer Research, Am. Soc. Biol. Chemists. Republican. Current work: Development of a cancer detection test, identification of natural anticarcinogens and studies into the regulation of genetic expression. Subspecialties: Biochemistry (medicine); Cancer research (medicine). Home: 2050 Nayland Rd Columbus OH 43220 Office: Ohio State U Coll Medicine 333 W 10th Ave Columbus OH 43210

WEBB, WATTS RANKIN, surgeon, educator; b. Columbia, Ky., Sept. 8, 1922; s. Frank Elbert and Susan Josephine (Rankin) W.; m. Frances Luella Cooke, Aug. 19, 1944; children—Gordon Lewis, Harvey Elbert, Paul Alan, Andrew Michael. B.A., U. Miss., 1942; M.D., John Hopkins U., 1945. Diplomate Am. Bd. Surgery, Am. Bd. Thoracic Surgery. Intern, Barnes Hosp., St. Louis, 1945-46, resident in gen. and thoracic surgery, 1948-52; chief surgeon Miss. State Sanitorium, 1952-63; instr. U. Miss. Sch. Medicine, Jackson, 1955-56, asst. prof., 1956-58, prof. surgery, 1958-63; prof., chmn. div. thoracic and cardiovascular surgery U. Tex. Southwestern Med. Sch. Dallas, 1964-70; prof., chmn. dept. surgery SUNY-Upstate Med. Ctr., Syracuse, 1970-77; prof., chmn. dept. surgery Tulane U. Sch. Medicine, New Orleans, 1977—; cons. Wilford Hall USAF Hosp., Lackland AFB, Tex., 1966—, thoracic surgery, Brooke Army Hosp., 1967—; part-time staff pediatric surgeon Dept. Health and Human Resources, Handicapped Children's Program, New Orleans Dist., 1978—, staff cardiac surgeon, 1983—. Author: (with others) A Programmed Instruction Text: Cardiac Surgery rev. edit., 1983. Editor: (with others) Aneurysms, 1983, Vascular Trauma, 1984; Surgery in Acute Coronary Problems; The Surgical Clinics of North America, 1974. Contbr. articles to profl. jours. Mem. various com. VA, mem. Inter-Soc. Commn. Heart Disease; mem. cardiac adv. com. N.Y. State Dept. Health, 1971-77; med. adv. bd. Edn. Film Prodn., 1971-77; mem. various coms., exec. com. Council Cardiovascular Surgery, Am. Heart Assn., 1975—; bd. dirs. New Orleans Area Soc. Parental and Enteral Nutrition, 1984—. Served to capt. AUS, 1946-48. Recipient Silver medal Am. Heart Assn., 1963, Hadassah award, 1965, Outstanding Clin. dept. award Tulane U. Sch. Medicine, 1979, Outstanding Teaching Dept. award Tulane U. Sch. Medicine, 1980, 1983; grantee Miss. Heart Assn., Nat. Inst. Arthritis and Metabolic Diseases, Nat. Heart Inst., Tex. Heart Assn., Nat. Inst. Gen. Med. Scis., Dallas Heart Assn., Heart Assn. Upstate N.Y., Burn Resuscitation Study Group. Fellow Am. Coll. Chest Physicians (cardiovascular council 1965—), A.C.S. (trauma com. 1963-70, cardiovascular com. 1969-75, La. Dist. #1 com. on applicants 1979—); mem. Am. Assn. Thoracic Surgery (grad. med. edn. nat. adv. com. 1979—), Am. Coll. Cardiology, AMA, Am. Surg. Assn., Am. Thoracic Soc., Soc. Cryobiology, New Orleans Surg. Soc. (pres. 1983—), Surg. Assn. La. (pres. 1984—), So. Med. Assn., So. Thoracic Soc., Sigma Xi, others. Current work: Shock, cardiac and pulmonary transplantation, hypothermic preservation, cardiac metabolism. Subspecialties: Surgery; Cardiac surgery. Office: Dept Surgery Tulane Med Sch 1430 Tulane Ave Room 8513 New Orleans LA 70112

WEBER, ALFONS, physicist; b. Dortmund, Germany, Oct. 8, 1927. B.S., Ill. Inst. Tech., 1951, M.S., 1953, Ph.D., 1956. Asst. in physics Ill. Inst. Tech., Chgo., 1951-53, instr., 1953-56; NRC/Can. fellow U. Toronto, Ont., 1956-57; from asst. prof. to assoc. prof. physics Fordham U., Bronx, N.Y., 1957-66, prof., 1966-81, chmn. dept. physics, 1964-69; physicist Nat. Bur. Standards, Gaithersburg, Md., 1977—, chief molecular spectroscopy div., 1982—. Fellow Am. Phys. Soc.; mem. Optical Soc. Am., Am. Assn. Physics Tchrs. Current work: Raman and infrared spectroscopy; molecular mechanics; optics. Subspecialties: Atomic and molecular physics; Laser spectroscopy. Office: Nat Bur Standards Molecular Spectroscopy Div Gaithersburg MD 20899

WEBER, CARL JOSEPH, III, chemical researcher; b. Evanston, Ill., Nov. 7, 1954; s. Carl Joseph Jr. and Florence Dean (Woodman) W.; m. Judith Debra Malmin, Jan. 15, 1977; 1 child, Elizabeth Ann. B.S. in Chemistry, U. Calif.-Santa Barbara, 1976; M.S. in Inorganic Chemistry, U. Mass., 1980, Ph.D., 1981. Devel. engr. Thick Film Systems, Santa Barbara, 1976-78; postdoctoral assoc. U. Mass., Amherst, 1981; research chemist U.S. Borax Research Corp., Anaheim, Calif., 1981-85, mem. materials devel. staff Raychem Corp., Menlo Park, Calif., 1985—. Contbr. articles to profl. jours., also to Ullmanns Ency. of Indsl. Chemistry. U. Calif.-Santa Barbara scholar, 1972; Dow Chem. Co. fellow U. Mass., 1980. Mem. Am. Chem. Soc., AAAS, Sigma Xi. Democrat. Presbyterian. Current work: Polymeric materials development, inorganic synthesis and characterization, molybdenum chemistry, metal containing polymers, inorganic reaction kinetics, polymer characterization. Subspecialties: Inorganic chemistry; Polymer chemistry. Home: 43 Berkeley Ave Orinda CA 94563 Office: Raychem 300 Constitution Dr Menlo Park CA 94025

WEBER, DARRELL JACK, plant biochemist, pathologist, researcher; b. Thornton, Idaho, Nov. 16, 1933; s. John and LaNorma Anna (Severson) W.; m. Carolyn Foremaster, Aug. 24, 1962; children: Brad, Becky, Brian, Todd, Kelly, Jason, Trent. B.S., U. Idaho, 1958, M.S., 1959; Ph.D., U. Calif.-Davis, 1963. Postdoctoral fellow U. Wis.-Madison, 1963-65; asst. prof., then assoc. prof. U. Houston, 1965-69; prof. botany Brigham Young U., Provo, Utah, 1969—; postdoctoral fellow Mich. State U., 1975-76. Contbr. articles to sci. jours.; author of 3 books. Active Ch. Jesus Christ of Latter-day Saints. Recipient Karl G. Masear award, 1973; Utah Acad. Sci. fellow, 1974; grantee in field. Mem. Am.Inst. Biol. Scis., Am. Phytopath Soc., Am. Microbiology Soc., Am. Mycol. Soc., Sigma Xi. Republican. Current Work: Physiology of host parasite interaction; physiology of salt tolerance; fungal physiology. Subspecialties: Biochemistry (biology); Plant pathology. Home: 560 E Robin Orem UT 84057 Office: Brigham Young U Provo UT 84602

WEBER, DAVID ALEXANDER, medical physicist; b. Lockport, N.Y., Mar. 6, 1939; s. Fred Leonard and Catherine Gladys (Woodcock) W.; m. Sandra Watson, Aug. 26, 1961; children: Sarah D., David A. B.S., St. Lawrence U., 1960; Ph.D., U. Rochester, 1971. Grad. teaching asst. physics U. Buffalo, 1960-61; sr. research aide, research asst. biophysics div. Sloan-Kettering Research Inst., N.Y.C., 1961-68; asst. attending physicist, asst. physicist div. med. physics Meml. Hosp. Cancer and Allied Disease, N.Y.C., 1967-68, lab. chief radioactive isotopes sect. div. med. physics, 1967-68; AEC grad. lab. fellow dept. radiation biology and biophysics U. Rochester, N.Y., 1968-70, asst. prof. radiology, 1970-75, asst. prof. radiation biology and biophysics, 1970-81, acting chief div. nuclear medicine, 1974-75, assoc. prof. radiation biology and biophysics, 1981—, assoc. prof. radiology, 1975—; clin. faculty dept. clin. sci. Sch. Health Related Professions, Rochester (N.Y.) Inst. Tech., 1976—; sr. internat. fellow Fogarty Internat. Center, NIH, Bethesda, Md., 1978-79; sr. internat. fellow dept. orthopedic surgery Lundu. Hosp., Sweden, 1978-79. Recipient Vis. Scientist fellowship award Swedish Med. Research Council, Stockholm, Vis. Scientist fellowship award Lund U. Hosp., 1978-79. Mem. Soc.Nuclear Medicine, Am. Assn. Physicists in Medicine, Am. Coll. Nuclear Medicine, Health Physics Soc., Assn. Univ. Radiologists, Sigma Xi. Current Work: Design and evaluation of image storage, processing and display systems for nuclear medicine imaging; tracer kinetics, especially in the study of lung, heart and benign and malignant bone disease. Subspecialties: Nuclear medicine; Imaging technology. Office: U Rochester Div Nuclear Medicine 601 Elmwood Ave Rochester NY 14642

WEBER, DENNIS JOSEPH, analytical chemical research scientist; b. Kalamazoo, Mich., Mar. 30, 1934; s. Cleland Burton and Ellen Elizabeth (Rector) W.; children—Michael, Ann, Mark, Timothy, Thomas, Dennis II. B.S. in Chemistry, Western Mich. U., 1958, M.A. in Chemistry, 1962; Ph.D., U. Fla., 1967. Research asst. Upjohn Co., Kalamazoo, 1958-62, research scientist, 1970—; grad. fellow U. Fla., Gainesville, 1962-67; mgr. applications research, Syntex Labs., Palo Alto, Calif., 1967-70. Contbr. articles to profl. jours. Pres., Kalamazoo Male Chorus, 1978-82; treas. New Horizon Village Co-op, Kalamazoo, 1982. Mem. Am. Chem. Soc., Am. Pharm. Assn., Acad. Pharm. Scis., Royal Chem. Soc. Britian. Republican. Roman Catholic. Current work: Soluble anti-inflammatory steroids analysis and pharmacokinetics; esterase enzyme localization and specificity. Subspecialties: Pharmacokinetics; Analytical chemistry. Home: 901 Jenks Kalamazoo MI 49007 Office: Upjohn Co 301 Henrietta Kalamazoo MI 49001

WEBER, ERNST, electrical engineering educator; b. Vienna, Austria, Sept. 6, 1901; came to U.S., 1930; s. Hermann Rudolf and Josefine (Swoboda) W.; m. Irma Lintner, Jan. 18, 1925 (div. 1933); m. Charlotte Sonya Escherich, Aug. 7, 1936 (dec.); children—Hertha Emma Flack, Greta Neelsen. Diploma E.E., Tech. U., Vienna, 1924; Sc.D., 1927; Ph.D., U. Vienna, 1926. Research engr. elec. machinery Oesterreichische Siemens-Schuckert Werke, Vienna, Austria, 1924-29; design and research engr. elec. machinery Siemsns-Schuckert Werke, Berlin, 1929-30; adj. prof. Tech. U., Berlin-Charlottenburg, 1929-31; vis. prof. elec. engring. dept. Poly. Inst. Bklyn., 1930-31, research prof., 1931-41, prof., head grad. study and research, 1942-45, head dept. elec. engring., 1945-57, dir. Microwave Research Inst., 1943-47, SPL pres., 1957-69; dir. Poly. Research and Devel. Co., Inc., 1944-52, pres., 1952-59; cons. PRD Electronics div. Harris Corp., 1959-81; pres. emeritus Poly Inst. N.Y. (formerly Poly. Inst. Bklyn.), 1969—; chmn. div. engring. Nat. Research Council, Nat. Acad. Scis., Washington, 1969-74, acting exec. dir. Commn. on Sociotech. Systems, 1974-76, mem., 1974-78, cons., 1978-79; cons. Army Sci. Adv. Panel, 1957-69; mem. U.S.A. Electronics Command Adv. Group, 1965-70, vice chmn., 1968-70; mem. Defense Sci. Bd., 1963-66; mem. N.Y. State Adv. Council for Advancement of Indsl. Research and Devel., 1959-69. Author: Electromagnetic Theory, Static Fields and Their Mapping, 1965; Linear Transient Analysis, 2 vols., 1954-56. Contbr. tech. papers to profl. publs. Patentee in field. Recipient Presdl. Cert. Merit, 1948, Outstanding Civilian Service award U.S. Army, 1969, Disting. Service award Transp. Research Bd., Nat. Research Council, 1976, L.E. Grintee award Engrs.' Council for Profl. Devel., 1978. Fellow IEEE (pres. 1963, Edn. medal 1960, Founders award 1970, Am. Phys. Soc., N.Y. Acad. Scis., Am. Acad. Arts and Scis.; mem. Am. Soc. Engring. Edn., AAUP, AAAS (chmn. sect. engring. 1977-78, council del. 1978-79), N.Y. Elec. Soc. (pres. 1946-47, Engrs. Council for Profl. Devel. (bd. dirs. 1964-72, pres. 1968-70), Austrian Assns. Elec. Engrs. Republican. Clubs: University (N.Y.C.); Cosmos (Washington). Subspecialties: Electrical engineering; Microwaves.

WEBER, GEORGE, biochemist, cancer researcher; b. Budapest, Hungary, Mar. 29, 1922; came to U.S., 1959, naturalized, 1965; s. Salamon and Hajnalka (Arvai) W.; m. Catherine E. Forrest, June 30, 1958; children: Dolly, Julie, Jefferson. B.A., Queen's U. Kingston, Ont., Can., 1950; M.D., 1952; M.D. (hon.), Chieti (Italy) Med. Sch., 1979, U. Budapest, 1982. Lic. Med. Council Can. Postdoctorate fellow U. B.C., 1952-53; research assoc. Notre Dame Hosp.-Montreal Cancer Insti., U. Montreal, Que., Can., 1953-56, head sect. path. chemistry, 1956-59; vis. scientist Harvard U. Med. Sch., summer 1957; mem. faculty Ind. U. Med. Sch., 1959—, prof. pharmacology, 1961—, prof., dir. exptl. oncology, 1974—. Author numerous articles, book chpts. in field.; Editor: Advances in Enzyme Regulation, vols. 1-21, 1962—. Recipient Alecce prize cancer research Rome, 1971, SAMA award Student AMA, 1966, 68; hon. mem. All-Union Biochem. Soc.; hon. mem. Nat. Acad. Sci., USSR, 1981—. Fellow Royal Soc. Medicine; Mem. Am. Assn. Cancer Research (G.H.A. Clowes award 1982), Am. Soc. Pharmacology and Exptl. Therapeutics, Am. Physiol. Soc. Current Work: Biochemistry and pharmacology of cancer, chemotherapy and enzymology. Subspecialties: Cancer research (medicine); Molecular pharmacology. Home: 7307 Lakeside Dr Indianapolis IN 46278 Office: Room 337 Riley Cancer Wing Ind U Med Sch 1100 W Michigan St Indianapolis IN 46223

WEBER, HANS-JUERGEN, physics educator, nuclear theorist; b. Berlin, May 3, 1939; came to U.S., 1966; s. Hans Gustav Wilhelm and Hedwig Berta Elisabeth (Angermann) W.; m. Edith Elli Enzian; 1 son, Chris. M.A. in Math., Goethe U., Frankfurt, W.Ger., 1961, Ph.D. in Theoretical Physics, 1965. Research assoc. Goethe U., Frankfurt/Main, 1962-66, Duke U., Durham, N.C., 1966-67; research assoc., acting asst. prof. U. Va., Charlottesville, 1967-68, asst. prof., 1968-71, assoc. prof., 1971-77, prof. physics, 1977—; vis. prof., scientist Max-Planck Institue, Mainz, W.Ger., 1972-73, U. Mainz, 1977, 83, 84, U. Paris, Orsay, France, 1979, U. Lyon (France), 1977-78. NSF prin. investigator, grantee, 1971—. Mem. Am. Phys. Soc., AAAS, Am. Assn. Physics Tchrs. Lutheran. Current work: Quark model description of the nuclear forces. Subspecialties: Nuclear physics; Particle physics. Home: 1308 Lester Dr Charlottesville VA 22901 Office: Inst Nuclear and Particle Physics and Jesse W Beams Lab U Va Charlottesville VA 22901

WEBER, JAMES ALAN, physiological plant ecologist; b. Santa Monica, Calif., Mar. 16, 1944; s. Leo Andreas and Wilma Kathleen (Lewis) W.; m. Nancy Jane Smith, Apr. 18, 1970. Student, El Camino Coll., Torrance, Calif., 1962-65; A.B. in Botany, U. Calif.-Berkeley, 1966; A.M. in Botany, U. Mich., 1967, Ph.D. in Botany, 1973. Postdoctoral scholar Biol. Sta., U. Mich., Ann Arbor, 1973-79, asst. research scientist, 1979—. Co-editor: The Mich. Botanist, 1984—. Contbr. articles to profl. jours. Mem. exec. com. Mackinac chpt. Sierra Club, 1976-80. Mem. AAAS, Am. Inst. Biol. Scis., Am. Soc. Plant Physiologists, Internat. Soc. Ecol. Modelling, Bot. Soc. Am., Ecol. Soc. Am., Internat. Assn. Aquatic Vascular Plant Biologists, Sigma Xi. Current Work: Control of carbon dioxide exchange in leaves as a function of environmental variables; the relationships between net carbon gain and plant growth. Subspecialties: Plant physiology (biology); Ecology (environmental science). Office: Biological Station U Mich Ann Arbor MI 48109

WEBER, JOSEPH, physicist; b. Paterson, N.J., May 17, 1919; s. Jacob and Lena (Stein) W.; m. Anita Meinhardt Straus, Oct. 18, 1942; m. Virginia Louise Trimble, Mar. 16, 1972; children: Jonathan, Paul, James, David. B.S., U.S. Naval Acad., 1940; Ph.D. in Physics, Cath. U. Am., 1951. Physicist U.S. Navy Bur. Ships, 1945-48; U. Md., College Park, 1948—, U. Calif.-Irvine, 1973—; staff Inst. Advanced Study, Princeton, N.J., 1955-56, 62-63, 69-70. Author: Quantum Electronics, 1951, Gravitational Radiation Antennna, 1958. Served with USN, World War II. Guggenheim fellow, 1955, 62; NRC fellow, 1955-56; recipient First prize Gravity Research Found., 1959, Boris Pregel award N.Y. Acad. Scis., 1973. Fellow IEEE, Am. Phys. Soc. Current Work: Gravitaton, relativity, statistical physics, weak interactions, quantum electronics. Subspecialties: Relativity and gravitation; Statistical physics. Office: Physics Dept U Md College Park MD 20742

WEBER, MARVIN JOHN, physicist; b. Fresno, Calif., Feb. 26, 1932; s. John William and Louise (Grill) W.; m. Pauline Margaret Sikes, Feb. 2, 1957; children: Ann Hilary, Eve Kimberley. A.B., U. Calif., Berkeley, 1954, M.A., 1956, Ph.D., 1959. Research assoc. dept. physics U. Calif., Berkeley, 1959; prin. scientist Research Div., Raytheon Co., Waltham, Mass., 1960-73; vis. research assoc. dept. physics Stanford U., 1966; group leader Lawrence Livermore Nat. Lab., 1973-80, asst. assoc. program leader, 1980-83; with Office Basic Energy Scis. Dept Energy, 1984-85, Lawrence Livermore Nat. Lab., 1986—; editor-in-chief CRC Handbook Series of Laser Sci. and Tech., 1978—; assoc. editor Jour. Luminescence, 1985—; adv. editorial bd. Jour. Non-Crystalline Solids, 1981—; cons. NSF, 1973-76. Contbr. articles to profl. jours. Recipient IR 100 award Indsl. Research Mag., 1979, George W. Money award Am. Ceramics Soc., 1983. Fellow Am. Phys. Soc. Optical Soc. Am.; mem. Am. Ceramics Soc., Am. Assn. Crystal Growth, Fedn. Am. Scientists, Sigma Xi, Phi Beta Kappa. Current Work: Lasers, quantum electronics, luminescence, optical spectroscopy, optical materials. Subspecialties: Condensed matter physics; Laser spectroscopy. Home: 221 Loch Lomond Way Danville CA 94526 Office: PO Box 808 Livermore CA 94550

WEBER, PAUL EGON, consulting physicist; b. Jena, Germany, Nov. 8, 1913; came to U.S., 1953; naturalized, 1957; s. Paul Albin and Barbara Babette (Bouffier) W.; m. Gertrud Anna Brüningsen, Nov. 1, 1947; children—Norbert Paul, Dieter Erich. Ingenieur, Hoehere Tech. Staatslehranstalt Machinenwesen, Frankfurt on Main, Germany, 1935; Diplom Ingenieur, Fachhochschule Frankfurt on Main, 1983. Devel. engr. Am. Optical Co., Buffalo, 1953-54; research engr. Wollensak Optical Co., Rochester, N.Y., 1954-57; physicist Stromberg Carlson, Rochester, 1957-58; staff engr. AVCO Crosly Div., Cin., 1958-59; prin. engr. Bendix Corp., South Bend, Ind. and Ann Arbor, Mich., 1959-61; scientist Trion Instruments, Ann Arbor, 1961-65; pvt. cons., Ypsilanti, Mich., 1965-66; physicist Bell and Howell, Chgo., 1966-78; cons., Libertyville, Ill., 1979—. Internat. patentee in field. Contbr. articles to profl. jours. Recipient award for disting. work German Govt. 1945. Mem. Deutsche Gesellschaft fuer angewandte Optik, Optical Soc. Am., Am. Inst. Physics. Current work: Optical radiation physics. . Home and Office: 921 Bartlet Terr Libertyville IL 60048

WEBER, THOMAS RICHARD, pediatric surgery educator, researcher; b. Cleve., Feb. 19, 1945; s. Robert E. and Lois L. (Payne) W.; m. Suzanne M. Muehring, June 14, 1969; children: Amy, Jill, Patrick. B.A., Eastern Mich. U., 1967; M.D., Ohio State U., 1971. Diplomate: Am. Bd. Surgery. Intern U. Mich. Hosp., Ann Arbor, 1971-72, resident in surgery, 1972-77; resident in pediatric surgery Washington Children's Hosp., 1977-79; asst. prof. pediatric surgery Ind. U. Med. Ctr., Indpls., 1979—; attending surgeon Riley Children's Hosp., Indpls., 1979—. Fellow ACS; mem. Assn. Acad. Surgery (exec. council 1979-81), Am. Pediatric Surg. Assn. Current Work: Neonatal bowel ischemia, pediatric solid tumors, pediatric septic shock—pharmacologic support, pediatric liver disease. Subspecialties: Surgery; Cancer research (medicine). Office: Riley Childrens Hospital 702 Barnhill Dr Indianapolis IN 46223

WEBER, WALTER JACOB, JR., engineering educator; b. Pitts., June 16, 1934; s. Walter Jacob and Anne Mae (Chando) W.; m. Ruth L. Stryker, Dec. 17, 1955 (div. Jan. 1975); children: Wendilyn Ruth, Elizabeth Anne, Pamela Jean, Linda Lorraine; m. Patricia L. Nagel Braden, July 20, 1981. Sc.B., Brown U., 1956; M.S.E., Rutgers U., 1959; A.M., Harvard, 1961, Ph.D., 1962. Registered profl. engr. Diplomate Am. Acad. Environ. Engrs. Engr. Caterpillar Tractor Co., Peoria, Ill., 1956-57; instr. Rutgers U., 1957-59; engr. Soil Conservation Service, New Brunswick, N.J., 1957-59; research, teaching asso. Harvard, 1959-63; faculty U. Mich., Ann Arbor, 1963—, prof., chmn. water resources program, 1968—, Disting. prof., 1978—; Internat. cons. to industry, govt. Author: (with K.H. Mancy) Analysis of Industrial Wastewaters, 1971, Physicochemical Processes for Water Quality Control, 1972; editor-author: (with E. Matijevic) Adsorption from Aqueous Solution, 1968; Contbr. numerous articles and chpts. to tech., profl. jours. and books. Recipient Distinguished Faculty award U. Mich., 1967, 78; Faraday lectr. U. Mich., 1970; Engr. of Distinction, Engrs. Joint Council, 1973; Research Excellence award U. Mich., 1980. Mem. Am. Chem. Soc. (cert. of merit 1962, F. J. Zimmerman award 1982), Nat. Soc. Profl. Engrs., Am. Inst. Chem. Engrs., ASCE (Rudolph Hering medal 1980, Thomas R. Camp award 1982, Simon W. Freese award 1984, G. Brooks Ernest award 1985), Am. Water Works Assn. (Acad. Achievement award 1981), Assn. Environ. Engring. Profs. (Disting Faculty award 1968, Nalco research award 1979, Engring. Sci. research award 1984), Water Pollution Control Fedn. (John R. Rumsey Meml. award 1975, Willard F. Shephard award 1980), Nat. Acad. Engring., Tau Beta Pi, Sigma Xi, Chi Epsilon, Delta Omega. Subspecialty: Water supply and wastewater treatment. Home: 1700 South Grove Rd Ypsilanti MI 48197 Office: Water Resources Program Coll Engring U Mich Ann Arbor MI 48109

WEBSTER, EDWARD WILLIAM, medical physicist; b. London, Apr. 12, 1922; s. Edward and Bertha Louisa (Cornish) W.; m. Dorothea Anne Wood; children: John, Peter, Anne, Edward, Mark, Susan. B.Sc., U. London, 1943, Ph.D., 1946. Diplomate: Am. Bd. Radiology, Am. Bd. Health Physics. Research engr. English Electric Co., Stafford, Eng., 1945-49; research physicist div. indsl. cooperation M.I.T., 1950-52; lectr. nuclear energy and elec. engring. Queen Mary Coll., U. London, 1952-53; physicist, dir. radiol. scis. div. dept. radiology Mass. Gen. Hosp., Boston, 1953—, radiation safety officer, 1962-80; prof. radiology Harvard U., 1975—, prof. radiology Harvard-M.I.T. Health Scis. and Tech. Div., 1978—; examiner in physics Am. Bd. Radiology, 1958-78; dir. Nat. Council Radiation Protection, 1981—; mem. adv. com. on med. uses of isotopes U.S. Nuclear Regulatory Commn., 1971—; mem. com. on biol. effects of ionizing radiation U.S. Nat. Acad. Scis., 1977-80, mem. oversight com. on radioepidemiologic tables, 1982-83; mem. adv. com. on environ. hazards VA, 1985—; mem. com. on radiologic monitoring NRC, 1985—; cons. IAEA, 1960-61, WHO, 1964-67. Contbr. chpts. to books, articles to profl. jours. Robert Blair traveling fellow London County Council, 1949-50; USPHS fellow, 1965-66; NIH grantee. Mem. Radiol. Soc. N.Am. (v.p. 1977-78), Am. Assn. Physicists in Medicine (pres. 1963-64, Coolidge medal 1983), Soc. Nuclear Medicine (trustee 1970-71, 73-77), Am. Coll. Radiology, New Eng. Radiologic Physics Orgn. (chmn. 1970-73), New Eng. Roentgen Ray Soc. (hon. mem.), Radiation Research Soc., Health Physics Soc. (Landauer award 1985). Patentee in field of low energy x-ray shielding. Current Work: Low dose radiation imaging technology, radiation dosimetry, biological effects of radiation, radiation protection and shielding design, medical uses of radioisotopes. Subspecialties: Imaging technology; Medical physics. Office: Dept Radiology Mass Gen Hosp Boston MA 02114

WEBSTER, GEORGE CALVIN, biological sciences educator, researcher; b. South Haven, Mich., July 17, 1924; s. Eugene Homer Webster and Hazel Edna (Empson) Davis; m. Sandra Lee Whitman, Jan. 23, 1960; children: Jeffrey C., Kimberley Ann. B.S., Western Mich. U., 1948; M.S., U. Minn.-Mpls., 1949, Ph.D., 1952. Sr. research fellow Calif. Inst. Tech., 1952-55; assoc. prof. Ohio State U., 1955-61; vis. prof. U. Wis., Madison, 1961-64; chief environ. health lab., Cape Kennedy, Fla., 1964-70; prof. biol. scis. Fla. Inst. Tech., Melbourne, 1971—, head dept., 1971—, assoc. dean sci. and engring., 1985—. Author: Nitrogen Metabolism in Plants, 1959; Contbr. numerous articles to profl. jours. Served to 1st lt. USAF, 1942-45. Am. Heart Assn. investigator, 1963. Fellow AAAS; mem. Am. Soc. Biol. Chemists, Biochem. Soc. Gt. Britain, Am. Soc. Cell Biology, Gerontol. Soc. Democrat. Current Work: Research on the molecular basis of the aging process in animals, using recombinant DNA and related techniques. Subspecialties: Molecular biology; Genetics and genetic engineering (biology). Home: 532 Majorca Ct Satellite Beach FL 32937 Office: Dept Biol Sciences Florida Institute Technology 150 W University Blvd Melbourne FL 32901

WEBSTER, LESLIE TILLOTSON, JR., pharmacologist; b. N.Y.C., Mar. 31, 1926; s. Leslie Tillotson and Emily (de Forest) W.; m. Alice Katharine Holland, June 24, 1955; children—Katharine White, Susan Holland, Leslie Tillotson III, Romi Anne. B.A., Amherst Coll., 1947, Sc.D. (hon.), 1982; student, Union Coll., 1944; M.D., Harvard U., 1948. Diplomate: Am. Bd. Internal Medicine. Rotating intern Cleve. City Hosp., 1948-49, jr. asst. resident, 1949-50; asst. resident medicine Bellevue Hosp., N.Y.C., 1952-53; research fellow medicine Harvard and Boston City Hosp. Thorndike Meml. Lab., 1953-55; from demonstator to instr. medicine Case Western Res. U. Sch. Medicine, 1955-60, research assoc. to sr. instr. biochemistry, 1959-60, asst. prof. medicine, 1960-70, asst. prof. biochemistry, 1960-65, asst. prof. pharmacology, 1965-67, asso. prof., 1967-70, prof. pharmacology, 1976—, chmn. pharmacology dept., 1976—, prof. medicine, 1980—; prof., chmn. pharmacology dept. Northwestern U. Med. and Dental Sch., 1970-76; cons. NIH, WHO, Rockefeller Found. Contbr. articles to sci. and med. jours. Served to lt. USNR, 1950-52. Russell M. Wilder fellow Nat. Vitamin Found., 1956-59; Sr. USPHS Research fellow, 1959-61; Research Career Devel. awardee, 1961-69; Macy faculty scholar, 1980-81. Mem. Am. Assn. Study Liver Diseases, ACP (life), Central Soc. Clin. Research (emeritus), Am. Soc. Clin. Investigation (emeritus), Am. Soc. Biol. Chemists, Assn. Med. Sch. Pharmacology, Am. Soc. Pharmacology and Exptl. Therapeutics. Current Work: Molecular pharmacology and immunopharmacology; pharmacology of antiparasitic drugs. . Home: 2728 Leighton Rd Shaker Heights OH 44120 Office: Dept Pharmacology Case Western Res U Sch Med 2119 Abington Rd Cleveland OH 44106

WEBSTER, MURRAY ALEXANDER, JR., sociologist; b. Manila, Philippines, Dec. 10, 1941; s. Murray A. and Patricia (Morse) W. A.B., Stanford U., 1963, M.A., 1966, Ph.D., 1968. Instr., Coll. San Mateo, Calif., 1967; asst. prof. Johns Hopkins U., Balt., 1968-74; assoc. prof. U. S.C., Columbia, 1974-76, prof. sociology, 1976—, adj. prof. psychology, 1979—; vis. prof. Stanford U., 1981-82; session organizer Am. Sociol. Assn. and So. Sociol. Soc., 1974-80. Contbr. articles to profl. jours.; editorial bd.: Am. Jour. Sociology, 1977-80, Social Psychology Quar, 1976-79, 84—; assoc. editor: Social Sci. Research, 1976—; editor social psychology sect. newsletter Am. Sociol. Assn., 1984—; author: Sources of Self-Evaluation, 1974, Actions and Actors, 1975. NIH trainee, 1965; Wilson fellow, 1964; NIH grantee, 1966-68; Nat. Inst. Edn. grantee, 1968-74; NSF grantee, 1976—. Republican. Presbyterian. Current Work: Status cues and effects on behavior; physical attractiveness; interrelations of social processes (liking, control, status, love/committment). Subspecialty: Social psychology. Home: 1829 Senate St Apt 10A Columbia SC 29201 Office: Dept Sociology Univ SC Columbia SC 29208

WEBSTER, STEVEN CRAIG, electrical engineer, researcher; b. Mpls., Apr. 26, 1956; s. George Arden and Betty F. (Pedley) W.; m. Catherine Jean Roessler, June 9, 1979. B.S., M.S., MIT, 1979. Coop. edn. student RCA Astro-Electronics, Princeton, N.J., 1976-78; mem. tech. staff Bell Labs., Holmdel, N.J., 1979-81; research and devel. supr. 3M Co., St. Paul, 1981—. Active MIT Ednl. Council, Mpls., 1984—. Recipient Supervised Investors Service award MIT, 1979. Mem. IEEE, Inst. Computer Soc. Democrat. Current work: Electronic and computer systems for optical data storage.

especially real-time computer software and digital hardware; distributed processing; process control software. Subspecialties: Electrical engineering; Laser data storage and reproduction. Home: 14399 Chestnut Dr Eden Prairie MN 55344 Office: 3M Co 544-2N 3M Ctr St Paul MN 55144

WEBSTER, WILLIAM MERLE, JR., electronics company executive; b. Warsaw, N.Y., June 13, 1925; s. William Merle and Carrie Melinda (Luce) W.; m. Mary Lambert Tourison, May 3, 1947; children: Melissa, Cecelia. B.S. in Physics, Union Coll., Schenectady, 1945; Ph.D. in Elec. Engring, Princeton, 1954. With RCA Corp., 1946—, v.p. labs., Princeton, N.J., 1969-85, v.p., sr. tech. adviser, 1985—; dir. Horizon Bancorp., Princeton Bank & Trust Co. Served to lt. (j.g.) USNR, 1942-46. Fellow IEEE; mem. Nat. Acad. Engring., Sigma Xi. Current Work: Technical Management. Subspecialties: Electronics; Microelectronics. Home: 77 Cleveland Ln Princeton NJ 08540 Office: RCA Laboratories Princeton NJ 08540

WECHSLER, JAMES ALAN, molecular geneticist; b. Pitts., Oct. 26, 1940; s. Maurice B. and Pearl Janice (Wilner) W.; m. Josephine Ann Puddington, Feb. 2, 1963; children: Samantha Leigh, Jeremy Dylan. B.S., Yale U., 1962, Ph.D., 1968. Postdoctoral fellow U. Edinburgh, Scotland, 1968-70; asst. prof. Columbia U., 1970-75, assoc. prof., 1975-77; research assoc. prof. U. Utah, Salt Lake City, 1977-80; sr. scientist Pub. Health Research Inst. City N.Y., 1981—. Contbr. articles to profl. jours. USPHS Grad. fellow, 1964-68; Am. Cancer Soc. postdoctoral fellow, 1968-70; USPHS research grantee, 1971—. Mem. Am. Soc. Microbiology, AAAS, N.Y. Acad. Scis., Union of Concerned Scientists, Sierra Club, Fedn. Am. Scientists. Democrat. Club: Yale of Utah. Current Work: Analysis of chromosome replication in Escherichia coli. Regulation of genes and interaction of gene products involved in DNA replication. Subspecialties: Gene actions; Molecular biology. Home: 2475 Emerson Ave Salt Lake City UT 84108 Office: 455 1st Ave 11th Floor New York NY 10016

WECKER, LYNN, pharmacologist, educator; b. N.Y.C., Sept. 27, 1947; d. Frank L. and Sue (Levin) W. Ph.D. in Pharmacology, U. Fla., 1972. Postdoctoral fellow in pharmacology Vanderbilt U. Sch. Medicine, Nashville, 1973-75; asst. prof. med. chemistry and pharmacology Northeastern U., Boston, 1975-76; asst. prof. pharmacology Vanderbilt U. Sch. Medicine, 1976-78; asst. prof. pharmacology La. State U. Med. Center, New Orleans, 1978-80, assoc. prof., 1980-84, prof., 1984—, assoc. prof. psychiatry, 1980-84, prof., 1984—. Contbr. articles to profl. jours. Recipient Andrew Mellon Tchr.-Scientist award, 1975; Outstanding Young Scientist award SK&F Labs., 1979; NIMH grantee. Mem. Am. Soc. Neurochemistry, Am. Soc. Pharmacology and Exptl. Therapeutics, Soc. Neuroscience, Internat. Soc. Neurochemistry. Current Work: Mechanisms regulating the metabolism of acetylcholine in the nervous system. Subspecialties: Neuropharmacology; Neurochemistry. Office: Dept Pharmacology Louisiana State Univ Med Center 1901 Perdido St New Orleans LA 70112

WEDIG, JOHN H., toxicologist, pharmacologist; b. St. Louis, Dec. 25, 1941; s. John H. and Verla L. (Lampert) W.; married; children: Sarah, Alison, Meredith, Robert. A.B. in Zoology, Washington U., St. Louis, 1964; M.S. in Wildlife Mgmt, U. Mich., 1967, Ph.D. in Toxicology, 1971. Diplomate: Am. Bd. Toxicology. Cons. Olin Corp., New Haven, 1971—, sr. toxicologist, 1976—; environ. toxicology cons. Nilo Earms Shooting Preserve, div. Winchester-Western, 1971—; non-resident lectr. U. Mich. Contbr. chpts. to books, articles to profl. jours. Mem. Am. Coll. Vet. Toxicologists, Soc. Toxicology, Am. Soc. Pharmacology and Exptl. Therapeutics. Patentee in field. Current Work: Neurotoxicology, reproductive toxicology, ecological toxicology, dermato-toxicology. Subspecialties: Toxicology (medicine); Environmental toxicology. Office: 240 Greenwich Ave PO Box 1717 Greenwich CT 06830

WEED, HERMAN ROSCOE, biomedical engineering educator, consultant, researcher; b. Union City, Pa., Aug. 5, 1922; s. Roscoe Conklin and Leta Venettie (Bryner) W.; m. Sylvia Kathryn Yearick, Apr. 20, 1946; children: David Herman, Douglas Leonard, Kathryn Marie. B.S.E.E., Pa. State U., 1945; M.Sc., Ohio State U., 1948. Registered profl. engr., Ohio. Instr. Pa. State U., 1945-46; instr. Ohio State U., Columbus, 1946-49, asst. prof., 1949-55, assoc. prof., 1955-59, prof., elec. engring., 1959—; dir. Ohio State U. (Biomed. Engring. Ctr.), 1971—; dir. biomed. engring. Project Hope, Millwood, Va., 1985—; cons. HOPE, 1980—, others; vis. prof. Inst. Biocybernetics, U. Karlsruhe, W.Ger., 1979; UNESCO adv. Punjab (India) Agrl. U., 1978, 81, Ford Found. cons., 1966, 72, 78; guest Polish Acad. Sci. Biomed. Engring. Inst., Oct. 1975, French Ministry Industry and Research, Sept. 1975; vis. prof. U. Cairo, 1977. Contbr. numerous articles to sci. and tech. jours. Recipient Disting. Teaching award Eta Kappa Nu, 1965; cert. of commendation Ohio Ho. of Reps., 1977; Robert Critchfield award, 1968, 73. Mem. Internat. Fedn. Automatic Control (chmn. tech. com. systems bio med. engring.), Ohio Acad. Sci., Am. Soc. Engring. Edn. (chmn. COBECC), Alliance for Engring. in Medicine and Biology, Am. Automatic Control Council. Clubs: Ohio State U. Faculty, Photography. Current Work: Biomedical engineering with emphasis on muscle stimulation, physiological controls, heartsound analysis, developing technology. Subspecialty: Biomedical engineering. Office: Room 257 2015 Neil Ave Columbus OH 43210

WEEKES, TREVOR C., astrophysicist; b. Dublin, Ireland, May 21, 1940; came to U.S., 1966; s. Gerard C. and Florence (Murtagh) W.; m. Ann Katherine Owens, Sept. 30, 1964; children—Karina, Fiona, Lara. B.Sc., Univ. Coll. Dublin, 1962, Ph.D., 1966; D.Sc., Nat. U. Ireland, 1978. Lectr., Univ. Coll. Dublin, 1964-66; astrophysicist Smithsonian Instn., Amado, Ariz., 1966—; resident dir. Mt. Hopkins Obs., Ariz., 1969-76. Author: High Energy Astrophysics, 1970. Mem. Am. Astronom. Soc., Internat. Astronom Union. Democrat. Roman Catholic. Current work: Ground based gamma ray astronomy; clusters of galaxies; cosmic rays; optical transients. Subspecialties: Gamma ray high energy astrophysics; Optical astronomy. Home: 1132 Calle San Jose Sahuarita AZ 85629 Office: Whipple Obs Box 97 Amado AZ 85645

WEEKS, MAUREEN O'BRIEN, chemist; b. Boston, Feb. 20, 1954; d. Thomas Alexander and Helen Gorman (Buckley) O'B.; m. Lawrence C. Weeks, June 21, 1975 (div. 1985). B.A. in Chemistry, Wellesley Coll., 1975; Ph.D. in Chemistry, Am. U., 1983. Research assoc. Meloy Labs. Inc., Springfield, Va., 1975-76; chemist Lab. Tumor Virus Genetics, Nat. Cancer Inst., Bethesda, Md., 1976-83, Lab. Tumor Immunology and Biology, 1983—. Contbr. articles to profl. jours., chpts. in books. Recipient award for sci. excellence Bausch & Lomb, 1971; Wellesley Town scholar, 1971. Mem. Am. Chem. Soc., Am. Soc. Microbiology, AAAS, N.Y. Acad. Scis., Grad. Women in Sci. Roman Catholic. Club: Washington Wellesley. Current work: Biochemistry, biology and immunology of neoplastic states; characterization of monoclonal antibodies and oncogenes. Home: 2948 Schoolhouse Circle Silver Spring MD 20902 Office: Lab Tumor Immunology and Biology Nat Cancer Inst Bldg 10 Room 8B07 Bethesda MD 20205

WEEKS, STEPHAN JOHN, research analytical chemist; b. Mpls., Apr. 13, 1950; s. John Norman and Betty Jo Ann (Hemingway) W.; m. Jean Carol Seifert, Nov. 24, 1977; children: Erik, Mark. B.A., St. Olaf Coll., 1972; Ph.D., U. Fla., 1977. Chem. technician Minn. Dept. Health, Mpls., 1971; grad. research asst. U. Fla., Gainesville, 1972-77; NRC postdoctoral research fellow Nat. Bur. Standards, Washington, 1977-79, research chemist, 1979-84; research chemist Ames Lab., Iowa, 1984—. Contbr. articles to profl. jours. Mem. Am. Chem. Soc. (analytical div.), Soc. Applied Spectroscopy, ASTM. Lutheran. Current Work: Trace atomic and molecular analysis; petroleum analysis and characterization. Subspecialties: Analytical chemistry; Laser spectroscopy. Home: 1933 Maxwell Ave Ames IA 50010 Office: Ames Lab Ames IA 50011

WEEKS, WILFORD FRANK, glaciologist; b. Champaign, Ill., Jan. 8, 1929; s. Frank Cook and B. Caroline (Pool) W.; m. Beverly Jean Weeks, June 8, 1952 (div. 1984); children—Ellen Jean, Paul Russell; m. Marilyn Rupp McDonald, Dec. 29, 1984. B.S., U. Ill., 1951, M.S., 1953; Ph.D. in Geochemistry, U. Chgo., 1956. Glaciologist Air Force Cambridge Research Center, 1955-57; asst. prof. geology Washington U., 1957-62; glaciologist U.S. Army Cold Regions Research and Engring. Lab., Hanover, N.H., 1962—; adj. prof. earth scis. Dartmouth Coll., 1972—; Japan Soc. for Promotion Sci. prof. Inst. Low Temperature Sci., Hokkaido U., Japan, 1973; Office of Naval Research chair of arctic marine sci. Naval Postgrad. Sch., 1978-79; mem. numerous govt. and industry panels. Bassist, Dartmouth Symphony, Monterey Symphony, Hanover Chamber Orch.; Contbr. numerous articles to profl. jours. Served with USAF, 1955-57. Recipient research and devel. achievement award U.S. Army, 1967, 81. Fellow Arctic Inst. N.Am.; mem. Internat. Glaciological Soc. (pres. 1972-75), Am. Geophys. Union, Am. Polar Soc., Nat. Acad. Engring., Phi Beta Kappa, Phi Kappa Phi, Sigma Xi. Current Work: Geophysical characteristics of ice in the sea as they relate to offshore engineering; remote sensing and material sciences; general glaciology. Subspecialties: Geophysics; Oceanography. Office: Cold Regions Research and Engring Lab 72 Lyme Rd Hanover NH 03755

WEESE, JAMES LEIGHTON, surgical oncologist, immunologist, educator; b. Chgo., Apr. 22, 1949; s. Carlisle and Florence (Kales) W.; m. Barbara Fried, Mar. 26, 1977; children—Brooke Jennifer, Scott Bradley. B.A., U. Chgo., 1970, M.D., 1973. Diplomate Am. Bd. Surgery. Intern, U. Mich., Ann Arbor, 1973-74, resident in surgery, 1974-79; guest investigator lab. immuno-diagnosis Nat. Cancer Inst., Bethesda, Md., 1975-77; staff surgeon William Middleton VA Hosp., Madison, Wis.; asst. prof. surgery and human oncology U. Wis.-Madison, 1979-85, assoc. prof., 1985—; cons. Nat. Cancer Inst., 1981, 82, 84. Contbr. numerous articles to profl. publs., 1981-84. Recipient Jr. Clin. Faculty Fellowship award Am. Cancer Soc., 1981-84; VA grantee, 1980-85. Fellow ACS; mem. Soc. Univ. Surgeons, Am. Assn. Immunologists, Am. Soc. Clin. Oncologists, Soc. Surg. Oncology. Current work: Tumor immunology; immunotherapy; effects of operations on tumor growth. Subspecialties: Surgery; Cancer research (medicine). Home: 606 Ozark Trail Madison WI 53705 Office: U Wis 600 Highland Ave Madison WI 53792

WEETALL, HOWARD HAYYIM, biochemist, researcher; b. Chgo., Nov. 17, 1936; s. David Dale and Mina (Satin) W.; m. Billie Rosenberg, Nov. 2, 1962; children—Marla Lynn, Laurel Beth. B.A., UCLA, 1960, M.A., 1962. Research scientist Corning Glass Works, Corning, N.Y., 1967-75, research assoc., 1975-79, mgr., 1979-84, research fellow, Cambridge, Mass., 1984—. Patentee; editor: Enzyme Engineering, 1978; contbr. articles to profl. jours. Recipient USPHS award, 1978. Mem. Am. Assn. Immunology, Am. Soc. Biol. Chemistry, Am. Soc. Microbiology. Current work: Immobilized enzymes, antigenes and antibodies for diagnostic applications. Subspecialty: Enzyme technology. Office: Corning Biomed 1 Kendall Sq Cambridge MA 02139

WEG, JOHN GERARD, physician; b. N.Y.C., Feb. 16, 1934; s. Leonard and Pauline M. (Kanzleiter) W.; m. Mary Loretta Flynn, June 2, 1956; children—Diane Marie, Kathryn Mary, Carol Ann, Loretta Louise, Veronica Susanne, Michelle Celeste. B.A. cum laude, Coll. Holy Cross, Worcester, Mass., 1955; M.D., N.Y. Med. Coll., 1959. Diplomate: Am. Bd. Internal Medicine. Commd. 2nd lt. USAF, 1958, advanced through grades to capt., 1967; intern Walter Reed Gen. Hosp., Washington, 1959-60; resident, then chief resident in internal medicine Wilford Hall USAF Hosp., Lackland AFB, Tex., 1960-64, chief pulmonary sect., 1964-66, chief inhalation sect., 1964-66, chief pulmonary and infectious disease service, 1966-67, resigned, 1967; clin. dir. pulmonary disease div. Jefferson Davis Hosp., Houston, 1967-71; from asst. prof. to assoc. prof. medicine Baylor U. Coll. Medicine, Houston, 1967-71; assoc. prof. medicine U. Mich. Med. Sch. Univ. Hosp., Ann Arbor, 1971-74, prof., 1974—; physician-in-charge pulmonary div., 1971-81, physician-in-charge pulmonary and critical care med. div., 1981—; cons. Ann Arbor VA, Wayne County Gen. hosps.; advisory bd. Washtenaw County Health Dept., 1973—. Contbr. med. jours., reviewer, mem. editorial bds. Decorated Air Force Commendation medal; travelling fellow Nat. Tb and Respiratory Disease Assn., 1971; recipient Aesculpaius award Tex. Med. Assn., 1971. Fellow Am. Coll. Chest Physicians (chmn. bd. govs. 1976-79, gov. Mich. 1975-79, chmn. membership com. 1976-79, prof.-in-residence 1972—, chmn. critical care council 1982—), Am. Coll. Chest Physicians and Internat. Acad. Chest Physicians (exec. council 1976—), Internat. Acad. Chest Physicians unit of Am. Coll. Chest Physicians (pres. elect 1979-80, pres. 1980-81), ACP (chmn. Mich. program com. 1974); mem. AAAS, Am. Fedn. Clin. Research, AMA, Am. Thoracic Soc. (sec.-treas. 1974-76), Am. Assn. Inhalation Therapy, Air Force Soc. Internists and Allied Specialists, Soc. Med. Consultants to Armed Forces, Internat. Union Against Tb, Mich. Thoracic Soc. (pres. 1976-78), Mich. Lung Assn. (dir.), Am. Lung Assn., Research Club U. Mich., Assn. Advancement Med. Instrumentation, Central Soc. Clin. Research, Am. Bd. Internal Medicine (asso., subsplty. com. on pulmonary disease 1980), Alpha Omega Alpha. Current Work: Pulmonary pathophysiology, critical care medicine, education. Subspecialties: Pulmonary medicine; Internal medicine. Home: 3060 Exmoor St Ann Arbor MI 48104 Office: 1405 E Ann St Ann Arbor MI 48109

WEHAUSEN, JOHN VROOMAN, mathematician, educator; b. Duluth, Sept. 23, 1913; s. George W. and Elizabeth (Vroman) W.; m. Mary Katherine Wertime, Aug. 19, 1938; children—Sarah, Peter Vrooman, Julia, John David. B.S., U. Mich., 1934, M.S., 1935, Ph.D., 1938. Instr. math. Brown U., 1937-38, Columbia, 1938-40, U. Mo., 1940-44; mathematician David Taylor Model Basin, Carderock, Md., 1946-49; acting head mechanics br. Office Naval Research, 1949-50; exec. editor Math. Revs., 1950-56; asso. research mathematician Inst. Engring. Research, U. Calif. at Berkeley, 1956-57, research mathematician, 1957—, asso. prof. engring. sci., 1958-59, prof., 1959—; Fulbright lectr. U. Hamburg, 1960-61; Consultant Operations Research Group USN, 1944-46. Mem. Am. Math. Soc., Math. Assn. Am., Soc. Naval Architects and Marine Engrs., Soc. Naval Architects of Japan, Nat. Acad. Engring. Current Work: Ship hydrodynamics; water-wave theory. Subspecialty: Fluid mechanics. Home: 15 Hillside Ct Berkeley CA 94704

WEHINGER, PETER AUGUSTUS, astronomer, educator; b. Goshen, N.Y., Feb. 18, 1938; s. George Edward and Elizabeth Marie (Goode) W.; m. Susan Wyckoff, July 29, 1967. B.S. in Physics, Union Coll., Schenectady, N.Y., 1960; M.A. in Astronomy, Ind. U., Bloomington, 1962; Ph.D. in Astronomy (NASA predoctoral fellow), Case Inst. Tech., 1966. Instr. astronomy U. Mich., 1965-67, asst. prof., 1967-70; assoc. prof. physics and astronomy U. Kans., 1970-72; vis. assoc. prof., Smithsonian research fellow in physics and astronomy Tel Aviv U., 1972-75; U.K. Sci. Research Council prin. research fellow Royal Greenwich Obs., Eng., 1975-78; adj. prof. astronomy Sussex U., 1975-78; Max Planck Gesellschaft vis. sr. scientist Max Planck Institut für Astronomie, W. Ger., 1978-80; vis. sr. research assoc. astronomy Ohio State U., 1978-79; research prof. physics Ariz. State U., Tempe, 1981—; vis. research prof. physics No. Ariz. U., 1981-82, discipline scientist for spectroscopy and spectrophotometry Internat. Halley Watch, 1982—. Contbr. articles to profl. jours. Fellow Royal Astron. Soc. London; mem. Am. Astron. Soc., Astron. Soc. Pacific, Internat. Astron. Union, Sigma Xi (research prize 1960). Co-discoverer of ionized water in comets. Current Work: Detection of extended sodium torus associated with Io and Jupiter; imaging, surface photometry and spectroscopy of quasar galaxies; cometary spectroscopy. Subspecialty: Optical astronomy. Home: 2135 E Loma Vista Dr Tempe AZ 85282 Office: Astronomy Group Physics Dept Arizona State University Tempe AZ 85287

WEHNER, PAUL SHERMAN, physical chemist; b. Balt., Apr. 1, 1952; s. Andrew John and Mary K. (Sheldon) W.; m. Karen Bittner, Aug. 2, 1980; children—Jennifer, Amanda. B.A. magna cum laude, U. Md., 1974; M.S., U. Calif.-Berkeley, 1976, Ph.D., 1978. Research chemist Tenn. Eastman Co., Kingsport, 1978-80, sr. research chemist, 1980—. Mem. Am. Chem. Soc., Sigma Xi. Roman Catholic. Current work: Heterogeneous catalysis; surface sci; polymer surfaces. Subspecialty: Physical chemistry. Home: 4017 Lakewood Dr Kingsport TN 37663 Office: Tenn Eastman Co PO Box 1972 Kingsport TN 37662

WEI, JAMES, chemical engineering educator; b. Macao, China, Aug. 14, 1930; came to U.S., 1949, naturalized, 1960; s. Hsiang-chen and Nuen (Kwok) W.; m. Virginia Hong, Nov. 4, 1956; children: Alexander, Christina, Natasha, Randolph. B.S. in Chem. Engring, Ga. Inst. Tech., 1952; M.S., MIT, 1954, Sc.D., 1955; grad., Advanced Mgmt. Program Harvard, 1969. Research engr. to research asso. Mobil Oil, Paulsboro, N.J., 1956-62, sr. scientist, Princeton U., N.J., 1963-68, mgr. analysis, N.Y.C., 1969-70; Allan P. Colburn prof. U. Del., Newark, 1971-77; Sherman Fairchild disting. scholar Calif. Inst. Tech., 1977; Warren K. Lewis prof., head. dept. chem. engring. MIT, Cambridge, 1977—; vis. prof. Princeton, 1962-63, Calif. Inst. Tech., 1965; cons. Mobil Oil Corp., Milliken Corp.; cons. com. on motor vehicle emissions Nat. Acad. Sci., 1972-74, 79-80; mem. sci. adv. bd. EPA, 1976-79; mem. Presdl. Pvt. Sector Survey Task Force on Dept. Energy, 1982-83. Bd. editors: Chem. Tech, 1971—, Chem. Engring. Communications, 1972—; cons. editor chem. engring. series, McGraw-Hill, 1964—; editor-in-chief: Advances in Chemical Engineering, 1980; Contbr. papers, monographs to profl. lit., The Structure of Chemical Processing Industries, 1979. Recipient Am. Acad. Achievement Golden Plate award, 1966. Mem. Am. Inst. Chem. Engrs. (dir. 1970-72, Inst. lectr. 1968, Profl. Progress award 1970, Walker award 1980, Lewis award 1985), Am. Chem. Soc. (award in petroleum chemistry 1966), Nat. Acad. Engring. (nominating com. 1981, peer com. 1980-82, membership com. 1983—), AAAS, Am. Acad. Arts and Scis., Academica Sinica of Taiwan, Sigma Xi. Subspecialties: Chemical engineering; Catalysis chemistry. Home: 420 Waverley Ave Newton MA 02158 Office: Chem Engring Dept Mass Inst Tech Cambridge MA 02139

WEI, JENG SHU, clinical chemist; b. Hsin Chu, Taiwan, China, Oct. 16, 1942, came to U.S., 1969, naturalized, 1984; s. Bing Lang and Mangmei (Chen) W.; m. Cathy S.C. Chang, July 14, 1973; children—Kenan, Melvin. B.S., Nat. Taiwan U., Taipei, 1966, M.S., 1969; Ph.D., U. Calif.-Berkeley, 1975. Postdoctoral U. Calif.-San Francisco, 1975-76; vis. scientist Syva Syntex, Palo Alto, Calif., 1976-77; sr. scientist IDT Boehringer Ingelheim, Santa Clara, Calif., 1977-78; sr. scientist Technicon Instruments, Tarrytown, N.Y., 1978-80; sr. research scientist Fisher Sci. Co., Orangeburg, N.Y., 1980—; lectr. East West Acupuncture Research Ctr., N.Y.C., 1982-84. Contbr. articles to profl. jours. Served to 2d lt. Chinese Army, 1966-67. Mem. Am. Chem. Soc., Am. Assn. Clin. Chemistry, AAAS, Am. Acupuncture Assn., Chinese Biochemical Soc. Current work: Enzymology; hemoglobins; non-isotopic immunoassays; clinical research in acupuncture. Subspecialties: Clinical chemistry; Acupuncture. Home: 5 Douglas Dr Pleasantville NY 10570 Office: Fisher Diagnostics 526 Route 303 Orangeburg NY 10962

WEI, JIM P(IAU), mechanical engineer; b. Hsin-Chu, Taiwan, Feb. 25, 1940; came to U.S., 1968, naturalized, 1974; s. Bing-Lang and Mang-Mei (Chen) W.; m. Rose L. Tang, June 15, 1968; children: Tracy, Sherry. B.S., Nat. Cheng-Kung U., Tainan (Taiwan), 1963; M.A.Sc., U. B.C. (Can.), Vancouver, 1967; Ph.D., U.Md., 1972. Sr. Engr. Bechtel Inc., San Francisco, 1972-74; Sr. engr. advanced reactor systems dept. Gen. electric Co., Sunnyvale, Calif., 1974—. Mem. Am. Nuclear Soc. Democrat. Current Work: Liquid metal fast breeder reactor thermal-hydraulics and safety, especially in reactor core fluid flow and heat transfer. Subspecialties: Nuclear fission; Nuclear engineering. Office: Gen Electric Co/ARS 310 De Guigne Dr PO Box 508 Sunnyvale CA 94086

WEI, MILLET LUNCHIN, consulting engineer; b. Taiwan, July 1, 1937; came to U.S., 1962, naturalized, 1973; s. Yu Tzu and Mei (Cheng) W.; m. Betty Teresa Leung, June 3, 1967; children: Natalie Vennesa, Terence. B.S., Nat. Taiwan U., Taipei, 1960; M.S., U. R.I., Kingston, 1964; Ph.D., Carnegie-Mellon U., Pitts., 1967. Registered profl. engr., Pa. Research engr. Bethlehem Steel Co., Pa., 1967-73, project engr., 1973-74, cons. engr. tech. services, 1974—. Contbr. articles to profl. jours. Served to 2d lt. Chinese Marine Corps, 1960-61. Mem. Assn. Iron and Steel Engrs. (Kelly award 1981), AIME, ASME, ASCE, Chinese Inst. Engrs. U.S.A. (dir.). Republican. Roman Catholic. Club: Shepherd Hills Country (Wescosville, Pa.). Patentee in field. Current Work: Hardware technology for steelmaking in basic oxygen furnaces and electric furnaces, cooling technology for blast furnaces, modern technology for tall coke oven batteries, equipment technology for rolling mills, ladles, slag pots, heat exchangers, pressure vessels, reheat furnaces and continuous casters. Subspecialties: Civil engineering; Mechanical engineering. Home: 6106 Fairway Ln Wescosville PA 18106 Office: 1361 Martin Tower 8th Ave Bethlehem PA 18016

WEIDE, BRUCE WARREN, computer scientist; b. Toledo, Dec. 13, 1952; s. Harley Warren and Betty Jo Ann (Habig) W. B.S.E.E., U. Toledo, 1974; Ph.D., Carnegie-Mellon U., Pitts., 1978. Asst. prof. computer and info. sci. Ohio State U., Columbus, 1978-83, assoc. prof., 1983—. NSF grad. fellow, 1974-77; IBM grad. fellow, 1977-78; NSF grantee, 1979-81. Mem. Assn. Computing Machinery, IEEE. Current Work: Data structures, algorithms, process control systems design aids. Subspecialties: Algorithms; Software engineering. Home: 5425 Rockport St Columbus OH 43220 Office: 2036 Neil Ave Mall Columbus OH 43210

WEIDENSAUL, M T(HOMAS) CRAIG, plant pathology educator, researcher, consultant; b. Reedsville, Pa., Apr. 4, 1939; s. Thomson Becker and Grace Elizabeth (Kendig) W.; m. Martha Robertson, June 12, 1965; children—Thomas Luke, Susan Elizabeth, Daniel Josh. B.S., Gettysburg Coll., 1962; M.F., Duke U., 1963; Ph.D., Pa. State U., 1969. Forest pathologist U.S. Forest Service, Harrisonburg, Va., 1963-66; research asst. Pa. State U., University Park, 1966-70; prof. plant pathology, head of environ. studies lab. Ohio State U., Wooster, 1970—; owner, operator Tannenbaum Farms, Centre Hall, Pa., 1970—; prin. T.C. Weidensaul, Cons., Wooster, Ohio, 1966—. Assoc. editor Phytopathology Jour. Contbr. chpts. to books, articles to profl. jours. Deacon United Ch. Christ, Apple Creek, Ohio, 1977, elder, 1984; coach Triway Recreation Inc., Wooster, 1984, 85. Served with U.S. Army, 1963-64. Mem. Am. Phytopathol. Soc., Am. Soc. Agronomy, Pa. Christmas Tree Growers Assn. Republican. Subspecialty: Plant pathology. Office: Lab for Environ Studies Ohio Agrl Research and Devel Ctr Madison Ave Wooster OH 44691

WEIHAUPT, JOHN GEORGE, university administrator, geophysicist; b. LaCrosse, Wis., Mar. 5, 1930; s. John George and Gladys Mae (Ash) W.; m. Audrey Rae Reis, Jan. 28, 1961. B.S., U. Wis.-Madison, 1952, M.S., 1953, 71, Ph.D., 1973. Chmn. dept. phys. and biol. sci. U.S. Air Force Inst., Madison, 1963-73; asst. dean Grad. Sch., prof. geoscis. Purdue U., West Lafayette, Ind., 1973-78; assoc. dean acad. affairs Ind.-Purdue U., Indpls., 1973-78; prof. geology, assoc. acad. v.p. dean Grad. Sch., San Jose State U., Calif., 1978-82; vice chancellor acad. affairs U. Colo.-Denver, 1982—; cons. lectr. in field. Author: Exploration of the Oceans, 1979, Spanish edit., 1983. Contbr. articles to profl. jours. Served to 1st lt. U.S. Army, 1954-55, Korea. Mt. Weihaupt in Antartica named in his honor, 1965. Fellow Geol. Soc. Am., Explorers Club; mem. Am. Geophys. Union, AAAS, Am. Assn. Geographics. Co-discoverer USARP Mountain Range (Arctic Inst. Mountain Range) in Victoria Land, Antarctica, Wilkes Land Meteorite Crater, Antarctica. Current work: Planetary geology/geophysics; polar regions; oceanography; glaciology; climatology; meteorite impact phenomena. Subspecialties: Geophysics; Planetology. Office: U Colo 1100 14th St PO Box 137 Denver CO 80202

WEIKEL, MAURICE MARCEL, dental manufacturing company executive; b. Winnemucca, Nev., May 1, 1921; s. Charles Elmer and Julie (Sairde) W.; m. Lorraine H. Hansen, Sept. 1, 1944; children: Larry, Gary, Dennis, Kristi, Joni. B.S., U. Pacific, 1945; D.D.S., 1945. Owner Dental Clinic, San Diego, 1945-67; pres. CIA Minera Tecate, Tecate, Mex., 1955-58, N.K. Metals, San Diego, 1953-58, Am. Silver & Mercury, San Diego, 1966-73, Dispersalloy Inc., El Cajon, Calif., 1973-74, Koberly Inc., El Cajon, 1974—; dir. U. Pacific Dental Sch., San Francisco, 1969-72; cons. in field. Served to lt. USN, 1945-46. Mem. ADA, Internat. Assn. Dental Researchers, Am. Powder Mettallurgy Inst., PSI-Omega. Republican. Lodge: Kiwanis. Patentee: Dental Anchor Prothesis, 1976; Disposable Dental All Container, 1978; Dental Tablet and Mercury Dispenser, 1978; Sliding Dental Dispenser, 1982. Current Work: Dental filling material for posterior teeth. Subspecialty: Dental materials. Home: 3537 S Buena Vista Dr Las Vegas NC 89132 Office: Koberly Inc 1050 Greenfield Dr PO Drawer D El Cajon CA 92022

WEIL, ANDRE, mathematician; b. Paris, May 6, 1906; D.Sc., U. Paris, 1928. Prof. math. Aligarh Muslin U., India, 1930-32, U. Strasbourg, 1933-40; lectr. Haverford Coll. and Swarthmore Coll., 1941-42; prof. U. Sao Paulo, Brazil, 1945-47, U. Chgo., 1947-58, Sch. Math., Inst. for Advanced Study, Princeton, N.J., 1958—. Author: Number Theory, 1984. Mem. Math. Soc. France, Indian Math. Soc., Nat. Acad. Scis. (fgn. assoc.). Subspecialty: Algebra and number theory. Office: Inst for Advanced Study Princeton NJ 08540*

WEIL, MAX HARRY, medical educator, physician, researcher; b. Baden, Switzerland, Feb. 9, 1927; came to U.S., naturalized, 1944; s. Marcel and Gretel (Winter) W.; m. Marianne Judith Posner, Apr., 1955; children—Susan Margot, Carol Juliet. A.B., U. Mich., 1948; M.D., SUNY Coll. Medicine, N.Y.C., 1952; Ph.D., U. Minn., 1957. Diplomate Am. Bd. Internal Medicine, Am. Bd. Cardiovascular Diseases. Rotating intern Cin. Gen. Hosp., 1952-53; resident in internal medicine U. Minn. Hosps., Heart Hosp., and VA Hosp., Mpls., 1953-55; research fellow in medicine and physiology U. Minn., Mpls., 1955-56; Nat. Heart Inst. sr. fellow and spl. research fellow, fellow in cardiorespiratory physiology Mayo Clinic, Rochester, Minn., 1956-57; chief cardiology City of Hope Med. Ctr., Duarte, Calif., 1957-59; cons. for cardiology, 1959-63; asst. clin. prof. medicine U. So. Calif., Los Angeles, 1957-59, asst. prof., 1959-63, assoc. prof., 1963-71, prof. clin. medicine, 1971-81, prof. clin. biomed. engring., 1972-81, adj. prof. medicine, 1981—, dir. shock research unit, 1961-81, chmn. div. critical care medicine, 1978-81; attending cardiologist children's div. Los Angeles County/U. So. Calif. Med. Ctr., Los Angeles, 1958-65, sr. attending cardiologist children's div., 1968-73, attending physician internal medicine service, 1958-71, sr. attending physician internal medicine service, 1971-81; dir. Ctr. for Critically Ill, U. So. Calif. and Hollywood Presby. Med. Ctr., Los Angeles, 1968-80; prof. medicine, chmn. dept. medicine, prof. physiology and biophysics, chief div. cardiology U. Health Scis./Chgo. Med. Sch., North Chicago, Ill., 1982—; attending physician (on leave of absence) Cedars-Sinai Med. Ctr., Los Angeles; mem. courtesy med. staff (on leave of absence) Good Samaritan Hosp., Los Angeles; attending physician St. Mary of Nazareth Hosp. Ctr., Chgo.; cons. physician med. ctrs.; clin. prof. anesthesia UCLA, 1981—; vis. prof., spl. lectr. at numerous instns., 1964—, including: disting. alumnus lectr. SUNY Downstate Alumni Ctr., N.Y.C., 1967; vis. prof. anesthesiology/critical care medicine Pitts. Sch. Medicine, 1973—; honored lectr. 50th Japanese Congress Infectious Diseases, Tokyo, 1976; Royal Coll. Physicians lectr. U. Toronto, Ont., Can., 1976; 13th ann. Oscar Schwidetzky Meml. lectr. Internat. Anesthesia Research Soc., San Francisco, 1978; honored guest lectr. 5th Anniversary of Philippine Heart Ctr. for Asia Sci. Meetings, Manila, 1980; invited disting. prof. Beijing Heart Lung and Blood Vessel Med. Ctr. Symposium on Critical Care Medicine, China, 1984; dir. U. So. Calif. and Inst. Critical Care Medicine Ann. Symposium on Critical Care Medicine, 1963—; bd. dirs., pres. Inst. Critical Care Medicine, Los Angeles and Chgo., 1974—; tech. cons., adviser in field. Author, editor monographs; author/co-author numerous profl. publs. Editor-in-chief Acute Care, 1983—; assoc. editor Critical Care Medicine, 1973-74, editorial bd., 1974-80; sect. editor Archives Internal Medicine, 1983—; editorial bd. Am. Jour. Medicine, 1971-79, 81—, Methods of Info. in Medicine, 1977—, Circulatory Shock, 1979—, Clin. Engring. Newsletter, 1980—, Chest, 1980—; guest editor, editorial adv. bd. and reviewer various profl. jours. Patentee in field. Pres. brotherhood Wilshire Blvd. Temple, Los Angeles, 1967-68; mem. Los Angeles Olympic Citizens Adv. Commn., 1981-84; bd. dirs. Los Angeles affiliate Am. Heart Assn., 1962-67; Hollywood Presbyn. Med. Ctr., Los Angeles, 1976-81. Served with U.S. Army, 1936-47. Recipient Alumni medallion SUNY Downstate Med. Ctr., 1970; N.Y. State Regents' scholar SUNY Coll. Medicine, 1950-52; prin. investigator numerous grants. Fellow Am. Coll. Cardiology (chmn. emergency cardiac care com. 1978-81), ACP, Am. Coll. Chest Physicians (council on clin. cardiology, council on critical care medicine), Council on Circulation of Am. Heart Assn., N.Y. Acad. Sci.; mem. Council on Thrombosis of Am. Heart Assn., Council on Cardiopulmonary Diseases of Am. Heart Assn., AMA (jour. sect. editor 1969-72), Lake County Med. Assn., Los Angeles County Med. Assn., Am. Physiol. Soc., Am. Soc. Pharmacology and Exptl. Therapeutics, Am. Soc. Echocardiography, Am. Soc. Nephrology, Am. Thoracic Soc., Am. Trauma Soc. (founding), Assn. Computing Machinery, Assn. Profs. Medicine, Assn. Am. Med. colls., Assn. Programs Dirs. in Internal Medicine, Central Soc. Clin. Research, Chgo. Heart Assn. (bd. govs.), Chgo. Cardiol. Group (exec. com.), Chgo. Soc. Internal Medicine, Lake County Heart Assn. (bd. govs.), Intensive Care Soc. U.K., IEEE (sr.), Soc. Exptl. Biology and Medicine, Western Soc. Clin. Research, Fedn. Am. Socs. Exptl. Biology, Am. Soc. Parenteral and Enteral Nutriton, Chgo. Soc. Internal Medicine; hon. mem. Soc. Critical Care Medicine (founding pres. 1971-72, Disting. Service award and hon. membership 1984), Am. Assn. Critical Care Nurses, Mexican Soc. Intensive Care, Chilean Soc. Surgery; mem. Skull and Dagger, Sigma Xi, Alpha Omega Alpha. Lodge: Toastmasters (pres. local lodge 1965-66). Subspecialties: Cardiology; Critical care. Home: 3810 S Mission Hills Rd Apt 303 Northbrook IL 60062Office: U of Health Scis/Chgo Med Sch 3333 Green Bay Rd North Chicago IL 60064

WEILER, JOHN MAYER, physician, researcher; b. Erie, Pa., Mar. 19, 1945; s. Ad R. and Ruth (Schlosser) W. B.S., U. Mich, 1967; M.D., Temple U., 1971. Diplomate: Am. Bd. Internal Medicine. Intern Ind. U. Hosp., 1971-72; resident Kans. U. Med. Ctr., 1974-75; research fellow Harvard U., 1975-77; asst. prof. U. Iowa, Iowa City, 1977-83, assoc. prof., 1983—. Served with USPHS, 1972-74. Recipient Research Assoc. Career Devel. award VA, 1979-82; recipient Clin. Investigation Career award VA, 1983-85; NIH research career devel. awardee, 1983—. Fellow ACP, Am. Acad. Allergy; mem. Am. Assn. Immunologists, Am. Rheumatism Assn. Subspecialties: Immunology (medicine); Allergy. Office: SW34E GH U Iowa Iowa City IA 52242

WEILER, KURT WALTER, research astronomer; b. Phoenix, Mar. 16, 1943; s. Henry C. and Dorothy Marie (Esser) W.; m. Geertje Weiler-Stoelwinder, June 8, 1979. B.S., U. Ariz., 1964; Ph.D., Calif. Inst. Tech., 1970. Sr. sci. officer Westerbork Radio Obs., Dwingeloo, Netherlands, 1970-72; fgn. guest collaborator U. Groningen, Netherlands, 1972-74; sci. collaborator Laboratorio di Radioastronomia, Bologna, Italy, 1975-76; research assoc. Max Planck Inst. Radioastronomy, Bonn, W. Ger., 1976-79; program dir. NSF, Washington, 1979-85; radio astronomer Naval Research Lab., Washington, 1985—. Contbr. articles to profl. jours. Mem. Am. Astron. Soc., Royal Astron. Soc., Internat. Astron. Union, Nederlandse Astronomen Club. Patentee in field. Current Work: Astronomical research on supernovae, supernova remants. Subspecialties: High energy astrophysics; Radio and microwave astronomy. Office: NRL-Code 4131 Washington DC 20375

WEILER, LAWRENCE STANLEY, chemistry educator, consultant; b. Middleton, N.S., Can., July 11, 1942; s. Stanley Walter and Gladys Louise (Rowe) W.; m. Agnes McCallum, Aug. 1, 1964; children—Cathrine, Nancy Lynn, Patricia. B.S., U. Toronto, Can., 1964; Ph.D., Harvard U., 1968. Asst. prof. chemistry, U. B.C., Vancouver, Can., 1968-75, assoc. prof., 1975-80, prof., 1980—, head dept. chemistry, 1982—. Recipient Merck, Sharpe and Dohme award Chem. Inst. Can., 1984. Fellow Chem. Inst Can.; mem. Am. Chem. Soc., Chem. Soc. London, Swiss Chem. Soc. Current work: Organic synthesis and natural products chemistry. Subspecialty: Organic chemistry. Office: U BC Dept Chemistry Vancouver BC V6T 146 Canada

WEILL, HANS, physician, educator; b. Berlin, Germany, Aug. 31, 1933; came to U.S., 1939; s. Kurt and Gerda (Philipp) W.; m. Kathleen Burton, Apr. 3, 1958; children: Judith, Leslie, David. B.S., Tulane U., 1955, M.D., 1958. Diplomate Am. Bd. Internal Medicine (mem. pulmonary disease subsplty. bd. 1980-86, bd. govs. 1985—). Intern Mt. Sinai Hosp., N.Y.C., 1958-59; resident Tulane Med. Unit, Charity Hosp. La., New Orleans, 1959-60, chief resident, 1961-62, sr. vis. physician, 1972—; NIH research fellow dept. medicine and pulmonary lab. Sch. Medicine Tulane U., New Orleans, 1960-61, instr. in medicine, 1962-64, asst. prof. medicine, 1964-67, asso. prof., 1967-71, prof. medicine, 1971—; chief pulmonary diseases sect. Tulane Med. Center, 1980—; dir. interdisciplinary research group in occupational lung diseases Nat. Heart, Lung and Blood Inst., 1972—, chmn. pulmonary disease adv. com., 1982-84; active staff Tulane Med. Center Hosp., 1976—; cons. pulmonary diseases and medicine USPHS Hosp., New Orleans, 1964—; cons. pulmonary diseases Touro Infirmary, New Orleans, 1962—; cons. NIH, Nat. Inst. Occupational Safety and Health, Occupational Safety and Health Adminstrn., USN, Nat. Acad. Scis., U.S. EPA. Editorial bd. American Review of Respiratory Disease, 1980-85; editor Respiratory Diseases Digest, 1981; guest editor Byssinosis Conference Supplement, Chest, 1981; lectr. participant workshops and confs. profl. groups in field, U.S., France, Can., U.K. Fellow Am. Acad. Allergy, Royal Soc. Medicine, A.C.P.; mem. Am. Thoracic Soc. (pres. 1976), Am. Lung Assn. (bd. dirs. 1975-78), New Orleans Acad. Internal Medicine (sec., treas. 1973-75), Am. Coll. Chest Physicians (gov. for La. 1970-75), Am. Fedn. Clin. Research, So. Soc. Clin. Investigation, N.Y. Acad. Scis., Brit. Thoracic Assn., Internat. Epidemiol. Assn., Am. Heart Assn. (task force on environment and cardiovascular system 1978), Phi Beta Kappa, Alpha Omega Alpha. Current Work: Occupational lung dieases. Subspecialties: Pulmonary medicine; Epidemiology. Home: 333 Friedrichs Ave Metairie LA 70005 Office: 1700 Perdido St New Orleans LA 70012

WEIN, ALAN JEROME, urologist, educator, researcher; b. Newark, Dec. 15, 1941; s. Isadore R. and Jeannette Francis (Abrams) W.; m. Kristene E. Whitmore; children: Allison, Rebecca. A.B., Princeton U., 1962; M.D., U. Pa., 1966. Diplomate: Am. Bd. Urology. Instr. urology U. Pa., 1971-72, asst. prof. urology, 1974-76, assoc. prof., 1976-83, prof., 1983—, chmn. div. urology, 1980—. Contbr. articles to profl. jours. Served to maj., M.C. U.S. Army, 1972-74. NIH; VA grantee. Mem. ACS, Soc. Univ. Urologists, Soc. Univ. Surgeons, Am. Assn. Surgery Trauma, Am. Soc. Pharmacology and Exptl. Therapeutics, Am. Soc. Clin. Oncology, Am. Urologic Assn., Sigma Xi, Alpha Omega Alpha. Republican. Jewish. Lodge: Rotary. Current Work: Urology, neurophysiology and neuropharmacology of bladder function. Subspecialties: Urology; Neuropharmacology. Home: 502 Addison Ct Philadelphia PA 19147 Office: 5 Silverstein U Pa 3400 Spruce St Philadelphia PA 19104

WEIN, ROSS WALLACE, science educator; b. Exeter, Ont., Can., Oct. 29, 1940; s. Emerson and Lauren (Hirtzel) W.; m. Eleanor Elizabeth Schmidt, Sept. 16, 1967; children—Laurie Pauline, Daniel Emerson. B.S., U. Guelph, Ont., 1966, M.S., 1967; Ph.D., Utah State U., 1969. NRC postdoctoral fellow U. Alta., Edmonton, 1969-70; vis. asst. prof., 1970-71; asst. prof. to prof., U. N.B., Fredericton, 1972—; dir. Fire Sci. Ctr., 1978—. Editor: Role of Fire in Northern Circumpolar Ecosystems, 1983; Resources and Dynamics of the Zone, 1983. Mem. United Ch. of Can. Current work: Fire ecology, natural resource and fire management. Subspecialty: Resource management. Office: Fire Sci Ctr U NB Box 4400 Fredericton NB E3B 5A3 Canada

WEINBERG, RICHARD ALAN, computer scientist; b. Mpls., Sept. 7, 1951; s. Edward Maurice and June Adele (Lieberman) W. B.A., Cornell U., 1973; M.S., U. Minn.-Mpls., 1974-80. Electronics engr. NASA Johnson Space Ctr., Houston, 1977; engr. Lockheed Electronics, Houston, 1977-79; computer scientist Cray Research, Inc., Mpls., 1980—. Contbr. articles to Spl. Interest Group Computer Graphcs publs.; dir.: computer-animated film Euclidean Illusions, 1978 (Cine Golden Eagle 1978). Mem. Assn. Computing Machinery, Spl. Interest Group Computer Graphics, IEEE. Current Work: Research and development of high-speed computer architectures and algorithms for synthesis of complex computer graphics images; Very large scale integrated circuit architectures; computer-synthesized animation. Subspecialties: Graphics, image processing, and pattern recognition; Computer architecture. Office: Cray Research Inc 3416 S La Cienega Blvd Los Angeles CA 90016

WEINBERG, ROBERT ALLEN, biology educator; b. Pitts., Nov. 11, 1942; s. Fritz E. and Lore R. W.; m. Amy Shulman, Aug. 29, 1976; children: Aron, Leah Rosa. B.A., MIT, 1964, Ph.D., 1969. Postdoctoral fellow Weizmann Inst., Rehovoth, Israel, 1969-70, Salk Inst., La Jolla, Calif., 1970-72; research assoc. fellow MIT, 1972-73; asst. prof. biology dept. biology and MIT (Ctr. for Cancer Research), 1973-76, assoc. prof., 1976-79, prof., 1979—; research scholar Mass. div. Am. Cancer Soc., 1974-77. Named Scientist of Yr. Discover Mag., 1982; recipient nat. divisional award Mass. div. Am. Cancer Soc., 1982; U.S. Steel Found. award in molecular biology, 1984; Bristol-Myers award for disting. achievement in cancer research, 1984; Rita Allen Found. scholar, 1976-80. Mem. Nat. Acad. Scis. Current Work: Molecular basis of carcinogenesis; isolation and characterization of tumor oncogenes. Subspecialties: Molecular biology; Cell and tissue culture. Office: Center for Cancer Research MIT 77 Massachusetts Ave Cambridge MA 02139

WEINBERG, STEVEN, physicist, educator; b. N.Y.C., May 3, 1933; s. Fred and Eva (Israel) W.; m. Louise Goldwasser, July 6, 1954; 1 dau. B.A., Cornell U., 1954; postgrad., Copenhagen Inst. Theoretical Physics, 1954-55; Ph.D., Princeton U., 1957; A.M. (hon.), Harvard U., 1973; Sc.D. (hon.), Knox Coll., 1978, U. Chgo., 1978, U. Rochester, 1979, Yale U., 1979, CUNY, 1980, Clark U., 1982, Dartmouth Coll., 1984; Ph.D. (hon.), Weizmann Inst., 1985; D.Litt. (hon.), Washington Coll., 1985. Research asso., instr. Columbia U., 1957-59; research physicist Lawrence Radiation Lab., Berkeley, Calif., 1959-60; mem. faculty U. Calif.-Berkeley, 1960-69, prof. physics, 1964-69; vis. prof. MIT, 1967-69, prof. physics, 1969-73; Higgins prof. physics Harvard U., 1973-83; sr. scientist Smithsonian Astrophys. lab., 1973-83; Josey prof. sci. U. Tex.-Austin, 1982—; sr. cons. Smithsonian Astrophys. Obs., 1983—; cons. Inst. Def. Analyses, Washington, 1960-73, ACDA, 1970-73; mem. Pres.'s Com. on Nat. Medal of Sci., 1979-82, Council of Scholars, Library of Congress, 1983—; sr. adv. La Jolla Inst.; chair in physics Collège de France, 1971; mem. NRC Com. on Internat. Security and Arms Control, 1981; dir. Jerusalem Winter Sch. Theoretical Physics, 1983—; Silliman lectr. Yale U., 1977; Richtmeyer lectr., 1974; Scott lectr. Cavendish Lab., 1975; Lauritsen Meml. lectr. Calif. Inst. Tech., 1979; Bethe lectr. Cornell U., 1979; de Shalit lectr. Weizman Inst., 1979; Einstein lectr. Israel Acad. Arts and Scis., 1984; Hilldale lectr. U. Wis., 1985; Sloan fellow, 1961-65; Loeb lectr. in physics Harvard U., 1966-67; Cherwell-Simon lectr. Oxford U., 1983; Bampton lectr. Columbia U., 1983; Morris Loeb vis. prof. physics Harvard U., 1983—. Author: Gravitation and Cosmology: Principles and Applications of the General Theory of Relativity, 1972, The First Three Minutes: A Modern View of the Origin of the Universe, 1977, The Discovery of Subatomic Particles, 1982; research and publs. on elementary particles, quantum field theory, cosmology.; co-editor, Cambridge Univ. Press; Co-editor monographs on math. physics; editorial bd., Progress in Sci. Culture, Nuclear Physics B, U. Chgo. Press, series on theoretical astrophysics. Bd. overseers SSC Accelerator, 1984—; bd. advisers Santa Barbara Inst. Theoretical Physics, 1983—. Recipient J. Robert Oppenheimer meml. prize, 1973; recipient Dannie Heineman prize in math. physics, 1977, Am. Inst. Physics-U.S. Steel Found. sci. writing award, 1977; Nobel prize in physics, 1979; Elliott Cresson medal Franklin Inst., 1979. Mem. Am. Acad. Arts and Scis. (council), Am. Phys. Soc. (past councilor at large), Nat. Acad. Sci., Internat. Astron. Union, Council Fgn. Relations, Am. Philos. Soc., Am. Hist. Assn., Royal Soc. London (fgn. mem.), Am. Mediaeval Acad. Subspecialties: Theoretical physics; Theoretical astrophysics. Office: Dept Physics U Tex Austin TX 78712

WEINBERG, UZI, endocrinology and biology clin investigator; b. Tel Aviv, Israel, Apr. 19, 1939; came to U.S., 1972; s. Elimelech and Hava (Listek) W.; m. Nira Yaron, Apr. 4, 1967; children: Odealia, Maya. M.D., U. Paris, 1968. Lic. physician, N.Y. Extern Hospitaux de Paris, 1964; asst. prof. N.Y. U., 1976-77; asst. prof. medicine and neurology Albert Einstein Coll. Medicine, 1979-82, assoc. prof., 1982—; cons. Eli Lilly Co., 1980—. Contbr. articles profl. jours.; reviewer profl. jours. Served to capt. Israeli Def. Force, 1957-60. Ford Found. grantee, 1977-78; NIH grantee, 1979-82. Mem. Am. Endocrine Soc., Am. Fedn. Clin. Research, Internat. Soc. Internat., Soc. Sleep Research, Internat. Soc. Endocrinology. Inventor RIA for melatonin, discoverer novel biochemical mechanism concering puberty. Current Work: Developmental neurobiology and endocrinology. Subspecialties: Neuroendocrinology; Biochemistry (medicine).

WEINBERGER, NORMAN MALCOLM, biological sciences educator; b. Cleve., Aug. 10, 1935; s. Adolph Weinberger and Jean (Schneiderman) Wasserman; m. Jacqueline Denise Meckler, Sept. 3, 1954; children—Amy, Gregg, Eric, Tamara, Jennifer, Lisa, Andrea. B.A., Western Res. U., 1957, M.S., 1959, Ph.D., 1961. Asst. prof. U. Calif.-Irvine, 1965-68, assoc. prof., 1968-74, assoc. dean, 1975, assoc. dean for programs, 1979-80, acting dean for biol. sci., 1980-81, prof. neurosci., 1974—. Author: Neural Control of Behavior, 1970; Psychobiology: The Biological Bases of Behavior, 1967; editor: Neurobiology of Learning and Memory, 1984. Mem. editorial adv. bd. Behavioral and Neural Biology. Assoc. editor Exptl. Neurology. Mem. editorial bd. Neurosci. and Behavioral Physiology. Reviewer Behavioral Sci. Instrumentation and Methods. NIMH fellow, 1958, 62-64; recipient Outstanding Faculty Service award U. Calif.-Irvine, 1975. Mem. AAAS, Internat. Brain Research Orgn., Pavlovian Soc. Am., Soc. for Neurosci., N.Y. Acad. Scis. Current work: Neurobiology of learning and attention; neurophysiological and Behavioral plasticity; auditory system function. Subspecialty: Neurobiology. Home: 958 Sandcastle Dr Corona del Mar CA 92625 Office: Ctr for Neurobiology of Learning and Memory U Calif Irvine CA 92717

WEINER, MURRAY, physician, educator, cons. to pharm. industry; b. N.Y.C., Apr. 18, 1919; s. Samuel O. and Gussie (Begun) W.; m. Marilyn Rose, Jan. 14, 1951 (dec.); m. Helen Jane McNeely, June 15, 1976; children: Eve Gail Weiner Schauer, George Jay, Joan Sally. B.S., CCNY, 1939; M.S. in Biochemistry, M.D., NYU, 1943. Diplomate: Am. Bd. Internal Medicine. Intern Sinai Hosp., Balt., 1943-44; resident N.Y.U. Research Service, Goldwater Meml. Hosp., 1946-49; practice medicine specializing in internal medicine, N.Y.C., 1950-71; mem. faculty N.Y.U. Coll. Medicine, N.Y.C., 1946-71; v.p. biologic research, also other positions Geigy Pharms., N.Y.C., 1957-71; v.p. research and sci. affairs Merrell Research Center, Cin., 1971-81; clin. prof. medicine, dir. clin. pharmacology Coll. Medicine, U. Cin., 1981—; pres. Weiner Cons., Inc., Cin., 1981—. Author: Coagulation. Thrombosis, and Dicumarol, 1949, Nicotinic Acid: Nutrient/Co-factor/Drug, 1983; novel The Medicine Makers, 1979. Contbr. over 170 articles to sci. publs. Chmn. Cin. chpt. Project HOPE, 1979-81. Served to capt. M.C. U.S. Army, 1944-46, PTO. NIH, Am. Heart Assn., Nutrition Found. grantee; also others. Fellow ACP, N.Y. Acad. Scis., Am. Soc. for Pharmacology and Exptl. Therapeutics; mem. numerous other orgns. Current Work: Clinical pharmacology; drug disposition, safety, utility Subspecialties: Pharmacology; Internal medicine.

WEINFURTER, ERICH BRIAN, nuclear engineer; b. Appleton, Wis., Nov. 27, 1955; s. Robert Wayne and Cathryn Janice (Masterson) W. B.S. in Engring, Iowa State U., Ames, 1981. Tech. staff engr. Commonwealth Edison Co., Cordova, Ill., 1981—. Mem. Am. Nuclear Soc., Profl. Reactor Operator Soc. Current Work: Design and development of safety related systems for a nuclear power station. Subspecialty: Nuclear engineering. Home: 3441 60th St Apt 6C Moline IL 61252 Office: Commonwealth Edison Co 22710 206th Ave N Cordova IL 61242

WEINGAND, KURT WILLIAM, comparative atherobiologist, veterinary pathologist, educator; b. St. Louis, Oct. 25, 1955; s. William George and Arleen Marie (Ayers) W. D.V.M., U. Mo., 1980; Ph.D. in Pathology, Colo. State U., 1984. Practice vet. medicine specializing in companion animals Blue Springs Animal Clinic, Mo., 1980-81; pathology resident Colo. State U., Ft. Collins, 1981-84; instr. comparative medicine Bowman Gray Sch. Medicine, Winston-Salem, N.C., 1984—. Co-author: The Biology and Clinical Science of Atherosclerosis, 1984. Contbr. articles to profl. jours. Recipient Loren D. Kintner Vet. Diagnostic Lab. award U. Mo., 1980, Edgar F. Ebert Meml. award U. Mo., 1980. Mem. Am. Vet. Med. Assn., Am. Soc. Vet. Clin. Pathology, Am. Soc. Vet. Physiol. and Pharmacology, Phi Zeta. Current work: Comparative experimental atherosclerosis research; veterinary clinical pathology. Subspecialties: Pathology (veterinary medicine); Laboratory animal medicine. Office: Dept Comparative Medicine Bowman Gray Sch Medicine 300 S Hawthorne Rd Winston-Salem NC 27103

WEINHOUSE, SIDNEY, biochemist, educator; b. Chgo., May 21, 1909; s. Harry and Dora (Cutler) W.; m. Sylvia Krawitz, Sept. 15, 1935 (dec. Aug. 1957); children: Doris Joan, James Lester, Barbara May; m. Adele Klein, Dec. 27, 1969. B.S., U. Chgo., 1933, Ph.D., 1936; D.M.S. (hon.), Med. Coll. Pa., 1973; D.Sc. (hon.), Temple U., 1976. Eli Lilly fellow U. Chgo., 1936-38, Coman fellow, 1939-41; staff OSRD, 1941-44; with Houdry Process Corp., 1944-47; biochem. research dir. Temple U. Research Inst., 1947-50, prof. chemistry, 1952-77; emeritus prof. biochemistry Temple U. Med. Sch., 1977—; head dept. metabolic chemistry Lankenau Hosp. Research Inst. and Inst. Cancer Research, 1950-57; chmn. div. biochemistry Inst. Cancer Research, 1957-61; asso. dir. Fels Research Inst., Temple U. Med. Sch., Phila., 1961-64, dir., 1964-74; mem. bd. sci. advisers Inst. Environ. Health, NIH. Contbr. articles on original research to sci. jours.; editor: Jour. Cancer Research, 1969-79. Bd. dirs. Am. Cancer Soc. Mem. Am. Chem. Soc., Am. Soc. Biol. Chemists, Am. Assn. Cancer Research, Nat. Acad. Sci. Current Work: Enzyme studies in cancer as manitestations of abnormalities of general regulation. Subspecialties: Biochemistry (medicine); Cancer research (medicine). Home: 1919 Chestnut St Philadelphia PA 19103 Office: Fels Research Inst Temple U Sch Medicine Philadelphia PA 19140*

WEININGER, STEPHEN JOEL, chemistry educator; b. N.Y.C., Mar. 28, 1937; s. Isadore and Ruth (Hochman) W.; m. Jennifer Lynne Barkham, Oct. 15, 1961; children—Elliot, J. Daniel, David. B.A., Bklyn. Coll., 1957; Ph.D., U. Pa., 1964. Sr. demonstrator U. Durham, Eng., 1964-65; asst. prof. chemistry Worcester Poly. Inst., Mass., 1965-70, assoc. prof., 1970-77, prof., 1977—; vis. assoc. prof. Colo. State U., Fort Collins, 1976-78; cons. Natick Research Devel. Commn., U.S. Army, Mass., 1980—, Noramco, Inc., Worcester, Mass., 1984—. Author: Contemporary Organic Chemistry, 1972; Organic Chemistry, 1984. Mem. Am. Chem. Soc., AAUP. Current work: Reactive intermediates: carbenes, radical ions; synthesis and electronic properties of porphyrins and phthalocyanines. Subspecialty: Organic chemistry. Home: 18 Chiltern Hill Dr Worcester MA 01602 Office: Worcester Poly Inst Goddard Hall Worcester MA 01609

WEINLAND, STUART LOUIS, ceramic engineer; b. Dayton, Ohio, Sept. 25, 1940; s. Louis Albert and Hazel Clara (Schott) W. B.S., Alfred U., 1962; M.S., Miss. State U., 1965. Assoc. ceramic engr. Babcock and Wilcox Co., Alliance, Ohio, 1962-63; scientist Lockheed Missiles and Space Co., Sunnyvale, Calif., 1965-67; sr. engr. Martin Marietta Corp., Orlando, Fla., 1968-70; sr. sci. assoc. Lawrence Livermore Nat. Lab., Livermore, Calif., 1976—. Patentee Core removal U.S., 1972; contbr. articles to prof. jours. Mem. Am. Ceramic Soc. Current work: Ceramic powder technology; shock wave effects in materials. Subspecialties: Ceramic engineering; Ceramics. Office: Lawrence Livermore Nat Lab 7000 East Ave Livermore CA 94550

WEINRICH, BRIAN ERWIN, educator; b. Passaic, N.J., Jan. 8, 1952; s. Erwin H. and Ann E. (Gall) W. B.S., Pa. State U., 1974, M.A., 1978; M.S., Shippensburg State U., 1983. Mathematician U.S. Dept. Agr., SEA-ARS, Northeast Watershed Research Ctr., University Park, Pa., 1974-80; instr. math and computer sci. Shippensburg (Pa.) State U., 1980-84; asst. prof. math. and computer sci. California U. of Pa., 1984—; cons. in field. Author: (with A. S. Rogowski) Water Movement and Quality on Strip-Mined Lands: A Compilation of Computer Programs, 1983; contbg. author (Surface Mining) Edit, II, 1983; contbr. articles to profl. jours. Mem. Missions bd. Calvary Bapt. Ch., State College, Pa., 1975-80; visitation team Prince St. United Brethren Ch., Shippensburg, 1982-84. U.S. Dept. Agr. grantee, 1982—. Mem. Soc. for Indsl. and Applied Math., Math. Assn. Am., Am. Math. Soc., Assn. Computing Machinery. Republican. Current Work: Development of mathematical, statistical and numerical models and simulation techniques in hydrology, especially as applied to strip mining/erosion. Subspecialties: Mathematical software; Hydrology. Home: 988 Cross St Apt 34 California PA 15419 Office: Dept Math and Computer Sci California U Pa California PA 15419

WEINSTEIN, I. BERNARD, physician; b. Madison, Wis., Sept. 9, 1930; s. Max and Frieda (Blackman) W.; m. Joan Anker, Dec. 21, 1952; children: Tamara, Claudia, Matthew. B.S., U. Wis., 1952, M.D., 1955. Intern, then resident in medicine Montefiore Hosp., N.Y.C., 1955-57; clin. asso. NIH, 1957-59; research asso. Harvard U. Med. Sch., 1959-60, MIT, 1960-61; mem. faculty Columbia U. Coll. Physicians and Surgeons, 1961—, prof. medicine and pub. health, 1978—, also dir. Comprehensive Cancer Ctr., dir. environ. sci. Sch. Pub. Health; attending physician Presbyn. Hosp., N.Y.C.; cons. Nat. Cancer Inst., Am. Cancer Soc.; cons. Internat. Agy. Research Cancer, Chem. Industry's Inst of Toxicology. Author research papers biochemistry, genetics, cancer biology, chem. carcinogenesis. Served with USPHS, 1957-59. Recipient Meltzer medal Soc. Exptl. Biology and Medicine; European Molecular Biology Orgn. fellow Imperial Cancer Research Fund, London, 1970-71. Mem. Am. Soc. Microbiology, Am. Soc. Clin. Investigation, Am. Soc. Biol. Chemists, Am. Soc. Cell Biology, Internat. Soc. Quantum Biology, Am. Assn. Cancer Research, Inst. Medicine of U.S. Nat. Acad. Scis., Phi Beta Kappa, Sigma Xi, Alpha Omega Alpha. Jewish. Subspecialties: Oncology; Molecular biology. Home: 249 Chestnut St Englewood NJ 07631 Office: 701 W 168th St New York NY 10032

WEINSTEIN, MILTON CHARLES, educator; b. Brookline, Mass., July 14, 1949; s. William and Ethel (Rosenbloom) W.; m. Rhonda Kruger, June 14, 1970; children: Jeffrey William, Daniel Jay. A.B., A.M., Harvard U., 1970, M.P.P., 1972, Ph.D., 1973. Asst. prof. John F. Kennedy Sch. Govt., Harvard U., Cambridge, Mass., 1973-76, assoc. prof., 1976-80; prof. policy and decision scis. Harvard Sch. Pub. Health, Boston, 1980—; adj. prof. community and family medicine Dartmouth Med. Sch., Hanover, N.H., 1981—; cons. HHS, 1979—, EPA, 1978—, Battelle Human Affairs Research Ctr., Seattle, 1981—, Mass. Health Data Consortium, Waltham, Mass., 1983, Smith Kline and French Labs., Phila., 1983—, VA, 1984. Author: Clinical Decision Analysis, 1980, Hypertension: A Policy Perspective, 1976; editorial bd.: Med. Decision Making, 1981—. NSF fellow, 1972. Mem. Soc. Med. Decision Making (v.p. 1982-83, pres. 1984-85, trustee 1980-82), Soc. Risk Analysis, AAAS, Ops. Research Soc. Am., Phi Beta Kappa. Current Work: Evaluation medical technology; cost-benefit and cost-effectiveness analysis; medical decision making; health care policy; risk analysis. Subspecialties: Health services research; Operations research (mathematics). Office: 677 Huntington Ave Boston MA 02115

WEINSTEIN, ROY, college dean, physics researcher; b. N.Y.C., Apr. 21, 1927; s. Harry and Lillian (Ehrenberg) W.; m. Janet Spiller, Mar. 28, 1954; children—Lee, Sara. S.B., MIT, 1951, Ph.D., 1954; Sc.D. (hon.), Lycoming Coll., 1981. Instr. Brandeis U., 1954-55, asst. prof., 1955-56; asst. prof. MIT, Cambridge, 1956-59; assoc. prof. Northeastern U., Boston, 1960-63, prof., 1963-82, chmn. dept. physics, 1974-82; prof. physics, dean Coll. Natural Scis. and Math., U. Houston, 1982—; vis. scholar Stanford U., Calif., 1965-66, 68-69, 81-82; dir. Wincom, Woburn, Mass.; dir., mem. exec. com. Houston Area Research Corp., Woodlands, Tex. Author: Atomic Physics, 1964; Nuclear Physics, 1964; Interaction of Radiation and Matter, 1964. Editor textbooks, research compendium. Contbr. numerous research papers to profl. jours. Active Lexington Town Meeting, Mass., 1975-81. Served with USNR, 1945-46. Grantee NSF, 1960-85, U.S. Dept. Energy, 1963, 74, 77; fellow NSF, 1959, 68, Guggenheim Found., 1970. Fellow Am. Phys. Soc.; mem. Phi Kappa Phi (nat. triennial scholar 1979-82). Current work: Particle detectors, experiment design, quantum electrodynamics, chromodynamics, properties of quarks and leptons. Subspecialties: Atomic and molecular physics; Particle physics. Home: 4368 Fiesta Ln Houston TX 77004 Office: Coll Natural Scis and Math U Houston Central Campus Houston TX 77004

WEINTRAUB, MARVIN, plant virologist; b. Radom, Poland, Oct. 17, 1924; came to Can., 1930, naturalized, 1935; s. Abraham and Rachel Leah (Krygier) W.; m. Phyliss Rita Enushevsky, June 20, 1948; children—Laura, Mark, Lisa, John. B.A., U. Toronto, 1947, Ph.D., 1950. Research scientist Agr. Can., St. Catharines, Ont., 1950-59, research scientist, Vancouver, B.C., 1959-71, research dir., 1971—; research fellow, virus lab. U. Calif.-Berkeley, 1956-57; hon. prof. plant sci. U. B.C., Vancouver, 1971—. Author: Textbook of Botany, 1947. Asst. editor Virology, 1966-69. Contbr. articles to sci. jours. Mem. Provincial Com. on Edn., B.C., 1962-64; pres. Congregation Beth Israel, Vancouver, 1964-67, Pacific region Can. Jewish Congress, 1974-77. Ont. Sci. Found. fellow, 1950; recipient Queen's Jubilee medal, 1977. Fellow N.Y. Acad. Sci.; mem. Am. Phytopathol.. Soc., Can. Phytopathol Soc., Electron Microscopy Soc. Am., Am. Soc. Virology. Current work: correlation of ultra structuraland biochemical effects of plant virus infections; acquired immunity in plants; electron microscopy. Subspecialty: Plant virology. Office: Research Station Agriculture Canada 6660 NW Marine Dr Vancouver BC V6T 1X2 Canada

WEIR, BRUCE SPENCER, genetics educator; b. Christchurch, N.Z., Dec. 31, 1943; came to U.S., 1976; s. Gordon Ralph and Margaret Annie (Hodder) W.; m. Elizabeth Anna Swainson, Aug. 7, 1971; children: Claudia Beth, Henry Bruce. B.Sc. (hons.), U. Canterbury, 1964; Ph.D., N.C. State U., 1968. Reader Massey U., N.Z., 1970-76; prof. stats./genetics N.C. State U., Raleigh, 1976—. Contbr. articles to profl. jours. Mem. Am. Statis. Assn., Biometric Soc, Genetic Soc. Am., Soc. Study of Evolution. Current work: Statistical analysis of genetic data. Subspecialties: Genetics and genetic engineering (biology); Statistics. Home: 3328 Boulder Ct Raleigh NC 27067 Office: NC State Univ PO Box 8203 Raleigh NC 27695

WEIS, KONRAD MAX, chemical company executive; b. Leipzig, Germany, Oct. 10, 1928; came to U.S., 1971; s. Alfred and Margarete (Leipoldt) W.; m. Gisela Lueg, Aug. 3, 1956; children—Alfred, Bettina. Ph.D., U. Bonn, 1955. Joined Bayer AG, Leverkusen, W.Ger., 1956, mgmt./exec. positions, 1961-74; pres., chief exec. officer Mobay Chem. Corp. subs. Bayer AG, Pitts., 1974-81; chmn., pres., chief exec. officer (Mobay Chem. Corp. subs. Bayer AG), 1981—; vice chmn. Miles Labs. Inc.; dir. European Am. Bank, Cyclops Corp., Dravo Corp., Agfa-Gevaert, Inc.; Hon. consul Fed. Republic West Germany, Pitts., 1978—. Trustee, mem. exec. com. bd. trustees Carnegie-Mellon U., 1981—; trustee Carnegie Inst., 1984—; v.p. Allegheny Conf. on Community Devel., 1980—; mem. policy com. Bus. Council Pa., 1980—; bd. dirs. Pitts. Ballet Theatre, Inc., 1983—. Mem. Chem. Mfg. Assn. (dir., fin. com. 1985—), German Am. C. of C. (dir. 1981—), World Affairs Council Pitts (dir. 1983—). Clubs: Links (N.Y.C.); Pitts. Golf, Duquesne (Pitts.); Rolling Rock Country, Houston. Subspecialty: Organic chemistry. Address: Mobay Chem Corp Mobay Rd Pittsburgh PA 15205-9741

WEISBACH, JERRY ARNOLD, See *Who's Who in America,* 43rd edition.

WEISBERG, AARON, internist, gastroenterologist, consultant, research, educator; b. Bklyn., July 21, 1915; s. Joseph and Yetta (Weisberg) W.; m. Ruth Hannah Mintz, Feb. 7, 1949; children: Harlene Edith, Sharon Esta Weisberg Shapiro. B.A. in Chemistry, NYU, 1935; M.D., Cin. Eclectic Med. Coll., 1939. Diplomate: Am. Bd. Internal Medicine. Intern Coney Island Hosp., Bklyn., 1939-41, resident, 1941-42, attending physician, 1946-74, attending physician emeritus, 1974—; dir. medicine Carson C. Peck Meml. Hosp., Bklyn., 1954-70; chief of medicine Meth. Hosp. Bklyn., 1970-74, cons. in medicine and gastroenterology, 1974—; attending staff mem. in medicine and gastroenterology Tampa VA Hosp., 1974 —, St. Petersburg (Fla.) Gen. Hosp., 1974—, Palms Pasadena Hosp., St. Petersburg, 1974—; med. dir. Spery Gyroscope, Clearwater, Fla., 1975—; clin. asst. prof. internal medicine and gastroenterology and clin. asst. prof. comprehensive medicine U. South Fla., 1975—. Contbr. numerous articles on cardiology, gastroenterology and cancer to profl. jours.; editorial staff: Colon and Rectal Surgery, 1980—. Served to capt. M.C. U.S. Army, 1942-46. Recipient Gold Medal award Coney Island Hosp., 1972, Silver cert. Meth. Hosp., 1974. Fellow ACP, Am. Coll. Gastroenterology, Internat. Acad. Proctology, Royal Soc. Medicine, Am. Coll Nutrition; mem. Am. Fedn. Clin. Research (sr.), Am. Soc. Gastrointestinal Endoscopy, AMA, Pan Am. Soc., Occupational Med. Assn., Am. Chem. Soc., Am. Heart Assn., Phi Lambda Kappa. Clubs: NYU (N.Y.C.); Seminole Country and Golf. Current Work: Cancer research; thymus gland lymphocytes immunity. Subspecialties: Internal medicine; Gastroenterology.

WEISBORD, NORMAN EDWARD, invertebrate paleontology educator; b. Jersey City, Oct. 1, 1901; s. Edward and Clara (Mirsky) W.; m. Nettie S. Schein, Dec. 19, 1939. B.A., Cornell U., 1923, M.S., 1926. Geologist Atlantic Refining Co., Latin Am., 1923-33; sr. field geologist Standard Oil Co. N.J., Argentina and Bolivia, 1933-35; geologist to asst. chief geologist Standard Vacuum Oil Co., Java, Sumatra, Borneo and New Guinea, 1935-42; chief geologist Mobil Oil Corp., Venezuela, 1942-57; research assoc. in geology Fla. State U., Tallahassee, 1957-64, prof. geology, 1964—; occasional cons. oil cos. Author 38 articles and books on geology and paleontology, 1926-81. Mem. Paleontol. Research Instn. of Ithaca (charter and life mem., v.p. 1956-59, pres. 1959-61), Alpha Epsilon Pi. Current Work: Adviser to students; publishing on matters relating to geology and invertebrate paleontology. Subspecialties: Geology; Paleobiology. Home: 1910 Gibbs Dr Tallahassee FL 32303 Office: Dept Geology Fla State U Tallahassee FL 32306

WEISS, HOWARD JACOB, operations research educator; b. Phila., Sept. 18, 1950; s. Ernest D. and Charlotte M. (Silverman) W.; m. Lucia Beck, Aug. 17, 1975; children: Lisa, Ernest. B.Sc., Washington U., St. Louis, 1972; M.S., Northwestern U., 1973, Ph.D., 1975. Asst. prof. Western Ill. U., Macomb, 1975-76; asst. prof. Temple U., Phila., 1976-81; assoc. prof. dept. mgmt. Temple U. (Sch. Bus. Adminstrn.), 1981—; cons. USI, Inc., N.Y.C., 1982-83, Matlack, Inc., Lansdowne, Pa., 1982-83. Author: (with Ben Lev) Introduction to Mathematical Programming, 1982. Mem. Ops. Research Soc. Am./Inst. Mgmt. Sci., Ops. Research Soc. Phila. (pres. 1977-78). Current Work: Research interests in operations management, inventory, bulk service queues, job shop scheduling. Subspecialties: Operations research (engineering); Industrial engineering. Home: 2157 Woodlawn Ave Glenside PA 19038 Office: Dept Mgmt Temple U Sch Bus Adminstrn Philadelphia PA 19122

WEISS, NORMAN LOUIS, environmental planner; b. Phoenix, Jan. 21, 1951; s. Hyman and Hattie Ethyl (Merlinsky) W.; m. Robin Lee Byram, Aug. 16, 1985. A.A., Phoenix Coll., 1972; B.S., Ariz. State U., 1974, M.A., 1977, postgrad., 1977-81. Ptnr., Bioconn Environ. Studies, Phoenix, 1973-74; environ. research intern Ariz. State U., Tempe, 1975-76; environ. planner Ariz. Dept. Health Services, Phoenix, 1978-80, bur. planning dir., 1980-83, asst. legis. liaison, 1981—, chief bur. waste control, 1983-84, mgr. environ. programs, 1984—. EPA grantee, 1979—. Mem. Ariz. Pub. Health Assn. (bd. dirs. 1982, 83), Ariz. Environ. Health Assn. (bd. dirs 1981, 82, 85), Am. Planning Assn., Nat. Environ. Health Edn. Conf. (asst. state chmn.). Jewish. Current work: Hazardous waste facility siting; environmental regulation and public policy; environmental planning and land use management. Subspecialty: Hazardous waste disposal. Home: 830 E Flynn Ln Phoenix AZ 85014 Office: Ariz Dept Health Services 2005 N Central Ave Phoenix AZ 85004

WEISS, ROLAND GEORGE, electrical engineer, consultant; b. Milw., July 11, 1949; s. George William and Alice Edna (Wille) W. B.S., U. Wis.-Milw., 1972; M.S., Northwestern U., 1975, Ph.D., 1976. Ops. research analyst Nat. Bur. Standards, Washington, 1976-79; mem. tech staff Bell Labs., Lincroft, N.J., 1979-83; sr. engr. Ford Aerospace, College Park, Md., 1984—. Contbr. articles to profl. jours. Mem. IEEE, AIAA. Current work: Systems engineering of data processing, communications, and control systems including space station information system. Subspecialties: Systems engineering; Information systems, storage, and retrieval (computer science). Home: 44 Columbia Ave Takoma Park MD 20912 Office: Ford Aerospace & Communications 4920 Niagara Rd College Park MD 20740

WEISS, STEFAN ADAM, microbiologist; b. Jablonica, Poland, Dec. 25, 1936; came to U.S., 1966, naturalized, 1971; s. Antony Jan and Mary Helen (Malyszczuk) W.; married; children: Carl, Catherine, Tanya. M.S., Poly U. Lwow, Poland, 1955, 1957; postgrad., U. Toronto, 1962. Research assoc. Connaught Med. Research Labs., U. Toronto, 1959-62; virologist Food and Drug Directorate of Can. Dept. Nat. Health and Welfare, Ottawa, 1962-66; research virologist Bristol Labs., Syracuse, N.Y., 1966-69; virologist Alcon Labs., Inc., Ft. Worth, 1969-70; research virologist Monsanto Co., St. Louis, 1970-72; head cell culture and virology prodn. Inst. Molecular Virology, St. Louis U., 1972-73; sr. research virologist-microbiologist Dow Lepetit Ltd. of Dow Chem. Co., Indpls., 1973-75; mgr. tissue culture prodn. Litton Bionetics, Inc., Kensington, Md., 1975-77; head cell culture labs. microbiology and infectious diseases Southwest Found. Research and Edn., San Antonio, 1977—; cons. in field. Contbr. articles to profl. jours. Grantee in field. Mem. Am. Soc. Microbiology, Am. Tissue Culture Assn. Democrat. Roman Catholic. Lodge: KC. Patentee in field. Current Work: Virology, human, animal, insect, chemotherapy; viral insecticides, cell culture, large scale, bioengineering, genetic toxicology. Subspecialties: Tissue culture; Virology (biology). Office: W Loop 410 at Military Dr San Antonio TX 78284

WEISSBACH, ARTHUR, cell biologist, researcher, educator; b. N.Y.C., Aug. 27, 1927; s. Louis and Vivian W.; m. Joyce, Nov. 1, 1958; children: Lyle, Claudia. B.S., CCNY, 1947; Ph.D. (Life Ins. Med. Research Fund fellow), Columbia U., 1953. Nat. Found. Infantile Paralysis postdoctoral fellow NIH, 1953-55; NSF sr. postdoctoral fellow Institut Pasteur, Paris, 1959-60; research chemist in biochemistry Nat. Inst. Arthritis and Metabolic Diseases, NIH, 1960-68; head dept. cell biology Roche Inst. Molecular Biology, Nutley, N.J., 1968-83, assoc. dir., 1983—; adj. prof. human genetics and devel. Coll. Physicians and Surgeons, Columbia U., 1969-83; adj. prof. microbiology Univ. Medicine and Dentistry N.J., 1981—; lectr. in chemistry Georgetown U. Grad. Sch., 1957-58; vis. scientist Institut de Biologie Physico-chimique, Paris, 1968-69. Bd. dirs. Rapkine French Sci. Fund. Current Work: Enzymology and mechanism of DNA synthesis in mammalian and plant cells; control of viral and host DNA replication after infection with DNA containing viruses. Subspecialties: Cell and tissue culture; Biochemistry (biology). Office: Roche Inst Molecular Biology Nutley NJ 07110

WEISSBACH, HERBERT, biochemist; b. N.Y.C., Mar. 16, 1932; s. Louis and Vivan (Ruhalter) W.; m. Renee Kohl, Dec. 27, 1953; children: Lawrence, Marjorie, Nancy, Robert. B.S., CCNY, 1953; M.S. in Biochemistry, George Washington U., 1955, Ph.D., 1957. Chemist Lab. Clin. Biochemistry, NIH, Bethesda, Md., 1953-68, acting chief, 1968-69; asso. dir. Roche Inst. Molecular Biology, Nutley, N.J., 1969-83, dir., 1983—; v.p. Hoffmann La Roche, 1983—; adj. prof. dept. human genetics and devel. Columbia U., 1969-85; adj. prof. dept. microbiology N.J. Coll. Medicine and Dentistry, 1981—. Editor: (with S. Pestka) Molecular Mechanisms of Protein Biosynthesis, 1977, (with R. Kunz) Health Research: Search for the Medicines of Tomorrow, 1978, (with M.A.Q. Siddiqui and M. Krauskopf) Molecular Approaches to Gene Expression and Protein Synthesis. Recipient Superior Service award HEW, 1968. Mem. Nat. Acad. Scis., Am. Soc. Biol. Chemistry, Am. Chem. Soc. (Enzyme award 1970), AAAS, Am. Soc. Microbiology. Current Work: Regulation of gene expression. Subspecialties: Biochemistry (biology); Molecular biology. Home: 333 Crestmont Rd Cedar Grove NJ 07009 Office: Roche Inst Molecular Biology Nutley NJ 07110

WEISSKOPF, VICTOR FREDERICK, physicist; b. Vienna, Austria, Sept. 19, 1908; came to U.S., 1937, naturalized, 1942; s. Emil and Martha (Gut) W.; m. Ellen Tvede, Sept. 5, 1934; children: Thomas Emil, Karen Louise. Ph.D., U. Goettingen, Germany, 1931. Research asso. U. Copenhagen, Denmark, 1932-34, Inst. of Tech., Zûrich, Switzerland, 1934-37; asst. prof. physics U. Rochester, N.Y., 1937-43; with Manhattan Project, Los Alamos, N.M., 1943-46; prof. physics Mass. Inst. Tech., 1946-60; dir. gen. European Orgn. for Nuclear Research, Geneva, Switzerland, 1961-65; Inst. prof. Mass. Inst. Tech., 1965—; chmn. high energy physics adv. panel AEC, 1967-73. Author: (with J. Blatt) Theoretical Nuclear Physics, 1952, Knowledge and Wonder, 1962, Physics in the Twentieth Century, 1972; (with K. Gottfried) Concepts of Particle Physics; articles on nuclear physics, quantum theory, radiation theory, etc. in science jours. Recipient Max Planck medal Germany, 1956, Hi Majorana award, 1970, G. Gamov award, 1971, Boris Pregel award, 1971, Prix Mondial Cino del Duca France, 1972, L. Boltzmann prize Austria, 1977; Nat. Medal of Sci. U.S., 1980; Wolf prize Jerusalem, 1982. Fellow Am. Phys. Soc. (pres. 1960); mem. Nat. Acad. Scis., Am. Acad. Arts and Scis. (pres. 1975-79), French Academie des Scis. (corr.), Austrian Acad. Sci. (corr.), Danish Acad. Sci. (corr.), Bavarian Acad. Sci. (corr.), Scottish Acad. Sci. (corr.), Soviet Acad. Sci. (corr.), Pontifical Acad. Sci. Subspecialty: Nuclear physics. Home: 36 Arlington St Cambridge MA 02140

WEISSLER, GERHARD LUDWIG, physicist, educator; b. Eilenburg, Germany, Feb. 20, 1918; came to U.S., 1939, naturalized, 1944; s. Otto and Margret Louise (Wendt) W.; m. Claire Betty Weissler, Aug. 15, 1953; children: Roderick A., Robert Eric, Mark Gregory (dec.). B.S., Tech. U. Berlin, 1938; M.A., U. Calif.-Berkeley, 1941, Ph.D., 1942. Diplomate: Am. Bd. Radiology. Instr. radiol. physics U. Calif. Med. Sch.-San Francisco, 1942-44; asst. prof. physics U. So. Calif., Los Angeles, 1944-48, assoc. prof. physics, 1948-52, prof. physics, 1952—, chmn. dept. physics, 1951-56, dir. nuclear accelerator, 1955-65. Contbr. articles to sci. jours. Fellow Am. Phys. Soc. (chmn., mem. exec. com. div. electron and atomic physics), Optiocal Soc. Am., AAUP, Sigma Xi. Current Work: Vacuum ultraviolet and x-radiation interaction with gases and surfaces. Subspecialties: Atomic and molecular physics; Plasma physics. Office: University Park U So Calif Los Angeles CA 90089

WEITKAMP, WILLIAM GEORGE, nuclear physicist; b. Fremont, Nebr., June 22, 1934; s. Alvin Herman and Georgia Ann (Fuhrmeister) W.; m. Audrey Ann Jensen, June 2, 1956; children—Erick, Gretchen, Laurie. B.A., St. Olaf Coll., 1956; M.S., U. Wis., 1961, Ph.D., 1965. Research asst. prof. U. Wash., Seattle, 1965-67; asst. prof. U. Pitts., 1967-68; tech. dir., research prof. Nuclear Physics Lab., U. Wash., Seattle, 1968—. Served with USAF, 1956-59. acad. guest Eidgenossische Technische Hochschule Zurich, Switzerland, 1974-75. Mem. Am. Phys. Soc. Current Work: Polarization phenomena in nuclear reactions; Van de Graaff accelerator design and development; superconducting linac design and development. Subspecialties: Nuclear physics; Electrical engineering. Home: 2019 E Louisa St Seattle WA 98112 Office: Nuclear Physics Lab GL-10 U Wash Seattle WA 98195

WELCH, HERBERT EUGENE, electronics corporation executive, educator; b. Gainsville, Tex., Aug. 22, 1933; s. John Arthur and Virginia Pearl (White) W.; m. Nedra Jo Thorn, Sept. 15, 1951; children—Randy Eugene, Pamela Denise Welch Alcorn. B.S. in Physics, Tex. Tech. U., 1965, M.S. in Physics, 1968, Ph.D. in Physics, 1969. Sr. staff engr. Collins Radio, Dallas, 1969-72; dir. engring. Rockwell Internat., Dallas, 1972-80, Chgo., 1980-81, dir. product devel., Dallas, 1981-82; v.p. United Telecom/U.S. TEL, Dallas, 1982-84, Andrew Corp., Plano, Tex., 1984—; adj. assoc. prof. of elec. engring. U. Tex., Arlington, 1974—. Patentee in field. Contbr. articles to engring. jours. Mem. IEEE (chmn. nominating com., 1980-81, Dallas sect. 1979-80, exec. vice chmn. 1978-79, mem. steering com. 1982, edn. chmn. 1976-77), Am. Soc. of Engring. Edn. (Rockwell Internat. Corp. rep. 1978—), Nat. Mgmt. Assn. (charter), Am. Phys. Soc., AAUP, AAAS, Internat. Platform Assn., Sigma Pi Sigma, (sec., treas. 1964, pres. 1966, faculty prize for best student paper 1964), Inst. of Cert. Profl. Mgrs., Am. Mgmt. Assn. Democrat. Baptist. Club: Engineers (Dallas). Current work: Communications theory, digital telephony, fiber optics systems, network systems design. Subspecialties: Electronics; Fiber optics. Office: Andrew Corp Electronic Tech 1500 W Plano Pkwy Plano TX 75075

WELCH, LESTER CLINT, physicist, software engineer; b. Tucumcari, N.Mex., Mar. 27, 1941; s. Nelson Eldridge and Lydia Pawneee (Kenyon) W.; m. Dixie Jean, July 4, 1964 (div. Nov. 1984); children—Von, Kent. B.S. in Physics, N.Mex. Inst. Tech., 1962; M.A. in Physics, U. So. Calif.-Los Angeles, 1966, Ph.D. in Physics, 1970. Physicist, III Physics Inst. RWTH (CERN), Aachen, W.Ger., 1974-78; software physicist Ind. U. Cyclotron Faculty, Bloomington, 1978-82; systems mgr. Argonne Nat. Lab. Ill., 1982—; adj. faculty Coll. of St. Francis, Joliet, Ill., 1984—. Contbr. articles to physics jours. Mem. IEEE (sec. nuclear sci. tech. com. on computer applications in nuclear and plasma physics 1984—). Am. Phys. Soc. Unitarian. Current work: Parallel processing, data acquisition. Subspecialties: Nuclear physics; Programming languages. Home: 12A Kingery Qtr #102 Hinsdale IL 60521

WELDON, VIRGINIA V., pediatric endocrinologist, educator, medical administrator; b. Toronto, Ont., Can., Sept. 8, 1935; 2 children. A.B., Smith Coll., 1957; M.D., SUNY-Buffalo, 1962. Intern, then resident, then fellow Sch. Medicine, Johns Hopkins U. and Hosp., 1962-67; instr. pediatrics Johns Hopkins U., 1967-68; from instr. to assoc. prof. Washington U., St. Louis, 1968-79, prof. pediatrics, 1979—, asst. vice chancellor med. affairs, 1975-81, assoc. vice chancellor med. affairs, 1981-83, dep. vice chancellor for med. affairs, 1983—; v.p. Washington U. Med. Ctr., 1980—. co-dir. div. metabolism and endocrinology St. Louis Children's Hosp., 1973-77; cons. adv. com. endocrinology and metabolism FDA, 1973-76; mem. Mo. Health Manpower Planning Task Force, 1976—; mem. gen. clin. research ctr. adv. com. NIH, 1976-80, mem. nat. adv. research resources council, 1980-84. Fellow AAAS; mem. Endocrine Soc., Soc. Pediatric Research, Am. Pediatric Soc., Assn. Am. Med. Colls. (chmn. council acad. socs. 1984-85, chmn.-elect 1984-85, chmn. 1985-86), Inst. Medicine, Sigma Xi, Alpha Omega Alpha. Subspecialty: Pediatric endocrinology. Office: Washington U Sch Medicine PO Box 8106 660 S Euclid Ave Saint Louis MO 63110*

WELDON, WILLIAM FORREST, mechanical engineer, researcher, cons.; b. San Marcos, Tex., Jan. 12, 1945; s. Forrest Jackson and Rubie Mae (Wilson) W.; m. Morey Sheppard McGonigle, July 27, 1968; children: William Embree, Seth Forrest. B.S. in Engring. Sci, Trinity U., 1967; M.S. in Mech. Engring, U. Tex., 1970. Registered profl. engr., Tex. Engr. Cameron Iron Works, Houston, 1967-68; project engr. Glastron Boat Co., Austin, Tex., 1970-71; chief project engr. Nalle Plastics, Austin, 1971-73; chief engr. Energy Storage Group, U. Tex., Austin, 1973-76; tech. dir. Center for Electromechanics, 1976-85, dir. Ctr. for Electromechanics, 1985—, cons. to industry, govt. Contbr. numerous articles on pulsed power to profl. jours. Mem. ASME. Patentee homopolar generators and compulsators. Current Work: Electromechanical machine design, pulsed power, homopolar generator, compulsator. Subspecialties: Mechanical engineering; Fusion. Home: 4707 Peace Pipe Path Austin TX 78746 Office: Ctr Electromechanics U Tex Austin Balcomes Research Ctr 10100 Burnet Rd Austin TX 78758

WELLER, PETER FAHEY, physician, researcher, educator; b. Boston, May 5, 1946; s. Thomas Huckle and Kathleen (Fahey) W.; m. Anne Nicholson, May 26, 1979; children: Susan R., Nathaniel N. A.B., Harvard U., 1968, M.D., 1972. Diplomate: Am. Bd. Internal Medicine, Am. Bd. Allergy and Immunology. Intern Peter Bent Brigham Hosp., Boston, 1972-73, resident, 1973-74; clin. and research fellow in medicine, infectious diseases Mass. Gen. Hosp., 1976-77; asst. in medicine Brigham and Women's Hosp., Boston, 1977—; asst. prof. medicine Harvard U., 1979—; asst. physician Beth Israel Hosp., 1981—; cons. infectious diseases New Eng. Deaconess Hosp., Boston, 1980—. Contbr. articles to profl. jours. Served with USPHS, 1974-76. Fellow ACP, Am. Acad. Immunology, Infectious Disease Soc. Am.; mem. Am. Soc. Tropical Medicine and Hygiene (Janssen award 1979), Am. Soc. Microbiology, Royal Soc. Tropical Medicine and Hygiene, Am. Thoracic Soc., Am. Assn. Immunologists, Am. Fedn. Clin. Research, Phi Beta Kappa. Current Work: Immunology of eosinophils and host defense against parasitic infections. Subspecialties: Infectious diseases; Parasitology.

WELLER, RICHARD ELDON, veterinarian, researcher; b. Yakima, Wash., Mar. 22, 1947; s. Richard Clarence and Betty Lou (Palmer-Foulkes) W.; m. JoDeanna Rae Kenifel, Sept. 7, 1968; children—Carrie, Christin, Mark, David. B.S., U. Wash., 1969; D.V.M., Wash. State U., 1973. Diplomate Am. Coll. Veterinary Internal Medicine. Resident in oncology U. Calif.-Davis, 1976-78; asst. prof. U. Ill.-Urbana, 1978-79; assoc. veterinarian Veter Hosp., Yakima, Wash., 1979-80; research scientist Battelle Pacific Northwest Labs., Richland, Wash., 1980—; cons. U.S. Agy. Internat. Devel., Washington, 1983—. Contbr. articles to sci. jours. Author: Canine Haematopoietic Tumors, 1984. Bd. dirs. Humane Soc. Central Wash., 1984; den leader Cub Scouts Am., Selah, Wash., 1984. Served to capt. AUS, 1972-76. U.S. Agy. for Internat. Devel. grantee, 1984. Mem. Am. Veterinary Med. Assn., Wash. State Veterinary Med. Assn., Veterinary Cancer Soc. (treas. 1984—), Yakima Valley Veterinary Med. Assn., Found. Veterinary Med. Research of Washington (trustee), Am. Assn. Lab. Animal Sci. Democrat. Presbyterian. Lodge: Elks. Current work: Life-span studies for very long-term DOE-sponsored programs; beagle dogs exposed to radionuclides to determine dose-effect relationships; biomedical database for malaria research. Subspecialties: Cancer research (veterinary medicine); Radiation biology. Home: Route 4 Box 4038 Selah WA 98942 Office: Battelle Pacific Northwest Labs PO Box 999 Richland WA 99352

WELLER, THOMAS HUCKLE, physician, educator; b. Ann Arbor, Mich., June 15, 1915; s. Carl V. and Elsie A. (Huckle) W.; m. Kathleen R. Fahey, Aug. 18, 1945; children—Peter Fahey, Nancy Kathleen, Robert Andrew, Janet Louise. A.B., U. Mich., 1936; M.S., 1937; LL.D. (hon.), 1956; M.D., Harvard, 1940; Sc.D., Gustavus Adolphus U., 1975; L.H.D., Lowell U., 1977. Diplomate: Am. Bd. Pediatrics. Teaching fellow bacteriology Harvard Med. Sch., 1940-41, research fellow tropical medicine, pediatrics, 1947-48, instr. comparative pathology, tropical medicine, 1948-49, asst. prof. tropical pub. health, 1949-50, asso. prof., 1950-54, Richard Pearson Strong prof. tropical pub. health, 1954-85, emeritus, 1985—, head dept., 1954-81; intern bacteriology and pathology Children's Hosp., Boston, 1941, intern medicine, 1942, asst. resident medicine, 1946, asst. dir. research div. infectious diseases, 1949-55; mem. commn. parasitic diseases Armed Forces Epidemiol. Bd., 1953-72, dir., 1953-59; charge parasitology, bacteriology, virology sections Antilles Dept. Med. Lab., P.R. Author sci. papers. Served to maj. M.C. AUS, 1942-46. Recipient E. Mead Johnson award for devel. tissue culture procedures in study virus diseases Am. Acad. Pediatrics, 1953; Kimble Methodology award, 1954; Nobel prize in physiology and medicine, 1954; George Ledlie prize, 1963; Weinstein Cerebral Palsy award, 1973; Stern Symposium honoree, 1972; Bristol award infectious Diseases Soc. Am., 1980. Fellow Am. Acad. Arts and Scis.; mem. Harvey Soc., AMA, Am. Soc. Parasitologists, Am., Royal socs. tropical medicine and hygiene, Am. Pub. Health Assn., AAAS, Am. Epidemiological Soc., Nat. Acad. Scis., Am. Pediatric Soc., Assn. Am. Physicians, Soc. Exptl. Biology and Medicine, Am. Assn. Immunologists. Soc. Pediatric Research, Phi Beta Kappa, Sigma Xi, Alpha Omega Alpha. Current work: Growth of viruses in vitro; polio, varicella, cytomegalovivus, rubella. Culture of schistosomes. Subspecialties: Virology (medicine); Parasitology. Home: 56 Winding River Rd Needham MA 02192 Office: 665 Huntington Ave Boston MA 02115

WELLMAN, GEORGE ROBERT, process chemist; b. Detroit, Jan. 18, 1945; s. George Goodhugh and Barbara Janet (Hebinger) W.; m. Sara Jill Wilson, Dec. 17, 1966; children—Robert, Andrew. B.S., Kalamazoo Coll., 1967; M.S., Western Mich. U., 1969, Ph.D., 1972. Assoc. sr. investigator Smithkline Beckman, Phila., 1973-75, sr. investigator, 1976-77, asst. dir. process chemistry, 1977-79, assoc. dir., 1979-81, dir. synthetic chemistry, 1981—. Patentee in field. NIH fellow, 1972. Mem. Am. Chem. Soc., AAAS, N.Y. Acad. Sci., Am. Inst. Chem. Engrs., Phila. Organic Chemists Club. Current work: Process research and development in the pharmaceutical business, study of metal-ammonia reduction of heterocyclic esters. Subspecialties: Organic chemistry; Chemical engineering. Home: 320 Kerrwood Dr Wayne PA 19087Office: Smithkline Beckman 1500 Spring Garden PO Box 7929 Philadelphia PA 19101

WELLS, ALAN HARVEY, nuclear data corporation executive, computer science educator; b. Ancon, C.Z., July 5, 1948; m. Kathy Jane Melanson, Aug. 8, 1970; children: Chandra, Krista, Michael. B.S. in Physics, Stevens Inst. Tech., 1970; M.S., Tex. A&M U., 1975, Ph.D., 1978. Data processing mgr. Nuclear Assurance Corp., Atlanta, 1979-81, sr. engr., 1981-82, cons., 1982—; engring. devel. mgr. Nuclear Data, Inc., Smyrna, Ga., 1982—; cons. Los Alamos Sci. Lab., 1978-79; adj. prof. computer sci. Ga. Inst. Tech., Atlanta, 1982—. Contbr. articles to profl. jours. Served to capt. USAF, 1970-74. Mem. Am. Nuclear Soc. (program com. 1974—). Current Work: Nuclear criticality safety for power reactor fuel, nuclear reactor operator training using knowledge-based computer aided instruction, control room diagnostic computers. Subspecialties: Nuclear engineering; Artificial intelligence. Office: Nuclear Data Inc 2734 S Cobb Industrial Blvd Smyrna GA 30080

WELLS, DAVID LEE, mechanical engineering technology educator, manufacturing researcher; b. McKeesport, Pa., Oct. 21, 1936; s. Otis Henry and Ottilie Hilda (Bostak) W.; m. Phyllis Claire Burmester, Mar. 19, 1960 (div. 1972); m. Carol Louise Villars, Dec. 31, 1977; 1 dau., Tammie Jo. B.S. in Mech. Engring., Stanford U., 1958, M.S. in Mech. Engring., 1960. Cert. mfg. engr. Materials and mfg. cons. U.S. Air Force, Los Angeles, 1963-64; v.p. Universal Tech. Corp., Dayton, Ohio, 1964-69; pres. Delphi Corp., Dayton, 1969-73; mfg. cons., Wilmington, Ohio, 1973-78; prof. mech. engring. tech., head dept. U. Cin., 1978—; instr. civil and indsl. tech. So. State Coll., Ohio, 1977-78; acting asst. prof. physics Wilmington Coll., 1978; cons. in field. Contbr. articles to profl. jours. Served to 1st lt. USAF, 1960-63. Recipient Exemplary Leadership plaque Engrs. and Sci. Inst., Dayton, 1972. Mem. Soc. Mfg. Engrs., ASME (cert. appreciation 1983, chmn. adhoc task group on mech. engring. tech. accreditation criteria 1980—, bd. of engring. edn. 1981-84, strategic planning com. 1984), Am. Soc. for Engring. Edn. (chmn. mfg. constituent com. 1983—, dir. profl. interest council I 1984—), Computer and Automated Systems Assn. of Soc. Mfg. Engrs., Machine Vision Group of Soc. Mfg. Engrs., Robotics Inst. of Soc. Mfg. Engrs., Soc. for Advancement of Materials and Process Engring. (chmn. Midwest chpt. 1969-70), Tau Alpha Pi. Republican. Current work:

Unattended manufacturing; integrated automation technology; social ramifications of technology. Subspecialties: Mechanical engineering; Robotics. Office: Mech Engring Tech U Cin 100 E Central Pkwy Cincinnati OH 45210

WELLS, EDWARD CURTIS, consultant, retired engineering executive; b. Boise, Idaho, Aug. 26, 1910; s. Edward Lansing and Laura Alice (Long) W.; m. Dorothy Evangeline Ostlund, Aug. 25, 1934; children: Laurie Jo (Mrs. William Tull), Edward Elliott. Student, Willamette U., 1927-29, D.Sc. (hon.), 1963; B.A. with gt. distinction, Stanford, 1931; LL.D., U. Portland, 1946. Draftsman Boeing Co., Seattle, summer 1930, draftsman, engr., 1931-33, group engr., 1933-34, engr.-in-charge preliminary design Model 299, 1934-35, asst. project engr., 1934-37, chief preliminary desgin engr., 1937-38, chief project engr., 1938-39, asst. chief engr., 1939-43, chief engr., 1943-47, v.p., chief engr., 1947-48, v.p. engring., 1948-58, 59-61, v.p., gen. mgr. mil. aircraft systems div., 1961-63, v.p. product devel., 1963-65, 66-67, group v.p. airplanes, 1965-66, sr. v.p., 1967-71, ret., 1972; v.p., gen. mgr. Systems Mgmt. Office, 1958-59; cons., 1972—; vis. prof. Stanford U., 1969-70; State Adv. Council Atomic Energy, 1958-60. Life trustee Willamette U.; mem. adv. bd. Wash. State Inst. Tech., 1957-61; mem. adv. council Stanford Engring. Sch.; pres. bd. Ryther Child Center, 1961-67, dir., 1961-80; mem. Def. Sci. Bd., 1969-72. Recipient Lawrence Sperry award Inst. Aero. Scis. for outstanding contbns. to art airplane design with spl. reference to 4-engined aircraft, 1942; Fawcett Aviation award, 1944; Young Man of Year Seattle, 1943; Elder Statesman of Aviation award, 1978; Daniel Guggenheim medal award, 1980; Tony Jannus award, 1985. Fellow AIAA (hon.), Soc. Automotive Engrs., AAAS; mem. Nat. Acad. Engring., Phi Beta Kappa Assos., Phi Beta Kappa, Phi Delta Theta, Tau Beta Pi. Club: Tennis (Seattle). Subspecialty: Aeronautical engineering. Home: PO Box 2031 Bellevue WA 98009

WELLS, EDWIN BOYD, chemist, geologist; b. Dallas, June 6, 1955; s. Hubert Boyd and Roberta V. (Walker) W. B.S., Auburn U., 1979. Chemist, Charleston Naval Shipyard, S.C., 1980-81; pollution control specialist Ala. Dept. Environ. Mgmt., Montgomery, 1981; chemist aid U. Ala., Huntsville, 1982; engr. aid Army Corp. Engrs., Waterways Experience Sta., Vicksburg, Miss., 1982; hydrological technician U.S. Geol. Survey, Jackson, Miss., 1982-83; chemist Oklahoma City Air Logistics Ctr., Tinker AFB, 1984—. Mem. Geol. Soc. Am., Oklahoma City Geol. Soc., Mu Alpha Theta. Club: Auburn Alumni Assn. Subspecialties: Environmental chemistry; Hydrology. Home: 828 Mira Vista Dr SE Huntsville AL 35802-3222

WELLS, GARY LEROY, psychology educator; b. Hutchinson, Kan., Dec. 11, 1950; s. Richard J. and Bonnie (Wilson) W.; m. Teresa Diane Wilson, Nov. 2, 1968; children: Gary Jonathan, Kristopher Aaron. B.Sc., Kan. State U., 1973; M.Sc., Ohio State U., 1975, Ph.D., 1977. Instr. Ohio State U., Columbus, 1974-76; asst. prof. U. Alta., Edmonton, Can., 1977-80, assoc. prof., 1980-85, prof., 1985—, assoc. chmn. dept. psychology, 1982—; spl. cons. Law Reform Commn. of Can., Ottawa, 1982—; reviewer NSF, Washington, 1978—; cons. on memory Can. and U.S. cts., 1979—; cons. The Investigators, Edmonton, 1982—. Editor, author: Eyewitness Test: Psychological Perspectives, 1983; contbr. articles to profl. jours.; guest editor: Law and Human Behavior, 1980. Eloise Worthy scholar, 1971-73; Ohio State U. fellow, 1974-76; Social Sci. and Humanities Research Council grantee, 1981—. Mem. Soc. Exptl. Social Psychology, Am. Psychol. Assn. (fellow psychology and law div.). Current Work: Experimental research on eyewitness testimony, attitude change and propaganda; experimental research on rumor transmission. Subspecialties: Cognition; Social psychology. Office: Dept Psychology Univ Alta Edmonton AB T6G 2E9 Canada

WELLS, STEPHEN GENE, geology educator, researcher; b. Linton, Ind., Mar. 4, 1949; s. William Gene Wells and Mary Lou (Foster) Veit; m. Bethany Jean Grover, Dec. 14, 1974; 1 child, Christopher Ryan. B.S., Ind. U., 1971; M.S., U. Cin., 1973, Ph.D., 1976. Asst. prof. U. N.Mex., Albuquerque, 1976-82, assoc. prof. geology, 1982—; faculty U.S. Geol. Survey, Menlo Park, Calif., 1982—; cons. geologist Environ. Improvement Div., Santa Fe, 1979—; chief scientist Cave Research Found., Yellow Springs, Ohio, 1976-79. Editor: Environmental Geology and Hydrology in New Mexico, 1981; Origin and Evolution of Deserts, 1983; Chaco Canyon Country, 1983. Mem. editorial bd. Geology, 1984—. Contbr. articles to sci. jours. Bd. dirs. Montecello Community Cons., Bernalillo County, N.Mex., 1982-84. Research fellow U.S. Air Force/Am. Soc. Engring. Edn., 1977; Fenneman fellow U. Cin., 1973; grantee in field. Mem. Geol. Soc. Am. (div. panel mem. 1984—), N.Mex. Geol. Soc. (cert. recognition 1982), Brit. Geomorphological Research Group, Am. Geomorphological Field Group, Sigma Xi (research grantee 1975). Current work: Earth surface processes and hydrology, landscape stability applied to reclamation and hazardous waste disposal, impact of climatic changes on landscapes and geomorphic processes. Subspecialties: Geology; Hazardous waste disposal. Office: Dept Geology U NMex Northrop Hall Albuquerque NM 87131

WELLS, WILLIAM LOCHRIDGE, chemical engineer; b. Mayfield, Ky., Oct. 12, 1939; s. Kenneth Morgan and Sarah Elizabeth (Lochridge) W. Student Vanderbilt U., 1957-59; B.S. in Chem. Engring., U. Ky., 1962; M.S., U. Ill., 1964, Ph.D. in Chemistry, 1967; M.S. in Chem. Engring., U. S.C., 1974; M.B.A., U. Tenn.-Chattanooga, 1982. Registered profl. engr., Ky., S.C. Asst. prof. Murray State U., Ky., 1967-69; research assoc. Wayne State U., Detroit, 1969-71; asst. prof. S.W. Bapt. Coll., Bolivar, Mo., 1971-72; prof. Midlands Tech. Coll., Columbia, S.C., 1972-74; engr., mgr. TVA, Chattanooga, Tenn., 1975-83; dir. Ctr. for Research on Sulfur in Coal, Champaign, Ill., 1983—; cons. Contbr. articles to profl. publs. Co-inventor in field. Mem. Am. Inst. Chem. Engrs. (chmn. Chattanooga sect. 1978), Am. Inst. Indsl. Engrs. (sr.), Am. Chem. Soc., Nat. Soc. Profl. Engrs., Royal Soc. Chemistry (assoc.), Tau Beta Pi, Phi Lambda Upsilon, Sigma Iota Epsilon. Baptist. Current work: Technologies to desulfurize coal; fuel gas cleanup (scrubbers); solid waste disposal. Subspecialties: Chemical engineering; Fuels. Office: Center for Research on Sulfur in Coal 615 E Peabody Dr Champaign IL 61820

WELLS, WILLIAM TERRY, fireplace manufacturer, inventor; b. Elfrida, Ariz., Dec. 11, 1919; s. Reubin Garret and Delma Montez (Terry) W.; m. Ruth Crum, Sept. 5, 1964; children: Berna and Sheila (twins), Mary and Michelle (twins), Rhonda, Marsha and Rebecca (twins). Student, U. Ariz., 1938-42. Quality engr. Boeing Aircraft, Seattle, 1946-59, Hughes Aircraft, Tucson, 1946-59; inventor, 1960- ; devel. and mktg. energy-efficient fireplaces Wells Fireplaces, Tucson, 1976—, invented gearless automatic transmission and rotary engine. Served in USAF, 1942-45. Decorated Air medal (4). Mem. So. Ariz. Home Builders Assn., Tucson C. of C. Republican. Mormon. Patentee internal combusion engine, infinitely variable transmission, fireplaces. Current Work: Research and development of fireplaces, transmission and rotary engines. Subspecialties: Mechanical engineering; Theoretical and applied mechanics. Office: 1221 W Monte Vista PO Box 7097 Tucson AZ 85725

WELSCH, FRANK, pharmacologist, toxicologist; b. Berlin, Germany, Apr. 14, 1941; s. Rudolf K. and Ilse (Hohn) W.; m. Melissa G. Hutchinson, Aug. 30, 1968; 1 son, Derek. Dr. med. vet., Free U. Berlin, 1964. Diplomate: Am. Bd. Toxicology. Research assoc. vet. pharmacology Free U. Berlin, 1964-67; research assoc. in neurochemistry Columbia U., 1967-68; research assoc. in pharmacology Vanderbilt U., 1968-71; mem. faculty Mich. State U., East Lansing, 1971-82, prof., 1981-82; sr. scientist Chem. Industry Inst. Toxicology, Research Triangle Park, N.C., 1982—. Contbr. articles to profl. jours. NIH grantee, 1972-82; March of Dimes grantee, 1975-78; Alexander von Humboldt Found. research fellow, 1977-78. Mem. Am. Soc. Pharmacology and Exptl. Therapeutics, AAAS, Teratology Soc., Soc. Toxicology. Current Work: Effects of chemicals on reproduction, research in prenatal toxicology. Subspecialties: Teratology; Toxicology (medicine). Office: PO Box 12137 Research Triangle Park NC 27709

WEN, WEN-YANG, chemist, educator; b. Taiwan, China, Mar. 7, 1931; came to U.S., 1953, naturalized, 1973; s. Chi and Yueh-Er (Yu) W.; m. Sue Liu, Aug. 1, 1959; children: Lilian, Alvin. B.S., Nat. Taiwan U., 1953; Ph.D., U. Pitts., 1957. Research assoc. U. Pitts., 1957-58; postdoctoral fellow Northwestern U., 1958-60; asst. prof. chemistry DePaul U., 1960-62; asst. prof. Clark U., 1962-66, assoc. prof., 1966-73, prof., 1973—; Alexander von Humboldt fellow Universitat Karlsruhe, W. Ger., 1970-71, summer 1973; vis. prof. Drittes Physikalisches Institut, Universitat Gottingen, Ger., summer 1976; faculty research participant Morgantown Energy Tech. Ctr., Dept. Energy, 1978-79. Contbr. articles to profl. pubs. Li Found. fellow, 1953-55. Mem. AAUP, Am. Chem. Soc., AAAS. Democrat. Baptist. Current Work: Coal gasification; tar cracking. Subspecialties: Coal; Physical chemistry. Office: Clark U 950 Main St Worcester MA 01610

WENDELBERGER, JAMES GEORGE, statistician, consultant; b. Milw., Mar. 13, 1953; s. Joseph Martin and Elizabeth (Neimon) W. B.S. with distinction in Math. and Physics, U. Wis.-Madison, 1976, M.S. in Stats, 1978, Ph.D. in Stats, 1982. Research assoc. Space Sci. and Engring. Ctr., U Wis. - Madison, 1982-83; sr. research scientist math. dept. Gen. Motors Research Labs., Warren, Mich., 1983—. Mem. Inst. Math. Stats., Soc. Indsl. and Applied Math., Am. Statis. Assn., AAAS, Sigma Xi. Current Work: Consulting research statistician; multiple time series analysis, multidimentional spline smoothing, computer graphics. Subspecialties: Statistics; Mathematical software. Office: Math Dept Gen Motors Research Labs Warren MI 48090

WENG, CHENG-NAN, environmental engineer; b. Tainan, Taiwan, Republic of China, July 5, 1941; s. Yao-Tsung and Hsiu-Hsia (Wu) W.; m. Stella Fuh-Mei Liu, June 9, 1968; children—Francis, Patricia. B.S.C.E., Nat. Taiwan U., 1963, M.S.C.E., 1965; M.E. in Sanitary Engring., Manhattan Coll., 1968; Ph.D. in Sanitary Engring., NYU, 1972. Registered environ. engr., N.J., N.Y. Instr., Provincial Taipei Inst. Tech., 1965-66; research asst. Manhattan Coll., Bronx, N.Y., 1966-68; project engr. Lawler, Matusky & Skelly, Engrs., Pearl River, N.Y., 1968-73, Buck, Seifert & Jost, Inc., Paramus, N.J., 1973-75, assoc., 1975-80, v.p., 1981—; lectr. Fairleigh Dickinson U., Teaneck, N.J., 1976-77, adj. asst. prof., 1977-81, adj. assoc. prof., 1981-84. Contbr. articles to profl. jours. Recipient Founder's Day award NYU, 1972. Mem. Am. Acad. Environ. Engrs. (diplomate), ASCE, Am. Water Works Assn., Water Pollution Control Fedn. Republican. Current work: Research on water treatment using ozone and hydrogen peroxide. Subspecialties: Civil engineering; Water supply and wastewater treatment. Home: 64 Columbus Dr Tenafly NJ 07670 Office: Buck Seifert & Jost Inc 30 Park Pl Paramus NJ 07653

WENG, GEORGE JUENG-CIOUS, engineering educator; b. Taiwan, Oct. 8, 1944; s. Wan-Chung and Kuan-chia (Hsieh) W.; m. Shu-yu Huang, Oct. 26, 1949; children: Bruce, Joyce. B.S., Taiwan U., 1967; M.Phil., Yale U., 1971, Ph.D., 1974. Research fellow Delft (Netherlands) U. Tech., 1973-74; postdoctoral fellow Yale U., UCLA, 1974-76; sr. research engr. Gen. Motors Research Lab., Warren, Mich., 1976-77; asst. prof. mechanics and materials sci. Rutgers U., Piscataway, N.J., 1977-80, assoc. prof., 1980-84, prof., 1984—. Contbr. articles to profl. jours. NSF grantee, 1978, 80; U.S. Dept. Enrgy grantee, 1980. Mem. Am. Acad. Mechanics, ASME, AIME, Soc. Rheology, Sigma Xi. Current Work: Micromechanics of plastic deformation of metals, creep and fracture at elevated temperature, interfacial problems in continuum plasticity and mechanical metallurgy, mechanics of composite materials, theory of inclusions. Subspecialties: Solid mechanics; Metallurgical engineering. Home: 9 Langley Rd Kendall Park NJ 08824 Office: Coll Engring Rutgers U Piscataway NJ 08854

WENG, SHANG-LIN, physicist; b. Taipei, Taiwan; May 5, 1949; came to U.S., 1973; s. Kao-Hong and Hsu-Wei (Hsu) W.; m. Ming-Shan Yu, Aug. 20, 1977; 1 son, Philbert Leeying. B.S., Nat. Taiwan U., 1971; Ph.D., U. Pa., 1978. Postdoctoral mem. tech. staff AT&T Bell Labs., Murray Hill, N.J., 1978-79; assoc. physicist Brookhaven Nat. Lab., Upton, N.Y., 1979-83; research mgr., sr. engr. Varian Assocs., Inc. Central Research, Palo Alto, Calif., 1983—. Contbr. articles to physics jours. Recipient Wayne B. Nottingham prize Conf. on Phys. Electronics, 1977; Sigma Xi prize, 1978. Mem. Am. Phys. Soc., Am. Vacuum Soc. Current work: Molecular-beam epitaxy (MBE), III-V materials growth, characterization and processing, surface physics, photoemission, electron-stimulated desorption, synchrotron. Subspecialties: Condensed matter physics; Electronic materials. Home: 901 Cottonwood Dr Cupertino CA 95014 Office: Varian Assocs Research Ctr 611 Hansen Way M/S K-212 Palo Alto CA 94303

WENGER, GALEN ROSENBERGER, pharmacologist, educator, researcher; b. Sellersville, Pa., May 16, 1946; s. Warren Martin and Ethel Gargas (Rosenberger) W.; m. Carolyn Jean Liechty, Nov. 24, 1972; children: Alyssa Nicole, Aaron Joseph. B.A. in Biology, Goshen (Ind.) Coll., 1968; Ph.D., W.Va. U., 1971. Postdoctoral fellow dept. pharmacology U. Colo. Med. Center, Denver, 1972-73; research fellow Lab. Psychobiology dept. psychiatry Harvard U. Med. Sch., Boston, 1973-75, instr. pharmacology, 1975-78; asst. prof. pharmacology and interdisciplinary toxicology U. Ark. for Med. Sci., Little Rock, 1978-81, assoc. prof., 1981—; grant reviewer NIH, NSF, VA. Contbr. articles and abstracts to sci. publs., also monographs; reviewer: Jour. Pharmacology and Exptl. therapeutics, Psychopharmacology, Pharmacology Biochemistry and Behavior. Mem. Am. Soc. Pharmacology and Exptl. Therapeutics, Behavioral Pharmacology Soc., Neurobehavioral Toxicology Soc., Sigma Xi. Democrat. Mennonite. Current Work: Behavioral pharmacology of drug abuse, behavioral toxicology, operant conditioning. Subspecialties: Pharmacology; Behavioral psychology. Home: 18 Hayfield Dr Little Rock AR 72207 Office: 4301 W Markham St Mail Slot 638 Little Rock AR 72205

WENK, EDWARD, JR., civil engineer, policy analyst, educator; b. Balt., Jan. 24, 1920; s. Edward and Lillie (Heller) W.; m. Carolyn Frances Lyford, Dec. 21, 1941; children: Lawrence Shelley, Robin Edward Alexander, Terry Allan. B.E., Johns Hopkins U., 1940, D.Eng., 1950; M.Sc., Harvard U., 1947; D.Sc. (hon.), U. R.I., 1968. Head structures div. USN David Taylor Model Basin, Washington, 1942-56; chmn. dept. engring. mechanics S.W. Research Inst., San Antonio, 1956-59; sr. specialist sci. and tech. Legis. Reference Service, Library of Congress, Washington, 1959-61, chief sci. policy research div., 1964-66; tech. asst. to U.S. President's sci. adviser and exec. sec. Fed. Council for Sci. and Tech., White House, Washington, 1961-64; exec. sec. Nat. Council on Marine Resources and Engring. Devel., Exec. Office of Pres., Washington, 1966-70; prof. engring. and pub. affairs U. Wash., Seattle, 1970—, dir. program in social mgmt. tech., 1973-79; dir. URS Corp.; lectr. U. Md., Seattle U., Va. Poly. Inst., Colo. Sch. Mines. Cons. in pub. policy for environ. and tech. affairs, risk assessments, ocean engring. Nat. Adv. Com. on Oceans and Atmosphere, 1972-73; vice chmn. U.S. Congress Tech. Assessment Adv. Council, 1973-79; adviser Congress, GAO, U.N. Secretariat, Alaska, Wash. State, U.K., Sweden, Philippines, Australia, pub. interest groups; vis. scholar Woodrow Wilson Internat. Center for Scholars, 1970-72, Harvard, 1976, Woods Hole Oceanographic Instn., 1976, U. Sussex, 1977. Author: The Politics of the Ocean, 1972, Margins for Survival, 1979; Tradeoffs, in press. Editor: Engring. Mechanics Jour, 1958-60, Exptl. Mechanics Jour, 1954-56; mem. editorial bd.: Tech. Forecasting; Tech. in Soc.; contbr. articles to profl. jours. Bd. dirs. Human Interaction Research Inst., Smithsonian Sci. Info. Exchange., 1977-82. Served as ensign USNR, 1944-45. Recipient Navy Meritorious Civilian Service award, 1946; named Disting. Alumnus Johns Hopkins U., 1979; Tchr. of Yr. Wash. State Engrs., 1980; Ford Found. grantee, 1970; Rockefeller Found. fellow, 1976. Fellow ASME; mem. Soc. Exptl. Stress Analysis (past pres. William M. Murray lectr.), Internat. Assn. Impact Assessment (pres. 1981-82), Nat. Acad. Engring. (chmn. com. on pub. policy 1970-75), Nat. Acad. Pub. Adminstrn., Am. Soc. for Pub. Adminstrn. (chmn. com. on sci. and tech. in govt. 1974-78), Assembly Engring.-NRC, ASCE, Nat. Soc. Profl. Engrs., Nat. Oceanography Assn. (v.p. pub affairs 1970-72), Cousteau Soc. (chmn. adv. bd.), AAAS, Explorers Club, Sigma Xi (nat. lectr.), Tau Beta Pi, Chi Epsilon. Club: Cosmos (Washington). Designer Aluminaut submarine. Current Work: Technology policy; risk analysis; industrial productivity and economic vitality. Subspecialty: Technology assessment. Home: 15142 Beach Dr NE Seattle WA 98155

WENZ, MICHAEL FRANK, JR., nuclear engineer; b. Arlington, Va., Dec. 9, 1953; Michael Frank and Theo (Lambert) W. B.S. in Nuclear Engring, U. Va., 1975, B.S. in Applied Math., 1975, M.E. in Nuclear Engring, 1977. Nuclear engr. Naval Reactors, Naval Sea Systems Command, Washington, 1977-84; asst. to naval reactors rep. Nuclear Propulsion Directorate, Naval Sea Systems Command, 1984—. Mem. Am. Nuclear Soc., Tau Beta Pi. Current Work: Technical direction and surveillance of repairs, modifications, tests, refuelings and operations of Naval nuclear propulsion plants undergoing overhaul at Norfolk Naval Shipyard. Subspecialties: Nuclear engineering; Nuclear fission. Home: 4040 Oak Moss Ct Chesapeake VA 23321 Office: Naval Reactors Rep Office PO Box 848 Portsmouth VA 23705

WERBELOW, LAWRENCE GLEN, chemistry educator, researcher; b. Ross, Calif., Dec. 19, 1948; s. Arnold Glen and Helen Corrine (Freeburg) W.; m. Catherine Elizabeth Fouques, Dec. 28, 1979; children—Prisca, Guilhelm. B.Sc., Humboldt State U., 1970; Ph.D., U. B.C., 1974; D.Sc., U. Provence, Marseille, France, 1979. Research assoc. U. Utah, Salt Lake City, 1974-78; vis. prof. U. Provence, Marseille, 1978-79, Mont. State U., Bozeman, 1979-80; assoc. prof. chemistry N.Mex. Inst. Mining and Tech., Socorro, 1980—; vis.scientist Los Alamos Nat. Lab., 1980—. Contbr. chpts. to books, articles to profl. jours. Nat. Research Council Can. fellow, 1974; Am. Chem. Soc. grantee, 1980; NSF grantee, 1980; NATO grantee, 1982; Research Corp. grantee, 1983; Assoc. Western Univs. fellow, 1985. Mem. Internat. Soc. Magnetic Resonance. Current Work: Time-dependent aspects of nuclear paramagnetism; creation and dissipation of transient multipolar spin order; quantum theory angular momentum. Subspecialties: Nuclear magnetic resonance; Magnetic resonance imaging. Home: 907 Michigan St Socorro NM 87801 Office: Dept Chemistry N Mex Inst Mining and Tech Socorro NM 87801

WERES, OLEH, chemist, consultant; b. Grand Rapids, Mich., June 21, 1950; s. Roman and Eugenia (Sokolowski) W.; m. Nancy Henning, Sept. 2, 1974. B.S. in Chemistry, U. Chgo., 1972, Ph.D. in Theoretical Chemistry, 1972. Staff scientist Lawrence Berkeley Lab, Calif., 1974—. Contbr. chpts. in books, articles to profl. jours. Pres. no. Calif. br. Ukrainian Congress Com. of Am., 1980-84; v.p. Ukrainian Famine Commemoration Com. of no. Calif., San Francisco, 1983. Fellow Hertz Found., 1969-72, Miller Inst., U. Calif., Berkeley, 1972-74. Mem. Am. Chem. Soc., Nat. Assn. Corrosion Engrs. Democrat. Ukrainian Orthodox. Current work: Control of groundwater pollution; geothermal energy; air pollution control; high temperature aqueous chemistry; formation and migration of petroleum; corrosion prevention in nuclear plants. Subspecialties: Geothermal power; Geochemistry. Home: 6455 Irwin Ct Oakland CA 94609 Office: Lawrence Berkeley Lab 50E 1 Cyclotron Rd Berkeley CA 94720

WERGIN, WILLIAM P., research scientist; b. Manitowoc, Wis., Apr. 20, 1942; s. Eugene A. and Catherine A. (Virnoche) W.; m. Mary Ester Guse, Aug. 25, 1962; children: Anne Michele, W. Peter. B.S. in Genetics, U. Wis., 1964, Ph.D. in Botany, 1970. With Agrl. Research Service, U.S. Dept. Agr., 1970—; assigned to a Agrl. Research Service, U.S. Dept. Agr. (pathology lab.), 1970-72, Agrl. Research Service, U.S. Dept. Agr. (weed sci. lab.), 1972-74, Agrl. Research Service, U.S. Dept. Agr. (animal reprodn. lab.), 1974-78, Agrl. Research Service, U.S. Dept. Agr. (nematology lab.), 1974-79, Agrl. Research Service, U.S. Dept. Agr. (cell culture lab.), 1979; lab. chief Agrl. Research Service, U.S. Dept. Agr. (Plant Stress Lab.), Beltsville, Md., 1979—. Contbr. articles to profl. jours. H.S. Dept. Agr. grantee, 1977-79; Binat. Agrl. Research and Devel. Fund grantee, 1980-83. Mem. Am. Soc. Cell Biologists, AAAS, Am. Soc. Plant Physiology, Soc. Nematologists, Electron Microscopy Soc. Am., Helminthological Soc., Sigma Xi. Current Work: Ultrastructural alterations in plants that are subjected to environmental or biological stress. Subspecialties: Plant physiology (agriculture); Cell and tissue culture. Home: 10108 Towhee Ave Adelphi MD 20783 Office: US Dept Agr Plant Stress Lab Bldg 001 Room 206 BARC-W Beltsville MD 20783

WERNER, CHRISTIAN THOR, mechanical engineer; b. Chgo., Mar. 25, 1916; s. Thor Christian and Anna Hedvig (Engstrom) Rothstein; m. Barbara Ruth Schneck, July 20, 1957 (div. 1972); 1 child, Diane Lynn Werner Zink. B.S. in Aero. Engring, Aero. U., Chgo., 1937. Aero. engr. Boeing Aircraft Co., Seattle, 1938-43; aerodynamicist Republic Aviation Corp., Farmingdale, L.I., N.Y., 1944-46, sr. aerodynamicist, 1946-48; contract aerodynamics cons. Naval Air Devel. Ct., Johnsville, Pa., 1949-50; systems engr. Bendix Missile System Div., Mishawaka, Ind., 1951-57, sr. systems engr., 1958-67; sr. mech. engr. Sparton Electronics Div., Jackson, Mich., 1967-68, prin. mech. engr., 1968-69, lab. mgr., 1969-71, staff engr., 1972—; instr. Swedish Jackson Community Coll., 1976-80. Fellow AIAA (assoc.); mem. Marine Tech. Soc., Am. Def. Preparedness Assn. Club: Engineers of St. Joseph Valley (South Bend, Ind.). Current Work: Preliminary mechanical design and systems analysis of underwater anti-submarine and anti-surface vessel defense systems. Subspecialties: Fluid mechanics; Theoretical and applied mechanics. Home: 313 Tecumseh St Apt 4 Brooklyn MI 49230 Office: ASW Tech Ct Sparton Electronics Div 2400 E Ganson St Jackson MI 49202

WERNER, JOHN ELLIS, steel company executive, metallurgist; b. Erie, Pa., Oct. 25, 1932; s. Harold Douglas and Anne Mae (Ellis) W.; m. Marjorie Mae Wood, Apr. 27, 1957; children—John Preston, Jennifer Ann, Jessica Carol, Andrew Robert. B.S. in Metallurgy, Pa. State U., 1954, M.S., 1960. Engr., Bethlehem Steel Corp., Lackawanna, N.Y., 1954-58, research engr. steelmaking, Bethlehem, Pa., 1960-65, supr. steelmaking processes, 1965-66, asst. sect. mgr. steelmaking, 1966-69, sect. mgr. phys. metallurgy, 1969-74, asst. div. mgr. product research, 1974-76, asst. div. mgr. primary processes, 1976-78, mgr. raw materials and chem. processes, 1978-82, dir. research, 1982-84, dir. tech. transfer and ventures, 1984—; dir. Consep Membranes, Inc., Bend, Oreg., ABEC, Inc., Bethlehem. Served with U.S. Army, 1955-56. Mem. Metal Properties Council (bd. dirs. 1984—), Am. Soc. Metals (Bradley Stoughton award 1980), Am. Iron and Steel Inst. (bd. dirs. 1970-74), Am. Inst. Mining Metall. and Petroleum Engrs. (chmn. phys. chemistry of steelmaking 1970). Republican. Methodist. Club: Saucon Valley Country. Current work: Responsible for developing technology-based new ventures and transfer of technology to Bethlehem's businesses. Subspecialties: Metallurgy; Materials. Office: Bethlehem Steel Corp Homer Research Labs Bethlehem PA 18016

WERNICK, JACK HARRY, metallurgical engineer; b. St. Paul, May 19, 1923; s. Joseph and Eva (Legan) W.; married; children: Phyllis Roberta, Rosanne Pauline. B. in Metall. Engring., U. Minn., 1947, M.S., 1948; Ph.D., Pa. State U., 1954. Metallurgist Manhattan Project, Los Alamos, 1944-46; instr. Pa. State U., State College, 1949-54; mem. tech. staff Bell Labs., Murray Hill, N.J., 1954-64, head phys. metallurgy research dept., 1964-73, head solid state chemistry research dept., 1973-81, head device materials research dept., 1981-84; mgr. materials sci. research div. Bell Communications, 1984—. Contbr. articles on metall. engring. to profl. jours. Served with C.E. U.S. Army, 1944-46. Fellow Metall. Soc. of AIME, Am. Phys. Soc., N.Y. Acad. Scis.; mem. Nat. Acad. Engring., IEEE, AAAS, Am. Soc. for Metals, Electrochem. Soc. Patentee in field. Current Work: synthesis and study of new superconducting, semiconducting, and magnetic materials for possible use in optoelectronic, superconducting and magnetic devices. Subspecialties: Electronic materials; Metallurgy. Office: 600 Mountain Ave Murray Hill NJ 07974

WERT, CHARLES ALLEN, engineering educator; b. Battle Creek, Iowa, Dec. 31, 1919; s. John Henry and Anna (Spotts) W.; m. Lucille Vivian Mathena, Sept. 5, 1943; children: John Arthur, Sara Ann. B.A., Morningside Coll., Sioux City, 1941; M.S., State U. Iowa, 1943, Ph.D., 1948. Mem. staff Radiation Lab., Mass. Inst. Tech., 1943-45; instr. physics U. Chgo., 1948-50; mem. faculty U. Ill. at Urbana, 1950—, prof., 1955, head dept. metall. and mining engring., 1967—; cons. to industry. Author: Physics of Metals, 1970, Opportunities in Materials Science and Engineering, 1977; also articles.; Cons. editor, McGraw Hill Book Co. Recipient sr. scientist award von Humboldt-Stiftung, W. Ger. Fellow Am. Phys. Soc., Am. Soc. Metals, AAAS, AIME; mem. Sigma Xi. Current Work: Description of crystalline and chemical nature of fine-scale inclusions in metals and alloys; chemistry and structure of coal, especially as related to combustion and chemical conversion processes. Subspecialties: Metallurgy; Condensed matter physics. Home: 1708 W Green St Champaign IL 61820 Office: Metallurgy and Mining Bldg Univ Ill Urbana IL 61801

WERTHEIM, ROBERT HALLEY, aerospace company executive; b. Carlsbad, N.Mex., Nov. 9, 1922; s. Joseph and Emma (Vorenberg) W.; m. Barbara Louise Selig, Dec. 26, 1946; children—Joseph Howard, David Andrew. B.S., U.S. Naval Acad., 1945; M.S. in Physics, MIT, 1954. Commd. 2d lt. U.S. Navy, 1945, advanced through grades to rear adm., 1972, ret., 1980; sr. v.p. Lockheed Corp., Burbank, Calif., 1981—; adv. com. mem. Naval Research Adv. Commn., Washington, 1984—; mem. nat. security adv. com. Los Alamos Nat. Lab., N.Mex., 1981—; mem. sci. adv. group Joint Strategic Target Planning Group, Omaha, 1976—; industry adv. group mem. Nat. Soc. Profl. Engrs., Washington, 1983—; mem. Charles Stark Draper Lab., Inc., Cambridge, Mass., 1981—; mem. sci. adv. group Def. Nuclear Agy., Washington, 1981—. Trustee Naval Undersea Warfare Found., Washington, 1983—. Decorated Legion of Merit, Disting. Service medal U.S. Navy; recipient William S. Parsons award Navy League of U.S. Fellow AIAA; mem. Am. Soc. Naval Engrs. (hon. mem., Gold medal, 1972), Nat. Acad. Engring., Sigma Xi. Club: Woodland Hills Country (Calif.). Subspecialties: Aerospace engineering and technology; Nuclear engineering. Office: Lockheed Corp PO Box 551 Burbank CA 91520

WEST, JOHN BURNARD, physician, educator; b. Adelaide, Australia, Dec. 27, 1928; came to U.S., 1969; s. Esmond Frank and Meta Pauline (Spehr) W.; m. Penelope Hall Banks, Oct. 28, 1967; children—Robert Burnard, Joanna Ruth. M.B.B.S., Adelaide U., 1952, M.D., 1958, D.Sc., 1980; Ph.D., London U., 1960. Intern Royal Adelaide Hosp., 1952; resident Hammersmith Hosp.,

London, Eng., 1953-55; physiologist Sir Edmund Hillary's Himalayan Expdn., 1960-61; dir. respiratory research group Postgrad. Med. Sch., London, 1962-67, reader medicine, 1968; prof. medicine U. Calif. at San Diego, 1969—. Author: Ventilation/Blood Flow and Gas Exchange, 1965, Respiratory Physiology-The Essentials, 1974, Pulmonary Pathophysiology-The Essentials, 1977, also articles. Fellow Royal Coll. Physicians (London), Royal Australasian Coll. Physicians; Mem. AAAS, Am. Physiol. Soc., Am. Soc. Clin. Investigation, Brit. Physiol. Soc., Am., Brit. thoracic socs., Assn. Am. Physicians, Western Assn. Physicians, Western Soc. Clin. Research., Explorers Club. . Home: 9626 Blackgold Rd La Jolla CA 92037

WEST, PHILIP WILLIAM, chemist; b. Crookston, Minn., Apr. 12, 1913; s. William Leonard and Anne (Thompson) W.; m. Tenney Constance Johnson, July 5, 1935 (dec. Feb. 1964); children—Dorothy Anne West Farwell, Linda West Gueho, Patty West Elstrott; m. Foymae S. Kelso, July 1, 1964. B.S., U. N.D., 1935, M.S., 1936, D.Sc. (hon.), 1958; Ph.D., State U. Iowa, 1939; postgrad., Rio de Janeiro, 1946. Chemist N.D. Geol. Survey, 1935-36; research asst. san. chemistry U. Iowa, 1936-37; asst. chemist Iowa Dept. Health, 1937-40; research microchemist Econ. Lab., Inc., St. Paul, 1940; faculty La. State U., 1940-80, prof. chemistry, 1951-80, Boyd prof., 1953-80, emeritus, 1980—, chmn. ann. symposium modern methods of analytical chemistry, 1948-65, dir. Inst. for Environmental Scis., 1967-80; O.M. Smith lectr. Okla. State U., 1955; vis. prof. U. Colo., 1963, Rand Afrikaans U., 1980; adj. prof. EPA, 1969-80; founder Kem-Tech. Labs., Inc., Baton Rouge, 1954, chmn. bd., 1965-74; co-founder West-Paine Labs., Inc., Baton Rouge, 1978, chmn. bd., 1978—; mem. 1st working party sci. com. on problems of environment, 1971-74; Pres. analytical sect. Internat. Union Pure and Applied Chemistry, 1965-69, mem. sect. indsl. hygiene and toxicology, 1971-73, mem. air quality sect., 1973-75; mem. tech. adv. com. La. Air Pollution Control Com., 1979—; mem. Gov.'s Task Force Environ. Health, 1982—; mem. sci. adv. bd. EPA, 1983—; cons. WHO. Author: Chemical Calculations, 1948, (with Vick) Qualitative Analysis and Analytical Chemical Separations, 2d edit, 1959, (with Bustin) Experience Approach to Experimental Chemistry, 1975; Editor: (with Hamilton) Science of the Total Environment, 1973-78, (with Macdonald) Analytica Chimica Acta, 1959-78, Reagents and Reaction for Qualitative Inorganic Analysis; co-editor: Analytical Chemistry, 1963; asst. editor: Mikrochemica Acta, 1952-78, Michrochem. Jour, 1957-75; adv. bd.: Analytical Chemistry, 1959-60; publ. bd.: Jour. Chem. Edn, 1954-57; Contbr. articles to profl. jours. Recipient Honor Scroll award La. sect. Am. Inst. Chemistry, 1972. Fellow AAAS; mem. Am. Chem. Soc. (Southwest award 1954, Charles E. Coates award 1967, Analytical Chemistry award 1974, award for advances in environ. sci. and tech.), La. Acad. Sci., Air Pollution Control Assn., Am. Indsl. Hygiene Assn., Austrian Microchem. Soc. (hon.), Soc. of Analysts Eng. (hon.), Internat. Union Pure and Applied Chemistry (pres. commn. I), Japan Soc. for Analytical Chemistry (hon.), Sigma Xi, Phi Lambda Upsilon, Phi Kappa Phi, Alpha Epsilon Delta, Alpha Chi Sigma, Tau Kappa Epsilon. Subspecialties: Environmental chemistry; Analytical chemistry. Home: 605 Nelson Dr Baton Rouge LA 70808

WEST, ROBERT CULBERTSON, chemistry educator; b. Glen Ridge, N.J., Mar. 18, 1928; s. Robert C. and Constance (MacKinnon) W.; children: David Russell, Arthur Scott. B.A., Cornell U., 1950; A.M., Harvard U., 1952, Ph.D., 1954. Asst. prof. Lehigh U., 1954-56; mem. faculty U. Wis.-Madison, 1956—, prof. chemistry, 1963—, Eugene G. Rochow prof., 1980; indsl. and govt. cons., 1961—; Abbott lectr. U. N.D., 1964; Fulbright lectr. Kyoto U., 1964-65; vis. prof. U. Würzburg, 1968-69, Haile Selassie I U., 1972, U. Calif., Santa Cruz, 1977, U. Utah, 1981; Jean Day Meml. lectr. Rutgers U., 1973; Japan Soc. for Promotion Sci. vis. prof. Tohoku U., 1976; Lady Davis vis. prof. Hebrew U., 1979; Cecil and Ida Green honors prof. Tex. Christian U., 1983. Co-editor: Advances in Organometallic Chemistry, Vols. I-XXIII, 1964-83, Organometallic Chemistry—A Monograph Series, 1968—; contbr. articles to profl. jours. Pres. Madison Community Sch., 1970-71; bd. dirs. Women's Med. Fund, 1971—, Zero Population Growth, 1980—; bd. dirs., v.p. Protect Abortion Rights Inc., 1980; lay minister Prairie Unitarian Universalist Soc., 1982. Recipient F.S. Kipping award, 1970; Amoco Disting. Teaching award, 1974. Mem. Am. Chem. Soc., Chem. Soc. (London), Japan Chem. Soc., AAAS, Wis. Acad. Sci. Current Work: Discovered first compound containing a silicon-silicon double bond. Subspecialties: Inorganic chemistry; Organic chemistry. Home: 305 Nautilus Dr Madison WI 53705

WEST, THEODORE LEE, periodontist, educator; b. N.Y.C., July 26, 1934; s. Jacob Martin and Belle (Lasky) w.; m. Amy Mae Freedman, June 29, 1958; children: Miles Kirby, Andrew David, Sharyn Rebecca. Student, Brown U., Providence, R.I., 1952-54; D.D.S., U. Pa., 1958, M.S.D., 1961; certificate, Boston U., 1960. Instr. U. Pa., Phila., 1960-64; assoc. prof. Fairleigh Dickinson U., Hackensack, N.J., 1972—; pres. Periodontal Assocs., Englewood, N.J., 1963—. Contbr. research reports, clin. articles to profl. jours. Fellow Internat. Coll. Dentistry, Am. Coll. Dentistry; mem. Am. Acad. Periodontology, Northeastern Acad. Periodontology, Phila. Soc. Periodontics, Internat. Assn. Dental Research, Omicron Kappa Upsilon. Republican. Current Work: Wound healing; periodontal disease microbiology; genetic susceptibility to periodontal disease; bone transplants into periodontal defects; surgical and non-surgical periodontal therapy development. Subspecialty: Periodontics. Home: 1 McCain Ct Closter NJ 07624 Office: 1 Periodontal Assocs 97 N Dean St Englewood NJ 07631

WESTERFELDT, CHRISTOPHER RAY, physics researcher; b. Mauston, Wis., Sept. 17, 1952; s. Marvin Herbert Arthur and Francis Marion (Hanson) W. B.S., U. Wis.-River Falls, 1974; M.S., N.C. State U., 1977. Research assoc. Duke U., Durham, N.C., 1977—. Contbr. articles to physics jours. Mem. Am. Phys. Soc., AAAS, Sigma Pi Sigma. Current work: Ultra-high energy resolution proton resonance studies, development of accelerator and computer based techniques and instrumentation for experimental research program. Subspecialty: Nuclear physics. Home: Apt 20 1011 Morreene Rd Durham NC 27705 Office: Dept Physics Duke U Durham NC 27706

WESTERHOUT, GART, astronomer; b. The Hague, Netherlands, June 15, 1927; came to U.S., 1962, naturalized, 1967; s. Gerrit and Magdalena H.M. (Foppe) W.; m. Judith M. Monaghan, Nov. 14, 1956; children—Magda C., Gart T., Brigit M., Julian C., Anthony K. Cand, U. Leiden, Netherlands, 1950, Drs., 1954, Ph.D., 1958. Asst., Leiden U. Obs., 1952-56, sci. officer, 1956-59, chief sci. officer, 1959-62; prof., dir. astronomy U. Md., College Park, 1962-73, prof., 1973-77 chmn. div. math. and phys. scis. and engring., 1972-73; sci. dir. U.S. Naval Obs., Washington, 1977—; vis. astronomer Max Planck Inst. Radio Astronomy, Bonn, W. Ger., 1973-74; vice chmn., div. physics NRC, D.C., 1969-73; trustee Associated U. Inc., D.C., 1971-74. Contbr. articles to profl. jours. Fellow NATO, 1959, Commonwealth Sci. and Indsl. Research Orgn., Sydney, Australia, 1959. Recipient Teaching of Sci. award D.C. Acad. Sci., Humboldt award, 1973. Mem. Internat. Astron. Union (v.p. working group com. S 1979—), Internat. Sci. Radio Union (pres. com. J 1975-78), Am. Astron. Soc. (councillor 1975-78, v.p. 1985-87), Royal Astron. Soc., Sigma Xi. Roman Catholic. Current work: Positional astronomy; timekeeping; galactic structure; radio astronomy. Office: US Naval Obs 34th and Massachusetts Ave Washington DC 20390

WESTERMAN, DAVID SCOTT, geologist, educator; b. Ann Arbor, Mich., July 12, 1946; s. Harold Scott and Shirley Martha (Mackey) W.; m. Jenny Anne Swanson, Sept. 13, 1968 (div. 1980); children: Lisa Anne, Matthew Evan. B.S. in Geology, Allegheny Coll., 1969; M.S. in Geology, Lehigh U., 1971, Ph.D. in Geology, 1972. Lic. geologist Maine. Asst. prof. earth scis. Northeastern U., Boston, Mass., 1972-78; vis. asst. prof. geology U. So. Maine, Portland, 1978-79; asst. prof. geology U. Maine, Orono, 1980, Colby Coll., Waterville, Maine, 1980-82; assoc. prof. earth scis. Norwich U., Northfield, Vt., 1982—; field geologist Maine Geol. Survey. Editor: Maine Geology. Recipient research grants Lehigh U., 1971, research grants Northeastern U., 1976-77. Mem. Geol. Soc. Am., Geol. Soc. Maine (pres. 1978-80), Maine Minerals Resources Assn., Vt. Geol. Soc., Planetary Soc., Zero Population Growth (charter), Sigma Xi (grant-in-aid 1971). Unitarian. Current Work: analysis of rock structures to understand current seismic activity in regions of earthquake concentration; resolution of ancient stress fields; the persistence of large-scale tectonic parameters. Subspecialties: Tectonics; Petrology. Home: PO Box 457 Moretown VT 05660 Office: Norwich U Dept Physical Sciences Northfield VT 05663

WESTERVELT, PETER JOCELYN, physics educator; b. Albany, N.Y., Dec. 16, 1919; s. William Irving and Dorothy (Jocelyn) W.; m. Alice Francis Brown, June 2, 1956; children: Dirck Edgell, Abby Brown. B.S., MIT, 1947, M.S., 1949, Ph.D., 1951. Mem. staff radiation lab. MIT, 1940-41, underwater sound lab., 1941-45, asst. in physics, 1946-47, research asso., 1948-50; asst. prof. physics Brown U., 1951-58, asso. prof., 1958-63, prof., 1963—; mem. subcom. aircraft noise NASA, 1954-59; mem. com. hearing and bio-acoustics NRC, 1957-83, exec. council, 1960-61, 78-83, chmn., 1967-68, 80-83; mem. sonic boom com. Nat. Acad. Sci., 1968-71; mem. R.I. Atomic Energy Commn., 1968-73; cons. applied research lab. U. Tex., Austin, 1973—. Recipient Rayleigh medal Inst. Acoustics U.K., 1985. Fellow Am. Physics Soc., Acoustical Soc. Am. Current Work: Theory of nonlinear waves; acoustic and gravitational. Subspecialties: Acoustics; Relativity and gravitation. Home: 16 John St Providence RI 02906 Office: Brown U Dept Physics Providence RI 02912

WESTHEIMER, FRANK H(ENRY), chemistry educator; b. Balt., Jan. 15, 1912; s. Henry Ferdinand and Carrie (Burgunder) W.; m. Jeanne Friedmann, Aug. 30, 1937; children: Ruth, Ellen. A.B., Dartmouth Coll., 1932, D.Sc. (hon.), 1962; M.A., Harvard U., 1933, Ph.D., 1935; NRC fellow, Columbia U., 1935-36; Sc.D. (hon.), U. Chgo., 1973, U. Cin., 1976, Tufts U., 1978, U. N.C., 1983, Bard Coll., 1983. Instr. chemistry U. Chgo., 1936-41, asst. prof., 1941-44, assoc. prof., 1946-48, prof. chemistry, 1948-53; vis. prof. Harvard U., Cambridge, Mass., 1953-54, prof. chemistry, from 1954, now Morris Loeb prof. emeritus, chmn. dept., 1959-62; Overseas fellow Churchill Coll., Cambridge (Eng.) U., 1962-63; Harrison Howe lectr. U. Rochester, 1954; Stieglitz lectr. U. Chgo., 1956; Morrell lectr. Cambridge U., 1962; Alexander Todd lectr., 1976, Centenary lectr. Chemistry Soc., 1963; Folkers lectr. U. Wis., 1963; Baker lectr. Cornell U., 1964; Priestly lectr. Pa. State U., 1968; Morris S. Kharasch lectr. U. Chgo., 1969; David Rivett Meml. lectr. Canberra, Australia, 1969; DuPont lectr. U. Tenn., 1973; Bachmann lectr. U. Mich., 1974; Werner lectr. U. Kans., 1975; Kolthoff lectr. U. Minn., 1980; Disting. Scientist lectr. Bard Coll., 1982. Assoc. editor: Jour. Chem. Physics; editorial bd.: Jour. Am. Chem. Soc, 1960-69; contbr. articles to sci. jours. Mem. Pres.'s Sci. Adv. Com., 1967-70; research supr. Explosives Research Lab., Nat. Def. Research Com., 1944-45; chmn. com. survey chemistry Nat. Acad. Scis., 1964-65, mem. council, 1973-75, 76-78. Recipient Naval Ordnance Devel. award, 1946; Army-Navy cert. of appreciation, 1948; James Flack Norris award, 1970; Willard Gibbs medal, 1970; Theodore Richards medal, 1976; award in chem. scis. Nat. Acad. Sci., 1980; Richard Kokes, award, 1980; Charles Frederick Chandler medal Columbia U., 1980; Rosenstiel award Brandeis U., 1981; Guggenheim fellow, 1962-63; Fulbright-Hays fellow, 1974; Welch award Robert A. Welch Found., 1982; Nichols medal Am. Chem. Soc., 1982; Arthur C. Cope award, 1982. Fgn. mem. Royal Soc.; mem. Nat. Acad. Sci., Am. Philos. Soc., Am. Chem. Soc., Am. Acad. Arts and Scis., Phi Beta Kappa. Current Work: Calculations of electrostatic effects and of steric effects in organic chemistry; determination of mechanisms of chromic acid oxidation; enzymic and metal-ion promoted decarboxylation, biochemical oxidation-reduction reactions which require nicotine adenine dinucleotide as coenzyme; the mechanisms of the hydrolysis of phosphate esters and photoaffinity labeling. Subspecialties: Organic chemistry; Biochemistry (medicine). Office: Harvard U 12 Oxford St Cambridge MA 02138

WESTHEIMER, GERALD, physiology educator; b. Berlin, Germany, May 13, 1924, came to U.S., 1951, naturalized Australian citizen, 1945; s. Isaac and Ilse (Cohn) W.; B.Sc., Sydney U., Australia, 1947; Ph.D., Ohio State U., 1953. Optometric practice N.S.W., Australia, 1945-51; mem. faculty U. Houston, 1953-54, Ohio State U., Columbus, 1954-60; mem. faculty U. Calif.-Berkeley, 1960-67, prof. physiology, 1967—. Contbr. articles to profl. jours., chpts. to books. Recipient Proctor medal Assn. Research in Vision and Ophthomology, 1979. Fellow Optical Soc. Am. (Tillyer medal 1978), AAAS Royal Soc. London; mem. Soc. for Neurosci., Royal Soc. N.S.W., Internat. Brain Research Orgn. Jewish. Current work: Eye movements; ocular optics; visual acuity; stereoscopic vision. Subspecialties: Neurophysiology; Psychophysics. Home: 582 Santa Barbara Rd Berkeley CA 94707 Office: U Calif Dept Physiology-Anatomy Berkeley CA 94720

WESTMAN, WALTER EMIL, ecologist, environmental scientist; b. N.Y.C., Nov. 5, 1945; s. Joseph and Claire (Berkowitz) W. B.A. with high honors, Swarthmore Coll., 1966; M.S. with honors, Macquarie U., Sydney, Australia, 1969; Ph.D., Cornell U., 1971. Congl. fellow Am. Polit. Sci. Assn., Washington, 1971-72; lectr. botany U. Queensland, Brisbane, Australia, 1972-74; lectr. environ. planning and mgmt. UCLA, 1975-76, prof. geography, 1976-84; sr. research scientist NASA-Ames Research Ctr., Moffett Field, Calif., 1984—; mem. commn. on ecology Internat. Union for Conservation of Nature, 1981—. Author: (with D. Conn) Quantifying the Benefits of Pollution Control, 1976, Ecology, Impact Assessment and Environmental Planning, 1985. Contbr. sci. research articles to profl. jours. Grantee NSF, Nat. Park Service, EPA, others, 1975—. Mem. Ecol. Soc. Am., AAAS, Am. Assn. Geographers, Phi Beta Kappa, Sigma Xi, Phi Kappa Phi. Democrat. Current work: Effects of pollutants on ecosystems; plant community ecology; environmental assessment and public policy. Subspecialties: Ecology (environmental science); Remote sensing (geoscience). Office: Technicolor Govt Services Inc M S 242-4 Moffett Field CA 94035

WESTMORELAND, THOMAS DELBERT, JR., industrial chemist, researcher; b. Vivian, La., June 2, 1940; s. Thomas Delbert and Marguerite Beatrice (Moore) W.; m. Martha Verne Beard, Jan. 1, 1966; children—Anne Laura, Kyle Thomas. B.S., N. Tex. State U., 1963, M.S., 1965; Ph.D., La. State U., 1971. Chemistry tchr. Lewisville High Sch., Tex., 1964-65; research student Tex. Instruments Inc., Dallas, 1966-67; grad. student instr. La. State U., Baton Rouge, La., 1966-70, postdoctoral fellow, 1971-72; sr. exptl. engr. United Techs. Inc., S. Windsor, Conn., 1972-76; research assoc. Pennzoil Co., The Woodlands, Tex., 1976—; cons. Dixilyn Corp., Odessa, Tex., 1968. Contbr. articles to profl. jours. Recipient E.I. DuPont Teaching award La. State U., 1969. Mem. Jaycees (state dir., 1975, Govs. Civic Leadership award, 1976, One of Twelve Outstanding Jaycees, 1976), Am. Chem. Soc. (treas. 1978-79, chmn. 1979-80), Sigma Xi, Phi Eta Sigma (pres. 1959-60). Clubs: Golden Girl's Drill Team Booster (Conroe, Tex.). Lodge: Masons. Current work: Resolution of produced fluids from tertiary oil recovery; physical and chemical characterization of base stock and formulated lubricating oils. Subspecialty: Physical chemistry. Home: 143 Melmont Ln Conroe TX 77302Office: Pennzoil Products Co Tech Div PO Box 7569 The Woodlands TX 77387

WESTON, RALPH E., JR., chemist; b. San Francisco, Nov. 9, 1923; s. Ralph E. and Ruth (Fields) W.; m. Virginia Louise Priest, May 26, 1951; children—Judith, Joan, Barbara. B.S., U. Calif.-Berkeley, 1946; Ph.D., Stanford U., 1950. Research fellow Harvard U., Cambridge, Mass., 1949-51; chemist, sr. chemist, dep. dept. chmn. Brookhaven Nat. Lab., Upton, N.Y., 1951—; vis. scientist Nuclear Research Ctr., Saclay, France, 1960-61; vis. lectr. Hunter Coll., N.Y.C., 1962-63, Columbia U., N.Y.C., 1970-71, U. Calif.-Berkeley, 1968. Co-author: Chemical Kinetics, 1972. Contbr. articles to profl. jours. Mem., zone leader Suffolk County Democratic Com., Patchogue, N.Y., 1972—. Served to 1st lt. U.S. Army, 1944-46. Mem. Am. Chem. Soc., Sigma Xi, Phi Lambda Upsilon. Current work: Photochemistry and molecular energy transfer, emphasizing the use of lasers and synchrotron radiation. Subspecialties: Laser-induced chemistry; Photochemistry. Office: Chemistry Dept Brookhaven Nat Lab Bldg 555 Upton NY 11973

WESTRUM, EDGAR FRANCIS, JR., chemistry educator, researcher; b. Albert Lea, Minn., Mar. 16, 1919; s. Edgar Francis and Nora Dorothy (Kipp) W.; m. Florence Emily Barr, June 13, 1943; children: Ronald Mark, James Scott, Michael Lauren, Margaret Kristin. Student, Hamline U., 1936-38; B.Chemistry, U. Minn., 1940; Ph.D., U. Calif.-Berkeley, 1944. Scientist Metall. Lab., U. Chgo., 1944-45; scientist Radiation Lab., U. Calif., 1945; asst. prof. chemistry U. Mich., Ann Arbor, 1947-56, assoc. prof., 1956-62, prof., 1963—; sec. gen. com. on data for sci. and tech. Internat. Council Sci. Unions, 1973-82. Editor: Jour. of Chem. Thermodynamics, 1970-80, Bull. Chem. Thermodynamics, 1955-77, Codata Directory, 1982—; contbr. articles to profl. jours. Recipient Bausch and Lomb hon. sci. award, 1936. Fellow AAAS, Am. Inst. Chem. Engrs., Am. Phys. Soc.; mem. Am. Chem. Soc., Netherlands Phys. Soc. Presbyterian. Current Work: Cryogenic calorimetry, phase, ordering and electronic transitions, resolution of electronic and magnetic contributions. Subspecialties: Thermodynamics; Condensed matter physics. Home: 2019 Delaware Dr Ann Arbor MI 48103 Office: Department Chemistry University Michigan Ann Arbor MI 48109

WESTWATER, JAMES WILLIAM, chemical engineering educator; b. Danville, Ill., Nov. 24, 1919; s. John and Lois (Maxwell) W.; m. Elizabeth Jean Keener, June 9, 1942; children: Barbara, Judith, David, Beverly. B.S., U. Ill., 1941; Ph.D., U. Del., 1948. Mem. faculty U. Ill., Urbana, 1948—, prof. chem. engring., 1962—, head dept., 1962-80; papers chmn. 5th Nat. Heat Transfer Conf., Buffalo, 1960; chmn. 3d Internat. Heat Transfer Conf., Chgo., 1966; Reilly lectr. Notre Dame U., 1958; Donald L. Katz lectr. U. Mich., 1978. Contbr. articles profl. jours. Recipient Conf. award 8th Nat. Heat Transfer Conf., 1965. Mem. Am. Inst. Chem. Engrs. (dir., past div. chmn., Inst. lectr. 1964 named Eminent Chem. Engr., William H. Walker award 1966, Max Jakob award 1972, Founders award 1984), Am. Chem. Soc., ASME (Max Jakob award 1972), Am. Soc. Engring. Edn. (Vincent Bendix award 1974), Nat. Acad. Engring. Current Work: Heat transfer during boiling or condensation. Subspecialty: Chemical engineering. Home: 116 W Iowa St Urbana IL 61801

WESTWOOD, ALBERT RONALD CLIFTON, engineer; b. Birmingham, Eng., June 9, 1932; came to U.S., 1958, naturalized, 1974; s. Albert Sydney and Ena Emily (Clifton) W.; m. Jean Mavis Bullock, 1956; children—Abigail, Andrea. B.S. with honors, U. Birmingham, 1953, Ph.D. in Phys. Metallurgy, 1956, D.Sc. in Materials Sci., 1968. Chartered engr., U.K. Tech. officer research dept., metals div. Imperial Chem. Industries, Birmingham, 1956-58; scientist and sr. scientist Martin Marietta Labs. (formerly RIAS), Balt., 1958-64, asso. dir., head materials sci. dept., 1964-69, dep. dir., 1969-74, dir., 1974-84, corp. dir. research and devel., 1984—; Tewksbury lectr. U. Melbourne, 1974; mem. various govt., univ. and editorial coms. including Commn. on Engring. and Tech. Studies of NRC, 1985—; bd. dirs. Indsl. Research Inst., 1984—; mem. Md. Humanities Council, 1984—. Contbr. numerous articles to sci. jours. Recipient Disting. Young Scientist award Md. Acad. Scis., 1966; Beilby Gold medal Royal Inst. Chemistry, 1970. Fellow Am. Soc. Metals (Burgess lectr. 1984, Campbell meml. lectr. 1987), Instn. Metallurgists, Inst. Physics; mem. U.S. Nat. Acad. Engring., Metall. Soc. AIME (bd. dirs. 1985—), AAAS, Md. Acad. Scis. (mem. council), Md. Inst. Metals (pres.). Current work: Research and development management. Environment-sensitive mechanical behavior. Ceramics. Subspecialty: Metallurgy. Home: 908 E Joppa Rd Towson MD 21204 Office: 1450 S Rolling Rd Baltimore MD 21227

WETHERILL, GEORGE WEST, geophysicist; b. Phila., Aug. 12, 1925; s. George West and Leah Victoria (Hardwick) W.; m. Phyllis May Steiss, June 17, 1950; children—Rachel, George, Sarah. Ph.B., U. Chgo., 1948, S.B. in Physics, 1949, S.M., 1951, Ph.D. in Physics, 1953. Mem. staff dept. terrestrial magnetism Carnegie Instn., Washington, 1953-60; prof. geophysics and geology UCLA, 1960-75, chmn. dept. planetary and space sci., 1968-72; dir. dept. terrestrial magnetism Carnegie Instn., Washington, 1975—; cons. NASA, NSF, Nat. Acad. Sci. Contbr. articles to profl. jours. Served with USN, 1943-46. Recipient G. K. Gilbert award Geol. Soc. Am. Fellow Am. Acad. Arts and Scis., Am. Geophys. Union (pres. planetology sect. 1970-72), Meteoritical Soc. (v.p. 1971-74, 81-83, pres. 1983-85, Leonard medal 1981); mem. Geochem. Soc. (v.p. 1973-74, pres. 1974-75), Internat. Assn. Geochem. and Cosmochemistry (pres. 1977-80), Internat. Astron. Union, Am. Astron. Soc., Nat. Acad. Scis. Episcopalian. Current work: Origin, evolution and dynamics of the earth and solar system. Subspecialties: Planetology; Geochemistry. Office: 5241 Broad Branch Rd NW Washington DC 20015

WETMUR, JAMES GERARD, microbiologist; b. New Castle, Pa., July 1, 1941; s. Leon Gerard and Wilma Aileen (Lostetter) W.; m. Brigid M. Long, Sept. 4, 1965; children: Katherine, John, Tara. B.S., Yale U., 1963; Ph.D., Calif. Inst. Tech., 1967. Chief biochemistry U.S. Army Aeromed. Research Lab., Ft. Rucker, Ala., 1967-69; asst. prof. chemistry and biochemistry U. Ill., Urbana, 1969-74; assoc. prof. microbiology Mt. Sinai Sch. Medicine, CUNY, 1974-82, prof., 1982—. Contbr. articles to sci. jours. Served as capt. AUS, 1967-69. NIH grantee, 1969—. Mem. Am. Soc. Biol. Chemists, Am. Soc. Microbiology, Am. Chem. Soc., N.Y. Acad. Sci., Sigma Xi. Republican. Roman Catholic. Current Work: DNA reassociation kinetics; DNA protein interactions, equilibra and kinetics; recombination of DNAs. Subspecialties: Microbiology; Biophysical chemistry. Home: 994 Post Rd Scarsdale NY 10583 Office: Dept Microbiolog Mt Sinai Sch Medicine 1 Gustave Levy Pl New York NY 10029

WETSTEIN, LEWIS, cardio-thoracic surgeon, cardiac researcher, electro-physiologist; b. N.Y.C., June 23, 1947; s. Benjamin and Rose (Finkilstein) W.; married; children: Jennifer Sandra. B.A., Queens Coll, 1968; M.D., Autonoumous U., Barcelona, Spain, 1973. Diplomate: Am. Bd. Surgery, Am. Bd. Thoracic Surgery. Intern L.F. Jewish Hosp.-Hillside Med. Center, 1973-75; resident in surgery Kings County Hosp.-Downstate Med. Center, 1975-80; asst. instr. surgery Downstate Med. Ctr., Bklyn., 1975-80; instr. surgery U. Pa., Phila., 1980-82, research assoc., 1980-82; asst. prof. surgery Med. Coll. Pa., Phila., 1982-84; assoc. prof. surgery Med. Coll. Va., 1984—; chief thoracic surgery McGuire VA Med. Ctr.; cons. to surgeon gen. USAF, 1985—. Editor: (with P.D. Myerowitz) Latest Advances in Cardiac Surgery, 1985. Contbr. articles to profl. jours. Served to maj. USAFR, 1976—. Recipient postdoctoral research service award NIH, 1980-82, spl. investigatorship award Am. Heart Assn., 1983-85, research adv. award VA, 1985-86. Fellow Assn. Acad. Surgery, ACS, Am. Coll. Cardiology, Am. Coll. Chest Physicians., Soc. Thoracic Surgeons, Soc. Univ. Surgeons. Jewish. Current Work: Electrophysiology; development of the surgical therapy for cardiac arrhythnias. Subspecialties: Cardiac surgery; Surgery. Home: 4307 Oxford Circle West Richmond VA 23221 Office: Med Coll VA PO Box 68 MCV Sta 1200 E Broad St Richmond VA 23298

WETZEL, ROBERT GEORGE, botanist; b. Ann Arbor, Mich., Aug. 16, 1936; s. Wilhelm and Eugenia (Wagner) W.; m. Carol Ann Andree, Aug. 9, 1959; children—Paul Robert, Pamela Jeanette, Timothy Mark, Kristina Marie. B.S., U. Mich., 1958, M.S., 1959; Ph.D., U. Calif. at Davis, 1962, U. Uppsala (Sweden), 1984. Research asso. Ind. U., Bloomington, 1962-65; asst. prof. botany Mich. State U., Hickory Corners, 1965-68, asso. prof., 1968-71, prof., 1971—; cons. Internat. Biol. Program, London, 1967-75; chmn. Internat. Seagrass Commn., 1974-75. Author: Limnology, 1975, 2d rev. edit., 1983, Limnological Analyses, 1979, To Quench Our Thirst: Present and Future Freshwater Resources of the United States, 1983; editor: Periphyton of Freshwater Ecosystems, 1983; contbr. numerous articles on ecology and freshwater biol. systems to profl. jours.; mem. editorial bd.: Aquatic Botany, 1975—. Served with USNR, 1954-62. Recipient First T. Erlander Nat. professorship Swedish Nat. Research Council and U. Uppsala, 1982-83; AEC grantee, 1965-75; NSF grantee, 1962—; ERDA grantee, 1975-77; Dept. Energy grantee, 1978—. Fellow AAAS; mem. Am. Inst. Biol. Scis., Am. Soc. Limnology and Oceanography (editorial bd. 1971-74, v.p. 1979-80, pres. 1980-81), Aquatic Plant Mgmt. Soc., Ecol. Soc. Am., Internat. Assn. Ecology, Freshwater Biol. Assn. U.K., Internat. Assn. Theoretical and Applied Limnology (gen. sec., treas. 1968—), Internat. Phycological Soc., Mich. Acad. Scis., N. Am. Benthological Soc., Phycological Soc. Am., Internat. Assn. Great Lakes Research, Japanese Soc. Limnology, Mich. Bot. Soc., Internat. Assn. Aquatic Vascular Plant Biologists (founder, pres. 1979—), Sigma Xi, Phi Sigma. Current work: Botanical and chemical limnology; physiological ecology of algae and higher aquatic plants. Subspecialties: Limnology; Ecology (biology). Home: 15216 Marshfield Rd Hickory Corners MI 49060 Office: WK Kellogg Biol Sta Mich State U Hickory Corners MI 49060

WEVER, ERNEST GLEN, psychology educator; b. Benton, Ill., Oct. 16, 1902; s. Ernest Sylvester and Mary Jane (Shirtz) W.; m. Suzanne Rinehart. A.B., Ill. Coll., 1922; A.M., Harvard U., 1924, Ph.D., 1926; D.Sc. (hon.), U. Mich., 1981. Instr. U. Calif.-Berkeley, 1926-27; instr. Princeton U., 1927-29, asst. prof. psychology, 1929-31, assoc. prof., 1931-41, prof, 1941-71, prof. emeritus, sr. research psychologist, 1971—. Author: books The Reptile Ear, 1978, The Amphibian Ear; contbr. articles to profl. jours. Mem. Am. Psychol. Assn., Nat. Acad. Scis., Soc. Exptl. Psychology, Acoustical Soc. Am. (Silver medal 1981), Am. Otolaryngology Soc. (assoc.), Assn. Research in Otolaryngology (award of Merit 1983, hon. mem.). Current Work: The ear and hearing processes; evolution of vertebrate ear. Subspecialties: Physiological psychology; Sensory processes. Office: Princeton U 055 Green Hall Princeton NJ 08544

WHALEN, JAMES JOSEPH, electrical engineering educator, consultant; b. Meriden, Conn., Feb. 16, 1935; s. Lawrence William and Caroline (Barrette) W.; m. Barbara Ann Jakiel, July 11, 1959; children—Elizabeth Ann, Catherine Louise, Thomas Michael. B.E.E., Cornell U., 1958; M.S. in Engring., Johns Hopkins, 1962, Ph.D., 1969. Research staff assoc. Johns Hopkins U., Balt., 1961-70; asst. prof. SUNY-Buffalo, Amherst, 1970-77, assoc. prof., 1977-81, prof. elec. engring., 1981—; session organizer, chmn. 3rd-6th Symposium Electro Magnetic Compatibility, Zurich, Switzerland, 1979-85; cons. Southeastern Ctr. Elec. Engring. Edn., St. Cloud, Fla., 1977-85. Assoc. editor Trans. So. African Inst. Elec. Engrs., Pretoria, South Africa, 1984—. Contbr. articles to prof. jours. Served to lt. (j.g.) USN, 1958-61. Recipient Prize Paper award 3rd Symposium and Tech. Exhbn. EMC, Rotterdam, the Netherlands, 1979;

NSF grantee, 1971-73. Mem. IEEE (sr., bd. dirs. Buffalo sec. 1982-85), Am. Soc. Engring. Edn. Current work: Determining electro-magnetic interference (EMI) effects in silicon analog & digital microelectronics and damage effects in GaAs microwave transistors and integrated circuits caused by microwave overstress. Subspecialty: Semiconductors. Home: 5095 Alexander Dr Clarence New York NY 14031 Office: SUNY-Buffalo 215 Bonner Hall Amherst NY 14260

WHALEN, RICHARD EDWARD, psychologist; b. Holyoke, Mass., Mar. 29, 1934; s. John J. and Katheryn (O'Neil) W. A.B., Brown U., 1956; M.S., Yale U., 1957, Ph.D., 1960. Faculty UCLA, 1961-65; mem. faculty U. Calif., Irvine, 1965-79; prof. dept. psychiatry and behavioral sci. SUNY-Stony Brook, 1979-82; prof. psychology U. Calif., Riverside, 1982—. Contbr. articles to profl. jours. NIH, NIMH grantee, 1962—. Mem. Soc. Neurosci., Internat. Brain Research Orgn., Internat. Acad. Sex Research, Internat. Soc. Devel. Neurosci., Sigma Xi. Current Work: Hormone brain interactions in development and regulation of neuroendocrine function and behavior. Subspecialty: Psychobiology.

WHARTON, CHARLES BENJAMIN, electrical engineer, educator; b. Gold Hill, Oreg., Mar. 29, 1926; s. Howard Ervin and Ida Fay (Starns) W.; m. Gloria Jean Dorris, Aug. 16, 1953; children—Carl Gene, Kristi Anna, Mark Theodore. B.E.E., U. Calif.-Berkeley, 1950, M.E.E., 1952. Staff mem. Lawrence Livermore Lab., Calif., 1950-62, Gen. Atomic Co., San Diego, 1962-67; vis. scientist Max Planck Inst., Munich, Fed. Republic Germany, 1959-60, 73-74; vis. prof. Occidental Research Co., Irvine, Calif., 1979-81, Sandia Nat. Labs., Albuquerque, 1983-84; prof. Cornell U., Ithaca, N.Y., 1967—; cons. Los Alamos Nat. Lab., N.Mex., 1982-84, Naval Research Lab., Washington, 1971-76; dir. Internat. Sch., Varenna, Italy. Author: Plasma Diagnostics with Microwaves, 1965; also articles. Editor Proc. Diagnostics for Fusion, 1978, 82, 86. Patentee in microwave apparatus. Mem. planning commn. Alameda County, Pleasanton, Calif., 1957-61. Served with USN, 1944-46, PTO. Recipient Humboldt prize A. Von Humboldt Found., Bonn, Fed. Republic Germany, 1973. Fellow Am. Phys. Soc., IEEE; mem. Sierra (v.p. 1952-53), Tau Beta Pi (chpt. sec. 1948), Eta Kappa Nu (pres. chpt. 1949). Republican. Clubs: DeMolay (Medford, Oreg.). Current work: Techniques for measurements in plasma physics and high power microwaves and generation of high power microwaves. Subspecialty: Plasma physics. Home: 303 N Sunset Dr Ithaca NY 14850 Office: Cornell U Sch Elec Engring Phillips Hall Ithaca NY 14853

WHEATLEY, JOHN CHARLES, physicist; b. Tucson, Feb. 17, 1927; s. Robert C. and Grace (Nowell) W.; m. Martha Raup, Jan. 29, 1949; children—William, Benjamin, Jane (dec.). B.S. in Elec. Engring, U. Colo., 1947; Ph.D., U. Pitts., 1952; D.Sc. (hon.), Leiden (Netherlands) U., 1975. Mem. faculty U. Ill., 1952-67; prof. physics U. Calif., San Diego, 1967—; mem. staff Los Alamos Nat. Lab., 1981—; dir. Biomagnetic Techs. Inc. Contbr. articles to profl. jours. Served with USNR, 1944-46. Guggenheim fellow, 1954-55, 80-81; Fulbright fellow, Netherlands, 1954-55, Argentina, 1961-62; recipient Simon Meml. prize Low Temperature Group, Inst. Physics and Phys. Soc., Gt. Britain, 1966; Fritz London award at 14th Internat. Low Temperature Conf., 1975; Disting. Grad. award U. Pitts, 1984. Fellow AAAS Acoustical Soc. Am., Am. Phys. Soc.; mem. Nat. Acad. Scis., Acad. Finland. Current work: Natural heat engines, thermoacoustics, localized states in condensed matter, nonlinear dynamics in fluids, superfluid 3He, spin-polarized hydrogen isotopes. Subspecialties: Condensed matter physics; Low temperature physics. Office: Group P-10 MSK764 LANL Los Alamos NM 87545

WHEDON, GEORGE DONALD, medical administrator, researcher; b. Geneva, N.Y., July 4, 1915; s. George Dunton and Elizabeth (Crockett) W.; m. Margaret Brunssen, May 12, 1942 (div. Sept., 1982); children: Karen Anne, David Marshall. A.B., Hobart Coll., 1936, Sc.D. (hon.), 1967; M.D., U. Rochester, 1941, Sc.D. (hon.), 1978. Diplomate: Am. Bd. Internal Medicine, Am. Bd. Nutrition. Intern in medicine Mary Imogene Bassett Hosp., Cooperstown, N.Y., 1941-42; asst. in medicine U. Rochester Sch. Medicine; also asst. resident physician medicine Strong Meml. Hosp., Rochester, 1942-44; instr. medicine Cornell U. Med. Coll., 1944-50, asst. prof. medicine, 1950-52; chief metabolic diseases br. Nat. Inst. Arthritis, Diabetes, Digestive and Kidney Diseases, NIH, Bethesda, Md., 1952-65, asst. dir., 1956-62, dir., 1962-81, sr. sci. adviser, 1981-82; sr. assoc. dir. conf. program Kroc Found., Santa Ynez, Calif., 1982-84; adj. prof. medicine (endocrinology) UCLA Sch. Medicine, 1982-84; cons. med. research programs Shriners Hosps. for Crippled Children, Internat. Shrine Hdqrs., Tampa, Fla., 1984—; mem. subcom. on calcium, com. dietary allowances Food and Nutrition Bd., NRC, 1959-64; cons. to office manned space flight NASA, 1963—, chmn. Am. Inst. Biol. Scis. med. program adv. panel to NASA, 1971-75, chmn. life scis. com., 1974-78, mem. space program adv. council, 1974-78; cons. on endocrinology and metabolism adv. com. Bur. Drugs, FDA, 1977-82; mem. subcommn. on gravitational biology Com. on Space Research, 1979—; mem. research adv. bd. Shriners Hosps., 1981-84; cons. in medicine Wadsworth Gen. Hosp. VA Center, Los Angeles, 1982-84. Editorial bd.: Jour. Clin. Endocrinology and Metabolism, 1960-67; adv. editor: Calcified Tissue Research, 1967-76; Contbr. articles to profl. publs. Mem. med. alumni council U. Rochester Sch. Medicine, 1971-76; mem. trustees' council U. Rochester, 1971-76, vice chmn., 1973-74, chmn., 1974-75; trustee Dermatology Found., 1978-82. Recipient Superior Service award USPHS, 1967, Alumni citation U. Rochester, 1971; Ayerst award Endocrine Soc., 1974; Exceptional Sci. Achievement medal NASA, 1974. Mem. Am. Fedn. Clin. Research, Assn. Am. Physicians, Pan Am. Med. Assn., Aerospace Med. Assn. (Arnold D. Tuttle meml. award 1978), Am. Rheumatism Assn., Md. Acad. Scis. (mem. sci. council 1964-70, 81-82), Endocrine Soc. (Robert H. Williams Disting. Leadership award in endocrinology 1982), N.Y. Acad. Scis., AAAS, Am. Physiol. Soc., Am. Diabetes Assn., Am. Gasteroenterol. Assn., Gerontol. Soc., Am. Inst. Nutrition, Acad. Orthopaedic Surgeons (hon.), Am. Soc. for Bone and Mineral Research (public affairs and devel. com.), Orthopaedic Research Soc., Theta Delta Chi. Episcopalian. Subspecialty: Nutrition (medicine). Home: 880 Mandalay Ave Apt S 1002 Clearwater Beach FL 33515 Office: Internat Shrine Hdqrs 2900 Rocky Point Dr Tampa FL 33607

WHEELER, E(RNEST) JOSEPH, JR., marine technology company executive; b. Phila., Nov. 7, 1925; s. Ernest Joseph and Lottie Blance (Hyers) W.; m. Nancy Jane Radcliffe, June 4, 1979; children—Annette Louise, Rebecca Ellen, Christine Lynn, Ernest Joseph III, Daniel James, Dawn Virginia. B.S.E.E., Temple U., 1954; M.B.A., U. Pa., 1956. Pres. Wheeler Industries, Inc., Washington, 1966—; mem U.S. Congl. Adv. Bd., Washington, 1982—; corp. mem. Marine Tech. Soc., Navy League. Founder (with others) Lorton (Reformatory) (Va.) Spl. Olympics, 1974. Served with USAF, World War II, 1951-52; Korea. Recipient Jefferson award Am. Inst. Pub. Service, 1978, Outstanding Service award Kidney Found., 1979, Community Service award Sales and Mktg. Execs., 1979; named Vol. of Yr. D.C. Dept. Corrections, 1977. Mem. Undersea Med. Soc. (membership chmn. 1970-74), CEDAM Internat., Am. Soc. Naval Engrs., Nat. Football League Alumni Touchdown Club. Democrat. Club. Capital Yacht (Washington). Current work: Hands-on research aboard 90-foot motor yacht in engine oil filtration; marine sanitation; burglary, fire and medical systems. Subspecialty: Electrical engineering. Office: Wheeler Industries Inc 1120-19th St NW #700 Washington DC 20036

WHEELER, GLYNN PEARCE, biochemist; b. Milan, Tenn., Oct. 13, 1919; s. Hollis E. and Vera M. (Pearce) W.; m. Annie Ford Lester, Jan. 20, 1943; children: William H., Anne P. B.A., Vanderbilt U., 1941, Ph.D., 1950; M.S., U. Akron, 1947. Analytical chemist Tenn. Coal Iron & R.R. Co., Birmingham, Ala., 1941, Govt. Lab. Ala. Ordnance Works, Childersburg, 1942; research chemist B.F. Goodrich Co., Akron, Ohio, 1942-46; head cancer biochemistry div. So. Research Inst., Birmingham, 1946-48, 50-85; mem. ad hoc coms. Nat. Cancer Inst.; mem. chemotherapy and hematology rev. com. Am. Cancer Soc., 1980-84, chmn., 1984. Contbr. numerous articles in field to profl. jours. Trustee Homewood Pub. Library, Gorgas Scholarship Found. Inc. USPHS fellow, 1948-50. Mem. Am. Soc. Biol. Chemists, Am. Assn. Cancer Research, AAAS, Am. Chem. Soc., Ala. Acad. Sci., Cell Kinetics Soc., Southeastern Cancer Research Assn., Phi Beta Kappa, Sigma Xi. Methodist. Club: The Club (Birmingham). Current Work: Biochemistry related to cancer chemotherapy; mechanims of action of anticancer agents. Subspecialties: Cancer research (medicine); Chemotherapy. Office: PO Box 55305 Birmingham AL 35255

WHEELER, JOHN ARCHIBALD, scientist; b. Jacksonville, Fla., July 9, 1911; s. Joseph Lewis and Mabel (Archibald) W.; m. Janette Hegner, June 10, 1935; children: Isabel Letitia Wheeler Ufford, James English, Alison Christie Wheeler Ruml. Ph.D., Johns Hopkins U., 1933, LL.D., 1977; Sc.D., Western Res. U., 1958, U. N.C., 1959, U. Pa., 1968, Middlebury Coll., 1969, Rutgers U., 1969, Yeshiva U., 1973, Yale U., 1974, U. Uppsala, 1975, U. Md., 1977, Gustavus Adolphus U., 1981, Cath. U. Am., 1982, U. Newcastle-upon-Tyne, 1983. NRC fellow, N.Y., Copenhagen, 1933-35; asst. prof. physics U. N.C., 1935-38; asst. prof. physics Princeton U., 1938-42, asso. prof., 1945-47, prof., 1947-76, Joseph Henry prof. physics, 1966-76, Joseph Henry prof. physics emeritus, 1976—; prof. physics U. Tex., Austin, 1976—, dir. Ctr. for Theoretical Physics, 1976—, Ashbel Smith prof., 1979—, Blumberg prof., 1981—; cons. and physicist on atomic energy projects Princeton U., 1939-42, U. Chgo., 1942, E.I. duPont de Nemours & Co., Wilmington, Del., and Richland, Wash., 1943-45, Los Alamos, 1950-53; dir. project Matterhorn Princeton U., 1951-53; Guggenheim fellow, Paris and Copenhagen, 1949-50; summer lectr. U. Mich., U. Chgo., Columbia U.; Lorentz prof. U. Leiden, 1956; Fulbright prof. Kyoto U., 1962; 1st vis. fellow Clare Coll. Cambridge U., 1964; Ritchie lectr. Edinburgh, 1958; vis. prof. U. Calif.-Berkeley, 1960; Battelle prof. U. Wash., 1975; sci. adviser U.S. Senate del. to 3d ann. conf. NATO Parliamentarians, Paris, 1957; mem. adv. com. Oak Ridge Nat. Lab., 1957-65, U. Calif., Los Alamos and Livermore, 1972-77; v.p. Internat. Union Physics, 1951-54; chmn. joint com. Am. Phys. Soc. and Am. Philos. Soc. on history theoretical physics in 20th Century, 1960-72; sci. adv. bd. USAF, 1961, 62; chmn. Dept. Def. Advanced Research Projects Agy. Project, 1958; mem. U.S. Gen. Adv. Com. Arms Control and Disarmament, 1969-72, 74-77. Author: Geometrodynamics, 1962, Gravitation Theory and Gravitational Collapse, 1965, Spacetime Physics, 1966, Einstein's Vision, 1968, Gravitation, 1973, Black Holes, Gravitational Radiation and Cosmology, 1974, Frontiers of Time, 1979, (with W. Zurek) Quantum Theory and Measurement, 1983; contbr. articles to profl. jours. Trustee Battelle Meml. Inst., 1959—. Recipient A. Cressy Morrison prize N.Y. Acad. Sci. for work on nuclear physics, 1947; Albert Einstein prize Strauss Found., 1965; Enrico Fermi award AEC, 1968; Franklin medal Franklin Inst., 1969; Nat. medal of Sci., 1971; Herzfeld award, 1975; Outstanding Grad. Teaching award U. Tex., 1981; Niels Bohr Internat. Gold medal, 1982; Oersted medal Am. Assn. Physics Tchrs., 1983. Fellow AAAS (dir. 1965-68), Am. Phys. Soc. (pres. 1966); mem. Am. Math Soc., Internat. Astron. Union, Am. Acad. Arts and Scis., Nat. Acad. Sci., Am. Philos. Soc. (councillor 1963-66, 76—, v.p. 1971-73), Royal Danish Acad. Scis., Royal Acad. Sci. (Uppsala, Sweden), l'Académie Internationale de Philosophie des Sciences, Internat. Union Physics (v.p. 1951-54), Phi Beta Kappa, Sigma Xi. Unitarian (trustee 1965). Subspecialties: Relativity and gravitation; Theoretical physics. Home: 1410 Wildcat Hollow Austin TX 78746 Office: Physics Dept U Tex Austin TX 78712

WHETSELL, WILLIAM OTTO, JR., neuropathologist; b. Orangeburg, S.C., Sept. 25, 1940; s. William Otto and Margaret Elizabeth (Daniel) W.; m. Anne Elizabeth Rodgers, Oct. 14, 1967; children: William Otto III, Helen Fern Elizabeth. B.S., Wofford Coll., Spartanburg, S.C., 1961; M.S., Med. U. S.C., 1964, M.D., 1966. Diplomate: Am. Bd. Pathology, Sub-Bd. Neuropathology. Fellow in neurobiology, instr. Columbia U. Coll. Physicians and Surgeons, 1968-69; resident in neurology, pathology and neuropathology N.Y. Neurol. Inst. and Columbia U., 1971-75; asst. prof. pathology and neurology Mt. Sinai Sch. Medicine, N.Y.C., 1975-78, asso. prof., 1978-79, cons. dept. neurology, 1979—; adj. asst. prof. Rockefeller U., N.Y.C., 1975-78; prof. pathology, dir. neuropathology U. Tenn. Center Health Sci., Memphis, 1979—; chief neuropathology VA Hosp., Memphis, 1979—. Contbr. articles to profl. jours. Served to lt. comdr. USN, 1969-71. USPHS grantee, 1975—. Mem. Am. Assn. Anatomists, Am. Assn. Neuropathologists, Am. Acad. Neurology, Assn. Research in Nervous and Mental Disorders, Soc. Neuroscience, AMA, N.Y. Acad. Scis. Republican. Current Work: Development of exploitation of experimental models in organotypic nerve cell tissue culture for study of porphyrin-heme metabolism in nervous system, study of cellular mechanisms involved in neurodegenerative disorders of neostriatum. Subspecialty: Neuropathology. Office: 858 Madison Ave Memphis TN 38163

WHIDDEN, STANLEY JOHN, physiologist, physician; b. N.Y.C., Oct. 10, 1947; s. Stanley Graham and Maybell (Von Houten) W. A.S., Delgado Coll., 1969; B.S., Southeastern La. U., 1971, M.S., 1973; Ph.D., Auburn U., 1979; M.D., U. Auto. De Ciudad Juarex, Mex., 1984; postgrad. Hyperbaric Physicians Ctr., NOAA. Asst. head ops. Nuclear Sci. Ctr., Auburn U., Ala., 1976-78; lectr. physiology U. Wis.-Madison, 1978-79; asst. prof. U. New Orleans, 1979-80; postdoctoral fellow shock physiology La. State U. Med. Ctr., New Orleans, 1980-82; research, med. staff JESM Baromed. Inst., New Orleans, 1984—. Contbr. chpt. to book: Handbook of Shock and Trauma, 1983. Served to capt. USAR, 1966—. Mem. AAUP, AAAS, Am. Physiology Soc., Soc. Neurosci. Am. Chem. Soc., Am. Burn Assn., N.Y. Acad. Sci., Shock Soc., Undersea Med. Soc. Republican. Club: Spl. Forces assn. (New Orleans) (pres. 1983-84). Current work: Underlining cardiovascular and metabolic responses during shock with resuscitation and hyperbaric medical treatment. Subspecialties: Physiology (medicine); Space medicine. Home: 2917 Prytania New Orleans LA 70115 Office: JESM Baromed Research Inst 4444 Gen Meyer New Orleans LA 70114

WHINNERY, JOHN ROY, electrical engineering educator; b. Read, Colo., July 26, 1916; s. Ralph V. and Edith Mable (Bent) W.; m. Patricia Barry, Sept. 17, 1944; children—Carol Joanne, Catherine, Barbara. B.S. in Elec. Engring, U. Calif. at Berkeley, 1937, Ph.D., 1948. Student engr. Gen. Electric Co., 1937-40, supr. high frequency course advanced engring. program, 1940-42, research engr., 1942-46; part-time lectr. Union Coll., Schenectady, 1945-46; asso. prof. elec. engring. U. Calif.-Berkeley, 1946-52, prof., vice chmn. div. elec. engring., 1952-56, chmn., 1956-59; dean Coll. Engring. U. Calif-Berkeley, 1959-63, prof. elec. engring., 1963-80, Univ. prof. Coll. Engring., 1980—; vis. mem. tech. staff. Bell Telephone Labs., 1963-64; research sci. electron tubes Hughes Aircraft Co., Culver City, 1951-52; bd. editors I.R.E., 1956. Author: (with Simon Ramo) Fields and Waves in Modern Radio, 1944, (with D. O. Pederson and J. J. Studer) Introduction to Electronic Systems, Circuits and Devices; also tech. articles. Chmn. Commn. Engring. Edn., 1966-68; mem. sci. and tech. com. Manned Space Flight, NASA, 1963-69; mem. Pres.'s Com. on Nat. Sci. Medal, 1970-73, 79-80; standing com. controlled thermonuclear research AEC, 1970-73. Recipient Edn. medal IEEE, 1967; Lamme medal Am. Soc. Engring. Edn., 1975; Microwave Career award IEEE Microwave Theory and Techniques Soc., 1977; Engring Alumni award U. Calif. at Berkeley, 1980; named to Hall of Fame Modesto High Sch. (Calif.), 1983; Guggenheim fellow, 1959. Fellow I.R.E. (dir. 1956-59), Optical Soc. Am., Am. Acad. Arts and Scis.; mem. Nat. Acad. Engring., Nat. Acad. Scis., IEEE (dir. 1969-71, sec. 1971, medal of honor 1985), Phi Beta Kappa, Sigma Xi, Tau Beta Pi, Eta Kappa Nu. Conglist. Current Work: Generation and use of short optical pulses. Subspecialties: Electrical engineering; Fiber optics. Home: One Daphne Ct Orinda CA 94563 Office: U Calif Berkeley CA 94720

WHIPPLE, FRED LAWRENCE, astronomer; b. Red Oak, Iowa, Nov. 5, 1906; s. Harry Lawrence and Celestia (MacFarl) W.; m. Dorothy Woods, 1928 (div. 1935); 1 son, Earle Raymond; m. Babette F. Samelson, Aug. 20, 1946; children—Dorothy Sandra, Laura. Student, Occidental Coll., 1923-24; A.B., UCLA, 1927, Ph.D., at Berkeley, 1931; A.M. (hon.), Harvard, 1945; Sc.D., Am. Internat. Coll., 1958; D.Litt. (hon.), Northeastern U., 1961; D.Sc. (hon.), Temple U., 1961, U. Ariz., 1979; LL.D. (hon.), C.W. Post Coll., L.I. U., 1962. Teaching fellow U. Calif. at Berkeley, 1927-29; Lick Obs. fellow, 1930-31; instr. Stanford, summer 1929, U. Calif., summer 1931; staff mem. Harvard Obs., from 1931; instr. Harvard, 1932-38, lectr., 1938-45; research assoc. Radio Research Lab., 1942-45, assoc. prof. astronomy, 1945-50, prof. astronomy, from 1950, chmn. dept., 1949-56, Phillips prof. astronomy, 1968-77; dir. Smithsonian Astrophys. Obs., 1955-73, sr. scientist, from 1973, now supervising astrophysicist; mem. Rocket Research Panel U.S., from 1946; U.S. subcom NASA, 1946-52, U.S. Research and Devel. Bd. Panel, 1947-52; chmn. Tech. Panel on Rocketry; mem. Tech. Panel on Earth Satellite Program; other coms. Internat. Geophys. Year, 1955-59; mem., past officer Internat. Astron. Union; cons. missions to U.K. and MTO, 1944; del. Inter-Am. Astrophys. Congress, Mexico, 1942; active leader project on Upper-Atmospheric Research via Meteor Photog. sponsored by Bur. Ordnance, U.S. Navy, 1946-51; by Bur. Ordnance, U.S. Navy (Office Naval Research), 1951-57, USAF, 1948-62; mem. com. meteorology, space sci. bd., com. on atmospheric scis. Nat. Acad. Scis.-NRC, 1958-65; project dir. Harvard Radio Meteor Project, from 1958; adviser Sci. Adv. Bd., USAF, 1963-67; spl. cons. com. Sci. and Astronautics U.S. Ho. Reps., 1960-73; chmn. Gordon Research Confs., 1963; dir. Optical Satellite Tracking Project, NASA, 1958-73; project dir. Orbiting Astron. Obs., 1958-72; dir. Meteorite Photography and Recovery Program, 1962-73, cons. planetary atmospheres, 1962-69; mem. space scis. working group on Orbiting Astron. Observatories, 1959-70; chmn. sci. council geodetic uses artifical satellites Com. Space Research, from 1965. Author: Earth, Moon and Planets, rev. edit, 1968, Orbiting The Sun: Planets and Satellites of The Solar System; co-author: Survey of the Universe; Contbr.: sci. papers on astron. and upper atmosphere to Ency. Brit; mags., other publs.; Asso. editor: Astronomical Jour, 1954-56, from 64; editor: Smithsonian Contributions to Astrophysics, 1956-73, Planetary and Space Science, from 1958, Science Revs, from 1961; editorial bd.: Earth and Planetary Sci. Letters; inventor tanometer, meteor bumper; a developer window as radar countermeasure, 1944. Decorated comdr. Order of Merit for research and invention, Esnault-Pelterie award France; recipient Donohue medals for ind. discovery of 6 new comets; Presdl. Cert. of Merit for sci. work during, World War II; J. Lawrence Smith medal Nat. Acad. Scis. for research on meteors, 1949; medal for astron. research U. Liege, 1960; Space Flight award Am. Astronautical Soc., 1961; Disting. Fed. Civilian Service award, 1963; Space Pioneers medallion for contbns. to fed. space program, 1968; Public Service award for contbns. to OAO2 devel. NASA, 1969; Leonard medal Meteoritical Soc., 1970; Kepler medal AAAS, 1971; Career Service award Nat. Civil Service League, 1972; Henry medal Smithsonian Instn., 1973; Alumnus of Yr. Achievement award UCLA, 1976; Golden Plate award Am. Acad. Achievement, 1981; Benjamin Franklin fellow Royal Soc. Arts, London, 1968—. Fellow Am. Astron. Soc. (v.p. 1962-64), Am. Rocket Soc., Am. Geophys. Union; asso. Royal Astron. Soc.; mem. Nat. Acad. Scis., AIAA Astronautics (aerospace tech. panel space physics 1960-63), Astronautical Soc. Pacific, Solar Assos., Internat. Sci. Radio Union (U.S.A. nat. com. 1949-61), Am. Meteoritical Soc., Am. Standards Assn., Am. Acad. Arts and Scis., Am. Philos. Soc. (councillor sect. astronomy and erth scis. 1966—), Royal Soc. Scis. Belgium (corr.), Internat. Acad. Astronautics (sci. advisory com. 1962—), Internat. Astronautical Fedn., AAAS, Am. Meteorol. Soc., Royal Astron. Soc. (asso.), Phi Beta Kappa, Sigma Xi, Pi Mu Epsilon. Clubs: Examiner (Boston); Cosmos (Washington). Subspecialty: Optical astronomy. Home: 35 Elizabeth Rd Belmont MA 02178 Office: 60 Garden St Cambridge MA 02138

WHITAKER, EWEN ADAIR, astronomer; b. London, June 22, 1922; came to U.S., 1958; s. George Frederick and Gladys Emily (Johnstone) W.; m. Beryl Joyce Horswell, June 22, 1946; children: Malcolm John, Graham David, Fiona Carolyn. Higher nat. cert. in mech. engring, Woolwich Poly., London, 1944. Spectrographer, analytical chemist Siemens Bros. Co., Ltd., London, 1940-49; exptl. officer Royal Greenwich Obs., London, 1949-56, Herstmonceux Castle, Sussex, 1956-58; research assoc. Yerkes Obs., Williams Bay, Wis., 1958-60; assoc. research scientist Lunar & Planetary Lab., U. Ariz., Tucson, 1960—. Author: Photographic Lunar Atlas, 1960, Orthographic Atlas of the Moon, 1961, Rectified Lunar Atlas, 1963, Consolidated Lunar Atlas, 1967; author: NASA Catalogue of Lunar Nomenclature, 1982; The University of Arizona's Lunar and Planetary Laboratory-It's Founding and Early Years, 1985; contbr. articles to profl. jours. Recipient Walter Goodacre medal and gift Brit. Astron. Assn., 1982. Fellow Royal Astron. Soc.; mem. Am. Astron. Soc., Internat. Astron. Union. Current Work: Lunar surface topography, physics/chemistry, evolution; history of lunar observations, cartography and nomenclature. Subspecialty: Planetary science. Home: 4332 E 6 St Tucson AZ 85711 Office: Lunar & Planetary Lab U Ariz Tucson AZ 85721

WHITCOMB, BRUCE MAGILL, electro-optic scientist; b. Manhattan, Kans., June 9, 1943; s. Stuart Estes and Katherine (Magill) W.; m. Trudi Lillian Carley, Aug. 5, 1967 (div. Aug. 6, 1975); children—Tara Brandylane, Heathera Paige, Hans-David Christian. B.A. in Physics, Earlham Coll., 1965; M.S. in Physics, U. Mo.-Rolla, 1967; postgrad. U. Nev., Reno, 1974-80. Grad. teaching asst. dept. physics U. Mo.-Rolla, 1965-67, Purdue U., West Lafayette, Ind., 1967-69; research assoc. TPRC, West Lafayette, 1969-72; grad. teaching asst. dept. physics U. Nev., Reno, 1974-77; research assoc. Desert Research Inst., Reno, 1977-81; sci. specialist EG&G/Energy Measurements, Las Vegas, 1981—. Contbr. articles to profl. jours., papers to symposia. Mem. Optical Soc. Am., Soc. Photo-Optical Instrumentation Engrs., Sigma Xi, Sigma Pi Sigma. Current work: Development of electro-optical systems for diagnostics of fast phenomena in radiation environments. Subspecialty: Fiber optics. Office: EG&G/Energy Measurements PO Box 1912 M/S S-08 Las Vegas NV 89125

WHITE, BENJAMIN STEVEN, mathematician, researcher; b. Boston, Sept. 29, 1945; s. Norman Kenneth White and Mildred Ruth (Silverman) Segal; m. Helen Katherine Frazer, June 12, 1966; children—Adam Frazer, Ethan Abraham. S.B., MIT, 1967; M.A., U. Ariz., 1968; Ph.D., Courant Inst., NYU, 1974. Sr. mathematician Raytheon Co., Newport, R.I., 1969-70; systems analyst Time-Sharing Resources, N.Y.C., 1970-71; vis. mem. Courant Inst., NYU, 1974-75; instr. applied math. Calif. Inst. Tech., Pasadena, 1975-78; mem. tech. staff Jet Propulsion Lab., Pasadena, 1978-81; research assoc. Exxon Research and Engring. Co., Annandale, N.J., 1981—; instr. NYU, Bronx, 1971-72; v.p. Perceptive Systems, Inc., Pasadena, 1980-81. Contbr. articles to profl. jours. Mem. Soc. for Indsl. and Applied Math., Am. Math. Soc., N.Y. Acad. Scis. Democrat. Current work: Applied mathematics, applications of stochastic processes; wave propagation in random media. Subspecialties: Applied mathematics; Probability. Home: 345 Shunpike Rd Chatham Township NJ 07928 Office: Exxon Research and Engring Co Route 22 East Annandale NJ 08801

WHITE, CHARLES OLDS, aerospace engineer; b. Beirut, Lebanon, Apr. 2, 1931; came to U.S., 1945; s. Frank Laurence and Dorothy Alice (Olds) W.; m. Mary Carolyn Liechty, Sept. 3, 1955; children: Charles Cameron, Bruce Blair. B.S., MIT, 1953, M.S., 1954. Aero. engr. Douglas Aircraft Co., Long Beach, Calif., 1954-60; sr. engring. specialist Ford Aerospace & Communications Corp., Newport Beach, Calif., 1969-79, staff office gen. mgr., 1979-80, tech. mgr., 1981-82; supr. design and analysis DIVAD div., 1982—. Prin. collaborator: handbook USAF Stability and Control Methods; contbr. articles to profl. jours. Recipient Sigma Gamma Tau award MIT, 1953. Mem. AIAA, Nat. Mgmt. Assn., Am. Aviation Hist. Soc. Republican. Presbyterian. Clubs: Newport Beach and Tennis, Masters Swimming. Current Work: High temperature fluid mechanics, aerodynamic heating, propellants, materials, system dynamics. Subspecialties: Fluid mechanics; Aerospace engineering and technology. Home: 2857 Alta Vista Dr Newport Beach CA 92660 Office: Ford Aerospace and Communications Corp Ford Rd Newport Beach CA 92660

WHITE, DAVID CLEAVELAND, microbial ecologist, toxicologist, educator; b. Moline Ill., May 18, 1929; s. Fredrick Berryhill and Dorothy (Cleaveland) W.; m. Sandra Shoults, July 7, 1957; children—Winifred S., Christopher C., Andrew B. A.B., Dartmouth Coll., 1951; M.D., Tufts U., 1955; Ph.D., Rockefeller U., 1962. Intern Hosp. of U. Pa., Phila., 1955-56; prof. U. Ky. Med. Ctr., Lexington, 1962-72; prof. biol. scis. Fla. State U., Tallahassee, 1972—; pres. Impact Cons., Inc., Tallahassee, 1984—; mem. adv. bd. Ctr. for Theol. Inquiry, Princeton, N.J., 1984—; mem. adv. panel NRC, Washington, 1982—. Author: SFX, Drugs and Pollution, 1955, also articles. Editor-in-chief Jour. Microbiol. Methods, 1983—. Served to lt. USN, 1956-58. Recipient P.R. Edwards award Am. Soc. Microbiology, 1981; Winzler award Fla. State U.; Burroughs Welcome fellow, 1984. Democrat. Presbyterian. Current work: Use chemical analysis to describe biomass, community structure, nutritional status and metabolic activities of microbial consortia and biofilms related to environmental contamination, fermentations and corrosion. Subspecialty: Environmental chemistry. Office: Fla State U 310 Nuclear Research Bldg Tallahassee FL 32306

WHITE, DONALD HERBERT, See *Who's Who in America,* 43rd edition.

WHITE, HELEN LYNG, biochemist, pharmacologist; b. Oceanside, N.Y., Oct. 25, 1930; d. James and Irene Genevieve (Dilzer) Lyng; m. James Rushton White, Jan. 15, 1955; children: Jennifer, John Nelson. B.A., Russell Sage Coll., 1952; M.S., U. Del., 1963; Ph.D. (NASA fellow), U. N.C., 1967. Chemist E.I. duPont de Nemours & Co., Wilmington, Del., 1952-56; research assoc. dept. medicinal chemistry U. N.C., Chapel Hill, 1967-70; sr. research pharmacologist Wellcome Research Labs., Research Triangle Park, N.C., 1970—; ad hoc reviewer for several sci. jours. and NSF. Contbr. over 100 articles and abstracts to sci. publs. Recipient Crockett Alumnae award Russell Sage Coll., 1972. Mem. Am. Soc. for Pharmacology and Exptl. Therapeutics, Am. Soc. Biol. Scis., Am. Chem. Soc. (medicinal chemistry div.), Soc. for Neurosci., Sigma Xi. Patentee in field. Current Work: Enzyme inhibitors; neurochemistry; prostaglandins; monoamine oxidase; drug development for therapeutic purposes. Subspecialties: Biochemistry (biology); Pharmacology. Office: Wellcome Research Labs Research Triangle Park NC 27709

WHITE, JOHN FRANCIS, corporate executive; b. Madison, Wis., Dec. 2, 1929; s. Francis Bernard and Helen Margaret (Brown) W.; 1 dau., Susan Jeanne. B.S., U. Wis., 1951; grad., Harvard U. Advanced Mgmt. Program, 1974. With Kraft Inc., 1954—, v.p., dir. research and devel., Glenview, Ill., 1974—. Served with AUS, 1951-53. Mem. Inst. Food Technologists, Am. Chem. Soc., AAAS. Republican. Roman Catholic. Club: North Shore Country

(Glenview). Current work: Food processing and packaging. Subspecialty: Food science and technology. Home: 1439 Pebble Creek Dr Glenview IL 60025 Office: Kraft Inc 801 Waukegan Rd Glenview IL 60025

WHITE, KEITH D., psychologist. Assoc. prof. psychology U. Fla., Gainesville. Recipient Troland award Nat. Acad. Scis., 1985. Subspecialty: Physiological psychology. Office: U Fla Dept Psychology Gainesville FL 32611

WHITE, KING PRESTON, JR., engineering educator, researcher, consultant; b. Port Chester, N.Y., Dec. 31, 1948; s. King Preston and Emily Rosamond (Conley) W.; m. Charlotte Rebekah O'Cain, Apr. 9, 1977; children—William Preston, B.S.E., Duke U., 1970, M.S., 1972, Ph.D., 1976. Asst. prof. Poly. Inst. N.Y., Bklyn., 1975-77, Carnegie-Mellon U., Pitts., 1977-79; asst. prof. U. Va., Charlottesville, 1979-85, assoc. prof., 1985—; cons. TRW, Inc., Redondo Beach, Calif., 1978, Contraves Goerz, Inc., Pitts., 1979, City of Richmond, Va., 1982-84, Gen. Electric Co., Charlottesville, 1985—. Author book chpts. Contbr. numerous articles to tech. jours. Mem. IEEE, Ops. Research Soc. Am., Am. Soc. Engring. Edn., Soc. Automotive Engrs. (Teetor ednl. award 1985), Systems, Man, and Cybernetics Soc., Control Systems Soc., Sigma Xi, Tau Beta Pi, Pi Tau Sigma, Omega Rho. Current work: modeling, simulation, analysis, and control of dynamic systems; sequencing and scheduling; database and knowledge-based systems for decision support. Subspecialties: Systems engineering; Operations research (engineering). Home: Rt #1 Box 132 Shipman VA 22971 Office: Dept Systems Engring Thornton Hall U Va Charlottesville VA 22901

WHITE, MARY-ALICE, psychologist, educator; b. Washington, Mar. 18, 1920; d. Charles Stanley and Blanche M. (Strong) W.; m. Edward N. Kimball, Mar. 27, 1949 (div. 1968); children: Christopher, Katharine. B.A., Vassar Coll., 1941; Ph.D., Columbia U., 1948. Head dept. psychology Westchester div. N.Y. Hosp., White Plains, 1948-60; psychol. cons. Pelham (N.Y.) Sch. System, 1953-62; assoc. prof. Tchrs. Coll., Columbia U., N.Y.C., 1966-67, prof. psychology, 1967—; dir. Electronic Learning Lab., 1977—. Author: (with others) Parents Guide to School Testing, 1982; editor: (with others) Future of Electronic Learning, 1983; Contbr. (with others) articles to profl. jours. NIMH grantee, 1966-82. Fellow Am. Psychol. Assn. (pres. div. 1967, Disting. Service award 1971). Democrat. Current Work: Development of electronic learning psychology—how humans learn from electronic communications and information technology. Subspecialties: Psychology of electronic learning; Psychology of computer learning. Home: Box 426 Salisbury CT 06068 Office: Tchrs Coll Columbia New York NY 10027

WHITE, MITCHELL RAY, chemist; b. San Antonio, May 4, 1952; s. Clifford Lee and Sarah Alpha (Jones) W.; m. Lydia Lynn Biegert, Aug. 27, 1977 (div. 1983). B.S., Tex. Luth. Coll., 1976; Ph.D., U. Utah, 1983. Sr. research chemist Dow Chem. Co., Freeport, Tex., 1983—. Contbr. articles to profl. jours. Mem. Am. Chem. Soc., AAAS. Presbyterian. Current work: Reactive intermediates in catalysis, computer modelling and chemical process in-situ analysis. Subspecialties: Organometallics; Analytical chemistry. Home: 420 Garland Dr Apt 410 Lake Jackson TX 77566 Office: Dow Chem Co Bldg B2406 Freeport TX 77541

WHITE, RAYMOND PETRIE, JR., dentist; b. N.Y.C., Feb. 13, 1937; s. Raymond Petrie and Mabel Sarah (Shutze) W.; m. Betty Pritchett, Dec. 27, 1961; children—Karen Elizabeth, Michael Wood. Student, Washington and Lee U., 1955-58; D.D.S., Med. Coll. Va., 1962, Ph.D., 1967. Diplomate: Am. Bd. Oral and Maxillofacial Surgery. Postdoctoral fellow anatomy Med. Coll. Va., Richmond, 1962-67, resident in oral surgery, 1964-67; asst. prof. U. Ky., Lexington, 1967-70, asso. prof., 1970-71, chmn. dept. oral surgery, 1969-71; prof., asst. dean adminstrn. Va. Commonwealth U., Richmond, 1971-74; prof. Sch. Dentistry, U. N.C., Chapel Hill, 1974—, dean, 1974-81; assoc. dean Sch. Medicine, U. N.C., 1981—; cons. Portsmouth Naval Hosp., Fayetteville VA; mem. staff N.C. Meml. Hosp., mem. exec. com., 1974—, sec., 1977-78, asso. chief of staff, 1981—; mem. rev. com. health manpower br. USPHS, 1974-76; mem. rev. com. VA Health Manpower Tng. Assistance, 1976-79. Author: (with E.R. Costich) Fundamentals of Oral Surgery, 1971, (with Bell and Proffit) Surgical Correction of Dentofacial Deformities, 1980; contbr. sci. articles to profl. jours. Recipient A.D. Williams award for highest class standing Med. Coll. Va., 1962, Outstanding Tchr. award U. Ky., 1971. Mem. Am. Dental Assn., N.C. Dental Soc., Am. Acad. Oral Pathology, Atwood Wash Oral Surgery Soc., AAAS, Internat. Assn. for Dental Research (pres. Ky. sect. 1970), Inst. of Medicine of Nat. Acad. Scis., Chalmers J. Lyons Acad. Oral Surgery, Am. Assn. Oral and Maxillofacial Surgeons (gen. chmn. sci. sessions com. 1974-76, Outstanding Service award as committeeman 1976), N.C. Soc. Oral and Maxillofacial Surgeons, Sigma Xi, Psi Omega, Delta Tau Delta, Psi Omega (Scholarship award 1962), Omicron Kappa Upsilon. Roman Catholic. Current Work: Facial growth and development; effects of treatment of dentofacial deformity; health services research and policy analysis in dentistry. Subspecialties: Oral and maxillofacial surgery; Health services research. Home: 1506 Velma Rd Chapel Hill NC 27514 Office: Dept Oral and Maxillofacial Surgery Univ NC Sch Dentistry Chapel Hill NC 27514

WHITE, RICHARD ALAN, botanist; b. Phila., Oct. 25, 1935; s. Alpheus Rayburn and Kathryn (Mulhanney) W.; m. Norma Marie Blackburn, June 12, 1965; children—Richard, Karen, Susan. B.S., Temple U., 1957, M.S., 1957; M.A., U. Mich., 1960, Ph.D., 1962. Asst. prof. botany Duke U., Durham, N.C., 1963-68, assoc. prof., 1968-73, prof., 1973-84, chmn. dept., 1978-84, now dean Arts and Scis., dean Trinity Coll. mem. exec. com., bd. dirs. Orgn. of Tropical Studies. NSF fellow, 1962-63; Danforth fellow, 1957-62. Mem. Bot. Soc. Am., Internat. Soc. Plant Morphologists. Torrey Bot. Club, Am. Fern Soc., AAAS. Subspecialties: Morphology; Developmental biology. Office: Dean Arts and Scis and Dean Trinity Coll 104 Allen Bldg Duke U Durham NC 27706

WHITE, RICHARD EDWARD, astronomer, educator; b. Chgo., Jan. 18, 1944; s. Edward Joseph and Eileen Dorothy (Prendergast) W.; m. Penny Conrad, Sept. 5, 1970 (div. July 1981). B.S. summa cum laude, St. Joseph's Coll., 1965; Ph.D., Columbia U., 1971. Carnegie fellow Hale Obs. Pasadena, Calif., 1970-72; resident research assoc. NASA Goddard Inst. for Space Studies, N.Y.C., 1972-74; adj. asst. prof. Columbia U., 1974; asst. prof. astronomy Smith Coll., Northampton, Mass., 1974-75, 76-82, lectr., 1975-76, assoc. prof., 1982—; vis. astronomer F.L. Whipple Obs., Smithsonian Instn., Amado, Ariz., 1980, 82, 83, 84; mem. users adv. com. Kitt Peak Nat. Obs., 1977-79. Contbr. articles to profl. jours. NSF grantee, 1978-80; Am. Astron. Soc. grantee, 1981. Mem. Am. Astron. Soc., Astron. Soc.Pacific, AAAS, Sigma Xi. Democrat. Current Work: Optocal studies of interstellar clouds. Subspecialty: Optical astronomy.

WHITE, RICHARD MAHAFFEY, systems architect, management technology, company executive, consultant; b. N.Y.C., June 14, 1944; s. Richard Thornton and Anna M. (Mahaffey) W. B.S. in Systems Analysis, Miami U., Oxford, Ohio, 1972, M.S. in Stats. cum laude, 1972. Cons. Ops. Analysis and Research, Washington, 1978—; dir. The OAR Corp., Washington, 1979—; cons. Naval Space and Surface Systems Command, 1978—. Served to lt. comdr. USN, 1965-78; lt. comdr. USNR, 1978—. Mem. Soc. Indsl. and Applied Math., Math Assn. Am., U.S. Naval Inst., Soc. Old Crows, Smithsonian Assocs., Cultural Alliance Greater Washington, Corcoran Assocs., Phi Beta Kappa, Pi Mu Epsilon. Current Work: Undersea acoustics research, space technology, Navy command and control systems, world wide communications architectures, astrodynamics, operations research, expert systems, multi-sensor correlation, large screen displays, multi-channel telemetry. Subspecialty: Cryptography and data security. Office: Operations Analysis and Research 6005 Milo Dr Washington DC 20816

WHITE, ROBERT CARL, physicist; b. Tachikawa AFB, Japan, June 15, 1958; s. Robert David and Mavis (Graham) W. B.S. in Physics, B.A. in Math., U. Calif.-Santa Barbara, 1980; M.S. in Applied Sci., U. Calif.-Davis, 1982. Physicist Lawrence Livermore Nat. Lab., Calif., 1980—. Mem. Am. Phys. Soc. Current work: Study of nonlinear resonances in Hamiltonian systems with applications to confinement and heating in magnetic fusion experiments. Subspecialties: Fusion; Plasma physics. Home: 278 Elvira St Livermore CA 94550 Office: Lawrence Livermore Nat Lab L 630 Livermore CA 94550

WHITE, ROBERT GEORGE, research fish biologist, fishery educator; b. Gilman City, Mo., July 21, 1940; s. Russel Dale and Ethel Christina (Davisson) W.; m. Barbara Ann Odom, June 2, 1968; children—Jennifer, Brian, Jason. B.S. in Edn., N.E. Mo. State U., 1962, M.A. in Edn., 1963; Ph.D. in Fisheries, Utah State U., 1974. Sci. tchr. Braymer C-4 Sch., Mo., 1963-68; asst. dir. Bear Lake Lab., Utah State U., Logan, 1968-70; asst. leader Idaho Coop. Fisheries Research Unit, U.S. Fish and Wildlife Service, Moscow, 1974-80, leader Mont. Coop. Fisheries Research Unit, Bozeman, 1980—. Contbr. articles to profl. jours. Advisor Mont. council Boy Scouts Am., 1984—. NDEA fellow, 1968-71. Mem. Am. Fisheries Soc. (life, 2d v.p. 1985-86, program chmn. 1984-85, best poster award 1973, chmn. steering com. small hydro fish symposium Bio-engring. sect. Western Div., 1982-85, pres. Western div. 1980-81, pres. Idaho chpt. 1975-77), Sigma Xi (grantee 1972), Phi Delta Kappa. Current work: Evaluation of effects of habitat alterations, especially as related to habitat utilization by fishes and species interactions. Subspecialties: Ecology (biology); Population biology. Home: 1111 Tayabeshockup Rd Bozeman MT 59715 Office: Mont Coop Fishery Research Unit Biology Dept Mont State Univ Bozeman MT 59717

WHITE, ROBERT J., educator, neurosurgeon, neuroscientist; b. Duluth, Minn., Jan. 21, 1926; married 1950; children: Robert, Christopher, Patricia, Michael, Daniel, Pamela, James, Richard, Marguerite, Ruth. B.S., Coll. St. Thomas, U. Minn., 1951, Ph.D. in Neurosurg. Physiology, 1962; M.D., Harvard, 1953; D.Sc. (hon.), John Carroll U., 1979, Cleve. State U., 1981. Intern surgery Peter Bent Brigham Hosp., Boston, 1953-54; resident Boston Children's Hosp. and Peter Bent Brigham Hosp., 1954-55; fellow neurosurgery Mayo Clinic, 1955-58, asst. to staff, 1958-59, research asso. neuro physiol., 1959-61; mem. faculty Case Western Res. U. Sch. Medicine, 1961—, prof. neurosurgery, 1966—, co-dir. neurosurgery, 1972, co-chmn. neurosurgery, 1973—; dir. neurosurg. and brain research lab. Cleve. Met. Gen. Hosp., 1961—; neurosurgeon Univ. Hosps.; also sr. attending neurosurgeon VA Hosp., 1961—; lectr. USSR, 1966, 68, 70, 72, 73, 78, 79, People's Republic China, 1977, 81. Gen. editor: Internat. Soc. Angiol. Jour, 1966; editor: Western Hemisphere Jour. Resuscitation, 1971—, Surg. Neurology, Resuscitation, Jour. of Trauma; co-editor: Surg. Neurology, 1973—; Contbr. numerous articles to profl. jours. Served with AUS, 1944-46. Recipient Mayo Clinic Research award, 1958; Med. Mut. Honor award, 1975; L.W. Freeman award PF, 1977. Mem. ACS (com. on trauma task force), Harvey Cushing Soc., Soc. Univ. Surgeons, Am. Physiol. Soc., Soc. Univ. Neurosurgeons (pres. 1978-79), Ohio Neurosurg. Soc. (pres. 1975), Northeast Ohio Neurosurg. Soc. (pres. 1971), Soc. Exptl. Biology, Internat. Soc. Cybernetic Medicine (mem. internat. bd. 1971—), Internat. Soc. Surgery, Soc. Neurol. Surgeons, Neurosurg. Soc. Am., A.C.S., AMA, Acad. Medicine Cleve. (dir., pres. 1978-79). Developed 1st isolated brain models; pioneered brain and cephalon transplant in animals, deep hypothermia techniques in brain and spinal surgery. Current Work: Operative brain surgery; brain transplantation; neurochemistry; neuroimmuology; head injury; spinal cord injury. Subspecialties: Neurochemistry; Neurophysiology. Address: 3395 Scranton Rd Cleveland OH 44109

WHITE, ROBERT M., association executive; b. Boston, Feb. 13; m. Mavis Edwina Seagle, children—Richard H., Edwina J. B.A., Harvard U., 1944; M.S., MIT, 1949, Sc.D., 1950. Research scientist Atmospheric Analysis Lab., Air Force Cambridge Research Ctr., 1950-52, dir. Meteorology Devel. Lab., 1952-59; research assoc. MIT, Cambridge, 1959; assoc. dir. research Travelers Ins. Co., Hartford, Conn., 1959-60; pres. Travelers Research Ctr. Inc., Hartford, 1960-63, Joint Oceanographic Instns. Inc., Washington, 1977-79, Univ. Corp. for Atmospheric Research, Boulder, Colo., 1980-83, Washington, 1980-83, Nat. Acad. Engring., 1983—; chief U.S. Weather Bur., Dept. Commerce, Washington, 1963-65; adminstr. Environ. Sci. Services, Dept. Commerce, Washington, 1963-65; adminstr. Environ. Sci. Services, Dept. Commerce, Washington, 1965-70, Nat. Oceanic and Atmospheric Adminstrn., Dept. Commerce, 1970-77; chmn. Climate Research Bd., Nat. Research Council, Nat. Acad. Scis., Washington, 1977-79; mem. Nat. Adv. Com. Oceans and Atmosphere, Washington, 1979—, Dept. State Adv. Com. Oceans and Internat. Environmental and Sci. Affairs, 1979—, Woods Hole Oceanograhic Instn. Corp. (Mass.), 1980—; bd. dirs. Resources for Future, Washington, 1980—, Draper Labs., Cambridge, 1983—; mem. vis. com. Sch. Engring., U. Okla., 1968-71; mem. adv. com. Ctr. Ocean Law and Policy, U. Va., Charlottesville, 1975-78; chmn. vis. com. Mus. Comparative Zoology, Harvard U., 1977-79, mem. bd. overseers, 1977-79; mem. vis. com. John F. Kennedy Sch. Govt., 1978-82, mem. vis. com. div. applied scis., 1979—; mem., vice chmn. bd. trustees Univ. Corp. Atmospheric Research, Boulder, 1977-80; mem. vis. com. Ctr. for Earth Scis, MIT, 1968-81; U.S. chmn. U.S.-France Coop. Program in Oceanography, 1973-77, U.S.-U.S.S.R. Joint Commn. for Exploration of World Oceans, 1974-77; mem. exec. com. World Meteorol. Orgn., Geneva, Switzerland, 1963-78; chmn. Climate Coordinating Group, Internat. Council Sci. Unions, Geneva, 1979, World Climate Conf., World Meteorol. Orgn., 1979. Served to capt. USAF, 1945. Decorated Chevalier Legion of Honor; recipient Internat. Conservation Nat. Wildlife Fedn., Washington, 1977, Neptune award for contributions to marine affairs Am. Oceanic Orgn., Washington, 1977, Charles Franklin Brooks Am. Meteorol. Soc., 1978, Internat. Meteorol. Orgn. prize World Meteorol. Orgn., 1980, Fahrney Franklin Inst., 1983. Fellow Am. Geophys. Union, Am. Meteorol. Soc. (pres. 1980); mem. Sci. Adv. Council, Marine Tech. Soc. (v.p. 1975-77), AAAS. Club: Cosmos (Washington). Subspecialties: Climatology; Oceanography. Office: Nat Acad Engring 2101 Constitution Ave NW Washington DC 20488

WHITE, R(OBERT) STEPHEN, physics educator, researcher; b. Ellsworth, Kans., Dec. 28, 1920; s. Byron F. and Sebina (Leighty) W.; m. Freda Marie Bridgewater, Aug. 30, 1942; children—Nancy Lynn, Margaret Diane, John Stephen, David Bruce. A.B., Southwestern Coll., 1942, D.Sc. (hon.), 1971; M.S., U. Ill., 1943; Ph.D., U. Calif.-Berkeley, 1951. Physicist, Lawrence Radiation Lab. U. Calif.-Berkeley and Livermore, 1948-61; head dept. particles and fields Space Physics Lab., Aerospace Corp., El Segundo, Calif., 1962-67; prof. physics U. Calif.-Riverside, 1967—, assoc. dir. Inst. Geophysics and Planetary Physics, 1967—, chmn. dept. physics, 1970-73. Author: Space Physics, 1970, Contbr. articles to profl. jours. Served to lt. (j.g.), USN, 1944-46. NSF fellow, 1961-62; grantee in field. Fellow Am. Phys. Soc. (exec. com. 1972-74), Am. Geophys. Union; mem. Am. Astron. Soc., AAAS, AAUP. Republican. Methodist. Current work: Studies of broad gamma ray lines, continuous spectra, and time distributions from galactic pulsars, black holes and other compact objects and extragalactic sources such as quasars and active galaxies with gamma rays of 1-30 MeV observed with the UCR double scatter gamma ray telescope to extend our knowledge of high energy astrophysics. Subspecialties: Gamma ray high energy astrophysics; High energy astrophysics. Office: Inst Geophysics and Planetary Physics U Calif Riverside CA 92521

WHITE, ROLFE DOWNING, medical educator; b. Annapolis, Md., Sept. 9, 1949; s. John and Jane (Angus) W.; m. Sarah Elizabeth Haughton, June 4, 1978; children—Kathryn Diane, Bryan Rolfe. B.S., Va. Mil. Inst., 1971; postgrad., George Washington U. Sch. Medicine, 1970; M.D., Med. Coll. Va., 1975. Diplomate: Nat. Bd. Med. Examiners, Am. Bd. Ob-Gyn. Resident in ob-gyn Naval Regional Med. Ctr., Portsmouth, Va., 1975-79; attending physician in gynecol. urology Nat. Naval Med. Ctr., Bethesda, Md., 1980-81; cons. in gynecol. urology Walter Reed Army Med. Ctr., Washington, 1980-81; chmn. dept. ob-gyn U.S. Naval Hosp., Patuxent River, Md., 1980-81; pres. Va. Urodynamics Labs., Virginia Beach, Va., 1982—; asst. prof. Eastern Va. Med. Sch., Norfolk, 1981—. Contbr. articles to profl. jours. Served to lt. comdr. USNR, 1975-81. Recipient Physicians Recognition award AMA, 1983; Cert. of Achievement NASA, 1970. Fellow Am. Coll. Ob-Gyn, Am. Soc. Abdominal Surgeons, Southeastern Surg. Conf.; mem. Am. Fertility Soc., Gynecol. Urology Soc., Am. Assn. Mil. Surgeons U.S., Am. Fedn. for Clin. Research. Republican. Episcopalian. Current Work: Utilization of real-time ultrasonography for the evaluation of the lower urinary tract successfully adapted commonly used obstetric technology (fetal monitor systems) for electronic cystourethrometrics (bladder testing). Subspecialties: Obstetrics and gynecology; Gynecologic urology. Office: Va Urodynamics Labs 3386 Holland Rd Suite 205 Virginia Beach VA 23452

WHITE, STEPHEN HALLEY, biophysicist, educator; b. Wewoka, Okla., May 14, 1940; s. James Halley and Gertrude June (Wyatt) W.; m. Buff Ertl, Aug. 20, 1961; children: Saill, Shell, Storn, Sharr, Skye, Sunde; m. Jackie M. Dooley, Apr. 14, 1984. B.S., U. Colo., 1963; M.S., U. Wash., 1965, Ph.D., 1969; grad., Mgmt. Inst., U. Calif., 1981. Asst. prof. dept. physiology and biophysics U. Calif.-Irvine, 1972-75, assoc. prof., 1975-78, prof., 1978—, vice chmn., 1974-75, chmn., 1977—; guest biophysicist Brookhaven Nat. Lab., Upton, N.Y., 1977—. Contbr. articles to profl. jours. Mem. adv. panel on molecular biology NSF. Served to capt. U.S. Army, 1969-71. Recipient Excellence in Teaching award Kaiser Permanente Found., 1975; Research Career Devel. award NIH, 1976; USPHS fellow, 1971. Mem. Biophys. Soc. (council 1981, exec. bd. 1981-83, program chmn. 1985). Am. Physiol. Soc. (editorial bd. 1981—), Soc. Gen. Physiologists (treas. 1985-88). Democrat. Current Work: Structure and physical chemistry of cell membranes. Subspecialties: Biophysics (biology); Physical chemistry. Office: Dept Physiology U Calif Irvine CA 92717

WHITE, TIMOTHY PETER, physical education educator; b. Buenos Aires, Argentina, July 9, 1949; came to U.S., 1957, naturalized, 1969; s. Anthony Robert and Mary (Weston) W.; m. Nina Marie Kasper, Oct. 11, 1981. B.A. magna cum laude, Fresno State U., 1970; M.S., Calif. State U.-Hayward, 1972; Ph.D., U. Calif.-Berkeley, 1977; postgrad., U. Mich., 1976-78. Asst. prof. dept. phys. edn. U. Mich., Ann Arbor, 1978-82, assoc. prof., 1982-83; assoc. prof. dept. phys. edn. U. Calif.-Berkeley, 1983—. Fellow Am. Coll. Sports Medicine (New Investigator award 1981); mem. Am. Physiol. Soc., Phi Kappa Phi. Current Work: Research on the mechanisms by which exercise influences morphological, biochemical and physiological variables of normal and regenerating skeletal muscle. Subspecialty: Physiology (biology). Home: 112 Patterson Blvd Pleasant Hill CA 94523 Office: Dept Physical Education University of California 103 Harmon Gym Berkeley CA 94720

WHITECAR, JOHN P., JR., medical oncologist; b. Phila., July 17, 1939; s. John P. and Patience (Daven) W.; m. Kathleen L. Hemelt, Dec. 3, 1966; children: Linnane Rene, John P. III, Michael Anthony, Colleen Jeanette. B.A. magna cum laude, LaSalle Coll., 1960; M.D., Jefferson Med. Coll., 1964. Diplomate: Am. Bd. Internal Medicine, Am. Bd. Med. Oncology. Intern U. Minn. Hosp., Mpls., 1964-65, resident in medicine, 1965-66, 67-68; USPHS trainee in hematology 1966-67; clin. fellow Am. Cancer Soc., 1967-68; faculty assoc., chief leukemia and hematology sect., dept. devel. therapeutics U. Tex.-M.D. Anderson Hosp. and Tumor Inst., Houston, 1970-71; prin. investigator S.W. Oncology Group, San Antonio, 1971-74; clin. assoc. prof./dept. medicine U. Tex. Health Sci. Center, San Antonio, 1972-79, clin. prof. medicine (oncology), 1979-80; prin. investigator clin. oncology S.W. Tex. Methodist Hosp., San Antonio, 1977-79; practice med. oncology S.W. Oncology Assocs. (P.A.), San Antonio, 1974—. Contbr. articles to profl. jours. Served with M.C., U.S. Army, 1971-74. Recipient Anatomy prize Jefferson Med. Coll., 1961, Henry M. Phillips prizes in medicine and surgery, 1964, Edward J. Moore prize, 1964. Fellow ACP; mem. N.Y. Acad. Scis., AAAS, Tex. Med. Assn., Bexar County Med. Soc., AMA, Am. Fedn. Clin. Research, Am. Soc. Hematology, Am. Assn. Cancer Research, Am. Soc. Clin. Oncology, Am. Soc. Internal Medicine, So. Med. Assn., AAMD, Am. Mgmt. Assn., San Antonio Club Internal Medicine (sec.-treas. 1980—, pres. 1985-86), Alpha Omega Alpha. Current Work: Clinical research in cancer therapy. Subspecialties: Chemotherapy; Hematology. Home: Route 1 Box 24 Helotes TX 78023 Office: 1303 McCullough 348 San Antonio TX 78212

WHITEHEAD, FRANK ROGER, physicist, researcher; b. Biloxi, Miss., May 19, 1944; s. Thomas Frank and Willa (Robertson) W.; m. Ann Marie Tram, Apr. 25, 1971; children: Pamela, Brian. B.S. in Physics, Hamline U., 1966; M.S. in Optical Scis, U. Ariz., 1975, Ph.D. in Optical Scis, 1976. Prin. research physicist Searle Diagnostics, Des Plaines, Ill., 1973-79; systems engr. Gen. Electric Ultrasound, Rancho Cordova, Calif., 1979-81; staff scientist Siemens Gammasonics, Des Plaines, 1981-83; research scientist Sound Imaging, Folsom, Calif., 1983-84; lectr. in field. Contbr. chpt., articles to profl. publs. Mem. Soc. Nuclear Medicine. Republican. Methodist. Current Work: Development of medical imaging systems; special interest in analysis and testing of imaging systems, performance and optimization of image display systems. Subspecialties: Imaging technology; Electronics. Home and Office: 8610 Gaines Ave Orangevale CA 95662

WHITEHEAD, GEORGE WILLIAM, mathematician; b. Bloomington, Ill., Aug. 2, 1918; s. George W. and Mary (Gutschlag) W.; m. Kathleen E. Butcher, June 7, 1947. B.S., U. Chgo., 1937, M.S., 1938, Ph.D., 1941. Instr. Purdue U., 1941-45; mathematician Aberdeen Proving Ground, 1945; instr. Princeton U., 1945-47, vis. prof., 1958-59; asst. prof. Brown U., 1947-48, asso. prof., 1948-49; asst. prof. Mass Inst. Tech., 1949-51, asso. prof., 1951-57, prof. math., 1957—; vis. research fellow Birkbeck Coll., U. London, 1973, U. London, Oxford U., 1981. Author: Homotopy Theory, 1965, Recent Advances in Homotopy Theory, 1970, Elements of Homotopy Theory, 1978. Guggenheim fellow, Fulbright research scholar, 1955-56; NSF sr. postdoctoral fellow, 1965-66. Fellow Am. Acad. Arts and Scis.; mem. Am. Math. Soc. (v.p. 1978-79), Math. Assn. Am., London Math. Soc., Nat. Acad. Scis., Phi Beta Kappa, Sigma Xi. Current Work: Homotopy theory; particularly stable homotopy and generalized homology theories. Subspecialty: Topology and foundations. Home: 25 Bellevue Rd Arlington MA 02174 Office: Room 2-284 Mass Inst Tech Cambridge MA 02139

WHITEHEAD, JOHN JED, medical information company executive; b. N.Y.C., June 1, 1945; s. Edwin Carl and Constance Rosemary (Raywid) W. B.A., Williams Coll., 1967; postgrad., Case Western Res. U., 1967-68. Dir. chem. mktg., chem. div. Technicon Corp., Tarrytown, N.Y., 1969-70, sr. v.p., gen. mgr. indsl. div., 1970-71, sr. v.p. clin. div., 1971-74, sr. v.p. corp. planning, 1974-75, sr. v.p. research and devel., 1975-81, sr. v.p. bus. devel. and market planning, 1981-83, pres. diagnostic systems div., 1983-85, also dir.; pres. Technicon Data Systems Corp., 1985—; pres., dir. PJS Contractors Inc., 1978—; v.p., dir. Saint Paul Prodns., Inc., 1978—; dir. Whitehead Assocs., Inc.; Mem. adv. council Nat. Inst. Environ. Health Scis., NIH, 1971-73. Mem. Rockefeller adv. group to Pres.'s 1976 Bicentennial Planning Commn., 1971-72; Bd. dirs. Westchester Urban League, 1973-74, Whitehead Biomed. Research Inst., 1974—. Subspecialty: Information systems (Information science). Home: 167 Cantitoe Rd Katonah NY 10536 Office: 3255-1 Scott Blvd Santa Clara CA 95051

WHITELEY, STEPHEN ROBERT, electronics company manager, researcher; b. Dayton, Ohio, June 9, 1955; s. Benjamin Robert and Elaine M. (Yunker) W. B.S., U. Calif.-Berkeley, 1977, Ph.D., 1982. Engr., Tektronix, Inc., 1982-83; research and devel. mgr., Hypres, Inc., Elmsford, N.Y., 1983—. Contbr. articles to profl. jours. Mem. IEEE, Am. Phys. Soc. Current work: Design of circuitry based on superconducting elements for use in measurement or computational equipment. Subspecialties: Superconductors; Integrated circuits. Office: Hypres Inc 175 Clearbrook Rd Elmsford NY 10523

WHITFIELD, JACK DUANE, technology company executive, consultant; b. Paoli, Okla., May 16, 1928; s. Lloyd H. and Ethel (Wigley) W.; m. Marcheta Rae Steward, Sept. 11, 1949; children: Donna, Jeffrey, Karen. B.S.A.E., U. Okla., 1951; M.S.M.E., U. Tenn., 1960; D.Sc., Royal Inst. Tech., Stockholm, 1972. Registered profl. engr., Tenn. Dir. von Karman Gas Dynamics Facility, Arnold Engring. Devel. Cent., 1968-75; dir. Engine Test Facility, Arnold Engring. Devel. Ctr., 1975-76; exec. v.p. Sverdrup/ARO, Inc. and successor firm, Sverdrup Tech., Inc., Tullahoma, Tenn., 1974-81, pres., dir., 1981—; exec. v.p. Sverdrup Corp.; dir. Sverdrup & Parcel & Assocs., Sverdrup & Parcel Constrn. Mgmt., Nine Ten North Eleventh, Hotel Equity, Ltd., Conv. Plaza, W., Sverdrup & Parcel, Inc. Real Estate; chmn. corp. prins. Reviewer: Heat Transfer and Fluid mechanics. Recipient Gen. H.H. Arnold award, 1968. Fellow AIAA (Simulation and Ground Testing award 1979); mem. Sigma Xi, Tau Beta Pi, Tau Omega. Current Work: Design and development of environmental ground test facilities, executive corporate management, project direction on major design or developement projects, advanced planning for corporate advanced technology programs. Subspecialties: Fluid mechanics; Aeronautical engineering. Home: Route 2 Box 150A Wartrace TN 37183 Office: Sverdrup Technology Inc 600 William Northern Blvd PO Box 884 Tullahoma TN 37388

WHITFORD, WALTER GEORGE, ecology educator; b. Providence, June 12, 1936; s. Walter Albert and Mary Helen (Gravier) W.; m. Ann Edith Rowley, Jan. 1959 (div. Jan. 1968); children—William Brett, Eric Ian; m. Linda Claire Grist, June 16, 1969; children—Colleen Adelia (dec.), Andrea Susanna. B.A., U. R.I., 1961, Ph.D., 1964. Mem. faculty biology dept. N.Mex. State U., Las Cruces, 1964—, prof., 1971—; cons. in field. Editor Soil Biology and Fertility, 1984. NSF grantee, 1971—; recipient Westhafer research award N.Mex. State U., 1984. Fellow AAAS, Herpetologists League; mem. Am. Soc. Mammalogists, Ecol. Soc. Am., Brit. Ecol. Soc. Current work: Research focus on desert ecosystems, nutrient cycling processes, social insects, soil biota. Office: New Mexico State U Biology Dept Box 3AF Las Cruces NM 88003

WHITLEY, ROBERT DAVID, veterinary ophthalmologist; b. Decatur, Ala., Mar. 30, 1953; s. Jean Felton and Willadean (Minter) W.; m. Susan Jane Kalway, Oct. 20, 1979 (div. 1984). D.V.M., Auburn U., 1977, M.Sc., 1981. Diplomate Am. Coll. Vet. Ophthalmologists. Intern, U. Mo.-Columbia, 1977-78; resident in ophthalmology, U. Fla.-Gainesville, 1978-79, asst. prof., 1984—; instr. Auburn U., 1979-81, asst. prof., 1982; asst. prof. vet. ophthalmology U. Wis.-Madison, 1982-84. Contbr. articles to profl. jours., chpts. to books. Mem. Am. Coll. Vet. Ophthalmologists, AVMA, Am. Soc. Vet. Ophthalmology, Internat. Soc. Vet. Ophthalmology, Assn. Research in Vision and Ophthalmology, Phi Zeta, Phi Kappa Phi, Phi Theta Kappa. Republican. Baptist. Clubs: Lions, Zeta. Current work: Animal and comparative ophthalmology; ocular pathology; cataracts, glaucoma and diseases of the cornea; corneal and cataract surgery; diseases and surgery of the horse and dog eye; corneal pathology. Subspecialties: Veterinary ophthalmology; Ophthalmology. Home: 610 S Boundary St Archer FL 32618 Office: Dept Comparative Ophthalmology U Fla Box J-115 JHMHC Gainesville FL 32610

WHITLOCK, LEE RONALD, chemist; b. Canton, Pa., July 6, 1944; s. Joseph H. and Margaret (Burnham) W.; m. Carol Bauer, Aug. 17, 1968; children—Terri, Eric. B.S., Pa. State U., 1966; M.S., U. Mass., 1968, Ph.D., 1970, postgrad., 1971-72. Research chemist Eastman Kodak, Rochester, N.Y., 1972-78, research assoc., 1979—. Contbr. articles to profl. jours. Mem. Am. Chem. Soc., Sigma Xi. Current work: Research in new methods polymer characterization and separation science. Subspecialties: Analytical chemistry; Polymer chemistry. Home: 4 Cavan Way Pittsford NY 14534 Office: Eastman Kodak Research Labs Kodak Park Rochester NY 14650

WHITMAN, PATRICK GENE, physicist, educator; b. Beaumont, Tex., Sept. 30, 1944; s. Norman L. and Roberta M. (Wright) W.; m. Darla J. Mason, Aug. 25, 1973; children: Jeremy A., Leslie A. B.Sc., Lamar Inst. Tech., 1970; M.Sc. in Math., Lamar U., 1971; postgrad., U. Tex.-Dallas, 1971-74; Ph.D., North Tex. State U., 1978. Asst. prof. physics Benedictine Coll., Atchison, Kans., 1978-79; Asst. prof. physics U. Southwestern La., Lafayette, 1979-85, assoc. prof., 1985—, mem. grad. council, 1981—. Contbr. articles to profl. jours. Welch Found. predoctoral fellow, 1976-77. Mem. Am. Inst. Physics, Am. Phys. Soc., Am. Astron. Soc. Democrat. Current Work: Exact solutions in general relativity; orbital mechanics. Subspecialties: Relativity and gravitation; Theoretical astrophysics.

WHITMAN, ROBERT VAN DUYNE, civil engineer; b. Pitts., Feb. 2, 1928; s. Edwin A. and Elsie (Van Duyne) W.; m. Elizabeth Cushman, June 19, 1954; children—Jill Martyne, Martha Allerton (dec.), Gweneth Giles. B.S., Swarthmore Coll., 1948; S.M., Mass. Inst. Tech., 1949, Sc.D., 1951. Mem. faculty Mass. Inst. Tech., 1953—, prof. civil engring., 1963—, head structural engring., 1970-74, head soil mechanics div., 1970-72; vis. scholar U. Cambridge, Eng., 1976-77; cons. to govt. and industry, 1953—. Author: (with T. W. Lambe) Soil Mechanics. Mem. Town Meeting Lexington, Mass., 1962-76, 85—, mem. permanent bldg. com., 1968-75, mem. bd. appeals, 1979-81, 85—. Served to lt. (j.g.) USNR, 1954-56. Mem. Am. Soc. Civil Engrs. (Research award, 1962, Terzaghi Lecture 1981), Boston Soc. Civil Engrs. (Structural sect. prize 1963, Desmond Fitzgerald medal 1973, Ralph W. Horne Fund award 1977), Internat. Soc. Soil Mechanics and Found. Engrs., Seismol. Soc. Am., Nat. Acad. Engring., Earthquake Engring. Research Inst. (dir. 1978-81, 84— v.p. 1979-81, pres. 1985—). Research in soil mechanics, soil dynamics and earthquake engring. Current Work: Earthquake engineering; permanent deformations of soil; seismic hazard analysis. Subspecialty: Civil engineering. Home: 9 Demar Rd Lexington MA 02173 Office: Mass Inst Tech Cambridge MA 02139

WHITMORE, FRANK CLIFFORD, JR., geologist, paleontologist; b. Cambridge, Mass., Nov. 17, 1915; s. Frank Clifford and Marion Gertrude (Mason) W.; m. Martha Burling Kremers, June 24, 1939; children—Geoffrey, John, Katherine, Susan. B.A., Amherst Coll., 1938; M.S., Pa. State U., 1939; M.A., Harvard U., 1941, Ph.D., 1942. Teaching fellow Harvard U., Cambridge, 1940-42; instr. geology R.I. State Coll., Kingston, 1942-44; geologist U.S. Geol. Survey, Washington, 1944—; research assoc. Smithsonian Inst., Washington, 1967—. Editor: Resources for the 21st Century (Blue Pencil award), 1982. Contbr. articles to profl. jours. Bd. dirs. Prince George's County Boys Club, Md., 1954-56; chmn. Green Meadows Boys Club, West Hyattsville, Md., 1950-56. Decorated Medal of Freedom. Fellow Geol. Soc. Am., AAAS (sec. sect. E 1957-60, chmn. 1972); mem. Geol. Soc. Washington (pres. 1970; Great Dane 1980, 81), Soc. Vertebrate Paleontology (exec. com. 1960-62, charter mem.); Sigma Xi. Republican. Clubs; Midriver (pres. 1976-80), Pick and Hammer (chmn. 1955-56) (Washington). Current work: Mammalian paleontology, especially the evolution and paleogeography of fossil whales. Subspecialties: Paleobiology; Paleontology, paleoecology. Home: 20 Woodmoor Dr Silver Spring MD 20901 Office: Nat Mus Natural History 10th St and Constitution Ave Washington DC 20560

WHITMORE, JACOB LESLIE, III, tropical forester, researcher, consultant; b. Pontiac, Mich., Jan. 21, 1939; s. Jacob Leslie and Grace Mae (Wall) W.; m. Menandra Sabina Mosquera Moreno, Jan. 7, 1965; children—Jacqueline Grace, Michelle Jacinta. B.S., U. Mich., 1961, M.F., 1968; postgrad., U. Wash., 1968-69. Forester Am. Friends Service Com., San Martin, Mex., 1962-64; instr., researcher silviculture and tree improvement Tropical Agrl. Research and Tng. Ctr., Turrialba, Costa Rica, 1974-76; research forester Inst. Tropical Forestry, USDA Forest Service, Rio Piedras, P.R., 1969-74, 76-80, internat. forester, U.S. Dept. Agr., Forest Service, Washington, 1980—; U.S. Del. Latin Am. Forestry Commn., Mex., 1980, Com. on Forest Devel. in the Tropics, Rome, 1983; rapporteur N. Am. Forestry Commn., El Paso, 1984; USDA Forest Service liaison to FAO, Peace Corps and Mex. Forest Service 1982—; Asia coordinator, 1981-82; coordinator Man and the Biosphere Program, 1980-81; cons. in field. Mem. editorial bd. Jour. of Forestry, 1985—. Contbr. articles to profl. jours. Grantee Block Drug Co., Costa Rica, 1967, Orgn. Tropical Studies, Costa Rica, 1967, U. P.R., 1979. Mem. Soc. Am. Foresters, Ecol. Soc. Am., Internat. Soc. Tropical Foresters (membership chmn. 1983—), Internat. Union for Forestry Research Orgns. (working party chmn. 1978—), Orgn. Profl. Employees of Dept. Agr. (local chpt. v.p. 1984—), Soc. of Les Voyageurs. Current work: Technology transfer through research networks, species and provenance trials, seed acquisition and production, management of tropical forest by natural regeneration. Office: USDA Forest Service Internat Forestry 1621 N Kent St Rosslyn VA 22209

WHITMORE, L. DAMON, electrical engineer; b. Dayton, Ohio, May 1, 1936; s. L. Damon and Lois Rebecca (Keiser) W.; m. Waltraud H. Schuffler, Feb. 1, 1973; children—Mark, Heidi, Kirstin, Hetty. B.S. in Elec. Engring., Purdue U., 1958; M.A.E., Chrysler Inst., 1960. Engr., Chrysler Corp., Detroit, 1958-61, Burroughs Corp., Detroit, 1961-66; engring. mgr., project engr. Control Data, Mpls., 1966-77; internat. engring. mgr. Litton Microwave, Mpls., 1977-82; design engring. mgr. Nortronics Co., Inc., Mpls., 1982-85; mgr. devel. engring. Zytec Corp., Eden Prairie, Minn., 1985—; instr. Detroit Inst. Tech., 1961-62. Patentee in field. Mem. IEEE, Purdue Alumni Assn. (life), Tau Beta Pi (life; essay award 1958). Methodist. Clubs: Western Saddle Assn., Silver Buckle Saddle. Current work: Managing electronic power supply and development group including transformer design; using a computer to aid in the development. Subspecialties: Applied magnetics; Electrical engineering. Home: 5115 Vicksburg Ln Plymouth MN 55446 Office: Zytec Corp 7575 Marketplace Dr Eden Prairie MN 55344

WHITNEY, HASSLER, mathematics educator; b. N.Y.C., Mar. 23, 1907; married, 1930 and 1955; 2 children. Ph.B., Yale U., 1928, Mus.B., 1929; Ph.D., Harvard U., 1932; Sc.D. (hon.), Yale U., 1947. Instr. math. Harvard U., 1930-31, NRC lectr. and fellow, 1931-33, from instr. to prof., 1933-52, prof., 1952-77; Emer prof. math. Inst. Advanced Study, Princeton, N.J., 1977—. Mem. math. panel Nat. Def. Research Com., 1943-45. Recipient Wolf prize, 1982; Nat. medal of Sci., 1976. Mem. Nat. Acad. Sci., Am. Math. Soc. (v.p. 1948-50), Am. Philos. Soc. Subspecialty: Topology and foundations. Office: Sch Math Inst Advanced Study Princeton NJ 08540*

WHITTEN, BERTWELL KNEELAND, biological sciences educator, research institute administrator; b. Boston, Apr. 1, 1941; s. Bertwell M. and Phyllis (Kneeland) W.; m. Hope Ford, Aug. 11, 1962; children—Steven, Ellen, Richard. A.B., Middlebury Coll., 1962; M.S., Purdue U., 1964, Ph.D., 1966. Research physiologist USARNL, Fitzsimons Gen. Hosp., Denver, 1966-68; sr. research physiologist Army Inst. Environ. Medicine, Natick, Mass., 1968-70; assoc. prof. Mich. Technol. U., Houghton, 1972-74, prof. biol. scis., 1974—; head dept., 1981—; adj. prof. Mich. State U, East Lansing, 1974—, Wayne State U., Detroit, 1978, 77, 80. Contbr. articles to profl. jours. Coach Am. Legion Baseball Team, Houghton, 1984-85. Served to capt. Med. Service Corps, U.S. Army, 1966-68. Mem. Am. Physiol. Soc., AAAS, Sigma Xi. Lodge: Lions (pres.). Subspecialties: Physiology (biology); Biochemistry (biology). Office: Dept Biol Scis Mich Technol U Houghton MI 49931

WHITTEN, CHARLES ALEXANDER, JR., educator; b. Harrisburg, Pa., Jan. 20, 1940; s. Charles Alexander and Helen (Shoop) W.; m. Joan Emann, Nov. 20, 1965; 1 son, Charles Alexander. B.S. summa cum laude, Yale U., 1961; Ph.D. in Physics, Princeton U., 1966. Research asso. A.W. Wright Nuclear Structure Lab., Yale U., 1966-68; asst. prof. physics UCLA, 1968-74, asso. prof., 1974-80, prof., 1980—; vis. scientist Centre d'Etudes Nucléaires de Saclay-Moyenne Energie, 1980-81. Contbr. articles to profl. jours. Mem. Am. Phys. Soc., Sigma Pi Sigma, Phi Beta Kappa. Current Work: Intermediate energy physics using high energy particles as probes of nuclear structure; polarized proton-nucleus scattering; small angle nucleon-nucleon scattering. Subspecialties: Nuclear physics; Particle physics. Home: 9844 Vicar St Los Angeles CA 90034 Office: Dept Physics U Calif 405 Hilgard Ave Los Angeles CA 90024

WHITTEN, ERIC HAROLD TIMOTHY, geologist, university official; b. Ilford, Essex, Eng., July 26, 1927; came to U.S., 1958; s. Charles Alexander and Muriel Gladys (Smith) W.; m. Mary Cleopha Staciva, Feb. 28, 1976; children: Catherine, Peter, Jennifer, Adam, Joshua. B.Sc. with gen. honors, U. London, 1948, B.Sc. in Geology, 1948, Ph.D. in Geology, 1952, D.Sc. in Geology, 1968. Clk. Rex Thomas (Ins.) Ltd., London, 1943-45; lectr. in geology Queen Mary Coll., London U., 1948-58; asso. prof. geology Northwestern U., 1958-63, prof., 1963-81, chmn. dept. geol. scis., 1977-81; v.p. for acad. affairs Mich. Technol. U., Houghton, 1981—. Author: Structural Geology of Folded Rocks, 1966, Quantitative Studies in the Geological Sciences, 1975. Geol. Soc. London Daniel Pidgeon Fund grantee, 1954. Fellow Geol. Soc. London, Geol. Soc. Am., AAAS; mem. Internat. Assn. Math. Geology (past pres.). Geologists' Assn. (London), Queen Mary Coll. Student Union Soc. (hon. life), English Speaking Union (life). Clubs: Hope Town Sailing (Abaco, Bahama Islands); Onigaming Yacht (Houghton). Lodge: Rotary. Current Work: Quantitative variability and petrogenetic evolution of the granitoids of the Lachlan Fold Belt, S.E. Australia. Subspecialty: Petrology. Office: Office Acad Affairs Mich Technol U Houghton MI 49931

WIBERG, JOHN SAMUEL, molecular geneticist; b. Plaistow, N.H., Dec. 4, 1930; s. Hugo William and Mary Josephine (Loeffler) W.; m. Elsie Nelson, Nov. 22, 1952; children: Kristina, Karl, Derek. B.S., Trinity Coll., 1952; Ph.D., U. Rochester, 1956. USPHS postdoctoral fellow M.I.T., 1959-60, research asso., 1961-63; asst. prof. radiation biology and biophysics U. Rochester, 1963-70, assoc. prof., 1970—. Contbr. articles to sci. jours.; Editorial bd.: Jour. of Virology, 1970-79. Served with USAF, 1957-58. Mem. Am. Chem. Soc., AAAS, Am. Soc. Biol. Chemists, Genetics Soc. Am., Am. Soc. Microbiology, Fedn. Am. Scientists, Am. Soc. Virology. Current Work: Regulation of protein synthesis by bacteriophage; nucleic acid metabolism. Subspecialties: Molecular biology; Virology (biology). Home: 8 Woodside Ln Pittsford NY 14534 Office: RBB Dept U Rochester Med Sch Rochester NY 14642

WIBERG, KENNETH BERLE, educator, chemist; b. Bklyn., Sept. 22, 1927; s. Dan and Solveig Berle W.; m. Marguerite Koch, Mar. 18, 1951; children—Patricia, Robert, William. B.S., Mass. Inst. Tech., 1948; Ph.D., Columbia, 1950. Mem. faculty U. Wash., 1950-62, prof. chemistry, 1958-62, Yale, 1962—, Whitehead prof., 1968—, chmn. chem. dept., 1968-71; Boomer lectr. U. Alta., Can., 1959; Mem. chemistry advisory panel Air Force Office Sci. Research, 1960-66, NSF, 1965-68, chmn., 1967-68. Author: Laboratory Technique in Organic Chemistry, 1960, Interpretation of NMR Spectra, 1962, Physical Organic Chemistry, 1964, Computer Programming for Chemists, 1966, also articles.; Editor: Oxidation in Organic Chemistry, 1966, Sigma M.O. Theory, 1970; mem. editorial bd.: Organic Syntheses, 1963-71, Jour. Organic Chemistry, 1968-72; bd. editors: Jour. Am. Chem. Soc, 1969-72. Recipient James Flack Norris award, 1973; Sloan Found. fellow, 1958-62; Guggenheim fellow, 1961-62. Mem. Nat. Acad. Scis., Am. Acad. Arts and Scis., Am. Chem. Soc. (exec. com. organic div. 1961-63, Calif. sect. award 1963). Current Work: Small ring chemistry; thermochemistry; spectroscopy and theoretical calculations related to the above. Subspecialties: Organic chemistry; Theoretical chemistry. Home: 160 Carmalt Rd Hamden CT 06517 Office: Chemistry Dept Yale U New Haven CT 06520

WICKER, ED FRANKLIN, research plant pathologist; b. Upper Tygart, Ky., Aug. 21, 1930; s. Leslie and Bessie Mae (Hamilton) W.; m. Veneta Carol Law, Dec. 20, 1953; children: Cynthia, Sonja. B.S. in Forestry, Wash. State U., Pullman, 1959, Ph.D. in Plant Pathology, 1965. Research forester Intermountain Forest and Range Expt. Sta., USDA Forest Service, Spokane, Wash., 1959-63, plant physiologist, 1963-78; staff research plant pathologist USDA Forest Service, Washington, 1978-82; asst. dir. Rocky Mountain Forest and Range Expt. Sta., Fort Collins, Colo., 1982—; vis. scientist sch. botany Cambridge (Eng.) U., 1970-71. Contbr. articles to profl. jours. Served with USAF, 1950-54. Recipient Research award Govt. of Japan, 1974. Mem. Am. Phytopathol. Soc., Soc. Am. Foresters, Mycol. Soc. Am. Current Work: Biology, ecology, and control of dwarf mistletoes; biology of conifer stem rusts; biological control of forest tree diseases. Subspecialties: Plant pathology; Resource conservation. Home: 4118 Attleboro Ct Fort Collins CO 80525 Office: 240 W Prospect St Fort Collins CO 80526

WICKHAM, MARGARET EDNA, spectrometrist, chemist; b. Kansas City, Mo., June 7, 1956; d. Ronald Lee and Mary Ann (Nicholas) W.; B.S. in Chemistry, St. Mary Coll., Leavenworth, Kans., 1978. Analytical chemist Midwest Research Inst., Kansas City, Mo., 1978-80, mass spectrometrist, 1980—; vol. lab. tchr. Kans. U. Med. Ctr., Kansas City, Kans., 1973; student intern FDA, Kansas City, Mo., 1977; research participant Argonne Nat. Lab., Ill., 1978. Mem. St. Peter's Catholic Ch. Choir, Kansas City, Mo., 1980-85, St. Bernadette's Cath. Ch. Choir, Raytown, Mo., 1978-80; troop sec. Midcontinent council Girl Scouts U.S., 1978—. Mem. Am. Chem. Soc. (sect. offices), Am. Soc. Mass Spectrometry, Kappa Gamma Pi, Delta Epsilon Sigma. Current work: Determination and quantitation of chlorinated dibenzodioxins, dibenzofurans, and biphenyls (PCDD, PCDF, and PCB respectively) in various media. Determination and quantitution of volatile organics in water, sludge, and air. Determination of impurities in various samples by gas chromatography/mass spectrometry and mass spectrometry. Subspecialties: Mass spectrometry; Environmental chemistry. Office: Midwest Research Inst 425 Volker Blvd Kansas City MO 64110

WICKRAMASEKERA, (IAN EDWARD WICKRAM), psychiatry and behavioral sciences educator, clinical psychologist and psychophysiologist; b. Colombo, Ceylon, Oct. 23, 1939; came to U.S., 1959, naturalized, 64; s. Harry Stanley and Maude M. (Robinson) W.; married; children: Melissa, Edward. B.A., Friend's U., 1961; student, London U., U.K., 1956-58; M.A., Roosevelt U., 1965; Ph.D., U. Ill., 1969. Diplomate: Am. Bd. Clin. Psychology, Am. Bd. Psychol. Hypnosis. Intern East Moline (Ill.) State Hosp., 1964-65, staff psychologist, 1965-66; research asst. Children's Research Center, Urbana, Ill., 1966-67; staff psychologist Peoria (Ill.) Mental Health Clinic, 1969-75; assoc. prof. psychiatry and behavioral medicine U. Ill. Med. Sch., Peoria, 1971-81; prof. psychiatry Eastern Va. Med. Sch., Norfolk, 1981—; cons. VA, Iowa City, 1974-80, Chgo., 1978-79. Author, editor: Biofeedback Behavior Therapy and Hypnosis, 1976; also articles; mem. editorial bd.: Behavior Therapy, 1975-78. Clin. fellow Behavior Therapy and Research Soc.; fellow Am. Psychol. Assn.; mem. AAAS, Ill. Psychol. Assn. (pres. 1980), Biofeedback Soc. Am. (dir. 1978-80). Roman Catholic. Current Work: Risk factors for psychophysiological disorders placebo effect, hypnosis. Subspecialties: Psychophysiology; Psychobiology. Home: 922 W Ocean View Norfolk VA 23503 Office: Eastern VA Med Sch 700 Olney Rd PO Box 1980 Norfolk VA 23501

WIDDER, KENNETH JON, pathologist, company executive; b. Chgo., Jan. 14, 1953; s. Alan A. and Edith Widder. B.A., Carleton Coll., 1974; M.D., Northwestern U., 1979. Intern, Duke U., Durham, N.C., 1979-80, resident in pathology, 1979-81; asst. clin. prof. U. Calif.-San Diego, 1981-84, assoc. clin. prof., 1984—; chmn., chief exec. officer Molecular Biosystems, Inc., San Diego, 1981—; cons. Eli Lilly & Co., Indpls., 1978—. Patentee in field; editor: Methods in Enzymology: Drug and Enzyme Targeting, 1985. Mem. adv. com. Congl. Sci. and Tech. Com., Washington, 1985. Recipient Wiley J. Forbus award N.C. Soc. Pathology, 1981. Mem. AAAS, Am. Soc. Clin Pathologists, Sigma Xi. Current work: Drug delivery and drug targeting; aids research. Subspecialties: Drug delivery systems; Pathology (medicine). Office: Molecular Biosystems Inc 11180 Roselle St San Diego CA 92121

WIDDOES, LAWRENCE CURTIS, oil service company executive, consultant; b. Spokane, Wash., Nov. 10, 1919; s. Curtis E. and Hazel A. (North) W.; m. Marcella Elizabeth Maize, Feb. 28, 1942; children: Bonni, Patricia, Lawrence. B.S., Calif. Inst. Tech., 1941; M.S.E., U. Mich., 1947. Registered profl. engr., Calif., N.Y., Mo., Tex. Reseach engr. Nat. Dairy Co., Idlewild, N.Y., 1947-50; project mgr. Monsanto Co., St. Louis, 1950-56; pres. Internuclear Co., Clayton, Mo., 1956-60; dir. research Petrolite Corp., Webseter Groves, Mo., 1960-66; pres. Conresco Corp., Stamford, Conn., 1966-72; v.p. devel. Magna Corp., Houston, 1972—. Served to lt. comdr. USN, 1942-46, PTO. Fellow Am. Inst. Chem. Engrs. Republican. Club: Petroleum (Houston). Current Work: Development of enhanced oil recovery techniques and application thereof. Subspecialties: Fuels; Petroleum engineering. Home: 5877 Sugar Hill Houston TX 77057 Office: PO Box 33387 Houston TX 77233

WIDERA, G.E.O., mechanical engineering educator, consultant; b. Dortmund, Germany, Feb. 16, 1938; came to U.S., 1950; s. Otto and Gertrude (Yzermann) W.; m. Kristel Kornas, June 21, 1974; 1 dau., Erika. B.S., U. Wis., 1960, M.S., 1962, Ph.D., 1965. Asst. prof., then prof. materials engring. dept. U. Ill.-Chgo., 1965-82, prof. mech. engring., 1982—, head dept., 1983—; gastdozent U. Stuttgart, W.Ger., 1968; vis. prof. U. Wis.-Milw., 1973-74, Marquette U., Milw., 1978-79; cons. Ladish Co., Cudahy, Wis., 1967-76, Howmedica, Inc., Chgo., 1972-75, Sargent & Lundy, Chgo., 1970—, Nat. Bur. Standards, 1980; vis. scientist Argonne Nat. Lab., Ill., 1968. Editor: Procs. Innovations in Structural Engring, 1974; assoc. editor: Pressure Vessel Tech, 1977-81; editorial bd.: Pressure Vessels and Piping Design Technology, 1982; tech. editor: Pressure Vessel Technology, 1983—. Standard Oil Co. Calif. fellow, 1961-63; NASA fellow, 1966; Nat. Acad. Scis. travel grantee Russia, 1972; von Humboldt fellow W.Ger., 1968-69. Mem. ASME (chmn. (research com. pressure vessels 1982—, chmn. design and analysis com. pressure vessel and piping div. 1980-83, chmn. jr. awards com. applied mechanics div. 1973-76, chmn. machine design div. of Chgo. sect. 1967-68, editor newsletter 1971-73, exec. com. Chgo. sect. 1970-73), ASCE (sec.-treas. structural div. of Ill. sect. 1972-73, chmn. div. 1976-77), Internat. Assn. Dental Research, Gesellschaft für Angewandte Mathematik und Mechanik, Am. Acad. Mechanics. Current Work: Mechanics of composite materials, plates and shells, asymptotic methods in elasticity, pressure vessels and piping, mechanics of deformation processing. Subspecialties: Solid mechanics; Composite materials. Home: 345 Greenleaf Wilmette IL 60091 Office: PO Box 4348 Chicago IL 60680

WIDOM, BENJAMIN, physical chemist, educator, researcher; b. Newark, Oct. 13, 1927; married, 1953; 3 children. A.B., Columbia U., 1949; Ph.D. in Chemistry, Cornell U., 1953. Research assoc. in chemistry U. N.C., 1952-54; instr. Cornell U., 1954-55, from asst. prof. to assoc. prof., 1955-63, prof. chemistry, 1963—; van der Waals prof. U. Amsterdam, 1972; IBM prof. Oxford U., 1978; Lorentz prof. Leiden U., 1985. Guggenheim and Fulbright fellow, 1961-62; NSF sr. fellow, 1965; Guggenheim fellow, 1969. Mem. Nat. Acad. Sci., Am. Phys. Soc., Am. Acad. Arts and Scis., Am. Chem. Soc. Subspecialties: Physical chemistry; Statistical mechanics. Office: Dept Chemistry Cornell U Ithaca NY 14853*

WIEBE, LEONARD IRVING, university dean; b. Swift Current, Sask., Can., Oct. 14, 1941; s. Cornelius C. and Margaret (Teichroeb) W.; m. Grace E. McIntyre, Sept. 5, 1964; children—Glenis J., Kirsten B., Megan C. B.S. in Pharmacy, U. Sask., 1963, M.S., 1966; Ph.D., U. Sydney, Australia, 1970. Pharm. chemist, Sask.; lic. Pharmacy Bd. New South Wales. Assoc. prof. U Alta.-Slowpoke Reactor, Edmonton, 1974-79, chmn., 1974—; vis. scientist German Cancer Research Ctr., Heidelberg, 1976-77; research assoc. Cross Cancer Inst., Edmonton, 1978—; prof. nuclear medicine U. Alta., Edmonton, 1979—, asst. dean for research, 1984—; radiopharmacy cons. Australian Atomic Energy Commn., 1984; vis. prof., W.Ger., Eng., 1976; Med. Research Council Can. vis. scientist, W.Ger., Australia, 1983. Editor: (with A. Noujaim and C. Ediss) Liquid Scintillation, 1976; (with C. Ediss and S. McQuarrie) Scintillation Counting, 1983. Contbr. articles to profl. jours. Co-inventor bromocholesterols. Recipient U.K. Commonwealth Univs. travel award, 1966; Humboldt Founds. fellow, 1976. Mem. Soc. Nuclear Medicine (sec.-treas. 1983-84). Mennonite. Club: Faculty (U. Alta) (pres. 1985-86). Current work: Chemical synthesis of radiolabelled biochemicals/drugs; metabolism of xenobiotics in man and in animals using animal models (oncology, virology). Subspecialties: Nuclear chemistry; Drug metabolism. Office: Faculty of Pharmacy U Alta Edmonton AB T6G 2N8 Canada

WIEBE, MICHAEL EUGENE, microbiologist, educator; b. Newton, Kans., Oct. 1, 1942; s. Austin Roy and Ruth Fern (Stucky) W.; m. Rebecca Ann Wiebe, June 12, 1965. B.S., Sterling Coll., 1965; Ph.D. in Microbiology, U. Kans., 1971. Research assoc. Duke U., 1971-73; asst. prof. microbiology Cornell U., 1973-81, assoc. prof., 1980-83, dir. leukocyte products, 1983—; assoc. dir. research and devel. N.Y. Blood Center, N.Y.C., 1980—. Contbr. articles to profl. jours. NIH fellow, 1971-73; recipient Alumni award Sterling Coll., 1979. Mem. Am. Soc. Microbiology, Am. Soc. Virology, Am. Soc. Tropical Medicine and Hygiene, Soc. Exptl. Biology and Medicine, N.Y. Acad. Sci. Democrat. Presbyterian. Current Work: Human interferon and lymphokine induction, synthesis and regulation, molecular virology. Subspecialties: Virology (medicine); Cell biology (medicine). Home: 83 Haviland Ct Stamford CT 06903 Office: 310 E 67th St New York NY 10021

WIEGERT, RICHARD GEORGE, zoology educator; b. Toledo, Sept. 9, 1932; s. Arthur E. and Helen M. (Bremforder) W.; m. Patricia Ann Bernhardt, Feb. 19, 1955; (div. 1985); children—Lisa, Karla. B.S., Adrian Coll., 1954, D.S.C. (hon.), 1976; M.S., Mich. State U., 1958; Ph.D., U. Mich., 1962. Teaching fellow U. Mich., Ann Arbor, 1958-59, instr., 1961-62; asst. prof. dept. zoology U. Ga., Athens, 1962-66, assoc. prof., 1966-71, prof., 1971—; mem. panel NSF, 1980-82; ecology editor McGraw-Hill Co., N.Y.C., 1975—. Author: Ecological Energetics, 1976; Ecology of a Salt Marsh, 1982. Editor Ecol. Monographs, Durham, N.C., 1976-77. Served with U.S. Army, 1954-56. Grantee: Nat. Sea Grant Coll. Program, Dept. State, NSF, 1982—. Mem. Am. Soc. Mammalogists, Ecol. Soc. Am., Am. Soc. Limnology and Oceanography, Sigma Xi, Phi Kappa Phi. Current work: Ecosystem analysis and modeling, energetics and material fluxes, theoretical investigations of competition and predation and plant-herbivore interactions, carbon flow in coastal salt marshes. Subspecialties: Ecology (biology); Ecosystems analysis. Office: Dept Zoology U Ga Athens GA 30602

WIELAND, STEVEN JOSEPH, neurobiologist; b. Lakewood, Ohio, Dec 5, 1948; s. Steven Joseph and Elvira (Almassy) W.; m. Susan Elizabeth Barr, Oct. 2, 1977; 1 son, Benjamin. B.S. in Physics, U. Notre Dame, 1970; Ph.D., Harvard U., 1979. Research fellow dept. neurosci. Children's Hosp. Med. Center, Boston, 1979-80; research assoc. dept. biology Princeton U., 1980-83; asst. prof. dept. anatomy Hahnemann U., 1983—. World Book Yearbook Nat. Merit scholar, 1966-70. Mem. Soc. Neurosci., AAAS, Phi Beta Kappa. Current Work: Neuronal plasticity; hormone interactions with the nervous system;; neuromodulators, learning and memory. Subspecialties: Neurobiology; Neurophysiology. Office: Dept Anatomy Hahnemann U Broad and Vine Sts Philadelphia PA 19102

WIERNIK, PETER HARRIS, physician; b. Crocket, Tex., June 16, 1939; s. Harris and Molly (Emmerman) W.; m. Roberta Joan Fuller, Sept. 6, 1961; children: Julie Anne, Lisa Britt, Peter Harrison. B.A. with distinction, U. Va., 1961, M.D., 1965; Dr. h.c., U of Republic, Montevideo, Uruguay, 1982. Diplomate: Am. Bd. Internal Medicine, Sub-Bd. Med. Oncology. Intern, Cleve. Met. Gen. Hosp., 1965-66, resident, 1969-70, Osler Service Johns Hopkins Hosp., Balt., 1970-71; sr. asst. surgeon USPHS, 1966, advanced through grades to med. dir., 1976; sr. staff asso. Balt. Cancer Research Center, 1966-71, chief sect. med. oncology, 1971-76, chief clin. oncology br., 1976-81, dir., 1976-82, asso. dir. div. cancer treatment, Nat. Cancer Inst., 1976-81; asst. prof. medicine U. Md. Hosp., Balt., 1971-74, asso. prof., 1974-76, prof., 1976-82; Gutman prof., chmn. dept. oncology Montefiore Med. Ctr., 1982—; head div. med. oncology Albert Einstein Coll. Medicine, 1982—; assoc. dir. Albert Einstein Cancer Ctr., 1982—; bd. dirs. Balt. City unit Am. Cancer Soc., 1971-78, chmn. patient care com., 1972-75; mem. med. adv. com. Nat. Leukemia Assn., 1976—; chmn. adult leukemia com. Cancer and Leukemia Group B, 1976-82; prin. investigator Eastern Corp. Oncology Group, 1982—. Editor: Controversies in Oncology, 1982, Supportive Care of the Cancer Patient, 1983, Leukemia and Lymphoma, 1985, Neoplastic Diseases of the Blood, 1985; mem. editorial bd.: Cancer Treatment Reports, 1972-76, Leukemia Research, 1976—, Cancer Clin. Trials, 1977—, Hosp. Practice, 1979—, Am. Jour. Clin. Oncology, 1981—, Jour. Cancer Research and Clin. Oncology, Cancer Investigation, 1985—; sect. editor antineoplastic drugs Jour. Clin. Pharmacology, 1985; co-editor: Am. Jour. Med. Scis., 1976-81; also articles, chpts. in books. Recipient Z Soc. award U. Va., 1961, Byrd S. Leavell Hematology award U. Va. Sch. Medicine, 1965. Fellow AAAS, Am. Coll. Clin. Pharmacology, Internat. Soc. Hematology, Royal Soc. Medicine (London), ACP; mem. Am. Soc. Clin. Investigation, Am.

Soc. Clin. Oncology (chmn. edn. and tng. com. 1976-79, 84, subcom. on clin. investigation 1980-82), Am. Assn. Cancer Research, Am. Soc. Hematology, Am. Fedn. Clin. Research, Am. Acad. Clin. Toxicology, Internat. Soc. Exptl. Hematology, N.Y. Acad. Sci., Am. Soc. Hosp. Pharmacy, Am. Soc. Clin. Pharmacology and Therapeutics, Am. Radium Soc., Phi Beta Kappa, Sigma Xi, Alpha Omega Alpha, Phi Sigma (award 1961). Current Work: New treatments for cancer, especially leukemia and lymphoma. Subspecialties: Cancer research (medicine); Hematology. Home: 43 Longview Ln Chappaqua NY 10514 Office: Montefiore Med Ctr 111 E 210th St New York NY 10467

WIERS, BRANDON HELMHOLZ, chemist, research and development manager; b. San Francisco, July 31, 1934; s. Walter Benjamin Wiers and Grace Elizabeth (Pleune) MacNaughton; m. Patricia Joan Hollingsworth, May 14, 1960; children—Matthew Dirk, Suesann Elizabeth, Carl John. B.A., Calvin Coll., 1957; Ph.D., U. Minn., 1964. Staff chemist research and devel. dept. Procter & Gamble, Cin., 1964-69, sect. head internat. div., 1969-74, group leader packaged soap detergent div., 1974-78, sect. head research and devel. services and research adminstrn., 1979—; instr. phys. chemistry Colo. State Coll., Greeley, 1961, Xavier U., Cin., 1966-67. Contbr. articles to profl. jours. Patentee in field. Council mem., mayor, Forest Park, Ohio, 1976-85; mem. Hamilton County Devel. Co., Cin., 1983—; bd. dirs. Community Housing Resources Bd., Cin., 1982—, Charter Com. Greater Cin., 1985—. Recipient Fair Housing award Community Housing Resources Bd., 1984. Mem. Am. Chem. Soc., Am. Statis. Soc., AAAS, Leadership Cin., Phi Lambda Upsilon. Presbyterian. Club: Forest Park Run/Walk (Ohio). Current work: Chemical modeling/speciation of aqueous systems; coordination chemistry/ion exchange; precipitation/dissolution of inorganic salts/minerals; surface chemistry of clays/clay minerals. Subspecialties: Physical chemistry; Computational chemistry. Home: 11261 Hanover Rd Forest Park OH 45240 Office: Procter & Gamble Co Miami Valley Labs PO Box 39175 Cincinnati OH 45247

WIESE, WOLFGANG LOTHAR, physicist; b. Tilsit, Germany, Apr. 21, 1931; came to U.S., 1957, naturalized, 1965; s. Werner Max and Charlotte (Donath) W.; m. Gesa Ladehoff, Oct. 12, 1957; children: Margrit, Cosima. B.S., U. Kiel, W.Ger., 1954, Ph.D., 1957. Research assoc. U. Md., 1958-59; research physicist Nat. Bur. Standards, Washington, 1960-62, chief plasma spectroscopy sect., 1962-77, chief atomic and plasma radiation div., 1977-; lectr. UCLA, summers 1963, 64; Guggenheim fellow Max-Planck Inst., Munich, W.Ger., 1966-67. Prin. author: Atomic Transition Probabilities, Vol. I, 1966, Vol. II, 1969; asso. ed.: Jour. of Quantitative Spectroscopy and Radiative Transfer, 1971—; contbr. numerous articles to profl. jours. Recipient Dept. Commerce Silver medal, 1962, Gold medal, 1971. Fellow Am. Phys. Soc., Optical Soc. Am.; mem. Internat. Astron. Union, Fusion Power Assos., Sigma Xi. Current Work: Atomic processes in high temperature plasmas; atomic transition probabilities; spectral line broadening by plasmas. Subspecialties: Atomic and molecular physics; Plasma physics. Home: 8229 Stone Trail Dr Bethesda MD 20817 Office: Nat Bur Standards Room A267 Bldg 221 Gaithersburg MD 20899

WIESEL, TORSTEN NILS, neurobiologist, educator; b. Upsala, Sweden, June 3, 1924; came to U.S., 1955; s. Fritz Samuel and Anna-Lisa Elisabet (Bentzer) W.; 1 dau., Sara Elisabet. M.D., Karolinska Inst., Stockholm, 1954; A.M. (hon.), Harvard U., 1967. Instr. physiology Karolinska Inst., 1954-55; asst. dept. child psychiatry Karolinska Hosp., 1954-55; fellow in ophthalmology Johns Hopkins U., 1955-58, asst. prof. ophthalmic physiology, 1958-59; assoc. in neurophysiology and neuropharmacology Harvard U. Med. Sch., Boston, 1959-60, asst. prof. neurophysiology and neuropharmacology, 1960-64, asst. prof. neurophysiology, dept. psychiatry, 1964-67, prof. physiology, 1967-68, prof. neurobiology, 1968-74, Robert Winthrop prof. neurobiology, 1974-83, chmn. dept. neurobiology, 1973-82; prof. neurobiology Rockefeller U., N.Y.C., 1983—; Ferrier lectr. Royal Soc. London, 1972; NIH lectr., 1975; Grass lectr. Soc. Neurosci., 1976; lectr. Coll. de France, 1977; Hitchcock prof. U. Calif.-Berkeley, 1980; Sharpey-Schafer lectr. Phys. Soc. London; George Cotzias lectr. Am. Acad. Neurology, 1983. Contbr. numerous articles to profl. jours. Recipient Jules Stein award Trustees for Prevention Blindness, 1971, Lewis S. Rosenstiel prize Brandeis U., 1972, Friedenwald award Trustees of Assn. for Research in Vision and Ophthalmology, 1975, Karl Spencer Lashley prize Am. Philos. Soc., 1977, Louisa Gross Horwitz prize Columbia U., 1978, Dickson prize U. Pitts., 1979, Nobel prize in Physiology/Medicine, 1981. Mem. Am. Physiol. Soc., Am. Philos. Soc., AAAS, Am. Acad. Arts and Scis., Nat. Acad. Arts and Scis., Swedish Physiol. Soc., Soc. Neurosci. (pres. 1978-79), Royal Soc. (fgn. mem.), Physiol. Soc. (Eng.) (hon. mem.). Subspecialty: Neurobiology. Office: Rockefeller U York Ave and 66th Streets New York NY 10021

WIESNER, JEROME BERT, engineering educator and researcher, former university president; b. Detroit, May 30, 1915; s. Joseph and Ida (Friedman) W.; m. Laya Wainger, Sept. 1, 1940; children: Stephen Jay, Zachary Kurt, Elizabeth Ann, Joshua A. B.S., U. Mich., 1937, M.S., 1938, Ph.D., 1950. Assoc. dir. U. Mich. Broadcasting Service, 1937-40; chief engr. Acoustical Record Lab., Library of Congress, 1940-42; staff Mass. Inst. Tech. Radiation Lab., 1942-45, U. of Calif. Los Alamos Lab., 1945-46; mem. faculty Mass. Inst. Tech., 1946-71, dir. research lab. of electronics, 1952-61, head dept. elec. engring., 1959-60, dean of sci., 1964-66, provost, 1966-71, pres., 1971-80, Inst. researcher and prof., 1980—; spl. asst. to Pres. on sci. and tech., 1961-64; chmn. Pres.'s Sci. Adv. Com., 1961-64; chmn. tech. assessment adv. council Office Tech. Assessment, U.S. Congress, 1976-79; Dir. Automatix, Damon Biotech., New Eng. TV Corp., Schlumberger Ltd., Raychem Corp. Author: Where Science and Politics Meet, 1965, ABM—An Evaluation, 1969. Bd. govs. Weizmann Inst. Sci., MacArthur Found.; trustee Woods Hole Oceanographic Inst., Kennedy Meml. Trust. Fellow IEEE, Am. Acad. Arts and Scis.; mem. Am. Philos. Soc., AAUP, Am. Geophys. Union, Acoustical Soc. Am., Nat. Acad. Engring., Nat. Acad. Scis., Sigma Xi, Phi Kappa Phi, Eta Kappa Nu, Tau Beta Pi. Subspecialty: Electrical engineering. Office: Mass Inst Tech Cambridge MA 02139

WIEWIOROWSKI, EDWARD IGNACY, chemical engineer, researcher, consultant; b. Gdansk, Poland, May 1932; s. Karol Ignacy and Gertrude Victoria (Pluszkiewicz) W.; m. Irena Sobolewska, June 24, 1956; children—Martin, Maria. B.S. in Chem. Engring., Inst. Tech., Gdansk, 1956, M.S., 1956, Ph.D., 1963. Registered profl. engr., La. Asst., Inst. Tech., Gdansk, 1954-63; mem. faculty, 1966-72; pvt. practice chem. engring. cons., Warsaw, 1964-72; research and devel. engr. Amax, Braithwaite, La., 1973-77, sr. research and devel. engr., 1977—. Contbr. articles to profl. jours. Patentee in field of chem. engring., metallurgy, pollution abatement. Recipient Humanitarian award U.S. Catholic Conf., 1983. Mem. Nat. Soc. Profl. Engrs., La. Engring. Soc., AIME, Am. Inst. Chem. Engrs. Clubs: Dolphin Speakers Toastmasters, Aurora Country (New Orleans). Current work: Hydrometallurgy, chemical engineering, pollution abatement. Subspecialties: Chemical engineering; Metallurgical engineering. Office: Amax Nickel Inc R&D PO Box 1336 Braithwaite LA 11724*

WIGLER, MICHAEL, molecular biologist. With Cold Spring Harbor Lab., N.Y. Subspecialty: Molecular biology. Office: Cold Spring Harbor Lab Mammalian Cell Genetics Sect Cold Spring Harbor NY 11724

WIGNER, EUGENE PAUL, retired educator; b. Budapest, Hungary, Nov. 17, 1902; came to U.S., 1930, naturalized, 1937; s. Anthony and Elisabeth (Einhorn) W.; m. Amelia Z. Frank, Dec. 23, 1936 (dec. 1937); m. Mary Annette Wheeler, June 4, 1941 (dec. Nov. 1977); children: David Wheeler, Martha Faith; m. Eileen C.P. Hamilton, 1979. Chem. Engr. and Dr. Engring., Technische Hochschule, Berlin, 1925; hon. D.Sc., U. Wis., 1949, Washington U., 1950, Case Inst. Tech., 1956, U. Chgo., 1957, Colby Coll., 1959, U. Pa., 1961, Thiel Coll., 1964, U. Notre Dame, 1965, Technische Universität Berlin, 1966, Swarthmore Coll., 1966, Université de Louvain, Belgium, 1967; Dr.Jr., U. Alta., 1957; L.H.D., Yeshiva U., 1963; hon. degrees, U. Liège, 1967, U. Ill., 1968, Seton Hall U., 1969, Catholic U., 1969, Rockefeller U., 1970, Israel Inst. Tech., 1973, Lowell U., 1976, Princeton U., 1976, U. Tex., 1978, Clarkson Coll., 1979, Allegheny Coll., 1979. Lectr. Princeton U., 1930, halftime prof. math. physics, 1931-36; prof. physics U. Wis., 1936-38; Thomas D. Jones prof. theoretical physics Princeton U., 1938-71; on leave of absence, 1942-45; at Metall. Lab., U. Chgo., 1946-47; as dir. research and devel. Clinton Labs.; dir. CD Research Project, Oak Ridge, 1964-65; Lorentz lectr. Inst. Lorentz, Leiden, 1957; cons. prof. La. State U., 1971—; mem. gen. adv. com. AEC, 1952-57, 59-64; mem. math. panel NRC, 1952-54; physics panel NSF, 1953-56; vis. com. Nat. Bur. Standards, 1947-51. Decorated medal of Merit, 1946; recipient Franklin medal Franklin Inst., 1950, citation N.J. Tchrs. Assn., 1951, Enrico Fermi award AEC, 1958, Atoms for Peace award, 1960, Max Planck medal German Phys. Soc., 1961, Nobel prize for physics, 1963, George Washington award Am. Hungarian Studies Found., 1964, Semmelweiss medal Am. Hungarian Med. Assn., 1965, Nat. Sci. medal, 1969, Pfizer award, 1971, Albert Einstein award, 1972, Golden Plate medal Am. Acad. Achievement, 1974, Disting. Achievement award La. State U., 1977, Wigner medal, 1978, Founders medal Internat. Cultural Found., 1982, Medal of the Hungarian Central Research Inst., Medal of the Autonomous Univ. Barcelona; named Nuclear Pioneer Soc. Nuclear Medicine, 1977, Colonel Gov. of La., 1983. Mem. Royal Soc. Eng. (fgn.), Royal Netherlands Acad. Sci. and Letters, Am. Nuclear Soc., Am. Phys. Soc. (v.p. 1955, pres. 1956), Am. Math. Soc., Am. Assn. Physics Tchrs., Am. Acad. Arts and Scis., Am. Philos. Soc., Nat. Acad. Scis., N.Y. Acad. Scis. (hon. life mem.), Austrian Acad. Scis., German Phys. Soc., Franklin Inst., AAAS, Sigma Xi, Acad. Sci., Gottingen, Germany (corr.), Hungarian Acad. Sci. (hon.), Austrian Acad. Scis. (hon.), Hungarian L. Eötvös Phys. Soc. (hon.). Subspecialties: Theoretical physics; Statistical physics.

WIIG, KARL MARTIN, artificial intelligence executive; b. Karasjok, Norway, Feb. 8, 1934; came to U.S., 1957, naturalized, 1970; s. Alf Kristian Theodor and Margarethe Haerem (Soylann) W.; m. Elisabeth Hemmersam, June 10, 1958; children—Charlotte Elisabeth, Erik Daniel. B.S.M.E., Case Inst. Tech., 1959, M.S. in Instumentation, 1964. Research physicist Christian Michelsen Inst., Bergen, Norway, 1960-64; system engr. Bunker Ramo/G.E., Cleve., 1964-66; mgr. systems engring. Dundee Cement Co., Mich., 1966-70; mgr. systems and policy analysis Arthur D. Little, Inc., Cambridge, Mass., 1970-81, dir. artificial intelligence program, 1983—; chmn. Abacus Alpha, Inc., Newton, Mass., 1981-82. Author: Economic Offshore Oil and Gas Supply, 1977. Contbr. articles to profl. jours. Patentee variable ratio power steering. Served to cpl. Norwegian Army, 1953-54. Mem. IEEE, Am. Assn. Artificial Intelligence, AAAS, Ops. Research Soc. Am., Inst. Mgmt. Sci. (chmn. local chpt. 1977-78). Democrat. Lutheran. Current work: Application of artificial intelligence and advanced systems science technology to management of knowledge used in organizations and for cognitive support of professional work functions including decision making and planning. Subspecialties: Artificial intelligence; Operations research (engineering). Home: 63 Oakwood Rd Newtonville MA 02160 Office: Arthur D Little Inc Acorn Park Cambridge MA 02140

WIKEL, STEPHEN KENNETH, immunologist, educator; b. York, Pa., Apr. 11, 1945; s. Kenneth Brown and Sarah Elizabeth (Young) W.; m. Kathleen Patricia Guedo, June 8, 1978; children—Sarah, Kurtis. B.A., Shippensburg State Coll., 1967; M.Sc., Vanderbilt U., 1973; Ph.D., U. Sask., 1976. Staff fellow NIH, Bethesda, Md., 1977-79; asst. prof. to assoc. prof. immunology U. S.D., Vermillion, 1979-83; assoc. prof. Sch. of Medicine, U. N.D., Grand Forks, 1983—; cons. U.S. Dept. Agr., Kerrville, Tex., 1977—. Editor: Insect Allergy, 1985. Contbr. articles to profl. jours. Deacon Congregational Ch., Vermillion, 1981-83. Recipient grants U.S. Dept. Agr., others. Mem. Am. Assn. Immunologists, Am. Soc. Parasitologists, Am. Soc. Tropical Medicine and Hygiene., Sigma Xi. Current work: Immunoparasitology, antigen identification and isolation; molecular biology; immunogenetics; vaccine development. Subspecialties: Immunology (medicine); Infectious diseases. Office: Dept Microbiology and Immunology Med Sch Univ ND Grand Forks ND 58202

WILBER, CHARLES GRADY, forensic science educator, consultant; b. Waukesha, Wis., June 18, 1916; s. Charles Bernard and Charlotte Agnes (Grady) W.; m. Ruth Mary Bodden, July 12, 1944 (dec. 1950); children: Maureen, Charles Bodden, Michael; m. Clare Marie O'Keefe, June 14, 1952; children: Thomas Grady (dec.), Kathleen, Aileen, John Joseph. B.Sc., Marquette U., 1938; M.A., Johns Hopkins U., 1941; Ph.D., Johns Hopkins, 1942. Asst. prof. physiology Fordham U., 1945-49; assoc. prof. physiology, dir. biol. labs. St. Louis U., 1949-52; leader Arctic expdns., 1943-44, 48, 50, 51; physiologist Chem. Corps, U.S. Army, 1952-61; assoc. physiology and pharmacology U. Pa., 1953-61, chief comparative physiology, 1956-61; profl. lectr. biol. scis. Loyola Coll., Balt., 1957-61; dir. Loyola Coll. (In-Service Inst. Sci. Tchrs.), 1958-61; prof. biol. scis., univ. research coordinator, dean Grad. Sch., Kent State U., 1961-64; dir. marine laboratories U. Del., 1964-67; chmn. prof. dept. zoology Colo. State U., 1967-73, prof., 1973—, also dir. forensic sci. lab.; Welcome vis. prof. Ohio U. Med. Sch., 1983-84; dep. coroner, Larimer County, Colo.; Wellcome vis. prof. basic med. scis. Ohio U. Med. Sch., Columbus, 1983-84; mem. Center for Human Identification; expert witness fed. and state cts. on poisons, firearms, others. mem. Marine Biol. Lab., Woods Hole, Mass., 1947—; mem. U.S. Army Panel Environ. Physiology, 1952-61; mem. study group Nat. Acad. Scis.-USAF, 1958-61. Author: Biological Aspects of Water Pollution, 2d edit, 1971, Japanese edit., 1970, Forensic Biology for the Law Enforcement Officer, 1975, Contemporary Violence, 1975, Ballistic Science for the Law Enforcement Officer, 1977, Medicolegal Investigation of The President John F. Kennedy Murder, 1978, Chemical Trauma from Pesticides, 1979, Forensic Toxicology, 1980, Beryllium, 1980, Agent Orange, 1980; Author: Turbidity, 1983, Selenium, 1983; contbr. articles to profl. jours.; exec. editor: Adaption to the Environment, vol. in series, 1962; editor: Am. Lecture Series in Environ. Studies; mem. editorial bd.: Am. Jour. Forensic Medicine and Pathology; contbr.: Harper Ency. Nat; vis. lectr.: Am. Inst. Biol. Scis, 1957—. Served to capt. USAAF, 1942-46; col., ret. USAF. Fellow N.Y. Acad. Scis., Am. Acad. Forensic Sci.; mem. Am. Physiol. Soc., Phi Beta Kappa, Sigma Xi, Phi Sigma, Gamma Alpha. Republican. Catholic. Club: Cosmos (Washington). Current Work: Energy effect relations in wound ballistics, chemical trauma from pesticides; toxicology and biology of selenium. Subspecialties: Physiology (biology); Toxicology (medicine). Home: 900 Edwards St Fort Collins CO 80524 Office: Dept Zoology Colo State U Fort Collins CO 80523

WILBUR, DWIGHT LOCKE, retired internal medicine educator; b. Horrow-on-the-Hill, U.K., Sept. 18, 1903; s. Ray Lyman and Marguerite May (Blake) W.; m. Ruth Esther Jordan, Oct. 20, 1928; children—Dwight L. III, Jordan R., Gregory F. A.B. with distinction, Stanford U., 1923; M.D. with honors, U. Pa., 1926; M.S. in Medicine, U. Minn., 1933; Sc.D. (hon.), Dartmouth Coll., 1973. Diplomate Am. Bd. Internal Medicine. Mem. med. staff Mayo Clinic, Rochester, Minn., 1931-37; clin. prof. medicine Stanford U., Calif., 1949-68, prof. emeritus, 1968—; practice medicine specializing in internal medicine, gastroenterology, San Francisco, 1937-83. Author: (with John R. Gamble) Chemistry of Digestive Diseases, 1961; Current Concepts of Gastroenterology, 1965. Trustee, Mayo Found., 1950-73. Served to comdr. USNR, 1942-46. Mem. Am. Gastroenterological Assn. (pres. 1954-55), Am. Coll. Physicians (pres. 1958-59), AMA (pres. 1968-69), Calif. Med. Assn. (hon. past pres. 1964—), Phi Beta Kappa, Sigma Xi, Alpha Omega Alpha. Republican. Clubs: Commonwealth, Bohemian (San Francisco). Current work: medical practice and education. Subspecialty: Gastroenterology.

WILBUR, JAMES M(YERS), JR., chemist, educator, researcher; b. Phila., Oct. 31, 1929; s. James M. and Mary E. (Scherer) W.; m. Ann J.; children: Kirsten, Karen, Eric. B.S., Muhlenberg Coll., 1951; Ph.D. in Chemistry, U. Pa., Phila., 1959. Chemist J. T. Baker Chem. Co., Phillipsburg, N.J., 1951-53; postdoctoral fellow U. Minn., Mpls., 1958-60; research chemist E. I. duPont de Nemours & Co., Wilmington, Del., 1960-62; postdoctoral fellow U. Ariz., Tucson, 1962-63; prof. chemistry S.W. Mo. State U., 1963—. Served with Signal Corps U.S. Army, 1954-56. Mem. Am. Chem. Soc., Chem. Soc. (London), AAAS. Current Work: Polymer synthesis; chemotherapy. Subspecialties: Organic chemistry; Polymer chemistry. Home: 1715 S National Springfield MO 65804 Office: 905 S National Springfield MO 65802

WILBUR, LYMAN DWIGHT, civil engineer; b. Los Angeles, Apr. 27, 1900; s. Curtis Dwight and Olive (Doolittle) W.; m. Henrietta Shattuck, July 6, 1925; children: Olive Wilbur Gamble; m. Pauline Jordan, Apr. 26, 1985. A.B. in Civil Engring, Stanford U., 1921; LL.D. (hon.), Coll. Idaho, 1962; Dr.Sci. (hon.), U. Idaho, 1967. Registered civil engr., Calif., Idaho, Wash., Ariz. Field engr. City of San Francisco, 1921-24; designer Merced Irrigation Dist., Calif., 1924-26; design engr. East Bay Mcpl. Utility Dist., Oakland, Calif., 1926-29; asst. to chief consulting engr. Middle Asia Water Ecology Service USSR, 1929-31; engr. to v.p. and dir. Morrison-Knudsen Co., Inc., Los Angeles and Boise, Idaho, 1932-70; concurrently exec. v.p. to chmn. Internat. Engring. Co., Inc., San Francisco, constrn. mgr. and resident ptnr. joint ventures; self employed cons. engr., Boise, 1971—. Contbr. articles to profl. jours. Pres. Good Samaritan League, 1982—; bd. dirs. Bench Sewer Dist., 1978-85, St. Alphonsus Hosp. Found., Blue Cross of Idaho Health Services, Univ/Community Health Scis. Assn.; trustee Coll. Idaho. Served with U.S. Army, 1918. Recipient Golden Beaver award The Beavers, 1962; Constrn. Man of Yr. Engring. News Record, 1966; award for disting. humanitarian accomplishments through engring. Idaho Soc. Profl. Engrs., 1967; John Fritz medal Five Founder Engring. Socs., 1973; Moles award for outstanding achievement in constrn., 1974; ann. award Nat. Soc. Profl. Engrs., 1974; others. Mem. Nat. Acad. Engring., ASCE, Idaho Soc. Profl. Engrs., Nat. Soc. Profl. Engrs., Soc. Am. Mil. Engrs. Republican. Presbyterian. Clubs: Hillcrest, Arid. Patentee in field. Current Work: Consulting and helping with civic and non-profit orgns. Subspecialty: Civil engineering. Address: 4502 Hillcrest Dr Boise ID 83705

WILCOX, PATTI MARIE, nurse, clinician and clinical researcher; b. River Falls, Wis., Jan. 24, 1946; d. David Arthur Sr. and Patti Marie (Gambrell) W.; m. dau., Amanda. Diploma, Johns Hopkins Hosp. Sch. Nursing, 1967; cert., Johns Hopkins Sch. Health Services, 1976. Cert. adult nurse practitioner. Head nurse Johns Hopkins Hosp., Balt., 1964-70, Man Alive Research Inst., Balt., 1970-71; Head nurse Johns Hopkins Oncology Ctr., 1971-75, adult nurse practitioner, 1976—; health care coordinator Threshold Inc., Balt., 1978-81; dir., developer NEED, Balt., 1979—; coordinator breast cancer program Am. Cancer Soc., Balt., 1978-80. Author, editor: NEED Co-leader Handbook, 1982. Active Big sister Big Bros./Big Sisters; bd. dirs. YWCA Greater Balt. Area, Inc. Recipient cert. merit Am. Cancer Soc., 1981; volo. of yr. award YWCA, 1982. Mem. Oncology Nursing Soc., Md. Oncology Nursing Soc. (pres. 1980-81), Am. Cancer Soc.; affiliate mem. Am. Soc. Clin. Oncology. Democrat. Methodist. Current Work: Breast cancer-primary, metastic, reconstruction after, adjuvant chemotherapy, nausea and vomiting-anticipatory; alopecia-2 chemotherapy; psychosocial issues following mastectomy; body image after mastectomy; support groups; patient education. Subspecialty: Oncology. Home: 2809 Southern Ave Baltimore MD 21214 Office: Johns Hopkins Oncology Ctr B-111 600 N Wolfe St Baltimore MD 21205

WILCOX, ROBERT HOWARD, engineering company executive; b. Lockport, N.Y., Aug. 21, 1930; s. Robert Herrick and Ruth Beatrice (Cullingford) W.; m. Doris Marie Gillis, June 19, 1955; children—Susan Marie Wilcox-Harris, Janet Patricia, Robert Allen, Heather Ruth. M.E., Stevens Inst. Tech., 1952; M.S. in Nuclear Engring., MIT, 1958. Registered profl. engr., Va. Mech. and service engr. Babcock & Wilcox, Barberton, Ohio, 1952-57; reactor engr. AEC, Germantown, Md., 1958-63; asst. to exec. sec. Adv. Com. Reactor Safeguards, Washington, 1963-67, sci. rep., Brazil and Europe, 1967-73; sci. and tech. counselor Dept. State, Argentina and Mex., 1973-81; project mgr. Stone & Webster, Boston, 1981—. Bd. dirs. Lincoln Sch., Buenos Aires, Argentina, 1974-77; mem. Friends of Endicott Estate, 1984—. Recipient meritorious service award Dept. State, 1981; Charles Hayden scholar, 1948-52; AEC spl. fellow, 1957-58. Mem. Am. Nuclear Soc. (pub. info. chmn. northeastern sect. 1984—), ASME, Project Mgmt. Inst. Republican. Roman Catholic. Club: Falmouth Men's (Mass.). Current work: Management of international energy projects--nuclear, solids circulation boiler, plant services, technical assistance, technology transfer. Subspecialties: Nuclear fission; Nuclear engineering. Office: Stone & Webster 245 Summer St Boston MA 02210

WILCOX, W(EBSTER) WAYNE, forest products pathologist; b. Berkeley, Calif., Oct. 28, 1938; s. Webster Williamson, Jr. and Edith Jeanette (LaBelle) W.; m. Margaret Ruth Starkweather, Aug. 7, 1960; children: Melissa Margaret, Wynn William. B.S. in Forestry, U. Calif., Berkeley, 1960; M.S., U. Wis., 1962, Ph.D. in Plant Pathology, 1965. Plant pathologist U.S. Forest Products Lab., Madison, Wis., 1960-64; mem. faculty U. Calif., Berkeley, also U. Calif. Forest Product Lab., 1964—, forest products pathologist, prof. forestry, 1977—; cons. in field; mem. Calif. Structural Pest Control Bd., 1979-81. Fulbright-Hays sr. postdoctoral fellow, 1973-74. Fellow Internat. Acad. Wood Sci.; mem. Forest Products Research Soc. (Wood award 1965), Soc. Wood Sci. and Tech., Am. Inst. Biol. Scis., Sigma Xi, Xi Sigma Pi. Subspecialty: Plant pathology. Office: Forest Products Lab U Calif 47th and Hoffman Blvd Richmond CA 94804

WILD, JAMES ROBERT, research scientist; b. Sedalia, Mo., Nov. 24, 1945; s. Robert Lee and Frances Elleta (Wheeler) W.; m. Ann Lynn Brenner, Aug. 1, 1973. B.S., U. Calif.-Davis, 1967; Ph.D., U. Calif.-Riverside, 1971. Teaching asst. dept. biology U. Calif.-Riverside, 1967-71; asst. prof. genetics dept. plant sci. Tex. A&M U., 1975-80, assoc. prof. biochemistry and genetics, dept. biochemistry and biophysics, 1980-84, prof., chmn. faculty genetics, 1984—. Contbr. numerous articles to profl. jours. Served with USNR, 1972-75. NIH grantee, 1981—; NSF grantee, 1981—; Robert A. Welch Found. grantee, 1982—. Mem. Am. Soc. Biol. Chemists, Am. Soc. Microbiology, AAAS, Genetics Soc. Am., Sigma Xi, Phi Sigma. Current Work: Analysis of gene structure-function; regulation of gene expression enzymology, molecular genetics, development metabolism, biochemical analogues, gene amplification and restructuring. Subspecialty: Genetics and genetic engineering (agriculture). Home: 1606 Todd Trail College Station TX 77840 Office: Dept Biochemistry and Biophysics Tex A&M U College Station TX 77843

WILDENTHAL, BRYAN HOBSON, physicist; b. San Marcos, Tex., Nov. 4, 1937; 3 children. B.A., Sul Ross State Coll., 1958; Ph.D. in Physics, U. Kans., 1964. Research assoc. physics Rice U., 1964-66; fellow AEC Oak Ridge Nat. Lab., 1966-68; asst. prof. Tex A&M U., 1968-69; assoc. prof. Mich. State U., 1969-72, prof. physics, 1972-84; head physics and atmospheric scis dept. Drexel U., Philad, 1985—; sr. U.S. fellow Humboldt Found. U. Munich, 1973; vis. scientist Brookhaven Nat. Lab., 1974, Max Planck Inst. Nuclear Physics, Heidelberg, 1976, Gesellschaft fur Schwereionforschung, Darmstadt, 1977; vis. prof. U. Paris, 1977; program assoc. physics div. NSF, 1978. Fellow John Simon Guggenheim Meml. Found., 1977. Subspecialty: Nuclear physics. Office: Drexel U Physics and Atmospheric Scis Dept Philadelphia PA 19104*

WILDENTHAL, C(LAUD) KERN, university dean; b. San Marcos, Tex., July 1, 1941; s. Bryan and Doris (Kellam) W.; m. Margaret Dehlinger, Oct. 15, 1964; children—Pamela, Catharine. B.A., Sul Ross Coll., 1960; M.D., U. Tex., Dallas, 1964; Ph.D., U. Cambridge, Eng., 1970. Intern Bellevue Hosp., N.Y.C., 1964-65; resident in medicine, fellow cardiology Parkland Hosp., Dallas, 1965-67; research fellow Nat. Heart Inst., Bethesda, Md., 1967-68; vis. research fellow Strangeways Research Lab., Cambridge, 1968-70; asst. prof. to prof. internal medicine and physiology U. Tex., Dallas, 1970-76, prof., dean Grad. Sch., 1976-80; prof., dean Southwestern Med. Sch., 1980—; sci. cons. Strangeways Research Lab.; chmn. research rev. com. Nat. Heart, Lung and Blood Inst. Mem. Health Awards Com., Met. Life Found. Author: Regulation of Cardiac Metabolism, 1976, Degradative Processes in Heart and Skeletal Muscle, 1980; contbr. articles to profl. jours. Bd. dirs. Tex. br. Am. Heart Assn., 1978—. USPHS spl. research fellow, 1968-70; recipient Research Career Devel. award NIH, 1972, Sybil Eastwood research award, 1976; John Simon Guggenheim Meml. fellow, 1975-76. Mem. Am. Soc. Clin. Investigation, Am. Coll. Cardiology, Royal Soc. Medicine Gt. Britain, Assn. Am. Physicians, Am. Physiol. Soc., Internat. Soc. Heart Research (Am. sect. pres. 1982-85), Am. Fedn. Clin. Research (So. sect. pres. 1979-80), Assn. Am. Med. Colls., AMA. Current Work: Cardiac cellular physiology and metabolism; lysosomes; protein turnover. Subspecialties: Physiology (medicine); Cell biology (medicine). Home: 4128 Southwestern Blvd Dallas TX 75225 Office: 5323 Harry Hines Blvd Dallas TX 75235

WILDER, DAVID GOULD, biomechanics researcher, mechanical engineering consultant; b. Neptune, N.J., July 24, 1952; s. Charles Moulton Gould and Christine Bayard (Clark) W.; m. Kathleen Mary Hill, July 11, 1981. B.S. in Mech. Engring., U. Vt., 1974, M.S. in Mech. Engring., 1978. Registered profl. engr., Vt. Grad. research asst. dept. orthopedics and rehab. U. Vt., Burlington, 1974-79, research assoc., 1979—. Contbr. articles to profl. jours. Recipient Volvo award, New Orleans, 1980. Mem. ASME, Am. Soc. Biomechanics, AAAS, Orthopaedic Research Soc., Nat. Soc. Profl. Engrs., Sigma Xi. Episcopalian. Current work: Study of low back pain as a mechanical problem connected with seating and vibration (work) environments. Subspecialties: Biomedical engineering; Mechanical engineering. Office: Univ Vermont Dept Orthopaedics & Rehab Given Bldg Burlington VT 05405

WILDER, JAMES ANDREW, JR., research engineer; b. Washington, Dec. 19, 1950; s. James Andrew and Margaret Elizabeth (Bell) W.; m. Diane Jean Krop, June 16, 1973; children—Derek James, Jennifer Lynn. B.S. in Engring., Cath. U. Am., 1973, M.S. in Engring., 1975, Ph.D., 1977. Research asst. Cath. U. Am., Washington, 1971-77; mem. tech. staff Sandia Nat. Labs., Albuquerque, 1977—. Contbr. articles to profl. publs. Patentee glassy composition for hermitic seals. Mem. Am. Ceramic Soc. (chmn. rules com. 1980), Optical Soc. Am., IEEE, Soc. Photo-optical Engrs. Republican. Lutheran. Current work: Optoelectronics and nonreciproal devices for microwave, mm wave and optical frequency applications. Subspecialties: Ceramics; Optical signal processing. Home: 1459 Bluebell Dr NE Albuquerque NM 87122 Office: Sandia Nat Labs PO Box 5800 Albuquerque NM 87185

WILENSKY, ROBERT J., information scientist. Asst. prof. computer science U.Calif., Berkeley. Office: U Calif Dept Elec Engring and Computer Scis Berkeley CA 94720*

WILEY, RONALD GORDON, neurologist, neurobiologist; b. Akron, Ohio, Mar. 21, 1947; s. H.J. and Sara T. (Moore) W.; m. Karen Sue Steffy, July 24, 1970; children: Elizabeth Ann, Kathleen Sara, Allison Christine. B.S., Northwestern U., 1972, Ph.D., 1975, M.D. with distinction, 1975. Diplomate: Am. Bd. Psychiatry and Neurology, Am. Bd. Internal Medicine. Intern, then jr. asst. resident in medicine Peter Bent Brigham Hosp., Boston, 1975-77; resident in neurology N.Y. Hosp., N.Y.C., 1977-80; fellow Lab. Neurobiology, Cornell U. Med. Coll., 1980-82; assoc. attending neurologist La Guardia Hosp., N.Y.C., 1980-82; asst. prof. neurology, instr. pharmacology Vanderbilt U. Med. Sch., Nashville, 1982—; attending neurologist VA Med. Center, Nashville, 1982—; vis. staff in neurology Vanderbilt U. Hosp., 1984—; chief neuro-oncology service Vanderbilt U. Med. Ctr., 1984—. Contbr. articles to sci. publs. Recipient Roche awards in neurosci., G.D. Searle award for research; Tchr. of Yr. award Ill. Coll. Optometry, 1972. Mem. AAAS, Am. Acad. Neurology, Soc. Neurosci., N.Y. Acad. Scis., Sigma Xi (research award), Alpha Omega Alpha. Current Work: Development of suicide transport agents; axonal transport; mechanisms of neurotransmitter secretion, particularly role of synaptic vesicles. Subspecialties: Neurology; Neurobiology. Office: 1310 24th Ave S Nashville TN 37203

WILEY, WILLIAM R., research director; b. Oxford, Miss., Sept. 5, 1931; s. William Russell and Edna Alberta (Threlkeld) W.; m. Myrtle Louise Smith, Nov. 10, 1952; 1 child, Johari. B.S., Tougaloo Coll., 1954; M.S. (Rockefeller Found. fellow), U. Ill., Urbana, 1960; Ph.D., Wash. State U., 1965. Mgr. cellular and molecular biology sect. Battelle-Northwest, Richmond, Wash., 1969-72, mgr. biology dept., 1974-79, dir. research, 1979—; coordinator Battelle Inst. Life Scis. Program, Richland, 1972-74; George Washington Carver Lectr. Tuskegee Inst., 1967; lectr. Black Exec. Exchange Program. Co-author 2 books; editor: Methods in Enzymology, 1974; contbr. articles to sci. publs. Trustee Gonzaga U., 1982—, bd. regents, 1968-81; bd. dirs. Richland City Library, chmn. bd., 1970-71; trustee Kadlec Hosp., 1972-74. Served with U.S. Army, 1954-56. Mem. Am. Soc. Microbiology, AAAS, Soc. Exptl. Biology and Medicine. Lodge: Kiwanis. Current Work: Mgmt. research and devel. environ., health, geoscis., space scis. and engring. Subspecialties: Cell biology; Biochemistry (biology). Office: Battelle-NW PO Box 999 Richland WA 99352

WILHELM, WILBERT E., industrial engineer, educator; b. Oct. 24, 1942; married; 2 children. B.S. in Mech. Engring., W.Va. U., 1964; M.S. in Indsl. Engring., Va. Tech. U., 1970, Ph.D., 1972. Registered profl. engr., Ohio. Maintenance engr. E.I. DuPont, Belle, W.Va., 1963; mfg. mgmt. staff Gen. Electric Co., various locations, 1964-67, specialist mfg. adminstrn., Salem, Va., 1967-69; asst. prof. dept. indsl. and systems engring. Ohio State U., Columbus, 1972-78, assoc. prof., 1978—; cons. and lectr. in field. Author 1 book. Contbr. articles to profl. jours. Chmn., participant profl. confs. Recipient numerous awards for excellence in engring. and edn. including Ralph Boyer award, 1984, Ohio State U. Research award, 1985; NSF fellow, 1970-71. Mem. Op. Research Soc. of Am., Soc. Mfg. Engrs., Am. Inst. Indsl. Engrs. (various coms., editorial bd. 1977—), Alpha Pi Mu, Phi Kappa Phi. Current work: Material flow management in small-lot assembly systems. Subspecialties: Operations research (engineering); Systems engineering. Home: 6745 Merwin Pl Worthington OH 43085

WILKE, CHARLES ROBERT, chemical engineer, educator, investment adviser; b. Dayton, Ohio, Feb. 4, 1917; s. Otto Alexander and Stella M. (Dodge) W.; m. Bernice Lucille Arnett, June 19, 1946. B. Chem. Engring., U. Dayton, 1940; M.S. in Chemistry, State Coll. Wash., 1942; Ph.D. in Chem. Engring, U. Wis., 1944. Asso. engr. Union Oil Co. of Calif., 1944-45, cons., 1952—; instr. chem. engring. Wash. State Coll., 1945-46; instr. chem. engring. U. Calif. at Berkeley, 1946-47, asst. prof., 1947-51, asso. prof., 1951-53, prof., 1953—, chmn. dept. chem. engring., 1953-63, asst. to chancellor acad. affairs, 1967-69, prin. investigator Lawrence Berkeley Lab., 1950—, indsl. cons., 1952—; chmn. bd. C.R. Wilke Internat. Corp., 1970—; cons. editor Reinhold Pub. Co., 1958-64; mem. Calif. Bd. Registration Civil and Profl. Engrs., 1964-72, pres., 1967-69. Contbr. articles to profl. jours. Recipient Walker award Am. Inst. Chem. Engrs., 1965, Colburn award, 1951; Disting. Alumnus award U. Dayton, 1984. Fellow Am. Inst. Chem. Engrs. (past chmn. No. Calif. sect.); mem. Soc. Applied Bacteriology, Am. Chem. Soc., Electrochem. Soc., Nat. Acad. Engring., Am. Soc. Engring. Edn. (Chem. Engring. lecture award 1964), Am. Soc. Microbiology, Sigma Xi, Tau Beta Pi. Clubs: Commonwealth of California, World Trade of San Francisco. Current Work: Production of chemicals by microbial processes, mircobial and enzyne reactor design, enzymatic conversion processes. Subspecialties: Chemical engineering; Enzyme technology. Home: 1327 Contra Costa Dr El Cerrito CA 94530

WILKENING, LAUREL LYNN, dean, planetary science educator, researcher; b. Richland, Wash., Nov. 23, 1944; d. Marvin H. and Ruby A. (Barks) W.; m. Godfrey T. Sill, May 18, 1974. B.A., Reed Coll., 1966; Ph.D., U. Calif.-San Diego, 1970. Research assoc. Enrico Fermi Inst., 1972-73; research assoc. chem. dept; U. Chgo., 1972-73; asst. prof. planetary sci. U. Ariz., Tucson, 1973-78, assoc. prof., 1978-83, prof., 1983—, dept. head, 1981-83, acting dean scis., 1982; dir. Lunar and Planetary Lab., 1981-83, vice provost, 1983-85, v.p. for research, dean Grad. Coll., 1985—; div. scientist planetary div. NASA Hdqrs., Washington, 1980. Editor: Comets, 1982; contbr. sci. articles to profl. publs. Recipient Ninenger Meteorite award, 1971. Mem. Am. Geophys. Union, Am. Astron. Soc. (div. planetary sci.), Internat. Astron. Union, Meteoritical Soc., AAAS, Phi Beta Kappa. Current Work: Meteorites, asteroids, comets. Subspecialties: Planetary science; Space chemistry. Office: U Ariz 601 Adminstrn Bldg Tucson AZ 85721

WILKERSON, SUSAN MCCASLAND, optical scientist, astronomer; b. San Diego, Nov. 8, 1953; d. Elmer Davis and Dyxie Dathyne (Canaday) W.; m. William Neil McCasland, 1985. B.A., U. Calif., San Diego, 1975; Ph.D., U. Ariz., 1979. Grad. research asst Steward Obs., U. Ariz., Tucson, 1975-77; research asst. Kitt Peak Nat. Obs., Tucson, 1977-79; commd. 2d lt. U.S. Air Force, 1980, advanced through grades to capt., 1984; sci. sr. staff Sacramento Peak Obs., Sunspot, N.Mex., 1980-81; chief, laser recorder systems br., dir. advanced studies Hdqrs. Space Div./YBE, Los Angeles, 1981-85; mem. tech. staff Analytic Scis. Corp., Reading, Mass., 1985—. Contbr. articles to profl. jours. Mem. Am. Astron. Soc., Astron. Soc. of Pacific. Current work: Defense related studies and analyses in optical sciences, image processing and image quality, space-based optical systems. Subspecialties: Optical astronomy; Optical image processing. Home: 18 Samson Rd Medford MA 02155 Office: Analytic Scis Corp One Jacob Way Reading MA 01867

WILKES, H(ILBERT) GARRISON, biologist, educator, plant breeder; b. Los Angeles, Oct. 2, 1937; s. Hilbert Garrison and Margret Lee (Boggs) W.; m. Susan Kreps Redwood, May 29, 1965; m. Marie Dalton Gibby, Apr. 9, 1978; children: Nathan, Jennifer, Andrew, Katharan. B.A., Pomona Coll., 1959; Ph.D., Harvard U., 1966. Asst. prof. Tulane U., 1966-70; assoc. prof. biology U. Mass., Boston, 1970-83, prof., 1983—; cons. tropical biology, plant genetic resources, maize germplasm; Fulbright fellow, India, 1959-60, Harvard travelling fellow, C. Am., 1963-64, Indo-Am. fellow, India, 1978-79; mem. exec. com. Assembly Life Sci., Nat. Acad. Sci., 1973-77. Contbr. numerous articles on maize evolution, econ. botany, plant genetic resources to profl. jours. Woodrow Wilson fellow, 1960-61; NSF grantee, 1968-70, 72, 74-78. Mem. Am. Bot. Soc., Soc. Econ. Botany, Soc. Study Evolution, Linnean Soc. Current Work: Evolution under domesticization; genetic resources; econ. botany; evolution crop plants, especially maize and its wild relatives; conservation of plant genetic resources; gene banks. Subspecialties: Plant genetics; Evolutionary biology.

WILKINSON, ARTHUR FREDERICK, biomedical research engineer; b. London, Aug. 28, 1918; came to U.S., 1954, naturalized, 1962; s. Frederick F. and Marian (Scott) W.; m. Elizabeth Law, Nov. 25, 1939; children—Yvonne, Barbara. Telephone engr. Reliance Telephone Co, London, 1938-39, 46-52; electronics engr. Middlesex Hosp. Med. Sch., Eng., 1952-54, Latter-day Saints Hosp. and U. Utah, Salt Lake City, 1954-57; biomed. research engr. Maine Med. Ctr., Portland, 1957—. Contbr. articles to profl. jours. Served with RAF, 1939-46, NATOUSA, ETO. Mem. IEEE, Biophys. Soc. (charter), Portland YMCA. Club: Regent Polytechnic (London). Current work: Design, construction, modification and calibration of electronic and mechanical equipment used for research; assisting in cardiology research; design, construction and repair of surgical instruments. Subspecialties: Biomedical engineering; Electronics. Office: 22 Bramhall St Portland ME 04102

WILKINSON, DAVID STANLEY, pathologist, consultant, researcher; b. Richmond, Va., Feb. 2, 1945; s. Herbert Carroll and Hattie Mae (Vaughan) W.; m. Judith Farish Pace, June 16, 1967; children: Jill Marie, Julie Lynne, Virginia Ann. B.S. in Chemistry, Va. Mil. Inst., Lexington, 1967; Ph.D. in Exptl. Oncology and Pathology, U. Wis.-Madison, 1971; M.D., U. Miami, 1978. Diplomate: Am. Bd. Pathology. Commd. 2d lt. U.S. Army, 1967, advanced through grades to maj., 1982; fellow McArdle Lab. Cancer Research U. Wis., 1967-71; asst. prof. biochemistry U. South Fla., Tampa, 1972-76; resident in pathology Walter Reed Army Med. Ctr., Washington, 1978-82; instr. pathology Uniformed Services U. of Health Scis., Bethesda, 1979-82; chief clin. pathology Eisenhower Army Med. Ctr., Ft. Gordon, Ga., 1982—; mem. clin. faculty Med. Coll. Ga. Augusta; lectr. in field. Contbr. articles to profl. jours. Damon Runyon-Walter Winchell Cancer Fund grantee, 1973; Am. Cancer Soc. grantee, 1973; Nat. Cancer Inst. grantee, 1975. Mem. Am. Assn. Cancer Research, Soc. Exptl. Biology and Medicine, Am. Soc. Clin. Pathologists. Republican. Club: VMI Keydet (Lexington, Va.). Current Work: Biochemical pathology, experimental cancer chemotherapy, mechanisms of action of antitumor agents, therapeutic drug monitoring. Subspecialties: Pathology (medicine); Cancer research (medicine). Office: Department Pathology Dwight D Eisenhower Army Medical Center Fort Gordon GA 30905

WILKINSON, GRANT ROBERT, pharmacologist, educator; b. Derby, Eng., Aug. 27, 1941; s. Arthur Henry and Gwendoline Mary (Fox) W.; m. Margaret Kay Fletcher, Aug. 8, 1964 (div. 1978); children: Grant R., Nicole E.; m. June Zoe Dass, July 12, 1978; children: Tracey A., Erika L. B.Sc., U. Manchester, Eng., 1963; Ph.D., U. London, 1966. Postdoctoral fellow dept. pharmacology U. Calif., San Francisco, 1966-68; asst. prof. Coll. Pharmacy, U. Ky., Lexington, 1968-71; asst. prof. dept. pharmacology Vanderbilt U., Nashville, 1971-73, assoc. prof., 1973-78, prof., 1978—; assoc. dir. Ctr. for Clin. Pharmacology, 1980—; cons. NIH; indsl. cons. Fellow AAAS; mem. Am. Soc. for Pharmacology and Exptl. Therapeutics, Am. Soc. Clin. Pharmacology and Therapeutics. Current Work: Drug disposition in man; factors affecting this such as genetics, disease-states, aging, drug interactions. Pharmacokinetics. Bioanalysis. Subspecialties: Pharmacology; Pharmacokinetics. Office: Dept Pharmacology Vanderbilt U Nashville TN 37232

WILKINSON, NANCY M., flavor chemist; b. Kalamazoo, Sept. 8, 1947; d. Varl O. and Nancy (Buben) W. B.S., Central Mich. U., Mt. Pleasant, 1969. Product devel. technician Kalsec Inc., Kalamazoo, 1971-75; flavor chemist Frostie Enterprises, Camden, N.J., 1976-80; flavor chemist Northville Labs., Mich., 1980-82, 85—; flavor analyst Faygo Beverages, Detroit, 1982-84. Flutist Plymouth Community Band, Mich., 1976—. Mem. Inst. Food Tech., Soc. Flavor Chemists. Subspecialty: Food science and technology. Home: 41162 Southwind Canton MI 48188

WILKINSON, THOMAS ALLAN, engineering geologist; b. Fort Worth, Jan. 6, 1932; s. Joseph Ackinson and Grace (Wythe) W.; m. Rosalyn Sarah Schilz, Dec. 21, 1959; children—Kris Allan, Nachelle Marie, Tedric Gordon. B.S. in Geology, U. Okla., 1954, M.S. in Geology, 1956, postgrad., 1958-59. Registered geologist, Calif. Cert. Engring. Geologist, Calif. Engring. geologist Corps of Engrs., Kansas City, Mo., 1959-64, project geologist, Stockton, Mo., 1964-65, dist. geologist, Buffalo, 1965-71, chief geotech. br., 1971—; lectr. in geology Canisius Coll., Buffalo, 1971-72, Waterways Expt. Sta., Vicksburg, Miss., 1982—; cons. in engring. geology NRC, Bethesda, Md., 1978-82, Dept of Energy, Columbus, Ohio, 1984—. Contbr. articles to profl. jours. Pres. Willow Ridge PTA, Amherst, N.Y., 1976; umpire Little League Baseball, Amherst, 1978; sports photographer Sweet Home High Sch., Amherst, 1980—; lectr. various civic orgns., western N.Y., 1965—. Served to lt. U.S. Army, 1955-57, Kansas City Assn. Trustee Found. scholar, 1960-61. Mem. Assn. Engring. Geologists, Geol. Soc. Am., Soc. Am. Mil. Engrs. (bd. dirs. 1983—), Sigma Xi. Republican. Unitarian. Current work: Manage engineers and geologists in geotechnical design of harbor, navigation, and flood control projects in New York, Pennsylvania, and Ohio. Subspecialty: Engineering geology. Home: 41 Willow Ln Amherst NY 14150 Office: US Army Engr Dist Buffalo 1776 Niagara St Buffalo NY 14207

WILL, LOREN AUGUST, veterinarian, epidemiologist, researcher; b. Mpls., Dec. 31, 1942; s. Vernon Eugene and Lillian Dorothy (LaFore) W.; m. Joan Heather Allibone, June 13, 1964; children: Heather, Michelle, Christina, Davina, John, Geoffrey. B.A., St. Mary's Coll., Winona, Minn., 1965; B.S., U. Minn., St. Paul, 1967, D.V.M., 1969; M.P.H., U. Minn., Mpls., 1975. Tchr. St. Josephs Sch., Vanderhoof, B.C., 1963-64; vet. clinician, Prince George, B.C., 1969-70; environ. health and cancer research scientist U. Iowa, Iowa City, 1974-78; asst. prof. pub. health coll. Vet. Medicine, Iowa State U., Ames, 1978—; vet. pub. health specialist Pan Am. Health Orgn. WHO, Bridgetown, Barbados, 1985—. Pack chmn. Cub Scouts. Mem. AAAS, Assn. Animal Allergic Veterinarians (founder , dir., newsletter pub.), Assn. Tchrs. of Vet. Pub. Health and Preventive Medicine, Assn. Am. Vet. Med. Colls.; Mem Acad. Vet. Allergy. Roman Catholic. Current Work: Allergy to animals in occupational groups, nature of the problem, its extent, its medical, physiologic, and social consequences. Subspecialties: Allergy; Epidemiology. Home: 1910 George Allen Dr Ames IA 50010 Office: 2116 Veterinary Medicine Iowa State University Ames IA 50011 Also: Pan Am Health Orgn WHO PO Box 508 Bridgetown Barbados

WILLARDSON, ROBERT KENT, physicist, consultant; b. Gunnison, Utah, July 11, 1923; s. Anthony Robert and Alice Eva (Pierce) W.; m. Beth Marie Bennett, Sept. 12, 1947; children—Amanda Marie Ballou, Elizabeth Ann Engar, Jennie Lynette. B.S. in Physics, Brigham Young U., 1949; M.S. in Solid State Physics, Iowa State U., 1951. Asst. chief physicist chem. div. Batelle Meml. Inst., Columbus, Ohio, 1951-60; gen. mgr. Bell & Howell Co., Pasadena, Calif., 1960-72; pres. Electronic Material Corp., Pasadena, 1973; sr. scientist Cominco Elec. Material, Spokane, Wash., 1973-82; pres. Willardson Cons., Spokane, 1982-84, Cryscon Tech. Inc., Phoenix, 1984—; dir. Ohio Semicondrs. Inc., Columbus, 1956-58, Cryscon Techs. Inc., Phoenix, 1984—. Editor: Compound Semiconductors, 1962, Semiconductors and Semimetals, 1966—. Patentee in field. Contbr. articles to profl. jours. Served with USAF, 1942-46. Mem. IEEE (sr. mem.), Am. Phys. Soc., Am. Chem. Soc., Electrochem. Soc., Internat. Soc. Hybird Microelectronics, Components, Hybirds, and Mfg. Tech. (chmn. TC-5 1980—). Current work: Crystal growth; electronic, optical & magnetic properties of solids, impurities, crystal defects, radiation damage, chemical analysis, high purity metals, compound semiconductors. Subspecialties: Semiconductors; Electronic materials. Home: E 12722 23rd Ave Spokane WA 99216Office: Cryscon Technologies Inc 21002 N 19th Ave Bldg A-7 Phoenix AZ 85027

WILLCOX, PHILLIP JAMES, project engineer, scientific consultant; b. Winterset, Iowa, June 28, 1935; s. Irl F. and Margaret J. (Perry) W.; m. Marlene N. Clark, June 18, 1955 (dec. Feb. 1982); children: James M., John A. B.S. in Math, Ind. Inst. Tech., Ft. Wayne, 1961, B.S. in Physics, 1962; M.S. in Physics, Akron U., 1965; postgrad. in astrophysics and philosophy, UCLA and U. Calif.-Berkeley, 1972-78. Staff scientist Goodyear Aerospace Co., Akron, Ohio, 1962-65; sr. staff scientist Heliodyne Corp., Norton AFB, Calif., 1965-66; project engr., sect. mgr. TRW DSSG, Redondo Beach, Calif., 1966-79; ind. cons. Magnavox, TRW, 1979-82; project engr. Magnavox GIEC, Ft. Wayne, 1982—; cons. TRW DSSG, 1979—; instr. physics and math. Huntingdon Cath. High Sch., Ind. Inst. Tech., 1979-82; Assoc. fellow AIAA; guest lectr. Author: The UFO Question, 1976, Modern Cosmology, 1982, High Energy Astronomy, in preparation; contbr. articles tech. jours. Served with USMC, 1952-55. Mem. AAAS, Planetary Soc. (charter). Democrat. Current Work: Military communications systems, high energy astrophysics, scientific education. Subspecialties: Electrical engineering; High energy astrophysics. Home: 11902 Winterthur Ln Reston VA 22091

WILLEMS, WILLIAM JOSEPH, neurology educator, neurophysiology researcher; b. Paris, Ark., Sept. 1, 1943; s. Aloys Jacob and Anne Rose (Wagner) W.; m. Margot Wilma Alexander, Aug. 17, 1968; children—Heidi Rose, Wendy Therese, Michael Alexander. B.S. in C.E., Marquette U., 1965; M.D., Med. Coll. Wis., 1970, M.S., 1970. Diplomate Am. Bd. Psychiatry and Neurology. Intern, Milw. Affiliated Hosps., 1970-71, resident in neurology, 1975-76; sr. resident, 1977-78; neurology research Cleve. Clinic, 1976-77; asst. prof. neurology Med. Coll. Wis., 1978—. Contbr. articles to sci. jours. Am. Heart Assn. Research grantee, 1983-84; Veterans Hosps. Merit Rev. grantee, 1981-84, Career Devel. grantee, 1981—. Mem. Am. Acad. Neurology, Am. Physiologic Soc., Soc. Neurosci., AMA, Sigma Xi. Roman Catholic. Current work: Electrophysiologic measurements of intracellular membrane potential in cells of blood vessels "in vivo" to measure effects of innervation in normo tension, hypotension and hypertension. Subspecialties: Neurology; Physiology (medicine). Home: 4911 W Sunnyside Dr Milwaukee WI 53208 Office: Research VA Hosp 5000 W National Ave Milwaukee WI 53208

WILLEMSEN, JORGE FERNANDO, physicist; b. Guatemala, Nov. 1, 1945; s. Fernando Edgar Willemsen and Graciela (Granados) Snitzler; m. Susan Mary Kilcourse, Aug. 31, 1984; children—Jorge Alberto, Keagan Gaitley. B.A. with honors, U. Chgo., 1967, M.S., 1968, Ph.D., 1972. Research assoc. Stanford Linear Accelerator Ctr. (Calif.), 1972-74, Ctr. for Theoretical Physics MIT, Cambridge, 1974-77; asst. prof. in residence U. Calif. Santa Cruz, 1977-80; mem. profl. staff Schlumberger-Doll Research, Ridgefield, Conn., 1980—. Mem. Am. Phys. Soc., Sigma Xi (assoc.). Current work: Dynamics of systems involving many relevant spatial and temporal scales: flow in porous media, dielectric properties of composites. Subspecialties: Theoretical physics; Statistical physics. Home: 6 Briar Ridge Rd Danbury CT 06810 Office: Schlumberger-Doll Research Old Quarry Rd Ridgefield CT 06877

WILLENBROCK, FREDERICK KARL, engineer, educator; b. N.Y.C., July 19, 1920; s. Berthold Daniel and Anna Marie (Koniger) W.; m. Mildred Grace White, Dec. 20, 1944. Sc.B., Brown U., 1942; M.A., Harvard U., 1947, Ph.D., 1950. Research fellow, lectr. and asso. dean Harvard U., Cambridge, Mass., 1950-67; provost, prof. faculty engring. and applied sci. SUNY, Buffalo, 1967-70; dir. Inst. Applied Tech., Nat. Bur. Standards, Washington, 1970-76; dean Sch. Engring. and Applied Sci., So. Meth. U., Dallas, 1976-81, Cecil H. Green prof. engring., 1976—. Contbr. articles to profl. jours. Served with USN, 1943-46. Recipient Disting. engring. award Brown U., 1962; Gold medal U.S. Dept. Commerce, 1975. Fellow IEEE, AAAS; mem. Nat. Acad. Engring., Am. Phys. Soc., Am. Soc. for Engring. Edn., ASTM, Sigma Xi, Tau Beta Phi. Office: Sch of Engring and Applied Sci So Meth Univ Dallas TX 75275

WILLFORD, WAYNE ALAN, federal government research chemist; b. Canton, Minn., Dec. 9, 1941; s. Ward Eugene and Ethel Irene (Reed) W.; m. Judeen Marie Walters, May 29, 1965; children—Douglas Alan, Tracy Lynn. B.A., Winona State Coll., 1963; postgrad. Wis. State U.-LaCrosse, 1968-69. Research chemist Fish Control Lab., Fish and Wildlife Service, U.S. Dept Interior, LaCrosse, 1963-70, supervisory research chemist, Gt. Lakes Fishery Lab., Ann Arbor, Mich., 1970—, sect. chief, 1975—; mem. Upper Lakes Reference Group, Internat. Joint Commn., Windsor, Ont., Can., 1974-77, mem. surveillance subcom., 1976-80, mem. dredging subcom., 1982—; chmn. Fish Community Health Task Group, Gt. Lakes Fishery Commn., Ann Arbor, 1984—; invited participant USSR-U.S. EPA Sci. Exchange, Borok, USSR, 1979. Contbr. articles to profl. jours. Recipient Moffett publ. award Fish and Wildlife Service, 1976. Mem. Am. Fisheries Soc., Am. Chem. Soc., Internat. Assn. for Gt. Lakes Research. Current work: Types, amounts and effects of chemical contaminants in Great Lakes fisheries. Subspecialties: Analytical chemistry; Environmental toxicology. Office: Great Lakes Fishery Lab Fish and Wildlife Service US Dept Interior 1451 Green Rd Ann Arbor MI 48105

WILLIAMS, ALBERT LYNN, JR., investment corporation executive; b. Harrisburg, Pa., Aug. 26, 1935; s. Albert Lynn and Ruth (Bloom) W.; m. Catherine Cranford, July 25, 1961 (div. 1965); m. Warrene Thompson, Jan. 10, 1983; 1 child, Gail Whitney. B.A., Yale U., 1957. Lectr. Nanyang U., Singapore, 1960-61; investment research officer J.P. Morgan Co., N.Y.C., 1969-70; chmn. bd. Cutler Williams, Inc., Dallas, 1970-75; pres. 313 William St. Corp., Key West, Fla., 1975—; pres. Albert L. Williams Found., Key West, 1966—. Served with U.S. Army, 1957-60. Mem. AIAA, Space Studies Inst., Am. Astronautical Soc., Am. Interstellar Soc., Am. Assn. Artificial Intelligence, L-5 Soc. Clubs: Links; Am. Yacht (Rye, N.Y.). Current work: Medical application of artificial intelligence, economic and political systems simulation, genetic engineering, maglev transportation, solar cells. Subspecialties: Artificial intelligence; Space industrialization. Home and Office: PO Box 2 Key West FL 33041

WILLIAMS, AUBREY JAMES, electrical engineer, consultant; b. Kingston, Ont., Can., Aug. 29, 1930; came to U.S., 1965, naturalized, 1971; s. James and Sarah Jane (Gamble) W.; m. Alice Teresa Moore, Oct. 26, 1957; children—Myra Leslie, Kevin Hugh, Nancy Ann, Kelly Lynn. B.S.E.E., Queen's U., Kingston, 1957. Registered profl. engr., Que., Ga. Elec. engr. Iron Ore Co. of Can., Schefferville, Que., 1957-65; sr. engr. Bechtel Corp., Gaithersburg, Md., 1965-68; chief elec. engr. DeLeuw Cather & Co., Washington, 1968-73, MetroAtlanta, 1973-79; engring. mgr. Niagara Frontier Transp. Authority, Buffalo, 1979-81; project mgr. systems Parsons Brinckerhoff, Atlanta, 1981—, cons. 1981—. Mem. Nat. Soc. Profl. Engrs., Ga. Soc. Profl. Engrs., IEEE. Roman Catholic. Current work: Systems and subsystems for transit (railsystems) including people movers, light rail systems, heavy rail systems and high speed rail systems; evaluation of energy applications and cost. Subspecialties: Electrical engineering; Systems engineering. Home: 2828 Livsey Ct Tucker GA 30084

WILLIAMS, CARROLL MILTON, biologist, entomologist; educator; b. Richmond, Va., Dec. 2, 1916; s. George Leslie and Jessie Ann (Henricks) W.; m. Muriel Anne Voter, June 26, 1944; children: John Leslie (dec.), Wesley Conant, Peter Glenn (dec.), Roger Lee. B.S., U. Richmond, 1937, D.Sc. (hon.), 1960; A.M., Harvard U., 1938, Ph.D., 1941, M.D., 1946. Jr. prize fellow Harvard U., Cambridge, Mass., 1941-46, asst. prof. biology, 1946-48, assoc. prof. biology, 1943-53, prof. biology, 1953-65, Benjamin Bussey prof. biology, 1965—, chmn. dept. biology, 1959-62; chmn. Harvard U. Sci. Ctr., 1975-79; cons. in field. Author, co-author numerous papers in sci. jours. Mem. ACLA, Planned Parenthood, Zero Population Growth, Citizens for a Livable World. Cambridge U. Guggenheim fellow, 1955-56; recipient Harvard U. Med. Sch. Boylston medal, 1961, Harvard U. George Ledlie award, 1967, U. Chgo. Howard Taylor Ticketts award, 1969. Fellow Am. Acad. Arts and Scis., AAAS (council 1952-55, 74-77, Newcomb Cleveland prize 1950); mem. Nat. Acad. Scis. (chmn. zoology and anatomy sect. 1970-73, council 1973-76, 85—, chmn. biol. sci. 1981-84), Am. Philos. Soc., Inst. Medicine, Phi Beta Kappa, Sigma Xi. Democrat. Clubs: Harvard Faculty, Examiner, Cambridge Scientific, Signet Soc. Current Work: Endocrinology and developmental biology of insects. Subspecialty: Developmental biology. Home: 27 Eliot Rd Lexington MA 02173 Office: Harvard Biological Laboratories 16 Divinity Ave Cambridge MA 02138

WILLIAMS, CHARLES EDWARD, ceramic engineer; b. Warsaw, N.Y., July 9, 1939; s. Charles Dwight and Oletha (Davenport) W.; m. Grace Robertson, June 30, 1963 (div. May 1971); m. Virginia Vee Perkins, May 3, 1980. B.S. in Ceramic Engring., Alfred U., 1961; M.S. in Phys. Metallurgy, Denver U., 1968. Ceramic engr. Dow Chem. Co., Rocky Flats, Colo., 1961-65; devel. engr. Coors Porcelain Co., Golden, Colo., 1965-69; ceramic engr. Fairchild Semicondr., San Diego, 1969-71; sales engr. Otto Jahnke Assocs., El Cajon, Calif., 1971-72; plant engr. Temple Industries, Tecate, Mexico, 1972-73; sr. ceramic engr. Ceramic div. Buckbee Mears Co., El Cajon, 1973-75; process engr., mem. tech. staff Tex. Instruments, Dallas, 1975—, process engr. Hybrid Lab., 1983—; cons. ceramic capacitors, San Diego, 1971-75; pres. Lafitte Ceramics, Dallas, 1981—. Author, patentee in field. Campaign worker Com. to Re-elect Steve Bartlett to Congress, Dallas, 1984. Mem. Am. Ceramic Soc., Internat. Electronic Packaging Soc., Nat. Rifle Assn., Dallas Fencers Club (sec. 1984-85). Republican. Presbyterian. Current work: Development of new electronic packages and packaging methods; modification and development of new ceramic materials and metals for use in electronic packages and other applications; develop new glazes and ceramic bodies for pottery and decorative ceramics. Subspecialties: Ceramic engineering; Ceramics. Home: 6230 Ellsworth St Dallas TX 75214 Office: Tex Instruments M/S 88 PO Box 660246 Dallas TX 75266

WILLIAMS, CURTIS ALVIN, JR., educator, researcher, editor; b. Moorestown, N.J., June 26, 1927; s. Curtis A. and Nola Allen (Johnson) W.; m. Marjorie R. King, Jan. 20, 1960; children: Jennifer, Scott, Elisabeth. Student, Swarthmore Coll., 1946-49; B.S., Pa. State U., 1950; Ph.D., Rutgers U., 1954. Fellow Pasteur Inst., Paris, 1952-54, Carlsberg Lab., Copenhagen, 1954-56; research assoc. Rockefeller U., 1955-60, asst. prof., 1960-65, assoc. prof., 1965-70, adj. prof., 1970-78; prof. biology SUNY, Purchase, 1969—; dean SUNY (Natural Scis.), 1969-80. Editor: Methods in Immunology and Immunochemistry, Volumes I-V; contbr. numerous articles in field. Grantee in field. Mem. Am. Assn. Immunology, Soc. Neurosci., Am. Soc. Microbiology, Electrophoresis Soc. (recipient Founders award 1982). Current Work: Research on animal models and mechanism for neuropsychiat. disorders associated with autoimmune diseases. Subspecialties: Neuroimmunology; Neurochemistry. Home: 436 Manor Ridge Rd Pelham NY 10803 Office: Division of Natural Science State University of New York Purchase NY 10577

WILLIAMS, DANIEL FRANK, zoology educator; b. Redmond, Oreg., Nov. 20, 1942; s. John Frank and Margaret Lucille (Zehner) W.; m. Susan Diane Waltman, Nov. 28, 1981; children by previous marriage: Matthew, Amy. B.A., Central Wash. State Coll., 1966; M.S., U. N.Mex., 1968, Ph.D., 1971. Lab. technician Shell Oil Co., Seattle, 1962-63; grad. teaching asst. U. N.Mex., Albuquerque, 1966-71; asst. prof. biology Calif. State U.-Stanislaus, 1971-75, assoc. prof., 1975-80, prof. zoology, 1980—; postdoctoral fellow Carnegie Inst., Pitts., 1977-78, research assoc., 1978—; dir. Inst. Ecology, Calif. State Coll., 1977-82; cons. Forest Service, U.S. Dept. Agr., Berkeley, Calif., 1977—. Author: Systematics and Ecogeographic Variation of the Apache Pocket Mouse, 1978, Mammalian Species of Special Concern in California, California Wildlife and Their Habitats, 1980; Editor: (with Sydney Anderson) Mammalian Species, 1978-82. NDEA Title IV fellow HEW, 1966-69; Ford Found. fellow, 1964-66; U.S. Dept. Agr. grantee, 1977—. Mem. Am. Soc. Mammalogists, Soc. Study of Evolution, Soc. Systematic Zoology, Ecol. Soc. Am., Wildlife Soc., Phi Sigma. Current Work: Management and conservation of nongame wildlife species; ecology, evolution and systematics of mammals; habitat inventory of small mammals; cytoegenetics. Subspecialties: Resource management; Evolutionary biology. Office: Calif State Univ Dept Biology Turlock CA 95380

WILLIAMS, DONALD JOHN, research physicist; b. Fitchburg, Mass., Dec. 25, 1933; s. Toivo John and Ina (Kokkinen) W.; m. Priscilla Mary Gagnon, July 4, 1953; children: Steven John, Craig Mitchell, Eino Stenroos. B.S., Yale U., 1955, M.S., 1958, Ph.D., 1962. Sr. staff physicist Applied Physics Lab., Johns Hopkins U., 1961-65; head particle physics br. Goddard Space Flight Center, NASA, 1965-70; dir. Space Environ. Lab., NOAA, Boulder, Colo., 1970-82; prin. investigator Energetic Particles expt. NASA Galileo Mission, 1977—; research physicist Johns Hopkins U. Applied Physics Lab., 1982—; mem. nat. and internat. sci. planning coms. Author: (with L.R. Lyons) Quantitative Aspects of Magnetospheric Physics, 1983; assoc. editor: Jour. Geophys. Research, 1967-69, Revs. of Geophysics and Space Research, 1984—; editor: (with G.D. Mead) Physics of the Magnetosphere, 1969, Physics of Solar-Planetary Environments, 1976; mem. editorial bd.: Space Sci. Revs., 1975—; contbr. articles to profl. jours. Served to lt. USAF, 1955-57. Recipient Sci. Research award, 1974; Disting. Authorship award, 1976. Mem. AAAS, Am. Geophys. Soc., Am. Phys. Soc. Current Work: Research in space plasma physics applied to solar system physics, solar-terrestrial physics and planetary environments including the earth. Subspecialties: Satellite studies; Planetary science. Home: 5611 Suffield Court Columbia MD 21044

WILLIAMS, GARY MURRAY, biomedical researcher; b. Regina, Sask., Can., May 7, 1940; s. Murray Austin and Selma Ruby (Domstad) W.; m. Christine Lundberg, Nov. 26, 1966; children: Walter, Jeffrey, Ingrid. B.A., Washington and Jefferson Coll., 1963; M.D., U. Pitts., 1967. Diplomate: Am. Bd. Pathology, Am. Bd. Toxicology. Intern, then resident Mass. Gen. Hosp., Boston, 1967-69; staff assoc. Nat. Cancer Inst., Bethesda, Md., 1969-71; asst. prof. Temple U., 1971-75; chief div. pathology and toxicology Naylor Dana Inst. Disease Prevention, Valhalla, N.Y., 1979-80, chief div. pathology and toxicology and assoc. dir. inst., 1980—; research prof. N.Y. Med. Coll. Contbr. articles to profl. jours. Served with USPHS, 1969-71. Recipient Sheard-Sandford award Am. Soc. Clin. Pathologists, 1967; Arnold J. Lehman award Soc. Toxicology, 1982. Mem. Am. Assn. Cancer Research, Am. Assn. Pathologists, Internat. Acad. Pathology, Environ. Mutagen Soc., Soc. Toxicology; mem. Assn. Univ. Pathologists; mem. Soc. Toxicologic Pathologists; mem. Mem. Phi Beta Kappa, Alpha Omega Alpha. Lutheran. Club: Vasa Order. Current Work: Mechanism of action of chemical carcinogens. Subspecialties: Pathology (medicine); Cell study oncology. Home: 8 Elm Rd Scarsdale NY 10583 Office: Naylor Dana Inst Am Health Found 1 Dana Rd Valahalla NY 10595

WILLIAMS, GERALD ALBERT, internist, educator; b. Plankinton, S.D., Apr. 1, 1921; s. Albert Thomas and Leila Belle (Morehead) W.; m. Dorothy Jayne Burks, Aug. 12, 1950; children—Jeffrey B., Douglas A., Jonathon G. B.S., S.D. State U., 1945; M.D., George Washington U., 1949. Diplomate Am. Bd. Internal Medicine. Intern U.S. Navy, Phila., 1949-50; resident VA, Washington, 1950-55; fellow dept. endocrinology U. Va., Charlottsville, 1955-57, instr., 1957-59; chief sect. endocrinology and nuclear medicine VA West Side Hosp., Chgo., 1959—; chief sect. endocrinology and nuclear medicine, attending physician U. Ill. Coll. Medicine, Chgo., 1959—. Contbg. author chpts. to various books in field. Contbr. articles to profl. jours. Served to lt. USNR, 1949-50. Recipient Research award VA, 1959—; NIH grantee, 1962-66. Fellow ACP; mem. Endocrine Soc., Soc. Exptl. Biology and Medicine, Central Soc. Clin. Research, Chgo. Endocrine Club (pres. 1960-64). Republican. Methodist. Current work: Evaluation of hormonal control calcium metabolism, especially factors in parathyroid hormone cacitonin secretion. Subspecialties: Endocrinology; Nuclear medicine. Home: 734 N Elmwood Ave Oak Park IL 60302 Office: VA Wet Side Med Ctr PO Box 8195 MP 115 Chicago IL 60680

WILLIAMS, GORDON LEE, research molecular geneticist, genetic engr., educator; b. Mechanicsburg, Pa., Sept. 9, 1947; s. Frank B. and Eva M. (Bowman) W.; m. Phyllis Jaye Reynolds, June 14, 1969; children: Eric Alan, Paul Andrew, Jennifer Lynn. B.A. with honors in Biology and Psychology, Lehigh U., 1969; Ph.D. in Genetics (Alumni research fellow), U. N.H., 1972. Asst. prof. biology Wilmington (Ohio) Coll., 1972-76; asst. prof. biology, coordinator biomed. scis. SUNY, Fredonia, 1976-79, asso. prof., chmn. biology dept., dir. biomed. scis., 1979-80; sr. research scientist, project mgr. molecular genetics Battelle Pacific N.W. Labs., Richland, Wash., 1980-83; research and devel. mgr. Northwest Biotech., Inc., 1983—; cons. Jamestown (N.Y.) Gen. Hosp., 1977-80; adj. prof. grad. genetics Wash. State U., Pullman, 1982—; mem. oil shale task force U.S. Dept. Energy, 1980-81. Contbr. articles to profl. jours.; patentee in field; discovered Quasmid DNA in bacteria, 1983. Bd. dirs. S.W. N.Y. Chpt. Am. Cancer Soc., 1978-80; mem. research bd. Western N.Y. chpt. Am. Heart Assn., 1979-80. NIMH fellow, 1968-69; grantee N.Y. Dept. Public Health; grantee SUNY Research Corp.; grantee NSF; grantee Sigma Xi; recipient citation for program excellence Am. Soc. Allied Health Professions, 1978, Chancellor's award SUNY, 1979. Mem. N.Y. Acad. Scis., Ohio Acad. Scis., Genetics Soc. Am., Am. Soc. Microbiology, Sigma Xi. Current Work: Applied and basic recombinant DNA research; genetic engineering of microorganisms and eucaroyotes; genetic transformation; proprietary gene exchange systems. Subspecialties: Genetics and genetic engineering (biology); Molecular biology. Home: 741 Grosscup Blvd West Richland WA 99352 Office: Battelle Pacific NW Lab Richland WA 99352

WILLIAMS, HAROLD LLOYD, research chemist; b. Houston, May 6, 1932; s. John Luther Williams and Inez (Clifford) Owens; m. Essie Lee Daniels, Dec. 19, 1954; children—Byron Keith, Belden Norman, Bruce Clifford. B.S., Tex. Coll., 1953; M.S., Tex. So. U., 1959; Ed.D., George Washington U., 1983. Instr., Tex. So. U., Houston, 1959-61; research chemist Walter Reed Army Inst. Research, Washington, 1959—. Contbr. biochem. and med. articles to profl. jours. Sci. coordinator Sch. Without Walls, D.C. Pub. Schs., 1974-84, recipient Appreciation letters; treas. Candidates for Howard County Sch. Bd., Columbia, Md., 1980; chmn. bd. deacons St. John Baptist Ch., Columbia, 1980-84, named Man of Year 1983; v.p. Columbia Tots and Teens, 1983-84, pres., 1985-86. Named Sci. Coordinator of Year Joint Bd. Sci. Educators, 1971; recipient Outstanding Performance award Walter Reed Army Inst. Research, 1985. Mem. Am. Assn. Clin. Chemistry, Am. Chem. Soc., AAAS, Nat. Orgn. Black Chemists and Chem. Engrs., Nat. Orgn. Black Scientists, Am. Assn. Ednl. Adminstrs., Alpha Phi Alpha. Democrat. Baptist. Current work: Studies on red cell metabolism and enzymology related to blood and blood disorders. Subspecialties: Biochemistry (medicine); Analytical chemistry. Home: 4953 W Running Brook Rd Columbia MD 21044 Office: Walter Reed Army Inst Research 6800 Georgia Ave NW Washington DC 20307

WILLIAMS, JACK MARVIN, chemist; b. Delta, Colo., Sept. 26, 1938; s. John Davis and Ruth Emma (Gallup) W.; m. Joan Marlene Davis, Mar. 7, 1958; 3 children. B.S. with honors, Lewis and Clark Coll., 1960; M.S., Wash. State U., 1964, Ph.D., 1966. Postdoctoral fellow Argonne (Ill.), Nat. Lab., 1966-68, asst. chemist, 1968-70, assoc. chemist, 1970-72, chemist, 1972-77, sr. chemist, group leader, 1977—; vis. guest prof. U. Mo., Columbia, 1980, 81, U. Copenhagen, 1980, 83, 85. Bd. editors: Inorganic Chemistry, 1979—; assoc. editor, 1982—. Crown-Zellerbach scholar, 1959-60; NDEA fellow, 1960-63. Mem. Am. Crystallographic Assn., Am. Chem. Soc. (treas. inorganic div. 1982), Am. Phys. Soc., AAAS. Current work: Organic conductors and superconductors. Subspecialties: Inorganic chemistry; Crystallography. Office: Chemistry Div 9700 S Cass Ave Argonne IL 60439

WILLIAMS, JAMES GERARD, astronomer, researcher; b. New Kensington, Pa., Apr. 12, 1941; s. James Emerson and Mary Frances (Bolick) W. B.S., Calif. Inst. Tech., 1963; Ph.D., UCLA, Westwood, 1969. Mem. tech. staff N.Am. Rockwell, Downey, Calif., 1962-68; research scientist, mem. tech. staff Jet Propulsion Lab., Pasadena, Calif., 1969—. Contbr. articles to profl. jours. Recipient Exceptional Sci. Achievement medal NASA, 1976. Mem. Am. Astron. Soc., Am. Geophys. Union, Internat. Astron. Union. Current Work: Analysis of lunar laser range data; orbit of moon; rotations of Earth and moon; dynamical evolution of asteroid orbits; planet crossing asteroids; asteroid families and main belt morphology. Subspecialties: Astronautics; Geophysics. Office: Jet Propulsion Lab 264/700 4800 Oak Grove Dr Pasadena CA 91109

WILLIAMS, JAMES HENRY, JR., mechanical engineer, educator, cons.; b. Newport News, Va., Apr. 4, 1941; s. James H. Williams and Margaret L. (Holt) Mithcell; 1 son, James Henry III. Mech. designer (Homer L. Ferguson scholar), Newport News Apprentice Sch., 1965; S.B., M.I.T., 1967, S.M., 1968; Ph.D., Trinity Coll., Cambridge U., 1970. Sr. design engr. Newport News Shipyard, 1960-70; asst. prof. mech. engring. M.I.T., 1970-74, assoc. prof., 1974-81, prof., 1981—, duPont prof., 1973, Edgerton prof., 1974-76; head M.I.T. (Composite Materials and Nondestructive Evaluation Lab.), 1974—, cons. engring. to numerous cos. Contbr. numerous articles on stress analysis, vibration, fracture mechanics, composite materials and nondestructive testing to profl. jours. Recipient Charles F. Bailey Bronze medal, 1961, Charles F. Bailey Silver medal, 1962, Charles F. Bailey Gold medal, 1963, Baker award M.I.T., 1973, Den Hartog Disting. Educator award M.I.T., 1981. Mem. ASME, Am. Soc. Nondestructive Testing, Nat. Tech. Assn. Subspecialties: Theoretical and applied mechanics; Composite materials. Office: 77 Massachusetts Ave Room 3-360 Cambridge MA 02139

WILLIAMS, JERRY ALBERT, consulting meteorologist; b. St. Petersburg, Fla., Dec. 1, 1933; s. Arthur William and Beulah Gladys (Atherton) W.; m. Adele Mae Cooper, Sept. 11, 1954; children: Jerry Martin, Alan James, Reed Edward (dec.). B.G.S., U. Nebr.-Omaha, 1974. Weather observer/forecaster USAF, Air Weather Service, 1953-74; meteorologist Bechtel, Inc., Fairbanks, Alaska, 1974-75, Oceanroutes, Inc., Palo Alto, Calif., 1976—. Leader Boy Scouts Am., Big Spring, Tex., 1964-67, Eielson AFB, Alaska, 1967-70; commr. Offutt AFB, Omaha, 1970-76; commr., dist. chmn. Eielson AFB, San Jose, Calif., 1976-82. Served with USAF, 1953-74. Mem. Am. Meteorol. Soc. (v.p. farthest north chpt. 1967-70). Republican. Congregationalist. Current Work: Meteorology/oceanography consulting for offshore construction and petroleum industry, operational offshore forecasting. Subspecialties: Meteorology; Climatology. Office: Oceanroutes Inc 3260 Hillview Ave Palo Alto CA 95117

WILLIAMS, JOHN MICHAEL, computer scientist; b. Hollywood, Calif., Aug. 17, 1938; s. Earl Bryan and Genevieve (Donovan) W.; m. Ann Furlong, Apr. 27, 1959 (div. 1968); children—Brian Hilary, Genevieve Alice, Paul Michael, John Michael, Jr.; m. Roxanne Rosse, May 24, 1969. Nat. account mgr. Sperry (Univac), Washington, 1957-67; sr. computer scientist Computer Scis. Corp., Falls Church, Va., 1967-77; dir. security systems System Devel. Corp., McLean, Va., 1977—. Contbr. articles to profl. jours. Mem. IEEE (sr.), Computer Soc. of IEEE, Assn. Computer Machinery, AAAS, Armed Forces Communication Electronics Assn. Current work: Secure computers and networks and large information systems for defense, intelligence, and commercial applications. Subspecialties: Cryptography and data security; Information systems, storage, and retrieval (computer science). Home: 6210 Leeke Forest Ct Bethesda MD 20817 Office: System Devel Corp 7929 Westpark Dr McLean VA 22102

WILLIAMS, J(OHN) W(ARREN), retired chemistry educator; b. Woburn, Mass., Feb. 10, 1898; s. Charles Sampson and Genevieve (Allen) W.; m. Lois Mary Andrews (dec.); 1 child, Janet Andrews. Student Trinity Coll., Hartford, Conn., 1915-17; B.S., Worcester Poly. Inst., 1921; M.S., U. Wis.-Madison, 1922, Ph.D., 1925. Instr. dept. chemistry U. Wis.-Madison, 1925-27, asst. prof. 1927-32, assoc. prof., 1932-38, prof. chemistry, 1938-1968, prof. emeritus, 1968—; fellow NRC, Copenhagen and Leipsig, 1927-28, Internat. Edn. Bd., Upsala, 1934-35, Guggenheim Meml. Found., Oxford, Copenhagen, and Pasadena, 1956-57; vis. prof. chemistry Calif. Inst. Tech,, 1946-47. Author: Experimental Physical Chemistry (with others) 1929, 6th rev. edition 1962. Assoc. editor Jour. Phys. and Colloid Chemistry, 1947-53; Annual Reviews of Phys. Chemistry, 1949-55; editor Ultracentrifugal Analysis in theory and Experiment, 1963. Patentee in field. Served with USN, 1918; served as investigator Office Sci. Research and Devel., 1941-46. Mem. Am. Chem. Soc. (sec., vice chmn. and chmn. div. phys. and inorganic chemistry, 1934-36, vice chmn. and chmn. div. colloid chemistry, 1937-38, chmn. nat. colloid symposium 1947-52, Kendall award 1955), Nat. Acad. Scis., Am. Soc. Biol. Chemists, Sigma Xi, Tau Beta Pi, Phi Gamma Delta. Congregationalist. Subspecialty: Physical chemistry. Office: Dept Chemistry U Wis 1101 University Ave Madison WI 53706

WILLIAMS, KEITH ALAN, electronics engineer; b. Indpls., June 7, 1951; s. Herbert Otto and Gladys A. (Ruff) W.; m. Kimberly S. Anderson, May 6, 1978; children—Kassandra Ann, Kenneth Andrew, Katherine Amelia. B.S. in Chemistry, Purdue U., 1976, B.S. in Engring., 1984. Research technician Oral Health Research Inst., Indpls., 1977-79, sr. research technologist, 1979-84; electronics engr. Naval Avionics Ctr., Indpls., 1984—. Contbr. articles in field to profl. jours. Mem. IEEE, IEEE Computer Soc. Current work: Logic design of a high-speed, fault-tolerant digital data multiplexer/demultiplexer. Subspecialties: Computer-aided design; Communications systems. Home: 1326 N Ewing Indianapolis IN 46201 Office: Naval Avionics Ctr Applied Research Dept 6000 E 21st St Indianapolis IN 46219-2189

WILLIAMS, LESLEY LATTIN, educator; b. New Bedford, Mass., Aug. 10, 1939; d. Bruce Wallace and Lesley (Olcott) W.; m. Felix Schreiner, July 12, 1969. A.B., Hollins Coll., 1961; Ph.D., U. Wis., 1968. Asst. prof. dept. phys. scis. Chgo. State U., 1968-73, assoc. prof. chemistry, 1973-78, prof., 1978—; lectr. chemistry U. Md. Munich Campus, 1971-72; faculty research participant Argonne Nat. Lab., 1978. Mem. Am. Phys. Soc., Am. Fedn. Tchrs., Sigma Xi, Sigma Delta Epsilon. Current Work: Teacher physical chemistry, instrumental analysis, research interests in radiochemistry, NMR relaxation mechanisms in liquids, physics of music. Subspecialty: Physical chemistry. Office: Chicago State U Dept Phys Scis Chicago IL 60628

WILLIAMS, MARSHALL HENRY, JR., physician, educator; b. New Haven, July 15, 1924; s. Marshall Henry and Henrietta (English) W.; m. Mary Butler, Aug. 27, 1948; children: Stuart, Patricia, Marshall, Frances, Richard. Grad., Pomfret Sch., 1942; B.S., Yale, 1945, M.D., 1947. Diplomate: Nat. Bd. Med. Examiners, Am. Bd. Internal Medicine. Intern Presbyn. Hosp., N.Y.C., 1947-48, asst. resident medicine, 1948-49, New Haven Hosp., 1949-50, asst. in medicine, 1950; trainee Nat. Heart Inst., 1950; practice medicine, specializing in internal medicine, Bronx, N.Y.; chief respiratory sect., dept. cardiorespiratory diseases Army Med. Service Grad. Sch., Walter Reed Army Med. Center, 1953-55; dir. cardiorespiratory lab. Grasslands Hosp., Valhalla, N.Y., 1955-59; dir. chest service Bronx Municipal Hosp. Center, 1959; vis. asst. prof. physiology Albert Einstein Coll. Medicine, Bronx, N.Y., 1955-59, assoc. prof. medicine and physiology, 1959-66, prof. medicine, 1966—; dir. pulmonary div. Albert Einstein Coll. Medicine—Montefiore Hosp. and Med. Ctr., 1966—. Author: Clinical Applications of Cardiopulmonary Physiology, 1960, Essentials of Pulmonary Medicine, 1982; Contbr. articles to profl. jours. Served from 1st lt. to capt. U.S. Army, 1950-52. Mem. Am. Physiol. Soc., A.A.A.S., Am., Westchester (past pres.) heart assns., Am. Thoracic Soc., Am. Fedn. Clin. Research, N.Y. Acad. Sci., N.Y. Trudeau Soc. (past pres.), Am. Soc. Clin. Investigation, Soc. Urban Physicians (past pres.), N.Y. Tb. and Health Assn. (past dir.), Alpha Omega Alpha. Subspecialty: Pulmonary medicine. Home: 13 Colvin Rd Scarsdale NY 10583 Office: Albert Einstein Coll Medicine Bronx NY 10461

WILLIAMS, MARTHA ETHELYN, educator; b. Chgo., Sept. 21, 1934; d. Harold Milton and Alice Rosemond (Fox) W. B.A., Barat Coll., 1955; M.A., Loyola U., 1957. With IIT Research Inst., Chgo., 1957-72, mgr. info. scis., 1962-72, mgr. computer search center, 1968-72; adj. asso. prof. sci. info. Ill. Inst. Tech., Chgo., 1965-73, lectr. chemistry dept., 1968-70; research prof. info. sci., coordinated sci. lab. (Coll. Engring.); also dir. info. retrieval research lab., affiliate computer sci. dept. U. Ill., Urbana, 1972—; chmn. large data base conf. Nat. Acad. Sci./NRC, 1974, mem. ad hoc panel on info. storage and retrieval, 1977, numerical data adv. bd., 1979-82; mem. task force on sci. info. activities NSF, 1977; U.S. rep. review com. for project on broad system of ordering, UNESCO, Hague, Netherlands, 1974; vice chmn. Gordon Research Conf. on Sci. Info. Problems in Research, 1978, chmn., 1980; cons. to numerous cos. and research founds. Contbr. numerous articles to profl. jours.; editor-in-chief: Computer-Readable Databases—A Directory and Data Sourcebook, 1976; editor, Ann. Rev. Info. Sci. and Tech., 1976—, Online Rev., 1979—; contbg. editor: column on Databases to Bull. Am. Soc. Info. Sci., 1974-78. Trustee Engring. Index, 1974-83, bd. dirs., 1976—, chmn. bd. dirs., 1982-84, v.p., 1978-79, pres., 1980-81; regent Nat. Library Medicine, 1978-82, chmn. bd. regents, 1981. Recipient best paper of year award H. W. Wilson Co., 1975; NSF travel grantee Luxembourg, 1972; NSF travel grantee Honolulu, 1973; NSF travel grantee Tokyo, 1973; NSF travel grantee Mexico City, 1975; NSF travel grantee Scotland, 1976. Fellow AAAS (computers, info. and communication mem.-at-large 1978-81, nominating com. 1983); Mem. Am. Chem. Soc., Am. Soc. Info. Sci. (councilor 1971-72, chmn. networks com. 1973-74, chmn. spl. interest group on SDI 1974-75), Assn. for Computing Machinery (pub. bd. 1972-76), Assn. Sci. Info. Dissemination Centers (v.p. 1971-73, pres. 1975-77), Nat. Acad. Sci. (joint com. with NRC on chem. info. 1971-73), U.S. Nat. Com. for Internat. Fedn. for Documentation. Current Work: Information Science, storage and retrieval databases; online systems; systems analysis and design. Subspecialties: Information systems (Information science); Information systems, storage, and retrieval (computer science). Home: Route 1 Monticello IL 61856 Office: Univ of Ill CSL 5-135 1101 W Springfield St Urbana IL 61801

WILLIAMS, MARVIN WRIGHT, clinical psychologist, educator, researcher; b. Houston, May 10, 1949; s. Marvin Wright and Mary Katherine (Lacey) W. B.A., U.Tex.-Austin, 1971; M.S., Fla. State U., 1976, Ph.D., 1978. Lic. and cert. in psychology, Tex. Staff psychologist VA Med. Ctr., Houston, 1979—; adj. asst. prof. Baylor Coll. Medicine, Houston, 1980—; adj. asst. prof. psychology U. Houston, 1982—. USPHS fellow NIMH, 1973-76; recipient cert. of recognition DAV, 1980. Mem. Am. Psychol. Assn. (cert. of recognition for pub. service 1981), Southeastern Psychol. Assn., Am. Group Psychotherapy Assn., Am. Assn. Correctional Psychologists. Current Work: Dangerous behavior, the law/psychology interface, neuropsychology. Currently involved in clinical work, research, teaching and training in a large VA Medical Center. Office: VA Medical Ctr Psychology Service 2002 Holcombe Blvd Houston TX 77211

WILLIAMS, NORRIS HAGAN, plant taxonomist; b. Birmingham, Ala., Mar. 31, 1943; s. Norris H. and Ernestyne E. (Brown) W.; m. Nancy Fraser, June 26, 1970; children—Matthew Ian, Luke Fraser. B.S., U. Ala., 1964; postgrad. Washington U., St. Louis, 1964-65; M.S., U. Ala., 1967; Ph.D., U. Miami (Fla.), 1971. Asst. prof. Fla. State U., Tallahassee, 1973-78, assoc. prof., 1978-81; assoc. curator Fla. State Mus., U. Fla., Gainesville, 1981-84, curator, joint prof. botany, 1984—, chmn. dept. natural scis., 1985—. Mem. Bot. Soc. Am., Am. Chem. Soc., Am. Assn. Plant Taxonomists, Internat. Assn. for Plant Taxonomy, Assn. for Tropical Biology. Current work: Systematics and evolution of Orchidaceae, chemical attraction of insects to plants, pollen morphology of Gesneriaceae. Subspecialties: Taxonomy; Evolutionary biology. Home: 2430 NW 38th St Gainesville FL 32605 Office: Fla State Museum Univ of Fla Gainesville FL 32611

WILLIAMS, PETER MACLELLAN, nuclear engineer, project manager; b. N.Y.C., Aug. 30, 1931; s. Gilbert Harris and Evelyn (Buss) W.; m. Lois Crane, Oct. 9, 1956; children: Jane, Gilbert, Katherine, Anne, Louise, Robert. B. Chem. Engring., Cornell U., 1954; M.S., MIT, 1957; Ph.D., U. Md., 1971. Engr. Dupont Savannah River, Aiken, S.C., 1954-55; task engr. AGN, San Ramon, Calif., 1957-60; project mgr. Am. Machine & Foundry, Greenwich, Conn., 1960-62; research staff mem. Princeton U., 1962-67; sr. project mgr. U.S. Nuclear Regulatory Comm., Washington, 1967—. Scoutmaster Boy Scouts Am., Potomac, Md., 1972; pres. Winston Churchill High Sch. PTA, Potomac, 1981. Recipient U.S. Nuclear Regulatory Commn. High Quality Service award, 1982. Mem. ASME, Am. Nuclear Soc., Sigma Xi. Democrat. Unitarian. Patentee liquid core nuclear rocket. Current Work: High temperature gas cooled ractors for commercial power, safety and licensing requirements. Subspecialties: Nuclear fission; Fluid mechanics. Home: 9418 Thrush Ln Potomac MD 20854 Office: US Nuclear Regulatory Commn Washington DC 20555

WILLIAMS, RICHARD, research physical chemist; b. Chgo., Aug. 5, 1927; s. Frank B. and Nadia (Mortimer) W.; m. Alma Maria Eusebietti, Sept. 2, 1961; children—Elena, Christina, Matthew. A.B. in Chemistry, Miami U., Oxford, Ohio, 1950; Ph.D. in Chemistry, Harvard U., 1954. Instr. chemistry Harvard U., Cambridge, Mass., 1955-58; mem. tech. staff RCA Labs., Princeton, N.J., 1958—; Fulbright lectr. Escola de Engenharia, Sao Carlos, Brazil, 1969; vis. prof. Instituto Politecnico Nacional, Mex., 1972. Author: Fisica de Aislantes, 1971. Mem. editorial bd. Jour. Applied Physics, 1980-83. Patentee in field. Mem. N.J. Sc. Adv. Council, Trenton, 1983-84. Served with U.S. Army, 1954-55. Recipient Callinan award Electrochem. Soc., 1978. Fellow Am. Phys. Soc.; mem. Brazilian Acad. Sci. (corr.). Current work: Physical chemistry of interfaces, electrical properties of insulators, capillary phenomena, solar energy utilization. Subspecialties: Photochemistry; Condensed matter physics. Office: RCA Labs Princeton NJ 08540

WILLIAMS, RONALD OSCAR, systems engineer; b. Denver, May 10, 1940; s. Oscar H. and Evelyn (Johnson) W. B.S. in Applied Math, Colo., Coll. Engring., U. 1964, also postgrad.; postgrad. U. Denver, George Washington U. Computer programmer Apollo systems dept. Missile & Space div. Gen. Electric Co., Kennedy Space Center, Fla., 1965-67, Manned Spacecraft Ctr., Houston, 1967-68; computer programmer U. Colo., Boulder, 1968-73; computer programmer analyst Def. Systems div. System Devel. Corp., N.Am. Aerospace Def. Command, Colorado Springs, Colo., 1974-75; engr. Def. Systems div. and Command and Info. Systems div. Martin Marietta Aerospace, Denver, 1976-80; systems engr. Space and Communications group Def. Systems div. Hughes Aircraft Co., Aurora, Colo., 1980—. Vol. fireman Clear Lake City Fire Dept., Tex., 1968; Officer, rescue squadman Boulder Emergency Squad, 1969-76, liaison officer to cadets, 1971, personnel officer, mem. exec. bd., 1971-76; emergency med. technician, 1973—; spl. police officer Boulder Police Dept., 1970-75; spl. dep. sheriff Boulder County Sheriff's Dept., 1970-71; mem. nat. adv. bd. Am. Security Council, Coalition of Peace through Strength, 1979—; mem. Republican Nat. Com., Rep. nat. Senatorial Com. Served with USMCR, 1958-66. Mem. AAAS, Math. Assn. Am., Am. Math. Soc., Soc. Indsl. and Applied Math., AIAA, Armed Forces Communications and Electronics Assn., Assn. Old Crows, Am. Def. Preparedness Assn., Marine Corps Assn., Air Force Assn., Colo. Hist. Soc., Historic Denver Inc., Historic Boulder, Nat. Geog. Soc., Smithsonian Assocs., Met. Opera Guild, Am. Mensa Ltd., Denver Mile Hi Mensa, Denver Art Mus., Denver Bot. Gardens, Denver Mus. Natural History, Denver Zool. Found. Lutheran. Club: Eagles. Subspecialty: Systems engineering. Home: 7504 W Quarto Ave Littleton CO 80123 Office: Hughes Aircraft Co PO Box 31979 Aurora CO 80041

WILLIAMS, T. H. LEE, geography educator; b. Deganwy, Wales, U.K., May 31, 1951; came to U.S., 1976; m. Trevor Glynne and Grace Myfanwy (Owen) W.; m. D.M. Naila Mendes, Apr. 14, 1973; children—Owen-John Roderiques, Samantha Louise. B.Sc. with honors, U. Bristol, Eng., 1972; Ph.D. in Geography, 1977. Tchr. sci. Antigua (W.I.) Grammar Sch., 1972-73; vis. research assoc. U. Okla., Norman, 1976-77; asst. prof. geography U. Kans., Lawrence, 1977-81, assoc. prof., 1981—, mem. Radar Systems and Remote Sensing Lab., 1984—; assoc. fellow Inst. Math. and Its Applications, Eng., 1978; cons. UNESCO, 1978-79, Nat. Park Services, 1979. Mem. Am. Soc. Photogrammetry and Remote Sensing, IEEE. Current Work: Active microwave sensors in arctic sea ice, forestry and image analysis. Subspecialties: Remote sensing (geoscience); Graphics, image processing, and pattern recognition. Home: 1022 Wellington St Lawrence KS 66044 Office: Radar Systems and Remote Sensing Lab Space Tech Ctr U Kans Lawrence KS 66045

WILLIAMS, THEODORE JOSEPH, engineering educator; b. Black Lick, Pa., Sept. 2, 1923; s. Theodore Finley and Mary Ellen (Shields) W.; m. Isabel Annette McAnulty, July 18, 1946; children: Theodore Joseph, Mary Margaret, Charles Augustus, Elizabeth Ann. B.S.Ch.E., Pa. State U., 1949, M.S.Ch.E., 1950, Ph.D., 1955; M.S. in Elec. Engring., Ohio State U., 1956. Research fellow Pa. State U., University Park, 1947-51; asst. prof. Air Force Inst. Tech., 1953-56; technologist Monsanto Co., 1956-57, sr. engring. supr., 1957-65; vis. prof. Washington U., St. Louis, 1962-65; prof engring., dir. control and information systems lab. Purdue U., Lafayette, Ind., 1965-66; dir. Purdue Lab. Applied Indsl. Control, 1966—. Author: Systems Engineering for the Process Industries, 1961, Automatic Control of Chemical and Petroleum Processes, 1961, Progress in Direct Digital Control, 1969, Interfaces with the Process Control Computer, 1971, Modeling and Control of Kraft Production Systems, 1975, Modelling, Estimation and Control of the Soaking Pit, 1983, The Use of Digital Computers in Process Control, 1983; editor: Computer Applications in Shipping and Shipbuilding, 6 vols., 1973-79, Proceedings Advanced Control Confs., 11 vols., 1974-85. Served to 1st lt. USAAF, 1942-45; to capt. USAF, 1951-56. Decorated Air medal with 3 oak leaf clusters. Fellow Instrument Soc. America (pres. 1968-69), Am. Inst. Chemists, Am. Inst. Chem. Engrs., Inst. Measurement and Control (London), AAAS; sr. mem. IEEE; mem. Am. Chem. Soc., Am. Automatic Control Council (pres. 1965-67), Am. Fedn. Info. Processing Socs. (pres. 1976-78), Sigma Xi, Tau Beta Pi, Phi Kappa Phi, Phi Lambda Upsilon. Current Work: Industrial automation; hierarchical computer control systems; mathematical modeling of industrial processes for automatic control. Subspecialties: Distributed systems and networks; Systems engineering. Home: 208 Chippewa St West Lafayette IN 47906 Office: Purdue Lab Applied Indsl Control Potter Research Ctr Purdue Univ Lafayette IN 47907

WILLIAMS, THOMAS FRANKLIN, physician, medical institute director; b. Belmont, N.C., Nov. 26, 1921; s. T.F. and Mary L. (Deaton) W.; m. Catharine Carter Catlett, Dec. 15, 1951; children—Mary Wright, Thomas Nelson. B.S., U. N.C., 1942; M.A., Columbia U., 1943; M.D., Harvard U., 1950. Diplomate: Am. Bd. Internal Medicine. Intern Johns Hopkins, Balt., 1950-51, asst. resident physician, 1951-53; resident physician Boston VA Hosp., 1953-54; research fellow U. N.C., Chapel Hill, 1954-56, instr. dept. medicine and preventive medicine, 1956-57, asst. prof., 1957-61, asso. prof., 1961-68, prof., 1968; attending physician Strong Meml. Hosp., Rochester, N.Y., 1968—; cons. physician Genesee Hosp., 1973—, St. Mary's Hosp., 1974—, Highland Hosp., 1973; all Rochester; prof. medicine, preventive medicine and community health U. Rochester, 1968-83, also prof. radiation biology and biophysics, 1968-82, mem. adv. bd., 1968-83; dir. Nat. Inst. on Aging NIH, 1983—; med. dir. Monroe Community Hosp., Rochester, 1968-83; Mem. rev. coms. Nat. Center for Health Services Research; mem. adv. bd. St. Ann's Home; mem. governing bd. NRC, 1981-83. Contbr. articles on endocrine disorders, diabetes, health care delivery in chronic illness and aging to profl. publs. Served with USNR, 1943-46. USPHS fellow, 1966-67; Markle scholar, 1957-61. Fellow Am. Pub. Health Assn., A.C.P.; mem. N.Y. State, Monroe County med. socs., Inst. Medicine, Nat. Acad. Scis. (council 1980—), Am. Diabetes Assn. (dir. 1974—), AAAS, Am. Fedn. Clin. Research, Soc. Exptl. Biology and Medicine, Rochester Regional Diabetes Assn. (pres. 1977-79), N.C. Council for Human Relations (chmn. 1963-66). Episcopalian. Subspecialty: Gerontology. Office: Nat Inst on Aging NIH Bldg 31 9000 Rockville Pike Bethesda MD 20892

WILLIAMS, WALTER JACKSON, JR., engineer; b. Elkhart, Ind., Jan. 17, 1925; s. Walter Jackson and Mary (Delcamp) W.; m. Helen L. Evans, July 20, 1944; children—David, Eileen, Valerie; m. Evelyn M. Bowyer, May, 1984. B.S. in Elec. Engring, Purdue U., 1948, M.S., 1950; Ph.D., 1954. From grad. asst. to instr. Purdue U., Layfayette, Ind., 1948-54; jr. engr. Argonne Nat. Lab., 1950, Naval Ordnance Plant, Indpls., 1951; engr. Internat. Tel. & Tel. Co., Ft. Wayne, Ind., 1954-60, cons., 1961-63, sr. tech. advisor, 1975-80, tech. dir., 1980—; chmn. dept. elec. engring. Ind. Inst. Tech., Ft. Wayne, 1961-65, dean engring., 1963-67, v.p., acad. dean, 1967-75, interim pres., 1970-72; cons. in field, 1960—. Bd. dirs. Associated Chs., Ft. Wayne, 1965-67. Served with AUS, 1943-46. Mem. IEEE (sr.; chmn. Ft. Wayne sect. 1984-85, dir. 1985—), Am. Soc. Engring. Edn., Nat. Soc. Profl. Engrs., Ind. Soc. Profl. Engrs. (dir. Ft. Wayne 1968-70), Ft. Wayne Engrs. Club (pres. 1967-68, dir. 1969-71), Sigma Xi, Tau Beta Pi, Eta Kappa Nu. Patentee in field. Current work: Providing technical direction and expertise in control systems, spread spectrum communications, and ESM receivers. Subspecialties: Systems engineering; Electronics. Home: 6518 DuMont Dr Fort Wayne IN 46815

WILLIAMS, WENDELL STERLING, materials scientist, educator. Prof. U. Ill., Urbana. Subspecialty: Materials. Office: U Ill Materials Research Lab Urbana IL 61801

WILLIAMSON, HAROLD EMANUEL, pharmacologist; b. Racine, Wis., Aug. 8, 1930; s. Harold E. and Grace Mae (McIntyre) W.; m. Joan Louise Chase, Apr. 28, 1957; children: Timothy, Julie, Eric. B.S., U. Wis., 1953, Ph.D., 1959. Project assoc. pharmacology U. Wis.-Madison, 1959-60; instr. to prof. U. Iowa, Iowa City, 1960—. Contbr. articles on pharmacology to profl. jours. Fellow Am. Coll. Clin. Pharmacology; mem. Am. Soc. for Pharmacology and Exptl. Therapeutics, Am. Soc. Nephrology, Soc. for Exptl. Biology and Medicine, Internat. Soc. Nephrology, Am. Heart Assn., Am. Fedn. for Clin. Research, AAAS. Current Work: Research in renal pharmacology and physiology, mechanisms of action and toxicity of diuretic agents, factor influencing renal blood flow. Subspecialty: Pharmacology. Home: 131 S Mt Vernon Dr Iowa City IA 52240 Office: 2-252 BSB U Iowa Iowa City IA 52242

WILLIAMSON, JAMES LAWRENCE, agricultural company executive; b. Rebecca, Ga., Feb. 28, 1929; s. George Lafayette and Clarice Elizabeth (Livingston) W.; m. Renee Lucille Johnson, Dec. 4, 1949; children—Renee E. Williamson Godbey, Lisa M. Williamson Wichern, Rise M. B.S. in Agr., U. Ga., 1951; M.S., U. Ill., 1952, Ph.D., 1957. Cert. animal scientist. Mgr. beef cattle and sheep research Chow Div., Ralston Purina, St. Louis, 1957-63, mgr. livestock research 1963-64, dir. research, 1964-65, div. v.p., 1965-83; sr. v.p. tech. devel. Purina Mills, Inc., St. Louis, 1983—; mem. adv. com. U.S. Dept. Agr., Washington, 1983—, FDA, Washington, 1985—. Served to capt. USAF, 1951-55, maj. Res. Mem. Am. Soc. Animal Sci. (bd. dirs. 1976-78), Am. Dairy Assn., Poultry Sci. Assn., Agrl. Research Inst. (chmn. 1984), Indsl. Research Inst., U.S. Power Squadron. Republican. Methodist. Current work: Research management; product acquisition; business development. Subspecialty: Animal nutrition. Office: Purina Mills Inc Checkerboard Sq Saint Louis MO 63188

WILLIS, ISAAC, dermatologist; b. Albany, Ga., July 13, 1940; s. R.L. and Susie M. (Miller) W.; m. Alliene Horne, June 12, 1965; children: Isaac Horne, Alliric Isaac. B.S., Morehouse Coll., 1961; M.D., Howard U., 1965. Diplomate: Am. Bd. Dermatology. Intern Phila. Gen. Hosp., 1965-66; fellow Howard U., Washington, 1966-67; resident, fellow U. Pa., Phila., 1967-69, assoc. in dermatology, 1969-70; instr. dept. dermatology U. Calif.-San Francisco, 1970-72; asst. prof. Johns Hopkins U. and Johns Hopkins Hosp., Balt., 1972-73; asst. prof. Emory U., Atlanta, 1973-77, assoc. prof., 1977-82; prof. Morehouse Sch. Medicine, Atlanta, 1982—; attending staff Phila. Gen. Hosp., 1969-70, Moffit Hosp., U. Calif., 1970-72, Johns Hopkins Hosp., Balt. City Hosp., Good Samaritan Hosp., 1972-74, Crawford W. Long Meml. Hosp., Atlanta, 1974—, West Paces Ferry Hosp., Atlanta, 1974—, others; mem. Group A Medicine Study Sect. NIH, 1985—; cons. in field. Author: Textbook of Dermatology, 1971—; Contbr. articles to profl. jours. Chmn. bd. med. dirs. Lupus Erythematosus Found., Atlanta, 1975-83; bd. dirs. Jacquelyn McClure Lupus Erythematosus Clinic, 1982—; bd. med. dirs. Skin Cancer Found., 1980—; trustee Friendship Bapt. Ch., Atlanta, 1980—. Nat. Cancer Inst. grantee, 1974-77, 78—; EPA grantee, 1980—, 82—. Fellow Am. Acad. Dermatolgy, Am. Dermtol. Assn.; mem. Soc. Investigative Dermatology, Am. Fedn. Clin. Research, AAAS, Am. Soc. Photobiology, Am. Med. Assn., Nat. Med. Assn., Internat. Soc. Tropical Dermatology, Pan Am. Med. Assn., Phi Beta Kappa. Clubs: Frontiers Internat, Sportsman Internat. Current Work: Clinical therapy and research in dermatology and photomedicine including cancer research. Subspecialties: Dermatology; Cancer research (medicine). Home: 1141 Regency Rd NW Atlanta GA 30327 Office: NW Med Center Suite 342 3280 Howell Mill Rd NW Atlanta GA 30327

WILLIS, JOHN PATRICK, chemist; b. Albany, N.Y., Mar. 10, 1947; s. John James and Mary Catherine (Varden) W.; m. Tientje Jane Dirzuweit, July 22, 1972. B.S., Iona Coll., 1969; M.S., SUNY-Oswego, 1974; Ph.D., U. Conn., 1977. Prodn. chemist Winthrop Labs., Rensselaer, N.Y., 1970-72; research chemist Uniroyal, Inc., Middlebury, Conn., 1977-79; research assoc. U. Minn., Mpls., 1979-80; mgr. chem. research NOVA Biomed. Corp., Newton, Mass., 1980-83; chmn., tech. dir. Insenco, Inc., Woburn, Mass., 1983-84; chmn., tech. dir. ILEX Corp., Woburn, 1985—. Contbr. articles to profl. jours. Patentee in field. U. Conn. fellow, 1977. Mem. Am. Chem. Soc., Am. Assn. Clin. Chemistry, N.Y. Acad. Sci., Electrochem. Soc., Am. Inst. Chemists, Phi Kappa Phi, Sigma Xi. Democrat. Roman Catholic. Current work: Research in bioelectrochemistry; applications of biosensors in medicine and biomimetic membranes. Subspecialties: Organic chemistry; Biochemistry (medicine).

WILLMAN, MICHAEL KAREL, radiologist; b. Detroit, Feb. 6, 1941; s. Michael Joseph and Minnie Ann (Simerka) W.; m. Janet Faye Burchett, May 20, 1965; children: Michael, Paul, Amy. D.O., Kansas City Coll. Osteopathic Medicine, 1965. Family practice osteopathic medicine, Rochester, Mich., 1966-67; resident in radiology Kirksville (Mo.) Coll. Osteopathic Medicine, 1969-72, radiologist, 1972—. Bd. dirs. YMCA, 1972-81, pres., 1979. Served to maj. AUS, 1967-69, Vietnam. Decorated Bronze Star. Mem. Am. Osteopathic Coll. Radiology (sec. 1975-82, v.p. 1982-83), Am. Osteopathic Assn., Mo. Assn. Osteopathic Physicians and Surgeons, Northeast Assn. Osteopathic Physicians and Surgeons, Radiol. Soc. N. Am. Club: Kirksville Country (pres. 1980-81). Subspecialties: Diagnostic radiology; Radiology in nuclear medicine. Home: East Hwy 6 Kirksville MO 63501 Office: Kirksville Osteopathic Health Center 800 W Jefferson St Kirksville MO 63501

WILLOUGHBY, NANCY BHARUCHA, nuclear engineer, consultant; b. Aug. 6, 1945; came to U.S., 1959; d. Pesi N. and Tehmi (Mistry) Bharucha; m. James Willoughby, 1962 (div. 1963); 1 son, Scot Cleon. B.S., Royal Inst. Sci., 1958; A.T.C.L., Trinity Coll. Music, London; S.M., Harvard U., 1961; postgrad., N.C. State Coll.-Raleigh, 1961-62, 63-65. Registered profl. engr., N.Y., Md. Nuclear engr. Babcock & Wilcox Co., Lynchburg, Va., 1962-63; research/teaching asst. N.C. State U., Raleigh, 1963-65; physicist Picatinny Arsenal, Dover, N.J., 1965-68; nuclear/environ. supr. Consol. Edison, N.Y.C., 1968-70; asst. dir. nuclear tech. N.Y. State Atomic and Space Devel., N.Y.C., 1970-71; project engr. Bechtel Corp., Gaithersburg, Md., 1972—; chmn. standard com. Am. Nat. Standards Inst., 1979—. Contbr. articles to profl. jours. N.C. State U. fellow, 1961, 63, 64; recipient award of merit Bechtel Corp., 1975, 80; Pres. of Year award Exptl. Aircraft Assn., 1972. Mem. Am. Nuclear Soc. (sec. 1977-79, exec. com. 1977-82), ASME, AAAS, IEEE, Exptl. Aircraft Assn. (pres. 1970-80). Zoroastrian. Club: Harvard Engring. (N.Y.C.). Current Work: Reactor safety, radiation protection, aircraft construction. Subspecialties: Nuclear engineering; Environmental engineering. Home: 18700 Walker's Choice Rd Gaithersburg MD 20879 Office: Bechtel Corp 19760 Shady Grove Rd Gaithersburg MD 20877

WILLOWS, ARTHUR OWEN DENNIS, neurobiologist, zoology educator; b. Winnipeg, Man., Can., Mar. 26, 1941; came to U.S., 1959; s. Danby and Laura Beatrice (Bumstead) W.; m. Shirley Alice Stratton, June 15, 1963; children—Kurt Danby, Keith Stratton, Amy Margaret. B.S., Yale U., 1963; Ph.D., U. Oreg., 1967. Asst. prof. U. Wash., Seattle, 1969-72, assoc. prof., 1972-75, prof. zoology, 1975—, chmn. dept., 1979—; dir. Friday Harbor Labs., Wash., 1973—. Editor: Invertebrate Learning, 2 vols., 1973, Neurobiology and Behavior, 2 vols., 1985, Marine Behavior and Physiology. Guggenheim fellow, 1976. Mem. Soc. for Neurosci., Am. Soc. Zoologists, Western Soc. Naturalists, Am. Soc. Physiologists. Subspecialty: Neurobiology. Office: Dept Zoology U Wash Seattle WA 98195

WILLSON, MARY F., ecology educator; b. Madison, Wis., July 28, 1938; d. Gordon L. and Sarah (Loomans) W. B.A. with honors, Grinnell Coll., 1960; Ph.D., U. Wash., 1964. Asst. prof. U. Ill., Urbana, 1965-71, assoc. prof., 1971-76, prof. ecology, 1976—. Author: Plant Reproductive Ecology, 1983, Vertebrate Natural History, 1983; co-author: Mate Choice in Plants, 1983. Fellow Am. Ornithologists Union; mem. Soc. for Study Evolution, Am. Soc. Naturalists, Ecol. Soc. Am. (assoc. editor 1974-78), Brit. Ecol. Soc. Current work: Reproductive ecology in plants. Subspecialty: Ecology (biology). Office: 606 E Healey St Champaign IL 61820

WILLSON, RICHARD CLAYTON, solar radiation scientist; b. Austin, May 18, 1937; s. Richard James and Evelyn Ann W.; m. Marie Elizabeth, Aug. 20, 1977. B.S., U. Colo., 1960, M.S., 1963; Ph.D., UCLA, 1975. Research engr. Jet Propulsion Lab., Calif. Inst. Tech., Pasadena, 1963-65, sr. engr., 1966-75, sr. scientist, 1975-81, mem. tech. staff, 1981—; prin. investigator solar irradiance monitoring NASA. Contbr. numerous sci. articles to profl. publs. Recipient Exceptional Sci. Achievement medal NASA, 1982, others. Mem. Am. Geophys. Union, Am. Meteorol. Soc. Club: Pasadena Athletic. Developed active cavity radiometer instrumentation approach. Current Work: The link between solar irradiance variability and the earth's climate; solar-terrestrial relationships; solar total irradiance variability; measurements of solar irradiance in space flight experiments; weather and climate response to solar variability. Subspecialties: Solar-terrestrial relationships; Solar physics. Office: 4800 Oak Grove Dr 171-400 Pasadena CA 91109

WILSON, ALLAN CHARLES, biochemist; b. Ngaruawahia, N.Z., Oct. 18, 1934; married, 1958; 2 children. B.Sc., U. Otago, N.Z., 1955; M.S., Wash. State U., 1957; Ph.D. in Biochemistry, U. Calif.-Berkeley, 1961. Fellow in biochemistry Brandeis U., 1961-64; from asst. prof. to assoc. prof. U. Calif.-Berkeley, 1964-72, prof. biochemistry, 1972—; mem. Alpha Helix Expdn., New Guinea, 1969. Assoc. editor: Biochemical Genetics, from 1975, Jour. Molecular Evolution, from 1978. Recipient Guggenheim Meml. Found. award Weizmann Inst. Sci., U. Nairobi, 1972-73; grantee NSF, from 1965, NIH, from 1974, MacArthur Found., 1984. Mem. Am. Soc. Biol. Chemistry, Soc. Systematic Zoology. Subspecialty: Genetics and genetic engineering (biology). Office: U Calif Biochemistry Bldg Berkeley CA 94720*

WILSON, ANDREW STEPHEN, astronomer; b. Doncaster, Eng., Mar. 26, 1947; s. Norman and Mary Alice (Beckett) W.; m. Kaija Annikki, Oct. 4, 1975; children: Daniel Marcus, Caroline Johanna. B.A. with 1st class honors, U. Cambridge, 1969, M.A., Ph.D., 1973. Royal Soc. European Program fellow Leiden (Netherlands) Obs., 1973-75; research fellow U. Sussex, Eng., 1975-78; asst. prof. astronomy U. Md., College Park, 1978-81, assoc. prof., 1981—. Contbr. articles to profl. jours. Grantee NASA, NSF, 1979—. Fellow Royal Astron. Soc.; mem. Internat. Astron. Union, Am. Astron. Soc. Current Work: Active galactic nuclei, supernova remnants. Subspecialties: High energy astrophysics; Optical astronomy. Office: Astronomy Program University of Maryland College Park MD 20742

WILSON, ARTHUR JESS, clinical psychologist, consultant; b. Yonkers, N.Y., Oct. 25, 1910; s. Samuel Louis and Anna Lee (Gilbert) W.; m. Lillian Moss, Sept. 16, 1941; children: Warren David, Anton Francis. B.S., NYU, 1935, M.A., 1949, Ph.D., 1961; LL.B., St. Lawrence U., 1940; J.D., Bklyn. Law Sch., 1967. Supr. rehab. N.Y. State Edn. Dept., N.Y.C., 1942-44; rehab. field sec. N.Y. Health Assn., N.Y.C., 1946-48; dir. rehab. Westchester County Med. Ctr., Valhalla, N.Y., 1948-67; dir. N.Y. State Drug Abuse Rehab. Ctr, N.Y.C., 1967-68; clin. psychologist F D Roosevelt VA Hosp., Montrose, N.Y., 1968-72; pvt. practice clin. psychology, Yonkers, 1972—; instr. in psychology Westchester Community Coll., 1966-67; dir. Manhattan Narcotic Rehab. Ctr., 1967-68; cons. in field; participant Clin. Study Tour of mental health facilities in Mainland China, 1980. Author: Emotional Life of the Ill and Injured, 1950. Served with USN, 1944-46. Recipient Founders Day award NYU, 1961; honored as Westchester author Westchester County Hist. Soc. at Washington Irving Celebration, 1957; named Pioneer N.Y. State Narcotic Addiction Control Commn. Mem. N.Y. Acad. Scis., Am. Psychol. ASsn., N.Y. State Psychol. Assn., Internat. Mark Twain Soc. (hon.), Kappa Delta Pi, Phi Dela Kappa, Epsilon Pi Tau. Current Work: Intensive research in psychotherapeutic techniques involving eidetic imagery; application of research to psychotherapy in private practice. Subspecialties: Physical medicine and rehabilitation; Clinical psychology. Home: 487 Park Ave Yonkers NY 10703

WILSON, DAVID BUCKINGHAM, biochemist, educator; b. Cambridge, Mass., Jan. 15, 1940; s. E. Bright and Emily (Buckingham) W.; m. Nancy Jane Heffelfinger, Dec. 23, 1962; children: Allison K., Ashley L., Laurie E. B.A., Harvard U., 1961; Ph.D., Stanford U., 1966. Postdoctoral fellow Johns Hopkins U. Med. Sch., Balt., 1966-67; asst. prof. biochemistry Cornell U., Ithaca, N.Y., 1967-73, assoc. prof., 1973-83, prof., 1984—. Bd. mgrs. Tompkins Community Hosp. Mem. Am. Soc. Biol. Chemists, Am. Soc. Microbiology, AAAS. Democrat. Current Work: Ecoli inner membrane; enzymology of cellulose degradation and genetic engineering of cellulase genes. Subspecialties: Biochemistry (biology); Biomass (energy science and technology). Home: 232 Troy Rd Ithaca NY 14850 Office: Dept Biochemistry Cornell U Ithaca NY 14853

WILSON, EDGAR BRIGHT, chemistry educator; b. Gallatin, Tenn., Dec. 18, 1908; s. Edgar Bright and Alma (Lackey) W.; m. Emily Buckingham, June 15, 1935 (dec. 1954); children: Kenneth, David, Nina (Nina W. Cornell); m. Therese Bremer, July 25, 1955; children: Anne, Paul, Steven. B.S., Princeton U., 1930, A.M., 1931; Ph.D., Calif. Inst. Tech., 1933; A.M., Harvard, 1942; D. honoris causa, U. Brussels, 1975; D.Sc. (hon.), Dickinson Coll., 1976, Columbia U., 1979, Princeton U., 1981, Clarkson Coll., 1983, Harvard U., 1983; Dr. Chem., U. Bologna, 1976. Research fellow Calif. Inst. Tech., 1933-34; jr. fellow Soc. of Fellows Harvard U., 1934-36, asst. prof. chemistry, 1936-39, asso. prof., 1939-46, prof., 1946-79, Theodore William Richards prof. chemistry, 1947-79, prof. emeritus, 1979—; research dir. Underwater Explosives Research Lab., 1942-44; chief div. 2 Nat. Def. Research Com., 1944-46; research dir., weapons systems evaluation group Dept. Def., 1952-53. Author: (with Linus Pauling) Introduction to Quantum Mechanics, 1935, Introduction to Scientific Research, 1952, (with P.C. Cross, J.C. Decius) Molecular Vibrations, 1955. Hon. trustee Woods Hole Oceanographic Instn., 1979—. Recipient Am. Chem. Soc. award, 1937, medal for Merit U.S. govt., 1948, Debye award, 1962; Distinguished Service award Calif. Inst. Tech., 1966; Pauling award, 1972; Rumford medal, 1973; Nat. Medal Sci., 1976; Feltrinelli award, 1976; Ferst award Sigma Xi, 1977; Pitts. Spectroscopy award, 1978; Robert A. Welch award, 1978; Willard Gibbs award, 1979; Lippincott medal, 1979; Guggenheim fellow, 1949-50, 70-71; Fulbright grantee Queen's Coll., Oxford, Eng., 1949-50. Mem. Am. Chem. Soc. (Norris award N.E. sect. 1966, Lewis award Calif. sect. 1969, T.W. Richards medal N.E. sect. 1978), Am. Phys. Soc. (Plyler award 1978), Am. Philos. Soc., Am. Acad. Arts and Scis., Internat. Acad., Quantum Molecular Scis., Nat. Acad. Scis., Phi Beta Kappa. Current Work: Molecular spectroscopy and structure. Subspecialty: Physical chemistry. Office: 12 Oxford St Cambridge MA 02138

WILSON, EDWARD OSBORNE, entomology educator; b. Birmingham, Ala., June 10, 1929; s. Edward Osborne and Inez (Freeman) W.; m. Irene Kelley, Oct. 30, 1955; 1 dau., Catherine Irene. B.S., U. Ala., 1949, M.S., 1950; Ph.D., Harvard U., 1955; D.Sc. (hon.), Duke U., Grinnell Coll., Lawrence U., U. West Fla.; L.H.D., U. Ala.; LL.D., Simon Fraser U. Jr. fellow Soc. Fellows, Harvard, 1953-56, mem. faculty, 1956—, Baird prof. sci., 1976—, curator entomology, 1971—. Author: The Insect Societies, 1971, Sociobiology: The New Synthesis, 1975, On Human Nature, 1978, Promethean Fire, 1983, Biophilia, 1984. Recipient Nat. Medal Sci., 1976; Pulitzer prize for nonfiction, 1979; Leidy medal Acad. Natural Sci., Phila., 1979; Disting. Service award Am. Inst. Biol. Scis., 1976; Mercer award Ecol. Soc. Am., 1971; Founders Meml. award Entomol. Soc. Am., 1972; Archie Carr medal U. Fla., 1978; Disting. Service award Am. Humanist Soc., 1982; Tyler ecology prize, 1984; L.O. Howard award Entomol. Soc. Am., 1985; others. Fellow Am. Acad. Arts and Scis., Am. Phil. Soc., Deutsche Akad. Naturforsch.; mem. Nat. Acad. Sci. Subspecialties: Sociobiology; Evolutionary biology. Home: 9 Foster Rd Lexington MA 02173 Office: Mus Comparative Zoology Harvard Univ Cambridge MA 02138

WILSON, GABRIEL HENRY, radiologist; b. Caruthersville, Mo., Jan. 30, 1929; s. Michael Earl and Alma Alberta (Cecil) W. Student, St. Mary's Coll., 1946-48, UCLA, 1952-53; B.S., Loyola U., Chgo., 1955; M.D., Creighton U., 1959. Diplomate: Nat. Bd. Med. Examiners, Am. Bd. Radiology. Rotating intern Los Angeles County Harbor Gen. Hosp., Torrance, Calif., 1959-60, resident in radiology, 1960-63, staff radiologist, 1963-64, 65-66, vis. physician in neuroradiology, 1964-67, instr. in radiology, 1963-64, asst. prof., 1964-66; asst. prof. radiology UCLA, 1966-70, asso. prof., 1970-74, prof., 1974—, chmn. dept. radiol. scis., 1973-84; med. staff sec. UCLA Hosp. and Clinics, 1978-80, chief of staff, 1980-82; cons. neuroradiology VA Hosp., Long Beach, Calif., 1965-66, cons., Los Angeles, 1965—. Served with USNR, 1948-52. Fellow Am. Coll. Radiology (councilor 1976-81, chancellor 1981—); mem. AMA, Calif. Med. Assn. (asst. sec. sect. on radiology 1970-71, sec. 1971-72, chmn. 1972-74, chmn. adv. panel radiology 1972-73, 76-82), Calif. Radiol. Soc. (exec. com. 1976—, pres. 1980-81), Los Angeles Radiol. Soc. (exec. com. 1971—, treas. 1971-72, sec. 1972-73, pres. 1974-75), Los Angeles County Med. Assn. (councilor 1985—), Calif. (bd. dirs. 1976-83, sec.-treas. 1979-80, pres.-elect 1980-81, pres. 1981-82), Radiol. Soc. N.Am. (councilor 1976-81), Am. Soc. Neuroradiology (v.p. 1979-80, pres.-elect 1980-81, pres. 1981-82), Western Neuroradiol. Soc. (pres. 1968-70, chmn. nominating com. 1971-72, chmn. membership com. 1974), Fedn. Western Socs. Neurol. Sci. (bd. dirs. 1968-76, chmn. nominating com. 1968-69, chmn. auditing com. 1969-70, sec.-treas. 1971-73, chmn. 1973-75), Inter-Am. Fedn. Neuroradiology, Los Angeles Soc. Neurology and Psychiatry, Soc. Chairmen of Acad. Radiology Depts., Am. Roentgen Ray Soc., Alpha Omega Alpha. Current Work: Magnetic resonance. Subspecialties: Diagnostic radiology; Imaging technology. Home: 4009 Ocean Front Walk Venice CA 90292 Office: U California Dept of Radiological Sciences Center for Health Sciences Los Angeles CA 90024

WILSON, GEOFFREY LEONARD, engineer, educator; b. London, Oct. 26, 1924; came to U.S., 1959, naturalized, 1965; s. Percy and Dorothy Jennett (Kingston) W.; m. Patricia Winfred Pankhurst, Dec. 17, 1955; children—Anthony John, Nigel David. B.A. in Physics, Oxford U., 1945, M.A. in Physics, 1949, M.Sc. in Physics, 1949; Ph.D. in Elec. Engring., Loughborough U., Eng., 1975. Registered profl. engr., Pa. Chartered elec. engr., U.K. Sci. officer Royal Naval Sci. Service, U.K., 1948-53; design engr. Can. Westinghouse Co., Hamilton, Ont., 1953-59; asst. prof. engring research Pa. State U., University Park, 1959, assoc. prof., 1965-85, mem. grad. faculty in acoustics, 1975-85; SOHIO prof. math. and physics Johnson C. Smith U., Charlotte, N.C., 1985—; vis. research fellow Loughborough U., 1968-69; vis. sci. Inst. Nat. des Sci. Appliquées, Lyon, France, 1982. Contbr. articles to profl. jours. Patentee in field. Com. troop chmn. Juniata Valley Council Boy Scouts Am., 1975-81. Grantee NSF. Fellow Audio Engring. Soc., Inst. Acoustics, Inst. Elec. Engrs.; mem. IEEE (sr.; Centennial Medal 1984), Acoustical Soc. Am. Lodge: Rotary. Current work: Acoustics, underwater; electroacoustic transducers and arrays; acoustical holography; materials for vibration control; audio tech. Subspecialties: Acoustical engineering; Acoustics. Home: 527 W Fairmount Ave State College PA 16801 Office: Johnson C Smith U 100 Beatties Ford Rd Charlotte NC 28216

WILSON, GREGORY BRUCE, medical educator, consultant; b. Columbus, Ohio, Oct. 15, 1948; s. Bruce N. and Miriam J. (Allen) W.; m. Nancy Lee Maddux, Apr. 13, 1975 (div. June 1978); m. Judy Hunter Jennings, Dec. 4, 1982. B.A. in Zoology, UCLA, 1971, Ph.D. in Biology, 1974. Research asst. UCLA, 1972-74, postdoctoral research fellow dept. biology, 1974; postdoctoral research fellow dept. medicine U. Calif.-San Francisco, 1974-75; assoc. dept. basic and clin. immunology and microbiology Med. U. S.C., Charleston, 1975-76, asst. prof., 1976-79, assoc. prof., 1979—, assoc. prof. dept. pediatrics, 1982—; cons. Intron, Inc., Charleston, 1982—. Co-editor: Immunological Aspects of Cystic Fibrosis, 1983; contbr. numerous articles and revs. to sci. jours. Pres. regional council Cystic Fibrosis Found., 1982—, state bd. dirs., 1979—, numerous other coms.; county mem. med. adv. com. Nat. Found. March of Dimes, 1977-81. Nat. Cystic Fibrosis Found. research fellow, 1974-76; Nat. Found. March of Dimes Basil O'Connor grantee, 1976-79; Nat. Cystic Fibrosis Found. grantee, 1980—. Mem. AAAS, Soc. Exptl. Biology and Medicine, Reticuloendothelial Soc., N.Y. Acad. Scis., Am. Fedn. Clin. Research, Electrophoresis Soc., Soc. Am. Inventors, Sigma Xi. Patentee method of diagnosing cystic fibrosis patients and asymptomatic carriers of the CF gene, 1982. Current Work: Immunoregulation - development of immunotherapeutic and immunoprophylactic agents and regimens for treatment of immunodeficiency diseases; development of immunoassays for detection of subjects with genetic diseases and probes for elucidation of their basic genetic defect(s). Subspecialties: Genetics and genetic engineering (medicine); Immunology (medicine). Office: 171 Ashley Ave Charleston SC 29425

WILSON, JEAN DONALD, physician; b. Wellington, Tex., Aug. 26, 1932; s. J. D. and Maggie E. (Hill) W. B.A. in Chemistry, U. Tex., 1951, M.D., 1955. Diplomate: Am. Bd. Internal Medicine. Intern, then resident in internal medicine Parkland Meml. Hosp., Dallas, 1955-58; clin. assoc. Nat. Heart Inst., Bethesda, Md., 1958-60; instr. internal medicine U. Tex. Southwestern Med. Sch., Dallas, 1960-61, prof., 1968—. Editor: Jour. Clin. Investigation, 1972-77. Served as sr. asst. surgeon USPHS, 1958-60. Recipient Oppenheimer award Endocrine Soc., 1972; Amory prize Am. Acad. Arts and Scis., 1977; Fuller prize Am. Urol. Assn., 1983. Mem. Am. Fedn. Clin. Research, Am. Soc. Clin. Investigation, Soc. Exptl. Biology and Medicine, Am. Soc. Biol. Chemists, Endocrine Soc., Assn. Am. Physicians., Am. Acad. Arts and Scis., Nat. Acad. Scis. Current Work: The molecular mechanisms of normal androgen action in the developing male embryo and in postembryonic life and investigation of clinical disorders that impair androgen action and cause abnormal sexual development. Subspecialty: Receptors. Home: 4517 Watauga Rd Dallas TX 75209 Office: Dept Internal Medicine U Tex Health Sci Center Dallas TX 75235

WILSON, JOHN SHERIDAN, chem. engr.; b. Morgantown, W.Va., June 17, 1944; s. Jack Belmont and Vivian Jean (Fike) W.; m. Diane Barbara Wilson, July 14, 1944; children: David Bailey, Kevin Mark, Matthew Joseph, Adam

Jason. B.S. in Chem. Engring, W.Va. U., 1966, M.S. in Nuclear Engring, 1968, Ph.D. in Chem. Engring, 1975. Project leader and project engr. Bur. Mines, U.S. Dept. Interior, Morgantown, W.Va., 1968-76; project mgr. combustion research and devel. br. Morgantown Energy Research Center, ERDA, 1976, research supr., 1976-77; asst. dir. energy conversion and utilization div. Morgantown (W.Va.) Energy Tech. Center, U.S. Dept. Energy, 1977-79, dir. coal projects mgmt. div., 1979—. Contbr. articles to profl. jours. Bd. dirs. Morgantown Hockey Assn. Mem. Am. Chem. Soc., ASME, Sigma Xi. Baptist. Current Work: Coal combustion and gasification processes along with environmental aspects of coal use; utilization of coal and coal-derived fuels in gas turbines, fuel cells and boilers. Subspecialties: Coal; Chemical engineering. Office: PO Box 880 Morgantown WV 26505

WILSON, KENNETH GEDDES, physical science educator; b. Waltham, Mass., June 8, 1936; s. Edgar Bright and Emily Fisher (Buckingham) W.; m. Alison Brown, Oct. 1982. A.B., Harvard U., 1956, Ph.D. (hon.), 1981; Ph.D., Calif. Tech. U., 1961; Ph.D. (hon.), U. Chgo., 1976. Asst. prof. to prof. phys. sci. Cornell U., Ithaca, N.Y., 1963—. Contbr. articles to profl. jours., conf. presentations on theoretical physics. Recipient Nobel Prize, 1982; Frankin medal, 1983. Current Work: Elementary particles theory; statistical mechanics; large scale scientific computing. Subspecialty: Theoretical physics. Office: Cornell U 316 Newman Lab Ithaca NY 14853

WILSON, LEONARD RICHARD, geologist, consultant; b. Superior, Wis., July 23, 1906; s. Ernest and Sarah Jane (Cooke) W.; m. Marian Alice DeWilde, Sept. 1, 1930; children—Richard Graham, Marcia Graham. Ph.B., U. Wis.-Madison, 1930, Ph.M., 1932, Ph.D., 1935. Research assoc. Wis. Geol. and Nat. Hist. Survey, Trout Lake, Wis., 1932-36; instr. to prof. geology Coe Coll., Cedar Rapids, Iowa, 1934-46; head dept. geology and mineralogy U. Mass., Amherst, 1946-56; leader Greenland Ice Cap Am. Geog. Soc., N.Y.C., 1953; prof. geology NYU, N.Y.C., 1956-57; prof. to George L. Cross research prof. geology and geophysics U. Okla., Norman, 1957-77, prof. emeritus, 1977—; geologist Okla. Geol. Survey, Norman, 1957-77, ret. 1977—; cons. in field; research assoc., mem. edn. bd. Mus. Nat. Hist., N.Y.C., 1956-77; curator paleobotany Stovall Mus. Sci. and History, Norman, 1968—. Contbr. articles to profl. jours. Editor proceedings Iowa Acad. Sci., 1936-46. Melhaup fellow Ohio State U., 1939-40; NSF grantee, 1959-65. Fellow AAAS, Geol. Soc. Am., Palynological Soc. India (Erdtman Internat. medal 1973); mem. Am. Assn. Petroleum Geologists, Am. Assn. Stratigraphic Palynologists (hon.), Nat. Assn. Geology Tchrs. (hon. life), Audubon Soc. (pres. Norman br. 1982-83), Explorers Club, Sigma Xi, Phi Beta Kappa, Phi Kappa Phi. Current work: Stratigraphic research in Paleozoic palynology as it relates to hydrocarbon maturation and associated strata. Subspecialties: Geology; Chronobiology. Office: Stovall Mus Sci and History U Okla Norman OK 73019

WILSON, LOUIS FREDERICK, ecologist; b. Milw., Nov. 22, 1932; s. Frederick and Colette (Greif) W.; m. Diane Helen Schwedler, Dec. 29, 1956; children—Barbara and Scott (twins), Daniel, Glenn. B.S., Marquette U., 1955, M.S., 1957; Ph.D., U. Minn., 1962. Forest entomologist U.S. Dept. Agr. Forest Service, St. Paul, 1958-62, research entomologist, East Lansing, Mich., 1962-65, project leader, 1965—; faculty Mich. State U., East Lansing, 1967—, prof. forestry, 1967—, prof. entomology, 1969—. Contbr. articles to profl. jours. Mem. Mich. Entomol. Soc., Entomol. Soc. Am., Entomol. Soc. Can., Sigma Xi. Current work: Pest management, insect behavior, forest insect control, insect biology and models of management of pests and systems. Subspecialties: Behavioral ecology; Integrated pest management. Home: 900 Longfellow Dr East Lansing MI 48823 Office: US Dept Agr Forest Service North Central Forest Experiment Sta 1407 S Harrison Rd Room 20 East Lansing MI 48823

WILSON, MARJORIE PRICE, physician, epidemiology educator, university dean; b. Pitts.; m. Lynn Minford Wilson, Sept. 15, 1951; children: Lynn Deyo, Liza Price. Student, Bryn Mawr Coll., 1942-45; M.D., U. Pitts., 1949. Intern U. Pitts. Med. Center Hosps., 1949-50; resident Children's Hosp. U. Pitts., 1950-51, Jackson Meml. Hosp., U. Miami Sch. Medicine, 1954-56; chief residency and internship div. edn. service Office of Research and Edn., VA, Washington, 1956, chief profl. tng. div., 1956-60, asst. dir. edn. service, 1960; chief tng. br. Nat. Inst. Arthritis and Metabolic Disease, NIH, 1960-63; asst. to asso. dir. for tng. Office of Dir. NIH, 1963-64; asso. dir. extramural programs Nat. Library Medicine, 1964-67; asso. dir. program devel. OPPD NIH, 1967-69, asst. dir. program planning and evaluation NIH, Bethesda, Md., 1969-70; dir. dept. instl. devel. Assn. Am. Med. Colls., Washington, 1970-81; sr. assoc. dean U. Md. Sch. Medicine, Balt., 1981—; mem. Inst. Medicine, Nat. Acad. Scis., 1974—; bd. visitors U. Pitts. Sch. Medicine, 1974—; mem. adv. com. Md. Cancer Registry; mem. Gov.'s Commn. on Toxic Wastes. Contbr. articles to profl. jours. Mem. governing bd. Robert Wood Johnson Health Policy Fellowships, 1975—; trustee Analytic Services, Inc., Falls Church, Va., 1976—. Mem. Nat. Bd. Med. Examiners (mem.-at-large), Assn. Am. Med. Colls., Am. Fedn. Clin. Research, AAAS, IEEE. Episcopalian. Current Work: Research and teaching in management of medical systems, medical center organization and management; medical education; information sciences. Subspecialty: Health/medical systems, management. Office: Univ Maryland Sch Medicine Baltimore MD 21201

WILSON, MARK WAYNE, research physicist; b. Chgo., Sept. 14, 1955; s. William O. and Mary Elizabeth (Carroll) W.; m. Michele Marie Marcheschi, Sept. 26, 1956; children—Jennifer Ada, Matthew Christopher, Rebecca Anne Marie. B.S., Ill. Benedictine Coll., 1977; M.S., U. Ill.-Chgo., 1979, Ph.D., 1982. Research physicist SRI Internat., Menlo Park, Calif., 1982—. Contbr. articles to profl. jours. Mem. IEEE, Optical Soc. Am., Sigma Pi Sigma. Democrat. Current work: Investigation and application of integrated optic and fiber optic devices for data handling and transmission. Office: SRI Internat M/S GT2 333 Ravenswood Ave Menlo Park CA 94025

WILSON, MICHAEL JOHN, research biochemist; b. Iowa City, June 3, 1942; s. James H. and Doris E. (Lachender) W.; m. Martha J. Swartzwelter, June 7, 1969; 1 son, Matthew J. A.A., Divine Word Coll., 1962; B.A., St. Ambrose Coll., 1964; M.S., U. Iowa, 1967, Ph.D., 1971. Postdoctoral fellow Harvard Med. Sch., Boston, 1971-73; research assoc. U. Minn., Mpls., 1973-75, asst. prof., 1975-82, assoc. prof., 1982—; research biochemist VA Med. Ctr., Mpls., 1976—. Contbr. articles to profl. jours. Chmn. Spl. Edn. Adv. Council, St. Paul Pub. Schs., 1982—; bd. dirs. United Cerebral Palsy of Minn., 1985—. Grantee VA 1980—, Nat. Cancer Inst., 1984. Mem. Am. Soc. Study Cell Biology, Ednocrine Soc., Am. Physiol. Soc., Am. Soc. Zoologists. Roman Catholic. Current work: Male reproductive biology; studies of prostate cancer and male infertility. Subspecialties: Cell biology (medicine); Andrology. Home: 2053 Dayton Ave St Paul MN 55104 Office: VA Med Ctr 54th & 48th Aves Minneapolis MN 55417

WILSON, OLIN C(HADDOCK), astronomer; b. San Francisco, Jan. 13, 1909; s. Olin C. and Sophie (Clary) W.; m. Katherine E. Johnson, Sept. 3, 1943; children: Nicole Wilson McMillin, Randall S. A.B., U. Calif.-Berkeley, 1930; Ph.D., Calif. Inst. Tech., 1934. Asst. Mt. Wilson Obs., Pasadena, Calif., 1931-36; astronomer Mt. Wilson Obs., Palomar Obs., Pasadena, 1936-74, emeritus astronomer, 1975—. Recipient Bruce medal Astron. Soc. of Pacific, 1984. Mem. Nat. Acad. Sci., Am. Astron. Soc. (Henry Norris Russell lectr. 1977). AAAS. Democrat. Current Work: Stellar chromospheres, activity cycles in stars. Subspecialty: Optical astronomy. Office: 813 Santa Barbara St Pasadena CA 91101

WILSON, RAYMOND HIRAM, JR., astronomer, mathematician; b. Gap, Pa., Feb. 14, 1911; s. Raymond Hiram and Agnes (Wright) W.; m. Irene Gladys Louise Hansing, Aug. 21, 1940; 1 dau., Kristin Marie Wilson Young. A.B., Swarthmore Coll., 1931; A.M., U. Pa., 1933, Ph.D., 1935, postgrad., 1950-51; postgrad., Harvard U., 1937. Research asso., instr. math. and astronomy various colls., 1929-40; astronomer Naval Obs., 1940-42; prin. investigator contracts Office Naval Research, 1949-52; asst. prof. math. and astronomy, cons. research inst. Temple U., 1946-51; asst. prof. math. U. Louisville, 1951-54; physicist Naval Research Lab. and Project Vanguard, 1954-58; applied mathematician Goddard Space Flight Center, 1958-71; chief applied math. br. NASA Hdqrs., Washington, 1962-69; profl. lectr. astronomy Georgetown U. Grad. Sch., Washington, 1962-68; prof. astronomy and applied math., dir. obs. U. Aegean, Turkey, 1971-74, 77-80; astronomer Armagh Obs., No. Ireland, 1974-77, self-employed, 1980—; liaison com. mem. div. math. Nat. Acad. Sci., 1963-68. Contbr. articles in field to profl. jours. Served to comdr. USNR, 1942-46. Recipient Incentive award NASA, 1963. Fellow AAAS; mem. Internat. Astron. Union, Am. Astron. Soc. (grant 1981), Math. Assn. Am., Rittenhouse Astron. Soc. (pres. 1949), Sigma Xi, Sigma Pi Sigma. Democrat. Episcopalian. Clubs: Bolling Officers' (Washington); Kings Ridge Swim (Fairfax, Va.). Patentee in field. Current Work: Measurement of visual double stars and computation of their orbits for publication. Subspecialties: Optical astronomy; Applied mathematics. Home: 5325 Gainsborough Dr Fairfax VA 22032

WILSON, RICHARD, physicist, educator; b. London, Eng., Apr., 29, 1926; came to U.S., 1950; s. Percy and Dorothy (Kingston) W.; m. Andrée Desirée DuMond, Jan. 6, 1952; children—Arthur Christopher, Michael Thomas, Nicholas Graham, Elaine Susan, Annette Adele, Peter James. B.A., Christ Church, Oxford U., 1946, M.A., D.Phil., 1949; M.A., Harvard U., 1957. Research lectr. Christ Ch., Oxford U., 1948-53, research officer Dept. Sci. and Indsl. Research, 1953-55; research asso. U. Rochester, 1950-51, Stanford U., 1951-52; asst. prof. Harvard U., 1955-57, asso. prof., 1957-61, prof., 1961—, Mallinchrodt prof. physics, 1982—, chmn. dept. physics, 1982-85, asso. Adams House, 1971—; cons. NRC, Oak Ridge Nat. Lab., Los Alamos Sci. Lab. Asst. editor: Annals of Physics, 1956-84; author 4 books; contbr. articles to sci. jours. Guggenheim fellow, 1961, 69; Fulbright fellow, 1959, 69. Fellow Am. Phys. Soc.; mem. N.Y. Acad. Scis., Am. Acad. Arts and Scis., Soc. Psychical Research (London), Explorers Club, Newton Conservators. Current work: Colliding beams of electrons and protons; assessment of hazards in life. Subspecialties: Particle physics; Environmental toxicology. Home: 15 Bracebridge Rd Newton MA 02159 Office: Lyman Lab Harvard University Cambridge MA 02138

WILSON, ROBERT LEE, geologist; b. Peoria, Ill., Dec. 16, 1918; s. Harry James and Alta May (Mathews) W.; m. Annabell June Tullis, May 25, 1941; children—Cheryl Diane, Sandra Jean, David Lee. Geol.E., Colo. Sch. Mines, 1941; postgrad. U. Colo., 1946; Ph.D., U. Ariz., 1956. Registered geologist, Calif.; cert. engring geologist. Asst. regional geologist U.S. Bur. Reclamation, Boulder City, Nev., 1946-51; dist. geologist Corps. of Engrs., Savannah, Ga., 1951-54; chief geologist Kaiser Steel Corp., Fontana, Calif., 1956-68, exploration mgr., Oakland, Calif., 1968-84; cons., Lafayette, Calif., 1984—. Contbr. articles to profl. jours. Served to maj. U.S. Army, 1941-46, PTO. Indian Service fellow U. Ariz., 1953-55. Mem. Geol. Soc. Am., Soc. Econ. Geologists, AIME, Am. Inst. Profl. Geologists, Sigma Xi. Current work: Western U.S. and Canada coal deposits, southern California geology, limestone, mineral property evaluation. Subspecialty: Geology. Home and Office: 3153 Windsor Ct Lafayette CA 94549

WILSON, ROBERT MARIS, consulting engineer; b. Evanston, Ill., July 22, 1928; s. Leroy Clark and Dorothy Wainright (Ross) W.; m. Winifred Engeman, June 29, 1957; children—Roderick, Frederick, Edward. B.S., U.S. Mil. Acad., 1950, M.S. in Civil Engring., MIT, 1956; M.S. in Pub. Adminstrn., Shippensburg State Coll., 1971; Ph.D. in M.E., Lehigh U., 1973. Registered profl. engr., D.C. Commd. 2d lt. U.S. Army, 1950; advanced through grades to col.; ret., 1971; prof. engring. U.S. Mil. Acad., West Point, N.Y., 1971-83; cons. engr. Am. Standards Testing Bur., Inc., N.Y.C., 1984—. Mem. ASME, Am. Soc. Engring. Edn., AAAS, Soc. Am. Mil. Engrs. Office: Am Standards Testing Bur Inc 40 Water St New York NY 10004

WILSON, ROBERT R., physicist; b. Frontier, Wyo., Mar. 4, 1914; s. Platt E. and Edith W. (Rathbun) W.; m. Jane Scheyer, Aug. 20, 1940; children: Daniel, Jonathan, Rand. A.B., U. Calif., Berkeley, 1936, Ph.D., 1940; hon. degrees, U. Bonn., W.Ger., U. Notre Dame. Instr., asst. prof. Princeton U., 1940-43; head cyclotron group and research div. Los Alamos Nat. Lab., 1943-46; assoc. prof. physics Harvard U., 1946-47; dir. Lab. Nuclear Studies, Cornell U., Ithaca, N.Y., 1947-67, Fermi Lab., Batavia, Ill., 1967-78; prof. U. Chgo., 1967-80; prof. physics Columbia U., 1980—. Recipient Elliott Cresson medal Franklin Inst., Nat. medal of Sci., 1973, Fermi award, 1984. Mem. Am. Phys. Soc. (pres. 1985), Nat. Acad., Scis., Am. Acad. Scis., Philos. Soc. Sculpture exhibited Inst. Advanced Studies, Princeton, N.J., Harvard Sci. Ctr., Fermi Lab. Subspecialty: Nuclear physics. Home: 916 Stewart Ave Ithaca NY 14850 Office: Newman Lab Cornell U Ithaca NY 14853

WILSON, ROBERT WOODROW, radio astronomer; b. Houston, Jan. 10, 1936; s. Ralph Woodrow and Fannie May (Willis) W.; m. Elizabeth Rhoads Sawin, Sept. 4, 1958; children—Philip Garrett, Suzanne Katherine, Randal Woodrow. B.A. with honors in Physics, Rice U., 1957; Ph.D., Calif. Inst. Tech., 1962. Research fellow Calif. Inst. Tech., Pasadena, 1962-63; mem. tech. staff Bell Labs., Holmdel, N.J., 1963-76, head radio physics research dept., 1976—. Recipient Henry Draper medal Royal Astron. Soc., London, 1977, Herschel medal Nat. Acad. Scis., 1977; Nobel prize in physics, 1978; NSF fellow, 1958-61; Cole fellow, 1957-58. Mem. Am. Astron. Soc., Internat. Astron. Union, Am. Phys. Soc., Internat. Sci. Radio Union, Nat. Acad. Scis., Phi Beta Kappa, Sigma Xi. Discoverer of 3 deg. k Microwave Background Radiation, 1965; discoverer of CO and other molecules in interstellar space using their millimeter wavelength radiation. Current Work: Structure of interstellar clouds and galaxies using the radiation from simple molecules. Subspecialty: Radio and microwave astronomy. Home: 9 Valley Point Dr Holmdel NJ 07733 Office: Bell Labs HOH L239 Holmdel NJ 07733

WILSON, THOMAS LEON, physicist; b. Alpine, Tex., May 21, 1942; s. Homer Marvin and Ogarita Maude (Bailey) W.; m. Joyce Ann Krevosky, May 7, 1978; 1 son, Kenneth Edward Byron. B.A., Rice U., 1964, B.S., 1965, M.A., 1974, Ph.D., 1976. With NASA, Houston, 1965—; astronaut instr. NASA (U.S. Apollo and Skylab manned spacecraft programs), 1965-74; high-energy theoretical physicist NASA (Johnson Space Center), 1969—. Contbr. articles in field to profl. jours. Recipient Hugo Gernsback award IEEE, 1964; NASA fellow, 1969-76. Mem. Am. Phys. Soc., AAAS, N.Y. Acad. Scis., Am. Assn. Physicists in Medicine. Patentee in field. Current Work: Theoretical work in grand unified field theory, relativistic quantum field theory, quantum chromodynamics, supergravity, cosmology, astrophysics, deep inelastic scattering, authority on neutrino tomography, discoverer classical uncertainty principle. Subspecialties: Relativity and gravitation; High energy astrophysics. Home: 206 Woodcombe Dr Houston TX 77062 Office: NASA Johnson Space Center Houston TX 77058

WILSON, THORNTON ARNOLD, airplane company executive; b. Sikeston, Mo., Feb. 8, 1921; s. Thornton Arnold and Daffodil (Allen) W.; m. Grace Miller, Aug. 5, 1944; children: Thornton Arnold III, Daniel Allen, Sarah Louise Wilson Anderson. Student, Jefferson City (Mo.) Jr. Coll., 1938-40; B.S., Iowa State Coll., 1943; M.S., Calif. Inst. Tech., 1948; M.S. Sloan fellow, MIT, 1952-53. With Boeing Co., Seattle, 1943—, asst. chief tech. staff, project engring. mgr., 1957-58, v.p., mgr. Minuteman br. aerospace div., 1962-64, v.p. ops. and planning, 1964-66, exec. v.p., dir., 1966-68, pres., 1968—, chief exec. officer, 1969, chmn. bd., 1972—; dir. PACCAR, Inc., Seattle-First Nat. Bank, Weyerhaeuser Co., U.S. Steel Co. Bd. govs. Iowa State U. Found.; mem. Bus. Council; trustee Seattle U. Mem. Aerospace Industries Assn. Subspecialty: Aeronautical engineering. Office: The Boeing Co PO Box 3707 Seattle WA 98124

WILSON, VICTOR JOSEPH, educator; b. Berlin, Germany, Dec. 24, 1928; s. Andrew A. and Lydia (Yampolsky) W.; m. Isa Hermer, June 7, 1953; children—Janet, Denise. B.S., Tufts Coll., 1948, M.S., 1949; research student, U. Cambridge, Eng., 1949-50; Ph.D., U. Ill., 1953. Research asso. Rockefeller U., N.Y.C., 1953-58, asst. prof., 1958-62, assoc. prof., 1962-69, prof. neurophysiology, 1969—. Served to 1st lt. U.S. Army, 1954-56. Mem. Am. Physiol. Soc., Soc. Neurosci., Harvey Soc., Sigma Xi, Phi Beta Kappa. Research physiology central nervous system. Current Work: Neurophysiological analysis of postural reflexes; study of vestibular system and spinal cord. Subspecialties: Neurobiology; Physiology (biology). Home: 4525 Henry Hudson Pkwy New York NY 10471

WILSON, W. R. D., mechanical engineering educator. B.S. in Mech. Engring., Queen's U., Belfast, Northern Ireland, 1963, Ph.D., 1967. Sr. research scientist Battelle Lab., Columbus, Ohio, 1967-71; faculty U. Mass., Amherst, 1971-81; prof. mech. and nuclear engring., Northwestern U., Evanston, Ill., 1981—. Contbr. articles to profl. jours. Assoc. editor (past) Jour. Lubrication Tech., Transactions Jour. Mem. ASME (research com. lubrication). Office: Northwestern U Dept Mech & Nuclear Engring Evanston IL 60201

WILSON, WALTER ERVIN, physicist; b. Salem, Oreg., Apr. 1, 1934; s. Ralph A. and Erma L. (Simmons) W.; m. Connie Sue Harding, May 2, 1939; children: Bruce, Douglas, Gregory, DeeAnn. B.A., Willamette U., 1956; M.S., U. Wis., 1958, Ph.D., 1961. Sr. scientist Battelle N.W., Richland, Wash., 1965—; adj. asst. prof. radiol. physics Joint Center Grad. Studies, Richland, 1977—. Mem. Am. Phys. Soc., Radiation Research Soc., Am. Assn. Physicists in Medicine, Health Physics Soc. Current Work: Research in effects of radiation. Subspecialties: Atomic and molecular physics; Numerical analysis (computer science). Office: PO Box 999 Richland WA 99352

WILSON, WILLIAM JOHN, microwave research engineer; b. Spokane, Wash., Dec. 16, 1939; s. William Edward and Margret Avis (Drury) W.; m. Julia Ann Haselton, Aug. 7, 1982; children by previous marriage: Elizabeth Joan, Amy Kathleen. B.S.E.E., U. Wash., 1961; M.S.E.E., M.I.T., 1963, Ph.D., 1970. Research asst. M.I.T., Cambridge, 1967-70; sect. mgr. Aerospace Corp., El Segundo, Calif., 1970-76, 77-80; asst. prof. elec. engring. U. Tex., Austin, 1976-77; group supr. microwave advanced systems Jet Propulsion Lab., Pasadena, 1980—. Contbr. articles to profl. jours. Served to capt. USAF, 1964-67. Decorated Air Force Commendation medal.; Whitney fellow, 1961. Mem. IEEE, Am. Astron. Soc., Internat. Union Radio Sci., Internat. Astron. Union. Current Work: Development of low-noise millimeter-wave radiometers and systems, including mixers, solid state sources and quasi-optical components. Subspecialties: Electronics; Radio and microwave astronomy. Office: 4800 Oak Grove 168-327 Pasadena CA 91109

WILSON, WILLIAM STANLEY, oceanographer; b. Alexander City, Ala., June 5, 1938. B.S., Coll. William and Mary, 1959, M.A., 1964; Ph.D., Johns Hopkins U., 1972. Program mgr. phys. oceanography Office Naval Research, 1972-79; chief oceanic processes br. NASA Hdqrs., Washington, 1979—. Recipient Superior Civilian Service award Dept. Navy, 1979; Exceptional Sci. Achievement medal NASA, 1981. Mem. Am. Geophys. Union (Ocean Scis. award 1984), Am. Meteorol. Soc. Sigma Xi. Current Work: Oceanography from space. Subspecialties: Oceanography; Satellite studies.

WINARSKI, DANIEL JAMES, mechanical engineer; b. Toledo, Dec. 16, 1948; s. Daniel Edward and Marguerite (Pietersien) W.; m. Donna Ilene Robinson, Oct. 10, 1970; 1 child, Tyson York. B.S.M.E., U. Mich., 1970; M.S.M.E., U. Colo., 1973; Ph.D., U. Mich., 1976. Registered profl. engr., Ariz., Colo. Research engr. Exxon Prodn. Research, Houston, 1976-77; staff engr. gen. products div. IBM, Boulder, Colo., 1977-78, Tucson, 1978—, staff engr. computer peripherals devel., 1978-84, adv. engr., 1984—; instr. U.S. Mil. Acad., West Point, 1980—; instr. Computer Camp for Minorities, No. Ariz. U., Flagstaff, 1983-85. Co-v.p. Gale Sch. PTA, 1979-80, co-pres., 1981-82. Served to maj. C.E., U.S. Army, 1970-85. Recipient Invention Achievement awards IBM, 1981, 82; NSF fellow, 1973-76; Nat. Student Dissertation grantee U. Mich., 1975-76. Mem. ASME, Soc. Lunar and Planetary Observers. Republican. Methodist. Patentee in field. Current Work: Computer data archive and retrival systems, design and development, design artificial leg, study of knee stresses. Subspecialties: Information systems, storage, and retrieval (computer science); Biomedical engineering. Home: 647 S Woodstock Dr Tucson AZ 85710 Office: IBM 75R/071-2 Tucson AZ 85744

WINBURY, MARTIN MAURICE, pharmacologist, pharm. co. exec.; b. N.Y.C., Aug. 4, 1918; s. Ervin and Helen (Stein) WINBURY.; m. Blanche M. Simons, July 11, 1942; children: Nancy E. Winbury Griffith, Gail E. B.S., L.I.U., 1940; M.S., U. Md., 1942; Ph.D., N.Y.U., 1951. Research fellow Merck Dohme Co., 1944-47; pharmacologist Searle Co., 1947-55; dir. pharmacology Schering Co., 1955-61; dir. pharmacology Warner-Lambert Co., Ann Arbor, Mich., 1961-79, dir. sci. devel., 1979—; organizer symposia and workshops. Contbr. articles to profl. jours., chpts. to books. Mem. Am. Soc. Pharmacology and Exptl. Therapeutics, AAAS, Soc. Exptl. Biology and Medicine, Am. Coll. Cardiology, Am. Heart Assn., Sigma Xi. Current Work: Action of drugs for coronary disease; locate, identify and evaluate new therapeutic agents and technologies. Subspecialties: Pharmacology; Cardiology. Home: 3600 Windemere Dr Ann Arbor MI 48105 Office: Warner Lambert 2800 Plymouth Rd Ann Arbor MI 48105

WINDELS, CAROL ELIZABETH, plant pathologist; b. Long Prairie, Minn., July 12, 1948; d. Jerome Joseph and Genevieve Anna Marie (Clasemann) Schrenk; m. Mark Bernard Windels, Apr. 4, 1970. B.A. in Biology, St. Cloud State U., 1970; M.S. in Plant Pathology, U. Minn., 1972, Ph.D., 1980. Asst. scientist dept. plant pathology U. Minn.-St. Paul, 1974-77, assoc. scientist, 1977-80, scientist, 1980-84, asst. prof., 1984—. Co-editor: Biological Control on the Phylloplane, 1985. Contbr. chpts. to books, articles to profl. jours. Mem. Am. Phytopathol. Soc., Can. Phytopath. Soc., Internat. Soc. Plant Pathology, Mycol. Soc. Am., AAAS, Sigma Xi, Gamma Sigma Delta, Sigma Delta Epsilon. Roman Catholic. Current Work: Soil microbiology; biology and control of soilborne pathogens of sugarbeets and cereals. Subspecialties: Plant pathology; Biological control. Home: 121 Mill St Crookston MN 56716 Office: U Minn Northwest Expt Sta Crookston MN 56716

WINER, JANE LOUISE, psychology educator; b. Albany, N.Y., Nov. 1, 1947; d. Harold and Elizabeth Gertrude (Jensen) W.; m. Monty Joseph Strauss, Nov. 4, 1978. B.A., SUNY-Albany, 1969, M.L.S., 1970; M.A., Ohio State U., 1971, Ph.D., 1975. Lic. psychologist, Tex.; registered psychologist Nat. Register Health Service Providers in Psychology. Asst. prof. psychology Tex. Tech U., Lubbock, 1975-81, assoc. prof., 1981—, dir. counseling psychology program, 1984—. Contbr. articles to profl. jours. NSF grad. trainee Ohio State U., 1970-73. Mem. Am. Psychol. Assn., Southwestern Psychol. Assn., Tex. Psychol. Assn., Am. Personnel and Guidance Assn., Assn. Women in Sci. Democrat. Jewish. Current Work: Vocational psychology, including vocational choice, person-environment congruence, computer literacy and applications. Home: 7010 Nashville Dr Lubbock TX 79413 Office: Dept Psychology Tex Tech U PO Box 4100 Lubbock TX 79409

WINFREE, ARTHUR TAYLOR, biophysicist, educator; b. St. Petersburg, Fla., May 15, 1942; s. Charles Van and Dorothy Rose (Scheb) W.; children—Rachael, Erik.; m. Ji-Yun Yang, June 18, 1983. B.Engring. Physics, Cornell U., 1965; Ph.D. in Biology, Princeton U., 1970. Lic. pvt. pilot. Asst. prof. theoretical biology U. Chgo., 1969-72; asso. prof. biology Purdue U., West Lafayette, Ind., 1972-79, prof., 1979—; pres., dir. research Inst. Natural Philosophy, Inc., 1979—. Author: The Geometry of Biological Time, 1980. Recipient MacArthur prize, 1984—; Guggenheim Meml. fellow, 1982-83. Recipient Career Devel. award NIH, 1973-78; NSF grantee, 1966—. Current work: chemical and electrical waves in excitable media such as heart muscle. Biological oscillators. Circadian rhythms. Subspecialties: Chronobiology; Psychophysiology. Office: Biological Sciences Purdue University West Lafayette IN 47907

WING, EDWARD JOSEPH, physician, educator; b. Mineola, N.Y., June 19, 1945; s. Maurice J. and Frances (Elliott) W.; m. Rena Rimsky, Aug. 27, 1967; children: Jonathan, Kenneth. B.A., Williams Coll., 1967; M.D., Harvard U., 1971. Diplomate: Am. Bd. Internal Medicine, Am. Bd. Infectious Diseases, Nat. Bd. Med. Examiners. Med. intern, asst. resident Peter Bent Brigham Hosp., Boston, 1971-73; fellow in infectious diseases Stanford U. and Palo Alto (Calif.) Med. Research Found.; clin. instr. medicine Harvard U., 1971-73; clin. instr. medicine U. Pitts., 1973-75, asst. prof., 1977-82, assoc. prof., 1982—. Contbr. numerous articles to profl. jours. Served with USPHS, 1973-75. Mem. Am. Soc. Microbiology, Am. Assn. Immunologists, Am. Fedn. Clin. Research, Infectious Diseases Soc. Am., Reticuloendothelial Soc., Central Soc. Clin. Research, Phi Beta Kappa. Current Work: Immunology of infectious dieseases, macrophage physiology, nutrition. Subspecialties: Infectious diseases; Immunology (medicine). Office: Montefiore Hosp Pittsburgh PA 15213

WINICK, MYRON, pediatrician, educator; b. N.Y.C., May 4, 1929; s. Charles B. and Ruth E. (Gesser) W.; m. Elaine L. Lasky, Sept. 19, 1964; children—Jonathan, Stephen. A.B., Columbia U., 1951; M.S., U. Ill., 1952; M.D., SUNY, 1956. Intern U. Pa., Phila., 1956-57; asst. resident pediatrics Cornell U. Med. Coll., N.Y.C., 1957-59, chief resident, 1959-60; attending pediatrician Stanford U. Hosp., 1963-64; asst. prof. pediatrics Cornell U. Med. Coll., N.Y.C., 1964-68, asso. prof. pediatrics and nutrition, 1968-70, prof., 1970-71; prof. pediatrics, dir. Inst. Human Nutrition, Columbia, 1972—, R.R. Williams prof. nutrition, 1973—; dir. Center for Nutrition, Genetics and Human Devel., 1975—; Vis. prof. pediatrics U. Chile, Santiago, 1967; asst. attending pediatrician N.Y. Hosp., N.Y.C., 1964-68, asso. attending pediatrician, 1968-70, attending pediatrician, 1970-71, Presbyn. Hosp., N.Y.C., 1972—; cons. Pan Am. Health Orgn., 1966—. Author: Malnutrition and Brain Development, 1976; textbook Nutrition in Health and Disease, 1980; Growing Up Healthy; A Parent's Guide to Good Nutrition, 1982; author: For Mothers and Daughters: A Guide to Good Nutrition for Women, 1983; Your Personalized Health Profile: Choosing the Diet That's Right for You, 1985;

Editor: textbook Current Concepts in Nutrition, 1972—, Nutrition: Pre- and Postnatal Development, Vol. I; Human Nutrition: A Comprehensive Treatise, 1979; contbg. editor Nutrition Revs., 1969-76; editorial bd.: Jour. Nutrition, 1972-76, 82—, The Year in Metabolism (now Contemporary Metabolism), 1975—. Trustee Found. for Internat. Child Health; mem. nutrition interdisciplinary cluster Pres.' Biomed. Research Panel, 1975; mem. panel on infants and children Pres.' Commn. on Mental Health, 1977; cons. Office of Tech. Assessment, U.S. Congress, 1976-78; mem. Food and Nutrition Bd. NRC, 1982—. Served with USNR, 1960-62. Bank of Am.-Gianini Found. fellow Stanford, 1962; NIH Spl. fellow, 1963; recipient NIH Career Devel. award, 1968-71; Fogarty sr. internat. fellow, 1978; E. Mead Johnson award pediatric research, 1970; Osborne and Mendel award Am. Inst. Nutrition, 1976; Agnes Higgins award March of Dimes Found., 1983. Fellow Royal Soc. Health, Am. Acad. Pediatrics; mem. AAAS, Am. Soc. Cell Biology, Soc. Developmental Biology, Harvey Soc., Soc. Pediatric Research, Brit. Nutrition Soc., Am. Inst. Nutrition, Am. Soc. Clin. Nutrition, N.Y. Acad. Scis., N.Y. Acad. Medicine, Soc. for Exptl. Biology and Medicine, Soc. for Neurosci. Current work: Nutrition and brain development; nutrition and pregnancy. Subspecialties: Nutrition (medicine); Pediatrics. Office: Inst Human Nutrition Columbia U 701 W 168th St New York NY 10032

WINICOV, ILGA BUTELIS, biochemist, educator; b. Riga, Latvia, May 16, 1935; d. Arturs and Zenta (Gutmanis) Butelis; m. Herbert B. Winicov, Aug. 30, 1958; children: Eric, Mark; m. Rodney E. Harrington, Jan. 26, 1979. M.S., U. Wis-Madison, 1958; A.B., U. Pa., 1956, Ph.D., 1971. Postdoctoral fellow Inst. for Cancer Research, Phila., 1972-74, research assoc., 1974-76; research asst. prof. biochemistry Fels Research Inst., Temple U. Sch. Medicine, Phila., 1976-78; asst. prof. biochemistry U. Nev. Sch. Medicine, Reno, 1979-85, assoc. prof., 1985—; cons. in field. Contbr. numerous sci. articles to profl. publs. NSF grantee, 1978-83; NIH grantee, 1980-83. Mem. Am. Soc. Biol. Chemists, Am. Soc. Microbiology, Am. Assn. Cancer Research. Current Work: Research in gene expression at the transcriptional and RNA processing level of eucaryotic cells using genetic engineering technology; also the effect of chemical carcinogens on this process. Subspecialties: Biochemistry (medicine); Molecular biology. Office: U Nev Biochemistry Dept Reno NV 89557

WINJE, RUSSELL A., electrical engineer. With Tokamak Fusion Reactor Project, Princeton U. Plasma Physics Lab., N.J. Subspecialties: Nuclear fusion; Electrical engineering. Office: Princeton U Plasma Physics Lab Princeton NJ 08544

WINKELSTEIN, WARREN, JR., educator, physician; b. Syracuse, N.Y., July 1, 1922; s. Warren and Evelyn (Neiman) W.; m. Veva Kerrigan, Feb. 14, 1976; children by previous marriage: Rebecca Winkelstein Yamin, Joshua, Shoshana. B.A., U. N.C., 1942; M.D. cum laude, Syracuse U., 1947; M.P.H., Columbia U., 1950. Diplomate: Am. Bd. Preventive Medicine. Intern Charity Hosp., New Orleans, 1947-48; with I.C.A., Vietnam, 1951-53; dir. div. communicable disease control to 1st dep. commr. local and environmental health services Erie County Health Dept., 1953-62; assoc. prof. to prof. SUNY-Buffalo, 1962-68; prof. epidemiology, dean pub. health U. Calif., 1972-82. Author: Basic Readings in Epidemiology, 1972; Contbr. articles profl. jours. Served with AUS, 1944-46. Mem. Am. Pub. Health Assn., AAAS, Internat., Am. epidemiol. socs., Am. Heart Assn. Subspecialty: Epidemiology. Home: 560 Washington Ave Point Richmond CA 94801

WINKER, DAVID M(ICHAEL), physicist; b. Mpls., Aug. 28, 1954; s. James A. and Marlene J. (Modjeske) W. B.Physics, U. Minn., Mpls., 1977; M.S., U. Ariz., 1982, Ph.D., 1984. Research asst. Optical Sci. Ctr., U. Ariz., 1977-79; research assoc. Inst. Atmospheric Physics, 1979-84; research physicist Air Force Weapons Lab., 1984—. Mem. Optical Soc. Am., Tau Beta Pi. Current Work: Research on characteristics of optical propagation through the atmosphere. Subspecialty: Remote sensing (atmospheric science). Office: AFW-L/ARBA KAFB Albuquerque NM 87117

WINKLER, PETER, physicist; b. Zwickau, Germany, Feb. 2, 1937; s. Robert Gotthard and Martha Ida (Franz) W.; m. Erika Caecilie Bock, Feb. 21, 1962; children: Michael, Ulrike. Diploma in Physics, Universitaet Frankfurt am Main, W.Ger., 1966; Dr. rer. nat., U. Erlangen-Nuernberg, W.Ger., 1969, Dr. rer. nat. habil, 1977. Asst. U. Erlangen-Nuernberg, 1966-72; Max-Kade fellow SUNY, Stony Brook, 1972-74; asst. U. Erlangen-Nurnberg, 1974-77, sr. research assoc., 1977-79; assoc. prof. physics U. Nev., Reno, 1979-85, prof., 1985—. Contbr. articles to profl. jours. Mem. Am. Phys. Soc., AAAS, Am. Fedn. Musicians, Deutsche Physikalische Gesellschaft, Sigma Pi Sigma. Current Work: Theory of resonances; new mathematical methods in physics; theoretical atomic, molecular and chemical physics. Subspecialties: Theoretical physics; Atomic and molecular physics. Office: Dept Physics U Nev Reno NV 89557

WINN, RICHARD EARL, physician, educator; b. Houston, Aug. 21, 1950; s. Earl Hardy and Elvera Elayne (Balas) W.; m. Sandra Lee Sutterfield, Sept. 14, 1974; children: Sara Sutterfield, Alice Lee Sutterfield. B.S., U.S. Air Force Acad., 1972; M.D., U. Ariz., 1975. Diplomate: Am. Bd. Internal. Am. Bd. Medicine, Infectious Diseases, Am. Bd. Pathology, Am. Bd. Microbiology. Resident in internal medicine David Grant Med. Ctr., Fairfield, Calif., 1975-78; fellow in infectious diseases U. Oreg., Portland, 1978-80; staff infectious diseases Wilford Hall Med. Ctr., San Antonio, 1980—, asst. chief infectious diseases, 1980-84, chief infectious diseases, 1984—, dir. infectious diseases research lab., 1980-82; asst. prof. Uniformed Services U. Health Scis., Washington, 1981—; clin. asst. prof. U. Tex.-San Antonio, 1981—. Served to maj. USAF, 1972—. Fellow ACP; mem. Am. Soc. Microbiology, Soc. Air Force Physicians, Tex. Soc. Infectious Diseases. Current Work: Mechanisms of human fungal infections, mucormycosis, staphylococcal bacterial diseases, osteomyelitis. Subspecialties: Internal medicine; Infectious diseases. Home: 10806 Whisper Valley San Antonio TX 78230 Office: Wilford Hall Med Ctr Lackland AFB TX 78236

WINOGRAD, SHMUEL, mathematician; b. Tel Aviv, Jan. 4, 1936; came to U.S., 1956, naturalized, 1965; s. Pinchas Mordechai and Rachel W.; m. Elaine Ruth Tates, Jan. 5, 1958; children—Danny H., Sharon A. B.S. in Elec. Engring, M.I.T., M.S. in Elec. Engring; Ph.D. in Math, NYU, 1968. Mem. research staff IBM, Yorktown Heights, N.Y., 1961-70, dir. math. sci. dept., 1970-74, IBM fellow, 1972—; permanent vis. prof. Technion, Israel. Author: (with J.D. Cowan) Reliable Computations in the Presence of Noise. Fellow IEEE (W. Wallace McDowell award 1974); mem. Am. Math. Soc., Math. Assn. Am., Assn. Computing Machines, Nat. Acad. Scis., Soc. Indsl. and Applied Math. Research on complexity of computations. Subspecialty: Applied mathematics. Home: 235 Glendale Rd Scarsdale NY 10483 Office: IBM Research PO Box 218 Yorktown Heights NY 10598

WINOGRAD, TERRY ALLEN, computer science educator, consultant; b. Takoma Park, Md., Feb. 24, 1946; s. Harold S. and Florence L. (Winograd); m. Carol Hutner, Aug. 24, 1968; children: Shoshana, Avra. B.A. in Math, Colo. Coll., 1966; postgrad., Univ. Coll., London, 1967; Ph.D. in Applied Math, MIT, 1970. Research programmer Penrose Hosp., Colorado Springs, Colo., 1965-66; instr. math. MIT, Cambridge, 1970-71, asst. prof. elec. engring., 1971-74; vis. asst. prof. computer sci. and linguistics Stanford (Calif.) U., 1973-74, asst. prof., 1974-79, assoc. prof., 1979—; cons. Xerox Palo Alto Research Ctr., 1972—, Hermenet, Inc., San Francisco, 1981—; spl. cons. to French Govt., 1981, Fuji Xerox, Japan, 1982; mem. govt. panels and other panels in field; advisor Cognitive Sci. Program U. Calif.-San Francisco, 1979—; dir. Live Oak Inst., Berkeley, Calif., 1980—. Author: Language as a Cognitive Process: Vol. I—Syntax, 1983, Understanding Natural Language, 1972; contbr. numerous articles on liguistics and computer sci. to profl. jours.; mem. editoral bd.: Artificial Intelligence, 1973—, Am. Jour. Computational Linguistics, 1974-77, Cognitive Sci, 1977-80, Discourse Processes, 1978—, Behaviorial and Brain Scis. (commentator), 1978—. Recipient Dean's award Stanford U., 1977; Danforth fellow, 1967-70; NSF (hon.) fellow, 1966; Woodrow Wilson fellow (hon.), 1966; Fulbright fellow, 1966-67; Boettcher scholar, 1962-66; NSF grantee, 1975-77, 1982-83; ARPA grantee, 1969-73, 73-75; Xerox grantee, 1975-80; Sloan Found. grantee, 1978—; System Devel. Found. grantee, 1982-83; Mellon Jr. Faculty fellow, 1977. Mem. Assn. for Computational Linguistics, Linguistics Soc. Am., Am. Assn. Artificial Intelligence (nat. bd. dirs. 1979-81), Union Concerned Scientists, Computer Profls. for Social Responsibility. Current Work: The development of system description languages. Subspecialties: Artificial intelligence; Software engineering. Office: Stanford U Stanford CA 94305

WINOKUR, GEORGE, psychiatrist, educator; b. Phila., Feb. 10, 1925; s. Louis and Vera P. W.; m. Betty Stricklin, Sept. 15, 1951; children: Thomas, Kenneth, Patricia. A.B., Johns Hopkins U., 1944; M.D., U. Md., 1947. Intern Church Home and Hosp., Balt., 1947-48; asst. resident Seton Inst., Balt., 1948-50; assoc. Washington U., St. Louis, 1950-51; resident in neuropsychiatry Barnes Hosp., St. Louis, 1950-51; asst. prof. psychiatry Washington U., St. Louis, 1955-59, asso. prof., 1959-66, prof., 1966-71; asso. psychiatrist Barnes Hosp., 1963-71; cons. in psychiatry Homer G. Phillips Hosp., 1954-64; instr. psychiatry Meharry Med. Coll., Nashville, 1954-55; prof., head dept. psychiatry U. Iowa, 1971—; dir. Iowa Psychiat. Hosp. Author: Manic Depressive Illness, 1969, Depression: The Facts, 1981; chief Am. editor: Jour. Affective Disorders, 1979—; editorial bd. 8 profl. jours.; contbr. numerous articles on clin. genetics of affective disorders, alcoholism and schizophrenia to profl. jours. Served to capt. M.C. USAF, 1952-54. Recipient Anna-Monika 1st prize award, 1973, Hofheimer prize, 1972, Samuel W. Hamilton award, 1977, Leonard Crammer Meml. award, 1980, Paul Hoch award, 1981; Vol. Service award Nat. Council Alcoholism, 1974. Fellow Am. Psychiat. Assn.; Mem. Am. Psychopath. Assn. (pres. 1975-77), Am. Soc. Human Genetics, Internat. Group Study of Affective Disorders, Psychiat. Research Soc., Am. Fedn. Clin. Research, Assn. Research in Nervous and Mental Disorders, Sigma Xi. Club: Tudor and Stewart (Balt.). Current Work: Epidemiology, genetics and classification of affective disorders, alcoholism and schizophrenia; treatment studies in depression. Subspecialties: Psychiatry; Genetics and genetic engineering (medicine). Office: 500 Newton Rd Iowa City IA 52242

WINT, DENNIS MICHAEL, museum director; b. Macon, Ga., Mar. 17, 1943; s. Paul Kenneth and Mary (McClure) W.; m. Patricia McLaughlin, Dec. 27, 1970; children—Laurel, Julia. B.S., U. Mich., 1965; tchr.'s cert. Lake Erie Coll., 1970; Ph.D., Case Western Res. U., 1977. Dir. environ. edn. Wiloughby Eastlake City Schs., 1968-70; dir. Ctr. for Devel. Environ. Curiculum, 1970-75; cons. Ohio Dept. Edn., 1975-77; dir. mus. and edn. Acad. Natural Scis., Phila., 1977-79, v.p., dir. natural history mus., 1979-82; dir. Cranbrook Inst. Sci., Bloomfield Hills, Mich., 1982—; adj. asst. prof. Temple U. Grantee in field. Mem. Am. Assn. Museums (accreditation commn.), Assn. Sci.-Tech. Ctrs. (bd. dirs.), Mich. Museums Assn. (bd. dirs.). Subspecialty: Environmental Education.

WINTER, ARTHUR, neurosurgeon; b. Newark, Sept. 7, 1922; s. Benjamin and Rose W.; m. Ruth N. Grosman, June 16, 1956; children: Robin, Craig, Grant. B.A., Drew U., 1947; P.C.B. cum laude, U. Montreal, 1948, M.D., 1953. Cert. physician, N.Y. Cert. physician, N.J. Intern U. Montreal Hosps., 1952-53; resident Newark Beth Israel Hosp., 1953-55; resident in neurol. surgery Baylor Med. Coll.-Tex. Med. Center, Houston, 1955-56, Albert Einstein Med. Center, 1956-59; practice medicine specializing in neurol. surgery, Livingston, N.J.; attending staff St. Barnabas Med. Center, Hosp. Center at Orange (N.J.), N.J. Orthopedic Hosp., VA Hosp.; cons. numerous hosps. and rehab. insts.; clin. instr. N.J. Coll. Medicine and Dentistry. Author: The Moment of Death, 1969, Surgical Control of Behavior, 1971, Life and Death Decisions; also numerous articles; developer Winter head dressing, microsug. brain retractor, pupicon; patent pending: multilevel thermistor for microwave control, array plug for Stereotaxic implant in the brain. Served with U.S. Army, 1943-46, ETO. Decorated Purple Heart; decorated Battle Stars (3); grantee Multiple Sclerosis Research Fund, 1974, N.J. Dept. Health Beth Israel Hosp. Fellow Am. Acad. Neurol. Sand Orthopedic Surgeons, Am. Coll. Emergency Physicians, N.J. Acad. Medicine, Royal Soc. Health; mem. AMA, EEG Soc. (assoc.), AAAS, Congress of Neurol. Surgeons, Essex County Med. Assn., Soc. Neurosci., Am. Soc. Stereotactic and Functional Neurosurgery, others. Current Work: Research in cancer (microwaves), multiple sclerosis (amino acids) and brain and spinal cord injury' central nervous system functions and dysfunctions and applied research. Subspecialties: Neurology; Neurophysiology. Office: 22 Old Short Hills Rd Suite 110 Livingston NJ 07039

WINTER, PETER MICHAEL, physician, anesthesiologist, educator; b. Sverdlovsk, Russia, Aug. 5, 1934; came to U.S., 1938, naturalized, 1944; s. George and Anne W.; m. Madge Sato, Aug. 22, 1964; children: Karin Anne, Christopher George. B.A., Cornell U., 1958; M.D., U. Rochester, 1962. Intern U. Utah, Salt Lake City, 1962-63; resident in anesthesiology Mass. Gen. Hosp., Boston, 1963-65; USPHS fellow Harvard U. Med. Sch., 1964-66; Buswell fellow dept. physiology, asst. prof. SUNY, Buffalo, 1966-69; asso. prof. dept. anesthesiology Sch. Medicine, U. Wash., Seattle, 1969-74, prof., 1974-79; prof., chmn. dept. anesthesiology U. Pitts. Sch. Medicine, 1979—; cons. Union Carbide Corp., NIH; med. officer Tektite II (underwater habitation project); anesthesiologist in chief Univ. Health Center Hosps., Pitts. Mem. editorial bd.: Jour. Critical Care Medicine; editorial cons.: Anesthesiology; contbr. chpts. to books, papers and abstracts on anesthesia, environ. phys. pharmacology and med. edn. to publs. Served with U.S. Army, 1953-56. Recipient NIH career devel. award, 1971. Mem. AMA, Am. Coll. Chest Physicians, Am. Soc. Anesthesiologists, N.Y. Acad. Scis., Undersea Med. Soc. Internat. Anesthesia Research Soc., Soc. Acad. Anesthesia Chairmen, Assn. Univ. Anesthetists. Current Work: Anesthesiology; mechanism of action of central nervous system depressants; environmental physiology. Subspecialties: Anesthesiology; Physiology (medicine). Office: 1385 E Scaife Hall Univ Pittsburgh School Medicine Pittsburgh PA 15260

WINTER, THOMAS GUSTAV, physicist; b. N.Y.C., Jan. 14, 1946; s. Henry Ernest and Caroline G. (Kunkel) W.; m. Janis Rae Bruehl, June 11, 1967; 1 child, John Thomas. B.A. magna cum laude, Queens Coll. City N.Y., 1967; Ph.D., U. Wis.-Madison, 1972. Teaching asst. U. Wis.-Madison, 1967-70, research asst., 1970-72; univ. fellow Queen's U., Belfast, No. Ireland, 1972-73; research assoc. Rice U., Houston, 1973-76; asst. prof. physics Pa. State U., Wilkes-Barre, Pa., 1976-81, assoc. prof., 1981—; vis. assoc. prof. Kans. State U., 1983; sr. research assoc. Rice U., 1984. Referee Phys. Review, 1973—, U.S. Dept. Energy, 1981—, NSF, 1982—. Contbr. articles to profl. jours. Mem. Union Concerned Scientists, Fedn. Am. Scientists, Citizen's Recycling Com., Wilkes-Barre, Wyo. Valley Peace Com., Wilkes-Barre, Mem. Am. Physical Soc., Phi Beta Kappa. Clubs: Wyoming Valley Striders (Wilkes-Barre); N.Y. Rd. Runners. Current work: Atom scattering (theory); electron transfer, excitation and ionization in ion-atom and atom-atom collisions, electron-molecule scattering. Subspecialty: Atomic and molecular physics. Home: 90 E Franklin St Shavertown PA 18708 Office: Pa State U Dept Physics Wilkes-Barre Campus Lehman PA 18627

WINTERFELDT, ESTHER, nutrition educator; b. Stigler, Okla., July 27, 1926; d. Walter William and Elsie P. (Wells) W. B.S., Okla. State U., 1948, M.S., 1957; Ph.D., Ohio State U., 1970. Registered dietitian, Okla. Chief dietitian Children's Hosp., Louisville, 1949-52; asst. dir. dietary U. Chgo. Hosps., 1953-56, 57-60; dir. dietary dept. Ohio State U. Hosps., Columbus, 1960-67; prof., head nutrition Okla. State U., Stillwater, 1970—; nutritionist, food scientist Coop. State Research Service, Dept. Agr., Washington, 1979-80, adminstr. Human Nutrition Info. Service, 1981-82. Recipient Disting. Alumni award Coll. Agr. and Home Econs., Ohio State U., 1981. Mem. Am. Dietetic Assn. (pres. 1979-80), Am. Home Econs. Assn., Sigma Xi, Phi Kappa Phi. Republican. Subspecialty: Nutrition (medicine). Address: 563 Greenbriar Crescent Stillwater OK 74078

WINTROBE, MAXWELL MYER, medical educator; b. Halifax, N.S., Can., Oct. 27, 1901; came to U.S., 1927, naturalized, 1933; s. Herman and Ethel (Swerling) W.; m. Becky Zanphir, Jan. 1, 1928; children: Susan Hope, Paul William H. (dec.). B.A., U. Man., Can.), Winnipeg, 1921, M.D., 1926, B.Sc. in Medicine, 1927, D.Sc. (hon.), 1958; Ph.D., Tulane U., 1929; D.Sc. (hon.), U. Utah, 1967, Med. Coll. Wis., Milw., 1974; M.D. (hon.), U. Athens, 1981. Diplomate Am. Bd. Internal Medicine. Gordon Bell fellow, Manitoba, 1926-27; instr. in medicine Tulane U., 1927-30; also asst. vis. physician Charity Hosp., New Orleans; instr. medicine Johns Hopkins, 1930-35, asso. in medicine, 1935-43, also asso. physician, 1935-43; physician in charge, clinic for nutritional, gastro-intestinal and hemopoietic disorders Johns Hopkins Hosp., 1941-43; prof. medicine U. Utah, 1943-70, Disting. prof. internal medicine, 1970—, head dept. medicine, 1943-67, dir. cardiovascular research and tng. inst., 1969-73; physician-in-chief Salt Lake Gen. Hosp., 1943-65, U. Utah Med. Center, 1965-67; cons. to surgeon-gen. U.S. Army; chief cons. Va Hosp., Salt Lake City; dir. lab. for study of hereditary and metabolic disorders U. Utah, 1945-73; spl. cons. nutritional anemias WHO; UN. Council mem. Nat. Adv. Arthritis and Metabolic Diseases Council, USPHS, 1950-54, chmn. hematology study sect., 1956-59; council mem. Nat. Allergy and Infectious Disease Council, 1967-70; mem. com. research in life scis. Nat. Acad. Sci., 1966-69; chmn. sci. adv. bd. Scripps Clinic and Research Found., 1964-74; med. cons. AEC; mem., then chmn. adv. council Life Ins. Med. Research Fund, 1949-53; dir. Am. Soc. Human Genetics, 1948; chmn. hematology com. Research and Devel. Command Surg. Gen.'s U.S. Army; cons. FDA, Dept. Health, Edn. and Welfare; vis. prof. numerous univs. including Rochester, Vanderbilt, Marquette, N.Y., Tufts, Johns Hopkins, Tulane, U. Calif. at San Diego, Brown U., N.C., Emory, U. Fla., Gainesville, Ala., Southwestern at Dallas, Harvard, UCLA, U. Toronto, Ottawa, U. B.C., McGill U., Dalhousie U. Mng. editor: Bull. Johns Hopkins Hosp, 1942-43; asso. editor: Nutrition Revs, Boston, 1943-49; adv. editor: Tice Practice of Medicine, 1943-76; asso. editor: Internat. Med. Digest, 1944- 58, Blood, 1945-75, Am. Jour. Medicine, 1946-56, Medicine, Cancer, Jour. Clin. Pathology; editorial bd.: Jour. Clin. Investigation, 1948-49, Gen. Practitioner, 1949-59, Jour. Clin. Nutrition, 1952-65, Jour. Chronic Diseases, 1955-75; Author: Clinical Hematology, 1942, 8th edit., 1981; Blood, Pure and Eloquent, 1980; Hematology, The Blossoming of a Science, A Story of Inspiration and Effort, 1985; also numerous sci. articles.; Editor: Harrison's Principles of Internal Medicine, 1950; editor-in-chief, 6th edit., 1970, 7th edit., 1974. Bd. dirs., v.p. Salt Lake Chamber Music Soc.; nat. adv. bd. Utah Symphony Orch.; bd. dirs. Pro-Utah.; Mem. Anti-Anemia Preparations adv. bd., U.S. Pharmacopeia, 1941-49, com. revision, 1950-60. Recipient gold medals in polit. econs. and French, 1921, Isbister prizes, 1920-25; all U. Man.).; Recipient Physician of Excellence award Med. Times, 1979. Fellow A.C.P. (John Philips Meml. award 1967, master 1973), Am. Inst. Nutrition; corr. mem. Italian, Swiss, German. socs. hematology, Brit. Assn. Clin. Pathology, Nat. Acad. Medicine (Buenos Aires); mem. Am. Soc. Hematology (pres. 1971-72), AMA (vice chmn. council on drugs 1964-68, chmn. sect. on adverse reactions), Assn. Am. Physicians (Kober medal 1974, councillor 1957-63, pres. 1964-65), Assn. Profs. Medicine (Robert H. Williams award 1973, councillor 1962-63, pres. 1965-66), Western Assn. Physicians (pres. 1956-57), Am. Soc. Exptl. Pathology, AAAS, Nat. Acad. Scis. (sec. med. scis. 1974-77, com. on sci. and public policy, 1975-80, chmn. sect. on human genetics, hematology and oncology 1977-80), Soc. Exptl. Biology and Medicine, Leukemia Soc. (chmn. nat. med. adv. bd.), Pacific Interurban Clin. Club, Western Soc. Clin. Research (Mayo Soley award 1970), European Soc. Hematology (corr.), Internat. Soc. Hematology (councillor-at-large 1972-74, v.p. 1976-78, pres. 1978-80, Ferrata award Rome 1958), Harvey Soc. (hon.), Assn. Clin. Pathologists (Eng.) (corr.), Am. Fedn. Clin. Research, Phi Beta Kappa (hon.), Sigma Xi, Alpha Omega Alpha, Sigma Alpha Mu; hon. mem. Chilean, Peruvian, Venezuelan, Uruguayan Socs. hematology. Current Work: Internal medicine; hematology; medical education; history of medicine; especially hematology. Subspecialty: Internal medicine. Home: 5882 Brentwood Dr Salt Lake City UT 84121 Office: U Utah Med Center Salt Lake City UT 84132

WINTZ, JOSEPH ANTHONY, III, consulting engineer, researcher; b. Phila., July 25, 1946; s. Joseph Anthony, Jr. and Margaret Jeannette (Stoner) W.; m. Nina Leigh Fuhst, June 14, 1969; children—Joseph Anthony IV, Carey Leigh. B.S.C.E., U. Va., 1970; M.S., George Washington U., 1974. Registered profl. engr., D.C., Pa., Va., W. Va. Student asst. Va. Hwy. Research Council, Charlottesville, 1969-70; structural engr. Fortune, Downey & Elliott Ltd., Alexandria, Va., 1970-74; sr. structural engr. Bernard Johnson, Inc., Washington, 1974-75, Airways Engring. Corp., Washington, 1975-76; asst. chief engr. Brick Inst. Am., McLean, Va., 1976-84; pres., sr. cons. Joseph Wintz, Ltd., Falls Church, Va., 1984—. Editor Proc. of 5th Internat. Brick Masonry Conf., 1982. Contbr. articles on masonry to profl. jours. Mem. Am. Ceramic Soc., Am. Concrete Inst., ASCE, ASTM, Brit. Ceramic Soc., Constrn. Specifications Inst., Earthquake Engring. Research Inst., Internat. Council Bldg. Research, Studies and Documentation, Masonry Soc., Nat. Inst. Bldg. Scis., Nat. Soc. Profl. Engrs., Nat. Trust Hist. Preservation, N.Z. Nat. Soc. Earthquake Engrs. Current work: Properties and performance of masonry assemblages and materials, especially in their application to design, construction and maintenance of masonry systems in architectural structures. Subspecialty: Structural engineering. Home: 3250 Annandale Rd Falls Church VA 22042 Office: Joseph Wintz Ltd PO Box 2257 Falls Church VA 22042

WIREN, ROBERT CRAIG, electronics firm nuclear engineer-designer; b. Seattle, Apr. 23, 1954; s. Robert and Agnes (Selle) W. B.S. Engring., U. Wash., 1976, M.S., 1979. Engr. Gen. Electric Co., San Jose, Calif., 1979-81, Electronic Assocs., West Long Branch, N.J., 1981—. Mem. Nat. Republican Congl. Com., 1981-82. Mem. Am. Nuclear Soc. Mem. Ch. of Scientology. Current Work: Increasing the ability of reactor operators, exteriorization in the control room and operator processing to clear and operating thetan, BWR ECCS logic systems simulation, reactor protection system simulation for boiling water reactors. Subspecialties: Nuclear engineering; Nuclear fission.

WISE, GARY LAMAR, electrical engineering and mathematics educator, researcher; b. Texas City, Tex., July 29, 1945; s. Calder Lamar and Ruby Lavon (Strom) W.; m. Mary Estella Warren, Dec. 28, 1974; 1 dau., Tanna Estella. B.A., Rice U., 1971; M.S.E., Princeton U., 1973, M.A., 1973, Ph.D., 1974. Postdoctoral research assoc. Princeton (N.J.) U., 1974; asst. prof. Tex. Tech U., Lubbock, 1975-76; asst. prof. U. Tex.-Austin, 1976-80, assoc. prof. elec. engring. and math., 1980-84, prof. elec. and computer engring. and math., 1984—; tech. reviewer Army Research Office, Durham, N.C., 1976, Air Force Office Sci. Research, Washington, 1980, 83, 84, 85, Harper and Row, N.Y.C., 1982-83, NSF, Washington, 1984-85; speaker tech. confs. Contbr. chpts., numerous articles to profl. publs. Air Force Office Sci. Research grantee, 1976—; Carroll D. Simmons Centennial teaching fellow in engring. U. Tex.-Austin, 1982-84. Mem. IEEE, Soc. Indsl. and Applied Math., Am. Math. Soc., Inst. Math. Stats., Phi Beta Kappa, Tau Beta Pi. Methodist. Current Work: Statistical communication theory, random processes, signal processing, signal detection and estimation, quantization theory, computer communication and applied mathematics. Subspecialties: Electrical engineering; Probability. Home: 8705 Collingwood Dr Austin TX 78748 Office: Dept Elec and Computer Engring U Tex Austin TX 78712

WISE, ROBERT EDWARD, radiologist; b. Pitts., May 21, 1918; s. Joseph Frank and Victoria Rose (Conley) W.; m. Yvonne Burkhard, Mar. 27, 1943; children—Lynne Dailey, Robert Edward, John Burkhard. B.S., U. Pitts., 1941; M.D., U. Md., 1943. Intern U.S. Naval Hosp., Phila., 1943-44; fellow in radiology Cleve. Clin. Found., 1947-49; radiologist Cleve. Clinic, 1949-52; practice medicine specializing in radiology, Pitts., 1952-53; radiologist Lahey Clinic Found., Boston, 1953—, chief exec. officer, chmn. bd. govs., 1975—; instr. radiology U. Pitts., 1971-72; clin. prof. radiology Sch. Medicine, Boston U.; dir. Bay State Skills Corp., Boston., Optronics Internat. Inc. Author: Intravenous Cholangiography, 1962, Accessory Digestive Organs, 1973, Radiology, Gallbladder and Bile Ducts. Trustee Boston Ballet Co., Eleanor Naylor Dana Trust, Middlesex Community Coll., Lahey Clinic Found., Lahey Clinic Hosp., L.C.F. Found.; mem. corp. New Eng. Bapt. Hosp., New Eng. Deaconess Hosp., Boston. Served in M.C. USN, 1943-47. Mem. Am. Coll. Radiology (pres. 1975), Radiol. Soc. N.Am. (pres. 1974), New Eng. Roentgen Ray Soc. (pres. 1963), AMA, Mass. Med. Soc. Mass. Radiol. Soc. (pres. 1973), Eastern Radiol. Soc. (pres. 1965), Beacon Soc. Boston. Roman Catholic. Clubs: Algonquin (Boston) (dir.); Brae Burn Country (West Newton, Mass.). Home: 155 Cliff Rd Wellesley Hills MA 02181 Home: Marshalls Point Rd Kennebunkport ME Office: 605 Commonwealth Ave Boston MA 02215

WIST, ABUND OTTOKAR, biomedical engineer, educator; b. Vienna, Austria, May 23, 1926; came to U.S., 1959; naturalized, 1964; s. Engelbert Johannes and Augusta Barbara (Ungewitter) W.; m. Suzanne Gregson Smiley, Nov. 30, 1963; children—John Joseph, Bundy Charles. B.S. in Engring. Physics, Eng U., Graz, Austria, 1948; M.S. in Edn., U. Vienna, 1950, Ph.D. in Physics, 1951. Cert. computer mfg. engineer. Research and devel. engr. Hornyphon A.G., Vienna, 1952-54, Siemens and Halske A.G., Munich, W. Ger., 1954-59; dir. research Brinkmann Instruments Inc., Westbury, L.I., N.Y., 1959-64; sr. scientist Fisher Sci. Inc., Pitts., 1964-70; research assoc. U. Pitts., 1970-73; mem. faculty dept. radiology Med. Coll. Va., Richmond, 1973—; dir. Symposium on Computer Applications Med. Care, D.C.; grant reviewer NIH; adv. Preston Coll., Columbia, S.C., 1984. Author: Microprocessor Based Instrumentation and Control Systems, 1985. Contbr. numerous articles to profl. jours. Patentee in field. Fellow NASA-ASEE, 1975. Mem. Biomed. Engr. Soc., IEEE (sr.), N.Y. Acad. Scis., Am. Chem. Soc., ASTM, Club: Toastmasters Internat. (pres. chpt.). Richmond Computer Club (pres.). Roman Catholic. Current work: Biomedical engineering; use of microcomputers to improve medical laboratory experimentation; cognitive psychology; improve information transfer from computer to medical scientists; catalysis chemistry; find catalysts in coal. Subspecialties: Agricultural engineering; Catalysis chemistry. Home: 9304 Farmington Dr Richmond VA 23229 Office: Med Coll Va 1101 E Marshall St Richmond VA 23298

WITHAM, PHILLIP ROSS, biological scientist, consultant; b. Stuart, Fla., Apr. 11, 1917; s. Paul Witham and Lucille (Ross) Zeigler; m. Mabel Josephine Blasko, May 27, 1945; children—Chester Randolph, Steven Paul, Timothy Dean, Julie Ann. B. of Ind. Studies, U. South Fla., 1973; M. of Liberal Studies, U. Okla., 1976. Aviation machinest mate U.S. Navy, 1934-44, civilian, 1949-52; tollkeeper Fla. Turnpike, Palm City, 1956-58; hydroponics supr. Pub. Health Found. for Blood Pressure and Cancer Research, Stuart, Fla., 1959-63; project leader Fla. Dept. Natural Resources, Stuart, 1963—; team mem. U.S. Fish and Wildlife Service and Nat. Marine Fisheries Service, St. Petersburg, Fla., 1979—, U.S. Corps Engrs., Jacksonville, Fla., 1982—; cons. in field. Author: (with others) Turtles: Extinction or Survival, 1974. Fellow Explorers Club; mem. Am. Soc. Zoologists, Ecol. Soc. Am., Am. Inst. Fisheries Research Biologists, Fla. Acad. Scis., Izaak Walton League. Lodge: Masons. Current work: Seaturtles, secondary interest in spiny lobsters; oceanic dispersal, growth and survival of head started (pen-reared) yearlings; management of turtle populations in highly developed area. Subspecialties: Marine biology; Behavioral ecology. Home: 1457 NW Lake Point Stuart FL 33494 Office: Fla Dept Natural Resources PO Box 941 Jensen Beach FL 33457

WITHERS, HUBERT RODNEY, radiobiologist; b. Stanthorpe, Queensland, Australia, Sept. 21, 1932; came to U.S., 1966; s. Hubert and Gertrude Ethel (Tremayne) W.; 1 child, Genevieve. M.B.B.S., U. Queensland, 1956; Ph.D., U. London, 1965; D.Sc., U. London, 1982. Diplomate: Am. Bd. Radiology, Royal Australasian Coll. Radiology. Radiotherapist Prince of Wales Hosp., Randwick, Sydney, Australia, 1966; vis. research scientist Lab. Physiology, Nat. Cancer Inst., Bethesda, Md., 1966-68; assoc. radiotherapist, assoc. prof. radiotherapy sect. exptl. radiotherapy U. Tex. System Cancer Center, M.D. Anderson Hosp and Tumor Inst., Houston, 1968-71, radiotherapist, prof. radiotherapy, chief sect., 1971-80; assoc. grad. faculty U. Tex. Grad. Sch. Biomed. Scis., Houston, 1969-73, mem. grad. faculty, 1973-80; prof. dept. radiotherapy U. Tex. Health Sci. Center, Houston, 1975-80; prof., dir. exptl. radiation oncology, dept. radiation oncology UCLA Med. Ctr., 1980—; cons. ad hoc revs. div. research grants Nat. Cancer Inst., 1969—, cons. clin. cancer centers program project rev. com., 1976-79; cons. clin. cancer centers program project rev. com. Nat. Surg. Adjuvant Breast and Bowel Program, 1976-81; mem. radiation study sect. NIH, 1970-74; mem. Internat. Com. on Radiation Protection Task Force on Non-Stochastic Effects of Radiation, 1980—, Com. on Radiation Oncology Studies, Subcom. on Particle Therapy, 1979-81. Assoc. editor: Radiation Research, 1973-76, Internat. Jour. Radiation Oncology Biology Physics, 1977—, Year Book of Cancer, 1972—, Radiotherapy and Oncology, 1983—; contbr. articles in field to profl. jours. Recipient Finzi Bequest prize Brit. Inst. Radiology, 1974; Commemorative medal of achievement U. Tex. System Cancer Center, 1981; Gaggin fellow cancer research U. Queensland, 1963-66. Fellow Royal Australasian Coll. Radiologists; mem. Radiation Research Soc. (pres. 1982-83), Am. Soc. Therapeutic Radiologists (bd. dirs. 1982— mem. com. on long-range planning, sci. program com.), Am. Coll. Radiology (mem. com. on radiotherapeutic devel., radiotherapy written exams. com.), Radiation Therapy Oncology Group (mem. radiobiology com.), Am. Radium Soc., Brit. Inst. Radiology. Current Work: Radiation biology in cancer treatment. Subspecialties: Cancer research (medicine); Radiology. Office: Dept Radiation Oncology UCLA Med Ctr Los Angeles CA 90024

WITKOP, BERNHARD, chemist; b. Freiburg, Baden, Germany, May 9, 1917; came to U.S., 1947, naturalized, 1953; s. Philipp W. and Hedwig M. (Hirschhorn) W.; m. Marlene Prinz, Aug. 8, 1945; children: Cornelia Johanna, Phyllis, Thomas. Diploma, U. Munich, 1938, Ph.D., 1940; Sc.D., Privat-Dozent, 1947. Matthew T. Mellon research fellow Harvard U., 1947-48, mem. faculty, 1948-50; spl. USPHS fellow Nat. Heart Inst., NIH, 1950-52; vis. scientist Nat. Inst. Arthritis and Metabolic Diseases, 1953, chemist, 1954-55, chief sect. metabolites, 1956—, chief lab. chemistry, 1957—; vis. prof. U. Kyoto, Japan, 1961, U. Freiburg, Germany, 1962; adj. prof. U. Md. Med. Sch., Balt., Nobel symposium lectr., Stockholm-Karlskoga, 1981; mem. bd. Internat. Sci. Exchange, 1974; mem. exec. com. NRC, 1975; mem. Com. Internat. Exchange, 1977, Paul Ehrlich Award Com., Frankfurt, 1980. Editor: Fedn. European Biochem. Soc. Letters, 1979—. Recipient Superior Service award USPHS, 1967; Paul Karrer gold medal U. Zurich, 1971; Kun-ni-to (medal of sci. and culture 2d class) Emperor of Japan, 1975; Alexander von Humboldt award for sr. U.S. scientists, 1978. Mem. Am. Chem. Soc. (Hillebrand award 1958), Nat. Acad. Scis., Am. Acad. Arts and Sci., Acad. Leopoldina (fgn.), Pharm. Soc. Japan (hon.), Chem. Soc. Japan (hon.), Japanese Biochem. Soc. (hon.). Current Work: Natural toxins, receptors, drugs, neurotransmitters. Subspecialties: Organic chemistry; Biochemistry (medicine). Office: Nat Insts Health Bethesda MD 20205

WITORSCH, RAPHAEL JAY, physiology educator, researcher; b. N.Y.C., Dec. 12, 1941; s. Benjamin and Sarah (Etkin) W.; m. Barbara Diane Margolis, Dec. 26, 1964; children—Benjamin, Marc. B.A., NYU, 1963; M.S., Yale U., 1965, Ph.D., 1968. Postdoctoral fellow U. Va., Charlottesville, 1968-70; asst. prof. physiology Med. Coll. Va., Va. Commonwealth U., Richmond, 1970-79, assoc. prof., 1979—; cons. Ctr. for Environ. Health and Human Toxicology, Washington, 1984—. Contbr. chpt. to book, articles to profl. publs. Recipient awards for excellence in teaching Med. Coll. Va., 1971, 73, 79, 84; NIH/Nat. Cancer Inst. grantee, 1978-84. Mem. Endocrine Soc., Soc. for Exptl. Biology and Medicine, Histochem. Soc., Am. Physiol. Soc., Am. Soc. Andrology, AAAS. Jewish. Current work: Role of prolactin in prostate physiology; mechanism of action of prolactin at the molecular level; toxicology of endocrine-reproductive system. Subspecialties: Endocrinology; Receptors. Office: Va Commonwealth U Med Coll Va Dept Physiology and Biophysics Snager Hall 3-038 Richmond VA 23298

WITTE, KURT ALLEN, electronics engineer; b. Mpls., May 27, 1949; s. Elmer Reinhardt and Thelma Anna (Tessmer) W.; m. Randi Elaine Johnson, June 27, 1969; m. Mary Lynne Bundy, Dec. 16, 1978; children—David Francis, Kevin Matthew. B.A. in Math, U. Minn., 1972, B.A. in Psychology, 1974. Instrumentation engr. Metallurgical, Inc., Mpls., 1977; supr. spl. products dept. Mobile Radio Engring., Inc., Mpls., 1978; design engr. research dept. CPT Corp., Mpls., 1978-82; electronics design engr. Solid Controls, Inc., Mpls., 1982-84; design engr. Ciprico, Inc., Plymouth, Minn., 1984—. Mem. IEEE, Assn. Computing Machinery, Mensa. Current Work: Multimicroprocessor systems architecture and software design. Subspecialties: Information systems, storage, and retrieval (computer science); Computer engineering. Home: 225 Monroe Ave N Hopkins MN 55343 Office: 2955 Xenium Ln Plymouth MN 55441

WITTE, MICHAEL, chemist, consultant, solar energy researcher; b. Poland, Mar. 15, 1911; s. Jake and Rose (Schlesinger) W.; m. Louise, Dec. 21, 1940; children: Michael S., Janet L., Lois J., John C. B.S., Loyola U., Chgo., 1937; M.S., U. Ill., 1938, Ph.D., 1941. Asst. chemistry dept. U. Ill., 1938-41; research chemist Nat. Aniline div. Allied Chem. Corp., Buffalo, 1941-47; product supr. Gen. Aniline & Film Corp., Rensselaer, N.Y., 1947-53, product mgr., Linden, N.J., 1953-56; pres. Simpson Labs. Inc., Newark, 1957-59, Carnegies Fine Chems. div. Rexall Drug & Chem. Corp., Kearny, N.J., 1959-60, M. Witte Assocs., Chatham, N.J., 1960—; cons., dir. Tennant Devel. Corp., N.Y.C., 1961-65. Explorer chmn. Boy Scouts Am., Berkeley Heights, N.J., 1959-60. Dept. Energy grantee, 1980-81. Mem. Am. Chem. Soc., Sigma Xi. Patenteein field (U.S. and fgn). Current Work: Organic syntheses of polarizing crystals; solar energy absorption; sulfur dioxide absorption; basic and applied chemical process and research development; research in dyestuff mfg., pharm. intermediates, organic chems. Subspecialties: Organic chemistry; Solar energy. Home and Office: 420 River Rd C-11 Chatham NJ 07928

WITTEN, LOUIS, physics educator; b. Balt., Apr. 13, 1921; s. Abraham and Bessie (Perman) W.; m. Lorraine Wollach, Mar. 27, 1949; children: Edward, Celia, Matthew, Jesse. B.E., Johns Hopkins U., 1941, Ph.D. in Physics, 1951; B.S. in Meteorology, NYU, 1944. Research assoc. Princeton U., 1951-53, U. Md., College Park, 1953-54; staff scientist Lincoln Lab., MIT, 1954-55; assoc. dir. Martin-Marietta Research Lab., Balt., 1955-68; prof. physics U. Cin., 1968—; v.p. Gravity Research Found., 1967—. Editor: Gravitation: An Introduction to Current Research, 1962, Relativity, 1964, Asymptotic Structure of Space-Time, 1977; contbr. articles to profl. jours.; patentee in field. Served to 1st lt. USAAF, 1942-46. Fulbright lectr. Weizmann Inst. Sci., Rehovot, Israel, 1963-64; NSF grantee; Dept. Def. grantee. Fellow Am. Phys. Soc.; mem. Internat. Astron. Union, Am. Astron. Soc., Am. Math. Soc., Am. Assn. Physics Tchrs., AAAS. Patentee in field. Current Work: Theory of supergravity—an attempt to unite general theory of relativity with theory of elementary particles. Subspecialties: Relativity and gravitation; Particle physics. Home: 7920 Rollingknolls Dr Cincinnati OH 45237 Office: Dept Physics U Cin Cincinnati OH 45221

WITTENBORN, JOHN RICHARD, psychology educator, clinical researcher, consultant; b. Ft. Gage, Ill., May 22, 1915; s. Richard Edward and Mabel (Mulholl) W.; m. Sarah Elizabeth Alwood, Apr. 29, 1938; children: Sarah Elizabeth, Gretchen Ann, Richard, Christopher Dirk. Ed.B., So. Ill. U., 1937; M.S., U. Ill., 1939, Ph.D., 1942. Instr. Yale U., New Haven, 1942-45, asst. prof., 1945-50, assoc. prof., 1950-54, clin. psychologist dept. univ. health, 1942-46; Univ. prof. psychology and edn. Rutgers U., New Brunswick, N.J., 1954—, dir. interdisciplinary research ctr., 1958-80; adv. com. psychopharmacology FDA, Washington, 1970-73, cons. pharm. industries. Author: Wittenborn Psychiatric Rating Scale, 1955, rev., 1964, Clinical Pharmacology of Anxiety, 1966, Placement of Adoptive Children, 1957, Guidelines for Clinical Trials of Psychotropic Drugs, 1977. USPHS fellow, 1948-50; recipient disting. teaching and research award Rutgers U., 1961; Devel. Sch. Psychology award N.J. Assn. Sch. Psychologists, 1973. Fellow Am. Coll. Neuropsychopharmacology (sec.-treas. 1964-72, pres. 1973, Paul Hoch Disting. Service award 1968), Collegium International Neuropsychopharmacologicum (v.p. 1982—), Am. Psychol. Assn. Club: Cosmos (Washington). Current Work: Design of clinical investigations of behavior disorders and their evaluation and treatment, age-related behavior changes. Subspecialties: Psychopharmacology; Psychopathology. Office: Rutgers U 13 Senior St New Brunswick NJ 07979

WITTIE, LARRY DAWSON, computer scientist, educator; b. Bay City, Tex., Mar. 9, 1943; s. L.D. and Mildred (Brown) W.; m. Diane M. Fischer, July 15, 1972; children: Lea D.F., Loren D.F. B.S., Calif. Inst. Tech., 1966; M.S., U. Wis., 1967, Ph.D., 1973. Systems programmer Calif. Inst. Tech., Pasadena, 1963-66, IBM, Sunnyvale, Calif., 1966; NASA trainee in computer sci. U. Wis., Madison, 1966-69, research asst., 1969-72; vis. asst. prof. computer sci. Purdue U., Lafayette, Ind., 1972-73; asst. prof. computer sci. SUNY, Buffalo, 1973-79, assoc. prof., 1979-82, assoc. prof. computer sci., Stony Brook, 1982—; tech. adviser Boeing, M. Wile & Co., Raytheon, Calspan, U.S. Army, NIH. Contbr. articles to profl. publs. Research grantee NSF; Research grantee USAF; Research grantee NASA; Research grantee U.S. Army. Mem. Assn. Computing Machinery, IEEE, Soc. Neurosci., Sigma Xi. Designer MICRONET computer and MICROS distributed operating system. Current Work: Distributed information processing in large networks: portable distributed operating systems for network computers and efficient interconnection topologies for networks of millions of computers. Subspecialties: Distributed systems and networks; Operating systems. Home: 7 Woodhull Rd East Setauket NY 11733 Office: Computer Sci Dept Room 1426 Lab Office Bldg SUNY Stony Brook NY 11794

WITTWER, SYLVAN HAROLD, research administrator, horticulture educator; b. Hurricane, Utah, Jan. 17, 1917; s. Joseph and Mary Ellen (Stucki) W.; m. Maurine Cottle, July 27, 1938; children: La Ree Wittwer Farrar, Alice Wittwer Sowards, Arthur John, Carl Thomas. B.S., Utah State Coll., 1939; Ph.D., U. Mo., 1943; D.Sc. (hon.), Utah State U., 1981. Instr. horticulture U. Mo., 1943-46; asst. prof. horticulture Mich. State U., 1964-68, East Lansing assoc. prof., 1948-50, prof., 1950—; dir. Mich. State U. (Agrl. Expt. Sta.), 1965-83; assoc. dean Coll. Agr. and Natural Resources Mich. State U., 1982—; hon. prof. N.E. Agrl. Coll., Harbin, China; sr. sci. advisor Heilongjiang Acad. Agrl. Sci., Jiangsu Acad. Agrl. Scis. Contbr. numerous articles on horticulture, plant physiology, agrl. tech., agrl. communications, priorities in agrl. research, food policy and agrl. policy, and sci. and tech. for food prodn. in 21st century to profl. publs. Recipient Disting. Faculty award Mich. State U., 1965; Benjamin Duggar award in plant physiology Auburn U., 1967; Disting. Service to Agr. award Mich. Farm Bur., 1976; James E. Talmage Sci. Achievement award Brigham Young U., 1977; citation of merit Coll. Agr., U. Mo.; Achievement award Am. Farm Bur. Fedn., 1983. Mem. Am. Soc. Hort. Sci., AAAS, Am. Soc. Plant Physiologists, Bot. Soc. Am., Soc. Devel. Biology, V.I. Lenin All Union Acad. Agrl. Scis. (USSR). Mormon. Current Work: Biological limits in crop and livestock productivity; telecommunication and electronic communications; genetic engineering, research priorities in food and agriculture, science and technology-the further frontiers in food production for the 21st century. Subspecialties: Plant physiology (agriculture); Plant physiology (biology). Office: Mich State U 108 Agr Hall East Lansing MI 48824

WNEK, GARY EDMUND, science educator; b. Amsterdam, N.Y., Sept. 9, 1955; s. Edmund J. and Joan (Malicki) W.; m. Maria Dufresne, June 17, 1978; children—Janice, Christine. B.S.Ch.E., Worcester Poly. Inst., 1977; Ph.D. in Polymer Sci., U. Mass., 1980. Asst. prof. dept. materials sci. MIT, Cambridge, 1980-85, assoc. prof., 1985—. NSF undergrad. research fellow SUNY-Albany, 1975. Mem. Am. Chem. Soc. (polymer div. speakers bur. chmn. 1983), Am. Phys. Soc., AAAS. Roman Catholic. Current Work: Synthesis modification and characterization of electrically conductive polymers, sythesis of new polymers, ion implantation of polymers. Subspecialties: Polymer chemistry; Electronic materials. Home: 45 Shore Rd Ashland MA 01721 Office: MIT 77 Massachusettes Ave Rm 13-5094 Cambridge MA 02139

WNUK, MICHAEL PETER, mechanics engineering educator; b. Katowice, Poland, Sept. 12, 1936; came to U.S., 1966, naturalized, 1972; s. Marian and Helena (Zaluska) W.; m. Renata Budzilowicz, June 7, 1964; 1 dau., Jennifer. M.S. in Mechanics, Tech. U. Krakow, Poland, 1959, Ph.D. in Theoretical and Applied Mechanics, 1962; M.S. in Physics, Jagiellonian U.-Krakow, 1965. Disting. vis. scholar U. Cambridge, Eng., 1970; sr. research fellow Calif. Inst. Tech., Pasadena, 1967-68; asst. prof. mech. engring. S.D. State U., Brookings, 1966-67, assoc. prof., 1968-76, prof., 1976-82; prof. engring. mechanics U. Wis.-Milw., 1982—. Author: Introduction to Fracture Mechanics, 1977; editor: Proceedings 1st Yugoslav Summer Sch. on Fracture Mechanics, 1980. Mem. Cambridge Philos. Soc., N.Y. Acad. Scis. (life), Sigma Xi. Roman Catholic. Current Work: Stability problems in elastic-plastic fracture; numerical methods in continuum mechanics. Subspecialties: Mechanical engineering; Applied mathematics. Home: 3436 N Dousman St Milwaukee WI 53201 Office: U Wis Coll of Engring and Applied Scis 1530 Cramer St Milwaukee WI 53201

WOBUS, REINHARD ARTHUR, geologist, educator; b. Norfolk, Va., Jan. 11, 1941; s. Reinhard Schaffer and Oral (Phares) W.; m. Sheridan Whitcher, Mar. 18, 1967; children—Erik Reinhard, Cameron Wright. B.A., Washington U., St. Louis, 1962; M.A., Harvard U., 1963; Ph.D., Stanford U., 1966. Asst. prof. geology Williams Coll., 1966-72, assoc. prof., 1972-78, prof., 1978—; geologist U.S. Geol. Survey, Denver, 1967—; vis. prof. Colo. Coll., Colorado Springs, 1976, 82-83, Colo. State U., Ft. Collins, summers 1977-84; staff geologist Colo. Outdoor Edn. Ct., Florissant, Colo., summers 1983-84. Contbr. maps and articles on Precambrian geology of so Rocky Mountains to profl. jours. NSF fellow, 1962-66. Fellow Geol. Soc. Am.; mem. Nat. Assn. Geology Tchrs., Colo. Sci. Soc., Phi Beta Kappa, Sigma Xi. Current work: Petrology and geochronology of Precambrian igneous and metamorphic rocks, southern Rocky Mountains. Subspecialties: Petrology; Geology. Home: 20 Grandview Dr Williamstown MA 01267 Office: Dept Geology Williams College Williamstown MA 01267

WOGAN, GERALD NORMAN, educator; b. Altoona, Pa., Jan. 11, 1930; s. Thomas B. and Florence E. (Corl) W.; m. Henrietta E. Hoenicke, Aug. 24, 1957; children—Christine F., Eugene E. B.S., Juniata Coll., 1951; M.S., U. Ill., 1953, Ph.D., 1957. Asst. prof. physiology Rutgers U., New Brunswick, N.J., 1957-61; asst. prof. toxicology Mass. Inst. Tech., Cambridge, 1962-65, assoc. prof., 1965-69, prof., 1969—, head dept. applied biol. scis., 1979—; cons. to nat. and internat. govt. agys., industries. NIH grantee, 1963—. Mem. editorial bd.: Cancer Research, 1971—, Applied Microbiology, 1971—, Chem.-Biol. Interactions, 1975—, Toxicology, Environ. Health, 1974—; Contbr. articles and revs. to profl. jours. NSF grantee, 1965-68. Mem. Nat. Acad. Scis. U.S., Am. Assn. Cancer Research, Am. Soc. Pharmacology and Exptl. Therapeutics, Am. Soc. Microbiology, Soc. Toxicology, Am. Inst. Nutrition, AAAS, Sigma Xi. Current Work: Mechanisms of chemical carcinogenesis; identification of carcinogens. Subspecialties: Cancer research (medicine); Biochemistry (medicine). Home: 125 Claflin St Belmont MA 02178 Office: Dept Applied Biol Scis Mass Inst Tech Cambridge MA 02139

WOHLFEIL, PAUL FREDERICK, health maintenance organization counselor; b. Saginaw, Mich., Aug. 28, 1934; s. Herman Frederick and Rose (Kueffner) W.; m. Shirli Jean Setzer, July 20, 1976; children: Paul John, Ondria Rose. B.A., Mich. State U., 1962; M.A., Eastern Mich. U., 1966; Ph.D., Independence (Mo.) U., 1973; postgrad., Rutgers U., 1974. Lic. psychologist, marriage counselor, Mich., cert. social worker, lic. marriage and family therapist, cert. clin. mental health counselor, Fla. Psychologist Boys Tng. Sch., Whitmore Lake, Mich., 1962-65; psychologist, assoc. dir. Whaley Home for Disturbed Children, Flint, Mich., 1963-68; psychologist Adult Mental Health Clinic, Bay City, Mich., 1968-73, Salman Psychiat. Clinic, Bay City, 1973-79; dir. counseling Group Health Services of Mich., Saginaw, 1978—; cons. Saginaw Steering Gear, 1973—, Gen. Electric Corp., Pittsfield, Mass., 1978-79, Gratiot Community Mental Health, Alma, Mich., 1969-71; dir. Personal Growth, Inc., Saginaw, 1975—. Author: (1977.) Awareness Counseling for Nurses. Served with AUS, 1954-56. Recipient award Bay City Bd. Commrs., 1971, award Flint (Mich.) Bd. Dirs., 1963. Mem. Am. Assn. Marriage and Family Therapists, Mich. Assn. Marriage and Family Therapists, Mich. Psychol. Assn., Am. Psychol. Assn. (assoc.), Mich. Assn. Group Psychotherapy. Lutheran. Club: Riverview Rod and Gun (Grayling, Mich.). Current Work: Psychological and physiological aspects in the health care field, using computer data-based information for counseling development. Subspecialties: Health psychology; Cognition. Home: 3102 Sharon Rd Midland MI 48640 Office: Group Health Service Mich 4200 Fashion Square Blvd Saginaw MI 48603

WOHLGEMUTH, JOHN H., solid state physicist, researcher; b. N.Y.C., Dec. 20, 1946; s. Harold Vincent and Joan Gladys (Purvey) W.; m. Bethany H. Hubbard, June 23, 1973; children—Edward J., Robert B. B.S., Rensselaer Poly. Inst., 1968, M.S., 1972, Ph.D., 1973. Postdoctoral research U. Waterloo, Ont., Can., 1973-75, U. Pa., Phila., 1975-76; mgr. advanced devel. Solarex Corp., Rockville, Md., 1976-83; solid state sci. group leader Cabot Corp., Billerica, Mass., 1983—; sec. exec. com. Ghemini Technologies, Salem, Mass., 1983—. Contbr. articles to profl. jours. Mem. Am. Phys. Soc., IEEE, Materials Research Soc., Sigma Pi Sigma. Current work: Gas Crystal growth, electronic ceramics (packaging and capacitors), semiconductor materials, photovoltaic devices and systems. Subspecialties: Electronic materials; Ceramics. Home: 30 Agawan Rd Acton MA 01720 Office: Cabot Corp Concord Rd Billerica MA 01821

WOHLSEN, ROBERT COBB, computer scientist, mechanical engineer; b. Phila., July 14, 1950; s. Herman Fredrick and Jean (Dithridge) W.; m. Linda Ann Broughton, Sept. 8, 1979. B.S.M.E., Heald Engring. Coll., San Francisco, 1975. Registered profl. engr., Calif. Research engr. Skyway Products, San Fernando, Calif., 1975-76; design engr. Peterbilt Motors, Newark, Calif., 1976-78; project mgr. Go-Power Corp., Palo Alto, Calif., 1978-82; engring. mgr. Clement Designlabs, Mountain View, Calif., 1982-84; computer scientist SRI Internat., Menlo Park, Calif., 1984—. Mem. Robotic Soc. Am. (v.p. 1984—), Robotics Internat., IEEE, ASME. Quaker. Current work: Development of artificial intelligence techniques for use in manufacturing and mechanical engineering applications; planning systems, expert systems. Subspecialties: Artificial intelligence; Robotics. Office: SRI Internat Advanced Computer Systems Dept 333 Ravenswood Ave Menlo Park CA 94025

WOHLTJEN, HENRY, III, research chemist; b. S.I., N.Y., July 20, 1950; s. Henry, II, and Elizabeth (Bronner) W.: m. Sharon Mutter, May 2, 1980. B.S. in Chemistry, CUNY, 1972, B.S. in Engring. Sci., 1974; Ph.D. in Chemistry, Va. Poly. Inst. and State U., 1978. Post-doctoral fellow IBM Research, Yorktown Heights, N.Y., 1978-79, Zurich, Switzerland, 1979-80; research chemist U.S. Naval Research Lab., Washington, 1980-85; founder, pres. Microsensor Systems, Inc., Fairfax, Va., 1985—. Patentee in field. Contbr. articles to profl. jours. Mem. IEEE, Am. Chem. Soc. Current work: Surface acoustic wave devices, langmuir-blodgett film chemiresistors and optical waveguide spectrometers for microfabricated chemical sensors and micro instrumentation. Subspecialties: Analytical chemistry; Microchip technology (materials science).

WOJCICKI, STANLEY G., physicist; b. Warsaw, Poland, Mar. 30, 1937; U.S. citizen; married. A.B., Harvard U., 1957; Ph.D., in Physics, U. Calif.-Berkeley, 1962. Physicist Lawrence Radiation Lab., U. Calif., 1961-66; from asst. prof. to assoc. prof. physics Stanford U., Calif., 1966-74, prof., 1974—; chmn. HEPAP panel Dept. Energy, Washington. NSF fellow, 1964-65; Alfred P. Sloan Found. fellow, 1968-72; Guggenheim fellow, 1973-74; recipient Alexander von Humnoldt sr. scientist award, 1980. Fellow Am. Phys. Soc. Subspecialty: Particle physics. Office: Stanford U Dept Physics Stanford CA 94305*

WOLANSKY, BONNIE KAY, digital design engineer; b. Syracuse, N.Y.; d. Abraham Ghemey and Roslyn Leonore (Olum) G. B.S., Ohio State U., 1980; M.S. in Elec. Engring., Syracuse U., 1983; postgrad. Upstate Med. Ctr., 1981-82. Summer fellow Masonic Med. Research Lab., Utica, N.Y., 1981; teaching asst. Syracuse U., 1981-82; project engr. Dynamics Research, Wilmington, Mass., 1983-84; systems engr. AT&T Info. Systems Lab., Holmdel, N.J., 1984-85; digital design engr. Goodyear Aerospace Corp., Akron, Ohio, 1985—. Mem. IEEE, Engring. Medicine and Biology Assn., Nat. Assn. Female Execs. Current work: Digital Designer for VHSIC/VLSI circuits, developing cell libraries for a wide spectrum of usage; work with the hardware development group for digital defense systems. Subspecialty: Systems engineering. Home: 6 Kimberly Ct 73 Red Bank NJ 07701 Office: AT&T Info Systems Crawfords Corner Rd Holmdel NJ 07733

WOLBARSHT, MYRON LEE, biophysicist, educator, researcher; b. Balt., Sept. 18, 1924; s. Samuel and Rose (Levine) W.; children: Seth, Selah, Jeremy. A.B., St. John's Coll., 1950; Ph.D., Johns Hopkins U., 1958. Research assoc. Psychiat. Inst., U. Md., 1954-60; research cons. neurology U. Md. Med. Sch., 1960-63; research fellow Johns Hopkins U., Balt., 1959-68; research cons. neurology York (Pa.) Hosp., 1963-68; physicist Naval Med. Research Inst., Bethesda, Md., 1958-68, head biophysics div., 1966-68; prof. ophthalmology and biomed. engring. Duke U., Durham, N.C., 1968—, assoc. prof. physiology, lectr. psychology; cons. in field of laser safety. Author: (with D.H. Sliney) Safety with Lasers and Opther Optical Sources, 1980; assoc. editor: Quar. Rev. Biology, 1963-68, IRE-IEEE Transactions on Biomed. Electronics, 1961-69; contbr. chpts. to books, articles to profl. jours. Served with USAAF, 1943-46. Mem. Am. Nat. Standards Inst. (chmn. eye hazards subcom. 1969—), U.S. Nat. Com. Photobiology, Laser Inst. Am. (pres. 1983), Am. Soc. Laser Medicine and Surgery (bd. dirs., editor jour.), Armed Forces-NRC Com. on Vision, Am. Physiol. Soc., Am. Soc. Photobiology, Assn. Research in Vision and Ophthalmology, Biophys. Soc., IEEE, Soc. Gen. Physiologists, N.Y. Acad. Scis., Optical Soc. Am., Soc. Photo-Optical Instrumentation Engrs., Royal Soc. Medicine, Sigma Xi. Club: Cosmos (Washington). Patentee in field. Current Work: Research in laser tissue interaction, vascular complications of diabetes, laser safety, automated visual function testing. Subspecialties: Neurophysiology; Ophthalmology. Office: Dept Psychology Duke U Durham NC 27706

WOLBER, WILLIAM GEORGE, instrumentation engineer, consultant; b. Detroit, Feb. 19, 1927; s. Joseph Gregory Wolber and Theresa Wolber Quardt; m. Velma Faye Campbell, June 17, 1950; children—Paul K., William George, Teresa Ann Wolber-Eustis, Robert A., Andrew J. B.S.Ch.E., U. Mich., 1949, B.S. in Engring. Math., 1949, M.S. in Physics, 1950. Registered profl. engr., Mich., Ind. With UniRoyal Process Devel., Detroit, 1950-54, divisional group leader, 1952-54; with Bendix Research, Southfield, Mich., 1954-81, sr. prin. engr., 1979-81; sr. tech. adviser, electronics systems div. Cummins Engine Co., Columbus, Ind., 1981—; cons., speaker in field. Served with USN, 1945-46. Mem. Instrument Soc. Am., Soc. Automotive Engrs. (sr.; Best Oral award 1983), IEEE (sr.), Tau Beta Pi. Roman Catholic. Current work: Measurement science; armored force vehicles; sensors for diesel engine electronic control; advanced propulsion system controls for armored force vehicles. Subspecialties: Microelectronics; Systems engineering. Home: 3151 Sumac Ct Columbus IN 47203 Office: Cummins Engine Co Electronics Systems Div Mail Stop 95032 PO Box 3005 Columbus IN 47202

WOLEN, ROBERT LAWRENCE, pharmacologist, educator; b. N.Y.C., May 20, 1928; s. Albert and Yetta W.; m. Marion Jacobs, Apr. 9, 1953; children: Sonya M., Y. Rosalind. B.S., West Chester State U., 1950; M.S., U. Del., 1951, Ph.D., 1961. Lectr. Oak Ridge Inst. Nuclear Studies, 1961-62; research scientist St. Joseph Hosp., Lancaster, Pa., 1962-63; sr. biochemist Eli Lilly & Co., Indpls., 1963-66, sr. clin. biochemist, 1966-68, research scientist, 1968-69, chief clin. chemistry and drug metabolism dept., 1969-75, research assoc., 1975-79, research adv., 1979—. Served to lt. USN, 1951-55. Mem. Am. Chem. Soc., Am. Soc. Pharmacology and Exptl. Therapeutics, Am. Soc. Clin. Pharmacology and Therapeutics, Am. Assn. Clin. Chemists. Jewish. Current Work: Drug metabolism and pharmacokinetics. Subspecialties: Pharmacology; Biochemistry (medicine). Office: 307 E McCarty St Indianapolis IN 46285

WOLF, BARBARA ANNE, research administrator, educator; b. N.Y.C., July 24, 1947; d. Boris and Molly (Gruberg) W.; m. Robert, Spiel, Aug. 25, 1977. B.A. in Chemistry, Queens Coll., CUNY, 1968; Ph.D. in Biology, M.I.T., 1973. Research asst. Sloan-Kettering Inst. Cancer Research, Rye, N.Y., 1967; undergrad. researcher Queens Coll., 1968; teaching asst. M.I.T., 1969-70, 72-73; research asst. in virology Rockefeller U., 1973-75; fellow Nat. Cancer Inst., 1975-77, research assoc., 1977; mgr. biol. services Revlon Research Ctr., Bronx, N.Y., 1977-80, dir. biol. scis., 1981—; attendee U. Tex., 1979; assoc. prof. St. John's U., 1981—. Contbr. articles to profl. jours. Recipient Stanley Koncal award, 1968; N.Y. State Regents scholar, 1964-68. Mem. Environ. Mutagen Soc., Genetic Toxicology Assn., Am. Coll. Toxicology, Soc. Toxicology, N.Y. Acad. Scis., AAAS, Am. Soc. Microbiologists, Soc. Cosmetic Chemists, N.Y . Soc. Electron Microscopists, Phi Beta Kappa, Sigma Xi, Beta Delta Chi. Current Work: Animal toxicology, genotoxicity (mutagenicity), clinical testing, antimicrobial testing. Subspecialties: Toxicology (medicine); Cell biology (medicine).

WOLF, JACK KEIL, electrical engineering educator, consultant; b. Newark, Mar. 14, 1935; s. Joseph and Rosaline M. (Keil) W.; m. Toby Katz, Sept. 10, 1955; children—Joseph M., Jay S., Sarah K. B.S.E.E., U. Pa., 1956; M.S.E., Princeton U., 1957, M.A., 1958, Ph.D., 1960. Assoc. prof. elec. engring. NYU, 1963-65; from assoc. prof. to prof. Poly. Inst. Bklyn., 1965-73; prof. U. Mass., Amherst, 1973-85, U. Calif.-San Diego, La Jolla, 1985—; cons. in field, 1963—; pres. Jack Keil Wolf Inc., La Jolla, 1982—. Contbr. articles to profl. jours. Served to lt. USAF, 1960-63. NSF sr. postdoctoral fellow, 1971; Guggenheim fellow, 1979. Fellow IEEE; mem. IEEE Info. Theory Group (pres. 1974, Prize Paper award 1975), AAAS, Sigma Xi, Sigma Tau, Eta Kappa Nu, Pi Mu Epsilon, Tau Beta Pi. Current work: High density digital magnetic recording and computer-communication networks. Subspecialties: Computer engineering; Information systems (Information science). Office: U Calif-San Diego Ctr for Magnetic Rec Research La Jolla CA 92093

WOLF, JOSEPH ALLEN, JR., mechanical engineer; b. Tacoma, Nov. 26, 1933; s. Joseph Allen and Wilma Audrey (Murphy) W.; m. Sally Blackwood Doyle, June 25, 1960; 1 son, Joseph Allen. M.E. with honor, Stevens Inst. Tech., 1955; M.S. in Applied Physics, UCLA, 1957; Sc.D. in Mech. Engring. (NSF fellow), M.I.T., 1967. Registered profl. engr., Calif. Mem. tech. staff Hughes Aircraft Co., Culver City, Calif., 1955-62; asst. prof. engring. and applied sci. UCLA, 1966-71; staff research engr. dept. engring. mechanics Gen. Motors Research Labs., Warren, Mich., 1971—. Co-author and co-editor: Modern Automotive Structural Analysis, 1982; contbr. articles, chpts. to profl. publs. Mem. ASME, Soc. Automotive Engrs., Am. Soc. Engring. Edn., Sigma Xi, Tau Beta Pi. Republican. Episcopalian. Current Work: Dynamics, mechanical and structural vibrations, and structural analysis of automotive components and structures. Subspecialties: Theoretical and applied mechanics; Acoustical engineering. Home: 438 S Glenhurst Birmingham MI 48009 Office: Engring Mechanics Dept Gen Motors Research Labs Warren MI 48090

WOLF, NANCY GAIL, behavioral ecologist, educator; b. Cleve., Nov. 18, 1954; d. Milton Albert and Roslyn (Zehman) W. A.B. summa cum laude, Harvard U., 1977; diploma Oxford U., 1978; Ph.D. in Ecology, Evolutionary Biology, Cornell U., 1983. Teaching asst. Harvard U., Cambridge, Mass., 1977, Cornell U., Ithaca, N.Y., 1979-82; postdoctoral fellow Woods Hole Oceanographic Inst., Mass., 1983-84; NATO postdoctoral fellow McGill U., Montreal, Que., Can., 1984—; assoc. ichthyology Harvard U., Cambridge, 1984—; aquanaut NOAA, St. Croix, V.I., 1979-80. NSF grantee, 1982-84. Mem. Am. Soc. Zoologists, Am. Soc. Ichthyologists and Herpetologists (Raney award 1979), Ecol. Soc. Am., Am. Soc. Naturalists, Animal Behavior Soc., Sigma Xi. Club: Harvard (N.Y.C.). Current work: Effects of respiratory mode and oxygen concentration on risk of predation in fishes. Subspecialties: Behavioral ecology; Marine biology. Office: Biology Dept McGill U 1205 Ave Dr Penfield Montreal PQ H3A 1B1 Canada

WOLF, RICHARD CLARENCE, educator; b. Lancaster, Pa., Nov. 28, 1926; s. Clarence Lester and Bertha Mae (Felker) W.; m. Marilyn Jean Miller, Aug. 23, 1952; children—Mark, Eric. B.S., Franklin and Marshall Coll., 1950; Ph.D., Rutgers U., 1954. Faculty dept. physiology U. Wis.-Madison, 1957—, prof., 1966—, chmn., 1971—, mem. endocrinology-reproductive physiology program, 1963—, co-dir., 1968-70, dir., 1970—; Cons. NIH; Cons. Ford Found.; mem. sci. bd. Yerkes Regional Primate Center, Emory U., 1972-78. Contbr. articles to profl. jours. Served with AUS, 1945-46. Waksman-Merck fellow Rutgers U., 1954-55; Milton fellow Harvard, 1955-56; USPHS fellow, 1956-57. Fellow N.Y. Acad. Scis.; Mem. Endocrine Soc., Am. Physiol. Soc., Soc. for Endocrinology (Gt. Britain), Soc. Exptl. Biology and Medicine (sec. Wis.), Soc. Study Fertility, Internat. Soc. for Research in Biology of Reproduction, Soc. for Study Reproduction, Sigma Xi., Phi Beta Pi. Lutheran. Club: Masons. Current Work: Reproductive biology; follicle growth and implantation. Subspecialty: Endocrinology. Home: 4205 Manitou Way Madison WI 53711

WOLF, WERNER PAUL, educator, physicist; b. Vienna, Austria, Apr. 22, 1930; came to U.S., 1963, naturalized, 1977; s. Paul and Wilhelmina (Wagner) W.; m. Elizabeth Eliot, Sept. 23, 1954; children: Peter Paul, Mary-Anne Githa. B.A., Oxford (Eng.) U., 1951, D.Phil, 1954, M.A., 1954; M.A. (hon.), Yale U., 1965. Research fellow Harvard U., 1956-57; Fulbright travelling fellow, 1956-57; Imperial Chem. Industries research fellow Oxford U., 1957-59, univ. demonstrator, lectr., 1959-63; lectr. New Coll., 1957-63; faculty Yale U., 1963—, prof. physics and applied sci., 1965—, dir. grad. studies dept. engring. and applied sci., 1973-76, Becton prof., 1976—, chmn. dept. engring. and applied sci., 1976-81, chmn. council engring., 1981—; cons. to industry, 1957—; Sigma Xi vis. prof. Technische Hochschule, Munich, Germany, 1969; Sci. Research Council sr. vis. fellow Oxford U., 1980; mem. program com. Conf. Magnetism and Magnetic Materials, 1963, 65, chmn., 1968, mem. adv. com., 1964-65, 70-76, chmn., 1972, steering com., 1970-71, conf. gen. chmn., 1971; mem. organizing, program coms. Internat. Congress on Magnetism, 1967, internat. program com., 1978-79, planning com., 1979; vis. physicist Brookhaven Nat. Lab., 1966, 68, vis. sr. physicist, 1970, research collaborator, 1972, 74, 75, 77, 80; mem. vis. com. dept. physics U. Del., 1980—. Contbr. papers on magnetic materials and low temperature physics. Fellow IEEE, Am. Phys. Soc. (edn. com. 1977-80, program dir. Indsl. Grad. Intern Program 1978—, chmn. fellowship com. 1981, mem. exec. com. Div. Condensed Material Physics 1980-83); mem. Am. Assn. Crystal Growers, Conn. Acad. Sci. and Engring., Yale U. Sci. and Engring. Assn. (hon. v.p. 1976). Current Work: Properties of magnetic materials, especially rare earth compounds, at low temperatures; phase transitions and critical phenomena. Subspecialty: Magnetic physics. Office: Becton Center Yale U New Haven CT 06520

WOLFE, BRADLEY ALLEN, electrical engineer; b. Seattle, Nov. 1, 1935; s. Adolph Edward and Bernice Eleanor (Younglowe) W.; m. Louis Mae Weber, Feb. 14, 1974; 1 stepdau., Kimberly Mae; m. Zelma Jean Harvey, Apr. 2, 1955 (div. Nov. 1973); children: Scott Bradley, Colleen Jean, Cynthia Joann. B.S.E.E., Heald Engring Coll., San Francisco, 1959. Registered profl. engr., Calif. Lead design engr. Boeing Co., Seattle, 1959-61, research and devel. mgr., Oak Ridge, 1965-78; project engr. Collins Radio Co., Cedar Rapids, Iowa, 1961-63; systems engr. Sperry Rand Corp., St. Paul, 1963-65; div. mgr. Sci. Applications, Inc., Oak Ridge, 1978-81; group mgr., projects mgr. Rockwell Internat., Richland, Wash., 1981—. Contbr. articles to profl. jours. Chmn. citizens adv. council Granite Falls (Wash.) Sch. Dist., 1972. Served with USN, 1953-56. Recipient Apollo Medallion NASA/Boeing, 1967; Outstanding Achievement award U.S. Dept. Energy, 1976. Mem. System Safety Soc. (chmn. N.W. chpt. 1967-68), IEEE (vice chmn, engring. mgmt. 1971-72), N.Y. Acad Scis., Am. Nuclear Soc., Nat. Mgmt. Assn. Current Work: Application of step-by-step planning methods for conduct of complex projects in efficient and effective manner. Effective application of computers to petro-chemical process monitor and control. Subspecialties: Systems engineering; Operating systems. Home: 7015 W 8th St Kennewick WA 99336 Office: Rockwell Internat PO Box 800 Richland WA 99352

WOLFE, DOUGLAS ARTHUR, pollution ecologist; b. Dayton, Ohio, July 6, 1939; s. Ranald Milton and Julia Marie (Good) W.; m. Nancy Suzanne Meeker, June 13, 1959; children—Cynthia Marie, Nicholas Arden. Catherine Ann. B.Sc., Ohio State U., 1959, M.Sc., 1961, Ph.D. (NIH fellow), 1964; M.Sc., Stanford U., 1981. Grad. teaching asst. physiol. chemistry Ohio State U., 1959-62, research asst., 1962-63; chief program biogeochemistry Bur. Comml. Fisheries Radiobiol. Lab., Beaufort, N.C., 1964-69; chief scientist I program marine biology div. radioecology P.R. Nuclear Center, Mayaguez, 1969-70; leader program elemental cycling Nat. Marine Fisheries Service Center for Estuarine and Menhaden Research, Beaufort, 1969-72; dir. div. ecology Atlantic Estuarine Fisheries Center, Beaufort, 1972-75; liaisson scientist Nat. Marine Fisheries Service, 1975-77; dep. dir. Outer Continental Shelf Environ. Assessment Program, NOAA Boulder, Colo., 1977-81; dir. operational programs Office Marine Pollution Assessment, Rockville, Md., 1981-84; chief scientist Ocean Assessments div. NOAA, 1984—; tng. assignment Stanford U. dept. engring.-econ. systems, 1980-81; adj. asso. prof. zoology N.C. State U., 1966-75; cons. Nat. Acad. Scis. Contbg. author: Handbook of Biochemistry and Biophysics, 1966, Impingement of Man on the Ocean, 1971, Coastal Ecological Systems of the U.S, 1974, Estuarine Research, 1975; Wastes in the Ocean, 1985; Oceanic Processes in Marine Pollution, 1986. Editor: Fate and Effects of Petroleum Hydrocarbons in Marine Ecosystems and Organisms, 1977. Recipient Superior Performance award Nat. Marine Fisheries Service, 1974; Spl. Achievement award NOAA, 1981. Mem. Am. Littoral Soc., Atlantic Estuarine Research Soc., Estuarine Research Fedn., Am. Chem. Soc., Am. Soc. Limnology Oceanography, Cave Research Found., Ecol. Soc. Am., Am. Malacological Union, N.C. Shell Club (v.p. 1971, 85, pres. 1972, 73), Sigma Xi, Phi Eta Sigma Phi Lambda Upsilon. Research, publs. on trace metals, radioactivity, pesticides and petroleum in marine organisms and ecosystems, and on biology of molluscs. Current work: Analysis and evaluation of environmental consequences of marine pollution. Subspecialties: Ecology (environmental science); Environmental chemistry. Home: 9101 Rosemont Dr Gaithersburg MD 20877 Office: NOAA Ocean Assessments Div Rockville MD 20852

WOLFE, HOWARD FRANCIS, mechanical and aeronautical engineer, research administrator; b. Dayton, Ohio, Feb. 17, 1938; s. Marion Francis and Ethel Louella (Dempsey) W.; m. Phyllis Ann, June 17, 1961; children: Timothy, Douglas, Brian, Gregory, Elizabeth, Matthew. B.M.E., U. Dayton, 1961; M.S.M.E., Ohio State U., 1970. Registered profl. engr., Ohio. Aerospace engr. Air Force Wright-Aero. Lab., Wright-Patterson AFB, Ohio, 1964-77; tech. mgr. Acoustics and Sonic Fatigue Group, 1977—. Mem. Beavercreek (Ohio) Music Parents Assn., 1979—, chmn. band camp, 1981. Served to 1st lt. Ordnance Corps U.S. Army, 1961-64. Decorated Army Commendation medal. Mem. ASME (Dayton sect. Outstanding Achievement award 1980), Nat. Mgmt. Assn. Roman Catholic. Patentee wide band siren system. Current Work: Acoustic fatigue of structures, acoustics, structural dynamics, random vibration, modal analysis, fatigue behavior. Subspecialties: Aerospace engineering and technology; Mechanical engineering. Home: 2834 Southfield Dr Xenia OH 45385 Office: Air Force Wright-Aero Lab/FIBGD Wright-Patterson AFB OH 45433

WOLFE, JAMES ALVIS, soil conservationist, consultant; b. Rogersville, Tenn., Aug. 16, 1931; s. William Alvis and Hazel (Looney) W.; m. Phyllis Jean Williams, Aug. 3, 1968. B.S., Carson-Newman Coll., 1953; M.S., U. Tenn., 1956, Ph.D., 1967. Health physicist Oak Ridge Nat. Lab., Tenn., 1959-60; research technician U. Tenn., Knoxville, 1960-64; asst. prof. biology Campbellsville Coll., Ky., 1968-72; soil scientist USDA Soil Conservation Service, DeLand, Fla., 1973-77, LaBelle, Fla., 1977-80, plant materials specialist, Jackson, Miss., 1980—. Contbr. articles to profl. jours. Served with U.S. Army, 1956-58. Recipient Achievement award Soil Conservation Service, DeLand, 1975, Jackson, 1983. Mem. Ecol. Soc. Am., Am. Soc. Agronomy, Am. Hort. Soc., Soil Conservation Soc. Am. Current work: Soil-plant relationships, selection of plants to vegetate soils damaged by erosion and toxic materials. Subspecialties: Resource conservation; Soil science. Home: 1711 Wood Glen Dr Jackson MS 39204 Office: Soil Conservation Service 100 W Capitol St Jackson MS 39269

WOLFE, MICHAEL DAVID, mathematician; b. Houston, Feb. 16, 1950; s. Alfred Sigmund and Raquel (Azcarraga) W. B.S., U. Tex.-Austin, 1972, Ph.D., 1978; postgrad., Cambridge (Eng.) U., 1974. Asst. instr. U. Tex.-Austin, 1972-77; lectr. U. Tex.-San Antonio, 1978; staff mem. BDM Corp., Albuquerque, 1978-80; scientist Mission Research Corp., Albuquerque, 1980-83; mem. tech. staff Rocketdyne div. Rockwell Internat. Corp., Albuquerque, 1983—. Author: Long Range Potential Scattering, 1978. Mem. Am. Math. Soc., Soc. Indsl. and Applied Math., IEEE, Inst. Mgmt. Sci., Phi Kappa Phi. Clubs: N.Mex. Orchid Soc. (state fair chmn. 1981), Sierra. Current Work: Mathematics of nuclear effects, electromagnetic pulse theory, measurement of efficiency, scheduling algorithms, scattering theory. Subspecialties: Mathematical software; Operations research (mathematics). Home: 4016 Douglas Macarthur NE Albuquerque NM 87110 Office: Rocketdyne Div Rockwell Internat Corp PO Box 5670 Kirkland AFB NM 87185

WOLFE, RALPH STONER, microbiologist, educator; b. New Windsor, Md., July 18, 1921; s. Marshall Richard and Jennie Naomi (Weybright) W.; m. Gretka Margaret Young, Sept. 9, 1950; children—Daniel Binns, Jon Marshall, Sylvia Suzanne. B.S., Bridgewater (Va.) Coll., 1942; M.S., U. Pa., 1949, Ph.D., 1953. Mem. faculty U. Ill., 1953—, prof. microbiology, 1961—; cons. USPHS, Nat. Inst. Gen. Med. Scis. Author research papers microbial physiology, biochemistry. Guggenheim fellow, 1961, 75; USPHS spl. postdoctoral fellow, 1967; recipient Pasteur award Ill. Soc. for Microbiology, 1974. Mem. Nat. Acad. Scis., Am. Acad. Arts and Scis., Am. Soc. Microbiology (Carski Disting. Teaching award 1971), Am. Soc. Biol. Chemists. Subspecialty: Microbiology. Address: Univ Ill Dept Microbiology Urbana IL 61801

WOLFENSTEIN, LINCOLN, physicist, educator; b. Cleve., Feb. 10, 1923; s. Leo and Anna (Koppel) W.; m. Wilma Caplin, Feb. 3, 1957; children: Frances, Leonard, Miriam. S.B., U. Chgo., 1943, S.M., 1944, Ph.D., 1949. Physicist Nat. Adv. Com. Aeros., 1944-46; mem. faculty dept. physics Carnegie-Mellon U., Pitts., 1948—, asso. prof., 1957-60, prof., 1960-78, Univ. prof., 1978—. Contbr. articles to profl. jours. Guggenheim fellow, 1973, 83. Mem. Am. Phys. Soc., Fedn. Am. Scientists, AAAS, Nat. Acad. Sci. Current Work: Theory of weak interactions; neutrino theory. Subspecialty: Particle physics. Office: Carnegie Mellon U Pittsburgh PA 15213

WOLFF, FREDERICK WILLIAM, medical scientist, educator, researcher, consultant; b. Berlin, Aug. 21, 1920; came to U.S., 1959, naturalized, 1967; s. Bruno and Elizabeth (Landau) W.; m. Catherine M. Chura, Feb. 14, 1967; children: Susan, Peter, Catherine. M.B., B.S., U. Durham, Eng., 1947, M.D., 1957. Resident, chief resident teaching hosps. of Newcastle and London, 1946-58; asst. prof. Johns Hopkins Hosp., Balt., 1959-64; prof. medicine Sch. Medicine, George Washington U., Washington, 1965—; pres. Inst. for Drug Devel., Washington, 1979—; vis. scientist Nat. Heart Inst., NIH, 1982—; cons. in field. Contbr. numerous articles to sci. and med. jours. Served with RAF, 1950-52. Named hon. diplomate Georgian Acad. Scis., 1981. Mem. Am. Diabetes Assn., Am. Heart Assn., Soc. Pharmacology and Exptl. Therapeutics, Am. Soc. for Clin. Pharmacology, Brit. Pharm. Soc., Brit. Med. Assn., Am. Fedn. for Clin. Research, AAAS, AAUP, UN Assn. (bd. dirs. Nat. Capital area 1982—). Club: Cosmos (Washington). Current Work: New drug development; organization of interdisciplinary pharmaceutical research. Subspecialties: Pharmacology; Endocrinology. Home and Office: 800 Notley Rd Silver Spring MD 20904

WOLFF, GEORGE LOUIS, biologist, researcher; b. Hamburg, Germany, Aug. 24, 1928; came to U.S., 1940, naturalized, 1946; s. Adolf and Eva (Nathan) W.; m. Eleanor Herstein, Aug. 30, 1953; children: David B., Adrienne A. B.S cum laude, Ohio State U., 1950; Ph.D., U. Chgo., 1954. Postdoctoral fellow Nat. Cancer Inst., 1954-56, biologist, 1956-58; research assoc., supr. animal colony Inst. Cancer Research, Phila., 1958-63, asst. mem., supr. animal colony, 1963-68, asst. mem., geneticist, 1968-72; chief mammalian genetics br. Nat. Center Toxicol Research, 1972-73, chief div. mutagenic research, 1973-79; sr. sci. coordinator genetics, research biologist Nat. Center Toxicol. Research, 1979—; coordinator Interdisciplinary Toxicology Program, 1982—; adj. asst. prof. dept. biochemistry U. Ark. for Med. Scis., 1973-81, adj. assoc. prof. dept. biochemistry and div. toxicology dept. pharmacology, 1981—. Contbr. articles to sci. publs. Mem. Genetics Soc., Am. Genetic Assn., Soc. Toxicology, Am. Assn. Cancer Research, Soc. Exptl. Biology and Medicine, Environ. Mutagen Soc. Current Work: Definition of metabolic bases for differential susceptibility of inbred strains, F-1 hybrids and mutant experimental animals to induction of toxicologic endpoints. Characterization of inbred strains, etc. for metabolic characteristics of importance in in vivo toxicologic assays; design and testing of improved toxicologic assays. Subspecialties: Animal genetics; Toxicology (medicine). Office: Nat Center Toxicological Research Jefferson AR 72079

WOLFF, GUNTHER ARTHUR, electronics consulting firm executive, scientist; b. Essen, W.Ger., Mar. 31, 1918; came to U.S., 1953; s. Joseph and Anna (Breidecker) W.; m. Gertrude A. Stalte, Feb. 27, 1945; children—Christinane, Francis. Abitur, Humboldt-Oberreal, Essen, 1937; student Tuebingen U., Ger., 1941-43; B.S., Berlin U., 1944, M.S., 1945; Sc.D., Tech. U. Berlin, 1948. Sr. group leader Harshaw Chem. Co., Cleve., 1960-63; dir. materials research Erie Tech. Products, Pa., 1963-64; prin. scientist Tyco Labs., Waltham, Mass., 1964-70; cons. chemist Gen. Electric, Cleve., 1970-77; sr. staff engr. Nat. Semiconductor, Los Angeles, 1977-81; pres. G.A. Cons., NPO, Cleveland Heights, Ohio, 1982—; chmn. Gordon Conf., Providence, 1965; Am. rep. internat. com. Internat. Union Crystallography, 1966-75. Contbr. articles to profl. jours. Patentee in field. Fellow Am. Inst. Chemists, Mineral. Soc. Am.; mem. Electrochem. Soc., N.Y. Acad. Sci., Am. Chem. Soc., Am. Crystallographic Assn. Methodist. Current work: Solid state science; material purification; material properties; crystallography. Subspecialties: Materials; Single crystal growth. Office: GA Cons NPO 3776 Northampton Rd Cleveland Heights OH 44121

WOLFF, JAMES ALEXANDER, physician, emeritus educator; b. N.Y.C., June 19, 1914; s. William F. and Blanch R. W.; m. Janet Wolff, June 24, 1946; children: James A., John, Barbara, Timothy. B.A., Harvard U., 1935; M.D., N.Y.U., 1940. Diplomate: Am. Bd. Pediatrics. Prof. pediatrics Coll. Physicians and Surgeons, Columbia U., N.Y.C., 1972-82, prof. emeritus, 1982—; dir. Valerie Fund Children's Ctr., N.Y.C., 1981—. Contbr. articles to profl. jours. Served to capt., M.C. U.S. Army, 1942-45. Decorated Silver Star. Mem. Soc. Pediatric Research, Am. Pediatric Soc., Am. Soc. Pediatric Hematology and Oncology, Internat. Soc. Pediatric Oncology. Current Work: Research on childhood cancer, disorders of the blood. Subspecialties: Cancer research (medicine); Hematology. Office: Valerie Childrens Center Overlook Hosp Summit NJ 07901

WOLFF, PETER ADALBERT, physicist, educator; b. Oakland, Calif., Nov. 15, 1923; s. Adalbert and Ruth Margaret W.; m. Catherine C. Carroll, Sept. 11, 1948; children: Catherine Mia, Peter Whitney. A.B. in Physics, U. Calif., Berkeley, 1945, Ph.D. in Physics, 1951. Research scientist Lawrence Radiation Lab., 1951-52; staff scientist Bell Telephone Lab., Murray Hill, N.J., 1952-63, dept. head, dir. electronic research lab., 1964-70; prof. physics U. Calif., San Diego, 1963-64; prof. physics, head solid state and atomic physics div., asso. dir. material sci. center M.I.T., Cambridge, 1970-76, prof. physics, 1976—, dir. research lab. of electronics, 1976-81; dir. Francis Bitter Nat. Magnet Lab., 1981—; dir. Draper Lab. Contbr. articles to profl. jours. Served with C.E. U.S. Army, 1945-46. Mem. Am. Phys. Soc., Am. Acad. Arts and Scis. Subspecialty: Theoretical physics. Office: MIT 77 Massachusetts St Cambridge MA 02139

WOLFF, SHELDON, radiobiologist, educator; b. Peabody, Mass., Sept. 22, 1928; s. Henry Herman and Goldie (Lipchitz) W.; m. Frances Faye Farbstein, Oct. 23, 1954; children: Victor Charles, Roger Kenneth, Jessica Raye. B.S. magna cum laude, Tufts U., 1950; M.A., Harvard U., 1951, Ph.D., 1953. Teaching fellow Harvard U., 1951-52; sr. research staff biology div. Oak Ridge Nat. Lab., 1953-66; prof. cytogenetics U. Calif., San Francisco, 1966—, dir. Lab. Radiobiology and Environ. Health, 1983—; Vis. prof. radiation biology U. Tenn., 1962, lectr., 1953-65; cons. several fed. sci. agys. Editor: Chromosoma, 1983—; assoc. editor: Cancer Research, 1983—; Editorial bd.: Radiation Research, 1968-72, Photochemistry and Photobiology, 1962-72, Radiation Botany, 1964—, Mutation Research, 1964—, Caryologia, 1967—, Radiation Effects, 1969-81, Genetics, 1972—; Contbr. articles to sci. jours. Recipient E.O. Lawrence meml. award U.S. AEC, 1973. Mem. Genetics Soc. Am., Radiation Research Soc. (counselor for biology 1968-72), Am. Soc. Naturalists, Am. Soc. Cell Biology, Environmental Mutagen Soc. (council 1972—, pres.-elect 1979, pres. 1980-81), Internat. Assn. Environ. Mutagen Socs. (treas. 1978—), Sigma Xi. Democrat. Current Work: Radiation mutagenesis, environmental mutagenesis, cytogenetics. Subspecialties: Genome organization; Cell and tissue culture. Home: 41 Eugene St Mill Valley CA 94941 Office: Lab Radiobiology U Calif San Francisco CA 94143

WOLFF, SIDNEY CARNE, astronomer; b. Sioux City, Iowa, June 6, 1941; d. George Albert and Ethel Larose (Smith) Carne; m. Richard James Wolff, Oct. 7, 1940. B.A., Carleton Coll., 1962; Ph.D., U. Calif-Berkeley, 1966. Astronomer Inst. Astronomy, U. Hawaii, Honolulu, 1967-82, assoc. dir., from 1976. Mem. Am. Astron. Soc., Astron. Soc. Pacific, Internat. Astron. Union. Subspecialty: Optical astronomy. Office: Kitt Peak National Observatory Tucson AZ 85726

WOLLEY, ELDEN DUANE, semiconductor device physicist; b. Dodge City, Kans., Mar. 25, 1930; s. Henry William and Clara Ione (Hubbard) W.; m. Margaret Jane Carder, June 6, 1954 (div. Nov. 1972); children—Susan Elizabeth, Steven Henry, Anne Margaret; m. Cynthia Lee Lent, Aug. 20, 1977. B.S., Kans. State U., 1952, M.S., 1953; postgrad. Purdue U., 1953-55. Sr. engr. Westinghouse Research Co., Pitts., 1955-67; mgr. engring. Westinghouse Semicondr. Co., Youngwood, Pa., 1967-69; mem. tech. staff Gen. Electric Co., Syracuse, N.Y., 1969—. Contbr. articles to profl. jours., 1958-81. Patentee in field. Mem. IEEE (sr.; newsletter editor 1972-77, papers chmn. 1974-75; Best Paper award 1973). Current work: Design and characterization of power diodes, thyristors, gate turn-off thyristors and transistors. Subspecialties: Semiconductors; Condensed matter physics. Home: 1 Highland St Auburn NY 13021 Office: Gen Electric Co Electronics Park Syracuse NY 13221

WOLLMAN, HARRY, medical educator; b. Bklyn., Sept. 26, 1932; s. Jacob and Florence Roslyn (Hoffman) W.; m. Anne Carolyn Hamel, Feb. 16, 1957; children—Julie Ellen, Emily Jane, Diana Leigh. A.B. summa cum laude (hon. John Harvard scholar 1950-53, hon. Harvard Coll. scholar 1953-54, Detur award 1951), Harvard, 1954, M.D., 1958. Diplomate: Am. Bd. Anesthesiology. Intern U. Chgo. Clinics, 1958-59; resident U. Pa., 1959-63, asso. in anesthesia, 1963-65, mem. faculty, 1965—, prof. anesthesia, 1970—, prof. pharmacology, 1971—, Robert Dunning Dripps prof., chmn. dept. anesthesia, 1972—; prin. investigator Anesthesia Research Center, 1972-78; program dir. Anesthesia Research Tng. Grant, 1972—; Mem. anesthesia drug panel, drug efficacy study, com. on anesthesia Nat. Acad. Scis.-NRC, 1970-71, com. on adverse reactions to anesthesia drugs, 1971-72; mem. pharm. and toxicology tng. grants com. NIH, 1966-68, anesthesia tng. grants com., 1971-73, surgery, anesthesia and trauma study sect., 1974-78; chmn. com. on studies involving human beings U. Pa., 1972-76, chmn. clin. practice exec. com., 1976-80. Asso. editor for revs.: Anesthesiology, 1970-75; Contbr. and editor books. NIH research traineeship fellow, 1959-63; Pharm. Mfg. Assn. fellow, 1960-61. Mem. Pa. Soc. Anesthesiologists (pres. 1972-73), Am. Physiol. Soc., Assn. Univ. Anesthetists (exec. council 1971-74, chmn. sci. adv. bd. 1975-77), Soc. Acad. Anesthesia Chairmen (chmn. com. on financial resources 1973-77, pres.-elect 1976-77, pres. 1977-78), Am. Soc. Anesthesiologists, Am. Dental Soc. of Anesthesiology (adv. bd. 1985—), Phila. Soc. Anesthesiologists, AMA, Pa. Med. Soc., Phila. County Med. Soc., John Morgan Soc., Coll. Physicians Phila., Phi Beta Kappa, Sigma Xi. Republican. Unitarian. Current Work: Anesthesiology and critical care. Subspecialties: Anesthesiology; Critical care. Home: 2203 Delaney Pl Philadelphia PA 19103 Office: Dept Anesthesia Hosp University Pa 3400 Spruce St Philadelphia PA 19104

WOLMAN, M. GORDON, geography educator; b. Balt., Aug. 16, 1924; s. Abel and Anna (Gordon) W.; m. Elaine Mielke, June 20, 1951; children: Elsa Anne, Abel Gordon, Abby Lucille, Fredericka Jeannette. Student, Haverford Coll.; A.B. in Geology, Johns Hopkins U., 1949; M.A. in Geology, Harvard U., 1951, Ph.D., 1953. Geologist U.S. Geol. Survey, 1951-58, part-time, 1958—; assoc. prof. geography Johns Hopkins U., Balt., 1958-62; prof. Johns Hopkins, 1962—; chmn. dept. geography and environ. engring., 1958—; Mem. adv. com. geography U.S. Office Naval Research; mem. exec. com. Div. Earth Sci., NRC; mem. com. internat. environ. programs, mem. environ. studies bd.; mem. com. water Nat. Acad. Sci.; mem. exec. com. Earth Sci. div., Nat. Acad. Scis., mem. com. mineral resources and environment, chmn. nat. commn. water quality policy; cons. in field to, City of Balt., Balt. County, State of Md.; Mem. Balt. City Charter Revision Commn.; mem. Community Action Com., Balt. Author: Fluvial Processes in Geomorphology, 1964; Editorial bd.: Science mag. Trustee Park Sch., Balt., Md. Acad. Scis.; v.p. bd. trustees Sinai Hosp., Balt.; pres. bd. dirs. Resources for Future.; mem. adv. com. Inst. Nuclear Power Ops., 1982—. Served with USNR, 1943-46. Recipient Meritorious Contribution award Assn. Am. Geographers, 1972. Fellow Am. Acad. Arts and Scis.; mem. Am. Geophys. Union (chmn. subcom. sedimentation, pres. hydrol. sect.), Geol. Soc. Am. (v.p. 1983, pres. 1984), Washington Geol. Soc., ASCE, Agrl. Hist. Soc., Am. Geog. Soc. (councilor 1965-70), Assn. Am. Geographers, Phi Beta Kappa, Sigma Xi, Md. Acad. Scis. (mem. exec. com.). Current Work: Geomorphology, alluvial river channel processes, hydrology, quaternary geology, physical geography, environmental change and natural processes, energy and environmental policy. Subspecialties: Geology; Hydrology. Home: 2104 W Rogers Ave Baltimore MD 21209

WOLMAN, SANDRA R., pathologist, geneticist, educator, researcher; b. N.Y.C., Nov. 23, 1933; d. Alexander J. and Sophie (Raffel) Rosman; m. Eric Wolman, July 27, 1963; children: Karin, Alec. B.A. cum laude, Radcliffe Coll., 1955; M.D., N.Y.U., 1959. Diplomate: Am. Bd. Pathology, Am. Bd. Med. Genetics. Intern Bellevue Hosp., N.Y.C., 1959-60, resident, 1960-63; USPHS fellow; instr. N.Y.U. Med. Ctr., 1962-64; asst. pathologist Morristown (N.J.) Meml. Hosp., 1964-66, Monmouth (N.J.) Med. Ctr., 1966-67; asst. prof. pathology N.Y.U. Sch. Medicine, 1967-76, assoc. prof., 1976-84, prof., 1984—; dir. cytogenetics NYU Med. Ctr., 1967—; mem. staff Bellevue Hosp., Univ. Hosp.; cons. NIH, mem. pathology B study sect., 1976-80; chairperson faculty council NYU, 1985-86. Research numerous publs. in field; editorial reviewer: for various jours., including Cancer Research. Mem. adv. bd. Women's Center, Brookdale Community Coll., 1975—; mem. bd. Planned Parenthood Monmouth County, 1980—, chmn. nominating com., 1981, 82. Recipient Merit award Monmouth County Bd. Chosen Freeholders, 1976. Mem. Am. Assn. Cancer Research, Am. Assn. Pathologists, Am. Soc. Clin. Pathologists, Am. Soc. Human Genetics, AAAS, Genetic Toxicology Assn. (bd. dirs. 1984—), Environ. Mutagen Soc., Tissue Culture Assn., Harvey Soc., Somatic Cell Genetics, Internat. Soc. Exptl. Hematology. Clubs: Radcliffe (N.Y.C.); Sea Bright Beach. Current Work: Cytogenetics of cancer cells; mutation testing. Subspecialties: Cancer research (medicine); Genetics and genetic engineering (medicine). Office: 550 1st Ave New York NY 10016

WOMBLES, ROBERT HUSTON, chemist; b. Covington, Ky., Dec. 3, 1951; s. Worden Huston and Jewell Lee (Conley) W.; m. Lois Ann Phillips, Aug. 18, 1973; 1 child, Andrew David. B.S. in Math. summa cum laude, Georgetown Coll., 1973; M.S. in Chemistry, Vanderbilt U., 1975. Chemist Ashland Oil, Inc., Ky., 1975-78, research chemist, 1978-80, sr. research chemist, 1980-81, group leader, 1981-84, group mgr., 1984—. Contbr. articles to profl. publs. Patentee in field. Hon. scholor Georgetown Coll., 1969-73. Mem. Am. Chem. Soc., (Petroleum div.), ASTM. Baptist. Lodge: Elks. Current work: Chemistry of residual petroleum materials such as asphalt, reduced crude and petroleum pitch. Subspecialties: Fuels; Organic chemistry. Home: Route 2 Box 726 Worthington KY 41183 Office: Ashland Oil Inc PO Box 391 Ashland KY 41114

WONG, DAVID T., biochemist; b. Hong Kong, Nov. 6, 1935; s. Chi-Keung and Pui-King W.; m. Christina lee, Dec. 28, 1963; children: Conrad, Melvin, Vincent. Student, Nat. U. Taiwan, 1955-56; B.S., Seattle Pacific Coll., 1960; M.S., Oreg. State U., 1964; Ph.D., U. Oreg., 1966. Postdoctoral fellow U. Pa., Phila., 1966-68; sr. biochemist Lilly Research Labs., Indpls., 1968-72, research biochemist, 1973-77, research asso., 1978—. Contbr. numerous articles to sci. jours. Mem. Am. Soc. Pharmacology and Exptl. Therapeutics, Internat. Soc. Neurochemistry, Am. Soc. Neurochemistry, Biophys. Soc., Soc. Neurosci., N.Y. Acad. Scis., Sigma Xi. Current Work: Biochemistry and pharmacology of neurotransmission; discovery of the first selective inhibitor of serotonin uptake and development of new type of antidepressive drug, Fluoxetine and a selective inhibitor of norepinephrine uptake, Tomoxetine; studies of potentially useful substances which activate transmission of norepinephrine, dopamine, serotonin, acetylcholine and GABA-neurons; studies of natural products led to the discovery of carboxylic ionophores: Narasin, A28695 and A204, which increase transport of cations across biomembranes. Subspecialties: Neurochemistry; Neuropharmacology. Office: Lilly Research Labs Indianapolis IN 46285

WONG, EDWARD CHOR-CHEUNG, computer engineer; b. Hong Kong, Jan. 16, 1952; s. Kan-Wen and Wai-Ying (Ip) W.; m. Rosaline Kowk-Chun, Aug. 4, 1973; children: Duane, Fun-wah, Edward Chiu-Wah, Elliott Chun-Wah. B.A., Fordham U., 1973; B.S., Columbia U., 1974, M.S., 1974, Computer Systems Engr., 1980. With IBM, Poughkeepsie, N.Y., 1974—, staff engr., devel. engring. mgr., 1979-85, hdqrs. tech. staff data system div., 1985—; Adj. lectr. Columbia U., 1982; adj. prof. Marist Coll., 1983. Mem. IEEE (sr.), Assn. Computing Machinery, Soc. Indsl. and Applied Math. Democrat. Patentee cache control for concurrent access. Current Work: Error detection fauly isolation technique, with incorporation into design automation; algorithms, cyrptology and switching circuit theory application on designs. Subspecialties: Computer architecture; Logic design. Home: PO Box 1909 Poughkeepsie NY 12601 Office: IBM PO Box 390 Poughkeepsie NY 12602

WONG, HANS KUOMIN, chemist; b. Canton, Kwangtung, China, Apr. 30, 1936; came to U.S., 1947, naturalized, 1972; s. Yelk Ng and Thru Kin (Tang) W.; m. Frances Kwai Fu Tang, Mar. 25, 1967; children—Wilbur, Alan. B.S. in Chemistry, N.D. State U., 1959; Ph.D. in Phys. Chemistry, U. Minn., 1965. Sr. chemist Itek Corp., Lexington, Mass., 1965-70, Olivetti Corp., N.Y.C., 1971-80, Bacharach Instruments, Pitts., 1980-82; asst. prof. Cumberland Coll., Williamsburg, Ky., 1983-84; sr. chemist Hunt Chem., Palisades Park, N.J., 1984—. Contbr. articles to profl. jours. Patentee in field. Mem. Am. Chem. Soc. Current work: Electrophotography: characterization and evaluation of toners, developments and photoconductors. Subspecialties: Photographic science; Physical chemistry. Office: Philip A Hunt Chem Corp 200 Roosevelt Pl Palisades Park NJ 07650

WONG, JESSE KWOK-KEUNG, organic chemist, basic researcher; b. Hunan, China, Dec. 31, 1947; came to U.S., 1972, naturalized, 1982; s. Jen-Ren and Yi-Cheng (Wang) W.; m. Anna Chin, Jan. 6, 1977; children—Timothy Tien-Long, Cynthia Sum-Sien. B.S., Rutgers U., 1976, M.S., 1979, Ph.D., 1984. Scientist, Hoffmann La-Roche, Nutley, N.J., 1979-80, Schering-Plough, Bloomfield, N.J., 1980—. Martin Frieman scholar, 1984. Mem. Am. Chem. Soc., Am. Soc. Clin. Pathologists. Subspecialties: Organic chemistry; Synthetic chemistry. Home: 547 Andress Terr Union NJ 07083 Office: Schering Plough Bloomfield NJ 07003

WONG, JULIUS PAN, engineering educator, consultant; b. Shanghai, China, May 8, 1937; came to U.S., 1960, naturalized, 1973; s. Kai S. and Po L. (Hsu) W. B.S., Hong Kong Bap. Coll., 1960; M.S., La. Tech. U., 1962; Ph.D., Okla. State U.-Stillwater, 1966. Analytical specialist Bendix Corp., South Bend, Ind., 1966-69; assoc. prof. engring. U. Louisville, 1970-80, prof., 1980—. Contbr. articles to profl. jours. Recipient Outstanding Faculty award Tau Beta Pi, 1976; Outstanding Tchr. award, 1982. Mem. ASME, Am. Soc. Engring. Edn., Am. Acad. Mechanics, Soc. Indsl. and Applied Math., AAUP. Current Work: Stress analysis, optimal design, computer-aided engineering. Subspecialties: Theoretical and applied mechanics; Mechanical engineering. Office: U Louisville Louisville KY 40292

WONG, PATRICK YUI-KWONG, biochemistry and pharmacology educator; b. Kiangsai, China, Nov. 25, 1944; came to U.S., 1969, naturalized, 1983; s. Kuan Kuen and Bai Chei (Cheng) W.; m. Patsy H-W Chao, Sept. 26, 1969. B.Sc., Nat. Taiwan Normal U., 1967; Ph.D., U. Vt., 1974. Postdoctoral fellow Med. Coll. Wis., Milw., 1974-75; instr. pharmacology U. Tenn. Med. Center, Memphis, 1975-78, asst. prof., 1978-79; assoc. prof. pharmacology N.Y. Med. Coll., Valhalla, 1979-85, prof., 1985—. Contbr. chpts. to books, articles to profl. jours. Recipient Young Investigator award NIH, 1978-80, Research Career Devel. award, 1981-85; spl. dental award Nat. Inst. Dental Research, 1978-81; NIH grantee, 1980—. Mem. Am. Soc. Biol. Chemists, Am. Soc. Pharmacology and Exptl. Therapeutics, Am. Heart Assn. (high blood pressure council, thrombosis council). Current Work: Relationship of prostaglandins in hypertension; prostaglandins, leukotrienes; calcium and calmodulin; hypertension and thrombosis. Subspecialties: Biochemistry (medicine); Cellular pharmacology. Home: 2307 William Ct Yorktown Hwights NY 10598 Office: Dept Pharmacology NY Med Coll Valhalla NY 10595

WONG, PO KEE, mathematician; b. Canton City, China, May 5, 1934; came to U.S., 1959, naturalized, 1971; s. K. F. and W. C. (Lam) W.; m. Ruby Ching, Aug. 18, 1965; children: Adam, Anita. B.Sc., Cheng-Kung U., 1956; Engr., U. Utah, 1961; M.M.E., Calif. Inst. Tech., 1966; Ph.D., Stanford U., 1970. Registered profl. engr., Taiwan. cert. tchr., Mass. Teaching asst. Cheng-Kung U., 1958-59; tchr. math. and sci. Hong Kong YMCA Coll., 1959; research-/teaching asst. U. Utah, 1959-61, Calif. Inst. Tech., Pasadena, 1961-65; sr. scientist Lockheed Missiles & Space Co., Palo Alto, Calif., 1966-68; research asst. Stanford U., 1968-70; instr., researcher U. Santa Clara, 1970-71; staff Moffet Field, Calif. Ames Center, NASA, 1970; engr. I, dept. breeder reactors Gen. Electric Co., Sunnyvale, Calif., 1972-73; specialist engr. Nuclear Service Co., Campbell, Calif., 1973; engr. Stone & Webster Engring. Co., Boston, 1974; tchr. math. and sci. Boston Pub. Schs., 1979—; pres., chief exec. officer Systems Research Co., Brookline, Mass., 1976—. Reviewer: Applied Mechanics Rev, 1972—; contbr. articles to profl. jours. Mem. ASME, Am. Acad. Mechanics, Sigma Xi. Current Work: Initiated trajectory solid angle to solve the P2 problem of statis. mechanics, three dimensional unsteady stream functions, magnetovisco-elastodynamics; formulated phys. econ. model via solution of indeterminate structure problem; provided formulation and solution of multireservoir transient problem. Subspecialties: Theoretical physics; Applied mathematics. Address: 238 Cypress St S3 Brookline MA 02146

WONG, ROBERT KING-SUEN, neuroscientist; b. Chungsha, Hunan, China., May 25, 1946; came to U.S., 1975; s. Kai and Edith (Wu) Wang; m. Ruth Lo-Nor Wong, Mar. 30, 1974; 1 son, Andrew. B.S., McGill U., 1970; Ph.D., U. Alta., 1975; postdoctoral student, Stanford U., 1975-79. Asst. prof. La. State U., Shreveport, 1979-81; asst. prof. U. Tex. Med. Br., Galveston, 1981-83, assoc. prof. dept. physiology, 1983—. Contbr. chpt. to book, articles to profl. jours. Research grantee NIH, 1980—; Research grantee Am. Heart Assn., 1981—; neurosci. fellow Ester and John Klingenstein Found., 1981—. Mem. Soc. for Neurosci., Am. Physiol. Soc. Current Work: Basic mechanism of epilepsy using electrophysiological studies on In Vitro brain slices; biophysics of mammalian brain cells using individual neurons isolated from the cerebral cortex. Subspecialties: Physiology (medicine); Neurophysiology. Home: 16451 Parksley Houston TX 77059 Office: Univ Tex Med Br Galveston TX 77550

WONG, STEWART, pharmacologist; b. Toronto, Ont., Can., Jan. 2, 1930; came to U.S., 1960; s. Sai Moy and Mabel (Mar) W.; married; children: John, Clifford. B.A., U. Toronto, 1958; M.A. in Physiology, 1960; Ph.D. in Biochem. Pharmacognosy, Purdue U., 1963. Asso. prof. pharmacology N.D. State U., Fargo, 1963-65; instr., postdoctoral trainee dept. pharamcology U. Iowa, Iowa City, 1965-67; head pharmacology sect. Applied Sci. div. Litton Industries, Inc., Bethesda, Md., 1968; head cardiovascular sect. dept. pharmacology Union Carbide Co., 1968-69; group leader exptl. diseases dept. pharmacology McNeil Labs., Inc., Ft. Washington, Pa., 1969-78, research fellow in immunopharmacology, 1978; group leader dept. pharmacology Boehringer-Ingelheim Ltd., Ridgefield, Conn., 1979—; mem. adv. bd. Lupus Research Inst., 1980—. Contbr. articles to sci. jours., chpt. to book. Recipient medal Rotary Club, 1952. Mem. Inflammation Research Assn. (treas. 1975-80, pres. 1980), Am. Soc. Pharmacology and Exptl. Therapeutics, Am. Chem. Soc. (medicinal chemistry div.), AAAS, N.Y. Acad. Scis., Am. Coll. Toxicology. Current Work: Immunomodulation for anti-rheumatic diseases; immunopharmacology and immunotoxicology; etiology of rheumatic diseases. Subspecialties: Immunopharmacology; Immunotoxicology. Home: 6 Elbow Hill Rd Brookfield CT 06804 Office: Boehringer Ingelheim Ltd PO Box 368 Ridgefield CT 06877

WONG, THOMAS TANG YUM, engineering educator, researcher; b. Hong Kong, July 27, 1952; came to U.S., 1976, naturalized, 1984; s. Kwai Sun and Yee Yuen (Fung) W.; m. Min-I Lee, June 9, 1984. B.Sc. in Engring., U. Hong Kong, 1975; M.S., Northwestern U., 1978, Ph.D., 1981. Product engr. Motorola Semicondr., Inc., Hong Kong, 1975-76; teaching asst. Northwestern U., Evanston, Ill., 1976-78, research engr., 1978-80, postdoctoral fellow, 1980-81; asst. prof. elec. engring. Ill. Inst. Tech., Chgo., 1981—; cons. to pvt. industry, 1981—. Gen. Electric fellow, 1983. Mem. IEEE, Am. Phys. Soc. Current work: Device physics and modeling of microwave semiconductor devices and integrated circuits; pulse propagation in dissipative medium. Subspecialties: Semiconductors; Applied magnetics. Office: Dept of ECE Ill Inst Tech IIT Ctr Chicago IL 60616

WOO, KA-CHIU, physicist; b. Hong Kong, Feb. 6, 1951. B.S., Cornell U., 1973; Ph.D, U. Ill.-Urbana, 1978. Research assoc. Brown U., 1978-80; postdoctoral fellow U. Pa.-Phila., 1980-82; asst. prof. physics U. Ill.-Chgo., 1982—. Mem. Am. Phys. Soc. Current work: Properties of two-dimensional systems. Subspecialty: Condensed matter physics. Office: Univ Ill Dept Physics Chicago IL 60680

WOO, RICHARD, radio scientist; b. Portland, Oreg., June 24, 1941; s. Robert P.Y. and Lilliam H. (Ho) W.; m. Bobbie Wong, Dec. 20, 1964; 1 son, Dennis. B.S.E.E., U. Wash., 1962, M.S.E.E., 1964. Engr. Jet Propulsion Lab., Pasadena, Calif., 1964-68, sr. engr., 1968-73, mem. tech. staff, 1973-79, research scientist engr., 1979—; guest lectr. Calif. Inst. Tech., 1982. Contbr. articles to profl. jours. Recipient Exceptional Sci. Achievement medal NASA, 1979. Mem. Am. Astron. Soc., Am. Geophys. Union, Internat. Radio Sci. Union. Patentee in field. Current Work: Wave propagation theory; remote sensing of planetary atmospheres and the solar wind with radio wave; radio scintillations. Subspecialties: Planetary atmospheres; Solar wind.

WOO, SAVIO LAU CHING, molecular medical geneticist; b. Shanghai, China, Dec. 20, 1944; came to U.S., 1966; s. Kwok-Cheung and Fun-Sin (Yu) W.; m. Emily H. Chang, July 14, 1973; children: Audrey C. C., Brian Y.H. B.Sc., Loyola Coll., Montreal, Can., 1966; Ph.D., U. Wash., 1971. Asst. prof. cell biology Baylor Coll. Medicine, Houston, 1975-78, assoc. prof., 1979-83, prof., 1983—; assoc. investigator Howard Hughes Med. Inst., Coconut Grove, Fla., 1977-79, investigator, 1979—; cons. Cooper Lab., Palo Alto, Calif., 1982-84, Zymos Corp., Seattle, 1982—; 1st chmn. Gordon Conf. Molecular Genetics, 1985. Contbr. sci. articles to profl. jours. Recipient Noel Raine Meml. award Soc. Study Inborn Errors of Metabolism, 1983. Mem. bd. dirs. March of Dimes Birth Defects Found., Met. Houston chpt., 1979—. Mem. Am. Soc. Human Genetics, Am. Soc. Biol. Chemists, Am. Soc. Cell Biology. Current Work: Development of methodologies using recombinant DNA technology for prenatal diagnosis and somatic gene therapy of human genetic disorders. Subspecialties: Genetics and genetic engineering (medicine); Gene actions.

WOOD, DAVID DUDLEY, medical research immunologist; b. Wilmington, Del., May 3, 1943; s. William Herman and Barbara Emma (Rose) W.; m. Carole Lee Putnam, Sept. 5, 1964; children: Kristen Elizabeth, Whitney Lynn. B.A., Harvard U., 1965; Ph.D., Rockefeller U., 1970. Helen Hay Whitney fellow Harvard U. Med. Sch., Boston, 1970-72; sr. research immunologist Merck, Sharp and Dohme Research Labs., Rahway, N.J., 1972-76, research fellow, 1976-82, sr. research fellow, assoc. dir., 1982-83; dir. immunology Ayerst Research Labs., Princeton, N.J., 1983—. Contbr. articles to profl. jours. Mem. Summit Bd. Edn., 1979-81. Mem. N.Y. Acad. Scis., Am. Assn. Immunology. Current Work: Biochemistry and biology of interleukin-1; immunoregulation; natural resistance. Subspecialties: Immunobiology and immunology; Immunopharmacology. Home: 12 Meadow Ln Pennington NJ 08534 Office: Ayerst Research Lab CN 8000 Princeton NJ 08540

WOOD, DIXON LEE, geologist; b. Annapolis, Md., Apr. 27, 1953; s. Irving Lee and Alta Joy (Dixon) W. B.S., James Madison U., 1982. Substitute tchr. Anne Arundel County Schs., Annapolis, 1983-84; geologist Century Engring., Inc., Towson, Md., 1984—. Mem. Geol. Soc. Am., Anne Arundel Gem and Mineral Club. Democrat. Methodist. Current work: Site geologist at the Choptank River Bridge Project, Cambridge, Maryland; producing sediment profiles and cross-sections to determine pile lengths and probable depth at bearing of piles; in charge of sediment control for the project. Subspecialties: Geology; Coastal zones. Home: 964 Mount Airy Rd Davidsonville MD 21035 Office: Century Engring 32 West Rd Towson MD 21204

WOOD, HARLAND GOFF, biochemist, emeritus educator; b. Delavan, Minn., Sept. 2, 1907; s. William C. and Inez (Goff) W.; m. Mildred Lenora Davis, Sept. 14, 1929; children: Donna, Beverly, Louise. A.B., Macalester Coll., 1931, D.Sc. (hon.), 1946; Ph.D., Iowa State Coll., 1935; D.Sc., Northwestern U., 1972, U. Cin., 1982. Fellow NRC, biochem. dept. U. Wis., 1935-36; asst. prof. bacteriology dept. Iowa State Coll., 1936-43; assoc. prof. physiol. chemistry dept. U. Minn., 1943-46; prof., dir. biochemistry dept. Case Western Res. U., Cleve., 1946-65, prof. biochemistry, 1965-78, dean scis., 1967-69, Univ. prof., 1970-78, prof. emeritus, 1978—; chmn. isotope panel com. on growth NRC, 1947-48; adv. council Life Ins. Med. Research Fund, 1957-62; mem. tng. grant com. NIH, 1965-69; adv. bd. Case Inst. Tech., 1971-78; adv. com. div. biology and medicine U.S. AEC, 1967-72; mem. Presdl. Sci. Adv. Com., Washington, 1968-72, mem. physiol. chemistry study sect., 1973-77. Recipient Eli Lilly research award in bacteriology, 1942, Carl Neuberg award Nat. Acad. Scis., 1953, Glycerine award, 1954, Modern Med. award for disting. achievement, 1968; Lynen lectr. and medal, 1972; Humbolt prize as sr. U.S. scientist W. Ger., 1979; Fulbright fellow, 1955; Guggenheim fellow, 1962. Mem. Am. Acad. Arts and Scis., Am. Heart Assn. (research com. 1949), Am. Chem. Soc., Am. Soc. Biol. Chemists (pres. 1959), Biochem. Soc. Gt. Britain, Biochem. Soc. Japan (hon.), N.Y. Acad. Scis., Am. Cancer Soc. (adv. bd. 1965-69), Internat. Union Biochemistry (mem. council 1967-76, sec. gen. 1970-73, pres. 1979-85), Soc. Am. Bacteriologists, Sigma Xi; corr. mem. Der Bayerischen Akademie der Wissenschaften. Methodist. Current Work: Mechanism of enzyme reactions; synthesis of acetate by bacteria from CO or CO2 and H2; role of inorganic polyphosphate and pyrophosphate in metabolism. Subspecialties: Microbiology; Biochemistry (medicine). Office: care Western Res U Dept Biochemistry 2109 Adelbert Rd Cleveland OH 44106*

WOOD, JOHN ARMSTEAD, geochemist, geology educator; b. Roanoke, Va., July 28, 1932; s. John Armstead and Lillian Cary (Hall) W.; m. Elisabeth Mathilde Heuser, June 12, 1958 (div.); children—Crispin S., Georgia K. B.S. in Geology, Va. Polytech. Inst., 1954, Ph.D., Mass. Inst. Tech., 1958; post-doctoral study, U. Cambridge, Eng., 1959-60. Staff scientist Smithsonian Astrophys. Obs., Cambridge, Mass., 1959, 61-62, 65—; research asso. Enrico Fermi Inst. U. Chgo., 1962-65; prof. dept. geol. scis. Harvard, 1976—; asso. dir. Harvard-Smithsonian Center for Astrophysics, 1981—; Vice chmn. Lunar Sample Analysis Planning Team, 1971-72. Author: Meteorites and the Origin of Planets, 1968, The Solar System, 1979. Recipient NASA medal for exceptional sci. achievement, 1973; J.L. Smith medal Nat. Acad. Scis., 1976. Fellow Am. Geophys. Union, Meteoritical Soc. (pres. 1971-72, Leonard medal 1980), AAAS; mem. Internat. Astron. Union. Current work: Meteorite and lunar sample studies as a key to the origin and early evolution of the planets. Subspecialty: Planetary science. Home: 375 Harvard St Cambridge MA 02138 Office: 60 Garden St Cambridge MA 02138

WOOD, OBERT REEVES, II, laser researcher; b. Sacramento, Jan. 18, 1943; s. Obert Reeves and Marietta (Korff) W.; m. Nancy Jean Stanger, Apr. 21, 1973; 1 son, Obert Reeves III. B.S., U. Calif.-Berkeley, 1964, M.S., 1965, Ph.D., 1969. Research asst. Electronics Research Lab., U. Calif.-Berkeley, 1965-69; mem. tech. staff Bell Labs., Holmdel, N.J., 1969—; Cons. on carbon dioxide laser eye surgery N.Y. Hosp.-Cornell U. Med. Ctr., N.Y.C., 1978—. Contbr. articles to profl. jours. Mem. Am. Phys. Soc., Optical Soc. Am., IEEE, AAAS, N.Y. Acad. Scis., Sigma Xi, Tau Beta Pi, Eta Kappa Nu. Patentee quantum electronics, optics, atomic physics and laser fields. Current Work: Research on short-wave length lasers and laser-produced plasmas; involved in experimental tests of quantum electrodynamics and use of lasers in medicine. Subspecialties: Atomic and molecular physics; Laser research. Home: 19 Fox Hill Dr Little Silver NJ 07739 Office: Bell Labs Room 4C434 Holmdel NJ 07747

WOOD, THOMAS H., physicist; b. Mineola, N.Y., Apr. 17, 1953; Sc.B., Brown U., 1975; M.S., U. Ill., 1976, Ph.D., 1980. Mem. tech. staff AT&T Bell Labs., Holmdel, N.J., 1980—. Contbr. articles to profl. jours. Mem. Am. Phys. Soc., IEEE, Optical Soc. Am., Am. Vacuum Soc. Current work: Optoelectronic properties of semiconductor multiple quantum wells; optical fiber local area networks. Subspecialties: Fiber optics; Condensed matter physics. Office: AT&T Bell Labs PO Box 400 Holmdel NJ 07733

WOOD, WILLIAM BARRY, III, biologist, educator; b. Balt., Feb. 19, 1938; s. William Barry, Jr. and Mary Lee (Hutchins) W.; m. Marie-Elisabeth Renate Hartisch, June 30, 1961; children: Oliver Hartisch, Christopher Barry. A.B., Harvard U., 1959; Ph.D., Stanford U., 1963. Asst. prof. biology Calif. Inst. Tech., Pasadena, 1965-68, assoc. prof., 1968-69, prof. biology, 1970-77; prof. molecular, cellular and developmental biology U. Colo., Boulder, 1977—, chmn. dept., 1978-83; mem. panel for developmental biology NSF, 1970-72; physiol. chemistry study sect. NIH, 1974-78, mem. cellular and molecular basis of disease rev. com., 1984—; mem. com. on sci. and public policy Nat. Acad. Scis., 1979-80. Author: (with J.H. Wilson, R.M. Benbow, L.E. Hood) Biochemistry: A Problems Approach, 2d edit, 1981, (with L.E. Hood and J.H. Wilson) Molecular Biology of Eucaryotic Cells, 1975, (with L.E. Hood and I.L. Weissman) Immunology, 1978, (with L.E. Hood, I.L. Weissman, and J.H. Wilson) Immunology, 2d edit., 1984, (with L.E. Hood and I.L. Weissman) Concepts in Immunology, 1978. Assoc. editor Cell, 1985—; bd. reviewing editors Science, 1985—. Contbr. articles to profl. jours. Recipient U.S. Steel Molecular Biology award, 1969; NIH research grantee, 1965—; Guggenheim fellow, 1975-76. Mem. Nat. Acad. Scis., Am. Acad. Arts and Scis., Am. Soc. Biol. Chemists, Soc. for Developmental Biology, Soc. Nematology, Am. Soc. Virology, AAAS. Current Work: Genetic control of invertebrate development; genetic control of virus assembly. Subspecialties: Gene actions; Developmental biology. Office: Dept MCD Biology Box 347 U Colorado Boulder CO 80309

WOODALL, MILTON ANDREW, II, physicist; b. Port Arthur, Tex., Feb. 14, 1956; s. Milton Andrew and Georgia Belle (Hackney) W. m. Darla Lane, Aug. 1, 1981. B.S. in Physics, Lamar U., 1978; M.S. in Physics, N. Tex. State U., 1981, Ph.D. in Physics, 1985. Lab. instr. Lamar U., Beaumont, Tex., 1976-78; teaching asst. N. Tex. State U., Denton, 1978-80, research fellow, 1980-84; systems design engr. Tex. Instruments, Dallas, 1984—. Contbr. papers and articles to profl. confs. and jours. NSF grantee, 1973; Welch Found. fellow, 1981-84. Mem. Optical Soc. Am., Lasers and Electro-optics Soc. of IEEE, Am. Phys. Soc., Soc. Photo-Instrumentation Engrs. Phi Kappa Phi, Sigma Pi Sigma (chpt. v.p. 1981-83). Current work: Applied nonliner optics, electro-optic countermeasures and EOCCM, ultrasensitive laser spectroscopy, optical power limiters, optical phase conjugation, ultrafast phenomena and EO system design. Subspecialties: Condensed matter physics; Infrared spectroscopy. Home: PO Box 742493 Dallas TX 75374 Office: Texas Instruments 8505 Forest Ln PO Box 660246 MS 3122 Dallas TX 75266

WOODBURY, CHARLES PUTNAM, JR., chemistry educator; b. El Paso, Tex., Apr. 6, 1949; s. Charles Putnam and Dorothy Jean (Calvin) W.; m. Martha Lee Bryan, June 20, 1970; children—Katherine Lee, Geoffrey Kirk. B.S., U. Wash., 1971; Ph.D., U. Wis.-Madison, 1975. Research assoc. molecular biology U. Oreg., Eugene, 1975-79; asst. prof. medicinal chemistry U. Ill., Chgo., 1979—. Contbr. articles to profl. jours. Bd. dirs. Nat. Assn. Down's Syndrome, Chgo., 1980-84, Down's Syndrome Research Fund, Chgo., 1984. NIH fellow, 1977-79; NSF grantee, 1984. Mem. Biophys. Soc., Am. Soc. Biol. Chemists, Am. Chem. Soc., Sigma Xi. Current work: Statistical mechanics of electrolyte and polyelectrolyte solutions; protein-nucleic acid interactions; drug-nucleic acid and drug-membrane binding. Subspecialties: Biophysics (biology); Molecular biology. Home: 332 S Edson St Lombard IL 60148 Office: U Ill Dept Medicinal Chemistry 833 S Wood St Chicago IL 60680

WOODE, GERALD NOTTIDGE, veterinarian, educator; b. Hartlepool, Eng., July 16, 1934; came to U.S., 1978; s. Meredith Marshall and Evelyn Grace (Baker) W.; m. Shirley Wilkin, July 4, 1959; children: Clair, Lindsay, Mary. B.Vet. Med., U. London, 1960, D.Vet. Med., 1978. Gen practive veterinary medicine, Ashford, Eng., 1961-62; virologist Glaxo, Ltd., Eng., 1962-66; lectr. Royal Sch. Veterinary Studies, Edinburgh, 1966-71; prin. veterinary research officer Inst. Research on Animal Diseases, Eng., 1971-77; prof. veterinary medicine Iowa State U., 1978—; cons. in field. Contbr. to profl. jours. Served with Brit. Army, 1953-55. U.S. Dept. Agr. grantee, 1979-82; Nat. Pork Producers Council grantee, 1979-81; State of Iowa grantee, 1978-82. Mem. Am. Soc. Virology, WHO, Royal Coll. Veterinary Surgeons. Current Work: Virus infections of the intestinal tract causing diarrhea and death in children: calves, piglets, horses, lambs, dogs. Subspecialties: Animal virology; Virology (veterinary medicine). Office: Department Veterinary Microbiology College of Veterinary Medicine Iowa State University Ames IA 50011

WOODFORD, WARREN JAMES, research chemist, forensics consultant; b. Roanoke, Va., Mar. 18, 1946; s. Warren Rucker Woodford. B.S., East Carolina U., 1968; M.S., Emory U., 1970, Ph.D., 1973. Postdoctoral fellow dept. medicinal chemistry U. Kans., Lawrence, 1973-74; dir. Web of Research, Atlanta, 1975—; instr. clin. chemistry Branan Drug and Toxicology Lab., Atlanta, 1978; vis. scientist, guest speaker Scotland Yard's Met. Police Forensic Sci. Labs. Contbr. articles to profl. jours. Bd. dirs. Met. Atlanta Council on Alcohol and Drugs, 1978—. Recipient Research award Nat. Cancer Inst., 1973. Mem. Am. Chem. Soc., AAAS. Current work: Medicinal chemistry and analysis of evidence for court purposes. Subspecialties: Toxicology (medicine); Analytical chemistry. Office: Web of Research PO Box 5437 Atlanta GA 30307

WOODHOUR, ALLEN FRANCIS, microbiologist; b. Newark, Feb. 21, 1930; s. Frank E. and Alice (Rawa) W.; m. Rosamond C. Woodhour, Nov. 5, 1955 (dec. Sept. 1982); 1 child, Rosamond M.; m. Deanna Arner, Apr. 7, 1984; children—Valerie A. Fisher, Richard Arner. A.B., St. Vincent Coll., Latrobe, Pa., 1952; M.S., Cath. Univ. Am., 1954; Ph.D., Cath. U. Am., 1956. Microbiologist Walter Reed Army Inst. Research, Washington, 1956-57; Microbiologist, Chas. Pfizer & Co., Inc., Terre Haute, Ind., 1957-60; with Merck & Co., Inc., West Point, Pa., 1960—; sr. dir. regulatory affairs Merck Sharp & Dohme Research Labs., 1984—. Contbr. articles to sci. jours. Mem. Am. Soc. Microbiology, AAAS, Internat. Assn. Biol. Standardization, Am. Soc. Immunologists, Sigma Xi. Patentee in field (5). Current Work: Biologics and pharmaceutical regulatory matters. Subspecialties: Microbiology (medicine); Virology (medicine). Home: PO Box 187 Brandon Dr Lederach PA 19450 Office: Merck Labs West Point PA 19406

WOODLEY, DAVID TIMOTHY, dermatology educator; b. St. Louis, Aug. 1, 1946; s. Raoul Ramos-Mimosa and Marian (Schlueter) W.; m. Christina Paschall Prentice, May 4, 1974; 1 son, David Thatcher. A.B., Washington U., St. Louis, 1968; M.D., U. Mo., 1973. Diplomate: Am. Bd. Internal Medicine, Am. Bd. Dermatology, Nat. Bd. Internal Medicine. Intern Beth Israel Med. Center, Mt. Sinai Sch. Medicine, N.Y. Hosp., Cornell U. Sch. Medicine, N.Y.C., 1973-74; resident in internal medicine U. Nebr., Omaha, 1974-76; resident in dermatology U.N.C., Chapel Hill, N.C., 1976-78, asst. prof. dept. dermatology, 1983-85, assoc. prof. dept. dermatology, 1985—; research fellow U. Paris, 1978-80; expert NIH, Bethesda, Md., 1980-82; cons. VA Med. Ctr., AHEC Med. Ctr., Fayetteville, N.C., 1983—. Contbr. chpts. to books and articles in field to profl. jours. Mem. Clean Water Action Project, Washington, 1982-83; mem. Potomac Albicore Fleet, 1982-83, Friends of the Art Sch., Chapel Hill, 1983—, Jungian Soc. Triangle Area, 1983—. Fellow Am. Acad. Dermatology; mem. Dermatology Found., Soc. Investigative Dermtology, ACP (assoc.), Assn. Physican Poets. Current Work: The biochemistry of basement membrane molecules in skin and the influence of these molecules on epidermal cells. Subspecialties: Dermatology; Cell biology (medicine). Home: 46 Laurel Ridge Apts Chapel Hill NC 27514 Office: U NC Med Sch Dept Dermatology Rm 137 NC Meml Hosp Chapel Hill NC 27514

WOODRING, JOHN HOWELL, diagnostic radiology educator, physician; b. Louisville, Sept. 10, 1951; s. Franklyn Howell and Dorothy Moore (McInteer) W.; m. Catherine Anne Martin, Aug. 27, 1977; children—Paul Martin, Mark Reynolds. B.S., U. Louisville, 1973; M.D., U. Ky., 1976. Diplomate: Am. Bd. Radiology. Intern Louisville Gen. Hosp., 1976-77; resident in radiology U. Ky. Med. Center, Lexington, 1977-80; asst. prof. diagnostic radiology U. Ky. Coll. Medicine, Lexington, 1980-84, assoc. prof., 1984—, chest radiologist, dept. diagnostic radiology, 1980—. Fellow U. Ky. Fellows; mem. Am. Coll. Radiology, Radiol. Soc. N.Am., Assn. Univ. Radiologists, Soc. Thoracic Radiology, Bluegrass Radiol. Soc., Soc. Thoracic Radiology, Phi Kappa Phi. Methodist. Current Work: Research and teaching chest trauma, carcinoma of the lung, adult respiratory distress syndrome, computed tomography of the chest, mycobacterial and fungal diseases of the lung. Home: 162 N Arcadia Park Lexington KY 40503 Office: Dept Diagnostic Radiology HX315B U Ky Med Ctr 800 Rose St Lexington KY 40536

WOODROOFE, MICHAEL BARRETT, statistician; b. Corvallis, Oreg., Mar. 17, 1940; s. Robin Russell and Helen Lucille (Barrett) W.; m. Frances Smock, July 6, 1974; children—Russell, Carolyn, Blake. B.S. in Math, Stanford U., 1962; M.A. in Math, U. Oreg., 1964, Sc. in Math, 1965. Research asso. Stanford U., 1965-66; asst. prof. stats. Carnegie Mellon U., 1966-68; mem. faculty U. Mich., 1968—, prof. math. and stats., 1973-83, chmn. dept. stats., 1977-83; prof. stats. Rutgers U., 1983—; vis. assoc. prof. Columbia U., 1970-71; vis. prof. MIT, 1976-77. Author: Probability with Application, 1974, Non Linear Renewal Theory in Sequential Analysis, 1982. Grantee NIH; Grantee NSF; Grantee U.S. Army. Mem. Am. Math. Soc., Inst. Math. Stats., Phi Beta Kappa. Current Work: Sequential analysis; repeated significance tests; non linear renewal theory; optimal stopping; sequential estimation. Subspecialties: Probability; Statistics. Home: 707 Abbott St Highland Park NJ 80903 Office: Stats Dept Rutgers U New Brunswick NJ

WOODROW, JAMES EUGENE, chemist, researcher; b. Eugene, Oreg., May 30, 1942; s. John Eugene and Wanda Vee (Keaton) W.; m. Rosemary Sherry, June 21, 1968. B.A., U. Calif.-Berkeley, 1966; M.S., San Jose State U., 1970. Chemist, Shell Devel., Emeryville, Calif., 1966-68; staff research assoc., U. Calif.-Davis, 1972—. Contbr. articles to profl. jours. Recipient Outstanding Performance award U. Calif., 1984. Fellow Am. Inst. Chemists; mem. Am. Chem. Soc., AAAS, N.Y. Acad. Sci., Sigma Xi. Current work: Environmental fate of pesticides; air sampling; mathematical modeling of environmental processes. Subspecialties: Analytical chemistry; Environmental chemistry. Home: 738 W Cross St Woodland CA 95695 Office: Dept Environ Toxicology U Calif Davis CA 95616

WOODRUFF, NEIL PARKER, civil engineer, consultant; b. Clyde, Kans., July 25, 1919; s. Charles Scott and Myra (Christian) W.; m. Dorothy Adele Russ, June 15, 1952; children—Timothy C., Thomas S. B.S. in Agrl. Engring., Kans. State U., 1949, M.S. in Agrl. Engring., 1953; post-grad. Iowa State U., 1959. Cert. in exec. devel. U.S. Dept. Agr. Agrl. engr. Agrl. Research Service, U.S. Dept. Agr., Manhattan, Kans., 1949-68, research leader, 1968-75; cons. Nat. Acad. Sci., Washington, 1975-77; civil engr. Kans. Dept. Transp., Topeka, 1977-79, Kans. State U., Manhattan, 1979-84; freelance cons., Manhattan, 1984—; mem. adv. com. research project assessment of research on natural hazards NSF, 1972-75; mem. sci. exchange team to Soviet Union, 1974; mem. panel V com. on climate and weather fluc Nat. Acad. Sci., 1975-76. Contbr. articles, reports and book chpts. on wind erosion, aerodynamics, tillage and soil conservation to profl. publs. Served to tech. sgt. USAF, 1941-45. Fellow Am. Soc. Agrl. Engrs. (chmn. fellow screening com., chmn. soil and water com., recipient Hancor Soil and Water Engring. award 1976); mem. Soil Conservation Soc. Am., Sigma Xi, Gamma Sigma Delta. Republican. Current work: Wind erosion control: consulting and editing; civil engineering: water systems, drainage, lawn irrigation systems. Subspecialties: Agricultural engineering; Civil engineering. Home: 3115 Heritage Ct Manhattan KS 66502

WOODRUFF-PAK, DIANA STENEN, psychologist, educator; b. Pasadena, Calif., Apr. 10, 1946; d. Norman Hanson and Ruth Lee (Helsel) Stenen; m. Hyung Woong Pak, Aug. 5, 1975; children: Jonathan Tong-Hee, Michelle Hyun-Mi. A.B. magna cum laude, UCLA, 1968; A.M., U. So. Calif., 1970, Ph.D., 1972. Research asst. dept. psychology UCLA, 1972-74; asst. prof. psychology U. So. Calif., Los Angeles, 1974-75; asst. prof. psychology Temple U., Phila., 1975-77, assoc. prof., 1977-83, prof., 1983—; vis. prof. psychology Stanford U., 1983-85. Author: Can You Live to Be 100? , 1977, (with others) Developmental Psychology: A Life-Span Approach, 1981; editor: (with James E. Birren) Aging: Scientific Perspectives and Social Issues, 1st edit, 1975, 2d edit., 1983; Contbr. articles to profl. jours. Nat. Inst. Aging research awardee, 1979-81; sr. fellow, 1983-85. Fellow Am. Psychol. Assn., Gerontol. Soc. Am.; Mem. Soc. for Psychophysiol. Research (chmn. ethics com. 1980-83), Soc. for Neurosci., Phi Beta Kappa. Current Work: Learning and memory in aging animals; behavioral neuroscience. Subspecialties: Developmental psychology; Physiological psychology. Home: 1015 Sharpless Rd Philadelphia PA 19126 Office: Dept Psychology Temple U Philadelphia PA 19122

WOODS, CHARLES ARTHUR, zoology educator, curator; b. Sherman, Tex., Dec. 23, 1940; s. Hicks Arthur and Janice (Gertrude) (McCallum) W.; m. Ellen Stott Woods, Mar. 23 1963; children: C. Stott, Patricia, Bryan. Student, Middlebury Coll., 1959-62; B.A., U. Denver, 1964; Ph.D., U. Mass., 1970. Asst. prof. biology U. Denver, 1970-71; asst. prof. zoology U. Vt., 1971-76, assoc. prof., 1976-79; prof. zoology U. Fla., 1979—, assoc. curator, 1979-82, curator, 1982—, chmn., 1979—. Contbr. articles to profl. jours. Served with USMC Res., 1962-68. NSF fellow, 1977-79. Mem. Am. Soc. Mammalogists, Am. Soc. Naturalists, Soc. Study Evolution, Soc. Vertebrate Paleontologists, Sigma Xi. Current Work: Functional biology, evolution and systematics of mammals with an emphasis on rodents; conservation of island mammals. Subspecialties: Evolutionary biology; Systematics. Home: PO Box 218 Micanopy FL 32667 Office: Florida State Museum Gainesville FL 32611

WOODS, DELMA MARIA, psychologist; b. N.Y.C., June 11; d. Edmund and Maria Williams (Tucker) Prioleau; m. Roy Woods, Mar. 17, 1974; children: Roy, Edmund, Delma. M.S., Howard U., 1971. Tchr. emotionally disturbed children D.C. Pub. Schs., Washington, 1964-66, psychologist, 1967-74, 76-78; clin. psychologist Head Start, Washington, 1969, psychol. cons., 1973; 76-78; psychologist Dade County (Fla.) Schs., Miami, 1974-76; cons. Roy Woods, Charleston, S.C., 1979—; guardian ad-litem for neglected and abused children, Charleston County, S.C., 1979-82; mem. chmn. Charleston County Multidisciplinary Commn., 1978-79; coordinator The Health Line, Sta. WPAL, Charleston, S.C., 1979—. Chmn. Jack and Jill Am., Inc., Charleston, 1979—; co-chmn, youth leadership com. Alpha Kappa Alpha, Charleston, 1979-80, co-chmn. health edn. com., 1979-80; founder Morris Brown Players, Charleston, 1982; bd. dirs. Pam Robinson Contemporary Sch. Performing Arts, 1982—. Recipient Achievement awards Washington Sch. Psychiatry, 1972, Achievement awards Children's Hosp. Nat. Ctr., 1973. Mem. Am. Psychol. Assn., Assn. Black Psychologists, AAAS, S.C. Assn. Black Psychologists, Charleston County Med. Soc. Aux. (sec.), Palmetto Med. Soc. Aux. (exec. bd.). Current Work: The interrelationships between physical and psychological disorders, behavior modification in young children. Subspecialty: Behavioral psychology. Home: 1106 Woodhaven Dr Charleston SC 29407 Office: 19 Hagood Ave Suite 901 Charleston SC 29407

WOODS, EUGENE FRANCIS, health care products corporation executive; b. Richmond, Va., June 29, 1931; s. Edward Joseph and Wilhelmena (Walker) W.; m. E. Ruth Butler, Oct. 30, 1951 (div. Nov. 1980); children: Janet, Ralph, Randolph; m. Janet M. Scolari, Apr. 3, 1982. Faculty mem. Med. U. S.C., Charleston, 1957-75, prof. pharmacology, 1975; dir. pharmacology Baxter Travenol Inc., Morton Grove, Ill, 1975-79, dir. safety assessment, 1979—. Served to maj. U.S. Army Res., 1950-67. Recipient USPHS (NIH) Research Career Devel. award, 1960-70; NIH, Am. Heart Assn., S.C. Heart Assn. research grantee, 1960-75. Mem. Am. Soc. Pharmacology and Exptl. Therapeutics, Am. Physiol. Soc., Am. Soc. for Artificial Internal Organs. Current Work: Research and administration in broad areas of medical devices and drug agents. Subspecialties: Pharmacology; Toxicology (medicine). Office: Baxter Travenol Inc 6301 Lincoln Ave Morton Grove IL 60053

WOODS, GEORGE THEODORE, veterinarian, epidemiologist; b. Tyro, Kans., Aug. 21, 1924; s. Samuel Branchford and Harriett (Crawford) W.; m. Helen Louise Jordan, June 20, 1948; children—David, Jeffrey, Linda. D.V.M., Kans. State U.-Manhattan, 1946; M.P.H., U. Calif.-Berkeley, 1959; M.S., Purdue U., 1960. Field veterinarian Ill. Dept. Agr., Danville, 1946-47; supr. lab. animals Northwestern U. Med. Sch., Chgo., 1947-48; pvt. practice veterinary medicine, Shelbyville, Ill., 1948-49; extension veterinarian U. Ill.-Urbana, 1949-59, teaching and research, 1959—, prof. veterinary microbiology and pub. health, 1966—; cons. Nat. Specific Pathogen Free Swine Certification Agy., Conrad, Iowa, 1970-83, chmn. adv. com., 1980-83. Contbr. numerous articles to profl. jours. Chmn. Ednl. Com., Champaign County Health Dept., 1965-67. Served to capt. USAF, 1954-56. Mem. AVMA (mem. exec. com. 1979-84, recipient Service award 1983), Am. Pub. Health Assn., Am. Assn. Food Hygiene Veterinarians, Am. Assn. Tchrs. Veterinary Pub. Health (pres. 1971-73), Am. Assn. Swine Practitioners. Republican. Methodist. Current work: The role of mixed microbial infections in acute respiratory disease in cattle and swine and their relationship to human pathogens. Subspecialties: Preventive medicine (veterinary medicine); Epidemiology. Office: Coll Veterinary Medicine U Ill 2001 S Lincoln St Urbana IL 61801

WOODS, GORDON LEON, veterinary science educator; b. Colfax, Wash., July 14, 1952; s. Leo Carlon Woods and Gale Marie (Shearer) Woods Sego; m. Shauna Joan Vail, Aug. 17, 1972; children—Stephanie, Jonathan, Benjamin, Elizabeth. Student Ricks Coll., Rexburg, Idaho, 1970-71; B.S., U. Idaho, 1974; D.V.M., Colo. State U., 1978; M.S., U. Wis.-Madison, 1982, Ph.D., 1983. Diplomate Am. Coll. Theriogenologists. Practice vet. medicine McIntosh Vet. Clinic, Lewiston, Idaho, 1978-79; resident in large animal reprodn. U. Pa., Kennett Square, 1979-80; instr. Cornell U., Ithaca, N.Y., 1983-84, asst. prof. reproductive physiology of equine, 1984—, dir. Lab. of Equine Growth and Devel., 1984—. Author lit. on theriogenology. Recipient Burr A. Beach award Wis. Vet. Med. Assn., 1984. Mem. AVMA, Am. Assn. Equine Practitioners, Soc. Theriogenology, Internat. Embryo Transfer Soc., Soc. Studs of Reprodn. Republican. Mormon. Subspecialties: Embryo transplants (veterinary medicine); Genetics and genetic engineering (veterinary medicine). Home: 1436 Hanshaw Rd Ithaca NY 14850 Office: 431 VRT Cornell U Ithaca NY 14880

WOODS, JOHN GALLOWAY, mechanical engineer, high technology manufacturing company executive; b. N.Y.C., July 21, 1926; s. John Burrows Collings and Elizabeth (Galloway) W.; m. Merilyn Baron, Sept. 15,1948; children: Anne Helen, Elizabeth Ruth. B.M.E., Cornell U., 1949; M.S.M.E., Drexel U., 1958. Registered profl. engr., Pa. Test engr. Babcock & Wilcox Co., Alliance, Ohio, 1949-51; sr. engr. Philco Corp., Phila., 1951-54; sr. devel. engr. IRC Inc., Phila., 1954-69; sr. devel. engr. TRW Inc. (merger IRC Inc. with TRW Inc.), 1969-79, sr. project engr., 1979-81, program mgr. Electronic Components Group, Research and Devel. Labs., 1981-82; chief engr. Fiber Optic Products Electronic Components Group, Research and Devel. Labs., 1983—. Asst. treas. Awbury Arboretum Neighbors Assn., Phila., 1979-82. Served with USN, 1945—46. Mem. Nat. Soc. Profl. Engrs. (vice chmn. Profl. Engrs. in Industry 1977-79, Outstanding Service award 1979, nat. dir. 1983-86), Pa. Soc. Profl. Engrs. (pres. Phila. chpt. 1979-80, v.p. S.E. Pa. region 1980-83, state pres. 1984-85, Disting. Service award Profl. in Industry 1979), ASME, Soc. Photo-Instrumentation Engrs., IEEE. Patentee electronic components. Current Work: Fiber optic interconnections and sensors. Subspecialties: Fiber optics; Electronic materials. Home: 5928 Devon Pl Philadelphia PA 19138 Office: TRW 401 N Broad St Philadelphia PA 19108

WOODS, ROY, internist, immunologist; b. Birmingham, Ala., Mar. 25, 1938; s. Abraham Lincoln and Maggie Rosalee (Wallace) W.; m. Delma Maria Prioleau, Mar. 17, 1974; children: Roy, Edmund Prioleau, Delma Maria. A.B., Miles Coll., 1958; M.S., U. Wis.-Madison, 1960, Ph.D., 1963; M.D., U. Miami, Fla., 1976. Diplomate: Am. Bd. Medical Examiners. Assoc. prof. biology Miles Coll., Birmingham, 1963-64; postdoctoral research fellow U. Uppsala, Sweden, 1964-66, Stanford (Calif.) U., 1966-67; sr. scientist, dir. immunoglogulin reference Ctr. Nat. Cancer Inst., Springfield, Va., 1967-74, practice medicine specializing in internal medicine and immunology, Charleston, S.C., 1979—; mem. staff Roper Hosp., St. Francis-Xavier Hosp., Charleston.; cons., prin. investigator WHO. Author: Qualitation and Quantitation of the Immunoglobulins, 1972; columnist: Charleston Chronicle; contbr. numerous articles top profl. jours.; panel host Health Line, Sta. WPAL. NIH grantee. Mem. Nat. Med. Assn., AMA, Am. Assn. Immunologists, AAAS, N.Y. Acad. Scis., S.C. Med. Assn., Charleston County Med. Soc. Baptist. Club: Whist (Charleston). Current Work: Private practice of internal medicine and the investigation of immunodeficiency syndromes. Subspecialties: Internal medicine; Immunology (medicine). Home: 1106 Woodhaven Dr Charleston SC 29407 Office: 19 Hagood Ave Suite 901 Charleston SC 29403

WOODS, WALTER ABNER, marketing executive, educator, consumer behavior researcher; b. Lingle, Wyo., Jan. 16, 1915; s. James Abner and Mazeppa (Israel) W.; m. Margaret C. Edmiston, June 15, 1955 (div. 1974); 1 dau., Dana Jeanne. A.B., U. Wyo., 1937; M.A., Syracuse U., 1942; Ph.D., Columbia U., 1952; student, Art Students League, N.Y.C., 1946-47. Research psychologist Art Sch., Pratt Inst., Bklyn., 1948-51; assoc. prof. psychology Richmond (Va.) Profl. Inst., 1952-55; v.p., sr. dir. research Nowland & Co., Greenwich, Ct., 1955-61; pres., sr. researcher Products & Concepts Research Inc., Sparta, (N.J.), Brussels, Sydney, 1961—; prof. mktg. West Ga. Coll., Carrollton, 1971-85, prof. emeritus, 1985—; dir. Prognosis S.A., Brussels, 1963—; cons. in field. Author: Consumer Behavior, 1980. County chmn. Ford for Pres., Carroll County, Ga., 1976; coordinator Anderson for Pres. campaign, Ga., 1980. Served to lt. USNR, 1942-46. Recipient disting. mktg. service award Sales Execs. Club of N.Y., 1968; named Outstanding Educator of Am., 1973. Fellow Acad. Mktg. Sci.; mem. Am. Psychol. Assn., Am. Mktg. Assn., Internat. Assn. for Empirical Aesthetics, AAAS. Developer: personality test Polychrome Index, 1954; color aptitude test, 1951; originator product concept research; cooriginator positioning strategy. Current Work: Supra level purposes and motives in consuming behavior motivation and perception in art experiencing. Subspecialties: Behavioral psychology; Cognition. Home: 389 Smyrna Church Rd Carrollton GA 30117 Office: West Ga Coll Carrollton GA 30118

WOODS, WALTER RALPH, animal scientist; b. Grant, Va., Dec. 2, 1931; s. John Wythe and Hazel Gladys (Hash) W.; m. Jacqulyn Rose Miller, Sept. 14, 1953; children: Neal Ralph, Diana Lyn. B.S., Murray (Ky.) State U., 1954; M.S., U. Ky., 1955; Ph.D., Okla. State U., 1957. Instr. animal sci. Okla. State U., 1956-57; asst. prof., then assoc. prof. Iowa State U., 1957-62; assoc. prof., then prof. U. Nebr., 1962-71; prof. animal sci., head dept. Purdue U., 1971-85; dean agr., dir. agr. expt. sta. Kans. State U., 1985—; pres. Am. Registry Profl. Animal Scientists, 1984-85. Author papers, articles in field. Bd. dirs. Ind. 4-H Found., 1979-81. Recipient Disting. Agrl. Alumni award Murray State U., 1969, Meritorious Service award Ind. Pork Producers Assn., 1975. Mem. Am. Soc. Animal Sci. (sec.-treas. Midwest sect. 1979-81, pres. Midwest sect. 1983-84), Am. Inst. Nutrition, Am. Dairy Sci. Assn., Poultry Sci. Assn., Ind. Beef Cattle Assn. (dir. 1973-85), Sigma Xi, Gamma Sigma Delta. Baptist. Club: Lafayette Rotary (dir. 1976-79). Current Work: Director of research in agriculture and responsibility for teaching and extension. Subspecialty: Animal nutrition. Home: 2818 Tatairax Dr Manhattan KS 66502 Office: Waters Hall 114 Kansas State U Manhattan KS 66506

WOODS, WALTER THOMAS, JR., physiologist, consultant, educator; b. Nashville, Mar. 13, 1947; s. Walter Thomas and Evelyn Eugenia (Cooper) W.; m. Kathleen Gage Frye, Aug. 23, 1969; children: Thomas Cooper, Kathleen Gage, Helen Frye. B.A., U. of the South, Sewanee, Tenn., 1969; M.A., Appalachian State U., 1971; Ph.D., Bowman Gray Sch. Medicine Wake Forest U., 1975. With dept. physiology and biophysics, div. cardiovascular disease and cardiovascular research and tng. ctr. U. Ala., Birmingham, 1975—, asst. prof., 1971-84, assoc. prof., 1984—; outside expert in cardiac electrophysiology Med. Research Council, Can., 1983—. Contbr. articles to profl. jours. NSF trainee, 1973-74; Am. Heart Assn. grantee, 1981; Lilly Research Labs. grantee, 1982; NIH grantee, 1983; Army Med. Research and Devel. Command grantee, 1983—. Fellow Council Circulation Am. Heart Assn., Am. Physiol. Soc. (fellow sect. on heart and circulatory physiology). Republican. Episcopalian. Club: Mt. Brook (Birmingham). Current Work: Having located and isolated in vitro the cells that initiate each heartbeat, present effort is to determine how membrane proteins in these cells regulate their firing rate. Subspecialties: Cell biology; Physiology (biology). Home: PO Box 7662A Birmingham AL 35253 Office: U Ala Birmingham Sch Medicine University Station Birmingham AL 35294

WOODSON, HERBERT HORACE, electrical engineering educator; b. Stamford, Tex., Apr. 5, 1925; s. Herbert Viven and Floy (Tunnell) W.; m. Blanche Elizabeth Sears, Aug. 17, 1951; children: William Sears, Robert Sears, Bradford Sears. S.B., S.M., M.I.T., 1952, Sc.D. in Elec. Engring, 1956. Registered profl. engr., Tex., Mass. Instr. elec. engring., also project leader magnetics div. Naval Ordnance Lab., 1952-54; mem. faculty M.I.T., 1956-71, prof. elec. engring., 1965-71, Philip Sporn prof. energy processing, 1967-71; prof. elec. engring., chmn. dept. U. Tex., Austin, 1971-81, Alcoa Found. prof., 1972-75, Ernest H. Cockrell Centennial prof. engring., 1982—, dir. Center for Energy Studies, 1973—, Tex. Atomic Energy Research Found. prof. engring., 1980-82; staff engr. elec. engring. div. AEP Service Corp., N.Y.C., 1965-66; cons. to industry, 1956—. Author: (with others) Electromechanical Dynamics, parts I, II, III. Served with USNR, 1943-46. Fellow IEEE (pres. Power Engring. Soc. 1978-80); mem. Am. Soc. Engring. Edn., Nat. Acad. Engring., AAAS. Patentee in field. Current Work: Electromechanical pulse power supplies and their application to industrial processes; military systems and fusion research. Subspecialties: Electrical engineering; Fusion. Home: 7603 Rustling Rd Austin TX 78731

WOODWARD, JAMES FRANKLIN, history educator; b. Boston, Dec. 22, 1941; s. William Redin and Edith (Jones) W.; m. Paulette Grignon, Oct. 16, 1966. A. B., Middlebury Coll., 1964; M.S., N.Y.U., 1969; Ph.D., U. Denver, 1972. Asst. prof. history Calif. State U., Fullerton, 1972-76, assoc. prof., 1976-80, prof., 1980—, chmn. dept., 1982—, adj. prof. physics, 1980—. Contbr. articles to profl. jours. Mem. Internat. Soc. on Gen. Relativity and Gravitation, N.Y. Acad. Scis., AAAS, Phi Alpha Theta. Current Work: Experimental work on the coupling of the electromagnetic and gravitational fields. Theoretical work on the evolution of pulsars and quasars. Subspecialties: Relativity and gravitation; Theoretical astrophysics. Office: Calif State U Fullerton CA 92634

WOODWARD, PAUL RALPH, computational physicist, astrophysicist; b. Rockville Centre, N.Y., Aug. 25, 1946; s. William Redin and Edith (Jones) W.; m. Judith Hansburg, Jan. 5, 1973; 1 son, Thomas Christopher. B.A., Cornell U., Ithaca, N.Y., 1967; Ph.D. in Physics (Woodrow Wilson fellow), U. Calif.-Berkeley, 1973. Research assoc. Nat. Radio Astronomy Obs., Charlottesville, Va., 1974-75, Leiden U. Obs., Netherlands, 1975-78; computational physicist Lawrence Livermore (Calif.) Nat. Lab., 1978-85; prof. astronomy, fellow Supercomputer Inst., U. Minn., 1985—. Mem. Internat. Astron. Union, Am. Astron. Soc. Co-developer Piecewise-Parabolic Method, technique for calculating fluid flow with computers. Current Work: Simulation of astrophysical systems on computers for study of evolution of spiral galaxies, formation of stars, and propagation of supersonic galactic jets. Subspecialties: Theoretical astrophysics; Algorithms. Office: U Minn Dept Astronomy 116 Church St SE Minneapolis MN 55455

WOODWELL, GEORGE MASTERS, ecologist, educator; b. Cambridge, Mass., Oct. 23, 1928; s. Philip McIntire and Virginia (Sellers) W.; m. Alice Katharine Rondthaler, June 23, 1955; children—Caroline Alice, Marjorie Virginia, Jane Katharine, John Christopher. A.B., Dartmouth Coll., 1950; A.M., Duke U., 1956, Ph.D., 1958; D.Sc. (hon.), Williams Coll., 1977, Miami U., Oxford, Ohio, 1984. Mem. faculty U. Maine, 1957-61, assoc. prof. botany, 1960-61; vis. asst. ecologist, biology dept. Brookhaven Nat. Lab., Upton, N.Y., 1961-62, ecologist, 1965-67, sr. ecologist, 1967-75; founder, dir. Ecosystems Center, 1975-85; dep. and asst. dir. Marine Biol. Lab., Woods Hole, Mass., 1975-76; founder, dir. Woods Hole Research Ctr., 1985—. Lectr. Yale Sch. Forestry, 1967—; chmn. Conf. on Long Term Biol. Consequences of Nuclear War, 1983—. Editor: Ecological Effects of Nuclear War, 1965, Diversity and Stability in Ecological Systems, 1969, (with E.V. Pecan) Carbon and the Biosphere 1973, The Role of Terrestrial Vegetation in the Global Carbon Cycle: Measurement by Remote Sensing, 1984. Founding trustee Environ. Def. Fund, 1967; founding trustee Natural Resources Def. Council, 1970—, vice chmn., 1974—; founding trustee World Resources Inst., 1982—; bd. dirs. World Wildlife Fund, 1970-84, chmn., 1980-84; bd. dirs. Conservation Found., 1975-77, Ruth Mott Fund, 1984—. Fellow AAAS, Am. Acad. Arts and Scis.; mem. Brit. Ecol. Soc., Ecol. Soc. Am. (v.p. 1966-67, pres. 1977-78), Sea Edn. Assn. (bd. dirs. 1980—), Sigma Xi. Research, pub. on structure and function of natural communities, biotic impoverishment, especially ecological effects of ionizing radiation, effects of persistent toxins, world carbon cycle. . Office: Woods Hole Research Center PO Box 296 Woods Hole MA 02543

WOOLDRIDGE, DEAN EVERETT, scientist, executive; b. Chickasha, Okla., May 30, 1913; s. Auttie Noonan and Irene Amanda (Kerr) W.; m. Helene Detweiler, Sept. 1936; children—Dean Edgar, Anna Lou, James Allan. A.B., U. Okla., 1932, M.S., 1933; Ph.D., Calif. Inst. Tech., 1936. Mem. tech. staff Bell Telephone Labs., N.Y.C., 1936-46; co-dir. research and devel. labs Hughes Aircraft Co., Culver City, Calif., 1946-51, dir., 1951-52, v.p. research and devel., 1952-53; pres., dir. Ramo-Wooldridge Corp., Los Angeles, 1953-58, Thompson Ramo Wooldridge, Inc., Los Angeles, also Cleve., 1958-62; research assoc. Calif. Inst. Tech., 1962-80. Author: The Machinery of the Brain, 1963, The Machinery of Life, 1966, Mechanical Man, 1968, Sensory Processing in the Brain, 1979, also articles. Recipient citation of Honor Air Force Assn., 1950, Raymond E. Hackett award, 1955, Westinghouse Sci. Writing award AAAS, 1963. Fellow Am. Acad. Arts and Sci., Am. Phys. Soc., IEEE, Am. Inst. Aeros. and Astronautics; mem. Nat. Acad. Scis., Nat. Acad. Engring., Calif. Inst. Assos., Am. Inst. Physics, AAAS, Phi Beta Kappa, Sigma Xi, Tau Beta Pi, Phi Eta Sigma, Eta Kappa Nu. Subspecialty: Electrical engineering. Address: 4545 Via Esperanza Santa Barbara CA 93110

WOOLF, HARRY, historian of science, educational administrator; b. N.Y.C., Aug. 12, 1923; s. Abraham and Anna (Frankman) W.; m. Patricia A. Kelsh; children—Susan Deborah, Alan, Aaron, Sara Anna. B.S., U. Chgo., 1948, M.A., 1949; Ph.D., Cornell U., 1955; D.Sc. (hon.), Whitman Coll., 1979, Am. U., 1982; L.H.D., Johns Hopkins U., 1983. Instr. physics Boston U., 1953-55; instr. history Brandeis U., 1954-55; asst. prof. history U. Wash., 1955-58, assoc. prof., 1958-59, prof. history of science, 1959-61; Willis K. Shepard prof. history of sci. Johns Hopkins U., 1961-76, chmn. dept. history of sci., 1961-72, provost, 1972-76; pres., chmn. bd. Johns Hopkins Program for Internat. Edn. in Gynecology and Obstetrics, Inc., 1973-76, trustee, 1976—; dir. Inst. for Advanced Study, Princeton, N.J., 1976—; trustee Cluster C Funds, Merrill Lynch Open-End Investment Cos., 1982—; chmn. sci. adv. council Merrill Lynch Sci./Tech. Holdings, Inc., 1983—; Mem. adv. council Sch. Advanced Internat. Studies, Washington, 1973-76; adv. bd. Smithsonian Research awards, 1975-79; trustee Asso. Univs., Inc., Brookhaven Nat. Labs., 1972-82; mem. vis. com. student affairs Mass. Inst. Tech., 1973-77, mem. corp. vis. com. dept. linguistics and philosophy, 1977-83, mem. corp. vis. com. dept. physics, 1979; mem. Nat. Advisory Child Health and Human Devel. Council NIH, 1977-80; mem. vis. com. Research Center for Lang. Scis., Ind. U., 1977-80; com. visitors Vanderbilt Grad. Sch., Nashville, Tenn., 1977-79; adv. council dept. philosophy Princeton U., 1980-84, adv. council dept. comparative lit., 1982—. Author: Transits of Venus, 1959, 81, Quantification, 1961, Science as a Cultural Force, 1964, Some Strangeness in the Proportion, 1980, The Analytic Spirit, 1981; Contbr. articles, revs. to profl. publs.; Editor: rev. devoted to history of sci. and its cultural influences Isis Internat, 1958-64; series editor: The Sources of Science, 1964—; Asso. editor: Dictionary of Scientific Biography, 1970-80; Editorial bd.: Interdisciplinary Sci. Revs., 1975—; editorial adv. bd.: The Writings of Albert Einstein, 1977—. Trustee Hampshire Coll., Amherst, Mass., 1977-79, Winterthur Mus., 1978-83; bd. govs. Tel-Aviv U., 1977—; trustee-at-large Univs. Research Assn., Inc., 1978—, chmn. bd., 1979—; mem.

adv. council John F. Kennedy Inst. for Handicapped Children, 1979—; mem. Internat. Research and Exchanges Bd., 1980—; chmn. MX Missile basing adv. panel Office of Tech. Assessment, Congress of U.S., 1980-81; mem. adv. bd. New Perspective Fund, Inc., 1980-83; trustee Rockefeller Found., 1984—; bd. dirs. Alex. Brown Cash Res. Fund, Inc., Balt., 1981—; dir. at large Am. Cancer Soc., 1982—; mem. sci. adv. bd. Wissenschaftskolleg zu Berlin, Ger., 1981—; mem. adv. bd. mem. adv. panel WGBH, Nova, Boston, 1978—, Stanford Humanities Ctr., 1981—; bd. dirs. W. Alton Jones Cell Sci. Ctr., 1982—. Served with AUS, 1943-46. NSF sr. postdoctoral fellow, Europe, 1961-62. Fellow AAAS (v.p. 1960); mem. History of Sci. Soc. (council), Acad. Internat. d'Histoire des Sciences, Am. Philos. Soc., Council on Fgn. Relations. Am. Acad. Arts and Scis., Phi Beta Kappa, Sigma Xi, Phi Alpha Theta. Address: Inst for Advanced Study Olden Ln Princeton NJ 08540

WOOLFORD, THOMAS LANEY, mathematical physicist, aerospace engineer, researcher; b. Potosi, Mo., Mar. 22, 1937; s. William Tyler and Currie Roberta (Laney) W.; m. Barbara Joanne Biggs, June 29, 1968. B.A. in Chemistry, N. Mex. Highlands U., 1958; M.S. in Physics, Ariz. State U., Tempe, 1969, postgrad., 1969-71; postgrad., U. Houston, 1978-83. Research aerospace engr. U.S. Army Missile Command, Redstone Arsenal, Ala., 1962-66; research physicist U.S. Dept. Agr. Forest Service, Tempe, 1972-73; prin. engr. Link div. Singer Corp., Houston, 1974-78; sr. engr. Computer Sci. Corp., Houston, 1978-81; prin. scientist Lockheed-EMSCO, Houston, 1981—. Mem. Houston Mus. Find Arts, 1980—. Served with U.S. Army, 1960-62. Recipient NASA ALT Award, 1978. Mem. AIAA, AAAS, Am. Phys. Soc., Soc. Indsl. and Applied Math., Am. Soc. Photogrammetry. Designer Shuttle Mission Simulator astrodynamics and rigid body motion simulation software, 1976-78. Current Work: Research remote sensing of agricultural crop cover and condition: specializing in visible and infrared interactions, plant growth models and radiative transfer theorgy; work in fluid and flight dynamics, aerospace systems analysis, guidance and navigation, microwave-plasma interactions, and combustion. Subspecialty: Biophysics (physics). Home: 734 Ramada Dr Houston TX 77062 Office: Lockheed EMSCO 1830 NASA Rd 1 Houston TX 77058

WOOLMAN, MYRON, psychologist; b. Phila., Jan. 18, 1917; s. Irvin and Rose (Goldberg) W.; m. Eugenia Marr Johnston, Nov. 1, 1941; children—Marcia Isabel, Bruce Douglas, Diana Eugenia. B.S. magna cum laude, Columbia, 1950, M.A. (Pres.'s scholar), 1951, Ph.D. in Psychology, 1955. Chief proficiency measurements, McConnell AFB, Kans., 1952-56; sr. scientist Human Resources Office, George Washington U., 1956-61; dir., prin. investigator Inst. Ednl. Research, 1961—; cons., prin. investigator for major projects U.S. Dept. Labor, NIMH, OEO, Office Child Devel., govts. Nigeria and Ghana, 1961—; pres. Myron Woolman, Inc., 1969—; William H. Robinson lectr. Hampton (Va.) Coll., 1978; systems cons. Nat. Urban League, 1979, U.S. Dept. Agr./AID, 1979; adviser to mayor of Detroit in riot prevention, 1967, prin. investigator, designer manpower devel. and learning systems for edn., govt. and industry in, U.S. and abroad, 1967—; designer quantified impact evaluation method USAID, 1982-83; Founder Interactional Learning. Inc., 1984; project leader Virtuoso micro-computer software simulation method, 1984-85. Author numerous papers in field; patentee in field. Bd. dirs. James Farmer Center Community Action, 1964-65; mem. Consortium Developmental Continuity Coll. Human Ecology, Cornell U. Served with USAAF, 1942-46. Menninger Found. fellow, 1980. Mem. Am. Psychol. Assn., AAAS, Am. Assn. Mental Deficiency, AAUP, Council Exceptional Children, Kappa Delta Pi, Phi Delta Kappa. Current Work: Computerized accelerated learning environments, management information systems, accelerated learning/training methods for international development. Subspecialties: Learning; Information systems, storage, and retrieval (computer science). Home: 10649 Montrose Ave Bethesda MD 20814

WOOLSEY, CLINTON NATHAN, neurophysiology educator, consultant; b. Bklyn., Nov. 30., 1904; s. Joseph Woodhull and Matilda (Aichholz) W.; m. Harriet Runion, May 24, 1942; children: Thomas Allen, John David, Edward Alexander. A.B., Union Coll., 1928, Sc.D. (hon.), 1968; M.D., Johns Hopkins U., 1933. Asst. in physiology, assoc. prof. physiology Johns Hopkins U. Sch. Medicine, 1933-48; Charles Sumner Slichter research prof. neurophysiology, dir. Lab. Neurophysiology, U. Wis., Madison, 1948-75; coordinator biomed. research unit Lab. Neurophysiology, U. Wis. (Waisman Center), 1973-80, Slichter prof. emeritus, 1975—; trainer grad. students and postdoctoral fellows in neurosci. NIH Exchange Mission to Russia, 1958. NIH grantee, 1948-75. Mem. Nat. Acad. Scis., Am. Physiol. Soc., AAAS, Soc. for Neurosci. (Ralph Gerard award 1982), Internat. Brain Research Orgn. Democrat. Current Work: Research on animals and man on cerebral cortical localization; present efforts devoted to preparing for publication of several studies not previously published. Subspecialties: Animal physiology; Neurobiology. Home: 106 Virginia Terr Madison WI 53705 Office: U Wis 627 Waisman Center Madison WI 53706

WOOLVERTON, DALTON LEO, general contractor, mechanical engineer; b. New Orleans, May 25, 1938; s. Nicholas Winnot and Marie Mandevilla (Viosca) W.; m. Marilyn Ann Ciaccio, Dec. 29, 1960; children—Gregory, Douglas, David, Stephen. B.S. in M.E., Tulane U., 1960; M.S. in M.E., 1962; M.B.A., Loyola U., New Orleans, 1966. Registered profl. engr., La. Research engr. Boeing Co., New Orleans, 1962-65; v.p. Rumold, Inc., Metairie, La., 1965-78, pres., 1978—; pres., dir. Woolcarr Investments, Inc., Metairie, 1983—; dir. Rumold Mech. Inc., New Orleans, State-Investors Savs. & Loan, New Orleans. Mem. New Orleans Mech. Inspection Bd., 1978—; bd. dirs. Christian Bros. Found., New Orleans, 1975-82. Mem. New Orleans C. of C., La. Assn. Bus. and Industry, Assoc. Gen. Contractors (vice-chmn. 1982—), Assoc. Builders and Contractors (dir.), ASME, La. Engring. Soc., Nat. Soc. Profl. Engrs., Soc. War of 1812, Soc. Founders City of New Orleans, La. Soc. SAR, Soc. Tulane Engrs., ASHRAE, Constrn. Specifications Inst., La. Engring. Soc. Club: City (New Orleans). Current work: Management of businesses and research into geothermal heat exchangers for use in heat pump systems. Subspecialties: Mechanical engineering; Fluid mechanics. Home: 2464 Killdeer St New Orleans LA 70122 Office: Rumold Inc 2001 Ridgelake Dr Metairie LA 70001

WOOSLEY, STANFORD EARL, astrophysicist, educator; b. Texarkana, Tex., Dec. 8, 1944; s. Homer Earl and Wanda Faye (Fisher) W. B.S. in Physics, Rice U., 1966, Ph.D. in Astrophysics, 1971. Research assoc. Kellogg Radiation Lab., Calif. Inst. Tech., Pasadena, 1973-75; asst. prof. astronomy and astrophysics U. Calif.-Santa Cruz, 1975-78, assoc. prof., 1978-83, prof., 1983—; cons., part-time employee Lawrence Livermore (Calif.) Nat. Lab. Contbr. writings in field to profl. publs. NSF and NASA grantee. Mem. Am. Astron. Soc., Am. Phys. Soc., Internat. Astron. Union. Current Work: Nucleosynthesis (origin of the elements); supernova models, models for X-ray and gamma-ray bursts; nuclear astrophysics. Subspecialties: High energy astrophysics; Nuclear physics. Home: 115 Auburn Ave Santa Cruz CA 95060 Office: Lick Obs U Calif Santa Cruz CA 95064

WOOSTER, WARREN S(CRIVER), marine educator; b. Westfield, Mass., Feb. 20, 1921; s. Harold Abbott and Violet (Scriver) W.; m. Clarissa Pickles, Sept. 13, 1948; children: Susan Wooster Allen, Daniel, Dana Wooster Pawka. Sc.B., Brown U., 1943; M.S., Calif. Inst. Tech., 1947; Ph.D., UCLA, 1953. From research asst. to prof. Scripps Instn. Oceanography, U. Calif., 1948-73; dir. UNESCO Office Oceanography, 1961-63; dean Rosenstiel Sch. Marine Atmospheric Sci., U. Miami, 1973-76; prof. marine studies and fisheries U. Wash., Seattle, 1976—. Contbr. to books, profl. jours. Served with USNR, 1943-46. Fellow Am. Geophys. Union, Am. Meterol Soc.; mem. Sci. Com. Oceanic Research, Sigma Xi. Current Work: Establishing abiotic variability effects on fish stock abundance in ocean. Subspecialty: Oceanography. Office: U Wash Inst for Marine Studies Seattle WA 98105

WORLEY, S. D., chemistry educator; b. Russellville, Ala., Jan. 31, 1942; s. Shelby L. and Betty (Davis) W.; m. Karen H., June 20, 1964; children: Christopher G., Brian S. B.S., Auburn U., 1964; Ph.D., U. Tex. Austin, 1969. Research chemist NASA Manned Spacecraft Center, Houston, 1969-72; asst. prof. chemistry Cleve. State U., 1972-73; sci. officer Office of Naval Research, Arlington, Va., 1973-74; asst. prof. chemistry Auburn (Ala.) U., 1974-78, assoc. prof., 1978—, Alumni prof. chemistry, 1982 . Contbr. numerous articles on chemistry to profl. jours. Served to capt. U. S. Army, 1969-72. Research Corp. grantee, 1975, 81; grantee NSF, 1981, U.S. Army/U.S. Air Force, 1983, U.S. Navy, 1983. Mem. Am. Chem. Soc. Current Work: Infrared and photoelecton spectroscopy, water disinfection, catalysis, theoretical chemistry. Subspecialties: Catalysis chemistry; Physical chemistry. Office: Chemistry Dept Auburn U Auburn AL 36849

WORSHAM, JAMES E., See *Who's Who in America,* 43rd edition.

WORTH, JAMES JUDSON BLACKLEY, meteorologist; b. Charleston, W.Va., Dec. 11, 1927; s. John Clifford and Madalyn Alice (Tonkin) W.; m. Sarah Ellen Shoemaker, Apr. 5, 1952; children—James C.B., Judson L.B., Rebecca B. B.S. in Meteorology, Pa. State U., 1952; M.S., U. Mich., 1957; postgrad., U. N.C., 1964-68. Indsl. engr. Armstrong Cork Co., Lancaster, Pa., also, Fulton, N.Y., 1952-56; research meteorologist U. Mich. Engring. Research Inst., Ann Arbor, 1956-57; asst. gen. mgr., dir. program mgmt. Bendix Systems div., Ann Arbor, 1957-64; with Research Triangle Inst., Research Triangle Park, N.C., 1962—, dir. indsl. deve., 1970-71, v.p., 1971-83; pres. Camp Minnehaha Enterprises, Minnehaha Springs, W.Va., 1969—; pres. Am. Biogenics Corp., 1984—; v.p. Bio assay Systems Corp., 1984— mem. vis. council U. N.C., Chapel Hill, 1964-69; Mem. adv. com. Water Resources Research Inst., 1965-70; mem. State of N.C. Gov.'s Energy Task Force, 1977; mem. bd. sci. advisers N.C. Energy Inst., 1980—. Contbr. chpt. to text. Served with USAAF, 1945-47. Mem. Am. Meteorol. Soc., Royal Meteorol. Soc., Geophys. Union, Explorers Club. Club: Space Pioneers. Home: 731 Millstream #2 Decatur IL 62521 Office: Am Biogenics Corp 1800 E Pershing Rd Decatur IL 62526

WOSILAIT, WALTER DANIEL, pharmacologist; b. Racine, Wis., Feb. 4, 1924; s. Julius George and Louise (Kalweit) W.; m. Marilyn Anne, Aug. 14, 1948; 1 dau., Karen Anne. Ph.D., Johns Hopkins U., 1953. Research assoc. Western Res. U., 1953-56; asst. prof. and assoc. prof. SUNY Downstate Med. Center, Bklyn., 1956-65; prof. pharmacology U. Mo. Sch. Medicine Columbia, 1965—. Pres. Columbia Art League. Served with USN, 1943-46. Mem. Am. Soc. Biol. Chemists, Am. Soc. Pharmacology and Exptl. Therapeutics, AAAS. Current Work: Mathematical modeling and computer simulations of drug interactions affecting anticoagulants and antineoplastic drugs. Subspecialties: Pharmacology; Pharmacokinetics.

WOSKIE, SUSAN RENEE, industrial hygiene researcher; b. Washington, May 5, 1953; d. William Henry and Coyla Renee (Gagnon) W. B.S. summa cum laude, U. Mass., 1977. Indsl. hygiene chemist Mass. Div. Occupational Hygiene, 1980; staff indsl. hygienist Harvard U. Sch. Pub. Health, Boston, 1981-85; indsl. hygiene researcher U. Mass. Med. Ctr., Worcester, 1985—; cons. New Eng. Safety and Health Assocs., Arlington, Mass., 1983—. Contbr. chpts. to books. Mem. adv. bd. Nine to Five Women Office Workers Orgn., Boston, 1981—, Mass. Right To Know Project, Boston, 1984—; mem. Mass. Coalition for Occupational Safety and Health, Boston, 1981—. Mem. Am. Indsl. Hygiene Assn., Am. Conf. Govt. Indsl. Hygienists, Harriet Hardy Inst. (com. chmn. 1983—, bd. dirs.), Nat. Assn. Pub. Policy (council sec. 1984—). Democrat. Mem. Soc. of Friends. Current work: Investigation of potential occupational health and safety hazards; development of toxicological models correlating occupational exposures with biological dose; statistical applications in industrial hygiene. Subspecialty: Environmental toxicology. Home: 66 Cleveland St Arlington MA 02174 Office: Dept Family and Community Medicine U Mass Med Ctr 55 Lake Ave N Worcester MA 01605

WOSKOBOINIKOW, PAUL PETER, physicist; b. Watkins Glen, N.Y., Apr. 23, 1950; s. Tichon and Julia (Marchenko) W.; m. Constance Ann Golba, Aug. 29, 1976. B.S., Rensselaer Poly. Inst., 1972, M.S. in Elec. Engring, 1974, Ph.D. in Electrophysics, 1976. Postdoctoral fellow Francis Bitter Nat. Magnet Lab., M.I.T., Cambridge, 1976-77, staff scientist, 1977-80; project leader Plasma Fusion Ctr., 1980—. Mem. Am. Phys. Soc., IEEE. Current Work: Infrared, far infrared, millimeter high power source development including lasers and gyrotrons; application of far-infrared technology to fusion plasma diagnostics. Subspecialties: Laser research; Plasma physics. Office: Mass Inst Tech NW16-134 Cambridge MA 02139

WOSNICK, MICHAEL ALAN, research scientist; b. Toronto, Ont., Can., Nov. 3, 1951; s. Hyman L. and Bella (Levy) W.; m. Katherine J. Wosnick, May 30, 1973; 1 dau., Allison. B.Sc., U. Toronto, 1974; Ph.D., Queens U., Kingston, Ont., 1978. Fellow U. Calgary, Alta., 1978-81; research scientist Connaught Research Inst., Toronto, 1981—. Contbr. numerous articles in field to profl. jours. Med. Research Council Can. fellow, 1978-81; Govt. Ont. scholar, 1976-77; Nat. Research Council Can. scholar, 1977. Mem. AAAS, Canadian Soc. Cell Biology, Genetics Soc. Am. Current Work: Genetic engineering, recombinant DNA technology, expression of genes in foreign hosts, regulation of gene expression. Subspecialties: Genetics and genetic engineering (biology); Molecular biology. Office: 1755 Steeles Ave W Willowdale ON M2R 3T4 Canada

WOTIZ, HERBERT HENRY, biochemist, educator; b. Vienna, Austria, Oct. 8, 1922; came to U.S., 1938, naturalized, 1944; s. Edward and Irene (Politzer) Wottitz; m. Miriam S. Rose, June 15, 1947; children: Sue W. Goldstein, Robert P., Richard A. B.Sc., Providence Coll., 1944; Ph.D., Yale U., 1951. Asst. prof. biochemistry Boston U. Sch. Medicine, 1951-55, assoc. prof., 1955-63, research prof. urology, 1978—, prof. biochemistry, 1963—; dep. dir. H. H. Humphrey Cancer Research Center, Boston U., 1981-84, dir., 1984—; cons. and dir. Seragen, Inc., Boston, 1979-85. Mem. Milton (Mass.) Sch. Com., 1959-65, 66-69. Mem. editorial bd.: Chem. Abstracts, 1969—, mem. editorial bd. Steroids, 1956-85; assoc. editor, 1985—; mem. editorial bd. Jour. Chromatographic Sci, 1963-85; assoc. editor steroids, 1985—. Served with U.S. Army, 1944-45. NIH sr. research fellow, 1960-65; career devel. fellow, 1965-70. Mem. Am. Chem. Soc., Endocrine Soc., Am. Soc. Biol. Chemists, Soc. Exptl. Biology and Medicine, AAAS, Am. Assn. Cancer Research. Current Work: The role of hormones in cancer, mechanism of estrogen action, analysis of hormone receptors, role of estriol in carcinogenesis. Subspecialties: Receptors; Cancer research (medicine). Home: 9 Cape Cod Ln Milton MA 02187 Office: 80 E Concord St Boston MA 02118

WOYCZYNSKI, WOJBOR ANDRZEJ, mathematician, research, educator, administrator; b. Czestochowa, Poland, Oct. 24, 1943; came to U.S., 1970; s. Eugeniusz and Otylia Sabina (Borkiewicz) W.; m. Aleksandra Henryka Krasna, May 25, 1976; 1 son, Martin Wojbor. M.Sc. in Elec. Engring, Wroclaw (Poland) U., 1966, Ph.D. in Math, 1968. Teaching asst. Wroclaw U., 1966-68, asst. prof., 1968-72, assoc. prof., 1972-77; postdoctoral fellow Carnegie-Mellon U., 1970-72; prof. math. and stats. Cleve. State U., 1977-82; prof., chmn, dept. math. and stats. Case Western Res. U., 1982—; vis. prof. U. Paris, 1974, U. Wis.-Madison, 1976, Northwestern U., 1976-77, U.S.C., 1979, U. Göttingen, 1985. Author: Geometry and Martingales in Banach Spaces, part I, 1975, Part II, 1979; editor: Martingale theory in harmonic analysis and Banach spaces, 1982; (with J.A. Chao) Probability Theory and Harmonic Analysis, 1985. NSF grantee, 1970, 71, 76, 77, 81; Polish Acad. Scis. grantee, 1972-76; Office Naval Research grantee, 1985. Mem. Polish Math. Soc. (v.p. br. 1973-75, Gt. prize 1973), Inst. Math. Stats., Am. Math. Soc., Wroclaw Sci. Soc. Roman Catholic. Clubs: Park East Racquet (Beechwood, Ohio); Acad. Sports (Wroclaw). Current Work: Probability theory on infinite dimensional spaces, stochastic processes, harmonic analysis, functional analysis, theory of martingales. Subspecialty: Probability. Home: 18147 Scottsdale Blvd Shaker Heights OH 44122 Office: Dept Math and Stats Case Western Res U University Circle Cleveland OH 44106

WRAY, JOHN LAWRENCE, mechanical engineer; b. Maryville, Mo., June 17, 1935; s. Lawrence Paul and Roberta Inez (Cook) W.; m. Sally Blair Gerdes, Dec. 27, 1958; children: Mary, Nancy, Carolyn. B.S., U. Mo., 1957; M.S., Stanford U., 1958; M.B.A., U. Santa Clara, 1966. Registered profl. engr., N.Y., Ill., Mo., Pa., others. Instr. George Mason U., Arlington, Va., 1961-62; with Gen. Electric Co., San Jose, Calif., 1962-78, mgr. product planning and market research, 1972-76, mgr. market research and planning, 1977-78; v.p. engring. Quadrex Corp., Campbell, Calif., 1978-82, v.p. computer systems and ops., 1982—; dir., treas. Mich. Nuclear Services Corp., Detroit, 1982—; dir. Quadrex FLIC Computer Systems, Inc., Princeton, N.J. Mem. fin. com. Elem. Sch. Dist., Saratoga, Calif., 1974-78. Served to capt. USAF, 1958-62. AEC fellow, 1957-58. Mem. Am. Nuclear Soc., ASME, Stanford U. Alumni Club (pres. 1970-71), Beta Theta Phi. Republican. Club: Brookside Swim and Tennis (pres., dir. 1974-75). Lodge: Masons. Current Work: Computer systems applied to process control industry. Subspecialties: Information systems, storage, and retrieval (computer science); Systems engineering. Home: 14961 Haun Ct Saratoga CA 95070 Office: Quadrex Corp 1700 Dell Ave Campbell CA 95008

WRAY, JOHN ROBERT, health physics engineer; b. Passaic, N.J., June 24, 1951; s. Arthur and Mary (DeLeo) W.; m. Marybeth Glasheen, July 17, 1976. B.S., Rensselaer Poly. Inst., 1973; M.S., Northeastern U., 1978. Registered profl. engr., Mass. cert. health physicist. Radiation protection engr. Stone & Webster Engring. Co., Boston, 1973-78; health physics inspr. U.S. Nuclear Regulatory Commn., Atlanta, 1979—. Recipient Cert. of Appreciation U.S. Nuclear Regulatory Commn., 1980, 82, 83, Cert. of Recognition, 1981. Mem. Am. Nuclear Soc., Health Physics Soc. Current Work: Inspection and evaluation of radiation protection and radioactive waste management programs at nuclear power plants, research and test reactors, and fuel facilities. Respond to nuclear power reactor plant emergencies. Subspecialty: Nuclear fission. Home: 1740 Charmeth Rd Lithonia GA 30058 Office: US Nuclear Regulatory Commn 101 Marietta St Suite 2900 Atlanta GA 30303

WRIGHT, CREIGHTON BOLTER, medical educator, cardiovascular surgeon; b. Washington, Jan. 29, 1939; s. Benjamin W. and Catherine B. (Zeller) W.; m. Carolyn Eleanor Craver, Jan. 29, 1966; children: Creighton, Benson, Kathryn, Elizabeth. B.A. in Chemistry, Duke U., 1961, M.D., 1965. Diplomate: Am. Bd. Surgery, Am. Bd. Thoracic Surgery, Gen. Vascular Surgery. Intern Duke U., 1965; resident U. Va., 1966-71; chief cardiovascular physiology Walter Reed Inst. Research, Washington, 1971-74; assoc. prof. George Washington U. and chief cardiovascular surgery Washington VA Med. Ctr., both Washington, 1974-76; prof. surgery U. Iowa, Iowa City, 1976-81; also chief surgery VA Med. Ctr., 1979-81; prof. surgery U. Cin. and staff Christ and Jewish hosps., Cin., 1982—; cons. VA Med. Ctr., Cin., 1982—. Editor: Vascular Grafting: Clinical Application and Techniques, 1983; co-editor: Venous Trauma: Pathophysiology Diagnosis and Surgical Management, 1983, Vascular Occlusive Disorders: Medical and Surgical Management, 1981; contbr. chpts. to books, articles to profl. jours. Served to col., M.C. USAR, 1966—. Recipient Kindred award U. Va., 1967; Meritorious Service medal U.S. Army, 1974; Golden Apple award Georgetown U. Students Assn., 1975. Fellow ACS; mem. Assn. Acad. Surgery (pres. and council 1979-80), Muller Surg. Soc. (v.p. 1981 83, pres. 1985-87), Soc. Vascular Surgery (program chmn. 1980), Alpha Omega Alpha. Current Work: Clinical and experimental cardiovascular research; teaching and active thoracic and cardiovascular surgeon. Subspecialties: Surgery; Cardiac surgery. Home: 1242 Edwards Rd Cincinnati OH 45208 Office: 2139 Auburn Ave Cincinnati OH 45219

WRIGHT, EDWARD STEWART, mechanical engineer, consultant; b. Englewood, N.J., Jan. 18, 1930; s. William H. and Mildred (Stewart) W.; m. Lenaire Jean Botting, Oct. 21, 1951; children—Jeffry, Jody, William. B.S. in Agr., Rutgers U., 1951; B.S. in Aero-Mech. Engring., Air Force Inst. Tech., 1960; M.S. in Aero-Engring., Princeton U., 1965. Commd. 2d lt. U.S. Air Force, 1951, advanced through grades to capt., 1963; chief systems analyst United Techs. Research Ctr., East Hartford, Conn., 1963-73, mgr. energy systems, 1973-79; mgr. components product planning Deere and Co., Moline, Ill., 1979-83, dir. govt. products, 1983—; pres. Wis. Internat. Engring. Ltd., Racine, 1975—; cons. Fed. Energy Office, Washington, 1973-74. Author course Introduction to Gas Turbine, 1976-80. Contbr. articles to profl. jours. Fellow ASME (chmn. gas turbine div. 1975-79); mem. Soc. Automotive Engrs. (chmn. Iowa, Ill. sect. 1984—), Am. Soc. Agrl. Engrs. Clubs: Short Hills Country (Moline); Baldwin Yacht (Old Saybrook, Conn.). Current work: Direct all activities in research and development of John Deere stratified charge omnivorous rotary engines. Subspecialties: Mechanical engineering; Systems engineering. Home: 917 48th St A Moline IL 61265 Office: Govt Products Ops John Deere Rd Moline IL 61265

WRIGHT, FRED CARL, research chemist; b. Uvalde, Tex., May 8, 1938; s. Frank Theodore and Estella Hilda (Doerr) W.; m. Ora Gradene Rogers, Aug. 29, 1959; children—Michelle Phay, Courtney D'Ann. B.S., Southwest Tex. State U., 1960, M.A., 1961. Chemist, Dow Chem. Co., Freeport, Tex., 1961-63; chemist Agrl. Research Service, U.S. Dept. Agr., Kerrville, Tex., 1963-68, research chemist, 1968—. Contbr. chpt. to book, articles to profl. publs. Patentee latexes, alkyl amine acaricides, carbamate acaricides (invention award U.S. Dept. Agr. 1984). Adult dir., pres. Hill Country Youth Rodeo Assn., 1981-83. Southwest Tex. State U. fellow, 1960. Mem. Am. Chem. Soc., Entomol. Soc. Am., Acarological Soc. Am., Southwestern Entomol. Soc., Am. Assn. Vet. Parasitologists. Club: Buck and Bull. Current work: Ticks and psoroptic scabies of cattle, control, and related biochemical and analytical determinations. Subspecialties: Analytical chemistry; Biochemistry (biology). Home: 1114 Barbara Ann Kerrville TX 78028 Office: Agrl Research Service US Dept Agr PO Box 232 Kerrville TX 78029-0232

WRIGHT, GEORGE G(REEN), microbiologist; b. Ann Arbor, Mich., Aug. 17, 1916; s. George Green and May (Bradbeer) W.; m. Marjory Gray Hawley, 1941; 1 son, George; m. Mary Griffith West, 1957; children: Laurence, Mary. B.A., Olivet Coll., Mich., 1936; Ph.D. in Microbiology, U. Chgo., 1941. Instr. immunology U. Chgo., 1941-42; research fellow Calif. Inst. Tech., Pasadena, 1942-46; with CIA, 1946-48; chief immunology br. Dept. Army, Ft. Detrick, Frederick, Md., 1948-71; asst. dir. Mass. Pub. Health Biologic Labs., Boston, 1971-77, dir., 1977-82; research asst. prof. dept. internal medicine U. Va. Sch. Medicine, 1983—; lectr. medicine Tufts U., 1972-83; vis. lectr. applied microbiology Harvard U. Sch. Pub. Health, 1972-83. Contbr. chpts. to books, articles to sci. jours. Recipient Ricketts prize U. Chgo., 1941; Exceptional Civilian Service award Dept. Army, 1954; Sec. Army fellow Oxford U., 1957-58. Mem. Am. Assn. Immunologists, Soc. Exptl. Biology and Medicine, Am. Soc. Microbiology. Methodist. Current Work: Research on mode of action of bacterial Toxins on mammalian cells. Subspecialties: Immunology (medicine); Microbiology (medicine). Office: Div Infectious Disease Box 385 U Va Sch Medicine Charlottesville VA 22908

WRIGHT, HERBERT E(DGAR), JR., geologist; b. Malden, Mass., Sept. 13, 1917; s. Herbert E. and Annie M. (Richardson) W.; m. Rhea Jane Hahn, June 21, 1943; children—Richard, Jonathan, Stephen, Andrew, Jeffrey. A.B., Harvard U., 1939; M.A., 1941; Ph.D., 1943; D.Sc. (hon.), Trinity Coll., Dublin, Ireland, 1966. Instr. Brown U., 1946-47; asst. prof. geology U. Minn., Mpls., 1947-51, assoc. prof., 1951-59, prof., 1959-74 Regents' prof. geology, ecology and botany, 1974—; dir. Limnological Research Center, 1963—. Served to maj. USAAF, 1942-45. Decorated D.F.C., Air medal with 6 oak leaf clusters; Guggenheim fellow, 1954-55; Wenner-Gren fellow, 1954-55. Fellow Geol. Soc. Am., AAAS, Scientists Inst. Pub. Info.; mem. Ecol. Soc. Am., Am. Soc. Limnology, Oceanography, Am. Quaternary Assn., Arctic Inst., Brit. Ecol. Soc., Internat. Glaciological Soc., Nat. Acad. Scis. Research on Quaternary geology, paleoecology, paleolimnology and environ. archaeology in Minn., New Mex., Yukon, Labrador, Peru, eastern Mediterranean. Subspecialty: Paleontology, paleoecology. Office: 221 Pillsbury Hall U of Minn 310 Pillsbury Dr SE Minneapolis MN 55455

WRIGHT, JOHN RICKEN, chemist, educator, cons.; b. Batesville, Ark., Jan. 3, 1939; s. John Adam and Alice Lanelle (Burge) W.; m. Barbara Ruth Martin; 1 child, Karen Elizabeth. Student, Ark. Coll., Batesville, 1956-57; B.S., Ark. State U., Jonesboro, 1960; M.S., U. Miss., 1967, Ph.D., 1971. High sch. sci. tchr., Wynne, Ark., 1960-61; research asst. Washington U., St. Louis, 1967-68; postdoctoral research assoc. in chemistry Fla. State U., Tallahassee, 1972-73; assoc. prof. chemistry Southeastern Okla. State U., Durant, prof.; cons. Dept. Energy, NASA. Contbr. chem. articles to profl. jours. Served to capt. USAF, 1961-65. NIH grantee, 1974—. Mem. Sigma Xi. Lodge: Kiwanis. Current Work: Development of anticancer immunotoxins which double as staining agents for light and electron microscopy. Copper cluster chemistry. Subspecialties: Inorganic chemistry; Immunobiology and immunology. Office: Southeastern Okla State U Box 4181 Sta A Durant OK 74701

WRIGHT, LYNNE C., strategic defense analyst and scientist; b. Gadsden, Ala., Jan. 19, 1954; d. William Earl and Pauline (Hill) W. B.S., U. Ala., 1974, M.A., 1976, Ph.D., 1978. Inst. U. Ala., University, 1974-79; program mgr. Analytic Services, Inc., Arlington, Va., 1979-83; div. mgr. TITAN Systems, Inc., Vienna, Va., 1983—. Contbr. articles to profl. jours. First soprano soloist ch. choir, Falls Church, Va., 1969—, mem. fin. com., 1980-83, sec. fin. com., 1983-84. Recipient Outstanding Tech. Service commendation U.S. Air Force, 1982; named Most Valuable Performer, TITAN Systems, Inc., 1984. Mem. Am. Math. Soc., Math. Assn. Am., Am. Astronautical Soc., Women in Math., Mortar Bd., Phi Mu Epsilon, Delta Gamma (chmn. fashion bd. 1973). Baptist. Current work: Space surveillance, mathematical and computer modelling, development of requirements for operational space programs, President's Strategic Defense Initiative. Subspecialties: Applied mathematics; Aerospace engineering and technology. Home: 6644 Fisher Ave Falls Church VA 22046 Office: TITAN Systems Inc 1950 Gallows Rd Suite 600 Vienna VA 22180

WRIGHT, RICHARD KENNETH, comparative immunologist; b. Richmond, Ind., Sept. 22, 1939; s. Willard Kenneth and Dorothy Janelle (Moon) W. B.S., San Diego State U., 1967, M.S., 1970; Ph.D., U. Calif.-Santa Barbara,

1973. Teaching asst. San Diego State U., 1967-69; assoc. biol. scis. U. Calif., Santa Barbara, 1971-73; USPHS postdoctoral fellow UCLA, 1973-75, asst. research anatomist, 1975-81, assoc. research anatomist, 1981-84; dir. research and devel. Physicians Labs., Inc., 1984—. Author: Phylogeny of Thymus and Bone Marrow-Bursa Cells, 1976; contbr. articles to profl. jours. Served with USN, 1960-64. Mem. Am. Assn. Immunologists, Internat. Soc. Devel. and Comparative Immunology, Am. Soc. Zoologists, AAAS, Sigma Xi. Republican. Current Work: Assays for determining food sensitivities and allergies. Subspecialties: Immunobiology and immunology; Immunology (medicine). Home: 1315 Stanford St #1 Santa Monica CA 90404 Office: Physicians Labs Inc Century City Med Plaza 2080 Century Park East Suite 1201 Los Angeles CA 90067

WRIGHT, RICHARD NEWPORT, III, civil engr., govt. ofcl.; b. Syracuse, N.Y., May 17, 1932; s. Richard Newport and Carolyn (Baker) W.; m. Teresa Rios, Aug. 23, 1959; children—John Stannard, Carolyn Maria, Elizabeth Rebecca, Edward Newport. B.C.E., Syracuse U., 1953, M.C.E. (Parcel fellow), 1955; Ph.D., U. Ill., 1962. Jr. engr. Pa. R.R., Phila., 1953-55; instr. civil engring. U. Ill. at Urbana, 1957-62, asst. prof., 1962-65, asso. prof., 1965-70, prof., 1970-74, adj. prof., 1974-79; chief structures sect. Bldg. Research div. U.S. Bur. Standards, Washington, 1971-72; dep. dir. tech. Center Bldg. Tech., 1972-73, dir., 1974—. Pres. Internat. Council for Bldg. Research, Studies and Documentation. Contbr. articles to profl. jours. Served with AUS, 1955-57. Fellow ASCE (tech. activities com. 1979-80). Subspecialties: Structural engineering; Computer-aided design. Home: 20081 Doolittle St Gaithersburg MD 20879 Office: Center Building Technology National Bureau Standards Gaithersburg MD 20899

WRIGHT, ROBERT JAMES, geoscience association executive; technical advisor, b. Bridgewater, Va., Dec. 16, 1918; s. Frank James and Anna Catherine (Zigler) W.; m. Dorothy Lawrene Burnham, Oct. 26, 1946; children—Nancy G., Anne L., Lawrence J., Sara E. B.A., Denison U., 1940; M.A., Columbia U., 1942, Ph.D., 1947. Prof., St. Lawrence U., Canton, N.Y., 1947-49; staff geologist US AEC, Grand Junction, Colo, 1949-54; chief geologist Climax Uranium Co., Grand Junction, 1954-58; mgr. western exploration Amax Inc., Denver, 1958-65; v.p. Amax Exploration Co., N.Y.C., 1965-73; cons. geologist Roan Consol. Mines, Lusaka, Zambia, 1973-75; chief geologist for uranium US Dept Energy, Washington, 1975-79; sr. tech. advisor, high level waste, US NRC, Washington, 1979—. Contbr. articles to profl. jours. Served to lt. (j.g.) USN, 1944-46. Recipient Alumni citation Denison U., 1974. Fellow Geol. Soc. Am.; mem. Soc. Econ. Geologists, AIME, Phi Beta Kappa, Sigma Xi. Current work: Disposal of high-level radioactive waste; uranium resources. Subspecialties: Fuels and sources; Hazardous waste disposal. Home: 5 Goshen Ct Gaithersburg MD 20879 Office: US NRC 623-SS Washington DC 20555

WRIGHT, SEWALL, geneticist, educator; b. Melrose, Mass., Dec. 21, 1889; s. Philip and Elizabeth (Sewall) W.; m. Louise Lane Williams, Sept. 10, 1921; children: Richard, Robert, Elizabeth Quincy (Mrs. John Rose). B.S., Lombard Coll., Galesburg, Ill., 1911; M.S., U. Ill., 1912, Sc.D. (hon.), 1961; Sc.D., Harvard U., 1915; hon. Sc.D., U. Rochester, 1942, Yale U., 1949, Knox Coll., 1957, Western Res. U., 1958, U. Chgo., 1959, U. Wis., 1965; LL.D. (hon.), Mich. State U., 1955. Sr. animal husbandman U.S. Dept. Agr., Washington, 1915-25; assoc. prof. zoology U. Chgo., 1926-29, prof., 1930-37, Eernest D. Burton Disting. Service prof., 1938-54; Leon J. Cole prof. genetics U. Wis., Madison, 1955-60, prof. emeritus, 1960—; Hitchcock prof. U. Calif., Berkeley, spring 1943; Fulbright prof. U. Edinburgh, Scotland, 1949-50; pres. 10th Internat. Congress Genetics, 1958. Author: Evolution and the Genetics of Populations, 4 vols, 1968-78; over 200 articles. Recipient Weldon Meml. medal Oxford (Eng.) U., 1947; Nat. medal of Sci., 1966; Darwin medal Royal Soc. London, 1980; Thomas Hunt Morgan medal Genetics Soc. Am., 1982; Balzan prize Balzan Found., Rome, 1984. Mem. Nat. Acad. Sci. (Girard Elliott medal 1945, Kimber Genetics award 1956), Am. Soc. Zoologists (pres. 1934), Genetics Soc. Am. (pres. 1944), Am. Philos. Soc. (Lewis prize 1950), Am. Soc. Naturalists (pres. 1952), AAAS, Soc. Study of Evolution (pres. 1955), Royal Soc. Edinburgh (hon.), Royal Soc. London, Royal Danish Acad. Arts and Sci., others. Democrat. Unitarian. Club: Universrity (Madison). Current Work: Theory of evolution. Subspecialties: Animal genetics; Evolutionary biology. Office: U Wis Madison WI 53706

WRIGHTON, MARK STEPHEN, chemistry educator; b. Jacksonville, Fla., June 11, 1949; s. Robert D. and Doris (Cutler) W.; m. Deborah Ann Wiseman, Aug. 10, 1968; children: James Joseph, Rebecca Ann. B.S., Fla. State U., 1969; Ph.D., Calif. Inst. Tech., 1972; D.Sc. (hon.), U. West Fla., 1983. Asst. prof. chemistry M.I.T., 1972-76, assoc. prof., 1976-77, prof., 1977—, Frederick G. Keyes prof. chemistry, 1981—; cons. Gen. Electric; Alfred P. Sloan fellow, 1974-76. Author: Organometallic Photochemistry, 1979; editor books in field; cons. editor, Houghton-Mifflin. Recipient Herbert Newby McCoy award Calif. Inst. Tech., 1972; E.O. Lawrence award Dept. Energy, 1983; Fresemius award Phi Lambda Upsilon, 1984; Halpern award in photochemistry N.Y. Acad. Scis., 1983; Dreyfus Tchr.-Scholar, 1975-80; MacArthur fellow, 1983—. Mem. Am. Chem. Soc. (award in pure chemistry 1981), Electrochem. Soc., AAAS. Current Work: Energy conversion, catalysis, photochemistry, molecular electronics. Subspecialties: Inorganic chemistry; Photochemistry. Office: Dept Chemistry MIT Cambridge MA 02139

WRONSKI, CHRISTOPHER ROMAN, physicist; b. Warsaw, Poland, Mar. 2, 1939; came to U.S., 1963, naturalized, 1971; s. Bohdan Walerian and Irene Maria (Zawisza) W.; m. Lia Maira Verbeek, July 25, 1963; children—Christopher John, Antonia, Helena, Paola. B.Sc., Inperial Coll., London U., 1960, Assoc. Royal Coll. Sci., 1960, diploma, 1963, Ph.D., 1963. Mem. tech. staff MMM Research Labs., St. Paul, 1963-67, RCA Research Lab., Princeton, N.J., 1967-78; mem. tech. staff Corp. Research Labs., Exxon Research and Engring. Co., Annandale, N.J., 1978—, research assoc., 1982—. Contbr. papers to profl. publs., chpts. to books. Patentee in field. Fellow Am. Phys. Soc.; mem. IEEE (sr. mem.; Morris N. Liebman Meml. award 1984). Roman Catholic. Current work: Optoelectronic properties of semiconductors and in particular of amorphous thin films, device physics of thin film, solar cells, especially as related to improvements in power conversion efficiencies. Subspecialties: Solar energy; Electronic materials. Office: Exxon Research and Engring Hwy 22 E Annandale NJ 08801

WU, CHIH, mechanical engineer, educator, researcher; b. Changsha, Hunan, China, Apr. 13, 1936; came to U.S., 1961, naturalized, 1973; s. K.T. and D.R. W.; m. Holly H.Y., Jan. 27, 1966; children: Anna, Joy, Sheree, Patricia. B.S., Cheng Kung U., Taiwan, 1957; Ph.D. in Mech. Engring., U. Ill., Urbana, 1966. Asst. prof. to prof. mech. engring. U.S. Naval Acad., Annapolis, Md., 1966—; prof. evening coll. Johns Hopkins U., Balt., 1969—, prof. Whiting Engring. Sch., 1982—. Contbr. articles to profl. jours. Mem. ASME, Am. Soc. Engring. Edn. Current Work: Thermodynamics, fluid dynamics, heat transfer, energy conversion, statistics, computer application, education. Subspecialty: Mechanical engineering. Home: 1705 Tarleton Way Crofton MD 21114 Office: Dept Mech Engring US Naval Acad Annapolis MD 21402

WU, CHI-HAUR, educator robotics, consultant; b. Taipei, China, May 9, 1951; came to U.S., 1975, naturalized, 1985; s. Mu-Chiai and Po-Lun (Chang) W.; m. Miao-Ying Yeh, Jan. 22, 1977; 1 child, Alexander. B.S., Nat. Taiwan U. (China), 1973; M.S., Va. Poly. Inst. and State U., 1977; Ph.D., Purdue U., 1980. Sr. engr. Unimation Inc., Denbury, Conn., 1981-83, cons., 1983—; asst. prof. elec. engring. and computer sci. Northwestern U., Evanston, Ill., 1983—. Engring. Found. Research Initiation grantee, 1984; NSF grantee, 1985. Mem. IEEE, Robotics Internat. of Soc. Mfg. Engrs. (Outstanding Young Mfg. Engr. award 1985). Current work: Robotics, manipulators control and programming, robotic vision and sensory control pattern recognition, integrated computer-control systems, and industrial automation. Subspecialties: Robotics; Computer engineering. Office: Dept Elec Engring and Computer Sci Northwestern U Evanston IL 60201

WU, CHING-KUEI, biology educator; b. Chiensei, Hopei, China, Feb. 26, 1919; came to U.S., 1961, naturalized, 1972; s. Muching and Chi (Lu) W.; m. Shun Chi, Jan. 8, 1938; children—Fenny Chang, Sendy Gan, Wendy. B.S., Peking Cath. U., 1941, M.S., 1943; cert. advanced study No. Ill. U., 1963; Ph.D., Brown U., 1965. Asst. in biology Peking Cath. U., 1941-43; high sch. tchr., Kaifun, Honan, China, 1943-45; asst. prof. Kaifun Med. Coll., 1945-47; lectr. Taiwan U., Taipei, 1947-60; mem. faculty Adrian Coll., Mich., 1967-79, prof. genetics, 1979-85, prof. emeritus, 1985—. Mem. AAAS, Genetics Soc. Am., Am. Genetic Assn. Current work: Induction of lethality and chromosome damages in Brosophila melanogaster by artificial sweetners and other chemicals. Subspecialties: Cytology and histology; Animal genetics. Home: 1099 Trevino Dr Troy MI 48098

WU, CHING-SHENG, physics educator; b. Nanjing, China, Nov. 11, 1929; came to U.S., 1954, naturalized, 1963; s. Shao-Ling Wu and Chen-Fang Pan; m. Lucia Zah-Chien Moh, Aug. 12, 1961; 1 child, Bryant C.Y. B.S., Nat. Taiwan U., China, 1953; M.S., Va. Poly. Inst., 1956; Ph.D., Princeton U., 1959. Sr. scientist Jet Propulsion Lab., Pasadena, Calif., 1959-69; research prof. U. Md. Inst. Phys. Sci. and Tech., College Park, 1969—; cons. NASA, Washington, 1977-82; hon. prof. Chinese Acad. Sci., Beijing, China, 1979—. Assoc. editor: Jour. Geophys. Research, 1984—. Fellow Am. Physics Soc.; mem. Am. Geophys. Union, Internat. Union Radio Sci., N.Y. Acad. Sci., Sigma Xi. Current work: Study of important plasma processes in solar-terrestrial environment; basic plasma physics problems relevant to laboratory experiments. Subspecialty: Plasma physics. Office: Inst Phys Sci and Tech U Md College Park MD 20742

WU, CHUEN-SHANG CHUNG, biochemist; b. Pintung, Taiwan, China, July 10, 1932; came to U.S. 1960, naturalized 1974; d. Jen-Sou and Yun-Hwa (Lin) Chung; m. Teng-Chung Wu, Oct. 21, 1967; 1 child, Yeeling Wu. Ph.D., U. Calif.-Berkeley, 1967. Research chemist USDA Western Research Lab., Albany, Calif., 1967-69; asst. research biochemist U. Calif.-Berkeley, 1969; asst. research biochemist U. Calif.-San Francisco, 1975-83, assoc. research biochemist, 1983—. Contbr. articles to profl. jours. Mem. Am. Chem. Soc., Am. Soc. Biol. Chemists. Current work: Biochemical research in protein structure and function. Subspecialties: Biochemistry (medicine); Biophysical chemistry. Home: 1004 Rudgear Rd Walnut Creek CA 94596 Office: Univ Calif 3d and Parnassus San Francisco CA 94143

WU, CHUN-FANG, biology educator; b. Fujian, China, Feb. 4, 1947; came to U.S., 1970; s. Chung-Chuen and Yun (Chen) W.; m. Mei-Lien Lin, Sept. 25, 1971; children: Daw-An, Yusing, Dawin. B.S., Tunghai U., Taiwan, 1969; Ph.D., Purdue U., 1976. Research asst. Purdue U., West Lafayette, Ind., 1971-76, research assoc., 1976; research fellow Calif. Inst. Tech., Pasadena, 1976-79; asst. prof. U. Iowa, Iowa City, 1979-83, assoc. prof., 1983—. Contbr. articles to profl. jours. Searle scholar, 1981-84; Spencer research fellow, 1976-78; recipient Research Career Devel. award NIH, 1982-87. Mem. Soc. Neurosci., Biophys. Soc., AAAS, Phi Kappa Phi. Current Work: Genetic dissection of nerve and muscle membrane excitability in Drosophila. Subspecialties: Neurobiology; Neurophysiology. Office: Dept Biology U Iowa Iowa City IA 52242

WU, HAI-PING, biomedical engineer, researcher; b. Kaoshung, Taiwan, Republic of China, June 19, 1949; came to U.S., 1973, naturalized, 1980; s. Kuo-Chang and Yue-Ho (Shu) W.; m. Teh-Hsin Kung, Aug. 9, 1974; children—Shyanshi Shane, Jane. B.S., Tunghai U., Taiwan, 1971; M.S., U. N.C., 1976, Ph.D., 1984. Teaching asst. U. N.C., Chapel Hill, 1974-79, research asst., 1979-81; physicist Becton Dickinson & Co., Research Triangle Park, N.C., 1981-85, RCA/David Sarnoff Research Ctr., Princeton, N.J., 1985—. Patentee in field. Contbr. article to profl. jour. Sec., Triangle Area Chinese Am. Soc., Raleigh, N.C., 1984. Mem. IEEE. Buddhist. Clubs: Ridgewood (Chapel Hill), SPA Health. Current work: Pattern recognition in cell classification using flow cytometry; research in signal processing, image processing and pattern recognition. Subspecialties: Biomedical engineering; Graphics, image processing, and pattern recognition. Home: 5 Braemar Dr Princeton Junction NJ 08550 Office: RCA/David Sarnoff Research Ctr Princeton NJ 08540

WU, JOHN NAICHI, electric products manufacturing executive; b. Soochow, China, Sept. 10, 1932; m. Mary C. Chan; children: Winthrop J., Jarvis C. Ph.D., U. Fla., 1965. Sr. research specialist Alliance Research Center, Babcock & Wilcox Co., Alliance, Ohio, 1962-66, group supr., 1967-77; mngr. Materials and Processes Lab., Transp. System Bus. Operation, Gen. Electric Co., Erie, Pa., 1977—, chmn. research and tech. papers com., 1980—, engring. design rev. coordinator, 1981—, chmn. div. wire and cable com., 1982—. Contbr. articles to profl. jours. Bd. dirs. Erie Internat. Inst., 1981—; pres. Erie Chinese Assn., 1982. Mem. Am. Acad. Mechanics, ASME, Acoustic Soc. Am., Am. Metals Engring., Phi Kappa Phi. Current Work: Applied mechanics; shock and vibrations; management information system. Subspecialties: Theoretical and applied mechanics; Software engineering. Home: 139 Putnam Dr Erie PA 16511 Office: 2901 E Lake Rd Erie PA 16531

WU, PO-SHUN, biochemist; b. Taipei, Republic of China, July 26, 1947; came to U.S., 1969; s. Ann-Pan and Zuei-Mei (Lee) W.; m. Susan Chen, Jan. 4, 1980. B.S., Nat. Taiwan U., 1969; M.S., U. Akron, 1971, M.S. in Chemistry, 1972; Ph.D., Georgetown U., 1977. Postdoctoral fellow Albert Einstein Coll. Medicine, Bronx, 1977-79, Calif. Inst. Tech., Pasadena, 1980-82; asst. prof. Calif. State U., Los Angeles, 1982; research scientist Inst. Cancer Research, San Francisco, 1982-84; o.c. tech. service mgr. Xoma Corp., Berkeley, Calif., 1984—. Contbr. articles to profl. jours. Author: (with others) Liposome Technology, 1984. Mem. Am. Chem. Soc., AAAS, Phi Sigma. Current work: Immunotoxin for cancer therapeutics. Subspecialties: Biochemistry (medicine); Enzyme technology. Home: 267 25th Ave San Francisco CA 94121 Office: Xoma Corp 2840 8th St Berkeley CA 94710

WU, RAYMOND KEE-KIN, medical radiation physicist, educator; b. Canton, China, Feb. 4, 1948; came to U.S., 1969, naturalized, 1983; s. Leung and Wai-Tak (Chow) W.; m. Dulcie W. Wu, Apr. 20, 1975; 1 son, Jeffrey Kai. B.Sc. in Physics, Chinese U. Hong Kong, 1969; Ph.D., Dartmouth Coll., 1973. Diplomate: Am. Bd. Radiology. Med. physicist Dept. Radiation Therapy, Thomas Jefferson U. Hosp., Phila., 1973-75; dir. Div. Med. Physics, St. Joseph Hosp., Milw., 1975-77; asst. prof., dir. radiation therapy physics Temple U. Hosp., Phila., 1977-78, assoc. prof., 1978-85; dep. dir. dept. radiation oncology, 1982-83; prof., dir. div. physics dept. radiation oncology and biophysics Eastern Va. Med. Sch., 1985—; cons. physicist dept. radiation oncology Chang Gung Meml. Hosp., Taipei, Taiwan, 1978; mem. adv. com. AEC, Republic of China, 1981—. Contbr. articles to profl. jours. Mem. Am. Assn. Physicists in Medicine (pres. Delaware Valley chpt.), Am. Soc. Therapeutic Radiologists, Am. Coll. Radiology. Republican. Club: Chinese Community Center of South Jersey. Current Work: Radiation therapy physics, radiation dosimetry in therapeutic radiology and nuclear medicine. Subspecialties: Radiology; Biophysics (physics). Office: Radiation Oncology Dept Eastern Va Med Sch Norfolk VA 23507

WU, SHANG-REN, chemist, researcher; b. Taipei, Republic of China, Sept. 9, 1950; came to U.S., 1974; s. Hsi-Huang and Chun-Tao (Chuang) W. B.S., Chung-Hsing U., Republic of China, 1973; Ph.D., Ohio State U., 1979; postdoctoral U. Md., 1979-81. Sr. research chemist Henkel Corp., Mpls., 1981—. Contbr. articles to profl. jours. Procter & Gamble fellow, 1977. Mem. Am. Chem. Soc., Phi Kappa Phi. Current work: Polysaccharide modification, structure determination, hydrogel formation, process development. Subspecialties: Organic chemistry; Polymer chemistry. Home: 4094 Foss Rd St Anthony MN 55421 Office: Henkel Corp 2010 E Hennepin Ave Minneapolis MN 55413

WU, STEPHEN HONG-WEI, biophysical chemist; b. Taiwan, China, July 28, 1945; came to U.S. 1968, naturalized 1980; m. An Chen, Sept. 7, 1975; children—Christine, Esther, Victor. B.S., Nat. Taiwan U., Taipei, 1967; M.S., East Tenn. State U., 1970; Ph.D., Stanford U., 1974. Sr. research chemist Eastman Kodak Co., Kingsport, Tenn., 1974—. Contbr. articles to profl. jours., chpts. to books. Patentee in field. Mem. Am. Chem. Soc., Controlled Release Soc. Current work: Controlled release of bioactive materials, rumen-stable delivery systems, water-dispersible polymeric coatings, coated seeds, oral delivery dosage forms. Subspecialties: Biophysical chemistry; Drug delivery systems. Home: 1104 Meadow Ln Kingsport TN 37663 Office: Research Labs B-150 B Eastman Chemicals Div Kingsport TN 37663

WU, STEVE, mechanical engineer; b. Macau, Nov. 11, 1923; came to U.S., 1959, naturalized, 1968; s. Pak Tin and Shio Chi (Soo) W.; married; 1 dau., Theresa. B.S.M.S., Aero. Inst., Chung King, China, 1947; M.S.M.E., U. Portland, 1976. Registered profl. engr., Oreg. Mem. tech. staff Civil Air Transport, China, 1953-60; engr. Cascade Corp., Portland, Oreg., 1960-79; asst. prof. mech. engring. Portland State U., 1979-80; pres. Wemco Crang Co., Portland, 1980—; adj. prof. mech. engring. Portland State U. and U. Portland, 1970-79; cons. in field. Mem. ASME. Patentee hydraulic crane, hydraulic seal, rotating mechanism; developed formulas for critical load of n-sects. column, 180 degree phase error in direction finding for aircraft. Current Work: Hydraulic machinery; mechanic robot. Subspecialties: Fluid mechanics; Theoretical and applied mechanics. Home: 11740 SE Salmon St Portland OR 97216

WU, THEODORE YAO-TSU, engineer; b. Changchow, Kiangsu, China, Mar. 20, 1924; came to U.S., 1948, naturalized, 1962; s. Ren Fu and Gee-Ing (Shu) W.; m. Chin-Hua Shih, June 17, 1950; children—Fonda Bai-yueh, Melba Bai-chin. B.S., Chiao-Tung U., 1946; M.S., Iowa State U., 1948; Ph.D., Calif. Inst. Tech., 1952. Mem. faculty Calif. Inst. Tech., Pasadena, 1952—, asso. prof., 1957-61, prof. engring. sci., 1961—; vis. prof. Hamburg (Germany) U., 1964-65; cons. numerous indsl. firms. Editorial bd.: Advances in Applied Mechanics series, 1970; Contbr. profl. jours. Guggenheim fellow, 1964-65. Fellow Am. Phys. Soc., AIAA (asso.); mem. Sigma Xi, Nat. Acad. Engring., Phi Tau Phi. Office: Calif Inst Tech Pasadena CA 91125*

WU, WILLIAM W., engineering researcher, educator; b. Nanking, China, Nov. 2, 1934; came to U.S., 1955; s. Hsing-Ling and Sophia (Pan) W.; m. Margaret C. Wu, July 9, 1962; children—Mars, Bechien. B.S. in Elec. Engring., Purdue U., 1961; M.S. in Elec. Engring., MIT, 1967; Ph.D., Johns Hopkins U., 1976. Product engr. semicondr. div. Raytheon Co., Newton, Mass., 1961-63; design engr. Hewlett Packard, Waltham, Mass., 1963-65; sr. staff scientist COMSAT, Washington, 1967-79; mem. sr. staff INTELSAT, Washington, 1979—; grant reviewer NSF, Washington, 1978—; mem. NASA Coding Standard Commn., 1981—. Author: Elements of Digital Satellite Communications, Vol. I, 1984, Vol. II, 1985; (with others) Satellite Trans. Engineering, 1985. Editor book series: Advances in Satellite Communications, 1986. Mem. IEEE (chmn. info. theory 1975-76). Current work: Design, analyze, propose, evaluate, optimize satellite communication systems and subsystems. Subspecialties: Satellite studies; Telecommunications. Office: Internat Telecommunication Satellite Orgn 3400 International Dr NW Washington DC 20008

WUEST, CRAIG RICHARD, experimental high energy physicist; b. San Jose, Calif., Sept. 29, 1956; s. Alan Richard and Barbara Jean (Albo) W.; m. Dawn Ann Clements, Nov. 1, 1980. A.S., West Valley Community Coll., Saratoga, Calif., 1976; B.A. in Physics, U. Calif.-Irvine, 1978, M.S., 1980, Ph.D., 1983. Research asst. Lawrence Berkeley Lab., Berkeley, Calif., 1977, Fermilab., U. Calif.-Irvine, also Batavia, Ill., 1977-78; teaching asst. U. Calif.-Irvine, 1978-79, research asst., 1979-83; postdoctoral physicist Lawrence Livermore Lab., Calif., 1983—. Contbr. articles to sci. jours. Patentee high altitude thermometer (recipient 1st prize Instrument Soc. Am.). Mem. Am. Phys. Soc., Sigma Pi Sigma, Beta Theta Pi (past sec.). Current work: Quark searches in bulk matter using high volume liquid drop technique; proton decay searches using H2O Cherenkov detectors; neutrino oscillations measurements. Subspecialty: Particle physics. Office: Lawrence Livermore Nat Lab PO Box 808 L495 Livermore CA 94550

WULFMAN, CARL EUGENE, physics educator, researcher; b. Detroit, Nov. 29, 1930; s. Eugene Jacob and Laura Jean (Swinton) W.; m. Constance Ann Hart, Sept. 6, 1952; children—Michael, Peter, Andrew, Edward. B.S. cum laude, U. Mich., 1953; Ph.D., U. London, 1957. Instr. dept. chemistry U. Tex., Austin, 1955-57; chmn. dept. chemistry Defiance Coll., Ohio, 1957-61; chmn. dept. physics U. Pacific, Stockton, Calif., 1961-73, 81—, prof. physics, 1961—. Author: (with others) Group Theory and its Applications, 1971; Recent Advances in Group Theory, 1979; Symmetries in Science, 1980. NSF grantee, 1963-83; U. Mich. fellow, 1952; NSF fellow, 1968; Fulbright scholar, 1953-55. Mem. Am. Phys. Soc. Current work: Transformation groups admitted by differential equations of physics and chemistry; determination of the groups and the laws they imply using expert artificial intelligence systems. Subspecialties: Theoretical physics; Artificial intelligence. Office: U Pacific Dept Physics Stockton CA 95211

WUNDERLE, JOSEPH MACKIE, JR., zoology educator, researcher; b. Abington, Pa., Jan. 27, 1949; s. Joseph Mackie and Mary T. (Maier) W.; m. Deborah Jean Lodge, June 4, 1983. B.S. in Biology with distinction, U. Maine, 1971; M.S. in Ecology and Behavior, U. Minn., 1976, Ph.D., 1980. Instr. ecology and evolution Canadian Jr. Coll., Carriacou, Grenada, W.I., 1975-76, dir., headmaster, 1977-78; co-coordinator Organ. Tropical Studies Inc. Tropical Biology Course, Costa Rica, 1979, coordinator grad. tropical biology, 1982; vis. asst. prof. zoology N.C. State U., 1980-81; asst. prof. biology U. P.R., Cayey, 1982-85, assoc. prof., 1985—; cons. hepetology Internat. Species Inventory, Mpls., 1979-80; adj. research scientist Ctr. Energy and Environ. Research, San Juan, P.R., 1984. Contbr. articles to profl. jours. Grantee NSF, 1985, Nat. Geog. Soc., 1981, Am. Mus. Natural History, 1974-78. Mem. AAAS, Am. Ornithologists Union (grant 1975), Animal Behavior Soc., Cooper Ornithol. Soc., Ecol. Soc. Am., Assn. Tropical Biology, Wilson Ornithol. Soc. (grant 1981), Puerto Rican Natural History Soc., Nat. Audubon Soc. Current work: Behavioral ecology of Caribbean birds, foraging behavior, learning and risk aversion in the nectarivorous Bananaquit, teaching of vertebrate behavior, ecology and evolution. Subspecialties: Behavioral ecology; Evolutionary biology. Office: Departamento de biologia Colegio Universitario de Cayey Universidad de PR Cayey PR 00633

WUNSCH, CARL ISAAC, oceanographer, educator; b. Bklyn., May 5, 1941; s. Harry and Helen (Gellis) W.; m. Marjory Markel, June 6, 1970; children—Jared, Hannah. S.B., MIT, 1962, Ph.D., 1967. Asst. prof. phys. oceanography M.I.T., 1967-70, assoc. prof., 1970-75, prof., 1975-76, Cecil and Ida Green prof., 1976—, Sec. of Navy prof. oceanography, 1985—, head dept. earth and planetary scis., 1977-81; sr. vis. fellow U. Cambridge, Eng., 1969, 74-75, 81-82; cons. NASA, NSF, Nat. Acad. Scis. Asso. editor: Jour. Phys. Oceanography, 1977-80, Revs. of Geophysics and Space Physics, 1981—; co-editor: Evolution of Physical Oceanography, 1981; contbr. articles to profl. jours. Recipient Tex. Instruments Found. Founders prize, 1975; Fulbright sr. scholar, 1981-82; Guggenheim fellow, 1981-82. Fellow Am. Geophys. Union (James R. Macelwane award 1971), Royal Astron. Soc., Am. Acad. Arts and Scis.; mem. Nat. Acad. Scis. Current Work: Study of ocean circulation using satellite altimetry and scatterometry, ocean acoustic tomography and inverse methods. Subspecialty: Oceanography. Home: 16 Crescent St Cambridge MA 02138 Office: Department of Earth Atmospheric and Planetary Sciences Massachusetts Institute Technology Cambridge MA 02139

WURSTER, DALE ERWIN, university dean, educator; b. Sparta, Wis., Apr. 10, 1918; s. Edward Emil and Emma Sophia (Steingraeber) W.; m. June Margaret Peterson, June 16, 1944; children—Dale Eric, Susan Gay. B.S., U. Wis., 1942, Ph.D., 1947. Faculty, U. Wis. Sch. Pharmacy, 1947-71, prof., 1958-71; prof., dean N.D. State U. Coll. Pharmacy, 1971-72; prof. U. Iowa Coll. Pharmacy, Iowa City, 1972—, dean, 1972-84, dean emeritus, 1984—, Hancher Finkbinc Medallion prof., 1984; George B. Kaufman Meml. lectr. Ohio State U., 1968; cons. in field; phys. sci. adminstr. U.S. Navy, 1960-63; sci. adviser Wis. Alumni Research Found., 1968-72; mem. revision com. U.S. Pharmacopoeia, 1961-70; mem. pharmacy rev. com. USPHS, 1966-72. Contbr. articles to profl. jours., chpts. to books. Patentee in field, inventor air-suspension coating, granulation and microencapsulation process. Served as officer USNR, 1944-46. Recipient Superior Achievement citation Navy Dept., 1964, merit citation U. Wis., 1976, Disting. Alumni award U. Wis. Sch. Pharmacy, 1984. Mem. Am. Assn. Colls. Pharmacy (exec. com. 1964-66, chmn. conf. tchrs. 1960-61, vis. scientist 1963-70, Disting. Educator award 1983), Acad. Pharm. Scis. (exec. com. 1967-70, chmn. basic pharmaceutics sect. 1965-67, pres. 1975, indsl. pharm. tech. award 1980), Am. Pharm. Assn. (chmn. sci. sect. 1964-65, Research achievement award 1965), Wis. Pharm. Assn. (Disting. Service award 1971), Iowa Pharm. Assn. (Pharmacist of Yr. 1983), Wis. Acad. Scis., Arts and Letters, Soc. Investigative Dermatology, Rumanian Soc. Med. Sci. (hon.), Sigma Xi, Kappa Psi (past officer), Rho Chi, Phi Lambda Upsilon, Phi Sigma. Current work: Research in dissolution kinetics, drug diffusion through skin and other biological membranes, drug formulation. Subspecialties: Physical chemistry; Molecular pharmacology. Home: Rural Route 6 16 Brickwood Knoll River Heights Iowa City IA 52242 Office: U Iowa Coll Pharmacy Iowa City IA 52242

WURTMAN, RICHARD JAY, physician, educator; b. Phila., Mar. 9, 1936; s. Samuel Richard and Hilda (Schreiber) W.; m. Judith Joy Hirschhorn, Nov. 15, 1959; children: Rachael Elisabeth, David Franklin. A.B., U. Pa., 1956; M.D., Harvard U., 1960. Intern, Mass. Gen. Hosp., 1960-61, resident, 1961-62, fellow medicine, 1965-66; research asso., med. research officer NIMH, 1962-67; mem. faculty MIT, 1967—, prof. endocrinology and metabolism, 1970-80, prof. neuroendocrine regulation, 1980—; lectr. medicine Harvard Med. Sch., 1969—; prof. Harvard-MIT Div. Health Scis. and Tech., 1978—; dir. MIT Clin. Research Ctr., 1985—; clin. assoc. in medicine Mass. Gen. Hosp., 1985—; sci. dir. Ctr. for Brain Scis. and Metabolism Charitable Trust, 1981—; invited prof. U. Geneva, 1981; Sterling vis. prof. Boston U., 1981; mem. small grants study sect. NIMH, 1967-69, preclin. psychopharmacolgy study sect., 1971-75; behavioral biology adv. panel NASA, 1969-72; council basic sci. Am. Heart

Assn., 1969-74; research adv. bd. Parkinson's Disease Found., 1972-80, Am. Parkinson's Disease Assn., 1978—; com. phototherapy in newborns NRC-Nat. Acad. Scis., 1972-74, com. nutrition, brain devel. and behavior, 1976, mem. space applications bd., 1976-80; mem. task force on drug devel. Muscular Dystrophy Assn., 1980-85; chmn. life scis. adv. com. NASA, 1979-84; mem. adv. bd. Alzheimer's Disease Assn., 1981-85; asso. neuroscis. research program MIT, 1974-82; Bennett lectr. Am. Neurol. Assn., 1974; Flexner lectr. U. Pa., 1975. Author: Catecholamines, 1966, (with others) The Pineal, 1968; editor: (with Judith Wurtman) Nutrition and the Brain, Vols. I and II, 1977, Vols. III, IV, V, 1979, Vol. VI, 1983, Vol. VII, 1985; also articles.; editorial bd.: Endocrinology, 1967-73, Jour. Pharmacology and Exptl. Therapeutics, 1968-75, Jour. Neural Transmission, 1969—, Neuroendocrinology, 1969-72, Metabolism, 1970-80, Circulation Research, 1972-77, Jour. Neurochemistry, 1973-82, Life Scis., 1973-81, Brain Research, 1977—. Patentee in uses of drugs and nutrients in brain disorders. Recipient Alvarenga prize and lectureship Phila. Coll. Physicians, 1970. Mem. Am. Soc. Clin. Investigation, Endocrine Soc. (Ernst Oppenheim award 1972), Am. Physiol. Soc., Am. Soc. Biol. Chemists, Am. Soc. Pharmacology and Exptl. Therapeutics (John Jacob Abel award 1968), Am. Soc. Neurochemistry, Soc. Neuroscis., Am. Soc. Clin. Nutrition. Club: Harvard (Boston). Current Work: Amino acid metabolism; neurotransmitters; drug development ; appetite; memory disorders; pineal gland. Subspecialties: Neurochemistry; Neuroendocrinology. Home: 193 Marlborough St Boston MA 02116 Office: Mass Inst Tech E25-604 Cambridge MA 02139

WYATT, RICHARD JED, physician; b. Los Angeles, June 5, 1939; m. Rollyn Simon, Sept. 11, 1966; children—Elizabeth, Christopher, Justin. B.A., Johns Hopkins U., 1961, M.D., 1964; M.D. (hon.), Central U. Venezuela, 1977. Intern in pediatrics Western Res. U. Hosp., Cleve., 1964-65; resident psychiatry Mass. Mental Health Center, Boston, 1965-67; with NIMH, 1967—, assoc. dir. for research St. Elizabeth's Hosp., chief Neuropsychiatry br., intramural research program NIMH, Washington, 1983—, also dir. div., 1977—; clin. prof. psychiatry Stanford U. Med. Sch., 1973-74, Duke U. Med. Sch., 1975—, Uniformed Services Sch. Medicine, 1980—; practice medicine specializing in psychiatry, Washington, 1968—; cons. in field. Exec. editorial bds. profl. jours. Recipient Harry Solomon Research award Mass. Mental Health Center, 1968; A.E. Bennett award Soc. Biol. Psychiatry, 1971; Psychopharm. award Am. Psychol. Assn., 1971; Superior Achievement award USPHS, 1980; Dean award Am. Coll. Psychiatrists. Fellow Am. Psychiat. Assn., Am. Coll. Neuropsychopharmacology; mem. Washington Psychiat. Assn., Soc. Psychophysiol. Study Sleep, Soc. Biol. Psychology, Am. Assn. Geriatric Psychiatry, Psychiat. Research Soc., Soc. Neuroscis., AMA. Office: WAW Bldg Room 536 St Elizabeths Hosp Washington DC 20032

WYLIE, EVAN BENJAMIN, engineer. Chmn. dept. civil engring. U. Mich., Ann Arbor. Subspecialty: Civil engineering. Office: U Mich Coll Engring Ann Arbor MI 48109

WYLLIE, PETER JOHN, geologist, educator; b. London, Feb. 8, 1930; U.S., 1961; s. George William and Beatrice Gladys (Weaver) W.; m. Francis Rosemary Blair, June 9, 1956; children—Andrew, Elizabeth (dec.), Lisa, John. B.Sc. in Geology and Physics, U. St. Andrews Scotland, 1952, 1955, Ph.D. in Geology, 1958, D.Sc. (hon.), 1974 Glaciologist Brit. W. Greenland Expdn., 1950; geologist Brit. N. Greenland Expdn., 1952-54; asst. lectr. geology U. St. Andrews, 1955-56; research asst. geochemistry Pa. State U., State College, 1956-58 asst. prof. geochemistry, 1958-59, asso. prof. petrology, 1961-65, acting head, dept. geochemistry mineralogy, 1962-63; research fellow chemistry Leeds (Eng.) U., 1959-60, lectr. exptl. petrology, 1960-61; prof. petrology geochemistry U. Chgo., 1965-77, Homer J. Livingston prof., 1978-83, chmn. dept. geophys. scis., 1979-83, master phys. scis. collegiate div., asso. dean coll., asso. dean phys. scis. div., 1972-73; chmn. div. geol. and planetary scis. Calif. Inst. Tech., Pasadena, 1983—; mem. commn. exptl. petrology high pressures temperatures Internat. Union Geol. Scis.; mem. adv. panel earth scis. NSF, 1975-78, chmn. adv. com. earth scis. div., 1979-82; mem. U.S. Nat. Com. on Geology, 1978-82; mem. U.S. nat. com. Internat. Union Geodesy and Geophysics, 1980-84. Author: The Dynamic Earth, 1971, The Way the Earth Works, 1976; editor and contbr.: Ultramafic and Related Rocks, 1967; editor: Jour. Geology, 1967-83, Series in Intermediate Geology, 1978—; editor-in-chief: Minerals Rocks (monograph series), 1967—. Served with RAF, 1948-49. Fellow Am. Acad. Arts and Scis., Royal Soc. London, Edinburgh geol. Soc. (corr.). Recipient Polar medal H.M. Queen Elizabeth, Eng.; Quantrell award, 1979; Wollaston medal Geol. Soc. London, 1982. Mem. Mineral. Soc. Am. (award 1965, pres. 1977-78), Internat. Mineral. Assn. (2d v.p. 1978-82, 1st v.p. 1982—), Am. Acad. Scis. (fgn. asso.). Current work: Heterogeneous phase equilibrium studies on minerals and rock at high pressures and temperatures, simulating deep-earth processes. Subspecialties: Petrology; Geochemistry. Office: Calif Inst Tech Pasadena CA 91125

WYMAN, ROBERT J., neurophysiologist; b. Syracuse, N.Y., June 8, 1940; s. Ralph and Selma (Franklin) W. A.B., Harvard U., 1960; M.S., U. Calif., Berkeley, 1963, Ph.D., 1965; M.A. (hon.), Yale U., 1980. Math. analyst Tech. Research Group, 1959; NSF research fellow Calif. Inst. Tech., 1966; asst. prof. Yale U., 1966-71, assoc. prof., 1971-80, prof., 1980—; vis. scientist Nobel Inst., Stockholm, 1970-71, Med. Research Council, Cambridge, Eng., 1974, U. Basel, Switzerland, 1977. Bd. dirs. Urban League; bd. sponsors Nat. Com. for an Effective Congress. Mem. Soc. Neurosci., Internat. Brain Research Orgn., Soc. Exptl. Biology, Sigma Xi. Current Work: Genes which specify development of the nervous system. Subspecialties: Comparative neurobiology; Genetics and genetic engineering (biology). Home: 11J Cedar Ct East Haven CT 06513 Office: Dept Biology 646 KBT Yale U New Haven CT 06511

WYNER, AARON DANIEL, mathematician, researcher; b. N.Y.C., Mar. 17, 1939; s. Alvin and Mary (Jacobson) W.; m. Nusha Zukerman, June 9, 1962; children—Tamar, Abraham, Dena, Yael. B.S., Queens Coll., 1960; B.E.E., Columbia U., 1960, M.E.E., 1961, Ph.D., 1963. Asst. prof. elec. engring. Columbia U., N.Y.C., 1963, vis. prof., 1965-69, 72; vis. prof. Princeton U., N.J., 1983, Technion, Haifa, Israel, 1969-70, Polytech. Inst. N.Y., Bklyn., 1971, 75; mem. tech. staff ATT Bell Labs, Murray Hill, N.J., 1963—. Contbr. numerous articles to profl. jours. Patentee in field. Guggenheim Found. fellow, 1966. Fellow IEEE (pres. inform. theory group 1976, editor-in-chief transactions on info. theory, centennial medal 1984). Current work: Information theory and congnate mathematical problems. Subspecialties: Applied mathematics; Computer engineering. Home: 33 Oakview Ave Maplewood NJ 07040 Office: ATT Bell Labs Murray Hill NJ 07974

WYNGAARDEN, JAMES BARNES, physician; b. East Grand Rapids, Mich., Oct. 19, 1924; s. Martin Jacob and Johanna (Kempers) W.; m. Ethel Vredevoogd, June 20, 1946 (div. 1977); children: Patricia Wyngaarden Fitzpatrick, Joanna Wyngaarden Gandy, Martha Wyngaarden Krauss, Lisa Wyngaarden Rolland, James Barnes. Student, Calvin Coll., 1942-43, Western Mich. U., 1943-44; M.D., U. Mich., 1948, Sc.D. (hon.), 1980; Sc.D. (hon.), U. Ohio, 1984, U. Ill., 1985. Diplomate: Am. Bd. Internal Medicine. Intern Mass. Gen. Hosp., Boston, 1948-49, resident, 1949-51; vis. investigator Pub. Health Research Inst., N.Y.C., 1952-53; investigator NIH, USPHS, Bethesda, Md., 1953-56; assoc. prof. medicine and biochemistry Duke Med. Sch., 1956-61, prof., 1961-65; prof., chmn. dept. medicine U. Pa. Med. Sch., 1965-67; Frederic M. Hanes prof., chmn. dept. medicine Duke Med. Sch., 1967-82; dir. NIH, Bethesda, MD, 1982—; mem. staff Duke, VA, Durham County hosps.; cons. Office Sci. and Tech., Exec. Office of President, 1966-72; Mem. President's Sci. Adv. Com., 1972-73; mem. Pres.'s Com. for Nat. Medal of Sci., 1977-80; mem. adv. com. biology and medicine AEC, 1966-68; mem. bd. sci. counselors NIH, 1971-74; mem. adv. bd. Howard Hughes Med. Inst., 1969-82; mem. adv. council Life Ins. Med. Research Fund, 1967-70; adv. bd. Sci. Yr., 1977-81; vice chmn. Com. on Study Nat. Needs for Biomed. and Behavioral Research Personnel, NRC, 1977-81. Author: (with W.N. Kelley) Gout and Hyperuricemia, 1976; Mem. editorial bd.: Jour. Biol. Chemistry, 1971-74, Arthritis and Rheumatism, 1959-66, Jour. Clinical Investigation, 1962-66, Ann. Internal Medicine, 1964-74, Medicine, 1963—; editor: (with J.B. Stanbury, D.S. Fredrickson) The Metabolic Basis of Inherited Disease, 1960, 66, 72, 78, 83, (with O. Sperling and A. DeVries) Purine Metabolism in Man, 1974, (with L.H. Smith, Jr.) Cecil Textbook of Medicine, 17th edit., 1985, (with L.H. Smith Jr.) Rev. of Gen. Internal Medicine: A Self-Assessment Guide, 3d edit., 1985. Bd. dirs. Royal Soc. Medicine Found., 1971-76, The Robert Wood Johnson Found. Clin. Scholar Program., 1973-78. Served with USNR, 1943-46; sr. surgeon USPHS, 1951-56. Recipient Borden Undergrad. Research award U. Mich., 1948; Dalton scholar in medicine Mass. Gen. Hosp., 1950; vis. scientist Inst. de Biologie-Physicochemique Paris, France, 1963-64; Recipient N.C. Gov.'s award for sci., 1974. Fellow Royal Coll. Physicians; mem. Am. Rheumatism Assn., Am. Fedn. Clin. Research, So. Soc. Clin. Investigation (pres. 1974, founder's medal 1978), A.C.P. (Phillips medal 1980), Am. Soc. Clin. Investigation, AAAS, Am. Soc. Biol. Chemists, Assn. Am. Physicians (councillor 1973-77, pres. 1978), Endocrine Soc., Nat. Acad. Sci., Am. Acad. Arts and Sci., Inst. Medicine, Sigma Xi. Club: Interurban Clinical (Balt.). Subspecialties: Biochemistry (medicine); Medical research administration. Office: Nat Inst Health 9000 Rockville Pike Bethesda MD 20892

WYSOLMERSKI, THERESA, biology educator, nun; b. West Rutland, Vt., Oct. 25, 1932; d. John and Rose (Sasinowska) W. B.S., Coll. St. Rose, 1959; M.S. in Biology, U. Notre Dame, 1961; postgrad. Ind. U., 1965-67; Ph.D., Rutgers U., 1973. Tchr. chemistry and biology St. John the Evangelist Acad., Syracuse, N.Y., 1955-59; instr. biology Coll. St. Rose, Albany, N.Y., 1959—, pre-med. advisor, 1975—. Insp., Republican Party, Albany, 1984—. NSF Devel. grantee Dartmouth Coll., 1981-82; recipient Disting. Faculty Excellence in Tchg. award Coll St. Rose, 1983. Mem. Am. Inst. Biol. Scis., Ecol. Soc., Sigma Xi, Delta Kappa Gamma, Delta Epsilon Sigma. Current work: Teaching zoology, anatomy and related areas; research contractile proteins. Subspecialties: Developmental biology; Anatomy and embryology. Home: 432 Western Ave Albany NY 12203 Office: Coll St Rose 432 Western Ave Albany NY 12203

WYSS, JAMES MICHAEL, anatomist; b. Ft. Wayne, Ind., Mar. 11, 1948; s. Alen George and Anne (Winicker) W.; m. Gloria F. Wyss, Apr. 25, 1973; children: Dana Ann, William Alen. A.A., Concordia Coll., Ann Arbor, Mich., 1968; B.A., Concordia Coll., Ft. Wayne, 1970; M.Div., Luth. Sch. Theology, Chgo., 1974; Ph.D., Washington U., St. Louis, 1976. Sloan postdoctoral fellow Washington U., St. Louis, 1976-79, instr. anatomy, 1976-79; asst. prof. cell biology and anatomy U. Ala., Birmingham, 1979-83, assoc. prof., 1983—; mem. Neurosci. Research Ctr., 1979—, Cardiovascular Research and Tng. Ctr., 1980—. Contbr. articles to profl. jours. Ordained to ministry Lutheran Ch., 1976; dir. alcholism and youth services Project Promised Land, St. Louis, 1974-79; Chmn. Law Enforcement Assistance Adminstrn. Regional Program, North St. Louis, 1974-77. Washington U. fellow, 1975; NIH fellow, 1977-79. Mem. AAAS, Soc. Neurosci., Am. Heart Assn. (fellow Council for High Blood Pressure Research), Am. Assn. Anatomists. Current Work: Determination of structure and function of various cerebral cortex regions, especially limbic cortex regions and neurogenic control of blood pressure and heart rate. Subspecialties: Neurobiology; Cardiology. Home: 1925 Old Creek Trail Vestavia Hills AL 35216 Office: Dept Anatomy Univ Ala Birmingham AL 35294

YACOWITZ, HAROLD, nutritionist; b. N.Y.C., Feb. 17, 1922; s. Louis and Clara (Kurtzberg) Y.; m. Ann Ruth Barnett, Dec. 31, 1941; children—Caryn, Richard, Suzanne. B.S., Cornell U., 1947, M.Nutritional Sci., 1948, Ph.D., 1950. Research biochemist Parke Davis Co., Detroit, 1950-51; assoc. prof. biochemistry Ohio State U., Columbus, 1951-55; head nutrition dept. Squibb Inst., New Brunswick, N.J., 1955-59; research assoc. Fairleigh Dickinson U., Madison, N.J., 1961-81; pres. AIMS, Inc., Piscataway, N.J., 1979—. Contbr. articles to profl. jours. Patentee in field. Served with U.S. Army, 1943-46. Fellow N.Y. Acad. Scis.; mem. Am. Chem. Soc., Inst. Nutrition, Am. Assn. Lab. Animal Sci. Jewish. Club: Bohemia River Sailing. Current work: Biochemist in calcium and lipid metabolism and laboratory animal care. Subspecialties: Animal nutrition; Biochemistry (biology). Home: 221 2nd Ave Piscataway NJ 08854 Office: AIMS Inc 221 2nd Ave Piscataway NJ 08854

YAFFE, SUMNER JASON, pediatrician, devel. and pediatric pharmacologist; b. Boston, May 9, 1923; s. Henry H. and Ida E. (Fisher) Y.; married; children: Steven, Kris, Jason, Noah. A.B., Harvard U., 1945; M.A., 1950; M.D., U. Vt., 1954. Diplomate: Am. Bd. Pediatrics. Intern Children's Hosp., Boston, 1954-55; resident 1955-56; exchange resident St. Mary's Hosp., London, 1956-57; asst. prof. pediatrics Stanford U., Palo Alto, Calif., 1960-63; assoc. prof. pediatrics SUNY, Buffalo, 1963-66, prof., 1966-75; dir. Poison Control Center, Children's Hosp., Buffalo, 1967-75; prof. pediatrics and pharmacology U. Pa., Phila., 1975-81; dir. Ctr. for Research for Mothers and Children, Nat. Inst. Child Health and Human Devel., NIH, Bethesda, Md., 1981—; vis. prof. pharmacology Karolinska Inst., Stockholm, 1969-70; Wall Meml. lectr. Children's Hosp., Washington, 1968; Dr, W.E. Upjohn lectr. Can. Med. Assn., 1974; William N. Creasy vis. prof. clin. pharmacology SUNY, Buffalo, 1976; mem. expert adv. panel on maternal and child health WHO; cons. Am. Found. for Maternal and Child Health, Inc.; dir. div. clin. pharmacology Children's Hosp., Phila., 1975-81; mem. adv. panel in pediatrics U.S. Pharmacopeia. Editor-in-chief: Pediatric Pharmacology; mem. editorial bd.: Pharmacology, Developmental Pharmacology and Therapeutics; contbr. articles to profl. jours. Served with U.S. Army, 1943-44. Recipient Lederle Med. Faculty award, 1962; Fulbright scholar Eng., 1956-57. Mem. Am. Pharm. Assn., Am. Soc. Clin. Pharmacology and Therapeutics (dir.), Am. Soc. Pharmacology and Exptl. Therapeutics, Acad. Pharm. Scis., Am. Acad. Pediatrics, AAAS, Am. Assn. Poison Control Centers, AAUP, Am. Pediatric Soc., Soc. Pediatric Research, Wilderness Soc. Current Work: Direct program of research in biomedical and behavioral sciences with special emphasis on pregnancy, perinatal biology ad human biological and behavioral development from conception through adolescence to maturity. Subspecialties: Pediatrics; Pharmacology. Home: 8144 Inverness Ridge Rd Potomac MD 20854 Office: NIH Room 7C03 Landow Bldg 7910 Woodmont Ave Bethesda MD 20205

YAGIELA, JOHN ALLEN, dental educator, researcher; b. Washington, July 23, 1947; s. Stanley and Kathryn (Gilkeson) Y.; m. Dolores Jean Mitchell, Mar. 21, 1970; children: Gregory Mitchell, Leanne Elizabeth. D.D.S., UCLA, 1971; Ph.D. in Pharmacology, U. Utah, 1975. Asst. prof. dept. oral biology Emory U. Sch. Dentistry, Atlanta, 1975-78, assoc. prof., 1978-82; prof. UCLA Sch. Dentistry, 1982—, coordinator anesthesia and pain control, 1982—, assoc. dean acad. affairs, 1985—; cons. Astra Pharm. Co., Worcester, Mass., 1981—, C.V. Mosby Co., St. Louis, 1981—; outside reviewer U.S. Pharmacopeia Dispensing Info., 1981—. Co-author: Regional Anesthesia of the Oral Cavity, 1981; co-editor: Pharmacology and Therapeutics for Dentistry, 1980, 2d edit., 1985. Recipient award of achievement Am. Coll. Dentists, 1971; regents scholar UCLA, 1969-71. Fellow Am. Dental Soc. Anesthesiology; Mem. Internat. Assn. Dental Research (sec. Atlanta sect. 1979-81, pres. so. Calif. sect. 1983—), Am. Assn. Dental Schs. (chmn. sect. pharmacology and therapeutics 1982), Dental Research Inst. (UCLA), Omicron Kappa Upsilon, Alpha Omega. Methodist. Current Work: Research concerning local and systemic toxicity of local anesthetic drugs; application of therapeutic agents for pain control in dentistry. Subspecialties: Oral biology; Pharmacology. Home: 7956 Glade Ave Canoga Park CA 91304 Office: UCLA Sch Dentistry Center for Health Scis Los Angeles CA 90024

YAHIL, AMOS, astrophysicist, educator; b. Tel Aviv, Nov. 28, 1943, came to U.S., 1966; s. Chaim and Helena (Westphal) Y.; m. Jane Elisabeth Graber, Jan. 1, 1972; children—Edna Ruth, Ron Jonathan. B.Sc., Hebrew U., Jerusalem, Israel, 1966; Ph.D., Calif. Inst. Tech., 1970. Mem. staff Inst. for Advanced Study, Princeton, N.J., 1971-73; lectr. Tel Aviv U., 1970-71, 73-75, sr. lectr., 1975-77; asst. prof. astrophysics SUNY-Stony Brook, 1977-79, assoc. prof., 1979-83, prof., 1983—. Recipient Fullam award Dudley Obs., 1982; Guggenheim fellow, 1984. Mem. Am. Astron. Soc., Internat. Astron. Union. Current work: Cosmology; dynamics and clustering of galaxies; nuclear astrophysics; stellar collapse; supernovae; molecular clouds. Subspecialties: Theoretical astrophysics; Cosmology. Home: 9 Story Book Ln East Setauket NY 11733 Office: Astronomy Program SUNY Stony Brook NY 11794

YALOW, ROSALYN SUSSMAN, medical physicist; b. N.Y.C., July 19, 1921; d. Simon and Clara (Zipper) Sussman; m. A. Aaron Yalow, June 6, 1943; children: Benjamin, Elanna. A.B., Hunter Coll., 1941; M.S., U. Ill., Urbana, 1942, Ph.D., 1945; D.Sc. (hon.), U. Ill., Chgo., 1974, Phila. Coll. Pharmacy and Sci., 1976, N.Y. Med. Coll., 1976, Med. Coll. Wis., Milw., 1977, Yeshiva U., 1977, Southampton (N.Y.) Coll., 1978, Bucknell U., 1978, Princeton U., 1978, Jersey City State Coll., 1979, Med. Coll. Pa., 1979, Manhattan Coll., 1979, U. Vt., 1980, U. Hartford, 1980, Rutgers U., 1980, Rensselaer Poly. Inst., 1980, Colgate U., 1981, U. So. Calif., 1981, Clarkson Coll., 1982, U. Miami, 1983, Washington U., St. Louis, 1983, Adelphi U., 1983, U. Alta. (Can.), 1983, Columbia U., 1984, SUNY, 1984, Tel Aviv U., 1985; L.H.D. (hon.), Hunter Coll., 1978, Sacred Heart U., Conn., 1978, St. Michael's Coll., Winooski Park, Vt., 1979, Johns Hopkins U., 1979; D. honoris causa, U. Rosario, Argentina, 1980, U. Ghent, Belgium, 1984. Diplomate: Am. Bd. Sci. Lectr., asst. prof. physics Hunter Coll., 1946-50; physicist, asst. chief radiosotope service VA Hosp., Bronx, N.Y., 1950-70, chief nuclear medicine, 1970-80, acting chief radiosotope service, 1968-70; research prof. Mt. Sinai Sch. Medicine, City U. N.Y., 1968-74, Disting. Service prof., 1974-79; Disting. prof.-at-large Albert Einstein Coll. Medicine, Yeshiva U., 1979—; chmn. dept. clin. Scis. Albert Einstein Coll. Medicine, Montefiore Med. Center, Bronx, 1980—; cons. Lenox Hill Hosp., N.Y.C., 1956-62, WHO, Bombay, 1978; sec. U.S. Nat. Com. on Med. Physics, 1963-67; mem. nat. com. Radiation Protection, Subcom. 13, 1957—; mem. Pres.'s Study Group on Careers for Radiation Women, 1966—; sr. med. investigator VA, 1972; dir. Solomon A. Berson Research Lab., VA Hosp., Bronx, N.Y., 1973. Co-editor: Hormone and Metabolic Research, 1973-79; editorial adv. council: Acta Diabetologica Latina, 1975-77, Ency. Universalis, 1978—; editorial bd.: Mt. Sinai Jour. Medicine, 1976-79, Diabetes, 1976—, Endocrinology, 1967-72; contbr. numerous articles to profl. jours. Bd. dirs. N.Y. Diabetes Assn., 1974. Recipient VA William S. Middleton Med. Research award, 1960; Eli Lilly award Am. Diabetes Assn., 1961; Van Slyke award N.Y. met. sect. Am. Assn. Clin. Chemists, 1968; award A.C.P., 1971; Dickson prize U. Pitts., 1971; Howard Taylor Ricketts award U. Chgo., 1971; Gairdner Found. Internat. award, 1971; Commemorative medallion Am. Diabetes Assn., 1972; Bernstein award Med. Soc. State N.Y., 1974; Boehringer-Mannheim Corp. award Am. Assn. Clin. Chemists, 1975; Sci. Achievement award AMA, 1975; Exceptional Service award VA, 1975; A. Cressy Morrison award N.Y. Acad. Scis., 1975; sustaining membership award Assn. Mil. Surgeons, 1975; Distinguished Achievement award Modern Medicine, 1976; Albert Lasker Basic Med. Research award, 1976; La Madonnina Internat. prize Milan, 1977; Golden Plate award Am. Acad. Achievement, 1977; Nobel prize for medicine and physiology, 1977; citation of esteem St. John's U., 1979; G. von Hevesy medal, 1978; Rosalyn S. Yalow Research and Devel. award established Am. Diabetes Assn., 1978; Banting medal, 1978; Torch of Learning award Am. Friends Hebrew U., 1978; Virchow gold medal Virchow-Pirquet Med. Soc., 1978; Gratum Genus Humanum gold medal World Fedn. Nuclear Medicine or Biology, 1978; Jacobi medallion Asso. Alumni Mt. Sinai Sch. Medicine, 1978; Jubilee medal Coll. of New Rochelle, 1978; VA Exceptional Service award, 1978; Fed. Woman's award, 1961; Harvey lectr., 1966; Am. Gastroenterol. Assn. Meml. lectr., 1972; Joslyn lectr. New Eng. Diabetes Assn., 1972; Franklin I. Harris Meml. lectr., 1973; 1st Hagedorn Meml. lectr. Acta Endocrinologica Congress, 1973; Sarasota Med. award for achievement and excellence, 1979; gold medal Phi Lambda Kappa, 1980; Achievement in Life award Ency. Brit., 1980; Theobald Smith award, 1982; Pres.'s Cabinet award U. Detroit, 1982; John and Samuel Bard award in medicine and sci. Bard Coll., 1982; Disting. Research award Dallas Assn. Retarded Citizens, 1982; numerous others. Fellow N.Y. Acad. Scis. (chmn. biophysics div. 1964-65), Am. Coll. Radiology (asso. in physics), Clin. Soc. N.Y. Diabetes Assn.; mem. Nat. Acad. Scis., Am. Acad. Arts and Scis., Am. Phys. Soc., Radiation Research Soc., Am. Assn. Physicists in Medicine, Biophys. Soc., Soc. Nuclear Medicine, Endocrine Soc. (Koch award 1972, pres. 1978), Am. Physiol. Soc., Phi Beta Kappa, Sigma Xi, Sigma Pi Sigma, Pi Mu Epsilon, Sigma Delta Epsilon. Current Work: Radioimmunoassay. Subspecialties: Neuroendocrinology; Gastroenterology. Office: 130 W Kingsbridge Rd Bronx NY 10468

YAMADA, MASAAKI, physicist; b. Kitami, Japan, Aug. 9, 1942; came to U.S., 1969; s. Tomaji and Hatsue (Mayanagi) Y.; m. JoAnn M. Nojiri, Nov. 6, 1971; children—Masahiro, Hideki. B.S., U. Tokyo, 1966, M.S., 1968; Ph.D. in Physics, U. Ill., 1973. Research assoc. Plasma Physics Lab., Princeton U., N.J., 1973-75, mem. research staff, 1975-78, research physicist, 1978-82, prin. research physicist, 1982—. Co-editor spheromak symposia. Patentee spheromak formations. Mem. Am. Phys. Soc., Japanese Phys. Soc. Current work: Experimental research on magnetic fusion devices, spheromaks, tokamaks, RFP's and stellarator; head S-1 spheromak research. Subspecialties: Fusion; Plasma physics. Home: 6 Larkspur Ln Lawrenceville NJ 08648Office: Plasma Physics Lab Princeton U PO Box 4512 Princeton NJ 08544

YAMADA, TETSUJI, atmospheric scientist; b. Osaka, Japan, May 9, 1942; came to U.S., 1967, naturalized, 1983; s. Kozo and Kamiko (Juen) Y.; m. Sueko Fukumoto, Nov. 1, 1967; children—Sayuri, Tetsuhiro. B.E., Osaka U., 1965, M.E., 1967; Ph.D., Colo. State U., 1971. Research staff Princeton U., 1972-76; meteorologist Argonne Nat. Lab., 1976-81; staff mem. Los Alamos Nat. Lab., 1981—. Contbr. articles to profl. jours. Fulbright grantee, 1967-71. Mem. Am. Meteorol. Soc., Meteorol. Soc. Japan (award 1984), Royal Meteorol. Soc., Sigma Xi. Current work: Development and application of computer models for mesoscale atmospheric turbulent flows; transport/diffusion of air pollutants in complex terrain. Subspecialty: Mesoscale meteorology. Office: Los Alamos Nat Lab PO Box 1663 Los Alamos NM 87545

YAMAGISHI, TOMEJIRO, physicist; b. Kawaguchi, Japan, Jan. 13, 1938; came to U.S., 1976, naturalized, 1982; s. Umekichi and Rieko (Murata) Y.; m. Emiko Amasaki, Nov. 26, 1974; children—Kenichi, Mihoko. B.S., Tohoku U. (Japan), 1962; Ph.D., Osaka U., Japan, 1973. Systems engr. Japan IBM, Tokyo, 1962-64; research assoc. Osaka U., 1965-76; sr. scientist Gen. Atomic Tech. Inc. San Diego, 1976—. Contbr. theoretical papers to profl. jours. Grantee Sakkokai Found. 1969, Ministry Edn. Japan 1973. Mem. Am. Phys. Soc. Current work: Magnetohydrodynamic plasma equilibrium, magnetohydrodynamic and kinetic plasma stability, anamalous plasma transport, study of non linear problems, plasma confinement. Subspecialties: Plasma physics; Nuclear fusion. Office: Gen Atomic Tech Inc PO Box 85608 San Diego CA 92138

YAMAGUCHI, SHOGO, botanist, former educator; b. Gresham, Oreg., Mar. 29, 1916; s. Tokuji and Shina (Watanabe) Y.; m. Elizabeth May Hughes, May 30, 1928; children: Nichola, Matthew, Theodore. Ph.D. in Bot. Scis, UCLA, 1954. Asst. to plant anatomist U. Calif.-Riverside, 1953; herbicide researcher U. Calif.-Davis, 1954-65; assoc. prof. Tuskegee Inst., 1966-81. Author: (with A.S. Crafts) Autoradiography of Plant Materials, 1964. Served to sgt. U.S. Army, 1941-45. Decorated Bronze Star.; Recipient W. Kelly Mosley Environ. award Ala. Coop. Extension Service, Auburn U., 1980; Agrl. Research Service grantee, 1967-71. Democrat. Roman Catholic. Subspecialty: Plant physiology (biology). Home: 1031 Hughes Ln Fallbrook CA 92028

YAMAGUCHI, YUKIO, chemistry research scientist; b. Hiroshima, Japan, Feb. 22, 1941; came to U.S., 1970; s. Tameo and Miyuki (Kodama) Y. B.Engring., Kyushu U., Fukuoka, Japan, 1964, M.Engring., 1966; Ph.D., U. Tex.-Austin, 1978. Research assoc. Kyushu U., 1966-70; postdoctoral fellow U. Tex., 1979-80; postdoctoral fellow U. Calif. and Lawrence Berkeley Lab, Berkeley, 1980-82, sr. research scientist chemistry, 1982—. Contbr. articles to profl. jours. Mem. Am. Chem. Soc., Chem. Soc. Japan. Subspecialties: Physical chemistry; Theoretical chemistry. Office: Univ Calif Dept Chemistry Berkeley CA 94720

YAMAMOTO, RICHARD KUMEO, physics educator; b. Honolulu, June 29, 1935; s. Minoru and Edith Hatsuko (Ogawa) Y.; m. Lily Marie Chin, June 11, 1961; children—Cara-Jean, Lani, Sharon. S.B., MIT, 1957, Ph.D., 1963. Research assoc. MIT, Cambridge, 1963-64, instr. physics, 1964-65, asst. prof., 1965-68, assoc. prof., 1968-75, prof., 1975—. Fellow Am. Phys. Soc.; mem. AAAS. Current work: Weak, electromagnetic and strong interactions at high energy accelerators, electronic and visual detectors. Subspecialty: Particle physics. Office: Room 409 MIT 575 Technology Sq Cambridge MA 02139

YAMANIS, JEAN, chemical engineer; b. Nea Makri, Attica, Greece, May 11, 1941; came to U.S., 1975; s. Michael and Thespina Yamanis; m. Donna Mae Edwards, Mar. 15, 1969; children—Thespina Jeanne, Monica Jeanne. Dipl. Chem. Eng., Nat. Tech. U. Athens, 1964; M.Eng. in Chem. Engring., McMaster U., 1970; Ph.D., U. Windsor, 1975. Research assoc. U. Windsor, Ont., Can., 1970-71, sessional instr., 1974; asst. prof. U. Ky., Lexington, 1975-81, assoc. prof., 1981; sr. research engr. Allied Corp., Morristown, N.J., 1981-85, group leader, 1985—. Contbr. articles to profl. jours. Patentee in field. Coach Morristown United Soccer League, 1984—. Mem. Am. Inst. Chem. Engrs., Am. Chem. Soc., Chem. Inst. Can., Can. Soc. Chem. Engrs., Catalysis Soc. Met. N.Y. (treas.), Catalysis Soc., Am. Chem. Soc. Subspecialties: Chemical engineering; Catalysis chemistry. Office: Allied Corp PO Box 1021 R Morristown NJ 07960

YAMANOUCHI, TAIJI, physicist; b. Tokyo, Aug. 16, 1931; married; 2 children. B.S., Tokyo U., 1953, M.S., 1955; Ph.D. in Physics, U. Rochester, 1960. Research assoc. physics U. Rochester, 1960-65, sr. research assoc., 1965-69; physicist Fermi Nat. Accelerator Lab., 1969-84, asst. dir., 1985—. Recipient Nishina Meml. Prize, 1983. Mem. Am. Phys. Soc. Subspecialty: Particle physics. Office: Fermilab PO Box 500 Batavia IL 60510*

YAN, MAN FEI, material scientist; b. Nam Po, China, Dec. 26, 1948; came to U.S., 1968, naturalized, 1982; s. Wing Lam and Chiu (Chan) Y.; m. Su Su

Goon, Sept. 18, 1977; children—Victor, Leo, Oscar. B.S., MIT, 1970, Sc.D., 1976; M.S., U. Calif.-Berkeley, 1971. Mem. tech. staff AT&T Bell Labs., Murray Hill, N.J., 1976—. Editor: Character of Grain Boundaries, 1983; Additives and Interfaces in Electronic Ceramics, 1983. Patentee in field. Recipient Ross Coffin Purdy award Am. Ceramic Soc., 1980. Current work: Electronic ceramics, capacitors, ferrites, fiber optics, grain boundary phenomena, sintering, grain growth, phosphor. Subspecialties: Ceramics; Electronic materials.

YAN, TUNG-MOW, physicist, educator; b. Keeling, Taiwan, Nov. 27, 1936; s. Chang-Nan and Chih (Chen) Y.; m. Ren-Huei Lu, Sept. 16, 1964; children—Thomas, Anthony. B.S., Nat. Taiwan U., Taipei, 1960; M.S., Nat. Tsing-Hua U., Hsinchu, Taiwan, 1962; Ph.D. in Physics, Harvard U., 1968. Research assoc. Stanford Linear Accelerator Ctr., Stanford U., Calif., 1968-70; asst. prof. physics Cornell U., Ithaca, N.Y., 1970-76, assoc. prof., 1976-81, prof., 1981—; sci. assoc. CERN, Geneva, 1977-78. Contbr. articles to profl. publs. Alfred Sloan fellow, 1974-78. Mem. Am. Phys. Soc. Current work: Quantum field theory and structure of elementary particles. Subspecialties: Particle physics; Theoretical physics. Home: 136 Simsbury Dr Ithaca NY 14850 Office: Newman Lab Cornell U Ithaca NY 14853

YANCEY, ASA GREENWOOD, physician; b. Atlanta, Aug. 19, 1916; s. Arthur H. and Daisy L. (Sherard) Y.; m. Carolyn E. Dunbar, Dec. 28, 1944; children: Arthur H. II, Carolyn L., Caren L., Asa Greenwood. B.S., Morehouse Coll., 1937; M.D., U. Mich., 1941. Diplomate: Am. Bd. Surgery. Intern City Hosp., Cleve., 1941-42; resident Freedmen's Hosp., Washington, 1942-45, U.S. Marine Hosp., Boston, 1945; instr. surgery Meharry Med. Coll., 1946-48; chief surgery VA Hosp., Tuskegee, Ala., 1948-58; practice medicine specializing in surgery, Atlanta, 1958—; med. dir. Grady Meml. Hosp., Atlanta, 1972—; mem. staff Hughes Spalding, St. Joseph, hosps.; asst. prof. surgery Emory U., 1958-72, prof., 1975—, assoc. dean Sch. Medicine, 1972—. Contbr. articles to profl. jours. Mem. Atlanta Bd. Edn., 1967-77; trustee Ga. chpt. Am. Cancer Soc. Served to 1st lt. M.C., AUS, 1942. Fellow ACS, Am. Surg. Assn.; mem. Nat. Med. Assn. (trustee 1960-66, editorial bd. jour. 1964-80), Inst. Medicine of Nat. Acad. Scis. Baptist. Subspecialty: Surgery. Home: 2845 Engle Rd NW Atlanta GA 30318 Office: Grady Meml Hosp Atlanta GA 30303

YANDERS, ARMON FREDERICK, research administrator, researcher; b. Lincoln, Nebr., Apr. 12, 1928; s. Fred Westamer and Neva Beatrice (Pate) Y.; m. Evelyn Louise Gatz, Aug. 1, 1948; children—Mark Frederick, Kent Michael. A.B., Nebr. State Coll., 1948; M.S., U. Nebr., 1950, Ph.D., 1953. Research assoc. Oak Ridge Nat. Lab. and Northwestern U., Evanston, Ill., 1953-54; assoc. geneticist Argonne Nat. Lab., Ill., 1958-69; prof., asst. dean Mich. State U., East Lansing, 1959-69; dean arts and sci. U. Mo., Columbia, 1969-82, dir. Environ. Trace Substances Research Ctr. and Sinclair Comparative Medicine Research Farm, 1983—; pres., chmn. bd. Argonne Univs. Assocs., 1970-77; mem. Mo. Dioxin Adv. Com., Jefferson City, 1984—; mem. adv. com. on environ. hazards VA, Washington, 1985—; bd. dirs. Council Colls. of Arts and Scis., 1980-82. Author: papers in field. Bd. dirs. United Way, Columbia, 1971-75. Served to lt. USN, 1954-58. Recipient Robert W. Martin Acad. Freedom award, AAUP, 1981. Fellow AAAS; mem. Environ. Mutagen Soc., Genetics Soc. Am., Radiation Research Soc., Sigma Xi. Current work: Conducting and administering research on mutagenic, carcinogenic and toxic effects of extremely hazardous chemicals and radiation. Subspecialties: Environmental toxicology; Genetics and genetic engineering (biology). Home: 2405 Ridgefield Rd Columbia MO 65203 Office: Environ Trace Substances Research Ctr and Sinclair Comparative Medicine Research Farm Univ Mo Columbia MO 65203

YANG, CHEN NING, physicist, educator; b. Hefei, Anhwei, China, Sept. 22, 1922; naturalized, 1964; s. Ke Chuan and Meng Hwa Lo; m. Chih Li Tu, Aug. 26, 1950; children—Franklin, Gilbert, Eulee. B.Sc., Nat. S.W. Asso. U., China, 1942; Ph.D., U. Chgo., 1948; D.Sc. (hon.), Princeton U., 1958, Bklyn. Poly. Inst., 1965, U. Wroclaw, Poland, 1974, Gustavus Adolphus Coll., 1975, U. Md., 1979, U. Durham, Eng., 1979. Instr., U. Chgo., 1948-49; mem. Inst. Advanced Study, Princeton U., 1949-55, prof., 1955-66; Albert Einstein prof. SUNY, Stony Brook, 1966—, dir., 1966—. Trustee Rockefeller U., 1970-76, Salk Inst., 1978—, Ben Gurion U., 1980—. Recipient Albert Einstein Commemorative award in sci., 1957; Nobel prize for physics, 1957; Rumford prize, 1980. Mem. Am. Phys. Soc., Nat. Acad. Scis., Brazilian Acad. Scis., Venezuelan Acad. Scis., Royal Spanish Acad. Scis., Am. Philos. Soc., AAAS (bd. dirs. 1975-79), Sigma Xi. . Office: Physics Dept State U NY Stony Brook NY 11794*

YANG, CHUNG SHU, biochemist, educator; b. Beijing, China, Aug. 8, 1941; came to U.S., 1963, naturalized, 1970; s. Su Chuan and Sue Fen (Li) Y.; m. Sue Pai, June 25, 1966; children: Arlene, Jenny. B.S., Nat. Taiwan U., 1962; M.N.S., Cornell U., 1965, Ph.D., 1967. Mem. faculty U. Medicine and Dentistry N.J.-N.J. Med. Sch., 1971—, prof. biochemistry, 1979—; mem. pathology study sect. NIH, 1979; mem. spl. rev. com. (site visit) Nat. Cancer Inst., 1979, 80. Author papers in field. Recipient Faculty Research award Am. Cancer Soc., 1971; Future Leaders award Nutrition Found., 1973; Internat. Union Against Cancer award to visit Cancer Inst. of Chinese Acad. Med. Scis. Peking, 1979; research scholar (China) Nat. Acad. Scis., 1980. Mem. Am. Soc. Biol. Chemists, Soc. Pharmacology and Exptl. Therapeutics, Am. Inst. Nutrition, Am. Assn. Cancer Research. Current Work: Biochemistry of cytochrome P-450 and carcinogen activation, cancer etiology and modification of carcinogenesis. Subspecialties: Biochemistry (medicine); Cancer research (medicine). Office: Dept Biochemistry NJ Med Sch Newark NJ 07103

YANG, HENRY WU-HSIANG, scientist, researcher; b. Hsinchu, Taiwan, June 18, 1947; came to U.S., 1972, naturalized, 1980; s. Liang Kway and Show May (Peng) Y.; m. Claudia T.H. Hsu; children—Stephen, Stephanie. B.S. in Chem. Engring., Nat. Taiwan U., 1970; Ph.D. in Chemistry, Dartmouth Coll., 1976. Research assoc. U. Mass., Amherst, 1976-78, B.F. Goodrich Co., Avon Lake, Ohio, 1978—. Contbr. articles to profl. jours. Served to 2d lt. Chinese Army, 1970-71. Dartmouth fellow, 1972. Mem. Am. Chem. Soc., N.Y. Acad. Scis., Sigma Xi. Current work: Polymer synthesis, characterization and structure-properties relationship; polymer applications in agricultural seed coatings and plant protections against environmental stresses such as water, temperature, insects and emmissions. Subspecialties: Polymer chemistry; Plant physiology (agriculture). Home: 32411 Orchard Park Dr Avon Lake OH 44012 Office: BF Goodrich Chem Co PO Box 122 Avon Lake OH 44012

YANG, JEN TSI, biochemistry educator; b. Shanghai, China, Mar. 18, 1922; came to U.S., 1947; s. Dao-Kai and Ho-Ching (Yu) Y.; m. Yee-Mui Lee, Aug. 8, 1949; children: Janet, Frances. B.S., Nat. Central U., Nanking, China, 1944; Ph.D., Iowa State U., 1952, postdoctoral, 1952-54; postdoctoral, Harvard U., 1954-56. Research chemist Am. Viscose Corp., Marcus Hook, Pa., 1956-59; assoc. prof. Dartmouth Med. Sch., Hanover, N.H., 1959-60; assoc. prof. U. Calif.-San Francisco, 1960-64, prof. biochemistry, 1964—; Vis. prof. Japan Soc. for Promotion of Sci., 1975; Guggenheim fellow, 1959, Commonwealth Fund fellow, 1967. Mem. Am. Chem. Soc., Am. Soc. Biol. Chemists, Biophys. Soc., AAAS. Current Work: Chiroptical properties of biopolymers; conformation of macromolecules; structure-function relationship of proteins. Subspecialty: Biophysical chemistry. Home: 1375 20th Ave San Francisco CA 94122 Office: Dept Biochemistry and Biophysics U Calif San Francisco San Francisco CA 94143

YANG, RALPH TZU-BOW, chemical engineering educator; b. Chung King, China, Sept. 18, 1942; came to U.S., 1965; s. Chen Pei and Wei G. (Gee) Y.; m. Frances Chang, Dec. 23, 1972; children—Michael, Robert. B.S., Nat. Taiwan U., Taipei, 1964; M.S., Yale U., 1968, Ph.D., 1971. Research assoc. NYU, N.Y.C., 1971-72, Argonne Nat. Lab., Ill., 1972-73; scientist Alcoa, Pitts., 1973-74; group leader Brookhaven Nat. Lab., Upton, N.Y., 1974-78, cons., 1979-80; assoc. prof. chem. engring. SUNY-Buffalo, 1978-82, prof., 1982—; cons. Combustion Engring., Wellsville, N.Y., 1979-84, Sundstrand Corp., Rockford, Ill., 1984—. Contbr. articles to profl. jours. Patentee in field. Grantee NSF, 1980-82, 82-85, Dept. Energy, 1980-82, 80-84. Mem. Am. Inst. Chem. Engrs., Am. Chem. Soc., Am. Carbon Soc., Am. Soc. for Engring. Edn., Sigma Xi. Current work: Chemical kinetics, catalysis, chemical engineering, gas separation, coal gasification, carbon, physical chemistry, surface chemistry. Subspecialty: Chemical engineering. Office: Dept Chem Engring SUNY Buffalo NY 14260

YANG, SHANG FA, plant physiology educator, plant physiology researcher; b. Tainan, Taiwan, Nov. 10, 1932; came to U.S., 1959, naturalized, 1971; s. Chian-Zuei and En-Liu (Lu) Y.; m. Eleanor Shou-yuan Liu, Sept. 16, 1964; children—Albert, Bryant. B.S., Nat. Taiwan U., 1956, M.S., 1958; Ph.D., Utah State U., 1962. Research assoc. U. Calif.-Davis, 1962-63, NYU, 1963-64, U. Calif.-San Diego, 1964-66; asst. biochemist U. Calif.-Davis, 1966-69, assoc. biochemist, 1969-74, prof., biochemist, 1974—; vis. prof. U. Konstanz, Germany, 1974, Nat. Taiwan U., Taipei, 1983, U. Cambridge, U.K., 1983; mem. editorial bd. Plant Physiology, 1974—; assoc. editor Jour. Plant Growth Regulation, 1981—. Recipient Campbell award Am. Inst. Biol. Scis., 1969; NSF grantee, 1967—, U.S.-Israel Agrl. Research and Devel. Found. grantee, 1981—; Guggenheim fellow, 1982. Mem. Am. Soc. Plant Physiologists (chmn. western sect. 1982-84), Am. Soc. of Biol. Chemists, Am. Soc. Hort. Sci. Current work: Biosynthesis and action of plant hormones, particularly ethylen; postharvest physiology and biochemistry of fruits and vegetables; plant senesence. Subspecialties: Plant physiology (agriculture); Biochemistry (biology). Home: 1118 Villanova Dr Davis CA 95616 Office: Mann Lab U Calif-Davis Davis CA 95616

YANG, WEN-CHING, chemical engineer; b. Taipei, Taiwan, China, Nov. 11, 1939; came to U.S. 1964, naturalized 1972; s. Ting-Lien and Ho (Lee) Y.; m. Rae Tien, Aug. 24, 1968; children—Evonne R., Peter T. B.S. in Chem. Engring., Nat. Taiwan U., Taipie, 1962; M.S. in Chem. Engring. U. Calif.-Berkeley, 1965; Ph.D. in Chem. Engring., Carnegie-Mellon U., 1968. Sr. engr. Research and Devel. Ctr. Westinghouse Electric Corp., Pitts., 1968-76, fellow engr., 1976—; guest lectr. U. Pitts., 1980, 83; Ph.D. adviser Lehigh U., Bethlehem, Pa., 1981-84. Contbr. articles to profl. jours. and books. Patentee in field. Mem. Am. Chem. Soc., Am. Inst. Chem. Engrs. (program vice chmn 1984-85, program chmn. 1986-87). Current work: Chemical engineering application on energy systems; fluidization and fluid-particles systems. Subspecialties: Chemical engineering; Fuels. Home: 236 Vernon Ave Export PA 15632 Office: Westinghouse Elec Corp Research and Devel Ctr Beulah Rd Pittsburgh PA 15235

YANG, YEE-HONG, electrical engineer, computer scientist; b. Hong Kong, Feb. 29, 1952; came to U.S., 1977; s. Yuan-Yung and Wai-King (Lau) Y.; m. Evelyn Lai-Ngor Hui, May 31, 1975. B.Sc. with honors, U. Hong Kong, 1974; M.Sc., Simon Fraser U., 1977; M.S.E.E., U. Pitts., 1980, Ph.D., 1982. Teaching asst. Simon Fraser U., Burnaby, Vancouver, Can., 1974-77; staff engr. Pattern Recognition Lab., U. Pitts., 1977-80; scientist Mellon Inst. Computer Engring. Ctr., Pitts., 1980—. Contbr. articles to profl. jours. Mem. IEEE, Assn. Computing Machinery, Am. Phys. Soc. Current Work: Image processing, hardware descriptive languages, simulation, language design, very high speed computation and computer architecture. Subspecialties: Computer engineering; Graphics, image processing, and pattern recognition. Office: Mellon Inst Computer Engring Ctr 4616 Henry St Pittsburgh PA 15213

YANOFSKY, CHARLES, educator; b. N.Y.C., Apr. 17, 1925; s. Frank and Jennie (Kopatz) Y.; m. Carol Cohen, June 19, 1949; children—Stephen David, Robert Howard, Martin Fred. B.S., Coll. City N.Y., 1948; M.S., Yale, 1950, Ph.D., 1951, D.Sc. (hon.), 1981; D.Sc. (hon.), U. Chgo., 1980. Research Asst. Yale, 1951-54; asst. prof. microbiology Western Res. U. Med. Sch., 1954-57; mem. faculty Stanford, 1958—, prof. biology, 1961—. Career investigator Am. Heart Assn., 1969—. Served with AUS, 1944-46. Recipient Lederle Med. Faculty award, 1957, Eli Lilly award bacteriology, 1959, U.S. Steel Co. award molecular biology, 1964, Howard Taylor Ricketts award U. Chgo., 1966, Albert and Mary Lasker award, 1971; Townsend Harris medal Coll. City N.Y., 1973; Louisa Gross Horwitz prize in biology and biochemistry Columbia U., 1976; V.D. Mattia award Roche Inst., 1982; medal Genetics Soc. Am., 1983, internat. award Gardiner Found., 1985. Mem. Nat. Acad. Scis. (Selman A. Waksman award in microbiology 1972), Am. Acad. Arts and Scis., Genetics Soc. Am. (pres. 1969), Am. Soc. Biol. Chemists (pres. 1984). Current Work: Regulation of gene expression; evolution of genes, proteins and regulatory regions. Subspecialty: Molecular biology. Home: 725 Mayfield Ave Stanford CA 94305

YAO, JAMES TSU-PING, civil engineering educator; b. Shanghai, China, July 7, 1933; came to U.S., 1953, naturalized, 1969; s. C.C. and M.J. (Wang) Y.; m. Anna Lee, June 14, 1958; children—Tina Lee, Timothy H.J., Shana Lynn. B.S. with honors, U. Ill., 1957, M.S., 1958, Ph.D., 1961; postgrad. Columbia U., 1964-65. Registered profl. engr., N.Mex. Research asst. U. Ill., Urbana, 1957-61; asst. prof. civil engring. U. N.Mex., Albuquerque, 1961-64, assoc. prof., 1965-69, prof., 1969-71; prof. civil engring. Purdue U., West Lafayette, Ind., 1971—, asst. head Sch. Civil Engring., 1983, asst. dean Grad. Sch., 1984, postdoctoral preceptor Columbia U., 1964-65; guest worker Nat. Bur. Standards, summers 1974-75; vis. scholar U. Calif.-Berkeley, 1977-78, UCLA, 1978; vis. prof. Engring. Inst., Mex., 1977; vis. assoc. earthquake engring. Calif. Inst. Tech., 1978. Mem. editorial bd. Solid Mechanics Archives, 1980-85, Internat. Jour. Soil Dynamics and Earthquake Engring., 1980—, Jour. Structural Mechanics, 1981, Jour. Civil Engring. Systems, 1982—, Pitman Adv. Pub. Program/Monographs and Surveys in Structural Engring. and Structural Mechanics, 1982—, Jour. Probabilistic Engineering Mechanics, 1984—. Contbr. articles to profl. jours. Recipient Harold Munson Outstanding Tchr. Civil Engring. award, Ross Judson Buck 1907 Meml. Best Counselor Civil Engring. award Purdue U., 1982. Fellow ASCE (State-of-Art Civil Engring. awards 1973, 83, publ. sec. adminstrv. com. on structural div. safety and reliability 1980-82, chmn. 1982-85; chmn. programs com. engring. mechanics div. 1982-86); mem. Am. Concrete Inst. (chmn. com. 348 on structural safety 1982-86), Am. Soc. for Engring. Edn., Am. Acad. Mechanics (founder mem.), AAUP, Internat. Assn. for Bridge and Structural Engring., Sigma Xi, Chi Epsilon, Phi Tau Phi, Tau Beta Pi, Sigma Tau. Current work: Structural safety and reliability Subspecialties: Structural engineering; Civil engineering. Home: 201 E Lutz Ave West Lafayette IN 47906 Office: Sch Civil Engring Purdue Univ West Lafayette IN 47907

YAO, LUN-SHIN, mechanical engineer, educator; b. Chang King, China, Oct. 25, 1943; came to U.S., 1967; s. Shin-Yung and Ya-Yun (Wu) Y.; m. Susan C.C. Hsu, Dec. 25, 1967 (div. 1976); m. Jeannie J. Chen, Nov. 4, 1978; children—Mike, Dwight, Alice. B.B.E., Cheng-King U., Republic of China, 1966; M.S., U. Tex., 1968; Ph.D., U. Calif.-Berkeley, 1974. Engr. Lockheed Aircraft Co., Marrietta, Ga., 1968-69, Gen. Electric Co. Sunnyvale, Calif., 1974-75; research staff Rand Corp., Santa Monica, Calif., 1975-78; asst. prof. U. Ill., Urbana, 1978-81; prof. mech. engring., Ariz. State U., Tempe, 1981—; cons. U.S. Nuclear Regulatory Commn., Washington, 1977-81, Argonne Nat. lab., Argonne, 1979; research fellow Calif. Inst. Tech., Pasadena, 1978. Contbr. articles to profl. jours. Served to lt. USAF, 1966-67. Grantee U.S. Navy, 1981; Allen Wilson fellow U. of Calif.-Berkeley, 1970. Mem. ASME. Republican. Current work: Conduct research in thermofluid mechanics with moving boundaries; applications of theory to transport phenomena and various subfields in mechanics physics, materials, electronics, others. Subspecialties: Theoretical and applied mechanics; Applied mathematics. Office: Ariz State U Tempe AZ 85287

YAO, SHI CHUNE, mechanical engineering educator; b. Taiwan, Republic of China, Dec. 31, 1946; came to U.S., 1969; m. Tai-Ti; children—Shu-Hone, Shu-Dan. B.S., Nat. Tsing Hua U., Taiwan, 1969; M.S., U. Calif.-Berkeley, 1971, Ph.D., 1974. Registered mech. engr., Pa. Engr., Argonne Nat. Lab., Ill., 1974-77; from asst. to prof. mech. engring. Carnegie-Mellon U., Pitts., 1977—. Editor books. Contbr. articles to profl. jours. Mem. ASME, Combustion Inst. Current work: Two phase heat transfer, two phase combustion; numerical heat transfer. Subspecialties: Mechanical engineering; Nuclear engineering. Office: Dept Mech Engring Carnegie-Mellon Univ Pittsburgh PA 15213

YAO, SHI-KAY, electro-optics engineer; b. Shanghai, China, June 30, 1945; came to U.S., 1968, naturalized, 1981; s. Shu-Chien and U-Wen (Wu) Y.; m. Jin-Wen Liu, Oct. 6, 1973; children—Shu-Ann, Shu-Yeah. B.S.E.E., Nat. Taiwan U., 1967; M.S.E.E., Carnegie-Mellon U., 1969, Ph.D., 1974. Research assoc. Carnegie-Mellon U., Pitts., 1973-74; group leader Harris Corp., Melbourne, Fla., 1974-76; dept. mgr. Rockwell-Electronics Research Ctr., Anaheim, Calif., 1976-80; lab. mgr. TRW Electro-Optics Research Ctr., El Segundo, Calif., 1980-85; optics engring. mgr. TRE Semicondr. Equipment Corp., Woodland Hills, Calif., 1985—. Editor: Optics Technology for Microwave Applications, 1984. Contbr. articles to profl. jours. Patentee in field. Recipient various research grants; Buhl fellow, 1971-72. Fellow Inst. for Advancement Profl. Engring.; mem. IEEE, Quantum Electronics Soc. of IEEE (chmn. Los Angeles chpt. 1984—), Optical Soc. Am., Soc. Photo-optical Instrument Engrs. Current work: Acousto-optics and waveguide optics devices and signal processing systems for communication, microwave signal processing and semiconductor photolithography. Subspecialties: Optical signal processing; Fiber optics. Home: 4071 Towhee Dr Calabasas CA 91302 Office: TRE Semicondr Equipment Corp Woodland Hills CA 91367

YAP, WILLIAM TAN, research chemist; b. Amoy, Fookien, China, Aug. 10, 1934; came to U.S., 1953; s. Lian Du and So Choon (Tan) Y.; m. Lung Wen Chiao, May 30, 1969; children—Elisabeth, Priscilla. B.S. in Chem. Engring., MIT, 1956, M.S. in Nuclear Engring., 1958, Ph.D. in Phys. Chemistry, 1964. Research assoc. MIT, 1964; research chemist Hercules Inc., Wilmington, Del., 1964-68; vis. assoc. NIH, 1968-71; research chemist Nat. Bur. of Standards, Gaithersburg, Md., 1972—. Contbr. articles to profl. jours. Current work: Macromolecular solutions, charge transport at polymer coated electrode; electroanalytical chemistry of organic compounds. Subspecialties: Physical chemistry; Analytical chemistry. Home: 6204 Mori St McLean VA 22101 Office: Nat Bur of Standards Gaithersburg MD 20899

YARDLEY, JAMES THOMAS, research scientist; b. Taft, Calif., May 15, 1942; s. James Thomas and Irene (Blackledge) Y.; m. Serena Savage, Sept. 6, 1966 (dec. Dec. 1971); m. Anne Bagnall, Jan. 2, 1976; children—William Blackledge, Margaret Bagnall, Jonathan Turner. B.S., Rice U., 1964; Ph.D., U. Calif.-Berkeley, 1967. Asst. prof. U. Ill., Urbana, 1967-73, assoc. prof., 1973-77; Research scientist Allied Corp. Research, Morristown, N.J., 1977-81, research mgr., 1981-84, assoc. dir., 1984—. Author: Introduction to Molecular Energy Transfer, 1978. Current work: Molecular energy transfer, photochemistry. Subspecialties: Physical chemistry; Photochemistry. Home: 40 Macculloch Ave Morristown NJ 07960 Office: Allied Corp Box 1021 R Morristown NJ 07960

YARDLEY, JOHN FINLEY, aerospace engineer; b. St. Louis, Feb. 1, 1925; s. Finley Abna and Johnnie (Patterson) Y.; m. Phyllis Steele, July 25, 1946; children—Kathryn, Robert, Mary, Elizabeth, Susan. B.S., Iowa State Coll., 1944; M.S., Washington U., St. Louis, 1950. Structral and aero. engr. McDonnell Aircraft Corp., St. Louis, 1946-55, chief strength engr., 1956-57; project engr. Mercury spacecraft design, 1958-60; launch ops. mgr. Mercury and Gemini spacecraft, Cape Canaveral, Fla., 1960-64, Gemini tech. dir., 1964-67; v.p., dep. gen. mgr. Eastern div. McDonnell Douglas Astronautics, 1968-72, v.p., gen. mgr., 1973-74, pres., 1981—; asso. adminstr. for manned space flight NASA, Washington, 1974-81. Served to ensign USNR, 1943-46. Recipient Achievement award St. Louis sect. Inst. Aerospace Scis., 1961; John J. Montgomery award, 1963; Pub. Service award NASA, 1963, 66; Engr. of yr. NASA, 1982; profl. achievement citation Iowa State Coll., 1970; Spirit of St. Louis medal, 1973; Alumni citation Washington U., 1975; Disting. Achievement citation Iowa State U., 1976; Presdl. citation as meritorious exec. Sr. Exec. Service, 1980; NASA Disting. Service medal, 1981; Goddard Meml. trophy, 1983; Achievement award, Washington U. Engring. Alumni, 1983. Fellow AIAA (Goddard award 1982), Am. Astronautical Soc. (Space Flight award 1978); mem. Nat. Acad. Engring., Tau Beta Pi, Phi Kappa Phi, Phi Eta Sigma, Phi Mu Epsilon. Presbyterian. Subspecialty: Aerospace engineering and technology. Office: McDonnell Douglas Astronautics Office of Pres PO Box 516 Saint Louis MO 63166*

YARMUSH, MARTIN LEON, chemical engineer; b. Bklyn., Oct. 8, 1952; s. Rubin and Rosalyn (Mann) Y.; m. Deborah Rachel Weisfogel, Apr. 2, 1978; children—Rubin Samuel, Gabriel Adam. B.A., Yeshiva U., 1975; Ph.D., Rockefeller U., 1979; M.D., Yale U., 1984; postgrad. MIT, 1982-83. Research chemist NIH, Bethesda, Md., 1978-79; sr. lectr. biology dept. So. Conn. State U., New Haven, 1980-81; adj. asst. prof. dept. pathobiology U. Pa., Phila., 1980—; vis. scientist MIT, Cambridge, 1983-84, prin. research assoc. dept. chem. engring., 1984—; cons. Evreka, Inc., Bergenfield, N.J., 1983—, Sepracor, Inc., Princeton, N.J., 1985. Mem. Am. Chem. Soc., Am. Assn. Immunologists, Am. Soc. for Artificial Internal Organs, AMA, Sigma Xi. Current work: Applied immunology, biotechnology and artificial internal organs. Subspecialties: Biomedical engineering; Biophysical chemistry. Home: 35 Cheryl Dr Sharon MA 02067 Office: MIT Dept Chem Engring 77 Massachusetts Ave Room 66-425 Cambridge MA 02139

YARYMOVYCH, MICHAEL IHOR, aerospace engineer; b. Bialystok, Poland, Oct. 13, 1933; came to U.S. 1951, naturalized, 1956; s. Nicholas Joseph and Olga (Kruckowy) Y.; m. Roxolana Abramiuk, Nov. 21, 1959; children—Tatiana M., Nicholas A. B.S. in Aero. Engring., NYU, 1955; M.S., Columbia U., 1956, Ph.D. in Engring. Mechanics, 1960. Dep. asst. sect. research and devel. U.S. Air Force, Washington, 1962-70, chief scientist, 1973-75; dir. adv. group for aerospace research and devel. NATO, Paris, 1970-73; asst. adminstr. field ops. U.S. Energy Research and Devel. Adminstrn., Washington, 1975-77; v.p. engring. aerospace Rockwell Internat., El Segundo, Calif., 1977-81, v.p. advanced systems devel., 1981—; dir. Inst. for Large Scale Programs, Austin, Tex.; chief scientist Air Force Assn., Washington, 1983-84; advisor Calif. State U.-Long Beach, 1982-83. Contbr. articles to profl. jours. Recipient Exceptional Civilian Service award U.S. Air Force, 1968, 73, 75; Disting. Service award Energy Research and Devel. Adminstrn., 1977. Fellow AIAA (pres. 1982-83); mem. Internat. Acad. Astronautics, Am. Astronautical Soc., AAAS, Nat. Mgmt. Assn., Sigma Xi, Tau Beta Pi. Current work: Conceptual engineering and operations analysis of space systems with particular interest in manned space flight, space studies and strategic defense. Subspecialties: Aeronautical engineering; Aerospace engineering and technology. Office: Rockwell Internat 2230 E Imperial Hwy El Segundo CA 90245

YASUDA, NAOKI, endocrinologist, medical educator; b. Tokyo, Mar. 12, 1945; came to U.S., 1972; m. Yuko Hoshino, May 1, 1971; children: Hajime, Makiko, Tsutomu. M.D., Tokyo Med. and Dental U., 1969. Intern Mercy Hosp. and Med. Ctr., Chgo., 1972-73; resident in medicine Toranomon Hosp., Tokyo, 1970-72; fellow in endocrinology Oreg. Health Scis. U., Portland, 1973-76, asst. prof. medicine, 1976-82, assoc. prof., 1982—. Tartar Research fellow Med. Research Found. Oreg., Portland, 1980; NIH grantee, 1982. Mem. Am. Endocrine Soc., Am. Fedn. Clin. Research, Western Soc. Clin. Research, N.Y. Acad. Sci., AAAS, Internat. Soc. Neuroendocrinology, AMA. Current Work: Neuroendocrine mechanism regulating AC TH secretion. Subspecialty: Neuroendocrinology. Home: 2634 SW Boundary St Portland OR 97201 Office: Oreg Health Scis U Endocrinology Div 3181 SW Sam Jackson Park Rd Portland OR 97201

YATANI, ATSUKO, physiology educator, researcher; b. Kagoshima, Japan, Mar. 29, 1947; came to U.S., 1980; d. Susumu and Masako Yatani. B.S., Kyushu U., Fukuoka, Japan, 1969, Ph.D., 1978. Research asst. prof. Kyushu U., 1972-80, asst. prof., 1982-83; research asst. prof. physiology U. Tex. Med. Br., Galveston, 1980-82, asst. prof., 1983—; counselor Physiology Soc., Japan, 1978—. Contbr. articles to profl. jours. Current work: Cariac electrophysiology (Ca channel current and Na channel current which are closely related to cariac arhythmia). Subspecialty: Physiological psychology. Home: 300 Strand Apt 200 Galveston TX 77550 Office: Physiology and Biophysics Dept U Tex Med Branch Galveston TX 77550

YATES, GEORGE THOMAS, mechanical engineer, researcher; b. Youngstown, Ohio, Jan. 28, 1949; s. Horace Thomas and Verna (Hughes) Y. B.S., Purdue U., 1971; M.S., Calif. Inst. Tech., 1972, Ph.D., 1976. Research fellow Calif. Inst. Tech., Pasadena, 1976-78, lectr., 1980-82, sr. research fellow, 1978—. Contbr. articles to profl. jours. Mem. ASME, Calif. Inst. Tech. Ice Hockey Club (pres. 1977—), So. Calif. Collegiate Hockey Assn. (treas. 1984—), Sigma Xi. Current work: Unsteady fluid dynamics; slender-body theory applied to vehicle dynamics and propulsion; mechanics and physiology of aquatic and aerial animal locomotion; muco-ciliary transport; free surface flows (water waves). Subspecialties: Fluid mechanics; Biomedical engineering. Home: 3831 Blanche St Pasadena CA 91107 Office: Engring Sci Dept 104-44 Calif Inst Tech Pasadena CA 91125

YATES, JOHN HARRY, programmer analyst; systems manager, research chemist, educator; b. Atlantic City, N.J., Oct. 12, 1948; s. Charles S. and Lillian I. (Sears) Y. B.S., Case Western Res. U., 1970; M.S. in X-Ray Crystallography, Ohio State U., 1973, Ph.D. in Theoretical Chemistry, 1976. Research assoc. dept. crystallography U. Pitts., 1977-79, research asst. prof. chemistry and crystallography, 1982-84; dir. computing facility dept. chemistry U. Pa.,1985—; research assoc. dept. chemistry and chem. engring. Stevens Inst. Tech., Hoboken, N.J., 1980-82. Contbr. articles to profl. jours. Mem. Am. Chem. Soc., Am. Inst. Physics, Am. Crystallographic Assn., AAAS, Am. Phys. Soc. Current Work: Accurate molecular structure determination using state-of-the-art methods, both theoretical and crystallographic, with extensive use of computers; fundamental research in theoretical chemistry and x-ray crystallography. Subspecialties: Theoretical chemistry; X-ray crystallography.

Home: 1600 Garrett Rd C-108 Upper Darby PA 19082 Office: Dept Chemistry U Pa Philadelphia PA 19104

YATES, KEITH, chemistry educator; b. Preston, Eng., Oct. 22, 1928; came to Can., 1948, naturalized, 1959; s. Harold and Elizabeth Ann (Wilson) Y.; m. Norma June Charter, Aug. 21, 1953; children—Alison, Robyn, Nicola. B.A., U. B.C., 1956, M.Sc., 1957, Ph.D., 1959; D.Phil., Oxford U., Eng., 1961. Asst. prof. U. Toronto, Ont., Can., 1961-64, assoc. prof., 1964-68, prof. chemistry, 1968—, chmn. dept., 1974-85. Author: Hückel Molecular Orbital Theory, 1977. Contbr. articles to sci. jours. Served with Royal Navy, 1946-48. Fellow Royal Soc. Can., Chem. Inst. Can. (Syntex award 1948). Current work: Mechanistic photochemistry. Subspecialty: Theoretical chemistry. Office: Dept Chemistry U Toronto Toronto ON M5S 1A1 Canada

YATES, PETER, chemistry educator; b. Wanstead, Eng., Aug. 26, 1924; s. Harold Andrew and Kathryn (Yexley) Y.; m. Mary Ann Palmer, Sept. 9, 1950; 1 son, John Anthony; stepchildren—William Palmer Franklin, Thomas Jay Franklin. B.Sc., U. London, Eng., 1946; M.Sc., Dalhousie U., 1948; Ph.D., Yale U., 1951. Postdoctoral fellow Harvard U., 1950-51, mem. faculty, 1952-60; instr. Yale U., 1951-52, vis. prof., 1966; prof. chemistry U. Toronto, Ont., Can., 1960—; vis. prof. Princeton U., 1977. Fellow Royal Soc. Can., Chem. Inst. Can. (Merck, Sharp & Dohme lectr. 1963; medalist 1984); mem. Am. Chem. Soc., Royal Soc. Chemistry. Research and publs. on structure, synthesis and reactions of natural products, photochem. products, heterocyclic compounds, and aliphatic diazo compounds. Current work: Synthesis of sesquiterpenes, alkaloids, steroids, antibiotics, and mutagenic polyenes; new organic synthetic methods. Subspecialties: Photochemistry; Synthetic chemistry. Office: U Toronto Dept Chemistry Toronto ON M5S 1A1 Canada

YAZULLA, STEPHEN, neuroscientist, educator; b. Jersey City, Sept. 3, 1945; s. Stephen and Elsie Alvina (Smith) Y.; m. Margarett Ann Stanley; children: Lisa, Debra, stepchildren: Caroline, Marie. B.S., U. Scranton, Pa., 1967; M.A., U. Del., 1969, Ph.D., 1971. Asst. prof. biology SUNY-Stony Brook, 1974-79, assoc. prof. neurobiology, 1979—. Contbr. articles in field to profl. jours. NASA fellow, 1967-70; NIH fellow, 1972, 73-74; NIH grantee, 1976-79, 1979—. Mem. AAAS, Assn. Research in Vision and Ophthalmology, Soc. Neuroscience, Internat. Soc. Eye Research, Sigma Xi. Current Work: Vertebrate retina, synaptic transmission, electrophysiology, electron microscopical autoradiography and immunohistochemistry, neurochemistry. Subspecialties: Neurobiology; Neurophysiology. Office: Dept Neurobiology and Behavior SUNY Stony Brook NY 11794

YEACK-SCRANTON, CELIA ELIZABETH, applied physicist, researcher; b. Toledo, Jan. 23, 1952; d. William Robert and Dorothy Elizabeth (Davison) Yeack; m. Robert Alan Scranton, Apr. 25, 1981. B.S. in Physics, Washington U., St. Louis, 1974; Ph.D., Stanford U., 1980. Summer student Xerox Palo Alto Research, Calif., 1973; mem. research staff IBM Corp., Yorktown Heights, N.Y., 1979-83, mgr. recording transducers, 1983—. Contbr. articles to Jour. Applied Physics, IBM Tech. Disclosure Bull. Bd. dirs. Twin Lakes Water Works, South Salem, N.Y., 1984—. Recipient Outstanding Innovation award IBM Corp., 1983, 1st Invention Plateau award, 1984, Invention Achievement award, 1984. Mem. Am. Phys. Soc., IEEE (3M steering com. 1985—), Sigma Xi. Current work: Non-destructive testing, particularly acoustic-related; magnetic recording novel device design. Subspecialties: Non-destructive testing; Device design for magnetic recording. Office: IBM Corp PO Box 218 Yorktown Heights NY 10598

YEAGER, ERNEST BILL, chemistry educator, administrator, consultant; b. Orange, N.J., Sept. 26, 1924; s. Ernest F. and Olga S. (Wittwer) Y.; B.A. summa cum laude Montclair State Coll., 1945, hon. degree, 1983; M.S. in Chemistry, Case Western Res. U., 1946, Ph.D. in Phys. Chemistry, 1948. Teaching asst. Western Res. U., Cleve., 1945-47, Coffin fellow, 1947-48, instr. chemistry, 1948-51, asst. prof., 1951-53, assoc. prof., 1953-58, prof., 1958—, acting chmn. chemistry dept., 1964-65, chmn. 1969-72, chmn. faculty senate, 1972-73, dir. Case Ctr. for Electrochem. Scis., 1976—; vis. prof. chemistry U. Southampton, Eng., 1968; mem. com. on undersea warfare NRC, 1959-73, rep. mem., 1969-73; mem. Commn. on Electrochemistry, Internat. Union Pure and Applied Chemistry, 1972-76; mem. tech. power panel Advanced Research Project Agy., 1972-75; mem. vis. com. Brookhaven Nat. Lab., 1978-81; mem. vis. com. chemistry Montclair State Coll., 1978; mem. adv. com. on Soviet and Eastern Europe exchange program NRC, 1978-85; U.S. coordinator U.S.-Argentina Workshop in Electrocatalysis, 1978; advisor to electrolytic tech. adv. com. Dept. Energy, 1978-81; mem. com. on battery materials tech., nat. materials adv. bd. NRC, 1979-81, mem. com. on fuel cells for vehicle application, 1979-81; mem. advanced fuel cell working group U.S. Dept. Energy, 1984—; mem. rev. com. for chem. tech. div. Argonne Nat. Lab., Ill., 1984—; cons. Union Carbide Corp., Gen. Motors Corp. Editor: Trans. Symposium on Electrode Processes, 1961; (with others) Electrode Processes, 1966; Techniques of Electrochemistry, Vols. 1-3, 1972, 73, 77; Proc. of 3d Symposium on Electrode Processes, 1980; Comprehensive Treatise on Electrochemistry, 10 vols., 1980-84; Electrochemistry in Industry: New Directions, 1982; sect. editor Electrochem. Physics, Electrochimica Acta, 1972-76. Recipient Tech. award Cleve. Tech. Socs. Council, 1954, ann. award Chem. Profession Cleve., 1959, alumni citation Montclair State Coll., 1968, Case Western Res. U., 1968, commendation U.S. Navy, 1972, Disting. Service award Cleve. Tech. Socs., 1982; medal for Disting. Achievement, Western Res. Coll., 1982. Fellow Acoustical Soc. Am. (v.p. 1967-68, Biennial award 1956); mem. Electrochem. Soc. (hon.; v.p. 1962-65, pres. 1965, Heise award Cleve. sect. 1974, Acheson medal 1980), Internat. Soc. Electrochemistry (v.p. 1967-68, pres. 1969-71), Am. Chem. Soc. (Morley award Cleve. sect. 1981), Soc. Applied Spectroscopy, Sigma Xi. Presbyterian. Current work: Electrocatalysis; electrode kinetics; physical acoustics applied to electrolytic solutions. Subspecialties: Physical chemistry; Surface chemistry. Home: 2051 Lee Blvd East Cleveland OH 44112 Office: Chemistry Dept Case Western Reserve Univ Cleveland OH 44106

YEEND, WARREN ERNEST, geologist; b. Colfax, Wash., May 14, 1936; s. Kenneth Edward Yeend and Frances (Lynch) Benner; m. Nancy Eloise Neal, June 6, 1964 (div. Dec. 1980); 1 dau., Erica. B.S. in Geology, Wash. State U., 1948; M.S., U. Colo., 1961; Ph.D., U. Wis., 1965. Geologist, U.S. Geol. Survey, Denver, 1965-66, Menlo Park, Calif., 1967—. Contbr. articles to profl. jours. Recipient Outstanding Teaching award U. Wis., 1964; Spl. Achievement award U.S. Geol. Survey, 1975, 80. Mem. Geol. Soc. Am., Am. Quaternary Assn., History of Earth Sci. Soc. Current work: Geology of placer deposits in Alaska; Quarternary geology in Alaska and California. Subspecialties: Geology; Arctic studies. Office: US Geol Survey 345 Middlefield Rd Menlo Park CA 94025

YEGIAN, MISHAC K., civil engineering educator, consultant; b. Beirut, May 3, 1947; came to U.S. 1971, naturalized 1983; s. Kevork and Sara (Govgasian) Y.; m. Karen Brehm, Aug. 12, 1984. B.S.C.E., Am. U. Beirut, 1971; M.S.C.E., U. Tex., 1973; Ph.D., MIT, 1976. Registered profl. engr., Mass. Assoc. prof. civil engring. Northeastern U., Boston, 1976—, chmn. dept., 1983—; cons. Weston Geophys. Co., Westboro, Mass., 1982—, Metcalf & Eddy, Boston, 1982—. Contbr. articles to tech. jours. Mem. ASCE, Boston Soc. Civil Engrs., Earthquake Engring. Research Inst., Internat. Soc. Soil Mechanics, Sigma Xi. Current work: Soil dynamics, soil mechanics, earthquake engineering, risk analysis. Subspecialty: Civil engineering. Office: Civil Engring Dept Northeastern Univ 360 Huntington Ave Boston MA 02115

YEH, BILLY KUO-JIUN, cardiologist, pharmacologist; b. Foochow, China, Aug. 28, 1937; came to U.S., 1962, naturalized, 1973; s. Shin-Hwa and Que-Lu (Mao) Y.; m. Lydia Lo-Pi Ou, Aug. 21, 1965; children: Elizabeth Shih-I, Brian Shih-Heng, William Shih-Tseng. M.D., Nat. Taiwan U., 1961; M.S., U. Okla., 1963; Ph.D., Columbia U., 1967. Diplomate: Am. Bd. Internal Medicine, Sub-Bd. Cardiovascular Disease. Intern Nat. Taiwan U., Taipei, 1960-61; resident Emory U. Affiliated Hosps., Atlanta, 1967-69; sect. chief clin. pharmacology, also chief hypertension clinic, attending cardiologist Mt. Sinai Med. Center of Greater Miami, 1969-71; acting co-dir. Heart Sta., Jackson Meml. Hosp., Miami, 1972-73; assoc. dir. div. clin. investigation Miami Heart Inst., 1973-76; asst. prof. medicine U. Miami Sch. Medicine, 1970-76, assoc. clin. prof. medicine, 1976—, practice medicine specializing in internal medicine and cardiology, Coral Gables, Fla., 1976—; cons. clin. cardiologist and pharmacologist to several maj. med. centers and pharm. firms. Contbr. articles to profl. publs.; mem. editorial bd.: Miami Medicine, 1978—. Fellow ACP, Am. Coll. Cardiology; mem. Am. Heart Assn. (fellow council on clin. cardiology, past mem. bd. dirs. Miami chpt.), Am. Physiol. Soc., Am. Soc. Pharmacology and Exptl. Therapeutics, Fla. Heart Assn. (profl. edn. com.). Presbyterian. Current Work: Mechanisms and therapies of cardiac arrhythmias; ambulatory monitor of blood pressures; efficacy and safety of new antihypertensive and antiarrhythmic drugs. Subspecialties: Cardiology; Pharmacology. Home: 7110 SW 148 Terr Miami FL 33158 Office: 315 Palermo Ave Coral Gables FL 33134

YEH, EDWARD HSIN-YANG, physicist, educator; b. Hsin-chu, Republic of China, Jan. 1, 1930; came to U.S., 1958; s. Sun-teh and Siang-hua (Tsai) Y.; m. Gretchen C. Y. Lo, June 17, 1967; children—Henry, Daniel. B.S., Nat. Taiwan U., 1952; M.S., Kyushu U., Fukuoka, Japan, 1957; Ph.D., U. N.C., 1960. Research physicist Nat. Acad. Scis., NRC, Washington, 1960-61; sr. scientist Edgerton Germeshausen & Grier, Inc., Boston, 1961-63; research scholar Dublin Inst. Advanced Studies, Ireland, 1963-66; prof. physics and astronomy Moorehead State U., Minn., 1966—; physicist Naval Weapons Ctr., China Lake, Calif., 1984—. Contbr. articles to sci. publs.; reviewer math. articles. Mem. Am. Phys. Soc., Sigma Xi, Sigma Pi Sigma. Current work: Quantum electrodynamics; electromagnetic waves scattering. Subspecialties: Theoretical physics; Nuclear physics. Home: 628 S Gemstone St Ridgecrest CA 93555 Office: Code 3313 Naval Weapons Ctr China Lake CA 93555

YEH, HORNG-CHIN GENE, polymer chemist; b. Chia-Yi, Taiwan, May 10, 1948; s. Tien Y. and Shin Kai (Lee) Y.; m. Anna S. Tsai, June 19, 1977; 1 child, Joanna. B.S., Cheng-Kung U., 1970; M.A., Wake Forest U., 1976; Ph.D., U. Wash., 1980. Research chemist Phillips Petroleum Co., Bartlesville, Okla., 1980—. Recipient Best Paper award, Am. Chem. Soc. Rubber Div., 1984. Mem. Am. Chem. Soc. Current work: Polymer synthesis and characterization; Ziegler-Natta polymerization, anionic polymerization and water soluble polymers. Subspecialty: Polymer chemistry. Home: 319 SE Fenway Ave Bartlesville OK 74006 Office: Phillips Petroleum Co 251 CPL Bartlesville OK 74004

YEH, JAMES TEHCHENG, chemical engineer, research scientist; b. Fuzhou, China, Apr. 19, 1933; came to U.S. 1958, naturalized 1973; s. Shusheng and Huihua (Wu) Yeh; m. Nov. 18, 1967; 1 child, Theresa. B.S., Cheng Kung U., 1956; M.S., U. Detroit, 1961; Ph.D., Stevens Inst. Tech., 1970. Asst. prof. math., chemistry Philander Smith Coll., Little Rock, 1963-66; chem. engr. Procedyne Corp., New Brunswick, N.J., 1968-69, U.S. Dept. Energy, Pitts., 1974—; sr. chem. engr. Princeton Aqua Sci., New Brunswick, 1970-74; dir. modeling studies Environ. Assessment Council, Inc., New Brunswick, 1973-74; staff systems engr. Singer Simulation, Silver Spring, Md., 1974. Contbr. articles to profl. jours. Patentee in field. Treas., bd. dirs. Organ. Chinese Ams. Chinese Sch. Pitts., 1983—. Mem. Am. Inst. Chem. Engrs. (sessions chmn. Fluegas Cleanup nat. mtgs. 1985), Air Pollution Control Assn. (lectr. continuing educ. ann. mtgs. 1983—), Am. Chem. Soc., Instrument Soc. Am. Current work: Coal combustion fluegas cleanup process research and development, solid-gas reaction kinetics, process simulation. Subspecialties: Environmental engineering; Combustion processes. Home: 5705 Glen Hill Dr Bethel Park PA 15102

YEH, KEMING WAYNE, microelectronics technologist, technology manager; b. Honan, China, Mar. 3, 1947; s. Huai-Tsen and Yu (Chao) Y. B.S., Cheng-Kung U., Tainan, Taiwan, 1968; M.S., UCLA, 1972; Ph.D., U. Calif.-Berkeley, 1976. Research asst. dept. elec. engring. UCLA, 1969-72, U. Calif.-Berkeley, 1972-76; mgr. tech. Xerox Corp., El Segundo Calif., 1976-82; dir. tech. Commodore Internat., Ltd., West Chester, Pa., 1982—; participant profl. workshops and meetings. Patentee in field of integrated circuit device and fabrication tech.; contbr. papers on microchip tech. and home computer applications to profl. publs. Recipient Pres.'s Achievement award Xerox Corp., 1979. Mem. IEEE, Sigma Xi. Current work: Very large scale integrated circuits—device and fabrication technology, design and manufacturing automation technology; microcomputer technology applications. Subspecialties: Microchip technology (engineering); Integrated circuits. Home: 319 Headhouse Ct Wayne PA 19087 Office: Commodore Internat Inc 1200 Wilson Dr West Chester PA 19380

YEH, KUNG CHIE, electrical engineering educator, radio propagation researcher, consultant; b. Hangchow, China, Aug. 4, 1930; came to U.S. 1950; s. S.J. and A. (Hsu) H.; m. Margaret M. Yung, Sept. 14, 1957; children—Joanna, Lisa, David, Richard. B.S., U. Ill., 1953; M.S., Stanford U., 1954, Ph.D., 1958. Teaching asst. Stanford U., Calif., 1953-54, research asst., 1954-58; research assoc. U. Ill., Urbana, 1958-59, asst. prof. elec. engring., 1959-62, assoc. prof. 1962-67, prof., 1967—; head, vis. prof. Nat. Sun Yat-sen U., Kaohsiung, Taiwan, 1981-82; vis. scientist Max-Panck Inst. Aeronomy, Katlenburgh-Lindau, Fed. Republic Germany, 1979; invited lectr. Space Research Ctr. Polish Acad. Scis., Warsaw, Poland, 1977; U.S. mem. electromagnetic wave propagation panel adv. group for aerospace research and devel. NATO, 1984-86; assoc. Ctr. for Advanced Study, U. Ill., 1973-74; vice chmn. Commn. G, Internat. Union Radio Sci., 1981-84, chmn., 1985—, mem. U.S. nat. com., Commn. H. Author: Theory of Ionopheric Waves, 1972. Assoc. editor Radio Sci., 1979-81, editor, 1983-86; guest editor spl. issue Radio Sci., 1980. Grantee NSF, NASA, Army Research Office, Air Force Geophysics Lab. Fellow IEEE; mem. Am. Geophys. Union, Am. Phys. Soc., Am. Meteorol. Soc. Current work: Wave propagation in random media, radio beacon studies of the ionophere, propagation of acoustic-gravity waves. Subspecialties: Remote sensing (geoscience); Satellite studies. Home: 4 Regent Ct Champaign IL 61820 Office: Univ Ill 1406 W Green St Urbana IL 61801

YEH, YEA-CHUAN MILTON, electronic engineer; b. Szu-Chuan, China, Apr. 16, 1943; came to U.S., 1967, naturalized, 1977; s. Sing-Min and Dah-Chwen (Wang) Y.; m. Grace Ching-Hsia Shen, June 7, 1969; children—Caroline, Christopher. B.S.E.E., Nat. Taiwan U., 1965; M.S., UCLA, 1969, Ph.D., 1973. Head Radio Multiplex Relay Sta., Taiwan, 1965-66; asst. instr. Nat. Taiwan U., 1966-67; teaching assoc. UCLA, 1967-72; mem. tech. staff Jet Propulsion Lab., Pasadena, Calif., 1972-82; dir. adv. research Applied Solar Energy Corp., Industry, Calif., 1982—; pres. MYK Tech. Inc., Industry, 1983—. Contbr. articles to profl. jours. Patentee method of fabricating schottky barrier solar cell. Recipient cert. of recognition NASA, 1976, 77, 81, 82; UCLA disting. fellow, 1969-70. Mem. IEEE, Internat. Solar Energy Soc., Sigma Xi. Current work: Solar cells and electronic devices made of III-V compounds. Subspecialties: Solar energy; Semiconductors.

YELON, WILLIAM B., physics educator; b. Bklyn., Aug. 23, 1944; s. Martin and Fanny (Salzman) Y.; m. Harriet Gale Most, July 16, 1978; 1 child, Sasha Max; children by previous marriage—Joshua, Rachel. Staff scientist Nat. Bur. Standards, Washington, summers 1960-66; postdoctoral researcher Brookhaven Nat. Lab., Upton, N.Y., 1970-72; staff physicist Inst. Lave Langevin, Grenoble, France, 1972-75; mem. faculty U. Mo., Columbia, 1975—, now prof. physics, group leader neutron scattering, cons. Gen. Motors Corp., Warren, Mich., 1977—, McDonnell Douglas Corp., St. Louis, 1981—. Contbr. chpts. to books, numerous sci. articles to profl. jours. Grantee NSF, Dept. Energy, NATO, others. Mem. Am. Phys. Soc., Am. Crystallographic Soc., Neutron Diffraction Commn., Internat. Union Crystallographers. Current work: Neutron and gamma ray scattering from condensed matter; electron density studies; magnetic structures; powder diffraction; other experimental methods in nuclear condensed matter science. Subspecialties: Condensed matter physics; Crystallography. Home: 1309 Overhill Ct Columbia MO 65203 Office: Univ Missouri Reactor Research Park Columbia MO 65211

YEN, WILLIAM MAO-SHUNG, physics educator, consultant; b. Nanking, China, Apr. 5, 1935; came to U.S. 1952; s. Wanli and Jane (Jing) Y.; m. Laurel Frances Curtis, Aug. 18, 1978; 1 child, Jan Lushan Bess. B.S., U. Redlands, 1956; Ph.D., Washington U., St. Louis, 1962; prof. honorario U. St. Antonio Abad De Cusco, Peru, 1982. Research assoc. Stanford U., Calif., 1962-65; asst. prof. physics U. Wis., Madison, 1965-68, assoc. prof., 1968-72, prof., 1972—; cons. Varian Assocs., Palo Alto, Calif., 1963-65, Argonne Nat. lab., Ill., 1977-81, Lawrence Livermore Lab., Calif., 1975—. Co-editor: Laser Spectroscopy of Solids, 1981. Contbr. numerous articles to profl. jours. Recipient Humboldt prize, 1984; fellow Washington U., 1961, J.S. Guggenheim Found., 1979. Fellow Am. Phys. Soc., Am. Optical Soc., AAAS; mem. Electrochem. Soc., Laser Inst. Am. Current work: Application of lasers to the study of solids, free electron laser applications. Subspecialties: Condensed matter physics; Laser spectroscopy. Home: 500 County Trunk M Middleton WI 53562 Office: Dept Physics Univ Wis 1150 University Ave Madison WI 53706

YENSEN, RICHARD, psychologist, computer cons.; b. Washington, Aug. 28, 1949; s. Elwood and Maria Amalia (Perez-Venero) Y.; m. Joyce Marie Compton, May 1972; 1 son, John Alexander. B.A., U. Calif.-Irvine, 1971, B.A. in Social Ecology, 1972, M.A. in Social Scis, 1975, Ph.D. in Psychology, 1975. Lic. psychologist, Md. Research fellow clin. scis. div. Md. Psychiat. Research Ctr., Balt., 1972-76; mem. core faculty in applied behavioral scis. Johns Hopkins U., Balt., 1976—; pvt. practice psychology, Balt., 1976—; dir. Inst. for Human Devel., Balt., 1980—; adj. prof. Union Grad. Sch., Yellow Springs, Ohio, 1980—; cons.-clinician Ctr. for Vaccine Devel., U. Md., Balt., 1978—, Grassroots Crisis Ctr., Columbia, Md., 1976—, Oldfields Sch. for Girls, Sparks, Md., 1979—. Creator, producer multimedia prodns. and video tapes. Bd. dirs., pres. Brotherhood of Man Counseling Ctr., Towson, Md., 1976-77; bd. dirs. Grassroots Crisis Ctr., 1976-77. Mem. Assn. for Computing Machinery, Am. Psychol. Assn., Md. Psychol. Assn., World Future Soc., Internat. Transpersonal Assn., N.Y. Acad. Scis., AAAS. Current Work: Psychedelic drugs as adjuncts to psychotherapy. Use of computer technology to manage audio-visual database generated environments. Use of audiovisual environments for consciousness alteration and psychotherapy; clinical research with psychedelic drugs and psychotherapy. Subspecialties: Psychotherapy/personality/consciousness; Clinical psychology. Office: Inst for Human Devel 2403 Talbot Rd Baltimore MD 21216

YEOMANS, DONALD KEITH, astronomer; b. Rochester, N.Y., May 3, 1942; s. George E. and Jessie (Sutherl) Y.; m. Laurie Ernst, June 20, 1970; children Sarah K., Keith A. B.S., Middlebury Coll., 1964; M.S., U. Md., 1967, Ph.D., 1970. Tech. supr. Computer Scis. Corp., Silver Spring, Md., 1972-76; mem. tech. staff Jet Propulsion Lab., Pasadena, Calif., 1976—; mem. NASA sci. working groups to study space missions to comets and asteroids, discipline specialist for astrometry within Internat. Halley Watch orgn., 1982. Contbr. articles to profl. jours. Mem. Internat. Astron. Union, Am. Astron. Soc., History of Sci. Soc., Explorer's Club. Democrat. Current Work: Research on long-term motion and behavior of comet Halley. Support of European, Japanese and Russian space missions to comet Halley. Subspecialty: Planetary science. Home: 833 Chehalem Rd La Canada CA 91011 Office: Jet Propulsion Lab 264-664 Pasadena CA 91109

YERGIN, PAUL FLOHR, physicist, educator; b. N.Y.C., Apr. 21, 1923; s. Howard Vernon and Ida (Flohr) Y.; m. Eunice Carlson, June 14, 1947; children—Ann, Susan. Student CCNY, 1939-41; B.S., Union Coll., Schenectady, N.Y., 1944; M.S., Columbia U., 1949, Ph.D., 1953. Instr. U. Pa., Phila., 1952-54, asst. prof., 1954-56; asst. prof. physics Rensselaer Poly. Inst., Troy, N.Y.C., 1956-57, assoc. prof., 1957-74, prof., 1974—. Contbr. numerous articles to profl. jours. Mem. Am. Phys. Soc., Am. Assn. Physics Tchrs., Sigma Xi. Current work: Nuclear physics, intermediate energy, photonuclear reactions, photo-production of pions on nuclei. Subspecialty: Nuclear physics. Home: 326 State St Albany NY 12210 Office: Physics Dept Rensselaer Poly Inst Troy NY 12181

YESAIR, DAVID WAYNE, pharmaceutical research company executive, consultant biomolecular sciences; b. Newbury, Mass., Sept. 9, 1932; s. Wayne and Roma E. (Arlin) Y.; m. Ruth Elizabeth Avery, June 6, 1954; children—Karen E. Catherine E., Peter D. B.S. in Chemistry, Math., U. Mass., 1954; Ph.D. in Biochemistry, Cornell U., 1958; NSF postdoctoral fellow Nat. Research Inst., Reading, England, 1961-62; sabbatical leave Institute de Substances Naturelles, France, 1971-72. Scientist Am. Cyanamid, Pearl River, N.Y., 1959-61; biochemist Arthur D. Little, Inc., Cambridge, Mass., 1962-66, biochemistry, pharmacology group leader, 1966-77, biomolecular sci. sect. mgr., 1977-82, v.p., 1978-84; founding pres., chief exec. officer BioMolecular Products, Inc., Byfield, Mass., 1984—; guest lectr., mem. doctoral research com. MIT, 1972—; mem. Devel. Therapeutic Com. Div. Cancer Treatment Nat. Cancer Inst. NIH, 1975-78. Contbr. articles to profl. jours. and chpts. to books. Patentee drug delivery systems, 1981, 1983. Served to 2nd lt. U.S. Chem. Corps, 1958. Fellow NIH, NSF, Leukemia Soc. Am., Nat. Cancer Inst. Fellow Am. Inst. Chemists; mem. Am. Soc. Pharmacology and Exptl. Therapeutics, Am. Soc. Toxicology, Am. Soc. Cancer Research, N.Y. Acad. Scis., Am. Chem. Soc. (Div. Biol. Chemistry), AAAS, Mass. Inst. Chemists (sec. 1970-71, bd. dirs., 1976-79, chmn. student award com. 1972-79, mem. Nat. Mktg. Orgn. 1975), Internat. Soc. for Studying Xenobiotics (organizer, treas. 1984—), Sigma Xi, Gordon Conf. on Drug Metabolism (chmn. Xenobiotic Interactions, 1974, chmn. 1983, vice chmn. 1982). Current work: Molecular lipid systems for use in oral drug formulations and in nutrition; evaluation of nuclear macromolecular lipids as targets for design of new drugs. Subspecialties: Biochemistry (medicine); Drug delivery systems. Home: 6 Johnson Ln Byfield MA 01922 Office: BioMolecular Products Inc PO Box 347 Byfield MA 01922

YESNER, RAYMOND, pathologist, researcher; b. Columbus, Ga., Apr. 18, 1914; s. Benjamin Nabrisky and Anna (Tolbert) Y.; m. Bernice Lieberman, Feb. 16, 1947; children—David Raymond, Donna Lee, Steven Charles. A.B., Harvard U., 1935; M.D., Tufts U., 1941; hon. M.A., Yale U., 1972. Diplomate Am. Bd. Pathology. Chief lab. service VA Hosp., Newington, Conn., 1947-52; chief lab. service VA Med. Ctr., West Haven, Conn., 1952-74, chief staff, 1968-74, dir. pathol. anatomy, 1974—; assoc. dean Yale Med. Sch., New Haven, 1968-74; chmn. pathology panel VA Lung Group, 1958-78; cons., chmn. WHO Lung Cancer Panel, Geneva, Switzerland, 1976-78; cons. Radiation Theroncology Group, 1980—. Editor: Handbook Service Pathology, 1978; WHO Nomenclature, 1981. Bd. govs. Conn. chpt. Am. Cancer Soc., New Haven ARC. Served to capt. AUS, 1944-47. Recipient Heath Meml. award U. Tex., 1984. Fellow emeritus Internat. Acad. Pathology, Am. Coll. Pathology; mem. Conn. Thoracic Soc. (life mem.), Conn. Pathology Soc., Am. Assn. Pathology, Arthur P. Stout Surg. Pathology Soc. Current work: Lung cancer; histopathology, epidemiology, and biology, with clinical and therapeutic implications. Subspecialties: Pathology (medicine); Cancer research (medicine). Home: 16 Sunbrook Rd Woodbridge CT 06525 Office: VA Med Ctr W Spring St West Haven CT 06516

YESSIOS, CHRIS IOANNIS, architecture and computer-aided design educator, architect, planner, consultant; b. Edessa, Greece, Aug. 10, 1938; came to U.S., 1968, naturalized, 1979; s. Ioannis C. and Aikaterini (Papachristou) Y.; m. Alexandra Varsamis, Sept. 1, 1971; children: Yiannis, Katerina, Dorina, Christina. Diploma in Law, Aristotelian U., Thesaloniki, Greece, 1962, diploma in Architecture, 1967; Ph.D., Carnegie-Mellon U., 1973. Tech. dir., ptnr. Gorgo: Workshop for Interior Designs and Popular Crafts, Athens and Thessaloniki, Greece, 1960-62, with various archtl. and planning firms, 1962-73, pvt. practice architecture specializing in single family houses and apt. bldgs., Thessaloniki and Columbus, Ohio, 1974—; teaching asst. dept. urban affairs U. Pitts., 1968; teaching and research assoc. dept. architecture Carnegie-Mellon U., 1969-71, lectr., 1971-73; asst. prof. architecture Ohio State U., 1973-79, assoc. prof. architecture and computer-aided design, 1979-83, prof., 1983—, cons. in computer-aided design and computer graphics techiques for practice architecture and planning, 1975—. Research publs. and presentations in field; author user manuals of implemented systems. Recipient Best Research Paper Contest citation 15th Design Automation Conf., Las Vegas, Nev., 1978, Mayor's prize for Vernacular Theme Mayor Thessaloniki, 1962; IBM grantee, 1982—. Mem. Greek Inst. Architects, Tech. Chamber Greece, Environ, Design and Research Assn., Design Methods Group, Assn. Computer Aided Design in Architecture, Assn. Computing Machinery, Spl. Interest Group for Computer Graphics, Spl. Interest Group for Design Automation, Nat. Computer Graphics Assn., Anatolia Coll. Alumni Assn., Carnegie-Mellon U. Alumni Assn. Greek Orthodox. Current Work: Development of innovative techniques for use of computer (primarily computer graphics) in environmental design (computer-aided architectural design). Subspecialties: Graphics, image processing, and pattern recognition; Computer-aided design. Home: 4367 Mumford Dr Columbus OH 43220Office: Dept Architecture Ohio State U 190 W 17th Ave Columbus OH 43210

YEUNG, EDWARD SZESHING, chemistry educator, researcher; b. Hong Kong, Feb. 17, 1948; came to U.S., 1965, naturalized, 1979; s. Yu Long and King Mai (Luk) Y.; m. Anna Kunkwok Seto, Sept. 18, 1971; children—Rebecca, Amanda. A.B., Cornell U., 1968; Ph.D., U. Calif.-Berkeley, 1972. Instr. chemistry Iowa State U., Ames, 1972-74, asst. prof., 1974-77, assoc. prof., 1977-81, prof., 1981—; sr. chemist Ames Lab., Iowa, 1981—; hon. prof. Zhengzhau U., 1983. Patentee in field. Alfred P. Sloan Found. fellow 1974. Mem. Am. Chem. Soc. (local chmn. 1978), Soc. Photo-Optical Instrumentation Engrs. Current work: Laser applications in chemistry, spectroscopy, photochemistry. Subspecialties: Analytical chemistry; Physical chemistry. Office: Iowa State U Gilman Hall Ames IA 50011

YIELDING, K. LEMONE, physician, educator; b. Auburn, Ala., Mar. 25, 1931; s. Riley LaFayette and Bertie (Dees) Y.; m. Mildred Louise Schell, Apr. 14, 1950 (div. 1973); children—K. Lemone, Michael Lafon, Teresa Louise, Riley LaFayette; Lerena Wade Hauge, Dec. 8, 1973; 1 child, Katrina Elizabeth. B.S., Auburn U., 1949; M.S., U. Ala., 1952, M.D., 1954. Intern U. Hosp., Birmingham, 1954-55; clin. assoc. Nat. Inst. Arthritis and Metabolic Diseases, NIH, Bethesda, Md., 1955-57, sr. investigator, 1958-64, cons., 1965-68, 75-80;

resident USPHS Hosp., Balt., 1957-58; prof. biochemistry, assoc. prof. medicine, dir. molecular biology U. Ala., Birmingham, 1964-80; prof., chmn. dept. Anatomy U. So. Ala., Mobile, 1980—. Contbr. articles to profl. jours. Served to sr. surgeon USPHS, 1955-64. Grantee NIH, Am. Cancer Soc., Nat. Found. March of Dimes, U.S. Army, Mem. Am. Soc. Biol. Chemists, Am. Assn. Pathologists, Am. Soc. Pharmacology and Exptl. Therapeutics, Am. Assn. Anatomy, Am. Soc. Cell Biologists, Am. Assn. Cancer Research, Am. Soc. Photobiology, Am. Heart Assn. (cons.), Arthritis Found. (cons.). Lutheran. Current work: DNA damage repair; photo affinity labeling of drug receptors. Subspecialties: Molecular biology; Internal medicine. Home: 4617 Bit and Spur Rd Mobile AL 36608 Office: Dept Anatomy U So Ala Coll Medicine Mobile AL 36688

YIH, CHIA-SHUN, mechanical engineering educator; b. Kweiyang, Kweichow, China, July 25, 1918; s. Ting-Chien and Wan-Lan (Shiao) Y.; m. Shirley Gladys Ashman, Feb. 17, 1949; children—Yiu-Yo, Yuen-Ming David, Weiling Katherine. B.S., Nat. Central U., 1942; M.S., U. Iowa, 1947, Ph.D., 1948. Instr. Nat. Kweichow U., 1944-45; instr. math. U. Wis., 1948-49; lectr. U. B.C., 1949-50; assoc. prof. Colo. State U., 1950-52; research engr. U. Iowa, 1952-54, assoc. prof., 1954-56, U. Mich., Ann Arbor, 1956-58, prof., 1958—, Stephen P. Timoshenko univ. prof. fluid mechanics, 1968—, Henry Russel lectr., 1974; vis. prof. U. Paris, France, 1970-71; cons. Huyck Felt Co., 1960-64; Trustee Rocky Mountain Hydraulic Lab.; Attaché de Recherche in Math. French Govt., 1951-52. Author: Dynamics of Nonhomogeneous Fluids, 1965, Fluid Mechanics, An Introduction to the Theory, 1969, 79, Stratified Flows, 1980; Editor: Advances in Applied Mechanics, 1970-82; Contbr. articles to profl. jours. Recipient Achievement award Chinese Inst. Engrs. N.Y., 1968, Chinese Engrs. and Scientists Assn. So. Calif., 1973; Sr. Scientist award Humboldt Found., W. Ger., 1977; Theodore von Kármán medal ASCE, 1981; S.S. Attwood award U. Mich., 1984; sr. postdoctoral fellow NSF, 1959-60; Guggenheim fellow, 1964. Fellow Am. Phys. Soc. (Fluid Dynamics prize 1985), Mich. Soc. Fellows (sr.); mem. U.S. Nat. Acad. Engring., Academia Sinica, Internat. Assn. Hydraulic Research, Sigma Xi, Pi Mu Epsilon, Tau Beta Pi, Phi Kappa Phi. Current work: Flows of fluids stratified in density or entropy, wave motion of fluids, hydrodynamic stability, geophysical fluid dynamics, and applied mathematics in general. Subspecialties: Fluid mechanics; Applied mathematics. Home: 3530 W Huron River Dr Ann Arbor MI 48103

YIM, GEORGE KWOCK WAH, pharmacology educator; b. Honolulu, Jan. 7, 1930; s. George Goon-Hop and Josephine (Lau) Y.; m. Ramona Leiahina Lew, Aug. 9, 1952; children—Paula Kehaulani, Donna Lehua, Marsha Haunani, David Andrew, Jonathan Paul. B.S., U. Iowa, 1952, M.S., 1954, Ph.D., 1956. Asst. prof. Purdue U. Sch. Pharmacy, West Lafayette, Ind., 1956-61, assoc. prof., 1962-68, prof., 1969—, chmn. dept. pharmacy, 1983—; vis. prof. McGill U., Montreal, 1966-67. Mem. Soc. for Neurosci., Am. Soc. Pharmacology and Exptl. Therapeutics, Soc. Toxicology. Mem. Reorganized Ch. of Jesus Christ of Latter-day Saints. Current work: Endogenous opioids in stress-induced diseases (obesity, gallstones, atherosclerosis); mechanisms of cancer anorexia, cachexia. Subspecialty: Pharmacology. Office: Dept Pharmacology and Toxicology Sch Pharmacy and Pharmacal Scis Purdue U West Lafayette IN 47907

YIM, KALVIN WALKIN, biochemistry researcher; b. Hong Kong, Apr. 15, 1949; came to U.S. 1968; s. Shui Hsiang and Annie (Wai) Y.; m. Mary Manman Tsui, May 25, 1979. B.S., U. Ill., 1972, M.S., 1975, Ph.D., 1978. Research assoc. MIT, Cambridge, Mass., 1978-79; scientist Ortho Pharm. Corp., Raritan, N.J., 1979-81, sr. research scientist, 1981—. Sloan Found. scholar U. Calif.-San Diego, 1972. Mem. Am. Chem. Soc., Sigma Xi, Phi Eta Sigma, Phi Lambda Epsilon. Current work: Research and development of methodologies for the characterization and production of drugs, particularly those proteins and peptides from biotechnology. Subspecialty: Analytical chemistry. Home: 2 Candlewood Dr Princeton NJ 08550 Office: Ortho Pharm Corp Route 202 Raritan NJ 08869

YIN, MINGTANG THOMAS, electronic engineer; b. Taipei, Republic of China, Jan. 10, 1952; came to U.S., 1975, naturalized, 1985; s. Charles Tsai-Chien and Tzu-Yun (Wei) Y.; m. Cynthia Tsun Chang, Feb. 15, 1980; 1 child, David. B.S., Nat. Taiwan U., Taipei, 1973; A.M., Harvard U., 1976; Ph.D., U. Calif.-Berkeley, 1981. Cert. electronic engr., Republic of China. Mem. tech. staff AT&T Bell Labs., Murray Hill, N.J., 1981-84; computer-aided design program mgr. ECAD, Inc., Santa Clara, Calif., 1984—. Contbr. articles to profl. jours. Served to ensign Navy of Republic of China, 1973-75. Mem. IEEE, Am. Phys. Soc., Chinese Inst. Engrs. (regional program chmn. 1984—), Current work: VLSI design methodology; computer-aided design; physical design automation; modeling, simulation and analysis of integrated circuits. Subspecialties: Microelectronics; Condensed matter physics. Home: 13080 Anza Dr Saratoga CA 95070 Office: ECAD Inc 2455 Augustine Dr Santa Clara CA 95054

YING, SHUH-PAN, acoustician, physicist, consultant, researcher; b. Shaohsing, China, July 12, 1929; came to U.S., 1960, naturalized, 1972; s. Hok-Song and Yen-Yun (Fan) Y.; m. Tienchu Chen, Sept. 23, 1956; children—Ramona, John, William. B.S. in Physics, Nat. Taiwan U., Republic of China, 1959; M.S. in Physics, U. Mass., 1962; Ph.D. in Physics, U. Mich., 1969. Registered profl. engr., N.Y., Mich., N.C. Sr. research engr. Southwest Research Inst., San Antonio, 1970-76; project mgr., prin. cons. Gilbert/Commonwealth, Jackson, Mich., 1976-84, sect. mgr., project mgr., cons., 1984—. Patentee pulsed acoustic image tube. Author tech. papers. Served to capt. Chinese Air Force, 1947-55. Fellow Acoustical Soc. Am. (com. mem. 1978—); mem. Am. Nat. Standards Inst. (chmn. sub-com. 1978—), Am. Phys. Soc., Am. Soc. Nondestructive Testing, Nat. Soc. Profl. Engrs. (chpt. v.p. 1982-83), Phi Kappa Phi. Club: Toastmasters (pres. 1981). Current work: Acoustical technology applied to machinery diagnosis, human effects in sound, and non-destructive testing. Subspecialties: Acoustics; Non-destructive testing. Home: 3378 Vrooman Rd Jackson MI 49201 Office: Gilbert/Commonwealth Inc PO Box 1498 Reading PA 19603

YOCUM, RONALD HARRIS, chemical company executive; b. Darby, Pa., June 2, 1939; s. Jacob Harris and Gladys (Phillips) Y.; m. Martha Virginia Meitzner, July 6, 1963; children—Beth Ann, James Eric. B.A., Gettysburg (Pa.) Coll., 1961; Ph.D., U. Pa., 1965. With Dow Chem. Co., 1965—, dir. research and devel. Dow Latin Am., Coral Gables, Fla., 1973-77, dir. research and devel. designed products dept., Midland, Mich., 1977-78, dir. product research Dow USA, Midland, 1978-80, dir. research Mich. div., 1980—. Editor: (with others) Functional Monomers, Vols. I and II, 1974. Active Boy Scouts Am. Mem. Am. Chem. Soc. Republican. Episcopalian. Current work: Research management. Subspecialties: Organic chemistry; Polymer chemistry. Office: 566 Bldg Bay City Rd Midland MI 48640

YODER, HATTEN SCHUYLER, JR., petrologist; b. Cleve., Mar. 20, 1921; s. Hatten Schuyler and Elizabeth Katherine (Knieling) Y.; m. Elizabeth Marie Bruffey, Aug. 1, 1959; children: Hatten Schuyler III, Karen. A.A., U. Chgo., 1940, S.B., 1941; student, U. Minn., summer 1941; Ph.D., Mass. Inst. Tech., 1948; Dr. h.c., U. Paris VI, 1981. Petrologist Geophys. Lab., Carnegie Instn., Washington, 1948-71, dir., 1971—. Author: Generation of Basaltic Magma, 1976; Editor: The Evolution of the Igneous Rocks: Fiftieth Anniversary Perspectives; co-editor: Jour. of Petrology, 1959-69; asso. editor: Am. Jour. Sci, 1972—; Contbr. articles to sci. jours. Served to lt. comdr. USNR, 1942-46. Recipient award Mineral. Soc. Am., 1954, Bicentennial medal Columbia, 1954; Arthur L. Day medal Geol. Soc. Am., 1962; A.L. Day prize and lectureship Nat. Acad. Sci., 1972; A.G. Werner medal German Mineral. Soc., 1972; Golden Plate award Am. Acad. Achievement, 1973; Wollaston medal Geol. Soc. London, 1979; mineral, Yoderite, named in his honor. Fellow Geol. Soc. Am. (mem. council 1966-68), Mineral. Soc. Am. (council 1962-64, 69-73, pres. 1971-72), Am. Geophys. Union (pres. volcanology, geochemistry and petrology sect. 1962-64); mem. Mineral Soc. London (hon. 1983—), Geol. Soc. Edinburgh (corr.), Geol. Soc. Finland, All-Union Mineral. Soc. USSR (hon.), Geochem. Soc. (council 1956-58), Am. Chem. Soc., Mineral. Assn. Can., Nat. Acad. Sci. (chmn. geology sect. 1973-76), Washington Acads. Sci., Geol. Soc. Washington, Chem. Soc. Washington, Am. Philos. Soc. (council 1982-85), Am. Acad. Arts and Scis., Explorers Club, Sigma Xi, Phi Delta Theta. Current Work: Experimental petrology; mineral stability; high-pressure synthesis; heat and mass transfer; phase equilibria. Subspecialties: Petrology; Geophysics. Address: 2801 Upton St NW Washington DC 20008

YODER, JOHN MONLEY, medical laboratory executive; b. Fort Wayne, Ind., Oct. 4, 1931; s. Dorsa M. and Hermione (Brunk) Y.; m. Lois L. Baker, June 8, 1960; children—Lynne L., Lora J. B.S., Purdue U., 1953, Ph.D., 1962. Research and devel. staff Miles Lab., Elkhart, Ind., 1962—. Author: (with others) Column Chromatography Proteins, 1964. Patentee in field. Treas. Ch. Community Services, Elkhart, 1974; tchr. Trinity United Meth. Ch., Elkhart, 1982; group leader Non-Denominational Fellowship, Elkhart, 1984. Served with U.S. Army, 1954-56. Mem. Am. Chem. Soc. Current work: Diagnostic assays in endrocrinology immunology; purification and characterization of proteins. Subspecialties: Immunology (medicine); Biochemistry (medicine). Home: 26221 Bell Elkhart IN 46514 Office: Ames Div Miles Lab Box 70 Elkhart IN 46515

YODZIS, PETER PAUL, biomathematics educator, researcher; b. Balt., July 10, 1943; s. Peter Paul and Florence Proxella (Kopitsky) Y.; m. Karin Barbara Henke, Aug. 20, 1964; 1 child, Hans Christoph. B.S., Duke U., 1964; Ph.D., N.Mex. State U., 1969. Scholar Dublin Inst. Advanced Studies, Ireland, 1970-72; postdoctoral fellow U. Hamburg, Germany, 1972-74; asst. U. Bern, Switzerland, 1974-79; lehrbeauftragte U. Zurich, Switzerland, 1978-79; prof. U. Guelph, Ont., Can., 1979—; cons. Ont. Ministry Natural Resources, Maple, 1981-83. Author: Competition for Space and the Structure of Ecological Communities, 1978; Introduction to Theoretical Ecology, 1985. Mem. Ecol. Soc. Am. Current work: All aspects of mathematical modelling in ecology, competition for space, food web structure, the influence of predation or harvesting on competitive systems. Subspecialties: Theoretical ecology; Applied mathematics. Office: Dept Zoology U Guelph Guelph ON N1G 2W1 Canada

YOERGER, ROGER RAYMOND, agrl. engr., educator; b. LeMars, Iowa, Feb. 17, 1929; s. Raymond Herman and Crystal Victoria (Ward) Y.; m. Barbara M. Ellison, Feb. 14, 1953; 1 dau., Karen Lynne; m. Laura M. Summitt, Dec. 23, 1971; stepchildren—Daniel L. Summitt, Linda Summitt Canull, Anita Summitt Smith. B.S., Iowa State U., 1949, M.S., 1951, Ph.D., 1957. Registered profl. engr., Ill., Pa., Iowa. Instr., asst. prof. agrl. engring. Iowa State U., 1949-56; asso. prof. agrl. engring. Pa. State U., 1956-58; prof. agrl. engring. U. Ill., Urbana, 1959—, head agrl. engring. dept., 1978—. Contbr. articles to profl. jours. Mem. Ill. Noise Task Force, 1974—. Fellow Am. Soc. Agrl. Engrs.; mem. Am. Soc. Engring. Edn., AAAS, Phi Kappa Phi (dir. fellowships, dir. 1971—). Roman Catholic. Clubs: Rotary, Moose. Patentee in field. Current Work: Administration of an educational and research program in agricultural engineering. Subspecialties: Agricultural engineering; Acoustical engineering. Home: 107 W Holmes Urbana IL 61801 Office: 1304 W Pennsylvania Ave Urbana IL 61801

YOKEL, ROBERT ALLEN, pharmacologist, researcher, educator; b. Rockford, Ill., June 22, 1945; s. Edward Clarence and Lilyann Lucille (Ehlert) Y.; m. Susan Jeanne Brown, Dec. 27, 1969; children: Erich Matthew, Kimberly Allison. B.S. in Pharmacy, U. Wis., 1968; Ph.D. in Pharmacology, U. Minn., 1973. Registered pharmacist, Wis., Ohio. Postdoctoral research assoc. Corcordia U., Montreal, Que., Can., 1973-75; asst. prof. pharmacology U. Cin., 1975-79; asst. prof. Coll. Pharmacy, U. Ky., Lexington, 1979-84, assoc. prof., 1984—. Contbr. articles to sci. publs., chpts. to books. Mem. Soc. Neurosci., Behavioral Pharmacology Soc., Am. Soc. Pharmacology and Exptl. Therapeutics, AAAS. Current Work: Neurobehavioral toxicology; aluminum toxicology; developmental toxicology; aluminum analysis. Subspecialties: Psychopharmacology; Toxicology (medicine).

YOKELL, MICHAEL DAVID, economist, consultant; b. Plattsburgh, N.Y., Nov. 21, 1946; s. Stanley and Edith Helen (Gersen) Y.; m. Jane Bunin, Apr. 13, 1946. B.Sc. in Physics, MIT, 1968; M.A. in Econs, U. Colo., 1973, Ph.D. in Econs, 1975. Instr. math. econs. U. Colo., 1975; asst. prof. money and banking Wash. State U., 1976; vis. asst. prof., NSF research fellow U. Calif.-Berkeley, 1977; sr. economist Solar Energy Research Inst., 1977-79; pres. Energy & Resource Cons., Inc., Boulder, Colo., 1979—; arbitrator Am. Arbitration Assn.; cons., lectr., speaker profl. meetings. Author: (with Geoff Sanders) The Economics of Minerals Reclamation, 1981, The Environmental Benefits and Costs of Solar Energy, 1980, Yellowcake: The International Uranium Cartel, (with June Taylor), 1979. Mem. Am. Econ. Assn., AAAS, Nat. Assn. Bus. Economists, Fedn. Am. Scientists, Am. Arbitration Assn. (arbitrator), Internat. Assn. Energy Economists. Club: Am. Alpine. Current Work: Research and cons. in mgmt. of energy and natural resources. Subspecialties: Resource management; Fuels.

YOKOYAMA, SHOZO, population geneticist; b. Miyazaki, Japan, Jan. 15, 1946; s. Iwanori and Masu Y.; m. Ruth Weaver. B.S., Miyazaki U., 1968; M.S., Kyushu U., 1971; Ph.D., U. Wash., 1977. Research assoc. U. Tex., Houston, 1977-78; instr. depts. psychiatry and genetics Washington U., St. Louis, 1978-79, asst. prof. dept. psychiatry, 1980—, asst. prof. dept. genetics, 1981—, asst. prof. dept. biology, 1982—. Contbr. articles to sci. jours. NIH grantee, 1981—. Mem. Soc. Study of Evolution, Genetics Soc. Japan, Genetics Soc. Am., AAAS, Am. Soc. Human Genetics, Am. Soc. Naturalists. Current Work: Population genetics; evolution; human genetics; molecular biology; mathematical models; deleterious genes; mutation; recombinant DNA. Subspecialties: Population biology; Genome organization. Home: 7405 Melrose Saint Louis MO 63130 Office: Washington U Saint Louis MO 63110

YONAS, GEROLD, physicist; b. Cleve., Dec. 8, 1939; married; 2 children. B.S., Cornell U., 1962; Ph.D. in Engring. Sci., Calif. Inst. Tech., 1966. Physicist and mgr. electron beam research dept Physics Internat. Co., 1967-72, div. supr., 1972-73, dept. mgr. fusion research, 1973-78; dir. pulsed energy programs Sandia Labs., N.Mex., 1978-84; chief scientist strategic def. initiative program Dept. Def., Washington, 1984—. Subspecialties: Fusion; Laser technology. Office: Office of the Sec Dept Def SDI Orgn Washington DC 20301*

YONG, RAYMOND NEN-YIU, civil engineer; b. Singapore, Apr. 10, 1929; naturalized, 1966; s. Ngim Djin and Lucy (Loh) Y.; m. Florence Lechensky, July 8, 1961; children—Raymond T.M., Christopher T.K. B.A. in Math. and Physics, Washington and Jefferson Coll., 1950; B.S., M.I.T., 1952; M.S., Purdue U., 1954; M.Engring., McGill U., Montreal, Que., Can., 1958, Ph.D., 1960. Mem. faculty McGill U., 1959—, prof. civil engring., 1965—, William Scott prof. civil engring. and applied mechanics, dir. Geotech. Research Centre, 1973—. Decorated chevalier Order of Que. Author: Soil Properties and Behavior, 1975 (Japanese edit. 1977), Introduction to Soil Behavior, 1966 (Japanese edit. 1974). Mem. ASCE, Instn. Civil Engrs., Order Engrs. Que., Soc. Rheology, Clay Minerals Soc., Internat. Soc. Terrain-Vehicle Systems, Can. Geotech. Soc., ASTM. Current work: Biotechnical and geo-environmental engineering; containment transport in substrata; operations research. Subspecialties: Civil engineering; Water supply and wastewater treatment. Office: 817 Sherbrooke St W Montreal PQ H3A 2K6 Canada

YONKERS, THOMAS DARRELL, veterinarian; b. Lake Odessa, Mich., Oct. 23, 1943; s. Lester Randolph and Virginia Irene (Goodsell) Y.; m. Patricia Ann Thiery, Aug. 1, 1964; children—Christopher Paul, Taleese Kay, Trena Eileen. B.S., Mich. State U., 1966, M.S., 1971, D.V.M., 1974. Tchr. Lakewood Pub. Sch., Lake Odessa, 1966-71; vet. assoc. Clark Vet. Hosp., Hastings, Mich., 1974-77; veterinarian Thornapple Valley Animal Hosp., Middleville, Mich., 1977-78; tech. services veterinarian Upjohn Co., Kalamazoo, Mich., 1978-81, head animal regulatory services, 1981-84, program mgr. tech. services, 1984—; rep. Animal Health Inst., Alexandria, Va., 1983—, Nat. Mastitis Council, Arlington, Va., 1984—. Author: (with others) Poultry Diseases and Management, 1984. Contbr. articles to profl. jours. Leader 4-H Vet. Sci. Program, Barry County, Mich., 1978-82. Mem. Am. Vet. Med. Assn., Christian Vet. Mission (state rep. 1984-85). Republican. Methodist. Clubs: Ducks Unlimited (Long Grove, Ill), Mich. United Conservation (Lansing, Mich.). Current work: Involves application of state of the art technology to practical animal agriculture, and relating this information to practicing veterinarians and farmers. Home: 3209 Buehler Rd Hastings MI 49085 Office: Upjohn Co 9661-190-44 Kalamazoo MI 49001

YOO, DAL, physician, medical researcher, educator; b. Kwang-Ju, Korea, Nov. 20, 1943; came to U.S., 1967, naturalized, 1972; s. Bong Soo and Yang Hee (Kim) Y.; m. Charlotte M. Nordanlycke, Apr. 14, 1974; children: Derek Torgny, Nora Ottilia. B.S., Seoul (Korea) Nat. U., 1963, M.D., 1967. Diplomate: Am. Bd. Internal Medicine, Am. Bd. Hematology, Am. Bd. Med. Oncology. Intern St. Luke's Hosp., Newburgh, N.Y., 1967-68, asst. resident in internal medicine, 1968, resident in anatomic pathology, 1968-69; resident Thomas Jefferson U. Hosp., 1969-70; resident George Washington U. Hosp., 1970-71, fellow in hematology and oncology, 1971-72, 74-75, assoc. clin. prof. medicine, 1975—; fellow in blood banking and immunochematology ARC, Washington, 1975; practice medicine specializing in internal medicine, hematology and med. oncology, Washington, 1975—; sr. attending physician Washington Hosp. Ctr., 1975—; mem. active staff Providence Hosp., Washington, chief hematology-oncology sect., 1984—; mem. active staff Capitol Hill Hosp., Washington; mem. courtesy staff Suburban Hosp., Washington Adventist Hosp., Holy Cross Hosp. Contbr. articles to profl. jours. Served to maj. U.S. Army, 1972-74. Fellow ACP; mem. Med. Soc. D.C., Washington Blood Club, Washington Soc. Oncology, Am. Soc. Hematology, Am. Soc. Clin. Oncology. Presbyterian. Current Work: Clincial and laboratory research of hematology and medical oncology. Subspecialties: Hematology; Oncology. Home: 5102 Wessling Ln Bethesda MD 20814 Office: Providence Hosp 1150 Varnum St NE Washington DC 20017

YOO, HEE JU, chemical engineer; b. Sungnamsi, Korea, Dec. 21, 1947; came to U.S., 1976; s. Duk Keun and Hee Gap (Lee) Y.; m. Haeseon Lee, Jan. 21, 1980; 1 child, Charles Sungdo. B.S., Seoul Nat. U., (Korea), 1971; M.S., Poly. Inst. N.Y., 1977, Ph.D., 1980. Supr. Korea Gen. Chem. Co., Chungju, 1971-75; design engr. Daelim Engring., Seoul, Korea, 1976; assoc. chem. engr. Brookhaven Nat. Lab., Upton, N.Y., 1980-83; research engr. Himont USA, Wilmington, Del., 1983—. Contbr. articles to profl. jours. Mem. Soc. Rheology, Soc. Plastics Engrs., Sigma Xi. Current work: Polymer rheology and its application to polymer processing operations polymer characterization. Subspecialty: Chemical engineering. Home: 5424 Crestline Rd Wilmington DE 19808 Office: Himont USA 800 Greenbank Rd Wilmington DE 19808

YOON, JI-WON, microbiologist; b. Korea, Mar. 28, 1939; came to U.S., 1969, naturalized, 1977; s. Bakin and Ducksoon Y.; m. Chungja Rhim, Aug. 17, 1968; children: John, James. M.S., U. Conn., 1971, Ph.D., 1973. Asst. prof. microbiology Chosun U., Kwangju, Korea, 1965-67; assoc. prof. microbiology Chosun U. (Med. Sch.), 1967-69; staff fellow NIH, Bethesda, Md., 1974-76, sr. staff fellow, 1976-78, sr. investigator, 1978-84, mem. faculty Grad. Sch., 1983-84; prof., chief div. virology Faculty of Medicine Health Sci. Ctr., U. Calgary, Alta., Can., 1984— dir. Lab. Viral and Immunopathogenesis of Diabetes, 1984—, adj. prof. microbiology and immunology Chgo. Med. Sch., 1984—. Recipient NIH Dir.'s award, 1984. Mem. Am. Soc. Microbiology, N.Y. Acad. Sci., Am. Tissue Culture Assn., AAAS, Am. Diabetes Assn. Baptist. Current Work: Role of viruses and autoimmunity in pathogenesis of diseases in man and animal; virus-induced diabetes mellitus. Subspecialties: Virology (biology); Virology (medicine). Office: Div Virology M/D Health Sci Ctr U Calgary 3330 Hospital Dr NW Calgary AB T2N 4N1 Canada

YOON, JONG SIK, geneticist; b. Suwon, Korea, Jan. 25, 1937; s. Ki and Pil (Kang) Y.; m. Kyung-soon A. Yoon, Sept. 10, 1962; children: Edward, Mimi, Sunny. B.S., Yonsei U., Seoul, 1961; M.A., U. Tex., Austin, 1964, Ph.D., 1965. Research scientist U. Tex., Austin, 1965-68; research scientist, faculty mem., 1971-78; asst. prof. Yonsei U., 1968-71; assoc. prof. Bowling Green (Ohio) State U., 1978-83, prof., 1983—. Contbr. articles to profl. jours. Served with Korean Army, 1958-60. China Med. Bd. N.Y. fellow, 1968-70; Baylor Coll. Medicine research fellow, 1970; recipient Young Scientist award Internat. Union Against Cancer, 1970; NIH grantee, 1976-77; NSF grantee, 1976—; Ohio Bd. Regents grantee, 1980-82. Fellow Tex. Acad. Sci.; mem. Genetics Soc. Am., Am. Genetic Assn., Soc. Study Evolution, Am. Soc. Naturalists, AAAS, Environ. Mutagen Soc., Tex. Assn. Radiation Research, Ohio Acad. Sci., Sigma Xi. Current Work: Research in cytogenetics, mutations, oncogenetics, genome organization and genetic engineering. Subspecialties: Genetics and genetic engineering (biology); Genome organization. Home: 4 Picardie Ct Bowling Green OH 43402 Office: Dept Biol Scis Bowling Green State U Bowling Green OH 43403

YOON, SOO CHARLES, ceramic engineer, researcher; b. Andong, Korea, June 11, 1941; came to U.S., 1969, naturalized, 1979; s. Sung Sool and Keum-Ee (Choi) Y.; m. Helen Choo, Dec. 23, 1972; children—Janet and Joann. B.E., Hanyang U., Seoul, Korea, 1964; M.S., Rutgers U., 1971, Ph.D., 1973. Research intern Rutgers U., New Brunswick, N.J., 1970-74; material specialist Foseco Inc., Cleve., 1975-77; mgr. research and devel. Leco Inc., St. Joseph, Mich., 1977-79; research engr. Sherwood-TRW, Cleve., 1979-81, Ferro Engring., Cleve., 1981—. Mem. Am. Ceramic Soc., Korean Ceramic Soc. Current work: Research abd development of inorganic and organic material systems. Subspecialties: Ceramic engineering; Ceramics. Home: 5628 Bay Ct Willoughby OH 44094 Office: Ferro Engr 3289 E 80th St Cleveland OH 44104

YORK, JOHN LOUIS, JR., engineer, diversified company executive; b. Robstown, Tex., June 16, 1948; s. John Louis and Lorine M. (Hoelscher) Y.; married; children—Richard, Johnathon, Robert. B.S.E.E., U. Tex., 1972. Registered profl. engr., Tex.; cert. mfg. engr, Tex. Engr. TRW, Houston, 1972-82; pres. York Assoc., Inc., Houston, 1982—, MDSoft Inc., Houston, 1984—; dir. CHUG Inc., Houston, 1984. Mem. IEEE, Soc. Mfg. Engrs. Roman Catholic. Current work: Factory automation; medical laboratory automation. Subspecialties: Computer engineering; Bioinstrumentation. Office: York Assocs Inc 5860 Sampley Way Houston TX 77092

YORK, JOHN LYNDAL, biochemistry educator, researcher; b. Morton, Tex., Aug. 14, 1936; s. James Lee and Jewell Fern (Braden) Y.; m. Cynthia Carolyn Giles, June 29, 1958; children—John Lee, Michelle Annette. B.S., Harding Coll., 1958; Ph.D., Johns Hopkins U., 1962. Biochemist, Stanford Research Inst., Menlo Park, Calif., 1964-65; asst. prof. U. Tenn. Med. Sch., Memphis, 1965-68; assoc. prof. U. Ark. Med. Coll., Little Rock, 1968-77, prof., 1977—. Author: Review of Biolchemistry, 1969; Porphyrias, 1972; also abstracts and articles. Bd. dirs. Pulaski Heights United Meth. Ch., Little Rock, 1981-84. NIH Predoctoral fellow, 1958-62; grants NIH, NSF, 1965-84; Swedish Med. Research Council fellow, 1974. Mem. Am. Chem. Soc. (vice chmn. Central Ark. sect. 1971-72, chmn. 1972-73), Am. Soc. Biol. Chemists, AAUP, AAAS, Sigma Xi. Club: Audubon Soc. (pres. 1970-72, treas. 1977-83). Current work: Structure and function of blood clotting factors especially fibrinogen and thrombin; structure and function of bone marrow growth factors and growth inhibitors and their regulation. Subspecialty: Biochemistry (medicine). Home: 42 Pine Manor Dr Little Rock AR 72207 Office: U Ark Med Sci 4301 W Markham Little Rock AR 72205

YORKE, CALLYN DENNIS, zoology educator; b. San Mateo, Calif., June 30, 1950; s. Elliott Byron and Lois Jean (Deeds) Y.; m. Karen Elaine Maia, Feb. 29, 1970 (div. Oct. 1972); 1 child, Jennifer Lynda. B.S., Calif. State U.-Hayward, 1975, M.A., 1976; Ph.D., U. Ark., 1983. Lectr. zoology Nat. U. Malaysia, Kuala Lumpur, 1977-80; grad. teaching asst. U. Ark., 1980-83; instr. zoology Monterey Peninsula Coll., 1984; asst. prof. zoology Antelope Valley Coll., Lancaster, Calif., 1984—; instr. ornithology Open Edn. Exchange, Berkeley, Calif., 1976-77; research avian paleontologist U.S. Nat. Mus., Washington, 1983—. Contbr. articles to profl. jours. Mem. Am. Ornithologists Union, Cooper Ornithol. Soc., Soc. for Study Reptiles and Amphibians, Sigma Xi. Current work: Avian paleontology; man's impact on bird distributions in southeast Asia. Subspecialties: Evolutionary biology; Behavioral ecology. Office: Antelope Valley Coll 3041 West Ave K Lancaster CA 93534

YOSHIKAWA, SHOICHI, physicist, educator; b. Tokyo, Apr. 9, 1935; came to U.S., 1958; s. Haruhisa and Eiko (Inouye) Y.; m. Hiroko Inouye, Apr. 9, 1960 (div. 1984); children—Yoko, Machiko, Aiko; m. Elinor Doris Sussman, Oct. 20, 1984. B.S., U. Tokyo, 1958; M.S., MIT, 1960, Ph.D., 1961. Prin. research physicist Plasma Physics Lab., Princeton U., N.J., 1961—, lectr. with rank prof. dept. astrophys. scis., 1966—; prof. U. Tokyo, 1973-75; chmn. bd. dirs. Princeton Sci. Cons., 1979—. Author: Challenge of Nuclear Fusion, 1974 (award 1974). Contbr. papers to profl. publs. Patentee in field. Fellow Am. Phys. Soc. Presbyterian. Current work: Fusion-related sciences, especially physics, designs, energy policies, teaching. Subspecialties: Fusion; Plasma physics. Home: 302 Hartley Ave Princeton NJ 08540 Office: Princeton Plasma Physics Lab PO Box 451 Princeton NJ 08544

YOST, WILLIAM ALBERT, psychology educator, hearing researcher; b. Dallas, Sept. 21, 1944; s. William Jacque and Gladys (Funk) Y.; m. Lee Prater, June 15, 1969; children—Kelley Ann, Alyson Leigh. B.A. in Psychology, Colo. Coll., 1966; Ph.D., Ind. U., 1970. Asst. prof. psychology U. Fla., Gainesville, 1971-75, assoc. prof., 1975-77; prof. psychology Loyola U., Chgo., 1977—, dir. Parmly Hearing Inst., 1977—; program dir. NSF, Washington, 1982-83, ad hoc reviewer, 1973—. Author: (with Donald W. Nielsen) Fundamentals of Hearing, 1977, 84; also many jour. articles, book chpts. Editor: (with George Gourevitch) Directional Hearing, 1985; cons. editor Coll. div. Random House, N.Y.C., 1980—. Grantee for hearing research NSF, 1974—, NIH, 1975—. Fellow Acoustical Soc. Am. (chmn. standards com. on bioacoustics 1978-84, assoc. editor jour. 1983—); mem. N.Y. Acad. Scis., Assn. for Research in

Otolaryngology (sec.-treas. 1984-87), Nat. Acad. Scis. (exec. com. on hearing, bioacoustics, biomechanics 1981—), Evanston Tennis Assn. (pres. 1984). Current work: Basic research concerning hearing and auditory information processing. Subspecialties: Sensory processes; Neurophysiology. Office: Parmly Hearing Inst Loyola U 6525 N Sheridan Rd Chicago IL 60626

YOU, KWAN-SA, biochemist, cell biologist; b. Seoul, Korea, Oct. 26, 1941; came to U.S., 1966, naturalized, 1977; s. Jae-rock and Byung-sook (Lee) Y.; m. Hwa Yung Yu, Jan. 31, 1973; children—Young Nathan, Jiyoung Jennifer. B.S., Seoul U., 1966; Ph.D., Brandeis U., 1971. Post-doctoral fellow Scripps Clinic and Research Found., La Jolla, Calif., 1971-73; postgrad. research chemist U. Calif.-San Diego, La Jolla, 1973-77; asst. prof. Duke U., Durham, N.C., 1977-83; vis. scientist W. Alton Jones Cell Sci. Ctr., Lake Placid, N.Y., 1984—; grant reviewer NSF Molecular Biology Sect., Washington, 1984—. Patentee Salicylate Quantification, 1985; editor; The Pyridine Nucleotide Coenzymes, 1982; contbr. revs. and research articles to profl. jours.; articles referee various jours. Mem. AAAS, Am. Soc. Biol. Chemists, Tissue Culture Assn., Am. Assn. Clin. Chemistry, Am. Chem. Soc., Am. Soc. Microbiology, Biophys. Soc., Internat. Soc. Clin. Enzymologists. Current work: Mechanism of enzyme action; cancer chemotherapy; regulation of cell growth; development of analytical methods; mass purification of biomaterials; enzymatic diagnosis of diseases; energy transducing membrane. Subspecialties: Biochemistry (medicine); Cell biology (medicine). Home: Mt Vista Ave Lake Placid NY 12946 Office: W Alton Jones Cell Sci Ctr 10 Old Barn Rd Lake Placid NY 12946

YOUD, THOMAS LESLIE, civil engineering educator; s. Spanish Fork, Utah, Apr. 2, 1938; s. Thomas Leslie and Mary (Evans) Y.; m. Denice Porter, June 26, 1962; children—Verlin, Lance, Melinda, Thomas, Emily. B.E.S., Brigham Young U., 1964; Ph.D., Iowa State U., 1967; postgrad. Imperial Coll., London, 1975-76. Research civil engr. U.S. Geol. Survey, Menlo Park, Calif., 1967-84; assoc. prof. civil engring. Brigham Young U., Provo, Utah, 1984—. Contbr. articles to profl. jours. Mem. ASCE, Internat. Soc. Soil Mechanics and Found. Engring., Earthquake Engring. Research Inst., Seismol. Soc. Am., NRC (com. natural disasters 1982). Current work: Liquefaction and ground failure caused by earthquakes, methods for mapping potential ground failure hazards. Subspecialties: Civil engineering; Geology. Home: 1132 E 1010 N St Orem UT 84057 Office: Brigham Young Univ 368 Clyde Bldg Provo UT 84602

YOUM, YOUNGIL, mechanical engineering educator; b. Seoul, Korea, Jan. 2, 1942; s. Jin-Mo and Su-up (Ahn) Y.; m. Whaja Lee, Mar. 18, 1968; children—Julie, Ann, Robyn. B.S. in Mech. Engring., Utah State U., 1968; M.S. in Mech. Engring., U. Wis.-Madison, 1970, M.S. in Engring. Mechanics, 1973, Ph.D., 1976. Registered profl. engr., Washington. Research asst. U. Wis.-Madison, 1968-73; research scientist, asst. prof. U. Iowa-Iowa City, 1974-78; dir. biomechanics, assoc. prof. Catholic U. Am., 1978—; adj. assoc. prof. U. Md. Med. Sch., 1982—, The Uniformed Service U., Bethesda, Md., 1981—; cons. Walter Reed Army Med. Ctr., Washington, 1980—. Patentee wrist prosthesis. NIH grantee, 1974-78, Nat. Bur. Standards grantee, 1981, NSF grantee, 1982. Mem. Am. Soc. Biomechanics, ASME. Roman Catholic. Current work: Kinematics of mechanisms and robotics; biomechanics. Subspecialties: Mechanical engineering; Biomedical engineering. Home: 310 Vierling Dr Silver Spring MD 20904 Office: Catholic U Am Washington DC 20064

YOUN, SO YOUNG, engineer; b. Seoul, Korea, Nov. 20, 1941; came to U.S., 1972; s. Tai Ku Youn and Kil (Soon) Kim; m. Young Mee Youn, Apr. 12, 1972; 1 dau., H. Grace. B.S. in Elec. Engring., Yonsei U., Seoul, 1965; M.S. in Elec. Engring., U. Mo., 1975; M.S. in Computer Engring., So. Meth. U., 1980. Research assoc. Yonsei U., 1965-67; fellow UN (I.T.U.), Geneva, 1969-71; engr. Mostek Corp. subs. United Technologies, Carrollton, Tex., 1980-83; sr. engr. Fairchild Semiconductor Div., Mountain View, Calif., 1984-85; prin. CMOS prodn. engr. solid state div. research and devel. Honeywell Inc., Plymouth, Minn., 1985—. Mem. IEEE (Electron Devices Soc.), IEEE (Solid State Circuit Soc.), IEEE VLSI subcom. 1982-83). Current work: CMOS gate array integrated circuit; submicron device characterization and debugging; device modeling. Subspecialties: Microchip technology (engineering); Microelectronics. Home: 3099 Alexander Ln Mound MN 55364 Office: Honeywell Inc Research and Devel 12001 State Hwy St Plymouth MN 55441

YOUNG, ARTHUR, astrophysicist, astronomy educator; b. N.Y.C., Jan. 4, 1940; m. Ruth M. McRoberts, Aug. 15, 1960 (div. June 1977); children—Gregory, Bruce; m. Carole A. Lee, June 1, 1979. B.S. in Physics, Allegheny Coll., 1960; M.A. in Astronomy, Ind. U., 1965, Ph.D. in Astronomy, 1967. Prof. San Diego State U., 1967—; vis. prof. U. Boulder, Colo., 1981-82, 84—. Contbr. articles to profl. jours. Served to 1st lt. USAF, 1960-63. Mem. Am. Astron. Soc., Astron. Soc. of Pacific, Internat. Astron. Union. Current work: Solar-stellar relations; interacting binaries; pulsating hot stars. Subspecialty: Optical astronomy. Office: Astronomy Dept San Diego State U San Diego CA 92182

YOUNG, AUSTIN HARRY, manufacturing company executive, researcher, consultant; b. Brighton, Mass., Oct. 25, 1928; s. Austin Stanley and Anna (Linfield) Y.; m. Elizabeth Frank, Jan. 18, 1958; children—Katherine Anne, Diane Elizabeth. B.S. in Chemistry, Tufts U., 1950; Ph.D. in Phys. Chemistry, U. Wis.-Madison, 1958. Chemist E.I. Du Pont De Nemours & Co., Fabrics and Finishes dept., Phila., 1950-51; supv. E.I. Du Pont De Nemours & Co. Explosives dept., Newport, Ind., 1951-52; research chemist to research assoc. A.E. Staley Mfg. Co., Decatur, Ill, 1958-78, sr. scientist, mgr. material research, 1978-84, mgr., tech. group polymerizable products dept, 1984—. Author: (with others) Chemistry and Properties of Crosslinked Polymers, 1977; Starch, 1984. Patentee in field. Sec. ch. council First Lutheran Ch., Decatur, 1973-79, coordinator growth div., 1984—. Served to cpl. Army Chem. Ctr., U.S. Army, 1953-54. Recipient IR-100 award Indsl. Research and Devel., Mus. Sci. and Industry, 1978. Standard Oil Ind. Found. fellowship U. Wis-Madison, 1957. Mem. Am. Chem. Soc. (chmn. Decatur-Springfield chpt. 1968), Am. Assn. Cereal Chemists, AAAS, Sigma Xi, Phi Lambda Upsilon. Republican. Starch, colloid, polymer and radiation chemistry; polymerizable acrylamidomethyl carbohydrates for radiation and thermal cure coatings, adhesives, fiber reinforced plastics. Subspecialties: Physical chemistry; Polymer chemistry. Home: 151 Point Bluff Dr Decatur IL 62521Office: A E Staley Mfg Co 2200 E Eldorado St Decatur IL 62521

YOUNG, CHUNG CHANG, biomedical company chemist; b. Taichung, Taiwan, Dec. 20, 1941; came to U.S., 1965, naturalized, 1975; m. Meei-Meei Liao, May 6, 1969; children—Connie, James. B.S. in Chemistry, Nat. Taiwan U., 1964; M.S. in Analytic Chemistry, U. Ill., 1967, Ph.D., 1970. Research chemist Owens-Ill., Inc., Toledo, 1971-75; dir. sensor devel. Orion Research Inc., Cambridge, Mass., 1975-76; v.p. research Nova Biomed. Corp., Waltham, Mass., 1976—, also dir. Inventor in field. Mem. Am. Chem. Soc., Am. Assn. Clin. Chemistry. Current work: Clinical instruments; electrochemistry; ion-selective electrode. Subspecialties: Analytical chemistry; Clinical chemistry. Home: 145 Buckskin Dr Weston MA 02193 Office: Nova Biomed Corp 200 Prospect St Waltham MA 02254

YOUNG, DONALD CLIFFORD, chemist; b. Paducah, Ky., Feb. 25, 1933; s. John Clifford and Lillian (Dougherty) Y.; m. Geraldine Lee Wallace, July 7, 1951; children—Martha, Rachel, Steven, Mark. B.A., U. Calif.-Riverside, 1962, Ph.D. in Inorganic Chemistry, 1966. Staff cons. Union Oil Co., Brea, Calif., 1980—. Patentee in field. Mem. Am. Chem. Soc. (Service Through Chemistry award 1984). Current work: Synthesis of new fertilizer, pesticides and plant growth regulators. Subspecialty: Inorganic chemistry. Office: Union Oil Sci and Tech 376 Valencia Ave Brea CA 92621

YOUNG, DONALD FRANCIS, mathematician, educator; b. Washington, Oct. 26, 1944; s. Martin Greene and Alberta Elizabeth (Francis) Y. B.S., Duke U., 1966; M.S., U. Va., 1972, Ph.D., 1975. Asst. prof. U S.C., Columbia, 1975-78; asst. prof. math. Agnes Scott Coll., Decatur, Ga., 1978-83; asst. prof. Oxford (Ga.) Coll., 1983-84; asst. prof. So. Tech. Inst., Marietta, Ga., 1984—. Served to lt. USN, 1966-71. Mem. Am. Math. Soc., Math. Assn. Am., Soc. Indsl. and Applied Math., Phi Beta Kappa. Unitarian Universalist. Current Work: Controllability and optimal control of systems governed by linear and non-linear functional equations. Subspecialty: Applied mathematics. Home: 3223-C Post Woods Dr NW Atlanta GA 30339 Office: Dept Math Southern Tech Inst Marietta GA 30060

YOUNG, DONALD REEDER, physicist; b. Logan, Utah, July 21, 1921; s. Ernest Thomas and Artencia Ruth (Reeder) Y.; m. Anne Watson, June 16, 1946; children—Reed Thomas, Ralph Watson, Frances Anne, Elaine. B.S., Utah State U., 1942; Ph.D., MIT, 1949. Staff mem. MIT, Cambridge, 1942-45, research asst., 1945-49; staff mem. IBM Research Lab., Yorktown Heights, N.Y., 1949—; adj. prof. Lehigh U., 1982—. Recipient U.S. Sr. Scientist award Humboldt Found., 1981-82. Fellow Am. Phys. Soc., IEEE. Mem. Ch. of Jesus Christ of Latter-day Saints. Current work: Charge transport in MOS structures. Subspecialties: Condensed matter physics; Semiconductors. Office: IBM Research ctr PO Box 218 Yorktown Heights NY 10598

YOUNG, DOUGLAS WILFORD, operations research analyst; b. Salt Lake City, July 9, 1944; s. Wilford T. and Ada J. (Asper) Y.; m. Crystal Jean Burrup, Dec. 2, 1968; children: Gregory, Kimberly, Wendy, Brenda, Linda. B.S., U. Utah, 1967, M.B.A., 1970. Cert. cost analyst. Ops. research analyst U.S. Army Info. Services Command, Ft. Huachuca, Ariz., 1979-80, 80-81, 82—, budget analyst, 1971-79, U.S. Air Traffic Control Ctr., Ft. Huachuca, 1980; program analyst Dugway Proving Ground, Utah, 1981-82. Served with U.S. Army, 1968-70, Vietnam. Recipient profl. awards. Mem. Ops. Research Soc. Am. (assoc.), Am. Soc. Mil. Comptrollers (award 1975). Subspecialty: Operations research (mathematics). Office: US Army Info Services Command Fort Huachuca AZ 85613

YOUNG, EVIE FOUNTAIN, JR., horticulturist, researcher; b. Baton Rouge, Sept. 9, 1928; s. Evie Fountain and Ettie Inez (Morgan) Y.; m. Sarah Davis, Aug. 10, 1957; children—Kathryn, Eric, Brett. B.S., La. State U., 1951; M.S., 1953; Ph.D., Okla. State U., 1964. Asst., prof. La. State U., Baton Rouge, 1956-59; research agronomist Agr. Research Service U.S. Dept. Agr. El Paso, Tex., 1963-79, Phoenix, 1980-83, horticulturist, Brownwood, Tex., 1983—. Served with U.S. Army, 1946-48, PTO. Mem. Am. Soc. Agronomists, Sigma Xi. Pecan breeding and performance testing; pecan germ plasm clonal repository. Subspecialty: Plant genetics. Home: 3318 Drumond El Paso TX 79925

YOUNG, FRANCIS ALLAN, psychologist; b. Utica, N.Y., Dec. 29, 1918; s. Frank Allan and Julia Mae (McOwen) Y.; m. Judith Wadsworth Wright, Dec. 21, 1945; children—Francis Allan, Thomas Robert. B.S., U. Tampa, 1941; M.A., Western Res. U., 1945; Ph.D., Ohio State U., 1949. Instr. Wash. State U., Pullman, 1948-50, asst. prof., 1950-56, assoc. prof., 1956-61, prof. psychology, 1961—, dir. primate research center, 1957—; vis. prof. ophthalmology U. Oreg., Portland, 1964; vis. prof. pharmacology U. Uppsala (Sweden) Med. Sch., 1971; vis. prof. optometry U. Houston, 1979-80. Editor: (with Donald B. Lindsley) Early Experience and Visual Information Processing in Perceptual and Reading Disorders, 1970. Named Disting. Psychologist State of Wash., Wash. Psychol. Assn., 1973; recipient Paul Yarwood Meml. award Calif. Optometric Assn., 1978; Apollo award Am. Optometric Assn., 1980; Nat. Acad. Sci.-NRC sr. postdoctoral fellow in physiol. psychology U. Wash., 1956-57; research grantee NSF, 1950-53; research grantee USAF, 1965-72; research grantee NIH, 1960-78. Fellow Am. Acad. Optometry, Am. Pychol. Assn. ((pres. Div. 31) 1974-75); mem. Common Cause, Ams. Dem. Action, Assn. Research in Vision and Ophthalmology, Internat. Soc. Myopia Research (sec.-treas. 1978—), AAAS, Psychonomic Soc., Wash. State Psychol. Assn. (exec. sec. 1965-77), Western Psychol. Assn.; Mem. N.Y. Acad. Scis.; mem. Sigma Xi, Psi Chi (nat. pres. 1968-70). Current Work: Role of behavior and genetics in development of myopia including influence of accomodation and convergence; its morbidity and prevention and epidemiological character. Subspecialties: Sensory processes; Physiological psychology. Home: NW 344 Webb St Pullman WA 99163 Office: Wash State U Pullman WA 99164

YOUNG, FRANK N(ELSON), JR., biology educator, entomologist, parasitologist; b. Oneonta, Ala., Nov. 2, 1915; s. Frank N. and Mary Ellen (Loe) Y.; m. Frances Elizabeth Norman, July 2, 1943; children—Frances Elizabeth Young VonHerrmann, Frank Nelson. B.S., U. Fla., 1938, M.S. in Biology, 1940, Ph.D. in Entomology, 1942. Asst. prof. biology dept. Univ. Coll., U. Fla., Gainesville, 1946-49; asst. prof. Ind. U., Bloomington, 1949-51, assoc. prof., 1951-62, prof. biology, 1963—. Author: Water Beetles of Florida, 1954; contbr. articles to jours. Served to col. Med. Service Corps, U.S. Army, 1943-70. Guggenheim fellow, 1960-61, La. State U. fellow in tropical medicine, West Indies, 1963; recipient Phi Sigma Medal for Research, U. Fla., 1938. Fellow Ind. Acad. Sci.; mem. Am. Inst. Biol. Sci., AAAS, Sigma Xi (pres. Ind. chpt. 1967-68). Democrat. Baptist. Current work: Taxonomy and ecology of aquatic Coleoptera and land snails, human parasites. Subspecialties: Taxonomy; Parasitology. Office: Biology Dept Inc Univ Bloomington IN 47405

YOUNG, FRANKLIN, nutritional biochemist, educator; b. Beijing, China, Feb. 1, 1928; came to U.S., 1950. A.B., Mercer U., 1951; B.S.A. magna cum laude, U. Fla., 1952, M.Agr., 1954, Ph.D., 1960. Grad. research fellow U. Fla., Gainesville, 1958-60, postdoctoral research fellow, 1960-61; research assoc. Bowman Gray Sch. Medicine, Wake Forest U., Winston-Salem, N.C., 1961-65; research assoc. instr., 1965-66; assoc. prof. nutritional biochemistry U. Hawaii, Honolulu, 1966-83; prof., chmn. foods and nutrition Coll. Health, U. Utah, Salt Lake City, after 1983; now with dept. health West Chester U., Pa.; judge sci. fair Hawaii Acad. Sci., Honolulu, 1967-71; supr. high sch. students' sci. research (sponsored by NSF and Hawaii Heart Assn.), Honolulu, 1967-71. Contbr. articles to profl. jours. Supr. State Farm Fairs, Honolulu, 1971-74, Sci. Career Day Exhibit, Honolulu, 1976-78. Grantee fed. govt. agys. and local med. and instl. agys. Mem. Am. Inst. Nutrition, Am. Chem. Soc., Sigma Xi (charter), Gamma Sigma Delta (treas. Hawaii chpt. 1970-71), Phi Sigma, Phi Kappa Phi. Current work: Lipidmetabolism, atherosclerosis, and hypertension. Subspecialties: Biochemistry (biology); Nutrition (biology). Office: Dept Health West Chester U West Chester PA 19383

YOUNG, FREDERICK JOHN, electodynamicist; b. Buffalo, May 19, 1931; s. Frederick John and Marie T. (Brown) Y.; m. Beverly Mae Hall, June 4, 1954; children—John, James, Jeffrey. B.S., Carnegie Inst. Tech., 1953, M.S., 1954, Ph.D., 1956. Registered profl. engr., Pa. Prof. elec. engring. Carnegie Mellon U., Pitts., 1956-74, cons. Westinghouse Research Lab., Pitts., 1957-80; prof. elec. engring. Pa. State U., State Coll., 1974-80; pres. Frontier Timber Co., Bradford, Pa., 1974—; cons. E.I. DuPont Co., Camp Hill, Pa., 1980—. Author: Electrical Engineering Problems, 1959; EMD of Fluids, 1965; also articles; patentee. Scoutmaster, Boy Scouts Am., Pitts., 1969-73. Mem. IEEE, Eta Kappa Nu (award 1963). Current work: Electromagnetic propulsion, computer interconnections. Subspecialties: Computer engineering; Distributed systems and networks. Home: 800 Minard Run Rd Bradford PA 16701 Office: Frontier Timber Co 800 Minard Run Rd Bradford PA 16701

YOUNG, GARRY GEAN, nuclear/licensing engr.; b. Ft. Smith, Ark., Sept. 7, 1951; s. Lee Leonard and Lola Belle (Bartlett) Y.; m. Patricia Ann Farmer, June 24, 1977; 1 dau., Kathryn Elizabeth. B.S. in M.E, U. Ark., 1974, M.S., 1975. Registered profl. engr., Ark., D.C. Prodn. engr. Ark. Power & Light Co., Little Rock, 1975-79; fellow Adv. Com. on Reactor Safeguards, Washington, 1979-80, reactor engr., 1980-81; supervising engr. United Energy Services Corp., Atlanta, 1981—. Author tech. papers. Youth leader, Sunday Sch. tchr. Knollwood Bapt. Ch., Burke, Va., 1980-81; co-dir. children's ch. First Bapt. Ch. of Pelham, Ala., 1982. Mem. ASME, Am. Nuclear Soc., Health Physics Soc., Pi Tau Sigma. Current Work: Commercial nuclear power plant technical reviews and evaluation of engineered safety features and reactor protection systems. Subspecialties: Nuclear fission; Mechanical engineering.

YOUNG, GLENN REID, nuclear physicist; b. Kingsport, Tenn., Aug. 22, 1951; s. Howard Seth and Anne Reid (Maven) Y.; m. Katherine Ann Geoffroy, Sept. 28, 1980; children—Meredith Elaine, Lianne Rebecca. B.A., U. Tenn., 1973; Ph.D., MIT, 1977. Postdoctoral fellow MIT, 1977-78; postdoctoral fellow Oak Ridge Nat. Lab., 1978-80, research physicist, 1980—. Contbr. articles to profl. jours. Mem. Am. Phys. Soc., Sigma Xi, Phi Beta Kappa. Current work: Heavy ion reaction mechanisms, relativistic heavy ion reactions, heavy ion synchrotrons. Subspecialty: Nuclear physics. Home: 110 A Newell Ln Oak Ridge TN 37830 Office: Oak Ridge Nat Lab Bldg 6003 Oak Ridge TN 37830

YOUNG, GREGORY ODD, electronics engineer, physicist; b. Spokane, Wash., Apr. 20, 1922; s. Odd O. and Maude Ida (Gregory) Y.; m. Dolores Sophia Weeks, Apr. 17, 1948; children—Garth, Victoria, Guy, Grant, Viveca. B.S. in Elec. Engring., Calif. Inst. Tech., 1944, M.S. in Elec. Engring., 1947; Ph.D. in Elec. Engring., U. So. Calif., 1956. Sr. staff engr. Hughes Aircraft Co., El Segundo, Calif., 1947-77; prof. elec. engring. U. So. Calif., Los Angeles, 1956-64; dean engring. Northrop U., Los Angeles, 1977-80; project engr. TRW, San Bernardino, Calif., 1980—; cons. in field. Contbr. articles to tech. jours. Patentee in field. Served to capt. AUS, 1943-46, ETO. Mem. IEEE (sr. mem.), Sigma Xi, Eta Kappa Nu, Tau Beta Pi. Republican. Episcopalian. Lodge: Elks. Current work: Radar guilded missiles, smart reentry vehicles, ground (intrusion) radar, antenna, antenna window/plasma design and analysis, communications systems design. Subspecialties: Electronics; Systems engineering. Home: PO Box 1038 552 S Santa Barbara Ave Sugarloaf CA 92386 Office: TRW-Norton AFB PO Box 1310 San Bernardino CA 92402

YOUNG, JAMES ALLAN, physicist; b. Hamilton, Ont., Can., Mar. 9, 1934; came to U.S., 1957, naturalized, 1967; s. Jack and May (Jones) Y.; m. Tanis Ruth Dalrymple, June 26, 1982; children—Carol Darlene, Kathryn Joan. B.S., McMaster U., 1957; Ph.D., U. Calif.-Berkeley, 1961. Physicist Gen. Electric Co., Pleasanton, Calif., 1960-63; asst. chmn. accelerator physics dept. Gen. Atomic, San Diego, 1963-68; sci. asst. to dep. dir. sci. and tech. Def. Nuclear Agy., Washington, 1968-70; mgr. theoretical div. Sci. Applications, Inc., La Jolla, Calif., 1970-75; pres., chmn. bd. Jaycor, San Diego, 1975—. Author: Aswan High, 1983. Mem. Chancellor's Assn., U. Calif.-San Diego, 1983—. Episcopalian. Subspecialty: Fluid mechanics. Office: PO Box 85154 San Diego CA 92138

YOUNG, JAMES FORREST, elec. engr., educator; b. Meadville, Pa., June 22, 1943; s. David George and Carolyn Hope (Spinney) Y.; m. Cecily Sweet, June 10, 1971. B.S., M.I.T., 1965, M.S., 1966; Ph.D. in Elec. Engring, Stanford U., 1970. Research assoc. Stanford U., 1970-75, prof. elec. engring., 1975—; asst. dir. tech. ops. Stanford U. (Ginzton Lab.), 1977-83, assoc. dir. Ginzton Lab., 1983—; cons. Bell Telephone Labs, Spectra-Physics, Quanta-Ray, Coherent. Contbr. articles to profl. jours. Fellow Optical Soc. Am.; mem. IEEE, Fedn. Am. Scientists, Tau Beta Pi. Current Work: Research and development of new lasers, short wave length sources and new laser applications. Subspecialties: Optical engineering; Laser spectroscopy. Home: 940 Cottrell Way Stanford CA 94305 Office: Ginzton Lab Stanford CA 94305

YOUNG, JAMES FRANCIS, engineering educator; b. Palmerston North, N.Z., Jan. 6, 1940; came to U.S., 1969; s. Robert Oswald and June Lifford (Hewitt) Y.; m. Heather June McQuarrie, July 21, 1964; children—Warwick Evan, Helen Claire. B.Sc., U. N.Z., Christchurch, 1960, M.Sc. with honors, 1961; Ph.D., Imperial Coll., London, 1965. Scientist, Dept. Sci. Indsl. Research, Willington, N.Z., 1961-69; research chemist Portland Cement Assn., Skokie, Ill., 1969-70; asst. prof. engring. U. Ill., Urbana, 1970-74, assoc. prof., 1974-77, prof., 1977—; cons. Elkem Chems., Kristiansand, Norway, 1983—, U.S. Army Engrs., Champaign, Ill., 1984—. Co-author: Concrete, 1981. Editor: (serial publ.) Cements Research Progress, 1974—. 1851 Exhbn. scholar, 1962-65. Fellow Am. Ceramic Soc. (div. chmn. 1977-78, trustee 1984—); mem. Am. Concrete Inst., ASTM (P.H. Bates award 1974), Chi Epsilon (faculty mem.). Current work: Cement manufacture, concrete admixtures, concrete properties, new cement-based materials. Subspecialties: Civil engineering; Materials (engineering). Home: 1006 S Orchard Urbana IL 61801 Office: Dept Civil Engring U Ill 208 N Romine Urbana IL 61801

YOUNG, JERRY WESLEY, nutrition educator; b. Mulberry, Tenn., Aug. 19, 1934; s. Rufus William and Annie Jewell (Sweeney) Y.; m. Charlotte Sullenger, July 8, 1959; children: David Wesley, Jeretha Lynn. B.S., Berry Coll., 1957; M.S., N.C. State U.-Raleigh, 1959, Ph.D., 1963. Research asst. N.C. State U., Raleigh, 1957-63; NIH fellow U. Wis., Madison, 1963-65; asst. prof. animal sci Iowa State U., Ames, 1965-71, assoc. prof., 1971-74, prof., 1974 . Contbr. numerous articles to profl. publs. NIH grantee, 1966-69, 71-78; U.S. Dept. Agr. grantee, 1979-82. Mem. Am. Inst. Nutrition, Am. Dairy Sci. Assn., Am. Soc. Animal Sci., Sigma Xi, Phi Kappa Phi. Democrat. Baptist. Current Work: Metabolism and kinetics of glucose in cattle; ketosis in lactating cows; digestive physiology and metabolism of ruminants. Subspecialties: Animal nutrition; Nutrition (biology). Home: 1515 20th St Ames IA 50010 Office: Iowa State U 313 Kildee Hall Ames IA 50011

YOUNG, JOHN ALAN, See *Who's Who in America,* 43rd edition.

YOUNG, JOHN EDWARD, chemist; b. Sioux Falls, S.D., Nov. 24, 1940; s. John E. and Dorothy H. (Rost) Y.; m. Natalie Brodzinsky, June 8, 1969; children—H. Daniel, Charles J. B.S., Iowa State U., 1962; Ph.D., Cornell U., 1970. Chemist Gulf Research and Devel. Co., Pitts., 1970-75, Argonne Nat. Lab., Ill., 1975—. Patentee in field (6). Contbr. articles to tech. jours. Chmn. Energy & Environment Commn., Woodridge, Ill., 1979—. Mem. Am. Chem. Soc., AAAS, Chgo. Catalyst Soc., Sigma Xi. Current work: Conversion of municipal solid waste to liquid fuels, chemical coal cleaning, coal conversion processes. Subspecialties: Catalysis chemistry; Kinetics. Home: 6701 King Ct Woodridge IL 60517 Office: 9700 S Cass Bldg 205 Argonne IL 60439

YOUNG, JOHN FALKNER, research biologist, educator; b. Tyler, Tex., Apr. 3, 1940; s. Cuthbert Benjamin and Vivian Irene (Falkner) Y.; m. Victoria Mary Molter, Aug. 27, 1977; 1 child, Christopher Benjamin. B.A., N. Tex. State U., 1963; B.S., U. Houston, 1966; M.S., U. Fla., 1969, Ph.D., 1973. Research biologist Nat. Ctr. for Toxicol. Research, Jefferson, Ark., 1973—, acting div. dir., 1980-82, div. dir., 1982—; adj. asst. prof. pharmacy and interdisciplinary toxicology U. Ark. for Med. Sci., Little Rock, 1979—; adj. assoc. prof. pharmacy U Tenn. Ctr. Health Scis., 1982—. Recipient Commendable Service awards FDA, 1974, 82. Mem. Am. Pharm. Assn., Soc. Applied Spectroscopy, Soc. for Computer Simulation, AAAS, Teratology Soc., Little Rock Jaycees, (pres. 1975), Sigma Xi. Club: Twin City Rugby (Little Rock). Current work: Pharmacokinetics/pharmacodynamics; predictive mathematical relationships between teratogenic endpoints and pharmacokinetic parameters. Subspecialties: Pharmacokinetics; Teratology. Office: Div Reproductive and Developmental Toxicology HFT-130 Nat Ctr for Toxicol Research Jefferson AR 72079

YOUNG, KEVIN NORMAN, research meteorologist; b. Reading, Pa., Nov. 11, 1956; s. Kenneth Norman and Ruth Rose (Wentzel) Y. B.S. in Astronomy, Villanova U., 1978; M.S. in Atmospheric Physics, Drexel U., 1980. Research asst. Drexel U., 1979-82; research meteorologist FAA Tech. Ctr., Atlantic City, 1982—. Contbr. articles to profl. jours. Mem. Am. Meteorol. Soc., Am. Astron. Soc., U.S. Ski Assn., U.S. Recreational Ski Assn. Current work: Severe local storm research, automation of mesoscale analysis, numerical weather prediction on the mesoscale. Subspecialty: Meteorology. Office: Fed Aviation Adminstrn FAA Tech Ctr ACT110 Atlantic City NJ 08405

YOUNG, LAURENCE RETMAN, biomedical engineer, educator; b. N.Y.C., Dec. 19, 1935; s. Benjamin and Bess (Retman) Y.; m. Joan Marie Fisher, June 12, 1960; children—Eliot Fisher, Leslie Ann, Robert Retman. A.B., Amherst Coll., 1957; S.B., MIT, 1957; S.M., Mass. Inst. Tech., 1959, Sc.D., 1962; Certificat de License (French Govt. fellow), Faculty of Sci. U. of Paris, France, 1958. Registered profl. engr., Mass. Engr. Sperry Gyroscope Co., Great Neck, N.Y., 1957; engr. Instrumentation Lab., Mass. Inst. Tech., 1958-60, asst. prof. aero. and astronautics, 1962-67, asso. prof., 1967-70, prof., 1970—; summer lectr. U. Ala., Huntsville, 1966-68; lectr. Med. Sch. Harvard U., 1970-78; mem. tng. com. biomed. engring. NIH, 1971-73; mem. com. space medicine and biology Space Sci. Bd., Nat. Acad. Scis., 1974—, chmn. vestibular panel summer study of life scis. in space, 1977; mem. com. engring. and clin. care Nat. Acad. Engring., 1970; mem. Air Force Sci. Adv. Bd., 1979—; vis. prof. Swiss Fed. Inst. Tech., Zurich, 1972-73, Conservatoire Nationale des Arts and Metiers, Paris, 1972-73; vis. scientist Kantonsspital Zurich, 1972-73; prin. investigator vestibular expts. on Spacelabs—1, 4 and D-1, 1977—; cons. Arthur D. Little, NASA, Gulf & Western, Link div. Singer Co., Boeing Corp. Contbg. author: chpt. on vestibular system Medical Physiology, 1974; Editorial bd.: chpt. on vestibular system Internat. Jour. Man-Machine Studies, 1966-75, Neurosci, 1976—; Contbr. numerous articles to profl. jours. Fellow IEEE (Franklin V. Taylor award 1963); mem. Nat. Acad. Engring., Biomed. Engring. Soc. (founding/charter mem., dir. 1972-75, pres. 1979-80), Aerospace Med. Assn., ASTM (com. sports safety, subcom. skiing safety, chmn. skiing statistics subcom. 1975—), Internat. Fedn. Automatic Control (tech. com. biomed. engring. 1975—), AIAA (working group for simulator facilities 1976—, Dryden lectr. in research 1982), Internat. Soc. Skiing Safety (dir. 1977—), Barany Soc., Tau Beta Pi. Inventor eye movement monitor. Current Work: Human adaptation to weightlessness; human factors. Subspecialties: Biomedical engineering; Space medicine. Home: 8 Devon Rd Newton Centre MA 02159 Office: Mass Inst Tech Dept Aeros and Astronautics Cambridge MA 02139

YOUNG, LLOYD MARTIN, physicist; b. Merricourt, N.D., Nov. 9, 1942; s. Stanley Clyde and Grace L. (Olsen) Y.; m. Linda Kay Heuer, Mar. 8, 1966; children—Christopher Lee, Daniel Lloyd. B.S., U. N.D., 1965, M.S., 1966; Ph.D., U. Ill., 1972. Asst. research prof. U. Ill., Urbana, 1972-75, research physicist, 1975-79; project leader Los Alamos Nat. Lab., 1979—. Mem. Am. Phys. Soc., AAAS. Current work: Design and build racetrack microtrons, free electron lasers and medical accelerators. Subspecialty: Free-electron lasers. Office: MS H 817 Los Alamos Nat Lab Los Alamos NM 87545

YOUNG, LOUISE GRAY, planetary astronomer, educator; b. Los Angeles, Oct. 4, 1935; d. Frank Elliot and Ruth Alice (Davis) Dillon; m. Bruce Everett Gray, Nov., 1953 (div. 1959); children—Gregory, Elizabeth; m. Andrew Tipton Young, Dec. 14, 1968. B.S., UCLA, 1958, M.S., 1959; Ph.D., Calif. Tech., 1963. Sr. scientist Jet Propulsion Lab., Pasadena, Calif., 1963-73; research assoc. Tex. A&M U., College Station, 1973-80; adj. prof. San Diego State U., Calif., 1980—. Exchange scientist Nat. Acad. Sci., Poland, 1974, USSR, 1980. Fellow Optical Soc. Am.; mem. Internat. Astron. Union, Am. Astron. Soc., Am. Meteorol. Soc. Current work: Planetary atmospheres; remote sensing; atomic and molecular physics. Home: 4906 63rd St San Diego CA 92115 Office: San Diego State U Astronomy Dept San Diego CA 92182

YOUNG, MICHAEL WARREN, geneticist; b. Miami, Fla., Mar. 28, 1949; s. Lloyd G. and Mildred L. (Tillery) Y.; m. Laurel Ann Eckhardt, Dec. 27, 1978. B.A., U. Tex., 1971, Ph.D., 1975. Postdoctoral fellow Stanford U., 1975-77; asst. prof. genetics Rockefeller U., N.Y.C., 1978-84, assoc. prof., 1984—; adv. panel for genetic biology NSF, 1984—. Contbr. articles to profl. jours. Meyer Found. fellow, 1978—. Mem. Genetics Soc. Am., AAAS. Current Work: Eukaryote chromosome organization, transposable elements, genes controlling development and behavior. Subspecialties: Gene actions; Genome organization. Office: Rockefeller U 1230 York Ave New York NY 10021

YOUNG, ORAN REED, educator, political scientist; b. Yonkers, N.Y., Mar. 15, 1941; s. John A. and Eleanor (Wiggin) Y.; 1 dau., Linda Katrin. A.B., Harvard U., 1962; M.A., Yale U., 1964, Ph.D., 1965. Mem. staff Hudson Inst., 1962-64; research asso. Harvard, 1965; prof. polit. sci. Princeton, 1966-71; prof. govt. U. Tex., Austin, 1972-76; prof. govt. and politics U. Md., College Park, 1976-82; co-dir. Center for No. Studies, 1980-82, dir., 1983—. Author: The Intermediaries: Third Parties in International Crises, 1967, Systems of Political Science, 1968, (with others) Neutralization and World Politics, 1968, The Politics of Force: Bargaining During International Crises, 1968, (with others) Political Leadership and Collective Goods, 1971, Bargaining: Formal Theories of Negotiation, 1975, Resource Management at the International Level, 1977, Compliance and Public Authority, A Theory with Applications to International Politics, 1979, Natural Resources and the State: The Political Economy of Resource Management, 1981, Resource Regimes: Natural Resources and Social Institutions, 1982; Sr. editor: World Politics, 1968-76; mem. editorial bd.: Internat. Orgn., 1968-76. Mem. Internat. Studies Assn., Am. Soc. Polit. and Legal Philosophy, Public Choice Soc. Club: Cosmos. Current work: Designing institutional arrangements to govern the human use of natural resources and natural environments. Subspecialty: Resource management. Home: East Hill Wolcott VT 05680

YOUNG, PEGGY SANBORN, psychologist; b. Painesville, Ohio, Aug. 25, 1926; d. Philip Harold and Josephine Diana (Masters) Sanborn; m. Philip Percy Young, Nov. 14, 1947 (div. Sept. 1968); children: Philip Harold, Timothy Mark, Don Sanborn. B.S. Ed., Baldwin Wallace Coll., 1956; M.A., Case Western Res. U., 1963; Ph.D., Kent State U., 1977. Tchr. spl. edn. Willoughby (Ohio) East Schs., 1960-61; vocat. counseling psychologist Salvation Army Hosp., Cleve., 1961-62; psychologist Willoughby Eastlake Schs.(Ohio), 1962-63, Mentor (Ohio) Pub. Schs., 1963-65, Tuslaw and Fairless Local Schs., Stark County, Ohio, 1965-67; chief psychologist Mentor (Ohio) Pub. Schs., 1967-75; coordinator spl. edn. and related services, 1975—; dir. ops. (Body Wrap of Mentor), 1981—; mem. adv. bd. Comprehensive Program for Hearing Impaired, Mayfield, Ohio, 1975; mem. Lake County Welfare Bd. Childrens Services, Painesville, 1979-82. Mem. Am. Psychol. Assn., Nat. Assn. Sch. Psychologists, Ohio Psychol. Assn., Ohio Assn. Sch. Psychologists, Cleve. Area Sch. Psychologists. Republican. Episcopalian. Current Work: Handicapped children, personnel psychology, personnel selection, body image and self concept; obesity. Subspecialties: Learning; Behavioral psychology. Home: 9956 Johnnycake Ridge C-5 Painesville OH 44077 Office: Mentor Exempted Village Schs 6451 Center St Mentor OH 44060

YOUNG, RICHARD ALAN, editor, environmental consultant; b. Oak Park, Ill., Mar. 17, 1935; s. Harry Alfred and L. Claribel (Yoss) Y.; m. Carol Ann Schellinger, June 28, 1958; children—Steven Scott, Karen Ann, Christopher Alan. Student Colo. Sch. Mines, 1954-56; B.S. U. Iowa, 1958. Registered profl. engr. Chief designer Cardox Corp., Chgo., 1958-61; asst. chief engr. Goodman Mfg., Chgo., 1961-64; project mgr. Signode Corp., Glenview, Ill., 1964-69; editor Pollution Engring. Mag., Northbrook, Ill., 1969—; v.p. Young Environ. Services, Glenview, 1972—. Author-editor 26 textbooks and reference books on environ. engring. Contbr. articles to profl. jours. Patentee in field. Mem. Inst. Hazardous Materials Mgmt. (bd. dirs.), Nat. Soc. Profl. Engrs., Air Pollution Control Assn., Water Pollution Control Fedn., Assn. Local Air Pollution Control Ofcls. (com. chmn.). Current work: Study of new technologies for control of industrial and municipal environmental pollutants. Subspecialties: Environmental engineering; Water supply and wastewater treatment. Home: 1253 Roosevelt Ave Glenview IL 60025 Office: Pollution Engring 1935 Shermer Rd Northbrook IL 60062

YOUNG, ROBERT JOHN, emeritus animal science educator; b. Calgary, Alta., Canada, Feb. 10, 1923; came to U.S., 1956, naturalized, 1965; s. Harold P. and Kate A. (Thomson) Y.; m. Greta G. Milne, June 16, 1950; children—Kenneth W., Donna E. B.S.A. with honors, U. B.C., 1950; Ph.D., Cornell U., 1953. Research asso. dept. med. research Banting & Best, Toronto, Ont., Can., 1953-56; research chemist Internat. Minerals and Chem. Corp., Skokie, Ill., 1956-58, Proctor and Gamble Co., Cin., 1958-60; prof. animal nutrition Cornell U., 1960-85, chmn. dept. poultry sci., 1965-76, chmn. dept. animal sci., 1976-83, assoc. dir. research, 1983-84, assoc. dean Coll. Agr. and Life Scis., 1984-85, emeritus prof. animal sci., 1985, coordinator phys. space, 1985—. Author: (with M.L. Scott, M.C. Nesheim) Nutrition of the Chicken, 1976; Contbr. articles to profl. jours. Served with RCAF, 1942-45. Mem. Am. Inst. Nutrition, Poultry Sci. Assn., Am. Soc. Animal Sci., Am. Soc. Dairy Sci. Current Work: Poultry nutrition. Subspecialty: Animal nutrition. Office: Roberts Hall Cornell U Ithaca NY 14853

YOUNG, ROY ALTON, plant research institute administrator; b. McAlister, N.Mex., Mar. 1, 1921; s. John Arthur and Etta Julia (Sprinkle) Y.; m. Marilyn Ruth Sandman, May 22, 1950; children: Janet Elizabeth, Randall Owen. B.S., N.Mex. A&M Coll., 1941; M.S., Iowa State U., 1942, Ph.D., 1948; LL.D. (hon.), N.Mex. State U., 1978. Teaching fellow Iowa State U., 1941-42, instr., 1946-47, Indsl. fellow, 1947-48; asst. prof. Oreg. State U., 1948-50, asso. prof., 1950-53, prof., 1953-76, head dept. botany and plant pathology, 1958-66, dean research, 1966-70, acting pres., 1969-70, v.p. for research and grad. studies, 1970-76; chancellor U. Nebr., Lincoln, 1976-80; mng. dir. Boyce Thompson Inst. Plant Research, Cornell U., Ithaca, N.Y., 1980—; Dir. Pacific Power & Light Co., First Bank of Ithaca.; Mem. Commn. on Undergrad. Edn. in Biol. Scis., 1963-68; cons. State Expt. Stas. div. U.S. Dept. Agr.; chmn. subcom. plant pathogens, agr. bd. Nat. Acad. Scis.-NRC, 1965-68, mem. exec. com. study on problems of pest control, 1972-75; mem. exec. com. Nat. Govs.' Council on Sci. and Tech., 1970-74; mem. U.S. com. man and biosphere UNESCO, from 1973; mem. com. to rev. U.S. component Internat. Biol. Program, Nat. Acad. Scis., 1974-76; mem. adv. panel on post-doctoral fellowships in environ. sci. Rockefeller Found., 1974-78; bd. dirs. Boyce Thompson Inst. Plant Research, 1975—, Boyce Thompson Southwestern Arboretum, 1981—; mem. adv. com. Directorate for Engring. and Applied Sci., NSF, 1977-81, mem. sea grant adv. panel, 1978-80. Trustee Ithaca Coll., 1982—. Served to lt. USNR, 1943-46. Fellow AAAS (exec. com. Pacific div. 1963-67, pres. div. 1971), Am. Phytopath Soc. (pres. Pacific div. 1957); mem. Oreg. Acad. Sci., Nat. Assn. State Univs. and Land Grant Colls. (chmn. council for research policy and adminstrn. 1970, chmn. standing com. on environment and energy 1974-82), Sigma Xi, Phi Kappa Phi, Phi Sigma, Sigma Alpha Epsilon. Subspecialty: Plant pathology. Office: Boyce Thompson Inst Tower Rd Cornell U Ithaca NY 14853

YOUNG, STEPHEN KWOK-WAI, physicist; b. Hong Kong, Dec. 28, 1946; came to U.S., 1966, naturalized, 1976; s. Augustine Chi-Yet and Maria Oi-Wan (Chow) Y.; m. Mary Helen Whisenant, Jan. 23, 1971; children—Jeffrey Christopher, Stephanie Caroline. B.S. summa cum laude in Physics, St. Joseph's U., Phila., 1969; M.S. in Physics, U. Md., 1971, Ph.D. in Physics, 1973. Adj. asst. prof. UCLA, 1973-76; mem. staff Los Alamos Nat. Lab, 1976-77; mem. tech. staff Def. Systems Group, TRW, Redondo Beach, Calif., 1977-82, sect. head Energy Technology Div., 1982-83, asst. dept. mgr., 1983—, sr. scientist, 1984—; vis. staff mem. Los Alamos Nat. Lab., 1977-79; vis. scientist UCLA, 1976-78. Author scholarly papers. Recipient award for teaching excellence U. Md., 1971. Mem. Am. Phys. Soc. Current work: Research in plasma separation of isotopes, ion cyclotron resonance heating, high power microwave technology, scattering theory, 3-body methods in nuclear reaction theories, muon-catalyzed fusion. Subspecialties: Plasma (energy science and technology); Nuclear physics. Office: TRW Energy Technology Div R1/2020 One Space Park Redondo Beach CA 90278

YOUNG, WEI, biophysicist; b. Loting, Hopei, China, Feb. 10, 1919; came to U.S., 1949, naturalized, 1961; s. Shu-Tong Yang and Hai-Lan Chang; m. Ho Lee, Dec. 28, 1949; 1 dau., Linda. B.S., Cath. U. Peking, 1943; Ph.D., U. Calif.-Berkeley, 1957. Instr. Med. Coll., Shanghai, China, 1945-49; biophysicist U. Calif.-Berkeley, 1957-63, sr. biophysicist, 1979—; biophysicist-8 U. Calif. Livermore Lab., 1963-70; sr. fellow Nat. Research Council (Moffett, Calif.), 1971-73; adj. research prof. San Jose State U., Calif., 1975-79. Author: Biological Effects of Magnetic Fields, 1969; Contbr. articles to profl. publs. Ames/NASA NRC Grantee, 1971-73, 1975-78, 1976—. Mem. Am. Physiol. Soc., AAAS, N.Y. Acad. Sci., Cryobiology Assn. (charter). Democrat. Current Work: Interaction of microwave/laser on biomembrane energy barrier, zero magnetic field on Ga-As Microcuits; membrane bound enzyme kinetics; microwave reflectometry for arteriosclerosis. Subspecialties: Biophysics (biology); Comparative neurobiology. Home: 5978 Greenridge Rd Castro Valley CA 94546 Office: U Calif Berkeley CA 94720

YOUNG, WILLIAM ROBERT, air force officer, meteorologist; b. Foxboro, Mass., Dec. 27, 1947; s. Robert Benjamin and Margaret Louise (Moore) Y.; m. Deanna Louise McConnell Lusk, June 13, 1982. B.S. in Social Sci, Colo. State U., 1969; M. Meteorology, Tex. A&M U., 1977. Cert. meteorologist. Commd. 2d lt. U.S. Air Force, 1969, advanced through grades to maj., 1982; weather forecaster (Detachment 31 15 Weather SQ, Dobbins AFB), Marietta, Ga., 1971-73; asst. team chief,global team (Air Force Global Weather Central), Offutt AFB, Nebr., 1973-76; staff meteorologist space shuttle (Space Div.), El Segundo, Calif., 1978-81; comdr. (Detachment 10, 7th Weather SQ), Giebelstadt AAF, W. Ger., 1981—. Decorated Air Force Commendation Medal, 1973, 76; Meritorious Service Medal, 1981. Mem. Air Force Assn., AIAA. Republican. Methodist. Current Work: Forecasting of freezing precipitation types in attempt to develop a decision graph. Subspecialty: Synoptic meteorology. Home: 12002 Dunklee Ln Garden Grove CA 92640

YOUNGER, MELANIE MOORE, veterinarian, educator; b. Cookeville, Tenn., Feb. 6, 1950; d. William F. and Betty (Fickel) Moore; m. George Winston Younger, Mar. 15, 1975; children: Katherine Moore, Elizabeth Sims. B.A., Ohio Wesleyan U., 1972; D.V.M., Auburn U., 1975. Lic. veterinarian, Tenn., Ala., Ohio, Ky., La. Instr. Auburn U., 1975-76; staff veterinarian Grady Vet. Hosp., Cin., 1976-77, Brentwood Vet. Hosp., Tenn., 1979-80; asst. prof. dept. agr. Northwestern State U., Natchitoches, La., 1980—, pvt. practice vet. medicine, 1981—. Vol. Natchitoches Animal Shelter. Named to Athletic Hall of Fame Ohio Wesleyan U., 1979. Mem. Central La. Vet. Medicine, La. Vet. Medicine Assn., Am. Assn. Animal Tech. Educators, AAUW, Bus. and Profl. Women. (local pres.). Methodist. Subspecialties: Preventive medicine (veterinary medicine); Internal medicine (veterinary medicine). Home: 1405 Barclay Narchitoches LA 71457 Office: Small Animal Clinic 126 Touline St Natchitoches LA 71457 Agr Dept Vet Tech Program Northwestern State U 126 Touline St Natchitoches LA 71457

YOUNGS, ROBERT LELAND, forestry educator; b. Pittsfield, Mass., Feb. 10, 1924; s. Frank Leland and Florence Catherine (Wilcox) Y.; m. Esther Louise Stevenson, June 11, 1949; children—Susan, Karen, Steven, Rebecca, Sarah. B.S., Syracuse U., 1948; M.W.T., U. Mich., 1950; Ph.D., Yale U., 1957. Researcher U.S. Forest Service, Dept. Agr., Madison, Wis., 1951-66, research adminstr., Washington, 1966-70, 72-75, research adminstr., New Orleans, 1970-72, research adminstr., Madison, 1975-85; prof. dept. forest products Va. Poly. Inst. and State U., Blacksburg, 1985—; cons. AID, 1984-85. Contbr. articles to profl. jours. Leader Combined Fed. Campaign, Madison, 1976-83. C.S. Chapman fellow Yale U., 1953; recipient Disting. Service award Dept. Agr., 1981; Sr. Exec. Service Presdl. award, 1984. Fellow Internat. Acad. Wood Sci. (exec. bd. 1983—); mem. Forest Products Research Soc. (Wood award 1957), Soc. Wood Sci. Tech. (pres. 1960-61), Soc. Am. Foresters, Sigma Xi. Clubs: Cosmos (Washington); University (Blacksburg). Current work: International forestry; forestry for social and economic development. Subspecialty: Forestry. Office: Va Poly Inst and State U 210 Cheatham Hall Blacksburg VA 24061

YOUNOS, TAMIM M., agricultural engineering educator; b. Kabul, Afghanistan, Nov. 3, 1947; came to U.S., 1977, s. Mohammed and Setara Younos; m. Yumiko Ohno, July 1, 1973; children—Ken, Rona. B.S., Tohoku U., Sendai, 1971; M.S. in Engring., U. Tokyo, 1973. D. Engring., 1976. Postdoctoral assoc. Cornell U., Ithaca, N.Y., 1977-78; research assoc. Va. Poly. Inst., Blacksburg, 1979-80, asst. prof. agrl. engring., 1980—. Contbr. articles to profl. jours. Grantee Va. State Water Control Bd. 1983, Mining & Mineral Resources Research Inst. 1984-85, Va. Water Resources Research Ctr., 1985. Mem. ASCE, Am. Soc. Agrl. Engrs., Water Pollution Control Fedn., Soil Conservation Soc. Am., Inter-Am. Assn. Sanitary Engrs. Current work: Land application of sludge; nonpoint source pollution; subsurface flow. Subspecialties: Water supply and wastewater treatment; Agricultural engineering. Office: Dept Agrl Engring Va Poly Inst and State U 304 Seitz Hall Blacksburg VA 24061

YOUNT, DAVID EUGENE, physics educator, physics and physiology researcher; b. Prescott, Ariz., June 5, 1935; s. Robert Ephram and Jeannette Francis (Judson) Y.; m. Christel Marlene Notz, Feb. 22, 1975; children—Laura Christine, Gregory Gordon, Steffen Jurgen Robert, Sonja Kate Jeannette. B.S. in Physics, Calif. Inst. Tech., 1957; M.S. in Physics, Stanford U., 1959, Ph.D. in Physics, 1963. Instr., asst. prof. Princeton U., N.J., 1962-64; NSF postdoctoral fellow U. Paris, Orsay, France, 1964-65; research assoc. Stanford U., Calif., 1965-69; asst. prof. physics U. Hawaii, Honolulu, 1969-73, prof., 1973—, chmn. dept. physics and astronomy, 1979—. Editor: Proc. 4th Topical Conf. in Particle Physics, 1971. Contbr. articles to profl. jours. Minn. and Mining & Mfg. fellow, 1963; U. Hawaii grantee, 1974—. Mem. Am. Phys. Soc., Am. Chem. Soc., Undersea Med. Soc., AAUP, Sigma Xi. Republican. Lutheran. Current work: Positron-electron colliding beams, photoproduction of elementary particles, diving medicine, decompression sickness, gas bubble nucleation, diving tables. Subspecialties: Particle physics; Physiology (medicine). Office: Dept Physics and Astronomy U Hawaii 2505 Correa Rd Honolulu HI 96822

YOUSIF, SALAH MOHAMMAD, engineering educator, consultant, researcher; b. Burin, Palestine, Nov. 15, 1938; came to U.S., 1965, naturalized, 1974; s. Mohammad Yousif Ibrahim and Aisha (Saber) Darwish; m. Nancy Lou de Manigold, June 28, 1967; children—Mariam, Dina, Leila. B.S.E.E., U. Alexandria, Arab Republic of Egypt, 1962; M.S.E.E., Middle East Tech. U., Ankara, Turkey, 1964; Ph.D. in Elec. Engring., Oreg. State U., 1969. Registered profl. engr., Calif. Elec. engr. Govt. of Jordan, Amman, 1962-63; chief elec. engr. Govt. Kuwait, Kuwait, 1964-65; instr. elec. engring. Mich. State U., East Lansing, 1966-68; instr. Oreg. State U., Corvallis, 1968-69; prof., Calif. State U., Sacramento, 1969—; cons. Sacramento Utility Dist., 1969-70, Devel. and Resources Corp., Sacramento, 1972-79, Energy Commn., Sacramento, 1976-82. Contbr. articles to profl. jours. Fellow UN, Arab. Republic of Egypt, 1957-62; Fulbright scholar Council for Exchange of Scholars, Washington, D.C., 1981-82. Mem. IEEE, Soc. Indsl. and Applied Math. Muslim. Current work: Control systems, power system planning, computer operation and control of power systems. Subspecialty: Computer engineering. Home: 1707 Cathay Way Sacramento CA 95864 Office: Calif State U 6000 J St Sacramento CA 95819

YOUSSEF, MAHMOUD Z. HASSAN, research engineer; b. Cairo, Egypt, Oct. 9, 1945; came to U.S., 1974; s. Hassan M. and S. (Youssef) Y.; m. Mona A. Ismail, Jan. 23, 1974; children: Amr M., Susan. B.Sc., U. Alexandria, Egypt, 1967, M.Sc., 1973; M.Sc., U. Wis., 1976, Ph.D. in Nuclear Engring, 1980. Teaching asst. Atomic Energy Authority, Cairo, Egypt, 1971-74; research asst. Nuclear Study Ctr. of Casaccia, Rome, Italy, 1974; research asst. dept. nuclear engring. U. Wis., Madison, 1974-80; research engr. Sch. Engring. and Applied Sci., UCLA, 1980—; cons. TRW, Redondo Beach, Calif., 1981—. Contbr. articles to profl. jours. IAEA fellow, 1974. Mem. Am. Nuclear Soc. Current Work: Fusion and fusion-fission engineering; cross-section processing; sensitivity analysis; perturbation theory. Subspecialties: Nuclear fusion; Nuclear fission. Office: UCLA Sch Engring & Applied Sci Los Angeles CA 90024

YOZAWITZ, ALLAN, neuropsychologist; b. Bklyn., Jan. 8, 1949; s. Louis and Sylvia Claire Y.; m. Arlene Susan Greenfield, Jan. 20, 1973; children: Elissa Gayle, Justin Mark. B.S., Poly. Inst. Bklyn., 1970; M.A., Queens Coll. CUNY, 1973; Ph.D., CUNY, 1977. Diplomate in clin. neuropsychology Am. Bd. Profl. Psychology, Am. Bd. Clin. Neuropsychology. Asst. research scientist biometrics N.Y. State Dept. Mental Hygiene, N.Y.C., 1970-77; trainee clin. neuropsychology Montefiore Hosp. and Med. Center, Bronx, N.Y., 1974-75; cons. gerontology sect. N.Y. State Psychiat. Inst., N.Y.C., 1975-76; dir. neuropsychology lab. Hutchings Psychiat. Center, N.Y. State Office Mental Health, Syracuse, 1977—; asst. prof. psychology Med. Coll. SUNY Upstate Med. Center, Syracuse, 1979—; adj. asst. prof. psychology Syracuse U., 1979—; cons. Syracuse Devel. Center, 1979-83, Benjamin Rush Center, Syracuse, 1980—; pvt. practice, Syracuse, 1979—; mem. profl. adv. bd. N.Y. State Head Injury Assn., 1984—. Cons. editor: Jour. Clin. and Exptl. Neuropsychology, 1983—. Contbr. articles to profl. jours. NIMH grantee, 1974-77, 79-82. Mem. AAAS, Am. Psychol. Assn. (charter mem. div. clin. neuropsychology 1979—), Internat. Neuropsychol. Soc. (task force on edn., accreditation and credentialing 1979—, dir. continuing edn. 1985—), N.Y. State Psychol. Assn., N.Y. Acad. Scis., Soc. Neuroscience. Current Work: Cognitive rehabilitation of psychiatric patients based on neuropsychological diagnosis, computer software design for cognitive rehabilitation, theories of neuropsychological basis of psychiatric disorder. Subspecialties: Neuropsychology; Psychiatry. Home: 150 Brookside Ln Fayetteville NY 13066 Office: Hutchings Psychiat Center Neuropsychology Unit Syracuse NY 13210

YPHANTIS, DAVID ANDREW, biophysicist, educator; b. Boston, July 14, 1930; s. K. Paul and Beatrice (Hanson) Y.; m. Lorna Ruth Nickerson, June 4, 1953; children—Sandra, Peter, Susan, Kim, Diana. A.B., Harvard U., 1952; Ph.D., MIT, 1955. Fellow Am. Cancer Soc., MIT, Cambridge, 1955-56; from asst. to assoc. biophysicist Argonne Nat. Lab., Ill., 1956-58, 58; from asst. prof. to assoc. prof. Rockefeller U., N.Y.C., 1958-64, 64-65; prof. biology SUNY-Buffalo, 1965-68, chmn. biology, 1967-68; prof. biology U. Conn., Storrs, 1968—; cons., vis. investigator Argonne Nat. Lab., 1958-62, 66-67; cons. NIH, Bethesda, Md., 1967-80, Xenogen, Inc., Mansfield, Conn., 1982—; instr. physiology Marine Biol. Lab., Woods Hole, Mass., 1968-73. Editorial bd. profl. jours. Mem. Am. Chem. Soc., Am. Soc. Biol. Chemists, Biophys. Soc. Current work: Protein physical chemistry; instrumentation for biophysical chemistry; ultracentrifugation; data acquisition techniques. Subspecialties: Biophysics (biology); Biochemistry (biology). Home: 99 River Rd Mansfield Center CT 06250 Office: U Conn Biochemistry and Biophysics Sect Box U-125 Storrs CT 06268

YU, CHENG WOU, human genetics educator; b. Kwangtong, China, Apr. 10, 1942; came to U.S., 1969, naturalized, 1983; s. Jang Jong and Feng Tze (Pang) Y.; m. Kathy Lin Ling, May 20, 1972; children—Ivy I-Hua, Victor I-Bing. B.S. in Agronomy, Nat. Taiwan U., Taipei, 1965; M.S. in Plant Sci., Mont. State U., 1971, Ph.D. in Genetics, 1975. Diplomate Am. Bd. Med. Genetics. Postdoctoral fellow Johns Hopkins Med. Sch., 1975-77; sr. assoc. Emory U., 1977-79; asst. prof. La. State U., 1979-83, assoc. prof. Med. Ctr., 1983-84; dir. lab. Calif. Prenatal Diagnosis Inst., San Jose, Calif., 1984—, also dir. Contbr. articles (25) to profl. jours. Recipient So. Med. Assn. Research award, 1980, Biomed. Research award La. Med. Sch., 1980; Bd. of Regents La. State U. Research grantee, 1982. Mem. AAAS, Am. Soc. Human Genetics, Tissue Culture Assn., Am. Soc. Genetics, Assn. Cytogenetic Technologists. Current work: Sequence of DNA replication in human X chromosomes, human chondrocyte culture study, prenatal diagnosis (amniocentesis and chorionic villi biopsy). Subspecialties: Genetics and genetic engineering (medicine); Cell and tissue culture. Home: 414 Crystalline Dr Fremont CA 94539 Office: Calif Prenatal Diagnosis Inst 1390 S Winchester Blvd San Jose CA 95128

YU, FRANCIS TIONG SUY, electrical engineer, educator; b. Amoy, China, Nov. 12, 1932; came to U.S., 1956, naturalized, 1965; s. Kim Tiao and Chang (Go) Y.; m. Lucy Cha, June 16, 1962; children—Peter T., Ann G., Edward H. B.S. in Elec. Engring., Mapua Inst. Tech. (Philippines), 1956; M.S. in Engring., U. Mich., 1958, Ph.D., 1964. Instr. dept. elec. engring. U. Mich., Ann Arbor, 1961-64, lectr., 1964-66; asst. prof. dept. elec. engring. Wayne State U., Detroit, 1966-69, assoc. prof., 1969-76, prof., 1976-80; prof. dept. elec. engring. Pa. State U., University Park, 1980—; consulting engr. Elec. Optics div. Bendix Corp., Ann Arbor, 1966-67; research cons. Gen. Motors Research Lab., Warren, Mich., 1969-70; cons. Inst. Def. Analysis, Arlington, Va., 1970-71. Contbr. to books. Fellow Optical Soc. Am.; mem. IEEE (sr.). Current work: Optical signal processing, holography, information theory. Home: 355 Carogin Dr State College PA 16803 Office: Pa State U Elec Engring Dept University Park PA 16802

YU, JIA-HUEY, pharmacologist, researcher; b. Taiwan, China, May 16, 1941; came to U.S., 1969, naturalized, 1976; d. Te-Fang and Chin-Len (Chang) Lin; m. Henry Hongjen Ye, June 22, 1968; children: Deborah, Tyson. D.D.S., Nat. Taiwan U., Taipei, 1966; M.S., U. Alta., Can.), Edmonton, 1968; Ph.D., U. Mich., 1973. Research assoc. Food and Drug Directorate, Ottawa, Ont., Can., 1968-69; lectr. U. Mich., 1973-74; research asst. prof. Boston U., 1974-77; research asst. prof. physiology U. Ala.-Birmingham, 1977—. Recipient Spl. Dental Research award Nat. Inst. Dental Research, 1980—; Nat. Inst. Dental Research postdoctoral fellow, 1971-73. Mem. Internat. Assn. Dental Reseearch, AAAS, Sigma xi. Current Work: Modulating roles of prostaglandins in regulating secretory activities of salivary glands during stimulation of autonomic innvervations. Subspecialties: Pharmacology; Physiology (medicine). Office: U Ala 1600 University Blvd Birmingham AL 35294

YU, SIMON SHYI-JIAN, insect toxicologist, researcher, educator; b. Ilan, Taiwan, Sept. 11, 1935; came to Can., 1963, came to U.S., 1968; s. Song-Wei and Ah-So (Liaw) Y.; m. Rachel Ruey-Chih Yeh, Sept. 16, 1967; children:Robert, Edmund P. B.S., Nat. Taiwan U., 1959; M.S., McGill U., 1965, Ph.D., 1968. Research entomologist Taiwan Sugar Co., Kaohsiung, 1961-62; research asst. McGill U., Montreal, Que., Can., 1963-68; postdoctoral fellow Cornell U., Ithaca, N.Y., 1968-69; research assoc. Oreg. State U., Corvallis, 1969-74, asst. prof., 1974-79; asst. and assoc. prof. dept. entomology and nematology U. Fla., Gainesville, 1980—, prin. investigator, 1980—. Grantee NIH, 1979—; Grantee EPA, 1981; Grantee U.S. Dept. Agr., 1982—. Mem. Entomol. Soc. Am., AAAS, Am. Chem. Soc., Fla. Entomol. Soc., Sigma Xi. Current Work: Insecticide toxicology, biochemical toxicology, detoxication mechanisms, insecticide resistance, pest management. Subspecialties: Toxicology (agriculture); Environmental toxicology. Home: 3560 NW 30th Blvd Gainesville FL 32605 Office: Dept Entomology and Nematology Univ Fla Gainesville FL 32611

YU, YI-YUAN, academic dean, mechanical and aerospace engineer; b. Tientsin, China, Jan. 29, 1923; came to U.S., 1947, naturalized, 1962; s. Tsi-Chi and Hsiao-Kung (Wang) Y.; m. Eileen Wu, June 14, 1952; children: Yolanda, Lisa. B.S., Tientsin U., 1944; M.S., Northwestern U., 1950, Ph.D., 1951. Asst. prof. applied mechanics Washington U., St. Louis, 1951-54; assoc. prof. mech. engring. Syracuse U., 1954-57; prof. mech. engring. Poly. Inst. Bklyn., 1957-66; cons. engr. Space div. Gen. Electric Co., Valley Forge, Pa., 1966-71; Disting. prof. aero. engring. Wichita State U., 1972-75; mgr. components and analysis Rocketdyne div. Rockwell Internat., Canoga Park, Calif., 1975-79; exec. engr. Rocketdyne div. Rockwell Internat. (Energy Systems Group), 1979-81; dean engring. Newark Coll. Engring., N.J. Inst. Tech., 1981—; vis. prof. Cambridge (Eng.) U., 1960; lectr. Gen. Electric Modern Engring. Course, 1963-73; adv. Middle East Tech. U., Ankara, Turkey, 1966; cons. Chinese U. Devel. Project., 1983; cons. to govt. agys., industry; prin. investigator research grants Air Force Office Sci. Research, 1956-66, NASA Marshall Space Flight Center, 1967-69, NASA Langeley Research Center, 1974-75. Contbr.: chpt. to Handbook of Engineering Mechanics; articles to profl. publs.; reviewer tech., sci. jours. Guggenheim fellow, 1959-60. Fellow AIAA (assoc.); mem. ASME, Am. Soc. Engring Edn., N.Y. Acad. Scis., Sigma Xi, Phi Kappa Phi, Pi Tau Sigma, Tau Beta Pi. Current Work: Dynamics, structural mechanics, wind turbine. Subspecialties: Theoretical and applied mechanics; Aerospace engineering and technology. Home: 22 Linden Aven West Orange NJ 07052 Office: 323 High Street Newark NJ 07102

YUE, MIKE YUAN, nuclear engineer; b. Chungking, Szechuan, China, June 6, 1941; came to U.S., 1964, naturalized, 1976; s. Chien-nan and Fong-shan (Young) L.; m. Anna Mo-Chee Fung, June 5, 1976; children: Vincent John, Joey John. B.S. in Mech. Engring, Nat. Cheng Kung U., Taiwan, 1963; M.S. in Mech. Engring, N.C. State U., 1968, M.S. in nuclear engring, 1972, postgrad., 1969-72. Engr. The Babcock & Wilcox Inc., Lynchburg, Va., 1966-69; sr. nuclear steam supply system engr. Combustion Engring. Inc.,

Windsor, Conn., 1972-76; advanced engr. Westinghouse Hanford Co., Richland, Wash., 1976-82; sr. core analysis engr., supr. Duquesne Light Co., Pitts., 1982—. Contbr. articles to profl. jours. Mem. Am. Nuclear Soc. Baptist. Current Work: Senior core analysis engineering supervisor; core analysis and safety licensing group supervisor; supervise core physics personnel and safety analysis personnel to perform analysis and research to support Beaver Valley nuclear reactors safety analysis activities and fast breeder reactor core physics research. Subspecialties: Nuclear fission; Nuclear engineering. Office: Duquesne Light Company 435 6th Ave Pittsburgh PA 15219

YUEN, HORACE P., electrical engineering and computer science educator; b. Hong Kong, Aug. 3, 1946. B.S. in Elec. Engring., MIT, 1967, M.S., 1967, Ph.D. in Elec. Engring., 1970. Mem. tech. staff exploratory transmission media dept. Bell Telephone Labs., Murray Hill, N.J., 1970-72; engr. Systems Control Inc., Palo Alto, Calif., 1972-73; research scientist Research Lab. Electronics MIT, Cambridge, 1973-80; assoc. prof. Northwestern U., Evanston, Ill., 1980-84, prof. dept. elec. engring. and computer sci., 1984—. Contbr. numerous articles to profl. jours. Current work: Quantum optics and quantum measurement theory; probability theory and applications. Subspecialties: Electrical engineering; Theoretical physics. Home: 2732 Hampton Pkwy # E-1 Evanston IL 60201 Office: Northwestern U Dept Elec Engring and Computer Sci Evanston IL 60201

YUEN, MAN-CHUEN, mechanical and nuclear engineering educator. B.S., Purdue U., 1956; M.S., MIT, 1958; Ph.D., Harvard U., 1965. Structural engr. A.E. Stinson & Assoc., Columbus, Ohio, 1966; research asst. MIT, Cambridge, 1956-58; Harvard U., 1961-64; asst. prof. Northwestern U., Evanston, Ill., 1964-68, assoc. prof., 1968-75; vis. scientist Factory Mutual Research Corp., Norwood, Mass., summer 1970-71; vis. engr. Nat. Bur. Standards, Washington, summer 1973; prof. dept. mech. engring. and astronautical scis., Northwestern U., Evanston, 1975—; vis. engr. Argonne Nat. Lab., Chgo., summer 1976; prof. nuclear engring., Northwestern U., Evanston, 1976—, chmn. dept. mech. engring. and astronautical scis., 1978-79, chmn. dept. mechanical nuclear engring., 1979—. Contbr. numerous articles to profl. jours. Mem. ASME, Combustion Inst., Sigma Xi, Tau Beta Pi. Current work: Heat transfer; fluid dynamics; combustion. Office: Northwestern U Dept Mech and Nuclear Engring Evanston IL 60201

YUNG, SHU-CHIEN, nuclear energy corporation engineer, engineering educator; b. Ching-tu, Szechwan, China, Nov. 13, 1936; came to U.S., 1963, naturalized, 1972; s. Fu-Min and Ching-Dir (Ho) Y.; m. Shu-Shih Chu, Mar. 25, 1967; children: Jane, Delphine, Irene. B.S., Nat. Taiwan U., 1959; M.S., U. Mo.-Rolla, 1966; Ph.D., U. Ill.-Chgo., 1973. Registered profl. engr., N.J., N.Y. Mgr. quality control China Textile Ind. Corp., Nayli, Taiwan, 1961-63; assoc. engr. Allis-Chalmers Mfg. Co., Harvey, Ill., 1965-66; sr. engr. Curtiss-Wright Corp., Wood-Ridge, N.J., 1973-75, Westinghouse Hanford Co., Richland, Wash., 1975-84, Rockwell Hanford Ops., Richland, 1984—; research asst. U. Ill.-Chgo., 1966-73; lectr. Joint Ctr. for Grad. Study, Richland, 1977—. Contbr. papers in field to profl. jours. Am. Nuclear Soc. Current Work: Performance, reliability and safety analyses for high-level nuclear waste in basalt geologic repository, ground-water resaturation time study; intrasubassembly incoherencies studies on liquid metal fast breeder reactor in unprotected transient overpower accidents, sodium fire modelling, nuclear reactor core debris and substrates interaction modelling, containment code development. Subspecialties: Nuclear fission; Nuclear engineering. Home: 2133 Cascade Ct Richland WA 99352 Office: Rockwell Hanford Ops PO Box 800 Richland WA 99352

YUNGER, LIBBY MARIE, pharmacologist; b. East Cleveland, Ohio, Feb. 20, 1944; d. Ladimer and Eleanore Wilma (Svasek) Y.; m. Richard D. Cramer III, May 22, 1979. B.A., Earlham Coll., 1966; postgrad., U. Chgo., 1967-68; M.A., U. Iowa, 1971, Ph.D., 1974. Nat. Inst. Neurol. and Communicable Diseases and Stroke postdoctoral fellow U. Pitts., 1974-75; research biochemist Lederle Labs., Pearl River, N.Y., 1975-78; assoc. sr. investigator Smith Kline & French Labs., Phila., 1978-83; mgr. bioanalytical research Internat. Minerals & Chem. Corp., 1983—. Contbr. articles to profl. jours. Mem. AAAS, Am. Chem. Soc., Soc. Neurosci. N.Y. Acad. Scis., Internat. Soc. Immunopharmacology, Sigma Xi, Phi Beta Kappa. Current Work: Production of polyclonal and monoclonal antibodies to, and development of immunoassays and receptor binding assays for neurotransmitters and other chemical mediators of cellular functions; using cells in culture to model the metabolism and mechanism of action of these mediators in vivo. Subspecialties: Immunopharmacology; Neurochemistry. Office: Dept Chem Research Internat Minerals and Chem Corp Box 207 Terre IN 47808

YUNIS, JORGE JOSÉ, geneticist, pathologist; b. Sincelejo, Colombia; m. Mary Brogmus. M.D., Central U. Madrid, 1956. Gen. practice medicine, Barranquilla, Colombia, 1957-59; resident in clin. pathology, U. Minn., Mpls., 1959-62, resident in anatomical pathology, 1962-64, faculty, 1965—, prof., 1969—, dir. grad. studies in lab. medicine, 1969-74, dir. grad. studies in pathology, 1972-74. Author: Human Chromosome Method, 1965, 75; New Chromosomal Syndromes, 1977; Molecular Structure of Human Chromosomes, 1977. Contbr. over 200 articles to profl. jours. Mem. Leukemia Soc. Am. (trustee 1983—). Current work: Study of chromosome, fragile sites and oncogene defects in human cancer; development and application of high resolution chromosome techniques for diagnosing cancer and birth defects; development of simple blood test for detecting cancer susceptibility through chromosomal fragile sites. Office: U Minn Hosps Box 198 Med Sch Minneapolis MN 55455

YUSPA, STUART HOWARD, cancer research scientist, physician; b. Balt., July 19, 1941; s. Michael and Rose Y.; m. Eleanor M. Hecht, Aug. 1, 1965; children: Catharine, Margaret. B.S., Johns Hopkins U., 1962; M.D., U. Md., 1966. Diplomate: Am. Bd. Internal Medicine. Intern and resident in medicine Hosp. of U. Pa., Phila., 1966-67, 1970-72; commd. med. officer USPHS, HEW, 1972-75; sr. scientist Nat. Cancer Inst., Bethesda, Md., 1972-75, sect.chief, 1975-80; lab. chief Nat. Cancer Inst. (Lab. of Cellular Carcinogenesis and Tumor Promotion), 1980—. Contbr. articles to profl. jours. Served with USPHS, 1967-70. Recipient Balder prize U. Md. Med. Sch., 1966; recipient Commendation medal USPHS, 1978. Mem. Am. Assn. for Cancer Research, AAAS, Am. Soc. Cell Biology. Current Work: Chemical carcinogenesis, cellular differentiation. Subspecialties: Cancer research (medicine); Cell biology. Office: Nat Cancer Inst Bethesda MD 20205

ZABEL, HARTMUT, physics educator, researcher; b. Radolfzell, Fed. Republic of Germany, Mar. 21, 1946; came to U.S., 1978; s. Gerhard and Klara (Hirling) Z.; m. Rosemarie Havers, Dec. 12, 1973; children—Cordula Daphne, Astrid Mirijam, Julia Elisabeth. B.S., U. Bonn, 1969; M.S., Tech. U. Munich, 1973; Ph.D., U. Munich, 1978. Research assoc. U. Houston, 1978-79; asst. prof. physics U. Ill., Urbana, 1979-83, assoc. prof., 1983—. Contbr. numerous articles to profl. jours. Mem. Deutsche Physikalische Gesellschaft, Am. Phys. Soc., Materials Research Soc., AAAS. Current work: X-ray and neutron scattering; lattice dynamics; structural and magnetic phase transitions; solid state diffusion; graphite-intercalation compounds; metal-and semiconductor superlattices. Subspecialty: Condensed matter physics.

ZACH, RETO, environmental scientist, radioecologist, biologist, zoologist; b. Davos, Switzerland, Dec. 17, 1940; came to Can., 1962, naturalized, 1967; s. Hans and Alouisa (Bettschart) Z.; m. Margrith Cysouw, Mar. 5, 1966; 1 child, Tammy. B.Sc. with honors, U. Alta., Edmonton, Can., 1972; Ph.D., U. Toronto, Ont., Can., 1977. Postdoctoral fellow U. B.C., Vancouver, Can., 1977-78; research officer Atomic Energy of Can. Ltd., Pinawa, Man., Can., 1978—. Contbr. articles to profl. jours. Mem. Ecol. Soc. Am., Can. Soc. Zoology, Cooper Ornithol. Soc., Am. Ornithol. Union. Current work: Environmental assessments, radioecology, radiation biology, ornithology, environmental stress, food chains. Subspecialties: Ecology (environmental science); Radiation biology. Home: Box 89 Pinawa MB R0E 1L0 Canada Office: Atomic Energy of Can Ltd Pinawa MB R0E 1L0 Canada

ZACHARIN, ALEXEY THEODORE, mechanical engineer; b. Beograd, Yugoslavia, Oct. 26, 1933; came to U.S., 1950, naturalized, 1955; s. Feodor F. and Olga N. (Zelensky) Z.; m. Valentina V. Skarupka, June 14, 1959; children—Tatiana, Natalia. B.M.E., CCNY, 1964. Design engr. Farrand, Bronx, 1964-65, Picatinny ARS, Dover, 1965-67; project leader ARRADCOM, Dover, 1967-71, sr. project leader, 1971-83; chief concepts group ARDC, Dover, 1983—, also cons., 1971—. Contbr. articles to profl. jours. Patentee in field. Dir. St. George Pathfinders of Am., N.Y., 1974—. Recipient Meritorious Civil Service medal U.S. Army, 1983, Spl. Act award U.S. Army, 1979, Research & Devel. award U.S. Army, 1975, Six Commendation awards U.S. Army, 1970-80. Mem. ASME, Am. Def. Preparedness Assn. Russian Orthodox. Current work: Fuze, fuze systems and ancillary devices for ordnance. Subspecialty: Mechanical engineering. Office: ARDC SMCAR-LCN-C Dover NJ 07801-5001

ZACHERT, VIRGINIA, psychologist, educator; b. Jacksonville, Ala., Mar. 1, 1920; d. R.E. and Cora H. (Massee) Z. Student, Norman Jr. Coll., 1937; A.B., Ga. State Woman's Coll., 1940; M.A., Emory U., 1947; Ph.D., Purdue U., 1949. Diplomate: Am. Bd. Profl. Psychologists. Statistician Davison-Paxon Co., Atlanta, 1941-44; research psychologist Mil. Contracts, Auburn Research Found., Ala. Poly. Inst.; indsl. and research psychologist Sturm & O'Brien (cons. engrs.), 1958-59; research project dir. Western Design, Biloxi, Miss., 1960-61, self-employed cons. psychologist, Norman Park, Ga., 1961-71, Good Hope, Ga., 1971—; research assoc. med. edn. Med. Coll. Ga., Augusta, 1963-65, assoc. prof., 1965-70, research prof., 1970-84, research prof. emerita, 1984—, chief learning materials div., 1973-84, mem. faculty senate, 1976-84, mem. acad. council, 1976-82, pres. acad. council, 1983, sec., 1978; mem. Ga. Bd. Examiners of Psychologists, 1974-79, v.p., 1977, pres., 1978; Mem. adv. bd. Comdr. Gen. ATC USAF, 1967-70; cons. Ga. Legislature, 1980. Author: (with P.L. Wilds) Essentials of Gynecology-Oncology, 1967, Applications of Gynecology-Oncology, 1981. Del. White House Conf. on Aging, 1981. Served as aerologist USN, 1944-46; aviation psychologist USAF, 1949-54. Fellow Am. Psychol. Assn.; mem. Am. Statis. Assn., AAUP (chpt. pres. 1977-80), Sigma Xi. (chpt. pres. 1980-81). Baptist. Current Work: Use of multi-media techniques to instruct students in cognative aspects of subject matter; self-teaching or training; all ages, especially elderly. Subspecialties: Learning; Obstetrics and gynecology. Home: 1126 Highland Ave Augusta GA 30904 Office: Dept Obstetrics and Gynecology Med Coll Ga Augusta GA 30912

ZACHOS, COSMAS K., theoretical physicist; b. Athens, Greece, Sept. 8, 1951; came to U.S., 1970, s. Kyriacoulis and Evangelie (Spanidou) Z. A.B. in Physics, Princeton U., 1974; Ph.D. in Physics, Calif. Inst. Tech., 1979. Research assoc. in theoretical physics U. Wis., Madison, 1979-81, Fermi Nat. Accelerator Lab., Batavia, Ill., 1981-83; asst. physicist Argonne Nat. Lab., Ill., 1983—. Editor: Conf. Proc. Gauge Theory on a Lattice, 1984. Contbr. articles to profl. jours. Mem. Am. Phys. Soc., Phi Beta Kappa, Sigma Xi. Current work: Theoretical high energy physics, supergravity. Subspecialty: Particle physics. Home: 232 N Oak Park Ave Oak Park IL 60302 Office: HEP 362 Argonne Nat Lab Argonne IL 60439

ZADJURA, RICHARD EDWARD, research chemist; b. N.Y.C., Sept. 19, 1951; s. Edward A. and Veronica (Dolinich) Z. A.S., Kingsborough Community Coll., Bklyn., 1970; B.S., Bklyn. Coll., 1972; Ph.D., CUNY, 1977. Research chemist Am. Cyanamid Co., Bound Brook, N.J., 1977-82; sr. chemist Berlex Labs., Cedar Knolls, N.J., 1982-84; project supr. Nat. Starch & Chem. Co., Bridgewater, N.J., 1984—. Contbr. articles to profl. jours. Mem. Am. Chem. Soc. Current work: Applications of nuclear magnetic resonance to structural identifications, investigations using two dimensional and solid state nuclear magnetic resonance. Subspecialties: Analytical chemistry; Nuclear magnetic resonance. Home: 264 Prospect St Westfield NJ 07090 Office: Nat Starch & Chem Co Finderne Ave Bridgewater NJ 08807

ZAHLER, STANLEY ARNOLD, geneticist; b. N.Y.C., May 28, 1926; s. Irving and Clara (Heimowitz) Z.; m. Eleanor Janette Haugness, Nov. 1, 1952; children: Kathy Ann, Diane Louise, Peter Irving. A.B., N.Y.U., 1948; M.S., U. Chgo., 1950, Ph.D., 1952. Postdoctoral fellow U. Ill., Urbana, 1952-54; asst. prof. U. Wash., Seattle, 1954-59, W.Va. U., Morgantown, 1959; asst. prof. Cornell U., Ithaca, N.Y., 1959-64, assoc. prof., 1964-80, assoc. dir. div. biol. sci., 1976-79, prof. microbiology sect. genetics and devel., 1980—; cons. in field. Assoc. editor: Jour. Bacteriology, 1968-74, Applied & Environ. Microbiology, 1980—. Served with USNR, 1944-46. Mem. AAAS, Am. Soc. Microbiology, Genetics Soc. Am., Soc. Gen. Microbiology. Current Work: Genetics and genetic engineering of Bacillus and its bacteriophages. Subspecialties: Genetics and genetic engineering (biology); Molecular biology. Office: Cornell Univ 317 Bradfield Hall Ithaca NY 14853

ZAK, BENNIE, chemistry educator; b. Detroit, Sept. 29, 1919; s. Morris and Lena (Snyder) Z.; m. Doris Kitty Zak, Sept. 7, 1946; children—Steven Dennis, Marsha, Deborah. B.S. in Chemistry, Wayne State U., 1948, Ph.D., 1952. Jr. assoc. in biochemistry Detroit Receiving Hosp., 1951-57; asst. prof. pathology Wayne State U., Detroit, 1957-61, assoc. prof. pathology, 1961-65, assoc. in biochemistry, 1965—, prof. pathology, 1965—; cons. in field. Contbr. articles to profl. jours. Served to 1st lt. USAAF, 1941-45. Recipient Faculty Research award Sigma Xi, 1973; Benedetti-Pichler award Am. Microchem. Soc., 1984; Disting. Service award Wayne State U., 1983. Mem. Am. Assn. Clin. Chemistry (Ames award 1974) Am. Chem. Soc., Nat. Acad. Clin. Biochemistry, Fedn. Am. Soc. for Exptl. Biology. Jewish. Current work: Trace metal analysis, electrophoresis and densitometry, lipid biochemistry and analysis, peroxidase coupled indicator reactions, microchemistry. Subspecialties: Analytical chemistry; Clinical chemistry. Office: Wayne State Univ Sch Medicine 540 E Canfield Detroit MI 48201

ZAK, STANISLAW HENRYK, electrical engineering educator, automatic control researcher; b. Darstkowo, Poland, June 4, 1950; came to U.S., Sept. 1980; s. Konstanty and Janina (Gryka) Z. Elec. engr. Tech. U. Warsaw, Poland, 1974, MSEE, 1974, Ph.D., 1977. Asst. prof. Tech. U. Warsaw, 1977-80; vis. asst. prof. U. Minn., Mpls., 1980-83, Purdue U., West Lafayette, Ind., 1984—; cons. Ministry of Transp., Warsaw, 1978-80. Author: (with others) Topics in Control Theory, 1984. Contbr. articles to profl. jours. Mem. IEEE, Soc. for Indsl. and Applied Math. Roman Catholic. Current work: Linear and nonlinear systems, algebraic systems theory, systolic architectures. Subspecialties: Electrical engineering; Computer engineering. Home: 709 N 6th St Apt 2 Lafayette IN 47901 Office: Purdue Univ Sch of Elec Engring Room 374 B Potter Bldg West Lafayette IN 47907

ZAKIN, JACQUES LOUIS, chemical engineering educator; b. N.Y.C., Jan. 28, 1927; s. Mordecai and Ada Davies (Fishbein) Z.; m. Laura Pienkny, June 11, 1950; children: Richard Joseph, David Fredric, Barbara Ellen, Emily Anne, Susan Beth. B.Chem. Engring., Cornell U., 1949; M.S. in Chem. Engring., Columbia U., 1950; D.Engring. Sci. (Socony-Mobil Employee Incentive fellow), N.Y. U., 1959. Chem. engr. Flintkote Research Labs., Whippany, N.J., 1950-51; research technologist, research dept. Socony-Mobil, Bklyn., 1951-53, sr. research technologist, 1953-56, supervising technologist, 1959-62; asso. prof. chem. engring. U. Mo., Rolla, 1962-65, prof., 1965-77, dir. minority engring. program, 1974-77, dir. women in engring. program, 1975-77; chmn. dept. chem. engring. Ohio State U., Columbus, 1977—. Co-editor: Proc. Turbulence Symposium, 1969, 71, 73, 75, 77, 79, 81-83; contbr. articles to profl. jours. Bd. dirs. Rolla Community Concert Assn., 1966-77, 2d v.p., 1975-77; bd. dirs. Ozark Mental Health Assn., 1976-77; trustee Ohio State Hillel Found., 1981-84, treas., 1984—; trustee Congregation Beth T.Kvah, 1983-85; co-chmn. Concerned Academics and Scientists for Soviet Refuseniks; chmn. sci. manpower and resources com. Council for Chem. Research, 1984—. Served with USNR, 1945-46. Recipient Outstanding Research award U. Mo., Rolla, 1970; Am. Chem. Soc. Petroleum Research Fund Internat. fellow, 1968-69. Mem. Am. Inst. Chem. Engrs., Am. Chem. Soc., Soc. of Rheology, Am. Soc. Engring. Edn., Sigma Xi, Phi Lambda Upsilon, Phi Eta Sigma, Alpha Chi Sigma, Tau Beta Pi. Jewish. Patentee in field. Current Work: Turbulent drag reduction; rheology of dilute polymer solutions; rtransport of viscous crude oil as oil in water emulsions. Subspecialty: Chemical engineering. Office: 140 W 19th Ave Ohio State U Columbus OH 43210

ZAKKAY, VICTOR H., aeronautical engineering educator; b. Baghdad, Iraq, Sept. 8, 1927; came to U.S., 1946, naturalized, 1955; s. Haron and Massouda Isac (David) Z. B.Ae.E., Poly. Inst. Bklyn., 1952, M.S. Ae.E., 1953, Ph.D., 1959. Research asst. prof. Poly. Inst. Bklyn., 1959-62, research assoc. prof., 1962-64; assoc. prof. aeronaut. engring. N.Y.U., N.Y.C., 1964-65, prof., 1965—; asst. dir. Antonio Ferri Labs., 1970-76, dir., 1976—, chmn. dept. applied sci., 1977-84; cons. to various orgns. Contbr. articles to profl. jours. NSF grantee India, 1982. Mem. AIAA (fluid dynamics tech. adv. panel 1972-75), Sigma Xi, Tau Beta Pi, Sigma Gamma Tau. Current Work: Research in fluid mechanics, turbulence, oil combustion, and fluidized bed coal combustion. Subspecialties: Fluid mechanics; Combustion processes. Office: 425 Merrick Ave Westbury NY 11590

ZALESKI, MAREK BOHDAN, immunologist, researcher, educator; b. Krzemieniec, Poland, Oct. 18, 1936; came to U.S., 1969, naturalized, 1977; s. Stanislaw and Jadwiga (Zienkowicz) Z. M.D., Sch. Medicine, Warsaw, 1960, Dr. Med. Sci., 1963. Instr. dept. histology Sch. Medicine, Warsaw, 1955-60, asst. prof., 1960-69; research asst. prof. (Henry C. and Bertha H. Buswell fellow) dept. microbiology SUNY, Buffalo, 1969-72, assoc. prof., 1976-78, prof., 1978—; bd. dirs. Ctr. Polish Studies, SUNY; permanent chair Polish Culture Canisius Coll., Buffalo; vis. scientist Inst. Exptl. Biology and Genetics, Czechoslovac Acad. Sci., Prague, 1965; Brit. Council's scholar, research lab. Queen Victoria Hosp., East Grinstead, Eng., 1966-67; asst. prof. dept. anatomy Mich. State U., East Lansing, 1972-75, assoc. prof., 1975-76; rep. Fund for Continuity of Polish Lit. and Humanities. Contbg. author: Transplantation and Preservation of Tissues in Human Clinic, 1966, The Man, 1968, Cytophysiology, 1970, Principles of Immunology, 1978, Medical Microbiology, 1982, Molecular Immunology, 1984. Co-author: Immunogenetics, 1983; co-editor: Immunobiology of Major Histocompatibility Complex, 1981; co-transl.: (J. Tischner) Spirit of Solidarity; editorial com.: Investigations and Research Notes in Immunology; contbr. articles to med. jours. NIH grantee, 1976—; NEH grantee, 1985. Mem. Transplantation Soc., Internat. Soc. Exptl. Hematology, Ernest Witebsky Center Immunology, Am. Assn. Immunologists, Buffalo Collegium of Immunology, N.Y. Acad. Scis., Solidarity and Human Rights Assn., Ctr. Polish Studies, SUNY. Roman Catholic. Current Work: Genetic regulation of the immune response to normal and neoplastic cell-surface alloantigens. Subspecialties: Immunogenetics; Transplantation. Office: Dept Microbiology SUNY Buffalo NY 14214

ZAMECNIK, PAUL CHARLES, physician; b. Cleve., Nov. 22, 1912; s. John C. and Mary (McCarthy) Z.; m. Mary Connor, Oct. 10, 1936; children—Karen, John, Elizabeth. A.B., Dartmouth, 1933; M.D., Harvard U., 1936, D.Sc. (hon.), 1982; D.Sc. (hon.), U. Utrecht, 1966, Columbia, 1971, Roger Williams U., 1983. Resident medicine Huntington Hosp., Harvard, 1936-37, Collis P. Huntington prof. oncologic medicine, 1956-79; prin. scientist Worcester Found. Exptl. Biology, Shrewsbury, Mass., 1979—; intern medicine U. Hosps. of Cleve., 1938-39; fellow Carlsberg Lab., Copenhagen, Denmark, 1939-40, Rockefeller Inst., N.Y.C., 1941-42; physician Mass. Gen. Hosp., 1956-79, hon. physician, 1983—; dir. J.C. Warren Labs., Harvard and Mass. Gen. Hosp., 1956-79; Mem. staff OSRD, World War II. Recipient John Collins Warren Triennial prize, 1946, 50; James Ewing award, 1963; Borden award in med. scis., 1965; Am. Cancer Soc. award, 1967; Passano award, 1970; Fogarty scholar NIH, 1975, 78-79. Mem. Royal Danish Acad. Scis. (fgn. hon.), Am. Acad. Arts and Scis., Assn. Am. Physicians, Am. Assn. Biol. Chemists, Am. Assn. Cancer Research (pres. 1964-65), Nat. Acad. Sci. Home: 65 Commons Dr Shrewsbury Commons Shrewsbury MA 01545 Office: Worcester Found Exptl Biology 222 Maple St Shrewsbury MA 01545

ZAMENHOF, ROBERT GEORGE, med. physicist; b. Tanganyika, East Africa, Oct. 24, 1946; s. Julian and Olga Eugenia (Nietupska) Z.; m. Ruth Lilian Dlugi, Apr. 19, 1949. B.Sc., Poly. N. London, 1970; M.Sc., U. Strathclyde, Glasgow, Scotland, 1972; Ph.D., M.I.T., 1977. Research fellow in radiology Harvard Med. Sch., 1977-79; asst. prof. engring. Boston U., 1978-80; asst. prof. therapeutic and diagnostic radiology Tufts U. Sch. Medicine, Boston, 1979-82, assoc. prof., 1982—. Contbr. articles to profl. jours. Brit. Sci. Research Council scholar, 1971-72; Harvard-M.I.T. Health Scis. and Tech. fellow, 1972-74; M.I.T. Health Scis. Fund fellow, 1975-77; Nat. Cancer Inst. tng. fellow, 1978-79. Mem. Am. Assn. Physicists in Medicine (pres. New Eng. chpt. 1982-83), Biomedical Engring. Soc., Roentgen Ray Soc., Inst. Electronic and Radio Engrs., Nat. Commn. Radiation Protection. Current Work: Digital imaging, activation analysis, clinical physics. Subspecialty: Medical physics. Home: 129 Clinton Rd Brooklin MA 02146 Office: 171 Harrison Ave Boston MA 02111

ZAMENHOF, STEPHEN, biochemist, educator; b. Warsaw, Poland, June 12, 1911; s. Henry Gregory and Sabina (Szpinak) Z.; m. Patrice J. Driskell, May 2, 1961. Ph.D. in Biochemistry, Columbia U., 1949. Asst. prof., assoc. prof. biochemistry UCLA, 1951-64, prof. microbial genetics and biol. chemistry, 1964—, prof. emeritus, 1978, recalled for active duty. Author: The Chemistry of Heredity, 1959. Contbr. 221 articles to profl. jours. Guggenheim fellow, 1958-59. Mem. Am. Soc. Biol. Chemists, Am. Soc. Neurochemistry, Am. Inst. Nutrition, Am. Soc. Anatomists, Soc. Neurosci., Internat. Soc. Devel. Psychobiology, Internat. Soc. Neurochemistry, Sigma Xi. Current Work: Neuroscience; factors affecting prenatal brain development. Subspecialties: Biochemistry (biology); Neurochemistry. Home: 333 Medio Dr Los Angeles CA 90049 Office: UCLA Sch Medicine Los Angeles CA 90024

ZAMMUTO, RICHARD MICHAEL, ecologist, researcher; b. Waltham, Mass., Apr. 21, 1953; s. Joseph John and Leona (LeBlanc) Z.; m. Julie Grace Ezinicki, Nov. 20, 1976. A.S., Essex Tech. Inst., 1973; B.S., U. Mass., 1976; M.S., Western Ill. U., 1978; Ph.D., U. Western Ont., 1983. Biol. aide Mass. Coop. Fish Unit, Amherst, 1975; grad. tchr. asst. Western Ill. U., Macomb, 1977-78; grad. tchr. assoc. U. Ark., Fayetteville, 1978-79; grad. demonstrator U. Western Ont., London, Can., 1979-82, lectr., 1982; postdoctoral fellow U. Calgary, Alta., Can., 1983—, asst. field sta. mgr., 1984—. Asst. editor Fedn. Alta. Naturalists, 1982—. Contbr. articles to profl. jours. Tuition-waiver awards U. Mass, Western Ill. U., U. Western Ont., 1974-79; Ont. grad. scholar U. Western Ont., 1981-82; Nat. Sci. tng. grantee U. Western Ont., 1980-81; Can. Nat. Sportsmen's Fund postdoctoral fellow, 1983-84. Mem. Wildlife Soc. (pres. Western Ont. chpt. 1980-81, Western Ill. U. chpt. 1976-78), Am. Ornithologists Union, Am. Soc. Mammalogists, Am. Soc. Naturalists, Can. Soc. Zoologists, Cooper Ornithol. Soc., Ecol. Soc. Am., Northeastern Bird-Banding Assn., Ottawa Field Naturalists' club, Soc. Can. Ornithologists, Soc. Study of Evolution, Soc. Systematic Zoologists, Can. Soc. Zoologists (wildlife biology sect.), Wildlife Soc. Can., Wilson Ornithol. Soc. Relationships among varying environmental conditions and life histories of mammal and bird populations; evolutionary population ecology of vertebrates. Subspecialties: Theoretical ecology; Evolutionary biology. Home and Office: Kananaskis Ctr for Environ Research Univ of Calgary Seebe AB T0L 1X0 Canada

ZAMORA, ANTONIO, computer and chemical information systems scientist; b. Nuevo Laredo, Mex., Dec. 6, 1942; came to U.S., 1957, naturalized, 1965; s. Antonio and Clementina (Garza) Z.; m. Elena, June 26, 1981; children—Lev, Antonio M., Maria G. B.S., U. Tex., 1962; M.S., Ohio State U., 1969. Sr. scientist Chem. Abstracts Service, Columbus, Ohio, 1965-81; mgr. linguistics IBM, Gaithersburg, Md., 1982—. Contbr. articles to profl. jours. Mem. adv. bd. Jour. Chem. Info. and Computer Scis., 1976—. Served with U.S. Army, 1962-65. Mem. Am. Soc. for Info. Sci. (best paper award 1972), Assn. for Computing Machinery, Am. Chem. Soc., Computational Linguistics Soc. Current work: Techniques for manipulating and understanding natural language using computers. Subspecialties: Automated language processing; Chemical information. Office: IBM 201 Perry Pkwy Gaithersburg MD 20877

ZAND, ROBERT, biophysical and polymer chemistry educator; b. N.Y.C., Jan. 7, 1930; s. Morris and Gussie (Lassman) Z.; m. Charlene Ross Rooth, June 14, 1952; children—Martin Stuart, Joel Raphael, Dina Jane. B.S., U. Mo., 1951; M.S., Poly. Inst. Bklyn., 1954; Ph.D., Brandeis U., 1961. Chemist, Irvington Varnish (N.J.), 1954; postdoctoral fellow Brandeis U., Waltham, Mass., 1961-63, Harvard U. Med. Sch., Boston, 1961-63; asst. research biophysicist U. Mich., Ann Arbor, 1963-68, asst. prof. biochemistry, 1968-73, assoc. prof., assoc. researcher biophysics, 1973—; cons., tech. dir. Med. Products div. Recreational Innovations, South Lyo, Mich., 1981; cons. Covalent Tech., Ann Arbor, 1984, Meridian Instruments Inc., Okemos, Mich., 1984. Contbr. articles to sci. jours. Pres., Washtenaw Jewish Community Council, Ann Arbor, 1971-72; chmn. Washtenaw County United Jewish Appeal, 1966-67. NIH, NSF grantee, 1964—; NIH fellow, 1961-63. Mem. Am. Chem. Soc., Biophys. Soc., Am. Soc. Biol. Chemists, Am. Soc. Neurochemistry (pub. policy com. 1983), Internat. Soc. for Neurochemistry, Sigma Xi (north central region dir. 1981-84, 84—, mem. coms., bd. dirs.). Current work: Synthesis, structure and properties of biological and synthetic macromolecules. Subspecialties: Biophysical chemistry; Polymer chemistry. Office: U Mich Biophysics Research Div 2200 Bonisteel Blvd Ann Arbor MI 48109

ZANDER, DONALD VICTOR, veterinary medicine researcher, avian pathologist; b. Bellingham, Wash., Feb. 15, 1916; m. Verna Mare Mace, Aug. 17, 1945; children—Linda Jo, David Lee, Arnold Alan. B.S., U. Calif.-Berkeley, 1941; M.S., Colo. State U., 1945, D.V.M., 1950; Ph.D., U. Calif.-Davis, 1953. Research asst. Colo. State U., Ft. Collins, 1942-45; research specialist U. Calif.-Davis, 1950-53, asst. prof., 1953-55; dir. health research and service H & N Inc., Redmond, Wash., 1955—; western states rep. Nat. Poultry

Improvement Plan, 1980-82. Served to 1st lt., U.S. Army, 1945-47. Recipient Disting. Service award Washington Poultry Industry Assn., 1982, Dist. award of merit Boy Scouts Am., Seattle, 1979. Mem. Am. Vet. Med. Assn., Am. Assn. Avian Pathologists (pres. 1964-65, dir. western dist. 1983—), Poultry Sci. Assn., World's Poultry Sci. Assn., World's Poultry Vet. Assn., Western Poultry Disease Conf. (pres. 1956-57). Lodge: Kiwanis (pres. 1962, Disting. Service award 1968). Current work: Diseases of domestic poultry. Subspecialty: Avian pathology. Office: H & N Inc 15305 NE 40th St Redmond WA 98052

ZANDI, IRAJ, educator; b. Tehran, Iran, June 30, 1931; came to U.S., 1962; s. Housain and Ahtram (Batmaghelidj) Z.; m. Annette M. Grantham, June 20, 1958; children: Mark M., Richard H., Miriam R., Karl D., Peter P. B.S. in Electro-Mech. Engring, U. Tehran, 1952; M.S. in Civil Engring, U. Okla., 1957; Ph.D., Ga. Inst. Tech., 1959; M.A. (hon.), U. Pa., 1971. Dir. Dept. Environ. Engring., Ministry of Health, Tehran, 1961; asso. prof. Abadan Inst. Tech., 1962; asst. prof. U. Del., Newark, 1962-66; asso. prof. U. Pa., Phila., 1966-69, prof. dept. civil engring., 1969-81; prof. dept. civil engring. and dept. social scis. (Wharton). U. Pa. (Nat. Center Resource Mgmt. and Tech.), 1981—, chmn. Nat. Center Energy Mgmt. and Power, 1971-72; partner Resoumetric U.S.A., Inc., Radnor, Pa., 1975—; sci. cons. U.S. Congressman Lawrence R. Coughlin, 1973. Editor: Jour. Pipelines, Jour. Resource Mgmt. and Tech.; Contbr. articles to various publs. Recipient M.A. Ferst award Sigma Xi, Ga. Inst. Tech., 1960. Mem. ASCE, Am. Inst. Chem. Engrs. Subspecialties: Environmental engineering; Resource management. Home: 260 Highview Dr Radnor PA 19087 Office: Dept Civil Engring U Pa Philadelphia PA 19104

ZANNUCCI, JOSEPH SALVATORE, chemist, researcher; b. Highland, N.Y., Jan. 30, 1937; m. Iris Ann Maddy, June 23, 1963; children—Joseph Paul, David Maddy. B.S., U. Ala., 1955-59; Ph.D., Northeastern U., 1967. Biochemist, U.S. Govt., Frederick, Md., 1962-63; research chemist Tenn. Eastman Co., Kingsport, 1967-69, sr. research chemist, 1969-82, research assoc., 1982—. Contbr. to profl. sci. publs. Patentee in field. Served with U.S. Army, 1960-62. Mem. Am. Chem. Soc., Sigma Xi. Club: Cherokee Rod and Gun. Lodge: Eagles. Research or work interests: Photochemical and thermal reactions of monomers and polymers; stabilization of polymers; lightfastness of dyes; chromatography. Subspecialties: Organic chemistry; Analytical chemistry. Home: 1112 Buchelew Dr Kingsport TN 37663 Office: Tenn Eastman Co PO Box 1972 Kingsport TN 37662

ZANZUCCHI, PAUL E., physicist; b. Syracuse, N.Y., Sept. 20, 1947; s. John and Lina (Pietrantoni) Z.; m. Judith Elaine Kozel, July 5, 1980; children—Leah, Eric. B.S., LeMoyne Coll., 1970; Ph.D., U. Va., 1976. Postdoctoral researcher U. Md., College Park, 1976-77, U. Ky., Lexington, 1978-79; research assoc. Case Western Res. U., Cleve., 1979-80; physicist Ocean Systems div. Gould Inc., Celve., 1980—. Patentee optical fiber magnetometer, 1981. Served with U.S. Army, 1970-72. Mem. Am. Phys. Soc. Current work: Magnetic field sensor research, optical fiber sensor research, structural vibration analysis. Subspecialties: Magnetic physics; Fiber optics. Home: 1453 E 174th St Cleveland OH 44110 Office: Ocean Systems Div Gould Inc Dept 721 18901 Euclid Ave Celveland OH 44117

ZAPOL, WARREN MYRON, anesthesiologist, researcher, educator; b. N.Y.C., Mar. 16, 1942; s. Bernard and Florence (Rothlein) Z.; m. Nikki Jane Kaplan, Sept. 15, 1968; children—David, Elisabeth. B.S., MIT, 1962; M.D., U. Rochester, 1966. Diplomate Am. Bd. Anesthesiologists. Research assoc. Nat. Heart Inst., Bethesda, Md., 1967-70; resident in anesthesiology Mass. Gen. Hosp., Boston, 1970-72, staff, 1972—; asst. prof. anesthesia Harvard U. Med. Sch., Boston, 1972-77, assoc. prof. anesthesia, 1977-85, prof. anesthesia, 1985—. Editor: Artificial Lungs for Acute Respiratory Failure, 1977; Acute Respiratory Failure, 1985. Served with USPHS, 1967-70. Recipient Antarctic Service medal NSF, 1979. Fellow Explorers Club. Current work: Clinical and experimental studies of acute respiratory failure aimed at developing and testing new therapies; studies of diving physiology, particularly Antarctic seals. Subspecialties: Anesthesiology; Comparative physiology. Home: 182 Holden Wood Rd Concord MA 01742 Office: Dept Anesthesia Mass Gen Hosp Fruit St Boston MA 02114

ZARATZIAN, VIRGINIA LOUISE, pharmacologist; b. Highland Park, Mich., Nov. 15, 1918; d. Vahan Oskihan and Makrouhie (Kevorkian) Z. B.S., U. Mich., 1942, B.S. in Pharmacy, 1946, M.S., 1949; Ph.D., Wayne State U., 1956. Research assoc. U. Ill. Coll. Medicine, Chgo., 1956-59; pharmacologist, acting chief, pesticide sect. FDA, HEW, Washington, 1959-61; research pharmacologist, acting chief, pharmacology sect., div. air pollution USPHS, HEW, Cin., 1961-63; pharmacologist, chief pharmacology br. U.S. Environ. Hygiene Agy., Edgewood Arsenal, Md., 1963-66; pharmacologist pesticides regulation U.S. Dept. Agr., Washington, 1966-68, toxicologist, food safety inspection service, 1978—; pharmacologist, psychopharmacology research br. div. NIMH, Rockville, MD., 1968-78, toxicologist, food safety inspection service, 1978—. Contbr. articles to profl. jours. Mem. Am. Chem. Soc., AAAS, Internat. Soc. Study Zenobiotics, Soc. Toxicology, Pan Am. Med. Soc., Toxicology Forum. Iota Sigma Pi. Current Work: Researcher in toxicology. Subspecialties: Toxicology (agriculture); Neurobiology. Home: PO Box 2217 Gaithersburg MD 20879 Office: US Dept Agriculture Cotton Annex 300 12th St SW Washington DC 20250

ZARCO, ROMEO M., immunologist; b. Caloocan, Rizal, Philippines, Oct. 7, 1920; s. Pablo V. and Marciana (Morales) Z.; m. Soledad Arcenas, Jan. 31, 1948; children: Cynthia, David, Sylvia. M.D., U. Philippines, 1943; M.P.H., Johns Hopkins U., 1954. Prof. microbiology U. Philippines, Manila, 1946-66; asst. dir. Howard Hughes Med. Inst., Miami, Fla., 1964-67; asst. prof. U. Miami, Fla., 1964—; with Cordis Labs., Inc., Miami, 1967—, pres., 1980—. WHO fellow, 1953; USPHS fellow, 1959. Mem. Am. Assn. Immunologists, Filipino-Am. Assn. Fla. (pres. 1982), Philippine-Am. Acad. Sci. and Engring. (chmn. 1982-83), Phi Sigma. Republican. Subspecialty: Immunobiology and immunology. Office: 2140 N Miami Ave Miami FL 33127

ZARE, RICHARD NEIL, chemistry educator; b. Cleve., Nov. 19, 1939; s. Milton and Dorothy Sylvia (Amdur) Z.; m. Susan Leigh Shively, Apr. 20, 1963; children—Bethany Jean, Bonnie Sue, Rachel Amdur. B.A., Harvard, 1961; postgrad., U. Calif. at Berkeley, 1961-63; Ph.D. (NSF predoctoral fellow), Harvard, 1964. Postdoctoral fellow Harvard, 1964; postdoctoral research asso. Joint Inst. for Lab. Astrophysics, 1964-65; asst. prof. chemistry Mass. Inst. Tech., 1964-66; asst. prof. dept. physics and astrophysics U. Colo., 1965-68, assoc. prof. physics and astrophysics, asso. prof. chemistry, 1968-69; prof. chemistry Columbia, 1969-77, Higgins prof. natural sci., 1975-77; prof. Stanford U., 1977—, Shell Disting. prof. chemistry, 1980-85; Christensen fellow St. Catherine's Coll., Oxford U., 1982; Cons. Aeronomy Lab., NOAA, 1966-77, radio standards physics div. Nat. Bur. Standards, 1968-77, Lawrence Livermore Lab., U. Calif., 1974—, Stanford Research Inst., 1974—, Los Alamos Sci. Lab., U. Calif., 1975—; mem. IBM Sci. Advisory Com., 1977—. Recipient Fresenius award Phi Lambda Upsilon, 1974; Michael Polanyi medal, 1979; award Spectroscopy Soc. Pitts., 1983, Nat. Medal of Sci., 1985; Nonresident fellow Joint Inst. for Lab. Astrophysics, 1970—; Alfred P. Sloan fellow, 1967-69; Christensen fellow St. Catherine's Coll., Oxford U., 1982. Mem. Nat. Acad. Sci., Am. Acad. Arts and Scis., AAAS, Am. Phys. Soc. (Earle K. Plyler prize 1981, Irving Langmuir prize in chem. physics 1985), Am. Chem. Soc., Chem. Soc. London, Phi Beta Kappa. Research and publs. on molecular luminescence, photochemistry and chem. physics. Current Work: Reaction dynamics. Subspecialties: Physical chemistry; Laser-induced chemistry. Office: Dept Chemistry Stanford U Stanford CA 94305

ZARET, BARRY LEWIS, medical educator, cardiologist; b. N.Y.C., Oct. 3, 1940; s. Irving and Beatrice (Fader) Z.; m. Myrna Zimmerman, June 23, 1963; children—Adam L., Elliot C., Owen M. B.S., Queens Coll., 1962; M.D., NYU, 1966; M.A. (hon.), Yale U., 1982. Intern, Bellevue Hosp., N.Y.C., 1966-67, resident, 1967-69; research fellow Johns Hopkins U., 1969-71; asst. prof. medicine Yale U., New Haven, 1973-76, assoc. prof. medicine and diagnostic radiology, 1976, 80-82, prof., 1982—, Robert W. Berliner prof. medicine, 1984—, chief sect. cardiology, 1978—; mem. nuclear medicine and diagnostic radiology study sect., 1979-83. Mem. editorial bd. Circulation, 1977-80, 81-83, Am. Jour. Cardiology, 1977—; assoc. editor: Yearbook of Nuclear Medicine, 1980—. Contbr. numerous chpts. to books, articles to profl. jours. Served to maj. USAF, 1971-73. Recipient Casimir Funk award Soc. Mil. Surgeons U.S., 1973. Fellow Am. Heart Assn. (established investigator 1977-78), Am. Physiol. Soc., Am. Coll. Cardiology; mem. Am. Fedn. Clin. Research, Soc. Nuclear Medicine (Herrman Blumgart Pioneer award New Eng. chpt. 1978), Internat. Soc. and Fedn. Cardiology (council on clin. cardiology 1983—). Current work: Nuclear cardiology, cardiac metabolism; ventricular function Subspecialties: Cardiology; Nuclear medicine. Home: 15 Cassway Rd Woodbridge CT 06525 Office: Yale Univ Sch Medicine 333 Cedar St New Haven CT 06510

ZARTMAN, DAVID LESTER, geneticist; b. Albuquerque, July 6, 1940; s. Lester Grant and Mary Elizabeth (Kitchel) Z.; m. Micheal Aline Zartman, July 6, 1963; children: Kami Renee, Dalan Lee. B.Sc., N.Mex. State U., 1962; M.Sc., Ohio State U., 1966, Ph.D., 1968. Jr. partner Marlea Guernsey Farm, Albuquerque, 1962-64; research asst. Ohio State U., Columbus, 1964-68; asst. prof. N.Mex. State U., Las Cruces, 1968-71, assoc. prof., 1971-78, prof., 1978-84; prof., chmn. dept. dairy sci. Ohio State U., Columbus, 1984—; pres. Mary K. Zartman, Inc., Albuquerque, 1977-84; lectr. in field; Fulbright Hayes lectr., Malaysia, 1976. Contbr. articles to profl. jours.; patentee in field. Supt. dairy div. So. N.Mex. State Fair, 1978-84; judge 4-H. NIH fellow, 1973; Fulbright grantee, 1976. Recipient Outstanding Research award coll. agrl. N.Mex. State U., 1984. Fellow AAAS; mem. Am. Inst. Biol. Sci., Am. Dairy Sci. Assn., Am. Soc. Animal Sci., Sigma Xi, Phi Kappa Phi. Republican. Current Work: Bio-engineering of farm animals, genetic improvement of livestock. Subspecialties: Biomedical engineering; Genetics and genetic engineering (agriculture). Office: 2027 Coffey Rd Ohio State U Columbus OH 43210

ZAWADA, EDWARD THADDEUS, JR., physician; b. Chgo., Oct. 3, 1947; s. Edward Thaddeus and Evelyn Mary (Kovarek) Z.; m. Nancy Ann Stephen, Mar. 26, 1976; children—Elizabeth Ann, Nicholas Edward. B.S., Loyola U., 1969, M.D., 1973. Intern UCLA Hosps. and Clinics, 1973-74, resident, 1974-78; asst. prof. medicine UCLA, 1978-79; chief nephrology SLC VA Hosp., Salt Lake City, 1980-81; asst. prof. medicine U. Utah, Salt Lake City, 1979-81; asst. chief medicine McGuire VA Hosp., Richmond, Va., 1981-83; assoc. prof. medicine Med. Coll. Va., Richmond, 1981-83; chief nephrology and hypertension U.S.D. Sch. Medicine and R.C. Johnson VA Hosp., S.D., 1983—. cons. in field. Contbr. articles to profl. jours. Recipient VA Merit Rev., 1982—. Fellow ACP, Am. Coll. Chest Physicians, Am. Coll. Nutrition; mem. Am. Soc. Pharm. and Exptl. Therapeutics, Alpha Omega Alpha. Roman Catholic. Current Work: Role of calcium in blood pressure regulation; prostaglandins in renal physiology. Subspecialties: Internal medicine; Nephrology. Home: 1608 Cedar Ln Sioux Falls SD 57103 Office: U SD Sch Medicine 2501 W 22d St Sioux Falls SD 57705

ZAWADZKI, ZBIGNIEW APOLINARY, physician; b. Sosnowiec, Poland, July 23, 1921; s. Stanislaw and Sabina (Paliga) Z.; m. Danuta Irena Nowotczynska, Oct. 15, 1947; children: Barbara E., Joanna K. M.D., Sch. Medicine U. Warsaw, Poland, 1947, Dr.Sci., 1951; A.M. (hon.), Brown U., 1975. Asst. prof. Inst. Hematology, Warsaw, 1951-60; fellow in hematology New Eng. Ctr. Hosp., 1957-59; research assoc. VA Hosp., Pitts., 1961-67, chief hematology and oncology sect., 1961-67; asst. prof. U. Pitts., 1967-72, assoc. prof. medicine, 1972-74, Brown U., 1974—; dir. div. clin. immunology and oncology Meml. Hosp., Pawtucket, R.I., 1974—. Contbr. articles to profl. jours. Mem. AMA, Am. Assn. Immunologists, Am. Soc. Clin. Oncology, Am. Soc. Hematology, Am. Rheumatism Assn., R.I. Med. Soc., Sigma Xi. Roman Catholic. Club: Brown U. Faculty. Current Work: Study of paraproteinemias and the immunologic aspects of cancer disease. Subspecialties: Oncology; Immunology (medicine). Home: 21 Wingate Rd Providence RI 02906 Office: Meml Hosp Pawtucket RI 02860

ZEE, PAULUS, pediatrician; b. Amsterdam, Netherlands, 1928; came to U.S., 1954, naturalized, 1961; m. V.A. Carlock; 4 children. M.D., U. Amsterdam, 1954; Ph.D., Tulane U., 1965. Diplomate Am. Bd. Pediatrics. Intern, Trinity Luth. Hosp., Kansas City, Mo., 1954-55; resident in pediatrics The Children's Mercy Hosp., Kansas City, 1956-58; fellow in diabetes and metabolism U. Mo., Columbia, 1958-59; fellow in nutrition and metabolism Tulane U., New Orleans, 1959-63; mem. staff St. Jude Children's Hosp., Memphis, 1963—, chmn. pediatrics, 1981—; mem. active staff St. Joseph Hosp., Memphis. Contbr. articles to profl. jours. Fellow Am. Acad. Pediatrics; mem. Am. Inst. Nutrition, Am. Soc. Clin. Nutrition, Am. Oil Chemists Soc., Memphis Med. Soc., Shelby County Med. Soc. Current work: Community nutrition, nutritional and metabolic problems of newborns and children with cancer. Subspecialties: Pediatrics; Nutrition (biology). Office: St Jude Children's Research Hosp PO Box 318 Memphis TN 38101

ZEIDMAN, BENJAMIN, physicist; b. N.Y.C., Oct. 6, 1931; s. Sam and Eve Zeidman; m. Anne Jo Macfarland, June 3, 1972; children—Michael, William, Katherine. B.S., CCNY, 1952; Ph.D., Washington U., St. Louis, 1957. Sr. physicist Argonne Nat. Lab. (Ill.), 1957—, mem. various adv. coms. Los Alamos Nat. Lab. 1968—; vis. prof. SUNY-Stony Brook, 1972. Contbr. articles to sci. jours. Humboldt fellow Max Planck Inst., Heidelberg, W.Ger., 1975; Ford fellow Niels Bohr Inst., Copenhagen, 1963-64. Fellow Am. Phys. Soc.; mem. AAAS. Current work: Nuclear physics research utilizing medium and high energy probes. Subspecialty: Nuclear physics. Home: 354 Cumnor Ave Glen Ellyn IL 60137 Office: Physics Div Argonne Nat Lab Argonne IL 60439

ZEIKUS, J. GREGORY, bacteriologist, institute director. Dir. Mich. Biotech. Inst., Mich. State U., East Lansing. Subspecialty: Biotechnology administration. Office: Mich State U Mich Biotech Inst East Lansing MI 48824

ZEISSIG, GUSTAVE ALEXANDER, systems engineer; b. Ithaca, N.Y., June 2, 1940; s. Alexander and Edith M. (Cuervo) Z.; m. Olga I. Rodriguez, May 3, 1969; children: Gustavo A., Walesca, Eric G., Karl A. B.E.E., Cornell U., 1964, Ph.D., 1971. Assoc. prof. physics dept. U. P.R., Rio Piedras, 1971-78; tech. staff M.I.T./Lincoln Lab., Lexington, Mass., 1978-85; asst. leader, leader TRADEX, Kiernan Reentry Measurements Site, Kwajalein, Marshall Islands, 1982-83; mem. dept. staff MITRE Corp., Bedford, Mass., 1985—. Contbr. articles to profl. jours. Mem. Am. Astron. Soc., N.Y. Acad. Scis., Sigma Xi. Clubs: Littleton Soccer, Harvard Sportsmen's. Current Work: Radar systems, radar imaging, multi-static radar systems, pattern recognition (as applied to imaging techniques), simulation techniques, coherent radar processing techniques. Subspecialties: Systems engineering; Radio and microwave astronomy. Home: 216 Harwood Ave Littleton MA 01460 Office: MITRE Corp Middlesex Turnpike Bedford MA 02173

ZELIBOR, JOSEPH LOUIS, JR., research microbiologist; b. Coronado, Calif., Oct. 20, 1953; s. Joseph Louis and Mavie Rita (Ames) Z.; m. Brenda Kay Rexrode, Jan. 20, 1979; children—Joseph Louis III, Jason Warren. Assoc. Sci., No. Va. Community Coll., 1974; B.S., Purdue U., 1976; postgrad. U. Md., 1976—. Sci. cons. Systems Integration & Research, Inc., Arlington, Va., 1975-76, dir. sci. research, 1976-77; research microbiologist U.S. Geol. Survey, Reston, Va., 1977-83, safety officer, 1978-83; faculty U. Md., College Park, 1983—. Contbr. articles to profl. jours. Inventor in field. Supr.-asst. Fairfax County Recreation Dept., Va., 1973-74. Served with USN, 1971-72. Grantee ERDA, 1977, U.S. Geol. Survey, 1984. Mem. AAAS, Am. Chem. Soc. (symposium co-chmn. 1982), Am. Soc. Microbiology (regional sci. judge 1984-85), Nat. Rifle Assn., Sigma Xi. Roman Catholic. Current work: Microbial origin of humic substances; genetic probes applied to the study of geomicrobiological processes; redox cells applied to geomicrobiology. Subspecialties: Genetics and genetic engineering (biology); Geochemistry. Home: 3149 Bayswater Ct Fairfax VA 22031 Office: U Md Dept Microbiology College Park MD 20742

ZEMCOV, ALEXANDER, biomedical research engineer, educator; b. Berlin, Germany, Feb. 9, 1944; came to U.S., 1962, naturalized, 1985; s. Boris and Olga (Romanov) Z.; m. Laurie Barclay, June 11, 1978. B.Engring., NYU, 1967, M.S., 1969; D.Sc., Columbia U., 1980. Asst. prof. CUNY Tech. Coll., Bklyn., 1969-80; asst. prof. neurology Cornell U. Med. Coll., N.Y.C., 1981—; dir. computer ops. Burke Rehab. Ctr., White Plains, N.Y., 1981—. Contbr. articles to profl. jours. Mem. IEEE, Soc. Indsl. and Applied Math. N.Y. Acad. Sci., Sigma Xi, Sigma Pi Sigma. Current work: Utilization of cerebral imaging in the diagnosis of dementing diseases; study of the epidemiology of dementing diseases; computer applications to medicine. Subspecialty: Biomedical engineering. Office: Burke Rehab Ctr 785 Mameroneck Ave White Plains NY 10605

ZEN, E-AN, research geologist; b. Peking, China, May 31, 1928; came to U.S., 1946, naturalized, 1963; s. Hung-chun and Heng-chi'h (Chen) Z. A.B., Cornell U., 1951; M.A., Harvard U., 1952, Ph.D., 1955. Research fellow Woods Hole Oceanographic Inst., 1955-56, research asso., 1956-58; asst. prof. U. N.C., 1958-59; geologist U.S. Geol. Survey, 1959-80, research geologist, 1981—; vis. asso. prof. Calif. Inst. Tech., 1962; Crosby vis. prof. M.I.T., 1973; Harry H. Hess sr. vis. fellow Princeton U., 1981. Contbr. articles to profl. jours. Fellow Geol. Soc. Am. (council 1985—), AAAS, Am. Acad. Arts and Scis., Mineral. Soc. Am. (council 1975-77, pres. 1975-76); mem. Geol. Soc. Washington (pres. 1973), Nat. Acad. Scis., Mineral. Assn. Can. Subspecialty: Petrology. Office: Mail Stop 959 US Geol Survey Nat Center Reston VA 22092

ZENSER, TERRY VERNON, research biochemist, geriatric and gerontology research coordinator; b. Port Clinton, Ohio, Aug. 1, 1945; s. Vernon S. and Hazel Z.; m. Barbara Jean Morrison, Aug. 10, 1968; children: Nathan, Jason. B.S. in Biol. Scis, Ohio State U., 1967; Ph.D. in Biochemistry, U. Mo., 1971. Lectr. Hood Coll., 1974-75; renal research VA Med. Center, Pitts., 1975-76; adj. asst. prof. biochemistry U. Pitts., 1975-76; asst. prof. biochemistry and medicine St. Louis U., 1976-80, assoc. prof., 1980-85, prof., 1985—; core coordinator Geriatric Research, Edn. and Clin. Center, VA Med. Center, St. Louis, 1976—. Contbr. numerous articles to profl. jours., chpts. to books. Served to capt., Med. Service Corps U.S. Army, 1971-75. VA grantee, 1976—; Am. Cancer Soc. grantee, 1981—; Nat. Cancer Inst. grantee, 1980—; EPA grantee, 1980-81. Mem. Am. Chem. Soc., Am. Fedn. Clin. Research, Gerontol. Soc., Am. Soc. Biol. Chemists, Am. Soc. Pharmacology and Exptl. Therapeutics, Sigma Xi. Current Work: Biology of aging and drug metabolism; investigating mechanism of initiation of toxic and carcinogenic effects of certain chemicals and renal metabolism. Subspecialties: Biochemistry (medicine); Cancer research (medicine). Home: 1200 Dunloe Rd Manchester MO 63011 Office: VA Med Center GRECC 111G-JB Saint Louis MO 63125

ZENTMYER, GEORGE AUBREY, JR., plant pathology educator; b. North Platte, Nebr., Aug. 9, 1913; s. George Aubrey and Mary Elizabeth (Strahorn) Z.; m. Dorothy Anne Dudley, May 24, 1941; children: Elizabeth Zentmyer Dossa, Jane Zentmyer Fernald, Susan Dudley. A.B., UCLA, 1935; M.S., U. Calif., 1936, Ph.D., 1938. Asst. forest pathologist U.S. Dept. Agr., San Francisco, 1937-40; asst. pathologist Conn. Agrl. Expt. Sta., New Haven, 1940-44; asst. plant pathologist to plant pathologist U. Calif. at Riverside, 1944-62, prof. plant pathology, 1962-81, prof. emeritus, 1981—, chmn. dept., 1968-73; cons. NSF, Trust Ter. of Pacific Islands, 1964, 66, Commonwealth of Australia Forest and Timber Bur., 1968, AID, Ghana and Nigeria, 1969, Govt. of South Africa, 1980, Govt. of Israel, 1983, Israel Phytopath. Soc., 1983, Govt. Western Australia, 1983. Author: Plant Disease Development and Control, 1968, Recent Advances in Pest Control, 1957, Plant Pathology, an Advanced Treatise, 1977, The Soil-Root Interface, 1979, Phytophthora: Its Biology, Taxonomy, Ecology and Pathology, 1983; Ecology and Management of Soilborne Plant Pathogens, 1985—; assoc. editor: Ann. Rev. of Phytopathology, 1971—; Jour. Phytopathology, 1951-54; contbr. articles to profl. jours. Bd. dirs. Riverside YMCA, 1949-58; pres. Town and Gown Orgn., Riverside, 1962; mem. NRC, 1968-73; bd. dirs. Riverside Hospice, 1982—, pres. bd. dirs., 1984-85; bd. dirs. Friends of Mission Inn, 1981—. Guggenheim fellow Australia, 1964-65; NATO sr. sci. fellow Eng., 1971; recipient award of honor Calif. Avocado Soc., 1954, 81; NSF research grantee, 1963, 68, 71, 74, 78. Fellow Am. Phytopath. Soc. (pres. 1966, pres. Pacific div. 1955, award of distinction 1983), AAAS (pres. Pacific div. 1974-75); mem. Nat. Acad. Scis., Mycol. Soc. Am., Am. Inst. Biol. Scis., Bot. Soc. Am., Brit. Mycol. Soc., Australian Plant Pathology Soc., Philippine Phytopath. Soc., Indian Phytopath. Soc., Assn. Tropical Biology, Internat. Soc. Plant Pathology (councilor 1973-78), Explorers Club, Sigma Xi, Gamma Sigma Delta. Gamma Sigma Delta. Current Work: The genus phytophthora-biology; physiology, control, ecology; diseases of subtropical and tropical plants; especially avocado and cacao; soil-borne pathogens; fungicides. Subspecialty: Plant pathology. Home: 3892 Chapman Pl Riverside CA 92506

ZEPPETELLA, ANTHONY JOHN, actuary; b. Bklyn., Dec. 26, 1949; s. Michael Lucio and Filemena (Peluso) Z.; m. Barbara Bahna, July 9, 1972; children: Peter, Thomas. B.S., Bklyn. Coll., CUNY, 1971; M.S., Courant Inst., N.Y.C., 1973, Ph.D., 1976. Asst. prof. math. NYU, N.Y.C., 1975-76, Clarkson Coll., Potsdam, N.Y., 1976-81; asst. actuarial dir. Mut. Life Ins. Co. N.Y., N.Y.C., 1980-82; actuary McKay-Barlow Co., Butler, N.J., 1982-83; assoc. actuary Mut. Life Ins. Co. N.Y., N.Y.C., 1983—. Research asst. Courant Inst., 1973-76; research grantee NIH, NSF, 1979-81. Fellow Soc. Actuaries (assoc., instr. risk theory 1982); Mem. Soc. for Indsl. and Applied Math., Pi Mu Epsilon. Club: N.Y. Actuaries (instr. risk theory 1982—). Current Work: Mathematical risk thoery. Subspecialty: Mathematical biology. Home: 540 75th St Brooklyn NY 11209 Office: MONY 1740 Broadway New York NY 10019

ZERGUINI, TAHA HOUSSINE, nuclear engineering educator, researcher, consultant; b. Constantine, Algeria, Aug. 29, 1953; came to U.S., 1977; s. Kamel and Ourida (Hadjout) Z. DES, U. Algiers, Algeria, 1976; M. Nuclear Engrng., U. Wash., 1979, Ph.D. in Nuclear Engring., 1983. Research assoc. U. Wash., Seattle, 1977-83; asst. prof. nuclear engrng. U. Ill., Urbana, 1983—; cons. Lawrence Livermore Lab., Calif., 1979-83, McDonald Douglas, St. Louis, 1983-84. Mem. Am. Nuclear Soc. (Best Paper award 1982), Am. Phys. Soc., IEEE. Current work: Numerical methods in particle transport, fusion plasma science and engineering, fusion reactor design. Subspecialties: Nuclear engineering; Fusion. Home: 702 Crescent Dr #2 Champaign IL 61821 Office: U Ill 103 S Goodwin Ave Urbana IL 61801

ZEROKA, DANIEL, chemistry educator; b. Plymouth, Pa., June 22, 1941; s. Michael and Mary (Klimchak) Z.; m. Alexandra S. Kotulak, May 27, 1967; children: Daniel M., Andrea M. B.S. in Chemistry, Wilkes Coll., 1963; Ph.D. in Chemistry, U. Pa., 1966. Asst. prof. chemistry Lehigh U., Bethlehem, Pa., 1967-74, assoc. prof., 1974—. Author research publs. in field. NSF postdoctoral fellow, 1966-67. Mem. Am. Chem. Soc., Am. Phys. Soc., Combustion Inst., Sigma Xi. Current Work: Quantum chemistry; statistical thermodynamics; effect of magnetic and electric fields on matter. Subspecialties: Physical chemistry; Theoretical chemistry. Office: Dept Chemistry Lehigh U Bethlehem PA 18015

ZETLIN, LEV, civil engineer, educator; b. Namangan, Russia, July 14, 1918; s. Mark and Alexandra (Senelnikoff) Z.; m. Eve Shmueli, Jan. 24, 1946; children—Alexandria, Thalia, Michael Steven. Diploma, Higher Tech. Inst., Palestine, 1939; M.C.E., Cornell U., 1951, Ph.D., 1953. Research asso., asst. prof. civil engring. Cornell U., 1951-55; disting. prof. civil engring. Pratt Inst., N.Y.C., 1956—; vis. prof. civil engring. Manhattan Coll., N.Y.C., 1957-59; guest lectr. Columbia, U. Minn., U. Va., 1955-63; Univ. prof. engring. and architecture U. Va., 1967; cons. engr.; pres. Zetlin-Argo Liaison & Guidance Corp., Lev Zetlin Cons., Spl. Structural Systems, Inc.; mem. Internal Bd. Engring.; Cons. to James Bay Energy Corp., Can., Montreal Olympics Stadium.; Mem. Concrete Industry Bd. N.Y.C.; former mem. adv. panel GSA, housing tech. joint panel Dept. Commerce-Dept. Housing and Urban Devel.; mem. planning com. bldg. research adv. bd. Nat. Acad. Scis.; past. pres. Internat. Tech. Cooperation Centre. Mem. editorial adv. bd. Bldg.: Constrn. Mag, 1962—; Author: Reinforced Concrete Design, Standard Handbook for Engineers, 1968, Suspension Structures, Structural Engineering Handbook, 1968; Contbr. articles to profl. jours.; chpt. on stadiums Ency. Brit. Trustee, chmn. consultor com. Manhattan Coll. Sacred Heart, N.Y.; mem. N.Y. State Council on Arts, 1978. Decorated Knight of honour Mil. and Hospitaler Order St. John of Jerusalem, Knight of Malta; recipient Prestressed Concrete Inst. award for N.Y. State Observation Towers N.Y. Worlds Fair, 1964; Gold medal Société Arts, Sciences, Lettres, 1969; named to Profl. and Exec. Hall of Fame. Fellow ASCE; mem. Soc. Am. Mil. Engrs., Internat. Assn. Bridge and Structural Engrs., Inst. Structural Engrs. (Eng.), N.Y. Acad. Scis., Am. Concrete Inst., Sigma Xi, Phi Kappa Phi, Chi Epsilon. Inventor prestressed runways, light gage airplane hangars, cable suspension structures, systems bldgs.; cons. Montreal Olympics Stadium, investigator major structural collapses such as Hayatt Regency,; Kansas City, Mo., Mianus Bridge, Conn. Home: 6 Fairway Dr Manhasset NY 11030 Office: 60 E 42d St New York NY 10017

ZHOU, FENG-CHIAO, neuroscience educator; b. Taiwan, Republic of China, Aug. 8, 1951; came to U.S., 1978; s. Ying-sen and Giu-Ying (Huang) Z.; m. Paula Chi Mo, Oct. 16, 1982. B.S., Taiwan Normal U., 1975; M.Ph., City Univ. N.Y., 1982; Ph.D., Mount Sinai Sch. Medicine, 1983. Instr. anatomy N.Y. Coll. Podiatric Medicine, N.Y.C., 1981-83, asst. prof., 1983-85; fellow in neurobiology NYU, 1983-85, adj. asst. prof., 1984—; asst. research anatomist UCLA, 1985—. Contbr. articles to profl. jours. Served to 2d lt. U.S. Army, 1975-77. Mem. Am. Assn. Colls. Podiatric Medicine, Am. Bur. Med. Advancement in China, N.Y. Acad. Scis., Soc. for Neurosci., Chinese in Neurosci., Internat. Brain Research Orgn. Current work: Plasticity in central nervous system as result of trauma, the effect of neurotrophic factors, brain/neurontransplant for traumatic brain. Subspecialties: Anatomy and embryology; Neurobiology.

Office: Mental Retardation Research Ctr UCLA Sch Medicine NPI 58-258 760 Westwood Plaza Los Angeles CA 90024

ZHOU, ZONG-YUAN, physicist, educator; b. Nin Bo, Zhejiang, China, Mar. 22, 1942; s. Zheng-Yuan and Su-Zheng (Chan) Z.; m. Bi-He Wu, Oct. 1, 1967; children—Jin-Song, Nin. Diploma, Nanjing U., 1964. Teaching asst. Nanjing U., People's Republic of China, 1964-80, lectr., 1980-85, assoc. prof., 1985—, also dir. neutron lab., 1978-81; research asst. Qinghua U., Beijing, People's Republic of China, 1965-66; researcher Atomic Energy Inst., Beijing, 1979; vis. scholar Lawrence Berkeley Lab., U. Calif., 1981—. Cooperator new discovery Beta-delayed two-proton decay 22A1 and 26P, 1983; Discoverer new weak protons of 21Mg, 25Si, 29S and 41Ti, 1984. Mem. Chinese Physics Soc., Am. Physics Soc. (nuclear sci. div.). Current work: Study of exotic nuclei far from the beta stability and description of heavy ion reaction mechanism. Subspecialty: Nuclear physics. Home: Dept Physics Nanjing U Nanjing JiangSu People's Republic of China Office: Room 210 Bldg 88 Lawrence Berkeley Lab U California 1 Cyclotron Rd Berkeley CA 94720

ZHU, NAI JUE, chemist; b. Zun Yi, Guizhou, China, Jan. 24, 1942; s. Shi Kai and Boruo (Pan) Z.; m. Li Liang, Dec. 21, 1967; children: Nan Zhu, Hua Zhu. B.S., Peking U., Beijing, 1965. Research asst. Inst. Chemistry, Beijing, China, 1965-78, research assoc., group leader, 1979—; cons. Beijing Grad. Sch., Wuhan Geol. Coll., 1980; vis. scholar SUNY-Buffalo, 1980-82. Recipient Inst. Chemistry, Academia Sinica invention award, 1979. Mem. Chinese Chem. Soc., Am. Crystallographic Soc. Current Work: Electron density distributions and chemical bond, using x-ray diffractometer at low temperatures, relationship between molecular structure and properties for novel materials and organometallic compounds, metallic clusters structures. Subspecialties: Crystallography; X-ray crystallography. Office: Inst Chemistry Academia Sinica Zhong Guan Dun Beijing People's Republic of China

ZIEGLER, DANIEL MARTIN, chemistry educator, biochemistry researcher; b. Quinter, Kans., July 6, 1927; s. Anton T. and Clara (Weissbeck) Z.; m. Mary Alice Weir, Aug. 19, 1952; children—Daniel L., Paul W., Mary Claire, James M. B.S. in Chemistry, St. Benedict's Coll., 1949; Ph.D. in Chemistry, Loyola U., Chgo., 1955. Asst. prof. chemistry U. Wis., Madison, 1959-61; asst. prof. chemistry U. Tex.-Austin, 1961-62, assoc. prof., 1962-69, prof., 1969—; mem. study sect. NIH, 1983—. Mem. editorial bd. Jour. Biological Chemistry, 1977—; contbr. articles to sci. jours. USPHS Career Devel. awardee, 1965-75; established investigator Am. Heart Assn., 1960-65. Mem. AAAS, Am. Chem. Soc., Am. Soc. Biol. Chemists, Am. Soc. Pharmacology and Exptl. Therapeutics, N.Y. Acad. Scis., Sigma Xi. Current work: Drug metabolism, chemical carcinogenesis and metabolic control mechanisms. Subspecialties: Biochemistry (biology); Pharmacology. Home: 6704 Shoalcreek Blvd Austin TX 78731 Office: Clayton Found Biochem Inst U Tex Austin TX 78712

ZIELINSKI, PAUL BERNARD, civil engineering educator; b. West Allis, Wis., Sept. 9, 1932; s. Stanley Charles and Lottie Caroline (Pliszkiewicz) Z.; m. Monica Theresa Beres, July 13, 1957; children: Daniel Paul, Gregory John, Robert Mathias, Sarah Ann. B.S.C.E., Marquette U., 1956; M.S., U. Wis-Madison, 1961, Ph.D., 1965. Registered profl. engr., Wis., S.C. Asst. instr. Marquette U., Milw., asst. prof., 1964-67; instr. U. Wis.-Madison, 1959-64; from asst. prof. to prof. civil engring. dept. Clemson (S.C.) U., 1967—; dir. Water Resources Research Inst., Clemson, 1978—; cons. Am. Pub. Works Assn., Chgo., 1974-78. Mem. S.C. Water Resources Commn., Columbia, 1978—; chmn. Clemson City Planning Commn., 1971-74. Mem. ASCE, Am. Soc. Engring. Edn., Sigma Xi. Roman Catholic. Lodge: Sertoma (pres. 1979-80). Current Work: consultant on several hydraulic laboratory and field demonstration projects of swirl chamber as a storm water separator, a primary sedimentation chamber and a soil erosion control device. Subspecialties: Water supply and wastewater treatment; Fluid mechanics. Office: Civil Engring Dept Clemson U Clemson SC 29631

ZIMM, BRUNO HASBROUCK, physical chemistry educator; b. Woodstock, N.Y., Oct. 31, 1920; s. Bruno L. and Louise S. (Hasbrouck) Z.; m. Georgianna S. Grevatt, June 17, 1944; children: Louis H., Carl B. Grad., Kent (Conn.) Sch., 1938; A.B., Columbia, 1941, M.S., 1943, Ph.D., 1944. Research asso. Columbia, 1944; research asso., instr. Polytech. Inst. Bklyn., 1944-46; instr. chemistry U. Calif. at Berkeley, 1946-47, asst. prof., 1947-50, asso. prof., 1950-51; vis. lectr. Harvard, 1950-51; research asso. research lab. Gen. Electric Co., 1951-60; prof. chemistry U. Calif., La Jolla, 1960—. Asso. editor: Jour. Chem. Physics, 1947-49; adv. bd.: Jour. Polymer Sci, 1953-62, Jour. Bio-Rheology, 1962-73, Jour. Biopolymers, 1963—, Jour. Phys. Chemistry, 1963-68, Jour. Biophys. Chemistry, 1973—. Recipient Bingham Medal Soc. Rheology, 1960—, also the High Polymer Physics prize from Am. Phys. Soc., 1963. Mem. Biophys. Soc., Am. Soc. Biol. Chemists, Am. Chem. Soc. (Baekeland award 1957), Nat. Acad. Scis. (award in Chem. Scis. 1981), Am. Acad. Arts and Scis., Am. Phys. Soc. Current Work: Theory of macromolecular solutions; properties and structure of biopolymers. Subspecialties: Biophysical chemistry; Theoretical chemistry. Home: 2522 Horizon Way La Jolla CA 92037

ZIMMANCK, FRANK ROBERT, JR., nuclear reactor operator; b. St. Petersburg, Fla., Feb. 5, 1950; s. Frank Robert and Helen E. (Warns) Z.; m. Naoma Lee Kinsman, May 17, 1974; children: Leesa, Patricia, Frank. Cert. sr. reactor operator. Aux. operator Fla. Power Corp., Crystal River, 1975-77, reactor operator, 1977-80, sr. reactor operator, 1980-81, nuclear tech. support analyst, 1981-84, nuclear modification functional test supr., 1984-85; pres. Perspective Cons. Services, Inc., 1985—. Mem. PowerPAC, St. Petersburg, 1982—; bd. dirs. Fla. Power Employees Fed. Credit Union, 1982—. Mem. Am. Nuclear Soc. Democrat. Mem. Ch. of God/Ind. Current Work: Supervising the operational testing of PWR nuclear power plant modifications. Subspecialty: Nuclear fission. Home: 5533 S Power Terr Homosassa FL 32646 Office: 5533 S Power Terr Homosassa FL 32646

ZIMMERMAN, HOWARD ELLIOT, chemist, educator; b. N.Y.C., July 5, 1926; s. Charles and May (Cohen) Z.; m. Jane Kirschenheiter, June 3, 1950 (dec. Jan. 1975); children: Robert, Steven, James; m. Martha L. Bailey Kaufman, Nov. 7, 1975; stepchildren: Peter and Tanya Kaufman. B.S., Yale U., 1950, Ph.D., 1953. NRC fellow Harvard U., 1953-54; faculty Northwestern U., 1954-60, asst. prof., 1955-60; assoc. prof. U. Wis., Madison, 1960-61, prof. chemistry, 1961—, Arthur C. Cope prof. chemistry, 1975—; Chmn. 4th Internat. Union Pure and Applied Chemistry Symposium on Photochemistry, 1972. Author: Quantum Mechanics for Organic Chemists, 1975; Mem editorial bd. Jour. Organic Chemistry, 1967-71, Molecular Photochemistry, 1969-80, Jour. Am. Chem. Soc., 1982-85. Contbr. articles to profl. jours. Recipient Halpern award for photochemistry N.Y. Acad. Scis., 1979. Mem. Am. Chem. Soc. (James Flack Norris award 1976), Chem. Soc. London, German Chem. Soc., Inter-Am. Photochemistry Assn. (co-chmn. organic div. 1977-79, exec. com. 1979—), Nat. Acad. Scis., Phi Beta Kappa, Sigma Xi. Current Work: Organic photochemical research to explore reactivity of electronically excited organic molecules; search for new organic photochemical reactions and theory; study of unusual reactions and mechanisms; synthesis of unusual organic molecules. Subspecialties: Organic chemistry; Photochemistry. Home: 1 Oconto Ct Madison WI 53705

ZIMMERMAN, HYMAN JOSEPH, physician, educator; b. Rochester, N.Y., July 14, 1914; s. Philip and Rachel (Marine) Z.; m. Kathrin J. Jones, Feb. 28, 1943; children: Philip M., David J., Robert L., Diane E. A.B., U. Rochester, 1936; M.A., Stanford, 1938, M.D., 1942. Diplomate: Am. Bd. Internal Medicine. Intern Stanford U. Hosp., 1942-43; resident George Washington U. div. Gallinger Municipal Hosp., 1946-48; clin. instr. medicine George Washington U. div. Gallinger Municipal Hosp. (Sch. Medicine), 1948-51; practice medicine, specializing in internal medicine, Washington, 1948-49; asst. chief med. service VA Hosp., Washington, 1949-51; dir. Liver and Metabolic Research Lab., 1965-68, chief med. service, 1971-78, sr. clinician, 1978-80, disting. physician, 1984—; asst. prof. medicine Coll. Medicine U. Nebr.; also chief med. service VA Hosp., Omaha, 1951-53; chief med. service West Side VA Hosp., Chgo.; also clin. asso. prof. medicine Coll. Medicine U. Ill., 1953-57; prof., chmn. dept. medicine Chgo. Med. Sch.; also chmn. dept. medicine Mt. Sinai Hosp., Chgo., 1957-65; prof. medicine George Washington Sch. of Medicine, Washington, 1965-68, 71—; chief med. service Boston VA Hosp., 1968-71; prof. medicine Boston U. Sch. Medicine, 1968-71; lectr. medicine Tufts U. Sch. Medicine, 1968-71; chief med. service VA Hosp., Washington, 1971-78, sr. clinician, 1978—; prof. medicine George Washington Sch. Medicine, 1971—; clin. prof. medicine Georgetown U., 1971—, Howard U., 1971—, Uniformed Services U. Health Scis., 1978—. Contbr. numerous articles to med. jours. Served to maj. AUS, 1943-46. Fellow ACP; mem. AMA (council on drugs, gastroenterology panel 1968-70), AAAS, Am. Fedn. for Clin. Research, Am. Diabetes Assn., Endocrine Soc., Assn. for Study Liver Diseases, Am. Soc. Clin. Investigation, N.Y. Acad. Scis., Central Soc. Clin. Research, Soc. for Exptl. Biology and Medicine, Am. Soc. for Pharmacology and Therapeutics, Am. Gastroenterol. Assn., Sigma Xi, Alpha Omega Alpha. Subspecialty: Gastroenterology. Home: 7913 Charleston Ct Bethesda MD 20817 Office: 50 Irving St Washington DC 20422

ZIMMERMAN, JOHN THOMAS, neuroscientist, educator; b. Denver, Feb. 27, 1949; s. Richard Gordon Zimmerman and Neva-Jeanne (Bloom) Lavine; m. Marlene Sanae Yamada, Feb. 20, 1970 (div. 1980). B.A. cum laude, U. Colo., 1972, M.A., 1978, Ph.D., 1981. Lab. dir. U. Colo. Sch. Medicine, 1968-72, research asst., 1979-80, research assoc., 1981-83, asst. prof. psychiatry, 1983—; cons. Sleep Disorders Lab., Presbyn. Hosp., Denver, 1980-83; co-dir. Sleep Disorders Ctr., Colo. Psychiat. Hosp., 1983—; pres. Bioelectromagnetics, Inc., Denver, 1983—. Mem. Joint Bd. Student Health Services, U. Colo.-Boulder, 1969-71. Mem. Clin. Sleep Soc., Sleep Research Soc., Assn. Polysomnographic Technologists, Psi Chi. Current work: Developing a biomagnetic imaging system to visualize the dynamically changing biomagnetic field patterns associated with sensation, thought processes and energy field medicine. Subspecialties: Bioinstrumentation; Psychobiology. Home: 3710 Chase St Wheat Ridge CO 80212 Office: U Colo Sch Medicine 4200 E 9th Ave Box C268 Denver CO 80262

ZIMMERMAN, RICHARD CARL, marine biologist, oceanographer; b. Honolulu, Apr. 14, 1953; s. Richard Eugene and Catherine Ruby (Yost) Z.; m. Audrey Ann Burdekin, Aug. 9, 1975. B.S., U. So. Calif., 1975, M.S., 1979, Ph.D., 1983. Asst. marine scientist U. So. Calif., Los Angeles, 1975-76, grad. teaching asst., 1976-81, grad. res. asst., 1982, postdoctoral res. assoc., 1983—; cons. 1975—. Contbr. (with others) articles to profl. jours. Author (with others) (computer software) CRUNCH—A Statistical Package, 1984. Grantee Sigma Xi, 1978, 79; recipient research scholarship Achievement Rewards for Coll. Scientists Found., 1980-83. Mem. AAAS, Ecol. Soc. Am., Am. Soc. Limnology & Oceanography, Am. Phycol. Soc., Sigma Xi. Current work: Regulation of primary production in ecosystems, computer simulation of energy flow, and material cycling within ecosystems. Subspecialties: Marine biology; Ecology (biology). Home: 301 Sapphire #A Redondo Beach CA 90277 Office: Allan Hancock Foundation Univ So California Los Angeles CA 90089-0371

ZIMMERMAN, THOMAS PAUL, research biochemist; b. Plainfield, N.J., Sept. 3, 1942; s. Carl Paul and Anna Marie (Deere) Z.; m. Barbara Ann Ouimet, June 18, 1966; children: Michael Thomas, Catherine Ann. B.S. in Chemistry, Providence Coll., 1964; Ph.D. in Biochemistry, Brown U., 1969. USPHS postdoctoral fellow Brown U., Providence, R.I., 1969-71; sr. research biochemist Burroughs Wellcome Co., Research Triangle Park, N.C., 1971—, principal scientist, 1984—. Mem. adv. com. on chemotherapy and hematology Am. Cancer Soc., 1983—. Contbr. articles to sci. publs. Mem. Am. Soc. Pharmacology and Exptl. Therapeutics, Am. Assn. Cancer Research, Internat. Soc. Immunopharmacology, Am. Assn. Cancer Research. Roman Catholic. Patentee in field. Current Work: Metabolic studies of purine antimetabolites, determination of mechanisms by which pharmacological agents modulate immune and inflammatory cell function; nucleoside transport. Subspecialties: Biochemistry (biology); Molecular pharmacology. Home: 1415 Brunson Ct Cary NC 27511 Office: 3030 Cornwallis Rd Research Triangle Park NC 27709

ZINCONE, ROBERT, aerospace company executive; b. N.Y.C., Apr. 11, 1934; s. Nicholas Zincone and Josephine (DeBoli) Zincone Ferri; m. Irene Beyer, Feb. 15, 1958. B.S. in Mech. Engring., U. Bridgeport, 1964; M.S., Columbia U., 1968. Engr., Sikorsky Aircraft Co., Stratford, Conn., 1955—, chief engr., 1975-79, v.p. engring., 1979-82, sr. v.p. research and engring., 1982-83, exec. v.p., 1983—. Contbr. articles to aerospace jours. Patentee devices in field of helicopter rotor systems. Served with USAF, 1957. Recipient George Meade Achievement award United Technologies Corp., 1972, 76. Mem. Am. Helicopter Soc. (pres. 1985—), Army Aircraft Assn. Am., AIAA, Soc. Automotive Engrs., Am. Soc. Metals, ASME. Current work: Management of technology growth and micro digital electronic applications to rotary wing vehicles of future; relativity and gravitation. Subspecialties: Aeronautical engineering; Composite materials. Office: Sikorsky Aircraft Co North Main St Stratford CT 06601

ZINDER, NORTON DAVID, geneticist, educator; b. N.Y.C., Nov. 7, 1928; s. Harry Jean and (Gottesman) Z.; m. Marilyn Estreicher, Dec. 24, 1949; children—Stephen, Michael. A.B., Columbia U., 1947; M.S., U. Wis., 1949, Ph.D., 1952. Asst. Rockefeller U., N.Y.C., 1952-56, asso., 1956-58, asso. prof. genetics, 1958-64, prof., 1964—, John D. Rockefeller Jr. prof., 1977—; Cons. genetic-biology NSF, 1962—; chmn. ad hoc com. to rev. viral cancer program Nat. Cancer Inst., 1973-74; Mem. vis. com. dept. biology Harvard U., 1975—; sect. virology Yale U., 1975—; dept. biochemistry Princeton U., 1975—. Asso. editor: Virology. Recipient Eli Lilly award in microbiology and immunology, 1962; U.S. Steel Found. award in molecular biology, 1966; medal of excellence Columbia U., 1969. Fellow Am. Acad. Arts and Scis.; mem. Nat. Acad. Scis. (exec. com. Assembly of Life Scis. 1975—), Soc. Am. Biol. Chemists, Genetics Soc. Am., Am. Soc. for Microbiology, Harvey Soc., Sigma Xi. Spl. research in microbial genetics. Subspecialty: Genetics and genetic engineering (biology). Home: 450 E 63d St New York NY 10021 Office: Rockefeller U 66th St and York Ave New York NY 10021

ZINGG, WALTER, surgeon, educator; b. Kloten, Zurich, Switzerland, Mar. 29, 1924; came to Can., 1954, naturalized, 1959; s. Ernst J. and Ida (Haab) Z.; m. Regula L. Zollinger, June 25, 1949; children—Claudia E., Jeannette R., Esther A., David W., Tracy Bill. M.D., U. Zurich, 1951; M.Sc., U. Man., 1952. Intern, Bethesda Hosp., Cin., 1950-51; resident Zurich Gen. Hosp., 1949-50, Winterthur Gen. Hosp., 1952-54, Deer Lodge Vets. Hosp., Winnipeg, Man., Can., 1954-55, Winnipeg Children's Hosp., 1955-56; mem. faculty U. Man., Winnipeg, 1956-64, assoc. prof., 1964; head div. surgery Research Inst., Hosp. for Sick Children, Toronto, Ont., 1964—; asst. prof. U. Toronto, 1964-68, assoc. prof., 1968-78, prof. surgery and biomed. engring., 1978—, assoc. dir. Inst. Biomed. Engring., 1975-83, dir., 1983—; dir. MediPro Scis. Ltd., Toronto; chmn. bd. dirs. Conn Smythe Research Found. for Crippled Children, Toronto, 1980-85. Contbr. articles to profl. jours. Patentee. Fellow Royal Coll. Physicians and Surgeons Can., ACS, Am. Coll. Cardiology; mem. Can. Med. Biol. Engring. Soc. (pres. 1984—), Am. Soc. Artificial Internal Organs, Internat. Soc. Artificial Organs, European Soc. Artificial Organs. Current work: Artificial organs; surgical research; biomaterials. Subspecialties: Artificial organs and prostheses; Biomedical engineering. Office: Inst Biomed Engring U Toronto Rosebrugh Bldg Toronto ON M5S 1A4 Canada

ZINN, GENE MARVIN, veterinarian, educator; b. Kellerton, Iowa, Apr. 9, 1932; s. Raymond Bryon and Pearl Lavon (Watts) Z.; m. Muriel Lue McLain, June 16, 1957; children: Karl Gene, Kurt Ray, Sandra Lee, Eric Marvin. D.V.M., Iowa State U., 1956; Ph.D., U. Mo., 1970. Gen. practice vet. medicine, Bethany, Mo., 1956-65; 70-78, Gallatin, Mo., 1966-67; instr. large animal surgery Kans. State U., Manhattan, 1965-66; research assoc. dept. vet. physiology and pharmacology U. Mo., Columbia, 1967-70; asst. prof. food animal medicine and surgery U. Mo. (Coll. Vet. Medicine), 1979—. Contbr. articles to profl. jours. County chmn. Harrison County Republican Central Com., 1972-76. Recipient various awards. Mem. AVMA, Am. Assn. Bovine Practitioners, Am. Assn. Swine Practitioners, Mo. Vet. Med. Assn., Am. Acad. Vet. Nutrition, Am. Assn. Vet. Clinicians, Am. Soc. Animal Sci., Council for Agr. Sci. and Tech. Methodist. Current Work: Swine disease, swine nutrition. Subspecialties: Food animal medicine and surgery; Animal nutrition. Home: 1204 Longwell Dr Columbia MO 65201 Office: 1600 E Rollins Rd Columbia MO 65211

ZIRKER, JACK BERNARD, solar astronomer; b. Bklyn., July 19, 1927; s. Joseph and Rose Z.; m. Lorette Zuckerman, Jan. 21, 1951; children—Robin, Alizon, Pamela. B.M.E., CCNY, 1948; M.S., N.Y. U., 1953; Ph.D., Harvard U., 1956. Scientist Sacramento Peak Obs., Sunspot, N.Mex., 1956-64, dir. obs., 1976-84; solar astronomer U. Hawaii, 1964-76, prof., 1965-76; cons. NASA. Served with U.S. Army, 45-47. Mem. Am. Astron. Soc., Internat. Astron. Union. Subspecialty: Solar physics.

ZISK, STANLEY HARRIS, research scientist; b. Boston, July 11, 1931; s. Morris and Edith (Lewenberg) Z.; married; children: Jonathan Lee, Stephen Robert, Matthew Bruce. B.S., M.I.T., 1953, M.S., 1953; Ph.D., Stanford U., 1965. Faculty dept. elec. engring. M.I.T., Cambridge, 1965-68; staff scientist, head cryogenics sect. Haystack Obs., Westford, 1968—; cons. in field; lectr. in field. Contbr. articles to profl. jours. Served with USNR, 1956-59. NASA grantee, 1968—. Mem. Am. Astron. Soc., Am. Geophys. Union, Union Radio Sci. Internat., IEEE. Current Work: Remote sensing of planetary surfaces; maser amplifier development. Subspecialties: Planetary science; Cryogenics. Address: MIT Haystack Obs Westford MA 01886

ZOGRAFI, GEORGE D., pharm. scientist, university administrator; b. N.Y.C., Mar. 13, 1936; s. Elias D. and Parashgeva Z.; m. Dorothy Ann Gordon, June 16, 1957; children—Thomas E., Paul M., Anna J., Ellyn J. B.S., Columbia U., 1956, D.Sc. (hon.), 1976; M.S., U. Mich., 1958, Ph.D., 1961. Asst. prof. pharmacy Columbia U., 1961-64; asst. prof. U. Mich., 1964-67, asso. prof., 1967-72; prof. U. Wis., Madison, 1972—, dean, 1975-80; cons. to industry. Contbr. numerous articles to profl. publs. Am. Found. Pharm. Edn. Gustavus Pfieffer research fellow, 1970-71. Mem. Am. Chem. Soc., AAAS, Am. Pharm. Assn., Am. Assn. Colls. Pharmacy, Am. Inst. History Pharmacy. Unitarian. Current work: Basic surface chemical research related to the development and operation of drug delivery systems. Subspecialties: Drug delivery systems; Surface chemistry. Home: 1037 Seminole Hwy Madison WI 53711 Office: U Wis Sch Pharmacy Madison WI 53706

ZOLLER, BROC GERALD, agricultural consultant, consulting firm executive; b. Oakland, Calif., Apr. 17, 1944; s. Dudley Francis and Edcil Fitzgerald (Doerr) Z.; m. Sharron Ann Higgins, July 31, 1971; children: Molly Elizabeth, Zachary Joseph, Analiese Maria. Student, Georg August U., Goettingen, W. Ger., 1965-66; B.S. in Plant Pathology with highest honors, U. Calif.-Davis, 1966, Ph.D. in Plant Pathology, 1972. Agrl. cons. Agrl. Advs., Inc., Yuba City, Calif., 1972-79; agrl . cons., pres. Pear Doctor, Inc., Yuba City, 1979—. Contbr. articles, abstracts to profl. publs. Served with U.S. Army, 1967-69. Recipient departmental citation, dept. plant pathology U. Calif.-Davis, 1966; Achievement award Lake County Farm Bur., 1982; Title IV fellow, 1969. Mem. Am. Phytopathol. Soc. (chmn. pvt. practice com.), Assn. Applied Insect Ecologists (dir. 1978-82, program chmn. 1980, pres. 1981, treas. 1985), Nat. Alliance Ind. Crop Cons., Sierra Club, Phi Beta Kappa, Sigma xi. Current Work: Economics and application of integrated pest management in deciduous tree fruit crops; agricultural loss investigation and expert testimony; disease control in deciduous tree crops; production of deciduous tree crops. Subspecialties: Integrated pest management; Plant pathology. Office: PO Box 952 1441 Garden Hwy Yuba City CA 95992

ZOLLWEG, ROBERT JOHN, physicist; b. Medina, N.Y., Aug. 1, 1924; s. Louis August and Martina Mildred (Lagasse) Z.; m. Aileen Boules, Sept. 7, 1946; children: Lynn. Vicky. B.S., Northwestern U., 1949, M.S., 1950; Ph.D., Cornell U., 1955. Research physicist Westinghouse Research & Devel. Center, Pitts., 1954-67, fellow scientist, 1967-68, adv. scientist, 1968-80, cons. scientist, 1980—. Contbr. articles to profl. jours. Served with USN, 1943-46. Mem. Am. Phys. Soc. Patentee in field. Current Work: Research in high temperature plasmas, arc modeling, arc lamps, plasma chemistry, electrodes. Subspecialties: Atomic and molecular physics; High temperature chemistry. Home: 4560 Bulltown Rd Murrysville PA 15668 Office: Westinghouse Research and Development Center 1310 Beulah Rd Pittsburgh PA 15235

ZRAKET, CHARLES ANTHONY, See *Who's Who in America,* 43rd edition.

ZUCCARELLI, ANTHONY JOSEPH, microbiologist, educator, researcher; b. N.Y.C., Aug. 11, 1944; s. Anthony D. and Rose Marie (Lisanti) Z.; m. Sharron Adele Ames, Dec. 23, 1968; children: Cara Nicole, Anthony Alexander. B.S. (Roberts scholar), Cornell U., 1966; M.A., Loma Linda U., 1968; Ph.D., Calif. Inst. Tech., 1973. Am. Cancer Soc. postdoctoral fellow U. Konstanz, W.Ger., 1974-76; asst. prof. biology Loma Linda U., 1976-80, assoc. prof. microbiology, 1980—. Research publs. on genetics. NSF grantees, 1977, 78-79; Loma Linda U. Research Adv. Com. grantee, 1978-79. Mem. Am. Soc. Microbiology, AAAS, Sigma Xi. Adventist. Current Work: Genetic engring. of small DNA viruses; protein-DNA interactions; site-specific mutagenesis; enzymology of DNA replication in E. coli. Subspecialties: Genetics and genetic engineering (biology); Molecular biology. Home: 22255 Mavis St Grand Terrace CA 92324 Office: Dept Microbiology Loma Linda U Loma Linda CA 92350

ZUIDEMA, GEORGE DALE, surgeon; b. Holland, Mich., Mar. 8, 1928; s. Jacob and Reka (Dalman) Z.; m. Joan K. Houtman, June 2, 1953; children—Karen Sue, David Jay, Nancy Ruth, Sarah Kay. A.B., Hope Coll., 1949, D.Sc. (hon.), 1969; M.D., Johns Hopkins U., 1953. Diplomate; Am. Bd. Surgery. Intern Mass. Gen. Hosp., 1953-54, asst. resident surgeon, then chief resident surgeon, 1954, 57, 58, 59; asst. prof. surgery, then assoc. prof. U. Mich. Sch. Medicine, 1960-64; prof. surgery, dir. dept. Johns Hopkins Sch. Medicine; also surgeon in chief Johns Hopkins Hosp., 1964-84; vice provost med. affairs U. Mich., 1984—; Cons. Walter Reed Army Med. Center, Sinai Hosp., Balt., Balt. City Hosp., Clin. Center of NIH; chmn. Study on Surg. Services for U.S., 1970-75. Editor: (with O. H. Gauer) Gravitational Stress in Aerospace Medicine, 1961, (with G. L. Nardi) Surgery-A Concise Guide to Clinical Practice, 1961, 4th edit., 1982, (with R.D. Judge and F. Fitzgerald) Physical Diagnosis, 1963, 4th edit., 1982, (with W.F. Ballinger and R.B. Rutherford) Management of Trauma, 1968, 4th edit., 1985, (with L. Schlossberg) Atlas of Human Functional Anatomy, 1977, 3d edit., 1985; editor Jour. Surg. Research, 1966-72; asso. editor, editorial bd., 1972—; mem. editorial bd.: Surgery Ann., 1968—, Surgery, 1970—; co-editor in chief, 1975—. Bd. dirs. Md. div. Am. Cancer Soc., 1964—. Served to capt. M.C., USAF, 1954-56. John and Mary R. Markle scholar academic medicine, 1961-66; recipient Henry Russell award U. Mich., 1963. Fellow ACS, Royal Coll. Surgeons Ireland (hon.); mem. Assn. Am. Med. Colls., Central Soc. Clin. Research, Soc. Univ. Surgeons, Am., So. surg. assns., Soc. Clin. Surgery, Soc. Vascular Surgery, Internat. Cardiovascular Surgery, Halsted Soc., Nat. Inst. Medicine, Assn. Acad. Surgeons (pres. 1967-69), Allen O. Whipple Soc., Phi Beta Kappa, Tri Beta, Alpha Omega Alpha. Home: 443 Huntington Pl Ann Arbor MI 48104 Office: M3246 Med Sci I 1301 Catherine Rd Ann Arbor MI 48109

ZUMINO, BRUNO, physicist. Prof. dept. physics U. Calif.-Berkeley. Mem. Nat. Acad. Scis., Am. Acad. Arts and Scis. Subspecialty: Relativity and gravitation. Office: U Calif-Berkeley Dept Physics Berkeley CA 94720

ZUNDE, PRANAS, information science educator, researcher; b. Kaunas, Lithuania, Nov. 26, 1923; came to U.S., 1960, naturalized, 1964; s. Pranas and Elzbieta (Lisajevic) Z.; m. Alge R. Bizauskas, May 29, 1945; children: Alge R., Audronis K., Aurelia R., Aidis L., Gytis J. Dipl. Ing., Hanover Inst. Tech., 1947; M.S., George Washington U., 1965; Ph.D., Ga. Inst. Tech., 1968. Project dir. Documentation, Inc., Bethesda, Md., 1961-64, mgmt. info. system mgr., 1964-65; sr. research scientist Ga. Inst. Tech., Atlanta, 1965-68, assoc. prof., 1968-72, prof. dept. computer sci., 1973—; cons. UNESCO, Caracas, Venezuela, 1970-72, Esquela Polit. Nacional, Quito, Ecuador, 1974-75, State of Ga., Atlanta, 1976-78; Fulbright prof. Nat. Acad. Sci., 1975; vis. prof. Simon Bolivar U., Caracas, 1976, J. Kepler U., Austria, 1981. Author: Agriculture in Soviet Lithuania, 1962; Editor: Procs. Information Utilities, 1974, Procs. Foundations of Information and Software Science, 1983. Mem. Am. Soc. Info. Sci., Semiatic Soc. Am. Roman Catholic. Current Work: Theoretical foundations of information and software sciences, system theory, information systems design, mathematical modeling, pattern recognition. Subspecialty: Software engineering. Home: 1808 Timothy Dr NE Atlanta GA 30329 Office: Ga Inst Tech North Ave Atlanta GA 30332

ZURAWSKI, VINCENT RICHARD, JR., biotechnology company executive, researcher; b. Irvington, N.J., June 10, 1946; s. Vincent Richard and Norma Mary (Alliston) Z.; m. Mary Rita Stanziola, Aug. 18, 1968; children: Daniel Vincent, John Alliston. B.A., Montclair State Coll., 1968; Ph.D., Purdue U., 1973. Research fellow dept. medicine Harvard U.- Mass. Gen. Hosp., 1975-78, instr., 1978-79; co-founder, v.p., tech. dir. Centocor, Malvern, Pa., 1979-82, sr. v.p., 1982-83, exec. v.p, tech. dir., 1983—; lectr. dept. ob-gynec Harvard U. Med. Sch. Contbr. articles to profl. jours., books and mags. Served with USAR, 1969-79. NIH fellow, 1976-78; Med. Found. research fellow, 1978-79. Mem. AAAS, Am. Chem. Soc., Am. Soc. Microbiologists, Am. Assn. Immunologists, Am. Soc. Biol. Chemists. Patentee in field. Subspecialties: Biochemistry (biology); Immunobiology and immunology. Office: 244 Great Valley Pkwy Malvern PA 19355

ZURIER, ROBERT BURTON, rheumatologist, medical educator; b. Passaic, N.J., Feb. 19, 1934; s. Milton and Lillian (Matzner) Z.; m. Catherine Elizabeth Miers, June 3, 1962; 1 child, Adam Wheaton. B.S., Rutgers U., 1955; M.D. U.

Tex. Southwestern Med. Sch., 1962. Intern, resident med. services Boston City Hosp., 1962-64; resident, fellow in medicine St. Luke's Hosp. Ctr., N.Y., 1964-66; practice medicine specializing in internal medicine Holden Hosp., Mass., 1967-70; Rheumatic Diseases Study Group fellow NYU Sch. Medicine, 1970-71, instr., 1971-73; asst. prof. U. Conn. Sch. Medicine, Farmington, 1973-76, assoc. prof., 1976-80, prof. medicine, chief rheumatology sect. U. Pa. Sch. Medicine, Phila., 1980—; rev. com. NIH, Bethesda, Md., 1978—. Editorial bd. Arthritis and Rheumatism 1980—, Jour. Immunology, 1982-84; ad hoc reviewer manuscripts for several jours. Contbr. chpts. to books, tech. articles, revs., abstracts to profl. jours. Mem. Am. Fedn. for Clin. Research, Am. Rheumatism Assn., Ea. Pa. Arthritis Found., Phila. Rheumatism Soc., Am. Assn. Immunologists, Am. Soc. for Clin. Investigation. Served to capt. AUS, 1955-56. NIH grantee, 1974—. Current work: Role of phospholipid metabolites in inflammation and immune responses, especially as related to rheumatic diseases. Subspecialties: Rheumatology; Cell biology (medicine). Office: Rheumatology Sect Hosp of U Pa 3400 Spruce St Philadelphia PA 19104

ZUSPAN, FREDERICK PAUL, physician, educator; b. Richwood, Ohio, Jan. 20, 1922; s. Irl Goff and Kathryn (Speyer) Z.; m. Mary Jane Cox, Nov. 23, 1943; children: Mark Frederick, Kathryn Jane, Bethany Anne. B.A., Ohio State U., 1947, M.D., 1951. Intern Univ. Hosps., Columbus, Ohio, 1951-52, resident, 1952-54, Western Res. U., Cleve., 1954-56, Oblebay fellow, 1958-60, asst. prof., 1958-60; chmn. dept. ob-gyn McDowell (Ky.) Meml. Hosp., 1956-58, chief clin. services, 1957-58; prof., chmn. dept. ob-gyn Med. Coll. Ga., Augusta, 1960-66; Joseph Boliver DeLee prof. ob-gyn, chmn. dept. U. Chgo., 1966-75; obstetrician, gynecologist in chief Chgo. Lying-In Hosp., 1966-75; prof., chmn. dept. ob-gyn Ohio State U. Sch. Medicine, Columbus, 1975—; Richard L. Meiling prof. ob-gyn, 1984—. Founding editor: Lying In, Jour. Reproductive Medicine; editor: (with Lindheimer and Katz) Hypertension in Pregnancy, 1976, Current Developments in Perinatology, 1977, (with Quilligan) Operative Obstetrics, 1981, Manual of Practical Obstetrics, 1981, Am. Jour. Ob-Gyn, Clin. and ExpH. Hypertension in Pregnancy, (with Rayburn) Drug Therapy in Ob-Gyn, 1981; Mem. editorial bd.: Exerpta Medica; editor: (with Christian) Controversies in Obstetrics and Gynecology; contbr. articles to med. jours., chpts. to books. Pres. Barren Found., 1974-76. Served with USNR, 1942-43; to 1st lt. USMCR, 1943-45. Decorated DFC, Air medal with 10 oak leaf clusters. Mem. Soc. Gynecol. Investigation, Chgo. Gynecol. Soc., Am. Assn. Ob-Gyn, Am. Acad. Reproductive Medicine (pres.), Am. Coll. Obstetricians and Gynecologists, Assn. Profs. Gynecology and Obstetrics (pres. 1972), South Atlantic Assn. Obstetricians and Gynecologists (Found. prize for research 1962). Central Assn. Ob-Gyn (cert. of merit, research prize 1970), Am. Soc. Clin. Exptl. Hypnosis (exec. sec. 1968, v.p. 1970), So. Gynecol. Soc., Internat. Soc. Study Hypertension in Pregnancy (pres. 1981-84), Sigma Xi, Alpha Omega, Alpha Kappa Kappa. Current Work: Catecholamine research on hypertension in pregnancy and fetal neuroendocrine regulation. Subspecialties: Obstetrics and gynecology; Maternal and fetal medicine. Home: 2400 Coventry Rd Upper Arlington Columbus OH 43211

ZUZOLO, RALPH CARMINE, biologist, educator, researcher; b. Dente Cane, Avellino, Italy, Sept. 5, 1929; came to U.S., 1930; s. Antonio and Assunta (Nardone) Z.; m. Betty Ann Fong, July 22, 1972. B.A. in Biology, N.Y.U., 1956, MS. in Cell Physiology, 1960, Ph.D. in cell physiology and Micro-Surgery, 1965. Asst. prof. CCNY of CUNY, 1965, assoc. prof., 1975—; co-dir. Robert Chambers Lab., 1978—, Sch. Gen. Studies supr. dept. biology, 1968—; adj. research sci. N.Y.U., 1965-78. Served to cpl. USMC, 1951-52, Korea. Recipient NYU Founders Day award, 1965; U. Tex. research fellow, 1966-68. Mem. AAAS, N.Y. Acad. Sci., Soc. Applied Spectroscopy, AAUP, Sigma Xi. Current Work: Continue developing Robert Chambers Lab for cellular

microsurgery; produce simplified instrumentations and methods for mechanical microinjection of macromolecules into single cells; serve as a center for other interested scientist. Office: CCNY of CUNY Convent Ave at 138th St New York NY 10031

ZWANZIG, ROBERT WALTER, physical chemist; b. Bklyn., Apr. 9, 1928; s. Walter and Bertha (Weil) Z.; m. H. Frances Ryder, June 6, 1953; children—Elizabeth Ann, Carl Philip. B.S., Poly. Inst Bklyn., 1948; M.S., U. So. Calif., 1950; Ph.D., Calif. Inst. Tech., 1952. Research assoc. Yale, 1951-54; asst. prof. Johns Hopkins, 1954-58; phys. chemist Nat. Bur. Standards, 1958-66; research prof. U. Md., College Park, 1966—, Disting. prof. phys. sci., 1980—. Asso. editor: Jour. of Chem. Physics, 1965-67, Jour. of Math. Physics, 1968-70, Transport Theory and Statistical Physics, 1970, Collective Phenomena, 1972—, Chem. Physics, 1973—; Contbr. articles profl. jours. Dept. Commerce Silver medal, 1965. Fellow Am. Phys. Soc., Am. Acad. Arts and Scis., mem. Nat. Acad. Scis., Am. Chem. Soc. (Peter Debye award in phys. chemistry 1976, Langmuir award in chem. physics 1984). Subspecialty: Physical chemistry. Home: 5314 Sangamore Rd Bethesda MD 20816 Office: Inst for Physical Sciences and Tech U Md College Park MD 20742

ZWEBEN, STUART HARVEY, computer science educator; b. Bronx, N.Y., June 13, 1971; 1 child, Naomi. B.S., CCNY, 1968; M.S., Purdue U., 1971, Ph.D., 1974. Systems analyst IBM, Kingston, N.Y., 1969, 70; grad. research asst. Purdue U., West Lafayette, Ind., 1971-74, instr. computer sci., 1974; asst. prof. computer sci. Ohio State U., Columbus, 1974-80, assoc. prof., 1980—, acting chmn. computer sci., 1983-84. Contbr. articles to profl. publs. Grantee: NSF, Army Research Office, Dow Chem. USA, AT&T, Dept. Edn. Mem. Assn. for Computing Machinery (Recognition Service award 1980) chmn. chapters bd. 1982-85, regional rep. to council 1982—), IEEE Computer Soc. Democrat. Jewish. Current work: Software engineering; programming methodology. Subspecialty: Software engineering. Office: Ohio State U 2036 Neil Ave Columbus OH 43210

ZWEIFACH, BENJAMIN WILLIAM, bioengineering educator; b. N.Y.C., Nov. 27, 1910; s. Max N. and Paula (Zucker) Z.; m. Beatrice F. Brustein, June 17, 1937; children—Paula, Marilyn, Mark. B.S., CUNY, 1931; M.S., NYU, 1933, Ph.D., 1936. Asst. prof. physiology NYU Sch., N.Y.C., 1941-50; assoc. prof. biology NYU, N.Y.C. 1950-55, prof. pathology, 1955-66; prof. bioengring. U. Calif.-San Diego, La Jolla, 1966-82, emeritus prof, 1982—; mem. cardiovascular study sect. NIH, 1964-68; mem. surgery adv. com. U.S. Army Research and Devel. Command, San Francisco, 1981-84. Recipient Claude Bernarde medal Montreal U., 1960. Fellow Am. Heart Assn. (career investigator 1955-59), U.S.A. Microcirculatory Soc. (pres. 1961, Landis award 1971), N.Y. Acad. Scis.; mem. Am. Physiology Soc. Jewish. Current work: Behavior of microcirculation in health and disease; biomechanics; pathogenesis of hypertension and diabetes. Subspecialty: Physiology (biology). Office: U Calif-San Diego M-005 Bioengineering La Jolla CA 92093

ZWEIG, JOSEPH B., psychologist, consultant; b. N.Y.C., Mar. 29, 1949; s. Milton and Rose (Engelson) Z.; m. Michelle Bonnie Bloch, Dec. 19, 1970; children: Jeremy, Samantha. B.A., SUNY-Stony Brook, 1969; M.A., Fairleigh Dickinson U., 1970; Ph.D., Hofstra U., 1980. Diplomate: Am. Acad. Behavioral Medicine; cert. psychologist, biofeedback therapist, rehab. counselor. Psychologist Bergen Pines County Hosp., Paramus, N.J., 1970-72, Jewish Vocat. Services, East Orange, N.J., 1972-74; program dir. East Plains Mental Health Services, Hicksville, N.Y., 1974-80; psychologist Rockland Ctr. for Physically Handicapped, New City, N.Y., 1980—; dir./ptnr. Rockland

Psychol. Assocs., Pomona, N.Y., 1981—; adj. faculty Hofstra U., Hempstead, N.Y., 1982—; steering com. Mothers' Ctr., Hicksville, 1975-78. Bd. Edn. citizens adv. com. mem., Clarkstown, N.Y., 1980. Mem. Am. Psychol. Assn., Biofeedback Soc. Am., Soc. for Psychosomatic Obs/Gyn. Jewish. Current Work: Stress management; biofeedback: first study of use of electromyography biofeedback in preparation for childbirth. Subspecialty: Behavioral psychology. Office: Rockland Psychol Assocs Route 45 Pomona NY 10970

ZWEIMAN, BURTON, physician, scientist, educator; b. N.Y.C., June 7, 1931; s. Charles and Gertrude (Levine) Z.; m. Claire Traig, Dec. 30, 1962; children: Amy Beth, Diane Susan. A.B., U. Pa., 1952, M.D., 1956. Intern Mt. Sinai Hosp., N.Y.C.; resident in medicine Hosp. U. Pa., Bellevue Hosp. Center, 1957-60; fellow NYU Sch. Medicine, 1960-61; mem. faculty dept. medicine U. Pa. Sch. Medicine, Phila., 1963—, prof. medicine, chief allergy and immunology sect., 1969—; cons. U.S. Army, NIH; co-chmn. Am. Bd. Allergy and Immunology, 1979-81. Contbr. articles to med. jours. Served with M.C., USNR, 1961-63. Allergy Found. Am. fellow, 1959-61. Fellow Am. Acad. Allergy, A.C.P.; mem. Am. Assn. Immunologists, Am. Fedn. Clin. Research, Phi Beta Kappa, Alpha Omega Alpha. Current Work: Immune and inflammatory mechanisms in allergic connective tissue and neurologic disorders. Subspecialties: Allergy; Immunology (medicine). Office: 512 Johnson Pavilion 36th and Hamilton Walk Philadelphia PA 19104

ZWICKER, GARY MICHAEL, veterinary pathologist, consultant; b. Lewiston, Idaho, June 20, 1937; s. Warren August and Marie Adelia (Gonser) Z.; m. Geraldine J. Newby, Feb. 10, 1962; children—Randy, Thomas, Karen, Debra. B.S., Washington State U., 1960, D.V.M., 1962; M.S., Purdue U., 1970, Ph.D., in Vet. Pathology, 1973. Diplomate Am. Coll. Vet. Pathology. Vet. pathologist DuPont's Haskell Lab., Newark, Del., 1964-67, toxicology dept. E.R. Squibb Corp., New Brunswick, N.J., 1967-70; research assoc. biology dept. Battelle's Pacific Northwest Lab., Richland, Wash., 1973-78; sr. sect. mgr. toxicology dept. Stauffer Chem. Co., Farmington, Conn., 1978—; cons. inhalation toxicology Can. Nat. Sci. Engring. Research Grant Rev., Montreal, PQ, Can., 1984. Contbr. articles to profl. jours. Mem. exec. bd. YMCA, Richland, 1976-78. Served to capt. Vet. Corps, U.S. Army, 1962-64. Named clin. assoc. U. Conn. Sch. Medicine, 1978—; Elks scholar, 1965, Wash. Intercollegiate Knights, 1957; NCI spl. postdoctoral fellow, 1972. Mem. Am. Vet. Med. Assn., Am. Coll. Vet. Pathologists, Soc. Toxicology, Internat. Acad. Pathology, Am. Assn. Pathologists, Sigma Xi, Phi Zeta. Clubs: Golf, Charter Oak Aquatic (pres. 1984). Current work: Toxicologic pathology; inhalation toxicology; reproductive toxicology; chemical carcinogenicity; aquatic species toxicology. Subspecialties: Pathology (veterinary medicine); Environmental toxicology. Home: 89 Coldspring Rd Avon CT 06010 Office: Stauffer Chem Co Toxicology Dept 400 Farmington Ave Farmington CT 06032

ZYSKIND, JUDITH WEAVER, biologist, educator, researcher; b. Cin., July 2, 1939; d. Max Correy and Mary Catherine (Landis) Weaver; m. George Zyskind, May 12, 1964 (dec. 1974); children: Aviva Deborah, Joy Esther; m. Douglas Wemp Smith, Aug. 16, 1975. B.S., U. Dayton, 1961; M.S., Iowa State U., 1964, Ph.D. (USPHS predoctoral fellow, 1965-67), 1968. Postdoctoral research assoc. dept. genetics Iowa State U., Ames, 1970-71, vis. asst. prof. dept. genetics, 1971-73, postdoctoral research assoc. dept. biochemistry, 1973-74; NIH postdoctoral research fellow dept., biology U. Calif., San Diego, 1974-77, asst. research biologist, 1977-82; assoc. prof. biology San Diego State U., 1982—; prin. investigator research NIH. Contbr. articles to sci. jours. Mem. Am. Soc. Microbiology, AAAS, Genetics Soc. Am., Sigma Xi. Current Work: Initiation of DNA replication in bacteria: components and control. Subspecialties: Genetics and genetic engineering (biology); Molecular biology.

Index

Fields and Subspecialties

Plant pathology
Aist, James Robert
Alcorn, Stanley Marcus
Alexander, Samuel Adam
Allen, Thomas Cort, Jr.
Alves, Leo Manuel
Anderson, Neil Albert
Aube, Claude B.
Barnes, George Lewis
Bateman, Durward Franklin
Bergstrom, Gary Carlton
Bloom, James Richard
Brennan, Eileen G.
Bushnell, William Rodgers
Cameron, H. Ronald
Castello, John Donald
Cheo, Pen Ching
Coakley, Stella Melugin
Cobb, William Thompson
Crall, James Monroe
Crossan, Donald Franklin
Csinos, Alexander Stephen
Currier, William Wesley
Davis, Michael Jay
Davis, Robert Gene
Diener, Theodor Otto
Douglas, Dexter Richard
Dueck, John
Duniway, John M.
Engelhard, Arthur William
Essenberg, Margaret Kottke
Feldman, Albert William
Fett, William Frederick
Ford, Richard Earl
Gough, Francis Jacob
Gregory, Garold Fay
Hagedorn, Donald James
Harman, Gary Elvan
Harrison, Martin Bernard
Heidrick, Lee Edward
Helton, Audus Winzle
Herr, Leonard Jay
Himelick, Eugene Bryson
Holcomb, Gordon Ernest
Hollis, John Percy, Jr.
Hooker, Arthur Lee
Hooper, Gary Ray
Huber, Don Morgan
Humaydan, Hasib Shaheen
Hunter, Richard Edmund
Israel, Herbert William
Jedlinski, Henryk
Jones, John Paul
Joshi, Madan Mohan
Keen, Noel Thomas
Kelman, Arthur
Kiesling, Richard Lorin
Kliejunas, John Thomas
Knott, Douglas Ronald
Kommedahl, Thor
Krausz, Joseph Philip
Lai, Carl Mingtan
Lamey, Howard Arthur
Lawrence, Gary Wright
Leath, Kenneth Thomas
Lindow, Steven E.
Lister, Richard Malcolm
Litton, Columbus C.
Livingston, Clark H.
Lowe, Sunny Ken
Lukezic, Felix Lee
MacSwan, Iain Christie
Marion, Daniel Francis
Martinson, Charlie Anton
Matthysse, Ann Gale
Mayol, Pete Syting
McIntyre, Gary Allen
McLaughlin, Michael Ray
Melouk, Hassan Aly
Miller, Raymond Michael
Mircetich, Srecko Mirko
Moody, Arnold Ralph
Moore, John Duain
Moore, Laurence D.
Ogawa, Joseph Minoru
Overman, Amegda Jack
Petersen, Lawrence John
Politis, Demetrios John
Quinn, James Allen
Raghunathan, Rengachari
Rich, Jimmy Ray
Roelfs, Alan Paul
Rogers, Jack David
Ruppel, Earl George
Schadler, Daniel Leo
Schafer, John Francis
Scheffer, Robert Paul
Skinner, Daniel Zolek
Smith, Samuel Howard
Sommer, Noel Frederick
Spalding, Donald Hood
Spencer, James Alphus
Staples, Richard Cromwell
Stavely, Joseph Rennie
Steadman, James Robert
Stoner, Martin Franklin
Thomas, Claude Earle
Timian, Roland Gustav
Tsai, James Hsi-cho
Tweedy, Billy G.
Van Alfen, Neal K.
Waggoner, Paul Edward
Walker, Jerry Tyler
Wallin, Jack Robb
Weaver, Michael John
Weber, Darrell Jack
Weidensaul, M, T(homas) Craig
Wicker, Ed Franklin
Wilcox, W(ebster) Wayne
Windels, Carol Elizabeth
Young, Roy Alton
Zentmyer, George Aubrey, Jr.
Zoller, Broc Gerald

Plant physiology. *See also* BIOLOGY.
Akers, Stuart William
Alder, Edwin Francis
App, Alva Agee
Bare, Charles Edgar
Bass, Louis Nelson
Bateman, Durward Franklin
Bogorad, Lawrence
Bovey, Rodney William
Burton, Glenn Willard
Bushnell, William Rodgers
Campbell, Wilbur Harold
Christiansen, Meryl Naeve
Cohen, Jerry David
De Hertogh, August Albert
Duniway, John M.
Emino, Everett Raymond
Epstein, Emanuel
Feldman, Albert William
Fett, William Frederick
Finkle, Bernard Joseph
French, Charles Stacy
Funt, Richard Clair
Gatherum, Gordon Elwood
Gorski, Stanley Francis
Gossett, Dorsey McPeake
Graham, Terrence Lee
Green, Victor Eugene, Jr.
Greenwood, Michael Sargent
Hanson, Kenneth Warren
Hardy, Ralph W.F.
Hatzios, Kriton Kleanthis
Heidrick, Lee Edward
Helton, Audus Winzle
Hodges, Thomas Kent
Homann, Peter Hinrich Fritz
Hrazdina, Geza
Inglett, George Everett
Jensen, Richard Grant
Johnson, Virgil Allen
Kozlowski, Theodore Thomas
Kramer, Paul Jackson
Krikorian, Abraham Der
Kurtzman, Ralph Harold, Jr.
Laing, Frederick Mitchell
Lambeth, Victor Neal
Larson, Philip Rodney
Lay, Ming-muh
Leone, Ida A.
Marini, Richard Paul
McArdle, Richard Neff
McNulty, Irving Bazil
Moore, Laurence D.
Nelson, Neil Douglas
Nickell, Louis G.
Obendorf, Ralph Louis
Ohki, Kenneth
Oliver, Craig Stanley
Prange, Robert Keith
Proebsting, Edward Louis
Putnam, Alan R.
Ries, Stanley K.
Roberts, Bruce Roger
Rouse, Roy Dennis
Snyder, Freeman Woodrow
Spomer, Louis Arthur
Stewart, Ivan
Sung, Zinmay Renee
Syvertsen, James Patrick
Teramure, Alan Hiroshi
Wadleigh, Cecil Herbert
Wagner, George Joseph
Wergin, William P.
Wittwer, Sylvan Harold
Yang, Henry Wu-Hsiang
Yang, Shang Fa

Plant virology
Agrios, George N.
Allen, Thomas Cort, Jr.
Brakke, Myron Kendall
Cameron, H. Ronald
Cheo, Pen Ching
Diener, Theodor Otto
Edwardson, John Richard
Ford, Richard Earl
Hall, Timothy C.
Hartman, Robert Dale
Hooper, Gary Ray
Horst, Ralph Kenneth
Hsu, Hei-ti
Jedlinski, Henryk
Lister, Richard Malcolm
Livingston, Clark H.
McLaughlin, Michael Ray
Petersen, Lawrence John
Raghavendra, Krishnamurthy
Ruppel, Earl George
Smith, Samuel Howard
Sun, Mike
Timian, Roland Gustav
Tsai, James Hsi-cho
Weintraub, Marvin

Resource conservation
Allen, Durward Leon
Anderson, Richard Orr
Baker, Paul Manuel Aviles
Bass, Louis Nelson
Becker, Donald August
Bradley, Katharine Tryon
Coate, Barrie Douglas
Cook, Maurice Gayle
Davis, John Rowland
Dixon, Robert Morton
Finkle, Bernard Joseph
Flikke, Arnold Maurice
Frasier, Gary Wayne
Fredrickson, Leigh Harry
Granger, Clark Allen
Keran, Douglas Charles
Laycock, William Anthony
Lee, Harry William
LeFebvre, Eugene Allen
Little, Terry William
McGinnies, William Grovernor
Moldenhauer, William Calvin
Montalbano, Frank, III
Nickerson, Norton Hart
Oglesby, Ray Thurmond
Parr, James Floyd, Jr.
Rudis, Victor Augustine
Safley, John Marcus, Jr.
Saunders, Paul Richard
Schuster, William Stanley Fallon
Scifres, Charles Joel
Talbot, Lee Merriam
Wadleigh, Cecil Herbert
Wicker, Ed Franklin
Wolfe, James Alvis

Soil science
Allen, Arthur L.
Andreis, Henry Jerome
Barrows, Harold Lindsey
Bennett, William F., Sr.
Bremner, John MCColl
Calvert, David Victor
Cheng, H(wei)-H (sien)
Dixon, Robert Morton
Doll, Eugene Carter
Gast, Robert G.
Gifford, Gerald F.
Groff, Donald William
Grunes, David Leon
Hagood, Melvin Ardene
Hensel, Dale Robert
Johnson, Arthur H.
Kreh, Richard Edward
Lomen, David Orlando
Lucas, Robert Elmer
Lunt, Owen Raynal
MacLeod, Lloyd Beck
Malcolm, John Lowrie
Mausel, Paul Warner
McFadden, Leslie David
McFee, William Warren
Menzel, Ronald George
Meyer, (Lawrence) Donald
Moldenhauer, William Calvin
Mulkey, James Robert, Jr.
Parr, James Floyd, Jr.
Pietz, Richard Irwin
Ritchie, Jerry Carlyle
Rouse, Roy Dennis
Secor, Jack Behrent
Smika, Darryl Eugene
Wolfe, James Alvis

Solar Energy. *See* ENERGY SCIENCE.

Toxicology. *See also* ENVIRONMENTAL SCIENCE, **Environmental toxicology.**
Ansari, Ghulam A. S.
Asquith, Richard LaVerne
Beier, Ross Carlton
Bell, Marvin Carl
Benezet, Herman Joseph
Bennett, Jesse Harland
Clarkson, Thomas William
Clemens, George Ronald
Davis, Brian Kent
DeCaprio, Anthony Paul
Dhar, Amiya Kanti
Dickerson, Charlesworth Lee
Floyd, Robert A.
Freed, Virgil Haven
Grosch, Daniel Swartwood
Guthrie, Frank Edwin
Harroff, H(omer) Hugh, Jr.
Homburger, Freddy
Ivie, Glen Wayne
Kawalek, Joseph Casimir
Mehendale, Harihara Mahadeva
Miller, Edward Phillip
Safe, Stephen Harvey
Schmidt, Richard Ralph
Schneider, Norman Richard
Stahr, Henry Michael
Stannard, James Newell
Wagner, George Joseph
Yu, Simon Shyi-Jian
Zaratzian, Virginia Louise

Other
Allen, Arthur L., *Agricultural research administration*
Armistead, Willis William, *Agricultural research, administration*
Baumgardt, Billy R., *Agricultural research administration*
Bay, Roger Rudolph, *Forestry*
Benezet, Herman Joseph, *Entomology*
Bennett, Billy Wayne, *Agricultural administration*
Bentley, Orville George, *Agricultural research administration*
Bloom, James Richard, *Nematology*
Blum, Barton Morrill, *Silviculture*
Bowden, David Merle, *Agricultural research administration*
Bukovac, Martin J., *Horticulture*
Cheng, Lanna
Cobb, William Thompson, *Weed science*
Colvin, Lonnie Benard, *Aquaculture*
Cooper, Arthur Wells, *Forestry*
D'Appolonia, Bert Luigi
Donoho, Clive Wellington, Jr., *Agricultural administration*
Dorrell, Douglas Gordon, *Agricultural research administration*
Drawe, Dale Lynn
Elmstrom, Gary William, *Agricultural research administration*
Fischer, Hans-Peter, *Horticultural technology assessment*
Forshey, Chester Gene, *Pomology*
Gardner, Charles Olda, *Plant breeding*
Gifford, Gerald F., *Range management*
Gorski, Stanley Francis, *Weed science*
Gowe, Robb Shelton, *Animal research administration*
Green, Victor Eugene, Jr., *Sunflower crop production*
Hammer, Paul Allen, *Horticulture*
Hilton, James Lee, *Herbicides*
Johnson, George Robert, *Animal science administration*
Johnson, Richard James, *Agricultural research administration*
Kazam, Abdul Raoof
Kiil, Dave Ain
Kinney, Terry B., Jr., *Animal research administration*
Knipling, Edward Fred
Kommedahl, Thor, *Biological control*
Kraeuter, John Norman, *Aquaculture*
Kramer, Paul Jackson, *Physiology of plant stress*
Kreh, Richard Edward, *Forestry*
Kuhns, John Farrell, *Fisheries science*
Laben, Robert Cochrane, *Animal production*
La Ferney, Preston E., *Agricultural research administration*
Laidlaw, Harry Hyde, Jr.
Lawler, George Herbert, *Fisheries science*
Laycock, William Anthony, *Range management*
Lembersky, Mark Raphael, *Forestry*
Leonard, David Edmund, *Entomology*
McSorley, Robert
Miller, Regis Bolden
Moore, Raymond Franklin
Muniappan, Rangaswamy Naicker, *Biological control*
Newman, James Edward, *Agricultural meteorology*
Norton, Robert Alan, *Horticulture*
Parker, George Ralph, *Forestry*
Pollett, Frederick C.
Princen, Lambertus H(enricus), *Science administration*
Proebsting, Edward Louis, *Pomology*
Rich, Jimmy Ray, *Nematology*
Rudis, Victor Augustine
Ryan, James Bernard, *Weed science; Agriculture chemicals development*
Saladini, John Louis, *Agrichemicals*
Schmidt, Wyman Carl, *Silviculture*
Schultheis, Robert Arthur, *Extension service*
Smith, Thomas Lloyd, *Urban forest resource management*
Sommer, Noel Frederick, *Postharvest pathology*
Stout, Benjamin Boreman, *Silviculture*
Taber, Steve
Thomas, Claude Earle
Torrey, John Gordon, *Forestry*
Weaver, Michael John, *Agriculture information systems*
Whitmore, Jacob Leslie, III
Young, Donald Clifford
Youngs, Robert Leland, *Forestry*

ASTRONOMY. *See also* SPACE SCIENCE.

Cosmology
Barnes, Ronnie Clay
Borra, Ermanno Franco
Burbidge, Geoffrey
Chaisson, Eric Joseph
Chincarini, Guido Ludovico
De Vaucouleurs, Gerard Henri
Emslie, A. Gordon
Ettrick, Marco Antonio
Fox, Kenneth
Giacconi, Riccardo
Gott, John Richard, III
Gudehus, Donald Henry
Gunn, James Edward
Guth, Alan Harvey
Hu, Bei-Lok Bernard
Mather, John Cromwell
McGraw, John Thomas
Moody, Elizabeth Anne
Morabito, David Dominic
Motz, Lloyd
Nanos, George Peter, Jr.
Noonan, Thomas Wyatt
Pagels, Heinz Rudolf
Partridge, Robert Bruce
Penzias, Arno Allan
Press, William Henry
Sagan, Carl Edward
Sandage, Allan Rex
Schramm, David Norman
Smalley, Larry Lee
Stecker, Floyd William
Tipler, Frank Jennings, III
Tryon, Edward Polk
Vilenkin, Alexander
Vona, Daniel O'Neal, III
Yahil, Amos

General relativity
Brecher, Kenneth
Chandrasekhar, Subrahmanyan
Gott, John Richard, III
Hacyan, Shahen
Hill, Henry Allen
Laubscher, Roy Edward
Pechenick, Kay Rhoda
Tipler, Frank Jennings, III

High energy astrophysics
Baum, Peter Joseph
Brecher, Kenneth
Bridge, Herbert Sage
Burbidge, Geoffrey
Burns, Jack O'Neal, Jr.
Burrows, Adam Seth
Colgate, Stirling A.
Fan, Chang-Yun
Fichtel, Carl Edwin
Garmire, Gordon Paul
Gould, Robert Joseph
Harding, Alice Kust
Holt, Stephen S.
Kafatos, Minas
Keel, William Clifford
Koga, Rokutaro
Kraushaar, William Lester
Kronberg, Philipp Paul
McDiarmid, Ian Bertrand
Meekins, John Fred
Morrison, Philip
Ormes, Jonathan F.
Osterbrock, Donald Edward
Ostriker, Jeremiah Paul
Rose, William Kenneth
Shapiro, Maurice Mandel
Shapiro, Stuart Louis
Shen, Benjamin Shih-Ping
Smarr, Larry Lee
Starrfield, Sumner Grosby
Terrell, (Nelson) James
Terzian, Yervant
Tucker, Wallace Hampton
Weiler, Kurt Walter
White, R(obert) Stephen
Willcox, Phillip James
Wilson, Andrew Stephen
Wilson, Thomas Leon
Woosley, Stanford Earl

High energy astrophysics, cosmic ray
Adams, James Hall, Jr.
Chasson, Robert Lee
Chenette, David Louis
Davis, Raymond, Jr.
Doolittle, Robert F., II
Firor, John William
Greisen, Kenneth Ingvard
Hadler, Herbert Isaac
Leighton, Robert Benjamin
Marshak, Marvin Lloyd
McDonald, Frank Bethune
Ormes, Jonathan F.
Parnell, Thomas Alfred
Pomerantz, Martin Arthur
Price, Paul Buford
Rossi, Bruno
Shapiro, Maurice Mandel
Silberberg, Rein
Stone, Edward Carroll, Jr.
Tornabene, Hugh Salvatore
Van Allen, James Alfred
Vogt, Rochus Eugen
Waddington, Cecil Jacob

High energy astrophysics, gamma ray
Cline, Thomas Lytton
Doolittle, Robert F., II
Fichtel, Carl Edwin
Fishman, Gerald Jay
Gehrels, Neil
Greisen, Kenneth Ingvard
Kane, Sharad Ramchandra
Lamb, Richard Compton
MacCallum, Crawford John
March, Robert Herbert
Metzger, Albert Emanuel
Nolan, Patrick Lee
Parnell, Thomas Alfred
Ulmer, Melville Paul
Vogt, Rochus Eugen
Weekes, Trevor C.
White, R(obert) Stephen

High energy astrophysics, ultraviolet
Ahmad, Imad Al Dean
Augensen, Harry John
Basri, Gibor Broitman
Bolton, Charles Thomas
Brugel, Edward William
Cordova, France Anne-Dominic
Davidsen, Arthur Falnes
Davis, Robert James
Ferland, Gary Joseph
Green, Richard Frederick
Gull, Theodore Raymond
Hobbs, Lewis Mankin
Hutchings, John Barrie
Johnson, Hollis Ralph
Kondo, Yoji
Macchetto, Ferdinando Duccio
Maran, Stephen Paul
Michalitsianos, Andrew Gerasimos
Moos, Henry Warren
Olson, Gordon Lee
Plavec, Mirek Josef
Shipman, Harry Longfellow

High energy astrophysics, X-ray
Ahmad, Imad Al Dean
Ayasli, Serpil
Belian, Richard Duane
Bleach, Richard David
Boldt, Elihu A.
Bradt, Hale Van Dorn
Buff, James Steve
Burrows, David Nelson
Canizares, Claude Roger
Clark, George Whipple
Cordova, France Anne-Dominic
Davis, John Moulton
Dolan, Joseph Francis
Feigelson, Eric Dennis
Garmire, Gordon Paul
Giacconi, Riccardo
Gorenstein, Paul
Haisch, Bernhard Michael
Harris, Daniel Everett
Holt, Stephen S.
Kowalski, Michael Paul
Kylafis, Nikolaos Dimitriou
Malina, Roger Frank
Margon, Bruce H.
Mastronardi, Richard
McDonald, Frank Bethune
Meekins, John Fred
Nolan, Patrick Lee
Parsignault, Daniel Raymond
Pradhan, Anil Kumar
Sanders, Wilton Turner, III
Tucker, Wallace Hampton
Ulmer, Melville Paul

Infrared astronomy
Bartel, Norbert Harald
Bell, Roger Alistair
Bentley, Alan Frank
Briotta, Daniel A., Jr.
Carney, Bruce William
Christy, James Walter
Clark, Thomas Alan
Craine, Eric Richard
Cudaback, David Dill
Daehler, Mark
Dinerstein, Harriet
Evans, Neal John, II
Gehrz, Robert Douglas
Gezari, Daniel Ysa
Goorvitch, David
Grasdalen, Gary Lars
Guetter, Harry Hendrik
Harper, Doyal Alexander, Jr.
Houck, James Richard
Lebofsky, Larry Allen
Leighton, Robert Benjamin
Lo, Kwok-Yung
Martin, Terry Zachry
Mather, John Cromwell
Ney, Edward Purdy
Odenwald, Sten Felix, Jr.
Price, R(ichard) Marcus
Russell, Ray William
Sargent, Anneila Isabel
Seab, C(harles) Gregory
Shivanandan, Kandiah
Shoore, Joseph David
Smith, Sheldon Magill
Telesco, Charles Michael
Thompson, Rodger Irwin
Townes, Charles Hard

Optical astronomy
Adelman, Saul Joseph
Aikman, George Christopher Lawrence
Aller, Lawrence Hugh
Andersen, Per Holme
Augensen, Harry John
Babcock, Horace Welcome
Beckers, Jacques Maurice
Benedict, George Frederick

Bidelman, William Pendry
Boeshaar, Patricia Chikotas
Bolton, Charles Thomas
Bradt, Hale Van Dorn
Breakiron, Lee Allen
Brugel, Edward William
Bryan, James Thomas, Jr.
Bump, Frederick H.
Burbidge, E. Margaret
Butcher, Harvey Raymond, III
Campbell, Donald Bruce
Canizares, Claude Roger
Carney, Bruce William
Chaffee, Frederic H.
Chambliss, Carlson Rollin
Chincarini, Guido Ludovico
Clements, Gregory Leland
Connolly, Leo Paul
Conti, Peter Selby
Corwin, Harold Glenn, Jr.
Cowie, Lennox Lauchlan
Crawford, David Livingston
Cudworth, Kyle McCabe
Daehler, Mark
Davis, Robert James
De Vaucouleurs, Gerard Henri
Dickel, Helene Ramsever
Dolan, Joseph Francis
Dressler, Alan
Dube, Roger Raymond
Elliot, James Ludlow
Evans, David Stanley
Filippenko, Alexei Vladimir
Flower, Phillip John
Fontaine, Gilles Joseph
Fredrick, Laurence William
Garrison, Robert Frederick
Green, Richard Frederick
Greenstein, Jesse Leonard
Gudehus, Donald Henry
Guetter, Harry Hendrik
Gull, Theodore Raymond
Hardorp, Johannes C.
Harris, Alan William
Havlen, Robert James
Hazen, Martha L(ocke)
Hemenway, Mary Kay
Herr, Richard Baessler
Hesser, James E(dward)
Hiltner, William Albert
Hobbs, Lewis Mankin
Hoffleit, Ellen Dorrit
Houston, Walter Scott
Howard, Robert Franklin
Hube, Douglas Peter
Hutchings, John Barrie
Ianna, Philip A.
Illingworth, Garth D.
Irvine, Cynthia Emberson
Keel, William Clifford
King, Ivan Robert
Kowal, Charles Thomas
Kowalski, Michael Paul
Landstreet, John Darlington
Lanning, Howard Hugh
Lester, John Bernard
Lindenblad, Irving Werner
Linnell, Albert Paul
Lippincott, Sarah Lee
Livingston, William Charles
Luft, Herbert Arthur
Lutz, Barry Lafean
Lutz, Julie Haynes
Lynds, Clarence Roger
Macchetto, Ferdinando Duccio
Malkan, Matthew Arnold
Maran, Stephen Paul
Margon, Bruce H.
Mattei, Janet Akyuz
McCollough, Michael Leon
McCracken, Robert Henry
McGraw, John Thomas
Mc Millan, Robert Scott
Meinel, Aden Baker
Meisel, David Dering
Michalitsianos, Andrew Gerasimos
Moffat, Anthony Frederick John
Mohler, Orren Cuthbert
Morgan, William Wilson
Murray, Stephen S.
Newkirk, Gordon Allen, Jr.
Newsom, Gerald Higley
Odell, Andrew Paul
Oliver, John Parker
Olson, Edward Cooper
Osborn, Wayne Henry
Osterbrock, Donald Edward
Page, Thornton Leigh
Percy, John Rees
Peterson, Bradley Michael
Pfeiffer, Raymond John
Poland, Arthur Ira
Prince, Helen Dodson
Ratnatunga, Kavan Upajiva
Rhodes, Edward Joseph, Jr.
Romanishin, William
Sadun, Alberto Carlo
Sandage, Allan Rex
Schoening, William Edward
Schweighauser, Charles Arthur
Schweizer, Francois
Seidelmann, P. Kenneth
Shipman, Harry Longfellow
Shull, Peter Otto, Jr.
Smith, Harlan James
Spitzer, Lyman, Jr.
Sumners, Carolyn Taylor
Tandberg-Hanssen, Einar Andreas
Upgren, Arthur Reinhold, Jr.
van den Bergh, Sidney
Vilkki, Erkki Uuno
Vogt, Steven Scott
Weekes, Trevor C.
Wehinger, Peter Augustus
Whipple, Fred Lawrence
White, Richard Edward
Wilkerson, Susan McCasland
Wilson, Andrew Stephen
Wilson, Olin C(haddock)
Wilson, Raymond Hiram, Jr.
Wolff, Sidney Carne
Young, Arthur

Planetary science
Appleby, John Frederick
Backus, George Edward
Blanford, George Emmanuel, Jr.

Boss, Alan Paul
Brecher, Aviva
Brunk, William Edward
Burgess, Eric
Burns, Joseph Arthur
Cameron, Alastair Graham Walter
Christy, James Walter
Cordell, Bruce Monteith
Davies, Merton Edward
Davis, Raymond, Jr.
El-Baz, Farouk
Elliot, James Ludlow
Eshleman, Von Russel
Esposito, Larry Wayne
Gehrels, Tom
Goldreich, Peter Martin
Hapke, Bruce William
Harris, Alan William
Horanyi, Mihaly
Irvine, William Michael
Irving, Donald J.
James, Philip Benjamin
Khare, Bishun Narain
Kliore, Arvydas Joseph
Krimigis, Stamatios Mike
Lambert, John Vincent
Lebofsky, Larry Allen
Levy, David Howard
Lutz, Barry Lafean
Martin, Terry Zachry
McDonough, Thomas Redmond
Metzger, Albert Emanuel
Misconi, Nebil Yousif
Nelson, Robert M.
Owen, Tobias Chant
Penzias, Arno Allan
Pettengill, Gordon H(emenway)
Pomphrey, Richard Bryan
Sagan, Carl Edward
Sandel, Bill Roy
Schultz, Alfred Bernard
Seidelmann, P. Kenneth
Shoemaker, Eugene Merle
Smith, Bradford A.
Smith, Dale Wilford
Smith, Harlan James
Smoluchowski, Roman
Stone, Edward Carroll, Jr.
Sullivan, Roger John
Whitaker, Ewen Adair
Wilkening, Laurel Lynn
Williams, Donald John
Wood, John Armstead
Yeomans, Donald Keith
Zisk, Stanley Harris

Radio and microwave astronomy
Backer, Donald Charles
Bally, John
Bartel, Norbert Harald
Bash, Frank Ness
Blitz, Leo
Bowers, Phillip Frederick
Brocka, Bruce
Burns, Jack O'Neal, Jr.
Burton, William Butler
Carter, William Eugene
Chaisson, Eric Joseph
Cowan, John James
Cudaback, David Dill
Deguchi, Shuji
Dickel, Helene Ramsever
Dickman, Robert Laurence
Doiron, David John
Donivan, Frank Forbes, Jr.
Douglas, James Nathaniel
Drake, Frank Donald
Ekers, Ronald David
Elitzur, Moshe
Evans, Neal John, II
Ewing, Martin Sipple
Feigelson, Eric Dennis
Galt, John Alexander
Gary, Dale Everett
Gergely, Tomas Esteban
Gold, Thomas
Gordon, Mark Aitken
Gottesman, Stephen Thancy
Hankins, Timothy Hamilton
Hansen, Stanley Severin, II
Harris, Daniel Everett
Havlen, Robert James
Hjellming, Robert Michael
Irvine, William Michael
Irving, Donald J.
Johnson, Donald Rex
Kliore, Arvydas Joseph
Kronberg, Philipp Paul
Kundu, Mukul R.
Kwok, Sun
Kylafis, Nikolaos Dimitriou
Lewis, Brian Murray
Lo, Kwok-Yung
Marsh, Kenneth Albert
Meeks, Marion Littleton
Mirabel, Igor Felix
Morabito, David Dominic
Myers, Philip Cherdak
Newell, Robert Terry
Odenwald, Sten Felix, Jr.
Papagiannis, Michael D.
Partridge, Robert Bruce
Price, R(ichard) Marcus
Ratner, Michael Ira
Roberts, Morton Spitz
Rodriguez, Luis Felipe
Rubin, Robert Howard
Safko, John Loren
Salpeter, Edwin Ernest
Shapiro, Irwin Ira
Shomer, John Edward
Swanson, Paul Norman
Tarter, Jill Cornell
Terzian, Yervant
Tyler, George Leonard
Unwin, Stephen Charles
Vanden Bout, Paul Adrian
Weiler, Kurt Walter
Wilson, Robert Woodrow
Wilson, William John
Zeissig, Gustave Alexander

Theoretical astrophysics
Andersen, Per Holme
Arnett, William David
Ayasli, Serpil
Barnes, Aaron

Bash, Frank Ness
Baym, Gordon Alan
Becker, Stephen Allan
Bell, Roger Alistair
Bentley, Alan Frank
Borra, Ermanno Franco
Boss, Alan Paul
Brunish, Wendee M.
Burrows, Adam Seth
Cameron, Alastair Graham Walter
Chandrasekhar, Subrahmanyan
Chanmugam, Ganesar
Cheng, Andrew Francis
Cohen, Jeffrey M.
Comins, Neil Francis
Cowan, John James
Cowie, Lennox Lauchlan
Cox, Arthur Nelson
Dalgarno, Alexander
Deupree, Robert Gaston
DeYoung, David Spencer
Dicus, Duane Alfred
Elitzur, Moshe
Endal, Andrew Samson
Felton, James Edgar
Ferland, Gary Joseph
Field, George Brooks
Flower, Phillip John
Fontaine, Gilles Joseph
Gilliland, Ronald Lynn
Greenberg, Philip Joel
Greenstein, Jesse Leonard
Haisch, Bernhard Michael
Harding, Alice Kust
Held, Ronald Dennis
Hills, Jack Gilbert
Hinata, Satoshi
Hjellming, Robert Michael
Holt, Alan Craig
Horanyi, Mihaly
Hughes, Philip Alfred
Iben, Icko, Jr.
Ionson, James
Johnson, Hollis Ralph
Kafatos, Minas
Kwok, Sun
Kyrala, Ali
Lamb, Donald Quincy
Larson, Richard Bondo
Lee, Martin Alan
Lewis, Brian Murray
Liebovitch, Larry S.
Linnell, Albert Paul
Littleton, John Edward
Marks, Dennis William
Mazurek, Thaddeus John
McCollough, Michael Leon
McDonald, Keith Leon
Mihalas, Dimitri Manuel
Miller, Glenn Edward
Mitalas, Romas
Newell, Robert Terry
Nickas, George Demosthenes
Odell, Andrew Paul
Olson, Gordon Lee
Ostriker, Jeremiah Paul
Parker, Eugene Newman
Parks, Allen Danforth
Petschek, Albert George
Pines, David
Plavec, Mirek Josef
Press, William Henry
Purcell, Edward Mills
Rose, William Kenneth
Rubin, Robert Howard
Sadun, Alberto Carlo
Salpeter, Edwin Ernest
Schramm, David Norman
Schwartz, Sandra
Seab, C(harles) Gregory
Seiden, Philip Edward
Shull, Peter Otto, Jr.
Simon, Sheridan Alan
Smith, Dean F.
Spitzer, Lyman, Jr.
Sreenivasan, S. Ranga
Starrfield, Sumner Grosby
Stecker, Floyd William
Sturrock, Peter Andrew
Taam, Ronald Everett
Tarter, C. Bruce
Terrell, (Nelson) James
Thompson, Rodger Irwin
Thorne, Kip Stephen
Van Hoven, Gerard
Villere, Karen R.
Wagoner, Robert Vernon
Weinberg, Steven
Whitman, Patrick Gene
Woodward, James Franklin
Woodward, Paul Ralph
Yahil, Amos

Other
Aller, Lawrence Hugh
Barnes, Ronnie Clay, *Binary stars*
Bidelman, William Pendry, *Spectral classification, astronomical data*
Bryan, James Thomas, Jr., *Supernovae*
Carlson, John B., *Archaeoastronomy; Extragalactic astronomy*
de la Zerda, Alberto, *Cosmic rays*
Duley, Walter Winston, *Laboratory astrophysics*
Evans, David Stanley, *History of astronomy*
Filippenko, Alexei Vladimir
Gatewood, George David, *Astrometry*
Hall, Donald Norman Blake, *Astronomical research administration*
Harrington, Robert Sutton, *Astrometry*
Hemenway, Mary Kay
Houston, Walter Scott
Ianna, Philip A., *Astrometry*
Jordan, Stuart Davis, *Solar, stellar astrophysics*
Lester, John Bernard, *Stellar composition*
Levy, David Howard, *Astronomy journalism*
Lindenblad, Irving Werner, *Geodetic astronomy*
Lippincott, Sarah Lee
Mathews, Grant James, *Nuclear astrophysics*
Mattei, Janet Akyuz, *Variable stars*
McCarthy, Dennis Dean, *Astrometry*

McDonough, Thomas Redmond, *Search for extraterrestrial intelligence*
Miller, Freeman Devold, *Cometary physics*
Mitalas, Romas, *Nucleosynthesis*
Murawski, Walter Ted
Oesterwinter, Claus, *Celestial mechanics*
Oliver, John Parker, *Astronomical instruments*
Olson, Edward Cooper, *Close binary stars*
Sargent, Anneila Isabel, *Millimeter/submillimeter wave astrophysics*
Shapiro, Lee Tobey
Sinclair, Rolf Malcolm, *Archaeoastronomy*
Synek, M., *Intelligent life in the universe.*
Tarter, Jill Cornell, *Search for extraterrestrial intelligence*
Teem, John McCorkle, *Astronomical research administration*
Tilak, Manohar Anant
Toomre, Alar

ASTROPHYSICS. See ASTRONOMY.

ATMOSPHERIC SCIENCE. See also ENVIRONMENTAL SCIENCE.

Aeronomy
Akasofu, Syun-Ichi
Benesch, William
Bering, Edgar Andrew, III
Bowhill, Sidney Allan
Brown, Neal Boyd
Caledonia, George Ernest
Cartwright, David Chapman
Evans, John Vaughan
Ferguson, Eldon Earl
Fremouw, Edward Joseph
Johnson, Francis Severin
Kuhn, William Richard
Torr, Marsha Russell

Atmospheric chemistry
Appel, Bruce Richard
Boron, David John
Duce, Robert Arthur
Dunker, Alan Melvin
Ferguson, Ronald Max
Fogg, Thomas Robert
Gaffney, Jeffrey Steven
Grosjean, Daniel
Heicklen, Julian Phillip
Holton, Gregory Allan
Japar, Steven Martin
Kaye, Jack Alan
Kelly, Nelson Allen
Kolb, Charles Eugene
Machta, Lester
Martin, L(aurence) Robbin
McMurry, Peter Howard
Newman, Leonard
Saxena, Vinod Kumar
Sedlacek, William Adam
Tang, Ignatius Ning-Bang
Van Valin, Charles Carroll
Wang, Pao-Kuan

Climatology
Barnett, Tim P.
Barry, Roger Graham
Bryson, Reid Allen
Bushnell, Robert Hempstead
Coakley, Stella Melugin
Dando, William Arthur
Decker, Wayne Leroy
Donn, William L.
Donnelly, Richard Frank
Endal, Andrew Samson
Essenwanger, Oskar Maximilian Karl
Firor, John William
Gates, William Lawrence
Glatzmaier, Gary Andrew
Hadeen, Kenneth Doyle
James, Philip Benjamin
Kellogg, William Welch
Kuhn, William Richard
Landsberg, Helmut E(rich)
Larsen, James Arthur
Mitchell, John Murray, Jr.
Newman, James Edward
Rampino, Michael Robert
Reifsnyder, William Edward
Roberts, Walter Orr
Rosenberg, Norman Jack
Schneider, Stephen Henry
Smagorinsky, Joseph
Trapasso, Louis Michael
Untersteiner, Norbert
Waite, Paul Junior
Wang, Wei-Chyung
White, Robert M.
Williams, Jerry Albert

Meteorology
Atlas, David
Bonner, William Darrell
Boyd, John Philip
Brown, Neal Boyd
Byers, Horace Robert
Cerni, Todd Andrew
Coulson, Kinsell Leroy
Cox, Stephen Kent
Dutton, John Altnow
Epstein, Edward S.
Frank, Neil LaVerne
Fujita, Tetsuya Theodore
Gates, William Lawrence
Gaut, Norman Eugene
Goldman, Joseph L.
Hadeen, Kenneth Doyle
Hess, Wilmot Norton
Hosler, Charles Luther, Jr.
Houghton, David Drew
Kellogg, William Welch
Kessler, Edwin
Liou, Kuo-Nan
Long, Robert Radcliffe
Moe, Roderick Donald, Sr.
Norment, Hillyer Gavin
Ostby, Frederick Paul, Jr.
Peterson, Vern LeRoy

Pfeffer, Richard Lawrence
Pitts, David Eugene
Reifsnyder, William Edward
Rosen, Richard David
Ruggles, Kenneth Warren
Shuman, Frederick Gale
Smagorinsky, Joseph
Tang, M, Chung-Muh
Theon, John Speridon
Vaughan, William Walton
Wang, Pao-Kuan
Wang, Wei-Chyung
Williams, Jerry Albert
Young, Kevin Norman

Meteorology, meteorologic instrumentation
Berry, Edwin X
Bouillant, Alain Marcel
Cerni, Todd Andrew
Greenfield, Stanley Marshall
Moe, Roderick Donald, Sr.
Pallmann, Albert Josef
Saxena, Vinod Kumar
Siam, Monir Ahmed
Simpson, Joanne Malkus
Smith, James Gilbert
Ussailis, James Stewart

Meteorology, micrometeorology
Blackadar, Alfred Kimball
Hatfield, Jerry Lee
Kanemasu, Edward Tsukasa
Kelley, Neil Davis
Landsberg, Helmut E(rich)
Lumley, John Leask
Rosenberg, Norman Jack

Meteorology, synoptic meteorology
Almeyda, Guillermo Felix
Blackadar, Alfred Kimball
Gaffney, Paul Golden, II
Gannon, Patrick Thomas
Tang, M, Chung-Muh
Young, William Robert

Planetary atmospheres
Appleby, John Frederick
Barth, Charles Adolph
Cloutier, Paul Andrew
Jastrow, Robert
Moore, Thomas Earle
Owen, Tobias Chant
Pallmann, Albert Josef
Poultney, Sherman King
Sandel, Bill Roy
Scattergood, Thomas W.
Trafton, Laurence Munro
Travis, Larry Dean
Woo, Richard

Remote sensing
Atlas, David
Barnett, Tim P.
Bauer, Marvin Eugene
Bevan, Thomas Edward
Booker, Henry George
Bowhill, Sidney Allan
Brook, Marx
Coulson, Kinsell Leroy
Cox, Stephen Kent
Dando, William Arthur
Davidson, Gilbert
Evans, John Vaughan
Hall, Freeman Franklin, Jr.
Hatfield, Jerry Lee
Herget, William Frederick
Hilgeman, Theodore William
Jory, Virginia Vickery
Kanemasu, Edward Tsukasa
Karl, Robert Raymond, Jr.
Killinger, Dennis Karl
LaPorte, Daniel D'Arcy
Liou, Kuo-Nan
Meeks, Marion Littleton
Pitts, David Eugene
Post, Madison John
Poultney, Sherman King
Sawyer, Constance Bragdon
Simpson, Joanne Malkus
Theon, John Speridon
Trapasso, Louis Michael
Winker, David M(ichael)

Other
Carswell, Allan Ian, *Atmospheric physics*
Chuan, Raymond Lu-po
Cramer, Harrison Emery
Decker, Wayne Leroy
Gannon, Patrick Thomas
Goldman, Joseph L.
Haurwitz, Bernhard, *Dynamic meteorology*
Helsdon, John Hebard, Jr., *Atmospheric electricity; Cloud physics*
Mooers, Christopher Northrup Kennard
Orlanski, Isidoro, *Mesoscale meteorology*
Saint-Amand, Pierre, *Weather modification*
Schryer, David Richard, *Heterogeneous processes*
Spiegel, Stanley Lawrence
Yamada, Tetsuji, *Mesoscale meteorology*

BIOLOGY

Behaviorism
Arave, Clive Wendell
Day, Stacey Biswas
Konishi, Masakazu
Kristal, Mark Bennett
Novak, John Allen
Russell-Hunter, W(illiam) D(evigne)
Ward, Angus Lorin

Biochemistry. See also MEDICINE.
Adler, Julius
Agosin, Moises K.
Allen, Howard Joseph
Ames, Bruce N(athan)
Anderson, Lucy Macdonald
Anfinsen, Christian Boehmer
Ansari, Ghulam A. S.
Apirion, David
Applewhite, Thomas Hood
Armstrong, Donald
Atkinson, Mark Arthur Leonard
Aull, John Louis

Azhir, Arasteh
Ball, Laurence Andrew
Bamburg, James Robert
Banerjee, Sipra
Banik, Narendra Lal
Barden, Roland Eugene
Beaucage, Serge Laurent
Beck, William Samson
Belman, Sidney
Bender, Myron Lee
Benson, Andrew Alm
Berg, Paul
Berg, Richard Alan
Bessman, Samuel Paul
Bhavanandan, Veerasingham P.
Bieber, Mark Allan
Bietz, Jerold Allen
Blau, Lea
Bloch, Konrad
Bobst, Albert Max
Bockstahler, Larry Earl
Boeker, Elizabeth Anne
Bonaventura, Celia Jean
Bonaventura, Joseph
Boyer, Herbert Wayne
Boyer, Paul D.
Braatz, James Anthony
Bradford, Marion McKinley
Brakke, Myron Kendall
Brouwer, Marius
Brown, Kenneth Lawrence
Bundy, Hallie Flowers
Burleigh, Bruce Daniel
Burris, Robert Harza
Bustin, Michael
Callewaert, Denis Marc
Campbell, Wilbur Harold
Carubelli, Raoul
Castellino, Francis Joseph
Cathou, Renata Egone
Chalmers, John H., Jr.
Chalovich, Joseph Michael
Chan, Phillip C.
Chang, Kwen-Jen
Chase, John William
Chatterjee, Sunil Kumar
Christman, Judith Kershaw
Chuang, Ronald Y(an-li)
Chytil, Frank
Clarke, Steven Gerard
Cohen, Seymour Stanley
Coligan, John Ernest
Collins, James Francis
Cook, Elton Straus
Cooper, Alan Douglas
Costa, Max
Counselman, Clarence James
Cummings, Richard Dale
Cushman, David Wayne
Day, Richard Allen
Dean, David Devereaux
DeBari, Vincent Anthony
Decker, Richard Henry
de Duve, Christian Rene
DeFrank, Joseph John
De Luca, Luigi Maria
de Luque, Orlando Rafael
Denton, Arnold Eugene
De Vries, George Henry
Dickerman, Herbert W
Dilley, Richard A.
Dixon, Jack E.
Dolak, Terence Martin
Dudock, Bernard Samuel
Duffy, Lawrence Kevin
Duker, Nahum Johanan
Dunlap, R. Bruce
Eagon, Robert Garfield
Edmonds, Mary Patricia
Edsall, John Tileston
Ehrenfeld, Elvera
Ellsworth, Jeff Lynn
Etzler, Marilynn Edith
Fain, John Nicholas
Floyd, Robert A.
Forbes, Richard Mather
Forrest, Hugh Sommerville
Frear, Donald Stuart
Fresco, Jacques Robert
Fukuda, Minoru
Ganesan, Adayapalam Tyagarajan
Ganis, Frank Michael
Gawienowski, Anthony M(ichael)
Gelboin, Harry Victor
Gerwin, Brenda Isen
Ginzler, Edward Richard
Glassman, Edward
Godfrey, Henry Philip
Goll, Darrel Eugene
Golub, Ellis Eckstein
Graham, Terrence Lee
Gross, Paul Randolph
Grossman, Lawrence
Gumport, Richard I.
Hadler, Herbert Isaac
Hagedorn, Scott Richard
Hammes, Gordon G.
Harrington, Rodney Elbert
Harris, Don Navarro
Hascall, Vincent Charles, Jr.
Hathaway, Gary Michael
Hayes, Dora Kruse
Herr, Earl Binkley, Jr.
Herrmann, Klaus Manfred
Hershberger, Charles Lee
Hess, George P.
Hierholzer, John Charles
Hitchings, George Herbert
Hoagland, Mahlon Bush
Holzman, Thomas Fredric
Horecker, Bernard Leonard
Horwitt, Max Kenneth
Hwang, San-Bao
Idler, David Richard
Inman, Franklin Pope
Jackson, David Stanley
Jackson, Richard Lee
Jacob, Gary Steven
Jacobson, Gary R(onald)
Jeanloz, Roger William
Jernigan, Howard Maxwell, Jr.
Johnson, Lee F(rederick)
Johnston, Laurance Scott
Kaczorowski, Gregory John
Kaiser, Armin Dale
Kalra, Vijay Kumar
Kang, Sungzong
Kaplan, Stanley Albert
Karavolas, Harry J(ohn)
Kasarda, Donald David
Kaufman, Seymour
Keen, Noel Thomas
Keller, John Mahlon
Kennedy, Eugene Patrick
Khorana, Har Gobind
Kindt, Thomas James
Klibanov, Alexander Maxim
Knowles, Jeremy Randall
Kordonowy, Rhoda Klempel
Korn, Edward David
Kreimer-Birnbaum, F
Kritchevsky, David
Lacks, Sanford Abraham
Lai, Ching-San
Larson, Bruce L.
Laskowski, Michael, Jr.
Lata, Gene Frederick
Lawton, Richard Graham
Lay, Ming-muh
Lee, Chuan-pu
Lehninger, Albert Lester
Lerner, Pauline
Levin, Wayne
Li, Choh Hao
Liang, Tehming
Liao, Shutsung
Light, Albert
Lin, Tsau-Yen
Lipmann, Fritz (Albert)
Litov, Richard Emil
Liu, Yung-Pin
Lodish, Harvey Franklin
Lorance, Elmer Donald
Lornitzo, Frank Adam
Lundblad, Roger Lauren
Lygre, David Gerald
Macara, Ian Gregory
MacColl, Robert
MacCoss, Malcolm
MacFarlane, Robert Bruce
Machlin, Lawrence Judah
Maier, Robert James
Mangano, Richard Michael
Marcoullis, George Panayiotis
Marcus, Frank
Margoliash, Emanuel
Marks, Neville
Marsh, Benjamin Bruce
Marshall, Wayne Edward
Martin, David Lee
Martinez-Carrion, Marino
Massaro, Edward Joseph
Matheson, Alastair Taylor
Max, Stephen Richard
Mc Elroy, William David
McGeachin, Robert Lorimer
McLaughlin, Calvin S.
Merrifield, Robert Bruce
Meselson, Matthew Stanley
Michaeli, Dov
Miljanich, George Paul
Misra, Hara Prasad
Mitchell, Earl Douglass, Jr.
Model, Peter
Mohammad, Syed Fazal
Moody, Terry William
Moore, Peter Bartlett
Mooz, Elizabeth Dodd
Morre, D. James
Moskowitz, Gerard J.
Murray, Allen Ketcik
Na, George Chao
Nandi, Jyotirmoy
Natelson, Samuel
Newman, David John
Newman, David William
Nicholas, Harold Joseph
Nickerson, Kenneth Warwick
Nicolau, Gabriela
Nirenberg, Marshall Warren
O'Brien, Paul Joseph
O'Connor, Timothy E.
Oeltmann, Thomas Napier
Olson, Mark Obed Jerome
Oro, Juan
Pan, Huo-Ping
Pardee, Arthur Beck
Parham, Peter
Passwater, Richard Albert
Pattee, Harold Edward
Pettit, Flora Hunter
Phillips, George Neal, Jr.
Phillips, Lawrence Richard
Pomeranz, Yeshajahu
Ponnamperuma, Cyril Andrew
Powers, Dennis Alpha
Price, Alan Roger
Prigge, Edward Christian, Jr.
Privett, Orville Samuel
Ptashne, Mark Stephen
Pullman, Maynard Edward
Rabinowitz, Israel Nathan
Rabovsky, Jean
Radhakrishnamurthy, Bhandaru
Reazin, George Harvey, Jr.
Rebeiz, Constantin Anis
Rebello, Tessio Estevam
Reddy, Chinthamani Channa
Reed, Lester James
Richman, Joseph Ben
Rizack, Martin Arthur
Robakis, Nikolaos Konstantinou
Roberts, John D.
Robinson, James Lawrence
Roelofs, Wendell Lee
Rogers, Sam
Rosen, Martin Howard
Rothfus, John Arden
Rotruck, John Truman
Rudney, Harry
Rutman, Robert J.
Rutter, William J.
Sabban, Esther Louise
Sabol, Steven Layne
Sachan, Dileep S.
Samy, Anantha T. S.
Sanders, Robert Burnett
Sani, Brahma P.
Sarich, Vincent M.
Schacht, Jochen Heinrich
Schlenk, Hermann
Schmidgall, Robert Lee
Schooley, David Allan
Segal, Joseph
Shapiro, Irving Meyer
Shatkin, Aaron Jeffrey
Shelton, Damon Charles
Shemin, David
Shih, Jason Chia-Hsing
Shihabi, Zakariya Kamel
Siedler, Arthur James
Silverman, Richard Bruce
Simmons, William Howard
Sink, John Davis
Skipski, Vladimir P(avlovich)
Smith, Emil L.
Smith, Leonard Charles
Snyder, Fred Leonard
Spitsberg, Vitaly Lev
Spremulli, Linda Lucy
Stadtman, Earl Reece
Stadtman, Thressa Campbell
Steck, Theodore Lyle
Steinback, Katherine Ellen
Steiner, Robert Frank
Stewart, Ivan
Stowe, Bruce Bernot
Strauss, Phyllis R.
Strobel, Rudolf Gottfried Karl
Stromer, Marvin Henry
Stryer, Lubert
Tabachnick, Joseph
Takemoto, Dolores Jean
Tallent, William Hugh
Tanaka, Nobumasa
Tarnowski, Stanley Joseph, Jr.
Taylor, Eric Robert
Thomas, Fairwell
Thomas, William Eric
Thompson, David Jerome
Tischler, Marc Eliot
Tökés, Zoltán András
Tropp, Burton E.
Tsang, Joseph Chiao-Liang
Turco, Salvatore Joseph
Tweedy, Billy G.
Underwood, Arthur Louis, Jr.
Vaishnav, Dinesh Divakarrai
Valassi, Kyriake Vlassios
Valenzuela, Pablo De Tarso
Vanaman, Thomas C.
VanderMeulen, David Lee
Vary, James Corydon
Vasington, Frank Daniel
Vehar, Gordon Allen
Veis, Arthur
Vickers, Stanley
Volanakis, John Emmanuel
Volcani, Benjamin Elazari
Vold, Barbara Schneider
Volsky, David Julian
Wakil, Salih Jawad
Wald, George
Walker, Thomas Eugene
Wallace, Garn Arthur
Walsh, John Stuart
Wampler, John Edward
Wang, Chi-Sun
Wang, Dalton Ta Tung
Watts, Tania Helen
Weber, Darrell Jack
Weissbach, Arthur
Weissbach, Herbert
White, Helen Lyng
Whitten, Bertwell Kneeland
Wiley, William R.
Wilson, David Buckingham
Wright, Fred Carl
Yacowitz, Harold
Yang, Shang Fa
Young, Franklin
Yphantis, David Andrew
Zamenhof, Stephen
Ziegler, Daniel Martin
Zimmerman, Thomas Paul
Zurawski, Vincent Richard, Jr.

Biophysics
Abercrombie, Ronald Ford
Absolom, Darryl Robin
Alexander, Nelson Eugene
Atwater, Illani Jeanne
Azhir, Arasteh
Baylor, Stephen Murray
Bendet, Irwin Jacob
Berg, Howard Curtis
Boeker, Elizabeth Anne
Brink, Peter Richards
Carstensen, Edwin Lorenz
Caspar, Donald Louis Dvorak
Chance, Britton
Cheung, Herbert Chiu-Ching
Corey, David Paul
Cranefield, Paul Frederic
D'Arrigo, Joseph Salvatore
Davis, Brian Keith
DeLisi, Charles
Dunham, Philip Bigelow
Dusenbery, David Brock
Eckert, Roger Otto
Fabiato, Alexandre
Fine, Samuel
Ford, George D
Goldman, Lawrence
Goldstein, David Arthur
Goll, Darrel Eugene
Gross, Leo
Haselkorn, Robert
Haynes, Robert Hall
Helgerson, Sam Leland
Hollander, Lewis E., Jr.
Hruby, Victor Joseph
Hwang, San-Bao
Jakobsson, Eric Gunnar
Jankelson, Bernard
Justesen, Don Robert
Karle, Isabella Lugoski
Kessel, David
Kirkpatrick, Francis H(ubbard), Jr.
Kohen, Elli
Krishna, Nepalli Rama
Krohmer, Jack Stewart
Kroon, Paulus Arie
La Celle, Paul Louis
Lai, Ching-San
Lamvik, Michael Kasper
Leblanc, Roger Maurice
Lee, Chin Ok
Lee, Chuan-pu
Leibovic, K. Nicholas
Levine, Rhea Joy Cottler
Llinas, Rodolfo Riascos
Loewenstein, Werner Randolph
Lontz, John Frank
Lucas, William John
Makinen, Marvin William
Martinez-Carrion, Marino
Mazur, Peter
McClellan, George Baird
Merilan, Charles Preston
Morse, Philip Dexter, II
Nacht, Sergio
Nagy, Béla Ferenc
Papahadjopoulos, Demetrios P.
Pattabiraman, Nagarajan
Phillips, George Neal, Jr.
Piette, Lawrence Hector
Powell, Michael Robert
Powers, Linda Sue
Purcell, Edward Mills
Quintanilha, Alexandre Tiedtke
Rakowski, Robert Frank
Recktenwald, Diether Joseph
Redgrave, Trevor Gordon
Salzberg, Brian Matthew
Salzman, Gary Clyde
Schroeder, LeRoy William
Schwan, Herman Paul
Setlow, Richard Burton
Shamoo, Adil E(lias)
Smith, George David
Smith, Ian Cormack Palmer
Song, Chang Won
Stevens, Charles F.
Taylor, Eric Robert
Tien, H. Ti
Ts'o, Paul On-Pong
VanderMeulen, David Lee
Van Dilla, Marvin Albert
Wald, George
Wallace, Bonnie Ann
White, Stephen Halley
Woodbury, Charles Putnam, Jr.
Young, Wei
Yphantis, David Andrew

Cell biology. ***See also*** **MEDICINE.**
Abrams, Thomas William
Adlakha, Ramesh Chander
Aist, James Robert
Allen, Howard Joseph
Arch, Stephen William
Atkinson, Mark Arthur Leonard
Bamburg, James Robert
Bechtel, Donald Bruce
Benjamini, Eliezer
Billen, Daniel
Bleyman, Lea Kanner
Blystone, Robert Vernon
Bregman, Allyn Aaron
Brown, R. Malcolm, Jr.
Bryan, John Henry Donald
Bustin, Michael
Byers, Breck Edward
Chalovich, Joseph Michael
Chapman, Russell Leonard
Crick, Francis Harry Compton
Danielli, James Frederic
de Duve, Christian Rene
DeLisi, Charles
DiPaolo, Joseph Amedeo
Diwan, Joyce Johnson
Draznin, Boris
Dritschilo, Anatoly
Dute, Roland Roy
Edelson, Paul Jeffrey
Forer, Arthur Hanan
Forman, David Sholem
Fox, C. Fred
Gale, Robert Peter
Goldstein, Lester
Harper, Jeffrey Frederick
Hartter, Daryl Edward
Haywood, Anne Mowbray
Herlyn, Meenhard Folkeus
Herman, William Sparkes
Higgins, Paul Joseph
Hikida, Robert Seiichi
Horvitz, Howard Robert
Howse, Harold Darrow
Jessup, John Milburn
Johnson, John Edlin, Jr.
Jurand, Arthur
Kikkawa, Yutaka
Kohen, Elli
Kramarsky, Bernhard
LaChance, Leo Emery
La Claire, John Willard, II
Ledbetter, Myron Calvert
Leif, Robert Cary
Levine, Rhea Joy Cottler
Lipton, Allan
Lodish, Harvey Franklin
Maguire, Marjorie Paquette
Malamed, Sasha
Mazia, Daniel
Mazur, Peter
Meyer, Dale R.
Miller, Morton W(illiam)
Nacht, Sergio
Nicklas, Robert Bruce
Nicolson, Garth L.
O'Brien, Paul Joseph
Olson, Mark Obed Jerome
Painter, Richard Grant
Palade, George Emil
Pardee, Arthur Beck
Pardue, Mary Lou
Parthasarathy, Mandayam Veerambhudi
Pelus, Louis Martin
Pfenninger, Karl Hans
Politis, Demetrios John
Powers, Edward Lawrence
Reddi, A(kepati) Hari
Reynafarje, Baltazar Davila
Ribak, Charles Eric
Ris, Hans
Robbins, Robert Raymond
Roseman, Saul
Ruddle, Francis Hugh
Rudney, Harry
Sabatini, David Domingo
Sanadi, D. Rao
Santos, Eugenio Miguel
Scharff, Matthew Daniel
Schvartzman, Jorge Bernardo
Segal, Joseph
Siekevitz, Philip
Sivak, Andrew
Stromer, Marvin Henry
Stryer, Lubert
Tamm, Igor
Tchen, Tche-Tsing
Thompson, Elizabeth Barnes
Toback, F(rederick) Gary
Tytell, Michael
Wiley, William R.
Woods, Walter Thomas, Jr.
Yuspa, Stuart Howard

Cell biology, cell and tissue culture. ***See also*** **AGRICULTURE, Plant cell and tissue culture.**
Abid, Syed Hasan
Andrews, Peter Walter
Avner, Barry Paul
Barald, Katharine Francesca
Becker, Robert Otto
Berg, Richard Alan
Berliner, Martha D.
Birckbichler, Paul Joseph
Breitman, Theodore Ronald
Briggs, Robert Wilbur
Broadhurst, John Henry
Bronson, David Lee
Buchanan, Judith Ann
Burleigh, Bruce Daniel
Chopra, Dharam Pal
Chou, Iih-Nan
Crang, Richard Francis Earl
Cronshaw, James
Culp, Lloyd Anthony
Dickinson, Winifred Ball
Dow, Lois Weyman
Duff, Ronald George
Egan, Marianne Louise
Engle, Michael J(ean)
Eppstein, Deborah Anne
Etzler, Marilynn Edith
Fox, Michael Henry
Fried, Jerrold
Gardner, Eldon John
Gentile, Arthur Christopher
Glick, J. Leslie
Goldfeder, Anna
Goodheart, Clyde Raymond
Gross, Nicholas Jabob
Gurney, Elizabeth Tucker Guice
Han, Stella C.
Hanley, Kevin Joseph
Hathaway, Gary Michael
Hayflick, Leonard
Haynes, Lynn O.
Hill, Ray Allen
Hoegerman, Stanton Fred
Holley, Robert William
Horner, Harry Theodore
Huberman, Eliezer
Iannaccone, Philip Monroe
Jaffe, Eric Allen
Johnson, John Morris
Ledbetter, Mary Lee Stewart
Ledinko, Nada
Leung, Benjamin Shuet-kin
Lostroh, Ardis June
Mahlberg, Paul Gordon
Moehring, Joan Marquart
Moldenhauer, Jeanne Elisabeth
Monette, Francis C.
Moore, George Eugene
Munro, Hamish Nisbet
Oberley, Terry De Wayne
Opel, William
Park, Chan Hyung
Patterson, Rosalyn Victoria Mitchell
Pollard, Harvey Bruce
Riser, Mary Elizabeth
Rost, Thomas Lowell
Seraydarian, Marie Wargon
Shafi, Muhammad Iqbal
Shapiro, Burton Leonard
Shires, Thomas Kay
Silver, Robert Benjamin
Stabler, Timothy Allen
Steuer, Anton Francis
Stevenson, Robert Edwin
Thompson, Edward Ivins Bradbridge
Ting, Yu-Chen
Topper, Yale J.
Trowbridge, Richard Stuart
Van De Water, Thomas Roger
Wagner, Carmen Machado
Washington, Linda Phaire
Weinberg, Robert Allen
Weissbach, Arthur
Wergin, William P.
Wolff, Sheldon
Yu, Cheng Wou

Chronobiology
Beljan, John Richard
Evans, James Warren
Guillaume, Germaine Gabrielle Cornelissen
Hayes, Dora Kruse
Hrushesky, William John Michael
Kafka, Marian Adele Stern
King-Smith, Eric Alfred
Lai, Por-Hsiung
Morin, Lawrence Porter
Morris, Ralph William
Pauly, John Edward
Perlow, Mark Jacob
Repenning, Charles Albert
Smolensky, Michael Hale
Sturtevant, Frank Milton
Sturtevant, Ruthann Patterson
Takahashi, Joseph S.
Wainwright, Stanley Dunstan
Wilson, Leonard Richard
Winfree, Arthur Taylor

Developmental biology
Alessi, Norman Emil
Andrews, Peter Walter
Bechtel, Donald Bruce
Benbow, Robert Michael
Blystone, Robert Vernon
Bohn, Martha D.
Bonner, John Tyler
Brown, Donald David
Chang, Ernest Sun-Mei
Cunningham, Bruce Arthur
Davidson, Eric Harris
Dawid, Igor Bert

Smith, Gerald Ralph
Steitz, Joan Argetsinger
Sutton, Harry Eldon
Timberlake, William Edward
Van Houten, Judith Lee
Waelsch, Salome Gluecksohn
Walters, Ronald Arlen
Wechsler, James Alan
Woo, Savio Lau Ching
Wood, William Barry, III
Young, Michael Warren

Genetics, genome organization
Asato, Yukio
Basilico, Claudio
Betterley, Donald Alan
Bouillant, Alain Marcel
Bregman, Allyn Aaron
Bullas, Leonard Raymond
Campbell, Allan McCulloch
Cantor, Charles R.
Carrano, Anthony Vito
Catlin, B. Wesley
Cohen, Stanley Norman
Dingle, Richard Douglas Hugh
Dutta, Sisir Kamal
Endrizzi, John E.
Farmer, James Lee
Flagg, Raymond Osbourn
Flory, Walter S., Jr.
Garon, Claude Francis
Gerwin, Brenda Isen
Gray, Joe William
Grossman, Lawrence I.
Gustafson, John Perry
Han, Stella C.
Henderson, Ann Shirley
Hickey, Donal Aloysius
Jackson, Raymond Carl
Jeffery, Duane Eldro
Jenkins, Edmund Charles
Johnson, Edward Michael
Kao, Fa-Ten
Kellogg, Scott Thomas
Lewin, Benjamin
Lin, Yue Jee
Lingrel, Jerry B.
Mage, Rose Goldman
Maroni, Gustavo Primo
Martin, Scott McClung
Mc Kusick, Victor Almon
Mickey, George Henry
Miksche, Jerome Phillip
Narang, Sudhir Karl
Patterson, Rosalyn Victoria Mitchell
Powers, Dennis Alpha
Price, Harold James
Robbins, Leonard G(ilbert)
Rubin, Gerald M.
Schvartzman, Jorge Bernardo
Sheffer, Richard Douglas
Singer, Maxine Frank
Staub, Rick Walter
Villa-Komaroff, Lydia
Vodkin, Michael Harold
Ward, Oscar G., Jr.
Wolff, Sheldon
Yokoyama, Shozo
Yoon, Jong Sik
Young, Michael Warren

Gravitational biology. *See* SPACE SCIENCE.

Immunobiology and immunology
Alevy, Yael Gris
Anderson, Gary Allan
Angus, Robert Dale
Arnaout, M. Amin
Austen, K(arl) Frank
Baltimore, David
Barisas, Bernard George, Jr.
Barrett, James Thomas
Beck, Lee Randolph
Beller, David I.
Benacerraf, Baruj
Benjamini, Eliezer
Bice, David E.
Bloom, Eda Terri
Bona, Constantin A(tanasie)
Braciale, Vivian Lam
Brown, Stephen James
Brunda, Michael John
Bykowsky, Michael John
Callewaert, Denis Marc
Carlo, Jaime Rafael
Carlson, George Alfred, Jr.
Carrier, E. Bernard
Castro, Alberto
Cathou, Renata Egone
Cerini, Costantino Peter
Chengappa, Muckatira Madaiah
Chi, David S.
Chused, Thomas M.
Clark, Edward Alan
Cleveland, William Louis
Coligan, John Ernest
Collins, Bobby Ray
Conway, Thomas Patrick
Conway de Macario, Everly
David, Gary Samuel
Day, Eugene Davis
Duffey, Paul Stephen
Dusanic, Donald Gabriel
Dyminski, John W(ladyslaw)
Ebert, James David
Egan, Marianne Louise
Erlanger, Bernard Ferdinand
Ettinger, Anna Marie
Fernandez-Cruz, Eduardo P.
Fidler, John Michael
Field, Arthur Kirk
Finkelstein, Richard Alan
Fitch, Frank Wesley
Fuccillo, David Anthony
Gefter, Malcolm Lawrence
Gleicher, Norbert
Goodman, Joel Warren
Goust, Jean-Michel Christian
Graziano, Kenneth Donald
Halonen, Marilyn Jean
Hillis, William Daniel, Sr.
Hogan, Yvonne Holland
Hokama, Yoshitsugi
Hood, Leroy Edward
Hsu, Clement C.S.
Hsu, Hei-ti
Huard, Thomas King
Inman, Franklin Pope
Irigoyen, Oscar Horacio
Iverson, Gilbert Michael
Jacobs, Diane Margaret
Kahn, Carolyn Robin
Kaplan, Alan Marc
Kapp-Pierce, Judith Anne
Kaufman, Leo
Kim, Byung Suk
Kim, Yoon Berm
Kobilinsky, Lawrence
Koo, Peter Hung-Kwan
Koprowski, Hilary
Koshland, Marian Elliott
Ladisch, Stephan
Lamm, Michael Emanuel
Laux, David Charles
Lawrence, David A.
Lehrer, Samuel B.
Leong, Stanley Pui-Lock
Liao, Shuen-Kuei
Lornitzo, Frank Adam
Loughman, Barbara Ellen Evers
Mage, Rose Goldman
Makinodan, Takashi
Mason, Margaret Jeanne
McNamara, T(homas) F(rancis)
Meggs, William Joel
Michael, Jacob Gabriel
Mickelson, Claudia A(nn)
Mickley, Harold Somers
Moody, Charles Edward, Jr.
Mosmann, Timothy Richard
Nisonoff, Alfred
Paque, Ronald Edward
Paul, William Erwin
Pearson, Terry William
Perryman, Lance Edward
Pistole, Thomas Gordon
Platsoucas, Chris Dimitrios
Pollack, Sylvia Byrne
Previte, Joseph James
Ramsey, Robert Bruce
Ray, Prasanta Kumar
Reed, Norman Duane
Reed, Steven Gregory
Roberts, Robert Russell
Scharff, Matthew Daniel
Schreiber, Hans
Segre, Mariangela
Sell, Stewart
Senter, Peter Dana
Sidky, Younan Abdel-Malik
Sigal, Nolan Howard
Sindelar, William Francis
Stanton, Glennon John
Strelkauskas, Anthony James
Strober, Samuel
Talmage, David Wilson
Tartof, David
Till, Gerd Oskar
Tonegawa, Susumu
Tse, Harley Y.
Tseng, Jeenan
Van Alten, Pierson Jay
Vilcek, Jan Tomas
Volkman, Alvin
Washington, Linda Phaire
Watson, Ronald Ross
Wood, David Dudley
Wright, John Ricken
Wright, Richard Kenneth
Zarco, Romeo M.
Zurawski, Vincent Richard, Jr.

Immunocytochemistry
Brown, Hannah R(eeva)
Carlo, Jaime Rafael
Duke, Scherer Preston Sanders
Ho, Raymond How-Chee
Iverson, Gilbert Michael
Khachaturian, Henry
Lambris, John Dimitrios
Lee, Sin Hang
McGinty, Jacqueline Frances
McNeill, Thomas Hugh
Mrema, John E. K.
Nilaver, Gajanan
Reiss, Errol
Stuart, William Dorsey, Jr.

Limnology
Addis, James Theodore
Bartos, Leonard Francis
Beeton, Alfred Merle
Brugam, Richard Blair
Chimney, Michael John
Cole, Jonathan Jay
Coleman, James Mark
Eberly, William Robert
Edmondson, W(allace) Thomas
Elmore, James Lewis
Erickson, J(ohn) Mark
Francko, David Alex
Gannon, John Edward
Gerritsen, Jeroen
Gibbons, Harry Lawrence, Jr.
Goldner, Laurie Linda
Gregory, Jean Winfrey
Grossnickle, Nevin Edwin
Hamelink, Jerry Lee
Harman, Willard Nelson
Harper, Carol Lynn Mount
Hart, Robert Joseph
Kaczynski, Victor Walter
Keating, Kathleen Irwin
Kelly, Mahlon George, Jr.
Kilham, Peter
Kosinski, Robert Joseph
Lisiecki, Jerry Boyd
Makarewicz, Joseph Chester
Maly, Edward John
Moore, John Robert
Ohlhorst, Sharon Lee
Patrick, Ruth (Mrs. Charles Hodge)
Pollman, Curtis Devin
Polls, Irwin
Porter, Karen Glaus
Shubeck, Paul Peter
Soltero, Raymond Arthur
Stoermer, Eugene Filmore
Sullivan, Carl Rollynn, Jr.
Vallentyne, John Reuben Way (Johnny Biosphere)
Van Landingham, Samuel Leighton
Wetzel, Robert George

Marine biology
Auster, Peter Jay
Backman, Thomas William Hightower
Blinks, Lawrence Rogers
Buroker, Norman Everett
Capriles, Victor Antonio
Caruso, John Howard
Cheng, Lanna
Costlow, John DeForest
Digby, Peter Saki Bassett
Dorsey, John Henry
Gibbs, Robert Henry, Jr.
Gruber, Samuel Harvey
Guist, Guyer Gordon, Jr.
Harman, Willard Nelson
Hay, Mark Edward
Laurence, Geoffrey Cameron
Lee, John Joseph
Levin, Jack
Littler, Mark Masterton
MacFarlane, Robert Bruce
Mason, John Montgomery, Jr.
Mohr, John Luther
Moore, Richard Harlan
Ohlhorst, Sharon Lee
Orsi, James John
Palmer, Allison Richard
Paull, Charles
Perkins, Frank Overton
Provasoli, Luigi
Ropes, John Warren
Sedberry, George R., III
Sellner, Kevin Gregory
Somero, George Nicholls
Stein, Jeffrey Lee
Stobo, Wayne Thomas
Sullivan, Carl Rollynn, Jr.
Thom, Ronald Mark
VanBlaricom, Glenn Richard
Van Dolah, Robert Frederick
Witham, Phillip Ross
Wolf, Nancy Gail
Zimmerman, Richard Carl

Membrane biology
Aberg, Gunnar A.K.
Al-Bazzaz, Faiq Jaber
Andrew, Clifford George
Arnaout, M. Amin
Birckbichler, Paul Joseph
Bradley, Ronald James
Candia, Oscar A.
Chacko, George Kutty
Cone, Robert Edward
Conway, Thomas Patrick
Diwan, Joyce Johnson
Dubinsky, William Paul, Jr.
Earhart, Charles Franklin, Jr.
Eaton, Barbara Ruth
Farquhar, Marilyn Gist
Fox, C. Fred
Goldfeder, Anna
Goldin, Stanley Michael
Goodman, David Barry Poliakoff
Goodman, Steven Richard
Hester, Richard Kelly
Hong, Jen-shiang
Jacobson, Gary R(onald)
Jakobsson, Eric Gunnar
Janis, Ronald Allen
Kaczorowski, Gregory John
Kennedy, Eugene Patrick
Kimelberg, Harold Keith
Kornel, Ludwig
Ledbetter, Mary Lee Stewart
Morre, D. James
Morse, Philip Dexter, II
Nandi, Jyotirmoy
Narahara, Hiromichi Tsuda
Neuhaus, Otto W.
Olson, Erik Joseph
Packer, Lester
Painter, Richard Grant
Parks, Leo W.
Pullman, Maynard Edward
Rakowski, Robert Frank
Rasenick, Mark Mitchell
Ray, Tushar Kanti
Ritter, Carl Alan
Rodbell, Martin
Roseman, Saul
Schroeder, Friedhelm
Segrest, Jere Palmer
Steck, Theodore Lyle
Takemoto, Dolores Jean
Troy, Frederic Arthur, II
Tu, Shu-I
Vanatta, John Crothers, III
Van Houten, Judith Lee
Varki, Ajit Pothan
Vasington, Frank Daniel
Wakil, Salih Jawad
Wang, Howard Hao
Watts, Tania Helen

Microbiology. *See also* MEDICINE.
Anderson, Mauritz Gunnar
Bader, Fredric George
Barrett, James Thomas
Berg, Howard Curtis
Berliner, Martha D.
Bernstein, Carol
Bertani, Giuseppe
Betterley, Donald Alan
Boston, Penelope Jane Ashley
Brenchley, Jean Elnora
Bulla, Lee Austin, Jr.
Carrier, E. Bernard
Catlin, B. Wesley
Chakrabarty, Ananda Mohan
Champe, Sewell Preston
Chang, Te-Wen
Chengappa, Muckatira Madaiah
Chesney, Robert Harold
Cohen, Joel Ralph
Combes, Richard Willard
Conti, Samuel Francis
Crang, Richard Francis Earl
Cronholm, Lois S.
Curtiss, Roy, III
Daoust, Donald Roger
deFiebre, Conrad William
Dehority, Burk Allyn
Demain, Arnold Lester
DiRienzo, Joseph Michael
Docherty, John Joseph
Doi, Roy Hiroshi
Domer, Judith Elaine
Dougherty, Robert Malvin
Drexler, Henry
Eagar, Robert Gouldman, Jr.
Eagon, Robert Garfield
Earhart, Charles Franklin, Jr.
Ely, Berten E., III
Essex, Myron Elmer
Ferchau, Hugo Alfred
Finkelstein, Richard Alan
Finnerty, William Robert
Foster, Edwin Michael
Founds, Henry William, Jr.
Fox, Eugene Noah
Friedman, Selwyn Marvin
Frisell, Wilhelm Richard
Garfinkle, Barry David
Geiger, Jon Ross
Gerhardt, Philipp
Ginsberg, Harold Samuel
Gleicher, Norbert
Goldberg, Ivan D.
Gowans, Charles Shields
Grogan, James Bigbee
Hagen, Charles Alfred
Hammill, Terrence Michael
Hammond, Benjamin Franklin
Hanson, Richard Steven
Harman, Gary Elvan
Hemmingsen, Barbara Bruff
Herscowitz, Herbert Bernard
Hochstadt, Joy
Horn, Dennis Lee
Huber, Don Morgan
Humphrey, Ronald De Vere
Ingraham, John Lyman
Ippen-Ihler, Karin Ann
Johnson, F. Brent
Joshi, Madan Mohan
Kasai, George Joji
Kashket, Eva Ruth
Kellogg, Scott Thomas
Kelman, Arthur
Kline, Ellis Lee
Kohlhepp, Sue Joanne
Laux, David Charles
Leath, Kenneth Thomas
Lerner, Stephen Alexander
Leslie, John Franklin
Lipmann, Fritz (Albert)
Lippincott, James Andrew
Litchfield, John Hyland
Lukezic, Felix Lee
Luria, Salvador Edward
Maier, Robert James
Maramorosch, Karl
Marchin, George L.
Margulis, Lynn
Marinucci, Andrew Carmen
Martin, Scott McClung
Masker, Warren Edward
Mayol, Pete Syting
Mc Elroy, William David
McNamara, T(homas) F(rancis)
Mehta, Bipin Mohanlal
Mendelson, Neil Harland
Moehring, Joan Marquart
Mohney, Leone Laura
Moody, Arnold Ralph
Moody, Charles Edward, Jr.
Morris, J(oseph) Anthony
Neidhardt, Frederick Carl
Newell, Steven Young
Newman, David John
Ng, Thomas K.
Nickerson, Kenneth Warwick
Orland, Frank Jay
Pappenheimer, Alwin M(ax), Jr.
Parks, Leo W.
Phillip, Michael J.
Pistole, Thomas Gordon
Pollard, Morris
Pun, Pattle Pak Toe
Raju, Namboori Bhaskara
Reiss, Errol
Roberts, Robert Russell
Rogolsky, Marvin
Salzman, Gary Clyde
Samuelson, Don Arthur
Sapp, Danny Lee
Sarachek, Alvin
Savageau, Michael Antonio
Schadler, Daniel Leo
Schaechter, Moselio
Schoknecht, Jean Donze
Sebek, Oldrich Karel
Setliff, Edson Carmack
Shan, Hsin-Tsan Grace
Shanmugam, Keelnatham Thirunavukkarasu
Shapiro, James Alan
Sherris, John Charles
Shih, Jason Chia-Hsing
Singh, Shiva Pujan
Six, Howard Ronald
Spizizen, John
Stadtman, Earl Reece
Stadtman, Thressa Campbell
Staubus, John Reginald
Stevens, Roy Harris
Strandberg, Gerald William
Tanaka, Nobumasa
Taylor, Bernard Franklin
Thomas, Donald Charles
Torriani, Annamaria Gorini
Tropp, Burton E.
Tzianabos, Theodore
Underdahl, Norman Russell
Vaishnav, Dinesh Divakarrai
Vary, James Corydon
Vilcek, Jan Tomas
Volcani, Benjamin Elazari
Wetmur, James Gerard
Wolfe, Ralph Stoner
Wood, Harland Goff

Molecular biology
Abelson, John N.
Adler, Julius
Amer, M. Samir
Anderson, Carl William
Anderson, W. French
Asato, Yukio
Baltimore, David
Banerjee, Amiya Kumar
Bean, William Joseph, Jr.
Becker, Michael McClellan
Benade, Leonard Edward
Benbow, Robert Michael
Berg, Patricia E.
Bernstein, Carol
Bernstein, Harris
Billingsley, Melvin Lee
Bogorad, Lawrence
Bond, Clifford Walter
Bonner, James
Bonner, James Jose
Brown, Gregory Gaynor
Calame, Kathryn Lee
Camiolo, Sarah May
Campbell, Judith Lynn
Cantor, Charles R.
Carlson, Marian Bille
Carroll, Dana
Carter, Timothy Howard
Chalmers, John H., Jr.
Cooper, Geoffrey Mitchell
Cozzarelli, Nicholas Robert
Croce, Carlo Maria
Crooke, Stanley Thomas
Cunningham, Bruce Arthur
Dahlberg, James Eric
Dahms, Arthur Stephen
Davidson, Eric Harris
Davidson, Norman Ralph
Dawid, Igor Bert
Denhardt, David Tilton
Dinarello, Charles A.
DiRienzo, Joseph Michael
Dixon, Gordon Henry
Dixon, Jack E.
Doi, Roy Hiroshi
Donnellan, James Edward, Jr.
Duker, Nahum Johanan
Dutko, Francis Joseph, Jr.
Edelman, Gerald Maurice
Edenberg, Howard Joseph
Edmonds, Mary Patricia
Efcavitch, J. William
Eichhorn, Gunther Louis
Engelking, Henry Mark
Ennis, Herbert L.
Enquist, Lynn William
Fedoroff, Nina Vserolod
Fernandes, Daniel James
Flanegan, James Bert
Fowler, Elizabeth
Fox, George Edward
Fraenkel-Conrat, Heinz
Fresco, Jacques Robert
Furth, John Jacob
Galas, David John
Ganesan, Adayapalam Tyagarajan
Gartland, William Joseph
Gefter, Malcolm Lawrence
Geiduschek, E(rnest) Peter
Gelfand, David H.
Ghangas, Gurdev S.
Gilbert, Walter
Gillespie, David Hutton
Goeddel, David Van Norman
Goldstein, David Arthur
Goodman, Howard M.
Goodman, Joel Warren
Green, Harry
Grossman, Lawrence I.
Grubman, Marvin
Hamilton, Leonard Derwent
Hanafusa, Hidesaburo
Harriman, Philip Darling
Harrington, Rodney Elbert
Hawley, Robert John
Henderson, Ann Shirley
Herrmann, Klaus Manfred
Higuchi, Russell Gene
Hong, Jen-shiang
Horecker, Bernard Leonard
Iglewski, Wallace Joseph
Jaworski, Ernest George
Jernigan, Robert Lee
Johnson, Lee F(rederick)
Karawya, Essam Mohamed
Kashmiri, Syed V.S.
Kettlewell, Neil MacKewan
Knudson, Gregory Blair
Kohlhepp, Sue Joanne
Kopecko, Dennis J.
Kramer, Fred Russell
Krause, James Edward
Kroon, Paulus Arie
Kuemmerle, Nancy Benton Stevens
Kung, Shain-dow
Lapeyre, Jean-Numa
Leamnson, Robert Neal
Lederberg, Joshua
Ledinko, Nada
Lerman, Michael Isaac
Levine, Arthur Samuel
Lewis, Robert Mason
Livingston, David Morse
Lovett, Paul Scott
Lu, Ponzy
Mahler, Inga R.
Maniloff, Jack
Marchin, George L.
Margoliash, Emanuel
Marrs, Barry Lee
Marsh, Max Martin
Marx, Kenneth Allan
Masker, Warren Edward
Matheson, Alastair Taylor
Matthews, Brian Wesley
Matthysse, Ann Gale
McCandliss, Russell John
McCorkle, George Maston
McKelvy, Jeffrey Forrester
Meehan, Thomas
Messing, Joachim W.
Meyerowitz, Elliot Martin
Modak, Mukund Janardan
Model, Peter
Motzkin, Shirley Mittman
Nayak, Debi Prosad
Neidhardt, Frederick Carl
Nomura, Masayasu
Novick, Richard Paul
Novotny, Jiri
Ochoa, Severo
Oeltmann, Thomas Napier
Ohi, Seigo
Oiler, Larry Wayne
Pabo, Carl Ogren
Pardue, Mary Lou
Pearson, Mark Landell

Pestka, Sidney
Polatnick, Jerome
Potel, Michael John
Price, Carl Arthur
Procunier, James Douglas
Ptashne, Mark Stephen
Reed, Lester James
Reed, Steven Gregory
Reynafarje, Baltazar Davila
Robakis, Nikolaos Konstantinou
Roberts, Richard John
Rosenkranz, Herbert S.
Rownd, Robert Harvey
Rubin, Gerald M.
Sabol, Steven Layne
Salzman, Steven Kerry
Samuel, Charles E.
Sancar, Aziz
Santos, Eugenio Miguel
Sarkar, Nurul Haque
Schaechter, Moselio
Schuster, Todd Mervyn
Sehgal, Pravinkumar Bhagatram
Serwer, Philip
Shatkin, Aaron Jeffrey
Sherman, Fred
Sherman, Louis Allen
Shine, John
Shinnick, Thomas Michael
Silverstein, Emanuel
Singer, Maxine Frank
Sinsheimer, Robert Louis
Smith, Cassandra L.
Smith, Emil L.
Smith, Gerald Ralph
Spradling, Allan C.
Spremulli, Linda Lucy
Stahl, Franklin William
Steely, H(enry) Thomas, Jr.
Steitz, Joan Argetsinger
Stent, Gunther Siegmund
Strauss, Bernard S.
Sukow, Wayne William
Tobin, Allan Joshua
Tonegawa, Susumu
Torriani, Annamaria Gorini
Verma, Desh Pal Singh
Vold, Barbara Schneider
Volsky, David Julian
von Hippel, Peter Hans
Vovis, Gerald Francis
Walker, James Roy
Wallace, Douglas Cecil
Walters, Ronald Arlen
Waters, David John
Watson, James Dewey
Webster, George Calvin
Wechsler, James Alan
Weinberg, Robert Allen
Weinstein, I. Bernard
Weissbach, Herbert
Wiberg, John Samuel
Wigler, Michael
Williams, Gordon Lee
Winicov, Ilga Butelis
Woodbury, Charles Putnam, Jr.
Wosnick, Michael Alan
Yanofsky, Charles
Yielding, K. Lemone
Zahler, Stanley Arnold
Zuccarelli, Anthony Joseph
Zyskind, Judith Weaver

Morphology
Adler, Irving
Archibald, Patricia A.
Bock, Walter J(oseph)
Byrne, John Maxwell
Clark, George Alfred, Jr.
Commisso, Franklyn W.
Daily, Fay Kenoyer
Doyle, William Thomas
Emino, Everett Raymond
Gans, Carl
Gensel, Patricia Gabbey
Ghoshal, Nani Gopal
Griffiths, Thomas Alan
Hickey, Leo Joseph
Johnson, John Edlin, Jr.
Koutnik, Daryl Lee
Lim, David Jong Jai
McConnell, Dennis Brooks
McHenry, Henry Malcolm
Morey, Elsie D.
Naples, Virginia L.
Olive, Lindsay Shepherd
Rembert, David Hopkins, Jr.
Rennels, Marshall Leigh
Rogers, Donald Philip
Schwartz, Ilsa Roslow
Varkey, Alexander
White, Richard Alan

Neurobiology
Abercrombie, Ronald Ford
Agrawal, Harish Chandra
Aitken, Peter Gil
Allen, Theresa Ohotnicky
Andrew, Clifford George
Aprison, Morris Herman
Asanuma, Hiroshi
Barald, Katharine Francesca
Beach, Robert Leigh
Beck, Mary McLean
Beitz, Alvin James
Bekoff, Anne C.
Berger, Theodore William
Bernstein, Jerald J(ack)
Bishop, Beverly P(etterson)
Bizzi, Emilio
Bloom, Floyd Elliott
Bodian, David
Bohn, Martha D.
Boulton, Alan Arthur
Bower, James Mason
Bradley, Ronald James
Breedlove, Stephen Marc
Broadwell, Richard Dow
Brown, Paul Burton
Burgess, Joseph Wesley, Jr.
Busis, Neil Amdur
Campbell, Carlos Boyd Godfrey
Caspary, Donald Michel
Castellucci, Vincent Francois
Caviness, Verne Strudwick, Jr.
Chamberlain, Steven Craig
Chang, Kwen-Jen
Cheng, Mei-Fang Hsieh
Church, Allen Charles
Cohen, David Harris
Coleman, Paul D.
Corey, David Paul
Cowan, William Maxwell
Crain, Barbara Jean
Crick, Francis Harry Compton
Dafny, Nachum Frenkel
Davis, Leonard George
de Lanerolle, Nihal Chandra
de la Torre, Jack Carlos
Demeter, Steven
De Vries, George Henry
Dibner, Mark Douglas
Dubin, Mark William
Dubois Dalcq, Monique Elizabeth
Dusenbery, David Brock
Earle, Alvin Mathews
Easter, Stephen Sherman, Jr.
Eckert, Roger Otto
Egger, Maurice David
Ehrenpreis, Seymour
Erlanger, Bernard Ferdinand
Etgen, Anne Marie
Faber, Donald Stuart
Finch, Caleb Ellicott
Fite, Katherine Virginia
Flexner, Louis Barkhouse
Flood, Dorothy Garnett
Forman, David Sholem
Friedhoff, Arnold
Friesen, Wolfgang Otto
Furshpan, Edwin Jean
Gershon, Michael David
Ghetti, Bernardino
Gilmore, Shirley Ann
Glaser, Donald A(rthur)
Goldberg, Alan Marvin
Goldin, Stanley Michael
Grobstein, Paul
Haigler, Henry James
Hamill, Robert Wallace
Hernandez, Daniel E.
Herrup, Karl
Ho, Raymond How-Chee
Horwitz, Alan F.
Hyson, Michael Terry
Jen, Philip Hung Sun
Johnson, Anne Bradstreet
Kaczmarek, Leonard Konrad
Kafka, Marian Adele Stern
Kandel, Eric Richard
Kennedy, Linda Mann
Khachaturian, Henry
Kimelberg, Harold Keith
Kornguth, Steven Edward
Korr, Irvin Morris
Krause, James Edward
Krebs, Helmut Waldemar Graf von Thorn
Kvist, Tage Nielsen
Lake, David Allen
Leibovic, K. Nicholas
Levitan, Herbert
Levy, Nelson Louis
Lewis, Edwin Reynolds
Lewis, James Alexander
Light, Alan Ray
Liu, Hsiang Mei
Loewenstein, Werner Randolph
Loh, Yoke Peng
Luckenbill-Edds, Louise
Lynch, Robert Emmett, Jr.
Malmgren, Leslie Theodore, Jr.
Mann, Michael David
Masland, Richard Harry
McBride, William Joseph, Jr.
McGinty, Jacqueline Frances
McKelvy, Jeffrey Forrester
McLoon, Linda Kirschen
McNamara, James O'Connell
McNeill, Thomas Hugh
Mellin, Theodore Nelson
Mendelson, Thea
Messing, Rita Bailey
Monjan, Andrew Arthur
Moore, Robert Yates
Morest, Donald Kent
Mountcastle, Vernon Benjamin, Jr.
Neary, Joseph Thomas
Newman, John Dennis
Nicklas, William John
Ochs, Sidney
Olsen, Kathie Lynn
Park, Dong Hwa
Pearlman, Alan Lee
Perlow, Mark Jacob
Pfenninger, Karl Hans
Pitts, Nathaniel Gilbert
Provine, Robert Raymond
Purpura, Dominick Paul
Rennels, Marshall Leigh
Reppert, Steven Marion
Ribak, Charles Eric
Rockland, Kathleen Skiba
Román, Gustavo Campos
Rotter, Andrej
Ruggero, Mario Alfredo
Salcman, Michael
Salzberg, Brian Matthew
Saneto, Russell Patrick
Schneider, Richard Joel
Schwartz, Ilsa Roslow
Sheffield, Joel B.
Sherman, S. Murray
Shinowara, Nancy Lee
Shucard, David William
Silberberg, Donald H.
Spencer, Robert Frederick
Sprague, James Mather
Stach, Robert William
Stefano, George B.
Stent, Gunther Siegmund
Stern-Tomlinson, Wendy Barbara
Streicher, Eugene
Sur, Mriganka
Suzuki, Kinuko
Swarz, Jeffrey Robert
Takahashi, Joseph S.
Thompson, Elizabeth Barnes
Tobin, Allan Joshua
Tolbert, Leslie Page
Trubatch, Janett
Tucker, Gail Susan
Tuttle, Jeremy Ballou
Tweedle, Charles David
Tytell, Michael
Ueda, Tetsufumi
Ulinski, Philip Steven
Uyeki, Edwin M.
Viveros, Osvaldo Humberto
Wainwright, Stanley Dunstan
Walsh, Patrick Robert
Wang, Howard Hao
Weinberger, Norman Malcolm
Wieland, Steven Joseph
Wiesel, Torsten Nils
Wiley, Ronald Gordon
Willows, Arthur Owen Dennis
Wilson, Victor Joseph
Woolsey, Clinton Nathan
Wu, Chun-Fang
Wyss, James Michael
Yazulla, Stephen
Zaratzian, Virginia Louise
Zhou, Feng-Chiao

Neurobiology, comparative
Adams, David Bachrach
Alley, Keith Edward
Dallos, Peter
De Blas, Angel Luis
Fite, Katherine Virginia
Greenberg, Neil
Griffin, Donald R(edfield)
Heisey, S. Richard
Jennings, Kent Richard
Kennedy, Michael Craig
Kicliter, Ernest Earl, Jr.
Koestner, Adalbert
Mann, Michael David
Martin, George Franklin
Partridge, Brian Lloyd
Price, David Alan
Root, Thomas Michael
Salmoiraghi, Gian Carlo
Scharrer, Berta Vogel
Sharma, Sansar C.
Tsin, Andrew Tsang Cheung
Ulinski, Philip Steven
Wyman, Robert J.
Young, Wei

Nutrition
Anderson, Jay Oscar
Aurand, Leonard William
Buskirk, Elsworth Robert
Caldwell, Elwood Fleming
Calloway, Doris Howes
Chen, Tung-Shan
Crnic, Linda Sue Smith
Del Valle, Francisco Rafael
Dreizen, Samuel
Giannetta, Carl Lee
Harrell, Ruth Flinn
Hegsted, David Mark
Iacono, James M.
King, James Roger
Kirk, James Robert
Koldovsky, Otakar
Kritchevsky, David
Labuza, Theodore Peter
Litov, Richard Emil
Machlin, Lawrence Judah
Mertz, Walter
Mitchell, George Ernest, Jr.
Moore, Jerry Lamar
Munro, Hamish Nisbet
Passwater, Richard Albert
Rebello, Tessio Estevam
Reber, Elwood F.
Robinson, James Lawrence
Rogers, Quinton Ray
Romney, Seymour Leonard
Rotruck, John Truman
Ruberg, Robert Lionel
Rusoff, Irving I(sadore)
Shamberger, Raymond Joseph, Jr.
Smith, Leonard Charles
Sunde, Milton L.
Tumbleson, M.E.
Wallace, Garn Arthur
Watson, Ronald Ross
Young, Franklin
Young, Jerry Wesley
Zee, Paulus

Parasitology. *See* **MEDICINE.**

Photosynthesis
Bowes, George Ernest
Dilley, Richard A.
Duke, Stephen Oscar
French, Charles Stacy
Greenbaum, Elias
Hatzios, Kriton Kleanthis
Henderson, Robert Edward
Homann, Peter Hinrich Fritz
Izawa, Seikichi
Jensen, Richard Grant
Lawrence, William Thomas, Jr.
Mooney, Harold Alfred
Newman, David William
Prange, Robert Keith
Sherman, Louis Allen
Spreitzer, Robert Joseph
Steinback, Katherine Ellen

Physiology. *See also* **MEDICINE.**
Albers, Henry Elliott
Anderson, Donald Keith
Beard, Elizabeth Letitia
Berne, Robert Matthew
Bishop, Beverly P(etterson)
Brenner, Barry Morton
Brown, Paul Burton
Burke, Robert Emmett
Buskirk, Elsworth Robert
Butler, James Preston
Carson, Virginia Rosalie Gottschall
Chowdhury, Parimal
Corradino, Robert A.
Davis, James (Othello)
Diamond, Jared Mason
DuBois, Arthur Brooks
Dunham, Philip Bigelow
Fabiato, Alexandre
Francis, Kennon Thompson
Fray, John Cordell Spencer
Harris, Thomas R.
Hartter, Daryl Edward
Heistad, Donald Dean
Heller, Lois Jane
Hoffman, Eric Alfred
Intaglietta, Marcos
Jankelson, Bernard
Karagueuzian, Hrayr Sevag
Katz, Ann Harris
Kelsen, Steven Gus
Kerr, Janet Spence
Koldovsky, Otakar
Korr, Irvin Morris
La Barbera, Andrew Richard
La Farge, Christopher Grant C.
Lee, Chung
Levinsky, Norman George
Lieber, Richard Louis
Liebovitch, Larry S.
Maack, Thomas Michael
Mason, Charles Perry
Masoro, Edward Joseph
McAllister, Chris Thomas
McMahon, Robert Francis
Metcalf, John Franklin
Michelson, Eric Lee
Moore, Earl Neil
Moore-Ede, Martin Christopher
Oatley, David Herbert
Ohata, Carl Andrews
Oyama, Jiro
Pace, Nello
Petrofsky, Jerrold Scott
Phillips, Richard Dean
Previte, Joseph James
Quintanilha, Alexandre Tiedtke
Reid, Michael Baron
Roberts, Michael Foster
Roelofs, Wendell Lee
Rosen, Martin Howard
Russell-Hunter, W(illiam) D(evigne)
Samaras, George Michael
Scherlag, Benjamin Jacob
Schloerb, Paul Richard
Sillman, Arnold Joel
Simmons, William Howard
Smolensky, Michael Hale
Snyder, Ann Catherine
Sokoloff, Louis
Spaet, Theodore Herzl
Taylor, Charles Richard
Tenney, Stephen Marsh
Tobe, Stephen Solomon
Tsin, Andrew Tsang Cheung
Waitzman, Morton Benjamin
Walgenbach-Telford, Susan Carol
Wasserman, Martin Allan
White, Timothy Peter
Whitten, Bertwell Kneeland
Wilber, Charles Grady
Wilson, Victor Joseph
Woods, Walter Thomas, Jr.
Zweifach, Benjamin William

Physiology, comparative
Baust, John G.
Bito, Laszlo Z.
Burggren, Warren William
Caire, William
Carey, Cynthia
Chou, Shyan-Yih
Donovan, John Charles
Ewald, Bruce Harold
Gootman, Phyllis Myrna
Gur, David
Hainsworth, F. Reed
Harmon, John Watson
Huey, Raymond Brunson
King, James Roger
Malanga, Carl Joseph
Moon, Thomas William
Nagy, Kenneth A.
Parrish, John Wesley, Jr.
Rahn, Hermann
Schmidt-Nielsen, Knut
Schneider, Richard Joel
Umminger, Bruce Lynn
Venkataramiah, Amaraneni
Zapol, Warren Myron

Plant growth
Bennett, William F., Sr.
Coate, Barrie Douglas
Forshey, Chester Gene
Funt, Richard Clair
Green, Paul Barnett
Greene, Duane Wesley
Grunes, David Leon
Hensel, Dale Robert
Larson, Philip Rodney
Ledbetter, Myron Calvert
Maravolo, Nicholas C.
Marx, Donald Henry
McConnell, Dennis Brooks
Miller, Carlos Oakley
Minore, Don
Ohki, Kenneth
Phinney, Bernard Orrin
Postlethwait, Samuel Noel
Rost, Thomas Lowell
Ruddat, Manfred
Salters, Grace Heyward
Schwartzkopf, Steven Henry
Seago, James Lynn, Jr.
Serwer, Philip
Smith, Thomas Lloyd
Spiess, Luretta D(avis)
Strader, Herman Lee
Thomas, Robert James
Walker, Dan Berne

Plant physiology. *See also* **AGRICULTURE.**
Alves, Leo Manuel
Bennett, Jesse Harland
Blinks, Lawrence Rogers
Briggs, Winslow Russell
Doyle, William Thomas
Drew, Allan Pierce
Duke, Stephen Oscar
Einhellig, Frank Arnold
Francko, David Alex
Frear, Donald Stuart
Gentile, Arthur Christopher
Gibbs, Martin
Goodin, Joe Ray
Gregory, Garold Fay
Hill, Ray Allen
Hirsch, Ann Mary
Hunt, Earle Raymond, Jr.
Jensen, William August
Kaufman, Peter Bishop
Kennedy, Robert Alan
Lippincott, James Andrew
Lockhart, James Arthur
Lucas, William John
Lunt, Owen Raynal
McClendon, John Haddaway
McNulty, Irving Bazil
Miller, Carlos Oakley
Myers, Jack Edgar
Nobel, Park S.
Oechel, Walter Clarence
Pattee, Harold Edward
Price, Carl Arthur
Prien, Samuel David
Reazin, George Harvey, Jr.
Ruddat, Manfred
Ruesink, Albert William
Scheffer, Robert Paul
Snyder, Freeman Woodrow
Staples, Richard Cromwell
Stowe, Bruce Bernot
Thomas, Robert James
Tolbert, Nathan Edward
Weber, James Alan
Wittwer, Sylvan Harold
Yamaguchi, Shogo

Population biology
Aarssen, Lonnie William
Abrahamson, Warren Gene, II
Anderson, Stanley Helmer
Archer, Steven Ronald
Berry, James Frederick
Best, Troy Lee
Brynjolfsson, Ari
Christian, John Jermyn
Clay, Keith Andrew
Dahlsten, Donald Lee
Ehrlich, Paul Ralph
Ellstrand, Norman Carl
Fairbairn, Daphne Janice
Grant, Verne Edwin
Kinney, Terry B., Jr.
Kozloff, Lloyd M.
Lieberman, Diana Dale
Little, Terry William
Lockhart, James Arthur
Lutz, Paul Eugene
Mack, Richart Norton
Martin, Bradford Douglas
Matzinger, Dale Frederick
Namkoong, Gene
Nichols, James Dale
Pfahler, Paul Leighton
Pianka, Eric Rodger
Pitelka, Louis Frank
Pollard, Arthur Joseph, II
Quinn, James Amos, Jr.
Rabinowitz, Deborah
Robel, Robert Joseph
Ropes, John Warren
Schemnitz, Sanford David
Schowalter, Timothy Duane
Sedinger, James Stone
Shan, Robert Kuocheng
Smith, Eric Peter
Snell, Terry Wayne
Springer, Joseph Tucker
Tamarin, Robert Harvey
Turkington, Robert (Roy) Albert
White, Robert George
Yokoyama, Shozo

Psychobiology. *See* **PSYCHOLOGY.**

Radiation biology
Bockstahler, Larry Earl
Cockerham, Lorris G.
Cronkite, Eugene Pitcher
Dicello, John Francis, Jr.
Donnellan, James Edward, Jr.
Failla, Patricia McClement
Fornace, Albert Joseph, Jr.
Glicksman, Arvin Sigmund
Greenstock, Clive Lewis
Hickey, Richard James
Kimler, Bruce Franklin
Luckinbill, Leo Stephen
Miller, Morton W(illiam)
Musacchia, X. J.
Powers, Edward Lawrence
Stannard, James Newell
Wald, Niel
Weller, Richard Eldon
Zach, Reto

Reproductive biology
Baker, Irene
Benseler, Rolf Wilhelm
Buss, Edward George
Chung, Melvin Chung-Hing
Coleman, Marilyn Ruth Adams
Davis, Brian Keith
Dickerman, Herbert W
Edgren, Richard Arthur
Evans, James Warren
Fabricant, Jill Diane
Fahim, Mostafa Safwat
Ford, Stephen Paul
Garrett, Gary Pace
Harper, Michael John Kennedy
Hawk, Harold William
Herr, John Mervin, Jr.
Hoar, Richard Morgan
Kalra, Satya Paul
Krapu, Gary Lee
Lerner, Leonard Joseph
Leto, Salvatore
Little, Robert John, Jr.
Lu, John Kuew-Hsiung
McClure, Michael Edward
Menino, Alfred Rodrigues, Jr.
Parrish, John Wesley, Jr.
Phemister, Robert David
Pieper, David Robert
Pineda, Mauricio Hernan
Reel, Jerry Royce
Robbins, Robert Raymond
Sanderson, Glen Charles
Szabo, Kalman Tibor
Tobe, Stephen Solomon
Turner, Terry Tomo
Wagner, William Charles

Sociobiology
Haubrich, Robert Rice
Howard, Lauren Davis
Kaufmann, John Henry
Kistner, David Harold
Michener, Charles Duncan
Michod, Richard Earl
Morrison, Douglas Wildes
Wilson, Edward Osborne

Species interaction
Aarssen, Lonnie William
Andersen, Douglas Craig
Berkland, James Omer
Cates, Rex Gordon
Garrett, Gary Pace
Hamon, Danny Joe
Hibbs, David Edgemon
Layne, James Nathaniel
Meinwald, Jerrold
Moll, Don L.
Ordway, Ellen
Robbins, Chandler Seymour
Siddiqi, Shaukat Mahmood

Systematics
Anderson, Gregory Joseph
Archibald, James David
Best, Troy Lee
Carpenter, James Michael
Caruso, John Howard
Chambers, Kenton Lee
Choate, Jerry Ronald
Fairbanks, H. Lee
Flagg, Raymond Osbourn
Fox, George Edward
Funk, Vicki Ann
Genoways, Hugh Howard
George, Sarah Brewster
Hafner, John Christopher
Henrickson, James Solberg
Herr, John Mervin, Jr.
Hershkovitz, Philip
Highton, Richard Taylor
Jackson, Raymond Carl
Jones, Claris Eugene, Jr.
Keeley, Sterling Carter
Kirtley, David Warren
Kohn, Alan Jacobs
Koutnik, Daryl Lee
Levin, Michael Howard
Littler, Mark Masterton
Michener, Charles Duncan
Munroe, Eugene Gordon
Novak, John Allen
Opler, Paul Alexander
Phillips, Raymond Bruce
Prothero, Donald Ross
Radford, Albert Ernest
Raven, Peter Hamilton
Rollins, Reed Clark
Rozen, Jerome George, Jr.
Savage, Jay Mathers
Schaeffer, Robert L., Jr.
Schultes, Richard Evans
Severinghaus, William Daniel
Sheffer, Richard Douglas
Shetler, Stanwyn Gerald
Smith, Albert Charles
Spencer, Lorraine Barney
Steiner, William Wallace Mokahi
Stoermer, Eugene Filmore
Stuessy, Tod Falor
Turner, Bruce Jay
Varkey, Alexander
Woods, Charles Arthur

Taxonomy
Balick, Michael Jeffrey
Baranov, Andrey I(ppolitovich)
Bazinet, Lester
Carpenter, James Michael
Curry, Mary Grace
Daily, Fay Kenoyer
Dehgan, Bijan
deLaubenfels, David John
Dorsey, John Henry
Eleuterius, Lionel Numa
Fairbanks, H. Lee
Fryxell, Paul Arnold
Genoways, Hugh Howard
George, Sarah Brewster
Gibbs, Robert Henry, Jr.
Howard, Lauren Davis
Hudson, William Donald, Jr.
Korf, Richard Paul
Lellinger, David Bruce
Little, Elbert Luther, Jr.
MacBryde, Bruce
Manley, Donald Gene
Miller, Regis Bolden
Olive, Lindsay Shepherd
Parker, Frank(lin) Downs
Phillips, Raymond Bruce
Radford, Albert Ernest
Rogers, Donald Philip
Sailer, Reece Ivan
Salamun, Peter J(oseph)
Schaeffer, Robert L., Jr.
Schultes, Richard Evans
Sharp, Aaron John
Siddiqi, Shaukat Mahmood
Sipple, William Stanton
Smith, Clifford Winston
Spencer, Lorraine Barney
Williams, Norris Hagan
Young, Frank N(elson), Jr.

Tissue culture
Behbehani, Abbas M.
Biemer, Thomas Anthony
Cleveland, William Louis
Goodin, Joe Ray
Noga, Edward Joseph
Oberley, Terry De Wayne
Weiss, Stefan Adam

Virology. See also MEDICINE.
Anderson, Carl William
Ball, Laurence Andrew
Basilico, Claudio
Bean, William Joseph, Jr.
Biswal, Nilambar
Bond, Clifford Walter
Campbell, Allan McCulloch
Carter, Timothy Howard
Cerini, Costantino Peter

Choppin, Purnell Whittington
Docherty, John Joseph
Dougherty, Robert Malvin
Dubes, George Richard
Dubois Dalcq, Monique Elizabeth
Duff, James Thomas
Duff, Ronald George
Dutko, Francis Joseph, Jr.
Ehrenfeld, Elvera
Engelking, Henry Mark
Eppstein, Deborah Anne
Field, Arthur Kirk
Flanegan, James Bert
Founds, Henry William, Jr.
Fuccillo, David Anthony
Gale, Charles
Garfinkle, Barry David
Garon, Claude Francis
Geiduschek, E(rnest) Peter
Ginsberg, Harold Samuel
Goodheart, Clyde Raymond
Grubman, Marvin
Haselkorn, Robert
Hillis, William Daniel, Sr.
Hsiung, Gueh-Djen
Johnson, F. Brent
Kasel, Julius Albert
Koprowski, Hilary
Kozloff, Lloyd M.
Kramarsky, Bernhard
Leamnson, Robert Neal
Lewis, Andrew Morris, Jr.
Maniloff, Jack
Martignoni, Mauro Emilio
Melnick, Joseph L.
Miller, Lois Kathryn
Morris, J(oseph) Anthony
Nayak, Debi Prosad
Ozer, Harvey Leon
Person, Donald Ames
Polatnick, Jerome
Potash, Louis
Price, Alan Roger
Quinnan, Gerald Vincent
Rapp, Ulf Ruediger
Roane, Philip Ransom, Jr.
Samuel, Charles E.
Schooley, Robert Turner
Schwabel, Mary Jane
Sidwell, Robert William
Singh, Shiva Pujan
Stanton, Glennon John
Tamm, Igor
Taylor, Bernard Franklin
Thomas, Donald Charles
Thormar, Halldor
Trowbridge, Richard Stuart
Tzianabos, Theodore
Varmus, Harold Eliot
Waters, David John
Weiss, Stefan Adam
Wiberg, John Samuel
Yoon, Ji-Won

Other
Albers, Peter Heinz, *Wildlife management*
Alderson, Louis Everett
Amirkhanian, John David, *Mutagenesis*
Archibald, Patricia A., *Phycology (Algology)*
Arnold, Dean Edward
Balick, Michael Jeffrey, *Economic botany*
Bandurski, Bruce Lord, *Transdisciplinary ecomanagement*
Bane, Gilbert Winfield, Jr., *Fishery biology*
Baranov, Andrey I(ppolitovich), *Ethnobotany*
Benfield, Ernest Frederick, *Stream ecology*
Benson, Andrew Alm, *Marine metabolism*
Biber, Michael Peter, *Sleep disorders*
Briggs, Winslow Russell, *Photobiology*
Bundy, Hallie Flowers, *Enzymology*
Butcher, James Walter, *Entomology*
Carey, Cynthia
Caspar, Donald Louis Dvorak
Challinor, David, *Administration*
Chovnick, Arthur, *Intragenic recombination*
Collins, Margaret Strickland, *Entomology*
Cranefield, Paul Frederic, *Electrophysiology*
Delevoryas, Theodore, *Botany*
Dickerson, Richard Earl, *Molecular evolution*
Elwell, Lynn Paul, *Recombinant DNA technology*
Emmons, Louise Hickok, *Tropical ecology*
Folsome, Clair Edwin, *Closed system ecology*
Fritts, Harold Clark, *Dendroclimatology*
Garland, Bernard William
Gerking, Shelby Delos
Gifford, Ernest Milton, Jr., *Plant anatomy*
Golub, Ellis Eckstein, *Biochemical computing*
Guthrie, Frank Edwin, *Entomology*
Halstead, Bruce Walter, *Biotoxicology*
Harshbarger, John Carl, Jr., *Pathobiology*
Hickey, Joseph James
Hudecki, Michael Stephen, *Muscle pathology*
Hutchison, Jay Bryson, Jr., *Fishery biology*
James, Frances Crews, *Ornithology*
Jensh, Ronald Paul, *Teratology*
Kashket, Eva Ruth
Kaufman, Leo, *Medical mycology*
Korf, Richard Paul, *Mycology*
Kurtzman, Ralph Harold, Jr., *Mycology*
La Claire, John Willard, II, *Marine phycology*
Laudenslayer, William Franklin, Jr., *Wildlife management*
Lestrel, Pete Ernest, *Morphometrics*
Little, Robert John, Jr., *Botany*
Masoro, Edward Joseph
Matin, Abdul, *Microbial physiology*
Maxson, Linda Ellen, *Molecular systematics*

McAllister, Chris Thomas, *Herpetology*
McMahon, Robert Francis
Mech, Lucyan David, *Wildlife biology*
Michaeli, Dov
Misra, Hara Prasad, *Free radical biology*
Mittler, Sidney, *Radiation biology*
Myhre, Byron Arnold
Parker, Frank(lin) Downs
Plonsey, Robert, *Cardiac electrophysiology*
Powell, Thomas Edward, III, *Biological supplies company management*
Ragotzkie, Robert Austin, *Aquatic ecology*
Rembert, David Hopkins, Jr., *Botanical history*
Revelle, Roger Randall Dougan
Salmoiraghi, Gian Carlo, *Research management*
Sanderson, Glen Charles, *Wildlife biology*
Schemnitz, Sanford David
Schmid-Schoenbein, Geert Wilifried
Schonewald-Cox, Christine Micheline, *Conservation biology*
Snyder, Ann Catherine
Snyder, Arnold Peter, *Analytical microbiology*
Spitsberg, Vitaly Lev, *Biochemical evolution*
Starr, Richard Cawthon
Stickney, Robert Roy
Stobo, Wayne Thomas, *Fishery biology*
Strain, Boyd Ray, *Botany*
Tempel, Ann, *Opiate receptor regulation*
Udvardy, Miklos Dezso Ferenc
Vadas, Robert Louis, *Phycology*
Vagelos, Pindaros Roy, *Biomedical research management*
Vuilleumier, Francois, *Biogeography*
Wagner, Warren Herbert, *Botany*
Watt, Doris Jane, *Ornithology*
Weathersby, A(ugustus) Burns, *Entomology*
White, Timothy Peter
Williams, Carroll Milton
Windels, Carol Elizabeth, *Biological control*
Zeppetella, Anthony John, *Mathematical biology*
Zuzolo, Ralph Carmine

BIOTECHNOLOGY

Artificial organs and prostheses. See also MEDICINE, Surgery.
Aberman, Harold Mark
Ackerman, Roy Alan
Chandran, Krishnan B.
Chang, Thomas Ming Swi
Cheng, Kevin K. T.
Daniel, Michael Andrew
de Luque, Orlando Rafael
DeVore, Dale Paul
Eckstein, Eugene Charles
Eyerly, Robert Michael
Galletti, Pierre Marie
Jacobsen, Stephen Charles
Jaron, Dov
Kraus, Menahem Alfred
Love, Jerry Thorton
Miller, Irving Franklin
Patel, Anil S.
Pierce, William Schuler
Price, Howard Charles
Ulrich, Robert David
Watson, John Thomas
Zingg, Walter

Bioinstrumentation
Ahnell, Joseph Eugene
Alexander, Nelson Eugene
Bakuzonis, Craig William
Bradley, A. Freeman, Jr.
Brown, Charles Eric
Caruolo, Edward Vitangelo
Chait, Edward Martin
Chang, Wei
Chilcoat, Robert Talmadge
Combs, Claud Steve
David, Yadin
Del Guercio, Louis Richard Maurice
Ellis, Donald Griffith
Fernández, Salvador M.
Fidel, Howard
Friesen, Wolfgang Otto
Gallant, Nanette
Guvenis, Albert
Jaszczak, Ronald Jack
King-Smith, Eric Alfred
Knoll, Glenn Frederick
Lai, Por-Hsiung
Leif, Robert Cary
Lieber, Richard Louis
Mummert, Thomas Allen
Patti, Robert Dale
Pykett, Ian Lewis
Royds, Robert B.
Rugh, John Douglas
Schultz, Jerome Samson
Shamos, Morris Herbert
Shapiro, Howard Maurice
Walker, Cedric Frank
Wang, Carl Chang-Tao
York, John Louis, Jr.
Zimmerman, John Thomas

Biomaterials. See MATERIALS SCIENCE.

Biomedical engineering. See also ENGINEERING.
Ackerman, Michael Jan
Altschuler, Martin David
Anderson, Thomas Edward
Attinger, Ernst Otto
Babb, Albert Leslie
Bak, Martin Joseph
Bakuzonis, Craig William
Becker, Robert Otto
Bischoff, Kenneth Bruce
Boston, John Robert
Bradley, A. Freeman, Jr.
Buchwald, Henry
Carstensen, Edwin Lorenz
Cetas, Thomas Charles
Chandran, Krishnan B.

Chen, Ching-Nien
Cox, Jerome Rockhold, Jr.
Daley, Michael Leo
Daniel, Alex Van
DiBianca, Frank Anthony
Drzewiecki, Gary Michael
Eberhart, Robert Clyde
Findl, Eugene
Fine, Samuel
Finney, Roy Pelham
Fischell, Robert Ellentuch
Garfinkel, David
Glantz, Stanton Arnold
Gold, Michael Nathan
Gradijan, Jack Robertson
Greer, James Alan
Harris, Thomas R.
Heimer, Malcolm Lee
Hovnanian, H. Philip
Humphrey, Arthur Earl
Huntsman, Lee L.
Jain, Rakesh Kumar
Jarisch, Wolfram Rudolf
Jarvik, Robert K.
Jenkins, James Thomas
Johnson, Patrick Woodruff
Knowles, Lloyd George
Krag, Martin Hans
Kydd, George Herman
Laing, Ronald Albert
Latham, Allen, Jr.
Lee, George C.
Lee, Wylie In-Wei
Leifer, Larry
Levin, Stephen Michael
Lewis, Edwin Reynolds
Lichtenberg, Byron K.
Liebig, William John
Lin, Heh-Sen
Love, Jerry Thorton
Lyman, John
Mow, Van C.
Mulcihy, Casey Thomas
Murdock, Wilbert Quinc
Murphy, Eugene Francis
Myers, Philip Cherdak
Nelson, Alan Caril
Newman, Arnold Lewis
Nobel, Joel J.
Nunan, Craig Spencer
Ollapally, Philip Joseph
Oman, Charles McMaster
Opel, William
Page, Michael Gerald
Papahadjopoulos, Demetrios P.
Patel, Anil S.
Petrofsky, Jerrold Scott
Saha, Subrata
Sandhu, Taljit Singh
Schmid-Schoenbein, Geert Wilifried
Schwan, Herman Paul
Severns, Matthew Lincoln
Sherif, Mostafa Hashem
Spector, Andrew Lawrence
Suydam, Peter R.
Tackel, Ira Stuart
Tang, John Chu-Tay
Tsitlik, Joshua E.
Vogelman, Joseph Herbert
Von Gierke, Henning Edgar
Walker, Cedric Frank
Wang, Carl Chang-Tao
Weed, Herman Roscoe
Wilder, David Gould
Wu, Hai-Ping
Yarmush, Martin Leon
Young, Laurence Retman

Enzyme technology
Ackerman, Roy Alan
Baldwin, Thomas Oakley
Bassi, Sukh Dev
Bollon, Arthur Peter
Cannon, John Joseph
Chang, Thomas Ming Swi
Chase, John William
Cheryan, Munir
Chuang, Ronald Y(an-li)
Copeland, James Clinton
DeFrank, Joseph John
Evans, Harold J.
Gum, Ernest Kemp, Jr.
Gunner, Haim Bernard
Han, Youn Woo
Hanson, Richard Steven
Hirasuna, Thomas Jyun
Huang, Hsing T.
Jones, Mary Ellen
Kempe, Lloyd Lute
Klibanov, Alexander Maxim
Koshland, Daniel Edward, Jr.
Kuan, Shia Shiong
Kupper, Robert Joe
Ladisch, Michael R.
Loftfield, Robert Bernard
Mateles, Richard Isaac
Moskowitz, Gerard J.
Murray, Allen Ketcik
Ng, Thomas K.
Ortiz-Suarez, Humberto Jose
Pettit, Flora Hunter
Quinn, John Albert
Raman, Jay
Reilly, Peter John
Roberts, Joseph
Royer, Garfield Paul
Scandella, Carl John
Schultz, Jerome Samson
Sebek, Oldrich Karel
Shemin, David
Subramanian, Sethuraman
Tarnowski, Stanley Joseph, Jr.
Wang, Ching-Tso
Wang, Dalton Ta Tung
Weetall, Howard Hayyim
Wilke, Charles Robert
Wu, Po-shun

Genetics and genetic engineering. See BIOLOGY, MEDICINE.

Imaging technology, CAT scan
Brundage, Bruce Howard
George, Ajax Elis
Lim, Chun Bin
Naeser, Margaret Ann
Pollack, R. Stuart

Prior, Fred William
Vitola, Jack Joseph

Imaging technology, magnetic resonance imaging. See also CHEMISTRY, Nuclear magnetic resonance.
Aull, John Louis
Bradley, William Guerin, Jr.
Chance, Britton
Haacke, Ewart Mark
Lasker, Leslie
Markley, John Lute
Nelson, Alan Caril
Pykett, Ian Lewis
Raudkivi, Uno
Rocca, Jeffrey John
Schenck, John F.
Schultz, Sheldon
Werbelow, Lawrence Glen

Imaging technology, mass spectrometry
Djerassi, Carl
Green, Donald Eugene
Korfmacher, Walter Averill
Noonan, James Stephen

Imaging technology, PET scan
Bennett, Gerald William
Brownell, Gordon Lee
Farukhi, Mohammad Rahimullah
Gur, Ruben C.
Guvenis, Albert
Lim, Chun Bin
Mullani, Nizar Abdul

Ultrasound
Beigel, Michael Lee
Bond, Meredith Gene
Ensminger, Dale
Fidel, Howard
Huntsman, Lee L.
Powers, Jeffry Earl
Rosenberg, Eric Ronald
Sabbagha, Rudy E.
Taenzer, Jon Charles

Other
Bader, Fredric George
Baust, John G.
Bone, Donald Robert, *Hybridoma technology*
Busby, John Carroll, *Biotechnology administration*
Chilton, Mary-Dell, *Biotechnology research and development*
Datta, Rathin, *Fermentation technology*
David, Gary Samuel, *Hybridoma technology*
Dean, Nathan Wesley, *Biotechnology administration*
Donaldson, Terrence Lee, *Biochemical Engineering*
Esposito, Vito M., *Biotechnology research and development*
Evans, David Alan, *Biotechnology research and development*
Feder, Ralph
Fildes, Robert Anthony
Forman, J(oseph) Charles
Fox, Michael Henry
Ginsburg, Arthur Phillip, *Vision research*
Jervis, Herbert Hunter, *Biotechnology patents*
Kirkpatrick, Francis H(ubbard), Jr., *Biotechnology research and development*
Kobayashi, Hester Atsuko, *Waste and waste water treatment.*
Lamvik, Michael Kasper
McKell, Cyrus Milo
Mou, Duen-Gang
Murdock, Wilbert Quinc, *Real-time video motion analysis*
Nebert, Daniel Walter
Pass, Franklin, *Biotechnology administration*
Patwardhan, Bhalchandra Hari
Pearson, Terry William
Pitcher, Wayne Harold, Jr., *Biotechnology research and development*
Raab, G. Kirk, *Biotechnology administration*
Seiders, Barbara Ann Bornemeier
Strandberg, Gerald William, *Applied microbiology*
Yim, Kalvin Walkin
Zeikus, J. Gregory, *Biotechnology administration*

BOTANY. See BIOLOGY.

CHEMISTRY

Analytical chemistry
Abidi, Sharon Low
Abrahamson, Earl Arthur
Alkalay, David
Allan, Barry David
Anderson, Craig Jay
Annino, Raymond
Armstrong, Andrew Thurman
Baedecker, Philip Ackerman
Banerjee, Sujit
Bard, Allen Joseph
Bauman, Albert Joseph
Becker, Donald Arthur
Benson, Royal Henry
Berni, Ralph John
Bible, Roy Henderson, Jr.
Biemer, Thomas Anthony
Bietz, Jerold Allen
Blotcky, Alan Jay
Brody, Stuart Martin
Brooks, Marvin Alan
Browning, Sterling Edwin, II.
Bullock, Kevin Edward
Burke, Jerry Alan
Burrows, Elizabeth Parker
Bushaw, Thomas Henry
Caduff, Noralynn Jo
Caduto, Ralph
Caldwell, Karin Maria Elisabet

Chadwick, Robert William
Chait, Edward Martin
Chan, Kwan Ming
Chao, Mou Shu
Chen, Gloria Chao
Chesler, Stephen Norman
Cohen, Jerry David
Coleman, Walden Emile
Corsini, Alfio
Craft, Charles Douglas
Dahlgran, James Robert
Davis, Robert Edgar
Davis, Thomas Paul
Dessy, Raymond Edwin
Dickerson, Dean Stuart
Downing, Robert Gregory
Dunn, Danny LeRoy
Easton, Myriam Perdices
Edelson, Martin Charles
Elkin, Robert Glenn
Ettre, Leslie Stephen
Evans, Frederick E.
Evans, William Frederick
Fales, Henry Marshall
Fateley, William Gene
Faulkner, Larry Ray
Faust, Robert Jeffrey
Ferguson, Ronald Max
Finn, James Walter
Firestone, David
Fletcher, Aaron Nathaniel
Foreman, Fredrick
Fornshell, Randall Douglas
Freiser, Ben Sherman
Frye, Herschel Gordon
Gaarenstroom, Stephen William
Gaeke, Gottlieb Charles
Gaffney, Jeffrey Steven
Garrett, Howard Leroy
Giddings, John Calvin
Gill, Jasbir Singh
Ginzler, Edward Richard
Goldstein, Henry
Golightly, Danold Wayne
Goyal, Greesh Chand
Greco, Gary
Green, David William
Grob, Robert Lee
Guilbault, George Gerald
Haaland, David Michael
Haberman, John Phillip
Hackleman, David Eugene
Haidle, Rudy Henry
Hanson, Ray Lorain
Hass, Alan Joseph
Hass, James Ronald
Hausmann, Werner Karl
Heeschen, Jerry Parker
Henry, Norman Whitfield, III
Heydegger, H(elmut) Roland
Hill, Walter Edward, Jr.
Hinze, Willie Lee
Hirschfeld, Tomas Beno
Hobbs, John Robert
Huang, Shyhchang Strong
Hubbard, Harold Mead
Irgolic, Kurt Johann
Ito, Yoichiro
Janghorbani, Morteza
Johnson, Deadre Jeanne
Johnson, Greg Willard
Johnson, Pratt Deen
Juvet, Richard Spalding, Jr.
Kabra, Pokar Mal
Kadish, Karl Mitchell
Kalita, Chabi Chandra
Katz, Hyman Bernard
Kaykaty, Maurice
Kohl, Paul Albert
Korfmacher, Walter Averill
Krause, Richard Theodore
Krebs, Herman Allen
Krull, Ira Stanley
Kuan, Shia Shiong
Laitinen, Herbert August
Landsberg, Johanna Dobrot
Lasoski, Bernard Albert
Laub, Richard James
Law, Stephen LeRoy
Lindauer, Maurice William
Macdonald, James Ross
MacFadden, Kenneth Orville
Malbica, Joseph Orazio
Malinowski, Edmund Robert
Marcott, Curtis Allen
Margerum, Dale William
Margolis, Sam Aaron
Marvasti, Setareh Alim
Matthews, Dwight Earl
Mayer, William John
McLafferty, Fred Warren
Michaels, Adlai Eldon
Micheli, Roger Paul
Middleditch, Brian Stanley
Miller, Sidney Israel
Mosier, Benjamin
Murray, Royce Wilton
Newmark, Richard Alan
Nichiporuk, Walter
Niegisch, Walter Dietrich
Nisbet, Phillip Clark
Nogar, Nicholas Stephen
Noonan, James Stephen
Nowicki, Henry George
Obremski, Robert John
O'Donovan, Patrick Alexander
Ogden, Roger Wayne
Ohnesorge, William Edward
Okinaka, Yutaka
Page, Mary Michael
Parent, Douglas John
Parrish, Milton Earl
Parsons, Michael L.
Pease, David Nathaniel
Phillips, Sidney Leon
Pierre, Harvey Harold
Preiss, Ivor Louis
Privett, Orville Samuel
Purdy, William Crossley
Rabenstein, Dallas Leroy
Rebbert, Richard Edward
Reddy, Thomas Bradley
Riley, John Thomas
Rothbart, Herbert L.
Rousch, Patricia Marie Barry
Saalfeld, Fred Eric
Schure, Mark Richard
Scypinski, Stephen
Seeley, James Lewis
Sherren, Anne Terry
Shinn, Michael Howard
Sivertson, John Neilos
Srinivasan, Brihmadesam Narasimhan
Stahr, Henry Michael
Stewart, Kent Kallam
Stranz, David Donald
Strojny, Norman
Sutherland, James Milton
Swarin, Stephen John
Swarts, E(llywn) Lowell
Szalecki, Wojciech Josef
Tang, Lucia Chia-Lu
Thompson, James Earl
Thompson, Richard David
Tivin, Fred
Toome, Voldemar
Tou, James Chieh
Underwood, Arthur Louis, Jr.
van Til, Alan Everett
Van Valin, Charles Carroll
Varma, Asha
Walters, Douglas Bruce
Waltking, Arthur Ernest
Warner, Ray Allen
Weber, Dennis Joseph
Weeks, Stephan John
West, Philip William
White, Mitchell Ray
Whitlock, Lee Ronald
Willford, Wayne Alan
Williams, Harold Lloyd
Wohltjen, Henry, III
Woodford, Warren James
Woodrow, James Eugene
Wright, Fred Carl
Yap, William Tan
Yeung, Edward Szeshing
Yim, Kalvin Walkin
Young, Chung Chang
Zadjura, Richard Edward
Zak, Bennie
Zannucci, Joseph Salvatore

Archaeological chemistry
Harbottle, Garman
Lewis, Donald Richard
Olin, Jacqueline Smith

Biophysical chemistry
Alger, Jeffry Roy
Babu, Uma Mahesh
Benkovic, Stephen J.
Berg, Paul
Berger, Robert Lewis
Bettelheim, Frederick Abraham
Birnbaum, Edward R.
Blau, Lea
Brouwer, Marius
Caldwell, Karin Maria Elisabet
Case, George David
Castellino, Francis Joseph
Chen, Holly Ho
Cheung, Herbert Chiu-Ching
Chiang, Joseph Fei
Clementi, Enrico
Cohn, Mildred
Cooper, Alan Douglas
Day, Richard Allen
Dickerson, Richard Earl
Dickinson, Leonard Charles
Dill, Kenneth Austin
Duffy, Thomas Hyatt
Eanes, Edward David
Edsall, John Tileston
Epstein, Irving Robert
Eran, Harutyun
Ford, George D
Fried, Josef
Fu, Shou-Cheng Joseph
Gaber, Bruce Paul
Glusker, Jenny Pickworth
Goyal, Greesh Chand
Grossman, Steven Harris
Hammes, Gordon G.
Harrison, John Henry, IV
Haurowitz, Felix
Hess, George P.
Holcomb, David Nelson
Holzman, Thomas Fredric
Hou, Kenneth Chiang
Johnson, Charles Sidney, Jr.
Kasarda, Donald David
Kim, Sung-Hou
Klotz, Irving Myron
Kopple, Kenneth David
Koshland, Daniel Edward, Jr.
Kraus, Marjorie Patt
Kwiram, Alvin L.
Laskowski, Michael, Jr.
Lehninger, Albert Lester
Lerman, Sidney
Levin, Ira William
Lin, Tsung-I George
Live, David Harris
Lu, Ponzy
Madison, Vincent Stewart
Markley, John Lute
Marx, Kenneth Allan
McConnell, Harden Marsden
McLendon, George Leland
Miller, Kenneth John
Moore, Peter Bartlett
Myers, William Graydon
Na, George Chao
Nielsen, Harald Christian
O'Brien, David Frank
Ocone, Luke Ralph
Oeswein, James Quentin
Pabo, Carl Ogren
Parr, Gary Raymond
Pauling, Linus Carl
Pfeffer, Philip Elliot
Pimentel, George Claude
Polefka, Thomas Gregory
Raghavendra, Krishnamurthy
Rothfus, John Arden
Schachman, Howard Kapnek
Scheraga, Harold Abraham
Schroeder, Friedhelm
Schroeder, LeRoy William
Schurr, John Michael
Schuster, Todd Mervyn
Scovell, William Martin
Seeman, Nadrian Charles
Shore, Joseph David
Steiner, Robert Frank
Sturtevant, Julian Munson
Su, Lao-Sou
Subramanian, Sethuraman
Sweet, Robert Mahlon
Thomas, George Joseph, Jr.
Tinoco, Ignacio, Jr.
Tu, Shu-I
Vallee, Bert Lester
Veis, Arthur
von Hippel, Peter Hans
Wallace, Bonnie Ann
Wetmur, James Gerard
Wu, Chuen-Shang Chung
Wu, Stephen Hong-wei
Yang, Jen Tsi
Yarmush, Martin Leon
Zand, Robert
Zimm, Bruno Hasbrouck

Catalysis chemistry
Angell, Charles Leslie
Baetzold, Roger Charles
Bloch, Herman Samuel
Brumberger, Harry
Burrington, James David
Butt, John B.
Carrick, Wayne Lee
Chan, Albert Sun Chi
Chen, Hoffman Hor-Fu
Cratty, Leland Earl, Jr.
Current, Steven Paul
Daly, Francis Patrick
Davies, Geoffrey
Duncan, Thomas Michael
Edmondson, Morris Stephen
Ellgen, Paul Clifford
Falk, Charles David
Farcasiu, Dan Alexandru
Gassman, Paul George
Gates, Bruce Clark
Goddard, William Andrew, III
Good, Mary Lowe
Habermann, Clarence Edward
Habib, Mohammad Munir
Halpern, Jack
Hansen, Robert Suttle
Harris, Thomas Van
Heinemann, Heinz
Hemstock, Glen Alton
Henry, Patrick M.
Hettinger, William Peter, Jr.
Hoare, James Patrick
Hofer, Lawrence John Edward
Iyengar, Doreswamy Raghavachar
Jezl, James Louis
Kasai, Paul Haruo
Katz, Thomas Joseph
Kennedy, James Vern
Klotz, Irving Myron
Kutz, Nancy Ann
Labinger, Jay Alan
LaCava, Alberto Ignacio
Mack, Mark Philip
Mao, Chung-Rei
Marder, Todd Benjamin
Mares, Frank
Masilamani, Divakar
Orchin, Milton
Oyekan, Soni Olufemi
Peri, John Bayard
Peterson, Alan Herbert
Poutsma, Marvin Lloyd
Rathke, Jerome William
Reagan, William Joseph
Richard, Michael Alan
Sachtler, Wolfgang Max Hugo
Samoilov, Sergey Michael
Schoonover, Michael Wayne
Schwank, Johannes Walter
Sewchok, Michael George
Sinfelt, John Henry
Somorjai, Gabor A(rpad)
Staley, Ralph Horton
Storm, David Anthony
Suslick, Kenneth Sanders
Taylor, Dennis Riley
Teller, Raymond Gene
Wei, James
Wist, Abund Ottokar
Worley, S. D.
Yamanis, Jean
Young, John Edward

Clinical chemistry
Achter, Eugene Kenneth
Bhattacharya, Syamal Kanti
Bruns, David Eugene
Brynes, Paul Jeffrey
Canova-Davis, Eleanor
Carakostas, Michael Charles
Chen, Shuenn-Tzong
Cornatzer, William Eugene
DeBari, Vincent Anthony
Dhar, Amiya Kanti
Forman, Donald T.
Gershbein, Leon Lee
Giannetta, Carl Lee
Gress-Gordon, Jean Anne
Grossman, Steven Harris
Guilbault, George Gerald
Gupta, Satyendra Kumar
Guthermann, Howard Edgar
Hankes, Lawrence Valentine
Hinze, Willie Lee
Johnson, Lavell R.
Kabra, Pokar Mal
Kachmar, John Frederick
Kahn, Stephen Ellsworth
LeBlanc, Robert Bruce
Loor, Rueyming
Mericle, David Allen
Mickelson, Kenneth Eugene
Naito, Herbert K.
Natelson, Samuel
Polz-Schaerffenberg, Erika
Purdy, William Crossley
Shamberger, Raymond Joseph, Jr.
Shihabi, Zakariya Kamel
Tarnowski, Thomas Lynn
Thomas, John Joseph
Wei, Jeng Shu
Young, Chung Chang
Zak, Bennie

Crystallography
Abrahams, Sidney Cyril
Azaroff, Leonid Vladimirovitch
Balascio, Joseph Francis
Camerman, Arthur
Frazier, Alva William
Freeman, Wade Austin
Hutchison, Clyde Allen, Jr.
Jacobson, Robert Andrew
Kaduk, James Albert
Karle, Jerome
Koetzle, Thomas Frederick
Kvick, Åke Harry
Newnham, Robert Everest
Rotella, Frank J.
Seeman, Nadrian Charles
Teller, Raymond Gene
Veidis, Mikelis Valdis
Williams, Jack Marvin
Yelon, William B.
Zhu, Nai Jue

Crystallography, X-ray
Blackwell, John
Broach, Robert William
Cotton, Frank Albert
DeBoer, Barry Goodwin
Diaddario, Leonard Lawrence, Jr.
Flippen-Anderson, Judith Lee
Freeman, Wade Austin
Frueh, Alfred Joseph
Glusker, Jenny Pickworth
Karle, Isabella Lugoski
Love, Warner Edwards
Margulis, Thomas N.
Shoemaker, David Powell
Smith, George David
Sweet, Robert Mahlon
Yates, John Harry
Zhu, Nai Jue

Electron spin resonance
Barber, Michael James
Chisholm, William Preston
Dickinson, Leonard Charles
Gutierrez, Peter Luis
Irwin, Peter Lloyd
Kasai, Paul Haruo
Lang, Conrad Marvin
Mao, Chung-Rei
McBay, Henry Cecil
McCalley, Roderick Canfield
Mercer, Kermit Ray
Mossoba, Magdi Michel
Schwartz, Robert Nelson

High temperature chemistry
Ames, Lynford Lenhart
Bamberger, Carlos Enrique Leopoldo
Barbee, Steven George
Barnes, Hubert Lloyd
Bennett, Stephen Lawrence
Brittain, Robert Dameron
Brown, Paul Edmund
Dean, Anthony Marion
Folweiler, Robert Cooper
Green, David William
Haupin, Warren Emerson
Krikorian, Oscar Harold
Lipschutz, Michael Elazar
Muan, Arnulf
Pfender, Emil
Selover, Theodore Britton, Jr.
Shackelford, Scott Addison
Zollweg, Robert John

Immunocytochemistry. *See* **BIOLOGY.**

Inorganic chemistry
Alper, Howard
Bamberger, Carlos Enrique Leopoldo
Barber, Eugene John
Basolo, Fred
Bauman, John E., Jr.
Broach, Robert William
Brown, Paul Edmund
Burow, Duane Frueh
Carlin, Richard Lewis
Carter, John Paul
Carter, Robert Lawrence
Caslavska, Vera Barbara
Chalilpoyil, Purush
Chan, Albert Sun Chi
Chang, James C.
Chisholm, Malcolm Harold
Choppin, Gregory Robert
Cotton, Frank Albert
Cratty, Leland Earl, Jr.
Davies, Geoffrey
DeBoer, Barry Goodwin
Dhara, Sudhir Chandra
Diamond, Herbert
Dodson, Charles Leon, Jr.
Dorogy, William Eugene, Jr.
Eanes, Edward David
Earley, Joseph Emmet
Eaton, Gareth Richard
Ellgen, Paul Clifford
Falk, Charles David
Feeney, Jospeh John
Fields, Paul Robert
Fischer, Albert Karl
Fonseca, Anthony Gutierre
Frazier, Alva William
Gallagher, Patrick Kent
Gladfelter, Wayne Lewis
Gray, Harry Barkus
Gray, Leonard Wesley
Hagen, Arnulf Peder
Halpern, Jack
Hanson, John Elbert
Harrington, Roy Victor
Herron, Norman
Ibers, James Arthur
Ingle, William Martell
Interrante, Leonard Vincent
Irgolic, Kurt Johann
Johnson, Jack Wayne
Kaduk, James Albert
Karas, Bradley Ross
Kargol, Joseph Anthony, Jr.
Keller, Oswald Lewin, Jr.
Kenney, John William, III
Kutz, Nancy Ann
Kvick, Åke Harry
Landis, Michael Eugene
Landolt, George Robert
Lippard, Stephen James
Long, Gary John
Longhi, Raymond
Luehrs, Dean Carl
MacInnes, David Fenton, Jr.
Makinen, Marvin William
Margerum, Dale William
Mason, Caroline Faith Vibert
McLendon, George Leland
Milburn, Ronald McRae
Mislankar, Dattatraya Ghanshyam
Morrow, Scott Imlay
Moyer, John Raymond
Nechamkin, Howard
Netzel, Thomas Leonard
Nikles, David Eugene
Ozin, Geoffrey A.
Papke, Brian Lee
Pearson, Ralph Gottfrid
Porterfield, William Wendell
Puddephatt, Richard John
Rabinovich, Eliezer M.
Radtke, Schrade Fred
Reagan, William Joseph
Rice, Gary Wayne
Rotella, Frank J.
Samuels, George Joseph
Sapp, Danny Lee
Schoonover, Michael Wayne
Scovell, William Martin
Self, James Maurice
Sewchok, Michael George
Sherren, Anne Terry
Silver, Gary Lee
Simmons, George Allen
Spiro, Clifford Lawrence
Squillante, Michael Robert
St. George, George Michael
Stucky, Galen Dean
Suslick, Kenneth Sanders
Taube, Henry
Telkes, Maria
Thompson, Mary Eileen
Thompson, Richard Claude
Trevorrow, LaVerne Everett
Wagner, Louis Frank
Wartik, Thomas
Weber, Carl Joseph, III
West, Robert Culbertson
Williams, Jack Marvin
Wright, John Ricken
Wrighton, Mark Stephen
Young, Donald Clifford

Kinetics
Anderson, James Gilbert
Bauer, Simon Harvey
Benson, Sidney William
Birely, John Horton
Braun, Charles Louis
Caduto, Ralph
Calvert, Jack George
Daly, Francis Patrick
Datz, Sheldon
Diaddario, Leonard Lawrence, Jr.
Dorko, Ernest A(lexander)
Dunker, Alan Melvin
Earley, Joseph Emmet
Epstein, Irving Robert
Gardner, Michael Patrick
Jacob, Adir
Kirkien-Rzeszotarski, Alicja Maria
Lampe, Frederick Walter
Larter, Raima Marzee
Lee, Yuan Tseh
Lin, Ming-Chang
Litt, Morton Herbert
LuValle, James Ellis
Marcus, Rudolph Arthur
Martin, L(aurence) Robbin
Meisels, Gerhard George
Miller, Raymond Earl, Jr.
Moran, Thomas Francis
Muschlitz, Earle Eugene, Jr.
Noyes, Richard Macy
Okabe, Hideo
Oldenborg, Richard Charles
Parr, Gary Raymond
Raw, Cecil John Gough
Rhinesmith, Robert J.
Root, John Walter
Ross, John
Sahyun, Melville Richard Valde
Scaiano, Juan Cesar
Slichter, William Pence
Taube, Henry
Thompson, Richard Claude
Wang, Chi-Sun
Young, John Edward

Laser-induced chemistry. *See* **LASER.**

Neurochemistry. *See* **NEUROSCIENCE.**

Nuclear chemistry
Alexander, John Macmillan
Apt, Kenneth Ellis
Basolo, Fred
Batzel, Roger Elwood
Becker, Donald Arthur
Coleman, Charles F(ranklin)
Dahl, J(ohn) Robert
Diamond, Herbert
Downing, Robert Gregory
Evans, William Frederick
Fields, Paul Robert
Filby, Royston Herbert
Fink, Richard W(alter)
Friedlander, Gerhart
Griffin, Henry Claude
Harbottle, Garman
Hoffman, Darleane Christian
Holub, Robert F(rantisek)
Hopke, Philip Karl
Hulet, E. Kenneth
Kalbach, Constance
Keller, Oswald Lewin, Jr.
Lin, Chien-Chang
McHarris, William Charles
Pacer, John Charles
Pierce, Elliot Stearns
Scott, David Knight
Seaborg, Glenn Theodore
Sedlacek, William Adam
Steinberg, Ellis Philip
Turkevich, Anthony Leonid
Ussery, Larry Eugene

Ward, Thomas Edmund
Wiebe, Leonard Irving

Nuclear magnetic resonance. ***See also*** **BIOTECHNOLOGY, Imaging technology.**

Alger, Jeffry Roy
Bailey, William F.
Baldeschwieler, John Dickson
Bible, Roy Henderson, Jr.
Bovey, Frank Alden
Brey, Wallace Siegfried
Browning, Sterling Edwin, II.
Carr, Thomas Michael
Chen, Ching-Nien
Cohn, Mildred
Cunningham, Clarence Marion
Duffy, Thomas Hyatt
Duncan, Thomas Michael
Dybowski, Cecil Ray
Eckman, Richard Raymond
Eliel, Ernest Ludwig
Evans, Frederick E.
Faehl, Larry Gene
Greiner, Jack Volker
Gutowsky, Herbert Sander
Heeschen, Jerry Parker
Highet, Robert John
Holecek, Dale Robert
Irwin, Peter Lloyd
Jacob, Gary Steven
Jonas, Jiri
Karabatsos, Gerasimos John
Komoroski, Richard Andrew
Kopple, Kenneth David
Krishna, Nepalli Rama
Mc Dowell, Charles Alexander
Nagel, Donald Lewis
Newmark, Richard Alan
Paudler, William Wolfgang
Pfeffer, Philip Elliot
Rabenstein, Dallas Leroy
Sardella, Dennis Joseph
Schuh, Joseph Randolph
Scott, Alastair Ian
Slichter, William Pence
Smith, Ian Cormack Palmer
Stary, Frank Edward
Taber-Maier, Katherine Helen
Tanner, John Eyer, Jr.
Thyvelikakath, George Xavier
Traficante, Daniel Dominick
Walker, Thomas Eugene
Werbelow, Lawrence Glen
Zadjura, Richard Edward

Organic chemistry

Abidi, Sharon Low
Abou-Gharbia, Magid Abdel-Megeid
Agosta, William Carleton
Aguiar, Adam Martin
Alper, Howard
Anderson, Albert Gordon
Angeles, Marshall Robert
Ault, Addison
Bahner, Carl Tabb
Bailey, William F.
Bak, David Arthur
Baker, William Ray
Banitt, Elden Harris
Baran, John Stanislaus
Barborak, James Carl
Barnabeo, Austin Emidio
Bartlett, Paul Doughty
Barton, Thomas Jackson
Baumgarten, Reuben Lawrence
Baxter, Gene Francis
Becker, Ernest I.
Behnke, Walter Eric
Beier, Ross Carlton
Bender, Myron Lee
Benson, Royal Henry
Bergman, Robert George
Berson, Jerome Abraham
Bezoari, Massimo Daniel
Bierenbaum, Richard Elliot
Bloomfield, Jordan Jay
Bluestein, Bernard R.
Boden, Richard Mark
Bodine, Richard Shearon
Bodor, Nicholas Stephen
Boekelheide, Virgil Carl
Borchardt, John Keith
Borowitz, Grace Burchman
Brauman, John I.
Breslow, Ronald Charles
Brook, Adrian Gibbs
Broom, Arthur Davis
Brown, Herbert Charles
Brunelle, Daniel Joseph
Buchman, Russell
Buncel, Erwin
Bunnett, Joseph Frederick
Burgoyne, William Franklin, Jr.
Burke, Luke Anthony
Burrington, James David
Burrows, Elizabeth Parker
Burton, Donald Joseph
Bush, James Hastings
Cairns, Theodore LeSueur
Carlson, Kenneth T.
Carroll, Felix Alvin, Jr.
Catena, Robert John
Catt, John David
Chapman, Orville Lamar
Chen, Hoffman Hor-Fu
Cobb, R(aymond) Lynn
Cohen, Irwin
Cohen, Noal
Combes, Richard Willard
Cook, Clarence Edgar
Cook, Elton Straus
Coover, Harry Wesley
Counts, Wayne Boyd
Covington, Edward Royals
Cox, James Carl, Jr.
Cram, Donald James
Cristol, Stanley Jerome
Current, Steven Paul
Currie, Bruce Lamonte
Dauben, William Garfield
Dean, William Dennis
DeBoer, Edward Dale
DeGooyer, William Jay
de Mayo, Paul
DePompei, Michael Frederick
Djerassi, Carl
Dolak, Terence Martin
Eagar, Robert Gouldman, Jr.
Eaton, Philip Eugene
Efcavitch, J. William
Eliel, Ernest Ludwig
Elliott, William Hueckel
Fales, Henry Marshall
Farcasiu, Dan Alexandru
Fatiadi, Alexander Johann
Felix, Arthur Martin
Figuly, Garret Daniel
Filbey, Allen Howard
Fischer, Hans-Peter
Fisher, Charles Harold
Floyd, Middleton Brawner, Jr.
Flynn, Daniel Lee
Fodor, Gabor Bela
Foreman, Fredrick
Fox, Marye Anne
Frank, Dieter
Freedman, Leon David
Fried, Josef
Friedman, Howard Stephen
Gaa, Peter Charles
Gandler, Joseph Rubin
Gandour, Richard David
Ganguly, Ashit Kumar
Gassman, Paul George
Gates, Marshall DeMotte, Jr.
Gerek, James Michael
Gilliom, Richard D.
Glamkowski, Edward Joseph
Gless, Richard Douglas, Jr.
Goe, Gerald Lee
Goldstein, Henry
Gooden, Robert
Graham, Donald Lee
Graham, William Hardin
Griller, David
Grim, Michael David
Haire, Michael Joseph
Hall, Stan S.
Hansch, Corwin Herman
Hartman, Robert John
Hausmann, Werner Karl
Helsley, Grover Cleveland
Henderson, Roseta McKinley
Hill, Marion Elza
Hoch, Paul Edward
Holmes, Jerry Dell
Hruby, Victor Joseph
Hudgin, Donald Edward
Hutchins, Charles William
Ingham, Robert Kelly
Ingram, Alvin Richard
Ireland, Chris Michael
Iyengar, Bhashyam Srinivasa
Jaynes, Edgar Norris
Jencks, William Platt
Jensen, Norman Peter
Jezl, James Louis
Jiang, Jack Bau-Chien
Johns, William Francis
Johnson, Christopher Peter, III
Juster, Norman Joel
Kagan, Fred
Kalita, Chabi Chandra
Kam, Sheung-Tsam
Kaplan, Martin Louis
Karabatsos, Gerasimos John
Katz, Thomas Joseph
Kauer, James Charles
Keehn, Philip Moses
Kelsey, Donald Ross
Khanna, Pyare Lal
Khorana, Har Gobind
Kingsbury, William Dennis
Klayman, Daniel Leslie
Klein, Jack S.
Knowles, Jeremy Randall
Konecky, Milton Stuart
Kovac, Pavol
Krull, Ira Stanley
Kupper, Robert Joe
Lakshmikantham, Maduraivas Venugopal
LaMattina, John Lawrence
Landis, Michael Eugene
Lasoski, Bernard Albert
Law, Kock-Yee
Lawson, David F.
Lawton, Richard Graham
Lazarus, Allan K.
Lee, James Travis, Jr.
Lee, John Yuchu
Lee, Yong-Jai
Lemieux, Raymond Urgel
Leonard, Nelson Jordan
Lin, Chiu-Hong
Lipschutz, Bruce Howard
Liu, Kou-chang
Loeb, Melvin Lester
Logullo, Francis Mark
Lokensgard, Jerrold Paul
Lorance, Elmer Donald
Lyle, Robert Edward, Jr.
MacCoss, Malcolm
MacDonald, Donald MacKenzie
MacMillan, John Harry
Macnair, Richard Nelson
Mandava, Naga Bhushan
Mao, Chung-Ling
Marfat, Anthony
Masilamani, Divakar
McBay, Henry Cecil
McClure, David Earl
McKenna, James Emmet
McKeon, James Edward
Mehta, Nariman Bomanshaw
Meinwald, Jerrold
Meyers, Albert Irving
Meyers, Cal Yale
Micheli, Roger Paul
Miljkovic, Momcilo
Miller, Duane Douglas
Miller, Sidney Israel
Millich, Frank
Mislankar, Dattatraya Ghanshyam
Mislow, Kurt Martin
Mitscher, Lester Allen
Moore, Gordon George
Moore, Patrick David
Moos, Walter Hamilton
Mowery, Dwight Fay
Muccino, Richard Robert
Mundell, Brian Lee
Nace, Harold Russ
Nachman, Ronald James
Nagasawa, Herbert Tsukasa
Nagel, Donald Lewis
Nakanishi, Koji
Natale, Nicholas Robert
Nechamkin, Howard
Neumeyer, John Leopold
Newman, Melvin Spencer
Nicolae, Gheorghe
Niederhauser, Warren Dexter
Noceti, Richard Paul
Occolowitz, John Lewis
Ocone, Luke Ralph
Ojakaar, Leo
Olah, George Andrew
Olson, Gary Lee
Oro, Juan
Paciorek, Kazimiera Jola Liliana
Pappas, James John
Pappas, Socrates Peter
Parham, Marc Ellous
Parks, Carl Ramsey
Parliment, Thomas Holden
Pastor, Stephen Daniel
Patwardhan, Bhalchandra Hari
Paudler, William Wolfgang
Peterson, William Robert, Jr.
Pettit, George Robert
Phillips, Lawrence Richard
Pomerantz, Martin
Ponpipom, Mitree Michael
Pop, Emil
Poutsma, Marvin Lloyd
Powell, Richard Grant
Press, Jeffery Bruce
Preus, Martin William
Prince, Martin Irwin
Rajanbabu, T. V.
Ranken, Paul Frederick
Ray, Wesley Carl
Regelman, Dale Francis
Reichmanis, Elsa
Riordan, James Michael
Rislove, David Joel
Rizvi, Syed Qalab Abbas
Roberts, John D.
Robins, Morris Joseph
Rockwell, Ned Miles
Rondestvedt, Christian S(criver)
Rosenbrook, William, Jr.
Saam, John Carlton
Saegebarth, Klaus Arthur
Saeva, Franklin D.
Saggiomo, Andrew Joseph
Salsbury, Jason Melvin
Sardella, Dennis Joseph
Sarno, Maria Erlinda Co
Sauer, Robert Jay
Schlenk, Hermann
Schlosberg, Richard Henry
Schmidgall, Robert Lee
Schroeck, Calvin William
Schroeder, Leland Roy
Schuda, Paul Francis
Schultz, Frederick John
Schwab, Arthur William
Scott, Alastair Ian
Seemuth, Paul Douglas
Senter, Peter Dana
Shackelford, Scott Addison
Shibata, Tomoo
Shih, David Houng-min
Shusterman, Alan Jeffrey
Simon, Myron Sydney
Sogah, Dotsevi Yao
Stamoudis, Vassilis Christos
Stang, Peter John
Starnes, William Herbert, Jr.
Steele, Gerald Hicks
St. George, George Michael
Stille, John Kenneth
Stork, Gilbert (Josse)
Streitwieser, Andrew, Jr.
Sund, Eldon H(arold)
Tam, Steve Yik-Kai
Tarbell, Dean Stanley
Tarnowski, Thomas Lynn
Taylor, Edward Curtis
Taylor, Lloyd David
Thomas, Fairwell
Thyvelikakath, George Xavier
Tilley, Jefferson Wright
Tishler, Max
Toomey, Joseph Edward, Jr.
Townsend, Leroy B.
Trachtenberg, Edward Norman
Traficante, Daniel Dominick
Trost, Barry Martin
Ukachukwu, Victoria Chikaodili
Ulrich, Henri
Upton, Charles Joseph
Vail, Sidney Lee
Valenty, Vivian Briones
Vander Meer, Robert Kenneth
Vandesteeg, Gregg Alan
Vargas, Luis Alberto
Vercellotti, John Raymond
Viola, Alfred
Voaden, Denys John
Wade, James Joseph
Wade, Peter Allen
Wagenknecht, John Henry
Walba, David Mark
Walling, Cheves Thomson
Wanat, Stanley Frank
Wang, Chia-Lin Jeffrey
Wang, Nai-Yi
Wang, Richard Hsu-Shien
Watts, Michelle Marie
Weiler, Lawrence Stanley
Weininger, Stephen Joel
Weis, Konrad Max
Wellman, George Robert
West, Robert Culbertson
Westheimer, Frank H(enry)
Wiberg, Kenneth Berle
Wilbur, James M(yers), Jr.
Willis, John Patrick
Witkop, Bernhard
Witte, Michael
Wombles, Robert Huston
Wong, Jesse Kwok-Keung
Wu, Shang-Ren
Yocum, Ronald Harris
Zannucci, Joseph Salvatore
Zimmerman, Howard Elliot

Organometallics

Angeles, Marshall Robert
Anglin, James Richard
Barborak, James Carl
Barton, Thomas Jackson
Bauer, Dennis Paul
Bergman, Robert George
Brown, Kenneth Lawrence
Buncel, Erwin
Card, Roger John
Carr, Thomas Michael
Chen, Kon Swee
Chisholm, Malcolm Harold
Filbey, Allen Howard
Freedman, Leon David
Gaa, Peter Charles
Gladfelter, Wayne Lewis
Habib, Mohammad Munir
Hall, Stan S.
Harris, Thomas Van
Hoeg, Donald Francis
Ingham, Robert Kelly
Kaesz, Herbert David
Kang, Jung Wong
Labinger, Jay Alan
Marder, Todd Benjamin
Marks, Tobin Jay
Natale, Nicholas Robert
Pastor, Stephen Daniel
Pearson, Anthony John
Peterson, William Robert, Jr.
Prince, Martin Irwin
Puddephatt, Richard John
Rajanbabu, T. V.
Rathke, Jerome William
Shusterman, Alan Jeffrey
Streitwieser, Andrew, Jr.
Stucky, Galen Dean
Vollhardt, Kurt Peter Christian
Wade, Peter Allen
Wagman, Gerald H(oward)
White, Mitchell Ray

Photochemistry

Agosta, William Carleton
Araujo, Roger Jerome
Baum, Thomas Hall
Bloomfield, Jordan Jay
Calvert, Jack George
Calvin, Melvin
Carroll, Felix Alvin, Jr.
Chen, Eng Ming
Cristol, Stanley Jerome
Dauben, William Garfield
de Mayo, Paul
Dorko, Ernest A(lexander)
Eaton, David Fielder
Figard, Joseph Emerson
Fox, Marye Anne
Freiser, Ben Sherman
Gaylord, Norman Grant
Gooden, Robert
Gray, Harry Barkus
Halpern, Arthur M(errill)
Japar, Steven Martin
Juvet, Richard Spalding, Jr.
Kaplan, Michael
Kelly, Nelson Allen
Kohl, Paul Albert
Law, Kock-Yee
Lerman, Sidney
Lin, Sheng Hsien
Liu, Kou-chang
Meisel, Dan
Molina, Luisa Tan
Nauman, Robert Vincent
Nottorf, Robert William
Okabe, Hideo
Pappas, Socrates Peter
Parkinson, Bruce Alan
Ruzo, Luis Octavio
Saeva, Franklin D.
Sahyun, Melville Richard Valde
Scaiano, Juan Cesar
Strickler, Stewart Jeffery
Trozzolo, Anthony Marion
Turro, Nicholas John
Wanat, Stanley Frank
Weston, Ralph E., Jr.
Williams, Richard
Wrighton, Mark Stephen
Yardley, James Thomas
Yates, Peter
Zimmerman, Howard Elliot

Photochemistry, laser

Berry, Michael James
Brack, Karl
Butler, James Ehrich
Delap, James Harve
Donohue, Terence
Earl, Boyd Lorel
Flynn, George William
Greene, John Philip
Grossweiner, Leonard Irwin
Halpern, Arthur M(errill)
Kliger, David Saul
Lampe, Frederick Walter
Lyman, John Leslie
McLaughlin, Donald Reed
Micha, David Allan
Netzel, Thomas Leonard
Oldenborg, Richard Charles
Rettner, Charles Thomas
Robinson, Dean Wentworth
Spiglanin, Thomas Arthur

Physical chemistry

Addy, John Keith
Albertson, Clarence Elmo, Jr
Allan, Barry David
Amero, Bernard Alan
Ames, Lynford Lenhart
Anderson, James Emmons
Antcliff, Richard Raymond
Apkarian, Vartkess Ara
Axe, John Donald
Baer, Eric
Baes, Charles Frederick, Jr.
Bahe, Lowell Warren
Baldeschwieler, John Dickson
Barber, Eugene John
Bard, Allen Joseph
Bates, Richard Doane, Jr.
Bauer, Simon Harvey
Benerito, Ruth Rogan
Benson, Sidney William
Benzinger, William D(onald)
Bernheim, Robert Allan
Bernstein, Richard Barry
Berry, Richard Stephen
Berry, Robert Walter
Bigeleisen, Jacob
Birely, John Horton
Bocko, Peter Lawrence
Boggs, James Ernest
Bohme, Diethard Kurt
Bondybey, Vladimir Edmund
Bowen, Lawrence Hoffman
Bramwell, Fitzgerald Burton
Brauer, Beth-Ellen
Brauman, John I.
Braun, Charles Louis
Braun, Richard
Brion, Christopher Edward
Brittain, Robert Dameron
Brooks, Philip Russell
Brumberger, Harry
Burow, Duane Frueh
Butler, James Ehrich
Cady, Wayne Allen
Campbell, John Hyde
Cha, Charles Young
Chao, Mou Shu
Charney, Elliot
Chen, Holly Ho
Cheney, Brigham Vernon
Chiang, Joseph Fei
Chu, Benjamin
Clark, Roy White
Clifton, David Geyer
Cole, Terry
Coleman, Charles F(ranklin)
Cox, Hollace Lawton, Jr.
Crawford, Bryce Low, Jr.
Criss, Cecil M.
Cunningham, Clarence Marion
Curl, Robert Floyd, Jr.
Dai, Hai-Lung
Davis, Howard Ted
Dean, Anthony Marion
Delap, James Harve
Denio, Allen A(lbert)
Dennis, Kent Seddens
Dodson, Charles Leon, Jr.
Donnelly, Timothy Christopher
Drickamer, Harry George
Dybowski, Cecil Ray
Dykstra, Clifford Elliot
Eastman, Michael Paul
Eaton, Gareth Richard
Ebdon, David William
Eckhardt, Craig Jon
Eckman, Richard Raymond
Ellison, Frank Oscar
El-Sayed, Mostafa Amr
Eyler, John Robert
Fateley, William Gene
Faust, Robert Jeffrey
Findley, Gary Lee
Fischer, Albert Karl
Fleming, Hubert Loy
Fletcher, Aaron Nathaniel
Flynn, George William
Force, Carlton Gregory
Freund, Robert Stanley
Fried, Vojtech
Friedlander, Gerhart
Gaines, George Loweree, Jr.
Gamble, Fred Ridley, Jr.
Gardner, Michael Patrick
Gayles, Joseph Nathan Webster, Jr.
Gill, Jasbir Singh
Glasser, Julian
Glatz, Alfred Christian
Goffman, Martin
Goldberg, Robert Nathan
Goldstein, Mark Kingston Levin
Goodfriend, Paul Louis
Gopikanth, Mysore Laxmikanth
Gouterman, Martin Paul
Graybeal, Jack Daniel
Gulari, Erdogan
Gur, Turgut Mehmet
Haaland, David Michael
Hackleman, David Eugene
Haller, Ivan
Harker, Alan Butler
Harris, Harold Hart
Harrison, Anna Jane
Haslam, John Lee
Healey, Frank Henry
Heller, Adam
Hernandez, Samuel P.
Higuchi, Takeru
Hobbs, John Robert
Hodge, Ian Moir
Holly, Frank Joseph
Hsia, Yu-Ping
Hutchison, Clyde Allen, Jr.
Ingold, Keith Usherwood
Jacob, Adir
Jacobson, Robert Andrew
Johnson, Charles Sidney, Jr.
Johnson, Donald Rex
Kaplan, Michael
Kargol, Joseph Anthony, Jr.
Karl, Robert Raymond, Jr.
Karlicek, Robert Frank, Jr.
Katz, Joseph Jacob
Kauzmann, Walter Joseph
Kemp, Marwin King
Kennedy, James Vern
Kenney, John William, III
Kenyon, Allen Stewart
Kinsey, James Lloyd
Kirkien-Rzeszotarski, Alicja Maria
Klein, Ralph
Knoot, Peter Anton
Koetzle, Thomas Frederick
Kolb, Charles Eugene
Krishnan, Pallassana Narayanier
Kuffner, Roy Joseph
Kunzler, John Eugene
Kwiram, Alvin L.
Laane, Jaan
Ladanyi, Branka Maria
Lagunas-Solar, Manuel Claudio
Lambrecht, Richard M(erle)
Landolt, George Robert
Lang, Conrad Marvin
Lang, John Calvin
Lange, Klaus Robert
Lassettre, Edwin Nichols

Laub, Richard James
Lee, Yuan Tseh
Leibowitz, Leonard
Leung, Wing Hai
Levin, Ira William
Levy, Donald Harris
Li, Ying-Sing
Light, John C.
Lim, Edward Chol
Lin, Chien-Chang
Lin, Sheng Hsien
Lindauer, Maurice William
Lipscomb, William Nunn, Jr.
Lissant, Kenneth Jordan
Litovchenko, Vladimir Alexei
Littauer, Ernest Lucius
Long, Franklin A.
Longeway, Paul Allen
Lonsdale, Harold Kenneth
LuValle, James Ellis
Maahs, Howard Gordon
MacColl, Robert
MacFadden, Kenneth Orville
Maclay, William Nevin
MacPhail, Richard Allyn
Mahy, Tyler Xerez
Malinowski, Edmund Robert
Mandelkern, Leo
Marchetti, Alfred Paul
Marcott, Curtis Allen
Mark, James Edward
Marsh, Max Martin
Martin, Richard Lee
McAfee, Kenneth Bailey, Jr.
McAtee, James Lee, Jr.
McBreen, James
McCalley, Roderick Canfield
Mc Dowell, Charles Alexander
McKee, Douglas William
Meeks, James Laverne
Meisel, Dan
Meisels, Gerhard George
Meiser, John Henry
Melton, Charles Estel
Michaels, Adlai Eldon
Michl, Josef
Miller, Raymond Earl, Jr.
Miner, Bryant Albert
Molina, Luisa Tan
Moore, John Hays
Moran, Thomas Francis
Morris, George Vincent
Morrow, Scott Imlay
Mortensen, Earl Miller
Mortimer, Robert George
Moyer, John Raymond
Muschlitz, Earle Eugene, Jr.
Myers, Howard
Nauman, Robert Vincent
Navangul, Himanshoo Vishnu
Nelson, Robert Norton
Newton, Amos Sylvester
Nottorf, Robert William
Oblad, Alexander Golden
Obremski, Robert John
O'Donovan, Patrick Alexander
Okinaka, Yutaka
O'Neil, James Richard
Orwoll, Robert Arvid
Osterhoudt, Hans Walter
Palke, William E.
Pardini, Steven Peter
Parkinson, Bruce Alan
Parreira, Helio Correa
Pauling, Linus Carl
Person, Willis Bagley
Pitzer, Kenneth S.
Polestak, Walter John Stephen
Popowicz, Anthony Michael
Powell, George Louis
Powers, Robert William
Pudzianowski, Andrew Thaddeus
Pye, Earl Louis
Rao, Gopalakrishna M.
Raw, Cecil John Gough
Rebbert, Richard Edward
Reddy, Thomas Bradley
Rentzepis, Peter M.
Rhinesmith, Robert J.
Rice, Stuart Alan
Richard, Michael Alan
Roberts, George Philip
Rollino, John
Root, John Walter
Ross, John
Rossington, David Ralph
Rubin, Robert Joshua
Ruch, Richard Julius
Rush, Richard Marion
Russell, Allen Stevenson
Saalfeld, Fred Eric
Safron, Sanford Alan
Sage, Gloria Welt
Samuel, Aryeh Hermann Albert
Sarada, Thyagaraja
Schellman, John Anthony
Scheraga, Harold Abraham
Schryer, David Richard
Schuhmann, Reinhardt, Jr.
Schuler, Robert Hugo
Schurr, John Michael
Schwab, Arthur William
Scott, Robert Lane
Seegmiller, David William
Selby, Theodore William
Shaub, Walter Michael
Shaw, Robert Wilson
Shirley, David Arthur
Shoup, Robert Donald
Shubert, Fred George
Spiglanin, Thomas Arthur
Spindel, William
Srinivasan, Brihmadesam Narasimhan
Staley, Ralph Horton
St. Louis, Robert Vincent
Stockmayer, Walter Hugo
Storm, Roger S.
Strickler, Stewart Jeffery
Su, Lao-Sou
Sullivan, Edward Maurice
Swarts, E(lywn) Lowell
Symes, Marion Ernest
Takano, Masaharu
Tanner, John Eyer, Jr.
Taylor, Robert Cooper
Telkes, Maria
Terner, James
Thompson, Joseph Kyle
Thompson, Mary Eileen
Toome, Voldemar
Tou, James Chieh
Trajmar, Sandor
Tyrrell, James
Verdier, Peter Howard
Vernardakis, Theodore Galaction
Vijh, Ashok Kumar
Wahnsiedler, Walter Edward
Wall, Frederick Theodore
Waltking, Arthur Ernest
Waugh, John Stewart
Weatherford, Charles Albert
Wehner, Paul Sherman
Wen, Wen-Yang
Westmoreland, Thomas Delbert, Jr.
White, Stephen Halley
Widom, Benjamin
Wiers, Brandon Helmholz
Williams, J(ohn) W(arren)
Williams, Lesley Lattin
Wilson, Edgar Bright
Wong, Hans Kuomin
Worley, S. D.
Wurster, Dale Erwin
Yamaguchi, Yukio
Yap, William Tan
Yardley, James Thomas
Yeager, Ernest Bill
Yeung, Edward Szeshing
Young, Austin Harry
Zare, Richard Neil
Zeroka, Daniel
Zwanzig, Robert Walter

Polymer chemistry
Addy, John Keith
Albright, Robert Lee
Aldissi, Mahmoud
Allcock, Harry Rex
Anderson, James Emmons
Baer, Eric
Bahary, William Shaul
Bailey, Frederick Eugene, Jr.
Barnabeo, Austin Emidio
Baxter, Gene Francis
Benerito, Ruth Rogan
Benzinger, William D(onald)
Berry, Guy Curtis
Bezoari, Massimo Daniel
Bikales, Norbert M.
Billmeyer, Fred Wallace, Jr.
Bock, Jan
Borchardt, John Keith
Bovey, Frank Alden
Brack, Karl
Brauer, Gerhard Max
Carrick, Wayne Lee
Catena, Robert John
Cha, Charles Young
Chang, Tiang-Shing
Chen, Kon Swee
Claiborne, C. Clair
Class, Jay Bernard
Coleman, Michael Murray
Counselman, Clarence James
Covington, Edward Royals
Cox, James Carl, Jr.
Cummin, Alfred S(amuel)
Darsey, Jerome Anthony
Das, Pankaj Kumar
Das, Sajal
DeBoer, Edward Dale
DeGooyer, William Jay
Denio, Allen A(lbert)
Dennis, Kent Seddens
Desai, Kirit Navnitrai
Dorogy, William Eugene, Jr.
Edmondson, Morris Stephen
Eirich, Frederick Roland
Elias, Hans Georg
Ferry, John Douglass
Figuly, Garret Daniel
Fisher, Charles Harold
Force, Carlton Gregory
Frank, Dieter
Fulton, Christopher
Gaylord, Norman Grant
Germroth, Ted Calvin
Gibbs, William Eugene
Gooch, Jan Woodall
Graham, William Hardin
Hardin, Ian Russell
Harris, Milton
Hartman, Robert John
Harvey, Leonard A.
Hawkins, Walter Lincoln
Henderson, Douglas James
Hoeg, Donald Francis
Holecek, Dale Robert
Horowitz, Carl
Huang, Shyhchang Strong
Huang, Sun-Yi
Hudgin, Donald Edward
Ingram, Alvin Richard
Jacobs, Howard Larkin
Jelinski, Lynn W.
Jernigan, Robert Lee
Jones, Rufus Sidney, Jr.
Kafrawy, Adel
Kang, Jung Wong
Kaplan, Martin Louis
Katz, Manfred
Katz, Martin
Kelsey, Donald Ross
Kenyon, Allen Stewart
Koenig, Jack Leonard
Komoroski, Richard Andrew
Kratzer, Reinhold Hermann
Kraus, Menahem Alfred
Kresge, Edward Nathan
Kwiatkowski, George Thomas
Kwok, Wo Kong
Kwolek, Stephanie Louise
Lal, Joginder
Lambuth, Alan Letcher
Landoll, Leo M.
Lawson, David F.
LeBlanc, Robert Bruce
Levine, Leon
Levy, Alan Joel
Lin, Ju-Chui
Lin, Shaow Burn
Litt, Morton Herbert
Live, David Harris
Logullo, Francis Mark
Longhi, Raymond
MacDonald, Donald MacKenzie
MacInnes, David Fenton, Jr.
Mack, Mark Philip
Maclay, William Nevin
MacMillan, John Harry
Macnair, Richard Nelson
Mandelkern, Leo
Mao, Chung-Ling
Mares, Frank
Mark, James Edward
Marvasti, Setareh Alim
Mauter, Warren Eugene
Menyhert, William Robert
Millich, Frank
Monaghan, Leo John
Morgan, Paul Winthrop
Mosier, Benjamin
Mundell, Brian Lee
Nagarajan, Madukkarai Krishnarao
Neidlinger, Hermann Heinrich
Nemphos, Speros Peter
Niederhauser, Warren Dexter
Ojakaar, Leo
O'Malley, James J.
Orwoll, Robert Arvid
Osterhoudt, Hans Walter
Paciorek, Kazimiera Jola Liliana
Pardini, Steven Peter
Pariser, Rudolph
Parks, Carl Ramsey
Patterson, Donald Duke
Pearson, James Murray
Polestak, Walter John Stephen
Preus, Martin William
Ray, Wesley Carl
Regelman, Dale Francis
Restaino, Alfred Joseph
Rhein, Robert Alden
Roberts, George Philip
Robertson, James Richard, Jr.
Rondestvedt, Christian S(criver)
Ropp, Walter Shade
Rosthauser, James William
Rotenberg, Don Harris
Saam, John Carlton
Salame, Morris
Salsbury, Jason Melvin
Samoilov, Sergey Michael
Sarkar, Nitis
Sau, Arjun Chandra
Schwarz, Richard Anton
Senich, George A.
Sexsmith, Frederick Hamilton
Shah, Kishore Ramanlal
Shibata, Tomoo
Shu, Peter Hua-Cheng
Silverman, Joseph
Simha, Robert
Sogah, Dotsevi Yao
Stahl, Joel S.
Starnes, William Herbert, Jr.
Stary, Frank Edward
St. Clair, Anne King
Stein, Richard Stephen
Stille, John Kenneth
Stockmayer, Walter Hugo
Symes, Marion Ernest
Taylor, Lloyd David
Thompson, Larry Flack
Tucker, Robert J.
Turner, Derek Terence
Van De Mark, Michael Roy
Vijayendran, Bheema Rao
Vogl, Otto
Wagner, Herman Leon
Wagner, Melvin Peter
Walsh, William Kershaw
Walters, Sandra Jean
Wang, Richard Hsu-Shien
Warchol, Joseph Frederick
Webb, John Day, III
Weber, Carl Joseph, III
Whitlock, Lee Ronald
Wilbur, James M(yers), Jr.
Wnek, Gary Edmund
Wu, Shang-Ren
Yang, Henry Wu-Hsiang
Yeh, Horng-Chin Gene
Yocum, Ronald Harris
Young, Austin Harry
Zand, Robert

Solid state chemistry
Baglio, Joseph Anthony
Baker, William Oliver
Balascio, Joseph Francis
Beyer, Klaus Dietrich
Bowen, Lawrence Hoffman
Bramwell, Fitzgerald Burton
Chen, Shuenn-Tzong
Dunn, Bruce Sidney
Eckhardt, Craig Jon
Gallagher, Patrick Kent
Gallagher, Sarah Ann
Giessen, Bill Cormann
Hochmann, Petr Tomás
Ibers, James Arthur
Interrante, Leonard Vincent
Johnson, Jack Wayne
Juster, Norman Joel
Laudise, Robert Alfred
Leary, David Joseph
Long, Gary John
Longeway, Paul Allen
Meiser, John Henry
Metzger, Robert Melville
Nassau, Kurt
Ovshinsky, Stanford Robert
Parker, Sidney Glenn
Sarma, Abul Chandra
Sato, Hiroshi
Shoemaker, David Powell
Tanner, David Burnham
Trozzolo, Anthony Marion
Wagner, James Bruce, Jr.
Wang, Chih-Chun
Ward, John William

Space chemistry. *See* SPACE SCIENCE.

Statistical mechanics
Adelman, Steven A.
Araujo, Roger Jerome
Desai, Rashmi C.
Fixman, Marshall
Freeman, David Laurence
Fried, Vojtech
Johnson, Elijah
Ladanyi, Branka Maria
Lee, John Francis
Mazo, Robert Marc
Mortimer, Robert George
Ohmine, Iwao
Prigogine, Ilya
Stillinger, Frank Henry
Widom, Benjamin

Surface chemistry
Anderson, Alfred Bennett
Andres, Ronald Paul
Angell, Charles Leslie
Babchin, Alexander Joseph
Bock, Jan
Boll, David Jackson
Boudart, Michel
Braun, Richard
Brey, Wallace Siegfried
Clippinger, Everett
D'Arrigo, Joseph Salvatore
Davis, Robert Edgar
Davison, Sydney George
Deviney, Marvin Lee, Jr.
Doering, Dale Larry
Donohue, Terence
Dresser, Miles Joel
Ebdon, David William
Egelhoff, William Frederick, Jr.
Eirich, Frederick Roland
Evans, Willis Thomas
Fabish, Thomas John
Facci, John Stephen
Fogler, Hugh Scott
Franses, Elias I.
Franz, Helmut
Fuerstenau, Douglas Winston
Gaines, George Loweree, Jr.
Gomer, Robert
Good, Mary Lowe
Handy, Lyman Lee
Hansen, Robert Suttle
Harker, Alan Butler
Healey, Frank Henry
Hemstock, Glen Alton
Hofer, Lawrence John Edward
Holly, Frank Joseph
Ignatiev, Alex
Iyengar, Doreswamy Raghavachar
Jaynes, Edgar Norris
Katz, William
Kellogg, Gary Lee
Klein, Ralph
Koenig, Jack Leonard
Krauss, Alan Robert
Kuffner, Roy Joseph
Lange, Klaus Robert
Larach, Simon
Lauer, James Lothar
Leblanc, Roger Maurice
Leidheiser, Henry, Jr.
Leung, Wing Hai
Lissant, Kenneth Jordan
Lorenz, Philip Boalt
Lynn, Jesse Lynch, Jr.
Madey, Theodore Eugene
Marton, Joseph
McAtee, James Lee, Jr.
McKee, Douglas William
Merrill, Robert Perkins
Misra, Dwarika Nath
Morrison, Stanley Roy
Moudgil, Brij Mohan
Nagarajan, Madukkarai Krishnarao
Papke, Brian Lee
Parreira, Helio Correa
Peri, John Bayard
Powell, George Louis
Rhodin, Thor Nathaniel
Ropp, Walter Shade
Rounds, Fred Grafton
Ruch, Richard Julius
Sachtler, Wolfgang Max Hugo
Sarada, Thyagaraja
Sarkar, Nitis
Seemuth, Paul Douglas
Shirley, David Arthur
Shoup, Robert Donald
Shubert, Fred George
Shustorovich, Evgeny
Shuttleworth, Derek
Somasundaran, Ponisseril
Somorjai, Gabor A(rpad)
St. Louis, Robert Vincent
Taber, Joseph J.
Taylor, Dennis Riley
Thomas, H. Ronald
Tuul, Johannes
Ueda, Issaku
Van De Mark, Michael Roy
Vernardakis, Theodore Galaction
Vijayendran, Bheema Rao
Vijh, Ashok Kumar
Wachs, Israel Ephraim
Warchol, Joseph Frederick
Ward, John William
Yeager, Ernest Bill
Zografi, George D.

Synthetic chemistry
Abou-Gharbia, Magid Abdel-Megeid
Albright, Robert Lee
Attard, John
Banitt, Elden Harris
Bauer, Dennis Paul
Beaucage, Serge Laurent
Becker, Ernest I.
Behnke, Walter Eric
Boden, Richard Mark
Bodine, Richard Shearon
Brown, Herbert Charles
Brunelle, Daniel Joseph
Brynes, Paul Jeffrey
Buchman, Russell
Burgoyne, William Franklin, Jr.
Burton, Donald Joseph
Catt, John David
Cheng, Chia-Chung
Cobb, R(aymond) Lynn
Cohen, Noal
Counts, Wayne Boyd
Dean, William Dennis
Eaton, Philip Eugene
Fatiadi, Alexander Johann
Felix, Arthur Martin
Fodor, Gabor Bela
Fox, Jack Jay
Gates, Marshall DeMotte, Jr.
Gerek, James Michael
Germroth, Ted Calvin
Ginos, James Zissis
Gless, Richard Douglas, Jr.
Gupta, Satyendra Kumar
Haire, Michael Joseph
Harbert, Charles Armon
Hill, Marion Elza
Huang, Sun-Yi
Jerina, Donald Michael
Jiang, Jack Bau-Chien
Johnson, Christopher Peter, III
Katner, Allen Samuel
Kingsbury, William Dennis
Koenig, Karl Eric
Kovac, Pavol
Lakshmikantham, Maduraivas Venugopal
Lee, John Yuchu
Lin, Chiu-Hong
Lipschutz, Bruce Howard
Lokensgard, Jerrold Paul
McGorrin, Robert Joseph
McKenna, James Emmet
Mehrotra, Ashok Kumar
Meyers, Albert Irving
Miljkovic, Momcilo
Natansohn, Samuel
Newman, Melvin Spencer
Nicolae, Gheorghe
Ogilvie, Kelvin K.
Pearson, Anthony John
Ponpipom, Mitree Michael
Reynolds, John Gordon
Rhein, Robert Alden
Rislove, David Joel
Rizvi, Syed Qalab Abbas
Roberts, John Lawson
Rosenbrook, William, Jr.
Sau, Arjun Chandra
Schuda, Paul Francis
Shen, Tsung Ying
Simon, Myron Sydney
Sund, Eldon H(arold)
Szalecki, Wojciech Josef
Taylor, Edward Curtis
Trost, Barry Martin
Vail, Sidney Lee
Vargas, Luis Alberto
Vlattas, Isidoros
Wade, James Joseph
Wang, Chia-Lin Jeffrey
Wang, Ching-Tso
Wong, Jesse Kwok-Keung
Yates, Peter

Theoretical chemistry
Adams, William Henry
Adelman, Steven A.
Alder, Berni Julian
Alexander, Millard Henry
Alldredge, Gerald Palmer
Anderson, Alfred Bennett
Baetzold, Roger Charles
Bicerano, Jozef
Boggs, James Ernest
Brumer, Paul William
Bunge, Carlos Federico
Burke, Luke Anthony
Clementi, Enrico
Cohen, Irwin
Combs, Leon Lamar
Del Bene, Janet Elaine
Delos, John Bernard
Duffey, George Henry
Dykstra, Clifford Elliot
Ellison, Frank Oscar
Fixman, Marshall
Freed, Karl Frederick
Freeman, David Laurence
Gilliom, Richard D.
Gimarc, Benjamin Maurice
Gislason, Eric Arni
Goddard, William Andrew, III
Goodfriend, Paul Louis
Gouterman, Martin Paul
Guberman, Steven Lawrence
Hochmann, Petr Tomás
Hoffmann, Roald
Hopfield, John Joseph
Hopper, Darrel Gene
Horne, Frederick Herbert
Kaye, Jack Alan
Keller, Jaime
Konowalow, Daniel Dimitri
Langhoff, Peter Wolfgang
Larter, Raima Marzee
Lassettre, Edwin Nichols
Light, John C.
Madison, Vincent Stewart
Marcus, Rudolph Arthur
Martin, Richard Lee
Mason, Edward Allen
McLaughlin, Donald Reed
Meeks, James Laverne
Metzger, Robert Melville
Micha, David Allan
Mortensen, Earl Miller
Noid, Donald William
O'Donnell, Terence John
Ohmine, Iwao
Pack, Russell T.
Palke, William E.
Pan, Yuh Kang
Parr, Robert Ghormley
Pearson, Ralph Gottfrid
Pitzer, Kenneth S.
Pudzianowski, Andrew Thaddeus
Reynolds, Peter James
Rice, Stuart Alan
Richardson, James Wyman
Sandorfy, Camille
Seiders, Barbara Ann Bornemeier
Shustorovich, Evgeny
Stillinger, Frank Henry
Tanner, Anthony Charles
Tenney, Agnes
Tyrrell, James
Wall, Frederick Theodore
Wasserman, Zelda Rakowitz
Wiberg, Kenneth Berle
Yamaguchi, Yukio
Yates, John Harry
Yates, Keith

Zeroka, Daniel
Zimm, Bruno Hasbrouck

Thermodynamics
Baes, Charles Frederick, Jr.
Bahe, Lowell Warren
Barron, Saul
Bauman, John E., Jr.
Clifton, David Geyer
Criss, Cecil M.
Fletcher, Edward Abraham
Germano, Don Joseph
Goldberg, Robert Nathan
Gorges, Heinz A.
Gupta, Vijay Kumar
Gyftopoulos, Elias Panayiotis
Hall, Kenneth Richard
Higuchi, Takeru
Horne, Frederick Herbert
Kellogg, Herbert Humphrey
Krikorian, Oscar Harold
Lang, John Calvin
Lee, John Francis
Mason, Caroline Faith Vibert
Miner, Bryant Albert
Parrish, William Rutledge
Phillips, Sidney Leon
Prigogine, Ilya
Selover, Theodore Britton, Jr.
Sengers, Jan Vincent
Serrin, James Burton
Sturtevant, Julian Munson
Westrum, Edgar Francis, Jr.

Other
Angus, John Cotton, *Electrochemistry*
Bagby, Marvin Orville
Bahary, William Shaul, *Electrochemistry*
Bartlett, Paul Doughty, *Reaction mechanisms*
Bersohn, Richard
Blakeslee, A. Eugene, *Crystal growth*
Bluestein, Bernard R. (Metal Plating and Metal finishing)
Bolker, Henry Irving, *Wood chemistry*
Brooks, John Bill
Brown, Glenn Halstead, *Liquid crystals*
Bushaw, Thomas Henry
Caduff, Noralynn Jo, *Radiochemistry*
Cleland, W(illiam) Wallace, *Biochemistry*
Cobb, Carolus Melville, *Chemistry research management*
Crawford, Bryce Low, Jr., *Molecular spectroscopy*
Daniel, Samuel Henderson, III, *Nuclear power plant chemistry*
Dey, Arabinda Narayan
Evans, Dennis Hyde, *Electrochemistry*
Facci, John Stephen, *Electroanalytical chemistry*
Faehl, Larry Gene, *Agricultural chemistry*
Faulkner, Larry Ray
Fields, Ellis Kirby
Folkers, Karl August, *Biomedical research administration*
Folsome, Clair Edwin, *Chemistry of the origin of life*
Frye, Herschel Gordon, *Forensic chemistry*
Gardner, Marjorie Hyer, *Chemical education*
Goebel, Walther Frederick, *Immunochemistry*
Goetz, Frank, *Propellant chemistry*
Guist, Guyer Gordon, Jr.
Gutowsky, Herbert Sander
Haberman, John Phillip, *Chemistry of oil and gas production*
Hagen, Arnulf Peder
Harris, Milton, *Natural and synthetic fibers*
Harris, Ronald Lee
Hesselberth, John Frederic, *Chemistry and engineering research administration*
Hoare, James Patrick, *Electrochemistry*
Hopgood, David
Hopke, Philip Karl
Hoseney, Russell Carl
Jenkins, Alexander, III, *Research and development management*
Johnson, Greg Willard, *Atomic spectroscopy*
Jonas, Jiri, *High pressure techniques*
Kaiser, Emil Thomas, *Bio-organic chemistry*
Karas, Bradley Ross, *Electrochemistry*
Kaykaty, Maurice, *Drug metabolism*
Keil, Klaus, *Cosmochemistry*
Kliem, Peter Otto, *Photographic science*
Krogh, Lester Christensen, *Research and development management*
Kwolek, Stephanie Louise
Laitinen, Herbert August, *Electrochemistry*
Lazarus, Allan K., *Synthetic lubricants*
Lim, Edward Chol
Losin, Edward Thomas
MacKay, Kenneth Donald, *Chemistry research administration*
Magee, John Lafayette
Mayer, William John, *Separation science.*
McKillip, William James, *Research and development management*
Mehrotra, Ashok Kumar
Menyhert, William Robert, *Conductive polymers*
Morris, Robert Scott, *Separation science*
Mossoba, Magdi Michel
Occolowitz, John Lewis, *Mass spectrometry*
Ojima, Iwao
Olhoeft, Gary Roy, *Electrochemistry*
Pan, Huo-Ping, *Radiation chemistry*
Pappas, James John, *Graphic arts chemistry*
Parsons, Michael L.
Porter, Walter James, Jr.
Princen, Lambertus H(enricus), *Science administration*
Puchtler, Holde, *Histochemistry*
Riley, John Thomas, *Coal chemistry*
Rousch, Patricia Marie Barry
Rudys, Stasys Kestutis
Sasse, Ronald Anthony, *Radiation chemistry; Propellant chemistry*

Schachman, Howard Kapnek, *Biochemistry*
Schroeder, Leland Roy, *Carbohydrate chemistry*
Schuler, Robert Hugo, *Radiation chemistry*
Scotti, Vincent Guy, *Radiochemistry*
Segar, Douglas Allan
Spenser, Ian Daniel
Spindel, William, *Science policy, chemical science administration*
Steele, Gerald Hicks
Sullivan, Edward Maurice, *Quality assurance*
Tang, Lucia Chia-Lu
Taylor, Robert Cooper, *Spectroscopy and molecular structure*
Throdahl, Monte Corden, *Chemical research management*
Tobias, Charles William
Toomey, Joseph Edward, Jr.
Upton, Charles Joseph
Varma, Asha, *Atomic spectroscopy*
Vining, Leo Charles, *Bio-organic chemistry*
Viola, Victor E., Jr.
Wagenknecht, John Henry
Wagman, Gerald H(oward)
Walters, Douglas Bruce, *Chemical health and safety*
Watras, Ronald Edward, *Chemical education*
Westmoreland, Thomas Delbert, Jr.
Wickham, Margaret Edna, *Mass spectrometry*
Wiers, Brandon Helmholz, *Computational chemistry*
Wong, Hans Kuomin, *Photographic science*
Zamora, Antonio, *Chemical information*

COGNITIVE SCIENCE. *See* PSYCHOLOGY, Cognition.

COMPUTER SCIENCE. *See also* ENGINEERING, Electrical.

Algorithms
Afshar, Siroos K.
Aliphas, Amnon
Banerjee, Utpal
Bauer, Michael Anthony
Baybars, Ilker
Brown, R(oy) Leonard
Chandra, Ashok Kumar
Corder, Michael Paul
Datta, Biswa Nath
Decker, James Frederick
Delashmit, Walter Howard, Jr.
Dobkin, David Paul
Doster, Joseph Michael
Fienup, James Ray
Fishman, Robert Sumner
Franco, John Vincent
Frank, Ellen Ryan
Frederickson, Paul Oliver
Garzia, Ricardo Francisco
Girou, Michael
Hale, William Kent
Jasiulek, Joachim Norbert
Kameda, Tiko
Karmarkar, Narenda
Kesler, Stanislav Branko
Kleiman, Howard
Klema, Virginia C.
Knuth, Donald Ervin
Kobler, Virginia Ponds
Kondilis, Francis Nicholas, Jr.
Koskelo, Markku Juhani
Krisnamoorthy, Mukkai Subramaniam
Lakshmivarahan, Sivaramakrishnan
Leifman, Lev Jacob
Levin, Joshua Zev
Lin, Shen
Lincoln, Walter Butler, Jr.
Mandelbaum, David Michael
Manning, Ruth Ann
Marquardt, Donald Wesley
Morgan, Stephen Lyle
Newman, Morris
Oliver, Carl Edward
Rabin, Michael O.
Rosen, Judah Ben
Sadowsky, John
Samn, Sherwood
Sappington, John Oliver
Schwartz, Jacob Theodore
Sullivan, Francis Edward
Tarjan, Robert Endre
Urry, Vern William
Weide, Bruce Warren
Woodward, Paul Ralph

Artificial intelligence
Affatato, Joseph Frank
Aliphas, Amnon
Amarel, Saul
Anderson, John Robert
Andria, George Daniel
Anselmo, Victor John
Apple, Martin Allen
Ball, Larry Lennox
Barstow, David Robbins
Berliner, Hans Jack
Bezdek, James Christian
Binford, Thomas Oriel
Boyle, Brian John
Briggs, Arthur Brailsford, Jr.
Brode, John
Chandrasekaran, Balakrishnan
Conners, Richard William
Conway, Lynn Ann
Corff, Nicholas J.
Daly, John Anthony
Decker, Bruce Michael
De Jong, Gerald
Dlhopolsky, Joseph Gerald
Evens, Martha Walton
Feigenbaum, Edward Albert
Gajski, Daniel Danko
Galambos, James Andrew
Goyal, Shri Krishna
Griffiths, John David
Hansen, James Vernon
Hayes-Roth, Frederick

Hecht, Lee Martin
Heilmeier, George Harry
Hofstadter, Douglas Richard
Holtzman, Samuel
Jarisch, Wolfram Rudolf
Kasdan, Harvey Lee
Kasturi, Rangachar
Kawamura, Kazuhiko
Kirsch, Russell Andrew
Kobler, Virginia Ponds
Krug, Harry Everistus Peter, Jr.
Kurzweil, Raymond C.
LaBonte, Anton Edward
Lapen, Robert Joseph
Lauzzana, Raymond Guido
Leibholz, Stephen Wolfgang
Ligomenides, Panos Aristides
Loatman, Robert Bruce
Mackworth, Alan Keith
Malkoff, Donald Burton
Marcot, Bruce Gregory
McArthur, Wilson Cooper
Meystel, Alexander Michael
Michalski, Ryszard Spencer
Minker, Jack
Minsky, Marvin Lee
Moody, Daniel
Moravec, Hans Peter
Moses, Joel
Negoita, Constantin Virgil
Nelson, Richard D.
Nirenburg, Sergei
Park, Ok-Choon
Parker, Alice Cline
Pesch, William Allan
Popov, Dan
Powell, Edward Gordon
Power, Daniel Joseph
Radzikowski, Pawel
Reddy, D. Raj
Rosen, C(harles) A.
Rosenfeld, Azriel
Sage, Andrew Patrick, Jr.
Schvaneveldt, Roger Wayne
Shortliffe, Edward Hance
Siegel, Melvin Walter
Steinman, Stuart Leonard
Szilagyi, Mike Nicholas
Tanimoto, Steven Larry
Triffet, Terry
Turchin, Valentin Fedorovich
Utting, Kenneth
Van Winkle, Edgar Walling
Wells, Alan Harvey
Wiig, Karl Martin
Williams, Albert Lynn, Jr.
Winograd, Terry Allen
Wohlsen, Robert Cobb
Wulfman, Carl Eugene

Computer architecture
Amdahl, Gene Myron
Amundsen, Keith Byron
Arvind
Aupperle, Kenneth Robert
Banerjee, Utpal
Bartlett, Peter Greenough
Bell, Chester Gordon
Belle Isle, Albert Pierre
Bertrand, John
Bic, Lubomir
Boyd, Edward Lee
Brooks, Frederick Phillips, Jr.
Carter, William Caswell
Chen, Steve S.
Cheung, John Yan-Poon
Childs, Jeffrey John
Conway, Lynn Ann
Cotton, John M.
Cox, Jerome Rockhold, Jr.
Cray, Seymour R.
Davis, Alan Lynn
Decker, James Frederick
Denning, Peter James
Donnelley, James Ellis
Feigenbaum, Edward Albert
Fleck, David Charles
Girou, Michael
Gordon, Edward Barry
Gray, Festus Gail
Greco, Richard James
Hammer, Carl
Heard, Harry Gordon
Kavipurapu, Krishna M.
Kuck, David Jerome
Liang, Tom Yuan-Tong
Lombardi, Fabrizio
Mac Laren, Malcolm Donald
Magar, Surendar Singh
Maguire, Gerald Quentin, Jr.
Mooney, James Donald
Myers, Wade Hampton, Jr.
Pahwa, Ashok
Patton, Peter Clyde
Peparata, Franco Paolo
Quek, Swee-Meng
Riganati, John Philip
Schwartz, Jacob Theodore
Slowinski, David Allen
Stewart, Robert Murray, Jr.
Stock, Rodney Dennis
Svarrer, Robert W.
Walsh, Jacqueline Ann
Wang, Pong-Sheng
Weinberg, Richard Alan
Wong, Edward Chor-Cheung

Cryptography and data security
Absalom, Constance Mary
Blakley, George Robert, Jr.
Denning, Dorothy Elizabeth
Figueres, Maurice Christian
Hammer, Carl
Linn, John
Makar, Boshra Halim
Miller, James Edward
Myers, Eugene Dolan
Palazzo, Reginaldo, Jr.
Parker, Donn Blanchard
Rabin, Michael O.
Richards, Roger Thomas
Wagner, Raymond Lee
White, Richard Mahaffey
Williams, John Michael

Database systems
Bic, Lubomir
Breitbart, Yuri Jacob
Carino, Felipe, Jr.
Cox, Steven Willard
Dougherty, George John
Duncan, Doris Gottschalk
Flum, Robert Samuel, Sr.
Fry, James Palmer
Hanson, Trevor Russell
Hoplin, Herman Peter
Howard, Jay Lloyd
Hudgins, Archibald Perrin, II
Jennings, Larry Eugene
Jones, Donald Leroy
Kameda, Tiko
Kellner, Richard George
Lawrence, David Delbert
Lee, Edward Yue Shing
Levy, David Edward
Li, Victor On-Kwok
Martin-Robinson, Kera Gayle
Massey, James Kendall
Minker, Jack
Moore, Patrick David
Nigam, Rajendra C.
Pahwa, Ashok
Rose, Glenn Robert
Scheuermann, Peter I.
Shan, Hsin-Tsan Grace
Shay, William Albert
Sokol, Robert James
Stewart, David Harry
Tenopir, Carol
Valencis, Janet Margaret

Distributed systems and networks
Amar, Amar Dev
Amundsen, Keith Byron
Arns, Robert George
Avadian, John Mark
Bedrosian, Samuel Der
Borochoff, Robert M.
Breitbart, Yuri Jacob
Brody, Stuart Martin
Cape, Robert E.
Carson, George Stephen
Carter, Jeff Crossett
Christ, Duane Marland
Curtis, Ronald Sanger
Dessy, Raymond Edwin
Doherty, Mark Fitzgerald
Donahue, Michael James
Donnelley, James Ellis
Dougherty, George John
Dunbar, Geoffrey Thorne
Farah, Badie Naiem
Ferrari, Domenico
Fry, James Palmer
Gable, Ralph Kirkland
Gladney, Henry Martin
Grand, Diana Leigh
Green, Paul Eliot, Jr.
Hale, William Kent
Hall, Nancy Rose
Heinicke, Peter Hart
Katz, Alan R.
Kellner, Richard George
Kleinrock, Leonard
Krutz, Ronald L.
Lakshmivarahan, Sivaramakrishnan
Lee, Edward Yue Shing
Li, Victor On-Kwok
Linn, John
Lloyd, Evan Elliott Morgan
Lu, Chun Chian
Malfara, David Joseph
Meditch, James Stephen
Myers, Eugene Dolan
Myers, Wade Hampton, Jr.
Nelson, Larry Dean
Ng, Peter Ann-Beng
Nikora, Allen Peter
Perry, Dennis Gordon
Perry, Dwight
Robinson, James Robert
Scheuermann, Peter I.
Schwartz, Mischa
Shreve, Gregory Monroe
Siegel, Eric David
Simpson, W(ilburn) Dwain
Skinner, Thomas Paul
Springer, Donald Harold
Stein, Scott Allen
Stewart, Robert Murray, Jr.
Storozum, Steven Lee
Sweeney, Patrick J.
Thompson, Kenneth Lane
Unger, Brian William
Wang, Pong-Sheng
Williams, Theodore Joseph
Wittie, Larry Dawson
Young, Frederick John

Foundations of computer science
Backus, John
Clark, Gary Edwin
Codd, Edgar Frank
Hartmanis, Juris
Krisnamoorthy, Mukkai Subramaniam
Rogers, Edwin Henry
Warfield, John Nelson

Graphics, image processing, and pattern recognition
Amero, Bernard Alan
Asher, Robert Bernard
Bardwell, Steven Jack
Barsky, Brian Andrew
Bedrosian, Samuel Der
Benedict, George Frederick
Bezdek, James Christian
Binford, Thomas Oriel
Bitzer, Donald Lester
Bowyer, Allen Frank
Bridges, Alan Lynn
Brooks, Frederick Phillips, Jr.
Brooks, Richard Cavett
Carberry, James Joseph
Carino, Felipe, Jr.
Carson, George Stephen
Chakravarty, Indranil
Chandrasekaran, Balakrishnan
Chang, Shi-Kuo
Chappell, Gary Alan
Chittineni, Chittibabu
Clark, Alan Lee

Cohen, Edgar Allan, Jr.
Conners, Richard William
Cooper, (Howard) Gordon
Corff, Nicholas J.
Croft, Thomas A(rthur)
Crowe, Devon George
Dean, Edwin Becton
Delashmit, Walter Howard, Jr.
Dertouzos, Michael Leonidas
Dobkin, David Paul
Doherty, Mark Fitzgerald
Dusko, Harold George
Eigen, Daryl Jay
Elmaghraby, Adel Said
El Shazly, Hassan
Fakharzadeh, Ali M.
Fischell, David Ross
Franzblau, Daniel Eric
Gaber, Bruce Paul
Garfield, Alan J.
Gentleman, Jane F.
Ghanta, Babu Madhur
Glackin, David Langdon
Gordon, Mark Gardiner
Grace, Thomas Peter
Greco, Richard James
Gur, Yigal
Hansche, Bruce David
Hasegawa, Tony Seisuke
Hayes, Monson Henry, III
Henderson, Floyd Merl
Hughett, Paul William
Jenkins, Arnold Milton
Jones, Walter William
Kasdan, Harvey Lee
Kashyap, Rangasami L.
Kasturi, Rangachar
Kelley, Michael Stephen
Kiefhaber, Nikolaus Josef
Kim, Yongmin
Kirsch, Russell Andrew
Knowles, Richard James Robert
Kratz, Lawrence John
LaBonte, Anton Edward
Lahart, Martin Joseph
Landgrebe, David Allen
Latta, John Neal
Lauzzana, Raymond Guido
Legters, George Richard
Levin, Joshua Zev
Ligler, George Todd
Liles, Clifton Roy
Lopez, Hector
Lowinger, Thomas
Maguire, Gerald Quentin, Jr.
Maiman, Theodore Harold
Marsh, Kenneth Albert
Marshall, Garland Ross
Martin-Robinson, Kera Gayle
Meagher, Donald Joseph
Merrill, Marshall Leigh
Michalski, Ryszard Spencer
Mitchell, Nancy Brown
Morgan, Stephen Lyle
Oldroyd, L(awrence) Andrew
Paluzzi, Peter Ronald
Panda, Durga Prasad
Pintsov, Leon Aron
Poltorak, Alexander (Israel)
Pomalaza Raez, Carlos Arturo
Potel, Michael John
Pschigoda, Loraine Mae
Rabin, Monroe Stephen Zane
Ratnatunga, Kavan Upajiva
Raudkivi, Uno
Ritter, Gerhard X.
Rosenfeld, Azriel
Sadjadi, Firooz Ahmadi
Salari, Ezzatollah
Schueler, Carl Frederick
Schweizer, Francois
Shneier, Michael Oliver
Shrier, Stefan
Sidlinger, Bruce Douglas
Stevens, Donald Meade
Stock, Rodney Dennis
Stranz, David Donald
Tanimoto, Steven Larry
Tobler, Waldo Rudolph
Toga, Arthur Warren
Trivedi, Manmohan Manubhai
Utting, Kenneth
Vesel, Richard Warren
Walkup, John Frank
Wang, Patrick Shen-pei
Weinberg, Richard Alan
Williams, T. H. Lee
Wu, Hai-Ping
Yang, Yee-Hong
Yessios, Chris Ioannis

Information systems, storage, and retrieval. *See also* INFORMATION SCIENCE.
Abrahamson, Earl Arthur
Allen, Robert Burnell
Beiser, Leo
Blakley, George Robert, Jr.
Bookstein, Abraham
Borochoff, Robert M.
Branscomb, Lewis McAdory
Braun, Stephen Hughes
Bridges, Alan Lynn
Brinson, Donald Edward
Burford, Hugh Jonathan
Cazes, Albert N.
Chi, Chao Shu
Cole, Irad Dean
Cummings, Martin Marc
Demmerle, Alan Michael
Du Wors, Robert Jerome
Everett, Robert Rivers
Findeisen, Heinz H.
Fisher, H. Leonard
Fried, Jerrold
Gardin, T. Hershel
Gill, Hardayal Singh
Hagel, Andrew Richard
Hamblen, John Wesley
Heard, Harry Gordon
Ho, Thomas Inn Min
Hollaar, Lee Allen
Hoye, Robert Earl
Huang, Shiezen
Hudgins, Archibald Perrin, II
Jackson, Douglas Webster
Jacobs, Keith William

Jaffe, Norman J.
Johnson, Clark Eugene, Jr.
Kraft, Donald H.
Kricka, Hanna Halyna
Lesko, Robert Joseph
Ligomenides, Panos Aristides
Livingston, John David
Lurix, Paul Leslie, Jr.
Martin, Richard Douglas
Massey, James Kendall
Maxwell, Donald Lee
Mayer, Dieter Heinz Hermann
Miller, James Edward
Moody, Daniel
Ngo, Peter Dinh-Tuan
Packer, Katherine Helen
Pesch, William Allan
Pollock, Roy Van Horn
Pratt, Arnold W.
Pribor, Hugo Casimer
Pritchard, Lois Breur
Rush, Richard William
Sachs, Lester Marvin
Sahni, Omesh
Schniederjans, Marc James
Schroer, Bernard Jon
Shannon, Claude Elwood
Smith, David William
Smith, Robert David
Stewart, David Harry
Summit, Roger Kent
Sweeney, Urban Joseph
Tucker, Marc Stephen
Vinson, John Wilmot
Watkins, Paul Roger
Weaver, Christopher Scot
Weiss, Roland George
Williams, John Michael
Williams, Martha Ethelyn
Winarski, Daniel James
Witte, Kurt Allen
Woolman, Myron
Wray, John Lawrence

Mathematical software
Altschuler, Martin David
Anderson, James Bryan
Andria, George Daniel
Bickart, Theodore Albert
Bradford, Bert Larue
Brown, R(oy) Leonard
Burr, Baldwin Gwynne
Chang, Albert Fuwu
Clay, Charles George, Jr.
Craig, Richard G.
Dediu, Mihai Michael
Diaz, Julio Cesar
Dixon, Wilfrid Joseph
Driessel, Kenneth R.
Ford, Byron Milton
Frauenthal, James Clay
Garzia, Ricardo Francisco
Grace, Thomas Peter
Harbaugh, John Warvelle
Heath, Larry Francis
Heath, Michael Thomas
Held, Ronald Dennis
Kootsey, Joseph Mailen
Ley, Richard Wayne
Lin, Shen
Ling, Robert F.
Litvak, Boris Lvovich
Lupash, Lawrence O(vidiu)
Markatos, Nicolas-Christos Gregory
McCall, Edward Huffaker
Meisel, David Dering
Minkoff, Michael
Mochizuki, Leslie Yasuko
Moses, Joel
Mowery, Dwight Fay
Nguyen, Chinh Trung
Pool, James Christopher Thomas
Prior, Fred William
Salane, Douglas Edward
Sheridan, Robert Emmett, Jr.
Stahl, Raymond Earl
Tretter, Marietta Joan
Tsay, Yih Tsong
Tyson, Robert Karl
Van Winkle, Edgar Walling
Ward, Robert C.
Wasserman, Zelda Rakowitz
Weinrich, Brian Erwin
Wendelberger, James George
Wolfe, Michael David

Numerical analysis. ***See also* MATHEMATICS.**
Ancona, Antonio
Anderson, James Bryan
Andrushkiw, Roman Ihor
Basehore, Kerry Lee
Blackburn, Jacob Floyd
Bober, William
Bramble, James Henry
Branco, Maria dos Milagres
Burton, Howard Alan
Carasso, Alfred Sam
Carter, Leland LaVelle
Chang, Albert Fuwu
Concordia, Charles
Cooley, Donald Wayne
Diaz, Julio Cesar
Di Donato, Armido Richard
Dietenberger, Mark Anthony
Doster, Joseph Michael
Du, Sen-Wo
Edwards, Bruce Haven
Felippa, Carlos Alberto
Fix, George Joseph
Gallie, Thomas Muir, Jr.
Gilmartin, Amy Jean
Glimm, James Gilbert
Grimm, Louis J.
Gropp, William Douglas
Hakala, Reino William
Hauptman, John Michael
Heath, Michael Thomas
Hoagland, Gordon Wood
Jasiulek, Joachim Norbert
Jedruch, Jacek
Kadi, Kamal Sif-el
Kaufman, Edwin H., Jr.
Kearfott, Ralph Baker
Kratz, Lawrence John
Lax, Peter David
Leventhal, Stephen Henry
Lu, Allen An-hua
Manning, Ruth Ann
McAuley, Van Alfon
Meenakshi Sundaram, Kandasamy
Mehra, Raman Kumar
Minkoff, Michael
Molz, Fred John, III
Monash, Ellis Alan
Neuberger, John William
Neumann, Herschel
Nguyen, Vietchau
Oliver, Carl Edward
Orszag, Steven Alan
Rheinboldt, Werner Carl
Rosen, Judah Ben
Schneider, Gerald Elmore
Shay, William Albert
Steihaug, Trond
Thompson, Sylvester
Wahnsiedler, Walter Edward
Wilson, Walter Ervin

Operating systems
Brinson, Donald Edward
Brower, Joseph Gilbert
Carter, Jeff Crossett
Du Wors, Robert Jerome
Ferrari, Domenico
Friedberg, Carl E.
Hanson, Trevor Russell
Hume, James Nairn Patterson
Kelley, Michael Stephen
Mayes, Leslie William
Merrill, Marshall Leigh
Merritt, David Alan
Moldenhauer, Jeanne Elisabeth
Mooney, James Donald
Paris, Steven Mark
Schwetman, Herbert De Witt, Jr.
Schwetman, Herbert Dewitt
Sherman, Gordon Rae
Sidlinger, Bruce Douglas
Skinner, Thomas Paul
Slowinski, David Allen
Stein, Scott Allen
Walsh, Jacqueline Ann
Wittie, Larry Dawson
Wolfe, Bradley Allen

Programming languages
Arvind
Backus, John
Bergquist, James William
Bondy, Jonathan
Chirlian, Paul M.
Cohen, David Marshall
Council, Edward Latimer
Curtis, Ronald Sanger
Dediu, Mihai Michael
Garfield, Alan J.
Gladney, Henry Martin
Hume, James Nairn Patterson
Jaffe, Norman J.
Knuth, Donald Ervin
Lee, Van Ming
Mac Laren, Malcolm Donald
Mall, Vance Austin
Mayes, Leslie William
Perlis, Alan J.
Randolph, Lynwood Parker
Sammet, Jean E.
Schuman, Gail Isherwood
Shah, Babubhai Vadilal
Sowers, Joseph Louis
Thompson, James Earl
Tucker, Allen Brown, Jr.
Turchin, Valentin Fedorovich
Wallace, Robert Bruce, Jr.
Welch, Lester Clint

Software engineering
Afshar, Siroos K.
Avadian, John Mark
Barstow, David Robbins
Bauer, Michael Anthony
Bayer, Jesse Abraham
Bondy, Jonathan
Briggs, Arthur Brailsford, Jr.
Brocka, Bruce
Brody, Steven
Brower, Joseph Gilbert
Burgess, Eric
Chamis, Christos Constantinos
Christian, John Thomas
Clay, Charles George, Jr.
Clements, Gregory Leland
Cole, Irad Dean
Cook, Joseph Marion
Council, Edward Latimer
D'Entremont, Edward Joseph
Fakharzadeh, Ali M.
Farah, Badie Naiem
Figueres, Maurice Christian
Franzblau, Daniel Eric
Fries, Richard Cyril
Fritz, Frank Mark
Galbiati, Louis Joseph
Geary, William Charles
Ghanta, Babu Madhur
Gordon, Edward Barry
Gradijan, Jack Robertson
Grand, Diana Leigh
Hagel, Andrew Richard
Hall, David Lee
Hall, Nancy Rose
Heinicke, Peter Hart
Jackson, Glen Leon
Karasik, Myron Solomon
Kavipurapu, Krishna M.
Kelsoe, Lynda Carol
Kiefhaber, Nikolaus Josef
Kuck, David Jerome
Ligler, George Todd
Liotine, Frank James, Jr.
Ljung, Donovan Allen
Loftus, Margaret A.
Mall, Vance Austin
Martin, Paul Joseph
McGill, Scott Douglas
McMillen, Sandra Lee
Mehra, Raman Kumar
Merlin, Howard Eliot
Merritt, David Alan
Miller, Robert Alan
Mochizuki, Leslie Yasuko
Ng, Peter Ann-Beng
Nieh, Bill
Nikora, Allen Peter
Parent, Douglas John
Paris, Steven Mark
Park, William Harold
Parrish, Mark David
Patton, Peter Clyde
Pearce, William Julian
Pemble, Kim Russell
Perlis, Alan J.
Perry, Dennis Gordon
Perry, Dwight
Petras, Charles Edward
Pohl, Jens Gerhard
Rocca, Jeffrey John
Ross, Douglas Taylor
Rothrock, Ray Alan
Sammet, Jean E.
Schuman, Gail Isherwood
Schure, Mark Richard
Shih, Charles Chien
Simon, Sheridan Alan
Smith-Vaniz, William Reid
Sossamon, David Baine
Spital, Robin David
Springer, Donald Harold
Su, Stanley Y. W.
Sweeney, Patrick J.
Thulin, Frederick Adolph, Jr.
Toth, Joseph William
Town, Donald Earl
Tramontozzi, Louis Robert
Vogelman, Joseph Herbert
Wagner, Raymond Lee
Wallace, Robert Bruce, Jr.
Wang, Patrick Shen-pei
Weide, Bruce Warren
Winograd, Terry Allen
Wu, John Naichi
Zunde, Pranas
Zweben, Stuart Harvey

Theoretical computer science
Amarel, Saul
Bedinger, Joseph Arnold
Brakefield, James Charles
Cenzer, Douglas Alfred
Chandra, Ashok Kumar
Cohen, David Marshall
Cook, Stephen Arthur
Franco, John Vincent
Goldstine, Herman Heine
Gross, Jonathan Light
Hartmanis, Juris
Kannan, Ravindran
Killian, Barbara Germain
Lamport, Leslie
Lloyd, Evan Elliott Morgan
Loui, Michael Conrad
Meinel, Carolyn Pettit
Pemble, Kim Russell
Peparata, Franco Paolo
Purdom, Paul Walton, Jr.
Seadler, Stephen Edward
Sherman, Gordon Rae

Other
Atal, Bishnu Saroop, *Man machine communication by voice*
Bennett, John Roscoe, *Computer company management*
Berliner, Hans Jack
Briotta, Daniel A., Jr., *Laboratory microcomputing*
Brown, Stephen Woody, *Computer applications in education and psychology*
Buzen, Jeffrey Peter, *Computer performance*
Carlton-Foss, John Andrew
Carter, William Caswell
Chase, Robert Arthur, *Computers in medicine*
Clark, Alan Lee, *Geometric modelling of solids*
Conrad, Michael, *Computers and biological systems*
Danaher, Brian Grayson, *Computer-based instruction*
Dean, Nathan Wesley, *Research administration*
Dertouzos, Michael Leonidas, *Personal computers*
Dupree, Samuel Hardy, Jr., *Scientific computing*
Everett, Robert Rivers, *Digital computer design*
Farrington, Thomas Alex, *Computer services management*
Flippen-Anderson, Judith Lee
Gajski, Daniel Danko
Gatewood, George David, *Computer interfacing*
Goffman, Martin
Hamid, Mohamed Ahmed-Abdel
Hards, Kathryn Elisa
Inman, Bobby Ray, *Computer technology research and development management*
Javel, Eric
Jennings, Larry Eugene
Jones, Alfred Welwood
Kahn, Robert Elliot, *Research administration*
Kobayashi, Hisashi, *Research administration*
Laxer, Cary
Levine, Randolph Herbert, *Computer education*
Maish, F(rederic) Michael
Merlin, Howard Eliot
Murawski, Walter Ted
Nadin, Mihai, *Semiotics of computer use and applied artificial intelligence*
Nagy, Denes
Navangul, Himanshoo Vishnu, *Use of computers in education*
Oettinger, Anthony Gervin, *Information resources policy*
Pattabiraman, Nagarajan
Peli, Eliezer, *Computerized image enhancement*
Perkins, Glenn Richard, *Data management*
Pinney, Frank Batchelder, *Computer-aided manufacturing*
Purdom, Paul Walton, Jr., *Compiler design*
Recktenwald, Diether Joseph
Rice, Stephen Landon, *CAD/CAM*
Rogers, Edwin Henry
Rollwagen, John A., *Computer company management*
Schwetman, Herbert De Witt, Jr.
Shneier, Michael Oliver
Smith, Robert David, *Human resource information systems*
Snyder, James Newton, *Administration*
Sowers, Joseph Louis, *Simulation*
Tang, John Theodore
Tarjan, Robert Endre, *Group theory, data structures*
Tidball, Charles Stanley
Tripathy, Sukant Kishore
Wagner, Lorry Yale
White, Mary-Alice, *Psychology of computer learning*
White, Richard Mahaffey
Wong, Edward Chor-Cheung, *Logic design*

DENTISTRY AND ODONTOLOGY

Cariology
Gantt, David Graham
Hein, John William
Hicks, M. John
Levy, John Stuart
Mallatt, Mark Edward
Pape, Harry Rudolph, Jr.
Parkins, Frederick Milton
Shrestha, Buddhi Man

Dental growth and development
Doyle, Walter Arnett
Duperon, Donald Francis
Garner, LaForrest Dean
Goldsmith, Douglas Howard
Hicks, M. John
Lestrel, Pete Ernest
Malhotra, Shyam Kumar
Nahoum, Henry Isaac
Nakamoto, Tetsuo
Owen, David Gray
Peterson, Thomas Mark
Schwartz, Jeffrey Hugh
Siebert, Joseph Robert
Wang, Teen-Meei Thomas

Dental materials
Bowen, Jeffrey Louis
Brauer, Gerhard Max
Chang, Tiang-Shing
Ciancio, Sebastian Gene
Civjan, Simon
Gandt, Jerome Otto
Gavelis, Jonas Rimvydas
Heyde, John Bradley
Lund, Melvin Robert
Malhotra, Manohar Lal
Misra, Dwarika Nath
Mueller, Herbert Joseph
Panzera, Carl
Rogers, Sam
Valega, Thomas Michael
Vandesteeg, Gregg Alan
Washburn, John Garrett
Weikel, Maurice Marcel

Endodontics
Block, Robert Michael
Cappuccino, Carleton C.
DePalma, Robert Anthony
Heuer, Michael Alexander
Lin, Louis Min-Tsu
Taintor, Jerry Frank

Implantology
Chappell, Robert Paul
Cranin, Abraham Norman
Nery, Edmundo Barbin
Sendax, Victor Irven
Stallard, Richard Elgin
Valega, Thomas Michael

Oral and maxillofacial surgery
Beirne, Owen Ross
Clayman, Lewis
Cranin, Abraham Norman
DeVore, Duane Thomas
Goldsmith, Douglas Howard
Gotcher, Jack Everett, Jr.
Gross, Bob Dean
Laskin, Daniel M.
Leake, Donald Lewis
Mc Leran, James Herbert
Mercier, Paul
Petri, William Henry, III
Steelman, Robert Joe
Waite, Daniel Elmer
White, Raymond Petrie, Jr.

Oral biology
Alley, Keith Edward
Avery, James Knuckey
Boyan, Barbara Dale
Cappuccino, Carleton C.
Ciarlone, Alfred Edward
Davenport, William Daniel, Jr.
Dirksen, Thomas Reed, II
Fine, Albert S.
Gaffar, Maria Corazon Solis
Gangaros, Louis Paul, Sr.
Gantt, David Graham
Gaynor, Harold Marvin
Goepp, Robert August
Golub, Lorne Malcolm
Orland, Frank Jay
Rao, Gopal Subba
Rifkin, Barry Richard
Scott, David Bytovetzski
Sessle, Barry John
Siegel, Ivens Aaron
Slomiany, Bronislaw Leszek
Stevens, Roy Harris
Taubman, Martin Arnold
Termine, John David
Van Dyke, Thomas Elliott
Yagiela, John Allen

Oral pathology
Alexander, William Nebel
Fullmer, Harold Milton
Lin, Louis Min-Tsu
Lynch, Denis Patrick
Nelson, John Franklin

Orthodontics
Cantor, Benjamin Boruch
Di Salvo, Nicholas Armand
Doyle, Walter Arnett
Garner, LaForrest Dean
Hanley, Kevin Joseph
Legan, Harry Lewis
Litton, Stephen Frederick
Malhotra, Shyam Kumar
Nahoum, Henry Isaac
Nikolai, Robert Joseph
Peterson, Thomas Mark

Periodontics
Buchanan, Judith Ann
Chilton, Neal W(arwick)
Ciancio, Sebastian Gene
Cohen, David Walter
Cohen, Ronald Alex
Cox, Donald Stephen
De Marco, Thomas Joseph
Eggert, Frank Michael
Evian, Cyril Ian
Gandt, Jerome Otto
Gaynor, Harold Marvin
Gher, Marlin Eugene, Jr.
Golub, Lorne Malcolm
Kaslick, Ralph Sidney
Löe, Harald
Lopatin, Dennis Edward
Marks, Sandy Cole, Jr.
Mehta, Noshir Rustom
Narayanan, A. Sampath
Nery, Edmundo Barbin
Offenbacher, Steven
Page, Roy Christopher
Schifter, Catherine Crutchfield
Suzuki, Jon Byron
Van Dyke, Thomas Elliott
West, Theodore Lee

Preventive dentistry
Caslavska, Vera Barbara
Christen, Arden Gale
Dunning, James Morse
Faunce, Frank Roland
Greene, John Clifford
Grover, Pushpinder Singh
Kaslick, Ralph Sidney
Mallatt, Mark Edward
Pape, Harry Rudolph, Jr.
Parkins, Frederick Milton
Stallard, Richard Elgin

Prosthodontics
Asawa, George Nobuo
Baxter, Joann Crystal
Cheng, Kevin K. T.
Cohen, Ronald Alex
Gavelis, Jonas Rimvydas
Javid, Nikzad Sabet
Lenchner, Nathaniel Herbert
Sakaguchi, Ronald Louis
Schwartzman, Boris
Sendax, Victor Irven

Other
Alexander, William Nebel, *Oral Medicine*
Bastawi, Aly Eloui, *Pedodontics*
Campbell-Smith, Rosemary Gilles, *Dental practice consulting*
Cordova-Salinas, Maria Asuncion
Crim, Gary Allen, *Operative dentistry*
DeVincenzi, Ronald George
Douglas, William Hugh, *Restorative dentistry*
Duperon, Donald Francis, *Pediatric dentistry*
Gage, Tommy Wilton
Greene, John Clifford, *Epidemiology*
Grembowski, David Emil
Lee, Mickey Mitchell
Lipton, James Abbott, *Facial pain*
Löe, Harald, *Dental research institute administration*
Lund, Melvin Robert, *operative dentistry*
Mehta, Noshir Rustom, *Cranio-mandibular cervical pain and dysfunction*
Nelson, John Franklin, *Oral medicine*
Nylen, Marie Ussing, *Dental research institute administration*
Olsen, Norman Harry, *Pediatric dentistry*
Pierce, Calvin Judson, *Behavioral dentistry/medicine*
Re, Gerald James
Riviere, George Robert, *Pediatric dentistry*
Schifter, Catherine Crutchfield
Schoen, Max Howard, *Public health*
Solberg, William Knott, *Temporomandibular joint and facial pain*
Stannard, Jan Gregory
Weikel, Maurice Marcel

ENERGY SCIENCE AND TECHNOLOGY

Biomass. ***See also*** **AGRICULTURE.**
Abeles, Tom Peter
Antal, Michael Jerry, Jr.
Archer, Richard Earl
Bagby, Marvin Orville
Barnett, Stockton Gordon
Basic, John Nicholas, Sr.
Bassi, Sukh Dev
Boubel, Richard William
Flikke, Arnold Maurice
Hamrick, Joseph Thomas
Henry, Patrick M.
Hiler, Edward Allan
Ingram, Lonnie O'Neal
Irgon, Joseph
Klausmeier, William Hilton
Li, Chung-Hsiung
MacKay, G. David MacIvor
Paisley, Mark Alan
Rockwood, Donald Lee
Thomas, John Joseph
Wilson, David Buckingham

Combustion processes

Agnew, William George
Audette, Louis Girard, II
Avery, William Hinckley
Basic, John Nicholas, Sr.
Berman, Herbert L(awrence)
Bly, Lloyd George, Jr.
Carrier, George Francis
Churchill, Stuart Winston
Davis, Lewis Berkley, Jr.
Detra, Ralph William
Dolan, Linda Sutliff
Emmons, Howard Wilson
Friedman, Raymond
Gelinas, Robert Joseph
Gilmour, William Alexander
Glassman, Irvin
Gollahalli, Subramanyam Ramappa
Hamrick, Joseph Thomas
Hjertager, Bjorn Helge
Hochwalt, Carroll Alonzo, Jr.
Jenkins, Donald Ralph
Kanury, (Anjaneya) Murty
Kassoy, David R.
Kruger, Charles Herman, Jr.
Lefebvre, Arthur Henry
Levine, Robert Sidney
Longwell, John Ploeger
Lortie, John William
Loth, John Lodewyk
McGowan, Jon Gerald
Myers, Phillip Samuel
Nagamatsu, Henry Takeshi
Olmstead, William Edward
Penner, Stanford Solomon
Proctor, Charles Lafayette, II
Rosenberg, Robert Brinkmann
Santoro, Robert John
Schmieder, Robert William
Shipman, Charles William
Sirignano, William Alfonso
Slaminski, John Michael
Strain, John Willard
Summerfield, Martin
Suzuki, Tateyuki
Talley, Robert Lee
van Til, Alan Everett
Yeh, James Tehcheng
Zakkay, Victor H.

Fuels

Anglin, James Richard
Attilio, Donald Ernest
Bloch, Herman Samuel
Bodily, David Martin
Burnham, ALan Kent
Cassidy, Martin Macdermott
Chronic, Byron John
Creagan, Robert Joseph
Dolan, Linda Sutliff
Epperly, William Robert
Folk, Stewart Huntley
Gelbard, Fred
Glassman, Irvin
Gollahalli, Subramanyam Ramappa
Harbay, Edward William
Harmon, David E., Jr.
Hoffman, Edward Jack
Jawetz, Pincas
Kratzer, Reinhold Hermann
Lauth, Robert Edward
Lefebvre, Arthur Henry
Linden, Henry Robert
Longwell, John Ploeger
Lowe, Phillip A(rnold)
Marsden, Sullivan Samuel, Jr.
Mc Afee, Jerry
McCoy, Alexander Watts, III
Mc Ketta, John J., Jr.
Merriam, Daniel F(rancis)
Meyers, Robert Allen
Miernyk, William Henry
Morgan, William Andrew
Myers, Phillip Samuel
Olsen, David Kenneth
Page, Mary Michael
Rosenberg, Robert Brinkmann
Schlosberg, Richard Henry
Shen, Sin-Yan
Taylor, William Francis
Thomas, John Richard
Watney, Willard Lynn
Wells, William Lochridge
Widdoes, Lawrence Curtis
Wombles, Robert Huston
Yang, Wen-Ching
Yokell, Michael David

Fuels, coal

Agarwal, Ashok Kumar
Aldridge, Melvin Dayne
Austin, Steven Arthur
Bodily, David Martin
Boron, David John
Boshkov, Stefan Hristov
Brecher, Lee Edward
Carlton, Donald Morrill
Cheeseman, Ray
Cohen, Arthur David
Crelling, John Crawford
Fonseca, Anthony Gutierre
Frölicher, Franz
Garg, Diwakar
Hochwalt, Carroll Alonzo, Jr.
Hopkins, M. E.
Hsia, Yu-Ping
Jansen, George James
Kottlowski, Frank Edward
Losin, Edward Thomas
Maas, Dana Jon
Mathewson, Christopher Colville
Meyer, Edmond Gerald
Miernyk, William Henry
Nichols, Duane Guy
Paisley, Mark Alan
Papamarcos, John
Parks, Oattis Elwyn
Reinemund, John Adam
Spiro, Clifford Lawrence
Sprouse, Kenneth Michael
Squires, Arthur Morton
Thompson, Richard Rogers
Wen, Wen-Yang
Wilson, John Sheridan

Fuels, oil shale

Alexander, Peter
Brecher, Lee Edward
Moore, Richard Owen, Jr.
Park, U-Sun
Pei, Richard Yusien
Pforzheimer, Harry, Jr.

Fuels, other fuels and sources

Audette, Louis Girard, II
Bowden, Bryant Baird
Cunningham, Raymond Leo
Fan, Liang-tseng
Gupta, Vijay Kumar
Hatchell, William O'Donald
Jackson, Michael Dean
Leber, Ralph Eric
Loring, Thomas Joseph
Lortie, John William
Lumb, Ralph Francis
Marchaj, Tadeusz Jozef
McEldowney, Roland Conant
Papamarcos, John
Penner, Stanford Solomon
Scott, David
Starr, Chauncey
Thomason, Harry Jack Lee, Jr.
Veziroglu, Turhan Nejat
Waitzman, Donald Anthony
Wright, Robert James

Fusion. See also LASER.

Auer, Peter Louis
Berry, Lee Allen
Burrell, Charles Frederick
Bussard, Robert William
Campbell, Philip Montgomery, Jr.
Cary, John Robert
Corvin, Wayne Clay
Ellis, William R.
Finn, Patricia Ann
Fleischmann, Hans Hermann
Furth, Harold Paul
George, Thycodam Varkkey
Gilleland, John Rogers
Hammer, David Andrew
Hart, Roger Douglas
Hicks, Harry Richard
Izzo, Ralph
Jensen, Richard Alan
Jesser, William Augustus
Kaita, Robert
Kusse, Bruce Raymond
Kyrala, George Amine
Lazar, Norman H(enry)
Levine, Jerry David
Miley, George Hunter
Miller, Robert Alan
Niimura, Masanobu
Schlachter, Alfred Simon
Shkarofsky, Issie Peter
Stevens, James Everell
Takeda, Harunori
Taylor, Lyle Herman
Weldon, William Forrest
White, Robert Carl
Woodson, Herbert Horace
Yamada, Masaaki
Yonas, Gerold
Yoshikawa, Shoichi
Zerguini, Taha Houssine

Geothermal power

Goldsberry, Fred Lynn
Haskins, Roger Allen
Icerman, Larry
Luth, William Clair
McMurdie, Dennis Stoddard
Philbrick, David Alan
Rinehart, John Sargent
Russell, Eugene A.
Salisbury, John William
Schriener, Alexander, Jr.
Weres, Oleh

Nuclear fission

Abdou, Mohamed Aziz
Adams, James Paul
Alapour, Adel
Albaugh, Fred William
Alexeff, Igor
Allman, Norris C.
Austin, Edward Marvin
Babb, Albert Leslie
Bankoff, Seymour George
Barsky, Arnold M(ilton)
Bartine, David Elliott
Bauer, Richard Carlton
Beach, Louis Andrew
Beckjord, Eric Stephen
Bell, Barbara Jean
Benedict, Manson
Bickel, John Henry
Block, Robert Charles
Blomeke, John Otis
Booth, James Albert
Burge, Charles Arthur
Cacuci, Dan Gabriel
Carter, Robert LeRoy
Chan, Shih Hung
Chandler, John Christopher
Chao, Jiatsong Jason
Chewning, June Spangler
Choppin, Gregory Robert
Chung, Chien
Chung, Hee Mok
Cohen, Karl Paley
Cole, Thomas Earle
Crawley, Paul F.
Critoph, Eugene
Culler, Floyd LeRoy, Jr.
Cullingford, Hatice S(adan)
Detterman, Robert Linwood
Dickens, Justin Kirk
Dickson, Paul Wesley, Jr.
Difilippo, Felix Carlos
Dolan, Linda Capano
Duda, Richard Frank
Edlund, Milton Carl
Einziger, Robert Emanuel
Feinberg, Robert Jacob
Fellows, W(alter) Scott, Jr.
Ferer, Kenneth Michael
Flanagan, Charles Allen
Fluegge, Ronald Marvin
Frantz, Frederick Strassner, Jr.
Gabor, John Dewain

Garlid, Kermit Leroy
Garrick, B. John
Gilligan, John Gerard
Goldsmith, William Alee
Goldstein, Mark Kingston Levin
Goode, Glenn Amos, Jr.
Gowda, Byre Venkataramana
Griffin, Henry Claude
Groenier, William Samuel
Hagmann, Dean Berry
Haire, Marvin Jonathan
Haler, Lawrence Eugene
Halverson, Thomas George
Harms, Archie Arkadius
Heckman, Richard Ainsworth
Hickman, Jack William
Higgins, Patrick John, Jr.
Hildebrandt, Thomas Owen
Hofmann, Peter Ludwig
Holzer, Joseph Mano
Huang, Hai Chow
Huberman, Benjamin
Hurd, Edward Nelson, III
Ibrahim, Shawki Amin
Ireland, John Richard
Jaquess, James Fletcher
Jergins, Colvin Edward
Joksimovich, Vojin
Jones, David Hunter
Kasper, Raphael Goldsmith
Kempe, Robert Aron
Kerr, William
Kikuchi, Chihiro
Koussa, Harold Alan
Kouts, Herbert John Cecil
Kreid, Dennis Karl
Larrimore, James Abbott
Lauzon, Thomas Andrew
Lee, Mike Yuan
Leibowitz, Leonard
Levine, Samuel Harold
Little, Robert Narvaez, Jr.
Liu, Yung Yuan
Lorenzini, Paul Gilbert
Maceda, Edward Louis
Maxwell, Donald Lee
McArthur, Wilson Cooper
McIntyre, Brian Arch
Meem, James Lawrence, Jr.
Misra, Balabhadra
Neely, Horace Hollis
Nicaise, Walter Ferdinand
Oakes, Lester Cornelius
Oatley, David Herbert
Okrent, David
Pagel, Deborah Joanne
Park, U-Sun
Parry, John O.
Paustian, Harold Herman
Pense, Alan Wiggins
Rao, Surendar Purushothay
Redmond, Robert Francis
Richman, Jack William
Rose, David John
Rose, Ronald Palmer
Roush, Marvin Leroy
Saluja, Jagdish Kumar
Schaeffer, Norman M.
Shum, Raymond Hing-Yan
Stewart, James Edmund, III
Tomlinson, Richard Lee
Turinsky, Paul Josef
Umek, Anthony M.
Varley, Ronald Arthur
Vest, Anthony Leon
Wachter, William John
Way, Richard A(lvord)
Wei, Jim P(iau)
Wenz, Michael Frank, Jr.
Wilcox, Robert Howard
Williams, Peter MacLellan
Wiren, Robert Craig
Wray, John Robert
Young, Garry Gean
Youssef, Mahmoud Z. Hassan
Yue, Mike Yuan
Yung, Shu-Chien
Zimmanck, Frank Robert, Jr.

Nuclear fusion

Abdou, Mohamed Aziz
Attaya, Hosny M(oustafa)
Bellan, Paul Murray
Block, Robert Charles
Carter, Robert LeRoy
Chang, Choong-Seock
Chao, Jiatsong Jason
Cheng, Edward Teh-Chang
Cullingford, Hatice S(adan)
Davis, Jay Clarence
Draper, Ernest Linn, Jr.
Flanagan, Charles Allen
Fonck, Raymond John
Furth, Harold Paul
Gaffey, John Dean, Jr.
Gibbs, Garry Wayne
Gilligan, John Gerard
Godlove, Terry F.
Gohar, Mohamed Yousry Ahmed
Harms, Archie Arkadius
Hovingh, Jack
Kim, Jinchoon
Krauss, Alan Robert
Kreisler, Michael Norman
Kribel, Robert Edward
Liu, Yung Yuan
Maceda, Edward Louis
Maglich, Bogdan C.
Massey, Robert Stewart
Mazarakis, Michael Gerassimos
McGuire, Kevin Marian
McNally, James Rand, Jr.
Mense, Allan Tate
Miley, George Hunter
Misra, Balabhadra
Olson, Richard Edward
Pietrzyk, Zbigniew Adam
Politzer, Peter Alexander
Ragheb, Magdi
Ribe, Fred Linden
Richman, Jack William
Robertson, James Craig
Rose, Ronald Palmer
Roth, J(ohn) Reece
Saylor, William Wardell
Seraydarian, Raymond Paul
Simon, Albert

Sinclair, Rolf Malcolm
Starr, Chauncey
Sudan, Ravindra Nath
Taylor, Gary
Thomas, Dan McDougal
Wachter, William John
Wagner, Carl Ernest
Winje, Russell A.
Yamagishi, Tomejiro
Youssef, Mahmoud Z. Hassan

Ocean energy conversion

Attilio, Donald Ernest
Avery, William Hinckley
Berry, William Benjamin Newell
Reid, Allen Francis
Venkataramiah, Amaraneni

Plasma. See also ENGINEERING, PHYSICS.

Alexeff, Igor
Bellan, Paul Murray
Chen, Hollis Ching
Gilleland, John Rogers
Mihas, Faquir Ullah
Ohkawa, Tihiro
Pfender, Emil
Soures, John Michael
Trivelpiece, Alvin William
Young, Stephen Kwok-Wai

Solar energy

Abeles, Tom Peter
Abernathy, Bill J.
Amick, James Albert
Anderson, Lynn M.
Antal, Michael Jerry, Jr.
Archer, Richard Earl
Backus, Charles Edward
Bauch, Tamil Daniel
Beard, James Taylor
Berry, William Bernard
Bhardwaj, Brahm Dev
Bier, Charles James
Block, David Lester
Blue, Todd Irwin
Boehm, Robert Foty
Böer, Karl Wolfgang
Broadbent, Donald Clarence
Bull, Stanley Raymond
Burr, Baldwin Gwynne
Bush, George Edward
Bushnell, Robert Hempstead
Carlson, David Emil
Casperson, Richard L.
Choi, Michael Kam-Wah
Clausing, Arthur Marvin
Cockshutt, Eric Philip
Craine, Eric Richard
Dean, Thomas Scott
DeBlasio, Richard
DeMeo, Edgar Anthony
Duffie, John Atwater
Ebenezer, Job Selvarayan
Eltimsahy, Adel H.
Farber, Joseph
Figard, Joseph Emerson
Fletcher, Edward Abraham
Fulton, Christopher
Gay, Charles Francis
Glaser, Peter Edward
Greenbaum, Elias
Groumpos, Peter
Henderson, Robert Edward
Hildebrandt, Alvin Frank
Holloway, Dennis Robert
Howe, Arthur Trevor
Hubbard, Harold Mead
Icerman, Larry
Irgon, Joseph
Johnson, Douglas Blaikie
Jordan, Richard Charles
Kadaba, Prasanna Venkatarama
Kokoropoulos, Panos
Lampert, Seymour
Lampkin, Curtis Magill
Levine, Jules David
Lillywhite, Malcolm Alden
Loeb, William A.
Lorenzen, Robert T.
Machovec, George Stephen
Madan, Arun
Makofske, William Joseph
Mallmann, Alexander James
Manalis, Melvyn Samuel
Martin, Jose Ginoris
McDaniels, David Keith
McGarity, Arthur Edwin
McKee, James Stanley Colton
McKown, Cora F.
Miluschewa, Sima
Morse, Frederick H.
Nash, Jonathon Michael
Neidlinger, Hermann Heinrich
Newman, Jerry Okey
Philbrick, David Alan
Pohl, Jens Gerhard
Prince, Morton Bronenberg
Rao, Gopalakrishna M.
Rapp, Donald
Remo, John Lucien
Rosenberg, Paul
Russell, Eugene A.
Saluja, Jagdish Kumar
Shahryar, Ishaq M.
Shing, Yuh-Han
Shkedi, Zvi
Smith, Otto J.M.
Stange, James Henry
Stone, Jack Lee
Sumners, Carolyn Taylor
Taylor, Roger William
Thomas, Carlton Eugene
Tien, H. Ti
Wald, Fritz Veit
Washom, Byron John
Watson, Donald Ralph
Watt, Mamadou Hamé
Webb, John Day, III
Witte, Michael
Wronski, Christopher Roman
Yeh, Yea-Chuan Milton

Wind power

Berry, Edwin X
Brooks, Richard Cavett
Clews, Henry Madsion

DeMeo, Edgar Anthony
Kelley, Neil Davis
Kempf, Gary William
Liu, Chang Yu
Manalis, Melvyn Samuel
McGowan, Jon Gerald
Miller, Rene Harcourt
Moretti, Peter Marc Allan
Reitan, Daniel Kinseth
Riegler, Gerold Ernst
Sheff, James Robert
Smith, Otto J.M.

Other

Abraham, Kuzhikalail Mathew, *Electrochemical energy storage and conversion*
Ackermann, Norbert Joseph, Jr.
Aggarwal, Mahesh Chand
Agrawal, Ram Kumar
Baen, Spencer R., *Research and development management*
Balzhiser, Richard Earl, *Energy research management*
Bauch, Tamil Daniel, *Energy conservation*
Bonnet, Juan Amedee, *Energy research administration*
Carlson, Kenneth T.
Chen, Ching Jen, *Heat transfer processes*
Chewning, June Spangler, *Employment aspects of energy production*
Claassen, Richard Strong
Clippinger, Everett, *Enhanced oil recovery*
Cockshutt, Eric Philip
Coleman, James Stafford, *Energy research management*
Culler, Floyd LeRoy, Jr.
Daugherty, Jack D., *Research and development management*
Dean, Thomas Scott, *Energy conservation*
Dean, William Evans, *Energy research administration*
Dey, Arabinda Narayan
Dorgan, Charles Edward
Ebenezer, Job Selvarayan, *Pedal power*
Edwards, William Charles
Eggers, Alfred John, Jr., *Energy research administration*
Freiwald, David Allen
Green, Ralph Ellis, *Nuclear energy research management*
Groff, Gerald Charles, *Energy systems in buildings*
Gross, William Allen, *Renewable energy*
Gyftopoulos, Elias Panayiotis, *Energy conservation*
Hamilton, Leonard Derwent, *Environmental effects of energy technologies*
Hart, Roger Douglas
Hester, Jarrett Charles, *Energy systems policy*
Hoffman, Kenneth Charles, *Resource policy*
Hollander, Milton Bernard
Jaquess, James Fletcher, *Nuclear power generation-quality engineering*
Jordan, Carl Harvey, *Energy systems in buildings*
Kerr, Donald MacLean, Jr., *Energy research and development administration*
Klock, Peter Illitch, Jr., *Energy conservation*
Koomanoff, Frederick Alan
Kovach, Paul Joseph, *Applied health physics*
Krachman, Howard Ellis, *Energy management*
Kraushaar, Jack Jourdan, *Energy and society*
Lee, Bernard Shing-Shu, *Energy research management*
Lee, Thomas Henry, *Energy systems*
Mahy, Tyler Xerez, *Electrochemical energy storage and conversion*
Marquet, Louis Carl
Mathiprakasam, B., *Thermoelectrics*
Mayo, Howard Armstrong, Jr., *Hydro power systems*
McBreen, James
Meyer, Edmond Gerald
Mills, Randall Adrain, *Natural gas from coal seams*
Morrison, David Lee, *Energy research administration*
Morse, Richard Stetson, *Batteries and industrial instruments; Management of new enterprises*
Murray, Peter, *Nuclear energy research and development administration*
Neely, Horace Hollis, *Heat transfer*
Othmer, Donald Frederick
Pigeaud, Adolph
Pratt, Jeremy, *Energy and society.*
Rathjens, George William
Raymond, Delmar Richard
Reuther, James Joseph, *Fire suppression*
Roddis, Louis Harry, Jr., *Energy research and development*
Rose, David John, *Energy policy and technology assessment*
Russell, B. Don, *Power and energy transmission*
Sadhal, Satwindar Singh
Scherrer, James Sydney
Schultz, Frederick H. C., *Energy sources and uses*
Shanker, Roy James, *Regulated utilities*
Shelnutt, James William, III, *Energy systems in buildings*
Sherman, Max Howard
Siri, William Emil
Snow, Joel Alan, *Energy research management*
Spielvogel, Lawrence George
Staszesky, Francis Myron, *Energy consulting*
Sterling, Raymond Leslie, *Earth-sheltered buildings*
Thompson, Benny Louis, *Gasification*
Thornton, Gunnar
Tien, Chang Lin, *Heat transfer*
Timmerman, Robert Wilson
Walter, Donald Kenneth
Watras, Ronald Edward, *Energy education*

ENGINEERING. *See also* BIOTECHNOLOGY, COMPUTER SCIENCE, ENERGY SCIENCE, ENVIRONMENTAL SCIENCE, GEOSCIENCE, INFORMATION SCIENCE, LASER, MATERIALS SCIENCE, OPTICS, PHYSICS, SPACE SCIENCE.

Acoustical
Buck, Otto
Campbell, Colin Kydd
Cyr, Reginald John
Ehrlich, Stanley L(eonard)
Eldred, Kenneth McKechnie
Eriksson, Larry John
Fischell, David Ross
Greenspan, Martin
Harari, Azriel
Harris, Cyril Manton
Harris, Wesley Leroy
Hellman, Rhona Phyllis
Johnson, Glen Eric
Kremkau, Frederick W.
Lang, William Warner
Malosh, James Boyd
Marshall, Steven Edwin
Munson, John Christian
Pierce, John Robinson
Schlegel, Ronald Gene
Shah, Surendra Poonamchand
Walker, Eric Arthur
Wilson, Geoffrey Leonard
Wolf, Joseph Allen, Jr.
Yoerger, Roger Raymond

Aeronautical
Adamczak, Robert Leonard
Ashley, Holt
Bedford, Anthony
Bogdonoff, Seymour Moses
Brilliant, Howard Michael
Caughey, David Alan
Chow, Chuen-Yen
Coles, Donald Earl
Covert, Eugene Edzards
Davenport, Arthur K.
Dolling, David Stanley
Donaldson, Coleman duPont
Dring, Robert Paul
Duffy, Robert Aloysius
Dvorak, Frank Arthur
Fung, Kee-Ying
Gasich, Welko Elton
Gessow, Alfred
Goland, Martin
Gregoriou,, Gregor Georg
Greywall, Mahesh
Haberman, Charles Morris
Hall, Charles Frederick
Harris, Wesley Leroy
Hawkins, Willis Moore
Hoff, Nicholas John
Holtby, Kenneth Fraser
Hsia, Henry Tao-sze
Hsieh, Tsuying Carl
Hua, Hsichun Mike
Hughett, Paul William
Jones, Robert Thomas
Kerrebrock, Jack Leo
Killian, Barbara Germain
Lederer, Jerome Fox
Lewis, David Sloan, Jr.
Liepmann, Hans Wolfgang
Liu, Chen-Huei
Loewy, Robert Gustav
Long, Lyle Norman
Lund, Charles Edward
Malvern, Donald
Marvin, Joseph George
Mc Carthy, John Francis, Jr.
Mikulla, Volker
Morino, Luigi
Moulden, Trevor Holmes
Nomura, Yasumasa
Oman, Charles McMaster
Oved, Yoel
Pai, Shih I.
Perkins, Courtland Davis
Puckett, Allen Emerson
Puskas, Elek
Rae, William Howard, Jr.
Reshotko, Eli
Roache, Patrick John
Rubin, Stanley Gerald
Russell, David Allison
Rutan, Burt
Savage, William Frederick
Schaufele, Roger Donald
Scheuing, Richard Albert
Schmit, Lucien André , Jr.
Schwanhausser, Robert Rowland
Seamans, Robert Channing, Jr.
Sears, William Rees
Sellars, John Randolph
Shank, Maurice Edwin
Shannon, Jack
Siuru, William Dennis, Jr.
Stever, Horton Guyford
Sun, John
Syvertson, Clarence Alfred
Vaicaitis, Rimas
Van Dyke, Milton Denman
Wang, Charles P.
Wells, Edward Curtis
Whitfield, Jack Duane
Wilson, Thornton Arnold
Yarymovych, Michael Ihor
Zincone, Robert

Aerospace. *See* SPACE SCIENCE.

Agricultural
Bockhop, Clarence William
Bondurant, Byron Lee
Bornstein, Joseph
Bouwer, Herman
Boyd, Landis Lee
Bubenzer, Gary Dean
Buelow, Frederick Henry
Davis, John Rowland
Divine, Theodore Emry
Driggers, Louis Bynum
Foster, Neil Robert
Garvey, Peter Medford
Haan, Charles Thomas
Hagen, Lawrence Jacob
Hagood, Melvin Ardene
Hahn, George LeRoy
Hall, Carl William
Hiler, Edward Allan
Hulsman, Robert Bruce
Jacobson, Larry Dean
James, Larry George
Jarrett, Albert Russell
Johnson, Arthur Thomas
Johnson, Howard Paul
Kendrick, David Richard
Larson, Dennis L.
Lorenzen, Robert T.
Meyer, (Lawrence) Donald
Mickelson, Rome Huebert
Nelson, Gordon Leon
Newman, Jerry Okey
Nieber, John Little
Peterson, Charles
Pratt, George L.
Reddell, Donald Lee
Robbins, Jackie Wayne Darmon
Rochester, Eugene Wallace, Jr.
Rubin, A(lbert) Robert
Schultheis, Robert Arthur
Sewell, John Ike
Shoup, William David
Splinter, William Eldon
Thomas, Adrian Wesley
Tollner, Ernest William
Von Bernuth, Robert Dean
Waitzman, Donald Anthony
Wist, Abund Ottokar
Woodruff, Neil Parker
Yoerger, Roger Raymond
Younos, Tamim M.

Applied mathematics. *See* MATHEMATICS.

Biomedical. *See also* BIOTECHNOLOGY; MEDICINE, Physical medicine, Radiology.
Abbrecht, Peter Herman
Abel, Larry Allen
Achter, Eugene Kenneth
Ackerman, Michael Jan
Ahlen, John William, III
Alexander, Harold
Anderson, David Walter
Barton, Kenneth E., Jr.
Battocletti, Joseph Henry
Berkwits, Leland
Bilotto, Gerardo
Boyle, Brian John
Brighton, John Austin
Brown, Richard Hart
Chen, Michael Ming
Cholvin, Neal Robert
Clark, Howard Garmany
Cokelet, Giles Roy
Colahan, Patrick Timothy
Crane, Robert
Csermely, Thomas John
Curran, Bruce Howlett
Darrah, Mark Irwin
David, Yadin
Dean, Robert Charles, Jr.
Del Guercio, Louis Richard Maurice
Delliosso, Louis Frank
De Luca, Carlo John
Doubek, Clifford James
Eckstein, Eugene Charles
Ellis, Donald Griffith
Epstein, Benjamin Ross
Eyerly, Robert Michael
Findl, Eugene
Fraden, Jacob
Francis, John Elbert
Fries, Richard Cyril
Galanopoulos, Kelly
Gezari, Daniel Ysa
Ghoshal, Nani Gopal
Goodenough, Samuel Henry
Gough, David Arthur
Grant, John Wallace, Jr.
Grotberg, James Bernard
Guthermann, Howard Edgar
Hagmann, Mark Joseph
Haque, Promod
Hefzy, Mohamed Samir W. M.
Intaglietta, Marcos
Jacobs, John Edward
Jaron, Dov
Johnson, Arthur Thomas
Katz, J. Lawrence
Kipp, John Edward
Klitzman, Bruce Maurice
Kun, Luis Guillermo
Lafferty, James Francis
Lakes, Roderic Stephen
Laxer, Cary
Lenchner, Nathaniel Herbert
Lichtenberg, Byron K.
Lin, James C.
Lin, Pei-Jan Paul
Llaurado, Josep G.
Macovski, Albert
Mann, Robert Wellesley
McDonagh, Paul Francis
McElhaney, James Harry
McGrath, Thomas John, Jr.
McNeal, Donald Richard
Mendelson, Yitzhak
Miller, Irving Franklin
Mummert, Thomas Allen
Nelson, Clifford Vincent
Nobel, Joel J.
Nunan, Craig Spencer
Nyquist, Gerald Warren
Page, Michael Gerald
Partridge, Lloyd D(onald)
Peli, Eliezer
Petit, Parker Holmes
Pierson, Richard Norris, Jr.
Plonsey, Robert
Pollack, Gerald Harvey
Ragsdale, Charles William
Ramon, Ceon
Rathod, Mulchand Shamjibhai
Reddy, Narander Pabbathi
Reswick, James Bigelow
Reynolds, Larry Owen
Richardson, Peter Damian
Rothe, Carl Frederick
Rudy, Yoram
Ryu, Jai Hyun
Sabbah, Hani Naief
Saha, Subrata
Sakaguchi, Ronald Louis
Samaras, George Michael
Schreck, David Michael
Schultz, Albert Barry
Seitman, David T.
Shapiro, Ascher Herman
Shen, Chiayi
Sheppard, Louis Clarke
Skalak, Richard
Smiley, Parker Clark
Smith, Kirby
Solomonow, Moshe
Spector, Andrew Lawrence
Suydam, Peter R.
Tackel, Ira Stuart
Taylor, Leonard Stuart
Udwadia, Firdaus Erach
Vaishnav, Ramesh Navalshanker
Wampler, John Edward
Washburn, John Garrett
Wasserman, Jack Frederick
Wilkinson, Arthur Frederick
Winarski, Daniel James
Yates, George Thomas
Youm, Youngil
Zartman, David Lester
Zemcov, Alexander
Zingg, Walter

Ceramic
Allis, Deo G.
Arthur, Michael Edward
Bergeron, Clifton George
Bly, Lloyd George, Jr.
Brockmeyer, Jerry W.
Brubaker, Burton Dale
Cherry, John Thomas
Cook, Lee Melbourne
Crowley, Michael Summers
Duckworth, Winston Howard
Ellis, Howard Franklin
Engel, Alan James
Fay, Wayne Xalpha
Forchheimer, Otto L.
Frechette, Van Derck
Freeman, Stephen Morrison
Givan, Guy Van
Glaeser, Andreas Michael
Gonczy, Stephen Thomas
Holcombe, Cressie Earl, Jr.
Horton, Robert Andrew
Insley, Robert Hiteshew
Johnson, James Robert
Kielmeyer, William Henry
Kingery, William David
Kohut, William
Logan, Kathryn Vance
McGee, Thomas Donald
Moody, Willis Elvis, Jr.
Moore, Francis Mears
Ramey, Roy Richard
Readey, Dennis William
Rossington, David Ralph
Schroth, Peter
Sevier, James Rollins
Shoot, Lyle Edward
Shumate, Monroe William
Smiley, Parker Clark
Spriggs, Richard Moore
Stadler, Henry Lewis
Thompson, Gregory Robert
Tummala, Rao Ramamohana
Valent, Francis Samuel
Viechnicki, Dennis John
Weinland, Stuart Louis
Williams, Charles Edward
Yoon, Soo Charles

Chemical
Agarwal, Ashok Kumar
Anderson, Donald Keith
Andres, Ronald Paul
Angelo, Michael James
Angus, John Cotton
Aris, Rutherford
Ayers, Arnold Leslie, Sr.
Bankoff, Seymour George
Barron, Saul
Beck, Theodore Richard
Benedict, Manson
Benzing, Walter Charles
Berman, Herbert L(awrence)
Bhagat, Phiroz Maneck
Bischoff, Kenneth Bruce
Blakely, John Paul
Board, William Jesse, Jr.
Boehmer, Matthew Anthony
Boundy, Ray Harold
Brenner, Howard
Brown, Glenn Robbins, Jr.
Burnet, George, Jr.
Butt, John B.
Cannon, John Joseph
Caplan, John DAvid
Carr, William Hoge, Jr.
Characklis, William Gregory
Cheremisinoff, Paul Nicholas
Churchill, Stuart Winston
Cohen, Robert Edward
Couper, James Riley
Cronauer, Donald Charles
Dahlstrom, Donald Albert
Datta, Rathin
Davis, Howard Ted
Donaldson, Terrence Lee
Doubek, Clifford James
Drew, Bruce Arthur
Duda, Richard Frank
Duffie, John Atwater
Dunigan, Paul Francis Xavier
Eagleton, Lee Chandler
Eckert, Charles Alan
Elliott, Martin Anderson
Epperly, William Robert
Erdogan, Haydar
Fair, James Rutherford, Jr.
Fan, Liang-tseng
Fisher, Harold Wallace
Fleming, Hubert Loy
Fogler, Hugh Scott
Forman, J(oseph) Charles
Franses, Elias I.
Friedlander, Sheldon Kay
Frumerman, Robert
Gabor, John Dewain
Garlid, Kermit Leroy
Gates, Bruce Clark
Gautreaux, Marcelian Francis, Jr.
Gauvin, William Henry
Gavalas, George Rousetos
Gelbard, Fred
Goldstein, Paul
Graham, Donald Lee
Greenkorn, Robert Albert
Groenier, William Samuel
Gulari, Erdogan
Hackman, E(lmer) Ellsworth, III
Hall, Kenneth Richard
Halligan, James Edmund
Hanratty, Thomas Joseph
Harkness, John Barrett Long
Harris, Ronald David
Haupin, Warren Emerson
Hauser, Ray Louis
Heckman, Richard Ainsworth
Hoffman, Edward Jack
Hulburt, Hugh McKinney
Isakoff, Sheldon Erwin
Ito, Yoichiro
Jansson, Robert Edward
Katz, Donald L.
Kempe, Lloyd Lute
King, Cary Judson, III
Klausmeier, William Hilton
Koerner, Ernest Lee
Kohn, James Paul
Krumrine, Paul Henry, III
LaCava, Alberto Ignacio
Ladisch, Michael R.
Levine, Robert Sidney
Linden, Henry Robert
Long, Robert B.
Loven, Andrew Witherspoon
Luus, Rein
Macaraeg, Michele Gay
MacKay, G. David MacIvor
Marchaterre, John Frederick
Markatos, Nicolas-Christos Gregory
Mc Afee, Jerry
McHenry, Keith Welles, Jr.
Mc Ketta, John J., Jr.
Meenakshi Sundaram, Kandasamy
Mensah, Thomas
Meyer, Walter
Meyers, Robert Allen
Mickley, Harold Somers
Mills, Patrick Leo
Moore, Richard Owen, Jr.
Muller, Rolf Hugo
Nemeth, Edward Joseph
Nichols, Duane Guy
Nobe, Ken
Oblad, Alexander Golden
Olien, Neil Arnold
Othmer, Donald Frederick
Oyekan, Soni Olufemi
Parrish, William Rutledge
Pearson, Dale Sheldon
Periasamy, Ravindran
Perlmutter, Daniel D.
Pickard, David Kenneth
Poettmann, Fred Heinz
Price, Charles Ronald
Quinn, John Albert
Reid, Allen Francis
Reid, Robert Lelon
Reilly, Peter John
Reklaitis, Gintaras Victor
Remer, Donald Sherwood
Robb, Walter Lee
Robins, Norman Alan
Rockwell, Ned Miles
Rothe, Erhard William
Santoro, Robert John
Schowalter, William Raymond
Schwank, Johannes Walter
Schwing, Richard Charles
Scinta, James
Selm, Robert Prickett
Shipman, Charles William
Silas, Cecil Jesse
Smith, Joe Mauk
Sohn, Hong Yong
Song, Leila Shia
Squires, Arthur Morton
Stewart, Warren Earl
Stockinger, Siegfried Ludwig
Storm, David Anthony
Swanson, William Mason
Takano, Masaharu
Talty, Robert Dean
Tang, Ignatius Ning-Bang
Taylor, William Francis
Thomas, Leo John
Timmerhaus, Klaus Dieter
Tobias, Charles William
Varma, Arvind
Venkatesan, Valadi Nataraj
Wei, James
Wellman, George Robert
Wells, William Lochridge
Westwater, James William
Wiewiorowski, Edward Ignacy
Wilke, Charles Robert
Wilson, John Sheridan
Yamanis, Jean
Yang, Ralph Tzu-bow
Yang, Wen-Ching
Yoo, Hee Ju
Zakin, Jacques Louis

Civil
Abdel-Ghaffar, Ahmed Mansour
Adeli, Hojjat
Arnold, Orville Edward
Astenah-Asl, Abolhassan
Atchley, Bill Lee
Bacon, Vinton Walker
Beard, Leo Roy
Bechtel, Stephen Davison, Jr.
Beedle, Lynn Simpson
Bellport, Bernard Philip
Benzley, Steven Edward
Blue, Todd Irwin
Blume, John August
Bondurant, Byron Lee
Bovay, Harry Elmo, Jr.
Brannon, H(ezzie) Raymond, Jr.
Breen, John Edward
Brown, John Eros
Caspe, Marc S.
Cermak, Jack Edward
Chen, Wai-Fah
Chesson, Eugene, Jr.
Christian, John Thomas
Clemente, Frank Massimino, Jr.
Clough, Ray William, Jr.
Cohen, Edward
Cooper, James Daniel
Culver, Charles George
D'Appolonia, Elio
Davy, Philip Sheridan
Denton, Richard Andrew
Donaldson, David
Doyle, Earl Howard, Jr.
Drown, Eugene Ardent
Durgun, Kanat
Dym, Clive Lionel
Ebeling, Dick Winfield
Ellingwood, Bruce Russell
Eng, Norman
Ewing, Benjamin Baugh
Fadum, Ralph Eigil
Fairhurst, Charles
Falvey, Henry Thomas
Fazio, Paul
Gaither, William Samuel
Gallagher, Richard Hugo
Garbarini, Edgar Joseph
Gere, James Monroe
Gergely, Peter
Goodyear, Wayne David
Gould, Phillip Louis
Goyal, Satish Chandra
Graham, Frederick Mitchell
Gupta, Ajaya Kumar
Halasi-Kun, George Joseph
Hall, William Joel
Halpin, Daniel William
Harris, Lee Errol
Hawkins, Neil Middleton
Heiberg, Elvin Ragnvald, III
Hoel, Lester A.
Hognestad, Eivind
Hradilek, Peter Jaroslav
Hughes, Thomas Joseph
Hulsman, Robert Bruce
Inyang, Hilary
Johnson, James Allen
Johnston, Bruce Gilbert
Jolly, Edward Martin
Kausel, Eduardo
Kelly, William Edward
Kesler, Clyde Ervin
Kuesel, Thomas Robert
Kunze, Walter Edward, Jr.
Kuroiwa, Julio
Ladd, Charles Cushing, III
Lai, James Shau-Yan
Lambe, Thomas William
Lee, Griff Calicutt
Lee, Harry William
Lundgren, James Reinhold
Lynn, Walter Royal
Makdisi, Faiz Isbir
Mangus, Alfred Ring
McCann, Martin William, Jr.
McNair, John William, Jr
Michel, Bernard
Minor, Joseph Edward
Mitchell, James Kenneth
Monismith, Carl Leroy
Nadel, Norman Allen
Nguyen, Duc Thai
O'Rourke, Thomas Denis
Papastamatiou, Dimitri
Parsons, William Andrews
Pearson, Samuel Dibble, III
Peck, Ralph Brazelton
Peltier, Eugene Joseph
Penzien, Joseph
Pfrang, Edward Oscar
Popov, Egor Paul
Potter, Miles Buttles
Prakash, Shamsher
Pratt, Benjamin Cabell
Price, Bobby Earl
Ramanuja, Teralandur Krishnaswamy
Resnick, Sol Donald
Richart, Frank Edwin, Jr.
Robers, Jonathan David
Rolfe, Stanley Theodore
Saada, Adel Selim
Saiidi, Mehdi
Salomone, William Gerald
Salvatorelli, Joseph J.
Sauter, Franz Fabian
Saxena, Surendra Kumar
Schad, Theodore MacNeeve
Schmidt, Robert
Schmit, Lucien André , Jr.
Schuster, Robert Lee
Scordelis, Alexander Costicas
Seth, Baldev Raj
Siess, Chester Paul
Singh, Jogeshwar Preet
Turner, Earl James
Vaicaitis, Rimas
Vanmarcke, Erik Hector
Vanoni, Vito August
Viest, Ivan M(iroslav)
Vinogradov, Aleksandra M.
Wagner, Aubrey Joseph
Watson, Edward Fisk
Wei, Millet Lunchin
Weng, Cheng-Nan
Whitman, Robert Van Duyne
Wilbur, Lyman Dwight
Woodruff, Neil Parker
Wylie, Evan Benjamin
Yao, James Tsu-Ping
Yegian, Mishac K.
Yong, Raymond Nen-Yiu
Youd, Thomas Leslie
Young, James Francis

Civil, water supply and wastewater treatment. *See* ENGINEERING, Environmental.

Computer-aided design
Adeli, Hojjat
Alig, Roger Casanova
Beadle, Charles Wilson
Bedinger, Joseph Arnold
Benzley, Steven Edward
Bhattacharyya, Shankar

Chua, Leon Ong
Clayton, David Lawrence
Donahue, Michael James
Dorgan, Charles Edward
El-Mansy, Youssef Aly
Frisch, Joseph
Gruber, Sheldon
Gummel, Hermann Karl
Gwyn, Charles William
Horman, Melvin Herbert
Horstmann, Paul William
Johnson, Bruce Paul
Kim, Jin Koo
Koford, James Shingle
Kostem, Celal Nizamettin
Lombardi, Fabrizio
Lupash, Lawrence O(vidiu)
McDonald, John Francis Patrick
Meagher, Donald Joseph
Migliore, Herman James
Naqvi, Iqbal Mehdi
Nguyen, Duc Thai
Orthwein, William Coe
Parker, Alice Cline
Pister, Karl Stark
Reynolds, Harold Gene
Sadler, Stanley Gene
Saiidi, Mehdi
Schumaker, Larry Lee
Smith, Kevin Richard
Speciale, Ross Aldo
Su, Stanley Y. W.
Szilagyi, Mike Nicholas
Talukdar, Sarosh N.
Trimberger, Stephen Mathias
VanDell, William Ronald
Waldron, Kenneth John
Wang, Cheh Cheng
Wasserman, Jack Frederick
Williams, Keith Alan
Wright, Richard Newport, III
Yessios, Chris Ioannis

Computer engineering. *See* **COMPUTER SCIENCE; ENGINEERING, Electrical.**

Corrosion
Baboian, Robert
Beck, Theodore Richard
Boehmer, Matthew Anthony
Carter, John Paul
Dabkowski, John
Dandapani, Bala Subramaniam
Daniel, Samuel Henderson, III
French, David Nichols
Leidheiser, Henry, Jr.
Marek, Miroslav I.
Niesse, John Edgar
Nobe, Ken
Nowak, Welville Berenson
Pearl, Wesley Lloyd
Pickering, Howard William
Pierce, Robert Raymond
Promisel, Nathan E.
Pye, Earl Louis
Radtke, Schrade Fred
Salensky, George
Schwartz, (Ellen) Shirley Eckwall
Shieh, Wei Tong
Verink, Ellis Daniel, Jr.
von Fraunhofer, Joseph Anthony
Wang, Rong

Cryogenics
Barron, Randall Franklin
Birmingham, Bascom Wayne
Coombe, John Raymond
Geist, Jacob Myer
Klockzien, Vernon George
Marchaj, Tadeusz Jozef
Rahm, David Charles
Singhal, Anil Kumar
Timmerhaus, Klaus Dieter
Zisk, Stanley Harris

Electrical
Abbey, George William Samuel
Abend, Kenneth
Aldridge, Melvin Dayne
Asmussen, Jes, Jr.
Bailey, Jake S.
Balanis, George Nick
Barnard, Thomas Elliot
Barney, Diane Jean
Barton, Kenneth E., Jr.
Battocletti, Joseph Henry
Baum, Carl Edward
Beckjord, Eric Stephen
Benedict, Anthony Gorman
Berger, Robert Law
Bjorndahl, David Lee
Blachman, Nelson M(erle)
Blanck, A.R.
Boerner, Wolfgang Martin
Brown, George Harold
Burdick, Glenn Arthur
Caimi, Frank Michael
Carroll, Lee Francis
Cermak, Ivan Anthony
Chandler, Edward William
Chang, William Shen Chie
Chen, Kun-Mu
Chen, Wai-Kai
Chirlian, Paul M.
Chua, Leon Ong
Cohen, Haggai
Cohn, Nathan
Collin, Robert Emanuel
Collins, James Joseph
Cook, Gerald
Cookson, Albert Ernest
Cooley, Donald Wayne
Cooper, Robert Shanklin
Corry, Andrew Francis
Crenner, James Charles
Cruz, Jose Bejar
Curry, James Regnald
Dabkowski, John
Daley, Michael Leo
Darlington, Sidney
David, Edward Emil, Jr.
DeBlasio, Richard
de Wolf, David Alter
Dickinson, Bradley William
Dinneen, Gerald Paul
Donalek, Peter John
Edgerton, Harold Eugene
Egner, John David, Jr.
Einspruch, Norman Gerald
Eltimsahy, Adel H.
Epstein, Benjamin Ross
Eriksson, Larry John
Everitt, William Littell
Fink, Lester Harold
Flanagan, James Loton
Fraden, Jacob
Friberg, Emil Edwards
Fung, Adrian Kin-Chiu
Gandhi, Shirish Manilal
George, Thycodam Varkkey
Gilkeson, Robert Fairbairn
Gordon, Eugene Irving
Gowen, Richard Joseph
Gray, Paul Edward
Greenwood, Allan Nunns
Groumpos, Peter
Gupta, Madhu Sudan
Hagmann, Mark Joseph
Harrington, Dean Butler
Hayes, Monson Henry, III
Helliwell, Robert Arthur
Hickey, Roger Lee
Higgins, Patrick John, Jr.
Hoffman, Graham Walter
Holmes, Dyer Brainerd
Huang, Tsou-Chiang
Huggins, William Herbert
Irwin, John David
Ishii, Thomas Koryu
Jackson, William David
Jacobs, John Edward
Joel, Amos Edward, Jr.
Johnson, Ingolf Birger
Joshi, Chandrashekhar Janardan
Kazek, Gregory Joseph
Kennedy, Wilbert Keith, Jr.
Kong, Jin Au
Kopplin, Julius Otto
Kuh, Ernest Shinu-Jen
Kumar, Mahesh
Kusko, Alexander
Lafferty, James Martin
Lanzkron, Rolf Wolfgang
Lauzon, Thomas Andrew
Lee, Thomas Henry
Levine, William Silver
Li, Tingye
Lin, James C.
Lischer, Ludwig Frederick
LoCicero, Joseph Lawrence
Lonngren, Karl Erik
Mandelbaum, David Michael
Manitius, Andrzej Zdzislaw
Marcuse, Dietrich
Marcuvitz, Nathan
Mayo, John Sullivan
McGregor, Dennis Nicholas
McMillan, Robert Walker
McWright, Glen Martin
Mehravari, Nader
Melcher, James Russell
Melsa, James Louis
Merewether, David Evan
Meystel, Alexander Michael
Miller, Stewart Edward
Mitchell, James Thomas
Mohanty, Nirode Chandra
Moore, Richard Kerr
Mueller, George E.
Namkung, Won
Nemarich, Joseph
Novotny, Donald Wayne
Nunn, Walter Melrose, Jr.
Oakes, Lester Cornelius
Olsen, Kenneth Harry
Packard, David
Paulk, Charles Jasper, Jr.
Pearse, James Newburg
Pedersen, Charles Russell
Peebles, Peyton Zimmerman, Jr.
Pierce, John Robinson
Pierre, Donald Arthur
Poularikas, Alexander Demitrios
Pravda, Milton Frank
Presley, Joe Andrew, Jr.
Preuss, Robert David
Quate, Calvin Forrest
Rabinow, Jacob
Rabow, Gerald
Rahman, Iftekhar
Ramon, Ceon
Ramos-Lorenzi, Jorge Ramon
Randa, James Paul
Rauch, Herbert Emil
Ream, Gregory Lawrence
Rechtin, Eberhardt
Reinman, Robert Andrew
Reitan, Daniel Kinseth
Rice, Bart Francis
Robertson, Lawrence Marshall
Ross, Hugh Courtney
Ross, Ian Munro
Rowe, Joseph Everett
Rugh, Wilson John, II
Rumsey, Victor Henry
Russell, B. Don
Ryaciotaki-Boussalis, Helen Alexandra
Ryan, Daniel Joseph
Sabbagh, Harold Abraham
Sadjadi, Firooz Ahmadi
Sandberg, Irwin Walter
Schoenbach, Karl Heinz
Schramm, Frederic Bernard
Sebo, Stephen Andrew
Senior, Thomas Bryan Alexander
Sethares, James Costas
Shank, Charles Vernon
Shepherd, Mark, Jr.
Shoucair, Farid Sami
Shum, Raymond Hing-Yan
Sites, Kenneth Ronald
Slemon, Gordon Richard
Slepian, David
Smith, James Gilbert
South, Hugh Miles
Spiro, Julius
Staszesky, Francis Myron
Stein, David Eric
Steinway, William Joseph
Stern, Arthur Paul
Stone, Jack Lee
Stubberud, Allen Roger
Suciu, Spiridon N.
Sullivan, Roger John
Talley, Thomas James
Talukdar, Sarosh N.
Tatchyn, Roman Orest
Taylor, Barry Norman
Taylor, Herbert Lyndon
Taylor, Leonard Stuart
Tourtellotte, Mills Charlton
Turin, George Lewis
Ulaby, Fawwaz Tayssir
Ulland, Paul David
Vaks, Yefim Elias
Vanderbilt, Vern Corwin
Van Lint, Victor Anton Jacobus
Verriest, Erik Isidoor
Vitkovitsky, Ihor Myron
Vitola, Jack Joseph
Von Tersch, Lawrence Wayne
Wagers, Robert Shelby
Wait, James Richard
Walker, Eric Arthur
Walquist, Robert Louis
Warzecha, Ladislaus William
Weber, Ernst
Webster, Steven Craig
Weitkamp, William George
Wheeler, E(rnest) Joseph, Jr.
Whinnery, John Roy
Whitmore, L. Damon
Wiesner, Jerome Bert
Willcox, Phillip James
Williams, Aubrey James
Winje, Russell A.
Wise, Gary Lamar
Woodson, Herbert Horace
Wooldridge, Dean Everett
Yuen, Horace P.
Zak, Stanislaw Henryk

Electrical, applied magnetics
Allan, James Clark
Avery, Robert Tolman
Bainbridge, Kenneth Tompkins
Bajpai, Shyam N
Barney, Diane Jean
Bauman, Albert Joseph
Boerner, Wolfgang Martin
Braddock, Peter Samuel
Chew, Weng Cho
Chi, Chao Shu
Felix, Michael O(tto)
Fielder, Louis Dunn
Frink, Richard Clark
Fritz, Frank Mark
Gage, Donald Shepard
Gattozzi, Angelo Luciano
Gill, Hardayal Singh
Godlewski, Harry Henry, Jr.
Gogue, George Paul
Graneau, Peter
Green, Jerome Joseph
Green, Michael I(rving)
Gross, Thomas Alfred Otto
Jaeger, Klaus Bruno
Jocic, Dusan
Kolm, Henry Herbert
Lopez, Orlando
Luborsky, Fred Everett
Mazur, Alexander
McWhirter, James Herman
Moskowitz, Ronald
Owens, James Arthur, Jr.
Petrarca, Bruce Frederick
Reynolds, Larry Owen
Sethares, James Costas
Underhill, Earl Marvin
Van der Poel, Jan M.
Whitmore, L. Damon
Wong, Thomas Tang Yum

Electrical, computer engineering
Abraham, George
Adams, Karyl Ann
Amdahl, Gene Myron
Anderson, Richard Cooper
Aupperle, Kenneth Robert
Basar, Tamer
Batchelder, Michael Jack
Baylis, Charles Merritt
Bell, Chester Gordon
Berlekamp, Elwyn Ralph
Bertrand, John
Bickart, Theodore Albert
Bitzer, Donald Lester
Bloch, Erich
Braddock, Peter Samuel
Brakefield, James Charles
Branscomb, Lewis McAdory
Brick, Donald Bernard
Bush, George Edward
Cermak, Ivan Anthony
Chakravarty, Indranil
Chan, Kam Hang
Chen, Hollis Ching
Chen, Hsiang Tsun
Cheng, Peter Yu-Hung
Cheung, John Yan-Poon
Childs, Jeffrey John
Chitsaz, Sirus
Cooper, (Howard) Gordon
Copeland, John Alexander, III
Csermely, Thomas John
Decker, Bruce Michael
Dhadesugoor, Vaman Rao
Dixit, Sudhir Sharan
Drozd, Andrew Louis Stephan
Elmaghraby, Adel Said
Evans, Bob Overton
Ewing, Martin Sipple
Fleck, David Charles
Ghausi, Mohammed Shuaib
Goodman, Nancy B.
Gray, Festus Gail
Hankins, Timothy Hamilton
Hedges, Harry George
Horstmann, Paul William
Inada, Hitoshi
Jaluria, Rajiv
Kahn, Robert Elliot
Kesler, Stanislav Branko
Keyes, Robert William
Kim, Yongmin
Klassen, Klaas Berend
Kopplin, Julius Otto
Krutz, Ronald L.
Landauer, Rolf William
Legters, George Richard
Levine, William Silver
Levitin, Lev Berovich
LoCicero, Joseph Lawrence
Lucky, Robert Wendell
Mann, John Bunyan
Marr, James Douglas
Masiello, Ralph D.
McAulay, Alastair D.
McDonald, John Francis Patrick
Meditch, James Stephen
Mergler, Harry Winston
Mickle, Marlin Homer
Mondal, Kalyan
Nguyen, Chinh Trung
Nguyen, Dung Chi
Niederjohn, Russell James
Ollapally, Philip Joseph
Ong, Chong Kok
Osborne, Adam
Panda, Durga Prasad
Pattipati, Krishna Rao
Plunkett, Joseph Charles
Porskievies, Thomas Anthony
Prada, Kenneth Edwin
Quek, Swee-Meng
Rabiner, Lawrence Richard
Riganati, John Philip
Sahely, Camille
Schneider, Kenneth Stuart
Schueler, Carl Frederick
Sedlak, Richard John
Seth, Sharad Chandra
Sheppard, Albert Parker, Jr.
Sherif, Mostafa Hashem
Silvern, Leonard Charles
Slaughter, John Brooks
Smith-Vaniz, William Reid
Stenger, Ralph L., Jr.
Svarrer, Robert W.
Talley, Thomas James
Trivedi, Manmohan Manubhai
Varshney, Pramod Kumar
Von Tersch, Lawrence Wayne
Witte, Kurt Allen
Wolf, Jack Keil
Wu, Chi-haur
Wyner, Aaron Daniel
Yang, Yee-Hong
York, John Louis, Jr.
Young, Frederick John
Yousif, Salah Mohammad
Zak, Stanislaw Henryk

Electrical, microchip technology. *See also* **MATERIALS SCIENCE.**
Akcasu, Osman Ersed
Armstrong, John Allan
Banerjee, Sanjay Kumar
Beyer, Klaus Dietrich
Bower, Robert William
Chen, Teh-Yi James
Copeland, John Alexander, III
Cronquist, Brian Edward
Detterman, Robert Linwood
Doodlesack, Gary Abbott
Early, James Michael
Einspruch, Norman Gerald
Ellis, Jack Gerald
Eng, Lawrence (Larry) Phillip
Fair, Richard Barton
Gillespie, Sherry Jacqueline
Glendinning, William Bernard
Goronkin, Herbert
Greene, Richard Melvyn
Hawley, Sandra Sue
Heath, Barbara Anita
Hsieh, Kuan Hsiung
Hutchison, Robert Vern
Ibrahim, Ali Abd-El-Fattah
Joy, Richard Carleton
Kapoor, Ashok Kumar
Kestenbaum, Ami
Kilby, Jack St. Clair
Kressel, Henry
Kumar, Mahesh
Lancaster, Arthur Lewis
Law, Hsiang-Yi David
Lin, Mou-Shiung
Mai, Chao Chen
Maloney, Timothy James
Miracky, Robert Foster
Moore, Gordon E.
Moysenko, Andrew Edward
Mukherjee, Satyen
Nakada, Yoshinao
Nalamwar, Ashok Laxmanrao
Nguyen, Nhiem Yinh
Oleszek, Gerald Michael
Packwood, Donald Lee
Pease, Roger Fabian Wedgwood
Pechar, Henry William
Pfeifer, Robert Frederick
Phillips, Alfred, Jr.
Reddy, Chitranjan
Rutledge, James Luther
Sack, Edgar Albert, Jr.
Sai-Halasz, George Anthony
Spicer, William Edward, III
Sweet, Alexander
Tang, Denny Duan-Lee
Tenedorio, Jaime Gonsalves
Wallace, John Robert
Yeh, Keming Wayne
Youn, So Young

Electrical, semiconductors
Aghevli, Reza
Alexander, Michael Norman
Anderson, Richard Louis
Ashok, S.
Banerjee, Sanjay Kumar
Barnes, Frank Stephenson
Bate, Robert Thomas
Bedair, Salah Mohamed
Bharat, Ramasesha
Bhardwaj, Brahm Dev
Bhattacharyya, Anjan
Blair, John
Bube, Richard Howard
Buckman, A(lvin) Bruce
Burrus, Charles Andrew, Jr.
Butler, Jack Fairchild
Bylander, Ernest Gerald
Casey, H. Craig, Jr.
Chaundhari, Pundlik Kashiram
Chen, Daniel Ray
Christianson, Keith Alan
Chu, Ting L.
Cole, Lee Arthur
Conwell, Esther Marly
Cregger, Barton Bentley
Crossley, Ian
Dacey, George Clement
Das, Pankaj K.
Dhong, Sang Hoo
Doodlesack, Gary Abbott
Dow, Daniel Gould
Dupuis, Russell Dean
Ellis, Jack Gerald
Erickson, Robert Arlen
Fair, Richard Barton
Ferry, David Keane
Galloway, Kenneth Franklin
Gildenblat, Gennady
Gillespie, Sherry Jacqueline
Glascock, Homer Hopson, II
Gray, Peter Vance
Green, Jonathan Bregstone
Gutmann, Ronald Jay
Gwo, Tai-Chuan
Haddad, George Ilyas
Harris, James Stewart, Jr.
Hawkins, Gilbert A.
Hawrylo, Frank Zygmunt
Heilmeier, George Harry
Hickmott, Thomas Ward
Holonyak, Nick, Jr.
Holton, William Coffeen
Jayadev, Tumkur Shiva
Kapoor, Ashok Kumar
Kennedy, Wilbert Keith, Jr.
Khan, Abdul Azim
Kiehl, Richard Arthur
Krowne, Clifford Mitchell
Kwok, Hoi-Sing
Larrabee, Robert Dean
Larson, Donald Clayton
Liu, Hua-Kuang
Liu, Yet-zen
Look, David Charles
LoVecchio, Paul
Ma, Tso-Ping
Majidi-Ahy, Gholamreza
Maloney, Timothy James
Manley, Martin Harold
Martin, Paul Alan
Martin, Thomas Lyle, Jr.
Mayer, James Walter
McWhirter, James Herman
Moore, Gordon E.
Moustakas, Theodore Demetri
Nguyen, Nhiem Yinh
Noyce, Robert Norton
O'Clock, George Daniel, Jr.
Oguz, Suha
Oliver, James D., Jr.
Pai, Damodar Mangalore
Park, Yoon Soo
Pfeifer, Robert Frederick
Pierret, Robert Francis
Polgar, Leslie George
Polinsky, Murray Arthur
Rabii, Sohrab
Rabson, Thomas Avelyn
Ransom, Craig Mitchell
Rezek, Edward Anthony
Rumennik, Vladimir
Sah, Chih-Tang
Schechter, Daniel
Scholl, Frederick William
Schroder, Dieter Karl
Seiter, Gary Joseph
Serreze, Harvey B.
Shockley, William Bradford
Shrivastava, Ritu
Slade, Bernard Newton
Sollner, Traugott Carl Ludwig Gerhard
Su, Kung-Yen
Tabak, Mark David
Tauc, Jan
Tenedorio, Jaime Gonsalves
Tennant, William Emerson
Tsang, Dean Zensh
Valsamakis, Emmanuel Anthony
VanDell, William Ronald
Van de Walle, Chris Gilbert
Van Vliet, Carolyn Marina
Varshney, Ramesh Chandra
Wang, Shyh
Wang, Wen I.
Whalen, James Joseph
Willardson, Robert Kent
Wolley, Elden Duane
Wong, Thomas Tang Yum
Yeh, Yea-Chuan Milton
Young, Donald Reeder

Electrical, superconductors
Campbell, Colin Kydd
Coleman, John Howard
Dhong, Sang Hoo
Gattozzi, Angelo Luciano
Hsu, Yarsun
Jablonski, Daniel Gary
Kressel, Henry
Piore, Emanuel Ruben
Strauss, Bruce Paul
Tinkham, Michael
Whiteley, Stephen Robert

Electronics
Adler, Robert
Adrian, Donald James
Allen, Jonathan
Bailey, Jake S.
Bak, Martin Joseph
Baksay, Laszlo Andrew
Bartlett, Peter Greenough
Beigel, Michael Lee
Blythe, Cleveland Henry
Brandinger, Jay Jerome
Brick, Donald Bernard
Bridge, Charles Sommers
Bridges, Jack E(dgar)
Brown, George Harold
Brumm, Douglas Bruce
Burkhart, James Nelson, Jr.
Bussgang, Julian Jakob
Button, Kenneth J(ohn)
Chen, Kun-Mu
Chynoweth, Alan Gerald
Clark, Richard James
Collin, Robert Emanuel
Collins, James Joseph

Croft, Thomas A(rthur)
Cyr, Reginald John
Damon, Richard Winslow
Dick, Robert James
Dow, Daniel Gould
Eernisse, Errol Peter
Egner, John David, Jr.
Emming, Jan Goossem
Farago, George
Fielder, Louis Dunn
Forney, George David, Jr.
Fowler, Charles Albert
Friedrich, Otto Martin, Jr.
Fukui, Hatsuaki
Gablehouse, Reuben Harold
Galbiati, Louis Joseph
Gard, Michael Floyd
Gearing, Alan Eugene
Gewartowski, James Walter
Gibbons, James F.
Ginzton, Edward Leonard
Godlewski, Harry Henry, Jr.
Gordon, Eugene Irving
Gray, Eoin Wedderburn
Green, Samuel Isaac
Greenberg, Harold Paul
Groeber, Edward Otto, Jr.
Gross, Al
Gross, Leo
Gross, Thomas Alfred Otto
Grove, Andrew S.
Hammond, Donald L.
Hanisko, John-Cyril Patrick
Hannay, N(orman) Bruce
Haque, Promod
Hartig, Elmer Otto
Haus, Hermann Anton
Heller, Douglas Max
Hewlett, William (Redington)
House, Charles H.
Hull, Harvard Leslie
Irwin, John David
Ishii, Thomas Koryu
Jablonski, Daniel Gary
Jackson, Glen Leon
Jordan, Arthur Kent
Jordan, Edward Conrad
Kabell, Jack
Kang, Min Ho
Keiser, Bernhard Edward
Kennedy, Eldredge Johnson
Kravitz, David William
Kravitz, Lawrence Charles
Kusko, Alexander
Lafferty, James Martin
Liotine, Frank James, Jr.
Lipsky, Stephen Edward
Lytle, James Mark
Martin, Thomas Lyle, Jr.
McCracken, Robert Henry
McGrath, Thomas John, Jr.
Mehring, James Warren
Meitzler, Allen Henry
Messenger, George Clement
Minter, Jerry Burnett
Mitchell, Michael Eugene
Moore, Robert Avery
Morris, Charles Reginald
Morrow, Walter Edwin, Jr.
Naqvi, Iqbal Mehdi
Newman, Arnold Lewis
Nichols, Warren De Forrest
Nunn, Walter Melrose, Jr.
Pande, Krishna Prasad
Patti, Robert Dale
Pearson, Ronald Korin
Perrella, Anthony Joseph
Powers, Jeffry Earl
Preschutti, Joseph Paul
Prince, John Luther, III
Ragsdale, Charles William
Rathbun, Edwin Roy
Rhodes, Donald Frederick
Riebman, Leon
Rose, Albert
Ross, Hugh Courtney
Salvatori, Vincent Louis
Schipper, Lawrence J.
Schramm, Frederic Bernard
Sensiper, Samuel
Shapiro, Jonathan Salem
Sheppard, Albert Parker, Jr.
Shinners, Stanley Marvin
Shoot, Lyle Edward
Skolnik, Merrill I.
Smith, Wayne D.
Sorger, Gunther Urban
Speciale, Ross Aldo
Spellman, Donald Jerome
Spencer, Edson White
Sprott, Julien Clinton
Steinway, William Joseph
Stern, Arthur Paul
Stone, Gregory Michael
Stone, William Ross
Taylor, George William
Thompson, Fred Clayton
Townsend, Marjorie Rhodes
Tracy, Joseph Charles
Ulland, Paul David
Van de Vaart, Herman
Vollmer, James
Webster, William Merle, Jr.
Welch, Herbert Eugene
Whitehead, Frank Roger
Wilkinson, Arthur Frederick
Williams, Walter Jackson, Jr.
Wilson, William John
Young, Gregory Odd

Electronics, integrated circuits

Abraham, George
Anderson, Richard Cooper
Belle Isle, Albert Pierre
Burghard, Ronald Albert
Chan, Kam Hang
Chen, Wai-Kai
Cheng, Peter Yu-Hung
Choma, John, Jr.
Das, Pankaj K.
de Wit, Michiel
Dyck, Rudolph Henry
El-Mansy, Youssef Aly
Eng, Lawrence (Larry) Phillip
Gage, Donald Shepard
Geller, Bernard Dov
Ghausi, Mohammed Shuaib
Glendinning, William Bernard
Gray, Paul Russell
Greene, Richard Melvyn
Grove, Andrew S.
Guttag, Karl Marion
Gwo, Tai-Chuan
Gwyn, Charles William
Heath, Barbara Anita
Heimer, Malcolm Lee
Hickernell, Fred Slocum
Ibrahim, Ali Abd-El-Fattah
Ipri, Alfred Charles
Jenne, Frederick Benjamin
Joy, Richard Carleton
Kennedy, Eldredge Johnson
Kim, Jin Koo
Klassen, Klaas Berend
Knoot, Peter Anton
Krinsky, Jeffrey Alan
Krowne, Clifford Mitchell
Kuo, Clinton Chang-Kiang
Lancaster, Arthur Lewis
Leary, David Joseph
Leung, Chung Wai
Libby, Vibeke
Lim, Teong Cheng
Linvill, John Grimes
Lu, Chih-Yuan
Magar, Surendar Singh
Mai, Chao Chen
Majidi-Ahy, Gholamreza
Manley, Martin Harold
Manor, Robert Edward
Meindl, James Donald
Moll, John Lewis
Mondal, Kalyan
Murphy, Bernard T.
Nalamwar, Ashok Laxmanrao
Nelson, Richard D.
Oleszek, Gerald Michael
O'Neil, Vernon Patrick, II
Pande, Krishna Prasad
Park, Hee Kyun
Patel, Vipinchandra Natwarlal
Perez, Ricardo
Plunkett, Joseph Charles
Polinsky, Murray Arthur
Polkinghorn, Robert William
Prather, Lawrence Albert
Rajeevakumar, T. V.
Reddy, Chitranjan
Sah, Chih-Tang
Schober, Robert Charles
Shah, Rajiv Rajaram
Shibib, Muhammed Ayman
Shoucair, Farid Sami
Siddiqui, Saeed Hasan
Slade, Bernard Newton
Stach, Joseph
Stoebe, Thomas Gaines
Sweet, Alexander
Tang, Denny Duan-Lee
Taylor, Herbert Lyndon
Trimberger, Stephen Mathias
Valsamakis, Emmanuel Anthony
Varshney, Ramesh Chandra
Wallace, John Robert
Whiteley, Stephen Robert
Yeh, Keming Wayne

Electronics, microelectronics

Abraham-Shrauner, Barbara Wayne
Aghevli, Reza
Anderson, Richard Louis
Ashok, S.
Bajpai, Shyam N
Berger, Robert Law
Boesch, Harold Edwin, Jr.
Bower, Robert William
Brown, Michael Gregory
Chaundhari, Pundlik Kashiram
Chen, Teh-Yi James
Cheung, W(ah-Kwan) Stephen
Choma, John, Jr.
Clark, Richard James
Cregger, Barton Bentley
Crossley, Ian
Dirks, Leslie Chant
Divine, Theodore Emry
Early, James Michael
Feinstein, Joseph
Fetterman, Harold Ralph
Galloway, Kenneth Franklin
Gupta, Madhu Sudan
Gutmann, Ronald Jay
Haddad, George Ilyas
Harman, George Gibson
Harris, James Stewart, Jr.
Holonyak, Nick, Jr.
Hsieh, Kuan Hsiung
Hsu, Yarsun
Hutchison, Robert Vern
Ipri, Alfred Charles
Jackel, Lawrence David
Jenne, Frederick Benjamin
Johnson, Bruce Paul
Johnson, Patrick Woodruff
Kabell, Jack
Kuo, Clinton Chang-Kiang
Lam, Hon Wai
Leheny, Robert Francis
Leung, Chung Wai
Lim, Teong Cheng
Lin, Mou-Shiung
Liu, Yung Sheng
Ma, David I.
Martin, Frederick Wight
Meitzler, Allen Henry
Michalak, Edward Michael
Michener, John Russell
Miracky, Robert Foster
Mitchell, James Thomas
Morrison, Roderick Gordon
O'Clock, George Daniel, Jr.
Oliver, James D., Jr.
O'Neil, Vernon Patrick, II
Orr, William Harold
Patel, Vipinchandra Natwarlal
Pearse, James Newburg
Pease, Roger Fabian Wedgwood
Perez, Ricardo
Prince, John Luther, III
Rao, Kameswara Kolla
Raschke, Curt Robert
Reche, John Joseph
Rumennik, Vladimir
Rutledge, James Luther
Sack, Edgar Albert, Jr.
Schroder, Dieter Karl
Sedlak, Richard John
Sergent, Jerry Elden
Shibib, Muhammed Ayman
Shrivastava, Ritu
Siddiqui, Saeed Hasan
Singh, Rajendra
Stach, Joseph
Stroscio, Michael Anthony
Tien, Ping King
Wade, Thomas Edward
Wang, Andrew Chi Mo
Webster, William Merle, Jr.
Wolber, William George
Yin, Mingtang Thomas
Youn, So Young

Environmental

Amar, Praveen Kumar
Armstrong, Neal Earl
Baer, Thomas Strickland
Betts, Austin Wortham
Bolch, William Emmett, Jr.
Boubel, Richard William
Bregman, Jacob Israel
Cline, James Gerard
Coate, Lester Edwin
deMonsabert, Winston Russel, Jr.
Donaldson, David
Edwards, Ray Conway
Fausett, Robert Julian
Friedlander, Sheldon Kay
Ganley, Mary Constance
Giardina, Paul Anthony
Goldsmith, William Alee
Goldstein, Paul
Grosjean, Daniel
Happ, Stafford Coleman
Hart, Fred Clinton
Jackson, Michael Dean
Jester, William Andrew
Kathren, Ronald Laurence
Kaylor, Frank Baad
Kim, Geung-Ho
Kokoropoulos, Panos
Kolaz, David James
Kovach, Bela Joseph
Kuehn, Thomas Howard
Lauber, Jack David
Lieberman, Joseph Abraham
Liebman, Jon Charles
Loven, Andrew Witherspoon
Ludwig, John Howard
Lyon, Walter Alphons
McMurry, Peter Howard
Middleditch, Brian Stanley
Moeller, Dade William
Morey, Philip Richard
Nelson, Gordon Leon
Noll, Charles Gordon
O'Shaughnessy, James Colin
Pavia, Edgar Hugo
Perdue, Philip Taw
Perrine, Richard Leroy
Putnam, Hugh Dyer
Rinehart, David Alan
Salvatorelli, Joseph J.
Schwing, Richard Charles
Shelley, Philip Eugene
Stange, James Henry
Stockinger, Siegfried Ludwig
Teletzke, Gerald Howard
Tollner, Ernest William
Uicker, Joseph Bernard
Vaughan, Richard Dugger
Vijayakumar, Rajagopal
Ward, Robert Carl
Willoughby, Nancy Bharucha
Yeh, James Tehcheng
Young, Richard Alan
Zandi, Iraj

Environmental, water supply and wastewater treatment

Bacon, Vinton Walker
Berger, Bernard Ben
Bouwer, Herman
Bregman, Jacob Israel
Brooks, Norman Herrick
Cawley, William Arthur
Chambers, James Vernon
Characklis, William Gregory
Cronholm, Lois S.
Davy, Philip Sheridan
de la Noue, Joel Jean-Louis
deMonsabert, Winston Russel, Jr.
Eaton, David J.
Eckenfelder, W. Wesley
Engelbrecht, Richard Stevens
Erdogan, Haydar
Ewing, Benjamin Baugh
Frasier, Gary Wayne
Gloyna, Earnest Frederick
Hamilton, Joseph Hants, Jr.
Horn, Dennis Lee
Jaske, Robert Theodore
Johnson, James Allen
Kendrick, David Richard
Kerfoot, William Buchanan, Jr.
Kilner, Suzanne Miiller
Koerner, Ernest Lee
Kraus, Marjorie Patt
Kumar, Shailendra
La Motta, Enrique Jaime
Levin, Paul
Long, David Ainsworth
Ludwig, John Howard
Luthy, Richard Godfrey
Malinowski, Leonard Chester
McNair, John William, Jr
Miller, Herbert Irving
Myrick, Henry Nugent
Noceti, Richard Paul
Ogle, Dale Francis
Okun, Daniel Alexander
Olesen, Douglas Eugene
O'Shaughnessy, James Colin
Pope, Theodore Campbell, Jr.
Potter, Miles Buttles
Probstein, Ronald Filmore
Rao, Serin Rangeneni
Roe, Sheldon Ford, Jr.
Roman, Ian Charles
Roop, Robert Dickinson
Rubin, A(lbert) Robert
Selm, Robert Prickett
Semmens, Michael John
Seneff, James Orin
Wang, Tsen Chen
Watson, Edward Fisk
Weber, Walter Jacob, Jr.
Weng, Cheng-Nan
Yong, Raymond Nen-Yiu
Young, Richard Alan
Younos, Tamim M.
Zielinski, Paul Bernard

Fusion. *See* ENERGY SCIENCE, LASER.

Human factors

Allen, Robert Burnell
Baise, Walker Nathan
Bashinski, Howard Stewart
Bell, Barbara Jean
Bevan, Thomas Edward
Boff, Kenneth Richard
Boggs, George Johnson
Cahill, Mary-Carol
Carley, John Wesley, III
Carr, Gerald Paul
Cogbill, Charles Lipscomb, III
Cohen, Edwin
Davies, Ivor Kevin
Dlhopolsky, Joseph Gerald
Eigen, Daryl Jay
Frandsen, Walter James
Gatchell, Susanne Marie
Goldman, Alexander
Hoeller, Louise
Jesson, Joseph Edward
Johnston, Dorothy Mae
Jones, Daniel Todd
Loeffler, William Robert
Lund, Arnold Milton, Jr.
Lyman, John
Mitchell, Nancy Brown
Onorato, Howard Louis
Peterson, James Robert
Pulling, Nathaniel H(osler)
Reed, Adam Victor
Rohles, Frederick Henry, Jr.
Schurman, Donald Lee
Shea, Daniel Joseph
Sheridan, Thomas Brown
Singer, Timothy James
Smith, Wayne D.
Tepas, Donald Irving
Tiedemann, Edward Eric
Valfer, Ernst Siegmar
Von Gierke, Henning Edgar

Industrial

Amar, Amar Dev
Bishop, Albert Bentley, III
Bovay, Harry Elmo, Jr.
Burge, Charles Arthur
Burnham, Donald Clemens
Dizer, John Thomas, Jr.
Frassanito, John Robert
Gatchell, Susanne Marie
Hedstrom, Joseph Charles
Hwang, Ching-Lai
Johnson, Harold Arthur
Kapur, Kailash Chander
Katz, Hyman Bernard
Litzenberg, David P.
Majewski, Frank Thomas
Marshall, Harry Dwight
McKee, Keith Earl
Meier, Wilbur Leroy, Jr.
Paté-Cornell, Marie-Elisabeth
Schowalter, William Raymond
Schroer, Bernard Jon
Stanislao, Joseph
Thompson, David Alfred
Weiss, Howard Jacob

Materials. *See also* MATERIALS SCIENCE.

Albertson, Clarence Elmo, Jr
Amick, James Albert
Antler, Morton
Bailey, Stuart Lohr
Baker, William Oliver
Bauman, Thomas Charles
Carpenter, Joseph Andrew, Jr.
Chen, Jesse Hsiang
Chin, Gilbert Yukyu
Chubb, Walston
Dai-Shu-Ho
De Vries, Kenneth Lawrence
Dresselhaus, Mildred Spiewak
Drucker, Daniel Charles
Eiber, Robert James
Finn, Patricia Ann
Fiore, Nicholas Francis
Flemings, Merton Corson
Gallagher, Joseph Patrick
Goins, William (Doris), III
Grace, Richard Edward
Green, Robert Edward, Jr.
Haggag, Fahmy Mahmoud
Hasson, Dennis Francis
Irwin, George Rankin
Jansson, Robert Edward
Johnson, James Robert
Jordan, Charles Ralph
Kapp, Joseph Alexander
Kesler, Clyde Ervin
Koenig, John Richard
Kwon, Young Doo
Lal, Brij Bihari
Loss, Frank J.
Megget, Leslie Makepeace
Mordfin, Leonard
Morrow, JoDean
Orr, William Harold
Pai, Damodar Mangalore
Payne, Robert William
Polonis, Douglas Hugh
Promisel, Nathan E.
Restaino, Alfred Joseph
Ruud, Clayton Olaf
Sahely, Camille
Sardar, Dhiraj Kumar
Schuler, Robert Hans
Selby, Theodore William
Shahinpoor, Mohsen
Shirkey, William Dan
Strauss, Bruce Paul
Stregowski, Thomas John
Tallan, Norman M.
Teller, Cecil Martin, II
Ting, Robert Yen-Ying
Uhlir, Donald Andrew
Van Vlack, Lawrence Hall
Verink, Ellis Daniel, Jr.
Walton, Lewis Anthony
Young, James Francis

Mechanical

Agnew, William George
Agrawal, Ram Kumar
Alexander, Dennis Jay
Ascher, Michael Charles
Atkinson, Steven Albert
Avery, Robert Tolman
Avitzur, Betzalel
Bachman, Walter Crawford
Bailey, Stuart Lohr
Bair, Scott Slaybaugh, III
Ban, Stephen Dennis
Barkan, Philip
Baron, Seymour
Barron, Randall Franklin
Basu, Amiya
Batcha, George
Baumer, (Andrew) Ronald
Beachley, Norman Henry
Beadle, Charles Wilson
Beard, James Taylor
Beggs, James Montgomery
Benedict, Anthony Gorman
Bhagat, Phiroz Maneck
Binns, Jack Neville
Birmingham, Bascom Wayne
Blackwell, Arlyn Navet
Bodenheimer, Bert Arno
Boehm, Robert Foty
Boulger, Francis William
Bowden, Bryant Baird
Brasher, John Odus, Jr.
Brighton, John Austin
Bromberg, Yury
Bujtas, Mark Steven
Calder, Clarence Andrew
Calvert, Glenn Spencer
Caplan, John DAvid
Carroll, Dyer Edmund
Castelvecchi, John Patrick
Chao, Bei Tse
Chateau, Georges Michel
Chattopadhyay, Somnath
Chen, Chih Ping
Chen, Kuan
Chen, Michael Ming
Cho, Soung Moo
Choi, Michael Kam-Wah
Clausing, Arthur Marvin
Coburn, Herbert Dightman, Jr.
Cole, Kenneth Dean
Copes, John Carson, III
Cornell, Robert Witherspoon
Cross, Ralph Emerson
Cugini, Edward Thomas
Cummings, Garth Ellis
Cunningham, James Thomas
Cwycyshyn, Walter
Czernik, Daniel Edward
Daily, James Wallace
Dai-Shu-Ho
Damianov, Vladimir Blagoi
Dasgupta, Aaron
Davis, Lewis Berkley, Jr.
Dean, Robert Charles, Jr.
De Vries, Kenneth Lawrence
DeVries, Marvin Frank
DiOrio, Mark Lewis
Dizer, John Thomas, Jr.
Drake, Michael Lee
Dring, Robert Paul
Eberhardt, Allen Craig
Eckert, Ernst R. G.
Ehrlich, Ira Robert
Eiss, Norman Smith, Jr.
Engen, Byron Wayne
Faccini, Ernest Carlo
Faeth, Gerard Michael
Fischer, Traugott Erwin
Flack, Ronald Dumont, Jr.
Foley, Cray Lyman
Forkel, Curt Emil
Foti, John Thomas
Francis, John Elbert
Friberg, Emil Edwards
Frisch, Joseph
Gaddis, M. Francis
Gaines, Albert Lowery
Gaither, Robert Barker
Gajewski, Walter Michael
Gandhi, Shirish Manilal
Gannatal, Joseph Paul
Garcia, Nicholas Flores
Garg, Devendra Prakash
Geary, William Charles
Glickman, Myron
Glower, Donald Duane
Goldstein, Richard Jay
Goodenough, Samuel Henry
Gorenc, Edward Joseph
Gorges, Heinz A.
Gouse, S. William, Jr.
Grant, Donald Andrew
Greywall, Mahesh
Groff, Gerald Charles
Guill, Frederick Charles
Haberman, Charles Morris
Hagmann, Dean Berry
Hall, Carl William
Hartman, Patrick James
Heckman, Thomas Paul
Hester, Jarrett Charles
Hester, Lawrence Ray, II
Hoffman, John Robert, Jr.
Hopkins, Stephen William
Hovingh, Jack
Hrones, John Anthony
Hrycak, Peter
Hudelson, George David
Hughes, Thomas Joseph
Incropera, Frank Paul
Jacobsen, Stephen Charles
Jensen, Richard Alan
Jergins, Colvin Edward
Johnson, Douglas Blaikie
Johnson, Glen Eric
Johnson, Harold Arthur
Johnson, Stephen Thomas
Jordan, Carl Harvey

Jordan, Richard Charles
Kadaba, Prasanna Venkatarama
Kautz, David Johnathan
Kemelhor, Robert Elias
Kempf, Gary William
Kestin, Joseph
Kirk, James Allen
Kline, Stephen Jay
Kobayashi, Shiro
Korwin, Paul
Kovacs, Gyula
Kreid, Dennis Karl
Kuehn, Thomas Howard
Kumar, Shailendra
Kusuda, Tamami
Kwik, Robert Julius
Lafferty, James Francis
Lahoti, Goverdhan Das
Lai, Ying-San
Latham, Allen, Jr.
Lau, Henry
Laurenson, Robert Mark
Laydon, James Robert
Leitmann, George
Lewis, James Bryson
Lewis, Michael Dolan
Lilje, Karl David
Litzenberg, David P.
Lochte, Glen Elgin
Long, Leonard Michael
Look, Dwight Chester, Jr.
Lowe, Phillip A(rnold)
Lund, Charles Edward
Lundgren, James Reinhold
Macke, Harry Jerry
Maier, Leo Robert, Jr.
Majewski, Frank Thomas
Manvi, Ramachandra
Mapother, Dillon Edward
Margolis, Donald Lee
Mark, William David
Marshall, Harry Dwight
Marshall, Steven Edwin
Mathiprakasam, B.
Mayo, Howard Armstrong, Jr.
McClure, Carl Kenneth
McFadden, Peter William
McFadden, Terry Ted
McGean, Thomas James
McKey, Paul Michael
McLerran, Archie Ralph
McMenamin, Edward William
Melcher, James Russell
Merchant, Mylon Eugene
Merilo, Mati
Migliore, Herman James
Miller, Paul Leroy, Jr.
Min, Tony Charles
Minkowycz, W(olodymyr) J(ohn)
Moretti, Peter Marc Allan
Morris, Robert Howard
Nagy, Denes
Nakos, James Thomas
Narayana, Anand Deo
Netzel, James Phillip
Nichols, Paul Arthur
O'Brien, Kenneth Stanley
Olsen, Joseph Carl
Orthwein, William Coe
Ovens, William George
Owens, James Arthur, Jr.
Park, U. Young
Park, William Harold
Paul, Frank Waters
Pavia, Edgar Hugo
Phillips, William Evans
Phillips, Winfred Marshall
Pope, Theodore Campbell, Jr.
Powe, Ralph Elward
Psaros, George Emanuel
Rabinow, Jacob
Rabins, Michael Jerome
Rathod, Mulchand Shamjibhai
Reddy, Narander Pabbathi
Reed, Helen Louise
Reid, Robert Lelon
Reswick, James Bigelow
Reynolds, Harold Gene
Reynolds, William Craig
Richter, George Brownell
Rocco, Vincent Anthony
Roe, Kenneth Keith
Rohsenow, Warren Max
Rowlands, Robert Edward
Rubin, Carol Ann
Sabin, Cullen Milo
Schiller, Roger William
Schlegel, Ronald Gene
Schmidt, William Frederick
Schneider, Robert William
Schoen, George Janssen
Schultz, Albert Barry
Sciandra, Luigi Claudio
Seely, John Henry
Shahinpoor, Mohsen
Shank, Maurice Edwin
Shaw, Milton Clayton
Shelnutt, James William, III
Silsby, Graham Forbes
Simonetti, Joseph Lawrence
Singhal, Anil Kumar
Siuru, William Dennis, Jr.
Smallwood, Donald Lee
Smith, Kevin Richard
Snyder, Glenn Jacob
Solberg, Ruell Floyd, Jr.
Spielvogel, Lawrence George
Sprouse, Kenneth Michael
Stalker, Kenneth Walter
Steinitz, Louis Joseph
Sternlicht, Beno
Stumpe, Warren Robert
Suciu, Spiridon N.
Suh, Nam Pyo
Swenson, Donald Otis
Szewczyk, Albin Anthony
Taraman, Khalil Showky
Taylor, Robert P.
Tejwani, Gopal Das
Tellep, Daniel Michael
Teller, Cecil Martin, II
Thomas, Gary Charles
Thompson, Jack Mansfield, Jr.
Thornburg, Dale Lynn
Timmerman, Robert Wilson
Tome, Richard Earle
Tonda, Richard Dale
Tourtellotte, Mills Charlton
Uicker, Joseph Bernard
Umek, Anthony M.
Urquhart, James Burwell, III
Vachon, Reginald Irenee
Valencis, Janet Margaret
Valentine, Daniel Thomas
Vest, Charles Marstiller
Veziroglu, Turhan Nejat
Vigil, Manuel Gilbert
Vijayakumar, Rajagopal
Viswanathan, K.
Walton, Lewis Anthony
Wang, Cheh Cheng
Warder, Richard Currey, Jr.
Watkins, Louie W(illard)
Watson, Gary Edward
Wei, Millet Lunchin
Weldon, William Forrest
Wells, David Lee
Wells, William Terry
Wilder, David Gould
Wnuk, Michael Peter
Wolfe, Howard Francis
Wong, Julius Pan
Woolverton, Dalton Leo
Wright, Edward Stewart
Wu, Chih
Yao, Shi Chune
Youm, Youngil
Young, Garry Gean
Zacharin, Alexey Theodore

Mechanics, fluid
Abramson, Hyman Norman
Andersen, Cyril F.
Babchin, Alexander Joseph
Bair, Scott Slaybaugh, III
Bird, Robert Byron
Blair, Michael Francis
Blais, Roger Nathaniel
Bober, William
Brilliant, Howard Michael
Broersma, Sybrand
Bromberg, Yury
Brooks, Norman Herrick
Carelli, Mario Domenico
Carrier, George Francis
Carrigan, Charles Roger
Cartlidge, Edward Sutterley
Caughey, David Alan
Caulk, David Allen
Cermak, Jack Edward
Chan, Shih Hung
Chao, Bei Tse
Chawla, Tara (Tilak)
Chen, Ching Jen
Chen, Kuan
Coles, Donald Earl
Collins, Frank Gibson
Covert, Eugene Edzards
Criminale, William Oliver, Jr.
Daily, James Wallace
Dallman, John Clay
Damianov, Vladimir Blagoi
Darden, Christine Mann
Davis, Stephen Howard
Deissler, Robert George
Denysyk, Bohdan
Donnelly, Russell James
Dukler, Abraham Emanuel
Dvorak, Frank Arthur
Eaton, John Kelly
Emmons, Howard Wilson
Falvey, Henry Thomas
Flack, Ronald Dumont, Jr.
Fornberg, Bengt
Freiwald, David Allen
Goldschmied, Fabio Renzo
Gorenc, Edward Joseph
Green, Geoffrey Francis
Grossman, Bernard
Grotberg, James Bernard
Handler, Robert Alphonse
Hanratty, Thomas Joseph
Hjertager, Bjorn Helge
Horn, Stanislav Václav
Hrycak, Peter
Hsu, Ming-Teh
Jawad, Sarim Najim
Kamm, Roger Dale
Kandil, Osama Abdel-Mohsin
Kantrowitz, Arthur
Kassoy, David R.
Kennedy, John Fisher
Kipp, John Edward
Klebanoff, Philip Samuel
Kline, Stephen Jay
Lampert, Seymour
Landweber, Louis
Li, Chung-Hsiung
Liepmann, Hans Wolfgang
Liu, Chang Yu
Liu, Chen-Huei
Liu, Paul Chi
Long, Lyle Norman
Long, Robert Radcliffe
Lumley, John Leask
Marvin, Joseph George
McDonough, James Michael
McIntyre, Brian Arch
Merilo, Mati
Mikulla, Volker
Miller, Harvey Philip
Minkowycz, W(olodymyr) J(ohn)
Muirhead, Vincent Uriel
Neitzel, G(eorge) Paul, Jr.
Norment, Hillyer Gavin
O'Brien, Morrough Parker
Orszag, Steven Alan
Ostrach, Simon
Oved, Yoel
Paul, John Francis
Phillips, Winfred Marshall
Powe, Ralph Elward
Probstein, Ronald Filmore
Proctor, Charles Lafayette, II
Raichel, Daniel Richter
Ramos, Juan Ignacio
Randall, John Douglas
Reed, Helen Louise
Reshotko, Eli
Reynolds, William Craig
Riahi, Nourollah
Riegler, Gerold Ernst
Rivlin, Ronald Samuel
Rosensweig, Ronald Ellis
Rouhani, Sayd Zia
Rudavsky, Alexander Bohdan
Sabin, Cullen Milo
Sadhal, Satwindar Singh
Salwen, Harold
Schaufele, Roger Donald
Scheuing, Richard Albert
Schneider, Gerald Elmore
Schwarz, Klaus W.
Sears, William Rees
Shapiro, Ascher Herman
Sheridan, Robert Emmett, Jr.
Siegel, Robert
Sieracki, Leonard Mark
Siginer, Aydeniz
Sirignano, William Alfonso
Smith, Raymond Virgil
Soo, Shao Lee
Stahl, Charles Drew
Street, Robert Lynnwood
Suzuki, Tateyuki
Szewczyk, Albin Anthony
Tai, Tsze Cheng
Tankus, Harry
Taylor, Robert P.
Tellep, Daniel Michael
Thomas, John Howard
Turinsky, Paul Josef
Vafai, Kambiz
Valentine, Daniel Thomas
Van Dyke, Milton Denman
Vigil, Manuel Gilbert
Waldo, George Van Pelt, Jr.
Warder, Richard Currey, Jr.
Wehausen, John Vrooman
Werner, Christian Thor
White, Charles Olds
Whitfield, Jack Duane
Williams, Peter MacLellan
Woolverton, Dalton Leo
Wu, Steve
Yates, George Thomas
Yih, Chia-Shun
Young, James Allan
Zakkay, Victor H.
Zielinski, Paul Bernard

Mechanics, fracture
Advani, Sunder Hashmatrai
Apostal, Michael Christopher
Atluri, Satya Nadham
Caddell, Robert Macormac
Chen, Er-Ping
Coffin, Louis Fussell, Jr.
Duckworth, Winston Howard
Dunayevsky, Victor Arkady
Eiber, Robert James
Frechette, Van Derck
Gallagher, Joseph Patrick
Hopkins, Stephen William
Irwin, George Rankin
Jespersen, Niels Vestergaard
Jones, Douglas Linwood
Kapp, Joseph Alexander
Kobayashi, Albert S.
Lange, Eugene Albert
Lewis, James Bryson
Loss, Frank J.
Marshall, David Bruce
Michener, John Russell
Morrow, JoDean
Nagar, Arvind Kumar
Needleman, Alan
Pindera, Jerzy Tadeusz
Rolfe, Stanley Theodore
Saada, Adel Selim
Salama, Mamdouh M.
Sciammarella, Cesar Augusto
Shieh, Wei Tong
Smith, C. William
Stout, Robert Daniel
Sun, Chang-Tsan
Swedlow, Jerold Lindsay
Tramontozzi, Louis Robert
Tseng, Ampere An-Pei

Mechanics, solid
Adams, Donald Frederick
Altan, Taylan
Antman, Stuart Sheldon
Caddell, Robert Macormac
Calder, Clarence Andrew
Carroll, William Finch
Chen, Er-Ping
Chen, Wai-Fah
Chiang, Fu-pen
de Richemond, Albert Leo
Dunayevsky, Victor Arkady
Durelli, August Joseph
Eberhardt, Allen Craig
Fabrikant, Valery Isaac
Foral, Ralph Francis
Freund, Lambert Ben
Gallagher, Richard Hugo
Gould, Phillip Louis
Hodge, Philip Gibson, Jr.
Iannuzzelli, Raymond Joseph
Kim, Kyung-Suk
Kunin, Isaak A.
Lahoti, Goverdhan Das
Lakes, Roderic Stephen
Lardner, Thomas Joseph
Maier, Leo Robert, Jr.
McClure, Carl Kenneth
Nagar, Arvind Kumar
Narayana, Anand Deo
Narayanaswamy, Onbathiveli Subrahmanyan
Nariboli, Gundo Annacharya
Nash, William Arthur
Needleman, Alan
Nikolai, Robert Joseph
Noor, Ahmed Khairy
Nordgren, Ronald Paul
Pollak, Henry Lewis
Popov, Egor Paul
Rice, James Robert
Rinehart, John Sargent
Rivlin, Ronald Samuel
Rowlands, Robert Edward
Sancaktar, Erol
Schey, John Anthony
Schmidt, Robert
Schmidt, William Frederick
Shaw, Milton Clayton
Smith, C. William
Sun, Chang-Tsan
Swedlow, Jerold Lindsay
Tao, Li-Chung
Tepera, Joseph Edward
Tseng, Ampere An-Pei
Tso, Wai Keung
Vargas, John David
Vinogradov, Aleksandra M.
Wang, Leon Ru-Liang
Weng, George Jueng-cious
Widera, G.E.O.

Mechanics, theoretical and applied
Abramson, Hyman Norman
Achenbach, Jan Drewes
Adbel-Ghaffar, Ahmed Mansour
Advani, Sunder Hashmatrai
Alexander, Leckie Frederick
Andersen, Cyril F.
Apostal, Michael Christopher
Arkilic, Galip Mehmet
Atluri, Satya Nadham
Barfield, Walter David
Bedford, Anthony
Belytschko, Ted B.
Benjamin, Roland John
Block, David Lester
Boley, Bruno Adrian
Boyd, Landis Lee
Bryant, Michael David
Bryson, Arthur Earl, Jr.
Burns, Joseph Arthur
Buske, Norman L.
Carey, Graham Francis
Carson, James Matthew
Casperson, Richard L.
Caulk, David Allen
Chamis, Christos Constantinos
Chattopadhyay, Somnath
Chiu, Kao Ding
Chow, Pao-Liu
Cohen, Harley
Czernik, Daniel Edward
Dafermos, Constantine Michael
Dasgupta, Aaron
Datta, Subhendu K(umar)
Den Hartog, Jacob Pieter
de Richemond, Albert Leo
Dick, William Allen
Dowell, Earl Hugh
Drucker, Daniel Charles
Dym, Clive Lionel
Ericksen, Jerald Laverne
Fistedis, Stanley H.
Fitzgerald, Edwin Roger
Gerstle, Frank P., Jr.
Gipson, Gary Steven
Goland, Martin
Goyal, Satish Chandra
Graham, Frederick Mitchell
Grant, Donald Andrew
Grant, John Wallace, Jr.
Gross, William Allen
Gulati, Suresh Thakurdas
Hahn, Hong Thomas
Hall, William Joel
Handler, Robert Alphonse
Harari, Azriel
Hefzy, Mohamed Samir W. M.
Hemp, Gene W(illard)
Hodge, Philip Gibson, Jr.
Holmes, Philip John
Howland, Robert Alden, Jr.
Hunter, Thomas Alexander, III
Jenkins, James Thomas
Kausel, Eduardo
Keil, Alfred Adolf Heinrich
Kim, Kyung-Suk
Kobayashi, Albert S.
Kunar, Roy Rajpaul
Laheru, Ken Liem
Landweber, Louis
Lardner, Thomas Joseph
Leipholz, Horst Hermann Eduard
Levinson, David Alan
Macke, Harry Jerry
Malosh, James Boyd
Man, Chi-Sing
Mark, William David
Mindlin, Raymond David
Mordfin, Leonard
Mow, Van C.
Nash, William Arthur
Nguyen, Vietchau
Norwood, Frederick Reyes
Nyquist, Gerald Warren
Peng, Steven Tsu Jiunn
Pindera, Jerzy Tadeusz
Pister, Karl Stark
Plunkett, Robert
Rubin, Carol Ann
Sciammarella, Cesar Augusto
Sidorowicz, Kenneth Joseph
Sierakowski, Robert Leon
Siginer, Aydeniz
Simitses, George John
Sinha, Bikash Kumar
Solberg, Ruell Floyd, Jr.
Tang, Ruen C.
Triffet, Terry
Udwadia, Firdaus Erach
Vaishnav, Ramesh Navalshanker
Viest, Ivan M(iroslav)
Wan, Frederic Yui-Ming
Wang, Tsuey Tang
Wells, William Terry
Werner, Christian Thor
Williams, James Henry, Jr.
Wolf, Joseph Allen, Jr.
Wong, Julius Pan
Wu, John Naichi
Wu, Steve
Yao, Lun-Shin
Yu, Yi-Yuan

Metallurgical. *See also* **MATERIALS SCIENCE.**
Aukrust, Egil
Avitzur, Betzalel
Bauman, Thomas Charles
Beaton, Michael Steve
Berardi, Matteo P.
Birkle, A(dolph) John
Bush, Spencer Harrison
Canonico, Domenic Andrew
Carroll, Dyer Edmund
Chang, Ji Young
Cribb, Walter Raymond
Dahlstrom, Donald Albert
Dalgarno, Alexander
Duerr, J. Stephen
Einziger, Robert Emanuel
Elliott, John Frank
Fiore, Nicholas Francis
Fuerstenau, Douglas Winston
Gibson, George William
Glasser, Julian
Glodowski, Robert John
Goins, William (Doris), III
Grace, Richard Edward
Habermann, Clarence Edward
Kellogg, Herbert Humphrey
Khare, Ashok K.
Kleinsorge, William Peter
Lange, Eugene Albert
Lautzenheiser, Clarence Eric
Lewis, Michael Dolan
Luerssen, Frank Wonson
McEvily, Arthur Joseph
Moudgil, Brij Mohan
Mullins, William Wilson
Niederkorn, Ioan Stefan
Olson, Ferron Allred
Payne, Robert William
Robins, Norman Alan
Schuhmann, Reinhardt, Jr.
Schultz, Clifford William
Schwer, Roger Edwin
Shirley, Joseph Floyd
Somasundaran, Ponisseril
Spachner, Sheldon Arthur
Spisak, John Francis
Stalker, Kenneth Walter
Stout, Robert Daniel
Tomonto, Charles Vincent
Wadsworth, Milton Elliot
Wayne, Steven Falko
Weng, George Jueng-cious
Wiewiorowski, Edward Ignacy

Non-destructive testing
Djordjevic, Borislav Boro
Ensminger, Dale
Kleinsorge, William Peter
Koenig, John Richard
Nakos, James Thomas
Nicaise, Walter Ferdinand
Perkins, Glenn Richard
Rae, William Howard, Jr.
Sabbagh, Harold Abraham
Tomonto, Charles Vincent
Yeack-Scranton, Celia Elizabeth
Ying, Shuh-Pan

Nuclear. *See also* **ENERGY SCIENCE, Nuclear.**
Abrams, Richard Francis
Ackermann, Norbert Joseph, Jr.
Alapour, Adel
Alexander, Dennis Jay
Amer, Ahmad (El Sayed)
Arnold, William Howard
Atkinson, Steven Albert
Attaya, Hosny M(oustafa)
Ayers, Arnold Leslie, Sr.
Baer, Thomas Strickland
Baron, Seymour
Barsky, Arnold M(ilton)
Bartine, David Elliott
Basehore, Kerry Lee
Batcha, George
Bauer, Richard Carlton
Beakes, John Herbert
Beaton, Roy Howard
Bevelacqua, Joseph John
Bickel, John Henry
Bigeleisen, Jacob
Blomeke, John Otis
Bolch, William Emmett, Jr.
Booth, James Albert
Branco, Maria dos Milagres
Bridgman, Charles James
Brown, Steven Harry
Bush, Spencer Harrison
Card, Darrell Holder
Carelli, Mario Domenico
Carter, Benjamin Dudley
Carter, Leland LaVelle
Casey, Leslie Anne
Chandler, John Christopher
Chawla, Tara (Tilak)
Chen, Chih Ping
Cheng, Edward Teh-Chang
Cho, Soung Moo
Choi, Seung Hoon
Chung, Chien
Cogbill, Charles Lipscomb, III
Cohen, Karl Paley
Colby, Nathaniel Fred
Cole, Thomas Earle
Coombe, John Raymond
Crawley, Paul F.
Cummings, Garth Ellis
Cuttler, Jerry Milton
DeMott, Diana L(ynn)
Dickson, Paul Wesley, Jr.
Difilippo, Felix Carlos
Doerner, Robert Carl
Dolan, Linda Capano
Draper, Ernest Linn, Jr.
Dunigan, Paul Francis Xavier
Dunn, Michael James
Ebert, Marlin J.
Eichholz, Geoffrey G.
Eng, Norman
Fistedis, Stanley H.
Fleming, Karl Neill
Fluegge, Ronald Marvin
Forkel, Curt Emil
Gaines, Albert Lowery
Gajewski, Walter Michael
Garrick, B. John
Gibson, George William
Glower, Donald Duane
Gohar, Mohamed Yousry Ahmed
Goode, Glenn Amos, Jr.
Goodman, Julius
Goodwin, Richard Clarke
Green, Ralph Ellis
Groeber, Edward Otto, Jr.
Haggag, Fahmy Mahmoud
Haire, Marvin Jonathan
Halsey, William Guy
Halverson, Thomas George
Hansen, Kent Forrest

Hanson, John Edward
Harbay, Edward William
Hendrie, Joseph Mallam
Hendron, John Alden
Hoffman, John Robert, Jr.
Hofmann, Peter Ludwig
Holzer, Joseph Mano
Hootman, Harry Edward
Hsia, Henry Tao-sze
Hsu, Ming-Teh
Huang, Hai Chow
Hurd, Edward Nelson, III
Huston, Norman Earl
Ireland, John Richard
Jacovitch, John
Jaske, Robert Theodore
Jasny, George Roman
Jedruch, Jacek
Jester, William Andrew
Joksimovich, Vojin
Jones, David Hunter
Kerr, William
Klema, Ernest Donald
Knoll, Glenn Frederick
Koskelo, Markku Juhani
Koussa, Harold Alan
Kouts, Herbert John Cecil
Kovach, Bela Joseph
Krug, Harry Everistus Peter, Jr.
Kunar, Roy Rajpaul
Kwik, Robert Julius
Larrimore, James Abbott
Lester, Richard Keith
Levenson, Milton
Levine, Jerry David
Levine, Samuel Harold
Levy, Salomon
Li, Xing Zhong
Lineberry, Michael J.
Lischer, Ludwig Frederick
Lorenzini, Paul Gilbert
Lumb, Ralph Francis
Lundin, Bruce Theodore
Marchaterre, John Frederick
Martin, Jose Ginoris
Martin, Lawrence Ronald
Mason, Edward Archibald
McGuire, Stephen Craig
Meem, James Lawrence, Jr.
Meyer, Walter
Morris, Charles Reginald
Morris, Robert Howard
Morrison, Roderick Gordon
Nichols, Kenneth David
Nichols, Paul Arthur
Niederkorn, Ioan Stefan
Okrent, David
Onorato, Howard Louis
Osborn, Daniel Cargill, III
Pagel, Deborah Joanne
Palladino, Nunzio Joseph
Park, U. Young
Parry, John O.
Pastorelle, Peter John
Paustian, Harold Herman
Pearson, John Stuart
Pearson, Samuel Dibble, III
Perry, Nelson Allen
Pigford, Thomas Harrington
Podowski, Michael Zbigniew
Pravda, Milton Frank
Prelas, Mark Anthony
Radford, Kenneth Charles
Ragheb, Magdi
Randall, John Del
Rao, Surendar Purushothay
Redmond, Robert Francis
Roberds, Richard Mack
Robertson, James Craig
Roe, Kenneth Keith
Rothrock, Ray Alan
Rouhani, Sayd Zia
Roush, Marvin Leroy
Savage, William Frederick
Schaeffer, Norman M.
Scotti, Vincent Guy
Sheff, James Robert
Shih, Charles Chien
Sholtis, Joseph Arnold, Jr.
Siess, Chester Paul
Silverman, Joseph
Simon, Albert
Speis, Themis P.
Spellman, Donald Jerome
Stephenson, Thomas Edgar
Stewart, James Edmund, III
Tiedemann, Edward Eric
Tomlinson, Richard Lee
Uhrig, Robert Eugene
Varley, Ronald Arthur
Vaurio, Jussi Kalervo
Wagner, Aubrey Joseph
Warren, Holland Douglas
Way, Richard A(lvord)
Wei, Jim P(iau)
Weinfurter, Erich Brian
Wells, Alan Harvey
Wenz, Michael Frank, Jr.
Wertheim, Robert Halley
Wilcox, Robert Howard
Willoughby, Nancy Bharucha
Wiren, Robert Craig
Yao, Shi Chune
Yue, Mike Yuan
Yung, Shu-Chien
Zerguini, Taha Houssine

Operations research. *See also* **MATHEMATICS.**
Alexander, Ronald Clifford
Berkman, Herman Gerald
Blanchard, Susan Manning
Carberry, James Joseph
Chesser, Nancy Jean
Cooper, William Wager
Eaton, David J.
Eidson, Robert Ansel
Engel, Lars Norlick
Fang, Shu-Cherng
Fariss, Thomas Lee
Ferchek, Gary Randall
Frank, Ellen Ryan
Gross, Donald
Hedstrom, Joseph Charles
Holtzman, Samuel
Horvath, William John
Hwang, Ching-Lai
Jewell, William Sylvester
Jones, James Thomas, Jr.
Kapur, Kailash Chander
Karroll, Joseph E.
Kocaoglu, Dundar F.
Kushner, Harvey David
Lee, William Wai Lim
Levary, Reuven Robert
Levis, Alexander Henry
Liang, Tom Yuan-Tong
Liebman, Jon Charles
Luus, Rein
Lynn, Walter Royal
Magnanti, Thomas Lee
Makowski, Armand Maurice
McGarity, Arthur Edwin
Meier, Wilbur Leroy, Jr.
Meredith, Orsell Montgomery
Miller, Herbert Irving
Miller, Trudi Claire
Miser, Hugh Jordan
Muckstadt, John A.
Mulvey, John Michael
Nieh, Bill
Samuel, Aryeh Hermann Albert
Shea, Daniel Joseph
Stanford, Robert Ernest
Steinberg, Frederick
Vasko, Francis Joseph
Verry, William Robert
Wagner, Daniel Hobson
Weiss, Howard Jacob
White, King Preston, Jr.
Wiig, Karl Martin
Wilhelm, Wilbert E.

Optical. *See also* **OPTICS.**
Adhav, Ratnakar Shankar
Axelrod, Norman Nathan
Babish, Richard Constantine
Brown, Gordon M(arshall)
Caimi, Frank Michael
Church, Eugene Lent
Crawford, David Livingston
Crowe, Devon George
Devereux, William Patrick
Dowley, Mark William
Dumas, Herbert Monroe, (Jr.)
Dunn, Anne Roberts
Durelli, August Joseph
Dyck, Rudolph Henry
Fein, Michael E.
Gelles, Rubin
Gill, Dennis Howard
Gould, Gordon
Gundersen, Martin Adolph
Hall, Freeman Franklin, Jr.
Hammond, Thomas Joseph
Hansche, Bruce David
Hilgeman, Theodore William
Iverson, Mark Vernon
Johnson, Peter Dexter
Kornstein, Edward
Lamberts, Robert Lewis
Little, Gordon Rice
Liu, Hua-Kuang
Marshall, Gerald Francis
Meinel, Aden Baker
Miles, Richard Bryant
Olszewski, Jerzy Adam
Ong, Hiap Liew
Paranto, Joseph Nolan
Post, Madison John
Ruterbusch, Paul Hugo
Saleh, Bahaa E. A.
Sappington, John Oliver
Skelton, Dennis Lee
Spoelhof, Charles P.
Task, Harry Lee
Thompson, Brian John
Tucker, Robert J.
Young, James Forrest

Petroleum. *See also* **GEOSCIENCE, Oceanography; ENERGY SCIENCE, Fuels.**
Ayoub, George Tanios
Blais, Roger Nathaniel
Brannon, H(ezzie) Raymond, Jr.
Carson, David Brooks
Chateau, Georges Michel
Chilingarian, George Varos
Coburn, Herbert Dightman, Jr.
Coburn, Timothy Craig
Coons, William Ray, Jr.
Coonts, Harvey Lee
DiFoggio, Rocco
Dorfman, Myron Herbert
Fisher, James Harold
Frederickson, Arman Frederick
Geer, Ronald Lamar
Glimm, James Gilbert
Goldsberry, Fred Lynn
Greenkorn, Robert Albert
Halbouty, Michel Thomas
Handy, Lyman Lee
Hartmann, Dan John
Heinemann, Heinz
Henderson, William David
Hettinger, William Peter, Jr.
Hopgood, David
Huff, Kenneth O.
Kadi, Kamal Sif-el
Kleinberg, Robert Leonard
Knight, Wilbur Hall
Krumrine, Paul Henry, III
Lacy, Lewis Lee
Leventhal, Stephen Henry
Litvak, Boris Lvovich
Lochte, Glen Elgin
Long, Robert B.
Lorenz, Philip Boalt
Luttrell, Eric Martin
Maderak, Marion Louis
Marsden, Sullivan Samuel, Jr.
Nordgren, Ronald Paul
Olsen, David Kenneth
Pestak, Mark William
Poettmann, Fred Heinz
Powers, Richard Wallace
Reynolds, John Gordon
Sammon, Peter
Smith, Joe Mauk
Sprunt, Eve Silver
Stahl, Charles Drew
Taber, Joseph J.
Taylor, Larry Don
Urschel, Stephen Francis
Venkatesan, Valadi Nataraj
Waid, Margaret Cowsar
Walker, George Pinckney, III
Wayland, Russell Gibson, Jr.
Widdoes, Lawrence Curtis

Plasma. *See also* **ENERGY SCIENCE.**
Anderson, John Melvin
Houlberg, Wayne Arthur
Kazek, Gregory Joseph
Kruger, Charles Herman, Jr.
Martin, Richard Douglas
Mense, Allan Tate
Schoenbach, Karl Heinz
Seidl, Milos
Wagner, Carl Ernest

Polymer
Bamji, Soli Shavax
Cohen, Robert Edward
Elias, Hans Georg
Gupta, Bhupender Singh
Hardin, Ian Russell
Kwon, Young Doo
Lawson, Kenneth Robert
Lee, Michael Ching Hsueh
Lin, Kenneth Shou-Chein
Lustig, Stanley
Malloy, Jr. Donald Edwin
Monaghan, Leo John
Nakajima, Nobuyuki
Peng, Steven Tsu Jiunn
Sarjeant, Walter James
Shu, Peter Hua-Cheng
Sutherland, James Milton
Tehon, Stephen Whittier
Weaver, James Clyde

Robotics
Anselmo, Victor John
Batchelder, Michael Jack
Bollinger, John Gustave
Cwycyshyn, Walter
Engelberger, Joseph Frederick
Fodor, Magda Maria
Gelles, Rubin
Green, Robert G.
Hanifin, Leo Eugene
Hawkes, Graham Sidney
Hogan, Neville
Horn, Berthold Klaus Paul
Hull, Harvard Leslie
Jawad, Sarim Najim
Kawamura, Kazuhiko
Luo, Ren-Chyuan
Lytle, James Mark
Margolis, Donald Lee
Maynard, Kenneth Baker
McKee, Keith Earl
Mergler, Harry Winston
Miluschewa, Sima
Moravec, Hans Peter
Nevins, James Lawrence, Jr.
Nitzan, David
Ogata, Katsuhiko
Oldroyd, L(awrence) Andrew
Oppenheim, Irving Jeffrey
Paul, Frank Waters
Rechnitzer, Andreas Buchwald
Reddy, D. Raj
Robinson, James Robert
Schiller, Roger William
Severns, Matthew Lincoln
Sheridan, Thomas Brown
Siegel, Melvin Walter
Simonds, J(ohn) Todd
Stanislao, Joseph
Stone, Gregory Michael
Taenzer, Jon Charles
Thompson, Jack Mansfield, Jr.
Tiras, Herbert Gerald
Vesel, Richard Warren
Wagner-Bartak, Claus Gunther Johann
Waldron, Kenneth John
Wang, Paul Keng-Chieh
Warnat, Winifred Irene
Wells, David Lee
Wohlsen, Robert Cobb
Wu, Chi-haur

Solar
Basu, Amiya
Hermann, Allen Max
Jayadev, Tumkur Shiva
Kohn, James Paul
Lau, Henry
Laydon, James Robert
McNabb, John Leland
Thomason, Harry Jack Lee, Jr.

Structural
Astenah-Asl, Abolhassan
Belytschko, Ted B.
Brown, John Eros
Carroll, William Finch
Chiu, Kao Ding
Clemente, Frank Massimino, Jr.
Cooper, James Daniel
Culver, Charles George
Cunningham, James Thomas
Ebeling, Dick Winfield
Engen, Byron Wayne
Felippa, Carlos Alberto
Fowler, Timothy John
Gere, James Monroe
Gergely, Peter
Gupta, Ajaya Kumar
Gurfinkel, German Ruben
Huang, Jiin-Long
Jespersen, Niels Vestergaard
Johnston, Bruce Gilbert
Ketchum, Milo Smith
Kostem, Celal Nizamettin
Kunze, Walter Edward, Jr.
Kuo, Pao-Tsin
Lai, James Shau-Yan
Lee, George C.
Mangus, Alfred Ring
Megget, Leslie Makepeace
Meirovitch, Leonard
Minor, Joseph Edward
Oppenheim, Irving Jeffrey
Pall, Avtar Singh
Pazargadi, Shayan
Pinkham, Clarkson Wilfred
Porter, Max Lee
Robertson, Leslie Earl
Scawthorn, Charles
Schuler, Robert Hans
Seth, Baldev Raj
Tepera, Joseph Edward
Thulin, Frederick Adolph, Jr.
Tso, Wai Keung
Wang, Leon Ru-Liang
Wintz, Joseph Anthony, III
Wright, Richard Newport, III
Yao, James Tsu-Ping

Systems engineering
Abend, Kenneth
Adrian, Donald James
Alexander, Ronald Clifford
Appelbaum, Joel A(lan)
Asher, Robert Bernard
Attinger, Ernst Otto
Austin, Edward Marvin
Bayer, Jesse Abraham
Betts, Austin Wortham
Beutler, Frederick Joseph
Beyster, John Robert
Bhattacharyya, Shankar
Bishop, Albert Bentley, III
Black, Edward Partridge
Bodenheimer, Bert Arno
Bollinger, John Gustave
Braden, Charles Hosea
Burnham, Donald Clemens
Busch, Allen Cyril
Bussgang, Julian Jakob
Carlton-Foss, John Andrew
Chestnut, Harold
Christ, Duane Marland
Cohen, Edwin
Cohn, Nathan
Concordia, Charles
Cordero, Julio
Cruz, Jose Bejar
Cullen, Donald Lee
Darlington, Sidney
Davis, Dean Earl
Dick, Robert James
Dickinson, Bradley William
Donalek, Peter John
Drozd, Andrew Louis Stephan
Dunn, Michael James
Emanuel, William Robert
Farber, Joseph
Fish, Andrew Joseph, Jr.
Fishman, Robert Sumner
Fletcher, James Chipman
Frosch, Robert Alan
Gaither, William Samuel
Garg, Devendra Prakash
Garzia, Mario Ricardo
Glickman, Myron
Goldschmied, Fabio Renzo
Gollobin, Leonard Paul
Gordon, Mark Gardiner
Gouse, S. William, Jr.
Griffiths, John David
Guastaferro, Angelo
Halpin, Daniel William
Harris, James Ridout
Hawkes, Graham Sidney
Hester, Lawrence Ray, II
Hoag, David Garratt
Hoffman, Kenneth Charles
Huang, Richard Shih-Chiu
Jaluria, Rajiv
Jenkins, Donald Ralph
Johnson, Jeffrey Paul
Jones, Daniel Todd
Kahne, Stephen James
Karasik, Myron Solomon
Karpetsky, Timothy Paul
Karroll, Joseph E.
Keehn, Neil Francis
Keil, Alfred Adolf Heinrich
Kelley, Albert Joseph
Key, Michael Leon
Knowles, Lloyd George
Koci, Bruce R.
Kushner, Harvey David
Lapen, Robert Joseph
Lautzenheiser, Clarence Eric
Leber, Ralph Eric
Leibholz, Stephen Wolfgang
Levis, Alexander Henry
Lewis, Frank Leroy
Lincoln, Walter Butler, Jr.
Lindberg, Eric Kent
Loeb, William A.
Mak, Sioe Tho
Manvi, Ramachandra
Marks, Robert Jackson, II
Maynard, Kenneth Baker
McCalla, Thomas Mark, Jr.
McGean, Thomas James
McGurrin, Michael Francis
McNabb, John Leland
Meinel, Carolyn Pettit
Meisner, James Edward
Michels, David Barry
Mitzel, Glenn Earle
Myers, Howard
Nash, Jonathon Michael
Nelson, Larry Dean
O'Neill, Russell Richard
Pazargadi, Shayan
Petras, Charles Edward
Porskievies, Thomas Anthony
Powers, William Francis
Purser, Paul Emil
Rabins, Michael Jerome
Rabow, Gerald
Rapp, Paul Ernest
Rathjens, George William
Reinhold, Richard Clarke
Reklaitis, Gintaras Victor
Roberts, Edward Baer
Roberts, Liona Russell, Jr.
Robertson, Lawrence Marshall
Ross, Ian Munro
Rugh, Wilson John, II
Sage, Andrew Patrick, Jr.
Salant, Abner Samuel
Salvatori, Vincent Louis
Sargent, Ernest Douglas
Satzer, William Joseph, Jr.
Saylor, William Wardell
Schaefer, Jacob Wernli
Scholz, Lawrence Charles
Schwartz, Jay William
Seifer, Arnold David
Shelley, Edwin Freeman
Shinners, Stanley Marvin
Shoup, William David
Shursky, Stanley James
Silvern, Leonard Charles
Simms, James Robert
Skalafuris, Angelo James
Skolnik, Merrill I.
Snyder, Glenn Jacob
Sorace, Ronald Eugene
Spoelhof, Charles P.
Staehle, Charles Michael
Steinberg, Frederick
Stonebraker, Jeffrey Scot
Stumpe, Warren Robert
Summers, George Donald
Todd-Spring, Deborah Ann
Toomey, John Patrick, III
Tsay, Yih Tsong
Uda, Robert Takeo
Vasko, Francis Joseph
Verriest, Erik Isidoor
Verry, William Robert
Vollmer, James
Wagner, Lorry Yale
Walton, Vincent Michael
Wang, Paul Keng-Chieh
Warfield, John Nelson
Warzecha, Ladislaus William
Washom, Byron John
Weiss, Roland George
White, King Preston, Jr.
Wilhelm, Wilbert E.
Williams, Aubrey James
Williams, Ronald Oscar
Williams, Theodore Joseph
Williams, Walter Jackson, Jr.
Wolansky, Bonnie Kay
Wolber, William George
Wolfe, Bradley Allen
Wray, John Lawrence
Wright, Edward Stewart
Young, Gregory Odd
Zeissig, Gustave Alexander

Telecommunications
Atal, Bishnu Saroop
Baer, Walter S.
Cape, Robert E.
Chandler, Edward William
Charyk, Joseph Vincent
Chaudhuri, Siddheswar
Chitsaz, Sirus
Coggeshall, Ivan Stoddard
Coleman, Jeffrey Owen
Colmenares, Narses Jose
Cook, James Howell, Jr.
Cotton, John M.
Crombie, Douglass Darnill
Dixit, Sudhir Sharan
Eaves, Reuben Elco
Everitt, William Littell
Farago, George
Felix, Michael O(tto)
Fine, Terrence Leon
Flom, Terrence Edsel Flom
Fukui, Hatsuaki
Gearing, Alan Eugene
Gross, Al
Helstrom, Carl Wilhelm
Jesson, Joseph Edward
Kasper, Bryon Lynn
Kay, Steven Michael
Keiser, Bernhard Edward
Keiser, Gerd Emdo
Krawarik, Peter Heinz
Ljung, Donovan Allen
Makowski, Armand Maurice
Malfara, David Joseph
Mann, John Bunyan
Marshalek, Robert Gerald
McGregor, Dennis Nicholas
Mickle, Marlin Homer
Mitchell, Michael Eugene
Olszewski, Jerzy Adam
Ong, Chong Kok
Palazzo, Reginaldo, Jr.
Perrella, Anthony Joseph
Pintsov, Leon Aron
Pomalaza Raez, Carlos Arturo
Preschutti, Joseph Paul
Sayegh, Soheil I(skandar)
Schillebeeckx, Dirk Johan
Schwartz, Jay William
Schwartz, Mischa
Siegel, Eric David
Sossamon, David Baine
Utlaut, William Frederick
Van Slyke, Richard Maurice
Viterbi, Andrew James
Wu, William W.

Other
Aggarwal, Mahesh Chand
Alexander, William Davidson, III, *Transportation engineering*
Anders, James Edward, *Power hydraulics*
Auburg, C(harles) Douglas, *Energy conservation engineering*
Baciocco, Albert Joseph, Jr., *Research administration*
Bell, Grant Richard, *Construction inspection, testing-failure analysis, mgmt. orgn. (organizational behavior)*
Bernitsas, Michael Marinos, *Marine engineering*
Berry, Maurice Robert, Jr.
Blasingame, Benjamin Paul, *Aeronautical instrumentation*
Blythe, Cleveland Henry
Boundy, Ray Harold, *International research management*
Bull, Stanley Raymond, *Engineering physics*
Burnett, James Robert
Cartner, John Aubrey, *Naval architecture and marine engineering*
Catton, Ivan, *Heat transfer*
Cole, Kenneth Dean
Collier, John Walter
Cook, James Howell, Jr.
Cookson, Albert Ernest
Crowl, Daniel A., *Oil shale technology*
Deissler, Robert George, *Heat transfer*

De Lauer, Richard D., *Research engineering administration*
DeVries, Marvin Frank, *Manufacturing engineering*
Duffy, Robert Aloysius, *Research administration*
Edwards, Ray Conway, *Heat transfer*
Eiss, Norman Smith, Jr.
Ellingwood, Bruce Russell, *Structural reliability*
Elliott, David LeRoy, *Control system theory*
Faccini, Ernest Carlo, *Explosives phenomena*
Fairhurst, Charles, *Mining engineering*
Fenton, Noel John, *Electronics company management*
Flaschen, Steward Samuel, *Research and development management*
Fleming, Karl Neill
Friedman, Edward Alan, *Technological education*
Fung, Yuan-Cheng Bertram, *Biomechanics*
Geller, Bernard Dov, *Microwave circuits*
German, Richard Barry, *Mining engineering*
Ginwala, Kymus, *Research and development management.*
Gogue, George Paul, *Power electronics*
Goodyear, Wayne David, *Dynamics*
Greenberg, Harold Paul, *Quality engineering*
Griffith, James Edward, *Space heating and cooling.*
Guill, Frederick Charles
Hall, Jerome William
Hanifin, Leo Eugene, *Manufacturing productivity*
Helliwell, Robert Arthur, *Radioscience*
Herbich, John Bronislaw, *Coastal engineering*
Hilbertz, Wolf Hartmut, *Marine architecture*
Hillier, James, *Technology transfer*
Ho, Cho-Yen, *Thermophysics*
Hoff, Marcian Edward, Jr., *Electronics industry research and development management.*
Hollander, Milton Bernard
Hou, Kenneth Chiang
Hradilek, Peter Jaroslav, *Earthquake engineering*
Hunter, Thomas Alexander, III
Jackson, James Oswald, *Industrial hygiene engineering*
Jacobs, Joseph Donovan, *Construction engineering*
Jasny, George Roman, *Engineering and computing organization management*
Jayne, Theodore Douglas, *Research and development management*
Jones, Roger Clyde
Jordan, Arthur Kent, *Inversion methods*
Jordan, Charles Ralph, *Naval engineering*
Kanury, (Anjaneya) Murty, *Heat and mass transfer*
Kirk, James Allen, *Automobile accident reconstruction*
Kocaoglu, Dundar F., *Engineering management*
Kuhn, Alan Karl, *Geological engineering*
Kulicke, Charles Scott, *Equipment engineering company management*
Kuo, Pao-Tsin
Larson, Clarence Edward, *Engineering consulting*
Levy, Salomon, *Heat transfer*
Lofting, Everard Mervyn
Lou, Jack Yung Kia
Love, Tom Jay, Jr., *Heat transfer*
Lupo, Michael Vincent, *Reliability and maintainability*
Lyons, John W(inship), *Engineering research administration*
Makdisi, Faiz Isbir
Marash, Stanley Albert, *Quality assurance*
Mc Cune, William James, Jr., *Manufacturing, engineering administration*
McFadden, Terry Ted
McKey, Paul Michael
Mettler, Ruben Frederick, *Electronics, engineering management*
Miller, Lee Stephen
Min, Tony Charles, *Heat transfer*
Moore, F. Richard
Morelli, Ugo
Mou, Duen-Gang
Nicholson, Christopher, *Submersible vehicle design*
Nuzzo, Salvatore Joseph, *Electronics company management*
O'Brien, Kenneth Stanley, *Quality assurance*
Ogata, Katsuhiko
Ogden, Roger Wayne, *Pulp and paper engineering*
O'Shea, Patrick Gerard
Owen, Daniel Lee
Ozdemir, Levent, *Mining engineering*
Pall, Avtar Singh, *Earthquake engineering*
Parsignault, Daniel Raymond
Polay, Janet Skinner
Pulling, Nathaniel H(osler)
Radcliff, Roger Dale, *Electromagnetic theory*
Ramo, Simon, *Engineering management*
Remer, Donald Sherwood, *Engineering economics*
Roberts, Edward Baer, *Management of technology*
Rounds, Fred Grafton
Rubin, Lawrence G(ilbert), *Cryogenic thermometry.*
Saperstein, Lee Waldo, *Mining engineering*
Saville, Thorndike, Jr., *Coastal, port, harbor engineering*
Schmitt, Roland Walter, *Research management*
Schwartz, (Ellen) Shirley Eckwall, *Lubrication*
Sebo, Stephen Andrew, *High voltage*
Shock, D'Arcy Adriance, *Solution mining*
Siegel, Robert
Silsby, Graham Forbes
Simpson, John A., *Manufacturing engineering*
Slaughter, John Brooks, *Control systems theory*
Slemon, Gordon Richard, *Electrical propulsion*
Smallwood, Donald Lee, *Rehabilitation Engineering*
Smith, Raymond Virgil
Speis, Themis P., *Nuclear power plant risk assessment.*
Sterling, Raymond Leslie, *Underground engineering*
Stonebraker, Jeffrey Scot
Swanson, David Henry, *Technology transfer administration*
Todd-Spring, Deborah Ann, *Power engineering*
Toomey, III John Patrick, *Radar, sonar*
Ungar, Edward William, *Research and development management*
Vafai, Kambiz, *Heat transfer*
Vanderslice, Thomas Aquinas, *Electrical research; manufacturing management*
Viswanathan, K., *Materials handling*
Wakeland, Howard Leslie, *Engineering education*
Weber, Ernst, *Microwaves*
Wenk, Edward, Jr., *Technology assessment*
Whalen, James Joseph
Wharton, Charles Benjamin
Williams, Keith Alan, *Communications systems*
Wintz, Joseph Anthony, III
Wu, Theodore Yao-Tsu
Yeack-Scranton, Celia Elizabeth, *Device design for magnetic recording*

ENVIRONMENTAL SCIENCE. *See also* ATMOSPHERIC SCIENCE.

Ecology. *See also* BIOLOGY.
Adams, David Arthur
Alderfer, Ronald Godshall
Anderson, Roger Clark
Armstrong, Neal Earl
Arnold, Dean Edward
Baker, Herbert George
Becker, Donald August
Beeton, Alfred Merle
Berkson, Harold
Berry, James Frederick
Bliss, Lawrence Carroll
Blum, Barton Morrill
Breininger, David Robert
Brugam, Richard Blair
Buffington, John Douglas
Cates, Rex Gordon
Chittenden, Mark Eustace, Jr.
Colinvaux, Paul Alfred
Coney, Charles Clifton
Cooper, Arthur Wells
Curry, Mary Grace
Dahlsten, Donald Lee
Diamond, Jared Mason
Earle, Sylvia Alice
Eberly, William Robert
Edwards, William Charles
Ehrlich, Paul Ralph
Eisner, Thomas
Eleuterius, Lionel Numa
Fawcett, Michael Harold
Ferchau, Hugo Alfred
Forest, Herman Silva
Fredrickson, Leigh Harry
French, Norman Roger
Frost, Melvin Jesse
Gammon, James Robert
Gannon, John Edward
Gates, David Murray
Graham, Harry Morgan
Harper, Carol Lynn Mount
Hasler, Arthur Davis
Henderson, Carrol LaVerne
Herricks, Edwin Eugene
Hinckley, Alden Dexter
Holloway, Harry Lee, Jr.
Hughes, Eric Hill
Hulbert, Lloyd Clair
Hurt, Valina Kay
Hutchison, Jay Bryson, Jr.
Ibrahim, Shawki Amin
Ilg, Ronald Jon
Johnson, Philip Lewis
Keeley, Sterling Carter
Kennish, Michael Joseph
Kevan, Peter Graham
Kistner, David Harold
Kohn, Alan Jacobs
Kosinski, Robert Joseph
Kunz, Thomas Henry
Landis, Wayne G.
LaRoche, Germain
Lee, John Joseph
Lees, Lester
Leighton, Mark
Levin, Michael Howard
London, Mark David
Lyon, L. Jack
Mackie, Richard John
Marcot, Bruce Gregory
Marino, Mary Lou
Marion, Wayne Richard
Marten, Gordon Cornelius
Mason, Charles Perry
Maughan, O. Eugene
McNaughton, Samuel Joseph
McVoy, Gary Richard
Mertz, David Byron
Miller, Lee N.
Mitsch, William Joseph
Moll, Don L.
Mooney, Harold Alfred
Morgan, Eric Lee
Mountainspring, Stephen
Murdoch-Doty, Lynne Frances
Nabholz, Joseph Vincent
Nickerson, Norton Hart
Oliver, Kelly Hoyet, Jr.
Oswald, Edward Theodore
Page, Thomas Lee
Peterle, Tony John
Pitelka, Louis Frank
Polls, Irwin
Quinn, James Amos, Jr.
Rapport, David Joseph
Ritchie, Jerry Carlyle
Robel, Robert Joseph
Robertson, Andrew
Rochow, John Joseph
Roop, Robert Dickinson
Ruibal, Rodolfo
Salamun, Peter J(oseph)
Sanderson, H. Reed
Schreiber, Richard Kent
Schreiner, Stephen Philip
Sellner, Kevin Gregory
Sells, Saul B.
Severinghaus, William Daniel
Sharp, Aaron John
Smith, Clifford Winston
Springer, Joseph Tucker
Strader, Herman Lee
Talbot, Lee Merriam
Tiffney, Wesley Newell, Jr.
Tourangeau, Phillip Clifford
Turner, Robert Eugene
Ungar, Irwin A.
Vadala, Frank Rocco
Vallentyne, John Reuben Way (Johnny Biosphere)
Vinyard, Timothy Wayne
Vollenweider, Richard
Wali, Mohan Kishen
Ward, F(raser) Prescott
Watson, Annetta Paule
Weber, James Alan
Westman, Walter Emil
Wolfe, Douglas Arthur
Zach, Reto

Environmental chemistry
Anderson, Craig Jay
Banerjee, Sujit
Barrows, Harold Lindsey
Bradford, Wesley Lamont
Chen, Eng Ming
Chen, Gloria Chao
Coleman, Walden Emile
Craft, Charles Douglas
Dasch, Jean Muhlbaier
Davies, Patrick Hanlon
Drever, James Irving
Duce, Robert Arthur
Easton, Myriam Perdices
Eckenfelder, W. Wesley
Farrier, Noel John
Fornshell, Randall Douglas
Hanson, Ray Lorain
Hass, James Ronald
Helz, George Rudolph
Henry, Norman Whitfield, III
Hilton, James Lee
Holdren, George R., Jr.
Huang, Cheng Schen
Ivie, Glen Wayne
Johnson, Pratt Deen
Kenaga, Eugene Ellis
Krause, Richard Theodore
Kresse, Herman Joseph
Kuhns, John Farrell
Landrum, Peter Franklin
Landsberg, Johanna Dobrot
Law, Stephen LeRoy
McArdle, Richard Neff
Menzel, Ronald George
Newman, Leonard
Newton, Amos Sylvester
Nowicki, Henry George
Nyssen, Gerard Allan
Pietz, Richard Irwin
Pollman, Curtis Devin
Rast, Walter, Jr.
Robertson, Andrew
Rose, Arthur William
Sage, Gloria Welt
Shaw, Robert Wilson
Song, Leila Shia
Stamoudis, Vassilis Christos
Teal, John M.
Wakeham, Stuart Glenwood
Walsh, Ted William
Wang, Tsen Chen
Wells, Edwin Boyd
West, Philip William
White, David Cleaveland
Wickham, Margaret Edna
Wolfe, Douglas Arthur
Woodrow, James Eugene

Environmental toxicology. *See also* AGRICULTURE, toxicology.
Albers, Peter Heinz
Alderfer, Ronald Godshall
Amirkhanian, John David
Anderson, Robert Simpers
Atallah, Yousef Hanna
Brown, Steven Harry
Case, George David
Chanana, Arjun Dev
Chandler, Jerry LeRoy
Cheng, H(wei)-H (sien)
Chowdhury, Parimal
Clark, Donald Ray, Jr.
Clarkson, Thomas William
Claxton, Larry Davis
Coleman, Ronald L.
Couse, Nancy Lee
Dalvi, Ramesh R.
Davies, Patrick Hanlon
DeCaprio, Anthony Paul
Dunbar, Jan Robert
Edwards, Gordon Stuart
Ehrlich, Richard
Eisenbud, Merril
Failla, Patricia McClement
Folinsbee, Lawrence John
Fouts, James Ralph
Freed, Virgil Haven
Giesy, John Paul
Gift, James Joseph
Goldberg, Alan Marvin
Gorham, Eville
Groopman, John Davis
Gurtoo, Hira L.
Hamelink, Jerry Lee
Harrison, Keith Graham
Heicklen, Julian Phillip
Hutchinson, Thomas Cuthbert
Jones, Maurice (Mo), Jr.
Kallman, Mary Jeanne
Kenaga, Eugene Ellis
Koschier, Francis Joseph, III
Kresse, Herman Joseph
Kulle, Thomas John
Landis, Wayne G.
Landrum, Peter Franklin
Leone, Ida A.
Lipnick, Robert Louis
Malins, Donald Clive
Meeks, Robert G.
Mehendale, Harihara Mahadeva
Melancon, Mark John
Morgan, Eric Lee
Nabholz, Joseph Vincent
Nakatani, Roy Eiji
Neel, James Van Gundia
Oliver, Kelly Hoyet, Jr.
Owen, David Gray
Peterle, Tony John
Phillips, Richard Dean
Pilson, Michael Edward Quinton
Rabovsky, Jean
Rao, Serin Rangeneni
Reddy, Chinthamani Channa
Rocco, Vincent Anthony
Roth, Robert Andrew, Jr.
Ruzo, Luis Octavio
Safe, Stephen Harvey
Seckar, Joel Andreas
Shaikh, Zahir Ahmad
Shapiro, Irving Meyer
Sigman, Caroline Compton
Singh, Jarnall
Sutton, Harry Eldon
Tilson, Hugh Arval, Jr.
Wedig, John H.
Willford, Wayne Alan
Wilson, Richard
Woskie, Susan Renee
Yanders, Armon Frederick
Yu, Simon Shyi-Jian
Zwicker, Gary Michael

Gas cleaning systems
Abrams, Richard Francis
Brook, Marx
Carlton, Donald Morrill
Hall, Herbert Joseph
Harkness, John Barrett Long
McIver, Samuel Hodgeden
Moeller, Dade William
Noll, Charles Gordon
Swenson, Donald Otis
Thompson, Benny Louis

Hazardous waste disposal
Baumer, (Andrew) Ronald
Boateng, Kwasi
Boland, J. Robert
Borns, David James
Boyd, James
Carr, William Hoge, Jr.
Cawley, William Arthur
Cheremisinoff, Paul Nicholas
Choi, Seung Hoon
Clapham, Wentworth Beggs, Jr.
Cline, James Gerard
Costello, Richard James
Dunbar, Jan Robert
Fradkin, Larry
Gaddis, M. Francis
Hackman, E(lmer) Ellsworth, III
Hinckley, Alden Dexter
Holloway, John Thomas
Holton, Gregory Allan
Jackson, Douglas Webster
Kaczynski, Victor Walter
Kobayashi, Hester Atsuko
Kuhn, Alan Karl
Lauber, Jack David
Levin, Paul
Luthy, Richard Godfrey
Malinowski, Kenneth Chester
Maslansky, Steven Paul
Mote, Peter Allen
Neiheisel, James
Parsons, William Andrews
Peck, John Hazen
Rinehart, David Alan
Roe, Sheldon Ford, Jr.
Russell, Virginia Willis
Shaub, Walter Michael
Shinn, Michael Howard
Shock, D'Arcy Adriance
Stiller, David Martin
Teletzke, Gerald Howard
Trevorrow, LaVerne Everett
Weiss, Norman Louis
Wells, Stephen Gene
Wright, Robert James

Resource management
Adams, David Arthur
Adams, James Rolf
Addis, James Theodore
Agnew, Douglas Craig
Alexander, Peter John
Barrett, Izadore
Bassin, N. Jay
Berkman, Herman Gerald
Bier, Charles James
Boyd, James
Boyd, William Edward
Bradley, Katharine Tryon
Bradley, Michael Douglas
Brant, Russell Alan
Buffington, John Douglas
Burnet, George, Jr.
Burroughs, Richard H., III
Carpenter, Richard Amon
Clapham, Wentworth Beggs, Jr.
Coate, Lester Edwin
Cook, Maurice Gayle
Drawe, Dale Lynn
Drown, Eugene Ardent
Fradkin, Larry
Frost, Melvin Jesse
Garland, Bernard William
Gatherum, Gordon Elwood
Gaut, Norman Eugene
Gibbons, Harry Lawrence, Jr.
Gilliam, James Karl
Hamon, Danny Joe
Haug, Peter Tiffany
Henderson, Carrol LaVerne
Herricks, Edwin Eugene
Holland, Majorie Miriam
Hughes, Eric Hill
Hurt, Valina Kay
Ilg, Ronald Jon
Jacoby, Henry Donnan
Jarrett, Albert Russell
Jayne, Benjamin Anderson
Johnson, Howard A(rthur)
Karr, James Richard
Kaylor, Frank Baad
Keran, Douglas Charles
Kilner, Suzanne Miiller
Lee, William Wai Lim
Levary, Reuven Robert
Lieberman, Joseph Abraham
Maley, Terry Samuel
Manus, Andrew Theodore
Marino, Mary Lou
Marion, Wayne Richard
Marx, Donald Henry
Mason, John Montgomery, Jr.
McVoy, Gary Richard
Monash, Ellis Alan
Montalbano, Frank, III
Mountainspring, Stephen
Myrick, Henry Nugent
Nakatani, Roy Eiji
Oglesby, Ray Thurmond
Parker, Garald Gordon
Parker, Robert Hallett
Pease, David Nathaniel
Psuty, Norbert Phillip
Renard, Kenneth George
Resler, Steven Charles
Salwasser, Hal James
Sather, John Henry
Schuh, G(eorge) Edward
Scott, Morris Douglas
Spiegel, Zane
Stoltenberg, Carl Henry
Ursic, Stanley John
Vane, Sylvia Brakke
Vaughan, Richard Dugger
Ward, Robert Carl
Watt, Mamadou Hamé
Wein, Ross Wallace
Williams, Daniel Frank
Yokell, Michael David
Young, Oran Reed
Zandi, Iraj

Wastewater treatment systems. *See* ENGINEERING, Environmental.

Other
Amar, Praveen Kumar, *Acid rain*
Berkson, Harold
Cain, William S., *Environmental health*
Chirnside, Anastasia Elizabeth McHugh
deLaubenfels, David John, *Biogeography*
Den Hartog, Jacob Pieter
Ellison, Alfred Harris, *Environmental science research administration*
Evans, Gary William
Foti, John Thomas, *Solid waste management*
Giardina, Paul Anthony
Glenn, Robert Edward, *Industrial hygiene*
Greenfield, Stanley Marshall, *Air pollution dispersion*
Hawkinson, Thomas Edwin, *Industrial hygiene*
Kolaz, David James, *Ambient air sampling and measurement*
MacBryde, Bruce
Mayfield, Donald Lewis, *Radiological protection*
McIver, Samuel Hodgeden
Miles, Edward Lancelot, *Marine studies*
Mohr, John Luther
Moore, Barbara S. P.
Murdoch-Doty, Lynne Frances, *Environmental health protection*
Nichols, Grady Barney
O'Brien, Keran
Orloff, Neil, *Environmental research management*
Parkhurst, David Frank, *Environmental risk and decision analysis*
Pilson, Michael Edward Quinton, *Marine ecosystems*
Resler, Steven Charles, *Marine environmental sciences*
Sanderson, H. Reed, *Range and wildlife habitat*
Schneider, Stephen Henry, *Environmental policy*
Schwickert, Russell Charles
Tourangeau, Phillip Clifford
White, David Cleaveland
Whitmore, Jacob Leslie, III
Wint, Dennis Michael, *Environmental Education*
Worth, James Judson Blackley
Woskie, Susan Renee

GENETICS. *See* AGRICULTURE, BIOLOGY, MEDICINE, VETERINARY MEDICINE.

GEOSCIENCE

Arctic studies
Anderson, Duwayne Marlo
Collin, Arthur Edwin
Comiso, Josefino Cacas
Elliot, David H.
Faure, Gunter
Koci, Bruce R.
Linder, Gerhard Martin
Meier, Mark Frederick
Nichols, Donald Ray
Walters, James Carter
Yeend, Warren Ernest

Coastal zones
Brickman, Eugene
Finkl, Charles William, Jr.
Heron, S(tephen) Duncan, Jr.
Ingram, Roy Lee
Leatherman, Stephen Parker

Manus, Andrew Theodore
McCloy, James Murl
Pilkey, Orrin H.
Seibel, Erwin
Tanner, William Francis, Jr.
Turner, Robert Eugene
Wasserburg, Gerald Joseph
Wood, Dixon Lee

Geochemistry
Allen, Gary Curtiss
Anderson, Duwayne Marlo
Baedecker, Philip Ackerman
Banaszak, Konrad Joseph
Barden, Roland Eugene
Barnes, Hubert Lloyd
Biscaye, Pierre Eginton
Bishop, Richard Stearns
Brimhall, George H.
Brown, Harrison Scott
Buseck, Peter R.
Drever, James Irving
Eastman, Michael Paul
Eastoe, Christopher John
Edmond, John Marmion
Ehlers, Ernest George
Epstein, Samuel
Ernst, Wallace Gary
Faure, Gunter
Filby, Royston Herbert
Filipek, Lorraine Henrietta
Fish, Ferol Fredric
Frost, John Elliott
Garrels, Robert Minard
Goldberg, Edward David
Goodell, Horace Grant
Grossman, Lawrence
Hare, Ben Dean
Helz, George Rudolph
Hem, John David
Heydegger, H(elmut) Roland
Hill, Walter Edward, Jr.
Holdren, George R., Jr.
Kauzmann, Walter Joseph
Kemp, Marwin King
Kutina, Jan
Laughlin, Alexander William
Lewis, Donald Richard
Light, Thomas Dale
Lofgren, Gary Ernest
Luth, William Clair
MacGregor, Ian Duncan
Malcolm, Ronald Lee
Mason, Brian Harold
Maywood, Paul Stanley
Meyers, Philip Alan
Miller, Donald Spencer
Moore, Carleton Bryant
Murthy, Varanasi Rama
Nisbet, Phillip Clark
O'Hara, Patrick Francis
O'Neil, James Richard
Osborn, Elburt Franklin
Perdue, Philip Taw
Pierre, Harvey Harold
Pigott, John Dowling
Raedeke, Linda Dismore
Rice, Donald Lester
Riese, Walter Charles
Rose, Arthur William
Ruckmick, John Christian
Savin, Samuel Marvin
Schrader, Edward Leon
Schwarcz, Henry Philip
Seeley, James Lewis
Shaw, Denis Martin
Skinner, Brian John
Temples, Tom J.
Thompson, Keith Francis MacKechnie
Tillman, James Edward
Turekian, Karl Karekin
Ulmer, Gene C.
Van Patter, Douglas Macpherson
Veizer, Ján
Wahl, Floyd Michael
Wakeham, Stuart Glenwood
Walls, Richard Alan
Waslenchuk, Dennis Grant
Weres, Oleh
Wetherill, George West
Wyllie, Peter John
Zelibor, Joseph Louis, Jr.

Geology
Absalom, Constance Mary
Aronow, Saul
Austin, Steven Arthur
Bagwell, Joyce Marie Burris
Ballmann, Donald Lawrence
Berg, Henry Clay
Berkland, James Omer
Bettis, Patricia Karen
Bishop, Richard Stearns
Borns, David James
Bourgeois, Joanne
Boyer, Robert Ernst
Brabb, Earl Edward
Braumiller, Allen Spooner
Briskin, Madeleine
Brooks, Harold Kelly
Brooks, Howard Claude
Brooks, James Elwood
Brophy, Gerald Patrick
Brown, Jim McCaslin
Bruce, Clemont Hughes
Burke, Kevin Charles Antony
Calkin, Parker Emerson
Campbell, Russell Harper
Carter, William Douglas
Cassidy, Martin Macdermott
Cheeseman, Ray
Chenoweth, Philip Andrew
Chilingarian, George Varos
Churnet, Habte Giorgis
Clark, Sandra Helen Becker
Clay, Vickie Lynn
Clopine, Gordon Alan
Cohen, Arthur David
Coleman, James Malcom
Cox, Steven Willard
Craddock, Campbell
Craig, Richard G.
Cramer, Howard Ross
Crelling, John Crawford
Dean, John David
Donath, Fred Arthur
Doyle, Frank Lawrence
DuBar, Jules Ramon
DuMontelle, Paul Bertrand
Eastoe, Christopher John
Ehlen, Judy
Elam, Jack Gordon
Epstein, Samuel
Felts, Wayne Moore
Finch, Warren Irvin
Finkl, Charles William, Jr.
Flax, Philip Daniel
Folger, David Winslow
Folk, Stewart Huntley
Force, Eric Ronald
Fritz, William Jon
Gabelman, John Warren
Galey, John Taylor
Ganley, Mary Constance
Garman, Phyllis Metrolis
Garrels, Robert Minard
Grossman, Irving Gross
Haeberle, Frederick Roland
Halbouty, Michel Thomas
Hall, Stephen A.
Harmon, David E., Jr.
Hartmann, Dan John
Hatton, Kay Smith
Heinrichs, Walter Emil, Jr.
Hopkins, M. E.
Hubbert, Marion King
Huff, Kenneth O.
Hulburt, Margery Ann
Huntsman, John Robert
Ivosevic, Stanley Wayne
James, Harold Lloyd
Jamison, Harrison Clyde
Judson, Sheldon
Keenmon, Kendall Andrews
Kirtley, David Warren
Kluth, Charles Frederick
Knight, Wilbur Hall
Knutson, Carroll Field
Kottlowski, Frank Edward
Kuroiwa, Julio
Lauth, Robert Edward
Lee Roark, Carol Kindle
Leighton, Morris Wellman
Lienhart, David Arthur
Light, Thomas Dale
Lucchitta, Baerbel Koesters
MacGregor, Ian Duncan
Maley, Terry Samuel
Maness, Lindsey Vance, Jr.
Marston, Richard Alan
Marvin, Richard Frederick
Masursky, Harold
Mathewson, Christopher Colville
McCoy, Alexander Watts, III
McEldowney, Roland Conant
McFadden, Leslie David
McGregor-Dawson, James Lindsay
Mc Laren, Digby Johns
McMurdie, Dennis Stoddard
Merriam, Daniel F(rancis)
Metsger, Robert William
Milling, Marcus Eugene
Mills, Randall Adrain
Mitchell, Albert Wallace, III
Moore, Carla Jean
Moore, Henry John, II
Moore, James Robert
More, Syver Wakeman
Morrison, Roger Barron
Mote, Peter Allen
Mullen, Ellen D.
Myers, Donald Arthur
Naeser, Nancy Dearien
Namy, Jerome N.
Narasimhan, Thiruppudaimarudhur Narayanaiyer
Neiheisel, James
Nunan, Adrienne Nichola
O'Connor, Howard Grant
O'Rourke, Thomas Denis
Ovens, Stephen Alexander
Ovenshine, A(lexander) Thomas
Peck, Dallas Lynn
Peck, John Hazen
Pees, Samuel Thomas
Percival, Stephen Francis, Jr.
Péwé , Troy Lewis
Pilkey, Orrin H.
Ponder, Herman
Popp, John Thomas
Porter, Stephen Cummings
Powers, Richard Wallace
Pray, Lloyd Charles
Price, William Charles
Ranney, Wayne Donald
Reinemund, John Adam
Reynolds, Mitchell William
Riese, Walter Charles
Riggs, Karl A., Jr.
Riley, Patrick Paul
Roberts, Ralph Jackson
Rochet, Jean Paul
Rodgers, John
Rosenfeld, John Lang
Rosenshein, Joseph Samuel
Ruckmick, John Christian
Ruppel, Edward Thompson
Rutford, Robert Hoxie
Saint-Amand, Pierre
Schmidt, Ruth A.M.
Schmitz, Darrel Wayne
Schneider, Allan Frank
Schuster, Robert Lee
Servos, Kurt
Sevon, William David
Shaffer, Paul Raymond
Shipman, Ross Lovelace
Shoemaker, Eugene Merle
Short, Nicholas Martin
Sonnenberg, Stephen Arnold
Stead, Frederick Lee
St. John, Bill
Stott, Donald Franklin
Stuart, Robert James
Sullivan, Neil Maxwell
Sundell, Kent Allan
Swann, Gordon Alfred
Tanaka, Stephanie Masae
Taylor, Charles LaVerne
Temples, Tom J.
Thompson, Keith Francis MacKechnie
Thompson, Woodrow Burr
Thorson, Robert Mark
Toth, Margo Irene
Turner, Mortimer Darling
Twiss, Page Charles
Vineyard, Jerry D.
Wallace, Robert Earl
Walters, James Carter
Walton, Paul Talmage
Weisbord, Norman Edward
Wells, Stephen Gene
Wilson, Leonard Richard
Wilson, Robert Lee
Wobus, Reinhard Arthur
Wolman, M. Gordon
Wood, Dixon Lee
Yeend, Warren Ernest
Youd, Thomas Leslie

Geology, mineralogy
Barton, Paul Booth, Jr.
Bassett, William Akers
Brophy, Gerald Patrick
Bundy, Wayne Miley
Buseck, Peter R.
Chamberlain, Steven Craig
Davies, David Keith
Dietrich, Richard Vincent
Frederickson, Arman Frederick
Frueh, Alfred Joseph
Gregory, Joel Patrick
Jansen, George James
Kim, Hae Soo
Klein, Cornelis
Kutina, Jan
Leonard, Benjamin Franklin, III
Powell, Benjamin Neff
Servos, Kurt
Skinner, Brian John
Sullivan, Kathryn D.
Thompson, James Burleigh, Jr.
Wadsworth, William Bingham
Wahl, Floyd Michael

Geology, petrology
Albee, Arden Leroy
Allen, Gary Curtiss
Bird, John Malcolm
Brett, Robin
Brimhall, George H.
Churnet, Habte Giorgis
Dick, Henry Jonathan Biddle
Dietrich, Richard Vincent
Ehlers, Ernest George
Elliot, David H.
Felts, Wayne Moore
Fisher, George Wescott
Gregg, Jay Mason
Hare, Ben Dean
Inyang, Hilary
Isachsen, Yngvar William
James, Harold Lloyd
Kays, M(arvin) Allan
Klein, Cornelis
Lofgren, Gary Ernest
Meinert, Lawrence David
Miller, William Lawrence
Miyashiro, Akiho
Mullen, Ellen D.
Murthy, Varanasi Rama
Nichols, Kathryn Marion
O'Hara, Patrick Francis
Oman, Paul Richard
Peterson, Donald William
Powell, Benjamin Neff
Rall, Elizabeth Pretzer
Rosenfeld, John Lang
Schreiber, B. Charlotte
Shaw, Denis Martin
Simkin, Thomas Edward
Thompson, James Burleigh, Jr.
Toth, Margo Irene
Treves, Samuel Blain
Ulmer, Gene C.
Usdansky, Steven Ira
Vanko, David Alan
Wadsworth, William Bingham
Walker, David
Warwick, Peter Delawet
Westerman, David Scott
Whitten, Eric Harold Timothy
Wobus, Reinhard Arthur
Wyllie, Peter John
Yoder, Hatten Schuyler, Jr.
Zen, E-an

Geology, sedimentology
Anderson, Franz Elmer
Babuin, Michael Louis
Bettis, Patricia Karen
Bloomer, Richard Rodier
Bourgeois, Joanne
Braumiller, Allen Spooner
Brooks, James Elwood
Carozzi, Albert Victor
Chamberlain, Charles Franklin
Clopine, Gordon Alan
Cloud, Preston
Coleman, James Malcom
Creager, Joe Scott
Davies, David Keith
De Keyser, Thomas Lee
Dorfman, Myron Herbert
Eby, David Eugene
Field, Michael Ehrenhart
Fields, Robert William
Fillon, Richard Henry
Fisher, James Harold
Flax, Philip Daniel
Friedman, Gerald Manfred
Fritz, William Jon
Gaffey, Susan Jenks
Gregg, Jay Mason
Groff, Donald William
Happ, Stafford Coleman
Hatchell, William O'Donald
Hay, William Winn
Heron, S(tephen) Duncan, Jr.
Hixon, Sumner Best (Dave)
Ingram, Roy Lee
John, Chacko Joseph
Jorstad, Thomas Floyd
Kaplan, Sanford Sandy
Keller, George Henrik
Klein, George deVries
Kornfeld, Itzchak E.
Leinen, Margaret Sandra
Lighty, Robin Greg
Linder, Gerhard Martin
Lowe, Donald Ray
Luttrell, Eric Martin
Maywood, Paul Stanley
Milling, Marcus Eugene
Morgan, William Andrew
Nelson, Alan Robert
Oaks, Robert Quincy, Jr.
O'Kelley, Joseph Charles
Osterman, Lisa Ellen
Pacht, Jory Allen
Parker, Robert Hallett
Parks, Oattis Elwyn
Peterson, Robert Michael
Pettijohn, Francis John
Pigott, John Dowling
Popp, John Thomas
Pray, Lloyd Charles
Psuty, Norbert Phillip
Richnafsky, Albert Michael
Root, Samuel I.
Sabel, Joseph Morris
Schreiber, B. Charlotte
Shukla, Vijai
Simkin, Thomas Edward
Sonnenberg, Stephen Arnold
Stanley, Daniel Jean
Sukup, James Walter
Sullivan, Neil Maxwell
Tanner, William Francis, Jr.
Twiss, Page Charles
Urschel, Stephen Francis
Veizer, Ján
Visher, Glenn Shillington
Walker, Kenneth Russell
Walls, Richard Alan
Warwick, Peter Delawet
Watney, Willard Lynn

Geology, tectonics
Allen, Clarence Roderic
Alvarez, Walter
Berg, Henry Clay
Bird, John Malcolm
Bloomer, Richard Rodier
Bruce, Clemont Hughes
Burke, Kevin Charles Antony
Channell, James Essex Trevelyan
Chapin, Charles Edward
Cohen, Curtis Rae
Diment, William Horace
Drake, Avery Ala, Jr.
Dutch, Steven Ian
Elam, Jack Gordon
Ernst, Wallace Gary
Fink, Jonathan Harry,
Fisher, George Wescott
Flinn, Edward Ambrose, III
Friedman, Melvin
Gallagher, John Joseph, Jr.
Golombek, Matthew Philip
Gregory, Joel Patrick
Irving, Edward
Isachsen, Yngvar William
Kaplan, Sanford Sandy
Karachewski, John Andrew
Kelm, Donald Lewis
Kluth, Charles Frederick
Laughlin, Alexander William
Lienkaemper, James Julius
Liu, Han-Shou
Meyerhoff, Arthur Augustus
Moore, Gregory Frank
Morrison, Roger Barron
Naeser, Charles Wilbur
Nance, Richard Damian
Nelson, Alan Robert
Ness, Gordon Everett
Nolen-Hoeksema, Richard Clarence
Oaks, Robert Quincy, Jr.
Oliver, Jack Ertle
Page, Robert Alan, Jr.
Prager, Gerald David
Reynolds, Mitchell William
Ritchie, Alexander Webb
Rodgers, John
Root, Samuel I.
Ruppel, Edward Thompson
Rush, Richard William
Seeger, Charles Ronald
St. John, Bill
Sun, Albert Yen
Swann, Gordon Alfred
Sykes, Lynn Ray
Tanaka, Stephanie Masae
Taylor, Charles LaVerne
Thompson, George Albert
Tillman, James Edward
Treves, Samuel Blain
Turcotte, Donald Lawson
Van Der Voo, Rob
Wallace, Robert Earl
Westerman, David Scott

Geophysics
Allen, Clarence Roderic
Alvarez, Walter
Anderle, Richard John
Anderson, Don Lynn
Ayoub, George Tanios
Backus, George Edward
Bentley, Charles Raymond
Blanck, Eugene Louis, Jr.
Bolt, Bruce Alan
Bufe, Charles Glenn
Bull, Colin Bruce Bradley
Cantor, Murray Robert
Carrigan, Charles Roger
Carson, David Brooks
Channell, James Essex Trevelyan
Cohen, Curtis Rae
Cordell, Bruce Monteith
Danes, Zdenko Frankenberger
Decker, Robert Wayne
Diment, William Horace
Donath, Fred Arthur
Dreschhoff, Gisela Auguste Marie
Dziewonski, Adam Marian
Falzone, Anthony Joseph
Fanchi, John Richard
Fischetti, Thomas Louis
Fish, Ferol Fredric
Flinn, Edward Ambrose, III
Gallagher, John Joseph, Jr.
Gard, Michael Floyd
Gedney, Larry Daniel
Gold, Thomas
Goody, Richard Mead
Green, Harry Western, II
Hadidi, Mohamed Taher
Hamilton, Robert Morrison
Hastings, David Alan
Heinrichs, Walter Emil, Jr.
Hubbert, Marion King
Hugg, James William
Irving, Edward
Jeanloz, Raymond
Kamb, Walter Barclay
Kanamori, Hiroo
Kelm, Donald Lewis
Khan, Mohammad Asad
Kleinberg, Robert Leonard
Kober, Carl Leopold
Kominz, Michelle Anne
Kyrala, Ali
LeSchack, Leonard Albert
Lienkaemper, James Julius
Liu, Han-Shou
Luyendyk, Bruce Peter
Mac Donald, Gordon James Fraser
Malinconico, Lawrence Lorenzo, Jr.
Mateker, Emil Joseph, Jr.
Maxwell, Arthur Eugene
Mc Evilly, Thomas Vincent
Melton, Charles Estel
Meyerhoff, Arthur Augustus
Miles, John Wilder
Moore, Gregory Frank
Munk, Walter Heinrich
Ness, Gordon Everett
Ney, Edward Purdy
Nolen-Hoeksema, Richard Clarence
Noltimier, Hallan Costello
Nunan, Adrienne Nichola
Nuttli, Otto William
Olhoeft, Gary Roy
Oliver, Jack Ertle
Pacht, Jory Allen
Paillet, Frederick Lawrence
Perlovsky, Leonid Isaacovich
Pounder, Elton Roy
Press, Frank
Price, William Charles
Reiter, Leon
Rice, James Robert
Riley, Patrick Paul
Rochet, Jean Paul
Romney, Carl F.
Rundle, John Belting
Sabel, Joseph Morris
Seeger, Charles Ronald
Sprunt, Eve Silver
Sriram, K(aushik) P.
Taranik, James Vladimir
Thompson, George Albert
Turcotte, Donald Lawson
Van Der Voo, Rob
Walker, Robert Mowbray
Wall, Robert Ecki
Ward-McLemore, Ethel
Wasserburg, Gerald Joseph
Weeks, Wilford Frank
Weihaupt, John George
Williams, James Gerard
Yoder, Hatten Schuyler, Jr.

Hydrology
Abrahams, Athol Denis
Beard, Leo Roy
Belt, Charles Banks, Jr.
Bradford, Wesley Lamont
Bryant, Charles Thomas
Cohen, Philip
Doyle, Frank Lawrence
Eagleson, Peter Sturges
Fenske, Paul Roderick
Filipek, Lorraine Henrietta
Foley, Michael Glen
Goodell, Horace Grant
Grossman, Irving Gross
Haan, Charles Thomas
Halasi-Kun, George Joseph
Hammond, Weldon Woolf, Jr.
Hart, Robert Joseph
Hem, John David
Hillel, Daniel
Hulburt, Margery Ann
Kelly, William Edward
Kennedy, John Fisher
Kerfoot, William Buchanan, Jr.
Knutson, Carroll Field
Kornfeld, Itzchak E.
Linsley, Ray Keyes
Lu, Allen An-hua
Maderak, Marion Louis
Malcolm, Ronald Lee
Marine, I. Wendell
Marston, Richard Alan
Martin, Jeffrey Donald
Maslansky, Steven Paul
Metsger, Robert William
Molz, Fred John, III
Monte, Judith Ann
Moody, David Wright
Narasimhan, Thiruppudaimarudhur Narayanaiyer
Nieber, John Little
O'Connor, Howard Grant
Paillet, Frederick Lawrence
Parker, Garald Gordon
Powell, John Edward
Price, Bobby Earl
Rast, Walter, Jr.
Reddell, Donald Lee
Renard, Kenneth George
Resnick, Sol Donald
Rhodes, Dallas D.
Richnafsky, Albert Michael
Rosenshein, Joseph Samuel
Rudavsky, Alexander Bohdan
Schad, Theodore MacNeeve
Scherrer, James Sydney
Schmitz, Darrel Wayne
Seneff, James Orin
Shelley, Philip Eugene
Shipman, Ross Lovelace
Spiegel, Zane
Stiller, David Martin
Street, Robert Lynnwood
Ursic, Stanley John
VanAlstyne, Frederick Earl
Vineyard, Jerry D.
Weinrich, Brian Erwin
Wells, Edwin Boyd
Wolman, M. Gordon

Oceanography. See also ENERGY SCIENCE, Ocean energy conversion; ENGINEERING, Petroleum.

Anderson, Franz Elmer
Atwood, Donald Keith
Baker, Donald James
Bascom, Willard Newell
Bassin, N. Jay
Biscaye, Pierre Eginton
Boyd, John Philip
Briskin, Madeleine
Burroughs, Richard H., III
Byrne, John Vincent
Carton, James Alfred
Chan, Kwan Ming
Chittenden, Mark Eustace, Jr.
Collin, Arthur Edwin
Creager, Joe Scott
Dunn, Dean Alan
Edmond, John Marmion
Etter, Paul Courtney
Field, Michael Ehrenhart
Folger, David Winslow
Fye, Paul McDonald
Gaffney, Paul Golden, II
Greenberg, David Alexander
Gross, M. Grant
Hayes, John George
Jennings, Feenan Dee
John, Chacko Joseph
Kana, Timothy William
Kennish, Michael Joseph
Klein, George deVries
Leatherman, Stephen Parker
Leinen, Margaret Sandra
Lighty, Robin Greg
Loomis, Harold George
Menzel, David Washington
Meyers, Philip Alan
Munk, Walter Heinrich
Nierenberg, William Aaron
Paul, John Francis
Paull, Charles
Pedlosky, Joseph
Pounder, Elton Roy
Presley, Joe Andrew, Jr.
Ragotzkie, Robert Austin
Reid, Joseph Lee
Revelle, Roger Randall Dougan
Rice, Donald Lester
Sancetta, Constance Antonina
Savin, Samuel Marvin
Seibel, Erwin
Shear, Nathaniel
Spiess, Fred Noel
Stanley, Daniel Jean
Steele, John Hyslop
Stommel, Henry Melson
Untersteiner, Norbert
Visher, Glenn Shillington
Wall, Robert Ecki
Walsh, Ted William
Waslenchuk, Dennis Grant
Watson, Kenneth Marshall
Weeks, Wilford Frank
White, Robert M.
Wilson, William Stanley
Wooster, Warren S(criver)
Wunsch, Carl Isaac

Oceanography, deep-sea biology

Chen, Chin
Duguay, Linda Emma
Earle, Sylvia Alice

Oceanography, ocean engineering

Bachman, Walter Crawford
Bernitsas, Michael Marinos
Cibosky, William
Clayton, David Lawrence
Daniel, Alex Van
Davis, Mark Hezekiah, Jr.
Doyle, Earl Howard, Jr.
Ehrlich, Stanley L(eonard)
El-Hawary, Ferial Mohamed
El-Tahan, Mona Salah
Ferer, Kenneth Michael
Gannatal, Joseph Paul
German, Richard Barry
Gerwick, Ben Clifford, Jr.
Harris, Lee Errol
Hartman, Patrick James
Herbich, John Bronislaw
Jennings, Feenan Dee
Keller, George Henrik
Kemelhor, Robert Elias
Liu, Paul Chi
Moore, Barbara S. P.
Prada, Kenneth Edwin
Rainnie, William Ogg, Jr.
Rechnitzer, Andreas Buchwald
Shursky, Stanley James
Sieracki, Leonard Mark
Spiess, Fred Noel
Staehle, Charles Michael
Venezia, William Albert

Oceanography, offshore technology

Cartner, John Aubrey
Chamberlain, Charles Franklin
El-Tahan, Mona Salah
Gerwick, Ben Clifford, Jr.
Jones, Maurice (Mo), Jr.
Man, Chi-Sing
McLerran, Archie Ralph
Muggeridge, Derek Brian
Peterson, Melvin Norman Adolph
Taylor, Larry Don
Venezia, William Albert

Oceanography, sea floor spreading

Atwood, Donald Keith
Dick, Henry Jonathan Biddle
El-Hawary, Ferial Mohamed
Emery, Kenneth Orris
Luyendyk, Bruce Peter
Maxwell, Arthur Eugene
Nance, Richard Damian
Sigurdsson, Haraldur
Vanko, David Alan

Paleontology

Abbott, William Harold, Jr.
Barnett, Stockton Gordon
Berdan, Jean Milton
Boaz, Noel Thomas
Chronic, Byron John

Cisne, John Luther
Cramer, Howard Ross
Delevoryas, Theodore
Frederiksen, Norman Oliver
Hay, William Winn
Howells, William White
Jablonski, David
Johanson, Donald Carl
Knoll, Andrew Herbert
Langenheim, Ralph Louis, Jr.
Mc Laren, Digby Johns
Percival, Stephen Francis, Jr.
Pilbeam, David Roger
Raup, David Malcolm
Sancetta, Constance Antonina
Schoch, Robert Milton
Schwimmer, David Richard
Smiley, Charles Jack
Srivastava, Satish Kumar
Sukup, James Walter
Tischler, Herbert
Valentine, James William
Van Landingham, Samuel Leighton

Paleontology, paleobiology

Archibald, James David
Colbert, Edwin H.
Conroy, Glenn C.
Crane, Peter R.
Dilcher, David Leonard
Fields, Robert William
Finks, Robert Melvin
Frederiksen, Norman Oliver
Galton, Peter Malcolm
Gensel, Patricia Gabbey
Gould, Stephen Jay
Hickey, Leo Joseph
Higuchi, Russell Gene
Leary, Richard Lee
Matten, Lawrence Charles
McGhee, George Rufus, Jr.
Morey, Elsie D.
Naples, Virginia L.
Oliver, William Albert, Jr.
Pachut, Joseph Francis, Jr.
Padian, Kevin
Prothero, Donald Ross
Repenning, Charles Albert
Rose, Kenneth David
Smith, Bruce David
Stanton, Robert James, Jr.
Tiffney, Bruce Haynes
Ubelaker, Douglas Henry
Weisbord, Norman Edward
Whitmore, Frank Clifford, Jr.

Paleontology, paleoecology

Abbott, William Harold, Jr.
Benninghoff, William Shiffer
Berdan, Jean Milton
Bukry, J(ohn) David
Chen, Chin
De Keyser, Thomas Lee
DuBar, Jules Ramon
Dunn, Dean Alan
Eby, David Eugene
Erickson, J(ohn) Mark
Fields, Patrick F.
Fillon, Richard Henry
Finks, Robert Melvin
Frölicher, Franz
Fulmer, Charles Virgil
Hall, Stephen A.
Kerfoot, Wilson Charles
Leary, Richard Lee
Loeb, Robert Eli
Luchterhand, Kubet Emil
McGhee, George Rufus, Jr.
Noble, Mark Gregory
Olsson, Richard Keith
Osterman, Lisa Ellen
Pachut, Joseph Francis, Jr.
Peterson, Robert Michael
Sandberg, Charles Albert
Schmidt, Ruth A.M.
Scudder, Harvey Israel
Srivastava, Satish Kumar
Stanton, Robert James, Jr.
Walker, Kenneth Russell
Whitmore, Frank Clifford, Jr.
Wright, Herbert E(dgar), Jr.

Planetology

Albee, Arden Leroy
Arvidson, Raymond Ernst
Blanford, George Emmanuel, Jr.
Bogard, Donald Dale
Boyce, Joseph Micheal
Brett, Robin
Clark, Pamela Elizabeth
Golombek, Matthew Philip
Grossman, Lawrence
Head, James W.
Lucchitta, Baerbel Koesters
Moore, Henry John, II
Sanger, Gary Edward
Strain, Priscilla Logan
Thompson, Thomas William
Walker, David
Weihaupt, John George
Wetherill, George West

Remote sensing

Arvidson, Raymond Ernst
Baker, Donald James
Baumgardner, Marion Fisher
Boyd, William Edward
Brooks, Harold Kelly
Brown, Jim McCaslin
Carter, William Douglas
Chittineni, Chittibabu
Clark, Bill Pat
Clark, Pamela Elizabeth
Comiso, Josefino Cacas
Conrow, Edmund Henry
Davies, Merton Edward
Dusko, Harold George
Ehlen, Judy
El Shazly, Hassan
Eshleman, Von Russel
Foley, Michael Glen
Fung, Adrian Kin-Chiu
Gabelman, John Warren
Gaffey, Susan Jenks
Hastings, David Alan
Hatton, Kay Smith
Hayes, John George

Henderson, Floyd Merl
Hixon, Sumner Best (Dave)
Hogg, Howard Carl
Holter, Marvin Rosenkrantz
Keenmon, Kendall Andrews
Kober, Carl Leopold
Kong, Jin Au
LeSchack, Leonard Albert
Lienhart, David Arthur
Maness, Lindsey Vance, Jr.
Mateker, Emil Joseph, Jr.
Matson, Lawrence Robert
Mausel, Paul Warner
Monte, Judith Ann
Mower, Roland Deloy
Murdoch, Bruce Thomas
Oman, Paul Richard
Paluzzi, Peter Ronald
Pees, Samuel Thomas
Perry, David R.
Pettengill, Gordon H(emenway)
Porter, John Robert, Jr.
Radcliff, Roger Dale
Rodrigue, Christine M.
Rosenberg, Paul
Salisbury, John William
Sanger, Gary Edward
Short, Nicholas Martin
Strain, Priscilla Logan
Taranik, James Vladimir
Thomas, Garland Leon
Thompson, Thomas William
Tiras, Herbert Gerald
Townsend, John William, Jr.
Ulaby, Fawwaz Tayssir
Vanderbilt, Vern Corwin
Westman, Walter Emil
Williams, T. H. Lee
Yeh, Kung Chie

Seismology

Bagwell, Joyce Marie Burris
Banister, John Robert
Berg, Eduard
Bufe, Charles Glenn
Hamilton, Robert Morrison
Hill, David Paul
Huang, Jiin-Long
Marine, I. Wendell
Page, Robert Alan, Jr.
Papastamatiou, Dimitri
Reiter, Leon
Rice, James Allen
Rundle, John Belting
Scawthorn, Charles
Singh, Jogeshwar Preet
Sykes, Lynn Ray

Volcanology

Chapin, Charles Edward
Decker, Robert Wayne
Fink, Jonathan Harry,
Hill, David Paul
McGee, Kenneth A.
Park, Steven Lynn
Peterson, Donald William
Sigurdsson, Haraldur
Sundell, Kent Allan

Other

Abrahams, Athol Denis, Geomorphology
Aronow, Saul, Geomorphology.
Babuin, Michael Louis, Tropical geomorphology
Banaszak, Konrad Joseph, Hydrogeology
Barry, Roger Graham
Barton, Paul Booth, Jr.
Bascom, Willard Newell, Archaeology
Belt, Charles Banks, Jr.
Berry, William Benjamin Newell, Paleo oceanography
Blanck, Eugene Louis, Jr., Engineering geology
Boateng, Kwasi, Ground water geology
Bogard, Donald Dale, Meteorites
Brabb, Earl Edward, Engineering geology
Bradley, Michael Douglas, Water resources policy
Brant, Russell Alan
Brickman, Eugene, Engineering geology
Bukry, J(ohn) David, Oceanography, biochronology
Bull, Colin Bruce Bradley, Glaciology
Campbell, Russell Harper, Engineering geology
Carozzi, Albert Victor
Carter, William Eugene, Geodesy
Catacosinos, Paul Anthony, Stratigraphy
Cemen, Ibrahim
Cisne, John Luther, Stratigraphy
Clewell, Dayton Harris, Petroleum research management
de Laguna, Frederica
Donn, William L., Atmospheric infrasound
DuMontelle, Paul Bertrand
Fields, Patrick F., Paleobotany
Finch, Warren Irvin
Fogg, Thomas Robert, Chemical oceanography
Frost, John Elliott, Geoscience management
Garman, Phyllis Metrolis, Hydrogeology
Gupta, Bhupender Singh
Harbaugh, John Warvelle, Mathematical geology
Harris, DeVerle Porter, Mineral and energy resources
Harrison, J(ames) M(erritt), Economic geology
Haskins, Roger Allen
Hulke, Steven Delbert, Petroleum exploration; Petroleum geology
Jorstad, Thomas Floyd
Judson, Sheldon, Geomorphology
Kamb, Walter Barclay, Glaciology
Kana, Timothy William
Kanamori, Hiroo
Keil, Klaus, Meteoritics
Khan, Mohammad Asad
Koucky, Frank Louis, Archaeogeology
Langenheim, Ralph Louis, Jr.
Leonard, Benjamin Franklin, III, Ore or mineral deposits
Matson, Lawrence Robert, Geomorphology

McBryde, Felix Webster, Geography, space relationship analysis; Thematic cartography, cartographic design
McCarthy, Dennis Dean, Geodesy
Meinert, Lawrence David
Meisner, James Edward
Moore, Carla Jean, Geological systems development and data base management
More, Syver Wakeman, Mineral exploration and development
Myers, Donald Arthur, Biostratigraphy
Naeser, Charles Wilbur, Geochronology
Naeser, Nancy Dearien, Geochronology
Nichols, Donald Ray, Environmental geology
Nichols, Kathryn Marion
O'Kelley, Joseph Charles, Precambrian geology
Olsson, Richard Keith, Biostratigraphy
Ovens, Stephen Alexander, Petroleum exploration
Park, Steven Lynn
Perry, David R.
Peterson, Melvin Norman Adolph
Pettijohn, Francis John, Precambrian geology
Prager, Gerald David, Petroleum geology
Pyle, Gerald Fredric, Urban geography
Raedeke, Linda Dismore
Rall, Elizabeth Pretzer, Stratigraphy
Rhodes, Dallas D., Geomorphology
Roberts, Ralph Jackson
Rodrigue, Christine M., Economic Geography
Rutford, Robert Hoxie, Geomorphology
Saville, Thorndike, Jr., Nearshore oceanography
Scheid, Vernon Edward, Economic geology
Schrader, Edward Leon, Ore deposit origins, distributions
Schwarcz, Henry Philip, Archeometry
Schweitzer, Jeffrey Stewart, Nuclear well logging
Schwimmer, David Richard
Segar, Douglas Allan
Stead, Frederick Lee, Petroleum geology
Thompson, Woodrow Burr, Glacial stratigraphy.
Thorson, Robert Mark, Geological hazards
Tischler, Herbert, Stratigraphy
Toth, Joseph William, Geodetic analysis
Usdansky, Steven Ira
Van Burkalow, Anastasia, Geomorphology; Medical geography
Wait, James Richard
Walker, George Pinckney, III, Petroleum geology
Wayland, Russell Gibson, Jr.
Wilkinson, Thomas Allan, Engineering geology

INFORMATION SCIENCE

Automated language processing

Borko, Harold
Charniak, Eugene
Cooper, Franklin Seaney
Evens, Martha Walton
Niederjohn, Russell James
Nirenburg, Sergei
Oettinger, Anthony Gervin
Shreve, Gregory Monroe
Slocum, Jonathan
Tucker, Allen Brown, Jr.
Zamora, Antonio

Information systems. See also COMPUTER SCIENCE, Information systems.

Bailey, William James
Baise, Walker Nathan
Baker, Dale B
Barbieri, Richard Charles
Beakes, John Herbert
Borgman, Christine L.
Borko, Harold
Chang, Shi-Kuo
Cummings, Martin Marc
Day, Stacey Biswas
Dunbar, Geoffrey Thorne
Duncan, Doris Gottschalk
Edelman, Ann Lynn
Edwards, Carl Normand
Elion, Herbert Aaron
Farmer, Nick A.
Fiene, Richard John
Goldstein, Charles M.
Goyal, Shri Krishna
Hadidi, Mohamed Taher
Haeberle, Frederick Roland
Hansen, Grant Lewis
Hansen, James Vernon
Harris, James Ridout
Ho, Thomas Inn Min
Hoplin, Herman Peter
House, Charles H.
Howard, Jay Lloyd
Hoye, Robert Earl
Jenkins, Arnold Milton
Kashyap, Rangasami L.
Key, Michael Leon
Kraft, Donald H.
Krawarik, Peter Heinz
Kricka, Hanna Halyna
Landgrebe, David Allen
Lide, David Reynolds, Jr.
Lindberg, Donald A.B.
Livingston, John David
Lovell, James Frederick
Lukasik, Stephen Joseph
Lundeen, Gerald Wayne
Machovec, George Stephen
McGill, Michael John
McGill, Scott Douglas
Melichar, Joseph Frank
Meyer, Fred Lewis
Mohanty, Nirode Chandra
Nadin, Mihai
Packer, Katherine Helen
Penniman, W. David
Powell, James Charles
Power, Daniel Joseph

Pratt, Allan Daniel
Ritt, Paul Edward
Robinson, Earl James
Rogers, Steven Ray
Rusch, Peter F.
Schmerling, Erwin Robert
Shelley, Edwin Freeman
Sigman, Caroline Compton
Simms, James Robert
Stenger, Ralph L., Jr.
Summit, Roger Kent
Sweeney, Urban Joseph
Teddlie, Charles Benton
Tenopir, Carol
Tucker, Marc Stephen
Tummala, V. M. Rao
Turek, Jeffery Lee
Turin, George Lewis
Wagner, William Gerard
Whitehead, John Jed
Williams, Martha Ethelyn
Wolf, Jack Keil

Other

Ahlen, John William, III, Human information processing
Bhathena, Sam Jehangirji
Davis, Charles Hargis, Library and information science education administration
Fisher, H. Leonard, Societal effects of information technology
Fujimura, Osamu, Linguistics and speech science
Jahiel, René I.
Konecky, Milton Stuart
Miller, Trudi Claire
Patterson, Robert Logan, Library systems automation
Ross, Douglas Taylor, Systems analysis
Sahni, Omesh, Electron devices
Schroeder, James Ernest, Computer-assisted training and simulation
Small, Henry Gilbert
Swanson, David Henry
Vavra, Terry Gwyn
Zunde, Pranas

LASER. See also OPTICS.

Data storage and reproduction

Axelrod, Norman Nathan
Barnes, Frank Stephenson
Beiser, Leo
Derderian, George
Findeisen, Heinz H.
Jones, Rufus Sidney, Jr.
Lang, James Edward
Maiman, Theodore Harold
Miceli, Joseph James, Jr.
Nikles, David Eugene
Reche, John Joseph
Sari, Seppo Oliver
Szabo, Alexander
Tomlinson, W. John
Weaver, Christopher Scot
Webster, Steven Craig

Excimers

Asmus, John Fredrich
Bigio, Irving Joseph
Cordero, Julio
Dharamsi, Amin Nurdin
Kraemer, Arthur Robert
Litzenberger, Leonard Nelson

Free-electron lasers

Elias, Luis
Freund, Henry Phillip
Gold, Steven Harvey
Sessler, Andrew Marienoff
Takeda, Harunori
Young, Lloyd Martin

Fusion. See also ENERGY.

Ahearne, Daniel Paul
Barish, Samuel Joseph
Burnham, ALan Kent
Devaney, Joseph James
Gibbs, Garry Wayne
Gitomer, Steven Joel
Glass, Alexander Jacob
Grun, Jacob
Kopp, Roger Alan
Kyrala, George Amine
Larsen, Jon Thorsten
Manor, Robert Edward
Mason, Rodney Jackson
McWright, Glen Martin
Mueller, Marvin Martin
Olson, Richard Edward
Soures, John Michael

Laser-induced chemistry

Apkarian, Vartkess Ara
Bates, Richard Doane, Jr.
Baum, Thomas Hall
Bel Bruno, Joseph J(ames)
Beri, Avinash Chandra
Berry, Michael James
Bhatnagar, Ravi
Brooks, Philip Russell
Caird, John Allyn
Cantrell, Cyrus Duncan, III
Clark, John Hamilton
Cox, Hollace Lawton, Jr.
Dai, Hai-Lung
Dobbs, Gregory Melville
Earl, Boyd Lorel
Eyler, John Robert
Gill, Dennis Howard
Grant, Edward Robert
Harmon, Gary R.
Heller, Donald Franklin
Keehn, Philip Moses
Kwok, Hoi-Sing
Lau, Albert Man-Fai
Lin, Ming-Chang
Lyman, John Leslie
Moseley, John Travis
Rettner, Charles Thomas
Rice, Gary Wayne
Robinson, Dean Wentworth
Rothe, Erhard William
Sell, Jeffrey Alan
Weston, Ralph E., Jr.
Zare, Richard Neil

Medicine
Abela, George Samih
Bellina, Joseph Henry
Bennett, William Ralph, Jr.
Choy, Daniel Shu Jen
Clayman, Lewis
Cosman, Bard
Curry, Stephen Martindale
Donnelly, Timothy Christopher
Evans, James Thomas
Fernández, Salvador M.
Fisher, John Courtney
Goldbaum, Michael Henry
Gruhn, John George
Haidle, Rudy Henry
Hovnanian, H. Philip
Jako, Geza Julius
Joffe, Stephen Neal
Lee, Garrett
Lee, Wylie In-Wei
LoCicero, Joseph, III
Marhic, Michel Edmond
Newell, Frank William
Parkin, James Lamar
Pepine, Carl John
Sliney, David Hammond
Solon, Leonard R(aymond)
Tai, Selwyn Clarke

Semiconductor lasers
Agrawal, Govind Prasad
Botez, Dan
Burroughs, Mark Scott
Butler, Jack Fairchild
Casey, H. Craig, Jr.
Lax, Benjamin
Liu, Yet-zen
Logan, Ralph Andre
Nahory, Robert Edward
Ryan, Daniel Joseph
Scarl, Donald
Tsang, Dean Zensh
van der Ziel, Jan Peter
Wang, Shing Chung

Spectroscopy
Antcliff, Richard Raymond
Armstrong, John Allan
Barisas, Bernard George, Jr.
Birnbaum, Edward R.
Bloembergen, Nicolaas
Brauer, Beth-Ellen
Brink, Gilbert O.
Cantrell, Cyrus Duncan, III
Carter, Robert Lawrence
Chisholm, William Preston
Compaan, Alvin Dell
Cone, Rufus Lester
Cooper, Charles Dewey
Curl, Robert Floyd, Jr.
Curry, Stephen Martindale
Dallman, John Clay
Dharamsi, Amin Nurdin
Dobbs, Gregory Melville
Dugan, Charles Hammond
Duley, Walter Winston
Edelson, Martin Charles
Fairbank, William Martin, Jr.
Farley, John William
Gayles, Joseph Nathan Webster, Jr.
Grant, Edward Robert
Hall, John Lewis
Hanley, Stephen Thure
Harris, Harold Hart
Hilborn, Robert Clarence
Hirschfeld, Tomas Beno
Jackson, Warren Bruce
Kabler, Milton Norris
Kinsey, James Lloyd
Kliger, David Saul
Kocher, Carl Alvin
Kramer, Steven David
Krishnan, Pallassana Narayanier
Laane, Jaan
Lapatovich, Walter Peter
Lawler, James Edward
Lee, Long C.
Liao, Paul F(oo-Hung)
Littman, Michael Geist
Mack, Michael Edward
Miles, Richard Bryant
Miniscalco, William Joseph
Moerner, William Esco
Nelson, Robert Norton
Nogar, Nicholas Stephen
Oelfke, William Clarence
Oka, Takeshi
Orlowski, Thomas Edward
O'Shea, Donald Charles
Paddock, Carolyn Allison
Parrish, Milton Earl
Patel, Chandra Kumar Naranbhai
Person, Willis Bagley
Quivers, William Wyatt, Jr.
Radziemski, Leon Joseph
Rand, Stephen Colby
Rast, Howard Eugene, Jr.
Roessler, David Martyn
Sardar, Dhiraj Kumar
Schawlow, Arthur Leonard
Sell, Jeffrey Alan
Smyth, Kermit Campbell
Snyder, James Jacob
Sorokin, Peter Pitirimovich
Stone, Julian
Szabo, Alexander
Terner, James
Thomas, George Joseph, Jr.
Weber, Alfons
Weber, Marvin John
Weeks, Stephan John
Yen, William Mao-shung
Young, James Forrest

X-ray lasers
Chapline, George Frederick, Jr.
Matthews, Dennis Lee
Mc Ilrath, Thomas James
Rhodes, Charles Kirkham
Suckewer, Szymon

Other
Birkitt, John Clair, *High energy chemical lasers*
Bridges, William Bruce, *Physics research*
Carswell, Allan Ian, *Laser radar*
Carter, Benjamin Dudley
Carter, William Harold, *Laser research*
Clark, Roy
Craik, Gary C., Sr., *Carbon dioxide lasers*
Deb, Krishna K.
Decker, Charles David
Degnan, John James, III
De Maria, Anthony J., *Laser physics*
Dixon, Richard Wayne, *Laser research and development*
Dowley, Mark William, *Laser research*
Eggers, David Frank
Fader, Walter John
Fein, Michael E., *Laser design*
Feinstein, Joseph, *Laser power generation*
Figueira, Joseph F.
Fisher, Robert Alan, *Nonlinear laser optics; Optical phase conjugation*
Flom, Terrence Edsel Flom, *Laser communications*
Friedrich, Otto Martin, Jr., *Laser research*
Fuhs, Allen Eugene
Gerstenberger, David Charles, *Gas lasers*
Geslicki, Mark Louis, *Laser scanning systems*
Goodwin, Richard Clarke, *Laser physics*
Gregson, Victor Gregory, *Industrial laser processing*
Grischkowsky, Daniel, *Ultrafast lasers*
Gunter, William Dayle, Jr.
Hammer, Jacob Meyer
Hansch, Theodor Wolfgang, *Dye lasers*
Hansler, Richard Lowell, *Laser processing*
Hauck, James Pierre, *Laser gyroscopes and radars*
Haun, Robert Dee, Jr., *Laser research*
Heller, Donald Franklin, *Laser physics*
Hertzberg, Abraham, *Laser research and development*
Hill, Alan Eugene, *Laser research and development*
Hirleman, Edwin Daniel, Jr., *Laser instrumentation*
Hochuli, Urs Erwin
Holmes, Dale Arthur, *High energy laser systems*
Hyman, Howard Allan, *Laser physics*
Ippen, Erich Peter, *Ultrashort pulse lasers*
Johannsen, David Charles
Jones, Roger Clyde
Kantrowitz, Arthur, *High energy lasers*
Kestenbaum, Ami, *Laser applications*
Killinger, Dennis Karl
Klaiber, Robert, *Laser applications*
Konopnicki, Marek Jan
Krinsky, Jeffrey Alan, *Laser efficiency*
Lampkin, Curtis Magill
Lin, Chinlon, *Laser technology*
Linder, Solomon Leon, *Guidance systems*
Linz, Arthur, *Laser research*
Litzenberger, Leonard Nelson
Liu, Yung Sheng, *Laser optics*
Mandel, Leonard, *Laser optics*
Marshall, Gerald Francis, *Laser alignment*
Martin, Lawrence Ronald, *Laser applications*
Massey, Gail Austin, *Laser instrumentation*
McArthur, David Alexander
Melville, Richard Devern Samuels, Jr., *Laser technology*
Meth, Sheldon Zalmen, *Military applications of lasers*
Mollenauer, Linn Frederick
Nanos, George Peter, Jr., *Laser physics*
Nelson, Donald Frederick, *Laser research*
Paddock, Carolyn Allison
Paranto, Joseph Nolan, *Laser devices*
Pearson, James Edward, *High energy lasers*
Pernick, Benjamin, *Laser research*
Remo, John Lucien, *Lasers/resonator theory*
Roberts, Thomas George, *Laser physics*
Seegmiller, David William
Shah, Rajiv Rajaram
Shannon, Robert Rennie, *Laser research management*
Sidorowicz, Kenneth Joseph, *Laser welding stress analysis*
Smith, Peter William, *Laser research*
Snyder, Arnold Peter, *Laser biochemistry*
Synek, M., *Laser-active materials*
Teague, James Ralph, *Laser technology*
Tomren, Douglas Roy, *Laser research*
Turner, Mortimer Darling
Urquhart, James Burwell, III, *Laser wave optics*
Vander Sluis, Kenneth L., *Laser systems*
Wang, Charles P., *Laser research*
Whitcomb, Bruce Magill
Wood, Obert Reeves, II, *Laser research*
Woskoboinikow, Paul Peter, *Laser research*
Yonas, Gerold, *Laser technology*

MATERIALS SCIENCE. *See also* **ENGINEERING, Materials.**

Biomaterials
Aberman, Harold Mark
Absolom, Darryl Robin
Apostolou, Spyridon F.
Bapna, Mahendra Singh
Chappell, Robert Paul
Chuang, Hanson Yii-Kuan
Civjan, Simon
Crim, Gary Allen
Doane, William McKee
Doremus, Robert Heward
Douglas, William Hugh
Eberhart, Robert Clyde
Faunce, Frank Roland
Filisko, Frank Edward
Galletti, Pierre Marie
Hall, C(harles) William
Harms, Weldon Menno
Heuer, Michael Alexander
Horowitz, Emanuel
Jackson, David Stanley
Kumar, Binod
Leake, Donald Lewis
Lee, Eun Soo
Lee, Stuart Milton
Morris, Robert Scott
Mueller, Herbert Joseph
O'Brien, David Frank
Polay, Janet Skinner
Robertson, James Richard, Jr.
Rothschild, Kenneth Joseph
Salamone, Joseph Charles
Shah, Kishore Ramanlal
Stannard, Jan Gregory
Stith, William Joseph
Thomas, Mathew
von Fraunhofer, Joseph Anthony
Ward, F(raser) Prescott

Ceramics
Allis, Deo G.
Bates, John Bryant
Beaton, Michael Steve
Becker, Paul Robin
Bergeron, Clifton George
Bocko, Peter Lawrence
Bray, Philip James
Brockmeyer, Jerry W.
Brun, Milivoj Konstantin
Card, Roger John
Cherry, John Thomas
Cohen, Jerome Bernard
Cook, Lee Melbourne
Crabtree, Jerome Otto
Doman, Robert Charles
Doremus, Robert Heward
Economos, George
Ellis, Howard Franklin
Franz, Helmut
Gonczy, Stephen Thomas
Graff, William Arthur
Green, Robert Lester
Gulati, Suresh Thakurdas
Herman, Herbert
Holcombe, Cressie Earl, Jr.
Insley, Robert Hiteshew
Kielmeyer, William Henry
Kim, Hae Soo
Kingery, William David
Kohut, William
Kumar, Ananda Hosakere
Kumar, Binod
Kumar, Kaplesh
Lanford, William Armistead
Lang, James Edward
Lay, Kenneth Wilbur
Logan, Kathryn Vance
MacKenzie, John Douglas
Marchant, David Dennis
Marshall, David Bruce
Moore, Francis Mears
Moss, Herbert Irwin
O'Bryan, Henry Miles, Jr.
Osborn, Elburt Franklin
Palilla, Frank Charles
Panzera, Carl
Pask, Joseph Adam
Peterson, Norman Lee
Pincus, Alexis George
Pollock, E. Kears
Rabinovich, Eliezer M.
Radford, Kenneth Charles
Ramey, Roy Richard
Rankin, David Thomas
Rawal, Bharat Singh
Rossi, Ronald Charles
Rothman, Steven John
Roy, Rustum
Schneider, Samuel James, Jr.
Sheinberg, Haskell
Shukla, Vishwa Nath
Singh, Raj Narain
Slayton, Michael Henry
Spriggs, Richard Moore
Stewart, Ronald Leroy
Stoddard, Stephen Davidson
Storm, Roger S.
Tallan, Norman M.
Taylor, Thomas Alan
Thomas, Mathew
Topping, John Allan
Uhlmann, Donald Robert
Van Vlack, Lawrence Hall
Viechnicki, Dennis John
Vogel, Eva Milar
Wachtman, John Bryan, Jr.
Wagner, James Bruce, Jr.
Weinland, Stuart Louis
Wilder, James Andrew, Jr.
Williams, Charles Edward
Wohlgemuth, John H.
Yan, Man Fei
Yoon, Soo Charles

Materials
Allen, Douglas Mark
Baboian, Robert
Bapna, Mahendra Singh
Barrett, Charles Sanborn
Beasley, Wayne Machon
Bever, Berliner Michael
Bhattacharya, Rabi Sankar
Blakely, John McDonald
Blanck, A.R.
Board, William Jesse, Jr.
Boatner, Lynn Allen
Boyd, Edward Lee
Bujtas, Mark Steven
Carson, James Matthew
Cohen, Jerome Bernard
Cohen, Morris
Dandapani, Bala Subramaniam
Davis, Guy Donald
Djordjevic, Borislav Boro
DuPlessis, John Joseph
Eades, John Alwyn
Fausett, Robert Julian
Fontana, Mars Guy
Freund, Lambert Ben
Frohnsdorff, Geoffrey James Carl
Glosser, Robert
Green, Robert Edward, Jr.
Hannay, N(orman) Bruce
Harrington, Roy Victor
Hasson, Dennis Francis
Hayner, George Oliver
Herman, Herbert
Horowitz, Emanuel
Hwang, Jennie Shilan
Jennings, Laurence Duane
Jensen, Barbara Lynne
Karpetsky, Timothy Paul
Kumar, Kaplesh
Lal, Brij Bihari
Lee, Stuart Milton
Loeffler, William Robert
Luborsky, Fred Everett
Morris, George Vincent
Myers, Samuel Maxwell
Ong, Hiap Liew
Painter, Gayle Stanford
Pehlke, Robert Donald
Peterson, Norman Lee
Phillips, Julia Mae
Pierce, Robert Raymond
Pinizzotto, Russell Felix
Plunkett, Robert
Powers, Robert William
Ritt, Paul Edward
Rotenberg, Don Harris
Sagalyn, Paul Leon
Salama, Kamel
Salensky, George
Sales, Brian Craig
Samuels, George Joseph
Sannella, Joseph Lee
Sari, Seppo Oliver
Seely, John Henry
Seitz, Frederick
Sellers, Gregory Jude
Thrower, Peter Albert
Tibbetts, Gary George
Turner, Derek Terence
Tyndall, Bruce Mapes
Van Uitert, LeGrand Gerard
Wachs, Israel Ephraim
Werner, John Ellis
Williams, Wendell Sterling
Wolff, Gunther Arthur

Materials, composite
Adams, Donald Frederick
Alper, Allen Myron
Beck, Warren Randall
Chow, Tsu Sen
Davis, LeRoy Wellington
De, Bibhas Ranjan
DeRudder, James Louis
Deviney, Marvin Lee, Jr.
Dick, William Allen
Diefendorf, Russell Judd
Doman, Robert Charles
Fabish, Thomas John
Foral, Ralph Francis
Freeman, Stephen Morrison
Gerstle, Frank P., Jr.
Gujrati, Bitthal Das
Hahn, Hong Thomas
Hong, Su-Don
Hoover, William Leichliter
Jayne, Benjamin Anderson
Jin, Sungho
Jones, Douglas Linwood
Katz, Manfred
Lee, Charles Ying-Cheung
Little, Gordon Rice
Mak, Sioe Tho
Marcus, Harris Leon
Pearce, Malcolm Bulkeley, Jr.
Pipes, Robert Byron
Powers, Joseph
Rangaswamy, Subramaniam
Riggs, Dennis Michael
Robertson, Richard Earl
Sauer, Robert Jay
Schultz, Jerold Marvin
Seferis, James Constantine
Self, James Maurice
Stewart, Ronald Leroy
Tang, Ruen C.
Tao, Li-Chung
Thrower, Peter Albert
Tonda, Richard Dale
Uhlir, Donald Andrew
Watkins, Louie W(illard)
Widera, G.E.O.
Williams, James Henry, Jr.
Zincone, Robert

Materials, electronic
Albert, Paul Andre
Arthur, Michael Edward
Bagley, Brian G.
Baglio, Joseph Anthony
Berger, Lev Isaac
Berry, William Bernard
Blair, John
Botez, Dan
Brown, Michael Gregory
Bube, Richard Howard
Bylander, Ernest Gerald
Chandler, Thomas Clinton
Christianson, Keith Alan
Chu, Ting L.
Chu, Wei-Kan
Curelaru, Irina Mariana
Dalbec, Paul Euclide
Deb, Krishna K.
Delfino, Michelangelo
Desai, Kirit Navnitrai
Dickens, Elmer Douglas, Jr.
Dunn, Bruce Sidney
Dupuis, Russell Dean
Economos, George
Falco, Charles Maurice
Forman, Richard Allan
Fradin, Frank Yale
Goldenberg, Barbara L.
Graff, William Arthur
Haacke, Gottfried
Haller, Ivan
Heller, Adam
Howe, Arthur Trevor
Hubbard, G(regory) Scott
Hwang, Jennie Shilan
Ingle, William Martell
Jackson, Kenneth Arthur
Jaworowski, Andrzej Edward
Jin, Sungho
Johnson, Robert E.
Kamieniecki, Emil
Karlicek, Robert Frank, Jr.
Katz, William
Kennedy, Thomas Albert, Jr.
Khan, Abdul Azim
Lagally, Max Gunter
Lam, Hon Wai
Laudise, Robert Alfred
Levine, Jules David
Logan, Ralph Andre
Lu, Chih-Yuan
Malloy, Jr. Donald Edwin
Margaritondo, Giorgio
Mayer, James Walter
Michalak, Edward Michael
Michalchik, Michael
Moss, Herbert Irwin
Mulay, Laxman N.
Nakada, Yoshinao
Narayan, Jagdish
Nowak, Welville Berenson
O'Bryan, Henry Miles, Jr.
O'Handley, Robert Charles
Olego, Diego Jose
Palilla, Frank Charles
Parker, Sidney Glenn
Pearson, James Murray
Pierret, Robert Francis
Raschke, Curt Robert
Roberts, Cornelius Sheldon
Ronsheim, Paul Andrew
Salerno, Jack Peter
Sarjeant, Walter James
Schuller, Ivan Kohn
Sergent, Jerry Elden
Shin, Sung-Chul
Shing, Yuh-Han
Shukla, Vishwa Nath
Spencer, Edward G.
Spitzer, William George
Squillante, Michael Robert
Stoebe, Thomas Gaines
Taylor, George William
Tran, Nang Tri
Treacy, Michael Matthew John
Wang, Chih-Chun
Wang, James Cheng-Koung
Weaver, Carson Edgar
Weng, Shang-Lin
Wernick, Jack Harry
Willardson, Robert Kent
Wnek, Gary Edmund
Wohlgemuth, John H.
Woods, John Galloway
Wronski, Christopher Roman
Yan, Man Fei

Materials, high-temperature
Abraham, Marvin Meyer
Alexander, Leckie Frederick
Alper, Allen Myron
Ansell, George Stephen
Beasley, Wayne Machon
Becker, Paul Robin
Boone, Donald H(erbert)
Brun, Milivoj Konstantin
Cezairliyan, Ared
Chang, Ji Young
Chubb, Walston
Coffin, Louis Fussell, Jr.
Crowley, Michael Summers
Diefendorf, Russell Judd
Elliott, John Frank
Ernst, Donald Martin
Forchheimer, Otto L.
Friedman, Melvin
Gallagher, Sarah Ann
Gowda, Byre Venkataramana
Green, Harry Western, II
Hanson, John Edward
Hoch, Michael
Kim, Jonathan Jang-Ho
Korwin, Paul
Maahs, Howard Gordon
Marchant, David Dennis
Muan, Arnulf
Phillips, William Evans
Pigeaud, Adolph
Rangaswamy, Subramaniam
Riggs, Dennis Michael
Roy, Rustum
Sarma, Abul Chandra
Schneider, Samuel James, Jr.
Schroth, Peter
Schwer, Roger Edwin
Shumate, Monroe William
Stoddard, Stephen Davidson
Swift, Robert Anton
Taylor, Thomas Alan
Valent, Francis Samuel

Materials processing
Altan, Taylan
Amer, Ahmad (El Sayed)
Appleton, B. R.
Bennett, Stephen Lawrence
Boulger, Francis William
Cullen, Donald Lee
Dhara, Sudhir Chandra
DuPlessis, John Joseph
Flinn, Richard Aloysius
Folweiler, Robert Cooper
Glaeser, Andreas Michael
Gregson, Victor Gregory
Gujrati, Bitthal Das
Hoch, Michael
Hoover, William Leichliter
Jellison, Gerald Earle, Jr.
Kim, Jonathan Jang-Ho
Kuhn, Howard Arthur
Lacy, Lewis Lee
Michalchik, Michael
Moody, Willis Elvis, Jr.
Narayanaswamy, Onbathiveli Subrahmanyan
Natansohn, Samuel
Ovens, William George
Pask, Joseph Adam
Pinney, Frank Batchelder
Ponder, Herman
Rankin, David Thomas
Rivkin, Maxcy Calvin
Roberts, Cornelius Sheldon
Ronsheim, Paul Andrew
Schey, John Anthony
Sharma, Yadunandan Prasad
Shirkey, William Dan
Simmons, George Allen
Stregowski, Thomas John
Swift, Robert Anton
Taraman, Khalil Showky
Tran, Nang Tri
Valyi, Emery I.

Vogel, Eva Milar
Ward, H. Blair, Jr.
Weaver, Carson Edgar

Metallurgy
Ansell, George Stephen
Azaroff, Leonid Vladimirovitch
Beck, Paul Adams
Bennett, Lawrence Herman
Berardi, Matteo P.
Bever, Berliner Michael
Boone, Donald H(erbert)
Bruner, Ralph Clayburn
Buck, Otto
Bush, James Hastings
Chin, Gilbert Yukyu
Chung, Hee Mok
Cohen, Morris
Conrad, Hans
Crabtree, Jerome Otto
Davis, LeRoy Wellington
DiOrio, Mark Lewis
Driscoll, Timothy John
Duerr, J. Stephen
Evans, Willis Thomas
Fine, Morris Eugene
Flinn, Richard Aloysius
French, David Nichols
Gagnebin, Albert Paul
Giessen, Bill Cormann
Glodowski, Robert John
Hart, Raymond Kenneth
Hawrylo, Frank Zygmunt
Hayner, George Oliver
Horton, Robert Andrew
Jaffee, Robert Isaac
Jesser, William Augustus
Kautz, David Johnathan
Khare, Ashok K.
Koucky, Frank Louis
Littauer, Ernest Lucius
Livingston, James Duane
Lucas, William Ray
Malhotra, Manohar Lal
Marcus, Harris Leon
Marek, Miroslav I.
McGee, Thomas Donald
Mc Mahon, Charles Joseph, Jr.
McMenamin, Edward William
McPherson, Donald J.
Miller, William Lawrence
Olson, Ferron Allred
Opie, William Robert
Parker, Earl Randall
Paxton, Harold William
Pehlke, Robert Donald
Pense, Alan Wiggins
Pickering, Howard William
Polonis, Douglas Hugh
Rothman, Steven John
Russell, Allen Stevenson
Ruud, Clayton Olaf
Salama, Kamel
Salama, Mamdouh M.
Saw, Cheng-Kiong
Sciandra, Luigi Claudio
Sheinberg, Haskell
Sohn, Hong Yong
Swalin, Richard Arthur
Swanson, William Mason
Teleshak, Stephen
Thomas, Gareth
Veidis, Mikelis Valdis
Wang, James Cheng-Koung
Wang, Rong
Watts, Michelle Marie
Werner, John Ellis
Wernick, Jack Harry
Wert, Charles Allen
Westwood, Albert Ronald Clifton

Microchip technology. See also ENGINEERING, Electrical.
Baird, Richard William
Barbee, Steven George
Baylis, Charles Merritt
Burghard, Ronald Albert
Cady, Wayne Allen
Craighead, Harold G.
Cronquist, Brian Edward
De Hodgins, Ofelia Canales
Flinn, Paul Anthony
Harman, George Gibson
Kumar, Ananda Hosakere
Kwok, Thomas Yu-Kiu
Lanford, William Armistead
Larrabee, Robert Dean
Ma, Tso-Ping
Packwood, Donald Lee
Park, Hee Kyun
Pinizzotto, Russell Felix
Pritchard, Lois Breur
Ransom, Craig Mitchell
Rossi, Ronald Charles
Salerno, Jack Peter
Singh, Raj Narain
Singh, Rajendra
Tanielian, Minas Hagop
Thompson, Larry Flack
Wade, Thomas Edward
Wohltjen, Henry, III

Polymers
Aldissi, Mahmoud
Belton, Daniel James
Bikales, Norbert M.
Blackwell, John
Borch, Jens
Boyer, Raymond Foster
Brown, Charles Eric
Brubaker, Burton Dale
Claiborne, C. Clair
Class, Jay Bernard
Das, Sajal
DeRudder, James Louis
Doane, William McKee
Eckhardt, Helmut Karl
Ferry, John Douglass
Filisko, Frank Edward
Finegold, Leonard X.
Fuzek, John Frank
Garrett, Howard Leroy
Germano, Don Joseph
Guttman, Charles Martin
Hauser, Ray Louis
Hawkins, Walter Lincoln
Hoffman, John Drake

Jacobs, Howard Larkin
Johnson, Dee Lynn
Kresge, Edward Nathan
Kwok, Wo Kong
Landel, Robert Franklin
Lando, Jerome B.
Lawson, Kenneth Robert
Lee, Charles Ying-Cheung
Lee, Michael Ching Hsueh
Lin, Kenneth Shou-Chein
Lin, Shaow Burn
Lustig, Stanley
Mauter, Warren Eugene
Morgan, Paul Winthrop
Nakajima, Nobuyuki
Niegisch, Walter Dietrich
Pearson, Dale Sheldon
Penn, Benjamin Grant
Prest, William Marchant, Jr.
Preston, Jack
Price, Howard Charles
Reichmanis, Elsa
Rosthauser, James William
Salame, Morris
Sancaktar, Erol
Sanchez, Isaac Cornelius
Sannella, Joseph Lee
Schultz, Jerold Marvin
Seferis, James Constantine
Sellers, Gregory Jude
Senich, George A.
Shen, Chiayi
Shuttleworth, Derek
Skotheim, Terje Asbjorn
Stahl, Joel S.
St. Clair, Anne King
Swarin, Stephen John
Uhlmann, Donald Robert
Ulrich, Robert David
Valyi, Emery I.
Wagner, Herman Leon
Wagner, Melvin Peter
Walsh, William Kershaw
Ward, H. Blair, Jr.
Watson, Gary Edward
Weaver, James Clyde

Other
Adhav, Ratnakar Shankar
Antler, Morton, *Electrical contacts and tribology*
Beck, Paul Adams
Beck, Warren Randall, *Glass technology*
Blakeslee, A. Eugene, *Semiconductors*
Bragg, Robert Henry
Califano, Joseph Michael, *Filtration membranes*
Ellison, Michael Scot
Ericksen, Jerald Laverne, *Theories of crystals*
Gur, Turgut Mehmet, *Solid state ionics*
Halemane, Thirumala Raya
Halsey, William Guy
Harms, Weldon Menno
Hilbertz, Wolf Hartmut
Jenkinson, Howard Acis, *Semiconductors*
Kuhn, Howard Arthur, *Powder metallurgy*
Lambuth, Alan Letcher, *Wood treatment, modification*
Marlow, William Henry, *Aerosol applications*
Penz, P. Andrew
Pollock, E. Kears
Primak, William L.
Rice, Stephen Landon, *Wear of materials*
Rudys, Stasys Kestutis, *Infrared spectroscopy*
Sherwood, Gerald E.
Steiner, Bruce Watson
Teleshak, Stephen, *Failure anaylsis*
Topping, John Allan
Vook, Richard Werner, *Thin films and surfaces*
Wolff, Gunther Arthur, *Single crystal growth*

MATHEMATICS. See also COMPUTER SCIENCE.

Algebra and number theory
Bass, Hyman
Dynkin, Eugene B. (Evgenii Borisovich)
Goldhaber, Jacob Kopel
Jain, S(urender) K(umar)
Kleiman, Howard
Lam, Tsit-Yuen
Lusztig, George
Maxson, Carlton James
Minassian, Donald Paul
Sadowsky, John
Swan, Richard Gordon
Weil, Andre

Analysis
Cain, Bryan Edmund
Cesari, Lamberto
Coleman, Courtney Stafford
Du, Sen-Wo
Frederickson, Paul Oliver
Hausrath, Alan Richard
Heath, Larry Francis
Horn, Roger Alan
Hutzler, Erich Kurt
John, Fritz
Jorgensen, Palle Erik Tikob
Levine, Howard Allen
Lieb, Elliott Hershel
Loud, Warren Simms
Medhin, Negash Gabre
Morino, Luigi
Neuberger, John William
Neuringer, Joseph Louis
Pollak, Henry Otto
Renardy, Michael
Robinson, Clark
Schrader, Keith William
Sheehy, Jerome Joseph
Shiffman, Max
Trench, Wiliam Frederick
Walter, Gilbert Gustav
Warga, Jack

Applied
Ablowitz, Mark Jay
Achenbach, Jan Drewes
Adler, Irving
Akcasu, Osman Ersed
Ames, William Frances
Andrushkiw, Roman Ihor
Antman, Stuart Sheldon
Aris, Rutherford
Arkilic, Galip Mehmet
Balanis, George Nick
Barnard, Thomas Elliot
Barshinger, Richard N
Basar, Tamer
Birnbaum, Zygmunt William
Blackburn, Jacob Floyd
Bojadziev, George Nikolov
Boley, Bruno Adrian
Bolt, Bruce Alan
Bramble, James Henry
Bryant, Michael David
Byrne, George Dennis
Cacuci, Dan Gabriel
Calter, Paul
Campbell, Russell Bruce
Cantor, Murray Robert
Carasso, Alfred Sam
Carey, Graham Francis
Carr, Ralph W.
Cazes, Albert N.
Censor, Yair
Cerceo, John Michael
Chow, Pao-Liu
Clarke, Frank H.
Cohen, Donald Sussman
Cohen, Harley
Cohen, Michael Paul
Coleman, Courtney Stafford
Colvin, Burton Houston
Cook, Joseph Marion
Corduneanu, Constantin C.
Dafermos, Constantine Michael
Danes, Zdenko Frankenberger
Darden, Christine Mann
Datta, Subhendu K(umar)
Davis, Stephen Howard
D'Entremont, Edward Joseph
Dergarabedian, Paul
Dhaliwal, Ranjit Singh
Di Donato, Armido Richard
Driessel, Kenneth R.
Durgun, Kanat
Dutton, John Altnow
Elliott, David LeRoy
Fabrikant, Valery Isaac
Farr, Edwin H.
Fish, Andrew Joseph, Jr.
Fix, George Joseph
Follingstad, Henry George
Fowler, Howland Auchincloss
Frauenthal, James Clay
Freiberger, Walter Frederick
Fung, Kee-Ying
Garabedian, Paul Roesel
Garzia, Mario Ricardo
Gibbs, David Eugene
Gilbert, Robert Pertsch
Gipson, Gary Steven
Goldstine, Herman Heine
Gomory, Ralph Edward
Grimm, Louis J.
Gur, Yigal
Hamilton, Eugene Phillip
Hariharan, Subramaniya Iyer
Hasimoto, Hidenori
Hausrath, Alan Richard
Hemp, Gene W(illard)
Herrmann, Robert Arthur
Hoagland, Gordon Wood
Holland, Robert Louis
Holmes, Philip John
Holt, William R.
Hoppensteadt, Frank Charles
Howland, Robert Alden, Jr.
Iannuzzelli, Raymond Joseph
Irwinsky, Larry Don
Jerome, Joseph Walter
John, Fritz
Johnsen, Eugene Carlyle
Jorgensen, Palle Erik Tikob
Jory, Virginia Vickery
Katz, I. Norman
Kays, James Lee
Khan, Winston
Kimme, Ernest Godfrey
Kockinos, Constantin Neophytos
Kravitz, David William
Krumhansl, James Arthur
Kruskal, Martin David
Kunin, Isaak A.
Langford, William Finlay
Lavery, John Edward
Lax, Peter David
Leipholz, Horst Hermann Eduard
Levine, Howard Allen
Levitin, Lev Berovich
Liniger, Werner
Lomen, David Orlando
Loomis, Harold George
Loud, Warren Simms
Lu, Kau U.
Mandelbrot, Benoit B.
Manitius, Andrzej Zdzislaw
Matkowsky, Bernard Judah
McGehee, Richard Paul
McLenithan, Kelly Daniel
Medhin, Negash Gabre
Mickens, Ronald Elbert
Miles, John Wilder
Miller, Harvey Philip
Miller, Wilbur Charles
Miller, Willard, Jr.
Mills, Patrick Leo
Mityagin, Boris Samuel
Mitzel, Glenn Earle
Morawetz, Cathleen Synge
Moulden, Trevor Holmes
Nagurney, Anna Bobiak
Nanzetta, Philip Newcomb
Nariboli, Gundo Annacharya
Neitzel, G(eorge) Paul, Jr.
Newman, Morris
Norwood, Frederick Reyes
Olmstead, William Edward
Ostrach, Simon
Pearson, Ronald Korin
Peatman, John Gray
Perlovsky, Leonid Isaacovich

Persek, Stephen Charles
Podowski, Michael Zbigniew
Pollak, Henry Lewis
Pollak, Henry Otto
Preuss, Robert David
Puri, Pratap
Ramos, Juan Ignacio
Randall, John Douglas
Renardy, Michael
Renardy, Yuriko
Rheinboldt, Werner Carl
Riahi, Nourollah
Rice, Bart Francis
Ritter, Gerhard X.
Rivkin, Maxcy Calvin
Roache, Patrick John
Sammon, Peter
Samn, Sherwood
Sandberg, Irwin Walter
Satzer, William Joseph, Jr.
Savageau, Michael Antonio
Scarf, Herbert Eli
Schneider, Harold
Schrader, Keith William
Schumaker, Larry Lee
Seebass, Alfred Richard, III
Seifer, Arnold David
Serrin, James Burton
Shannon, Claude Elwood
Shiffman, Max
Skalafuris, Angelo James
Sorace, Ronald Eugene
Sriram, K(aushik) P.
Stakgold, Ivar
Stehney, Ann Kathryn
Strauss, Walter Alexander
Sullivan, Francis Edward
Thompson, Sylvester
Toomre, Alar
Trench, Wiliam Frederick
Tretter, Marietta Joan
Turner, Malcolm Elijah, Jr.
Tyndall, Bruce Mapes
Underhill, Earl Marvin
Vargas, John David
Victory, Harold Dean, Jr.
Wagner, Daniel Hobson
Wahba, Grace
Waid, Margaret Cowsar
Wan, Frederic Yui-Ming
Warga, Jack
White, Benjamin Steven
Wilson, Raymond Hiram, Jr.
Winograd, Shmuel
Wnuk, Michael Peter
Wong, Po Kee
Wright, Lynne C.
Wyner, Aaron Daniel
Yao, Lun-Shin
Yih, Chia-Shun
Yodzis, Peter Paul
Young, Donald Francis

Numerical analysis. See also COMPUTER SCIENCE.
Ames, William Frances
Bradford, Bert Larue
Byrne, George Dennis
Calter, Paul
Cassity, C. R.
Datta, Biswa Nath
Edwards, Bruce Haven
Fornberg, Bengt
Hariharan, Subramaniya Iyer
Hobbs, Willard Earl, Jr.
Jerome, Joseph Walter
Jones, Donald Leroy
Katz, I. Norman
Kearfott, Ralph Baker
Klema, Virginia C.
Lavery, John Edward
Liniger, Werner
Macaraeg, Michele Gay
McCarthy, William James
McDonough, James Michael
Salane, Douglas Edward
Shrier, Stefan
Silver, Gary Lee
Victory, Harold Dean, Jr.
Ward, Robert C.

Operations research. See also ENGINEERING.
Abrahams, Clark Richard
Albers, Walter Anthony, Jr
Arrow, Kenneth Joseph
Baybars, Ilker
Bookstein, Abraham
Christman, Arthur Castner, Jr.
Cooper, William Wager
Daly, John Anthony
Dean, Edwin Becton
Farr, Edwin H.
Ford, Byron Milton
Gollobin, Leonard Paul
Hannan, Edward Lees
Hansen, Morris Howard
Hunter, John Stuart
Irwinsky, Larry Don
Johnson, Howard A(rthur)
Jones, Alfred Welwood
Kannan, Ravindran
Knowlden, Norman Francis
Leifman, Lev Jacob
Lembersky, Mark Raphael
Lin, Winston T.
Lucantoni, David Michael
Magnanti, Thomas Lee
McCall, Edward Huffaker
Meyer, Fred Lewis
Mulvey, John Michael
Nagurney, Anna Bobiak
Pattipati, Krishna Rao
Pei, Richard Yusien
Persek, Stephen Charles
Peters, Charles William
Pettey, Dix Hayes
Portare, Anthony Frank
Radzikowski, Pawel
Roberts, Fred Stephen
Samuelson, Douglas Alan
Scarf, Herbert Eli
Schniederjans, Marc James
Shanker, Roy James
Shapley, Lloyd Stowell
Shear, Nathaniel

Spoeri, Randall Keith
Stanford, Robert Ernest
Steihaug, Trond
Van Slyke, Richard Maurice
Weinstein, Milton Charles
Wolfe, Michael David
Young, Douglas Wilford

Probability
Beutler, Frederick Joseph
Blume, John August
Chernick, Michael Ross
Cohen, Edgar Allan, Jr.
Colberg, Magda
Doob, Joseph Leo
Dynkin, Eugene B. (Evgenii Borisovich)
Fine, Terrence Leon
Gleason, Andrew Mattei
Griffith, William Schuler
Gross, Donald
Heller, Barbara Ruth
Jones, James Thomas, Jr.
Kimme, Ernest Godfrey
Lebowitz, Joel Louis
Ley, Richard Wayne
Lucantoni, David Michael
McCann, Martin William, Jr.
Mehravari, Nader
Owen, Daniel Lee
Paté-Cornell, Marie-Elisabeth
Pickard, David Kenneth
Reinman, Robert Andrew
Robbins, Herbert Ellis
Rota, Gian-Carlo
Samuelson, Douglas Alan
Sawyer, Stanley Arthur
Slepian, David
Vanmarcke, Erik Hector
Vaurio, Jussi Kalervo
White, Benjamin Steven
Wise, Gary Lamar
Woodroofe, Michael Barrett
Woyczynski, Wojbor Andrzej

Statistics
Abrahams, Clark Richard
Barbieri, Richard Charles
Berger, Philip Jeffrey
Bickel, Peter John
Birnbaum, Zygmunt William
Blachman, Nelson M(erle)
Box, George Edward Pehhem
Brillinger, David Ross
Busch, Allen Cyril
Califano, Joseph Michael
Chernick, Michael Ross
Chiang, Chin Long
Chilton, Neal W(arwick)
Choi, Sung Chil
Coburn, Timothy Craig
Cohen, Michael Paul
Colmenares, Narses Jose
Cox, Lawrence Henry
Crain, Chester Raymond
David, Herbert Aron
Deming, William Edwards
Dixon, Wilfrid Joseph
Drew, Bruce Arthur
Efron, Bradley
Essenwanger, Oskar Maximilian Karl
Freiberger, Walter Frederick
Gaines, James Abner
Gaylor, David William
Gentleman, Jane F.
Gibbs, David Eugene
Girden, Ellen Robinson
Grandon, Gary Michael
Grembowski, David Emil
Grenander, Ulf
Griffith, William Schuler
Grossman, Michael
Guillaume, Germaine Gabrielle Cornelissen
Hall, William Jackson
Hansen, Morris Howard
Harris, Dewey Lynn
Heller, Barbara Ruth
Hogg, Robert Vincent, Jr.
Holley, Charles DeWayen
Holt, William R.
Horvitz, Daniel Goodman
Hunter, John Stuart
Jewell, William Sylvester
Karantinos, Andrew E.
Kay, Steven Michael
Kim, Geung-Ho
Knowlden, Norman Francis
Ku, Harry Hsien H.
Land, Margaret F.
Lehmann, Erich Leo
Lin, Winston T.
Ling, Robert F.
London, Mark David
Mac Donald, Gordon James Fraser
Mahan, Harry Clinton
Marash, Stanley Albert
Marquardt, Donald Wesley
Martin, Jeffrey Donald
Mason, David Dickenson
Miser, Hugh Jordan
Mosteller, Frederick
Norton, Julia Anne
Novick, Melvin Robert
Nyquist, Wyman Ellsworth
Ockerman, Herbert Wood
Parzen, Emanuel
Pauls, John Frederick
Peatman, John Gray
Perrin, Edward Burton
Phillips, Donald Lundahl
Richter, George Brownell
Robbins, Herbert Ellis
Rosenblatt, Murray
Rossing, Robert Grangaard
Scott, Elizabeth Leonard
Shah, Babubhai Vadilal
Sivertson, John Neilos
Slack, Nelson Hosking
Smith, Eric Peter
Smith, William Boyce
Spoeri, Randall Keith
Stahl, Raymond Earl
Stalnaker, John Marshall
Town, Donald Earl
Tummala, V. M. Rao
Turner, Malcolm Elijah, Jr.
Vaks, Yefim Elias

Wahba, Grace
Walter, Gilbert Gustav
Ward-McLemore, Ethel
Weir, Bruce Spencer
Wendelberger, James George
Woodroofe, Michael Barrett

Topology and foundations
Gross, Jonathan Light
Montgomery, Deane
Seadler, Stephen Edward
Whitehead, George William
Whitney, Hassler

Other
Ablowitz, Mark Jay
Brandt, Edward Newman, Jr., *Biostatistics*
Brode, John, *Stochastic processes*
Calabi, Eugenio
Carr, Ralph W., *Differential and integral equations*
Cenzer, Douglas Alfred
Chern, Shiing-Shen, *Differential geometry*
Gehring, Frederick William, *Complex analysis*
Gleason, Andrew Mattei, *Abstract analysis*
Greenberg, David Alexander, *Numerical modelling*
Grenander, Ulf, *Pattern theory*
Halberstam, Heini, *Number theory*
Hale, Jack K., *Differential equations*
Herrmann, Robert Arthur
Horn, Roger Alan
Imbrie, John Z(eller), *Mathematical physics*
Karantinos, Andrew E.
Kaufman, Edwin H., Jr.
Land, Margaret F., *Quality control*
Landau, Henry J., *Harmonic analysis*
Makar, Boshra Halim, *Theory of functions and functional analysis*
Middleton, David
Miller, Willard, Jr., *Group theory*
Minassian, Donald Paul, *Actuarial science*
Mityagin, Boris Samuel, *Functional analysis and its applications*
Mostow, George Daniel, *Group theory*
Negoita, Constantin Virgil
Pettey, Dix Hayes
Roberts, Fred Stephen, *Discrete mathematics*
Rossa, Robert Frank
Simon, Barry
Staley, Frederick Joseph, *Foundations of mathematics*
Stehney, Ann Kathryn
Stout, Benjamin Boreman, *Biostatistics*
Tobler, Waldo Rudolph, *Mathematical geography*
Young, Douglas Wilford
Zeppetella, Anthony John

MEDICINE

Allergy
Abdou, Nabih I.
Adkinson, N. Franklin, Jr.
Altman, Leonard
Bardana, Emil John, Jr.
Bernstein, I. Leonard
Buchholz, Donna Marie
Fauci, Anthony Stephen
Fleisch, Jerome Herbert
Frank, Michael M.
Gillespie, Elizabeth
Hoffman, Donald Richard
Kagey-Sobotka, Anne
Kirkpatrick, Charles Harvey
Kulczycki, Anthony, Jr.
Lewis, Alan James
Mathews, Kenneth Pine
Metzger, W. James
Michael, Jacob Gabriel
Middleton, Elliott, Jr
Nelson, Harold Stanley
Norman, Philip Sidney
Parker, Charles Ward
Santilli, John, Jr.
Scott, Roland Boyd
Talmage, David Wilson
Valentine, Martin Douglas
Vaughan, John Heath
Wayne, Steven Falko
Weiler, John Mayer
Will, Loren August
Zweiman, Burton

Anatomy and embryology
Adams, Donald Robert
Beitz, Alvin James
Conroy, Glenn C.
Cotter, William Bryan, Jr.
Davenport, William Daniel, Jr.
Dung, H.C.
Ettinger, Anna Marie
Flood, Dorothy Garnett
Gibbons, Michael Francis, Jr.
Gilmore, Shirley Ann
Goodrich, James Tait
Gotcher, Jack Everett, Jr.
Greulich, Richard Curtice
Hendrickx, Andrew George
Kennedy, Michael Craig
Krauthamer, Gunter Michael (George)
Leung, Christopher Chung-Kit
Liszczak, Theodore Michael
Litton, Stephen Frederick
Marks, Sandy Cole, Jr.
Martin, George Franklin
Morest, Donald Kent
Norvell, John Edmondson, III
Odend'hal, Stewart
Overman, Dennis Orton
Palay, Sanford Louis
Pauly, John Edward
Rose, Kenneth David
Sawyer, Charles Henry
Siebert, Joseph Robert
Spencer, Robert Frederick
Sprague, James Mather
Stephens, Trent Dee
Sturtevant, Ruthann Patterson
Tobin, Gordon Ross
Wang, Teen-Meei Thomas
Wysolmerski, Theresa
Zhou, Feng-Chiao

Anesthesiology
Acosta, Gustavo
Bendixen, Henrik Holt
Carr, Daniel Barry
Chen, Richard Yuan Zin
Chilcoat, Robert Talmadge
Combs, Claud Steve
Gandolfi, Allen Jay
Hornbein, Thomas F.
Khambatta, Hoshang Jal
Marcella, Kenneth Louis
Miletich, David John
Philbin, Daniel Michael
Seeler, David Charles
Seitman, David T.
Skarda, Roman Thomas
Ueda, Issaku
Winter, Peter Michael
Wollman, Harry
Zapol, Warren Myron

Biochemistry. *See also* **BIOLOGY.**
Abdel-Latif, Ata Abdel-hafez
Allen, Charles Marshall, Jr
Allen, Donald Orrie
Allen, Robert Charles
Allmann, David William
Atlas, Steven Alan
Babitch, Joseph Aaron
Baldwin, Thomas Oakley
Balinsky, Doris
Banks, William Louis, Jr.
Barber, Michael James
Bernstein, Isadore Abraham
Bezkorovainy, Anatoly
Bhalla, Vinod K.
Bishop, John Michael
Bistrian, Bruce Ryan
Black, Arthur Leo
Blair, Donald George Ralph
Bole, Giles G.
Boyan, Barbara Dale
Brady, Roscoe O.
Braughler, J(ohn) Mark
Breslow, Jan Leslie
Bucovaz, Edsel T.
Carroll, Kenneth Kitchener
Carsten, Mary E.
Cash, Derek John
Chacko, George Kutty
Chan, Pak Hoo
Chargaff, Erwin
Chasin, Mark
Chaudry, Irshad Hussain
Chen, Kirk Ching Shyong
Chen, Yu Min
Chiang, John Young Ling
Chinn, Kenneth Sai-Keung
Chou, Albert Chung-Ho
Christensen, Mary Lucas
Chuang, Hanson Yii-Kuan
Cohn, David V(alor)
Collins, John H.
Conn, Rex Boland, Jr.
Conney, Allan Howard
Cooper, David Young
Cooper, Herbert Asel
Cornatzer, William Eugene
Creighton, Donald John
Cunningham, Earlene Brown
Dahms, Arthur Stephen
Darby, William Jefferson, Jr.
Dawson, Earl Bliss
Dean, David Devereaux
Dearborn, Dorr Gellatly
Deibel, Martin Robert, Jr.
DeVore, Dale Paul
Di Pasquale, Gene
Dirksen, Thomas Reed, II
Doellgast, George John
Dombro, Roy Sandor
Donnelly, Thomas Edward, Jr.
Dubinsky, William Paul, Jr.
Dudock, Bernard Samuel
Duerre, John Arden
Duffy, Lawrence Kevin
Eaton, Barbara Ruth
Ebner, Kurt Ewald
el Kouni, Mahmoud Hamdi
Ellenbogen, Leon
Elliott, William Hueckel
Engle, Michael J(ean)
Essenberg, Margaret Kottke
Estabrook, Ronald Winfield
Falcone, Alfonso Benjamin
Fine, Albert S.
Foote, J(oel) Lindsley
Fowler, Bruce Andrew
Free, Charles Alfred
Fridovich, Irwin
Friedenson, Bernard Allen
Frisell, Wilhelm Richard
Fu, Shou-Cheng Joseph
Gabriel, Othmar
Garfinkel, David
Gershbein, Leon Lee
Ghebrehiwet, Berhane
Giles, Ralph Edson
Glas-Greenwalt, Pia
Goh, Edward Hua Seng
Goldstein, Jack
Goldyne, Marc Ellis
Goodman, DeWitt Stetten
Griffin, John Henry
Grinnan, Edward Leonard
Gurd, Ruth Sights
Guttman, Helene Nathan
Haas, Erwin
Hager, Chester Bradley
Hanson, Douglas M.
Harlow, Robert Dean
Harmon, Frederick Robert
Harrison, John Henry, IV
Harrison, Yvonne Elois
Hart, Lawrence Austin
Hawkins, Edward Frederick
Heinrich, Milton Rollin
Henshaw, Edgar Cummings
Hill, Robert Lee
Holleman, William H.
Hollenberg, Paul Frederick
Hollis, Bruce Warren
Holloway, Caroline Tobia
Holman, Ralph Theodore
Hommes, Fritz Aukustinus
Hostetler, Karl Yoder
Hougland, Arthur Eldon
Hsu, Ih-Chang
Hugli, Tony Edward
Inagami, Tadashi
Iqbal, Zafar
Iqbal, Zafar Mohd
Irimura, Tatsuro
Jackson, Richard Lee
Jeanloz, Roger William
Jencks, William Platt
Johnson, Deadre Jeanne
Johnston, Laurance Scott
Jones, Mary Ellen
Kachmar, John Frederick
Kahn, Stephen Ellsworth
Kaistha, Krishan, Kumar
Kalra, Vijay Kumar
Kaltenbach, John Paul
Kao, Winston Whei-Yang
Kaplan, Ann Esther
Kefalides, Nicholas Alexander
Kim, Jin Kyung
Klingman, Jack Dennis
Kokatnur, Mohan Gundo
Korn, Edward David
Krasny, Harvey Charles
Kumar, Sudhir
Kumar, Vijaya Buddhiraju
Kuntzman, Ronald Grover
Kuo, Jyh-Fa
Lands, William Edward Mitchell
Lane, Daniel McNeel
Lazicki-Lakshmanan, Florence Mary
Le, Hung Van
Lei, David K.Y.
Lester, David
Leung, Philip Min-Bun
Lieberman, Seymour
Light, Albert
Lis, Adam Wiktor
Litchfield, William John
Loftfield, Robert Bernard
Malbica, Joseph Orazio
Malik, Mazhar Nasir
Malins, Donald Clive
Malkinson, Alvin Maynard
Maniatis, Thomas Peter
Mansour, Tag Eldin
Margolis, Frank Leonard
Margolis, Sam Aaron
Markland, Francis Swaby, Jr.
McCarty, Kenneth Scott
McGeachin, Robert Lorimer
Medzihradsky, Fedor
Meister, Alton
Meyer, Ralph Roger
Mickelson, Kenneth Eugene
Miller, Francis Peter
Mittal, Chandra Kant
Moore, Robert Blaine
Morgan, Howard Edwin
Munns, Theodore W.
Murayama, Makio
Mushinski, J. Frederic
Nagy, Béla Ferenc
Najjar, Victor Assad
Narayanan, A. Sampath
Neary, Joseph Thomas
Neuhaus, Otto W.
Newman, Jack Huff
Niedermeier, William
Noble, Nancy Lee
Nordlie, Robert Conrad
O'Connor, Daniel Thomas, Jr.
Offenbacher, Steven
Ohno, Mikio
Okerholm, Richard Arthur
O'Leary, Gerard Paul, Jr.
Parham, Marc Ellous
Patsch, Josef Rudolf
Peanasky, Robert Joseph
Peterson, Rudolph Nicholas
Pezzuto, John Michael
Pfefferkorn, Elmer Roy
Pilgeram, Laurence Oscar
Pizzo, Salvatore Vincent
Polefka, Thomas Gregory
Pollard, Thomas Dean
Polz-Schaerffenberg, Erika
Pories, Walter J.
Prager, Morton David
Radhakrishnamurthy, Bhandaru
Rall, Joseph Edward
Rawat, Arun Kumar
Ray, Richard Schell
Reichle, Frederick Adolph
Reitz, Ronald Charles
Richardson, Carol Lynn
Richardson, Charles Clifton
Rosenkrantz, Harris
Russ, Wesley Dale
Sacks, William
Sahu, Saura Chandra
Salvo, Rino Anthony
Samuel, Paul
Sancar, Aziz
Sanders, Robert Burnett
Sanslone, William Robert
Sarno, Maria Erlinda Co
Saryan, Leon Aram
Scandella, Carl John
Schlesinger, David Harvey
Schrohenloher, Ralph Edward
Schuh, Joseph Randolph
Schwartz, Edith Richmond
Seetharam, Bellur
Segrest, Jere Palmer
Shamoo, Adil E(lias)
Sharpless, Nansie Sue
Shore, Joseph David
Skare, Kevin Lynn
Sky-Peck, Howard H.
Snyderman, Selma E(leanore)
Sourkes, Theodore Lionel
Strauss, Elliott William
Subbiah, Ravi Mandepanda Thimmiah
Sun, Albert Yung-Kwang
Sun, Grace Yan Chi
Tabachnick, Joseph
Tanaka, Kay
Tchen, Tche-Tsing
Termine, John David
Tilak, Manohar Anant
Tischler, Marc Eliot
Tolman, Edward Laurie
Tsang, Joseph Chiao-Liang
Tulp, Orien Lee
Tumbleson, M.E.
Turco, Salvatore Joseph
Uitto, Jouni Jorma
Vanaman, Thomas C.
Vatsis, Kostas Petros
Venter, J. Craig
Vercellotti, John Raymond
Wacker, Warren Ernest Clyde
Wang, Jerry Hsueh-Ching
Wang, Taitzer
Webb, Thomas Evan
Weinberg, Uzi
Weinhouse, Sidney
Westheimer, Frank H(enry)
Williams, Harold Lloyd
Willis, John Patrick
Winicov, Ilga Butelis
Witkop, Bernhard
Wogan, Gerald Norman
Wolen, Robert Lawrence
Wong, Patrick Yui-Kwong
Wood, Harland Goff
Wu, Chuen-Shang Chung
Wu, Po-shun
Wyngaarden, James Barnes
Yang, Chung Shu
Yesair, David Wayne
Yoder, John Monley
York, John Lyndal
You, Kwan-sa
Zenser, Terry Vernon

Biofeedback
Doerr, Robert Douglas
Eberstein, Arthur
Engel, Bernard Theodore
Green, Elmer Ellsworth
King, Dennis R.
Tansey, Michael Anselme
Verma, Ram Sagar

Cancer research. *See also* **Oncology.**
Ablashi, Dharam Vir
Ablin, Richard Joel
Agrawal, Krishna Chandra
Aisenberg, Alan C.
Aisner, Joseph
Albano, William A.
Allaudeen, Hameedsulthan Sheik
Al-Sarraf, Muhyi
Anderson, Lucy Macdonald
Archer, Michael Christopher
Arseneau, James Charles
Auerbach, Oscar
Baker, Laurence Howard
Balbinder, Elias
Balinsky, Doris
Banerjee, Sipra
Baron, Jeffrey
Bast, Robert Clinton, Jr.
Beattie, Craig Warren
Beirne, Owen Ross
Belman, Sidney
Benade, Leonard Edward
Berlin, Nathaniel Isaac
Bernacki, Ralph James
Bhavanandan, Veerasingham P.
Bichsel, Hans
Birt, Diane Feickert
Biswal, Nilambar
Blair, Donald George Ralph
Blitzer, Andrew
Bloom, Eda Terri
Borden, Ernest Carleton
Boyd, Ann Lewis
Bradner, William Turnbull
Brady, Luther W., Jr.
Brattain, Michael G.
Bronson, David Lee
Brown, Jay Clark
Buchsbaum, Donald Jay
Bucovaz, Edsel T.
Buehler, Robert John
Bunn, Paul Axtell, Jr.
Burdette, Walter James
Burt, Michael Edward
Burzynski, Stanislaw Rajmund
Camiolo, Sarah May
Cardiff, Robert Darrell
Carrano, Anthony Vito
Carubelli, Raoul
Castro, Joseph Ronald
Cave, William Thompson, Jr.
Cavins, John Alexander
Chan, Po Chuen
Chandra, Satish
Chavin, Walter
Chechik, Boris E.
Chernicoff, David Paul
Chin, Hong W.
Chiu, Jen-Fu
Chiuten, Delia Fung She
Chou, Iih-Nan
Chou, Ting-Chao
Clapp, Neal Keith
Cohen, Samuel M.
Coleman, C. Norman
Conney, Allan Howard
Cooper, Robert Arthur, Jr.
Crabtree, Gerald Winston
Creech, Richard Hearne
Cromwell, Norman H
Cummings, Richard Dale
Dalla-Favera, Riccardo
Datta, Surjit Kumar
Day, Calvin Lee, Jr.
Dean, Judith Carol Hickman
DelVillano, Bert C., Jr.
DeVita, Vincent Theodore, Jr.
DeWys, William Dale
Diamandopoulos, George Theodore
Dicello, John Francis, Jr.
DiPaolo, Joseph Amedeo
Diwan, Bhalchandra Apparao
Douglas, J. Fielding
Dow, Lois Weyman
Drewinko, Benjamin
Duff, James Thomas
Ebert, Paul Stoudt
Eble, John Nelson
Edwards, Gordon Stuart
el Kouni, Mahmoud Hamdi
Epstein, Alan Lee
Epstein, Lois Barth
Essex, Myron Elmer
Evans, Charles Hawes
Evans, James Thomas
Evans, William Edward
Everson, Richard Bernard
Fabian, Carol J.
Fairchild, Ralph Grandison
Feinerman, Burton
Fernandes, Daniel James
Fine, Donald Lee
Frank, Irwin Norman
Fraumeni, Joseph Francis, Jr.
Freedman, Herbert Allen
Fu, Karen King-Wah
Fukuda, Minoru
Gale, Robert Peter
Gallo, Robert Charles
Geran, Ruth I.
Gifford, George Edwin
Glasgow, Glenn Patrick
Golberg, Leon
Golomb, Frederick Martin
Gordon, Robert Thomas
Gosalvez, Mario
Gray, Joe William
Greenstock, Clive Lewis
Greenwald, Edward S.
Grimm, Elizabeth Ann
Groopman, John Davis
Gross, Ludwik
Grossweiner, Leonard Irwin
Hager-Rich, Jean Carol
Hall, Thomas Christopher
Hampar, Berge
Hampton, James Wilburn
Hanafusa, Hidesaburo
Hanna, Michael George, Jr.
Harlow, Robert Dean
Hedgcoth, Charles
Henderson, Isaac Craig
Henshaw, Edgar Cummings
Herlyn, Meenhard Folkeus
Higgins, Paul Joseph
Hillman, Elizabeth Ann
Hoge, Arthur Franklin, Jr.
Hokama, Yoshitsugi
Houghton, Janet Anne
Houghton, Peter James
Howell, Stephen Barnard
Hrushesky, William John Michael
Hsu, Ih-Chang
Huberman, Eliezer
Huebner, Robert Joseph
Hueser, James Nicholas
Hutchison, Dorris Jeannette
Iannaccone, Philip Monroe
Iqbal, Zafar Mohd
Irimura, Tatsuro
Jacobs, Jerome Barry
Jain, Rakesh Kumar
Jensen, Elwood Vernon
Jensen, Keith Edwin
Jerina, Donald Michael
Jessup, John Milburn
Johnson, Frank Edward
Johnson, Irving Stanley
Jones, Lawrence William
Jones, Russell Allen
Jordan, V. Craig
Kamiyama, Mikio
Kaplan, Ann Esther
Kaplan, Richard Stephen
Kapp, John Paul
Kellen, John Andrew
Kennedy, Byrl James
Kennett, Roger Howard
Kessel, David
Kim, Jae Ho
Kim, Yoon Berm
Kim, Yung Dai
Kimler, Bruce Franklin
King, (Mary) Margaret
Kirkman, Hadley
Kithier, Karel
Knudson, Alfred George, Jr.
Kodama, Toshiko
Koo, Peter Hung-Kwan
Kori, Shashidhar Halappa
Krause, Charles Joseph
Kreimer-Birnbaum, F
Krown, Susan Ellen
Kumar, Prasanna K.
Ladisch, Stephan
Lamon, Eddie William
Lapeyre, Jean-Numa
Lawrence, David Delbert
Lazo, John Stephen
Lee, Ching-Li
Lee, Francis Him
Lee, Lihsyng Stanford
Leon, Shalom A.
Leong, Stanley Pui-Lock
Lerch, Irving Abram
Lerman, Michael Isaac
Leventhal, Brigid Gray
Levy, Ronald
Li, Jonathan J.
Liao, Shuen-Kuei
Lipkin, George
Livingston, David Morse
London, William Thomas
Longnecker, Daniel Sidney
Loor, Rueyming
Lotlikar, Prabhakar Dattaram
Luderer, Albert August
Ludlum, David Blodgett
Lupulescu, Aurel Peter
Lvovsky, Edward Abraham
Macara, Ian Gregory
Maki, Takashi
Malkinson, Alvin Maynard
Malsky, Stanley Joseph
Margulis, Thomas N.
Markland, Francis Swaby, Jr.
Marton, Laurence Jay
Maruyama, Yosh
Mayhew, Eric George
Mc Credie, Kenneth Blair
McCully, Kilmer Serjus
McDonald, Hemprova Ghosh
McGovren, James Patrick
Meehan, Thomas
Mehta, Rajendra G.
Meyer, Ralph Roger
Michaels, Howard Brian
Milman, Harry Abraham
Milner, John A.

Min, Kyung-Whan
Mirand, Edwin Albert
Moertel, Charles George
Mohla, Suresh
Morrison, Francis Secrest
Morrow, Gary Robert
Murphy, Gerald Patrick
Nag, Subir K.
Nettesheim, Paul
Newton, William Allen, Jr.
Nichols, Warren Wesley
Nicolson, Garth L.
Nomura, Abraham Michael Yozaburo
Ochoa, Manuel, Jr.
O'Connor, Timothy E.
Oettgen, Herbert F.
Ohno, Mikio
Ohnuma, Takao
Old, Lloyd John
Oldham, James Warren
Opler, Stanley Ronal
Oppenheim, Joost J.
Ove, Peter
Packer, Lester
Papsidero, Lawrence Dean
Patterson, David
Pereira, Michael Alan
Pettit, George Robert
Pezzuto, John Michael
Piette, Lawrence Hector
Pollack, Sylvia Byrne
Pong, Raymond S.
Popescu, Nicolae Constantin
Potter, Michael
Pour, Parviz M.
Poydock, Mary Eymard
Prager, Morton David
Preffer, Frederic Ira
Presant, Cary A.
Press, Michael Fredrick
Puck, Theodore Thomas
Randerath, Kurt
Ratajczak, Helen Vosskuhler
Ray, Prasanta Kumar
Reif, Arnold Eugene
Rhim, Johng Sik
Riordan, James Michael
Robertson, James Bragg
Romney, Seymour Leonard
Rosenkranz, Herbert S.
Rothenberg, Sheldon Philip
Rowley, Janet Davison
Roy-Burman, Pradip
Russo, Irma Haydee Alvarez
Saffiotti, Umberto
Samaan, Naguib Abdelmalik
Saravis, Calvin Albert
Sarkar, Nurul Haque
Sartiano, George P.
Sartorelli, Alan Clayton
Saslaw, Leonard David
Schultz, Richard Michael
Schwartz, Arthur Gerald
Sears, Henry Francis, II
Sell, Stewart
Sethi, Vidya Sagar
Setlow, Richard Burton
Shah, Sudhir Amratlal
Shapiro, Howard Maurice
Shertzer, Howard Grant
Shug, Austin Leo
Shuster, Joseph
Sidky, Younan Abdel-Malik
Silver, Hulbert Keyes Belford
Silver, Robert Benjamin
Simpson, Larry Dean
Singhakowinta, Amnuay
Sinkovics, Joseph G.
Sirica, Alphonse Eugene
Skipski, Vladimir P(avlovich)
Sky-Peck, Howard H.
Slack, Nelson Hosking
Smith, Barry Hamilton
Soloway, Albert Herman
Sommers, Sheldon Charles
Song, Chang Won
Spratt, John Stricklin
Steckel, Richard J.
Steeves, Richard Allison
Steplewski, Zenon
Sternhagen, Charles James
Stolinsky, David C.
Stone, Marvin Jules
Stowell, Robert Eugene
Strauss, Bernard S.
Sudilovsky, Oscar
Sunkara, Sai Prasad
Szal, Marcel Michael
Szent-Gyorgyi, Albert
Talbot, Jr. Timothy Ralph
Tannock, Ian Frederick
Tejada, Francisco
Terman, David Stephen
Testa, Joseph Robert
Tew, Kenneth David
Todaro, George Joseph
Tökés, Zoltán András
Tom, Baldwin H.
Tormey, Douglass C.
Townsend, Leroy B.
Trosko, James Edward
Trown, Patrick Willoughby
Troy, Frederic Arthur, II
Tsang, Alfred Kwong-Y
Tyre, Timothy Edward
Ultmann, John Ernest
Urano, Muneyasu
Vallera, Daniel Attilio
Van Echo, David Andrew
van Nagell, John Rensselaer, Jr.
Varki, Ajit Pothan
Varmus, Harold Eliot
Veltri, Robert William
Vogel, Charles Lewis
Wade, Adelbert Elton
Waldmann, Thomas Alexander
Walia, Amrik Singh
Wallace, Harold James, Jr.
Wang, Nancy
Warrell, Raymond Paul
Webb, Thomas Evan
Weber, George
Weber, Thomas Richard
Weese, James Leighton
Weinhouse, Sidney
Wheeler, Glynn Pearce
Wiernik, Peter Harris
Wilkinson, David Stanley
Willis, Isaac
Withers, Hubert Rodney
Wogan, Gerald Norman
Wolff, James Alexander
Wolman, Sandra R.
Wotiz, Herbert Henry
Yang, Chung Shu
Yesner, Raymond
Yuspa, Stuart Howard
Zenser, Terry Vernon

Cardiology
Abdulla, Abdulla Mohammed
Abela, George Samih
Alexander, Jonathan
Alikhan, Mahmood
Antzelevitch, Charles
Arnsdorf, Morton Frank
Banka, Vidya Sagar
Berger, Harvey James
Bilitch, Michael
Bing, Richard John
Blanchard, Susan Manning
Blomquist, Carl Gunnar
Bloomfield, Daniel Kermit
Boudoulas, Harisios
Bowyer, Allen Frank
Braunwald, Eugene
Brooks, Harold Lloyd
Bruce, Thomas Allen
Brundage, Bruce Howard
Bulkley, Bernardine Healy
Burton, Karen Poliner
Castle, Charles Hilmon
Cha, Se Do
Coffman, Jay Denton
Cooper, Theodore
Covit, Andrew B.
Cudkowicz, Leon
Deedwania, Prakash Chandra
Desser, Kenneth Barry
Diana, John Nicholas
DuCharme, Donald Walter
Elkayam, Uri
Engel, Toby Ross
Ettinger, Philip Owen
Farshidi, Ardeshir B.
Franciosa, Joseph Anthony
Frankl, William Stewart
Freis, Edward David
Frohlich, Edward David
Gaffney, Francis Andrew
Ganguly, Sunilendu Narayan
Gardin, Julius Markus
Gheorghiade, Mihai
Gillette, Paul Crawford
Glantz, Stanton Arnold
Goldman, Lee
Gomoll, Allen Warren
Greene, Murray A.
Gupta, Prem Kamal
Han, Jaok
Harrison, Donald Carey
Hayes, Arthur Hull, Jr.
Haywood, L. Julian
Heistad, Donald Dean
Hejtmancik, Milton Rudolph
Hyman, Albert Lewis
James, Thomas Naum
Johannsen, Ulmer James
Johns, Dearing Ward
Kannel, William Bernard
Kaplan, Kenneth Charles
Klausner, Steven Charles
Knoebel, Suzanne Buckner
Kun, Luis Guillermo
Kupersmith, Joel
Laddu, Atul Ramchandra
La Farge, Christopher Grant C.
Laks, Michael Milton
Lee, Garrett
Levy, Robert Isaac
Lichstein, Edgar
Little, Robert Colby
Lust, Robert Maurice
Lutas, Elizabeth M.
Mahapatra, Rajat Kanti
Manger, William Muir
Marshall, Franklin Nick
McCampbell, Stanley Reid
Michelson, Eric Lee
Mikat, Eileen Marie
Mohiuddin, Syed Maqdoom
Morganroth, Joel
Murray, Raymond Harold
Mustafa, Syed Jamal
Nair, Chandra Kunju
Nelson, Clifford Vincent
Noordergraaf, Abraham
Nora, James Jackson
Okada, Robert Dean
Pepine, Carl John
Pitt, Bertram
Proakis, Anthony George
Ribeiro, Lair G(eraldo) T(heodoro)
Richardson, David Walthall
Rosenfeld, Isadore
Sabbah, Hani Naief
Saffitz, Jeffrey Ernest
Samuel, Paul
Sanders, Charles Addison
Schelbert, Heinrich Ruediger
Scherlag, Benjamin Jacob
Schober, Robert Charles
Schwartz, Mortimer Leonard
Segal, Bernard Louis
Sherry, Sol
Shug, Austin Leo
Singh, Bramah Nand
Sintetos, Anthony Lee
Slutsky, Robert Allen
Smith, Thomas Woodward
Sobol, Bruce J.
Sparks, Harvey Vise, Jr.
Strom, Joel Andrew
Sullivan, Jay Michael
Thind, Guadarshan Singh
Tilton, Ronald Gene
Tsitlik, Joshua E.
Veray, Francisco X.
Wackers, Frans Jozef Thomas
Waller, Bruce Frank
Wann, Lee Samuel
Warltier, David Charles
Weil, Max Harry
Winbury, Martin Maurice
Wyss, James Michael
Yeh, Billy Kuo-Jiun
Zaret, Barry Lewis

Cell biology. *See also* **BIOLOGY.**
Adlakha, Ramesh Chander
Albrecht, Thomas Blair
Allison, David Coulter
Al Saadi, Abdul Amir
Benditt, Earl Philip
Bianco, Celso
Bonventre, Joseph Vincent
Brattain, Michael G.
Broadwell, Richard Dow
Brody, Jerome Saul
Chandra, Satish
Chew, Catherine Strong
Chopra, Dharam Pal
Clark, James Henry
Clowes, Alexander Whitehill
Cohn, Zanvil A.
Crews, Harold Richardson
Cuatrecasas, Pedro Martin
Duerre, John Arden
Ellsworth, Jeff Lynn
Farquhar, Marilyn Gist
Friedman, Harold Ira
Goldfischer, Sidney Leo
Goodman, Steven Richard
Haudenschild, Christian C.
Helgerson, Sam Leland
Horwitz, Alan F.
Howard-Peebles, Patricia Nell
Inagami, Tadashi
Insel, Paul Anthony
Isselbacher, Kurt Julius
Jacobs, Jerome Barry
Kaltenbach, John Paul
Kao, Winston Whei-Yang
Knowles, Barbara B.
Korn, Joseph H.
Lagunoff, David
LaVail, Matthew Maurice
Leblond, Charles Philipps
Lebo, Roger Van
Lin, Hsiu-San
Lubiniecki, Anthony Stanley
Madri, Joseph Anthony
Margolius, Harry Stephen
Martinez, Irving Ricardo, Jr.
O'Leary, Gerard Paul, Jr.
Ove, Peter
Pilgeram, Laurence Oscar
Pollard, Thomas Dean
Ross, Russell
Ryan, Una Scully
Sajdel-Sulkowska, Elizabeth Maria
Saunders, Robert Norman
Schilling, John Albert
Schreiber, Sidney S.
Schultz, Stanley George
Sherman, James Howe
Shinowara, Nancy Lee
Simons, Roy Kenneth
Somlyo, Avril Virginia
St. Clair, Richard William
Sunkara, Sai Prasad
Tan, Eng Meng
Tomanek, Robert Joseph
Velardo, Joseph Thomas
Wiebe, Michael Eugene
Wildenthal, C(laud) Kern
Wilson, Michael John
Wolf, Barbara Anne
Woodley, David Timothy
You, Kwan-sa
Zurier, Robert Burton

Cytology and histology
Babrakzai, Noorullah
Bodian, David
Farber, Phillip Andrew
Ferraro, Bernadette Angela
Howse, Harold Darrow
Inhorn, Stanley Lee
Kirkman, Hadley
Koss, Leopold G.
Mickey, George Henry
Mowry, Robert Wilbur
Norton, William Nicholson, Jr.
Stumpf, Walter Erich
Tomanek, Robert Joseph
Wu, Ching-Kuei

Critical care
Baxter, Charles Rufus
Crowe, Dennis Timothy, Jr.
Reitz, Richard Elmer
Schwab, C. William
Smith, Joseph Lorenzo
Steinman, Stuart Leonard
Weil, Max Harry
Wollman, Harry

Dermatology
Bernstein, Joel Edward
Bystryn, Jean-Claude
Callen, Jeffrey Phillip
Cripps, Derek J.
Day, Calvin Lee, Jr.
Folse, Dean Sydney
Freedberg, Irwin Mark
Goldstein, Norman
Goldyne, Marc Ellis
Goltz, Robert William
Hu, Chung-Hong
Lipkin, George
Maibach, Howard I.
Martinez, Irving Ricardo, Jr.
Mihm, Martin Charles, Jr.
Montagna, William
Mukhtar, Hasan
Reisner, Ronald Morton
Smith, Jesse Graham, Jr.
Uitto, Jouni Jorma
Willis, Isaac
Woodley, David Timothy

Endocrinology
Anderson, Ralph Robert
Atlas, Steven Alan
August, Gilbert Paul
Barbosa-Saldivar, Jose Luis
Bardin, Clyde Wayne
Baxter, John Darling
Biglieri, Edward George
Bransome, Edwin Dagobert, Jr.
Brosnihan, K. Bridget
Brown, Keith Irwin
Burrell, Craig Donald
Cahill, George Francis, Jr.
Carew, Lyndon Belmont, Jr.
Carlson, Harold Ernest
Castro, Alberto
Cave, William Thompson, Jr.
Challoner, David Reynolds
Chan, W. Y.
Chang, Ernest Sun-Mei
Chavin, Walter
Cohn, David V(alor)
Corradino, Robert A.
Dietrich, John William
Draznin, Boris
Ertel, Norman H.
Fajans, Stefan Stanislaus
Falcone, Alfonso Benjamin
Finkelstein, Michael
Fortier, Claude
Fray, John Cordell Spencer
Galton, Valerie Anne
Ganis, Frank Michael
Gaut, Zane Noel
Genest, Jacques
Goldman, Allen Seymour
Goodman, David Barry Poliakoff
Grinnan, Edward Leonard
Gueriguian, John Leo
Hamilton, Carlos Robert, Jr.
Hertz, Roy
Hogness, John Rusten
Holtkamp, Dorsey E(mil)
Horwitz, David Larry
Hostetler, Karl Yoder
Jackson, Ivor
Jewelewicz, Raphael
Jöchle, Wolfgang Johannes
Jordan, V. Craig
Kabadi, Udaya Manohar
Kalu, Dike Ndukwe
Kenny, Alexander Donovan
Kodama, Toshiko
Komanicky, Pavel
Kostyo, Jack Lawrence
Laychock, Suzanne Gale
Lerner, Leonard Joseph
Li, Choh Hao
Liao, Shutsung
Lieberman, Seymour
Lipsett, Mortimer Broadwin
Lostroh, Ardis June
Lupulescu, Aurel Peter
Malamed, Sasha
Maloff, Bruce L
Mohla, Suresh
Nachreiner, Raymond Francis
Nichols, George
Nocenti, Mero Raymond
Pak, Charles Y.C.
Peck, William Arno
Pento, J. Thomas
Plymate, Stephen Rex
Rall, Joseph Edward
Reel, Jerry Royce
Rich, Clayton
Riggs, Byron Lawrence, Jr.
Rooks, Wendell Hofma, II
Roth, Jesse
Rubenstein, Arthur Harold
Salans, Lester Barry
Schultz, Alvin Leroy
Segal, Barry M.
Sherwin, Joseph Richard
Solomon, David Harris
Steiner, Donald Frederick
Theoharides, Theoharis Constantin
Umminger, Bruce Lynn
Urquhart, John
Walsh, Patrick Craig
Ward, Walter F(rederick)
Williams, Gerald Albert
Witorsch, Raphael Jay
Wolf, Richard Clarence
Wolff, Frederick William

Endocrinology, neuroendocrinology
Abrams, Gary Mitchell
Albers, Henry Elliott
Aronin, Neil
Atwater, Illani Jeanne
Badger, Thomas Mark
Baksi, Samarendra Nath
Beck, Lyle Vibert
Bell, Norman Howard
Berlind, Allan
Beyer-Mears, Annette
Brito, Gilberto Ottoni
Brooks, David Patrick
Brosnihan, K. Bridget
Bryson, George Gardner
Buckman, Maire Tults
Carr, Daniel Barry
Cheng, Mei-Fang Hsieh
Chretien, Michel
Chung, Melvin Chung-Hing
Cone, Ric Ian
Critchlow, B(urtis) Vaughn
Dunn, Adrian John
Edgren, Richard Arthur
Einhorn, Daniel
Eldridge, John Charles
Ellis, LeGrande Clark
Etgen, Anne Marie
Fernstrom, John Dickson
Fortier, Claude
Gambert, Steven Ross
Gawienowski, Anthony M(ichael)
Gorbman, Aubrey
Grota, Lee James
Guillemin, Roger
Halbreich, Uriel
Hatton, Glenn Irwin
Hawkins, Edward Frederick
Herman, William Sparkes
Hernandez, Daniel E.
Holaday, John Waldron
Jackson, Ivor
Johnson, David Gregory
Johnston, Craig Alan
Kalra, Satya Paul
Kant, Gloria Jean
Keefer, Donald Ashby
Lisk, Robert Douglas
Loh, Yoke Peng
Loosen, Peter Thomas
Lu, John Kuew-Hsiung
Manger, William Muir
McGuire, John L.
McIntosh, Tracy Kahl
McMillin, John Michael
Mellin, Theodore Nelson
Ney, Robert Leo
Nilaver, Gajanan
Olsen, Kathie Lynn
Phelps, Carol Jo
Phillips, Michael Ian
Plotsky, Paul Mitchell
Porter, Johnny R.
Raff, Hershel
Ragavan, Vanaja Vijaya
Reddy, Vangala Venkatarami
Samaan, Naguib Abdelmalik
Sartin, James Lewis, Jr.
Sawyer, Charles Henry
Schally, Andrew Victor
Scharrer, Berta Vogel
Schlesinger, David Harvey
Schwartz, William Joseph
Shambaugh, George Elmer, III
Sladek, Celia Davis
Stumpf, Walter Erich
Tweedle, Charles David
Uno, Hideo
Van de Kar, Louis D.
Van Loon, Glen Richard
Velardo, Joseph Thomas
Verbalis, Joseph George
Viveros, Osvaldo Humberto
Weinberg, Uzi
Wurtman, Richard Jay
Yalow, Rosalyn Sussman
Yasuda, Naoki

Endocrinology, receptors
Archer, Juanita Almetta Hinnant
Bardin, Clyde Wayne
Beattie, Craig Warren
Bhalla, Vinod K.
Bhathena, Sam Jehangirji
Clark, James Henry
Fain, John Nicholas
Galton, Valerie Anne
Gurd, Ruth Sights
Jacobs, Steven Jay
Jaffe, Randal Craig
Jensen, Elwood Vernon
Keefer, Donald Ashby
Kornel, Ludwig
La Barbera, Andrew Richard
Lata, Gene Frederick
Lee, Chung
Leung, Benjamin Shuet-kin
Li, Jonathan J.
Liang, Tehming
Mehta, Rajendra G.
Meyers, Cal Yale
Raam, Shanthi
Read, George Wesley
Reitz, Richard Elmer
Rodbell, Martin
Singhakowinta, Amnuay
Varga, Janos M.
Venter, J. Craig
Wilson, Jean Donald
Witorsch, Raphael Jay
Wotiz, Herbert Henry

Epidemiology
Alderman, Michael Harris
Alexander, Edward Russell
Benenson, Abram Salmon
Beran, George Wesley
Brandt, Carl David
Breslow, Lester
Burridge, Michael John
Buttery, Christopher M. G.
Caldwell, Glyn Gordon
Craven, Donald Edward
Denny, Floyd Wolfe, Jr.
Densen, Paul Maximillian
Eisenberg, Leon
Emanuel, Irvin
Everson, Richard Bernard
Farrier, Noel John
Feinstein, Alvan Richard
Ferris, Benjamin Greeley, Jr.
Franti, Charles Elmer
Fraumeni, Joseph Francis, Jr.
Gable, Carol Brignoli
Gardner, John Willard
Glenn, Robert Edward
Goldstein, Murray
Grayston, J. Thomas
Gross, Peter Alan
Haughee, Sharon Marie
Holmberg, Scott A.
Huebner, Robert Joseph
Jordan, William Stone, Jr.
Kannel, William Bernard
Kass, Edward Harold
London, William Thomas
Lyman, Gary Herbert
Mahboubi, Ezzat Ollah
Mattson, Margaret Ellen
Mortimer, James Arthur
Neuhauser, Duncan von Briesen
Nomura, Abraham Michael Yozaburo
Parsons, James Eugene
Robins, Lee Nelken
Shelokov, Alexis
Sheps, Cecil George
Stallones, Reuel Arthur
Starfield, Barbara Helen
Urquhart, John
van Riper, Charles, III
Watson, Annetta Paule
Weill, Hans
Will, Loren August
Winkelstein, Warren, Jr.
Woods, George Theodore

Family practice
Black, David Joseph
Burket, George Edward, Jr.
Shahady, Edward John
TePoorten, Bernard A.

Gastroenterology
Achord, James Lee
Alphin, Reevis Stancil
Anuras, Sinn
Brooks, Frank Pickering

Caplan, Daniel Bennett
Carey, Martin Conrad
Chalmers, Thomas Clark
Dearing, William Hill
Deschner, Eleanor Elizabeth
Dienstag, Jules Leonard
Dietschy, John Maurice
El-Ackad, Tarek M.
Euler, Arthur Ray
Farmer, Richard Gilbert
Gidda, Jaswant Singh
Gottlieb, Leonard Solomon
Goyal, Raj K.
Groszmann, Roberto Jose
Hoyumpa, Anastacio Maningo
Innes, David Lyn
Isselbacher, Kurt Julius
Katz, Julian
Kirsner, Joseph Barnett
MacDermott, Richard Pratt
Mellinkoff, Sherman Mussoff
Mortillaro, Nicholas A.
Pitchumoni, Capecomorin S.
Plaut, Andrew George
Post, Joseph
Rajan, Kannan Ramalingam
Reichen, Juerg
Reitemeier, Richard Joseph
Robert, Andre
Roth, Harold P.
Roth, James Luther Aumont
Schade, Robert Richard
Schuster, Marvin Meier
Scott, Gerald William
Seetharam, Bellur
Shearin, Nancy Louise
Shorter, Roy Gerrard
Shriver, David Allen
Slomiany, Bronislaw Leszek
Stein, George Nathan
Stern, Robert Morris
Szabo, Sandor
Tache, Yvette France
Weisberg, Aaron
Wilbur, Dwight Locke
Yalow, Rosalyn Sussman
Zimmerman, Hyman Joseph

Genetics and genetic engineering. ***See also*** **BIOLOGY.**
Allen, Robert Carter
Al Saadi, Abdul Amir
Anderson, W. French
Anuras, Sinn
Axel, Richard
Baron, Miron
Bearn, Alexander Gordon
Bender, Harvey Alan
Benz, Edward John, Jr.
Bieber, Frederick Robert
Blumberg, Baruch Samuel
Bowman, James Edward
Brady, Roscoe O.
Breslow, Jan Leslie
Brown, Michael Stuart
Brown, William Ted
Burdette, Walter James
Chan, Wai-Yee
Chandler, Jerry LeRoy
Choudary, Prabhakara Velagapudi
Cline, Martin Jay
Dahlberg, James Eric
D'Ambrosio, Steven Mario
Desnick, Robert John
Dorn, Gordon Lee
Duckworth, Donna Hardy
Frias, Jaime Luis
Friedman, Orrie Max
Goldstein, David Joel
Goldstein, Joseph Leonard
Graham, John Borden
Hansen, Carl Tams
Hauswirth, William Walter
Hommes, Fritz Aukustinus
Howard-Peebles, Patricia Nell
Huang, Eng-Shang
Joklik, Wolfgang Karl
Kan, Yuet Wai
Kark, Pieter Robert Adriaan
Kennett, Roger Howard
Knudson, Alfred George, Jr.
Kopecko, Dennis J.
Le, Hung Van
Lebo, Roger Van
Lee, Ching Y.
Littlefield, John Walley
Low, Kenneth Brooks, Jr.
Lowy, Douglas Ronald
Lubiniecki, Anthony Stanley
Maniatis, Thomas Peter
Marinus, Martin Gerard
McCandliss, Russell John
Motulsky, Arno Gunther
Mukherjee, Anil Baran
Murphree, Alan Linn
Murray, Robert Fulton, Jr.
Nebert, Daniel Walter
Neel, James Van Gundia
Nightingale, Elena Ottolenghi
Nitowsky, Harold Martin
Nora, James Jackson
Opitz, John Marius
Parisi, Joseph Thomas
Pelzer, Charles Francis
Pestka, Sidney
Popescu, Nicolae Constantin
Richardson, Charles Clifton
Rimoin, David Lawrence
Robbins, Leonard G(ilbert)
Rosenberg, Leon Emanuel
Rothschild, Henry
Salvo, Rino Anthony
Scriver, Charles Robert
Seide, Rochelle Karen
Shalev, Moshe
Shapiro, Burton Leonard
Shaw, Margery Wayne Schlamp
Shine, John
Siminovitch, Louis
Steiner, Donald Frederick
Tanaka, Kay
Testa, Joseph Robert
Thirion, Jean-Paul Joseph
Thompson, Edward Ivins Bradbridge
Tobias, Lawrence Damian
Trosko, James Edward
Vesell, Elliot Saul

Wang, Nancy
Wilson, Gregory Bruce
Winokur, George
Wolman, Sandra R.
Woo, Savio Lau Ching
Yu, Cheng Wou

Gerontology
Alikhan, Mahmood
Aronson, Miriam Klausner
Bartus, Raymond T.
Baxter, Joann Crystal
Branch, Laurence George
Brown, William Ted
Butler, Robert Neil
Calkins, Evan
Chesky, Jeffrey Alan
Dean, Reginald Langworthy, III
Dimant, Jacob
Finch, Caleb Ellicott
Gambert, Steven Ross
Greulich, Richard Curtice
Hayflick, Leonard
Johnson, Thomas Eugene
Kaszniak, Alfred Wayne
Kay, Marguerite M. Boyle
Kenney, Richard Alec
Makinodan, Takashi
Martinson, Ida Marie
Masters, Robert Edward Lee
Rothschild, Henry
Schwartz, Arthur Gerald
Solomon, David Harris
Uno, Hideo
Volicer, Ladislav
Williams, Thomas Franklin

Gynecology. ***See*** **Obstetrics.**

Health services research
Appel, Antoinette Ruth
Babayan, Vigen Khachig
Baker, Herman
Branch, Laurence George
Connelly, John Peter
Costello, Richard James
Densen, Paul Maximillian
Donabedian, Avedis
Edwards, Carl Normand
Frazier, Howard Stanley
Gardin, T. Hershel
Greenlick, Merwyn Ronald
Hannan, Edward Lees
Hoeller, Louise
Horvath, William John
Kennedy, Clive Dale
Lambird, Perry Albert
Lashof, Joyce R. Cohen
Lev, Maurice
Lovell, James Frederick
Morey, Philip Richard
Naito, Herbert K.
Nelson, Bernard William
Neuhauser, Duncan von Briesen
Newman, Jack Huff
Perrin, Edward Burton
Reichgott, Michael J.
Rich, Clayton
Rotenberg, Keith Saul
Sheppard, Louis Clarke
Starfield, Barbara Helen
Stark, Jack Alan
Szlyk, Patricia Carol
Taylor, Roger Norris
Thomas, Charles Samuel
Weinstein, Milton Charles
White, Raymond Petrie, Jr.

Hematology
Akbar, Huzoor
Alcena, Valiere
Amjad, Hassan
Andreeff, Michael
Balcerzak, Stanley Paul
Barger, James Daniel
Beck, William Samson
Benz, Edward John, Jr.
Berlin, Nathaniel Isaac
Bond, William Holmes
Boxer, Laurence Alan
Brinkhous, Kenneth Merle
Brown, Loren Dennis
Bull, Brian Stanley
Burd, Robert M.
Case, Delvyn Caedren, Jr.
Cavins, John Alexander
Chanana, Arjun Dev
Chang, Jae Chan
Chernoff, Amoz Immanuel
Chou, Albert Chung-Ho
Cline, Martin Jay
Conrad, Marcel Edward
Cooper, Herbert Asel
Cooper, Richard Alan
Costea, Nicolas Vincent
Cowan, Dale Harvey
Crews, Harold Richardson
Cronkite, Eugene Pitcher
Dalla-Favera, Riccardo
Davila, Enrique
DeVita, Vincent Theodore, Jr.
Fadulu, Sunday O.
Fairbanks, Grant
Fisher, James W.
Fleming, James Stuart, Jr.
Frenkel, Eugene Phillip
Giblett, Eloise Rosalie
Glas-Greenwalt, Pia
Golde, David William
Goldstein, Jack
Griffin, John Henry
Hampton, James Wilburn
Hauer, Jerome Maurice
Haynes, Duncan Harold
Hoovis, Marvin Lorin
Hyman, Carol Brach
Iatridis, Panayotis George
Jacobson, Leon Orris
Jaffe, Eric Allen
Jain, Sushil Kumar
Joishy, Suresh K.
Joist, Johann Heinrich
Kan, Yuet Wai
Kang, Sungzong
Kasimis, Basil Spiros
Kyle, Robert Arthur
La Celle, Paul Louis

Lawrason, F. Douglas
Levin, Jack
Levin, William Cohn
Lichtman, Marshall A.
Liu, Yung-Pin
London, Irving Myer
Longenecker, Gesina (Louise) Lizana
Louis, John
Lubin, Bertram Harold
Marcoullis, George Panayiotis
Masouredis, Serafeim P.
McDonald, Hemprova Ghosh
McIntyre, Oswald Ross
Mirand, Edwin Albert
Mohammad, Syed Fazal
Monette, Francis C.
Moore, Robert Blaine
Morrison, Francis Secrest
Mrema, John E. K.
Naughton, Brian Arthur
Nelson, Eric Charles
Norton, James Michael
Oishi, Noboru
Omura, George Adolf
Pelus, Louis Martin
Pirofsky, Bernard
Prasad, Ananda Shiva
Rassiga, Anne Louise
Ratnoff, Oscar Davis
Rausen, Aaron Reuben
Rigby, Perry Gardner
Rothenberg, Sheldon Philip
Rowley, Janet Davison
Scott, Roland Boyd
Senhauser, Donald Albert
Shapiro, Donald Michael
Sherry, Sol
Smith, John Bryan
Spaet, Theodore Herzl
Sprague, Charles Cameron
Stein, Ira David
Sydorak, Jaroslava Kuzmycz
Vietti, Teresa Jane
Warth, James Arthur
Whitecar, John P., Jr.
Wiernik, Peter Harris
Wolff, James Alexander
Yoo, Dal

Hematology, marrow transplant
Armitage, James Olen
Robers, Jonathan David
Santos, George Wesley
Strong, Douglas Michael
Thomas, Edward Donnall
Trigg, Michael Edward

Immunology
Abdou, Nabih I.
Ablin, Richard Joel
Adkinson, N. Franklin, Jr.
Albini, Boris
Alspaugh, Margaret Ann
Altman, Leonard
Amos, Dennis Bernard
Archer, Robert Allen
Ariano, Marjorie A.
Bankhurst, Arthur Dale
Bardana, Emil John, Jr.
Barriga, Omar Oscar
Beck, Lee Randolph
Beller, David I.
Bernstein, I. Leonard
Bianco, Celso
Blaese, (Robert) Michael
Boyle, Michael Dermot
Brown, Eric Reeder
Buchholz, Donna Marie
Buehler, Robert John
Bystryn, Jean-Claude
Cavallaro, Joseph John
Chechik, Boris E.
Chen, Yi-Hsiang (Alan)
Chen, Yu Min
Chi, David S.
Chiorazzi, Nicholas
Chused, Thomas M.
Clinton, James Michael
Coe, John Emmons
Collison, Betty Christine
Conway de Macario, Everly
Cox, Donald Stephen
Crowle, Alfred John
Davis, John Mihran
DelVillano, Bert C., Jr.
Dixon, Frank James
Doellgast, George John
Duncan, Robert Leon, Jr.
Duque, Richaro Ernesto
Dyminski, John W(ladyslaw)
Eggert, Frank Michael
Ennis, Francis A.
Epstein, Lois Barth
Foster, Charles Stephen
Fremount, Henry Neil
Friedenson, Bernard Allen
Fu, Shuman
Fudenberg, H. Hugh
Ghebrehiwet, Berhane
Giblett, Eloise Rosalie
Gifford, George Edwin
Goebel, Walther Frederick
Goldman, Armond Samuel
Grimm, Elizabeth Ann
Grogan, James Bigbee
Gusdon, John Paul, Jr.
Hager, Chester Bradley
Hager-Rich, Jean Carol
Halme, Jouko Kalervo
Hamburger, Max I.
Hanna, Michael George, Jr.
Hildreth, Eugene A.
Hillyer, George Van Zandt
Hoffman, Donald Richard
Jain, Naresh Kumar
Jarrett, Mark Paul
Jennette, John Charles
Kabat, Elvin Abraham
Kagey-Sobotka, Anne
Kamiyama, Mikio
Kaplan, Melvin H.
Kellen, John Andrew
Khanna, Pyare Lal
Kier-Schroeder, Ann B.
Kierszenbaum, Felipe
Kim, Yung Dai
Kind, Phyllis Dawn

Kite, Joseph Hiram, Jr.
Kobilinsky, Lawrence
Korn, Joseph H.
Kreft, Anthony Frank, III
Krown, Susan Ellen
Kulczycki, Anthony, Jr.
Kung, Patrick Chung-Shu
Kyle, Robert Arthur
Lamon, Eddie William
Lee, Ching-Li
Leon, Shalom A.
Leung, Christopher Chung-Kit
Levy, Nelson Louis
Litchfield, William John
Lopatin, Dennis Edward
Luderer, Albert August
Lum, Lawrence George
MacDermott, Richard Pratt
Marshall, Gailen Daugherty, Jr.
Marx, James John, Jr.
Masouredis, Serafeim P.
Mathur, Subbi
McCalmon, Robert Thomas, Jr.
McConahey, Patricia Jane
McDevitt, Hugh O'Neill
Meggs, William Joel
Mellors, Robert Charles
Mills, John Alexander
Mitchell, Malcolm Stuart
Morse, Stephen Scott
Munns, Theodore W.
Narahara, Hiromichi Tsuda
Nash, Donald Robert
Naughton, Brian Arthur
Niedermeier, William
Nowell, Peter Carey
Oppenheim, Joost J.
Papsidero, Lawrence Dean
Parker, Charles Ward
Peri, Barbara Ann
Pinnas, Jacob Louis
Pirofsky, Bernard
Plotz, Paul Hunter
Rabin, Bruce S.
Ratajczak, Helen Vosskuhler
Reif, Arnold Eugene
Riviere, George Robert
Rommel, Frederick Allen
Rothberg, Richard Martin
Salvaggio, John Edmond
Saunders, George Cherdron
Schlager, Seymour Irving
Schrohenloher, Ralph Edward
Schur, Peter Henry
Schwartz, Anthony
Shuster, Joseph
Sizemore, Robert Carlen
Smith, Jackson Bruce
Spitzer, Roger Earl
Steinman, Charles Robert
Stone, Marvin Jules
Strober, Samuel
Suzuki, Jon Byron
Taubman, Martin Arnold
Taylor, Roger Norris
Terman, David Stephen
Tsang, Alfred Kwong-Y
Uhr, Jonathan W.
Valentine, Martin Douglas
Vaughan, John Heath
Veltri, Robert William
Volanakis, John Emmanuel
Waldmann, Thomas Alexander
Walia, Amrik Singh
Warren, Kenneth S.
Weiler, John Mayer
Wikel, Stephen Kenneth
Wilson, Gregory Bruce
Wing, Edward Joseph
Woods, Roy
Wright, George G(reen)
Wright, Richard Kenneth
Yoder, John Monley
Zawadzki, Zbigniew Apolinary
Zweiman, Burton

Immunology, cellular engineering
Attallah, Abdelfattah
Bone, Donald Robert
Gillis, Steven
Graziano, Kenneth Donald
Heil, Matthew Francis
Kim, Byung Suk
Lotze, Michael Thomas
Milani, Cyrus Saeed
Moticka, Edward J.
Nathanson, S. David
Paque, Ronald Edward
Reckel, Rudolph Peter
Santos, George Wesley
Seide, Rochelle Karen
Shevach, Ethan Menahem
Steele, Glenn Daniel, Jr.
Steplewski, Zenon
Tom, Baldwin H.
Tsoi, Mang-So
Wagner, Carmen Machado

Immunology, immunogenetics
Babcock, George Francis
Bach, Marilyn Lee
Benacerraf, Baruj
Calame, Kathryn Lee
Carlson, George Alfred, Jr.
Carpenter, Charles Bernard
Clark, Edward Alan
Cohen, Nicholas
Datta, Syamal Kumar
Dixon, Frank James
Fathman, Charles Garrison
Freedman, Herbert Allen
Frelinger, Jeffrey Allen
Fudenberg, H. Hugh
Garovoy, Marvin R.
Gill, Thomas James, III
Kaplan, Alan Marc
Kapp-Pierce, Judith Anne
Kindt, Thomas James
Knowles, Barbara B.
Krause, Richard Michael
Lewis, Alan James
McBride, Raymond Andrew
Mushinski, J. Frederic
Nathenson, Stanley Gail
Pandey, Janardan Prasad
Parham, Peter
Paul, William Erwin

Schanfield, Moses Samuel
Sears, Duane William
Shevach, Ethan Menahem
Solinger, Alan Michael
Sondel, Paul M.
Zaleski, Marek Bohdan

Immunology, immunopharmacology
Attallah, Abdelfattah
Avner, Barry Paul
Bankhurst, Arthur Dale
Bast, Robert Clinton, Jr.
Beaven, Michael Anthony
Benet, Leslie Zachary
Borden, Ernest Carleton
Brunda, Michael John
Cabrera, Edelberto Jose
Evans, Charles Hawes
Feinerman, Burton
Fidler, John Michael
Gillespie, Elizabeth
Gillis, Steven
Godfrey, Henry Philip
Good, Robert Alan
Halonen, Marilyn Jean
Hastings, Robert Clyde
Herscowitz, Herbert Bernard
Huard, Thomas King
Jensen, Keith Edwin
Johnson, Herbert Gardner
Kolodny, Abraham Lewis
Loughman, Barbara Ellen Evers
Loveless, Scott Edward
Lvovsky, Edward Abraham
Mathews, Kenneth Pine
Medzihradsky, Joseph Ladislas
Middleton, Elliott, Jr
Misfeldt, Michael Lee
Norman, Philip Sidney
Page, Michel
Schlager, Seymour Irving
Schrier, Denis J.
Schultz, Richard Michael
Schwartz, Anthony
Sigal, Nolan Howard
Sizemore, Robert Carlen
Stinnett, Jimmy Dwight
Tarr, Melinda Jean
Trigg, Michael Edward
Wong, Stewart
Wood, David Dudley
Yunger, Libby Marie

Immunology, immunotoxicology
Bice, David E.
Duke, Scherer Preston Sanders
Gainer, Joseph Henry
Lawrence, David A.
Megel, Herbert
Northup, Sharon Joan
Olenchock, Stephen Anthony
Pazdernik, Thomas Lowell
Sandusky, Jr. George Earl
Shands, Joseph Walter, Jr.
Sonnenfeld, Gerald
Tarr, Melinda Jean
Vallera, Daniel Attilio
Wong, Stewart

Immunology, infectious diseases
Allen, Robert Charles
Apicella, Michael Allen
Austrian, Robert
Babcock, George Francis
Benenson, Abram Salmon
Blacklow, Neil Richard
Cabrera, Edelberto Jose
Carpenter, Charles Colcock Jones
Cavallaro, Joseph John
Chang, Te-Wen
Choppin, Purnell Whittington
Coe, John Emmons
Cohn, Zanvil A.
Collins, Frank Miles
Cooney, Marion Kathleen
Cramblett, Henry Gaylord
Craven, Donald Edward
Crowle, Alfred John
Cukor, George
Decker, Richard Henry
Diggs, Carter Lee
Domer, Judith Elaine
Dowdle, Walter Reid
Duncan, Robert Leon, Jr.
Edelson, Paul Jeffrey
Ennis, Francis A.
Fadulu, Sunday O.
Fauci, Anthony Stephen
Fenwick, Bradley Willard
Forghani, Bagher
Fox, Eugene Noah
Frank, Michael M.
Friedman, Harvey Michael
Gallin, John I.
Gerety, Robert John
Grayston, J. Thomas
Gross, Peter Alan
Hamburger, Max I.
Harford, Carl Gayler
Harmon, Frederick Robert
Hendley, Joseph Owen
Higashi, Gene Isao
Hirsch, Martin Stanley
Hsu, Clement C.S.
Jacobs, Barbara Beaman
Jain, Naresh Kumar
James, Stephanie Lynn
Jensen, James Burt
Joshi, Jai H.,
Kass, Edward Harold
Katz, Samuel Lawrence
Kirkpatrick, Charles Harvey
Kohl, Steve
Krugman, Saul
Larson, Vivian M.
Lawrence, Henry Sherwood
Maas, Synthea Jean
Marquardt, Warren William
McCarty, Maclyn
McHenry, Martin Christopher
Merigan, Thomas Charles, Jr.
Monjan, Andrew Arthur
Morse, Stephen Scott
Muchmore, Harold Gordon
Neurath, Alexander Robert
O'Connor, G(eorge) Richard
Pan, In-Chang

Parker, John Clarence
Paterson, Philip Y.
Peri, Barbara Ann
Petersdorf, Robert George
Pfau, Charles Julius
Plaut, Andrew George
Quinnan, Gerald Vincent
Reckel, Rudolph Peter
Sanford, Jay Philip
Schooley, Robert Turner
Sinkovics, Joseph G.
Six, Howard Ronald
Sonnenfeld, Gerald
Targowski, Stanislaw Pytkowski
Volkman, Alvin
Walker, David Hughes
Weller, Peter Fahey
Wikel, Stephen Kenneth
Wing, Edward Joseph
Winn, Richard Earl

Immunology, neuroimmunology
Calabrese, Vincent Paul
Cohen, Nicholas
Cook, Stuart Donald
Dafny, Nachum Frenkel
Day, Eugene Davis
del Cerro, Manuel
Grota, Lee James
Hafler, David Allen
Korenyi-Both, Andras Levente
Kori, Shashidhar Halappa
Lees, Marjorie Berman
Lisak, Robert Philip.
Lublin, Fred David
Lyons, Michael Joseph
McIntosh, Tracy Kahl
Misfeldt, Michael Lee
Paterson, Philip Y.
Resch, Joseph Anthony
Shearer, David Ross
Sydorak, Jaroslava Kuzmycz
Williams, Curtis Alvin, Jr.

Immunology, transplantation
Alexander, James Wesley
Amos, Dennis Bernard
Bach, Marilyn Lee
Carpenter, Charles Bernard
Chatterjee, Satya Narayan
Cone, Robert Edward
Datta, Surjit Kumar
Donawick, William Joseph
Fawwaz, Rashid Adib
Garovoy, Marvin R.
Gill, Thomas James, III
Jacobs, Barbara Beaman
Jacobson, Leon Orris
Joison, Julio
Kung, Patrick Chung-Shu
Lafferty, Kevin J
Lawrence, Henry Sherwood
Lobo, Peter Isaac
Lum, Lawrence George
Maki, Takashi
Mathur, Subbi
Medzihradsky, Joseph Ladislas
Montefusco, Cheryl Marie
Munda, Rino
Nathenson, Stanley Gail
Oh, Jung Hee
Preffer, Frederic Ira
Rabin, Bruce S.
Rapaport, Felix Theodosius
Rearden, Carole Ann
Sears, Duane William
Simonian, Simon John
Stiller, Calvin Ralph
Strom, Terry Barton
Strong, Douglas Michael
Tsoi, Mang-So
Zaleski, Marek Bohdan

Internal medicine
Aagaard, George Nelson
Achord, James Lee
Alderman, Michael Harris
Alexander, Jonathan
Apicella, Michael Allen
Archer, Juanita Almetta Hinnant
Austen, K(arl) Frank
Azarnoff, Daniel Lester
Barbosa-Saldivar, Jose Luis
Becker, E(rnest) Lovell
Bedell, George Noble
Bell, Norman Howard
Bennett, Joe Claude
Biglieri, Edward George
Bilitch, Michael
Blewitt, George Augustine
Bloomfield, Saul S.
Blythe, William Brevard
Boudoulas, Harisios
Braunwald, Eugene
Briggs, Arthur Harold
Bulger, Roger James
Burrell, Craig Donald
Burwell, Edward Langdon
Burzynski, Stanislaw Rajmund
Caldwell, Glyn Gordon
Calesnick, Benjamin
Calkins, Evan
Callen, Jeffrey Phillip
Carbone, Paul Peter
Carpenter, Charles Colcock Jones
Castle, Charles Hilmon
Cha, Se Do
Challoner, David Reynolds
Charan, Nirmal Biswas
Chase, John David
Cherkasky, Martin
Chernoff, Amoz Immanuel
Cheung, Joseph Yat-sing
Chiorazzi, Nicholas
Clark, Mervin Leslie
Cluff, Leighton Eggertsen
Cohn, Major Lloyd
Conn, Jerome W.
Cooper, Edward Sawyer
Costanza, Mary E.
Crane, Robert
Curd, John Gary
Dearing, William Hill
Deedwania, Prakash Chandra
Desser, Kenneth Barry
Dickie, Helen Aird
Dietschy, John Maurice
Dimant, Jacob
Dougherty, Joseph Charles
Drayer, Jan Ignatius
Einhorn, Daniel
Ertel, Norman H.
Ettinger, David Seymour
Ettinger, Philip Owen
Farber, Saul Joseph
Farmer, Richard Gilbert
Farshidi, Ardeshir B.
Fathman, Charles Garrison
Feinstein, Alvan Richard
Felts, William Robert, Jr.
Franciosa, Joseph Anthony
Frazier, Howard Stanley
Frei, Emil, III
Frohlich, Edward David
Frommer, J. Pedro
Gallin, John I.
Ganguly, Sunilendu Narayan
Garcia, Julio M.
Gault, N.L., Jr.
Gheorghiade, Mihai
Giorgi, Elsie Agnes
Goldberg, Leon Isadore
Goldman, Lee
Goldsmith, Stanley Joseph
Graham, David Tredway
Grenfell, Raymond Frederic
Grob, David
Hadler, Nortin M.
Hadlock, Daniel C.
Hamilton, Carlos Robert, Jr.
Haviland, James West
Herbert, Victor
Hildreth, Eugene A.
Hogness, John Rusten
Hoyumpa, Anastacio Maningo
Hunter, Harry Laymond
Hyman, Edward Sidney
Iatridis, Panayotis George
James, Thomas Naum
Johns, Dearing Ward
Johnson, David Gregory
Kabadi, Udaya Manohar
Kahn, Thomas
Kaplan, Kenneth Charles
Kassan, Stuart S.
Kay, Marguerite M. Boyle
Kefalides, Nicholas Alexander
Kirsner, Joseph Barnett
Klausner, Steven Charles
Kolodny, Abraham Lewis
Komanicky, Pavel
Krothapalli, Radha Krishna
Krupp, Marcus Abraham
Kushner, Irving
Laddu, Atul Ramchandra
Laskin, Oscar Larry
Lawrason, F. Douglas
Leaf, Alexander
Levy, Robert Isaac
London, Irving Myer
Lopez-Ovejero, Jorge Andres
Lutas, Elizabeth M.
Lyons, Kenneth Paul
Macdonald, John Stephen
Mahapatra, Rajat Kanti
Marshall, Gailen Daugherty, Jr.
McHenry, Martin Christopher
Metzger, W. James
Mills, John Alexander
Mitchell, Jere Holloway
Mohiuddin, Syed Maqdoom
Motz, Robin Owen
Muchmore, Harold Gordon
Mukherjee, Anil Baran
Murray, John Frederic
Murray, Robert Fulton, Jr.
Murthy, Vishnubhakta Shrinivas
Naides, Stanley Jay
Nelson, Harold Stanley
Okada, Robert Dean
Olson, Kenneth Barrie
Orloff, Jack
Overweg, Norbert Ido Albert
Pagano, Joseph Stephen
Patsch, Josef Rudolf
Petersdorf, Robert George
Pettinger, William A.
Pinnas, Jacob Louis
Plotz, Paul Hunter
Plymate, Stephen Rex
Post, Joseph
Rajan, Kannan Ramalingam
Reidenberg, Marcus Milton
Relman, Arnold Seymour
Richardson, David Walthall
Richardson, Joseph Hill
Rigby, Perry Gardner
Rimoin, David Lawrence
Rosenberg, Leon Emanuel
Roth, Harold P.
Rubenstein, Arthur Harold
Rubenstein, Edward
Salvaggio, John Edmond
Sandstead, Harold Hilton
Sanford, Jay Philip
Schade, Robert Richard
Schmid, Rudi Rudolf
Schreck, David Michael
Schreiber, Sidney S.
Schultz, Alvin Leroy
Schwartz, Mortimer Leonard
Schwarz, Anton J.
Scribner, Belding Hibbard
Segal, Bernard Louis
Seldin, Donald Wayne
Shambaugh, George Elmer, III
Shortliffe, Edward Hance
Silverstein, Emanuel
Smith, Jackson Bruce
Smith, Lynwood Herbert
Smith, Thomas Woodward
Soskel, Norman Terry
Spilker, Bert
Stambaugh, John Edgar, Jr.
Steinman, Charles Robert
Stemmler, Edward Joseph
Summers, William Koopmans
Sutnick, Alton Ivan
Thier, Samuel Osiah
Thomas, Lewis
Thompson, Alvin Jerome
Thompson, Wilmer Leigh
Tisi, Gennaro Michael
Tuma, Samir Naif
Vaziri, Nostratola Dabir
Veray, Francisco X.
Verbalis, Joseph George
Wacker, Warren Ernest Clyde
Wann, Lee Samuel
Wanner, Adam
Ward, John Robert
Ward, Louis Emmerson
Weg, John Gerard
Weiner, Murray
Weisberg, Aaron
Winn, Richard Earl
Wintrobe, Maxwell Myer
Woods, Roy
Yielding, K. Lemone
Zawada, Edward Thaddeus, Jr.

Laser. *See* **LASER, Medicine.**

Microbiology. *See also* **BIOLOGY.**
Ahnell, Joseph Eugene
Albach, Richard Allen
Albrecht, Thomas Blair
Alexander, Edward Russell
Austrian, Robert
Bezkorovainy, Anatoly
Boyle, Michael Dermot
Bradner, William Turnbull
Brown, Jay Clark
Chen, Kirk Ching Shyong
Clinton, James Michael
Collins, Frank Miles
Collins, Michael Thomas
Consigli, Richard Albert
Cornett, James Bryce
Diggs, Carter Lee
Dorn, Gordon Lee
Duffey, Paul Stephen
Ehrlich, Richard
Elwell, Lynn Paul
Fine, Donald Lee
Francis, Robert Dorl
Gabriel, Othmar
Georgiades, Jerzy Alexander
Gerhardt, Philipp
Guttman, Helene Nathan
Hawley, Robert John
Hughes, John Henry
Hutchison, Dorris Jeannette
Kilbourne, Edwin Dennis
Kim, Charles Wesley
Kite, Joseph Hiram, Jr.
Kohn, Dennis Fredrich
Kumar, Vijaya Buddhiraju
Lehman, John Michael
Levner, Mark Henry
Macasaet, Francisco Friginal
McCarty, Maclyn
Miller, Richard Lynn
Moe, James Burton
Nash, Donald Robert
Novick, William Joseph, Jr.
Olenchock, Stephen Anthony
Parisi, Joseph Thomas
Parker, John Clarence
Parsons, James Eugene
Pirtle, Eugene Claude
Read, Ralston Baker
Reed, Norman Duane
Richardson, Carol Lynn
Robinson, Harry John
Rommel, Frederick Allen
Smith, Ralph Earl
Stewart, John Alvin
Tseng, Jeenan
Walker, Clay Brown
Woodhour, Allen Francis
Wright, George G(reen)

Microscopy
Anderson, Mauritz Gunnar
Bertalanffy, Felix Dionysius
Fremount, Henry Neil
Hart, Raymond Kenneth
Hillman, Elizabeth Ann
Leblond, Charles Philipps
Lee, Tony Jer-Fu
Mc Gregor, Douglas Hugh
Miskimen, George William
Murayama, Makio
Norton, William Nicholson, Jr.
Prewitt, Russell Lawrence
Prien, Samuel David
Schoknecht, Jean Donze
Steinbach, Arden Lynn
Strauss, Elliott William

Nephrology
Albini, Boris
Beck, Nama
Becker, E(rnest) Lovell
Bello-Reuss, Elsa N.
Berlyne, Geoffrey Merton
Berndt, William Oscar
Blythe, William Brevard
Bonventre, Joseph Vincent
Brautbar, Nachman
Brenner, Barry Morton
Butkus, Donald Eugene
Carter, Mary Kathleen
Cavallo, Tito
Chan, Yun Lai
Chevalier, Robert Louis
Chou, Shyan-Yih
Covit, Andrew B.
Davis, James (Othello)
Dougherty, Joseph Charles
Duarte, Cristobal G.
DuBose, Thomas Durward, Jr.
Falk, Sandor A.
Farber, Saul Joseph
Frommer, J. Pedro
Genest, Jacques
Giebisch, Gerhard Hans
Goldfarb, Stanley
Huang, Chia Ming
Kahn, Thomas
Kim, Jin Kyung
Klahr, Saulo
Krothapalli, Radha Krishna
Leaf, Alexander
Levinsky, Norman George
Lobo, Peter Isaac
Maack, Thomas Michael
Malluche, Hartmut Horst
Mandal, Anil Kumar
Metcoff, Jack
Michael, Alfred Frederick
Misra, Raghunath Prasad
O'Connor, Daniel Thomas, Jr.
Oh, Jung Hee
Orloff, Jack
Pak, Charles Y.C.
Rabkin, Ralph
Seldin, Donald Wayne
Selkurt, Ewald Erdman
Smith, Lynwood Herbert
Spitzer, Adrian
Spitzer, Roger Earl
Stiller, Calvin Ralph
Tannen, Richard Laurence
Thier, Samuel Osiah
Toback, F(rederick) Gary
Tuma, Samir Naif
Vaziri, Nostratola Dabir
Walser, Mackenzie
Zawada, Edward Thaddeus, Jr.

Neurology
Abrams, Gary Mitchell
Ackerman, Robert Harold
Allocca, John Anthony
Asbury, Arthur Knight
Barnett, Henry Joseph Macauley
Bates, Stephen Roger Denis
Bergey, Gregory Kent
Biber, Michael Peter
Brooke, Michael Howard
Busis, Neil Amdur
Cahill, David Wooding
Caviness, Verne Strudwick, Jr.
Cedarbaum, Jesse Michael
Chu, Nai-Shin
Conomy, John Paul
Cook, Stuart Donald
Davis, James Norman
Demeter, Steven
Deshmukh, Vinod Dhundiraj
Duchowny, Michael Samuel
Elble, Rodger Jacob, Jr.
Elizan, Teresita S.
Fahn, Stanley
Ferrendelli, James Anthony
Fromm, Gerhard Hermann
Galaburda, Albert Mark
Gallagher, Brian Boru
Gilman, Sid
Glaser, Gilbert Herbert
Goldstein, Murray
Goust, Jean-Michel Christian
Hafler, David Allen
Hallett, Mark
Hamill, Robert Wallace
Harter, Donald Harry
Hekmatpanah, Javad
Henderson, Victor Warren
Heyer, Eric John
Hogan, Edward Leo
Housepian, Edgar Minas
Hsu, Chung Y.
Hughes, John Russell
Kasarskis, Edward Joseph
Kennedy, Charles
Kraig, Richard Paul
Krall, Ronald Lee
Kuncl, Ralph William
Levy, David Edward
Lisak, Robert Philip.
Lublin, Fred David
Malkoff, Donald Burton
Manyam, Bala Venktesha
Marwah, Joe
Mayer, Richard Frederick
McLean, John Robert
McNamara, James O'Connell
Mesulam, M. Marsel
Mitsumoto, Hiroshi
Moore, Robert Yates
Nathanson, Morton
Ng, Lorenz Keng Yong
Ohata, Carl Andrews
Pearlman, Alan Lee
Philippart, Michel
Pickett, Jackson Brittain Elbridge
Resch, Joseph Anthony
Rimel, Rebecca Webster
Roel, Lawrence Edmund
Rosen, Arthur D.
Ross, Diana Lynn
Rowland, Lewis Phillip
Ruff, Robert Louis
Sainati, Stephen Mitchell
Sanders, Donald Benjamin
Schwartz, William Joseph
Seil, Fredrick John
Sheridan, Philip Henry
Silberberg, Donald H.
Slevin, John Thomas
Swaiman, Kenneth Fred
Tourtellotte, Wallace William
Traub, Roger Dennis
Wiley, Ronald Gordon
Willems, William Joseph
Winter, Arthur

Neuroscience. *See* **NEUROSCIENCE.**

Nuclear medicine. *See also* **Radiology.**
Buchsbaum, Donald Jay
Chaudhuri, Tapan Kumar
Clanton, Jeffrey Alan
Donati, Robert Mario
Ebert, Marlin J.
Evens, Ronald Gene
Fawwaz, Rashid Adib
Freeman, Leonard Murray
Ginos, James Zissis
Glassman, Armand Barry
Goldsmith, Stanley Joseph
Grissom, Michael Phillip
Holman, B. Leonard
Llaurado, Josep G.
Loken, Merle Kenneth
Luckett, Larry Wayne
Lyons, Kenneth Paul
MacIntyre, William James
Malamud, Herbert
McCombs, Rollin Koenig
McEllistrem, Marcus Thomas
Mericle, David Allen
Myers, William Graydon
Opler, Stanley Ronal
Oster, Zvi Herman
Pierson, Richard Norris, Jr.
Pollack, R. Stuart
Rao, Dandamudi Vishnuvardhana
Schelbert, Heinrich Ruediger
Seevers, Robert Harmon, Jr.
Segal, Barry M.
Siegel, Michael Elliot
Smith, Charles Irvel
Verstandig, Charles Coleman
Wackers, Frans Jozef Thomas
Weber, David Alexander
Williams, Gerald Albert
Zaret, Barry Lewis

Nutrition
Babayan, Vigen Khachig
Badger, Thomas Mark
Baker, Herman
Bartel, Lavon Lee
Bernardis, Lee Livius
Bessman, Samuel Paul
Bieber, Mark Allan
Birt, Diane Feickert
Bistrian, Bruce Ryan
Black, Arthur Leo
Brautbar, Nachman
Bull, Leonard Seth
Carroll, Kenneth Kitchener
Chan, Wai-Yee
Childs, Marian Tolbert
Chinn, Kenneth Sai-Keung
Crosby, Lon Owen
Darby, William Jefferson, Jr.
Dawson, Earl Bliss
DeWys, William Dale
Ellenbogen, Leon
Gable, Carol Brignoli
Gaut, Zane Noel
Hankes, Lawrence Valentine
Hegsted, David Mark
Herbert, Victor
Hodges, Robert Edgar
Holloway, Caroline Tobia
Holman, Ralph Theodore
Horwitz, David Larry
Jain, Sushil Kumar
Janghorbani, Morteza
Johnson, Wayne Allan
Kokatnur, Mohan Gundo
Kramer, Lois Beth
Lands, William Edward Mitchell
Lazicki-Lakshmanan, Florence Mary
Lei, David K.Y.
Leung, Philip Min-Bun
Lieberman, Harris Ritchie
Madura, James Anthony
Matthews, Dwight Earl
Mendeloff, Albert Irwin
Metcoff, Jack
Milner, John A.
Morgan, Brian Leslie Gordon
Nakamoto, Tetsuo
Nichols, Buford Lee, Jr.
Nordlie, Robert Conrad
O'Dell, Boyd Lee
Omaye, Stanley Teruo
Oser, Bernard Levussove
Pitchumoni, Capecomorin S.
Poydock, Mary Eymard
Prasad, Ananda Shiva
Purvis, George Allen
Radcliffe, John David
Rassin, David Keith
Resnick, Oscar
Rogers, Quinton Ray
Sachan, Dileep S.
Sandstead, Harold Hilton
Sanslone, William Robert
Shank, Robert Ely
Shanklin, Douglas Radford
Sisson, Thomas Randolph Clinton
Spiller, Gene Alan
Stinnett, Jimmy Dwight
Sudweeks, Earl Max
Tamura, Tsunenobu
Tulp, Orien Lee
Walser, Mackenzie
Whedon, George Donald
Winick, Myron
Winterfeldt, Esther

Obstetrics and gynecology
Bellina, Joseph Henry
Gusdon, John Paul, Jr.
Hollis, Bruce Warren
Jewelewicz, Raphael
Jones, Howard Wilbur, Jr.
Kirschbaum, Thomas Harry
Lee, Si Gaph
Prystowsky, Harry
Stenchever, Morton Albert
Toth, Attila
White, Rolfe Downing
Zachert, Virginia
Zuspan, Frederick Paul

Obstetrics, gynecological oncology. *See also* **Oncology.**
Abdulhay, Gazi
Pattillo, Roland A.
Peterson, Rudolph Nicholas
Prem, Konald Arthur
Thigpen, James Tate
van Nagell, John Rensselaer, Jr.

Obstetrics, maternal and fetal medicine
Case, Marvin Theodore
Cohen, Wayne Roy
Fabro, Sergio Edigio
Hess, Orvan Walter
Kretchmer, Norman
Maulik, Debabrata
Miller, Richard Kermit
Mueller-Heubach, Eberhard August
Sokol, Robert James
Towbin, Abraham
Zuspan, Frederick Paul

Obstetrics, reproductive biology
Abel, Ernest Lawrence
Cohen, Wayne Roy
Fabro, Sergio Edigio
Fahim, Mostafa Safwat
Fajer, Abram Bencjan
Gustafsson, Borje Karl
Halme, Jouko Kalervo
Harper, Michael John Kennedy
Mueller-Heubach, Eberhard August

Naftolin, Frederick
Pattillo, Roland A.
Sairam, Malur Ramaswamy
Sturtevant, Frank Milton

Obstetrics, reproductive endocrinology
Carsten, Mary E.
Chatterton, Robert Treat, Jr.
Eldridge, John Charles
Lee, Si Gaph
Nachreiner, Raymond Francis
Penn, Benjamin Grant
Reddy, Vangala Venkatarami
Sairam, Malur Ramaswamy
Shah, Surendra Poonamchand

Oncology. ***See also*** **Cancer research.**
Abdulhay, Gazi
Aisenberg, Alan C.
Aisner, Joseph
Amols, Howard Ira
Armitage, James Olen
Banks, William Louis, Jr.
Bitran, Jacob David
Brown, Eric Reeder
Brown, Loren Dennis
Bunn, Paul Axtell, Jr.
Burd, Robert M.
Cabanillas, Fernando
Carbone, Paul Peter
Case, Delvyn Caedren, Jr.
Castro, Joseph Ronald
Chang, Jae Chan
Chatterjee, Sunil Kumar
Chernicoff, David Paul
Chin, Hong W.
Chung, Chung-Taik
Cole, Jack Westley
Coleman, C. Norman
Conrad, Marcel Edward
Corder, Michael Paul
Costanza, Mary E.
Creech, Richard Hearne
Davis, Thomas Edward
Donegan, William Laurence
Drago, Joseph Rosario
Drapkin, Robert L.
Dreizen, Samuel
Dutcher, Janice Phillips
Erturk, Erdogan
Ettinger, David Seymour
Fabian, Carol J.
Frenkel, Eugene Phillip
Friedman, Nathan Baruch
Fu, Karen King-Wah
Gensler, Helen Lynch
Glicksman, Arvin Sigmund
Golde, David William
Goldsmith, Michael Allen
Golomb, Frederick Martin
Greenwald, Edward S.
Haas, Thomas Stewart
Hadlock, Daniel C.
Harshbarger, John Carl, Jr.
Henderson, Isaac Craig
Hoge, Arthur Franklin, Jr.
Holder, Walter Dalton, Jr.
Hoopes, Paul Jack
Hoovis, Marvin Lorin
Hunter, Harry Laymond
Hyman, Carol Brach
Joishy, Suresh K.
Joshi, Jai H.,
Kaplan, Richard Stephen
Kashmiri, Syed V.S.
Kasimis, Basil Spiros
Kennedy, Byrl James
Lane, Daniel McNeel
Lee, Yeu-Tsu Margaret
Levin, William Cohn
Levine, Arthur Samuel
Long, Harry Joseph
Lotlikar, Prabhakar Dattaram
Lyman, Gary Herbert
Marchetta, Frank Carmelo
Marks, Paul Alan
Maruyama, Yosh
Mc Credie, Kenneth Blair
McIntyre, Oswald Ross
Miller, Elizabeth Cavert
Miller, James Alexander
Mitchell, Malcolm Stuart
Moertel, Charles George
Nag, Subir K.
Nathanson, Larry
Nathanson, S. David
Neidhart, James Allen
Nelson, Diana Furst
Ochoa, Manuel, Jr.
Oettgen, Herbert F.
Oishi, Noboru
Olsson, Carl Alfred
Omura, George Adolf
Oster, Martin William
Park, Chan Hyung
Petrakis-Pawson, Stella
Pitot, Henry Clement
Poiesz, Bernard Joseph
Preston, Frederick Willard
Raam, Shanthi
Rassiga, Anne Louise
Rausen, Aaron Reuben
Salcman, Michael
Schally, Andrew Victor
Shnider, Bruce I.
Siegel, Stuart Elliott
Silver, Hulbert Keyes Belford
Sondel, Paul M.
Steeves, Richard Allison
Stehlin, John Sebastian, Jr.
Sternhagen, Charles James
Sugarbaker, Everett Van Dyke
Talbot, Jr. Timothy Ralph
Taren, James Arthur
Tefft, Melvin
Temple, Walley John
Thigpen, James Tate
Thomas, Edward Donnall
Tormey, Douglass C.
Umsawasdi, Theera
Urano, Muneyasu
Van Echo, David Andrew
Vaughn, Clarence Benjamin
Vietti, Teresa Jane
Weinstein, I. Bernard
Wilcox, Patti Marie
Yoo, Dal
Zawadzki, Zbigniew Apolinary

Oncology, chemotherapy
Alcena, Valiere
Al-Sarraf, Muhyi
Amjad, Hassan
Arseneau, James Charles
Bahner, Carl Tabb
Baker, Laurence Howard
Barber, Ann McDonald
Bitran, Jacob David
Bond, William Holmes
Buckman, Robert William
Cabanillas, Fernando
Chiuten, Delia Fung She
Cowan, Dale Harvey
Crabtree, Gerald Winston
Davila, Enrique
Davis, Thomas Edward
Drapkin, Robert L.
Frei, Emil, III
Fujimoto, Takeo
Garcia, Julio M.
Geran, Ruth I.
Goldsmith, Michael Allen
Hall, Thomas Christopher
Hande, Kenneth Robert
Houghton, Janet Anne
Houghton, Peter James
Howell, Stephen Barnard
Jones, Russell Allen
Korytnyk, Wsewolod
Lipton, Allan
Long, Harry Joseph
Louis, John
Loveless, Scott Edward
Luce, James Kent
Macdonald, John Stephen
Magrath, Ian Trevor
Marx, James John, Jr.
Merrin, Claude Emile Andre
Morris, Don Melvin
Nathanson, Larry
Nelson, Eric Charles
Ohnuma, Takao
Olson, Kenneth Barrie
Oster, Martin William
Petrakis-Pawson, Stella
Presant, Cary A.
Reitemeier, Richard Joseph
Roberts, Joseph
Rutman, Robert J.
Samy, Anantha T. S.
Sartiano, George P.
Shapiro, Donald Michael
Shnider, Bruce I.
Stefanini, Mario
Stewart, David James
Stolinsky, David C.
Tannock, Ian Frederick
Trown, Patrick Willoughby
Ultmann, John Ernest
Vaughn, Clarence Benjamin
Vogel, Charles Lewis
Wallace, Harold James, Jr.
Warrell, Raymond Paul
Watanabe, Kouichi
Wheeler, Glynn Pearce
Whitecar, John P., Jr.

Oncology, cell study
Andreeff, Michael
Breitman, Theodore Ronald
Busch, Harris
Chen, Yi-Hsiang (Alan)
Culp, Lloyd Anthony
Deschner, Eleanor Elizabeth
Dwivedi, Chandradhar
Ebert, Paul Stoudt
Epstein, Alan Lee
Ferraro, Bernadette Angela
Fisher, Paul B.
Glaser, Ronald
Heil, Matthew Francis
Lehman, John Michael
Lewis, Andrew Morris, Jr.
Magrath, Ian Trevor
Matchett, Arnett
Rapp, Ulf Ruediger
Robberson, Donald L.
Tejada, Francisco
Tomei, L. David
Williams, Gary Murray

Ophthalmology
Armstrong, Donald
Bazan, Nicholas Guillermo
Bettelheim, Frederick Abraham
Beyer-Mears, Annette
Bores, Leo Daniel
Campbell, Charles John
Candia, Oscar A.
Colasanti, Brenda Karen
Crenner, James Charles
Dawkins, Barry Gilbert
del Cerro, Manuel
Foster, Charles Stephen
Gills, James Pitzer
Goldbaum, Michael Henry
Goodman, Arden Patricia
Gragoudas, Evangelos Stelios
Green, Keith
Greiner, Jack Volker
Jernigan, Howard Maxwell, Jr.
Kaplan, Henry Jerrold
Kulkarni, Prasad Shrikrishna
Kupfer, Carl
Laing, Ronald Albert
LaVail, Matthew Maurice
Leon, Judith Merer
Lotti, Victor Joseph
Morse, Peter Hodges
Murphree, Alan Linn
Newell, Frank William
O'Connor, G(eorge) Richard
Reaves, Troy Albert, Jr.
Records, Raymond Edwin
Sadun, Alfredo Arrigo Umberto
Samuelson, Don Arthur
Shoch, David Eugene
Streeten, Barbara Anne Wiard
Tripathi, Ramesh Chandra
Waitzman, Morton Benjamin
Whitley, Robert David
Wolbarsht, Myron Lee

Orthopedics
Brown, Richard Hart
Chan, Donald Pin Kwan
Compere, Clinton Lee
Cooper, Reginald Rudyard
Cruess, Richard Leigh
Frankel, Victor Hirsch
Friedlaender, Gary Elliott
Greer, James Alan
Hargens, Alan Robert
Herndon, James Henry
Ingram, Alvin John
Jay, Richard Martin
Krag, Martin Hans
Levin, Stephen Michael
Matthews, Leslie Scott
Opgrande, John Donald
Reider, Bruce
Salter, Robert B.
Schwartz, Edith Richmond
Stith, William Joseph
Walter, Thomas Harry

Otorhinolaryngology
Bernstein, Joel M.
Black, Franklin Owen
Blitzer, Andrew
Cummings, Charles William
Dormer, Kenneth John
Farmer, Joseph Clarence, Jr.
Hast, Malcolm Howard
Homburger, Freddy
Jako, Geza Julius
Krause, Charles Joseph
Lim, David Jong Jai
Ludlow, Christy Leslie
Malmgren, Leslie Theodore, Jr.
Mc Cabe, Brian Francis
Nielsen, Donald Wayne
Parkin, James Lamar
Schacht, Jochen Heinrich
Sismanis, Aristides
Stockwell, Charles Warren

Pathology
Abrams, Gerald David
Allen, Robert Carter
Arenberg, Irving Kaufman
Aronson, Stanley Maynard
Auerbach, Oscar
Barger, James Daniel
Benditt, Earl Philip
Benz, Edward John
Bond, Meredith Gene
Bowman, James Edward
Brinkhous, Kenneth Merle
Brown, Arnold Lanehart, Jr.
Bruns, David Eugene
Bull, Brian Stanley
Cardiff, Robert Darrell
Cavallo, Tito
Chedid, Antonio
Cohen, Samuel M.
Conn, Rex Boland, Jr.
Cooper, Robert Arthur, Jr.
Crain, Barbara Jean
Damjanov, Ivan
Diamandopoulos, George Theodore
Duque, Richaro Ernesto
Eble, John Nelson
Elliott, George Algimon
Fitch, Frank Wesley
Folse, Dean Sydney
Forman, Donald T.
Fornace, Albert Joseph, Jr.
Frenkel, Jacob Karl
Friedman, Nathan Baruch
Fullmer, Harold Milton
Furth, John Jacob
Ghetti, Bernardino
Glassman, Armand Barry
Goldfischer, Sidney Leo
Goltz, Robert William
Gottlieb, Leonard Solomon
Gown, Allen Michael
Gruhn, John George
Haas, Thomas Stewart
Hammond, Mary Elizabeth Hale
Handorf, Charles Russell
Haudenschild, Christian C.
Heffner, Reid Russell, Jr.
Hellstrom, H. Richard
Hu, Chung-Hong
Inhorn, Stanley Lee
Jennette, John Charles
Johnson, Anne Bradstreet
Joist, Johann Heinrich
Kashgarian, Michael
Kikkawa, Yutaka
Kirschstein, Ruth L.
Kithier, Karel
Koestner, Adalbert
Korenyi-Both, Andras Levente
Koss, Leopold G.
Lagunoff, David
Lambird, Perry Albert
Lamm, Michael Emanuel
Lane, Bernard Paul
Lee, Sin Hang
Lev, Maurice
Liotta, Lance A.
Longnecker, Daniel Sidney
Lynch, Denis Patrick
Macasaet, Francisco Friginal
Mandal, Anil Kumar
McBride, Raymond Andrew
McClure, Harold Monroe
McCully, Kilmer Serjus
Mc Gregor, Douglas Hugh
Mellors, Robert Charles
Mihm, Martin Charles, Jr.
Mikat, Eileen Marie
Milani, Cyrus Saeed
Min, Kyung-Whan
Misra, Raghunath Prasad
Mowry, Robert Wilbur
Nettesheim, Paul
Newton, William Allen, Jr.
Normann, Sigurd Johns
Nowell, Peter Carey
O'Donoghue, John (Lipomi)
Page, Roy Christopher
Pavelic, Zlatko Paul
Pertschuk, Louis Philip
Pitot, Henry Clement
Pizzo, Salvatore Vincent
Pour, Parviz M.
Powell, Henry Caleb
Press, Michael Fredrick
Pribor, Hugo Casimer
Puchtler, Holde
Race, George Justice
Rifkin, Barry Richard
Robert, Andre
Ross, Russell
Roth, Sanford Irwin
Rowlands, David Thomas
Russo, Irma Haydee Alvarez
Rust, John Howard
Saffiotti, Umberto
Saffitz, Jeffrey Ernest
Sandusky, Jr. George Earl
Saunders, George Cherdron
Senhauser, Donald Albert
Shanklin, Douglas Radford
Shorter, Roy Gerrard
Shrestha, Buddhi Man
Sirica, Alphonse Eugene
Sogandares-Bernal, Franklin
Sommers, Sheldon Charles
St. Clair, Richard William
Stefanini, Mario
Stout, Landon Clarke, Jr.
Stowell, Robert Eugene
Streeten, Barbara Anne Wiard
Sudilovsky, Oscar
Swarm, Richard Lee
Szabo, Sandor
Till, Gerd Oskar
Tilton, Ronald Gene
Toth, Attila
Towbin, Abraham
Townsend, Frank Marion
Tripathi, Ramesh Chandra
Upton, Arthur Canfield
Uzman, Betty Geren
Walker, David Hughes
Waller, Bruce Frank
Ward, Peter Allan
Widder, Kenneth Jon
Wilkinson, David Stanley
Williams, Gary Murray
Yesner, Raymond

Parasitology
Agosin, Moises K.
Albach, Richard Allen
Barriga, Omar Oscar
Beaver, Paul Chester
Brown, Stephen James
Courtney, Charles Hill, III
Dusanic, Donald Gabriel
Ferris, Deam Hunter
Frenkel, Jacob Karl
Gaafar, Sayed M.
Healey, Mark Calvin
Higashi, Gene Isao
Hillyer, George Van Zandt
Hogan, Yvonne Holland
Holloway, Harry Lee, Jr.
Honigberg, Bronislaw Mark
James, Stephanie Lynn
Jensen, James Burt
Kazacos, Kevin Robert
Kierszenbaum, Felipe
Kim, Charles Wesley
Langlands, Robert Phelan
Miller, Lynne Cathy
Nogueira, Nadia
Peanasky, Robert Joseph
Pfefferkorn, Elmer Roy
Poinar, George Orlo, Jr.
Race, George Justice
Rapmund, Garrison
Rota, Gian-Carlo
Silverman, Paul Hyman
Sogandares-Bernal, Franklin
Vande Hey, Robert Clarence
Weller, Peter Fahey
Weller, Thomas Huckle
Young, Frank N(elson), Jr.

Pediatrics
Abel, Ernest Lawrence
August, Gilbert Paul
Baird, Henry Welles, III
Bates, Stephen Roger Denis
Behrman, Richard Elliot
Blaese, (Robert) Michael
Blim, Richard Don
Boxer, Laurence Alan
Caplan, Daniel Bennett
Chevalier, Robert Louis
Connelly, John Peter
Cooper, Louis Zucker
Cramblett, Henry Gaylord
Dearborn, Dorr Gellatly
Deibel, Rudolf
Denny, Floyd Wolfe, Jr.
Euler, Arthur Ray
Frias, Jaime Luis
Fujimoto, Takeo
Gartner, Lawrence Mitchel
Gerety, Robert John
Goldman, Armond Samuel
Goldstein, David Joel
Good, Robert Alan
Hendley, Joseph Owen
Hersher, Leonard
Izant, Robert James, Jr.
Jay, Richard Martin
Katz, Michael
Katz, Samuel Lawrence
Kohl, Steve
Kretchmer, Norman
Krugman, Saul
Leventhal, Brigid Gray
Littlefield, John Walley
Lubin, Bertram Harold
Martinson, Ida Marie
Michael, Alfred Frederick
Miller, C. Arden
Mulcihy, Casey Thomas
Nadler, Henry Louis
Najjar, Victor Assad
Nguyen, Dung Chi
Nichols, Buford Lee, Jr.
Nitowsky, Harold Martin
Oh, William
Pachman, Lauren Merle
Person, Donald Ames
Polgar, George
Reppert, Steven Marion
Richmond, Julius Benjamin
Robbins, Frederick Chapman
Ross, Diana Lynn
Sheridan, Philip Henry
Sidbury, James Buren
Siegel, Stuart Elliott
Silver, Henry K.
Snyderman, Selma E(leanore)
Spitzer, Adrian
Tamura, Tsunenobu
Top, Franklin Henry, Jr.
Winick, Myron
Yaffe, Sumner Jason
Zee, Paulus

Pediatrics, neonatology
Behrman, Richard Elliot
Clements, John Allen
Egan, Edmund A.
Gartner, Lawrence Mitchel
Hess, Orvan Walter
Hodgman, Joan Elizabeth
Kotas, Robert Vincent
Lawson, Edward Earle
Nightingale, Elena Ottolenghi
Oh, William
Paxson, Charles L., Jr.
Sisson, Thomas Randolph Clinton

Pharmacology
Aagaard, George Nelson
Aberg, Gunnar A.K.
Ackerman, Neil Richard
Adams, Max D.
Akbar, Huzoor
Akera, Tai
Alkadhi, Karim Abdel
Altura, Burton Myron
Ambre, John Joseph
Amer, M. Samir
Aronson, Carl Edward
Axelrod, Julius
Azarnoff, Daniel Lester
Balazs, Tibor
Barnett, Allen
Baughman, Robert A., Jr.
Beaven, Michael Anthony
Bernacki, Ralph James
Berndt, William Oscar
Bernstein, Jerrold
Bernstein, Joel Edward
Besch, Henry Roland, Jr.
Bito, Laszlo Z.
Bleiberg, Marvin Jay
Bloomfield, Saul S.
Blumberg, Harold
Borgstedt, Harold Heinrich
Borzelleca, Joseph Francis
Bosin, Talmage Raymond
Braughler, J(ohn) Mark
Brodie, Harlow Keith Hammond
Brody, Theodore Meyer
Brooks, Harold Lloyd
Buchanan, Robert Alexander
Buckley, Joseph Paul
Buckman, Robert William
Burford, Hugh Jonathan
Burkman, Allan Maurice
Busch, Harris
Calesnick, Benjamin
Carson, Steven
Carter, Mary Kathleen
Castronovo, Frank Paul, Jr.
Catterall, William A.
Chan, Arthur Wing Kay
Chan, W. Y.
Chang, Richard Li-chai
Chasin, Mark
Chaturvedi, Arvind Kumar
Chung, Ho
Cluff, Leighton Eggertsen
Cohen, Marlene Lois
Collins, John H.
Concannon, James Thomas
Cook, Clarence Edgar
Cooper, Theodore
Cosmides, George James
Crawford, Lester Mills, Jr.
Davis, Lloyd Edward
De Salva, Salvatore Joseph
Di Pasquale, Gene
Dixon, Robert L.
Dombro, Roy Sandor
Domer, Floyd Ray
Downey, James Merritt
Drayer, Jan Ignatius
DuCharme, Donald Walter
Duckles, Sue Piper
El-Ackad, Tarek M.
Emele, Jane Frances
Engel, Toby Ross
Eshelman, Fred Neville
Feigen, Larry Philip
Ferko, Andrew Paul
Findlay, John William Addison
Fleisch, Jerome Herbert
Fleming, James Stuart, Jr.
Fouts, James Ralph
Frankl, William Stewart
Freeman, Julia Berg
Freis, Edward David
Fuller, Ray Ward
Gage, Tommy Wilton
Gallardo-Carpentier, Adriana
Gangaros, Louis Paul, Sr.
Garg, Lal Chand
Gautieri, Ronald Francis
Giles, Ralph Edson
Gilman, Alfred G.
Glassman, Jerome Martin
Goh, Edward Hua Seng
Goldberg, Leon Isadore
Goldstein, Sidney
Gomoll, Allen Warren
Greenbaum, Lowell Marvin
Greenberg, Stan Shimen
Guarino, Anthony Michael
Gueriguian, John Leo
Hall, Edward Dallas
Hancock, John Charles
Hande, Kenneth Robert
Harakal, Concetta
Harris, Louis Selig
Harrison, Steadman Darnell, Jr.
Harrison, Yvonne Elois
Harvey, Terence
Hastings, Robert Clyde
Hatch, Roger Conant

Hayes, Arthur Hull, Jr.
Haynes, Duncan Harold
Heffner, Thomas Gary
Hirsh, Kenneth Roy
Hofmann, Lorenz Martin
Holtkamp, Dorsey E(mil)
Horakova, Zdenka Zahutova
Horovitz, Zola Philip
Hudak, William John
Hyman, Albert Lewis
Imondi, Anthony Rocco
Isom, Gary Eugene
Jandhyala, Bhagavan Srikrishna
Jöchle, Wolfgang Johannes
Johnson, Herbert Gardner
Kamerling, Steven Glenn
Karagueuzian, Hrayr Sevag
Kau, Sen T.
Kenny, Alexander Donovan
Keplinger, Moreno L.
King, (Mary) Margaret
Kinnard, William James, Jr.
Kiplinger, Glenn Francis
Kohli, Jai Dev
Kosersky, Donald S.
Kulkarni, Prasad Shrikrishna
Kuntzman, Ronald Grover
Kupersmith, Joel
Lasagna, Louis Cesare
Laskin, Oscar Larry
Lazo, John Stephen
Lee, Cheng-Chun
Lee, Francis Him
Lee, Tony Jer-Fu
Leon, Judith Merer
Lerner, Stephen Alexander
Lester, David
Levin, Wayne
Levy, Gerhard
Lin, Tsung-Min
Lish, Paul Merrill
Liu, Ching-Tong
Longenecker, Gesina (Louise) Lizana
Ludlum, David Blodgett
MacFarlane, Malcolm David
Mackerer, Carl Robert
Maickel, Roger Philip
Malanga, Carl Joseph
Malone, Marvin Herbert
Mandel, H(arold) George
Marshall, Franklin Nick
Martin, Billy R.
Maxwell, Donald Robert
Mayhew, Eric George
McColl, John Duncan
McConnell, William Ray
McDermott, Daniel Joseph
McGovren, James Patrick
Melancon, Mark John
Miller, Francis Peter
Miller, Lynne Cathy
Miller, Richard Kermit
Misra, Anand Lal
Mokler, Corwin Morris
Moore, Alan Frederic
Morris, Ralph William
Mullane, John Francis
Murthy, Vishnubhakta Shrinivas
Mustafa, Syed Jamal
Novick, William Joseph, Jr.
Nwangwu, Peter Uchenna
Ochillo, Richard Frederick
Ogilvie, Richard Ian
Omaye, Stanley Teruo
Osterberg, Arnold Curtis
Overweg, Norbert Ido Albert
Pandya, Krishnakant Hariprasad
Pavelic, Zlatko Paul
Pento, J. Thomas
Perel, James Maurice
Pettinger, William A.
Prabhu, Venkatray G.
Proakis, Anthony George
Quebbemann, Aloysius John
Quirion, Remi
Rao, Gopal Subba
Ray, Richard Schell
Reichen, Juerg
Reichgott, Michael J.
Reidenberg, Marcus Milton
Reinke, Lester Allen
Ress, Rudyard Joseph
Reyes, Edward
Reynolds, Robert Donald
Rheinstein, Peter Howard
Ribiero, Lair G(eraldo) T(heodoro)
Rifkind, Arleen B.
Rosen, Michael Robert
Rosenberg, Howard Charles
Rosenberg, Philip
Rosenkranz, Roberto Pedro
Royds, Robert B.
Rubin, Bernard
Rudzik, Allan D.
Ruffolo, Robert Richard, Jr.
Russell, Robert Lee
Rust, John Howard
Salafsky, Bernard P.
Sanner, John Harper
Sartorelli, Alan Clayton
Saunders, Robert Norman
Sethi, Vidya Sagar
Sevy, Roger Warren
Shargel, Leon David
Shepherd, Alexander M.M.
Shriver, David Allen
Siegel, Ivens Aaron
Slikker, William, Jr.
Smith, Emil Richard
Smith, Roger Powell
Sofia, Robert Duane
Somani, Satu Motilal
Spector, Reynold
Spilker, Bert
Spratt, James Leo
Steinfeis, George Francis
Stewart, David James
Su, Che
Taber, Robert Irving
Thompson, Wilmer Leigh
Thurman, Ronald Glenn
Tobias, Lawrence Damian
Turlapaty, Prasad Durga Mallikharjuna Vara
Ventura, William Paul
Verebey, Karl G.
Vesell, Elliot Saul
Vick, Robert Lore
Vincenzi, Frank Foster
Volicer, Ladislav
Waddell, William Joseph
Ward, John Wesley
Wardell, Joe Russell, Jr.
Waritier, David Charles
Wasserman, Martin Allan
Way, James Leong
Weiner, Murray
Wenger, Galen Rosenberger
White, Helen Lyng
Wilkinson, Grant Robert
Williamson, Harold Emanuel
Winbury, Martin Maurice
Wolen, Robert Lawrence
Wolff, Frederick William
Woods, Eugene Francis
Wosilait, Walter Daniel
Yaffe, Sumner Jason
Yagiela, John Allen
Yeh, Billy Kuo-Jiun
Yim, George Kwock Wah
Yu, Jia-Huey
Ziegler, Daniel Martin

Pharmacology, cellular
Allen, Donald Orrie
Beck, Lyle Vibert
Bosin, Talmage Raymond
Bowen, John Metcalf
Chaudry, Irshad Hussain
Drewinko, Benjamin
Fisher, James W.
Greenberg, Stan Shimen
Haigler, Henry James
Hester, Richard Kelly
Johanson, Conrad Earl
Laychock, Suzanne Gale
Lee, Insu Peter
Maloff, Bruce L
Margolius, Harry Stephen
Reasor, Mark J.
Ritter, Carl Alan
Rizack, Martin Arthur
Robison, G(eorge) Alan
Russell, Robert Lee
Salganicoff, Leon
Sevy, Roger Warren
Smith, John Bryan
Theoharides, Theoharis Constantin
Tolman, Edward Laurie
Uyeki, Edwin M.
Ward, Patrick E.
Wong, Patrick Yui-Kwong

Pharmacology, molecular
Abood, Leo George
Agrawal, Krishna Chandra
Allaudeen, Hameedsulthan Sheik
Alphin, Reevis Stancil
Alvares, Alvito Peter
Baksi, Samarendra Nath
Billingsley, Melvin Lee
Briggs, Arthur Harold
Bylund, David B.
Camerman, Arthur
Chignell, Colin Francis
Cho, Arthur Kenji
Chou, Ting-Chao
Cooper, Jack Ross
Corbascio, Nicola Aldo
Creveling, Cyrus Robbins
Cuatrecasas, Pedro Martin
Cushman, David Wayne
Donnelly, Thomas Edward, Jr.
Eldefrawi, Amira Toppozada
Enna, Salvatore Joseph
Free, Charles Alfred
Greenbaum, Lowell Marvin
Gurtoo, Hira L.
Gutierrez, Peter Luis
Harper, Jeffrey Frederick
Harris, Don Navarro
Insel, Paul Anthony
Janis, Ronald Allen
Jarboe, Charles Harry
Kam, Sheung-Tsam
Kellar, Kenneth Jon
Kuo, Jyh-Fa
Lasslo, Andrew
Levitt, Morton
Long, John Paul
Makar, Adeeb Bassili
Mansour, Tag Eldin
Mantione, Charles Ross
Marshall, Garland Ross
Medzihradsky, Fedor
Mieyal, John Joseph
Miller, Kenneth John
Mittal, Chandra Kant
Morgan, John Paul
Randerath, Kurt
Read, George Wesley
Robinson, Harry John
Robison, G(eorge) Alan
Salganicoff, Leon
Scheibel, Leonard William
Shires, Thomas Kay
Soliman, Magdi Ramzi Iskandar
Stebbing, Nowell
Stefano, George B.
Stohs, Sidney John
Tew, Kenneth David
Vatsis, Kostas Petros
Vincenzi, Frank Foster
Wade, Adelbert Elton
Ward, Patrick E.
Watanabe, Kouichi
Weber, George
Wurster, Dale Erwin
Zimmerman, Thomas Paul

Pharmacology, neuropharmacology. *See* NEUROSCIENCE.

Physical medicine and rehabilitation
Alexander, James L.
Berkwits, Leland
Betts, Henry Brognard
Compere, Clinton Lee
Gersten, Jerome William
Goodman, Arden Patricia
Lake, David Allen
McNeal, Donald Richard
Sanders, Gloria Tolson
Wilson, Arthur Jess

Physiology. *See also* **BIOLOGY.**
Abbrecht, Peter Herman
Alexander, Harold
Altura, Burton Myron
Antzelevitch, Charles
Barker, Harold Grant
Baylor, Stephen Murray
Bello-Reuss, Elsa N.
Bennett, Peter Brian
Berliner, Robert William
Berlyne, Geoffrey Merton
Berne, Robert Matthew
Brobeck, John Raymond
Brooks, Chandler McCuskey
Brooks, David Patrick
Brooks, Frank Pickering
Bulkley, Gregory Bartlett
Bunger, Rolf
Burton, Karen Poliner
Butkus, Donald Eugene
Cahill, George Francis, Jr.
Chan, Yun Lai
Chesky, Jeffrey Alan
Cheung, Joseph Yat-sing
Chew, Catherine Strong
Clements, John Allen
Cordova-Salinas, Maria Asuncion
Cournand, Andre F.
Crawford, Lester Mills, Jr.
Crosby, Lon Owen
Cserr, Helen FitzGerald
Diana, John Nicholas
Dormer, Kenneth John
Downey, James Merritt
DuBois, Arthur Brooks
DuBose, Thomas Durward, Jr.
Edelman, Norman H.
Egan, Edmund A.
Falk, Sandor A.
Feigen, Larry Philip
Fettman, Martin Joseph
Folinsbee, Lawrence John
Foreman, Robert Dale
Francis, Kennon Thompson
Gaudino, Mario
Giebisch, Gerhard Hans
Gilboe, David Dougherty
Gladfelter, Wilbert Eugene
Gold, Michael Nathan
Goldfarb, Stanley
Gottschalk, Carl William
Green, Howard
Green, Keith
Greene, Murray A.
Hales, Charles Albert
Han, Jaok
Hauer, Jerome Maurice
Heisey, S. Richard
Heller, Lois Jane
Hendler, Edwin
Hertz, Roy
Hitzig, Bernard Michael
Hockel, Gregory Martin
Innes, David Lyn
Jaffe, Randal Craig
Jayaweera, Ananda Ranjith
Johannsen, Ulmer James
Johnson, John Marshall
Kalu, Dike Ndukwe
Kao, Race L.
Kashgarian, Michael
Kellogg, Ralph Henderson
Kenney, Richard Alec
Kerr, Janet Spence
Khambatta, Hoshang Jal
Klahr, Saulo
Klitzman, Bruce Maurice
Kootsey, Joseph Mailen
Lacy, Priti Sheila
Laragh, John Henry
Lawson, Edward Earle
Lee, Chin Ok
Levitsky, Sidney
Lichtman, Marshall A.
Lin, Tsung-Min
Little, Robert Colby
Liu, Ching-Tong
Loeppky, Jack Albert
Lust, Robert Maurice
Martin, Paul Joseph
McClellan, George Baird
McDermott, Daniel Joseph
McDonagh, Paul Francis
McIlreath, Fred J.
Miletich, David John
Milic-Emili, Joseph
Miller, Michael James
Miller, Thomas Allen
Millhorn, David Eugene
Mitchell, Jere Holloway
Moe, Gordon Kenneth
Mokler, Corwin Morris
Montefusco, Cheryl Marie
Morgan, Howard Edwin
Mortillaro, Nicholas A.
Musacchia, X. J.
Nair, Pankajam K(arunakaran)
Nocenti, Mero Raymond
Norton, James Michael
Pace, Nello
Pearce, William Julian
Petri, William Henry, III
Pitts, Grover Cleveland
Pollack, Gerald Harvey
Porter, Johnny R.
Powell, Michael Robert
Powers, Scott Kline
Prewitt, Russell Lawrence
Rabkin, Ralph
Raff, Hershel
Randall, David Clark
Randall, Walter C(lark)
Redgrave, Trevor Gordon
Reid, Michael Baron
Rennie, Ian Drummond
Ress, Rudyard Joseph
Reynolds, Robert Donald
Rhoades, Rodney Allen
Rode, Andris
Rosen, Michael Robert
Rothe, Carl Frederick
Rottenberg, David Allan
Ruff, Robert Louis
Ruwe, William David
Schultz, Stanley George
Schwartz, Marshall Zane
Selkurt, Ewald Erdman
Shah, Sudhir Amratlal
Shearin, Nancy Louise
Sherman, James Howe
Sherwin, Joseph Richard
Silver, Donald
Sintetos, Anthony Lee
Skoryna, Stanley Constantine
Solomon, Sidney
Sparks, Harvey Vise, Jr.
Spiller, Gene Alan
Spitzer, John J.
Szlyk, Patricia Carol
Tai, Yuan-Heng
Tannen, Richard Laurence
Taylor, Aubrey Elmo
Turlapaty, Prasad Durga Mallikharjuna Vara
Vanatta, John Crothers, III
Van Beaumont, Karel Willem
Vassalle, Mario
Vick, Robert Lore
Vogel, James Alan
Vogel, Thomas Timothy
Walgenbach-Telford, Susan Carol
Ward, Walter F(rederick)
Warth, James Arthur
Watson, John Thomas
Whidden, Stanley John
Wildenthal, C(laud) Kern
Willems, William Joseph
Winter, Peter Michael
Wong, Robert King-Suen
Yount, David Eugene
Yu, Jia-Huey

Physiology, neurophysiology. *See* **NEUROSCIENCE.**

Physiology, psychophysiology
Bastawi, Aly Eloui
Cacioppo, John Terrance
Chen, Richard Yuan Zin
del Regato, Juan Angel
Dixen, Jean Marie
Eisdorfer, Carl
Eisenberg, M(yron) Michael
Engel, Bernard Theodore
Feuerstein, Michael
Fotopoulos, Sophia Strathopoulos
Graham, David Tredway
Green, Elmer Ellsworth
Kety, Seymour S(olomon)
Lee, Richard M
London, Ray William
Odom, James Vernon
Patterson, Michael Milton
Pivik, Rudolph Terry
Randall, David Clark
Schwartz, Irving Leon
Silverman, Albert Jack
Wagman, Althea M.I.
Wickramasekera, (Ian Edward Wickram)
Winfree, Arthur Taylor

Preventive medicine. *See also* **Epidemiology.**
Adams, John David
Aronson, Stanley Maynard
Bailey, William James
Barker, Lewellys Franklin
Bloomfield, Daniel Kermit
Breslow, Lester
Buttery, Christopher M. G.
Charlesworth, Edward Allison
Cherkasky, Martin
Deuschle, Kurt Walter
Farquhar, John William
Ferris, Benjamin Greeley, Jr.
Gardner, John Willard
Greenwald, Peter
Halstead, Bruce Walter
Hinman, Edward John
Jordan, William Stone, Jr.
Lashof, Joyce R. Cohen
Mahboubi, Ezzat Ollah
Mason, James Ostermann
Matsumoto, Teruo
Miller, C. Arden
Ng, Lorenz Keng Yong
Rode, Andris
Scheibel, Leonard William
Schwabel, Mary Jane
Shank, Robert Ely
Shearer, David Ross
Sheps, Cecil George
Stewart, John Alvin
Tidball, Charles Stanley

Psychiatry
Abuzzahab, Faruk Said, Sr.
Acosta, Gustavo
Baron, Miron
Butler, Robert Neil
Crawshaw, Ralph
DePaulo, Joseph Raymond, Jr.
Docherty, John Patrick
Eisdorfer, Carl
Eisenberg, Leon
Figley, Charles Ray
Frazier, Sherbert Hughes, Jr.
Gaudino, Mario
Goodwin, Frederick K.
Guze, Samuel Barry
Halaris, Angelos
Hobson, J. Allan
Jacobs, Roland William
Jandhyala, Bhagavan Srikrishna
Kadushin, Phineas
Kandel, Eric Richard
Katz, Jay
Loosen, Peter Thomas
Mallinger, Alan Gary
McCarley, Robert William
Menninger, William Walter
Pettinati, Helen Marie
Pope, Harrison Graham, Jr.
Rakoff, Vivian Morris
Richmond, Julius Benjamin
Robertson, Brian Max
Robins, Lee Nelken
Sarma, P.S. Bala
Schuster, Marvin Meier
Shamoian, Charles A.
Silver, Larry Bernard
Silverman, Albert Jack
Solnit, Albert Jay
Uhlenhuth, Eberhard Henry
Visotsky, Harold Meryle
Wallerstein, Robert Solomon
Winokur, George
Yozawitz, Allan

Psychiatry, psychopharmacology
Abuzzahab, Faruk Said, Sr.
Alessi, Norman Emil
Appel, James Barry
Balster, Robert Louis
Borison, Richard Lewis
Boulton, Alan Arthur
Brown, Gerald LaVonne
Buckman, Maire Tults
Byrd, Larry Donald
Chan, Arthur Wing Kay
Clark, Mervin Leslie
DeMet, Edward Michael
DePaulo, Joseph Raymond, Jr.
Freedman, Daniel X.
Gershon, Elliot Sheldon
Giambalvo, Cecilia Tang
Giannini, A. James
Goldstein, Jeffrey Marc
Halaris, Angelos
Halbreich, Uriel
Hartmann, Ernest Louis
Huang, Chuong Chun
Hui, Koon-Sea
Johnson, David Norseen
Kety, Seymour S(olomon)
Kim, S. Peter
Koslow, Stephen Hugh
Lake, Charles Raymond
Lal, Harbans
Lawson, William Bradford
Lucot, James Bernard
Maas, James Weldon
Malitz, Sidney
Mallinger, Alan Gary
Mendels, Joseph
Menon, Madhavan Krishna
Messiha, Fathy Sabry
Nemeroff, Charles Barnet
Pollard, Gerald Tilman
Pope, Harrison Graham, Jr.
Pottash, A.L.C.
Pozuelo, Jose
Ramos-Lorenzi, Jorge Ramon
Reiser, Morton Francis
Roffman, Mark
Sanberg, Paul Ronald
Schechter, Martin David
Shamoian, Charles A.
Skolnick, Phil
Snyder, Solomon Halbert
Spohn, Herbert Emil
Stern, Warren Charles
Tamminga, Carol Ann
Uhlenhuth, Eberhard Henry
Uyeno, Edward Teiso
Wittenborn, John Richard
Yokel, Robert Allen

Pulmonary medicine
Adams, Donald Robert
Al-Bazzaz, Faiq Jaber
Bedell, George Noble
Boushey, Homer Astley, Jr.
Brody, Jerome Saul
Charan, Nirmal Biswas
Collins, James Francis
Cudkowicz, Leon
Edelman, Norman H.
Fishman, Alfred Paul
Gross, Nicholas Jabob
Hales, Charles Albert
Hooper, Robert George
Kelsen, Steven Gus
Kotas, Robert Vincent
Kulle, Thomas John
Mayock, Robert Lee
Metcalf, John Franklin
Michels, David Barry
Milic-Emili, Joseph
Miller, Michael James
Murray, John Frederic
Newman, John Hughes
O'Neil, John James
Pack, Allan Ian
Polgar, George
Rhoades, Rodney Allen
Rossing, Robert Grangaard
Rothberg, Richard Martin
Russ, Wesley Dale
Ryan, Una Scully
Smith, Joseph Lorenzo
Sobol, Bruce J.
Soskel, Norman Terry
Stemmler, Edward Joseph
Taylor, Aubrey Elmo
Tisi, Gennaro Michael
Wanner, Adam
Weg, John Gerard
Weill, Hans
Williams, Marshall Henry, Jr.

Radiology
Amols, Howard Ira
Berger, Harvey James
Brady, Luther W., Jr.
Cano, Elmer Raul
Chen, Tao-seng
del Regato, Juan Angel
DeWerd, Larry A.
Dritschilo, Anatoly
Evens, Ronald Gene
Goepp, Robert August
Hevezi, James Michael
Hubbard, Lincoln Beals
Jacobson, Harold Gordon
Lerch, Irving Abram
Lin, Hsiu-San
Littleton, Jesse Talbot, III
McCombs, Rollin Koenig
Moyer, Robert Findley
Narayanan, C. S.
Nibhanupudy, Jagannadha Rao
Orton, Colin George
Perry, Nelson Allen
Rollo, F. David
Sakover, Raymond Paul
Seaman, William Bernard
Seydel, Horst Gunter
Siegel, Michael Elliot
Sontag, Marc Robert

Szal, Marcel Michael
Tefft, Melvin
Withers, Hubert Rodney
Wu, Raymond Kee-Kin

Radiology, diagnostic
Ackerman, Robert Harold
Alfidi, Ralph Joseph
Andre, Michael
Axel, Leon
Baum, Stanley
Burrell, Morton I
Carroll, Barbara Anne
Courtney,, John Vincent
Doi, Kunio
Eisenberg, Ronald Lee
Figley, Melvin Morgan
Fischer, Harry W.
George, Ajax Elis
Graham, Leslie Stephen
Gratt, Barton Michael
Jacobson, Harold Gordon
Jereb, Marjan Josip
Larach, Simon
Lodwick, Gwilym Savage
Meyers, Morton Allen
Moseley, Robert David, Jr.
Rapport, Robert
Rosenberg, Eric Ronald
Seaman, William Bernard
Steckel, Richard J.
Stein, George Nathan
Tortorici, Marianne Rita
Verstandig, Charles Coleman
Willman, Michael Karel
Wilson, Gabriel Henry

Radiology, imaging technology. See also
BIOTECHNOLOGY.
Agard, Eugene Theodore
Alfidi, Ralph Joseph
Axel, Leon
Banjavic, Richard Alan
Carroll, Barbara Anne
Carson, Paul Langford
Censor, Yair
Chang, Wei
Clanton, Jeffrey Alan
Danos, Michael
DiBianca, Frank Anthony
Dick, Charles Edward
Doi, Kunio
Gratt, Barton Michael
Grissom, Michael Phillip
Gur, David
Hoffman, Eric Alfred
Holman, B. Leonard
Jaszczak, Ronald Jack
Knowles, Richard James Robert
Kremkau, Frederick W.
Krohmer, Jack Stewart
Lin, Pei-Jan Paul
Lodwick, Gwilym Savage
Luckett, Larry Wayne
MacIntyre, William James
Macovski, Albert
Malamud, Herbert
Metz, Charles Edgar
Minter, Jerry Burnett
Mooney, Richard T.
Moseley, Robert David, Jr.
Rao, Dandamudi Vishnuvardhana
Renner, Wendel Dean
Revesz, George
Rollo, F. David
Rottenberg, David Allan
Rubenstein, Edward
Shapiro, Jonathan Salem
Slutsky, Robert Allen
Strom, Joel Andrew
Van Metter, Richard Lawrence
Weber, David Alexander
Webster, Edward William
Whitehead, Frank Roger
Wilson, Gabriel Henry

Radiology, nuclear medicine. See also
Nuclear medicine.
Castronovo, Frank Paul, Jr.
Croft, Barbara Yoder
Farukhi, Mohammad Rahimullah
Freeman, Leonard Murray
Harris, Gale Ion
Loken, Merle Kenneth
Mooney, Richard T.
Pastorelle, Peter John
Ruegsegger, Donald Ray, Jr.
Sakover, Raymond Paul
Willman, Michael Karel

Rheumatology
Ackerman, Neil Richard
Alspaugh, Margaret Ann
Archer, Robert Allen
Bennett, Joe Claude
Bole, Giles G.
Curd, John Gary
Hadler, Nortin M.
Hicks, John Trimmer
Irigoyen, Oscar Horacio
Kaplan, Melvin H.
Kassan, Stuart S.
Krakauer, Randall Sheldon
Kushner, Irving
Naides, Stanley Jay
Pachman, Lauren Merle
Schur, Peter Henry
Shulman, Lawrence Edward
Solinger, Alan Michael
Tan, Eng Meng
Tartof, David
Ward, John Robert
Ward, Louis Emmerson
Zurier, Robert Burton

Space medicine. See SPACE SCIENCE.

Surgery
Albano, William A.
Allison, David Coulter
Austen, W(illiam) Gerald
Baker, Daniel Clifton
Barker, Harold Grant
Barone, Robert Michael

Baue, Arthur Edward
Buchwald, Henry
Bulkley, Gregory Bartlett
Burt, Michael Edward
Campbell, Gilbert Sadler
Chase, Robert Arthur
Choy, Daniel Shu Jen
Clowes, Alexander Whitehill
Coran, Arnold Gerald
Cosman, Bard
Davis, John Mihran
De Bakey, Michael Ellis
Donegan, William Laurence
Dos, Serge Jacques
Eisenberg, M(yron) Michael
Farmer, Joseph Clarence, Jr.
Fisher, John Courtney
Friedman, Harold Ira
Harmon, John Watson
Hirose, Teruo Terry
Holder, Walter Dalton, Jr.
Housepian, Edgar Minas
Hutchinson, William Burke
Imbembo, Anthony Louis
Izant, Robert James, Jr.
Jackson, Benjamin Taylor
Jamplis, Robert Warren
Joffe, Stephen Neal
Johnson, Frank Edward
Joison, Julio
Lee, James Travis, Jr.
Lee, Yeu-Tsu Margaret
Lotze, Michael Thomas
Madura, James Anthony
Marchetta, Frank Carmelo
Mason, George Robert
Mathes, Stephen John
Matsumoto, Teruo
McCarthy, Joseph Gerald
Miller, Thomas Allen
Moore, George Eugene
Morris, Don Melvin
Munster, Andrew Michael
Nahrwold, David Lange
Nichols, Walter Kirt
Pories, Walter J.
Preston, Frederick Willard
Prout, George Russell, Jr.
Pruitt, Basil Arthur
Reemtsma, Keith
Reichle, Frederick Adolph
Ruberg, Robert Lionel
Sabiston, David Coston, Jr.
Schenck, Robert Roy
Schilling, John Albert
Schloerb, Paul Richard
Schwartz, Marshall Zane
Sears, Henry Francis, II
Secord, David Cartwright
Silver, Donald
Sindelar, William Francis
Sollinger, Hans Werner
Spratt, John Stricklin
Starzl, Thomas Earl
Stehlin, John Sebastian, Jr.
Sugarbaker, Everett Van Dyke
Temple, Walley John
Tobin, Gordon Ross
Turcotte, Jeremiah George
Vogel, Thomas Timothy
Watkins, David Hyder
Webb, Watts Rankin
Weber, Thomas Richard
Weese, James Leighton
Wetstein, Lewis
Wright, Creighton Bolter
Yancey, Asa Greenwood

Surgery, artificial organs and prostheses.
See also BIOTECHNOLOGY.
DeVries, William Castle
Hall, C(harles) William
Imbembo, Anthony Louis
Jarvik, Robert K.
Kantrowitz, Adrian
Kolff, Willem Johan
Litwak, Philip
Mendenhall, Harlan Vincent
Toledo-Pereyra, Luis Horacio
Watkins, David Hyder

Surgery, cardiac
Bailey, Leonard Lee
Barner, Hendrick Boyer
Baue, Arthur Edward
De Bakey, Michael Ellis
DeVries, William Castle
Dos, Serge Jacques
Frazier, Oscar Howard
Geha, Alexander Salim
Gordon, Robert Thomas
Gott, Vincent Lynn
Hirose, Teruo Terry
Kantrowitz, Adrian
Kao, Race L.
Kilman, James William
Levitsky, Sidney
LoCicero, Joseph, III
Lowe, James Edward
Mc Goon, Dwight Charles
Myerowitz, P. David
Pierce, William Schuler
Reitz, Bruce Arnold
Sones, Jr. F. Mason
Watson, Donald Charles
Webb, Watts Rankin
Wetstein, Lewis
Wright, Creighton Bolter

Surgery, microsurgery
Baker, Daniel Clifton
DeVore, Duane Thomas
Gallant, Nanette
Kleinert, Harold Earl
Mathes, Stephen John
Mullan, John Francis
Opgrande, John Donald
Schenck, Robert Roy
Shaw, William Wei-Lien
Shons, Alan Rance

Surgery, neurosurgery
Bering, Edgar Andrew, Jr.
Black, Peter McLaren
Borges, Lawrence Francis
Brodner, Robert Albert
Cahill, David Wooding
Campbell, James Norman
Chou, Shelley Nien-chun
Fessler, Richard Glenn
Hekmatpanah, Javad
Javid, Manucher J.
Kapp, John Paul
Levy, Walter Joseph, Jr.
Liszczak, Theodore Michael
McQuarrie, Irvine Gray
Miller, Carole Ann
Mullan, John Francis
Ojemann, George Alvin
Ortiz-Suarez, Humberto Jose
Osterholm, Jewell L.
Simpson, Richard Kendall, Jr.
Smith, Barry Hamilton
Taren, James Arthur
Velasco-Suarez, Manual M.

Surgery, transplants
Alexander, James Wesley
Bailey, Leonard Lee
Baxter, Charles Rufus
Chatterjee, Satya Narayan
Czitrom, Andrei Alexander
Frazier, Oscar Howard
Friedlaender, Gary Elliott
Geha, Alexander Salim
Hardy, Mark Adam
Munda, Rino
Myerowitz, P. David
Najarian, John Sarkis
Rapaport, Felix Theodosius
Shaw, William Wei-Lien
Shons, Alan Rance
Simonian, Simon John
Sollinger, Hans Werner
Starzl, Thomas Earl
Toledo-Pereyra, Luis Horacio
Turcotte, Jeremiah George
Veith, Frank James
Watson, Donald Charles

Teratology
Bieber, Frederick Robert
Damjanov, Ivan
Daniel, Michael Andrew
Diwan, Bhalchandra Apparao
D'Ver, Abbott Simon
Friedler, Gladys
Gautieri, Ronald Francis
Goldman, Allen Seymour
Hardin, Bryan David
Hendrickx, Andrew George
Hicks, Heraline Elaine
Hoar, Richard Morgan
John-Greene, Jacqueline Ann
Johnson, Elmer Marshall
Kelman, Bruce Jerry
Kille, John William
Overman, Dennis Orton
Schardein, James Loren
Singh, Jarnall
Slikker, William, Jr.
Stephens, Trent Dee
Szabo, Kalman Tibor
Voehees, Charles Van
Welsch, Frank
Young, John Falkner

Toxicology
Aaroe, William Henry
Adams, Max D.
Akera, Tai
Allen, Henry Leigh
Alvares, Alvito Peter
Ambre, John Joseph
Anderson, Rebecca J.
Archer, Michael Christopher
Aronson, Carl Edward
Atallah, Yousef Hanna
Baker, Thomas
Balazs, Tibor
Baron, Jeffrey
Bernstein, Isadore Abraham
Besch, Henry Roland, Jr.
Bleiberg, Marvin Jay
Borgstedt, Harold Heinrich
Borzelleca, Joseph Francis
Carson, Steven
Chadwick, Robert William
Chang, Ming Jen Wu
Chaturvedi, Arvind Kumar
Chesney, Charles Frederic
Chung, Ho
Coleman, Ronald L.
Cooper, David Young
Cosmides, George James
Dalvi, Ramesh R.
D'Ambrosio, Steven Mario
Davis, Wilbur Marvin
Decker, Walter Johns
Desaiah, Durisala
De Salva, Salvatore Joseph
Deutsch, Dale George
Dickerson, Charlesworth Lee
Dixon, Robert L.
Dolenz, John Joseph
Donzanti, Bruce Armand
Douglas, J. Fielding
D'Ver, Abbott Simon
Dyer, Robert Stritzinger
Elliott, George Algimon
Emele, Jane Frances
Fowler, Bruce Andrew
Gandolfi, Allen Jay
Glassman, Jerome Martin
Golberg, Leon
Gress-Gordon, Jean Anne
Guarino, Anthony Michael
Hanson, Douglas M.
Hardin, Bryan David
Harrison, Steadman Darnell, Jr.
Hatch, Roger Conant
Hayes, Wayland Jackson, Jr.
Hollenberg, Paul Frederick
Horakova, Zdenka Zahutova
Isom, Gary Eugene
Jarboe, Charles Harry
Jayasekara, Upali Matheskankanange
John-Greene, Jacqueline Ann

Johnson, Elmer Marshall
Joy, Robert McKernon
Kaistha, Krishan, Kumar
Kelman, Bruce Jerry
Keplinger, Moreno L.
Kille, John William
Koschier, Francis Joseph, III
Lee, Cheng-Chun
Lee, Insu Peter
Levin, Stuart
Lipnick, Robert Louis
Lish, Paul Merrill
Loomis, Ted Albert
Mackerer, Carl Robert
Madissoo, Harry
Maibach, Howard I.
Makar, Adeeb Bassili
Malone, Marvin Herbert
Mayer, Ramona Ann
McColl, John Duncan
McConnell, William Ray
Medhi, Nabeel Abdel-Qadir
Meeks, Robert G.
Messiha, Fathy Sabry
Meyer, Dale R.
Milman, Harry Abraham
Mukhtar, Hasan
Northup, Sharon Joan
Nwangwu, Peter Uchenna
O'Callaghan, James Patrick
Ochillo, Richard Frederick
O'Donoghue, John (Lipomi)
Olajos, Eugene Julius
Oldham, James Warren
Oser, Bernard Levussove
Pereira, Michael Alan
Rall, David Platt
Reasor, Mark J.
Rifkind, Arleen B.
Robertson, James Bragg
Robinson, Farrel Richard
Rosenkrantz, Harris
Roth, Robert Andrew, Jr.
Ruben, Zadok
Saryan, Leon Aram
Saslaw, Leonard David
Schardein, James Loren
Schechter, Martin David
Seckar, Joel Andreas
Shaikh, Zahir Ahmad
Shargel, Leon David
Sharma, Raghubir Prasad
Shertzer, Howard Grant
Sivak, Andrew
Skare, Kevin Lynn
Smith, Emil Richard
Smith, Frank Ackroyd
Smith, Roger Powell
Sofia, Robert Duane
Somani, Satu Motilal
Swarm, Richard Lee
Talbot, Richard Burritt
Tepper, Lloyd Barton
Tyler, Tipton Ransom
Valdes, James John
Ventura, William Paul
Verebey, Karl G.
Waddell, William Joseph
Ward, John Wesley
Way, James Leong
Wedig, John H.
Welsch, Frank
Wilber, Charles Grady
Wolf, Barbara Anne
Wolff, George Louis
Woodford, Warren James
Woods, Eugene Francis
Yokel, Robert Allen

Urology
Drago, Joseph Rosario
Finney, Roy Pelham
Frank, Irwin Norman
Grayhack, John Thomas
Merrin, Claude Emile Andre
Murphy, Gerald Patrick
Olsson, Carl Alfred
Pong, Raymond S.
Prout, George Russell, Jr.
Turner, Terry Tomo
Walsh, Patrick Craig
Wein, Alan Jerome

Virology. See also BIOLOGY.
Ablashi, Dharam Vir
Behbehani, Abbas M.
Bishop, John Michael
Blacklow, Neil Richard
Blumberg, Baruch Samuel
Boyd, Ann Lewis
Brandt, Carl David
Christensen, Mary Lucas
Cooney, Marion Kathleen
Cooper, Louis Zucker
Cukor, George
Datta, Syamal Kumar
Deibel, Rudolf
Fields, Bernard Nathan
Fisher, Paul B.
Forghani, Bagher
Francis, Robert Dorl
Friedman, Harvey Michael
Funk, Glenn Albert
Gajdusek, Daniel Carleton
Georgiades, Jerzy Alexander
Glaser, Ronald
Gross, Ludwik
Hampar, Berge
Harford, Carl Gayler
Harter, Donald Harry
Haywood, Anne Mowbray
Hicks, John Trimmer
Hierholzer, John Charles
Hirsch, Martin Stanley
Hougland, Arthur Eldon
Hsiung, Gueh-Djen
Huang, Eng-Shang
Iglewski, Wallace Joseph
Joklik, Wolfgang Karl
Kasai, George Joji
Kilbourne, Edwin Dennis
Larson, Vivian M.
Lowy, Douglas Ronald
Lyons, Michael Joseph
Mayor, Heather Donald
Melnick, Joseph L.
Merigan, Thomas Charles, Jr.

Michalski, Frank Joseph
Miller, Richard Lynn
Neurath, Alexander Robert
O'Callaghan, Dennis John
Ohi, Seigo
Pagano, Joseph Stephen
Parrott, Robert Harold
Pfau, Charles Julius
Potash, Louis
Rhim, Johng Sik
Roane, Philip Ransom, Jr.
Roizman, Bernard
Roy-Burman, Pradip
Schmidt, Nathalie Joan
Schwartz, Steven Otto
Schwarz, Anton J.
Seto, Joseph Tobey
Shelokov, Alexis
Smith, Ralph Earl
Stebbing, Nowell
Top, Franklin Henry, Jr.
Weller, Thomas Huckle
Wiebe, Michael Eugene
Woodhour, Allen Francis
Yoon, Ji-Won

Other
Anderson, Robert Simpers, *Immunotoxicology*
Arnsdorf, Morton Frank
Attix, Frank Herbert, *Radiation dosimetry*
Baldonado, Ardelina-Erika Albano, *Research methodology*
Barone, Robert Michael, *Head and neck surgery*
Berliner, Robert William, *Circulatory system*
Bernardis, Lee Livius
Bertalanffy, Felix Dionysius
Bliznakov, Emile George, *Medical research administration*
Bois, Pierre, *Medical research administration*
Bondurant, Stuart, *Medical institution administration*
Brandt, Edward Newman, Jr., *Public policy in health*
Breuer, Charles Benedict, *Medical products research and development management*
Brodner, Robert Albert, *Fetal surgery*
Bunger, Rolf, *Bioenergetics of heart*
Cangialosi, Charles Philip, *Podiatry; podiatric surgery*
Chase, John David, *Medical institution administration*
Chedid, Antonio, *Hepatology*
Choi, Sung Chil, *Biostatistics*
Chung, Chung-Taik
Collen, Morris Frank, *Medical research administration*
Cronkhite, Leonard Wolsey, Jr., *Medical institution administration*
Dean, Richard H., *Vascular surgery*
Delliosso, Louis Frank, *Neuro-ophthalmology*
Dienstag, Jules Leonard
Dishman, Rodney King, *Sports medicine*
Donabedian, Avedis, *Health care organization and administration*
Eichholz, Geoffrey G., *Radiation protection*
Enoch, Jay Martin
Ewing, June Swift, *Electron microscopy*
Farber, Phillip Andrew, *Cytogenetics*
Feeney, Jospeh John
Franti, Charles Elmer
Freeman, Julia Berg
Friedler, Gladys
Garg, Lal Chand, *Renal pharmacology*
Gault, N.L., Jr., *Medical education*
Gibson, Sam Thompson, *Regulatory medicine*
Gillette, Paul Crawford
Goldstein, Norman, *Medical photography*
Goodman, DeWitt Stetten, *Arteriosclerosis*
Grenfell, Raymond Frederic
Groszmann, Roberto Jose
Grouse, Lawrence Douglas, *Medical education*
Hammond, Mary Elizabeth Hale
Hardy, Mark Adam, *Vascular surgery*
Henderson, Donald Ainslie, *Public health education administration*
Huber, Ivan
Hudecki, Michael Stephen, *Muscular dystrophy*
Ingram, Alvin John, *Health care delivery*
Jahiel, René I.
Jirousek, Ludek
Katz, Michael, *Tropical medicine*
Kau, Sen T., *Renal physiology*
Kerns, William David, *Vascular disease, atherosclerosis*
Kindwall, Eric Post, *Hyperbaric medicine*
Kohli, Jai Dev, *Cardiovascular pharmacology*
Krevans, Julius Richard, *Educational administration*
Lazarus, Steven
Leevy, Carroll Moton, *Hepatology*
Leto, Salvatore, *Andrology*
Liebig, William John, *Medical instrumentation*
Lipton, James Abbott, *Medical sociology*
Lopez-Ovejero, Jorge Andres
Loucks, Vernon Reece, Jr., *Medical products research and development management*
Lynn, George Leslie
Mackaness, George Bellamy, *Medical research management*
Maricq, Hildegard Rand, *Interdisciplinary clinical research*
Marton, Laurence Jay
Maulik, Debabrata, *Perinatal diagnosis and therapy*
Michaels, Howard Brian
Mustard, James Fraser, *Arteriosclerosis; Research administration*
Nath, Ravinder, *Radiological physics*
Nelson, Diana Furst
O'Neil, John James

Philbin, Daniel Michael, *Cardiovascular physiology*
Pratt, Arnold W., *Computers in medicine*
Prystowsky, Harry, *Medical administration*
Purpura, Dominick Paul, *Medical education and research adminstration*
Rabkin, Mitchell Thornton, *Medical administration*
Radcliffe, John David, *Atherosclerosis*
Reider, Bruce
Rheinstein, Peter Howard, *Legal medicine*
Rooks, Wendell Hofma, II
Ruegsegger, Donald Ray, Jr., *Radiation therapy*
Ruegsegger, Paul Melchior, *Thermography of diseases*
Salafsky, Bernard P., *Tropical medicine*
Selikoff, Irving John, *Environmental medicine*
Seto, Joseph Tobey
Shaw, Margery Wayne Schlamp, *Health law*
Slack, Stephen Thomas, *Radiation safety*
Sprague, Charles Cameron, *Medical administration*
Steele, Glenn Daniel, Jr., *Surgical oncology*
Stenchever, Morton Albert, *Perinatal diagnosis and therapy*
Stinchcomb, Thomas Glenn
Strom, Terry Barton
Sullivan, Carole A., *Radiation oncology*
Sutnick, Alton Ivan
Suzuki, Kinuko
Tai, Selwyn Clarke, *Podiatric medicine and surgery*
Tepper, Lloyd Barton, *Environmental medicine*
Thind, Guadarshan Singh, *Hypertension*
Trudeau, Francis Berger, *Sports medicine*
Ubelaker, Douglas Henry, *Forensic anthropology*
Wald, Niel
Walter, Thomas Harry, *Bioelectricity*
Warren, Kenneth S., *Tropical medicine*
Wei, Jeng Shu, *Acupuncture*
Weldon, Virginia V., *Pediatric endocrinology*
White, Rolfe Downing, *Gynecologic urology*
Wilcox, Patti Marie
Wilson, Marjorie Price
Wilson, Michael John, *Andrology*
Woodring, John Howell
Wyngaarden, James Barnes, *Medical research administration*

NEUROSCIENCE

Neurobiology. *See* **BIOLOGY.**

Neurochemistry
Abood, Leo George
Abou-Donia, Martha May
Agnew, William Scott
Agrawal, Harish Chandra
Aprison, Morris Herman
Arch, Stephen William
Ariano, Marjorie A.
Babitch, Joseph Aaron
Banik, Narendra Lal
Bautz, Gordon Thomas
Bazan, Nicholas Guillermo
Beach, Robert Leigh
Bidlack, Jean Marie
Calabrese, Vincent Paul
Cash, Derek John
Chan, Pak Hoo
Cohn, Major Lloyd
Cone, Ric Ian
Cooper, Jack Ross
Coscina, Donald Victor
Craig, Charles Robert
Davis, Leonard George
De Blas, Angel Luis
DeMet, Edward Michael
Dettbarn, Wolf-Dietrich
Deutsch, Dale George
Dora, Eors Istvan
Dunn, Adrian John
Dwivedi, Chandradhar
Ehrlich, Yigal H.
Frey, William Howard II
Giambalvo, Cecilia Tang
Gilboe, David Dougherty
Green, Harry
Grouse, Lawrence Douglas
Hanin, Israel
Harris-Warrick, Ronald Morgan
Hogan, Edward Leo
Hoss, Wayne P.
Hui, Koon-Sea
Iqbal, Zafar
Jennings, Kent Richard
Johanson, Conrad Earl
Johnston, Craig Alan
Kant, Gloria Jean
Kark, Pieter Robert Adriaan
Kasarskis, Edward Joseph
Kauer, James Charles
Kaufman, Seymour
Kinnier, William James
Klingman, Gerda Isolde
Klingman, Jack Dennis
Kochman, Ronald Lawrence
Koslow, Stephen Hugh
Kumar, Sudhir
Lajtha, Abel
Larrabee, Martin Glover
Ledeen, Robert Wagner
Lee, Ching Y.
Lees, Marjorie Berman
Lerner, Pauline
Levitt, Morton
Lin, Shih-chia Chen
Lolley, Richard Newton
London, Edythe Danick
Mangano, Richard Michael
Marangos, Paul Jerome
Margolis, Frank Leonard
Marks, Neville
Marrazzi, Mary Ann
Martin, David Lee
Mason, Norman Ronald
Max, Stephen Richard
McBride, William Joseph, Jr.
McMorris, F(rederick) Arthur
Mehta, Nariman Bomanshaw
Miljanich, George Paul
Moody, Terry William
Morley, Barbara Jane
Nachman, Ronald James
Nicholas, Harold Joseph
Nicklas, William John
Olajos, Eugene Julius
Park, Dong Hwa
Philippart, Michel
Pozuelo, Jose
Prentky, Robert Alan
Price, David Alan
Rassin, David Keith
Rebec, George Vincent
Reis, Donald Jeffery
Resnick, Oscar
Riker, Donald Kay
Roel, Lawrence Edmund
Rosenberg, Philip
Sacks, William
Sajdel-Sulkowska, Elizabeth Maria
Schooley, David Allan
Scott, Irena McCammon
Severson, James Alan
Seyfried, Thomas Neil
Sharpless, Nansie Sue
Shih, Tsung-Ming Anthony
Sourkes, Theodore Lionel
Spector, Reynold
Squires, Richard Felt
Stach, Robert William
St. Omer, Vincent Edmund Victor
Streicher, Eugene
Sun, Albert Yung-Kwang
Sun, Grace Yan Chi
Taylor, Duncan Paul
Thomas, William Eric
Tjioe, Sarah Archambault
Ueda, Tetsufumi
Wang, Taitzer
Wecker, Lynn
White, Robert J.
Williams, Curtis Alvin, Jr.
Wong, David T.
Wurtman, Richard Jay
Yunger, Libby Marie
Zamenhof, Stephen

Neuroendocrinology. *See* **MEDICINE, Endocrinology.**

Neuroimmunology. *See* **MEDICINE, Immunology.**

Neuropharmacology
Abou-Donia, Martha May
Alford, Geary Simmons
Alkana, Ronald Lee
Anderson, Rebecca J.
Anisman, Hymie
Baker, Thomas
Barnes, Charles Dee
Barnett, Allen
Bartus, Raymond T.
Bautz, Gordon Thomas
Berney, Stuart Alan
Bidlack, Jean Marie
Bloom, Floyd Elliott
Blum, Kenneth
Blumberg, Harold
Borison, Richard Lewis
Brown, Gerald LaVonne
Browne, Ronald Gregory
Burkman, Allan Maurice
Bylund, David B.
Carson, Virginia Rosalie Gottschall
Caspary, Donald Michel
Cedarbaum, Jesse Michael
Chesire, Rebecca Martha
Chiodo, Louis Anthony
Chu, Nai-Shin
Church, Allen Charles
Chute, Douglas Lawrence
Chweh, Andrew Young Chul
Ciarlone, Alfred Edward
Cohen, Marlene Lois
Colasanti, Brenda Karen
Concannon, James Thomas
Craig, Charles Robert
Creese, Ian Nigel Richard
Creveling, Cyrus Robbins
Davis, Michael
Davis, Thomas Paul
Davis, Wilbur Marvin
Dean, Reginald Langworthy, III
Desaiah, Durisala
Dettbarn, Wolf-Dietrich
Dibner, Mark Douglas
Domer, Floyd Ray
Donzanti, Bruce Armand
Duckles, Sue Piper
Edmonds, Harvey Lee, Jr.
Ehrenpreis, Seymour
Eison, Michael Steven
Eldefrawi, Amira Toppozada
Enna, Salvatore Joseph
Fahn, Stanley
Faingold, Carl Lawrence
Ferko, Andrew Paul
Fernstrom, John Dickson
Ferrendelli, James Anthony
Fessler, Richard Glenn
Franz, Donald Norbert
Freedman, Daniel X.
Friedhoff, Arnold
Fromm, Gerhard Hermann
Fuller, Ray Ward
Gallagher, Brian Boru
Gallardo-Carpentier, Adriana
Goe, Don Richard
Goldstein, Jeffrey Marc
Graedon, Joe David
Hackman, John Clement
Hall, Edward Dallas
Hancock, John Charles
Hanin, Israel
Hansl, Nikolaus Rudolf
Harris, Louis Selig
Hartmann, Ernest Louis
Heffner, Thomas Gary
Hirsh, Kenneth Roy
Holaday, John Waldron
Hollister, Leo Edward
Hoss, Wayne P.
Hsu, Chung Y.
Jenden, Donald James
Jensen, Robert Alan
Johnson, David Norseen
Joy, Robert McKernon
Kaczmarek, Leonard Konrad
Kallman, Mary Jeanne
Kamerling, Steven Glenn
Kellar, Kenneth Jon
Khavari, Khalil Akhtar
Khazan, Naim
Kinnier, William James
Klingman, Gerda Isolde
Kochman, Ronald Lawrence
Kornetsky, Conan
Kosersky, Donald S.
Krall, Ronald Lee
Krnjevic, Kresimir Ivan
Lake, Charles Raymond
Lakoski, Joan Marie
Lal, Harbans
Levin, Harvey Steven
Levitan, Herbert
Lin, Shih-chia Chen
London, Edythe Danick
Long, John Paul
Lotti, Victor Joseph
Lucot, James Bernard
Maas, James Weldon
Mabry, Paul Davis, Jr.
Mantione, Charles Ross
Manyam, Bala Venktesha
Maran, Janice Wengerd
Marangos, Paul Jerome
Marrazzi, Mary Ann
Marwah, Joe
Mason, Norman Ronald
Matsuzaki, Masaji
Maxwell, Donald Robert
Mc Elligott, James George
McLean, John Robert
Menon, Madhavan Krishna
Messing, Rita Bailey
Morley, Barbara Jane
Murrin, Leonard Charles, II
Myslinski, Norbert Raymond
Narahashi, Toshio
Nemeroff, Charles Barnet
Novack, Gary Dean
O'Callaghan, James Patrick
Osterberg, Arnold Curtis
Paule, Merle Gale
Pazdernik, Thomas Lowell
Phillis, John Whitfield
Pottash, A.L.C.
Prabhu, Venkatray G.
Quirion, Remi
Raja, Srinivasa N.
Rasenick, Mark Mitchell
Rawat, Arun Kumar
Rebec, George Vincent
Reitz, Ronald Charles
Reyes, Edward
Richter, Judith Anne
Riker, Donald Kay
Roffman, Mark
Rose, Gregory Mancel
Rosenberg, Howard Charles
Rosenkranz, Roberto Pedro
Rotter, Andrej
Rudzik, Allan D.
Ruwe, William David
Schlesinger, Edward Bruce
Severson, James Alan
Shih, Tsung-Ming Anthony
Skolnick, Phil
Sladek, Celia Davis
Slevin, John Thomas
Snyder, Solomon Halbert
Soliman, Magdi Ramzi Iskandar
Squires, Richard Felt
Steinfels, George Francis
Stern, Warren Charles
Strahlendorf, Jean Carol
Summers, William Koopmans
Tamminga, Carol Ann
Taylor, Charles Price, Jr.
Taylor, Duncan Paul
Tempel, Ann
Tjioe, Sarah Archambault
Valdes, James John
Van de Kar, Louis D.
Van Loon, Glen Richard
Vaupel, Donald Bruce
Wecker, Lynn
Wein, Alan Jerome
Wong, David T.

Neurophysiology
Abel, Larry Allen
Abrams, Thomas William
Aitken, Peter Gil
Alberts, Walter Watson
Alkadhi, Karim Abdel
Alkon, Daniel Leon
Allen, Gary Irving
Allen, Gil C.
Anderson, James Alfred
Anderson, Thomas Edward
Asanuma, Hiroshi
Baird, Henry Welles, III
Baldo, George Jesse
Ball, Larry Lennox
Barnes, Charles Dee
Beck, Mary McLean
Bekoff, Anne C.
Berger, Theodore William
Bergey, Gregory Kent
Berlind, Allan
Bernstein, Jerrold
Bhattacharya, Syamal Kanti
Bilotto, Gerardo
Bizzi, Emilio
Black, Franklin Owen
Boston, John Robert
Bowen, John Metcalf
Bower, James Mason
Brink, Peter Richards
Brobeck, John Raymond
Brooks, Chandler McCuskey
Brown, Thomas Huntington
Buchwald, Jennifer Sullivan
Burke, Robert Emmett
Campbell, James Norman
Chiodo, Louis Anthony
Chou, Shelley Nien-chun
Cockerham, Lorris G.
Cohen, David Harris
Coleman, James R.
Costanzo, Richard Michael
Crampton, George Harris
de la Torre, Jack Carlos
De Luca, Carlo John
Deshmukh, Vinod Dhundiraj
Dora, Eors Istvan
Dyer, Robert Stritzinger
Eberstein, Arthur
Egger, Maurice David
Elble, Rodger Jacob, Jr.
Emerson, Robert Charles
Ewing, June Swift
Faber, Donald Stuart
Faingold, Carl Lawrence
Foreman, Robert Dale
Franz, Donald Norbert
Furshpan, Edwin Jean
Gabriel, Michael
Gardner, Jill Christopher
Giannini, A. James
Gidda, Jaswant Singh
Gilman, Sid
Gladfelter, Wilbert Eugene
Goe, Don Richard
Gonzalez-Lima, Francisco Maria
Gootman, Phyllis Myrna
Grob, David
Hackman, John Clement
Hallett, Mark
Hamid, Mohamed Ahmed-Abdel
Harrison, Jean Burch
Harris-Warrick, Ronald Morgan
Hatton, Glenn Irwin
Heyer, Eric John
Hobson, J. Allan
Huang, Chuong Chun
Hughes, John Russell
Jacobs, Roland William
Javel, Eric
Jen, Philip Hung Sun
Kennedy, Philip Richard
Kraig, Richard Paul
Krauthamer, Gunter Michael (George)
Krnjevic, Kresimir Ivan
Kukulka, Carl George
Lakoski, Joan Marie
Larrabee, Martin Glover
Lawrence, Merle
Lee, Mary Bronwyn
Light, Alan Ray
Lindsley, Donald Benjamin
Llinas, Rodolfo Riascos
Low, Walter Cheney
Maran, Janice Wengerd
Marshall, Louise Hanson
Masland, Richard Harry
Matsuzaki, Masaji
Mayer, David Jonathan
Mayer, Richard Frederick
Mc Cabe, Brian Francis
McCarley, Robert William
Millhorn, David Eugene
Mortimer, James Arthur
Moss, Robert Louis
Mountcastle, Vernon Benjamin, Jr.
Movshon, J(oseph) Anthony
Myslinski, Norbert Raymond
Nair, Pankajam K(arunakaran)
Narahashi, Toshio
Nathanson, Morton
Nelson, Jeremiah I.
Newton, Roberta Ann
Ochs, Sidney
Pack, Allan Ian
Pagala, Murali Krishna
Partridge, Lloyd D(onald)
Patterson, Terence Edward
Phillips, Michael Ian
Phillis, John Whitfield
Pitts, Nathaniel Gilbert
Pivik, Rudolph Terry
Plotsky, Paul Mitchell
Puente, Antonio Enrique
Raja, Srinivasa N.
Randall, Walter C(lark)
Rapp, Paul Ernest
Ratliff, Floyd
Ray, Richard Hallett
Reaves, Troy Albert, Jr.
Reis, Donald Jeffery
Rockland, Kathleen Skiba
Rosen, Arthur D.
Ruggero, Mario Alfredo
Ryu, Jai Hyun
Sainati, Stephen Mitchell
Salzman, Steven Kerry
Sanders, Donald Benjamin
Schlesinger, Edward Bruce
Scott, Irena McCammon
Scott, Thomas Russell, Jr.
Sessle, Barry John
Sharma, Sansar C.
Sillman, Arnold Joel
Simpson, Richard Kendall, Jr.
Smith, Robert L.
Solomonow, Moshe
Sparks, David Lee
Stephens, Philip John
Stern-Tomlinson, Wendy Barbara
Stevens, Charles F.
Stockwell, Charles Warren
Strahlendorf, Jean Carol
Sur, Mriganka
Taber-Maier, Katherine Helen
Tache, Yvette France
Taylor, Charles Price, Jr.
Thompson, Richard Frederick
Toga, Arthur Warren
Tourtellotte, Wallace William
Traub, Roger Dennis
Trehub, Arnold
Trubatch, Janett
Tuttle, Jeremy Ballou
Walsh, Patrick Robert
Westheimer, Gerald
White, Robert J.
Wieland, Steven Joseph
Winter, Arthur
Wolbarsht, Myron Lee
Wong, Robert King-Suen
Wu, Chun-Fang
Yazulla, Stephen
Yost, William Albert

Neuropsychology
Allen, Robert Arthur
Anisman, Hymie
Anson, James Greg
Appel, Antoinette Ruth
Bauer, Richard Henry
Berg, Richard Alan
Berman, Marlene Oscar
Bigler, Erin David
Bodnar, Richard Julius
Braggio, John Thomas
Brito, Gilberto Ottoni
Brodie, Harlow Keith Hammond
Brooker, Alan Edward
Brown, Thomas Huntington
Bryant, James Winston, Jr.
Bryden, Mark Philip
Bryson, George Gardner
Buchtel, Henry Augustus, IV
Buck, Ross Workman
Burton, Howard Alan
Campbell-Smith, Rosemary Gilles
Chute, Douglas Lawrence
Cleeland, Charles Samuel
Coutts, Robert LaRoy
Crown, Barry Michael
Dalby, (John) Thomas
Davis, Michael
Dolenz, John Joseph
Donchin, Emanuel
Duncan, Constance Catharine
Dunlop, Terrence Ward
Eckardt, Michael Jon
Fisher, Jerid Martin
Gallo, Mario Martin
Gardner, Jill Christopher
Gasparrini, William Gerard
Goldman, Alexander
Greenblatt, Samuel Harold
Gur, Ruben C.
Hamning, Richard Rudolph
Hebb, Donald Olding
Hill, A. Lewis
Holmstrom, Valerie Louise
Howard, James Lawrence
Hursh, Steven Rawlings
Jackson, Thomas Larry
Jones, Ben Morgan
Kamback, Marvin Carl
Karrer, Rathe Stevens
Kaszniak, Alfred Wayne
Kettlewell, Neil MacKewan
Kodanaz, Hatice Altan
Lansdell, Herbert Charles
Lee, Mary Bronwyn
Levin, Harvey Steven
Levinthal, Charles Frederick
Lieberman, Harris Ritchie
Litle, Patrick Alan
Lloyd, John Tracy
Lubar, Joel Fredric
Ludlow, Christy Leslie
MacDonald, G(eorge) Wayne
Mahan, Harry Clinton
Malitz, Sidney
Masters, Robert Edward Lee
Matarazzo, Joseph Dominic
Mc Elligott, James George
McSweeny, Austin John
Miller, Nancy E(llen)
Miller, Patricia Lynn
Naranjo, Jennings Neal
Neff, William Duwayne
Ojemann, George Alvin
Olton, David Stuart
Pagnoncelli, Giacomo
Patterson, Terence Edward
Pavlidis, George Theophilou
Peniston, Eugene G.
Perez, Francisco Ignacio
Pitcher, Georgia Ann
Plakosh, Paul, Jr.
Podbros, Linda Zoe
Puente, Antonio Enrique
Reitan, Ralph Meldahl
Rose, Gregory Mancel
Ruegsegger, Paul Melchior
Sachs, Benjamin David
Sbordone, Robert Joseph
Silverman, Hirsch Lazaar
Soper, Henry Victor
Stapleton, Leroy Earl
Stewart, Larry Gene
Tansey, Michael Anselme
Vicente, Peter James
Wagman, Althea M.I.
Yozawitz, Allan

Regeneration
Bernstein, Jerald J(ack)
Borges, Lawrence Francis
Creese, Ian Nigel Richard
Davis, James Norman
Easter, Stephen Sherman, Jr.
Fiori, Mario Giuseppe
Goodrich, James Tait
Krebs, Helmut Waldemar Graf von Thorn
Kromer, Lawrence Frederick
Liu, Hsiang Mei
McQuarrie, Irvine Gray
Mendelson, Thea
Norvell, John Edmondson, III
Phelps, Carol Jo
Román, Gustavo Campos
Seil, Fredrick John
Uzman, Betty Geren

Other
Adelman, George, *Interdisciplinary neuroscience*
Berg, Richard Alan, *Pediatric neuropsychology*
Brick, John
Buchwald, Jennifer Sullivan, *Electrophysiology*
Coleman, James R., *Developmental neuroscience*
Earle, Alvin Mathews
Elizan, Teresita S., *Neurovirology*
Emerson, Robert Charles, *Neuroanatomy*
Fiori, Mario Giuseppe
Fotopoulos, Sophia Strathopoulos

Gonzalez-Lima, Francisco Maria
Henkel, Craig Kenneth, *Neuroanatomy*
Hoop, Bernard
Hope, George Marion, *Visual neuroscience*
Hopfield, John Joseph, *Neural modelling*
Isaacson, Robert Lee
Kennedy, Charles, *Brain energy metabolism*
Kromer, Lawrence Frederick, *Neurodevelopment*
Lacy, Priti Sheila, *Neural aspects of stroke*
Low, Walter Cheney, *Neural transplantation*
Mesulam, M. Marsel, *Neuroanatomy*
Miskimen, George William
Mitsumoto, Hiroshi, *Neuropathology*
Naeser, Margaret Ann, *Acupuncture research for stroke cases with paralysis*
Pagala, Murali Krishna
Palay, Sanford Louis
Pietsch, Paul Andrew
Rimel, Rebecca Webster
Romagnano, Mary Ann Antoinette
Sadun, Alfredo Arrigo Umberto, *Neuroanatomy*
Sherman, S. Murray
St. Omer, Vincent Edmund Victor
Swaiman, Kenneth Fred, *Developmental neuroscience*
Tilson, Hugh Arval, Jr., *Neurotoxicology*
Wagner, William Gerard
Whetsell, William Otto, Jr., *Neuropathology*

OPERATIONS RESEARCH. *See* ENGINEERING, MATHEMATICS.

OPTICS. *See also* LASER.

Fiber optics
Affatato, Joseph Frank
Bagley, Brian G.
Berry, Robert Walter
Brumm, Douglas Bruce
Buckman, A(lvin) Bruce
Burroughs, Mark Scott
Burrus, Charles Andrew, Jr.
Cuomo, Frank William
Dakss, Mark Ludmer
Davis, Mark Hezekiah, Jr.
Dyott, Richard Burnaby
Edahiro, Takao
Fang, Shu-Cherng
Gewartowski, James Walter
Gould, Gordon
Green, Samuel Isaac
Hammer, Jacob Meyer
Hasegawa, Akira
Hoffman, Graham Walter
Kang, Min Ho
Kao, Charles Kuen
Kapron, Felix Paul
Kasper, Bryon Lynn
Keiser, Gerd Emdo
Kim, Kwang-Seok
Kovacs, Gyula
Kraemer, Arthur Robert
Law, Hsiang-Yi David
LeMay, Charlotte Zihlman
Li, Tingye
Lin, Chinlon
Marcuse, Dietrich
Marhic, Michel Edmond
Marshalek, Robert Gerald
McMahon, Donald Howland
Mensah, Thomas
Miller, Stewart Edward
Mollenauer, Linn Frederick
Morton, Randall Eugene
Myer, Jon H(arold)
Newton, Steven Arthur
Pincus, Alexis George
Rast, Howard Eugene, Jr.
Rezek, Edward Anthony
Scholl, Frederick William
Schwickert, Russell Charles
Shorthill, Richard Warren
Stone, Julian
Storozum, Steven Lee
Tien, Ping King
Welch, Herbert Eugene
Whinnery, John Roy
Whitcomb, Bruce Magill
Wood, Thomas H.
Woods, John Galloway
Yao, Shi-Kay
Zanzucchi, Paul E.

Holography
Aldrich, Ralph Edward
Attwood, David Thomas
Broadbent, Donald Clarence
Brown, Gordon M(arshall)
Bryan, David A.
Chang, B(yung) Jin
Erf, Robert K.
Lamberts, Robert Lewis
Latta, John Neal
Leibhardt, Edward
Leith, Emmett Norman
Mueller, Peter Francis
Owen, Robert Barry
Prikryl, Ivan
Reynolds, George Owen
Ruterbusch, Paul Hugo
Thompson, Brian John
Tomren, Douglas Roy
Upatnieks, Juris
Vest, Charles Marstiller

Infrared spectroscopy
Curnutte, Basil, Jr.
Degnan, John James, III
Dionne, Gerald Francis
Eggers, David Frank
Garing, John Seymour
Gilmour, William Alexander
Han, Ki Sup
Hanley, Stephen Thure
Herget, William Frederick
Herzberg, Gerhard
Koos, Gregory Lee
LaPorte, Daniel D'Arcy
Lauer, James Lothar
Li, Ying-Sing
Lurix, Paul Leslie, Jr.
McCubbin, Thomas King, Jr.
Nee, Tsu-Wei
Shoore, Joseph David
Woodall, Milton Andrew, II

Optical image processing
Casasent, David Paul
Derderian, George
Fienup, James Ray
Kornstein, Edward
Lahart, Martin Joseph
Leith, Emmett Norman
McMahon, Donald Howland
Mc Millan, Robert Scott
Melville, Richard Devern Samuels, Jr.
Mueller, Peter Francis
Pederson, Donald Otis
Revesz, George
Reynolds, George Owen
Saleh, Bahaa E. A.
Schultz, Alfred Bernard
Smith, Donald Eugene
Tomei, L. David
Wilkerson, Susan McCasland

Optical signal processing
Bryan, David A.
Casasent, David Paul
Chang, B(yung) Jin
Chen, Hsiang Tsun
Gibbs, Hyatt McDonald
Guenther, Bob Dean
Haus, Hermann Anton
Helstrom, Carl Wilhelm
Kondilis, Francis Nicholas, Jr.
Lieberman, Alfred George
Lopez, Hector
Marks, Robert Jackson, II
McAulay, Alastair D.
Meeks, Steven Wayne
Myer, Jon H(arold)
Newton, Steven Arthur
Pernick, Benjamin
Poularikas, Alexander Demitrios
Rabson, Thomas Avelyn
Reinhold, Richard Clarke
Smith, Peter William
Soffer, Bernard H.
Teague, James Ralph
Upatnieks, Juris
Walkup, John Frank
Wang, Shing Chung
Wang, Shyh
Wilder, James Andrew, Jr.
Yao, Shi-Kay

Other
Aldrich, Ralph Edward
Anderson, Albert Gordon, *Electro-optics*
Benjamin, Roland John, *Optical aspheric surfaces*
Bigio, Irving Joseph, *Nonlinear optics*
Bottema, Murk, *Optical design*
Carter, William Harold, *Optics research*
Chiang, Fu-pen, *Stress analysis*
Clark, Roy
Dunn, Anne Roberts, *Infrared technology*
Enoch, Jay Martin
Fader, Walter John
Fennelly, Alphonsus John, *General optics.*
Franken, Peter Alden
Freniere, Edward Richard
Garnett, Robert William
Geslicki, Mark Louis, *Laser optics design*
Gunter, William Dayle, Jr.
Hansch, Theodor Wolfgang, *Spectroscopy*
Herriott, Donald Richard, *Optical instrumentation*
Hirleman, Edwin Daniel, Jr., *Optical instrumentation*
Holmes, Dale Arthur, *Laser optics*
Jacobsen, Edward Hastings, *Electron optics*
Jenkinson, Howard Acis, *Integrated optics*
Klaiber, Robert, *Applied optics*
Konopnicki, Marek Jan
Leibhardt, Edward, *Diffraction Gratings*
Lilje, Karl David, *Opto-mechanics consulting*
Linder, Solomon Leon, *Electro-optical systems*
Mallmann, Alexander James
Massey, Gail Austin, *Nonlinear optics*
McConkey, John William
McManamon, Paul Francis, *Thermal imaging*
Moody, John Chrystor, *Remote sensor optics and systems*
Moore, Duncan Thomas, *Gradient-index optics*
Muller, Rolf Hugo, *Thin film optical research*
Offner, Abe
O'Shea, Donald Charles, *Optical design*
Owen, Robert Barry, *Optical measurement systems*
Pearson, James Edward, *Applied optics*
Prikryl, Ivan, *Optical information processing*
Primak, William L.
Rand, Stephen Colby
Rockensies, Kenneth Jules, *Physical optics*
Schaefer, Albert Russell, *Photo-optical instrumentation*
Schultz, Frederick H. C., *Polarized infrared absorption and reflection*
Shannon, Robert Rennie, *Optical research management*
Steiner, Bruce Watson
Swenson, George Warner, Jr., *Optics*
Task, Harry Lee
Tatchyn, Roman Orest, *X-Ray Optics*
Teegarden, Kenneth James, *Optical research management*
Tomlinson, W. John, *Optics research*
Tyson, Robert Karl, *Theoretical optics*
Vander Sluis, Kenneth L.
Van Metter, Richard Lawrence
Wang, Ru Tsang
Weber, Paul Egon
Wilson, Mark Wayne

PHARMACEUTICS

Drug delivery systems
Amidon, Gregory Everett
Canova-Davis, Eleanor
Das, Pankaj Kumar
Fisher, Richard Keith
Fraser, Clarence Malcolm
Greco, Gary
Haslam, John Lee
Haynes, Lynn O.
Johnson, Dee Lynn
Kafrawy, Adel
Katz, Martin
Lee, Eun Soo
Lee, Yong-Jai
Page, Michel
Valvani, Shri Chand
Van Campen, Lynn
Widder, Kenneth Jon
Wu, Stephen Hong-wei
Yesair, David Wayne
Zografi, George D.

Drug design
Bransome, Edwin Dagobert, Jr.
Cheney, Brigham Vernon
Demerson, Christopher Alex
Fox, Jack Jay
Ganguly, Ashit Kumar
Gosalvez, Mario
Hockel, Gregory Martin
Holleman, William H.
Jensen, Norman Peter
Kenakin, Terrence Peter
King, James Wesley
Kuyper, Lee Frederick
Lazer, Edward Stephen
Martin, Lawrence Leo
McFarland, James William
Michne, William Francis
Miller, Edward Phillip
Moore, Michael Lee
O'Donnell, Terence John
Olson, Gary Lee
Ondetti, Miguel Angel
Pschigoda, Loraine Mae
Shealy, Y. Fulmer
Unger, Stefan Howard
Valvani, Shri Chand
Van Campen, Lynn
Vinson, John Wilmot

Medicinal chemistry
Aguiar, Adam Martin
Attard, John
Baran, John Stanislaus
Bloom, Barry Malcolm
Bodor, Nicholas Stephen
Broom, Arthur Davis
Cates, Lindley Addison, Jr.
Cheng, Chia-Chung
Chignell, Colin Francis
Cho, Arthur Kenji
Cromwell, Norman H
Currie, Bruce Lamonte
Demerson, Christopher Alex
Douglas, Bryce
Floyd, Middleton Brawner, Jr.
Flynn, Daniel Lee
Glamkowski, Edward Joseph
Green, Donald Eugene
Grim, Michael David
Handorf, Charles Russell
Harbert, Charles Armon
Helsley, Grover Cleveland
Hutchins, Charles William
Iyengar, Bhashyam Srinivasa
Jenden, Donald James
Jirousek, Ludek
Johns, William Francis
Kagan, Fred
Katner, Allen Samuel
King, James Wesley
Klayman, Daniel Leslie
Koonse, Howard Joseph
Korytnyk, Wsewolod
Kreft, Anthony Frank, III
Kuyper, Lee Frederick
LaMattina, John Lawrence
Langeland, William Enberg
LaRocca, Joseph Paul
Lasslo, Andrew
Lazer, Edward Stephen
Lee, Henry Joung
Lunsford, Carl Dalton
Lyle, Robert Edward, Jr.
Marfat, Anthony
Martin, Lawrence Leo
McClure, David Earl
McFarland, James William
Michne, William Francis
Miller, Duane Douglas
Misra, Anand Lal
Moore, Michael Lee
Moos, Walter Hamilton
Nagasawa, Herbert Tsukasa
Neumeyer, John Leopold
O'Brien, Jay Philip
Ondetti, Miguel Angel
Pars, Harry George
Paul, Ara Garo
Pop, Emil
Prabhu, Vilas Anandrao
Press, Jeffery Bruce
Roberts, John Lawson
Robins, Morris Joseph
Rodriguez, Eloy
Saggiomo, Andrew Joseph
Seevers, Robert Harmon, Jr.
Shealy, Y. Fulmer
Shen, Tsung Ying
Shih, David Houng-min
Silverman, Richard Bruce
Smith, Charles Irvel
Smith, David William
Soloway, Albert Herman
Stohs, Sidney John
Thompson, Richard David
Tilley, Jefferson Wright
Tishler, Max
Unger, Stefan Howard
Verghese, Chacko Perakathu
Vlattas, Isidoros
Walsh, John Stuart

Pharmacognosy
Brady, Lynn Robert
Paul, Ara Garo
Powell, Richard Grant
Rhodes, Charles Kirkham
Rodriguez, Eloy
Staba, Emil John

Pharmacokinetics
Alkalay, David
Angelo, Michael James
Baughman, Robert A., Jr.
Benet, Leslie Zachary
Berney, Stuart Alan
Block, Lawrence Howard
Doluisio, James Thomas
Eshelman, Fred Neville
Evans, William Edward
Findlay, John William Addison
Galinsky, Raymond Ethan
Goyan, Jere Edwin
Grindel, Joseph Michael
Hofmann, Lorenz Martin
Imondi, Anthony Rocco
Kaplan, Stanley Albert
Krasny, Harvey Charles
Levy, Gerhard
Mayock, Robert Lee
Mehta, Bipin Mohanlal
Mendels, Joseph
Mitchell, George Bert
Nicolau, Gabriela
Okerholm, Richard Arthur
Perel, James Maurice
Richman, Joseph Ben
Rotenberg, Keith Saul
Seeler, David Charles
Singhvi, Sampat Manakchand
Stambaugh, John Edgar, Jr.
Sullivan, Hugh Richard, Jr.
Tyler, Tipton Ransom
Vickers, Stanley
Walker, Clay Brown
Weber, Dennis Joseph
Wilkinson, Grant Robert
Wosilait, Walter Daniel
Young, John Falkner

Other
Amidon, Gordon Lewis, *Pharmaceutical research and development*
Block, Lawrence Howard
Buchanan, Robert Alexander, *Clinical research*
Cartlidge, Edward Sutterley
Gaffar, Maria Corazon Solis
Goldstein, Sidney
Grindel, Joseph Michael
Johnson, Irving Stanley, *Pharmaceutical research and development*
Kenakin, Terrence Peter, *Drug receptor kinetics*
Langeland, William Enberg
Lunsford, Carl Dalton, *Pharmaceutical research*
McIlreath, Fred J., *Pharmaceutical research and development*
Megel, Herbert, *Pharmaceutical toxicology*
Oeswein, James Quentin
Rippie, Edward Grant
Singhvi, Sampat Manakchand
Stoll, Roger G., *Pharmaceutical research and development*
Stucki, Jacob Calvin, *Pharmaceutical research and development*
Sullivan, Hugh Richard, Jr.
Tivin, Fred, *Pharmaceutical quality assurance*
Van Ryzin, Robert Joseph, *Pharmaceutical toxicology*
Verghese, Chacko Perakathu, *Drug metabolism*
Wardell, Joe Russell, Jr., *Pharmacological research and administration*
Wiebe, Leonard Irving, *Drug metabolism*

PHYSICS

Acoustics
Adler, Robert
Banjavic, Richard Alan
Barger, James Edwin
Cerceo, John Michael
Cuomo, Frank William
Dunn, Floyd
Eby, Ronald K.
Eldred, Kenneth McKechnie
Erf, Robert K.
Etter, Paul Courtney
Fujimura, Osamu
Gibbons, Michael Francis, Jr.
Griffy, Thomas Alan
Harris, Cyril Manton
Johnson, David Linton
Kaufman, Charles
Kays, James Lee
Lang, William Warner
Maris, Humphrey John
Meeks, Steven Wayne
Mintzer, David
Munson, John Christian
Raichel, Daniel Richter
Ream, Gregory Lawrence
Richards, Roger Thomas
Rosario-Garcia, Efraín
Rudnick, Isadore
Sablik, Martin John
Shen, Sin-Yan
Shivanandan, Kandiah
Sinha, Bikash Kumar
Slayton, Michael Henry
South, Hugh Miles
Stevens, Donald Meade
Swenson, George Warner, Jr.
Tam, Andrew Ching
Tehon, Stephen Whittier
Ting, Robert Yen-Ying
Uberall, Herbert Michael Stefan
Wagers, Robert Shelby
Westervelt, Peter Jocelyn
Wilson, Geoffrey Leonard
Ying, Shuh-Pan

Astrophysics. *See* **ASTRONOMY.**

Atomic and molecular physics
Alexander, Millard Henry
Andrews, Roger Charles
Aubel, Joseph Lee
Azziz, Nestor Jalil
Bashkin, Stanley
Baylis, William Eric
Bel Bruno, Joseph J(ames)
Benesch, William
Bennett, William Ralph, Jr.
Berney, Charles V.
Berry, Richard Stephen
Bichsel, Hans
Bloembergen, Nicolaas
Bondybey, Vladimir Edmund
Brewer, Richard George
Brink, Gilbert O.
Brion, Christopher Edward
Brody, Burton Alan
Brown, Ellen Ruth
Bruch, Reinhard Frank
Brumer, Paul William
Bunge, Carlos Federico
Burns, Jay, III
Burr, Alexander Fuller
Caird, John Allyn
Caledonia, George Ernest
Callaway, Joseph
Cartwright, David Chapman
Chang, Tu-Nan
Cheng, Kwok-Tsang
Childs, William Jeffries
Chupp, Timothy Edward
Church, David Arthur
Cohen, James Samuel
Conway, John G.
Cooper, Charles Dewey
Cowan, Robert Duane
Cox, Arthur Nelson
Crasemann, Bernd
Curnutte, Basil, Jr.
Curtis, Lorenzo Jan
Dang, Richard Kaoyu
Datz, Sheldon
Davidson, Gilbert
Decker, Charles David
Dehmelt, Hans Georg
Delos, John Bernard
de Wit, Michiel
Dick, Charles Edward
Dugan, Charles Hammond
Dunning, Frank Barry
Fairbank, William Martin, Jr.
Fano, Ugo
Farley, John William
Feld, Michael Stephen
Fetterman, Harold Ralph
Findley, Gary Lee
Fite, Wade Lanford
Fonck, Raymond John
Fontana, Peter Robert
Fox, Kenneth
Franken, Peter Alden
Freed, Karl Frederick
Freund, Robert Stanley
Fuhr, Jeffrey Robert
Fystrom, Dell Orren
Gallagher, Thomas Francis
Galt, John Alexander
Garing, John Seymour
Gay, Timothy James
George, James
Gillespie, George Hubert
Ginter, Marshall Lloyd
Gislason, Eric Arni
Golden, David Edward
Goorvitch, David
Gordy, Walter
Greene, Arthur Edward
Greene, Chris H.
Greene, John Philip
Gregory,, Donald CliffordDOnald CliffordDk
Guenther, Bob Dean
Gupta, Rajendra
Hall, John Lewis
Hanson, Harold Palmer
Haun, Robert Dee, Jr.
Hayden, Howard Corwin, Jr.
Heer, Clifford V.
Herzberg, Gerhard
Hilborn, Robert Clarence
Hodges, Ronald Vernon
Hopper, Darrel Gene
Huang, Keh-Ning
Hyman, Howard Allan
Islam, Muhammad Azadul
Jaduszliwer, Bernardo
Jakas, Mario Mateo
Johnson, Peter Dexter
Johnson, Robert E.
Judd, Brian Raymond
Karo, Arnold Mitchell
Kerwin, Larkin
Kessler, Karl G.
Kleppner, Daniel
Knight, Walter David
Kobe, Donald Holm
Kocher, Carl Alvin
Konowalow, Daniel Dimitri
Kramer, Steven David
Krause, Manfred Otto
Kusch, Polykarp
Langhoff, Peter Wolfgang
Lapatovich, Walter Peter
Lapicki, Gregory
Larsen, Jon Thorsten
Lau, Albert Man-Fai
Lawler, James Edward
Lee, Long C.
Levin, Frank S.
Li, Ming Chiang
Lide, David Reynolds, Jr.
Lim, Teck-Kah
Lin, Chun Chia
Lindau, Ingolf Evert
Littleton, John Edward
Littman, Michael Geist
Lodhi, Sattar Khan
Lu, Chun Chian
Lubell, Michael Stephen
Lucatorto, Thomas Benjamin
MacArthur, Duncan Whittemore
Mack, Michael Edward
Madison, Don Harvey
Magnuson, Gustav Donald
Mandel, Leonard

Manson, Steven Trent
Martin, Frederick Wight
Mason, Edward Allen
Mavroyannis, Constantine
McAfee, Kenneth Bailey, Jr.
McArthur, David Alexander
McClelland, Jabez Jenkins
McCubbin, Thomas King, Jr.
McFarland, Robert Harold
McGregor, Wheeler Kesey, Jr.
McGuire, James Horton
Mc Ilrath, Thomas James
McLaughlin, William Lowndes
Meyerhof, Walter Ernst
Miers, Richard Ernest
Moore, (Edwin) Neal
Moore, John Hays
Moseley, John Travis
Neumann, Herschel
Newsom, Gerald Higley
Nitz, David Edwin
Noid, Donald William
Norcross, David Warren
Oka, Takeshi
O'Malley, Thomas Francis
Orel, Ann Elizabeth
Pack, Russell T.
Park, John Thornton
Parr, Albert Clarence
Patel, Chandra Kumar Naranbhai
Pfeiffer, Raymond John
Pierce, Elliot Stearns
Piore, Emanuel Ruben
Pollak, Gregory Daniel
Postma, Herman
Pradhan, Anil Kumar
Pratt, Richard Houghton
Radziemski, Leon Joseph
Ramsey, Norman
Randall, Russel R.
Rapp, Donald
Reading, John Frank
Reber, Jerry Donald
Richardson, James Wyman
Robinson, Edward J.
Roy, Denis L.
Ryan, Stewart Richard
Sachs, Lester Marvin
Safron, Sanford Alan
Saha, Bidhan Chandra
Saloman, Edward Barry
Samson, James Alexander Ross
Sarachman, Theodore Nicholas
Scarl, Donald
Schaefer, Albert Russell
Schawlow, Arthur Leonard
Schlachter, Alfred Simon
Schmieder, Robert William
Shah, Saiyid Masroor
Sharpton, Francis Arthur
Smyth, Kermit Campbell
Snow, William Rosebrook
Sorokin, Peter Pitirimovich
Stroscio, Michael Anthony
Sung Ho, (Salk)
Tai, Chen-Yu
Tam, Andrew Ching
Taylor, Lyle Herman
Taylor, William Leroy
Tejwani, Gopal Das
Temkin, Richard Joel
Thomas, Dan McDougal
Townes, Charles Hard
Trajmar, Sandor
Van Brunt, Richard Joseph
Varney, Robert Nathan
Wang, Wen I.
Weatherford, Charles Albert
Weber, Alfons
Weinstein, Roy
Weissler, Gerhard Ludwig
Wiese, Wolfgang Lothar
Wilson, Walter Ervin
Winkler, Peter
Winter, Thomas Gustav
Wood, Obert Reeves, II
Zollweg, Robert John

Biophysics
Agard, Eugene Theodore
Alberts, Walter Watson
Alfano, Robert Richard
Allocca, John Anthony
Alpen, Edward Lewis
Alvarez, Luis W.
Anderson, David Walter
Banerjee, Krishnadas
Bearden, Alan Joyce
Beetz, Charles Pershing, Jr.
Benedek, George Bernard
Berger, Robert Lewis
Bigler, Rodney E.
Brownell, Gordon Lee
Butler, James Preston
Carey, Martin Conrad
Charney, Elliot
Chu, William Tongil
Cohen, Morrel Herman
Cokelet, Giles Roy
Dunn, Floyd
Fairchild, Ralph Grandison
Feinberg, Robert Jacob
Finegold, Leonard X.
Giaever, Ivar
Gordy, Walter
Harth, Erich
Hitzig, Bernard Michael
Hobbie, Russell Klyver
Huang, Cheng Schen
Hyman, Edward Sidney
Jayaweera, Ananda Ranjith
Katz, J. Lawrence
Krimm, Samuel
Lin, Tsung-I George
Lis, Adam Wiktor
Malsky, Stanley Joseph
Marden, Michael Charles
Marino, Andrew Anthony
Mercer, Kermit Ray
Meredith, Orsell Montgomery
Noordergraaf, Abraham
Powers, Linda Sue
Redfield, Alfred Guillou
Ritz-Gold, Caroline Joyce
Roper, Leon David
Rothschild, Kenneth Joseph
Rudy, Yoram
Sandhu, Taljit Singh
Schwartz, Irving Leon
Shamos, Morris Herbert
Sharma, Ram Ratan
Shulman, Robert Gerson
Simpson, Larry Dean
Sliney, David Hammond
Somlyo, Avril Virginia
Steely, H(enry) Thomas, Jr.
Sukow, Wayne William
Tai, Yuan-Heng
Woolford, Thomas Laney
Wu, Raymond Kee-Kin

Condensed matter physics
Abraham, Marvin Meyer
Abrahams, Sidney Cyril
Albers, Robert Charles
Albers, Walter Anthony, Jr
Alexander, Michael Norman
Alfano, Robert Richard
Alig, Roger Casanova
Allan, Douglas Clippinger
Alldredge, Gerald Palmer
Alterovitz, Samuel Adar
Ambler, Ernest
Anderson, Ansel Cochran
Andrews, Hugh Robert
Appelbaum, Joel A(lan)
Appleton, B. R.
Arai, Tadashi
Arakawa, Edward Takashi
Ashcroft, Neil William
Aubel, Joseph Lee
Bardeen, John
Bate, Robert Thomas
Bates, John Bryant
Batterman, Boris William
Beetz, Charles Pershing, Jr.
Berger, Lev Isaac
Beri, Avinash Chandra
Bharat, Ramasesha
Bhattacharya, Rabi Sankar
Bhattacharyya, Anjan
Bicerano, Jozef
Biswas, Rana
Blakely, John McDonald
Blessinger, Michael Anthony
Blume, Martin
Boatner, Lynn Allen
Böer, Karl Wolfgang
Boesch, Harold Edwin, Jr.
Bray, Philip James
Brewer, Richard George
Burns, Jay, III
Butler, William Hill
Button, Kenneth J(ohn)
Cain, Laurence Sutherland
Callaway, Joseph
Carlson, David Emil
Cezairliyan, Ared
Chabal, Yves Jean
Chan, Iu-Yam
Chaudhuri, Siddheswar
Chen, Daniel Ray
Chen, Tao-seng
Ching, Wai-Yim
Chu, Wei-Kan
Chynoweth, Alan Gerald
Claassen, Richard Strong
Clark, Bill Pat
Clark, Clifton Bob
Cohen, Morrel Herman
Coleman, Charles Clyde
Compaan, Alvin Dell
Cone, Rufus Lester
Connolly, John William
Conway, John G.
Conwell, Esther Marly
Craighead, Harold G.
Curelaru, Irina Mariana
Dacey, George Clement
Dalbec, Paul Euclide
Davis, Guy Donald
Davison, Sydney George
Delfino, Michelangelo
DeLong, Lance Eric
Doering, Dale Larry
Dreschhoff, Gisela Auguste Marie
Dresselhaus, Mildred Spiewak
Dresser, Miles Joel
Drickamer, Harry George
Druger, Stephen David
Dunning, Frank Barry
Eades, John Alwyn
Eckhardt, Helmut Karl
Edahiro, Takao
Eernisse, Errol Peter
Egelhoff, William Frederick, Jr.
Esaki, Leo
Falco, Charles Maurice
Falzone, Anthony Joseph
Family, Fereydoon
Fariss, Thomas Lee
Farmer, John William
Fischer, Traugott Erwin
Fisher, David George
Flinn, Paul Anthony
Foner, Simon
Forman, Richard Allan
Fowler, Howland Auchincloss
Fradin, Frank Yale
Galt, John Kirtland
Gamble, Fred Ridley, Jr.
Garland, James C.
Giaever, Ivar
Gibbs, Hyatt McDonald
Gildenblat, Gennady
Glascock, Homer Hopson, II
Glicksman, Maurice
Glosser, Robert
Goldenberg, Barbara L.
Gomer, Robert
Goodman, Nancy B.
Goronkin, Herbert
Gossard, Arthur Charles
Gray, Peter Vance
Green, Jonathan Bregstone
Griffiths, Robert B.
Haacke, Gottfried
Hakala, Reino William
Hall, Herbert Joseph
Hallock, Robert Bruce
Halperin, Bertrand Israel
Harmon, Bruce N.
Hawkins, Gilbert A.
Hermann, Allen Max
Herring, William Conyers
Hess, George Burns
Hickernell, Fred Slocum
Hickmott, Thomas Ward
Himpsel, Franz Josef
Hirsch, Jorge Eduardo
Hollander, Lewis E., Jr.
Holton, William Coffeen
Hope, Lawrence Latimer
Huang, Shiezen
Huse, David Alan
Ignatiev, Alex
Ippen, Erich Peter
Iverson, Mark Vernon
Jackel, Lawrence David
Jackson, Kenneth Arthur
Jackson, Shirley Ann
Jackson, Warren Bruce
Jacobsen, Edward Hastings
Jaffe, John Edward
James, Ralph Boyd
Jaworowski, Andrzej Edward
Jeanloz, Raymond
Jellison, Gerald Earle, Jr.
Jennings, Laurence Duane
Jensen, Barbara Lynne
Johanson, William Richard
Johnson, David Linton
Jona, Franco Paul
Kabler, Milton Norris
Kadanoff, Leo Philip
Kadin, Alan Mitchell
Kamieniecki, Emil
Kardar, Mehran
Karo, Arnold Mitchell
Keller, Jaime
Kellogg, Gary Lee
Kennedy, Thomas Albert, Jr.
Keyes, Robert William
Kiehl, Richard Arthur
Kim, Young Hwa
King, James Claude
Kleban, Peter Henry
Kliewer, Kenneth Lee
Knight, Walter David
Koehler, Wallace Conrad
Kohn, Stanley Erwin
Koos, Gregory Lee
Kortan, Ahmet Refik
Kouvel, James Spyros
Krumhansl, James Arthur
Kupferberg, Lenn Carl
Kurtze, Douglas Alan
Kwok, Thomas Yu-Kiu
Lagally, Max Gunter
Landauer, Rolf William
Lander, Gerard H.
Langenberg, Donald Newton
Larson, Donald Clayton
Lax, Benjamin
Leheny, Robert Francis
Lehnen, Alfred Paul
LeMay, Charlotte Zihlman
Lhota, James Raymond, II
Liao, Paul F(oo-Hung)
Libby, Vibeke
Lin, Chun Chia
Lindau, Ingolf Evert
Liu, Samuel Hsi-peh
Livingston, James Duane
Look, David Charles
Lynch, David William
Lynn, Jeffrey Whidden
Ma, David I.
Macdonald, James Ross
MacPhail, Richard Allyn
Madan, Arun
Madey, Theodore Eugene
Mahan, Gerald D.
Maki, Kazumi
Mandelbrot, Benoit B.
Marchetti, Alfred Paul
Margaritondo, Giorgio
Martin, Paul Alan
Martin, Paul Cecil
Martino, Frank
Massey, Walter Eugene
Mavroyannis, Constantine
McMillan, Robert Walker
Mehran, Farrokh
Mermin, N. David
Miller, William Robert, Jr.
Miniscalco, William Joseph
Moerner, William Esco
Moriarty, John Alan
Moss, Marvin
Moustakas, Theodore Demetri
Moy, Dan
Moysenko, Andrew Edward
Myers, Samuel Maxwell
Nagel, David Joseph
Nagel, Sidney Robert
Nahory, Robert Edward
Nam, Sang Boo
Narayan, Jagdish
Narayanamurti, Venkatesh
Nassau, Kurt
Nee, Tsu-Wei
Nelson, Donald Frederick
Nemarich, Joseph
Ngai, Kia Ling
Nicastro, Anthony Joseph
O'Connell, Robert Francis
Oguz, Suha
O'Handley, Robert Charles
O'Hare, J. Michael
Olego, Diego Jose
Orlowski, Thomas Edward
Overhauser, Albert Warner
Painter, Gayle Stanford
Pakulis, Elga
Park, Yoon Soo
Peak, David
Pederson, Donald Otis
Penz, P. Andrew
Perdew, John Paul
Pestak, Mark William
Phillips, Alfred, Jr.
Phillips, Julia Mae
Pierce, Daniel Thornton
Pines, David
Polgar, Leslie George
Pomerantz, Melvin
Preston, Richard Swain
Price, David Cecil Long
Price, Peter J.
Prince, Morton Bronenberg
Pryor, Roger Welton
Rabii, Sohrab
Rabin, Herbert
Rajeevakumar, T. V.
Rao, Kameswara Kolla
Ratnam, Bharati Asoka
Reinecke, Thomas Leonard
Reynolds, Peter James
Rhodin, Thor Nathaniel
Rice, Michael John
Richardson, Robert Coleman
Ritz-Gold, Caroline Joyce
Rodriguez, Sergio
Roessler, David Martyn
Rubinstein, Michael
Safran, Samuel Abraham
Sagalyn, Paul Leon
Sai-Halasz, George Anthony
Salamon, Myron Ben
Sales, Brian Craig
Sander, Leonard Michael
Sarachik, Myriam Paula
Sato, Hiroshi
Satterthwaite, Cameron B.
Saw, Cheng-Kiong
Schechter, Daniel
Schroeder, Peter Allan
Schuller, Ivan Kohn
Schultz, Sheldon
Schwartz, Robert Nelson
Seiden, Philip Edward
Serreze, Harvey B.
Sharma, Ram Ratan
Sharma, Yadunandan Prasad
Shin, Sung-Chul
Shockley, William Bradford
Simmons, Ralph Oliver
Slichter, Charles Pence
Smoluchowski, Roman
Sneddon, Leigh
Snow, Joel Alan
Sokoloff, Jeffrey Bruce
Sollner, Traugott Carl Ludwig Gerhard
Spencer, Edward G.
Spicer, William Edward, III
Spitzer, William George
Stadler, Henry Lewis
Stearns, Mary Beth
Stein, Konrad Mark
Sullivan, Neil Samuel
Surko, Clifford Michael
Swenson, Clayton A.
Tabak, Mark David
Takeuchi, Takao
Tanielian, Minas Hagop
Tannenwald, Peter Ernest
Tanner, David Burnham
Tanttila, Walter Hjalmer
Tauc, Jan
Taylor, R(aymond) Dean Taylor
Tedrow, Paul Muller
Tennant, William Emerson
Tibbetts, Gary George
Treacy, Michael Matthew John
Trullinger, Steven Eugene
Tsong, Tien Tzou
Tucker, John R.
Tuul, Johannes
Ukleja, Paul
Vaishnava, Prem Prakash
van der Ziel, Jan Peter
Van de Walle, Chris Gilbert
Van Driel, Henry Martin
Vanfleet, Howard Bay
Van Ostenburg, Donald Ora
van Roosbroeck, Willy Werner
Van Zytveld, John Bos
Vineyard, George Hoagland
Wachtman, John Bryan, Jr.
Wang, Ching-Ping Shih
Weber, Marvin John
Weng, Shang-Lin
Wert, Charles Allen
Westrum, Edgar Francis, Jr.
Wheatley, John Charles
Williams, Richard
Wolley, Elden Duane
Woo, Ka-Chiu
Wood, Thomas H.
Woodall, Milton Andrew, II
Yelon, William B.
Yen, William Mao-shung
Yin, Mingtang Thomas
Young, Donald Reeder
Zabel, Hartmut

Low temperature physics
Alterovitz, Samuel Adar
Ambler, Ernest
Anderson, Ansel Cochran
Bardeen, John
Brody, Burton Alan
Brooks, Walter Fanger
Cabrera, Blas
DeLong, Lance Eric
Donnelly, Russell James
Duffy, William Thomas, Jr.
Garland, James C.
Geballe, Theodore Henry
Gehrz, Robert Douglas
Greytak, Thomas John
Hallock, Robert Bruce
Hess, George Burns
Jakas, Mario Mateo
Johanson, William Richard
Kadin, Alan Mitchell
King, James Claude
Langenberg, Donald Newton
Lee, David Morris
Maki, Kazumi
Mapother, Dillon Edward
Maris, Humphrey John
McGurrin, Michael Francis
Moy, Dan
Narayanamurti, Venkatesh
Noltimier, Hallan Costello
Paik, Ho Jung
Perry, Theodore Sonne
Ratnam, Bharati Asoka
Richards, Paul Linford
Richardson, Robert Coleman
Rivier, Nicolas Yves
Rudnick, Isadore
Satterthwaite, Cameron B.
Schooley, James Frederick
Schroeder, Peter Allan
Schwarz, Klaus W.
Simmons, Ralph Oliver
Sullivan, Neil Samuel
Swenson, Clayton A.
Taylor, Barry Norman
Taylor, Gerald Reed, Jr.
Taylor, R(aymond) Dean Taylor
Tedrow, Paul Muller
Tepley, Norman
Tinkham, Michael
Tucker, John R.
Vaishnava, Prem Prakash
Wheatley, John Charles

Magnetic physics
Albert, Paul Andre
Allan, James Clark
Bennett, Lawrence Herman
Broersma, Sybrand
Dionne, Gerald Francis
Duffy, William Thomas, Jr.
Foner, Simon
Graneau, Peter
Green, Jerome Joseph
Green, Michael I(rving)
Gross, Dan Arthur
Harmon, Bruce N.
Holt, Alan Craig
Johnson, Clark Eugene, Jr.
Kikuchi, Chihiro
Kupferberg, Lenn Carl
Leifer, Mark Curtis
Lhota, James Raymond, II
Lopez, Orlando
Magnuson, Gustav Donald
Mehran, Farrokh
Mulay, Laxman N.
Petrarca, Bruce Frederick
Pomerantz, Melvin
Rosensweig, Ronald Ellis
Sablik, Martin John
Salamon, Myron Ben
Sarachik, Myriam Paula
Schenck, John F.
Slichter, Charles Pence
Stearns, Mary Beth
Van de Vaart, Herman
Wanderer, Peter John, Jr.
Wang, Ching-Ping Shih
Wolf, Werner Paul
Zanzucchi, Paul E.

Medical physics
Ahluwalia, Bhagwat Datta
Alessandro, Daniel
Andre, Michael
Attix, Frank Herbert
Bennett, Gerald William
Cetas, Thomas Charles
Curran, Bruce Howlett
Dahl, J(ohn) Robert
Datta, Ratna
DeWerd, Larry A.
Gibson, Jean M.
Hsieh, Jen-shu
Koch, H(erman) William
Leifer, Mark Curtis
Lowinger, Thomas
Manlulu, Higinio Y(abut)
McCullough, Edwin Charles
Meeker, Ralph Dennis
Metz, Charles Edgar
Mistry, Vitthalbhai Dahyabhai
Moyer, Robert Findley
Murphy, Bernard T.
Nalcioglu, Orhan
Nibhanupudy, Jagannadha Rao
Nosil, Josip
Orton, Colin George
Renner, Wendel Dean
Sashin, Donald
Shah, Saiyid Masroor
Slack, Stephen Thomas
Steinbach, Arden Lynn
Sullivan, Carole A.
Webster, Edward William
Zamenhof, Robert George

Nuclear physics
Aaroe, William Henry
Adair, Robert Kemp
Adams, James Paul
Agnew, Harold Melvin
Alburger, David Elmer
Alexander, John Macmillan
Ammar, Raymond G.
Ancona, Antonio
Andrews, Hugh Robert
Andrews, Roger Charles
Armstrong, Dale Dean
Arns, Robert George
Azziz, Nestor Jalil
Bainbridge, Kenneth Tompkins
Bartlett, Albert Allen
Beach, Louis Andrew
Becchetti, Frederick Daniel, Jr.
Becker, Stephen Allan
Benenson, Walter
Bertozzi, William
Bevelacqua, Joseph John
Biedenharn, Lawrence Christian, Jr.
Bigler, Rodney E.
Blotcky, Alan Jay
Bodek, Arie
Boehm, Felix Hans
Boudrie, Richard Lynn
Braden, Charles Hosea
Braun-Munzinger, Peter
Broadhurst, John Henry
Bromley, David Allan
Brynjolfsson, Ari
Burrows, Thomas Wesley
Caldwell, David Orville
Chamberlain, Owen
Childs, Wendell Arthur
Choudhury, Deo Chand
Clark, Gary Edwin
Clarke, Robert Francis
Conzett, Homer Eugene
Craik, Gary C., Sr.
Crane, Horace Richard
Creutz, Edward Chester
Crewe, Albert Victor
Curry, James Regnald
Cuttler, Jerry Milton
Daehnick, Wilfried Wolfgang
Danos, Michael
Deci, Eugene Clark

Degnan, James Henry
Devons, Samuel
Dickens, Justin Kirk
Doerner, Robert Carl
Dombeck, Thomas Walter
Donnelly, Thomas William
Elminyawi, Imam Mohamed
Elmore, David
Enge, Harald Anton
Engel, Lars Norlick
Erskine, John Robert
Evans, Patrick James
Fadner, Willard Lee
Fai, George
Ferry, James Allen
Feshbach, Herman
Fink, Richard W(alter)
Fivozinsky, Sherman Paul
Flanz, Jacob B.
Fowler, William Alfred
Franco, Victor
Freed, Norman
Fricke, Martin Paul
Gai, Moshe
Garnett, Robert William
Gelbke, Claus-Konrad
Glasgow, Glenn Patrick
Glashausser, Charles Michael
Goldhaber, Maurice
Goldman, Terrance Jack
Goodman, Charles David
Gorenstein, Paul
Gove, Harry Edmund
Greene, Steven Joseph
Griffy, Thomas Alan
Halbert, Melvyn Leonard
Hamilton, Joseph Hants, Jr.
Hardekopf, Robert A(llen)
Harris, Gale Ion
Hausman, Hershel Judah
Hendrie, Joseph Mallam
Henley, Ernest Mark
Herb, Raymond George
Hill, David Lawrence
Hoffman, Cyrus Miller
Holloway, John Thomas
Holmgren, Harry D.
Holub, Robert F(rantisek)
Horen, Daniel Joseph
Hulet, E. Kenneth
Humanic, Thomas John
Jackson, Harold Edward, Jr.
Jacovitch, John
Kalbach, Constance
Kammeraad, Judith Ellen
Kasper, Raphael Goldsmith
Keyworth, George A., II
Klema, Ernest Donald
Ko, Che Ming
Koch, H(erman) William
Komorek, Michael, Jr.
Kraushaar, Jack Jourdan
Kumar, Krishna
Kumar, Prasanna K.
Lederman, Leon Max
Leiss, James Elroy
Levin, Frank S.
Levy, Paul Henrie
Lewis, Harold Walter
Lindsay, William Francis
Little, Robert Narvaez, Jr.
Liu, Keh-Fei Frank
Lodhi, Sattar Khan
MacArthur, Duncan Whittemore
Makofske, William Joseph
Manley, Donald Mark
Manlulu, Higinio Y(abut)
Mathews, Grant James
McClelland, John Benjamin
McDaniels, David Keith
McEllistrem, Marcus Thomas
McGuire, Stephen Craig
McHarris, William Charles
McKee, James Stanley Colton
McLaughlin, William Lowndes
Mc Millan, Edwin Mattison
McNally, James Henry
Medicus, Heinrich Adolf
Meeker, Ralph Dennis
Meier, Michael McDaniel
Messenger, George Clement
Minehart, Ralph Conrad
Mischke, Richard Evans
Mistry, Vitthalbhai Dahyabhai
Mitchell, Gary Earl
Moniz, Ernest Jeffrey
Moszkowski, Steven Alexander
Mueller, Dennis
Murdoch, Bruce Thomas
Nann, Hermann
Negele, John William
Nierenberg, William Aaron
O'Brien, Keran
O'Connell, James Sheridan
Parker, Peter Donald MacDougall
Paul, Ronald Stanley
Paulk, Charles Jasper, Jr.
Pella, Peter John
Peters, Charles William
Pieper, George F(rancis)
Portare, Anthony Frank
Preiss, Ivor Louis
Price, Paul Buford
Rabi, Isidor Isaac
Randall, Russel R.
Rapkin, Marwin Joel
Rathbun, Edwin Roy
Reading, John Frank
Reber, Jerry Donald
Redish, Edward Frederick
Rees, Lawrence Brent
Rhodes, Donald Frederick
Roberds, Richard Mack
Roberts, Bradley Lee
Robinson, Russell Lee
Rosario-García, Efraín
Rosen, Louis
Saperstein, Alvin Martin
Satchler, George Raymond
Saxon, David Stephen
Schwarzschild, Arthur Zeiger
Schweitzer, Jeffrey Stewart
Scott, David Knight
Seagondollar, Lewis Worth
Sebhatu, Mesgun
Segrè , Emilio
Selove, Walter

Serot, Brian David
Sharon (Schwadron), Yitzhak Yaakov
Sholtis, Joseph Arnold, Jr.
Silberberg, Rein
Simpson, W(ilburn) Dwain
Sites, Kenneth Ronald
Sperber, Daniel
Spinka, Harold Matthew, Jr.
Sprung, Donald Whitfield Loyal
Steadman, Stephen Geoffrey
Stephenson, Thomas Edgar
Teller, Edward
Thiessen, Henry Archer
Ting, Samuel Chao Chung
Townsend, Lawrence Willard
Uberall, Herbert Michael Stefan
Udagawa, Takeshi
Ussery, Larry Eugene
Van Bibber, Karl Albert
Van Lint, Victor Anton Jacobus
Van Patter, Douglas Macpherson
Vary, James Patrick
Viola, Victor E., Jr.
Waddington, Cecil Jacob
Walecka, John Dirk
Ward, Thomas Edmund
Warner, Ray Allen
Warren, Holland Douglas
Weber, Hans-Juergen
Weisskopf, Victor Frederick
Weitkamp, William George
Welch, Lester Clint
Westerfeldt, Christopher Ray
Whitten, Charles Alexander, Jr.
Wildenthal, Bryan Hobson
Wilson, Robert R.
Woosley, Stanford Earl
Yeh, Edward Hsin-Yang
Yergin, Paul Flohr
Young, Glenn Reid
Young, Stephen Kwok-Wai
Zeidman, Benjamin
Zhou, Zong-Yuan

Particle physics

Adair, Robert Kemp
Adler, Stephen Louis
Albright, John Rupp
Aldinger, Randolph Rhett
Alvarez, Luis W.
Ammar, Raymond G.
Ayres, David Smith
Baksay, Laszlo Andrew
Bander, Myron
Bardeen, William A.
Barish, Samuel Joseph
Basri, Saul Abraham
Behrends, Ralph Eugene
Beier, Eugene William
Biedenharn, Lawrence Christian, Jr.
Bodek, Arie
Boehm, Felix Hans
Borenstein, Jeffrey Mark
Bridgewater, Albert Louis
Caldwell, David Orville
Choudhury, Abdul Latif
Chu, William Tongil
Chung, Suh-Urk
Cihangir, Selcuk
Coleman, Sidney Richard
Cool, Rodney Lee
Corvin, Wayne Clay
Coward, David Hand
Cronin, James Watson
Das, Ashok Kumar
Davis, Jay Clarence
Dehmelt, Hans Georg
Deser, Stanley
Dicus, Duane Alfred
Dombeck, Thomas Walter
Dowd, John Peter
Drell, Sidney David
Ebel, Marvin Emerson
Ehlers, Kenneth Warren
Field, Robert Clive
Finn, James Edward
Fitch, Val Logsdon
Ford, William Tibbets
Frampton, Paul Howard
Friedberg, Carl E.
Frisch, Henry Jonathan
Georgi, Howard Mason, III
Goldberger, Marvin L.
Goldman, Terrance Jack
Good, Roland Hamilton, Jr.
Goulianos, Konstantin
Greene, Steven Joseph
Gross, Dan Arthur
Gross, David Jonathan
Guth, Alan Harvey
Haacke, Ewart Mark
Haber, Howard Eli
Hamber, Herbert Walter
Han, Ki Sup
Han, Moo-Young
Hanson, Gail Gulledge
Harris, Frederick Allan
Hauptman, John Michael
Hiller, John Richard
Hoffman, Cyrus Miller
Hugg, James William
Hulsizer, Robert Inslee
Jackson, (John) David
Jaeger, Klaus Bruno
Johannsen, David Charles
Johnson, David Edwin
Jones, Lawrence William
Kane, Gordon L.
Kinnison, Willard Wayne
Kostoulas, Ioannis Georgiou
Kovacs, Eve Veronika Elizabeth
Kreisler, Michael Norman
Lach, Joseph T(heodore)
Lamb, Richard Compton
Levy, Paul Henrie
Lichtenberg, Don Bernett
Lindsay, William Francis
Litke, Alan Michael
Liu, Keh-Fei Frank
Lott, Fredrick Wilbur, III
Lubatti, Henry Joseph
Lubell, Michael Stephen
Lynn, Jeffrey Whidden
MacLachlan, James Angell
Makarowitz, Lloyd
Malamud, Ernest I.
Manley, Donald Mark

March, Robert Herbert
Margulies, Seymour
Marshak, Marvin Lloyd
Marshak, Robert Eugene
Marx, Jay Neil
McDaniel, Boyce Dawkins
McLerran, Larry Dean
Minehart, Ralph Conrad
Mischke, Richard Evans
Moffat, John William
Moneti, Giancarlo
Nappi, Chiara Rosanna
Nepomechie, Rafael I.
Ng, Yee Jack
Oakes, Robert J.
Oehme, Reinhard
O'Halloran, Thomas A.
Okobu, Susumu
Ong, Rene Ashwin
Overseth, Oliver Enoch
Paar, Hans Peter
Pagels, Heinz Rudolf
Pais, Abraham
Pakvasa, Sandip Sirish
Panofsky, Wolfgank Kurt Hermann
Parker, Sherwood I
Pearson, John Stuart
Peaslee, David Chase
Peoples, John, Jr.
Periasamy, Ravindran
Perl, Martin Lewis
Pollak, Gregory Daniel
Rabin, Monroe Stephen Zane
Radford, Stanley Fritz
Rahm, David Charles
Ramsey, Norman
Randa, James Paul
Rebbi, Claudio
Reines, Frederick
Rice, James Allen
Richter, Burton
Roberts, Bradley Lee
Roper, Leon David
Rosen, Louis
Sachs, Robert Green
Sakita, Bunji
Samios, Nicholas Peter
Samuel, Mark Aaron
Schnitzer, Howard Joel
Sebhatu, Mesgun
Selove, Walter
Shapero, Donald Campbell
Shrauner, James Ely
Smith, Wesley Harold
Spinka, Harold Matthew, Jr.
Spiro, Julius
Steiner, Robert Victor
Tannenbaum, Michael J(ay)
Teng, Lee Chang-Li
Thiessen, Henry Archer
Tornabene, Hugh Salvatore
Tryon, Edward Polk
Umland, Eric Alexander
van Nieuwenhuizen, Peter
Vary, James Patrick
Vaughn, Michael Thayer
Wanderer, Peter John, Jr.
Wang, Chia Ping
Weber, Hans-Juergen
Weinstein, Roy
Whitten, Charles Alexander, Jr.
Wilson, Richard
Witten, Louis
Wojcicki, Stanley G.
Wolfenstein, Lincoln
Wuest, Craig Richard
Yamamoto, Richard Kumeo
Yamanouchi, Taiji
Yan, Tung-Mow
Yount, David Eugene
Zachos, Cosmas K.

Plasma physics. *See also* ENERGY SCIENCE AND TECHNOLOGY.

Abraham-Shrauner, Barbara Wayne
Ahearne, Daniel Paul
Ahluwalia, Harjit Singh
Akasofu, Syun-Ichi
Alfven, Hannes Olof Gosta
Ali, Abdul Wahab
Anderson, John Melvin
Armstrong, Thomas Peyton
Attwood, David Thomas
Auer, Peter Louis
Bardwell, Steven Jack
Bleach, Richard David
Booker, Henry George
Bruch, Reinhard Frank
Buff, James Steve
Burrell, Charles Frederick
Cary, John Robert
Chang, Choong-Seock
Cloutier, Paul Andrew
Coleman, John Howard
Davidson, Ronald Crosby
Dawson, John Myrick
Degnan, James Henry
Detra, Ralph William
Eames, David Robson
Eccleshall, Donald
Edwards, William Farrell
Ehlers, Kenneth Warren
Ellis, William R.
Figueroa-Viñas, Adolfo
Fleischmann, Hans Hermann
Forrester, A(lvin) Theodore
Forslund, David Wallace
Freeman, Bruce L., Jr.
Freund, Henry Phillip
Gaffey, John Dean, Jr.
Gitomer, Steven Joel
Gold, Steven Harvey
Gray, Eoin Wedderburn
Greene, Arthur Edward
Grun, Jacob
Hammer, David Andrew
Hammond, Thomas Joseph
Hansler, Richard Lowell
Harmon, Gary R.
Hasegawa, Akira
Hauck, James Pierre
Hickok, Robert Lyman, Jr.
Hicks, Harry Richard
Hobbs, Willard Earl, Jr.
Hollweg, Joseph Vincent
Houlberg, Wayne Arthur
Izzo, Ralph

Jahn, Robert George
Kaita, Robert
Kammeraad, Judith Ellen
Kan, Joseph R.
Kim, Jinchoon
Kim, Kwang-Seok
Krall, Nicholas Anthony
Krapchev, Vladimir Bogdanov
Kribel, Robert Edward
Kusse, Bruce Raymond
Kuswa, Glenn Wesley
Lazar, Norman H(enry)
Li, Xing Zhong
Lonngren, Karl Erik
Lucatorto, Thomas Benjamin
Marcuvitz, Nathan
Mason, Rodney Jackson
Massey, Robert Stewart
McCann, Robert Thomas
McFarland, Robert Harold
McGuire, Kevin Marian
McNally, James Henry
McNally, James Rand, Jr.
Meyerand, Russell Gilbert, Jr.
Miller, Hillard Craig
Moore, Thomas Earle
Moos, Henry Warren
Motz, Robin Owen
Mueller, Dennis
Mueller, Marvin Martin
Namkung, Won
Nation, John Arthur
Nicholson, Dwight Roy
Niimura, Masanobu
Ohkawa, Tihiro
Oleson, Norman Lee
Olness, Robert James
O'Shea, Patrick Gerard
Parker, Eugene Newman
Perry, Theodore Sonne
Pietrzyk, Zbigniew Adam
Politzer, Peter Alexander
Postma, Herman
Prelas, Mark Anthony
Pritchett, Philip Lentner
Radoski, Henry Robert
Ribe, Fred Linden
Roberts, Thomas George
Rosenbluth, Marshall Nicholas
Roth, J(ohn) Reece
Rothwell, Harold Leroy, Jr.
Seidl, Milos
Shkarofsky, Issie Peter
Shumaker, Dana Edward
Snow, William Rosebrook
Sprott, Julien Clinton
Sreenivasan, S. Ranga
Stevens, James Everell
Sturrock, Peter Andrew
Sudan, Ravindra Nath
Surko, Clifford Michael
Tajima, Toshiki
Takahashi, Hironori
Tang, John Theodore
Taylor, Gary
Taylor, Gerald Reed, Jr.
Temkin, Richard Joel
Trivelpiece, Alvin William
Van Brunt, Richard Joseph
Van Hoven, Gerard
Varney, Robert Nathan
Vitkovitsky, Ihor Myron
Weissler, Gerhard Ludwig
Wharton, Charles Benjamin
White, Robert Carl
Wiese, Wolfgang Lothar
Woskoboinikow, Paul Peter
Wu, Ching-Sheng
Yamada, Masaaki
Yamagishi, Tomejiro
Yoshikawa, Shoichi

Polymer physics. *See also* MATERIALS SCIENCE.

Apostolou, Spyridon F.
Bailey, Frederick Eugene, Jr.
Bamji, Soli Shavax
Belton, Daniel James
Berney, Charles V.
Berry, Guy Curtis
Borch, Jens
Boyer, Raymond Foster
Chow, Tsu Sen
Chu, Benjamin
Darsey, Jerome Anthony
Dickens, Elmer Douglas, Jr.
Dill, Kenneth Austin
Eby, Ronald K.
Ellison, Michael Scot
Family, Fereydoon
Fitzgerald, Edwin Roger
Fuzek, John Frank
Gonzalez Flores, Agustin Eduardo
Guttman, Charles Martin
Hodge, Ian Moir
Hoffman, John Drake
Hong, Su-Don
Kim, Young Hwa
Kogowski, Gary John
Kuo, Cheng-Yih
Landel, Robert Franklin
Lando, Jerome B.
Lin, Ju-Chui
Lohse, David John
Lontz, John Frank
McKenna, Gregory Born
Ngai, Kia Ling
O'Malley, James J.
Powers, Joseph
Prest, William Marchant, Jr.
Robertson, Richard Earl
Rubinstein, Michael
Sanchez, Isaac Cornelius
Simha, Robert
Skotheim, Terje Asbjorn
Sung Ho, (Salk)
Thomas, H. Ronald
Tripathy, Sukant Kishore
Verdier, Peter Howard
Walters, Sandra Jean
Wang, Tsuey Tang

Psychophysics

Bashinski, Howard Stewart
Boggs, George Johnson
Borresen, C. Robert
Boynton, Robert Merrill

Chastain, Garvin
Cooper, Franklin Seaney
Davis, Elizabeth Emily Louise Thorpe
Drum, Bruce Alan
Garner, Wendell Richard
Glaser, Donald A(rthur)
Hart, John Birdsall
Hirsh, Ira Jean
Hubbard, G(regory) Scott
Jameson, Dorothea
Kenshalo, Daniel Ralph
Kicliter, Ernest Earl, Jr.
Luce, (Robert) Duncan
Luria, Saul Martin
Makous, Walter
Marks, Lawrence Edward
Movshon, J(oseph) Anthony
Raslear, Thomas Gregory
Riggs, Lorrin Andrews
Roederer, Juan Gualterio
Staley, Frederick Joseph
Swets, John Arthur
Verrillo, Ronald Thomas
Westheimer, Gerald

Relativity and gravitation

Ashtekar, Abhay Vasant
Buske, Norman L.
Cheung, W(ah-Kwan) Stephen
Chupp, Timothy Edward
Cohen, Jeffrey M.
Deser, Stanley
Dube, Roger Raymond
Follingstad, Henry George
Greenberg, Philip Joel
Hu, Bei-Lok Bernard
Israel, Werner
Lott, Fredrick Wilbur, III
Maglich, Bogdan C.
Malin, Shimon
Marks, Dennis William
Moffat, John William
Motz, Lloyd
Ng, Yee Jack
Noonan, Thomas Wyatt
Oelfke, William Clarence
Paik, Ho Jung
Poltorak, Alexander (Israel)
Safko, John Loren
Schwebel, Solomon Lawrence
Smalley, Larry Lee
Snider, Joseph Lyons
Stachel, John Jay
Tangherlini, Frank Robert
Unruh, William George
van Nieuwenhuizen, Peter
Vilenkin, Alexander
Wagoner, Robert Vernon
Weber, Joseph
Westervelt, Peter Jocelyn
Wheeler, John Archibald
Whitman, Patrick Gene
Wilson, Thomas Leon
Witten, Louis
Woodward, James Franklin
Zumino, Bruno

Solar physics. *See* SPACE SCIENCE.

Solid state physics. *See* **Condensed matter physics.**

Statistical physics

Alder, Berni Julian
Bander, Myron
Basu, Pankaj Kumar
Blume, Martin
Carruthers, Peter Ambler
Desai, Rashmi C.
Dowell, Flonnie
Ettrick, Marco Antonio
Evans, Patrick James
George, James
Gonzalez Flores, Agustin Eduardo
Griffiths, Robert B.
Heer, Clifford V.
Henderson, Douglas James
Hirsch, Jorge Eduardo
Huse, David Alan
Imbrie, John Z(eller)
Kardar, Mehran
Kleban, Peter Henry
Kurtze, Douglas Alan
Lebowitz, Joel Louis
Lehnen, Alfred Paul
Martin, Paul Cecil
Mazo, Robert Marc
Mintzer, David
Nicholson, Dwight Roy
Olness, Robert James
Peak, David
Perdew, John Paul
Price, Peter J.
Ramshaw, John David
Rivier, Nicolas Yves
Rubin, Robert Joshua
Safran, Samuel Abraham
Sander, Leonard Michael
Sengers, Jan Vincent
Tanttila, Walter Hjalmer
Tarter, C. Bruce
Van Vliet, Carolyn Marina
Waldo, George Van Pelt, Jr.
Weber, Joseph
Wigner, Eugene Paul
Willemsen, Jorge Fernando

Theoretical physics

Adler, Stephen Louis
Agrawal, Govind Prasad
Albers, Robert Charles
Albright, John Rupp
Aldinger, Randolph Rhett
Ali, Abdul Wahab
Anderson, Philip Warren
Arai, Tadashi
Ashcroft, Neil William
Ashtekar, Abhay Vasant
Bardeen, William A.
Baylis, William Eric
Baym, Gordon Alan
Behrends, Ralph Eugene
Berger, Steven Barry
Bergmann, Peter G(abriel)
Bethe, Hans Albrecht
Biswas, Rana
Brown, Ellen Ruth

Burdick, Glenn Arthur
Burt, Philip Barnes
Campbell, Philip Montgomery, Jr.
Carruthers, Peter Ambler
Chang, Tu-Nan
Chapline, George Frederick, Jr.
Charpie, Robert Alan
Cheng, Kwok-Tsang
Ching, Wai-Yim
Choudhury, Abdul Latif
Choudhury, Deo Chand
Cohen, James Samuel
Cole, Lee Arthur
Coleman, Sidney Richard
Cooper, Leon N.
Cowan, Robert Duane
Das, Ashok Kumar
Devaney, Joseph James
de Wolf, David Alter
Donnelly, Thomas William
Dowell, Flonnie
Drell, Sidney David
Duffey, George Henry
Dyson, Freeman John
Ebel, Marvin Emerson
Edwards, William Farrell
Elminyawi, Imam Mohamed
Evenson, William Edwin
Fai, George
Fanchi, John Richard
Fano, Ugo
Feigenbaum, Mitchell Jay
Feinberg, Gerald
Fennelly, Alphonsus John
Feshbach, Herman
Feynman, Richard Phillips
Fontana, Peter Robert
Forslund, David Wallace
Franco, Victor
Freed, Norman
Freedman, Daniel Z.
Gell-Mann, Murray
Georgi, Howard Mason, III
Gillespie, George Hubert
Glashow, Sheldon Lee
Goldberger, Marvin L.
Good, Roland Hamilton, Jr.
Goodman, Julius
Gould, Robert Joseph
Greene, Chris H.
Gross, David Jonathan
Haber, Howard Eli
Halemane, Thirumala Raya
Hamber, Herbert Walter
Han, Moo-Young
Hanisko, John-Cyril Patrick
Hasimoto, Hidenori
Henley, Ernest Mark
Herring, William Conyers
Hill, David Lawrence
Hope, Lawrence Latimer
Huang, Keh-Ning
Hutzler, Erich Kurt
Iberall, Arthur Saul
Israel, Werner
Jackson, (John) David
Jackson, Shirley Ann
Jaffe, John Edward
James, Ralph Boyd
Judd, Brian Raymond
Kadanoff, Leo Philip
Katz, Alan R.
Kaufman, Charles
Kliewer, Kenneth Lee
Kobe, Donald Holm
Kockinos, Constantin Neophytos
Kovacs, Eve Veronika Elizabeth
Krapchev, Vladimir Bogdanov
Kumar, Krishna
Kursunoglu, Behram N.
Lam, Kui-chuen
Lamb, Donald Quincy
Lamb, Willis Eugene, Jr.
Langer, James S.
Lapicki, Gregory
Lasker, Leslie
Lee, Tsung-Dao
Li, Ming Chiang
Lieb, Elliott Hershel
Lieberman, Alfred George
Lim, Teck-Kah
Litovchenko, Vladimir Alexei
Liu, Samuel Hsi-peh
Low, Francis Eugene
Malin, Shimon
Manning, Irwin
Mansfield, John Edward
Manson, Steven Trent
Marshak, Robert Eugene
Martino, Frank
Massey, Walter Eugene
Mazurek, Thaddeus John
McDonald, Keith Leon
McGuire, James Horton
McLenithan, Kelly Daniel
McLerran, Larry Dean
Moniz, Ernest Jeffrey
Moszkowski, Steven Alexander
Nam, Sang Boo
Nappi, Chiara Rosanna
Negele, John William
Nepomechie, Rafael I.
Nickas, George Demosthenes
Norcross, David Warren
Oakes, Robert J.
Oehme, Reinhard
O'Hare, J. Michael
Overhauser, Albert Warner
Pais, Abraham
Pakvasa, Sandip Sirish
Peaslee, David Chase
Peshkin, Murray
Pratt, Richard Houghton
Pryor, Roger Welton
Quivers, William Wyatt, Jr.
Radford, Stanley Fritz
Rebbi, Claudio
Redish, Edward Frederick
Reinecke, Thomas Leonard
Rice, Michael John
Robinson, Edward J.
Rodriguez, Sergio
Rosenkilde, Carl Edward
Rowe, David John
Russell, Virginia Willis
Sachs, Robert Green
Saha, Bidhan Chandra
Sakita, Bunji
Salingaros, Nikos Angelos
Salwen, Harold
Samuel, Mark Aaron
Saperstein, Alvin Martin
Satchler, George Raymond
Saxon, David Stephen
Schnitzer, Howard Joel
Schrieffer, John Robert
Schwebel, Solomon Lawrence
Schwinger, Julian
Seitz, Frederick
Serot, Brian David
Sessler, Andrew Marienoff
Shapero, Donald Campbell
Shrauner, James Ely
Simon, Barry
Sneddon, Leigh
Sperber, Daniel
Spital, Robin David
Sprung, Donald Whitfield Loyal
Stachel, John Jay
Stein, David Eric
Stone, William Ross
Takahashi, Yasushi
Tangherlini, Frank Robert
Teller, Edward
Thorne, Kip Stephen
Townsend, Lawrence Willard
Umland, Eric Alexander
Unruh, William George
van Roosbroeck, Willy Werner
Vaughn, Michael Thayer
Vineyard, George Hoagland
Vona, Daniel O'Neal, III
Von Baeyer, Hans Christian
Watson, Kenneth Marshall
Weinberg, Steven
Wheeler, John Archibald
Wigner, Eugene Paul
Willemsen, Jorge Fernando
Wilson, Kenneth Geddes
Winkler, Peter
Wolff, Peter Adalbert
Wong, Po Kee
Wulfman, Carl Eugene
Yan, Tung-Mow
Yeh, Edward Hsin-Yang
Yuen, Horace P.

Other
Apel, John Ralph, *Physics laboratory administration*
Armstrong, Dale Dean
Banerjee, Krishnadas, *Radiological physics*
Banister, John Robert, *Fluid dynamics*
Barfield, Walter David, *Radiative transfer*
Bartlett, Albert Allen
Baum, Carl Edward
Belian, Richard Duane
Berman, Alan, *Research management*
Bhatnagar, Jagdish Prasad, *Radiological physics*
Bilderback, Donald Heywood, *X-ray physics*
Bragg, Robert Henry
Brecher, Aviva, *Applied physics*
Bridges, William Bruce, *Microwaves*
Brown, Harold, *National security policy*
Burstein, Elias, *Solid state physics*
Burstein, Paul Harris, *X-Ray applications*
Burt, Philip Barnes
Carson, Paul Langford
Chahine, Moustafa Toufic, *Physics of fluids*
Chesser, Nancy Jean
Childs, Wendell Arthur, *Physics education*
Christman, Arthur Castner, Jr.
Chughtai, Gul Muhammad
Church, David Arthur
Cipolla, Sam Joseph, *Radiation physics and radiation dosimetry*
Crombie, Douglass Darnill, *Electromagnetic wave propagation*
Davis, L(loyd) Wayne, *Nuclear weapons effects*
Deupree, Robert Gaston, *Nuclear shock effects*
Devons, Samuel
DiFoggio, Rocco, *Petrophysics*
Driscoll, Timothy John, *Surface physics*
Eccleshall, Donald
Eden, William Murphey, *Health physics*
Fadner, Willard Lee
Feigenbaum, Mitchell Jay, *Chaotic phenomena*
Fisher, David George
Fite, Wade Lanford, *Mass spectrometry*
Flanz, Jacob B.
Flum, Robert Samuel, Sr., *Anti-submarine warfare*
Freeman, Bruce L., Jr., *Explosive pulsed power*
Frosch, Robert Alan
Gelinas, Robert Joseph, *Non-equilibrium fluid dynamics*
Godlove, Terry F.
Grunder, Hermann August, *Accelerator physics*
Gundersen, Martin Adolph, *Quantum electronics*
Hammond, Donald L., *Research administration*
Hardekopf, Robert A(llen), *Accelerator physics*
Hart, John Birdsall, *Operational general physics*
Hausman, Hershel Judah, *Nuclear astrophysics*
Hayden, Howard Corwin, Jr., *Ion implantation*
Hellwarth, Robert Willis, *Optical physics*
Hevezi, James Michael
Hickey, Roger Lee
Hill, Thomas Westfall, *Space plasma physics*
Hofstadter, Robert, *High energy physics*
Hogg, David Clarence, *Radiophysics*
Hoop, Bernard
Huppe, Francis Frowin
Huston, Norman Earl, *Instrumentation*
Jackson, Harold Edward, Jr.
Jaffe, Arthur Michael, *Mathematical physics*
Johnson, David Edwin, *Accelerator physics*
Jones, Walter William, *Numerical fluid dynamics*
Karle, Jerome, *Diffraction physics*
Kathren, Ronald Laurence, *Health physics*
Kerr, Donald MacLean, Jr., *Physics research and development administration*
Khan, Winston, *Physics of fluids*
Koehler, Wallace Conrad, *Neutron scattering*
Kutzscher, Edgar Walter, *Infrared detectors and technology*
Land, Edwin Herbert, *Photographic science*
Landers, Roy Eslyn, Jr., *Therapeutic radiological physics*
Leiss, James Elroy
Lukasik, Stephen Joseph, *Fluid dynamics*
Makarowitz, Lloyd, *Physics education*
Marlow, William Henry, *Aerosol micro physics*
Martin, Lee David
Mayfield, Donald Lewis, *Health physics*
Mazarakis, Michael Gerassimos
McKenna, Gregory Born
Medicus, Heinrich Adolf
Meth, Sheldon Zalmen, *Advanced technology assessment*
Middleton, David
Minichiello, Lee P.
Moneti, Giancarlo
Mooers, Christopher Northrup Kennard
Morrison, Stanley Roy
Narayanan, C. S., *Medical radiation physics*
Pake, George Edward, *Research management*
Parker, Sherwood I
Peoples, John, Jr., *Particle accelerator design*
Petschek, Albert George, *Applied physics*
Prasad, Satish Chandra
Ramshaw, John David
Rogers, Steven Ray
Rosenkilde, Carl Edward, *Fluid dynamics*
Rubin, Lawrence G(ilbert), *Instrument and measurement science*
Ryan, Stewart Richard, *Applied physics*
Saloman, Edward Barry, *Radiometry*
Seraydarian, Raymond Paul, *Visible and ultraviolet spectroscopy*
Sherman, Max Howard
Silk, John Kevin
Soffer, Bernard H.
Solon, Leonard R(aymond), *Health physics*
Sontag, Marc Robert
Sparks, Ronald Wayne, *Enhanced heat transfer*
Sternick, Edward Selby
Stillwagon, Gary Bouldin
Stinchcomb, Thomas Glenn
Talley, Robert Lee, *Aerosol and small macroscopic particle physics*
Tannenwald, Peter Ernest, *Quantum electronics*
Teng, Lee Chang-Li
Tepley, Norman
Thornton, Gunnar
Tigner, Maury, *Accelerator physics*
Tsong, Tien Tzou
Ussailis, James Stewart, *Electromagnetic propagation*
Wang, Chia Ping, *Thermal physics*
Wang, Ru Tsang
Waugh, John Stewart, *Magnetic resonance*
Weber, Paul Egon
Woolford, Thomas Laney
Wuest, Craig Richard
Young, Lloyd Martin

PSYCHOLOGY

Behavioral
Alford, Geary Simmons
Anderson, Eric Edward
Annis, Lawrence Vincent, Jr.
Appel, James Barry
Axelrood, Helen Blau
Baldonado, Ardelina-Erika Albano
Bedell, Ralph Clairon
Belding, Hiram Hurlburt, IV
Bloom, Richard Fredric
Boor, Myron Vernon
Bootzin, Richard Ronald
Borresen, C. Robert
Bradshaw, Howard Holt
Bratter, Thomas Edward
Brooker, Alan Edward
Bufford, Rodger Keith
Carr, Edward Gary
Casler, Lawrence
Charlesworth, Edward Allison
Chermol, Brian Hamilton
Christian, Barry Theodore
Cleeland, Charles Samuel
Clifford, Margaret Louise
Coché, Erich Henry Ernst
Cohen, Ira Larry
Collins, William Edward
Crown, Barry Michael
Cullari, Salvatore Santino
Dalby, (John) Thomas
Danaher, Brian Grayson
D'Errico, Albert Pasquale, Jr.
Dixen, Jean Marie
Dreyfus, Edward A.
Dunlop, Terrence Ward
Ebert-Flattau, Pamela
Elliott, Charles H.
Eurich, Alvin Christian
Force, Ronald C(larence)
Foxx, Richard Michael
Frandsen, Walter James
Frey, William Howard II
Gallatin, Judith Estelle
Gasparrini, William Gerard
Goh, David Shuh Jen
Goldstein, Steven Edward
Gray, Philip Howard
Hall, Howard Ralph
Hickis, Charles Francis
Hirsch, Jerry
Holmstrom, Valerie Louise
Humphries, Joan Ropes
Hursh, Steven Rawlings
Ince, Laurence Peter
Jackson, Thomas Larry
Jacobs, Keith William
Johnson, Richard Frederick
Kamback, Marvin Carl
Kennedy, Clive Dale
Klarreich, Samuel Henry
Krass, Alvin
Lardy, Henry Arnold
Lazarus, Arnold Allan
Lent, Robert William
Lichtman, Robert Mark
Litle, Patrick Alan
Litrownik, Alan Jay
Lofquist, Lloyd Henry
Lundin, Robert William
Lupiani, Donald Anthony
Luria, Saul Martin
MacDonald, G(eorge) Wayne
Mattson, Margaret Ellen
Mayo, Clyde Calvin
McAbee, Thomas Allen
McCraw, Ronald Kent
McGuigan, Frank Joseph
Mills, Harry Lee, Jr.
Montgomery, Robert Lew
Moore, Benjamin L.
Morrow, Gary Robert
Mulick, James Anton
Nezu, Arthur Maguth
O'Farrell, Timothy James
Painter, Genevieve
Pazzaglini, Mario Peter
Peniston, Eugene G.
Perez, Francisco Ignacio
Plakosh, Paul, Jr.
Pollard, Gerald Tilman
Raslear, Thomas Gregory
Reisman, Scott
Rodin, Judith
Sells, Saul B.
Smith, John Philip
Stallworth, Charles Dorothea, Jr.
Stapleton, Leroy Earl
Stark, Jack Alan
Suedfeld, Peter
Thompson, William Warren
Tolchinsky, Paul D.
Trzasko, Joseph Anthony
Tyre, Timothy Edward
Uhlaner, Julius Earl
Uyeno, Edward Teiso
Walls, Betty L.
Wenger, Galen Rosenberger
Woods, Delma Maria
Woods, Walter Abner
Young, Peggy Sanborn
Zweig, Joseph B.

Clinical
Braun, Stephen Hughes
Brown, Stephen Woody
Bruhn, Arnold Rahn, Jr.
Capanzano, Charles Thomas
Carr, Edward Gary
Cleveland, Sidney Earl
Coché, Erich Henry Ernst
Cullari, Salvatore Santino
Davis, Thompson Elder, Jr.
Dewart, Dorothy Boardman
Domino, George
Dunn, William Lawrence
Felner, Robert David
Ferraio, Nicholas LaVerne
Feuerstein, Michael
Fisher, Jerid Martin
Gallo, Mario Martin
Graham, Kenneth Robert
Llorca, Arthur Lee
Lupiani, Donald Anthony
McDowell, David Jamison
Pazzaglini, Mario Peter
Pierce, Calvin Judson
Pine, Charles Joseph
Rubert, Mary Lou
Seay, Thomas Austin
Seligson, M. Ross
Traynham, Richard Neville
Wilson, Arthur Jess
Yensen, Richard

Cognition
Anderson, James Alfred
Anderson, John Robert
Anson, James Greg
Beach, Lee Roy
Bergquist, James William
Berninger, Virginia Wise
Blechner, Mark J.
Brown, Robert Michael
Brown, Roger William
Bruhn, Arnold Rahn, Jr.
Bryden, Mark Philip
Cahill, Mary-Carol
Carlson, Roger David
Carroll, John Stephen
Chappell, Gary Alan
Chastain, Garvin
Cole, Michael
Davies, Ivor Kevin
D'Errico, Albert Pasquale, Jr.
Dreyfus, Edward A.
Duncan, Starkey Davis, Jr.
Dutch, Susan Elaine
Ellis, Henry Carlton
Estes, William Kaye
Federico, Pat-Anthony
Foulkes, David
Freedle, Roy Omer
Fulkerson, Samuel Cole
Fuller, Renee Nuni
Galambos, James Andrew
Gallatin, Judith Estelle
Garner, Wendell Richard
Getzels, Jacob Warren
Gibson, Eleanor Jack
Goh, David Shuh Jen
Gooding, Charles Thomas
Greenfield, Patricia Ann Marks
Hansl, Nikolaus Rudolf
Harkins, Stephen Wayne
Herrmann, Douglas J.
Hilgard, Ernest Ropiequet
Hilliard, Asa Grant, III
Holley, Charles DeWayen
Jensen, Arthur Robert
Jones, Ben Morgan
Jordan, Theresa Joan
Karpicke, John Arthur
Kessen, William
Kiesler, Charles Adolphus
Klarreich, Samuel Henry
Krippner, Stanley Curtis
Landauer, Thomas K.
Lazarus, Arnold Allan
Lichtman, Robert Mark
Litrownik, Alan Jay
Lloyd, John Tracy
Locher, Paul John
Loftus, Elizabeth F.
London, Ray William
Lund, Arnold Milton, Jr.
MacLachlan, James Morrill
Mallory-Barkley, Barbara Zommer
Metzl, Marilyn Newman
Muller, John Paul
Muse, Mark Dana
Nezu, Arthur Maguth
Pettinati, Helen Marie
Powell, James Charles
Reed, Adam Victor
Sbordone, Robert Joseph
Schunk, Dale Hansen
Schurman, Donald Lee
Schvaneveldt, Roger Wayne
Shade, Barbara Jean
Silverman, Hirsch Lazaar
Stallworth, Charles Dorothea, Jr.
Straussner, Joel Harvey
Suedfeld, Peter
Teevan, Richard Collier
Trehub, Arnold
Tversky, Amos
Vandendorpe, Mary Moore
Velk, Robert James
Watkins, Paul Roger
Wells, Gary Leroy
Wohlfeil, Paul Frederick
Woods, Walter Abner

Developmental
Anderson, Eric Edward
Atwood, Joan Dolores
Berninger, Virginia Wise
Brannigan, Gary G(eorge)
Brown, Robert Michael
Carlson, Roger David
Chibucos, Thomas Robert
Childers, John Stephen
Cleland, Charles Carr
Clifford, Margaret Louise
Cohen, Ira Larry
Cummings, Edward Mark
El Ghatit, Zeinab Mohammed
Felner, Robert David
Feshbach, Seymour
Fiene, Richard John
Fouts, Gregory Taylor
Fuller, Renee Nuni
Gibson, Eleanor Jack
Grallo, Richard Martin
Greenfield, Patricia Ann Marks
Grimley, Liam Kelly
Gutierrez, Fernando Jose
Hall, William Sterling
Holtzman, Wayne Harold
Hunt, Elizabeth Hope
Jones, Molly Modrall
Jordan, Theresa Joan
Karrer, Rathe Stevens
Kessen, William
Kurtz, Theodore Stephen
Lorion, Raymond Paul
Lyons-Ruth, Karlen
Maccoby, Eleanor Emmons
Machtiger, Harriet Gordon
Massad, Carolyn Emrick
Melichar, Joseph Frank
Metzl, Marilyn Newman
Miller, Nancy E(llen)
Moore, Benjamin L.
Murray, John Patrick
Netzer, Carol
Pacheco-Maldonado, Angel Manuel
Painter, Genevieve
Pavlidis, George Theophilou
Pitcher, Georgia Ann
Robin, Mitchell Wolfe
Ross, John Munder
Rubert, Mary Lou
Safarjan, William Robert
Spear, Norman Eberman
Suomi, Stephen John
Tough, Allen M(ac Neill)
Tramill, James Louis
Vandendorpe, Mary Moore
Violato, Claudio
Warshaw, Rhoda
Woodruff-Pak, Diana Stenen

Learning
Brannigan, Gary G(eorge)
Bratter, Thomas Edward
Carney, Richard Edward
Christian, Barry Theodore
Clemens, William Jenkins
Colotla, Victor Adolfo
Drummond, Robert John
Ellis, Henry Carlton
Estes, William Kaye
Eurich, Alvin Christian
Federico, Pat-Anthony
Fouts, Gregory Taylor
Foxx, Richard Michael
Freedle, Roy Omer
Gabriel, Michael
Gardner, Marjorie Hyer
Gooding, Charles Thomas
Grallo, Richard Martin
Harrell, Ruth Flinn
Humphries, Joan Ropes
Jensen, Arthur Robert
Karpicke, John Arthur
Krass, Alvin
Loftus, Elizabeth F.
Lundin, Robert William
Lynch, Robert Emmett, Jr.

Mallory-Barkley, Barbara Zommer
Miller, D. Merrily
Mills, Harry Lee, Jr.
Overmier, James Bruce
Park, Ok-Choon
Rescorla, Robert Arthur
Safarjan, William Robert
Sanders, Gilbert Otis
Schroeder, James Ernest
Schunk, Dale Hansen
Spear, Norman Eberman
Straub, Richard Otto
Tough, Allen M(ac Neill)
Walls, Betty L.
Warnat, Winifred Irene
Warshaw, Rhoda
Woolman, Myron
Young, Peggy Sanborn
Zachert, Virginia

Neuropsychology. *See* NEUROSCIENCE.

Physiological
Adams, David Bachrach
Andreassi, John L(awrence)
Balster, Robert Louis
Bauer, Richard Henry
Berman, Marlene Oscar
Bodnar, Richard Julius
Braggio, John Thomas
Carney, Richard Edward
Cheal, MaryLou
Chesire, Rebecca Martha
Clemens, William Jenkins
Coscina, Donald Victor
Doerr, Robert Douglas
Don, Norman Stanley
Eison, Michael Steven
Everly, George Stotelmyer, Jr.
Goodman, Irving Jack
Goy, Robert William
Grossman, George Samuel
Grossman, Sebastian Peter
Hassett, Carol Alice
Howard, James Lawrence
Ince, Laurence Peter
Jones, Molly Modrall
Julesz, Bela
Justesen, Don Robert
Khavari, Khalil Akhtar
Kornetsky, Conan
Lansdell, Herbert Charles
Lavond, David Gerard
Levinthal, Charles Frederick
Lindsley, Donald Benjamin
Lubar, Joel Fredric
McGuigan, Frank Joseph
Olton, David Stuart
Patterson, Michael Milton
Ratliff, Floyd
Reitan, Ralph Meldahl
Rohles, Frederick Henry, Jr.
Rugh, John Douglas
Smith, Kirby
Soper, Henry Victor
Sparks, David Lee
Stern, Robert Morris
Tramill, James Louis
Wever, Ernest Glen
White, Keith D.
Woodruff-Pak, Diana Stenen
Yatani, Atsuko
Young, Francis Allan

Psychobiology
Alkana, Ronald Lee
Allen, Robert Arthur
Bigler, Erin David
Breedlove, Stephen Marc
Brick, John
Buchtel, Henry Augustus, IV
Byrd, Larry Donald
Cheal, MaryLou
Chennault, Madelyn Joanne
De Haan, Henry John
Dillon, Donald Joseph
Donchin, Emanuel
Ehrlich, Yigal H.
Everly, George Stotelmyer, Jr.
Glazer, Howard Irwin
Goodman, Irving Jack
Grayson, Henry
Grossman, Sebastian Peter
Harkins, Stephen Wayne
Hellman, Rhona Phyllis
Hersher, Leonard
Hickis, Charles Francis
Isaacson, Robert Lee
Jensen, Robert Alan
Kristal, Mark Bennett
Lavond, David Gerard
Lawson, William Bradford
Lee, Richard M
Lisk, Robert Douglas
Lynds-Cherry, Patricia Gail
Matarazzo, Joseph Dominic
Maxson, Stephen Clark
Mayer, David Jonathan
Morin, Lawrence Porter
Overmier, James Bruce
Prentky, Robert Alan
Provine, Robert Raymond
Reiser, Morton Francis
Rescorla, Robert Arthur
Richter, Curt Paul
Sachs, Benjamin David
Sanberg, Paul Ronald
Shucard, David William
Sperry, Roger Wolcott
Straub, Richard Otto
Suomi, Stephen John
Thompson, Richard Frederick
Voehees, Charles Van
Whalen, Richard Edward
Wickramasekera, (Ian Edward Wickram)
Zimmerman, John Thomas

Psychophysics. *See* PHYSICS.

Sensory processes
Andreassi, John L(awrence)
Bedair, Salah Mohamed
Boff, Kenneth Richard
Boynton, Robert Merrill
Cain, William S.
Collins, William Edward
Corso, John Fiermonte
Crampton, George Harris
Davis, Elizabeth Emily Louise Thorpe
Dillon, Donald Joseph
Drum, Bruce Alan
Dunn, William Lawrence
Harth, Erich
Hirsh, Ira Jean
Hope, George Marion
Jameson, Dorothea
Johnston, Dorothy Mae
Kennedy, Linda Mann
Kenshalo, Daniel Ralph
Lawrence, Merle
Luo, Ren-Chyuan
Makous, Walter
Marks, Lawrence Edward
Neff, William Duwayne
Nelson, Jeremiah I.
Nielsen, Donald Wayne
Odom, James Vernon
Ray, Richard Hallett
Riggs, Lorrin Andrews
Smith, Robert L.
Swets, John Arthur
Trybus, Raymond J.
Verrillo, Ronald Thomas
Wever, Ernest Glen
Yost, William Albert
Young, Francis Allan

Social psychology
Adams, John David
Adler, Leonore Loeb
Atwood, Joan Dolores
Beach, Lee Roy
Billington, Randall John
Blake, Brian Francis
Boor, Myron Vernon
Brown, Roger William
Brunson, Bradford Ira
Buck, Ross Workman
Bush, David Frederic
Cacioppo, John Terrance
Carducci, Bernardo Joseph
Carroll, John Stephen
Carsrud, Alan Lee
Casler, Lawrence
Chennault, Madelyn Joanne
Chermol, Brian Hamilton
Childers, John Stephen
Cohen, Sheldon Avery
Diener, Edward Francis
Doehrman, Steven R(alph)
Drummond, Robert John
Edelman, Ann Lynn
Figley, Charles Ray
Franklin, Paula Anne
Gable, Ralph Kirkland
Garland, Howard
Getzels, Jacob Warren
Graham, Kenneth Robert
Grosser, George Samuel
Gutierrez, Fernando Jose
Hatcher, John Christopher
Hilton, Thomas Frederick
Holtzman, Wayne Harold
Hull, Diana
Kiesler, Charles Adolphus
Kilmann, Ralph Herman
Lasry, Jean-Claude Maurice
McCombs, Harriet G.
Montgomery, Robert Lew
Murray, John Patrick
Pacheco-Maldonado, Angel Manuel
Prewitt-Diaz, Joseph Orlando
Rosnow, Ralph L(eon)
Seay, Thomas Austin
Shaffer, Howard Jeffrey
Sirgy, Magdy Joseph
Smith, John Philip
Sparacino, Jack Robert
Spence, Janet Taylor
Stevens, Gwendolyn Ruth
Teddlie, Charles Benton
Teevan, Richard Collier
Valfer, Ernst Siegmar
Violato, Claudio
Webster, Murray Alexander, Jr.
Wells, Gary Leroy

Other
Adler, Leonore Loeb, *Comparative psychology*
Andrysco, Robert Michael, *Human/animal bond*
Bach, Deborah, *Clinical psychology*
Bedell, Ralph Clairon, *Counseling psychology*
Bell, Charolette Renee, *Testing and evaluation*
Blake, Brian Francis
Blanchard, Ray Milton, *Gender identity disorders*
Blechner, Mark J.
Bloom, Richard Fredric, *Psychotherapy*
Bradley, John Michael, *Reading-related cognition and perception*
Brunson, Bradford Ira, *Counseling psychology*
Bryant, James Winston, Jr.
Bufford, Rodger Keith, *Psychology and religion*
Bush, David Frederic, *Health psychology*
Carducci, Bernardo Joseph, *Personality*
Carsrud, Alan Lee, *Applied social/personality psychology*
Chibucos, Thomas Robert, *Child development and family studies*
Colberg, Magda
Colotla, Victor Adolfo, *Behavioral toxicology*
Corso, John Fiermonte, *Aging*
Cournand, Andre F.
Crnic, Linda Sue Smith
Cupchik, William, *Psychotherapy*
Dean, Judith Carol Hickman, *Oncology counseling psychology*
De Haan, Henry John, *Perception*
deTorres, Cory Delgado, *Neurolinguistic programming*
Dewart, Dorothy Boardman, *Diagnosis and control of chronic pain*
Dishman, Rodney King, *Exercise and sport psychology*
Doehrman, Steven R(alph), *Health psychology*
Don, Norman Stanley, *Consciousness*
Dreitlein, Raymond Paul, *Alcoholism rehabilitation counseling*
Duncan, Starkey Davis, Jr.
Eckardt, Michael Jon, *Medical psychology*
El Ghatit, Zeinab Mohammed, *Clinical psychology*
Elkins, Gary Ray
Elliott, Charles H., *Pediatric psychology*
Evans, Gary William, *Environmental psychology*
Fedner, Mark Lee
Feher, Leslie, *Perinatal psychology*
Feshbach, Seymour, *Personality*
Force, Ronald C(larence), *Corrections psychology*
Franklin, Paula Anne
Franklin, Randall Morrow
Garland, Howard, *Organizational psychology*
Girden, Ellen Robinson, *Research design*
Glazer, Howard Irwin, *Clinical/organizational psychology*
Goldstein, Steven Edward, *Stress management*
Grandon, Gary Michael, *Educational measurement*
Grayson, Henry
Greuling, Jacquelin Wren, *Health psychology*
Hamning, Richard Rudolph
Hards, Kathryn Elisa
Hayek, Theodore Craig, *Human resources management and development; Organizational and industrial psychology*
Hill, A. Lewis
Hilliard, Asa Grant, III, *Cultural bias and testing*
Hilton, Thomas Frederick, *Health psychology*
Hull, Diana, *Population and environment, media psychology*
Hunt, Elizabeth Hope
Jeong, Tung Hon
Johnson, Richard Frederick, *Human factors psychology*
Jones, Lyle Vincent, *Psychometrics*
Kadushin, Phineas
Kilmann, Ralph Herman, *Organizational sciences*
Kim, S. Peter, *Trans/cross-cultural medical psychology*
King, Dennis R., *Pain management*
Kodanaz, Hatice Altan, *Clinical-behavioral studies*
Komechak, Marilyn Gilbert, *Psychotherapy*
Kopelman, Richard Eric, *Industrial and organizational psychology*
Krippner, Stanley Curtis
Kupst, Mary Jo, *Psychological aspects of illness*
Landauer, Thomas K., *Human factors psychology*
Lasry, Jean-Claude Maurice, *Psychotherapy*
Lawlor, Evelyn Davis
Leddick, George Russell, *Counseling psychology*
Lee, Mickey Mitchell
Linville, Malcolm Eugene, Jr., *Counseling psychology*
Llorca, Arthur Lee
Lofquist, Lloyd Henry, *Vocational psychology*
Lorion, Raymond Paul
Louttit, Richard Talcott, *Behavioral sciences program administration*
Luce, (Robert) Duncan
Lynds-Cherry, Patricia Gail, *School psychology*
Lynn, George Leslie
Machtiger, Harriet Gordon, *Psychotherapy*
Massad, Carolyn Emrick, *Psychometrics*
Mayo, Clyde Calvin, *Industrial/organizational psychology*
McAbee, Thomas Allen, *Community psychology*
Miner, John Burnham, *Organizational psychology*
Mulick, James Anton, *Mental retardation*
Muller, John Paul, *Psychoanalysis*
Novick, Melvin Robert, *Psychometrics*
O'Farrell, Timothy James
Paarfus, Barbara Leidholdt, *Educational psychology*
Patterson, Robert Logan, *Psychotherapy*
Paule, Merle Gale, *Behavioral pharmacology/toxicology*
Pine, Charles Joseph, *Health psychology*
Popov, Dan, *Organizational/Clinical Psychology*
Prewitt-Diaz, Joseph Orlando
Ross, John Munder
Sanders, Gilbert Otis
Schwarzbeck, Charles
Seligson, M. Ross
Shaffer, Howard Jeffrey, *Substance use and abuse*
Shepard, Roger Newland, *Experimental psychology*
Sirgy, Magdy Joseph, *Consumer psychology*
Solomon, Richard Lester, *Experimental psychology*
Sparacino, Jack Robert
Spohn, Herbert Emil, *Experimental psychopathology*
Stalnaker, John Marshall
Stevens, Gwendolyn Ruth
Stewart, Larry Gene
Straussner, Joel Harvey, *Educational psychology*
Tepas, Donald Irving
Thompson, William Warren, *Educational psychology*
Torigoe, Rodney Yoshito
Traynham, Richard Neville
Trybus, Raymond J.
Trzasko, Joseph Anthony
Tzeng, Oliver Chun Shun, *Cross-cultural Psychology; Psychosemantics*
Uhlaner, Julius Earl
Urry, Vern William, *Test theory*
Vavra, Terry Gwyn
Waldron, Joseph Anthony
Wass, Hannelore Lina
White, Mary-Alice, *Psychology of electronic learning*
Winer, Jane Louise
Wittenborn, John Richard, *Psychopathology*
Wohlfeil, Paul Frederick, *Health psychology*
Yensen, Richard, *Psychotherapy/personality/consciousness*
Zweig, Joseph B.

SPACE SCIENCE. *See also* ASTRONOMY, ENGINEERING, PHYSICS.

Aerospace engineering and technology
Abbey, George William Samuel
Adamczak, Robert Leonard
Adams, Karyl Ann
Allen, Douglas Mark
Androulakis, John George
Ashley, Holt
Asmussen, Jes, Jr.
Babish, Richard Constantine
Bareiss, Lyle Eugene
Bastedo, William Gardner
Battin, Richard Horace
Beggs, James Montgomery
Bekey, Ivan
Bertrando, Bertrand Robert
Birkitt, John Clair
Blasingame, Benjamin Paul
Boll, David Jackson
Bottema, Murk
Bourgeois, Sidney V., Jr.
Brody, Steven
Brooks, Walter Fanger
Buddington, Patricia Arrington
Bussard, Robert William
Calvert, Glenn Spencer
Carr, Gerald Paul
Chuan, Raymond Lu-po
Cibosky, William
Cipriano, Leonard Francis
Clarke, Larry Denman
Cloud, James Douglas
Cohen, Aaron
Cohen, Edward
Cohen, Haggai
Cole, Terry
Coleman, Jeffrey Owen
Collins, Frank Gibson
Conrow, Edmund Henry
Cornell, Robert Witherspoon
Cramer, Harrison Emery
Currie, Malcolm Roderick
Davis, Dean Earl
De, Bibhas Ranjan
Dean, William Evans
Dergarabedian, Paul
Devereux, William Patrick
Dietenberger, Mark Anthony
Dirks, Leslie Chant
Dolling, David Stanley
Dowell, Earl Hugh
Drake, Michael Lee
Duggin, Michael John
Eaves, Reuben Elco
Eggers, Alfred John, Jr.
Emming, Jan Goossem
Ernst, Donald Martin
Faeth, Gerard Michael
Fellows, W(alter) Scott, Jr.
Ferguson, Jackson Robert, Jr.
Fodor, Magda Maria
Foley, Cray Lyman
Frazier, William Earl
Friesen, Larry Jay
Frink, Richard Clark
Fuhs, Allen Eugene
Gaffney, Francis Andrew
Garneau, Marc
Gartrell, Charles Frederick
Gessow, Alfred
Gilruth, Robert Rowe
Glaser, Peter Edward
Goetz, Frank
Gould, Charles Laverne
Grady, Arthur Lynn
Griffin, Gerald Duane
Grossman, Bernard
Guastaferro, Angelo
Gunn, Charles Rowley
Hall, Charles Frederick
Hansen, Grant Lewis
Hansen, Stanley Severin, II
Harford, James Joseph
Hart, Lawrence Austin
Hartig, Elmer Otto
Hasegawa, Tony Seisuke
Heller, Douglas Max
Hendron, John Alden
Hertzberg, Abraham
Hnatiuk, Bohdan Taras
Hoag, David Garratt
Hoff, Nicholas John
Holmes, Dyer Brainerd
Horman, Melvin Herbert
Hsieh, Tsuying Carl
Huang, Richard Shih-Chiu
Huang, Tsou-Chiang
Huberman, Benjamin
Hurley, Francis Xavier
Jahn, Robert George
Johnson, Jeffrey Paul
Jones, Robert Thomas
Kandil, Osama Abdel-Mohsin
Kelley, Albert Joseph
Kelsoe, Lynda Carol
Kerrebrock, Jack Leo
Khadduri, Farid Majid
Klockzien, Vernon George
Kolm, Henry Herbert
Kostoulas, Ioannis Georgiou
Krachman, Howard Ellis
Laheru, Ken Liem
Lam, Kui-chuen
Laurenson, Robert Mark
Lindberg, Eric Kent
Loewy, Robert Gustav
Loth, John Lodewyk
Lucas, William Ray
Lundin, Bruce Theodore
Mastronardi, Richard
McAuley, Van Alfon
Mc Carthy, John Francis, Jr.
McGregor, Wheeler Kesey, Jr.
McMillen, Sandra Lee
Mettler, Ruben Frederick
Mihas, Faquir Ullah
Miller, Rene Harcourt
Moody, Elizabeth Anne
Moody, John Chrystor
Morton, Randall Eugene
Muirhead, Vincent Uriel
Nagamatsu, Henry Takeshi
Naugle, John Earl
Neuringer, Joseph Louis
Nomura, Yasumasa
Noor, Ahmed Khairy
Osborn, Daniel Cargill, III
Pagano, Frank Paul
Pai, Shih I.
Park, Chul
Pearce, Malcolm Bulkeley, Jr.
Pearson, Jerome
Pechenick, Kay Rhoda
Peebles, Peyton Zimmerman, Jr.
Peterson, James Robert
Petrone, Rocco A.
Pickering, William Hayward
Pollock, R. Donald
Pomphrey, Richard Bryan
Porter, Frederick Charles
Powers, William Francis
Pownall, Thomas Gilmore
Psaros, George Emanuel
Purser, Paul Emil
Puskas, Elek
Randolph, James Eugene
Randolph, Lynwood Parker
Rubin, Stanley Gerald
Ryker, Norman Jenkins, Jr.
Sadler, Stanley Gene
Santi, Gino P.
Sargent, Ernest Douglas
Schairer, George Swift
Schneider, Harold
Scholz, Lawrence Charles
Schwanhausser, Robert Rowland
Seamans, Robert Channing, Jr.
Sesak, John Robert
Sheehy, Jerome Joseph
Shkedi, Zvi
Shomer, John Edward
Silveira, Milton Anthony
Simitses, George John
Simonetti, Joseph Lawrence
Singer, Timothy James
Skurla, George Martin
Slaminski, John Michael
Slayton, Donald Kent
Smith, Donald Eugene
Smith, Richard Graham
Stever, Horton Guyford
Stofan, Andrew J.
Strain, John Willard
Stubberud, Allen Roger
Swanson, Paul Norman
Syvertson, Clarence Alfred
Szebehely, Victor G.
Tai, Tsze Cheng
Tapley, Byron Dean
Thomas, Garland Leon
Townsend, John William, Jr.
Townsend, Marjorie Rhodes
Turner, Earl James
Uda, Robert Takeo
Vaughan, William Walton
Vlay, George John
von Tiesenhausen, Georg F.
Wagner-Bartak, Claus Gunther Johann
Walquist, Robert Louis
Walton, Vincent Michael
Wattendorf, Frank Leslie
Wertheim, Robert Halley
White, Charles Olds
Wolfe, Howard Francis
Wright, Lynne C.
Yardley, John Finley
Yarymovych, Michael Ihor
Yu, Yi-Yuan

Astronautics
Anderle, Richard John
Armstrong, Neil A.
Berger, Steven Barry
Danby, J(ohn) M(ichael) Anthony
Donivan, Frank Forbes, Jr.
Ferguson, Jackson Robert, Jr.
Fisher, Anna
Fletcher, James Chipman
Frazier, William Earl
Garneau, Marc
Gilruth, Robert Rowe
Harford, James Joseph
Hnatiuk, Bohdan Taras
Holland, Robert Louis
Jastrow, Robert
Levinson, David Alan
Manion, David Edward
Miller, Jay
Nigam, Rajendra C.
Oesterwinter, Claus
Pearson, Jerome
Randolph, James Eugene
Rauch, Herbert Emil
Ride, Sally Kristen
Schairer, George Swift
Sullivan, Kathryn D.
Szebehely, Victor G.
Williams, James Gerard

Gravitational biology
Cipriano, Leonard Francis
Heinrich, Milton Rollin
Hoffman, Ronald Bruce
Kaufman, Peter Bishop
Loeppky, Jack Albert
Oyama, Jiro

Satellite studies
Androulakis, John George
Arnold, James Richard
Bareiss, Lyle Eugene
Barkley, Linda Dorothy
Bertrando, Bertrand Robert
Cahill, Laurence James, Jr.
Chenette, David Louis
Duggin, Michael John

SPACE SCIENCE

Dumas, Herbert Monroe, (Jr.)
El-Baz, Farouk
Fremouw, Edward Joseph
Gartrell, Charles Frederick
Gould, Charles Laverne
Hall, David Lee
Hernandez, Samuel P.
Hyson, Michael Terry
Inada, Hitoshi
Johnson, Francis Severin
Kondo, Yoji
Lambert, John Vincent
Landecker, Peter Bruce
Largman, Kenneth
Laubscher, Roy Edward
Lockwood, John Alexander
Lupo, Michael Vincent
Lynch, John Patrick
Masursky, Harold
Mehring, James Warren
Murray, Stephen S.
Nelson, Robert M.
Page, Thornton Leigh
Papagiannis, Michael D.
Parks, Allen Danforth
Peterson, Vern LeRoy
Pieper, George F(rancis)
Porter, John Robert, Jr.
Rabin, Herbert
Radoski, Henry Robert
Schlussel, Neil
Schwartz, Sandra
Schwartzkopf, Steven Henry
Shorthill, Richard Warren
Spiegel, Stanley Lawrence
Tapley, Byron Dean
Torr, Marsha Russell
Tousey, Richard
Travis, Larry Dean
Vaeth, Joseph Gordon
Van Allen, James Alfred
Vlay, George John
Williams, Donald John
Wilson, William Stanley
Wu, William W.
Yeh, Kung Chie

Solar physics

Anderson, Kinsey A.
Bai, Taeil
Bame, Samuel Jarvis, Jr.
Barnes, Aaron
Baum, Peter Joseph
Beckers, Jacques Maurice
Brunish, Wendee M.
Chasson, Robert Lee
Claflin, Robert Malden
Clark, Thomas Alan
Cook, John W.
Davis, John Moulton
de la Zerda, Alberto
Doiron, David John
Donnelly, Richard Frank
Emslie, A. Gordon
Fan, Chang-Yun
Gary, Dale Everett
Gergely, Tomas Esteban
Gilliland, Ronald Lynn
Glackin, David Langdon
Glatzmaier, Gary Andrew
Gosling, John Thomas
Hill, Henry Allen
Hinata, Satoshi
Hollweg, Joseph Vincent
Howard, Robert Franklin
Jefferies, John Trevor
Jordan, Stuart Davis
Kan, Joseph R.
Kane, Sharad Ramchandra
Koga, Rokutaro
Kopp, Roger Alan
Krieger, Allen Stephen
Kundu, Mukul R.
Landecker, Peter Bruce
Lee, Martin Alan
Levine, Randolph Herbert
Livingston, William Charles
Lockwood, John Alexander
Mac Queen, Robert Moffat
Mendis, D(evamitta) Asoka
Mohler, Orren Cuthbert
Moore, Ronald Lee
Newkirk, Gordon Allen, Jr.
Poland, Arthur Ira
Pomerantz, Martin Arthur
Prince, Helen Dodson
Rhodes, Edward Joseph, Jr.
Roberts, Walter Orr
Sawyer, Constance Bragdon
Skelton, Dennis Lee
Smith, Dean F.
Smith, Sheldon Magill
Snider, Joseph Lyons
Tajima, Toshiki

Tandberg-Hanssen, Einar Andreas
Thomas, John Howard
Tousey, Richard
Willson, Richard Clayton
Zirker, Jack Bernard

Space chemistry

Anderson, James Gilbert
Bohme, Diethard Kurt
Khare, Bishun Narain
Lipschutz, Michael Elazar
Moore, Carleton Bryant
Nichiporuk, Walter
Ponnamperuma, Cyril Andrew
Scattergood, Thomas W.
Turkevich, Anthony Leonid
Wilkening, Laurel Lynn

Space medicine

Beljan, John Richard
Buchanan, Paul
Darrah, Mark Irwin
Donati, Robert Mario
Graybiel, Ashton
Hargens, Alan Robert
Hendler, Edwin
Hoffman, Ronald Bruce
Moore-Ede, Martin Christopher
Thornton, William E.
Townsend, Frank Marion
Whidden, Stanley John
Young, Laurence Retman

Other

Adelman, Saul Joseph
Allen, Lew, Jr., *Space science research management.*
Armstrong, Thomas Peyton
Bame, Samuel Jarvis, Jr., *Space plasma physics*
Barth, Charles Adolph, *Space physics*
Bering, Edgar Andrew, III
Boston, Penelope Jane Ashley
Cahill, Laurence James, Jr., *Space physics*
Carley, John Wesley, III
Clarke, Robert Francis
Dessler, Alex J., *Space physics*
Feinberg, Gerald, *Extraterrestrial life*
Figueroa-Viñas, Adolfo
Frassanito, John Robert, *Space habitat design*
Friesen, Larry Jay
Fulda, Michael, *Space policy*
Garcia, Nicholas Flores, *Large space structures*
Gosling, John Thomas, *Space plasma physics*
Grosch, Daniel Swartwood, *Space biology*
Hannah, David, Jr., *Space launch service*
Hesser, James E(dward), *Space astronomy*
Hinners, Noel W., *Space flight center adminstration*
Hlass, I. Jerry, *Space technology management*
Keehn, Neil Francis, *National security space systems*
Kessler, Donald Joe, *Orbital debris studies.*
Khadduri, Farid Majid, *Solid rocket propulsion*
Krimigis, Stamatios Mike, *Space plasma physics*
Largman, Kenneth, *Military space systems*
Lederer, Jerome Fox, *Aerospace safety*
McDiarmid, Ian Bertrand, *Government space program administration*
Mendis, D(evamitta) Asoka, *Cometary physics.*
Pritchett, Philip Lentner, *Magnetospheric physics*
Roederer, Juan Gualterio, *Space physics*
Schlussel, Neil
Sesak, John Robert
Soffen, Gerald Alan, *Government space program administration*
Tien, Chang Lin, *Thermophysics*
Williams, Albert Lynn, Jr., *Space industrialization*
Willson, Richard Clayton, *Solar-terrestrial relationships*
Woo, Richard, *Solar wind*

VETERINARY MEDICINE. See also
AGRICULTURE.

Biomedical engineering. See
ENGINEERING, Biomedical.

Cancer research

Bankert, Richard Burton
Benjamin, Stephen Alfred
Chang, Ming Jen Wu
Chang, Richard Li-chai
Diters, Richard William
Koller, Loren D.
Lozano-Alarcon, Fernando
MacCoy, Douglas Maidlow
Mayer, Ramona Ann
McCoy, John R(oger)
McGill, Lawrence David
Purchase, Harvey Graham
Szebenyi, Emil Steven
Weller, Richard Eldon

Embryo transplants. *See also*
AGRICULTURE, Animal breeding,
embryo transplants.

Dawson, Lionel James
Donaldson, Lloyd Eric
Neely, Dean Philip
Phatak, Arun
Woods, Gordon Leon

Genetics and genetic engineering. *See also*
AGRICULTURE, BIOLOGY.

Bachrach, Howard L.
Gibbs, E(dward) Paul J(ohnson)
Healey, Mark Calvin
Palmer, Guy Hughes
Woods, Gordon Leon

Internal medicine

Breitschwerdt, Edward Bealmear
Chastain, Claud Blankenhorn
Davis, Lloyd Edward
Detweiler, David Kenneth
Foreman, Jonathan Hale
Fraser, Clarence Malcolm
Harvey, Terence
Lee, Hazel Ann
Leib, Michael Samuel
Maplesden, Douglas Cecil
Marshak, Robert Reuben
Mohanty, Sashi B.
Peterson, Mark Earl
Ross, Linda Anne
Scarratt, William Kent
Younger, Melanie Moore

Laboratory animal medicine

Baas, Ervin Junior
Black, David Joseph
Bowman, Teresa Ann
Chacko, Jacob
Clarke, George Lee
Collins, Bobby Ray
Dawkins, Barry Gilbert
Donovan, John Charles
Ewald, Bruce Harold
Harroff, H(omer) Hugh, Jr.
Hunt, Ronald Duncan
Klein, Hilton James
Kohn, Dennis Fredrich
Lipman, Neil Scott
Loew, Franklin Martin
Marcella, Kenneth Louis
Melby, Edward Carlos, Jr.
Miller, Carl Edward
Peterson, Mark Earl
Secord, David Cartwright
Shalev, Moshe
Szabo, Tibor
Szczepanski, Marek Michal
Van Pelt, Lloyd Franklin
Weingand, Kurt William

Microbiology

Angus, Robert Dale
Bairey, Miles Huxtable
Bell, C. Thomas
Claflin, Robert Malden
Collins, Michael Thomas
Dardiri, Ahmed Hamed
Dua, Suresh Kumar
Eberhart, Robert James
Ferris, Deam Hunter
Klein, Hilton James
Klesius, Phillip Harry
Maas, Synthea Jean
McAllister, Harold Antonio
McLennan, Jean Glinn
Myers, Lyle Leslie
Nicoletti, Paul
Paul, Prem Sagar
Shadduck, John Allen
Sharma, Jagdev Mittra
Siam, Monir Ahmed
Stoddard, Patricia Ann
Targowski, Stanislaw Pytkowski
Walton, Thomas Edward

Pathology

Alden, Carl Leslie
Allen, Henry Leigh
Anderson, Gary Allan
Anderson, Wayne Ian
Baas, Ervin Junior
Barnes, Harold John
Benjamin, Stephen Alfred
Bertram, Timothy Allyn
Bossart, Gregory Dana
Brobst, Duane Franklin
Buergelt, Claus Dietmar
Carakostas, Michael Charles
Case, Marvin Theodore
Cera, Lee Marie
Chacko, Jacob
Chesney, Charles Frederic
Cheville, Norman Frederick
Clapp, Neal Keith
Clarke, George Lee
Diters, Richard William
Dua, Suresh Kumar
Fenwick, Bradley Willard
Fettman, Martin Joseph
Gooneratne, Sarojith Ravi
Greve, John Henry
Hall, LeRoy Brooks, Jr.
Hartmann, William Lawrence
Haschek-Hock, Wanda Maria
Hoopes, Paul Jack
Hunt, Ronald Duncan
Jayasekara, Upali Matheskankanange
Jenson, Alfred Bennett
Kazacos, Kevin Robert
Kerns, William David
Kier-Schroeder, Ann B.
Kim, Hyun Young
Knobloch, Cheryl Porter
Koller, Loren D.
Levin, Stuart
Lozano-Alarcon, Fernando
Madissoo, Harry
McAllister, Harold Antonio
McCoy, John R(oger)
McGill, Lawrence David
Melby, Edward Carlos, Jr.
Miller, Lyle Devon
Moe, James Burton
Montgomery, Donald Lee
Neely, Dean Philip
Nielsen, Niels Ole
Olson, David Peter
Palmer, Guy Hughes
Perryman, Lance Edward
Phemister, Robert David
Robinson, Farrel Richard
Ruben, Zadok
Schwartz, Leland Dwight
Shadduck, John Allen
Tasker, John Baker
Torres-Medina, Alfonso
Van Ryzin, Robert Joseph
Weingand, Kurt William
Zwicker, Gary Michael

Preventive medicine

Asquith, Richard LaVerne
Bailey, Alfred William
Bennett, Billy Wayne
Beran, George Wesley
Burridge, Michael John
Courtney, Charles Hill, III
Eberhart, Robert James
Fisher, Richard Keith
Francis, Marlan Lanning
Haughee, Sharon Marie
Hutchinson, Lawrence Jay
Johnson, Daryl Clyde
Meyerholz, George William
Myers, Lyle Leslie
Odend'hal, Stewart
Olson, David Peter
Scott, Robert Glenn (Bob), Jr.
Shor, Aaron Louis
Smith, Robert Johnie
Sprinkle, Fredrick Preston
Sweat, Robert Lee
Szabo, Tibor
Underdahl, Norman Russell
Woods, George Theodore
Younger, Melanie Moore

Surgery

Benedetti, Latayah McClellan
Bramlage, Lawrence Robert
Cholvin, Neal Robert
Colahan, Patrick Timothy
Cooper, Robert Carl, Jr.
Crowe, Dennis Timothy, Jr.
Donawick, William Joseph
Lee, Hazel Ann
Litwak, Philip
MacCoy, Douglas Maidlow
Mendenhall, Harlan Vincent
Pearson, Phillip Theodore

Pathology (continued)

Probst, Curtis Ware
Raffe, Marc Roye
Ramey, David William
Skoryna, Stanley Constantine
Szczepanski, Marek Michal
Tangner, Cecil Herman, Jr.

Virology

Banerjee, Amiya Kumar
Gainer, Joseph Henry
Gibbs, E(dward) Paul J(ohnson)
Jenson, Alfred Bennett
Kim, Hyun Young
Luchsinger, Donald Wayne
Marquardt, Warren William
Mohanty, Sashi B.
Pan, In-Chang
Paul, Prem Sagar
Pollock, Roy Van Horn
Purchase, Harvey Graham
Sidwell, Robert William
Sweat, Robert Lee
Torres-Medina, Alfonso
Walton, Thomas Edward
Woode, Gerald Nottidge

Other

Alden, Carl Leslie
Armistead, Willis William, *Veterinary medical research, administration*
Barnes, Harold John, *Poultry medicine*
Barta, Ota, *Clinical immunology*
Beaver, Bonnie Veryle
Bossart, Gregory Dana, *Diseases of aquatic animals*
Brown, Connell J.
Cooper, Robert Carl, Jr.
Czarnecki, Caroline Mary Anne, *Veterinary anatomy*
Dawson, Lionel James, *Theriogenology*
Diesem, Charles David, *Ophthalmology*
Drummond, Roger Otto, *Veterinary acarology*
Ekperigin, Henry Eyituoyo
Feeney, Daniel Arthur
Feller, Douglas Lee, *Physiology; Veterinary pharmacology*
Gaafar, Sayed M., *Veterinary Parasitology*
Greve, John Henry
Gustafsson, Borje Karl, *Theriogenology*
Hansel, William
Holmes, Robert Antell
Hooser, Stephen Blair, *Veterinary toxicology*
Houdeshell, Jesse William, *Veterinary pharmacology; Clinical veterinary medicine*
Johnson, Daryl Clyde, *Veterinary Epidemiology*
Kawalek, Joseph Casimir, *Drug metabolism in food producing animals*
Kazam, Abdul Raoof
Klide, Alan Marshall, *Veterinary Anesthesiology*
Luchsinger, Donald Wayne, *Diagnostic veterinary medicine*
Mason, Margaret Jeanne, *Clinical veterinary medicine*
Massaro, Edward Joseph
Medhi, Nabeel Abdel-Qadir, *Mycotoxicosis*
Memon, Mushtaq Ahmed
Meyerholz, George William
Mitchell, George Bert
Moore, Earl Neil, *Cardiology*
Noga, Edward Joseph, *Diseases of aquatic animals*
Oliver, Jack (Wallace), *Veterinary pharmacology*
Paddleford, Robert Ray, *Veterinary anesthesiology*
Pineda, Mauricio Hernan, *Animal contraception*
Schlafer, Donald Hughes, *Theriogenology*
Schneider, Norman Richard, *Diagnostic veterinary toxicology*
Schwartz, Leland Dwight
Skarda, Roman Thomas, *Veterinary anesthesiology*
Talbot, Richard Burritt, *Veterinary physiology*
Tangner, Cecil Herman, Jr.
Tasker, John Baker, *Veterinary medicine education*
Whitley, Robert David, *Veterinary ophthalmology*
Yonkers, Thomas Darrell
Zander, Donald Victor, *Avian pathology*
Zinn, Gene Marvin, *Food animal medicine and surgery*

ZOOLOGY. See BIOLOGY.